WHITAKER'S
2019

AN

Almanack

For the Year of Our Lord

2019

ESTABLISHED 1868

BY

JOSEPH WHITAKER, FSA

CONTAINING AN ACCOUNT OF THE

ASTRONOMICAL AND OTHER PHENOMENA

AND

A vast Amount of INFORMATION respecting the

GOVERNMENT, FINANCES, POPULATION,

COMMERCE, and GENERAL STATISTICS of

the various Nations of the WORLD

with an INDEX containing

nearly 7,500

References

LONDON

OFFICE: 50 BEDFORD SQUARE

LONDON WC1B 3DP

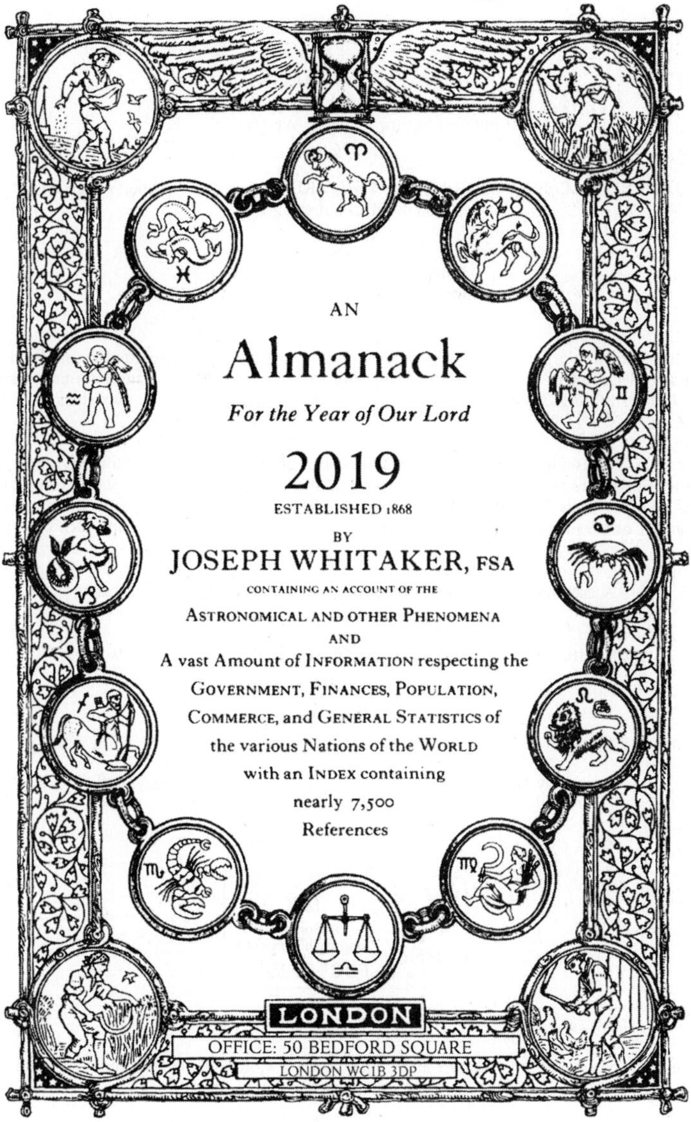

The traditional design of the title page for Whitaker's Almanack which has appeared in each edition since 1868

BLOOMSBURY YEARBOOKS

LONDON • OXFORD • NEW YORK • NEW DELHI • SYDNEY

BLOOMSBURY YEARBOOKS
Bloomsbury Publishing Plc
50 Bedford Square, London, WC1B 3DP, UK

BLOOMSBURY, BLOOMSBURY YEARBOOKS, WHITAKER'S, and the Whitaker's logo are trademarks of
Bloomsbury Publishing Plc

Published annually since 1868
151st edition © Bloomsbury Publishing Plc, 2018

A catalogue record for this book is available from the British Library

ISBN: HB: 978-1-4729-4752-9; CONCISE EDITION: 978-1-4729-5909-6

2 4 6 8 10 9 7 5 3 1

Typeset by DLxml, a division of RefineCatch Limited, Bungay, Suffolk
Printed and bound in Italy by L.E.G.O. S.p.A.

MIX
Paper from
responsible sources
FSC® C023419

To find out more about our authors and books visit www.bloomsbury.com and sign up for our
newsletters

CONTENTS

4

THE WORLD

THE YEAR 2017–18

TIME AND SPACE

5

PREFACE

Our main image on the front cover this year shows an ordinary session of the European Parliament back in 2011 when it was 'business as usual' and here in the UK we had no inkling we would soon be leaving the European Union. Read our Parliament article for a full record of day-to-day parliamentary business in our section 'The Year 2017–18' and see our special feature detailing all the debates of the European Union (Withdrawal) Bill. Also read about the effects of Brexit on the insurance industry in our Banking and Finance chapter.

It's safe to say that we'll soon be waving goodbye to our European Parliament chapter in our governance section and this edition marks its last appearance in *Whitaker's*, but we have plenty of other chapters to keep you occupied. European Union will, of course, remain in our 'World' section.

For something completely different, why not dip your toes into our year in review articles? We have two new contributors this year for our Dance and Film articles, plus our Archaeology article features a fascinating re-look at Hadrian's Wall – was it '...effectively a bureaucratic soft border primarily designed to regulate and tax the peaceful movement of people...' or '...a hard border capable of repulsing full-scale barbarian invasions'? – and some original research by the contributor himself. There is a detailed write-up of the new V&A Dundee, with accompanying illustration, in the Architecture review 2017–18.

But let us not forget the staples of *Whitaker's*: Royalty, The Government, Churches, and the Peerage and Baronetage. Completely updated as always, you will notice that Peerage and Baronetage this year is sporting some smart new graphics illustrating the coronets and badges of the peers and orders of chivalry.

For those of you that would like more, don't forget you can now subscribe to www.whitakersalmanack.com which is continually updated throughout the year. Subscribe to the website using discount code **WhitA2019Print** for 25% off your individual annual subscription.

Interested in an institutional subscription for your library or organisation? Please do get in touch to discuss your requirements.

We hope you enjoy the wide and varied content *Whitaker's* has to offer, and please do feel free to contact us with comments and suggestions, which are always very welcome.

Ruth Northey
Executive Editor
whitakersalmanackteam@bloomsbury.com
www.whitakersalmanack.com

6

COVER PHOTOGRAPHS

Main image: European Parliament: members of the European Parliament vote during a session at the European Parliament in Strasbourg, eastern France in June 2011 © Getty Images

Top, from left to right:
1. Hillside fire on Llantysilio Mountain in Llangollen, Wales during UK prolonged dry spell in July 2018 © Getty Images
2. Former Secretary-General of the United Nations Kofi Annan attends a honorary dinner in March 2018 © Getty Images
3. British cyclist Geraint Thomas competes on the Champs-Elysees avenue before winning the Tour de France in July 2018 © Getty Images
4. Prince Harry, Duke of Sussex and Meghan, Duchess of Sussex, emerge from the West Door of St George's Chapel, Windsor Castle after their wedding in May 2018 © Getty Images

SOURCES
Whitaker's was compiled with the assistance of HM Revenue and Customs; The Met Office; Oxford Cartographers; Press Association; UK Hydrographic Office; and The World Bank.

Material was reproduced from (in addition to that indicated): *Abolitionist and Retentionist Countries* © Amnesty International 2018 (**W** www.amnesty.org); *CIA World Factbook 2018; Corruption Perceptions Index 2017* © Transparency International licensed under CC BY-ND 4.0 DE (**W** www.transparency.org); *Human Development Indicators* published by the UN Development Programme and *UN Statistics* published by UN data; *World Press Freedom Score 2018* © Reporters Without Borders; Stockholm International Peace Research Institute (SIPRI) 2017; *World Development Indicators 2017* published by The World Bank; *World*

Economic Outlook Database 2017 © International Monetary Fund; UNESCO Institute for Statistics (UIS) 2018 (**W** www.uis.unesco.org/datacentre); Crown copyright material is reproduced with the permission of the Controller of Her Majesty's Stationery Office.

Government cabinet lists are sourced from *People in Power* © Cambridge International Reference on Current Affairs Ltd (**W** www.circaworld.com). People in Power provides a constantly updated service at **W** www.peopleinpower.com

EDITORIAL STAFF
Executive Editor: Ruth Northey
Project Editor: James Robinson
Editorial Assistants: Alexandru Ciobanu; Kayla McCrary; Kat Taylor
Head of Yearbooks: Katy McAdam

Thanks to Lucy Beevor, John Bromham, Nathan Coonan-Joyce; Rob Hardy, Stephen Kershaw, Elizabeth Kingston, Hilary Marsden, Katie Rome

CONTRIBUTORS (where not listed)
Sheridan Williams, Graham Relf (Astronomy); Adam McKie (Countries of the World); Anthea Lipsett, Caroline Macready (Education); Graham Bartram (Flags); Clive Longhurst (Insurance), Amy Carter, Richard McMeeken, Chris Priestley (Legal Notes); Sarah Perkins (Taxation); and Sean Clarke (Weather)

Terrestrial Magnetism data supplied by Dr Susan Macmillan of the British Geological Survey

Night Sky data supplied by John Flannery of the Irish Astronomical Society

THE YEAR 2019

THE YEAR 2019

CHRONOLOGICAL CYCLES AND ERAS

Dominical Letter	F
Epact	24
Golden Number (Lunar Cycle)	VI
Julian Period	6732
Roman Indiction	12
Solar Cycle	12

	Beginning
*Muslim year AH 1440	11 Sep 2018
†Japanese year Heisei 31	1 Jan–30 Apr
Roman year 2772 AUC	14 Jan
Chinese year of the Pig	5 Feb
Regnal year 68	6 Feb
Sikh new year	14 Mar
Indian (Saka) year 1941	22 Mar
Hindu new year (Chaitra)	6 Apr
*Jewish year AM 5780	30 Sep

* Year begins at sunset on the previous day
† The Heisei epoch will end on 30 April on the abdication of Emperor Akihito. The new era begins when Crown Prince Naruhito ascends the throne on 1 May 2019. The name of the new epoch is to be announced on 1 April 2019.

RELIGIOUS CALENDARS

CHRISTIAN

Epiphany	6 Jan
Presentation of Christ in the Temple	2 Feb
Ash Wednesday	6 Mar
The Annunciation	25 Mar
Palm Sunday	14 Apr
Maundy Thursday	18 Apr
Good Friday	19 Apr
Easter Day (western churches)	21 Apr
Easter Day (Eastern Orthodox)	28 Apr
Rogation Sunday	26 May
Ascension Day	30 May
Pentecost (Whit Sunday)	9 Jun
Trinity Sunday	16 Jun
Corpus Christi	20 Jun
All Saints' Day	1 Nov
Advent Sunday	1 Dec
Christmas Day	25 Dec

HINDU

Makar Sankranti	14 Jan
Vasant Panchami (Sarasvati Puja)	10 Feb
Shivaratri	5 Mar
Holi	20 Mar
Chaitra (Spring new year)	6 Apr
Rama Navami	13 Apr
Raksha Bandhan	14 Aug
Krishna Janmashtami	23 Aug
Ganesh Chaturthi, first day	2 Sep
Navratri festival (Durga Puja), first day	29 Sep
Dussehra	8 Oct
Diwali (New Year festival of lights), first day	27 Oct

JEWISH

Purim	21 Mar
Pesach (Passover), first day	20 Apr
Shavuot (Feast of Weeks), first day	9 Jun
Rosh Hashanah (Jewish new year)	30 Sep
Yom Kippur (Day of Atonement)	9 Oct
Sukkot (Feast of Tabernacles), first day	14 Oct
Hanukkah (Festival of Lights), first day	23 Dec

MUSLIM‡

Al-Hijra (Muslim new year)	12 Sep 2018
Ashura	21 Sep 2018
Ramadan, first day	6 May
Eid-ul-Fitr	5 Jun
Hajj, first day	10 Aug
Eid-ul-Adha	12 Aug

SIKH

Birthday of Guru Gobind Singh Ji	5 Jan
1 Chet (Sikh new year)	14 Mar
§Hola Mohalla	21 Mar
Vaisakhi	14 Apr
Martyrdom of Guru Arjan Dev Ji	16 Jun
§Birthday of Guru Nanak Dev Ji	12 Nov
Martyrdom of Guru Tegh Bahadur Ji	24 Nov

‡ The Islamic calendar is lunar so religious dates may vary by one or two days locally and according to when the new Moon is first seen
§ Currently celebrated according to the lunar, rather than Nanakshahi, calendar, so the date varies annually

CIVIL CALENDAR

Duchess of Cambridge's birthday	9 Jan
Countess of Wessex's birthday	20 Jan
Accession of the Queen	6 Feb
Duke of York's birthday	19 Feb
St David's Day	1 Mar
Earl of Wessex's birthday	10 Mar
Commonwealth Day	11 Mar
St Patrick's Day	17 Mar
Birthday of the Queen	21 Apr
St George's Day	23 Apr
Europe Day	9 May
Coronation Day	2 Jun
The Queen's Official Birthday	8 Jun
Duke of Edinburgh's birthday	10 Jun
Duke of Cambridge's birthday	21 Jun
Duchess of Cornwall's birthday	17 Jul
Princess Royal's birthday	15 Aug
Lord Mayor's Day	9 Nov
Remembrance Sunday	10 Nov
Prince of Wales' birthday	14 Nov
Wedding Day of the Queen	20 Nov
St Andrew's Day	30 Nov

LEGAL CALENDAR

LAW TERMS

Hilary Term	11 Jan to 17 Apr
Easter Term	30 Apr to 24 May
Trinity Term	4 Jun to 31 Jul
Michaelmas Term	1 Oct to 21 Dec

QUARTER DAYS (England, Wales & Northern Ireland)	TERM DAYS (Scotland)
Lady – 25 Mar	Candlemas – 28 Feb
Midsummer – 24 Jun	Whitsunday – 28 May
Michaelmas – 29 Sep	Lammas – 28 Aug
Christmas – 25 Dec	Martinmas – 28 Nov

2019

JANUARY							FEBRUARY							MARCH						
Sunday		6	13	20	27		Sunday		3	10	17	24		Sunday		3	10	17	24	31
Monday		7	14	21	28		Monday		4	11	18	25		Monday		4	11	18	25	
Tuesday	1	8	15	22	29		Tuesday		5	12	19	26		Tuesday		5	12	19	26	
Wednesday	2	9	16	23	30		Wednesday		6	13	20	27		Wednesday		6	13	20	27	
Thursday	3	10	17	24	31		Thursday		7	14	21	28		Thursday		7	14	21	28	
Friday	4	11	18	25			Friday	1	8	15	22			Friday	1	8	15	22	29	
Saturday	5	12	19	26			Saturday	2	9	16	23			Saturday	2	9	16	23	30	

APRIL						MAY							JUNE						
Sunday		7	14	21	28	Sunday		5	12	19	26		Sunday		2	9	16	23	30
Monday	1	8	15	22	29	Monday		6	13	20	27		Monday		3	10	17	24	
Tuesday	2	9	16	23	30	Tuesday		7	14	21	28		Tuesday		4	11	18	25	
Wednesday	3	10	17	24		Wednesday	1	8	15	22	29		Wednesday		5	12	19	26	
Thursday	4	11	18	25		Thursday	2	9	16	23	30		Thursday		6	13	20	27	
Friday	5	12	19	26		Friday	3	10	17	24	31		Friday		7	14	21	28	
Saturday	6	13	20	27		Saturday	4	11	18	25			Saturday	1	8	15	22	29	

JULY						AUGUST							SEPTEMBER						
Sunday		7	14	21	28	Sunday		4	11	18	25		Sunday	1	8	15	22	29	
Monday	1	8	15	22	29	Monday		5	12	19	26		Monday	2	9	16	23	30	
Tuesday	2	9	16	23	30	Tuesday		6	13	20	27		Tuesday	3	10	17	24		
Wednesday	3	10	17	24	31	Wednesday		7	14	21	28		Wednesday	4	11	18	25		
Thursday	4	11	18	25		Thursday	1	8	15	22	29		Thursday	5	12	19	26		
Friday	5	12	19	26		Friday	2	9	16	23	30		Friday	6	13	20	27		
Saturday	6	13	20	27		Saturday	3	10	17	24	31		Saturday	7	14	21	28		

OCTOBER							NOVEMBER							DECEMBER						
Sunday		6	13	20	27		Sunday		3	10	17	24		Sunday	1	8	15	22	29	
Monday		7	14	21	28		Monday		4	11	18	25		Monday	2	9	16	23	30	
Tuesday	1	8	15	22	29		Tuesday		5	12	19	26		Tuesday	3	10	17	24	31	
Wednesday	2	9	16	23	30		Wednesday		6	13	20	27		Wednesday	4	11	18	25		
Thursday	3	10	17	24	31		Thursday		7	14	21	28		Thursday	5	12	19	26		
Friday	4	11	18	25			Friday	1	8	15	22	29		Friday	6	13	20	27		
Saturday	5	12	19	26			Saturday	2	9	16	23	30		Saturday	7	14	21	28		

PUBLIC HOLIDAYS	England and Wales	Scotland	Northern Ireland
New Year	1 January†	1, 2† January	1 January†
St Patrick's Day	—	—	18 March
*Good Friday	19 April	19 April	19 April
Easter Monday	22 April	—	22 April
Early May	6 May†	6 May	6 May†
Spring	27 May	27 May†	27 May
Battle of the Boyne	—	—	12 July‡
Summer	26 August	5 August	26 August
St Andrew's Day	—	2 December§	—
*Christmas	25, 26 December	25†, 26 December	25, 26 December

* In England, Wales and Northern Ireland, Christmas Day and Good Friday are common law holidays

† Subject to royal proclamation

‡ Subject to proclamation by the Secretary of State for Northern Ireland

§ The St Andrew's Day Holiday (Scotland) Bill was approved by parliament on 29 November 2006; it does not oblige employers to change their existing pattern of holidays but provides the legal framework in which the St Andrew's Day bank holiday could be substituted for an existing local holiday from another date in the year

Note: In the Channel Islands, Liberation Day is a bank and public holiday

2020

JANUARY
Sunday   5 12 19 26
Monday   6 13 20 27
Tuesday   7 14 21 28
Wednesday 1 8 15 22 29
Thursday   2 9 16 23 30
Friday   3 10 17 24 31
Saturday   4 11 18 25

FEBRUARY
Sunday   2 9 16 23
Monday   3 10 17 24
Tuesday   4 11 18 25
Wednesday   5 12 19 26
Thursday   6 13 20 27
Friday   7 14 21 28
Saturday   1 8 15 22 29

MARCH
Sunday   1 8 15 22 29
Monday   2 9 16 23 30
Tuesday   3 10 17 24 31
Wednesday 4 11 18 25
Thursday   5 12 19 26
Friday   6 13 20 27
Saturday   7 14 21 28

APRIL
Sunday   5 12 19 26
Monday   6 13 20 27
Tuesday   7 14 21 28
Wednesday 1 8 15 22 29
Thursday   2 9 16 23 30
Friday   3 10 17 24
Saturday   4 11 18 25

MAY
Sunday   3 10 17 24 31
Monday   4 11 18 25
Tuesday   5 12 19 26
Wednesday   6 13 20 27
Thursday   7 14 21 28
Friday   1 8 15 22 29
Saturday   2 9 16 23 30

JUNE
Sunday   7 14 21 28
Monday   1 8 15 22 29
Tuesday   2 9 16 23 30
Wednesday 3 10 17 24
Thursday   4 11 18 25
Friday   5 12 19 26
Saturday   6 13 20 27

JULY
Sunday   5 12 19 26
Monday   6 13 20 27
Tuesday   7 14 21 28
Wednesday 1 8 15 22 29
Thursday   2 9 16 23 30
Friday   3 10 17 24 31
Saturday   4 11 18 25

AUGUST
Sunday   2 9 16 23 30
Monday   3 10 17 24 31
Tuesday   4 11 18 25
Wednesday   5 12 19 26
Thursday   6 13 20 27
Friday   7 14 21 28
Saturday   1 8 15 22 29

SEPTEMBER
Sunday   6 13 20 27
Monday   7 14 21 28
Tuesday   1 8 15 22 29
Wednesday 2 9 16 23 30
Thursday   3 10 17 24
Friday   4 11 18 25
Saturday   5 12 19 26

OCTOBER
Sunday   4 11 18 25
Monday   5 12 19 26
Tuesday   6 13 20 27
Wednesday   7 14 21 28
Thursday   1 8 15 22 29
Friday   2 9 16 23 30
Saturday   3 10 17 24 31

NOVEMBER
Sunday   1 8 15 22 29
Monday   2 9 16 23 30
Tuesday   3 10 17 24
Wednesday 4 11 18 25
Thursday   5 12 19 26
Friday   6 13 20 27
Saturday   7 14 21 28

DECEMBER
Sunday   6 13 20 27
Monday   7 14 21 28
Tuesday   1 8 15 22 29
Wednesday 2 9 16 23 30
Thursday   3 10 17 24 31
Friday   4 11 18 25
Saturday   5 12 19 26

PUBLIC HOLIDAYS	England and Wales	Scotland	Northern Ireland
New Year	1 January†	1, 2† January	1 January†
St Patrick's Day	—	—	17 March
*Good Friday	10 April	10 April	10 April
Easter Monday	13 April	—	13 April
Early May	4 May†	4 May	4 May†
Spring	25 May	25 May†	25 May
Battle of the Boyne	—	—	13 July‡
Summer	31 August	3 August	31 August
St Andrew's Day	—	30 November§	—
*Christmas	25, 28 December	25†, 28 December	25, 28 December

* In England, Wales and Northern Ireland, Christmas Day and Good Friday are common law holidays
† Subject to royal proclamation
‡ Subject to proclamation by the Secretary of State for Northern Ireland
§ The St Andrew's Day Holiday (Scotland) Bill was approved by parliament on 29 November 2006; it does not oblige employers to change their existing pattern of holidays but provides the legal framework in which the St Andrew's Day bank holiday could be substituted for an existing local holiday from another date in the year
Note: In the Channel Islands, Liberation Day is a bank and public holiday

FORTHCOMING EVENTS

* Provisional dates

JANUARY 2019

11–20	London Short Film Festival
15–17	UK Open Dance Championships, Bournemouth
16–20	London Art Fair, Business Design Centre
17–3 Feb	Celtic Connections Music Festival, Glasgow
26–28	RSPB Big Garden Birdwatch

FEBRUARY

2	World Wetlands Day
6–24	Leicester Comedy Festival
10	British Academy Film Awards, Royal Opera House, London
24	Academy Awards, Los Angeles

MARCH

3	World Wildlife Day
7	World Book Day
7–10	Crufts Dog Show, NEC, Birmingham
8	International Women's Day
8–13	Belfast Children's Festival
*17	St Patrick's Day Parade, Piccadilly, London
20–26	BADA Antiques and Fine Art Fair, Duke of York Square, London
21	World Poetry Day
22–7 Apr	Ideal Home Show, Olympia, London
30–7 Apr	Oxford Literary Festival

APRIL

12–14	London Book Fair, Olympia, London
22	Earth Day
28–5 May	Stratford-upon-Avon Literary Festival

MAY

17–26	Bath Festival
18 May–25 Aug	Glyndebourne Festival
21–25	RHS Chelsea Flower Show, Royal Hospital, London
23–2 Jun	Hay Festival of Literature and the Arts, Hay-on-Wye

JUNE

1	Strawberry Fair, Cambridge
5–9	RHS Chatsworth Flower Show, Derbyshire
8	Trooping the Colour, Horse Guards Parade, London
13–16	Isle of Wight Festival
20–23	Royal Highland Show, Edinburgh
26–30	Glastonbury Festival of Contemporary Performing Arts, Somerset

JULY

2–7	RHS Hampton Court Palace Flower Show, Surrey
5–14	Cheltenham Music Festival
6	Pride Parade, London
*12–7 Sep	BBC Promenade Concerts, Royal Albert Hall, London
17–21	RHS Flower Show, Tatton Park, Cheshire
20–27	The Welsh Proms, St David's Hall, Cardiff
25–28	WOMAD Festival, Charlton Park, Wiltshire
26–3 Aug	Three Choirs Festival, Gloucester

AUGUST

1–4	Cambridge Folk Festival
2–4	Brighton Pride, Brighton and Hove
2–10	National Eisteddfod of Wales, Conwy County
2–24	Edinburgh Military Tattoo, Edinburgh Castle
2–26	Edinburgh International Festival
*24–26	Notting Hill Carnival, London
*30–4 Nov	Blackpool Illuminations, Blackpool Promenade

SEPTEMBER

7	Braemar Royal Highland Gathering, Aberdeenshire
8	International Literacy Day
*8–11	TUC Annual Congress
14–17	Liberal Democrat Party Conference
Sep–Oct	Labour Party Conference
Sep–Oct	Conservative Party Conference

OCTOBER

Early Oct	Frieze Art Fair, Regent's Park, London
Mid Oct	Booker Prize Awards
Mid Oct	BFI London Film Festival

NOVEMBER

9 Nov	Lord Mayor's Procession and Show, City of London
Mid Nov	CBI Annual Conference

SPORTS EVENTS

JANUARY 2019

5–13	Darts: BDO World Darts Championship, Lakeside
10–27	Bowls: World Indoor Bowls Championships, Hopton on Sea
13–20	Snooker: Masters, Alexandra Palace, London
14–27	Tennis: Australian Open, Melbourne, Australia

FEBRUARY

1–16 Mar	Rugby Union: Six Nations Championship, Europe
3	American Football: Super Bowl 53, Atlanta, Georgia, USA
12–17	Squash: British National Championships, Nottingham
24	Football: EFL Cup Final, Wembley Stadium, London
27–3 Mar	Cycling: UCI Track Cycling World Championships, Pruszków, Poland

MARCH
28–29 Sep   Baseball: Major League Baseball Season

APRIL
4–6   Horse Racing: Grand National, Aintree, Liverpool
7   Rowing: The Boat Race, Putney to Mortlake, London
11–14   Golf: Masters, Augusta, Georgia, USA
20–6 May   Snooker: World Championship, Crucible Theatre, Sheffield
21–28   Table Tennis: World Championships, Budapest, Hungary
28   Athletics: London Marathon

MAY
1–5   Equestrian: Badminton Horse Trials, Badminton
3–4   Horse Racing: Kentucky Derby, Louisville, Kentucky, USA
8–12   Equestrian: Royal Windsor Horse Show, Home Park, Windsor
10   Rugby Union: European Rugby Challenge Cup Final, St James's Park, Newcastle
11   Rugby Union: European Rugby Champions Cup Final, St James's Park, Newcastle
18   Football: FA Cup Final, Wembley Stadium, London
25   Football: Scottish Cup Final, Hampden Park, Glasgow
26   Motor Racing: Indianapolis 500, Indiana, USA
26–9 Jun   Tennis: French Open, Paris, France
29   Football: UEFA Europa League Final, Baku, Azerbaijan
30–14 July   Cricket: World Cup, England and Wales

JUNE
1   Football: UEFA Champions League Final, Estadio Metropolitano, Madrid, Spain
1   Horse Racing: The Derby, Epsom Downs
7–7 July   Football: FIFA Women's World Cup, France
13–16   Golf: US Open, Pebble Beach, Florida, USA
18–22   Horse Racing: Royal Ascot

JULY
1–14   Tennis: Wimbledon Championships, All England Lawn Tennis Club, London
3–7   Rowing: Henley Royal Regatta, Henley-on-Thames
6–28   Cycling: Tour de France
12–21   Netball: Netball World Cup, Liverpool
12–28   Aquatics: World Championships, Gwangju, South Korea
15–23   Fencing: World Championships, Budapest, Hungary
18–21   Golf: Open Championship, Royal Portrush, Northern Ireland
26–27   Horse Racing: King George VI and Queen Elizabeth Diamond Stakes, Ascot

AUGUST
1–16 Sep   Cricket: Ashes Test series, England vs Australia

9–25   Swimming: World Championships, Gwangju, South Korea
14   Football: UEFA Super Cup final, Istanbul, Turkey
15–18   Golf: US PGA Championship, Bethpage State Park, New York, USA
25–1 Sep   Rowing: World Championships, Linz Ottensheim, Austria
26–9 Sep   Tennis: US Open, New York

SEPTEMBER
5–8   Equestrian: Burghley Horse Trials, Stamford, Lincolnshire
Early Sep   Horse Racing: St Leger, Doncaster
Early Sep–Late Dec   American Football: NFL Season
8   Athletics: Great North Run, Newcastle
20–2 Nov   Rugby Union: Rugby World Cup, Japan
28–6 Oct   Athletics: IAAF World Championships, Qatar

OCTOBER
Late Oct–Early Nov   Baseball: World Series

NOVEMBER
3   Athletics: New York City Marathon, New York, USA
11–17   Tennis: ATP World Tour Finals, O2 Arena, London
18–24   Tennis: Davis Cup Finals, Madrid, Spain

DECEMBER
9–15   Golf: Presidents Cup, Melbourne, Australia

CENTENARIES

2018

1518
29 Sep — Tintoretto, Italian painter, born
3 Oct — Cardinal Wolsey's Treaty of London temporarily assured peace in Europe

1618
20 Feb — Philip William, Prince of Orange, died
23 May — The Thirty Years War began, initiated by the Second Defenestration of Prague
29 Oct — Sir Walter Raleigh, English explorer, writer and courtier, executed on charges of treason

1718
7 May — The city of New Orleans was founded by Jean-Baptiste Le Moyne de Bienville
5 Jun — Thomas Chippendale, English furniture maker, born
18 Nov — Voltaire's first play, *Oedipe,* premiered in Paris
22 Nov — Edward Teach, English pirate known as 'Blackbeard', died
17 Dec — France, Britain, the Dutch Republic and the Holy Roman Empire declared war on Spain (War of the Quadruple Alliance 1718–20)

1818
11 Jan — Percy Bysshe Shelley's poem 'Ozymandias' was published under a pseudonym in *The Examiner*
12 Feb — Chile proclaimed independence from the Spanish Empire
14 Feb — Adopted birthday of Frederick Douglass, African American abolitionist author and statesman
11 Mar — Mary Shelley's novel *Frankenstein* was published anonymously
8 Apr — King Christian IX of Denmark, born
5 May — Karl Marx, German political philosopher, born
30 Jul — Emily Brontë, English novelist and author of *Wuthering Heights,* born
24 Dec — The Christmas Carol 'Silent Night' (*'Stille Nacht'*) was performed for the first time in Austria

1918
25 Jan — The Ukranian People's Republic declared independence from Russia
1 Feb — Muriel Spark, Scottish author, born
6 Feb — The Representation of the People Act gave most UK women the vote
6 Feb — Gustav Klimt, Austrian painter, died
3 Mar — The Treaty of Brest-Litovsk was signed, ending Russian involvement in the First World War
25 Mar — Claude Debussy, French composer, died
1 Apr — The Royal Air Force was formed
8 Apr — Betty Ford, US First Lady, born
16 Apr — Spike Milligan, comedian, writer and actor, born
21 Apr — Manfred von Richthofen, German fighter pilot known as 'the Red Baron', died in combat
17 Jul — Tsar Nicholas II and his family were executed at Yekaterinburg, ending the Romanov dynasty
18 Jul — Nelson Mandela, South African president, born
29 Sep — Allied forces breached the German Hindenburg Line
17 Oct — Rita Hayworth, American actor, born
3 Nov — Poland declared independence from Russia
11 Nov — An armistice between the Allies and Germany was signed at Compiègne, France, ending the First World War
13 Nov — Allied occupation of Constantinople began
11 Dec — Aleksandr Solzhenitsyn, Russian writer, born
28 Dec — David Lloyd George's coalition government won the UK general election, while Sinn Fein claimed a landslide victory in Ireland

2019

1519
13 Mar — Conquistador Hernán Cortés landed in Mexico
2 May — Leonardo da Vinci, Italian painter, sculptor, architect and engineer, died
28 Jun — Charles V became Holy Roman Emperor
30 Nov — Michael Wolgemut, German painter, died

1619
7 Jan — Nicholas Hilliard, painter, died
18 May — Hugo de Groot was given life imprisonment
30 Jul — First elected legislative assembly in the New World convened in Jamestown, Virginia
5 Nov — Philips Koninck, Dutch painter, born
10 Nov — Rene Descartes had dreams that inspired *Meditations on First Philosophy*

1719
23 Jan — The principality of Liechtenstein was established
25 Apr — Daniel Defoe published *Robinson Crusoe*
17 Jun — Joseph Addison, essayist, poet and dramatist, died
20 Aug — Christian Mayer, astronomer, born
19 Sep — Jan Weenix, Dutch painter, buried
11 Dec — A sighting of aurora borealis was recorded for the first time

1819
19 Feb — William Smith discovered the South Shetland Islands in Antarctica
22 Feb — The USA purchased Florida from Spain
2 Mar — USA passed its first federal legislation on immigration
11 Mar — Sir Henry Tate, founder of the Tate Gallery, born
22 May — SS *Savannah* departed on the first steam propelled journey across the Atlantic Ocean
24 May — Queen Victoria, born
31 May — Walt Whitman, American poet, born
19 Aug — James Watt, developer of the steam engine, died
22 Nov — George Eliot, novelist, born
14 Dec — Alabama became the 22nd state of the Union

1919
1 Jan — Jerome Salinger, novelist, born
6 Jan — Theodore Roosevelt, 26th US President, died
21 Jan — Sinn Féin created its own parliament
25 Jan — The League of Nations was established
5 Feb — The American film and television studio United Artists was created
19 Feb — W. E. B. Du Bois convened the first Pan-African Congress in Paris
26 Feb — The United States Congress passed the act that established the Grand Canyon National Park
14 Mar — Max Brand published his first novel, *The Untamed*
17 Mar — Nat King Cole, American jazz pianist and vocalist, born
23 Mar — Benito Mussolini formed Fasci Italiani di Combattimento
13 Apr — The Amritsar massacre took place

7 May	Eva Perón, First Lady of Argentina (1946–52), born
29 May	Arthur Eddington validated Albert Einstein's theory of general relativity
28 Jun	The First World War officially ended with the signing of the Treaty of Versailles
19 Jul	The Cenotaph war monument, designed by Edwin Lutyens, was unveiled in Whitehall
20 Jul	Edmund Hillary, explorer and mountaineer, born
11 Aug	Germany established parliamentary democracy
19 Aug	Adolf Hitler joined the German Workers' Party
12 Sep	Afghanistan became independent
22 Oct	Doris Lessing, Nobel Prize winning author, born
3 Dec	Pierre-Auguste Renoir, painter, died

2020

1520

7 Jun	A summit between England and France began in the Field of the Cloth of Gold
30 Sep	Suleiman the Magnificent succeeded his father Selim I as Ottoman Sultan
21 Oct	The islands of St Pierre and Miquelon were discovered by explorer Joao Alvares Fagundes
28 Nov	Ferdinand Magellan and his fleet became the first Europeans to sail into the Pacific Ocean

1620

24 Apr	John Graunt, statistician, born
16 May	William Adams, navigator, died
7 Aug	Johannes Kepler's mother was arrested for witchcraft
20 Oct	Aelbert Cuyp, Dutch painter, baptised
8 Nov	Catholic forces were victorious in the Battle of White Mountain (Thirty Years' War 1618–48)
11 Nov	The *Mayflower* anchored at Cape Cod
31 Oct	John Evelyn, writer, born

1720

27 Jan	Samuel Foote, actor and playwright, baptised
10 Feb	Edmond Halley was appointed the second Astronomer Royal at the Greenwich Observatory
17 Feb	The War of the Quadruple Alliance ended with the Treaty of The Hague
6 Mar	Pieter van Bloemen, Flemish painter, died
6 Apr	The South Sea bill was passed in the House of Lords
25 May	The ship *Grand-Saint-Antoine* arrived in Marseille, bringing Europe's last major plague outbreak, which killed around 100,000
5 Aug	Anne Finch, Countess of Winchilsea, poet, died
15 Nov	Female pirates Anne Bonny and Mary Read are captured in Jamaica along with Captain 'Calico Jack' Rackham and his crew
29 Dec	Theatre Royal Haymarket, then called the 'Hay Market', opens with the play *La Fille à la Mode*

1820

17 Jan	Anne Brontë, novelist and poet, born
29 Jan	King George IV ascended to the throne on the death of his father George III, ending the English Regency
30 Jan	Captain Edward Bransfield became the first person to sight the Antarctic mainland
28 Feb	John Tenniel, illustrator, born

10 Mar	The Royal Astronomical Society was founded in London
15 Mar	Maine became the 23rd state of the Union, following the Missouri Compromise
11 May	HMS *Beagle,* the ship that carried Charles Darwin on his scientific voyage, was launched
12 May	Florence Nightingale, social reformer and statistician, born
19 Jun	Joseph Banks, naturalist and botanist
26 Jul	Union Bridge, crossing the River Tweed between England and Scotland, opened
1 Aug	The second half of the Regent's Canal in London, from Camden to Limehouse, was completed
3 Sep	Benjamin Henry Latrobe, architect, died
28 Nov	Friedrich Engels, German political philosopher, born

1920

2 Jan	Isaac Asimov, American writer and biochemist, born
6 Jan	John Maynard Smith, biologist, born
10 Jan	The Covenant of the League of Nations came into force
16 Jan	Alcohol Prohibition came into effect nationwide in the USA
23 Jan	Queen Wilhelmina of the Netherlands refused to extradite former German Kaiser Wilhelm II
24 Jan	Amedeo Modigliani, Italian painter and sculptor, died
2 Feb	Soviet Russia recognised the independence of the Republic of Estonia in the Treaty of Tartu
3 Feb	Henry Heimlich, American physician, born
14 Mar	Dorothy Tyler, Olympic high jumper, born
5 Apr	Arthur Hailey, British-Canadian novelist, born
14 Apr	John George Bartholomew, cartographer, died
9 May	Richard Adams, novelist, born
16 May	Joan of Arc (Jeanne d'Arc) was canonised by Pope Benedict XV
18 May	John Paul II, Pope of the Catholic Church (1978–2005), born
21 May	Mexican President Venustiano Carranza was executed by army generals
4 Jun	The Allied Powers defined the borders of the Kingdom of Hungary at the Treaty of Trianon
12 Jul	Soviet Russia recognised the sovereignty of Lithuania
10 Aug	The Treaty of Sèvres abolished the Ottoman Empire
11 Aug	Soviet Russia recognised Latvia's independence in the Treaty of Riga
14 Aug	The Games of the VII Olympiad opened in Antwerp, Belgium
16 Aug	Charles Bukowski, American writer, born
18 Aug	The 19th Amendment to the US Constitution was ratified, granting American women the right to vote
1 Sep	Greater Lebanon was declared a state under the French Mandate for Syria and the Lebanon
29 Sep	Peter D. Mitchell, Nobel Prize winning biochemist, born
2 Nov	Warren G. Harding was elected President of the USA
10 Dec	The Nobel Peace Prize was awarded to US president Woodrow Wilson

THE UNITED KINGDOM

THE UK IN FIGURES

The United Kingdom comprises Great Britain (England, Wales and Scotland) and Northern Ireland. The Isle of Man and the Channel Islands are Crown dependencies with their own legislative systems and are not part of the UK.

ABBREVIATIONS
ONS   Office for National Statistics
NISRA   Northern Ireland Statistics and Research Agency

All data is for the UK unless otherwise stated.

AREA OF THE UNITED KINGDOM

	Sq. km	Sq. miles
United Kingdom	243,122	93,870
England	130,280	50,301
Wales	20,733	8,005
Scotland	77,958	30,100
Northern Ireland	14,150	5,463

Source: ONS (Crown copyright)

POPULATION

The first official census of population in England, Wales and Scotland was taken in 1801 and a census has been taken every ten years since, except in 1941 when there was no census because of the Second World War. The last official census in the UK was taken on 27 March 2011.

The first official census of population in Ireland was taken in 1841. However, all figures given below refer only to the area which is now Northern Ireland. Figures for Northern Ireland in 1921 and 1931 are estimates based on the censuses taken in 1926 and 1937 respectively.

Estimates of the population of England before 1801, calculated from the number of baptisms, burials and marriages, are:

1570	4,160,221	1670	5,773,646
1600	4,811,718	1700	6,045,008
1630	5,600,517	1750	6,517,035

Further details are available on the ONS website (W www.ons.gov.uk).

CENSUS RESULTS *(THOUSANDS)*

	United Kingdom			England and Wales			Scotland			Northern Ireland		
	Total	Male	Female	Total	Male	Female	Total	Male	Female	Total	Male	Female
1801	–	–	–	8,893	4,255	4,638	1,608	739	869	–	–	–
1811	13,368	6,368	7,000	10,165	4,874	5,291	1,806	826	980	–	–	–
1821	15,472	7,498	7,974	12,000	5,850	6,150	2,092	983	1,109	–	–	–
1831	17,835	8,647	9,188	13,897	6,771	7,126	2,364	1,114	1,250	–	–	–
1841	20,183	9,819	10,364	15,914	7,778	8,137	2,620	1,242	1,378	1,649	800	849
1851	22,259	10,855	11,404	17,928	8,781	9,146	2,889	1,376	1,513	1,443	698	745
1861	24,525	11,894	12,631	20,066	9,776	10,290	3,062	1,450	1,612	1,396	668	728
1871	27,431	13,309	14,122	22,712	11,059	11,653	3,360	1,603	1,757	1,359	647	712
1881	31,015	15,060	15,955	25,974	12,640	13,335	3,736	1,799	1,936	1,305	621	684
1891	34,264	16,593	17,671	29,003	14,060	14,942	4,026	1,943	2,083	1,236	590	646
1901	38,237	18,492	19,745	32,528	15,729	16,799	4,472	2,174	2,298	1,237	590	647
1911	42,082	20,357	21,725	36,070	17,446	18,625	4,761	2,309	2,452	1,251	603	648
1921	44,027	21,033	22,994	37,887	18,075	19,811	4,882	2,348	2,535	1,258	610	648
1931	46,038	22,060	23,978	39,952	19,133	20,819	4,843	2,326	2,517	1,243	601	642
1951	50,225	24,118	26,107	43,758	21,016	22,742	5,096	2,434	2,662	1,371	668	703
1961	52,709	25,481	27,228	46,105	22,304	23,801	5,179	2,483	2,697	1,425	694	731
1971	55,515	26,952	28,562	48,750	23,683	25,067	5,229	2,515	2,714	1,536	755	781
1981	55,848	27,104	28,742	49,155	23,873	25,281	5,131	2,466	2,664	*1,533	750	783
1991	56,467	27,344	29,123	49,890	24,182	25,707	4,999	2,392	2,607	1,578	769	809
2001	58,789	28,581	30,208	52,042	25,327	26,715	5,062	2,432	2,630	1,685	821	864
2011	63,182	31,028	32,153	56,076	27,574	28,502	5,295	2,567	2,728	1,810	887	923

* Figure includes 44,500 non-enumerated persons

ISLANDS

	Isle of Man			Jersey			Guernsey		
	Total	Male	Female	Total	Male	Female	Total	Male	Female
1901	54,752	25,496	29,256	52,576	23,940	28,636	40,446	19,652	20,794
1921	60,284	27,329	32,955	49,701	22,438	27,263	38,315	18,246	20,069
1951	55,123	25,749	29,464	57,296	27,282	30,014	43,652	21,221	22,431
1971	56,289	26,461	29,828	72,532	35,423	37,109	51,458	24,792	26,666
1991	69,788	33,693	36,095	84,082	40,862	43,220	58,867	28,297	30,570
2001	76,315	37,372	38,943	87,186	42,485	44,701	59,807	29,138	30,669
2006	80,058	39,523	40,535	–	–	–	–	–	–
2011	84,497	41,971	42,526	97,857	48,296	49,561	62,915	31,025	31,890

Source: Guernsey Annual Publication Bulletin, Isle of Man Government, States of Jersey Statistics Unit

RESIDENT POPULATION

ACTUAL AND PROJECTED BY COUNTRY
people, thousands

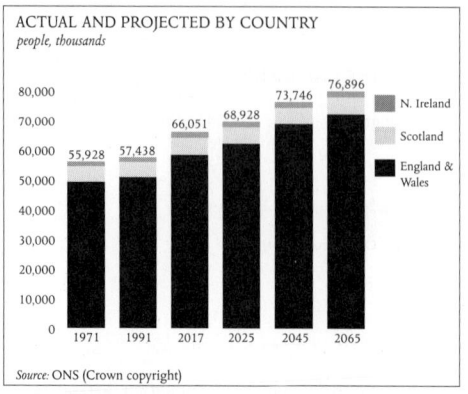

Source: ONS (Crown copyright)

PROJECTED AGE DISTRIBUTION, 2017 AND 2065
percentage

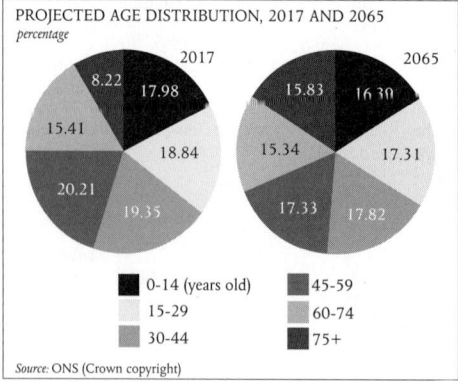

■ 0-14 (years old)	■ 45-59
15-29	■ 60-74
■ 30-44	■ 75+

Source: ONS (Crown copyright)

NON-UK BORN RESIDENTS BY COUNTRY OF BIRTH
thousands

	2004	2017
Poland	94	922
India	505	829
Pakistan	285	522
Romania	–	390
Republic of Ireland	453	390
Germany	276	318
Bangladesh	228	263
Italy	–	232
South Africa	181	228
China	152	216

Source: ONS (Crown Copyright)

BY AGE AND SEX (UK), 2017
people, thousands

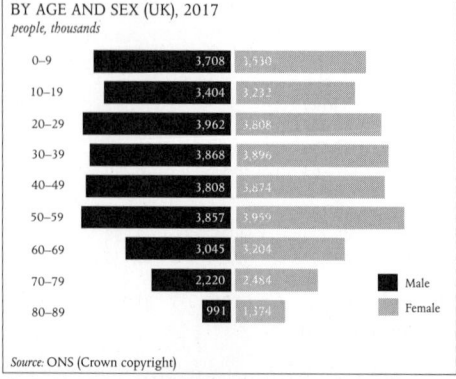

■ Male
Female

Source: ONS (Crown copyright)

ASYLUM

NATIONALITIES APPLYING FOR UK ASYLUM
year ending in March

Top 5 Nationalities	2016	2017
1) Iran	4,192	2,570
2) Pakistan	2,857	2,495
3) Iraq	2,666	1,712
4) Afghanistan	2,341	1,326
5) Bangladesh	1,939	1,712

Source: Home Office, National Statistics: Asylum

BIRTHS

	Live births 2017	Birth rate* 2017
United Kingdom†	756,107	10.7
England and Wales	679,106	9.3
Scotland	52,911	9.8
Northern Ireland†	24,090	13.0

* Live births per 1,000 population
† 2016 figures for Northern Ireland
Source: General Register Office for Scotland, NISRA, ONS (Crown copyright)

FERTILITY RATES
Total fertility rate is the average number of children which would be born to a woman if she experienced the age-specific fertility rates of the period in question throughout her child-bearing life span. The figures for the years 1960–2 are estimates.

	1960–2	2000	2016
United Kingdom	3.07	1.62	1.76
England and Wales	2.77	1.65	1.80
Scotland	2.98	1.48	1.52
Northern Ireland	3.47	1.75	1.95

Source: General Register Office for Scotland, NISRA, ONS (Crown copyright)

MATERNITY RATES FOR ENGLAND AND WALES 2016

	All maternities*	Singleton	All multiple†	Twins	Triplets
All ages	688,262	677,311	10,951	10,786	160
>20	22,404	22,220	184	182	2
20–24	102,090	101,059	1,031	1,023	8
25–29	194,328	191,753	2,575	2,541	33
30–34	217,343	213,750	3,593	3,542	49
35–39	123,106	120,462	2,644	2,607	36
40–44	26,882	26,142	740	720	19
45+	2,109	1,925	184	171	13

* Includes stillbirths
† Total includes rates for twins, triplets, quads and above
Source: ONS (Crown copyright)

TOP TEN BABY NAMES (ENGLAND AND WALES)

	1914		2016	
	Girls	Boys	Girls	Boys
1	Mary	John	Olivia	Oliver
2	Margaret	William	Amelia	Harry
3	Doris	George	Emily	George
4	Dorothy	Thomas	Isla	Jack
5	Kathleen	James	Ava	Jacob
6	Florence	Arthur	Isabella	Noah
7	Elsie	Frederick	Lily	Charlie
8	Edith	Albert	Jessica	Muhammad
9	Elizabeth	Charles	Ella	Thomas
10	Winifred	Robert	Mia	Oscar

Source: ONS (Crown copyright)

LIVE BIRTHS (ENGLAND AND WALES)
by age of mother

Year	under 20	20-29	30-39	40+	All ages
1947	27,747	509,052	309,531	34,696	881,026
1957	41,228	442,219	218,883	21,051	723,381
1967	84,542	535,458	193,364	18,800	832,164
1977	54,447	382,460	126,334	5,988	569,259
1987	57,545	432,161	183,162	8,643	681,511
1997	46,372	321,381	262,428	12,914	643,095
2007	44,805	313,354	306,504	25,350	690,013
2017	20,358	287,534	341,901	29,313	679,106

Source: ONS (Crown copyright)

MARRIAGE AND DIVORCE

	Marriages 2016	Divorces 2016
England and Wales	*239,020	106,559
Scotland	†28,440	7,938
Northern Ireland	8,306	2,572

* 2015 figure
† 2017 figure
Source: NISRA, ONS (Crown copyright), Scottish Government

LEGAL ABORTIONS

	2005	2017
England and Wales	186,416	189,859
Scotland	12,665	12,212

Source: Department of Health, NHS Scotland

DEATHS

INFANT MORTALITY RATE 2016*
United Kingdom	4.3
England and Wales	3.8
Scotland	3.3
Northern Ireland	5.0

* Deaths of infants under one year of age per 1,000 live births
Source: NISRA, ONS (Crown copyright), Scottish Government

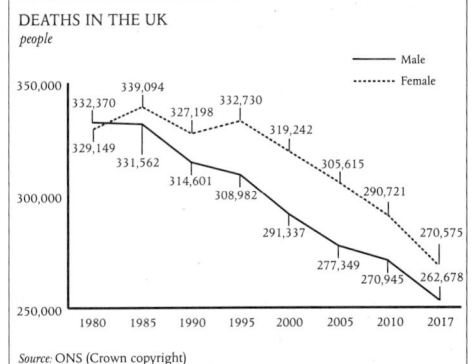

DEATHS IN THE UK
people
Source: ONS (Crown copyright)

EMPLOYMENT

MEDIAN FULL-TIME GROSS ANNUAL EARNINGS BY REGION (£)

Region	2005	2015
UK	22,888	27,645
England	23,280	27,872
North East	20,263	25,346
North West	21,777	25,681
Yorkshire and the Humber	21,506	25,180
East Midlands	21,494	25,003
West Midlands	21,447	25,779
East	22,883	27,299
London	29,882	35,333
South East	24,229	29,036
South West	21,279	25,982
Wales	20,634	24,733
Scotland	21,312	27,710
Northern Ireland	20,060	25,847

Source: ONS (Crown Copyright)

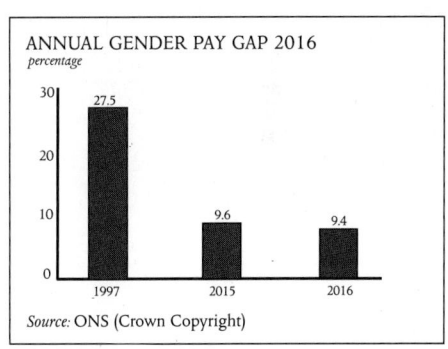

ANNUAL GENDER PAY GAP 2016
percentage
Source: ONS (Crown Copyright)

OVERSEAS VISITS TO THE UK

Year	Visits (thousands)	Spending (£m)
1980	12,419	2,961
1985	14,450	5,442
1990	18,017	7,748
1995	23,538	11,762
2000	25,207	12,806
2005	29,970	14,247
2010	29,804	16,714
2011	30,798	17,998
2012	31,085	18,640
2013	32,689	21,259
2014	34,380	21,851
2015	36,115	22,072
2016	37,610	22,544
2017	39,214	24,507

DEATHS BY CAUSE, 2017

	England and Wales	Scotland	N. Ireland*
Total deaths	533,253	57,883	15,433
Deaths from natural causes	512,027	54,731	14,764
Certain infectious and parasitic diseases	5,368	686	175
Intestinal infectious diseases	1,259	128	53
Respiratory and other tuberculosis	153	10	6
Meningococcal infection	49	1	1
Viral hepatitis	179	28	2
Human immunodeficiency virus (HIV)	162	6	1
Neoplasms	149,652	16,558	4,666
Malignant neoplasms	146,269	16,207	4,539
Malignant neoplasm of trachea, bronchus and lung	30,131	4,069	990
Malignant melanoma of skin	2,106	185	63
Malignant neoplasm of breast	10,219	954	293
Malignant neoplasm of cervix uteri	730	105	19
Malignant neoplasm of prostate	10,755	986	262
Leukaemia	4,315	387	139
Diseases of the blood and blood-forming organs and certain disorders involving the immune mechanism	1,099	98	39
Endocrine, nutritional and metabolic diseases	8,435	1,330	294
Diabetes mellitus	6,046	1,016	160
Mental and behavioural disorders	50,765	4,591	1,392
Vascular and unspecified dementia	49,057	4,161	1,267
Diseases of the nervous system	33,051	3,976	925
Meningitis (excluding meningococcal)	154	19	2
Alzheimer's disease	17,984	2,388	493
Diseases of the circulatory system	133,511	15,114	3,630
Ischaemic heart diseases	57,923	6,727	1,825
Cerebrovascular diseases	31,713	3,927	988
Diseases of the respiratory system	73,455	136	1,973
Influenza	454	1,735	10
Pneumonia	27,181	1,800	794
Bronchitis, emphysema and other chronic obstructive pulmonary diseases	28,597	3,449	819
Asthma	1,320	106	44
Diseases of the digestive system	25,627	3,134	776
Gastric and duodenal ulcer	1,866	121	28
Diseases of the liver	8,450	1,063	304
Diseases of the skin and subcutaneous tissue	2,132	188	24
Diseases of the musculo-skeletal system and connective tissue	3,751	388	120
Osteoporosis	810	70	13
Diseases of the genitourinary system	9,106	957	251
Complications of pregnancy, childbirth and the puerperium	26	5	2
Certain conditions originating in the perinatal period*	188	98	66
Congenital malformations, deformations and chromosomal abnormalities†	1,414	192	72
Symptoms, signs and abnormal findings not classified elsewhere	12,448	587	161
Senility	7,666	227	136
Sudden infant death syndrome	78	15	4
Deaths from external causes	21,226	3,152	773
Suicide and intentional self-harm	3,930	587	305
Assault	‡269	56	30

* 2016 data

† Excludes neonatal deaths (those at age under 28 days): for England and Wales neonatal deaths are included in the total number of deaths but excluded from the cause figures

‡ This will not be a true figure as registration of homicide and assault deaths in England and Wales is often delayed by adjourned inquests

Source: General Register Office for Scotland, NISRA, ONS (Crown copyright)

THE NATIONAL FLAG

The national flag of the United Kingdom is the Union Flag, generally known as the Union Jack.

The Union Flag is a combination of the cross of St George, patron saint of England, the cross of St Andrew, patron saint of Scotland and the cross of St Patrick, patron saint of Ireland.

Cross of St George: cross Gules in a field Argent (red cross on a white ground)

Cross of St Andrew: saltire Argent in a field Azure (white diagonal cross on a blue ground)

Cross of St Patrick: saltire Gules in a field Argent (red diagonal cross on a white ground)

A flag combining the cross of St George and the cross of St Andrew was first introduced by royal decree in 1606 following the conjoining of the English and Scottish crowns in 1603. In 1707 this flag became the flag of Great Britain after the parliaments of the two kingdoms were united. The cross of St Patrick was added in 1801 after the union of Great Britain and Ireland.

FLYING THE UNION FLAG

The correct orientation of the Union Flag when flying is with the broader diagonal band of white uppermost in the hoist (ie near the pole) and the narrower diagonal band of white uppermost in the fly (ie furthest from the pole).

The flying of the Union Flag on government buildings is decided by the Department for Digital Culture, Media and Sport (DCMS) at the Queen's command. There is no formal definition of a government building but it is generally accepted to mean a building owned or used by the Crown and/or predominantly occupied or used by civil servants or the Armed Forces.

The Scottish or Welsh governments are responsible for drawing up their own flag-flying guidance for their buildings. In Northern Ireland, the flying of flags is constrained by The Flags Regulations (Northern Ireland) 2000 and the Police Emblems and Flag Regulations (Northern Ireland) 2002. Individuals, local authorities and other organisations may fly the Union Flag whenever they wish, subject to compliance with any local planning requirement.

FLAGS AT HALF-MAST

Flags are flown at half-mast (ie two-thirds up between the top and bottom of the flagstaff) on the following occasions:
- from the announcement of the death of the sovereign until the funeral
- the death or funeral of a member of the royal family*
- the funerals of foreign rulers*
- the funerals of prime ministers and ex-prime ministers of the UK*
- the funerals of first ministers and ex-first ministers of Scotland, Wales and Northern Ireland (unless otherwise commanded by the sovereign, this only applies to flags in their respective countries)*
- other occasions by special command from the Queen

* By special command from the Queen in each case

DAYS FOR FLYING FLAGS

On 25 March 2008 the DCMS announced that UK government departments in England, Scotland and Wales may fly the Union Flag on their buildings whenever they choose and not just on the designated days listed below. In addition, on the patron saints' days of Scotland and Wales, the appropriate national flag may be flown alongside the Union Flag on UK government buildings in the wider Whitehall area. When flying on designated days flags are hoisted from 8am to sunset.

Duchess of Cambridge's birthday	9 Jan
Countess of Wessex's birthday	20 Jan
Accession of the Queen	6 Feb
Duke of York's birthday	19 Feb
St David's Day (in Wales only)*	1 Mar
Earl of Wessex's birthday	10 Mar
Commonwealth Day (2019)	11 Mar
St Patrick's Day (in Northern Ireland only)†	17 Mar
The Queen's birthday	21 Apr
St George's Day (in England only)*	23 Apr
Europe Day†	9 May
Coronation Day	2 Jun
The Queen's official birthday (2019)	8 Jun
Duke of Edinburgh's birthday	10 Jun
Duke of Cambridge's birthday	21 June
Duchess of Cornwall's birthday	17 Jul
Princess Royal's birthday	15 Aug
Remembrance Day (2019)	10 Nov
Prince of Wales' birthday	14 Nov
Wedding Day of the Queen	20 Nov
St Andrew's Day (in Scotland only)*	30 Nov

Opening of parliament by the Queen‡
Prorogation of parliament by the Queen‡

* The appropriate national flag, or the European flag, may be flown in addition to the Union Flag (where there are two or more flagpoles), but not in a superior position
† Only the Union Flag should be flown
‡ Only in the Greater London area, whether or not the Queen performs the ceremony in person

THE ROYAL STANDARD

The Royal Standard comprises four quarterings – two for England (three lions passant), one for Scotland* (a lion rampant) and one for Ireland (a harp).

The Royal Standard is flown when the Queen is in residence at a royal palace, on transport being used by the Queen for official journeys and from Victoria Tower when the Queen attends parliament. It may also be flown on any building (excluding ecclesiastical buildings) during a visit by the Queen. If the Queen is to be present in a building, advice on flag flying can be obtained from the DCMS.

The Royal Standard is never flown at half-mast, even after the death of the sovereign, as the new monarch immediately succeeds to the throne.

* In Scotland a version with two Scottish quarterings is used

THE ROYAL FAMILY

THE SOVEREIGN

ELIZABETH II, by the Grace of God, of the United Kingdom of Great Britain and Northern Ireland and of her other Realms and Territories Queen, Head of the Commonwealth, Defender of the Faith
Her Majesty Elizabeth Alexandra Mary of Windsor, elder daughter of King George VI and of HM Queen Elizabeth the Queen Mother
Born 21 April 1926, at 17 Bruton Street, London W1
Ascended the throne 6 February 1952
Crowned 2 June 1953, at Westminster Abbey
Married 20 November 1947, in Westminster Abbey, HRH the Prince Philip, Duke of Edinburgh
Official residences Buckingham Palace, London SW1A 1AA; Windsor Castle, Berks; Palace of Holyroodhouse, Edinburgh
Private residences Sandringham, Norfolk; Balmoral Castle, Aberdeenshire

HUSBAND OF THE QUEEN

HRH THE PRINCE PHILIP, DUKE OF EDINBURGH, KG, KT, OM, GCVO, GBE, Royal Victorian Chain, AK, QSO, PC, Ranger of Windsor Park
Born 10 June 1921, son of Prince and Princess Andrew of Greece and Denmark, naturalised a British subject 1947, created Duke of Edinburgh, Earl of Merioneth and Baron Greenwich 1947

CHILDREN OF THE QUEEN

HRH THE PRINCE OF WALES (Prince Charles Philip Arthur George), KG, KT, GCB, OM and Great Master of the Order of the Bath, AK, QSO, PC, ADC(P)
Born 14 November 1948, created Prince of Wales and Earl of Chester 1958, succeeded as Duke of Cornwall, Duke of Rothesay, Earl of Carrick and Baron Renfrew, Lord of the Isles and Great Steward of Scotland 1952
Married (1) 29 July 1981 Lady Diana Frances Spencer (Diana, Princess of Wales) (1961–97), youngest daughter of the 8th Earl Spencer and the Hon. Mrs Shand Kydd), marriage dissolved 1996; (2) 9 April 2005 Mrs Camilla Rosemary Parker Bowles, now HRH the Duchess of Cornwall, GCVO, PC (*born* 17 July 1947, daughter of Major Bruce Shand and the Hon. Mrs Rosalind Shand)
Residences Clarence House, London SW1A 1BA; Highgrove, Doughton, Tetbury, Glos GL8 8TN; Birkhall, Ballater, Aberdeenshire
Issue
1. HRH the Duke of Cambridge (Prince William Arthur Philip Louis), KG, KT, PC *born* 21 June 1982, *created* Duke of Cambridge, Earl of Strathearn and Baron Carrickfergus 2011 *married* 29 April 2011 Catherine Elizabeth Middleton, now HRH the Duchess of Cambridge (*born* 9 January 1982, elder daughter of Michael and Carole Middleton), and has issue, HRH Prince George of Cambridge (Prince George Alexander Louis), *born* 22 July 2013; HRH Princess Charlotte of Cambridge (Princess Charlotte Elizabeth Diana), *born* 2 May 2015; HRH Prince Louis of Cambridge (Prince Louis Arthur Charles), *born* 23 April 2018 *Residence* Kensington Palace, London W8 4PU; Anmer Hall, Norfolk PE31 6RW
2. HRH the Duke of Sussex (Prince Henry Charles Albert David), KCVO *born* 15 September 1984, *created* Duke of Sussex, Earl of Dumbarton and Baron Kilkeel 2018 *married* 19 May 2018 (Rachel) Meghan Markle, now HRH the Duchess of Sussex (*born* 4 August 1981, daughter of Thomas Markle and Doria Ragland) *Residence* Nottingham Cottage, Kensington Palace, London W8 4PU

HRH THE PRINCESS ROYAL (Princess Anne Elizabeth Alice Louise), KG, KT, GCVO
Born 15 August 1950, declared the Princess Royal 1987
Married (1) 14 November 1973 Captain Mark Anthony Peter Phillips, CVO (*born* 22 September 1948); marriage dissolved 1992; (2) 12 December 1992 Vice-Adm. Sir Timothy James Hamilton Laurence, KCVO, CB, ADC (P) (*born* 1 March 1955)
Residence Gatcombe Park, Minchinhampton, Glos GL6 9AT
Issue
1. Peter Mark Andrew Phillips, *born* 15 November 1977, *married* 17 May 2008 Autumn Patricia Kelly, and has issue, Savannah Phillips, *born* 29 December 2010; Isla Elizabeth Phillips, *born* 29 March 2012
2. Zara Anne Elizabeth Tindall, MBE, *born* 15 May 1981, *married* 30 July 2011 Michael James Tindall, MBE, and has issue, Mia Grace Tindall, *born* 17 January 2014; Lena Elizabeth Tindall, *born* 18 June 2018

HRH THE DUKE OF YORK (Prince Andrew Albert Christian Edward), KG, GCVO, ADC(P)
Born 19 February 1960, created Duke of York, Earl of Inverness and Baron Killyleagh 1986
Married 23 July 1986 Sarah Margaret Ferguson, now Sarah, Duchess of York (*born* 15 October 1959, younger daughter of Major Ronald Ferguson and Mrs Hector Barrantes), marriage dissolved 1996
Residence Royal Lodge, Windsor Great Park, Berks
Issue
1. HRH Princess Beatrice of York (Princess Beatrice Elizabeth Mary), *born* 8 August 1988
2. HRH Princess Eugenie, Mrs Jack Brooksbank (Princess Eugenie Victoria Helena), *born* 23 March 1990, *married* 12 October 2018 Jack Brooksbank

HRH THE EARL OF WESSEX (Prince Edward Antony Richard Louis), KG, GCVO, ADC(P)
Born 10 March 1964, created Earl of Wessex, Viscount Severn 1999
Married 19 June 1999 Sophie Helen Rhys-Jones, now HRH the Countess of Wessex, GCVO (*born* 20 January 1965, daughter of Mr and Mrs Christopher Rhys-Jones)
Residence Bagshot Park, Bagshot, Surrey GU19 5HS
Issue
1. Lady Louise Mountbatten-Windsor (Louise Alice Elizabeth Mary Mountbatten-Windsor), *born* 8 November 2003
2. Viscount Severn (James Alexander Philip Theo Mountbatten-Windsor), *born* 17 December 2007

NEPHEW AND NIECE OF THE QUEEN

Children of HRH the Princess Margaret, Countess of Snowdon and the Earl of Snowdon (*see* House of Windsor):
EARL OF SNOWDON (DAVID ALBERT CHARLES ARMSTRONG-JONES), *born* 3 November 1961, *married* 8 October 1993 Hon. Serena Alleyne Stanhope, and has issue, Viscount Linley (Charles Patrick Inigo Armstrong-Jones), *born* 1 July 1999; Lady Margarita Armstrong-Jones (Margarita Elizabeth Alleyne Armstrong-Jones), *born* 14 May 2002
LADY SARAH CHATTO (Sarah Frances Elizabeth), *born* 1 May 1964, *married* 14 July 1994 Daniel Chatto, and has issue, Samuel David Benedict Chatto, *born* 28 July 1996; Arthur Robert Nathaniel Chatto, *born* 5 February 1999

COUSINS OF THE QUEEN

Child of HRH the Duke of Gloucester and HRH Princess Alice, Duchess of Gloucester (*see* House of Windsor):
HRH THE DUKE OF GLOUCESTER (Prince Richard Alexander Walter George), KG, GCVO, Grand Prior of the Order of St John of Jerusalem
Born 26 August 1944
Married 8 July 1972 Birgitte Eva van Deurs, now HRH the Duchess of Gloucester, GCVO (*born* 20 June 1946, daughter of Asger Henriksen and Vivian van Deurs)
Residence Kensington Palace, London W8 4PU
Issue
1. Earl of Ulster (Alexander Patrick Gregers Richard), *born* 24 October 1974 *married* 22 June 2002 Dr Claire Alexandra Booth, and has issue, Lord Culloden (Xan Richard Anders), *born* 12 March 2007; Lady Cosima Windsor (Cosima Rose Alexandra), *born* 20 May 2010
2. Lady Davina Lewis (Davina Elizabeth Alice Benedikte), *born* 19 November 1977 *married* 31 July 2004 Gary Christie Lewis, and has issue, Senna Kowhai Lewis, *born* 22 June 2010; Tane Mahuta Lewis, *born* 25 May 2012
3. Lady Rose Gilman (Rose Victoria Birgitte Louise), *born* 1 March 1980 *married* 19 July 2008 George Edward Gilman, and has issue, Lyla Beatrix Christabel Gilman, *born* 30 May 2010; Rufus Gilman, *born* 2 November 2012

Children of HRH the Duke of Kent and Princess Marina, Duchess of Kent (*see* House of Windsor):
HRH THE DUKE OF KENT (Prince Edward George Nicholas Paul Patrick), KG, GCMG, GCVO, ADC(P)
Born 9 October 1935
Married 8 June 1961 Katharine Lucy Mary Worsley, now HRH the Duchess of Kent, GCVO (*born* 22 February 1933, daughter of Sir William Worsley, Bt.)
Residence Wren House, Palace Green, London W8 4PY
Issue
1. Earl of St Andrews (George Philip Nicholas), *born* 26 June 1962, *married* 9 January 1988 Sylvana Tomaselli, and has issue, Lord Downpatrick (Edward Edmund Maximilian George), *born* 2 December 1988; Lady Marina-Charlotte Windsor (Marina-Charlotte Alexandra Katharine Helen), *born* 30 September 1992; Lady Amelia Windsor (Amelia Sophia Theodora Mary Margaret), *born* 24 August 1995
2. Lady Helen Taylor (Helen Marina Lucy), *born* 28 April 1964, *married* 18 July 1992 Timothy Verner Taylor, and has issue, Columbus George Donald Taylor, *born* 6 August 1994; Cassius Edward Taylor, *born* 26 December 1996; Eloise Olivia Katharine Taylor, *born* 3 March 2003; Estella Olga Elizabeth Taylor, *born* 21 December 2004
3. Lord Nicholas Windsor (Nicholas Charles Edward Jonathan), *born* 25 July 1970, *married* 4 November 2006 Princess Paola Doimi de Lupis Frankopan Subic Zrinski, and has issue, Albert Louis Philip Edward Windsor, *born* 22 September 2007; Leopold Ernest Augustus Guelph Windsor, *born* 8 September 2009; Louis Arthur Nicholas Felix Windsor, *born* 27 May 2014

HRH PRINCESS ALEXANDRA, THE HON. LADY OGILVY (Princess Alexandra Helen Elizabeth Olga Christabel), KG, GCVO
Born 25 December 1936
Married 24 April 1963 the Rt. Hon. Sir Angus Ogilvy, KCVO (1928–2004), second son of 12th Earl of Airlie
Residence Thatched House Lodge, Richmond Park, Surrey TW10 5HP
Issue
1. James Robert Bruce Ogilvy, *born* 29 February 1964, *married* 30 July 1988 Julia Rawlinson, and has issue, Flora Alexandra Ogilvy, *born* 15 December 1994; Alexander Charles Ogilvy, *born* 12 November 1996
2. Marina Victoria Alexandra Ogilvy, *born* 31 July 1966, *married* 2 February 1990 Paul Julian Mowatt (marriage dissolved 1997), and has issue, Zenouska May Mowatt, *born* 26 May 1990; Christian Alexander Mowatt, *born* 4 June 1993

HRH PRINCE MICHAEL OF KENT (Prince Michael George Charles Franklin), GCVO
Born 4 July 1942
Married 30 June 1978 Baroness Marie-Christine Agnes Hedwig Ida von Reibnitz, now HRH Princess Michael of Kent (*born* 15 January 1945, daughter of Baron Gunther von Reibnitz)
Residence Kensington Palace, London W8 4PU
Issue
1. Lord Frederick Windsor (Frederick Michael George David Louis), *born* 6 April 1979, *married* 12 September 2009 Sophie Winkleman, and has issue, Maud Elizabeth Daphne Marina Windsor, *born* 15 August 2013; Isabella Alexandra May Windsor, *born* 16 January 2016
2. Lady Gabriella Windsor (Gabriella Marina Alexandra Ophelia), *born* 23 April 1981

ORDER OF SUCCESSION

The Succession to the Crown Act 2013 received royal assent on 25 April 2013 and made provision for the order of succession to the Crown not to be dependent on gender and for those members of the royal family married to a Roman Catholic to retain the right of succession to the throne. The provisions of the Act came into force on 26 March 2015, following its ratification by all 16 Realms of the Commonwealth.

On the Act's commencement HRH Prince Michael of Kent and the Earl of St Andrews were restored to the succession. In addition, all male members of the royal family born after 28 October 2011 no longer precede any elder female siblings; and their place in the order of succession changed accordingly.

The following list includes all living descendants of the sons of King George V eligible to succeed to the Crown under the current legislation. Lord Nicholas Windsor, Lord Downpatrick and Lady Marina-Charlotte Windsor renounced their rights to the throne on converting to Roman Catholicism in 2001, 2003 and 2008 respectively. Their children remain in succession provided that they are in communion with the Church of England.

1	HRH the Prince of Wales	30	Lady Davina Lewis
2	HRH the Duke of Cambridge	31	Senna Lewis
3	HRH Prince George of Cambridge	32	Tane Lewis
4	HRH Princess Charlotte of Cambridge	33	Lady Rose Gilman
5	HRH Prince Louis of Cambridge	34	Lyla Gilman
6	HRH the Duke of Sussex	35	Rufus Gilman
7	HRH the Duke of York	36	HRH the Duke of Kent
8	HRH Princess Beatrice of York	37	Earl of St Andrews
9	HRH Princess Eugenie of York	38	Lady Amelia Windsor
10	HRH the Earl of Wessex	39	Albert Windsor
11	Viscount Severn	40	Leopold Windsor
12	Lady Louise Mountbatten-Windsor	41	Louis Windsor
13	HRH the Princess Royal	42	Lady Helen Taylor
14	Peter Phillips	43	Columbus Taylor
15	Savannah Phillips	44	Cassius Taylor
16	Isla Phillips	45	Eloise Taylor
17	Zara Tindall	46	Estella Taylor
18	Mia Tindall	47	HRH Prince Michael of Kent
19	Lena Tindall	48	Lord Frederick Windsor
20	Earl of Snowdon	49	Maud Windsor
21	Viscount Linley	50	Isabella Windsor
22	Lady Margarita Armstrong-Jones	51	Lady Gabriella Windsor
23	Lady Sarah Chatto	52	HRH Princess Alexandra, the Hon. Lady Ogilvy
24	Samuel Chatto	53	James Ogilvy
25	Arthur Chatto	54	Alexander Ogilvy
26	HRH the Duke of Gloucester	55	Flora Ogilvy
27	Earl of Ulster	56	Marina Ogilvy
28	Lord Culloden	57	Christian Mowatt
29	Lady Cosima Windsor	58	Zenouska Mowatt

THE ROYAL HOUSEHOLD

The PRIVATE SECRETARY is responsible for:
- informing and advising the Queen on constitutional, governmental and political matters in the UK, her other Realms and the wider Commonwealth, including communications with the prime minister and government departments
- organising the Queen's domestic and overseas official programme
- the Queen's speeches, messages, patronage, photographs, portraits and official presents
- communications in connection with the role of the royal family
- dealing with correspondence to the Queen from members of the public
- royal travel policy
- coordinating and initiating research to support engagements by members of the royal family

The DIRECTOR OF ROYAL COMMUNICATIONS is in charge of Buckingham Palace's communications office and reports to the Private Secretary. The director is responsible for:
- developing communications strategies to enhance the public understanding of the role of the monarchy
- briefing the British and international media on the role and duties of the Queen and issues relating to the royal family
- responding to media enquiries
- arranging media facilities in the UK and overseas to support royal functions and engagements
- the management of the royal website

The Private Secretary is keeper of the royal archives and is responsible for the care of the records of the sovereign and the royal household from previous reigns, preserved in the royal archives at Windsor. As keeper, it is the Private Secretary's responsibility to ensure the proper management of the records of the present reign with a view to their transfer to the archives as and when appropriate. The Private Secretary is an *ex officio* trustee of the Royal Collection Trust.

The KEEPER OF THE PRIVY PURSE AND TREASURER TO THE QUEEN is responsible for:
- the Sovereign Grant, which is the money paid from the government's Consolidated Fund to meet official expenditure relating to the Queen's duties as Head of State and Head of the Commonwealth and is provided by the government in return for the net surplus from the Crown Estate and other hereditary revenues (*see also* Royal Finances)
- through the Director of Human Resources, the planning and management of personnel policy across the royal household, the allocation of employee and pensioner housing and the administration of all its pension schemes and private estates employees
- information systems and telecommunications
- property services at occupied royal palaces in England, comprising Buckingham Palace, St James's Palace, Clarence House, Marlborough House Mews, the residential and office areas of Kensington Palace, Windsor Castle and buildings in the Home and Great Parks of Windsor and Hampton Court Mews and Paddocks
- audit services
- health and safety; insurance matters
- the Privy Purse, which is mainly financed by the net income of the Duchy of Lancaster, and meets both official and private expenditure incurred by the Queen
- liaison with other members of the royal family and their households on financial matters

- the Queen's private estates at Sandringham and Balmoral, the Queen's Racing Establishment and the Royal Studs and liaison with the Ascot Authority
- the Home Park at Windsor and liaison with the Crown Estate Commissioners concerning the Home Park and the Great Park at Windsor
- the Royal Philatelic Collection
- administrative aspects of the Military Knights of Windsor
- administration of the Royal Victorian Order, of which the Keeper of the Privy Purse is secretary, Long and Faithful Service Medals, and the Queen's cups, medals and prizes, and policy on commemorative medals

The Keeper of the Privy Purse is one of three royal trustees (in respect of his responsibilities for the Sovereign Grant) and is Receiver-General of the Duchy of Lancaster and a member of the Duchy's Council.

The Keeper of the Privy Purse is an *ex officio* trustee of the Royal Collection Trust.

The DIRECTOR OF THE PROPERTY SECTION has day-to-day responsibility for the royal household's property section:
- fire and health and safety
- repairs and refurbishment of buildings and new building work
- utilities and telecommunications
- putting up stages, tents and other work in connection with ceremonial occasions, garden parties and other official functions

The property section is also responsible, on a sub-contract basis from the DCMS, for the maintenance of Marlborough House (which is occupied by the Commonwealth Secretariat).

The MASTER OF THE HOUSEHOLD is responsible for:
- delivering the majority of the official and private entertaining in the Queen's annual programme across all the occupied palaces and residences in the UK when required
- periodic support for entertaining by all other members of the royal family
- furnishings and internal decorative refurbishment of all the occupied palaces in the UK in conjunction with the Director, Royal Collection Trust
- all operational, domestic and kitchen staff in the royal household

The COMPTROLLER, LORD CHAMBERLAIN'S OFFICE is responsible for:
- the organisation of all ceremonial engagements, including state visits to the Queen in the UK, royal weddings and funerals, the state opening of parliament, Guards of Honour at Buckingham Palace, investitures, and the Garter and Thistle ceremonies
- garden parties at Buckingham Palace and the Palace of Holyroodhouse
- the Crown Jewels, which are part of the Royal Collection, when they are in use on state occasions
- coordination of the arrangements for the Queen to be represented at funerals and memorial services and at the arrival and departure of visiting heads of state
- delivery of all official and approved travel operations
- advising on matters of precedence, style and titles, dress, flying of flags, gun salutes, mourning and other ceremonial issues
- supervising the applications for Royal Warrants of Appointment
- advising on the commercial use of royal emblems and contemporary royal photographs

- the ecclesiastical household, the medical household, the bodyguards and certain ceremonial appointments such as Gentlemen Ushers and Pages of Honour
- the Lords in Waiting, who represent the Queen on various occasions and escort visiting heads of state during incoming state visits
- the Queen's bargemaster and watermen and the Queen's swans
- the Royal Almonry and Royal Maundy Service

The Comptroller is also responsible for the Royal Mews, assisted by the CROWN EQUERRY, who has day-to-day responsibility for:

- the provision of carriage processions for the state opening of parliament, state visits, Trooping of the Colour, Royal Ascot, the Garter Ceremony, the Thistle Service, the presentation of credentials to the Queen by incoming foreign ambassadors and high commissioners, and other state and ceremonial occasions
- the provision of chauffeur-driven cars
- coordinating travel arrangements by road in respect of the royal household
- supervision and administration of the Royal Mews at Buckingham Palace, Windsor Castle, Hampton Court and the Palace of Holyroodhouse

The Comptroller also has overall responsibility for the MARSHAL OF THE DIPLOMATIC CORPS, who is responsible for the relationship between the royal household and the Diplomatic Heads of Mission in London; and the SECRETARY OF THE CENTRAL CHANCERY OF THE ORDERS OF KNIGHTHOOD, who administers the Orders of Chivalry, makes arrangements for investitures and the distribution of insignia, and ensures the proper public notification of awards through *The London Gazette;* and the DIRECTOR OF OPERATIONS, ROYAL TRAVEL, who is responsible for the provision of travel arrangements by air and rail.

The DIRECTOR, ROYAL COLLECTION TRUST is responsible for:

- the administration and custodial control of the Royal Collection in all royal residences
- the care, display, conservation and restoration of items in the collection
- initiating and assisting research into the collection and publishing catalogues and books on the collection
- making the collection accessible to the public and educating and informing the public about the collection

The Royal Collection, which contains a large number of works of art, is held by the Queen as sovereign in trust for her successors and the nation and is not owned by her as an individual. The administration, conservation and presentation of the Royal Collection are funded by the Royal Collection Trust solely from income from visitors to Windsor Castle, Buckingham Palace and the Palace of Holyroodhouse. The Royal Collection Trust is chaired by the Prince of Wales. The Lord Chamberlain, the Private Secretary and the Keeper of the Privy Purse are *ex officio* trustees and there are three external trustees appointed by the Queen.

The Director, Royal Collection Trust is also at present the SURVEYOR OF THE QUEEN'S WORKS OF ART, responsible for paintings, miniatures and works of art on paper, including the watercolours, prints and drawings in the Print Room at Windsor Castle, and for the books, manuscripts, coins, medals and insignia in the Royal Library.

Royal Collection Enterprises Limited is the trading subsidiary of the Royal Collection Trust. The company, whose chair is the Keeper of the Privy Purse, is responsible for:

- managing access by the public to Windsor Castle (including Frogmore House), Buckingham Palace (including the Royal Mews and the Queen's Gallery) and the Palace of Holyroodhouse (including the Queen's Gallery)
- running shops at each location
- managing the images and intellectual property rights of the Royal Collection

The Director, Royal Collection Trust is also an *ex officio* trustee of Historic Royal Palaces.

PRIVATE SECRETARIES

THE QUEEN
Office: Buckingham Palace, London SW1A 1AA T 020-7930 4832
Private Secretary to The Queen, Rt. Hon. Edward Young, CVO

PRINCE PHILIP, THE DUKE OF EDINBURGH
Office: Buckingham Palace, London SW1A 1AA T 020-7930 4832
Private Secretary, Brig. Archie Miller-Bakewell

THE PRINCE OF WALES AND THE DUCHESS OF CORNWALL
Office: Clarence House, London SW1A 1BA T 020-7930 4832
Principal Private Secretary, Clive Alderton, LVO

THE DUKE AND DUCHESS OF CAMBRIDGE
Office: Kensington Palace, Palace Green, London W8 4PU
T 020-7930 4832
Private Secretary to the Duke of Cambridge, Simon Case, CVO
Private Secretary to the Duchess of Cambridge, Catherine Quinn

THE DUKE AND DUCHESS OF SUSSEX
Office, Kensington Palace, Palace Green, London W8 4PU
T 020-7930 4832
Interim Private Secretary to the Duke and Duchess of Sussex,
  Samantha Cohen

THE DUKE OF YORK
Office: Buckingham Palace, London SW1A 1AA T 020-7024 4227
Private Secretary, Amanda Thirsk, LVO

THE EARL AND COUNTESS OF WESSEX
Office: Bagshot Park, Surrey GU19 5PL T 01276-707040
Private Secretary, Tim Roberts

THE PRINCESS ROYAL
Office: Buckingham Palace, London SW1A 1AA T 020-7024 4199
Private Secretary, Capt. N. P. Wright, CVO, RN

THE DUKE AND DUCHESS OF GLOUCESTER
Office: Kensington Palace, London W8 4PU T 020-7368 1000
Private Secretary, Lt.-Col. Alastair Todd

THE DUKE OF KENT
Office: York House, St James's Palace, London SW1A 1BQ
T 020-7930 4872
Private Secretary, Nicholas Marden

PRINCE AND PRINCESS MICHAEL OF KENT
Office: Kensington Palace, London W8 4PU
W www.princemichael.org.uk
Private Secretary, Camilla Rogers

PRINCESS ALEXANDRA, THE HON. LADY OGILVY
Office: Buckingham Palace, London SW1A 1AA
T 020-7024 4270
Private Secretary, Diane Duke, LVO

SENIOR MANAGEMENT OF THE ROYAL HOUSEHOLD

Lord Chamberlain, Earl Peel, GCVO, PC

HEADS OF DEPARTMENT
Private Secretary to The Queen, Rt. Hon. Edward Young, CVO
Keeper of the Privy Purse, Sir Michael Stevens, KCVO
Master of the Household, Vice-Adm. Tony Johnstone-Burt, CB, OBE
Comptroller, Lord Chamberlain's Office, Lt.-Col. Sir Andrew Ford, KCVO
Director of the Royal Collection, Tim Knox

NON-EXECUTIVE MEMBERS
Private Secretary to the Duke of Edinburgh, Brig. Archie Miller-Bakewell
Principal Private Secretary to the Prince of Wales and the Duchess of Cornwall, Clive Alderton, LVO

ASTRONOMER ROYAL

The post of Astronomer Royal dates back to 1675, when astronomy had many practical applications in navigation. Today the post is largely honorary, although the Astronomer Royal is expected to be available for consultation on scientific matters for as long as the holder remains a professional astronomer. The Astronomer Royal receives a stipend of £100 a year and is a member of the royal household.

Astronomer Royal, Lord Rees of Ludlow, OM, *apptd* 1995

MASTER OF THE QUEEN'S MUSIC

The office of Master of the Queen's Music is an honour conferred on a musician of great distinction. The office was first created in 1626, when the master was responsible for the court musicians. Since the reign of King George V, the position has had no fixed duties, although the Master may choose to produce compositions to mark royal or state occasions. The Master of the Queen's Music is paid an annual stipend of £15,000. In 2004 the length of appointment was changed from life tenure to a ten-year term.

Master of the Queen's Music, Judith Weir, CBE, *apptd* 2014

POET LAUREATE

The post of Poet Laureate was officially established when John Dryden was appointed by royal warrant as Poet Laureate and Historiographer Royal in 1668. The post is attached to the royal household and was originally conferred on the holder for life; in 1999 the length of appointment was changed to a ten-year term. It is customary for the Poet Laureate to write verse to mark events of national importance. The postholder currently receives an honorarium of £5,750 a year.

The Poet Laureate, Dame Carol Ann Duffy, DBE, *apptd* 2009

ROYAL FINANCES

Dating back to the late 17th century the Civil List was originally used by the sovereign to supplement hereditary revenues for paying the salaries of judges, ambassadors and other government officers as well as the expenses of the royal household. In 1760, on the accession of George III, it was decided that the Civil List would be provided by parliament to cover all relevant expenditure in return for the king surrendering the hereditary revenues of the Crown. At that time parliament undertook to pay the salaries of judges, ambassadors etc. In 1831 parliament agreed also to meet the costs of the royal palaces in return for a reduction in the Civil List.

Until 1 April 2012 the Civil List met the central staff costs and running expenses of the Queen's official household. Annual grants-in-aid provided for the maintenance of the occupied royal palaces (*see* Royal Household for a list of occupied palaces) and royal travel.

THE SOVEREIGN GRANT

Under the Sovereign Grant Act 2011, which came into force on 1 April 2012, the funding previously provided by the Civil List and the grants-in-aid was consolidated in the Sovereign Grant. It is provided by HM Treasury from public funds in exchange for the surrender by the Queen of the revenue of the Crown Estate.

For 2016–17 the Sovereign Grant was calculated based on 15 per cent of the income account net surplus of the Crown Estate for the financial year two years previous. From 2017–18 this increased to 25 per cent, providing for a Sovereign Grant of £76.1m in 2017–18. The additional grant generated (£30.4m) will be used to fund the reservicing of Buckingham Palace over a ten-year period.

Official expenditure met by the Sovereign Grant in 2017–18 amounted to £47.4m. Royal travel accounted for £4.7m of the expenditure and property maintenance for £22.6m. The excess of Sovereign Grant over expenditure of £28.7m was transferred to the Sovereign Grant reserve.

The legislative requirement is for Sovereign Grant accounts to be audited by the Comptroller and Auditor-General, scrutinised by the National Audit Office, and submitted to parliament annually. They are subjected to the same scrutiny as for any other government department. The annual report for the year to 31 March 2018 was published in June 2018.

£m	2016–17	2017–18
Sovereign Grant	42.8	76.1
Core	–	45.7
Buckingham Palace	–	30.4
Transfer to the reserve	(0.9)	(28.7)
Core	–	(2.4)
Buckingham Palace	–	(26.3)
Net Expenditure	41.9	47.4

PARLIAMENTARY ANNUITIES

The Civil List acts provided for other members of the royal family to receive annuities from government funds to meet the expenses of carrying out their official duties. Since 1993 these annuities the Queen reimbursed HM Treasury for all of them except those paid to the late Queen Elizabeth the Queen Mother and the Duke of Edinburgh. The Sovereign Grant Act 2011 repealed all parliamentary annuities paid to the royal family, with the exception of that paid to the Duke of Edinburgh (£359,000). This is now paid directly from the Consolidated Fund.

THE PRIVY PURSE

The funds received by the Privy Purse pay for official expenses incurred by the Queen as head of state and for some of the Queen's private expenditure. The revenues of the Duchy of Lancaster are the principal source of income for the privy purse. The revenues of the Duchy were retained by George III in 1760 when the hereditary revenues were surrendered. The Duchy Council reports to the Chancellor of the Duchy of Lancaster, who is accountable directly to the sovereign rather than to parliament. However the chancellor does answer parliamentary questions on matters relating to the Duchy's responsibilities.

THE DUCHY OF LANCASTER, 1 Lancaster Place, London WC2E 7ED
Chancellor of the Duchy of Lancaster, Rt. Hon. David Lidington, CBE, MP, *apptd* 2018
Chair of the Council, Sir Alan Reid, GCVO
Chief Executive and Clerk, Nathan Thompson
Receiver-General, Sir Alan Reid, GCVO
Attorney-General, Robert Miles, QC

PERSONAL INCOME
The Queen's personal income derives mostly from investments, and is used to meet private expenditure.

PRINCE OF WALES' FUNDING

The Duchy Estate was created in 1337 by Edward III for his son Prince Edward (the Black Prince) who became the Duke of Cornwall. The Duchy's primary function is to provide an income from its assets for the Prince of Wales. Under a 1337 charter, confirmed by subsequent legislation, the Prince of Wales is not entitled to the proceeds or profit on the sale of Duchy assets but only to the annual income which is generated. The Duchy is responsible for the sustainable and commercial management of its properties, investment portfolio and 53,266 hectares of land, based mostly in the south-west of England. The Prince of Wales has chosen to use a proportion of his income to meet the cost of his public and charitable work. The Duchy also funds the public, charitable and private activities of the Duchess of Cornwall, the Duke and Duchess of Cambridge and the Duke and Duchess of Sussex.

THE DUCHY OF CORNWALL, 10 Buckingham Gate, London SW1E 6LA T 020-7834 7346 W www.duchyofcornwall.org
Lord Warden of the Stannaries, Sir Nicholas Bacon, Bt., OBE
Receiver-General, Hon. James Leigh-Pemberton, CVO
Attorney-General, Jonathan Crow, QC
Secretary and Keeper of the Records, Alastair Martin

TAXATION

The sovereign is not legally liable to pay income tax or capital gains tax, but since 6 April 1993 has paid both on a voluntary basis. The main provisions for the Queen and the Prince of Wales to pay tax are set out in a Memorandum of Understanding on Royal Taxation presented to parliament on 11 February 1993. The Queen pays income and capital gains tax in respect of her private income and assets, and on the proportion of the income and capital gains of the Privy Purse used for private purposes. Inheritance tax will be paid on the Queen's assets, except for those which pass to the next sovereign, whether automatically or by gift or bequest. The Prince of Wales pays income tax on income from the Duchy of Cornwall used for private purposes.

ROYAL SALUTES

ENGLAND

The basic royal salute is 21 rounds with an extra 20 rounds fired at Hyde Park because it is a royal park. At the Tower of London 62 rounds are fired on royal anniversaries (21 plus a further 20 because the Tower is a royal palace and a further 21 'for the City of London') and 41 on other occasions. When the Queen's official birthday coincides with the Duke of Edinburgh's birthday, 124 rounds are fired from the Tower (62 rounds for each birthday). Gun salutes occur on the following royal anniversaries:

- Accession Day
- The Queen's birthday
- Coronation Day
- Duke of Edinburgh's birthday
- The Queen's Official Birthday
- The Prince of Wales' birthday
- State opening of parliament

Gun salutes also occur when parliament is prorogued by the sovereign, on royal births and when a visiting head of state meets the sovereign in London, Windsor or Edinburgh.

In London, salutes are fired at Hyde Park and the Tower of London although on some occasions (state visits, state opening of parliament and the Queen's birthday parade) Green Park is used instead of Hyde Park. Other military saluting stations in England are at Colchester, Dover, Plymouth, Woolwich and York.

Constable of the Royal Palace and Fortress of London, Gen. Lord Houghton of Richmond, GCB, CBE

Lieutenant of the Tower of London, Lt.-Gen. Sir Simon Mayall, KBE, CB

Master Gunner of St James's Park, Lt.-Gen. Sir Andrew Gregory, KBE, CB

Resident Governor and Keeper of the Jewel House, Col. Richard Harrold, OBE

SCOTLAND

Royal salutes are authorised at Edinburgh Castle and Stirling Castle. A salute of 21 guns is fired on the following occasions:

- the anniversaries of the birth, accession and coronation of the sovereign
- the anniversary of the birth of the Duke of Edinburgh

A salute of 21 guns is fired in Edinburgh on the occasion of the opening of the general assembly of the Church of Scotland. A salute of 21 guns may also be fired in Edinburgh on the arrival of HM The Queen or a member of the royal family who is a Royal Highness on an official visit.

Military saluting stations are also situated at Cardiff Castle in Wales, Hillsborough Castle in Northern Ireland and in Gibraltar.

MILITARY RANKS AND TITLES

THE QUEEN

ARMY
Colonel-in-Chief
The Life Guards; The Blues and Royals (Royal Horse Guards and 1st Dragoons); The Royal Scots Dragoon Guards (Carabiniers and Greys); The Royal Lancers; The Royal Tank Regiment; Corps of Royal Engineers; Grenadier Guards; Coldstream Guards; Scots Guards; Irish Guards; Welsh Guards; The Royal Regiment of Scotland; The Duke of Lancaster's Regiment (King's, Lancashire and Border); The Royal Welsh; Adjutant General's Corps; The Governor General's Horse Guards (of Canada); The King's Own Calgary Regiment (Royal Canadian Armoured Corps); Canadian Forces Military Engineering Branch; Le Royal 22e Regiment (of Canada); The Governor General's Foot Guards (of Canada); The Canadian Grenadier Guards; The Stormont, Dundas and Glengarry Highlanders; Le Régiment de la Chaudière (of Canada); The Royal New Brunswick Regiment; The North Shore (New Brunswick) Regiment; 48th Highlanders of Canada; The Argyll and Sutherland Highlanders of Canada (Princess Louise's); The Calgary Highlanders; Royal Australian Engineers; Royal Australian Infantry Corps; Royal Australian Army Ordnance Corps; Royal Australian Army Nursing Corps; The Corps of Royal New Zealand Engineers; Royal New Zealand Infantry Regiment; Malawi Rifles

Affiliated Colonel-in-Chief
The Queen's Gurkha Engineers

Captain-General
Royal Regiment of Artillery; The Honourable Artillery Company; Combined Cadet Force; Royal Regiment of Canadian Artillery; Royal Regiment of Australian Artillery; Royal Regiment of New Zealand Artillery; Royal New Zealand Armoured Corps

Royal Colonel
Balaklava Company, 5th Battalion The Royal Regiment of Scotland

Patron
Royal Army Chaplains' Department

ROYAL AIR FORCE
Air Commodore-in-Chief
Royal Auxiliary Air Force; Royal Air Force Regiment; Air Reserve (of Canada); Royal Australian Air Force Reserve; Territorial Air Force (of New Zealand)

Commandant-in-Chief
RAF College, Cranwell

Royal Honorary Air Commodore
RAF Marham; 603 (City of Edinburgh) Squadron Royal Auxiliary Air Force

TRI-SERVICE
Colonel-in-Chief
The Canadian Armed Forces Legal Branch

PRINCE PHILIP, DUKE OF EDINBURGH

ROYAL NAVY
Lord High Admiral of the United Kingdom
Admiral of the Fleet
Admiral of the Fleet, Royal Australian Navy
Admiral of the Fleet, Royal New Zealand Navy
Admiral, Royal Canadian Navy
Admiral, Royal Canadian Sea Cadets

ARMY
Field Marshal
Field Marshal, Australian Military Forces
Field Marshal, New Zealand Army
General, Royal Canadian Army
Colonel-in-Chief
The Queen's Royal Hussars (Queen's Own and Royal Irish); The Rifles; Corps of Royal Electrical and Mechanical Engineers; Intelligence Corps; Army Cadet Force Association; The Royal Canadian Regiment; The Royal Hamilton Light Infantry (Wentworth Regiment of Canada); The Cameron Highlanders of Ottawa; The Queen's Own Cameron Highlanders of Canada; The Seaforth Highlanders of Canada; The Royal Canadian Army Cadets; The Royal Australian Corps of Electrical and Mechanical Engineers; The Australian Army Cadet Corps

Royal Colonel
The Highlanders, 4th Battalion The Royal Regiment of Scotland

Honorary Colonel
The Trinidad and Tobago Regiment

Member
Honourable Artillery Company

ROYAL AIR FORCE
Marshal of the Royal Air Force
Marshal of the Royal Australian Air Force
Marshal of the Royal New Zealand Air Force
General, Royal Canadian Air Force
Air Commodore-in-Chief
Royal Canadian Air Cadets

Honorary Air Commodore
RAF Northolt

THE PRINCE OF WALES

ROYAL NAVY
Admiral of the Fleet
Admiral of the Fleet, Royal New Zealand Navy
Vice-Admiral
Royal Canadian Navy

Commodore-in-Chief
Royal Naval Command Plymouth; Fleet Atlantic, Royal Canadian Navy

ARMY
Field Marshal
Field Marshal, New Zealand Army
Lieutenant-General
Canadian Army

Colonel-in-Chief
The Royal Dragoon Guards; The Parachute Regiment; The Royal Gurkha Rifles; Army Air Corps; The Royal Canadian Dragoons; Lord Strathcona's Horse (Royal Canadians); The Royal Regiment of Canada; Royal Winnipeg Rifles; Royal Australian Armoured Corps; The Royal Pacific Islands Regiment; 1st The Queen's Dragoon Guards; The Black Watch (Royal Highland Regiment) of Canada; The Toronto Scottish Regiment (Queen Elizabeth The Queen Mother's Own); The Mercian Regiment; 2nd Battalion The Irish Regiment of Canada

Royal Colonel
The Black Watch, 3rd Battalion The Royal Regiment of Scotland; 51st Highland, 7th Battalion The Royal Regiment of Scotland

Colonel
The Welsh Guards

Royal Honorary Colonel
The Queen's Own Yeomanry

ROYAL AIR FORCE
Marshal of the RAF
Marshal of the Royal New Zealand Air Force
Lieutenant-General
   Royal Canadian Air Force
Honorary Air Commodore
   RAF Valley
Air Commodore-in-Chief
   Royal New Zealand Air Force
Colonel-in-Chief
   Air Reserve Canada

THE DUCHESS OF CORNWALL

ROYAL NAVY
Commodore-in-Chief
   Royal Naval Medical Services; Naval Chaplaincy Services

ARMY
Colonel-in-Chief
   Queen's Own Rifles of Canada; Royal Australian Corps of Military Police
Royal Colonel
   4th Battalion The Rifles

ROYAL AIR FORCE
Honorary Air Commodore
   RAF Halton; RAF Leeming

THE DUKE OF CAMBRIDGE

ROYAL NAVY
Lieutenant Commander
Commodore-in-Chief
   Scotland Command; Submarines Command

ARMY
Colonel
   Irish Guards
Major
   The Blues and Royals (Royal Horse Guards and 1st Dragoons)

ROYAL AIR FORCE
Squadron Leader
Honorary Air Commandant
   RAF Coningsby

THE DUCHESS OF CAMBRIDGE

ROYAL AIR FORCE
Honorary Air Commandant
   Air Cadets

THE DUKE OF SUSSEX

ROYAL NAVY
Lieutenant-Commander
Commodore-in-Chief
   Small Ships and Diving Command

ROYAL MARINES
Captain-General

ARMY
Major
   The Blues and Royals (Royal Horse Guards and 1st Dragoons)

ROYAL AIR FORCE
Squadron Leader
Honorary Air Commandant
   RAF Honington

THE DUKE OF YORK

ROYAL NAVY
Vice-Admiral
Commodore-in-Chief
   Fleet Air Arm
Admiral of the Marine Society and Sea Cadets

ARMY
Colonel-in-Chief
   The Royal Irish Regiment (27th (Inniskilling), 83rd, 87th and The Ulster Defence Regiment); The Yorkshire Regiment (14th/15th, 19th and 33rd/76th Foot); Small Arms School Corps; The Queen's York Rangers (First Americans); Royal New Zealand Army Logistics Regiment; The Royal Highland Fusiliers of Canada; The Princess Louise Fusiliers (Canada)
Deputy Colonel-in-Chief
   The Royal Lancers (Queen Elizabeths' Own)
Colonel
   Grenadier Guards
Royal Colonel
   The Royal Highland Fusiliers, 2nd Battalion The Royal Regiment of Scotland

ROYAL AIR FORCE
Honorary Air Commodore
   RAF Lossiemouth

THE EARL OF WESSEX

ROYAL NAVY
Commodore-in-Chief
   Royal Fleet Auxiliary
Patron
   Royal Fleet Auxiliary Association

ARMY
Colonel-in-Chief
   Hastings and Prince Edward Regiment; Saskatchewan Dragoons; Prince Edward Island Regiment
Royal Colonel
   2nd Battalion, The Rifles
Royal Honorary Colonel
   Royal Wessex Yeomanry; The London Regiment

ROYAL AIR FORCE
Honorary Air Commodore
   RAF Waddington

THE COUNTESS OF WESSEX

ARMY
Colonel-in-Chief
   Corps of Army Music; Queen Alexandra's Royal Army Nursing Corps; The Lincoln and Welland Regiment; South Alberta Light Horse Regiment
Royal Colonel
   5th Battalion, The Rifles
Patron
   Queen Alexandra's Royal Army Nursing Corps Association

ROYAL AIR FORCE
Honorary Air Commodore
   RAF Wittering

ROYAL NAVY
Sponsor
   HMS *Daring*

THE PRINCESS ROYAL

ROYAL NAVY
Admiral (Chief Commandant for Women in the Royal Navy)
Commodore-in-Chief
   HM Naval Base Portsmouth; Fleet Pacific, Royal Canadian
   Navy

ARMY
Colonel-in-Chief
   The King's Royal Hussars; Royal Corps of Signals; Royal
   Logistic Corps; The Royal Army Veterinary Corps; 8th
   Canadian Hussars (Princess Louise's); Royal Newfoundland
   Regiment; Canadian Forces Communications and
   Electronics Branch; The Grey and Simcoe Foresters; The
   Royal Regina Rifles; Canadian Forces Medical Branch;
   Royal Canadian Hussars; Royal Australian Corps of Signals;
   Royal Australian Corps of Transport; Royal New Zealand
   Corps of Signals; Royal New Zealand Nursing Corps
Affiliated Colonel-in-Chief
   The Queen's Gurkha Signals; The Queen's Own Gurkha
   Transport Regiment
Royal Colonel
   The Royal Scots Borderers, 1st Battalion The Royal
   Regiment of Scotland, 52nd Lowland, 6th Battalion The
   Royal Regiment of Scotland
Colonel
   The Blues and Royals (Royal Horse Guards and 1st
   Dragoons)
Honorary Colonel
   University of London Officers' Training Corps
Commandant-in-Chief
   First Aid Nursing Yeomanry (Princess Royal's Volunteer
   Corps)

ROYAL AIR FORCE
Honorary Air Commodore
   RAF Brize Norton; University of London Air Squadron

THE DUKE OF GLOUCESTER

ARMY
Colonel-in-Chief
   The Royal Anglian Regiment; Royal Army Medical Corps;
   Royal New Zealand Army Medical Corps
Deputy Colonel-in-Chief
   The Royal Logistic Corps
Royal Colonel
   6th Battalion, The Rifles
Royal Honorary Colonel
   Royal Monmouthshire Royal Engineers (Militia)

ROYAL AIR FORCE
Honorary Air Marshal
Honorary Air Commodore
   RAF Odiham; No. 501 (County of Gloucester) Logistic
   Support Squadron

THE DUCHESS OF GLOUCESTER

ARMY
Colonel-in-Chief
   Royal Army Dental Corps; Royal Australian Army
   Educational Corps; Royal New Zealand Army Educational
   Corps; Royal Canadian Dental Corps; The Bermuda
   Regiment

Deputy Colonel-in-Chief
   Adjutant General's Corps
Royal Colonel
   7th Battalion, The Rifles
Vice-Patron
   Adjutant General's Corps Regimental Association
Patron
   Royal Army Educational Corps Association; Army Families
   Federation

THE DUKE OF KENT

ARMY
Field Marshal
Colonel-in-Chief
   The Royal Regiment of Fusiliers; Lorne Scots (Peel, Dufferin
   and Hamilton Regiment)
Deputy Colonel-in-Chief
   The Royal Scots Dragoon Guards (Carabiniers and Greys)
Royal Colonel
   1st Battalion The Rifles
Colonel
   Scots Guards

ROYAL AIR FORCE
Honorary Air Chief Marshal

THE DUCHESS OF KENT

ARMY
Honorary Major-General
Deputy Colonel-in-Chief
   The Royal Dragoon Guards; Adjutant General's Corps; The
   Royal Logistic Corps

PRINCE MICHAEL OF KENT

ROYAL NAVY
Honorary Vice-Admiral of the Royal Naval Reserves
Commodore-in-Chief of the Maritime Reserves

ARMY
Colonel-in-Chief
   Essex and Kent Scottish Regiment (Ontario)
Royal Honorary Colonel
   Honourable Artillery Company
Senior Colonel
   King's Royal Hussars

ROYAL AIR FORCE
Honorary Air Marshal
   RAF Benson

PRINCESS ALEXANDRA, THE HON. LADY OGILVY

ROYAL NAVY
Patron
   Queen Alexandra's Royal Naval Nursing Service

ARMY
Colonel-in-Chief
   The Canadian Scottish Regiment (Princess Mary's)
Deputy Colonel-in-Chief
   The Royal Lancers
Royal Colonel
   3rd Battalion The Rifles
Royal Honorary Colonel
   The Royal Yeomanry

ROYAL AIR FORCE
Patron and Air Chief Commandant
   Princess Mary's RAF Nursing Service

KINGS AND QUEENS

ENGLISH KINGS AND QUEENS 927–1603

HOUSES OF CERDIC AND DENMARK

927–939 **ÆTHELSTAN**
Son of Edward the Elder, by Ecgwynn, and grandson of Alfred *acceded* to Wessex and Mercia *c.*924, established direct rule over Northumbria 927, effectively creating the Kingdom of England *reigned* 15 years

939–946 **EDMUND I**
born 921, son of Edward the Elder, by Eadgifu *married* (1) Ælfgifu (2) Æthelflæd *killed* aged 25 *reigned* 6 years

946–955 **EADRED**
Son of Edward the Elder, by Eadgifu *reigned* 9 years

955–959 **EADWIG**
born before 943, son of Edmund and Ælfgifu *married* Ælfgifu *reigned* 3 years

959–975 **EDGAR I**
born 943, son of Edmund and Ælfgifu *married* (1) Æthelflæd (2) Wulfthryth (3) Ælfthryth *died* aged 32 *reigned* 15 years

975–978 **EDWARD I (the Martyr)**
*born c.*962, son of Edgar and Æthelflæd *assassinated* aged *c.*16 *reigned* 2 years

978–1016 **ÆTHELRED (the Unready)**
born 968/969, son of Edgar and Ælfthryth *married* (1) Ælfgifu (2) Emma, daughter of Richard I, Count of Normandy, 1013–14 dispossessed of kingdom by Swegn Forkbeard (King of Denmark 987–1014) *died* aged *c.*47, *reigned* 38 years

1016 **EDMUND II (Ironside)**
(Apr–Nov) *born* before 993, son of Æthelred and Ælfgifu *married* Ealdgyth *died* aged over 23 *reigned* 7 months

1016–1035 **CNUT (Canute)**
*born c.*995, son of Swegn Forkbeard, King of Denmark, and Gunhild *married* (1) Ælfgifu (2) Emma, widow of Æthelred the Unready. Gained submission of West Saxons 1015, Northumbrians 1016, Mercia 1016, King of all England after Edmund's death, King of Denmark 1019–35, King of Norway 1028–35 *died* aged *c.*40 *reigned* 19 years

1035–1040 **HAROLD I (Harefoot)**
born 1016/17, son of Cnut and Ælfgifu *married* Ælfgifu 1035 recognised as regent for himself and his brother Harthacnut; 1037 recognised as king *died* aged *c.*23 *reigned* 4 years

1040–1042 **HARTHACNUT (Harthacanute)**
*born c.*1018, son of Cnut and Emma. Titular king of Denmark from 1028, acknowledged King of England 1035–7 with Harold I as regent; effective king after Harold's death *died* aged *c.*24 *reigned* 2 years

1042–1066 **EDWARD II (the Confessor)**
born between 1002 and 1005, son of Æthelred the Unready and Emma *married* Eadgyth, daughter of Godwine, Earl of Wessex *died* aged over 60 *reigned* 23 years

1066 **HAROLD II (Godwinesson)**
(Jan–Oct) *born c.*1020, son of Godwine, Earl of Wessex, and Gytha *married* (1) Eadgyth (2) Ealdgyth *killed* in battle aged *c.*46 *reigned* 10 months

THE HOUSE OF NORMANDY

1066–1087 **WILLIAM I (the Conqueror)**
born 1027/8, son of Robert I, Duke of Normandy; obtained the Crown by conquest *married* Matilda, daughter of Baldwin, Count of Flanders *died* aged *c.*60, *reigned* 20 years

1087–1100 **WILLIAM II (Rufus)**
born between 1056 and 1060, third son of William I; succeeded his father in England only *killed* aged *c.*40 *reigned* 12 years

1100–1135 **HENRY I (Beauclerk)**
born 1068, fourth son of William I *married* (1) Edith or Matilda, daughter of Malcolm III of Scotland (2) Adela, daughter of Godfrey, Count of Louvain *died* aged 67 *reigned* 35 years

1135–1154 **STEPHEN**
born not later than 1100, third son of Adela, daughter of William I, and Stephen, Count of Blois *married* Matilda, daughter of Eustace, Count of Boulogne. Feb–Nov 1141 held captive by adherents of Matilda, daughter of Henry I, who contested the Crown until 1153 *died* aged over 53 *reigned* 18 years

THE HOUSE OF ANJOU (PLANTAGENETS)

1154–1189 **HENRY II (Curtmantle)**
born 1133, son of Matilda, daughter of Henry I, and Geoffrey, Count of Anjou *married* Eleanor, daughter of William, Duke of Aquitaine, and divorced queen of Louis VII of France *died* aged 56 *reigned* 34 years

1189–1199 **RICHARD I (Coeur de Lion)**
born 1157, third son of Henry II *married* Berengaria, daughter of Sancho VI, King of Navarre *died* aged 42 *reigned* 9 years

1199–1216 **JOHN (Lackland)**
born 1167, fifth son of Henry II *married* (1) Isabella or Avisa, daughter of William, Earl of Gloucester (divorced) (2) Isabella, daughter of Aymer, Count of Angoulême *died* aged 48 *reigned* 17 years

1216–1272 **HENRY III**
born 1207, son of John and Isabella of Angoulême *married* Eleanor, daughter of Raymond, Count of Provence *died* aged 65 *reigned* 56 years

1272–1307 **EDWARD I (Longshanks)**
born 1239, eldest son of Henry III *married* (1) Eleanor, daughter of Ferdinand III, King of Castile (2) Margaret, daughter of Philip III of France *died* aged 68 *reigned* 34 years

1307–1327 **EDWARD II**
born 1284, eldest surviving son of Edward I and Eleanor *married* Isabella, daughter of Philip IV of France *deposed* Jan 1327 *killed* Sep 1327 aged 43 *reigned* 19 years

1327–1377 **EDWARD III**
born 1312, eldest son of Edward II *married* Philippa, daughter of William, Count of Hainault *died* aged 64 *reigned* 50 years

1377–1399 **RICHARD II**
born 1367, son of Edward (the Black Prince), eldest son of Edward III *married* (1) Anne, daughter of Emperor Charles IV (2) Isabelle, daughter of Charles VI of France *deposed* Sep 1399 *killed* Feb 1400 aged 33 *reigned* 22 years

THE HOUSE OF LANCASTER

1399–1413   HENRY IV
born 1366, son of John of Gaunt, fourth son of Edward III, and Blanche, daughter of Henry, Duke of Lancaster *married* (1) Mary, daughter of Humphrey, Earl of Hereford (2) Joan, daughter of Charles, King of Navarre, and widow of John, Duke of Brittany *died* aged c.47 *reigned* 13 years

1413–1422   HENRY V
born 1387, eldest surviving son of Henry IV and Mary *married* Catherine, daughter of Charles VI of France *died* aged 34 *reigned* 9 years

1422–1471   HENRY VI
born 1421, son of Henry V *married* Margaret, daughter of René, Duke of Anjou and Count of Provence *deposed* Mar 1461 *restored* Oct 1470 *deposed* Apr 1471 *killed* May 1471 aged 49 *reigned* 39 years

THE HOUSE OF YORK

1461–1483   EDWARD IV
born 1442, eldest son of Richard of York (grandson of Edmund, fifth son of Edward III; and son of Anne, great-granddaughter of Lionel, third son of Edward III) *married* Elizabeth Woodville, daughter of Richard, Lord Rivers, and widow of Sir John Grey *acceded* Mar 1461 *deposed* Oct 1470 *restored* Apr 1471 *died* aged 40 *reigned* 21 years

1483   EDWARD V
(Apr–Jun) *born* 1470, eldest son of Edward IV *deposed* Jun 1483, *died* probably Jul–Sep 1483, aged 12 *reigned* 2 months

1483–1485   RICHARD III
born 1452, fourth son of Richard of York *married* Anne Neville, daughter of Richard, Earl of Warwick, and widow of Edward, Prince of Wales, son of Henry VI *killed* in battle aged 32 *reigned* 2 years

THE HOUSE OF TUDOR

1485–1509   HENRY VII
born 1457, son of Margaret Beaufort (great-granddaughter of John of Gaunt, fourth son of Edward III) and Edmund Tudor, Earl of Richmond *married* Elizabeth, daughter of Edward IV *died* aged 52 *reigned* 23 years

1509–1547   HENRY VIII
born 1491, second son of Henry VII *married* (1) Catherine, daughter of Ferdinand II, King of Aragon, and widow of his elder brother Arthur (divorced) (2) Anne, daughter of Sir Thomas Boleyn (executed) (3) Jane, daughter of Sir John Seymour (died in childbirth) (4) Anne, daughter of John, Duke of Cleves (divorced) (5) Catherine Howard, niece of the Duke of Norfolk (executed) (6) Catherine, daughter of Sir Thomas Parr and widow of Lord Latimer *died* aged 55 *reigned* 37 years

1547–1553   EDWARD VI
born 1537, son of Henry VIII and Jane Seymour *died* aged 15 *reigned* 6 years

1553   JANE
***(6/10–** *born* 1537, daughter of Frances (daughter of Mary Tudor, the younger daughter of Henry VII) and Henry Grey, Duke of Suffolk *married* Lord Guildford Dudley, son of the Duke of Northumberland *deposed* Jul 1553 *executed* Feb 1554 aged 16 *reigned* 13/9 days

1553–1558   MARY I
born 1516, daughter of Henry VIII and Catherine of Aragon *married* Philip II of Spain *died* aged 42 *reigned* 5 years

1558–1603   ELIZABETH I
born 1533, daughter of Henry VIII and Anne Boleyn *died* aged 69 *reigned* 44 years

* Depending on whether the date of her predecessor's death (6 July) or that of her official proclamation as Queen (10 July) is taken as the beginning of her reign

BRITISH KINGS AND QUEENS SINCE 1603

THE HOUSE OF STUART

1603–1625   JAMES I (VI OF SCOTLAND)
born 1566, son of Mary, Queen of Scots (granddaughter of Margaret Tudor, elder daughter of Henry VII), and Henry Stewart, Lord Darnley *married* Anne, daughter of Frederick II of Denmark *died* aged 58 *reigned* 22 years

1625–1649   CHARLES I
born 1600, second son of James I *married* Henrietta Maria, daughter of Henry IV of France *executed* 1649 aged 48 *reigned* 23 years

INTERREGNUM 1649–1660
1649–1653   Government by a council of state
1653–1658   Oliver Cromwell, Lord Protector
1658–1659   Richard Cromwell, Lord Protector

1660–1685   CHARLES II
born 1630, eldest son of Charles I *married* Catherine, daughter of John of Portugal *died* aged 54 *reigned* 24 years

1685–1688   JAMES II (VII OF SCOTLAND)
born 1633, second son of Charles I *married* (1) Lady Anne Hyde, daughter of Edward, Earl of Clarendon (2) Mary, daughter of Alphonso, Duke of Modena. Reign ended with flight from kingdom Dec 1688 *died* 1701 aged 67 *reigned* 3 years

INTERREGNUM 11 Dec 1688 to 12 Feb 1689

1689–1702   WILLIAM III
born 1650, son of William II, Prince of Orange, and Mary Stuart, daughter of Charles I *married* Mary, elder daughter of James II *died* aged 51 *reigned* 13 years

and
1689–1694   MARY II
born 1662, elder daughter of James II and Anne *died* aged 32 *reigned* 5 years

1702–1714   ANNE
born 1665, younger daughter of James II and Anne *married* Prince George of Denmark, son of Frederick III of Denmark *died* aged 49 *reigned* 12 years

THE HOUSE OF HANOVER

1714–1727 **GEORGE I (Elector of Hanover)**
born 1660, son of Sophia (daughter of Frederick, Elector Palatine, and Elizabeth Stuart, daughter of James I) and Ernest Augustus, Elector of Hanover *married* Sophia Dorothea, daughter of George William, Duke of Lüneburg-Celle *died* aged 67 *reigned* 12 years

1727–1760 **GEORGE II**
born 1683, son of George I *married* Caroline, daughter of John Frederick, Margrave of Brandenburg-Anspach *died* aged 76 *reigned* 33 years

1760–1820 **GEORGE III**
born 1738, son of Frederick, eldest son of George II *married* Charlotte, daughter of Charles Louis, Duke of Mecklenburg-Strelitz *died* aged 81 *reigned* 59 years

REGENCY 1811–1820
Prince of Wales regent owing to the insanity of George III

1820–1830 **GEORGE IV**
born 1762, eldest son of George III *married* Caroline, daughter of Charles, Duke of Brunswick-Wolfenbüttel *died* aged 67 *reigned* 10 years

1830–1837 **WILLIAM IV**
born 1765, third son of George III *married* Adelaide, daughter of George, Duke of Saxe-Meiningen *died* aged 71 *reigned* 7 years

1837–1901 **VICTORIA**
born 1819, daughter of Edward, fourth son of George III *married* Prince Albert of Saxe-Coburg and Gotha *died* aged 81 *reigned* 63 years

THE HOUSE OF SAXE-COBURG AND GOTHA

1901–1910 **EDWARD VII**
born 1841, eldest son of Victoria and Albert *married* Alexandra, daughter of Christian IX of Denmark *died* aged 68 *reigned* 9 years

THE HOUSE OF WINDSOR

1910–1936 **GEORGE V**
born 1865, second son of Edward VII *married* Victoria Mary, daughter of Francis, Duke of Teck *died* aged 70 *reigned* 25 years

1936 **EDWARD VIII**
(20 Jan–11 Dec) born 1894, eldest son of George V *married* (1937) Mrs Wallis Simpson *abdicated* 1936 *died* 1972 aged 77 *reigned* 10 months

1936–1952 **GEORGE VI**
born 1895, second son of George V *married* Lady Elizabeth Bowes-Lyon, daughter of 14th Earl of Strathmore and Kinghorne *died* aged 56 *reigned* 15 years

1952– **ELIZABETH II**
born 1926, elder daughter of George VI *married* Philip, son of Prince Andrew of Greece

KINGS AND QUEENS OF SCOTS 1016–1603

1016–1034 **MALCOLM II**
born c.954, son of Kenneth II *acceded* to Alba 1005, secured Lothian c.1016, obtained Strathclyde for his grandson Duncan c.1016, thus reigning over an area approximately the same as that governed by later rulers of Scotland *died* aged c.80 *reigned* 18 years

THE HOUSE OF ATHOLL

1034–1040 **DUNCAN I**
son of Bethoc, daughter of Malcolm II, and Crinan, Mormaer of Atholl *married* a cousin of Siward, Earl of Northumbria *reigned* 5 years

1040–1057 **MACBETH**
born c.1005, son of a daughter of Malcolm II and Finlaec, Mormaer of Moray *married* Gruoch, granddaughter of Kenneth III *killed* aged c.52 *reigned* 17 years

1057–1058 **LULACH**
(Aug–Mar) born c.1032, son of Gillacomgan, Mormaer of Moray, and Gruoch (and stepson of Macbeth) *died* aged c.26 *reigned* 7 months

1058–1093 **MALCOLM III (Canmore)**
born c.1031, elder son of Duncan I *married* (1) Ingibiorg (2) Margaret (St Margaret), granddaughter of Edmund II of England *killed* in battle aged c.62 *reigned* 35 years

1093–1097 **DONALD III BÁN**
born c.1033, second son of Duncan I *deposed* May 1094 *restored* Nov 1094 *deposed* Oct 1097 *reigned* 3 years

1094 **DUNCAN II**
(May–Nov) born c.1060, elder son of Malcolm III and Ingibiorg *married* Octreda of Dunbar *killed* aged c.34 *reigned* 6 months

1097–1107 **EDGAR**
born c.1074, second son of Malcolm III and Margaret *died* aged c.32 *reigned* 9 years

1107–1124 **ALEXANDER I (the Fierce)**
born c.1077, fifth son of Malcolm III and Margaret *married* Sybilla, illegitimate daughter of Henry I of England *died* aged c.47 *reigned* 17 years

1124–1153 **DAVID I (the Saint)**
born c.1085, sixth son of Malcolm III and Margaret *married* Matilda, daughter of Waltheof, Earl of Huntingdon *died* aged c.68 *reigned* 29 years

1153–1165 **MALCOLM IV (the Maiden)**
born c.1141, son of Henry, Earl of Huntingdon, second son of David I *died* aged c.24 *reigned* 12 years

1165–1214 **WILLIAM I (the Lion)**
born c.1142, brother of Malcolm IV *married* Ermengarde, daughter of Richard, Viscount of Beaumont *died* aged c.72 *reigned* 49 years

1214–1249 **ALEXANDER II**
born 1198, son of William I *married* (1) Joan, daughter of John, King of England (2) Marie, daughter of Ingelram de Coucy *died* aged 50 *reigned* 34 years

1249–1286 **ALEXANDER III**
born 1241, son of Alexander II and Marie *married* (1) Margaret, daughter of Henry III of England (2) Yolande, daughter of the Count of Dreux *killed* accidentally aged 44 *reigned* 36 years

1286–1290 **MARGARET (the Maid of Norway)**
born 1283, daughter of Margaret (daughter of Alexander III) and Eric II of Norway *died* aged 7 *reigned* 4 years

FIRST INTERREGNUM 1290–1292
Throne disputed by 13 competitors. Crown awarded to John Balliol by adjudication of Edward I of England

THE HOUSE OF BALLIOL

1292–1296   **JOHN (Balliol)**
born c.1250, son of Dervorguilla, great-great-granddaughter of David I, and John de Balliol married Isabella, daughter of John, Earl of Surrey abdicated 1296 died 1313 aged c.63 reigned 3 years

SECOND INTERREGNUM 1296–1306
Edward I of England declared John Balliol to have forfeited the throne for contumacy in 1296 and took the government of Scotland into his own hands

THE HOUSE OF BRUCE

1306–1329   **ROBERT I (Bruce)**
born 1274, son of Robert Bruce and Marjorie, Countess of Carrick, and great-grandson of the second daughter of David, Earl of Huntingdon, brother of William I married (1) Isabella, daughter of Donald, Earl of Mar (2) Elizabeth, daughter of Richard, Earl of Ulster died aged 54 reigned 23 years

1329–1371   **DAVID II**
born 1324, son of Robert I and Elizabeth married (1) Joanna, daughter of Edward II of England (2) Margaret Drummond, widow of Sir John Logie (divorced) died aged 46 reigned 41 years

1332   Edward Balliol, son of John Balliol
(Sep–Dec)
1333–1336   Edward Balliol

THE HOUSE OF STEWART

1371–1390   **ROBERT II (Stewart)**
born 1316, son of Marjorie (daughter of Robert I) and Walter, High Steward of Scotland married (1) Elizabeth, daughter of Sir Robert Mure of Rowallan (2) Euphemia, daughter of Hugh, Earl of Ross died aged 74 reigned 19 years

1390–1406   **ROBERT III**
born c.1337, son of Robert II and Elizabeth married Annabella, daughter of Sir John Drummond of Stobhall died aged c.69 reigned 16 years

1406–1437   **JAMES I**
born 1394, son of Robert III married Joan Beaufort, daughter of John, Earl of Somerset assassinated aged 42 reigned 30 years

1437–1460   **JAMES II**
born 1430, son of James I married Mary, daughter of Arnold, Duke of Gueldres killed accidentally aged 29 reigned 23 years

1460–1488   **JAMES III**
born 1452, son of James II married Margaret, daughter of Christian I of Denmark assassinated aged 36 reigned 27 years

1488–1513   **JAMES IV**
born 1473, son of James III married Margaret Tudor, daughter of Henry VII of England killed in battle aged 40 reigned 25 years

1513–1542   **JAMES V**
born 1512, son of James IV married (1) Madeleine, daughter of Francis I of France (2) Mary of Lorraine, daughter of the Duc de Guise died aged 30 reigned 29 years

1542–1567   **MARY**
born 1542, daughter of James V and Mary married (1) the Dauphin, afterwards Francis II of France (2) Henry Stewart, Lord Darnley (3) James Hepburn, Earl of Bothwell abdicated 1567, prisoner in England from 1568, executed 1587 reigned 24 years

1567–1625   **JAMES VI (and I of England)**
born 1566, son of Mary, Queen of Scots, and Henry, Lord Darnley acceded 1567 to the Scottish throne reigned 58 years succeeded 1603 to the English throne, so joining the English and Scottish crowns in one person. The two kingdoms remained distinct until 1707 when the parliaments of the kingdoms became conjoined

WELSH SOVEREIGNS AND PRINCES

Wales was ruled by sovereign princes from the earliest times until the death of Llywelyn in 1282. The first English Prince of Wales was the son of Edward I, who was born in Caernarvon town on 25 April 1284. According to a discredited legend, he was presented to the Welsh chieftains as their prince, in fulfilment of a promise that they should have a prince who 'could not speak a word of English' and should be native born. This son, who afterwards became Edward II, was created 'Prince of Wales and Earl of Chester' at the Lincoln Parliament on 7 February 1301.

The title Prince of Wales is borne after individual conferment and is not inherited at birth, though some Princes have been declared and styled Prince of Wales but never formally so created (s.). The title was conferred on Prince Charles by the Queen on 26 July 1958. He was invested at Caernarvon on 1 July 1969.

INDEPENDENT PRINCES AD 844 TO 1282

844–878	Rhodri the Great
878–916	Anarawd, son of Rhodri
916–950	Hywel Dda, the Good
950–979	Iago ab Idwal (or Ieuaf)
979–985	Hywel ab Ieuaf, the Bad
985–986	Cadwallon, his brother
986–999	Maredudd ab Owain ap Hywel Dda
999–1005	Cynan ap Hywel ab Ieuaf
1005–1018	Aeddan ap Blegywyrd
1018–1023	Llywelyn ap Seisyll
1023–1039	Iago ab Idwal ap Meurig
1039–1063	Gruffydd ap Llywelyn ap Seisyll
1063–1075	Bleddyn ap Cynfyn
1075–1081	Trahaern ap Caradog
1081–1137	Gruffydd ap Cynan ab Iago
1137–1170	Owain Gwynedd
1170–1194	Dafydd ab Owain Gwynedd
1194–1240	Llywelyn Fawr, the Great
1240–1246	Dafydd ap Llywelyn
1246–1282	Llywelyn ap Gruffydd ap Llywelyn

ENGLISH PRINCES SINCE 1301

1301	Edward (Edward II)
1343	Edward the Black Prince, son of Edward III
1376	Richard (Richard II), son of the Black Prince
1399	Henry of Monmouth (Henry V)
1454	Edward of Westminster, son of Henry VI
1471	Edward of Westminster (Edward V)
1483	Edward, son of Richard III (d. 1484)
1489	Arthur Tudor, son of Henry VII
1504	Henry Tudor (Henry VIII)
1610	Henry Stuart, son of James I (d. 1612)
1616	Charles Stuart (Charles I)
c.1638 (s.)	Charles Stuart (Charles II)
1688 (s.)	James Francis Edward Stuart (The Old Pretender), son of James II (d. 1766)
1714	George Augustus (George II)
1729	Frederick Lewis, son of George II (d. 1751)
1751	George William Frederick (George III)
1762	George Augustus Frederick (George IV)
1841	Albert Edward (Edward VII)
1901	George (George V)
1910	Edward (Edward VIII)
1958	Charles, son of Elizabeth II

PRINCESSES ROYAL

The style Princess Royal is conferred at the sovereign's discretion on his or her eldest daughter. It is an honorary title, held for life, and cannot be inherited or passed on. It was first conferred on Princess Mary, daughter of Charles I, in approximately 1642.

c.1642	Princess Mary (1631–60), daughter of Charles I
1727	Princess Anne (1709–59), daughter of George II
1766	Princess Charlotte (1766–1828), daughter of George III
1840	Princess Victoria (1840–1901), daughter of Victoria
1905	Princess Louise (1867–1931), daughter of Edward VII
1932	Princess Mary (1897–1965), daughter of George V
1987	Princess Anne (b. 1950), daughter of Elizabeth II

DESCENDANTS OF QUEEN VICTORIA

I. HRH Princess Victoria Adelaide Mary Louisa, Princess Royal (1840–1901) *m* Friedrich III (1831–88), later German Emperor

II. HRH Prince Albert Edward (HM KING EDWARD VII) (1841–1910) *succeeded* 22 Jan 1901 *m* HRH Princess Alexandra of Denmark (1844–1925)

III. HRH Princess Alice Maud Mary (1843–78) *m* Prince Ludwig (1837–92), later Grand Duke of Hesse

IV. HRH Prince Alfred Ernest Albert, Duke of Edinburgh (1844–1900) *succeeded* as Duke of Saxe-Coburg and Gotha 1893 *m* Grand Duchess Marie Alexandrovna of Russia (1853–1920)

I.

1. HIM Wilhelm II (1859–1941), later German Emperor *m* (1) Princess Augusta Victoria of Schleswig-Holstein-Sonderburg-Augustenburg (1858–1921) (2) Princess Hermine of Reuss (1887–1947). *Issue* Wilhelm (1882–1951); Eitel-Friedrich (1883–1942); Adalbert (1884–1948); August Wilhelm (1887–1949); Oskar (1888–1958); Joachim (1890–1920); Viktoria Luise (1892–1980)

2. Charlotte (1860–1919) *m* Bernhard, Duke of Saxe-Meiningen (1851–1928). *Issue* Feodora (1879–1945)

3. Heinrich (1862–1929) *m* Princess Irene of Hesse (*see* III.3). *Issue* Waldemar (1889–1945); Sigismund (1896–1978); Heinrich (1900–4)

4. Sigismund (1864–6)

5. Victoria (1866–1929) *m* (1) Prince Adolf of Schaumburg-Lippe (1859–1916) (2) Alexander Zubkov (1900–36)

6. Waldemar (1868–79)

7. Sophie (1870–1932) *m* Constantine I (1868–1923), later King of the Hellenes. *Issue* George II (1890–1947); Alexander I (1893–1920); Helena (1896–1982); Paul I (1901–64); Irene (1904–74); Katherine (1913–2007)

8. Margarethe (1872–1954) *m* Prince Friedrich Karl of Hesse (1868–1940). *Issue* Friedrich Wilhelm (1893–1916); Maximilian (1894–1914); Philipp (1896–1980); Wolfgang (1896–1989); Richard (1901–69); Christoph (1901–43)

II.

1. Albert Victor, Duke of Clarence and Avondale (1864–92)

2. George (HM KING GEORGE V) (1865–1936) (*see* House of Windsor)

3. Louise (1867–1931), later Princess Royal *m* 1st Duke of Fife (1849–1912). *Issue* Alexandra (1891–1959); Maud (1893–1945)

4. Victoria (1868–1935)

5. Maud (1869–1938) *m* Prince Carl of Denmark (1872–1957), later King Haakon VII of Norway. *Issue* Olav V (1903–91)

6. Alexander (6–7 Apr 1871)

III.

1. Victoria (1863–1950) *m* Prince Louis of Battenberg (1854–1921), later 1st Marquess of Milford Haven. *Issue* Alice (1885–1969); Louise (1889–1965); George (1892–1938); Louis (1900–79)

2. Elizabeth (1864–1918) *m* Grand Duke Sergius of Russia (1857–1905)

3. Irene (1866–1953) *m* Prince Heinrich of Prussia (*see* I.3)

4. Ernst Ludwig (1868–1937), Grand Duke of Hesse, *m* (1) Princess Victoria Melita of Saxe-Coburg (see IV.3) (2) Princess Eleonore of Solms-Hohensolms-Lich (1871–1937). *Issue* Elizabeth (1895–1903); George (1906–37); Ludwig (1908–68)

5. Frederick William (1870–3)

6. Alix (Tsaritsa of Russia) (1872–1918) *m* Nicholas II, Tsar of All the Russias (1868–1918). *Issue* Olga (1895–1918); Tatiana (1897–1918); Marie (1899–1918); Anastasia (1901–18); Alexis (1904–18)

7. Marie (1874–8)

QUEEN VICTORIA (Alexandrina Victoria) (1819–1901) *succeeded* 20 Jun 1837 *m* (Francis) Albert Augustus Charles Emmanuel, Duke of Saxony, Prince of Saxe-Coburg and Gotha (HRH Albert, Prince Consort) (1819–61)

VI. HRH Princess Louise Caroline Alberta (1848–1939) *m* Marquess of Lorne (1845–1914), later 9th Duke of Argyll

VII. HRH Prince Arthur William Patrick Albert, Duke of Connaught (1850–1942) *m* Princess Louisa of Prussia (1860–1917)

VIII. HRH Prince Leopold George Duncan Albert, Duke of Albany (1853–84) *m* Princess Helena of Waldeck (1861–1922)

IX. HRH Princess Beatrice Mary Victoria Feodore (1857–1944) *m* Prince Henry of Battenberg (1858–96)

1. Alfred, Prince of Saxe-Coburg (1874–99)

2. Marie (1875–1938) *m* Ferdinand (1865–1927), later King of Roumania. *Issue* Carol II (1893–1953); Elisabeth (1894–1956); Marie (1900–61); Nicolas (1903–78); Ileana (1909–91); Mircea (1913–16)

3. Victoria Melita (1876–1936) *m* (1) Grand Duke Ernst Ludwig of Hesse (*see* III.4) (2) Grand Duke Kirill of Russia (1876–1938). *Issue* Marie (1907–51); Kira (1909–67); Vladimir (1917–92)

4. Alexandra (1878–1942) *m* Ernst, Prince of Hohenlohe Langenburg (1863–1950). *Issue* Gottfried (1897–1960); Maria (1899–1967); Alexandra (1901–63); Irma (1902–86)

5. Beatrice (1884–1966) *m* Alfonso of Orleans, Infante of Spain (1886–1975). *Issue* Alvaro (1910–97); Alonso (1912–36); Ataulfo (1913–74)

1. Margaret (1882–1920) *m* Crown Prince Gustaf Adolf (1882–1973), later King of Sweden. *Issue* Gustaf Adolf (1906–47); Sigvard (1907–2002); Ingrid (1910–2000); Bertil (1912–97); Count Carl Bernadotte (1916–2012)

2. Arthur (1883–1938) *m* HH Duchess of Fife (1891–1959). *Issue* Alastair Arthur (1914–43)

3. (Victoria) Patricia (1886–1974) *m* Adm. Hon. Sir Alexander Ramsay (1881–1972). *Issue* Alexander (1919–2000)

1. Alice (1883–1981) *m* Prince Alexander of Teck (1874–1957), later 1st Earl of Athlone. *Issue* May (1906–94); Rupert (1907–28); Maurice (Mar–Sep 1910)

2. Charles Edward (1884–1954), Duke of Albany until title suspended 1917, Duke of Saxe-Coburg-Gotha *m* Princess Victoria Adelheid of Schleswig-Holstein-Sonderburg-Glücksburg (1885–1970). *Issue* Johann Leopold (1906–72); Sibylla (1908–72); Dietmar Hubertus (1909–43); Caroline (1912–83); Friedrich Josias (1918–98)

1. Alexander, 1st Marquess of Carisbrooke (1886–1960) *m* Lady Irene Denison (1890–1956). *Issue* Iris (1920–82)

2. Victoria Eugénie (1887–1969) *m* Alfonso XIII, King of Spain (1886–1941). *Issue* Alfonso (1907–38); Jaime (1908–75); Beatriz (1909–2002); Maria (1911–96); Juan (1913–93); Gonzalo (1914–34)

3. Maj. Lord Leopold Mountbatten (1889–1922)

4. Maurice (1891–1914)

V. HRH Princess Helena Augusta Victoria (1846–1923) *m* Prince Christian of Schleswig-Holstein-Sonderburg-Augustenburg (1831–1917)

1. Christian Victor (1867–1900)

2. Albert (1869–1931), later Duke of Schleswig-Holstein

3. Helena (1870–1948)

4. Marie Louise (1872–1956), *m* Prince Aribert of Anhalt (1864–1933)

5. Harold (12–20 May 1876)

THE HOUSE OF WINDSOR

King George V assumed by royal proclamation (17 July 1917) for his House and family, as well as for all descendants in the male line of Queen Victoria who are subjects of these realms, the name of Windsor.

KING GEORGE V

(George Frederick Ernest Albert), second son of King Edward VII *born* 3 June 1865 *married* 6 July 1893 HSH Princess Victoria Mary Augusta Louise Olga Pauline Claudine Agnes of Teck (Queen Mary *born* 26 May 1867 *died* 24 March 1953) *succeeded* to the throne 6 May 1910 *died* 20 January 1936. *Issue*

1. HRH PRINCE EDWARD Albert Christian George Andrew Patrick David *born* 23 June 1894 *succeeded* to the throne as King Edward VIII, 20 January 1936 *abdicated* 11 December 1936 *created* Duke of Windsor 1937 (Duke of Windsor 1937 Mrs Wallis Simpson (Her Grace The Duchess of Windsor *born* 19 June 1896 *died* 24 April 1986) *died* 28 May 1972

2. HRH PRINCE ALBERT Frederick Arthur George *born* 14 December 1895 *created* Duke of York 1920 *married* 26 April 1923 Lady Elizabeth Bowes-Lyon, youngest daughter of the 14th Earl of Strathmore and Kinghorne (HM Queen Elizabeth the Queen Mother *born* 4 August 1900 *died* 30 March 2002) *succeeded* to the throne as King George VI, 11 December 1936 *died* 6 February 1952. *Issue*
   (1) HRH Princess Elizabeth Alexandra Mary *succeeded* to the throne as Queen Elizabeth II, 6 February 1952 (*see* Royal Family)
   (2) HRH Princess Margaret Rose (later HRH The Princess Margaret, Countess of Snowdon) *born* 21 August 1930 *married* 6 May 1960 Antony Charles Robert Armstrong-Jones, GCVO *created* Earl of Snowdon 1961 (1930–2017), *marriage dissolved* 1978, *died* 9 February 2002, having had issue (*see* Royal Family)

3. HRH PRINCESS (Victoria Alexandra Alice) MARY *born* 25 April 1897 *created* Princess Royal 1932 *married* 28 February 1922 Viscount Lascelles, later the 6th Earl of Harewood (1882–1947) *died* 28 March 1965. *Issue:*

(1) George Henry Hubert Lascelles, 7th Earl of Harewood, KBE *born* 7 February 1923 *died* 11 July 2011 *married* (1) 1949 Maria (Marion) Stein (marriage dissolved 1967) *issue (a)* David Henry George, 8th Earl of Harewood *born* 1950 *(b)* James Edward *born* 1953 *(c)* (Robert) Jeremy Hugh *born* 1955 (2) 1967 Patricia Tuckwell *issue (d)* Mark Hubert *born* 1964
(2) Gerald David Lascelles *born* 21 August 1924 *died* 27 February 1998 *married* (1) 1952 Angela Dowding (marriage dissolved 1978) *issue (a)* Henry Ulick *born* 1953 (2) 1978 Elizabeth Collingwood (Elizabeth Colvin) *issue (b)* Martin David *born* 1962

4. HRH PRINCE HENRY William Frederick Albert *born* 31 March 1900 *created* Duke of Gloucester, Earl of Ulster and Baron Culloden 1928 *married* 6 November 1935 Lady Alice Christabel Montagu-Douglas-Scott, daughter of the 7th Duke of Buccleuch and Queensberry (HRH Princess Alice, Duchess of Gloucester *born* 25 December 1901 *died* 29 October 2004) *died* 10 June 1974. *Issue*
   (1) HRH Prince William Henry Andrew Frederick *born* 18 December 1941 *killed* 28 August 1972
   (2) HRH Prince Richard Alexander Walter George (HRH The Duke of Gloucester, *see* Royal Family)

5. HRH PRINCE GEORGE Edward Alexander Edmund *born* 20 December 1902 *created* Duke of Kent, Earl of St Andrews and Baron Downpatrick 1934 *married* 29 November 1934 HRH Princess Marina of Greece and Denmark (*born* 30 November 1906 *died* 27 August 1968) *killed* on active service 25 August 1942. *Issue*
   (1) HRH Prince Edward George Nicholas Paul Patrick (HRH The Duke of Kent, *see* Royal Family)
   (2) HRH Princess Alexandra Helen Elizabeth Olga Christabel (HRH Princess Alexandra, the Hon. Lady Ogilvy, *see* Royal Family)
   (3) HRH Prince Michael George Charles Franklin (HRH Prince Michael of Kent, *see* Royal Family)

6. HRH PRINCE JOHN Charles Francis *born* 12 July 1905 *died* 18 January 1919

PRECEDENCE

ENGLAND AND WALES

The Sovereign
The Prince Philip, Duke of Edinburgh
The Prince of Wales
The Sovereign's younger sons
The Sovereign's grandsons
The Sovereign's cousins
Archbishop of Canterbury
Lord High Chancellor
Archbishop of York
The Prime Minister
Lord President of the Council
Speaker of the House of Commons
Speaker of the House of Lords
President of the Supreme Court
Lord Chief Justice of England and
  Wales
Lord Privy Seal
Ambassadors and High Commissioners
Lord Great Chamberlain
Earl Marshal
Lord Steward of the Household
Lord Chamberlain of the Household
Master of the Horse
Dukes, according to their patent of
  creation:
  1. of England
  2. of Scotland
  3. of Great Britain
  4. of Ireland
  5. those created since the Union
Eldest sons of Dukes of the Blood
  Royal
Ministers, Envoys, and other important
  overseas visitors
Marquesses, according to their patent
  of creation:
  1. of England
  2. of Scotland
  3. of Great Britain
  4. of Ireland
  5. those created since the Union
Dukes' eldest sons
Earls, according to their patent of
  creation:
  1. of England
  2. of Scotland
  3. of Great Britain
  4. of Ireland
  5. those created since the Union
Younger sons of Dukes of Blood
  Royal

Marquesses' eldest sons
Dukes' younger sons
Viscounts, according to their patent of
  creation:
  1. of England
  2. of Scotland
  3. of Great Britain
  4. of Ireland
  5. those created since the Union
Earls' eldest sons
Marquesses' younger sons
Bishop of London
Bishop of Durham
Bishop of Winchester
Other English Diocesan Bishops,
  according to seniority of
  consecration
Retired Church of England Diocesan
  Bishops, according to seniority of
  consecration
Suffragan Bishops, according to
  seniority of consecration
Secretaries of State, if of the degree of
  a Baron
Barons, according to their patent of
  creation:
  1. of England
  2. of Scotland (Lords of Parliament)
  3. of Great Britain
  4. of Ireland
  5. those created since the Union,
    including Life Barons
Master of the Rolls
Deputy President of the Supreme
  Court
Justices of the Supreme Court,
  according to seniority of
  appointment
Treasurer of the Household
Comptroller of the Household
Vice-Chamberlain of the Household
Secretaries of State under the degree of
  Baron
Viscounts' eldest sons
Earls' younger sons
Barons' eldest sons
Knights of the Garter
Privy Counsellors
Chancellor of the Order of the Garter
Chancellor of the Exchequer
Chancellor of the Duchy of Lancaster
President of the Queen's Bench
  Division
President of the Family Division

Chancellor of the High Court
Lord Justices of Appeal, according to
  seniority of appointment
Judges of the High Court, according to
  seniority of appointment
Viscounts' younger sons
Barons' younger sons
Sons of Life Peers
Baronets, according to date of patent
Knights of the Thistle
Knights Grand Cross of the Bath
Knights Grand Cross of St Michael
  and St George
Knights Grand Cross of the Royal
  Victorian Order
Knights Grand Cross of the British
  Empire
Knights Commanders of the Bath
Knights Commanders of St Michael
  and St George
Knights Commanders of the Royal
  Victorian Order
Knights Commanders of the British
  Empire
Knights Bachelor
Circuit Judges, according to priority
  and order of their respective
  appointments
Master of the Court of Protection
Companions of the Bath
Companions of St Michael and St
  George
Commanders of the Royal Victorian
  Order
Commanders of the British Empire
Companions of the Distinguished
  Service Order
Lieutenants of the Royal Victorian
  Order
Officers of the British Empire
Companions of the Imperial Service
  Order
Eldest sons of younger sons of peers
Baronets' eldest sons
Eldest sons of knights, in the same
  order as their fathers
Members of the Royal Victorian Order
Members of the British Empire
Baronets' younger sons
Knights' younger sons, in the same
  order as their fathers
Esquires
Gentlemen

WOMEN

Women take the same rank as their husbands or as their brothers; but the daughter of a peer marrying a commoner retains her title as Lady or Honourable. Daughters of peers rank next immediately after the wives of their elder brothers, and before their younger brothers' wives. Daughters of peers marrying peers of a lower degree take the same order of precedence as that of their husbands; thus the daughter of a Duke marrying a Baron becomes of the rank of Baroness only, while her sisters married to commoners retain their rank and take precedence over the Baroness. Merely official rank on the husband's part does not give any similar precedence to the wife.

Peeresses in their own right take the same precedence as peers of the same rank, ie from their date of creation.

SCOTLAND

The Sovereign
The Prince Philip, Duke of Edinburgh
The Lord High Commissioner to the General Assembly of the Church of Scotland (while that assembly is sitting)
The Duke of Rothesay (eldest son of the Sovereign)
The Sovereign's younger sons
The Sovereign's grandsons
The Sovereign's nephews
Lord-Lieutenants
Lord Provosts, during their term of office*
Sheriffs Principal, during their term of office and within the bounds of their respective sheriffdoms
Lord Chancellor of Great Britain
Moderator of the General Assembly of the Church of Scotland
Keeper of the Great Seal of Scotland (the First Minister)
Presiding Officer
The Secretary of State for Scotland
Hereditary High Constable of Scotland
Hereditary Master of the Household in Scotland
Dukes, as in England
Eldest sons of Dukes of the Blood Royal

Marquesses, as in England
Dukes' eldest sons
Earls, as in England
Younger sons of Dukes of Blood Royal
Marquesses' eldest sons
Dukes' younger sons
Lord Justice General
Lord Clerk Register
Lord Advocate
The Advocate General
Lord Justice Clerk
Viscounts, as in England
Earls' eldest sons
Marquesses' younger sons
Lords of Parliament or Barons, as in England
Eldest sons of Viscounts
Earls' younger sons
Eldest sons of Lords of Parliament or Barons
Knights and Ladies of the Garter
Knights and Ladies of the Thistle
Privy Counsellors
Senators of the College of Justice (Lords of Session)
Viscounts' younger sons
Younger sons of Lords of Parliament or Barons
Baronets
Knights and Dames Grand Cross of orders, as in England

Knights and Dames Commanders of orders, as in England
Solicitor-General for Scotland
Lord Lyon King of Arms
Sheriffs Principal, when not within own county
Knights Bachelor
Sheriffs
Companions of Orders, as in England
Commanders of the Royal Victorian Order
Commanders of the British Empire
Lieutenants of the Royal Victorian Order
Companions of the Distinguished Service Order
Officers of the British Empire
Companions of the Imperial Service Order
Eldest sons of younger sons of peers
Eldest sons of baronets
Eldest sons of knights, as in England
Members of the Royal Victorian Order
Members of the British Empire
Baronets' younger sons
Knights' younger sons
Queen's Counsel
Esquires
Gentlemen

* The Lord Provosts of Aberdeen, Dundee, Edinburgh and Glasgow are Lord-Lieutenants for these cities *ex officio* and take precedence as such

THE PEERAGE

ABBREVIATIONS AND SYMBOLS

S.	Scottish title	§	life peer disqualified from sitting in the House of
I.	Irish title		Lords as a member of the judiciary
**	hereditary peer remaining in the House of Lords	ℂ	life peer who has resigned permanently from the
°	there is no 'of' in the title		House of Lords
b.	born	E.	life peer expelled for absenteeism under section 2
s.	succeeded		of the House of Lords Reform Act 2014 (*see*
m.	married		below)
c.p.	civil partnership	F_	represents forename
w.	widower or widow	S_	represents surname
M.	minor	†	heir not ascertained at time of going to press
cr.	created	‡	title not ascertained at time of going to press

The rules which govern the creation and succession of peerages are extremely complicated. There are, technically, five separate peerages, the Peerage of England, of Scotland, of Ireland, of Great Britain, and of the United Kingdom. The Peerage of Great Britain dates from 1707 when an Act of Union combined the two kingdoms of England and Scotland and separate peerages were discontinued. The Peerage of the United Kingdom dates from 1801 when Great Britain and Ireland were combined under an Act of Union. Some Scottish peers have received additional peerages of Great Britain or of the UK since 1707, and some Irish peers additional peerages of the UK since 1801.

The Peerage of Ireland was not entirely discontinued from 1801 but holders of Irish peerages, whether pre-dating or created subsequent to the Union of 1801, were not entitled to sit in the House of Lords if they had no additional English, Scottish, Great Britain or UK peerage. However, they were eligible for election to the House of Commons and to vote in parliamentary elections. An Irish peer holding a peerage of a lower grade which enabled him to sit in the House of Lords was introduced there by the title which enabled him to sit, though for all other purposes he was known by his higher title.

In the Peerage of Scotland there is no rank of Baron; the equivalent rank is Lord of Parliament, abbreviated to 'Lord' (the female equivalent is 'Lady').

All peers of England, Scotland, Great Britain or the UK who were 21 years or over, and of British, Irish or Commonwealth nationality were entitled to sit in the House of Lords until the House of Lords Act 1999, when hereditary peers lost the right to sit. However, section two of the act provided an exception for 90 hereditary peers plus the holders of the office of Earl Marshal and Lord Great Chamberlain to remain as members of the House of Lords for their lifetime or pending further reform. Of the 90 hereditary peers, 75 were elected by the hereditary peers in their political party, or Crossbench grouping, and the remaining 15 by the whole house. Until 7 November 2002 any vacancy arising due to the death of one of the 90 excepted hereditary peers was filled by the runner-up to the original election. From 7 November 2002 any vacancy due to a death – or, from 2014, a permanent retirement – has been filled by holding a by-election. By-elections are conducted in accordance with arrangements made by the Clerk of the Parliaments and have to take place within three months of a vacancy occurring. If the vacancy is among the 75, only the excepted hereditary peers in the relevant party or Crossbench grouping are entitled to vote. If the vacancy is among the other 15, the whole house is entitled to vote.

In the list below, peers currently holding one of the 92 hereditary places in the House of Lords are indicated by **.

HEREDITARY WOMEN PEERS

Most hereditary peerages pass on death to the nearest male heir, but there are exceptions, and several are held by women.

A woman peer in her own right retains her title after marriage, and if her husband's rank is the superior she is designated by the two titles jointly, the inferior one second. Her hereditary claim still holds good in spite of any marriage whether higher or lower. No rank held by a woman can confer any title or even precedence upon her husband but the rank of a hereditary woman peer in her own right is inherited by her eldest son (or in some cases daughter).

After the Peerage Act 1963, hereditary women peers in their own right were entitled to sit in the House of Lords, subject to the same qualifications as men, until the House of Lords Act 1999.

LIFE PEERS

From 1876 to 2009 non-hereditary or life peerages were conferred on certain eminent judges to enable the judicial functions of the House of Lords to be carried out. These lords were known as Lords of Appeal in Ordinary or law lords. The judicial role of the House of Lords as the highest appeal court in the UK ended on 30 July 2009 and since 1 October 2009, under the Constitutional Reform Act 2005, any peer who holds a senior judicial office is disqualified from sitting in the House of Lords until they retire from that office. In the list of life peerages which follows, members of the judiciary who are currently disqualified from sitting and voting in the House of Lords until retirement, are marked by a '§'.

Under the Constitutional Reform and Governance Act 2010, five peers permanently resigned from the House of Lords.

Since 1958 life peerages have been conferred upon distinguished men and women from all walks of life, giving them seats in the House of Lords in the degree of Baron or Baroness. They are addressed in the same way as hereditary lords and barons, and their children have similar courtesy titles.

HOUSE OF LORDS REFORM ACT 2014

The House of Lords Reform Act 2014 makes provision for a member of the House of Lords who is a peer to retire or resign by giving notice in writing to the Clerk of Parliaments. Resignations may not be rescinded. A number of life peers and elected hereditary peers have already retired permanently under this provision. The Act also makes provision for the expulsion of peers who do not attend the House of Lords for an entire parliamentary session which is longer than six months (indicated by an 'E.' in the following list). Peers on leave of absence or subject to a suspension or disqualification which results in absenteeism for an entire session will not be expelled. The House can also resolve that a peer should not be expelled by reason of special circumstances.

All life peers who have resigned permanently from the House of Lords are indicated by a '**℃**' in the following list.

PEERAGES EXTINCT SINCE 31 AUGUST 2017
BARONY: Melchett (cr. 1928)
EARLDOM: Lovelace (cr. 1838)
VISCOUNTCIES: Alanbrooke (cr. 1946); Churchill (cr. 1902)
LIFE PEERAGES: Barber of Tewkesbury (cr. 1992); Browne-Wilkinson (cr. 1991); Carington Of Upton (cr. 1999); Crickhowell (cr. 1987); Dean of Thornton-le-Fylde (cr. 1993); Farrington of Ribbleton (cr. 1994); Gibson of Market Rasen (cr. 2000); Howie of Troon (cr. 1978); Hutchinson of Lullington (cr. 1978); Imbert (cr. 1999); Jowell (cr. 2015); Laird (cr. 1999); Mackay of Drumadoon (cr. 1995); Martin of Springburn (cr. 2009); Nicol (cr. 1982); Quirk (cr. 1994); Richard (cr. 1990); Stewartby (cr. 1992); Steyn (cr. 1995); Sutherland of Houndwood (cr. 2001); Temple-Morris (cr. 2001); Thomas of Macclesfield (cr. 1997); Turner of Camden (cr. 1985); Vincent of Coleshill (cr. 1996); Wade of Chorlton (cr. 1990)

DISCLAIMER OF PEERAGES
The Peerage Act 1963 enables peers to disclaim their peerages for life. Peers alive in 1963 could disclaim within twelve months after the passing of the act (31 July 1963); a person subsequently succeeding to a peerage may disclaim within 12 months (one month if an MP) after the date of succession, or of reaching 21, if later. The disclaimer is irrevocable but does not affect the descent of the peerage after the disclaimant's death, and children of a disclaimed peer may, if they wish, retain their precedence and any courtesy titles and styles borne as children of a peer. The disclaimer permitted the disclaimant to sit in the House of Commons if elected as an MP. As the House of Lords Act 1999 removed the automatic right of hereditary peers to sit in the House of Lords, they are now entitled to sit in the House of Commons without having to disclaim their titles.

The following peerages are currently disclaimed:
EARLDOM: Selkirk (1994)
BARONIES: Sanderson of Ayot (1971); Silkin (2002)
PEERS WHO ARE MINORS (ie under 21 years of age)
EARLDOM: St Germans (b. 2004)
BARONY: Rodney (b. 1999)

FORMS OF ADDRESS
Forms of address are given under the style for each individual rank of the peerage. Both formal and social forms of address are given where usage differs; nowadays, the social form is generally preferred to the formal, which increasingly is used only for official documents and on very formal occasions.

ROLL OF THE PEERAGE
Crown Office, House of Lords, London SW1A 0PW
T 020-7219 4687 **E** hereditary.claims@gmail.com

The Roll of the Peerage is kept at the Crown Office and maintained by the Registrar and Assistant Registrar of the Peerage in accordance with the terms of a 2004 royal warrant. The roll records the names of all living life peers and hereditary peers who have proved their succession to the satisfaction of the Lord Chancellor. The Roll of the Peerage is maintained in addition to the Clerk of the Parliaments' register of hereditary peers eligible to stand for election in House of Lords' by-elections.

A person whose name is not entered on the Roll of the Peerage can not be addressed or mentioned by the title of a peer in any official document.

Registrar, Mrs Ceri King

HEREDITARY PEERS

PEERS OF THE BLOOD ROYAL

Style, His Royal Highness the Duke of _/His Royal Highness the Earl of_/His Royal Highness the Lord_
Style of address (formal) May it please your Royal Highness; *(informal)* Sir

Created	Title, order of succession, name, etc	Heir
	Dukes	
1947	Edinburgh (1st), HRH the Prince Philip, Duke of Edinburgh	The Prince of Wales *
1337	Cornwall, HRH the Prince of Wales, s. 1952	‡
1398 S.	Rothesay, HRH the Prince of Wales, s. 1952	‡
2011	Cambridge (1st), HRH Prince William of Wales	HRH Prince George of Cambridge
2018	Sussex (1st), HRH Prince Henry of Wales	None
1986	York (1st), Prince Andrew, HRH the Duke of York	None
1928	Gloucester (2nd), Prince Richard, HRH the Duke of Gloucester, s. 1974	Earl of Ulster
1934	Kent (2nd), Prince Edward, HRH the Duke of Kent, s. 1942	Earl of St Andrews
	Earl	
1999	Wessex (1st), Prince Edward, HRH the Earl of Wessex	Viscount Severn

* In June 1999 Buckingham Palace announced that the current Earl of Wessex will be granted the Dukedom of Edinburgh when the title reverts to the Crown. The title will only revert to the Crown on both the death of the current Duke of Edinburgh and the Prince of Wales' succession as king
‡ The title is held by the sovereign's eldest son from the moment of his birth or the sovereign's accession

DUKES

Coronet, Eight strawberry leaves

Style, His Grace the Duke of _
Envelope (formal), His Grace the Duke of _; *(social)*, The Duke of _. *Letter (formal)*, My Lord Duke; *(social)*, Dear Duke. *Spoken (formal)*, Your Grace; *(social)*, Duke
Wife's style, Her Grace the Duchess of _
Envelope (formal), Her Grace the Duchess of _; *(social)*, The Duchess of _. *Letter (formal)*, Dear Madam; *(social)*, Dear Duchess. *Spoken*, Duchess
Eldest son's style, Takes his father's second title as a courtesy title (*see* Courtesy Titles)
Younger sons' style, 'Lord' before forename (F_) and surname (S_)
Envelope, Lord F_ S_. *Letter (formal)*, My Lord; *(social)*, Dear Lord F_. *Spoken (formal)*, My Lord; *(social)*, Lord F_
Daughters' style, 'Lady' before forename (F_) and surname (S_)
Envelope, Lady F_ S_. *Letter (formal)*, Dear Madam; *(social)*, Dear Lady F_. *Spoken*, Lady F_

Created	Title, order of succession, name, etc	Heir
1868 I.	*Abercorn (5th)*, James Hamilton, KG, *b.* 1934, *s.* 1979, *m.*	Marquess of Hamilton, *b.* 1969
1701 S.	*Argyll (13th)*, Torquhil Ian Campbell, *b.* 1968, *s.* 2001 *m.*	Marquess of Lorne, *b.* 2004
1703 S.	*Atholl (12th)*, Bruce George Ronald Murray, *b.* 1960, *s.* 2012, *m.*	Marquis of Tullibardine, *b.* 1985
1682	*Beaufort (12th)*, Henry John Fitzroy Somerset, *b.* 1952, *s.* 2017, *m.*	Marquess of Worcester, *b.* 1989
1694	*Bedford (15th)*, Andrew Ian Henry Russell, *b.* 1962, *s.* 2003, *m.*	Marquess of Tavistock, *b.* 2005
1663 S.	*Buccleuch (10th)* and *Queensberry (12th)* (*S. 1684*), Richard Walter John Montagu Douglas Scott, KT, KBE, *b.* 1954, *s.* 2007, *m.*	Earl of Dalkeith, *b.* 1984
1694	*Devonshire (12th)*, Peregrine Andrew Morny Cavendish, KCVO, CBE, *b.* 1944, *s.* 2004, *m.*	Earl of Burlington, *b.* 1969
1900	*Fife (4th)*, David Charles Carnegie, *b.* 1961, *s.* 2015, *m.*	Earl of Southesk, *b.* 1989
1675	*Grafton (12th)*, Henry Oliver Charles FitzRoy, *b.* 1978, *s.* 2011, *m.*	Earl of Euston, *b.* 2012
1643 S.	*Hamilton (16th)* and *Brandon (13th)* (*1711*), Alexander Douglas Douglas-Hamilton, *b.* 1978, *s.* 2010, *m. Premier Peer of Scotland*	Marquess of Douglas and Clydesdale, *b.* 2012
1766 I.	*Leinster (9th)*, Maurice FitzGerald, *b.* 1948, *s.* 2004, *m. Premier Duke, Marquess and Earl of Ireland*	Edward F., *b.* 1988
1719	*Manchester (13th)*, Alexander Charles David Drogo Montagu, *b.* 1962, *s.* 2002, *m.*	Lord Kimble W. D. M., *b.* 1964
1702	*Marlborough (12th)*, Charles James Spencer-Churchill, *b.* 1955, *s.* 2014, *m.*	Marquess of Blandford, *b.* 1992
1707 S. **	*Montrose (8th)*, James Graham, *b.* 1935, *s.* 1992, *w.*	Marquis of Graham, *b.* 1973
1483 **	*Norfolk (18th)*, Edward William Fitzalan-Howard, *b.* 1956, *s.* 2002, *m. Premier Duke and Earl Marshal*	Earl of Arundel and Surrey, *b.* 1987
1766	*Northumberland (12th)*, Ralph George Algernon Percy, *b.* 1956, *s.* 1995, *m.*	Earl Percy, *b.* 1984
1675	*Richmond (11th)*, *Gordon (6th)* (*1876*) and *Lennox (11th)* (*S. 1675*), Charles Henry Gordon Lennox, *b.* 1955, *s.* 2017, *m.*	Earl of March and Kinrara, *b.* 1994
1707 S.	*Roxburghe (10th)*, Guy David Innes-Ker, *b.* 1954, *s.* 1974, *m. Premier Baronet of Scotland*	Marquis of Bowmont and Cessford, *b.* 1981
1703	*Rutland (11th)*, David Charles Robert Manners, *b.* 1959, *s.* 1999, *m.*	Marquess of Granby, *b.* 1999
1684	*St Albans (14th)*, Murray de Vere Beauclerk, *b.* 1939, *s.* 1988, *m.*	Earl of Burford, *b.* 1965
1547 **	*Somerset (19th)*, John Michael Edward Seymour, *b.* 1952, *s.* 1984, *m.*	Lord Seymour, *b.* 1982
1833	*Sutherland (7th)*, Francis Ronald Egerton, *b.* 1940, *s.* 2000, *m.*	Marquess of Stafford, *b.* 1975
1814 **	*Wellington (9th)*, Arthur Charles Valerian Wellesley, OBE, *b.* 1945, *s.* 2014, *m.*	Marquess of Douro, *b.* 1978
1874	*Westminster (7th)* and *9th Marquess of Westminster (1831)*, Hugh Richard Louis Grosvenor, *b.* 1991, *s.* 2016	To Marquessate only, Earl of Wilton (*see* that title)

MARQUESSES

Coronet, Four strawberry leaves alternating with four silver balls

Style, The Most Hon. the Marquess (of) _ . In Scotland the spelling 'Marquis' is preferred for pre-Union creations
Envelope (formal), The Most Hon. the Marquess of _; *(social),* The Marquess of _. *Letter (formal),* My Lord; *(social),* Dear Lord _.
Spoken (formal), My Lord; *(social),* Lord _

Wife's style, The Most Hon. the Marchioness (of) _
Envelope (formal), The Most Hon. the Marchioness of _; *(social),* The Marchioness of _. *Letter (formal),* Madam; *(social),* Dear
Lady _. *Spoken,* Lady _

Eldest son's style, Takes his father's second title as a courtesy title (*see* Courtesy Titles)

Younger sons' style, 'Lord' before forename and surname, as for Duke's younger sons

Daughters' style, 'Lady' before forename and surname, as for Duke's daughter

Created	Title, order of succession, name, etc	Heir
1915	*Aberdeen and Temair (7th),* Alexander George Gordon, *b.* 1955, *s.* 2002, *m.*	Earl of Haddo, *b.* 1983
1876	*Abergavenny (6th) and 10th Earl of Abergavenny (1784),* Christopher George Charles Nevill, *b.* 1955, *s.* 2000, *m.*	To Earldom only, David M, R, N, *b.* 1941
1821	*Ailesbury (8th),* Michael Sidney Cedric Brudenell-Bruce, *b.* 1926, *s.* 1974	Earl of Cardigan, *b.* 1952
1831	*Ailsa (9th),* David Thomas Kennedy, *b.* 1958, *s.* 2015, *m.*	Earl of Cassilis, *b.* 1995
1815	*Anglesey (8th),* Charles Alexander Vaughan Paget, *b.* 1950, *s.* 2013, *m.*	Earl of Uxbridge, *b.* 1986
1789	*Bath (7th),* Alexander George Thynn, *b.* 1932, *s.* 1992, *m.*	Viscount Weymouth, *b.* 1974
1826	*Bristol (8th),* Frederick William Augustus Hervey, *b.* 1979, *s.* 1999, *m.*	Timothy H. H., *b.* 1960
1796	*Bute (7th),* John Colum Crichton-Stuart, *b.* 1958, *s.* 1993, *m.*	Earl of Dumfries, *b.* 1989
1812 °	*Camden (6th),* David George Edward Henry Pratt, *b.* 1930, *s.* 1983	Earl of Brecknock, *b.* 1965
1815 **	*Cholmondeley (7th),* David George Philip Cholmondeley, KCVO, *b.* 1960, *s.* 1990, *m. Lord Great Chamberlain*	Earl of Rocksavage, *b.* 2010
1816 I. °	*Conyngham (8th),* Henry Vivian Pierpoint Conyngham, *b.* 1951, *s.* 2009, *m.*	Earl of Mount Charles, *b.* 1975
1791 I.	*Donegall (8th),* Arthur Patrick Chichester, *b.* 1952, *s.* 2007, *m.*	Earl of Belfast, *b.* 1990
1789 I.	*Downshire (9th),* (Arthur Francis) Nicholas Wills Hill, *b.* 1959, *s.* 2003, *m.*	Earl of Hillsborough, *b.* 1996
1801 I.	*Ely (9th),* Charles John Tottenham, *b.* 1943, *s.* 2006, *m.*	Lord Timothy C. T., *b.* 1948
1801	*Exeter (8th),* (William) Michael Anthony Cecil, *b.* 1935, *s.* 1988, *m.*	Lord Burghley, *b.* 1970
1800 I.	*Headfort (7th),* Thomas Michael Ronald Christopher Taylour, *b.* 1959, *s.* 2005, *w.*	Earl of Bective, *b.* 1989
1793	*Hertford (9th),* Henry Jocelyn Seymour, *b.* 1958, *s.* 1997, *m.*	Earl of Yarmouth, *b.* 1993
1599 S.	*Huntly (13th),* Granville Charles Gomer Gordon, *b.* 1944, *s.* 1987, *m. Premier Marquess of Scotland*	Earl of Aboyne, *b.* 1973
1784	*Lansdowne (9th),* Charles Maurice Mercer Nairne Petty-Fitzmaurice, LVO, *b.* 1941, *s.* 1999, *m.*	Earl of Kerry, *b.* 1970
1902	*Linlithgow (4th),* Adrian John Charles Hope, *b.* 1946, *s.* 1987, *m.*	Earl of Hopetoun, *b.* 1969
1816 I.	*Londonderry (10th),* Frederick Aubrey Vane-Tempest-Stewart, *b.* 1972, *s.* 2012	Lord Reginald A. V.-T.-S., *b.* 1977
1701 S.	*Lothian (13th) and Baron Kerr of Monteviot (life peerage, 2010),* Michael Andrew Foster Jude Kerr (Michael Ancram), PC, QC, *b.* 1945, *s.* 2004, *m.*	Lord Ralph W. F. J. K., *b.* 1957
1917	*Milford Haven (4th),* George Ivar Louis Mountbatten, *b.* 1961, *s.* 1970, *m.*	Earl of Medina, *b.* 1991
1838	*Normanby (5th),* Constantine Edmund Walter Phipps, *b.* 1954, *s.* 1994, *m.*	Earl of Mulgrave, *b.* 1994
1812	*Northampton (7th),* Spencer Douglas David Compton, *b.* 1946, *s.* 1978, *m.*	Earl Compton, *b.* 1973
1682 S.	*Queensberry (12th),* David Harrington Angus Douglas, *b.* 1929, *s.* 1954, *m.*	Viscount Drumlanrig, *b.* 1967
1926	*Reading (4th),* Simon Charles Henry Rufus Isaacs, *b.* 1942, *s.* 1980, *m.*	Viscount Erleigh, *b.* 1986
1789	*Salisbury (7th) and Baron Gascoyne-Cecil (life peerage, 1999),* Robert Michael James Gascoyne-Cecil, KCVO, PC, *b.* 1946, *s.* 2003, *m.*	Viscount Cranborne, *b.* 1970
1800 I.	*Sligo (12th),* Sebastian Ulick Browne, *b.* 1964, *s.* 2014, *m.*	Earl of Altamont, *b.* 1988
1787 °	*Townshend (8th),* Charles George Townshend, *b.* 1945, *s.* 2010, *m.*	Viscount Raynham, *b.* 1977
1694 S.	*Tweeddale (14th),* Charles David Montagu Hay, *b.* 1947, *s.* 2005	(Lord) Alistair J. M. H., *b.* 1955
1789 I.	*Waterford (9th),* Henry Nicholas de la Poer Beresford, *b.* 1958, *s.* 2015, *m.*	Earl of Tyrone, *b.* 1987
1551	*Winchester (18th),* Nigel George Paulet, *b.* 1941, *s.* 1968, *m. Premier Marquess of England*	Earl of Wiltshire, *b.* 1969
1892	*Zetland (4th),* Lawrence Mark Dundas, *b.* 1937, *s.* 1989, *m.*	Earl of Ronaldshay, *b.* 1965

EARLS

Coronet, Eight silver balls on stalks alternating with eight gold strawberry leaves

Style, The Rt. Hon. the Earl (of) _
Envelope (formal), The Rt. Hon. the Earl (of) _; *(social),* The Earl (of) _. *Letter (formal),* My Lord; *(social),* Dear Lord _. *Spoken (formal),* My Lord; *(social),* Lord _.
Wife's style, The Rt. Hon. the Countess (of) _
Envelope (formal), The Rt. Hon. the Countess (of) _; *(social),* The Countess (of) _. *Letter (formal),* Madam; *(social),* Lady _. *Spoken (formal),* Madam; *(social),* Lady _.
Eldest son's style, Takes his father's second title as a courtesy title (*see* Courtesy Titles)
Younger sons' style, 'The Hon.' before forename and surname, as for Baron's children
Daughters' style, 'Lady' before forename and surname, as for Duke's daughter

Created	Title, order of succession, name, etc	Heir
1639 S.	*Airlie (13th),* David George Coke Patrick Ogilvy, KT, GCVO, PC, Royal Victorian Chain, *b.* 1926, *s.* 1968, *m.*	Lord Ogilvy, *b.* 1958
1696	*Albemarle (10th),* Rufus Arnold Alexis Keppel, *b.* 1965, *s.* 1979	Viscount Bury, *b.* 2003
1952 °	*Alexander of Tunis (2nd),* Shane William Desmond Alexander, *b.* 1935, *s.* 1969, *m.*	Hon. Brian J. A., CMG, *b.* 1939
1662 S.	*Annandale and Hartfell (11th),* Patrick Andrew Wentworth Hope Johnstone, *b.* 1941, *s.* 1983, *m.* claim established 1985	Lord Johnstone, *b.* 1971
1789 I. °	*Annesley (12th),* Michael Robert Annesley, *b.* 1933, *s.* 2011, *m.*	Viscount Glerawly, *b.* 1957
1785 I.	*Antrim (9th),* Alexander Randal Mark McDonnell, *b.* 1935, *s.* 1977, *m.*	Viscount Dunluce, *b.* 1967
1762 I. **	*Arran (9th) and 5th UK Baron Sudley (1884),* Arthur Desmond Colquhoun Gore, *b.* 1938, *s.* 1983, *m.*	To Earldom only, William H. G., *b.* 1950
1955 ° **	*Attlee (3rd),* John Richard Attlee, *b.* 1956, *s.* 1991, *m.*	None
1714	*Aylesford (12th),* Charles Heneage Finch-Knightley, *b.* 1947, *s.* 2008, *m.*	Lord Guernsey, *b.* 1985
1937 °	*Baldwin of Bewdley (4th),* Edward Alfred Alexander Baldwin, *b.* 1938, *s.* 1976, *w.*	Viscount Corvedale, *b.* 1973
1922	*Balfour (5th),* Roderick Francis Arthur Balfour, *b.* 1948, *s.* 2003, *m.*	Charles G. Y. B., *b.* 1951
1772 °	*Bathurst (9th),* Allen Christopher Bertram Bathurst, *b.* 1961, *s.* 2011, *m.*	Lord Apsley, *b.* 1990
1919 °	*Beatty (3rd),* David Beatty, *b.* 1946, *s.* 1972, *m.*	Viscount Borodale, *b.* 1973
1797 I.	*Belmore (8th),* John Armar Lowry-Corry, *b.* 1951, *s.* 1960, *m.*	Viscount Corry, *b.* 1985
1739 I.	*Bessborough (12th),* Myles Fitzhugh Longfield Ponsonby, *b.* 1941, *s.* 2002, *m.*	Viscount Duncannon, *b.* 1974
1815	*Bradford (7th),* Richard Thomas Orlando Bridgeman, *b.* 1947, *s.* 1981, *m.*	Viscount Newport, *b.* 1980
1469 S.	*Buchan (17th),* Malcolm Harry Erskine, *b.* 1930, *s.* 1984, *m.*	Lord Cardross, *b.* 1960
1746	*Buckinghamshire (10th),* (George) Miles Hobart-Hampden, *b.* 1944, *s.* 1983, *m.*	Sir John V. Hobart, Bt., *b.* 1945
1800 °	*Cadogan (8th),* Charles Gerald John Cadogan, KBE, *b.* 1937, *s.* 1997, *m.*	Viscount Chelsea, *b.* 1966
1878 °	*Cairns (6th),* Simon Dallas Cairns, CVO, CBE, *b.* 1939, *s.* 1989, *m.*	Viscount Garmoyle, *b.* 1965
1455 S. **	*Caithness (20th),* Malcolm Ian Sinclair, PC, *b.* 1948, *s.* 1965, *w.*	Lord Berriedale, *b.* 1981
1800 I.	*Caledon (7th),* Nicholas James Alexander, KCVO, *b.* 1955, *s.* 1980, *m.*	Viscount Alexander, *b.* 1990
1661	*Carlisle (13th),* George William Beaumont Howard, *b.* 1949, *s.* 1994	Hon. Philip C. W. H., *b.* 1963
1793	*Carnarvon (8th),* George Reginald Oliver Molyneux Herbert, *b.* 1956, *s.* 2001, *m.*	Lord Porchester, *b.* 1992
1748 I.	*Carrick (11th),* Arion Thomas Piers Hamilton Butler, *b.* 1975, *s.* 2008, *m.*	Hon. Piers E. T. L. B., *b.* 1979
1800 I.°	*Castle Stewart (8th),* Arthur Patrick Avondale Stuart, *b.* 1928, *s.* 1961, *m.*	Viscount Stuart, *b.* 1953
1814 ° **	*Cathcart (7th),* Charles Alan Andrew Cathcart, *b.* 1952, *s.* 1999, *m.*	Lord Greenock, *b.* 1986
1647 I.	*Cavan (13th),* Roger Cavan Lambart, *b.* 1944, *s.* 1988 (claim to the peerage not yet established)	Cavan C. E. L., *b.* 1957
1827 °	*Cawdor (7th),* Colin Robert Vaughan Campbell, *b.* 1962, *s.* 1993, *m.*	Viscount Emlyn, *b.* 1998
1801	*Chichester (9th),* John Nicholas Pelham, *b.* 1944, *s.* 1944, *m.*	Richard A. H. P., *b.* 1952
1803 I. **	*Clancarty (9th),* Nicholas Power Richard Le Poer Trench, *b.* 1952, *s.* 1995, *m.*	None
1776 I.	*Clanwilliam (8th),* Patrick James Meade, *b.* 1960, *s.* 2009, *m.*	Lord Gillford, *b.* 1998
1776	*Clarendon (8th),* George Edward Laurence Villiers, *b.* 1976, *s.* 2009, *m.*	Lord Hyde, *b.* 2008
1620 I. **	*Cork and Orrery (15th),* John Richard Boyle, *b.* 1945, *s.* 2003, *m.*	Viscount Dungarvan, *b.* 1978
1850	*Cottenham (9th),* Mark John Henry Pepys, *b.* 1983, *s.* 2000, *m.*	Hon. Sam R. P., *b.* 1986
1762 I. **	*Courtown (9th),* James Patrick Montagu Burgoyne Winthrop Stopford, *b.* 1954, *s.* 1975, *m.*	Viscount Stopford, *b.* 1988
1697	*Coventry (13th),* George William Coventry, *b.* 1939, *s.* 2004, *m.*	David D. S. C., *b.* 1973

1857 °	*Cowley (8th)*, Garret Graham Wellesley, *b.* 1965, *s.* 2016, *m.*	Viscount Dangan, *b.* 1991
1892	*Cranbrook (5th)*, Gathorne Gathorne-Hardy, *b.* 1933, *s.* 1978, *m.*	Lord Medway, *b.* 1968
1801	*Craven (9th)*, Benjamin Robert Joseph Craven, *b.* 1989, *s.* 1990	Rupert J. E. C., *b.* 1926
1398 S.	*Crawford (29th) and Balcarres (12th) (S. 1651) and Baron Balniel (life peerage, 1974)*, Robert Alexander Lindsay, KT, GCVO, PC, *b.* 1927, *s.* 1975, *m.* Premier Earl on Union Roll	Lord Balniel, *b.* 1958
1861	*Cromartie (5th)*, John Ruaridh Blunt Grant Mackenzie, *b.* 1948, *s.* 1989, *m.*	Viscount Tarbat, *b.* 1987
1901	*Cromer (4th)*, Evelyn Rowland Esmond Baring, *b.* 1946, *s.* 1991, *m.*	Viscount Errington, *b.* 1994
1633 S.	*Dalhousie (17th)*, James Hubert Ramsay, *b.* 1948, *s.* 1999, *m. Lord Steward*	Lord Ramsay, *b.* 1981
1725 I.	*Darnley (12th)*, Ivo Donald Stuart Bligh, *b.* 1968, *s.* 2017, *m.*	Lord Clifton, *b.* 1999
1711	*Dartmouth (10th)*, William Legge, MEP, *b.* 1949, *s.* 1997, *m.*	Hon. Rupert L., *b.* 1951
1761 °	*De La Warr (11th)*, William Herbrand Sackville, *b.* 1948, *s.* 1988, *m.*	Lord Buckhurst, *b.* 1979
1622	*Denbigh (12th) and Desmond (11th) (I. 1622)*, Alexander Stephen Rudolph Feilding, *b.* 1970, *s.* 1995, *m.*	Viscount Feilding, *b.* 2005
1485	*Derby (19th)*, Edward Richard William Stanley, *b.* 1962, *s.* 1994, *m.*	Lord Stanley, *b.* 1998
1553 **	*Devon (19th)*, Charles Peregrine Courtenay, *b.* 1975, *s.* 2015, *m.*	Lord Courtenay, *b.* 2009
1800 I.	*Donoughmore (8th)*, Richard Michael John Hely-Hutchinson, *b.* 1927, *s.* 1981, *w.*	Viscount Suirdale, *b.* 1952
1661 I.	*Drogheda (12th)*, Henry Dermot Ponsonby Moore, *b.* 1937, *s.* 1989, *m.*	Viscount Moore, *b.* 1983
1837	*Ducie (7th)*, David Leslie Moreton, *b.* 1951, *s.* 1991, *m.*	Lord Moreton, *b.* 1981
1860	*Dudley (5th)*, William Humble David Jeremy Ward, *b.* 1947, *s.* 2013	Hon. Leander G. D. W., *b.* 1971
1660 S. **	*Dundee (12th)*, Alexander Henry Scrymgeour, *b.* 1949, *s.* 1983, *m.*	Lord Scrymgeour, *b.* 1982
1669 S.	*Dundonald (15th)*, Iain Alexander Douglas Blair Cochrane, *b.* 1961, *s.* 1986, *m.*	Lord Cochrane, *b.* 1991
1686 S.	*Dunmore (12th)*, Malcolm Kenneth Murray, *b.* 1946, *s.* 1995, *m.*	Hon. Geoffrey C. M., *b.* 1949
1833	*Durham (7th)*, Edward Richard Lambton *b.* 1961, *s.* 2006, *m.*	Viscount Lambton, *b.* 1985
1643 S.	*Dysart (13th)*, John Peter Grant of Rothiemurchus, *b.* 1946, *s.* 2011, *m.*	Lord Huntingtower, *b.* 1977
1837	*Effingham (7th)*, David Mowbray Algernon Howard, *b.* 1939, *s.* 1996, *m.*	Lord Howard of Effingham, *b.* 1971
1507 S.	*Eglinton (19th) and Winton (10th) (S. 1600)*, Hugh Archibald William Montgomerie, *b.* 1966, *s.* 2018, *m.*	Lord Montgomerie, *b.* 2007
1821	*Eldon (6th)*, John Francis Thomas Marie Joseph Columba Fidelis Scott, *b.* 1962, *s.* 2017, *m.*	Viscount Encombe, *b.* 1996
1633 S.	*Elgin (11th) and Kincardine (15th) (S. 1647)*, Andrew Douglas Alexander Thomas Bruce, KT, *b.* 1924, *s.* 1968, *m.*	Lord Bruce, *b.* 1961
1789 I.	*Enniskillen (7th)*, Andrew John Galbraith Cole, *b.* 1942, *s.* 1989, *m.*	Berkeley A. C., *b.* 1949
1789 I.	*Erne (7th)*, John Henry Michael Ninian Crichton, *b.* 1971, *s.* 2016	Charles D. B. C., *b.* 1953
1452 S. **	*Erroll (24th)*, Merlin Sereld Victor Gilbert Hay, *b.* 1948, *s.* 1978, *m. Hereditary Lord High Constable and Knight Marischal of Scotland*	Lord Hay, *b.* 1984
1661	*Essex (11th)*, Frederick Paul de Vere Capell, *b.* 1944, *s.* 2005	William J. C., *b.* 1952
1711 °	*Ferrers (14th)*, Robert William Saswalo Shirley, *b.* 1952, *s.* 2012, *m.*	Viscount Tamworth, *b.* 1984
1789 °	*Fortescue (8th)*, Charles Hugh Richard Fortescue, *b.* 1951, *s.* 1993, *m.*	John A. F. F., *b.* 1955
1841	*Gainsborough (6th)*, Anthony Baptist Noel, *b.* 1950, *s.* 2009, *m.*	Viscount Campden, *b.* 1977
1623 S.	*Galloway (13th)*, Randolph Keith Reginald Stewart, *b.* 1928, *s.* 1978, *w.*	Andrew C. S., *b.* 1949
1703 S.**	*Glasgow (10th)*, Patrick Robin Archibald Boyle, *b.* 1939, *s.* 1984, *m.*	Viscount of Kelburn, *b.* 1978
1806 I.	*Gosford (7th)*, Charles David Nicholas Alexander John Sparrow Acheson, *b.* 1942, *s.* 1966, *m.*	Nicholas H. C. A., *b.* 1947
1945	*Gowrie (2nd)*, Alexander Patrick Greysteil Hore Ruthven, PC, *b.* 1939, *s.* 1955, *m.*	Viscount Ruthven of Canberra, *b.* 1964
1684 I.	*Granard (10th)*, Peter Arthur Edward Hastings Forbes, *b.* 1957, *s.* 1992, *m.*	Viscount Forbes, *b.* 1981
1833 °	*Granville (6th)*, Granville George Fergus Leveson-Gower, *b.* 1959, *s.* 1996, *m.*	Lord Leveson, *b.* 1999
1806 °	*Grey (7th)*, Philip Kent Grey, *b.* 1940, *s.* 2013, *m.*	Viscount Howick, *b.* 1968
1752	*Guilford (10th)*, Piers Edward Brownlow North, *b.* 1971, *s.* 1999, *m.*	Lord North, *b.* 2002
1619 S.	*Haddington (14th)*, George Edmund Baldred Baillie-Hamilton, *b.* 1985, *s.* 2016	Thomas R. Hamilton-Baillie, *b.* 1948
1919 °	*Haig (3rd)*, Alexander Douglas Derrick Haig, *b.* 1961, *s.* 2009, *m.*	None
1944	*Halifax (3rd)*, Charles Edward Peter Neil Wood, *b.* 1944, *s.* 1980, *m.*	Lord Irwin, *b.* 1977
1754	*Hardwicke (10th)*, Joseph Philip Sebastian Yorke, *b.* 1971, *s.* 1974, *m.*	Viscount Royston, *b.* 2009
1812	*Harewood (8th)*, David Henry George Lascelles, *b.* 1950, *s.* 2011, *m.*	Viscount Lascelles, *b.* 1978
1742	*Harrington (12th)*, Charles Henry Leicester Stanhope, *b.* 1945, *s.* 2009, *m.*	Viscount Petersham, *b.* 1967
1809	*Harrowby (8th)*, Dudley Adrian Conroy Ryder, *b.* 1951, *s.* 2007, *m.*	Viscount Sandon, *b.* 1981
1605 S. **	*Home (15th)*, David Alexander Cospatrick Douglas-Home, KT, CVO, CBE, *b.* 1943, *s.* 1995, *m.*	Lord Dunglass, *b.* 1987
1821 ° **	*Howe (7th)*, Frederick Richard Penn Curzon, PC, *b.* 1951, *s.* 1984, *m.*	Viscount Curzon, *b.* 1994
1529	*Huntingdon (16th)*, William Edward Robin Hood Hastings-Bass, LVO, *b.* 1948, *s.* 1990, *m.*	Hon. John P. R. H. H.-B., *b.* 1954
1885	*Iddesleigh (5th)*, John Stafford Northcote, *b.* 1957, *s.* 2004, *m.*	Viscount St Cyres, *b.* 1985
1756	*Ilchester (10th)*, Robin Maurice Fox-Strangways, *b.* 1942, *s.* 2006, *m.*	Lord Stavordale, *b.* 1972
1929	*Inchcape (4th)*, (Kenneth) Peter (Lyle) Mackay, *b.* 1943, *s.* 1994, *m.*	Viscount Glenapp, *b.* 1979
1919	*Iveagh (4th)*, Arthur Edward Rory Guinness, *b.* 1969, *s.* 1992, *m.*	Viscount Elveden, *b.* 2003

1925 °	*Jellicoe (3rd),* Patrick John Bernard Jellicoe, *b.* 1950, *s.* 2007	Hon. Nicholas C. J., *b.* 1953
1697	*Jersey (10th),* George Francis William Child Villiers, *b.* 1976, *s.* 1998, *m.*	Viscount Villiers, *b.* 2015
1822 I.	*Kilmorey (6th),* Sir Richard Francis Needham, PC, *b.* 1942, *s.* 1977, *m.* (Does not use title)	Viscount Newry and Mourne, *b.* 1966
1866	*Kimberley (5th),* John Armine Wodehouse, *b.* 1951, *s.* 2002, *m.*	Lord Wodehouse, *b.* 1978
1768 I.	*Kingston (12th),* Robert Charles Henry King-Tenison, *b.* 1969, *s.* 2002, *m.*	Viscount Kingsborough, *b.* 2000
1633 S. **	*Kinnoull (16th),* Charles William Harley Hay, *b.* 1962, *s.* 2013, *m.*	Viscount Dupplin, *b.* 2011
1677 S.	*Kintore (14th),* James William Falconer Keith, *b.* 1976, *s.* 2004, *m.*	Lord Inverurie, *b.* 2010
1624 S.	*Lauderdale (18th),* Ian Maitland, *b.* 1937, *s.* 2008, *m.*	Viscount Maitland, *b.* 1965
1837	*Leicester (8th),* Thomas Edward Coke, *b.* 1965, *s.* 2015, *m.*	Viscount Coke, *b.* 2003
1641 S.	*Leven (15th) and Melville (14th) (S. 1690),* Alexander Ian Leslie Melville, *b.* 1984, *s.* 2012	Hon. Archibald R. L. M., *b.* 1957
1831	*Lichfield (6th),* Thomas William Robert Hugh Anson, *b.* 1978, *s.* 2005, *m.*	Viscount Anson, *b.* 2011
1803 I.	*Limerick (7th),* Edmund Christopher Pery, *b.* 1963, *s.* 2003, *m.*	Viscount Glentworth, *b.* 1991
1572	*Lincoln (19th),* Robert Edward Fiennes-Clinton, *b.* 1972, *s.* 2001	Hon. William J. Howson, *b.* 1980
1633 S. **	*Lindsay (16th),* James Randolph Lindesay-Bethune, *b.* 1955, *s.* 1989, *m.*	Viscount Garnock, *b.* 1990
1626	*Lindsey (14th) and Abingdon (9th) (1682),* Richard Henry Rupert Bertie, *b.* 1931, *s.* 1963, *m.*	Lord Norreys, *b.* 1958
1776 I.	*Lisburne (9th),* David John Francis Malet Vaughan, *b.* 1945, *s.* 2014, *m.*	Hon. Michael J. W. M. V., *b.* 1948
1822 I.**	*Listowel (6th),* Francis Michael Hare, *b.* 1964, *s.* 1997, *m.*	Hon. Timothy P. H., *b.* 1966
1905 **	*Liverpool (5th),* Edward Peter Bertram Savile Foljambe, *b.* 1944, *s.* 1969, *m.*	Viscount Hawkesbury, *b.* 1972
1945 °	*Lloyd George of Dwyfor (4th),* David Richard Owen Lloyd George, *b.* 1951, *s.* 2010, *m.*	Viscount Gwynedd, *b.* 1986
1785 I.	*Longford (8th),* Thomas Frank Dermot Pakenham, *b.* 1933, *s.* 2001, *m.* (Does not use title)	Edward M. P., *b.* 1970
1807	*Lonsdale (8th),* Hugh Clayton Lowther, *b.* 1949, *s.* 2006, *m.*	Hon. William J. L., *b.* 1957
1633 S.	*Loudoun (15th),* Simon Michael Abney-Hastings, *b.* 1974, *s.* 2012, *m.*	Hon. Marcus W. A.-H., *b.* 1981
1795 I.	*Lucan (8th),* George Charles Bingham, *b.* 1967, *s.* 2016, *m.*	Hon. Hugh B., *b.* 1939
1880 **	*Lytton (5th),* John Peter Michael Scawen Lytton, *b.* 1950, *s.* 1985, *m.*	Viscount Knebworth, *b.* 1989
1721	*Macclesfield (9th),* Richard Timothy George Mansfield Parker, *b.* 1943, *s.* 1992, *m.*	Hon. J. David G. P., *b.* 1945
1800	*Malmesbury (7th),* James Carleton Harris, *b.* 1946, *s.* 2000, *m.*	Viscount FitzHarris, *b.* 1970
1776	*Mansfield (8th) and Mansfield (9th) (1792),* Alexander David Mungo Murray, *b.* 1956, *s.* 2015, *m.*	Viscount Stormont, *b.* 1988
1565 S.	*Mar (14th) and Kellie (16th) (S. 1616) and Baron Erskine of Alloa Tower (life peerage, 2000),* James Thorne Erskine, *b.* 1949, *s.* 1994, *m.*	Hon. Alexander D. E., *b.* 1952
1785 I.	*Mayo (11th),* Charles Diarmuidh John Bourke, *b.* 1953, *s.* 2006, *m.*	Lord Naas, *b.* 1985
1627 I.	*Meath (15th),* John Anthony Brabazon, *b.* 1941, *s.* 1998, *m.*	Lord Ardee, *b.* 1977
1766 I.	*Mexborough (8th),* John Christopher George Savile, *b.* 1931, *s.* 1980, *m.*	Viscount Pollington, *b.* 1959
1813	*Minto (7th),* Gilbert Timothy George Lariston Elliot-Murray-Kynynmound, *b.* 1953, *s.* 2005, *m.*	Viscount Melgund, *b.* 1984
1562 S.	*Moray (21st),* John Douglas Stuart, *b.* 1966, *s.* 2011, *m.*	Lord Doune, *b.* 2002
1815	*Morley (7th),* Mark Lionel Parker, *b.* 1956, *s.* 2015, *m.*	Hon. Nigel G. P., *b.* 1931
1458 S.	*Morton (22nd),* John Stewart Sholto Douglas, *b.* 1952, *s.* 2016, *m.*	Lord Aberdour, *b.* 1986
1789	*Mount Edgcumbe (8th),* Robert Charles Edgcumbe, *b.* 1939, *s.* 1982	Piers V. E., *b.* 1946
1947 °	*Mountbatten of Burma (3rd),* Norton Louis Philip Knatchbull, *b.* 1947, *s.* 2017, *m.*	Lord Brabourne, *b.* 1981
1805 °	*Nelson (10th),* Simon John Horatio Nelson, *b.* 1971, *s.* 2009, *m.*	Viscount Merton, *b.* 2010
1660 S.	*Newburgh (12th),* Don Filippo Giambattista Camillo Francesco Aldo Maria Rospigliosi, *b.* 1942, *s.* 1986, *m.*	Princess Donna Benedetta F. M. R., *b.* 1974
1827 I.	*Norbury (7th),* Richard James Graham-Toler, *b.* 1967, *s.* 2000	None
1806 I.	*Normanton (6th),* Shaun James Christian Welbore Ellis Agar, *b.* 1945, *s.* 1967, *m.*	Viscount Somerton, *b.* 1982
1647 S.	*Northesk (15th),* Patrick Charles Carnegy, *b.* 1940, *s.* 2010, *m.*	Hon. Colin D. C., *b.* 1942
1801	*Onslow (8th),* Rupert Charles William Bullard Onslow, *b.* 1967, *s.* 2011, *m.*	Anthony E. E. O., *b.* 1955
1696 S.	*Orkney (9th),* (Oliver) Peter St John, *b.* 1938, *s.* 1998, *m.*	Viscount Kirkwall, *b.* 1969
1328 I.	*Ormonde and Ossory (I. 1527),* The 25th/18th Earl (7th Marquess) died in 1988	†Viscount Mountgarret *b.* 1961 (*see* that title)
1925 **	*Oxford and Asquith (3rd),* Raymond Benedict Bartholomew Michael Asquith, OBE, *b.* 1952, *s.* 2011, *m.*	Viscount Asquith, *b.* 1979
1929 ° **	*Peel (3rd),* William James Robert Peel, GCVO, PC, *b.* 1947, *s.* 1969, *m.* Lord Chamberlain	Viscount Clanfield, *b.* 1976
1551	*Pembroke (18th) and Montgomery (15th) (1605),* William Alexander Sidney Herbert, *b.* 1978, *s.* 2003, *m.*	Lord Herbert, *b.* 2012
1605 S.	*Perth (18th),* John Eric Drummond, *b.* 1935, *s.* 2002, *m.*	Viscount Strathallan, *b.* 1965
1905	*Plymouth (4th),* Ivor Edward Other Windsor-Clive, *b.* 1951, *s.* 2018, *m.*	Viscount Windsor, *b.* 1981
1785 I.	*Portarlington (7th),* George Lionel Yuill Seymour Dawson-Damer, *b.* 1938, *s.* 1959, *m.*	Viscount Carlow, *b.* 1965
1689	*Portland (12th),* Count Timothy Charles Robert Noel Bentinck, MBE, *b.* 1953, *s.* 1997, *m.*	Viscount Woodstock, *b.* 1984
1743	*Portsmouth (10th),* Quentin Gerard Carew Wallop, *b.* 1954, *s.* 1984, *m.*	Viscount Lymington, *b.* 1981

1804	*Powis (8th)*, John George Herbert, *b.* 1952, *s.* 1993, *m.*	Viscount Clive, *b.* 1979
1765	*Radnor (9th)*, William Pleydell-Bouverie, *b.* 1955, *s.* 2008, *m.*	Viscount Folkestone, *b.* 1999
1831 I.	*Ranfurly (7th)*, Gerald Françoys Needham Knox, *b.* 1929, *s.* 1988, *m.*	Viscount Northland, *b.* 1957
1771 I.	*Roden (10th)*, Robert John Jocelyn, *b.* 1938, *s.* 1993, *m.*	Viscount Jocelyn, *b.* 1989
1801	*Romney (8th)*, Julian Charles Marsham, *b.* 1948, *s.* 2004, *m.*	Viscount Marsham, *b.* 1977
1703 S.	*Rosebery (7th)*, Neil Archibald Primrose, *b.* 1929, *s.* 1974, *m.*	Lord Dalmeny, *b.* 1967
1806 I.	*Rosse (7th)*, William Brendan Parsons, *b.* 1936, *s.* 1979, *m.*	Lord Oxmantown, *b.* 1969
1801 **	*Rosslyn (7th)*, Peter St Clair-Erskine, CVO, QPM, *b.* 1958, *s.* 1977, *m.*	Lord Loughborough, *b.* 1986
1457 S.	*Rothes (22nd)*, James Malcolm David Leslie, *b.* 1958, *s.* 2005, *m.*	Hon. Alexander J. L., *b.* 1962
1861 °	*Russell (7th)*, John Francis Russell, *b.* 1971, *s.* 2014, *m.*	None
1915 °	*St Aldwyn (3rd)*, Michael Henry Hicks Beach, *b.* 1950, *s.* 1992, *m.*	Hon. David S. H. B., *b.* 1955
1815 M.	*St Germans (11th)*, Albert Charger Eliot, *b.* 2004, *s.* 2016	Hon. Louis R. E., *b.* 1968
1660 **	*Sandwich (11th)*, John Edward Hollister Montagu, *b.* 1943, *s.* 1995, *m.*	Viscount Hinchingbrooke, *b.* 1969
1690	*Scarbrough (13th)*, Richard Osbert Lumley, *b.* 1973, *s.* 2004, *m.*	Hon. Thomas H. L., *b.* 1980
1701 S.	*Seafield (13th)*, Ian Derek Francis Ogilvie-Grant, *b.* 1939, *s.* 1969, *m.*	Viscount Reidhaven, *b.* 1963
1882 **	*Selborne (4th)*, John Roundell Palmer, GBE, *b.* 1940, *s.* 1971, *m.*	Viscount Wolmer, *b.* 1971
1646 S.	*Selkirk (11th)*, Disclaimed for life 1994 (*see* Lord Selkirk of Douglas, Life Peers)	Master of Selkirk, *b.* 1978
1672	*Shaftesbury (12th)*, Nicholas Edmund Anthony Ashley-Cooper, *b.* 1979, *s.* 2005, *m.*	Lord Ashley, *b.* 2011
1756 I.	*Shannon (10th)*, Richard Henry John Boyle, *b.* 1960, *s.* 2013	Robert F. B., *b.* 1930
1442 **	*Shrewsbury and Waterford (22nd) (I. 1446)*, Charles Henry John Benedict Crofton Chetwynd Chetwynd-Talbot, *b.* 1952, *s.* 1980, *m. Premier Earl of England and Ireland*	Viscount Ingestre, *b.* 1978
1961	*Snowdon (2nd)*, David Albert Charles Armstrong-Jones, *b.* 1961, *s.* 2017, *m.*	Viscount Linley, *b.* 1999
1765 °	*Spencer (9th)*, Charles Edward Maurice Spencer, *b.* 1964, *s.* 1992, *m.*	Viscount Althorp, *b.* 1994
1703 S.	*Stair (14th)*, John David James Dalrymple, *b.* 1961, *s.* 1996, *m.*	Viscount Dalrymple, *b.* 2008
1984	*Stockton (2nd)*, Alexander Daniel Alan Macmillan, *b.* 1943, *s.* 1986, *m.*	Viscount Macmillan of Ovenden, *b.* 1974
1821	*Stradbroke (6th)*, Robert Keith Rous, *b.* 1937, *s.* 1983, *m.*	Viscount Dunwich, *b.* 1961
1847	*Strafford (9th)*, William Robert Byng, *b.* 1964, *s.* 2016, *m.*	Viscount Enfield, *b.* 1998
1606 S.	*Strathmore and Kinghorne (19th) (S. 1677)*, Simon Patrick Bowes Lyon, *b.* 1986, *s.* 2016	Hon. John F. B. L., *b.* 1988
1603	*Suffolk (21st) and Berkshire (14th) (1626)*, Michael John James George Robert Howard, *b.* 1935, *s.* 1941, *m.*	Viscount Andover, *b.* 1974
1955	*Swinton (3rd)*, Nicholas John Cunliffe-Lister, *b.* 1939, *s.* 2006, *m.*	Lord Masham, *b.* 1970
1714	*Tankerville (10th)*, Peter Grey Bennet, *b.* 1956, *s.* 1980	Adrian G. B., *b.* 1958
1822 °	*Temple of Stowe (9th)*, James Grenville Temple-Gore-Langton, *b.* 1955, *s.* 2013, *m.*	Hon. Robert C. T.-G.-L., *b.* 1957
1815	*Verulam (7th)*, John Duncan Grimston, *b.* 1951, *s.* 1973, *m.*	Viscount Grimston, *b.* 1978
1729 °	*Waldegrave (13th)*, James Sherbrooke Waldegrave, *b.* 1940, *s.* 1995, *m.*	Viscount Chewton, *b.* 1986
1759	*Warwick (9th) and Brooke (9th) (1746)*, Guy David Greville, *b.* 1957, *s.* 1996, *m.*	Lord Brooke, *b.* 1982
1633 S.	*Wemyss (13th) and March (9th) (S. 1697)*, James Donald Charteris, *b.* 1948, *s.* 2008, *m.*	Lord Elcho, *b.* 1984
1621 I.	*Westmeath (13th)*, William Anthony Nugent, *b.* 1928, *s.* 1971, *m.*	Sean C. W. N., *b.* 1965
1624	*Westmorland (16th)*, Anthony David Francis Henry Fane, *b.* 1951, *s.* 1993, *m.*	Hon. Harry St C. F., *b.* 1953
1876	*Wharncliffe (5th)*, Richard Alan Montagu Stuart Wortley, *b.* 1953, *s.* 1987, *m.*	Viscount Carlton, *b.* 1980
1801	*Wilton (8th)*, Francis Egerton Grosvenor, *b.* 1934, *s.* 1999, *m.*	Viscount Grey de Wilton, *b.* 1959
1628	*Winchilsea (17th) and Nottingham (12th) (1681)*, Daniel James Hatfield Finch Hatton, *b.* 1967, *s.* 1999, *m.*	Viscount Maidstone, *b.* 1998
1766 I. °	*Winterton (8th)*, (Donald) David Turnour, *b.* 1943, *s.* 1991, *m.*	Robert C. T., *b.* 1950
1956	*Woolton (3rd)*, Simon Frederick Marquis, *b.* 1958, *s.* 1969, *m.*	None
1837	*Yarborough (8th)*, Charles John Pelham, *b.* 1963, *s.* 1991, *m.*	Lord Worsley, *b.* 1990

COUNTESSES IN THEIR OWN RIGHT

Style, The Rt. Hon. the Countess (of) _
Envelope (formal), The Rt. Hon. the Countess (of) _; *(social),* The Countess (of) _. *Letter (formal),* Madam; *(social),* Lady _. *Spoken (formal),* Madam; *(social),* Lady _.
Husband, Untitled
Children's style, As for children of an Earl
In Scotland, the heir to a Countess may be styled 'The Master/Mistress of _ (title of peer)'

Created	Title, order of succession, name, etc	Heir
c.1115 S. **	*Mar (31st),* Margaret of Mar, *b.* 1940, *s.* 1975, *m. Premier Earldom of Scotland*	Mistress of Mar, *b.* 1963
c.1235 S.	*Sutherland (24th),* Elizabeth Millicent Sutherland, *b.* 1921, *s.* 1963, *w.*	Lord Strathnaver, *b.* 1947

VISCOUNTS

Coronet, Sixteen silver balls

Style, The Rt. Hon. the Viscount _
Envelope (formal), The Rt. Hon. the Viscount _; *(social),* The Viscount _. *Letter (formal),* My Lord; *(social),* Dear Lord _. *Spoken,* Lord _.
Wife's style, The Rt. Hon. the Viscountess _
Envelope (formal), The Rt. Hon. the Viscountess _; *(social),* The Viscountess _. *Letter (formal),* Madam; *(social),* Dear Lady _. *Spoken,* Lady _.
Children's style, 'The Hon.' before forename and surname, as for Baron's children
In Scotland, the heir to a Viscount may be styled 'The Master/Mistress of _ (title of peer)'

Created	Title, order of succession, name, etc	Heir
1945	*Addison (4th),* William Matthew Wand Addison, *b.* 1945, *s.* 1992, *m.*	Hon. Paul W. A., *b.* 1973
1919	*Allenby (4th),* Henry Jaffray Hynman Allenby, *b.* 1968, *s.* 2014, *m.*	Hon. Harry M. E. A., *b.* 2000
1911	*Allendale (4th),* Wentworth Peter Ismay Beaumont, *b.* 1948, *s.* 2002, *m.*	Hon. Wentworth A. I. B., *b.* 1979
1642 S.	*of Arbuthnott (17th),* John Keith Oxley Arbuthnott, *b.* 1950, *s.* 2012, *m.*	Master of Arbuthnott, *b.* 1977
1751 I.	*Ashbrook (11th),* Michael Llowarch Warburton Flower, *b.* 1935, *s.* 1995, *m.*	Hon. Rowland F. W. F., *b.* 1975
1917 **	*Astor (4th),* William Waldorf Astor, *b.* 1951, *s.* 1966, *m.*	Hon. William W. A., *b.* 1979
1781 I.	*Bangor (8th),* William Maxwell David Ward, *b.* 1948, *s.* 1993, *m.*	Hon. E. Nicholas W., *b.* 1953
1925	*Bearsted (5th),* Nicholas Alan Samuel, *b.* 1950, *s.* 1996, *m.*	Hon. Harry R. S., *b.* 1988
1963	*Blakenham (3rd),* Caspar John Hare, *b.* 1972, *s.* 2018, *m.*	Hon. Inigo H., *b. c.*2006
1935	*Bledisloe (4th),* Rupert Edward Ludlow Bathurst, *b.* 1964, *s.* 2009, *m.*	Hon. Benjamin B., *b.* 2004
1712	*Bolingbroke (9th) and St John (10th) (1716),* Nicholas Alexander Mowbray St John, *b.* 1974, *s.* 2011, *m.*	German A. St J., *b.* 1980
1960	*Boyd of Merton (2nd),* Simon Donald Rupert Neville Lennox-Boyd, *b.* 1939, *s.* 1983, *m.*	Hon. Benjamin A. L.-B., *b.* 1964
1717 I.	*Boyne (11th),* Gustavus Michael Stucley Hamilton-Russell, *b.* 1965, *s.* 1995, *m.*	Hon. Gustavus A. E. H.-R., *b.* 1999
1929	*Brentford (4th),* Crispin William Joynson-Hicks, *b.* 1933, *s.* 1983, *m.*	Hon. Paul W. J.-H., MBE, *b.* 1971
1929 **	*Bridgeman (3rd),* Robin John Orlando Bridgeman, *b.* 1930, *s.* 1982, *m.*	Hon. Luke R. O. B., *b.* 1971
1868	*Bridport (4th) and 7th Duke, Bronte in Sicily, 1799,* Alexander Nelson Hood, *b.* 1948, *s.* 1969, *m.*	Hon. Peregrine A. N. H., *b.* 1974
1952 **	*Brookeborough (3rd),* Alan Henry Brooke, KG, *b.* 1952, *s.* 1987, *m.*	Hon. Christopher A. B., *b.* 1954
1933	*Buckmaster (4th),* Adrian Charles Buckmaster, *b.* 1949, *s.* 2007, *m.*	Hon. Andrew N. B., *b.* 1980
1939	*Caldecote (3rd),* Piers James Hampden Inskip, *b.* 1947, *s.* 1999, *m.*	Hon. Thomas J. H. I., *b.* 1985
1941	*Camrose (5th),* Jonathan William Berry, *b.* 1970, *s.* 2016, *m.*	Hon. Hugo W. B., *b.* 2000
1954	*Chandos (3rd) and Baron Lyttelton of Aldershot (life peerage, 2000),* Thomas Orlando Lyttelton, *b.* 1953, *s.* 1980, *m.*	Hon. Oliver A. L., *b.* 1986
1665 I.	*Charlemont (15th),* John Dodd Caulfeild, *b.* 1966, *s.* 2001, *m.*	Hon. Shane A. C., *b.* 1996

1921	*Chelmsford (4th)*, Frederic Corin Piers Thesiger, *b.* 1962, *s.* 1999, *m.*	Hon. Frederic T., *b.* 2006
1717 I.	*Chetwynd (11th)*, Adam Douglas Chetwynd, *b.* 1969, *s.* 2015, *m.*	Hon. Connor A. C., *b.* 2001
1911	*Chilston (4th)*, Alastair George Akers-Douglas, *b.* 1946, *s.* 1982, *m.*	Hon. Oliver I. A.-D., *b.* 1973
1718	*Cobham (12th)*, Christopher Charles Lyttelton, *b.* 1947, *s.* 2006, *m.*	Hon. Oliver C. L., *b.* 1976
1902 **	*Colville of Culross (5th)*, Charles Mark Townshend Colville, *b.* 1959, *s.* 2010	Master of Colville, *b.* 1961
1826	*Combermere (6th)*, Thomas Robert Wellington Stapleton-Cotton, *b.* 1969, *s.* 2000, *m.*	Hon. Laszlo M. W. S.-C., *b.* 2010
1917	*Cowdray (4th)*, Michael Orlando Weetman Pearson, *b.* 1944, *s.* 1995, *m.*	Hon. Peregrine J. D. P., *b.* 1994
1927 **	*Craigavon (3rd)*, Janric Fraser Craig, *b.* 1944, *s.* 1974	None
1943	*Daventry (4th)*, James Edward FitzRoy Newdegate, *b.* 1960, *s.* 2000, *m.*	Hon. Humphrey J. F. N., *b.* 1995
1937	*Davidson (3rd)*, Malcolm William Mackenzie Davidson, *b.* 1934, *s.* 2012, *m.*	Hon. John N. A. D., *b.* 1971
1956	*De L'Isle (2nd)*, Philip John Algernon Sidney, MBE, *b.* 1945, *s.* 1991, *m.*	Hon. Philip W. E. S., *b.* 1985
1776 I.	*de Vesci (7th)*, Thomas Eustace Vesey, *b.* 1955, *s.* 1983, *m.*	Hon. Oliver I. V., *b.* 1991
1917	*Devonport (3rd)*, Terence Kearley, *b.* 1944, *s.* 1973, *m.*	Chester D. H. K., *b.* 1932
1964	*Dilhorne (2nd)*, John Mervyn Manningham-Buller, *b.* 1932, *s.* 1980, *m.*	Hon. James E. M.-B., *b.* 1956
1622 I.	*Dillon (22nd)*, Henry Benedict Charles Dillon, *b.* 1973, *s.* 1982	Thomas A. L. D., *b.* 1983
1785 I.	*Doneraile (10th)*, Richard Allen St Leger, *b.* 1946, *s.* 1983, *m.*	Hon. Nathaniel W. R. St J. St L., *b.* 1971
1680 I.	*Downe (12th)*, Richard Henry Dawnay, *b.* 1967, *s.* 2002	Thomas P. D., *b.* 1978
1959	*Dunrossil (3rd)*, Andrew William Reginald Morrison, *b.* 1953, *s.* 2000, *m.*	Hon. Callum A. B. M., *b.* 1994
1964 **	*Eccles (2nd)*, John Dawson Eccles, CBE, *b.* 1931, *s.* 1999, *m.*	Hon. William D. E., *b.* 1960
1897	*Esher (5th)*, Christopher Lionel Baliol Brett, *b.* 1936, *s.* 2004, *m.*	Hon. Matthew C. A. B., *b.* 1963
1816	*Exmouth (10th)*, Paul Edward Pellew, *b.* 1940, *s.* 1970, *m.*	Hon. Edward F. P., *b.* 1978
1620 S.**	*of Falkland (15th)*, Lucius Edward William Plantagenet Cary, *b.* 1935, *s.* 1984, *m, Premier Scottish Viscount on the Roll*	Master of Falkland, *b.* 1963
1720	*Falmouth (9th)*, George Hugh Boscawen, *b.* 1919, *s.* 1962, *w.*	Hon. Evelyn A. H. B., *b.* 1955
1720 I.	*Gage (8th)*, (Henry) Nicolas Gage, *b.* 1934, *s.* 1993, *m.*	Hon. Henry W. G., *b.* 1975
1727 I.	*Galway (13th)*, John Philip Monckton-Arundell, *b.* 1952, *s.* 2017, *m.*	Alan S. Monckton, *b.* 1934
1478 I.	*Gormanston (17th)*, Jenico Nicholas Dudley Preston, *b.* 1939, *s.* 1940, *m.* Premier Viscount of Ireland	Hon. Jenico F. T. P., *b.* 1974
1816 I.	*Gort (9th)*, Foley Robert Standish Prendergast Vereker, *b.* 1951, *s.* 1995, *m.*	Hon. Robert F. P. V., *b.* 1993
1900 **	*Goschen (4th)*, Giles John Harry Goschen, *b.* 1965, *s.* 1977, *m.*	Hon. Alexander J. E. G., *b.* 2001
1849	*Gough (5th)*, Shane Hugh Maryon Gough, *b.* 1941, *s.* 1951	None
1929	*Hailsham (3rd) and Baron Hailsham of Kettlethorpe (life peerage, 2015)*, Douglas Martin Hogg, PC, QC, *b.* 1945, *s.* 2001, *m.*	Hon. Quintin J. N. M. H., *b.* 1973
1891	*Hambleden (5th)*, William Henry Bernard Smith, *b.* 1955, *s.* 2012, *m.*	Hon. Bernardo J. S., *b.* 1957
1884	*Hampden (7th)*, Francis Anthony Brand, *b.* 1970, *s.* 2008, *m.*	Hon. Lucian A. B., *b.* 2005
1936 **	*Hanworth (3rd)*, David Stephen Geoffrey Pollock, *b.* 1946, *s.* 1996, *m.*	Harold W. C. P., *b.* 1988
1791 I.	*Harberton (11th)*, Henry Robert Pomeroy, *b.* 1958, *s.* 2004, *m.*	Hon. Patrick C. P., *b.* 1995
1846	*Hardinge (8th)*, Thomas Henry de Montarville Hardinge, *b.* 1993, *s.* 2014	Hon. Jamie A. D. H., *b.* 1996
1791 I.	*Hawarden (9th)*, (Robert) Connan Wyndham Leslie Maude, *b.* 1961, *s.* 1991, *m.*	Hon. Varian J. C. E. M., *b.* 1997
1960	*Head (2nd)*, Richard Antony Head, *b.* 1937, *s.* 1983, *m.*	Hon. Henry J. H., *b.* 1980
1550	*Hereford (19th)*, Charles Robin de Bohun Devereux, *b.* 1975, *s.* 2004, *m.* Premier Viscount of England	Hon. Henry W. de B. D., *b.* 2015
1842	*Hill (9th)*, Peter David Raymond Charles Clegg-Hill, *b.* 1945, *s.* 2003, *m.*	Hon. Michael C. D. C.-H., *b.* 1988
1796	*Hood (8th)*, Henry Lyttelton Alexander Hood, *b.* 1958, *s.* 1999, *m.*	Hon. Archibald L. S. H., *b.* 1993
1945	*Kemsley (3rd)*, Richard Gomer Berry, *b.* 1951, *s.* 1999, *m.*	Hon. Luke G. B., *b.* 1998
1911	*Knollys (3rd)*, David Francis Dudley Knollys, *b.* 1931, *s.* 1966, *m.*	Hon. Patrick N. M. K., *b.* 1962
1895	*Knutsford (6th)*, Michael Holland-Hibbert, *b.* 1926, *s.* 1986, *m.*	Hon. Henry T. H.-H., *b.* 1959
1954	*Leathers (3rd)*, Christopher Graeme Leathers, *b.* 1941, *s.* 1996, *m.*	Hon. James F. L., *b.* 1969
1781 I.	*Lifford (9th)*, (Edward) James Wingfield Hewitt, *b.* 1949, *s.* 1987, *m.*	Hon. James T. W. H., *b.* 1979
1921	*Long (5th)*, James Richard Long, *b.* 1960, *s.* 2017	None
1957	*Mackintosh of Halifax (3rd)*, (John) Clive Mackintosh, *b.* 1958, *s.* 1980, *m.*	Hon. Thomas H. G. M., *b.* 1985
1955	*Malvern (3rd)*, Ashley Kevin Godfrey Huggins, *b.* 1949, *s.* 1978	Hon. M. James H., *b.* 1928
1945	*Marchwood (3rd)*, David George Staveley Penny, *b.* 1936, *s.* 1979, *w.*	Hon. Peter G. W. P., *b.* 1965
1942	*Margesson (3rd)*, Richard Francis David Margesson, *b.* 1960, *s.* 2014, *m.*	None
1660 I.	*Massereene (14th) and Ferrard (7th) (I. 1797)*, John David Clotworthy Whyte-Melville Foster Skeffington, *b.* 1940, *s.* 1992, *m.*	Hon. Charles J. C. W.-M. F. S., *b.* 1973
1802	*Melville (10th)*, Robert Henry Kirkpatrick Dundas, *b.* 1984, *s.* 2011	Hon. James D. B. D., *b.* 1986
1916	*Mersey (5th) and 14th Lord Nairne (S. 1681)*, Edward John Hallam Bigham, *b.* 1966, *s.* 2006, *m.*	Hon. David E. H. B., *b.* 1938 (to Viscountcy); Mistress of Nairne, *b.* 2003 (to Lordship of Nairne)
1717 I.	*Midleton (12th)*, Alan Henry Brodrick, *b.* 1949, *s.* 1988, *m.*	Hon. Ashley R. B., *b.* 1980
1962	*Mills (3rd)*, Christopher Philip Roger Mills, *b.* 1956, *s.* 1988, *m.*	None
1716 I.	*Molesworth (12th)*, Robert Bysse Kelham Molesworth, *b.* 1959, *s.* 1997	Hon. William J. C. M., *b.* 1960
1801 I.	*Monck (7th)*, Charles Stanley Monck, *b.* 1953, *s.* 1982 (Does not use title)	Hon. George S. M., *b.* 1957
1957	*Monckton of Brenchley (3rd)*, Christopher Walter Monckton, *b.* 1952, *s.* 2006, *m.*	Hon. Timothy D. R. M., *b.* 1955

1946	*Montgomery of Alamein (2nd)*, David Bernard Montgomery, CMG, CBE, *b. 1928, s. 1976, m.*	Hon. Henry D. M., *b.* 1954
1550 I.	*Mountgarret (18th)*, Piers James Richard Butler, *b.* 1961, *s.* 2004, *m.*	Hon. Theo O. S. B., *b.* 2015
1952	*Norwich (3rd)*, Jason Charles Duff Bede Cooper, *b.* 1959, *s.* 2018	None
1651 S.	*of Oxfuird (14th)*, Ian Arthur Alexander Makgill, *b.* 1969, *s.* 2003, *m.*	Master of Oxfuird, *b.* 2012
1873	*Portman (10th)*, Christopher Edward Berkeley Portman, *b.* 1958, *s.* 1999, *m.*	Hon. Luke O. B. P., *b.* 1984
1743 I.	*Powerscourt (11th)*, Mervyn Anthony Wingfield, *b.* 1963, *s.* 2015, *m.*	To Viscountcy only, Patrick N. W., *b.* 1934
1900 **	*Ridley (5th)*, Matthew White Ridley, *b.* 1958, *s.* 2012, *m.*	Hon. Matthew W. R., *b.* 1993
1960	*Rochdale (3rd)*, Jonathan Hugo Durival Kemp, *b.* 1961, *s.* 2015, *m.*	George T. K., *b.* 2001
1919	*Rothermere (4th)*, (Harold) Jonathan Esmond Vere Harmsworth, *b.* 1967, *s.* 1998, *m.*	Hon. Vere R. J. H. H., *b.* 1994
1937	*Runciman of Doxford (3rd)*, Walter Garrison (Garry) Runciman, CBE, *b.* 1934, *s.* 1989, *m.*	Hon. David W. R., *b.* 1967
1918	*St Davids (4th)*, Rhodri Colwyn Philipps, *b.* 1966, *s.* 2009, *m.*	Hon. Roland A. J. E. P., *b.* 1970
1801	*St Vincent (8th)*, Edward Robert James Jervis, *b.* 1951, *s.* 2006, *m.*	Hon. James R. A. J., *b.* 1982
1937	*Samuel (5th)*, Jonathan Herbert Samuel, *b.* 1965, *s.* 2014, *m.*	Hon. Benjamin A. S., *b.* 1983
1911	*Scarsdale (4th)*, Peter Ghislain Nathaniel Curzon, *b.* 1949, *s.* 2000, *m.*	Hon. David J. N. C., *b.* 1958
1905	*Selby (6th)*, Christopher Rolf Thomas Gully, *b.* 1993, *s.* 2001	Hon. (James) Edward H. G. G., *b.* 1945
1805	*Sidmouth (8th)*, Jeremy Francis Addington, *b.* 1947, *s.* 2005, *w.*	Hon. John A., *b.* 1990
1940 **	*Simon (3rd)*, Jan David Simon, *b.* 1940, *s.* 1993, *m.*	None
1960 **	*Slim (2nd)*, John Douglas Slim, OBE, *b.* 1927, *s.* 1970, *m.*	Hon. Mark W. R. S., *b.* 1960
1954	*Soulbury (4th)*, Oliver Peter Ramsbotham, *b.* 1943, *s.* 2010, *m.*	Hon. Edward H. R., *b.* 1966
1776 I.	*Southwell (7th)*, Pyers Anthony Joseph Southwell, *b.* 1930, *s.* 1960, *m.*	Hon. Richard A. P. S., *b.* 1956
1942	*Stansgate (3rd)*, Stephen Michael Wedgwood Benn, *b.* 1951, *s.* 2014, *m.*	Hon. Daniel J. W. B., *b.* 1991
1959	*Stuart of Findhorn (3rd)*, Dominic Stuart, *b.* 1948, *s.* 1999, *m.*	Hon. Andrew M. S., *b.* 1957
1957	*Tenby (3rd)*, William Lloyd George, *b.* 1927, *s.* 1983, *m.*	Hon. Timothy H. G. L. G., *b.* 1962
1952 **	*Thurso (3rd)*, John Archibald Sinclair, PC, *b.* 1953, *s.* 1995, *m.*	Hon. James A. R. S., *b.* 1984
1721	*Torrington (11th)*, Timothy Howard St George Byng, *b.* 1943, *s.* 1961, *m.*	Colin H. Cranmer-Byng, *b.* 1960
1936 **	*Trenchard (3rd)*, Hugh Trenchard, *b.* 1951, *s.* 1987, *m.*	Hon. Alexander T. T., *b.* 1978
1921 **	*Ullswater (2nd)*, Nicholas James Christopher Lowther, LVO, PC, *b.* 1942, *s.* 1949, *m.*	Hon. Benjamin J. L., *b.* 1975
1642 I.	*Valentia (16th)*, Frances William Dighton Annesley, *b.* 1959, *s.* 2005, *m.*	Hon. Peter J. A., *b.* 1967
1952 **	*Waverley (3rd)*, John Desmond Forbes Anderson, *b.* 1949, *s.* 1990, *m.*	Hon. Forbes A. R. A., *b.* 1996
1938	*Weir (3rd)*, William Kenneth James Weir, *b.* 1933, *s.* 1975, *m.*	Hon. James W. H. W., *b.* 1965
1918	*Wimborne (4th)*, Ivor Mervyn Vigors Guest, *b.* 1968, *s.* 1993, *m.*	Hon. Ivor N. G. I G., *b.* 2016
1923 **	*Younger of Leckie (5th)*, James Edward George Younger, *b.* 1955, *s.* 2003, *m.*	Hon. Alexander W. G. Y., *b.* 1993

BARONS/LORDS

Coronet, Six silver balls

Style, The Rt. Hon. the Lord _
  Envelope (formal), The Rt. Hon. Lord _; *(social),* The Lord _. *Letter (formal),* My Lord; *(social),* Dear Lord _. *Spoken,* Lord _.
In the Peerage of Scotland there is no rank of Baron; the equivalent rank is Lord of Parliament and Scottish peers should always be styled 'Lord', never 'Baron'.

Wife's style, The Rt. Hon. the Lady _
Envelope (formal), The Rt. Hon. Lady _; *(social),* The Lady _. *Letter (formal),* My Lady; *(social),* Dear Lady _. *Spoken,* Lady _
Children's style, 'The Hon.' before forename (F_) and surname (S_)
Envelope, The Hon. F_ S_. *Letter,* Dear Mr/Miss/Mrs S_. *Spoken,* Mr/Miss/Mrs S_
In Scotland, the heir to a Lord may be styled 'The Master/Mistress of _ (title of peer)'

Created	*Title, order of succession, name, etc*	*Heir*
1911	*Aberconway (4th)*, (Henry) Charles McLaren, *b.* 1948, *s.* 2003, *m.*	Hon. Charles S. M., *b.* 1984
1873 **	*Aberdare (5th)*, Alastair John Lyndhurst Bruce, *b.* 1947, *s.* 2005, *m.*	Hon. Hector M. N. B., *b.* 1974
1835	*Abinger (9th)*, James Harry Scarlett, *b.* 1959, *s.* 2002, *m.*	Hon. Peter R. S., *b.* 1961
1869	*Acton (5th)*, John Charles Ferdinand Harold Lyon-Dalberg-Acton, *b.* 1966, *s.* 2010, *m.*	Hon. Robert P. L.-D.-A., *b.* 1946
1887 **	*Addington (6th)*, Dominic Bryce Hubbard, *b.* 1963, *s.* 1982, *m.*	Hon. Michael W. L. H., *b.* 1965

1896	*Aldenham (6th) and Hunsdon of Hunsdon (4th) (1923)*, Vicary Tyser Gibbs, *b.* 1948, *s.* 1986, *m.*	Hon. Humphrey W. F. G., *b.* 1989
1962	*Aldington (2nd)*, Charles Harold Stuart Low, *b.* 1948, *s.* 2000, *m.*	Hon. Philip T. A. L., *b.* 1990
1945	*Altrincham (3rd)*, Anthony Ulick David Dundas Grigg, *b.* 1934, *s.* 2001, *m.*	Hon. (Edward) Sebastian G., *b.* 1965
1929	*Alvingham (2nd)*, Maj.-Gen. Robert Guy Eardley Yerburgh, CBE, *b.* 1926, *s.* 1955, *m.*	Capt. Hon. Robert R. G. Y., *b.* 1956
1892	*Amherst of Hackney (5th)*, Hugh William Amherst Cecil, *b.* 1968, *s.* 2009, *m.*	Hon. Jack W. A. C., *b.* 2001
1881	*Ampthill (5th)*, David Whitney Erskine Russell, *b.* 1947, *s.* 2011, *m.*	Hon. Anthony J. M. R., *b.* 1952
1947	*Amwell (3rd)*, Keith Norman Montague, *b.* 1943, *s.* 1990, *m.*	Hon. Ian K. M., *b.* 1973
1863	*Annaly (6th)*, Luke Richard White, *b.* 1954, *s.* 1990, *m.*	Hon. Luke H. W., *b.* 1990
1885	*Ashbourne (4th)*, Edward Barry Greynville Gibson, *b.* 1933, *s.* 1983, *m.*	Hon. Edward C. d'O. G., *b.* 1967
1835	*Ashburton (7th)*, John Francis Harcourt Baring, KG, KCVO, *b.* 1928, *s.* 1991, *m.*	Hon. Mark F. R. B., *b.* 1958
1892	*Ashcombe (5th)*, Mark Edward Cubitt, *b.* 1964, *s.* 2013, *m.*	Hon. Richard R. A. C., *b.* 1995
1911 **	*Ashton of Hyde (4th)*, Thomas Henry Ashton, *b.* 1958, *s.* 2008, *m.*	Hon. John E. A., *b.* 1966
1800 I.	*Ashtown (8th)*, Roderick Nigel Godolphin Trench, *b.* 1944, *s.* 2010, *m.*	Hon. Timothy R. H. T., *b.* 1968
1956 **	*Astor of Hever (3rd)*, John Jacob Astor, PC, *b.* 1946, *s.* 1984, *m.*	Hon. Charles G. J. A., *b.* 1990
1789 I.	*Auckland (10th) and Auckland (10th) (1793)*, Robert Ian Burnard Eden, *b.* 1962, *s.* 1997, *m.*	Henry V. E., *b.* 1958
1313	*Audley*, Barony in abeyance between three co-heiresses since 1997	
1900	*Avebury (5th)*, Lyulph Ambrose Lubbock, *b.* 1954, *s.* 2016, *m.*	Hon. Alexander L. R. L., *b.* 1985
1718 I.	*Aylmer (14th)*, (Anthony) Julian Aylmer, *b.* 1951, *s.* 2006, *m.*	Hon. Michael H. A., *b.* 1991
1929	*Baden-Powell (3rd)*, Robert Crause Baden-Powell, *b.* 1936, *s.* 1962, *w.*	Hon. David M. B.-P., *b.* 1940
1780	*Bagot (10th)*, (Charles Hugh) Shaun Bagot, *b.* 1944, *s.* 2001, *m.*	Richard C. V. B., *b.* 1941
1953	*Baillieu (3rd)*, James William Latham Baillieu, *b.* 1950, *s.* 1973, *m.*	Hon. Robert L. B., *b.* 1979
1607 S.	*Balfour of Burleigh (8th)*, Robert Bruce, *b.* 1927, *s.* 1967, *m.*	Hon. Victoria B., *b.* 1973
1924	*Banbury of Southam (3rd)*, Charles William Banbury, *b.* 1953, *s.* 1981, *m.*	None
1698	*Barnard (12th)*, Henry Francis Cecil Vane, *b.* 1959, *s.* 2016, *m.*	Hon. William H. C. V., *b.* 2005
1887	*Basing (6th)*, Stuart Anthony Whitfield Sclater-Booth, *b.* 1969, *s.* 2007, *m.*	Hon. Luke W. S.-B., *b.* 2000
1917	*Beaverbrook (3rd)*, Maxwell William Humphrey Aitken, *b.* 1951, *s.* 1985, *m.*	Hon. Maxwell F. A., *b.* 1977
1647 S.	*Belhaven and Stenton (13th)*, Robert Anthony Carmichael Hamilton, *b.* 1927, *s.* 1961, *m.*	Master of Belhaven, *b.* 1953
1848 I.	*Bellew (8th)*, Bryan Edward Bellew, *b.* 1943, *s.* 2010, *m.*	Hon. Anthony R. B. B., *b.* 1972
1856	*Belper (5th)*, Richard Henry Strutt, *b.* 1941, *s.* 1999, *m.*	Hon. Michael H. S., *b.* 1969
1421	*Berkeley (18th) and Gueterbock (life peerage, 2000)*, Anthony Fitzhardinge Gueterbock, OBE, *b.* 1939, *s.* 1992, *m.*	Hon. Thomas F. G., *b.* 1969
1922 **	*Bethell (5th)*, James Nicholas Bethell, *b.* 1967, *s.* 2007, *m.*	Hon. Jacob N. D. B., *b.* 2006
1938	*Bicester (4th)*, Hugh Charles Vivian Smith, *b.* 1934, *s.* 2014	Charles J. V. S., *b.* 1963
1903	*Biddulph (5th)*, (Anthony) Nicholas Colin Maitland Biddulph, *b.* 1959, *s.* 1988, *m.*	Hon. Robert J. M. B., *b.* 1994
1958	*Birkett (3rd)*, Thomas Birkett, *b.* 1982, *s.* 2015	None
1907	*Blyth (5th)*, James Audley Ian Blyth, *b.* 1970, *s.* 2009, *m.*	Hon. Hugo A. J. B., *b.* 2006
1797	*Bolton (8th)*, Harry Algar Nigel Orde-Powlett, *b.* 1954, *s.* 2001, *w.*	Hon. Thomas O.-P., MC, *b.* 1979
1452 S.	*Borthwick (24th)*, John Hugh Borthwick, *b.* 1940, *s.* 1996, *m.*	Hon. James H. A. B. of Glengelt, *b.* 1940
1922 **	*Borwick (5th)*, (Geoffrey Robert) James Borwick, *b.* 1955, *s.* 2007, *m.*	Hon. Edwin D. W. B., *b.* 1984
1761	*Boston (11th)*, George William Eustace Boteler Irby, *b.* 1971, *s.* 2007, *m.*	Hon. Thomas W. G. B. I., *b.* 1999
1942 **	*Brabazon of Tara (3rd)*, Ivon Anthony Moore-Brabazon, PC, *b.* 1946, *s.* 1974, *m.*	Hon. Benjamin R. M.-B., *b.* 1983
1925	*Bradbury (3rd)*, John Bradbury, *b.* 1940, *s.* 1994, *m.*	Hon. John B., *b.* 1973
1962	*Brain (3rd)*, Michael Cottrell Brain, *b.* 1928, *s.* 2014, *m.*	Hon. Thomas R. B., *b.* 1965
1938	*Brassey of Apethorpe (4th)*, Edward Brassey, *b.* 1964, *s.* 2015, *m.*	Hon. Christian B., *b.* 2003
1788	*Braybrooke (11th)*, Richard Ralph Neville, *b.* 1977, *s.* 2017	Hon. Edward A. N., *b.* 2015
1957	*Bridges (3rd)*, Mark Thomas Bridges, CVO, *b.* 1954, *s.* 2017, *m.*	Hon. Nicholas E. B., *b.* 1956
1945	*Broadbridge (4th)*, Martin Hugh Broadbridge, *b.* 1929, *s.* 2000, *w.*	Air Vice-Marshal Hon. Richard J. M. B., CB, *b.* 1959
1933	*Brocket (3rd)*, Charles Ronald George Nall-Cain, *b.* 1952, *s.* 1967, *m.*	Hon. Alexander C. C. N.-C., *b.* 1984
1860 **	*Brougham and Vaux (5th)*, Michael John Brougham, CBE, *b.* 1938, *s.* 1967	Hon. Charles W. B., *b.* 1971
1776	*Brownlow (7th)*, Edward John Peregrine Cust, *b.* 1936, *s.* 1978, *m.*	Hon. Peregrine E. Q. C., *b.* 1974
1942	*Bruntisfield (3rd)*, Michael John Victor Warrender, *b.* 1949, *s.* 2007, *m.*	Hon. John M. P. C. W., *b.* 1996
1950	*Burden (4th)*, Fraser William Elsworth Burden, *b.* 1964, *s.* 2000, *m.*	Hon. Ian S. B., *b.* 1967
1529	*Burgh (8th)*, (Alexander) Gregory Disney Leith, *b.* 1958, *s.* 2001, *m.*	Hon. Alexander J. S. L., *b.* 1986
1903	*Burnham (7th)*, Harry Frederick Alan Lawson, *b.* 1968, *s.* 2005	None
1897	*Burton (4th)*, Evan Michael Ronald Baillie, *b.* 1949, *s.* 2013, *m.*	Hon. James E. B., *b.* 1975
1643	*Byron (13th)*, Robert James Byron, *b.* 1950, *s.* 1989, *m.*	Hon. Charles R. G. B., *b.* 1990
1937	*Cadman (3rd)*, John Anthony Cadman, *b.* 1938, *s.* 1966, *m.*	Hon. Nicholas A. J. C., *b.* 1977
1945	*Calverley (3rd)*, Charles Rodney Muff, *b.* 1946, *s.* 1971, *m.*	Hon. Jonathan E. Brown, *b.* 1975
1383	*Camoys (7th)*, (Ralph) Thomas Campion George Sherman Stonor, GCVO, PC, *b.* 1940, *s.* 1976, *m.*	Hon. R. William R. T. S., *b.* 1974

1715 I.	*Carbery (12th)*, Michael Peter Evans-Freke, b. 1942, s. 2012, m.	Hon. Dominic R. C. E.-F., b. 1969
1834 I.	*Carew (7th) and Carew (7th) (1838)*, Patrick Thomas Conolly-Carew, b. 1938, s. 1994, m.	Hon. William P. C.-C., b. 1973
1916	*Carnock (5th)*, Adam Nicolson, b. 1957, s. 2008, m.	Hon. Thomas N., b. 1984
1796 I.	*Carrington (7th) and Carrington (7th) (1797)*, Rupert Francis John Carington, b. 1948, s. 2018, m.	Hon. Robert C., b. 1990
1812 I.	*Castlemaine (8th)*, Roland Thomas John Handcock, MBE, b. 1943, s. 1973, m.	Hon. Ronan M. E. H., b. 1989
1936	*Catto (3rd)*, Innes Gordon Catto, b. 1950, s. 2001, m.	Hon. Alexander G. C., b. 1952
1918	*Cawley (4th)*, John Francis Cawley, b. 1946, s. 2001, m.	Hon. William R. H. C., b. 1981
1858	*Chesham (7th)*, Charles Gray Compton Cavendish, b. 1974, s. 2009, m.	Hon. Oliver N. B. C., b. 2007
1945	*Chetwode (2nd)*, Philip Chetwode, b. 1937, s. 1950, m.	Hon. Roger C., b. 1968
1945	*Chorley (3rd)*, Nicholas Rupert Debenham Chorley, b. 1966, s. 2016, m.	Hon. Patrick A. C. C., b. 2000
1815	*Churchill (6th)*, Richard Harry Ramsay Spencer, b. 1926, s. 2017, m.	Hon. Michael R. de C. S., b. 1960
1858	*Churston (5th)*, John Francis Yarde-Buller, b. 1934, s. 1991, m.	Hon. Benjamin F. A. Y.-B., b. 1974
1800 I.	*Clanmorris (8th)*, Simon John Ward Bingham, b. 1937, s. 1988, m.	Robert D. de B. B., b. 1942
1672	*Clifford of Chudleigh (14th)*, Thomas Hugh Clifford, b. 1948, s. 1988, m.	Hon. Alexander T. H. C., b. 1985
1299	*Clinton (22nd)*, Gerard Nevile Mark Fane Trefusis, b. 1934, s. 1965, m.	Hon. Charles P. R. F. T., b. 1962
1955	*Clitheroe (2nd)*, Ralph John Assheton, b. 1929, s. 1984, m.	Hon. Ralph C. A., b. 1962
1919	*Clwyd (4th)*, (John) Murray Roberts, b. 1971, s. 2006, m.	Hon. John D. R., b. 2006
1948	*Clydesmuir (3rd)*, David Ronald Colville, b. 1949, s. 1996, m.	Hon. Richard C., b. 1980
1960	*Cobbold (2nd)*, David Antony Fromanteel Lytton Cobbold, b. 1937, s. 1987, m.	Hon. Henry F. L. C., b. 1962
1919	*Cochrane of Cults (5th)*, Thomas Hunter Vere Cochrane, b. 1957, s. 2017, m.	Hon. Michael C. N. C., OBE, b. 1959
1954	*Coleraine (2nd)*, (James) Martin (Bonar) Law, b. 1931, s. 1980, m.	Hon. James P. B. L., b. 1975
1873	*Coleridge (5th)*, William Duke Coleridge, b. 1937, s. 1984, w.	Hon. James D. C., b. 1967
1946 **	*Colgrain (4th)*, Alastair Colin Leckie Campbell, b. 1951, s. 2008, m.	Hon. Thomas C. D. C., b. 1984
1917 **	*Colwyn (3rd)*, (Ian) Anthony Hamilton-Smith, CBE, b. 1942, s. 1966, m.	Hon. Craig P. H.-S., b. 1968
1956	*Colyton (2nd)*, Alisdair John Munro Hopkinson, b. 1958, s. 1996, m.	Hon. James P. M. H., b. 1983
1841	*Congleton (9th)*, John Patrick Christian Parnell, b. 1959, s. 2015, m.	Hon. Christopher J. E. P., b. 1987
1927	*Cornwallis (4th)*, Fiennes Wykeham Jeremy Cornwallis, b. 1946, s. 2010, m.	Hon. Fiennes A. W. M. C., b. 1987
1874	*Cottesloe (6th)*, Thomas Francis Henry Fremantle, b. 1966, s. 2018	Hon. Edward W. F., b. 1961
1929	*Craigmyle (4th)*, Thomas Columba Shaw, b. 1960, s. 1998, m.	Hon. Alexander F. S., b. 1988
1899	*Cranworth (3rd)*, Philip Bertram Gurdon, b. 1940, s. 1964, m.	Hon. Sacha W. R. G., b. 1970
1959 **	*Crathorne (2nd)*, Charles James Dugdale, KCVO, b. 1939, s. 1977, w.	Hon. Thomas A. J. D., b. 1977
1892	*Crawshaw (5th)*, David Gerald Brooks, b. 1934, s. 1997, m.	Hon. John P. B., b. 1938
1940	*Croft (3rd)*, Bernard William Henry Page Croft, b. 1949, s. 1997, m.	None
1797 I.	*Crofton (8th)*, Edward Harry Piers Crofton, b. 1988, s. 2007	Hon. Charles M. G. C., b. 1988
1375 **	*Cromwell (7th)*, Godfrey John Bewicke-Copley, b. 1960, s. 1982, m.	Hon. David G. B.-C., b. 1997
1947	*Crook (3rd)*, Robert Douglas Edwin Crook, b. 1955, s. 2001, m.	Hon. Matthew R. C., b. 1990
1920	*Cullen of Ashbourne (4th)*, Michael John Cokayne, b. 1950, s. 2016, m.	None
1914	*Cunliffe (3rd)*, Roger Cunliffe, b. 1932, s. 1963, m.	Hon. Henry C., b. 1962
1332	*Darcy de Knayth (19th)*, Caspar David Ingrams, b. 1962, s. 2008, m.	Hon. Thomas R. I., b. 1999
1927	*Daresbury (4th)*, Peter Gilbert Greenall, b. 1953, s. 1996, m.	Hon. Thomas E. G., b. 1984
1924	*Darling (3rd)*, (Robert) Julian Henry Darling, b. 1944, s. 2003, m.	Hon. Robert J. C. D., b. 1972
1946	*Darwen (4th)*, Paul Davies, b. 1962, s. 2011, m.	Hon. Oscar K. D., b. 1996
1932	*Davies (3rd)*, David Davies, b. 1940, s. 1944, m.	Hon. David D. D., b. 1975
1812 I.	*Decies (7th)*, Marcus Hugh Tristram de la Poer Beresford, b. 1948, s. 1992, m.	Hon. Robert M. D. de la P. B., b. 1988
1299	*de Clifford (27th)*, John Edward Southwell Russell, b. 1928, s. 1982, m.	Miles E. S. R., b. 1966
1851	*De Freyne (8th)*, Fulke Charles Arthur John French, b. 1957, s. 2009, m.	Hon. Alexander J. C. F., b. 1988
1821	*Delamere (5th)*, Hugh George Cholmondeley, b. 1934, s. 1979, m.	Hugh C., b. 1998
1838 **	*de Mauley (7th)*, Rupert Charles Ponsonby, b. 1957, s. 2002, m.	Ashley G. P., b. 1959
1937 **	*Denham (2nd)*, Bertram Stanley Mitford Bowyer, KBE, PC, b. 1927, s. 1948, m.	Hon. Richard G. G. B., b. 1959
1834	*Denman (6th)*, Richard Thomas Stewart Denman, b. 1946, s. 2012, m.	Hon. Robert D., b. 1995
1887	*De Ramsey (4th)*, John Ailwyn Fellowes, b. 1942, s. 1993, m.	Hon. Freddie J. F., b. 1978
1264	*de Ros (28th)*, Peter Trevor Maxwell, b. 1958, s. 1983, m. *Premier Baron of England*	Hon. Finbar J. M., b. 1988
1881	*Derwent (5th)*, Robin Evelyn Leo Vanden-Bempde-Johnstone, LVO, b. 1930, s. 1986, m.	Hon. Francis P. H. V.-B.-J., b. 1965
1831	*de Saumarez (7th)*, Eric Douglas Saumarez, b. 1956, s. 1991, m.	Hon. Victor T. S., b. 1956
1910	*de Villiers (4th)*, Alexander Charles de Villiers, b. 1940, s. 2001, m.	None
1930	*Dickinson (2nd)*, Richard Clavering Hyett Dickinson, b. 1926, s. 1943, m.	Hon. Martin H. D., b. 1961
1620 I.	*Digby (13th) and Digby (6th) (1765)*, Henry Noel Kenelm Digby, b. 1954, s. 2018, m.	Hon. Edward St V. K. D., b. 1985
1615	*Dormer (18th)*, William Robert Dormer, b. 1960, s. 2016, m.	Hon. Hugo E. G. D., b. 1995
1943	*Dowding (3rd)*, Piers Hugh Tremenheere Dowding, b. 1948, s. 1992, m.	Hon. Mark D. J. D., b. 1949
1439	*Dudley (15th)*, Jim Anthony Hill Wallace, b. 1930, s. 2002, m.	Hon. Jeremy W. G. W., b. 1964

1800 I.	*Dufferin and Clandeboye (11th)*, John Francis Blackwood, *b.* 1944, *s.* 1991, *m.* (claim to the peerage not yet established)	Hon. Francis S. B., *b.* 1979
1929	*Dulverton (3rd)*, (Gilbert) Michael Hamilton Wills, *b.* 1944, *s.* 1992, *m.*	Hon. Robert A. H. W., *b.* 1983
1800 I.	*Dunalley (7th)*, Henry Francis Cornelius Prittie, *b.* 1948, *s.* 1992, *m.*	Hon. Joel H. P., *b.* 1981
1324 I.	*Dunboyne (30th)*, Richard Pierce Theobald Butler, *b.* 1983, *s.* 2013, *m.*	Michael J. B., *b.* 1944
1892	*Dunleath (6th)*, Brian Henry Mulholland, *b.* 1950, *s.* 1997, *m.*	Hon. Andrew H. M., *b.* 1981
1439 I.	*Dunsany (21st)*, Randal Plunkett, *b.* 1983, *s.* 2011	Hon. Oliver P., *b.* 1985
1780	*Dynevor (10th)*, Hugo Griffith Uryan Rhys, *b.* 1966, *s.* 2008	Robert D. A. R., *b.* 1963
1963	*Egremont (2nd) and Leconfield (7th) (1859)*, John Max Henry Scawen Wyndham, *b.* 1948, *s.* 1972, *m.*	Hon. George R. V. W., *b.* 1983
1643 S.	*Elibank (15th)*, Robert Francis Alan Erskine-Murray, *b.* 1964, *s.* 2017, *m.*	Hon. Timothy A. E. E.-M. *b.* 1967
1802	*Ellenborough (9th)*, Rupert Edward Henry Law, *b.* 1955, *s.* 2013, *m.*	Hon. James R. T. L., *b.* 1983
1509 S.	*Elphinstone (19th) and Elphinstone (5th) (1885)*, Alexander Mountstuart Elphinstone, *b.* 1980, *s.* 1994, *m.*	Master of Elphinstone, *b.* 2011
1934 **	*Elton (2nd)*, Rodney Elton, TD, *b.* 1930, *s.* 1973, *m.*	Hon. Edward P. E., *b.* 1966
1627 S. **	*Fairfax of Cameron (14th)*, Nicholas John Albert Fairfax, *b.* 1956, *s.* 1964, *m.*	Hon. Edward N. T. F., *b.* 1984
1961	*Fairhaven (3rd)*, Ailwyn Henry George Broughton, *b.* 1936, *s.* 1973, *m.*	Maj. Hon. James H. A. B., *b.* 1963
1916	*Faringdon (3rd)*, Charles Michael Henderson, KCVO, *b.* 1937, *s.* 1977, *m.*	Hon. James H. H., *b.* 1961
1756 I.	*Farnham (13th)*, Simon Kenlis Maxwell, *b.* 1933, *s.* 2001, *w.*	Hon. Robin S. M., *b.* 1965
1856 I.	*Fermoy (6th)*, Maurice Burke Roche, *b.* 1967, *s.* 1984, *m.*	Hon. E. Hugh B. R., *b.* 1972
1826	*Feversham (7th)*, Jasper Orlando Slingsby Duncombe, *b.* 1968, *s.* 2009, *m.*	Hon. Orlando B. D., *b.* 2009
1798 I.	*ffrench (8th)*, Robuck John Peter Charles Mario ffrench, *b.* 1956, *s.* 1986, *m.*	None
1909	*Fisher (4th)*, Patrick Vavasseur Fisher, *b.* 1953, *s.* 2012, *m.*	Hon. Benjamin C. V. F., *b.* 1986
1295	*Fitzwalter (22nd)*, Julian Brook Plumptre, *b.* 1952, *s.* 2004, *m.*	Hon. Edward B. P., *b.* 1989
1776	*Foley (9th)*, Thomas Henry Foley, *b.* 1961, *s.* 2012	Rupert T. F., *b.* 1970
1445 S.	*Forbes (23rd)*, Malcolm Nigel Forbes, *b.* 1946, *s.* 2013, *m. Premier Lord of Scotland*	Master of Forbes, *b.* 1970
1821	*Forester (9th)*, Charles Richard George Weld-Forester, *b.* 1975, *s.* 2004, *m.*	Hon. Brook G. P. W.-F., *b.* 2014
1922	*Forres (4th)*, Alastair Stephen Grant Williamson, *b.* 1946, *s.* 1978, *m.*	Hon. George A. M. W., *b.* 1972
1917	*Forteviot (4th)*, John James Evelyn Dewar, *b.* 1938, *s.* 1993, *w.*	Hon. Alexander J. E. D., *b.* 1971
1951 **	*Freyberg (3rd)*, Valerian Bernard Freyberg, *b.* 1970, *s.* 1993, *m.*	Hon. Joseph J. F., *b.* 2007
1917	*Gainford (4th)*, George Pease, *b.* 1926, *s.* 2013, *m.*	Hon. Adrian C. P., *b.* 1960
1818 I.	*Garvagh (6th)*, Spencer George Stratford de Redcliffe Canning, *b.* 1953, *s.* 2013, *m.*	Hon. Stratford G. E. de R. C., *b.* 1990
1942 **	*Geddes (3rd)*, Euan Michael Ross Geddes, *b.* 1937, *s.* 1975, *m.*	Hon. James G. N. G., *b.* 1969
1876	*Gerard (5th)*, Anthony Robert Hugo Gerard, *b.* 1949, *s.* 1992, *m.*	Hon. Rupert B. C. G., *b.* 1981
1824	*Gifford (6th)*, Anthony Maurice Gifford, QC, *b.* 1940, *s.* 1961, *m.*	Hon. Thomas A. G., *b.* 1967
1917	*Gisborough (3rd)*, Thomas Richard John Long Chaloner, *b.* 1927, *s.* 1951, *m.*	Hon. T. Peregrine L. C., *b.* 1961
1899	*Glanusk (5th)*, Christopher Russell Bailey, *b.* 1942, *s.* 1997, *m.*	Hon. Charles H. B., *b.* 1976
1918 **	*Glenarthur (4th)*, Simon Mark Arthur, *b.* 1944, *s.* 1976, *m.*	Hon. Edward A. A., *b.* 1973
1911	*Glenconner (4th)*, Cody Charles Edward Tennant, *b.* 1994, *s.* 2010	Euan L. T., *b.* 1983
1964	*Glendevon (3rd)*, Jonathan Charles Hope, *b.* 1952, *s.* 2009	None
1922	*Glendyne (4th)*, John Nivison, *b.* 1960, *s.* 2008	None
1939	*Glentoran (3rd)*, (Thomas) Robin (Valerian) Dixon, CBE, *b.* 1935, *s.* 1995, *m.*	Hon. Daniel G. D., *b.* 1959
1909	*Gorell (5th)*, John Picton Gorell Barnes, *b.* 1959, *s.* 2007, *m.*	Hon. Oliver G. B., *b.* 1993
1953 **	*Grantchester (3rd)*, Christopher John Suenson-Taylor, *b.* 1951, *s.* 1995, *m.*	Hon. Jesse D. S.-T., *b.* 1977
1782	*Grantley (8th)*, Richard William Brinsley Norton, *b.* 1956, *s.* 1995	Hon. Francis J. H. N., *b.* 1960
1794 I.	*Graves (10th)*, Timothy Evelyn Graves, *b.* 1960, *s.* 2002, *m.*	None
1445 S.	*Gray (23rd)*, Andrew Godfrey Diarmid Stuart Campbell-Gray, *b.* 1964, *s.* 2003, *m.*	Master of Gray, *b.* 1996
1950	*Greenhill (3rd)*, Malcolm Greenhill, *b.* 1924, *s.* 1989	None
1927 **	*Greenway (4th)*, Ambrose Charles Drexel Greenway, *b.* 1941, *s.* 1975, *m.*	Nicholas W. P. G., *b.* 1988
1902	*Grenfell (3rd) and Grenfell of Kilvey (life peerage, 2000)*, Julian Pascoe Francis St Leger Grenfell, *b.* 1935, *s.* 1976, *m.*	Richard A. St L. G., *b.* 1966
1944	*Gretton (4th)*, John Lysander Gretton, *b.* 1975, *s.* 1989, *m.*	Hon. John F. B. G., *b.* 2008
1397	*Grey of Codnor (6th)*, Richard Henry Cornwall-Legh, *b.* 1936, *s.* 1996, *m.*	Hon. Richard S. C. C.-L., *b.* 1976
1955	*Gridley (3rd)*, Richard David Arnold Gridley, *b.* 1956, *s.* 1996, *m.*	Peter A. C. G., *b.* 1940
1964	*Grimston of Westbury (3rd)*, Robert John Sylvester Grimston, *b.* 1951, *s.* 2003, *m.*	Hon. Gerald C. W. G., *b.* 1953
1886	*Grimthorpe (5th)*, Edward John Beckett, *b.* 1954, *s.* 2003, *m.*	Hon. Harry M. B., *b.* 1993
1945	*Hacking (3rd)*, Douglas David Hacking, *b.* 1938, *s.* 1971, *m.*	Hon. Douglas F. H., *b.* 1968
1950	*Haden-Guest (5th)*, Christopher Haden-Guest, *b.* 1948, *s.* 1996, *m.*	Hon. Nicholas H.-G., *b.* 1951
1886	*Hamilton of Dalzell (5th)*, Gavin Goulburn Hamilton, *b.* 1968, *s.* 2006, *m.*	Hon. Francis A. J. G. H., *b.* 2009
1874	*Hampton (7th)*, John Humphrey Arnott Pakington, *b.* 1964, *s.* 2003, *m.*	Hon. Charles R. C. P., *b.* 2005
1939	*Hankey (3rd)*, Donald Robin Alers Hankey, *b.* 1938, *s.* 1996, *m.*	Hon. Alexander M. A. H., *b.* 1947
1958	*Harding of Petherton (3rd)*, William Allan John Harding, *b.* 1969, *s.* 2016, *m.*	Hon. Angus J. E. H., *b.* 2001
1910	*Hardinge of Penshurst (4th)*, Julian Alexander Hardinge, *b.* 1945, *s.* 1997, *m.*	Hon. Hugh F. H., *b.* 1948
1876	*Harlech (7th)*, Jasset David Cody Ormsby-Gore, *b.* 1986, *s.* 2016	None

1939	*Harmsworth (3rd)*, Thomas Harold Raymond Harmsworth, *b.* 1939, *s.* 1990, *m.*	Hon. Dominic M. E. H., *b.* 1973
1815	*Harris (8th)*, Anthony Harris, *b.* 1942, *s.* 1996, *m.*	Rear-Adm. Michael G. T. H., *b.* 1941
1954	*Harvey of Tasburgh (3rd)*, Charles John Giuseppe Harvey, *b.* 1951, *s.* 2010, *m.*	Hon. John H., *b.* 1993
1295	*Hastings (23rd)*, Delaval Thomas Harold Astley, *b.* 1960, *s.* 2007, *m.*	Hon. Jacob A. A., *b.* 1991
1835	*Hatherton (8th)*, Edward Charles Littleton, *b.* 1950, *s.* 1985, *m.*	Hon. Thomas E. L., *b.* 1977
1776	*Hawke (12th)*, William Martin Theodore Hawke, *b.* 1995, *s.* 2009	None
1927	*Hayter (4th)*, George William Michael Chubb, *b.* 1943, *s.* 2003, *m.*	Hon. Thomas F. F. C., *b.* 1986
1945	*Hazlerigg (3rd)*, Arthur Grey Hazlerigg, *b.* 1951, *s.* 2002, *m.*	Hon. Arthur W. G. H., *b.* 1987
1943	*Hemingford (3rd)*, (Dennis) Nicholas Herbert, *b.* 1934, *s.* 1982, *w.*	Hon. Christopher D. C. H., *b.* 1973
1906	*Hemphill (6th)*, Charles Andrew Martyn Martyn-Hemphill, *b.* 1954, *s.* 2012, *m.*	Hon. Richard P. L. M.-H., *b.* 1990
1799 I. **	*Henley (8th) and Northington (6th) (1885)*, Oliver Michael Robert Eden, PC, *b.* 1953, *s.* 1977, *m.*	Hon. John W. O. E., *b.* 1988
1800 I.	*Henniker (9th) and Hartismere (6th) (1866)*, Mark Ian Philip Chandos Henniker-Major, *b.* 1947, *s.* 2004, *m.*	Hon. Edward G. M. H.-M., *b.* 1985
1461	*Herbert (19th)*, David John Seyfried Herbert, *b.* 1952, *s.* 2002, *m.* Title called out of abeyance 2002	Hon. Oliver R. S. H., *b.* 1976
1935	*Hesketh (3rd)*, Thomas Alexander Fermor-Hesketh, KBE, PC, *b.* 1950, *s.* 1955, *m.*	Hon. Frederick H. F.-H., *b.* 1988
1828	*Heytesbury (7th)*, James William Holmes à Court, *b.* 1967, *s.* 2004, *m.*	Peter M. H. H. à. C., *b.* 1968
1886	*Hindlip (6th)*, Charles Henry Allsopp, *b.* 1940, *s.* 1993, *w.*	Hon. Henry W. A., *b.* 1973
1950	*Hives (3rd)*, Matthew Peter Hives, *b.* 1971, *s.* 1997	Hon. Michael B. H., *b.* 1926
1912	*Hollenden (4th)*, Ian Hampden Hope-Morley, *b.* 1946, *s.* 1999, *m.*	Hon. Edward H.-M., *b.* 1981
1897	*Holm Patrick (4th)*, Hans James David Hamilton, *b.* 1955, *s.* 1991, *m.*	Hon. Ion H. J. H., *b.* 1956
1797 I.	*Hotham (8th)*, Henry Durand Hotham, *b.* 1940, *s.* 1967, *m.*	Hon. William B. H., *b.* 1972
1881	*Hothfield (6th)*, Anthony Charles Sackville Tufton, *b.* 1939, *s.* 1991, *m.*	Hon. William S. T., *b.* 1977
1930	*Howard of Penrith (3rd)*, Philip Esme Howard, *b.* 1945, *s.* 1999, *m.*	Hon. Thomas P. H., *b.* 1974
1960	*Howick of Glendale (2nd)*, Charles Evelyn Baring, *b.* 1937, *s.* 1973, *m.*	Hon. David E. C. B., *b.* 1975
1796 I.	*Huntingfield (7th)*, Joshua Charles Vanneck, *b.* 1954, *s.* 1994, *w.*	Hon. Gerard C. A. V., *b.* 1985
1866 **	*Hylton (5th)*, Raymond Hervey Jolliffe, *b.* 1932, *s.* 1967, *m.*	Hon. William H. M. J., *b.* 1967
1933	*Iliffe (3rd)*, Robert Peter Richard Iliffe, *b.* 1944, *s.* 1996, *m.*	Hon. Edward R. I., *b.* 1968
1543 I.	*Inchiquin (18th)*, Conor Myles John O'Brien, *b.* 1943, *s.* 1982, *m.*	Conor J. A. O'B., *b.* 1952
1962	*Inchyra (3rd)*, Christian James Charles Hoyer Millar, *b.* 1962, *s.* 2011, *m.*	Hon. Jake C. R. M., *b.* 1996
1964 **	*Inglewood (2nd)*, (William) Richard Fletcher-Vane, *b.* 1951, *s.* 1989, *m.*	Hon. Henry W. F. F.-V., *b.* 1990
1919	*Inverforth (4th)*, Andrew Peter Weir, *b.* 1966, *s.* 1982, *m.*	Hon. Benjamin A. W., *b.* 1997
1941	*Ironside (2nd)*, Edmund Oslac Ironside, *b.* 1924, *s.* 1959, *w.*	Hon. Charles E. G. I., *b.* 1956
1952	*Jeffreys (3rd)*, Christopher Henry Mark Jeffreys, *b.* 1957, *s.* 1986, *m.*	Hon. Arthur M. H. J., *b.* 1989
1906	*Joicey (5th)*, James Michael Joicey, *b.* 1953, *s.* 1993, *m.*	Hon. William J. J., *b.* 1990
1937	*Kenilworth (4th)*, (John) Randle Siddeley, *b.* 1954, *s.* 1981, *m.*	Hon. William R. J. S., *b.* 1992
1935	*Kennet (3rd)*, William Aldus Thoby Young, *b.* 1957, *s.* 2009, *m.*	Hon. Archibald W. K. Y., *b.* 1992
1776 I.	*Kensington (8th) and Kensington (5th) (1886)*, Hugh Ivor Edwardes, *b.* 1933, *s.* 1981, *m.*	Hon. W. Owen A. E., *b.* 1964
1951	*Kenswood (3rd)*, Michael Christopher Whitfield, *b.* 1955, *s.* 2016, *m.*	Hon. Anthony J. W., *b.* 1957
1788	*Kenyon (6th)*, Lloyd Tyrell-Kenyon, *b.* 1947, *s.* 1993, *m.*	Hon. Lloyd N. T.-K., *b.* 1972
1947	*Kershaw (4th)*, Edward John Kershaw, *b.* 1936, *s.* 1962, *m.*	Hon. John C. E. K., *b.* 1971
1943	*Keyes (3rd)*, Charles William Packe Keyes, *b.* 1951, *s.* 2005, *m.*	Hon. (Leopold R.) J. K., *b.* 1956
1909	*Kilbracken (4th)*, Christopher John Godley, *b.* 1945, *s.* 2006, *m.*	Hon. James J. G., *b.* 1972
1900	*Killanin (4th)*, (George) Redmond Fitzpatrick Morris, *b.* 1947, *s.* 1999, *m.*	Hon. Luke M. G. M., *b.* 1975
1943	*Killearn (3rd)*, Victor Miles George Aldous Lampson, *b.* 1941, *s.* 1996, *m.*	Hon. Miles H. M. L., *b.* 1977
1789 I.	*Kilmaine (8th)*, John Francis Sandford Browne, *b.* 1983, *s.* 2013	Revd Aubrey R. C. B., *b.* 1931
1831	*Kilmarnock (8th)*, Dr Robin Jordan Boyd, *b.* 1941, *s.* 2009, *m.*	Hon. Simon J. B., *b.* 1978
1941	*Kindersley (4th)*, Rupert John Molesworth Kindersley, *b.* 1955, *s.* 2013, *m.*	Hon. Frederick H. M. K., *b.* 1987
1223 I.	*Kingsale (36th)*, Nevinson Mark de Courcy, *b.* 1958, *s.* 2005, *m. Premier Baron of Ireland*	Joseph K. C. de C., *b.* 1955
1902	*Kinross (5th)*, Christopher Patrick Balfour, *b.* 1949, *s.* 1985, *m.*	Hon. Alan I. B., *b.* 1978
1951	*Kirkwood (3rd)*, David Harvie Kirkwood, PHD, *b.* 1931, *s.* 1970, *m.*	Hon. James S. K., *b.* 1937
1800 I.	*Langford (10th)*, Owain Grenville Rowley-Conwy, *b.* 1958, *s.* 2017, *m.*	Hon. Thomas A. R.-C., *b.* 1987
1942	*Latham (2nd)*, Dominic Charles Latham, *b.* 1954, *s.* 1970	Anthony M. L., *b.* 1954
1431	*Latymer (9th)*, Crispin James Alan Nevill Money-Coutts, *b.* 1955, *s.* 2003, *m.*	Hon. Drummond W. T. M.-C., *b.* 1986
1869	*Lawrence (5th)*, David John Downer Lawrence, *b.* 1937, *s.* 1968	None
1947	*Layton (3rd)*, Geoffrey Michael Layton, *b.* 1947, *s.* 1989, *m.*	Jonathan F. L., *b.* 1942
1839	*Leigh (6th)*, Christopher Dudley Piers Leigh, *b.* 1960, *s.* 2003, *m.*	Hon. Rupert D. L., *b.* 1994
1962	*Leighton of St Mellons (3rd)*, Robert William Henry Leighton Seager, *b.* 1955, *s.* 1998, *m.*	Hon. Simon J. L. S., *b.* 1957
1797	*Lilford (8th)*, Mark Vernon Powys, *b.* 1975, *s.* 2005, *m.*	Robert C. L. P., *b.* 1930
1945	*Lindsay of Birker (3rd)*, James Francis Lindsay, *b.* 1945, *s.* 1994, *m.*	Alexander S. L., *b.* 1940

1758 I.	*Lisle (9th)*, (John) Nicholas Geoffrey Lysaght, *b.* 1960, *s.* 2003	Hon. David J. L., *b.* 1963
1850	*Londesborough (9th)*, Richard John Denison, *b.* 1959, *s.* 1968, *m.*	Hon. James F. D., *b.* 1990
1541 I.	*Louth (17th)*, Jonathan Oliver Plunkett, *b.* 1952, *s.* 2013, *m.*	Hon. Matthew O. P., *b.* 1982
1458 S.	*Lovat (16th) and Lovat (5th) (1837)*, Simon Fraser, *b.* 1977, *s.* 1995, *m.*	Hon. Jack F., *b.* 1984
1946	*Lucas of Chilworth (3rd)*, Simon William Lucas, *b.* 1957, *s.* 2001, *m.*	Hon. John R. M. L., *b.* 1995
1663 **	*Lucas (11th) and Dingwall (14th) (S. 1609)*, Ralph Matthew Palmer, *b.* 1951, *s.* 1991, *m.*	Hon. Lewis E. P., *b.* 1987
1929	*Luke (4th)*, Ian James St John Lawson Johnston, *b.* 1963, *s.* 2016, *m.*	Hon. Samuel A. J. St J. L. J., *b.* 2000
1859	*Lyveden (8th)*, Colin Ronald Vernon, *b.* 1967, *s.* 2017	Hon. Robert H. V., *b.* 1942
1959	*MacAndrew (3rd)*, Christopher Anthony Colin MacAndrew, *b.* 1945, *s.* 1989, *m.*	Hon. Oliver C. J. M., *b.* 1983
1776 I.	*Macdonald (8th)*, Godfrey James Macdonald of Macdonald, *b.* 1947, *s.* 1970, *m.*	Hon. Godfrey E. H. T. M., *b.* 1982
1937	*McGowan (4th)*, Harry John Charles McGowan, *b.* 1971, *s.* 2003, *m.*	Hon. Dominic J. W. M., *b.* 1951
1922	*Maclay (3rd)*, Joseph Paton Maclay, *b.* 1942, *s.* 1969, *m.*	Hon. Joseph P. M., *b.* 1977
1955	*McNair (3rd)*, Duncan James McNair, *b.* 1947, *s.* 1989, *m.*	Hon. William S. A. M., *b.* 1958
1951	*Macpherson of Drumochter (3rd)*, James Anthony Macpherson, *b.* 1979, *s.* 2008, *m.*	Hon. Daniel T. M., *b.* 2013
1937 **	*Mancroft (3rd)*, Benjamin Lloyd Stormont Mancroft, *b.* 1957, *s.* 1987, *m.*	Hon. Arthur L. S. M., *b.* 1995
1807	*Manners (6th)*, John Hugh Robert Manners, *b.* 1956, *s.* 2008, *m.*	Hon. John A. D. M., *b.* 2011
1922	*Manton (4th)*, Miles Ronald Marcus Watson, *b.* 1958, *s.* 2003, *m.*	Hon. Thomas N. C. D. W., *b.* 1985
1908	*Marchamley (4th)*, William Francis Whiteley, *b.* 1968, *s.* 1994, *m.*	Hon. Leon W., *b.* 2004
1965	*Margadale (3rd)*, Alastair John Morrison, *b.* 1958, *s.* 2003, *m.*	Hon. Declan J. M., *b.* 1993
1961	*Marks of Broughton (3rd)*, Simon Richard Marks, *b.* 1950, *s.* 1998, *m.*	Hon. Michael M., *b.* 1989
1964	*Martonmere (2nd)*, John Stephen Robinson, *b.* 1963, *s.* 1989, *m.*	Hon. James I. R., *b.* 2003
1776 I.	*Massy (10th)*, David Hamon Somerset Massy, *b.* 1947, *s.* 1995	Hon. John H. S. M., *b.* 1950
1935	*May (4th)*, Jasper Bertram St John May, *b.* 1965, *s.* 2006	None
1925	*Merrivale (4th)*, Derek John Philip Duke, *b.* 1948, *s.* 2007, *m.*	Hon. Thomas D., *b.* 1980
1911	*Merthyr (5th)*, David Trevor Lewis, *b.* 1977, *s.* 2015, *m.*	Hon. Peter H. L., *b.* 1937
1919	*Meston (3rd)*, James Meston, QC, *b.* 1950, *s.* 1984, *m.*	Hon. Thomas J. D. M., *b.* 1977
1838	*Methuen (8th)*, James Paul Archibald Methuen-Campbell, *b.* 1952, *s.* 2014	Thomas R. M. M.-C., *b.* 1977
1711	*Middleton (13th)*, Michael Charles James Willoughby, *b.* 1948, *s.* 2011, *m.*	Hon. James W. M. W., *b.* 1976
1939	*Milford (4th)*, Guy Wogan Philipps, QC, *b.* 1961, *s.* 1999, *m.*	Hon. Archie S. P., *b.* 1997
1933	*Milne (3rd)*, George Alexander Milne, *b.* 1941, *s.* 2005	Hon. Iain C. L. M., *b.* 1949
1951	*Milner of Leeds (3rd)*, Richard James Milner, *b.* 1959, *s.* 2003, *m.*	None
1947	*Milverton (2nd)*, Revd Fraser Arthur Richard Richards, *b.* 1930, *s.* 1978, *m.*	Hon. Michael H. R., *b.* 1936
1873	*Moncreiff (6th)*, Rhoderick Harry Wellwood Moncreiff, *b.* 1954, *s.* 2002, *m.*	Hon. Harry J. W. M., *b.* 1986
1884	*Monk Bretton (3rd)*, John Charles Dodson, *b.* 1924, *s.* 1933, *m.*	Hon. Christopher M. D., *b.* 1958
1885	*Monkswell (5th)*, Gerard Collier, *b.* 1947, *s.* 1984, *m.*	Hon. James A. C., *b.* 1977
1728	*Monson (12th)*, Nicholas John Monson, *b.* 1955, *s.* 2011, *m.*	Hon. Andrew A. J. M., *b.* 1959
1885	*Montagu of Beaulieu (4th)*, Ralph Douglas-Scott-Montagu, *b.* 1961, *s.* 2015, *m.*	Hon. Jonathan D. D.-S.-M., *b.* 1975
1839	*Monteagle of Brandon (7th)*, Charles James Spring Rice, *b.* 1953, *s.* 2013, *m.*	Hon. Michael S. R., *b.* 1935
1943	*Moran (3rd)*, James McMoran Wilson, *b.* 1952, *s.* 2014, *m.*	Hon. David A. M. W., *b.* 1990
1918	*Morris (4th)*, Thomas Anthony Salmon Morris, *b.* 1982, *s.* 2011	Hon. John M. M., *b.* 1983
1950	*Morris of Kenwood (3rd)*, Jonathan David Morris, *b.* 1968, *s.* 2004, *m.*	Hon. Benjamin J. M., *b.* 1998
1831	*Mostyn (7th)*, Gregory Philip Roger Lloyd-Mostyn, *b.* 1984, *s.* 2011	Roger H. L.-M., *b.* 1941
1933	*Mottistone (6th)*, Christopher David Peter Seely, *b.* 1974, *s.* 2013	Hon. Richard W. A. S., *b.* 1988
1945 **	*Mountevans (4th)*, Jeffrey Richard de Corban Evans, *b.* 1948, *s.* 2014, *m.*	Hon. Alexander R. A. E., *b.* 1975
1283	*Mowbray (27th), Segrave (28th) (1295) and Stourton (24th) (1448)*, Edward William Stephen Stourton, *b.* 1953, *s.* 2006, *m.*	Hon. James C. P. S., *b.* 1991
1932	*Moyne (3rd)*, Jonathan Bryan Guinness, *b.* 1930, *s.* 1992, *m.*	Hon. Valentine G. B. G., *b.* 1959
1929 **	*Moynihan (4th)*, Colin Berkeley Moynihan, *b.* 1955, *s.* 1997, *m.*	Hon. Nicholas E. B. M., *b.* 1994
1781 I.	*Muskerry (9th)*, Robert Fitzmaurice Deane, *b.* 1948, *s.* 1988, *m.*	Hon. Jonathan F. D., *b.* 1986
1627 S.	*Napier (15th) and Ettrick (6th) (1872)*, Francis David Charles Napier, *b.* 1962, *s.* 2012, *m.*	Master of Napier, *b.* 1996
1868	*Napier of Magdala (6th)*, Robert Alan Napier, *b.* 1940, *s.* 1987, *m.*	Hon. James R. N., *b.* 1966
1940	*Nathan (3rd)*, Rupert Harry Bernard Nathan, *b.* 1957, *s.* 2007, *m.*	Hon. Alasdair H. St J. N., *b.* 1999
1960	*Nelson of Stafford (4th)*, Alistair William Henry Nelson, *b.* 1973, *s.* 2006, *m.*	Hon. James J. N., *b.* 1947
1959	*Netherthorpe (3rd)*, James Frederick Turner, *b.* 1964, *s.* 1982, *m.*	Hon. Andrew J. E. T., *b.* 1993
1946	*Newall (2nd)*, Francis Storer Eaton Newall, *b.* 1930, *s.* 1963, *m.*	Hon. Richard H. E. N., *b.* 1961
1776 I.	*Newborough (8th)*, Robert Vaughan Wynn, *b.* 1949, *s.* 1998, *m.*	Antony C. V. W., *b.* 1949
1892	*Newton (5th)*, Richard Thomas Legh, *b.* 1950, *s.* 1992, *m.*	Hon. Piers R. L., *b.* 1979
1930	*Noel-Buxton (4th)*, Charles Connal Noel-Buxton, *b.* 1975, *s.* 2013, *m.*	Hon. Simon C. N.-B., *b.* 1943
1957	*Norrie (2nd)*, (George) Willoughby Moke Norrie, *b.* 1936, *s.* 1977, *m.*	Hon. Mark W. J. N., *b.* 1972
1884	*Northbourne (5th)*, Christopher George Walter James, *b.* 1926, *s.* 1982, *m.*	Hon. Charles W. H. J., *b.* 1960
1866 **	*Northbrook (6th)*, Francis Thomas Baring, *b.* 1954, *s.* 1990, *m.*	To the Baronetcy, Peter B., *b.* 1939
1878	*Norton (8th)*, James Nigel Arden Adderley, *b.* 1947, *s.* 1993, *m.*	Hon. Edward J. A. A., *b.* 1982

1906	*Nunburnholme (6th)*, Stephen Charles Yanath Wilson, *b.* 1973, *s.* 2000, *m.*	Hon. Charles T. C. W., *b.* 2002
1950	*Ogmore (3rd)*, Morgan Rees-Williams, *b.* 1937, *s.* 2004, *m.*	Hon. Tudor D. R.-W., *b.* 1991
1870	*O'Hagan (4th)*, Charles Towneley Strachey, *b.* 1945, *s.* 1961, *m.*	Hon. Richard T. S., *b.* 1950
1868	*O'Neill (4th)*, Raymond Arthur Clanaboy O'Neill, KCVO, TD, *b.* 1933, *s.* 1944, *w.*	Hon. Shane S. C. O'N., *b.* 1965
1836 I.	*Oranmore and Browne (5th) and Mereworth (3rd) (1926)*, Dominick Geoffrey Thomas Browne, *b.* 1929, *s.* 2002	Shaun D. B., *b.* 1964
1933 **	*Palmer (4th)*, Adrian Bailie Nottage Palmer, *b.* 1951, *s.* 1990, *m.*	Hon. Hugo B. R. P., *b.* 1980
1914	*Parmoor (5th)*, Michael Leonard Seddon Cripps, *b.* 1942, *s.* 2008, *m.*	Hon. Henry W. A. C., *b.* 1976
1937	*Pender (4th)*, Henry John Richard Denison-Pender, *b.* 1968, *s.* 2016, *m.*	Hon. Miles J. C. D.-P., *b.* 2000
1866	*Penrhyn (7th)*, Simon Douglas-Pennant, *b.* 1938, *s.* 2003, *m.*	Hon. Edward S. D.-P., *b.* 1966
1603	*Petre (18th)*, John Patrick Lionel Petre, KCVO, *b.* 1942, *s.* 1989, *m.*	Hon. Dominic W. P., *b.* 1966
1918	*Phillimore (5th)*, Francis Stephen Phillimore, *b.* 1944, *s.* 1994, *m.*	Hon. Tristan A. S. P., *b.* 1977
1945	*Piercy (3rd)*, James William Piercy, *b.* 1946, *s.* 1981	Hon. Mark E. P. P., *b.* 1953
1827	*Plunket (9th)*, Tyrone Shaun Terence Plunket, *b.* 1966, *s.* 2013, *m.*	Hon. Rory P. R. P., *b.* 2001
1831	*Poltimore (7th)*, Mark Coplestone Bampfylde, *b.* 1957, *s.* 1978, *m.*	Hon. Henry A. W. B., *b.* 1985
1690 S.	*Polwarth (11th)*, Andrew Walter Hepburne-Scott, *b.* 1947, *s.* 2005, *m.*	Master of Polwarth, *b.* 1973
1930	*Ponsonby of Shulbrede (4th) and Ponsonby of Roehampton (life peerage, 2000)*, Frederick Matthew Thomas Ponsonby, *b.* 1958, *s.* 1990, *m.*	Hon. Cameron J. J. P., *b.* 1995
1958	*Poole (2nd)*, David Charles Poole, *b.* 1945, *s.* 1993, *m.*	Hon. Oliver J. P., *b.* 1972
1852	*Raglan (6th)*, Geoffrey Somerset, *b.* 1932, *s.* 2010, *m.*	Inigo A. F. S., *b.* 2004
1932	*Rankeillour (5th)*, Michael Richard Hope, *b.* 1940, *s.* 2005, *m.*	Hon. James F. H., *b.* 1968
1953	*Rathcavan (3rd)*, Hugh Detmar Torrens O'Neill, *b.* 1939, *s.* 1994, *m.*	Hon. François H. N. O'N., *b.* 1984
1916	*Rathcreedan (3rd)*, Christopher John Norton, *b.* 1949, *s.* 1990, *m.*	Hon. Adam G. N., *b.* 1952
1868 I.	*Rathdonnell (5th)*, Thomas Benjamin McClintock-Bunbury, *b.* 1938, *s.* 1959, *m.*	Hon. William L. M.-B., *b.* 1966
1911	*Ravensdale (4th)*, Daniel Nicholas Mosley, *b.* 1982, *s.* 2017, *m.*	Hon. Matthew J. M., *b.* 1985
1821	*Ravensworth (9th)*, Thomas Arthur Hamish Liddell, *b.* 1954, *s.* 2004, *m.*	Hon. Henry A. T. L., *b.* 1987
1821	*Rayleigh (6th)*, John Gerald Strutt, *b.* 1960, *s.* 1988, *m.*	Hon. John F. S., *b.* 1993
1937 **	*Rea (3rd)*, John Nicolas Rea, MD, *b.* 1928, *s.* 1981, *m.*	Hon. Matthew J. R., *b.* 1956
1628 S.	*Reay (15th)*, Aeneas Simon Mackay, *b.* 1965, *s.* 2013, *m.*	Master of Reay, *b.* 2010
1902	*Redesdale (6th) and Mitford (life peerage, 2000)*, Rupert Bertram Mitford, *b.* 1967, *s.* 1991, *m.*	Hon. Bertram D. M., *b.* 2000
1940	*Reith (3rd)*, James Harry John Reith, *b.* 1971, *s.* 2016, *m.*	Hon. Harry J. J. R., *b.* 2006
1928	*Remnant (3rd)*, James Wogan Remnant, CVO, *b.* 1930, *s.* 1967, *m.*	Hon. Philip J. R., CBE, *b.* 1954
1806 I.	*Rendlesham (9th)*, Charles William Brooke Thellusson, *b.* 1954, *s.* 1999, *m.*	Hon. Peter R. T., *b.* 1920
1933	*Rennell (4th)*, James Roderick David Tremayne Rodd, *b.* 1978, *s.* 2006	None
1964	*Renwick (2nd)*, Harry Andrew Renwick, *b.* 1935, *s.* 1973, *m.*	Hon. Robert J. R., *b.* 1966
1885	*Revelstoke (7th)*, Alexander Rupert Baring, *b.* 1970, *s.* 2012	Hon. Thomas J. B., *b.* 1971
1905	*Ritchie of Dundee (6th)*, Charles Rupert Rendall Ritchie, *b.* 1958, *s.* 2008, *m.*	Hon. Sebastian R., *b.* 2004
1935	*Riverdale (3rd)*, Anthony Robert Balfour, *b.* 1960, *s.* 1998	Arthur M. B., *b.* 1938
1961	*Robertson of Oakridge (3rd)*, William Brian Elworthy Robertson, *b.* 1975, *s.* 2009, *m.*	None
1938	*Roborough (4th)*, Massey John Henry Lopes, *b.* 1969, *s.* 2015, *m.*	Hon. Henry M. P. L., *b.* 1997
1931	*Rochester (3rd)*, David Charles Lamb, *b.* 1944, *s.* 2017, *m.*	Hon. Daniel L., *b.* 1971
1934	*Rockley (4th)*, Anthony Robert Cecil, *b.* 1961, *s.* 2011, *m.*	Hon. William E. C., *b.* 1996
1782 M.	*Rodney (11th)*, John George Brydges Rodney, *b.* 1999, *s.* 2011	Nicholas S. H. R., *b.* 1947
1651 S.	*Rollo (14th) and Dunning (5th) (1869)*, David Eric Howard Rollo, *b.* 1943, *s.* 1997, *m.*	Master of Rollo, *b.* 1972
1959	*Rootes (3rd)*, Nicholas Geoffrey Rootes, *b.* 1951, *s.* 1992, *m.*	William B. R., *b.* 1944
1796 I.	*Rossmore (7th) and Rossmore (6th) (1838)*, William Warner Westenra, *b.* 1931, *s.* 1958, *m.*	Hon. Benedict W. W., *b.* 1983
1939 **	*Rotherwick (3rd)*, (Herbert) Robin Cayzer, *b.* 1954, *s.* 1996, *m.*	Hon. H. Robin C., *b.* 1989
1885	*Rothschild (4th)*, (Nathaniel Charles) Jacob Rothschild, OM, GBE, *b.* 1936, *s.* 1990, *m.*	Hon. Nathaniel P. V. J. R., *b.* 1971
1911	*Rowallan (4th)*, John Polson Cameron Corbett, *b.* 1947, *s.* 1993, *m.*	Hon. Jason W. P. C. C., *b.* 1972
1947	*Rugby (3rd)*, Robert Charles Maffey, *b.* 1951, *s.* 1990, *m.*	Hon. Timothy J. H. M., *b.* 1975
1919 **	*Russell of Liverpool (3rd)*, Simon Gordon Jared Russell, *b.* 1952, *s.* 1981, *m.*	Hon. Edward C. S. R., *b.* 1985
1876	*Sackville (7th)*, Robert Bertrand Sackville-West, *b.* 1958, *s.* 2004, *m.*	Hon. Arthur S.-W., *b.* 2000
1964	*St Helens (2nd)*, Richard Francis Hughes-Young, *b.* 1945, *s.* 1980, *m.*	Hon. Henry T. H.-Y., *b.* 1986
1559 **	*St John of Bletso (21st)*, Anthony Tudor St John, *b.* 1957, *s.* 1978, *m.*	Hon. Oliver B. St J., *b.* 1995
1887	*St Levan (5th)*, James Piers Southwell St Aubyn, *b.* 1950, *s.* 2013, *m.*	Hon. Hugh J. St A., *b.* 1983
1885	*St Oswald (6th)*, Charles Rowland Andrew Winn, *b.* 1959, *s.* 1999, *m.*	Hon. Rowland C. S. H. W., *b.* 1986
1960	*Sanderson of Ayot (2nd)*, Alan Lindsay Sanderson, *b.* 1931, *s.* 1971, *m.* Disclaimed for life 1971.	Hon. Michael S., *b.* 1959
1945	*Sandford (3rd)*, James John Mowbray Edmondson, *b.* 1949, *s.* 2009, *m.*	Hon. Devon J. E., *b.* 1986
1871	*Sandhurst (6th)*, Guy Rees John Mansfield, QC, *b.* 1949, *s.* 2002, *m.*	Hon. Edward J. M., *b.* 1982
1888	*Savile (4th)*, John Anthony Thornhill Lumley-Savile, *b.* 1947, *s.* 2008, *m.*	Hon. James G. A. L.-S., *b.* 1975
1447	*Saye and Sele (21st)*, Nathaniel Thomas Allen Fiennes, *b.* 1920, *s.* 1968, *m.*	Hon. Martin G. F., *b.* 1961
1826	*Seaford (6th)*, Colin Humphrey Felton Ellis, *b.* 1946, *s.* 1999, *m.*	Hon. Benjamin F. T. E., *b.* 1976

1932 **	*Selsdon (3rd)*, Malcolm McEacharn Mitchell-Thomson, *b.* 1937, *s.* 1963, *m.*	Hon. Callum M. M. M.-T., *b.* 1969
1489 S.	*Sempill (21st)*, James William Stuart Whitemore Sempill, *b.* 1949, *s.* 1995, *m.*	Master of Sempill, *b.* 1979
1916	*Shaughnessy (5th)*, Charles George Patrick Shaughnessy, *b.* 1955, *s.* 2007, *m.*	David J. S., *b.* 1957
1946	*Shepherd (3rd)*, Graham George Shepherd, *b.* 1949, *s.* 2001, *m.*	Hon. Patrick M. S., *b.* 1980
1964	*Sherfield (3rd)*, Dwight William Makins, *b.* 1951, *s.* 2006, *m.*	None
1902	*Shuttleworth (5th)*, Charles Geoffrey Nicholas Kay-Shuttleworth, KG, KCVO, *b.* 1948, *s.* 1975, *m.*	Hon. Thomas E. K.-S., *b.* 1976
1950	*Silkin (3rd)*, Christopher Lewis Silkin, *b.* 1947, *s.* 2001. Disclaimed for life 2002.	Rory L. S., *b.* 1954
1963	*Silsoe (3rd)*, Simon Rupert Trustram Eve, *b.* 1966, *s.* 2005	Hon. Peter N. T. E., OBE, *b.* 1930
1947	*Simon of Wythenshawe (3rd)*, Matthew Simon, *b.* 1955, *s.* 2002, *w.* In dormancy since 2016 when the 3rd baron officially reassigned his gender.	Michael B. S., *b.* 1970
1449 S.	*Sinclair (18th)*, Matthew Murray Kennedy St Clair, *b.* 1968, *s.* 2004, *m.*	Master of Sinclair, *b.* 2007
1957	*Sinclair of Cleeve (3rd)*, John Lawrence Robert Sinclair, *b.* 1953, *s.* 1985, *m.*	None
1919	*Sinha (6th)*, Arup Kumar Sinha, *b.* 1966, *s.* 1999, *m.*	Hon. Dilip K. S., *b.* 1967
1828 **	*Skelmersdale (7th)*, Roger Bootle-Wilbraham, *b.* 1945, *s.* 1973, *m.*	Hon. Andrew B.-W., *b.* 1977
1916	*Somerleyton (4th)*, Hugh Francis Saville Crossley, *b.* 1971, *s.* 2012, *m.*	Hon. John de B. T. S. C., *b.* 2010
1784	*Somers (9th)*, Philip Sebastian Somers Cocks, *b.* 1948, *s.* 1995	Jonathan B. C., *b.* 1985
1780	*Southampton (7th)*, Edward Charles FitzRoy, *b.* 1955, *s.* 2015, *m.*	Hon. Charles E. M. F., *b.* 1983
1959	*Spens (4th)*, Patrick Nathaniel George Spens, *b.* 1968, *s.* 2001, *m.*	Hon. Peter L. S., *b.* 2000
1640	*Stafford (15th)*, Francis Melfort William Fitzherbert, *b.* 1954, *s.* 1986, *m.*	Hon. Benjamin J. B. F., *b.* 1983
1938	*Stamp (4th)*, Trevor Charles Bosworth Stamp, MD, *b.* 1935, *s.* 1987, *m.*	Hon. Nicholas C. T. S., *b.* 1978
1839	*Stanley of Alderley (9th), Sheffield (9th) (I. 1738) and Eddisbury (8th) (1848)*, Richard Oliver Stanley, *b.* 1956, *s.* 2013, *m.*	Hon. Charles E. S., *b.* 1960
1318	*Strabolgi (12th)*, Andrew David Whitley Kenworthy, *b.* 1967, *s.* 2010, *m.*	Hon. Joel B. K., *b.* 2004
1628	*Strange (17th)*, Adam Humphrey Drummond of Megginch, *b.* 1953, *s.* 2005, *m.*	Hon. John A. H. D. of M., *b.* 1992
1955	*Strathalmond (3rd)*, William Roberton Fraser, *b.* 1947, *s.* 1976, *m.*	Hon. William G. F., *b.* 1976
1936	*Strathcarron (3rd)*, Ian David Patrick Macpherson, *b.* 1949, *s.* 2006, *m.*	Hon. Rory D. A. M., *b.* 1982
1955 **	*Strathclyde (2nd)*, Thomas Galloway Dunlop du Roy de Blicquy Galbraith, CH, PC, *b.* 1960, *s.* 1985, *m.*	Hon. Charles W. du R. de B. G., *b.* 1962
1900	*Strathcona and Mount Royal (5th)*, Donald Alexander S Howard, *b.* 1961, *s.* 2018, *m.*	Hon. Donald A. R. H., *b.* 1994
1836	*Stratheden (7th) and Campbell (7th) (1841)*, David Anthony Campbell, *b.* 1963, *s.* 2011, *m.*	None
1884	*Strathspey (6th)*, James Patrick Trevor Grant of Grant, *b.* 1943, *s.* 1992	Hon. Michael P. F. G., *b.* 1953
1838	*Sudeley (7th)*, Merlin Charles Sainthill Hanbury-Tracy, *b.* 1939, *s.* 1941, *m.*	Nicholas E. J. H.-T., *b.* 1959
1786	*Suffield (13th)*, John Edward Richard Harbord-Hamond, *b.* 1956, *s.* 2016, *m.*	Hon. Sam C. A. H.-H., *b.* 1989
1893	*Swansea (5th)*, Richard Anthony Hussey Vivian, *b.* 1957, *s.* 2005, *m.*	Hon. James H. H. V., *b.* 1999
1907	*Swaythling (5th)*, Charles Edgar Samuel Montagu, *b.* 1954, *s.* 1998, *m.*	Rupert A. S. M., *b.* 1965
1919 **	*Swinfen (3rd)*, Roger Mynors Swinfen Eady, MBE, *b.* 1938, *s.* 1977, *m.*	Hon. Charles R. P. S. E., *b.* 1971
1831 I.	*Talbot of Malahide (11th)*, Richard John Tennant Arundell, *b.* 1957, *s.* 2016, *m.*	Hon. John R. A., *b.* 1998
1946	*Tedder (3rd)*, Robin John Tedder, *b.* 1955, *s.* 1994, *m.*	Hon. Benjamin J. T., *b.* 1985
1884	*Tennyson (6th)*, David Harold Alexander Tennyson, *b.* 1960, *s.* 2006	Alan J. D. T., *b.* 1965
1918	*Terrington (6th)*, Christopher Richard James Woodhouse, MB, *b.* 1946, *s.* 2001, *m.*	Hon. Jack H. L. W., *b.* 1978
1940	*Teviot (2nd)*, Charles John Kerr, *b.* 1934, *s.* 1968, *m.*	Hon. Charles R. K., *b.* 1971
1616	*Teynham (20th)*, John Christopher Ingham Roper-Curzon, *b.* 1928, *s.* 1972, *m.*	Hon. David J. H. I. R.-C., *b.* 1965
1964	*Thomson of Fleet (3rd)*, David Kenneth Roy Thomson, *b.* 1957, *s.* 2006, *m.*	Hon. Benjamin T., *b.* 2006
1792 **	*Thurlow (9th)*, Roualeyn Robert Hovell-Thurlow-Cumming-Bruce, *b.* 1952, *s.* 2013, *m.*	Hon. Nicholas E. H.-T.-C.-B., *b.* 1986
1876	*Tollemache (5th)*, Timothy John Edward Tollemache, KCVO, *b.* 1939, *s.* 1975, *m.*	Hon. Edward J. H. T., *b.* 1976
1564 S.	*Torphichen (15th)*, James Andrew Douglas Sandilands, *b.* 1946, *s.* 1975, *m.*	Robert P. S., *b.* 1950
1947 **	*Trefgarne (2nd)*, David Garro Trefgarne, PC, *b.* 1941, *s.* 1960, *m.*	Hon. George G. T., *b.* 1970
1921 **	*Trevethin (5th) and Oaksey (3rd) (1947)*, Patrick John Tristram Lawrence, QC, *b.* 1960, *s.* 2012, *m.*	Hon. Oliver J. T. L., *b.* 1990
1880	*Trevor (5th)*, Marke Charles Hill-Trevor, *b.* 1970, *s.* 1997, *m.*	Hon. Iain R. H.-T., *b.* 1971
1461 I.	*Trimlestown (21st)*, Raymond Charles Barnewall, *b.* 1930, *s.* 1997	None
1940	*Tryon (3rd)*, Anthony George Merrik Tryon, OBE, *b.* 1940, *s.* 1976, *w.*	Hon. Charles G. B. T., *b.* 1976
1935	*Tweedsmuir (4th)*, John William de l'Aigle (Toby) Buchan, *b.* 1950, *s.* 2008, *m.*	Hon. John A. G. B., *b.* 1986
1523 **	*Vaux of Harrowden (12th)*, Richard Hubert Gordon Gilbey, *b.* 1965, *s.* 2014, *m.*	Hon. Alexander J. C. G., *b.* 2000
1800 I.	*Ventry (8th)*, Andrew Wesley Daubeny de Moleyns, *b.* 1943, *s.* 1987, *m.*	Hon. Francis W. D. de M., *b.* 1965
1762	*Vernon (11th)*, Anthony William Vernon-Harcourt, *b.* 1939, *s.* 2000, *m.*	Hon. Simon A. V.-H., *b.* 1969

1922	*Vestey (3rd),* Samuel George Armstrong Vestey, KCVO, *b.* 1941, *s.* 1954, *m.*	Hon. William G. V., *b.* 1983
1841	*Vivian (7th),* Charles Crespigny Hussey Vivian, *b.* 1966, *s.* 2004, *m.*	Thomas C. B. V., *b.* 1971
1934	*Wakehurst (3rd),* (John) Christopher Loder, *b.* 1925, *s.* 1970, *m.*	Hon. Timothy W. L., *b.* 1958
1723	*Walpole (10th) and Walpole of Wolterton (8th) (1756),* Robert Horatio Walpole, *b.* 1938, *s.* 1989, *m.*	Hon. Jonathan R. H. W., *b.* 1967
1780	*Walsingham (9th),* John de Grey, MC, *b.* 1925, *s.* 1965, *m.*	Hon. Robert de G., *b.* 1969
1936	*Wardington (3rd),* William Simon Pease, *b.* 1925, *s.* 2005, *m.*	None
1792 I.	*Waterpark (8th),* Roderick Alexander Cavendish, *b.* 1959, *s.* 2013, *m.*	Hon. Luke F. C., *b.* 1990
1942	*Wedgwood (5th),* Antony John Wedgwood, *b.* 1944, *s.* 2014, *m.*	Hon. Josiah T. A. W., *b.* 1978
1861	*Westbury (6th),* Richard Nicholas Bethell, MBE, *b.* 1950, *s.* 2001, *m.*	Hon. Alexander B., *b.* 1986
1944	*Westwood (3rd),* (William) Gavin Westwood, *b.* 1944, *s.* 1991, *m.*	Hon. W. Fergus W., *b.* 1972
1544/5	*Wharton (12th),* Myles Christopher David Robertson, *b.* 1964, *s.* 2000, *m.*	Hon. Meghan Z. M. R., *b.* 2006
1935	*Wigram (3rd),* Andrew Francis Clive Wigram, MVO, *b.* 1949, *s.* 2017, *m.*	Hon. Harry R. C. W., *b.* 1977
1491 **	*Willoughby de Broke (21st),* Leopold David Verney, *b.* 1938, *s.* 1986, *m.*	Hon. Rupert G. V., *b.* 1966
1937	*Windlesham (4th),* James Rupert Hennessy, *b.* 1968, *s.* 2010, *m.*	Hon. George R. J. H., *b.* 2006
1951	*Wise (3rd),* Christopher John Clayton Wise, *b.* 1949, *s.* 2012, *m.*	Hon. Thomas C. C. W., *b.* 1989
1869	*Wolverton (8th),* Miles John Glyn, *b.* 1966, *s.* 2011	Jonathan C. G., *b.* 1990
1928	*Wraxall (4th),* Antony Hubert Gibbs, *b.* 1958, *s.* 2017, *m.*	Hon. Orlando H. G., *b.* 1995
1915	*Wrenbury (4th),* William Edward Buckley, *b.* 1966, *s.* 2014, *m.*	Hon. Jamie P. B., *b.* 2001
1838	*Wrottesley (6th),* Clifton Hugh Lancelot de Verdon Wrottesley, *b.* 1968, *s.* 1977, *m.*	Hon. Victor E. F. de V. W., *b.* 2004
1829	*Wynford (9th),* John Philip Robert Best, *b.* 1950, *s.* 2002, *m.*	Hon. Harry R. F. B., *b.* 1987
1308	*Zouche (18th),* James Assheton Frankland, *b.* 1943, *s.* 1965, *m.*	Hon. William T. A. F., *b.* 1984

BARONESSES/LADIES IN THEIR OWN RIGHT

Style, The Rt. Hon. the Lady _ , *or* The Rt. Hon. the Baroness _ , according to her preference. Either style may be used, except in the case of Scottish titles (indicated by S.), which are not baronies and whose holders are always addressed as Lady.

Envelope, may be addressed in same way as a Baron's wife or, if she prefers *(formal),* The Rt. Hon. the Baroness _; *(social),* The Baroness _. Otherwise as for a Baron's wife

Husband, Untitled

Children's style, As for children of a Baron

In Scotland, the heir to a Lady may be styled 'The Master/Mistress of _ (title of peer)'

Created	Title, order of succession, name, etc	Heir
1664	*Arlington (11th),* Jennifer Jane Forwood, *b.* 1939, *s.* 1999, *w.* Title called out of abeyance 1999	Hon. Patrick J. D. F., *b.* 1967
1455	*Berners (16th),* Pamela Vivien Kirkham, *b.* 1929, *s.* 1995, *m.* Title called out of abeyance 1995	Hon. Rupert W. T. K., *b.* 1953
1529	*Braye (8th),* Mary Penelope Aubrey-Fletcher, *b.* 1941, *s.* 1985, *m.*	Linda K. C. Fothergill, *b.* 1930
1321	*Dacre (29th),* Emily Beamish, *b.* 1983, *s.* 2014, *m.*	Three co-heiresses
1283	*Fauconberg (10th) and Conyers (16th) (1509),* Baronies in abeyance between two co-heiresses since 2013	
1490 S.	*Herries of Terregles (16th),* (Theresa) Jane Kerr, Marchioness of Lothian, *b.* 1945, *s.* 2017, *m.*	Lady Clare T. Hurd, *b.* 1979
1597	*Howard de Walden (10th),* Mary Hazel Caridwen Czernin, *b.* 1935, *s.* 2004, *m.* Title called out of abeyance 2004	Hon. Peter J. J. C., *b.* 1966
1602 S.	*Kinloss (13th),* Teresa Mary Nugent Freeman-Grenville, *b.* 1957, *s.* 2012	Mistress of Kinloss, *b.* 1960
1445 S.	*Saltoun (20th),* Flora Marjory Fraser, *b.* 1930, *s.* 1979, *w.*	Hon. Katharine I. M. I. F., *b.* 1957
1313	*Willoughby de Eresby (27th),* (Nancy) Jane Marie Heathcote-Drummond-Willoughby, *b.* 1934, *s.* 1983	Two co-heirs

LIFE PEERS

Style, The Rt. Hon. the Lord _ /The Rt. Hon. the Lady _ , *or* The Rt. Hon. the Baroness _ , according to her preference
Envelope (formal), The Rt. Hon. Lord _/Lady_/Baroness_; *(social),* The Lord _/Lady_/Baroness_ *Letter (formal),* My Lord/Lady; *(social),* Dear Lord/Lady _. *Spoken,* Lord/Lady _
Wife's style, The Rt. Hon. the Lady _
Husband, Untitled
Children's style, 'The Hon.' before forename (F_) and surname (S_)
  Envelope, The Hon. F_ S_. *Letter,* Dear Mr/Miss/Mrs S_. *Spoken,* Mr/Miss/Mrs S_

NEW LIFE PEERAGES
1 September 2017 to 31 August 2018:

Sir Theodore Thomas More Agnew; Sir David William Kinloch Anderson, KBE, QC; Diana Francesca Caroline Barran, MBE; Rosel Marie Boycott; Pauline Christina Bryan; Deborah Clare Bull, CBE; Rt. Hon. Sir Ian Duncan Burnett; Rt. Revd and Rt. Hon. Richard John Carew Chartres, KCVO; Rona Alison Fairhead, CBE; Rt. Hon. Sir Edward Henry Garnier, QC; Rt. Hon. Sir Christopher Geidt, GCVO, KCB, OBE; Rt. Hon. Sir Alan Gordon Barraclough Haselhurst; Sir Bernard Hogan-Howe, QPM; Gen. Sir John Nicholas Reynolds Houghton, GCB, CBE; Rt. Hon. Peter Bruce Lilley; Revd (Robert Thomas) William McCrea; Iain Mackenzie McNicol; Catherine Irene Jacqueline, Lady Meyer, CBE; Martha Osamor; Rt. Hon. Sir Eric (Jack) Pickles; Rt. Hon. Sir (Alexander) John Randall; Amanda Jacqueline Sater; Rt. Hon. Andrew Guy Tyrie

SYMBOLS
* Hereditary peer who has been granted a life peerage. For further details, please refer to the Hereditary Peers section. For example, life peer *Balniel* can be found under his hereditary title *Earl of Crawford and Balcarres*
§ Members of the Judiciary currently disqualified from sitting or voting in the House of Lords until they retire from that office. For further information *see* Law Courts and Offices
‡ Title not confirmed at time of going to press
⟮ Peer who has permanently resigned from the House of Lords
E. Peer who has been expelled for absenteeism, under section 2 of the House of Lords Reform Act 2014, for failing to attend a sitting of the House during a session lasting six months or longer *see* The Peerage, introduction

CREATED UNDER THE APPELLATE JURISDICTION ACT 1876 (AS AMENDED)

BARONS
Created
2004   *Brown of Eaton-under-Heywood,* Simon Denis Brown, PC, *b.* 1937, *m.*
2004   *Carswell,* Robert Douglas Carswell, PC, *b.* 1934, *m.*
2009   *Collins of Mapesbury,* Lawrence Antony Collins, PC, *b.* 1941
1995   *Hoffmann,* Leonard Hubert Hoffmann, PC, *b.* 1934, *m.*
1997   ⟮*Hutton,* (James) Brian (Edward) Hutton, PC, *b.* 1931, *m.*
2009   §*Kerr of Tonaghmore,* Brian Francis Kerr, PC, *b.* 1948, *m.*
1993   ⟮*Lloyd of Berwick,* Anthony John Leslie Lloyd, PC, *b.* 1929, *m.*

2005   *Mance,* Jonathan Hugh Mance, PC, *b.* 1943, *m.*
1998   ⟮*Millett,* Peter Julian Millett, PC, *b.* 1932, *m.*
2007   *Neuberger of Abbotsbury,* David Edmond Neuberger, PC, *b.* 1948, *m.*
1994   ⟮*Nicholls of Birkenhead,* Donald James Nicholls, PC, *b.* 1933, *m.*
1999   *Phillips of Worth Matravers,* Nicholas Addison Phillips, KG, PC, *b.* 1938, *m.*
1997   *Saville of Newdigate,* Mark Oliver Saville, PC, *b.* 1936, *m.*
2000   ⟮*Scott of Foscote,* Richard Rashleigh Folliott Scott, PC, *b.* 1934, *m.*
2003   *Walker of Gestingthorpe,* Robert Walker, PC, *b.* 1938, *m.*
1992   *Woolf,* Harry Kenneth Woolf, CH, PC, *b.* 1933, *m.*

BARONESSES
2004   §*Hale of Richmond,* Brenda Marjorie Hale, DBE, PC, *b.* 1945, *m. President of the Supreme Court*

CREATED UNDER THE LIFE PEERAGES ACT 1958

BARONS
Created
2001   *Adebowale,* Victor Olufemi Adebowale, CBE, *b.* 1962
2005   *Adonis,* Andrew Adonis, PC, *b.* 1963, *m.*
2017   *Agnew of Oulton,* Theodore Thomas More Agnew, *b.* 1961, *m.*
2011   *Ahmad of Wimbledon,* Tariq Mahmood Ahmad, *b.* 1968, *m.*
1998   *Ahmed,* Nazir Ahmed, *b.* 1957, *m.*
1996   *Alderdice,* John Thomas Alderdice, *b.* 1955, *m.*
2010   *Allan of Hallam,* Richard Beecroft Allan, *b.* 1966
2013   *Allen of Kensington,* Charles Lamb Allen, CBE, *b.* 1957
1998   *Alli,* Waheed Alli, *b.* 1964
2004   *Alliance,* David Alliance, CBE, *b.* 1932
1997   *Alton of Liverpool,* David Patrick Paul Alton, *b.* 1951, *m.*
2018   *Anderson of Ipswich,* David William Kinloch Anderson, KBE, QC, *b.* 1961, *m.*
2005   *Anderson of Swansea,* Donald Anderson, PC, *b.* 1939, *m.*
2015   *Arbuthnot of Edrom,* James Norwich Arbuthnot, PC, *b.* 1952, *m.*
1992   *Archer of Weston-super-Mare,* Jeffrey Howard Archer, *b.* 1940, *m.*
1988   *Armstrong of Ilminster,* Robert Temple Armstrong, GCB, CVO, *b.* 1927, *m.*
2000   ⟮*Ashcroft,* Michael Anthony Ashcroft, KCMG, PC, *b.* 1946, *m.*
2001   *Ashdown of Norton-sub-Hamdon,* Jeremy John Durham (Paddy) Ashdown, GCMG, CH, KBE, PC, *b.* 1941, *m.*
1998   *Bach,* William Stephen Goulden Bach, *b.* 1946, *m.*
1997   *Baker of Dorking,* Kenneth Wilfred Baker, CH, PC, *b.* 1934, *m.*
2013   *Balfe,* Richard Andrew Balfe, *b.* 1944, *m.*
1974   **Balniel,* The Earl of Crawford and Balcarres, KT, GCVO, PC, *b.* 1927, *m. (see* Hereditary Peers)
2013   *Bamford,* Anthony Paul Bamford, *b.* 1945, *m.*
2015   *Barker of Battle,* Gregory Leonard George Barker, PC, *b.* 1966, *m.*
1997   *Bassam of Brighton,* (John) Steven Bassam, PC, *b.* 1953
2008   *Bates,* Michael Walton Bates, PC, *b.* 1961
2010   *Beecham,* Jeremy Hugh Beecham, *b.* 1944, *m.*
2015   *Beith,* Alan James Beith, PC, *b.* 1943, *m.*

1998   *Bell,* Timothy John Leigh Bell, *b.* 1941, *m.*

2013   *Berkeley of Knighton,* Michael Fitzhardinge Berkeley, CBE, *b.* 1948, *m.*

2001   *Best,* Richard Stuart Best, OBE, *b.* 1945, *m.*

2007   *Bew,* Prof. Paul Anthony Elliott Bew, *b.* 1950, *m.*

2001   *Bhatia,* Amirali Alibhai Bhatia, OBE, *b.* 1932, *m.*

2004   *Bhattacharyya,* Prof. (Sushantha) Kumar Bhattacharyya, CBE, *b.* 1932, *m.*

2010   *Bichard,* Michael George Bichard, KCB, *b.* 1947

2006   *Bilimoria,* Karan Faridoon Bilimoria, CBE, *b.* 1961, *m.*

2015   *Bird,* John Anthony Bird, MBE, *b.* 1946, *m.*

2000   *Birt,* John Francis Hodgess Birt, *b.* 1944, *m.*

2010   *Black of Brentwood,* Guy Vaughan Black, *b.* 1964, *m.*

2001   *Black of Crossharbour,* Conrad Moffat Black, *b.* 1944, *m.*

1997   *Blackwell,* Norman Roy Blackwell, *b.* 1952, *m.*

2010   *Blair of Boughton,* Ian Warwick Blair, QPM, *b.* 1953, *m.*

2011   *Blencathra,* David John Maclean, PC, *b.* 1953

2015   *Blunkett,* David Blunkett, PC, *b.* 1947, *m.*

1995   €*Blyth of Rowington,* James Blyth, *b.* 1940, *m.*

2010   *Boateng,* Paul Yaw Boateng, PC, *b.* 1951, *m.*

2010   *Boswell of Aynho,* Timothy Eric Boswell, *b.* 1942, *m.*

2013   *Bourne of Aberystwyth,* Nicholas Henry Bourne, *b.* 1952

1996   *Bowness,* Peter Spencer Bowness, CBE, *b.* 1943, *m.*

2003   *Boyce,* Michael Boyce, KG, GCB, OBE, *b.* 1943, *m.*

2006   §*Boyd of Duncansby,* Colin David Boyd, PC, *b.* 1953, *m.*

2006   *Bradley,* Keith John Charles Bradley, PC, *b.* 1950, *m.*

1999   *Bradshaw,* William Peter Bradshaw, *b.* 1936, *m.*

1998   *Bragg,* Melvyn Bragg, CH, *b.* 1939, *m.*

1987   *Bramall,* Edwin Noel Westby Bramall, KG, GCB, OBE, MC, *b.* 1923, *w.*

2000   *Brennan,* Daniel Joseph Brennan, QC, *b.* 1942, *m.*

2015   *Bridges of Headley,* James George Robert Bridges, MBE, *b.* 1970, *m.*

2004   *Broers,* Prof. Alec (Nigel) Broers, *b.* 1938, *m.*

1997   *Brooke of Alverthorpe,* Clive Brooke, *b.* 1942, *m.*

2001   €*Brooke of Sutton Mandeville,* Peter Leonard Brooke, CH, PC, *b.* 1934, *m.*

1998   *Brookman,* David Keith Brookman, *b.* 1937, *m.*

2006   *Browne of Belmont,* Wallace Hamilton Browne, *b.* 1947

2010   *Browne of Ladyton,* Desmond Henry Browne, PC, *b.* 1952

2001   *Browne of Madingley,* Edmund John Phillip Browne, *b.* 1948

2015   *Bruce of Bennachie,* Malcolm Gray Bruce, PC, *b.* 1944, *m.*

2006   *Burnett,* John Patrick Aubone Burnett, *b.* 1945, *m.*

2017   §*Burnett of Maldon,* Ian Duncan Burnett, PC, *b.* 1958, *m. Lord Chief Justice of England and Wales*

1998   *Burns,* Terence Burns, GCB, *b.* 1944, *m.*

1998   *Butler of Brockwell,* (Frederick Edward) Robin Butler, KG, GCB, CVO, PC, *b.* 1938, *m.*

2016   *Caine,* Jonathan Michael Caine, *b.* 1966

2014   *Callanan,* Martin John Callanan, *b.* 1961, *m.*

2004   *Cameron of Dillington,* Ewen (James Hanning) Cameron, *b.* 1949, *m.*

1984   €*Cameron of Lochbroom,* Kenneth John Cameron, PC, *b.* 1931, *m.*

2015   *Campbell of Pittenweem,* (Walter) Menzies Campbell, CH, CBE, PC, QC, *b.* 1941, *m.*

2001   *Campbell-Savours,* Dale Norman Campbell-Savours, *b.* 1943, *m.*

2002   *Carey of Clifton,* Rt. Revd George Leonard Carey, PC, Royal Victorian Chain, *b.* 1935, *m.*

1999   *Carlile of Berriew,* Alexander Charles Carlile, CBE, QC, *b.* 1948, *m.*

2013   *Carrington of Fulham,* Matthew Hadrian Marshall Carrington, *b.* 1947, *m.*

2008   *Carter of Barnes,* Stephen Andrew Carter, CBE, *b.* 1964, *m.*

2004   *Carter of Coles,* Patrick Robert Carter, *b.* 1946, *m.*

2014   *Cashman,* Michael Maurice Cashman, CBE, *b.* 1950

1990   *Cavendish of Furness,* (Richard) Hugh Cavendish, *b.* 1941, *m.*

1996   *Chadlington,* Peter Selwyn Gummer, *b.* 1942, *m.*

1964   €*Chalfont,* (Alun) Arthur Gwynne Jones, OBE, MC, PC, *b.* 1919, *w.*

2017   *Chartres,* Rt. Revd Richard John Carew Chartres, KCVO, PC, *b.* 1947, *m.*

2005   *Chidgey,* David William George Chidgey, *b.* 1942, *m.*

1998   *Christopher,* Anthony Martin Grosvenor Christopher, CBE, *b.* 1925, *m.*

2001   *Clark of Windermere,* David George Clark, PC, PHD, *b.* 1939, *m.*

1998   *Clarke of Hampstead,* Anthony James Clarke, CBE, *b.* 1932, *m.*

2009   *Clarke of Stone-Cum-Ebony,* Anthony Peter Clarke, PC, *b.* 1943, *m.*

1998   *Clement-Jones,* Timothy Francis Clement-Jones, CBE, *b.* 1949, *m.*

1990   €*Clinton-Davis,* Stanley Clinton Clinton-Davis, PC, *b.* 1928, *m.*

2000   *Coe,* Sebastian Newbold Coe, CH, KBE, *b.* 1956, *m.*

2011   *Collins of Highbury,* Raymond Edward Harry Collins, *b.* 1954

2001   €*Condon,* Paul Leslie Condon, QPM, *b.* 1947, *m.*

2014   *Cooper of Windrush,* Andrew Timothy Cooper, *b.* 1963, *m.*

1997   *Cope of Berkeley,* John Ambrose Cope, PC, *b.* 1937, *m.*

2010   *Cormack,* Patrick Thomas Cormack, *b.* 1939, *m.*

2006   *Cotter,* Brian Joseph Michael Cotter, *b.* 1938, *m.*

1991   *Craig of Radley,* David Brownrigg Craig, GCB, OBE, *b.* 1929, *m.*

2006   *Crisp,* (Edmund) Nigel (Ramsay) Crisp, KCB, *b.* 1952, *m.*

2003   *Cullen of Whitekirk,* William Douglas Cullen, KT, PC, *b.* 1935, *m.*

2005   *Cunningham of Felling,* John Anderson Cunningham, PC, *b.* 1939, *m.*

1996   *Currie of Marylebone,* David Anthony Currie, *b.* 1946, *m.*

2011   *Curry of Kirkharle,* Donald Thomas Younger Curry, CBE, *b.* 1944, *m.*

2011   *Dannatt,* (Francis) Richard Dannatt, GCB, CBE, MC, *b.* 1950, *m.*

2015   *Darling of Roulanish,* Alistair Maclean Darling, PC, *b.* 1953, *m.*

2007   *Darzi of Denham,* Ara Warkes Darzi, OM, KBE, PC, *b.* 1960, *m.*

2006   *Davidson of Glen Clova,* Neil Forbes Davidson, QC, *b.* 1950, *m.*

2009   *Davies of Abersoch,* Evan Mervyn Davies, CBE, *b.* 1952, *m.*

1997   *Davies of Coity,* (David) Garfield Davies, CBE, *b.* 1935, *m.*

1997   *Davies of Oldham,* Bryan Davies, PC, *b.* 1939, *m.*

2010   *Davies of Stamford,* John Quentin Davies, *b.* 1944, *m.*

2006   *Dear,* Geoffrey (James) Dear, QPM, *b.* 1937, *m.*

2010   *Deben,* John Selwyn Gummer, PC, *b.* 1939, *m.*

2012   *Deighton,* Paul Clive Deighton, KBE, *b.* 1956, *m.*

1991   *Desai,* Prof. Meghnad Jagdishchandra Desai, PHD, *b.* 1940, *m.*

1997   *Dholakia,* Navnit Dholakia, OBE, PC, *b.* 1937, *m.*

1993   *Dixon-Smith,* Robert William Dixon-Smith, *b.* 1934, *m.*

2010   *Dobbs,* Michael John Dobbs, *b.* 1948, *m.*

1985   *Donoughue,* Bernard Donoughue, DPHIL, *b.* 1934

2004   *Drayson,* Paul Rudd Drayson, PC, *b.* 1960, *m.*

1994   *Dubs,* Alfred Dubs, *b.* 1932, *m.*

2017   *Duncan of Springbank,* Ian James Duncan, *b.* 1973

2015   *Dunlop,* Andrew James Dunlop, *b.* 1959, *m.*

2004   *Dykes,* Hugh John Maxwell Dykes, *b.* 1939, *m.*

1995   *Eames,* Rt. Revd Robert Henry Alexander Eames, OM, PHD, *b.* 1937, *m.*

1992   *Eatwell,* John Leonard Eatwell, PHD, *b.* 1945

1983   ℃*Eden of Winton,* John Benedict Eden, PC, *b.* 1925, *m.*

2011   ℃*Edmiston,* Robert Norman Edmiston, *b.* 1946, *m.*

1999   *Elder,* Thomas Murray Elder, *b.* 1950

1992   *Elis-Thomas,* Dafydd Elis Elis-Thomas, PC, *b.* 1946, *m.*

1981   *Elystan-Morgan,* Dafydd Elystan Elystan-Morgan, *b.* 1932, *w.*

2011   *Empey,* Reginald Norman Morgan Empey, OBE, *b.* 1947, *m.*

2000   ℃*Erskine of Alloa Tower,* Earl of Mar and Kellie, *b.* 1949, *m. (see* Hereditary Peers)

1998   *Evans of Watford,* David Charles Evans, *b.* 1942, *m.*

2014   *Evans of Weardale,* Jonathan Douglas Evans, KCB, *b.* 1958

1997   *Falconer of Thoroton,* Charles Leslie Falconer, PC, QC, *b.* 1951, *m.*

2014   *Farmer,* Michael Stahel Farmer, *b.* 1944, *m.*

1999   *Faulkner of Worcester,* Richard Oliver Faulkner, *b.* 1946, *m.*

2010   *Faulks,* Edward Peter Lawless Faulks, QC, *b.* 1950, *m.*

2001   ℃*Fearn,* Ronald Cyril Fearn, OBE, *b.* 1931, *m.*

1996   ℃*Feldman,* Basil Feldman, *b.* 1926, *m.*

2010   *Feldman of Elstree,* Andrew Simon Feldman, PC, *b.* 1966, *m.*

1999   *Fellowes,* Robert Fellowes, GCB, GCVO, PC, *b.* 1941, *m.*

2011   *Fellowes of West Stafford,* Julian Alexander Fellowes, *b.* 1949, *m.*

1999   *Filkin,* David Geoffrey Nigel Filkin, CBE, *b.* 1944

2011   *Fink,* Stanley Fink, *b.* 1957, *m.*

2013   *Finkelstein,* Daniel William Finkelstein, OBE, *b.* 1962, *m.*

2011   *Flight,* Howard Emerson Flight, *b.* 1948, *m.*

1999   *Forsyth of Drumlean,* Michael Bruce Forsyth, PC, *b.* 1954, *m.*

2015   *Foster of Bath,* Donald Michael Ellison Foster, PC, *b.* 1947, *m.*

2005   *Foster of Bishop Auckland,* Derek Foster, PC, *b.* 1937, *m.*

1999   ℃*Foster of Thames Bank,* Norman Robert Foster, OM, *b.* 1935, *m.*

2005   *Foulkes of Cumnock,* George Foulkes, PC, *b.* 1942, *m.*

2001   *Fowler,* (Peter) Norman Fowler, PC, *b.* 1938, *m. Lord Speaker*

2014   *Fox,* Christopher Francis Fox, *b.* 1957, *m.*

2011   *Framlingham,* Michael Nicholson Lord, *b.* 1938, *m.*

2016   *Fraser of Corriegarth,* (Alexander) Andrew (Macdonell) Fraser, *b.* 1946, *m.*

1997   *Freeman,* Roger Norman Freeman, PC, *b.* 1942, *m.*

2009   *Freud,* David Anthony Freud, PC, *b.* 1950, *m.*

2016   *Gadhia,* Jitesh Kishorekumar Gadhia, *b.* 1970, *m.*

2010   *Gardiner of Kimble,* John Gardiner, *b.* 1956, *m.*

1997   *Garel-Jones,* (William Armand Thomas) Tristan Garel-Jones, PC, *b.* 1941, *m.*

2018   *Garnier,* Edward Henry Garnier, PC, QC, *b.* 1952, *m.*

1999   ℃*Gascoyne-Cecil,* The Marquess of Salisbury, KCVO, PC, *b.* 1946, *m. (see* Hereditary Peers)

2017   *Geidt,* Christopher Edward Wollaston MacKenzie Geidt, GCB, GCVO, OBE, PC, *b.* 1961, *m.*

2010   *German,* Michael James German, OBE, *b.* 1945, *m.*

2004   *Giddens,* Prof. Anthony Giddens, *b.* 1938, *m.*

2015   *Gilbert of Panteg,* Stephen Gilbert, *b.* 1963

2011   *Glasman,* Maurice Mark Glasman, *b.* 1961, *m.*

2011   *Glendonbrook,* Michael David Bishop, CBE, *b.* 1942

2014   *Goddard of Stockport,* David Goddard, *b.* 1952

2011   *Gold,* David Laurence Gold, *b.* 1951, *m.*

1999   *Goldsmith,* Peter Henry Goldsmith, PC, QC, *b.* 1950, *m.*

2005   *Goodlad,* Alastair Robertson Goodlad, KCMG, PC, *b.* 1943, *m.*

1997   *Gordon of Strathblane,* James Stuart Gordon, CBE, *b.* 1936, *m.*

1999   *Grabiner,* Anthony Stephen Grabiner, QC, *b.* 1945, *m.*

2011   *Grade of Yarmouth,* Michael Ian Grade, CBE, *b.* 1943, *m.*

1983   *Graham of Edmonton,* (Thomas) Edward Graham, PC, *b.* 1925, *m.*

2000   *Greaves,* Anthony Robert Greaves, *b.* 1942, *m.*

2014   *Green of Deddington,* Andrew Fleming Green, KCMG, *b.* 1941, *m.*

2010   *Green of Hurstpierpoint,* Stephen Keith Green, *b.* 1948, *m.*

2000   ℃*Grenfell of Kilvey,* Lord Grenfell, *b.* 1935, *m. (see* Hereditary Peers)

2001   *Griffiths of Burry Port,* Revd Dr Leslie John Griffiths, *b.* 1942, *m.*

1991   *Griffiths of Fforestfach,* Brian Griffiths, *b.* 1941, *m.*

2001   *Grocott,* Bruce Joseph Grocott, PC, *b.* 1940, *m.*

2000   *Gueterbock,* Lord Berkeley, OBE, *b.* 1939, *m. (see* Hereditary Peers)

2000   *Guthrie of Craigiebank,* Charles Ronald Llewelyn Guthrie, GCB, LVO, OBE, *b.* 1938, *m.*

1995   *Habgood,* Rt. Revd John Stapylton Habgood, PC, PHD, *b.* 1927, *w.*

2015   *Hague of Richmond,* William Jefferson Hague, PC, *b.* 1961, *m.*

2015   *Hailsham of Kettlethorpe,* Viscount Hailsham, PC, QC, *b.* 1945, *m. (see* Hereditary Peers)

2015   *Hain,* Peter Gerald Hain, PC, *b.* 1950, *m.*

2010   *Hall of Birkenhead,* Anthony William Hall, CBE, *b.* 1951, *m.*

2007   *Hameed,* Dr Khalid Hameed, CBE, *b.* 1941, *m.*

2005   *Hamilton of Epsom,* Archibald Gavin Hamilton, PC, *b.* 1941, *m.*

2001   *Hannay of Chiswick,* David Hugh Alexander Hannay, GCMG, CH, *b.* 1935, *w.*

1998   *Hanningfield,* Paul Edward Winston White, *b.* 1940

1997   ℃*Hardie,* Andrew Rutherford Hardie, PC, QC, *b.* 1946, *m.*

2006   *Harries of Pentregarth,* Rt. Revd Richard Douglas Harries, *b.* 1936, *m.*

1998   *Harris of Haringey,* (Jonathan) Toby Harris, *b.* 1953, *m.*

1996   *Harris of Peckham,* Philip Charles Harris, *b.* 1942, *m.*

1999   *Harrison,* Lyndon Henry Arthur Harrison, *b.* 1947, *m.*

2018   *Haselhurst,* Alan Gordon Barraclough Haselhurst, PC, *b.* 1937, *m.*

1993   *Haskel,* Simon Haskel, *b.* 1934, *m.*

1998   *Haskins,* Christopher Robin Haskins, *b.* 1937, *m.*

2005   *Hastings of Scarisbrick,* Michael John Hastings, CBE, *b.* 1958, *m.*

1997   ℃*Hattersley,* Roy Sidney George Hattersley, PC, *b.* 1932

2013   *Haughey,* William Haughey, OBE, *b.* 1956, *m.*

2004   *Haworth,* Alan Robert Haworth, *b.* 1948, *m.*

2014   *Hay of Ballyore,* William Alexander Hay, *b.* 1950, *m.*

2015   *Hayward,* Robert Antony Hayward, OBE, *b.* 1949

2010   *Hennessy of Nympsfield,* Prof. Peter John Hennessy, *b.* 1947, *m.*

2001   *Heseltine,* Michael Ray Dibdin Heseltine, CH, PC, *b.* 1933, *m.*

1997   *Higgins,* Terence Langley Higgins, KBE, PC, *b.* 1928, *m.*

2010   *Hill of Oareford,* Jonathan Hopkin Hill, CBE, PC, *b.* 1960, *m.*

2000   *Hodgson of Astley Abbotts,* Robin Granville Hodgson, CBE, *b.* 1942, *m.*

2017   *Hogan-Howe,* Bernard Hogan-Howe, QPM, *b.* 1957, *m.*

1991   *Hollick,* Clive Richard Hollick, *b.* 1945, *m.*

2013   *Holmes of Richmond,* Christopher Holmes, MBE, *b.* 1971

1995   *Hope of Craighead,* (James Arthur) David Hope, KT, PC, *b.* 1938, *m.*

2005   ☾*Hope of Thornes,* Rt. Revd David Michael Hope, KCVO, PC, *b.* 1940

2013   *Horam,* John Rhodes Horam, *b.* 1939, *m.*

2017   *Houghton of Richmond,* John Nicholas Reynolds Houghton, GCB, CBE, *b.* 1954, *m.*

2010   *Howard of Lympne,* Michael Howard, CH, PC, QC, *b.* 1941, *m.*

2004   *Howard of Rising,* Greville Patrick Charles Howard, *b.* 1941, *m.*

2005   *Howarth of Newport,* Alan Thomas Howarth, CBE, PC, *b.* 1944

1997   *Howell of Guildford,* David Arthur Russell Howell, PC, *b.* 1936, *m.*

1997   *Hoyle,* (Eric) Douglas Harvey Hoyle, *b.* 1930, *w.*

1997   *Hughes of Woodside,* Robert Hughes, *b.* 1932, *m.*

2000   *Hunt of Chesterton,* Julian Charles Roland Hunt, CB, *b.* 1941, *m.*

1997   *Hunt of Kings Heath,* Philip Alexander Hunt, OBE, PC, *b.* 1949, *m.*

1997   *Hunt of Wirral,* David James Fletcher Hunt, MBE, PC, *b.* 1942, *m.*

1997   ☾*Hurd of Westwell,* Douglas Richard Hurd, CH, CBE, PC, *b.* 1930, *w.*

2011   *Hussain,* Qurban Hussain, *b.* 1956, *m.*

2010   *Hutton of Furness,* John Matthew Patrick Hutton, PC, *b.* 1955, *m.*

1997   ☾*Inge,* Peter Anthony Inge, KG, GCB, PC, *b.* 1935, *m.*

1987   *Irvine of Lairg,* Alexander Andrew Mackay Irvine, PC, QC, *b.* 1940, *m.*

2006   *James of Blackheath,* David Noel James, CBE, *b.* 1937, *m.*

2007   *Janvrin,* Robin Berry Janvrin, GCB, GCVO, PC, *b.* 1946, *m.*

2006   *Jay of Ewelme,* Michael (Hastings) Jay, GCMG, *b.* 1946, *m.*

2001   *Jones,* (Stephen) Barry Jones, PC, *b.* 1937, *m.*

2007   *Jones of Birmingham,* Digby Marritt Jones, *b.* 1955, *m.*

2005   *Jones of Cheltenham,* Nigel David Jones, *b.* 1948, *m.*

1997   *Jopling,* (Thomas) Michael Jopling, PC, *b.* 1930, *m.*

2000   *Jordan,* William Brian Jordan, CBE, *b.* 1936, *m.*

1991   *Judd,* Frank Ashcroft Judd, *b.* 1935, *m.*

2008   *Judge,* Igor Judge, PC, *b.* 1941, *m.*

2010   *Kakkar,* Prof. Ajay Kumar Kakkar, PC, *b.* 1964

2004   *Kalms,* Harold Stanley Kalms, *b.* 1931, *m.*

2015   *Keen of Elie,* Richard Sanderson Keen, PC, QC, *b.* 1954, *m.*

2010   *Kennedy of Southwark,* Roy Francis Kennedy, *b.* 1962, *m.*

2004   *Kerr of Kinlochard,* John (Olav) Kerr, GCMG, *b.* 1942, *m.*

2010   **Kerr of Monteviot,* Marquess of Lothian (Michael Ancram), PC, QC, *b.* 1945, *m. (see* Hereditary Peers*)*

2015   *Kerslake,* Robert Walter Kerslake, *b.* 1955, *m.*

2011   *Kestenbaum,* Jonathan Andrew Kestenbaum, *b.* 1959, *m.*

2001   *Kilclooney,* John David Taylor, PC (NI), *b.* 1937, *m.*

2001   *King of Bridgwater,* Thomas Jeremy King, CH, PC, *b.* 1933, *m.*

2013   *King of Lothbury,* Mervyn Allister King, KG, GBE, *b.* 1948

2005   *Kinnock,* Neil Gordon Kinnock, PC, *b.* 1942, *m.*

1999   *Kirkham,* Graham Kirkham, *b.* 1944, *m.*

1975   ☾*Kirkhill,* John Farquharson Smith, *b.* 1930, *m.*

2016   *Kirkhope of Harrogate,* Timothy John Robert Kirkhope, *b.* 1945, *m.*

2005   *Kirkwood of Kirkhope,* Archibald Johnstone Kirkwood, *b.* 1946, *m.*

2010   *Knight of Weymouth,* James Philip Knight, PC, *b.* 1965, *m.*

2007   *Krebs,* Prof. John (Richard) Krebs, FRS, *b.* 1945, *m.*

2004   ☾*Laidlaw,* Irvine Alan Stewart Laidlaw, *b.* 1942, *m.*

1998   *Laming,* (William) Herbert Laming, CBE, PC, *b.* 1936, *w.*

1998   *Lamont of Lerwick,* Norman Stewart Hughson Lamont, PC, *b.* 1942, *m.*

1997   *Lang of Monkton,* Ian Bruce Lang, PC, *b.* 1940, *m.*

2015   *Lansley,* Andrew David Lansley, CBE, PC, *b.* 1956, *m.*

1992   *Lawson of Blaby,* Nigel Lawson, PC, *b.* 1932, *m.*

2000   *Layard,* Peter Richard Grenville Layard, *b.* 1934, *m.*

1999   *Lea of Crondall,* David Edward Lea, OBE, *b.* 1937

2006   *Lee of Trafford,* John Robert Louis Lee, *b.* 1942, *m.*

2013   *Leigh of Hurley,* Howard Darryl Leigh, *b.* 1959, *m.*

2004   *Leitch,* Alexander Park Leitch, *b.* 1947, *m.*

2014   *Lennie,* Christopher John Lennie, *b.* 1953, *m.*

1993   *Lester of Herne Hill,* Anthony Paul Lester, QC, *b.* 1936, *m.*

1997   *Levene of Portsoken,* Peter Keith Levene, KBE, *b.* 1941, *m.*

1997   *Levy,* Michael Abraham Levy, *b.* 1944, *m.*

2010   *Lexden,* Alistair Basil Cooke, OBE, *b.* 1945

2010   *Liddle,* Roger John Liddle, *b.* 1947, *m.*

2018   *Lilley,* Peter Bruce Lilley, PC, *b.* 1943, *m.*

2010   *Lingfield,* Robert George Alexander Balchin, *b.* 1942, *m.*

1999   *Lipsey,* David Lawrence Lipsey, *b.* 1948, *m.*

2014   *Lisvane,* Robert James Rogers, KCB, *b.* 1950, *m.*

2015   *Livermore,* Spencer Elliot Livermore, *b.* 1975

2013   *Livingston of Parkhead,* Ian Paul Livingston, *b.* 1964, *m.*

2016   *Llewellyn of Steep,* Edward David Gerard Llewellyn, OBE, PC, *b.* 1965, *m.*

1997   ☾*Lloyd-Webber,* Andrew Lloyd Webber, *b.* 1948, *m.*

2011   *Loomba,* Rajinder Paul Loomba, CBE, *b.* 1943, *m.*

2006   *Low of Dalston,* Prof. Colin MacKenzie Low, CBE, *b.* 1942, *m.*

2000   *Luce,* Richard Napier Luce, KG, GCVO, PC, *b.* 1936, *m.*

2015   *Lupton,* James Roger Crompton Lupton, CBE, *b.* 1955, *m.*

2000   **Lyttelton of Aldershot,* The Viscount Chandos, *b.* 1953, *m. (see* Hereditary Peers*)*

2010   *McAvoy,* Thomas McLaughlin McAvoy, PC, *b.* 1943, *m.*

1989   *McColl of Dulwich,* Ian McColl, CBE, FRCS, FRCSE, *b.* 1933, *m.*

2010   *McConnell of Glenscorrodale,* Dr Jack Wilson McConnell, PC, *b.* 1960, *m.*

2018   *McCrea of Magherafelt and Cookstown,* Revd Dr (Robert Thomas) William McCrea, *b.* 1948, *m.*

2010   *Macdonald of River Glaven,* Kenneth Donald John Macdonald, QC, *b.* 1953, *m.*

1998   ☾*Macdonald of Tradeston,* Angus John Macdonald, CBE, PC, *b.* 1940, *m.*

2010   *McFall of Alcluith,* John Francis McFall, PC, *b.* 1944, *m.*

1991   ₵*Macfarlane of Bearsden,* Norman Somerville Macfarlane, KT, FRSE, *b.* 1926, *m.*

2001   *MacGregor of Pulham Market,* John Roddick Russell MacGregor, CBE, PC, *b.* 1937, *m.*

2016   *McInnes of Kilwinning,* Mark McInnes, CBE, *b.* 1976

1979   *Mackay of Clashfern,* James Peter Hymers Mackay, KT, PC, FRSE, *b.* 1927, *m.*

1999   *MacKenzie of Culkein,* Hector Uisdean MacKenzie, *b.* 1940

1998   *Mackenzie of Framwellgate,* Brian Mackenzie, OBE, *b.* 1943, *m.*

2004   *McKenzie of Luton,* William David McKenzie, *b.* 1946, *m.*

1996   ₵*MacLaurin of Knebworth,* Ian Charter MacLaurin, *b.* 1937, *m.*

2001   *Maclennan of Rogart,* Robert Adam Ross Maclennan, PC, *b.* 1936, *m.*

1995   *McNally,* Tom McNally, PC, *b.* 1943, *m.*

2018   *McNicol of West Kilbride,* Iain Mackenzie McNicol, *b.* 1969, *m.*

2016   *Macpherson of Earl's Court,* Nicholas Ian Macpherson, GCB, *b.* 1959, *m.*

2011   *Magan of Castletown,* George Morgan Magan, *b.* 1945, *m.*

2001   *Maginnis of Drumglass,* Kenneth Wiggins Maginnis, *b.* 1938, *m.*

2015   *Mair,* Prof. Robert James Mair, CBE, PHD, FRS, *b.* 1950, *m.*

2007   *Malloch-Brown,* George Mark Malloch Brown, KCMG, PC, *b.* 1953, *m.*

2008   *Mandelson,* Peter Benjamin Mandelson, PC, *b.* 1953

2011   *Marks of Henley-on-Thames,* Jonathan Clive Marks, QC, *b.* 1952, *m.*

2006   *Marland,* Jonathan Peter Marland, *b.* 1956, *m.*

1991   *Marlesford,* Mark Shuldham Schreiber, *b.* 1931, *m.*

2015   *Maude of Horsham,* Francis Anthony Aylmer Maude, TD, PC, *b.* 1953, *m.*

2005   *Mawhinney,* Brian Stanley Mawhinney, PC, *b.* 1940, *m.*

2007   *Mawson,* Revd Andrew Mawson, OBE, *b.* 1954, *m.*

2004   *Maxton,* John Alston Maxton, *b.* 1936, *m.*

2001   ₵*May of Oxford,* Robert McCredie May, OM, *b.* 1936, *m.*

2013   *Mendelsohn,* Jonathan Neil Mendelsohn, *b.* 1966, *m.*

2000   *Mitchell,* Parry Andrew Mitchell, *b.* 1943, *m.*

2000   **Mitford,* Lord Redesdale, *b.* 1967, *m.* (*see* Hereditary Peers)

2008   *Mogg,* John (Frederick) Mogg, KCMG, *b.* 1943, *m.*

2010   *Monks,* John Stephen Monks, *b.* 1945, *m.*

2005   *Moonie,* Dr Lewis George Moonie, *b.* 1947, *m.*

1992   *Moore of Lower Marsh,* John Edward Michael Moore, PC, *b.* 1937, *w.*

2000   *Morgan,* Kenneth Owen Morgan, *b.* 1934, *m.*

2001   *Morris of Aberavon,* John Morris, KG, PC, QC, *b.* 1931, *m.*

2006   *Morris of Handsworth,* William Manuel Morris, *b.* 1938, *m.*

2006   *Morrow,* Maurice George Morrow, *b.* 1948, *m.*

2015   *Murphy of Torfaen,* Paul Peter Murphy, PC, *b.* 1948

2008   *Myners,* Paul Myners, CBE, *b.* 1948, *m.*

1997   *Naseby,* Michael Wolfgang Laurence Morris, PC, *b.* 1936, *m.*

2013   *Nash,* John Alfred Stoddard Nash, *b.* 1949

1997   *Newby,* Richard Mark Newby, OBE, PC, *b.* 1953, *m.*

1994   ₵*Nickson,* David Wigley Nickson, KBE, FRSE, *b.* 1929, *m.*

1998   *Norton of Louth,* Philip Norton, *b.* 1951

2000   *Oakeshott of Seagrove Bay,* Matthew Alan Oakeshott, *b.* 1947, *m.*

2015   *Oates,* Jonathan Oates, *b.* 1969, *c.p.*

2012   *O'Donnell,* Augustine Thomas (Gus) O'Donnell, GCB, *b.* 1952, *m.*

2005   *O'Neill of Clackmannan,* Martin John O'Neill, *b.* 1945, *m.*

2015   *O'Neill of Gatley,* Terence James O'Neill, *b.* 1957, *m.*

2015   *O'Shaughnessy,* James Richard O'Shaughnessy, *b.* 1976, *m.*

2001   *Ouseley,* Herman George Ouseley, *b.* 1945, *m.*

1992   *Owen,* David Anthony Llewellyn Owen, CH, PC, *b.* 1938, *m.*

1999   *Oxburgh,* Ernest Ronald Oxburgh, KBE, FRS, PHD, *b.* 1934, *m.*

2013   *Paddick,* Brian Leonard Paddick, *b.* 1958, *m.*

2011   *Palmer of Childs Hill,* Monroe Edward Palmer, OBE, *b.* 1938, *m.*

1991   *Palumbo,* Peter Garth Palumbo, *b.* 1935, *m.*

2013   *Palumbo of Southwark,* James Rudolph Palumbo, *b.* 1963

2008   *Pannick,* David Philip Pannick, QC, *b.* 1956, *m.*

2000   *Parekh,* Bhikhu Chhotalal Parekh, *b.* 1935, *m.*

1999   *Patel,* Narendra Babubhai Patel, KT, *b.* 1938

2000   *Patel of Blackburn,* Adam Hafejee Patel, *b.* 1940

2006   *Patel of Bradford,* Prof. Kamlesh Kumar Patel, OBE, *b.* 1960, *m.*

1997   *Patten,* John Haggitt Charles Patten, PC, *b.* 1945, *m.*

2005   *Patten of Barnes,* Christopher Francis Patten, CH, PC, *b.* 1944, *m.*

1996   *Paul,* Swraj Paul, PC, *b.* 1931, *m.*

1990   *Pearson of Rannoch,* Malcolm Everard MacLaren Pearson, *b.* 1942, *m.*

2001   *Pendry,* Thomas Pendry, PC, *b.* 1934, *m.*

1998   ₵*Phillips of Sudbury,* Andrew Wyndham Phillips, OBE, *b.* 1939, *m.*

1992   *Plant of Highfield,* Prof. Raymond Plant, PHD, *b.* 1945, *m.*

1987   ₵*Plumb,* (Charles) Henry Plumb, *b.* 1925, *m.*

2015   *Polak,* Stuart Polak, CBE, *b.* 1961

2000   **Ponsonby of Roehampton,* Lord Ponsonby of Shulbrede, *b.* 1958, *m.* (*see* Hereditary Peers)

2010   *Popat,* Dolar Amarshi Popat, *b.* 1953, *m.*

2015   *Porter of Spalding,* Gary Andrew Porter, CBE, *b.* 1960, *m.*

2000   *Powell of Bayswater,* Charles David Powell, KCMG, *b.* 1941, *m.*

2010   *Prescott,* John Leslie Prescott, *b.* 1938, *m.*

2018   *Pickles,* Eric (Jack) Pickles, PC, *b.* 1952, *m.*

2016   *Price,* Mark Ian Price, CVO, *b.* 1961, *m.*

2015   *Prior of Brampton,* David Gifford Leathes Prior, *b.* 1954, *m.*

2013   *Purvis of Tweed,* Jeremy Purvis, *b.* 1974

1997   *Puttnam,* David Terence Puttnam, CBE, *b.* 1941, *m.*

2001   *Radice,* Giles Heneage Radice, PC, *b.* 1936, *m.*

2005   *Ramsbotham,* David John Ramsbotham, GCB, CBE, *b.* 1934, *m.*

2004   *Rana,* Dr Diljit Singh Rana, MBE, *b.* 1938, *m.*

2018   *Randall of Uxbridge,* (Alexander) John Randall, PC, *b.* 1955, *m.*

1997   *Razzall,* (Edward) Timothy Razzall, CBE, *b.* 1943, *m.*

2005   *Rees of Ludlow,* Prof. Martin John Rees, OM, *b.* 1942, *m.*

2010   *Reid of Cardowan,* Dr John Reid, PC, *b.* 1947, *m.*

1991   *Renfrew of Kaimsthorn,* (Andrew) Colin Renfrew, FBA, *b.* 1937, *m.*

1999   *Rennard,* Christopher John Rennard, MBE, *b.* 1960

1997   ₵*Renton of Mount Harry,* (Ronald) Timothy Renton, PC, *b.* 1932, *m.*

1997   ₵*Renwick of Clifton,* Robin William Renwick, KCMG, *b.* 1937, *m.*

2010   *Ribeiro,* Bernard Francisco Ribeiro, CBE, *b.* 1944, *m.*

2014   *Richards of Herstmonceux,* David Julian Richards, GCB, CBE, DSO, *b.* 1952, *m.*

2016   *Ricketts,* Peter (Forbes) Ricketts, GCMG, GCVO, *b.* 1952, *m.*

2010   *Risby,* Richard John Grenville Spring, *b.* 1946, *m.*

2015   *Robathan,* Andrew Robathan, PC, *b.* 1951, *m.*

2004   *Roberts of Llandudno,* Revd John Roger Roberts, *b.* 1935, *m.*

1999   *Robertson of Port Ellen,* George Islay MacNeill Robertson, KT, GCMG, PC, *b.* 1946, *m.*

1992   *Rodgers of Quarry Bank,* William Thomas Rodgers, PC, *b.* 1928, *w.*

1999   *Rogan,* Dennis Robert David Rogan, *b.* 1942, *m.*

1996   *Rogers of Riverside,* Richard George Rogers, CH, RA, RIBA, *b.* 1933, *m.*

2001   *Rooker,* Jeffrey William Rooker, PC, *b.* 1941, *m.*

2014   *Rose of Monewden,* Stuart Alan Ransom Rose, *b.* 1949

2004   *Rosser,* Richard Andrew Rosser, *b.* 1944, *m.*

2006   *Rowe-Beddoe,* David (Sydney) Rowe-Beddoe, *b.* 1937, *m.*

2004   *Rowlands,* Edward Rowlands, CBE, *b.* 1940, *m.*

1997   *Ryder of Wensum,* Richard Andrew Ryder, OBE, PC, *b.* 1949, *m.*

1996   *Saatchi,* Maurice Saatchi, *b.* 1946, *w.*

2009   *Sacks,* Chief Rabbi Dr Jonathan Henry Sacks, *b.* 1948, *m.*

1989   *Sainsbury of Preston Candover,* John Davan Sainsbury, KG, *b.* 1927, *m.*

1997   *Sainsbury of Turville,* David John Sainsbury, *b.* 1940, *m.*

1985   ℂ *Sanderson of Bowden,* Charles Russell Sanderson, *b.* 1933, *m.*

2010   *Sassoon,* James Meyer Sassoon, *b.* 1955, *m.*

1998   *Sawyer,* Lawrence (Tom) Sawyer, *b.* 1943

2014   *Scriven,* Paul James Scriven, *b.* 1966

1997   *Selkirk of Douglas,* James Alexander Douglas-Hamilton, PC, QC, *b.* 1942, *m.*

1996   ℂ *Sewel,* John Buttifant Sewel, CBE, *b.* 1946

2010   *Sharkey,* John Kevin Sharkey, *b.* 1947, *m.*

1999   ℂ *Sharman,* Colin Morven Sharman, OBE, *b.* 1943, *m.*

1994   ℂ *Shaw of Northstead,* Michael Norman Shaw, *b.* 1920, *m.*

2006   *Sheikh,* Mohamed Iltaf Sheikh, *b.* 1941, *m.*

2001   ℂ *Sheldon,* Robert Edward Sheldon, PC, *b.* 1923, *m.*

2013   *Sherbourne of Didsbury,* Stephen Ashley Sherbourne, CBE, *b.* 1945

2015   *Shinkwin,* Kevin Joseph Maximilian Shinkwin, *b.* 1971

2010   *Shipley,* John Warren Shipley, OBE, *b.* 1946

2000   *Shutt of Greetland,* David Trevor Shutt, OBE, PC, *b.* 1942

1997   ℂ *Simon of Highbury,* David Alec Gwyn Simon, CBE, *b.* 1939, *m.*

1997   ℂ *Simpson of Dunkeld,* George Simpson, *b.* 1942, *m.*

2011   *Singh of Wimbledon,* Indarjit Singh, CBE, *b.* 1932, *m.*

1991   *Skidelsky,* Robert Jacob Alexander Skidelsky, DPHIL, *b.* 1939, *m.*

1997   *Smith of Clifton,* Trevor Arthur Smith, *b.* 1937, *m.*

2005   *Smith of Finsbury,* Christopher Robert Smith, PC, *b.* 1951

2015   *Smith of Hindhead,* Philip Roland Smith, CBE, *b.* 1966

2008   *Smith of Kelvin,* Robert (Haldane) Smith, KT, CH, *b.* 1944, *m.*

1999   *Smith of Leigh,* Peter Richard Charles Smith, *b.* 1945, *m.*

2004   *Snape,* Peter Charles Snape, *b.* 1942, *m.*

2005   *Soley,* Clive Stafford Soley, *b.* 1939

2010   *Spicer,* (William) Michael Hardy Spicer, PC, *b.* 1943, *m.*

1997   *Steel of Aikwood,* David Martin Scott Steel, KT, KBE, PC, *b.* 1938, *m.*

2011   *Stephen,* Nicol Ross Stephen, *b.* 1960, *m.*

1991   *Sterling of Plaistow,* Jeffrey Maurice Sterling, GCVO, CBE, *b.* 1934, *m.*

2007   *Stern of Brentford,* Nicholas Herbert Stern, CH, *b.* 1946, *m.*

2005   *Stevens of Kirkwhelpington,* John Arthur Stevens, QPM, *b.* 1942, *m.*

1987   *Stevens of Ludgate,* David Robert Stevens, *b.* 1936, *m.*

2010   *Stevenson of Balmacara,* Robert Wilfrid Stevenson, *b.* 1947, *m.*

1999   *Stevenson of Coddenham,* Henry Dennistoun Stevenson, CBE, *b.* 1945, *m.*

2011   *Stirrup,* Graham Eric Stirrup, KG, GCB, AFC, *b.* 1949, *m.*

1983   *Stoddart of Swindon,* David Leonard Stoddart, *b.* 1926, *m.*

1997   *Stone of Blackheath,* Andrew Zelig Stone, *b.* 1942, *m.*

2011   *Stoneham of Droxford,* Benjamin Russell Mackintosh Stoneham, *b.* 1948, *m.*

2011   *Storey,* Michael John Storey, CBE, *b.* 1949, *m.*

2011   *Strasburger,* Paul Cline Strasburger, *b.* 1946 *m.*

2015   *Stunell,* Robert Andrew Stunell, OBE, PC, *b.* 1942, *m.*

2009   *Sugar,* Alan Michael Sugar, *b.* 1947, *m.*

2014   *Suri,* Ranbir Singh Suri, *b.* 1935

1971   ℂ *Tanlaw,* Simon Brooke Mackay, *b.* 1934, *m.*

1996   *Taverne,* Dick Taverne, QC, *b.* 1928, *m.*

2010   *Taylor of Goss Moor,* Matthew Owen John Taylor, *b.* 1963, *m.*

2006   *Taylor of Holbeach,* John Derek Taylor, CBE, PC, *b.* 1943, *m.*

1996   *Taylor of Warwick,* John David Beckett Taylor, *b.* 1952, *m.*

1992   *Tebbit,* Norman Beresford Tebbit, CH, PC, *b.* 1931, *m.*

2006   *Teverson,* Robin Teverson, *b.* 1952, *m.*

2013   *Thomas of Cwmgiedd,* Roger John Laugharne Thomas, PC, *b.* 1947, *m.*

1996   *Thomas of Gresford,* Donald Martin Thomas, OBE, QC, *b.* 1937, *m.*

1990   ℂ *Tombs,* Francis Leonard Tombs, FRENG, *b.* 1924, *w.*

1998   *Tomlinson,* John Edward Tomlinson, *b.* 1939

1994   *Tope,* Graham Norman Tope, CBE, *b.* 1943, *m.*

1981   ℂ *Tordoff,* Geoffrey Johnson Tordoff, *b.* 1928, *m.*

2010   *Touhig,* James Donnelly Touhig, PC, *b.* 1947, *m.*

2012   *Trees,* Alexander John Trees, PHD, *b.* 1946, *m.*

2004   *Triesman,* David Maxim Triesman, *b.* 1943

2006   *Trimble,* William David Trimble, PC, *b.* 1944, *m.*

2010   *True,* Nicholas Edward True, CBE, *b.* 1951, *m.*

2004   *Truscott,* Dr Peter Derek Truscott, *b.* 1959, *m.*

1993   *Tugendhat,* Christopher Samuel Tugendhat, *b.* 1937, *m.*

2004   *Tunnicliffe,* Denis Tunnicliffe, CBE, *b.* 1943, *m.*

2000   *Turnberg,* Leslie Arnold Turnberg, MD, *b.* 1934, *m.*

2005   *Turnbull,* Andrew Turnbull, KCB, CVO, PC, *b.* 1945, *m.*

2005   *Turner of Ecchinswell,* (Jonathan) Adair Turner, *b.* 1955, *m.*

2005   *Tyler,* Paul Archer Tyler, CBE, PC, *b.* 1941, *m.*

2018   *Tyrie,* Andrew Guy Tyrie, PC, *b.* 1957

2004   *Vallance of Tummel,* Iain (David Thomas) Vallance, *b.* 1943, *m.*

2013   *Verjee,* Rumi Verjee, CBE, *b.* 1957

1985   *Vinson,* Nigel Vinson, LVO, *b.* 1931, *m.*

1992   *Wakeham,* John Wakeham, PC, *b.* 1932, *m.*

1999   *Waldegrave of North Hill,* William Arthur Waldegrave, PC, *b.* 1946, *m.*

2007 *Walker of Aldringham,* Michael John Dawson Walker, GCB, CMG, CBE, *b.* 1944, *m.*

1995 *Wallace of Saltaire,* William John Lawrence Wallace, PC, PHD, *b.* 1941, *m.*

2007 *Wallace of Tankerness,* James Robert Wallace, PC, QC, *b.* 1954, *m.*

1998 *Warner,* Norman Reginald Warner, PC, *b.* 1940, *m.*

2011 *Wasserman,* Gordon Joshua Wasserman, *b.* 1938

1997 *Watson of Invergowrie,* Michael Goodall Watson, *b.* 1949, *m.*

1999 *Watson of Richmond,* Alan John Watson, CBE, *b.* 1941, *m.*

2015 *Watts,* David Leonard Watts, *b.* 1951, *m.*

2010 *Wei,* Nathanael Ming-Yan Wei, *b.* 1977, *m.*

2007 *West of Spithead,* Alan William John West, GCB, DSC, PC, *b.* 1948, *m.*

2013 *Whitby,* Michael John Whitby, *b.* 1948

1996 *Whitty,* John Lawrence (Larry) Whitty, PC, *b.* 1943, *m.*

2011 *Wigley,* Dafydd Wynne Wigley, PC, *b.* 1943, *m.*

2015 *Willetts,* David Lindsay Willetts, PC, *b.* 1956, *m.*

1985 *Williams of Elvel,* Charles Cuthbert Powell Williams, CBE, PC, *b.* 1933, *m.*

2013 *Williams of Oystermouth,* Rt. Revd Rowan Douglas Williams, PC, Royal Victorian Chain, DPHIL, *b.* 1950, *m.*

2010 *Willis of Knaresborough,* George Philip Willis, *b.* 1941, *m.*

2010 *Wills,* Michael David Wills, PC, *b.* 1952, *m.*

2002 *Wilson of Dinton,* Richard Thomas James Wilson, GCB, *b.* 1942, *m.*

1992 *Wilson of Tillyorn,* David Clive Wilson, KT, GCMG, PHD, *b.* 1935, *m.*

1995 *Winston,* Robert Maurice Lipson Winston, FRCOG, *b.* 1940, *m.*

2010 *Wolfson of Aspley Guise,* Simon Adam Wolfson, *b.* 1967, *m.*

1991 E. *Wolfson of Sunningdale,* David Wolfson, *b.* 1935, *m.*

2011 *Wood of Anfield,* Stewart Martin Wood, *b.* 1968, *m.*

1999 *Woolmer of Leeds,* Kenneth John Woolmer, *b.* 1940, *m.*

2013 *Wrigglesworth,* Ian William Wrigglesworth, *b.* 1939, *m.*

1994 *Wright of Richmond,* Patrick Richard Henry Wright, GCMG, *b.* 1931, *m.*

2015 *Young of Cookham,* George Samuel Knatchbull Young, CH, PC, *b.* 1941, *m.*

1984 *Young of Graffham,* David Ivor Young, CH, PC, *b.* 1932, *m.*

2004 *Young of Norwood Green,* Anthony (Ian) Young, *b.* 1942, *m.*

BARONESSES
Created

2005 *Adams of Craigielea,* Katherine Patricia Irene Adams, *b.* 1947, *w.*

2007 *Afshar,* Prof. Haleh Afshar, OBE, *b.* 1944, *m.*

2015 *Altmann,* Dr Rosalind Miriam Altmann, CBE, *b.* 1956, *m.*

1997 *Amos,* Valerie Ann Amos, CH, PC, *b.* 1954

2000 *Andrews,* Elizabeth Kay Andrews, OBE, *b.* 1943, *m.*

1996 *Anelay of St Johns,* Joyce Anne Anelay, DBE, PC, *b.* 1947, *m.*

2010 *Armstrong of Hill Top,* Hilary Jane Armstrong, PC, *b.* 1945, *m.*

1999 *Ashton of Upholland,* Catherine Margaret Ashton, GCMG, PC, *b.* 1956, *m.*

2011 *Bakewell,* Joan Dawson Bakewell, DBE, *b.* 1933, *w.*

2013 *Bakewell of Hardington Mandeville,* Catherine Mary Bakewell, MBE, *b.* 1949

1999 *Barker,* Elizabeth Jean Barker, *b.* 1961

2018 *Barran,* Diana Francesca Caroline Barran, MBE, *m.*

2010 *Benjamin,* Floella Karen Yunies Benjamin, OBE, *b.* 1949, *m.*

2011 *Berridge,* Elizabeth Rose Berridge, *b.* 1972

2016 *Bertin,* Gabrielle Louise Bertin, *b.* 1978, *m.*

2000 *Billingham,* Angela Theodora Billingham, DPHIL, *b.* 1939, *w.*

1987 *Blackstone,* Tessa Ann Vosper Blackstone, PC, PHD, *b.* 1942

1999 ☾*Blood,* May Blood, MBE, *b.* 1938

2016 *Bloomfield of Hinton Waldrist,* Olivia Caroline Bloomfield, *b.* 1960, *m.*

2004 *Bonham-Carter of Yarnbury,* Jane Bonham Carter, *b.* 1957, *w.*

2000 *Boothroyd,* Betty Boothroyd, OM, PC, *b.* 1929

2005 *Bottomley of Nettlestone,* Virginia Hilda Brunette Maxwell Bottomley, PC, *b.* 1948, *m.*

2015 *Bowles of Berkhamsted,* Sharon Margaret Bowles, *b.* 1953, *m.*

2018 *Boycott,* Rosel Marie Boycott, MBE, *b.* 1951, *m.*

2014 *Brady,* Karren Rita Brady, CBE, *b.* 1969, *m.*

2011 *Brinton,* Sarah Virginia Brinton, *b.* 1955, *m.*

2015 *Brown of Cambridge,* Prof. Julia Elizabeth King, DBE, PHD, FRENG, *b.* 1954, *m.*

2010 *Browning,* Angela Frances Browning, *b.* 1946, *m.*

2018 *Bryan of Partick,* Pauline Christina Bryan

2018 *Bull,* Deborah Clare Bull, CBE, *b.* 1963

2015 *Burt of Solihull,* Lorely Jane Burt, *b.* 1954, *m.*

1998 *Buscombe,* Peta Jane Buscombe, *b.* 1954, *m.*

2006 *Butler-Sloss,* (Ann) Elizabeth (Oldfield) Butler-Sloss, GBE, PC, *b.* 1933, *m.*

1996 *Byford,* Hazel Byford, DBE, *b.* 1941, *w.*

2008 *Campbell of Loughborough,* Susan Catherine Campbell, CBE, *b.* 1948

2007 *Campbell of Surbiton,* Jane Susan Campbell, DBE, *b.* 1959, *m.*

2016 *Cavendish of Little Venice,* Hilary Camilla Cavendish, *b.* 1968, *m.*

2016 *Chakrabarti,* Sharmishta Chakrabarti, PC, CBE, *b.* 1969

1992 *Chalker of Wallasey,* Lynda Chalker, PC, *b.* 1942

2014 *Chisholm of Owlpen,* Caroline Elizabeth (Carlyn) Chisholm, *b.* 1951, *m.*

2005 §*Clark of Calton,* Dr Lynda Margaret Clark, PC, *b.* 1949

2000 *Cohen of Pimlico,* Janet Cohen, *b.* 1940, *m.*

2005 *Corston,* Jean Ann Corston, PC, *b.* 1942, *w.*

2007 *Coussins,* Jean Coussins, *b.* 1950

2016 *Couttie,* Philippa Marion Roe, *b.* 1962, *m.*

1982 *Cox,* Caroline Anne Cox, *b.* 1937, *m.*

1998 *Crawley,* Christine Mary Crawley, *b.* 1950, *m.*

1990 *Cumberlege,* Julia Frances Cumberlege, CBE, *b.* 1943, *m.*

2005 *Deech,* Ruth Lynn Deech, DBE, *b.* 1943, *m.*

2010 *Donaghy,* Rita Margaret Donaghy, CBE, *b.* 1944, *m.*

2010 *Doocey,* Elizabeth Deirdre Doocey, OBE, *b.* 1948, *m.*

2010 *Drake,* Jean Lesley Patricia Drake, CBE, *b.* 1948

2004 *D'Souza,* Dr Frances Gertrude Claire D'Souza, CMG, PC, *b.* 1944, *m.*

1990 ☾*Dunn,* Lydia Selina Dunn, DBE, *b.* 1940, *m.*

2010 *Eaton,* Ellen Margaret Eaton, DBE, *b.* 1942, *m.*

1990 *Eccles of Moulton,* Diana Catherine Eccles, *b.* 1933, *m.*

1997 *Emerton,* Audrey Caroline Emerton, DBE, *b.* 1935

2014 *Evans of Bowes Park,* Natalie Jessica Evans, PC, *b.* 1975, *m.*

2017 *Fairhead,* Rona Alison Fairhead, CBE, *b.* 1961, *m.*

1974 *Falkender,* Marcia Matilda Falkender, CBE, *b.* 1932

2004 *Falkner of Margravine,* Kishwer Falkner, *b.* 1955, *m.*

2015 *Fall,* Catherine Susan Fall, *b.* 1967

2015 *Featherstone,* Lynne Choona Featherstone, PC, *b.* 1951

2001 *Finlay of Llandaff,* Ilora Gillian Finlay, *b.* 1949, *m.*

2015 *Finn,* Simone Jari Finn, *b.* 1968

1990 *Flather,* Shreela Flather, *b.* 1934, *w.*

1997 *Fookes,* Janet Evelyn Fookes, DBE, *b.* 1936

2006 *Ford,* Margaret Anne Ford, *b.* 1957, *m.*

2005 *Fritchie,* Irene Tordoff Fritchie, DBE, *b.* 1942, *m.*

1999 *Gale,* Anita Gale, *b.* 1940

2007 *Garden of Frognal,* Susan Elizabeth Garden, PC, *b.* 1944, *w.*

1981 *Gardner of Parkes,* (Rachel) Trixie (Anne) Gardner, *b.* 1927, *w.*

2013 *Goldie,* Annabel MacNicholl Goldie, *b.* 1950

2001 *Golding,* Llinos Golding, *b.* 1933, *w.*

1998 *Goudie,* Mary Teresa Goudie, *b.* 1946, *m.*

1993 *Gould of Potternewton,* Joyce Brenda Gould, *b.* 1932, *m.*

2001 *Greenfield,* Susan Adele Greenfield, CBE, *b.* 1950, *m.*

2000 *Greengross,* Sally Ralea Greengross, OBE, *b.* 1935, *w.*

2013 *Grender,* Rosalind Mary Grender, MBE, *b.* 1962

2010 *Grey-Thompson,* Tanni Carys Davina Grey-Thompson, DBE, *b.* 1969, *m.*

1991 *Hamwee,* Sally Rachel Hamwee, *b.* 1947

1999 *Hanham,* Joan Brownlow Hanham, CBE, *b.* 1939, *m.*

2014 *Harding of Winscombe,* Diana Mary (Dido) Harding, *b.* 1967, *m.*

1999 *Harris of Richmond,* Angela Felicity Harris, *b.* 1944

1996 *Hayman,* Helene Valerie Hayman, GBE, PC, *b.* 1949, *m.*

2010 *Hayter of Kentish Town,* Dr Dianne Hayter, *b.* 1949, *m.*

2010 *Healy of Primrose Hill,* Anna Healy, *b.* 1955, *m.*

2014 *Helic,* Arminka Helic, *b.* 1968

2004 *Henig,* Ruth Beatrice Henig, CBE, *b.* 1943, *m.*

1991 *Hilton of Eggardon,* Jennifer Hilton, QPM, *b.* 1936

2013 *Hodgson of Abinger,* Fiona Ferelith Hodgson, CBE, *b.* 1954, *m.*

1995 *Hogg,* Sarah Elizabeth Mary Hogg, *b.* 1946, *m.*

2010 *Hollins,* Prof. Sheila Clare Hollins, *b.* 1946, *m.*

1990 *Hollis of Heigham,* Patricia Lesley Hollis, PC, DPHIL, *b.* 1941, *m.*

1985 *Hooper,* Gloria Dorothy Hooper, CMG, *b.* 1939

2001 *Howarth of Breckland,* Valerie Georgina Howarth, OBE, *b.* 1940

2001 *Howe of Idlicote,* Elspeth Rosamond Morton Howe, CBE, *b.* 1932, *w.*

1999 *Howells of St Davids,* Rosalind Patricia-Anne Howells, OBE, *b.* 1931, *m.*

2010 *Hughes of Stretford,* Beverley Hughes, PC, *b.* 1950, *m.*

2013 *Humphreys,* Christine Mary Humphreys, *b.* 1947

2010 *Hussein-Ece,* Meral Hussein Ece, OBE, *b.* 1953

2014 *Janke,* Barbara Lilian Janke, *b.* 1947, *m.*

1992 *Jay of Paddington,* Margaret Ann Jay, PC, *b.* 1939, *m.*

2011 *Jenkin of Kennington,* Anne Caroline Jenkin, *b.* 1955, *m.*

2010 *Jolly,* Judith Anne Jolly, *b.* 1951, *m.*

2013 *Jones of Moulsecoomb,* Jennifer Helen Jones, *b.* 1949

2006 *Jones of Whitchurch,* Margaret Beryl Jones, *b.* 1955

2013 *Kennedy of Cradley,* Alicia Pamela Kennedy, *b.* 1969, *m.*

1997 *Kennedy of the Shaws,* Helena Ann Kennedy, QC, *b.* 1950, *m.*

2012 *Kidron,* Beeban Tania Kidron, OBE, *b.* 1961, *m.*

2011 *King of Bow,* Oona Tamsyn King, *b.* 1967, *m.*

2006 *Kingsmill,* Denise Patricia Byrne Kingsmill, CBE, *b.* 1947, *m.*

2009 *Kinnock of Holyhead,* Glenys Elizabeth Kinnock, *b.* 1944, *m.*

1997 ℭ*Knight of Collingtree,* (Joan Christabel) Jill Knight, DBE, *b.* 1927, *w.*

2010 *Kramer,* Susan Veronica Kramer, PC, *b.* 1950, *w.*

2013 *Lane-Fox of Soho,* Martha Lane Fox, CBE, *b.* 1973

2013 *Lawrence of Clarendon,* Doreen Delceita Lawrence, OBE, *b.* 1952

2010 *Liddell of Coatdyke,* Helen Lawrie Liddell, PC, *b.* 1950, *m.*

1997 ℭ*Linklater of Butterstone,* Veronica Linklater, *b.* 1943, *m.*

2011 *Lister of Burtersett,* Margot Ruth Aline Lister, CBE, *b.* 1949, *m.*

1978 ℭ*Lockwood,* Betty Lockwood, *b.* 1924, *w.*

1997 *Ludford,* Sarah Ann Ludford, *b.* 1951

2004 *McDonagh,* Margaret Josephine McDonagh, *b.* 1961

2015 *McGregor-Smith,* Ruby McGregor-Smith, CBE, *b.* 1963

1999 *McIntosh of Hudnall,* Genista Mary McIntosh, *b.* 1946

2015 *McIntosh of Pickering,* Anne Caroline Ballingall McIntosh, *b.* 1954, *m.*

1997 *Maddock,* Diana Margaret Maddock, *b.* 1945, *m.*

1991 *Mallalieu,* Ann Mallalieu, QC, *b.* 1945

2008 *Manningham-Buller,* Elizabeth (Lydia) Manningham-Buller, LG, DCB, *b.* 1948, *m.*

2013 *Manzoor,* Zahida Parveen Manzoor, CBE, *b.* 1958, *m.*

1970 *Masham of Ilton,* Susan Lilian Primrose Cunliffe-Lister, *b.* 1935, *w.*

1999 *Massey of Darwen,* Doreen Elizabeth Massey, *b.* 1938, *m.*

2006 *Meacher,* Molly Christine Meacher, *b.* 1940, *m.*

2018 *Meyer,* Catherine Irene Jacqueline Meyer, CBE, *b.* 1953, *m.*

1998 *Miller of Chilthorne Domer,* Susan Elizabeth Miller, *b.* 1954

2014 §*Mobarik,* Nosheena Shaheen Mobarik, CBE, MEP, *b.* 1957, *m.*

2015 *Mone,* Michelle Georgina Mone, OBE, *b.* 1971

2004 *Morgan of Drefelin,* Delyth Jane Morgan, *b.* 1961, *m.*

2011 *Morgan of Ely,* Mair Eluned Morgan, *b.* 1967, *m.*

2001 *Morgan of Huyton,* Sally Morgan, *b.* 1959, *m.*

2004 *Morris of Bolton,* Patricia Morris, OBE, *b.* 1953

2005 *Morris of Yardley,* Estelle Morris, PC, *b.* 1952

2004 *Murphy,* Elaine Murphy, *b.* 1947, *m.*

2004 *Neuberger,* Rabbi Julia (Babette Sarah) Neuberger, DBE, *b.* 1950, *m.*

2007 *Neville-Jones,* (Lilian) Pauline Neville-Jones, DCMG, PC, *b.* 1939

2013 *Neville-Rolfe,* Lucy Jeanne Neville-Rolfe, DBE, CMG, *b.* 1953, *m.*

2010 *Newlove,* Helen Margaret Newlove, *b.* 1961, *w.*

1997 *Nicholson of Winterbourne,* Emma Harriet Nicholson, *b.* 1941, *m.*

2000 *Noakes,* Sheila Valerie Masters, DBE, *b.* 1949, *m.*

2000 *Northover,* Lindsay Patricia Granshaw, PC, *b.* 1954

2010 *Nye,* Susan Nye, *b.* 1955, *m.*

1991 *O'Cathain,* Detta O'Cathain, OBE, *b.* 1938, *w.*

2009 *O'Loan,* Nuala Patricia O'Loan, DBE, *b.* 1951, *m.*

1999 *O'Neill of Bengarve,* Onora Sylvia O'Neill, CH, CBE, FRS, FBA, *b.* 1941

1989 *Oppenheim-Barnes,* Sally Oppenheim-Barnes, PC, *b.* 1930, *m.*

2018 ‡*Osamor,* Martha Osamor, *b.* 1940, *w.*

2006 ℭ*Paisley of St George's,* Eileen Emily Paisley, *b.* 1931, *w.*

2010 *Parminter,* Kathryn Jane Parminter, *b.* 1964, *m.*

1991 ℭ*Perry of Southwark,* Pauline Perry, *b.* 1931, *m.*

2015 *Pidding,* Emma Samantha Pidding, CBE, *b.* 1966

2014 *Pinnock,* Kathryn Mary Pinnock, *b.* 1946, *m.*

1997 *Pitkeathley,* Jill Elizabeth Pitkeathley, OBE, *b.* 1940

1999 *Prashar,* Usha Kumari Prashar, CBE, PC, *b.* 1948, *m.*

2015	*Primarolo*, Dawn Primarolo, DBE, PC, *b.* 1954, *m.*	1996	*Symons of Vernham Dean*, Elizabeth Conway Symons, PC, *b.* 1951, *w.*
2004	*Prosser*, Margaret Theresa Prosser, OBE, *b.* 1937		
2006	*Quin*, Joyce Gwendoline Quin, PC, *b.* 1944	2005	*Taylor of Bolton*, Winifred Ann Taylor, PC, *b.* 1947, *m.*
1996	*Ramsay of Cartvale*, Margaret Mildred (Meta) Ramsay, *b.* 1936	1994	**E.** *Thomas of Walliswood*, Susan Petronella Thomas, OBE, *b.* 1935, *m.*
2011	*Randerson*, Jennifer Elizabeth Randerson, *b.* 1948, *m.*	2006	*Thomas of Winchester*, Celia Marjorie Thomas, MBE, *b.* 1945
1994	*Rawlings*, Patricia Elizabeth Rawlings, *b.* 1939		
2014	*Rebuck*, Gail Ruth Rebuck, DBE, *b.* 1952, *w.*	2015	*Thornhill*, Dorothy Thornhill, MBE, *b.* 1955, *m.*
2015	*Redfern*, Elizabeth Marie Redfern, *b.* 1947	1998	*Thornton*, (Dorothea) Glenys Thornton, *b.* 1952, *m.*
1998	*Richardson of Calow*, Kathleen Margaret Richardson, OBE, *b.* 1938, *m.*	2005	*Tonge*, Dr Jennifer Louise Tonge, *b.* 1941, *m.*
2015	*Rock*, Kate Harriet Alexandra Rock, *b.* 1968, *m.*	1980	₵*Trumpington*, Jean Alys Barker, DCVO, PC, *b.* 1922, *w.*
2004	*Royall of Blaisdon*, Janet Anne Royall, PC, *b.* 1955, *m.*	2011	*Tyler of Enfield*, Claire Tyler, *b.* 1957
2018	*Sater*, Amanda Jacqueline Sater	1998	*Uddin*, Manzila Pola Uddin, *b.* 1959, *m.*
1997	*Scotland of Asthal*, Patricia Janet Scotland, PC, QC, *b.* 1955, *m.*	2007	*Vadera*, Shriti Vadera, PC, *b.* 1962
2015	*Scott of Bybrook*, Jane Antoinette Scott, OBE, *b.* 1947, *m.*	2005	*Valentine*, Josephine Clare Valentine, *b.* 1958, *m.*
		2016	*Vere of Norbiton*, Charlotte Sarah Emily Vere, *b.* 1969
2000	*Scott of Needham Market*, Rosalind Carol Scott, *b.* 1957	2006	*Verma*, Sandip Verma, *b.* 1959, *m.*
1991	*Seccombe*, Joan Anna Dalziel Seccombe, DBE, *b.* 1930, *w.*	2000	*Walmsley*, Joan Margaret Walmsley, *b.* 1943
		1985	₵*Warnock*, Helen Mary Warnock, CH, DBE, *b.* 1924, *w.*
2010	*Shackleton of Belgravia*, Fiona Sara Shackleton, LVO, *b.* 1956, *m.*	2007	*Warsi*, Sayeeda Hussain Warsi, PC, *b.* 1971
1998	₵*Sharp of Guildford*, Margaret Lucy Sharp, *b.* 1938, *m.*	1999	*Warwick of Undercliffe*, Diana Mary Warwick, *b.* 1945, *m.*
1973	₵*Sharples*, Pamela Sharples, *b.* 1923, *w.*	2015	*Watkins of Tavistock*, Mary Jane Watkins, PHD, *b.* 1955
2015	*Sheehan*, Shaista Ahmad Sheehan, *b.* 1959, *m.*	2010	*Wheatcroft*, Patience Jane Wheatcroft, *b.* 1951, *m.*
2005	*Shephard of Northwold*, Gillian Patricia Shephard, PC, *b.* 1940, *m.*	2010	*Wheeler*, Margaret Eileen Joyce Wheeler, MBE, *b.* 1949
2010	*Sherlock*, Maeve Christina Mary Sherlock, OBE, *b.* 1960	1999	*Whitaker*, Janet Alison Whitaker, *b.* 1936
2014	*Shields*, Joanna Shields, OBE, *b.* 1962, *m.*	1996	*Wilcox*, Judith Ann Wilcox, *b.* 1940, *w.*
2010	*Smith of Basildon*, Angela Evans Smith, PC, *b.* 1959, *m.*	1999	₵*Wilkins*, Rosalie Catherine Wilkins, *b.* 1946
		1993	₵*Williams of Crosby*, Shirley Vivien Teresa Brittain Williams, CH, PC, *b.* 1930, *w.*
1995	*Smith of Gilmorehill*, Elizabeth Margaret Smith, *b.* 1940, *w.*	2013	*Williams of Trafford*, Susan Frances Maria Williams, *b.* 1967, *m.*
2014	*Smith of Newnham*, Dr Julie Elizabeth Smith, *b.* 1969	2014	*Wolf of Dulwich*, Alison Margaret Wolf, CBE, *b.* 1949, *m.*
2010	*Stedman-Scott*, Deborah Stedman-Scott, OBE, *b.* 1955	2011	*Worthington*, Bryony Katherine Worthington, *b.* 1971, *m.*
1999	*Stern*, Vivien Helen Stern, CBE, *b.* 1941	2017	*Wyld*, Laura Lee Wyld, *b.* 1978
2011	*Stowell of Beeston*, Tina Wendy Stowell, MBE, PC, *b.* 1967	2004	*Young of Hornsey*, Prof. Margaret Omolola Young, OBE, *b.* 1951, *m.*
2015	*Stroud*, Philippa Claire Stroud, *b.* 1965, *m.*	1997	*Young of Old Scone*, Barbara Scott Young, *b.* 1948
2016	*Sugg*, Elizabeth Grace Sugg, CBE, *b.* 1977		
2013	*Suttie*, Alison Mary Suttie, *b.* 1968		

COURTESY TITLES

The heir apparent to a Duke, Marquess or Earl uses the highest of his father's other titles as a courtesy title. For example, the Marquess of Blandford is heir to the Dukedom of Marlborough, and Viscount Amberley to the Earldom of Russell. Titles of second heirs (when in use) are also given, and the courtesy title of the father of a second heir is indicated by * eg Earl of Mornington, eldest son of *Marquess of Douro.

The holder of a courtesy title is not styled 'the Most Hon.' or 'the Rt. Hon.', and in correspondence 'the' is omitted before the title. The heir apparent to a Scottish title may use the title 'Master'.

MARQUESSES
Blandford – *Marlborough, D.*
Bowmont and Cessford – *Roxburghe, D.*
Douglas and Clydesdale – *Hamilton and Brandon, D.*
*Douro – *Wellington, D.*
Graham – *Montrose, D.*
Granby – *Rutland, D.*
*Hamilton – *Abercorn, D.*
Lorne – *Argyll, D.*
Stafford – *Sutherland, D.*

Tavistock – *Bedford, D.*
Tullibardine – *Atholl, D.*
Worcester – *Beaufort, D.*

EARLS
*Aboyne – *Huntly, M.*
Altamont – *Sligo, M.*
Arundel and Surrey – *Norfolk, D.*
Bective – *Headfort, M.*
Belfast – *Donegall, M.*
Brecknock – *Camden, M.*

*Burford – *St Albans, D.*
*Burlington – *Devonshire, D.*
*Cardigan – *Ailesbury, M.*
Cassilis – *Ailsa, M.*
Compton – *Northampton, M.*
Dalkeith – *Buccleuch and Queensberry, D.*
Dumfries – *Bute, M.*
Euston – *Grafton, D.*
*Haddo – *Aberdeen and Temair, M.*
Hillsborough – *Downshire, M.*

*Hopetoun – *Linlithgow, M.*
Kerry – *Lansdowne, M.*
March and Kinrara – *Richmond, Gordon and Lennox, D.*
Medina – *Milford Haven, M.*
Mornington – *Douro, M.*
*Mount Charles – *Conyngham, M.*
Mulgrave – *Normanby, M.*
Percy – *Northumberland, D.*

Rocksavage – *Cholmondeley,*
M.
Ronaldshay – *Zetland, M.*
*St Andrews – *Kent, D.*
Southesk – *Fife, D.*
Tyrone – *Waterford, M.*
*Ulster – *Gloucester, D.*
Uxbridge – *Anglesey, M.*
*Wiltshire – *Winchester, M.*
Yarmouth – *Hertford, M.*

VISCOUNTS
Aithrie – *Hopetoun, E.*
Alexander – *Caledon, E.*
Althorp – *Spencer, E.*
Andover – *Suffolk and*
Berkshire, E.
Anson – *Lichfield, E.*
Asquith – *Oxford and Asquith,*
E.
Borodale – *Beatty, E.*
Bury – *Albemarle, E.*
Campden – *Gainsborough, E.*
Carlow – *Portarlington, E.*
Carlton – *Wharncliffe, E.*
Chelsea – *Cadogan, E.*
Chewton – *Waldegrave, E.*
Clanfield – *Peel, E.*
Clive – *Powis, E.*
Coke – *Leicester, E.*
Corry – *Belmore, E.*
Corvedale – *Baldwin of*
Bewdley, E.
Cranborne – *Salisbury, M.*
Curzon – *Howe, E.*
Dalrymple – *Stair, E.*
Dangan – *Cowley, E.*
Drumlanrig – *Queensberry, M.*
Duncannon – *Bessborough, E.*
Dungarvan – *Cork and Orrery,*
E.
Dunluce – *Antrim, E.*
Dunwich – *Stradbroke, E.*
Dupplin – *Kinnoull, E.*
Elveden – *Iveagh, E.*
Emlyn – *Cawdor, E.*
Encombe – *Eldon, E.*

Enfield – *Strafford, E.*
Erleigh – *Reading, M.*
Errington – *Cromer, E.*
Feilding – *Denbigh and*
Desmond, E.
FitzHarris – *Malmesbury, E.*
Folkestone – *Radnor, E.*
Forbes – *Granard, E.*
Formartine – *Haddo, E.*
Garmoyle – *Cairns, E.*
Garnock – *Lindsay, E.*
Glenapp – *Inchcape, E.*
Glentworth – *Limerick, E.*
Glerawly – *Annesley, E.*
Grey de Wilton – *Wilton, E.*
Grimston – *Verulam, E.*
Gwynedd – *Lloyd George of*
Dwyfor, E.
Hawkesbury – *Liverpool, E.*
Hinchingbrooke – *Sandwich,*
E.
Howick – *Grey, E.*
Ikerrin – *Carrick, E.*
Ingestre – *Shrewsbury and*
Waterford, E.
Jocelyn – *Roden, E.*
Kelburn – *Glasgow, E.*
Kingsborough – *Kingston, E.*
Kirkwall – *Orkney, E.*
Knebworth – *Lytton, E.*
Lambton – *Durham, E.*
Lascelles – *Harewood, E.*
Linley – *Snowdon, E.*
Lymington – *Portsmouth, E.*
Macmillan of Ovenden –
Stockton, E.
Maidstone – *Winchilsea and*
Nottingham, E.
Maitland – *Lauderdale, E.*
Marsham – *Romney, E.*
Melgund – *Minto, E.*
Merton – *Nelson, E.*
Moore – *Drogheda, E.*
Newport – *Bradford, E.*
Newry and Mourne –
Kilmorey, E.
Northland – *Ranfurly, E.*
Petersham – *Harrington, E.*

Pollington – *Mexborough, E.*
Raynham – *Townshend, M.*
Reidhaven – *Seafield, E.*
Royston – *Hardwicke, E.*
Ruthven of Canberra –
Gowrie, E.
St Cyres – *Iddesleigh, E.*
Sandon – *Harrowby, E.*
Savernake – *Cardigan, E.*
Severn – *Wessex, E.*
Slane – *Mount Charles, E.*
Somerton – *Normanton, E.*
Stopford – *Courtown, E.*
Stormont – *Mansfield and*
Mansfield, E.
Strabane – *Hamilton, M.*
Strathallan – *Perth, E.*
Stuart – *Castle Stewart, E.*
Suirdale – *Donoughmore, E.*
Tamworth – *Ferrers, E.*
Tarbat – *Cromartie, E.*
Villiers – *Jersey, E.*
Weymouth – *Bath, M.*
Windsor – *Plymouth, E.*
Wolmer – *Selborne, E.*
Woodstock – *Portland, E.*

BARONS (LORDS)
Aberdour – *Morton, E.*
Apsley – *Bathurst, E.*
Ardee – *Meath, E.*
Ashley – *Shaftesbury, E.*
Balniel – *Crawford and*
Balcarres, E.
Berriedale – *Caithness, E.*
Brabourne – *Mountbatten of*
Burma, E.
Brooke – *Warwick and Brooke,*
E.
Bruce – *Elgin and Kincardine,*
E.
Buckhurst – *De La Warr, E.*
Burghley – *Exeter, M.*
Cardross – *Buchan, E.*
Cavendish – *Burlington, E.*
Clifton – *Darnley, E.*
Cochrane – *Dundonald, E.*

Courtenay – *Devon, E.*
Culloden – *Ulster, E.*
Dalmeny – *Rosebery, E.*
Doune – *Moray, E.*
Downpatrick – *St Andrews, E.*
Dunglass – *Home, E.*
Elcho – *Wemyss and March, E.*
Gillford – *Clanwilliam, E.*
Greenock – *Cathcart, E.*
Guernsey – *Aylesford, E.*
Hay – *Erroll, E.*
Herbert – *Pembroke and*
Montgomery, E.
Howard of Effingham –
Effingham, E.
Huntingtower – *Dysart, E.*
Hyde – *Clarendon, E.*
Inverurie – *Kintore, E.*
Irwin – *Halifax, E.*
Johnstone – *Annandale and*
Hartfell, E.
Leveson – *Granville, E.*
Loughborough – *Rosslyn, E.*
Masham – *Swinton, E.*
Medway – *Cranbrook, E.*
Montgomerie – *Eglinton and*
Winton, E.
Moreton – *Ducie, E.*
Naas – *Mayo, E.*
Norreys – *Lindsey and*
Abingdon, E.
North – *Guilford, E.*
Ogilvy – *Airlie, E.*
Oxmantown – *Rosse, E.*
Porchester – *Carnarvon, E.*
Ramsay – *Dalhousie, E.*
St John – *Wiltshire, E.*
Scrymgeour – *Dundee, E.*
Seymour – *Somerset, D.*
Stanley – *Derby, E.*
Stavordale – *Ilchester, E.*
Strathavon – *Aboyne, E.*
Strathnaver – *Sutherland, C.*
Vere of Hanworth – *Burford,*
E.
Wodehouse – *Kimberley, E.*
Worsley – *Yarborough, E.*

PEERS' SURNAMES

The following symbols
indicate the rank of the peer
holding each title:

C. Countess
D. Duke
E. Earl
M. Marquess
V. Viscount
* Life Peer

Where no designation is
given, the title is that of a
hereditary Baron or Baroness.
Abney-Hastings – *Loudoun, E.*
Acheson – *Gosford, E.*
Adams – *A. of Craigielea*

Adderley – *Norton*
Addington – *Sidmouth, V.*
Agar – *Normanton, E.*
Agnew – *A. of Oulton*
Ahmad – *A. of Wimbledon*
Aitken – *Beaverbrook*
Akers-Douglas – *Chilston, V.*
Alexander – *A. of Tunis, E.*
Alexander – *A. Caledon, E.*
Allan – *A. of Hallam*
Allen – *A. of Kensington*
Allsopp – *Hindlip*
Alton – *A. of Liverpool*
Anderson – *A. of Ipswich*
Anderson – *A. of Swansea*
Anderson – *Waverley, V.*

Anelay – *A. of St Johns*
Annesley – *Valentia, V.*
Anson – *Lichfield, E.*
Arbuthnot – *A. of Edrom*
Archer – *A. of Weston-super-*
Mare
Armstrong – *A. of Hill Top*
Armstrong – *A. of Ilminster*
Armstrong-Jones – *Snowdon,*
E.
Arthur – *Glenarthur*
Arundell – *Talbot of Malahide*
Ashdown – *A. of Norton-sub-*
Hamdon
Ashley-Cooper – *Shaftesbury,*
E.

Ashton – *A. of Hyde*
Ashton – *A. of Upholland*
Asquith – *Oxford and Asquith,*
E.
Assheton – *Clitheroe*
Astley – *Hastings*
Astor – *A. of Hever*
Aubrey-Fletcher – *Braye*
Bailey – *Glanusk*
Baillie – *Burton*
Baillie Hamilton – *Haddington,*
E.
Baker – *B. of Dorking*
Bakewell – *B. of Hardington*
Mandeville
Balchin – *Lingfield*

Baldwin – *B. of Bewdley, E.*
Balfour – *Kinross*
Balfour – *Riverdale*
Bampfylde – *Poltimore*
Banbury – *B. of Southam*
Baring – *Ashburton*
Baring – *Cromer, E.*
Baring – *Howick of Glendale*
Baring – *Northbrook*
Baring – *Revelstoke*
Barker – *B. of Battle*
Barker – *Trumpington*
Barnes – *Gorell*
Barnewall – *Trimlestown*
Bassam – *B. of Brighton*
Bathurst – *Bledisloe, V.*
Beamish – *Dacre*
Beauclerk – *St Albans, D.*
Beaumont – *Allendale, V.*
Beckett – *Grimthorpe*
Benn – *Stansgate, V.*
Bennet – *Tankerville, E.*
Bentinck – *Portland, E.*
Beresford – *Decies*
Beresford – *Waterford, M.*
Berkeley – *B. of Knighton*
Berry – *Camrose, V.*
Berry – *Kemsley, V.*
Bertie – *Lindsey and Abingdon, E.*
Best – *Wynford*
Bethell – *Westbury*
Bewicke-Copley – *Cromwell*
Bigham – *Mersey, V.*
Bingham – *Clanmorris*
Bingham – *Lucan, E.*
Bishop – *Glendonbrook*
Black – *B. of Brentwood*
Black – *B. of Crossharbour*
Blackwood – *Dufferin and Clandeboye*
Blair – *B. of Boughton*
Bligh – *Darnley, E.*
Bloomfield – *B. of Hinton Waldrist*
Blyth – *B. of Rowington*
Bonham Carter – *B.-C. of Yarnbury*
Bootle-Wilbraham – *Skelmersdale*
Boscawen – *Falmouth, V.*
Boswell – *B. of Aynho*
Bottomley – *B. of Nettlestone*
Bourke – *Mayo, E.*
Bourne – *B. of Aberystwyth*
Bowes Lyon – *Strathmore and Kinghorne, E.*
Bowles – *B. of Berkhamsted*
Bowyer – *Denham*
Boyd – *B. of Duncansby*
Boyd – *Kilmarnock*
Boyle – *Cork and Orrery, E.*
Boyle – *Glasgow, E.*
Boyle – *Shannon, E.*
Brabazon – *Meath, E.*
Brand – *Hampden, V.*
Brassey – *B. of Apethorpe*
Bryan – *B. of Partick*
Brett – *Esher, V.*

Bridgeman – *Bradford, E.*
Brodrick – *Midleton, V.*
Brooke – *B. of Alverthorpe*
Brooke – *B. of Sutton Mandeville*
Brooke – *Brookeborough, V.*
Brooks – *Crawshaw*
Brougham – *Brougham and Vaux*
Broughton – *Fairhaven*
Brown – *B. of Eaton-under-Heywood*
Browne – *B. of Belmont*
Browne – *B. of Ladyton*
Browne – *B. of Madingley*
Browne – *Kilmaine*
Browne – *Oranmore and Browne*
Browne – *Sligo, M.*
Bruce – *Aberdare*
Bruce – *Balfour of Burleigh*
Bruce – *B. of Bennachie*
Bruce – *Elgin and Kincardine, E.*
Brudenell-Bruce – *Ailesbury, M.*
Buchan – *Tweedsmuir*
Buckley – *Wrenbury*
Burnett – *B. of Maldon*
Burt – *B. of Solihull*
Butler – *B. of Brockwell*
Butler – *Carrick, E.*
Butler – *Dunboyne*
Butler – *Mountgarret, V.*
Byng – *Strafford, E.*
Byng – *Torrington, V.*
Cameron – *C. of Dillington*
Cameron – *C. of Lochbroom*
Campbell – *Argyll, D.*
Campbell – *C. of Loughborough*
Campbell – *C. of Pittenweem*
Campbell – *C. of Surbiton*
Campbell – *Cawdor, E.*
Campbell – *Colgrain*
Campbell – *Stratheden and Campbell*
Campbell-Gray – *Gray*
Canning – *Garvagh*
Capell – *Essex, E.*
Carey – *C. of Clifton*
Carington – *Carrington*
Carlisle – *C. of Berriew*
Carnegie – *Fife, D.*
Carnegy – *Northesk, E.*
Carrington – *C. of Fulham*
Carter – *C. of Barnes*
Carter – *C. of Coles*
Cary – *Falkland, V.*
Caulfeild – *Charlemont, V.*
Cavendish – *C. of Furness*
Cavendish – *C. of Little Venice*
Cavendish – *Chesham*
Cavendish – *Devonshire, D.*
Cavendish – *Waterpark*
Cayzer – *Rotherwick*
Cecil – *Amherst of Hackney*
Cecil – *Exeter, M.*

Cecil – *Rockley*
Chalker – *C. of Wallasey*
Chaloner – *Gisborough*
Charteris – *Wemyss and March, E.*
Chetwynd-Talbot – *Shrewsbury and Waterford, E.*
Chichester – *Donegall, M.*
Child Villiers – *Jersey, E.*
Chisholm – *C. of Owlpen*
Cholmondeley – *Delamere*
Chubb – *Hayter*
Clark – *C. of Calton*
Clarke – *C. of Hampstead*
Clarke – *C. of Stone-Cum-Ebony*
Clegg-Hill – *Hill, V.*
Clifford – *C. of Chudleigh*
Cochrane – *C. of Cults*
Cochrane – *Dundonald, E.*
Cocks – *Somers*
Cohen – *C. of Pimlico*
Cokayne – *Cullen of Ashbourne*
Coke – *Leicester, E.*
Cole – *Enniskillen, E.*
Collier – *Monkswell*
Collins – *C. of Highbury*
Collins – *C. of Mapesbury*
Colville – *Clydesmuir*
Colville – *C. of Culross, V.*
Compton – *Northampton, M.*
Conolly-Carew – *Carew*
Cooke – *Lexden*
Cooper – *C. of Windrush*
Cooper – *Norwich, V.*
Cope – *C. of Berkeley*
Corbett – *Rowallan*
Cornwall-Legh – *Grey of Codnor*
Courtenay – *Devon, E.*
Craig – *C. of Radley*
Craig – *Craigavon, V.*
Crichton – *Erne, E.*
Crichton-Stuart – *Bute, M.*
Cripps – *Parmoor*
Crossley – *Somerleyton*
Cubitt – *Ashcombe*
Cunliffe-Lister – *Masham of Ilton*
Cunliffe-Lister – *Swinton, E.*
Cunningham – *C. of Felling*
Currie – *C. of Marylebone*
Curry – *C. of Kirkharle*
Curzon – *Howe, E.*
Curzon – *Scarsdale, V.*
Cust – *Brownlow*
Czernin – *Howard de Walden*
Dalrymple – *Stair, E.*
Darling – *D. of Roulanish*
Darzi – *D. of Denham*
Daubeny de Moleyns – *Ventry*
Davidson – *D. of Glen Clova*
Davies – *Darwen*
Davies – *D. of Abersoch*
Davies – *D. of Coity*
Davies – *D. of Oldham*
Davies – *D. of Stamford*
Dawnay – *Downe, V.*

Dawson-Damer – *Portarlington, E.*
Deane – *Muskerry*
de Courcy – *Kingsale*
de Grey – *Walsingham*
Denison – *Londesborough*
Denison-Pender – *Pender*
Devereux – *Hereford, V.*
Dewar – *Forteviot*
Dixon – *Glentoran*
Dodson – *Monk Bretton*
Douglas – *Morton, E.*
Douglas – *Queensberry, M.*
Douglas-Hamilton – *Hamilton and Brandon, D.*
Douglas-Hamilton – *Selkirk, E.*
Douglas-Hamilton – *Selkirk of Douglas*
Douglas-Home – *Home, E.*
Douglas-Pennant – *Penrhyn*
Douglas-Scott-Montagu – *Montagu of Beaulieu*
Drummond – *Perth, E.*
Drummond of Megginch – *Strange*
Dugdale – *Crathorne*
Duke – *Merrivale*
Duncan – *D. of Springbank*
Duncombe – *Feversham*
Dundas – *Melville, V.*
Dundas – *Zetland, M.*
Eady – *Swinfen*
Eccles – *E. of Moulton*
Ece – *Hussein-Ece*
Eden – *Auckland*
Eden – *E. of Winton*
Eden – *Henley*
Edgcumbe – *Mount Edgcumbe, E.*
Edmondson – *Sandford*
Edwardes – *Kensington*
Egerton – *Sutherland, D.*
Eliot – *St Germans, E.*
Elliot-Murray-Kynynmound – *Minto, E.*
Ellis – *Seaford*
Erskine – *Buchan, E.*
Erskine – *Mar and Kellie, E.*
Erskine-Murray – *Elibank*
Evans – *E. of Bowes Park*
Evans – *E. of Watford*
Evans – *E. of Weardale*
Evans – *Mountevans*
Evans-Freke – *Carbery*
Eve – *Silsoe*
Fairfax – *F. of Cameron*
Falconer – *F. of Thoroton*
Falkner – *F. of Margravine*
Fane – *Westmorland, E.*
Faulkner – *F. of Worcester*
Feilding – *Denbigh and Desmond, E.*
Feldman – *F. of Elstree*
Fellowes – *De Ramsey*
Fellowes – *F. of West Stafford*
Fermor-Hesketh – *Hesketh*
Fiennes – *Saye and Sele*
Fiennes-Clinton – *Lincoln, E.*

Finch Hatton – *Winchilsea and Nottingham, E.*

Finch-Knightley – *Aylesford, E.*

Finlay – *F. of Llandaff*★

Fitzalan-Howard – *Norfolk, D.*

FitzGerald – *Leinster, D.*

Fitzherbert – *Stafford*

FitzRoy – *Grafton, D.*

FitzRoy – *Southampton*

FitzRoy Newdegate – *Daventry, V.*

Fletcher-Vane – *Inglewood*

Flower – *Ashbrook, V.*

Foljambe – *Liverpool, E.*

Forbes – *Granard, E.*

Forsyth – *F. of Drumlean*★

Forwood – *Arlington*

Foster – *F. of Bath*★

Foster – *F. of Bishop Auckland*★

Foster – *F. of Thames Bank*★

Foulkes – *F. of Cumnock*★

Fox-Strangways – *Ilchester, E.*

Frankland – *Zouche*

Fraser – *F. of Corriegarth*★

Fraser – *Lovat*

Fraser – *Saltoun*

Fraser – *Strathalmond*

Freeman-Grenville – *Kinloss*

Fremantle – *Cottesloe*

French – *De Freyne*

Galbraith – *Strathclyde*

Garden – *G. of Frognal*★

Gardiner – *G. of Kimble*★

Gardner – *G. of Parkes*★

Gascoyne-Cecil – *Salisbury, M.*

Gathorne-Hardy – *Cranbrook, E.*

Gibbs – *Aldenham*

Gibbs – *Wraxall*

Gibson – *Ashbourne*

Gilbert – *G. of Panteg*★

Gilbey – *Vaux of Harrowden*

Glyn – *Wolverton*

Goddard – *G. of Stockport*★

Godley – *Kilbracken*

Golding – *G. of Newcastle-under-Lyme*★

Gordon – *Aberdeen and Temair, M.*

Gordon – *G. of Strathblane*★

Gordon – *Huntly, M.*

Gordon Lennox – *Richmond, Gordon and Lennox, D.*

Gore – *Arran, E.*

Gould – *G. of Potternewton*★

Grade – *G. of Yarmouth*★

Graham – *G. of Edmonton*★

Graham – *Montrose, D.*

Graham-Toler – *Norbury, E.*

Granshaw – *Northover*★

Grant of Grant – *Strathspey*

Grant of Rothiemurchus – *Dysart, E.*

Green – *G. of Deddington*★

Green – *G. of Hurstpierpoint*★

Greenall – *Daresbury*

Greville – *Warwick and Brooke, E.*

Griffiths – *G. of Burry Port*★

Griffiths – *G. of Fforestfach*★

Grigg – *Altrincham*

Grimston – *G. of Westbury*

Grimston – *Verulam, E.*

Grosvenor – *Westminster, D.*

Grosvenor – *Wilton, E.*

Guest – *Wimborne, V.*

Gueterbock – *Berkeley*

Guinness – *Iveagh, E.*

Guinness – *Moyne*

Gully – *Selby, V.*

Gummer – *Chadlington*★

Gummer – *Deben*★

Gurdon – *Cranworth*

Guthrie – *G. of Craigiebank*★

Gwynne Jones – *Chalfont*★

Hague – *H. of Richmond*★

Hale – *H. of Richmond*★

Hall – *H. of Birkenhead*★

Hamilton – *Abercorn, D.*

Hamilton – *Belhaven and Stenton*

Hamilton – *H. of Dalzell*

Hamilton – *H. of Epsom*★

Hamilton – *Holm Patrick*

Hamilton-Russell – *Boyne, V.*

Hamilton-Smith – *Colwyn*

Hanbury-Tracy – *Sudeley*

Handcock – *Castlemaine*

Hannay – *H. of Chiswick*★

Harbord-Hamond – *Suffield*

Harding – *H. of Petherton*

Harding – *H. of Winscombe*★

Hardinge – *H. of Penshurst*

Hare – *Blakenham, V.*

Hare – *Listowel, E.*

Harmsworth – *Rothermere, V.*

Harries – *H. of Pentregarth*★

Harris – *H. of Haringey*★

Harris – *H. of Peckham*★

Harris – *H. of Richmond*★

Harris – *Malmesbury, E.*

Harvey – *H. of Tasburgh*

Hastings – *H. of Scarisbrick*★

Hastings Bass – *Huntingdon, E.*

Hay – *Erroll, E.*

Hay – *H. of Ballyore*★

Hay – *Kinnoull, E.*

Hay – *Tweeddale, M.*

Hayter – *H. of Kentish Town*★

Healy – *H. of Primrose Hill*★

Heathcote-Drummond-Willoughby – *Willoughby de Eresby*

Hely-Hutchinson – *Donoughmore, E.*

Henderson – *Faringdon*

Hennessy – *H. of Nympsfield*★

Hennessy – *Windlesham*

Henniker-Major – *Henniker*

Hepburne-Scott – *Polwarth*

Herbert – *Carnarvon, E.*

Herbert – *Hemingford*

Herbert – *Pembroke and Montgomery, E.*

Herbert – *Powis, E.*

Hervey – *Bristol, M.*

Hewitt – *Lifford, V.*

Hicks Beach – *St Aldwyn, E.*

Hill – *Downshire, M.*

Hill – *H. of Oareford*★

Hill-Trevor – *Trevor*

Hilton – *H. of Eggardon*★

Hobart-Hampden – *Buckinghamshire, E.*

Hodgson – *H. of Abinger*★

Hodgson – *H. of Astley Abbotts*★

Hogg – *Hailsham, V.*

Holland-Hibbert – *Knutsford, V.*

Hollis – *H. of Heigham*★

Holmes – *H. of Richmond*★

Holmes à Court – *Heytesbury*

Hood – *Bridport, V.*

Hope – *Glendevon*

Hope – *H. of Craighead*★

Hope – *H. of Thornes*★

Hope – *Linlithgow, M.*

Hope – *Rankeillour*

Hope Johnstone – *Annandale and Hartfell, E.*

Hope-Morley – *Hollenden*

Hopkinson – *Colyton*

Hore Ruthven – *Gowrie, E.*

Houghton – *H. of Richmond*★

Hovell-Thurlow-Cumming-Bruce – *Thurlow*

Howard – *Carlisle, E.*

Howard – *Effingham, E.*

Howard – *H. of Lympne*★

Howard – *H. of Penrith*

Howard – *H. of Rising*★

Howard – *Strathcona and Mount Royal*

Howard – *Suffolk and Berkshire, E.*

Howarth – *H. of Breckland*★

Howarth – *H. of Newport*★

Howe – *H. of Idlicote*★

Howell – *H. of Guildford*★

Howells – *H. of St. Davids*★

Hubbard – *Addington*

Huggins – *Malvern, V.*

Hughes – *H. of Stretford*★

Hughes – *H. of Woodside*★

Hughes-Young – *St Helens*

Hunt – *H. of Chesterton*★

Hunt – *H. of Kings Heath*★

Hunt – *H. of Wirral*★

Hurd – *H. of Westwell*★

Hutton – *H. of Furness*★

Ingrams – *Darcy de Knayth*

Innes-Ker – *Roxburghe, D.*

Inskip – *Caldecote, V.*

Irby – *Boston*

Irvine – *I. of Lairg*★

Isaacs – *Reading, M.*

James – *J. of Blackheath*★

James – *Northbourne*

Jay – *J. of Ewelme*★

Jay – *J. of Paddington*★

Jenkin – *J. of Kennington*★

Jervis – *St Vincent, V.*

Jocelyn – *Roden, E.*

Jolliffe – *Hylton*

Jones – *J. of Birmingham*★

Jones – *J. of Cheltenham*★

Jones – *J. of Moulsecoomb*★

Jones – *J. of Whitchurch*★

Joynson-Hicks – *Brentford, V.*

Kay-Shuttleworth – *Shuttleworth*

Kearley – *Devonport, V.*

Keith – *Kintore, E.*

Kemp – *Rochdale, V.*

Kennedy – *Ailsa, M.*

Kennedy – *K. of Cradley*★

Kennedy – *K. of Southwark*★

Kennedy – *K. of the Shaws*★

Kenworthy – *Strabolgi*

Keppel – *Albemarle, E.*

Kerr – *Herries of Terregles*

Kerr – *K. of Kinlochard*★

Kerr – *K. of Tonaghmore*★

Kerr – *Lothian, M. / K. of Monteviot*★

Kerr – *Teviot*

King – *Brown of Cambridge*★

King – *K. of Bow*★

King – *K. of Lothbury*★

King-Tenison – *Kingston, E.*

Kinnock – *K. of Holyhead*★

Kirkham – *Berners*

Kirkhope – *K. of Harrogate*★

Kirkwood – *K. of Kirkhope*★

Knatchbull – *Brabourne*

Knatchbull – *Mountbatten of Burma, E.*

Knight – *K. of Collingtree*★

Knight – *K. of Weymouth*★

Knox – *Ranfurly, E.*

Lamb – *Rochester*

Lambart – *Cavan, E.*

Lambton – *Durham, E.*

Lamont – *L. of Lerwick*★

Lampson – *Killearn*

Lane Fox – *L.-F. of Soho*★

Lang – *L. of Monkton*★

Lascelles – *Harewood, E.*

Law – *Coleraine*

Law – *Ellenborough*

Lawrence – *L. of Clarendon*★

Lawrence – *Trevethin and Oaksey*

Lawson – *Burnham*

Lawson – *L. of Blaby*★

Lawson Johnston – *Luke*

Lea – *L. of Crondall*★

Lee – *L. of Trafford*★

Legge – *Dartmouth, E.*

Legh – *Newton*

Leigh – *L. of Hurley*★

Leith – *Burgh*

Lennox-Boyd – *Boyd of Merton, V.*

Le Poer Trench – *Clancarty, E.*

Leslie – *Rothes, E.*

Leslie Melville – *Leven and Melville, E.*

Lester – *L. of Herne Hill*★

Levene – *L. of Portsoken*★

Leveson-Gower – *Granville, E.*

Lewis – *Merthyr*

Liddell – *L. of Coatdyke*★

Liddell – *Ravensworth*

Lindesay-Bethune – *Lindsay, E.*

Lindsay – *Crawford and Balcarres, E.*

Lindsay – *L. of Birker*

Linklater – *L. of Butterstone*

Lister – *L. of Burtersett*

Littleton – *Hatherton*

Livingston – *L. of Parkhead*

Llewellyn – *L. of Steep*

Lloyd – *L. of Berwick*

Lloyd George – *Lloyd George of Dwyfor, E.*

Lloyd George – *Tenby, V.*

Lloyd-Mostyn – *Mostyn*

Loder – *Wakehurst*

Lopes – *Roborough*

Lord – *Framlingham*

Low – *Aldington*

Low – *L. of Dalston*

Lowry-Corry – *Belmore, E.*

Lowther – *Lonsdale, E.*

Lowther – *Ullswater, V.*

Lubbock – *Avebury*

Lucas – *L. of Chilworth*

Lumley – *Scarbrough, E.*

Lumley-Savile – *Savile*

Lyon-Dalberg-Acton – *Acton*

Lysaght – *Lisle*

Lyttelton – *Chandos, V.*

Lyttelton – *Cobham, V.*

Lytton Cobbold – *Cobbold*

McClintock-Bunbury – *Rathdonnell*

McColl – *M. of Dulwich*

McConnell – *M. of Glenscorrodale*

McCrea – *M. of Magherafelt and Cookstown*

Macdonald – *M. of River Glaven*

Macdonald – *M. of Tradeston*

McDonnell – *Antrim, E.*

McFall – *M. of Alcluith*

Macfarlane – *M. of Bearsden*

MacGregor – *M. of Pulham Market*

McInnes – *M. of Kilwinning*

McIntosh – *M. of Hudnall*

McIntosh – *M. of Pickering*

Mackay – *Inchcape, E.*

Mackay – *M. of Clashfern*

Mackay – *Reay*

Mackay – *Tanlaw*

Mackenzie – *Cromartie, E.*

MacKenzie – *M. of Culkein*

Mackenzie – *M. of Framwellgate*

McKenzie – *M. of Luton*

Mackintosh – *M. of Halifax, V.*

McLaren – *Aberconway*

MacLaurin – *M. of Knebworth*

Maclean – *Blencathra*

Maclennan – *M. of Rogart*

Macmillan – *Stockton, E.*

McNicol – *M. of West Kilbride*

Macpherson – *M. of Drumochter*

Macpherson – *M. of Earl's Court*

Macpherson – *Strathcarron*

Maffey – *Rugby*

Magan – *M. of Castletown*

Maginnis – *M. of Drumglass*

Maitland – *Lauderdale, E.*

Makgill – *Oxfuird, V.*

Makins – *Sherfield*

Manners – *Rutland, D.*

Manningham-Buller – *Dilhorne, V.*

Mansfield – *Sandhurst*

Marks – *M. of Broughton*

Marks – *M. of Henley-on-Thames*

Marquis – *Woolton, E.*

Marsham – *Romney, E.*

Martyn-Hemphill – *Hemphill*

Massey – *M. of Darwen*

Masters – *Noakes*

Maude – *Hawarden, V.*

Maude – *M. of Horsham*

Maxwell – *de Ros*

Maxwell – *Farnham*

May – *M. of Oxford*

Meade – *Clanwilliam, E.*

Mercer Nairne Petty-Fitzmaurice – *Lansdowne, M.*

Methuen-Campbell – *Methuen*

Millar – *Inchyra*

Miller – *M. of Chilthorne Domer*

Milner – *M. of Leeds*

Mitchell-Thomson – *Selsdon*

Mitford – *Redesdale*

Monckton – *M. of Brenchley, V.*

Monckton-Arundell – *Galway, V.*

Money-Coutts – *Latymer*

Montagu – *Manchester, D.*

Montagu – *Sandwich, E.*

Montagu – *Swaythling*

Montagu Douglas Scott – *Buccleuch and Queensberry, D.*

Montagu Stuart Wortley – *Wharncliffe, E.*

Montague – *Amwell*

Montgomerie – *Eglinton and Winton, E.*

Montgomery – *M. of Alamein, V.*

Moore – *Drogheda, E.*

Moore – *M. of Lower Marsh*

Moore-Brabazon – *Brabazon of Tara*

Moreton – *Ducie, E.*

Morgan – *M. of Drefelin*

Morgan – *M. of Ely*

Morgan – *M. of Huyton*

Morris – *Killanin*

Morris – *M. of Aberavon*

Morris – *M. of Bolton*

Morris – *M. of Handsworth*

Morris – *M. of Kenwood*

Morris – *M. of Yardley*

Morris – *Naseby*

Morrison – *Dunrossil, V.*

Morrison – *Margadale*

Mosley – *Ravensdale*

Mountbatten – *Milford Haven, M.*

Muff – *Calverley*

Mulholland – *Dunleath*

Murphy – *M. of Torfaen*

Murray – *Atholl, D.*

Murray – *Dunmore, E.*

Murray – *Mansfield and Mansfield, E.*

Nall-Cain – *Brocket*

Napier – *Napier and Ettrick*

Napier – *N. of Magdala*

Needham – *Kilmorey, E.*

Nelson – *N. of Stafford*

Neuberger – *N. of Abbotsbury*

Nevill – *Abergavenny, M.*

Neville – *Braybrooke*

Nicholls – *N. of Birkenhead*

Nicolson – *Carnock*

Nicolson – *N. of Winterbourne*

Nivison – *Glendyne*

Noel – *Gainsborough, E.*

North – *Guilford, E.*

Northcote – *Iddesleigh, E.*

Norton – *Grantley*

Norton – *N. of Louth*

Norton – *Rathcreedan*

Nugent – *Westmeath, E.*

Oakeshott – *O. of Seagrove Bay*

O'Brien – *Inchiquin*

Ogilvie-Grant – *Seafield, E.*

Ogilvy – *Airlie, E.*

O'Neill – *O'N. of Bengarve*

O'Neill – *O'N. of Clackmannan*

O'Neill – *O'N. of Gatley*

O'Neill – *Rathcavan*

Orde-Powlett – *Bolton*

Ormsby-Gore – *Harlech*

Paget – *Anglesey, M.*

Paisley – *P. of St George's*

Pakenham – *Longford, E.*

Pakington – *Hampton*

Palmer – *Lucas and Dingwall*

Palmer – *P. of Childs Hill*

Palmer – *Selborne, E.*

Palumbo – *P. of Southwark*

Parker – *Macclesfield, E.*

Parker – *Morley, E.*

Parnell – *Congleton*

Parsons – *Rosse, E.*

Patel – *P. of Blackburn*

Patel – *P. of Bradford*

Patten – *P. of Barnes*

Paulet – *Winchester, M.*

Pearson – *Cowdray, V.*

Pearson – *P. of Rannoch*

Pease – *Gainford*

Pease – *Wardington*

Pelham – *Chichester, E.*

Pelham – *Yarborough, E.*

Pellew – *Exmouth, V.*

Penny – *Marchwood, V.*

Pepys – *Cottenham, E.*

Percy – *Northumberland, D.*

Perry – *P. of Southwark*

Pery – *Limerick, E.*

Philipps – *Milford*

Philipps – *St Davids, V.*

Phillips – *P. of Sudbury*

Phillips – *P. of Worth Matravers*

Phipps – *Normanby, M.*

Plant – *P. of Highfield*

Pleydell-Bouverie – *Radnor, E.*

Plumptre – *Fitzwalter*

Plunkett – *Dunsany*

Plunkett – *Louth*

Pollock – *Hanworth, V.*

Pomeroy – *Harberton, V.*

Ponsonby – *Bessborough, E.*

Ponsonby – *de Mauley*

Ponsonby – *P. of Shulbrede*

Porter – *P. of Spalding*

Powell – *P. of Bayswater*

Powys – *Lilford*

Pratt – *Camden, M.*

Preston – *Gormanston, V.*

Primrose – *Rosebery, E.*

Prittie – *Dunalley*

Purvis – *P. of Tweed*

Ramsay – *Dalhousie, E.*

Ramsay – *R. of Cartvale*

Ramsbotham – *Soulbury, V.*

Randall – *R. of Uxbridge*

Rees – *R. of Ludlow*

Rees-Williams – *Ogmore*

Reid – *R. of Cardowan*

Renfrew – *R. of Kaimsthorn*

Renton – *R. of Mount Harry*

Renwick – *R. of Clifton*

Rhys – *Dynevor*

Richards – *Milverton*

Richards – *R. of Herstmonceux*

Richardson – *R. of Calow*

Ritchie – *R. of Dundee*

Roberts – *Clwyd*

Roberts – *R. of Llandudno*

Robertson – *R. of Oakridge*

Robertson – *R. of Port Ellen*

Robertson – *Wharton*

Robinson – *Martonmere*

Roche – *Fermoy*

Rodd – *Rennell*

Rodgers – *R. of Quarry Bank*

Roe – *Couttie*

Rogers – *Lisvane*

Rogers – *R. of Riverside*

Roper-Curzon – *Teynham*

Rose – *R. of Monewden*

Rospigliosi – *Newburgh, E.*

Rous – *Stradbroke, E.*

Rowley-Conwy – *Langford*

Royall – *R. of Blaisdon*

Runciman – *R. of Doxford, V.*

Russell – *Ampthill*

Russell – *Bedford, D.*

Russell – *de Clifford*

Russell – *R. of Liverpool*

Ryder – *Harrowby, E.*

Ryder – *R. of Wensum*★
Sackville – *De La Warr, E.*
Sackville-West – *Sackville*
Sainsbury – *S. of Preston Candover*★
Sainsbury – *S. of Turville*★
St Aubyn – *St Levan*
St Clair – *Sinclair*
St Clair-Erskine – *Rosslyn, E.*
St John – *Bolingbroke and St John, V.*
St John – *St John of Bletso*
St Leger – *Doneraile, V.*
Samuel – *Bearsted, V.*
Sanderson – *S. of Ayot*
Sanderson – *S. of Bowden*★
Sandilands – *Torphichen*
Saumarez – *de Saumarez*
Savile – *Mexborough, E.*
Saville – *S. of Newdigate*★
Scarlett – *Abinger*
Schreiber – *Marlesford*★
Sclater-Booth – *Basing*
Scotland – *S. of Asthal*★
Scott – *Eldon, E.*
Scott – *S. of Bybrook*★
Scott – *S. of Foscote*★
Scott – *S. of Needham Market*★
Scrymgeour – *Dundee, E.*
Seager – *Leighton of St Mellons*
Seely – *Mottistone*
Seymour – *Hertford, M.*
Seymour – *Somerset, D.*
Shackleton – *S. of Belgravia*★
Sharp – *S. of Guildford*★
Shaw – *Craigmyle*
Shaw – *S. of Northstead*★
Shephard – *S. of Northwold*★
Sherbourne – *S. of Didsbury*★
Shirley – *Ferrers, E.*
Shutt – *S. of Greetland*★
Siddeley – *Kenilworth*
Sidney – *De L'Isle, V.*
Simon – *S. of Highbury*★
Simon – *S. of Wythenshawe*
Simpson – *S. of Dunkeld*★
Sinclair – *Caithness, E.*
Sinclair – *S. of Cleeve*
Sinclair – *Thurso, V.*
Singh – *S. of Wimbledon*★
Skeffington – *Massereene and Ferrard, V.*

Smith – *Bicester*
Smith – *Hambleden, V.*
Smith – *Kirkhill*★
Smith – *S. of Basildon*★
Smith – *S. of Clifton*★
Smith – *S. of Finsbury*★
Smith – *S. of Gilmorehill*★
Smith – *S. of Hindhead*★
Smith – *S. of Kelvin*★
Smith – *S. of Leigh*★
Smith – *S. of Newnham*★
Somerset – *Beaufort, D.*
Somerset – *Raglan*
Spencer – *Churchill*
Spencer-Churchill – *Marlborough, D.*
Spring – *Risby*★
Spring Rice – *Monteagle of Brandon*
Stanhope – *Harrington, E.*
Stanley – *Derby, E.*
Stanley – *S. of Alderley and Sheffield*
Stapleton-Cotton – *Combermere, V.*
Steel – *S. of Aikwood*★
Sterling – *S. of Plaistow*★
Stern – *S. of Brentford*★
Stevens – *S. of Kirkwhelpington*★
Stevens – *S. of Ludgate*★
Stevenson – *S. of Balmacara*★
Stevenson – *S. of Coddenham*★
Stewart – *Galloway, E.*
Stoddart – *S. of Swindon*★
Stone – *S. of Blackheath*★
Stoneham – *S. of Droxford*★
Stonor – *Camoys*
Stopford – *Courtown, E.*
Stourton – *Mowbray, Segrave and S.*
Stowell – *S. of Beeston*★
Strachey – *O'Hagan*
Strutt – *Belper*
Strutt – *Rayleigh*
Stuart – *Castle Stewart, E.*
Stuart – *Moray, E.*
Stuart – *S. of Findhorn, V.*
Suenson-Taylor – *Grantchester*
Symons – *S. of Vernham Dean*★
Taylor – *Kilclooney*★
Taylor – *T. of Bolton*★

Taylor – *T. of Goss Moor*★
Taylor – *T. of Holbeach*★
Taylor – *T. of Warwick*★
Taylour – *Headfort, M.*
Temple-Gore-Langton – *Temple of Stowe, E.*
Tennant – *Glenconner*
Thellusson – *Rendlesham*
Thesiger – *Chelmsford, V.*
Thomas – *T. of Cwmgiedd*★
Thomas – *T. of Gresford*★
Thomas – *T. of Walliswood*★
Thomas – *T. of Winchester*★
Thomson – *T. of Fleet*
Thynn – *Bath, M.*
Tottenham – *Ely, M.*
Trefusis – *Clinton*
Trench – *Ashtown*
Tufton – *Hothfield*
Turner – *Netherthorpe*
Turner – *T. of Ecchinswell*★
Turnour – *Winterton, E.*
Tyler – *T. of Enfield*★
Tyrell-Kenyon – *Kenyon*
Vallance – *V. of Tummel*★
Vanden-Bempde-Johnstone – *Derwent*
Vane – *Barnard*
Vane-Tempest-Stewart – *Londonderry, M.*
Vanneck – *Huntingfield*
Vaughan – *Lisburne, E.*
Vere – *V. of Norbiton*★
Vereker – *Gort, V.*
Verney – *Willoughby de Broke*
Vernon – *Lyveden*
Vesey – *de Vesci, V.*
Villiers – *Clarendon, E.*
Vivian – *Swansea*
Waldegrave – *W. of North Hill*★
Walker – *W. of Aldringham*★
Walker – *W. of Gestingthorpe*★
Wallace – *Dudley*
Wallace – *W. of Saltaire*★
Wallace – *W. of Tankerness*★
Wallop – *Portsmouth, E.*
Ward – *Bangor, V.*
Ward – *Dudley, E.*
Warrender – *Bruntisfield*
Warwick – *W. of Undercliffe*★
Watkins – *W. of Tavistock*★

Watson – *Manton*
Watson – *W. of Invergowrie*★
Watson – *W. of Richmond*★
Webber – *Lloyd-Webber*★
Weir – *Inverforth*
Weld-Forester – *Forester*
Wellesley – *Cowley, E.*
Wellesley – *Wellington, D.*
West – *W. of Spithead*★
Westenra – *Rossmore*
White – *Annaly*
White – *Hanningfield*★
Whiteley – *Marchamley*
Whitfield – *Kenswood*
Williams – *W. of Crosby*★
Williams – *W. of Elvel*★
Williams – *W. of Oystermouth*★
Williams – *W. of Trafford*★
Williamson – *Forres*
Willis – *W. of Knaresborough*★
Willoughby – *Middleton*
Wills – *Dulverton*
Wilson – *Moran*
Wilson – *Nunburnholme*
Wilson – *W. of Dinton*★
Wilson – *W. of Tillyorn*★
Windsor – *Gloucester, D.*
Windsor – *Kent, D.*
Windsor-Clive – *Plymouth, E.*
Wingfield – *Powerscourt, V.*
Winn – *St Oswald*
Wodehouse – *Kimberley, E.*
Wolf – *W. of Dulwich*★
Wolfson – *W. of Aspley Guise*★
Wolfson – *W. of Sunningdale*★
Wood – *Halifax, E.*
Wood – *W. of Anfield*★
Woodhouse – *Terrington*
Woolmer – *W. of Leeds*★
Wright – *W. of Richmond*★
Wyndham – *Egremont and Leconfield*
Wynn – *Newborough*
Yarde-Buller – *Churston*
Yerburgh – *Alvingham*
Yorke – *Hardwicke, E.*
Young – *Kennet*
Young – *Y. of Cookham*★
Young – *Y. of Graffham*★
Young – *Y. of Hornsey*★
Young – *Y. of Norwood Green*★
Young – *Y. of Old Scone*★
Younger – *Y. of Leckie, V.*

LORDS SPIRITUAL

The Lords Spiritual are the Archbishops of Canterbury and York and 24 other diocesan bishops of the Church of England. The Bishops of London, Durham and Winchester always have seats in the House of Lords; the other 21 seats were previously filled by the remaining diocesan bishops in order of seniority. However, the Lords Spiritual (Women) Act 2015 provides for vacancies among the remaining 21 places to be filled by any female diocesan bishop in office at the time and, only if there is no female diocesan bishop without a seat, by the longest serving male diocesan bishop. The provision will remain in place for ten years from 2015, equivalent to two fixed-term parliaments. At the end of this period, the provision under the Act will end and the previous arrangements under which vacancies are filled according to length of service as a diocesan bishop will be restored.

The Bishop of Sodor and Man and the Bishop of Gibraltar in Europe are not eligible to sit in the House of Lords.

ARCHBISHOPS

Style, The Most Revd and Rt. Hon, the Lord Archbishop of_
Addressed as Archbishop *or* Your Grace

INTRODUCED TO HOUSE OF LORDS
2012	*Canterbury* (105th), Justin Portal Welby, PC, *b.* 1956, *m., cons.* 2011, *elected* 2011, *trans.* 2013
2006	*York* (97th), John Mugabi Tucker Sentamu, PC, PHD, *b.* 1949, *m., cons.* 1996, *elected* 2002, *trans.* 2005

BISHOPS

Style, The Rt. Revd the Lord/Lady Bishop of _
Addressed as Bishop or My Lord/Lady
elected date of confirmation as diocesan bishop

INTRODUCED TO HOUSE OF LORDS
as at November 2018
2018	*London* (133rd), Dame Sarah Elisabeth Mullally, DBE, PC *b.* 1962, *m., cons.* 2015, *elected* 2018
2014	*Durham* (74th), Paul Roger Butler, *b.* 1955, *m., cons.* 2004, *elected* 2009, *trans.* 2014
2012	*Winchester* (97th), Timothy John Dakin, *b.* 1958, *m., cons.* 2012, *elected* 2011
2001	*Chester* (40th), Peter Robert Forster, PHD, *b.* 1950, *m., cons.* 1996, *elected* 1996
2004	*Norwich* (71st), Graham Richard James, *b.* 1951, *m., cons.* 1993, *elected* 1999
2010	*Birmingham* (9th), David Andrew Urquhart, KCMG, *b.* 1952, *cons.* 2000, *elected* 2006
2012	*Worcester* (113th), John Geoffrey Inge, PHD, *b.* 1955, *m., cons.* 2003, *elected* 2007
2013	*Coventry* (9th), Christopher John Cocksworth, PHD, *b.* 1959, *m., cons.* 2008, *elected* 2008
2013	*Oxford* (44th), Stephen John Lindsey Croft, PHD, *b.* 1957, *m., cons.* 2009, *elected* 2009, *trans.* 2016
2013	*Carlisle* (66th), James William Scobie Newcome, *b.* 1953, *m., cons.* 2002, *elected* 2009
2013	*St Albans* (10th), Alan Gregory Clayton Smith, PHD, *b.* 1957, *cons.* 2001, *elected* 2009
2014	*Peterborough* (38th), Donald Spargo Allister, *b.* 1952, *m., cons.* 2010, *elected* 2010
2014	*Portsmouth* (9th), Christopher Richard James Foster, *b.* 1953, *m., cons.* 2001, *elected* 2010
2014	*Chelmsford* (10th), Stephen Geoffrey Cottrell, *b.* 1958, *m., cons.* 2004, *elected* 2010
2014	*Rochester* (107th), James Henry Langstaff, *b.* 1956, *m., cons.* 2004, *elected* 2010
2014	*Ely* (69th), Stephen David Conway, *b.* 1957, *cons.* 2006, *elected* 2010
2014	*Southwark* (10th), Christopher Thomas James Chessun, *b.* 1956, *cons.* 2005, *elected* 2011
2015	*Leeds* (1st), Nicholas Baines, *b.* 1957, *m., cons.* 2003, *elected* 2011, *trans.* 2014
2015	*Salisbury* (78th), Nicholas Roderick Holtam, *b.* 1954, *m., cons.* 2011, *elected* 2011
2015	*Gloucester* (41st), Rachel Treweek, *b.* 1963, *m., cons.* 2015, *elected* 2015
2016	*Newcastle* (12th), Christine Elizabeth Hardman, *b.* 1951, *m., cons.* 2015, *elected* 2015
2017	*Lincoln* (72nd), Christopher Lowson, *b.* 1953, *m., cons.* 2011, *elected* 2011
2018	*Chichester* (103rd), Martin Clive Warner, PHD, *b.* 1958, *cons.* 2010, *elected* 2012
2018	*Bristol* (56th), Vivienne Frances Faull, *b.* 1955, *m. cons.* 2018, *elected* 2018

BISHOPS AWAITING SEATS, in order of seniority
as at November 2018

Blackburn (9th), Julian Tudor Henderson, *b.* 1954, *m., cons.* 2013, *elected* 2013
Manchester (12th), David Stuart Walker, *b.* 1957, *m., cons.* 2000, *elected* 2013
Bath and Wells (79th), Peter Hancock, *b.* 1955, *m., cons.* 2010, *elected* 2014
Exeter (71st), Robert Ronald Atwell, *b.* 1954, *cons.* 2008, *elected* 2014
Liverpool (8th), Paul Bayes, *b.* 1953, *m., cons.* 2010, *elected* 2014
Hereford (105th), Richard Michael Cokayne Frith, *b.* 1949, *m., cons.* 1998, *elected* 2014
Guildford (10th), Andrew John Watson *b.* 1961, *m., cons.* 2008, *elected* 2014
St Edmundsbury and Ipswich (11th), Martin Alan Seeley *b.* 1954, *m., cons.* 2015, *elected* 2015
Southwell and Nottingham (12th), Paul Gavin Williams, *b.* 1968, *m., cons.* 2009, *elected* 2015
Leicester (7th), Martyn James Snow, *b.* 1968, *m., cons.* 2013, *elected* 2016
Lichfield (99th), Michael Geoffrey Ipgrave, OBE, PHD, *b.* 1958, *m., cons.* 2012, *elected* 2016
Sheffield (8th), Peter Wilcox, DPHIL, *b.* 1961, *m., cons.* 2017, *elected* 2017
Truro (16th), Philip Ian Mountstephen, *b.* 1959, *m., cons.* 2018, *elected* 2018
Derby (8th), vacant

ORDERS OF CHIVALRY

THE MOST NOBLE ORDER OF THE GARTER (1348)

KG
Ribbon, Blue
Motto, Honi soit qui mal y pense (*Shame on him who thinks evil of it*)

The number of Knights and Ladies Companion is limited to 24

SOVEREIGN OF THE ORDER
The Queen

LADIES OF THE ORDER
HRH The Princess Royal, 1994
HRH Princess Alexandra, The Hon. Lady Ogilvy, 2003

ROYAL KNIGHTS
HRH The Prince Philip, Duke of Edinburgh, 1947
HRH The Prince of Wales, 1958
HRH The Duke of Kent, 1985
HRH The Duke of Gloucester, 1997
HRH The Duke of York, 2006
HRH The Earl of Wessex, 2006
HRH The Duke of Cambridge, 2008

EXTRA KNIGHTS COMPANION AND LADIES
Grand Duke Jean of Luxembourg, 1972
HM The Queen of Denmark, 1979
HM The King of Sweden, 1983
HM King Juan Carlos, 1988
HRH Princess Beatrix of the Netherlands, 1989
HIM The Emperor of Japan, 1998
HM The King of Norway, 2001
HM The King of Spain, 2017

KNIGHTS AND LADIES COMPANION
Lord Bramall, 1990
Lord Sainsbury of Preston Candover, 1992
Lord Ashburton, 1994
Sir Timothy Colman, 1996
Duke of Abercorn, 1999
Lord Inge, 2001
Sir Anthony Acland, 2001
Lord Butler of Brockwell, 2003
Lord Morris of Aberavon, 2003
Sir John Major, 2005

Lord Luce, 2008
Sir Thomas Dunne, 2008
Lord Phillips of Worth Matravers, 2011
Lord Boyce, 2011
Lord Stirrup, 2013
Baroness Manningham-Buller, 2014
Lord King of Lothbury, 2014
Lord Shuttleworth, 2016
Sir David Brewer, 2016
Viscount Brookeborough, 2018
Dame Mary Fagan, 2018

Prelate, Bishop of Winchester
Chancellor, Duke of Abercorn, KG
Register, Dean of Windsor, KCVO
Garter King of Arms, Thomas Woodcock, CVO
Lady Usher of the Black Rod, Sarah Clarke, OBE
Secretary, Patric Dickinson, LVO

THE MOST ANCIENT AND MOST NOBLE ORDER OF THE THISTLE (REVIVED 1687)

KT
Ribbon, Green
Motto, Nemo me impune lacessit (*No one provokes me with impunity*)

The number of Knights and Ladies of the Thistle is limited to 16

SOVEREIGN OF THE ORDER
The Queen

ROYAL KNIGHTS
HRH The Prince Philip, Duke of Edinburgh, 1952
HRH The Prince of Wales, Duke of Rothesay, 1977
HRH The Duke of Cambridge, Earl of Strathearn, 2012

ROYAL LADY OF THE ORDER
HRH The Princess Royal, 2000

KNIGHTS AND LADIES
Earl of Elgin and Kincardine, 1981
Earl of Airlie, 1985
Earl of Crawford and Balcarres, 1996
Lord Macfarlane of Bearsden, 1996
Lord Mackay of Clashfern, 1997
Lord Wilson of Tillyorn, 2000
Sir Eric Anderson, 2002

Lord Steel of Aikwood, 2004
Lord Robertson of Port Ellen, 2004
Lord Cullen of Whitekirk, 2007
Lord Hope of Craighead, 2009
Lord Patel, 2009
Earl of Home, 2013
Lord Smith of Kelvin, 2013
Duke of Buccleuch and Queensberry, 2017
Sir Ian Wood, 2018

Chancellor, Earl of Airlie, KT, GCVO, PC
Dean, Very Revd Prof. Sir Iain Torrance, TD
Secretary, Mrs Christopher Roads, LVO
Lord Lyon King of Arms, Dr Joseph Morrow, CBE, QC
Gentleman Usher of the Green Rod, Rear-Adm. Christopher Layman, CB, DSO, LVO

THE MOST HONOURABLE ORDER OF THE BATH (1725)

GCB *Military*   GCB *Civil*

GCB   Knight (or Dame) Grand Cross
KCB   Knight Commander
DCB   Dame Commander
CB   Companion

Ribbon, Crimson
Motto, Tria juncta in uno (*Three joined in one*)

Remodelled 1815, and enlarged many times since. The order is divided into civil and military divisions. Women became eligible for the order from 1 January 1971.

THE SOVEREIGN

GREAT MASTER AND FIRST OR PRINCIPAL KNIGHT GRAND CROSS
HRH The Prince of Wales, KG, KT, GCB, OM

Dean of the Order, Dean of Westminster
Bath King of Arms, Air Chief Marshal Sir Stephen Dalton, GCB
Registrar and Secretary, Rear-Adm. Iain Henderson, CB, CBE
Genealogist, Thomas Woodcock, CVO
Gentleman Usher of the Scarlet Rod, Maj.-Gen. James Gordon, CB, CBE

Deputy Secretary, Secretary of the Central Chancery of the Orders of Knighthood

Chancery, Central Chancery of the Orders of Knighthood, St James's Palace, London SW1A 1BH

THE ORDER OF MERIT (1902)

OM *Military*   OM *Civil*

OM
Ribbon, Blue and crimson

This order is designed as a special distinction for eminent men and women without conferring a knighthood upon them. The order is limited in numbers to 24, with the addition of foreign honorary members.

THE SOVEREIGN

HRH The Prince Philip, Duke of Edinburgh, 1968
Sir Michael Atiyah, 1992
Sir Aaron Klug, 1995
Lord Foster of Thames Bank, 1997
Prof. Sir Roger Penrose, 2000
Sir Tom Stoppard, 2000
HRH The Prince of Wales, 2002
Lord May of Oxford, 2002
Lord Rothschild, 2002
Sir David Attenborough, 2005
Baroness Boothroyd, 2005
Sir Michael Howard, 2005
Sir Timothy Berners-Lee, 2007
Lord Eames, 2007
Lord Rees of Ludlow, 2007
Rt. Hon. Jean Chrétien, QC, 2009
Robert Neil MacGregor, 2010
Hon. John Howard, 2011
David Hockney, 2011
Sir Simon Rattle, 2013
Prof. Sir Magdi Yacoub, 2013
Lord Darzi of Denham, 2016
Prof. Dame Ann Dowling, 2016
Sir James Dyson, 2016

Secretary and Registrar, Lord Fellowes, GCB, GCVO, PC, QSO

Chancery, Central Chancery of the Orders of Knighthood, St James's Palace, London SW1A 1BH

THE MOST DISTINGUISHED ORDER OF ST MICHAEL AND ST GEORGE (1818)

GCMG   KCMG

GCMG Knight (or Dame) Grand Cross
KCMG Knight Commander
DCMG Dame Commander
CMG   Companion

Ribbon, Saxon blue, with scarlet centre
Motto, Auspicium melioris aevi (*Token of a better age*)

THE SOVEREIGN

GRAND MASTER
HRH The Duke of Kent, KG, GCMG, GCVO, ADC

Prelate, Rt. Revd David Urquhart, KCMG
Chancellor, Lord Robertson of Port Ellen, KT, GCMG, PC
Secretary, Permanent Under-Secretary of State at the Foreign and Commonwealth Office and Head of the Diplomatic Service
Registrar, Sir David Manning, GCMG, KCVO
King of Arms, Sir Jeremy Greenstock, GCMG
Usher of the Blue Rod, Dame DeAnne Julius, DCMG, CBE
Dean, Dean of St Paul's
Deputy Secretary, Secretary of the Central Chancery of the Orders of Knighthood
Hon. Genealogist, Timothy Duke

Chancery, Central Chancery of the Orders of Knighthood, St James's Palace, London SW1A 1BH

THE IMPERIAL ORDER OF THE CROWN OF INDIA (1877) FOR LADIES

CI

Badge, the royal cipher of Queen Victoria in jewels within an oval, surmounted by an heraldic crown and attached to a bow of light blue watered ribbon, edged white

The honour does not confer any rank or title upon the recipient

No conferments have been made since 1947

HM The Queen, 1947

THE ROYAL VICTORIAN ORDER (1896)

GCVO   KCVO

GCVO Knight or Dame Grand Cross
KCVO Knight Commander
DCVO Dame Commander
CVO   Commander
LVO   Lieutenant
MVO   Member

Ribbon, Blue, with red and white edges

Motto, Victoria

THE SOVEREIGN

GRAND MASTER
HRH The Princess Royal, KG, KT, GCVO, QSO

Chancellor, Lord Chamberlain
Secretary, Keeper of the Privy Purse
Registrar, Secretary of the Central Chancery of the Orders of Knighthood
Chaplain, Chaplain of the Queen's Chapel of the Savoy
Hon. Genealogist, David White

THE MOST EXCELLENT ORDER OF THE BRITISH EMPIRE (1917)

GBE   KBE

The order was divided into military and civil divisions in December 1918

GBE Knight or Dame Grand Cross
KBE Knight Commander
DBE Dame Commander
CBE Commander
OBE Officer
MBE Member

Ribbon, Rose pink edged with pearl grey with vertical pearl stripe in centre (military division); without vertical pearl stripe (civil division)
Motto, For God and the Empire

THE SOVEREIGN

GRAND MASTER
HRH The Prince Philip, Duke of Edinburgh, KG, KT, OM, GCVO, GBE, PC

Prelate, Bishop of London
King of Arms, Lt.-Gen. Sir Robert Fulton, KBE
Registrar, Secretary of the Central Chancery of the Orders of Knighthood
Secretary, Secretary of the Cabinet and Head of the Home Civil Service
Dean, Dean of St Paul's
Lady Usher of the Purple Rod, Dame Amelia Chilcott Fawcett, DBE, CVO

Chancery, Central Chancery of the Orders of Knighthood, St James's Palace, London SW1A 1BH

ORDER OF THE COMPANIONS OF HONOUR (1917)

CH

Ribbon, Carmine, with gold edges

This order consists of one class only and carries with it no title. The number of awards is limited to 65 (excluding honorary members).

Amos, Baroness, 2016
Anthony, John, 1981
Ashdown of Norton-sub-Hamdon, Lord, 2014
Attenborough, Sir David, 1995
Baker, Dame Janet, 1993
Baker of Dorking, Lord, 1992
Birtwistle, Sir Harrison, 2000
Bragg, Lord, 2017
Brenner, Sydney, 1986
Brook, Peter, 1998
Brooke of Sutton Mandeville, Lord, 1992
Campbell of Pittenweem, Lord, 2013
Clarke, Kenneth, 2014
Coe, Lord, 2012
Conran, Sir Terence, 2017
De Chastelain, Gen. John, 1998
Dench, Dame Judi, 2005
Elder, Sir Mark, 2017
Eyre, Sir Richard, 2016
Fraser, Lady Antonia, 2017
Glennie, Dame Evelyn, 2016
Grey, Dame Beryl, 2017
Hannay of Chiswick, Lord, 2003
Henderson, Prof. Richard, 2018
Heseltine, Lord, 1997
Higgs, Prof. Peter, 2012
Hockney, David, 1997
Howard, Sir Michael, 2002
Howard of Lympne, Lord, 2011
Hurd of Westwell, Lord, 1995
Jeffreys, Sir Alec, 2016
King of Bridgwater, Lord, 1992

Lovelock, Prof. James, 2002
Lynn, Dame Vera, 2016
McCartney, Sir Paul, 2017
McKellen, Sir Ian Murray, 2007
McKenzie, Prof. Dan Peter, 2003
MacMillan, Prof. Margaret, 2017
Major, Sir John, 1998
O'Neill of Bengarve, Baroness, 2013
Osborne, George, 2016
Owen, Lord, 1994
Patten of Barnes, Lord, 1997
Peters, Dame Mary, 2014
Riley, Bridget, 1998
Rogers of Riverside, Lord, 2008
Rowling, Joanne, 2017
Serota, Sir Nicholas, 2013
Shirley, Dame Stephanie, 2017
Smith, Delia, 2017
Smith, Dame Margaret (Maggie), 2014
Smith of Kelvin, Lord, 2016
Somare, Sir Michael, 1978
Stern of Brentford, Lord, 2017
Strathclyde, Lord, 2013
Strong, Sir Roy, 2015
Te Kanawa, Dame Kiri, 2018
Tebbit, Lord, 1987
Warnock, Baroness, 2016
Williams of Crosby, Baroness, 2016
Woolf, Lord, 2015
Young of Cookham, Lord, 2012
Young of Graffham, Lord, 2014

Honorary Members, Bernard Haitink, 2002; Prof. Amartya Sen, 2000; Most Revd Desmond Tutu, 2015
Secretary and Registrar, Secretary of the Central Chancery of the Orders of Knighthood

THE DISTINGUISHED SERVICE ORDER (1886)

DSO

Ribbon, Red, with blue edges

Bestowed in recognition of especial services in action of commissioned officers in the Navy, Army and Royal Air Force and (since 1942) Mercantile Marine. The members are Companions only. A bar may be awarded for any additional act of service.

THE IMPERIAL SERVICE ORDER (1902)

ISO

Ribbon, Crimson, with blue centre

Appointment as companion of this order is open to members of the civil services whose eligibility is determined by the grade they hold. The order consists of the sovereign and companions to a number not exceeding 1,900, of whom 1,300 may belong to the home civil services and 600 to overseas civil services. The then prime minister announced in March 1993 that he would make no further recommendations for appointments to the order.

Secretary, Head of the Home Civil Service
Registrar, Secretary of the Central Chancery of the Orders of Knighthood

THE ROYAL VICTORIAN CHAIN (1902)

It confers no precedence on its holders

HM The Queen

HM The Queen of Denmark, 1974
HM The King of Sweden, 1975
HRH Princess Beatrix of the Netherlands, 1982
Gen. Antonio Eanes, 1985
HM King Juan Carlos, 1986
HM The King of Norway, 1994
Earl of Airlie, 1997
Rt. Revd and Rt. Hon. Lord Carey of Clifton, 2002
HRH Prince Philip, Duke of Edinburgh, 2007
HM The Sultan of Oman, 2010
Rt. Revd and Rt. Hon. Lord Williams of Oystermouth, 2012

BARONETAGE AND KNIGHTAGE

BARONETS

Style, 'Sir' before forename and surname, followed by 'Bt.'
   Envelope, Sir F_ S_, Bt. *Letter (formal),* Dear Sir; *(social),* Dear Sir F_. *Spoken,* Sir F_
Wife's style, 'Lady' followed by surname
   Envelope, Lady S_. *Letter (formal),* Dear Madam; *(social),* Dear Lady S_. *Spoken,* Lady S_
Style of Baronetess, 'Dame' before forename and surname, followed by 'Btss.' (*see also* Dames)

There are five different creations of baronetcies: Baronets of England (creations dating from 1611); Baronets of Ireland (creations dating from 1619); Baronets of Scotland or Nova Scotia (creations dating from 1625); Baronets of Great Britain (creations after the Act of Union 1707 which combined the kingdoms of England and Scotland); and Baronets of the United Kingdom (creations after the union of Great Britain and Ireland in 1801).

| *Badge of Baronets of the UK* | *Badge of Baronets of Nova Scotia* | *Badge of Ulster* |

   The patent of creation limits the destination of a baronetcy, usually to male descendants of the first baronet. In some cases, however, special remainders have allowed baronetcies to pass, in the absence of sons, to another relative. In the case of baronetcies of Scotland or Nova Scotia, a special remainder of 'heirs male and of tailzie' allows the baronetcy to descend to heirs general, including women. There are four existing Scottish baronetcies with such a remainder.
   The Official Roll of the Baronetage is kept at the Crown Office and maintained by the Registrar and Assistant Registrar of the Baronetage. Anyone who considers that he or she is entitled to be entered on the roll may apply through the Crown Office to prove their succession. Every person succeeding to a baronetcy must exhibit proofs of succession to the Lord Chancellor. A person whose name is not entered on the official roll will not be addressed or mentioned by the title of baronet or baroness in any official document, nor will he or she be accorded precedence as a baronet or baroness.
   The Standing Council of the Baronetage, established in 1898 as the Honourable Society of the Baronetage, is responsible for maintaining the interests of the Baronetage and for publishing the Official Roll of the Baronetage as established by royal warrant in 1910 (**W** www.baronetage.org/official-roll-of-the-baronets).

OFFICIAL ROLL OF THE BARONETAGE, Crown Office, House of Lords, London SW1A 0PW **T** 020-7219 4687
   E hereditary.claims@gmail.com
   Registrar, Mrs Ceri King

STANDING COUNCIL OF THE BARONETAGE, 1 Tarrel Farm Cottages, Portmahomack, Tain IV20 1SL
   E secretary@baronetage.org **W** www.baronetage.org
   Chair, Sir Nicholas Thompson, Bt.
   Secretary, Sarah Rawlings

BARONETCIES IDENTIFIED AS EXTINCT SINCE SEPTEMBER 2017
Hardy (cr. 1876); Williams (cr. 1798)

KNIGHTS

Style, 'Sir' before forename and surname, followed by appropriate post-nominal initials if a Knight Grand Cross or Knight Commander
   Envelope, Sir F_ S_. *Letter (formal),* Dear Sir; *(social),* Dear Sir F_. *Spoken,* Sir F_
Wife's style, 'Lady' followed by surname
   Envelope, Lady S_. *Letter (formal),* Dear Madam; *(social),* Dear Lady S_. *Spoken,* Lady S_

The prefix 'Sir' is not used by knights who are clerics of the Church of England, who do not receive the accolade. Their wives are entitled to precedence as the wife of a knight but not to the style of 'Lady'.

ORDERS OF KNIGHTHOOD
Knight Grand Cross and Knight Commander are the higher classes of the Orders of Chivalry (*see* Orders of Chivalry). Honorary knighthoods of these orders may be conferred on men who are citizens of countries of which the Queen is not head of state. As a rule, the prefix 'Sir' is not used by honorary knights.

KNIGHTS BACHELOR

The Knights Bachelor do not constitute a royal order, but comprise the surviving representation of the ancient state orders of knighthood. The Register of Knights Bachelor, instituted by James I in the 17th century, lapsed, and in 1908 a voluntary association under the title of the Society of Knights (now the Imperial Society of Knights Bachelor) was formed with the primary objectives of continuing the various registers dating from 1257 and obtaining the uniform registration of every created Knight Bachelor. In 1926 a design for a badge to be worn by Knights Bachelor was approved and adopted; in 1974 a neck badge and miniature were added.

THE IMPERIAL SOCIETY OF KNIGHTS BACHELOR, Magnesia House, 6 Playhouse Yard, London EC4V 5EX
   Knight Principal, Sir Colin Berry
   Prelate, Rt. Revd and Rt. Hon. Dame Sarah Mullally, DBE
   Registrar, Sir Michael Hirst
   Hon. Treasurer, Sir Clive Thompson
   Clerk to the Council, Col. Simon Doughty

LIST OF BARONETS AND KNIGHTS

as at 31 August 2018

†   Not registered on the Official Roll of the Baronetage
( )   The date of creation of the baronetcy is given in parentheses
I   Baronet of Ireland
NS   Baronet of Nova Scotia
S   Baronet of Scotland

A full entry in italic type indicates that the recipient of a knighthood died during the year in which the honour was conferred. The name is included for purposes of record. Peers are not included in this list.

Aaronson, Sir Michael John, Kt., CBE
†Abdy, Sir Robert Etienne Eric, Bt. (1850)
Abed, *Dr* Sir Fazle Hasan, KCMG
Abel, Sir Christopher Charles, Kt.
Acher, Sir Gerald, Kt., CBE, LVO
Ackroyd, Sir Timothy Robert Whyte, Bt. (1956)
Acland, Sir Antony Arthur, KG, GCMG, GCVO
Acland, *Lt.-Col.* Sir (Christopher) Guy (Dyke), Bt. (1890), LVO
Acland, Sir Dominic Dyke, Bt. (1678)
Adams, Sir Geoffrey Doyne, KCMG
Adams, Sir William James, KCMG
Adjaye, Sir David Frank, Kt., OBE
Adsetts, Sir William Norman, Kt., OBE
Adye, Sir John Anthony, KCMG
Aga Khan IV, HH Prince Karim, KBE
Agnew, Sir Crispin Hamlyn, Bt. (S. 1629)
Agnew, Sir George Anthony, Bt. (1895)
Agnew, Sir Rudolph Ion Joseph, Kt.
Agnew-Somerville, Sir James Lockett Charles, Bt. (1957)
Ah Koy, Sir James Michael, KBE
Aikens, *Rt. Hon.* Sir Richard John Pearson, Kt.
Ainslie, Sir Charles Benedict, Kt., CBE
†Ainsworth, Sir Anthony Thomas Hugh, Bt. (1917)
Aird, Sir (George) John, Bt. (1901)
Airy, *Maj.-Gen.* Sir Christopher John, KCVO, CBE
Aitchison, Sir Charles Walter de Lancey, Bt. (1938)
Ajegbo, Sir Keith Onyema, Kt., OBE
Akenhead, *Hon.* Sir Robert, Kt.
Akers-Jones, Sir David, KBE, CMG
Alberti, *Prof.* Sir Kurt George Matthew Mayer, Kt.
Albu, Sir George, Bt. (1912)
Alcock, *Air Chief Marshal* Sir (Robert James) Michael, GCB, KBE
Aldridge, Sir Rodney Malcolm, Kt., OBE
Alexander, *Rt. Hon.* Sir Daniel (Grian), Kt.
Alexander, Sir Douglas, Bt. (1921)
Alexander, Sir Richard, Bt. (1945)
Alghanim, Sir Kutayba Yusuf, KCMG
Allan, *Hon.* Sir Alexander Claud Stuart, KCB
Allen, Sir Errol Newton Fitzrose, KCMG

Allen, *Prof.* Sir Geoffrey, Kt., PHD, FRS
Allen, Sir Mark John Spurgeon, Kt., CMG
Allen, *Hon.* Sir Peter Austin Philip Jermyn, Kt.
Allen, Sir Thomas Boaz, Kt., CBE
Allen, *Hon.* Sir William Clifford, KCMG
Allen, Sir William Guilford, Kt.
Alleyne, Sir George Allanmoore Ogarren, Kt.
Alleyne, *Revd* John Olpherts Campbell, Bt. (1769)
Allinson, Sir (Walter) Leonard, KCVO, CMG
Allison, *Air Chief Marshal* Sir John Shakespeare, KCB, CBE
Altman, Sir Paul Bernard, Kt.
Amess, Sir David Anthony Andrew, Kt.
Amet, *Hon.* Sir Arnold Karibone, Kt.
Amory, Sir Ian Heathcoat, Bt. (1874)
Anderson, *Dr* Sir James Iain Walker, Kt., CBE
Anderson, Sir John Anthony, KBE
Anderson, Sir Leith Reinsford Steven, Kt., CBE
Anderson, *Prof.* Sir Roy Malcolm, Kt.
Anderson, *Air Marshal* Sir Timothy Michael, KCB, DSO
Anderson, Sir (William) Eric Kinloch, KT
Anderton, Sir (Cyril) James, Kt., CBE, QPM
Andrew, Sir Robert John, KCB
Andrew, Sir Warwick, Kt.
Andrews, Sir Ian Charles Franklin, Kt., CBE, TD
Angest, Sir Henry, Kt.
Annesley, Sir Hugh Norman, Kt., QPM
Anson, Sir John, KCB
Anson, Sir Philip Roland, Bt. (1831)
Anstruther, Sir Sebastian Paten Campbell, Bt. (S. 1694 and S. 1700)
Anstruther-Gough-Calthorpe, Sir Euan Hamilton, Bt. (1929)
Antrobus, Sir Edward Philip, Bt. (1815)
Appleyard, Sir Leonard Vincent, KCMG
Arbib, Sir Martyn, Kt.
Arbuthnot, Sir Keith Robert Charles, Bt. (1823)

Arbuthnot, Sir William Reierson, Bt. (1964)
Arbuthnott, *Prof.* Sir John Peebles, PHD, FRSE
†Archdale, Sir Nicholas Edward, Bt. (1928)
Arculus, Sir Thomas David Guy, Kt.
Armitage, *Air Chief Marshal* Sir Michael John, KCB, CBE
Armitt, Sir John Alexander, Kt., CBE
Armour, *Prof.* Sir James, Kt., CBE
Armstrong, Sir Christopher John Edmund Stuart, Bt. (1841), MBE
Armstrong, Sir Richard, Kt., CBE
Armytage, Sir John Martin, Bt. (1738)
Arnold, *Hon.* Sir Richard David, Kt.
Arnold, Sir Thomas Richard, Kt.
Arnott, Sir Alexander John Maxwell, Bt. (1896)
Arthur, *Lt.-Gen.* Sir (John) Norman Stewart, KCB, CVO
Arthur, Sir Michael Anthony, KCMG
†Arthur, Sir Benjamin Nathan, Bt. (1841)
Arulkumaran, *Prof.* Sir Sabaratnam, Kt.
Asbridge, Sir Jonathan Elliott, Kt.
Ash, *Prof.* Sir Eric Albert, Kt., CBE, FRS, FRENG
Ashburnham, Sir James Fleetwood, Bt. (1661)
Ashworth, *Dr* Sir John Michael, Kt.
Aske, Sir Robert John Bingham, Bt. (1922)
Askew, Sir Bryan, Kt.
Asquith, *Hon.* Sir Dominic Anthony Gerard, KCMG
Astill, *Hon.* Sir Michael John, Kt.
Astley-Cooper, Sir Alexander Paston, Bt. (1821)
Astwood, *Hon.* Sir James Rufus, KBE
Atiyah, Sir Michael Francis, Kt., OM, PHD, FRS
Atkins, *Rt. Hon.* Sir Robert James, Kt.
Atkinson, Sir William Samuel, Kt.
Atopare, Sir Sailas, GCMG
Attenborough, Sir David Frederick, Kt., OM, CH, CVO, CBE, FRS
Aubrey-Fletcher, Sir Henry Egerton, Bt. (1782)
Audland, Sir Christopher John, KCMG
Augier, *Prof.* Sir Fitzroy Richard, Kt.
Auld, *Rt. Hon.* Sir Robin Ernest, Kt.
Austin, Sir Peter John, Bt. (1894)
Austin, *Air Marshal* Sir Roger Mark, KCB, AFC

Austen-Smith, *Air Marshal* Sir Roy David, KBE, CB, CVO, DFC

Avei, Sir Moi, KBE

Ayaz, *Dr* Sir Iftikhar Ahmad, KBE

Ayckbourn, Sir Alan, Kt., CBE

Aykroyd, Sir Henry Robert George, Bt. (1920)

Aykroyd, Sir James Alexander Frederic, Bt. (1929)

Aylmer, Sir Richard John, Bt. (I. 1622)

Aylward, *Prof.* Sir Mansel, Kt., CB

Aynsley-Green, *Prof.* Sir Albert, Kt.

Bacha, Sir Bhinod, Kt., CMG

Backhouse, Sir Alfred James Stott, Bt. (1901)

Bacon, Sir Nicholas Hickman Ponsonby, Bt., OBE (1611 and 1627), *Premier Baronet of England*

Baddeley, Sir John Wolsey Beresford, Bt. (1922)

Badge, Sir Peter Gilmour Noto, Kt.

Bagge, Sir (John) Jeremy Picton, Bt. (1867)

Baggott, Sir Matthew David, Kt., CBE, QPM

Bagnall, *Air Chief Marshal* Sir Anthony, GBE, KCB

Bai, Sir Brown, KBE

Bailey, Sir Alan Marshall, KCB

Bailey, Sir Brian Harry, Kt., OBE

Bailey, Sir John Bilsland, KCB

Bailey, Sir John Richard, Bt. (1919)

Bailhache, Sir Philip Martin, Kt.

Bailhache, Sir William, Kt.

Baillie, Sir Adrian Louis, Bt. (1823)

Bain, *Prof.* Sir George Sayers, Kt.

Baird, Sir Charles William Stuart, Bt. (1809)

†Baird, Sir James Andrew Gardiner, Bt. (S. 1695)

Baird, *Air Marshal* Sir John Alexander, KBE

Baird, *Vice-Adm.* Sir Thomas Henry Eustace, KCB

Baker, *Hon.* Sir Andrew William, Kt.

Baker, Sir Bryan William, Kt.

Baker, *Hon.* Sir Jeremy Russell, Kt.

Baker, *Prof.* Sir John Hamilton, Kt., QC

Baker, Sir John William, Kt., CBE

Baker, *Rt. Hon.* Sir Jonathan Leslie, Kt.

Baker, *Rt. Hon.* Sir (Thomas) Scott (Gillespie), Kt.

Balasubramanian, *Prof.* Sir Shankar, Kt.

Baldry, Sir Antony Brian, Kt.

Baldwin, *Prof.* Sir Jack Edward, Kt., FRS

Ball, Sir Christopher John Elinger, Kt.

Ball, *Prof.* Sir John Macleod, Kt.

Ball, Sir Richard Bentley, Bt. (1911)

Ballantyne, *Dr* Sir Frederick Nathaniel, GCMG

Band, *Adm.* Sir Jonathon, GCB

Banham, Sir John Michael Middlecott, Kt.

Bannerman, Sir David Gordon, Bt. (S. 1682), OBE

Barber, Sir Brendan, Kt.

Barber, Sir Michael Bayldon, Kt.

Barber, Sir (Thomas) David, Bt. (1960)

Barclay, Sir Robert Colraine, Bt. (S. 1668)

Barclay, Sir David Rowat, Kt.

Barclay, Sir Frederick Hugh, Kt.

Baring, Sir John Francis, Bt. (1911)

Barker, *Hon.* Sir (Richard) Ian, Kt.

Barling, *Hon.* Sir Gerald Edward, Kt.

Barlow, Sir Christopher Hilaro, Bt. (1803)

Barlow, Sir Frank, Kt., CBE

Barlow, Sir James Alan, Bt. (1902)

Barlow, Sir John Kemp, Bt. (1907)

Barnes, Sir (James) David (Francis), Kt., CBE

Barnett, *Hon.* Sir Michael Lancelot Patrick, Kt.

Barnett, *Prof.* Sir Richard Robert, Kt.

†Barnewall, Sir Peter Joseph, Bt. (I. 1623)

†Barran, Sir John Ruthven, Bt. (1895)

Barrett, Sir Stephen Jeremy, KCMG

†Barrett-Lennard, Sir Peter John, Bt. (1001)

†Barrington, Sir Benjamin, Bt. (1831)

Barrington-Ward, *Rt. Revd* Simon, KCMG

Barron, Rt. Hon. Sir Kevin, Kt.

Barrons, *Gen.* Sir Richard, KCB, CBE, ADC

Barrow, Sir Anthony John Grenfell, Bt. (1835)

Barrow, Sir Timothy Earle, KCMG, LVO, MBE

Barry, Sir (Lawrence) Edward (Anthony Tress), Bt. (1899)

Barter, Sir Peter Leslie Charles, Kt., OBE

†Bartlett, Sir Andrew Alan, Bt. (1913)

Barttelot, *Col.* Sir Brian Walter de Stopham, Bt. (1875), OBE

Bate, *Prof.* Sir Andrew Jonathan, Kt., CBE

Bates, Sir James Geoffrey, Bt. (1880)

Bates, Sir Richard Dawson Hoult, Bt. (1937)

Batho, Sir Peter Ghislain, Bt. (1928)

Bathurst, *Admiral of the Fleet* Sir (David) Benjamin, GCB

Battishill, Sir Anthony Michael William, GCB

Baulcombe, *Prof.* Sir David Charles, Kt., FRS

Baxendell, Sir Peter Brian, Kt., CBE, FRENG

Bayley, Sir Hugh Nigel Edward, Kt.

Bayne, Sir Nicholas Peter, KCMG

Baynes, Sir Christopher Rory, Bt. (1801)

Bazalgette, Sir Peter Lytton, Kt.

Bazley, Sir Thomas John Sebastian, Bt. (1869)

Beach, *Gen.* Sir (William Gerald) Hugh, GBE, KCB, MC

Beache, *Hon.* Sir Vincent Ian, KCMG

Beale, *Lt.-Gen.* Sir Peter John, KBE, FRCP

Beamish, Sir Adrian John, KCMG

Beamish, Sir David Richard, KCB

Bean, *Dr* Sir Charles Richard, Kt.

Bean, *Rt. Hon.* Sir David Michael, Kt.

Bear, Sir Michael David, Kt.

Beatson, *Rt. Hon.* Sir Jack, Kt.

Beavis, *Air Chief Marshal* Sir Michael Gordon, KCB, CBE, AFC

Beck, Sir Edgar Philip, Kt.

Beckett, Sir Richard Gervase, Bt. (1921), QC

Beckett, *Lt.-Gen.* Sir Thomas Anthony, KCB, CBE

Beckwith, Sir John Lionel, Kt., CBE

Beddington, *Prof.* Sir John Rex, Kt., CMG

†Beecham, Sir Robert Adrian, Bt. (1914)

Beevor, Sir Antony James, Kt.

Beevor, Sir Thomas Hugh Cunliffe, Bt. (1784)

Behan, Sir David, Kt., CBE

Beldam, *Rt. Hon.* Sir (Alexander) Roy (Asplan), Kt.

Belgrave, *HE* Sir Elliott Fitzroy GCMG

Bell, Sir David Charles Maurice, Kt.

Bell, Sir David Robert, KCB

Bell, *Prof.* Sir John Irving, GBE

Bell, Sir John Lowthian, Bt. (1885)

Bell, *Prof.* Sir Peter Robert Frank, Kt.

Bell, *Hon.* Sir Rodger, Kt.

Bellamy, *Hon.* Sir Christopher William, Kt.

Bellingham, Sir Henry Campbell, Kt.

†Bellingham, Sir William Alexander Noel Henry, Bt. (1796)

Bender, Sir Brian Geoffrey, KCB

Benjamin, Sir George William John, Kt., CBE

Benn, Sir (James) Jonathan, Bt. (1914)

Bennett, *Air Vice-Marshal* Sir Erik Peter, KBE, CB

Bennett, *Hon.* Sir Hugh Peter Derwyn, Kt.

Bennett, *Gen.* Sir Phillip Harvey, KBE, DSO

Bennett, Sir Ronald Wilfrid Murdoch, Bt. (1929)

Benson, Sir Christopher John, Kt.

Beresford, Sir (Alexander) Paul, Kt.

Beresford-Peirse, Sir Henry Njers de la Poer, Bt. (1814)

Berghuser, *Hon.* Sir Eric, Kt., MBE

Beringer, *Prof.* Sir John Evelyn, Kt., CBE

Berman, Sir Franklin Delow, KCMG

Berners-Lee, Sir Timothy John, OM, KBE, FRS

Bernard, Sir Dallas Edmund, Bt. (1954)

Berney, Sir Julian Reedham Stuart, Bt. (1620)

Bernstein, Sir Howard, Kt.

Berragan, *Lt.-Gen.* Sir Gerald William, KBE, CB

Berridge, *Prof.* Sir Michael John, Kt., FRS

Berriman, Sir David, Kt.

Berry, *Prof.* Sir Colin Leonard, Kt., FRCPATH

Berry, *Prof.* Sir Michael Victor, Kt., FRS

Berthoud, Sir Martin Seymour, KCVO, CMG

Berwick, *Prof.* Sir George Thomas, Kt., CBE

Besley, *Prof.* Sir Timothy John, Kt., CBE

Best-Shaw, Sir Thomas Joshua, Bt. (1665)

Bethel, Sir Baltron Benjamin, KCMG

Bethlehem, Sir Daniel, KCMG

Bett, Sir Michael, Kt., CBE

Bettison, Sir Norman George, Kt., QPM

Bevan, Sir James David, KCMG

Bevan, Sir Martyn Evan Evans, Bt. (1958)

Bevan, Sir Nicolas, Kt., CB

Beverley, *Lt.-Gen.* Sir Henry York La Roche, KCB, OBE, RM

Bhadeshia, *Prof.* Sir Harshad Kumar Dharamshi, Kt., FRS

Bibby, Sir Michael James, Bt. (1959)

Biddulph, Sir Ian D'Olier, Bt. (1664)

Biggam, Sir Robin Adair, Kt.

Bilas, Sir Angmai Simon, Kt., OBE

Bill, *Lt.-Gen.* Sir David Robert, KCB

Billière, *Gen.* Sir Peter Edgar de la Cour de la, KCB, KBE, DSO, MC

Bindman, Sir Geoffrey Lionel, Kt.

Bingham, *Hon.* Sir Eardley Max, Kt.

Birch, Sir John Allan, KCVO, CMG

Birch, Sir Roger, Kt., CBE, QPM

Bird, *Prof.* Sir Adrian Peter, Kt., CBE, FRS, FRSE

Bird, Sir Richard Geoffrey Chapman, Bt. (1922)

Birkett, Sir Peter, Kt.

Birkin, Sir John Christian William, Bt. (1905)

Birkin, Sir (John) Derek, Kt., TD

Birkmyre, Sir James, Bt. (1921)

Birrell, Sir James Drake, Kt.

Birss, *Hon.* Sir Colin Ian, Kt.

Birt, Sir Michael, Kt.

Birtwistle, Sir Harrison, Kt., CH

Bischoff, Sir Winfried Franz Wilhelm, Kt.

Black, *Prof.* Sir Nicholas Andrew, Kt.

Black, Sir Robert David, Bt. (1922)

Blackburn, *Vice-Adm.* Sir David Anthony James, KCVO, CB

Blackburne, *Hon.* Sir William Anthony, Kt.

Blackett, Sir Hugh Francis, Bt. (1673)

Blackham, *Vice-Adm.* Sir Jeremy Joe, KCB

Blackman, Sir Frank Milton, KCVO, OBE

Blair, Sir Patrick David Hunter, Bt. (1786)

Blair, *Hon.* Sir William James Lynton, Kt.

†Blake, Sir Charles Valentine Bruce, Bt. (I. 1622)

Blake, Sir Francis Michael, Bt. (1907)

Blake, *Hon.* Sir Nicholas John Gorrod, Kt.

Blake, Sir Peter Thomas, Kt., CBE

Blake, Sir Quentin Saxby, Kt., CBE

Blakemore, *Prof.* Sir Colin Brian, Kt., FRS

Blaker, Sir John, Bt. (1919)

Blakiston, Sir Ferguson Arthur James, Bt. (1763)

Blanch, Sir Malcolm, KCVO

Bland, *Lt.-Col.* Sir Simon Claud Michael, KCVO

Blank, Sir Maurice Victor, Kt.

Blatherwick, Sir David Elliott Spiby, KCMG, OBE

Blavatnik, Sir Leonard, Kt.

Blennerhassett, Sir (Marmaduke) Adrian Francis William, Bt. (1809)

Blewitt, *Maj.* Sir Shane Gabriel Basil, GCVO

Blofeld, *Hon.* Sir John Christopher Calthorpe, Kt.

Blois, Sir Charles Nicholas Gervase, Bt. (1686)

Blom-Cooper, Sir Louis Jacques, Kt., QC

Blomefield, Sir Thomas Charles Peregrine, Bt. (1807)

Bloom, *Prof.* Sir Stephen Robert, Kt.

Bloomfield, Sir Kenneth Percy, KCB

Bundell, *Prof.* Sir Richard William, Kt., CBE, FBA

Blundell, Sir Thomas Leon, Kt., FRS

†Blunden, Sir Hubert Chisholm, Bt. (I. 1766)

Blunt, Sir David Richard Reginald Harvey, Bt. (1720)

Blyth, Sir Charles (Chay), Kt., CBE, BEM

Boardman, *Prof.* Sir John, Kt., FSA, FBA

Bodey, *Hon.* Sir David Roderick Lessiter, Kt.

Bodmer, Sir Walter Fred, Kt., PHD, FRS

Bogle, Sir Nigel, Kt.

Bogan, Sir Nagora, KBE

Boileau, Sir Nicolas Edmond George, Bt. (1838)

Boleat, Sir Mark John, Kt.

Boles, Sir Richard Fortescue, Bt. (1922)

Bollom, *Air Marshal* Sir Simon John, KBE, CB

Bona, Sir Kina, KBE

Bonallack, Sir Michael Francis, Kt., OBE

Bond, Sir John Reginald Hartnell, Kt.

Bond, *Prof.* Sir Michael Richard, Kt., FRCPSYCH, FRCPGLAS, FRCSE

Bone, *Prof.* Sir (James) Drummond, Kt., FRSE

Bone, Sir Roger Bridgland, KCMG

Bonfield, Sir Peter Leahy, Kt., CBE, FRENG

Bonham, Sir George Martin Antony, Bt. (1852)

Bonington, Sir Christian John Storey, Kt., CVO, CBE

Bonsor, Sir Nicholas Cosmo, Bt. (1925)

Boord, Sir Nicolas John Charles, Bt. (1896)

Boorman, *Lt.-Gen.* Sir Derek, KCB

Booth, Sir Clive, Kt.

Booth, Sir Douglas Allen, Bt. (1916)

Boothby, Sir Brooke Charles, Bt. (1660)

Bore, Sir Albert, Kt.

Boreel, Sir Stephan Gerard, Bt. (1645)

Borthwick, Sir Antony Thomas, Bt. (1908)

Borysiewicz, *Prof.* Sir Leszek Krzysztof, Kt.

Bosher, Sir Robin, Kt.

Bossano, *Hon.* Sir Joseph John, KCMG

Bossom, Sir Bruce Charles, Bt. (1953)

Boswell, *Lt.-Gen.* Sir Alexander Crawford Simpson, KCB, CBE

Botham, Sir Ian Terence, Kt., OBE

Bottomley, Sir Peter James, Kt.

Bottoms, *Prof.* Sir Anthony Edward, Kt.

Boughey, Sir John George Fletcher, Bt. (1798)

†Boulton, Sir John Gibson, Bt. (1944)

Bouraga, Sir Phillip, KBE

Bourn, Sir John Bryant, KCB

Bourne, Sir Matthew Christopher, Kt., OBE

Bowater, Sir Euan David Vansittart, Bt. (1939)

†Bowater, Sir Michael Patrick, Bt. (1914)

Bowden, Sir Andrew, Kt., MBE

Bowden, Sir Nicholas Richard, Bt. (1915)

Bowen, Sir Barry Manfield, KCMG

Bowen, Sir Geoffrey Fraser, Kt.

Bowen, Sir George Edward Michael, Bt. (1921)

Bowes Lyon, Sir Simon Alexander, KCVO

Bowlby, Sir Richard Peregrine Longstaff, Bt. (1923)

Bowman, Sir Edwin Geoffrey, KCB

Bowman, Sir Jeffery Haverstock, Kt.

Bowness, Sir Alan, Kt., CBE

Bowyer-Smyth, Sir Thomas Weyland, Bt. (1661)

Boyce, Sir Graham Hugh, KCMG

Boyce, Sir Robert Charles Leslie, Bt. (1952)

Boyd, Sir Alexander Walter, Bt. (1916)

Boyd, Sir John Dixon Iklé, KCMG

Boyd, Sir Michael, Kt.

Boyd, *Prof.* Sir Robert David Hugh, Kt.

Boyd-Carpenter, Sir (Marsom) Henry, KCVO

Boyd-Carpenter, *Lt.-Gen. Hon.* Sir Thomas Patrick John, KBE

Boyle, *Prof.* Sir Roger Michael, Kt., CBE

Boyle, Sir Simon Hugh Patrick, KCVO

Boyle, Sir Stephen Gurney, Bt. (1904)

Bracewell-Smith, Sir Charles, Bt. (1947)

Bradford, Sir Edward Alexander Slade, Bt. (1902)

Bradshaw, *Lt.-Gen.* Sir Adrian, KCB, OBE

Brady, Sir Graham Stuart, Kt.

Brady, *Prof.* Sir John Michael, Kt., FRS

Brailsford, Sir David John, Kt., CBE

Braithwaite, Sir Rodric Quentin, GCMG

Bramley, *Prof.* Sir Paul Anthony, Kt.

Branagh, Sir Kenneth Charles, Kt.

Branson, Sir Richard Charles Nicholas, Kt.

Bratza, *Hon.* Sir Nicolas Dušan, Kt.

Brazier, Sir Julian William Hendy, Kt., TD

Breckenridge, *Prof.* Sir Alasdair Muir, Kt., CBE

Brennan, *Hon.* Sir (Francis) Gerard, KBE

Brenton, Sir Anthony Russell, KCMG

Brewer, Sir David William, KG, CMG, CVO

Brierley, Sir Ronald Alfred, Kt.

Briggs, *Rt. Hon.* Sir Michael Townley Featherstone, Kt. (Lord Briggs of Westbourne)

Brighouse, *Prof.* Sir Timothy Robert Peter, Kt.

Bright, Sir Graham Frank James, Kt.

Bright, Sir Keith, Kt.

Brigstocke, *Adm.* Sir John Richard, KCB

Brinckman, Sir Theodore George Roderick, Bt. (1831)

†Brisco, Sir Campbell Howard, Bt. (1782)

Briscoe, Sir Brian Anthony, Kt.

Briscoe, Sir John Geoffrey James, Bt. (1910)

Brittan, Sir Samuel, Kt.

Britton, Sir Paul John James, Kt., CB

†Broadbent, Sir Andrew George, Bt. (1893)

Broadbent, Sir Richard John, KCB

Brocklebank, Sir Aubrey Thomas, Bt. (1885)

†Brodie, Sir Benjamin David Ross, Bt. (1834)

Bromhead, Sir John Desmond Gonville, Bt. (1806)

Bromley, Sir Michael Roger, KBE

†Bromley, Sir Charles Howard, Bt. (1757)

Bromley-Davenport, Sir William Arthur, KCVO

Brook, *Prof.* Sir Richard John, Kt., OBE

Brooke, Sir Alistair Weston, Bt. (1919)

Brooke, Sir Francis George Windham, Bt. (1903)

Brooke, Sir Richard Christopher, Bt. (1662)

Brooke, Sir Rodney George, Kt., CBE

Brooking, Sir Trevor David, Kt., CBE

Brooksbank, Sir (Edward) Nicholas, Bt. (1919)

Broomfield, Sir Nigel Hugh Robert Allen, KCMG

†Broughton, Sir David Delves, Bt. (1661)

Broughton, Sir Martin Faulkner, Kt.

Broun, Sir Wayne Hercules, Bt. (S. 1686)

Brown, Sir (Austen) Patrick, KCB

Brown, *Adm.* Sir Brian Thomas, KCB, CBE

Brown, Sir David, Kt.

Brown, Sir Ewan, Kt., CBE

Brown, Sir George Francis Richmond, Bt. (1863)

Brown, Sir Mervyn, KCMG, OBE

Brown, Sir Peter Randolph, Kt.

Brown, *Rt. Hon.* Sir Stephen, GBE

Brown, Sir Stephen David Reid, KCVO

Brownrigg, Sir Nicholas (Gawen), Bt. (1816)

Browse, *Prof.* Sir Norman Leslie, Kt., MD, FRCS

Bruce, Sir (Francis) Michael Ian, Bt. (s. 1628)

Bruce-Clifton, Sir Hervey Hamish Peter, Bt. (1804)

Bruce-Gardner, Sir Edmund Thomas Peter, Bt. (1945)

Brunner, Sir Hugo Laurence Joseph, KCVO

Brunner, Sir Nicholas Felix Minturn, Bt. (1895)

†Brunton, Sir James Lauder, Bt. (1908)

Bryan, *Hon.* Sir Simon James, Kt.

Bryant, *Air Chief Marshal* Sir Simon, KCB, CBE, ADC

Bubb, Sir Stephen John Limrick, Kt.

Buchan-Hepburn, Sir John Alastair Trant Kidd, Bt. (1815)

Buchanan, Sir Andrew George, Bt. (1878), KCVO

Buchanan-Jardine, Sir John Christopher Rupert, Bt. (1885)

Buckland, Sir Ross, Kt.

Buckley, *Dr* Sir George William, Kt.

Buckley, Sir Michael Sidney, Kt.

Buckley, *Lt.-Cdr.* Sir (Peter) Richard, KCVO

Buckley, *Hon.* Sir Roger John, Kt.

Bucknall, *Lt.-Gen.* Sir James Jeffrey Corfield, KCB, CBE

†Buckworth-Herne-Soame, Sir Richard John, Bt. (1697)

Budd, Sir Alan Peter, GBE

Budd, Sir Colin Richard, KCMG

Buffini, Sir Damon Marcus, Kt.

Bull, Sir George Jeffrey, Kt.

Bull, Sir Simeon George, Bt. (1922)

Bullock, Sir Stephen Michael, Kt.

Bultin, Sir Bato, Kt., MBE

Bunbury, Sir Michael William, Bt. (1681), KCVO

Bunyard, Sir Robert Sidney, Kt., CBE, QPM

Burbidge, Sir Peter Dudley, Bt. (1916)

Burden, Sir Anthony Thomas, Kt., QPM

Burdett, Sir Crispin Peter, Bt. (1665)

Burgen, Sir Arnold Stanley Vincent, Kt., FRS

Burgess, Sir (Joseph) Stuart, Kt., CBE, PHD, FRSC

Burgess, *Prof.* Sir Robert George, Kt.

Burke, Sir James Stanley Gilbert, Bt. (I. 1797)

Burke, Sir (Thomas) Kerry, Kt.

Burn, *Prof.* Sir John, Kt.

Burnell-Nugent, *Vice-Adm.* Sir James Michael, KCB, CBE, ADC

Burnett, Sir Charles David, Bt. (1913)

Burney, Sir Nigel Dennistoun, Bt. (1921)

Burns, *Dr* Sir Henry, Kt.

Burns, Sir (Robert) Andrew, KCMG

Burns, *Rt. Hon.* Sir Simon Hugh McGuigan, Kt.

Burnton, *Rt. Hon.* Sir Stanley Jeffrey, Kt.

Burrell, Sir Charles Raymond, Bt. (1774)

Burridge, *Air Chief Marshal* Sir Brian Kevin, KCB, CBE, ADC

Burton, *Lt.-Gen.* Sir Edmund Fortescue Gerard, KBE

Burton, Sir Graham Stuart, KCMG

Burton, *Hon.* Sir Michael John, Kt.

Burton, Sir Michael St Edmund, KCVO, CMG

Butcher, *Hon.* Sir Christopher John, Kt.

Butler, *Dr* Sir David Edgeworth, Kt., CBE

Butler, Sir Percy James, Kt., CBE

Butler, Sir Reginald Richard Michael, Bt. (1922)

Butler, Sir Richard Pierce, Bt. (I. 1628)

Butterfield, *Hon.* Sir Alexander Neil Logie, Kt.

Butterfill, Sir John Valentine, Kt.

Buxton, Sir Crispin Charles Gerard, Bt. (1840)

Buxton, *Rt. Hon.* Sir Richard Joseph, Kt.

Buzzard, Sir Anthony Farquhar, Bt. (1929)

Byatt, Sir Ian Charles Rayner, Kt.

Byron, *Rt. Hon.* Sir Charles Michael Dennis, Kt.

Cable, *Rt. Hon.* Sir (John) Vincent, Kt., PHD

†Cable-Alexander, Sir Patrick Desmond William, Bt. (1809)

Cadbury, Sir (Nicholas) Dominic, Kt.

Cadogan, *Prof.* Sir John Ivan George, Kt., CBE, FRS, FRSE

Cahn, Sir Albert Jonas, Bt. (1934)

Cahn, Sir Andrew Thomas, KCMG

Caine, Sir Michael (Maurice Micklewhite), Kt., CBE

Caines, Sir John, KCB

Cairns, *Very Revd* John Ballantyne, KCVO

Caldwell, Sir Edward George, KCB

Callaghan, Sir William Henry, Kt.

Callan, Sir Ivan Roy, KCVO, CMG

Callender, Sir Colin Nigel, Kt., CBE

Callman, *His Hon.* Sir Clive Vernon, Kt.

Calman, *Prof.* Sir Kenneth Charles, KCB, MD, FRCP, FRCS, FRSE

Calne, *Prof.* Sir Roy Yorke, Kt., FRS

Calvert-Smith, Sir David, Kt., QC

Cameron, Sir Hugh Roy Graham, Kt., QPM

Campbell, *Prof.* Sir Colin Murray, Kt.

Campbell, Sir Ian Tofts, Kt., CBE, VRD

Campbell, Sir James Alexander Moffat Bain, Bt. (S. 1668)

Campbell, Sir John Park, Kt., OBE

Campbell, Sir Lachlan Philip Kemeys, Bt. (1815)

Campbell, *Dr* Sir Philip Henry Montgomery, Kt.

Campbell, Sir Roderick Duncan Hamilton, Bt. (1831)

Campbell, Sir Louis Auchinbreck, Bt. (S. 1628)

Campbell, *Dr* Sir Simon Fraser, Kt., CBE

Campbell, *Rt. Hon.* Sir William Anthony, Kt.

†Campbell-Orde, Sir John Simon Arthur, Bt. (1790)

Cannadine, *Prof.* Sir David Nicholas, Kt.

Capewell, *Lt.-Gen.* Sir David Andrew, KCB, OBE, RM

†Carden, Sir Christopher Robert, Bt. (1887)

†Carden, Sir John Craven, Bt. (I. 1787)

Carew, Sir Rivers Verain, Bt. (1661)

Carey, Sir de Vic Graham, Kt.

Carleton-Smith, *Maj.-Gen.* Sir Michael Edward, Kt., CBE

Carlisle, Sir James Beethoven, GCMG

Carlisle, Sir John Michael, Kt.

Carlisle, Sir Kenneth Melville, Kt.

Carnegie, Sir Roderick Howard, Kt.

Carnwath, *Rt. Hon.* Sir Robert John Anderson, Kt., CVO (Lord Carnwath of Notting Hill)

Carr, *Hon.* Sir Henry James, Kt.

Carr, Sir Roger Martyn, Kt.

Carrick, Sir Roger John, KCMG, LVO

Carruthers, Sir Ian James, Kt., OBE

Carsberg, *Prof.* Sir Bryan Victor, Kt.

Carter, Sir Andrew Nicholas, Kt., OBE

Carter, Sir David Anthony, Kt.

Carter, *Prof.* Sir David Craig, Kt., FRCSE, FRCSGLAS, FRCPE

Carter, Sir Edward Charles, KCMG

Carter, Sir John Gordon Thomas, Kt.

Carter, *Lt.-Gen.* Sir Nicholas Patrick, KCB, CBE, DSO

Cartledge, Sir Bryan George, KCMG

Caruna, *Hon.* Sir Peter Richard, KCMG, QC

†Cary, Sir Nicholas Robert Hugh, Bt. (1955)

Cash, Sir Andrew John, Kt., OBE

Cash, Sir William Nigel Paul, Kt.

Cass, Sir Geoffrey Arthur, Kt.

Cassel, Sir Timothy Felix Harold, Bt. (1920)

Cassels, *Adm.* Sir Simon Alastair Cassillis, KCB, CBE

Cassidi, *Adm.* Sir (Arthur) Desmond, GCB

Castell, Sir William Martin, Kt.

Catto, *Prof.* Sir Graeme Robertson Dawson, Kt.

†Cave, Sir George Charles, Bt. (1896)

Cave-Browne-Cave, Sir John Robert Charles, Bt. (1641)

Cayley, Sir Digby William David, Bt. (1661)

Cazalet, *Hon.* Sir Edward Stephen, Kt.

Cazalet, Sir Peter Grenville, Kt.

Cenac, *HE* Sir (Emmanuel) Neville, GCMG

Chadwick, *Rt. Hon.* Sir John Murray, Kt.

Chadwick, Sir Joshua Kenneth Burton, Bt. (1935)

Chadwyck-Healey, Sir Charles Edward, Bt. (1919)

Chakrabarti, Sir Sumantra, KCB

Chalmers, Sir Iain Geoffrey, Kt.

Chalmers, Sir Neil Robert, Kt.

Chalstrey, Sir (Leonard) John, Kt., MD, FRCS

Chan, *Rt. Hon.* Sir Julius, GCMG, KBE

Chan, Sir Thomas Kok, Kt., OBE

Chance, Sir John Sebastian, Bt. (1900)

Chandler, Sir Colin Michael, Kt.

Chantler, *Prof.* Sir Cyril, GBE, MD, FRCP

Chaplin, Sir Malcolm Hilbery, Kt., CBE

Chapman, Sir David Robert Macgowan, Bt. (1958)

Chapman, Sir Frank, Kt.

Chapman, Sir George Alan, Kt.

Chapple, *Field Marshal* Sir John Lyon, GCB, GBE

Charles, *Hon.* Sir Arthur William Hessin, Kt.

Charlton, Sir Robert (Bobby), Kt., CBE

Charnley, Sir (William) John, Kt., CB, FRENG

†Chayter, Sir Bruce Gordon, Bt. (1831)

Checketts, *Sqn. Ldr.* Sir David John, KCVO

Checkland, Sir Michael, Kt.

Cheshire, Sir Ian Michael, Kt.

Cheshire, *Air Chief Marshal* Sir John Anthony, KBE, CB

Chessells, Sir Arthur David (Tim), Kt.

†Chetwynd, Sir Peter James Talbot, Bt. (1795)

Cheyne, Sir Patrick John Lister, Bt. (1908)

Chichester, Sir James Henry Edward, Bt. (1641)

Chilcot, *Rt. Hon.* Sir John Anthony, GCB

Chilcott, Sir Dominick John, KCMG

Child, Sir (Coles John) Jeremy, Bt. (1919)

Chinn, Sir Trevor Edwin, Kt., CVO

†Chinubhai, Sir Prashant, Bt. (1913)

Chipperfield, *Prof.* Sir David Alan, Kt., CBE

Chipperfield, Sir Geoffrey Howes, KCB

Chisholm, Sir John Alexander Raymond, Kt., FRENG

†Chitty, Sir Andrew Edward Willes, Bt. (1924)

Cholmeley, Sir Hugh John Frederick Sebastian, Bt. (1806)

Chope, Sir Christopher Robert, Kt., OBE

Choudhury, *Hon.* Sir Akhlaq Ur-Rahman, Kt.

Chow, Sir Chung Kong, Kt.

Chow, Sir Henry Francis, Kt., OBE

Christopher, Sir Duncan Robin Carmichael, KBE, CMG

Chung, Sir Sze-yuen, GBE, FRENG

Clark, *Prof.* Sir Christopher Munro, Kt.

Clark, Sir Francis Drake, Bt. (1886)

Clark, Sir Jonathan George, Bt. (1917)

Clark, Sir Terence Joseph, KBE, CMG, CVO

Clark, Sir Timothy Charles, KBE

Clarke, Sir (Charles Mansfield) Tobias, Bt. (1831)

Clarke, *Rt. Hon.* Sir Christopher Simon Courtenay Stephenson, Kt.

Clarke, *Hon.* Sir David Clive, Kt.

Clarke, Sir Jonathan Dennis, Kt.

Clarke, Sir Paul Robert Virgo, KCVO

Clarke, Sir Rupert Grant Alexander, Bt. (1882)

Clary, *Prof.* Sir David Charles, Kt.

Clay, Sir Edward, KCMG

Clay, Sir Richard Henry, Bt. (1841)

Clayton, Sir David Robert, Bt. (1732)

Cleaver, Sir Anthony Brian, Kt.

Clegg, *Rt. Hon.* Sir Nicholas William Peter, Kt.

Clementi, Sir David Cecil, Kt.

Clerk, Sir Robert Maxwell, Bt. (S. 1679), OBE

Clerke, Sir Francis Ludlow Longueville, Bt. (1660)

Clifford, Sir Roger Joseph, Bt. (1887)

Clifford, Sir Timothy Peter Plint, Kt.

Clifton-Brown, Sir Geoffrey Robert, Kt.

Coates, Sir Anthony Robert Milnes, Bt. (1911)

Coates, Sir David Frederick Charlton, Bt. (1921)

†Coats, Sir Alexander James Stuart, Bt. (1905)

Cobb, *Hon.* Sir Stephen William Scott, Kt.

Cochrane, Sir (Henry) Marc (Sursock), Bt. (1903)

†Cockburn, Sir Charles Christopher, Bt. (S. 1671)

Cockburn-Campbell, Sir Alexander Thomas, Bt. (1821)

Cockell, Sir Merrick, Kt.

Cockshaw, Sir Alan, Kt., FRENG.

Codrington, Sir Christopher George Wayne, Bt. (1876)

Codrington, Sir Giles Peter, Bt. (1721)

Codron, Sir Michael Victor, Kt., CBE
Coghill, Sir Patrick Kendal Farley, Bt. (1778)
Coghlin, *Rt. Hon.* Sir Patrick, Kt.
Cohen, Sir Ivor Harold, Kt., CBE, TD
Cohen, *Hon.* Sir Jonathan Lionel, Kt.
Cohen, *Prof.* Sir Philip, Kt., PHD, FRS
Cohen, Sir Ronald, Kt.
Cole, Sir (Robert) William, Kt.
Coleman, Sir Robert John, KCMG
Coleridge, *Hon.* Sir Paul James Duke, Kt.
Coles, Sir (Arthur) John, GCMG
Colfox, Sir Philip John, Bt. (1939)
Collas, Sir Richard John, Kt.
Collett, Sir Ian Seymour, Bt. (1934)
Collier, Sir Paul, Kt., CBE
Collins, Sir Alan Stanley, KCVO, CMG
Collins, *Hon.* Sir Andrew David, Kt.
Collins, Sir Bryan Thomas Alfred, Kt., OBE, QFSM
Collins, *Dr* Sir David John, Kt., CBE
Collins, Sir John Alexander, Kt
Collins, Sir Kenneth Darlingston, Kt.
Collins, *Dr* Sir Kevan Arthur, Kt
Collins, *Prof.* Sir Rory Edwards, Kt.
Collyear, Sir John Gowen, Kt.
Colman, Sir Michael Jeremiah, Bt. (1907)
Colman, Sir Timothy, KG
Colquhoun of Luss, Sir Malcolm Rory, Bt. (1786)
Colt, Sir Edward William Dutton, Bt. (1694)
Colthurst, Sir Charles St John, Bt. (I. 1744)
Colton, *Hon.* Sir Adrian George Patrick, Kt.
Conant, Sir John Ernest Michael, Bt. (1954)
Conner, *Rt Revd* David John, KCVO
Connery, Sir Sean, Kt.
Connolly, William (Billy), Kt., CBE
Connor, Sir William Joseph, Kt.
Conran, Sir Terence Orby, Kt., CH
Cons, *Hon.* Sir Derek, Kt.
Constantinou, Sir Kosta George, Kt., OBE
Constantinou, Sir Theophilus George, Kt., OBE
Conway, *Prof.* Sir Gordon Richard, KCMG, FRS
Cook, Sir Andrew, Kt., CBE
Cook, Sir Christopher Wymondham Rayner Herbert, Bt. (1886)
Cook, *Prof.* Sir Peter Frederic Chester, Kt.
Cooke, *Hon.* Sir Jeremy Lionel, Kt.
Cooke, *Prof.* Sir Ronald Urwick, Kt.
Cooke-Yarborough, Sir Anthony Edmund, Bt. (1661)
Cooksey, Sir David James Scott, GBE
Cooper, *Prof.* Sir Cary Lynn, Kt., CBE
Cooper, *Gen.* Sir George Leslie Conroy, GCB, MC
Cooper, Sir Richard Adrian, Bt. (1905)
Cooper, Sir Robert Francis, KCMG, MVO

Cooper, *Maj.-Gen.* Sir Simon Christie, GCVO
Cooper, Sir William Daniel Charles, Bt. (1863)
Coote, Sir Nicholas Patrick, Bt. (I. 1621), *Premier Baronet of Ireland*
Corbett, *Maj.-Gen.* Sir Robert John Swan, KCVO, CB
Corder, Vice-Adm. Sir Ian Fergus, KBE, CB
Cordy-Simpson, *Lt.-Gen.* Sir Roderick Alexander, KBE, CB
Corness, Sir Colin Ross, Kt.
Corry, Sir James Michael, Bt. (1885)
Cory, Sir (Clinton Charles) Donald, Bt. (1919)
Cory-Wright, Sir Richard Michael, Bt. (1903)
Cossons, Sir Neil, Kt., OBE
Cotter, Sir Patrick Laurence Delaval, Bt. (I. 1763)
Cotterell, Sir Henry Richard Geers, Bt. (1805), OBE
†Cotts, Sir Richard Crichton Mitchell, Bt. (1921)
Coulson, *Rt. Hon.* Sir Peter David William, Kt.
Couper, Sir James George, Bt. (1841)
Courtenay, Sir Thomas Daniel, Kt.
Cousins, *Air Chief Marshal* Sir David, KCB, AFC
Coville, *Air Marshal* Sir Christopher Charles Cotton, KCB
Cowan, *Gen.* Sir Samuel, KCB, CBE
Coward, *Lt.-Gen.* Sir Gary Robert, KBE, CB, OBE
Coward, *Vice-Adm.* Sir John Francis, KCB, DSO
Cowdery, Sir Clive, Kt.
Cowley, *Prof.* Sir Steven Charles, Kt., FRS, FRENG
Cowper-Coles, Sir Sherard Louis, KCMG, LVO
Cox, Sir Alan George, Kt., CBE
Cox, *Prof.* Sir David Roxbee, Kt.
Cox, Sir George Edwin, Kt.
Craft, *Prof.* Sir Alan William, Kt.
Cragg, *Prof.* Sir Anthony Douglas, Kt., CBE
Cragnolini, Sir Luciano, Kt.
Craig-Cooper, Sir (Frederick Howard) Michael, Kt., CBE, TD
Craig-Martin, Sir Michael, Kt., CBE
Crane, *Prof.* Sir Peter Robert, Kt.
Cranston, *Hon.* Sir Ross Frederick, Kt.
Craufurd, Sir Robert James, Bt. (1781)
Crausby, Sir David Anthony, Kt.
Craven, Sir John Anthony, Kt.
Craven, Sir Philip Lee, Kt., MBE
Crawford, *Prof.* Sir Frederick William, Kt., FRENG
Crawford, Sir Robert William Kenneth, Kt., CBE
Crawley-Boevey, Sir Thomas Michael Blake, Bt. (1784)
Cresswell, *Hon.* Sir Peter John, Kt.
Crew, Sir (Michael) Edward, Kt., QPM
Crewe, *Prof.* Sir Ivor Martin, Kt.
Crisp, Sir John Charles, Bt. (1913)

Critchett, Sir Charles George Montague, Bt. (1908)
Crittin, *Hon.* Sir John Luke, KBE
Croft, Sir Owen Glendower, Bt. (1671)
Croft, Sir Thomas Stephen Hutton, Bt. (1818)
Crofton, Sir Edward Morgan, Bt. (1801)
Crofton, Sir Julian Malby, Bt. (1838)
Crombie, Sir Alexander, Kt.
Crompton, Sir Dan, Kt., CBE, QPM
Cropper, Sir James Anthony, KCVO
Crosby, Sir Lynton Keith, Kt.
Crossley, Sir Sloan Nicholas, Bt. (1909)
Crowe, Sir Brian Lee, KCMG
Cruickshank, Sir Donald Gordon, Kt.
Cubie, *Dr* Sir Andrew, Kt., CBE
Cubitt, Sir Hugh Guy, Kt., CBE
Cubitt, *Maj.-Gen.* Sir William George, KCVO, CBE
Cullen, Sir (Edward) John, Kt., FRENG
Culme-Seymour, Sir Michael Patrick, Bt. (1809)
Culpin, Sir Robert Paul, Kt.
Cummins, Sir Michael John Austin, Kt.
Cunliffe, *Prof.* Sir Barrington, Kt., CBE
Cunliffe, Sir David Ellis, Bt. (1759)
Cunliffe, Sir Jonathan Stephen, Kt., CB
Cunliffe-Owen, Sir Hugo Dudley, Bt. (1920)
Cunningham, *Lt.-Gen.* Sir Hugh Patrick, KBE
Cunningham, *Prof.* Sir John, KCVO
Cunningham, Sir Roger Keith, Kt., CBE
Cunningham, Sir Thomas Anthony, Kt.
Cunynghame, Sir Andrew David Francis, Bt. (S. 1702)
Curran, *Prof.* Sir Paul James, Kt.
†Currie, Sir Bradley Mark Higgins, Bt. (1847)
Curtain, Sir Michael, KBE
Curtice, *Prof.* Sir John Kevin, Kt., FBA, FRSE
Curtis, Sir Barry John, Kt.
Curtis, *Hon.* Sir Richard Herbert, Kt.
Curtis, Sir Edward Philip, Bt. (1802)
Cuschieri, *Prof.* Sir Alfred, Kt.

Dain, Sir David John Michael, KCVO
Dales, Sir Richard Nigel, KCVO
Dalglish, Sir Kenneth, Kt., MBE
Dalrymple-Hay, Sir Malcolm John Robert, Bt. (1798)
†Dalrymple-White, Sir Jan Hew, Bt. (1926)
Dalton, Sir David Nigel, Kt.
Dalton, *Vice-Adm.* Sir Geoffrey Thomas James Oliver, GCB
Dalton, Sir Richard John, KCMG
Dalton, *Air Chief Marshal* Sir Stephen Gary George, GCB
†Dalyell, Sir Gordon Wheatley, Bt. (NS 1685)

Dancer, Sir Eric, KCVO, CBE

Daniel, Sir John Sagar, Kt., DSC

Darell, Sir Guy Jeffrey Adair, Bt. (1795)

Darrington, Sir Michael John, Kt.

Darroch, Sir Nigel Kim, KCMG

Dasgupta, *Prof.* Sir Partha Sarathi, Kt.

Dashwood, *Prof.* Sir (Arthur) Alan, KCMG, CBE, QC

Dashwood, Sir Edward John Francis, Bt. (1707), *Premier Baronet of Great Britain*

Dashwood, Sir Frederick George Mahon, Bt. (1684)

Daunt, Sir Timothy Lewis Achilles, KCMG

Davey, *Rt. Hon.* Sir Edward Jonathan, Kt.

Davidson, Sir Martin Stuart, KCMG

Davies, *Prof.* Sir David Evan Naughton, Kt., CBE, FRS, FRENG

Davies, Sir David John, Kt.

Davies, Sir Frank John, Kt., CBE

Davies, *Prof.* Sir Graeme John, Kt., FRENG

Davies, Sir John Howard, Kt.

Davies, Sir John Michael, KCB

Davies, Sir Raymond Douglas, Kt.

Davies, Sir Rhys Everson, Kt., QC

Davis, Sir Andrew Frank, Kt., CBE

Davis, Sir Crispin Henry Lamert, Kt.

Davis, Sir John Gilbert, Bt. (1946)

Davis, Sir Michael Lawrence, Kt.

Davis, *Rt. Hon.* Sir Nigel Anthony Lamert, Kt.

Davis, Sir Peter John, Kt.

Davis, *Hon.* Sir William Easthope, Kt.

Davis-Goff, Sir Robert (William), Bt. (1905)

Davson, Sir George Trenchard Simon, Bt. (1927)

Dawanincura, Sir John Norbert, Kt., OBE

Dawbarn, Sir Simon Yelverton, KCVO, CMG

Dawson, *Hon.* Sir Daryl Michael, KBE, CB

Dawson, Sir Nicholas Anthony Trevor, Bt. (1920)

Day, Sir Barry Stuart, Kt., OBE

Day, *Air Chief Marshal* Sir John Romney, KCB, OBE, ADC

Day, Sir Jonathan Stephen, Kt., CBE

Day, Sir (Judson) Graham, Kt.

Day, Sir Michael John, Kt., OBE

Day, Sir Simon James, Kt.

Day-Lewis, Sir Daniel Michael Blake, Kt.

Deane, *Hon.* Sir William Patrick, KBE

Dearlove, Sir Richard Billing, KCMG, OBE

Deaton, *Prof.* Sir Angus Stewart, Kt.

†Debenham, Sir Thomas Adam, Bt. (1931)

Deegan, Sir Michael, Kt., CBE

Deeny, *Rt. Hon.* Sir Donnell Justin Patrick, Kt.

De Haan, Sir Roger Michael, Kt., CBE

De Halpert, *Rear-Adm.* Sir Jeremy Michael, KCVO, CB

de Hoghton, Sir (Richard) Bernard (Cuthbert), Bt. (1611)

de la Rue, Sir Andrew George Ilay, Bt. (1898)

Dellow, Sir John Albert, Kt., CBE

Delves, *Lt.-Gen.* Sir Cedric Norman George, KBE

Denison-Smith, *Lt.-Gen.* Sir Anthony Arthur, KBE

Denny, Sir Charles Alistair Maurice, Bt. (1913)

Denny, Sir Piers Anthony de Waltham, Bt. (I. 1782)

Desmond, Sir Denis Fitzgerald, KCVO, CBE

de Trafford, Sir John Humphrey, Bt. (1841)

Devane, Sir Ciaran Gearoid, Kt.

Deverell, *Lt.-Gen.* Sir Christopher Michael, KCB, MBE

Deverell, *Gen.* Sir John Freegard, KCB, OBE

Devereux, Sir Robert, KCB

De Ville, Sir Harold Godfrey Oscar, Kt., CBE

Devine, *Prof.* Sir Thomas Martin, Kt., OBE, FRSE

Devitt, Sir James Hugh Thomas, Bt. (1916)

Dewey, Sir Rupert Grahame, Bt. (1917)

De Witt, Sir Ronald Wayne, Kt.

Diamond, *Prof.* Sir Ian David, Kt., FRSE

Dick-Lauder, Sir Piers Robert, Bt. (S. 1690)

Dilke, Revd Charles John Wentworth, Bt. (1862)

Dilnot, Sir Andrew William, Kt., CBE

Dillon, Sir Andrew Patrick, Kt., CBE

Dilley, Sir Philip Graham, Kt.

Dillwyn-Venables-Llewelyn, Sir John Michael, Bt. (1890)

Dingemans, *Hon.* Sir James Michael, Kt.

Dion, Sir Leo, KBE

Dixon, Sir Jeremy, Kt.

Dixon, Sir Jonathan Mark, Bt. (1919)

Dixon, *Dr* Sir Michael, Kt.

Dixon, Sir Peter John Bellett, Kt.

Djanogly, Sir Harry Ari Simon, Kt., CBE

Dobson, *Prof.* Sir Christopher Martin, Kt.

Dobson, *Vice-Adm.* Sir David Stuart, KBE

Dollery, Sir Colin Terence, Kt.

Don-Wauchope, Sir Roger (Hamilton), Bt. (S. 1667)

Donaldson, *Prof.* Sir Liam Joseph, Kt.

Donaldson, *Rt. Hon.* Sir Jeffrey Mark, Kt.

Donaldson, *Prof.* Sir Simon Kirwan, Kt.

Donnelly, Sir Joseph Brian, KBE, CMG

Donnelly, Sir Martin Eugene, KCB, CMG

Dorfman, Sir Lloyd, Kt., CBE

Dorman, Sir Philip Henry Keppel, Bt. (1923)

Douglas, *Prof.* Sir Neil James, Kt.

Douglas, *Hon.* Sir Roger Owen, Kt.

Dove, *Hon.* Sir Ian William, Kt.

Dowell, Sir Anthony James, Kt., CBE

Dowling, Sir Robert, Kt.

Downes, *Prof.* Sir Charles Peter, Kt., OBE, FRSE

Downey, Sir Gordon Stanley, KCB

Doyle, Sir Reginald Derek Henry, Kt., CBE

D'Oyly, Sir Hadley Gregory, Bt. (1663)

Drewry, *Lt.-Gen.* Sir Christopher Francis, KCB, CBE

Drinkwater, Sir John Muir, Kt., QC

Dryden, Sir John Stephen Gyles, Bt. (1733 and 1795)

Duberly, Sir Archibald Hugh, KCVO, CBE

Duckworth, Sir James Edward Dyce, Bt. (1909)

du Cros, Sir Julian Claude Arthur Mallet, Bt. (1916)

Dudley-Williams, Sir Alastair Edgcumbe James, Bt. (1964)

Duff, *Prof.* Sir Gordon William, Kt.

Duff-Gordon, Sir Andrew Cosmo Lewis, Bt. (1813)

Duffell, *Lt.-Gen.* Sir Peter Royson, KCB, CBE, MC

Duffy, Sir (Albert) (Edward) Patrick, Kt., PHD

Dugdale, Sir (William) Matthew Stratford, Bt. (1936)

Duggin, Sir Thomas Joseph, Kt.

Dunbar, Sir Edward Horace, Bt. (S. 1700)

Dunbar, Sir James Michael, Bt. (S. 1694)

Dunbar, Sir Robert Drummond Cospatrick, Bt. (S. 1698)

Dunbar of Hempriggs, Sir Richard Francis, Bt. (S. 1706)

Dunbar-Nasmith, *Prof.* Sir James Duncan, Kt., CBE

Duncan, *Rt. Hon.* Sir Alan James Carter, KCMG

Duncan, Sir James Blair, Kt.

Dunford, *Dr* Sir John Ernest, Kt., OBE

Dunlop, Sir Thomas, Bt. (1916)

Dunne, Sir Martin, KCVO

Dunne, Sir Thomas Raymond, KG, KCVO

Dunning, Sir Simon William Patrick, Bt. (1930)

Dunnington-Jefferson, Sir John Alexander, Bt. (1958)

Dunstone, Sir Charles William, Kt., CVO

Dunt, *Vice-Adm.* Sir John Hugh, KCB

†Duntze, Sir Daniel Evans, Bt. (1774)

Dupre, Sir Tumun, Kt., MBE

Durand, Sir Edward Alan Christopher David Percy, Bt. (1892)

Durie, Sir David Robert Campbell, KCMG

†Durrant, Sir David Alexander, Bt. (1784)

Duthie, Sir Robert Grieve (Robin), Kt., CBE

Dutton, *Lt.-Gen.* Sir James Benjamin, KCB, CBE

Dwyer, Sir Joseph Anthony, Kt.

Dyke, Sir David William Hart, Bt. (1677)

Dymock, *Vice-Adm.* Sir Anthony Knox, KBE, CB

Dyson, Sir James, Kt., OM, CBE

Dyson, *Rt. Hon.* Sir John Anthony, Kt. (Lord Dyson)

Eadie, Sir James Raymond, Kt., QC

Eady, *Hon.* Sir David, Kt.

†Eardley-Wilmot, Sir Benjamin John Assheton, Bt. (1821)

Earle, Sir (Hardman) George (Algernon), Bt. (1869)

Eastwood, *Prof.* Sir David Stephen, Kt.

Eaton, *Adm.* Sir Kenneth John, GBE, KCB

Ebdon, *Prof.* Sir Leslie Colin, Kt., CBE

Ebrahim, Sir (Mahomed) Currimbhoy, Bt. (1910)

Eddington, Sir Roderick Ian, Kt.

Eder, *Hon.* Sir Henry Bernard, Kt.

Edis, *Hon.* Sir Andrew Jeremy Coulter, Kt.

Edge, *Capt.* Sir (Philip) Malcolm, KCVO

†Edge, Sir William, Bt. (1937)

Edmonstone, Sir Archibald Bruce Charles, Bt. (1774)

Edward, *Rt. Hon.* Sir David Alexander Ogilvy, KCMG

Edwardes, Sir Michael Owen, Kt.

Edwards, Sir Christopher John Churchill, Bt. (1866)

Edwards, *Prof.* Sir Christopher Richard Watkin, Kt.

Edwards, Sir Gareth Owen, Kt., CBE

Edwards, Sir Llewellyn Roy, Kt.

Edwards, *Prof.* Sir Michael, OBE

Edwards, Sir Robert Paul, Kt.

†Edwards-Moss, Sir David John, Bt. (1868)

Edwards-Stuart, *Hon.* Sir Antony James Cobham, Kt.

Egan, Sir John Leopold, Kt.

Egerton, Sir William de Malpas, Bt. (1617)

Ehrman, Sir William Geoffrey, KCMG

Eichelbaum, *Rt. Hon.* Sir Thomas, GBE

Elder, Sir Mark Philip, Kt., CH, CBE

Eldon, Sir Stewart Graham, KCMG, OBE

Elias, *Rt. Hon.* Sir Patrick, Kt.

Eliott of Stobs, Sir Rodney Gilbert Charles, Bt. (S. 1666)

Elliott, Sir David Murray, KCMG, CB

†Elliott, Sir Ivo Antony Moritz, Bt. (1917)

Elliott, *Prof.* Sir John Huxtable, Kt., FBA

Ellis, Sir Herbert Douglas, Kt., OBE

Ellis, Sir Vernon James, Kt.

Ellwood, Sir Peter Brian, Kt., CBE

Elphinston, Sir Alexander, Bt. (S. 1701)

Elphinstone, Sir John Howard Main, Bt. (1816)

Elton, Sir Arnold, Kt., CBE

Elton, Sir Charles Abraham Grierson, Bt. (1717)

Elvidge, Sir John, KCB

Elwes, *Dr* Sir Henry William, KCVO

Elwes, Sir Jeremy Vernon, Kt., CBE

Elwood, Sir Brian George Conway, Kt., CBE

Elworthy, *Air Cdre Hon.* Sir Timothy Charles, KCVO, CBE

Enderby, *Prof.* Sir John Edwin, Kt. CBE, FRS

English, Sir Terence Alexander Hawthorne, KBE, FRCS

Ennals, Sir Paul Martin, Kt., CBE

Epstein, *Prof.* Sir (Michael) Anthony, Kt., CBE, FRS

Errington, Sir Robin Davenport, Bt. (1963)

Erskine, Sir (Thomas) Peter Neil, Bt. (1821)

Erskine-Hill, Sir Alexander Roger, Bt. (1945)

Esmonde, Sir Thomas Francis Grattan, Bt. (I. 1629)

†Esplen, Sir William John Harry, Bt. (1921)

Esquivel, *Rt. Hon.* Sir Manuel, KCMG

Essenhigh, *Adm.* Sir Nigel Richard, GCB

Etherington, Sir Stuart James, Kt.

Etherton, *Rt. Hon.* Sir Terence Michael Elkan Barnet, Kt.

Evans, *Rt. Hon.* Sir Anthony Howell Meurig, Kt., RD

Evans, *Prof.* Sir Christopher Thomas, Kt., OBE

Evans, *Air Chief Marshal* Sir David George, GCB, CBE

Evans, *Hon.* Sir David Roderick, Kt.

Evans, Sir Harold Matthew, Kt.

Evans, Sir John Stanley, Kt., QPM

Evans, Sir Malcolm David, KCMG, OBE

Evans, *Prof.* Sir Martin John, Kt., FRS

Evans, Sir Richard Harry, Kt., CBE

Evans, *Prof.* Sir Richard John, Kt.

Evans, Sir Robert, Kt., CBE, FRENG

Evans-Lombe, *Hon.* Sir Edward Christopher, Kt.

†Evans-Tipping, Sir David Gwynne, Bt. (1913)

Everard, Sir Henry Peter Charles, Bt. (1911)

Everard, *Lt.-Gen.* Sir James Rupert, KCB, CBE

Everington, *Dr* Sir Anthony Herbert, Kt., OBE

Every, Sir Henry John Michael, Bt. (1641)

Ewart, Sir William Michael, Bt. (1887)

Eyre, Sir Reginald Edwin, Kt.

Eyre, Sir Richard Charles Hastings, Kt., CH, CBE

†Fagge, Sir John Christopher Frederick, Bt. (1660)

Fahy, Sir Peter, Kt., QPM

Fairbairn, Sir Robert William, Bt. (1869)

Fairlie-Cuninghame, Sir Robert Henry, Bt. (S. 1630)

Fairweather, Sir Patrick Stanislaus, KCMG

Faldo, Sir Nicholas Alexander, Kt., MBE

†Falkiner, Sir Benjamin Simon Patrick, Bt. (I. 1778)

Fall, Sir Brian James Proetel, GCVO, KCMG

Fallon, *Rt. Hon.* Sir Michael Cathel, KCB

Fancourt, *Hon.* Sir Timothy Miles, Kt.

Fang, *Prof.* Sir Harry, Kt., CBE

Farah, Sir Mohamed (Mo) Muktar Jama, Kt., CBE

Fareed, Sir Djamil Sheik, Kt.

Farmer, Sir Thomas, Kt., CVO, CBE

Farquhar, Sir Michael Fitzroy Henry, Bt. (1796)

Farrell, Sir Terence, Kt., CBE

Farrer, Sir (Charles) Matthew, GCVO

Farrington, Sir Henry William, Bt. (1818)

Faull, Sir Jonathan Michael Howard, KCMG

Fay, Sir (Humphrey) Michael Gerard, Kt.

Feachem, *Prof.* Sir Richard George Andrew, KBE

Fean, Sir Thomas Vincent, KCVO

Feilden, Sir Henry Rudyard, Bt. (1846)

Feldmann, *Prof.* Sir Marc, Kt.

Fell, Sir David, KCB

Fender, Sir Brian Edward Frederick, Kt., CMG, PHD

Fenwick, Sir Leonard Raymond, Kt., CBE

Fergus, Sir Howard Archibald, KBE

Ferguson-Davie, Sir Michael, Bt. (1847)

Fergusson, *Rt. Hon.* Sir Alexander Charles Onslow, Kt.

Fergusson of Kilkerran, Sir Charles, Bt. (S. 1703)

Ferris, *Hon.* Sir Francis Mursell, Kt., TD

Fersht, *Prof.* Sir Alan Roy, Kt., FRS

ffolkes, Sir Robert Francis Alexander, Bt. (1774), OBE

Field, Sir Malcolm David, Kt.

Field, *Hon.* Sir Richard Alan, Kt.

Fielding, Sir Leslie, KCMG

Fields, Sir Allan Clifford, KCMG

Fiennes, Sir Ranulph Twisleton-Wykeham, Bt. (1916), OBE

Figgis, Sir Anthony St John Howard, KCVO, CMG

Finlay, Sir David Ronald James Bell, Bt. (1964)

Finlayson, Sir Garet Orlando, KCMG, OBE

Fish, *Prof.* Sir David Royden, Kt.

†Fison, Sir Charles William, Bt. (1905)

Fittall, Sir William Robert, Kt.

FitzGerald, Sir Adrian James Andrew Denis, Bt. (1880)

†Fitzgerald, Sir Andrew Peter, Bt. (1903)

FitzHerbert, Sir Richard Ranulph, Bt. (1784)

Fitzpatrick, *Air Marshal* Sir John Bernard, KBE, CB

Flanagan, Sir Ronald, GBE, QPM

Flaux, *Rt. Hon.* Sir Julian Martin, Kt.

Flint, Sir Douglas Jardine, Kt., CBE

Floud, *Prof.* Sir Roderick Castle, Kt.

Floyd, *Rt. Hon.* Sir Christopher David, Kt.

Floyd, Sir Giles Henry Charles, Bt. (1816)

Foley, *Lt.-Gen.* Sir John Paul, KCB, OBE, MC

Follett, *Prof.* Sir Brian Keith, Kt., FRS

†Forbes of Craigievar, Sir Andrew Iain Ochoncar, Bt. (S. 1630)

Forbes, *Adm.* Sir Ian Andrew, KCB, CBE

Forbes, Sir James Thomas Stewart, Bt. (1823)

Forbes, *Vice-Adm.* Sir John Morrison, KCB

Forbes, *Hon.* Sir Thayne John, Kt.

Forbes Adam, Revd Stephen Timothy Beilby, Bt. (1917)

Forbes-Leith, Sir George Ian David, Bt. (1923)

Ford, *Lt.-Col.* Sir Andrew Charles, KCVO

Ford, Sir Andrew Russell, Bt. (1929)

Forestier-Walker, Sir Michael Leolin, Bt. (1835)

Forrest, *Prof.* Sir (Andrew) Patrick (McEwen), Kt.

Forte, *Hon.* Sir Rocco John Vincent, Kt.

Forwood, *Hon.* Sir Nicholas James, Kt., QC

Forwood, Sir Peter Noel, Bt. (1895)

Foskett, *Hon.* Sir David Robert, Kt.

Foster, Sir Andrew William, Kt.

Foster, *Prof.* Sir Christopher David, Kt.

Foster, Sir Saxby Gregory, Bt. (1930)

Foulkes, Sir Arthur Alexander, GCMG

Fountain, *Hon.* Sir Cyril Stanley Smith, Kt.

Fowke, Sir David Frederick Gustavus, Bt. (1814)

Fowler, Sir (Edward) Michael Coulson, Kt.

Fox, Sir Christopher, Kt., QPM

Fox, Sir Paul Leonard, Kt., CBE

Francis, Sir Horace William Alexander, Kt., CBE, FRENG

Francis, *Hon.* Sir Peter Nicholas, Kt.

Francis, Sir Robert Anthony, Kt., QC

Frank, Sir Robert Andrew, Bt. (1920)

Franklin, Sir Michael David Milroy, KCB, CMG

Fraser, Sir Charles Annand, KCVO

Fraser, Sir Iain Michael Duncan, Bt. (1943)

Fraser, Sir James Murdo, KBE

Fraser, *Hon.* Sir Peter Donald, Kt.

Fraser, Sir Simon James, GCMG

Frayling, *Prof.* Sir Christopher John, Kt.

Frederick, Sir Christopher St John, Bt. (1723)

Freedman, *Rt. Hon. Prof.* Sir Lawrence David, KCMG, CBE

†Freeman, Sir James Robin, Bt. (1945)

French, *Air Marshal* Sir Joseph Charles, KCB, CBE

Frere, *Vice-Adm.* Sir Richard Tobias, KCB

Friend, *Prof.* Sir Richard Henry, Kt.

Froggatt, Sir Peter, Kt.

Fry, Sir Graham Holbrook, KCMG

Fry, *Lt.-Gen.* Sir Robert Allan, KCB, CBE

Fry, *Dr* Sir Roger Gordon, Kt., CBE

Fulford, *Rt. Hon.* Sir Adrian Bruce, Kt.

Fuller, Sir James Henry Fleetwood, Bt. (1910)

Fulton, *Lt.-Gen.* Sir Robert Henry Gervase, KBE

Furness, Sir Stephen Roberts, Bt. (1913)

Gage, *Rt. Hon.* Sir William Marcus, Kt, QC

Gains, Sir John Christopher, Kt.

Gainsford, Sir Ian Derek, Kt.

Gale, Sir Roger James, Kt.

Galsworthy, Sir Anthony Charles, KCMG

Galway, Sir James, Kt., OBE

Gamble, Sir David Hugh Norman, Bt. (1897)

Gambon, Sir Michael John, Kt., CBE

Gammell, Sir William Benjamin Bowring, Kt.

Gardiner, Sir John Eliot, Kt., CBE

Gardner, *Prof.* Sir Richard Lavenham, Kt.

Gardner, Sir Roy Alan, Kt.

Garland, *Hon.* Sir Patrick Neville, Kt.

Garland, *Hon.* Sir Ransley Victor, KBE

Garland, *Dr* Sir Trevor, KBE

Garnett, *Adm.* Sir Ian David Graham, KCB

Garnham, *Hon.* Sir Neil Stephen, Kt.

Garnier, *Rear-Adm.* Sir John, KCVO, CBE

Garrard, Sir David Eardley, Kt.

Garrett, Sir Anthony Peter, Kt., CBE

Garrick, Sir Ronald, Kt., CBE, FRENG

Garthwaite, Sir (William) Mark (Charles), Bt. (1919)

Garwood, *Air Marshal* Sir Richard Frank, KBE, CB, DFC

Gass, Sir Simon Lawrance, KCMG, CVO

Geim, *Prof.* Sir Andre Konstantin, Kt.

Geno, Sir Makena Viora, KBE

Gent, Sir Christopher Charles, Kt.

George, *Prof.* Sir Charles Frederick, Kt., MD, FRCP

Gerken, *Vice-Adm.* Sir Robert William Frank, KCB, CBE

Gershon, Sir Peter Oliver, Kt., CBE

Gethin, Sir Richard Joseph St Lawrence, Bt. (I. 1665)

Gibb, Sir Barry Alan Crompton, Kt., CBE

Gibbings, Sir Peter Walter, Kt.

Gibbons, Sir William Edward Doran, Bt. (1752)

Gibbs, *Hon.* Sir Richard John Hedley, Kt.

Gibbs, Sir Roger Geoffrey, Kt.

†Gibson, *Revd* Christopher Herbert, Bt. (1931)

Gibson, Sir Ian, Kt., CBE

Gibson, Sir Kenneth Archibald, Kt.

Gibson, *Rt. Hon.* Sir Peter Leslie, Kt.

Gibson-Craig-Carmichael, Sir David Peter William, Bt. (S. 1702 and 1831)

Gieve, Sir Edward John Watson, KCB

Giffard, Sir (Charles) Sydney (Rycroft), KCMG

Gifford, Sir Michael Roger, Kt.

Gilbert, *Air Chief Marshal* Sir Joseph Alfred, KCB, CBE

†Gilbey, Sir Walter Gavin, Bt. (1893)

Gill, Sir Anthony Keith, Kt.

Gill, Sir Robin Denys, KCVO

Gillam, Sir Patrick John, Kt.

Gillen, *Hon.* Sir John de Winter, Kt.

Gillett, Sir Nicholas Danvers Penrose, Bt. (1959)

Gillinson, Sir Clive Daniel, Kt., CBE

Gilmore, *Prof.* Sir Ian Thomas, Kt.

†Gilmour, *Hon.* Sir David Robert, Bt. (1926)

Gilmour, Sir John Nicholas, Bt. (1897)

Gina, Sir Lloyd Maepeza, KBE

Giordano, Sir Richard Vincent, KBE

Girolami, Sir Paul, Kt.

Girvan, *Rt. Hon.* Sir (Frederick) Paul, Kt.

Gladstone, Sir Charles Angus, Bt. (1846)

Glean, Sir Carlyle Arnold, GCMG

Globe, *Hon.* Sir Henry Brian, Kt.

Glover, Sir Victor Joseph Patrick, Kt.

Glyn, Sir Richard Lindsay, Bt. (1759 and 1800)

Gobbo, Sir James Augustine, Kt., AC

Godfray, *Prof.* Sir Hugh Charles Jonathan, Kt., CBE

Goldberg, *Prof.* Sir David Paul Brandes, Kt.

Goldring, *Rt. Hon.* Sir John Bernard, Kt.

Gomersall, Sir Stephen John, KCMG

Gonsalves-Sabola, *Hon.* Sir Joaquim Claudino, Kt

Gooch, Sir Arthur Brian Sherlock Heywood, Bt. (1746)

Gooch, Sir Miles Peter, Bt. (1866)

Good, Sir John James Griffen, Kt., CBE

Goodall, *Air Marshal* Sir Roderick Harvey, KBE, CB, AFC

Goode, *Prof.* Sir Royston Miles, Kt., CBE, QC

Goodenough, Sir Anthony Michael, KCMG

Goodenough, Sir William McLernon, Bt. (1943)

Goodhart, Sir Robert Anthony Gordon, Bt. (1911)

Goodison, Sir Nicholas Proctor, Kt.

Goodson, Sir Alan Reginald, Bt. (1922)

Goodwin, Sir Frederick, KBE

Goold, Sir George William, Bt. (1801)

Goose, *Hon.* Sir Julian Nicholas, Kt.

Gordon, Sir Donald, Kt.

Gordon, Sir Gerald Henry, Kt., CBE, QC

Gordon, Sir Robert James, Bt. (S. 1706)

Gordon-Cumming, Sir Alexander Alastair Penrose, Bt. (1804)

Gore, Sir Hugh Frederick Corbet, Bt. (I. 1622)

Gore-Booth, Sir Josslyn Henry Robert, Bt. (I. 1760)

Goring, Sir William Burton Nigel, Bt (1678)

Gormley, Sir Antony Mark David, Kt., OBE

Gormley, Sir Paul Brendan, KCMG, MBE

Goschen, Sir (Edward) Alexander, Bt. (1916)

Gosling, Sir (Frederick) Donald, KCVO

Goss, *Hon.* Sir James Richard William, Kt.

Goulden, Sir (Peter) John, GCMG

†Goulding, Sir (William) Lingard Walter, Bt. (1904)

Gourlay, Sir Simon Alexander, Kt.

Gowans, Sir James Learmonth, Kt., CBE, FRCP, FRS

Gowers, *Prof.* Sir William Timothy, Kt.

Gozney, Sir Richard Hugh Turton, KCMG

Graaff, Sir De Villiers, Bt. (1911)

Graham, Sir Alexander Michael, GBE

Graham, Sir James Bellingham, Bt. (1662)

Graham, Sir James Fergus Surtees, Bt. (1783)

Graham, Sir James Thompson, Kt., CMG

Graham, Sir John Alexander Noble, Bt. (1906), GCMG

Graham, Sir John Alistair, Kt.

Graham, Sir John Moodie, Bt. (1964)

Graham, Sir Peter, KCB, QC

Graham, *Lt.-Gen.* Sir Peter Walter, KCB, CBE

†Graham, Sir Ralph Stuart, Bt. (1629)

Graham-Moon, Sir Peter Wilfred Giles, Bt. (1855)

Graham-Smith, *Prof.* Sir Francis, Kt.

Grainge, Sir Lucian Charles, Kt., CBE

Grange, Sir Kenneth Henry, Kt., CBE

Grant, Sir Archibald, Bt. (S. 1705)

Grant, *Dr* Sir David, Kt., CBE

Grant, Sir Ian David, Kt., CBE

Grant, Sir John Douglas Kelso, KCMG

Grant, *Prof.* Sir Malcolm John, Kt., CBE

Grant, Sir Mark Justin Lyall, GCMG

Grant, Sir Patrick Alexander Benedict, Bt. (S. 1688)

Grant, Sir Paul Joseph Patrick, Kt.

Grant, *Lt.-Gen.* Sir Scott Carnegie, KCB

Grant-Suttie, Sir James Edward, Bt. (S. 1702)

Granville-Chapman, *Gen.* Sir Timothy John, GBE, KCB, ADC

Grattan-Bellew, Sir Henry Charles, Bt. (1838)

Gray, Sir Bernard Peter, Kt.

Gray, *Hon.* Sir Charles Anthony St John, Kt.

Gray, Sir Charles Ireland, Kt., CBE

Gray, *Prof.* Sir Denis John Pereira, Kt., OBE, FRCGP

Gray, *Dr* Sir John Armstrong Muir, Kt., CBE

Gray, Sir Robert McDowall (Robin), Kt.

Gray, Sir William Hume, Bt. (1917)

Graydon, *Air Chief Marshal* Sir Michael James, GCB, CBE

Grayson, Sir Jeremy Brian Vincent Harrington, Bt. (1922)

Green, Sir Allan David, KCB, QC

Green, Sir David John Mark, Kt., CB, QC

Green, Sir Edward Patrick Lycett, Bt. (1886)

Green, Sir Gregory David, KCMG

Green, *Hon.* Sir Guy Stephen Montague, KBE

Green, *Prof.* Sir Malcolm, Kt.

Green, *Rt. Hon.* Sir Nicholas Nigel, Kt.

Green, Sir Philip Green, Kt.

Green-Price, Sir Robert John, Bt. (1874)

Greenaway, *Prof.* Sir David, Kt.

Greenaway, Sir Thomas Edward Burdick, Bt. (1933)

Greener, Sir Anthony Armitage, Kt.

Greenstock, Sir Jeremy Quentin, GCMG

Greenwell, Sir Edward Bernard, Bt. (1906)

Greenwood, *Prof.* Sir Brian Mellor, Kt., CBE

Greenwood, *Prof.* Sir Christopher John, GBE, CMG

Gregory, *Lt.-Gen.* Sir Andrew Richard, KBE, CB

Gregory, *Prof.* Sir Michael John, Kt., CBE

Grey, Sir Anthony Dysart, Bt. (1814)

Grice, Sir Paul Edward, Kt.

Griffiths, Sir Michael, Kt.

Grigson, *Hon.* Sir Geoffrey Douglas, Kt.

Grimshaw, Sir Nicholas Thomas, Kt., CBE

Grimstone, Sir Gerald Edgar, Kt.

Grimwade, Sir Andrew Sheppard, Kt., CBE

Grose, *Vice-Adm.* Sir Alan, KBE

Gross, *Rt. Hon.* Sir Peter Henry, Kt.

Grossart, Sir Angus McFarlane McLeod, Kt., CBE

Grotrian, Sir Philip Christian Brent, Bt. (1934)

†Grove, Sir Charles Gerald, Bt. (1874)

Grundy, Sir Mark, Kt.

Guinness, Sir Howard Christian Sheldon, Kt., VRD

Guinness, Sir John Ralph Sidney, Kt., CB

Guinness, Sir Kenelm Edward Lee, Bt. (1867)

Guise, Sir Christopher James, Bt. (1783)

Gull, Sir Rupert William Cameron, Bt. (1872)

Gunning, Sir Charles Theodore, Bt. (1778)

Gunston, Sir John Wellesley, Bt. (1938)

Gurdon, *Prof.* Sir John Bertrand, Kt., DPHIL, FRS

Guthrie, Sir Malcolm Connop, Bt. (1936)

Habgood, Sir Anthony John, Kt.

Haddacks, *Vice-Adm.* Sir Paul Kenneth, KCB

Haddon-Cave, *Rt. Hon.* Sir Charles Anthony, Kt.

Hadlee, Sir Richard John, Kt., MBE

Hagart-Alexander, Sir Claud, Bt. (1886)

Haines, *Prof.* Sir Andrew Paul, Kt.

Haji-Ioannou, Sir Stelios, Kt.

Halberg, Sir Murray Gordon, Kt., MBE

Hall, *Dr* Sir Andrew James, Kt.

†Hall, Sir David Bernard, Bt. (1919)

Hall, Sir David Christopher, Bt. (1923)

Hall, *Prof.* Sir David Michael Baldock, Kt.

Hall, Sir Ernest, Kt., OBE

Hall, Sir Geoffrey, Kt.

Hall, Sir Graham Joseph, Kt.

Hall, Sir Iain Robert, Kt.

Hall, Sir John, Kt.

Hall, Sir John Douglas Hoste, Bt. (S. 1687)

Hall, HE *Prof.* Sir Kenneth Octavius, GCMG

Hall, Sir Peter Edward, KBE, CMG

Hall, *Revd* Wesley Winfield, Kt.

Hall, Sir William Joseph, KCVO

Halpern, Sir Ralph Mark, Kt.

Halsey, *Revd* John Walter Brooke, Bt. (1920)

Halstead, Sir Ronald, Kt., CBE

Ham, *Prof.* Sir Christopher John, Kt., CBE

Hamblen, *Rt. Hon.* Sir Nicholas Archibald, Kt.

Hambling, Sir Herbert Peter Hugh, Bt. (1924)

Hamilton, Sir Andrew Caradoc, Bt. (S. 1646)

Hamilton, Sir David, Kt.

Hamilton, Sir Nigel, KCB

Hamilton-Dalrymple, *Maj.* Sir Hew Fleetwood, Bt. (S. 1698), GCVO

Hamilton-Spencer-Smith, Sir John, Bt. (1804)

Hammick, Sir Jeremy Charles, Bt. (1834)

Hammond, Sir Anthony Hilgrove, KCB, QC

Hampel, Sir Ronald Claus, Kt.

Hampson, Sir Stuart, Kt., CVO

Hampton, Sir (Leslie) Geoffrey, Kt.

Hampton, Sir Philip Roy, Kt.

Hanham, Sir William John Edward, Bt. (1667)

Hankes-Drielsma, Sir Claude Dunbar, KCVO

Hanley, *Rt. Hon.* Sir Jeremy James, KCMG

Hanmer, Sir Wyndham Richard Guy, Bt. (1774)

Hannam, Sir John Gordon, Kt.

Hanson, Sir (Charles) Rupert (Patrick), Bt. (1918)

Harcourt-Smith, *Air Chief Marshal* Sir David, GBE, KCB, DFC

Hardie Boys, *Rt. Hon.* Sir Michael, GCMG

Harding, *Marshal of the Royal Air Force* Sir Peter Robin, GCB

Hardy, Sir David William, Kt.

Hardy, Sir James Gilbert, Kt., OBE

Hare, Sir David, Kt., FRSL

Hare, Sir Nicholas Patrick, Bt. (1818)

Haren, *Dr* Sir Patrick Hugh, Kt.

Harford, Sir Mark John, Bt. (1934)

Harington, Sir David Richard, Bt. (1611)

Harkness, *Very Revd* James, KCVO, CB, OBE

Harley, *Gen.* Sir Alexander George Hamilton, KBE, CB

Harman, *Hon.* Sir Jeremiah LeRoy, Kt.

Harman, Sir John Andrew, Kt.

†Harmsworth, Sir Hildebrand Harold, Bt. (1922)

Harper, *Air Marshal* Sir Christopher Nigel, KBE

Harper, Sir Ewan William, Kt., CBE

Harper, *Prof.* Sir Peter Stanley, Kt., CBE

Harris, Sir Christopher John Ashford, Bt. (1932)

Harris, *Air Marshal* Sir John Hulme, KCB, CBE

Harris, *Prof.* Sir Martin Best, Kt., CBE

Harris, Sir Michael Frank, Kt.

Harris, Sir Thomas George, KBE, CMG

Harrison, *Prof.* Sir Brian Howard, Kt.

Harrison, Sir David, Kt., CBE, FRENG

Harrison, *Hon.* Sir Michael Guy Vicat, Kt.

Harrison, Sir Michael James Harwood, Bt. (1961)

Harrison, Sir (Robert) Colin, Bt. (1922)

Harrison, Sir Terence, Kt., FRENG

Harrop, Sir Peter John, KCB

Hart, *Hon.* Sir Anthony Ronald, Kt.

Hart, Sir Graham Allan, KCB

Hartwell, Sir (Francis) Anthony Charles Peter, Bt. (1805)

Harvey, Sir Charles Richard Musgrave, Bt. (1933)

Harvey, Sir Nicholas Barton, Kt.

Harvie, Sir John Smith, Kt., CBE

Harvie-Watt, Sir James, Bt. (1945)

Harwood, Sir Ronald, Kt., CBE

Haslam, *Prof.* Sir David Antony, Kt., CBE

Hastie, *Cdre* Sir Robert Cameron, KCVO, CBE, RD

Hastings, Sir Max Macdonald, Kt.

Hastings, *Dr* Sir William George, Kt., CBE

Hatter, Sir Maurice, Kt.

Havelock-Allan, Sir (Anthony) Mark David, Bt. (1858), QC

Hawkes, Sir John Garry, Kt., CBE

Hawkhead, Sir Anthony Gerard, Kt., CBE

Hawkins, Sir Richard Caesar, Bt. (1778)

Hawley, Sir James Appleton, KCVO, TD

Haworth, Sir Philip, Bt. (1911)

Hay, Sir John Erroll Audley, Bt. (S. 1663)

†Hay, Sir Ronald Frederick Hamilton, Bt. (S. 1703)

Hayden, *Hon.* Sir Anthony Paul, Kt.

Hayes, Sir Brian, Kt., CBE, QPM

Hayes, Sir Brian David, GCB

Hayman-Joyce, *Lt.-Gen.* Sir Robert John, KCB, CBE

Hayter, Sir Paul David Grenville, KCB, LVO

Head, Sir Patrick, Kt.

Head, Sir Richard Douglas Somerville, Bt. (1838)

Heald, *Rt. Hon.* Sir Oliver, Kt.

Heap, Sir Peter William, KCMG

Heap, *Prof.* Sir Robert Brian, Kt., CBE, FRS

Hearne, Sir Graham James, Kt., CBE

Heathcote, Sir Simon Robert Mark, Bt. (1733), OBE

†Heathcote, Sir Timothy Gilbert, Bt. (1733)

Heber-Percy, Sir Algernon Eustace Hugh, KCVO

Hedley, *Hon.* Sir Mark, Kt.

Hegarty, Sir John Kevin, Kt.

Heiser, Sir Terence Michael, GCB

Helfgott, Sir Ber, Kt., MBE

Heller, Sir Michael Aron, Kt.

Hempleman-Adams, *Dr* Sir David Kim, KCVO, OBE

Henderson, *Rt Hon.* Sir Launcelot Dinadin James, Kt.

Henderson, *Maj.* Sir Richard Yates, KCVO

Hendrick, Sir Mark, Kt.

Hendry, *Prof.* Sir David Forbes, Kt.

Hendy, Sir Peter Gerard, Kt., CBE

Hennessy, Sir James Patrick Ivan, KBE, CMG

†Henniker, Sir Adrian Chandos, Bt. (1813)

Henniker-Heaton, Sir Yvo Robert, Bt. (1912)

Henriques, *Hon.* Sir Richard Henry Quixano, Kt.

Henry, Sir Lenworth George, Kt., CBE

†Henry, Sir Patrick Denis, Bt. (1923)

Henshaw, Sir David George, Kt.

Herbecq, Sir John Edward, KCB

Herbert, *Adm.* Sir Peter Geoffrey Marshall, KCB, OBE

Heron, Sir Conrad Frederick, KCB, OBE

†Heron-Maxwell, Sir Nigel Mellor, Bt. (S. 1683)

Hervey, Sir Roger Blaise Ramsay, KCVO, CMG

Hervey-Bathurst, Sir Frederick William John, Bt. (1818)

Heseltine, *Rt. Hon.* Sir William Frederick Payne, GCB, GCVO

Hewetson, Sir Christopher Raynor, Kt., TD

Hewett, Sir Richard Mark John, Bt. (1813)

Hewitt, Sir (Cyrus) Lenox (Simson), Kt., OBE

Hewitt, Sir Nicholas Charles Joseph, Bt. (1921)

Heygate, Sir Richard John Gage, Bt. (1831)

Heywood, Sir Jeremy John, KCB, CVO

Heywood, Sir Peter, Bt. (1838)

Hickey, Sir John Tongri, Kt., CBE

Hickinbottom, *Rt. Hon.* Sir Gary Robert, Kt.

Hickman, Sir (Richard) Glenn, Bt. (1903)

Hicks, Sir Robert, Kt.

Hielscher, Sir Leo Arthur, Kt.

Higgins, Sir David Hartmann, Kt.

Higgins, *Rt. Hon.* Sir Malachy Joseph, Kt.

Hildyard, *Hon.* Sir Robert Henry Thoroton, Kt.

Hill, *Rt. Revd Dr* Christopher John, KCVO

Hill, Sir James Frederick, Bt. (1917), OBE

Hill, Sir John Alfred Rowley, Bt. (I. 1779)

Hill, *Vice-Adm.* Sir Robert Charles Finch, KBE, FRENG

Hill-Norton, *Vice-Adm. Hon.* Sir Nicholas John, KCB

Hill-Wood, Sir Samuel Thomas, Bt. (1921)

Hillhouse, Sir (Robert) Russell, KCB

Hillier, *Air Marshal* Sir Stephen John, KCB, CBE, DFC

Hills, Sir John Robert, Kt., CBE

Hilly, Sir Francis Billy, KCMG

Hine, *Air Chief Marshal* Sir Patrick Bardon, GCB, GBE

Hintze, Sir Michael, Kt.

Hirsch, *Prof.* Sir Peter Bernhard, Kt., PHD, FRS

Hirst, Sir Michael William, Kt.

Hitchens, Sir Timothy Mark, KCVO, CMG, LVO

Hoare, *Prof.* Sir Charles Anthony Richard, Kt., FRS

Hoare, Sir Charles James, Bt. (I. 1784)

Hoare, Sir David John, Bt. (1786)

Hobart, Sir John Vere, Bt. (1914)

Hobbs, *Maj.-Gen.* Sir Michael Frederick, KCVO, CBE

Hobhouse, Sir Charles John Spinney, Bt. (1812)

†Hodge, Sir Andrew Rowland, Bt. (1921)

Hodge, Sir James William, KCVO, CMG

Hodgkinson, Sir Michael Stewart, Kt.

Hodson, Sir Michael Robin Adderley, Bt. (I. 1789)

Hogg, Sir Christopher Anthony, Kt.

Hogg, Sir Piers Michael James, Bt. (1846)

Hohn, Sir Christopher, KCMG

Holcroft, Sir Charles Anthony Culcheth, Bt. (1921)

Holden, Sir John David, Bt. (1919)

Holden, Sir Michael Peter, Bt. (1893)

Holder, Sir John Henry, Bt. (1898)

Holderness, Sir Martin William, Bt. (1920)

Holdgate, Sir Martin Wyatt, Kt., CB, PHD

Holgate, *Hon.* Sir David John, Kt.

Holland, *Hon.* Sir Christopher John, Kt.

Holland, Sir John Anthony, Kt.

Holm, Sir Ian (Holm Cuthbert), Kt.,CBE

Holman, *Hon.* Sir Edward James, Kt.

Holman, *Prof.* Sir John Stranger, Kt.

Holmes, Sir John Eaton, GCVO, KBE, CMG

Holroyd, Sir Michael De Courcy Fraser, Kt., CBE

Holroyde, *Rt. Hon.* Sir Timothy Victor, Kt.

Home, Sir William Dundas, Bt. (S. 1671)

Honywood, Sir Filmer Courtenay William, Bt. (1660)

†Hood, Sir John Joseph Harold, Bt. (1922)

Hooper, *Rt. Hon.* Sir Anthony, Kt.

Hope, Sir Alexander Archibald Douglas, Bt. (S. 1628), OBE

Hope-Dunbar, Sir David, Bt. (S. 1664)

Hopkin, *Prof.* Sir Deian Rhys, Kt.

Hopkin, Sir Royston Oliver, KCMG

Hopkins, Sir Anthony Philip, Kt., CBE

Hopkins, Sir Michael John, Kt., CBE, RA, RIBA

Hopwood, *Prof.* Sir David Alan, Kt., FRS

Hordern, *Rt. Hon.* Sir Peter Maudslay, Kt.

Horlick, *Vice-Adm.* Sir Edwin John, KBE, FRENG

Horlick, Sir James Cunliffe William, Bt. (1914)

Horn-Smith, Sir Julian Michael, Kt.

Horne, Sir Alan Gray Antony, Bt. (1929)

Horner, *Hon.* Sir Thomas Mark, Kt.

Horsbrugh-Porter, Sir Andrew Alexander Marshall, Bt. (1902)

Horsfall, Sir Edward John Wright, Bt. (1909)

Hort, Sir Andrew Edwin Fenton, Bt. (1767)

Hosker, Sir Gerald Albery, KCB, QC

Hoskins, *Prof.* Sir Brian John, Kt., CBE, FRS

Hoskyns, Sir Robin Chevallier, Bt. (1676)

Hotung, Sir Joseph Edward, Kt.

Hough, *Prof.* Sir James, Kt., OBE

Houghton, Sir John Theodore, Kt., CBE, FRS

Houghton, Sir Stephen Geoffrey, Kt., CBE

Houldsworth, Sir Richard Thomas Reginald, Bt. (1887)

Hourston, Sir Gordon Minto, Kt.

Housden, Sir Peter James, KCB

House, Sir Stephen, Kt., QPM

Houssemayne du Boulay, Sir Roger William, KCVO, CMG

Houstoun-Boswall, Sir (Thomas) Alford, Bt. (1836)

Howard, Sir David Howarth Seymour, Bt. (1955)

Howard, *Dr* Sir Laurence, KCVO, OBE

Howard, *Prof.* Sir Michael Eliot, Kt., OM, CH, CBE, MC

Howard-Lawson, Sir John Philip, Bt. (1841)

Howarth, Sir (James) Gerald Douglas, Kt.

Howells, Sir Eric Waldo Benjamin, Kt., CBE

Howes, Sir Christopher Kingston, KCVO, CB

Howlett, *Gen.* Sir Geoffrey Hugh Whitby, KBE, MC

Hoy, Sir Christopher Andrew, Kt., MBE

Hoyle, *Rt. Hon.* Sir Lindsay Harvey, Kt.

Hudson, Sir Mark, KCVO

Hugh-Jones, Sir Wynn Normington, Kt., LVO

Hughes, *Rt. Hon.* Sir Anthony Philip Gilson, Kt. (Lord Hughes of Ombersley)

Hughes, *Rt. Hon.* Sir Simon Henry Ward, Kt.

Hughes, Sir Thomas Collingwood, Bt. (1773)

Hughes-Hallett, Sir Thomas Michael Sydney, Kt.

Hughes-Morgan, Sir (Ian) Parry David, Bt. (1925)

Hull, *Prof.* Sir David, Kt.

Hulme, Sir Philip William, Kt.

Hulse, Sir Edward Jeremy Westrow, Bt. (1739)

Hum, Sir Christopher Owen, KCMG

Humphreys, *Prof.* Sir Colin John, Kt., CBE

Hunt, *Dr* Sir Richard Timothy, Kt.

Hunte, *Hon. Dr* Sir Julian Robert, KCMG, OBE

Hunter, Sir Alistair John, KCMG

Hunter, *Prof.* Sir Laurence Colvin, Kt., CBE, FRSE

Hunter, *Dr* Sir Philip John, Kt., CBE

Hunter, Sir Thomas Blane, Kt.

Huntington-Whiteley, Sir John Miles, Bt. (1918), VRD

Hurn, Sir (Francis) Roger, Kt.

Hurst, Sir Geoffrey Charles, Kt., MBE

Husbands, *Prof.* Sir Christopher Roy, Kt.

Hutchison, Sir Peter Craft, Bt. (1956), CBE

Hutchison, *Rt. Hon.* Sir Michael, Kt.

Hutchison, Sir Robert, Bt. (1939)

Hutt, Sir Dexter Walter, Kt.

Huxtable, *Gen.* Sir Charles Richard, KCB, CBE

Hytner, Sir Nicholas, Kt.

Iacobescu, Sir George, Kt., CBE

Ibbotson, *Vice-Adm.* Sir Richard Jeffrey, KBE, CB, DSC

Ife, *Prof.* Sir Barry William, Kt., CBE

Imbert-Terry, Sir Michael Edward Stanley, Bt. (1917)

Imray, Sir Colin Henry, KBE, CMG

Ingham, Sir Bernard, Kt.

Ingilby, Sir Thomas Colvin William, Bt. (1866)

†Inglis of Glencorse, Sir Ian Richard, Bt. (S. 1703)

Ingram, Sir James Herbert Charles, Bt. (1893)

Innes, Sir Alastair Charles Deverell, Bt. (NS 1686)

Innes of Edingight, Sir Malcolm Rognvald, KCVO

Innes, Sir Peter Alexander Berowald, Bt. (S. 1628)

Insall, Sir Donald William, Kt., CBE

Ipatas, *Hon.* Peter, KBE

Irvine, Sir Donald Hamilton, Kt., CBE, MD, FRCGP

Irving, *Prof.* Sir Miles Horsfall, Kt., MD, FRCS, FRCSE

Irwin, *Lt.-Gen.* Sir Alistair Stuart Hastings, KCB, CBE

Irwin, *Rt. Hon.* Sir Stephen John, Kt.

Isaacs, Sir Jeremy Israel, Kt.

Isham, Sir Norman Murray Crawford, Bt. (1627), OBE

Ishiguro, Sir Kazuo, Kt., OBE

Italeli, *HE* Sir Iakoba Taeia, GCMG

Ive, Sir Jonathan Paul, KBE

Ivory, Sir Brian Gammell, Kt., CBE

Jack, Sir Malcolm Roy, KCB

Jack, *Hon.* Sir Raymond Evan, Kt.

Jackling, Sir Roger Tustin, KCB, CBE

Jackson, Sir Barry Trevor, Kt.

Jackson, Sir Kenneth Joseph, Kt.

Jackson, *Gen.* Sir Michael David, GCB, CBE

†Jackson, Sir Neil Keith, Bt. (1815)

Jackson, Sir Nicholas Fane St George, Bt. (1913)

Jackson, *Rt. Hon.* Sir Peter Arthur Brian, Kt.

Jackson, *Rt. Hon.* Sir Rupert Matthew, Kt.

Jackson, Sir Thomas Saint Felix, Bt. (1902)

Jackson, Sir (William) Roland Cedric, Bt. (1869)

Jacob, *Rt. Hon.* Sir Robert Raphael Hayim (Robin), Kt.

Jacobi, Sir Derek George, Kt., CBE

Jacobs, Sir Cecil Albert, Kt., CBE

Jacobs, *Rt. Hon.* Sir Francis Geoffrey, KCMG, QC

Jacobs, *Dr* Sir Michael Graham, Kt.

Jacobs, *Hon.* Sir Richard David, Kt.

Jacomb, Sir Martin Wakefield, Kt.

Jaffray, Sir William Otho, Bt. (1892)

Jagger, Sir Michael Philip, Kt.

James, Sir Jeffrey Russell, KBE

James, Sir John Nigel Courtenay, KCVO, CBE

Jameson, *Brig.* Sir Melville Stewart, KCVO, CBE

Jardine, Sir Andrew Colin Douglas, Bt. (1916)

Jardine of Applegirth, Sir William Murray, Bt. (S. 1672)

Jarman, *Prof.* Sir Brian, Kt., OBE

Jarratt, Sir Alexander Anthony, Kt., CB

Jawara, *Hon.* Sir Dawda Kairaba, Kt.

Jay, *Hon.* Sir Robert Maurice, Kt.

Jeewoolall, Sir Ramesh, Kt.

Jeffery, Sir Thomas Baird, Kt., CB

Jeffrey, Sir William Alexander, KCB

Jeffreys, *Prof.* Sir Alec John, Kt., CH, FRS

Jeffries, *Hon.* Sir John Francis, Kt.

Jehangir, Sir Cowasji, Bt. (1908)

Jejeebhoy, Sir Jamsetjee, Bt. (1857)

Jenkin, *Hon.* Sir Bernard Christison, Kt.

Jenkins, Sir Brian Garton, GBE

Jenkins, Sir James Christopher, KCB, QC

Jenkins, Sir John, KCMG, LVO

Jenkins, *Dr* Sir Karl William Pamp, Kt., CBE

Jenkins, Sir Michael Nicholas Howard, Kt., OBE

Jenkins, Sir Simon, Kt.

Jenkinson, Sir John Banks, Bt. (1661)

Jenks, Sir (Richard) Peter, Bt. (1932)

Jenner, *Air Marshal* Sir Timothy Ivo, KCB

Jennings, Sir John Southwood, Kt., CBE, FRSE

Jennings, Sir Peter Neville Wake, Kt., CVO

Jephcott, Sir David Welbourn, Bt. (1962)

Jessel, Sir Charles John, Bt. (1883)

Jewkes, Sir Gordon Wesley, KCMG

Job, Sir Peter James Denton, Kt.

John, Sir David Glyndwr, KCMG

John, Sir Elton Hercules (Reginald Kenneth Dwight), Kt., CBE

Johns, *Vice-Adm.* Sir Adrian James, KCB, CBE, ADC

Johns, *Air Chief Marshal* Sir Richard Edward, GCB, KCVO, CBE

Johnson, Sir Colpoys Guy, Bt. (1755)

Johnson, *Gen.* Sir Garry Dene, KCB, OBE, MC

Johnson, Sir John Rodney, KCMG

†Johnson, Sir Patrick Eliot, Bt. (1818)

Johnson, *Hon.* Sir Robert Lionel, Kt.

Johnson-Ferguson, Sir Mark Edward, Bt. (1906)

Johnston, *Lt.-Gen.* Sir Maurice Robert, KCB, CVO, OBE

Johnston, Sir Thomas Alexander, Bt. (S. 1626)

Johnston, Sir William Ian Ridley, Kt., CBE, QPM

Johnstone, Sir Geoffrey Adams Dinwiddie, KCMG

Johnstone, Sir (George) Richard Douglas, Bt. (S. 1700)

Johnstone, Sir (John) Raymond, Kt., CBE

Jolliffe, Sir Anthony Stuart, GBE

Jolly, Sir Arthur Richard, KCMG

Jonas, Sir John Peter, Kt., CBE

Jones, Sir Alan Jeffrey, Kt.

Jones, Sir Bryn Terfel, Kt., CBE

Jones, Sir David Charles, Kt., CBE

Jones, Sir Derek William, KCB

Jones, Sir Harry George, Kt., CBE

†Jones, Sir James Peter Martin Benton, Bt. (1919)

Jones, *Rt. Revd* James Stuart, KBE

Jones, Sir John Francis, Kt.

Jones, Sir Kenneth Lloyd, Kt., QPM

Jones, Sir Lyndon, Kt.

Jones, Sir Mark Ellis Powell, Kt.

Jones, *Vice-Adm.* Sir Philip Andrew, KCB

Jones, Sir Richard Anthony Lloyd, KCB

Jones, Sir Robert Edward, Kt.

Jones, Sir Roger Spencer, Kt., OBE

†Joseph, *Hon.* Sir James Samuel, Bt. (1943)

Jowell, *Prof.* Sir Jeffrey Lionel, KCMG, QC

Jowitt, *Hon.* Sir Edwin Frank, Kt.

Jugnauth, *Rt. Hon.* Sir Aneerood, KCMG

Jungius, *Vice-Adm.* Sir James George, KBE

Kaberry, *Hon.* Sir Christopher Donald, Bt. (1960)

Kabui, Sir Frank Utu Ofagioro, GCMG, OBE

Kadoorie, *Hon.* Sir Michael David, Kt.

Kakaraya, Sir Pato, KBE

Kamit, Sir Leonard Wilson, Kt., CBE

Kao, *Prof.* Sir Charles Kuen, KBE

Kapoor, Sir Anish Mikhail, Kt., CBE

Kaputin, Sir John Rumet, KBE, CMG

Kavali, Sir Thomas, Kt., OBE

Kay, *Rt. Hon.* Sir Maurice Ralph, Kt.

Kay, Sir Nicholas Peter, KCMG

Kaye, Sir Paul Henry Gordon, Bt. (1923)

Keane, Sir John Charles, Bt. (1801)

Kearney, *Hon.* Sir William John Francis, Kt., CBE

Keegan, *Dr* Sir Donal Arthur John, KCVO, OBE

Keehan, *Hon.* Sir Michael Joseph, Kt.

Keene, *Rt. Hon.* Sir David Wolfe, Kt.

Keenlyside, Sir Simon John, Kt., CBE

Keith, *Hon.* Sir Brian Richard, Kt.

Keith, *Rt. Hon.* Sir Kenneth, KBE

†Kellett, Sir Stanley Charles, Bt. (1801)

Kelly, Sir Christopher William, KCB

Kelly, Sir David Robert Corbett, Kt., CBE

Kemakeza, Sir Allan, Kt.

Kemball, *Air Marshal* Sir (Richard) John, KCB, CBE

Kemp-Welch, Sir John, Kt.

Kendall, Sir Peter Ashley, Kt.

Kennaway, Sir John-Michael, Bt. (1791)

Kennedy, *Hon.* Sir Ian Alexander, Kt.

Kennedy, *Prof.* Sir Ian McColl, Kt.

†Kennedy, Sir George Matthew Rae, Bt. (1836)

Kennedy, *Rt. Hon.* Sir Paul Joseph Morrow, Kt.

Kenny, Sir Anthony John Patrick, Kt., DPHIL, DLITT, FBA

Kenny, Sir Paul Stephen, Kt.

Kentridge, Sir Sydney Woolf, KCMG, QC

Kenyon, Sir Nicholas Roger, Kt., CBE

Keogh, *Prof.* Sir Bruce Edward, KBE

Kere, *Dr* Sir Nathan, KCMG

Kerr, *Adm.* Sir John Beverley, GCB

Kerr, Sir Ronald James, Kt., CBE

Kerr, *Hon.* Sir Timothy Julian, Kt.

Kershaw, *Prof.* Sir Ian, Kt.

Keswick, Sir Henry Neville Lindley, Kt.

Keswick, Sir John Chippendale Lindley, Kt.

Kevau, *Prof.* Sir Isi Henao, Kt., CBE

Khaw, *Prof.* Sir Peng Tee, Kt.

Kikau, *Ratu* Sir Jone Latianara, KBE

Kimber, Sir Rupert Edward Watkin, Bt. (1904)

King, *Prof.* Sir David Anthony, Kt., FRS

King, Sir James Henry Rupert, Bt. (1888)

King, Sir Julian Beresford, KCVO, CMG

King, *Hon.* Sir Timothy Roger Alan, Kt.

King, Sir Wayne Alexander, Bt. (1815)

Kingman, *Prof.* Sir John Frank Charles, Kt., FRS

Kingman, Sir John Oliver Frank, KCB

Kingsley, Sir Ben, Kt.

Kinloch, Sir David, Bt. (S. 1686)

Kinloch, Sir David Oliphant, Bt. (1873)

Kipalan, Sir Albert, Kt.

Kirch, Sir David Roderick, KBE

Kirkpatrick, Sir Ivone Elliott, Bt. (S. 1685)

Kiszely, *Lt.-Gen.* Sir John Panton, KCB, MC

Kitchin, *Rt. Hon.* Sir David James Tyson, Kt.

Kitson, *Gen.* Sir Frank Edward, GBE, KCB, MC

Kitson, Sir Timothy Peter Geoffrey, Kt.

Kleinwort, Sir Richard Drake, Bt. (1909)

Klug, Sir Aaron, Kt., OM

Knight, *Rt. Hon.* Sir Gregory, Kt.

Knight, Sir Kenneth John, Kt., CBE, QFSM

Knight, *Air Chief Marshal* Sir Michael William Patrick, KCB, AFC

Knight, *Prof.* Sir Peter, Kt.

Knill, Sir Thomas John Pugin Bartholomew, Bt. (1893)

Knowles, Sir Charles Francis, Bt. (1765)

Knowles, *Hon.* Sir Julian Bernard, Kt.

Knowles, Sir Nigel Graham, Kt.

Knowles, *Hon.* Sir Robin St John, Kt.

Knox, Sir David Laidlaw, Kt.

Knox-Johnston, Sir William Robert Patrick (Sir Robin), Kt., CBE, RD

Koraea, Sir Thomas, Kt.

Kornberg, *Prof.* Sir Hans Leo, Kt., DSc, SCD, PHD, FRS

Korowi, Sir Wiwa, GCMG

Kulukundis, Sir Elias George (Eddie), Kt., OBE

Kulunga, Sir Toami, Kt., OBE, QPM

Kumar, Sir Harpal Singh, Kt.

Kwok-Po Li, *Dr* Sir David, Kt., OBE

Lachmann, *Prof.* Sir Peter Julius, Kt.

Lacon, Sir Edmund Richard Vere, Bt. (1818)

Lacy, Sir Patrick Brian Finucane, Bt. (1921)

Laing, Sir (John) Martin (Kirby), Kt., CBE

Lake, Sir Edward Geoffrey, Bt. (1711)

Lakin, Sir Richard Anthony, Bt. (1909)

Lamb, Sir Albert Thomas, KBE, CMG, DFC

Lamb, *Lt.-Gen.* Sir Graeme Cameron Maxwell, KBE, CMG, DSO

Lambert, *Vice-Adm.* Sir Paul, KCB

†Lambert, Sir Peter John Biddulph, Bt. (1711)

Lambert, Sir Richard Peter, Kt.

Lampl, Sir Peter, Kt., OBE

Lamport, Sir Stephen Mark Jeffrey, GCVO

Lancashire, Sir Steve, Kt.

Landau, Sir Dennis Marcus, Kt.

Lander, Sir Stephen James, KCB

Lane, Prof. Sir David Philip, Kt.

Lane, *Hon.* Sir Peter Richard, Kt.

Langham, Sir John Stephen, Bt. (1660)

Langley, *Hon.* Sir Gordon Julian Hugh, Kt.

Langrishe, Sir James Hercules, Bt. (I. 1777)

Langstaff, *Hon.* Sir Brian Frederick James, Kt.

Lankester, Sir Timothy Patrick, KCB

Lapli, Sir John Ini, GCMG

Lapthorne, Sir Richard Douglas, Kt., CBE

Large, Sir Andrew McLeod Brooks, Kt.

Latasi, *Rt. Hon.* Sir Kamuta, KCMG, OBE

Latham, *Rt. Hon.* Sir David Nicholas Ramsey, Kt.

Latham, Sir Richard Thomas Paul, Bt. (1919)

Laughton, Sir Anthony Seymour, Kt.

Laurence, *Vice-Adm.* Sir Timothy James Hamilton, KCVO, CB, ADC

Laurie, Sir Andrew Ronald Emilius, Bt. (1834)

Lavender, *Hon.* Sir Nicholas, Kt.

Lawrence, Sir Clive Wyndham, Bt. (1906)

Lawrence, Sir Edmund Wickham, GCMG, OBE

Lawrence, Sir Henry Peter, Bt. (1858)

Lawrence, Sir Ivan John, Kt., QC

†Lawrence, Sir Aubrey Lyttelton Simon, Bt. (1867)

Lawrence-Jones, Sir Christopher, Bt. (1831)

Laws, *Rt. Hon.* Sir John Grant McKenzie, Kt.

Laws, Sir Stephen Charles, KCB

Lawson, Sir Charles John Patrick, Bt. (1900)

Lawson, *Gen.* Sir Richard George, KCB, DSO, OBE

Lawson-Tancred, Sir Andrew Peter, Bt. (1662)

Lawton, *Prof.* Sir John Hartley, Kt., CBE, FRS

Layard, *Adm.* Sir Michael Henry Gordon, KCB, CBE

Lea, Sir Thomas William, Bt. (1892)

Leahy, Sir Daniel Joseph, Kt.

Leahy, Sir Terence Patrick, Kt.

Learmont, *Gen.* Sir John Hartley, KCB, CBE

Leaver, Sir Christopher, GBE

Lechler, *Prof.* Sir Robert Ian, Kt.

Lechmere, Sir Nicholas Anthony Hungerford, Bt. (1818)

†Leeds, Sir John Charles Hildyard, Bt. (1812)

Lees, Sir David Bryan, Kt.

Lees, Sir Christopher James, Bt. (1897), TD

Lees, Sir Thomas Harcourt Ivor, Bt. (1804)

Lees, Sir (William) Antony Clare, Bt. (1937)

Leese, Sir Richard Charles, Kt., CBE

Leeson, *Air Marshal* Sir Kevin James, KCB, CBE

le Fleming, Sir David Kelland, Bt. (1705)

Legard, Sir Charles Thomas, Bt. (1660)

Legg, Sir Thomas Stuart, KCB, QC

Leggatt, *Rt. Hon.* Sir Andrew Peter, Kt.

Leggatt, *Rt. Hon.* Sir George Andrew Midsomer, Kt.

Leggett, *Prof.* Sir Anthony James, KBE

Le Grand, *Prof.* Sir Julian Ernest, Kt.

Leigh, Sir Edward Julian Egerton, Kt.

Leigh, Sir Geoffrey Norman, Kt.

Leigh, *Dr* Sir Michael, KCMG

Leigh, Sir Richard Henry, Bt. (1918)

Leighton, Sir John Mark Nicholas, Kt.

Leighton, Sir Michael John Bryan, Bt. (1693)

†Leith-Buchanan, Sir Gordon Kelly McNicol, Bt. (1775)

Le Marchant, Sir Piers Alfred, Bt. (1841)

Lennox-Boyd, *Hon.* Sir Mark Alexander, Kt.

Leon, Sir John Ronald, Bt. (1911)

Lepani, Sir Charles Watson, KBE

†Leslie, Sir Shaun Rudolph Christopher, Bt. (1876)

Lester, Sir James Theodore, Kt.

Lethbridge, Sir Thomas Periam Hector Noel, Bt. (1804)

Letwin, *Rt. Hon.* Sir Oliver, Kt.

Lever, Sir Jeremy Frederick, KCMG, QC

Lever, Sir Paul, KCMG

Lever, Sir (Tresham) Christopher Arthur Lindsay, Bt. (1911)

Leveson, *Rt. Hon.* Sir Brian Henry, Kt.

Levi, Sir Wasangula Noel, Kt., CBE

Levinge, Sir Richard George Robin, Bt. (I. 1704)

Lewinton, Sir Christopher, Kt.

Lewis, *Hon.* Sir Clive Buckland, Kt.

Lewis, Sir David Thomas Rowell, Kt.

Lewis, Sir John Anthony, Kt., OBE

Lewis, Sir Leigh Warren, KCB

Lewis, Sir Martyn John Dudley, Kt., CBE

Lewis, Sir Terence Murray, Kt., OBE, GM, QPM

Lewison, *Rt. Hon.* Sir Kim Martin Jordan, Kt.

Ley, Sir Christopher Ian, Bt. (1905)

Li, Sir Ka-Shing, KBE

Lickiss, Sir Michael Gillam, Kt.

Liddington, Sir Bruce, Kt.

Lightman, *Hon.* Sir Gavin Anthony, Kt.

Lighton, Sir Thomas Hamilton, Bt. (I. 1791)

Likierman, *Prof.* Sir John Andrew, Kt.

Lilleyman, *Prof.* Sir John Stuart, Kt.

Lindblom, *Rt. Hon.* Sir Keith John, Kt.

†Lindsay, Sir James Martin Evelyn, Bt. (1962)

Lindsay, *Hon.* Sir John Edmund Frederic, Kt.

†Lindsay-Hogg, Sir Michael Edward, Bt. (1905)

Lipton, Sir Stuart Anthony, Kt.

Lipworth, Sir (Maurice) Sydney, Kt.

Lister, *Vice-Adm.* Sir Simon Robert, KCB, OBE

Lister-Kaye, Sir John Phillip Lister, Bt. (1812), OBE

Lithgow, Sir William James, Bt. (1925)

Llewellyn, Sir Roderic Victor, Bt. (1922)

Llewellyn-Smith, *Prof.* Sir Christopher Hubert, Kt.

Lloyd, *Prof.* Sir Geoffrey Ernest Richard, Kt., FBA

Lloyd, Sir Nicholas Markley, Kt.

Lloyd, *Rt. Hon.* Sir Peter Robert Cable, Kt.

Lloyd, Sir Richard Ernest Butler, Bt. (1960)

Lloyd, *Rt. Hon.* Sir Timothy Andrew Wigram, Kt.

Lloyd-Edwards, *Capt.* Sir Norman, KCVO, RD

Lloyd Jones, *Rt. Hon.* Sir David, Kt. (Lord Lloyd-Jones)

Loader, Air Marshal Sir Clive Robert, KCB, OBE

Lobban, Sir Iain Robert, KCMG, CB

Lockett, Sir Michael Vernon, KCVO

Lockhead, Sir Moir, Kt., OBE

Loder, Sir Edmund Jeune, Bt. (1887)

Logan, Sir David Brian Carleton, KCMG

Long, Sir Richard Julian, Kt., CBE

Longley, *Hon.* Sir Hartman Godfrey, Kt.

Longmore, *Rt. Hon.* Sir Andrew Centlivres, Kt.

Lorimer, *Lt.-Gen.* Sir John Gordon, KCB, MBE, DSO

Lorimer, Sir (Thomas) Desmond, Kt.

Los, *Hon.* Sir Kubulan, Kt., CBE

Loughran, Sir Gerald Finbar, KCB

Lourdenadin, Sir Ninian Mogan, KCMG, KBE

Lovestone, *Prof.* Sir Simon, Kt.

Lovill, Sir John Roger, Kt., CBE

Low, *Dr* Sir John Menzies, Kt., CBE

Lowa, *Rt. Revd* Sir Samson, KBE

Lowcock, Sir Mark Andrew, KCB

Lowe, Sir Frank Budge, Kt.

Lowe, Sir Philip Martin, KCMG

Lowe, Sir Thomas William Gordon, Bt. (1918), QC

Lowson, Sir Ian Patrick, Bt. (1951)

Lowther, *Col.* Sir Charles Douglas, Bt. (1824)

Lowy, Sir Frank, Kt.

Loyd, Sir Julian St John, KCVO

Lu, Sir Tseng Chi, Kt.

Lucas, *Prof.* Sir Colin Renshaw, Kt.

†Lucas, Sir Thomas Edward, Bt. (1887)

Lucas-Tooth, Sir (Hugh) John, Bt. (1920)

Luff, Sir Peter James, Kt.

Lumsden, Sir David James, Kt.

Lushington, Sir John Richard Castleman, Bt. (1791)

Lyall Grant, Sir Mark Justin, KCMG

Lyle, Sir Gavin Archibald, Bt. (1929)

Lynch-Blosse, *Capt.* Sir Richard Hely, Bt. (I. 1622)

Lynch-Robinson, Sir Dominick Christopher, Bt. (1920)

Lyne, *Rt. Hon.* Sir Roderic Michael John, KBE, CMG

Lyons, Sir John, Kt.

Lyons, Sir Michael Thomas, Kt.

McAlinden, *Hon.* Sir Gerry, Kt.

McAllister, Sir Ian Gerald, Kt., CBE

McAlpine, Sir Andrew William, Bt. (1918)

McCamley, Sir Graham Edward, KBE

McCanny, *Prof.* Sir John Vincent, Kt., CBE

McCarthy, Sir Callum, Kt.

McCartney, *Rt. Hon.* Sir Ian, Kt.

McCartney, Sir (James) Paul, Kt., CH, MBE

†Macartney, Sir John Ralph, Bt. (I. 1799)

McClement, *Vice-Admiral* Sir Timothy Pentreath, KCB, OBE

Macleod, Sir Iain, KCMG

McCloskey, *Hon.* Sir John Bernard, Kt.

McColl, Sir Colin Hugh Verel, KCMG

McColl, *Gen.* Sir John Chalmers, KCB, CBE, DSO

McCollum, *Rt. Hon.* Sir William, Kt.

McCombe, *Rt. Hon.* Sir Richard George Bramwell, Kt.

McConnell, Sir Robert Shean, Bt. (1900)

†McCowan, Sir David William, Bt. (1934)

McCoy, Sir Anthony Peter, Kt., OBE

McCullin, Sir Donald, Kt., CBE

MacCulloch, *Prof.* Sir Diarmaid Ninian John, Kt.

McCulloch, *Rt. Revd* Nigel Simeon, KCVO

McCullough, *Hon.* Sir (Iain) Charles (Robert), Kt.

MacDermott, *Rt. Hon.* Sir John Clarke, Kt.

Macdonald, Sir Alasdair Uist, Kt., CBE

MacDonald, *Hon.* Sir Alistair William Orchard, Kt.

Macdonald of Sleat, Sir Ian Godfrey Bosville, Bt. (S. 1625)

McDonald, *Prof.* Sir James, Kt.

Macdonald, Sir Kenneth Carmichael, KCB

McDonald, Sir Simon Gerard, KCMG, KCVO

McDonald, Sir Trevor, Kt., OBE

McDowell, Sir Eric Wallace, Kt., CBE

MacDuff, *Hon.* Sir Alistair Geoffrey, Kt.

Mace, *Lt.-Gen.* Sir John Airth, KBE, CB

McEwen, Sir John Roderick Hugh, Bt. (1953)

MacFadyen, *Air Marshal* Sir Ian David, KCVO, CB, OBE

McFarland, Sir John Talbot, Bt. (1914)

MacFarlane, *Prof.* Sir Alistair George James, Kt., CBE, FRS

McFarlane, *Rt. Hon.* Sir Andrew Ewart, Kt.

Macfarlane, Sir (David) Neil, Kt.

McGeechan, Sir Ian Robert, Kt., OBE

McGrath, Sir Harvey Andrew, Kt.

†Macgregor, Sir Ian Grant, Bt. (1828)

MacGregor of MacGregor, Sir Malcolm Gregor Charles, Bt. (1795)

McGrigor, Sir James Angus Rhoderick Neil, Bt. (1831)

McIntosh, Sir Neil William David, Kt., CBE

McIntosh, Sir Ronald Robert Duncan, KCB

McIntyre, Sir Donald Conroy, Kt., CBE

McIntyre, Sir Meredith Alister, Kt.

Mackay, *Hon.* Sir Colin Crichton, Kt.

MacKay, Sir Francis Henry, Kt.

McKay, Sir Neil Stuart, Kt., CB

McKay, Sir William Robert, KCB

Mackay-Dick, *Maj.-Gen.* Sir Iain Charles, KCVO, MBE

Mackechnie, Sir Alistair John, Kt.

McKellen, Sir Ian Murray, Kt., CH, CBE

†Mackenzie, Sir (James William) Guy, Bt. (1890)

Mackenzie, *Gen.* Sir Jeremy John George, GCB, OBE

†Mackenzie, Sir Peter Douglas, Bt. (S. 1673)

†Mackenzie, Sir Roderick McQuhae, Bt. (S. 1703)

Mackeson, Sir Rupert Henry, Bt. (1954)

Mackey, Sir Craig Thomas, Kt., QPM

McKibbin, *Dr* Sir Malcolm, KCB

McKillop, Sir Thomas Fulton Wilson, Kt.

McKinnon, *Rt. Hon.* Sir Donald Charles, GCVO

McKinnon, *Hon.* Sir Stuart Neil, Kt.

Mackintosh, Sir Cameron Anthony, Kt.

†Mackworth, Sir Alan Keith, Bt. (1776)

McLaughlin, Sir Richard, Kt.

Maclean of Dunconnel, Sir Charles Edward, Bt. (1957)

Maclean, *Hon.* Sir Lachlan Hector Charles, Bt., CVO (NS 1631)

Maclean, Sir Murdo, Kt.

†McLeod, Sir James Roderick Charles, Bt. (1925)

MacLeod, *Hon.* Sir (John) Maxwell Norman, Bt. (1924)

Macleod, Sir (Nathaniel William) Hamish, KBE

McLintock, Sir Michael William, Bt. (1934)

McLoughlin, Sir Francis, Kt., CBE

McLoughlin, *Rt. Hon.* Sir Patrick Allen, Kt.

Maclure, Sir John Robert Spencer, Bt. (1898)

McMahon, Sir Brian Patrick, Bt. (1817)

McMahon, Sir Christopher William, Kt.

McMaster, Sir Brian John, Kt., CBE

McMichael, *Prof.* Sir Andrew James, Kt., FRS

MacMillan, *Very Revd* Gilleasbuig Iain, KCVO

McMillan, Sir Iain Macleod, Kt., CBE

Macmillan, *Dr* Sir James Loy, Kt., CBE

MacMillan, *Lt.-Gen.* Sir John Richard Alexander, KCB, CBE

McMurtry, Sir David, Kt., CBE

Macnaghten, Sir Malcolm Francis, Bt. (1836)

McNair-Wilson, Sir Patrick Michael Ernest David, Kt.

McNee, Sir David Blackstock, Kt., QPM

McNulty, Sir (Robert William) Roy, Kt., CBE

MacPhail, Sir Bruce Dugald, Kt.

Macpherson of Cluny, *Hon.* Sir William Alan, Kt., TD

MacRae, Sir (Alastair) Christopher (Donald Summerhayes), KCMG

Macready, Sir Charles Nevil, Bt. (1923)

Mactaggart, Sir John Auld, Bt. (1938)

McVicar, Sir David, Kt.

McWilliam, Sir Michael Douglas, KCMG

McWilliams, Sir Francis, GBE

Madden, Sir Charles Jonathan, Bt. (1919)

Madden, Sir David Christopher Andrew, KCMG

Maddison, *Hon.* Sir David George, Kt.

Madejski, Sir John Robert, Kt., OBE

Madel, Sir (William) David, Kt.

Magee, Sir Ian Bernard Vaughan, Kt., CB

Magnus, Sir Laurence Henry Philip, Bt. (1917)

Maguire, *Hon.* Sir Paul Richard, Kt.

Mahon, Sir William Walter, Bt. (1819), LVO

Mahoney, Sir Paul John, KCMG

Maiden, Sir Colin James, Kt., DPHIL

Maini, *Prof.* Sir Ravinder Nath, Kt.

Maino, Sir Charles, KBE

†Maitland, Sir Charles Alexander, Bt. (1818)

Major, *Rt. Hon.* Sir John, KG, CH

Malbon, *Vice-Adm.* Sir Fabian Michael, KBE

Malcolm, Sir Alexander James Elton, Bt. (S. 1665), OBE

Malcolm, *Dr* Noel Robert, Kt., FBA

Malet, Sir Harry Douglas St Lo, Bt. (1791)

Males, *Rt. Hon.* Sir Stephen Martin, Kt.

Mallaby, Sir Christopher Leslie George, GCMG, GCVO

Mallick, *Prof.* Sir Netar Prakash, Kt.

Mallinson, Sir William James, Bt. (1935)

Malpas, Sir Robert, Kt., CBE

Mander, Sir (Charles) Nicholas, Bt. (1911)

Mann, *Hon.* Sir George Anthony, Kt.

Mann, Sir Rupert Edward, Bt. (1905)

Manning, Sir David Geoffrey, GCMG, KCVO

Mano, Sir Koitaga, Kt., MBE

Mans, *Lt.-Gen.* Sir Mark Francis Noel, KCB, CBE

Mansel, Sir Philip, Bt. (1622)

Manuella, Sir Tulaga, GCMG, MBE

Mara, Sir Nambuga, KBE

Margetson, Sir John William Denys, KCMG

Margetts, Sir Robert John, Kt., CBE

Markesinis, *Prof.* Sir Basil Spyridonos, Kt., QC

Markham, *Prof.* Sir Alexander Fred, Kt.

Markham, Sir (Arthur) David, Bt. (1911)

Marling, Sir Charles William Somerset, Bt. (1882)

Marmot, *Prof.* Sir Michael Gideon, Kt.

Marr, Sir Leslie Lynn, Bt. (1919)

Marsden, Sir Jonathan Mark, KCVO

†Marsden, Sir Tadgh Orlando Denton, Bt. (1924)

Marshall, Sir Michael John, Kt., CBE

Marshall, Sir Paul, Kt.

Marshall, Sir Peter Harold Reginald, KCMG

Marshall, *Prof. Emeritus* Sir Woodville Kemble, Kt.

Martin, Sir Clive Haydon, Kt., OBE

Martin, Sir Gregory Michael Gerard, Kt.

Martin, *Prof.* Sir Laurence Woodward, Kt.

Masefield, Sir Charles Beech Gordon, Kt.

Mason, *Hon.* Sir Anthony Frank, KBE

Mason, *Prof.* Sir David Kean, Kt., CBE

Mason, Sir Peter James, KBE

Mason, *Prof.* Sir Ronald, KCB, FRS

Massey, *Vice-Adm.* Sir Alan, KCB, CBE, ADC

Marsters, *HE* Sir Tom John, KBE

Matane, HE Sir Paulias Nguna, GCMG, OBE

Matheson of Matheson, Sir Alexander Fergus, Bt. (1882), LVO

Mathews, *Vice-Adm.* Sir Andrew David Hugh, KCB

Mathewson, Sir George Ross, Kt., CBE, PHD, FRSE

Matthews, Sir Terence Hedley, Kt., OBE

Maughan, Sir Deryck, Kt.

Mawer, Sir Philip John Courtney, Kt.

Maxwell, Sir Michael Eustace George, Bt. (S. 1681)

Maxwell Macdonald (formerly Stirling-Maxwell), Sir John Ronald, Bt. (NS 1682)

Maxwell-Scott, Sir Dominic James, Bt. (1642)

May, *Rt. Hon.* Sir Anthony Tristram Kenneth, Kt.

Mayall, *Lt.-Gen.* Sir Simon Vincent, KBE, CB

Mayfield, Sir Andrew Charles, Kt.

Meadow, *Prof.* Sir (Samuel) Roy, Kt., FRCP, FRCPE

Meale, Sir Joseph Alan, Kt.

Medlycott, Sir Mervyn Tregonwell, Bt. (1808)

Meeran, *His Hon.* Sir Goolam Hoosen Kader, Kt.

Meldrum, Sir Graham, Kt., CBE, QFSM

Melhuish, Sir Michael Ramsay, KBE, CMG

Mellars, *Prof.* Sir Paul Anthony, Kt., FBA

Mellon, Sir James, KCMG

Melmoth, Sir Graham John, Kt.

Melville, *Prof.* Sir David, Kt., CBE

Melville-Ross, Sir Timothy David, Kt., CBE

Merifield, Sir Anthony James, KCVO, CB

Messenger, *Gen.* Sir Gordon Kenneth, KCB, DSO, OBE

Metcalf, *Prof.* Sir David Harry, Kt., CBE

†Meyer, Sir (Anthony) Ashley Frank, Bt. (1910)

Meyer, Sir Christopher John Rome, KCMG

†Meyrick, Sir Timothy Thomas Charlton, Bt. (1880)

Miakwe, *Hon.* Sir Akepa, KBE

Michael, Sir Duncan, Kt.

Michael, *Dr* Sir Jonathan, Kt.

Michael, Sir Peter Colin, Kt., CBE

Michels, Sir David Michael Charles, Kt.

Middleton, Sir John Maxwell, Kt.

Middleton, Sir Peter Edward, GCB

Miers, Sir (Henry) David Alastair Capel, KBE, CMG

Milbank, Sir Edward Mark Somerset, Bt. (1882)

Milborne-Swinnerton-Pilkington, Sir Thomas Henry, Bt. (S. 1635)

Milburn, Sir Anthony Rupert, Bt. (1905)

†Miles, Sir Philip John, Bt. (1859)

Millais, Sir Geoffroy Richard Everett, Bt. (1885)

Millar, *Prof.* Sir Fergus Graham Burtholme, Kt.

Miller, Sir Donald John, Kt., FRSE, FRENG

Miller, *Air Marshal* Sir Graham Anthony, KBE

Miller, Sir Anthony Thomas, Bt. (1705)

Miller, Sir Jonathan Wolfe, Kt., CBE

Miller, Sir Robin Robert William, Kt.

Miller, Sir Ronald Andrew Baird, Kt., CBE

Miller of Glenlee, Sir Stephen William Macdonald, Bt. (1788)

Mills, Sir Ian, Kt.

Mills, Sir Jonathan Edward Harland (John), Kt., FRSE

Mills, Sir Keith Edward, GBE

Mills, Sir Peter Frederick Leighton, Bt. (1921)

Milman, Sir David Patrick, Bt. (1800)

Milne-Watson, Sir Andrew Michael, Bt. (1937)

Milner, Sir Timothy William Lycett, Bt. (1717)

Mitchell, *Rt. Hon.* Sir James FitzAllen, KCMG

Mitchell, *Very Revd* Patrick Reynolds, KCVO

Mitchell, *Hon.* Sir Stephen George, Kt.

Mitting, *Hon.* Sir John Edward, Kt.

Moate, Sir Roger Denis, Kt.

Moberly, Sir Patrick Hamilton, KCMG

Moir, Sir Christopher Ernest, Bt. (1916)

Molesworth-St Aubyn, Sir William, Bt. (1689)

Molony, Sir Peter John, Bt. (1925)

Moncada, *Prof.* Sir Salvador, Kt.

Montagu, Sir Nicholas Lionel John, KCB

†Montagu-Pollock, Sir Guy Maximilian, Bt. (1872)

Montague, Sir Adrian Alastair, Kt., CBE

Montgomery, Sir (Basil Henry) David, Bt. (1801), CVO

Montgomery, *Vice-Adm.* Sir Charles Percival Ross, KBE, ADC

Montgomery-Cuninghame, Sir John Christopher Foggo, Bt. (NS 1672)

Moody-Stuart, Sir Mark, KCMG

Moollan, Sir Abdool Hamid Adam, Kt.

†Moon, Sir Humphrey, Bt. (1887)

Moor, *Hon.* Sir Philip Drury, Kt.

Moorcroft, Sir William, KBE

Moore, *Most Revd* Desmond Charles, KBE

Moore, Sir Francis Thomas, Kt.

Moore, *Vice Adm.* Sir Michael Antony Claës, KBE, LVO

Moore, Sir Peter Alan Cutlack, Bt. (1919)

Moore, Sir William Roger Clotworthy, Bt. (1932), TD

Moore-Bick, *Rt. Hon.* Sir Martin James, Kt.

Morauta, Sir Mekere, KCMG

Mordaunt, Sir Richard Nigel Charles, Bt. (1611)

Morgan, *Vice-Adm.* Sir Charles Christopher, KBE

Morgan, *Rt. Hon.* Sir (Charles) Declan, Kt.

Morgan, Sir Graham, Kt.

Morgan, *Hon.* Sir Paul Hyacinth, Kt.

Morgan, Sir Terence Keith, Kt., CBE

Morison, *Hon.* Sir Thomas Richard Atkin, Kt.

Moritz, Sir Michael Jonathan, KBE

Morland, *Hon.* Sir Michael, Kt.

Morland, Sir Robert Kenelm, Kt.

Morpurgo, Sir Michael Andrew Bridge, Kt., OBE

†Morris, Sir Allan Lindsay, Bt. (1806)

Morris, Sir Andrew Valentine, Kt., OBE

Morris, *Air Marshal* Sir Arnold Alec, KBE, CB

Morris, Sir Derek James, Kt.

Morris, Sir Keith Elliot Hedley, KBE, CMG

Morris, *Prof.* Sir Peter John, Kt.

Morris, *Hon.* Sir Stephen Nathan, Kt.

Morris, Sir Trefor Alfred, Kt., CBE, QPM

Morrison, Sir (Alexander) Fraser, Kt., CBE

Morrison, Sir George Ivan, Kt., OBE

Morrison, Sir Howard Andrew Clive, KCMG, CBE

Morrison-Bell, Sir William Hollin Dayrell, Bt. (1905)

Morrison-Low, Sir Richard Walter, Bt. (1908)

Morritt, *Rt. Hon.* Sir (Robert) Andrew, Kt., CVO

Morse, Sir Amyas Charles Edward, KCB

Moses, *Rt. Hon.* Sir Alan George, Kt.

Moses, *Very Revd* Dr John Henry, KCVO

Moss, Sir David Joseph, KCVO, CMG

Moss, Sir Stephen Alan, Kt.

Moss, Sir Stirling Craufurd, Kt., OBE

Mostyn, *Hon.* Sir Nicholas Anthony Joseph Ghislain, Kt.

Mostyn, Sir William Basil John, Bt. (1670)

Motion, Sir Andrew, Kt.

Mott, Sir David Hugh, Bt. (1930)

Mottram, Sir Richard Clive, GCB

†Mount, Sir (William Robert) Ferdinand, Bt. (1921)

Mountain, Sir Edward Brian Stanford, Bt. (1922)

Mowbray, Sir John Robert, Bt. (1880)

Moylan, *Rt. Hon.* Sir Andrew John Gregory, Kt.

Moynihan, *Dr* Sir Daniel, Kt.

†Muir, Sir Richard James Kay, Bt. (1892)

Muir-Mackenzie, Sir Alexander Alwyne Henry Charles Brinton, Bt. (1805)

Mulcahy, Sir Geoffrey John, Kt.

Mummery, *Rt. Hon.* Sir John Frank, Kt.

Munby, *Rt. Hon.* Sir James Lawrence, Kt.

Munro, Sir Alan Gordon, KCMG

†Munro, Sir Ian Kenneth, Bt. (S. 1634)

Munro, Sir Keith Gordon, Bt. (1825)

Muria, *Hon.* Sir Gilbert John Baptist, Kt.

Murphy, Sir Jonathan Michael, Kt., QPM

Murray, Sir Andrew, Kt., OBE

Murray, Sir David Edward, Kt.

Murray, *Hon.* Sir Edward, Kt

Murray, Sir Nigel Andrew Digby, Bt. (S. 1628)

Murray, Sir Patrick Ian Keith, Bt. (S. 1673)

Murray, Sir Robert Sydney, Kt., CBE

Murray, Sir Robin MacGregor, Kt.

†Murray, Sir Rowland William, Bt. (S. 1630)

Muscatelli, *Prof.* Sir Vito Antonio, Kt., FRSE

Musgrave, Sir Christopher John Shane, Bt. (I. 1782)

Musgrave, Sir Christopher Patrick Charles, Bt. (1611)

Myers, Sir Derek John, Kt.

Myers, *Prof.* Sir Rupert Horace, KBE

Mynors, Sir Richard Baskerville, Bt. (1964)

Nairn, Sir Michael, Bt. (1904)

Naish, Sir (Charles) David, Kt.

Nalau, Sir Jerry Kasip, KBE

Nall, Sir Edward William Joseph, Bt. (1954)

Namaliu, *Rt. Hon.* Sir Rabbie Langanai, KCMG

Napier, Sir Charles Joseph, Bt. (1867)

Napier, Sir John Archibald Lennox, Bt. (S. 1627)

Narey, Sir Martin James, Kt.

Natzler, Sir David Lionel, KCB

Naylor, Sir Robert, Kt.

Naylor-Leyland, Sir Philip Vyvian, Bt. (1895)

Neal, Sir Eric James, Kt., CVO

Neave, Sir Paul Arundell, Bt. (1795)

†Nelson, Sir Jamie Charles Vernon Hope, Bt. (1912)

Nelson, *Hon.* Sir Robert Franklyn, Kt.

New, *Maj.-Gen.* Sir Laurence Anthony Wallis, Kt., CB, CBE

Newbigging, Sir David Kennedy, Kt., OBE

Newby, *Prof.* Sir Howard Joseph, Kt., CBE

Newey, *Rt. Hon.* Sir Guy Richard, Kt.

Newman, Sir Francis Hugh Cecil, Bt. (1912)

Newman, Sir Geoffrey Robert, Bt. (1836)

Newman, *Hon.* Sir George Michael, Kt.

Newman, *Vice-Adm.* Sir Roy Thomas, KCB

Newman Taylor, *Prof.* Sir Anthony John, Kt., CBE

Newsam, Sir Peter Anthony, Kt.

Newson-Smith, Sir Peter Frank Graham, Bt. (1944)

Newton, *Revd* George Peter Howgill, Bt. (1900)

Newton, Sir John Garnar, Bt. (1924)

Newton, *Lt.-Gen.* Sir Paul Raymond, KBE

Newton, *Hon.* Sir Roderick Brian, Kt.

Nice, Sir Geoffrey, Kt., QC

Nickell, *Prof.* Sir Stephen John, Kt., CBE, FBA

Nicklin, *Hon.* Sir Matthew James, Kt.

Nichol, Sir Duncan Kirkbride, Kt., CBE

Nicholas, Sir David, Kt., CBE

Nicholas, Sir John William, KCVO, CMG

Nicholson, Sir Bryan Hubert, GBE, Kt.

Nicholson, Sir Charles Christian, Bt. (1912)

Nicholson, Sir David, KCB, CBE

Nicholson, *Rt. Hon.* Sir Michael, Kt.

Nicholson, Sir Paul Douglas, KCVO, Kt.

Nicholson, Sir Robin Buchanan, Kt., PHD, FRS, FRENG

Nicol, *Hon.* Sir Andrew George Lindsay, Kt.

Nightingale, Sir Charles Manners Gamaliel, Bt. (1628)

†Nixon, Sir Simon Michael Christopher, Bt. (1906)

Noble, Sir David Brunel, Bt. (1902)

Noble, Sir Timothy Peter, Bt. (1923)

Nombri, Sir Joseph Karl, Kt., ISO, BEM

Norgrove, Sir David Ronald, Kt.

Norman, Sir Nigel James, Bt. (1915)

Norman, Sir Ronald, Kt., OBE

Norman, Sir Torquil Patrick Alexander, Kt., CBE

Normington, Sir David John, GCB

Norrington, Sir Roger Arthur Carver, Kt., CBE

Norris, *Hon.* Sir Alastair Hubert, Kt.

Norriss, *Air Marshal* Sir Peter Coulson, KBE, CB, AFC

North, *Air Marshal* Sir Barry Mark, KCB, OBE

North, Sir Peter Machin, Kt., CBE, QC, DCL, FBA

†North, Sir Jeremy William Francis, Bt. (1920)

Norton, Barry, Kt.

Norton, *Maj.-Gen.* Sir George Pemberton Ross, KCVO, CBE

Norton-Griffiths, Sir Michael, Bt. (1922)

Nossal, Sir Gustav Joseph Victor, Kt., CBE

Nott, *Rt. Hon.* Sir John William Frederic, KCB

Novoselov, *Prof.* Sir Konstantin, Kt.

Nugee, *Hon.* Sir Christopher George, Kt.

†Nugent, Sir Nicholas Myles John, Bt. (I. 1795)

Nugent, Sir Christopher George Ridley, Bt. (1806)

Nugent, Sir (Walter) Richard Middleton, Bt. (1831)

Nunn, Sir Trevor Robert, Kt., CBE

Nunneley, Sir Charles Kenneth Roylance, Kt.

Nursaw, Sir James, KCB, QC

Nurse, Sir Paul Maxime, Kt.

Nuttall, Sir Harry, Bt. (1922)

Nutting, Sir John Grenfell, Bt. (1903), QC

Oakeley, Sir Robert John Atholl, Bt. (1790)

Oakes, Sir Christopher, Bt. (1939)

Oakshott, Sir Thomas Hendrie, Bt. (1959)

O'Brien, Sir Robert Stephen, Kt., CBE

O'Brien, *Rt. Hon.* Sir Stephen Rothwell, KBE

†O'Brien, Sir Timothy John, Bt. (1849)

O'Brien, Sir William, Kt.

O'Connell, Sir Bernard, Kt.

O'Connell, Sir Maurice James Donagh MacCarthy, Bt. (1869)

O'Connor, Sir Denis Francis, Kt., CBE, QPM

Odell, Sir Stanley John, Kt.

Odgers, Sir Graeme David William, Kt.

O'Donnell, Sir Christopher John, Kt.

O'Donoghue, *Lt.-Gen.* Sir Kevin, KCB, CBE

O'Dowd, Sir David Joseph, Kt., CBE, QPM

Ogden, *Dr* Sir Peter James, Kt.

Ogden, Sir Robert, Kt., CBE

Ogilvy, Sir Francis Gilbert Arthur, Bt. (S. 1626)

Ogilvy-Wedderburn, Sir Andrew John Alexander, Bt. (1803)

Ognall, *Hon.* Sir Harry Henry, Kt.

Ohlson, Sir Peter Michael, Bt. (1920)

Oldham, *Dr* Sir John, Kt., OBE

Olisa, Sir Kenneth Aphunezi, Kt., OBE

Oliver, Sir Craig Stewart, Kt.

Oliver, Sir James Michael Yorrick, Kt.

Oliver, Sir Stephen John Lindsay, Kt., QC

O'Hara, *Hon.* Sir John Ailbe, Kt.

†O'Loghlen, Sir Michael, Bt. (1838)

O'Lone, Sir Marcus James, KCVO

Olver, Sir Richard Lake, Kt.

Omand, Sir David Bruce, GCB

Ondaatje, Sir Christopher, Kt., CBE

O'Nions, *Prof.* Sir Robert Keith, Kt., FRS, PHD

Onslow, Sir Richard Paul Atherton, Bt. (1797)

Oppenheimer, Sir Michael Bernard Grenville, Bt. (1921)

Openshaw, *Hon.* Sir Charles Peter Lawford, Kt.

O'Rahilly, *Prof.* Sir Stephen Patrick, Kt., FRS

Ord, Sir David Charles, Kt.

Orde, Sir Hugh Stephen Roden, Kt., OBE, QPM

O'Regan, *Dr* Sir Stephen Gerard (Tipene), Kt.

O'Reilly, Sir Anthony John Francis, Kt.

O'Reilly, *Prof.* Sir John James, Kt.

Orr-Ewing, *Hon.* Sir (Alistair) Simon, Bt. (1963)

Orr-Ewing, Sir Archibald Donald, Bt. (1886)

Osborn, Sir Richard Henry Danvers, Bt. (1662)

Osborne, Sir Peter George, Bt. (I. 1629)

O'Shea, *Prof.* Sir Timothy Michael Martin, Kt.

Osmotherly, Sir Edward Benjamin Crofton, Kt., CB

Oswald, Sir (William Richard) Michael, KCVO

Ottaway, *Rt. Hon.* Sir Richard Geoffrey James, Kt.

Otton, Sir Geoffrey John, KCB

Otton, *Rt. Hon.* Sir Philip Howard, Kt.

Ouseley, *Hon.* Sir Duncan Brian Walter, Kt.

Outram, Sir Alan James, Bt. (1858)

Owen, Sir Geoffrey, Kt.

Owen, *Prof.* Sir Michael John, Kt.

Owen, *Hon.* Sir Robert Michael, Kt.

Owen-Jones, Sir Lindsay Harwood, KBE

Packer, Sir Richard John, KCB

Paget, Sir Henry James, Bt. (1871)

Paget, Sir Richard Herbert, Bt. (1886)

Paice, Rt. Hon. Sir James Edward Thornton, Kt.

Paine, Sir Christopher Hammon, Kt., FRCP, FRCR

Pakenham, Hon. Sir Michael Aiden, KBE, CMG

Palin, Air Chief Marshal Sir Roger Hewlett, KCB, OBE

Palmer, Sir Albert Rocky, Kt.

Palmer, Sir (Charles) Mark, Bt. (1886)

Palmer, Sir Geoffrey Christopher John, Bt. (1660)

Palmer, Rt. Hon. Sir Geoffrey Winston Russell, KCMG

Palmer, Prof. Sir Godfrey Henry Oliver, Kt, OBE

Palmer, Sir John Edward Somerset, Bt. (1791)

Panter, Sir Howard Hugh, Kt.

Pappano, Sir Antonio, Kt.

Parbo, Sir Arvi Hillar, Kt.

Park, Hon. Sir Andrew Edward Wilson, Kt.

Parker, Sir Alan, Kt.

Parker, Sir Alan William, Kt., CBE

Parker, Rt. Hon. Sir Jonathan Frederic, Kt.

Parker, Hon. Sir Kenneth Blades, Kt.

Parker, Maj. Sir Michael John, KCVO, CBE

Parker, Gen. Sir Nicholas Ralph, KCB, CBE

Parker, Sir Richard (William) Hyde, Bt. (1681)

Parker, Sir (Thomas) John, GBE

Parker, Sir William Peter Brian, Bt. (1844)

Parkes, Sir Edward Walter, Kt., FRENG

Parkinson, Sir Michael, Kt., CBE

Parmley, Dr Sir Andrew Charles, Kt.

Parry, Prof. Sir Eldryd Hugh Owen, KCMG, OBE

Parry, Sir Emyr Jones, GCMG

Parry-Evans, Air Chief Marshal Sir David, GCB, CBE

Parsons, Sir John Christopher, KCVO

Partridge, Sir Michael John Anthony, KCB

Partridge, Sir Nicholas Wyndham, Kt., OBE

Pascoe, Gen. Sir Robert Alan, KCB, MBE

Pasley, Sir Robert Killigrew Sabine, Bt. (1794)

Paston-Bedingfeld, Sir Henry Edgar, Bt. (1661)

Patey, Sir William Charters, KCMG

Patten, Rt. Hon. Sir Nicholas John, Kt.

Pattie, Rt. Hon. Sir Geoffrey Edwin, Kt.

Pattison, Prof. Sir John Ridley, Kt., DM, FRCPATH

Pattullo, Sir (David) Bruce, Kt., CBE

Pauncefort-Duncombe, Sir David Philip Henry, Bt. (1859)

Payne, Prof. Sir David Neil, Kt., CBE, FRS

Peace, Sir John Wilfrid, Kt.

Peach, Air Chief Marshal Sir Stuart William, GBE, KCB, ADC

Pearce, Sir (Daniel Norton) Idris, Kt., CBE, TD

Pears, Sir Trevor Stephen, Kt., CMG

Pearse, Sir Brian Gerald, Kt.

Pearson, Sir David Lee, Kt., CBE

Pearson, Sir Francis Nicholas Fraser, Bt. (1964)

Pearson, Sir Keith, Kt.

Pearson, Gen. Sir Thomas Cecil Hook, KCB, CBE, DSO

Peart, Prof. Sir William Stanley, Kt., MD, FRS

Pease, Sir Joseph Gurney, Bt. (1882)

Pease, Sir Richard Thorn, Bt. (1920)

Peat, Sir Gerrard Charles, KCVO

Peat, Sir Michael Charles Gerrard, GCVO

Peckham, Prof. Sir Michael John, Kt.,

Peek, Sir Richard Grenville, Bt. (1874)

Pelgen, Sir Harry Friedrich, Kt., MBE

Pelham, Dr Sir Hugh Reginald Brentnall, Kt., FRS

Pelly, Sir Richard John, Bt. (1840)

Pendry, Prof. Sir John Brian, Kt., FRS

Penning, Rt. Hon. Sir Michael Allan, Kt.

Penny, Dr Nicholas Beaver, Kt., FBA

Penrose, Prof. Sir Roger, Kt., OM, FRS

Pepper, Dr Sir David Edwin, KCMG

Pepper, Prof. Sir Michael, Kt.

Pepys, Prof. Sir Mark Brian, Kt.

Perowne, Vice-Adm. Sir James Francis, KBE

Perring, Sir John Raymond, Bt. (1963), TD

Perris, Sir David (Arthur), Kt., MBE

Perry, Sir David Howard, KCB

Perry, Sir Michael Sydney, GBE

Pervez, Sir Mohammed Anwar, Kt., OBE

Petchey, Sir Jack, Kt., CBE

Peters, Prof. Sir (David) Keith, GBE, FRCP

Pethica, Prof. Sir John Bernard, Kt., FRS

Petit, Sir Dinshaw Manockjee, Bt. (1890)

Peto, Sir Francis Michael Morton, Bt. (1855)

Peto, Sir Henry Christopher Morton Bampfylde, Bt. (1927)

Peto, Prof. Sir Richard, Kt., FRS

Petrie, Sir Peter Charles, Bt. (1918), CMG

†Philipson-Stow, Sir (Robert) Matthew, Bt. (1907)

Phillips, Sir (Gerald) Hayden, GCB

Phillips, Sir John David, Kt., QPM

Phillips, Sir Jonathan, KCB

Phillips, Sir Peter John, Kt., OBE

Phillips, Sir Robin Francis, Bt. (1912)

Phillips, Hon. Sir Stephen Edmund, Kt.

Phillips, Sir Tom Richard Vaughan, KCMG

Pickard, Sir (John) Michael, Kt.

Picken, Hon. Sir Simon Derek, Kt.

Pickthorn, Sir James Francis Mann, Bt. (1959)

†Piers, Sir James Desmond, Bt. (I. 1661)

Piggott-Brown, Sir William Brian, Bt. (1903)

Pigot, Sir George Hugh, Bt. (1764)

Pigott, Lt.-Gen. Sir Anthony David, KCB, CBE

†Pigott, Sir David John Berkeley, Bt. (1808)

Pike, Lt.-Gen. Sir Hew William Royston, KCB, DSO, MBE

Pike, Sir Michael Edmund, KCVO, CMG

Pilditch, Sir John Richard, Bt. (1929)

Pile, Sir Anthony John Devereux, Bt. (1900), MBE

Pill, Rt. Hon. Sir Malcolm Thomas, Kt.

Pilling, Sir Joseph Grant, KCB

Pinsent, Sir Matthew Clive, Kt., CBE

Pinsent, Sir Thomas Benjamin Roy, Bt. (1938)

Pirmohamed, Prof. Sir Hussein Munir, Kt.

Pissarides, Prof. Sir Christopher Antoniou, Kt., FBA

Pitcher, Sir Desmond Henry, Kt.

Pitchers, Hon. Sir Christopher (John), Kt.

Pitoi, Sir Sere, Kt., CBE

Pitt, Sir Michael Edward, Kt.

Plastow, Sir David Arnold Stuart, Kt.

Platt, Sir Martin Philip, Bt. (1959)

Pledger, Air Chief Marshal Sir Malcolm David, KCB, OBE, AFC

Plender, Hon. Sir Richard Owen, Kt.

Plumbly, Sir Derek John, KCMG

Pocock, Dr Sir Andrew John, KCMG

Poffley, Lt.-Gen. Sir Mark William, KCB, OBE

Poh, Sir Sang Chung, Kt., MBE

Pohai, Sir Timothy, Kt., MBE

Pole, Sir (John) Richard (Walter Reginald) Carew, Bt. (1628), OBE

Pole, Sir John Chandos, Bt. (1791)

Poliakoff, Prof. Sir Martyn, Kt., CBE

Polkinghorne, Revd Canon John Charlton, KBE

Pollard, Sir Charles, Kt.

†Pollen, Sir Richard John Hungerford, Bt. (1795)

Pollock, Sir David Frederick, Bt. (1866)

Pomeroy, Sir Brian Walter, Kt., CBE

Ponder, Prof. Sir Bruce Anthony John, Kt.

Ponsonby, Sir Charles Ashley, Bt. (1956)

Poon, Sir Dickson, Kt., CBE

†Poore, Sir Roger Ricardo, Bt. (1795)

Popplewell, Hon. Sir Andrew John, Kt.

Popplewell, Hon. Sir Oliver Bury, Kt.

Porritt, Hon. Sir Jonathon Espie, Bt. (1963), CBE

Portal, Sir Jonathan Francis, Bt. (1901)

Porter, Prof. Sir Keith Macdonald, Kt.

Potter, Rt. Hon. Sir Mark Howard, Kt.

Pound, Sir John David, Bt. (1905)

Povey, Sir Keith, Kt., QPM

Powell, Sir Ian Clifford, Kt.

Powell, Sir John Christopher, Kt.

Powell, Sir Nicholas Folliott Douglas, Bt. (1897)

Power, Sir Alastair John Cecil, Bt. (1924)

Pownall, Sir Michael Graham, KCB

Poya, Sir Nathaniel, Kt.

Prance, Prof. Sir Ghillean Tolmie, Kt., FRS

Prendergast, Sir (Walter) Kieran, KCVO, CMG

Prescott, Sir Mark, Bt. (1938)

Preston, Prof. Sir Paul, Kt., CBE

Preston, Sir Philip Charles Henry Hulton, Bt. (1815)

Prevost, Sir Christopher Gerald, Bt. (1805)

Price, Sir Francis Caradoc Rose, Bt. (1815)

Price, Sir Frank Leslie, Kt.

†Prichard-Jones, Sir David John Walter, Bt. (1910)

†Primrose, Sir John Ure, Bt. (1903)

Pringle, Hon. Sir John Kenneth, Kt.

Pringle, Sir Norman Murray Archibald Macgregor, Bt. (S. 1683)

Proby, Sir William Henry, Bt. (1952), CBE

Proctor-Beauchamp, Sir Christopher Radstock, Bt. (1745)

Prosser, Sir David John, Kt.

Prosser, Sir Ian Maurice Gray, Kt.

Pryke, Sir Christopher Dudley, Bt. (1926)

Puapua, Rt. Hon. Sir Tomasi, GCMG, KBE

Pulford, Air Chief Marshal Sir Andrew Douglas, GCB, CBE, ADC

Purves, Sir William, Kt., CBE, DSO

Purvis, Vice-Adm. Sir Neville, KCB

Quan, Sir Henry (Francis), KBE

Quilter, Sir Guy Raymond Cuthbert, Bt. (1897)

Radcliffe, Sir Sebastian Everard, Bt. (1813)
Radda, Prof. Sir George Karoly, Kt., CBE, FRS
Rae, Sir William, Kt., QPM
Raeburn, Sir Michael Edward Norman, Bt. (1923)
Rake, Sir Michael Derek Vaughan, Kt.
Ralli, Sir David Charles, Bt. (1912)
Ramakrishnan, Dr Sir Venkatraman, Kt.
Ramdanee, Sir Mookteswar Baboolall Kailash, Kt.
Ramphal, Sir Shridath Surendranath, GCMG
Ramphul, Sir Baalkhristna, Kt.
Ramphul, Sir Indurduth, Kt.
Ramsay, Sir Alexander William Burnett, Bt. (1806)
Ramsay, Sir Allan John (Hepple), KBE, CMG
Ramsay-Fairfax-Lucy, Sir Edmund John William Hugh, Bt. (1836)
Ramsden, Sir David Edward John, Kt., CBE
Ramsden, Sir John Charles Josslyn, Bt. (1689)
Ramsey, Dr Sir Frank Cuthbert, KCMG
Ramsey, Hon. Sir Vivian Arthur, Kt.
Rankin, Sir Ian Niall, Bt. (1898)
Rasch, Sir Simon Anthony Carne, Bt. (1903)
Rashleigh, Sir Richard Harry, Bt. (1831)
Ratcliffe, Sir James Arthur, Kt.
Ratcliffe, Prof. Sir Peter John, Kt., FRS
Ratford, Sir David John Edward, KCMG, CVO
Rattee, Hon. Sir Donald Keith, Kt.
Rattle, Sir Simon Dennis, Kt., OM, CBE
Rawlins, Hon. Sir Hugh Anthony, Kt.
Rawlins, Prof. Sir Michael David, GBE, FRCP, FRCPED
Rawlinson, Sir Anthony Henry John, Bt. (1891)
Rea, Prof. Sir Desmond, Kt., OBE
Read, Prof. Sir David John, Kt.
Reardon-Smith, Sir (William) Antony (John), Bt. (1920)
Reddaway, Sir David Norman, KCMG, MBE
Redgrave, Sir Steven Geoffrey, Kt., CBE
Redmayne, Sir Giles Martin, Bt. (1964)
Redmond, Sir Anthony Gerard, Kt.
Redwood, Sir Peter Boverton, Bt. (1911)
Reed, Prof. Sir Alec Edward, Kt., CBE
Reedie, Sir Craig Collins, GBE
Rees, Sir David Allan, Kt., PHD, DSC, FRS
Rees, Sir Richard Ellis Meuric, Kt., CBE

Reffell, Adm. Sir Derek Roy, KCB
Reich, Sir Erich Arieh, Kt.
Reid, Sir Alexander James, Bt. (1897)
Reid, Sir David Edward, Kt.
Reid, Rt. Hon. Sir George, Kt.
Reid, Sir (Philip) Alan, GCVO
Reid, Sir Robert Paul, Kt.
Reid, Sir William Kennedy, KCB
Reiher, Sir Frederick Bernard Carl, KCMG, KBE
Renals, Sir Stanley, Bt. (1895)
Renouf, Sir Clement William Bailey, Kt.
Renshaw, Sir John David Bine, Bt. (1903)
Renwick, Sir Richard Eustace, Bt. (1921)
Reynolds, Sir James Francis, Bt. (1923)
Reynolds, Sir Peter William John, Kt., CBE
Rhodes, Sir John Christopher Douglas, Bt. (1919)
Ribat, Most Revd John Ribat, KBE
Rice, Prof. Sir Charles Duncan, Kt.
Rice, Maj.-Gen. Sir Desmond Hind Garrett, KCVO, CBE
Rice, Sir Timothy Miles Bindon, Kt.
Richard, Sir Cliff, Kt., OBE
Richards, Sir Brian Mansel, Kt., CBE, PHD
Richards, Rt. Hon. Sir David Anthony Stewart, Kt.
Richards, Sir David Gerald, Kt.
Richards, Sir Francis Neville, KCMG, CVO
Richards, Prof. Sir Michael Adrian, Kt., CBE
Richards, Sir Rex Edward, Kt., DSC, FRS
Richards, Rt. Hon. Sir Stephen Price, Kt.
Richardson, Sir Anthony Lewis, Bt. (1924)
Richardson, Sir John Patrick, KBE
Richardson, Sir Thomas Legh, KCMG
Richardson-Bunbury, Sir Thomas William, Bt. (I. 1787)
Richmond, Sir David Frank, KBE, CMG
Richmond, Prof. Sir Mark Henry, Kt., FRS
Ricketts, Sir Stephen Tristram, Bt. (1828)
Ricks, Prof. Sir Christopher Bruce, Kt.
Riddell, Sir Walter John Buchanan, Bt. (S. 1628)
Ridgway, Lt.-Gen. Sir Andrew Peter, KBE, CB
Ridley, Sir Adam (Nicholas), Kt.
Ridley, Sir Michael Kershaw, KCVO
Rifkind, Rt. Hon. Sir Malcolm Leslie, KCMG
Rigby, Sir Anthony John, Bt. (1929)
Rigby, Sir Peter, Kt.
Rimer, Rt. Hon. Sir Colin Percy Farquharson, Kt.
Ripley, Sir William Hugh, Bt. (1880)
Ritako, Sir Thomas Baha, Kt., MBE
Ritblat, Sir John Henry, Kt.

Ritchie, Prof. Sir Lewis Duthie, Kt., OBE
Rivett-Carnac, Sir Jonathan James, Bt. (1836)
Rix, Rt. Hon. Sir Bernard Anthony, Kt.
Robb, Sir John Weddell, Kt.
Roberts, Sir Derek Harry, Kt., CBE, FRS, FRENG
Roberts, Prof. Sir Edward Adam, KCMG
Roberts, Sir Gilbert Howland Rookehurst, Bt. (1809)
Roberts, Sir Hugh Ashley, GCVO
Roberts, Sir Ivor Anthony, KCMG
†Roberts, Sir James Elton Denby Buchanan, Bt. (1909)
Roberts, Dr Sir Richard John, Kt.
Roberts, Sir Samuel, Bt. (1919)
Roberts, Maj.-Gen. Sir Sebastian John Lechmere, KCVO, OBE
Robertson, Rt. Hon. Sir Hugh Michael, KCMG
Robertson, Sir Simon Manwaring, Kt.
Robey, Sir Simon Christopher Townsend, Kt.
Robins, Sir Ralph Harry, Kt., FRENG
Robinson, Sir Anthony, Kt.
Robinson, Sir Bruce, KCB
†Robinson, Sir Christopher Philipse, Bt. (1854)
Robinson, Sir Gerrard Jude, Kt.
Robinson, Sir Ian, Kt.
Robinson, Sir John James Michael Laud, Bt. (1660)
Robinson, Dr Sir Kenneth, Kt.
Robinson, Sir Peter Frank, Bt. (1908)
Robson, Sir Stephen Arthur, Kt., CB
Roch, Rt. Hon. Sir John Ormond, Kt.
Roche, Sir David O'Grady, Bt. (1838)
Roche, Sir Henry John, Kt.
Rodgers, Sir (Andrew) Piers (Wingate Aikin-Sneath), Bt. (1964)
Rogers, Air Chief Marshal Sir John Robson, KCB, CBE
Rogers, Sir Mark Ivan, KCMG
Rogers, Sir Peter, Kt.
Rollo, Lt.-Gen. Sir William Raoul, KCB, CBE
†Ropner, Sir Henry John William, Bt. (1952)
Ropner, Sir Robert Clinton, Bt. (1904)
Rose, Sir Arthur James, Kt., CBE
Rose, Rt. Hon. Sir Christopher Dudley Roger, Kt.
Rose, Sir Clive Martin, GCMG
†Rose, Sir David Lancaster, Bt. (1874)
Rose, Gen. Sir (Hugh) Michael, KCB, CBE, DSO, QGM
Rose, Sir John Edward Victor, Kt.
Rose, Sir Julian Day, Bt. (1872 and 1909)
Rosenthal, Sir Norman Leon, Kt.
Ross, Maj. Sir Andrew Charles Paterson, Bt. (1960)
Ross, Lt.-Gen. Sir Robert Jeremy, KCB, OBE
Ross, Lt.-Col. Sir Walter Hugh Malcolm, GCVO, OBE

Ross, Sir Walter Robert Alexander, KCVO

Rossi, Sir Hugh Alexis Louis, Kt.

Roth, Hon. Sir Peter Marcel, Kt.

Rothschild, Sir Evelyn Robert Adrian de, Kt.

Rowe, Rear-Adm. Sir Patrick Barton, KCVO, CBE

Rowe-Ham, Sir David Kenneth, GBE

Rowland, Sir Geoffrey Robert, Kt.

Rowland, Sir (John) David, Kt.

Rowley, Sir Mark Peter, Kt., QPM

Rowley, Sir Richard Charles, Bt. (1786 and 1836)

Rowling, Sir John Reginald, Kt.

Royce, Hon. Sir Roger John, Kt.

Royden, Sir John Michael Joseph, Bt. (1905)

Rubin, Prof. Sir Peter Charles, Kt.

Rudd, Sir (Anthony) Nigel (Russell), Kt.

Ruddock, Sir Paul, Kt.

Rudge, Sir Alan Walter, Kt., CBE, FRS

†Rugge-Price, Sir James Keith Peter, Bt. (1804)

Ruggles-Brise, Sir Timothy Edward, Bt. (1935)

Rumbold, Sir Henry John Sebastian, Bt. (1779)

Rushdie, Sir (Ahmed) Salman, Kt.

Russell, Sir Charles Dominic, Bt. (1916)

Russell, Sir George, Kt., CBE

Russell, Sir Muir, KCB

Russell, Sir Robert, Kt.

†Russell, Sir Stephen (Steve) Charles, Bt. (1812)

Rutnam, Sir Philip McDougall, KCB

Rutter, Prof. Sir Michael Llewellyn, Kt., CBE, MD, FRS

Ryan, Sir Derek Gerald, Bt. (1919)

Rycroft, Sir Richard John, Bt. (1784)

Ryder, Rt. Hon. Sir Ernest Nigel, Kt., TD

Sacranie, Sir Iqbal Abdul Karim Mussa, Kt., OBE

Sainsbury, Rt. Hon. Sir Timothy Alan Davan, Kt.

St Clair-Ford, Sir William Sam, Bt. (1793)

St George, Sir John Avenel Bligh, Bt. (I. 1766)

St John-Mildmay, Sir Walter John Hugh, Bt. (1772)

St Paul, Sir Lyle Kevin, KCMG

Sainty, Sir John Christopher, KCB

Sakora, Hon. Sir Bernard Berekia, KBE

Sales, Rt. Hon. Sir Philip James, Kt.

Salika, Sir Gibuna Gibbs, KBE

Salisbury, Sir Robert William, Kt.

Salt, Sir Patrick MacDonnell, Bt. (1869)

Salt, Sir (Thomas) Michael John, Bt. (1899)

Salusbury-Trelawny, Sir John William Richard, Bt. (1628)

Salz, Sir Anthony Michael Vaughan, Kt.

Samani, Prof. Sir Nilesh Jayantilal, Kt.

Sampson, Sir Colin, Kt., CBE, QPM

Samuel, Sir John Michael Glen, Bt. (1898)

Samuelson, Sir James Francis, Bt. (1884)

Samuelson, Sir Sydney Wylie, Kt., CBE

Samworth, Sir David Chetwode, Kt., CBE

Sanders, Sir Robert Tait, KBE, CMG

Sanders, Sir Ronald Michael, KCMG

Sanderson, Sir Frank Linton, Bt. (1920), OBE

Sands, Sir Roger Blakemore, KCB

Sants, Sir Hector William Hepburn, Kt.

Sargent, Sir William Desmond, Kt., CBE

Satchwell, Sir Kevin Joseph, Kt.

Saumarez Smith, Dr Sir Charles, Kt., CBE, FBA

Saunders, Sir Bruce Joshua, KBE

Saunders, Hon. Sir John Henry Boulton, Kt.

Savill, Prof. Sir John Stewart, Kt.

Savory, Sir Michael Berry, Kt.

Sawers, Sir Robert John, GCMG

Saxby, Prof. Sir Robin Keith, Kt.

Scarlett, Sir John McLeod, KCMG, OBE

Schama, Prof. Sir Simon, Kt., CBE, FBA

Schiemann, Rt. Hon. Sir Konrad Hermann Theodor, Kt.

Schiff, Sir András, Kt.

Scholar, Sir Michael Charles, KCB

Scholar, Sir Thomas Whinfield, KCB

Scholey, Sir David Gerald, Kt., CBE

Scipio, Sir Hudson Rupert, Kt.

Scott, Sir Anthony Percy, Bt. (1913)

Scott, Sir Christopher James Anderson, Bt. (1909)

Scott, Sir David Richard Alexander, Kt., CBE

Scott, Prof. Sir George Peter, Kt.

Scott, Sir James Jervoise, Bt. (1962)

Scott, Sir John Hamilton, KCVO

Scott, Sir Ridley, Kt.

Scott, Sir Robert David Hillyer, Kt.

Scott, Sir Walter John, Bt. (1907)

Scott-Lee, Sir Paul Joseph, Kt., QPM

Scruton, Prof. Sir Roger Vernon, Kt.

Seale, Sir Clarence David, Kt.

Seale, Sir John Robert Charters, Bt. (1838)

Sealy, Sir Austin Llewellyn, Kt.

Seaton, HE Sir Samuel Weymouth Tapley, GCMG, CVO

†Sebright, Sir Rufus Hugo Giles, Bt. (1626)

Sedley, Rt. Hon. Sir Stephen John, Kt.

Sedwill, Sir Mark, KCMG

Seely, Sir Nigel Edward, Bt. (1896)

Seeto, Sir Ling James, Kt., MBE

Seeyave, Sir Rene Sow Choung, Kt., CBE

Seldon, Dr Sir Anthony Francis, Kt.

Semple, Sir John Laughlin, KCB

Sergeant, Sir Patrick, Kt.

Serota, Hon. Sir Nicholas Andrew, Kt. CH

Setchell, Sir Marcus Edward, KCVO

†Seton, Sir Charles Wallace, Bt. (S. 1683)

Seton, Sir Iain Bruce, Bt. (S. 1663)

Seymour, Sir Julian Roger, Kt., CBE

Shadbolt, Prof. Sir Nigel Richard, Kt.

Shakerley, Sir Nicholas Simon Adam, Bt. (1838)

Shakespeare, Sir Thomas William, Bt. (1942)

Sharp, Sir Adrian, Bt. (1922)

Sharp, Sir Fabian Alexander Sebastian, Bt. (1920)

Sharp, Sir Leslie, Kt., QPM

Sharples, Sir James, Kt., QPM

Shaw, Sir Charles De Vere, Bt. (1821)

Shaw, Prof. Sir John Calman, Kt., CBE

Shaw, Sir Neil McGowan, Kt.

Shaw-Stewart, Sir Ludovic Houston, Bt. (S. 1667)

Shebbeare, Sir Thomas Andrew, KCVO

Sheehy, Sir Patrick, Kt.

Sheffield, Sir Reginald Adrian Berkeley, Bt. (1755)

Sheil, Rt. Hon. Sir John, Kt.

Sheinwald, Sir Nigel Elton, GCMG

Shelley, Sir John Richard, Bt. (1611)

Shepherd, Sir Colin Ryley, Kt.

Shepherd, Sir John Alan, KCVO, CMG

Shepherd, Sir Richard Charles Scrimgeour, Kt.

Sher, Sir Antony, KBE

Sherlock, Sir Nigel, KCVO, OBE

Sherston-Baker, Sir Robert George Humphrey, Bt. (1796)

Shiffner, Sir Henry David, Bt. (1818)

Shinwell, Sir (Maurice) Adrian, Kt.

Shirreff, Gen. Sir Alexander Richard David, KCB, CBE

Shortridge, Sir Jon Deacon, KCB

Shuckburgh, Sir James Rupert Charles, Bt. (1660)

Siedentop, Dr Sir Larry Alan, Kt., CBE

Sieff, Hon. Sir David, Kt.

Silber, Rt. Hon. Sir Stephen Robert, Kt.

Silk, Sir Evan Paul, KCB

Silverman, Prof. Sir Bernard Walter, Kt.

†Simeon, Sir Stephen George Barrington, Bt. (1815)

Simmonds, Rt. Hon. Dr Sir Kennedy Alphonse, KCMG

Simmons, Air Marshal Sir Michael George, KCB, AFC

Simms, Sir Neville Ian, Kt., FRENG

Simon, Rt. Hon. Sir Peregrine Charles Hugh, Kt.

Simonet, Sir Louis Marcel Pierre, Kt., CBE

Simpson, Sir Peter Austin, Kt., OBE

Simpson, Dr Sir Peter Jeffery, Kt.

Sims, Sir Roger Edward, Kt.

Sinclair, Sir Clive Marles, Kt.

Sinclair, Sir William Robert Francis, Bt. (S. 1704)

Sinclair, Sir Robert John, Kt.

Sinclair-Lockhart, Sir Simon John Edward Francis, Bt. (S. 1636)

Singer, Hon. Sir Jan Peter, Kt.

Singh, Sir Pritpal, Kt.

Singh, Rt. Hon. Sir Rabinder, Kt.

Singleton, Sir Roger, Kt., CBE

Sitwell, Sir George Reresby Sacheverell, Bt. (1808)

Skeggs, Sir Clifford George, Kt.

Skehel, Sir John James, Kt., FRS

Skingsley, Air Chief Marshal Sir Anthony Gerald, GBE, KCB

Skinner, Sir (Thomas) Keith (Hewitt), Bt. (1912)

Skipwith, Sir Alexander Sebastian Grey d'Estoteville, Bt. (1622)

Slack, Sir William Willatt, KCVO, FRCS

Slade, Rt. Hon. Sir Christopher John, Kt.

Slade, Sir Julian Benjamin Alfred, Bt. (1831)

Slater, Adm. Sir John (Jock) Cunningham Kirkwood, GCB, LVO

Sleight, Sir Richard, Bt. (1920)

Sloman, Sir David Morgan, Kt.

Smiley, Lt.-Col. Sir John Philip, Bt. (1903)

Smith, Prof. Sir Adrian Frederick Melhuish, Kt., FRS

Smith, Hon. Sir Andrew Charles, Kt.

Smith, Sir Andrew Thomas, Bt. (1897)

Smith, Sir David Iser, KCVO

Smith, Prof. Sir Eric Brian, Kt., PHD

Smith, Prof. Sir James Cuthbert, Kt., FRS

Smith, Sir John Alfred, Kt., QPM

Smith, Sir Joseph William Grenville, Kt.

Smith, Sir Kevin, Kt., CBE

Smith, Hon. Sir Marcus Alexander, Kt.

Smith, Sir Martin Gregory, Kt.

Smith, Sir Michael John Llewellyn, KCVO, CMG

Smith, Sir (Norman) Brian, Kt., CBE, PHD

Smith, Sir Paul Brierley, Kt., CBE

Smith, Hon. Sir Peter Winston, Kt.

Smith, Sir Robert Courtney, Kt., CBE

Smith, Sir Robert Hill, Bt. (1945)

Smith, Gen. Sir Rupert Anthony, KCB, DSO, OBE, QGM

Smith, Sir Steven Murray, Kt.

Smith-Dodsworth, Sir David John, Bt. (1784)

Smith-Gordon, Sir (Lionel) Eldred (Peter), Bt. (1838)

Smith-Marriott, Sir Peter Francis, Bt. (1774)

Smurfit, Dr Sir Michael William Joseph, KBE

Smyth, Sir Timothy John, Bt. (1956)

Smyth-Osbourne, Maj.-Gen. Sir Edward Alexander, KCVO, CBE

Snowden, Prof. Sir Christopher Maxwell, Kt.

Snowden, Hon. Sir Richard Andrew, Kt.

Snyder, Sir Michael John, Kt.

Soames, Rt. Hon. Sir (Arthur) Nicholas Winston, Kt.

Soar, Adm. Sir Trevor Alan, KCB, OBE

Sobers, Sir Garfield St Auburn, Kt.

Solomon, Sir Harry, Kt.

Somare, Rt. Hon. Sir Michael Thomas, GCMG, CH

Songo, Sir Bernard Paul, Kt., CMG, OBE

Soole, Hon. Sir Michael Alexander, Kt.

Sorabji, Prof. Sir Richard Rustom Kharsedji, Kt., CBE

Sorrell, Sir John William, Kt., CBE

Sorrell, Sir Martin Stuart, Kt.

Sosa, Sir Manuel, Kt.

Soulsby, Sir Peter Alfred, Kt.

Souter, Sir Brian, Kt.

Southby, Sir John Richard Bilbe, Bt. (1937)

Southern, Prof. Sir Edwin Mellor, Kt.

Southgate, Sir Colin Grieve, Kt.

Southgate, Sir William David, Kt.

Southward, Dr Sir Nigel Ralph, KCVO

Sowrey, Air Marshal Sir Frederick Beresford, KCB, CBE, AFC

Sparks, Prof. Sir Robert Stephen John, Kt., CBE

Sparrow, Sir John, Kt.

Spearman, Sir Alexander Young Richard Mainwaring, Bt. (1840)

Spencer, Sir Derek Harold, Kt., QC

Spencer, Hon. Sir Martin Benedict, Kt.

Spencer, Vice-Adm. Sir Peter, KCB

Spencer, Hon. Sir Robin Godfrey, Kt.

Spencer-Nairn, Sir Robert Arnold, Bt. (1933)

Spicer, Sir Nicholas Adrian Albert, Bt. (1906)

Spiegelhalter, Prof. Sir David John, Kt., OBE, FRS

Spiers, Sir Donald Maurice, Kt., CB, TD

Spooner, Sir James Douglas, Kt.

Spring, Sir Dryden Thomas, Kt.

Spurling, Sir John Damian, KCVO, OBE

Stacey, Air Marshal Sir Graham Edward, KBE, CB

Stadlen, Hon. Sir Nicholas Felix, Kt.

Stagg, Sir Charles Richard Vernon, KCMG

Staite, Sir Richard John, Kt., OBE

Stamer, Sir Peter Tomlinson, Bt. (1809)

Stanhope, Adm. Sir Mark, GCB, OBE, ADC

Stanier, Sir Beville Douglas, Bt. (1917)

Stanley, Rt. Hon. Sir John Paul, Kt.

Starkey, Sir John Philip, Bt. (1935)

Starkey, Sir Richard, Kt., MBE

Starmer, Rt. Hon. Sir Keir, KCB, QC

Stear, Air Chief Marshal Sir Michael James Douglas, KCB, CBE

Steel, Vice-Adm. Sir David George, KBE

Steel, Hon. Sir David William, Kt.

Steer, Sir Alan William, Kt.

Stephens, Sir (Edwin) Barrie, Kt.

Stephens, Sir Jonathan Andrew de Sievrac, KCB

Stephens, Rt. Hon. Sir (William) Benjamin Synge, Kt.

†Stephenson, Sir Henry Upton, Bt. (1936)

Stephenson, Sir Paul Robert, Kt., QPM

Stephenson, Prof. Sir Terence John, Kt.

Sterling, Sir Michael John Howard, Kt.

Stevens, Sir Michael John, KCVO

Stevenson, Sir Hugh Alexander, Kt.

Stewart, Sir Alan d'Arcy, Bt. (I. 1623)

Stewart, Sir Alastair Robin, Bt. (1960)

Stewart, Sir Brian John, Kt., CBE

Stewart, Sir David James Henderson, Bt. (1957)

Stewart, Sir David John Christopher, Bt. (1803)

Stewart, Sir James Moray, KCB

Stewart, Sir (John) Simon (Watson), Bt. (1920)

Stewart, Sir John Young, Kt., OBE

Stewart, Sir Patrick, Kt., OBE

Stewart, Lt.-Col. Sir Robert Christie, KCVO, CBE, TD

Stewart, Sir Roderick David, Kt., CBE

Stewart, Hon. Sir Stephen Paul, Kt.

Stewart, Prof. Sir William Duncan Paterson, Kt., FRS, FRSE

Stewart-Clark, Sir John, Bt. (1918)

Stewart-Richardson, Sir Simon Alaisdair Ian Neile, Bt. (S. 1630)

Stheeman, Sir Robert Alexander Talma, Kt., CB

Stilgoe, Sir Richard Henry Simpson, Kt., OBE

Stirling, Sir Angus Duncan Aeneas, Kt.

Stirling of Garden, Col. Sir James, KCVO, CBE, TD

Stirling-Hamilton, Sir Malcolm William Bruce, Bt. (S. 1673)

Stockdale, Sir Thomas Minshull, Bt. (1960)

Stoddart, Prof. Sir James Fraser, Kt.

Stoller, Sir Norman Kelvin, Kt., CBE

Stone, Sir Christopher, Kt.

Stonhouse, Revd Michael Philip, Bt. (1628 and 1670)

Stonor, Air Marshal Sir Thomas Henry, KCB

Stoppard, Sir Thomas, Kt., OM, CBE

Storey, Hon. Sir Richard, Bt., CBE (1960)

Stothard, Sir Peter Michael, Kt.

Stott, Sir Adrian George Ellingham, Bt. (1920)

Stoute, Sir Michael Ronald, Kt.

Stracey, Sir John Simon, Bt. (1818)

Strachan, Sir Curtis Victor, Kt., CVO

Strachan, Sir Hew Francis Anthony, Kt.

†Strachey, Sir Henry Leofric Benvenuto, Bt. (1801)

Straker, Sir Louis Hilton, KCMG

Strang, Prof. Sir John Stanley, Kt.

Strang Steel, Sir (Fiennes) Michael, Bt. (1938), CBE

Stratton, Prof. Sir Michael Rudolf, Kt., FRS

Strickland-Constable, Sir Frederic, Bt. (1641)

Stringer, Sir Donald Edgar, Kt., CBE

Stringer, Sir Howard, Kt.

Strong, Sir Roy Colin, Kt., CH, PHD, FSA

†Stronge, Sir James Anselan Maxwell, Bt. (1803)

†Stuart, Sir Geoffrey Phillip, Bt. (1660)

Stuart, Sir James Keith, Kt.

†Stuart-Forbes, Sir William Daniel, Bt. (S. 1626)

Stuart-Menteth, Sir Charles Greaves, Bt. (1838)

Stuart-Paul, Air Marshal Sir Ronald Ian, KBE

Stuart-Smith, Hon. Sir Jeremy Hugh, Kt

Stuart-Smith, Rt. Hon. Sir Murray, KCMG

Stubbs, Sir William Hamilton, Kt., PHD

Stucley, Lt. Sir Hugh George Coplestone Bampfylde, Bt. (1859)

Studd, Sir Edward Fairfax, Bt. (1929)

Studholme, Sir Henry William, Bt. (1956)

Sturridge, Sir Nicholas Anthony, KCVO

Stuttard, Sir John Boothman, Kt.

†Style, Sir William Frederick, Bt. (1627)

Sullivan, Rt. Hon. Sir Jeremy Mirth, Kt.

Sullivan, Sir Richard Arthur, Bt. (1804)

Sunderland, Sir John Michael, Kt.

Supperstone, Hon. Sir Michael Alan, Kt.

Sutherland, Sir John Brewer, Bt. (1921)

Sutherland, Sir William George MacKenzie, Kt.

Sutton, Sir Richard Lexington, Bt. (1772)

Swan, Sir Conrad Marshall John Fisher, KCVO, PHD

Swan, Sir John William David, KBE

Swann, Sir Michael Christopher, Bt. (1906), TD

Swayne, Rt. Hon. Sir Desmond, Kt., TD

Sweeney, Sir George, Kt.

Sweeney, Hon. Sir Nigel Hamilton, Kt.

Sweeting, Prof. Sir Martin Nicholas, Kt., OBE, FRS

Swinnerton-Dyer, Prof. Sir (Henry) Peter (Francis), Bt. (1678), KBE, FRS

Swinton, Maj.-Gen. Sir John, KCVO, OBE

Swire, Rt. Hon. Sir Hugo George William, KCMG

Sykes, Sir David Michael, Bt. (1921)

Sykes, Sir Francis John Badcock, Bt. (1781)

Sykes, Sir Hugh Ridley, Kt.

Sykes, Prof. Sir (Malcolm) Keith, Kt.

Sykes, Sir Richard, Kt.

Sykes, Sir Tatton Christopher Mark, Bt. (1783)

Symons, Vice-Adm. Sir Patrick Jeremy, KBE

Syms, Rt. Hon. Sir Robert Andrew Raymond, Kt.

†Synge, Sir Allen James Edward, Bt. (1801)

Tanner, Sir David Whitlock, Kt., CBE

Tantum, Sir Geoffrey Alan, Kt., CMG, OBE

Tapps-Gervis-Meyrick, Sir George Christopher Cadafael, Bt. (1791)

†Tate, Sir Edward Nicolas, Bt. (1898)

Taureka, Dr Sir Reubeh, KBE

Tauvasa, Sir Joseph James, KBE

Taylor, Sir Hugh Henderson, KCB

Taylor, Dr Sir John Michael, Kt., OBE

Taylor, Prof. Sir Martin John, Kt., FRS

Taylor, Sir Nicholas Richard Stuart, Bt. (1917)

Taylor, Prof. Sir William, Kt., CBE

Taylor, Sir William George, Kt.

Teagle, Vice-Adm. Sir Somerford Francis, KBE

Teare, Hon. Sir Nigel John Martin, Kt.

Teasdale, Prof. Sir Graham Michael, Kt.

Tebbit, Sir Kevin Reginald, KCB, CMG

Temple, Prof. Sir John Graham, Kt.

Temple, Sir Richard Carnac Chartier, Bt. (1876)

Temu, Hon. Dr Sir Puka, KBE, CMG

Tennyson-D'Eyncourt, Sir Mark Gervais, Bt. (1930)

Terry, Air Marshal Sir Colin George, KBE, CB

Thatcher, Hon. Sir Mark, Bt. (1990)

Thomas, Sir David John Godfrey, Bt. (1694)

Thomas, Sir Derek Morison David, KCMG

Thomas, Prof. Sir Eric Jackson, Kt.

Thomas, Sir Gilbert Stanley, Kt., OBE

Thomas, Sir Jeremy Cashel, KCMG

Thomas, Prof. Sir John Meurig, Kt., FRS

Thomas, Sir Keith Vivian, Kt.

Thomas, Dr Sir Leton Felix, KCMG, CBE

Thomas, Sir Philip Lloyd, KCVO, CMG

Thomas, Sir Quentin Jeremy, Kt., CB

Thomas, Sir William Michael, Bt. (1919)

Thompson, Sir Christopher Peile, Bt. (1890)

Thompson, Sir Clive Malcolm, Kt.

Thompson, Sir David Albert, KCMG

Thompson, Prof. Sir Michael Warwick, Kt., DSc

Thompson, Sir Nicholas Annesley, Bt. (1963)

Thompson, Sir Nigel Cooper, KCMG, CBE

Thompson, Sir Paul Anthony, Bt. (1963)

Thompson, Sir Peter Anthony, Kt.

Thompson, Dr Sir Richard Paul Hepworth, KCVO

Thompson, Sir Thomas d'Eyncourt John, Bt. (1806)

Thomson, Sir Adam McClure, KCMG

Thomson, Sir (Frederick Douglas) David, Bt. (1929)

Thomson, Sir Mark Wilfrid Home, Bt. (1925)

Thorne, Sir Neil Gordon, Kt., OBE, TD

Thornicroft, Prof. Sir Graham John, Kt.

Thornton, Air Marshal Sir Barry Michael, KCB

Thornton, Sir (George) Malcolm, Kt.

Thornton, Sir Peter Ribblesdale, Kt.

†Thorold, Sir (Anthony) Oliver, Bt. (1642)

Thorpe, Rt. Hon. Sir Mathew Alexander, Kt.

Thrift, Prof. Sir Nigel John, Kt.

Thurecht, Sir Ramon Richard, Kt., OBE

Thwaites, Sir Bryan, Kt., PHD

Tickell, Sir Crispin Charles Cervantes, GCMG, KCVO

Tidmarsh, Sir James Napier, KCVO, MBE

Tilt, Sir Robin Richard, Kt.

Tiltman, Sir John Hessell, KCVO

Timmins, Col. Sir John Bradford, KCVO, OBE, TD

Timpson, Sir William John Anthony, Kt., CBE

Tims, Sir Michael David, KCVO

Tindle, Sir Ray Stanley, Kt., CBE

Tirvengadum, Sir Harry Krishnan, Kt.

Tod, Vice-Adm. Sir Jonathan James Richard, KCB, CBE

Togolo, Sir Melchior Pesa, Kt.

Toka, Sir Mahuru Dadi, Kt., MBE

Tollemache, Sir Lyonel Humphry John, Bt. (1793)

Tomkys, Sir (William) Roger, KCMG

Tomlinson, Sir John Rowland, Kt., CBE

Tomlinson, Sir Michael John, Kt., CBE

Tomlinson, Rt. Hon. Sir Stephen Miles, Kt.

Tooke, Prof. Sir John Edward, Kt.

Tooley, Sir John, Kt.

ToRobert, Sir Henry Thomas, KBE

Torpy, Air Chief Marshal Sir Glenn Lester, GCB, CBE, DSO

Torrance, Very Revd Prof. Iain Richard, Kt.

Torry, Sir Peter James, GCVO, KCMG

†Touche, Sir Eric MacLellan, Bt. (1962)

Touche, Sir William George, Bt. (1920)

Tovadek, Sir Martin, Kt. CMG
Tovua, Sir Paul Joshua, KCMG
ToVue, Sir Ronald, Kt., OBE
Towneley, Sir Simon Peter Edmund Cosmo William, KCVO
Townsley, Sir John Arthur, Kt.
Traill, Sir Alan Towers, GBE
Trawen, Sir Andrew Sean, Kt., CMG, MBE
Trainor, Prof. Sir Richard Hughes, KBE
Treacy, Rt. Hon. Sir Colman Maurice, Kt.
Treacy, Hon. Sir (James Mary) Seamus, Kt.
Treisman, Sir Richard Henry, Kt., FRS
Treitel, Prof. Sir Guenter Heinz, Kt., FBA, QC
Trescowthick, Sir Donald Henry, KBE
†Trevelyan, Sir Peter John, Bt. (1662 and 1874)
Trezise, Sir Kenneth Bruce, Kt., OBE
Trippier, Sir David Austin, Kt., RD
Tritton, Sir Jeremy Ernest, Bt. (1905)
Trollope, Sir Anthony Simon, Bt. (1642)
Trotter, Sir Neville Guthrie, Kt.
Troubridge, Sir Thomas Richard, Bt. (1799)
Troup, Sir Edward Astley (John), Kt.
Trousdell, Lt.-Gen. Sir Philip Charles Cornwallis, KBE, CB
†Truscott, Sir Ralph Eric Nicholson, Bt. (1909)
Tsang, Sir Donald Yam-keun, KBE
Tuck, Sir Bruce Adolph Reginald, Bt. (1910)
Tucker, Sir Paul, Kt.
Tucker, Hon. Sir Richard Howard, Kt.
Tuckett, Sir Alan John, Kt., OBE
Tuckey, Rt. Hon. Sir Simon Lane, Kt.
Tugendhat, Hon. Sir Michael George, Kt.
Tuite, Sir Christopher Hugh, Bt. (I. 1622), PHD
Tully, Sir William Mark, KBE
Tunstall, Sir Craig, Kt.
†Tupper, Sir Charles Hibbert, Bt. (1888)
Turing, Sir John Dermot, Bt. (S. 1638)
Turnbull, Prof. Sir Douglass Matthew, Kt.
Turner, Hon. Sir Mark George, Kt.
Turner, Hon. Sir Michael John, Kt.
Turnquest, Sir Orville Alton, GCMG, QC
Tusa, Sir John, Kt.
Tweedie, Prof. Sir David Philip, Kt.
Tyrwhitt, Sir Reginald Thomas Newman, Bt. (1919)

Udny-Lister, Sir Edward Julian, Kt.
Ullmann, Sir Anthony James, Kt.
Underhill, Rt. Hon. Sir Nicholas Edward, Kt.
Underwood, Prof. Sir James Cressee Elphinstone, Kt.
Unwin, Sir (James) Brian, KCB

Ure, Sir John Burns, KCMG, LVO
Uren, Sir John Michael Leal, Kt., CBE
Urquhart, Sir Brian Edward, KCMG, MBE
Urquhart, Rt. Revd David Andrew, KCMG
Usher, Sir Andrew John, Bt. (1899)
Utting, Sir William Benjamin, Kt., CB

Vardy, Sir Peter, Kt.
Varney, Sir David Robert, Kt.
Vassar-Smith, Sir John Rathbone, Bt. (1917)
Vavasour, Sir Eric Michael Joseph Marmaduke, Bt. (1828)
Veness, Sir David, Kt., CBE, QPM
Vereker, Sir John Michael Medlicott, KCB
Verey, Sir David John, Kt., CBE
Verity, Sir Gary Keith, Kt.
Verney, Sir Edmund Ralph, Bt. (1818)
†Verney, Sir John Sebastian, Bt. (1946)
Vernon, Sir James William, Bt. (1914)
Vestey, Sir Paul Edmund, Bt (1921)
Vickers, Prof. Sir Brian William, Kt.
Vickers, Sir John Stuart, Kt.
Vickers, Lt.-Gen. Sir Richard Maurice Hilton, KCB, CVO, OBE
Vickers, Sir Roger Henry, KCVO
Viggers, Lt.-Gen. Sir Frederick Richard, KCB, CMG, MBE
Viggers, Sir Peter John, Kt.
Vincent, Sir William Percy Maxwell, Bt. (1936)
Vineall, Sir Anthony John Patrick, Kt.
Virdee, Prof. Sir Tejinder Singh, Kt.
Vos, Rt. Hon. Sir Geoffrey Charles, Kt.
Vuatha, Sir Tipo, Kt., LVO, MBE
†Vyvyan, Sir Ralph Ferrers Alexander, Bt. (1645)

Waena, Sir Nathaniel Rahumaea, GCMG
Waine, Rt. Revd John, KCVO
Wainwright, Sir Robert Mark, KCMG
Waite, Rt. Hon. Sir John Douglas, Kt.
Waka, Sir Lucas Joseph, Kt., OBE
Wake, Sir Hereward Charles, Bt. (1621)
Wakefield, Sir (Edward) Humphry (Tyrrell), Bt. (1962)
Wakefield, Sir Norman Edward, Kt.
Wakeford, Sir Geoffrey Michael Montgomery, Kt., OBE
Wakeham, Prof. Sir William Arnot, Kt.
†Wakeley, Sir Nicholas Jeremy, Bt. (1952)
Waksman, Hon. Sir David, Kt.
Wald, Prof. Sir Nicholas John, Kt.
Wales, Sir Robert Andrew, Kt.
Waley-Cohen, Sir Stephen Harry, Bt. (1961)
Walker, Gen. Sir Antony Kenneth Frederick, KCB
Walker, Sir Christopher Robert Baldwin, Bt. (1856)
Walker, Sir David Alan, Kt.

Walker, Air Vice-Marshal Sir David Allan, KCVO, OBE
Walker, Sir Harold Berners, KCMG
Walker, Sir John Ernest, Kt., DPHIL, FRS
Walker, Air Marshal Sir John Robert, KCB, CBE, AFC
Walker, Sir Malcolm Conrad, Kt., CBE
Walker, Sir Miles Rawstron, Kt., CBE
Walker, Sir Patrick Jeremy, KCB
Walker, Hon. Sir Paul James, Kt.
Walker, Sir Rodney Myerscough, Kt.
Walker, Sir Roy Edward, Bt. (1906)
Walker, Hon. Sir Timothy Edward, Kt.
Walker, Sir Victor Stewart Heron, Bt. (1868)
Walker-Okeover, Sir Andrew Peter Monro, Bt. (1886)
Walker-Smith, Hon. Sir John Jonah, Bt. (1960)
Wall, Sir (John) Stephen, GCMG, LVO
Wall, Gen. Sir Peter Anthony, GCB, CBE, ADC
Wallace, Prof. Sir David James, Kt., CBE, FRS
Waller, Rt. Hon. Sir (George) Mark, Kt.
Waller, Sir John Michael, Bt. (I. 1780)
Waller, Revd Dr Sir Ralph,
Wallis, Sir Peter Gordon, KCVO
Wallis, Sir Timothy William, Kt.
Walmsley, Vice-Adm. Sir Robert, KCB
Walport, Dr Sir Mark Jeremy, Kt.
†Walsham, Sir Gerald Percy Robert, Bt. (1831)
Walters, Sir Dennis Murray, Kt., MBE
Walters, Sir Frederick Donald, Kt.
Walters, Sir Peter Ingram, Kt.
Wamiri, Sir Akapite, KBE
Warby, Hon. Sir Mark David John, Kt.
Ward, Rt. Hon. Sir Alan Hylton, Kt.
Ward, Sir Austin, Kt., QC
Ward, Hon. Sir (Frederik) Gordon (Roy), Kt., OBE
Ward, Prof. Sir John MacQueen, Kt., CBE
Ward, Sir Joseph James Laffey, Bt. (1911)
Ward, Sir Timothy James, Kt.
†Wardlaw, Sir Henry Justin, Bt. (NS. 1631)
Waring, Sir (Alfred) Holburt, Bt. (1935)
Warmington, Sir Rupert Marshall, Bt. (1908)
Warner, Sir Gerald Chierici, KCMG
Warner, Sir Philip Courtenay Thomas, Bt. (1910)
Warren, Sir David Alexander, KCMG
Warren, Sir (Frederick) Miles, KBE
Warren, Sir Kenneth Robin, Kt.
Warren, Hon. Sir Nicholas Roger, Kt.
Waterlow, Sir Christopher Rupert, Bt. (1873)
Waterlow, Sir (Thomas) James, Bt. (1930)
Waters, Gen. Sir (Charles) John, GCB, CBE

Waters, Sir David Mark Rylance (Mark Rylance), Kt.

Waterstone, Sir Tim, Kt.

Wates, Sir Christopher Stephen, Kt.

Watson, Sir Graham Robert, Kt.

Watson, Sir (James) Andrew, Bt. (1866)

Watson, Prof. Sir Robert Tony, Kt., CMG

Watson, Sir Ronald Matthew, Kt., CBE

Watt, Gen. Sir Charles Redmond, KCB, KCVO, CBE, ADC

Watts, Sir Philip Beverley, KCMG

Weatherall, Prof. Sir David John, GBE, FRS

Weatherup, Hon. Sir Ronald Eccles, Kt.

Webb, Prof. Sir Adrian Leonard, Kt.

Webb, Rt. Hon. Sir Steven John, Kt.

Webb-Carter, Maj.-Gen. Sir Evelyn John, KCVO, OBE

Webster, Vice-Adm. Sir John Morrison, KCB

Wedgwood, Sir Ralph Nicholas, Bt. (1942)

Weekes, Sir Everton DeCourcey, KCMG, OBE

Weinberg, Sir Mark Aubrey, Kt.

Weir, Hon. Sir Reginald George, Kt.

Weir, Sir Roderick Bignell, Kt.

Welby, Sir (Richard) Bruno Gregory, Bt. (1801)

Welch, Sir John Reader, Bt. (1957)

Weldon, Sir Anthony William, Bt. (I. 1723)

Wellend, Prof. Sir Mark Edward, Kt.

Weller, Prof. Sir Ian Vincent Derrick, Kt.

Weller, Sir Nicholas John, Kt.

†Wells, Sir Christopher Charles, Bt. (1944)

Wells, Prof. Sir Stanley William, Kt., CBE

Wells, Sir William Henry Weston, Kt., FRICS

Wenge, Rt. Revd Girege, KBE

Wessely, Prof. Sir Simon Charles, Kt.

Westmacott, Sir Peter John, GCMG, LVO

Weston, Sir Michael Charles Swift, KCMG, CVO

Weston, Sir (Philip) John, KCMG

Whalen, Sir Geoffrey Henry, Kt., CBE

Wheeler, Rt. Hon. Sir John Daniel, Kt.

Wheeler, Sir John Frederick, Bt. (1920)

Wheeler, Gen. Sir Roger Neil, GCB, CBE

Wheler, Sir Trevor Woodford, Bt. (1660)

Whitaker, Sir John James Ingham (Jack), Bt. (1936)

Whitbread, Sir Samuel Charles, KCVO

Whitchurch, Sir Graeme Ian, Kt., OBE

White, Sir Adrian Edwin, Kt., CBE

White, Prof. Sir Christopher John, Kt., CVO

White, Sir David (David Jason), Kt., OBE

White, Sir David Harry, Kt.

White, Sir George Stanley James, Bt. (1904)

White, Sir John Woolmer, Bt. (1922)

White, Maj.-Gen. Sir Martin, KCVO, CB, CBE

White, Prof. Sir Nicholas John, KCMG, OBE

White, Sir Nicholas Peter Archibald, Bt. (1802)

White, Sir Willard Wentworth, Kt., CBE

White-Spunner, Lt.-Gen. Sir Barnabas William Benjamin, KCB, CBE

Whitehead, Sir Philip Henry Rathbone, Bt. (1889)

Whitfield, Sir William, Kt., CBE

Whitmore, Sir Clive Anthony, GCB, CVO

Whitmore, Sir Jason Kevin, Bt. (1954)

Whitson, Sir Keith Roderick, Kt.

Whittam Smith, Sir Andreas, Kt., CBE

Wickerson, Sir John Michael, Kt.

Wicks, Sir Nigel Leonard, GCB, CVO, CBE

Wigan, Sir Michael Iain, Bt. (1898)

Wiggin, Sir Richard Edward John, Bt. (1892)

Wiggins, Sir Bradley Marc, Kt., CBE

Wigram, Sir John Woolmore, Bt. (1805)

Wilbraham, Sir Richard Baker, Bt. (1776)

Wild, Sir John Ralston, Kt., CBE

Wiles, Prof. Sir Andrew John, KBE

Wilkie, Hon. Sir Alan Fraser, Kt.

Wilkins, Sir Michael, Kt.

Wilkinson, Sir (David) Graham (Brook) Bt. (1941)

Willcocks, Lt.-Gen. Sir Michael Alan, KCB, CVO

Williams, Sir Anthony Geraint, Bt. (1953)

Williams, Sir (Arthur) Gareth Ludovic Emrys Rhys, Bt. (1918)

Williams, Sir Charles Othniel, Kt.

Williams, Sir Daniel Charles, GCMG, QC

Williams, Hon. Sir David Basil, Kt.

Williams, Sir David Reeve, Kt., CBE

Williams, Sir Donald Mark, Bt. (1866)

Williams, Prof. Sir (Edward) Dillwyn, Kt., FRCP

Williams, Sir Francis Owen Garbett, Kt., CBE

Williams, Hon. Sir (John) Griffith, Kt.

Williams, Sir Nicholas Stephen, Kt.

Williams, Prof. Sir Norman Stanley, Kt.

Williams, Sir Paul Michael, Kt., OBE

Williams, Sir Peter Michael, Kt.

Williams, Sir (Robert) Philip Nathaniel, Bt. (1915)

Williams, HE Dr Sir Rodney Errey Lawrence, GCMG

Williams, Prof. Sir Roger, Kt.

Williams, Sir (William) Maxwell (Harries), Kt.

Williams, Hon. Sir Wyn Lewis, Kt.

Williams-Bulkeley, Sir Richard Thomas, Bt. (1661)

Williams-Wynn, Sir David Watkin, Bt. (1688)

Williamson, Sir George Malcolm, Kt.

Williamson, Sir Robert Brian, Kt., CBE

Willink, Sir Edward Daniel, Bt. (1957)

Wills, Sir David James Vernon, Bt. (1923)

Wills, Sir David Seton, Bt. (1904)

Wilmot, Sir Henry Robert, Bt. (1759)

Wilmut, Prof. Sir Ian, Kt., OBE

Wilsey, Gen. Sir John Finlay Willasey, GCB, CBE

Wilshaw, Sir Michael, Kt.

Wilson, Prof. Sir Alan Geoffrey, Kt.

Wilson, Sir David Mackenzie, Kt.

Wilson, Sir Franklyn Roosevelt Wilson, KCMG

Wilson, Sir James William Douglas, Bt. (1906)

Wilson, Brig. Sir Mathew John Anthony, Bt. (1874), OBE, MC

Wilson, Prof. Sir Robert James Timothy, Kt.

Wilson, Rt. Hon. Sir Nicholas Allan Roy, Kt. (Lord Wilson of Culworth)

Wilson, Sir Robert Peter, KCMG

Wilson, Air Chief Marshal Sir (Ronald) Andrew (Fellowes), KCB, AFC

Wilson, Sir Thomas David, Bt. (1920)

Winkley, Sir David Ross, Kt.

Winnington, Sir Anthony Edward, Bt. (1755)

Winship, Sir Peter James Joseph, Kt., CBE

Winsor, Sir Thomas Philip, Kt.

Winter, Dr Sir Gregory Winter, Kt., CBE

Winterton, Sir Nicholas Raymond, Kt.

Wiseman, Sir John William, Bt. (1628)

Witty, Sir Andrew, Kt.

Wolfendale, Prof. Sir Arnold Whittaker, Kt., FRS

†Wolseley, Sir James Douglas, Bt. (I. 1745)

†Wolseley, Sir Stephen Garnet Hugo Charles, Bt. (1628)

†Wombwell, Sir George Philip Frederick, Bt. (1778)

Womersley, Sir Peter John Walter, Bt. (1945)

Woo, Sir Leo Joseph, Kt., MBE

Woo, Sir Po-Shing, Kt.

Wood, Sir Alan Thorpe Richard, Kt., CBE

Wood, Sir Andrew Marley, GCMG

Wood, Sir Anthony John Page, Bt. (1837)

Wood, Sir Ian Clark, KT, GBE

Wood, Sir James Sebastian Lamin, KCMG

Wood, Sir Martin Francis, Kt., OBE

Wood, Sir Michael Charles, KCMG

Wood, Sir Peter John, Kt., CBE

Wood, Hon. Sir Roderic Lionel James, Kt.

Woodard, Rear Adm. Sir Robert Nathaniel, KCVO

Woodcock, Vice-Adm. Sir (Simon) Jonathan, KCB, OBE

Woodhead, Vice-Adm. Sir (Anthony) Peter, KCB

Woods, Prof. Sir Kent Linton, Kt.

Woods, Sir Robert Kynnersley, Kt., CBE

Woodward, Sir Clive Ronald, Kt., OBE

Woodward, Sir Thomas Jones (Tom Jones), Kt., OBE

Wootton, Sir David Hugh, Kt.

Wormald, Sir Christopher Stephen, KCB

Worsley, Sir William Ralph, Bt. (1838)

Worsthorne, Sir Peregrine Gerard, Kt.

Worthington, Sir Mark, Kt., OBE

Wratten, Air Chief Marshal Sir William John, GBE, CB, AFC

Wraxall, Sir Charles Frederick Lascelles, Bt. (1813)

Wrey, Sir George Richard Bourchier, Bt. (1628)

Wright, Sir Allan Frederick, KBE

Wright, Sir David John, GCMG, LVO

Wright, Hon. Sir (John) Michael, Kt.

Wright, Prof. Sir Nicholas Alcwyn, Kt.

Wright, Sir Peter Robert, Kt., CBE

Wright, Air Marshal Sir Robert Alfred, KBE, AFC

Wright, Sir Stephen John Leadbetter, KCMG

Wright, Dr Sir William Thompson, Kt., CBE

Wrightson, Sir Charles Mark Garmondsway, Bt. (1900)

Wrigley, Prof. Sir Edward Anthony (Sir Tony), Kt., PHD, PBA

Wrixon-Becher, Sir John William Michael, Bt. (1831)

Wroughton, Sir Philip Lavallin, KCVO

Wu, Sir Gordon Ying Sheung, KCMG

Wynne, Sir Graham Robert, Kt., CBE

Yacoub, Prof. Sir Magdi Habib, Kt., OM, FRCS

Yaki, Sir Roy, KBE

Yang, Hon. Sir Ti Liang, Kt.

Yarrow, Sir Alan Colin Drake, Kt.

Yarrow, Sir Eric Grant, Bt. (1916), MDE

Yassaie, Dr Sir Hossein, Kt.

Yoo Foo, Sir (François) Henri, Kt.

Young, Sir Colville Norbert, GCMG, MBE

Young, Sir Dennis Charles, KCMG

Young, Sir John Kenyon Roe, Bt. (1821)

Young, Sir John Robertson, GCMG

Young, Sir Leslie Clarence, Kt., CBE

Young, Sir Nicholas Charles, Kt.

Young, Sir Robin Urquhart, KCB

Young, Sir Stephen Stewart Templeton, Bt. (1945), QC

Young, Sir William Neil, Bt. (1769)

Younger, Capt. Sir John David Bingham, KCVO

Younger, Sir Julian William Richard, Bt. (1911)

Yuwi, Sir Matiabe, KBE

Zacaroli, Hon. Sir Antony James, Kt.

Zacca, Rt. Hon. Sir Edward, KCMG

Zahedi, Prof. Sir Mir Saeed, Kt., OBE

Zambellas, Adm. Sir George Michael, GCB, DSC, ADC

Zissman, Sir Bernard Philip, Kt.

Zumla, Prof. Sir Alimuddin, Kt.

Zunz, Sir Gerhard Jacob (Jack), Kt., FRENG

Zurenuoc, Sir Manasupe Zure, Kt., OBE

Zurenuoc, Sir Zibang, KBE

THE ORDER OF ST JOHN

THE MOST VENERABLE ORDER OF THE HOSPITAL OF ST JOHN OF JERUSALEM (1888)

GCStJ	Bailiff/Dame Grand Cross
KStJ	Knight of Justice/Grace
DStJ	Dame of Justice/Grace
CStJ	Commander
OStJ	Officer
SBStJ	Serving Brother
SSStJ	Serving Sister

Motto, Pro Fide, Pro Utilitate Hominum
(For the faith and in the service of humanity)

The Order of St John, founded in the early 12th century in Jerusalem, was a religious order with a particular duty to care for the sick. In Britain the order was dissolved by Henry VIII in 1540 but the British branch was revived in the early 19th century. The branch was not accepted by the Grand Magistracy of the Order in Rome but its search for a role in the tradition of the hospitallers led to the founding of the St John Ambulance Association in 1877 and later the St John Ambulance Brigade; in 1882 the St John Ophthalmic Hospital was founded in Jerusalem. A royal charter was granted in 1888 establishing the Order of St John as a British Order of Chivalry with the sovereign as its head.

Since October 1999 the whole order worldwide has been governed by a Grand Council which includes a representative from each of the 11 priories (England, Scotland, Wales, Hong Kong, Kenya, Singapore, South Africa, New Zealand, Canada, Australia and the USA). In addition there are also five commanderies in Northern Ireland, Jersey, Guernsey, the Isle of Man and Western Australia. There are also branches in about 30 other Commonwealth countries. Apart from St John Ambulance, the Order is also responsible for the Eye Hospital in Jerusalem. Admission to the order is usually conferred in recognition of service to either one of these institutions. Membership does not confer any rank, style, title or precedence on a recipient.

SOVEREIGN HEAD OF THE ORDER
HM The Queen

GRAND PRIOR
HRH The Duke of Gloucester, KG, GCVO

Lord Prior, Lt.-Col. Sir Malcolm Ross, GCVO, OBE
Prelate, Rt. Revd Timothy Stevens, CBE
Chancellor, Patrick Burgess, OBE
Sub-Prior, John Mah, QC
Secretary-General, Vice-Adm. Sir Paul Lambert, KCB

International Office, 3 Charterhouse Mews, London EC1M 6BB
T 020-7251 3292 W www.stjohninternational.org

DAMES

Style, 'Dame' before forename and surname, followed by appropriate post-nominal initials. Where such an award is made to a lady already in possession of a higher title, the appropriate initials follow her name
Envelope, Dame F_ S_, followed by appropriate post-nominal letters. *Letter (formal),* Dear Madam; *(social),* Dear Dame F_. *Spoken,* Dame F_
Husband, Untitled

Dame Grand Cross and Dame Commander are the higher classes for women of the Order of the Bath, the Order of St Michael and St George, the Royal Victorian Order, and the Order of the British Empire. Dames Grand Cross rank after the wives of Baronets and before the wives of Knights Grand Cross. Dames Commanders rank after the wives of Knights Grand Cross and before the wives of Knights Commanders.

Honorary damehoods may be conferred on women who are citizens of countries of which the Queen is not head of state.

LIST OF DAMES *as at 31 August 2018*
Women peers in their own right and life peers are not included in this list. Female members of the royal family are not included in this list; details of the orders they hold can be found within the Royal Family section.

If a dame has a double barrelled or hyphenated surname, she is listed under the first element of the name.

Abaijah, Dame Josephine, DBE
Abramsky, Dame Jennifer Gita, DBE
Acland Hood Gass, Lady (Elizabeth Periam), DCVO
Airlie, The Countess of, DCVO
Allen, *Hon.* Dame Anita Mildred, DBE
Allen, *Prof.* Dame Ingrid Victoria, DBE
Andrews, *Hon.* Dame Geraldine Mary, DBE
Andrews, Dame Julie, DBE
Angiolini, *Rt. Hon.* Dame Elish, DBE, QC
Anionwu, *Prof.* Dame Elizabeth Nneka, DBE
Anson, Lady (Elizabeth Audrey), DBE
Archer, *Dr* Dame Mary Doreen, DBE
Arden, *Rt. Hon.* Dame Mary Howarth (Mrs Mance), DBE
Ashcroft, *Prof.* Dame Frances Mary, DBE, FRS
Asplin, *Rt. Hon.* Dame Sarah Jane (Mrs Sherwin), DBE
Atkins, Dame Eileen, DBE
August, Dame Kathryn, DBE
Bacon, Dame Patricia Anne, DBE
Bailey, *Prof.* Dame Susan Mary, DBE
Baird, Dame Vera, DBE
Baker, Dame Janet Abbott (Mrs Shelley), CH, DBE
Barbour, Dame Margaret (Mrs Ash), DBE
Barker, Dame Katharine Mary, DBE
Barker-Welch, *Hon.* Dame Maizie Irene, DBE
Barrow, Dame Jocelyn Anita (Mrs Downer), DBE
Barstow, Dame Josephine Clare (Mrs Anderson), DBE
Bassey, Dame Shirley, DBE
Beale, Dame Inga Kristine, DBE
Beard, *Prof.* Dame (Winifred) Mary, DBE
Beasley, *Prof.* Dame Christine Joan, DBE
Beaurepaire, Dame Beryl Edith, DBE
Beckett, *Rt. Hon.* Dame Margaret Mary, DBE
Beer, *Prof.* Dame Gillian Patricia Kempster, DBE, FBA
Beer, *Prof.* Dame Janet Patricia, DBE
Begg, Dame Anne, DBE
Beral, *Prof.* Dame Valerie, DBE
Bertschinger, *Dr* Dame Claire, DBE
Bevan, Dame Yasmin, DBE
Bibby, Dame Enid, DBE

Black, *Prof.* Dame Carol Mary, DBE
Black, *Rt. Hon.* Dame Jill Margaret, DBE (Lady Black of Derwent)
Black, *Prof.* Dame Susan Margaret, DBE, FRSE
Blackadder, Dame Elizabeth Violet, DBE
Blaize, Dame Venetia Ursula, DBE
Blaxland, Dame Helen Frances, DBE
Blume, Dame Hilary Sharon Braverman, DBE
Booth, *Hon.* Dame Margaret Myfanwy Wood, DBE
Boulding, Dame Hilary, DBE
Bourne, Dame Susan Mary (Mrs Bourne), DBE
Bowe, *Dr* Dame (Mary) Colette, DBE
Bowtell, Dame Ann Elizabeth, DCB
Braddock, *Dr* Dame Christine, DBE
Brain, Dame Margaret Anne (Mrs Wheeler), DBE
Breakwell, *Prof.* Dame Glynis Marie, DBE
Brennan, Dame Maureen, DBE
Brennan, Dame Ursula, DCB
Brewer, *Dr* Dame Nicola Mary, DCMG
Bridges, Dame Mary Patricia, DBE
Brindley, Dame Lynne Janie, DBE
Brittan, Dame Diana (Lady Brittan of Spennithorne), DBE
Brooke, *Rt. Hon.* Dame Annette (Lesley), DBE
Bruce, Dame Susan Margaret, DBE
Bruce, *Prof.* Dame Victoria Geraldine, DBE, FBA, FRSE
Buckland, Dame Yvonne Helen Elaine, DBE
Burnell, *Prof.* Dame Susan Jocelyn Bell, DBE
Burslem, Dame Alexandra Vivien, DBE
Bussell, Dame Darcey Andrea, DBE
Butler, Dame Rosemary Janet Mair, DBE
Byatt, Dame Antonia Susan, DBE, FRSL
Cairncross, Dame Frances Anne, DBE, FRSE
Caldicott, Dame Fiona, DBE, FRCP, FRCPSYCH
Callil, Dame Carmen Thérèse, DBE
Cameron, *Prof.* Dame Averil Millicent, DBE
Campbell-Preston, Dame Frances Olivia, DCVO
Carew Pole, Lady Mary, DCVO
Carnall, Dame Ruth, DBE
Carnwath, Dame Alison Jane, DBE
Carr, *Hon.* Dame Sue Lascelles (Mrs Birch), DBE
Cartwright, Dame Silvia Rose, DBE
Casey, Dame Louise, DBE, CB
Chapman, *Prof.* Dame Hilary Anne, DBE
Cheema-Grubb, *Hon.* Dame Bobbie, DBE
Clancy, Dame Claire Elizabeth, DCB
Clark, *Prof.* Dame Jill MacLeod, DBE
Clark, *Prof.* Dame (Margaret) June, DBE, PHD
Cleverdon, Dame Julia Charity, DCVO, CBE
Coates, Dame Sally, DBE
Cockerill, *Hon.* Dame Sara Elizabeth, DBE
Coia, *Dr* Dame Denise Assunta, DBE
Collarbone, Dame Patricia, DBE
Collins, Dame Joan Henrietta, DBE
Connolly, Dame Sarah Patricia, DBE
Contreras, *Prof.* Dame Marcela, DBE
Corner, *Prof.* Dame Jessica Lois, DBE
Corsar, *Hon.* Dame Mary Drummond, DBE
Courtice, Dame Veronica Anne (Polly), DBE, LVO
Coward, Dame Pamela Sarah, DBE
Cowley, *Prof.* Dame Sarah Ann, DBE
Cox, *Hon.* Dame Laura Mary, DBE
Cramp, *Prof.* Dame Rosemary Jean, DBE
Cullum, *Prof.* Dame Nicola Anne, DBE
Cutts, *Hon.* Dame Johannah, DBE

Dacon, Dame Monica Jessie, DBE, CMG
Dacre, *Prof.* Dame Jane Elizabeth, DBE
Daniel, Dame Jacqueline Lesley, DBE
Davies, *Prof.* Dame Kay Elizabeth, DBE
Davies, Dame Laura Jane, DBE
Davies, *Rt. Hon.* Dame Nicola Velfor, DBE
Davies, *Prof.* Dame Sally Claire, DBE
Davies, Dame Wendy Patricia, DBE
Davis, Dame Karlene Cecile, DBE
Dawson, *Prof.* Dame Sandra Jane Noble, DBE
de Havilland, Dame Olivia Mary, DBE
De Souza, Dame Rachel Mary, DBE
Dean, *Prof.* Dame Caroline, DBE, FRS
Dell, Dame Miriam Patricia, DBE
Dench, Dame Judith Olivia (Mrs Williams), CH, DBE
Descartes, Dame Marie Selipha Sesenne, DBE, BEM
Dethridge, Dame Kate, DBE
Digby, The Lady, DBE
Dobbs, *Hon.* Dame Linda Penelope, DBE
Docherty, Dame Jacqueline, DBE
Dominiczak, *Prof.* Dame Anna Felicja, DBE, FRSE
Donald, *Prof.* Dame Athene Margaret, DBE, FRS
Dowling, *Prof.* Dame Ann Patricia, OM, DBE
Duffield, Dame Vivien Louise, DBE
Duffy, Dame Carol Ann, DBE
Dumont, Dame Ivy Leona, DCMG
Dunnell, Dame Karen, DCB
Dyche, Dame Rachael Mary, DBE
Elcoat, Dame Catherine Elizabeth, DBE
Ellison, Dame Jill, DBE
Ellman, Dame Louise Joyce, DBE
Elton, Dame Susan Richenda (Lady Elton), DCVO
Ennis-Hill, Dame Jessica, DBE
Esteve-Coll, Dame Elizabeth Anne Loosemore, DBE
Evans, Dame Anne Elizabeth Jane, DBE
Evans, Dame Madeline Glynne Dervel, DBE, CMG
Evans, Dame Oremi, DBE
Fagan, Dame (Florence) Mary, LG, DCVO
Fallowfield, *Prof.* Dame Lesley Jean, DBE
Falk, *Hon.* Dame Sarah, DBE
Farbey, *Hon.* Dame Judith Sarah, DBE
Farnham, Dame Marion (Lady Farnham), DCVO
Fawcett, Dame Amelia Chilcott, DBE
Fielding, Dame Pauline, DBE
Finch, *Prof.* Dame Janet Valerie, DBE
Fisher, *Prof.* Dame Amanda Gray, DBE
Fisher, Dame Jacqueline, DBE
Forgan, Dame Elizabeth Anne Lucy, DBE
Furse, Dame Clara Hedwig Frances, DBE
Fradd, Dame Elizabeth, DBE
Francis, *Prof.* Dame Jane Elizabeth, DCMG
Fraser, Lady Antonia, DBE, CH
Fraser, Dame Helen Jean Sutherland, DBE
Frost, Dame Barbara May, DBE
Fry, Dame Margaret Louise, DBE
Gai, *Prof.* Dame Pratibha Laxman (Mrs Gai-Boyes), DBE
Gaymer, Dame Janet Marion, DBE, QC
Ghosh, Dame Helen Frances, DCB
Gibb, Dame Moira Margaret, DBE
Gillian, *Rt. Hon.* Dame Cheryl Elise Kendall, DBE
Glenn, *Prof.* Dame Hazel Gillian, DBE
Glennie, *Dr* Dame Evelyn Elizabeth Ann, CH, DBE
Gloster, *Rt. Hon.* Dame Elizabeth (Lady Popplewell), DBE
Glover, Dame Audrey Frances, DBE, CMG
Glover, *Prof.* Dame Lesley Anne, DBE, FRSE
Goad, Dame Sarah Jane Frances, DCVO
Goodall, *Dr* Dame (Valerie) Jane, DBE
Goodfellow, *Prof.* Dame Julia Mary, DBE
Gordon, Dame Minita Elmira, GCMG, GCVO
Gordon, *Hon.* Dame Pamela Felicity, DBE

Gow, Dame Jane Elizabeth (Mrs Whiteley), DBE
Grafton, Ann, The Duchess of, GCVO
Grainger, *Dr* Dame Katherine Jane, DBE
Grant, Dame Mavis, DBE
Green, Dame Moya Marguerite, DBE
Green, Dame Pauline, DBE
Gretton, Lady Jennifer Ann, DCVO
Grey, Dame Beryl Elizabeth (Mrs Svenson), CH, DBE
Grimthorpe, Elizabeth, The Lady, DCVO
Guilfoyle, Dame Margaret Georgina Constance, DBE
Guthardt, *Revd Dr* Dame Phyllis Myra, DBE
Hackitt, Dame Judith Elizabeth, DBE
Hakin, *Dr* Dame Barbara Ann, DBE
Hall, *Prof.* Dame Wendy, DBE
Hallett, *Rt. Hon.* Dame Heather Carol, DBE
Hallett, Dame Nancy Karen, DBE
Hamilton, *Prof.* Dame Carolyn Paula, DBE
Harbison, Dame Joan Irene, DBE
Harper, Dame Elizabeth Margaret Way, DBE
Harris, Dame Pauline (Lady Harris of Peckham), DBE
Harris, Dame Philippa Jill Olivier, DBE
Hassan, Dame Anna Patricia Lucy, DBE
Hay, Dame Barbara Logan, DCMG, MBE
Henderson, Dame Fiona Douglas, DCVO
Hercus, *Hon.* Dame (Margaret) Ann, DCMG
Higgins, *Prof.* Dame Joan Margaret, DBE
Higgins, *Prof.* Dame Julia Stretton, DBE, FRS
Higgins, *Prof.* Dame Rosalyn, DBE, QC
Hill, *Air Cdre* Dame Felicity Barbara, DBE
Hill, *Prof.* Dame Judith Eileen, DBE
Hill, *Prof.* Dame Susan Lesley, DBE
Hine, Dame Deirdre Joan, DBE, FRCP
Hodge, *Rt. Hon.* Dame Margaret (Eve), DBE
Hodgson, Dame Patricia Anne, DBE
Hogg, *Hon.* Dame Mary Claire (Mrs Koops), DBE
Hollows, Dame Sharon, DBE
Holmes, Dame Kelly, DBE
Holroyd, Lady (Margaret Drabble), DBE
Holt, Dame Denise Mary, DCMG
Homer, Dame Linda Margaret, DCB
Hoodless, Dame Elisabeth Anne, DBE
Hoyles, *Prof.* Dame Celia Mary, DBE
Hudson, Dame Alice, DBE
Hufton, *Prof.* Dame Olwen, DBE
Humphrey, *Prof.* Dame Caroline (Lady Rees of Ludlow), DBE
Hunt, Dame Vivian, DBE
Husband, *Prof.* Dame Janet Elizabeth Siarey, DBE
Hussey, Dame Susan Katharine (Lady Hussey of North Bradley), GCVO
Hutton, Dame Deirdre Mary, DBE
Hyde, Dame Helen, DBE
Imison, Dame Tamsyn, DBE
Ion, *Dr* Dame Susan Elizabeth, DBE
Isaacs, Dame Albertha Madeline, DBE
James, Dame Naomi Christine (Mrs Haythorne), DBE
Jefford, *Hon.* Dame Nerys Angharad, DBE
Jiang, *Prof.* Dame Xiangqian (Jane), DBE
John, Dame Susan, DBE
Johnson, *Prof.* Dame Anne Mandall, DBE
Johnston, Dame Rotha Geraldine Diane, DBE
Jones, Dame Gwyneth (Mrs Haberfeld-Jones), DBE
Jordan, *Prof.* Dame Carole, DBE
Joseph, Dame Monica Theresa, DBE
Jowett, Dame Susan, DBE
Julius, *Dr* Dame DeAnne Shirley, DCMG, CBE
Karika, Dame Pauline Margaret Rakera George (Mrs Taripo), DBE
Keeble, *Dr* Dame Reena, DBE
Keegan, Dame Elizabeth Mary, DBE

Keegan, Dame Geraldine Mary Marcella, DBE
Keegan, *Hon.* Dame Siobhan Roisin, DBE
Keith, Dame Penelope Anne Constance (Mrs Timson), DBE
Kekedo, Dame Rosalina Violet, DBE
Kelleher, Dame Joan, DBE
Kelly, Dame Barbara Mary, DBE
Kelly, Dame Lorna May Boreland, DBE
Kendrick, Dame Fiona Marie, DBE
Kershaw, Dame Janet Elizabeth Murray (Dame Betty), DBE
Kharas, Dame Zarine, DBE
Khemka, Dame Asha, DBE
Kidu, Lady, DBE
King, *Rt. Hon.* Dame Eleanor Warwick, DBE
Kinnair, Dame Donna, DBE
Kirby, Dame Georgina Kamiria, DBE
Kirkby, Dame (Carolyn) Emma, DBE
Kirwan, *Prof.* Dame Frances Clare, DBE, FRS
Knowles, *Hon.* Dame Gwynneth Frances Dietinde, DBE
Kumar, *Prof.* Dame Parveen June (Mrs Leaver), DBE
La Grenade, *HE* Dame Cécile Ellen Fleurette, GCMG, OBE
Laine, Dame Cleo (Clementine) Dinah (Lady Dankworth), DBE
Laing, *Rt. Hon.* Dame Eleanor Fulton, DBE
Laing, *Hon.* Dame Elisabeth Mary Caroline, DBE
Lake-Tack, *HE* Dame Louise Agnetha, GCMG
Lamb, Dame Dawn Ruth, DBE
Lambert, *Hon.* Dame Christina Caroline, DBE
Lang, *Hon.* Dame Beverley Ann Mcnaughton, DBE
Lannon, *Dr* Dame Frances, DBE
Lansbury Shaw, Dame Angela Brigid, DBE
Lavender, *Prof.* Dame Tina, DBE
Leather, Dame Susan Catherine, DBE
Lee, *Prof.* Dame Hermione, DBE
Legge-Bourke, *Hon.* Dame Elizabeth Shân Josephine, DCVO
Lenehan, Dame Christine, DBE
Leslie, Dame Alison Mariot, DCMG
Leslie, Dame Ann Elizabeth Mary, DBE
Lewis, Dame Edna Leofrida (Lady Lewis), DBE
Leyser Day, *Prof.* Dame Henrietta Miriam Ottoline, DBE
Lively, Dame Penelope Margaret, DBE
Lott, Dame Felicity Ann Emwhyla (Mrs Woolf), DBE
Louisy, Dame (Calliopa) Pearlette, GCMG
Lynn, Dame Vera (Mrs Lewis), CH, DBE
MacArthur, Dame Ellen Patricia, DBE
McBride, *Hon.* Dame Denise Anne, DBE
McCall, Dame Carolyn Julia, DBE
McLean, *Prof.* Dame Angela Ruth, DBE
Macdonald, Dame Mary Beaton, DBE
McDonald, Dame Mavis, DCB
Mace, *Prof.* Dame Georgina, DBE
McGowan, *Hon.* Dame Maura Patricia, DBE
Macgregor, Dame Judith Anne, DCMG, LVO
McGuire, *Rt. Hon.* Dame Anne Catherine, DBE
MacIntyre, *Prof.* Dame Sarah Jane, DBE
Macur, *Rt. Hon.* Dame Julia Wendy, DBE
McVittie, Dame Joan Christine, DBE
Major, Dame Malvina Lorraine (Mrs Fleming), DBE
Major, Dame Norma Christina Elizabeth, DBE
Makin, *Dr* Dame Pamela Louise, DBE
Mantel, *Dr* Dame Hilary Mary, DBE
Manzie, Dame Stella Gordon, DBE
Marsden, *Dr* Dame Rosalind Mary, DCMG
Marsh, Dame Mary Elizabeth, DBE
Mason, *HE* Dame Sandra Prunella, DCMG
Marteau, *Prof.* Dame Theresa Mary, DBE
Marx, Dame Clare Lucy, DBE
Mason, Dame Monica Margaret, DBE
Massenet, Dame Natalie Sara, DBE
Matheson, Dame Jilian Norma, DCB
May, *Hon.* Dame Juliet Mary May, DBE

Mayhew Jonas, Dame Judith, DBE
Mellor, Dame Julie Thérèse, DBE
Metge, *Dr* Dame (Alice) Joan, DBE
Middleton, Dame Elaine Madoline, DCMG, MBE
Milburn, Dame Martina Jane, DCVO, CBE
Mills, *Prof.* Dame Anne Jane, DCMG, CBE
Mirren, Dame Helen, DBE
Monroe, *Prof.* Dame Barbara, DBE
Moore, Dame Henrietta Louise, DBE, FBA
Moore, Dame Julie, DBE
Moores, Dame Yvonne, DBE
Morgan, *Dr* Dame Gillian Margaret, DBE
Morgan, Dame Shan Elizabeth, DCMG
Morris, Dame Sylvia Ann, DBE
Morrison, *Hon.* Dame Mary Anne, GCVO
Morrissey, Dame Helena Louise, DBE
Moulder, *Hon.* Dame Jane Clare, DBE
Muirhead, Dame Lorna Elizabeth Fox, DCVO, DBE
Mullally, *Rt. Revd* Dame Sarah Elisabeth, DBE
Murray, Dame Jennifer Susan, DBE
Nelson, *Prof.* Dame Janet Laughland, DBE
Nelson-Taylor, Dame Nicola Jane, DBE
Neville, Dame Elizabeth, DBE, QPM
Newell, Dame Priscilla Jane, DBE
O'Brien, Dame Una, DCB
O'Farrell, *Hon.* Dame Finola Mary, DBE
Ogilvie, Dame Bridget Margaret, DBE, PHD, DSc
Oliver, Dame Gillian Frances, DBE
Owen, Dame Susan Jane, DCB
Owers, Dame Anne Elizabeth (Mrs Cook), DBE
Oxenbury, Dame Shirley Ann, DBE
Palmer, Dame Felicity Joan, DBE
Paraskeva, *Rt. Hon.* Dame Janet, DBE
Park, Dame Merle Florence (Mrs Bloch), DBE
Parker, *Hon.* Dame Judith Mary Frances, DBE
Partridge, *Prof.* Dame Linda, DBE
Patel, Dame Indira, DBE
Paterson, Dame Vicki, DBE
Pauffley, *Hon.* Dame Anna Evelyn Hamilton, DBE
Peacock, Dame Alison Margaret, DBE
Pearce, *Prof.* Dame Shirley, DBE
Pedder, Dame Angela Mary, DBE
Pereira, *Hon.* Dame Janice Mesadis, DBE
Penhaligon, Dame Annette (Mrs Egerton), DBE
Perkins, Dame Mary Lesley, DBE
Peters, Dame Mary Elizabeth, CH, DBE
Peyton-Jones, Dame Julia, DBE
Phillips, Dame Jane Elizabeth Ailwen (Sian), DBE
Pienaar, Dame Erica, DBE
Pierce, Dame Karen Elizabeth, DCMG
Pindling, Lady (Marguerite Matilda), GCMG
Platt, Dame Denise, DBE
Plotnikoff, Dame Joyce Evelyn, DBE
Plowright, Dame Joan Ann, DBE
Plunket Greene, Dame Barbara Mary, DBE
Poole, Dame Avril Anne Barker, DBE
Porter, Dame Shirley (Lady Porter), DBE
Powell, Dame Sally Ann Vickers, DBE
Pringle, Dame Anne Fyfe, DCMG
Proudman, *Hon.* Dame Sonia Rosemary Susan, DBE
Pugh, *Dr* Dame Gillian Mary, DBE
Rabbatts, Dame Heather Victoria, DBE
Rafferty, *Rt. Hon.* Dame Anne Judith, DBE
Rantzen, Dame Esther Louise (Mrs Wilcox), DBE
Rawson, *Prof.* Dame Jessica Mary, DBE
Rees, *Prof.* Dame Judith Anne, DBE
Rees, *Prof.* Dame Lesley Howard, DBE
Rees, *Prof.* Dame Teresa Lesley, DBE
Reeves, Dame Helen May, DBE
Refson, Dame Benita, DBE

DECORATIONS AND MEDALS

PRINCIPAL DECORATIONS AND MEDALS IN ORDER OF WEAR

VICTORIA CROSS (VC), 1856 (*see* below)
GEORGE CROSS (GC), 1940 (*see* below)

BRITISH ORDERS OF KNIGHTHOOD
(*see also* Orders of Chivalry)

Order of the Garter
Order of the Thistle
Order of St Patrick
Order of the Bath
Order of Merit
Order of the Star of India
Order of St Michael and George
Order of the Indian Empire
Order of the Crown of India
Royal Victorian Order (Classes I, II and III)
Order of the British Empire (Classes I, II and III)
Order of the Companions of Honour
Distinguished Service Order
Royal Victorian Order (Class IV)
Order of the British Empire (Class IV)
Imperial Service Order
Royal Victorian Order (Class V)
Order of the British Empire (Class V)

BARONET'S BADGE

KNIGHT BACHELOR'S BADGE

INDIAN ORDER OF MERIT (MILITARY)

DECORATIONS
Conspicuous Gallantry Cross (CGC), 1995
Royal Red Cross Class I (RRC), 1883
Distinguished Service Cross (DSC), 1914
Military Cross (MC), December 1914
Distinguished Flying Cross (DFC), 1918
Air Force Cross (AFC), 1918
Royal Red Cross Class II (ARRC)
Order of British India
Kaisar-i-Hind Medal
Order of St John

MEDALS FOR GALLANTRY AND DISTINGUISHED CONDUCT
Union of South Africa Queen's Medal for Bravery, in Gold
Distinguished Conduct Medal (DCM), 1854
Conspicuous Gallantry Medal (CGM), 1874
Conspicuous Gallantry Medal (Flying)
George Medal (GM), 1940
Queen's Police Medal for Gallantry
Queen's Fire Service Medal for Gallantry
Royal West African Frontier Force Distinguished Conduct Medal
King's African Rifles Distinguished Conduct Medal
Indian Distinguished Service Medal
Union of South Africa Queen's Medal for Bravery, in Silver
Distinguished Service Medal (DSM), 1914
Military Medal (MM), 1916
Distinguished Flying Medal (DFM), 1918
Air Force Medal (AFM)
Constabulary Medal (Ireland)

Medal for Saving Life at Sea (Sea Gallantry Medal)
Indian Order of Merit (Civil)
Indian Police Medal for Gallantry
Ceylon Police Medal for Gallantry
Sierra Leone Police Medal for Gallantry
Sierra Leone Fire Brigades Medal for Gallantry
Overseas Territories Police Medal for Gallantry
Queen's Gallantry Medal (QGM), 1974
Royal Victorian Medal (RVM), Gold, Silver and Bronze
British Empire Medal (BEM)
Canada Medal
Queen's Police Medal for Distinguished Service (QPM)
Queen's Fire Service Medal for Distinguished Service (QFSM)
Queen's Ambulance Service Medal
Queen's Volunteer Reserves Medal
Queen's Medal for Chiefs

CAMPAIGN MEDALS AND STARS
Including authorised United Nations, European Community/Union and North Atlantic Treaty Organisation medals (in order of date of campaign for which awarded).

Iraq Reconstruction Service Medal
Civilian Service Medal (Afghanistan)

POLAR MEDALS *in order of date*

IMPERIAL SERVICE MEDAL

POLICE MEDALS FOR VALUABLE SERVICE
Indian Police Medal for Meritorious Service
Ceylon Police Medal for Merit
Sierra Leone Police Medal for Meritorious Service
Sierra Leone Fire Brigades Medal for Meritorious Service
Overseas Territories Police Medal for Meritorious Service

BADGE OF HONOUR

JUBILEE, CORONATION AND DURBAR MEDALS
Queen Victoria, King Edward VII, King George V, King George VI, Queen Elizabeth II, Visit Commemoration and Long and Faithful Service Medals

EFFICIENCY AND LONG SERVICE DECORATIONS AND MEDALS
Medal for Meritorious Service
Accumulated Campaign Service Medal
Medal for Long Service and Good Conduct (Military)
Naval Long Service and Good Conduct Medal
Medal for Meritorious Service (Royal Navy 1918–28)
Indian Long Service and Good Conduct Medal
Indian Meritorious Service Medal
Royal Marines Meritorious Service Medal (1849–1947)
Royal Air Force Meritorious Service Medal (1918–1928)
Royal Air Force Long Service and Good Conduct Medal
Medal for Long Service and Good Conduct (Ulster Defence Regiment)
Indian Long Service and Good Conduct Medal
Royal West African Frontier Force Long Service and Good Conduct Medal
Royal Sierra Leone Military Forces Long Service and Good Conduct Medal
King's African Rifles Long Service and Good Conduct Medal
Indian Meritorious Service Medal

Police Long Service and Good Conduct Medal
Fire Brigade Long Service and Good Conduct Medal
African Police Medal for Meritorious Service
Royal Canadian Mounted Police Long Service Medal
Ceylon Police Long Service Medal
Ceylon Fire Services Long Service Medal
Sierra Leone Police Long Service Medal
Overseas Territories Police Long Service Medal
Sierra Leone Fire Brigades Long Service Medal
Mauritius Police Long Service and Good Conduct Medal
Mauritius Fire Services Long Service and Good Conduct Medal
Mauritius Prisons Service Long Service and Good Conduct Medal
Overseas Territories Fire Brigades Long Service Medal
Overseas Territories Prison Service Medal
Hong Kong Disciplined Services Medal
Army Emergency Reserve Decoration (ERD)
Volunteer Officers' Decoration (VD)
Volunteer Long Service Medal
Volunteer Officers' Decoration (for India and the Colonies)
Volunteer Long Service Medal (for India and the Colonies)
Colonial Auxiliary Forces Officers' Decoration
Colonial Auxiliary Forces Long Service Medal
Medal for Good Shooting (Naval)
Militia Long Service Medal
Imperial Yeomanry Long Service Medal
Territorial Decoration (TD), 1908
Ceylon Armed Services Long Service Medal
Efficiency Decoration (ED)
Territorial Efficiency Medal
Efficiency Medal
Special Reserve Long Service and Good Conduct Medal
Decoration for Officers of the Royal Navy Reserve (RD), 1910
Decoration for Officers of the Royal Naval Volunteer Reserve
     (VRD)
Royal Naval Reserve Long Service and Good Conduct Medal
Royal Naval Volunteer Reserve Long Service and Good Conduct
     Medal
Royal Naval Auxiliary Sick Berth Reserve Long Service and Good
     Conduct Medal
Royal Fleet Reserve Long Service and Good Conduct Medal
Royal Naval Wireless Auxiliary Reserve Long Service and Good
     Conduct Medal
Royal Naval Auxiliary Service Medal
Air Efficiency Award (AE), 1942
Volunteer Reserves Service Medal
Ulster Defence Regiment Medal
Northern Ireland Home Service Medal
Queen's Medal (for Champion Shots of the RN and RM)
Queen's Medal (for Champion Shots of the New Zealand
     Naval Forces)
Queen's Medal (for Champion Shots in the Military Forces)
Queen's Medal (for Champion Shots of the Air Forces)
Cadet Forces Medal, 1950
HM Coastguard Long Service and Good Conduct Medal
Special Constabulary Long Service Medal
Canadian Forces Decoration
Royal Observer Corps Medal
Civil Defence Long Service Medal
Ambulance Service (Emergency Duties) Long Service and Good
     Conduct Medal
Royal Fleet Auxiliary Service Medal
Prison Services (Operational Duties) Long Service and Good
     Conduct Medal
Jersey Honorary Police Long Service and Good Conduct Medal
Merchant Navy Medal for Meritorious Service
Ebola Medal for Service in West Africa

National Crime Agency Long Service and Good Conduct Medal
Rhodesia Medal
Royal Ulster Constabulary Service Medal
Northern Ireland Prison Service Medal
Union of South Africa Commemoration Medal
Indian Independence Medal
Pakistan Medal
Ceylon Armed Services Inauguration Medal
Ceylon Police Independence Medal (1948)
Sierra Leone Independence Medal
Jamaica Independence Medal
Uganda Independence Medal
Malawi Independence Medal
Fiji Independence Medal
Papua New Guinea Independence Medal
Solomon Islands Independence Medal
Service Medal of the Order of St John
Badge of the Order of the League of Mercy
Voluntary Medical Service Medal (1932)
Women's Royal Voluntary Service Medal
South African Medal for War Services
Overseas Territories Special Constabulary Medal

HONORARY MEMBERSHIP OF COMMONWEALTH
ORDERS

OTHER COMMONWEALTH MEMBERS' ORDERS,
DECORATIONS AND MEDALS

FOREIGN ORDERS

FOREIGN DECORATIONS

FOREIGN MEDALS

THE VICTORIA CROSS (1856)

FOR CONSPICUOUS BRAVERY

VC

Ribbon, Crimson, for all Services (until 1918 it was blue for
     the Royal Navy)

Instituted on 29 January 1856, the Victoria Cross was awarded
retrospectively to 1854, the first being held by Lt. C. D. Lucas,
RN, for bravery in the Baltic Sea on 21 June 1854 (gazetted
24 February 1857). The first 62 crosses were presented by
Queen Victoria in Hyde Park, London, on 26 June 1857.
 The Victoria Cross is worn before all other decorations, on
the left breast, and consists of a cross-pattée of bronze, 3.8cm
in diameter, with the royal crown surmounted by a lion in the
centre, and beneath there is the inscription *For Valour.* In July
2015 the tax-free annuity given to holders of the VC,
irrespective of need or other conditions, was increased to
£10,000. At the same time, further annual increases to the
annuity were linked to the CPI rate of inflation. In 1911, the
right to receive the cross was extended to Indian soldiers, and
in 1920 to matrons, sisters and nurses, the staff of the nursing
services and other services pertaining to hospitals and nursing,
and to civilians of either sex regularly or temporarily under the
orders, direction or supervision of the naval, military, or air
forces of the crown.

SURVIVING RECIPIENTS OF THE VICTORIA CROSS
as at 31 August 2018

Apiata, *Cpl.* B. H., VC (New Zealand Special Air Service)
2004 *Afghanistan*

Beharry, *LSgt* J. G., VC (Princess of Wales's Royal Regiment)
2005 *Iraq*

Cruickshank, *Flt Lt.* J. A., VC (RAFVR)
1944 *World War*

Donaldson, *Cpl.* M. G. S., VC (Australian Special Air Service)
2008 *Afghanistan*

Keighran, *Cpl.* D. A., VC (Royal Australian Regiment)
2012 *Afghanistan*

Leakey, *Lance Cpl.* J. M., VC (Parachute Regiment)
2015 *Afghanistan*

Payne, *WO* K., VC, DSC (USA) (Australian Army Training
Team)
1969 *Vietnam*

Rambahadur Limbu, *Capt.,* VC, MVO (10th Princess Mary's
Gurkha Rifles)
1965 *Sarawak*

Roberts-Smith, *Cpl.* B., VC (Australian Special Air Service)
2010 *Afghanistan*

THE GEORGE CROSS (1940)

FOR GALLANTRY

GC

Ribbon, Dark blue, threaded through a bar adorned with
laurel leaves
Instituted 24 September 1940 (with amendments,
3 November 1942)

The George Cross is worn before all other decorations (except
the VC) on the left breast (when worn by a woman it may be
worn on the left shoulder from a ribbon of the same width and
colour fashioned into a bow). It consists of a plain silver cross
with four equal limbs, the cross having in the centre a circular
medallion bearing a design showing St George and the
Dragon. The inscription *For Gallantry* appears round the
medallion and in the angle of each limb of the cross is the royal
cypher 'G VI' forming a circle concentric with the medallion.
The reverse is plain and bears the name of the recipient and the
date of the award. The cross is suspended by a ring from a bar
adorned with laurel leaves on dark blue ribbon 3.8cm wide.

The cross is intended primarily for civilians; awards to the
fighting services are confined to actions for which purely
military honours are not normally granted. It is awarded only
for acts of the greatest heroism or of the most conspicuous
courage in circumstances of extreme danger. In July 2015 the
tax-free annuity given to holders of the GC, irrespective of
need or other conditions, was increased to £10,000. At the
same time, further annual increases to the annuity were linked
to the CPI rate of inflation. The cross has twice been awarded
collectively rather than to an individual: to the island of Malta
(1942) and the Royal Ulster Constabulary (1999).

In October 1971 all surviving holders of the Albert Medal
and the Edward Medal exchanged those decorations for the
George Cross.

SURVIVING RECIPIENTS OF THE GEORGE CROSS
as at 31 August 2018

If the recipient originally received the Albert Medal (AM) or
the Edward Medal (EM), this is indicated by the initials in
parentheses.

Bamford, J., GC, 1952
Beaton, J., GC, CVO, 1974
Croucher, *Lance Cpl.* M., GC, 2008
Finney, C., GC, 2003
Flintoff, H. H., GC (EM), 1944
Gledhill, A. J., GC, 1967
Haberfield, *CSgt.* K. H., GC, 2005
Hughes, *WO2* K. S., GC, 2010
Johnson, *WO1* (*SSM*) B., GC, 1990
Lowe, A. R., GC (AM), 1949
Norton, *Maj.* P. A., GC, 2006
Pratt, M. K., GC, 1978
Purves, Mrs M., GC (AM), 1949
Raweng, Awang anak, GC, 1951
Shephard, S. J., GC, 2014
Stevens, H. W., GC, 1958
Troulan, D., GC, QGM, 2017
Walker, C., GC, 1972

THE ELIZABETH CROSS (2009)

EC

Instituted 1 July 2009

The Elizabeth Cross consists of a silver cross with a laurel
wreath passing between the arms, which bear the floral
symbols of England (rose), Scotland (thistle), Ireland
(shamrock) and Wales (daffodil). The centre of the cross bears
the royal cypher and the reverse is inscribed with the name of
the person for whom it is in honour. The cross is accompanied
by a memorial scroll and a miniature.

The cross was created to commemorate UK armed forces
personnel who have died on operations or as a result of an act
of terrorism. It may be granted to and worn by the next of kin
of any eligible personnel who died from 1 January 1948 to
date. It offers the wearer no precedence. Those that are eligible
include the next of kin of personnel who died while serving
on a medal earning operation, as a result of an act of terrorism,
or on a non-medal earning operation where death was caused
by the inherent high risk of the task.

The Elizabeth Cross is not intended as a posthumous medal
for the fallen but as an emblem of national recognition of the
loss and sacrifice made by the personnel and their families.

CHIEFS OF CLANS IN SCOTLAND

Only chiefs of whole Names or Clans are included, except certain special instances (marked *) who, though not chiefs of a whole Name, were or are for some reason (eg the Macdonald forfeiture) independent. Under decision (*Campbell-Gray*, 1950) that a bearer of a 'double or triple-barrelled' surname cannot be held chief of a part of such, several others cannot be included in the list at present.

THE ROYAL HOUSE: HM The Queen

AGNEW: Sir Crispin Agnew of Lochnaw, Bt., QC
ANSTRUTHER: Tobias Anstruther of Anstruther and Balcaskie
ARBUTHNOTT: Viscount of Arbuthnott
BANNERMAN: Sir David Bannerman of Elsick, Bt.
BARCLAY: Peter C. Barclay of Towie Barclay and of that Ilk
BORTHWICK: Lord Borthwick
BOYLE: Earl of Glasgow
BRODIE: Alexander Brodie of Brodie
BROUN OF COLSTOUN: Sir Wayne Broun of Colstoun, Bt.
BRUCE: Earl of Elgin and Kincardine, KT
BUCHAN: Charles Buchan of Auchmacoy
BURNETT: James C. A. Burnett of Leys
CAMERON: Donald Cameron of Lochiel, CVO
CAMPBELL: Duke of Argyll
CARMICHAEL: Richard Carmichael of Carmichael
CARNEGIE: Duke of Fife
CATHCART: Earl Cathcart
CHARTERIS: Earl of Wemyss and March
CLAN CHATTAN: K. Mackintosh of Clan Chattan
CHISHOLM: Hamish Chisholm of Chisholm (*The Chisholm*)
COCHRANE: Earl of Dundonald
COLQUHOUN: Sir Malcolm Rory Colquhoun of Luss, Bt.
CRANSTOUN: David Cranstoun of that Ilk
CUMMING: Sir Alastair Cumming of Altyre, Bt.
DARROCH: Duncan Darroch of Gourock
DAVIDSON OF DAVIDSTON: Grant Davidson of Davidston
DEWAR: Michael Dewar of that Ilk and Vogrie
DRUMMOND: Earl of Perth
DUNBAR: Sir James Dunbar of Mochrum, Bt.
DUNDAS: David Dundas of Dundas
DURIE: Andrew Durie of Durie, CBE
ELIOTT: Mrs Margaret Eliott of Redheugh
ERSKINE: Earl of Mar and Kellie
FARQUHARSON: Capt. Alwyne Farquharson of Invercauld, MC
FERGUSSON: Sir Charles Fergusson of Kilkerran, Bt.
FORBES: Lord Forbes
FORSYTH: Alistair Forsyth of that Ilk
FRASER: Lady Saltoun
*FRASER (OF LOVAT): Lord Lovat
GAYRE: Reinold Gayre of Gayre and Nigg
GORDON: Marquess of Huntly
GRAHAM: Duke of Montrose
GRANT: Lord Strathspey
GUNN: Iain Gunn of Gunn
GUTHRIE: Alexander Guthrie of Guthrie
HAIG: Earl Haig
HALDANE: Martin Haldane of Gleneagles
HANNAY: David Hannay of Kirkdale and of that Ilk
HAY: Earl of Erroll

HENDERSON: Alistair Henderson of Fordell
HUNTER: Pauline Hunter of Hunterston
IRVINE OF DRUM: David Irvine of Drum
JARDINE: Sir William Jardine of Applegirth, Bt.
JOHNSTONE: Earl of Annandale and Hartfell
KEITH: Earl of Kintore
KENNEDY: Marquess of Ailsa
KERR: Marquess of Lothian, PC
KINCAID: Madam Arabella Kincaid of Kincaid
LAMONT: Revd Peter Lamont of that Ilk
LEASK: Jonathan Leask of that Ilk
LENNOX: Edward Lennox of that Ilk
LESLIE: Earl of Rothes
LINDSAY: Earl of Crawford and Balcarres, KT, GCVO, PC
LIVINGSTONE (or MACLEA): Niall Livingstone of the Bachuil
LOCKHART: Ranald Lockhart of the Lee
LUMSDEN: Gillem Lumsden of that Ilk and Blanerne
MACALESTER: William St J. McAlester of Loup and Kennox
MACARTHUR; John MacArthur of that Ilk
MCBAIN: James H. McBain of McBain
MACDONALD: Lord Macdonald (*The Macdonald of Macdonald*)
*MACDONALD OF CLANRANALD: Ranald Macdonald of Clanranald
*MACDONALD OF KEPPOCH: Ranald MacDonald of Keppoch
*MACDONALD OF SLEAT (CLAN HUSTEAIN): Sir Ian Macdonald of Sleat, Bt.
*MACDONELL OF GLENGARRY: Ranald MacDonell of Glengarry
MACDOUGALL: Morag MacDougall of MacDougall
MACDOWALL: Fergus Macdowall of Garthland
MACGREGOR: Sir Malcolm MacGregor of MacGregor, Bt.
MACINTYRE: Donald MacIntyre of Glenoe
MACKAY: Lord Reay
MACKENZIE: Earl of Cromartie
MACKINNON: Anne Mackinnon of Mackinnon
MACKINTOSH: John Mackintosh of Mackintosh (*The Mackintosh of Mackintosh*)
MACLACHLAN: Euan MacLachlan of MacLachlan
MACLAINE: Lorne Maclaine of Lochbuie
MACLAREN: Donald MacLaren of MacLaren and Achleskine
MACLEAN: Hon. Sir Lachlan Maclean of Duart, Bt., CVO
MACLENNAN: Ruaraidh MacLennan of MacLennan
MACLEOD: Hugh MacLeod of MacLeod
MACMILLAN: George MacMillan of MacMillan
MACNAB: James W. A. Macnab of Macnab (*The Macnab*)
MACNAGHTEN: Sir Malcolm Macnaghten of Macnaghten and Dundarave, Bt.
MACNEACAIL: John Macneacail of Macneacail and Scorrybreac
MACNEIL OF BARRA: Rory Macneil of Barra (*The Macneil of Barra*)
MACPHERSON: Hon. Sir William Macpherson of Cluny, TD
MACTAVISH: Steven MacTavish of Dunardry
MACTHOMAS: Andrew MacThomas of Finegand
MAITLAND: Earl of Lauderdale
MAKGILL: Viscount of Oxfuird
MALCOLM (MACCALLUM): Robin N. L. Malcolm of Poltalloch

MAR: Countess of Mar
MARJORIBANKS: Andrew Marjoribanks of that Ilk
MATHESON: Sir Alexander Matheson of Matheson, Bt.
MENZIES: David Menzies of Menzies
MOFFAT: Madam Moffat of that Ilk
MONCREIFFE: Hon. Peregrine Moncreiffe of that Ilk
MONTGOMERIE: Earl of Eglinton and Winton
MORRISON: Dr John Ruairidh Morrison of Ruchdi
MUNRO: Hector Munro of Foulis
MURRAY: Duke of Atholl
NESBITT (or NISBET): Mark Nesbitt of that Ilk
OGILVY: Earl of Airlie, KT, GCVO, PC
OLIPHANT: Richard Oliphant of that Ilk
RAMSAY: Earl of Dalhousie
RIDDELL: Sir Walter Riddell of Riddell, Bt.
ROBERTSON: Alexander Robertson of Struan *(Struan-Robertson)*
ROLLO: Lord Rollo

ROSS: David Ross of that Ilk and Balnagowan
RUTHVEN: Earl of Gowrie, PC
SCOTT: Duke of Buccleuch and Queensberry, KT, KBE
SCRYMGEOUR: Earl of Dundee
SEMPILL: Lord Sempill
SHAW: Iain Shaw of Tordarroch
SINCLAIR: Earl of Caithness, PC
SKENE: Dugald Skene of Skene
STIRLING: Fraser Stirling of Cader
STRANGE: Maj. Timothy Strange of Balcaskie
SUTHERLAND: Countess of Sutherland
SWINTON: John Swinton of that Ilk
TROTTER: Alexander Trotter of Mortonhall, CVO
URQUHART: Wilkins F. Urquhart of Urquhart
WALLACE: Andrew Wallace of that Ilk
WEDDERBURN: The Master of Dundee
WEMYSS: Michael Wemyss of that Ilk

THE PRIVY COUNCIL

The sovereign in council, or Privy Council, was the chief source of executive power until the system of cabinet government developed in the 18th century. Now the Privy Council's main functions are to advise the sovereign and to exercise its own statutory responsibilities independent of the sovereign in council.

Membership of the Privy Council is automatic upon appointment to certain government and judicial positions in the UK, eg cabinet ministers must be Privy Counsellors and are sworn in on first assuming office. Membership is also accorded by the Queen to eminent people in the UK and independent countries of the Commonwealth of which she is Queen, on the recommendation of the prime minister. Membership of the council is retained for life, except for very occasional removals.

The administrative functions of the Privy Council are carried out by the Privy Council Office under the direction of the president of the council, who is always a member of the cabinet. (*see also* Parliament)

President of the Council, Rt. Hon. Andrea Leadsom, MP
Clerk of the Council, Richard Tilbrook

Style The Right (or Rt.) Hon._
Envelope, The Right (or Rt.) Hon. F_ S_. *Letter,* Dear Mr/Miss/Mrs S_. *Spoken,* Mr/Miss/Mrs S_

It is incorrect to use the letters PC after the name in conjunction with the prefix The Right Hon., unless the Privy Counsellor is a peer below the rank of Marquess and so is styled The Right Hon. because of his/her rank.

MEMBERS *as at 31 August 2018*

HRH The Duke of Edinburgh, 1951
HRH The Prince of Wales, 1977
HRH The Duke of Cambridge, 2016
HRH The Duchess of Cornwall, 2016

Abbott, Diane, 2017
Abernethy, *Hon.* Lord (Alastair Cameron), 2005
Adonis, Lord, 2009
Aikens, Sir Richard, 2008
Ainsworth, Robert, 2005
Airlie, Earl of, 1984
Alebua, Ezekiel, 1988
Alexander, Sir Danny, 2010
Alexander, Douglas, 2005
Amos, Baroness, 2003
Anderson of Swansea, Lord, 2000
Anelay of St Johns, Baroness, 2009
Angiolini, Dame Elish, 2006
Anthony, Douglas, 1971
Arbuthnot of Edrom, Lord, 1998
Arden, Dame Mary, 2000
Armstrong of Hill Top, Baroness, 1999
Arthur, *Hon.* Owen, 1995
Ashcroft, Lord, 2012
Ashdown of Norton-sub-Hamdon, Lord, 1989
Ashton of Upholland, Baroness, 2006
Asplin, Dame Sarah, 2017
Astor of Hever, Lord, 2015
Atkins, Sir Robert, 1995
Auld, Sir Robin, 1995
Baker, Sir Jonathan, 2018
Baker, Norman, 2014
Baker, Sir Thomas, 2002
Baker of Dorking, Lord, 1984
Baldry, Sir Tony, 2013
Balls, Ed, 2007
Barker of Battle, Lord, 2012
Barron, Sir Kevin, 2001
Barrow, Dean, 2016
Barwell, Gavin, 2017
Bassam of Brighton, Lord, 2009

Bates, Lord, 2015
Battle, John, 2002
Bean, Sir David, 2014
Beatson, Sir Jack, 2013
Beckett, Dame Margaret, 1993
Beith, Lord, 1992
Beldam, Sir Roy, 1989
Benn, Hilary, 2003
Benyon, Richard, 2017
Bercow, John, 2009
Birch, Sir William, 1992
Black of Derwent, Lady, 2010
Blackford, Ian, 2017
Blackstone, Baroness, 2001
Blair, Anthony, 1994
Blanchard, Peter, 1998
Blears, Hazel, 2005
Blencathra, Lord, 1995
Blunkett, Lord, 1997
Boateng, Lord, 1999
Bolger, James, 1991
Bonomy, *Hon.* Lord (Iain Bonomy), 2010
Boothroyd, Baroness, 1992
Bottomley of Nettlestone, Baroness, 1992
Boyd of Duncansby, Lord, 2000
Brabazon of Tara, Lord, 2013
Bracadale, *Hon.* Lord (Alastair Campbell), 2013
Bradley, Karen, 2016
Bradley, Lord, 2001
Bradshaw, Ben, 2009
Brake, Thomas, 2011
Briggs of Westbourne, Lord, 2013
Brodie, *Hon.* Lord (Philip Brodie), 2013
Brokenshire, James, 2015
Brooke, Dame Annette, 2014
Brooke of Sutton Mandeville, Lord, 1988
Brown, Gordon, 1996
Brown, Nicholas, 1997
Brown, Sir Stephen, 1983

Brown of Eaton-under-Heywood, Lord, 1992
Browne of Ladyton, Lord, 2005
Bruce of Bennachie, Lord, 2006
Burnett of Maldon, Lord, 2014
Burnham, Andy, 2007
Burns, Sir Simon, 2011
Burnton, Sir Stanley, 2008
Burstow, Paul, 2012
Burt, Alistair, 2013
Butler of Brockwell, Lord, 2004
Butler-Sloss, Baroness, 1988
Buxton, Sir Richard, 1997
Byers, Stephen, 1998
Byrne, Liam, 2008
Byron, Sir Dennis, 2004
Cable, Sir Vincent, 2010
Caborn, Richard, 1999
Cairns, Alun, 2016
Caithness, Earl of, 1990
Cameron, David, 2005
Cameron of Lochbroom, Lord, 1984
Camoys, Lord, 1997
Campbell, Alan, 2014
Campbell, Sir William, 1999
Campbell of Pittenweem, Lord, 1999
Canterbury, Archbishop of, 2013
Carey of Clifton, Lord, 1991
Carloway, *Hon.* Lord (Colin Sutherland), 2008
Carmichael, Alistair, 2010
Carnwath of Notting Hill, Lord, 2002
Carswell, Lord, 1993
Chadwick, Sir John, 1997
Chakrabarti, Baroness, 2018
Chalfont, Lord, 1964
Chalker of Wallasey, Baroness, 1987
Chan, Sir Julius, 1981
Chartres, Rt. Revd Lord, 1995
Chilcot, Sir John, 2004
Christie, Perry, 2004
Clark, Greg, 2010
Clark, Helen, 1990
Clark of Calton, Baroness, 2013

Clark of Windermere, Lord, 1997
Clarke, Charles, 2001
Clarke, Sir Christopher, 2013
Clarke, Kenneth, 1984
Clarke, *Hon.* Lord (Matthew Clarke), 2008
Clarke, Thomas, 1997
Clarke of Stone-Cum-Ebony, Lord, 1998
Clegg, Sir Nicholas, 2008
Clinton-Davis, Lord, 1998
Clwyd, Ann, 2004
Coghlin, Sir Patrick, 2009
Collins of Mapesbury, Lord, 2007
Cooper, Yvette, 2007
Cope of Berkeley, Lord, 1988
Corbyn, Jeremy, 2015
Corston, Baroness, 2003
Cosgrove, *Hon.* Lady (Hazel Cosgrove), 2003
Coulson, Sir Peter, 2018
Cox, Geoffrey, 2018
Crabb, Stephen, 2014
Crawford and Balcarres, Earl of, 1972
Creech, *Hon.* Wyatt, 1999
Cullen of Whitekirk, Lord, 1997
Cunningham of Felling, Lord, 1993
Curry, David, 1996
Darling of Roulanish, Lord, 1997
Darzi of Denham, Lord, 2009
Davey, Sir Edward, 2012
Davidson, Ruth, 2016
Davies, Denzil, 1978
Davies, Dame Nicola, 2018
Davies, Ronald, 1997
Davies of Oldham, Lord, 2006
Davis, David, 1997
Davis, Sir Nigel, 2011
Davis, Terence, 1999
de la Bastide, Michael, 2004
Deben, Lord, 1985
Deeny, Sir Donnell, 2017
Denham, John, 2000
Denham, Lord, 1981
Dholakia, Lord, 2010
Dobson, Frank, 1997
Dodds, Nigel, 2010
Donaldson, Sir Jeffrey, 2007
Dorrell, Stephen, 1994
Dorrian, *Hon.* Lady (Leona Dorrian), 2013
Douglas, *Dr* Denzil, 2011
Drayson, Lord, 2008
Drummond Young, *Hon.* Lord (James Drummond Young), 2013
D'Souza, Baroness, 2009
Duncan, Sir Alan, 2010
Duncan Smith, Iain, 2001
Dyson, Lord, 2001
Eassie, *Hon.* Lord (Ronald Mackay), 2006
East, Paul, 1998
Eden of Winton, Lord, 1972
Edward, Sir David, 2005
Eggar, Timothy, 1995
Eichelbaum, Sir Thomas, 1989
Elias, Sir Patrick, 2009
Elias, *Hon.* Dame Sian, 1999
Elis-Thomas, Lord, 2004
Ellwood, Tobias, 2017

Emslie, *Hon.* Lord (George Emslie), 2011
Esquivel, Manuel, 1986
Etherton, Sir Terence, 2008
Evans, Sir Anthony, 1992
Evans of Bowes Park, Baroness, 2016
Evennett, David, 2015
Falconer of Thoroton, Lord, 2003
Fallon, Sir Michael, 2012
Featherstone, Baroness, 2014
Feldman of Elstree, Lord, 2015
Fellowes, Lord, 1990
Field, Frank, 1997
Field, Mark, 2015
Flaux, Sir Julian, 2017
Flint, Caroline, 2008
Floyd, Sir Christopher, 2013
Forsyth of Drumlean, Lord, 1995
Foster, Arlene, 2016
Foster of Bath, Lord, 2010
Foster of Bishop Auckland, Lord, 1993
Foulkes of Cumnock, Lord, 2002
Fowler, Lord, 1979
Fox, Liam, 2010
Francois, Mark, 2010
Freedman, Sir Lawrence, 2009
Freeman, Lord, 1993
Freud, Lord, 2015
Fulford, Sir Adrian, 2013
Gage, Sir William, 2004
Garden of Frognal, Baroness, 2015
Garel-Jones, Lord, 1992
Garnier, Lord, 2015
Gauke, David, 2016
Geidt, Lord, 2007
George, Bruce, 2000
Gibb, Nicolas, 2016
Gibson, Sir Peter, 1993
Gill, *Hon.* Lord (Brian Gill), 2002
Gillan, Dame Cheryl, DBE, 2010
Gillen, Sir John, 2014
Girvan, Sir (Frederick) Paul, 2007
Glennie, *Hon.* Lord (Angus Glennie), 2016
Gloster, Dame Elizabeth, 2013
Goldring, Sir John, 2008
Goldsmith, Lord, 2002
Goodlad, Lord, 1992
Goodwill, Robert, 2018
Gove, Michael, 2010
Gowrie, Earl of, 1984
Graham, Sir Douglas, 1998
Graham of Edmonton, Lord, 1998
Grayling, Chris, 2010
Green, Damian, 2012
Green, Sir Nicholas, 2018
Greening, Justine, 2011
Grieve, Dominic, 2010
Grocott, Lord, 2002
Gross, Sir Peter, 2010
Gummer, Ben, 2016
Habgood, Lord, 1983
Haddon-Cave, Sir Charles, 2018
Hague of Richmond, Lord, 1995
Hailsham, Viscount, 1992
Hain, Lord, 2001
Hale of Richmond, Baroness, 1999
Halfon, Robert, 2015
Hallett, Dame Heather, 2005

Hamblen, Sir Nicholas, 2016
Hamilton, *Hon.* Lord (Arthur Hamilton), 2002
Hamilton of Epsom, Lord, 1991
Hammond, Philip, 2010
Hancock, Matthew, 2014
Hands, Gregory, 2014
Hanley, Sir Jeremy, 1994
Hanson, David, 2007
Hardie, Lord, 1997
Hardie Boys, Sir Michael, 1989
Harman, Harriet, 1997
Harper, Mark, 2015
Haselhurst, Lord, 1999
Hattersley, Lord, 1975
Hayes, John, 2013
Hayman, Baroness, 2000
Heald, Sir Oliver, 2016
Healey, John, 2008
Heath, David, 2015
Heathcoat-Amory, David, 1996
Henderson, Sir Launcelot, 2016
Hendry, Charles, 2015
Henley, Lord, 2013
Henry, John, 1996
Herbert, Nick, 2010
Heseltine, Lord, 1979
Heseltine, Sir William, 1986
Hesketh, Lord, 1991
Hewitt, Patricia, 2001
Hickinbottom, Sir Gary, 2017
Higgins, Lord, 1979
Higgins, Sir Malachy, 2007
Hill, Keith, 2003
Hill of Oareford, Lord, 2013
Hinds, Damian, 2018
Hodge, Dame Margaret, 2003
Hodge, Lord, 2013
Hoffmann, Lord, 1992
Hollis of Heigham, Baroness, 1999
Holroyde, Sir Timothy, 2018
Hoon, Geoffrey, 1999
Hooper, Sir Anthony, 2004
Hope of Craighead, Lord, 1989
Hope of Thornes, Lord, 1991
Hordern, Sir Peter, 1993
Howard of Lympne, Lord, 1990
Howarth, George, 2005
Howarth of Newport, Lord, 2000
Howe, Earl, 2013
Howell of Guildford, Lord, 1979
Howells, Kim, 2009
Hoyle, Sir Lindsay, 2013
Hughes, Sir Simon, 2010
Hughes of Ombersley, Lord, 2006
Hughes of Stretford, Baroness, 2004
Hunt, Jeremy, 2010
Hunt, Jonathon, 1989
Hunt of Kings Heath, Lord, 2009
Hunt of Wirral, Lord, 1990
Hurd, Nicholas, 2017
Hurd of Westwell, Lord, 1982
Hutchison, Sir Michael, 1995
Hutton, Lord, 1988
Hutton of Furness, Lord, 2001
Inge, Lord, 2004
Ingraham, Hubert, 1993
Ingram, Adam, 1999
Irvine of Lairg, Lord, 1997
Irwin, Sir Stephen, 2016

Jack, Michael, 1997
Jackson, Sir Peter, 2018
Jackson, Sir Rupert, 2008
Jacob, Sir Robert, 2004
Jacobs, Francis, 2005
Janvrin, Lord, 1998
Javid, Sajid, 2014
Jay of Paddington, Baroness, 1998
Johnson, Alan, 2003
Johnson, Boris, 2016
Jones, Carwyn, 2010
Jones, David, 2012
Jones, Kevan, 2018
Jones, Lord, 1999
Jopling, Lord, 1979
Judge, Lord, 1996
Jugnauth, Sir Aneerood, 1987
Kakkar, Lord, 2014
Kay, Sir Maurice, 2004
Keen of Elie, Lord, 2017
Keene, Sir David, 2000
Keith, Sir Kenneth, 1998
Kelly, Ruth, 2004
Kennedy, Jane, 2003
Kennedy, Sir Paul, 1992
Kerr of Tonaghmore, Lord, 2004
Khan, Sadiq, 2009
King, Dame Eleanor, 2014
King of Bridgwater, Lord, 1979
Kingarth, Hon. Lord (Derek Emslie), 2006
Kinnock, Lord, 1983
Kitchin, Sir David, 2011
Knight, Sir Gregory, 1995
Knight of Weymouth, Lord, 2008
Kramer, Baroness, 2014
Laing, Dame Eleanor, 2017
Lamb, Norman, 2014
Laming, Lord, 2014
Lammy, David, 2008
Lamont of Lerwick, Lord, 1986
Lancaster, Mark, 2017
Lang of Monkton, Lord, 1990
Lansley, Lord, 2010
Latasi, Sir Kamuta, 1996
Latham, Sir David, 2000
Laws, David, 2010
Laws, Sir John, 1999
Lawson of Blaby, Lord, 1981
Leadsom, Andrea, 2016
Leggatt, Sir Andrew, 1990
Leggatt, Sir George, 2018
Letwin, Sir Oliver, 2002
Leveson, Sir Brian, 2006
Lewis, Brandon, 2016
Lewis, Dr Julian, 2015
Lewison, Sir Kim, 2011
Liddell of Coatdyke, Baroness, 1998
Lidington, David, 2010
Lilley, Lord, 1990
Lindblom, Sir Keith, 2015
Llewellyn of Steep, Lord, 2015
Lloyd, Sir Peter, 1994
Lloyd, Sir Timothy, 2005
Lloyd of Berwick, Lord, 1984
Lloyd-Jones, Lord, 2012
Llwyd, Elfyn, 2011
Longmore, Sir Andrew, 2001
Lothian, Marquess of, 1996
Luce, Lord, 1986

Lyne, Sir Roderic, 2009
McAvoy, Lord, 2003
McCartney, Sir Ian, 1999
McCollum, Sir Liam, 1997
McCombe, Sir Richard, 2012
McConnell of Glenscorrodale, Lord, 2001
MacDermott, Sir John, 1987
McDonnell, John, 2016
Macdonald of Tradeston, Lord, 1999
McFadden, Patrick, 2008
McFall of Alcluith, Lord, 2004
McFarlane, Sir Andrew, 2011
MacGregor of Pulham Market, Lord, 1985
McGuire, Dame Anne, 2008
Macintosh, Kenneth, 2016
Mackay, Andrew, 1998
Mackay of Clashfern, Lord, 1979
McKinnon, Sir Donald, 1992
Maclean, Hon. Lord (Ranald MacLean), 2001
McLeish, Henry, 2000
Maclennan of Rogart, Lord, 1997
McLoughlin, Sir Patrick, 2005
McNally, Lord, 2005
McNulty, Anthony, 2007
Mactaggart, Fiona, 2015
Macur, Dame Julia, 2013
McVey, Esther, 2014
Major, Sir John, 1987
Malcolm, Hon. Lord (Colin Campbell), 2015
Males, Sir Stephen, 2018
Malloch-Brown, Lord, 2007
Mance, Lord, 1999
Mandelson, Lord, 1998
Marnoch, Hon. Lord (Michael Marnoch), 2001
Marwick, Tricia, 2012
Mates, Michael, 2004
Maude of Horsham, Lord, 1992
Mawhinney, Lord, 1994
May, Sir Anthony, 1998
May, Theresa, 2003
Mellor, David, 1990
Menzies, Hon. Lord (Duncan Menzies), 2012
Michael, Alun, 1998
Milburn, Alan, 1998
Miliband, David, 2005
Miliband, Ed, 2007
Miller, Maria, 2012
Millett, Lord, 1994
Milton, Anne, 2015
Mitchell, Andrew, 2010
Mitchell, Sir James, 1985
Mitchell, Dr Keith, 2004
Moore, Michael, 1990
Moore, Michael, 2010
Moore of Lower Marsh, Lord, 1986
Moore-Bick, Sir Martin, 2005
Mordaunt, Penny, 2017
Morgan, Sir Declan, 2009
Morgan, Nicky, 2014
Morris of Aberavon, Lord, 1970
Morris of Yardley, Baroness, 1999
Morritt, Sir Robert, 1994
Moses, Sir Alan, 2005
Moylan, Sir Andrew, 2017

Mulholland, Frank, 2011
Mullally, Rt. Revd Dame Sarah, 2018
Mummery, Sir John, 1996
Munby, Sir James, 2009
Mundell, David, 2010
Murphy, James, 2008
Murphy of Torfaen, Lord, 1999
Musa, Wilbert, 2005
Namaliu, Sir Rabbie, 1989
Naseby, Lord, 1994
Needham, Sir Richard, 1994
Neuberger of Abbotsbury, Lord, 2004
Neville-Jones, Baroness, 2010
Newby, Lord, 2014
Newey, Sir Guy, 2018
Nicholls of Birkenhead, Lord, 1995
Nicholson, Sir Michael, 1995
Nimmo Smith, Hon. Lord (William Nimmo Smith), 2005
Nokes, Caroline, 2018
Northover, Baroness, 2015
Nott, Sir John, 1979
O'Brien, Mike, 2009
O'Brien, Sir Stephen, 2013
Oppenheim-Barnes, Baroness, 1979
Osborne, George, 2010
Osborne, Hon. Lord (Kenneth Osborne), 2001
Ottaway, Sir Richard, 2013
Otton, Sir Philip, 1995
Owen, Lord, 1976
Paeniu, Bikenibeu, 1991
Paice, Sir James, 2010
Palmer, Sir Geoffrey, 1986
Paraskeva, Dame Janet, 2010
Parker, Sir Jonathan, 2000
Patel, Priti, 2015
Paterson, Owen, 2010
Paton, Hon. Lady (Ann Paton), 2007
Patten, Lord, 1990
Patten, Sir Nicholas, 2009
Patten of Barnes, Lord, 1989
Patterson, Percival, 1993
Pattie, Sir Geoffrey, 1987
Paul, Lord, 2009
Peel, Earl, 2006
Pendry, Lord, 2000
Penning, Sir Mike, 2014
Penrose, Hon. Lord (George Penrose), 2000
Perry, Claire, 2018
Peters, Winston, 1998
Philip, Hon. Lord (Alexander Philip), 2005
Phillips of Worth Matravers, Lord, 1995
Pickles, Lord, 2010
Pill, Sir Malcolm, 1995
Portillo, Michael, 1992
Potter, Sir Mark, 1996
Prashar, Baroness, 2009
Primarolo, Baroness, 2002
Puapua, Sir Tomasi, 1982
Purnell, James, 2007
Quin, Baroness, 1998
Raab, Dominic, 2018
Radice, Lord, 1999
Rafferty, Dame Anne, 2011
Ramsden, James, 1963
Randall of Uxbridge, Lord, 2010

Raynsford, Nick, 2001
Redwood, John, 1993
Reed, Lord, 2008
Reid, Sir George, 2004
Reid of Cardowan, Lord, 1998
Renton of Mount Harry, Lord, 1989
Richards, Sir David, 2016
Richards, Sir Stephen, 2005
Riddell, Peter, 2010
Rifkind, Sir Malcolm, 1986
Rimer, Sir Colin, 2007
Rix, Sir Bernard, 2000
Robathan, Lord, 2010
Robertson, Angus, 2015
Robertson, Sir Hugh, 2012
Robertson of Port Ellen, Lord, 1997
Robinson, Peter, 2007
Roch, Sir John, 1993
Rodgers of Quarry Bank, Lord, 1975
Rooker, Lord, 1999
Rose, Sir Christopher, 1992
Rose, Dame Vivien, 2018
Ross, *Hon.* Lord (Donald MacArthur), 1985
Royall of Blaisdon, Baroness, 2008
Rudd, Amber, 2015
Ruddock, Dame Joan, 2010
Ryan, Joan, 2007
Ryder, Sir Ernest, 2013
Ryder of Wensum, Lord, 1990
Sainsbury, Sir Timothy, 1992
Sales, Sir Philip, 2014
Salisbury, Marquess of, 1994
Salmond, Alex, 2007
Sandiford, Lloyd Erskine, 1989
Saville of Newdigate, Lord, 1994
Sawyer, Dame Joan, 2004
Schiemann, Sir Konrad, 1995
Scotland of Asthal, Baroness, 2001
Scott of Foscote, Lord, 1991
Seaga, Edward, 1981
Sedley, Sir Stephen, 1999
Selkirk of Douglas, Lord, 1996
Shapps, Grant, 2010
Sharp, Dame Victoria, 2013
Sheil, Sir John, 2005
Sheldon, Lord, 1977
Shephard of Northwold, Baroness, 1992
Shipley, Jennifer, 1998
Short, Clare, 1997
Shutt of Greetland, Lord, 2009
Simler, Dame Ingrid, 2018
Simmonds, Sir Kennedy, 1984
Simmonds, Mark, 2014
Simon, Sir Peregrine, 2015
Simpson, Keith, 2015

Sinclair, Ian, 1977
Singh, Sir Rabinder, 2018
Slade, Sir Christopher, 1982
Smith, Andrew, 1997
Smith, *Hon.* Lady (Anne Smith), 2013
Smith, Jacqueline, 2003
Smith, Dame Janet, 2002
Smith, Julian, 2017
Smith of Basildon, Baroness, 2009
Smith of Finsbury, Lord, 1997
Soames, Sir Nicholas, 2011
Somare, Sir Michael, 1977
Sopoaga, Enele, 2018
Soubry, Anna, 2015
Spellar, John, 2001
Spelman, Dame Caroline, 2010
Spicer, Lord, 2013
Stanley, Sir John, 1984
Starmer, Sir Keir, 2017
Steel of Aikwood, Lord, 1977
Stephens, Sir Benjamin, 2017
Stowell of Beeston, Baroness, 2014
Strang, Gavin, 1997
Strathclyde, Lord, 1995
Straw, Jack, 1997
Stride, Melvyn, 2017
Stuart, Freundel, 2013
Stuart, Gisela, 2015
Stuart-Smith, Sir Murray, 1988
Stunell, Lord, 2012
Sturgeon, Nicola, 2014
Sullivan, Sir Jeremy, 2009
Sumption, Lord, 2011
Sutherland, *Hon.* Lord (Ranald Sutherland), 2000
Swayne, Sir Desmond, 2011
Swire, Sir Hugo, 2010
Symons of Vernham Dean, Baroness, 2001
Taylor of Bolton, Baroness, 1997
Taylor of Holbeach, Lord, 2014
Tebbit, Lord, 1981
Thirlwall, Dame Kathryn, 2017
Thomas, Edmund, 1996
Thomas of Cwmgiedd, Lord, 2003
Thornberry, Emily, 2017
Thorpe, Sir Matthew, 1995
Thurso, Viscount, 2014
Timms, Stephen, 2006
Tipping, Andrew, 1998
Tomlinson, Sir Stephen, 2010
Touhig, Lord, 2006
Treacy, Sir Colman, 2012
Trefgarne, Lord, 1989
Trimble, Lord, 1997
Trumpington, Baroness, 1992
Truss, Elizabeth, 2014

Tuckey, Sir Simon, 1998
Turnbull, Lord, 2016
Tyler, Lord, 2014
Tyrie, Lord, 2015
Ullswater, Viscount, 1994
Underhill, Sir Nicholas, 2013
Upton, Simon, 1999
Vadera, Baroness, 2009
Vaizey, Ed, 2016
Vaz, Keith, 2006
Villiers, Theresa, 2010
Vos, Sir Geoffrey, 2013
Waite, Sir John, 1993
Wakeham, Lord, 1983
Waldegrave of North Hill, Lord, 1990
Walker of Gestingthorpe, Lord, 1997
Wallace, Ben, 2017
Wallace of Saltaire, Lord, 2012
Wallace of Tankerness, Lord, 2000
Waller, Sir Mark, 1996
Ward, Sir Alan, 1995
Warner, Lord, 2006
Warsi, Baroness, 2010
Weatherup, Sir Ronald, 2016
Webb, Sir Steven, 2014
Weir, Sir Reginald, 2016
West of Spithead, Lord, 2010
Wheatley, *Hon.* Lord (John Wheatley), 2007
Wheeler, Sir John, 1993
Whittingdale, John, 2015
Whitty, Lord, 2005
Widdecombe, Ann, 1997
Wigley, Lord, 1997
Willetts, Lord, 2010
Williams of Crosby, Baroness, 1974
Williams of Elvel, Lord, 2013
Williams of Oystermouth, Lord, 2002
Williamson, Gavin, 2015
Willott, Jennifer, 2014
Wills, Lord, 2008
Wilson, Brian, 2003
Wilson, Sammy, 2017
Wilson of Culworth, Lord, 2005
Wingti, Paias, 1987
Winterton, Dame Rosie, 2006
Wolffe, James, 2016
Woodward, Shaun, 2007
Woolf, Lord, 1986
Wright, Jeremy, 2014
York, Archbishop of, 2005
Young, Edward, 2017
Young of Cookham, Lord, 1993
Young of Graffham, Lord, 1984
Zacca, Sir Edward, 1992

PRIVY COUNCIL OF NORTHERN IRELAND

The Privy Council of Northern Ireland had responsibilities in Northern Ireland similar to those of the Privy Council in Great Britain until the Northern Ireland Act 1974. Membership of the Privy Council of Northern Ireland is retained for life. Since the Northern Ireland Constitution Act 1973 no further appointments have been made. The post-nominal initials PC (NI) are used to differentiate its members from those of the Privy Council.

MEMBERS *as at August 2018*
Bailie, Robin, 1971
Dobson, John, 1969
Kilclooney, Lord, 1970

PARLIAMENT

The UK constitution is not contained in any single document but has evolved over time, formed by statute, common law and convention. A constitutional monarchy, the UK is governed by ministers of the crown in the name of the sovereign, who is head both of the state and of the government.

The organs of government are the legislature (parliament), the executive and the judiciary. The executive comprises HM government (the cabinet and other ministers), government departments and local authorities (*see* the Government, Public Bodies and Local Government). The judiciary (*see* Law Courts and Offices) pronounces on the law, both written and unwritten, interprets statutes and is responsible for the enforcement of the law; the judiciary is independent of both the legislature and the executive.

THE MONARCHY

The sovereign personifies the state and is, in law, an integral part of the legislature, head of the executive, head of the judiciary, commander-in-chief of all armed forces of the crown and supreme governor of the Church of England. In the Channel Islands and the Isle of Man, which are crown dependencies, the sovereign is represented by a lieutenant-governor. In the member states of the Commonwealth of which the sovereign is head of state, her representative is a governor-general; in UK overseas territories the sovereign is usually represented by a governor, who is responsible to the British government.

Although in practice the powers of the monarchy are now very limited, and restricted mainly to the advisory and ceremonial, there are important acts of government which require the participation of the sovereign. These include summoning, proroguing and dissolving parliament, giving royal assent to bills passed by parliament, appointing important office-holders, eg government ministers, judges, bishops and governors, conferring peerages, knighthoods and other honours, and granting pardon to a person wrongly convicted of a crime. The sovereign appoints the prime minister; by convention this office is held by the leader of the political party which enjoys, or can secure, a majority of votes in the House of Commons. In international affairs the sovereign, as head of state, has the power to declare war and make peace, to recognise foreign states and governments, to conclude treaties and to annex or cede territory. However, as the sovereign entrusts executive power to ministers of the crown and acts on the advice of her ministers, which she cannot ignore, royal prerogative powers are in practice exercised by ministers, who are responsible to parliament.

Ministerial responsibility does not diminish the sovereign's importance to the smooth working of government. She holds meetings of the Privy Council (*see* below), gives audiences to her ministers and other officials at home and overseas, receives accounts of cabinet decisions, reads dispatches and signs state papers; she must be informed and consulted on every aspect of national life; and she must show complete impartiality.

COUNSELLORS OF STATE

If the sovereign travels abroad for more than a few days or suffers from a temporary illness, it is necessary to appoint members of the royal family, known as counsellors of state, under letters patent to carry out the chief functions of the monarch, including the holding of Privy Councils and giving royal assent to acts passed by parliament. The normal procedure is to appoint two or more members of the royal family remaining in the UK from among the sovereign's spouse and the four adults next in succession, provided they have reached the age of 21. There are currently four members of the royal family from which the counsellors of state are appointed: the Prince of Wales, the Duke of Cambridge, Prince Harry and the Duke of York.

In the event of the sovereign on accession being under the age of 18 years, or by infirmity of mind or body, rendered incapable of performing the royal functions, provision is made for a regency.

THE PRIVY COUNCIL

The sovereign in council, or Privy Council, was the chief source of executive power until the system of cabinet government developed. Its main function today is to advise the sovereign on the approval of various statutory functions and acts of the royal prerogative. These powers are exercised through orders in council and royal proclamations, approved by the Queen at meetings of the Privy Council. The council is also able to exercise a number of statutory duties without approval from the sovereign, including powers of supervision over the registering bodies for the medical and allied professions. These duties are exercised through orders of council.

Although appointment as a privy counsellor is for life, only those who are currently government ministers are involved in the day-to-day business of the council. A full council is summoned only on the death of the sovereign or when the sovereign announces his or her intention to marry. (For a full list of privy counsellors, *see* the Privy Council section.)

There are a number of advisory Privy Council committees whose meetings the sovereign does not attend. Some are prerogative committees, such as those dealing with legislative matters submitted by the legislatures of the Channel Islands and the Isle of Man or with applications for charters of incorporation; and some are provided for by statute, eg those for the universities of Oxford and Cambridge and some Scottish universities.

Administrative work is carried out by the Privy Council Office under the direction of the Lord President of the Council, a cabinet minister.

JUDICIAL COMMITTEE OF THE PRIVY COUNCIL
Supreme Court Building, Parliament Square, London SW1P 3BD
T 020-7960 1500 **W** www.jcpc.uk

The Judicial Committee of the Privy Council is the court of final appeal from courts of the UK dependencies, courts of independent Commonwealth countries which have retained the right of appeal and courts of the Channel Islands and the Isle of Man. It also hears very occasional appeals from a number of ancient and ecclesiastical courts.

The committee is composed of privy counsellors who hold, or have held, high judicial office. Only three or five judges hear each case, and these are usually justices of the supreme court.

Chief Executive, Mark Ormerod

PARLIAMENT

Parliament is the supreme law-making authority and can legislate for the UK as a whole or for any parts of it separately (the Channel Islands and the Isle of Man are crown dependencies and not part of the UK). The main functions of parliament are to pass laws, to enable the government to raise taxes and to scrutinise government policy and administration, particularly proposals for expenditure. International treaties and agreements are customarily presented to parliament before ratification.

Parliament can trace its roots to two characteristics of Anglo-Saxon rule: the *witan* (a meeting of the king, nobles and advisors) and the *moot* (county meetings where local matters were discussed). However, it was the parliament that Simon de Montfort called in 1265 that is accepted as the forerunner to modern parliament, as it included non-noble representatives from counties, cities and towns alongside the nobility. The nucleus of early parliaments at the beginning of the 14th century were the officers of the king's household and the king's judges, joined by such ecclesiastical and lay magnates as the king might summon to form a prototype 'House of Lords', and occasionally by the knights of the shires, burgesses and proctors of the lower clergy. By the end of Edward III's reign a 'House of Commons' was beginning to appear; the first known Speaker was elected in 1377.

Parliamentary procedure is based on custom and precedent, partly formulated in the standing orders of both houses of parliament. Each house has the right to control its own internal proceedings and to commit for contempt. The system of debate in the two houses is similar; when a motion has been moved, the Speaker proposes the question as the subject of a debate. Members speak from wherever they have been sitting. Questions are decided by a vote on a simple majority. Draft legislation is introduced, in either house, as a bill. Bills can be introduced by a government minister or a private member, but in practice the majority of bills which become law are introduced by the government. To become law, a bill must be passed by each house (for parliamentary stages, *see* Parliamentary Information) and then sent to the sovereign for the royal assent, after which it becomes an act of parliament.

Proceedings of both houses are public, except on extremely rare occasions. The minutes (called *Votes and Proceedings,* in the Commons and *House of Lords Minutes of Proceedings* in the Lords) and the speeches *(The Official Report of Parliamentary Debates,* Hansard) are published daily. Proceedings are also recorded for transmission on radio and television and stored in the Parliamentary Recording Unit before transfer to the British Library Sound Archive. Television cameras have been allowed into the House of Lords since 1985 and into the House of Commons since 1989; committee meetings may also be televised.

The Fixed Term Parliament Act 2011 fixed the duration of a parliament at five years in normal circumstances, the term being reckoned from the date given on the writs for the new parliament. The term of a parliament has been prolonged by legislation in such rare circumstances as the two World Wars (31 January 1911 to 25 November 1918; 26 November 1935 to 15 June 1945). The life of a parliament is divided into sessions, usually of one year in length, beginning and ending most often in May.

DEVOLUTION

The Scottish parliament and the National Assembly for Wales have legislative power over all devolved matters, ie matters not reserved to Westminster or otherwise outside its powers. The Northern Ireland Assembly has legislative authority in the fields previously administered by the Northern Ireland departments. The assembly was suspended in October 2002 and dissolved in April 2003, before being reinstated on 8 May 2007. Following a snap election in March 2017, negotiations to form an executive have failed and the Northern Ireland Assembly remains suspended. For further information, *see* Devolved Government

THE HOUSE OF LORDS

London SW1A 0PW
T 020-7219 3107
E hlinfo@parliament.uk W www.parliament.uk

The House of Lords is the second chamber, or 'Upper House', of the UK's bicameral parliament. Until the beginning of the 20th century, the House of Lords had considerable power, being able to veto any bill submitted to it by the House of Commons. Since the introduction of the Parliament Acts 1911 and 1949, however, it has no powers over money bills and its power of veto over public legislation has been reduced over time to the power to delay bills for up to one session of parliament (usually one year). Today the main functions of the House of Lords are to contribute to the legislative process, to act as a check on the government, and to provide a forum of expertise. Its judicial role as final court of appeal ended in 2009 with the establishment of a new UK Supreme Court (*see* Law Courts and Offices section).

The House of Lords has a number of select committees. Some relate to the internal affairs of the house – such as its House of Lords Commission – while others carry out important investigative work on matters of public interest. The main committees are: the Communications Committee; the Constitution Committee; the Economic Affairs Committee; the European Union Committee; and the Science and Technology Committee. House of Lords' investigative committees look at broad issues and do not mirror government departments as the select committees in the House of Commons do.

The Constitutional Reform Act 2005 significantly altered the judicial function of the House of Lords and the role of the Lord Chancellor as a judge and its presiding officer. The Lord Chancellor is no longer the presiding officer of the House of Lords nor head of the judiciary in England and Wales, but remains a cabinet minister (the Lord Chancellor and Secretary of State for Justice), and is currently a member of the House of Commons. The function of the presiding officer of the House of Lords was devolved to the newly created post of the Speaker of the House of Lords, commonly known as Lord Speaker. The first Lord Speaker elected by the House was the Rt. Hon. Baroness Hayman on 4 July 2006.

Membership of the House of Lords comprises mainly of life peers created under the Life Peerages Act 1958, along with 92 hereditary peers and a small number of Lords of Appeal in Ordinary, ie law lords, who were created under the Appellate Jurisdiction Act 1876*. The Archbishops of Canterbury and York, the Bishops of London, Durham and Winchester, and the 21 senior diocesan bishops of the Church of England are also members.

The House of Lords Act 1999 provides for 92 hereditary peers to remain in the House of Lords until further reform of the House has been carried out. Of these, 75 (42 Conservative, 28 crossbench, three Liberal Democrat and two Labour) were elected by hereditary peers in their political party or crossbench grouping. In addition, 15 office holders were elected by the whole house. Two hereditary peers with royal duties, the Earl Marshal and the Lord Great Chamberlain, have also remained members. Since November 2002, by-elections have been held to replace elected hereditary peers who have died, and since 2014 to replace those who retire permanently from the House. By-elections are held under the Alternative Vote System, and must take place within three months of a vacancy occurring. (*see also* The Peerage).

Peers are disqualified from sitting in the house if they are:
- absent for an entire parliamentary session which is longer than six months (under the House of Lords Reform Act 2014), unless they are on leave of absence (*see below*)

- aliens, ie any peer who is not a British citizen, a Commonwealth citizen (under the British Nationality Act 1981) or a citizen of the Republic of Ireland
- under the age of 21
- undischarged bankrupts or, in Scotland, those whose estate is sequestered
- holders of a disqualifying judicial office
- members of the European parliament
- convicted of treason

Bishops cease to be members of the house when they retire.

Members who do not wish to attend sittings of the House of Lords may apply for leave of absence for the duration of a parliament. Since the passage of the House of Lords Reform Act 2014, members of the House may also retire permanently by giving notice in writing to the Clerk of the Parliaments.

Members of the House of Lords, who are not paid a salary, may claim a daily allowance of £305 (or may elect to claim a reduced daily allowance of £153) per sitting day – but only if they attend a sitting of the House and/or committee proceedings.

* Although the office of Lord of Appeal in Ordinary no longer exists, law lords created under the Appellate Jurisdiction Act 1876 remain members of the House. Those in office at the time of the establishment of the Supreme Court became justices of the UK Supreme Court and are not permitted to sit or vote in the House of Lords until they retire.

COMPOSITION *as at September 2018*

Archbishops and bishops	25
Life peers under the Appellate Jurisdiction Act 1876 and the Life Peerages Act 1958*	676
Peers under the House of Lords Act 1999†	90
Total	791

* Excluding 17 peers on leave of absence
† Excluding one peer on leave of absence

STATE OF THE PARTIES* *as at September 2018*

Conservative	250
Labour	187
Liberal Democrat	98
Crossbench	185
Archbishops and bishops	25
Non-affiliated	29
Other parties	16
Total	791

* Excluding peers on leave of absence

HOUSE OF LORDS PAY FOR SENIOR STAFF 2017–18

Senior staff are placed in the following pay bands according to their level of responsibility and taking account of other factors such as experience and marketability.

Judicial group 4	£181,566
Senior band 3	£106,000–£139,829
Senior band 2	£87,000–£124,845
Senior band 1A	£75,956–£105,560
Senior band 1	£64,900–£93,380

OFFICERS AND OFFICIALS

The house is presided over by the Lord Speaker, whose powers differ from those of the Speaker of the House of Commons. The Lord Speaker has no power to rule on matters of order because the House of Lords is self-regulating. The maintenance of the rules of debate is the responsibility of all the members who are present.

A panel of deputy speakers is appointed by Royal Commission. The first deputy speaker is the Chair of Committees, a salaried officer of the house appointed at the beginning of each session. He or she chairs a number of 'domestic' committees relating to the internal affairs of the

house. The first deputy speaker is assisted by a panel of deputy chairs, headed by the salaried Principal Deputy Chair of Committees, who is also chair of the European Union Committee of the house.

The Clerk of the Parliaments is the accounting officer and the chief permanent official responsible for the administration of the house. The Lady Usher of the Black Rod is responsible for security and other services and also has royal duties as secretary to the Lord Great Chamberlain.

Lord Speaker (£102,101), Rt. Hon. Lord Fowler
Senior Deputy Speaker of the House of Lords (£84,524), Rt. Hon. Lord McFall of Alcluith
Principal Deputy Chair (£79,076), Lord Boswell of Aynho
Clerk of the Parliaments (Judicial Group 4), Edward Ollard
Clerk Assistant (Senior Band 3), Simon Burton
Reading Clerk and Clerk of the Overseas Office (Senior Band 3), Jake Vaughan
Lady Usher of the Black Rod (Senior Band 2), Sarah Clarke, OBE
Yeoman Usher of the Black Rod, Brig. Neil Baverstock
Commissioner for Lords' Standards, Lucy Scott-Moncrieff, CBE
Counsel to the Chair of Committees (Senior Band 2), J. Cooper
Registrar of Lords' Interests (Senior Band 1A), Tom Wilson
Clerk of Committees (Senior Band 2), Dr Philippa Tudor
Legal Adviser to the Human Rights Committee (Senior Band 2), Eleanor Hourigan
Director of Library Services (Senior Band 2), Patrick Vollmer
Director of Facilities (Senior Band 2), Carl Woodall
Finance Director (Senior Band 1A), Mostaque Ahmed
Director of Parliamentary Digital Service (Senior Band 1A), Tracey Jessup
Director of Human Resources (Senior Band 1A), Nigel Sully
Clerk of Legislation (Senior Band 1A), Andrew Makower
Principal Clerk of Select Committees (Senior Band 1A), Christopher Johnson, DPHIL
Director of Parliamentary Archives (Senior Band 1), Adrian Brown

LORD GREAT CHAMBERLAIN'S OFFICE
Lord Great Chamberlain, 7th Marquess of Cholmondeley, KCVO

SELECT COMMITTEES
The main House of Lords select committees, as at September 2018, are as follows:

Artificial Intelligence – Chair, Lord Clement-Jones, CBE; *Clerk,* Luke Hussey
Bribery Act 2010 – Chair, Rt. Hon. Lord Saville of Newdigate; *Clerk,* Michael Collon
Citizenship and Civic Engagement – Chair, Lord Hodgson of Astley Abbotts, CBE; *Clerk,* Michael Collon
Communications – Chair, Lord Gilbert of Panteg; *Clerk,* Theodore Pembroke
Constitution – Chair, Rt. Hon. Baroness Taylor of Bolton; *Clerk,* Matt Korris
Delegated Powers and Regulatory Reform – Chair, Rt. Hon Lord Blencathra
Economic Affairs – Chair, Rt. Hon. Lord Forsyth of Drumlean; *Clerk,* Luke Hussey
European Union – Chair, Lord Boswell of Aynho; *Principal Clerk,* Christopher Johnson; *Clerk,* Stuart Stoner
European Union – Sub-committees:
    Energy and Environment – Chair, Lord Teverson; *Clerk,* Alexandra McMillan
    External Affairs – Chair, Baroness Verma; *Clerk,* Jennifer Martin-Kohlmorgen
    Financial Affairs – Chair, Baroness Falkner of Margravine; *Clerk,* Matthew Manning

Home Affairs – Chair, Lord Jay of Ewelme, GCMG; *Clerk,* Tristan Stubbs

Internal Market – Chair, Rt. Hon. Lord Whitty; *Clerk,* Rosanna Barry

Justice – Chair, Baroness Kennedy of the Shaws, QC; *Clerk,* Simon Cran-McGrechin

Finance – Chair, Baroness Doocey, OBE; *Clerk,* Susannah Street

House – Chair, Rt. Hon. Lord Fowler; *Clerk,* Patrick Milner

Hybrid Instruments – Chair, Rt. Hon. Lord McFall of Alcluith

Intellectual Property (Unjustified Threats) Bill – Chair, Rt. Hon. Lord Saville of Newdigate; *Clerk,* Susannah Street

Intergenerational Fairness and Provision – Chair, Lord True, CBE; *Clerk,* Judith Brooke

International Relations – Chair, Rt. Hon. Lord Howell of Guildford; *Clerk,* Eva George

Liaison – Chair, Rt. Hon. Lord McFall of Alcluith; *Clerk,* Philippa Tudor

Long-Term Sustainability of the NHS – Chair, Lord Patel, KT; *Clerk,* Judith Brooke

Lords' Conduct – Chair, Rt. Hon. Lord Brown of Eaton-under-Heywood

Natural Environment and Rural Communities (NERC) Act 2006 – Chair, Lord Cameron of Dillington, FRICS; *Clerk,* Matthew Smith

Privileges and Conduct – Chair, Rt. Hon. Lord McFall of Alcluith; *Clerk,* Chloe Mawson

Procedure – Chair, Rt. Hon. Lord McFall of Alcluith; *Clerk,* Chloe Mawson

Regenerating Seaside Towns – Chair, Rt. Hon. Lord Bassam of Brighton; *Clerk,* Matthew Smith

Rural Economy – Chair, Rt. Hon. Lord Foster of Bath; *Clerk,* Simon Keal

Science and Technology – Chair, Lord Patel, KT; *Clerk,* Donna Davidson

Secondary Legislation Scrutiny – Chair, Rt. Hon. Lord Trefgarne

Selection – Chair, Rt. Hon. Lord McFall of Alcluith

Services – Chair, Rt. Hon. Lord Laming, CBE; *Clerk,* Susannah Street

Standing Orders (Private Bills) – Chair, Rt. Hon. Lord McFall of Alcluith

THE HOUSE OF COMMONS
London SW1A 0AA
T 020-7219 3000 W www.parliament.uk

HOUSE OF COMMONS ENQUIRY SERVICE
14 Tothill Street, London SW1H 9NB
T 020-7219 4272 E hcinfo@parliament.uk

The members of the House of Commons are elected by universal adult suffrage. For electoral purposes, the UK is divided into constituencies, each of which returns one member to the House of Commons, the member being the candidate who obtains the largest number of votes cast in the constituency. To ensure equitable representation, the four Boundary Commissions keep constituency boundaries under review and recommend any redistribution of seats which may seem necessary because of population movements etc. At the 2010 general election the number of seats increased from 646 to 650. Of the present 650 seats, there are 533 for England, 40 for Wales, 59 for Scotland and 18 for Northern Ireland.

NUMBER OF SEATS IN THE HOUSE OF COMMONS BY COUNTRY

	2005	2017
England	529	533
Wales	40	40
Scotland	59	59
Northern Ireland	18	18
Total	646	650

ELECTIONS
Elections are by secret ballot, each elector casting one vote; voting is not compulsory. (For entitlement to vote in parliamentary elections, *see* Legal Notes.) When a seat becomes vacant between general elections, a by-election is held.

British subjects and citizens of the Irish Republic can stand for election as MPs provided they are 18 or over and not subject to disqualification. Those disqualified from sitting in the house include:

- undischarged bankrupts
- people sentenced to more than one year's imprisonment
- members of the House of Lords (but hereditary peers not sitting in the Lords are eligible)
- holders of certain offices listed in the House of Commons Disqualification Act 1975, eg members of the judiciary, civil service, regular armed forces, police forces, some local government officers and some members of public corporations and government commissions

A candidate does not require any party backing but his or her nomination for election must be supported by the signatures of ten people registered in the constituency. A candidate must also deposit £500 with the returning officer, which is forfeit if the candidate does not receive more than 5 per cent of the votes cast. All election expenses at a general election, except the candidate's personal expenses, are subject to a statutory limit of £8,700, plus six pence for each elector in a borough constituency or nine pence for each elector in a county constituency.

See also members of parliament for a current alphabetical list.

STATE OF THE PARTIES *as at September 2018*

Party	Seats
Conservative*	315
Labour	257
Scottish National Party	35
Liberal Democrats	12
Democratic Unionist Party	9
Indepedent	9
Sinn Fein (have not taken their seats)	7
Plaid Cymru	4
Green	1
The Speaker	1
Total	650

* The Conservative Party have formed a minority government and have signed a 'confidence and supply' agreement with the Democratic Unionist Party

BUSINESS
The week's business of the house is outlined each Thursday by the leader of the house, after consultation between the chief government whip and the chief opposition whip. A quarter to a third of the time will be taken up by the government's legislative programme and the rest by other business. As a rule, bills likely to raise political controversy are introduced in the Commons before going on to the Lords, and the Commons claims exclusive control in respect of national taxation and expenditure. Bills such as the finance bill, which imposes taxation, and the consolidated fund bills, which authorise expenditure, must begin in the Commons. A bill of which the financial provisions are subsidiary may begin in the Lords, and the Commons may waive its rights in regard to Lords' amendments affecting finance.

The Commons has a public register of MPs' financial and certain other interests; this is published annually as a House of Commons paper. Members must also disclose any relevant financial interest or benefit in a matter before the house when taking part in a debate, in certain other proceedings of the house, or in consultations with other MPs, with ministers or with civil servants.

MEMBERS' PAY AND ALLOWANCES

Since 1911 members of the House of Commons have received salary payments; facilities for free travel were introduced in 1924. Salary rates for the last 30 years are as follows:

1988 Jan – £22,548	2003 Apr – £56,358
1989 Jan – £24,107	2004 Apr – £57,485
1990 Jan – £26,701	2005 Apr – £59,095
1991 Jan – £29,970	2006 Apr – £59,686
1992 Jan – £30,854	2007 Apr – £61,181
1993 Jan – £30,854	2008 Apr – £63,291
1994 Jan – £31,687	2009 Apr – £64,766
1995 Jan – £33,189	2010 Apr – £65,738
1995 Jan – £33,189	2011 Apr – £65,738
1996 Jan – £34,085	2012 Apr – £65,738
1996 Jul – £43,000	2013 Apr – £66,396
1997 Apr – £43,860	2014 Apr – £67,060
1998 Apr – £45,066	2015 May – £74,000
1999 Apr – £47,008	2016 Apr – £74,962
2000 Apr – £48,371	2017 Apr – £76,011
2001 Apr – £49,822	2018 Apr – £77,379
2002 Apr – £55,118	

The Independent Parliamentary Standards Authority (IPSA) was established under the Parliamentary Standards Act 2009 and is responsible for the independent regulation and administration of the MPs' Scheme of Business Costs and Expenses, as well as for paying the salaries of MPs and their staff members. Since May 2011, the IPSA has also been responsible for determining MPs' pay and setting the level of any increase to their salary.

For 2018–19, the office costs expenditure budget is £27,660 for London area MPs and £24,880 for non-London area MPs. The maximum annual staff budget for London area MPs is £164,460 and £153,620 for non-London area MPs.

Since 1972 MPs have been able to claim reimbursement for the additional cost of staying overnight away from their main residence while on parliamentary business. This is not payable to London area MPs and those MPs who reside in 'grace and favour' accommodation. Accommodation expenses for MPs claiming rental payments in the London area is capped at £22,850 a year; outside of the London area each constituency is banded according to rental values in the area and capped at £15,940. For MPs who own their own homes, mortgage interest and associated expenses up to £5,150 are payable.

For ministerial salaries see Government Departments.

MEMBERS' PENSIONS

Pension arrangements for MPs were first introduced in 1964. Under the Parliamentary Contributory Pension Fund CARE (career-averaged revalued earnings) scheme, MPs receive a pension on retirement based upon their salary in their final year, and upon accumulating proportions of pensionable earnings over each year of membership. MPs contributions are payable at a rate of 11.09 per cent of pay. Exchequer contributions are paid at a rate recommended by the Government Actuary and meet the balance of the cost of providing MP's retirement benefits. Pensions are normally payable upon retirement at age 65 to those who are no longer MPS. Abated pensions may be payable to members aged 55 or over. Pensions are also payable to spouses and other qualifying partners of deceased scheme members at the rate of three-eighths of the deceased member's pension. In the case of members who die in service, an enhanced spouse's or partner's pension and a lump sum equal to two times pensionable salary is payable. There are also provisions in place for dependants and MPs of any age who retire due to ill health. All pensions are CPI index-linked.

The House of Commons Members' Fund provides for annual or lump sum grants to ex-MPs, their widows or widowers, and children of those who either ceased to serve as an MP prior to the PCPF being established or who are experiencing hardship. Members contribute £24 a year and the Exchequer £215,000 a year to the fund.

HOUSE OF COMMONS PAY BANDS FOR SENIOR STAFF

Senior Staff are placed in the following Senior Civil Service pay bands. These pay bands apply to the most senior staff in departments and agencies.

Pay Band 1	£64,640–£118,978
Pay Band 1A*	£67,600–£128,900
Pay Band 2	£87,870–£164,125
Pay Band 3	£107,060–£210,181

* Pay Band 1A is now effectively a closed grade, although existing staff will remain on this grade

OFFICERS AND OFFICIALS

The House of Commons is presided over by the Speaker, who has considerable powers to maintain order. A deputy speaker, called the Chairman of Ways and Means, and two deputy chairs may preside over sittings of the House of Commons; they are elected by the house, and, like the Speaker, neither speak nor vote other than in their official capacity.

The staff of the house are employed by a commission chaired by the Speaker. The heads of the six House of Commons departments are permanent officers of the house, not MPs. The Clerk of the House is the principal adviser to the Speaker on the privileges and procedures of the house, the conduct of the business of the house, and committees. The Serjeant-at-Arms is responsible for security and ceremonial functions of the house.

Speaker (£150,236)*, Rt. Hon. John Bercow, MP
Chairman of Ways and Means (£107,108), Rt. Hon. Sir Lindsay Hoyle, MP
First Deputy Chairman of Ways and Means (£102,098), Rt. Hon. Dame Eleanor Laing, DBE, MP
Second Deputy Chairman of Ways and Means (£102,098), Rt. Hon. Dame Rosie Winterton, DBE, MP
House of Commons Commission, Rt, Hon. John Bercow, MP *(chair);* Ian Ailles *(Director-General of the House of Commons);* Sir Paul Beresford, MP; Rt. Hon. Tom Brake, MP; Dame Janet Gaymer, DBE *(external member);* Stewart Hosie, MP; Rt Hon. Andrea Leadsom, MP *(Leader of the House);* Jane McCall *(external member);* Sir David Natzler, KCB *(Clerk of the House);* Valerie Vaz, MP; Rt. Hon. Dame Rosie Winterton, DBE, MP
Secretary of the Commission, Marianne Cwynarski
Assistant Secretary, Rob Cope

* Salaries in parentheses are the maximum available. The Speaker and Deputies have opted not to take the statutory increases awarded to them each year as office holders.

OFFICE OF THE SPEAKER
Speaker's Secretary, Peter Barratt
Trainbearer, Jim Davey
Speaker's Counsel, Saira Salimi
Chaplain to the Speaker, Revd Rose Hudson-Wilkin

OFFICE OF THE CLERK OF THE HOUSE
Clerk of the House, Sir David Natzler, KCB

PARLIAMENTARY COMMISSIONER FOR STANDARDS
Parliamentary Commissioner for Standards, Kathryn Stone, OBE
Registrar of Members' Financial Interests, Heather Wood

PARLIAMENTARY SECURITY DIRECTOR
Parliamentary Security Director, Eric Hepburn, CBE

GOVERNANCE OFFICE
Head of Office, Marianne Cwynarski
Corporate Risk Management Facilitator, Rachel Harrison
Head of Central Communications, Lee Bridges
Strategy, Planning and Performance Manager, Jane Hough

DEPARTMENT OF CHAMBER AND COMMITTEE
SERVICES
Clerk Assistant and Managing Director, John Benger
Director of Departmental Services, Elizabeth Hunt

OVERSEAS OFFICE
Principal Clerk, Matthew Hamlyn
Delegation Secretary, Nick Wright
Inward Visits Manager, Alison Game, MBE
National Parliament Representative (Brussels), Alison Groves

COMMITTEE OFFICE
Clerk of Committees, Paul Evans
Principal Clerks of Select Committees, Sarah Davies; Tom
  Goldsmith; Crispin Poyser

DEPARTMENTAL SELECT COMMITTEES *as at
September 2018*
Administration – Chair, Sir Paul Beresford, MP; *Clerk,* Sarah
  Heath
Backbench Business – Chair, Ian Mearns, MP; *Clerk,* James
  Davies
Business, Energy and Industrial Strategy – Chair, Rachel Reeves,
  MP; *Clerk,* Chris Shaw
Defence – Chair, Rt. Hon. Dr Julian Lewis, MP; *Clerk,* Mark
  Etherton
Digital, Culture, Media and Sport – Chair, Damian Collins. MP;
  Clerk, Chloe Challender
Education – Chair, Robert Halfon, MP; *Clerk,* Richard Ward
Environment, Food and Rural Affairs – Chair, Neil Parish, MP;
  Clerk, Eliot Barrass
Environmental Audit – Chair, Mary Creagh, MP; *Clerk,* Lloyd
  Owen
European Scrutiny – Chair, Sir William Cash, MP; *Clerk,* Philip
  Aylett
Exiting the European Union – Chair, Rt. Hon. Hilary Benn, MP;
  Clerk, James Rhys
Finance – Chair, Chris Bryant, MP; *Clerk,* Rob Cope
Foreign Affairs – Chair, Tom Tugendhat, MP; *Clerk,* Tom
  Goldsmith
Health and Social Care – Chair, Dr Sarah Wollaston, MP; *Clerk,*
  Huw Yardley
High Speed Rail (West Midlands – Crewe) Bill – Chair, James
  Duddridge, MP
Home Affairs – Chair, Rt. Hon. Yvette Cooper, MP; *Clerk,*
  Elizabeth Hunt
Housing, Communities and Local Government, Chair, Clive Betts,
  MP, *Clerk* Edward Beale
International Development – Chair, Stephen Twigg, MP; *Clerk,*
  Fergus Reid
International Trade – Chair, Angus Brendan MacNeil, MP;
  Clerk, Joanna Welham
Justice – Chair, Robert Neill, MP; *Clerk,* Rhiannon Hollis
Liaison – Chair, Dr Sarah Wollaston, MP; *Clerk,* Lucinda Maer
Northern Ireland Affairs – Chair, Dr Andrew Murrison, MP;
  Clerk, Margaret McKinnon
Petitions – Chair, Helen Jones, MP
Privileges – Chair, Sir Kevin Barron, MP; *Clerk,* Robin James
Procedure – Chair, Charles Walker, MP; *Clerk,* Martyn Atkins
Public Accounts – Chair, Meg Hillier, MP; *Clerk,* Richard
  Cooke
Public Administration and Constitutional Affairs – Chair, Hon. Sir
  Bernard Jenkin, MP; *Clerks,* Libby Kurien; Dr Sarah
  Thatcher

Regulatory Reform – Chair, Stephen McPartland, MP; *Clerk,*
  Ben Sneddon
Science and Technology – Chair, Rt. Hon. Norman Lamb, MP;
  Clerk, Danielle Nash
Scottish Affairs – Chair, Pete Wishart, MP; *Clerk,* Ben Williams
Selection – Chair, Bill Wiggin, MP; *Clerks,* Gail Bartlett;
  Anwen Rees
Standards – Chair, Rt. Hon. Sir Kevin Barron, MP; *Clerk,*
  Robin James
Standing Orders (Private Bills) – Chair, Rt. Hon. Sir Lindsay
  Hoyle, MP
Statutory Instruments – Chair, Derek Twigg, MP; *Clerk,* Jeanne
  Delebarre
Transport – Chair, Lillian Greenwood, MP; *Clerk,* Gordon
  Clarke
Treasury – Chair, Rt. Hon. Nicky Morgan, MP; *Clerk,* Sarah
  Rees
Welsh Affairs – Chair, David T. C. Davies, MP; *Clerk,* Kevin
  Maddison
Women and Equalities – Chair, Rt. Hon. Maria Miller, MP;
  Clerk, Judith Boyce
Work and Pensions – Chair, Rt. Hon. Frank Field, MP; *Clerk,*
  Anne-Marie Griffiths

SCRUTINY UNIT
Head of Unit, David Lloyd
Head of Financial Security, Larry Honeysett
Public Bill Committees, Ian Hook

VOTE OFFICE
Deliver of the Vote, Catherine Fogarty
Deputy Deliverer of the Vote, Owen Sweeney
Head of Procedural Publishing, Tom McVeagh
Procedural Publishing Operations Manager, Stuart Miller

CHAMBER BUSINESS DIRECTORATE
Clerk of Legislation, Liam Laurence Smyth
Principal Clerks: Philippa Helme (Table Office); Paul Evans
  (Journals)

OFFICIAL REPORT DIRECTORATE
Editor, Alex Newton
Director of Broadcasting, John Angeli

SERJEANT-AT-ARMS DIRECTORATE
Serjeant-at-Arms, Kamal El-Hajji
Deputy Serjeant-at-Arms, Richard Latham
Assistant Serjeant-at-Arms, Lesley Scott

DEPARTMENT OF FACILITIES
Director-General, John Borley, CB
Director of Business Management, Della Herd
Parliamentary Director of Estates, Brian Finnimore
Director of Accommodation and Logistics Services, Fiona Channon
Executive Officer, Katie Phelan-Molloy
Director of Catering Services, Richard Tapner-Evans
Executive Chef, Mark Hill

DEPARTMENT OF FINANCE
Director of Finance, Myfanwy Barrett
Chief Accountant, Alex Mills
Head of Financial Planning and Performance, Philip Collins
Head of Financial Accounting, Debra Shirtcliffe
Head of Financial Services, Sam Rao

DEPARTMENT OF HUMAN RESOURCES AND
CHANGE
Director-General of HR and Change, Andrew Walker
Head of Safety, Dr Marianne McDougall

DEPARTMENT OF INFORMATION SERVICES
Director-General and Librarian, Penny Young
Curator of Works of Art, Malcolm Hay

Deputy Curator, Emma Gormley
Assistant Curators, James Ford; Sileas Wood
Registrar of Collections, Emily Green
Collections Care Manager, Caroline Babington
Collections Information Manager, Natasha Walsh
Administrators, Michelle Klein; Susan Reynolds
Head of Customer Services, Dr Patsy Richards

PARLIAMENTARY DIGITAL SERVICE (PDS)
Director of Parliamentary Digital Service, Tracey Jessup
Deputy Director, David Smith
Director of Technology, Sam Middleton
Director of Live Services, Rob Sanders
Director of Development, Emma Allen
Head of Information Systems, Sean van der Vyver
Head of the Strategy, Tracy Green

OTHER PRINCIPAL OFFICERS
Clerk of the Crown in Chancery, Richard Heaton, CB
Parliamentary and Health Service Ombudsman, Robert Behrens, CBE

NATIONAL AUDIT OFFICE
157–197 Buckingham Palace Road, London SW1W 9SP
T 020-7798 7000
E enquiries@nao.gsi.gov.uk W www.nao.org.uk

The National Audit Office came into existence under the National Audit Act 1983 to replace and continue the work of the former Exchequer and Audit Department. The act reinforced the office's total financial and operational independence from the government and brought its head, the Comptroller and Auditor-General, into a closer relationship with parliament as an officer of the House of Commons.

The National Audit Office (NAO) scrutinises public spending on behalf of parliament, helping it to hold government departments to account and helping public service managers improve performance and service delivery. The NAO audits the financial statements of all government departments and a wide range of other public bodies. It regularly publishes 'value for money' reports on the efficiency and effectiveness of how public resources are used.

Chair, Lord Bichard, KCB
Comptroller and Auditor-General, Sir Amyas Morse, KCB
Executive Leaders, Abdool Kara; Daniel Lambauer; Kate Mathers; Rebecca Sheeran; Stephen Smith; Max Tse; John Thorpe

PARLIAMENTARY INFORMATION

The following is a short glossary of aspects of the work of parliament. Unless otherwise stated, references are to House of Commons procedures.

BILL – Proposed legislation is termed a bill. The stages of a public bill (for private bills, *see* below) in the House of Commons are as follows:

First reading: This stage introduces the legislation to the house and, for government bills, merely constitutes an order to have the bill printed.

Second reading: The debate on the principles of the bill.

Committee stage: The detailed examination of a bill, clause by clause. In most cases this takes place in a public bill committee, or the whole house may act as a committee. Public bill committees may take evidence before embarking on detailed scrutiny of the bill. Very rarely, a bill may be examined by a select committee.

Report stage: Detailed review of a bill as amended in committee, on the floor of the house, and an opportunity to make further changes.

Third reading: Final debate on the full bill in the Commons.

Public bills go through the same stages in the House of Lords, but with important differences: the committee stage is taken in committee of the whole house or in a grand committee, in which any peer may participate. There are no time limits, all amendments are debated, and further amendments can be made at third reading.

A bill may start in either house, and has to pass through both houses to become law. Both houses have to agree the final text of a bill, so that amendments made by the second house are then considered in the originating house, and if not agreed, sent back or themselves amended, until agreement is reached.

CHILTERN HUNDREDS – A nominal office of profit under the crown, the acceptance of which requires an MP to vacate his/her seat. The Manor of Northstead is similar. These are the only means by which an MP may resign.

CONSOLIDATED FUND BILL – A bill to authorise the issue of money to maintain government services. The bill is dealt with without debate.

EARLY DAY MOTION – A motion put on the notice paper by an MP without, in general, the real prospect of its being debated. Such motions are expressions of back-bench opinion.

FATHER OF THE HOUSE – The MP whose continuous service in the House of Commons is the longest. The present Father of the House is the Rt. Hon. Kenneth Clarke, CH, QC, MP

GRAND COMMITTEES – There are three grand committees in the House of Commons, one each for Northern Ireland, Scotland and Wales; they consider matters relating specifically to that country. In the House of Lords, bills may be sent to a grand committee instead of a committee of the whole house (*see also* Bill).

HOURS OF MEETING – The House of Commons normally meets on Mondays at 2.30pm, Tuesdays and Wednesdays at 11.30am, Thursdays at 9.30am and some Fridays at 9.30am. (*See also* Westminster Hall Sittings, below.) The House of Lords normally meets at 2.30pm Mondays and Tuesdays, 3pm on Wednesdays and at 11am on Thursdays. The House of Lords occasionally sits on Fridays at 10am.

LEADER OF THE OPPOSITION – In 1937 the office of leader of the opposition was recognised and a salary was assigned to the post. In 2018–19 this is £141,408 (including a parliamentary salary of £77,379). The present leader of the opposition is the Rt. Hon. Jeremy Corbyn, MP.

THE LORD CHANCELLOR – The office of Lord High Chancellor of Great Britain was significantly altered by the Constitutional Reform Act 2005. Previously, the Lord Chancellor was (*ex officio*) the Speaker of the House of Lords, and took part in debates and voted in divisions in the House of Lords. The Department for Constitutional Affairs was created in 2003, and became the Ministry of Justice in 2007, incorporating most of the responsibilities of the Lord Chancellor's department. The role of Speaker has been transferred to the post of Lord Speaker. The Constitutional Reform Act 2005 also brought to an end the Lord Chancellor's role as head of the judiciary. A Judicial Appointments Commission was created in April 2006, and a supreme court (separate from the House of Lords) was established in 2009.

THE LORD GREAT CHAMBERLAIN – The Lord Great Chamberlain is a Great Officer of State, the office being hereditary since the grant of Henry I to the family of De Vere, Earls of Oxford. It is now a joint hereditary office rotating on the death of the sovereign between the Cholmondeley, Carington and Ancaster families.

The Lord Great Chamberlain, currently the 7th Marquess of Cholmondeley, is responsible for the royal apartments in the Palace of Westminster, the Royal Gallery, the administration of the Chapel of St Mary Undercroft and, in conjunction with the Lord Speaker and the Speaker of the House of Commons,

Westminster Hall. The Lord Great Chamberlain has the right to perform specific services at a coronation and has particular responsibility for the internal administrative arrangements within the House of Lords for state openings of parliament.

THE LORD SPEAKER – The first Lord Speaker of the House of Lords, the Rt. Hon. Baroness Hayman, took up office on 4 July 2006. The Lord Speaker is independent of the government and elected by members of the House of Lords rather than appointed by the prime minister. Although the Lord Speaker's primary role is to preside over proceedings in the House of Lords, she does not have the same powers as the Speaker of the House of Commons. For example, the Lord Speaker is not responsible for maintaining order during debates, as this is the responsibility of the house as a whole. The Lord Speaker sits in the Lords on one of the woolsacks, which are couches covered in red cloth and stuffed with wool.

MOTHER OF THE HOUSE – Introduced by Theresa May in 2017, the Mother of the House is the female MP whose continuous service is the longest. The inaugural and present Mother of the House is Rt. Hon. Harriet Harman, QC, MP.

OPPOSITION DAY – A day on which the topic for debate is chosen by the opposition. There are 20 such days in a normal session. On 17 days, subjects are chosen by the leader of the opposition; on the remaining three days by the leader of the next largest opposition party.

PARLIAMENT ACTS 1911 AND 1949 – Under these acts, bills may become law without the consent of the Lords, though the House of Lords has the power to delay a public bill for a parliamentary session.

PRIME MINISTER'S QUESTIONS – The prime minister answers questions from 12 to 12.30pm on Wednesdays.

PRIVATE BILL – A bill promoted by a body or an individual to give powers additional to, or in conflict with, the general law, and to which a special procedure applies to enable people affected to object.

PRIVATE MEMBER'S BILL – A public bill promoted by an MP or peer who is not a member of the government.

PRIVATE NOTICE QUESTION – A question adjudged of urgent importance on submission to the Speaker (in the Lords, the Lord Speaker), answered at the end of oral questions.

PRIVILEGE – The House of Commons has rights and immunities to protect it from obstruction in carrying out its duties. These are known as parliamentary privilege and enable Members of Parliament to debate freely. The most important privilege is that of freedom of speech. MPs cannot be prosecuted for sedition or sued for libel or slander over anything said during proceedings in the house. This enables them to raise in the house questions affecting the public good which might be difficult to raise outside owing to the possibility of legal action against them. The House of Lords has similar privileges.

QUESTION TIME – Oral questions are answered by ministers in the Commons from 2.30 to 3.30pm on Mondays, 11.30am to 12.30pm on Tuesdays and Wednesdays, and 9.30 to 10.30am on Thursdays. Questions are also taken for half an hour at the start of the Lords sittings.

ROYAL ASSENT – The royal assent is signified by letters patent to such bills and measures as have passed both Houses of Parliament (or bills which have been passed under the Parliament Acts 1911 and 1949). The sovereign has not given royal assent in person since 1854. On occasion, for instance in the prorogation of parliament, royal assent may be pronounced to the two houses by Lords Commissioners. More usually royal assent is notified to each house sitting separately in accordance with the Royal Assent Act 1967. The old French formulae for royal assent are then endorsed on the acts by the Clerk of the Parliaments.

The power to withhold assent resides with the sovereign but has not been exercised in the UK since 1707.

SELECT COMMITTEES – Consisting usually of 10 to 15 members of all parties, select committees are a means used by both houses in order to investigate certain matters.

Most select committees in the House of Commons are tied to departments: each committee investigates subjects within a government department's remit. There are other select committees dealing with matters such as public accounts (ie the spending by the government of money voted by parliament) and European legislation, and also committees advising on procedures and domestic administration of the house. Major select committees usually take evidence in public; their evidence and reports are published on the parliament website and in hard copy by The Stationery Office (TSO). House of Commons select committees are reconstituted after a general election.

In the House of Lords, select committees do not mirror government departments but cover broader issues. There is a select committee on the European Union (EU), which has six sub-committees dealing with specific areas of EU policy, a select committee on science and technology, a select committee on economic affairs and also one on the constitution. There is also a select committee on delegated powers and regulatory reform and one on privileges and conduct. In addition, *ad hoc* select committees have been set up from time to time to investigate specific subjects. There are also joint committees of the two houses, eg the committees on statutory instruments and on human rights.

THE SPEAKER – The Speaker of the House of Commons is the spokesperson and chair of the Chamber. He or she is elected by the house at the beginning of each parliament or when the previous Speaker retires or dies. The Speaker neither speaks in debates nor votes in divisions except when the voting is equal.

VACANT SEATS – When a vacancy occurs in the House of Commons during a session of parliament, the writ for the by-election is moved by a whip of the party to which the member whose seat has been vacated belonged. If the house is in recess, the Speaker can issue a warrant for a writ, should two members certify to him that a seat is vacant.

WESTMINSTER HALL SITTINGS – Following a report by the Modernisation of the House of Commons Select Committee, the Commons decided in May 1999 to set up a second debating forum. It is known as 'Westminster Hall' and sittings are in the Grand Committee Room on some Mondays from 4.30pm to 7.30pm, Tuesdays and Wednesdays from 9.30am to 11.30am and from 2.30pm to 5.30pm, and Thursdays from 1.30pm to 4.30pm. Sittings are open to the public at the times indicated.

WHIPS – In order to secure the attendance of members of a particular party in parliament, particularly on the occasion of an important vote, whips (originally known as 'whippers-in') are appointed. The written appeal or circular letter issued by them is also known as a 'whip', its urgency being denoted by the number of times it is underlined. Failure to respond to a three-line whip is tantamount in the Commons to secession (at any rate temporarily) from the party. Whips are provided with office accommodation in both houses, and government and some opposition whips receive salaries from public funds.

PARLIAMENTARY ARCHIVES
Houses of Parliament, London SW1A 0PW
T 020-7219 3074 E archives@parliament.uk W www.parliament.uk/archives

Since 1497, the records of parliament have been kept within the Palace of Westminster. They are in the custody of the Clerk of Parliaments. In 1946 the House of Lords Record Office, which became the Parliamentary Archives in 2006, was established to supervise their preservation and their availability to the public. Some 3 million documents are preserved, including acts of parliament from 1497, journals of the House of Lords from 1510, minutes and committee proceedings from 1610, and papers laid before parliament from 1531. Among the records are the Petition of Right, the death warrant of Charles I, the Declaration of Breda, and the Bill of Rights. Records are made available through a public search room.

Director of the Parliamentary Archives, Adrian Brown

GOVERNMENT OFFICE

The government is the body of ministers responsible for the administration of national affairs, determining policy and introducing into parliament any legislation necessary to give effect to government policy. The majority of ministers are members of the House of Commons but members of the House of Lords, or of neither house, may also hold ministerial responsibility. The prime minister is, by current convention, always a member of the House of Commons.

THE PRIME MINISTER

The office of prime minister, which had been in existence for nearly 200 years, was officially recognised in 1905 and its holder was granted a place in the table of precedence. The prime minister, by tradition also First Lord of the Treasury and Minister for the Civil Service, is appointed by the sovereign and is usually the leader of the party which enjoys, or can secure, a majority in the House of Commons. Other ministers are appointed by the sovereign on the recommendation of the prime minister, who also allocates functions among ministers and has the power to dismiss ministers from their posts.

The prime minister informs the sovereign on state and political matters, advises on the dissolution of parliament, and makes recommendations for important crown appointments, ie the award of honours, etc.

As the chair of cabinet meetings and leader of a political party, the prime minister is responsible for translating party policy into government activity. As leader of the government, the prime minister is responsible to parliament and to the electorate for the policies and their implementation.

The prime minister also represents the nation in international affairs, eg summit conferences.

THE CABINET

The cabinet developed during the 18th century as an inner committee of the Privy Council, which was the chief source of executive power until that time. The cabinet is composed of about 20 ministers chosen by the prime minister, usually the heads of government departments (generally known as secretaries of state unless they have a special title, eg Chancellor of the Exchequer), the leaders of the two houses of parliament, and the holders of various traditional offices.

The cabinet's functions are the final determination of policy, control of government and coordination of government departments. The exercise of its functions is dependent upon the incumbent party's (or parties') majority support in the House of Commons. Cabinet meetings are held in private, taking place once or twice a week during parliamentary sittings and less often during a recess. Proceedings are confidential, the members being bound by their oath as privy counsellors not to disclose information about the proceedings.

The convention of collective responsibility means that the cabinet acts unanimously even when cabinet ministers do not all agree on a subject. The policies of departmental ministers must be consistent with the policies of the government as a whole, and once the government's policy has been decided, each minister is expected to support it or resign.

The convention of ministerial responsibility holds a minister, as the political head of his or her department, accountable to parliament for the department's work. Departmental ministers

usually decide all matters within their responsibility, although on matters of political importance they normally consult their colleagues collectively. A decision by a departmental minister is binding on the government as a whole.

POLITICAL PARTIES

Before the reign of William and Mary, the principal officers of state were chosen by and were responsible to the sovereign alone, and not to parliament or the nation at large. Such officers acted sometimes in concert with one another but more often independently, and the fall of one did not, of necessity, involve that of others, although all were liable to be dismissed at any moment.

In 1693 the Earl of Sunderland recommended to William III the advisability of selecting a ministry from the political party which enjoyed a majority in the House of Commons, and the first united ministry was drawn in 1696 from the Whigs, to which party the king owed his throne. This group became known as the 'junto' and was regarded with suspicion as a novelty in the political life of the nation, being a small section meeting in secret apart from the main body of ministers. It may be regarded as the forerunner of the cabinet and in the course of time it led to the establishment of the principle of joint responsibility of ministers, so that internal disagreement caused a change of personnel or resignation of the whole body of ministers.

The accession of George I, who was unfamiliar with the English language, led to a disinclination on the part of the sovereign to preside at meetings of his ministers and caused the emergence of a prime minister, a position first acquired by Robert Walpole in 1721 and retained by him without interruption for 20 years and 326 days. The office of prime minister was formally recognised in 1905 when it was established by royal warrant.

DEVELOPMENT OF PARTIES

In 1828 the Whigs became known as Liberals, a name originally given by opponents to imply laxity of principles, but gradually accepted by the party to indicate its claim to be pioneers and champions of political reform and progressive legislation. In 1861 a Liberal Registration Association was founded and Liberal Associations became widespread. In 1877 a National Liberal Federation was formed, with its headquarters in London. The Liberal Party was in power for long periods during the second half of the 19th century and for several years during the first quarter of the 20th century, but after a split in the party in 1931, the numbers elected remained small. In 1988 a majority of the Liberals agreed on a merger with the Social Democratic Party under the title Social and Liberal Democrats; since 1989 they have been known as the Liberal Democrats. A minority continue separately as the Liberal Party.

Soon after the change from Whig to Liberal, the Tory Party became known as Conservative, a name believed to have been invented by John Wilson Croker in 1830 and to have been generally adopted around the time of the passing of the Reform Act of 1832 – to indicate that the preservation of national institutions was the leading principle of the party. After the Home Rule crisis of 1886 the dissentient Liberals entered into a compact with the Conservatives, under which the latter undertook not to contest their seats, but a separate Liberal Unionist organisation was maintained until 1912, when it was united with the Conservatives.

Labour candidates for parliament made their first appearance at the general election of 1892, when there were 27 standing as Labour or Liberal-Labour. In 1900 the Labour Representation Committee (LRC) was set up in order to establish a distinct Labour group in parliament, with its own whips, its own policy, and a readiness to cooperate with any party which might be engaged in promoting legislation in the direct interests of labour. In 1906 the LRC became known as the Labour Party.

The Green Party was founded in 1973 and campaigns for social and environmental justice. The party began as 'People', was renamed the Ecology Party, and became the Green Party in 1985.

The UK Independence Party (UKIP) was founded in 1993 by members of the Anti-Federalist League. It is a right-wing populist party with one key policy – to leave the European Union. In the 2014 European elections, UKIP became the first party, other than the Conservatives or Labour to win a national election in over a century.

Plaid Cymru was founded in 1926 to provide an independent political voice for Wales and to campaign for self-government in Wales.

The Scottish National Party (SNP) was founded in 1934 to campaign for independence for Scotland and a referendum on the subject was held in September 2014 which culminated in a 'no' to independence result.

The Social Democratic and Labour Party (SDLP) was founded in 1970, emerging from the civil rights movement of the 1960s, with the aim of promoting reform, reconciliation and partnership across the sectarian divide in Northern Ireland, and of opposing violence from any quarter.

The Democratic Unionist Party (DUP) was founded in 1971 to resist moves by the Ulster Unionist Party which were considered a threat to the Union. Its aim is to maintain Northern Ireland as an integral part of the UK.

Sinn Fein first emerged in the 1900s as a federation of nationalist clubs. It is a left-wing republican and labour party that seeks to end British governance in Ireland and achieve a 32-county republic.

GOVERNMENT AND OPPOSITION

The government is formed by the party which wins the largest number of seats in the House of Commons at a general election, or which has the support of a majority of members in the House of Commons. By tradition, the leader of the majority party is asked by the sovereign to form a government, while the largest minority party becomes the official opposition with its own leader and a shadow cabinet. Leaders of the government and opposition sit on the front benches of the Commons with their supporters (the back-benchers) sitting behind them.

FINANCIAL SUPPORT

Financial support for opposition parties in the House of Commons was introduced in 1975 and is commonly known as Short Money, after Edward Short, the leader of the house at that time, who introduced the scheme. Short Money is only payable to those parties that secured at least two seats, or one seat and more than 150,000 votes, at the previous general election and is only intended to provide assistance for parliamentary duties. The amount payable is around £17,000 for every seat won at the most recent general election plus £34 for every 200 votes gained by the party (the figures are uprated annually in line with CPI). Short Money allocations for 2017–18 were:

DUP	£217,021
Green	£130,938
Labour	£7,456,421
Liberal Democrats	£615,964
Plaid Cymru	£96,499
SDLP	£14,591
SNP	£873,216
UKIP	£43,774
UUP	£14,591

The sum paid to Sinn Fein and any other party that may choose not to take their seats in the House of Commons is

calculated on the same basis as Short Money, but is known as Representative Money. Sinn Fein's allocation in 2017–18 was £153,041.

For the financial year which commenced on 1 April 2016, the leader of the opposition's office was allocated £789,146 for running costs.

Financial support for opposition parties in the House of Lords was introduced in 1996 and is commonly known as Cranborne Money, after former leader of the house, Viscount Cranborne.

The following list of political parties are those with at least one MP or sitting member of the House of Lords in the present parliament.

CONSERVATIVE PARTY
Conservative Campaign Headquarters, 4 Matthew Parker Street, London SW1H 9HQ
T 020-7222 9000 W www.conservatives.com

Parliamentary Party Leader, Rt. Hon. Theresa May, MP
Leader in the Lords, Rt. Hon. Baroness Evans of Bowes Park
Leader in the Commons and Lord President of the Council, Rt. Hon. Andrea Leadsom, MP
Chair, Rt. Hon. Brandon Lewis, MP
Party Treasurer and Chief Executive, Sir Mick Davies

GREEN PARTY
The Biscuit Factory, Unit 201 A Block, 100 Clements Road, London SE16 4DG
T 020-3691 9400 E office@greenparty.org.uk
W www.greenparty.org.uk

Party Leaders, Sian Berry, AM and Jonathan Bartley
Deputy Leader, Amelia Womack
Chair (acting), Emma Carter
Finance Coordinator, Emma Carter

LABOUR PARTY
Labour Central, Kings Manor, Newcastle upon Tyne NE1 6PA
T 0845-092 2299 W www.labour.org.uk

General Secretary, Jennie Formby
General Secretary, Welsh Labour, Louise Magee
General Secretary, Scottish Labour Party, Brian Roy

SHADOW CABINET
Leader of the Opposition, Rt. Hon. Jeremy Corbyn, MP
Deputy Leader and Secretary of State for Digital, Culture, Media and Sport, Tom Watson, MP
Chancellor of the Exchequer, Rt. Hon. John McDonnell, MP
Foreign Secretary, Rt. Hon. Emily Thornberry, MP
Home Secretary, Rt. Hon. Diane Abbot, MP

Secretary of State for Business, Energy and Industrial Strategy, Rebecca Long-Bailey, MP
Secretary of State for Environment, Food and Rural Affairs, Sue Hayman, MP
Secretary of State for Communities and Local Government, Andrew Gwynne, MP
Secretary of State for Defence, Nia Griffith, MP
Secretary of State for Education, Angela Rayner, MP
Secretary of State for Exiting the European Union, Rt. Hon. Sir Keir Starmer, KCB, QC, MP
Secretary of State for Health, Jonathan Ashworth, MP
Secretary of State for Housing, Rt. Hon. John Healey, MP
Secretary of State for International Development, Kate Osamor, MP
Secretary of State for International Trade, Barry Gardiner, MP

Lord Chancellor and Secretary of State for Justice, Richard Burgon, MP
Secretary of State for Scotland, Lesley Laird, MP
Secretary of State for Transport, Andy McDonald, MP
Chief Secretary to the Treasury, Peter Dowd, MP
Secretary of State for Wales, Christina Rees, MP
Secretary of State for Northern Ireland, Tony Lloyd, MP
Secretary of State for Work and Pensions, Margaret Greenwood, MP
Minister for Diverse Communities, Dawn Butler, MP
Ministers for Mental Health and Social Care, Barbara Keeley, MP; Paula Sherriff, MP
Minister for Voter Engagement and Youth Affairs, Cat Smith, MP
Minister for Women and Equalities, Dawn Butler, MP
Chair and Co-National Campaign Co-ordinator, Ian Lavery, MP
Lord President of the Council and Minister for the Cabinet Office, Jon Trickett, MP
Leader of the House of Commons, Valerie Vaz, MP
Leader of the House of Lords, Rt. Hon. Baroness Smith of Basildon
Attorney General, Baroness Chakrabarti, CBE

LABOUR WHIPS
Chief Whip (Commons), Rt. Hon. Nick Brown, MP
Chief Whip (Lords), Rt. Hon. Lord McAvoy

LIBERAL DEMOCRATS
8–10 Great George Street, London SW1P 3AE
T 020-7022 0988 E info@libdems.org.uk W www.libdems.org.uk

Parliamentary Party Leader, Rt. Hon. Sir Vince Cable, MP
Deputy Party Leader, Jo Swinson, CBE, MP
Leader in the Lords, Rt. Hon. Lord Newby, OBE
President, Baroness Brinton

NORTHERN IRELAND DEMOCRATIC UNIONIST PARTY
91 Dundela Avenue, Belfast BT4 3BU
T 028-9047 1155
E info@mydup.com W www.mydup.com

Parliamentary Party Leader, Rt. Hon. Arlene Foster, MLA
Deputy Leader, Rt. Hon. Nigel Dodds, OBE, MP, MLA
Chair, Lord Morrow, MLA

PLAID CYMRU – THE PARTY OF WALES
Ty Gwynfor, Anson Court, Atlantic Wharf, Caerdydd CF10 4AL
T 029-2047 2272 E post@plaidcymru.org W www.partyof.wales

Party Leader, Leanne Wood, AM
Hon. Party President, Rt. Hon. Lord Wigley
Parliamentary Group Leader, Liz Saville Roberts, MP
Chair, Alun Ffred Jones
Chief Executive, Gareth Clubb

SCOTTISH NATIONAL PARTY
Gordon Lamb House, 3 Jackson's Entry, Edinburgh EH8 8PJ
T 0800-633 5432 E info@snp.org W www.snp.org

Westminster Parliamentary Party Leader, Rt. Hon. Ian Blackford, MP
Westminster Parliamentary Party Chief Whip, Patrick Grady, MP
First Minister of Scotland and Leader of the SNP, Rt. Hon. Nicola Sturgeon, MSP
Deputy Leader, Keith Brown, MSP
Party President, Ian Hudghton, MEP
National Treasurer, Colin Beattie, MSP
Chief Executive, Peter Murrell

SINN FEIN
53 Falls Road, Belfast BT12 4PD
T 028-9034 7350 E admin@sinnfein.ie W www.sinnfein.ie

Party President, Mary Lou McDonald, TD
Vice-President, Michelle O'Neill, MLA
Chair, Declan Kearney, MLA

MEMBERS OF PARLIAMENT *as at September 2018*

KEY
* Previously an MP for this seat in the 2015–17 parliament
† Previously an MP for this seat in any parliament prior to the 2015–17 parliament
‡ Previously an MP for a different seat in any previous parliament
§ Currently suspended from the parliamentary Conservative Party
℄ Currently suspended from the parliamentary Labour Party
** Elected via a by-election after the 2017 General Election

* **Abbott**, Rt. Hon. Diane (*b.* 1953) *Lab., Hackney North & Stoke Newington,* Maj. 35,139
* **Abrahams**, Debbie (*b.* 1960) *Lab., Oldham East & Saddleworth,* Maj. 8,182
* **Adams**, Nigel (*b.* 1966) *C., Selby & Ainsty,* Maj. 13,772
Afolami, Bim (*b.* 1986) *C., Hitchin & Harpenden,* Maj. 12,031
* **Afriyie**, Adam (*b.* 1965) *C., Windsor,* Maj. 22,384
* **Aldous**, Peter (*b.* 1961) *C., Waveney,* Maj. 9,215
* **Ali**, Rushanara (*b.* 1975) *Lab., Bethnal Green & Bow,* Maj. 35,393
* **Allan**, Lucy (*b.* 1964) *C., Telford,* Maj. 720
* **Allen**, Heidi (*b.* 1975) *C., Cambridgeshire South,* Maj. 15,952
* **Allin-Khan**, Dr Rosena (*b.* 1977) *Lab., Tooting,* Maj. 15,458
Amesbury, Mike (*b.* 1969) *Lab., Weaver Vale,* Maj. 3,928
* **Amess**, Sir David (*b.* 1952) *C., Southend West,* Maj. 10,000
* **Andrew**, Stuart (*b.* 1971) *C., Pudsey,* Maj. 331
Antoniazzi, Tonia (*b.* 1971) *Lab., Gower,* Maj. 3,269
* **Argar**, Edward (*b.* 1977) *C., Charnwood,* Maj. 16,341
* **Ashworth**, Jon (*b.* 1978) *Lab. Co-op, Leicester South,* Maj. 26,261
* **Atkins**, Victoria (*b.* 1976) *C., Louth & Horncastle,* Maj. 19,641
* **Austin**, Ian (*b.* 1965) *Lab., Dudley North,* Maj. 22
* **Bacon**, Richard (*b.* 1962) *C., Norfolk South,* Maj. 16,678
Badenoch, Kemi (*b.* 1980) *C., Saffron Walden,* Maj. 24,966
* **Bailey**, Adrian (*b.* 1945) *Lab. Co-op, West Bromwich West,* Maj. 4,460
* **Baker**, Steve (*b.* 1971) *C., Wycombe,* Maj. 6,578
* **Baldwin**, Harriett (*b.* 1960) *C., Worcestershire West,* Maj. 21,328
* **Barclay**, Stephen (*b.* 1972) *C., Cambridgeshire North East,* Maj. 21,270
* **Bardell**, Hannah (*b.* 1984) *SNP, Livingston,* Maj. 3,878
* **Baron**, John (*b.* 1959) *C., Basildon & Billericay,* Maj. 13,400
* **Barron**, Rt. Hon. Sir Kevin (*b.* 1946) *Lab., Rother Valley,* Maj. 3,882
* **Bebb**, Guto (*b.* 1968) *C., Aberconwy,* Maj. 635
* **Beckett**, Rt. Hon. Dame Margaret, DBE (*b.* 1943) *Lab., Derby South,* Maj. 11,248
** **Begley**, Órfhlaith (*b.* 1992) *SF, Tyrone West,* Maj. 7,956
* **Bellingham**, Sir Henry (*b.* 1955) *C., Norfolk North West,* Maj. 13,788
* **Benn**, Rt. Hon. Hilary (*b.* 1953) *Lab., Leeds Central,* Maj. 23,698
* **Benyon**, Rt. Hon. Richard (*b.* 1960) *C., Newbury,* Maj. 24,380
* **Bercow**, Rt. Hon. John (*b.* 1963) *Speaker, Buckingham,* Maj. 25,725
* **Beresford**, Sir Paul (*b.* 1946) *C., Mole Valley,* Maj. 24,137
* **Berger**, Luciana (*b.* 1981) *Lab. Co-op, Liverpool Wavertree,* Maj. 29,466
* **Berry**, Jake (*b.* 1978) *C., Rossendale & Darwen,* Maj. 3,216
* **Betts**, Clive (*b.* 1950) *Lab., Sheffield South East,* Maj. 11,798
* **Black**, Mhairi (*b.* 1994) *SNP, Paisley & Renfrewshire South,* Maj. 2,541

* **Blackford**, Rt. Hon. Ian (*b.* 1961) *SNP, Ross, Skye & Lochaber,* Maj. 5,919
* **Blackman**, Bob (*b.* 1956) *C., Harrow East,* Maj. 1,757
* **Blackman**, Kirsty (*b.* 1986) *SNP, Aberdeen North,* Maj. 4,139
* **Blackman-Woods**, Roberta, PHD (*b.* 1957) *Lab., Durham, City of,* Maj. 12,364
* **Blomfield**, Paul (*b.* 1953) *Lab., Sheffield Central,* Maj. 27,748
* **Blunt**, Crispin (*b.* 1960) *C., Reigate,* Maj. 17,614
* **Boles**, Nick (*b.* 1965) *C., Grantham & Stamford,* Maj. 20,094
* **Bone**, Peter (*b.* 1952) *C., Wellingborough,* Maj. 12,460
* **Bottomley**, Sir Peter (*b.* 1944) *C., Worthing West,* Maj. 12,090
Bowie, Andrew (*b.* 1988) *C., Aberdeenshire West & Kincardine,* Maj. 7,950
* **Brabin**, Tracy (*b.* 1961) *Lab. Co-op, Batley & Spen,* Maj. 8,961
Bradley, Ben (*b.* 1989) *C., Mansfield,* Maj. 1,057
* **Bradley**, Rt. Hon. Karen (*b.* 1970) *C., Staffordshire Moorlands,* Maj. 10,830
* **Bradshaw**, Rt. Hon. Ben (*b.* 1960) *Lab., Exeter,* Maj. 16,117
* **Brady**, Sir Graham (*b.* 1967) *C., Altrincham & Sale West,* Maj. 6,426
* **Brady**, Mickey (*b.* 1950) *SF, Newry & Armagh,* Maj. 12,489
* **Brake**, Rt. Hon. Tom (*b.* 1962) *LD, Carshalton & Wallington,* Maj. 1,369
* **Braverman**, Suella (*b.* 1980) *C., Fareham,* Maj. 21,555
* **Brennan**, Kevin (*b.* 1959) *Lab., Cardiff West,* Maj. 12,551
Brereton, Jack (*b.* 1991) *C., Stoke-on-Trent South,* Maj. 663
* **Bridgen**, Andrew (*b.* 1964) *C., Leicestershire North West,* Maj. 13,286
* **Brine**, Steve (*b.* 1974) *C., Winchester,* Maj. 9,999
* **Brock**, Deidre (*b.* 1961) *SNP, Edinburgh North & Leith,* Maj. 1,625
* **Brokenshire**, Rt. Hon. James (*b.* 1968) *C., Old Bexley & Sidcup,* Maj. 15,466
* **Brown**, Alan (*b.* 1970) *SNP, Kilmarnock & Loudoun,* Maj. 6,269
* **Brown**, Lyn (*b.* 1960) *Lab., West Ham,* Maj. 36,754
* **Brown**, Rt. Hon. Nick (*b.* 1950) *Lab., Newcastle upon Tyne East,* Maj. 19,261
* **Bruce**, Fiona (*b.* 1957) *C., Congleton,* Maj. 12,619
* **Bryant**, Chris (*b.* 1962) *Lab., Rhondda,* Maj. 13,746
* **Buck**, Karen (*b.* 1958) *Lab., Westminster North,* Maj. 11,512
* **Buckland**, Robert (*b.* 1968) *C., Swindon South,* Maj. 2,464
* **Burden**, Richard (*b.* 1954) *Lab., Birmingham Northfield,* Maj. 4,667
Burghart, Alex (*b.* 1977) *C., Brentwood & Ongar,* Maj. 24,002
* **Burgon**, Richard (*b.* 1980) *Lab., Leeds East,* Maj. 12,752
* **Burns**, Conor (*b.* 1972) *C., Bournemouth West,* Maj. 7,711
* **Burt**, Rt. Hon. Alistair (*b.* 1955) *C., Bedfordshire North East,* Maj. 20,862
* **Butler**, Dawn (*b.* 1969) *Lab., Brent Central,* Maj. 27,997
* **Byrne**, Rt. Hon. Liam (*b.* 1970) *Lab., Birmingham Hodge Hill,* Maj. 31,026
† **Cable**, Rt. Hon. Sir Vince, PHD (*b.* 1943) *LD, Twickenham,* Maj. 9,762
* **Cadbury**, Ruth (*b.* 1959) *Lab., Brentford & Isleworth,* Maj. 12,182
* **Cairns**, Rt. Hon. Alun (*b.* 1970) *C., Vale of Glamorgan,* Maj. 2,190
* **Cameron**, Dr Lisa (*b.* 1972) *SNP, East Kilbride, Strathaven & Lesmahagow,* Maj. 3,866
* **Campbell**, Rt. Hon. Alan (*b.* 1957) *Lab., Tynemouth,* Maj. 11,666
* **Campbell**, Gregory (*b.* 1953) *DUP, Londonderry East,* Maj. 8,842

* **Campbell**, Ronnie (*b.* 1943) *Lab., Blyth Valley*, Maj. 7,915

Carden, Dan (*b.* 1987) *Lab., Liverpool Walton*, Maj. 32,551

* **Carmichael**, Rt. Hon. Alistair (*b.* 1965) *LD, Orkney & Shetland*, Maj. 4,563

* **Cartlidge**, James (*b.* 1974) *C., Suffolk South*, Maj. 17,749

* **Cash**, Sir William (*b.* 1940) *C., Stone*, Maj. 17,495

* **Caulfield**, Maria (*b.* 1974) *C., Lewes*, Maj. 5,508

* **Chalk**, Alex (*b.* 1977) *C., Cheltenham*, Maj. 2,569

* **Champion**, Sarah (*b.* 1969) *Lab., Rotherham*, Maj. 11,387

* **Chapman**, Douglas (*b.* 1955) *SNP, Dunfermline & Fife West*, Maj. 844

* **Chapman**, Jenny (*b.* 1973) *Lab., Darlington*, Maj. 3,280

Charalambous, Bambos (*b.* 1967) *Lab., Enfield Southgate*, Maj. 4,355

* **Cherry**, Joanna (*b.* 1966) *SNP, Edinburgh South West*, Maj. 1,097

* **Chishti**, Rehman (*b.* 1978) *C., Gillingham & Rainham*, Maj. 9,430

* **Chope**, Sir Christopher, OBE (*b.* 1947) *C., Christchurch*, Maj. 25,171

* **Churchill**, Jo (*b.* 1964) *C., Bury St Edmunds*, Maj. 18,441

Clark, Colin (*b.* 1968) *C., Gordon*, Maj. 2,607

* **Clark**, Rt. Hon. Greg, PHD (*b.* 1967) *C., Tunbridge Wells*, Maj. 16,465

* **Clarke**, Rt. Hon. Kenneth, CH (*b.* 1940) *C., Rushcliffe*, Maj. 8,010

Clarke, Simon (*b.* 1984) *C., Middlesbrough South & Cleveland East*, Maj. 1,020

* **Cleverly**, James (*b.* 1969) *C., Braintree*, Maj. 18,422

* **Clifton-Brown**, Sir Geoffrey (*b.* 1953) *C., Cotswolds, The*, Maj. 25,499

* **Clwyd**, Rt. Hon. Ann (*b.* 1937) *Lab., Cynon Valley*, Maj. 13,238

* **Coaker**, Vernon (*b.* 1953) *Lab., Gedling*, Maj. 4,694

* **Coffey**, Ann (*b.* 1946) *Lab., Stockport*, Maj. 14,477

* **Coffey**, Therese, PHD (*b.* 1971) *C., Suffolk Coastal*, Maj. 16,012

* **Collins**, Damian (*b.* 1974) *C., Folkestone & Hythe*, Maj. 15,411

* **Cooper**, Julie (*b.* 1960) *Lab., Burnley*, Maj. 6,353

* **Cooper**, Rosie (*b.* 1950) *Lab., Lancashire West*, Maj. 11,689

* **Cooper**, Rt. Hon. Yvette (*b.* 1969) *Lab., Normanton, Pontefract & Castleford*, Maj. 14,499

* **Corbyn**, Rt. Hon. Jeremy (*b.* 1949) *Lab., Islington North*, Maj. 33,215

* **Costa**, Alberto (*b.* 1971) *C., Leicestershire South*, Maj. 18,631

* **Courts**, Robert (*b.* 1978) *C., Witney*, Maj. 21,241

* **Cowan**, Ronnie (*b.* 1959) *SNP, Inverclyde*, Maj. 384

* **Cox**, Rt. Hon. Geoffrey (*b.* 1960) *C., Devon West & Torridge*, Maj. 20,686

* **Coyle**, Neil (*b.* 1978) *Lab., Bermondsey & Old Southwark*, Maj. 12,972

* **Crabb**, Rt. Hon. Stephen (*b.* 1973) *C., Preseli Pembrokeshire*, Maj. 314

* **Crausby**, Sir David (*b.* 1946) *Lab., Bolton North East*, Maj. 3,797

* **Crawley**, Angela (*b.* 1987) *SNP, Lanark & Hamilton East*, Maj. 266

* **Creagh**, Mary (*b.* 1967) *Lab., Wakefield*, Maj. 2,176

* **Creasy**, Stella, PHD (*b.* 1977) *Lab. Co-op, Walthamstow*, Maj. 32,017

* **Crouch**, Tracey (*b.* 1975) *C., Chatham & Aylesford*, Maj. 10,458

* **Cruddas**, Jon (*b.* 1962) *Lab., Dagenham & Rainham*, Maj. 4,652

* **Cryer**, John (*b.* 1964) *Lab., Leyton & Wanstead*, Maj. 22,607

* **Cummins**, Judith (*b.* 1967) *Lab., Bradford South*, Maj. 6,700

* **Cunningham**, Alex (*b.* 1955) *Lab., Stockton North*, Maj. 8,715

* **Cunningham**, Jim (*b.* 1941) *Lab., Coventry South*, Maj. 7,947

** **Daby**, Janet (*b.* 1972) *Lab., Lewisham East*, Maj. 5,629

* **Dakin**, Nic (*b.* 1955) *Lab., Scunthorpe*, Maj. 3,431

† **Davey**, Rt. Hon. Sir Edward (*b.* 1965) *LD, Kingston & Surbiton*, Maj. 4,124

* **David**, Wayne (*b.* 1957) *Lab., Caerphilly*, Maj. 12,078

* **Davies**, Chris (*b.* 1967) *C., Brecon & Radnorshire*, Maj. 8,038

* **Davies**, David (*b.* 1970) *C., Monmouth*, Maj. 8,206

* **Davies**, Geraint (*b.* 1960) *Lab. Co-op, Swansea West*, Maj. 10,598

* **Davies**, Glyn (*b.* 1944) *C., Montgomeryshire*, Maj. 9,285

* **Davies**, Mims (*b.* 1975) *C., Eastleigh*, Maj. 14,179

* **Davies**, Philip (*b.* 1972) *C., Shipley*, Maj. 4,681

* **Davis**, Rt. Hon. David (*b.* 1948) *C., Haltemprice & Howden*, Maj. 15,405

* **Day**, Martyn (*b.* 1971) *SNP, Linlithgow & Falkirk East*, Maj. 2,919

De Cordova, Marsha (*b.* 1976) *Lab., Battersea*, Maj. 2,416

* **De Piero**, Gloria (*b.* 1972) *Lab., Ashfield*, Maj. 441

* **Debbonaire**, Thangam (*b.* 1966) *Lab., Bristol West*, Maj. 37,336

Dent Coad, Emma (*b.* 1954) *Lab., Kensington*, Maj. 20

Dhesi, Tanmanjeet (*b.* 1978) *Lab., Slough*, Maj. 16,998

* **Dinenage**, Caroline (*b.* 1971) *C., Gosport*, Maj. 17,211

* **Djanogly**, Jonathan (*b.* 1965) *C., Huntingdon*, Maj. 14,475

Docherty, Leo (*b.* 1976) *C., Aldershot*, Maj. 11,478

* **Docherty**, Martin (*b.* 1971) *SNP, Dunbartonshire West*, Maj. 2,288

Dockerill, Julia (*b.* 1984) *C., Hornchurch & Upminster*, Maj. 17,723

Dodds, Anneliese, PHD (*b.* 1978) *Lab. Co-op, Oxford East*, Maj. 23,284

* **Dodds**, Rt. Hon. Nigel (*b.* 1958) *DUP, Belfast North*, Maj. 2,081

* **Donaldson**, Rt. Hon. Sir Jeffrey (*b.* 1962) *DUP, Lagan Valley*, Maj. 19,229

* **Donelan**, Michelle (*b.* 1984) *C., Chippenham*, Maj. 16,630

* **Dorries**, Nadine (*b.* 1957) *C., Bedfordshire Mid*, Maj. 20,983

* **Double**, Steve (*b.* 1966) *C., St Austell & Newquay*, Maj. 11,142

* **Doughty**, Stephen (*b.* 1980) *Lab. Co-op, Cardiff South & Penarth*, Maj. 14,864

* **Dowd**, Peter (*b.* 1957) *Lab., Bootle*, Maj. 36,200

* **Dowden**, Oliver, CBE (*b.* 1978) *C., Hertsmere*, Maj. 16,951

* **Doyle-Price**, Jackie (*b.* 1969) *C., Thurrock*, Maj. 345

* **Drax**, Richard (*b.* 1958) *C., Dorset South*, Maj. 11,695

† **Drew**, David (*b.* 1952) *Lab. Co-op, Stroud*, Maj. 687

* **Dromey**, Jack (*b.* 1948) *Lab., Birmingham Erdington*, Maj. 7,285

* **Duddridge**, James (*b.* 1971) *C., Rochford & Southend East*, Maj. 5,548

Duffield, Rosie (*b.* 1971) *Lab., Canterbury*, Maj. 187

Duguid, David (*b.* 1970) *C., Banff & Buchan*, Maj. 3,693

* **Duncan**, Rt. Hon. Sir Alan, KCMG (*b.* 1957) *C., Rutland & Melton*, Maj. 23,104

* **Duncan Smith**, Rt. Hon. Iain (*b.* 1954) *C., Chingford & Woodford Green*, Maj. 2,438

* **Dunne**, Philip (*b.* 1958) *C., Ludlow*, Maj. 19,286

* **Eagle**, Angela (*b.* 1961) *Lab., Wallasey*, Maj. 23,320

* **Eagle**, Maria (*b.* 1961) *Lab., Garston & Halewood*, Maj. 32,149

* **Edwards**, Jonathan (*b.* 1976) *PC, Carmarthen East & Dinefwr*, Maj. 3,908

* **Efford**, Clive (*b.* 1958) *Lab., Eltham*, Maj. 6,296

* **Elliott**, Julie (*b.* 1963) *Lab., Sunderland Central*, Maj. 9,997

* **Ellis**, Michael (*b.* 1967) *C., Northampton North*, Maj. 807

* **Ellman**, Dame Louise, DBE (*b.* 1945) *Lab. Co-op, Liverpool Riverside*, Maj. 35,947

* **Ellwood**, Rt. Hon. Tobias (*b.* 1966) *C., Bournemouth East*, Maj. 7,937

* **Healey**, Rt. Hon. John (*b.* 1960) *Lab., Wentworth & Dearne,* Maj. 14,803
* **Heappey**, James (*b.* 1981) *C., Wells,* Maj. 7,582
* **Heaton-Harris**, Chris (*b.* 1967) *C., Daventry,* Maj. 21,734
* **Heaton-Jones**, Peter (*b.* 1963) *C., Devon North,* Maj. 4,332
* **Henderson**, Gordon (*b.* 1948) *C., Sittingbourne & Sheppey,* Maj. 15,211
* **Hendrick**, Sir Mark (*b.* 1958) *Lab. Co-op, Preston,* Maj. 15,723
* **Hendry**, Drew (*b.* 1964) *SNP, Inverness, Nairn, Badenoch & Strathspey,* Maj. 4,924
* **Hepburn**, Stephen (*b.* 1959) *Lab., Jarrow,* Maj. 17,263
* **Herbert**, Rt. Hon. Nick, CBE (*b.* 1963) *C., Arundel & South Downs,* Maj. 23,883
* **Hermon**, Lady (Sylvia) (*b.* 1955) *Ind., Down North,* Maj. 1,208
Hill, Mike *Lab., Hartlepool,* Maj. 7,650
* **Hillier**, Meg (*b.* 1969) *Lab. Co-op, Hackney South & Shoreditch,* Maj. 37,931
* **Hinds**, Rt. Hon. Damian (*b.* 1969) *C., Hampshire East,* Maj. 25,852
* **Hoare**, Simon (*b.* 1969) *C., Dorset North,* Maj. 25,777
Hobhouse, Wera (*b.* 1960) *LD, Bath,* Maj. 5,694
* **Hodge**, Rt. Hon. Dame Margaret, DBE (*b.* 1944) *Lab., Barking,* Maj. 21,608
* **Hodgson**, Sharon (*b.* 1966) *Lab., Washington & Sunderland West,* Maj. 12,940
* **Hoey**, Kate (*b.* 1946) *Lab., Vauxhall,* Maj. 20,250
* **Hollern**, Kate (*b.* 1955) *Lab., Blackburn,* Maj. 20,368
* **Hollingbery**, George (*b.* 1963) *C., Meon Valley,* Maj. 25,692
* **Hollinrake**, Kevin (*b.* 1963) *C., Thirsk & Malton,* Maj. 19,001
* **Hollobone**, Philip (*b.* 1964) *C., Kettering,* Maj. 10,562
* **Holloway**, Adam (*b.* 1965) *C., Gravesham,* Maj. 9,347
*⦗ **Hopkins**, Kelvin (*b.* 1941) *Lab., Luton North,* Maj. 14,364
* **Hosie**, Stewart (*b.* 1963) *SNP, Dundee East,* Maj. 6,645
* **Howarth**, Rt. Hon. George (*b.* 1949) *Lab., Knowsley,* Maj. 42,214
* **Howell**, John (*b.* 1955) *C., Henley,* Maj. 22,294
* **Hoyle**, Rt. Hon. Sir Lindsay (*b.* 1957) *Lab., Chorley,* Maj. 7,512
* **Huddleston**, Nigel (*b.* 1970) *C., Worcestershire Mid,* Maj. 23,326
Hughes, Eddie (*b.* 1968) *C., Walsall North,* Maj. 2,601
* **Hunt**, Rt. Hon. Jeremy (*b.* 1966) *C., Surrey South West,* Maj. 21,590
* **Huq**, Dr Rupa (*b.* 1972) *Lab., Ealing Central & Acton,* Maj. 13,807
* **Hurd**, Rt. Hon. Nick (*b.* 1962) *C., Ruislip, Northwood & Pinner,* Maj. 13,980
* **Hussain**, Imran (*b.* 1978) *Lab., Bradford East,* Maj. 20,540
Jack, Alister (*b.* 1964) *C., Dumfries & Galloway,* Maj. 5,643
* **James**, Margot (*b.* 1957) *C., Stourbridge,* Maj. 7,654
Jardine, Christine (*b.* 1960) *Edinburgh West,* Maj. 2,988
* **Jarvis**, Dan (*b.* 1972) *Lab., Barnsley Central,* Maj. 15,546
* **Javid**, Rt. Hon. Sajid (*b.* 1969) *C., Bromsgrove,* Maj. 16,573
* **Jayawardena**, Ranil (*b.* 1986) *C., Hampshire North East,* Maj. 27,772
* **Jenkin**, Hon. Sir Bernard (*b.* 1959) *C., Harwich & Essex North,* Maj. 14,356
* **Jenkyns**, Andrea (*b.* 1974) *C., Morley & Outwood,* Maj. 2,104
* **Jenrick**, Robert (*b.* 1982) *C., Newark,* Maj. 18,149
* **Johnson**, Rt. Hon. Boris (*b.* 1964) *C., Uxbridge & Ruislip South,* Maj. 5,034
* **Johnson**, Caroline (*b.* 1977) *C., Sleaford & North Hykeham,* Maj. 25,237
* **Johnson**, Diana (*b.* 1966) *Lab., Hull North,* Maj. 14,262
* **Johnson**, Gareth (*b.* 1969) *C., Dartford,* Maj. 13,186
* **Johnson**, Joseph (*b.* 1971) *C., Orpington,* Maj. 19,461

* **Jones**, Andrew (*b.* 1963) *C., Harrogate & Knaresborough,* Maj. 18,168
Jones, Darren (*b.* 1986) *Lab., Bristol North West,* Maj. 4,761
* **Jones**, Rt. Hon. David (*b.* 1952) *C., Clwyd West,* Maj. 3,437
* **Jones**, Gerald (*b.* 1970) *Lab., Merthyr Tydfil & Rhymney,* Maj. 16,334
* **Jones**, Graham (*b.* 1966) *Lab., Hyndburn,* Maj. 5,815
* **Jones**, Helen (*b.* 1954) *Lab., Warrington North,* Maj. 9,582
* **Jones**, Kevan (*b.* 1964) *Lab., Durham North,* Maj. 12,939
Jones, Sarah (*b.* 1972) *Lab., Croydon Central,* Maj. 5,652
* **Jones**, Susan Elan (*b.* 1968) *Lab., Clwyd South,* Maj. 4,356
* **Jones**, Marcus (*b.* 1974) *C., Nuneaton,* Maj. 4,739
* **Kane**, Mike (*b.* 1969) *Lab., Wythenshawe & Sale East,* Maj. 14,944
* **Kawczynski**, Daniel (*b.* 1972) *C., Shrewsbury & Atcham,* Maj. 6,627
Keegan, Gillian (*b.* 1968) *C., Chichester,* Maj. 22,621
* **Keeley**, Barbara (*b.* 1952) *Lab., Worsley & Eccles South,* Maj. 8,379
* **Kendall**, Liz (*b.* 1971) *Lab., Leicester West,* Maj. 11,060
* **Kennedy**, Seema (*b.* 1974) *C., South Ribble,* Maj. 7,421
Kerr, Stephen (*b.* 1960) *C., Stirling,* Maj. 148
Khan, Afzal, CBE (*b.* 1958) *Lab., Manchester Gorton,* Maj. 31,730
Killen, Ged (*b.* 1986) *Lab. Co-op, Rutherglen & Hamilton West,* Maj. 265
* **Kinnock**, Stephen (*b.* 1970) *Lab., Aberavon,* Maj. 16,761
* **Knight**, Rt. Hon. Sir Greg (*b.* 1949) *C., Yorkshire East,* Maj. 15,006
* **Knight**, Julian (*b.* 1972) *C., Solihull,* Maj. 20,571
* **Kwarteng**, Kwasi, PHD (*b.* 1975) *C., Spelthorne,* Maj. 13,425
* **Kyle**, Peter, DPHIL (*b.* 1970) *Lab., Hove,* Maj. 18,757
* **Laing**, Rt. Hon. Dame Eleanor, DBE (*b.* 1958) *C., Epping Forest,* Maj. 18,243
Laird, Lesley (*b.* 1958) *Lab., Kirkcaldy & Cowdenbeath,* Maj. 259
Lake, Ben (*b.* 1993) *PC, Ceredigion,* Maj. 104
* **Lamb**, Rt. Hon. Norman (*b.* 1957) *LD, Norfolk North,* Maj. 3,512
* **Lammy**, Rt. Hon. David (*b.* 1972) *Lab., Tottenham,* Maj. 34,584
Lamont, John (*b.* 1976) *C., Berwickshire, Roxburgh & Selkirk,* Maj. 11,060
* **Lancaster**, Rt. Hon. Mark (*b.* 1970) *C., Milton Keynes North,* Maj. 1,915
* **Latham**, Pauline, OBE (*b.* 1948) *C., Derbyshire Mid,* Maj. 11,616
* **Lavery**, Ian (*b.* 1963) *Lab., Wansbeck,* Maj. 10,435
* **Law**, Chris (*b.* 1969) *SNP, Dundee West,* Maj. 5,262
* **Leadsom**, Rt. Hon. Andrea, CBE (*b.* 1963) *C., Northamptonshire South,* Maj. 22,840
Lee, Karen (*b.* 1961) *Lab., Lincoln,* Maj. 1,538
* **Lee**, Dr Phillip (*b.* 1970) *C., Bracknell,* Maj. 16,016
* **Lefroy**, Jeremy (*b.* 1959) *C., Stafford,* Maj. 7,729
* **Leigh**, Sir Edward (*b.* 1950) *C., Gainsborough,* Maj. 17,023
* **Leslie**, Chris (*b.* 1972) *Lab. Co-op, Nottingham East,* Maj. 19,590
* **Letwin**, Rt. Hon. Sir Oliver, PHD (*b.* 1956) *C., Dorset West,* Maj. 19,091
* **Lewell-Buck**, Emma (*b.* 1978) *Lab., South Shields,* Maj. 14,508
Lewer, Andrew (*b.* 1971) *C., Northampton South,* Maj. 1,159
* **Lewis**, Rt. Hon. Brandon (*b.* 1971) *C., Great Yarmouth,* Maj. 7,973
* **Lewis**, Clive (*b.* 1971) *Lab., Norwich South,* Maj. 15,596
*⦗ **Lewis**, Ivan (*b.* 1967) *Lab., Bury South,* Maj. 5,965
* **Lewis**, Rt. Hon. Julian, DPHIL (*b.* 1951) *C., New Forest East,* Maj. 21,995

* **Liddell-Grainger**, Ian (*b.* 1959) *C., Bridgwater & Somerset West*, Maj. 15,448
* **Lidington**, Rt. Hon. David, CBE (*b.* 1956) *C., Aylesbury*, Maj. 14,696
Linden, David (*b.* 1990) *SNP, Glasgow East*, Maj. 75
Little Pengelly, Emma (*b.* 1979) *DUP, Belfast South*, Maj. 1,996
† **Lloyd**, Stephen (*b.* 1957) *LD, Eastbourne*, Maj. 1,609
‡ **Lloyd**, Tony (*b.* 1950) *Lab., Rochdale*, Maj. 14,819
* **Long Bailey**, Rebecca (*b.* 1979) *Lab., Salford & Eccles*, Maj. 19,132
* **Lopresti**, Jack (*b.* 1969) *C., Filton & Bradley Stoke*, Maj. 4,182
* **Lord**, Jonathan (*b.* 1962) *C., Woking*, Maj. 16,724
* **Loughton**, Tim (*b.* 1962) *C., Worthing East & Shoreham*, Maj. 5,106
* **Lucas**, Caroline, PHD (*b.* 1960) *Green, Brighton Pavilion*, Maj. 14,689
* **Lucas**, Ian (*b.* 1960) *Lab., Wrexham*, Maj. 1,832
* **Lynch**, Holly (*b.* 1986) *Lab., Halifax*, Maj. 5,376
* **McCabe**, Steve (*b.* 1955) *Lab., Birmingham Selly Oak*, Maj. 15,207
McCallion, Elisha (*b.* 1982) *SF, Foyle*, Maj. 169
* **McCarthy**, Kerry (*b.* 1965) *Lab., Bristol East*, Maj. 13,394
* **McDonagh**, Siobhain (*b.* 1960) *Lab., Mitcham & Morden*, Maj. 21,375
* **McDonald**, Andy (*b.* 1958) *Lab., Middlesbrough*, Maj. 13,873
* **McDonald**, Stewart (*b.* 1986) *SNP, Glasgow South*, Maj. 2,027
* **McDonald**, Stuart (*b.* 1978) *SNP, Cumbernauld, Kilsyth & Kirkintilloch East*, Maj. 4,264
* **McDonnell**, Rt. Hon. John (*b.* 1951) *Lab., Hayes & Harlington*, Maj. 18,115
* **McFadden**, Rt. Hon. Pat (*b.* 1965) *Lab., Wolverhampton South East*, Maj. 8,514
* **McGinn**, Conor (*b.* 1984) *Lab., St Helens North*, Maj. 18,406
* **McGovern**, Alison (*b.* 1980) *Lab., Wirral South*, Maj. 8,323
* **McInnes**, Liz (*b.* 1959) *Lab., Heywood & Middleton*, Maj. 7,617
* **Mackinlay**, Craig (*b.* 1966) *C., Thanet South*, Maj. 6,387
* **McKinnell**, Catherine (*b.* 1976) *Lab., Newcastle upon Tyne North*, Maj. 10,349
Maclean, Rachel (*b.* 1965) *C., Redditch*, Maj. 7,363
* **McLoughlin**, Rt. Hon. Sir Patrick (*b.* 1957) *C., Derbyshire Dales*, Maj. 14,327
* **McMahon**, Jim (*b.* 1980) *Lab. Co-op, Oldham West & Royton*, Maj. 17,198
McMorrin, Anna (*b.* 1971) *Lab., Cardiff North*, Maj. 4,174
* **McNally**, John (*b.* 1951) *SNP, Falkirk*, Maj. 4,923
* **MacNeil**, Angus (*b.* 1970) *SNP, Na h-Eileanan an Iar*, Maj. 1,007
* **McPartland**, Stephen (*b.* 1976) *C., Stevenage*, Maj. 3,384
‡ **McVey**, Rt. Hon. Esther (*b.* 1967) *C., Tatton*, Maj. 14,787
* **Madders**, Justin (*b.* 1972) *Lab., Ellesmere Port & Neston*, Maj. 11,390
* **Mahmood**, Khalid (*b.* 1961) *Lab., Birmingham Perry Barr*, Maj. 18,383
* **Mahmood**, Shabana (*b.* 1980) *Lab., Birmingham Ladywood*, Maj. 28,714
* **Main**, Anne (*b.* 1957) *C., St Albans*, Maj. 6,109
* **Mak**, Alan (*b.* 1983) *C., Havant*, Maj. 15,956
* **Malhotra**, Seema (*b.* 1972) *Lab. Co-op, Feltham & Heston*, Maj. 15,603
* **Malthouse**, Kit (*b.* 1966) *C., Hampshire North West*, Maj. 22,679
* **Mann**, John (*b.* 1960) *Lab., Bassetlaw*, Maj. 4,852
* **Mann**, Scott (*b.* 1977) *C., Cornwall North*, Maj. 7,200
* **Marsden**, Gordon (*b.* 1953) *Lab., Blackpool South*, Maj. 2,523
Martin, Sandy (*b.* 1957) *Lab., Ipswich*, Maj. 831

* **Maskell**, Rachael (*b.* 1972) *Lab. Co-op, York Central*, Maj. 18,575
* **Maskey**, Paul (*b.* 1967) *SF, Belfast West*, Maj. 21,652
Masterton, Paul (*b.* 1985) *C., Renfrewshire East*, Maj. 4,712
* **Matheson**, Chris (*b.* 1968) *Lab., Chester, City of*, Maj. 9,176
* **May**, Rt. Hon. Theresa (*b.* 1956) *C., Maidenhead*, Maj. 26,457
* **Maynard**, Paul (*b.* 1975) *C., Blackpool North & Cleveleys*, Maj. 2,023
* **Mearns**, Ian (*b.* 1957) *Lab., Gateshead*, Maj. 17,350
* **Menzies**, Mark (*b.* 1971) *C., Fylde*, Maj. 11,805
* **Mercer**, Johnny (*b.* 1981) *C., Plymouth Moor View*, Maj. 5,019
* **Merriman**, Huw (*b.* 1973) *C., Bexhill & Battle*, Maj. 22,165
* **Metcalfe**, Stephen (*b.* 1966) *C., Basildon South & Thurrock East*, Maj. 11,490
* **Miliband**, Rt. Hon. Edward (*b.* 1969) *Lab., Doncaster North*, Maj. 14,024
* **Miller**, Rt. Hon. Maria (*b.* 1964) *C., Basingstoke*, Maj. 9,466
* **Milling**, Amanda (*b.* 1975) *C., Cannock Chase*, Maj. 8,391
* **Mills**, Nigel (*b.* 1974) *C., Amber Valley*, Maj. 8,300
* **Milton**, Rt. Hon. Anne (*b.* 1955) *C., Guildford*, Maj. 17,040
* **Mitchell**, Rt. Hon. Andrew (*b.* 1956) *C., Sutton Coldfield*, Maj. 15,339
* **Molloy**, Francie (*b.* 1950) *SF, Ulster Mid*, Maj. 12,890
* **Monaghan**, Carol (*b.* 1972) *SNP, Glasgow North West*, Maj. 2,561
* **Moon**, Madeleine (*b.* 1950) *Lab., Bridgend*, Maj. 4,700
Moore, Damien (*b.* 1980) *C., Southport*, Maj. 2,914
Moran, Layla (*b.* 1982) *LD, Oxford West & Abingdon*, Maj. 816
* **Mordaunt**, Rt. Hon. Penny (*b.* 1973) *C., Portsmouth North*, Maj. 9,965
* **Morden**, Jessica (*b.* 1968) *Lab., Newport East*, Maj. 8,003
* **Morgan**, Rt. Hon. Nicky (*b.* 1972) *C., Loughborough*, Maj. 4,269
Morgan, Stephen (*b.* 1981) *Lab., Portsmouth South*, Maj. 1,554
* **Morris**, Anne Marie (*b.* 1957) *C., Newton Abbot*, Maj. 17,160
* **Morris**, David (*b.* 1966) *C., Morecambe & Lunesdale*, Maj. 1,399
* **Morris**, Grahame (*b.* 1961) *Lab., Easington*, Maj. 14,892
* **Morris**, James (*b.* 1967) *C., Halesowen & Rowley Regis*, Maj. 5,253
* **Morton**, Wendy (*b.* 1967) *C., Aldridge-Brownhills*, Maj. 14,307
* **Mundell**, Rt. Hon. David (*b.* 1962) *C., Dumfriesshire, Clydesdale & Tweeddale*, Maj. 9,441
* **Murray**, Ian (*b.* 1976) *Lab., Edinburgh South*, Maj. 15,514
* **Murray**, Sheryll (*b.* 1956) *C., Cornwall South East*, Maj. 17,443
* **Murrison**, Dr Andrew (*b.* 1961) *C., Wiltshire South West*, Maj. 18,326
* **Nandy**, Lisa (*b.* 1979) *Lab., Wigan*, Maj. 16,027
* **Neill**, Robert (*b.* 1952) *C., Bromley & Chislehurst*, Maj. 9,590
* **Newlands**, Gavin (*b.* 1980) *SNP, Paisley & Renfrewshire North*, Maj. 2,613
* **Newton**, Sarah (*b.* 1962) *C., Truro & Falmouth*, Maj. 3,792
* **Nokes**, Rt. Hon. Caroline (*b.* 1972) *C., Romsey & Southampton North*, Maj. 18,006
* **Norman**, Jesse (*b.* 1962) *C., Hereford & Herefordshire South*, Maj. 15,013
Norris, Alex (*b.* 1984) *Lab. Co-op, Nottingham North*, Maj. 11,160
O'Brien, Neil (*b.* 1978) *C., Harborough*, Maj. 12,429
* **Offord**, Matthew, PHD (*b.* 1969) *C., Hendon*, Maj. 1,072
* **O'Hara**, Brendan (*b.* 1963) *SNP, Argyll & Bute*, Maj. 1,328
O'Mara, Jared (*b.* 1981) *Ind., Sheffield Hallam*, Maj. 2,125
Onasanya, Fiona (*b.* 1983) *Lab., Peterborough*, Maj. 607
* **Onn**, Melanie (*b.* 1979) *Lab., Great Grimsby*, Maj. 2,565
* **Onwurah**, Chi (*b.* 1965) *Lab., Newcastle upon Tyne Central*, Maj. 14,937
* **Opperman**, Guy (*b.* 1965) *C., Hexham*, Maj. 9,236

* **Osamor**, Kate (*b.* 1968) *Lab. Co-op, Edmonton*, Maj. 21,115
* **Owen**, Albert (*b.* 1959) *Lab., Ynys Mon*, Maj. 5,259
* **Paisley**, Hon. Ian (*b.* 1960) *DUP, Antrim North*, Maj. 20,643
* **Parish**, Neil (*b.* 1956) *C., Tiverton & Honiton*, Maj. 19,801
* **Patel**, Rt. Hon. Priti (*b.* 1972) *C., Witham*, Maj. 18,646
* **Paterson**, Rt. Hon. Owen (*b.* 1956) *C., Shropshire North*, Maj. 16,355
* **Pawsey**, Mark (*b.* 1957) *C., Rugby*, Maj. 8,212
Peacock, Stephanie (*b.* 1986) *Lab., Barnsley East*, Maj. 13,283
* **Pearce**, Teresa (*b.* 1955) *Lab., Erith & Thamesmead*, Maj. 10,014
* **Penning**, Rt. Hon. Sir Mike (*b.* 1957) *C., Hemel Hempstead*, Maj. 9,445
* **Pennycook**, Matthew (*b.* 1982) *Lab., Greenwich & Woolwich*, Maj. 20,714
* **Penrose**, John (*b.* 1964) *C., Weston-Super-Mare*, Maj. 11,544
* **Percy**, Andrew (*b.* 1977) *C., Brigg & Goole*, Maj. 12,363
* **Perkins**, Toby (*b.* 1970) *Lab., Chesterfield*, Maj. 9,605
* **Perry**, Rt. Hon. Claire (*b.* 1964) *C., Devizes*, Maj. 21,136
* **Phillips**, Jess (*b.* 1981) *Lab., Birmingham Yardley*, Maj. 16,574
* **Phillipson**, Bridget (*b.* 1983) *Lab., Houghton & Sunderland South*, Maj. 12,341
* **Philp**, Chris (*b.* 1976) *C., Croydon South*, Maj. 11,406
Pidcock, Laura (*b.* 1988) *Lab., Durham North West*, Maj. 8,792
* **Pincher**, Christopher (*b.* 1969) *C., Tamworth*, Maj. 12,347
Platt, Jo (*b.* 1968) *Lab. Co-op, Leigh*, Maj. 9,554
Pollard, Luke (*b.* 1980) *Lab. Co-op, Plymouth Sutton & Devonport*, Maj. 6,002
* **Poulter**, Dr Dan (*b.* 1978) *C., Suffolk Central & Ipswich North*, Maj. 17,185
* **Pound**, Stephen (*b.* 1948) *Lab., Ealing North*, Maj. 19,693
* **Pow**, Rebecca (*b.* 1960) *C., Taunton Deane*, Maj. 15,887
* **Powell**, Lucy (*b.* 1974) *Lab. Co-op, Manchester Central*, Maj. 31,445
* **Prentis**, Hon. Victoria (*b.* 1971) *C., Banbury*, Maj. 12,399
* **Prisk**, Mark (*b.* 1962) *C., Hertford & Stortford*, Maj. 19,035
* **Pritchard**, Mark (*b.* 1966) *C., Wrekin, The*, Maj. 9,564
* **Pursglove**, Tom (*b.* 1988) *C., Corby*, Maj. 2,690
* **Quin**, Jeremy (*b.* 1968) *C., Horsham*, Maj. 23,484
* **Quince**, Will (*b.* 1982) *C., Colchester*, Maj. 5,677
* **Qureshi**, Yasmin (*b.* 1963) *Lab., Bolton South East*, Maj. 13,126
* **Raab**, Rt. Hon. Dominic (*b.* 1974) *C., Esher & Walton*, Maj. 23,298
Rashid, Faisal (*b.* 1972) *Lab., Warrington South*, Maj. 2,549
* **Rayner**, Angela (*b.* 1980) *Lab., Ashton Under Lyne*, Maj. 11,295
* **Redwood**, Rt. Hon. John, DPHIL (*b.* 1951) *C., Wokingham*, Maj. 18,798
* **Reed**, Steve (*b.* 1963) *Lab. Co-op, Croydon North*, Maj. 32,365
* **Rees**, Christina (*b.* 1954) *Lab. Co-op, Neath*, Maj. 12,631
* **Rees-Mogg**, Jacob (*b.* 1969) *C., Somerset North East*, Maj. 10,235
Reeves, Ellie *Lab., Lewisham West & Penge*, Maj. 23,162
* **Reeves**, Rachel (*b.* 1979) *Lab., Leeds West*, Maj. 15,965
* **Reynolds**, Emma (*b.* 1977) *Lab., Wolverhampton North East*, Maj. 4,587
* **Reynolds**, Jonathan (*b.* 1980) *Lab. Co-op, Stalybridge & Hyde*, Maj. 8,084
* **Rimmer**, Marie (*b.* 1947) *Lab., St Helens South & Whiston*, Maj. 24,343
* **Robertson**, Laurence (*b.* 1958) *C., Tewkesbury*, Maj. 22,574
* **Robinson**, Gavin (*b.* 1984) *DUP, Belfast East*, Maj. 8,474
* **Robinson**, Geoffrey (*b.* 1938) *Lab., Coventry North West*, Maj. 8,580
* **Robinson**, Mary (*b.* 1955) *C., Cheadle*, Maj. 4,507
Rodda, Matt (*b.* 1966) *Lab., Reading East*, Maj. 3,749
* **Rosindell**, Andrew (*b.* 1966) *C., Romford*, Maj. 13,778
Ross, Douglas (*b.* 1983) *C., Moray*, Maj. 4,159

Rowley, Danielle (*b.* 1990) *Lab., Midlothian*, Maj. 885
Rowley, Lee (*b.* 1980) *C., Derbyshire North East*, Maj. 2,861
† **Ruane**, Chris (*b.* 1958) *Lab., Vale of Clwyd*, Maj. 2,379
* **Rudd**, Rt. Hon. Amber (*b.* 1963) *C., Hastings & Rye*, Maj. 346
Russell-Moyle, Lloyd (*b.* 1986) *Lab. Co-op, Brighton Kemptown*, Maj. 9,868
* **Rutley**, David (*b.* 1961) *C., Macclesfield*, Maj. 8,608
* **Ryan**, Rt. Hon. Joan (*b.* 1955) *Lab., Enfield North*, Maj. 10,247
* **Sandbach**, Antoinette (*b.* 1969) *C., Eddisbury*, Maj. 11,942
* **Saville Roberts**, Liz (*b.* 1964) *PC, Dwyfor Meirionnydd*, Maj. 4,850
* **Scully**, Paul (*b.* 1968) *C., Sutton & Cheam*, Maj. 12,698
Seely, Bob (*b.* 1966) *C., Isle of Wight*, Maj. 21,069
* **Selous**, Andrew (*b.* 1962) *C., Bedfordshire South West*, Maj. 14,168
* **Shah**, Naz (*b.* 1973) *Lab., Bradford West*, Maj. 21,902
* **Shannon**, Jim (*b.* 1955) *DUP, Strangford*, Maj. 18,343
* **Shapps**, Rt. Hon. Grant (*b.* 1968) *C., Welwyn Hatfield*, Maj. 7,369
* **Sharma**, Alok (*b.* 1967) *C., Reading West*, Maj. 2,876
* **Sharma**, Virendra (*b.* 1947) *Lab., Ealing Southall*, Maj. 22,090
* **Sheerman**, Barry (*b.* 1940) *Lab. Co-op, Huddersfield*, Maj. 12,005
* **Shelbrooke**, Alec (*b.* 1976) *C., Elmet & Rothwell*, Maj. 9,805
* **Sheppard**, Tommy (*b.* 1959) *SNP, Edinburgh East*, Maj. 3,425
* **Sherriff**, Paula (*b.* 1975) *Lab., Dewsbury*, Maj. 3,321
* **Shuker**, Gavin (*b.* 1981) *Lab. Co-op, Luton South*, Maj. 13,925
* **Siddiq**, Tulip (*b.* 1982) *Lab., Hampstead & Kilburn*, Maj. 15,560
* **Simpson**, David (*b.* 1959) *DUP, Upper Bann*, Maj. 7,992
* **Simpson**, Rt. Hon. Keith (*b.* 1949) *C., Broadland*, Maj. 15,816
* **Skidmore**, Chris (*b.* 1981) *C., Kingswood*, Maj. 7,500
* **Skinner**, Dennis (*b.* 1932) *Lab., Bolsover*, Maj. 5,288
* **Slaughter**, Andy (*b.* 1960) *Lab., Hammersmith*, Maj. 18,651
* **Smeeth**, Ruth (*b.* 1979) *Lab., Stoke-on-Trent North*, Maj. 2,359
* **Smith**, Angela (*b.* 1961) *Lab., Penistone & Stocksbridge*, Maj. 1,322
* **Smith**, Cat (*b.* 1985) *Lab., Lancaster & Fleetwood*, Maj. 6,661
* **Smith**, Chloe (*b.* 1982) *C., Norwich North*, Maj. 507
Smith, Eleanor (*b.* 1957) *Lab., Wolverhampton South West*, Maj. 2,185
* **Smith**, Henry (*b.* 1969) *C., Crawley*, Maj. 2,457
* **Smith**, Jeff (*b.* 1963) *Lab., Manchester Withington*, Maj. 29,875
* **Smith**, Rt. Hon. Julian (*b.* 1971) *C., Skipton & Ripon*, Maj. 19,985
Smith, Laura (*b.* 1985) *Lab., Crewe & Nantwich*, Maj. 48
* **Smith**, Nick (*b.* 1960) *Lab., Blaenau Gwent*, Maj. 11,907
* **Smith**, Owen (*b.* 1970) *Lab., Pontypridd*, Maj. 11,448
* **Smith**, Royston (*b.* 1964) *C., Southampton Itchen*, Maj. 31
* **Smyth**, Karin (*b.* 1964) *Lab., Bristol South*, Maj. 15,987
* **Snell**, Gareth (*b.* 1986) *Lab. Co-op, Stoke-on-Trent Central*, Maj. 3,897
* **Soames**, Rt. Hon. Sir Nicholas (*b.* 1948) *C., Sussex Mid*, Maj. 19,673
Sobel, Alex (*b.* 1975) *Lab. Co-op, Leeds North West*, Maj. 4,224
* **Soubry**, Rt. Hon. Anna (*b.* 1956) *C., Broxtowe*, Maj. 863
* **Spellar**, Rt. Hon. John (*b.* 1947) *Lab., Warley*, Maj. 16,483
* **Spelman**, Rt. Hon. Dame Caroline, DBE (*b.* 1958) *C., Meriden*, Maj. 19,198
* **Spencer**, Mark (*b.* 1970) *C., Sherwood*, Maj. 5,198
* **Starmer**, Rt. Hon. Sir Keir, KCB (*b.* 1962) *Lab., Holborn & St Pancras*, Maj. 30,509
* **Stephens**, Chris (*b.* 1973) *SNP, Glasgow South West*, Maj. 60
* **Stephenson**, Andrew (*b.* 1981) *C., Pendle*, Maj. 1,279
* **Stevens**, Jo (*b.* 1966) *Lab., Cardiff Central*, Maj. 17,196
* **Stevenson**, John (*b.* 1963) *C., Carlisle*, Maj. 2,599

* **Stewart**, Bob, DSO (*b.* 1949) *C., Beckenham,* Maj. 15,087
* **Stewart**, Iain (*b.* 1972) *C., Milton Keynes South,* Maj. 1,725
* **Stewart**, Rory, OBE (*b.* 1973) *C., Penrith & The Border,* Maj. 15,910
Stone, Jamie (*b.* 1954) *LD, Caithness, Sutherland & Easter Ross,* Maj. 2,044
* **Streeter**, Gary (*b.* 1955) *C., Devon South West,* Maj. 15,816
* **Streeting**, Wes (*b.* 1983) *Lab., Ilford North,* Maj. 9,639
* **Stride**, Rt. Hon. Mel (*b.* 1961) *C., Devon Central,* Maj. 15,680
* **Stringer**, Graham (*b.* 1950) *Lab., Blackley & Broughton,* Maj. 19,601
* **Stuart**, Graham (*b.* 1962) *C., Beverley & Holderness,* Maj. 14,042
* **Sturdy**, Julian (*b.* 1971) *C., York Outer,* Maj. 8,289
* **Sunak**, Rishi (*b.* 1980) *C., Richmond (Yorks),* Maj. 23,108
* **Swayne**, Rt. Hon. Sir Desmond, TD (*b.* 1956) *C., New Forest West,* Maj. 23,431
Sweeney, Paul (*b.* 1989) *Lab. Co-op, Glasgow North East,* Maj. 242
† **Swinson**, Jo, CBE (*b.* 1980) *LD, Dunbartonshire East,* Maj. 5,339
* **Swire**, Rt. Hon. Sir Hugo, KCMG (*b.* 1959) *C., Devon East,* Maj. 8,036
* **Syms**, Sir Robert (*b.* 1956) *C., Poole,* Maj. 14,209
* **Tami**, Mark (*b.* 1962) *Lab., Alyn & Deeside,* Maj. 5,235
* **Thewliss**, Alison (*b.* 1982) *SNP, Glasgow Central,* Maj. 2,267
* **Thomas**, Derek (*b.* 1972) *C., St Ives,* Maj. 312
* **Thomas**, Gareth (*b.* 1967) *Lab. Co-op, Harrow West,* Maj. 13,314
* **Thomas-Symonds**, Nick (*b.* 1980) *Lab., Torfaen,* Maj. 10,240
Thomson, Ross (*b.* 1987) *C., Aberdeen South,* Maj. 4,752
* **Thornberry**, Rt. Hon. Emily (*b.* 1960) *Lab., Islington South & Finsbury,* Maj. 20,263
* **Throup**, Maggie (*b.* 1957) *C., Erewash,* Maj. 4,534
* **Timms**, Rt. Hon. Stephen (*b.* 1955) *Lab., East Ham,* Maj. 39,883
* **Tolhurst**, Kelly (*b.* 1978) *C., Rochester & Strood,* Maj. 9,850
* **Tomlinson**, Justin (*b.* 1976) *C., Swindon North,* Maj. 8,335
* **Tomlinson**, Michael (*b.* 1977) *C., Dorset Mid & Poole North,* Maj. 15,339
* **Tracey**, Craig (*b.* 1974) *C., Warwickshire North,* Maj. 8,510
* **Tredinnick**, David (*b.* 1950) *C., Bosworth,* Maj. 18,351
* **Trevelyan**, Anne-Marie (*b.* 1969) *C., Berwick-upon-Tweed,* Maj. 11,781
* **Trickett**, Jon (*b.* 1950) *Lab., Hemsworth,* Maj. 10,174
* **Truss**, Rt. Hon. Elizabeth (*b.* 1975) *C., Norfolk South West,* Maj. 18,312
* **Tugendhat**, Tom (*b.* 1973) *C., Tonbridge & Malling,* Maj. 23,508
* **Turley**, Anna (*b.* 1978) *Lab. Co-op, Redcar,* Maj. 9,485
* **Turner**, Karl (*b.* 1971) *Lab., Hull East,* Maj. 10,396
* **Twigg**, Derek (*b.* 1959) *Lab., Halton,* Maj. 25,405
* **Twigg**, Stephen (*b.* 1966) *Lab. Co-op, Liverpool West Derby,* Maj. 32,908
Twist, Liz (*b.* 1956) *Lab., Blaydon,* Maj. 13,477

* **Umunna**, Chuka (*b.* 1978) *Lab., Streatham,* Maj. 26,285
* **Vaizey**, Rt. Hon. Edward (*b.* 1968) *C., Wantage,* Maj. 17,380
* **Vara**, Shailesh (*b.* 1960) *C., Cambridgeshire North West,* Maj. 18,008
* **Vaz**, Rt. Hon. Keith (*b.* 1956) *Lab., Leicester East,* Maj. 22,428
* **Vaz**, Valerie (*b.* 1954) *Lab., Walsall South,* Maj. 8,892
* **Vickers**, Martin (*b.* 1950) *C., Cleethorpes,* Maj. 10,400
* **Villiers**, Rt. Hon. Theresa (*b.* 1968) *C., Chipping Barnet,* Maj. 353
* **Walker**, Charles, OBE (*b.* 1967) *C., Broxbourne,* Maj. 15,792
* **Walker**, Robin (*b.* 1978) *C., Worcester,* Maj. 2,508
Walker, Thelma (*b.* 1957) *Lab., Colne Valley,* Maj. 915
* **Wallace**, Rt. Hon. Ben (*b.* 1970) *C., Wyre & Preston North,* Maj. 12,246
* **Warburton**, David (*b.* 1965) *C., Somerton & Frome,* Maj. 22,906
* **Warman**, Matt (*b.* 1981) *C., Boston & Skegness,* Maj. 16,572
Watling, Giles (*b.* 1953) *C., Clacton,* Maj. 15,828
* **Watson**, Tom (*b.* 1967) *Lab., West Bromwich East,* Maj. 7,713
* **West**, Catherine (*b.* 1966) *Lab., Hornsey & Wood Green,* Maj. 30,738
Western, Matt (*b.* 1962) *Lab., Warwick & Leamington,* Maj. 1,206
* **Whately**, Helen (*b.* 1976) *C., Faversham & Kent Mid,* Maj. 17,413
* **Wheeler**, Heather (*b.* 1959) *C., Derbyshire South,* Maj. 11,970
* **Whitehead**, Alan, PHD (*b.* 1950) *Lab., Southampton Test,* Maj. 11,503
Whitfield, Martin (*b.* 1965) *Lab., East Lothian,* Maj. 3,083
* **Whitford**, Dr Philippa (*b.* 1958) *SNP, Ayrshire Central,* Maj. 1,267
* **Whittaker**, Craig (*b.* 1962) *C., Calder Valley,* Maj. 609
* **Whittingdale**, Rt. Hon. John, OBE (*b.* 1959) *C., Maldon,* Maj. 23,430
* **Wiggin**, Bill (*b.* 1966) *C., Herefordshire North,* Maj. 21,602
* **Williams**, Hywel (*b.* 1953) *PC, Arfon,* Maj. 92
Williams, Paul, PHD (*b.* 1972) *Lab., Stockton South,* Maj. 888
† **Williamson**, Chris (*b.* 1956) *Lab., Derby North,* Maj. 2,015
* **Williamson**, Rt. Hon. Gavin, CBE (*b.* 1976) *C., Staffordshire South,* Maj. 22,733
* **Wilson**, Phil (*b.* 1959) *Lab., Sedgefield,* Maj. 6,059
* **Wilson**, Rt. Hon. Sammy (*b.* 1953) *DUP, Antrim East,* Maj. 15,923
* **Winterton**, Rt. Hon. Dame Rosie, DBE (*b.* 1958) *Lab., Doncaster Central,* Maj. 10,131
* **Wishart**, Pete (*b.* 1962) *SNP, Perth & Perthshire North,* Maj. 21
* **Wollaston**, Dr Sarah (*b.* 1962) *C., Totnes,* Maj. 13,477
* **Wood**, Mike (*b.* 1976) *C., Dudley South,* Maj. 7,730
* **Woodcock**, John (*b.* 1978) *Ind., Barrow & Furness,* Maj. 209
* **Wragg**, William (*b.* 1987) *C., Hazel Grove,* Maj. 5,514
* **Wright**, Rt. Hon. Jeremy (*b.* 1972) *C., Kenilworth & Southam,* Maj. 18,086
Yasin, Mohammad (*b.* 1971) *Lab., Bedford,* Maj. 789
* **Zahawi**, Nadhim (*b.* 1967) *C., Stratford-on-Avon,* Maj. 20,958
* **Zeichner**, Daniel (*b.* 1956) *Lab., Cambridge,* Maj. 12,661

GENERAL ELECTION 2017 RESULTS

UK Turnout

Electorate (E.) 46,843,896 Turnout (T.). 32,181,757 (68.7%)

The results of voting in each of the 650 parliamentary constituencies at the general election on 8 June 2017 are given below.

KEY

* Previously an MP for this seat in the 2015–17 parliament

† Previously an MP for this seat in any parliament prior to the 2015–17 parliament

‡ Previously an MP for a different seat in any previous parliament

§ Currently suspended from the parliamentary Conservative Party

₵ By-election held since the 2017 General Election

swing N/A indicates a constituency for which the swing data cannot be calculated because one of the top two parties in the 2015 General Election did not field a candidate in the seat in 2017.

ABBREVIATIONS OF POLITICAL PARTIES

Active Dem.	Movement for Active Democracy	Good	The Common Good	Realist	The Realists' Party
AD	Apolitical Democrats	Green	Green Party	Rebooting	Rebooting Democracy
Alliance	Alliance Party of Northern Ireland	Green Soc.	Alliance for Green Socialism	Referendum	Scotland's Independence Referendum Party
AP	All People's Party	Guildford	Guildford Greenbelt Group	Respect	The Respect Party
APNI	APNI Party	Humanity	Humanity	Rochdale	Rochdale First Party
AWP	Animal Welfare Party	Ind.	Independent	Roman	The Roman Party
Blue	Blue Revolution	IPP	Immigrants Political Party	S. New	Something New
BNP	British National Party			SCP	Scottish Christian Party
Bournemouth	Bournemouth Independent Alliance	JACP	Justice & Anti-Corruption Party	SDLP	Social Democratic and Labour Party
BPE	Bus-Pass Elvis Party	Just	The Just Political Party	SF	Sinn Fein
Bradford	Better for Bradford	Lab.	Labour	SNP	Scottish National Party
Bristol	Independents for Bristol	Lab. Alt	Labour Alternative	Soc.	Socialist Party
C.	Conservative	Lab. Co-op	Labour and Co-operative	Soc. Dem.	Social Democratic Party
Change	Alter Change			Soc. Lab.	Socialist Labour Party
Ch. P.	The Christian Party	LD	Liberal Democrat	Southampton	Southampton Independents
CISTA	Cannabis is Safer than Alcohol	Lib.	The Liberal Party		
		Lib. GB	Liberty Great Britain	Southend	Southend Independent Association
Citizens	Citizens Independent Social Thought Alliance	Libertarian	Libertarian Party	Southport	The Southport Party
		Lincs Ind.	Lincolnshire Independents	Sovereign	Independent Sovereign Democratic Britain
Comm.	Communist Party of Britain	Loony	Monster Raving Loony Party	Space	Space Navies Party
Comm. Lge	Communist League	Love	One Love Party	Speaker	The Speaker
Community	Communities United Party	MC	The Magna Carta Party	SPGB	The Socialist Party of Great Britain
Compass	Compass Party	Money	Money Free Party	SSP	Scottish Socialist Party
Concordia	Concordia	ND	No description	Thanet	Party for a United Thanet
CPA	Christian Peoples Alliance	NE	The North East Party		
Croydon	Putting Croydon First	NF	National Front	TUSC	Trade Unionist and Socialist Coalition
CSP	Common Sense Party	NHAP	National Health Action Party	TUV	Traditional Unionist Voice
DDI	Demos Direct Initiative	North	Putting North of England People First	UKIP	UK Independence Party
Digital	Digital Democracy			UUP	Ulster Unionist Party
DUP	Democratic Unionist Party	Northern	Northern Party	Wessex Reg.	Wessex Regionalists
		Open	Open Borders Party	Wigan	Wigan Independents
DVP	Democrats and Veterans Party	Patria	Patria	Women	Women's Equality Party
		PBP	People Before Profit Alliance	Worth	The New Society of Worth
Eccentric	The Eccentric Party of Great Britain	PC	Plaid Cymru	WP	Workers' Party
Elmo	Give Me Back Elmo	Peace	Peace Party	WRP	Workers' Revolutionary Party
Elvis	Church of the Militant Elvis	PF	People First		
		Pilgrim	The Pilgrim Party	WVPTFP	War Veteran's Pro-Traditional Family Party
Eng. Dem.	English Democrats	Pirate	Pirate Party UK		
Eng. Ind.	English Independence	Poole	The Party for Poole People Ltd		
For Britain	The For Britain Movement			Yorks	Yorkshire First
Friends	Friends Party	Populist	Populist Party	Yorkshire	The Yorkshire Party
GM Homeless	Greater Manchester Homeless Voice	PUP	Progressive Unionist Party	Young	Young People's Party UK
		Radical	The Radical Party		

ENGLAND

ALDERSHOT
E. 76,205 T. 48,955 (64.24%)   C. hold
Leo Docherty, C.   26,955
Gary Puffett, Lab.   15,477
Alan Hilliar, LD   3,637
Roy Swales, UKIP   1,796
Donna Wallace, Green   1,090
C. majority 11,478 (23.45%)
4.41% swing C. to Lab.
(2015: C. majority 14,901 (32.26%))

ALDRIDGE-BROWNHILLS
E. 60,363 T. 40,235 (66.66%)   C. hold
*Wendy Morton, C.   26,317
John Fisher, Lab.   12,010
Ian Garrett, LD   1,343
Mark Beech, Loony   565
C. majority 14,307 (35.56%)
2.94% swing Lab. to C.
(2015: C. majority 11,723 (29.68%))

ALTRINCHAM & SALE WEST
E. 73,220 T. 52,790 (72.10%)   C. hold
*Graham Brady, C.   26,933
Andrew Western, Lab.   20,507
Jane Brophy, LD   4,051
Geraldine Coggins, Green   1,000
Neil Taylor, Lib.   299
C. majority 6,426 (12.17%)
7.07% swing C. to Lab.
(2015: C. majority 13,290 (26.31%))

AMBER VALLEY
E. 68,065 T. 45,811 (67.30%)   C. hold
*Nigel Mills, C.   25,905
James Dawson, Lab.   17,605
Kate Smith, LD   1,100
Matt McGuinness, Green   650
Daniel Bamford, Ind.   551
C. majority 8,300 (18.12%)
4.46% swing Lab. to C.
(2015: C. majority 4,205 (9.20%))

ARUNDEL & SOUTH DOWNS
E. 80,766 T. 60,256 (74.61%)   C. hold
*Nick Herbert, C.   37,573
Caroline Fife, Lab.   13,690
Shweta Kapadia, LD   4,783
Jo Prior, Green   2,542
John Wallace, UKIP   1,668
C. majority 23,883 (39.64%)
4.98% swing C. to Lab.
(2015: C. majority 26,177 (46.35%))

ASHFIELD
E. 78,099 T. 49,993 (64.01%) Lab. hold
*Gloria De Piero, Lab.   21,285
Tony Harper, C.   20,844
Gail Turner, Ind.   4,612
Ray Young, UKIP   1,885
Bob Charlesworth, LD   969
Arran Rangi, Green   398
Lab. majority 441 (0.88%)
8.86% swing Lab. to C.
(2015: Lab. majority 8,820 (18.60%))

ASHFORD
E. 87,396 T. 59,879 (68.51%)   C. hold
*Damian Green, C.   35,318
Sally Gathern, Lab.   17,840
Adrian Gee-Turner, LD   3,101
Gerald O'Brien, UKIP   2,218
Mandy Rossi, Green   1,402
C. majority 17,478 (29.19%)
2.41% swing C. to Lab.
(2015: C. majority 19,296 (33.63%))

ASHTON-UNDER-LYNE
E. 67,674 T. 39,773 (58.77%) Lab. hold
*Angela Rayner, Lab.   24,005
Jack Rankin, C.   12,710
Maurice Jackson, UKIP   1,878
Carly Hicks, LD   646
Andy Hunter-Rossall, Green   534
Lab. majority 11,295 (28.40%)
0.38% swing C. to Lab.
(2015: Lab. majority 10,756 (27.64%))

AYLESBURY
E. 82,546 T. 58,743 (71.16%)   C. hold
*David Lidington, C.   32,313
Mark Bateman, Lab.   17,617
Steven Lambert, LD   5,660
Vijay Srao, UKIP   1,296
Coral Simpson, Green   1,237
Kyle Michael, Ind.   620
C. majority 14,696 (25.02%)
5.26% swing C. to Lab.
(2015: C. majority 17,158 (30.96%))

BANBURY
E. 83,818 T. 61,562 (73.45%)   C. hold
*Victoria Prentis, C.   33,388
Sean Woodcock, Lab.   20,989
John Howson, LD   3,452
Dickie Bird, UKIP   1,581
Ian Middleton, Green   1,225
Roseanne Edwards, Ind.   927
C. majority 12,399 (20.14%)
5.79% swing C. to Lab.
(2015: C. majority 18,395 (31.71%))

BARKING
E. 77,020 T. 47,679 (61.90%) Lab. hold
*Margaret Hodge, Lab.   32,319
Minesh Talati, C.   10,711
Roger Gravett, UKIP   3,031
Shannon Butterfield, Green   724
Pauline Pearce, LD   599
Noel Falvey, Ind.   295
Lab. majority 21,608 (45.32%)
1.97% swing C. to Lab.
(2015: Lab. majority 15,272 (35.50%))

BARNSLEY CENTRAL
E. 64,204 T. 39,089 (60.88%) Lab. hold
*Dan Jarvis, Lab.   24,982
Amanda Ford, C.   9,436
Gavin Felton, UKIP   3,339
Richard Trotman, Green   572
David Ridgway, LD   549
Stephen Morris, Eng. Dem.   211
Lab. majority 15,546 (39.77%)
0.48% swing Lab. to C.
(2015: Lab. majority 12,435 (34.01%))

BARNSLEY EAST
E. 69,204 T. 40,776 (58.92%) Lab. hold
Stephanie Peacock, Lab.   24,280
Andrew Lloyd, C.   10,997
James Dalton, UKIP   3,247
Tony Devoy, Yorkshire   1,215
Nicola Turner, LD   750
Kevin Riddiough, Eng. Dem.   287
Lab. majority 13,283 (32.58%)
3.78% swing Lab. to C.
(2015: Lab. majority 12,034 (31.24%))

BARROW & FURNESS
E. 69,474 T. 47,590 (68.50%)
                      Lab. Co-op hold
*John Woodcock,
Lab. Co-op   22,592
Simon Fell, C.   22,383
Loraine Birchall, LD   1,278
Alan Piper, UKIP   962
Rob O'Hara, Green   375
Lab. Co-op majority 209 (0.44%)
0.70% swing Lab. to C.
(2015: Lab. Co-op majority 795
(1.84%))

BASILDON & BILLERICAY
E. 69,149 T. 44,918 (64.96%)   C. hold
*John Baron, C.   27,381
Kayte Block, Lab.   13,981
Tina Hughes, UKIP   2,008
Antonia Harrison, LD   1,548
C. majority 13,400 (29.83%)
0.41% swing Lab. to C.
(2015: C. majority 12,482 (29.01%))

BASILDON SOUTH & THURROCK EAST
E. 73,541 T. 47,120 (64.07%)   C. hold
*Stephen Metcalfe, C.   26,811
Byron Taylor, Lab.   15,321
Peter Whittle, UKIP   3,193
Reetendra Banerji, LD   732
Sim Harman, Green   680
Paul Borg, BNP   383
C. majority 11,490 (24.38%)
3.10% swing Lab. to C.
(2015: C. majority 7,691 (16.87%))

BASINGSTOKE
E. 81,873 T. 55,960 (68.35%)   C. hold
*Maria Miller, C.   29,510
Terry Bridgeman, Lab.   20,044
John Shaw, LD   3,406
Alan Stone, UKIP   1,681
Richard Winter, Green   1,106
Scott Neville, Libertarian   213
C. majority 9,466 (16.92%)
1.96% swing C. to Lab.
(2015: C. majority 11,063 (20.84%))

BASSETLAW
E. 78,535 T. 52,250 (66.53%) Lab. hold
*John Mann, Lab.   27,467
Annette Simpson, C.   22,615
Leon Duveen, LD   1,154
Nigel Turner, Ind.   1,014
Lab. majority 4,852 (9.29%)
4.33% swing Lab. to C.
(2015: Lab. majority 8,843 (17.94%))

BATH

E. 66,769   T. 49,582 (74.26%)   LD gain

Wera Hobhouse, LD	23,436
*Ben Howlett, C.	17,742
Joe Rayment, Lab.	7,279
Eleanor Field, Green	1,125

LD majority 5,694 (11.48%)
9.81% swing C. to LD
(2015: C. majority 3,833 (8.13%))

BATLEY & SPEN

E. 80,153   T. 53,780 (67.10%)

Lab. Co-op hold

*Tracy Brabin, Lab. Co-op	29,844
Ann Myatt, C.	20,883
John Lawson, LD	1,224
Aleks Lukic, Ind.	1,076
Alan Freeman, Green	695
Mohammed Hanif, Ind.	58

Lab. Co-op majority 8,961 (16.66%)
2.33% swing C. to Lab.
(2015: Lab. majority 6,057 (12.00%))
(2016: Lab. majority 16,537 (81.09%))

BATTERSEA

E. 77,572   T. 55,058 (70.98%)   Lab. gain

Marsha De Cordova, Lab.	25,292
*Jane Ellison, C.	22,876
Richard Davis, LD	4,401
Chris Coghlan, Ind.	1,234
Lois Davis, Green	866
Eugene Power, UKIP	357
Daniel Lambert, SPGB	32

Lab. majority 2,416 (4.39%)
9.97% swing C. to Lab.
(2015: C. majority 7,938 (15.56%))

BEACONSFIELD

E. 77,534   T. 56,028 (72.26%)   C. hold

*Dominic Grieve, C.	36,559
James English, Lab.	12,016
Peter Chapman, LD	4,448
Jon Conway, UKIP	1,609
Russell Secker, Green	1,396

C. majority 24,543 (43.80%)
4.01% swing C. to Lab.
(2015: C. majority 26,311 (49.49%))

BECKENHAM

E. 67,928   T. 51,630 (76.01%)   C. hold

*Bob Stewart, C.	30,632
Marina Ahmad, Lab.	15,545
Julie Ireland, LD	4,073
Ruth Fabricant, Green	1,380

C. majority 15,087 (29.22%)
4.31% swing C. to Lab.
(2015: C. majority 18,471 (37.85%))

BEDFORD

E. 71,829   T. 48,480 (67.49%)   Lab. gain

Mohammad Yasin, Lab.	22,712
*Richard Fuller, C.	21,923
Henry Vann, LD	2,837
Lucy Bywater, Green	1,008

Lab. majority 789 (1.63%)
2.00% swing C. to Lab.
(2015: C. majority 1,097 (2.38%))

BEDFORDSHIRE MID

E. 83,800   T. 63,148 (75.36%)   C. hold

*Nadine Dorries, C.	38,936
Rhiannon Meades, Lab.	17,953
Lisa French, LD	3,798
Gareth Ellis, Green	1,794
Ann Kelly, Loony	667

C. majority 20,983 (33.23%)
3.47% swing C. to Lab.
(2015: C. majority 23,327 (40.18%))

BEDFORDSHIRE NORTH EAST

E. 86,988   T. 64,220 (73.83%)   C. hold

*Alistair Burt, C.	39,139
Julian Vaughan, Lab.	18,277
Stephen Rutherford, LD	3,693
Duncan Strachan, UKIP	1,896
Philippa Fleming, Green	1,215

C. majority 20,862 (32.49%)
5.61% swing C. to Lab.
(2015: C. majority 25,644 (43.71%))

BEDFORDSHIRE SOUTH WEST

E. 79,670   T. 55,635 (69.83%)   C. hold

*Andrew Selous, C.	32,961
Daniel Scott, Lab.	18,793
Daniel Norton, LD	2,630
Morvern Rennie, Green	950
Morenike Mafoh, CPA	301

C. majority 14,168 (25.47%)
4.63% swing C. to Lab.
(2015: C. majority 17,813 (34.72%))

BERMONDSEY & OLD SOUTHWARK

E. 87,227   T. 58,521 (67.09%)   Lab. hold

*Neil Coyle, Lab.	31,161
Simon Hughes, LD	18,189
Siobhan Baillie, C.	7,581
Elizabeth Jones, UKIP	838
John Tyson, Green	639
James Clarke, Ind.	113

Lab. majority 12,972 (22.17%)
6.72% swing LD to Lab.
(2015: Lab. majority 4,489 (8.73%))

BERWICK-UPON-TWEED

E. 58,774   T. 42,212 (71.82%)   C. hold

*Anne-Marie Trevelyan, C.	22,145
Scott Dickinson, Lab.	10,364
Julie Porksen, LD	8,916
Thomas Stewart, Green	787

C. majority 11,781 (27.91%)
0.89% swing Lab. to C.
(2015: C. majority 4,914 (12.16%))

BETHNAL GREEN & BOW

E. 86,071   T. 59,825 (69.51%)   Lab. hold

*Rushanara Ali, Lab.	42,969
Charlie Chirico, C.	7,576
Ajmal Masroor, Ind.	3,888
William Dyer, LD	2,982
Alistair Polson, Green	1,516
Ian de Wulverton, UKIP	894

Lab. majority 35,393 (59.16%)
6.61% swing C. to Lab.
(2015: Lab. majority 24,317 (45.95%))

BEVERLEY & HOLDERNESS

E. 80,657   T. 55,678 (69.03%)   C. hold

*Graham Stuart, C.	32,499
Johanna Boal, Lab.	18,457
Denis Healy, LD	2,808
Lee Walton, Yorkshire	1,158
Richard Howarth, Green	756

C. majority 14,042 (25.22%)
1.03% swing Lab. to C.
(2015: C. majority 12,203 (23.17%))

BEXHILL & BATTLE

E. 78,512   T. 59,472 (75.75%)   C. hold

*Huw Merriman, C.	36,854
Christine Bayliss, Lab.	14,689
Joel Kemp, LD	4,485
Geoffrey Bastin, UKIP	2,006
Jonathan Kent, Green	1,438

C. majority 22,165 (37.27%)
1.69% swing C. to Lab.
(2015: C. majority 20,075 (36.36%))

BEXLEYHEATH & CRAYFORD

E. 65,315   T. 45,189 (69.19%)   C. hold

*David Evennett, C.	25,113
Stef Borella, Lab.	16,040
Mike Ferro, UKIP	1,944
Simone Reynolds, LD	1,201
Ivor Lobo, Green	601
Peter Finch, BNP	290

C. majority 9,073 (20.08%)
0.48% swing C. to Lab.
(2015: C. majority 9,192 (21.04%))

BIRKENHEAD

E. 64,484   T. 43,663 (67.71%)   Lab. hold

*Frank Field, Lab.	33,558
Stewart Gardiner, C.	8,044
Allan Brame, LD	1,118
Jayne Clough, Green	943

Lab. majority 25,514 (58.43%)
1.81% swing C. to Lab.
(2015: Lab. majority 20,652 (54.81%))

BIRMINGHAM EDGBASTON

E. 68,091   T. 43,612 (64.05%)

Lab. Co-op hold

Preet Gill, Lab. Co-op	24,124
Caroline Squire, C.	17,207
Colin Green, LD	1,564
Alice Kiff, Green	562
Dick Rodgers, Good	155

Lab. Co-op majority 6,917 (15.86%)
4.65% swing C. to Lab.
(2015: Lab. majority 2,706 (6.55%))

BIRMINGHAM ERDINGTON

E. 65,067   T. 37,217 (57.20%)   Lab. hold

*Jack Dromey, Lab.	21,571
Robert Alden, C.	14,286
Ann Holtom, LD	750
James Lovatt, Green	610

Lab. majority 7,285 (19.57%)
2.39% swing C. to Lab.
(2015: Lab. majority 5,129 (14.79%))

BIRMINGHAM HALL GREEN
E. 78,271 T. 54,310 (69.39%) Lab. hold
*Roger Godsiff, Lab.   42,143
Reena Ranger, C.   8,199
Jerry Evans, LD   3,137
Patrick Cox, Green   831
Lab. majority 33,944 (62.50%)
10.19% swing C. to Lab.
(2015: Lab. majority 19,818 (42.12%))

BIRMINGHAM HODGE HILL
E. 75,698 T. 46,394 (61.29%) Lab. hold
*Liam Byrne, Lab.   37,606
Ahmereen Reza, C.   6,580
Mohammed Khan, UKIP   1,016
Phil Bennion, LD   805
Clare Thomas, Green   387
Lab. majority 31,026 (66.88%)
4.97% swing C. to Lab.
(2015: Lab. majority 23,362 (56.93%))

BIRMINGHAM LADYWOOD
E. 70,023 T. 41,307 (58.99%) Lab. hold
*Shabana Mahmood, Lab.   34,166
Andrew Browning, C.   5,452
Lee Dargue, LD   1,156
Kefentse Dennis, Green   533
Lab. majority 28,714 (69.51%)
4.31% swing C. to Lab.
(2015: Lab. majority 21,868 (60.89%))

BIRMINGHAM NORTHFIELD
E. 72,322 T. 44,348 (61.32%) Lab. hold
*Richard Burden, Lab.   23,596
Meg Powell-Chandler, C.   18,929
Roger Harmer, LD   959
Eleanor Masters, Green   864
Lab. majority 4,667 (10.52%)
2.31% swing C. to Lab.
(2015: Lab. majority 2,509 (5.91%))

BIRMINGHAM PERRY BARR
E. 70,106 T. 44,197 (63.04%) Lab. hold
*Khalid Mahmood, Lab.   30,109
Charlotte Hodivala, C.   11,726
Harjun Singh, LD   1,080
Shangara Bhatoe, Soc. Lab.   592
Vijay Rana, Green   591
Harjinder Singh, Open   99
Lab. majority 18,383 (41.59%)
2.83% swing C. to Lab.
(2015: Lab. majority 14,828 (35.94%))

BIRMINGHAM SELLY OAK
E. 74,370 T. 48,985 (65.87%) Lab. hold
*Steve McCabe, Lab.   30,836
Sophie Shrubsole, C.   15,629
David Radcliffe, LD   1,644
Julien Pritchard, Green   876
Lab. majority 15,207 (31.04%)
6.20% swing C. to Lab.
(2015: Lab. majority 8,447 (18.65%))

BIRMINGHAM YARDLEY
E. 72,581 T. 44,502 (61.31%) Lab. hold
*Jess Phillips, Lab.   25,398
Mohammed Afzal, C.   8,824
John Hemming, LD   7,984
Paul Clayton, UKIP   1,916
Christopher Garghan, Green   280
Abu Nowshed, Ind.   100
Lab. majority 16,574 (37.24%)
4.81% swing C. to Lab.
(2015: Lab. majority 6,595 (16.03%))

BISHOP AUCKLAND
E. 67,661 T. 43,281 (63.97%) Lab. hold
*Helen Goodman, Lab.   20,808
Christopher Adams, C.   20,306
Ciaran Morrissey, LD   1,176
Adam Walker, BNP   991
Lab. majority 502 (1.16%)
3.87% swing Lab. to C.
(2015: Lab. majority 3,508 (8.91%))

BLACKBURN
E. 70,657 T. 47,512 (67.24%) Lab. hold
*Kate Hollern, Lab.   33,148
Bob Eastwood, C.   12,780
Duncan Miller, Ind.   875
Irfan Ahmed, LD   709
Lab. majority 20,368 (42.87%)
6.93% swing C. to Lab.
(2015: Lab. majority 12,760 (29.00%))

BLACKLEY & BROUGHTON
E. 71,648 T. 40,113 (55.99%) Lab. hold
*Graham Stringer, Lab.   28,258
David Goss, C.   8,657
Martin Power, UKIP   1,825
Charles Gadsden, LD   737
David Jones, Green   462
Abi Ajoku, CPA   174
Lab. majority 19,601 (48.86%)
0.99% swing C. to Lab.
(2015: Lab. majority 16,874 (45.47%))

BLACKPOOL NORTH & CLEVELEYS
E. 63,967 T. 41,007 (64.11%)   C. hold
*Paul Maynard, C.   20,255
Chris Webb, Lab.   18,232
Paul White, UKIP   1,392
Sue Close, LD   747
Duncan Royle, Green   381
C. majority 2,023 (4.93%)
1.77% swing C. to Lab.
(2015: C. majority 3,340 (8.48%))

BLACKPOOL SOUTH
E. 58,450 T. 34,953 (59.80%) Lab. hold
*Gordon Marsden, Lab.   17,581
Peter Anthony, C.   15,058
Noel Matthews, UKIP   1,339
Bill Greene, LD   634
John Peter Warnock, Green   341
Lab. majority 2,523 (7.22%)
0.38% swing Lab. to C.
(2015: Lab. majority 2,585 (7.97%))

BLAYDON
E. 68,459 T. 48,084 (70.24%) Lab. hold
Liz Twist, Lab.   26,979
Thomas Smith, C.   13,502
Jonathan Wallace, LD   4,366
Ray Tolley, UKIP   2,459
Paul McNally, Green   583
Michael Marchetti,
Libertarian   114
Lisabela Marschild, Space   81
Lab. majority 13,477 (28.03%)
1.84% swing Lab. to C.
(2015: Lab. majority 14,227 (31.66%))

BLYTH VALLEY
E. 63,371 T. 42,490 (67.05%) Lab. hold
*Ronnie Campbell, Lab.   23,770
Ian Levy, C.   15,855
Jeff Reid, LD   1,947
Dawn Furness, Green   918
Lab. majority 7,915 (18.63%)
2.99% swing Lab. to C.
(2015: Lab. majority 9,229 (24.00%))

BOGNOR REGIS & LITTLEHAMPTON
E. 75,827 T. 51,352 (67.72%)   C. hold
*Nick Gibb, C.   30,276
Alan Butcher, Lab.   12,782
Francis Oppler, LD   3,352
Paul Sanderson, Ind.   2,088
Patrick Lowe, UKIP   1,861
Andrew Bishop, Green   993
C. majority 17,494 (34.07%)
1.73% swing C. to Lab.
(2015: C. majority 13,944 (29.60%))

BOLSOVER
E. 73,429 T. 46,519 (63.35%) Lab. hold
*Dennis Skinner, Lab.   24,153
Helen Harrison, C.   18,865
Philip Rose, UKIP   2,129
Ross Shipman, LD   1,372
Lab. majority 5,288 (11.37%)
7.70% swing Lab. to C.
(2015: Lab. majority 11,778 (26.77%))

BOLTON NORTH EAST
E. 67,233 T. 45,183 (67.20%) Lab. hold
*David Crausby, Lab.   22,870
James Daly, C.   19,073
Harry Lamb, UKIP   1,567
Warren Fox, LD   1,316
Liz Spencer, Green   357
Lab. majority 3,797 (8.40%)
0.87% swing Lab. to C.
(2015: Lab. majority 4,377 (10.14%))

BOLTON SOUTH EAST
E. 68,886 T. 42,323 (61.44%) Lab. hold
*Yasmin Qureshi, Lab.   25,676
Sarah Pochin, C.   12,550
Jeff Armstrong, UKIP   2,779
Frank Harasiwka, LD   781
Alan Johnson, Green   537
Lab. majority 13,126 (31.01%)
0.45% swing C. to Lab.
(2015: Lab. majority 10,928 (26.82%))

BOLTON WEST
E. 72,797 T. 51,054 (70.13%)   C. hold
*Chris Green, C.   24,459
Julie Hilling, Lab.   23,523
Martin Tighe, UKIP   1,587
Rebecca Forrest, LD   1,485
C. majority 936 (1.83%)
0.09% swing Lab. to C.
(2015: C. majority 801 (1.65%))

BOOTLE
E. 72,872   T. 50,288 (69.01%)   Lab. hold
*Peter Dowd, Lab.   42,259
Charles Fifield, C.   6,059
David Newman, LD   837
Alison Gibbon, Green   709
Kim Bryan, Soc. Lab.   424
Lab. majority 36,200 (71.99%)
2.79% swing C. to Lab.
(2015: Lab. majority 28,704 (63.57%))

BOSTON & SKEGNESS
E. 68,391   T. 42,879 (62.70%)   C. hold
*Matt Warman, C.   27,271
Paul Kenny, Lab.   10,699
Paul Nuttall, UKIP   3,308
Philip Smith, LD   771
Victoria Percival, Green   547
Mike Gilbert, Blue   283
C. majority 16,572 (38.65%)
5.67% swing Lab. to C.
(2015: C. majority 4,336 (10.00%))

BOSWORTH
E. 80,633   T. 56,168 (69.66%)   C. hold
*David Tredinnick, C,   31,864
Chris Kealey, Lab.   13,513
Michael Mullaney, LD   9,744
Mick Gregg, Green   1,047
C. majority 18,351 (32.67%)
3.66% swing Lab. to C.
(2015: C. majority 10,988 (20.51%))

BOURNEMOUTH EAST
E. 74,591   T. 48,618 (65.18%)   C. hold
*Tobias Ellwood, C.   25,221
Mel Semple, Lab.   17,284
Jon Nicholas, LD   3,168
David Hughes, UKIP   1,405
Alasdair Keddie, Green   1,236
Kieron Wilson, Ind.   304
C. majority 7,937 (16.33%)
8.14% swing C. to Lab.
(2015: C. majority 14,612 (32.60%))

BOURNEMOUTH WEST
E. 73,195   T. 44,507 (60.81%)   C. hold
*Conor Burns, C.   23,812
David Stokes, Lab.   16,101
Phil Dunn, LD   2,929
Simon Bull, Green   1,247
Jason Halsey, Pirate   418
C. majority 7,711 (17.33%)
6.62% swing C. to Lab.
(2015: C. majority 12,410 (29.71%))

BRACKNELL
E. 79,199   T. 55,892 (70.57%)   C. hold
*Phillip Lee, C.   32,882
Paul Bidwell, Lab.   16,866
Patrick Smith, LD   4,186
Len Amos, UKIP   1,521
Olivio Barreto, Ind.   437
C. majority 16,016 (28.66%)
5.12% swing C. to Lab.
(2015: C. majority 20,650 (38.90%))

BRADFORD EAST
E. 70,389   T. 45,622 (64.81%)   Lab. hold
*Imran Hussain, Lab.   29,831
Mark Trafford, C.   9,291
David Ward, Ind.   3,576
Jonathan Barras, UKIP   1,372
Mark Jewell, LD   843
Paul Parkins, Bradford   420
Andy Stanford, Green   289
Lab. majority 20,540 (45.02%)
4.84% swing C. to Lab.
(2015: Lab. majority 7,084 (17.11%))

BRADFORD SOUTH
E. 67,752   T. 41,049 (60.59%)   Lab. hold
*Judith Cummins, Lab.   22,364
Tanya Graham, C.   15,664
Stephen Place, UKIP   1,758
Stuart Thomas, LD   516
Therese Hirst, Eng. Dem.   377
Darren Parkinson, Green   370
Lab. majority 6,700 (16.32%)
0.42% swing Lab. to C.
(2015: Lab. majority 6,450 (17.15%))

BRADFORD WEST
E. 67,568   T. 45,528 (67.38%)   Lab. hold
*Naz Shah, Lab.   29,444
George Grant, C.   7,542
Salma Yaqoob, ND   6,345
Derrick Hodgson, UKIP   885
Alun Griffiths, LD   712
Celia Hickson, Green   481
Hussain Khadim, ND   65
Muhammad Hijazi, Ind.   54
Lab. majority 21,902 (48.11%)
swing N/A
(2015: Lab. majority 11,420 (28.34%))

BRAINTREE
E. 75,316   T. 52,326 (69.48%)   C. hold
*James Cleverly, C.   32,873
Malcolm Fincken, Lab.   14,451
Peter Turner, LD   2,251
Richard Bingley, UKIP   1,835
Thomas Pashby, Green   916
C. majority 18,422 (35.21%)
0.07% swing C. to Lab.
(2015: C. majority 17,610 (35.02%))

BRENT CENTRAL
E. 80,845   T. 52,296 (64.69%)   Lab. hold
*Dawn Butler, Lab.   38,208
Rahoul Bhansali, C.   10,211
Anton Georgiou, LD   2,519
Shaka Lish, Green   802
Janice North, UKIP   556
Lab. majority 27,997 (53.54%)
5.88% swing C. to Lab.
(2015: Lab. majority 19,649 (41.78%))

BRENT NORTH
E. 82,556   T. 56,444 (68.37%)   Lab. hold
*Barry Gardiner, Lab.   35,496
Ameet Jogia, C.   18,435
Paul Lorber, LD   1,614
Michaela Lichten, Green   660
Elcena Jeffers, Ind.   239
Lab. majority 17,061 (30.23%)
4.74% swing C. to Lab.
(2015: Lab. majority 10,834 (20.74%))

BRENTFORD & ISLEWORTH
E. 85,151   T. 61,629 (72.38%)   Lab. hold
*Ruth Cadbury, Lab.   35,364
Mary Macleod, C.   23,182
Joe Bourke, LD   3,083
Lab. majority 12,182 (19.77%)
9.48% swing C. to Lab.
(2015: Lab. majority 465 (0.81%))

BRENTWOOD & ONGAR
E. 74,911   T. 52,910 (70.63%)   C. hold
Alex Burghart, C.   34,811
Gareth Barrett, Lab.   10,809
Karen Chilvers, LD   4,426
Michael McGough, UKIP   1,845
Paul Jeater, Green   915
Louca Kousoulou, Ind.   104
C. majority 24,002 (45.36%)
0.48% swing C. to Lab.
(2015: C. majority 21,810 (42.03%))

BRIDGWATER & SOMERSET WEST
E. 89,294   T. 58,267 (65.25%)   C. hold
*Ian Liddell-Grainger, C.   32,111
Wes Hinckes, Lab.   16,663
Marcus Kravis, LD   6,332
Simon Smedley, UKIP   2,102
Kay Powell, Green   1,059
C. majority 15,448 (26.51%)
0.91% swing C. to Lab.
(2015: C. majority 14,583 (26.78%))

BRIGG & GOOLE
E. 66,069   T. 45,057 (68.20%)   C. hold
*Andrew Percy, C.   27,219
Terence Smith, Lab.   14,856
David Jeffreys, UKIP   1,596
Jerry Lonsdale, LD   836
Isabel Pires, Green   550
C. majority 12,363 (27.44%)
0.81% swing Lab. to C.
(2015: C. majority 11,176 (25.83%))

BRIGHTON KEMPTOWN
E. 67,893   T. 49,207 (72.48%)
                                    Lab. Co-op gain
Lloyd Russell-Moyle,   28,703
Lab. Co-op
*Simon Kirby, C.   18,835
Emily Tester, LD   1,457
Doktor Haze, ND   212
Lab. Co-op majority 9,868 (20.05%)
10.79% swing C. to Lab.
(2015: C. majority 690 (1.52%))

BRIGHTON PAVILION
E. 75,486   T. 57,677 (76.41%)
                                        Green hold
*Caroline Lucas, Green   30,139
Solomon Curtis, Lab.   15,450
Emma Warman, C.   11,082
Ian Buchanan, UKIP   630
Nick Yeomans, Ind.   376
Green majority 14,689 (25.47%)
5.45% swing Lab. to Green
(2015: Green majority 7,967 (14.57%))

BRISTOL EAST
E. 72,414 T. 50,799 (70.15%) Lab. hold
*Kerry McCarthy, Lab.   30,847
Theo Clarke, C.   17,453
Chris Lucas, LD   1,389
Lorraine Francis, Green   1,110
Lab. majority 13,394 (26.37%)
8.88% swing C. to Lab.
(2015: Lab. majority 3,980 (8.61%))

BRISTOL NORTH WEST
E. 75,431 T. 54,096 (71.72%) Lab. gain
Darren Jones, Lab.   27,400
*Charlotte Leslie, C.   22,639
Celia Downie, LD   2,814
Sharmila Bousa, Green   1,243
Lab. majority 4,761 (8.80%)
9.17% swing C. to Lab.
(2015: C. majority 4,944 (9.54%))

BRISTOL SOUTH
E. 83,009 T. 54,382 (65.51%) Lab. hold
Karin Smyth, Lab.   32,666
Mark Weston, C.   16,679
Benjamin Nutland, LD   1,821
Ian Kealey, UKIP   1,672
Tony Dyer, Green   1,428
John Langley, Ind.   116
Lab. majority 15,987 (29.40%)
7.69% swing C. to Lab.
(2015: Lab. majority 7,128 (14.02%))

BRISTOL WEST
E. 92,986 T. 71,608 (77.01%) Lab. hold
*Thangam Debbonaire, Lab.   47,213
Annabel Tall, C.   9,877
Molly Scott Cato, Green   9,216
Stephen Williams, LD   5,201
Jodian Rodgers, Money   101
Lab. majority 37,336 (52.14%)
15.83% swing C. to Lab.
(2015: Lab. majority 5,673 (8.83%))

BROADLAND
E. 77,334 T. 55,971 (72.38%) C. hold
*Keith Simpson, C.   32,406
Iain Simpson, Lab.   16,590
Steve Riley, LD   4,449
David Moreland, UKIP   1,594
Andrew Boswell, Green   932
C. majority 15,816 (28.26%)
1.73% swing C. to Lab.
(2015: C. majority 16,838 (31.72%))

BROMLEY & CHISLEHURST
E. 65,113 T. 46,662 (71.66%) C. hold
*Robert Neill, C.   25,175
Sara Hyde, Lab.   15,585
Sam Webber, LD   3,369
Emmett Jenner, UKIP   1,383
Roisin Robertson, Green   1,150
C. majority 9,590 (20.55%)
5.11% swing C. to Lab.
(2015: C. majority 13,564 (30.78%))

BROMSGROVE
E. 73,571 T. 54,040 (73.45%) C. hold
*Sajid Javid, C.   33,493
Michael Thompson, Lab.   16,920
Neil Lewis, LD   2,488
Spoz Esposito, Green   1,139
C. majority 16,573 (30.67%)
0.48% swing C. to Lab.
(2015: C. majority 16,529 (31.64%))

BROXBOURNE
E. 73,502 T. 47,485 (64.60%) C. hold
*Charles Walker, C.   29,515
Selina Norgrove, Lab.   13,723
Tony Faulkner, UKIP   1,918
Andy Graham, LD   1,481
Tabitha Evans, Green   848
C. majority 15,792 (33.26%)
2.20% swing C. to Lab.
(2015: C. majority 16,723 (36.34%))

BROXTOWE
E. 74,017 T. 55,508 (74.99%) C. hold
*Anna Soubry, C.   25,983
Greg Marshall, Lab.   25,120
Tim Hallam, LD   2,247
Fran Loi, UKIP   1,477
Pat Morton, Green   681
C. majority 863 (1.55%)
3.23% swing C. to Lab.
(2015: C. majority 4,287 (8.02%))

BUCKINGHAM
E. 79,616 T. 52,679 (66.17%)
                           Speaker hold
*John Bercow, Speaker   34,299
Michael Sheppard, Green   8,574
Scott Raven, Ind.   5,638
Brian Mapletoft, UKIP   4,168
Speaker majority 25,725 (48.83%)
0.93% swing C. to Green
(2015: Speaker majority 22,942
(42.73%))

BURNLEY
E. 64,714 T. 40,290 (62.26%) Lab. hold
*Julie Cooper, Lab.   18,832
Paul White, C.   12,479
Gordon Birtwistle, LD   6,046
Tom Commis, UKIP   2,472
Laura Fisk, Green   461
Lab. majority 6,353 (15.77%)
4.16% swing Lab. to C.
(2015: Lab. majority 3,244 (8.16%))

BURTON
E. 73,954 T. 49,911 (67.49%) C. hold
*Andrew Griffiths, C.   28,936
John McKiernan, Lab.   18,889
Dominic Hardwick, LD   1,262
Simon Hales, Green   824
C. majority 10,047 (20.13%)
1.34% swing C. to Lab.
(2015: C. majority 11,252 (22.81%))

BURY NORTH
E. 67,587 T. 47,903 (70.88%) Lab. gain
James Frith, Lab.   25,683
*David Nuttall, C.   21,308
Richard Baum, LD   912
Lab. majority 4,375 (9.13%)
4.98% swing C. to Lab.
(2015: C. majority 378 (0.84%))

BURY ST EDMUNDS
E. 87,758 T. 62,160 (70.83%) C. hold
*Jo Churchill, C.   36,794
Bill Edwards, Lab.   18,353
Helen Korfanty, LD   3,565
Helen Geake, Green   2,596
Liam Byrne, Ind.   852
C. majority 18,441 (29.67%)
3.11% swing C. to Lab.
(2015: C. majority 21,301 (35.90%))

BURY SOUTH
E. 73,723 T. 50,990 (69.16%) Lab. hold
*Ivan Lewis, Lab.   27,165
Robert Largan, C.   21,200
Ian Henderson, UKIP   1,316
Andrew Page, LD   1,065
Peter Wright, Ind.   244
Lab. majority 5,965 (11.70%)
0.64% swing C. to Lab.
(2015: Lab. majority 4,922 (10.42%))

CALDER VALLEY
E. 79,045 T. 58,054 (73.44%) C. hold
*Craig Whittaker, C.   26,790
Josh Fenton-Glynn, Lab.   26,181
Janet Battye, LD   1,952
Paul Rogan, UKIP   1,466
Robert Holden, Ind.   1,034
Kieran Turner, Green   631
C. majority 609 (1.05%)
3.61% swing C. to Lab.
(2015: C. majority 4,427 (8.27%))

CAMBERWELL & PECKHAM
E. 85,586 T. 57,412 (67.08%) Lab. hold
*Harriet Harman, Lab.   44,665
Ben Spencer, C.   7,349
Michael Bukola, LD   3,413
Eleanor Margolies, Green   1,627
Ray Towey, CPA   227
Sellu Aminata, WRP   131
Lab. majority 37,316 (65.00%)
7.46% swing C. to Lab.
(2015: Lab. majority 25,824 (50.08%))

CAMBORNE & REDRUTH
E. 67,462 T. 48,456 (71.83%) C. hold
*George Eustice, C.   23,001
Graham Winter, Lab.   21,424
Geoff Williams, LD   2,979
Geoff Garbett, Green   1,052
C. majority 1,577 (3.25%)
6.01% swing C. to Lab.
(2015: C. majority 7,004 (15.27%))

CAMBRIDGE
E. 78,003 T. 55,934 (71.71%) Lab. hold
*Daniel Zeichner, Lab.   29,032
Julian Huppert, LD   16,371
John Hayward, C.   9,133
Stuart Tuckwood, Green   1,265
Keith Garrett, Reboot   133
Lab. majority 12,661 (22.64%)
10.74% swing LD to Lab.
(2015: Lab. majority 599 (1.16%))

CAMBRIDGESHIRE NORTH EAST
E. 84,404 T. 53,284 (63.13%) C. hold
*Stephen Barclay, C.   34,340
Ken Rustidge, Lab.   13,070
Darren Fower, LD   2,383
Robin Talbot, UKIP   2,174
Ruth Johnson, Green   1,024
Stephen Goldspink,   293
Eng. Dem.
C. majority 21,270 (39.92%)
0.37% swing C. to Lab.
(2015: C. majority 16,874 (32.59%))

CAMBRIDGESHIRE NORTH WEST
E. 93,223   T. 63,991 (68.64%)   C. hold
*Shailesh Vara, C.   37,529
Iain Ramsbottom, Lab.   19,521
Bridget Smith, LD   3,168
John Whitby, UKIP   2,518
Greg Guthrie, Green   1,255
C. majority 18,008 (28.14%)
3.23% swing C. to Lab.
(2015: C. majority 19,795 (32.40%))

CAMBRIDGESHIRE SOUTH
E. 85,257   T. 64,924 (76.15%)   C. hold
*Heidi Allen, C.   33,631
Dan Greef, Lab.   17,679
Susan van de Ven, LD   12,102
Simon Saggers, Green   1,512
C. majority 15,952 (24.57%)
4.45% swing C. to Lab.
(2015: C. majority 20,594 (33.46%))

CAMBRIDGESHIRE SOUTH EAST
E. 86,121   T. 63,002 (73.16%)   C. hold
*Lucy Frazer, C.   33,601
Huw Jones, Lab.   17,443
Lucy Nethsingha, LD   11,958
C. majority 16,158 (25.65%)
0.84% swing C. to Lab.
(2015: C. majority 16,837 (28.29%))

CANNOCK CHASE
E. 74,540   T. 47,872 (64.22%)   C. hold
*Amanda Milling, C.   26,318
Paul Dadge, Lab.   17,927
Paul Allen, UKIP   2,018
Paul Woodhead, Green   815
Nat Green, LD   794
C. majority 8,391 (17.53%)
3.54% swing Lab. to C.
(2015: C. majority 4,923 (10.45%))

CANTERBURY
E. 78,137   T. 56,800 (72.69%)   Lab. gain
Rosie Duffield, Lab.   25,572
*Julian Brazier, C.   25,385
James Flanagan, LD   4,561
Henry Stanton, Green   1,282
Lab. majority 187 (0.33%)
9.33% swing C. to Lab.
(2015: C. majority 9,798 (18.33%))

CARLISLE
E. 62,294   T. 43,056 (69.12%)   C. hold
*John Stevenson, C.   21,472
Ruth Alcroft, Lab.   18,873
Fiona Mills, UKIP   1,455
Peter Thornton, LD   1,256
C. majority 2,599 (6.04%)
0.24% swing C. to Lab.
(2015: C. majority 2,774 (6.51%))

CARSHALTON & WALLINGTON
E. 70,849   T. 50,753 (71.64%)   LD hold
*Tom Brake, LD   20,819
Matthew Maxwell Scott, C.   19,450
Emina Ibrahim, Lab.   9,360
Shasha Khan, Green   501
Nick Mattey, Ind.   434
Ashley Dickenson, CPA   189
LD majority 1,369 (2.70%)
0.24% swing LD to C.
(2015: LD majority 1,510 (3.17%))

CASTLE POINT
E. 69,470   T. 44,710 (64.36%)   C. hold
*Rebecca Harris, C.   30,076
Joe Cooke, Lab.   11,204
David Kurten, UKIP   2,381
Tom Holder, LD   1,049
C. majority 18,872 (42.21%)
2.59% swing Lab. to C.
(2015: C. majority 8,934 (19.66%))

CHARNWOOD
E. 78,071   T. 55,176 (70.67%)   C. hold
*Edward Argar, C.   33,318
Sean Kelly-Walsh, Lab.   16,977
Simon Sansome, LD   2,052
Victoria Connor, UKIP   1,471
Nick Cox, Green   1,036
Stephen Denham, BNP   322
C. majority 16,341 (29.62%)
1.39% swing C. to Lab.
(2015: C. majority 16,931 (32.40%))

CHATHAM & AYLESFORD
E. 70,419   T. 44,890 (63.75%)   C. hold
*Tracey Crouch, C.   25,587
Vince Maple, Lab.   15,129
Nicole Bushill, UKIP   2,275
Thomas Quinton, LD   1,116
Bernard Hyde, Green   573
John Gibson, CPA   260
C. majority 10,458 (23.30%)
1.65% swing C. to Lab.
(2015: C. majority 11,455 (26.59%))

CHEADLE
E. 72,780   T. 54,572 (74.98%)   C. hold
*Mary Robinson, C.   24,331
Mark Hunter, LD   19,824
Martin Miller, Lab.   10,417
C. majority 4,507 (8.26%)
1.95% swing C. to LD
(2015: C. majority 6,453 (12.15%))

CHELMSFORD
E. 81,045   T. 56,860 (70.16%)   C. hold
Vicky Ford, C.   30,525
Chris Vince, Lab.   16,953
Stephen Robinson, LD   6,916
Nigel Carter, UKIP   1,645
Hossain Reza, Green   821
C. majority 13,572 (23.87%)
5.02% swing C. to Lab.
(2015: C. majority 18,250 (33.91%))

CHELSEA & FULHAM
E. 63,728   T. 42,128 (66.11%)   C. hold
*Greg Hands, C.   22,179
Alan De'Ath, Lab.   13,991
Louise Rowntree, LD   4,627
Bill Cashmore, Green   807
Alasdair Seton-
Marsden, UKIP   524
C. majority 8,188 (19.44%)
10.20% swing C. to Lab.
(2015: C. majority 16,022 (39.83%))

CHELTENHAM
E. 78,875   T. 57,012 (72.28%)   C. hold
*Alex Chalk, C.   26,615
Martin Horwood, LD   24,046
Keith White, Lab.   5,408
Adam Van   943
Coevorden, Green
C. majority 2,569 (4.51%)
3.81% swing C. to LD
(2015: C. majority 6,516 (12.13%))

CHESHAM & AMERSHAM
E. 71,645   T. 55,252 (77.12%)   C. hold
*Cheryl Gillan, C.   33,514
Nina Dluzewska, Lab.   11,374
Peter Jones, LD   7,179
Alan Booth, Green   1,660
David Meacock, UKIP   1,525
C. majority 22,140 (40.07%)
3.13% swing C. to Lab.
(2015: C. majority 23,920 (45.36%))

CHESTER, CITY OF
E. 72,859   T. 56,421 (77.44%)   Lab. hold
*Chris Matheson, Lab.   32,023
Will Gallagher, C.   22,847
Linnie Jewkes, LD   1,551
Lab. majority 9,176 (16.26%)
8.04% swing C. to Lab.
(2015: Lab. majority 93 (0.18%))

CHESTERFIELD
E. 72,063   T. 47,927 (66.51%)   Lab. hold
*Toby Perkins, Lab.   26,266
Spencer Pitfield, C.   16,661
Tom Snowdon, LD   2,612
Stuart Bent, UKIP   1,611
David Wadsworth, Green   777
Lab. majority 9,605 (20.04%)
4.90% swing Lab. to C.
(2015: Lab. majority 13,598 (29.84%))

CHICHESTER
E. 84,996   T. 59,918 (70.50%)   C. hold
Gillian Keegan, C.   36,032
Mark Farwell, Lab.   13,411
Jonathan Brown, LD   6,749
Heather Barrie, Green   1,992
Andrew Moncreiff, UKIP   1,650
Andrew Emerson, Patria   84
C. majority 22,621 (37.75%)
3.89% swing C. to Lab.
(2015: C. majority 24,413 (42.73%))

CHINGFORD & WOODFORD GREEN
E. 66,078   T. 46,961 (71.07%)   C. hold
*Iain Duncan Smith, C.   23,076
Bilal Mahmood, Lab.   20,638
Deborah Unger, LD   2,043
Sinead King, Green   1,204
C. majority 2,438 (5.19%)
6.98% swing C. to Lab.
(2015: C. majority 8,386 (19.14%))

CHIPPENHAM
E. 76,432   T. 57,140 (74.76%)   C. hold
*Michelle Donelan, C.   31,267
Helen Belcher, LD   14,637
Andrew Newman, Lab.   11,236
C. majority 16,630 (29.10%)
5.46% swing LD to C.
(2015: C. majority 10,076 (18.19%))

CHIPPING BARNET
E. 77,020 T. 55,423 (71.96%) C. hold
*Theresa Villiers, C. 25,679
Emma Whysall, Lab. 25,326
Marisha Ray, LD 3,012
Phil Fletcher, Green 1,406
C. majority 353 (0.64%)
6.90% swing C. to Lab.
(2015: C. majority 7,656 (14.44%))

CHORLEY
E. 76,404 T. 55,634 (72.82%) Lab. hold
*Lindsay Hoyle, Lab. 30,745
Caroline Moon, C. 23,233
Stephen Fenn, LD 1,126
Peter Lageard, Green 530
Lab. majority 7,512 (13.50%)
2.37% swing C. to Lab.
(2015: Lab. majority 4,530 (8.76%))

CHRISTCHURCH
E. 70,329 T. 50,633 (71.99%) C. hold
*Christopher Chope, C. 35,230
Patrick Canavan, Lab. 10,059
Michael Cox, LD 4,020
Chris Rigby, Green 1,324
C. majority 25,171 (49.71%)
0.57% swing Lab. to C.
(2015: C. majority 18,224 (36.66%))

CITIES OF LONDON &
WESTMINSTER
E. 61,533 T. 38,654 (62.82%) C. hold
*Mark Field, C. 18,005
Ibrahim Dogus, Lab. 14,857
Bridget Fox, LD 4,270
Lawrence McNally, Green 821
Anil Bhatti, UKIP 426
Tim Lord, ND 173
Ankit Love The Maharaja of
Kashmir, Ind. 59
Benjamin Weenen, Young 43
C. majority 3,148 (8.14%)
9.29% swing C. to Lab.
(2015: C. majority 9,671 (26.73%))

CLACTON
E. 69,263 T. 44,145 (63.74%) C. gain
Giles Watling, C. 27,031
Tasha Osben, Lab. 11,203
Paul Oakley, UKIP 3,357
David Grace, LD 887
Chris Southall, Green 719
Caroline Shearer, Ind. 449
Robin Tilbrook, Eng. Dem. 289
Nick Martin, Ind. 210
C. majority 15,828 (35.85%)
30.70% swing UKIP to C.
(2015: UKIP majority 3,437 (7.77%))

CLEETHORPES
E. 73,047 T. 47,844 (65.50%) C. hold
*Martin Vickers, C. 27,321
Peter Keith, Lab. 16,921
Tony Blake, UKIP 2,022
Roy Horobin, LD 1,110
Loyd Emmerson, Green 470
C. majority 10,400 (21.74%)
2.12% swing Lab. to C.
(2015: C. majority 7,893 (17.51%))

COLCHESTER
E. 79,996 T. 53,545 (66.93%) C. hold
*Will Quince, C. 24,565
Tim Young, Lab. 18,888
Bob Russell, LD 9,087
Mark Goacher, Green 828
Robin Rennie, CPA 177
C. majority 5,677 (10.60%)
6.09% swing C. to Lab.
(2015: C. majority 5,575 (11.47%))

COLNE VALLEY
E. 84,381 T. 60,420 (71.60%) Lab. gain
Thelma Walker, Lab. 28,818
*Jason McCartney, C. 27,903
Cahal Burke, LD 2,494
Sonia King, Green 892
Patricia Sadio, Ind. 313
Lab. majority 915 (1.51%)
5.49% swing C. to Lab.
(2015: C. majority 5,378 (9.47%))

CONGLETON
E. 76,694 T. 56,231 (73.32%) C. hold
*Fiona Bruce, C. 31,830
Sam Corcoran, Lab. 19,211
Peter Hirst, LD 2,902
Mark Davies, UKIP 1,289
Alexander Heath, Green 999
C. majority 12,619 (22.44%)
5.23% swing C. to Lab.
(2015: C. majority 16,773 (32.90%))

COPELAND
E. 61,751 T. 42,927 (69.52%) C. hold
*Trudy Harrison, C. 21,062
Gillian Troughton, Lab. 19,367
Rebecca Hanson, LD 1,404
Herbert Crossman, UKIP 1,094
C. majority 1,695 (3.95%)
5.21% swing Lab. to C.
(2015: Lab. majority 2,564 (6.47%))
(2017: C. majority 2,147 (6.91%))

CORBY
E. 82,439 T. 59,997 (72.78%) C. hold
*Tom Pursglove, C. 29,534
Beth Miller, Lab. 26,844
Chris Stanbra, LD 1,545
Sam Watts, UKIP 1,495
Steven Scrutton, Green 579
C. majority 2,690 (4.48%)
0.09% swing Lab. to C.
(2015: C. majority 2,412 (4.29%))

CORNWALL NORTH
E. 68,850 T. 50,944 (73.99%) C. hold
*Scott Mann, C. 25,835
Daniel Rogerson, LD 18,635
Joy Bassett, Lab. 6,151
John Allman, CPA 185
Robert Hawkins, Soc. Lab. 138
C. majority 7,200 (14.13%)
0.20% swing LD to C.
(2015: C. majority 6,621 (13.72%))

CORNWALL SOUTH EAST
E. 71,896 T. 53,214 (74.02%) C. hold
*Sheryll Murray, C. 29,493
Gareth Derrick, Lab. 12,050
Phil Hutty, LD 10,336
Martin Corney, Green 1,335
C. majority 17,443 (32.78%)
4.23% swing C. to Lab.
(2015: C. majority 16,995 (33.65%))

COTSWOLDS, THE
E. 80,446 T. 59,702 (74.21%) C. hold
*Geoffrey Clifton-Brown, C. 36,201
Mark Huband, Lab. 10,702
Andrew Gant, LD 9,748
Sabrina Poole, Green 1,747
Chris Harlow, UKIP 1,197
Sandy Steel, ND 107
C. majority 25,499 (42.71%)
2.30% swing C. to Lab.
(2015: C. majority 21,477 (37.90%))

COVENTRY NORTH EAST
E. 75,792 T. 46,508 (61.36%) Lab. hold
*Colleen Fletcher, Lab. 29,499
Timothy Mayer, C. 13,919
Avtar Taggar, UKIP 1,350
Russell Field, LD 1,157
Matthew Handley, Green 502
Afzal Mahmood, Ind. 81
Lab. majority 15,580 (33.50%)
2.22% swing C. to Lab.
(2015: Lab. majority 12,274 (29.06%))

COVENTRY NORTH WEST
E. 75,214 T. 49,849 (66.28%) Lab. hold
*Geoffrey Robinson, Lab. 26,894
Resham Kotecha, C. 18,314
Michael Gee, UKIP 1,525
Andrew Hilton, LD 1,286
Ciaran Norris, Ind. 1,164
Stephen Gray, Green 666
Lab. majority 8,580 (17.21%)
3.62% swing C. to Lab.
(2015: Lab. majority 4,509 (9.97%))

COVENTRY SOUTH
E. 70,754 T. 47,009 (66.44%) Lab. hold
*Jim Cunningham, Lab. 25,874
Michelle Lowe, C. 17,927
Greg Judge, LD 1,343
Ian Rogers, UKIP 1,037
Aimee Challenor, Green 604
Sandra Findlay, Ind. 224
Lab. majority 7,947 (16.91%)
4.80% swing C. to Lab.
(2015: Lab. majority 3,188 (7.30%))

CRAWLEY
E. 73,424 T. 50,273 (68.47%) C. hold
*Henry Smith, C. 25,426
Tim Lunnon, Lab. 22,969
Marko Scepanovic, LD 1,878
C. majority 2,457 (4.89%)
4.28% swing C. to Lab.
(2015: C. majority 6,526 (13.44%))

CREWE & NANTWICH
E. 78,895   T. 55,027 (69.75%)   Lab. gain
Laura Smith, Lab.   25,928
*Edward Timpson, C.   25,880
Michael Stanley, UKIP   1,885
David Crowther, LD   1,334
Lab. majority 48 (0.09%)
3.67% swing C. to Lab.
(2015: C. majority 3,620 (7.26%))

CROYDON CENTRAL
E. 80,045   T. 57,091 (71.32%)   Lab. gain
Sarah Jones, Lab.   29,873
*Gavin Barwell, C.   24,221
Gill Hickson, LD   1,083
Peter Staveley, UKIP   1,040
Tracey Hague, Green   626
John Boadu, CPA   177
Don Locke, Ind.   71
Lab. majority 5,652 (9.90%)
5.11% swing C. to Lab.
(2015: C. majority 165 (0.31%))

CROYDON NORTH
E. 87,461   T. 59,623 (68.17%)
                              Lab. Co-op hold
*Steve Reed, Lab. Co-op   44,213
Samuel Kasumu, C.   11,848
Maltby Pindar, LD   1,656
Peter Underwood, Green   983
Michael Swadling, UKIP   753
Lee Berks, Ind.   170
Lab. Co-op majority 32,365 (54.28%)
7.18% swing C. to Lab.
(2015: Lab. Co-op majority 21,364
(39.92%))

CROYDON SOUTH
E. 83,518   T. 61,257 (73.35%)   C. hold
*Chris Philp, C.   33,334
Jennifer Brathwaite, Lab.   21,928
Anna Jones, LD   3,541
Catherine Shelley, Green   1,125
Kathleen Garner, UKIP   1,116
David Omamogho, CPA   213
C. majority 11,406 (18.62%)
5.54% swing C. to Lab.
(2015: C. majority 17,140 (29.70%))

DAGENHAM & RAINHAM
E. 70,620   T. 45,843 (64.92%)   Lab. hold
*Jon Cruddas, Lab.   22,958
Julie Marson, C.   18,306
Peter Harris, UKIP   3,246
Denis Breading, Green   544
Jonathan Fryer, LD   465
Paul Sturdy, BNP   239
Terence London, Concordia   85
Lab. majority 4,652 (10.15%)
3.45% swing Lab. to C.
(2015: Lab. majority 4,980 (11.57%))

DARLINGTON
E. 66,341   T. 44,817 (67.56%)   Lab. hold
*Jenny Chapman, Lab.   22,681
Peter Cuthbertson, C.   19,401
Kevin Brack, UKIP   1,180
Anne-Marie Curry, LD   1,031
Matthew Snedker, Green   524
Lab. majority 3,280 (7.32%)
0.18% swing Lab. to C.
(2015: Lab. majority 3,158 (7.68%))

DARTFORD
E. 78,506   T. 54,224 (69.07%)   C. hold
*Gareth Johnson, C.   31,210
Bachchu Kaini, Lab.   18,024
Ben Fryer, UKIP   2,544
Simon Beard, LD   1,428
Andrew Blatchford, Green   807
Ola Adewunmi, Ind.   211
C. majority 13,186 (24.32%)
0.38% swing Lab. to C.
(2015: C. majority 12,345 (23.55%))

DAVENTRY
E. 75,335   T. 55,663 (73.89%)   C. hold
*Chris Heaton-Harris, C.   35,464
Aiden Ramsey, Lab.   13,730
Andrew Simpson, LD   4,015
Ian Gibbins, UKIP   1,497
Jamie Wildman, Green   957
C. majority 21,734 (39.05%)
0.53% swing C. to Lab.
(2015: C. majority 21,059 (40.10%))

DENTON & REDDISH
E. 65,751   T. 39,599 (60.23%)   Lab. hold
*Andrew Gwynne, Lab.   25,161
Rozila Kana, C   11,081
Josh Seddon, UKIP   1,798
Catherine Ankers, LD   853
Gareth Hayes, Green   486
Farmin Lord Dave, Loony   217
Lab. majority 14,077 (35.55%)
4.19% swing C. to Lab.
(2015: Lab. majority 10,511 (27.17%))

DERBY NORTH
E. 69,919   T. 48,672 (69.61%)   Lab. gain
†Chris Williamson, Lab.   23,622
*Amanda Solloway, C.   21,607
Lucy Care, LD   2,262
Bill Piper, UKIP   1,181
Lab. majority 2,015 (4.14%)
2.12% swing C. to Lab.
(2015: C. majority 41 (0.09%))

DERBY SOUTH
E. 69,918   T. 45,306 (64.80%)   Lab. hold
*Margaret Beckett, Lab.   26,430
Evonne Williams, C.   15,182
Alan Graves, UKIP   2,011
Joe Naitta, LD   1,229
Ian Sleeman, Green   454
Lab. majority 11,248 (24.83%)
1.60% swing C. to Lab.
(2015: Lab. majority 8,828 (21.63%))

DERBYSHIRE DALES
E. 64,418   T. 49,571 (76.95%)   C. hold
*Patrick McLoughlin, C.   29,744
Andy Botham, Lab.   15,417
Andrew Hollyer, LD   3,126
Matthew Buckler, Green   1,002
Robin Greenwood,
Humanity   282
C. majority 14,327 (28.90%)
0.38% swing C. to Lab.
(2015: C. majority 14,044 (29.65%))

DERBYSHIRE MID
E. 67,466   T. 50,371 (74.66%)   C. hold
*Pauline Latham, C.   29,513
Alison Martin, Lab.   17,897
Adam Wain, LD   1,793
Sue Macfarlane, Green   1,168
C. majority 11,616 (23.06%)
1.85% swing C. to Lab.
(2015: C. majority 12,774 (26.76%))

DERBYSHIRE NORTH EAST
E. 72,097   T. 50,381 (69.88%)   C. gain
Lee Rowley, C.   24,784
*Natascha Engel, Lab.   21,923
James Bush, UKIP   1,565
David Lomax, LD   1,390
David Kesteven, Green   719
C. majority 2,861 (5.68%)
4.80% swing Lab. to C.
(2015: Lab. majority 1,883 (3.93%))

DERBYSHIRE SOUTH
E. 76,341   T. 52,631 (68.94%)   C. hold
*Heather Wheeler, C.   30,907
Robert Pearson, Lab.   18,937
Lorraine Johnson, LD   1,870
Marten Kats, Green   917
C. majority 11,970 (22.74%)
0.07% swing Lab. to C.
(2015: C. majority 11,471 (22.60%))

DEVIZES
E. 72,184   T. 50,593 (70.09%)   C. hold
*Claire Perry, C.   31,744
Imtiyaz Shaikh, Lab.   10,608
Christopher Coleman, LD   4,706
Timothy Page, UKIP   1,706
Emma Dawnay, Green   1,606
Jim Gunter, Wessex Reg.   223
C. majority 21,136 (41.78%)
1.49% swing C. to Lab.
(2015: C. majority 20,751 (42.34%))

DEVON CENTRAL
E. 74,370   T. 57,844 (77.78%)   C. hold
*Mel Stride, C.   31,278
Lisa Robillard Webb, Lab.   15,598
Alex White, LD   6,770
Andy Williamson, Green   1,531
Tim Matthews, UKIP   1,326
John Dean, NHAP   871
Lloyd Knight, Lib.   470
C. majority 15,680 (27.11%)
6.14% swing C. to Lab.
(2015: C. majority 21,265 (39.06%))

DEVON EAST
E. 82,382   T. 60,382 (73.30%)   C. hold
*Hugo Swire, C.   29,306
Claire Wright, Ind.   21,270
Jan Ross, Lab.   6,857
Alison Eden, LD   1,468
Brigitte Graham, UKIP   1,203
Peter Faithfull, Ind.   150
Michael Val Davies, Ind.   128
C. majority 8,036 (13.31%)
4.55% swing C. to Ind.
(2015: C. majority 12,261 (22.41%))

DEVON NORTH
E. 75,784   T. 55,705 (73.50%)   C. hold
*Peter Heaton-Jones, C.   25,517
Nick Harvey, LD   21,185
Mark Cann, Lab.   7,063
Stephen Crowther, UKIP   1,187
Ricky Knight, Green   753
C. majority 4,332 (7.78%)
2.74% swing C. to LD
(2015: C. majority 6,936 (13.26%))

DEVON SOUTH WEST
E. 71,262   T. 52,857 (74.17%)   C. hold
*Gary Streeter, C.   31,634
Philippa Davey, Lab. Co-op   15,818
Caroline Voaden, LD   2,732
Ian Ross, UKIP   1,540
Win Scutt, Green   1,133
C. majority 15,816 (29.92%)
5.00% swing C. to Lab.
(2015: C. majority 20,109 (39.92%))

DEVON WEST & TORRIDGE
E. 80,527   T. 59,480 (73.86%)   C. hold
*Geoffrey Cox, C.   33,612
Vince Barry, Lab. Co-op   12,926
David Chalmers, LD   10,526
Chris Jordan, Green   1,622
Robin Julian, Ind.   794
C. majority 20,686 (34.78%)
2.72% swing C. to Lab.
(2015: C. majority 18,403 (32.52%))

DEWSBURY
E. 81,338   T. 56,545 (69.52%)   Lab. hold
*Paula Sherriff, Lab.   28,814
Beth Prescott, C.   25,493
Ednan Hussain, LD   1,214
Simon Cope, Green   1,024
Lab. majority 3,321 (5.87%)
1.58% swing C. to Lab.
(2015: Lab. majority 1,451 (2.71%))

DON VALLEY
E. 73,988   T. 45,988 (62.16%)   Lab. hold
*Caroline Flint, Lab.   24,351
Aaron Bell, C.   19,182
Stevie Manion, Yorkshire   1,599
Anthony Smith, LD   856
Lab. majority 5,169 (11.24%)
4.84% swing C. to Lab.
(2015: Lab. majority 8,885 (20.91%))

DONCASTER CENTRAL
E. 71,716   T. 43,024 (59.99%)   Lab. hold
*Rosie Winterton, Lab.   24,915
Tom Hunt, C.   14,784
Chris Whitwood, Yorkshire   1,346
Eddie Todd, Ind.   1,006
Alison Brelsford, LD   973
Lab. majority 10,131 (23.55%)
2.40% swing Lab. to C.
(2015: Lab. majority 10,093 (24.97%))

DONCASTER NORTH
E. 72,372   T. 42,312 (58.46%)   Lab. hold
*Ed Miliband, Lab.   25,711
Shade Adoh, C.   11,687
Kim Parkinson, UKIP   2,738
Charlie Bridges, Yorkshire   741
Robert Adamson, LD   706
Frank Calladine, Ind.   366
David Allen, Eng. Dem.   363
Lab. majority 14,024 (33.14%)
0.48% swing Lab. to C.
(2015: Lab. majority 11,780 (29.82%))

DORSET MID & POOLE NORTH
E. 65,054   T. 48,254 (74.18%)   C. hold
*Michael Tomlinson, C.   28,585
Vikki Slade, LD   13,246
Steve Brew, Lab.   6,423
C. majority 15,339 (31.79%)
4.57% swing LD to C.
(2015: C. majority 10,530 (22.65%))

DORSET NORTH
E. 76,385   T. 55,724 (72.95%)   C. hold
*Simon Hoare, C.   36,169
Pat Osborne, Lab.   10,392
Thomas Panton, LD   7,556
John Tutton, Green   1,607
C. majority 25,777 (46.26%)
0.70% swing C. to Lab.
(2015: C. majority 21,118 (39.56%))

DORSET SOUTH
E. 72,323   T. 51,906 (71.77%)   C. hold
*Richard Drax, C.   29,135
Tashi Warr, Lab.   17,440
Howard Legg, LD   3,053
Jon Orrell, Green   2,278
C. majority 11,695 (22.53%)
1.07% swing C. to Lab.
(2015: C. majority 11,994 (24.68%))

DORSET WEST
E. 79,043   T. 59,598 (75.40%)   C. hold
*Oliver Letwin, C.   33,081
Andy Canning, LD   13,990
Lee Rhodes, Lab.   10,896
Kelvin Clayton, Green   1,631
C. majority 19,091 (32.03%)
1.73% swing LD to C.
(2015: C. majority 16,130 (28.57%))

DOVER
E. 74,564   T. 51,966 (69.69%)   C. hold
*Charlie Elphicke, C.   27,211
Stacey Blair, Lab.   20,774
Piers Wauchope, UKIP   1,722
Simon Dodd, LD   1,336
Beccy Sawbridge, Green   923
C. majority 6,437 (12.39%)
0.07% swing C. to Lab.
(2015: C. majority 6,294 (12.53%))

DUDLEY NORTH
E. 62,043   T. 38,910 (62.71%)   Lab. hold
*Ian Austin, Lab.   18,090
Les Jones, C.   18,068
Bill Etheridge, UKIP   2,144
Ben France, LD   368
Andrew Nixon, Green   240
Lab. majority 22 (0.06%)
5.47% swing Lab. to C.
(2015: Lab. majority 4,181 (11.00%))

DUDLEY SOUTH
E. 61,323   T. 38,244 (62.36%)   C. hold
*Mike Wood, C.   21,588
Natasha Millward, Lab.   13,858
Mitch Bolton, UKIP   1,791
Jon Bramall, LD   625
Jenny Maxwell, Green   382
C. majority 7,730 (20.21%)
4.52% swing Lab. to C.
(2015: C. majority 4,270 (11.18%))

DULWICH & WEST NORWOOD
E. 77,947   T. 56,143 (72.03%)   Lab. hold
*Helen Hayes, Lab.   39,096
Rachel Wolf, C.   10,940
Gail Kent, LD   4,475
Rashid Nix, Green   1,408
Robin Lambert, Ind.   121
Yen Lin Chong, Ind.   103
Lab. majority 28,156 (50.15%)
9.38% swing C. to Lab.
(2015: Lab. majority 16,122 (31.39%))

DURHAM, CITY OF
E. 71,132   T. 48,324 (67.94%)   Lab. hold
*Roberta Blackman-Woods,
Lab.   26,772
Richard Lawrie, C.   14,408
Amanda Hopgood, LD   4,787
Malcolm Bint, UKIP   1,116
Jonathan Elmer, Green   797
Jim Clark, Ind.   399
Jon Collings, Young   45
Lab. majority 12,364 (25.59%)
0.27% swing C. to Lab.
(2015: Lab. majority 11,439 (25.05%))

DURHAM NORTH
E. 66,970   T. 43,284 (64.63%)   Lab. hold
*Kevan Jones, Lab.   25,917
Laetitia Glossop, C.   12,978
Kenneth Rollings, UKIP   2,408
Craig Martin, LD   1,981
Lab. majority 12,939 (29.89%)
2.05% swing Lab. to C.
(2015: Lab. majority 13,644 (33.99%))

DURHAM NORTH WEST
E. 71,982   T. 47,902 (66.55%)   Lab. hold
Laura Pidcock, Lab.   25,308
Sally-Ann Hart, C.   16,516
Owen Temple, LD   3,398
Alan Breeze, UKIP   2,150
Dominic Horsman, Green   530
Lab. majority 8,792 (18.35%)
2.57% swing Lab. to C.
(2015: Lab. majority 10,056 (23.49%))

EALING CENTRAL & ACTON
E. 74,200   T. 55,342 (74.58%)   Lab. hold
*Rupa Huq, Lab.   33,037
Joy Morrissey, C.   19,230
Jon Ball, LD   3,075
Lab. majority 13,807 (24.95%)
12.21% swing C. to Lab.
(2015: Lab. majority 274 (0.54%))

EALING NORTH
E. 74,764   T. 52,516 (70.24%)   Lab. hold
*Stephen Pound, Lab.   34,635
Isobel Grant, C.   14,942
Humaira Sanders, LD   1,275
Peter McIlvenna, UKIP   921
Meena Hans, Green   743
Lab. majority 19,693 (37.50%)
6.04% swing C. to Lab.
(2015: Lab. majority 12,326 (25.41%))

EALING SOUTHALL
E. 65,188   T. 45,145 (69.25%)   Lab. hold
*Virendra Sharma, Lab.   31,720
Fabio Conti, C.   9,630
Nigel Bakhai, LD   1,892
Peter Ward, Green   1,037
John Poynton, UKIP   504
Arjinder Thiara, WRP   362
Lab. majority 22,090 (48.93%)
2.81% swing C. to Lab.
(2015: Lab. majority 18,760 (43.30%))

EASINGTON
E. 62,385   T. 36,364 (58.29%)   Lab. hold
*Grahame Morris, Lab.   23,152
Barney Campbell, C.   9,260
Susan McDonnell, NE   2,355
Allyn Roberts, UKIP   1,727
Tom Hancock, LD   460
Martie Warin, Green   410
Lab. majority 14,892 (40.95%)
3.57% swing Lab. to C.
(2015: Lab. majority 14,641 (42.29%))

EAST HAM
E. 83,827   T. 56,633 (67.56%)   Lab. hold
*Stephen Timms, Lab.   47,124
Kirsty Finlayson, C.   7,241
Daniel Oxley, UKIP   697
Glanville Williams, LD   656
Chidi Oti-Obihara, Green   474
Choudhry Afzal, Friends   311
Mirza Rahman, Ind.   130
Lab. majority 39,883 (70.42%)
2.46% swing C. to Lab.
(2015: Lab. majority 34,252 (65.50%))

EASTBOURNE
E. 78,754   T. 57,420 (72.91%)   LD gain
†Stephen Lloyd, LD   26,924
*Caroline Ansell, C.   25,315
Jake Lambert, Lab.   4,671
Alex Hough, Green   510
LD majority 1,609 (2.80%)
2.09% swing C. to LD
(2015: C. majority 733 (1.39%))

EASTLEIGH
E. 81,213   T. 57,280 (70.53%)   C. hold
*Mims Davies, C.   28,889
Mike Thornton, LD   14,710
Jill Payne, Lab.   11,454
Malcolm Jones, UKIP   1,477
Ron Meldrum, Green   750
C. majority 14,179 (24.75%)
4.14% swing LD to C.
(2015: C. majority 9,147 (16.48%))

EDDISBURY
E. 70,272   T. 51,319 (73.03%)   C. hold
*Antoinette Sandbach, C.   29,192
Cathy Reynolds, Lab.   17,250
Ian Priestner, LD   2,804
John Bickley, UKIP   1,109
Mark Green, Green   785
Morgan Hill, Pirate   179
C. majority 11,942 (23.27%)
2.06% swing C. to Lab.
(2015: C. majority 12,974 (27.40%))

EDMONTON
E. 65,705   T. 43,678 (66.48%)
                         Lab. Co-op hold
*Kate Osamor, Lab. Co-op   31,221
Gonul Daniels, C.   10,106
Nigel Sussman, UKIP   860
David Schmitz, LD   858
Benjamin Gill, Green   633
Lab. Co-op majority 21,115 (48.34%)
5.52% swing C. to Lab.
(2015: Lab. Co-op majority 15,419
(37.30%))

ELLESMERE PORT & NESTON
E. 68,666   T. 50,939 (74.18%)   Lab. hold
*Justin Madders, Lab.   30,137
Nigel Jones, C.   18,747
Ed Gough, LD   892
Fred Fricker, UKIP   821
Steven Baker, Green   342
Lab. majority 11,390 (22.36%)
4.47% swing C. to Lab.
(2015: Lab. majority 6,275 (13.43%))

ELMET & ROTHWELL
E. 80,291   T. 59,542 (74.16%)   C. hold
*Alec Shelbrooke, C.   32,352
David Nagle, Lab.   22,547
Stewart Golton, LD   2,606
Matthew Clover, Yorkshire   1,042
Dylan Brown, Green   995
C. majority 9,805 (16.47%)
0.89% swing Lab. to C.
(2015: C. majority 8,490 (14.69%))

ELTHAM
E. 64,474   T. 46,155 (71.59%)   Lab. hold
*Clive Efford, Lab.   25,128
Matt Hartley, C.   18,832
David Hall-Matthews, LD   1,457
John Clarke, BNP   738
Lab. majority 6,296 (13.64%)
3.70% swing C. to Lab.
(2015: Lab. majority 2,693 (6.24%))

ENFIELD NORTH
E. 68,454   T. 48,565 (70.95%)   Lab. hold
*Joan Ryan, Lab.   28,177
Nick de Bois, C.   17,930
Nicholas da Costa, LD   1,036
Deborah Cairns, UKIP   848
Bill Linton, Green   574
Lab. majority 10,247 (21.10%)
9.37% swing C. to Lab.
(2015: Lab. majority 1,086 (2.35%))

ENFIELD SOUTHGATE
E. 65,137   T. 48,328 (74.19%)   Lab. gain
Bambos Charalambous, Lab.   24,989
*David Burrowes, C.   20,634
Pippa Morgan, LD   1,925
David Flint, Green   780
Lab. majority 4,355 (9.01%)
9.69% swing C. to Lab.
(2015: C. majority 4,753 (10.38%))

EPPING FOREST
E. 74,737   T. 50,779 (67.94%)   C. hold
*Eleanor Laing, C.   31,462
Liam Preston, Lab.   13,219
Jon Whitehouse, LD   2,884
Patrick O'Flynn, UKIP   1,871
Simon Heap, Green   1,233
Thomas Hall, Young   110
C. majority 18,243 (35.93%)
1.35% swing C. to Lab.
(2015: C. majority 17,978 (36.43%))

EPSOM & EWELL
E. 80,029   T. 59,266 (74.06%)   C. hold
*Chris Grayling, C.   35,313
Ed Mayne, Lab.   14,838
Steve Gee, LD   7,401
Janice Baker, Green   1,714
C. majority 20,475 (34.55%)
4.11% swing C. to Lab.
(2015: C. majority 24,443 (42.78%))

EREWASH
E. 72,991   T. 49,781 (68.20%)   C. hold
*Maggie Throup, C.   25,939
Catherine Atkinson, Lab.   21,405
Martin Garnett, LD   1,243
Ralph Hierons, Green   675
Roy Dunn, Ind.   519
C. majority 4,534 (9.11%)
0.85% swing Lab. to C.
(2015: C. majority 3,584 (7.42%))

ERITH & THAMESMEAD
E. 69,724   T. 44,464 (63.77%)   Lab. hold
*Teresa Pearce, Lab.   25,585
Edward Baxter, C.   15,571
Ronie Johnson, UKIP   1,728
Simon Waddington, LD   750
Claudine Letsae, Green   507
Temi Olodu, CPA   243
Doro Oddiri, Ind.   80
Lab. majority 10,014 (22.52%)
0.09% swing C. to Lab.
(2015: Lab. majority 9,525 (22.35%))

ESHER & WALTON
E. 80,938   T. 59,842 (73.94%)   C. hold
*Dominic Raab, C.   35,071
Lana Hylands, Lab.   11,773
Andrew Davis, LD   10,374
Olivia Palmer, Green   1,074
David Ions, UKIP   1,034
Baron Badger, Loony   318
Della Reynolds, Ind.   198
C. majority 23,298 (38.93%)
5.65% swing C. to Lab.
(2015: C. majority 28,616 (50.22%))

EXETER
E. 77,329   T. 55,423 (71.67%)   Lab. hold
*Ben Bradshaw, Lab.   34,336
James Taghdissian, C.   18,219
Vanessa Newcombe, LD   1,562
Joe Levy, Green   1,027
Jonathan West, Ind.   212
Jonathan Bishop, ND   67
Lab. majority 16,117 (29.08%)
7.89% swing C. to Lab.
(2015: Lab. majority 7,183 (13.30%))

FAREHAM
E. 79,495   T. 57,014 (71.72%)   C. hold
*Suella Fernandes, C.   35,915
Matthew Randall, Lab.   14,360
Matthew Winnington, LD   3,896
Tony Blewett, UKIP   1,541
Miles Grindey, Green   1,302
C. majority 21,555 (37.81%)
2.02% swing C. to Lab.
(2015: C. majority 22,262 (40.70%))

FAVERSHAM & KENT MID
E. 76,008   T. 49,749 (65.45%)   C. hold
*Helen Whately, C.   30,390
Michael Desmond, Lab.   12,977
David Naghi, LD   3,249
Mark McGiffin, UKIP   1,702
Alastair Gould, Green   1,431
C. majority 17,413 (35.00%)
1.59% swing C. to Lab.
(2015: C. majority 16,652 (36.36%))

FELTHAM & HESTON
E. 81,707   T. 53,027 (64.90%)
                          Lab. Co-op hold
*Seema Malhotra, Lab. Co-   32,462
op
Samir Jassal, C.   16,859
Stuart Agnew, UKIP   1,510
Hina Malik, LD   1,387
Tony Firkins, Green   809
Lab. Co-op majority 15,603 (29.42%)
3.11% swing C. to Lab.
(2015: Lab. Co-op majority 11,463
(23.20%))

FILTON & BRADLEY STOKE
E. 72,569   T. 50,694 (69.86%)   C. hold
*Jack Lopresti, C.   25,331
Naomi Rylatt, Lab.   21,149
Eva Fielding, LD   3,052
Diana Warner, Green   1,162
C. majority 4,182 (8.25%)
5.89% swing C. to Lab.
(2015: C. majority 9,838 (20.04%))

FINCHLEY & GOLDERS GREEN
E. 73,138   T. 52,385 (71.62%)   C. hold
*Mike Freer, C.   24,599
Jeremy Newmark, Lab.   22,942
Jonathan Davies, LD   3,463
Adele Ward, Green   919
Andrew Price, UKIP   462
C. majority 1,657 (3.16%)
4.00% swing C. to Lab.
(2015: C. majority 5,662 (11.15%))

FOLKESTONE & HYTHE
E. 84,090   T. 58,875 (70.01%)   C. hold
*Damian Collins, C.   32,197
Laura Davison, Lab.   16,786
Lynne Beaumont, LD   4,222
Stephen Priestley, UKIP   2,565
Martin Whybrow, Green   2,498
David Plumstead, Ind.   493
Naomi Slade, Ind.   114
C. majority 15,411 (26.18%)
3.62% swing C. to Lab.
(2015: C. majority 13,797 (25.08%))

FOREST OF DEAN
E. 70,898   T. 51,767 (73.02%)   C. hold
*Mark Harper, C.   28,096
Shaun Stammers, Lab.   18,594
Janet Ellard, LD   2,029
James Greenwood, Green   1,241
Ernie Warrender, UKIP   1,237
Julian Burrett, Ind.   570
C. majority 9,502 (18.36%)
1.92% swing C. to Lab.
(2015: C. majority 10,987 (22.19%))

FYLDE
E. 65,937   T. 46,467 (70.47%)   C. hold
*Mark Menzies, C.   27,334
Jed Sullivan, Lab.   15,529
Freddie van Mierlo, LD   2,341
Tina Rothery, Green   1,263
C. majority 11,805 (25.41%)
2.48% swing C. to Lab.
(2015: C. majority 13,224 (30.36%))

GAINSBOROUGH
E. 75,893   T. 51,425 (67.76%)
*Edward Leigh, C.   31,790
Catherine Tite, Lab.   14,767
Lesley Rollings, LD   3,630
Vicky Pearson, Green   1,238
C. majority 17,023 (33.10%)
0.87% swing Lab. to C.
(2015: C. majority 15,449 (31.36%))

GARSTON & HALEWOOD
E. 75,248   T. 53,522 (71.13%)   Lab. hold
*Maria Eagle, Lab.   41,599
Adam Marsden, C.   9,450
Anna Martin, LD   1,723
Lawrence Brown, Green   750
Lab. majority 32,149 (60.07%)
2.32% swing C. to Lab.
(2015: Lab. majority 27,146 (55.42%))

GATESHEAD
E. 65,186   T. 42,103 (64.59%)   Lab. hold
*Ian Mearns, Lab.   27,426
Lauren Hankinson, C.   10,076
Mark Bell, UKIP   2,281
Frank Hindle, LD   1,709
Andy Redfern, Green   611
Lab. majority 17,350 (41.21%)
0.43% swing Lab. to C.
(2015: Lab. majority 14,784 (38.90%))

GEDLING
E. 71,221   T. 51,682 (72.57%)   Lab. hold
*Vernon Coaker, Lab.   26,833
Carolyn Abbott, C.   22,139
Lee Waters, UKIP   1,143
Robert Swift, LD   1,052
Rebecca Connick, Green   515
Lab. majority 4,694 (9.08%)
1.43% swing C. to Lab.
(2015: Lab. majority 2,986 (6.22%))

GILLINGHAM & RAINHAM
E. 72,903   T. 48,868 (67.03%)   C. hold
*Rehman Chishti, C.   27,091
Andrew Stamp, Lab.   17,661
Martin Cook, UKIP   2,097
Paul Chaplin, LD   1,372
Clive Gregory, Green   520
Roger Peacock, CPA   127
C. majority 9,430 (19.30%)
1.54% swing C. to Lab.
(2015: C. majority 10,530 (22.37%))

GLOUCESTER
E. 82,963   T. 54,071 (65.17%)   C. hold
*Richard Graham, C.   27,208
Barry Kirby, Lab.   21,688
Jeremy Hilton, LD   2,716
Daniel Woolf, UKIP   1,495
Gerald Hartley, Green   754
George Ridgeon, Loony   210
C. majority 5,520 (10.21%)
1.79% swing C. to Lab.
(2015: C. majority 7,251 (13.79%))

GOSPORT
E. 73,886   T. 49,481 (66.97%)   C. hold
*Caroline Dinenage, C.   30,647
Alan Durrant, Lab.   13,436
Bruce Tennent, LD   2,328
Chloe Palmer, UKIP   1,790
Monica Cassidy, Green   1,024
Jeffrey Roberts, Ind.   256
C. majority 17,211 (34.78%)
3.00% swing C. to Lab.
(2015: C. majority 17,098 (35.87%))

GRANTHAM & STAMFORD
E. 81,762   T. 56,593 (69.22%)   C. hold
*Nick Boles, C.   35,090
Barrie Fairbairn, Lab.   14,996
Anita Day, LD   3,120
Marietta King, UKIP   1,745
Tariq Mahmood, Ind.   860
Becca Thackray, Green   782
C. majority 20,094 (35.51%)
0.23% swing C. to Lab.
(2015: C. majority 18,989 (35.33%))

GRAVESHAM
E. 72,948   T. 48,997 (67.17%)   C. hold
*Adam Holloway, C.   27,237
Mandy Garford, Lab.   17,890
Emmanuel Feyisetan, UKIP   1,742
James Willis, LD   1,210
Marna Gilligan, Green   723
Michael Rogan, Ind.   195
C. majority 9,347 (19.08%)
1.18% swing Lab. to C.
(2015: C. majority 8,370 (16.71%))

GREAT GRIMSBY

E. 61,743 T. 35,521 (57.53%) Lab. hold
*Melanie Onn, Lab.   17,545
Jo Gideon, C.   14,980
Mike Hookem, UKIP   1,648
Steve Beasant, LD   954
Christina
McGilligan-Fell, Ind.   394
Lab. majority 2,565 (7.22%)
3.12% swing Lab. to C.
(2015: Lab. majority 4,540 (13.46%))

GREAT YARMOUTH

E. 71,408 T. 44,146 (61.82%) C. hold
*Brandon Lewis, C.   23,901
Mike Smith-Clare, Lab.   15,928
Catherine Blaiklock, UKIP   2,767
James Joyce, LD   987
Harry Webb, Green   563
C. majority 7,973 (18.06%)
2.11% swing Lab. to C.
(2015: C. majority 6,154 (13.84%))

GREENWICH & WOOLWICH

E. 77,190 T. 53,106 (68.80%) Lab. hold
*Matthew Pennycook, Lab.   34,215
Caroline Attfield, C.   13,501
Chris Adams, LD   3,785
Daniel Garrun, Green   1,605
Lab. majority 20,714 (39.01%)
6.72% swing C. to Lab.
(2015: Lab. majority 11,946 (25.57%))

GUILDFORD

E. 75,454 T. 55,509 (73.57%) C. hold
*Anne Milton, C.   30,295
Zoe Franklin, LD   13,255
Howard Smith, Lab.   10,545
Mark Bray-Parry, Green   1,152
John Morris, Peace   205
Semi Essessi, ND   57
C. majority 17,040 (30.70%)
5.44% swing C. to LD
(2015: C. majority 22,448 (41.58%))

HACKNEY NORTH & STOKE NEWINGTON

E. 83,955 T. 56,298 (67.06%) Lab. hold
*Diane Abbott, Lab.   42,265
Amy Gray, C.   7,126
Joe Richards, LD   3,817
Alastair Binnie-
Lubbock, Green   2,606
Jonathan Homan, AWP   222
Abraham Spielmann, Ind.   203
Coraline Corlis-
Khan, Friends   59
Lab. majority 35,139 (62.42%)
7.15% swing C. to Lab.
(2015: Lab. majority 24,008 (48.12%))

HACKNEY SOUTH & SHOREDITCH

E. 82,004 T. 55,354 (67.50%)
                       Lab. Co-op hold
*Meg Hillier, Lab. Co-op   43,974
Luke Parker, C.   6,043
Dave Raval, LD   3,168
Rebecca Johnson, Green   1,522
Vanessa Hudson, AWP   226
Russell Higgs, Ind.   143
Angel Watt, CPA   113
Jonty Leff, WRP   86
Hugo Sugg, Ind.   50
Dale Kalamazad, Ind.   29
Lab. Co-op majority 37,931 (68.52%)
8.80% swing C. to Lab.
(2015: Lab. Co-op majority 24,243
(50.92%))

HALESOWEN & ROWLEY REGIS

E. 68,856 T. 44,379 (64.45%) C. hold
*James Morris, C.   23,012
Ian Cooper, Lab.   17,759
Stuart Henley, UKIP   2,126
Jamie Scott, LD   859
James Robertson, Green   440
Tim Weller, Ind.   183
C. majority 5,253 (11.04%)
2.40% swing Lab. to C.
(2015: C. majority 3,082 (7.03%))

HALIFAX

E. 71,224 T. 48,276 (67.78%) Lab. hold
*Holly Lynch, Lab.   25,507
Chris Pearson, C.   20,131
Mark Weedon, UKIP   1,568
James Baker, LD   1,070
Lab. majority 5,376 (11.14%)
5.08% swing C. to Lab.
(2015: Lab. majority 428 (0.98%))

HALTEMPRICE & HOWDEN

E. 71,520 T. 51,440 (71.92%) C. hold
*David Davis, C.   31,355
Hollie Devanney, Lab.   15,950
David Nolan, LD   2,482
Diana Wallis, Yorkshire   942
Carole Needham, Green   711
C. majority 15,405 (29.95%)
1.63% swing C. to Lab.
(2015: C. majority 16,195 (33.22%))

HALTON

E. 73,457 T. 49,518 (67.41%) Lab. hold
*Derek Twigg, Lab.   36,115
Matthew Lloyd, C.   10,710
Glyn Redican, UKIP   1,488
Ryan Bate, LD   896
Vic Turton, Ind.   309
Lab. majority 25,405 (51.30%)
3.12% swing Lab. to C.
(2015: Lab. majority 20,285 (45.05%))

HAMMERSMITH

E. 72,803 T. 52,252 (71.77%) Lab. hold
*Andy Slaughter, Lab.   33,375
Charlie Dewhirst, C.   14,724
Joyce Onstad, LD   2,802
Alex Horn, Green   800
Jack Bovill, UKIP   507
Jagdeosingh Hauzaree, Ind.   44
Lab. majority 18,651 (35.69%)
11.05% swing C. to Lab.
(2015: Lab. majority 6,518 (13.59%))

HAMPSHIRE EAST

E. 74,148 T. 55,408 (74.73%) C. hold
*Damian Hinds, C.   35,263
Rohit Dasgupta, Lab.   9,411
Richard Robinson, LD   8,403
Richard Knight, Green   1,760
Susan Jerrard, JACP   571
C. majority 25,852 (46.66%)
1.95% swing C. to Lab.
(2015: C. majority 25,147 (48.69%))

HAMPSHIRE NORTH EAST

E. 75,476 T. 57,627 (76.35%) C. hold
*Ranil Jayawardena, C.   37,754
Barry Jones, Lab.   9,982
Graham Cockarill, LD   6,987
Chas Spradbery, Green   1,476
Mike Gascoigne, UKIP   1,061
Robert Blay, Ind.   367
C. majority 27,772 (48.19%)
3.94% swing C. to Lab.
(2015: C. majority 29,916 (55.40%))

HAMPSHIRE NORTH WEST

E. 81,430 T. 58,772 (72.17%) C. hold
*Kit Malthouse, C.   36,471
Andy Fitchet, Lab.   13,792
Alex Payton, LD   5,708
Roger Clark, UKIP   1,467
Dan Hill, Green   1,334
C. majority 22,679 (38.59%)
3.09% swing C. to Lab.
(2015: C. majority 23,943 (43.38%))

HAMPSTEAD & KILBURN

E. 82,957 T. 58,407 (70.41%) Lab. hold
*Tulip Siddiq, Lab.   34,464
Claire-Louise Leyland, C.   18,904
Kirsty Allan, LD   4,100
John Mansook, Green   742
Hugh Easterbrook, Ind.   136
Rainbow George Weiss, Ind.   61
Lab. majority 15,560 (26.64%)
12.27% swing C. to Lab.
(2015: Lab. majority 1,138 (2.11%))

HARBOROUGH

E. 78,647 T. 57,598 (73.24%) C. hold
Neil O'Brien, C.   30,135
Andy Thomas, Lab.   17,706
Zuffar Haq, LD   7,286
Teck Khong, UKIP   1,361
Darren Woodiwiss, Green   1,110
C. majority 12,429 (21.58%)
7.92% swing C. to Lab.
(2015: C. majority 19,632 (37.41%))

HARLOW

E. 67,697 T. 44,846 (66.25%) C. hold
*Robert Halfon, C.   24,230
Phil Waite, Lab.   17,199
Mark Gough, UKIP   1,787
Geoffrey Seeff, LD   970
Hannah Clare, Green   660
C. majority 7,031 (15.68%)
1.60% swing C. to Lab.
(2015: C. majority 8,350 (18.87%))

HARROGATE & KNARESBOROUGH
E. 77,265 T. 56,740 (73.44%) C. hold
*Andrew Jones, C. 31,477
Helen Flynn, LD 13,309
Mark Sewards, Lab. 11,395
Donald Fraser, Ind. 559
C. majority 18,168 (32.02%)
0.67% swing LD to C.
(2015: C. majority 16,371 (30.67%))

HARROW EAST
E. 71,757 T. 50,845 (70.86%) C. hold
*Bob Blackman, C. 25,129
Navin Shah, Lab. 23,372
Adam Bernard, LD 1,573
Emma Wallace, Green 771
C. majority 1,757 (3.46%)
3.13% swing C. to Lab.
(2015: C. majority 4,757 (9.71%))

HARROW WEST
E. 69,798 T. 50,355 (72.14%)
Lab. Co-op hold
*Gareth Thomas, Lab. Co-op 30,640
Hannah David, C. 17,326
Christopher Noyce, LD 1,267
Rowan Langley, Green 652
Rathy Alagaratnam, UKIP 470
Lab. Co-op majority 13,314 (26.44%)
10.85% swing C. to Lab.
(2015: Lab. Co-op majority 2,208 (4.74%))

HARTLEPOOL
E. 70,718 T. 41,835 (59.16%) Lab. hold
Mike Hill, Lab. 21,969
Carl Jackson, C. 14,319
Phillip Broughton, UKIP 4,801
Andy Hagon, LD 746
Lab. majority 7,650 (18.29%)
1.77% swing C. to Lab.
(2015: Lab. majority 3,024 (7.66%))

HARWICH & ESSEX NORTH
E. 71,294 T. 51,141 (71.73%) C. hold
*Bernard Jenkin, C. 29,921
Rosalind Scott, Lab. 15,565
Dominic Graham, LD 2,787
Aaron Hammond, UKIP 1,685
Blake Roberts, Green 1,042
Stephen Todd, CPA 141
C. majority 14,356 (28.07%)
1.63% swing C. to Lab.
(2015: C. majority 15,174 (31.33%))

HASTINGS & RYE
E. 78,298 T. 54,766 (69.95%) C. hold
*Amber Rudd, C. 25,668
Peter Chowney, Lab. 25,322
Nicholas Perry, LD 1,885
Michael Phillips, UKIP 1,479
Nicholas Wilson, Ind. 412
C. majority 346 (0.63%)
4.39% swing C. to Lab.
(2015: C. majority 4,796 (9.42%))

HAVANT
E. 72,464 T. 46,314 (63.91%) C. hold
*Alan Mak, C. 27,676
Graham Giles, Lab. 11,720
Paul Gray, LD 2,801
John Perry, UKIP 2,011
Tim Dawes, Green 1,122
Ann Buckley, Ind. 984
C. majority 15,956 (34.45%)
0.63% swing C. to Lab.
(2015: C. majority 13,920 (31.05%))

HAYES & HARLINGTON
E. 73,268 T. 47,802 (65.24%) Lab. hold
*John McDonnell, Lab. 31,796
Greg Smith, C. 13,681
Cliff Dixon, UKIP 1,153
Bill Newton Dunn, LD 601
John Bowman, Green 571
Lab. majority 18,115 (37.90%)
1.53% swing C. to Lab.
(2015: Lab. majority 15,700 (34.85%))

HAZEL GROVE
E. 62,684 T. 44,132 (70.40%) C. hold
*William Wragg, C. 20,047
Lisa Smart, LD 14,533
Nav Mishra, Lab. 9,036
Robbie Lee, Green 516
C. majority 5,514 (12.49%)
1.33% swing C. to LD
(2015: C. majority 6,552 (15.16%))

HEMEL HEMPSTEAD
E. 75,011 T. 52,282 (69.70%) C. hold
*Mike Penning, C. 28,735
Mandi Tattershall, Lab. 19,290
Sally Symington, LD 3,233
Sherief Hassan, Green 1,024
C. majority 9,445 (18.07%)
5.49% swing C. to Lab.
(2015: C. majority 14,420 (29.05%))

HEMSWORTH
E. 71,870 T. 45,944 (63.93%) Lab. hold
*Jon Trickett, Lab. 25,740
Mike Jordan, C. 15,566
David Dews, UKIP 2,591
Martin Roberts, Yorkshire 1,135
Joan MacQueen, LD 912
Lab. majority 10,174 (22.14%)
3.17% swing Lab. to C.
(2015: Lab. majority 12,078 (28.48%))

HENDON
E. 76,329 T. 52,215 (68.41%) C. hold
*Matthew Offord, C. 25,078
Mike Katz, Lab. 24,006
Alasdair Hill, LD 1,985
Carmen Legarda, Green 578
Sabriye Warsame, UKIP 568
C. majority 1,072 (2.05%)
2.73% swing C. to Lab.
(2015: C. majority 3,724 (7.50%))

HENLEY
E. 74,987 T. 57,099 (76.15%) C. hold
*John Howell, C. 33,749
Oliver Kavanagh, Lab. 11,455
Laura Coyle, LD 8,485
Robin Bennett, Green 1,864
Tim Scott, UKIP 1,154
Patrick Gray, Radical 392
C. majority 22,294 (39.04%)
3.45% swing C. to Lab.
(2015: C. majority 25,375 (45.94%))

HEREFORD & HEREFORDSHIRE SOUTH
E. 71,088 T. 50,484 (71.02%) C. hold
*Jesse Norman, C. 27,004
Anna Coda, Lab. 11,991
Jim Kenyon, Ind. 5,560
Lucy Hurds, LD 3,556
Diana Toynbee, Green 1,220
Gwyn Price, UKIP 1,153
C. majority 15,013 (29.74%)
5.02% swing C. to Lab.
(2015: C. majority 16,890 (35.74%))

HEREFORDSHIRE NORTH
E. 67,751 T. 50,177 (74.06%) C. hold
*Bill Wiggin, C. 31,097
Roger Page, Lab. 9,495
Jeanie Falconer, LD 5,874
Ellie Chowns, Green 2,771
Sasha Norris, Ind. 577
Arthur Devine, Ind. 363
C. majority 21,602 (43.05%)
0.59% swing C. to Lab.
(2015: C. majority 19,996 (41.64%))

HERTFORD & STORTFORD
E. 82,429 T. 59,992 (72.78%) C. hold
*Mark Prisk, C. 36,184
Katherine Chibah, Lab. 17,149
Mark Argent, LD 4,845
David Woollcombe, Green 1,814
C. majority 19,035 (31.73%)
3.25% swing C. to Lab.
(2015: C. majority 21,509 (38.22%))

HERTFORDSHIRE NORTH EAST
E. 75,967 T. 55,580 (73.16%) C. hold
*Oliver Heald, C. 32,587
Doug Swanney, Lab. 15,752
Nicky Shepard, LD 4,276
Tim Lee, Green 2,965
C. majority 16,835 (30.29%)
3.10% swing C. to Lab.
(2015: C. majority 19,080 (36.49%))

HERTFORDSHIRE SOUTH WEST
E. 80,293 T. 60,653 (75.54%) C. hold
*David Gauke, C. 35,128
Robert Wakely, Lab. 15,578
Christopher Townsend, LD 7,078
Paul De Hoest, Green 1,576
Mark Anderson, UKIP 1,293
C. majority 19,550 (32.23%)
4.19% swing C. to Lab.
(2015: C. majority 23,263 (40.62%))

HERTSMERE

E. 73,554 T. 52,253 (71.04%)   C. hold
*Oliver Dowden, C.   31,928
Fiona Smith, Lab.   14,977
Joe Jordan, LD   2,794
David Hoy, UKIP   1,564
Sophie Summerhayes, Green   990
C. majority 16,951 (32.44%)
2.21% swing C. to Lab.
(2015: C. majority 18,461 (36.85%))

HEXHAM

E. 61,012 T. 46,224 (75.76%)   C. hold
*Guy Opperman, C.   24,996
Stephen Powers, Lab.   15,760
Fiona Hall, LD   3,285
Wesley Foot, Green   1,253
Francis Miles, UKIP   930
C. majority 9,236 (19.98%)
3.89% swing C. to Lab.
(2015: C. majority 12,031 (27.76%))

HEYWOOD & MIDDLETON

E. 79,901 T. 49,865 (62.41%)   Lab. hold
*Liz McInnes, Lab.   26,578
Chris Clarkson, C.   18,961
Lee Seville, UKIP   3,239
Bill Winlow, LD   1,087
Lab. majority 7,617 (15.28%)
4.37% swing Lab. to C.
(2015: Lab. majority 5,299 (10.92%))

HIGH PEAK

E. 73,916 T. 53,853 (73.52%)   Lab. gain
Ruth George, Lab.   26,753
*Andrew Bingham, C.   24,431
Charles Lawley, LD   2,669
Lab. majority 2,322 (4.31%)
6.97% swing C. to Lab.
(2015: C. majority 4,894 (9.64%))

HITCHIN & HARPENDEN

E. 75,916 T. 58,783 (77.43%)   C. hold
Bim Afolami, C.   31,189
John Hayes, Lab.   19,158
Hugh Annand, LD   6,236
Richard Cano, Green   1,329
Ray Blake, Ind.   629
Sid Cordle, CPA   242
C. majority 12,031 (20.47%)
7.87% swing C. to Lab.
(2015: C. majority 20,055 (36.22%))

HOLBORN & ST PANCRAS

E. 88,088 T. 58,997 (66.98%)   Lab. hold
*Keir Starmer, Lab.   41,343
Tim Barnes, C.   10,834
Stephen Crosher, LD   4,020
Sian Berry, Green   1,980
Giles Game, UKIP   727
Janus Polenceus, Eng. Dem.   93
Lab. majority 30,509 (51.71%)
10.33% swing C. to Lab.
(2015: Lab. majority 17,048 (31.04%))

HORNCHURCH & UPMINSTER

E. 80,821 T. 56,107 (69.42%)   C. hold
Julia Dockerill, C.   33,750
Rocky Gill, Lab.   16,027
Lawrence Webb, UKIP   3,502
Jonathan Mitchell, LD   1,371
Peter Caton, Green   1,077
David Furness, BNP   380
C. majority 17,723 (31.59%)
1.36% swing Lab. to C.
(2015: C. majority 13,074 (23.67%))

HORNSEY & WOOD GREEN

E. 79,944 T. 62,293 (77.92%)   Lab. hold
*Catherine West, Lab.   40,738
Dawn Barnes, LD   10,000
Emma Lane, C.   9,246
Sam Hall, Green   1,181
Nimco Ali, Women   551
Ruth Price, UKIP   429
Helen Spiby-Vann, CPA   93
Anna Athow, WRP   55
Lab. majority 30,738 (49.34%)
15.10% swing LD to Lab.
(2015: Lab. majority 11,058 (19.14%))

HORSHAM

E. 82,773 T. 61,987 (74.89%)   C. hold
*Jeremy Quin, C.   36,906
Susannah Brady, Lab.   13,422
Morwen Millson, LD   7,644
Catherine Ross, Green   1,844
Roger Arthur, UKIP   1,533
James Smith, S. New   375
Jim Duggan, Peace   263
C. majority 23,484 (37.89%)
4.01% swing C. to Lab.
(2015: C. majority 24,658 (43.32%))

HOUGHTON & SUNDERLAND SOUTH

E. 68,123 T. 41,480 (60.89%)   Lab. hold
*Bridget Phillipson, Lab.   24,665
Paul Howell, C.   12,324
Michael Joyce, UKIP   2,379
Paul Edgeworth, LD   908
Richard Bradley, Green   725
Mick Watson, Ind.   479
Lab. majority 12,341 (29.75%)
3.46% swing Lab. to C.
(2015: Lab. majority 12,938 (33.61%))

HOVE

E. 74,236 T. 57,596 (77.58%)   Lab. hold
*Peter Kyle, Lab.   36,942
Kristy Adams, C.   18,185
Caroline Hynds, LD   1,311
Phelim Mac Cafferty, Green   971
Charley Sabel, Ind.   187
Lab. majority 18,757 (32.57%)
15.10% swing C. to Lab.
(2015: Lab. majority 1,236 (2.37%))

HUDDERSFIELD

E. 67,033 T. 43,834 (65.39%)
                          Lab. Co-op hold
*Barry Sheerman,
Lab. Co-op   26,470
Scott Benton, C.   14,465
Andrew Cooper, Green   1,395
Zulfiqar Ali, LD   1,155
Bikatshi Katenga, Yorkshire   274
Marteen
Thokkudubiyyapu, Ind.   75
Lab. Co-op majority 12,005 (27.39%)
4.62% swing C. to Lab.
(2015: Lab. Co-op majority 7,345 (18.15%))

HULL EAST

E. 65,959 T. 36,638 (55.55%)   Lab. hold
*Karl Turner, Lab.   21,355
Simon Burton, C.   10,959
Mark Fox, UKIP   2,573
Andrew Marchington, LD   1,258
Julia Brown, Green   493
Lab. majority 10,396 (28.37%)
3.72% swing Lab. to C.
(2015: Lab. majority 10,319 (29.36%))

HULL NORTH

E. 64,666 T. 37,102 (57.37%)   Lab. hold
*Diana Johnson, Lab.   23,625
Lia Nici-Townend, C.   9,363
Mike Ross, LD   1,869
John Kitchener, UKIP   1,601
Martin Deane, Green   644
Lab. majority 14,262 (38.44%)
0.32% swing Lab. to C.
(2015: Lab. majority 12,899 (36.50%))

HULL WEST & HESSLE

E. 60,181 T. 34,565 (57.44%)   Lab. hold
Emma Hardy, Lab.   18,342
Christine Mackay, C.   10,317
Claire Thomas, LD   2,210
Michelle Dewberry, Ind.   1,898
Gary Shores, UKIP   1,399
Mike Lammiman, Green   332
Will Taylor, Libertarian   67
Lab. majority 8,025 (23.22%)
4.25% swing Lab. to C.
(2015: Lab. majority 9,333 (29.35%))

HUNTINGDON

E. 84,320 T. 59,720 (70.83%)   C. hold
*Jonathan Djanogly, C.   32,915
Nik Johnson, Lab.   18,440
Rod Cantrill, LD   5,090
Paul Bullen, UKIP   2,180
Tom MacLennan, Green   1,095
C. majority 14,475 (24.24%)
5.23% swing C. to Lab.
(2015: C. majority 19,404 (34.70%))

HYNDBURN

E. 73,110 T. 45,202 (61.83%)   Lab. hold
*Graham Jones, Lab.   24,120
Kevin Horkin, C.   18,305
Janet Brown, UKIP   1,953
Les Jones, LD   824
Lab. majority 5,815 (12.86%)
1.30% swing C. to Lab.
(2015: Lab. majority 4,400 (10.26%))

ILFORD NORTH
E. 72,997   T. 52,941 (72.52%)   Lab. hold
*Wes Streeting, Lab.   30,589
Lee Scott, C.   20,950
Richard Clare, LD   1,034
Doris Osen, Ind.   368
Lab. majority 9,639 (18.21%)
8.50% swing C. to Lab.
(2015: Lab. majority 589 (1.20%))

ILFORD SOUTH
E. 85,358   T. 57,657 (67.55%)
                    Lab. Co-op hold
*Mike Gapes, Lab. Co-op   43,724
Chris Chapman, C.   12,077
Farid Ahmed, LD   772
Rosemary
Warrington, Green   542
Tariq Saeed, UKIP   477
Kane Khan, Friends   65
Lab. Co-op majority 31,647 (54.89%)
8.40% swing C. to Lab.
(2015: Lab. Co-op majority 19,777
(38.10%))

IPSWICH
E. 74,799   T. 51,137 (68.37%)   Lab. gain
Sandy Martin, Lab.   24,224
*Ben Gummer, C.   23,393
Tony Gould, UKIP   1,372
Adrian Hyyrylainen-Trett,
LD   1,187
Charlotte Armstrong, Green   840
David Tabane, Ind.   121
Lab. majority 831 (1.63%)
4.65% swing C. to Lab.
(2015: C. majority 3,733 (7.67%))

ISLE OF WIGHT
E. 110,697 T. 74,479 (67.28%)   C. hold
Bob Seely, C.   38,190
Julian Critchley, Lab.   17,121
Vix Lowthion, Green   12,915
Nick Belfitt, LD   2,740
Daryll Pitcher, UKIP   1,921
Julie Jones-Evans, Ind.   1,592
C. majority 21,069 (28.29%)
0.20% swing Lab. to C.
(2015: C. majority 13,703 (19.49%))

ISLINGTON NORTH
E. 74,831   T. 54,928 (73.40%)   Lab. hold
*Jeremy Corbyn, Lab.   40,086
James Clark, C.   6,871
Keith Angus, LD   4,946
Caroline Russell, Green   2,229
Keith Fraser, UKIP   413
Michael Foster, ND   208
Knigel Knapp, Loony   106
Susanne Cameron-Blackie,
Ind.   41
Bill Martin, SPGB   21
Andres Mendoza,
Comm. Lge   7
Lab. majority 33,215 (60.47%)
8.71% swing C. to Lab.
(2015: Lab. majority 21,194 (43.05%))

ISLINGTON SOUTH & FINSBURY
E. 69,534   T. 48,049 (69.10%)   Lab. hold
*Emily Thornberry, Lab.   30,188
Jason Charalambous, C.   9,925
Alain Desmier, LD   5,809
Benali Hamdache, Green   1,198
Pete Muswell, UKIP   929
Lab. majority 20,263 (42.17%)
6.73% swing C. to Lab.
(2015: Lab. majority 12,708 (28.71%))

JARROW
E. 64,828   T. 43,023 (66.36%)   Lab. hold
*Stephen Hepburn, Lab.   28,020
Robin Gwynn, C.   10,757
James Askwith, UKIP   2,338
Peter Maughan, LD   1,163
David Herbert, Green   745
Lab. majority 17,263 (40.13%)
0.77% swing C. to Lab.
(2015: Lab. majority 13,881 (35.99%))

KEIGHLEY
E. 71,429   T. 51,724 (72.41%)   Lab. gain
‡John Grogan, Lab.   24,066
*Kris Hopkins, C.   23,817
Paul Latham, UKIP   1,291
Matt Walker, LD   1,226
Ros Brown, Green   790
David Crabtree, Ind.   534
Lab. majority 249 (0.48%)
3.35% swing C. to Lab.
(2015: C. majority 3,053 (6.22%))

KENILWORTH & SOUTHAM
E. 66,323   T. 51,311 (77.37%)   C. hold
*Jeremy Wright, C.   31,207
Bally Singh, Lab.   13,121
Richard Dickson, LD   4,921
Rob Ballantyne, Green   1,133
Harry Cottam, UKIP   929
C. majority 18,086 (35.25%)
3.90% swing C. to Lab.
(2015: C. majority 21,002 (43.04%))

KENSINGTON
E. 60,594   T. 38,677 (63.83%)   Lab. gain
Emma Dent Coad, Lab.   16,333
*Lady (Victoria) Borwick, C.   16,313
Annabel Mullin, LD   4,724
Jennifer Nadel, Green   767
James Torrance, Ind.   393
Peter Marshall, Ind.   98
John Lloyd, Green Soc.   49
Lab. majority 20 (0.05%)
10.59% swing C. to Lab.
(2015: C. majority 7,361 (21.14%))

KETTERING
E. 71,523   T. 49,404 (69.07%)   C. hold
*Philip Hollobone, C.   28,616
Mick Scrimshaw, Lab.   18,054
Suzanna Austin, LD   1,618
Rob Reeves, Green   1,116
C. majority 10,562 (21.38%)
2.64% swing C. to Lab.
(2015: C. majority 12,590 (26.66%))

KINGSTON & SURBITON
E. 81,584   T. 62,178 (76.21%)   LD gain
†Edward Davey, LD   27,810
*James Berry, C.   23,686
Laurie South, Lab.   9,203
Graham Matthews, UKIP   675
Chris Walker, Green   536
Jason Chinnery, Loony   168
Michael Basman, Ind.   100
LD majority 4,124 (6.63%)
5.71% swing C. to LD
(2015: C. majority 2,834 (4.78%))

KINGSWOOD
E. 69,426   T. 48,741 (70.21%)   C. hold
*Chris Skidmore, C.   26,754
Mhairi Threlfall, Lab.   19,254
Karen Wilkinson, LD   1,749
Matt Furey-King, Green   984
C. majority 7,500 (15.39%)
1.66% swing C. to Lab.
(2015: C. majority 9,006 (18.71%))

KNOWSLEY
E. 81,751   T. 55,483 (67.87%)   Lab. hold
*George Howarth, Lab.   47,351
James Spencer, C.   5,137
Neil Miney, UKIP   1,285
Carl Cashman, LD   1,189
Steve Baines, Green   521
Lab. majority 42,214 (76.08%)
2.30% swing C. to Lab.
(2015: Lab. majority 34,655 (68.32%))

LANCASHIRE WEST
E. 73,258   T. 54,389 (74.24%)   Lab. hold
*Rosie Cooper, Lab.   32,030
Sam Currie, C.   20,341
Jo Barton, LD   1,069
Nate Higgins, Green   680
David Braid, WVPTFP   269
Lab. majority 11,689 (21.49%)
2.33% swing C. to Lab.
(2015: Lab. majority 8,360 (16.83%))

LANCASTER & FLEETWOOD
E. 67,171   T. 45,989 (68.47%)   Lab. hold
*Cat Smith, Lab.   25,342
Eric Ollerenshaw, C.   18,681
Robin Long, LD   1,170
Rebecca Novell, Green   796
Lab. majority 6,661 (14.48%)
5.73% swing C. to Lab.
(2015: Lab. majority 1,265 (3.03%))

LEEDS CENTRAL
E. 89,537   T. 47,673 (53.24%)   Lab. hold
*Hilary Benn, Lab.   33,453
Gareth Davies, C.   9,755
Bill Palfreman, UKIP   2,056
Ed Carlisle, Green   1,189
Andy Nash, LD   1,063
Alex Coetzee, CPA   157
Lab. majority 23,698 (49.71%)
6.02% swing C. to Lab.
(2015: Lab. majority 16,967 (37.66%))

LEEDS EAST

E. 65,950   T. 41,441 (62.84%)   Lab. hold
*Richard Burgon, Lab.   25,428
Matthew Robinson, C.   12,676
Paul Spivey, UKIP   1,742
Ed Sanderson, LD   739
Jaimes Moran, Green   434
John Otley, Yorkshire   422
Lab. majority 12,752 (30.77%)
1.02% swing Lab. to C.
(2015: Lab. majority 12,533 (32.81%))

LEEDS NORTH EAST

E. 70,112   T. 52,999 (75.59%)   Lab. hold
*Fabian Hamilton, Lab.   33,436
Ryan Stephenson, C.   16,445
Jon Hannah, LD   1,952
Ann Forsaith, Green   680
Tess Seddon, Yorkshire   303
Celia Foote, Green Soc.   116
Tim Mutamiri, CPA   67
Lab. majority 16,991 (32.06%)
8.52% swing C. to Lab.
(2015: Lab. majority 7,250 (15.01%))

LEEDS NORTH WEST

E. 68,152   T. 46,287 (67.92%)
                                Lab. Co-op gain
Alex Sobel, Lab. Co-op   20,416
*Greg Mulholland, LD   16,192
Alan Lamb, C.   9,097
Martin Hemingway, Green   582
Lab. Co-op majority 4,224 (9.13%)
7.92% swing LD to Lab.
(2015: LD majority 2,907 (6.70%))

LEEDS WEST

E. 67,955   T. 42,229 (62.14%)   Lab. hold
*Rachel Reeves, Lab.   27,013
Zoe Metcalfe, C.   11,048
Mark Thackray, UKIP   1,815
Andrew Pointon, Green   1,023
Alisdair McGregor, LD   905
Ed Jones, Yorkshire   378
Mike Davies, Green Soc.   47
Lab. majority 15,965 (37.81%)
4.94% swing C. to Lab.
(2015: Lab. majority 10,727 (27.92%))

LEICESTER EAST

E. 77,788   T. 52,424 (67.39%)   Lab. hold
*Keith Vaz, Lab.   35,116
Edward He, C.   12,688
Sujata Barot, Ind.   1,753
Nitesh Dave, LD   1,343
Melanie Wakley, Green   1,070
Ian Fox, Ind.   454
Lab. majority 22,428 (42.78%)
2.30% swing C. to Lab.
(2015: Lab. majority 18,352 (38.18%))

LEICESTER SOUTH

E. 75,534   T. 50,517 (66.88%)
                                Lab. Co-op hold
*Jon Ashworth, Lab. Co-op   37,157
Meera Sonecha, C.   10,896
Harrish Bisnauthsing, LD   1,287
Mags Lewis, Green   1,177
Lab. Co-op majority 26,261 (51.98%)
6.56% swing C. to Lab.
(2015: Lab. Co-op majority 17,845
(38.87%))

LEICESTER WEST

E. 64,834   T. 37,512 (57.86%)   Lab. hold
*Liz Kendall, Lab.   22,823
Jack Hickey, C.   11,763
Stuart Young, UKIP   1,406
Ian Bradwell, LD   792
Mel Gould, Green   607
David Bowley, Ind.   121
Lab. majority 11,060 (29.48%)
4.31% swing C. to Lab.
(2015: Lab. majority 7,203 (20.86%))

LEICESTERSHIRE NORTH WEST

E. 75,362   T. 53,541 (71.05%)   C. hold
*Andrew Bridgen, C.   31,153
Sean Sheahan, Lab.   17,867
Michael Wyatt, LD   3,420
Mia Woolley, Green   1,101
C. majority 13,286 (24.81%)
1.38% swing Lab. to C.
(2015: C. majority 11,373 (22.06%))

LEICESTERSHIRE SOUTH

E. 78,985   T. 56,689 (71.77%)   C. hold
*Alberto Costa, C.   34,795
Shabbir Aslam, Lab.   16,164
Gregory Webb, LD   2,403
Roger Helmer, UKIP   2,235
Mary Morgan, Green   1,092
C. majority 18,631 (32.87%)
0.83% swing Lab. to C.
(2015: C. majority 16,824 (31.20%))

LEIGH

E. 76,211   T. 46,874 (61.51%)
                                Lab. Co-op hold
Jo Platt, Lab. Co-op   26,347
James Grundy, C.   16,793
Mark Bradley, UKIP   2,783
Richard Kilpatrick, LD   951
Lab. Co-op majority 9,554 (20.38%)
5.43% swing Lab. to C.
(2015: Lab. majority 14,096 (31.24%))

LEWES

E. 70,947   T. 54,192 (76.38%)   C. hold
*Maria Caulfield, C.   26,820
Kelly-Marie Blundell, LD   21,312
Daniel Chapman, Lab.   6,060
C. majority 5,508 (10.16%)
4.01% swing LD to C.
(2015: C. majority 1,083 (2.14%))

LEWISHAM DEPTFORD

E. 78,472   T. 55,112 (70.23%)   Lab. hold
*Vicky Foxcroft, Lab.   42,461
Melanie McLean, C.   7,562
Bobby Dean, LD   2,911
John Coughlin, Green   1,640
Malcolm Martin, CPA   252
Laura McAnea, AWP   225
Jane Lawrence, Realist   61
Lab. majority 34,899 (63.32%)
8.98% swing C. to Lab.
(2015: Lab. majority 21,516 (45.37%))

LEWISHAM EAST

E. 68,126   T. 47,201 (69.28%)   Lab. hold
*Heidi Alexander, Lab.   32,072
Peter Fortune, C.   10,859
Emily Frith, LD   2,086
Storm Poorun, Green   803
Keith Forster, UKIP   798
Willow Winston, Ind.   355
Maureen Martin, CPA   228
Lab. majority 21,213 (44.94%)
5.77% swing C. to Lab.
(2015: Lab. majority 14,333 (33.39%))

LEWISHAM WEST & PENGE

E. 72,902   T. 53,196 (72.97%)   Lab. hold
Ellie Reeves, Lab.   35,411
Shaun Bailey, C.   12,249
John Russell, LD   3,317
Karen Wheller, Green   1,144
Hoong-Wai Cheah, UKIP   700
Katherine Hortense, CPA   325
Russell White, Populist   50
Lab. majority 23,162 (43.54%)
8.56% swing C. to Lab.
(2015: Lab. majority 13,714 (26.42%))

LEYTON & WANSTEAD

E. 65,285   T. 46,173 (70.73%)   Lab. hold
*John Cryer, Lab.   32,234
Laura Farris, C.   9,627
Ben Sims, LD   2,961
Ashley Gunstock, Green   1,351
Lab. majority 22,607 (48.96%)
6.15% swing C. to Lab.
(2015: Lab. majority 14,919 (36.65%))

LICHFIELD

E. 74,430   T. 53,524 (71.91%)   C. hold
*Michael Fabricant, C.   34,018
Chris Worsey, Lab.   15,437
Paul Ray, LD   2,653
Robert Pass, Green   1,416
C. majority 18,581 (34.72%)
0.31% swing C. to Lab.
(2015: C. majority 18,189 (35.34%))

LINCOLN

E. 73,111   T. 48,718 (66.64%)   Lab. gain
Karen Lee, Lab.   23,333
*Karl McCartney, C.   21,795
Nick Smith, UKIP   1,287
Caroline Kenyon, LD   1,284
Benjamin Loryman, Green   583
Phil Gray, Ind.   312
Iain Scott-Burdon, Ind.   124
Lab. majority 1,538 (3.16%)
3.12% swing C. to Lab.
(2015: C. majority 1,443 (3.08%))

LIVERPOOL RIVERSIDE

E. 76,332   T. 48,020 (62.91%)
                                Lab. Co-op hold
*Louise Ellman, Lab. Co-op   40,599
Pamela Hall, C.   4,652
Stephanie Pitchers, Green   1,582
Tom Sebire, LD   1,187
Lab. Co-op majority 35,947 (74.86%)
8.52% swing C. to Lab.
(2015: Lab. Co-op majority 24,463
(55.27%))

LIVERPOOL WALTON
E. 62,738 T. 42,197 (67.26%) Lab. hold
Dan Carden, Lab.   36,175
Laura Evans, C.   3,624
Terry May, Ind.   1,237
Kris Brown, LD   638
Colm Feeley, Green   523
Lab. majority 32,551 (77.14%)
0.27% swing C. to Lab.
(2015: Lab. majority 27,777 (72.33%))

LIVERPOOL WAVERTREE
E. 62,411 T. 43,640 (69.92%)
                        Lab. Co-op hold
*Luciana Berger, Lab. Co-op   34,717
Denise Haddad, C.   5,251
Richard Kemp, LD   2,858
Ted Grant, Green   598
Adam Heatherington, ND   216
Lab. Co-op majority 29,466 (67.52%)
4.10% swing C. to Lab.
(2015: Lab. Co-op majority 24,303
(59.31%))

LIVERPOOL WEST DERBY
E. 65,164 T. 45,163 (69.31%)
                        Lab. Co-op hold
*Stephen Twigg, Lab. Co-op   37,371
Paul Richardson, C.   4,463
Steve Radford, Lib.   2,150
Paul Parr, LD   545
Will Ward, Green   329
Graham Hughes, Ind.   305
Lab. Co-op majority 32,908 (72.86%)
2.15% swing C. to Lab.
(2015: Lab. Co-op majority 27,367
(66.70%))

LOUGHBOROUGH
E. 79,607 T. 54,148 (68.02%) C. hold
*Nicky Morgan, C.   27,022
Jewel Miah, Lab.   22,753
David Walker, LD   1,937
Andy McWilliam, UKIP   1,465
Philip Leicester, Green   971
C. majority 4,269 (7.88%)
4.88% swing C. to Lab.
(2015: C. majority 9,183 (17.65%))

LOUTH & HORNCASTLE
E. 79,006 T. 52,771 (66.79%) C. hold
*Victoria Atkins, C.   33,733
Julie Speed, Lab.   14,092
Jonathan Noble, UKIP   2,460
Lisa Gabriel, LD   1,990
The Iconic Arty-Pole, Loony   496
C. majority 19,641 (37.22%)
2.04% swing Lab. to C.
(2015: C. majority 14,977 (29.75%))

LUDLOW
E. 68,034 T. 49,970 (73.45%) C. hold
*Philip Dunne, C.   31,433
Julia Buckley, Lab.   12,147
Heather Kidd, LD   5,336
Hilary Wendt, Green   1,054
C. majority 19,286 (38.60%)
1.71% swing C. to Lab.
(2015: C. majority 18,929 (39.38%))

LUTON NORTH
E. 66,811 T. 46,622 (69.78%) Lab. hold
*Kelvin Hopkins, Lab.   29,765
Caroline Kerswell, C.   15,401
Rabi Martins, LD   808
Simon Hall, Green   648
Lab. majority 14,364 (30.81%)
4.24% swing C. to Lab.
(2015: Lab. majority 9,504 (22.33%))

LUTON SOUTH
E. 67,188 T. 46,133 (68.66%)
                        Lab. Co-op hold
*Gavin Shuker, Lab. Co-op   28,804
Dean Russell, C.   14,879
Andrew Strange, LD   1,056
Ujjawal Ub, UKIP   795
Marc Scheimann, Green   439
Abid Ali, Ind.   160
Lab. Co-op majority 13,925 (30.18%)
8.33% swing C. to Lab.
(2015: Lab. Co-op majority 5,711
(13.53%))

MACCLESFIELD
E. 75,228 T. 54,307 (72.19%) C. hold
*David Rutley, C.   28,595
Neil Puttick, Lab.   19,987
Richard Flowers, LD   3,350
James Booth, Green   1,213
Mark Johnson, Ind.   1,162
C. majority 8,608 (15.85%)
7.01% swing C. to Lab.
(2015: C. majority 14,811 (29.86%))

MAIDENHEAD
E. 76,276 T. 58,239 (76.35%) C. hold
*Theresa May, C.   37,718
Pat McDonald, Lab.   11,261
Tony Hill, LD   6,540
Derek Wall, Green   907
Gerard Batten, UKIP   871
Andrew Knight, AWP   282
Lord Buckethead, ND   249
Grant Smith, Ind.   152
Howling 'Laud'
Hope, Loony   119
Edmonds Victor, CPA   69
Julian Reid, Just   52
Yemi Hailemariam, Ind.   16
Bobby Smith, ND   3
C. majority 26,457 (45.43%)
4.26% swing C. to Lab.
(2015: C. majority 29,059 (53.96%))

MAIDSTONE & THE WEALD
E. 75,334 T. 51,696 (68.62%) C. hold
*Helen Grant, C.   29,136
Allen Simpson, Lab.   11,432
Emily Fermor, LD   8,455
Pamela Watts, UKIP   1,613
Stuart Jeffery, Green   888
Yolande Kenward, Ind.   172
C. majority 17,704 (34.25%)
0.35% swing C. to Lab.
(2015: C. majority 10,709 (21.41%))

MAKERFIELD
E. 74,259 T. 46,933 (63.20%) Lab. hold
*Yvonne Fovargue, Lab.   28,245
Adam Carney, C.   14,703
Bob Brierley, Ind.   2,663
John Skipworth, LD   1,322
Lab. majority 13,542 (28.85%)
1.71% swing Lab. to C.
(2015: Lab. majority 13,155 (29.37%))

MALDON
E. 66,960 T. 50,202 (74.97%) C. hold
*John Whittingdale, C.   34,111
Peter Edwards, Lab.   10,681
Zoe O'Connell, LD   2,181
Jesse Pryke, UKIP   1,899
Steven Betteridge, Green   1,073
Richard Perry, BNP   257
C. majority 23,430 (46.67%)
1.04% swing C. to Lab.
(2015: C. majority 22,070 (45.94%))

MANCHESTER CENTRAL
E. 90,261 T. 49,720 (55.08%)
                        Lab. Co-op hold
*Lucy Powell, Lab. Co-op   38,490
Xingang Wang, C.   7,045
John Bridges, LD   1,678
Kalvin Chapman, UKIP   1,469
Rachael Shah, Green   846
Neil Blackburn, Pirate   192
Lab. Co-op majority 31,445 (63.24%)
7.75% swing C. to Lab.
(2015: Lab. Co-op majority 21,639
(47.74%))

MANCHESTER GORTON
E. 75,362 T. 45,953 (60.98%) Lab. hold
Afzal Khan, Lab.   35,085
Shaden Jaradat, C.   3,355
George Galloway, Ind.   2,615
Jackie Pearcey, LD   2,597
Jess Mayo, Green   1,038
Phil Eckersley, UKIP   952
Kemi Abidogun, CPA   233
David Hopkins, Ind.   51
Peter Clifford, Comm. Lge   27
Lab. majority 31,730 (69.05%)
5.82% swing C. to Lab.
(2015: Lab. majority 24,079 (57.31%))

MANCHESTER WITHINGTON
E. 74,553 T. 53,602 (71.90%) Lab. hold
*Jeff Smith, Lab.   38,424
John Leech, LD   8,549
Sarah Heald, C.   5,530
Laura Bannister, Green   865
Sally Carr, Women   234
Lab. majority 29,875 (55.73%)
12.98% swing LD to Lab.
(2015: Lab. majority 14,873 (29.77%))

MANSFIELD
E. 77,811 T. 50,157 (64.46%) C. gain
Ben Bradley, C.   23,392
*Sir Alan Meale, Lab.   22,335
Sid Pepper, UKIP   2,654
Philip Shields, Ind.   1,079
Anita Prabhakar, LD   697
C. majority 1,057 (2.11%)
6.68% swing Lab. to C.
(2015: Lab. majority 5,315 (11.26%))

MEON VALLEY
E. 74,246   T. 54,192 (72.99%)   C. hold
*George Hollingbery, C.   35,624
Sheena King, Lab.   9,932
Martin Tod, LD   5,900
Paul Bailey, UKIP   1,435
Andrew Hayward, Green   1,301
C. majority 25,692 (47.41%)
1.36% swing C. to Lab.
(2015: C. majority 23,913 (46.24%))

MERIDEN
E. 81,437   T. 54,643 (67.10%)   C. hold
*Caroline Spelman, C.   33,873
Tom McNeil, Lab.   14,675
Antony Rogers, LD   2,663
Leslie Kaye, UKIP   2,016
Alison Gavin, Green   1,416
C. majority 19,198 (35.13%)
0.30% swing C. to Lab.
(2015: C. majority 18,795 (35.73%))

MIDDLESBROUGH
E. 61,114   T. 35,637 (58.31%)   Lab. hold
*Andy McDonald, Lab.   23,404
Jacob Young, C.   9,531
David Hodgson, UKIP   1,452
Terry Lawton, Ind.   632
Dawud Islam, LD   368
Carl Martinez, Green   250
Lab. majority 13,873 (38.93%)
0.71% swing Lab. to C.
(2015: Lab. majority 12,477 (38.15%))

MIDDLESBROUGH SOUTH & CLEVELAND EAST
E. 72,336   T. 47,620 (65.83%)   C. gain
Simon Clarke, C.   23,643
Tracy Harvey, Lab.   22,623
Chris Foote-Wood, LD   1,354
C. majority 1,020 (2.14%)
3.55% swing Lab. to C.
(2015: Lab. majority 2,268 (4.97%))

MILTON KEYNES NORTH
E. 89,272   T. 63,864 (71.54%)   C. hold
*Mark Lancaster, C.   30,307
Charlynne Pullen, Lab.   28,392
Imogen Shepherd-   2,499
Dubey, LD
Jeff Wyatt, UKIP   1,390
Alan Francis, Green   1,107
Venetia Sams, CPA   169
C. majority 1,915 (3.00%)
6.95% swing C. to Lab.
(2015: C. majority 9,753 (16.91%))

MILTON KEYNES SOUTH
E. 92,494   T. 64,486 (69.72%)   C. hold
*Iain Stewart, C.   30,652
Hannah O'Neill, Lab.   28,927
Tahir Maher, LD   1,895
Vince Peddle, UKIP   1,833
Graham Findlay, Green   1,179
C. majority 1,725 (2.67%)
6.07% swing C. to Lab.
(2015: C. majority 8,742 (14.81%))

MITCHAM & MORDEN
E. 68,705   T. 48,118 (70.04%)   Lab. hold
*Siobhain McDonagh, Lab.   33,039
Alicia Kearns, C.   11,664
Claire Mathys, LD   1,494
Richard Hilton, UKIP   1,054
Laura Collins, Green   644
Des Coke, CPA   223
Lab. majority 21,375 (44.42%)
3.47% swing C. to Lab.
(2015: Lab. majority 16,922 (37.49%))

MOLE VALLEY
E. 74,545   T. 56,726 (76.10%)   C. hold
*Paul Beresford, C.   35,092
Paul Kennedy, LD   10,955
Marc Green, Lab.   7,864
Jacquetta Fewster, Green   1,463
Judy Moore, UKIP   1,352
C. majority 24,137 (42.55%)
1.81% swing C. to LD
(2015: C. majority 25,453 (46.16%))

MORECAMBE & LUNESDALE
E. 66,838   T. 45,657 (68.31%)   C. hold
*David Morris, C.   21,773
Vikki Singleton, Lab.   20,374
Matthew Severn, LD   1,699
Robert Gillespie, UKIP   1,333
Cait Sinclair, Green   478
C. majority 1,399 (3.06%)
3.78% swing C. to Lab.
(2015: C. majority 4,590 (10.61%))

MORLEY & OUTWOOD
E. 76,495   T. 52,357 (68.44%)   C. hold
*Andrea Jenkyns, C.   26,550
Neil Dawson, Lab. Co-op   24,446
Craig Dobson, LD   1,361
C. majority 2,104 (4.02%)
1.57% swing Lab. to C.
(2015: C. majority 422 (0.87%))

NEW FOREST EAST
E. 72,602   T. 51,366 (70.75%)   C. hold
*Julian Lewis, C.   32,162
Julie Renyard, Lab.   10,167
David Harrison, LD   7,786
Henry Mellor, Green   1,251
C. majority 21,995 (42.82%)
0.63% swing C. to Lab.
(2015: C. majority 19,162 (38.75%))

NEW FOREST WEST
E. 68,787   T. 49,627 (72.15%)   C. hold
*Desmond Swayne, C.   33,170
Jo Graham, Lab.   9,739
Terry Scriven, LD   4,781
Janet Richards, Green   1,454
Des Hjerling, Pirate   483
C. majority 23,431 (47.21%)
0.95% swing C. to Lab.
(2015: C. majority 20,604 (43.46%))

NEWARK
E. 75,526   T. 55,042 (72.88%)   C. hold
*Robert Jenrick, C.   34,493
Chantal Lee, Lab.   16,344
David Watts, LD   2,786
Xandra Arundel, UKIP   1,419
C. majority 18,149 (32.97%)
1.17% swing C. to Lab.
(2015: C. majority 18,474 (35.32%))

NEWBURY
E. 82,923   T. 60,849 (73.38%)   C. hold
*Richard Benyon, C.   37,399
Judith Bunting, LD   13,019
Alex Skirvin, Lab.   8,596
Paul Field, Green   1,531
Dave Yates, AD   304
C. majority 24,380 (40.07%)
2.98% swing C. to LD
(2015: C. majority 26,368 (46.02%))

NEWCASTLE-UNDER-LYME
E. 65,540   T. 43,842 (66.89%)   Lab. hold
*Paul Farrelly, Lab.   21,124
Owen Meredith, C.   21,094
Nigel Jones, LD   1,624
Lab. majority 30 (0.07%)
0.72% swing Lab. to C.
(2015: Lab. majority 650 (1.51%))

NEWCASTLE UPON TYNE CENTRAL
E. 55,571   T. 37,094 (66.75%)   Lab. hold
*Chi Onwurah, Lab.   24,071
Steve Kyte, C.   9,134
Nick Cott, LD   1,012
David Muat, UKIP   1,482
Peter Thomson, Green   595
Lab. majority 14,937 (40.27%)
2.07% swing C. to Lab.
(2015: Lab. majority 12,673 (36.12%))

NEWCASTLE UPON TYNE EAST
E. 62,333   T. 41,637 (66.80%)   Lab. hold
*Nick Brown, Lab.   28,127
Simon Kitchen, C.   8,866
Wendy Taylor, LD   2,574
Tony Sanderson, UKIP   1,315
Alistair Ford, Green   755
Lab. majority 19,261 (46.26%)
7.20% swing C. to Lab.
(2015: Lab. majority 12,494 (31.85%))

NEWCASTLE UPON TYNE NORTH
E. 66,312   T. 48,288 (72.82%)   Lab. hold
*Catherine McKinnell, Lab.   26,729
Duncan Crute, C.   16,380
Anita Lower, LD   2,533
Timothy Marron, UKIP   1,780
Alison Whalley, Green   513
Brian Moore, North   353
Lab. majority 10,349 (21.43%)
0.59% swing Lab. to C.
(2015: Lab. majority 10,153 (22.62%))

NEWTON ABBOT
E. 71,722   T. 51,637 (72.00%)   C. hold
*§Anne Marie Morris, C.   28,635
James Osben, Lab.   11,475
Marie Chadwick, LD   10,601
Kathryn Driscoll, Green   926
C. majority 17,160 (33.23%)
2.12% swing C. to Lab.
(2015: C. majority 11,288 (23.42%))

NORFOLK MID
E. 80,026 T. 55,668 (69.56%)   C. hold
*George Freeman, C.   32,828
Sarah Simpson, Lab.   16,742
Fionna Tod, LD   2,848
Tracy Knowles, UKIP   2,092
Hannah Lester, Green   1,158
C. majority 16,086 (28.90%)
2.43% swing C. to Lab.
(2015: C. majority 17,276 (33.09%))

NORFOLK NORTH
E. 69,263 T. 52,188 (75.35%)   LD hold
*Norman Lamb, LD   25,260
James Wild, C.   21,748
Stephen Burke, Lab.   5,180
LD majority 3,512 (6.73%)
0.73% swing LD to C.
(2015: LD majority 4,043 (8.18%))

NORFOLK NORTH WEST
E. 72,062 T. 48,811 (67.73%)   C. hold
*Henry Bellingham, C.   29,408
Jo Rust, Lab.   15,620
Michael Stone, UKIP   1,539
Rupert Moss-Eccardt, LD   1,393
Andrew de Whalley, Green   851
C. majority 13,788 (28.25%)
0.60% swing C. to Lab.
(2015: C. majority 13,948 (29.44%))

NORFOLK SOUTH
E. 83,056 T. 61,111 (73.58%)   C. hold
*Richard Bacon, C.   35,580
Danielle Glavin, Lab.   18,902
Christopher Brown, LD   5,074
Catherine Rowett, Green   1,555
C. majority 16,678 (27.29%)
4.29% swing C. to Lab.
(2015: C. majority 20,493 (35.88%))

NORFOLK SOUTH WEST
E. 77,874 T. 52,416 (67.31%)   C. hold
*Elizabeth Truss, C.   32,894
Peter Smith, Lab.   14,582
David Williams, UKIP   2,575
Stephen Gordon, LD   2,365
C. majority 18,312 (34.94%)
0.64% swing Lab. to C.
(2015: C. majority 13,861 (27.66%))

NORMANTON, PONTEFRACT &
CASTLEFORD
E. 81,641 T. 49,191 (60.25%)   Lab. hold
*Yvette Cooper, Lab.   29,268
Andrew Lee, C.   14,769
Lewis Thompson, UKIP   3,030
Daniel Gascoigne, Yorkshire   1,431
Clarke Roberts, LD   693
Lab. majority 14,499 (29.47%)
2.31% swing Lab. to C.
(2015: Lab. majority 15,428 (33.61%))

NORTHAMPTON NORTH
E. 58,183 T. 40,378 (69.40%)   C. hold
*Michael Ellis, C.   19,065
Sally Keeble, Lab.   18,258
Jonathan Bullock, UKIP   1,404
George Smid, LD   1,015
Steve Miller, Green   636
C. majority 807 (2.00%)
3.12% swing C. to Lab.
(2015: C. majority 3,245 (8.23%))

NORTHAMPTON SOUTH
E. 60,993 T. 41,034 (67.28%)   C. hold
Andrew Lewer, C.   19,231
Kevin McKeever, Lab.   18,072
Rose Gibbins, UKIP   1,630
Jill Hope, LD   1,405
Scott Mabbutt, Green   696
C. majority 1,159 (2.82%)
3.47% swing C. to Lab.
(2015: C. majority 3,793 (9.75%))

NORTHAMPTONSHIRE SOUTH
E. 85,756 T. 64,998 (75.79%)   C. hold
*Andrea Leadsom, C.   40,599
Sophie Johnson, Lab.   17,759
Chris Lofts, LD   3,623
Nigel Wickens, UKIP   1,363
Denise Donaldson, Green   1,357
Josh Phillips, Ind.   297
C. majority 22,840 (35.14%)
4.13% swing C. to Lab.
(2015: C. majority 26,416 (43.40%))

NORWICH NORTH
E. 66,924 T. 45,895 (68.58%)   C. hold
*Chloe Smith, C.   21,900
Chris Jones, Lab.   21,393
Hugh Lanham, LD   1,480
Adrian Holmes, Green   782
Liam Matthews, Pirate   340
C. majority 507 (1.10%)
4.57% swing C. to Lab.
(2015: C. majority 4,463 (10.24%))

NORWICH SOUTH
E. 74,182 T. 51,359 (69.23%)   Lab. hold
*Clive Lewis, Lab.   31,311
Lana Hempsall, C.   15,715
James Wright, LD   2,841
Richard Bearman, Green   1,492
Lab. majority 15,596 (30.37%)
7.29% swing C. to Lab.
(2015: Lab. majority 7,654 (15.79%))

NOTTINGHAM EAST
E. 61,762 T. 39,327 (63.68%)
                              Lab. Co-op hold
*Chris Leslie, Lab. Co-op   28,102
Simon Murray, C.   8,512
Barry Holliday, LD   1,003
Robert Hall-Palmer, UKIP   817
Kat Boettge, Green   698
David Bishop, Elvis   195
Lab. Co-op majority 19,590 (49.81%)
8.02% swing C. to Lab.
(2015: Lab. Co-op majority 11,894
(33.78%))

NOTTINGHAM NORTH
E. 66,894 T. 38,319 (57.28%)
                              Lab. Co-op hold
Alex Norris, Lab. Co-op   23,067
Jack Tinley, C.   11,907
Stephen Crosby, UKIP   2,133
Tad Jones, LD   674
Kirsty Jones, Green   538
Lab. Co-op majority 11,160 (29.12%)
2.22% swing Lab. to C.
(2015: Lab. majority 11,860 (33.56%))

NOTTINGHAM SOUTH
E. 71,178 T. 48,129 (67.62%)   Lab. hold
*Lilian Greenwood, Lab.   30,013
Jane Hunt, C.   14,851
Tony Sutton, LD   1,564
David Hollas, UKIP   1,103
Adam McGregor, Green   598
Lab. majority 15,162 (31.50%)
7.77% swing C. to Lab.
(2015: Lab. majority 6,936 (15.96%))

NUNEATON
E. 69,201 T. 46,067 (66.57%)   C. hold
*Marcus Jones, C.   23,755
Philip Johnson, Lab.   19,016
Craig Carpenter, UKIP   1,619
Richard
Brighton-Knight, LD   914
Chris Brookes, Green   763
C. majority 4,739 (10.29%)
0.19% swing C. to Lab.
(2015: C. majority 4,882 (10.67%))

OLD BEXLEY & SIDCUP
E. 66,005 T. 48,042 (72.79%)   C. hold
*James Brokenshire, C.   29,545
Danny Hackett, Lab.   14,079
Freddy Vachha, UKIP   1,619
Drew Heffernan, LD   1,572
Derek Moran, Green   820
Michael Jones, BNP   324
Chinwe
Nwadikeduruibe, CPA   83
C. majority 15,466 (32.19%)
0.81% swing C. to Lab.
(2015: C. majority 15,803 (33.80%))

OLDHAM EAST & SADDLEWORTH
E. 72,223 T. 47,037 (65.13%)   Lab. hold
*Debbie Abrahams, Lab.   25,629
Kashif Ali, C.   17,447
Ian Bond, UKIP   2,278
Jonathan Smith, LD   1,683
Lab. majority 8,182 (17.39%)
1.95% swing C. to Lab.
(2015: Lab. majority 6,002 (13.49%))

OLDHAM WEST & ROYTON
E. 72,418 T. 45,788 (63.23%)
                              Lab. Co-op hold
*Jim McMahon, Lab. Co-op   29,846
Christopher Glenny, C.   12,648
Ruth Keating, UKIP   1,899
Garth Harkness, LD   956
Adam King, Green   439
Lab. Co-op majority 17,198 (37.56%)
0.88% swing C. to Lab.
(2015: Lab. majority 14,738 (34.17%))
(2015: Lab. majority 10,722 (38.70%))

ORPINGTON
E. 67,906 T. 50,461 (74.31%)   C. hold
*Joseph Johnson, C.   31,762
Nigel de Gruchy, Lab.   12,301
Alex Feakes, LD   3,315
Brian Philp, UKIP   2,023
Tamara Galloway, Green   1,060
C. majority 19,461 (38.57%)
1.63% swing C. to Lab.
(2015: C. majority 19,979 (40.75%))

OXFORD EAST
E. 78,360   T. 53,896 (68.78%)
Lab. Co-op hold
Anneliese Dodds,
Lab. Co-op   35,118
Suzanne Bartington, C.   11,834
Kirsten Johnson, LD   4,904
Larry Sanders, Green   1,785
Chaka Artwell, Ind.   255
Lab. Co-op majority 23,284 (43.20%)
6.53% swing C. to Lab.
(2015: Lab. majority 15,280 (30.14%))

OXFORD WEST & ABINGDON
E. 79,289   T. 60,020 (75.70%)   LD gain
Layla Moran, LD   26,256
*Nicola Blackwood, C.   25,440
Marie Tidball, Lab.   7,573
Alan Harris, UKIP   751
LD majority 816 (1.36%)
9.05% swing C. to LD
(2015: C. majority 9,582 (16.74%))

PENDLE
E. 64,963   T. 44,854 (69.05%)   C. hold
*Andrew Stephenson, C. 21,986
Wayne Blackburn, Lab.   20,707
Gordon Lishman, LD   941
Brian Parker, BNP   718
Ian Barnett, Green   502
C. majority 1,279 (2.85%)
4.71% swing C. to Lab.
(2015: C. majority 5,453 (12.27%))

PENISTONE & STOCKSBRIDGE
E. 71,293   T. 49,787 (69.83%)   Lab. hold
*Angela Smith, Lab.   22,807
Nicola Wilson, C.   21,485
John Booker, UKIP   3,453
Penny Baker, LD   2,042
Lab. majority 1,322 (2.66%)
5.85% swing Lab. to C.
(2015: Lab. majority 6,723 (14.35%))

PENRITH & THE BORDER
E. 65,139   T. 46,470 (71.34%)   C. hold
*Rory Stewart, C.   28,078
Lola McEvoy, Lab.   12,168
Neil Hughes, LD   3,641
Kerryanne Wilde, UKIP   1,142
Douglas Lawson, Green   1,029
Jonathan Davies, Ind.   412
C. majority 15,910 (34.24%)
5.53% swing C. to Lab.
(2015: C. majority 19,894 (45.29%))

PETERBOROUGH
E. 71,522   T. 47,738 (66.75%)   Lab. gain
Fiona Onasanya, Lab.   22,950
*Stewart Jackson, C.   22,343
Beki Sellick, LD   1,597
Fiona Radic, Green   848
Lab. majority 607 (1.27%)
2.68% swing C. to Lab.
(2015: C. majority 1,925 (4.09%))

PLYMOUTH MOOR VIEW
E. 69,342   T. 45,417 (65.50%)   C. hold
*Johnny Mercer, C.   23,567
Sue Dann, Lab.   18,548
Wendy Noble, UKIP   1,849
Graham Reed, LD   917
Joshua Pope, Green   536
C. majority 5,019 (11.05%)
4.32% swing Lab. to C.
(2015: C. majority 1,026 (2.41%))

PLYMOUTH SUTTON & DEVONPORT
E. 76,584   T. 44,621 (58.26%)
Lab. Co-op gain
Luke Pollard, Lab. Co-op   23,808
*Oliver Colvile, C.   17,806
Richard Ellison, UKIP   1,148
Henrietta Bewley, LD   1,106
Daniel Sheaff, Green   540
Danny Bamping, Ind.   213
Lab. Co-op majority 6,002 (13.45%)
7.27% swing C. to Lab.
(2015: C. majority 523 (1.09%))

POOLE
E. 73,011   T. 49,850 (67.54%)   C. hold
*Robert Syms, C.   28,888
Katie Taylor, Lab.   14,679
Mike Plummer, LD   4,433
Adrian Oliver, Green   1,299
Marty Caine, DDI   551
C. majority 14,209 (28.50%)
4.36% swing C. to Lab.
(2015: C. majority 15,789 (33.32%))

POPLAR & LIMEHOUSE
E. 87,274   T. 58,814 (67.39%)   Lab. hold
*Jim Fitzpatrick, Lab. 39,558
Christopher Wilford, C. 11,846
Elaine Bagshaw, LD   3,959
Oliur Rahman, Ind.   1,477
Bethan Lant, Green   989
Nicholas McQueen, UKIP   849
David Barker, ND   136
Lab. majority 27,712 (47.12%)
6.98% swing C. to Lab.
(2015: Lab. majority 16,924 (33.16%))

PORTSMOUTH NORTH
E. 71,374   T. 47,210 (66.14%)   C. hold
*Penny Mordaunt, C.   25,860
Rumal Khan, Lab.   15,895
Darren Sanders, LD   2,608
Mike Fitzgerald, UKIP   1,926
Ken Hawkins, Green   791
Joe Jenkins, Libertarian   130
C. majority 9,965 (21.11%)
1.05% swing C. to Lab.
(2015: C. majority 10,537 (23.21%))

PORTSMOUTH SOUTH
E. 69,785   T. 44,566 (63.86%)   Lab. gain
Stephen Morgan, Lab.   18,290
*Flick Drummond, C.   16,736
Robert Vernon-Jackson, LD 7,699
Kevan Chippindall-Higgin,
UKIP   1,129
Ian McCulloch, Green   712
Lab. majority 1,554 (3.49%)
9.38% swing C. to Lab.
(2015: C. majority 5,241 (12.51%))

PRESTON
E. 57,791   T. 35,597 (61.60%)
Lab. Co-op hold
*Mark Hendrick, Lab. Co-op   24,210
Kevin Beaty, C.   8,487
Simon Platt, UKIP   1,348
Neil Darby, LD   1,204
Anne Power, Green   348
Lab. Co-op majority 15,723 (44.17%)
4.06% swing C. to Lab.
(2015: Lab. Co-op majority 12,067 (36.05%))

PUDSEY
E. 72,622   T. 53,959 (74.30%)   C. hold
*Stuart Andrew, C.   25,550
Ian McCargo, Lab. Co-op 25,219
Allen Nixon, LD   1,761
Bob Buxton, Yorkshire   1,138
Michael Wharton, Ind.   291
C. majority 331 (0.61%)
4.11% swing C. to Lab.
(2015: C. majority 4,501 (8.84%))

PUTNEY
E. 65,026   T. 46,894 (72.12%)   C. hold
*Justine Greening, C.   20,679
Neeraj Patil, Lab.   19,125
Ryan Mercer, LD   5,448
Ben Fletcher, Green   1,107
Patricia Ward, UKIP   477
Lotta Quizeen, Ind.   58
C. majority 1,554 (3.31%)
10.23% swing C. to Lab.
(2015: C. majority 10,180 (23.78%))

RAYLEIGH & WICKFORD
E. 78,556   T. 55,323 (70.42%)   C. hold
*Mark Francois, C.   36,914
Mark Daniels, Lab.   13,464
Peter Smith, UKIP   2,326
Ron Tindall, LD   1,557
Paul Hill, Green   1,062
C. majority 23,450 (42.39%)
0.16% swing Lab. to C.
(2015: C. majority 17,230 (32.38%))

READING EAST
E. 75,522   T. 55,238 (73.14%)   Lab. gain
Matt Rodda, Lab.   27,093
*Rob Wilson, C.   23,344
Jenny Woods, LD   3,378
Kizzi Johannessen, Green 1,093
Michael Turberville, Ind. 188
Andy Kirkwood,
Active Dem.   142
Lab. majority 3,749 (6.79%)
9.85% swing C. to Lab.
(2015: C. majority 6,520 (12.91%))

READING WEST
E. 74,518   T. 51,766 (69.47%)   C. hold
*Alok Sharma, C.   25,311
Olivia Bailey, Lab.   22,435
Meri O'Connell, LD   3,041
Jamie Whitham, Green   979
C. majority 2,876 (5.56%)
4.09% swing C. to Lab.
(2015: C. majority 6,650 (13.74%))

REDCAR
E. 66,836   T. 42,560 (63.68%)
Lab. Co-op hold
*Anna Turley, Lab. Co-op   23,623
Peter Gibson, C.   14,138
Josh Mason, LD   2,849
Chris Gallacher, UKIP   1,950
Lab. Co-op majority 9,485 (22.29%)
2.68% swing Lab. to C.
(2015: Lab. Co-op majority 10,388 (25.39%))

REDDITCH
E. 64,334   T. 45,203 (70.26%)   C. hold
Rachel Maclean, C.   23,652
Rebecca Blake, Lab.   16,289
Neal Stote, NHAP   2,239
Paul Swansborough, UKIP   1,371
Susan Juned, LD   1,173
Kevin White, Green   380
Sally Woodhall, Ind.   99
C. majority 7,363 (16.29%)
0.15% swing Lab. to C.
(2015: C. majority 7,054 (16.00%))

REIGATE
E. 74,628   T. 53,823 (72.12%)   C. hold
*Crispin Blunt, C.   30,896
Toby Brampton, Lab.   13,282
Anna Tarrant, LD   5,889
Jonathan Essex, Green   2,214
Joseph Fox, UKIP   1,542
C. majority 17,614 (32.73%)
5.62% swing C. to Lab.
(2015: C. majority 22,334 (43.49%))

RIBBLE VALLEY
E. 77,968   T. 55,200 (70.80%)   C. hold
*Nigel Evans, C.   31,919
David Hinder, Lab.   18,720
Allan Knox, LD   3,247
Graham Sowter, Green   1,314
C. majority 13,199 (23.91%)
1.07% swing C. to Lab.
(2015: C. majority 13,606 (26.04%))

RICHMOND (YORKS)
E. 80,920   T. 57,013 (70.46%)   C. hold
*Rishi Sunak, C.   36,458
Dan Perry, Lab.   13,350
Tobie Abel, LD   3,360
Chris Pearson, Yorkshire   2,106
Fiona Yorke, Green   1,739
C. majority 23,108 (40.53%)
1.17% swing Lab. to C.
(2015: C. majority 19,550 (36.20%))

RICHMOND PARK
E. 80,025   T. 63,330 (79.14%)   C. gain
*Zac Goldsmith, C.   28,588
*Sarah Olney, LD   28,543
Cate Tuitt, Lab.   5,773
Peter Jewell, UKIP   426
C. majority 45 (0.07%)
19.44% swing C. to LD
(2015: C. majority 23,015 (38.94%))
(2016: LD majority 1,872 (4.53%))

ROCHDALE
E. 78,064   T. 50,044 (64.11%)   Lab. gain
‡Tony Lloyd, Lab.   29,035
Jane Howard, C.   14,216
Andy Kelly, LD   4,027
Christopher Baksa, UKIP   1,641
*Simon Danczuk, ND   883
Andy Littlewood,
GM Homeless   242
Lab. majority 14,819 (29.61%)
0.26% swing C. to Lab.
(2015: Lab. majority 12,442 (27.39%))

ROCHESTER & STROOD
E. 82,702   T. 53,769 (65.02%)   C. hold
*Kelly Tolhurst, C.   29,232
Teresa Murray, Lab.   19,382
David Allen, UKIP   2,893
Bart Ricketts, LD   1,189
Sonia Hyner, Green   781
Steve Benson, CPA   163
Primerose Chiguri, Ind.   129
C. majority 9,850 (18.32%)
2.98% swing C. to Lab.
(2015: C. majority 7,133 (13.58%))

ROCHFORD & SOUTHEND EAST
E. 73,501   T. 47,248 (64.28%)   C. hold
*James Duddridge, C.   23,013
Ashley Dalton, Lab.   17,465
Ron Woodley, Ind.   2,924
Neil Hookway, UKIP   1,777
Peter Gwizdala, LD   1,265
Simon Cross, Green   804
C. majority 5,548 (11.74%)
4.99% swing C. to Lab.
(2015: C. majority 9,476 (21.73%))

ROMFORD
E. 73,516   T. 49,944 (67.94%)   C. hold
*Andrew Rosindell, C.   29,671
Angelina
Leatherbarrow, Lab.   15,893
Andrew Beadle, UKIP   2,350
Ian Sanderson, LD   1,215
David Hughes, Green   815
C. majority 13,778 (27.59%)
1.25% swing C. to Lab.
(2015: C. majority 13,859 (28.18%))

ROMSEY & SOUTHAMPTON NORTH
E. 67,186   T. 50,168 (74.67%)   C. hold
*Caroline Nokes, C.   28,668
Catherine Royce, LD   10,662
Darren Paffey, Lab.   9,614
Ian Callaghan, Green   953
Don Jerrard, JACP   271
C. majority 18,006 (35.89%)
0.35% swing C. to LD
(2015: C. majority 17,712 (36.60%))

ROSSENDALE & DARWEN
E. 72,495   T. 50,156 (69.19%)   C. hold
*Jake Berry, C.   25,499
Alyson Barnes, Lab.   22,283
Sean Bonner, LD   1,550
John Payne, Green   824
C. majority 3,216 (6.41%)
2.56% swing C. to Lab.
(2015: C. majority 5,654 (11.53%))

ROTHER VALLEY
E. 75,230   T. 49,488 (65.78%)   Lab. hold
*Kevin Barron, Lab.   23,821
Bethan Eddy, C.   19,939
Lee Hunter, UKIP   3,704
Katie Pruszynski, LD   1,155
Paul Martin, Green   869
Lab. majority 3,882 (7.84%)
6.24% swing Lab. to C.
(2015: Lab. majority 7,297 (15.52%))

ROTHERHAM
E. 63,237   T. 37,923 (59.97%)   Lab. hold
*Sarah Champion, Lab.   21,404
James Bellis, C.   10,017
Allen Cowles, UKIP   3,316
Adam Carter, LD   1,754
Mick Bower, Yorkshire   1,432
Lab. majority 11,387 (30.03%)
5.09% swing Lab. to C.
(2015: Lab. majority 8,446 (22.33%))

RUGBY
E. 72,175   T. 51,336 (71.13%)   C. hold
*Mark Pawsey, C.   27,872
Claire Edwards, Lab.   19,660
Jerry Roodhouse, LD   2,851
Graham Bliss, Green   953
C. majority 8,212 (16.00%)
2.56% swing C. to Lab.
(2015: C. majority 10,345 (21.11%))

RUISLIP, NORTHWOOD & PINNER
E. 73,425   T. 53,382 (72.70%)   C. hold
*Nick Hurd, C.   30,555
Rebecca Lury, Lab.   16,575
Alex Cunliffe, LD   3,813
Sarah Green, Green   1,268
Richard Braine, UKIP   1,171
C. majority 13,980 (26.19%)
6.65% swing C. to Lab.
(2015: C. majority 20,224 (39.48%))

RUNNYMEDE & WEYBRIDGE
E. 74,887   T. 51,609 (68.92%)   C. hold
*Philip Hammond, C.   31,436
Fiona Dent, Lab.   13,386
John Vincent, LD   3,765
Nicholas Wood, UKIP   1,675
Lee-Anne Lawrance, Green   1,347
C. majority 18,050 (34.97%)
4.62% swing C. to Lab.
(2015: C. majority 22,134 (44.22%))

RUSHCLIFFE
E. 74,740   T. 58,311 (78.02%)   C. hold
*Kenneth Clarke, C.   30,223
David Mellen, Lab.   22,213
Jayne Phoenix, LD   2,759
George Mallender, Green   1,626
Matthew Faithfull, UKIP   1,490
C. majority 8,010 (13.74%)
5.67% swing C. to Lab.
(2015: C. majority 13,829 (25.07%))

RUTLAND & MELTON

E. 78,463 T. 57,569 (73.37%)   C. hold
*Alan Duncan, C.   36,169
Heather Peto, Lab.   13,065
Ed Reynolds, LD   4,711
John Scutter, UKIP   1,869
Alastair McQuillan, Green   1,755
C. majority 23,104 (40.13%)
0.08% swing C. to Lab.
(2015: C. majority 21,705 (39.75%))

SAFFRON WALDEN

E. 83,690 T. 60,911 (72.78%)   C. hold
Kemi Badenoch, C.   37,629
Jane Berney, Lab.   12,663
Mike Hibbs, LD   8,528
Lorna Howe, UKIP   2,091
C. majority 24,966 (40.99%)
2.21% swing C. to Lab.
(2015: C. majority 24,991 (43.42%))

ST ALBANS

E. 72,811 T. 56,998 (78.28%)   C. hold
*Anne Main, C.   24,571
Daisy Cooper, LD   18,462
Kerry Pollard, Lab.   13,137
Jack Easton, Green   828
C. majority 6,109 (10.72%)
8.71% swing C. to LD
(2015: C. majority 12,732 (23.39%))

ST AUSTELL & NEWQUAY

E. 78,618 T. 54,212 (68.96%)   C. hold
*Steve Double, C.   26,856
Kevin Neil, Lab.   15,714
Stephen Gilbert, LD   11,642
C. majority 11,142 (20.55%)
4.72% swing C. to Lab.
(2015: C. majority 8,173 (16.23%))

ST HELENS NORTH

E. 76,088 T. 50,222 (66.01%)   Lab. hold
*Conor McGinn, Lab.   32,012
Jackson Ng, C.   13,606
Peter Peers, UKIP   2,097
Tom Morrison, LD   1,287
Rachel Parkinson, Green   1,220
Lab. majority 18,406 (36.65%)
0.37% swing Lab. to C.
(2015: Lab. majority 17,291 (37.38%))

ST HELENS SOUTH & WHISTON

E. 79,036 T. 52,886 (66.91%)   Lab. hold
*Marie Rimmer, Lab.   35,879
Ed McRandal, C.   11,536
Brian Spencer, LD   2,101
Mark Hitchen, UKIP   1,953
Jess Northey, Green   1,417
Lab. majority 24,343 (46.03%)
1.07% swing C. to Lab.
(2015: Lab. majority 21,243 (43.89%))

ST IVES

E. 67,462 T. 51,226 (75.93%)   C. hold
*Derek Thomas, C.   22,120
Andrew George, LD   21,808
Christopher Drew, Lab.   7,298
C. majority 312 (0.61%)
2.25% swing C. to LD
(2015: C. majority 2,469 (5.11%))

SALFORD & ECCLES

E. 78,082 T. 47,619 (60.99%)   Lab. hold
*Rebecca Long Bailey, Lab.   31,168
Jason Sugarman, C.   12,036
Christopher Barnes, UKIP   2,320
John Reid, LD   1,286
Wendy Olsen, Green   809
Lab. majority 19,132 (40.18%)
5.59% swing C. to Lab.
(2015: Lab. majority 12,541 (28.99%))

SALISBURY

E. 72,892 T. 53,311 (73.14%)   C. hold
*John Glen, C.   30,952
Tom Corbin, Lab.   13,619
Paul Sample, LD   5,982
Dean Palethorpe, UKIP   1,191
Brig Oubridge, Green   1,152
King Arthur Pendragon, Ind.   415
C. majority 17,333 (32.51%)
3.88% swing C. to Lab.
(2015: C. majority 20,421 (40.27%))

SCARBOROUGH & WHITBY

E. 73,593 T. 50,449 (68.55%)   C. hold
*Robert Goodwill, C.   24,401
Eric Broadbent, Lab.   20,966
Sam Cross, UKIP   1,682
Robert Lockwood, LD   1,354
David Malone, Green   915
John Freeman, Ind.   680
Bill Black, Yorkshire   369
Gordon Johnson, Ind.   82
C. majority 3,435 (6.81%)
3.09% swing C. to Lab.
(2015: C. majority 6,200 (12.99%))

SCUNTHORPE

E. 61,578 T. 40,202 (65.29%)   Lab. hold
*Nic Dakin, Lab.   20,916
Holly Mumby-Croft, C.   17,485
Andy Talliss, UKIP   1,247
Ryk Downes, LD   554
Lab. majority 3,431 (8.53%)
0.03% swing C. to Lab.
(2015: Lab. majority 3,134 (8.48%))

SEDGEFIELD

E. 63,890 T. 41,591 (65.10%)   Lab. hold
*Phil Wilson, Lab.   22,202
Dehenna Davison, C.   16,143
John Grant, UKIP   1,763
Stephen Psallidas, LD   797
Melissa Wilson, Green   686
Lab. majority 6,059 (14.57%)
1.55% swing Lab. to C.
(2015: Lab. majority 6,843 (17.67%))

SEFTON CENTRAL

E. 69,019 T. 52,079 (75.46%)   Lab. hold
*Bill Esterson, Lab.   32,830
Jade Marsden, C.   17,212
Daniel Lewis, LD   1,381
Mike Carter, Green   656
Lab. majority 15,618 (29.99%)
2.91% swing C. to Lab.
(2015: Lab. majority 11,846 (24.17%))

SELBY & AINSTY

E. 75,765 T. 56,076 (74.01%)   C. hold
*Nigel Adams, C.   32,921
David Bowgett, Lab.   19,149
Callum Delhoy, LD   2,293
Tony Pycroft, UKIP   1,713
C. majority 13,772 (24.56%)
0.56% swing C. to Lab.
(2015: C. majority 13,557 (25.67%))

SEVENOAKS

E. 71,061 T. 51,218 (72.08%)   C. hold
*Michael Fallon, C.   32,644
Chris Clark, Lab.   10,727
Alan Bullion, LD   4,280
Graham Cushway, UKIP   1,894
Philip Dodd, Green   1,673
C. majority 21,917 (42.79%)
0.63% swing C. to Lab.
(2015: C. majority 19,561 (39.03%))

SHEFFIELD BRIGHTSIDE & HILLSBOROUGH

E. 70,344 T. 41,870 (59.52%)   Lab. hold
*Gill Furniss, Lab.   28,193
Michael Naughton, C.   9,058
Shane Harper, UKIP   2,645
Simon Clement-Jones, LD   1,061
Christine Gilligan
Kubo, Green   737
Mike Driver, WRP   137
Muzafar Rahman, Soc. Dem.   47
Lab. majority 19,143 (45.72%)
0.07% swing C. to Lab.
(2015: Lab. majority 13,807 (34.47%))
(2016: Lab. majority 9,590 (42.47%))

SHEFFIELD CENTRAL

E. 77,560 T. 47,877 (61.73%)   Lab. hold
*Paul Blomfield, Lab.   33,963
Stephanie Roe, C.   6,215
Natalie Bennett, Green   3,848
Shaffaq Mohammed, LD   2,465
Dominic Cook, UKIP   1,060
Jack Carrington, Yorkshire   197
Robert Moran, Pirate   91
Joe Westridge, Soc. Dem.   38
Lab. majority 27,748 (57.96%)
7.03% swing C. to Lab.
(2015: Lab. majority 17,309 (39.18%))

SHEFFIELD HALLAM

E. 73,455 T. 57,020 (77.63%)   Lab. gain
Jared O'Mara, Lab.   21,881
*Nick Clegg, LD   19,756
Ian Walker, C.   13,561
John Thurley, UKIP   929
Logan Robin, Green   823
Steven Winstone, Soc. Dem.   70
Lab. majority 2,125 (3.73%)
3.98% swing LD to Lab.
(2015: LD majority 2,353 (4.24%))

SHEFFIELD HEELEY

E. 68,040 T. 44,226 (65.00%)   Lab. hold
*Louise Haigh, Lab.   26,524
Gordon Gregory, C.   12,696
Joe Otten, LD   2,022
Howard Denby, UKIP   1,977
Declan Walsh, Green   943
Jaspreet Oberoi, Soc. Dem.   64
Lab. majority 13,828 (31.27%)
0.39% swing Lab. to C.
(2015: Lab. majority 12,954 (30.81%))

SHEFFIELD SOUTH EAST
E. 68,945 T. 43,596 (63.23%) Lab. hold
*Clive Betts, Lab. 25,520
Lindsey Cawrey, C. 13,722
Dennise Dawson, UKIP 2,820
Colin Ross, LD 1,432
Ishleen Oberoi, Soc. Dem. 102
Lab. majority 11,798 (27.06%)
3.50% swing Lab. to C.
(2015: Lab. majority 12,311 (29.53%))

SHERWOOD
E. 76,196 T. 53,364 (70.04%) C. hold
*Mark Spencer, C. 27,492
Mike Pringle, Lab. 22,294
Stuart Bestwick, UKIP 1,801
Becky Thomas, LD 1,113
Morris Findley, Green 664
C. majority 5,198 (9.74%)
0.29% swing Lab. to C.
(2015: C. majority 4,647 (9.17%))

SHIPLEY
E. 73,133 T. 53,395 (73.01%) C. hold
*Philip Davies, C. 27,417
Steve Clapcote, Lab. 22,736
Caroline Jones, LD 2,202
Sophie Walker, Women 1,040
C. majority 4,681 (8.77%)
5.14% swing C. to Lab.
(2015: C. majority 9,624 (19.04%))

SHREWSBURY & ATCHAM
E. 79,043 T. 58,203 (73.63%) C. hold
*Daniel Kawczynski, C. 29,073
Laura Davies, Lab. 22,446
Hannah Fraser, LD 4,254
Edward Higginbottom, UKIP 1,363
Emma Bullard, Green 1,067
C. majority 6,627 (11.39%)
3.15% swing C. to Lab.
(2015: C. majority 9,565 (17.68%))

SHROPSHIRE NORTH
E. 80,535 T. 55,599 (69.04%) C. hold
*Owen Paterson, C. 33,642
Graeme Currie, Lab. 17,287
Tom Thornhill, LD 2,948
Duncan Kerr, Green 1,722
C. majority 16,355 (29.42%)
0.98% swing C. to Lab.
(2015: C. majority 16,494 (31.37%))

SITTINGBOURNE & SHEPPEY
E. 81,715 T. 51,389 (62.89%) C. hold
*Gordon Henderson, C. 30,911
Mike Rolfe, Lab. 15,700
Mike Baldock, Ind. 2,133
Keith Nevols, LD 1,392
Mark Lindop, Green 558
Mad Mike Young, Loony 403
Lee McCall, Ind. 292
C. majority 15,211 (29.60%)
0.14% swing C. to Lab.
(2015: C. majority 12,168 (24.64%))

SKIPTON & RIPON
E. 78,108 T. 58,138 (74.43%) C. hold
*Julian Smith, C. 36,425
Alan Woodhead, Lab. 16,440
Andy Brown, Green 3,734
Jack Render, Yorkshire 1,539
C. majority 19,985 (34.38%)
1.84% swing C. to Lab.
(2015: C. majority 20,761 (38.05%))

SLEAFORD & NORTH HYKEHAM
E. 90,925 T. 65,797 (72.36%) C. hold
*Caroline Johnson, C. 42,245
Jim Clarke, Lab. 17,008
Ross Pepper, LD 2,722
Sally Chadd, UKIP 1,954
Fiona McKenna, Green 968
Paul Coyne, Ind. 900
C. majority 25,237 (38.36%)
0.29% swing C. to Lab.
(2015: C. majority 24,115 (38.93%))
(2016: C. majority 13,144 (40.03%))

SLOUGH
E. 83,272 T. 54,295 (65.20%) Lab. hold
Tan Dhesi, Lab. 34,170
Mark Vivis, C. 17,172
Tom McCann, LD 1,308
Karen Perez, UKIP 1,228
Paul Janik, Ind. 417
Lab. majority 16,998 (31.31%)
8.06% swing C. to Lab.
(2015: Lab. majority 7,336 (15.20%))

SOLIHULL
E. 77,784 T. 56,748 (72.96%) C. hold
*Julian Knight, C. 32,985
Nigel Knowles, Lab. 12,414
Ade Adeyemo, LD 8,901
Andrew Garcarz, UKIP 1,291
Max McLoughlin, Green 1,157
C. majority 20,571 (36.25%)
1.28% swing C. to Lab.
(2015: C. majority 12,902 (23.55%))

SOMERSET NORTH
E. 80,538 T. 61,994 (76.97%) C. hold
*Liam Fox, C. 33,605
Greg Chambers, Lab. 16,502
Richard Foord, LD 5,982
Donald Davies, Ind. 3,929
Charley Pattison, Green 1,976
C. majority 17,103 (27.59%)
5.80% swing C. to Lab.
(2015: C. majority 23,099 (39.19%))

SOMERSET NORTH EAST
E. 71,350 T. 54,043 (75.74%) C. hold
*Jacob Rees-Mogg, C. 28,992
Robin Moss, Lab. 18,757
Manda Rigby, LD 4,461
Sally Calverley, Green 1,245
Shaun Hughes, Ind. 588
C. majority 10,235 (18.94%)
3.00% swing C. to Lab.
(2015: C. majority 12,749 (24.94%))

SOMERTON & FROME
E. 84,435 T. 63,592 (75.31%) C. hold
*David Warburton, C. 36,231
Mark Blackburn, LD 13,325
Sean Dromgoole, Lab. 10,998
Theo Simon, Green 2,047
Richard Hadwin, Ind. 991
C. majority 22,906 (36.02%)
1.21% swing LD to C.
(2015: C. majority 20,268 (33.61%))

SOUTH HOLLAND & THE DEEPINGS
E. 76,381 T. 50,315 (65.87%) C. hold
*John Hayes, C. 35,179
Voyteck Kowalewski, Lab. 10,282
Nicola Smith, UKIP 2,185
Julia Cambridge, LD 1,433
Daniel Wilshire, Green 894
Rick Stringer, Ind. 342
C. majority 24,897 (49.48%)
1.19% swing Lab. to C.
(2015: C. majority 18,567 (37.73%))

SOUTH RIBBLE
E. 75,752 T. 54,834 (72.39%) C. hold
*Seema Kennedy, C. 28,980
Julie Gibson, Lab. 21,559
John Wright, LD 2,073
Mark Smith, UKIP 1,387
Andrew Wight, Green 494
Mark Jarnell, NHAP 341
C. majority 7,421 (13.53%)
1.09% swing Lab. to C.
(2015: C. majority 5,945 (11.35%))

SOUTH SHIELDS
E. 63,449 T. 40,772 (64.26%) Lab. hold
*Emma Lewell-Buck, Lab. 25,078
Felicity Buchan, C. 10,570
Richard Elvin, UKIP 3,006
Shirley Ford, Green 1,437
Gita Gordon, LD 681
Lab. majority 14,508 (35.58%)
0.46% swing C. to Lab.
(2015: Lab. majority 10,614 (29.27%))

SOUTHAMPTON ITCHEN
E. 71,716 T. 46,783 (65.23%) C. hold
*Royston Smith, C. 21,773
Simon Letts, Lab. 21,742
Eleanor Bell, LD 1,421
Kim Rose, UKIP 1,122
Rosie Pearce, Green 725
C. majority 31 (0.07%)
2.56% swing C. to Lab.
(2015: C. majority 2,316 (5.18%))

SOUTHAMPTON TEST
E. 70,194 T. 46,903 (66.82%) Lab. hold
*Alan Whitehead, Lab. 27,509
Paul Holmes, C. 16,006
Thomas Gravatt, LD 1,892
Andrew Pope, Southampton 816
Keith Morrell, Ind. 680
Lab. majority 11,503 (24.53%)
7.90% swing C. to Lab.
(2015: Lab. majority 3,810 (8.73%))

SOUTHEND WEST
E. 67,677 T. 47,191 (69.73%) C. hold
*David Amess, C.   26,046
Julian Ware-Lane, Lab.   16,046
Lucy Salek, LD   2,110
John Stansfield, UKIP   1,666
Dominic Ellis, Green   831
Tino Callaghan, Southend   305
Jason Pilley, Ind.   187
C. majority 10,000 (21.19%)
5.16% swing C. to Lab.
(2015: C. majority 14,021 (31.50%))

SOUTHPORT
E. 69,400 T. 47,956 (69.10%) C. gain
Damien Moore, C.   18,541
Liz Savage, Lab.   15,627
Sue McGuire, LD   12,661
Terry Durrance, UKIP   1,127
C. majority 2,914 (6.08%)
7.63% swing LD to C.
(2015: LD majority 1,322 (3.00%))

SPELTHORNE
E. 72,641 T. 50,115 (68.99%) C. hold
*Kwasi Kwarteng, C.   28,692
Rebecca Geach, Lab.   15,267
Rosamund Shimell, LD   2,755
Redvers Cunningham, UKIP   2,296
Paul Jacobs, Green   1,105
C. majority 13,425 (26.79%)
2.16% swing C. to Lab.
(2015: C. majority 14,152 (28.84%))

STAFFORD
E. 68,445 T. 51,924 (75.86%) C. hold
*Jeremy Lefroy, C.   28,424
David Williams, Lab.   20,695
Christine Tinker, LD   1,540
Tony Pearce, Green   1,265
C. majority 7,729 (14.89%)
1.97% swing C. to Lab.
(2015: C. majority 9,177 (18.82%))

STAFFORDSHIRE MOORLANDS
E. 66,009 T. 44,655 (67.65%) C. hold
*Karen Bradley, C.   25,963
Dave Jones, Lab.   15,133
Nicholas Sheldon, ND   1,524
Henry Jebb, LD   1,494
Mike Shone, Green   541
C. majority 10,830 (24.25%)
0.18% swing Lab. to C.
(2015: C. majority 10,174 (23.89%))

STAFFORDSHIRE SOUTH
E. 73,453 T. 51,109 (69.58%) C. hold
*Gavin Williamson, C.   35,656
Adam Freeman, Lab.   12,923
Hilary Myers, LD   1,348
Claire McIlvenna, Green   1,182
C. majority 22,733 (44.48%)
1.70% swing Lab. to C.
(2015: C. majority 20,371 (41.07%))

STALYBRIDGE & HYDE
E. 71,409 T. 42,457 (59.46%)
                          Lab. Co-op hold
*Jonathan Reynolds,
Lab. Co-op   24,277
Tom Dowse, C.   16,193
Paul Ankers, LD   996
Julie Wood, Green   991
Lab. Co-op majority 8,084 (19.04%)
1.37% swing C. to Lab.
(2015: Lab. Co-op majority 6,686
(16.29%))

STEVENAGE
E. 70,765 T. 49,329 (69.71%) C. hold
*Stephen McPartland, C.   24,798
Sharon Taylor, Lab. Co-op   21,414
Barbara Gibson, LD   2,032
Victoria Snelling, Green   1,085
C. majority 3,384 (6.86%)
1.75% swing C. to Lab.
(2015: C. majority 4,955 (10.37%))

STOCKPORT
E. 63,425 T. 41,544 (65.50%) Lab. hold
*Ann Coffey, Lab.   26,282
Daniel Hamilton, C.   11,805
Daniel Hawthorne, LD   1,778
John Kelly, UKIP   1,088
Gary Lawson, Green   591
Lab. majority 14,477 (34.85%)
4.74% swing C. to Lab.
(2015: Lab. majority 10,061 (25.38%))

STOCKTON NORTH
E. 66,279 T. 42,731 (64.47%) Lab. hold
*Alex Cunningham, Lab.   24,304
Mark Fletcher, C.   15,589
Ted Strike, UKIP   1,834
Sarah Brown, LD   646
Emma Robson, Green   358
Lab. majority 8,715 (20.40%)
0.37% swing Lab. to C.
(2015: Lab. majority 8,367 (21.14%))

STOCKTON SOUTH
E. 75,619 T. 53,824 (71.18%) Lab. gain
Paul Williams, Lab.   26,102
*James Wharton, C.   25,214
David Outterside, UKIP   1,186
Drew Durning, LD   951
Jo Fitzgerald, Green   371
Lab. majority 888 (1.65%)
5.70% swing C. to Lab.
(2015: C. majority 5,046 (9.74%))

STOKE-ON-TRENT CENTRAL
E. 58,196 T. 33,145 (56.95%)
                          Lab. Co-op hold
*Gareth Snell, Lab. Co-op   17,083
Daniel Jellyman, C.   13,186
Mick Harold, UKIP   1,608
Peter Andras, LD   680
Adam Colclough, Green   378
Barbara Fielding, Ind.   210
Lab. Co-op majority 3,897 (11.76%)
2.51% swing Lab. to C.
(2015: Lab. majority 5,179 (16.66%))
(2017: Lab. majority 2,620 (12.38%))

STOKE-ON-TRENT NORTH
E. 72,368 T. 41,786 (57.74%) Lab. hold
*Ruth Smeeth, Lab.   21,272
Ben Adams, C.   18,913
Richard Whelan, LD   916
Douglas Rouxel, Green   685
Lab. majority 2,359 (5.65%)
3.43% swing Lab. to C.
(2015: Lab. majority 4,836 (12.51%))

STOKE-ON-TRENT SOUTH
E. 66,046 T. 41,690 (63.12%) C. gain
Jack Brereton, C.   20,451
*Rob Flello, Lab.   19,788
Ian Wilkes, LD   808
Jan Zablocki, Green   643
C. majority 663 (1.59%)
4.04% swing Lab. to C.
(2015: Lab. majority 2,539 (6.49%))

STONE
E. 67,824 T. 50,032 (73.77%) C. hold
*William Cash, C.   31,614
Sam Hale, Lab. Co-op   14,119
Martin Lewis, LD   2,222
Edward Whitfield, UKIP   1,370
Samantha Pancheri, Green   707
C. majority 17,495 (34.97%)
0.21% swing Lab. to C.
(2015: C. majority 16,250 (34.55%))

STOURBRIDGE
E. 70,215 T. 47,135 (67.13%) C. hold
*Margot James, C.   25,706
Pete Lowe, Lab.   18,052
Glen Wilson, UKIP   1,801
Christoper Bramall, LD   1,083
Andi Mohr, Green   493
C. majority 7,654 (16.24%)
0.85% swing Lab. to C.
(2015: C. majority 6,694 (14.54%))

STRATFORD-ON-AVON
E. 72,609 T. 52,532 (72.35%) C. hold
*Nadhim Zahawi, C.   32,657
Jeff Kenner, Lab.   11,699
Elizabeth Adams, LD   6,357
Dominic Giles, Green   1,345
Jandy Spurway, Ind.   255
Tom Darwood, Ind.   219
C. majority 20,958 (39.90%)
2.40% swing C. to Lab.
(2015: C. majority 22,876 (44.45%))

STREATHAM
E. 78,532 T. 55,795 (71.05%) Lab. hold
*Chuka Umunna, Lab.   38,212
Kim Caddy, C.   11,927
Alex Davies, LD   3,611
Nicole Griffiths, Green   1,696
Robert Stephenson, UKIP   349
Lab. majority 26,285 (47.11%)
9.60% swing C. to Lab.
(2015: Lab. majority 13,934 (27.91%))

STRETFORD & URMSTON
E. 71,840 T. 50,191 (69.86%) Lab. hold
*Kate Green, Lab.   33,519
Lisa Cooke, C.   13,814
Andrew Beaumont, UKIP   1,094
Anna Fryer, LD   1,001
Michael Ingleson, Green   641
Rose Doman, CPA   122
Lab. majority 19,705 (39.26%)
7.03% swing C. to Lab.
(2015: Lab. majority 11,685 (25.19%))

STROUD
E. 82,849 T. 63,816 (77.03%)
                            Lab. Co-op gain
†David Drew, Lab. Co-op   29,994
*Neil Carmichael, C.   29,307
Max Wilkinson, LD   2,053
Sarah Lunnon, Green   1,423
Glenville Gogerly, UKIP   1,039
Lab. Co-op majority 687 (1.08%)
4.54% swing C. to Lab.
(2015: C. majority 4,866 (8.00%))

SUFFOLK CENTRAL & IPSWICH
NORTH
E. 78,116 T. 56,524 (72.36%) C. hold
*Dan Poulter, C.   33,992
Elizabeth Hughes, Lab.   16,807
Aidan Van de Weyer, LD   2,431
Regan Scott, Green   1,659
Stephen Searle, UKIP   1,635
C. majority 17,185 (30.40%)
3.42% swing C. to Lab.
(2015: C. majority 20,144 (37.24%))

SUFFOLK COASTAL
E. 79,366 T. 58,074 (73.17%) C. hold
*Therese Coffey, C.   33,713
Cameron Matthews, Lab.   17,701
James Sandbach, LD   4,048
Eamonn O'Nolan, Green   1,802
Philip Young, Ind.   810
C. majority 16,012 (27.57%)
3.16% swing C. to Lab.
(2015: C. majority 18,842 (33.89%))

SUFFOLK SOUTH
E. 75,967 T. 54,235 (71.39%) C. hold
*James Cartlidge, C.   32,829
Emma Bishton, Lab.   15,080
Andrew
Aalders-Dunthorne, LD   3,154
Robert Lindsay, Green   1,723
Aidan Powlesland, UKIP   1,449
C. majority 17,749 (32.73%)
0.54% swing C. to Lab.
(2015: C. majority 17,545 (33.80%))

SUFFOLK WEST
E. 76,984 T. 51,746 (67.22%) C. hold
*Matt Hancock, C.   31,649
Michael Jefferys, Lab.   14,586
Julian Flood, UKIP   2,396
Elfreda Tealby-Watson, LD   2,180
Donald Allwright, Green   935
C. majority 17,063 (32.97%)
0.86% swing C. to Lab.
(2015: C. majority 14,984 (30.44%))

SUNDERLAND CENTRAL
E. 72,728 T. 45,111 (62.03%) Lab. hold
*Julie Elliott, Lab.   25,056
Robert Oliver, C.   15,059
Gary Leighton, UKIP   2,209
Niall Hodson, LD   1,777
Rachel Featherstone, Green   705
Sean Cockburn, Ind.   305
Lab. majority 9,997 (22.16%)
2.30% swing Lab. to C.
(2015: Lab. majority 11,179 (26.77%))

SURREY EAST
E. 82,004 T. 59,203 (72.20%) C. hold
*Sam Gyimah, C.   35,310
Hitesh Tailor, Lab.   11,396
David Lee, LD   6,197
Andy Parr, Ind.   2,973
Helena Windsor, UKIP   2,227
Benedict Southworth, Green   1,100
C. majority 23,914 (40.39%)
2.60% swing C. to Lab.
(2015: C. majority 22,658 (40.39%))

SURREY HEATH
E. 80,537 T. 57,822 (71.80%) C. hold
*Michael Gove, C.   37,118
Laween Atroshi, Lab.   12,175
Anne-Marie Barker, LD   6,271
Sharon Galliford, Green   2,258
C. majority 24,943 (43.14%)
2.76% swing C. to Lab.
(2015: C. majority 24,804 (45.57%))

SURREY SOUTH WEST
E. 78,042 T. 60,432 (77.44%) C. hold
*Jeremy Hunt, C.   33,683
Louise Irvine, NHAP   12,093
David Black, Lab.   7,606
Ollie Purkiss, LD   5,967
Mark Webber, UKIP   1,083
C. majority 21,590 (35.73%)
7.83% swing C. to NHAP
(2015: C. majority 28,556 (49.99%))

SUSSEX MID
E. 83,747 T. 61,632 (73.59%) C. hold
*Nicholas Soames, C.   35,082
Greg Mountain, Lab.   15,409
Sarah Osborne, LD   7,855
Chris Jerrey, Green   1,571
Toby Brothers, UKIP   1,251
Baron Von
Thunderclap, Loony   464
C. majority 19,673 (31.92%)
5.16% swing C. to Lab.
(2015: C. majority 24,286 (42.24%))

SUTTON & CHEAM
E. 70,404 T. 51,970 (73.82%) C. hold
*Paul Scully, C.   26,567
Amna Ahmad, LD   13,869
Bonnie Craven, Lab.   10,663
Claire Jackson-Prior, Green   871
C. majority 12,698 (24.43%)
8.29% swing LD to C.
(2015: C. majority 3,921 (7.86%))

SUTTON COLDFIELD
E. 75,652 T. 52,858 (69.87%) C. hold
*Andrew Mitchell, C.   32,224
Rob Pocock, Lab.   16,885
Jennifer Wilkinson, LD   2,302
David Ratcliff, Green   965
Hannah Sophia, ND   482
C. majority 15,339 (29.02%)
1.63% swing C. to Lab.
(2015: C. majority 16,417 (32.28%))

SWINDON NORTH
E. 80,194 T. 54,911 (68.47%) C. hold
*Justin Tomlinson, C.   29,431
Mark Dempsey, Lab.   21,096
Liz Webster, LD   1,962
Steve Halden, UKIP   1,564
Andy Bentley, Green   858
C. majority 8,335 (15.18%)
3.69% swing C. to Lab.
(2015: C. majority 11,786 (22.56%))

SWINDON SOUTH
E. 72,391 T. 51,271 (70.83%) C. hold
*Robert Buckland, C.   24,809
Sarah Church, Lab. Co-op   22,345
Stan Pajak, LD   2,079
Martin Costello, UKIP   1,291
Talis Kimberley-Fairbourn,
Green   747
C. majority 2,464 (4.81%)
3.47% swing C. to Lab.
(2015: C. majority 5,785 (11.74%))

TAMWORTH
E. 71,319 T. 47,110 (66.06%) C. hold
*Christopher Pincher, C.   28,748
Andrew Hammond, Lab.   16,401
Jenny Pinkett, LD   1,961
C. majority 12,347 (26.21%)
1.13% swing Lab. to C.
(2015: C. majority 11,302 (23.96%))

TATTON
E. 67,874 T. 49,116 (72.36%) C. hold
‡Esther McVey, C.   28,764
Sam Rushworth, Lab.   13,977
Gareth Wilson, LD   4,431
Nigel Hennerley, Green   1,024
Quentin Abel, Ind.   920
C. majority 14,787 (30.11%)
5.08% swing C. to Lab.
(2015: C. majority 18,241 (40.27%))

TAUNTON DEANE
E. 85,466 T. 63,053 (73.78%) C. hold
*Rebecca Pow, C.   33,333
Gideon Amos, LD   17,446
Martin Jevon, Lab.   9,689
Alan Dimmick, UKIP   1,434
Clive Martin, Green   1,151
C. majority 15,887 (25.20%)
0.78% swing C. to LD
(2015: C. majority 15,491 (26.76%))

TELFORD
E. 68,164 T. 44,686 (65.56%) C. hold
*Lucy Allan, C.   21,777
Kuldip Sahota, Lab.   21,057
Susan King, LD   954
Luke Shirley, Green   898
C. majority 720 (1.61%)
0.09% swing C. to Lab.
(2015: C. majority 730 (1.80%))

TEWKESBURY
E. 81,442 T. 59,084 (72.55%) C. hold
*Laurence Robertson, C. 35,448
Manjinder Kang, Lab. 12,874
Cait Clucas, LD 7,981
Cate Cody, Green 1,576
Simon Collins, UKIP 1,205
C. majority 22,574 (38.21%)
0.75% swing C. to Lab.
(2015: C. majority 21,972 (39.70%))

THANET NORTH
E. 72,657 T. 48,325 (66.51%) C. hold
*Roger Gale, C. 27,163
Frances Rehal, Lab. 16,425
Clive Egan, UKIP 2,198
Martyn Pennington, LD 1,586
Ed Targett, Green 825
Iris White, CPA 128
C. majority 10,738 (22.22%)
4.44% swing C. to Lab.
(2015: C. majority 10,948 (23.27%))

THANET SOUTH
E. 72,342 T. 49,753 (68.77%) C. hold
*Craig Mackinlay, C. 25,262
Raushan Ara, Lab. 18,875
Stuart Piper, UKIP 2,997
Jordan Williams, LD 1,514
Trevor Roper, Green 809
Tim Garbutt, Ind. 181
Faith Fisher, CPA 115
C. majority 6,387 (12.84%)
0.77% swing C. to Lab.
(2015: C. majority 2,812 (5.69%))

THIRSK & MALTON
E. 78,670 T. 55,929 (71.09%) C. hold
*Kevin Hollinrake, C. 33,572
Alan Avery, Lab. 14,571
Dinah Keal, LD 3,859
Toby Horton, UKIP 1,532
Martin Brampton, Green 1,100
John Clark, Lib. 753
Philip Tate, Ind. 542
C. majority 19,001 (33.97%)
1.59% swing C. to Lab.
(2015: C. majority 19,456 (37.15%))

THORNBURY & YATE
E. 67,927 T. 50,690 (74.62%) C. hold
*Luke Hall, C. 28,008
Claire Young, LD 15,937
Brian Mead, Lab. 6,112
Iain Hamilton, Green 633
C. majority 12,071 (23.81%)
10.37% swing LD to C.
(2015: C. majority 1,495 (3.08%))

THURROCK
E. 78,153 T. 50,325 (64.39%) C. hold
*Jackie Doyle-Price, C. 19,880
John Kent, Lab. 19,535
Tim Aker, UKIP 10,112
Kevin McNamara, LD 798
C. majority 345 (0.69%)
0.20% swing C. to Lab.
(2015: C. majority 536 (1.08%))

TIVERTON & HONITON
E. 80,731 T. 57,815 (71.61%) C. hold
*Neil Parish, C. 35,471
Caroline Kolek, Lab. 15,670
Matthew Wilson, LD 4,639
Gill Westcott, Green 2,035
C. majority 19,801 (34.25%)
3.52% swing C. to Lab.
(2015: C. majority 20,173 (37.52%))

TONBRIDGE & MALLING
E. 77,234 T. 56,907 (73.68%) C. hold
*Tom Tugendhat, C. 36,218
Dylan Jones, Lab. 12,710
Keith Miller, LD 3,787
April Clark, Green 2,335
Colin Bullen, UKIP 1,857
C. majority 23,508 (41.31%)
1.97% swing C. to Lab.
(2015: C. majority 23,734 (44.22%))

TOOTING
E. 77,960 T. 58,171 (74.62%) Lab. hold
*Rosena Allin-Khan, Lab. 34,694
Dan Watkins, C. 19,236
Alexander Glassbrook, LD 3,057
Esther Obiri-Darko, Green 845
Ryan Coshall, UKIP 339
Lab. majority 15,458 (26.57%)
10.63% swing C. to Lab.
(2015: Lab. majority 2,842 (5.31%))
(2016: Lab. majority 6,357 (19.87%))

TORBAY
E. 75,936 T. 51,174 (67.39%) C. hold
*Kevin Foster, C. 27,141
Deborah Brewer, LD 12,858
Paul Raybould, Lab. 9,310
Tony McIntyre, UKIP 1,213
Sam Moss, Green 652
C. majority 14,283 (27.91%)
10.54% swing LD to C.
(2015: C. majority 3,286 (6.83%))

TOTNES
E. 68,913 T. 50,270 (72.95%) C. hold
*Sarah Wollaston, C. 26,972
Gerrie Messer, Lab. 13,495
Julian Brazil, LD 6,466
Jacqi Hodgson, Green 2,097
Steven Harvey, UKIP 1,240
C. majority 13,477 (26.81%)
6.72% swing C. to Lab.
(2015: C. majority 18,285 (38.82%))

TOTTENHAM
E. 72,883 T. 49,339 (67.70%) Lab. hold
*David Lammy, Lab. 40,249
Myles Stacey, C. 5,665
Brian Haley, LD 1,687
Jarelle Francis, Green 1,276
Patricia Rumble, UKIP 462
Lab. majority 34,584 (70.09%)
7.36% swing C. to Lab.
(2015: Lab. majority 23,564 (55.37%))

TRURO & FALMOUTH
E. 74,691 T. 56,647 (75.84%) C. hold
*Sarah Newton, C. 25,123
Jayne Kirkham, Lab. 21,331
Rob Nolan, LD 8,465
Duncan Odgers, UKIP 897
Amanda Pennington, Green 831
C. majority 3,792 (6.69%)
11.07% swing C. to Lab.
(2015: C. majority 14,000 (27.16%))

TUNBRIDGE WELLS
E. 75,138 T. 54,209 (72.15%) C. hold
*Greg Clark, C. 30,856
Charles Woodgate, Lab. 14,391
Rachel Sadler, LD 5,355
Chris Hoare, UKIP 1,464
Trevor Bisdee, Green 1,441
Celine Thomas, Women 702
C. majority 16,465 (30.37%)
7.05% swing C. to Lab.
(2015: C. majority 22,874 (44.48%))

TWICKENHAM
E. 83,161 T. 66,290 (79.52%) LD gain
†Vince Cable, LD 34,969
*Tania Mathias, C. 25,207
Katherine Dunne, Lab. 6,114
LD majority 9,762 (14.73%)
8.99% swing C. to LD
(2015: C. majority 2,017 (3.25%))

TYNEMOUTH
E. 77,434 T. 56,858 (73.43%) Lab. hold
*Alan Campbell, Lab. 32,395
Nick Varley, C. 20,729
John Appleby, LD 1,724
Stuart Houghton, UKIP 1,257
Julia Erskine, Green 629
Anthony The Durham
Cobbler Jull, ND 124
Lab. majority 11,666 (20.52%)
2.56% swing C. to Lab.
(2015: Lab. majority 8,240 (15.40%))

TYNESIDE NORTH
E. 78,914 T. 51,892 (65.76%) Lab. hold
*Mary Glindon, Lab. 33,456
Henry Newman, C. 14,172
Gary Legg, UKIP 2,101
Greg Stone, LD 1,494
Martin Collins, Green 669
Lab. majority 19,284 (37.16%)
0.22% swing C. to Lab.
(2015: Lab. majority 17,194 (36.73%))

UXBRIDGE & RUISLIP SOUTH
E. 69,938 T. 46,694 (66.76%)
*Boris Johnson, C. 23,716
Vincent Lo, Lab. 18,682
Rosina Robson, LD 1,835
Elizabeth Kemp, UKIP 1,577
Mark Keir, Green 884
C. majority 5,034 (10.78%)
6.54% swing C. to Lab.
(2015: C. majority 10,695 (23.87%))

VAUXHALL
E. 81,907 T. 55,042 (67.20%) Lab. hold
*Kate Hoey, Lab. 31,576
George Turner, LD 11,326
Dolly Theis, C. 10,277
Gulnar Hasnain, Green 1,152
Harini Iyengar, Women 539
Mark Chapman, Pirate 172
Lab. majority 20,250 (36.79%)
5.04% swing Lab. to LD
(2015: Lab. majority 12,708 (26.51%))

WAKEFIELD
E. 70,340 T. 46,284 (65.80%) Lab. hold
*Mary Creagh, Lab. 22,987
Antony Calvert, C. 20,811
Lucy Brown, Yorkshire 1,176
Denis Cronin, LD 943
Waj Ali, Ind. 367
Lab. majority 2,176 (4.70%)
0.69% swing Lab. to C.
(2015: Lab. majority 2,613 (6.08%))

WALLASEY
E. 67,454 T. 48,353 (71.68%) Lab. hold
*Angela Eagle, Lab. 34,552
Andy Livsey, C. 11,232
Debbie Caplin, UKIP 1,160
Paul Childs, LD 772
Lily Clough, Green 637
Lab. majority 23,320 (48.23%)
5.27% swing C. to Lab.
(2015: Lab. majority 16,348 (37.70%))

WALSALL NORTH
E. 67,309 T. 38,118 (56.63%) C. gain
Eddie Hughes, C. 18,919
*David Winnick, Lab. 16,318
Liz Hazell, UKIP 2,295
Isabelle Parasram, LD 586
C. majority 2,601 (6.82%)
6.04% swing Lab. to C.
(2015: Lab. majority 1,937 (5.25%))

WALSALL SOUTH
E. 67,417 T. 44,072 (65.37%) Lab. hold
*Valerie Vaz, Lab. 25,286
James Bird, C. 16,394
Derek Bennett, UKIP 1,805
Anna Wellings Purvis, LD 587
Lab. majority 8,892 (20.18%)
2.91% swing C. to Lab.
(2015: Lab. majority 6,007 (14.36%))

WALTHAMSTOW
E. 68,144 T. 48,143 (70.65%)
Lab. Co-op hold
*Stella Creasy, Lab. Co-op 38,793
Molly Samuel, C. 6,776
Ukonu Obasi, LD 1,384
Andrew Johns, Green 1,190
Lab. Co-op majority 32,017 (66.50%)
5.50% swing C. to Lab.
(2015: Lab. Co-op majority 23,195 (55.50%))

WANSBECK
E. 62,099 T. 42,454 (68.37%) Lab. hold
*Ian Lavery, Lab. 24,338
Chris Galley, C. 13,903
Joan Tebbutt, LD 2,015
Melanie Hurst, UKIP 1,483
Steven Leyland, Green 715
Lab. majority 10,435 (24.58%)
1.83% swing Lab. to C.
(2015: Lab. majority 10,881 (28.24%))

WANTAGE
E. 87,735 T. 63,602 (72.49%) C. hold
*Edward Vaizey, C. 34,459
Rachel Eden, Lab. Co-op 17,079
Chris Carrigan, LD 9,234
Sue Ap-Roberts, Green 1,546
David McLeod, UKIP 1,284
C. majority 17,380 (27.33%)
4.98% swing C. to Lab.
(2015: C. majority 21,749 (37.29%))

WARLEY
E. 63,724 T. 40,206 (63.09%) Lab. hold
*John Spellar, Lab. 27,004
Anthony Mangnall, C. 10,521
Darryl Magher, UKIP 1,349
Bryan Manley-Green, LD 777
Mark Redding, Green 555
Lab. majority 16,483 (41.00%)
1.07% swing C. to Lab.
(2015: Lab. majority 14,702 (38.86%))

WARRINGTON NORTH
E. 72,015 T. 48,517 (67.37%) Lab. hold
*Helen Jones, Lab. 27,356
Val Allen, C. 17,774
James Ashington, UKIP 1,561
Stefan Krizanac, LD 1,207
Lyndsay McAteer, Green 619
Lab. majority 9,582 (19.75%)
0.05% swing C. to Lab.
(2015: Lab. majority 8,923 (19.65%))

WARRINGTON SOUTH
E. 85,755 T. 61,995 (72.29%) Lab. gain
Faisal Rashid, Lab. 29,994
*David Mowat, C. 27,445
Bob Barr, LD 3,339
John Boulton, Ind. 1,217
Lab. majority 2,549 (4.11%)
4.37% swing C. to Lab.
(2015: C. majority 2,750 (4.63%))

WARWICK & LEAMINGTON
E. 74,237 T. 54,055 (72.81%) Lab. gain
Matt Western, Lab. 25,227
*Chris White, C. 24,021
Nick Solman, LD 2,810
Jonathan Chilvers, Green 1,198
Bob Dhillon, UKIP 799
Lab. majority 1,206 (2.23%)
7.65% swing C. to Lab.
(2015: C. majority 6,606 (13.06%))

WARWICKSHIRE NORTH
E. 72,277 T. 47,178 (65.27%) C. hold
*Craig Tracey, C. 26,860
Julie Jackson, Lab. 18,350
James Cox, LD 1,028
Keith Kondakor, Green 940
C. majority 8,510 (18.04%)
5.88% swing Lab. to C.
(2015: C. majority 2,973 (6.28%))

WASHINGTON & SUNDERLAND WEST
E. 67,280 T. 40,574 (60.31%) Lab. hold
*Sharon Hodgson, Lab. 24,639
Jonathan Gullis, C. 11,699
Bryan Foster, UKIP 2,761
Tom Appleby, LD 961
Michal Chantkowski, Green 514
Lab. majority 12,940 (31.89%)
2.10% swing Lab. to C.
(2015: Lab. majority 13,157 (35.31%))

WATFORD
E. 86,507 T. 58,610 (67.75%) C. hold
*Richard Harrington, C. 26,731
Chris Ostrowski, Lab. 24,639
Ian Stotesbury, LD 5,335
Ian Green, UKIP 1,184
Alex Murray, Green 721
C. majority 2,092 (3.57%)
6.94% swing C. to Lab.
(2015: C. majority 9,794 (17.44%))

WAVENEY
E. 80,784 T. 52,674 (65.20%) C. hold
*Peter Aldous, C. 28,643
Sonia Barker, Lab. 19,428
Bert Poole, UKIP 1,933
Elfrede Brambley-Crawshaw, Green 1,332
Jacky Howe, LD 1,012
Allyson Barron, Ind. 326
C. majority 9,215 (17.49%)
6.44% swing Lab. to C.
(2015: C. majority 2,408 (4.61%))

WEALDEN
E. 81,425 T. 60,464 (74.26%) C. hold
*Nus Ghani, C. 37,027
Angela Smith, Lab. 13,399
Chris Bowers, LD 6,281
Colin Stocks, Green 1,959
Nicola Burton, UKIP 1,798
C. majority 23,628 (39.08%)
3.56% swing C. to Lab.
(2015: C. majority 22,967 (40.28%))

WEAVER VALE
E. 69,016 T. 50,613 (73.34%) Lab. gain
Mike Amesbury, Lab. 26,066
*Graham Evans, C. 22,138
Paul Roberts, LD 1,623
Christopher Copeman, Green 786
Lab. majority 3,928 (7.76%)
4.74% swing C. to Lab.
(2015: C. majority 806 (1.72%))

WELLINGBOROUGH
E. 79,258 T. 53,240 (67.17%) C. hold
*Peter Bone, C. 30,579
Andrea Watts, Lab. 18,119
Allan Shipham, UKIP 1,804
Chris Nelson, LD 1,782
Jonathan Hornett, Green 956
C. majority 12,460 (23.40%)
4.58% swing C. to Lab.
(2015: C. majority 16,397 (32.51%))

WELLS
E. 82,449   T. 60,843 (73.79%)   C. hold
*James Heappey, C.   30,488
Tessa Munt, LD   22,906
Andy Merryfield, Lab.   7,129
Lorna Corke, CPA   320
C. majority 7,582 (12.46%)
0.43% swing C. to LD
(2015: C. majority 7,585 (13.33%))

WELWYN HATFIELD
E. 72,888   T. 51,669 (70.89%)   C. hold
*Grant Shapps, C.   26,374
Anawar Miah, Lab.   19,005
Nigel Quinton, LD   3,836
Dean Milliken, UKIP   1,441
Christianne Sayers, Green   835
Melvyn Jones, Ind.   178
C. majority 7,369 (14.26%)
4.97% swing C. to Lab.
(2015: C. majority 12,153 (24.21%))

WENTWORTH & DEARNE
E. 74,890   T. 43,947 (58.68%)   Lab. hold
*John Healey, Lab.   28,547
Steven Jackson, C.   13,744
Janice Middleton, LD   1,656
Lab. majority 14,803 (33.68%)
4.15% swing Lab. to C.
(2015: Lab. majority 13,838 (32.04%))

WEST BROMWICH EAST
E. 63,833   T. 39,098 (61.25%)   Lab. hold
*Tom Watson, Lab.   22,664
Emma Crane, C.   14,951
Karen Trench, LD   625
John Macefield, Green   533
Colin Rankine, Ind.   325
Lab. majority 7,713 (19.73%)
2.77% swing Lab. to C.
(2015: Lab. majority 9,470 (25.26%))

WEST BROMWICH WEST
E. 65,956   T. 36,094 (54.72%)
                     Lab. Co-op hold
*Adrian Bailey, Lab. Co-op   18,789
Andrew Hardie, C.   14,329
Star Anderton, UKIP   2,320
Flo Clucas, LD   333
Robert Buckman, Green   323
Lab. Co-op majority 4,460 (12.36%)
5.55% swing Lab. to C.
(2015: Lab. Co-op majority 7,742
(22.10%))

WEST HAM
E. 92,243   T. 60,708 (65.81%)   Lab. hold
*Lyn Brown, Lab.   46,591
Patrick Spencer, C.   9,837
Paul Reynolds, LD   1,836
Rosamund Beattie, UKIP   1,134
Michael Spracklin, Green   957
Kayode Shedowo, CPA   353
Lab. majority 36,754 (60.54%)
3.77% swing C. to Lab.
(2015: Lab. majority 27,986 (53.01%))

WESTMINSTER NORTH
E. 63,846   T. 43,295 (67.81%)   Lab. hold
*Karen Buck, Lab.   25,934
Lindsey Hall, C.   14,422
Alex Harding, LD   2,253
Emmanuelle Tandy, Green   595
Abby Dharamsey, ND   91
Lab. majority 11,512 (26.59%)
10.79% swing C. to Lab.
(2015: Lab. majority 1,977 (5.00%))

WESTMORLAND & LONSDALE
E. 66,391   T. 51,687 (77.85%)   LD hold
*Tim Farron, LD   23,686
James Airey, C.   22,909
Eli Aldridge, Lab.   4,783
Mr Fishfinger, Ind.   309
LD majority 777 (1.50%)
8.39% swing LD to C.
(2015: LD majority 8,949 (18.29%))

WESTON-SUPER-MARE
E. 82,160   T. 56,415 (68.66%)   C. hold
*John Penrose, C.   29,982
Timothy Taylor, Lab.   18,438
Mike Bell, LD   5,175
Helen Hims, UKIP   1,932
Suneil Basu, Green   888
C. majority 11,544 (20.46%)
4.62% swing C. to Lab.
(2015: C. majority 15,609 (29.70%))

WIGAN
E. 75,359   T. 47,542 (63.09%)   Lab. hold
*Lisa Nandy, Lab.   29,575
Alexander Williams, C.   13,548
Nathan Ryding, UKIP   2,750
Mark Clayton, LD   916
William Patterson, Green   753
Lab. majority 16,027 (33.71%)
1.14% swing C. to Lab.
(2015: Lab. majority 14,236 (31.43%))

WILTSHIRE NORTH
E. 71,408   T. 53,706 (75.21%)   C. hold
*James Gray, C.   32,398
Brian Mathew, LD   9,521
Peter Baldrey, Lab.   9,399
Phil Chamberlain, Green   1,141
Paddy Singh, UKIP   871
Lisa Tweedie, Ind.   376
C. majority 22,877 (42.60%)
0.48% swing LD to C.
(2015: C. majority 21,046 (41.63%))

WILTSHIRE SOUTH WEST
E. 76,898   T. 54,751 (71.20%)   C. hold
*Andrew Murrison, C.   32,841
Laura Pictor, Lab.   14,515
Trevor Carbin, LD   5,360
Christopher Walford, Green   1,445
Liam Silcocks, Ind.   590
C. majority 18,326 (33.47%)
2.87% swing C. to Lab.
(2015: C. majority 18,168 (35.18%))

WIMBLEDON
E. 66,771   T. 51,526 (77.17%)   C. hold
*Stephen Hammond, C.   23,946
Imran Uddin, Lab.   18,324
Carl Quilliam, LD   7,472
Charles Barraball, Green   1,231
Strachan McDonald, UKIP   553
C. majority 5,622 (10.91%)
7.57% swing C. to Lab.
(2015: C. majority 12,619 (26.06%))

WINCHESTER
E. 72,497   T. 57,156 (78.84%)   C. hold
*Steve Brine, C.   29,729
Jackie Porter, LD   19,730
Mark Chaloner, Lab.   6,007
Andrew Wainwright, Green   846
Martin Lyon, UKIP   695
Teresa Skelton, JACP   149
C. majority 9,999 (17.49%)
6.54% swing C. to LD
(2015: C. majority 16,914 (30.58%))

WINDSOR
E. 73,595   T. 53,921 (73.27%)   C. hold
*Adam Afriyie, C.   34,718
Peter Shearman, Lab.   12,334
Julian Tisi, LD   5,434
Fintan McKeown, Green   1,435
C. majority 22,384 (41.51%)
4.25% swing C. to Lab.
(2015: C. majority 25,083 (50.01%))

WIRRAL SOUTH
E. 57,670   T. 45,195 (78.37%)   Lab. hold
*Alison McGovern, Lab.   25,871
Adam Sykes, C.   17,548
Chris Carubia, LD   1,322
Mandi Roberts, Green   454
Lab. majority 8,323 (18.42%)
3.71% swing C. to Lab.
(2015: Lab. majority 4,599 (10.99%))

WIRRAL WEST
E. 55,995   T. 43,951 (78.49%)   Lab. hold
*Margaret Greenwood, Lab.   23,866
Tony Caldeira, C.   18,501
Peter Reisdorf, LD   1,155
John Coyne, Green   429
Lab. majority 5,365 (12.21%)
5.61% swing C. to Lab.
(2015: Lab. majority 417 (1.00%))

WITHAM
E. 69,137   T. 49,241 (71.22%)   C. hold
*Priti Patel, C.   31,670
Phil Barlow, Lab.   13,024
Jo Hayes, LD   2,715
James Abbott, Green   1,832
C. majority 18,646 (37.87%)
1.90% swing C. to Lab.
(2015: C. majority 19,554 (41.46%))

WITNEY
E. 82,727   T. 60,927 (73.65%)   C. hold
*Robert Courts, C.   33,839
Laetisia Carter, Lab.   12,598
Liz Leffman, LD   12,457
Claire Lasko, Green   1,053
Alexander Craig, UKIP   980
C. majority 21,241 (34.86%)
4.08% swing C. to Lab.
(2015: C. majority 25,155 (43.01%))
(2016: C. majority 5,702 (14.83%))

WOKING
E. 76,167   T. 55,246 (72.53%)   C. hold
*Jonathan Lord, C.   29,903
Fiona Colley, Lab.   13,179
Will Forster, LD   9,711
Troy De Leon, UKIP   1,161
James Brierley, Green   1,092
Hassan Akberali, Ind.   200
C. majority 16,724 (30.27%)
4.89% swing C. to Lab.
(2015: C. majority 20,810 (40.05%))

WOKINGHAM
E. 79,879   T. 59,690 (74.73%)   C. hold
*John Redwood, C.   33,806
Andy Croy, Lab.   15,008
Clive Jones, LD   9,512
Russell Seymour, Green   1,364
C. majority 18,798 (31.49%)
5.86% swing C. to Lab.
(2015: C. majority 24,197 (43.21%))

WOLVERHAMPTON NORTH EAST
E. 60,799   T. 36,508 (60.05%)   Lab. hold
*Emma Reynolds, Lab.   19,282
Sarah Macken, C.   14,695
Graham Eardley, UKIP   1,479
Ian Jenkins, LD   570
Clive Wood, Green   482
Lab. majority 4,587 (12.56%)
1.80% swing Lab. to C.
(2015: Lab. majority 5,495 (16.16%))

WOLVERHAMPTON SOUTH EAST
E. 69,951   T. 36,304 (51.90%)   Lab. hold
*Pat McFadden, Lab.   21,137
Kieran Mullan, C.   12,623
Barry Hodgson, UKIP   1,675
Ben Mathis, LD   448
Amy Bertaut, Green   421
Lab. majority 8,514 (23.45%)
3.78% swing Lab. to C.
(2015: Lab. majority 10,778 (31.00%))

WOLVERHAMPTON SOUTH WEST
E. 60,003   T. 42,346 (70.57%)   Lab. hold
Eleanor Smith, Lab.   20,899
Paul Uppal, C.   18,714
Rob Jones, UKIP   1,012
Sarah Quarmby, LD   784
Andrea Cantrill, Green   579
Jagmeet Singh, Ind.   358
Lab. majority 2,185 (5.16%)
1.58% swing C. to Lab.
(2015: Lab. majority 801 (1.99%))

WORCESTER
E. 72,815   T. 51,423 (70.62%)   C. hold
*Robin Walker, C.   24,731
Joy Squires, Lab.   22,223
Stephen Kearney, LD   1,757
Paul Hickling, UKIP   1,354
Louis Stephen, Green   1,211
Alex Rugg, Ind.   109
Mark Shuker, Compass   38
C. majority 2,508 (4.88%)
3.24% swing C. to Lab.
(2015: C. majority 5,646 (11.35%))

WORCESTERSHIRE MID
E. 76,065   T. 55,089 (72.42%)   C. hold
*Nigel Huddleston, C.   35,967
Fred Grindrod, Lab.   12,641
Margaret Rowley, LD   3,450
David Greenwood, UKIP   1,660
Fay Whitfield, Green   1,371
C. majority 23,326 (42.34%)
0.10% swing C. to Lab.
(2015: C. majority 20,532 (39.31%))

WORCESTERSHIRE WEST
E. 74,385   T. 56,471 (75.92%)   C. hold
*Harriett Baldwin, C.   34,703
Samantha Charles, Lab.   13,375
Edward McMillan-Scott, LD   5,307
Natalie McVey, Green   1,605
Mike Savage, UKIP   1,481
C. majority 21,328 (37.77%)
2.46% swing C. to Lab.
(2015: C. majority 22,578 (41.73%))

WORKINGTON
E. 60,256   T. 41,676 (69.16%)   Lab. hold
*Sue Hayman, Lab.   21,317
Clark Vasey, C.   17,392
George Kemp, UKIP   1,556
Phill Roberts, LD   1,133
Roy Ivinson, Ind.   278
Lab. majority 3,925 (9.42%)
1.38% swing Lab. to C.
(2015: Lab. majority 4,686 (12.18%))

WORSLEY & ECCLES SOUTH
E. 73,692   T. 45,642 (61.94%)   Lab. hold
*Barbara Keeley, Lab.   26,046
Iain Lindley, C.   17,667
Kate Clarkson, LD   1,087
Tom Dylan, Green   842
Lab. majority 8,379 (18.36%)
2.11% swing C. to Lab.
(2015: Lab. majority 5,946 (14.14%))

WORTHING EAST & SHOREHAM
E. 75,543   T. 53,117 (70.31%)   C. hold
*Tim Loughton, C.   25,988
Sophie Cook, Lab.   20,882
Oli Henman, LD   2,523
Mike Glennon, UKIP   1,444
Leslie Groves Williams, Green   1,273
Carl Walker, NHAP   575
Andy Lutwyche, Ind.   432
C. majority 5,106 (9.61%)
10.17% swing C. to Lab.
(2015: C. majority 14,949 (29.96%))

WORTHING WEST
E. 77,777   T. 54,503 (70.08%)   C. hold
*Peter Bottomley, C.   30,181
Beccy Cooper, Lab.   18,091
Hazel Thorpe, LD   2,982
Mark Withers, UKIP   1,635
Benjamin Cornish, Green   1,614
C. majority 12,090 (22.18%)
6.80% swing C. to Lab.
(2015: C. majority 16,855 (33.20%))

WREKIN, THE
E. 68,642   T. 49,523 (72.15%)   C. hold
*Mark Pritchard, C.   27,451
Dylan Harrison, Lab.   17,887
Denis Allen, UKIP   1,656
Rod Keyes, LD   1,345
Pat McCarthy, Green   804
Fay Easton, Ind.   380
C. majority 9,564 (19.31%)
2.17% swing C. to Lab.
(2015: C. majority 10,743 (23.64%))

WYCOMBE
E. 77,089   T. 53,493 (69.39%)   C. hold
*Steve Baker, C.   26,766
Rafiq Raja, Lab.   20,188
Steve Guy, LD   4,147
Richard Phoenix, UKIP   1,210
Peter Sims, Green   1,182
C. majority 6,578 (12.30%)
8.29% swing C. to Lab.
(2015: C. majority 14,856 (28.88%))

WYRE & PRESTON NORTH
E. 72,319   T. 52,646 (72.80%)   C. hold
*Ben Wallace, C.   30,684
Michelle Heaton-Bentley, Lab.   18,438
John Potter, LD   2,551
Ruth Norbury, Green   973
C. majority 12,246 (23.26%)
2.55% swing C. to Lab.
(2015: C. majority 14,151 (28.36%))

WYRE FOREST
E. 77,734   T. 51,129 (65.77%)   C. hold
*Mark Garnier, C.   29,859
Matthew Lamb, Lab.   16,525
Shazu Miah, LD   1,943
George Connolly, UKIP   1,777
Brett Caulfield, Green   1,025
C. majority 13,334 (26.08%)
0.02% swing Lab. to C.
(2015: C. majority 12,871 (26.03%))

WYTHENSHAWE & SALE EAST
E. 76,361   T. 45,846 (60.04%)   Lab. hold
*Mike Kane, Lab.   28,525
Fiona Green, C.   13,581
William Jones, LD   1,504
Mike Bayley-Sanderson, UKIP   1,475
Dan Jerrome, Green   576
Luckson Francis Augustine, Ind.   185
Lab. majority 14,944 (32.60%)
4.08% swing C. to Lab.
(2015: Lab. majority 10,569 (24.43%))

YEOVIL
E. 82,911   T. 59,404 (71.65%)   C. hold
*Marcus Fysh, C.   32,369
Jo Roundell Greene, LD   17,646
Ian Martin, Lab.   7,418
Robert Wood, Green   1,052
Katy Pritchard, Ind.   919
C. majority 14,723 (24.78%)
7.73% swing LD to C.
(2015: C. majority 5,313 (9.33%))

YORK CENTRAL
E. 77,315   T. 53,088 (68.66%)
Lab. Co-op hold
*Rachael Maskell, Lab. Co-op   34,594
Ed Young, C.   16,019
Nick Love, LD   2,475
Lab. Co-op majority 18,575 (34.99%)
10.45% swing C. to Lab.
(2015: Lab. Co-op majority 6,716 (14.09%))

YORK OUTER
E. 75,856   T. 57,427 (75.71%)   C. hold
*Julian Sturdy, C.   29,356
Luke Charters-Reid, Lab.   21,067
James Blanchard, LD   5,910
Bethan Vincent, Green   1,094
C. majority 8,289 (14.43%)
4.96% swing C. to Lab.
(2015: C. majority 13,129 (24.36%))

YORKSHIRE EAST
E. 81,065   T. 53,956 (66.56%)   C. hold
*Greg Knight, C.   31,442
Alan Clark, Lab.   16,436
Carl Minns, LD   2,134
Andrew Dennis, UKIP   1,986
Timothy Norman, Yorkshire   1,015
Michael Jackson, Green   943
C. majority 15,006 (27.81%)
1.03% swing C. to Lab.
(2015: C. majority 14,933 (29.87%))

WALES

ABERAVON
E. 49,891   T. 33,268 (66.68%)   Lab. hold
*Stephen Kinnock, Lab.   22,662
Sadie Vidal, C.   5,901
Andrew Bennison, PC   2,761
Caroline Jones, UKIP   1,345
Cen Phillips, LD   599
Lab. majority 16,761 (50.38%)
6.67% swing C. to Lab.
(2015: Lab. majority 10,445 (33.13%))

ABERCONWY
E. 45,251   T. 32,150 (71.05%)   C. hold
*Guto Bebb, C.   14,337
Emily Owen, Lab.   13,702
Wyn Jones, PC   3,170
Sarah Lesiter-Burgess, LD   941
C. majority 635 (1.98%)
5.64% swing C. to Lab.
(2015: C. majority 3,999 (13.26%))

ALYN & DEESIDE
E. 63,041   T. 44,760 (71.00%)   Lab. hold
*Mark Tami, Lab.   23,315
Laura Knightly, C.   18,080
Jacqui Hurst, PC   1,171
David Griffiths, UKIP   1,117
Pete Williams, LD   1,077
Lab. majority 5,235 (11.70%)
1.80% swing C. to Lab.
(2015: Lab. majority 3,343 (8.09%))

ARFON
E. 41,367   T. 28,208 (68.19%)   PC hold
*Hywel Williams, PC   11,519
Mary Griffiths Clarke, Lab.   11,427
Phillippa Parry, C.   4,614
Calum Davies, LD   648
PC majority 92 (0.33%)
6.67% swing PC to Lab.
(2015: PC majority 3,668 (13.67%))

BLAENAU GWENT
E. 51,227   T. 32,384 (63.22%)   Lab. hold
*Nick Smith, Lab.   18,787
Nigel Copner, PC   6,880
Tracey West, C.   4,783
Dennis May, UKIP   973
Vicki Browning, Ind.   666
Cameron Sullivan, LD   295
Lab. majority 11,907 (36.77%)
6.13% swing Lab. to PC
(2015: Lab. majority 12,703 (40.09%))

BRECON & RADNORSHIRE
E. 56,010   T. 41,334 (73.80%)   C. hold
*Chris Davies, C.   20,081
James Gibson-Watt, LD   12,043
Dan Lodge, Lab.   7,335
Kate Heneghan, PC   1,299
Peter Gilbert, UKIP   576
C. majority 8,038 (19.45%)
3.36% swing LD to C.
(2015: C. majority 5,102 (12.73%))

BRIDGEND
E. 62,185   T. 43,255 (69.56%)   Lab. hold
*Madeleine Moon, Lab.   21,913
Karen Robson, C.   17,213
Rhys Watkins, PC   1,783
Jonathan Pratt, LD   919
Alun Williams, UKIP   781
Isabel Robson, Ind.   646
Lab. majority 4,700 (10.87%)
2.99% swing C. to Lab.
(2015: Lab. majority 1,927 (4.88%))

CAERPHILLY
E. 64,381   T. 41,297 (64.14%)   Lab. hold
*Wayne David, Lab.   22,491
Jane Pratt, C.   10,413
Lindsay Whittle, PC   5,962
Liz Wilks, UKIP   1,259
Kay David, LD   725
Andrew Creak, Green   447
Lab. majority 12,078 (29.25%)
0.75% swing C. to Lab.
(2015: Lab. majority 10,073 (25.01%))

CARDIFF CENTRAL
E. 59,288   T. 40,367 (68.09%)   Lab. hold
*Jo Stevens, Lab.   25,193
Gregory Stafford, C.   7,997
Eluned Parrott, LD   5,415
Mark Hooper, PC   999
Benjamin Smith, Green   420
Sarul-Islam Mohammed, UKIP   343
Lab. majority 17,196 (42.60%)
8.64% swing C. to Lab.
(2015: Lab. majority 4,981 (12.89%))

CARDIFF NORTH
E. 67,221   T. 52,022 (77.39%)   Lab. gain
Anna McMorrin, Lab.   26,081
*Craig Williams, C.   21,907
Steffan Webb, PC   1,738
Matthew Hemsley, LD   1,714
Gary Oldfield, UKIP   582
Lab. majority 4,174 (8.02%)
6.10% swing C. to Lab.
(2015: C. majority 2,137 (4.18%))

CARDIFF SOUTH & PENARTH
E. 76,499   T. 50,736 (66.32%)
Lab. Co-op hold
*Stephen Doughty, Lab. Co-op   30,182
Bill Rees, C.   15,318
Ian Titherington, PC   2,162
Emma Sands, LD   1,430
Andrew Bevan, UKIP   942
Anthony Slaughter, Green   532
Jeb Hedges, Pirate   170
Lab. Co-op majority 14,864 (29.30%)
6.66% swing C. to Lab.
(2015: Lab. Co-op majority 7,453 (15.97%))

CARDIFF WEST
E. 67,221   T. 46,629 (69.37%)   Lab. hold
*Kevin Brennan, Lab.   26,425
Matt Smith, C.   13,874
Michael Deem, PC   4,418
Alex Meredith, LD   1,214
Richard Lewis, UKIP   698
Lab. majority 12,551 (26.92%)
5.71% swing C. to Lab.
(2015: Lab. majority 6,789 (15.50%))

CARMARTHEN EAST & DINEFWR
E. 55,976   T. 41,029 (73.30%)   PC hold
*Jonathan Edwards, PC   16,127
David Darkin, Lab.   12,219
Havard Hughes, C.   10,778
Neil Hamilton, UKIP   985
Lesley Prosser, LD   920
PC majority 3,908 (9.52%)
2.34% swing PC to Lab.
(2015: PC majority 5,599 (14.21%))

CARMARTHEN WEST & PEMBROKESHIRE SOUTH
E. 58,548   T. 42,226 (72.12%)   C. hold
*Simon Hart, C.   19,771
Marc Tierney, Lab.   16,661
Abi Thomas, PC   3,933
Alistair Cameron, LD   956
Phil Edwards, UKIP   905
C. majority 3,110 (7.37%)
3.82% swing C. to Lab.
(2015: C. majority 6,054 (15.00%))

CEREDIGION
E. 52,889   T. 39,767 (75.19%)   PC gain
Ben Lake, PC   11,623
*Mark Williams, LD   11,519
Dinah Mulholland, Lab.   8,017
Ruth Davis, C.   7,307
Tom Harrison, UKIP   602
Grenville Ham, Green   542
Crazed Sir Dudley, Loony   157
PC majority 104 (0.26%)
4.23% swing LD to PC
(2015: LD majority 3,067 (8.20%))

CLWYD SOUTH
E. 54,341   T. 37,474 (68.96%)   Lab. hold
*Susan Elan Jones, Lab.   19,002
Simon Baynes, C.   14,646
Christopher Allen, PC   2,293
Jeanette Bassford-Barton,
UKIP   802
Bruce Roberts, LD   731
Lab. majority 4,356 (11.62%)
2.39% swing C. to Lab.
(2015: Lab. majority 2,402 (6.85%))

CLWYD WEST
E. 58,263   T. 40,654 (69.78%)   C. hold
*David Jones, C.   19,541
Gareth Thomas, Lab.   16,104
Dilwyn Roberts, PC   3,918
Victor Babu, LD   1,091
C. majority 3,437 (8.45%)
4.62% swing C. to Lab.
(2015: C. majority 6,730 (17.70%))

CYNON VALLEY
E. 51,332   T. 31,802 (61.95%)   Lab. hold
*Ann Clwyd, Lab.   19,404
Keith Dewhurst, C.   6,166
Liz Walters, PC   4,376
Ian McLean, UKIP   1,271
Nicola Knight, LD   585
Lab. majority 13,238 (41.63%)
3.00% swing C. to Lab.
(2015: Lab. majority 9,406 (30.87%))

DELYN
E. 54,116   T. 39,418 (72.84%)   Lab. hold
*David Hanson, Lab.   20,573
Matt Wright, C.   16,333
Paul Rowlinson, PC   1,481
Tom Rippeth, LD   1,031
Lab. majority 4,240 (10.76%)
1.47% swing C. to Lab.
(2015: Lab. majority 2,930 (7.82%))

DWYFOR MEIRIONNYDD
E. 44,699   T. 30,348 (67.89%)   PC hold
*Liz Saville Roberts, PC   13,687
Neil Fairlamb, C.   8,837
Mathew Norman, Lab.   6,273
Stephen Churchman, LD   937
Frank Wykes, UKIP   614
PC majority 4,850 (15.98%)
1.11% swing PC to C.
(2015: PC majority 5,261 (18.20%))

GOWER
E. 62,163   T. 45,576 (73.32%)   Lab. gain
Tonia Antoniazzi, Lab.   22,727
*Byron Davies, C.   19,458
Harri Roberts, PC   1,669
Howard Evans, LD   931
Ross Ford, UKIP   642
Jason Winstanley, Pirate   149
Lab. majority 3,269 (7.17%)
3.62% swing C. to Lab.
(2015: C. majority 27 (0.06%))

ISLWYN
E. 56,256   T. 36,093 (64.16%)
                           Lab. Co-op hold
*Chris Evans, Lab. Co-op   21,238
Dan Thomas, C.   9,826
Darren Jones, PC   2,739
Joe Smyth, UKIP   1,605
Matthew Kidner, LD   685
Lab. Co-op majority 11,412 (31.62%)
1.10% swing Lab. to C.
(2015: Lab. Co-op majority 10,404
(29.39%))

LLANELLI
E. 59,434   T. 40,342 (67.88%)   Lab. hold
*Nia Griffith, Lab.   21,568
Stephen Davies, C.   9,544
Mari Arthur, PC   7,351
Ken Rees, UKIP   1,331
Rory Daniels, LD   548
Lab. majority 12,024 (29.81%)
1.40% swing C. to Lab.
(2015: Lab. majority 7,095 (18.39%))

MERTHYR TYDFIL & RHYMNEY
E. 55,463   T. 33,545 (60.48%)   Lab. hold
*Gerald Jones, Lab.   22,407
Pauline Jorgensen, C.   6,073
Amy Kitcher, PC   2,740
David Rowlands, UKIP   1,484
Bob Griffin, LD   841
Lab. majority 16,334 (48.69%)
2.45% swing C. to Lab.
(2015: Lab. majority 11,513 (35.19%))

MONMOUTH
E. 64,909   T. 49,734 (76.62%)   C. hold
*David Davies, C.   26,411
Ruth Jones, Lab.   18,205
Veronica German, LD   2,064
Carole Damon, PC   1,338
Ian Chandler, Green   954
Roy Neale, UKIP   762
C. majority 8,206 (16.50%)
3.32% swing C. to Lab.
(2015: C. majority 10,982 (23.14%))

MONTGOMERYSHIRE
E. 50,755   T. 34,891 (68.74%)   C. hold
*Glyn Davies, C.   18,075
Jane Dodds, LD   8,790
Iwan Jones, Lab.   5,542
Aled Hughes, PC   1,960
Richard Chaloner, Green   524
C. majority 9,285 (26.61%)
5.42% swing LD to C.
(2015: C. majority 5,325 (15.77%))

NEATH
E. 55,859   T. 38,285 (68.54%)
                           Lab. Co-op hold
*Christina Rees, Lab. Co-op   21,713
Orla Lowe, C.   9,082
Daniel Williams, PC   5,339
Richard Pritchard, UKIP   1,419
Frank Little, LD   732
Lab. Co-op majority 12,631 (32.99%)
2.25% swing C. to Lab.
(2015: Lab. majority 9,548 (25.71%))

NEWPORT EAST
E. 57,233   T. 36,820 (64.33%)   Lab. hold
*Jessica Morden, Lab.   20,804
Natasha Asghar, C.   12,801
Ian Gorman, UKIP   1,180
Pete Brown, LD   966
Cameron Wixcey, PC   881
Nadeem Ahmed, ND   188
Lab. majority 8,003 (21.74%)
4.17% swing C. to Lab.
(2015: Lab. majority 4,705 (13.40%))

NEWPORT WEST
E. 64,399   T. 43,438 (67.45%)   Lab. hold
*Paul Flynn, Lab.   22,723
Angela Jones-Evans, C.   17,065
Stan Edwards, UKIP   1,100
Morgan Bowler-Brown, PC   1,077
Sarah Lockyer, LD   976
Pippa Bartolotti, Green   497
Lab. majority 5,658 (13.03%)
2.16% swing C. to Lab.
(2015: Lab. majority 3,510 (8.70%))

OGMORE
E. 56,661   T. 37,204 (65.66%)   Lab. hold
*Chris Elmore, Lab.   23,225
Jamie Wallis, C.   9,354
Huw Marshall, PC   2,796
Glenda Davies, UKIP   1,235
Gerald Francis, LD   594
Lab. majority 13,871 (37.28%)
0.14% swing C. to Lab.
(2015: Lab. majority 13,043 (37.00%))
(2016: Lab. majority 8,575 (36.44%))

PONTYPRIDD
E. 60,566   T. 39,894 (65.87%)   Lab. hold
*Owen Smith, Lab.   22,103
Juliette Ash, C.   10,655
Fflur Elin, PC   4,102
Michael Powell, LD   1,963
Robin Hunter-Clarke, UKIP   1,071
Lab. majority 11,448 (28.70%)
2.49% swing C. to Lab.
(2015: Lab. majority 8,985 (23.72%))

PRESELI PEMBROKESHIRE
E. 58,540   T. 42,197 (72.08%)   C. hold
*Stephen Crabb, C.   18,302
Philippa Thompson, Lab.   17,988
Owain Williams, PC   2,711
Chris Overton, Ind.   1,209
Bob Kilmister, LD   1,106
Susan Bale, UKIP   850
Rodney Maile, Worth   31
C. majority 314 (0.74%)
5.75% swing C. to Lab.
(2015: C. majority 4,969 (12.25%))

RHONDDA
E. 50,513 T. 32,936 (65.20%) Lab. hold
*Chris Bryant, Lab.   21,096
Branwen Cennard, PC   7,350
Virginia Crosbie, C.   3,333
Janet Kenrick, UKIP   880
Karen Roberts, LD   277
Lab. majority 13,746 (41.74%)
9.05% swing PC to Lab.
(2015: Lab. majority 7,455 (23.64%))

SWANSEA EAST
E. 58,521 T. 35,159 (60.08%) Lab. hold
*Carolyn Harris, Lab.   22,307
Dan Boucher, C.   9,139
Steffan Phillips, PC   1,689
Clifford Johnson, UKIP   1,040
Charley Hasted, LD   625
Chris Evans, Green   359
Lab. majority 13,168 (37.45%)
0.11% swing Lab. to C.
(2015: Lab. majority 12,028 (35.78%))

SWANSEA WEST
E. 56,892 T. 37,282 (65.53%)
                        Lab. Co-op hold
*Geraint Davies, Lab. Co-op   22,278
Craig Lawton, C.   11,680
Rhydian Fitter, PC   1,529
Michael O'Carroll, LD   1,269
Mike Whittall, Green   434
Brian Johnson, SPGB   92
Lab. Co-op majority 10,598 (28.43%)
4.21% swing C. to Lab.
(2015: Lab. Co-op majority 7,036
(20.01%))

TORFAEN
E. 61,839 T. 38,429 (62.14%) Lab. hold
*Nick Thomas-Symonds,   22,134
Lab.
Graham Smith, C.   11,894
Jeff Rees, PC   2,059
Ian Williams, UKIP   1,490
Andrew Best, LD   852
Lab. majority 10,240 (26.65%)
2.56% swing C. to Lab.
(2015: Lab. majority 8,169 (21.53%))

VALE OF CLWYD
E. 56,890 T. 38,684 (68.00%) Lab. gain
†Chris Ruane, Lab.   19,423
*James Davies, C.   17,044
David Wyatt, PC   1,551
Gwyn Williams, LD   666
Lab. majority 2,379 (6.15%)
3.41% swing C. to Lab.
(2015: C. majority 237 (0.67%))

VALE OF GLAMORGAN
E. 73,958 T. 53,718 (72.63%) C. hold
*Alun Cairns, C.   25,501
Camilla Beaven, Lab.   23,311
Ian Johnson, PC   2,295
Jennifer Geroni, LD   1,020
Melanie Hunter-   868
Clarke, UKIP
Stephen Davis-Barker, Green   419
Sharon Lovell, Women   177
David Elston, Pirate   127
C. majority 2,190 (4.08%)
4.67% swing C. to Lab.
(2015: C. majority 6,880 (13.41%))

WREXHAM
E. 50,422 T. 35,092 (69.60%) Lab. hold
*Ian Lucas, Lab.   17,153
Andrew Atkinson, C.   15,321
Carrie Harper, PC   1,753
Carole O'Toole, LD   865
Lab. majority 1,832 (5.22%)
0.19% swing Lab. to C.
(2015: Lab. majority 1,831 (5.60%))

YNYS MON
E. 52,448 T. 37,367 (71.25%) Lab. hold
*Albert Owen, Lab.   15,643
Tomos Davies, C.   10,384
Ieuan Wyn Jones, PC   10,237
James Turner, UKIP   624
Sarah Jackson, LD   479
Lab. majority 5,259 (14.07%)
2.06% swing C. to Lab.
(2015: Lab. majority 229 (0.66%))

SCOTLAND

ABERDEEN NORTH
E. 62,130 T. 36,757 (59.16%)
                            SNP hold
*Kirsty Blackman, SNP   15,170
Orr Vinegold, Lab.   11,031
Grace O'Keeffe, C.   8,341
Isobel Davidson, LD   1,693
Richard Durkin, Ind.   522
SNP majority 4,139 (11.26%)
9.61% swing SNP to Lab.
(2015: SNP majority 13,396 (30.49%))

ABERDEEN SOUTH
E. 64,964 T. 44,483 (68.47%) C. gain
Ross Thomson, C.   18,746
*Callum McCaig, SNP   13,994
Callum O'Dwyer, Lab.   9,143
Jenny Wilson, LD   2,600
C. majority 4,752 (10.68%)
14.75% swing SNP to C.
(2015: SNP majority 7,230 (14.89%))

**ABERDEENSHIRE WEST &
KINCARDINE**
E. 72,477 T. 51,625 (71.23%) C. gain
Andrew Bowie, C.   24,704
*Stuart Donaldson, SNP   16,754
Barry Black, Lab.   5,706
John Waddell, LD   4,461
C. majority 7,950 (15.40%)
14.07% swing SNP to C.
(2015: SNP majority 7,033 (12.74%))

AIRDRIE & SHOTTS
E. 64,146 T. 38,002 (59.24%)
                            SNP hold
*Neil Gray, SNP   14,291
Helen McFarlane, Lab.   14,096
Jennifer Donnellan, C.   8,813
Ewan McRobert, LD   802
SNP majority 195 (0.51%)
9.66% swing SNP to Lab.
(2015: SNP majority 8,779 (19.82%))

ANGUS
E. 63,840 T. 40,192 (62.96%) C. gain
Kirstene Hair, C.   18,148
*Mike Weir, SNP   15,503
William Campbell, Lab.   5,233
Clive Sneddon, LD   1,308
C. majority 2,645 (6.58%)
15.91% swing SNP to C.
(2015: SNP majority 11,230 (25.24%))

ARGYLL & BUTE
E. 67,230 T. 48,069 (71.50%)
                            SNP hold
*Brendan O'Hara, SNP   17,304
Gary Mulvaney, C.   15,976
Alan Reid, LD   8,745
Michael Kelly, Lab.   6,044
SNP majority 1,328 (2.76%)
13.29% swing SNP to C.
(2015: SNP majority 8,473 (16.33%))

AYR, CARRICK & CUMNOCK
E. 71,241 T. 46,222 (64.88%) C. gain
Bill Grant, C.   18,550
*Corri Wilson, SNP   15,776
Carol Mochan, Lab.   11,024
Callum Leslie, LD   872
C. majority 2,774 (6.00%)
17.50% swing SNP to C.
(2015: SNP majority 11,265 (21.58%))

AYRSHIRE CENTRAL
E. 68,997 T. 45,087 (65.35%)
                            SNP hold
*Philippa Whitford, SNP   16,771
Caroline Hollins Martin, C.   15,504
Nairn McDonald, Lab.   11,762
Tom Inglis, LD   1,050
SNP majority 1,267 (2.81%)
16.51% swing SNP to C.
(2015: SNP majority 13,589 (26.76%))

AYRSHIRE NORTH & ARRAN
E. 73,174 T. 47,433 (64.82%)
                            SNP hold
*Patricia Gibson, SNP   18,451
David Rocks, C.   14,818
Chris Rimicans, Lab.   13,040
Mark Dickson, LD   1,124
SNP majority 3,633 (7.66%)
15.36% swing SNP to C.
(2015: SNP majority 13,573 (25.20%))

BANFF & BUCHAN
E. 67,601 T. 41,643 (61.60%) C. gain
David Duguid, C. 19,976
*Eilidh Whiteford, SNP 16,283
Caitlin Stott, Lab. 3,936
Galen Milne, LD 1,448
C. majority 3,693 (8.87%)
20.15% swing SNP to C.
(2015: SNP majority 14,339 (31.43%))

**BERWICKSHIRE, ROXBURGH &
SELKIRK**
E. 73,191 T. 52,367 (71.55%) C. gain
John Lamont, C. 28,213
*Calum Kerr, SNP 17,153
Ian Davidson, Lab. Co-op 4,519
Caroline Burgess, LD 2,482
C. majority 11,060 (21.12%)
10.86% swing SNP to C.
(2015: SNP majority 328 (0.60%))

**CAITHNESS, SUTHERLAND &
EASTER ROSS**
E. 46,868 T. 30,901 (65.93%) LD gain
Jamie Stone, LD 11,061
*Paul Monaghan, SNP 9,017
Struan Mackie, C. 6,990
Olivia Bell, Lab. 3,833
LD majority 2,044 (6.61%)
8.93% swing SNP to LD
(2015: SNP majority 3,844 (11.24%))

**COATBRIDGE, CHRYSTON &
BELLSHILL**
E. 71,198 T. 45,040 (63.26%) Lab. gain
Hugh Gaffney, Lab. 19,193
*Phil Boswell, SNP 17,607
Robyn Halbert, C. 7,318
David Bennie, LD 922
Lab. majority 1,586 (3.52%)
13.10% swing SNP to Lab.
(2015: SNP majority 11,501 (22.69%))

**CUMBERNAULD, KILSYTH &
KIRKINTILLOCH EAST**
E. 66,554 T. 43,833 (65.86%)
SNP hold
*Stuart McDonald, SNP 19,122
Elisha Fisher, Lab. 14,858
Stephen Johnston, C. 8,010
Rod Ackland, LD 1,238
Carl Pearson, UKIP 605
SNP majority 4,264 (9.73%)
10.07% swing SNP to Lab.
(2015: SNP majority 14,752 (29.87%))

DUMFRIES & GALLOWAY
E. 74,206 T. 51,599 (69.53%) C. gain
Alister Jack, C. 22,344
*Richard Arkless, SNP 16,701
Daniel Goodare, Lab. 10,775
Joan Mitchell, LD 1,241
Yen Hongmei Jin, ND 538
C. majority 5,643 (10.94%)
11.22% swing SNP to C.
(2015: SNP majority 6,514 (11.51%))

**DUMFRIESSHIRE, CLYDESDALE &
TWEEDDALE**
E. 67,672 T. 48,964 (72.35%) C. hold
*David Mundell, C. 24,177
Mairi McAllan, SNP 14,736
Douglas Beattie, Lab. 8,102
John Ferry, LD 1,949
C. majority 9,441 (19.28%)
8.88% swing SNP to C.
(2015: C. majority 798 (1.53%))

DUNBARTONSHIRE EAST
E. 66,300 T. 51,801 (78.13%) LD gain
†Jo Swinson, LD 21,023
*John Nicolson, SNP 15,684
Sheila Mechan, C. 7,563
Callum McNally, Lab. 7,531
LD majority 5,339 (10.31%)
7.13% swing SNP to LD
(2015: SNP majority 2,167 (3.95%))

DUNBARTONSHIRE WEST
E. 67,602 T. 44,083 (65.21%)
SNP hold
*Martin Docherty, SNP 18,890
Jean Anne Mitchell, Lab. 16,602
Penny Hutton, C. 7,582
Rebecca Plenderleith, LD 1,009
SNP majority 2,288 (5.19%)
11.26% swing SNP to Lab.
(2015: SNP majority 14,171 (27.71%))

DUNDEE EAST
E. 65,854 T. 42,928 (65.19%)
SNP hold
*Stewart Hosie, SNP 18,391
Eleanor Price, C. 11,746
Lesley Brennan, Lab. 11,176
Christopher McIntyre, LD 1,615
SNP majority 6,645 (15.48%)
14.63% swing SNP to C.
(2015: SNP majority 19,162 (39.77%))

DUNDEE WEST
E. 62,644 T. 38,677 (61.74%)
SNP hold
*Chris Law, SNP 18,045
Alan Cowan, Lab. 12,783
Darren Cormack, C. 6,257
Jenny Blain, LD 1,189
Sean Dobson, Ind. 403
SNP majority 5,262 (13.60%)
12.31% swing SNP to Lab.
(2015: SNP majority 17,092 (38.23%))

DUNFERMLINE & FIFE WEST
E. 75,672 T. 51,010 (67.41%)
SNP hold
*Douglas Chapman, SNP 18,121
Cara Hilton, Lab. Co-op 17,277
Belinda Hacking, C. 12,593
James Calder, LD 3,019
SNP majority 844 (1.65%)
8.43% swing SNP to Lab.
(2015: SNP majority 10,352 (18.52%))

**EAST KILBRIDE, STRATHAVEN &
LESMAHAGOW**
E. 80,442 T. 54,102 (67.26%)
SNP hold
*Lisa Cameron, SNP 21,023
Monique McAdams, Lab. 17,157
Mark McGeever, C. 13,704
Paul McGarry, LD 1,590
Janice MacKay, UKIP 628
SNP majority 3,866 (7.15%)
10.08% swing SNP to Lab.
(2015: SNP majority 16,527 (27.30%))

EAST LOTHIAN
E. 79,093 T. 55,878 (70.65%) Lab. gain
Martin Whitfield, Lab. 20,158
*George Kerevan, SNP 17,075
Sheila Low, C. 16,540
Elisabeth Wilson, LD 1,738
Mike Allan, Ind. 367
Lab. majority 3,083 (5.52%)
8.52% swing SNP to Lab.
(2015: SNP majority 6,803 (11.53%))

EDINBURGH EAST
E. 65,896 T. 43,523 (66.05%)
SNP hold
*Tommy Sheppard, SNP 18,509
Patsy King, Lab. 15,084
Katie Mackie, C. 8,081
Tristan Gray, LD 1,849
SNP majority 3,425 (7.87%)
5.73% swing SNP to Lab.
(2015: SNP majority 9,106 (19.34%))

EDINBURGH NORTH & LEITH
E. 79,473 T. 56,552 (71.16%)
SNP hold
*Deidre Brock, SNP 19,243
Gordon Munro, Lab. Co-op 17,618
Iain McGill, C. 15,385
Martin Veart, LD 2,579
Lorna Slater, Green 1,727
SNP majority 1,625 (2.87%)
3.39% swing SNP to Lab.
(2015: SNP majority 5,597 (9.65%))

EDINBURGH SOUTH
E. 64,553 T. 47,840 (74.11%) Lab. hold
*Ian Murray, Lab. 26,269
Jim Eadie, SNP 10,755
Stephanie Smith, C. 9,428
Alan Beal, LD 1,388
Lab. majority 15,514 (32.43%)
13.54% swing SNP to Lab.
(2015: Lab. majority 2,637 (5.35%))

EDINBURGH SOUTH WEST
E. 71,178 T. 49,390 (69.39%)
SNP hold
*Joanna Cherry, SNP 17,575
Miles Briggs, C. 16,478
Foysol Choudhury, Lab. 13,213
Aisha Mir, LD 2,124
SNP majority 1,097 (2.22%)
10.25% swing SNP to C.
(2015: SNP majority 8,135 (15.76%))

EDINBURGH WEST
E. 71,500   T. 52,795 (73.84%)

		LD gain
Christine Jardine, LD	18,108	
Toni Giugliano, SNP	15,120	
Sandy Batho, C.	11,559	
Mandy Telford, Lab.	7,876	
Mark Whittet, Referendum	132	

LD majority 2,988 (5.66%)
5.76% swing SNP to LD
(2015: SNP majority 3,210 (5.85%))

FALKIRK
E. 82,240   T. 53,809 (65.43%)

		SNP hold
*John McNally, SNP	20,952	
Craig Martin, Lab.	16,029	
Callum Laidlaw, C.	14,088	
Austin Reid, LD	1,120	
Debra Pickering, Green	908	
Stuart Martin, UKIP	712	

SNP majority 4,923 (9.15%)
11.75% swing SNP to Lab.
(2015: SNP majority 19,701 (32.65%))

FIFE NORTH EAST
E. 58,685   T. 41,822 (71.27%)

		SNP hold
*Stephen Gethins, SNP	13,743	
Janet Riches, LD	13,741	
Tony Miklinski, C.	10,088	
Rosalind Garton, Lab.	4,026	
Mike Scott-Hayward, Sovereign	224	

SNP majority 2 (0.00%)
4.80% swing SNP to LD
(2015: SNP majority 4,344 (9.60%))

GLASGOW CENTRAL
E. 64,346   T. 35,984 (55.92%)

		SNP hold
*Alison Thewliss, SNP	16,096	
Faten Hameed, Lab.	13,829	
Charlotte Fairbanks, C.	5,014	
Isabel Nelson, LD	1,045	

SNP majority 2,267 (6.30%)
6.59% swing SNP to Lab.
(2015: SNP majority 7,662 (19.49%))

GLASGOW EAST
E. 66,242   T. 36,175 (54.61%)

		SNP hold
David Linden, SNP	14,024	
Kate Watson, Lab.	13,949	
Thomas Kerr, C.	6,816	
Matthew Clark, LD	576	
John Ferguson, UKIP	504	
Karin Finegan, Ind.	158	
Steven Marshall, Soc. Dem.	148	

SNP majority 75 (0.21%)
12.14% swing SNP to Lab.
(2015: SNP majority 10,387 (24.49%))

GLASGOW NORTH
E. 53,863   T. 33,473 (62.14%)

		SNP hold
*Patrick Grady, SNP	12,597	
Pam Duncan-Glancy, Lab.	11,537	
Stuart Cullen, C.	4,935	
Patrick Harvie, Green	3,251	
Calum Shepherd, LD	1,153	

SNP majority 1,060 (3.17%)
11.00% swing SNP to Lab.
(2015: SNP majority 9,295 (25.17%))

GLASGOW NORTH EAST
E. 59,932   T. 31,775 (53.02%)

		Lab. Co-op gain
Paul Sweeney, Lab. Co-op	13,637	
*Anne McLaughlin, SNP	13,395	
Jack Wylie, C.	4,106	
Daniel Donaldson, LD	637	

Lab. Co-op majority 242 (0.76%)
12.56% swing SNP to Lab.
(2015: SNP majority 9,222 (24.36%))

GLASGOW NORTH WEST
E. 63,773   T. 38,844 (60.91%)

		SNP hold
*Carol Monaghan, SNP	16,508	
Michael Shanks, Lab.	13,947	
Christopher Land, C.	7,002	
James Speirs, LD	1,387	

SNP majority 2,561 (6.59%)
8.52% swing SNP to Lab.
(2015: SNP majority 10,364 (23.63%))

GLASGOW SOUTH
E. 69,126   T. 44,550 (64.45%)

		SNP hold
*Stewart McDonald, SNP	18,312	
Eileen Dinning, Lab.	16,285	
Taylor Muir, C.	8,506	
Ewan Hoyle, LD	1,447	

SNP majority 2,027 (4.55%)
10.30% swing SNP to Lab.
(2015: SNP majority 12,269 (25.15%))

GLASGOW SOUTH WEST
E. 62,991   T. 35,378 (56.16%)

		SNP hold
*Chris Stephens, SNP	14,386	
Matt Kerr, Lab. Co-op	14,326	
Thomas Haddow, C.	5,524	
Ben Denton-Cardew, LD	661	
Sarah Hemy, UKIP	481	

SNP majority 60 (0.17%)
12.07% swing SNP to Lab.
(2015: SNP majority 9,950 (24.32%))

GLENROTHES
E. 66,378   T. 40,399 (60.86%)

		SNP hold
*Peter Grant, SNP	17,291	
Altany Craik, Lab.	14,024	
Andrew Brown, C.	7,876	
Rebecca Bell, LD	1,208	

SNP majority 3,267 (8.09%)
10.55% swing SNP to Lab.
(2015: SNP majority 13,897 (29.20%))

GORDON
E. 78,531   T. 53,685 (68.36%)

		C. gain
Colin Clark, C.	21,861	
*Alex Salmond, SNP	19,254	
Kirsten Muat, Lab.	6,340	
David Evans, LD	6,230	

C. majority 2,607 (4.86%)
20.40% swing SNP to C.
(2015: SNP majority 8,687 (14.94%))

INVERCLYDE
E. 58,853   T. 39,093 (66.42%)

		SNP hold
*Ronnie Cowan, SNP	15,050	
Martin McCluskey, Lab.	14,666	
David Wilson, C.	8,399	
David Stevens, LD	978	

SNP majority 384 (0.98%)
11.91% swing SNP to Lab.
(2015: SNP majority 11,063 (24.80%))

INVERNESS, NAIRN, BADENOCH & STRATHSPEY
E. 76,844   T. 52,801 (68.71%)

		SNP hold
*Drew Hendry, SNP	21,042	
Nicholas Tulloch, C.	16,118	
Mike Robb, Lab.	8,552	
Ritchie Cunningham, LD	6,477	
Donald Boyd, SCP	612	

SNP majority 4,924 (9.33%)
17.41% swing SNP to C.
(2015: SNP majority 10,809 (18.76%))

KILMARNOCK & LOUDOUN
E. 73,327   T. 46,509 (63.43%)

		SNP hold
*Alan Brown, SNP	19,690	
Laura Dover, Lab.	13,421	
Alison Harper, C.	12,404	
Irene Lang, LD	994	

SNP majority 6,269 (13.48%)
5.91% swing SNP to Lab.
(2015: SNP majority 13,638 (25.30%))

KIRKCALDY & COWDENBEATH
E. 72,721   T. 46,193 (63.52%)   Lab. gain

Lesley Laird, Lab.	17,016	
*Roger Mullin, SNP	16,757	
Dave Dempsey, C.	10,762	
Malcolm Wood, LD	1,118	
David Coburn, UKIP	540	

Lab. majority 259 (0.56%)
9.71% swing SNP to Lab.
(2015: SNP majority 9,974 (18.86%))

LANARK & HAMILTON EAST
E. 77,313   T. 50,470 (65.28%)

		SNP hold
*Angela Crawley, SNP	16,444	
Poppy Corbett, C.	16,178	
Andrew Hilland, Lab.	16,084	
Colin Robb, LD	1,214	
Donald Mackay, UKIP	550	

SNP majority 266 (0.53%)
16.21% swing SNP to C.
(2015: SNP majority 10,100 (18.28%))

LINLITHGOW & FALKIRK EAST
E. 86,186   T. 56,094 (65.08%)

		SNP hold
*Martyn Day, SNP	20,388	
Joan Coombes, Lab.	17,469	
Charles Kennedy, C.	16,311	
Sally Pattle, LD	1,926	

SNP majority 2,919 (5.20%)
7.90% swing SNP to Lab.
(2015: SNP majority 12,934 (21.00%))

LIVINGSTON
E. 81,208   T. 52,505 (64.65%)

		SNP hold
*Hannah Bardell, SNP	21,036	
Rhea Wolfson, Lab.	17,158	
Damian Timson, C.	12,799	
Charles Dundas, LD	1,512	

SNP majority 3,878 (7.39%)
10.94% swing SNP to Lab.
(2015: SNP majority 16,843 (29.27%))

MIDLOTHIAN
E. 68,328   T. 45,273 (66.26%)   Lab. gain
Danielle Rowley, Lab.   16,458
*Owen Thompson, SNP   15,573
Chris Donnelly, C.   11,521
Ross Laird, LD   1,721
Lab. majority 885 (1.95%)
11.18% swing SNP to Lab.
(2015: SNP majority 9,859 (20.40%))

MORAY
E. 70,649   T. 47,605 (67.38%)   C. gain
Douglas Ross, C.   22,637
*Angus Robertson, SNP   18,478
Jo Kirby, Lab.   5,208
Alex Linklater, LD   1,078
Anne Glen, Ind.   204
C. majority 4,159 (8.74%)
13.57% swing SNP to C.
(2015: SNP majority 9,065 (18.39%))

MOTHERWELL & WISHAW
E. 68,215   T. 41,926 (61.46%)
                                   SNP hold
*Marion Fellows, SNP   16,150
Angela Feeney, Lab.   15,832
Meghan Gallacher, C.   8,490
Yvonne Finlayson, LD   920
Neil Wilson, UKIP   534
SNP majority 318 (0.76%)
11.95% swing SNP to Lab.
(2015: SNP majority 11,898 (24.67%))

NA H-EILEANAN AN IAR
E. 21,301   T. 14,818 (69.56%)
                                   SNP hold
*Angus MacNeil, SNP   6,013
Ealasaid MacDonald, Lab.   5,006
Dan McCroskrie, C.   2,441
John Cormack, SCP   1,108
James Paterson, LD   250
SNP majority 1,007 (6.80%)
9.47% swing SNP to Lab.
(2015: SNP majority 4,102 (25.74%))

OCHIL & PERTHSHIRE SOUTH
E. 76,767   T. 54,168 (70.56%)   C. gain
Luke Graham, C.   22,469
*Tasmina Ahmed-Sheikh,
SNP   19,110
Joanne Ross, Lab.   10,847
Iliyan Stefanov, LD   1,742
C. majority 3,359 (6.20%)
15.74% swing SNP to C.
(2015: SNP majority 10,168 (17.57%))

ORKNEY & SHETLAND
E. 34,164   T. 23,277 (68.13%)   LD hold
*Alistair Carmichael, LD   11,312
Miriam Brett, SNP   6,749
Robina Barton, Lab.   2,664
Jamie Halcro Johnston, C.   2,024
Robert Smith, UKIP   283
Stuart Hill, Ind.   245
LD majority 4,563 (19.60%)
8.00% swing SNP to LD
(2015: LD majority 817 (3.59%))

PAISLEY & RENFREWSHIRE
NORTH
E. 67,436   T. 46,615 (69.12%)
                                   SNP hold
*Gavin Newlands, SNP   17,455
Alison Taylor, Lab.   14,842
David Gardiner, C.   12,842
John Boyd, LD   1,476
SNP majority 2,613 (5.61%)
6.19% swing SNP to Lab.
(2015: SNP majority 9,076 (17.99%))

PAISLEY & RENFREWSHIRE
SOUTH
E. 61,344   T. 41,712 (68.00%)
                                   SNP hold
*Mhairi Black, SNP   16,964
Alison Dowling, Lab.   14,423
Amy Thomson, C.   8,122
Eileen McCartin, LD   1,327
Paul Mack, Ind.   876
SNP majority 2,541 (6.09%)
3.10% swing SNP to Lab.
(2015: SNP majority 5,684 (12.30%))

PERTH & PERTHSHIRE NORTH
E. 71,743   T. 51,525 (71.82%)
                                   SNP hold
*Pete Wishart, SNP   21,804
Ian Duncan, C.   21,783
David Roemmele, Lab.   5,349
Peter Barrett, LD   2,589
SNP majority 21 (0.04%)
8.87% swing SNP to C.
(2015: SNP majority 9,641 (17.79%))

RENFREWSHIRE EAST
E. 70,067   T. 53,738 (76.70%)   C. gain
Paul Masterton, C.   21,496
*Kirsten Oswald, SNP   16,784
Blair McDougall, Lab.   14,346
Aileen Morton, LD   1,112
C. majority 4,712 (8.77%)
13.68% swing SNP to C.
(2015: SNP majority 3,718 (6.55%))

ROSS, SKYE & LOCHABER
E. 53,638   T. 38,454 (71.69%)
                                   SNP hold
*Ian Blackford, SNP   15,480
Robert Mackenzie, C.   9,561
Jean Davis, LD   8,042
Peter O'Donnghaile, Lab.   4,695
Ronnie the Crofter   499
Campbell, Ind.
Stick Sturrock, S New   177
SNP majority 5,919 (15.39%)
13.26% swing SNP to C.
(2015: SNP majority 5,124 (12.26%))

RUTHERGLEN & HAMILTON WEST
E. 80,098   T. 50,872 (63.51%)
                              Lab. Co-op gain
Ged Killen, Lab. Co-op   19,101
*Margaret Ferrier, SNP   18,836
Ann Le Blond, C.   9,941
Robert Brown, LD   2,158
Caroline Santos, UKIP   465
Andy Dixon, Ind.   371
Lab. Co-op majority 265 (0.52%)
8.92% swing SNP to Lab.
(2015: SNP majority 9,975 (17.31%))

STIRLING
E. 66,415   T. 49,356 (74.31%)   C. gain
Stephen Kerr, C.   18,291
*Steven Paterson, SNP   18,143
Chris Kane, Lab.   10,902
Wendy Chamberlain, LD   1,683
Kirstein Rummery, Women   337
C. majority 148 (0.30%)
11.40% swing SNP to C.
(2015: SNP majority 10,480 (20.10%))

NORTHERN IRELAND

ANTRIM EAST
E. 62,908   T. 38,143 (60.63%)
                                   DUP hold
*Sammy Wilson, DUP   21,873
Stewart Dickson, Alliance   5,950
John Stewart, UUP   4,524
Oliver McMullan, SF   3,555
Margaret McKillop, SDLP   1,278
Mark Logan, C.   963
DUP majority 15,923 (41.75%)
10.30% swing Alliance to DUP
(2015: DUP majority 5,795 (17.30%))

ANTRIM NORTH
E. 75,657   T. 48,460 (64.05%)
                                   DUP hold
*Ian Paisley, DUP   28,521
Cara McShane, SF   7,878
Jackson Minford, UUP   3,482
Timothy Gaston, TUV   3,282
Patricia O'Lynn, Alliance   2,723
Declan O'Loan, SDLP   2,574
DUP majority 20,643 (42.60%)
5.83% swing SF to DUP
(2015:   DUP   majority   11,546
(27.55%))

ANTRIM SOUTH
E. 68,244   T. 43,170 (63.26%)
                                   DUP gain
Paul Girvan, DUP   16,508
*Danny Kinahan, UUP   13,300
Declan Kearney, SF   7,797
Neil Kelly, Alliance   3,203
Roisin Lynch, SDLP   2,362
DUP majority 3,208 (7.43%)
5.01% swing UUP to DUP
(2015: UUP majority 949 (2.60%))

BELFAST EAST
E. 63,495   T. 42,890 (67.55%)

		DUP hold
*Gavin Robinson, DUP		23,917
Naomi Long, Alliance		15,443
Hazel Legge, UUP		1,408
Mairead O'Donnell, SF		894
Georgina Milne, Green		561
Sheila Bodel, C.		446
Seamas de Faoite, SDLP		167
Bobby Beck, Ind.		54

DUP majority 8,474 (19.76%)
6.61% swing Alliance to DUP
(2015: DUP majority 2,597 (6.54%))

BELFAST NORTH
E. 68,249   T. 45,936 (67.31%)

		DUP hold
*Nigel Dodds, DUP		21,240
John Finucane, SF		19,159
Sam Nelson, Alliance		2,475
Martin McAuley, SDLP		2,058
Malachai O'Hara, Green		644
Gemma Weir, WP		360

DUP majority 2,081 (4.53%)
4.30% swing DUP to SF
(2015: DUP majority 5,326 (13.12%))

BELFAST SOUTH
E. 66,105   T. 43,705 (66.11%)

		DUP gain
Emma Little Pengelly, DUP		13,299
*Alasdair McDonnell, SDLP		11,303
Paula Bradshaw, Alliance		7,946
Mairtin O Muilleoir, SF		7,143
Clare Bailey, Green		2,241
Michael Henderson, UUP		1,527
Clare Salier, C.		246

DUP majority 1,996 (4.57%)
3.45% swing SDLP to DUP
(2015: SDLP majority 906 (2.33%))

BELFAST WEST
E. 62,423   T. 40,633 (65.09%)   SF hold

*Paul Maskey, SF	27,107
Frank McCoubrey, DUP	5,455
Gerry Carroll, PBP	4,132
Tim Attwood, SDLP	2,860
Sorcha Eastwood, Alliance	731
Conor Campbell, WP	348

SF majority 21,652 (53.29%)
3.45% swing DUP to SF
(2015: SF majority 12,365 (35.00%))

DOWN NORTH
E. 64,334   T. 39,185 (60.91%)   Ind. hold

*Lady (Sylvia) Hermon, Ind.	16,148
Alex Easton, DUP	14,940
Andrew Muir, Alliance	3,639
Steven Agnew, Green	2,549
Frank Shivers, C.	941
Therese McCartney, SF	531
Caoimhe McNeill, SDLP	400
Gavan Reynolds, Ind.	37

Ind. majority 1,208 (3.08%)
20.56% swing Ind. to Ind.
(2015: Ind. majority 9,202 (25.60%))

DOWN SOUTH
E. 75,685   T. 50,893 (67.24%)   SF gain

Chris Hazzard, SF	20,328
*Margaret Ritchie, SDLP	17,882
Diane Forsythe, DUP	8,867
Harold McKee, UUP	2,002
Andrew McMurray, Alliance	1,814

SF majority 2,446 (4.81%)
9.30% swing SDLP to SF
(2015: SDLP majority 5,891 (13.80%))

FERMANAGH & SOUTH TYRONE
E. 70,601   T. 53,481 (75.75%)   SF gain

†Michelle Gildernew, SF	25,230
*Tom Elliott, UUP	24,355
Mary Garrity, SDLP	2,587
Noreen Campbell, Alliance	886
Tanya Jones, Green	423

SF majority 875 (1.64%)
1.34% swing UUP to SF
(2015: UUP majority 530 (1.04%))

FOYLE
E. 70,324   T. 45,965 (65.36%)   SF gain

Elisha McCallion, SF	18,256
*Mark Durkan, SDLP	18,087
Gary Middleton, DUP	7,398
Shaun Harkin, PBP	1,377
John Doherty, Alliance	847

SF majority 169 (0.37%)
8.35% swing SDLP to SF
(2015: SDLP majority 6,046 (16.34%))

LAGAN VALLEY
E. 72,380   T. 44,926 (62.07%)

		DUP hold
*Jeffrey Donaldson, DUP		26,762
Robbie Butler, UUP		7,533
Aaron McIntyre, Alliance		4,996
Pat Catney, SDLP		3,384
Jacqui Russell, SF		1,567
Ian Nickels, C.		462
Jonny Orr, ND		222

DUP majority 19,229 (42.80%)
5.07% swing UUP to DUP
(2015: DUP majority 13,000 (32.67%))

LONDONDERRY EAST
E. 67,038   T. 41,030 (61.20%)

		DUP hold
*Gregory Campbell, DUP		19,723
Dermot Nicholl, SF		10,881
Stephanie Quigley, SDLP		4,423
Richard Holmes, UUP		3,135
Chris McCaw, Alliance		2,538
Liz St Clair-Legge, C.		330

DUP majority 8,842 (21.55%)
0.47% swing DUP to SF
(2015: DUP majority 7,804 (22.48%))

NEWRY & ARMAGH
E. 78,266   T. 53,579 (68.46%)   SF hold

*Mickey Brady, SF	25,666
William Irwin, DUP	13,177
Justin McNulty, SDLP	9,055
Sam Nicholson, UUP	4,425
Jackie Coade, Alliance	1,256

SF majority 12,489 (23.31%)
swing N/A
(2015: SF majority 4,176 (8.37%))

STRANGFORD
E. 64,327   T. 38,749 (60.24%)

		DUP hold
*Jim Shannon, DUP		24,036
Kellie Armstrong, Alliance		5,693
Mike Nesbitt, UUP		4,419
Joe Boyle, SDLP		2,404
Carole Murphy, SF		1,083
Ricky Bamford, Green		607
Claire Hiscott, C.		507

DUP majority 18,343 (47.34%)
8.39% swing Alliance to DUP
(2015: DUP majority 10,185 (30.02%))

TYRONE WEST ℂ
E. 64,009   T. 43,486 (67.94%)   SF hold

Barry McElduff, SF	22,060
Thomas Buchanan, DUP	11,718
Daniel McCrossan, SDLP	5,635
Alicia Clarke, UUP	2,253
Stephen Donnelly, Alliance	1,000
Ciaran McClean, Green	427
Barry Brown, Citizens	393

SF majority 10,342 (23.78%)
1.12% swing SF to DUP
(2015: SF majority 10,060 (26.03%))

ULSTER MID
E. 68,485   T. 46,694 (68.18%)   SF hold

*Francie Molloy, SF	25,455
Keith Buchanan, DUP	12,565
Malachy Quinn, SDLP	4,563
Mark Glasgow, UUP	3,017
Fay Watson, Alliance	1,094

SF majority 12,890 (27.61%)
3.88% swing SF to DUP
(2015: SF majority 13,617 (33.28%))

UPPER BANN
E. 80,168   T. 51,258 (63.94%)

		DUP hold
*David Simpson, DUP		22,317
John O'Dowd, SF		14,325
Doug Beattie, UUP		7,900
Declan McAlinden, SDLP		4,397
Tara Doyle, Alliance		2,319

DUP majority 7,992 (15.59%)
3.73% swing SF to DUP
(2015: DUP majority 2,264 (4.79%))

BY-ELECTIONS 2017–18

All UK parliament by-elections since the 2017 General Election. For a full list of party abbreviations *see* General Election 2017 results.

TYRONE WEST
3 May 2018
E. 64,178 T. 35,029 (54.58%)

		SF hold
Órfhlaith Begley, SF	16,346	
Thomas Buchanan, DUP	8,390	
Daniel McCrossan, SDLP	6,254	
Chris Smyth, UUP	2,909	
Stephen Donnelly, Alliance	1,130	

SF majority 7,956 (22.71%)
0.53% swing SF to DUP
(2017: SF. majority 10,342 (23.78%))

LEWISHAM EAST
14 June 2018
E. 66,140 T. 22,056 (33.35%)

		Lab. hold
Janet Daby, Lab.	11,033	
Lucy Salek, LD	5,404	
Ross Archer, C.	3,161	
Rosamund Adoo-Kissi-Debrah, Green	788	
Mandu Reid, Women	506	
David Kurten, UKIP	380	
Anne Marie Waters, For Britain	266	
Maureen Martin, CPA	168	
Howling Laud Hope, Looney	93	
Massimo DiMambro, DVP	67	
Sean Finch, Libertarian	38	
Charles Carey, Ind.	37	
Patrick Gray, Radical	20	
Thomas Hall, Young	18	

Lab majority 5,629 (25.61%)
19% swing Lab to LD
(2017: Lab. majority 21,123 (44.94%))

THE GOVERNMENT

THE CABINET

As at September 2018
Prime Minister, First Lord of the Treasury and Minister for the
　Civil Service
　Rt. Hon. Theresa May, MP
Chancellor of the Duchy of Lancaster and Minister for the Cabinet
　Office
　Rt. Hon. David Lidington, CBE, MP
Chancellor of the Exchequer
　Rt. Hon. Philip Hammond, MP
Secretary of State for the Home Department
　Rt. Hon. Sajid Javid, MP
Secretary of State for Foreign and Commonwealth Affairs
　Rt. Hon. Jeremy Hunt, MP
Secretary of State for Exiting the European Union
　Rt. Hon. Dominic Raab, MP
Secretary of State for Defence
　Rt. Hon. Gavin Williamson, CBE, MP
Lord Chancellor and Secretary of State for Justice
　Rt. Hon. David Gauke, MP
Secretary of State for Health and Social Care
　Rt. Hon. Matthew Hancock, MP
Secretary of State for Business, Energy and Industrial Strategy
　Rt. Hon. Greg Clark, MP
Secretary of State for Housing, Communities and Local Government
　Rt. Hon. James Brokenshire, MP
Secretary of State for International Trade and President of the Board
　of Trade
　Rt. Hon. Liam Fox, MP
Secretary of State for Education
　Rt. Hon. Damian Hinds, MP
Secretary of State for Environment, Food and Rural Affairs
　Rt. Hon. Michael Gove, MP
Secretary of State for Transport
　Rt. Hon. Chris Grayling, MP
Secretary of State for Work and Pensions
　Rt. Hon. Esther McVey, MP
Leader of the House of Lords and Lord Privy Seal
　Rt. Hon. Baroness Evans of Bowes Park
Secretary of State for Scotland
　Rt. Hon. David Mundell, MP
Secretary of State for Wales
　Rt. Hon. Alun Cairns, MP
Secretary of State for Northern Ireland
　Rt. Hon. Karen Bradley, MP
Secretary of State for International Development
　Rt. Hon. Penny Mordaunt, MP*
Secretary of State for Digital, Culture, Media and Sport
　Rt. Hon. Jeremy Wright, QC, MP
Minister without Portfolio
　Rt. Hon. Brandon Lewis, MP

ALSO ATTENDING CABINET MEETINGS
Chief Secretary to the Treasury
　Rt. Hon. Elizabeth Truss, MP
Leader of the House of Commons and Lord President of the Council
　Rt. Hon. Andrea Leadsom, CBE, MP
Parliamentary Secretary to the Treasury and Chief Whip
　Rt. Hon. Julian Smith, MP
Attorney-General
　Rt. Hon. Geoffrey Cox, QC, MP
Minister of State for Energy and Clean Growth
　Rt. Hon. Claire Perry, MP

Minister of State for Immigration
　Rt. Hon. Caroline Nokes, MP

* alongside role as Minister for Women and Equalities

LAW OFFICERS

As at September 2018
Attorney-General
　Rt. Hon. Geoffrey Cox, QC, MP
Solicitor-General
　Robert Buckland, QC, MP
Advocate-General for Scotland
　Rt. Hon. Lord Keen of Elie, QC

MINISTERS OF STATE

As at September 2018
Business, Energy and Industrial Strategy
　Sam Gyimah, MP*
　Rt. Hon. Claire Perry, MP
Defence
　Stuart Andrew, MP
　Rt. Hon. Earl Howe†
　Rt. Hon. Mark Lancaster, TD, MP
Digital, Culture, Media and Sport
　Margot James, MP
Education
　Rt. Hon. Nick Gibb, MP
　Sam Gyimah, MP‡
　Rt. Hon. Anne Milton, MP
Environment, Food and Rural Affairs
　George Eustice, MP
Exiting the European Union
　Lord Callanan
Foreign and Commonwealth Office
　Lord Ahmad of Wimbledon
　Harriett Baldwin, MP§
　Rt. Hon. Alistair Burt, MP§
　Rt. Hon. Sir Alan Duncan, KCMG, MP
　Rt. Hon. Mark Field MP
Health and Social Care
　Stephen Barclay, MP
　Caroline Dinenage, MP
Home Office
　Rt. Hon. Nick Hurd, MP
　Rt. Hon. Caroline Nokes, MP
　Rt. Hon. Ben Wallace, MP
　Baroness Williams of Trafford
Housing, Communities and Local Government
　Kit Malthouse, MP
International Development
　Rt. Hon. Lord Bates
　Rt. Hon. Harriett Baldwin, MP₵
　Rt. Hon. Alistair Burt, MP₵
International Trade
　George Hollingbery, MP
　Baroness Fairhead, CBE
Justice
　Rory Stewart, OBE, MP
Northern Ireland Office
　Shailesh Vara, MP
Transport
　Jo Johnson, MP

Work and Pensions
  Sarah Newton, MP
  Alok Sharma, MP

* position jointly held with the Department of Education
† alongside role as Deputy Leader of the House of Lords
‡ position jointly held with the Department of Business, Energy and Industrial Strategy
§ position jointly held with the Department of International Development
₵ position jointly held with the Foreign and Commonwealth Office

UNDER-SECRETARIES OF STATE

As at September 2018
Business, Energy and Industrial Strategy
  Richard Harrington, MP
  Kelly Tolhurst, MP
  Rt. Hon. Lord Henley
Defence
  Stuart Andrew, MP
  Rt. Hon. Tobias Ellwood, MP
Digital, Culture, Media and Sport
  Lord Ashton of Hyde
  Tracey Crouch, MP
  Michael Ellis, MP
Education
  Lord Agnew of Oulton
  Nadhim Zahawi, MP
Environment, Food and Rural Affairs
  Thérèse Coffey, MP
  David Rutley, MP*
  Lord Gardiner of Kimble
Exiting the European Union
  Suella Braverman, MP
  Christopher Heaton-Harris, MP
  Robin Walker, MP
Health and Social Care
  Steve Brine, MP
  Jackie Doyle-Price, MP
  Lord O'Shaughnessy
Home Office
  Victoria Atkins, MP
Housing, Communities and Local Government
  Jake Berry, MP
  Heather Wheeler, MP
  Nigel Adams, MP*
  Rishi Sunak, MP
  Lord Bourne of Aberystwyth†
International Trade
  Graham Stuart, MP
Justice
  Edward Argar, MP
  Lucy Frazer, QC, MP
Northern Ireland Office
  Lord Duncan of Springbank‡
Office of the Secretary of State for Scotland
  Lord Duncan of Springbank§
Transport
  Nusrat Ghani, MP*
  Jesse Norman, MP
  Baroness Sugg, CBE
Office of the Secretary of State for Wales
  Mims Davies, MP*
  Lord Bourne of Aberystwyth₵
Work and Pensions
  Baroness Buscombe

Justin Tomlinson, MP
Guy Opperman, MP

* position held alongside role as a Government Whip
† position jointly held with the Office of the Secretary of State for Wales
‡ position jointly held with the Office of the Secretary of State for Scotland
§ position jointly held with the Northern Ireland Office
₵ position jointly held with the Ministry of Housing, Communities and Local Government

OTHER MINISTERS

As at September 2018
Cabinet Office
  Oliver Dowden, CBE, MP *(Minister for Implementation and Parliamentary Secretary)*
  Chloe Smith, MP *(Minister for the Constitution and Parliamentary Secretary)*
Office of the Leader of the House of Lords
  Rt. Hon. Earl Howe *(Deputy Leader of the House of Lords)*
Treasury
  Rt. Hon. Mel Stride, MP *(Financial Secretary and Paymaster General)*
  John Glen, MP *(Economic Secretary)*
  Robert Jenrick, MP *(Exchequer Secretary)*

GOVERNMENT WHIPS

As at September 2018

HOUSE OF LORDS

Lords Chief Whip and Captain of the Honourable Corps of Gentlemen-at-Arms
  Rt. Hon. Lord Taylor of Holbeach, CBE
Deputy Chief Whip and Captain of the Queen's Bodyguard of the Yeomen of the Guard
  Earl of Courtown
Lords-in-Waiting
  Rt. Hon. Lord Young of Cookham, CH
  Viscount Younger of Leckie
Baronesses-in-Waiting
  Baroness Goldie
  Baroness Manzoor, CBE
  Baroness Stedman-Scott, OBE
  Baroness Vere of Norbiton

HOUSE OF COMMONS

Chief Whip and Parliamentary Secretary to the Treasury
  Rt. Hon. Julian Smith, MP
Deputy Chief Whip and Treasurer of HM Household
  Christopher Pincher, MP
Government Whip and Comptroller of HM Household
  Mark Spencer, MP
Government Whip and Vice-Chamberlain of HM Household
  Andrew Stephenson, MP
Lords Commissioners of HM Treasury (Whips)
  Nigel Adams, MP*; Mike Freer, MP; Rebecca Harris, MP; Paul Maynard, MP; David Rutley, MP†; Craig Whittaker, MP
Assistant Whips
  Jo Churchill, MP; Mims Davies, MP‡; Michelle Donelan, MP; Nusrat Ghani, MP§; Amanda Milling, MP; Wendy Morton, MP; Jeremy Quin, MP; Iain Stewart, MP

* alongside role as Under-Secretary of State at the Ministry of Housing, Communities and Local Government
† along role as Under-Secretary of State for Environment, Food and Rural Affairs
‡ alongside role as Under-Secretary of State at the Office of the Secretary of State for Wales
§ alongside role as Under-Secretary of State for Transport

GOVERNMENT DEPARTMENTS

THE CIVIL SERVICE

The civil service helps the government develop and deliver its policies as effectively as possible. It works in three types of organisations – departments, executive agencies, and non-departmental government bodies (NDPBs). Under the Next Steps programme, launched in 1988, many semi-autonomous executive agencies were established to carry out much of the work of the civil service. Executive agencies operate within a framework set by the responsible minister which specifies policies, objectives and available resources. All executive agencies are set annual performance targets by their minister. Each agency has a chief executive, who is responsible for the day-to-day operations of the agency and who is accountable to the minister for the use of resources and for meeting the agency's targets. The minister accounts to parliament for the work of the agency.

There are currently 331,392 civil servants on a full-time equivalent (FTE) basis and 430,676 on a headcount basis. FTE is a measure that counts staff according to the proportion of full-time hours that they work. Almost three-quarters of all civil servants work outside London and the south-east. All government departments and executive agencies are responsible for their own pay and grading systems for civil servants outside the senior civil service.

SALARIES 2018–19

MINISTERIAL SALARIES

Ministers who are members of the House of Commons receive a parliamentary salary of £77,379 in addition to their ministerial salary.

Prime minister	£75,440
Cabinet minister (Commons)	£67,505
Cabinet minister (Lords)	£101,038
Minister of state (Commons)	£31,680
Minister of state (Lords)	£78,891
Parliamentary under-secretary (Commons)	£22,375
Parliamentary under-secretary (Lords)	£68,710

SPECIAL ADVISERS' SALARIES

Special advisers to government ministers are paid out of public funds; their salaries are negotiated individually, but are usually in the range of £40,352 to £106,864.

CIVIL SERVICE SALARIES	
Senior Civil Servants	
Permanent secretary	£143,420–£202,000
Band 3	£107,060–£210,181
Band 2	£87,870–£164,125
Band 1	£64,640–£118,978

Staff are placed in pay bands according to their level of responsibility and taking account of other factors such as experience and marketability. Movement within and between bands is based on performance. Following the delegation of responsibility for pay and grading to government departments and agencies from 1 April 1996, it is no longer possible to show service-wide pay rates for staff outside the Senior Civil Service.

GOVERNMENT DEPARTMENTS

As at September 2018
For more information on government departments, *see* W www.gov.uk/government/organisations

ATTORNEY-GENERAL'S OFFICE

Attorney-General's Office, 5–8 The Sanctuary, London SW1P 3JS
T 020-7271 2492 E correspondence@attorneygeneral.gov.uk
W www.gov.uk/government/organisations/attorney-generals-office

The law officers of the crown for England and Wales are the Attorney-General and the Solicitor-General. The Attorney-General, assisted by the Solicitor-General, is the chief legal adviser to the government and is also ultimately responsible for all crown litigation. He has overall responsibility for the work of the Law Officers' Departments (the Treasury Solicitor's Department, the Crown Prosecution Service – incorporating the Revenue and Customs Prosecutions Office – and the Serious Fraud Office, and HM Crown Prosecution Service Inspectorate). The Attorney-General also oversees the armed forces' prosecuting authority and the government legal service. He has a specific statutory duty to superintend the discharge of their duties by the Director of Public Prosecutions (who heads the Crown Prosecution Service) and the Director of the Serious Fraud Office. The Attorney-General has specific responsibilities for the enforcement of the criminal law and also performs certain public interest functions, eg protecting charities and appealing unduly lenient sentences. He also deals with questions of law arising in bills and with issues of legal policy.

Following the devolution of power to the Northern Ireland Assembly on 12 April 2010, the assembly now appoints the Attorney-General for Northern Ireland. The Attorney-General for England and Wales holds the office of Advocate-General for Northern Ireland, with significantly reduced responsibilities in Northern Ireland. The Attorney-General's Office is supported by four executive agencies and public bodies.

Attorney-General, Rt. Hon. Geoffrey Cox, QC, MP
Parliamentary Private Secretary, vacant
Principal Private Secretary, Josh Dodd
Deputy Principal Private Secretary, Andrea Dowsett
Assistant Private Secretary, Leeann Thayalanayagam
Solicitor-General, Robert Buckland, QC, MP

MANAGEMENT BOARD
Director-General, Rowena Collins Rice
Deputy Legal Secretary and Head of Operations, Michelle Crotty

DEPARTMENT FOR BUSINESS, ENERGY AND INDUSTRIAL STRATEGY

1 Victoria Street, London SW1H 0ET
T 020-7215 5000 E enquiries@beis.gov.uk W www.gov.uk/government/organisations/department-for-business-energy-and-industrial-strategy

The Department for Business, Energy and Industrial Strategy (BEIS) was established in July 2016 following the appointment of Theresa May as prime minister. It merged the Department of Business, Innovation and Skills and the Department of Energy and Climate Change. BEIS brings together responsibilities for business, industrial strategy, science, innovation, energy and climate change, and is supported by 45 executive agencies and public bodies. It is responsible for:

developing and delivering a comprehensive industrial strategy and leading the government's relationship with business; ensuring that the UK has secure, reliable, affordable and clean energy supplies; ensuring the UK remains at the forefront of science, research and innovation; and tackling climate change.

Secretary of State for Business, Energy and Industrial Strategy,
Rt. Hon. Greg Clark, MP
Parliamentary Private Secretary, Alan Mak, MP
Special Advisers, Glen Hall; Guy Newey; Jacob Wilmer
Minister of State, Sam Gyimah, MP *(Universities, Science, Research and Innovation)**
Minister of State, Rt. Hon. Claire Perry, MP *(Energy and Clean Growth)*
Parliamentary Private Secretary, Mary Robinson, MP
Parliamentary Under-Secretary of State, Richard Harrington, MP *(Business and Industry)*
Parliamentary Under-Secretary of State, Rt. Hon. Lord Henley
Parliamentary Under-Secretary of State, Kelly Tolhurst, MP *(Small Business, Consumers and Corporate Responsibility)*
* Jointly with the Department for Education

MANAGEMENT BOARD
Permanent Secretary, Alex Chisholm
Members, Sam Beckett *(EU Exit and Analysis);* Julian Critchlow *(Energy Transformation and Clean Growth);* Gareth Davies *(Business and Science);* Sarah Harrison, MBE *(Corporate Services);* Prof. John Loughhead, CB, OBE *(BEIS Chief Scientific Adviser);* Jeremy Pocklington *(Energy and Security);* Jaee Samant *(Market Frameworks)*
Non-Executive Members, Archie Norman *(Lead);* Nigel Boardman; Stephen Carter; Dame Carolyn McCall, DBE; Leena Nair; Kathryn Parsons; Stuart Quickenden

BETTER REGULATION EXECUTIVE
1 Victoria Street, London SW1 0ET
T 020-7215 5000 E enquiries@beis.gov.uk
W www.gov.uk/government/policy-teams/
better-regulation-executive

The Better Regulation Executive (BRE) is a joint BEIS/ Cabinet Office unit which leads on delivering the government's manifesto commitment to reduce the overall burden on business, in order to increase growth and create jobs. Each government department is, however, responsible for delivering its part of the deregulation agenda within the framework put in place by the BRE.

Non-Executive Chair, Lord Curry of Kirkharle, CBE
Chief Executive, Graham Turnock

CABINET OFFICE
70 Whitehall, London SW1A 2AS
T 020-7276 1234
W www.gov.uk/government/organisations/cabinet-office

The Cabinet Office, alongside the Treasury, sits at the centre of the government, with an overarching purpose of making government work better. It supports the prime minister and the cabinet, helping to ensure effective development, coordination and implementation of policy and operations across all government departments. The Cabinet Office also leads work to ensure that the Civil Service provides the most effective and efficient support to the government to meet its objectives. The department is headed by the Minister for the Cabinet Office. The Cabinet Office is responsible for: supporting collective government; supporting the National Security Council and the Joint Intelligence Organisation, coordinating the government's response to crises and managing the UK's cyber security; promoting efficiency and

reform across government through innovation, better procurement and project management, and by transforming the delivery of services; promoting the release of government data, and making the way government works more transparent; improving the capability and effectiveness of the Civil Service; and political constitution and reform.

The priorities of the Cabinet Office include: supporting the prime minister and cabinet to deliver the government's programme; driving efficiencies and reforms to improve the government's performance; creating a more united democracy; and strengthening and securing the UK at home and abroad. The Cabinet Office employs around 2,050 staff and is supported by 20 executive agencies and public bodies.

Prime Minister, First Lord of the Treasury and Minister for the Civil Service, Rt. Hon. Theresa May, MP
Parliamentary Private Secretary, Seema Kennedy, MP
Principal Private Secretary, Peter Hill
Special Advisers, Gavin Barwell; Nikki Da Costa; Robbie Gibb; James Marshall; Joanna Penn
Special Adviser (Europe), Oliver Robbins
Chancellor of the Duchy of Lancaster and Minister for the Cabinet Office, Rt. Hon. David Lidington, CBE, MP
Parliamentary Private Secretary, Kevin Foster, MP
Special Advisers, Fraser Raleigh; James Wild
Lord President of the Council, Rt. Hon. Andrea Leadsom, MP
Parliamentary Private Secretary, Victoria Prentis, MP
Special Advisers, Lucia Hodgson; Marc Pooler
Minister without Portfolio, Rt. Hon. Brandon Lewis, MP
Parliamentary Private Secretary, Helen Whately, MP
Special Advisers, Anita Boateng; Hudson Roe; Zoe Thorogood
Parliamentary Under-Secretary of State, Chloe Smith, MP *(Constitution)*
Parliamentary Under-Secretary of State, Oliver Dowden, CBE, MP *(Implementation)*

MANAGEMENT BOARD
Permanent Secretary and Chief Executive of the Civil Service, John Manzoni
Cabinet Secretary and Head of the Civil Service, Sir Jeremy Heywood
First Parliamentary Counsel, Elizabeth Gardiner
Head of UK Governance Group, Philip Rycroft
Executive Director, Implementation Group, James Quinault
Chief Executive, Commonwealth Summit Unit, Sir Tim Hitchens, KCVO, CMG, LVO
Chief People Officer, Rupert McNeil
Director-General, Propriety and Ethics Team and Head of Private Offices Group, Helen MacNamara
National Security Adviser, Sir Mark Sedwill, KCMG
Deputy National Security Adviser, Dr Christian Turner, CMG
Chair of the Joint Intelligence Committee, Charles Farr
Director-General, Prime Minister's Office, Peter Hill
Government Chief Commercial Officer, Gareth Rhys Williams
Finance Director, Guy Lester
Human Resources Director, Rachel Coleman
Executive Director, Government Communications, Alex Aiken
Director-General, Government Digital Service, Kevin Cunnington
Director-General, Government Property, Mike Parsons
Director-General, UK Governance, Lucy Smith
Lead Non-Executive Director, Sir John Parker
Non-Executive Board Member, Sir Ian Cheshire

HONOURS AND APPOINTMENTS BOARD
Room G-39, Horse Guards Road, London SW1A 2HQ
T 020-7276 2777
Chair, Sir Jonathan Stephens, KCB

OFFICE OF THE LEADER OF THE HOUSE OF COMMONS
1 Horse Guards Road, London SW1A 2HQ
T 020-7276 1005 E commonsleader@cabinetoffice.gov.uk
W www.gov.uk/government/organisations/
the-office-of-the-leader-of-the-house-of-commons

The Office of the Leader of the House of Commons is responsible for the arrangement of government business in the House of Commons and for planning and supervising the government's legislative programme. The Leader of the House of Commons upholds the rights and privileges of the house and acts as a spokesperson for the government as a whole.

The leader reports regularly to the cabinet on parliamentary business and the legislative programme. In their capacity as leader of the house, they are a member of the House of Commons Commission. They also chair the cabinet committee on the legislative programme. As Lord President of the Council, they are a member of the cabinet and in charge of the Office of the Privy Council.

The Deputy Leader of the House of Commons supports the leader in handling the government's business in the house. They are responsible for monitoring MPs' and peers' correspondence.

Lord President of the Privy Council and Leader of the House of Commons, Rt. Hon. Andrea Leadsom, MP
Parliamentary Private Secretary, Victoria Prentis, MP
Special Advisers, Lucia Hodgson, Marc Pooler

OFFICE OF THE LEADER OF THE HOUSE OF LORDS
House of Lords, London SW1A 0PW
T 020-7219 3200 E pslseaderofthelords@cabinet-office.x.gsi.gov.uk
W www.gov.uk/government/organisations/
office-of-the-leader-of-the-house-of-lords

The Office of the Leader of the House of Lords provides support to the leader in their parliamentary and ministerial duties, which include leading the government benches in the House of Lords; the delivery of the government's business in the Lords; taking part in formal ceremonies such as the state opening of parliament; and giving guidance to the House of Lords on matters of procedure and order.

Lord Privy Seal and Leader of the House of Lords, Rt. Hon. Baroness Evans of Bowes Park
Parliamentary Private Secretary, Luke Hall, MP
Special Advisers, Annabelle Eyre; Katherine Howell; Thomas Pretty
Deputy Leader of the House of Lords, Rt. Hon. Earl Howe

PRIME MINISTER'S OFFICE
10 Downing Street, London SW1A 2AA
T 020-7930 4433
W www.number10.gov.uk

Prime Minister, Rt. Hon. Theresa May, MP
Parliamentary Private Secretary, Seema Kennedy, MP
Special Advisers, Gavin Barwell; Nikki Da Costa; Robbie Gibb; James Marshall; Joanna Penn
Special Adviser (Europe), Oliver Robbins
Principal Private Secretary, Peter Hill
Director of Communications, Robbie Gibb
Director of Policy, James Marshall
Prime Minister's Official Spokesman, James Slack
Prime Minister's Official Speech Writer, Jessica Cunliffe
Chief of Staff, Gavin Barwell
Deputy Chief of Staff, Joanna Penn
Press Secretary, James Slack
Head of Briefing, Edward de Minckwitz
Head of Features, Liz Sanderson
Head of Policy Unit, James Marshall
Head of Implementation Unit, Peter Hill

IMPLEMENTATION GROUP
Executive Director, James Quinault

PRIVATE OFFICES GROUP
Director-General, Propriety and Ethics and Head of Private Offices Group, Helen MacNamara

UK GOVERNANCE GROUP
Head of UK Governance Group, Philip Rycroft

CABINET OFFICE CORPORATE SERVICES
Executive Director, Government Communications, Alex Aiken
Finance Director, Guy Lester
Human Resources Director, Rachel Coleman

NATIONAL SECURITY
Comprises the National Security Secretariat and the Joint Intelligence Organisation. The National Security Secretariat is responsible for providing policy advice to the National Security Council, where ministers discuss national security issues at a strategic level; coordinating and developing foreign and defence policy across government; coordinating policy, ethical and legal issues across the intelligence community, managing its funding and priorities, and dealing with the Intelligence and Security Committee which calls it to account; developing effective protective security policies and capabilities for government; improving the UK's resilience to respond to and recover from emergencies, and maintaining facilities for the effective coordination of government response to crises; and providing strategic leadership for cyber security in the UK, in line with the National Cyber Security Strategy.

NATIONAL SECURITY SECRETARIAT
National Security Adviser, Sir Mark Sedwill, KCMG
Deputy National Security Advisers, Dr Christian Turner, CMG

JOINT INTELLIGENCE ORGANISATION
Chair, Joint Intelligence Committee, Charles Farr

INDEPENDENT OFFICES

CIVIL SERVICE COMMISSION
1 Horse Guards Road, London SW1A 2HQ
T 020-7271 0831
W www.civilservicecommission.independent.gov.uk

The Civil Service Commission regulates the requirement that selection for appointment to the Civil Service must be on merit on the basis of fair and open competition; the commission publishes its recruitment principles and audit departments and agencies' performance against these. Commissioners personally chair competitions for the most senior jobs in the civil service. In addition, the commission hears complaints from civil servants under the Civil Service Code.

The commission was established as a statutory body in November 2010 under the provisions of the Constitutional Reform and Governance Act 2010.

Commissioners, Jane Burgess; Jan Cameron; Natalie Campbell; Isabel Doverty; Margaret Edwards; Andrew Flanagan; Rosie Glazebrook; Sarah Laessig; June Milligan; Joe Montgomery; Ian Watmore; Kevin Woods

THE COMMISSIONER FOR PUBLIC APPOINTMENTS
G/8, 1 Horse Guards Road, London SW1A 2HQ
T 020-7271 0833 E publicappointments@csc.gov.uk
W http://publicappointmentscommissioner.independent.gov.uk

The Commissioner for Public Appointments is responsible for monitoring, regulating and reporting on ministerial appointments (including those made by Welsh government ministers) to public bodies. The commissioner can investigate complaints about the way in which appointments were made.

Commissioner for Public Appointments, Peter Riddell
Chief Executive Commission Secretariat, Peter Lawrence, OBE

OFFICE OF THE PARLIAMENTARY COUNSEL
1 Horse Guards Road, London SW1A 2HQ
T 02-7276 6586 E good.law@cabinetoffice.gov.uk W www.gov.uk/government/organisations/office-of-the-parliamentary-counsel

The Office of the Parliamentary Counsel is a group of government lawyers who specialise in drafting government bills; advising departments on the rules and procedures of Parliament; reviewing orders and regulations which amend Acts of Parliament; and assisting the government on a range of legal and constitutional issues.

First Parliamentary Counsel, Elizabeth Gardiner
Chief Executive, Jim Barron, CBE

MINISTRY OF DEFENCE
Main Building, Whitehall, London SW1A 2HB
T 020-7218 9000 W www.gov.uk/government/organisations/ministry-of-defence

For further information on the responsibilities and remit of the MoD *see* the Defence Chapter.

Secretary of State for Defence, Rt. Hon. Gavin Williamson, CBE, MP
Parliamentary Private Secretary, Will Quince, MP
Special Advisers, Eleanor Lyons; Robert Golledge
Minister of State, Rt. Hon. Earl Howe *(Lords)*
Minister of State, Rt. Hon. Mark Lancaster, TD, MP *(Armed Forces)*
Parliamentary Private Secretaries, Jack Lopresti, MP; Anne-Marie Trevelyan, MP
Parliamentary Under-Secretary of State and Minister for Defence People and Veterans, Rt. Hon. Tobias Ellwood, MP
Parliamentary Under-Secretary of State and Minister for Defence Procurement, Stuart Andrew, MP

CHIEFS OF STAFF
Chief of the Defence Staff, Gen. Sir Nick Carter, KCB, CBE, DSO, ADC
Vice-Chief of the Defence Staff, Gen. Sir Gordon Messenger, KCB, DSO*, OBE, ADC
Chief of the Naval Staff and First Sea Lord, Adm. Sir Philip Jones, KCB, ADC
Second Sea Lord and Deputy Chief of Naval Staff, Vice-Adm. Antony Radakin, CB
Chief of the General Staff, Gen. Mark Carleton-Smith, CBE
Assistant Chief of the General Staff, Maj.-Gen. Rupert Jones, CBE
Chief of the Air Staff, Air Chief Marshal Sir Stephen Hillier, KCB, CBE, DFC, ADC
Assistant Chief of the Air Staff, Air Vice-Marshal Gerard Mayhew, CBE

MANAGEMENT BOARD
Permanent Secretary, Stephen Lovegrove
Members, Lt.-Gen. Doug Chalmers *(Deputy Chief of Defence Staff (Military Strategy and Operations));* Prof. Hugh Durrant-Whyte *(Chief Scientific Adviser);* Charlie Forte *(Chief Information Officer);* Prof. Robin Grimes *(Chief Scientific Adviser (Nuclear));* Julian Kelly *(Nuclear);* Cat Little *(Finance);* Lt.-Gen. Richard Nugee, CVO, CBE *(Chief of Defence People);* Lt.-Gen. Mark Poffley, KCB, OBE *(Deputy Chief of Defence Staff (Financial and Military Capability));* Peter Watkins, CBE *(Strategy and International)*

Non-Executive Members, Sir Gerry Grimstone *(Lead);* Simon Henry; Danuta Gray; Paul Skinner, CBE

DEPARTMENT FOR DIGITAL, CULTURE, MEDIA AND SPORT
100 Parliament Street, London SW1A 2BQ
T 020-7211 6000 E enquiries@culture.gov.uk W www.gov.uk/government/organisations/department-for-digital-culture-media-sport

The Department for Digital, Culture, Media and Sport (DCMS) was established in July 1997 (as the Department for Culture, Media and Sport) and aims to improve the quality of life for all those in the UK through cultural and sporting activities while championing the tourism, creative and leisure industries. It is responsible for government policy relating to the arts, sport, the National Lottery, tourism, libraries, museums and galleries, broadcasting, creative industries – including film and the music industry – press freedom and regulation, licensing, gambling, the historic environment, telecommunications and online and media ownership and mergers. In July 2017, the department was rebranded to reflect its growing commitment and responsibility regarding digital infrastructure, communication and cyber security.

The department is also responsible for 43 agencies and public bodies that help deliver the department's strategic aims and objectives, the listing of historic buildings and scheduling of ancient monuments, the export licensing of cultural goods, and the management of the Government Art Collection and the Royal Parks (its sole executive agency). It has the responsibility for humanitarian assistance in the event of a disaster, as well as for the organisation of the annual Remembrance Day ceremony at the Cenotaph. In September 2012, the Government Equalities Office became part of DCMS, having previously been part of the Home Office.

Secretary of State for Digital, Culture, Media and Sport, Rt. Hon. Jeremy Wright, QC, MP
Parliamentary Private Secretary, Alex Burghart, MP
Special Advisers, Alexander Jackman; Lucy Noakes
Minister of State, Margot James, MP *(Digital and the Creative Industries)*
Parliamentary Under-Secretary of State, Tracey Crouch, MP *(Sport and Civil Society)*
Parliamentary Under-Secretary of State, Michael Ellis, MP *(Arts, Heritage and Tourism)*
Parliamentary Under-Secretary of State, Lord Ashton of Hyde

MANAGEMENT BOARD
Permanent Secretary, Dame Sue Owen, DCB
Members, Clare Dove, OBE *(Voluntary, Community and Social Enterprise Representative);* Matthew Gould *(Digital and Media);* Helen Judge *(Performance and Strategy);* Tim Sparrow *(Finance Director)*
Non-Executive Members, Charles Alexander *(Lead);* Matthew Campbell-Hill; Neil Mendoza; Fields Wicker-Miurin, OBE

DEPARTMENT FOR EDUCATION
20 Great Smith Street, London SW1P 3BT
T 0370-000 2288 W www.gov.uk/government/organisations/department-for-education

The Department for Education (DfE) was established in May 2010 in place of the Department for Children, Schools and Families (DCSF), in order to refocus the department on its core purpose of supporting teaching and learning. The department is responsible for education and children's services, while the Department for Business, Energy and

Industrial Strategy is responsible for higher education. The DfE is supported by 19 executive agencies and public bodies.

The department's objectives include the expansion of the academies programme, to allow schools to apply to become independent of their local authority, and the introduction of the free schools programme, to allow any suitable proposers, such as parents, businesses or charities, to set up their own school.

Secretary of State for Education, Rt. Hon. Damian Hinds, MP
Parliamentary Private Secretary, Simon Hoare, MP
Special Advisers, Meg Powell-Chandler; Jon Yates
Minister of State, Rt. Hon. Nick Gibb, MP *(School Standards)*
Minister of State, Sam Gyimah, MP *(Universities, Science, Research and Innovation)**
Minister of State, Rt. Hon. Anne Milton, MP *(Apprenticeships and Skills)*
Parliamentary Private Secretaries, Alex Chalk, MP; David Warburton, MP
Parliamentary Under-Secretary of State, Lord Agnew of Oulton *(School System)*
Parliamentary Under-Secretary of State, Nadhim Zahawi, MP *(Children and Families)*

* Jointly with the Department for Business, Energy and Industrial Strategy

MANAGEMENT BOARD
Permanent Secretary, Jonathan Slater
Members, Mike Green *(Chief Operating Officer, Insight, Resources and Transformation);* Paul Kett *(Director-General, Education Standards);* Philippa Lloyd *(Director-General, Higher and Further Education);* Andrew McCully *(Director-General, Infrastructure and Funding);* Indra Morris *(Director-General, Social Care, Mobility and Equalities);* Howard Orme, CB *(Chief Financial and Operating Officer, Insight, Resources and Transformation)*
Non-Executive Members, Richard Pennycook *(Lead);* Ian Ferguson, CBE; Baroness Ruby McGregor-Smith, CBE

GOVERNMENT EQUALITIES OFFICE
20 Great Smith Street, London SW1P 3BT
T 0370-000 2288 W www.gov.uk/government/organisations/government-equalities-office

The Government Equalities Office (GEO) is responsible for the government's overall strategy on equality. Its work includes leading the development of a more integrated approach on equality across government with the aim of improving equality and reducing discrimination and disadvantage for all. The office is also responsible for leading policy on gender equality, sexual orientation and transgender equality matters.

Minister for Women and Equalities, Rt. Hon. Penny Mordaunt, MP
Minister for Women, Victoria Atkins, MP
Minister for Equalities, Baroness Williams of Trafford
Director, Hilary Spencer

DEPARTMENT FOR ENVIRONMENT, FOOD AND RURAL AFFAIRS
Nobel House, 17 Smith Square, London SW1P 3JR
T 03459-335577 E defra.helpline@defra.gsi.gov.uk
W www.gov.uk/government/organisations/department-for-environment-food-rural-affairs

The Department for Environment, Food and Rural Affairs (DEFRA) is responsible for government policy on the environment, rural matters and farming and food production. In association with the agriculture departments of the Scottish government, the National Assembly for Wales and the Northern Ireland Office, the department is responsible for negotiations in the EU on the common agricultural and fisheries policies, and for single European market questions relating to its responsibilities. Its remit includes international agricultural and food trade policy.

The department's five strategic priorities are climate change adaptation; sustainable consumption and production; the protection of natural resources and the countryside; sustainable rural communities; and sustainable farming and food, including animal health and welfare. DEFRA, which is supported by 33 executive agencies and public bodies, is also the lead government department for emergencies in animal and plant diseases, flooding, food and water supply, dealing with the consequences of a chemical, biological, radiological or nuclear incident, and other threats to the environment.

Secretary of State for Environment, Food and Rural Affairs, Rt. Hon. Michael Gove, MP
Parliamentary Private Secretary, Kevin Hollinrake, MP
Special Advisers, Henry Cook; Josh Grimstone; James Starkie
Minister of State, George Eustice, MP *(Agriculture, Fisheries and Food)*
Parliamentary Private Secretary, Rebecca Pow, MP
Parliamentary Under-Secretary of State, Thérèse Coffey, MP *(Environment)*
Parliamentary Under-Secretary of State, David Rutley, MP
Parliamentary Under-Secretary of State, Lord Gardiner of Kimble *(Rural Affairs and Biosecurity)*

MANAGEMENT BOARD
Permanent Secretary, Clare Moriarty
Members, Betsy Bassis *(Chief Operating Officer);* Emma Howard Boyd; Prof. Ian Boyd *(Chief Scientific Adviser);* Tamara Finkelstein *(Strategy, EU Exit and Delivery);* David Kennedy *(Food, Farming and Biosecurity);* Sonia Phippard *(Environment, Rural and Marine);* Andrew Sells
Non-Executive Members, Henry Dimbleby *(Lead);* Elizabeth Buchanan; Colin Day; Ben Goldsmith

DEPARTMENT FOR EXITING THE EUROPEAN UNION
9 Downing Street, London SW1A 2AG
T 020-7276 0432 W www.gov.uk/government/organisations/department-for-exiting-the-european-union

The Department for Exiting the European Union (DEEU) was formed by the prime minister Theresa May in July 2016 after the UK voted to leave the European Union in a referendum on 23 June 2016. The DEEU is responsible for overseeing negotiations to leave the EU and establishing the future relationship of the UK with the EU.

The department has four main responsibilities: to support the UK's negotiations to leave the EU and to establish the future relationship between the UK and the EU; to work closely with the UK's devolved administrations, Parliament, and a range of other interested parties on the approach to the negotiations; to conduct the negotiations in support of the prime minister including supporting bilateral discussions on exiting the EU with other European countries; and to lead and coordinate cross-government work to seize the opportunities and ensure a smooth process of exit on positive terms.

Secretary of State for Exiting the European Union, Rt. Hon. Dominic Raab, MP
Parliamentary Private Secretary, vacant
Special Advisers, Nick de Bois; Stephanie Lis
Minister of State, Lord Callanan
Parliamentary Under-Secretary of State, Suella Braverman, MP
Parliamentary Under-Secretary of State, Christopher Heaton-Harris, MP
Parliamentary Under-Secretary of State, Robin Walker, MP

MANAGEMENT BOARD
Permanent Secretary, Philip Rycroft
Members, Matt Baugh *(Director of the Negotiation Coordination Unit);* Rhys Bowen *(International Agreements and Trade);* Simon Case *(Director-General);* Anna Clunes *(Institutions and Member States);* Alex Ellis, *(Director-General);* Sarah Healey *(Director-General);* Chris Hobley *(Director of Market Access and Budget);* Chris Jones *(Justice, Security and Migration);* Joanna Key *(Legislation and Constitution);* Helen Mills *(Human Resources and Corporate Centre);* Richard Ney *(Finance and Corporate Centre);* Eoin Parker *(Director of Market Access and Budget);* Nathan Phillips *(Planning and Analysis);* James Roscoe, MVO *(Communications and Stakeholders);* Tom Shinner *(Policy and Delivery Coordination);* Susannah Storey *(Acting Director-General)*
Non-Executive Members, Susan Hooper; Margaret Stephens

FOREIGN AND COMMONWEALTH OFFICE
King Charles Street, London SW1A 2AH
T 020-7008 1500 E fcocorrespondence@fco.gov.uk
W www.gov.uk/government/organisations/
foreign-commonwealth-office

The Foreign and Commonwealth Office (FCO) provides the means of communication between the British government and other governments – and international governmental organisations – on all matters falling within the field of international relations. The FCO employs over 14,000 people in nearly 270 places across the world through a network of embassies and consulates, which help to protect and promote national interests. FCO diplomats are skilled in understanding and influencing what is happening abroad, supporting British citizens who are travelling and living overseas, helping to manage migration into Britain, promoting British trade and other interests abroad and encouraging foreign investment in the UK. The FCO is supported by ten executive agencies and public bodies.

Secretary of State for Foreign and Commonwealth Affairs, Rt. Hon. Jeremy Hunt, MP
Parliamentary Private Secretary, vacant
Special Advisers, Ed Jones, Christina Robinson, Tim Smith
Minister of State, Rt. Hon. Sir Alan Duncan, KCMG, MP *(Europe and the Americas)*
Minister of State, Rt. Hon. Alistair Burt, MP *(Middle East)**
Minister of State, Rt. Hon. Harriett Baldwin, MP *(Africa)**
Minister of State, Rt. Hon Mark Field, MP *(Asia and the Pacific)*
Minister of State, Lord Ahmad of Wimbledon *(Commonwealth and the UN)*
Parliamentary Private Secretary, Robert Courts, MP
Special Representatives, Lord Ahmad of Wimbledon *(Prime Minister's Special Representative on Preventing Sexual Violence in Conflict);* Gareth Bayley *(Afghanistan and Pakistan);* Nick Bridge *(Climate Change);* Tim Cole *(Migration Envoy);* Prof. Robin Grimes *(Chief Scientific Adviser);* Simon Mustard *(Special Envoy for the African Great Lakes and Head of Southern and Central African Department);* Rt. Hon. Lord Pickles *(UK Special Envoy for Post-Holocaust Issues);* Joanna Roper, CMG *(Special Envoy for Gender Equality);* Chris Trott *(Sudan and South Sudan)*
* Jointly with the Department for International Development

MANAGEMENT BOARD
Permanent Under-Secretary and Head of the Diplomatic Service, Sir Simon McDonald, KCMG, KCVO
Members, Philip Barton, CMG *(Consular and Security);* Alison Blake, CMG *(Overseas Network Representative);* Deborah Bronnert, CMG *(Economic and Global Issues);* Lindsay Croisdale-Appleby *(EU Exit);* Jill Gallard *(Human Resources);* Peter Jones *(Chief Operating Officer);* Sir Iain

Macleod, KCMG *(Legal);* Andrew Sanderson *(Finance);* Liane Saunders *(Strategy and Strategic Programmes Coordinator);* Dr Christian Turner, CMG *(Deputy National Security Adviser);* Simon Wren, CBE *(Communications)*
Non-Executive Members, Miranda Curtis *(Lead);* Gaenor Bagley; Sir Edward Lister; Warren Tucker

DEPARTMENT OF HEALTH AND SOCIAL CARE
Richmond House, 79 Whitehall, London SW1A 2NS
T 020-7210 4850 W www.gov.uk/government/organisations/
department-of-health-and-social-care

The Department of Health and Social Care (DHSC) leads, shapes and funds health and social care in England, making sure people have the support, care and treatment they need and that this is delivered in a compassionate, respectful and dignified manner.

The DHSC leads across health and care by creating national policies and legislation to meet current and future challenges. It provides funding, assures the delivery and continuity of services and accounts to parliament in a way that represents the best interests of patients, the public and the taxpayer. The DHSC is supported by 28 executive agencies and public bodies.

Secretary of State for Health and Social Care, Rt. Hon. Matthew Hancock, MP
Parliamentary Private Secretary, Nigel Huddleston, MP
Special Advisers, Lottie Dominiczak: James Njoku-Goodwin
Minister of State, Stephen Barclay, MP *(Health)*
Minister of State, Caroline Dinenage, MP *(Care)*
Parliamentary Private Secretary, Maggie Throup, MP
Parliamentary Under-Secretary of State, Steve Brine, MP *(Public Health and Primary Care)*
Parliamentary Under-Secretary of State, Jackie Doyle-Price, MP *(Mental Health and Inequalities)*
Parliamentary Under-Secretary of State, Lord O'Shaughnessy *(Lords)*

DEPARTMENTAL BOARD
Permanent Secretary, Sir Chris Wormald, KCB
Members, Prof. Dame Sally Davies, DBE *(Chief Medical Officer);* Jonathan Marron *(Community and Social Care);* Lee McDonough *(Acute Care and Workforce);* Clara Swinson *(Global and Public Health);* Prof. Chris Whitty *(Chief Scientific Adviser);* David Williams *(Finance and Group Operations)*

HOME OFFICE
2 Marsham Street, London SW1P 4DF
T 020-7035 4848 E public.enquiries@homeoffice.gsi.gov.uk
W www.gov.uk/government/organisations/home-office

The Home Office deals with those internal affairs in England and Wales which have not been assigned to other government departments. The Secretary of State for the Home Department is the link between the Queen and the public, and exercises certain powers on her behalf, including that of the royal pardon.

The Home Office aims to build a safe, just and tolerant society and to maintain and enhance public security and protection; to support and mobilise communities so that they are able to shape policy and improvement for their locality, overcome nuisance and anti-social behaviour, maintain and enhance social cohesion and enjoy their homes and public spaces peacefully; to deliver departmental policies and responsibilities fairly, effectively and efficiently; and to make the best use of resources. These objectives reflect the priorities of the government and the home secretary in areas of crime, citizenship and communities, namely to work on the problems caused by illegal drug use; shape the alcohol strategy, policy and licensing conditions; keep the UK safe from the threat of terrorism; reduce and prevent crime, and ensure people feel safe in their homes and communities; secure the UK border and control immigration; consider applications to enter and stay in the UK; issue passports and visas; and to support visible, responsible and accountable policing by empowering the public and freeing up the police to fight crime.

The Home Office delivers these aims through the immigration services, its 31 executive agencies and non-departmental public bodies, and by working with partners in private, public and voluntary sectors, individuals and communities. The home secretary is also the link between the UK government and the governments of the Channel Islands and the Isle of Man.

Secretary of State for the Home Department, Rt. Hon. Sajid Javid, MP *(Ministerial Champion for the Midlands Engine)*
Parliamentary Private Secretary, Tom Pursglove, MP
Special Advisers, Samuel Coates; James Hedgeland; Salma Shah
Minister of State, Rt. Hon. Caroline Nokes, MP *(Immigration)*
Parliamentary Private Secretaries, Rachel McClean, MP; David Morris, MP
Minister of State, Rt. Hon. Ben Wallace, MP *(Security and Economic Crime)*
Minister of State, Rt. Hon. Nick Hurd, MP *(Policing and the Fire Service)*
Minister of State, Baroness Williams of Trafford* *(Countering Extremism)*
Parliamentary Under-Secretary of State, Victoria Atkins, MP† *(Crime, Safeguarding and Vulnerability)*

*Alongside role as Minister for Equalities
† Alongside role as Minister for Women

MANAGEMENT BOARD
Permanent Secretary, Sir Philip Rutnam, KCB
Second Permanent Secretary, Patsy Wilkinson
Members, Joanna Davinson *(Chief Digital, Data and Technology Officer)*; Peter Fish *(Legal)*; Charu Gorasia *(Capabilities and Resources)*; Tyson Hepple *(Immigration Enforcement)*; Tom Hurd *(Security and Counter-Terrorism)*; Paula Leach *(Chief People Officer)*; Paul Lincoln *(Border Force)*; Scott McPherson *(Crime, Policing and Fire Group)*; Mark Thomson *(UK Visas and Immigration; Director-General HM Passport Office)*; Andy Tighe *(Communications)*; Glyn Williams *(Boarders, Immigration and Citizenship)*
Non-Executive Members, Sue Langley, OBE *(Lead)*; Suzy Levy; Nicholas Shott; John Studzinski, CBE

MINISTRY OF HOUSING, COMMUNITIES AND LOCAL GOVERNMENT
2 Marsham Street, London SW1P 4DF
T 0303-444 0000 W www.gov.uk/government/organisations/ministry-of-housing-communities-and-local-government

The Ministry of Housing, Communities and Local Government was formed in January 2018 uniting housing, communities and civil renewal functions with responsibility for regeneration, neighbourhood renewal and local government. The ministry ensures that the Fire and Rescue services have the resources they need to reduce the number of deaths from fire, promote fire prevention activity and respond swiftly to national emergencies. The ministry is supported by 12 executive agencies and public bodies.

Secretary of State for Housing, Communities and Local Government, Rt. Hon. James Brokenshire, MP
Parliamentary Private Secretary, Chris Philp, MP

Special Advisers, Liam Booth-Smith; Peter Cardwell; Lee Scott
Minister of State, Kit Malthouse, MP *(Housing)*
Parliamentary Under-Secretary of State, Jake Berry, MP *(Northern Powerhouse and Local Growth)*
Parliamentary Under-Secretary of State, Heather Wheeler, MP *(Housing and Homelessness)*
Parliamentary Under-Secretary of State, Nigel Adams, MP
Parliamentary Under-Secretary of State, Rishi Sunak, MP *(Local Government)*
Parliamentary Under-Secretary of State, Lord Bourne of Aberystwyth *(Faith)**

* Jointly held with the Northern Ireland Office

MANAGEMENT BOARD
Permanent Secretary, Melanie Dawes, CB
Members, Lise-Anne Boissiere *(Director, Strategy, Communications and Private Office)*; Jo Farrar *(Director-General, Local Government and Public Services)*; Christine Hewitt *(Director, People, Capability and Change)*; Rachel McLean *(Director-General, Chief Financial Officer)*; Simon Ridley *(Director-General, Decentralisation and Growth)*
Non-Executive Members, Nick Markham *(Lead)*; Pam Chesters, CBE; Daniel Morley; Mary Ney

SPECIAL REPRESENTATIVES
UK Special Envoy for post-Holocaust Issues, Rt. Hon. Lord Pickles

DEPARTMENT FOR INTERNATIONAL DEVELOPMENT
22 Whitehall, London SW1A 2EG T 020-7023 0000
Abercrombie House, Eaglesham Road, East Kilbride, Glasgow G75 8EA T 01355-844000
Public Enquiries 0300-200 3343 E enquiry@dfid.gov.uk
W www.gov.uk/government/organisations/department-for-international-development

The Department for International Development (DFID) is responsible for promoting sustainable development and reducing poverty. The central focus of the government's policy is to honour the UK's international commitments and take action to achieve the United Nations' Global Goals. The DFID seeks to make British aid more effective by improving transparency, openness and value for money; target British international development policy on economic growth and wealth creation; improve the coherence and performance of British international development policy in fragile and conflict-affected countries; improve the lives of girls and women through better education and a greater choice on family planning; prevent violence against girls and women in the developing world; and help to prevent climate change and encourage adaptation and low-carbon growth in developing countries.

The DFID works in countries across Africa, Asia and the Middle East. It also has regional programmes in Africa, Asia and the Caribbean, and development relationships with 3 aid dependent UK Overseas Territories – St Helena, the Pitcairn Islands and Montserrat. In addition to working directly in countries, DFID also gives UK Aid through multi-country global programmes and core contributions to multilateral institutions, including the World Bank, United Nations agencies and the European Commission. The department, which is supported by three agencies and public bodies, has headquarters in London and East Kilbride, offices in many developing countries, and staff based in British embassies and high commissions around the world.

Secretary of State for International Development, Rt. Hon. Penny Mordaunt, MP*
Parliamentary Private Secretary, Michael Tomlinson, MP

Special Adviser, Laura Round
Minister of State, Rt. Hon. Harriett Baldwin, MP †
Minister of State, Rt. Hon. Alistair Burt, MP†
Minister of State, Rt. Hon. Lord Bates
Parliamentary Private Secretary, Craig Tracey, MP

* Alongside role as Minister for Women and Equalities
† Jointly with the Foreign and Commonwealth Office

MANAGEMENT BOARD
Permanent Secretary, Matthew Rycroft, CBE
Members, Lindy Cameron *(Country Programmes);* Juliet Chua *(Finance and Coperate Performance);* Nick Dyer *(Economic Development and International; Policy and Global Programmes)*
Non-Executive Members, Sally Jones-Evans; Richard Keys; Tim Robinson

CDC GROUP
123 Victoria Street, London SW1E 6DE
T 020-7963 4700 E enquiries@cdcgroup.com
W www.cdcgroup.com

Founded in 1948, CDC is the UK's Development Finance Institution wholly owned by the UK government. It invests to create jobs and build businesses in developing countries in Africa and South Asia. In 2017 CDC's new investment commitments totalled £1.05bn to 715 businesses in Africa and 338 businesses in South Asia, helping to create new jobs across these regions. CDC is a public limited company with net assets of £5.1bn.

Chair, Graham Wrigley
Chief Executive, Nick O'Donohoe

DEPARTMENT FOR INTERNATIONAL TRADE
King Charles Street, Whitehall, London SW1A 2AH
T 020-7215 5000 W www.gov.uk/government/organisations/department-for-international-trade

The Department for International Trade was formed by the prime minister Theresa May in July 2016 following the UK referendum to leave the European Union. The department is responsible for promoting British trade around the world, striking and extending trade agreements between the UK and non-EU states. It is supported by two executive agencies and public bodies.

Secretary of State for International Trade and President of the Board of Trade, Rt. Hon. Liam Fox, MP
Parliamentary Private Secretary, Michelle Donelan, MP
Special Advisers, David Goss; Amy Tinley
Minister of State, George Hollingbery, MP *(Trade Policy)*
Minister of State, Baroness Fairhead, CBE *(Trade and Export Promotion)*
Parliamentary Private Secretary, Mike Wood, MP
Parliamentary Under-Secretary of State, Graham Stuart, MP

MANAGEMENT BOARD
Permanent Secretary, Antonia Romeo
Second Permanent Secretary and Chief Trade Negotiation Adviser, Crawford Falconer
Members, John Alty *(Trade Policy);* John Mahon *(Exports);* Mark Slaughter *(Investment);* Louis Taylor *(Chief Executive, UK Export Finance);* Catherine Vaughan *(Chief Operating Officer)*
Non-Executive Members, Simon Walker *(Lead);* Julie Currie, Noel Harwerth, Dr Pippa Malmgren

MINISTRY OF JUSTICE
102 Petty France, London SW1H 9AJ
T 020-3334 3555
W www.gov.uk/government/organisations/ministry-of-justice

The Ministry of Justice (MoJ) was established in May 2007. MoJ is headed by the Lord Chancellor and Secretary of State for Justice who is responsible for improvements to the justice system so that it better serves the public. He is also responsible for some areas of constitutional policy.

The MoJ's key priorities are to reduce reoffending by using the skills of the public, private and voluntary sectors; reduce youth crime by putting education at the centre of youth justice; build a prison system that delivers maximum value for money; reduce the cost of legal aid and ensure it helps those cases that genuinely require it; and to improve the way the courts are run and put the needs of victims first. The MoJ has a budget of around £9bn and is supported by 33 executive agencies and public bodies to achieve its targets.

The Lord Chancellor and Secretary of State for Justice is the government minister responsible to parliament for the judiciary, the court system and prisons and probation. The Lord Chief Justice has been the head of the judiciary since 2006.

MoJ incorporates HM Prison and Probation Service; HM Courts and Tribunals Service; the Legal Aid Agency; and the Youth Justice Board.

Lord Chancellor and Secretary of State for Justice, Rt. Hon. David Gauke, MP
Parliamentary Private Secretary, Peter Heaton Jones, MP
Special Advisers, James Dowling; Idil Oyman
Minister of State, Rory Stewart, OBE, MP *(Prisons and Probation)*
Parliamentary Private Secretary, Julian Knight, MP
Parliamentary Under-Secretary of State, Edward Argar, MP *(Youth Justice, Victims, Female Offenders and Family Justice)*
Parliamentary Under-Secretary of State, Lucy Frazer, QC, MP *(Court Services)*
HM Advocate-General for Scotland and MoJ Spokesperson for the Lords, Rt. Hon. Lord Keen of Elie, QC

MANAGEMENT BOARD
Permanent Secretary, Richard Heaton
Members, Susan Acland-Hood *(Chief Executive and Board member, HM Courts and Tribunals Service);* Matthew Coats, CB *(Chief Operating Officer);* Mike Driver, CB *(Chief Financial Officer and Head of the Government Finance Function);* Justin Russell *(Prisons, Offender and Youth Justice Policy);* Mark Sweeney *(Justice and Courts Policy Group)*
Non-Executive Members, Mark Rawlinson *(Lead);* Nick Campsie; Shirley Cooper; Liz Doherty

NORTHERN IRELAND OFFICE
1 Horse Guards Road, London SW1A 2HQ
Stormont House, Stormont Estate, Belfast BT4 3SH
T 028-9052 0700 E comms@nio.gov.uk
W www.gov.uk/government/organisations/northern-ireland-office

The Northern Ireland Office was established in 1972, when the Northern Ireland (Temporary Provisions) Act transferred the legislative and executive powers of the Northern Ireland parliament and government to the UK parliament and a secretary of state. Under the terms of the 1998 Good Friday Agreement, power was devolved to the Northern Ireland Assembly in 1999. The assembly took on responsibility for the relevant areas of work previously undertaken by the departments of the Northern Ireland Office, covering agriculture and rural development, the environment, regional development, social development, education, higher education, training and employment, enterprise, trade and investment, culture, arts and leisure, health, social services, public safety and finance and personnel. In October 2002 the Northern Ireland Assembly was suspended and Northern Ireland returned to direct rule, but despite repeated setbacks, devolution was restored on 8 May 2007. On 9 January 2017 Martin McGuinness resigned as Deputy First Minister of Northern Ireland. Under the joint protocols that govern the power-sharing agreement, if either the first minister or the deputy resigns and a replacement is not nominated by the relevant party within seven days, then a snap election must be called. The assembly was formerly dissolved at midnight on 25 January 2017 and the most recent assembly elections were held on 2 March 2017. The assembly failed to appoint the executive committee of ministers in charge of the nine government departments within the three-week deadline following the election and, to date, the devolved government in Northern Ireland has yet to be restored. For further details, see Devolved Government.

The Northern Ireland Office is supported by three executive agencies and public bodies and is currently responsible for overseeing the devolution settlement; representing Northern Ireland interests within the UK government and similarly representing the UK government in Northern Ireland; working in partnership with the Northern Ireland Executive for a stable prosperous Northern Ireland; and supporting and implementing political agreements to increase stability.

Secretary of State for Northern Ireland, Rt. Hon. Karen Bradley, MP
Parliamentary Private Secretary, Matt Warman, MP
Special Advisers, Jonathan Caine; Romilly Dennys; Kris Hopkins
Minister of State, Shailesh Vara, MP
Parliamentary Under-Secretary of State, Lord Duncan of Springbank*
Permanent Secretary, Sir Jonathan Stephens

*Jointly with the Office of the Secretary of State for Scotland

OFFICE OF THE ADVOCATE-GENERAL FOR SCOTLAND

Dover House, Whitehall, London SW1A 2AU
T 020-7270 6770
Office of the Solicitor to the Advocate-General, Victoria Quay, Edinburgh EH6 6QQ T 0131-244 0359
E enquiries@advocategeneral.gsi.gov.uk
W www.gov.uk/government/organisations/ office-of-the-advocate-general-for-scotland

The Advocate-General for Scotland is one of the three law officers of the crown, alongside the Attorney-General and the Solicitor-General for England and Wales. He is the legal adviser to the UK government on Scottish law and is supported by staff in the Office of the Advocate-General for Scotland. The office is divided into the Legal Secretariat, based mainly in London, and the Office of the Solicitor to the Advocate-General, based in Edinburgh.

The post was created as a consequence of the constitutional changes set out in the Scotland Act 1998, which created a devolved Scottish parliament. The Lord Advocate and the Solicitor-General for Scotland then became part of the Scottish government and the Advocate-General took over their previous role as legal adviser to the UK government on Scots law. See also Devolved Government and Ministry of Justice.

HM Advocate-General for Scotland and MoJ Spokesperson for the Lords, Rt. Hon. Lord Keen of Elie, QC
Private Secretary, Craig Chalcraft

MANAGEMENT BOARD
Director and Solicitor to the Advocate-General, Neil Taylor
Members, Jim Logie (Head of HMRC Division); Ruaraidh Macniven (Head of Advisory and Legislation Division); Fiona Robertson (Head of Litigation Division)

OFFICE OF THE SECRETARY OF STATE FOR SCOTLAND

Dover House, Whitehall, London SW1A 2AU
1 Melville Crescent, Edinburgh EH3 7HW
T 0131-244 9010 E enquiries@scotlandoffice.gsi.gov.uk
W www.gov.uk/government/organisations/ office-of-the-secretary-of-state-for-scotland

The Office of the Secretary of State for Scotland represents Scottish interests within the UK government in matters reserved to the UK parliament. The Secretary of State for Scotland maintains the stability of the devolution settlement for Scotland; delivers secondary legislation under the Scotland Act 1998; is responsible for the conduct and funding of the Scottish parliament elections; manages the Scottish vote provision and authorises the monthly payment of funds from the UK consolidated fund to the Scottish consolidated fund; and publishes regular information on the state of the Scottish economy.

Matters reserved to the UK parliament include the constitution, foreign affairs, defence, international development, the civil service, financial and economic matters, national security, immigration and nationality, misuse of drugs, trade and industry, various aspects of energy regulation (eg coal, electricity, oil, gas and nuclear energy), various aspects of transport, social security, employment, abortion, genetics, surrogacy, medicines, broadcasting and equal opportunities. Devolved matters include health and social work, education and training, local government and housing, justice and police, agriculture, forestry, fisheries, the environment, tourism, sports, heritage, economic development and internal transport. It is supported by one public body. See also Devolved Government and Ministry of Justice.

Secretary of State for Scotland, Rt. Hon. David Mundell, MP
Parliamentary Private Secretary, Alberto Costa, MP
Special Advisers, Jennifer Donellan; Magnus Gardham
Principal Private Secretary, Victoria Jones
Parliamentary Under-Secretary of State, Rt. Hon. Lord Duncan of Springbank*

* Jointly with the Office of the Secretary of State for Northern Ireland

MANAGEMENT BOARD
Director, Gillian McGregor, CBE
Members, Victoria Bowman, (Corporate Services); Laura Crawforth (Joint Deputy Director, Constitutional Policy); Rebecca Hackett (Policy Delivery, Relationship Management); Rachel Irvine (Joint Deputy Director, Constitutional Policy); Flavia Paterson (Communications)

DEPARTMENT FOR TRANSPORT

Great Minster House, 33 Horseferry Road, London SW1P 4DR
T 0300-330 3000 W www.gov.uk/government/organisations/ department-for-transport

The Department for Transport (DfT) works with its agencies and partners to support the transport network that helps the UK's businesses and gets people and goods travelling around the country. The DfT plans and invests in transport infrastructure to keep the UK on the move. DfT is supported by 21 executive agencies and public bodies.

Secretary of State for Transport, Rt. Hon. Chris Grayling, MP
Parliamentary Private Secretary, James Heappey, MP
Special Advisers, Simon Jones; Emma Silver

Minister of State, Jo Johnson, MP *(London)*
Parliamentary Private Secretary, Chris Green, MP
Parliamentary Under-Secretary of State, Nusrat Ghani, MP
Parliamentary Under-Secretary of State, Jesse Norman, MP
Parliamentary Under-Secretary of State, Baroness Sugg, CBE

MANAGEMENT BOARD
Permanent Secretary, Bernadette Kelly, CB
Members, Prof. Phil Blythe *(Chief Scientific Adviser);* Lucy
  Chadwick *(International, Security and Environment Group);*
  Tricia Hayes *(Roads, Devolution and Motoring Group);* Nick
  Joyce *(Resources and Strategy Group);* Clive Maxwell *(High
  Speed Rail and Major Projects);* Polly Payne *(Rail Group);*
  Brett Welch *(Legal Director)*
Non-Executive Members, Ian King *(Lead);* Richard Aitken-
  Davies; Richard Keys; Tony Poulter; Tracy Westall

HM TREASURY
1 Horse Guards Road, London SW1A 2HQ
T 020-7270 5000 E public.enquiries@hmtreasury.gsi.gov.uk
W www.gov.uk/government/organisations/hm-treasury

HM Treasury is the country's economics and finance ministry, and is responsible for formulating and implementing the government's financial and economic policy. It aims to raise the rate of sustainable growth, boost prosperity, and provide the conditions necessary for universal economic and employment opportunities. The Office of the Lord High Treasurer has been continuously in commission for over 200 years. The Lord High Commissioners of HM Treasury are the First Lord of the Treasury (who is also the prime minister), the Chancellor of the Exchequer and five junior lords. This board of commissioners is assisted at present by the chief secretary, the parliamentary secretary (who is also the government chief whip in the House of Commons), the financial secretary, the economic secretary, the exchequer secretary and the commercial secretary. The prime minister as first lord is not primarily concerned with the day-to-day aspects of Treasury business; neither are the parliamentary secretary and the junior lords as government whips. Treasury business is managed by the Chancellor of the Exchequer and the other Treasury ministers, assisted by the permanent secretary.

The chief secretary is responsible for public expenditure, including spending reviews and strategic planning; in-year control; public-sector pay and pensions; Annually Managed Expenditure and welfare reform; efficiency in public services; procurement and capital investment. He also has responsibility for the Treasury's interest in devolution.

The financial secretary has responsibility for financial services policy including banking and financial services reform and regulation; financial stability; city competitiveness; wholesale and retail markets in the UK, Europe and internationally; and the Financial Services Authority. His other responsibilities include banking support; bank lending; UK Financial Investments; Equitable Life; and personal savings and pensions policy. He also provides support to the chancellor on EU and wider international finance issues.

The exchequer secretary is a title only used occasionally, normally when the post of paymaster-general is allocated to a minister outside of the Treasury. The exchequer secretary's responsibilities include strategic oversight of the UK tax system; corporate and small business taxation, with input from the commercial secretary; departmental minister for HM Revenue and Customs and the Valuation Office Agency; and lead minister on European and international tax issues.

The economic secretary's responsibilities include environmental issues such as taxation of transport, international climate change and energy; North Sea oil taxation; tax credits and child poverty; assisting the chief

secretary on welfare reform; charities and the voluntary sector; excise duties and gambling; stamp duty land tax; EU Budget; the Royal Mint; and departmental minister for HM Treasury Group.

HM Treasury is supported by 13 executive agencies and public bodies.

Prime Minister and First Lord of the Treasury, Rt. Hon. Theresa
  May, MP
Parliamentary Private Secretary, Seema Kennedy, MP
Special Advisers, Gavin Barwell; Nikki Da Costa; Robbie
  Gibb; James Marshall; Joanna Penn
Chancellor of the Exchequer, Rt. Hon. Philip Hammond, MP
Parliamentary Private Secretary, Kwasi Kwarteng, MP
Special Advisers, Duncan McCourt; Poppy Trowbridge; Giles
  Winn
Chief Secretary to the Treasury, Rt. Hon. Elizabeth Truss, MP
Parliamentary Private Secretary, Scott Mann, MP
Special Adviser, Kane Daniell
Financial Secretary to the Treasury and Paymaster General, Rt.
  Hon. Mel Stride, MP
Economic Secretary to the Treasury, John Glen, MP
Exchequer Secretary to the Treasury, Robert Jenrick, MP
Parliamentary Secretary to the Treasury (Chief Whip), Rt. Hon.
  Julian Smith, MP
Special Advisers, Simon Burton; Thomas Irven
Lords Commissioners of HM Treasury (Whips), Nigel Adams,
  MP*; Mike Freer, MP; Rebecca Harris, MP; Paul
  Maynard, MP; David Rutley, MP†; Craig Whittaker, MP
Assistant Whips, Jo Churchill, MP; Mims Davies, MP‡;
  Michelle Donelan, MP; Nusrat Ghani, MP§; Amanda
  Milling, MP; Wendy Morton, MP; Jeremy Quin, MP; Iain
  Stewart, MP

* alongside role as Under-Secretary of State at the Ministry of Housing, Communities and Local Government
† along role as Under-Secretary of State for Environment, Food and Rural Affairs
‡ alongside role as Under-Secretary of State at the Office of the Secretary of State for Wales
§ alongside role as Under-Secretary of State for Transport

MANAGEMENT BOARD
Permanent Secretary, Sir Tom Scholar, KCB
Second Permanent Secretary, Charles Roxburgh
Executive Members, James Bowler *(Public Spending);* Mark
  Bowman *(International and EU);* Katharine Braddick
  (Financial Services); Mike Driver *(Chief Financial Officer and
  Head of the Government Finance Function);* Clare Lombardelli
  (Director-General and Chief Economic Adviser); Beth Russell
  (Tax and Welfare)
Non-Executive Members, Richard Meddings; Tim Score

UK GOVERNMENT INVESTMENTS
1 Victoria Street, London SW1H 0ET
T 020-7638 9571 E ukgi@citigatedr.co.uk
W www.ukgi.org.uk/

UK Government Investments (UKGI) is the government's centre of expertise in corporate finance and corporate governance. UKGI Limited began operating on 1 April 2016 as a government company, wholly owned by HM Treasury, which brought together the functions of the Shareholder Executive (formerly part of the Department for Business, Energy and Industrial Strategy) and UK Financial Investments. UKGI's principle investments are to: prepare and execute all significant corporate asset sales by the UK government; advise on all major UK government financial interventions into corporate structures; act as shareholder for those arm's length bodies of the UK government that are structured to allow a meaningful shareholder function and for other UK government assets facing complex transformations; and to advise on major UK government negotiations with corporates.

Chief Executive, Mark Russell
Members, Tom Cooper; Michael Harrison; Oliver Holbourn; Henry Lloyd; Roger Lowe; Justin Manson; Candida Morley; Rachel Mortimer *(Chief Operating Officer);* Peter Norton; Robert Razzell *(Chief Financial Officer);* Conrad Smewing; Ceri Smith

OFFICE OF TAX SIMPLIFICATION

HM Treasury, 1 Horse Guards Road, London SW1A 2HQ
T 0300-0585 028 E ots@ots.gsi.gov.uk
W www.gov.uk/government/organisations/
office-of-tax-simplification

The chancellor and exchequer secretary to HM Treasury launched the Office of Tax Simplification (OTS) on 20 July 2010 to provide the government with independent advice on simplifying the UK tax system. The OTS is part of HM Treasury and provides the government with independent advice on simplifying the UK tax system. It carries out projects investigating complex areas of the tax system and makes recommendations to the chancellor in reports which are published on its website.

Chair, Angela Knight, CBE
Tax Director, Paul Morton

ROYAL MINT LTD

PO Box 500, Llantrisant, Pontyclun CF72 8YT
T 01443-222111 W www.royalmint.com

From 1975 the Royal Mint operated as a trading fund and was established as an executive agency in 1990. Since 2010 it has operated as Royal Mint Ltd, a company 100 per cent owned by HM Treasury, with an exclusive contract to supply all coinage for the UK.

The Royal Mint actively competes in world markets for a share of the available circulating coin business and about half of the coins and blanks it produces annually are exported. It is the leading export mint, accounting for around 15 per cent of the world market. The Royal Mint also manufactures special proof and uncirculated quality coins in gold, silver and other metals; military and civil decorations and medals; commemorative and prize medals; and royal and official seals.

Master of the Mint, Chancellor of the Exchequer *(ex officio)*
Chair, Peter Warry
Chief Executive, Anne Jessopp

UK EXPORT FINANCE

1 Horse Guards Road, London SW1A 2HQ
T 020-7271 8010 E customer.service@ukexportfinance.gov.uk
W www.gov.uk/government/organisations/uk-export-finance

UK Export Finance is the UK's export credit agency. It helps UK exporters by providing insurance to them and guarantees to banks to share the risks of providing export finance. Additionally, it can make loans to overseas buyers of goods and services from the UK. UK Export Finance is the operating name of the Export Credits Guarantee Department.

The priorities of UK Export Finance are to fulfil its statutory remit to support exports; operate within the policy and financial objectives established by the government, which includes international obligations; and to recover the maximum amount of debt in respect of claims paid, taking account of the government's policy on debt forgiveness. It is a ministerial department supported by one public body, the Export Guarantees Advisory Council.

Secretary of State for International Trade and President of the Board of Trade, Rt. Hon. Liam Fox, MP

Parliamentary Private Secretary, Michelle Donelan, MP
Special Advisers, David Goss; Amy Tinley
Minister of State, Baroness Fairhead, CBE *(Trade and Export Promotion)*

MANAGEMENT BOARD
Chief Executive, Louis Taylor
Chair, Noel Harwerth
Members, Cameron Fox *(Chief Finance and Operating Officer);* Shane Lynch *(Resources);* Davinder Mann *(Head of Legal Division);* Justin Manson *(UK Government Investments);* Samir Parkash *(Chief Risk Officer);* Gordon Welsh *(Head of the Business Group)*
Non-Executive Members, Shalini Khemka; Amin Mawji, OBE; Oliver Peterken; Lawrence Weiss

OFFICE OF THE SECRETARY OF STATE FOR WALES

Gwydyr House, Whitehall, London SW1A 2NP
T 029-2092 4228 E correspondence@walesoffice.gsi.gov.uk
W www.gov.uk/government/organisations/
office-of-the-secretary-of-state-for-wales

The Office of the Secretary of State for Wales, informally known as the Wales Office, was established in 1999 when most of the powers of the Welsh Office were handed over to the National Assembly for Wales. It is the department of the Secretary of State for Wales, who is the key government figure liaising with the devolved government in Wales and who represents Welsh interests in the cabinet and parliament. The secretary of state has the right to attend and speak at sessions of the National Assembly (and must consult the assembly on the government's legislative programme). *See also* Devolved Government *and* Ministry of Justice.

Secretary of State for Wales, Rt. Hon. Alun Cairns, MP
Parliamentary Private Secretary, Glyn Davies, MP
Special Advisers, Geraint Evans; Sophie Traherne
Principal Private Secretary, Michael Dynan-Oakley
Parliamentary Under-Secretary of State, Lord Bourne of Aberystwyth*
Parliamentary Under-Secretary of State, Mims Davies, MP
Parliamentary Private Secretary, Chris Davies, MP
Director, Glynne Jones
Deputy Director, Geth Williams *(Constitution and Policy)*
* Jointly with the Ministry of Housing, Communities and Local Government

DEPARTMENT FOR WORK AND PENSIONS

Caxton House, Tothill Street, London SW1H 9NA
T 020-3267 5144 E ministers@dwp.gsi.gov.uk
W www.gov.uk/government/organisations/
department-for-work-pensions

The Department for Work and Pensions was formed in June 2001 from parts of the former Department of Social Security, the Department for Education and Employment and the Employment Service. The department helps unemployed people of working age into work, helps employers to fill their vacancies and provides financial support to people unable to help themselves, through back-to-work programmes. The department also administers the child support system, social security benefits and the social fund. In addition, the department has reciprocal social security arrangements with other countries. The department is supported by 14 executive agencies and public bodies.

Secretary of State for Work and Pensions, Rt. Hon. Esther McVey
Parliamentary Private Secretary, Huw Merriman, MP
Special Adviser, Jean-André Prager

Minister of State, Alok Sharma, MP *(Employment)*
Minister of State, Sarah Newton, MP *(Disabled People, Health and Work)*
Parliamentary Private Secretary, Ranil Jayawardena, MP
Parliamentary Under-Secretary of State, Guy Opperman, MP *(Pensions and Financial Inclusion)*
Parliamentary Under-Secretary of State, Justin Tomlinson, MP *(Family Support, Housing and Child Maintenance)*
Parliamentary Under-Secretary of State, Baroness Buscombe *(Lords)*

MANAGEMENT BOARD
Permanent Secretary, Peter Schofield
Members, Debbie Alder *(Human Resources);* Neil Couling, CBE *(Universal Credit Programme);* John-Paul Marks *(Universal Credit Operations);* Jonathan Mills *(Strategy, Policy and Analysis);* Susan Park *(Operations);* Mayank Prakash *(Digital and Information Officer)*

EXECUTIVE AGENCIES

Executive agencies are well-defined business units that carry out services with a clear focus on delivering specific outputs within a framework of accountability to ministers. They can be set up or disbanded without legislation, and they are organisationally independent from the department they are answerable to. In the following list the agencies are shown in the accounts of their sponsor departments. Legally they act on behalf of the relevant secretary of state. Their chief executives also perform the role of accounting officers, which means they are responsible for the money spent by their organisations. Staff employed by agencies are civil servants.

DEPARTMENT FOR BUSINESS, ENERGY AND INDUSTRIAL STRATEGY

COMPANIES HOUSE
Crown Way, Cardiff CF14 3UZ
T 0303-123 4500 E enquiries@companies-house.gov.uk
W www.gov.uk/government/organisations/companies-house
Companies House incorporates and dissolves companies, examines and stores company information delivered under the Companies Act and related legislation; and makes this information available to the public.
Chief Executive, Louise Smyth

THE INSOLVENCY SERVICE
4 Abbey Orchard Street, London SW1P 2HT
T 020-7637 1110
E redundancypaymentsonline@insolvency.gsi.gov.uk
W www.gov.uk/government/organisations/insolvency-service
The role of the service includes administration and investigation of the affairs of bankrupts, individuals subject to debt relief orders, partnerships and companies in compulsory liquidation; dealing with the disqualification of directors in all corporate failures; authorising and regulating the insolvency profession; providing banking and investment services for bankruptcy and liquidation estate funds; assessing and paying statutory entitlement to redundancy payments when an employer cannot, or will not, pay its employees; and advising ministers on insolvency, redundancy and related issues. The service has around 1,700 staff, operating from 22 locations across Great Britain.
Inspector-General and Chief Executive, Sarah Albon

INTELLECTUAL PROPERTY OFFICE
Concept House, Cardiff Road, Newport NP10 8QQ
T 0300-300 2000 E information@ipo.gov.uk
W www.gov.uk/government/organisations/intellectual-property-office
The Intellectual Property Office (an operating name of the Patent Office) was set up in 1852 to act as the UK's sole office for the granting of patents. It was established as an executive agency in 1990 and became a trading fund in 1991. The office is responsible for the granting of intellectual property (IP) rights, which include patents, trade marks, designs and copyright.
Comptroller-General and Chief Executive, Tim Moss

MET OFFICE
FitzRoy Road, Exeter, Devon EX1 3PB
T 0370-900 0100 E enquiries@metoffice.gov.uk
W www.metoffice.gov.uk
The Met Office is the UK's National Weather Service, operating as an executive agency of BEIS, having transferred from the MoD to the Department for Business, Energy and Industrial Strategy in July 2011. It is a world leader in providing weather and climate services, using over 10 million weather observations a day, and employs more than 1,700 people at 60 locations throughout the world.
Interim Chief Executive, Nick Jobling
Chief Scientist, Prof. Stephen Belcher

UK SPACE AGENCY
Polaris House, North Star Avenue, Swindon, Wiltshire SN2 1SZ
T 020-7215 5000 E info@ukspaceagency.bis.gsi.gov.uk
W www.gov.uk/government/organisations/uk-space-agency
The UK Space Agency was established on 23 March 2010 and became an executive agency on 1 April 2011. It was created to provide a single voice for UK space ambitions, and is responsible for all strategic decisions on the UK civil space programme. Responsibilities of the UK Space Agency include coordinating UK civil space activity; supporting academic research; nurturing the UK space industry; raising the profile of UK space activities at home and abroad; working to increase understanding of space science and its practical benefits; and inspiring the next generation of UK scientists and engineers. It aims to capture 10 per cent of the global market for space by 2030.
Chief Executive, Graham Turnock

CABINET OFFICE

CROWN COMMERCIAL SERVICE
Floor 9, The Capital Building, Old Hall Street, Liverpool L3 9PP
T 0345-410 2222 E info@crowncommercial.gov.uk
W www.gov.uk/government/organisations/crown-commercial-service
The Crown Commercial Service (CCS) is an executive agency of the Cabinet Office, bringing together policy, advice and direct buying; providing commercial services to the public sector; and saving money for the taxpayer. The CCS works with over 17,000 customer organisations in the public sector. A major priority is helping government departments save more money, with a target of between £240m–£330m.
Interim Chief Executive, Simon Tse

MINISTRY OF HOUSING, COMMUNITIES AND LOCAL GOVERNMENT

PLANNING INSPECTORATE
Temple Quay House, 2 The Square, Temple Quay, Bristol BS1 6PN
T 0303-444 5000 E enquiries@pins.gsi.gov.uk
W www.gov.uk/government/organisations/planning-inspectorate
The main work of the inspectorate consists of national infrastructure planning under the Planning Act 2008 as amended by the Localism Act 2011, the processing of planning and enforcement appeals, and holding examinations into development plan documents. It also deals with listed building consent appeals; advertisement appeals; rights of way cases; cases arising from the Environmental Protection and Water

acts, the Transport and Works Act 1992 and other highways legislation; and reporting on planning applications called in for decision by the Ministry of Housing, Communities and Local Government and the Welsh government.
Chief Executive, Sarah Richards

THE QUEEN ELIZABETH II CONFERENCE CENTRE
Broad Sanctuary, London SW1P 3EE
T 020-7798 4000 W www.qeiicc.co.uk
The centre provides secure conference facilities for national and international government and private sector use.
Chief Executive, Mark Taylor

DEPARTMENT FOR DIGITAL, CULTURE, MEDIA AND SPORT

THE ROYAL PARKS
The Old Police House, Hyde Park, London W2 2UH
T 0300-061 2000 E hq@royalparks.gsi.gov.uk
W www.royalparks.org.uk
Royal Parks is responsible for maintaining and developing over 2,000 hectares (5,000 acres) of urban parkland contained within the eight royal parks in London: Bushy Park (with the Longford river); Green Park; Greenwich Park; Hyde Park; Kensington Gardens; Regent's Park (with Primrose Hill); Richmond Park and St James's Park.
Chief Executive, Andrew Scattergood

MINISTRY OF DEFENCE
See also Defence Chapter.

DEFENCE ELECTRONICS AND COMPONENTS AGENCY
Welsh Road, Deeside, Flintshire CH5 2LS T 01244-847694
E decainfo@deca.mod.uk
W www.gov.uk/government/organisations/
defence-electronics-and-components-agency
The Defence Electronics and Components Agency (DECA) provides maintenance, repair, overhaul, upgrade and procurement in avionics, electronics and components fields to support the MoD. As a 'trading' executive agency DECA is run along commercial lines, with funding for DECA's activities being generated entirely by payments for delivery of services provided to the MoD and other private sector customers. DECA currently has an annual turnover of around £25m and employs approximately 430 staff across its head office and main operating centre in North Wales, a site in Stafford and various deployed locations across the UK.
Chief Executive, Geraint Spearing

DEFENCE SCIENCE AND TECHNOLOGY LABORATORY
Porton Down, Salisbury, Wiltshire SP4 0JQ
T 01980-950000 E centralenquiries@dstl.gov.uk
W www.gov.uk/government/organisations/
defence-science-and-technology-laboratory
The Defence Science and Technology Laboratory (DSTL) supplies specialist science and technology services to the MoD and wider government.
Chief Executive, Gary Aitkenhead

UK HYDROGRAPHIC OFFICE
Admiralty Way, Taunton, Somerset TA1 2DN
T 01823-484444 E customerservices@ukho.gov.uk
W www.gov.uk/government/organisations/uk-hydrographic-office
The UK Hydrographic Office (UKHO) collects and supplies hydrographic and geospatial data for the Royal Navy and merchant shipping to protect lives at sea. Working with other national hydrographic offices, UKHO sets and raises global standards of hydrography, cartography and navigation.
Chief Executive, John Humphrey

DEPARTMENT FOR EDUCATION

THE EDUCATION AND SKILLS FUNDING AGENCY
Sanctuary Buildings, 20 Great Smith Street, London SW1P 3BT
T 0370-000 2288 W www.gov.uk/government/organisations/
education-and-skills-funding-agency
Formed on 1 April 2017 after a merger of the Education Funding Agency (EFA) and the Skills Funding Agency (SFA), the Education and Skills Funding Agency (ESFA) is the DfE's delivery agency for funding and compliance. It manages £63bn of funding each year to support all state-provided education and training for children and young people aged 3 to 19. The ESFA also supports the delivery of building and maintenance programmes for schools, academies, free schools and sixth-form colleges. It also administers the National Careers Service, the National Apprenticeship Service and the Learning Records Service.
Chief Executive, Eileen Milner

TEACHING REGULATION AGENCY
53–55 Butts Road, Earlsdon Park, Coventry CV1 3BH
T 0207-593 5394 E qts.enquiries@education.gov.uk
W www.gov.uk/government/organisations/
teaching-regulation-agency
On 1 April 2018 the Teaching Regulation Agency became operational. It is responsible for maintaining the database of qualified teachers in England and is the awarding body for Qualified Teacher Status (QTS).
Chief Executive, Alan Meyrick

STANDARDS AND TESTING AGENCY
53–55 Butts Road, Earlsdon Park, Coventry CV1 3BH
T 0300-303 3013 E assessments@education.gov.uk
W www.gov.uk/government/organisations/
standards-and-testing-agency
The Standards and Testing Agency (STA) opened on 1 October 2011 and is responsible for the development and delivery of all statutory assessments from early years to the end of Key Stage 2.
Chief Executive, Claire Burton

DEPARTMENT FOR ENVIRONMENT, FOOD AND RURAL AFFAIRS

ANIMAL AND PLANT HEALTH AGENCY
Woodham Lane, New Haw, Addlestone, Surrey KT15 3NB
T 020-8225 7611 E enquiries@apha.gsi.gov.uk
W www.gov.uk/government/organisations/
animal-and-plant-health-agency
The Animal and Plant Health Agency (APHA) was launched on 1 October 2014. It merged the former Animal Health and Veterinary Laboratories Agency with parts of the Food and Environment Research Agency responsible for plant and bee health to create a single agency responsible for animal, plant and bee health.

APHA is responsible for identifying and controlling endemic and exotic diseases and pests in animals, plants and bees, and surveillance of new and emerging pests and diseases; scientific research in areas such as bacterial, viral, prion and parasitic diseases, vaccines and food safety and act as an international reference laboratory for many farm animal diseases; facilitating international trade in animals, products of animal origin, and plants; protecting endangered wildlife through licensing and registration; managing a programme of apiary inspections, diagnostics, research and development, training and advice; and regulating the safe disposal of animal by-products to reduce the risk of potentially dangerous substances entering the food chain.

The agency provides all or some of these services to DEFRA and the Scottish and Welsh governments.
Chief Executive, Chris Hadkiss

CENTRE FOR ENVIRONMENT, FISHERIES AND AQUACULTURE SCIENCE (CEFAS)

Pakefield Road, Lowestoft, Suffolk NR33 0HT
T 01502-562244 W www.gov.uk/government/organisations/
centre-for-environment-fisheries-and-aquaculture-science
Established in April 1997, the agency provides research and consultancy services in fisheries science and management, aquaculture, fish health and hygiene, environmental impact assessment, and environmental quality assessment.
Chief Executive, Tom Karsten

RURAL PAYMENTS AGENCY

PO Box 69, Reading RG1 3YD
T 0300-0200 301 E ruralpayments@defra.gsi.gov.uk
W www.gov.uk/government/organisations/rural-payments-agency
The RPA was established in 2001. It pays out over £2bn each year to support the farming and food sector and is responsible for Common Agricultural Policy (CAP) schemes in England. In addition it manages over 40 other rural economy and community schemes. It is also responsible for operating cattle tracing services across Great Britain; conducting inspections of farms, processing plants and fresh produce markets in England; and managing the Rural Land Register.
Chief Executive, Paul Caldwell

VETERINARY MEDICINES DIRECTORATE

Woodham Lane, New Haw, Addlestone, Surrey KT15 3LS
T 01932-336911 E postmaster@vmd.defra.gsi.gov.uk
W www.gov.uk/government/organisations/
veterinary-medicines-directorate
The Veterinary Medicines Directorate is responsible for all aspects of the authorisation and control of veterinary medicines, including post-authorisation surveillance of residues in animals and animal products. It is also responsible for the development and enforcement of legislation concerning veterinary medicines and the provision of policy advice to ministers.
Chief Executive, Prof. Peter Borriello

FOREIGN AND COMMONWEALTH OFFICE

FCO SERVICES

Hanslope Park, Milton Keynes MK19 7BH
T 01908-515789 W www.fcoservices.gov.uk
FCO Services was established as an executive agency in April 2006 and became a trading fund in April 2008. It operates as the service delivery arm of the FCO, keeping their people, assets and information across the globe safe and secure from the threats they face. FCO Services also works with central government departments, law enforcement, HM government abroad, local government and the UK's critical national infrastructure.
Chief Executive, Danny Payne

WILTON PARK CONFERENCE CENTRE

Wiston House, Steyning, W. Sussex BN44 3DZ
T 01903-815020 W www.wiltonpark.org.uk
Wilton Park organises international affairs conferences and is hired out to government departments and commercial users.
Chair, Iain Ferguson
Chief Executive, Sharmila Nebhrajani, OBE

DEPARTMENT OF HEALTH AND SOCIAL CARE

MEDICINES AND HEALTHCARE PRODUCTS REGULATORY AGENCY (MHRA)

151 Buckingham Palace Road, London SW1W 9SZ
E info@mhra.gsi.gov.uk W www.gov.uk/government/organisations/
medicines-and-healthcare-products-regulatory-agency
The MHRA is a centre of the Medicines and Healthcare Products Regulatory Agency which also includes the National Institute for Biological Standards and Control (NIBSC) and the Clinical Practice Research Datalink (CPRD). The MHRA is responsible for regulating all medicines and medical devices in the UK by ensuring they work and are acceptably safe.
Chair, Prof. Sir Michael Rawlins, GBE
Chief Executive, Dr Ian Hudson

PUBLIC HEALTH ENGLAND

Wellington House, 133–155 Waterloo Road, London SE1 8UG
T 020-7654 8000 E enquiries@phe.gov.uk
W www.gov.uk/government/organisations/public-health-england
Public Health England (PHE) began operating on 1 April 2013 with a remit to protect and improve the health and wellbeing of people within the UK, and reducing health inequalities. PHE employs 5,500 staff who are mostly scientists, researchers and public health professionals. It has 8 local centres and four regions in England and works closely with public health professionals in Wales, Scotland, Northern Ireland and internationally.
Chief Executive, Duncan Selbie

MINISTRY OF JUSTICE

CRIMINAL INJURIES COMPENSATION AUTHORITY (CICA)

Alexander Bain House, Atlantic Quay, 15 York Street, Glasgow G2 8JQ T 0300-003 3601
W www.gov.uk/government/organisations/
criminal-injuries-compensation-authority
CICA is the executive agency responsible for administering the Criminal Injuries Compensation Scheme in England, Scotland and Wales (separate arrangements apply in Northern Ireland). CICA handles up to 40,000 applications for compensation each year, covering every aspect of compensation under the 1996, 2001 and 2008 Criminal Injuries Compensation Schemes. Appeals against decisions made by CICA can be put to the First-tier Tribunal (Criminal Injuries Compensation) *see* Tribunals.
Interim Chief Executive, Linda Brown

HM COURTS AND TRIBUNALS SERVICE

102 Petty France, London SW1H 9AJ
W www.gov.uk/government/organisations/
hm-courts-and-tribunals-service
HM Courts Service and the Tribunals Service merged on 1 April 2011 to form HM Courts and Tribunals Service, an integrated agency providing support for the administration of justice in courts and tribunals. As an agency within the MoJ it operates as a partnership between the Lord Chancellor, the Lord Chief Justice and the Senior President of Tribunals. It is responsible for the administration of the criminal, civil and family courts and tribunals in England and Wales and non-devolved tribunals in Scotland and Northern Ireland. The agency's work is overseen by a board headed by an independent chair working with non-executive, executive and judicial members.
Chief Executive, Susan Acland-Hood

HM PRISON AND PROBATION SERVICE

102 Petty France, London SW1H 9EX
T 01633-630941 E public.enquiries@noms.gsi.gov.uk
W www.gov.uk/government/organisations/
her-majestys-prison-and-probation-service
HM Prison and Probation Service (HMPPS) was established on 1 April 2017, responsible for the roll out of government policies concerning the welfare of offenders and communities, and for reducing levels of reoffending by the rehabilitation of offenders through education and training schemes. Through HM Prison Service, HMPPS manages public sector prisons and the contracts for private prisons in England and Wales.
Chief Executive, Michael Spurr

HM PRISON SERVICE

Clive House, 70 Petty France, London SW1H 9EX
T 0300-047 6325 E public.enquiries@noms.gsi.gov.uk
W www.gov.uk/government/organisations/hm-prison-service

As an executive agency of HM Prison and Probation Service, HM Prison Service is responsible for keeping those sentenced to prison in custody, helping them lead law-abiding and useful lives, both while they are in prison and after they have been released. HM Prison Service works alongside courts, police and local councils, in addition to voluntary organisations to achieve their aims. The agency runs 107 of the 120 prisons in England and Wales. HM Prison Service is further responsible for managing prison and probation services, and supporting effective offender management.
Chief Operating Officer, Phil Copple

LEGAL AID AGENCY

Berkley Way, Viking Business Park, Jarrow, South Tyneside NE31 1SF
T 0300-200 2020 E contactcivil@legalaid.gsi.gov.uk
W www.gov.uk/government/organisations/legal-aid-agency

The Legal Aid Agency provides civil and criminal legal aid and advice in England and Wales. Formed on 1 April 2013 as part of the Legal Aid, Sentencing and Punishment of Offenders Act 2012, the agency replaced the Legal Services Commission, a non-departmental public body of the MoJ.
Chief Executive, Shaun McNally, CBE

OFFICE OF THE PUBLIC GUARDIAN

PO Box 16185, Birmingham B2 2WH
T 0300-456 0300 E customerservices@publicguardian.gsi.gov.uk
W www.gov.uk/government/organisations/
office-of-the-public-guardian

The Office of the Public Guardian (OPG) works within the Mental Capacity Act 2005 to support and protect those who lack the mental capacity to make decisions for themselves. It supports the Public Guardian in the registration of Enduring Powers of Attorney (EPA) and Lasting Powers of Attorney (LPA), and the supervision of deputies appointed by the Court of Protection. The OPG also has responsibility for investigating and acting on allegations of abuse by attorneys and deputies. The OPG's responsibility extends across England and Wales.
Chief Executive and Public Guardian, Alan Eccles, CBE

DEPARTMENT FOR TRANSPORT

DRIVER AND VEHICLE LICENSING AGENCY (DVLA)

Longview Road, Swansea SA6 7JL
W www.gov.uk/government/organisations/
driver-and-vehicle-licensing-agency

The DVLA, established as an executive agency in 1990, maintains registers of drivers and vehicles in Great Britain. The information collated by the DVLA helps to improve road safety, reduce vehicle related crime, support environmental initiatives and limit vehicle tax evasion. The DVLA maintains over 48 million driver records and over 40 million vehicle records and collects over £6bn a year in vehicle tax.
Chief Executive, Julie Lennard

DRIVER AND VEHICLE STANDARDS AGENCY

Berkeley House, Croydon Street, Bristol BS5 0DA
T 0300-123 9000 E inform@vosa.gov.uk
W www.gov.uk/government/organisations/
driver-vehicle-standards-agency

Formed by the merger of the Driving Standards Agency and the Vehicle and Operator Services Agency in 2014, the Driver and Vehicle Standards Agency (DVSA) is responsible for improving road safety in the UK by setting standards for driving and motorcycling, and ensuring drivers, vehicle operators and MOT garages understand and comply with roadworthiness standards. It additionally provides a range of licensing, testing, education and enforcement services.
Chief Executive, Gareth Llewellyn

MARITIME AND COASTGUARD AGENCY

Spring Place, 105 Commercial Road, Southampton SO15 1EG
T 020-3817 2000 W www.gov.uk/government/organisations/
maritime-and-coastguard-agency

The agency's aims are to prevent loss of life, continuously improve maritime safety and protect the marine environment.
Chief Executive, Sir Alan Massey, KCB, CBE

VEHICLE CERTIFICATION AGENCY

1 Eastgate Office Centre, Eastgate Road, Bristol BS5 6XX
T 0300-330 5797 E enquiries@vca.gov.uk W www.dft.gov.uk/vca

The agency is the UK authority responsible for ensuring that new road vehicles, agricultural tractors, off-road vehicles and vehicle parts have been designed and constructed to meet internationally agreed standards of safety and environmental protection.
Chief Executive, Pia Wilkes

HM TREASURY

GOVERNMENT INTERNAL AUDIT AGENCY

1 Horse Guards Road, London SW1A 2HQ
E Correspondence@giaa.gsi.gov.uk W www.gov.uk/government/
organisations/government-internal-audit-agency

Launched on 1 April 2015, the Government Internal Audit Agency (GIAA) helps ensure government and the wider public sector provide services effectively. GIAA offers quality assurance on organisation's systems and processes, based on an objective assessment of the governance, risk management and control arrangements in place.
Chief Executive, Jon Whitfield

UK DEBT MANAGEMENT OFFICE

Eastcheap Court, 11 Philpot Lane, London EC3M 8UD
T 020-7862 6500 W www.dmo.gov.uk

The UK Debt Management Office (DMO) was launched as an executive agency of HM Treasury in April 1998. The Chancellor of the Exchequer determines the policy and financial framework within which the DMO operates, but delegates operational decisions on debt and cash management and the day-to-day running of the office to the chief executive. The DMO's remit is to carry out the government's debt management policy of minimising financing costs over the long term, and to minimise the cost of offsetting the government's net cash flows over time, while operating at a level of risk approved by ministers in both cases. The DMO is also responsible for providing loans to local authorities through the Public Works Loan Board, and for managing the assets of certain public-sector bodies through the Commissioners for the Reduction of the National Debt.
Chief Executive, Sir Robert Stheeman, CB

NON-MINISTERIAL GOVERNMENT DEPARTMENTS

Non-ministerial government departments are part of central government but are not headed by a minister and are not funded by a sponsor department. They are created to implement specific legislation, but do not have the ability to change it. Departments may have links to a minister, but the minister is not responsible for the department's overall performance. Staff employed by non-ministerial departments are civil servants.

CHARITY COMMISSION

PO Box 1227, Liverpool L69 3UG
T 0300-066 9197 W www.gov.uk/government/organisations/
charity-commission

The Charity Commission is established by law as the independent regulator and registrar of charities in England and Wales. Its aim is to provide the best possible regulation of these charities in order to ensure their legal compliance and increase their efficiency, accountability and effectiveness, as well as to encourage public trust and confidence in them. The commission maintains a register of 168,237 charities. It is accountable to both parliament and the First-tier Tribunal (Charity), and the chamber of the Upper Tribunal or high court for decisions made in exercising the commission's legal powers. The Charity Commission has offices in London, Liverpool, Taunton and Newport.

Chair, Rt. Hon. Baroness Stowell of Beeston, MBE
Chief Executive, Helen Stephenson, CBE

COMPETITION AND MARKETS AUTHORITY

Victoria House, Southampton Row, London WC1B 4AD
T 020-3738 6000 E general.enquiries@cma.gsi.gov.uk
W www.gov.uk/government/organisations/
competition-and-markets-authority

The Competition and Markets Authority (CMA) is the UK's primary competition and consumer authority. It is an independent non-ministerial government department with responsibility for carrying out investigations into mergers, markets and the regulated industries and enforcing competition and consumer law. From 1 April 2014 it took over the functions of the Competition Commission and the competition and certain consumer functions of the Office of Fair Trading under the Enterprise Act 2002, as amended by the Enterprise and Regulatory Reform Act 2013.

Chair, David Currie
Chief Executive, Dr Andrea Coscelli

CROWN PROSECUTION SERVICE

Rose Court, 2 Southwark Bridge Road, London SE1 9HS
T 020-3357 0899 E enquiries@cps.gsi.gov.uk W www.cps.gov.uk

The Crown Prosecution Service (CPS) is the independent body responsible for prosecuting people in England and Wales. The CPS was established as a result of the Prosecution of Offences Act 1985. It works closely with the police to advise on lines of inquiry and to decide on appropriate charges and other disposals in all but minor cases. *See also* Law Courts and Offices.

Director of Public Prosecutions, Alison Saunders, CB
Interim Chief Executive, Paul Staff

FOOD STANDARDS AGENCY

Aviation House, 125 Kingsway, London WC2B 6NH
T 020-7276 8829 E helpline@foodstandards.gsi.gov.uk
W www.food.gov.uk

Established in April 2000, the FSA is a UK-wide non-ministerial government body responsible for food safety and hygiene. The agency has the general function of developing policy in these areas and provides information and advice to the government, other public bodies and consumers. The FSA also works with local authorities to enforce food safety regulations and has staff working in UK meat plants to check that the requirements of the regulations are being met.

Chair, Heather Hancock
Chief Executive, Jason Feeney

FOOD STANDARDS AGENCY NORTHERN IRELAND,
10C Clarendon Road, Belfast BT1 3BG T 028-9041 7700
E infosani@foodstandards.gsi.gov.uk

FOOD STANDARDS AGENCY WALES, 11th Floor, South
Gate House, Wood Street, Cardiff CF10 1EW T 029-2067 8999
E walesadminteam@foodstandards.gsi.gov.uk

FORESTRY COMMISSION

620 Bristol Business Park, Coldharbour Lane, Bristol BS16 1EJ
T 0300-067 4000 E fe.england@forestry.gsi.gov.uk
Silvan House, 231 Corstorphine Road, Edinburgh EH12 7AT
T 0300-067 6156 E fcscotland@forestry.gsi.gov.uk
W www.forestry.gov.uk

The Forestry Commission is the government department responsible for forestry policy in England and Scotland. It is divided into Forestry Commission England and Forestry Commission Scotland, which report to forestry ministers (the Secretary of State for Environment, Food & Rural Affairs in the UK government, and to ministers in the Scottish government), to whom it is responsible for advice on and implementation of forestry policy. It has an agency, Forest Research, which carries out scientific research and technical development relevant to forestry. The public forests are managed through two additional executive agencies, known as Forest Enterprise England and Forest Enterprise Scotland.

On 1 April 2013 the functions of its Welsh division, Forestry Commission Wales, were subsumed into Natural Resources Wales, a new body established by the Welsh government to regulate and manage natural resources in Wales.

The commission's principal objectives are to protect and expand England's and Scotland's forests and woodlands; enhance the economic value of forest resources; conserve and improve the biodiversity, landscape and cultural heritage of forests and woodlands; develop opportunities for woodland recreation; and increase public understanding of, and community participation in, forestry. It does this by managing public forests in its care to implement these objectives; by supporting other woodland owners with grants, regulation, advice and tree felling licences; and, through its Forest Research agency, by carrying out scientific research and technical development in support of these objectives.

Chair (2014–20), Sir Harry Studholme, Bt.
Chief Executive, Forest Enterprise England, Simon Hodgson
Chief Executive, Forest Enterprise Scotland, Simon Hodge

GOVERNMENT ACTUARY'S DEPARTMENT

Finlaison House, 15–17 Furnival Street, London EC4A 1AB
T 020-7211 2601 E enquiries@gad.gov.uk
Elgin House, Haymarket Yards, Edinburgh EH12 5WN
T 0131-467 0324 E scottish-enquiries@gad.gov.uk
W www.gov.uk/government/organisations/
government-actuary-department

The Government Actuary's Department (GAD) was established in 1919 and provides actuarial advice to the public sector in the UK and overseas, and also to the private sector, where consistent with government policy. The GAD provides advice on occupational pension schemes, social security and National Insurance, investment and strategic risk management, insurance analysis and advice, financial risk management, and healthcare financing.

Government Actuary, Martin Clarke
Deputy Government Actuary, Colin Wilson

GOVERNMENT LEGAL DEPARTMENT

1 Kemble Street, London WC2B 4TS
T 020-7210 3000 E thetreasurysolicitor@governmentlegal.gov.uk
W www.gov.uk/government/organisations/
government-legal-department

The Treasury Solicitor's Department became the Government Legal Department (GLD) on 1 April 2015. The department provides legal advice to government on the development, design and implementation of government policies and decisions, and represents the government in court. It is superintended by the Attorney-General. The permanent secretary of the GLD, the Treasury Solicitor, is also the Queen's Proctor, and is responsible for collecting ownerless goods *(bona vacantia)* on behalf of the crown.

HM Procurator-General and Treasury Solicitor, Jonathan Jones
Directors-General, Stephen Braviner-Roman; Peter Fish, CB; Claire Johnston
Head of Bona Vacantia, Caroline Harold

HM LAND REGISTRY

Trafalgar House, 1 Bedford Park, Croydon CR0 2AQ
T 0300-006 0411
W www.gov.uk/government/organisations/land-registry

A government department and trading fund of BEIS, HM Land Registry maintains the Land Register – the definitive source of information for more than 25 million property titles in England and Wales. The Land Register has been open to public inspection since 1990.

Chief Land Registrar and Chief Executive, Graham Farrant

HM REVENUE AND CUSTOMS (HMRC)

100 Parliament Street, London SW1A 2BQ
Income Tax Enquiries 0300-200 3300
National Insurance Enquiries 0300-200 3500
VAT Enquiries 0300-200 3700
W www.gov.uk/government/organisations/hm-revenue-customs

HMRC was formed following the integration of the Inland Revenue and HM Customs and Excise, which was made formal by parliament in April 2005. It collects and administers direct taxes (capital gains tax, corporation tax, income tax, inheritance tax and national insurance contributions) and indirect taxes (excise duties, insurance premium tax, petroleum revenue tax, stamp duty, stamp duty land tax, stamp duty reserve tax and value-added tax). HMRC also pays and administers child benefit, tax credits and the Child Trust Fund, in addition to being responsible for environmental taxes, national minimum wage enforcement, recovery of student loans, the climate change levy and landfill tax. HMRC also administers the Government Banking Service.

Chief Executive and Permanent Secretary, Jon Thompson
Executive Chair and Permanent Secretary, vacant

VALUATION OFFICE AGENCY
Wingate House, 93–107 Shaftesbury Avenue, London W1D 5BU
T 0300-050 1501 W www.gov.uk/government/organisations/valuation-office-agency
Established in 1991, the Valuation Office is an executive agency of HM Revenue and Customs. It is responsible for compiling and maintaining the business rating and council tax valuation lists for England and Wales; valuing property throughout Great Britain for the purposes of taxes administered by HMRC; providing statutory and non-statutory property valuation services in England, Wales and Scotland; and giving policy advice to ministers on property valuation matters. In April 2009 the VOA assumed responsibility for the functions of The Rent Service, which provided a rental valuation service to local authorities in England, and fair rent determinations for landlords and tenants.
Chief Executive, Melissa Tatton

NATIONAL ARCHIVES

NATIONAL ARCHIVES
Kew, Richmond, Surrey TW9 4DU
T 020-8876 3444 W www.nationalarchives.gov.uk

The National Archives is a non-ministerial government department of the Ministry of Justice. It incorporates the Public Record Office, Historical Manuscripts Commission, Office of Public Sector Information and Her Majesty's Stationery Office. As the official archive of the UK government, it preserves, protects and makes accessible the historical collection of official records.

The National Archives also manages digital information including the UK government web archive which contains over one billion digital documents, and devises solutions for keeping government records readable now and in the future.

The organisation administers the UK's public records system under the Public Records Acts of 1958 and 1967. The records it holds span 1,000 years – from the Domesday Book to the latest government papers to be released – and fill more than 167km (104 miles) of shelving.

Chief Executive and Keeper, Jeff James

NATIONAL CRIME AGENCY

Units 1–6 Citadel Place, Tinworth Street, London SE11 5EF
T 0370-496 7622 E communication@nca.x.gsi.gov.uk
W www.nationalcrimeagency.gov.uk

The National Crime Agency (NCA) is an operational crime fighting agency introduced under the Crime and Courts Act 2013, which became fully operational in October 2013. The NCA's remit is to fight organised crime, strengthen UK borders, tackle fraud and cyber crime and protect children and young people. The agency employs over 4,200 officers and provides leadership through its organised crime, border policing, economic crime and Child Exploitation and Online Protection Centre commands, the National Cyber Crime Unit and specialist capability teams.

Director-General, Lynne Owens, CBE, QPM

NATIONAL SAVINGS AND INVESTMENTS

Glasgow G58 1SB
T 08085-007007 W www.nsandi.com

NS&I (National Savings and Investments) came into being in 1861 when the Palmerston government set up the Post Office Savings Bank, a savings scheme which aimed to encourage ordinary wage earners 'to provide for themselves against adversity and ill health'. NS&I was established as a government department in 1969. It is responsible for the design, marketing and administration of savings and investment products for personal savers and investors. It has over 25 million customers and more than £147bn invested.
See also Banking and Finance, National Savings.

Chief Executive, Ian Ackerley

OFFICE OF GAS AND ELECTRICITY MARKETS (OFGEM)

10 South Colonnade, Canary Wharf, London E14 4PU
T 020-7901 7000 W www.ofgem.gov.uk

OFGEM is the regulator for Britain's gas and electricity industries. Its role is to protect and advance the interests of consumers by promoting competition where possible, and through regulation only where necessary. OFGEM operates under the direction and governance of the Gas and Electricity Markets Authority, which makes all major decisions and sets policy priorities for OFGEM. OFGEM's powers are provided for under the Gas Act 1986 and the Electricity Act 1989, as amended by the Utilities Act 2000. It also has enforcement powers under the Competition Act 1998 and the Enterprise Act 2002.

Chair, David Gray
Chief Executive, Dermot Nolan

OFFICE OF RAIL AND ROAD
1 Kemble Street, London WC2B 4AN
T 020-7282 2000 W www.orr.gov.uk

The Office of the Rail and Road (ORR) is the operating name of the Office of Rail Regulation. The Office of Rail Regulation was established on 5 July 2004 under the Railways and Transport Safety Act 2003. It replaced the Office of the Rail Regulator.

On 1 April 2006, ORR assumed new responsibilities as a combined safety and economic regulator under the Railways Act 2005. It also has concurrent jurisdiction with the Competition and Market Authority under the Competition Act 1998 as the competition authority for the railways.

As the railway industry's independent health and safety and economic regulator, its principal functions are to: ensure that Network Rail and HS1 manage the national network efficiently and in a way that meets the needs of its users; encourage continuous health and safety performance; secure compliance with relevant health and safety law, including taking enforcement action as necessary; develop policy and enhance relevant railway health and safety legislation; and license operators of railway assets, setting the terms for access by operators to the network and other railway facilities, and enforce competition and consumer law in the rail sector.

On 1 April 2015, under the Infrastructure Act 2015, ORR assumed responsibility for monitoring Highways England's management and development of the strategic road network – the motorways and main 'A' roads in England. In this role ORR ensures that the network is managed efficiently, safely and sustainably, for the benefit of road users and the public.

On 16 March 2015, ORR signed an agreement with the French rail regulator ARAF to establish a collaborative regulatory approach for consistent independent regulation across the Channel tunnel network.

ORR is led by a board appointed by the Secretary of State for Transport.

Chair, Stephen Glaister
Chief Executive, Joanna Whittington

OFFICE OF QUALIFICATIONS AND EXAMINATIONS REGULATION (OFQUAL)
Spring Place, Herald Avenue, Coventry CV5 6UB
T 0300-303 3344 E public.enquiries@ofqual.gov.uk
W www.gov.uk/government/organisations/ofqual

OFQUAL became the independent regulator of qualifications, examinations and assessments on 1 April 2010. It is responsible for maintaining standards, improving confidence and distributing information about qualifications and examinations, as well as regulating general and vocational qualifications in England.

Chief Regulator, Sally Collier
Chair, Roger Taylor

OFFICE FOR STANDARDS IN EDUCATION, CHILDREN'S SERVICES AND SKILLS (OFSTED)
Piccadilly Gate, Store Street, Manchester M1 2WD
T 0300-123 1231 E enquiries@ofsted.gov.uk
W www.gov.uk/government/organisations/ofsted

Ofsted was established under the Education (Schools Act) 1992 and was relaunched on 1 April 2007 with a wider remit, bringing together four formerly separate inspectorates. It works to raise standards in services through the inspection and regulation of care for children and young people, and inspects education and training for children of all ages. *See also* Education.

HM Chief Inspector, Amanda Spielman
Chair, Prof. Julius Weinburg

ORDNANCE SURVEY
Adanac Drive, Southampton SO16 0AS
T 0345-605 0505 E customerservices@os.uk
W www.ordnancesurvey.co.uk

Ordnance Survey is the national mapping agency for Great Britain. It is a government department and executive agency operating as a trading fund since 1999.

Director-General and Chief Executive, Nigel Clifford

SERIOUS FRAUD OFFICE
2–4 Cockspur Street, London SW1Y 5BS
T 020-7239 7272 E public.enquiries@sfo.gsi.gov.uk
W www.sfo.gov.uk

The Serious Fraud Office is an independent government department that investigates and, where appropriate, prosecutes serious or complex fraud, bribery and corruption. It is part of the UK criminal justice system with jurisdiction over England, Wales and Northern Ireland but not Scotland, the Isle of Man or the Channel Islands. The office is headed by a director who is superintended by the Attorney-General.

Director, David Green, CB, QC

SUPREME COURT OF THE UNITED KINGDOM
Parliament Square, London SW1P 3BD
T 020-7960 1900 E enquiries@supremecourt.uk
W www.supremecourt.uk

The Supreme Court of the United Kingdom is the highest domestic judicial authority; it replaced the appellate committee of the House of Lords (the house functioning in its judicial capacity) on 1 October 2009. It is the final court of appeal for cases heard in Great Britain and Northern Ireland (except for criminal cases from Scotland). Cases concerning the interpretation and application of European Union law, including preliminary rulings requested by British courts and tribunals, are decided by the Court of Justice of the European Union (CJEU), and the supreme court can make a reference to the CJEU in appropriate cases. Additionally, in giving effect to rights contained in the European Convention on Human Rights, the supreme court must take account of any decision of the European Court of Human Rights.

The supreme court also assumed jurisdiction in relation to devolution matters under the Scotland Act 1998 (now partly superseded by the Scotland Act 2012), the Northern Ireland Act 1988 and the Government of Wales Act 2006; these powers were transferred from the Judicial Committee of the Privy Council. Ten of the 12 Lords of Appeal in Ordinary (Law Lords) from the House of Lords transferred to the 12-member supreme court when it came into operation (at the same time one law lord retired and another was appointed Master of the Rolls). All new justices of the supreme court are now appointed by an independent selection commission, and, although styled Rt. Hon. Lord, are not members of the House of Lords. Peers who are members of the judiciary are disqualified from sitting or voting in the House of Lords until they retire from their judicial office.

Chief Executive, Mark Ormerod, CB

UK STATISTICS AUTHORITY
1 Drummond Gate, London SW1V 2QQ
T 0845-604 1857 E authority.enquiries@statistics.gsi.gov.uk
W www.statisticsauthority.gov.uk

The UK Statistics Authority was established on 1 April 2008 by the Statistics and Registration Service Act 2007 as an independent body operating at arm's length from government, reporting to the UK parliament and the devolved legislatures. Its overall objective is to promote and safeguard the production and publication of official statistics and ensure their quality and comprehensiveness. The authority's main functions are the oversight of the Office for National Statistics (ONS); monitoring and reporting on all UK official statistics, which includes around 30 central government departments and the devolved administrations; and the production of a code of practice for statistics and the assessment of official statistics against the code.

BOARD

Chair, Sir David Norgrove

Board Members, Prof. Sir Adrian Smith, FRS *(Deputy Chair);* Jonathan Athow *(Deputy National Statistician for Economic Statistics);* Iain Bell *(Deputy National Statistician for Population and Public Policy);* Prof. David Hand, OBE, FBA; Prof. Jonathan Haskel; Ed Humpherson; Sian Jones; David Levy; Nora Nanayakkara; John Pullinger *(National Statistician);* Heather Savory *(Deputy National Statistician for Data Capability)*

OFFICE FOR NATIONAL STATISTICS (ONS)

Cardiff Road, Newport NP10 8XG

T 0845-601 3034 **E** info@ons.gsi.gov.uk **W** www.ons.gov.uk

The ONS was created in 1996 by the merger of the Central Statistical Office and the Office of Population Censuses and Surveys. On 1 April 2008 it became the executive office of the UK Statistics Authority. As part of these changes, the office's responsibility for the General Register Office transferred to HM Passport Office of the Home Office.

The ONS is responsible for preparing, interpreting and publishing key statistics on the government, economy and society of the UK. Its key responsibilities include designing, managing and running the Census and providing statistics on health and other demographic matters in England and Wales; the production of the UK National Accounts and other economic indicators; the organisation of population censuses in England and Wales and surveys for government departments and public bodies.

National Statistician, John Pullinger

Director-Generals, Jonathan Athow; Iain Bell; Heather Savory

WATER SERVICES REGULATION AUTHORITY (OFWAT)

Centre City Tower, 7 Hill Street, Birmingham B5 4UA

T 0121-644 7500 **E** mailbox@ofwat.gsi.gov.uk

W www.ofwat.gov.uk

OFWAT is the independent economic regulator of the water and sewerage companies in England and Wales. It is responsible for ensuring that the water industry in England and Wales provides household and business customers with a good quality service and value for money. This is done by ensuring that the companies provide customers with a good quality, efficient service at a fair price; limiting the prices companies can charge; monitoring the companies' performance and taking action, including enforcement, to protect customers' interests; setting the companies efficiency targets; making sure the companies deliver the best for consumers and the environment in the long term; and encouraging competition where it benefits consumers.

Chair, Jonson Cox

Chief Executive, Rachel Fletcher

PUBLIC BODIES

The following section is a listing of public bodies and other civil service organisations: it is not a complete list of these organisations.

Whereas executive agencies are either part of a government department or are one in their own right (*see* Government Departments), public bodies carry out their functions to a greater or lesser extent at arm's length from central government. Ministers are ultimately responsible to parliament for the activities of the public bodies sponsored by their department and in almost all cases (except where there is separate statutory provision) ministers make the appointments to their boards. Departments are responsible for funding and ensuring good governance of their public bodies.

The term 'public body' is a general one which includes public corporations, such as the BBC; NHS bodies; and non-departmental public bodies (NDPBs).

ADJUDICATOR'S OFFICE
PO Box 10280, Nottingham NG2 9PF
T 0300-057 1111 W www.adjudicatorsoffice.gov.uk

The Adjudicator's Office investigates complaints from individuals and businesses about the way that HM Revenue and Customs and the Valuation Office Agency have handled a person's affairs. The Adjudicator's Office will only consider a complaint after the respective organisation's internal complaints procedure has been exhausted.

The Adjudicator, Helen Megarry

ADVISORY, CONCILIATION AND ARBITRATION SERVICE (ACAS)
22nd Floor, Euston Tower, 286 Euston Road, London NW1 3JJ
T 0300-123 1100 W www.acas.org.uk

The Advisory, Conciliation and Arbitration Service was set up under the Employment Protection Act 1975 (the provisions now being found in the Trade Union and Labour Relations (Consolidation) Act 1992).

ACAS is largely funded by the Department for Business, Energy and Industrial Strategy. A council sets its strategic direction, policies and priorities, and ensures that the agreed strategic objectives and targets are met. It consists of a chair and 11 employer, trade union and independent members, appointed by the Secretary of State for Business, Energy and Industrial Strategy.

ACAS aims to improve organisations and working life through better employment relations, to provide up-to-date information, independent advice and high-quality training, and to work with employers and employees to solve problems and improve performance.

ACAS has regional offices in Birmingham, Bristol, Bury St Edmunds, Cardiff, Fleet, Glasgow, Leeds, Manchester, Newcastle-upon-Tyne and Nottingham. The head office is in London.

Chair, Sir Brendan Barber
Chief Executive, Anne Sharp, CBE

ADVISORY COUNCIL ON NATIONAL RECORDS AND ARCHIVES
The National Archives, Kew, Surrey TW9 4DU
T 020-8392 5337
E advisorycouncilsecretary@nationalarchives.gov.uk
W http://www.nationalarchives.gov.uk/about/our-role/advisory-council/

The Advisory Council on National Records and Archives advises the Secretary of State for Digital, Culture, Media and Sport on issues relating to public records that are over 20 years old including public access to them. The council meets four times a year, and its main task is to consider requests for the extended closure of public records; it also reaches decisions regarding government departments that want to keep records.

The Forum on Historical Manuscripts and Academic Research, a sub-committee of the Advisory Council, provides advice to the Chief Executive of The National Archives and Keeper of Public Records on matters relating to historical manuscripts, records and archives, other than public records.

Chair, Rt. Hon. Sir Terence Etherton *(Master of the Rolls)*

AGRICULTURE AND HORTICULTURE DEVELOPMENT BOARD
Stoneleigh Park, Kenilworth, Warwickshire CV8 2TL
T 02476-692051 E info@ahdb.org.uk W www.ahdb.org.uk

The Agriculture and Horticulture Development Board (AHDB) is funded by the agriculture and horticulture industries through statutory levies, with the duty to improve efficiency and competitiveness within six sectors: pig meat in England; milk in Great Britain; beef and lamb in England; commercial horticulture in Great Britain; cereals and oilseeds in the UK; and potatoes in Great Britain. The AHDB represents about 72 per cent of total UK agricultural output. Levies raised from the six sectors are ring-fenced to ensure that they can only be used to the benefit of the sectors from which they were raised.

Chair, Sir Peter Kendall
Independent members, Will Lifford; George Lyon
Sector members, Adam Quinney *(beef and lamb);* Meryl Ward, MBE *(pig meat);* Fiona Fell *(potatoes);* Paul Temple *(cereals and oilseeds);* Gwyn Jones *(milk)*
Chief Executive, Jane King

ARCHITECTURE AND DESIGN SCOTLAND
9 Bakehouse Close, 146 Canongate, Edinburgh EH8 8DD
T 0131-556 6699 E info@ads.org.uk W www.ads.org.uk

Architecture and Design Scotland (A&DS) was established in 2005 by the Scottish government as the national champion for good architecture, urban design and planning in the built environment; it works with a wide range of organisations at national, regional and local levels.

Chair, Karen Anderson
Chief Executive, Jim MacDonald

ARMED FORCES' PAY REVIEW BODY
8th Floor, Fleetbank House, 2-6 Salisbury Square, London EC4Y 8JX
T 020-7211 8315 W www.gov.uk/government/organisations/armed-forces-pay-review-body

The Armed Forces' Pay Review Body was appointed in 1971. It advises the prime minister and the Secretary of State for Defence on the pay and allowances of members of naval, military and air forces of the Crown.

Chair, Peter Maddison, QPM
Members, Brendan Connor, JP; Tim Flesher, CB; Prof. Ken Mayhew; Lesley Mercer; Vilma Patterson, MBE; Rear Admiral (retd) Jon Westbrook, CBE; Janet Whitworth

ARTS COUNCIL ENGLAND

21 Bloomsbury Street, London WC1B 3HF
T 0845-300 6200 W www.artscouncil.org.uk

Arts Council England is the national development agency for the arts in England. Using public money from government and the National Lottery, it supports a range of artistic activities, including theatre, music, literature, dance, photography, digital art, carnival and crafts. Between 2018 and 2022, Arts Council England is investing £1.45bn of public money from the government and around £860m from the National Lottery.

The governing body, the national council, comprises 14 members, who are appointed by the Secretary of State for Digital, Culture, Media and Sport usually for a term of four years. There are also five councils, responsible for the agreement of area strategies, plans and priorities for action within the national framework.

National Council Chair, Sir Nicholas Serota, CH
National Council Members, Maria Balshaw, CBE; Prof. Roni
 Brown; Michael Eakin; Sukhy Johal, MBE; David Joseph;
 Catherine Mallyon; Andrew Miller; George Mpanga;
 Elisabeth Murdoch; Paul Roberts, OBE; Tessa Ross; Dame
 Rosemary Squire; Veronica Wadley; Kate Willard
Chief Executive, Darren Henley, OBE

ARTS COUNCIL OF NORTHERN IRELAND

1 The Sidings, Antrim Road, Lisburn BT28 3AJ
T 028-9262 3555 E info@artscouncil-ni.org
W www.artscouncil-ni.org

The Arts Council of Northern Ireland is the prime distributor of government funds in support of the arts in Northern Ireland. It is funded by the Department for Communities and from National Lottery funds.

Chair, John Edmund
Members, David Alderdice; Anna Carragher; Roisin Erskine;
 Dr Siún Hanrahan; Dr Leon Litvack; Noelle McAlinden;
 Katherine McCloskey; Paul Mullan; Dr Katy Radford,
 MBE *(Vice-Chair);* Cian Smyth
Chief Executive, Roisin McDonough

ARTS COUNCIL OF WALES

Bute Place, Cardiff CF10 5AL
T 0845-873 4900 E comms@arts.wales W www.arts.wales

The Arts Council of Wales was established in 1994 by royal charter and is the development body for the arts in Wales. It funds arts organisations with funding from the Welsh government and is the distributor of National Lottery funds to the arts in Wales.

Chair, Phil George
Members, Iwan Bala; Andy Eagle; Kate Eden; Michael
 Griffiths; Melanie Hawthorne; Dr Lesley Hodgson;
 Andrew Miller; Rachel O'Riordan; Dafydd Rhys; Richard
 Turner; Alan Watkin; Marian Wyn Jones
Chief Executive, Nick Capaldi

AUDIT SCOTLAND

102 West Port, Edinburgh EH3 9DN
T 0131-625 1500 E info@audit-scotland.gov.uk
W www.audit-scotland.gov.uk

Audit Scotland was set up in 2000 to provide services to the Accounts Commission and the Auditor-General for Scotland. Together they help to ensure that public-sector bodies in Scotland are held accountable for the proper, efficient and effective use of public funds.

Audit Scotland's work covers bodies including local authorities; health boards; further education colleges; Scottish Water; the Scottish government; government agencies such as the Prison Service and non-departmental public bodies such as the Scottish Police Authority and the Scottish Fire and Rescue Service. The organisation audited 329 sets of accounts in 2016–17.

Audit Scotland carries out financial and regularity audits to ensure that public-sector bodies adhere to the highest standards of financial management and governance. It also carries out performance audits to ensure that these bodies achieve the best value for money. All of Audit Scotland's work in connection with local authorities is carried out for the Accounts Commission; its other work is undertaken for the Auditor-General.

Chair, Ian Leitch, CBE
Auditor-General, Caroline Gardner
Chair of the Accounts Commission, Dr Graham Sharp

BANK OF ENGLAND

Threadneedle Street, London EC2R 8AH
T 020-3461 4444 E enquiries@bankofengland.co.uk
W www.bankofengland.co.uk

The Bank of England was incorporated in 1694 under royal charter. It was nationalised in 1946 under the Bank of England Act of that year which gave HM Treasury statutory powers over the bank. It is the banker of the government and it manages the issue of banknotes. Since 1998 it has been operationally independent and its Monetary Policy Committee has been responsible for setting short-term interest rates to meet the government's inflation target. Its responsibility for banking supervision was transferred to the Financial Services Authority in the same year. As the central reserve bank of the country, the Bank of England keeps the accounts of British banks, and of most overseas central banks; the larger banks and building societies are required to maintain with it a proportion of their cash resources. The bank's core purposes are monetary stability and financial stability. The Banking Act 2009 increased the responsibilities of the bank, including giving it a new financial stability objective and creating a special resolution regime for dealing with failing banks.

In 2013, through the Prudential Regulation Authority (PRA), the bank became responsible for the prudential regulation and supervision of banks, building societies, credit unions, insurers and major investment firms.

Governor, Mark Carney
Deputy Governors, Dr Ben Broadbent; Sir Jon Cunliffe, CB; Sir
 Dave Ramsden; Sam Woods
Court of Directors, The Governor; Sir Anthony Habgood
 (Chair of Court); Dr Ben Broadbent; Sir John Cuncliffe;
 Bradley Fried; Tim Frost; Baroness Harding of
 Winscombe; Dave Prentis; Sir Dave Ramsden; Don
 Robert; Dorothy Thompson; Sam Woods
Financial Policy Committee, The Governor; Andrew Bailey;
 Alex Brazier; Dr Ben Broadbent; Sir Jon Cunliffe; Anil
 Kashyap; Donald Kohn; Sir Dave Ramsden; Charles
 Roxburgh; Richard Sharp; Elisabeth Stheeman; Martin
 Taylor; Sam Woods
Monetary Policy Committee, The Governor; Dr Ben Broadbent;
 Sir Jon Cunliffe; Andy Haldane; Ian McCafferty; Sir Dave
 Ramsden; Michael Saunders; Silvana Tenreyro; Dr Gertjan
 Vlieghe
General Counsel, Sonya Branch
Director for Banknotes and Chief Cashier, Victoria Cleland
The Auditor, Stephen Brown

BIG LOTTERY FUND

1 Plough Place, London EC4A 1DE
T 020-7211 1800 Advice Line 0345-410 2030
E general.enquiries@biglotteryfund.org.uk
W www.biglotteryfund.org.uk

The Big Lottery Fund is responsible for distributing 40 per cent of all funds raised for good causes by the National Lottery, amounting to around £670m to 12,000 projects a year across the UK. It is responsible for supporting health, education, environmental and charitable projects.

Chair, Peter Ainsworth
Vice-Chair, Tony Burton, CBE
Regional Chairs, Julie Harrison *(Northern Ireland);* Maureen McGinn *(Scotland);* Nat Sloane, CBE *(England);* Sir Adrian Webb *(Wales)*
Chief Executive, Dawn Austwick, OBE

BOUNDARY COMMISSIONS

ENGLAND
2nd Floor, 35 Great Smith Street, London SW1P 3BQ
T 020-7276 1102
E information@boundarycommissionengland.gov.uk
W http://boundarycommissionforengland.independent.gov.uk

Deputy Chair, Hon. Mr Justice Nichol

WALES
Hastings House, Fitzalan Court, Cardiff CF24 0BL
T 029-2046 4819 E bcomm.wales@wales.gsi.gov.uk
W www.bcomm-wales.gov.uk

Deputy Chair, Hon. Mr Justice Lewis

SCOTLAND
Thistle House, 91 Haymarket Terrace, Edinburgh EH12 5HD
T 0131-244 2001 E bcs@scottishboundaries.gov.uk
W www.bcomm-scotland.independent.gov.uk

Deputy Chair, Hon. Lord Matthews

NORTHERN IRELAND
The Bungalow, Stormont House, Stormont Estate, Belfast BT4 3SH
T 028-9052 7821 E contact@boundarycommission.org.uk
W www.boundarycommission.org.uk

Deputy Chair, Hon. Ms Justice McBride, DBE

The commissions, established in 1944, are constituted under the Parliamentary Constituencies Act 1986 (as amended). The Speaker of the House of Commons is the *ex officio* chair of all four commissions in the UK.

The next reviews of UK parliament constituencies will be undertaken using the electoral register from 1 December 2015; these reviews must be submitted before 1 October 2018.

BRITISH BROADCASTING CORPORATION (BBC)
BBC Broadcasting House, Portland Place, London W1A 1AA
W www.bbc.co.uk

The BBC was incorporated under royal charter in 1926 as successor to the British Broadcasting Company Ltd. The BBC's current charter, which came into force on 1 January 2017 and extends to 31 December 2027, recognises the BBC's editorial independence and sets out its public purposes. The BBC Board was formed under the new charter and is responsible for ensuring that the Corporation fulfils its mission and public purposes by setting the strategic direction of the BBC, establishing its creative remit, setting the budget and determining the framework for assessing performance. As part of the new charter, The Office of Communications (OFCOM) was awarded sole regulatory responsibility for the BBC. The BBC is financed by television licence revenue to ensure it remains independent from political control.

BBC BOARD

Chair, Sir David Clementi
Director-General, Lord Hall of Birkenhead, CBE

National Members, Steve Morrison *(Scotland);* Dr Ashley Steel *(England);* Elan Closs Stephens *(Wales)*
Members, Anne Bulford, OBE *(Deputy Director-General);* Simon Burke *(Senior Independent Director);* Tim Davie *(CEO BBC Studios);* Ken MacQuarrie *(Nations and Regions)*
Non-Executive Members, Baroness Grey-Thompson, DBE; Ian Hargreaves, CBE; Tom Ilube; Sir Nicholas Serota, CH

EXECUTIVE COMMITTEE
Director-General, Lord Hall of Birkenhead, CBE
Deputy Director-General, Anne Bulford, OBE
CEO BBC Worldwide, Tim Davie
Chief Technology and Product Officer, Matthew Postgate
Directors, Valerie Hughes D'Aeth *(Group HR);* Mark Linsey *(BBC Studios);* Ken MacQuarrie *(Nations and Regions);* Charlotte Moore *(Content);* James Purnell *(Radio and Education);* Francesca Unsworth *(News and Current affairs)*

CONTROLLERS
Director of BBC Content (BBC One), Charlotte Moore
BBC Two, Patrick Holland
BBC Three, Damian Kavanagh
CBBC, Cheryl Taylor
Comedy, Shane Allen
Daily News, Gavin Allen
Digital Distribution, Richard Cooper
Drama, Piers Wenger
English Regions, David Holdsworth
Entertainment, Kate Phillips
Factual, Alison Kirkham
Group Finance, Shirley Cameron
News Mobile and Online, Fiona Campbell
Programming and Daytime, Dan McGolpin
Research and Development, Andy Conroy
Director of BBC Radio and BBC Music, Bob Shennan
Radio 1, 1Xtra and Asian Network, Ben Cooper
Radio 2, Lewis Carnie
Radio 3, Alan Davey
Radio 4 and 4 Extra, Gwyneth Williams
Radio 5 Live and 5 Live Sports Extra, Jonathan Wall
Radio 6 Music, Paul Rodgers
Radio and Music Multiplatform, Mark Friend
World Service English, Mary Hockaday

BRITISH COUNCIL
Bridgewater House, 58 Whitworth Street, Manchester M1 6BB
T 0161-957 7755 E general.enquiries@britishcouncil.org
W www.britishcouncil.org

The British Council was established in 1934, incorporated by royal charter in 1940 and granted a supplemental charter in 1993. It is an independent, non-political organisation which promotes Britain abroad and is the UK's international organisation for educational and cultural relations. The British Council is represented in over 100 countries.

Chair, Christopher Rodrigues, CBE
Chief Executive, Sir Ciarán Devane

BRITISH FILM INSTITUTE
21 Stephen Street, London W1T 1LN
T 020-7255 1444 W www.bfi.org.uk

The BFI, established in 1933, offers opportunities for people throughout the UK to experience, learn and discover more about the world of film and moving image culture. It incorporates the BFI National Archive, the BFI Reuben Library, BFI Southbank, BFI Distribution, the annual BFI London Film Festival as well as the BFI FLARE: London LGBT Film Festival, and the BFI IMAX cinema. It also publishes the monthly *Sight and Sound* magazine and provides advice and support for regional cinemas and film festivals across the UK.

Following the closure of the UK Film Council in April 2011, the BFI became the lead body for film in the UK, in charge of allocating lottery money for the development and production of new British films.

Chair, Josh Berger, CBE
Chief Executive, Amanda Nevill

BRITISH LIBRARY

96 Euston Road, London NW1 2DB
T 020-7412 7676 E customer-services@bl.uk W www.bl.uk

The British Library was established in 1973. It is the UK's national library and one of the world's greatest research libraries. It aims to serve scholarship, research, industry, commerce and all other major users of information. The Library's collection has developed over 250 years and exceeds 150 million separate items, including books, journals, manuscripts, maps, stamps, music, patents, newspapers and sound recordings in all written and spoken languages. The library is now based at two sites: London St Pancras and Boston Spa, W. Yorks. The library's sponsoring department is the Department for Digital, Culture, Media and Sport. Up to 3 million digitised items are added to the collection each year.

BRITISH LIBRARY BOARD

Chair, Rt. Hon. Baroness Blackstone
Members, David Barclay; Dr Robert Black, CBE, FRSE; Jonathan Callaway; Tracy Chevalier, FRSL; Martin Dickson; Lord Janvrin, GCB, GCVO, QSO, PC; Roly Keating; Dr Stephen Page; Patrick Plant; Sir John Ritblat; Dr Simon Thurley, CBE; Prof. Dame Helen Wallace, DBE, CMG, FBA

EXECUTIVE
Chief Executive, Roly Keating
Chief Librarian, Caroline Brazier
Chief Operating Officer, Phil Spence

BRITISH LIBRARY, BOSTON SPA
Boston Spa, Wetherby, W. Yorks LS23 7BQ
T 01937-546070

BRITISH MUSEUM

Great Russell Street, London WC1B 3DG
T 020-7323 8000 E info@britishmuseum.org
W www.britishmuseum.org

The British Museum houses the national collection of antiquities, ethnography, coins and paper money, medals, prints and drawings. The British Museum dates from 7 June 1753, when parliament approved the holding of a public lottery to raise funds for the purchase of the collections of Sir Hans Sloane and the Harleian manuscripts, and for their proper housing and maintenance. The building (Montagu House) was opened in 1759. The existing buildings were erected between 1823 and the present day, and the original collection has increased to its current dimensions by gifts and purchases. Total government grant-in-aid for 2016–17 was £53.6m.

Chair, Sir Richard Lambert
Trustees, Hon. Nigel Boardman; Cheryl Carolus; Elizabeth Corley, CBE; Patricia Cumper, MBE; Clarissa Farr; Prof. Clive Gamble; Muriel Gray; Prof. Nicola Lacey, FBA; Sir Richard Lambert; Sir Deryck Maughan; John Micklethwait, CBE; Sir Paul Nurse, FRS; Gavin Patterson; Mark Pears, CBE; Grayson Perry, CBE, RA; Sir Paul Ruddock; Rt. Hon. Lord Sassoon, KT; Prof. Amartya Sen;

Dame Nemat (Minouche) Shafik; Ahdaf Soueif; Lord Turner of Ecchinswell, FRS; Baroness Wheatcroft

OFFICERS
Director, Dr Hartwig Fischer
Deputy Directors, Joanna Mackle; Jonathan Williams; Christopher Yates

KEEPERS
Keeper of Africa, Oceania and the Americas, Lissant Bolton
Keeper of Ancient Egypt and Sudan, Neal Spencer
Keeper of Asia, Jane Portal
Keeper of Coins and Medals, Philip Attwood
Keeper of Greece and Rome, J. Lesley Fitton
Keeper of the Middle East, Jonathan N. Tubb
Deputy Keeper of Britain, Europe and Prehistory, Jill Cook
Keeper of Prints and Drawings, Hugo Chapman

BRITISH PHARMACOPOEIA COMMISSION

151 Buckingham Palace Road, London SW1W 9SZ
T 020-3080 6561 E bpcom@mhra.gov.uk
W www.pharmacopoeia.com

The British Pharmacopoeia Commission sets standards for medicinal products used in human and veterinary medicines and is responsible for publication of *British Pharmacopoeia* (a publicly available statement of the standard that a medicinal substance or product must meet throughout its shelf-life), *British Pharmacopoeia (Veterinary)* and *British Approved Names.* It has 17 members, including two lay members, who are appointed on behalf of the Secretary of State for Health and Social Care by the Department of Health and Social Care.

Chair, Prof. Kevin Taylor
Vice-Chair, Prof. Alastair Davidson

CARE QUALITY COMMISSION

Citygate, Gallowgate, Newcastle upon Tyne NE1 4PA
T 0300-061 6161 E enquiries@cqc.org.uk W www.cqc.org.uk

The Care Quality Commission (CQC) is the independent regulator of health and adult social care services in England, ensuring health and social care services provide people with safe, effective, compassionate, high-quality care and encouraging them to improve. CQC monitors, inspects and regulates services to make sure they meet fundamental standards of quality and safety and publishes performance ratings to help people choose care.

Chair, Peter Wyman, CBE
Board Members, Prof. Louis Appleby, CBE; Prof. Ted Baker; Paul Corrigan, CBE; Prof. Steve Field, CBE; Sir Robert Francis, QC; Dr Malte Gerhold; Jora Gill; Jane Mordue; Sir John Oldham; Paul Rew; Mark Saton; Liz Sayce; Andrea Sutcliffe, CBE
Chief Executive, Sir David Behan, CBE

CENTRAL ARBITRATION COMMITTEE

Fleetbank House, 2-6 Salisbury Square, London EC4Y 8JX
T 0330-109 3610 E enquiries@cac.gov.uk
W www.gov.uk/government/organisations/
central-arbitration-committee

The Central Arbitration Committee (CAC) is a permanent independent body with statutory powers whose main function is to adjudicate on applications relating to the statutory recognition and de-recognition of trade unions for collective bargaining purposes, where such recognition or de-recognition cannot be agreed voluntarily. In addition, the CAC has a statutory role in determining disputes between trade unions and employers over the disclosure of information for collective bargaining purposes, and in resolving applications and complaints under the information and consultation regulations, and performs a similar role in relation to the legislation on the European Works Council, European companies, European cooperative societies and cross-border mergers. The CAC and its predecessors have also provided voluntary arbitration in collective disputes.

Chair, Stephen Redmond
Chief Executive, James Jacob

CERTIFICATION OFFICE FOR TRADE UNIONS AND EMPLOYERS' ASSOCIATIONS

Lower Ground Floor, Fleetbank House, 2-6 Salisbury Square, London EC4Y 8JX
T 0330-109 3602 E info@certoffice.org
W www.gov.uk/government/organisations/certification-officer

The Certification Office is an independent statutory authority. The Certification Officer is appointed by the Secretary of State for Business, Energy and Industrial Strategy and is responsible for maintaining a list of trade unions and employers' associations; ensuring compliance with statutory requirements and keeping available for public inspection annual returns from trade unions and employers' associations; determining complaints concerning trade union elections, certain ballots and certain breaches of trade union rules; ensuring observance of statutory requirements governing mergers between trade unions and between employers' associations; overseeing the political funds and finances of trade unions and employers' associations; and for certifying the independence of trade unions.

Certification Officer, Sarah Bedwell

CHURCH COMMISSIONERS

Church House, Great Smith Street, London SW1P 3AZ
T 020-7898 1135 E commissioners.enquiry@churchofengland.org
W www.churchofengland.org/about/leadership-and-governance/church-commissioners

The Church Commissioners were established in 1948 by the amalgamation of Queen Anne's Bounty (established 1704) and the Ecclesiastical Commissioners (established 1836). They are responsible for the management of some of the Church of England's assets, the income from which is predominantly used to help pay for the stipend and pension of the clergy and to support the church's work throughout the country. The commissioners own UK and global company shares, over 120,000 acres of forestry estate, a residential estate in central London, and commercial property across Great Britain, plus an interest in overseas property via managed funds. They also carry out administrative duties in connection with pastoral reorganisation and closed churches.

The 33 commissioners are: the Archbishops of Canterbury and of York; eleven people elected by the General Synod, comprising four bishops, three clergy and four lay persons; three Church Estates Commissioners; two cathedral deans; nine people appointed by the crown and the archbishops; six holders of state office, comprising the Prime Minister, the Lord Chancellor, the Lord President of the Council, the Secretary of State for Digital, Culture, Media and Sport, the Speaker of the House of Commons and the Lord Speaker.

CHURCH ESTATES COMMISSIONERS

First, Loretta Minghella, OBE
Second, Rt. Hon. Dame Caroline Spelman, DBE, MP
Third, Andrew Mackie

OFFICERS
Chief Executive, Andrew Brown
Official Solicitor, Stephen Slack

COAL AUTHORITY

200 Lichfield Lane, Mansfield, Notts NG18 4RG
T 0345-762 6848 E thecoalauthority@coal.gov.uk
W www.gov.uk/government/organisations/the-coal-authority

The Coal Authority was established under the Coal Industry Act 1994 to manage certain functions previously undertaken by British Coal, including ownership of unworked coal. It is responsible for licensing coal mining operations and for providing information on coal reserves and past and future coal mining. It settles subsidence damage claims which are not the responsibility of licensed coal mining operators. It deals with the management and disposal of property, and with surface hazards such as abandoned coal mine entries and mine water discharges. The Coal Authority's powers were extended alongside the Energy Act 2011 to enable it to deal with metal mine subsidence issues and deliver a metal mine water treatment programme.

Chair, Stephen Dingle
Chief Executive, Philip Lawrence

COMMITTEE ON STANDARDS IN PUBLIC LIFE

1 Horse Guards Road, London SW1A 2HQ
T 020-7271 2948 E public@public-standards.gov.uk
W www.gov.uk/government/organisations/the-committee-on-standards-in-public-life

The Committee on Standards in Public Life (CSPL) was set up in October 1994. It is formed of 8 people appointed by the prime minister, comprising the chair, three political members nominated by the leaders of the three main political parties and four independent members. The CSPL advises the prime minister on ethical standards across the whole of public life in the UK. It monitors and reports on issues relating to the standards of conduct of all public office holders. It is responsible for promoting the 7 principles of public life, being: selflessness; integrity; objectivity; accountability; openness; honesty; and leadership.

Chair, Lord Bew
Members, Rt. Hon. Dame Margaret Beckett, DBE, MP; Sheila Drew Smith, OBE; Simon Hart, MP; Dr Jane Martin, CBE; Dame Shirley Pearce, DBE; Jane Ramsey; Monisha Shah; The Rt. Hon. Lord Andrew Stunell, OBE

COMMONWEALTH WAR GRAVES COMMISSION

2 Marlow Road, Maidenhead, Berks SL6 7DX
T 01628-634221 E enquiries@cwgc.org W www.cwgc.org

The Commonwealth War Graves Commission (formerly Imperial War Graves Commission) was founded by royal charter in 1917. It is responsible for the commemoration of around 1.7 million members of the forces of the Commonwealth who lost their lives in the two world wars. More than one million graves are maintained in over 23,000 burial grounds across 154 countries. Over three-quarters of a million men and women who have no known grave or who were cremated are commemorated by name on memorials built by the commission.

The funds of the commission are derived from the six participating governments: the UK, Canada, Australia, New Zealand, South Africa and India.

President, HRH the Duke of Kent, KG, GCMG, GCVO, ADC
Chair, Secretary of State for Defence

Vice-Chair, Vice-Adm. Sir Tim Laurence, KCVO, CB, ADC(P)
Members, High Commissioners in London for Australia, Canada, India, New Zealand and South Africa; Edward Chaplin, CMG, OBE; Robert Fox, MBE; Kevan Jones, MP; Hon. Ros Kelly; Lt.-Gen. Sir William Rollo, KCB, CBE; Keith Simpson, MP; Prof. Sir Hew Strachan, FRSE; Air Marshal David Walker, CB, CBE, AFC, RAF (retd)
Director-General and Secretary to the Commission, Victoria Wallace

COMPETITION SERVICE

Victoria House, Bloomsbury Place, London WC1A 2EB
T 020-7979 7979 W www.catribunal.org.uk

The Competition Service is the financial corporate body by which the Competition Appeal Tribunal is administered and through which it receives funding for the performance of its judicial functions.

Registrar, Hon. Charles Dhanowa, OBE, QC

CONSUMER COUNCIL FOR WATER

Victoria Square House, Victoria Square, Birmingham, B2 4AJ
T 0300-034 2222 E enquiries@ccwater.org.uk
W www.ccwater.org.uk

The Consumer Council for Water was established in 2005 under the Water Act 2003 to represent consumers' interests in respect of price, service and value for money from their water and sewerage services, and to investigate complaints from customers about their water company. There are four regional committees in England and one in Wales.

Chair, Alan Lovell
Chief Executive, Tony Smith

CORPORATION OF TRINITY HOUSE

Trinity House, Tower Hill, London EC3N 4DH
T 020-7481 6900 E enquiries@trinityhouse.co.uk
W www.trinityhouse.co.uk

The Corporation of Trinity House of Deptford Strond is the UK's largest-endowed maritime charity, established formally by royal charter by Henry VIII in 1514, with statutory duties as the General Lighthouse Authority (GLA) for England, Wales, the Channel Islands and Gibraltar. Its remit is to assist the safe passage of a variety of vessels through some of the busiest sea-lanes in the world; it does this by deploying and maintaining over 600 aids to navigation, ranging from lighthouses to a satellite navigation service. The corporation also has certain statutory jurisdiction over aids to navigation maintained by local harbour authorities and is responsible for marking or dispersing wrecks dangerous to navigation, except those occurring within port limits or wrecks of HM ships.

The statutory duties of Trinity House are funded by the General Lighthouse Fund, which is provided from light dues levied on ships calling at ports of the UK and the Republic of Ireland. The corporation is a deep-sea pilotage authority, authorised by the Secretary of State for Transport to license deep-sea pilots. In addition, Trinity House is a charitable organisation that maintains a number of retirement homes for mariners and their dependants, funds a four-year training scheme for those seeking a career in the merchant navy, and also dispenses grants to a wide range of maritime charities. The charity work is wholly funded by its own activities.

The corporation is controlled by a court of 41 Elder Brethren; a separate board controls the Lighthouse Service. The Elder Brethren also act as nautical assessors in marine cases in the Admiralty Division of the High Court.

ELDER BRETHREN

Master, HRH the Princess Royal, KG, KT, GCVO
Deputy Master, Capt. Ian McNaught
Wardens, Capt. Nigel Palmer, OBE *(Rental);* Rear-Adm. David Snelson, CB *(Nether)*
Elder Brethren, HRH the Duke of Edinburgh, KG, KT, OM, GBE; HRH the Prince of Wales, KG, KT, GCB; HRH the Duke of York, KG, GCVO, ADC; Capt. Roger Barker; Adm. Lord Boyce, KG, GCB, OBE; Lord Browne of Madingley, FRS, FRENG; Capt. John Burton-Hall, RD; Lord Carrington, KG, GCMG, CH, MC, PC; Viscount Cobham; Cdre Robert Dorey; Capt. Sir Malcolm Edge, KCVO; Capt. Ian Gibb, MBE; Malcolm Glaister; Capt. Duncan Glass, OBE; Capt. Stephen Gobbi; Lord Greenway, Bt.; Rear-Adm. Sir Jeremy de Halpert, KCVO, CB; Capt. Nigel Hope, RD; Lord Mackay of Clashfern, KT; Sir John Major, KG, CH; Capt. Peter Mason, CBE; Cdre Peter Melson, CVO, CBE, RN; Capt. David Orr; Sir John Parker, GBE; Douglas Potter; Capt. Nigel Pryke; Richard Sadler; Capt. Derek Richards, RD; Lord Robertson of Port Ellen, KT, GCMG, PC; Rear-Adm. Sir Patrick Rowe, KCVO, CBE; Cdre James Scorer; Simon Sherrard; Adm. Sir Jock Slater, GCB, LVO; Cdre David Squire, CBE, RFA; Vice-Adm. Lord Sterling of Plaistow, GCVO, CBE, RNR; Capt. Colin Stewart, LVO; Sir Adrian Swire, AE; Capt. Thomas Woodfield, OBE; Capt. Richard Woodman, LVO; Cdre William Walworth, CBE; Adm. Sir George Zambellas, GCB, DSC

OFFICERS

Secretary, Thomas Arculus
Director of Business Services, Ton Damen, RA
Director of Navigational Requirements, Capt. Roger Barker
Director of Operations, Cdre Rob Dorey

CREATIVE SCOTLAND

Waverley Gate, 2–4 Waterloo Place, Edinburgh EH1 3EG
T 0330-333 2000 E enquiries@creativescotland.com
W www.creativescotland.com

Creative Scotland is the organisation tasked with leading the development of the arts, creative and screen industries across Scotland. It was created in 2010 as an amalgamation of the Scottish Arts Council and Scottish Screen, and it encourages and sustains the arts through investment in the form of grants, bursaries, loans and equity. It aims to invest in talent; artistic production; audiences, access and participation; and the cultural economy. Total Scottish government grant-in-aid for 2017–18 is £45.5m, while the funding from the National Lottery is £28m.

Chair, Robert Wilson
Board, Ian Aitchison; David Brew; Karen Forbes; Erin Forster; Sheila Murray; Cate Nelson-Shaw; Barclay Price; Karthik Subramanya
Chief Executive, Janet Archer

CRIMINAL CASES REVIEW COMMISSION

5 St Philip's Place, Birmingham B3 2PW
T 0121-233 1473 E info@ccrc.x.gsi.gov.uk W www.ccrc.gov.uk

The Criminal Cases Review Commission is the independent body set up under the Criminal Appeal Act 1995. It is a non-departmental public body reporting to parliament via the Lord Chancellor and Secretary of State for Justice. It is responsible for investigating possible miscarriages of justice in England, Wales and Northern Ireland, and deciding whether or not to refer cases back to an appeal court. Members of the commission are appointed in accordance with the Office of the Commissioner for Public Appointments' code of practice.

Chair, Richard Foster, CBE
Members, Liz Calderbank; Rachel Ellis; Jill Gramann; Celia
    Hughes; David James Smith; Stephen Leach, CB; Linda
    Lee; Alexandra Marks, CBE; Dr Sharon Persaud; Jennifer
    Portway; Andrew Rennison; Robert Ward, CBE
Chief Executive, Karen Kneller

CROFTING COMMISSION
Great Glen House, Leachkin Road, Inverness IV3 8NW
T 01463-663439 E info@crofting.scotland.gov.uk
W www.crofting.scotland.gov.uk

The Crofting Commission was established on 1 April 2012,
taking over the regulation of crofting from the Crofters
Commission. The aim of the Crofting Commission is to
regulate crofting, to promote the occupancy of crofts, active
land use, and shared management of the land by crofters, as a
means of sustaining and enhancing rural communities in
Scotland.

Chief Executive, Bill Barron

CROWN ESTATE
St James's Market, London SW1Y 4AH
T 020-7851 5000 E enquiries@thecrownestate.co.uk
W www.thecrownestate.co.uk

The Crown Estate is part of the hereditary possessions of the
sovereign 'in right of the crown', managed under the
provisions of the Crown Estate Act 1961. It had a capital value
of £13.1bn in 2017, and includes substantial blocks of urban
property, primarily in London, almost 95,000 hectares of rural
land, around half of the foreshore, and the seabed out to the
12 nautical mile territorial limit throughout the UK. The
Crown Estate has a duty to maintain and enhance the capital
value of estate and the income obtained from it. Under the
terms of the act, the estate pays its revenue surplus to the
Treasury every year.

Chair and First Commissioner, Robin Budenberg, CBE
Chief Executive and Second Commissioner, Alison Nimmo, CBE,
    FRICS

DISCLOSURE AND BARRING SERVICE
PO Box 3961, Royal Wootton Bassett SN4 4HF
T 0300-020 0190 E customerservices@dbs.gsi.gov.uk
W www.gov.uk/government/organisations/
disclosure-and-barring-service

The Disclosure and Barring Service (DBS) is an executive non-
departmental public body of the Home Office. It helps
employers make safer recruitment decisions and prevent
unsuitable people from working with vulnerable groups,
including children. It was formed on 1 December 2012 and
replaced the Criminal Records Bureau (CRB) and Independent
Safeguarding Authority (ISA). The DBS is responsible for the
children's barred list and adults' barred list for England, Wales
and Northern Ireland.

Chair, Bill Griffiths
Chief Executive, Adele Downey

ENVIRONMENT AGENCY
PO Box 544, Rotherham S60 1BY
T 0370-850 6506 E enquiries@environment-agency.gov.uk
Incident Hotline 0800-807060
W www.gov.uk/government/organisations/environment-agency

Established in 1996 under the Environment Act 1995, the
Environment Agency is a non-departmental public body
sponsored by the Department for Environment, Food and
Rural Affairs. On 1 April 2013, Natural Resources Wales took
over the Environment Agency's responsibilities in Wales.

Around 68 per cent of the agency's funding is from the
government, with the rest raised from various charging
schemes. The agency is responsible for pollution prevention
and control in England and for the management and use of
water resources, including flood defences, fisheries and
navigation. Its remit also includes: scrutinising potentially
hazardous business operations; helping businesses to use
resources more efficiently; taking action against those who do
not take environmental responsibilities seriously; looking after
wildlife; working with farmers; helping people get the most
out of their environment; and improving the quality of inner
city areas and parks by restoring rivers and lakes.

The Environment Agency has head offices in Bristol and
London, as well as offices across England, divided into 14
regions. Its total grant-in-aid for 2016–17 was £800m.

Chair, Emma Howard Boyd
Deputy Chair, Richard Macdonald
Board Members, Maria Adebowale-Schwarte; Peter Ainsworth;
    Judith Batchelar, OBE; Karen Burrows; Lynne Frostick;
    Robert Gould; John Lelliott, OBE; Caroline Mason, CBE;
    Joanne Segars, OBE; John Varley, OBE; Gill Weeks, OBE
Chief Executive, Sir James Bevan

EQUALITY AND HUMAN RIGHTS COMMISSION
Arndale House, The Arndale Centre, Manchester M4 3AQ
T 0161-829 8100 E correspondence@equalityhumanrights.com
W www.equalityhumanrights.com

The Equality and Human Rights Commission (EHRC) is a
statutory body, established under the Equality Act 2006 and
launched in October 2007. It inherited the responsibilities of
the Commission for Racial Equality, the Disability Rights
Commission and the Equal Opportunities Commission. The
EHRC's purpose is to reduce inequality, eliminate
discrimination, strengthen relations between people, and
promote and protect human rights. It enforces equality
legislation on age, disability, gender reassignment, marriage
and civil partnership, pregnancy and maternity, race, religion
or belief, sex and sexual orientation, and encourages
compliance with the Human Rights Act 1998 throughout
England, Wales and Scotland.

Chair, David Isaac, CBE
Deputy Chair, Caroline Waters, OBE
Commissioners, Susan Johnson, OBE; Lorna McGregor; June
    Milligan *(Wales Commissioner);* Dr Lesley Sawers, OBE
    (Scotland Commissioner); Prof. Swaran Singh
Chief Executive, Rebecca Hilsenrath

EQUALITY COMMISSION FOR NORTHERN IRELAND
Equality House, 7–9 Shaftesbury Square, Belfast BT2 7DP
T 028-9050 0600 Textphone 028-9050 0589
E information@equalityni.org W www.equalityni.org

The Equality Commission was set up in 1999 under the
Northern Ireland Act 1998 and is responsible for promoting
equality, keeping the relevant legislation under review,
eliminating discrimination on the grounds of age, race,
disability, sex and sexual orientation, gender (including marital
and civil partner status, gender reassignment, pregnancy and
maternity), religion and political opinion, and for overseeing
the statutory duties on public authorities to promote equality
of opportunity and good relations.

Chief Commissioner, Dr Michael Wardlow
Deputy Chief Commissioner, Revd Dr Lesley Carroll
Chief Executive, Dr Evelyn Collins, CBE

GAMBLING COMMISSION

Victoria Square House, Victoria Square, Birmingham B2 4BP
T 0121-230 6666 E info@gamblingcommission.gov.uk
W www.gamblingcommission.gov.uk

The Gambling Commission was established under the Gambling Act 2005, and took over the role previously occupied by the Gaming Board for Great Britain in regulating and licensing all commercial gambling – apart from spread betting and the National Lottery – ie casinos, bingo, betting, remote gambling, gaming machines and lotteries. It also advises local and central government on related issues, and is responsible for the protection of children and the vulnerable from being harmed by gambling. In October 2013, the Gambling Commission took over all the responsibilities of the National Lottery Commission in regulating the National Lottery. The commission is sponsored by the Department for Digital, Culture, Media and Sport, with its work funded by licence fees paid by the gambling industry.

Chair, Dr William Moyes
Interim Chief Executive, Neil McArthur, MBE

HEALTH AND SAFETY EXECUTIVE

Redgrave Court, Merton Road, Bootle, Merseyside L20 7HS
T 01519-514000 W www.hse.gov.uk

The Health and Safety Commission (HSC) and the Health and Safety Executive (HSE) merged on 1 April 2008 to form a single national regulatory body – the HSE – responsible for promoting the cause of better health and safety at work. The HSE is sponsored by the Department for Work and Pensions.

HSE regulates all industrial and commercial sectors except operations in the air and at sea. This includes agriculture, construction, manufacturing, services, transport, mines, offshore oil and gas, quarries and major hazard sites in chemicals and petrochemicals.

HSE is responsible for developing and enforcing health and safety law; providing guidance and advice; commissioning research; conducting inspections and accident and ill-health investigations; developing standards; and licensing or approving some work activities such as asbestos removal. The HSE's nuclear directorate merged with a number of other bodies on 1 April 2011 to form the Office for Nuclear Regulation, an agency of the HSE.

Chair, Martin Temple, CBE
Board Members, Nick Baldwin, CBE; Jonathan Baume; George Brechin; Janice Crawford; Martin Esom; Susan Johnson, OBE; Sarah Pinch; Ken Robertson; Kevin Rowan; Martyn Thomas
Chief Executive, Dr Richard Judge

HER MAJESTY'S OFFICERS OF ARMS

COLLEGE OF ARMS (HERALDS' COLLEGE)
130 Queen Victoria Street, London EC4V 4BT
T 020-7248 2762 W www.college-of-arms.gov.uk

The Sovereign's Officers of Arms (King's, Heralds and Pursuivants of Arms) were first incorporated by Richard III in 1484. The powers vested by the crown in the Earl Marshal (the Duke of Norfolk) with regard to state ceremonial are largely exercised through the college. The college is also the official repository of the arms and pedigrees of English, Welsh, Northern Irish and Commonwealth (except Canadian) families and their descendants, and its records include official copies of the records of the Ulster King of Arms, the originals of which remain in Dublin. The 13 officers of the college specialise in genealogical and heraldic work for their respective clients.

Arms have long been, and still are, granted by letters patent from the Kings of Arms. A right to arms can only be established by the registration in the official records of the College of Arms of a pedigree showing direct male line descent from an ancestor already appearing therein as being entitled to arms, or by making application through the College of Arms for a grant of arms. Grants are made to corporations as well as to individuals.

Earl Marshal, the Duke of Norfolk

KINGS OF ARMS
Garter, Thomas Woodcock, CVO, FSA
Clarenceux, Patric Dickinson, LVO
Norroy and Ulster, Timothy Duke

HERALDS
Lancaster, Robert Noel
Somerset, David White
Richmond, Clive Cheesman, FSA
York, Michael O'Donoghue, FSA
Chester, Hon. Christopher Fletcher-Vane
Windsor, vacant

PURSUIVANTS
Rouge Croix, John Allen-Petrie
Rouge Dragon, vacant
Bluemantle, vacant
Portcullis, vacant

COURT OF THE LORD LYON
HM New Register House, Edinburgh EH1 3YT
T 0131-556 7255 E lyonoffice@gov.scot
W www.courtofthelordlyon.scot

Her Majesty's Officers of Arms in Scotland perform ceremonial duties and, in addition, may be consulted by members of the public on heraldic and genealogical matters in a professional capacity.

KING OF ARMS
Lord Lyon King of Arms, Dr Joseph Morrow, QC

HERALDS
Rothesay, Sir Crispin Agnew of Lochnaw, Bt., QC
Snawdoun, Elizabeth Roads, LVO, FSA, FSA SCOT
Marchmont, The Hon. Adam Bruce, WS

PURSUIVANTS
Dingwall, Yvonne Holton
Unicorn, Liam Devlin
Carrick, George Way of Plean

EXTRAORDINARY OFFICERS
Orkney Herald Extraordinary, Sir Malcolm Innes of Edingight, KCVO, WS
Angus Herald Extraordinary, Robin Blair, CVO, WS
Islay Herald Extraordinary, David Sellar, MVO
Ross Herald Extraordinary, Mark Dennis
Linlithgow Pursuivant Extraordinary, John Stirling, WS
Falkland Pursuivant Extraordinary, Roderick Macpherson

HIGHLANDS AND ISLANDS ENTERPRISE

An Lòchran, 10 Inverness Campus, Inverness IV2 5NA
T 01463-245245 E info@hient.co.uk W www.hie.co.uk

Highlands and Islands Enterprise (HIE) was set up under the Enterprise and New Towns (Scotland) Act 1991. Its role is to deliver community and economic development in line with the Scottish government economic strategy. It focuses on four priorities: supporting businesses and social enterprises; strengthening communities and fragile areas; developing growth sectors; and creating the conditions for a competitive and low carbon region. HIE's draft budget for 2018–19 is £71.7m.

Chair, Prof. Lorne Crerar
Chief Executive, Charlotte Wright

HISTORIC ENGLAND
Cannon Bridge House, 25 Dowgate Hill, London EC4R 2YA
T 020-7973 3700 E customers@historicengland.org.uk
W www.historicengland.org.uk

Historic England was established as an executive non-departmental public body on 1 April 2015, having previously been known as English Heritage (following the National Heritage Act 1983). Its remit is to look after England's historic environment and has five key objectives: to champion historic places; to identify and protect England's heritage; to support change, including giving advice on over 20,000 applications each year for planning permission or listed building consent; to understand historic places; and to provide expertise at a local level. In 2016–17 Historic England received £87.8m in grant-in-aid from the Department for Digital, Culture, Media and Sport.

Chair, Sir Laurie Magnus
Commissioners, Sally Balcombe; Paul Baker; Alex Balfour; Nicholas Boys Smith; Prof. Martin Daunton; Sandra Dinneen; Paul Farmer; Prof. Michael Fulford, CBE; Victoria Harley; Rosemarie MacQueen, MBE; Neil Mendoza; Michael Morrison; Charles O'Brien; Susie Thornberry; Richard Upton
Chief Executive, Duncan Wilson, OBE

HISTORIC ENVIRONMENT SCOTLAND
Longmore House, Salisbury Place, Edinburgh EH9 1SH
T 0131-668 8600 W www.historicenvironment.scot

Historic Environment Scotland is the lead public body established to investigate, care for and promote Scotland's historic environment. It is the result of the bringing together of two of Scotland's leading heritage bodies, Historic Scotland and the Royal Commission on Ancient and Historical Monuments Scotland, and has been formed to help deliver the Our Place in Time strategy. It is responsible for more than 300 properties of national importance, including Edinburgh Castle, Skara Brae and Fort George, and for collections that include more than 5 million drawings, photographs, negatives and manuscripts, along with Scotland's National Collection of Aerial Photography, containing more than 26 million aerial images. The Historic Environment Scotland's draft budget from the Scottish government for 2018–19 is £41.1m.

Chair, Jane Ryder, OBE
Trustees, Ian Brennan; Dr Janet Brennan; Trudi Craggs; Andrew Holmes; Dr Coinneach Maclean; Dr Fiona McLean; Ian Robertson; Dr Paul Stollard; Dr Ken Thomson
Chief Executive, Alex Paterson

HISTORIC ROYAL PALACES
Apartment 39A, Hampton Court Palace, Surrey KT8 9AU
T 020-3166 6000 E operators@hrp.org.uk W www.hrp.org.uk

Historic Royal Palaces was established in 1998 as a royal charter body with charitable status and is contracted by the Secretary of State for Digital, Culture, Media and Sport to manage the palaces on his behalf. The palaces – the Tower of London, Hampton Court Palace, the Banqueting House, Kensington Palace and Kew Palace – are owned by the Queen on behalf of the nation. Since 1 April 2014, Historic Royal Palaces is also responsible for the management of Hillsborough Castle in Northern Ireland under contract with the Secretary of State for Northern Ireland.

The organisation is governed by a board comprising a chair and 11 non-executive trustees. The chief executive is accountable to the board of trustees and ultimately to parliament. Historic Royal Palaces receives no funding from the government or the Crown.

TRUSTEES
Chair, Rupert Gavin
Appointed by the Queen, Zeinab Badawi; Ajay Chowdhury; Tim Knox *(ex officio, Director of the Royal Collection Trust);* Sir Michael Stevens, KCVO *(ex officio, the Keeper of the Privy Purse)*
Appointed by the Secretary of State, Prof. Sir David Cannadine; Bruce Carnegie-Brown *(ex officio, the Chair of Historic Royal Palaces' Campaign Board);* Gen. Lord Houghton of Richmond, GCB, CBE *(ex officio, the Constable of the Tower of London);* Jane Kennedy; Carole Souter, CBE; Sue Wilkinson, MBE; Louise Wilson, FRSA

OFFICER
Chief Executive, John Barnes

HOMES ENGLAND
Fry Building, 2 Marsham Street, London SW1P 4DF
T 0300-123 4500 E enquiries@homesengland.gov.uk
W www.gov.uk/government/organisations/homes-england

Homes England is an executive non-departmental public body, sponsored by the Ministry of Housing, Communities and Local Government to facilitate delivery of sufficient new homes by bringing together land, money, expertise, planning and compulsory purchase powers. It replaced the Homes and Communities Agency in January 2018, adopting the new trading name Homes England. Along with it, its regulation directorate, which undertakes the functions of the Regulation Committee, refers to itself as the Regulator of Social Housing. Homes England invests mostly in building new homes, but also in creating employment floorspace nationwide, as well as bringing forward public land for development and increasing the speed with which it is made available.

Chair, Sir Edward Lister
Chief Executive, Nick Walkley

HUMAN TISSUE AUTHORITY (HTA)
151 Buckingham Palace Road, London SW1W 9SZ
T 020-7269 1900 E enquiries@hta.gov.uk W www.hta.gov.uk

The Human Tissue Authority (HTA) was established on 1 April 2005 under the Human Tissue Act 2004, and is sponsored and part-funded by the Department of Health and Social Care. It regulates organisations that remove, store and use tissue for research, medical treatment, post-mortem examination, teaching and display in public. The HTA also gives approval for organ and bone marrow donations from living people. Under the EU tissues and cells directives, the HTA is one of the two designated competent authorities for the UK responsible for regulating tissues and cells. The HTA is also the sole competent authority for the UK under the EU organ donation directive.

Chair, Nicola Blackwood
Chief Executive, Allan Marriott-Smith

IMPERIAL WAR MUSEUMS (IWM)
Lambeth Road, London SE1 6HZ
T 020-7416 5000 E contact@iwm.org.uk W www.iwm.org.uk

IWM is the world's leading authority on conflict and its impact, focusing on Britain, its former empire and the Commonwealth from the First World War to the present. IWM aims to enrich people's understanding of the causes, course and consequences of war and conflict.

IWM comprises the organisation's flagship, IWM London; IWM North in Trafford, Manchester; IWM Duxford in Cambridgeshire; the Churchill War Rooms in Whitehall; and HMS *Belfast* in the Pool of London.

The total grant-in-aid for 2018–19 is £19.74m.

OFFICERS

President, HRH the Duke of Kent, KG, GCMG, GCVO, ADC
Chair, Air Chief Marshal Sir Stuart Peach, GBE, KCB, ADC
Trustees, Rt. Hon. Lord Ashcroft, KCMG; Desmond Bowen, CBE; Hugh Bullock; HE Janice Charette; Elizabeth Cleaver; HE Hon. Alexander Downer; Lt.-Gen. Andrew Figgures, CBE; Rear-Adm. Amjad Hussain, CB; HE Syed Ibne Abbas; Tim Marlow; HE Rt. Hon. Sir Jerry Mateparae; HE Obed Mlaba; Suzanne Nicholas; HE Y. K. Sinha; Tamsin Todd; Mark Urban; Peter Watkins, CBE; Matthew Westerman; HE Amari Wijewardene
Director-General, Diane Lees, CBE
Directors, John Brown; Graeme Etheridge; Rohan Hewavisenti *(interim);* Gill Webber

INFORMATION COMMISSIONER'S OFFICE
Wycliffe House, Water Lane, Wilmslow, Cheshire SK9 5AF
T 0303-123 1113 W www.ico.org.uk

The Information Commissioner's Office (ICO) oversees and enforces the Freedom of Information Act 2000 and the Data Protection Act 1998, with the objective of promoting public access to official information and protecting personal information.

The Data Protection Act 1998 sets out rules for the processing of personal information and applies to records held on computers and some paper files. The Freedom of Information Act 2000 is designed to help end the culture of unnecessary secrecy and open up the inner workings of the public sector to citizens and businesses.

The ICO also enforces and oversees the privacy and electronic communications regulations 2003 and the environmental regulations 2004. It also has limited responsibilities under the INSPIRE regulations 2009 and DRR regulations 2014.

The Information Commissioner reports annually to parliament on the performance of his/her functions under the acts and has obligations to assess breaches of the acts. As of April 2010, the ICO has been able to fine organisations up to £500,000 for serious breaches of the Data Protection Act.

Information Commissioner, Elizabeth Denham

INDUSTRIAL INJURIES ADVISORY COUNCIL
First Floor, Caxton House, Tothill Street, London SW1H 9NA
T 020-7449 5618 E iiac@dwp.gsi.gov.uk
W www.gov.uk/government/organisations/
industrial-injuries-advisory-council

The Industrial Injuries Advisory Council was established under the National Insurance (Industrial Injuries) Act 1946, which came into effect on 4 July 1948. Statutory provisions governing its work are set out in the Social Security Administration Act 1992 and corresponding Northern Ireland legislation. The council currently consists of 17 members, including a chair, appointed by the Secretary of State for Work and Pensions, and has three roles: to advise on the prescription of diseases; to consider and advise on draft regulations and proposals concerning the industrial injuries disablement benefit scheme referred to it by the Secretary of State for Work and Pensions or the Department for Communities in Northern Ireland; and to advise on any other matter concerning the scheme or its administration.

Chair, Prof. Keith Palmer

JOINT NATURE CONSERVATION COMMITTEE
Monkstone House, City Road, Peterborough PE1 1JY
T 01733-562626 E comment@jncc.gov.uk
W www.jncc.defra.gov.uk

The committee was established under the Environmental Protection Act 1990 and was reconstituted by the Natural Environment and Rural Communities Act 2006. It advises the government and devolved administrations on UK and international nature conservation issues. Its work contributes to maintaining and enriching biological diversity, conserving geological features and sustaining natural systems.

Chair, Prof. Chris Gilligan, CBE
Chief Executive, Marcus Yeo

LAW COMMISSION
1st Floor, Tower, 52 Queen Anne's Gate, London SW1H 9AG
T 020-3334 0200 E enquiries@lawcommission.gsi.gov.uk
W www.lawcom.gov.uk

The Law Commission was set up under the Law Commissions Act 1965 to make proposals to the government for the examination of the law in England and Wales and for its revision where it is unsuited for modern requirements, obscure or otherwise unsatisfactory. It recommends to the lord chancellor programmes for the examination of different branches of the law and suggests whether the examination should be carried out by the commission itself or by some other body. The commission is also responsible for the preparation of Consolidation and Statute Law (Repeals) Bills.

Chair, Rt. Hon. Lord Justice Bean
Commissioners, Prof. Nicholas Hopkins; Stephen Lewis; Prof. David Ormerod, QC; Nicholas Paines, QC
Chief Executive, Phil Golding

NATIONAL ARMY MUSEUM
Royal Hospital Road, Chelsea, London SW3 4HT
T 020-7730 0717 E info@nam.ac.uk W www.nam.ac.uk

The National Army Museum shares the stories of the British Army and its soldiers. It was established by royal charter in 1960 and moved to its current site in Chelsea in 1971. The museum re-opened in spring 2017 following a major redevelopment project. The new museum features five state-of-the-art galleries, housing a wide array of artefacts, paintings, photographs, uniforms and equipment; a café; a shop; and learning and research facilities.

Chair, Gen. Sir Richard Shirreff, KCB, CBE
Council Members, Patrick Aylmer; Dr Jonathan Boff; Judith Donovan, CBE; John Duncan; Rt. Hon. Lord Hamilton of Epsom; Lt.-Gen. Sir Simon Mayall, KBE; Guy Perricone; Paul Schreier; Jessica Spungin; Sabine Vandenbroucke; William Wells
Director-General, Justin Maciejewski, MBE

NATIONAL GALLERIES OF SCOTLAND
73 Belford Road, Edinburgh EH4 3DS
T 0131-624 6200 E enquiries@nationalgalleries.org
W www.nationalgalleries.org

The National Galleries of Scotland comprise three galleries in Edinburgh: the National Gallery of Scotland, the Scottish National Portrait Gallery and the Scottish National Gallery of Modern Art. There are also partner galleries at Paxton House, Berwickshire, and Duff House, Banffshire. It also owns the Granton Centre for Art, a purpose built storage facility.

TRUSTEES
Chair, Benny Higgins
Trustees, Tricia Bey; Alistair Dodds; Edward Green; Lesley
  Knox; Tari Lang; Catherine Muirden; Prof. Nicholas
  Pearce; Willie Watt; Nicky Wilson

OFFICERS
Director-General, Sir John Leighton
Directors, Prof. Christopher Breward *(Collection and Research);*
  Nicola Catterall *(Chief Operating Officer);* Jo Coomber
  (Public Engagement); Jacqueline Ridge *(Conservation and
  Collection Management)*

NATIONAL GALLERY

Trafalgar Square, London WC2N 5DN
T 020-7747 2885 E information@ng-london.org.uk
W www.nationalgallery.org.uk

The National Gallery, which houses a collection of paintings
in the western European tradition from the 13th to the 20th
century, was founded in 1824, following a parliamentary grant
of £57,000 for the purchase of the Angerstein collection of
pictures. The present site was first occupied in 1838; an
extension to the north of the building with a public entrance
in Orange Street was opened in 1975; the Sainsbury Wing was
opened in 1991; and the Getty Entrance opened off Trafalgar
Square at the east end of the main building in 2004. Total
government grant-in-aid for 2016–17 was £24.1m.

BOARD OF TRUSTEES
Chair, Hannah Rothschild
Trustees, Lance Batchelor; Prof. Dexter Dalwood; Moya
  Greene; Katrin Henkel; Prof. Anya Hurlbert; Lord King of
  Lothbury, KG, GBE, FBA; Sir John Kingman; Rosemary
  Leith; David Marks; John Nelson; Charles Sebag-
  Montefiore; John Singer

OFFICERS
Director, Dr Gabriele Finaldi
Director of Public Engagement and Deputy Director, Dr Susan
  Foister
Director of Finance and Operations, Chris Walker
Director of Collections, Dr Larry Keith

NATIONAL HERITAGE MEMORIAL FUND

7 Holbein Place, London SW1W 8NR
T 020-7591 6044 E NHMF_Enquiries@nhmf.org.uk
W www.nhmf.org.uk

The National Heritage Memorial Fund was set up under the
National Heritage Act 1980 in memory of people who have
given their lives for the United Kingdom. The fund provides
grants to organisations based in the UK, mainly so that they
can buy items of outstanding interest and of importance to the
national heritage. These must either be at risk or have a
memorial character. The fund is administered by a chair and
12 trustees who are appointed by the prime minister.
  The National Heritage Memorial Fund receives an annual
grant from the Department for Digital, Culture, Media and
Sport. Under the National Lottery etc. Act 1993, the trustees
of the fund became responsible for the distribution of funds for
both the National Heritage Memorial Fund and the Heritage
Lottery Fund. Total annual government grant-in-aid is £5m.

Chair, Sir Peter Luff
Trustees, Baroness Andrews, OBE, FSA; Anna Carragher; Sir
  Neil Cossons, OBE; Sandie Dawe, CBE; Dr Angela Dean;
  Jim Dixon; Perdita Hunt, OBE; Steve Miller; Richard
  Morris, OBE; Atul Patel; Dame Seona Reid, DBE; Dr Tom
  Tew
Chief Executive, Ros Kerslake, OBE

NATIONAL LIBRARY OF SCOTLAND

George IV Bridge, Edinburgh EH1 1EW
T 0131-623 3700 E enquiries@nls.uk W www.nls.uk

The library, which was founded as the Advocates' Library in
1682, became the National Library of Scotland in 1925. It
contains over 24 million printed items: two million maps,
25,000 newspaper and magazine titles and over 100,000
manuscripts, including the John Murray Archive. The library
receives around 300,000 new items every year and has material
in 490 languages. It has an unrivalled Scottish collection as
well as online catalogues and digital resources which can be
accessed through the Library's website. Material can be
consulted in the library branches in Edinburgh and Glasgow,
which are open to anyone with a valid library card.
  The National Library of Scotland Act 2012 modernised the
make-up and responsibilities of the board. At present there are
12 members, plus an appointed Chair on the Library's Board.
All of them are appointed by the Scottish ministers.

Chair, Sir Kenneth Calman
Vice-Chairs, Sir Neil McIntosh; Fiona Robertson
Board members, Noreen Adams; Ruth Crawford; Helen
  Durndell; Dianne Haley; Simon Learoyd; Iain Marley;
  Prof. Adrienne Scullion; Amina Shah; Prof. Melissa Terras;
  Carmel Teusner
National Librarian and Chief Executive, Dr John Scally
Heads of Department, John Coll *(Access);* Graeme Forbes
  (Collections Management); Anthony Gillespie *(Business
  Support);* Stuart Lewis *(Digital);* Alexandra Miller *(External
  Relations & Governance);* Robin Smith *(Collections and
  Research)*

NATIONAL LIBRARY OF WALES/
LLYFRGELL GENEDLAETHOL CYMRU

Aberystwyth, Ceredigion, Wales SY23 3BU
T 01970-632800 E gofyn@llgc.org.uk W www.library.wales

The National Library of Wales was founded by royal charter
in 1907, and is funded by the Welsh government. It contains
about six million books and newspapers, 40,000 manuscripts,
four million deeds and documents, numerous maps, prints and
drawings, and a sound and moving image collection. It
specialises in manuscripts and books relating to Wales and the
Celtic peoples. It is the repository for pre-1858 Welsh probate
records, manorial records and tithe documents, and certain
legal records. Admission is by reader's ticket to the reading
rooms but entry to the exhibition programme is free.
  The draft budget from the Welsh government for 2018–19
is £10.8m.

Trustees, Lord Aberdare; Philip Cooper; Eleri Davies; Iwan
  Davies; Susan Davies; Richard Houdmont; Dyfrig Jones;
  Gwilym Dyfri Jones; Elizabeth Siberry; Hugh Thomas;
  Rhodri Thomas *(President);* Steve Williams; Lee Yale-
  Helms *(Treasurer)*
Librarian and Chief Executive, Linda Tomos

NATIONAL MUSEUM OF THE ROYAL
NAVY

HM Naval Base (PP66), Portsmouth PO1 3NH
T 023-9289 1370 W www.nmrn.org.uk

The National Museum of the Royal Navy comprises nine
museums: HMS *Victory,* HMS *Caroline,* HMS *M.33,* the
National Museum of the Royal Navy Portsmouth, the National
Museum of the Royal Navy Hartlepool, the Fleet Air Arm
Museum, the Royal Navy Submarine Museum, the Royal
Marines Museum and Explosion! Museum of Naval Firepower.
The Fleet Air Museum is located at RNAS Yeovilton, Somerset,

and HMS Caroline is located at Alexandra Dock, Belfast, while the other five are situated in Portsmouth and Gosport.

Chair, Adm. Sir Jonathon Band, GCB
Trustees, Michael Bedingfield; John Brookes, OBE; Capt. Dan Conley, OBE; Prof. John Craven, CBE; Sir Robert Crawford, CBE; Cllr Donna Jones; Mike Gambazzi; Vice-Adm. Sir Adrian Johns, KCB, CBE, ADC; Kimberley Marshall; Maj.-Gen. Jeffrey Mason, MBE; Tim Schadla-Hall; Gavin Whitter; Dr Caroline Williams, Charles Wilson
Director-General, Prof. Dominic Tweddle

NATIONAL MUSEUM WALES/ AMGUEDDFA CYMRU
Cathays Park, Cardiff CF10 3NP
T 0300-111 2333 W museum.wales

National Museum Wales (also known as Amgueddfa Cymru) is the body that runs Wales' seven national museums. It comprises National Museum Cardiff; St Fagans: National History Museum; Big Pit: National Coal Museum, Blaenafon; National Roman Legion Museum, Caerleon; National Slate Museum, Llanberis; National Wool Museum, Dre-fach Felindre; National Waterfront Museum, Swansea; and National Collections Centre, Nantgarw. The draft budget from the Welsh government for 2018-19 is £22.7m.

Trustees, Elisabeth Elias *(President);* Dr Carol Bell *(Vice President);* Laurence Pavelin, CBE *(Treasurer);* Baroness Andrews, OBE; Prof. Tony Atkins; Dr Caroline Duigan; Carys Howell; Rachel Hughes; Hywel John; Dr Glenda Jones; Dr Hywel Jones, CMG; Prof. Robert Pickard; Michael Prior; Victoria Provis; Jessica Seaton; Keshav Singhal, MBE
Director-General, David Anderson, OBE

NATIONAL MUSEUMS LIVERPOOL
127 Dale Street, Liverpool L2 2JH
T 0151-207 0001 W www.liverpoolmuseums.org.uk

National Museums Liverpool is a group of museums and collections including the World Museum, the Merseyside Maritime Museum (also home to the Border Force National Museum), the Lady Lever Art Gallery, the Walker Art Gallery, Sudley House, the International Slavery Museum and the Museum of Liverpool.

Chair, Sir David Henshaw
Trustees, Carmel Booth; Laura Carstensen; James Chapman; Heather Lauder; Andrew McCluskey; Philip Price; Ian Rosenblatt, OBE; Virginia Tandy; Dr Nicola Thorp
Interim Director, Louise Parnell
Director of Art Galleries, Sandra Penketh
Director, World Museum Liverpool, Steve Judd
Director, Museum of Liverpool, Janet Dugdale
Head of International Slavery Museum, Dr Richard Benjamin

NATIONAL MUSEUMS NORTHERN IRELAND
Cultra, Holywood, Northern Ireland BT18 0EU
T 0845-608 0000 E info@nmni.com W www.nmni.com

Across three unique sites National Museums Northern Ireland cares for and presents inspirational collections reflecting the creativity, innovation, history, culture and people of Northern Ireland and beyond.

Together the Ulster Museum, Ulster Folk and Transport Museum and Ulster American Folk Park offer a unique opportunity to experience the heritage and way of life of Northern Ireland.

Chair, Miceal McCoy
Vice-Chair, Dr Leon Litvack
Trustees, Prof. Michael Catto; Prof. Garth Earls; Prof. Karen Fleming; Hazel Francey; Daphne Harshaw; Dr Rosemary Kelly, OBE; Alan McFarland; Dr George McIlroy; Catherine Molloy; Annette Moor; Joseph Rice; Dr Margaret Ward
Chief Executive, Kathryn Thomson

NATIONAL MUSEUMS SCOTLAND
Chambers Street, Edinburgh EH1 1JF
T 0300-123 6789 E info@nms.ac.uk W www.nms.ac.uk

National Museums Scotland provides advice, expertise and support to the museums community across Scotland, and undertakes fieldwork that often involves collaboration at local, national and international levels. National Museums Scotland comprises the National Museum of Scotland, the National War Museum, the National Museum of Rural Life, the National Museum of Flight and the National Museums Collection Centre. Its collections represent more than two centuries of collecting and include Scottish and classical archaeology, decorative and applied arts, world cultures and social history and science, technology and the natural world.

Up to 15 trustees can be appointed by the Minister for Culture, Tourism and External Affairs for a term of four years, and may serve a second term.

Chair, Bruce Minto, OBE
Trustees, Ann Allen; Mary Bownes; Adam Bruce; Gordon Drummond; Chris Fletcher; Dr Brian Lang, CBE, FRSE; Lynda Logan; Dr Catriona Macdonald; Miller McLean, FCIBS, FIB; Prof. Walter Nimmo, CBE, MD, FRCP, FRCSED, FRCA, FRSE; Janet Stevenson; James Troughton, RIBA; Eilidh Wiseman
Director, Dr Gordon Rintoul, CBE

NATIONAL PORTRAIT GALLERY
St Martin's Place, London WC2H 0HE
T 020-7306 0055 W www.npg.org.uk

The National Portrait Gallery was established in 1856. Today the Gallery collects portraits of those who have made, or are making, a significant contribution to British history and culture. The Collection is free to visit, and includes works across all media, from painting and sculpture to photography and digital portraits. To complement the Collection, the Gallery stages exhibitions, displays, talks and events throughout the year which explore the nature of portraiture. The Gallery loans exhibitions, displays and individual portraits to organisations across the UK and internationally as part of its ongoing commitment to sharing the Collection as widely as possible.

Chair of the Board of Trustees, David Ross
Director, Dr Nicholas Cullinan

NATURAL ENGLAND
County Hall, Spetchley Road, Worcester WR5 2NP
T 0300-060 3900 E enquiries@naturalengland.org.uk
W www.gov.uk/government/organisations/natural-england

Natural England is the government's adviser on the natural environment, providing practical scientific advice on how to look after England's landscapes and wildlife.

The organisation's remit is to ensure sustainable stewardship of the land and sea so that people and nature can thrive.

Natural England works with farmers and land managers; business and industry; planners and developers; national and local government; charities and conservationists; interest groups and local communities to help them improve their local environment.

Chair, Andrew Sells
Chief Executive, James Cross

NATURAL HISTORY MUSEUM
Cromwell Road, London SW7 5BD
T 020-7942 5000 W www.nhm.ac.uk

The Natural History Museum, which houses 80 million natural history specimens, originates from the natural history departments of the British Museum, which grew extensively during the 19th century; in 1860 it was agreed that the natural history collections should be separated from the British Museum's collections of books, manuscripts and antiquities. Part of the site of the 1862 International Exhibition in South Kensington was acquired for the new museum, and the museum opened to the public in 1881. In 1963 the Natural History Museum became completely independent with its own board of trustees. The Natural History Museum at Tring, bequeathed by the second Lord Rothschild, has formed part of the museum since 1937. The Geological Museum merged with the Natural History Museum in 1986. In September 2009 the Natural History Museum opened the Darwin Centre, which contains public galleries, a high-tech interactive area known as the Attenborough Studio, scientific research facilities and storage for 28 million zoological specimens, 17 million entomology specimens and three million botanical specimens. Total budgeted government grant-in-aid for 2018–19 is £41.8m.

Chair, Lord Green of Hurstpierpoint
Trustees, Prof. Sir John Beddington, CMG, FRS; Dame Frances Cairncross, DBE, FRSE; Prof. Christopher Gilligan; Prof. Sir John Holman; Anand Mahindra; Hilary Newiss; Robert Noel; Simon Patterson; Prof. Stephen Sparks, FRS, CBE; Prof. Dame Janet Thornton, DBE, FRS, FMEDSCI; Dr Kim Winser, OBE
Museum Director, Sir Michael Dixon
Directors, Neil Greenwood *(Finance and Corporate Services);* Fiona McWilliams *(Development and Communications);* Prof. Ian Owens *(Science)*

NATURAL RESOURCES WALES
Ty Cambria, 29 Newport Road, Cardiff CF24 0TP
T 0300-065 3000 E enquiries@naturalresourceswales.gov.uk
W www.naturalresources.wales

Natural Resources Wales is the principal adviser to the Welsh government on the environment. It became operational on 1 April 2013 following a merger of the Countryside Council for Wales, Environment Agency Wales and the Forestry Commission Wales. It is responsible for ensuring that the natural resources of Wales are sustainably maintained, enhanced and used; now and in the future.

Chair, Diane McCrea, MBE
Deputy Chair, Dr Madeleine Harvard
Board Members, Karen Balmer; Chris Blake; Howard Davies; Dr Ruth Hall; Dr Elizabeth Haywood; Zoë Henderson; Andy Middleton; Clare Pillman; Nigel Reader, CBE; Sir Paul Williams, OBE
Chief Executive, Clare Pillman

NHS PAY REVIEW BODY
8th Floor, Fleetbank House, 2-6 Salisbury Square, London EC4Y 8JX
T 020-7211 8295 W www.gov.uk/government/organisations/nhs-pay-review-body

The NHS Pay Review Body (NHSPRB) advises the prime minister, Secretary of State for Health and ministers in Scotland, Wales and Northern Ireland on the remuneration of all paid staff under agenda for change and employed in the NHS. The review body was established in 1983 for nurses and allied health professionals. Its remit has since expanded to cover just under 1.5 million staff, ie almost all staff in the NHS, with the exception of dentists, doctors and very senior managers.

Chair, Philippa Hird
Members, Bronwen Curtis, CBE; Patricia Gordon; Joan Ingram, OBE; Shamaila Qureshi; Prof. David Ulph, CBE; Prof. Jonathan Wadsworth; Lorraine Zuleta

NORTHERN IRELAND HUMAN RIGHTS COMMISSION
Temple Court, 39 North Street, Belfast BT1 1NA
T 028-9024 3987 E info@nihrc.org W www.nihrc.org

The Northern Ireland Human Rights Commission is a non-departmental public body, established by the Northern Ireland Act 1998 and set up in March 1999. Its purpose is to protect and promote human rights in Northern Ireland. Its main functions include reviewing the law and practice relating to human rights, advising government and the Northern Ireland Assembly, and promoting an awareness of human rights. It can also investigate human rights violations and take cases to court. The members of the commission are appointed by the Secretary of State for Northern Ireland.

Chief Commissioner, Les Allamby
Commissioners, Helen Ferguson; Helena Macormac; Paul Mageean; John McCallister; Eddie Rooney; Graham Shields, OBE
Chief Executive, Dr David Russell

NORTHERN LIGHTHOUSE BOARD
84 George Street, Edinburgh EH2 3DA
T 0131-473 3100 E enquiries@nlb.org.uk W www.nlb.org.uk

The Northern Lighthouse Board is the general lighthouse authority for Scotland and the Isle of Man and owes its origin to an act of parliament passed in 1786. At present there are 19 commissioners who operate under the Merchant Shipping Act 1995.

The commissioners control 206 lighthouses, 165 lighted and unlighted buoys, four DGPS (differential global positioning system) stations and an ELORAN (long-range navigation) system. *See also* Transport.

Chair, Graham Crerar
Vice-Chair, Capt. Michael Brew
Commissioners, Lord Advocate; Solicitor-General for Scotland; Lord Provosts of Edinburgh, Glasgow and Aberdeen; Convener of Highland Council; Provost of Argyll and Bute Council; Sheriffs-Principal of North Strathclyde, Tayside, Central and Fife, Grampian, Highlands and Islands, South Strathclyde, Dumfries and Galloway, Lothian and Borders, and Glasgow and Strathkelvin; Capt. Alastair Beveridge; Capt. Alistair Mackenzie; Elaine Wilkinson; Rob Woodward
Chief Executive, Mike Bullock, MBE

NUCLEAR DECOMMISSIONING AUTHORITY
Herdus House, Westlakes Science and Technology Park, Moor Row, Cumbria CA24 3HU
T 01925-802077 E enquiries@nda.gov.uk
W www.gov.uk/government/organisations/nuclear-decommissioning-authority

The Nuclear Decommissioning Authority (NDA) was created under the Energy Act 2004. It is a strategic authority that owns 17 sites plus associated civil nuclear liabilities and assets of the public sector, previously under the control of the UK Energy Authority and British Nuclear Fuels. The NDA's responsibilities include decommissioning and cleaning up civil nuclear facilities; ensuring the safe management of waste products, both radioactive and non-radioactive; implementing government policy on the long-term management of nuclear waste; and developing UK-wide low-level waste strategy plans.

Total planned expenditure for 2018–19 is £3.146bn, with total grant-in-aid standing at £2.269bn. The remaining £0.877bn will come from commercial operations.

Chair, Tom Smith
Chief Executive, David Peattie

OFFICE FOR BUDGET RESPONSIBILITY

14T, 102 Petty France, London SW1H 9AJ
T 020-3334 6337 E OBR.Enquiries@obr.uk W www.obr.uk

The Office for Budget Responsibility (OBR) was created in 2010 to provide independent and authoritative analysis of the UK's public finances. It has five main roles: producing forecasts for the economy and public finances; judging progress towards the government's fiscal targets; evaluating fiscal risks; assessing the long-term sustainability of the public finances; and scrutinising HM Treasury's costing of tax and welfare spending measures.

Chair, Robert Chote
Committee Members, Prof. Sir Charles Bean; Graham Parker, CBE

OFFICE OF COMMUNICATIONS (OFCOM)

Riverside House, 2A Southwark Bridge Road, London SE1 9HA
T 0300-123 3000 W www.ofcom.org.uk

OFCOM was established in 2003 under the Office of Communications Act 2002 as the independent regulator and competition authority for the UK communications industries with responsibility, for television, video-on-demand, radio, telecommunications and wireless communications services.

Following the passing of the Postal Services Act 2011, OFCOM has assumed regulatory responsibility for postal services from Postcomm, the Postal Services Commission.

Chair, Lord Burns
Deputy Chair, Baroness Noakes, DBE
Board Members, Bob Downs *(Scotland);* Graham Mather; Jonathan Oxley; Nick Pollard; Dr Stephen Unger; Tim Suter; Ben Verwaayen
Chief Executive, Sharon White

OFFICE OF MANPOWER ECONOMICS (OME)

8th Floor, Fleetbank House, 2–6 Salisbury Square, London EC4Y 8JX
T 020-7211 8165 W www.gov.uk/government/organisations/office-of-manpower-economics

The Office of Manpower Economics (OME) was established in 1971. It is an independent non-statutory organisation responsible for servicing eight independent review bodies, which make recommendations impacting 2.5 million workers – around 45 per cent of public sector staff – and a pay bill of £100bn.

OME Director, Martin Williams
Directors, Mark Franks *(Chief Economist, Research and Analysis Group; Senior Salaries Review Body);* Stuart Sarson *(Prison Service Pay Review Body; Armed Forces' Pay Review Body; School Teachers' Review Body);* Edmund Quilty *(NHS Pay Review Body; Review Body on Doctors' and Dentists'*

Remuneration; National Crime Agency Remuneration Review Body; Police Remuneration Review Body)

PARADES COMMISSION

Andras House, 60 Great Victoria Street, Belfast BT2 7BB
T 028-9089 5900 E info@paradescommissionni.org
W www.paradescommission.org

The Parades Commission was set up under the Public Processions (Northern Ireland) Act 1998. Its function is to encourage and facilitate local accommodation of contentious parades; where this is not possible, the commission is empowered to make legal determinations about such parades, which may include imposing conditions on aspects of the notified parade (such as restrictions on routes/areas and exclusion of certain groups with a record of bad behaviour).

The chair and members are appointed by the Secretary of State for Northern Ireland; the membership must, as far as is practicable, be representative of the community in Northern Ireland.

Chair, Anne Henderson
Members, Sarah Havlin; Paul Hutchinson; Colin Kennedy; Anne Marshall; Geraldine McGahey

PAROLE BOARD FOR ENGLAND AND WALES

52 Queen Anne's Gate, London SW1H 9AG
T 020-3880 0885 E info@paroleboard.gov.uk
W www.gov.uk/government/organisations/parole-board

The Parole Board was established in 1968 under the Criminal Justice Act 1967 and became an independent executive non-departmental public body on 1 July 1996 under the Criminal Justice and Public Order Act 1994. It is the body that protects the public by making risk assessments about prisoners to decide who may safely be released into the community and who must remain in, or be returned to, custody. Board decisions are taken at two main types of panels of up to three members: 'paper panels' for the majority of cases, or oral hearings for decisions concerning prisoners serving life and indeterminate sentences for public protection. The budget for 2017–18 is £19.2m.

Chair, vacant
Chief Executive, Martin Jones

PAROLE BOARD FOR SCOTLAND

Saughton House, Broomhouse Drive, Edinburgh EH11 3XD
T 0131-244 8373 E paroleboardforscotland@gov.scot
W www.scottishparoleboard.gov.uk

The board directs and advises the Scottish ministers on the release of prisoners on licence, and related matters.

Chair, John Watt

PENSION PROTECTION FUND (PPF)

Renaissance, 12 Dingwall Road, Croydon CR0 2NA
T 0345-600 2541 E information@ppf.gsi.gov.uk
W www.pensionprotectionfund.org.uk

The PPF became operational in 2005. It was established to pay compensation to members of eligible defined-benefit pension schemes, when a qualifying insolvency event in relation to the employer occurs and where there is a lack of sufficient assets in the pension scheme. The PPF also administers the Financial Assistance Scheme, which helps members whose schemes wound-up before 2005. It is also responsible for the Fraud Compensation Fund (which provides compensation to occupational pension schemes that suffer a loss that can be attributed to dishonesty). The chair and board of the PPF are appointed by, and accountable to, the Secretary of State for

Work and Pensions, and are responsible for paying compensation, calculating annual levies (which help fund the PPF), and setting and overseeing investment strategy.

Chair, Arnold Wagner, OBE
Chief Executive, Oliver Morley, CBE

PENSIONS REGULATOR
Napier House, Trafalgar Place, Brighton BN1 4DW
T 0345-600 0707 E customersupport@tpr.gov.uk
W www.thepensionsregulator.gov.uk

The Pensions Regulator was established in 2005 as the regulator of work-based pension schemes in the UK, replacing the Occupational Pensions Regulatory Authority (OPRA). It aims to protect the benefits of occupational and personal pension scheme members by working with trustees, employers, pension providers and advisers. The regulator's work focuses on encouraging better management and administration of schemes, ensuring that final salary schemes have a sensible funding plan, and encouraging money purchase schemes to provide members with the information that they need to make informed choices about their pension fund. The Pensions Act 2004 and the Pensions Act 2008 gave the regulator a range of powers which can be used to protect scheme members, but a strong emphasis is placed on educating and enabling those responsible for managing pension schemes, and powers are used only where necessary. The regulator offers free online resources to help trustees, employers, professionals and advisers understand their role, duties and obligations.

Chair, Mark Boyle
Chief Executive, Lesley Titcomb

POLICE ADVISORY BOARD FOR ENGLAND AND WALES
Home Office, 6th Floor Fry, 2 Marsham Street, London SW1P 4DF
E PABEWsecretariat@homeoffice.gsi.gov.uk
W www.gov.uk/government/organisations/
police-advisory-board-for-england-and-wales

The Police Advisory Board for England and Wales was established in 1965 and provides advice to the home secretary on general questions affecting the police in England and Wales. It also considers draft regulations under the Police Act 1996 about matters such as recruitment, diversity and collaboration between forces.

Independent Chair, Elizabeth France

PRISON SERVICE PAY REVIEW BODY
8th Floor, Fleetbank House, 2-6 Salisbury Square, London EC4Y 8JX
T 020-7211 8259 W www.gov.uk/government/organisations/
prison-services-pay-review-body

The Prison Service Pay Review Body was set up in 2001. It makes independent recommendations on the pay of prison governors, operational managers, prison officers and related grades for the Prison Service in England and Wales, and for the Northern Ireland Prison Service.

Chair, Dr Peter Knight, CBE
Members, Roberta Brownlee; Nicholas Caton; Prof. Andy Dickerson; Leslie Manasseh, MBE; Paul West, QPM

PRIVY COUNCIL OFFICE
1 Horse Guards Road, London SW1A 2HQ
T 020-7271 3292 E enquiries@pco.gov.uk
W https://privycouncil.independent.gov.uk

The primary function of the office is to act as the secretariat to the Privy Council. It is responsible for the arrangements leading to the making of all royal proclamations and orders in council; for certain formalities connected with ministerial changes; for considering applications for the granting (or amendment) of royal charters; for the scrutiny and approval of by-laws and statutes of chartered institutions and of the governing instruments of universities and colleges; and for the appointment of high sheriffs and Privy Council appointments to governing bodies. Under the relevant acts, the office is responsible for the approval of certain regulations and rules made by the regulatory bodies of the medical and certain allied professions.

The Lord President of the Council is the ministerial head of the office and presides at meetings of the Privy Council. The Clerk of the Council is the administrative head of the Privy Council office.

Lord President of the Council and Leader of the House of Commons, Rt. Hon. Andrea Leadsom
Clerk of the Council, Richard Tilbrook
Head of Secretariat and Deputy Clerk, Ceri King
Deputy Clerk, Christopher Berry

REVIEW BODY ON DOCTORS' AND DENTISTS' REMUNERATION
8th Floor, Fleetbank House, 2-6 Salisbury Square, London EC4Y 8JX
T 020-7211 8300 W www.gov.uk/government/organisations/
review-body-on-doctors-and-dentists-remuneration

The Review Body on Doctors' and Dentists' Remuneration was set up in 1971. It advises the prime minister, the secretary of state for health and social care, first ministers in Scotland, Wales and Northern Ireland, and the ministers for Health and Social Care, in England, Scotland, Wales and Northern Ireland on the remuneration of doctors and dentists taking any part in the National Health Service.

Chair, Prof. Sir Paul Curran
Members, David Bingham; Mehrunnisa Lalani; Prof. Kevin Lee; Prof. James Malcomson; John Matheson, CBE; Nigel Turner, OBE; Jane Williams

ROYAL AIR FORCE MUSEUM
Grahame Park Way, London NW9 5LL
T 020-8205 2266 E london@rafmuseum.org
W www.rafmuseum.org.uk

The museum has two sites, one at the former airfield at Colindale, in North London, and the second at Cosford, in the West Midlands, both of which illustrate the development of aviation from before the Wright brothers to the present-day RAF. The museum's collection across both sites consists of over 170 aircraft, as well as artefacts, aviation memorabilia, fine art and photographs.

Chair, Air Chief Marshal Sir Glenn Torpy, GCB, CBE, DSO
Trustees, Peter Bateson; Laurie Benson; Dr Carol Cole; Alan Coppin; Dr Rodney Eastwood, MBE; Sir Gerry Grimstone; Richard Holman; Catriona Kempston; Julie McGarvey; Hon. John Michaelson; Andrew Reid; Nick Sanders; Michael Schindler; Robin Southwell, OBE; Alan Spence; Malcolm White, OBE
Chief Executive, Maggie Appleton, MBE

ROYAL BOTANIC GARDEN EDINBURGH
20A Inverleith Row, Edinburgh EH3 5LR
T 0131-552 7171 W www.rbge.org.uk

The Royal Botanic Garden Edinburgh (RBGE) originated as the Physic Garden, established in 1670 beside the Palace of Holyroodhouse. The garden moved to its present 28ha site at Inverleith, Edinburgh, in 1820. There are also three regional gardens: Benmore Botanic Garden, near Dunoon, Argyll; Logan Botanic Garden, near Stranraer, Wigtownshire; and

Dawyck Botanic Garden, near Stobo, Peeblesshire. Since 1986 RBGE has been administered by a board of trustees established under the National Heritage (Scotland) Act 1985. It receives an annual grant from the Scottish government's Environment and Forestry Directorate.

The RBGE is an international centre for scientific research on plant diversity and for horticulture education and conservation. It has an extensive library, a herbarium with almost three million preserved plant specimens, and over 15,000 species in the living collections.

Chair, Sir Muir Russell, KCB, FRSE
Trustees, Prof. Beverley Glover; Dr David Hamilton; Patricia Henton, FRSE; Prof. Thomas Meagher; Diana Murray; Prof. Ian Wall, FRSE; Chris Wallace
Regius Keeper and Queen's Botanist in Scotland, Simon Milne, MBE

ROYAL BOTANIC GARDENS, KEW

Kew Gardens, Richmond, Surrey TW9 3AB
T 020-8332 5655 E info@kew.org
Wakehurst, Ardingly, W. Sussex RH17 6TN
T 01444-894066 E wakehurst@kew.org
W www.kew.org

Kew Gardens was originally laid out as a private garden for the now demolished White House for George III's mother, Princess Augusta, in 1759. The gardens were much enlarged in the 19th century, notably by the inclusion of the grounds of the former Richmond Lodge. In 1965 Kew acquired the gardens at Wakehurst on a long lease from the National Trust. Under the National Heritage Act 1983 a board of trustees was set up to administer the gardens, which in 1984 became an independent body supported by grant-in-aid from the Department for Environment, Food and Rural Affairs. Total grant in aid for 2016–17 was £33m.

The functions of RBG, Kew are to carry out research into plant sciences, to disseminate knowledge about plants and to provide the public with the opportunity to gain knowledge and enjoyment from the gardens' collections. There are extensive national reference collections of living and preserved plants and a comprehensive library and archive. The main emphasis is on plant conservation and biodiversity; Wakehurst houses the Millennium Seed Bank Partnership, which is the largest *ex situ* conservation project in the world – its aim is to save seed from 25 per cent of the earth's wild plant species by 2020.

Chair, Marcus Agius
Trustees, Nick Baird; Prof. Liam Dolan; Catherine Dugmore; Sarah Flannigan; Valerie Gooding; Prof. Sue Hartley; Ian Karet; Jantiene Klein Roseboom van der Veer; Michael Lear; Sir Derek Myers; Prof. Malcolm Press
Director, Richard Deverell

ROYAL COMMISSION ON THE ANCIENT AND HISTORICAL MONUMENTS OF WALES

Ffordd Penglais, Aberystwyth SY23 3BU
T 01970-621200 E nmr.wales@rcahmw.gov.uk
W www.rcahmw.gov.uk

The Royal Commission on the Ancient and Historical Monuments of Wales, established in 1908, is the investigation body and national archive for the historic environment of Wales. It has the lead role in ensuring that Wales's archaeological, built and maritime heritage is authoritatively recorded, and seeks to promote the understanding and appreciation of this heritage nationally and internationally. The commission is funded by the Welsh government.

Chair, Dr Eurwyn Wiliam, FSA
Vice-Chair, Catherine Hardman, FSA
Commissioners, Neil Beagrie, FRSA; Chris Brayne; Caroline Crewe-Read, FRSA; Dr Louise Emanuel; Thomas Lloyd, OBE, FSA; Dr Mark Redknap, FSA; Prof. Christopher Williams, PHD, FRHISTS
Secretary, Christopher Catling

ROYAL MUSEUMS GREENWICH

National Maritime Museum, Greenwich, London SE10 9NF
T 020-8312 6565 E RMGenquiries@rmg.co.uk
W www.rmg.co.uk

Royal Museums Greenwich comprises the National Maritime Museum, the Queen's House and the Royal Observatory Greenwich. It also works in collaboration with the Cutty Sark Trust. The National Maritime Museum provides information on the maritime history of Great Britain and is the largest institution of its kind in the world, with over 1.5 million items in its collections related to seafaring, navigation and astronomy. Originally the home of Charles I's Queen, Henrietta Maria, the Queen's House was designed by Inigo Jones and built between 1616–18, although it was structurally altered between 1629–35. It now contains a fine-art collection. The Royal Observatory, Greenwich is the home of Greenwich Mean Time and the prime meridian of the world. It also contains London's only planetarium, Harrison's timekeepers and the UK's largest refracting telescope.

Chair, Sir Charles Dunstone, CVO
Trustees, Prof. Alison Bashford, CVO; Eleanor Boddington; Joyce Bridges, CBE; Dr Aminul Hoque, MBE; Prof. Christopher Lintott; Carol Marlow; Jeremy Penn; Eric Reynolds; Gerald Russell; Adm. Sir Mark Stanhope, GCB, OBE
Director, Kevin Fewster, FRSA

SCHOOL TEACHERS' REVIEW BODY

8th Floor, Fleetbank House, 2-6 Salisbury Square, London EC4Y 8JX
T 020-7211 8463 W www.gov.uk/government/organisations/school-teachers-review-body

The School Teachers' Review Body was set up under the School Teachers' Pay and Conditions Act 1991. It is required to examine and report on such matters relating to the statutory conditions of employment of school teachers in England and Wales as may be referred to it by the education secretary.

Chair, Dr Patricia Rice
Members, Peter Batley; Sir Robert Burgess; Ken Clark; John Lakin; Mike Redhouse; Jeanne Watson

SCIENCE MUSEUM GROUP

W https://group.sciencemuseum.org.uk

SCIENCE MUSEUM
Exhibition Road, London SW7 2DD
T 020-7942 4000 E info@sciencemuseum.ac.uk
W www.sciencemuseum.org.uk

MUSEUM OF SCIENCE AND INDUSTRY
Liverpool Road, Castlefield, Manchester M3 4FP
T 0161-832 2244 E contact@msimanchester.org.uk
W www.msimanchester.org.uk

NATIONAL RAILWAY MUSEUM AND LOCOMOTION
NRM York, Leeman Road, York YO26 4XJ
T 0333-016 1010 E nrm.visitorservices@nrm.org.uk
Locomotion, Shildon, Co. Durham DL4 2RE
T 01904-685780 E info@locomotion.org.uk
W www.nrm.org.uk

NATIONAL SCIENCE AND MEDIA MUSEUM

Pictureville, Bradford BD1 1NQ
T 0844-856 3797 E talk.nsmm@scienceandmediamuseum.org.uk
W www.scienceandmediamuseum.org.uk

The Science Museum Group (SMG) consists of the Science Museum; the Museum of Science and Industry, Manchester; the National Railway Museum, York; the National Science and Media Museum, Bradford; and Locomotion at Shildon. The Science Museum houses the national collections of science, technology, industry and medicine and attracts 3.3 million visits annually. The museum began as the science collection of the South Kensington Museum and first opened in 1857. In 1883 it acquired the collections of the Patent Museum and in 1909 the science collections were transferred to the new Science Museum, leaving the art collections with the Victoria and Albert Museum. The Wellcome Wing was opened in July 2000.

The Trustees of the Science Museum Group have statutory duties under the National Heritage Act 1983 for the general management and control of SMG.

Total government grant-in-aid for 2016–17 was £37.47m.

Chair, Dame Mary Archer, DBE
Trustees, Matthew D'Ancona; Prof. Brian Cantor; Dr Sarah Dry; Lord Faulkner of Worcester; Sharon Flood; Prof. Russell Foster, CBE, FRS, FMEDSCI; Andreas Goss; Lord Grade of Yarmouth, CBE; Prof. Ludmilla Jordanova, FRHS, FRSM; Simon Linnett; Lopa Patel; Prof. David Phoenix, OBE; Anton Valk, CBE; Rt. Hon. Lord Willetts; Dame Fiona Woolf, CBE
Director of Science Museum, Ian Blatchford
Director of Museum of Science & Industry, Sally MacDonald
Director of National Science and Media Museum, Jo Quinton-Tulloch
Director of National Railway Museum, Judith McNicol

SCOTTISH CRIMINAL CASES REVIEW COMMISSION

5th Floor, Portland House, 17 Renfield Street, Glasgow G2 5AH
T 0141-270 7030 E info@sccrc.org.uk W www.sccrc.org.uk

The commission is a non-departmental public body, funded by the Scottish Government Justice Directorate, and established by Act of Parliament in April 1999. It assumed the role previously performed by the Secretary of State for Scotland to consider alleged miscarriages of justice in Scotland and refer cases meeting the relevant criteria to the high court for determination. Members are appointed by the Queen on the recommendation of the first minister; senior executive staff are appointed by the commission.

Chair, Bill Matthews
Members, Dr Rajan Darjee; Colin Dunipace; Peter Ferguson, QC; Prof. Jim Fraser; Frances McMenamin, QC; Raymond McMenamin; Elaine Noad
Chief Executive, Gerard Sinclair

SCOTTISH ENTERPRISE

Atrium Court, 50 Waterloo Street, Glasgow G2 6HQ
T 0300-013 3385 E enquiries@scotent.co.uk
W www.scottish-enterprise.com

Scottish Enterprise was established in 1991 and its purpose is to stimulate the sustainable growth of Scotland's economy. It is mainly funded by the Scottish government and is responsible to the Scottish ministers. Working in partnership with the private and public sectors, Scottish Enterprise plan to invest £291.5m in 2017–18 to further the development of Scotland's economy by helping ambitious and innovative businesses grow and become more successful. Scottish Enterprise is particularly interested in supporting companies that provide renewable energy, encourage trade overseas, increase innovation, and those that will help Scotland become a low-carbon economy. Its anticipated grant-in-aid allocation (capital and resource allocation) for 2017–18 was £211.4m.

Chair, Bob Keiller
Chief Executive, Steve Dunlop

SCOTTISH ENVIRONMENT PROTECTION AGENCY (SEPA)

Erskine Court, Castle Business Park, Stirling FK9 4TZ
T 0300-099 6699 W www.sepa.org.uk

SEPA was established in 1996 and is the public body responsible for environmental protection in Scotland. It regulates potential pollution to land, air and water; the storage, transport and disposal of controlled waste; and the safekeeping and disposal of radioactive materials. It does this within a complex legislative framework of acts of parliament, EU directives and regulations, granting licences to operations of industrial processes and waste disposal. SEPA also operates Floodline (T 0345-988 1188), a public service providing information on the possible risk of flooding 24 hours a day, 365 days a year.

Chair, Bob Downes
Members, Franceska van Dijk; Dr Richard Dixon; Michelle Francis; Nicola Gordon; Martin Hill; Nick Martin; Prof. Bill McKelvey, OBE; Prof. Keith Nicholson; Dr Lesley Sawers
Chief Executive, Terry A'Hearn

SCOTTISH LAW COMMISSION

140 Causewayside, Edinburgh EH9 1PR
T 0131-668 2131 E info@scotlawcom.gsi.gov.uk
W www.scotlawcom.gov.uk

The Scottish Law Commission, established in 1965, keeps the law in Scotland under review and makes proposals for its development and reform. It is responsible to the Scottish ministers through the Scottish government constitution, law and courts directorate.

Chair, Hon. Lord Pentland
Commissioners, Caroline Drummond; David Johnston, QC; Dr Andrew Steven
Chief Executive, Malcolm McMillan

SCOTTISH LEGAL AID BOARD

Thistle House, 91 Haymarket Terrace, Edinburgh EH12 5HE
T 0131-226 7061 E general@slab.org.uk W www.slab.org.uk

The Scottish Legal Aid Board was set up under the Legal Aid (Scotland) Act 1986 to manage legal aid in Scotland. It reports to the Scottish government. Board members are appointed by Scottish ministers.

Chair, Ray MacFarlane
Members, Brian Baverstock; Rani Dhir; Marieke Dwarshuis; Stephen Humphreys; Tim McKay; Raymond McMenamin; Sheriff John Morris; Sarah O'Neill; Paul Reid; David Sheldon, QC; Lesley Ward
Chief Executive, Colin Lancaster

SCOTTISH NATURAL HERITAGE (SNH)

Great Glen House, Leachkin Road, Inverness IV3 8NW
T 01463-725000 E enquiries@snh.gov.uk W www.snh.gov.uk

SNH was established in 1992 under the Natural Heritage (Scotland) Act 1991. It is the government's adviser on all aspects of nature and landscape across Scotland and its role is to help the public understand, value and enjoy Scotland's nature, as well as to support those people and organisations that manage it.

Chair, Dr Mike Cantlay, OBE
Chief Executive and Accountable Officer, Francesca Osowska
Directors, Nick Halfhide *(Operations);* Sally Thomas *(Policy and Advice);* Jane Macdonald *(Interim, Corporate Services)*

SEAFISH

18 Logie Mill, Logie Green Road, Edinburgh EH7 4HS
T 0131-558 3331 E seafish@seafish.co.uk W www.seafish.org

Established under the Fisheries Act 1981, Seafish works with all sectors of the UK seafood industry to satisfy consumers, raise standards, improve efficiency and secure a sustainable and profitable future. Services range from research and development, economic consulting, market research and training and accreditation through to legislative advice for the seafood industry. It is sponsored by the four UK fisheries departments, which appoint the board, and receives 80 per cent of its funding through a levy on seafood.

Chair, Brian Young
Chief Executive, Marcus Coleman

SECURITY AND INTELLIGENCE SERVICES

GOVERNMENT COMMUNICATIONS HEADQUARTERS (GCHQ)
Hubble Road, Cheltenham GL51 0EX
T 01242-221491 W www.gchq.gov.uk

GCHQ produces signals intelligence in support of national security and the UK's economic wellbeing, and in the prevention or detection of serious crime. Additionally, in 2017 GCHQ launched the National Cyber Security Centre, NCSC, replacing the CESG, CCA, CERT UK and the cyber related responsibilities of CPNI. It is the national authority for cyber security, and provides advice and assistance to government departments, the armed forces and other national infrastructure bodies on the security of their communications and information systems. GCHQ was placed on a statutory footing by the Intelligence Services Act 1994 and is headed by a director who is directly accountable to the foreign secretary.

Director, Jeremy Fleming

SECRET INTELLIGENCE SERVICE (MI6)
PO Box 1300, London SE1 1BD
Anti-Terrorist Hotline 0800-789 321 W www.sis.gov.uk

Established in 1909 as the Foreign Section of the Secret Service Bureau, the Secret Intelligence Service produces secret intelligence in support of the government's security, defence, foreign and economic policies. It was placed on a statutory footing by the Intelligence Services Act 1994 and is headed by a chief, known as 'C', who is directly accountable to the foreign secretary.

Chief, Alex Younger

SECURITY SERVICE (MI5)
PO Box 3255, London SW1P 1AE
T 0800-111 4645 Anti-Terrorist Hotline 0800-789 321
W www.mi5.gov.uk

The Security Service is responsible for security intelligence work against covertly organised threats to the UK. It is organised into ten branches, each with dedicated areas of responsibility, which include countering terrorism, espionage and the proliferation of weapons of mass destruction. The Security Service also provides security advice to a wide range of organisations to help reduce vulnerability to threats from individuals, groups or countries hostile to UK interests. The

home secretary has parliamentary accountability for the Security Service. There is a network of regional offices around the UK, plus a Northern Ireland headquarters.

Director-General, Andrew Parker

SENIOR SALARIES REVIEW BODY
8th Floor, Fleetbank House, 2-6 Salisbury Square, London EC4Y 8JX
T 020-7211 8315 W www.gov.uk/government/organisations/review-body-on-senior-salaries

The Senior Salaries Review Body (formerly the Top Salaries Review Body) was set up in 1971 to advise the prime minister on the remuneration of the judiciary, senior civil servants, senior officers of the armed forces and very senior managers in the NHS. In 1993 its remit was extended to cover the pay, pensions and allowances of MPs, ministers and others whose pay is determined by the Ministerial and Other Salaries Act 1975, and also the allowances of peers. If asked, it advises on the pay of officers and members of the devolved parliament and assemblies.

Chair, Dr Martin Read, CBE
Members, Margaret Edwards; Sir Adrian Johns, KCB, CBE; David Lebrecht; John Steele; Dr Peter Westaway; Sharon Witherspoon

STUDENT LOANS COMPANY LTD
100 Bothwell Street, Glasgow G2 7JD
T 0300-100 0607 W www.slc.co.uk

The Student Loans Company (SLC) is owned by the Department for Education. It processes and administers financial assistance, in the form of grants and loans, for undergraduates who have secured a place at university or college. The SLC also provides loans for tuition fees, which are paid directly to the university or college. In 2016 the SLC introduced the provision of loans to postgraduates in accordance with government policy. The SLC supports around 1.8 million students per year.

Chair, Christian Brodie
Chief Executive, Peter Lauener *(interim)*

TATE
W www.tate.org.uk

TATE BRITAIN
Millbank, London SW1P 4RG
T 020-7887 8888 E visiting.britain@tate.org.uk

TATE MODERN
Bankside, London SE1 9TG
T 020-7887 8888 E visiting.modern@tate.org.uk

TATE LIVERPOOL
Albert Dock, Liverpool L3 4BB
T 015-1702 7400 E visiting.liverpool@tate.org.uk

TATE ST IVES
Porthmeor Beach, St Ives, Cornwall TR26 1TG
T 01736-796226 E visiting.stives@tate.org.uk

Tate comprises four art galleries: Tate Britain and Tate Modern in London, Tate Liverpool and Tate St Ives.

Tate Britain, which opened in 1897, displays the national collection of British art from 1500 to the present day – with special attention and dedicated space given to Blake, Turner and Constable. A £45m renovation of Tate Britain was completed in 2013.

Opened in May 2000, Tate Modern displays the Tate collection of international modern art dating from 1900 to the present day. It includes works by Dalí, Picasso, Matisse and Warhol, as well as many contemporary works. It is housed in the former Bankside Power Station in London, which was redesigned by the Swiss architects Herzog and de Meuron, and in the neighbouring and purpose-built Switch House, which was designed by Herzog and de Meuron and opened in 2016.

Tate Liverpool opened in 1988 and houses mainly 20th-century art, and Tate St Ives, which features work by artists from and working in St Ives and includes the Barbara Hepworth Museum and Sculpture Garden, opened in 1993.

BOARD OF TRUSTEES
Chair, Lionel Barber
Trustees, John Akomfrah, CBE; Dexter Dalwood; Tim Davie; Jayne-Anne Gadhia; Moya Greene; Maja Hoffman; Michael Lynton; Dame Seona Reid, DBE; Roland Rudd; James Timpson, CBE; Stephen Witherford

OFFICERS
Director, Tate, Maria Balshaw, CBE
Directors, Alex Farquharson *(Tate Britain);* Frances Morris *(Tate Modern);* Caroline Collier *(Partnerships and Programmes);* Anna Cutler *(Learning and Research);* Helen Legg *(Tate Liverpool);* Anne Barlow *(Tate St Ives)*

TOURISM BODIES

Visit Britain, Visit Scotland, Visit Wales and the Northern Ireland Tourist Board are responsible for developing and marketing the tourist industry in their respective regions. Visit Wales is not listed here as it is part of the Welsh government, within the Department for Heritage, and not a public body.

VISITBRITAIN
Sanctuary Buildings, 20 Great Smith Street, London SW1P 3BT
T 020-7578 1000 E industry.relations@visitbritain.org
W www.visitbritain.org
Chair, Steve Ridgway, CBE
Chief Executive, Sally Balcombe

VISITSCOTLAND
Ocean Point One, 94 Ocean Drive Edinburgh EH6 6JH
T 0131-472 2222 E info@visitscotland.com
W www.visitscotland.com
Chair, Lord Thurso
Chief Executive, Malcolm Roughead, OBE

NORTHERN IRELAND TOURIST BOARD
Floors 10–12, Linum Chambers, Bedford Square, Bedford Street, Belfast BT2 7ES T 028-9023 1221
E info@tourismni.com W www.tourismni.com
Chair, Terence Brannigan
Chief Executive, John McGrillen

TRANSPORT FOR LONDON (TFL)
4th Floor, 14 Pier Walk, London SE10 0ES
T 0343-222 1234 W www.tfl.gov.uk

TfL was created in July 2000 and is the integrated body responsible for the capital's transport system. Its role is to implement the Mayor of London's transport strategy and manage the transport services across London, for which the mayor has responsibility. These services include TfL Rail, London's buses, London Underground, London Overground, the Docklands Light Railway (DLR), Tramlink, London River Services and Victoria Coach Station. TfL also runs the Emirates Air Line and the London Transport Museum. In a joint venture with the Department for Transport, TfL is responsible for the construction of Crossrail – a new railway linking Maidenhead and Heathrow in the west, to Shenfield and Abbey Wood in the east. The central section of Crossrail is expected to be completed by the end of 2018. In 2017 TfL announced plans

for Crossrail 2, a railway running between Surrey and Hertfordshire.

TfL is responsible for managing the Congestion Charging scheme and for maintaining 360 miles (580km) of main roads and all of London's 6,000+ traffic lights. It also regulates the city's taxis and private hire vehicles. TfL runs the Santander Cycle Hire scheme, allowing customers to hire a bicycle from £2, and the Dial-a-ride scheme, a door-to-door service for disabled people unable to use buses, trams or the London Underground.

Chair, Rt. Hon. Sadiq Khan
Members, Kay Carberry, CBE; Prof. Greg Clark, CBE; Baroness Grey-Thompson, DBE; Bronwen Handyside; Ron Kalifa; Michael Liebreich; Anne McMeel; Dr Alice Maynard, CBE; Dr Mee Ling Ng, OBE; Dr Nelson Ogunshakin, OBE; Val Shawcross, CBE *(Deputy Chair);* Dr Nina Skorupska, CBE; Dr Lynn Sloman; Ben Story
Commissioner, Mike Brown, MVO

UK ATOMIC ENERGY AUTHORITY
Culham Science Centre, Abingdon, Oxfordshire OX14 3DB
T 01235-528822 W www.gov.uk/government/organisations/ uk-atomic-energy-authority

The UK Atomic Energy Authority (UKAEA) was established by the Atomic Energy Authority Act 1954 and took over responsibility for the research and development of the civil nuclear power programme. The UKAEA reports to the Department for Business, Energy and Industrial Strategy and is responsible for managing UK fusion research, including operating the Joint European Torus (JET) on behalf of the UKAEA's European partners at its site in Culham, Oxfordshire. Culham also houses the facilities for Materials Research, Remote Access in Challenging Environments and Oxford Advanced Skills. In October 2009, as part of the government's Operation Efficiency Programme, the authority sold its commercial arm, UKAEA Limited; as a result, the UKAEA no longer provides nuclear decommissioning services.

Chair, Prof. Roger Cashmore, CMG, FRS
Chief Executive, Prof. Ian Chapman

UK SPORT
21 Bloomsbury Street, London WC1B 3HF
T 020-7211 5100 E info@uksport.gov.uk W www.uksport.gov.uk

UK Sport was established by royal charter in 1997 and is accountable to parliament through the Department for Digital, Culture, Media and Sport. Its mission is to lead sport in the UK to world-class success. This means working with partner organisations to deliver medals at the Olympic and Paralympic Games and organising, bidding for and staging major sporting events in the UK; increasing the UK's sporting activity and influence overseas; and promoting sporting conduct, ethics and diversity in society. UK Sport is funded by a mix of grant-in-aid and National Lottery income.

Chair, Dame Katherine Grainger, DBE
Chief Executive, Liz Nicholl, OBE

VICTORIA AND ALBERT MUSEUM
Cromwell Road, London SW7 2RL
T 020-7942 2000 E contact@vam.ac.uk W www.vam.ac.uk

The Victoria and Albert Museum (V&A) is the national museum of art, design and performance. It descends directly from the Museum of Manufactures, which opened in Marlborough House in 1852 after the Great Exhibition of 1851. The museum was moved in 1857 to become part of the South Kensington Museum. It was renamed the Victoria and Albert

Museum in 1899. It also houses the National Art Library and Print Room.

The museum's collections span over 5,000 years of human creativity, including paintings, sculpture, architecture, ceramics, furniture, fashion and textiles, theatre and performance, photography, glass, jewellery and metalwork. Materials relating to childhood are displayed at the V&A Museum of Childhood at Bethnal Green, which opened in 1872 and is the most important surviving example of the type of glass and iron construction used by Joseph Paxton for the Great Exhibition. The V&A also houses the National Art Library, which holds over 950,000 books dedicated to the study of fine and decorative arts from around the world.

WALLACE COLLECTION

Hertford House, Manchester Square, London W1U 3BN
T 020-7563 9500 E collection@wallacecollection.org
W www.wallacecollection.org

The Wallace Collection was bequeathed to the nation by the widow of Sir Richard Wallace, in 1897, and Hertford House was subsequently acquired by the government. The collection contains works by Titian and Rembrandt, and includes porcelain, furniture and an array of arms and armour.

DEVOLVED GOVERNMENT

WALES

NATIONAL ASSEMBLY FOR WALES
Cardiff Bay, Cardiff CF99 1NA
T 0845-010 5500 W www.assemblywales.org

The National Assembly for Wales has been in existence since 1999, following a 'yes' vote in the 1997 referendum. However, the way the assembly is structured and its powers have changed over time.

The UK Act that created the assembly was the Government of Wales Act 1998. This stated that the Assembly was a 'corporate body' which meant that the Welsh government and the assembly were a single organisation. Also, it could not pass its own acts. It could, however make orders and regulations, known as secondary legislation.

The Government of Wales Act 2006 created a formal legal separation between:
- the legislative branch: the National Assembly for Wales, made up of 60 assembly members, and
- the executive branch: the Welsh government, made up of the First Minister, Welsh cabinet secretaries and the Counsel General

The act allowed the assembly to seek the power to make laws from the UK parliament. The laws were known as 'measures' of the National Assembly for Wales ('assembly measures'). The power to make laws ('legislative competence') was granted through clauses in Westminster bills or through legislative competence orders. These had to be approved by parliament and by the assembly. This is how the third assembly operated between 2007 and 2011.

The Government of Wales Act 2006 also contained provision for the assembly to make its own lawns without the permission of the UK parliament. These provisions could only be triggered by:
- two-thirds of all assembly members voting in favour of a referendum
- the approval of the UK government and parliament to hold a referendum
- a 'yes' vote in a referendum of the Welsh public

A referendum held on 3 March 2011 resulted in a 'yes' vote in favour of bringing into force part four of the Government of Wales Act 2006. This has meant that since the 2011 National Assembly of Wales election the assembly has been able to pass laws on all subjects in the devolved areas without first needing the agreement of the UK parliament.

During an assembly election, the people of Wales have two votes. One vote is for their constituency assembly member who represents local areas. Wales is divided into 40 constituencies and each is represented by one assembly member (AM).

The other vote is for a party or independent candidate to represent the voter's region. Wales is divided into five regions – North Wales, Mid and West Wales, South Wales West, South Wales East and South Wales Central.

This system means that the overall number of seats held by each political party more closely reflects the share of the vote that the party receives.

The 60 assembly members who are elected make decisions regarding many things that affect life in Wales – health, education, housing and transport. Their job is to make sure that the Welsh government's decisions are in the best interests of Wales and its people.

The National Assembly for Wales does this by:

- scrutinising the policies the Welsh government sets and the decisions it makes
- scrutinising suggestions for laws, proposing changes and voting on whether they should be passed
- asking questions to Welsh government and making suggestions about policies
- voting on how the Welsh government spends its budget every year

The assembly also makes laws for Wales. A law can be put forward by the Welsh government, an individual assembly member, or an assembly committee or the Assembly Commission. The majority of laws are put forward by the Welsh government.

The assembly operates in both Welsh and English and all its legislation is made bilingually.

In July 2018 the National Assembly of Wales Commission announced plans to lower the minimum voting age for assembly elections to 16 years. They also announced plans to change the name of the assembly to Welsh Parliament/ Senedd Cymru. The assembly intends to legislate both changes prior to the next assembly elections in 2021.

ASSEMBLY COMMISSION
The Assembly Commission was created under the Government of Wales Act 2006 to ensure that the assembly is provided with the property, staff and services required for it to carry out its functions. The commission also sets the National Assembly's strategic aims, objectives, standards and values. The Assembly Commission consists of the presiding officer, plus four other assembly members, one nominated by each of the four party groups. The five commissioners are accountable to the National Assembly.

Presiding Officer, Elin Jones, AM
Deputy Presiding Officer, Ann Jones, AM
Commissioners, Suzy Davies, AM; Adam Price, AM; Joyce Watson, AM
Chief Executive and Clerk of the Assembly, Manon Antoniazzi

ASSEMBLY COMMITTEES
The Business Committee, chaired by the Presiding Officer and established on 24 May 2016, is responsible for facilitating the effective organisation of assembly proceedings. The rest of the assembly committees *as at* August 2018 are:

Children, Young People and Education
  Chair, Lynne Neagle, AM
Climate Change, Environment and Rural Affairs
  Chair, Mike Hedges, AM
Constitutional and Legislative Affairs
  Chair, Mick Antoniw, AM
Culture, Welsh Language and Communications
  Chair, Bethan Sayed, AM
Economy, Infrastructure and Skills
  Chair, Russell George, AM
Equality, Local Government and Communities
  Chair, John Griffiths, AM
External Affairs and Additional Legislation
  Chair, David Rees, AM
Finance
  Chair, vacant
Health, Social Care and Sport
  Chair, Dai Lloyd, AM
Petitions
  Chair, David Rowlands, AM

Public Accounts
Chair, Nick Ramsay, AM
Scrutiny of the First Minister
Chair, Ann Jones, AM
Standards of Conduct
Chair, Jayne Bryant, AM

SALARIES* 2018–19

First Minister	£146,228
Presiding Officer	£109,671
Cabinet Secretary	£104,448
Minister/Deputy Presiding Officer	£88,781
Assembly Commissioners	£80,425
Assembly Member (AM)	£66,847

* All salaries include the AM salary

MEMBERS OF THE NATIONAL ASSEMBLY FOR WALES *as at 31 August 2018*

Antoniw, Mick, *Lab., Pontypridd,* Maj. 5,327
ap Iorwerth, Rhun, *PC, Ynys Môn,* Maj. 9,510
Asghar, Mohammad, *C., South Wales East region*
Bennett, Gareth, *UKIP, South Wales Central region*
Blythyn, Hannah, *Lab., Delyn,* Maj. 3,582
Bowden, Dawn, *Lab., Merthyr Tydfil and Rhymney,* Maj. 3,486
Brown, Michelle, *UKIP, North Wales region*
Bryant, Jayne, *Lab., Newport West,* Maj. 4,115
Burns, Angela, *C., Carmarthen West and South Pembrokeshire,* Maj. 3,373
David, Hefin, *Lab., Caerphilly,* Maj. 1,575
Davies, Alun, *Lab., Blaenau Gwent,* Maj. 650
Davies, Andrew R. T., *C., South Wales Central region*
Davies, Paul, *C., Preseli Pembrokeshire,* Maj. 3,930
Davies, Suzy, *C., South Wales West region*
Drakeford, Mark, *Lab., Cardiff West,* Maj. 1,176
* **Elis-Thomas**, Rt. Hon. Lord, *Ind., Dwyfor Meirionnydd,* Maj. 6,406
Evans, Rebecca, *Lab., Gower,* Maj. 1,829
Finch-Saunders, Janet, *C., Aberconwy,* Maj. 754
George, Russell, *C., Montgomeryshire,* Maj. 3,339
Gething, Vaughan, *Lab., Cardiff South and Penarth,* Maj. 6,921
Griffiths, John, *Lab., Newport East,* Maj. 4,896
Griffiths, Lesley, *Lab., Wrexham,* Maj. 1,325
Gruffydd, Llyr, *PC, North Wales region*
Gwenllian, Siân, *PC, Arfon,* Maj. 4,162
Hamilton, Neil, *UKIP, Mid and West Wales region*
Hedges, Mike, *Lab., Swansea East,* Maj. 7,452
Howells, Vikki, *Lab., Cynon Valley,* Maj. 5, 994
Hutt, Jane, *Lab., Vale of Glamorgan,* Maj. 777
Irranca-Davies, Huw, *Lab., Ogmore,* Maj. 9,468
Isherwood, Mark, *C., North Wales region*
James, Julie, *Lab., Swansea West,* Maj. 5,080
Jones, Ann, *Lab., Vale of Clwyd,* Maj. 768
Jones, Caroline, *UKIP, South Wales West region*
Jones, Rt. Hon. Carwyn, *Lab., Bridgend,* Maj. 5,623
Jones, Elin, *PC, Ceredigion,* Maj. 2,408
Jones, Helen Mary, *PC, Mid and West Wales region*
Jones, Mandy, *Ind., North Wales region*
Lewis, Steffan, *PC, South Wales East region*
Lloyd, Dai, *PC, South Wales West region*
* **McEvoy**, Neil, *Ind., South Wales Central region*
Melding, David, *C. South Wales Central region*
Miles, Jeremy, *Lab. Neath,* Maj. 2,923
Millar, Darren, *C., Clwyd West,* Maj. 5,063
Morgan, Eluned *Lab., Mid and West Wales region*

Morgan, Julie, *Lab., Cardiff North,* Maj. 3,667
Neagle, Lynne, *Lab., Torfaen,* Maj. 4,498
Passmore, Rhianon, *Lab., Islwyn,* Maj. 5,106
Price, Adam, *PC, Carmarthen East and Dinefwr,* Maj. 8,700
Ramsay, Nick, *C., Monmouth,* Maj. 5,147
Rathbone, Jenny, *Lab., Cardiff Central,* Maj. 817
† **Reckless**, Mark, *C., South Wales East*
Rees, David, *Lab, Aberavon,* Maj. 6,402
Rowlands, David J., *UKIP, South Wales East region*
Sargeant, Jack, *Lab., Alyn and Deeside* Maj. 5,364
Sayed, Bethan, *PC, South Wales West region*
Skates, Ken, *Lab., Clwyd South,* Maj. 3,016
Waters, Lee, *Lab., Llanelli,* Maj. 382
Watson, Joyce, *Lab., Mid and West Wales region*
Williams, Kirsty, *LD, Brecon and Radnorshire,* Maj. 8,170
Wood, Leanne, *PC, Rhondda,* Maj. 3,359

* Previously AM for PC
† Previously AM for UKIP

STATE OF THE PARTIES *as at 31 August 2018*

	Constituency AMs	Regional AMs	AM total
Labour (Lab.)	*27	2	29
Conservative (C.)	6	6	12
Plaid Cymru (PC)	5	5	10
UKIP	0	5	5
Independent (Ind.)	1	2	3
Liberal Democrats (LD)	1	0	1
Total	40	20	60

* Includes the Deputy Presiding Officer
† Includes the Presiding Officer

WELSH GOVERNMENT

Cathays Park, Cardiff CF10 3NQ
T 0300-060 3300 W www.gov.wales

The Welsh government is the devolved government of Wales. It is accountable to the National Assembly for Wales, the Welsh legislature which represents the interests of the people of Wales, and makes laws for Wales. The Welsh government and the National Assembly for Wales were established as separate institutions under the Government of Wales Act 2006.

The Welsh government comprises the first minister, who is usually the leader of the largest party in the National Assembly for Wales; up to 14 cabinet secretaries and ministers and deputy ministers; and a counsel general (the chief legal adviser).

Following the referendum on 3 March 2011 on granting further law-making powers to the National Assembly, the Welsh government's functions now include the ability to propose bills to the National Assembly on subjects within 20 set areas of policy. Subject to limitations prescribed by the Government of Wales Act 2006, acts of the National Assembly may make any provision that could be made by act of parliament. The 20 areas of responsibility devolved to the National Assembly for Wales (and within which Welsh ministers exercise executive functions) are: agriculture, fisheries, forestry and rural development; ancient monuments and historic buildings; culture; economic development; education and training; environment; fire and rescue services and promotion of fire safety; food; health and health services; highways and transport; housing; local government; the National Assembly for Wales; public administration; social welfare; sport and recreation; tourism; town and county planning; water and flood defence; and the Welsh language.

CABINET

First Minister of Wales, Rt. Hon. Carwyn Jones, AM
Cabinet Secretary for Economy and Transport, Ken Skates, AM
Cabinet Secretary Education, Kirsty Williams, AM
Cabinet Secretary for Energy, Planning and Rural Affairs, Lesley Griffiths, AM
Cabinet Secretary for Finance, Mark Drakeford, AM
Cabinet Secretary for Health and Social Services, Vaughan Gething, AM
Cabinet Secretary for Local Government and Public Services, Alun Davies, AM
Counsel-General for Wales, Jeremy Miles, AM
Leader of the House and Chief Whip, Julie James, AM

MINISTERS

Minister for Children, Older People and Social Care, Huw Irranca-Davies, AM
Minister for Culture, Tourism and Sport, Rt. Hon. Lord Elis-Thomas, AM
Minister for Environment, Hannah Blythyn, AM
Minister for Housing and Regeneration, Rebecca Evans, AM
Minister for Welsh Language and Lifelong Learning, Eluned Morgan, AM

MANAGEMENT BOARD

Permanent Secretary, Dame Shan Morgan, DCMG
Director-Generals, Tracey Burke *(Education and Public Services);* Desmond Clifford *(Office of the First Minister and Brexit);* Dr Andrew Goodall *(Health and Social Services);* Andrew Slade *(Economy, Skills and Natural Resources)*
Directors, Jeff Godfrey *(Legal Services);* Peter Kennedy *(HR);* David Richards *(Governance)*
Head of Organisational Development and Engagement, Natalie Pearson
Board Equality and Diversity Champion, Gillian Baranski
Chair of Operations Committee, vacant
Finance Director, Gawain Evans
Non-Executive Directors, Ellen Donovan; Jeff Farrar; Ann Keane; Gareth Lynn

DEPARTMENTS

Office of the First Minister and Cabinet Office
Education and Public Services
Health and Social Services
Economy, Skills and Natural Resources

NATIONAL ASSEMBLY ELECTION RESULTS *as at 5 May 2016*

Electorate (E.) 2,248,050 Turnout (T.) 45.3%
See General Election Results for a list of party abbreviations

ABERAVON (S. WALES WEST)
E. 49,074 T. 20,852 (42.49%)

David Rees, Lab.	10,578
Bethan Jenkins, PC	4,176
Glenda Davies, UKIP	3,119
David Jenkins, C.	1,342
Helen Ceri Clarke, LD	1,248
Jonathan Tier, Green	389

Lab. majority 6,402 (30.70%)
9.31% swing Lab. to PC

ABERCONWY (WALES N.)
E. 44,960 T. 22,038 (49.02%)

Janet Finch-Saunders, C.	7,646
Trystan Lewis, PC	6,892
Mike Priestley, Lab.	6,039
Sarah Lesiter-Burgess, LD	781
Petra Haig, Green	680

C. majority 754 (3.42%)
2.15% swing C. to PC

ALYN AND DEESIDE (WALES N.)
E. 62,697 T. 21,696 (34.60%)

Carl Sargeant, Lab.	9,922
Mike Gibbs, C.	4,558
Michelle Brown, UKIP	3,765
Jacqui Hurst, PC	1,944
Pete Williams, LD	980
Martin Bennewith, Green	527

Lab. majority 5,364 (24.72%)
0.11% swing C. to Lab.

ARFON (WALES N.)
E. 39,269 T. 19,994 (50.92%)

Sian Gwenllian, PC	10,962
Sion Jones, Lab.	6,800
Martin Peet, C.	1,655
Sara Lloyd Williams, LD	577

PC majority 4,162 (20.82%)
4.86% swing PC to Lab.

BLAENAU GWENT (S. WALES EAST)
E. 50,574 T. 21,291 (42.10%)

Alun Davies, Lab.	8,442
Nigel Copner, PC	7,792
Kevin Boucher, UKIP	3,423
Tracey West, C.	1,334
Brendan D'Cruz, LD	300

Lab. majority 650 (3.05%)
27.73% swing Lab. to PC

BRECON AND RADNORSHIRE (WALES MID AND W.)
E. 53,793 T. 30,367 (56.45%)

Kirsty Williams, LD	15,898
Gary Price, C.	7,728
Alex Thomas, Lab.	2,703
Thomas Turton, UKIP	2,161
Freddy Greaves, PC	1,180
Grenville Ham, Green	697

LD majority 8,170 (26.90%)
8.59% swing C. to LD

BRIDGEND (S. WALES WEST)
E. 60,195 T. 26,851 (44.61%)

Carwyn Jones, Lab.	12,166
George Jabbour, C.	6,543
Caroline Jones, UKIP	3,919
James Radcliffe, PC	2,569
Jonathan Pratt, LD	1,087
Charlie Barlow, Green	567

Lab. majority 5,623 (20.94%)
3.62% swing Lab. to C.

CAERPHILLY (S. WALES EAST)
E. 62,449 T. 27,115 (43.42%)

Hefin David, Lab.	9,584
Lindsay Whittle, PC	8,009
Sam Gould, UKIP	5,954
Jane Pratt, C.	2,412
Andrew Creak, Green	770
Aladdin Ayesh, LD	386

Lab. majority 1,575 (5.81%)
6.72% swing Lab. to PC

CARDIFF CENTRAL (S. WALES CENTRAL)
E. 57,177 T. 26,068 (45.59%)

Jenny Rathbone, Lab.	10,016
Eluned Parrott, LD	9,199
Joel Williams, C.	2,317
Glyn Wise, PC	1,951
Mohammed Islam, UKIP	1,223
Amelia Womack, Green	1,150
Jane Croad, Ind.	212

Lab. majority 817 (3.13%)
1.49% swing LD to Lab.

CARDIFF NORTH (S. WALES CENTRAL)
E. 65,927 T. 37,452 (56.81%)

Julie Morgan, Lab.	16,766
Jayne Cowan, C.	13,099
Haydn Rushworth, UKIP	2,509
Elin Walker Jones, PC	2,278
John Dixon, LD	1,130
Fiona Burt, Ind.	846
Chris von Ruhland, Green	824

Lab. majority 3,667 (9.79%)
2.31% swing C. to Lab.

CARDIFF SOUTH AND PENARTH (S. WALES CENTRAL)
E. 76,110 T. 30,276 (39.78%)

Vaughan Gething, Lab.	13,274
Ben Gray, C.	6,353
Dafydd Davies, PC	4,320
Hugh Moelwyn Hughes, UKIP	3,716
Nigel Howells, LD	1,345
Anthony Slaughter, Green	1,268

Lab. majority 6,921 (22.86%)
0.04% swing C. to Lab.

CARDIFF WEST (S. WALES CENTRAL)
E. 66,040 T. 31,960 (48.39%)

Mark Drakeford, Lab.	11,381
Neil McEvoy, PC	10,205
Sean Driscoll, C.	5,617
Gareth Bennett, UKIP	2,629
Hannah Pudner, Green	1,032
Cadan ap Tomos, LD	868
Eliot Freedman, Ind.	132
Lee Wools, FTC	96

Lab. majority 1,176 (3.68%)
11.71% swing Lab. to PC

CARMARTHEN EAST AND DINEFWR (WALES MID AND W.)
E. 55,395 T. 29,751 (53.71%)

Adam Price, PC	14,427
Stephen Jeacock, Lab.	5,727
Matthew Paul, C.	4,489
Neil Hamilton, UKIP	3,474
William Powell, LD	837
Freya Amsbury, Green	797

PC majority 8,700 (29.24%)
7.17% swing Lab. to PC

CARMARTHEN WEST AND SOUTH PEMBROKESHIRE (WALES MID AND W.)
E. 56,886 T. 29,237 (51.40%)

Angela Burns, C.	10,355
Marc Tierney, Lab.	6,982
Simon Thomas, PC	5,459
Allan Brookes, UKIP	3,300
Chris Overton, Ind.	1,638
Val Bradley, Green	804
Alistair Cameron, LD	699

C. majority 3,373 (11.54%)
3.10% swing Lab. to C.

CEREDIGION (WALES MID AND W.)
E. 51,230 T. 29,485 (57.55%)

Elin T Jones, PC	12,014
Elizabeth Evans, LD	9,606
Gethin James, UKIP	2,665
Felix Aubel, C.	2,075
Iwan Wyn Jones, Lab.	1,902
Brian Williams, Green	1,223

PC majority 2,408 (8.17%)
1.03% swing LD to PC

CLWYD SOUTH (WALES N.)
E. 54,185 T. 22,159 (40.90%)

Ken Skates, Lab.	7,862
Simon Baynes, C.	4,846
Mabon ap Gwynfor, PC	3,861
Mandy Jones, UKIP	2,827
Aled Roberts, LD	2,289
Duncan Rees, Green	474

Lab. majority 3,016 (13.61%)
0.17% swing C. to Lab.

CLWYD WEST (WALES N.)
E. 57,657 T. 26,226 (45.49%)

Darren Millar, C.	10,831
Llyr Gruffydd, PC	5,768
Jo Thomas, Lab.	5,246
David Edwards, UKIP	2,985
Victor Babu, LD	831
Julian Mahy, Green	565

C. majority 5,063 (19.31%)
0.52% swing C. to PC

CYNON VALLEY (S. WALES CENTRAL)
E. 50,292 T. 19,236 (38.25%)

Vikki Howells, Lab.	9,830
Cerith Griffiths, PC	3,836
Liz Wilks, UKIP	3,460
Lyn Hudson, C.	1,177
John Matthews, Green	598
Michael Wallace, LD	335

Lab. majority 5,994 (31.16%)
1.78% swing Lab. to PC

DELYN (WALES N.)
E. 53,490 T. 23,159 (43.30%)

Hannah Blythyn, Lab.	9,480
Huw Williams, C.	5,898
Nigel Williams, UKIP	3,794
Paul Rowlinson, PC	2,269
Tom Rippeth, LD	1,718

Lab. majority 3,582 (15.47%)
1.52% swing C. to Lab.

DWYFOR MEIRIONNYDD (WALES MID AND W.)
E. 43,304 T. 20,236 (46.73%)

Dafydd Elis-Thomas, PC	9,566
Neil Fairlamb, C.	3,160
Ian MacIntyre, Lab.	2,443
Frank Wykes, UKIP	2,149
Louise Hughes, Ind.	1,259
Steve Churchman, LD	916
Alice Hooker-Stroud, Green	743

PC majority 6,406 (31.66%)
2.77% swing C. to PC

GOWER (S. WALES WEST)
E. 60,631 T. 30,187 (49.79%)

Rebecca Evans, Lab.	11,982
Lyndon Jones, C.	10,153
Colin Beckett, UKIP	3,300
Harri Roberts, PC	2,982
Sheila Kingston-Jones, LD	1,033
Abi Cherry-Hamer, Green	737

Lab. majority 1,829 (6.06%)
6.05% swing Lab. to C.

ISLWYN (S. WALES EAST)
E. 54,465 T. 22,309 (40.96%)

Rhianon Passmore, Lab.	10,050
Joe Smyth, UKIP	4,944
Lyn Ackerman, PC	4,349
Paul Williams, C.	1,775
Matthew Kidner, LD	597
Katy Beddoe, Green	594

Lab. majority 5,106 (22.89%)

LLANELLI (WALES MID AND W.)
E. 59,651 T. 28,116 (47.13%)

Lee Waters, Lab.	10,267
Helen Mary Jones, PC	9,885
Ken Rees, UKIP	4,132
Stefan Ryszewski, C.	1,937
Sian Caiach, PF	1,113
Guy Smith, Green	427
Gemma Bowker, LD	355

Lab. majority 382 (1.36%)
0.53% swing PC to Lab.

MERTHYR TYDFIL AND RHYMNEY (S. WALES EAST)
E. 53,754 T. 20,683 (38.48%)

Dawn Bowden, Lab.	9,763
David Rowlands, UKIP	4,277
Brian Thomas, PC	3,721
Elizabeth Simon, C.	1,331
Bob Griffin, LD	1,122
Julie Colbran, Green	469

Lab. majority 5,486 (26.52%)

MONMOUTH (S. WALES EAST)
E. 64,197 T. 31,401 (48.91%)

Nick Ramsay, C.	13,585
Catherine Fookes, Lab.	8,438
Tim Price, UKIP	3,092
Debby Blakebrough, Ind.	1,932
Jonathan Clark, PC	1,824
Veronica German, LD	1,474
Chris Were, Green	910
Stephen Morris, Eng Dem	146

C. majority 5,147 (16.39%)
2.00% swing C. to Lab.

MONTGOMERYSHIRE (WALES MID AND W.)
E. 48,682 T. 23,600 (48.48%)

Russell George, C.	9,875
Jane Dodds, LD	6,536
Des Parkinson, UKIP	2,458
Aled Morgan Hughes, PC	2,410
Martyn Singleton, Lab.	1,389
Richard Chaloner, Green	932

C. majority 3,339 (14.15%)
2.01% swing LD to C.

NEATH (S. WALES WEST)
E. 55,395 T. 25,363 (45.79%)

Jeremy Miles, Lab.	9,468
Alun Llewelyn, PC	6,545
Richard Pritchard, UKIP	3,780
Peter Crocker-Jaques, C.	2,179
Steve Hunt, Ind.	2,056
Frank Little, LD	746
Lisa Rapado, Green	589

Lab. majority 2,923 (11.52%)
7.63% swing Lab. to PC

NEWPORT EAST (S. WALES EAST)
E. 55,499 T. 20,688 (37.28%)

John Griffiths, Lab.	9,229
James Peterson, UKIP	4,333
Munawar Mughal, C.	3,768
Paul Halliday, LD	1,481
Tony Salkeld, PC	1,386
Peter Varley, Green	491

Lab. majority 4,896 (23.67%)

NEWPORT WEST (S. WALES EAST)
E. 62,169 T. 27,751 (44.64%)

Jayne Bryant, Lab.	12,157
Matthew Evans, C.	8,042
Michael Ford, UKIP	3,842
Simon Coopey, PC	1,645
Liz Newton, LD	880
Pippa Bartolotti, Green	814
Bill Fearnley-Whittingstall, Ind.	333
Gruff Meredith, WSov	38

Lab. majority 4,115 (14.83%)
1.75% swing Lab. to C.

OGMORE (S. WALES WEST)
E. 54,502 T. 23,356 (42.85%)

Huw Irranca-Davies, Lab.	12,895
Tim Thomas, PC	3,427
Elizabeth Kendall, UKIP	3,233
Jamie Wallis, C.	2,587
Anita Davies, LD	698
Laurie Brophy, Green	516

Lab. majority 9,468 (40.54%)
3.36% swing Lab. to PC

PONTYPRIDD (S. WALES CENTRAL)
E. 58,277 T. 25,338 (43.48%)

Mick Antoniw, Lab.	9,986
Chad Rickard, PC	4,659
Joel James, C.	3,884
Edwin Allen, UKIP	3,322
Mike Powell, LD	2,979
Ken Barker, Green	508

Lab. majority 5,327 (21.02%)
8.18% swing Lab. to PC

PRESELI PEMBROKESHIRE (WALES MID AND W)
E. 56,414 T. 28,397 (50.34%)

Paul Davies, C.	11,123
Dan Lodge, Lab.	7,193
John Osmond, PC	3,957
Howard Lillyman, UKIP	3,286
Bob Kilmister, LD	1,677
Frances Bryant, Green	1,161

C. majority 3,930 (13.84%)
2.92% swing Lab. to C.

RHONDDA (S. WALES CENTRAL)
E. 49,758 T. 23,486 (47.20%)

Leanne Wood, PC	11,891
Leighton Andrews, Lab.	8,432
Stephen Clee, UKIP	2,203
Maria Hill, C.	528
Pat Matthews, Green	259
Rhys Taylor, LD	173

PC majority 3,459 (14.73%)
24.19% swing Lab. to PC

SWANSEA EAST (S. WALES WEST)
E. 57,589 T. 20,576 (35.73%)

Mike Hedges, Lab.	10,726
Clifford Johnson, UKIP	3,274
Dic Jones, PC	2,744
Sadie Vidal, C.	1,729
Charlene Webster, LD	1,574
Tony Young, Green	529

Lab. majority 7,452 (36.22%)

SWANSEA WEST (S. WALES WEST)
E. 54,593 T. 22,202 (40.67%)

Julie James, Lab.	9,014
Craig Lawton, C.	3,934
Dai Lloyd, PC	3,225
Rosie Irwin, UKIP	3,058
Chris Holley, LD	2,012
Gareth Tucker, Green	883
Brian Johnson, SPGB	76

Lab. majority 5,080 (22.88%)
0.77% swing C. to Lab.

TORFAEN (S. WALES EAST)
E. 60,246 T. 22,978 (38.14%)

Lynne Neagle, Lab.	9,688
Susan Boucher, UKIP	5,190
Graham Smith, C.	3,931
Matthew Woolfall-Jones, PC	2,860
Steve Jenkins, Green	681
Alison Willott, LD	628

Lab. majority 4,498 (19.58%)

VALE OF CLWYD (WALES N.)
E. 56,322 T. 24,183 (42.94%)

Ann Jones, Lab.	9,560
Sam Rowlands, C.	8,792
Paul Davies-Cooke, UKIP	2,975
Mair Rowlands, PC	2,098
Gwyn Williams, LD	758

Lab. majority 768 (3.18%)
7.11% swing Lab. to C.

VALE OF GLAMORGAN (S. WALES CENTRAL)
E. 71,177 T. 37,798 (53.10%)

Jane Hutt, Lab.	14,655
Ross England, C.	13,878
Ian Johnson, PC	3,871
Lawrence Andrews, UKIP	3,662
Denis Campbell, LD	938
Alison Haden, Green	794

Lab. majority 777 (2.06%)
4.65% swing Lab. to C.

WREXHAM (WALES N.)
E. 51,567 T. 20,354 (39.47%)

Lesley Griffiths, Lab.	7,552
Andrew Atkinson, C.	6,227
Carrie Harper, PC	2,631
Jeanette Bassford-Barton, UKIP	2,393
Beryl Blackmore, LD	1,140
Alan Butterworth, Green	411

Lab. majority 1,325 (6.51%)
5.67% swing Lab. to C.

YNYS MON (WALES N.)
E. 50,345 T. 25,167 (49.99%)

Rhun ap Iorwerth, PC	13,788
Julia Dobson, Lab.	4,278
Simon Wall, UKIP	3,212
Clay Theakston, C.	2,904
Gerry Wolff, Green	389
Thomas Crofts, LD	334
Daniel ap Eifion Jones, Ind.	262

PC majority 9,510 (37.79%)
11.29% swing Lab. to PC

REGIONS *as at 5 May 2016*
E. 2,248,050 T. 45.3%

MID AND WEST WALES
E. 425,355 T. 215,840 (50.74%)

PC	56,754	(26.29%)
C.	44,461	(20.60%)
Lab.	41,975	(19.45%)
UKIP	25,042	(11.60%)
LD	23,554	(10.91%)
Abolish	10,707	(4.96%)
Green	8,222	(3.81%)
PF	1,496	(0.69%)
Ch. P.	1,103	(0.51%)
Loony	1,071	(0.50%)
Loc. Ind.	1,032	(0.48%)
Welsh Comm	423	(0.20%)

PC majority 12,293 (5.70%)
2.02% swing C. to PC (2011 PC majority 3,479)

ADDITIONAL MEMBERS
Joyce Watson, *Lab.*
Eluned Morgan, *Lab.*
Simon Thomas, *PC*
Neil Hamilton, *UKIP*

NORTH WALES
E. 470,492 T. 204,490 (43.46%)

Lab.	57,528	(28.13%)
PC	47,701	(23.33%)
C	45,468	(22.23%)
UKIP	25,518	(12.48%)
Abolish	9,409	(4.60%)
LD	9,345	(4.57%)
Green	4,789	(2.34%)
Loc Ind.	1,865	(0.91%)
Loony	1,355	(0.66%)
Ind.	926	(0.45%)
Welsh Comm	586	(0.29%)

Lab. majority 9,827 (4.81%)
2.98% swing Lab. to PC (2011 Lab. majority 10,476)

ADDITIONAL MEMBERS
Mark Isherwood, *C.*
Llyr Gruffydd, *PC*
Nathan Gill, *UKIP*
Michelle Brown, *UKIP*

SOUTH WALES CENTRAL
E. 494,758 T. 231,133 (46.72%)

Lab.	78,366	(33.91%)
PC	48,357	(20.92%)
C.	42,185	(18.25%)
UKIP	23,958	(10.37%)
LD	14,875	(6.44%)
Abolish	9,163	(3.96%)
Green	7,949	(3.44%)
Women	2,807	(1.21%)
Loony	1,096	(0.47%)
TUSC	736	(0.32%)
Ind.	651	(0.28%)
Comm	520	(0.22%)
FTC	470	(0.20%)

Lab. majority 30,009 (12.98%)
7.24% swing Lab. to PC (2011 Lab. majority 39,694)

ADDITIONAL MEMBERS
Andrew Davies, *C.*
David Melding, *C.*
Neil McEvoy, *PC*
Gareth Bennett, *UKIP*

SOUTH WALES EAST
E. 463,353 T. 194,091 (41.89%)

Lab.	74,424	(38.34%)
UKIP	34,524	(17.79%)
C.	33,318	(17.17%)
PC	29,686	(15.29%)
Abolish	7,870	(4.05%)
LD	6,784	(3.50%)
Green	4,831	(2.49%)
Loony	1,115	(0.57%)
TUSC	618	(0.32%)
Welsh Comm	492	(0.25%)
NF	429	(0.22%)

Lab. majority 39,900 (20.56%)
9.93% swing Lab. to UKIP (2011 Lab. majority 47,240)

ADDITIONAL MEMBERS
Oscar Asghar, *C.*
Steffan Lewis, *PC*
Mark Reckless, *UKIP*
David Rowlands, *UKIP*

SOUTH WALES WEST
E. 391,979 T. 169,189 (43.16%)

Lab.	66,903	(39.54%)
PC	29,050	(17.17%)
C.	25,414	(15.02%)
UKIP	23,096	(13.65%)
LD	10,946	(6.47%)
Abolish	7,137	(4.22%)
Green	4,420	(2.61%)
Loony	1,106	(0.65%)
TUSC	686	(0.41%)
Welsh Comm	431	(0.25%)

Lab. majority 37,853 (22.37%)
5.17% swing Lab. to PC (2011 Lab. majority 44,309)

ADDITIONAL MEMBERS
Suzy Davies, *C.*
Bethan Jenkins, *PC*
Dai Lloyd, *PC*
Caroline Jones, *UKIP*

SCOTLAND

SCOTTISH PARLIAMENT

Edinburgh EH99 1SP
T 0131-348 5000/ 0800-092 7500
E info@parliament.scot
W www.parliament.scot

In July 1997 the government announced plans to establish a Scottish parliament. In a referendum on 11 September 1997 about 60 per cent of the electorate voted. Of those who voted, 74.3 per cent voted in favour of the parliament and 63.5 per cent voted in support of granting the parliament having tax-raising powers. Elections are normally held every four years, but the current session is scheduled to last for five years. The first elections were held on 6 May 1999, when around 59 per cent of the electorate voted. The first meeting was held on 12 May 1999 and the Scottish parliament was officially opened on 1 July 1999 at the Assembly Hall, Edinburgh. A new building to house the parliament was opened, in the presence of the Queen, at Holyrood on 9 October 2004. On 5 May 2016 the fifth elections to the Scottish parliament took place.

The Scottish parliament has 129 members (including the presiding officer), comprising 73 constituency members and 56 additional regional members, drawn from the party lists. It can introduce primary legislation and has the power to set rates and bands for income tax on non-savings and non-dividend income for Scottish taxpayers.

Members of the Scottish parliament are elected using the additional member system, the same system used to elect London Assembly and Welsh Assembly members. Under the additional member system the electorate has two votes; the first to elect their constituency member via the 'first past the post' method of voting and the second to elect their regional members. The 56 regional seats are filled proportionally from the parties' lists according to their share of the vote on the second ballot paper. By-elections are held for constituency seat vacancies but not for regional seat vacancies which are filled by the next candidate on the list from the same political party in which the vacancy arose.

The areas for which the Scottish parliament is responsible include: civil and criminal justice; education; health; environment; economic development; local government; housing; police; fire services; planning; financial assistance to industry; tourism; heritage and the arts; agriculture; social work; sports; public registers and records; forestry; food standards; some aspects of transport; and some areas of welfare.

SALARIES *as at 1 April 2018*

First Minister*	£90,030
Cabinet Secretary*	£46,705
Lord Advocate*	£61,017
Solicitor-General for Scotland*	£44,124
Minister*	£29,258
MSP†	£62,149
Presiding Officer*	£46,705
Deputy Presiding Officer*	£29,258

* In addition to the MSP salary
† Reduced by two-thirds if the member is also an MP or an MEP

MEMBERS OF THE SCOTTISH PARLIAMENT *as at 30 June 2018*

KEY
* Elected via by-election since the 2016 Scottish parliament election
† Replacement from the party list since the 2016 Scottish parliament election under the additional member system
‡ The Presiding Officer was elected as a regional member for Labour but has no party affiliation while in post

Adam, George, *SNP, Paisley*, Maj. 5,199
Adamson, Clare, *SNP, Motherwell and Wishaw*, Maj. 6,223
Allan, Alasdair, *SNP, Na h-Eileanan an Iar*, Maj. 3,496
Arthur, Tom, *SNP, Renfrewshire South*, Maj. 4,408
Baillie, Jackie, *Lab., Dumbarton*, Maj. 109
Baker, Claire, *Lab., Mid Scotland and Fife region*
Balfour, Jeremy, *C., Lothian region*
† **Ballantyne**, Michelle, *C., South Scotland region*
Beamish, Claudia, *Lab., South Scotland region*
Beattie, Colin, *SNP, Midlothian North and Musselburgh*, Maj. 7,035
Bibby, Neil, *Lab., West Scotland region*
† **Bowman**, Bill, *C., North East Scotland region*
Briggs, Miles, *C. Lothian region*
Brown, Keith, *SNP, Clackmannanshire and Dunblane*, Maj. 6,721
Burnett, Alexander, *C., Aberdeenshire West*, Maj. 900
Cameron, Donald, *C., Highlands and Islands region*
Campbell, Aileen, *SNP, Clydesdale*, Maj. 5,979
Carlaw, Jackson, *C., Eastwood*, Maj. 1,610
Carson, Finlay, *C., Galloway and West Dumfries*, Maj. 1,514
Chapman, Peter, *C., North East Scotland region*
Coffey, Willie, *SNP, Kilmarnock and Irvine Valley*, Maj. 11,194
Cole-Hamilton, Alex, *LD, Edinburgh Western*, Maj. 2,960
Constance, Angela, *SNP, Almond Valley*, Maj. 8,393
Corry, Maurice, *C., West Scotland region*
Crawford, Bruce, *SNP, Stirling*, Maj. 6,718
Cunningham, Roseanna, *SNP, Perthshire South and Kinross-shire*, Maj. 1,422
Davidson, Ruth, *C., Edinburgh Central*, Maj. 610
Denham, Ash, *SNP, Edinburgh Eastern*, Maj. 5,087
Dey, Graeme, *SNP, Angus South*, Maj. 4,304
Doris, Bob, *SNP, Glasgow Maryhill and Springburn*, Maj. 5,602
Dornan, James, *SNP, Glasgow Cathcart*, Maj. 9,390
Dugdale, Kezia, *Lab., Lothian region*
Ewing, Annabelle, *SNP, Cowdenbeath*, Maj. 3,041
Ewing, Fergus, *SNP, Inverness and Nairn*, Maj. 10,857
Fabiani, Linda, *SNP, East Kilbride*, Maj. 10,979
Fee, Mary, *Lab., West Scotland region*
Findlay, Neil, *Lab., Lothian region*
Finnie, John, *Green, Highlands and Islands region*
FitzPatrick, Joe, *SNP, Dundee City West*, Maj. 8,828
Forbes, Kate, *SNP, Skye, Lochaber and Badenoch*, Maj. 9,043
Fraser, Murdo, *C., Mid Scotland and Fife region*
Freeman, Jeane, *SNP, Carrick, Cumnock and Doon Valley*, Maj. 6,006
Gibson, Kenneth, *SNP, Cunninghame North*, Maj. 8,724
Gilruth, Jenny, *SNP, Mid Fife and Glenrothes*, Maj. 8,276
Golden, Maurice, *C., West Scotland region*
Gougeon, Mairi, *SNP, Angus North and Mearns*, Maj. 2,472
Grahame, Christine, *SNP, Midlothian South, Tweeddale and Lauderdale*, Maj. 5,868
Grant, Rhoda, *Lab., Highlands and Islands region*
Gray, Iain, *Lab., East Lothian*, Maj. 1,127
Greene, Jamie, *C., West Scotland region*
Greer, Ross, *Green, West Scotland region*

Griffin, Mark, *Lab., Central Scotland region*
† **Halcro Johnston**, Jamie, *C., Highlands and Islands region*
* **Hamilton**, Rachael, *C., Ettrick, Roxburgh and Berwickshire*, Maj. 9,338
Harper, Emma, *SNP, South Scotland region*
Harris, Alison, *C., Central Scotland region*
Harvie, Patrick, *Green, Glasgow region*
Haughey, Clare, *SNP, Rutherglen*, Maj. 3,743
Hepburn, Jamie, *SNP, Cumbernauld and Kilsyth*, Maj. 9,478
Hyslop, Fiona, *SNP, Linlithgow*, Maj. 9,335
Johnson, Daniel, *Lab., Edinburgh Southern*, Maj. 1,123
Johnstone, Alison, *Green, Lothian region*
Kelly, James, *Lab., Glasgow region*
Kerr, Liam, *C., North East Scotland region*
Kidd, Bill, *SNP, Glasgow Anniesland*, Maj. 6,153
Lamont, Johann, *Lab., Glasgow region*
Lennon, Monica, *Lab., Central Scotland region*
Leonard, Richard, *Lab., Central Scotland region*
Lindhurst, Gordon, *C., Lothian region*
Lochhead, Richard, *SNP, Moray*, Maj. 2,875
Lockhart, Dean, *C., Mid Scotland and Fife region*
Lyle, Richard, *SNP, Uddingston and Bellshill*, Maj. 4,809
McAlpine, Joan, *SNP, South Scotland region*
McArthur, Liam, *LD, Orkney Islands*, Maj. 4,534
MacDonald, Angus, *SNP, Falkirk East*, Maj. 8,312
MacDonald, Gordon, *SNP, Edinburgh Pentlands*, Maj. 2,456
Macdonald, Lewis, *Lab., North East Scotland region*
McDonald, Mark, *Ind., Aberdeen Donside*, Maj. 11,630
MacGregor, Fulton, *SNP, Coatbridge and Chryston*, Maj. 3,779
‡ **Macintosh**, Ken, *no party affiliation, West Scotland region*
Mackay, Derek, *SNP, Renfrewshire North and West*, Maj. 7,373
Mackay, Rona, *SNP, Strathkelvin and Bearsden*, Maj. 8,100
McKee, Ivan, *SNP, Glasgow Provan*, Maj. 4,783
McKelvie, Christina, *SNP, Hamilton, Larkhall and Stonehouse*, Maj. 5,437
McMillan, Stuart, *SNP, Greenock and Inverclyde*, Maj. 8,230
McNeill, Pauline, *Lab., Glasgow region*
Macpherson, Ben, *SNP, Edinburgh Northern and Leith*, Maj. 6,746
Maguire, Ruth, *SNP, Cunninghame South*, Maj. 5,693
Marra, Jenny, *Lab., North East Scotland region*
Martin, Gillian, *SNP, Aberdeenshire East*, Maj. 5,837
Mason, John, *SNP, Glasgow Shettleston*, Maj. 7,323
† **Mason**, Tom, *C., North East Scotland region*
Matheson, Michael, *SNP, Falkirk West*, Maj. 11,280
Mitchell, Margaret, *C., Central Scotland region*
Mountain, Edward, *C., Highlands and Islands region*
Mundell, Oliver, *C., Dumfriesshire*, Maj. 1,230
Neil, Alex, *SNP, Airdrie and Shotts*, Maj. 6,192
Paterson, Gil, *SNP, Clydebank and Milngavie*, Maj. 8,432
Rennie, Willie, *LD, North East Fife*, Maj. 3,465
Robison, Shona, *SNP, Dundee City East*, Maj. 10,898
Ross, Gail, *SNP, Caithness, Sutherland and Ross*, Maj. 3,913
Rowley, Alex, *Lab., Mid Scotland and Fife region*
Rumbles, Mike, *LD, North East Scotland region*
Ruskell, Mark, *Green, Mid Scotland and Fife region*
Russell, Michael, *SNP, Argyll and Bute*, Maj. 5,978
Sarwar, Anas, *Lab., Glasgow region*
Scott, John, *C., Ayr*, Maj. 750
Scott, Tavish, *LD, Shetland Islands*, Maj. 4,895
Simpson, Graham, *C., Central Scotland region*
Smith, Elaine, *Lab., Central Scotland region*
Smith, Liz, *C., Mid Scotland and Fife region*
Smyth, Colin, *Lab., South Scotland region*
Somerville, Shirley-Anne, *SNP, Dunfermline*, Maj. 4,558
Stevenson, Stewart, *SNP, Banffshire and Buchan Coast*, Maj. 6,583

Stewart, Alexander, *C., Mid Scotland and Fife region*
Stewart, David, *Lab., Highlands and Islands region*
Stewart, Kevin, *SNP, Aberdeen Central*, Maj. 4,349
Sturgeon, Nicola, *SNP, Glasgow Southside*, Maj. 9,593
Swinney, John, *SNP, Perthshire North*, Maj. 3,336
Todd, Maree, *SNP, Highlands and Islands region*
Tomkins, Adam, *C., Glasgow region*
Torrance, David, *SNP, Kirkcaldy*, Maj. 7,395
Watt, Maureen, *SNP, Aberdeen South and North Kincardine*, Maj. 2,755
Wells, Annie, *C., Glasgow region*
Wheelhouse, Paul, *SNP, South Scotland region*
White, Sandra, *SNP, Glasgow Kelvin*, Maj. 4,048
Whittle, Brian, *C., South Scotland region*
Wightman, Andy, *Green, Lothian region*
Yousaf, Humza, *SNP, Glasgow Pollok*, Maj. 6,482

The Presiding Officer, Ken Macintosh, MSP
Deputy Presiding Officers, Linda Fabiani, MSP; Christine Grahame, MSP

STATE OF THE PARTIES *as at 30 June 2018*

	Constituency MSPs	Regional MSPs	Total
Scottish National Party (SNP)	58	4	62
Scottish Conservative and Unionist Party (C.)	7	24	31
Scottish Labour Party (Lab.)	3	20	23
Scottish Green Party (Green)	0	6	6
Scottish Liberal Democrats (LD)	4	1	5
Independent (Ind.)	1	–	1
*Presiding Officer	–	1	1
Total	73	56	129

SCOTTISH GOVERNMENT

St Andrew's House, Regent Road, Edinburgh EH1 3DG
T 0300-244 4000
E ceu@gov.scot W www.gov.scot

The devolved government for Scotland is responsible for most of the issues of day-to-day concern to the people of Scotland, including health, education, justice, rural affairs and transport.

The Scottish government was known as the Scottish executive when it was established in 1999, following the first elections to the Scottish parliament. There has been a majority Scottish National Party administration since the elections in May 2011.

The government is led by a first minister who is nominated by the parliament and in turn appoints the other Scottish ministers who make up the cabinet.

Civil servants in Scotland are accountable to Scottish ministers, who are themselves accountable to the Scottish parliament.

CABINET

First Minister, Rt. Hon. Nicola Sturgeon, MSP
Deputy First Minister and Cabinet Secretary for Education and Skills, John Swinney, MSP
Cabinet Secretary for Communities, Social Security and Equalities Angela Constance, MSP
Cabinet Secretary for Culture, Tourism and External Affairs, Fiona Hyslop, MSP
Cabinet Secretary for Economy, Jobs and Fair Work, Keith Brown, MSP
Cabinet Secretary for the Environment, Climate Change and Land Reform, Roseanna Cunningham, MSP

Cabinet Secretary for Finance and the Constitution, Derek Mackay, MSP

Cabinet Secretary for Health and Sport, Shona Robison, MSP

Cabinet Secretary for Justice, Michael Matheson, MSP

Cabinet Secretary for Rural Economy and Connectivity, Fergus Ewing, MSP

Minister for Business, Innovation and Energy, Paul Wheelhouse, MSP

Minister for Community Safety and Legal Affairs, Annabelle Ewing, MSP

Minister for Employability and Training, Jamie Hepburn, MSP

Minister for Further Education, Higher Education and Science, Shirley-Anne Somerville, MSP

Minister for International Development and Europe, Alasdair Allan, MSP

Minister for Local Government and Housing, Kevin Stewart, MSP

Minister for Mental Health, Maureen Watt, MSP

Minister for Parliamentary Business, Joe Fitzpatrick, MSP

Minister for Public Health and Sport, Aileen Campbell, MSP

Minister for Social Security, Jeane Freeman, MSP

Minister for Transport and the Islands, Humza Yousaf, MSP

LAW OFFICERS
Lord Advocate, James Wolffe, QC
Solicitor-General for Scotland, Alison di Rollo

STRATEGIC BOARD
Permanent Secretary, Leslie Evans
Director-General Constitution and External Affairs, Ken Thomson
Director-General, Economy, Liz Ditchburn
Director-General, Education, Communities and Justice, Paul Johnston
Director-General, Scottish Exchequer, Alyson Stafford
Director-General, Health and Social Care, Paul Gray
Director-General, Organisational Development and Operations, Sarah Davidson

GOVERNMENT DEPARTMENTS

CONSTITUTION AND EXTERNAL AFFAIRS
St Andrew's House, Regent Road, Edinburgh EH1 3DG
Director-General, Ken Thomson
Directorates: External Affairs; Legal Services (Solicitor to the Scottish Government); Scottish Government EU Office; Strategy and Constitution; Parliamentary Counsel

ECONOMY
St Andrew's House, Regent Road, Edinburgh EH1 3DG
Director-General, Liz Ditchburn
Directorates: Agriculture and Rural Economy; Chief Economist; Chief Scientific Adviser for Rural Affairs, Food and the Environment; Culture, Tourism and Major Events; Economic Development; Energy and Climate Change; Environment and Forestry; Fair Work, Employability and Skills; International Trade and Investment; Marine Scotland; Scottish Development International

Executive Agencies
Accountant in Bankruptcy
Drinking Water Quality Regulator
Forestry Commission Scotland
James Hutton Institute
Moredun Research Institute
Scottish Agricultural College
Transport Scotland
Waterwatch Scotland

EDUCATION, COMMUNITIES AND JUSTICE
St Andrew's House, Regent Road, Edinburgh EH1 3DG
Director-General Paul Johnston

Directorates: Advance Learning and Science; Children and Families; Early Learning and Childcare Programme; Education Analytical Services; Housing and Social Justice; Justice; Learning; Local Government and Communities; Safer Communities

Executive Agencies
Disclosure Scotland
Education Scotland
HM Chief Inspector of Prosecution in Scotland
HM Inspectorate of Constabulary
HM Inspectorate of Prisons
Inspectorate of Prosecution in Scotland
Justice of the Peace Advisory Committee
Scottish Prison Service
Student Awards Agency for Scotland
Visiting Committees for Scottish Penal Establishments

SCOTTISH EXCHEQUER
Victoria Quay, Edinburgh, EH6 6QQ
Director-General, Alyson Stafford
Directorates: Budget and Sustainability; Financial Strategy; Internal Audit; Strategy, Performance and Outcomes

Executive Agencies, Audit Scotland; Scottish Public Pensions Agency

HEALTH AND SOCIAL CARE
St Andrew's House, Regent Road, Edinburgh EH1 3DG
Director-General Health and Social Care and Chief Executive NHS Scotland, Paul Gray
Directorates: Chief Medical Officer; Chief Nursing Officer; Health Finance; Health Workforce and Strategic Change; Health and Social Care Integration; Healthcare Quality and Improvement; Office of the Chief Executive NHS Scotland; Performance and Delivery; Population Health

Executive Agency, Scottish Children's Reporters Administration

ORGANISATIONAL DEVELOPMENT AND OPERATIONS
St Andrew's House, Regent Road, Edinburgh EH1 3DG
Directorates: Communications, Ministerial Support and Facilities; Digital; Financial Management; People; Social Security; Scottish Procurement and Commercial

NON-MINISTERIAL DEPARTMENTS
FOOD STANDARDS SCOTLAND
Pilgrim House, Old Ford Road, Aberdeen AB11 5RL **T** 01224-285100 **W** www.foodstandards.gov.scot
Chief Executive, Geoff Ogle
NATIONAL RECORDS OF SCOTLAND
General Register House, 2 Princes Street, Edinburgh EH1 3YY
T 0131-535 1314 **W** www.nrscotland.gov.uk
Registrar General and Keeper of the Records of Scotland, Tim Ellis
OFFICE OF THE SCOTTISH CHARITY REGULATOR
2nd Floor, Quadrant House, 9 Riverside Drive, Dundee DD1 4NY
T 01382-220446 **W** www.oscr.org.uk
Chief Executive, David Robb
REGISTERS OF SCOTLAND
Meadowbank House, 153 London Road, Edinburgh, Midlothian EH8 7AU **T** 0800-169 9391 **W** www.ros.gov.uk
Keeper, Jennifer Henderson
REVENUE SCOTLAND
PO Box 24068, Victoria Quay, Edinburgh EH6 9BR **T** 0300-020 0310 **W** www.revenue.scot
Chief Executive, Elaine Lorimer
SCOTTISH COURTS AND TRIBUNALS SERVICE
Saughton House, Broomhouse Drive, Edinburgh EH11 3XD
T 0131-444 3352 **W** www.scotcourts.gov.uk
Chief Executive, Eric McQueen
SCOTTISH HOUSING REGULATOR
Buchanan House, 58 Port Dundas Road, Glasgow G4 0HF
T 0141-242 5642 **W** www.scottishhousingregulator.gov.uk
Chief Executive, Michael Cameron

SCOTTISH PARLIAMENT ELECTION RESULTS *as at 5 May 2016*

Electorate (E.) 4,099,407 Turnout (T.) 55.6%
See General Election Results for a list of party abbreviations

ABERDEEN CENTRAL
(Scotland North East Region)
E. 57,195 T. 26,704 (46.69%)

Kevin Stewart, SNP	11,648
Lewis Macdonald, Lab.	7,299
Tom Mason, C.	6,022
Ken McLeod, LD	1,735

SNP majority 4,349 (16.29%)
6.92% swing Lab. to SNP

ABERDEEN DONSIDE
(Scotland North East Region)
E. 61,200 T. 30,981 (50.62%)

Mark McDonald, SNP	17,339
Liam Kerr, C.	5,709
Greg Williams, Lab.	5,672
Isobel Davidson, LD	2,261

SNP majority 11,630 (37.54%)
4.82% swing SNP to C.

ABERDEEN SOUTH & KINCARDINE NORTH
(Scotland North East Region)
E. 59,710 T. 32,340 (54.16%)

Maureen Watt, SNP	13,604
Ross Thomson, C.	10,849
Alison Evison, Lab.	5,603
John Waddell, LD	2,284

SNP majority 2,755 (8.52%)
9.49% swing SNP to C.

ABERDEENSHIRE EAST
(Scotland North East Region)
E. 62,844 T. 34,753 (55.30%)

Gillian Martin, SNP	15,912
Colin Clark, C.	10,075
Christine Jardine, LD	6,611
Sarah Flavell, Lab.	2,155

SNP majority 5,837 (16.80%)
16.90% swing SNP to C.

ABERDEENSHIRE WEST
(Scotland North East Region)
E. 59,576 T. 35,198 (59.08%)

Alexander Burnett, C.	13,400
Dennis Robertson, SNP	12,500
Mike Rumbles, LD	7,262
Sarah Christina Duncan, Lab.	2,036

C. majority 900 (2.56%)
12.03% swing SNP to C.

AIRDRIE & SHOTTS
(Scotland Central Region)
E. 53,899 T. 26,573 (49.30%)

Alex Neil, SNP	13,954
Richard Leonard, Lab.	7,762
Eric Holford, C.	4,164
Louise Young, LD	693

SNP majority 6,192 (23.30%)
7.46% swing Lab. to SNP

ALMOND VALLEY
(Lothian Region)
E. 64,901 T. 34,872 (53.73%)

Angela Constance, SNP	18,475
Neil Findlay, Lab.	10,082
Stephanie Smith, C.	5,308
Charles Dundas, LD	1,007

SNP majority 8,393 (24.07%)
3.02% swing Lab. to SNP

ANGUS NORTH & MEARNS
(Scotland North East Region)
E. 54,268 T. 29,379 (54.14%)

Mairi Evans, SNP	13,417
Alex Johnstone, C.	10,945
John Ruddy, Lab.	2,752
Euan Davidson, LD	2,265

SNP majority 2,472 (8.41%)
10.41% swing SNP to C.

ANGUS SOUTH
(Scotland North East Region)
E. 56,278 T. 31,929 (56.73%)

Graeme Dey, SNP	15,622
Kirstene Hair, C.	11,318
Joanne McFadden, Lab.	3,773
Clive Sneddon, LD	1,216

SNP majority 4,304 (13.48%)
12.40% swing SNP to C.

ARGYLL & BUTE
(Highlands and Islands Region)
E. 48,804 T. 29,476 (60.40%)

Michael Russell, SNP	13,561
Alan Reid, LD	7,583
Donald Cameron, C.	5,840
Mick Rice, Lab.	2,492

SNP majority 5,978 (20.28%)
9.07% swing SNP to LD

AYR
(Scotland South Region)
E. 61,558 T. 37,615 (61.10%)

John Scott, C.	16,183
Jennifer Dunn, SNP	15,433
Brian McGinley, Lab.	5,283
Robbie Simpson, LD	716

C. majority 750 (1.99%)
0.67% swing C. to SNP

BANFFSHIRE & BUCHAN COAST
(Scotland North East Region)
E. 59,155 T. 28,683 (48.49%)

Stewart Stevenson, SNP	15,802
Peter Chapman, C.	9,219
Nathan Morrison, Lab.	2,372
David Evans, LD	1,290

SNP majority 6,583 (22.95%)
12.96% swing SNP to C.

CAITHNESS, SUTHERLAND & ROSS
(Highlands and Islands Region)
E. 55,176 T. 32,207 (58.37%)

Gail Ross, SNP	13,937
Jamie Stone, LD	10,024
Struan Mackie, C.	4,912
Leah Franchetti, Lab.	3,334

SNP majority 3,913 (12.15%)
6.96% swing SNP to LD

CARRICK, CUMNOCK & DOON VALLEY
(Scotland South Region)
E. 58,548 T. 31,680 (54.11%)

Jeane Freeman, SNP	14,690
Carol Mochan, Lab.	8,684
Lee Lyons, C.	7,666
Dawud Islam, LD	640

SNP majority 6,006 (18.96%)
4.98% swing Lab. to SNP

CLACKMANNANSHIRE & DUNBLANE
(Mid Scotland and Fife Region)
E. 50,557 T. 29,746 (58.84%)

Keith Brown, SNP	14,147
Craig Miller, Lab.	7,426
Alexander Stewart, C.	6,915
Christopher McKinlay, LD	1,258

SNP majority 6,721 (22.59%)
4.72% swing Lab. to SNP

CLYDEBANK & MILNGAVIE
(Scotland West Region)
E. 54,761 T. 32,838 (59.97%)

Gil Paterson, SNP	16,158
Gail Casey, Lab.	7,726
Maurice Golden, C.	6,029
Frank Bowles, LD	2,925

SNP majority 8,432 (25.68%)
11.58% swing Lab. to SNP

CLYDESDALE
(Scotland South Region)
E. 58,471 T. 33,619 (57.50%)

Aileen Campbell, SNP	14,821
Alex Allison, C.	8,842
Claudia Beamish, Lab.	6,895
Danny Meikle, Ind.	1,332
Bev Gauld, CSSInd.	909
Jennifer Jamieson Ball, LD	820

SNP majority 5,979 (17.78%)
8.88% swing SNP to C.

COATBRIDGE & CHRYSTON
(Scotland Central Region)
E. 54,169 T. 28,334 (52.31%)

Fulton MacGregor, SNP	13,605
Elaine Smith, Lab.	9,826
Robyn Halbert, C.	2,868
John Wilson, Green	1,612
Jenni Lang, LD	423

SNP majority 3,779 (13.34%)
12.56% swing Lab. to SNP

COWDENBEATH
(Mid Scotland and Fife Region)
E. 54,596 T. 29,734 (54.46%)

Annabelle Ewing, SNP	13,715
Alex Rowley, Lab.	10,674
Dave Dempsey, C.	4,251
Bryn Jones, LD	1,094

SNP majority 3,041 (10.23%)
7.54% swing Lab. to SNP

CUMBERNAULD & KILSYTH
(Scotland Central Region)
E. 49,964 T. 28,308 (56.66%)

Jamie Hepburn, SNP	17,015
Mark Griffin, Lab.	7,537
Anthony Newman, C.	3,068
Irene Lang, LD	688

SNP majority 9,478 (33.48%)
9.89% swing Lab. to SNP

CUNNINGHAME NORTH
(Scotland West Region)
E. 55,647 T. 31,965 (57.44%)

Kenneth Gibson, SNP	16,587
Jamie Greene, C.	7,863
Johanna Baxter, Lab.	6,735
Charity Pierce, LD	780

SNP majority 8,724 (27.29%)
5.83% swing SNP to C.

CUNNINGHAME SOUTH
(Scotland South Region)
E. 50,215 T. 25,695 (51.17%)

Ruth Maguire, SNP	13,416
Joe Cullinane, Lab.	7,723
Billy McClure, C.	3,940
Ruby Kirkwood, LD	616

SNP majority 5,693 (22.16%)
5.76% swing Lab. to SNP

DUMBARTON
(Scotland West Region)
E. 55,098 T. 33,598 (60.98%)

Jackie Baillie, Lab.	13,522
Gail Robertson, SNP	13,413
Maurice Corry, C.	4,891
Aileen Morton, LD	1,131
Andrew Muir, Ind.	641

Lab. majority 109 (0.32%)
2.71% swing Lab. to SNP

DUMFRIESSHIRE
(Scotland South Region)
E. 60,698 T. 36,260 (59.74%)

Oliver Mundell, C.	13,536
Joan McAlpine, SNP	12,306
Elaine Murray, Lab.	9,151
Richard Brodie, LD	1,267

C. majority 1,230 (3.39%)
10.99% swing Lab. to C.

DUNDEE EAST
(Scotland North East Region)
E. 55,261 T. 28,437 (51.46%)

Shona Robison, SNP	16,509
Richard McCready, Lab.	5,611
Bill Bowman, C.	4,969
Craig Duncan, LD	911
Leah Ganley, TUSC	437

SNP majority 10,898 (38.32%)
1.57% swing SNP to Lab.

DUNDEE WEST
(Scotland North East Region)
E. 53,830 T. 27,788 (51.62%)

Joe FitzPatrick, SNP	16,070
Jenny Marra, Lab.	7,242
Nicola Ross, C.	2,826
Daniel Coleman, LD	1,008
Jim McFarlane, TUSC	642

SNP majority 8,828 (31.77%)
2.79% swing Lab. to SNP

DUNFERMLINE
(Scotland Mid and Fife Region)
E. 57,740 T. 32,909 (57.00%)

Shirley-Anne Somerville, SNP	14,257
Cara Hilton, Lab.	9,699
James Reekie, C.	5,797
James Calder, LD	3,156

SNP majority 4,558 (13.85%)
5.92% swing Lab. to SNP

EAST KILBRIDE
(Scotland Central Region)
E. 61,134 T. 34,629 (56.64%)

Linda Fabiani, SNP	19,371
LizAnne Handibode, Lab.	8,392
Graham Simpson, C.	5,857
Paul McGarry, LD	1,009

SNP majority 10,979 (31.70%)
12.59% swing Lab. to SNP

EAST LOTHIAN
(Scotland South Region)
E. 60,848 T. 37,913 (62.31%)

Iain Gray, Lab.	14,329
DJ Johnston-Smith, SNP	13,202
Rachael Hamilton, C.	9,045
Ettie Spencer, LD	1,337

Lab. majority 1,127 (2.97%)
1.25% swing SNP to Lab.

EASTWOOD
(Scotland West Region)
E. 53,085 T. 36,255 (68.30%)

Jackson Carlaw, C.	12,932
Stewart Maxwell, SNP	11,321
Ken Macintosh, Lab.	11,081
John Duncan, LD	921

C. majority 1,611 (4.44%)
5.70% swing Lab. to C.

EDINBURGH CENTRAL
(Lothian Region)
E. 59,581 T. 34,169 (57.35%)

Ruth Davidson, C.	10,399
Alison Dickie, SNP	9,789
Sarah Boyack, Lab.	7,546
Alison Johnstone, Green	4,644
Hannah Bettsworth, LD	1,672
Tom Laird, SLP	119

C. majority 610 (1.79%)
9.73% swing SNP to C.

EDINBURGH EASTERN
(Lothian Region)
E. 62,817 T. 35,397 (56.35%)

Ash Denham, SNP	16,760
Kezia Dugdale, Lab.	11,673
Nick Cook, C.	5,700
Cospatric D'Inverno, LD	1,264

SNP majority 5,087 (14.37%)
3.55% swing Lab. to SNP

EDINBURGH NORTHERN & LEITH
(Lothian Region)
E. 67,273 T. 37,102 (55.15%)

Ben Macpherson, SNP	17,322
Lesley Hinds, Lab.	10,576
Iain McGill, C.	6,081
Martin Veart, LD	1,779
Jack Caldwell, Ind.	1,344

SNP majority 6,746 (18.18%)
10.05% swing Lab. to SNP

EDINBURGH PENTLANDS
(Lothian Region)
E. 55,241 T. 33,353 (60.38%)

Gordon MacDonald, SNP	13,181
Gordon Lindhurst, C.	10,725
Blair Heary, Lab.	7,811
Emma Farthing-Sykes, LD	1,636

SNP majority 2,456 (7.36%)
0.76% swing C. to SNP

EDINBURGH SOUTHERN
(Lothian Region)
E. 59,587 T. 38,259 (64.21%)

Daniel Johnson, Lab.	13,597
Jim Eadie, SNP	12,474
Miles Briggs, C.	9,972
Pramod Subbaraman, LD	2,216

Lab. majority 1,123 (2.94%)
2.49% swing SNP to Lab.

EDINBURGH WESTERN
(Lothian Region)
E. 61,666 T. 39,766 (64.49%)

Alex Cole-Hamilton, LD	16,645
Toni Giugliano, SNP	13,685
Sandy Batho, C.	5,686
Cat Headley, Lab.	3,750

LD majority 2,960 (7.44%)
7.74% swing SNP to LD

ETTRICK, ROXBURGH &
BERWICKSHIRE
(Scotland South Region)
E. 54,506 T. 33,095 (60.72%)

John Lamont, C.	18,257
Paul Wheelhouse, SNP	10,521
Jim Hume, LD	2,551
Barrie Cunning, Lab.	1,766

C. majority 7,736 (23.38%)
2.43% swing SNP to C.

FALKIRK EAST
(Scotland Central Region)
E. 60,271 T. 32,524 (53.96%)

Angus MacDonald, SNP	16,720
Craig Martin, Lab.	8,408
Callum Laidlaw, C.	6,342
James Munro, LD	1,054

SNP majority 8,312 (25.56%)
6.50% swing Lab. to SNP

FALKIRK WEST
(Scotland Central Region)
E. 59,812 T. 32,083 (53.64%)

Michael Matheson, SNP	18,260
Mandy Telford, Lab.	6,980
Alison Harris, C.	5,877
Gillian Cole-Hamilton, LD	966

SNP majority 11,280 (35.16%)
7.39% swing Lab. to SNP

FIFE MID & GLENROTHES
(Scotland Mid and Fife Region)
E. 53,241 T. 28,547 (53.62%)

Jenny Gilruth, SNP	15,555
Kay Morrison, Lab.	7,279
Alex Stewart-Clark, C.	4,427
Jane-Ann Liston, LD	1,286

SNP majority 8,276 (28.99%)
6.54% swing Lab. to SNP

FIFE NORTH EAST
(Scotland Mid and Fife Region)
E. 54,052 T. 34,063 (63.02%)

Willie Rennie, LD	14,928
Roderick Campbell, SNP	11,463
Huw Bell, C.	5,646
Rosalind Garton, Lab.	2,026

LD majority 3,465 (10.17%)
9.45% swing SNP to LD

GALLOWAY & WEST DUMFRIES
(Scotland South Region)
E. 56,321 T. 33,363 (59.24%)

Finlay Carson, C.	14,527
Aileen McLeod, SNP	13,013
Fiona O'Donnell, Lab.	4,876
Andrew Metcalf, LD	947

C. majority 1,514 (4.54%)
0.83% swing SNP to C.

GLASGOW ANNIESLAND
(Glasgow Region)
E. 57,884 T. 29,016 (50.13%)

Bill Kidd, SNP	15,007
Bill Butler, Lab.	8,854
Adam Tomkins, C.	4,057
James Speirs, LD	1,098

SNP majority 6,153 (21.21%)
10.59% swing Lab. to SNP

GLASGOW CATHCART
(Glasgow Region)
E. 60,871 T. 30,637 (50.33%)

James Dornan, SNP	16,200
Soryia Siddique, Lab.	6,810
Kyle Thornton, C.	4,514
Margot Clark, LD	1,703
Brian Smith, TUSC	909
Chris Creighton, Ind.	501

SNP majority 9,390 (30.65%)
12.29% swing Lab. to SNP

GLASGOW KELVIN
(Glasgow Region)
E. 62,203 T. 28,442 (45.72%)

Sandra White, SNP	10,964
Patrick Harvie, Green	6,916
Michael Shanks, Lab.	5,968
Sheila Mechan, C.	3,346
Carole Ford, LD	1,050
Tom Muirhead, Ind.	198

SNP majority 4,048 (14.23%)

GLASGOW MARYHILL &
SPRINGBURN
(Glasgow Region)
E. 53,647 T. 23,612 (44.01%)

Bob Doris, SNP	13,109
Patricia Ferguson, Lab.	7,507
John Anderson, C.	2,305
James Harrison, LD	691

SNP majority 5,602 (23.73%)
15.01% swing Lab. to SNP

GLASGOW POLLOK
(Glasgow Region)
E. 61,350 T. 27,943 (45.55%)

Humza Yousaf, SNP	15,316
Johann Lamont, Lab.	8,834
Thomas Haddow, C.	2,653
Isabel Nelson, LD	585
Ian Leech, TUSC	555

SNP majority 6,482 (23.20%)
12.96% swing Lab. to SNP

GLASGOW PROVAN
(Glasgow Region)
E. 56,169 T. 24,077 (42.87%)

Ivan McKee, SNP	13,140
Paul Martin, Lab.	8,357
Annie Wells, C.	2,062
Tom Coleman, LD	518

SNP majority 4,783 (19.87%)
15.35% swing Lab. to SNP

GLASGOW SHETTLESTON
(Glasgow Region)
E. 58,021 T. 25,375 (43.73%)

John Mason, SNP	14,198
Thomas Rannachan, Lab.	6,875
Thomas Kerr, C.	3,151
Jamie Cocozza, TUSC	583
Giovanni Caccavello, LD	568

SNP majority 7,323 (28.86%)
13.05% swing Lab. to SNP

GLASGOW SOUTHSIDE
(Glasgow Region)
E. 52,141 T. 24,903 (47.76%)

Nicola Sturgeon, SNP	15,287
Fariha Thomas, Lab.	5,694
Graham Hutchison, C.	3,100
Kevin Lewsey, LD	822

SNP majority 9,593 (38.52%)
9.64% swing Lab. to SNP

GREENOCK & INVERCLYDE
(Scotland West Region)
E. 55,171 T. 31,725 (57.50%)

Stuart McMillan, SNP	17,032
Siobhan McCready, Lab.	8,802
Graeme Brooks, C.	4,487
John Watson, LD	1,404

SNP majority 8,230 (25.94%)
13.88% swing Lab. to SNP

HAMILTON, LARKHALL &
STONEHOUSE
(Scotland Central Region)
E. 57,656 T. 28,885 (50.10%)

Christina McKelvie, SNP	13,945
Margaret McCulloch, Lab.	8,508
Margaret Mitchell, C.	5,596
Eileen Baxendale, LD	836

SNP majority 5,437 (18.82%)
5.05% swing Lab. to SNP

INVERNESS & NAIRN
(Highlands and Islands Region)
E. 66,619 T. 38,317 (57.52%)

Fergus Ewing, SNP	18,505
Edward Mountain, C.	7,648
David Stewart, Lab.	6,719
Carolyn Caddick, LD	5,445

SNP majority 10,857 (28.33%)
5.80% swing SNP to C.

KILMARNOCK & IRVINE VALLEY
(Scotland South Region)
E. 62,620 T. 34,385 (54.91%)

Willie Coffey, SNP	19,047
Dave Meechan, Lab.	7,853
Brian Whittle, C.	6,597
Rebecca Plenderleith, LD	888

SNP majority 11,194 (32.55%)
6.87% swing Lab. to SNP

KIRKCALDY
(Scotland Mid and Fife Region)
E. 59,533 T. 31,108 (52.25%)

David Torrance, SNP	16,358
Claire Baker, Lab.	8,963
Martin Laidlaw, C.	4,568
Lauren Jones, LD	1,219

SNP majority 7,395 (23.77%)
11.56% swing Lab. to SNP

LINLITHGOW
(Lothian Region)
E. 71,434 T. 38,407 (53.77%)

Fiona Hyslop, SNP	19,362
Angela Moohan, Lab.	10,027
Charles Kennedy, C.	7,699
Dan Farthing-Sykes, LD	1,319

SNP majority 9,335 (24.31%)
6.17% swing Lab. to SNP

MIDLOTHIAN NORTH & MUSSELBURGH
(Lothian Region)
E. 63,360 T. 34,685 (54.74%)

Colin Beattie, SNP	16,948
Bernard Harkins, Lab.	9,913
Jeremy Balfour, C.	6,267
Jacquie Bell, LD	1,557

SNP majority 7,035 (20.28%)
5.12% swing Lab. to SNP

MIDLOTHIAN SOUTH, TWEEDDALE & LAUDERDALE
(Scotland South Region)
E. 60,204 T. 35,581 (59.10%)

Christine Grahame, SNP	16,031
Michelle Ballantyne, C.	10,163
Fiona Dugdale, Lab.	5,701
Kris Chapman, LD	3,686

SNP majority 5,868 (16.49%)
7.63% swing SNP to C.

MORAY
(Highlands and Islands Region)
E. 61,969 T. 33,421 (53.93%)

Richard Lochhead, SNP	15,742
Douglas Ross, C.	12,867
Sean Morton, Lab.	3,547
Jamie Paterson, LD	1,265

SNP majority 2,875 (8.60%)
14.83% swing SNP to C.

MOTHERWELL & WISHAW
(Scotland Central Region)
E. 57,045 T. 29,111 (51.03%)

Clare Adamson, SNP	15,291
John Pentland, Lab.	9,068
Meghan Gallacher, C.	3,991
Yvonne Finlayson, LD	761

SNP majority 6,223 (21.38%)
11.89% swing Lab. to SNP

NA H-EILEANAN AN IAR
(Highlands and Islands Region)
E. 21,695 T. 13,206 (60.87%)

Alasdair Allan, SNP	8,874
Rhoda Grant, Lab.	3,378
Ranald Fraser, C.	1,499
John Cormack, SCP	1,162
Ken MacLeod, LD	293

SNP majority 3,496 (26.47%)
5.10% swing SNP to Lab.

ORKNEY
(Highlands and Islands Region)
E. 16,997 T. 10,534 (61.98%)

Liam McArthur, LD	7,096
Donna Heddle, SNP	2,562
Jamie Halcro Johnston, C.	435
Gerry McGarvey, Lab.	304
Paul Dawson, Ind.	137

LD majority 4,534 (43.04%)
16.20% swing SNP to LD

PAISLEY
(Scotland West Region)
E. 51,673 T. 29,464 (57.02%)

George Adam, SNP	14,682
Neil Bibby, Lab.	9,483
Paul Masterton, C.	3,533
Eileen McCartin, LD	1,766

SNP majority 5,199 (17.65%)
8.34% swing Lab. to SNP

PERTHSHIRE NORTH
(Scotland and Mid Fife Region)
E. 54,255 T. 34,025 (62.71%)

John Swinney, SNP	16,526
Murdo Fraser, C.	13,190
Anna McEwan, Lab.	2,604
Peter Barrett, LD	1,705

SNP majority 3,336 (9.80%)
12.38% swing SNP to C.

PERTHSHIRE SOUTH & KINROSS-SHIRE
(Scotland and Mid Fife Region)
E. 59,397 T. 36,149 (60.86%)

Roseanna Cunningham, SNP	15,315
Liz Smith, C.	13,893
Scott Nicholson, Lab.	3,389
Willie Robertson, LD	3,008
Craig Finlay, Community	544

SNP majority 1,422 (3.93%)
9.51% swing SNP to C.

RENFREWSHIRE NORTH & WEST
(Scotland West Region)
E. 50,555 T. 30,807 (60.94%)

Derek Mackay, SNP	14,718
David Wilson, C.	7,345
Mary Fee, Lab.	7,244
Rod Ackland, LD	888
Jim Halfpenny, TUSC	414
Peter Morton, Ind.	198

SNP majority 7,373 (23.93%)
1.02% swing C. to SNP

RENFREWSHIRE SOUTH
(Scotland West Region)
E. 49,422 T. 29,681 (60.06%)

Thomas Arthur, SNP	14,272
Paul O'Kane, Lab.	9,864
Ann Le Blond, C.	4,752
Tristan Gray, LD	793

SNP majority 4,408 (14.85%)
12.21% swing Lab. to SNP

RUTHERGLEN
(Glasgow Region)
E. 60,702 T. 32,952 (54.28%)

Clare Haughey, SNP	15,222
James Kelly, Lab.	11,479
Taylor Muir, C.	3,718
Robert Brown, LD	2,533

SNP majority 3,743 (11.36%)
8.96% swing Lab. to SNP

SHETLAND ISLANDS
(Highlands and Islands Region)
E. 17,784 T. 11,041 (62.08%)

Tavish Scott, LD	7,440
Danus Skene, SNP	2,545
Robina Barton, Lab.	651
Cameron Smith, C.	405

LD majority 4,895 (44.33%)
4.45% swing SNP to LD

SKYE, LOCHABER & BADENOCH
(Highlands and Islands Region)
E. 59,537 T. 36,505 (61.31%)

Kate Forbes, SNP	17,362
Angela MacLean, LD	8,319
Robbie Munro, C.	5,887
Linda Stewart, Lab.	3,821
Ronnie Campbell, Ind.	1,116

SNP majority 9,043 (24.77%)
4.56% swing LD to SNP

STIRLING
(Scotland and Mid Fife Region)
E. 55,785 T. 34,189 (61.29%)

Bruce Crawford, SNP	16,303
Dean Lockhart, C.	9,585
Rebecca Bell, Lab.	6,885
Elisabeth Wilson, LD	1,416

SNP majority 6,718 (19.65%)
7.03% swing SNP to C.

STRATHKELVIN & BEARSDEN
(Scotland West Region)
E. 62,598 T. 39,188 (62.60%)

Rona Mackay, SNP	17,060
Andrew Polson, C.	8,960
Margaret McCarthy, Lab.	8,288
Katy Gordon, LD	4,880

SNP majority 8,100 (20.67%)
4.21% swing SNP to C.

UDDINGSTON & BELLSHILL
(Central Scotland Region)
E. 57,556 T. 29,543 (51.33%)

Richard Lyle, SNP	14,424
Michael McMahon, Lab.	9,615
Andrew Morrison, C.	4,693
Kaitey Blair, LD	811

SNP majority 4,809 (16.28%)
9.57% swing Lab. to SNP

REGIONS *as at 5 May 2016*
E. 4,099,407 T. 55.6%

GLASGOW
E. 522,988 T. 248,109 (47.44%)

SNP	111,101	(44.78%)
Lab.	59,151	(23.84%)
C.	29,533	(11.90%)
Green	23,398	(9.43%)
LD	5,850	(2.36%)
UKIP	4,889	(1.97%)
Solidarity	3,593	(1.45%)
RISE	2,454	(0.99%)
UP	2,453	(0.99%)
Women	2,091	(0.84%)
Animal	1,819	(0.73%)
SCP	1,506	(0.61%)
Ind.	271	(0.11%)

SNP majority 51,950 (20.94%)
8.05% swing Lab. to SNP (2011 SNP majority 10,078)
ADDITIONAL MEMBERS

Adam Tomkins, *C.*	James Kelly, *Lab.*
Annie Wells, *C.*	Pauline McNeill, *Lab.*
Anas Sarwar, *Lab.*	Patrick Harvie, *Green*
Johann Lamont, *Lab.*	

HIGHLANDS AND ISLANDS
E. 348,581 T. 205,313 (58.90%)

SNP	81,600	(39.74%)
C.	44,693	(21.77%)
LD	27,223	(13.26%)
Lab.	22,894	(11.15%)
Green	14,781	(7.20%)
UKIP	5,344	(2.60%)
Ind.	3,689	(1.80%)
SCP	3,407	(1.66%)
RISE	889	(0.43%)
Solidarity	793	(0.39%)

SNP majority 36,907 (17.98%)
8.95% swing SNP to C. (2011 SNP majority 59,198)
ADDITIONAL MEMBERS

Douglas Ross, *C.*	David Steward, *Lab.*
Edward Mountain, *C.*	Maree Todd, *SNP*
Donald Cameron, *C.*	John Finnie, *Green*
Rhoda Grant, *Lab.*	

LOTHIAN
E. 565,860 T. 327,178 (57.82%)

SNP	118,546	(36.23%)
C.	74,972	(22.91%)
Lab.	67,991	(20.78%)
Green	34,551	(10.56%)
LD	18,479	(5.65%)
UKIP	5,802	(1.77%)
Women	3,877	(1.18%)
RISE	1,641	(0.50%)
Solidarity	1,319	(0.40%)

SNP majority 43,574 (13.32%)
7.10% swing SNP to C. (2011 SNP majority 40,409)
ADDITIONAL MEMBERS

Miles Briggs, *C.*	Neil Findlay, *Lab.*
Gordon Lindhurst, *C.*	Alison Johnstone, *Green*
Jeremy Balfour, *C.*	Andy Wightman, *Green*
Kezia Dugdale, *Lab.*	

SCOTLAND CENTRAL
E. 511,506 T. 270,706 (52.92%)

SNP	129,082	(47.68%)
Lab.	67,103	(24.79%)
C.	43,602	(16.11%)
Green	12,722	(4.70%)
UKIP	6,088	(2.25%)
LD	5,015	(1.85%)
Solidarity	2,684	(0.99%)
SCP	2,314	(0.85%)
RISE	1,636	(0.60%)
Ind.	460	(0.17%)

SNP majority 61,979 (22.90%)
5.92% swing Lab. to SNP (2011 SNP majority 25,802)
ADDITIONAL MEMBERS

Margaret Mitchell, *C.*	Monica Lennon, *Lab.*
Graham Simpson, *C.*	Mark Griffin, *Lab.*
Alison Harris, *C.*	Elaine Smith, *Lab.*
Richard Leonard, *Lab.*	

SCOTLAND MID AND FIFE
E. 499,156 T. 291,172 (58.33%)

SNP	120,128	(41.26%)
C.	73,293	(25.17%)
Lab.	51,373	(17.64%)
LD	20,401	(7.01%)
Green	17,860	(6.13%)
UKIP	5,345	(1.84%)
RISE	1,073	(0.37%)
Solidarity	1,049	(0.36%)
SLP	650	(0.22%)

SNP majority 46,835 (16.08%)
7.50% swing SNP to C. (2011 SNP majority 52,068)
ADDITIONAL MEMBERS

Murdo Fraser, C.	Alex Rowley, Lab.
Liz Smith, C.	Claire Baker, Lab.
Dean Lockhart, C.	Mark Ruskell, Green
Alexander Stewart, C.	

SCOTLAND NORTH EAST
E. 579,317 T. 307,006 (52.99%)

SNP	137,086	(44.65%)
C.	85,848	(27.96%)
Lab.	38,791	(12.64%)
LD	18,444	(6.01%)
Green	15,123	(4.93%)
UKIP	6,376	(2.08%)
SCP	2,068	(0.67%)
Solidarity	992	(0.32%)
Nat Front	617	(0.20%)
RISE	599	(0.20%)
SLP	552	(0.18%)
Comm Brit	510	(0.17%)

SNP majority 51,238 (16.69%)
10.95% swing SNP to C. (2011 SNP majority 96,856)
ADDITIONAL MEMBERS

Alex Johnstone, C.	Jenny Marra, Lab.
Ross Thomson, C.	Lewis Macdonald, Lab.
Peter Chapman, C.	Mike Rumbles, LD
Liam Kerr, C.	

SCOTLAND SOUTH
E. 533,774 T. 314,192 (58.86%)

SNP	120,217	(38.26%)
C.	100,753	(32.07%)
Lab.	56,072	(17.85%)
Green	14,773	(4.70%)
LD	11,775	(3.75%)
UKIP	6,726	(2.14%)
CSSInd.	1,485	(0.47%)
Solidarity	1,294	(0.41%)
RISE	1,097	(0.35%)

SNP majority 19,464 (6.19%)
7.65% swing SNP to C. (2011 SNP majority 43,675)
ADDITIONAL MEMBERS

Rachel Hamilton, C.	Joan McAlpine, SNP
Brian Whittle, C.	Emma Harper, SNP
Claudia Beamish, Lab.	Paul Wheelhouse, SNP
Colin Smyth, Lab.	

SCOTLAND WEST
E. 538,225 T. 322,076 (59.84%)

SNP	135,827	(42.17%)
Lab.	72,544	(22.52%)
C.	71,528	(22.21%)
Green	17,218	(5.35%)
LD	12,097	(3.76%)
UKIP	5,856	(1.82%)
Solidarity	2,609	(0.81%)
SCP	2,391	(0.74%)
RISE	1,522	(0.47%)
SLP	484	(0.15%)

SNP majority 63,283 (19.65%)
5.44% swing Lab. to SNP (2011 SNP majority 24,776)
ADDITIONAL MEMBERS

Jamie Green, C.	Mary Fee, Lab.
Maurice Golden, C.	Ken Macintosh, Lab.
Maurice Corry, C.	Ross Greer, Green
Neil Bibby, Lab.	

NORTHERN IRELAND

NORTHERN IRELAND ASSEMBLY
Parliament Buildings, Stormont, Belfast BT4 3XX
T 028-9052 1137 E info@niassembly.gov.uk
W www.niassembly.gov.uk

The Northern Ireland Assembly was established as a result of the Belfast Agreement (also known as the Good Friday Agreement) in April 1998. The agreement was endorsed through a referendum held in May 1998 and subsequently given legal force through the Northern Ireland Act 1998.

The Northern Ireland Assembly has full legislative and executive authority for all matters that are the responsibility of the government's Northern Ireland departments – known as transferred matters. Excepted and reserved matters are defined in schedules 2 and 3 of the Northern Ireland Act 1998 and remain the responsibility of UK parliament.

The first assembly election occurred on 25 June 1998 and the 108 members elected met for the first time on 1 July 1998.

On 29 November 1999 the assembly appointed ten ministers as well as the chairs and deputy chairs for the ten statutory departmental committees. Devolution of powers to the Northern Ireland Assembly occurred on 2 December 1999, following several delays concerned with Sinn Fein's inclusion in the executive while Irish Republican Army (IRA) weapons were yet to be decommissioned.

Since the devolution of powers, the assembly has been suspended by the Secretary of State for Northern Ireland on four occasions. The first was between 11 February and 30 May 2000, with two 24-hour suspensions on 10 August and 22 September 2001 – all owing to a lack of progress in decommissioning. The final suspension took place on 14 October 2002 after unionists walked out of the executive following a police raid on Sinn Fein's office investigating alleged intelligence gathering.

The assembly was formally dissolved in April 2003 in anticipation of an election, which eventually took place on 26 November 2003. The results of the election changed the balance of power between the political parties, with an increase in the number of seats held by the Democratic Unionist Party (DUP) and Sinn Fein (SF), so that they became the largest parties. The assembly was restored to a state of suspension following the November election while political parties engaged in a review of the Belfast Agreement aimed at fully restoring the devolved institutions.

In July 2005 the leadership of the IRA formally ordered an end to its armed campaign; it authorised a representative to engage with the Independent International Commission on Decommissioning in order to verifiably put the arms beyond use. On 26 September 2005 General John de Chastelain, the chair of the commission, along with two independent church witnesses confirmed that the IRA's entire arsenal of weapons had been decommissioned.

Following the passing of the Northern Ireland Act 2006 the secretary of state created a non-legislative fixed-term assembly, whose membership consisted of the 108 members elected in the 2003 election. It first met on 15 May 2006 with the remit of making preparations for the restoration of devolved government; its discussions informed the next round of talks called by the British and Irish governments held at St Andrews. The St Andrews agreement of 13 October 2006 led to the establishment of the transitional assembly.

The Northern Ireland (St Andrews Agreement) Act 2006 set out a timetable to restore devolution, and also set the date for the third election to the assembly as 7 March 2007. The DUP and SF again had the largest number of Members of the Legislative Assembly (MLAs) elected, and although the initial restoration deadline of 26 March was missed, the leaders of the DUP and SF (Revd Dr Ian Paisley and Gerry Adams respectively) took part in a historic meeting and made a joint commitment to establish an executive committee in the assembly to which devolved powers were restored on 8 May 2007.

RECENT DEVELOPMENTS
Assembly elections took place on 5 May 2016 to elect the 108 members of the legislative assembly for a fifth term. This assembly collapsed on 9 January 2017 when Martin McGuinness resigned as Deputy First Minister. Under the joint protocols that govern the power-sharing agreement, if either the first minister or the deputy resigns and a replacement is not nominated by the relevant party within seven days, then a snap election must be called. The assembly was formerly dissolved at midnight on 25 January 2017 and the most recent assembly elections were held on 2 March 2017 to elect the 90 members of the legislative assembly. Under the Assembly Members (Reduction of Numbers) Act Northern Ireland 2016, the number of assembly members was reduced from 108 to 90 – five members to be elected by each constituency, rather than six.

Following the March 2017 election, negotiations to form an executive missed both the normal three week deadline and an extended deadline of 29 June 2017 set by the Secretary of State for Northern Ireland. As both deadlines have passed the Northern Ireland secretary has a duty to set a date for a new election. This duty is currently under review and the assembly remains suspended until an executive is formed.

THE SINGLE TRANSFERABLE VOTE SYSTEM
Members of the Northern Ireland Assembly are elected by the single transferable vote system from 18 constituencies – five per constituency. Under the single transferable vote system every voter has a single vote that can be transferred from one candidate to another. Voters number their candidates in order of preference. Where candidates reach their quota of votes and are elected, surplus votes are transferred to other candidates according to the next preference on each voter's ballot slip. The candidate in each round with the fewest votes is eliminated and their surplus votes are redistributed according to the voter's next preference. The process is repeated until the required number of members are elected.

SALARIES*

	2018–19
First Minister/Deputy First Minister	£121,500
Minister	£87,500
Junior Minister	£55,500
MLA	£49,500

*As there is currently no Executive, the planned £500 increase to all MLA salaries was not implemented on 1 April 2018

NORTHERN IRELAND ASSEMBLY
MEMBERS *as at August 2018*
KEY
* Replacement from the party list since the 2 March 2017 Northern Ireland Assembly election

Agnew, Steven, *Green, Down North*
Aiken, Steve, OBE, *UUP, Antrim South*
Allen, Andy, *UUP, Belfast East*
Allister, Jim, *TUV, Antrim North*
Archibald, Caoimhe, *SF, Londonderry East*
Armstrong, Kellie, *Alliance, Strangford*
Bailey, Clare, *Green, Belfast South*
Barton, Rosemary, *UUP, Fermanagh and South Tyrone*
Beattie, Doug, MC, *UUP, Upper Bann*
Beggs, Roy, *UUP, Antrim East*

* **Blair**, John, *Alliance, Antrim South*
Boylan, Cathal, *SF, Newry and Armagh*
Boyle, Michaela, *SF, Tyrone West*
Bradley, Maurice, *DUP, Londonderry East*
Bradley, Paula, *DUP, Belfast North*
Bradley, Sinéad, *SDLP, Down South*
Bradshaw, Paula, *Alliance, Belfast South*
Buchanan, Keith, *DUP, Ulster Mid*
Buchanan, Thomas, *DUP, Tyrone West*
Buckley, Jonathan, *DUP, Upper Bann*
Bunting, Joanne, *DUP, Belfast East*
Butler, Robbie, *UUP, Lagan Valley*
Cameron, Pam, *DUP, Antrim South*
Carroll, Gerry, *PBP, Belfast West*
Catney, Pat, *SDLP, Lagan Valley*
Chambers, Alan, *UUP, Down North*
* **Clarke**, Trevor, *DUP, Antrim South*
Dallat, John, *SDLP, Londonderry East*
Dickson, Stewart, *Alliance, Antrim East*
Dillon, Linda, *SF, Ulster Mid*
Dolan, Jemma, *SF, Fermanagh and South Tyrone*
Dunne, Gordon, *DUP, Down North*
Durkan, Mark, *SDLP, Foyle*
Easton, Alex, *DUP, Down North*
Eastwood, Colum, *SDLP, Foyle*
Ennis, Sinéad, *SF, Down South*
Farry, Dr Stephen, *Alliance, Down North*
Fearon, Megan, *SF, Newry and Armagh*
Flynn, Órlaithí, *SF, Belfast West*
Foster, Arlene, *DUP, Fermanagh and South Tyrone*
Frew, Paul, *DUP, Antrim North*
* **Gildernew**, Colm, *SF, Fermanagh and South Tyrone*
Givan, Paul, *DUP, Lagan Valley*
Hamilton, Simon, *DUP, Strangford*
Hanna, Claire, *SDLP, Belfast South*
Hilditch, David, *DUP, Antrim East*
Humphrey, William, *DUP, Belfast North*
Irwin, William, *DUP, Newry and Armagh*
Kearney, Declan, *SF, Antrim South*
Kelly, Dolores, *SDLP, Upper Bann*
Kelly, Gerry, *SF, Belfast North*
* **Kelly**, Catherine, *SF, Tyrone West*
Lockhart, Carla, *DUP, Upper Bann*
Long, Naomi, *Alliance, Belfast East*
Lunn, Trevor, *Alliance, Lagan Valley*
Lynch, Seán, *SF, Fermanagh and South Tyrone*
Lyons, Gordon, *DUP, Antrim East*
Lyttle, Chris, *Alliance, Belfast East*
McAleer, Declan, *SF, Tyrone West*
McCann, Fra, *SF, Belfast West*
McCartney, Raymond, *SF, Foyle*
McCrossan, Daniel, *SDLP, Tyrone West*
McGlone, Patsy, *SDLP, Ulster Mid*
McGrath, Colin, *SDLP, Down South*
McGuigan, Philip, *SF, Antrim North*
McIlveen, Michelle, *DUP, Strangford*
McNulty, Justin, *SDLP, Newry and Armagh*
Mallon, Nichola, *SDLP, Belfast North*
Maskey, Alex, *SF, Belfast West*
Middleton, Gary, *DUP, Foyle*
Milne, Ian, *SF, Ulster Mid*
* **Mullan**, Karen, *SF, Foyle*
Murphy, Conor, *SF, Newry and Armagh*
Nesbitt, Mike, *UUP, Strangford*
Newton, Robin, *DUP, Belfast East*
Ní Chuilín, Carál, *SF, Belfast North*
O'Dowd, John, *SF, Upper Bann*
O'Neill, Michelle, *SF, Ulster Mid*
Ó Muilleoir, Máirtín, *SF, Belfast South*

Poots, Edwin, *DUP, Lagan Valley*
Robinson, George, *DUP, Londonderry East*
* **Rogan**, Emma, *SF, Down South*
Sheehan, Pat, *SF, Belfast West*
Stalford, Christopher, *DUP, Belfast South*
Stewart, John, *UUP, Antrim East*
Storey, Mervyn, *DUP, Antrim North*
Sugden, Claire, *Ind., Londonderry East*
Swann, Robin, *UUP, Antrim North*
Weir, Peter, *DUP, Down North*
Wells, Jim, *DUP, Down South*

STATE OF THE PARTIES *as at 2 March 2017 election*

Party	Seats
Democratic Unionist Party (DUP)	28
Sinn Fein (SF)	27
Social Democratic and Labour Party (SDLP)	12
Ulster Unionist Party (UUP)	10
Alliance Party of Northern Ireland (Alliance)	8
Green Party (Green)	2
People Before Profit Alliance (PBP)	1
Traditional Unionist Voice (TUV)	1
Independents (Ind.)	1
Total	90

NORTHERN IRELAND EXECUTIVE

Stormont Castle, Stormont, Belfast BT4 3TT
T 028-9052 8400
W www.northernireland.gov.uk

The Northern Ireland Executive comprises the first minister, deputy first minister, two junior ministers and eight departmental ministers.

The executive exercises authority on behalf of the Northern Ireland Assembly, and takes decisions on significant issues and matters which cut across the responsibility of two or more ministers.

The executive also agrees proposals put forward by ministers for new legislation in the form of 'executive bills' for consideration by the assembly. It is also responsible for drawing up a programme for government and an agreed budget for approval by the assembly. Ministers of the executive are nominated by the political parties in the Northern Ireland Assembly. The number of ministers which a party can nominate is determined by its share of seats in the assembly. The first minister and deputy first minister are nominated by the largest and second largest parties respectively and act as chairs of the executive. Each executive minister has responsibility for a specific Northern Ireland government department.

EXECUTIVE COMMITTEE OF MINISTERS

There are currently no executive ministers in post since the most recent assembly elections which took place on 2 March 2017. Negotiations to appoint the executive committee of ministers in charge of the nine government departments failed to meet both the three-week deadline following the election and an extended deadline of 29 June 2017 set by the Secretary of State for Northern Ireland. The assembly remains suspended until an executive is formed.

NORTHERN IRELAND EXECUTIVE DEPARTMENTS

THE EXECUTIVE OFFICE, Stormont Castle, Stormont, Belfast BT4 3TT T 028-9052 8400 W www.executiveoffice-ni.gov.uk
DEPARTMENT OF AGRICULTURE, ENVIRONMENT AND RURAL AFFAIRS, Dundonald House, Upper Newtownards Road, Belfast BT4 3SB T 0300-200 7850 W www.daera-ni.gov.uk

DEPARTMENT FOR COMMUNITIES, Causeway Exchange, 1–7 Bedford Street, Belfast BT2 7EG T 028-9082 9000
W www.communities-ni.gov.uk
DEPARTMENT FOR THE ECONOMY, Netherleigh, Massey Avenue, Belfast BT4 2JP T 028-9052 9900
W www.economy-ni.gov.uk
DEPARTMENT OF EDUCATION, Rathgael House, Balloo Road, Bangor, Co. Down BT19 7PR T 028-9127 9279
W www.education-ni.gov.uk
DEPARTMENT OF FINANCE, Clare House, 303 Airport Road, Belfast BT3 9ED T 028-9185 8111 W www.finance-ni.gov.uk
DEPARTMENT OF HEALTH, Castle Buildings, Stormont, Belfast BT4 3SQ T 028-9052 0500 W www.health-ni.gov.uk
DEPARTMENT FOR INFRASTRUCTURE, Clarence Court, 10–18 Adelaide Street, Belfast BT2 8GB T 028-9054 0540
W www.infrastructure-ni.gov.uk
DEPARTMENT OF JUSTICE, Block B, Castle Buildings, Stormont Estate, Belfast BT4 3SG T 028-9076 3000
W www.justice-ni.gov.uk

NORTHERN IRELAND AUDIT OFFICE
106 University Street, Belfast BT7 1EU
T 028-9025 1000 E info@niauditoffice.gov.uk
W www.niauditoffice.gov.uk

The Northern Ireland Audit Office supports the Comptroller and Auditor-General in fulfilling his responsibilities. He is responsible for authorising the issue of money from central government funds to Northern Ireland departments and for both financial and value for money audits of central government bodies in Northern Ireland, including, Northern Ireland departments, executive agencies, executive non-departmental public bodies and health and social care bodies.

Comptroller and Auditor-General, Kieran Donnelly

OFFICE OF THE ATTORNEY-GENERAL FOR NORTHERN IRELAND
PO Box 1272, Belfast BT1 9LU
T 028-9072 5333 E contact@attorneygeneralni.gov.uk
W www.attorneygeneralni.gov.uk

With the devolution of justice responsibilities on 12 April 2010, the Justice (Northern Ireland) Act 2002 was enacted which established a new post of Attorney-General for Northern Ireland. The Attorney-General acts as the chief legal adviser to the Northern Ireland executive for both civil and criminal matters that fall within the devolved powers of the assembly. He is the executive's most senior representative in the courts and responsible for protecting the public interest in matters of law; overseeing the legal work of the in-house advisers to the executive and its departments; and for the appointment of the director and deputy director of the Public Prosecution Service for Northern Ireland. The Attorney-General participates in the assembly proceedings to the extent permitted by its standing orders, but does not vote in the assembly.

The post of Attorney-General is statutorily independent of the first minister, deputy first minister, the executive and the executive departments.

Attorney-General for Northern Ireland, John Larkin, QC

NORTHERN IRELAND ASSEMBLY ELECTION RESULTS *as at 2 March 2017*

Electorate (E.) 1,254,709 Turnout (T.) 64.8%
First = number of first-preference votes
See General Election Results for a list of party abbreviations

ANTRIM EAST
E. 62,933 T. 37,836 (60.12%)

	First	Round Elected
David Hilditch, DUP	6,000	3
Roy Beggs, UUP	5,121	6
Stewart Dickson, Alliance, DUP	4,179	6
Gordon Lyons, DUP	3,851	8
Oliver McMullan, SF	3,701	
John Stewart, UUP	3,377	9
Stephen Ross, DUP	3,313	
Danny Donnelly, Alliance	1,817	
Noel Jordan, UKIP	1,579	
Ruth Wilson, TUV	1,534	
Margaret McKillop, SDLP	1,524	
Dawn Patterson, Green	777	
Conor Sheridan, Lab. Alt	393	
Alan Dunlop, Lab. C	152	
Ricky Best, Ind.	106	

ANTRIM NORTH
E. 76,739 T. 48,518 (63.22%)

	First	Round Elected
Philip McGuigan, SF	7,600	6
Paul Frew, DUP	6,975	7
Mervyn Storey, DUP	6,857	7
Jim Allister, TUV	6,214	7
Robin Swann, UUP	6,022	6
Phillip Logan, DUP	5,708	
Connor Duncan, SDLP	3,519	
Patricia O'Lynn, Alliance	2,616	
Timothy Gaston, TUV	1,505	
Mark Bailey, Green	530	
Monica Digney, Ind.	435	
Adam McBride, Ind.	113	

ANTRIM SOUTH
E. 68,475 T. 42,726 (62.40%)

	First	Round Elected
Declan Kearney, SF	6,891	4
Steve Aiken, UUP	6,287	5
David Ford, Alliance	5,278	7
Paul Girvan, DUP	5,152	8
Pam Cameron, DUP	4,604	8
Trevor Clarke, DUP	4,522	
Roisin Lynch, SDLP	4,024	
Adrian Cochrane-Watson, UUP	2,505	
Richard Cairns, TUV	1,353	
Ivanka Antova, PBP	530	
David McMaster, Ind.	503	
Eleanor Bailey, Green	501	
Mark Logan, C.	194	

BELFAST EAST
E. 64,788 T. 40,828 (63.02%)

	First	Round Elected
Naomi Long, Alliance	7,610	1
Joanne Bunting, DUP	6,007	9
Andy Allen, UUP	5,275	9
Chris Lyttle, Alliance	5,059	8
Robin Newton, DUP	4,729	11
David Douglas, DUP	4,431	
John Kyle, PUP	2,658	
Georgina Milne, Green	1,447	
Mairead O'Donnell, SF	1,173	
Andrew Girvin, TUV.	917	
Courtney Robinson, CCLA	442	
Sheila Bodel, C.	275	
Séamas de Faoite, SDLP	250	
Jordy McKeag, Ind.	84	

BELFAST NORTH
E. 68,187 T. 42,119 (61.77%)

	First	Round Elected
Gerry Kelly, SF	6,275	7
Caral Ni Chuilin, SF	5,929	7
Nichola Mallon, SDLP	5,431	7
Paula Bradley, DUP	4,835	6
William Humphrey, DUP	4,418	6
Nelson McCausland, DUP	4,056	
Nuala McAllister, Alliance	3,487	
Robert Foster, UUP	2,418	
Julie-Anne Corr-Johnston, PUP	2,053	
Fiona Ferguson, PBP	1,559	
Malachai O'Hara, Green	711	
Gemma Weir, WP	248	
Adam Millar, Ind.	66	

BELFAST SOUTH
E. 61,309 T. 43,465 (70.89%)

	First	Round Elected
Mairtin O Muilleoir, SF	7,610	1
Claire Hanna, SDLP	6,559	6
Paula Bradshaw, Alliance	5,595	6
Christopher Stalford, DUP	4,529	9
Emma Little-Pengelly, DUP	4,446	
Clare Bailey, Green	4,247	9
Michael Henderson, UUP	3,863	
Emmet McDonough-Brown, Alliance	2,053	
Naomh Gallagher, SDLP	1,794	
Padraigin Mervyn, PBP	760	
John Hiddleston, TUV	703	
Sean Burns, Lab. Alt	531	
George Jabbour, C.	200	
Lily Kerr, WP	163	

BELFAST WEST
E. 61,309 T. 40,930 (66.76%)

	First	Round Elected
Orlaithi Flynn, SF	6,918	1
Alex Maskey, SF	6,346	3
Fra McCann, SF	6,201	4
Pat Sheehan, SF	5,466	4
Gerry Carroll, PBP	4,903	3
Frank McCoubrey, DUP	4,063	
Alex Attwood, SDLP	3,452	
Michael Collins, PBP	1,096	
Sorcha Eastwood, Alliance	747	
Fred Rodgers, UUP	486	
Connor Campbell, WP	415	
Ellen Murray, Green	251	

DOWN NORTH
E. 64,461 T. 38,174 (59.22%)

	First	Round Elected
Alex Easton, DUP	8,034	1
Alan Chambers, UUP	7,151	1
Stephen Farry, Alliance	7,014	1
Gordon Dunne, DUP	6,118	2
Steven Agnew, Green	5,178	7
Melanie Kennedy, Ind.	1,246	
William Cudworth, UUP	964	
Caoimhe McNeill, SDLP	679	
Frank Shivers, C.	641	
Kieran Maxwell, SF	591	
Chris Carter, Ind.	92	
Gavan Reynolds, Ind.	31	

DOWN SOUTH
E. 75,415 T. 49,934 (66.21%)

	First	Round Elected
Sinead Ennis, SF	10,256	1
Chris Hazzard, SF	8,827	1
Jim Wells, DUP	7,786	5
Sinead Bradley, SDLP	7,323	3
Colin McGrath, SDLP	5,110	7
Patrick Brown, Alliance	4,535	
Harold McKee, UUP	4,172	
Lyle Rea, TUV	630	
Hannah George, Green	483	
Patrick Clarke, Ind.	192	
Gary Hynds, C.	85	

FERMANAGH AND SOUTH TYRONE
E. 73,100 T. 53,075 (72.61%)

	First	Round Elected
Arlene Foster, DUP	8,479	2
Michelle Gildernew, SF	7,987	3
Jemma Dolan, SF	7,767	3
Maurice Morrow, DUP	7,102	
Sean Lynch, SF	6,254	4
Rosemary Barton, UUP	6,060	4
Richie McPhillips, SDLP	5,134	
Noreen Campbell, Alliance	1,437	
Alex Elliott, TUV	780	
Donal O'Cofaigh, Lab. Alt	643	
Tanya Jones, Green	550	
Ricahrd Dunn, C.	70	

FOYLE
E. 69,718 T. 45,317 (65.00%)

	First	Round Elected
Elisha McCallion, SF	9,205	1
Colum Eastwood, SDLP	7,240	3
Raymond McCartney, SF	7,145	2
Mark H. Durkan, SDLP	6,948	5
Gary Middleton, DUP	5,975	6
Eamon McCann, PBP	4,760	
Julia Kee, UUP	1,660	
Colm Cavanagh, Alliance	1,124	
Shannon Downey, Green	242	
John Lindsay, CISTA	196	
Stuart Canning, C.	77	
Arthur McGuinness, Ind.	44	

LAGAN VALLEY
E. 72,621 T. 45,440 (62.50%)

	First	Round Elected
Paul Givan, DUP	8,035	1
Robbie Butler, UUP	6,846	7
Trevor Lunn, Alliance	6,105	7
Edwin Poots, DUP	6,013	8
Brenda Hale, DUP	4,566	
Jenny Palmer, UUP	4,492	
Pat Catney, SDLP	3,795	8
Peter Doran, SF	1,801	
Samuel Morrison, TUV	1,389	
Dan Barrios-O'Neill, Green	912	
Jonny Orr, Ind.	856	
Matthew Robinson, C.	183	
Keith John Gray, Ind.	76	

LONDONDERRY EAST
E. 67,392 T. 42,248 (62.69%)

	First	Round Elected
Caoimhe Archibald, SF	5,851	12
Maurice Bradley, DUP	5,444	9
Cathal ohOisin, SF	4,953	
Claire Sugden, Ind.	4,918	8
George Robinson, DUP	4,715	9
Adrian McQuillan, DUP	3,881	
John Dallat, SDLP	3,319	12
William McCandless, UUP	2,814	
Chris McCaw, Alliance	1,841	
Gerry Mullan, Ind.	1,204	
Jordan Armstrong, TUV	1,038	
Russell Watton, PUP	879	
Gavin Campbell, PBP	492	
Anthony Flynn, Green	305	
David Harding, C.	219	

NEWRY AND ARMAGH
E. 80,140 T. 55,625 (69.41%)

	First	Round Elected
William Irwin, DUP	9,760	1
Cathal Boylan, SF	9,197	1
Justin McNulty, SDLP	8,983	2
Megan Fearon, SF	8,881	2
Conor Murphy, SF	8,454	3
Danny Kennedy, UUP	7,256	
Jackie Coade, Alliance	1,418	
Emmet Crossan, CISTA	704	
Rowan Tunnicliffe, Green	265	

STRANGFORD
E. 64,393 T. 39,239 (60.94%)

	First	Round Elected
Simon Hamilton, DUP	6,221	5
Kellie Armstrong, Alliance	5,813	4
Michelle McIlveen, DUP	5,728	9
Mike Nesbitt, UUP	5,323	9
Peter Weir, DUP	3,543	11
Joe Boyle, SDLP	3,045	
Philip Smith, UUP	2,453	
Jimmy Menagh, Ind.	1,627	
Jonathan Bell, Ind.	1,479	
Stephen Cooper, TUV	1,330	
Dermot Kennedy, SF	1,110	
Ricky Bamford, Green	918	
Scott Benton, C.	195	

TYRONE WEST
E. 64,258 T. 44,907 (69.89%)

	First	Round Elected
Thomas Buchanan, DUP	9,064	1
Michaela Boyle, SF	7,714	1
Barry McElduff, SF	7,573	1
Daniel McCrossan, SDLP	6,283	5
Declan McAleer, SF	6,034	5
Alicia Clarke, UUP	3,654	
Stephen Donnelly, Alliance	1,252	
Sorcha McAnespy, Ind.	864	
Charlie Chittick, TUV	851	
Ciaran McClean, Green	412	
Barry Brown, CISTA	373	
Corey French, Ind.	98	
Roisin McMackin, Ind.	85	
Susan-Anne White, Ind.	41	
Roger Lomas, C.	27	

ULSTER MID
E. 69,396 T. 50,228 (72.38%)

	First	Round Elected
Michelle, O'Neill, SF	10,258	1
Keith Buchanan, DUP	9,568	1
Ian Milne, SF	8,143	2
Linda Dillon, SF	7,806	2
Patsy McGlone, SDLP	6,419	5
Sandra Overend, UUP	4,516	
Hannah Loughrin, TUV	1,244	
Fay Watson, Alliance	1,017	
Hugh McCloy, Ind.	247	
Stefan Taylor, Green	243	
Hugh Scullion, WP	217	

UPPER BANN
E. 83,431 T. 52,174 (62.54%)

	First	Round Elected
Carla Lockhart, DUP	9,140	1
John O'Dowd, SF	8,220	5
Jonathan Buckley, DUP	7,745	4
Nuala Toman, SF	6,108	
Doug Beattie, UUP	5,467	5
Jo-Anne Dobson, UUP	5,132	
Dolores Kelly, SDLP	5,127	6
Tara Doyle, Alliance	2,720	
Roy Ferguson, TUV	1,035	
Simon Lee, Green	555	
Colin Craig, WP	218	
Ian Nickels, C.	81	

REGIONAL GOVERNMENT

LONDON

GREATER LONDON AUTHORITY (GLA)

City Hall, The Queen's Walk, London SE1 2AA
T 020-7983 4000 E mayor@london.gov.uk W www.london.gov.uk

On 7 May 1998 London voted in favour of the formation of the Greater London Authority (GLA). The first elections to the GLA took place on 4 May 2000 and the new authority took over its responsibilities on 3 July 2000. In July 2002 the GLA moved to one of London's most spectacular buildings, newly built on a brownfield site on the south bank of the Thames, adjacent to Tower Bridge. The fifth and most recent election to the GLA took place on 5 May 2016.

The structure and objectives of the GLA stem from its main areas of responsibility: transport, policing, fire and emergency planning, economic development, planning, culture and health. There are four functional bodies which form part of the wider GLA group and report to the GLA: the Mayor's Office for Policing and Crime (MOPAC), Transport for London (TfL), the London Fire Commissioner and the London Legacy Development Corporation.

The GLA consists of a directly elected mayor, the Mayor of London, and a separately elected assembly, the London Assembly. The mayor has the key role in decision making, with the assembly responsible for regulating and scrutinising these decisions, and investigating issues of importance to Londoners. In addition, the GLA has around 800 permanent staff to support the activities of the mayor and the assembly, which are overseen by a head of paid service. The mayor may appoint two political advisers and not more than ten other members of staff, though he does not necessarily exercise this power, but he does not appoint the chief executive, the monitoring officer or the chief finance officer. These must be appointed jointly by the assembly and the mayor.

Every aspect of the assembly and its activities must be open to public scrutiny and therefore accountable. The assembly holds the mayor to account through scrutiny of his strategies, decisions and actions. Mayor's Question Time, conducted on ten occasions a year at City Hall, is carried out by direct questioning at assembly meetings and by conducting detailed investigations in committee.

People's Question Time, held twice a year, and Talk London (W www.london.gov.uk/talk-london) give Londoners the chance to question and express their opinions to the mayor and the assembly about plans, priorities and policies for London.

The role of the mayor can be broken down into a number of key areas:

- to represent and promote London at home and abroad and speak up for Londoners
- to devise strategies and plans to tackle London-wide issues, such as crime, transport, housing, planning, economic development and regeneration, environment, public services, society and culture, sport and health; and to set budgets for TfL, MOPAC, London Fire Commissioner and the London Legacy Development Corporation
- the mayor is chair of TfL, and is responsible for the Metropolitan Police's priorities and performance

The role of the assembly can be broken down into a number of key areas:

- to hold the mayor to account by examining his decisions and actions

- to have the power to amend the mayor's budget by a majority of two-thirds
- to have the power to summon the mayor, senior staff of the GLA and functional bodies
- to investigate issues of London-wide significance and make proposals to appropriate stakeholders
- to examine the work of MOPAC and to review the police and crime plan for London through the Police and Crime Committee

MAYORAL TEAM
Mayor, Sadiq Khan
Deputy Mayors, Rajesh Agrawal *(Business);* Sophie Linden *(Policing and Crime);* Joanne McCartney, AM *(Education and Childcare);* James Murray *(Housing and Residential Development);* Jules Pipe *(Planning, Regeneration and Skills);* Matthew Ryder *(Social Integration, Social Mobility and Community Engagement);* Shirley Rodrigues *(Environment and Energy);* Heidi Alexander *(Transport);* Justine Simons, OBE *(Culture and the Creative Industries)*
Chief of Staff, David Bellamy
Directors, Nick Bowes *(Policy);* Patrick Hennessy *(Communications);* Leah Kreitzman *(External and International Affairs);* Jack Stenner *(Political and Public Affairs)*
Special Appointments, Dr Tom Coffey, OBE *(Health Adviser);* Kate Nicholls *(Chair of the Night Time Commission);* Amy Lamé *(Night Czar);* Dr Will Norman *(Walking and Cycling Commissioner);* Claire Waxman *(Victims Commissioner)*

ELECTIONS AND VOTING SYSTEMS
The assembly is elected every four years at the same time as the mayor, and consists of 25 members. There is one member from each of the 14 GLA constituencies topped up with 11 London-wide members who are either representatives of political parties or individuals standing as independent candidates. The last election was on 5 May 2016.

Two distinct voting systems are used to appoint the existing mayor and the assembly. The mayor is elected using the supplementary vote system (SVS). With SVS, electors have two votes: one to give a first choice for mayor and one to give a second choice; they cannot vote twice for the same candidate. If one candidate gets more than half of all the first-choice votes, he or she becomes mayor. If no candidate gets more than half of the first-choice votes, the two candidates with the most first-choice votes remain in the election and all the other candidates drop out. The second-choice votes on the ballot papers for the candidates who are then counted. Where these second-choice votes are for the two remaining candidates they are added to the first-choice votes these candidates already have. The candidate with the most first- and second-choice votes combined becomes the Mayor of London.

The assembly is appointed using the additional member system (AMS). Under AMS, electors have two votes. The first vote is for a constituency candidate. The second vote is for a party list or individual candidate contesting the London-wide assembly seats. The 14 constituency members are elected under the first-past-the-post system, the same system used in general and local elections. Electors vote for one candidate and the candidate with the most votes wins. The additional members are drawn from party lists or are independent candidates who stand as London members; they are chosen using a form of proportional representation.

The Greater London Returning Officer (GLRO) is the independent official responsible for running the election in

London. He is supported in this by returning officers in each of the 14 London constituencies.

GLRO for 2016 Election, Jeff Jacobs

TRANSPORT FOR LONDON (TFL)

TfL is the integrated body responsible for London's transport system. Its role is to implement the mayor's transport strategy for London and manage transport services across the capital for which the mayor has responsibility. TfL is directed by a management board whose members are chosen for their understanding of transport matters and are appointed by the mayor, who chairs the board. TfL's role is:

- to manage the London Underground, buses, Croydon Tramlink, London Overground and the Docklands Light Railway (DLR)
- to manage a 580km network of main roads and all 6,000 of London's traffic lights
- to regulate taxis and minicabs
- to run the London River Services, Victoria Coach Station and London Transport Museum
- to help to coordinate the Dial-a-Ride, Capital Call and Taxicard schemes for door-to-door services for transport users with mobility problems

The London Borough Councils maintain the role of highway and traffic authorities for 95 per cent of London's roads. A congestion charge for motorists driving into central London between the hours of 7am and 6.30pm, Monday to Friday (excluding public holidays) was introduced on 17 February 2003. On 19 February 2007, the charge zone roughly doubled in size after a westward expansion and the charging hours were shortened, to finish at 6pm. On 4 January 2011, the westward expansion was removed from the charging zone and an automated payment system was also introduced. As at September 2018 the daily congestion charge was £11.50 (£10.50 if paid via the automated service).

TfL introduced a low emission zone (LEZ) for London on 4 February 2008 which is in constant operation. Following tougher emissions standards introduced on 3 January 2012 there is a daily charge for polluting vehicles entering the zone (which covers most of Greater London) that do not meet Euro 3 or Euro 4 emissions standards. With the exception of minibuses, vehicles over three-and-a-half tonnes such as lorries, buses and coaches, face a daily charge of £200. Vehicles up to three-and-a-half tonnes and minibuses (with more than eight passenger seats) up to five tonnes pay a daily charge of £100. For further information *see* **W** www.tfl.gov.uk/lez

From 8 April 2019 new, ultra low emission zone (ULEZ) standards will affect petrol and diesel vehicles in central London. For further information *see* **W** www.tfl.gov.uk/modes/driving/ultra-low-emission-zone.

Since 2 January 2009, Londoners over pensionable age (or over 60 if born before 1950) and those with eligible disabilities are entitled to free travel on the capital's transport network at any time. War veterans who are receiving ongoing payments under the war pensions scheme, or those receiving guaranteed income payments under the armed forces compensation scheme can travel free at any time on bus, underground, DLR, tram and London Overground services and at certain times on National Rail services.

In the summer of 2010, the London cycle hire scheme launched with 6,000 new bicycles for hire from 400 docking stations across eight boroughs, the City and the Royal parks. The scheme has been expanded and there are now around 11,500 bicycles available and over 750 docking stations.

Commissioner of TfL, Mike Brown, MVO

MAYOR'S OFFICE FOR POLICING AND CRIME (MOPAC)

The Mayor's Office for Policing and Crime (MOPAC) was set up in response to the Police Reform and Social Responsibility Act 2011, replacing the Metropolitan Police Authority. MOPAC is headed by the mayor, or the appointed statutory deputy mayor for policing and crime. Operational responsibility for policing in London belongs to the Metropolitan Police Commissioner. The major areas of focus of MOPAC are:

- operational policing and crime reduction including counter terrorism
- ensuring the Metropolitan Police effectively reduce gang crime and violence in London and coordinating support for communities and local organisations to prevent gang activities
- criminal justice, including preventing reoffending, reducing crime and decreasing demand within the criminal justice system in addition to reducing alcohol and drug abuse.

The Police and Crime Committee consisting of nine elected members of the London Assembly scrutinises the work of MOPAC and meets regularly to hold to account the Deputy Mayor for Policing and Crime.

Deputy Mayor for Policing and Crime, Sophie Linden

LONDON FIRE COMMISSIONER

Under the Policing and Crime Act 2017, the London Fire Commissioner replaced the London Fire and Emergency Planning Authority (LFEPA) and was tasked with overseeing the London Fire Brigade, the fire and rescue authority for London. It consists of three main structural bodies: operational staff and firefighters, control staff and emergency responders, and a non-uniformed support team. Operational staff provide the only full-time fire service in the UK.

The Mayor of London sets its budget, approves its London Safety Plan, and can direct it to act. The London Fire Commissioner is further scrutinised by the Fire, Resilience and Emergency Planning (FREP) Committee of the London Assembly.

Commissioner, Dany Cotton, QFSM

LONDON LEGACY DEVELOPMENT CORPORATION

Following the London 2012 Olympic Games, the London Legacy Development Corporation was made responsible for the long-term planning, development, management and maintenance of the Queen Elizabeth Olympic Park (formerly the Olympic Park) and its facilities. The organisation is tasked with transforming the area into a thriving neighbourhood.

Chair, Sir Peter Hendy, CBE

SALARIES *as at September 2018*

Mayor	£146,804
Chief of Staff	£134,552
Deputy Mayors	
Housing and Residential Development	£127,513
Business	£127,513
Culture and the Creative Industries	£127,513
Transport	£127,513
Policing and Crime	£125,000
Education and Childcare	£108,180
(and Statutory Deputy Mayor)	
Chair of the Assembly	£67,498
Assembly Member	£56,270

LONDON ASSEMBLY COMMITTEES

Chair, Audit Panel, Peter Whittle

Chair, Budget and Performance Committee, Gareth Bacon

Chair, Budget Monitoring Sub-Committee, Gareth Bacon

Chair, Confirmation Hearings Committee, Andrew Boff
Chair, Economy Committee, Susan Hall
Chair, Education Panel, Jennette Arnold, OBE
Chair, Environment Committee, Caroline Russell
Chair, EU Exit Working Group, Len Duvall
Chair, GLA Oversight Committee, Gareth Bacon
Chair, Health Committee, Dr Onkar Sahota
Chair, Housing Committee, Sian Berry
Chair, Planning Committee, Nicky Gavron
Chair, Police and Crime Committee, Steve O'Connell
Chair, Regeneration Committee, Shaun Bailey
Chair, Transport Committee, Caroline Pidgeon, MBE

LONDON ASSEMBLY MEMBERS

as at September 2018

Arbour, Tony, *C., South West,* Maj. 21,444
Arnold, Jennette, OBE, *Lab., North East,* Maj. 101,742
Bacon, Gareth, *C., Bexley and Bromley,* Maj. 41,669
Bailey, Shaun, *C., London-wide*
Berry, Sian, *Green, London-wide*
Boff, Andrew, *C., London-wide*
Cooper, Leonie, *Lab., Merton and Wandsworth,* Maj. 4,301
Copley, Tom, *Lab., London-wide*
Desai, Unmesh, *Lab., City and East,* Maj. 89,629
Deverish, Tony, *C., West Central,* Maj. 14,564
Dismore, Andrew, *Lab., Barnet and Camden,* Maj. 16,240
Duvall, Len, *Lab., Greenwich and Lewisham,* Maj. 54,895
Eshalomi, Florence, *Lab., Lambeth and Southwark,* Maj. 62,243
Gavron, Nicky, *Lab., London-wide*
Hall, Susan, *C., London-wide*
Kurten, David, *UKIP, London-wide*
McCartney, Joanne, *Lab., Enfield and Haringey,* Maj. 51,152
O'Connell, Steve, *C., Croydon and Sutton,* Maj. 11,614
Pidgeon, Caroline, MBE, *LD, London-wide*
Prince, Keith, *C. Havering and Redbridge,* Maj. 1,438
Russell, Caroline, *Green, London-wide*
Sahota, Dr Onkar, *Lab., Ealing and Hillingdon,* Maj. 15,933
Shah, Navin, *Lab., Brent and Harrow,* Maj. 20,755
Twycross, Fiona, *Lab., London-wide*
Whittle, Peter, *UKIP, London-wide*

Chair of the London Assembly, Tony Arbour AM

STATE OF THE PARTIES *as at September 2018*

Party	Seats
Labour (Lab.)	12
Conservative (C.)	8
Green	2
UKIP	2
LD	1

MAYORAL ELECTION RESULTS

as at 5 May 2016

Electorate 5,739,011 Turnout 45.6%

First	Party	Votes	%
Sadiq Khan	Lab.	1,148,716	44.2
Zac Goldsmith	C.	909,755	35.0
Siân Berry	Green	150,673	5.8
Caroline Pidgeon	LD	120,005	4.6
Peter Whittle	UKIP	94,373	3.6
Sophie Walker	Women	53,055	2.0
George Galloway	Respect	37,007	1.4
Paul Golding	Brit. First	31,372	1.2
Lee Harris	CISTA	20,537	0.8
David Furness	BNP	13,325	0.5
Prince Zylinski	Ind.	13,202	0.5
Ankit Love	One Love	4,941	0.2

Second	Party	Votes	%
Sadiq Khan	Lab.	161,427	65.5
Zac Goldsmith	C.	84,859	34.5

LONDON ASSEMBLY ELECTION RESULTS *as at 5 May 2016*

E. Electorate T. Turnout
See General Election Results for a list of party abbreviations

CONSTITUENCIES
E. 5,739,011 T. 45.6%

BARNET AND CAMDEN
E. 387,844 T. 47.44%

Andrew Dismore, Lab.	81,482
Daniel Thomas, C.	65,242
Stephen Taylor, Green	16,996
Zack Polanski, LD	11,204
Joseph Langton, UKIP	9,057

Lab. majority 16,240

BEXLEY AND BROMLEY
E. 404,342 T. 46.94%

Gareth Bacon, C.	87,460
Sam Russell, Lab.	45,791
Frank Gould, UKIP	30,485
Roisin Robertson, Green	12,685
Julie Ireland, LD	12,145
Veronica Obadara, APP	1,243

C. majority 41,669

BRENT AND HARROW
E. 381,778 T. 45.76%

Navin Shah, Lab.	79,902
Joel Davidson, C.	59,147
Anton Georgiou, LD	11,534
Jafar Hassan, Green	9,874
Rathy Alagaratnam, UKIP	9,074
Akib Mahmood, Respect GG	5,170

Lab. majority 20,755

CITY AND EAST
E. 503,301 T. 42.01%

Unmesh Desai, Lab.	122,175
Chris Chapman, C.	32,546
Rachel Collinson, Green	18,766
Peter Harris, UKIP	18,071
Elaine Bagshaw, LD	10,714
Rayne Mickail, Respect GG	6,772
Amina Gichinga, TBTC	1,368
Aaron D'Souza, APP	1,009

Lab. majority 89,629

CROYDON AND SUTTON
E. 401,660 T. 45.29%

Steve O'Connell, C.	70,156
Marina Ahmad, Lab.	58,542
Amna Ahmad, LD	18,859
Peter Staveley, UKIP	18,338
Tracey Hague, Green	13,513
Madonna Lewis, APP	1,386
Richard Edmonds, NF	1,106

C. majority 11,614

EALING AND HILLINGDON
E. 444,168 T. 45.25%

Onkar Sahota, Lab.	86,088
Dominic Gilham, C.	70,155
Alex Nieora, UKIP	15,832
Meena Hans, Green	15,758
Francesco Fruzza, LD	13,154

Lab. majority 15,933

ENFIELD AND HARINGEY
E. 377,060 T. 44.73%

Joanne McCartney, Lab.	91,075
Linda Kelly, C.	39,923
Ronald Stewart, Green	15,409
Nicholas da Costa, LD	12,038
Neville Watson, UKIP	9,042
Godson Azu, APP	1,172

Lab. majority 51,152

GREENWICH AND LEWISHAM
E. 362,376 T. 45.08%

Len Duvall, Lab.	85,735
Adam Thomas, C.	30,840
Imogen Solly, Green	20,520
Paul Oakley, UKIP	13,686
Julia Fletcher, LD	11,303
Ajaratu Bangura, APP	1,275

Lab. majority 54,895

HAVERING AND REDBRIDGE
E. 383,234 T. 44.63%

Keith Prince, C.	64,483
Ivana Bartoletti, Lab.	63,045
Lawrence Webb, UKIP	26,788
Lee Burkwood, Green	9,617
Ian Sanderson, LD	7,105

C. majority 1,438

LAMBETH AND SOUTHWARK
E. 426,966 T. 43.98%

Florence Eshalomi, Lab.	96,946
Robert Flint, C.	34,703
Rashid Nix, Green	25,793
Michael Bukola, LD	21,489
Idham Ramadi, UKIP	6,591
Kevin Parkin, SPGB	1,333
Amadu Kanumansa, APP	906

Lab. majority 62,243

MERTON AND WANDSWORTH
E. 374,126 T. 49.56%

Leonie Cooper, Lab.	77,340
David Dean, C.	73,039
Esther Obiri-Darko, Green	14,682
Adrian Hyyrylainen-Trett, LD	10,732
Elizabeth Jones, UKIP	8,478
Thamilini Kulendran, Ind.	1,142

Lab. majority 4,301

NORTH EAST
E. 500,432 T. 45.72%

Jennette Arnold, Lab.	134,307
Sam Malik, C.	32,565
Samir Jeraj, Green	29,401
Terry Stacy, LD	14,312
Freddy Vachha, UKIP	11,315
Tim Allen, Respect GG	5,068
Bill Martin, SPGB	1,293
Jonathan Silberman, Comm L	536

Lab. majority 101,742

SOUTH WEST
E. 435,877 T. 49.04%

Tony Arbour, C.	84,381
Martin Whelton, Lab.	62,937
Rosina Robson, LD	30,654
Andree Frieze, Green	19,745
Alexander Craig, UKIP	14,983
Adam Buick, SPGB	1,065

C. majority 21,444

WEST CENTRAL
E. 348,740 T. 43.96%

Tony Devenish, C.	67,775
Mandy Richards, Lab.	53,211
Jennifer Nadel, Green	14,050
Annabel Mullin, LD	10,577
Clive Egan, UKIP	7,708

C. majority 14,564

LONDON-WIDE MEMBERS

Conservative Party	*Labour Party*
Kemi Badenoch	Fiona Twycross
Andrew Boff	Tom Copley
Shaun Bailey	Nicky Gavron

Green Party	*UKIP*
Sian Berry	Peter Whittle
Caroline Russell	David Kurten

Liberal Democrats
Caroline Pidgeon

EUROPEAN PARLIAMENT

European parliament elections take place at five-yearly intervals; on the current schedule the UK is due to withdraw from the EU on 29 March 2019. The next European parliament elections will take place 23–26 May 2019 and the current UK MEPs are expected to complete their mandates, remaining as members, until the European parliament's eighth term ends on 18 April 2019.

The first direct elections to the parliament were held in 1979. In mainland Britain, members of the European parliament (MEPs) were elected in all constituencies on a first-past-the-post basis until 1999, when a regional system of proportional representation was introduced; in Northern Ireland three MEPs have been elected by the single transferable vote system of proportional representation since 1979. Under the terms of the Lisbon Treaty, the UK gained an extra seat in December 2011, taking the total to 73. This seat was added to the West Midlands region and filled by the highest-ranked losing candidate standing for the region in the 2009 European parliament elections.

At the 2014 European parliament elections all UK MEPs were elected under a 'closed-list' regional system of proportional representation, with England being divided into nine regions (residents of Gibraltar vote in the South West region) and Scotland, Wales and Northern Ireland each constituting a single region. Parties submitted a list of candidates for each region in their own order of preference. Votes were cast for a party or an independent candidate, and the first seat in each region was allocated to the party or candidate with the highest number of votes. The rest of the seats in each region were then allocated broadly in proportion to each party's share of the vote. Each region returned the following number of members: East Midlands, 5; Eastern, 7; London, 8; North East, 3; North West, 8; South East, 10; South West, 6; West Midlands, 7; Yorkshire and the Humber, 6; Wales, 4; Northern Ireland, 3; Scotland, 6.

Following the UK's withdrawal from the EU, the total number of seats in the European parliament will be reduced from 751 to 705. with 27 of the current 73 UK seats redistributed among the 27 remaining member states. France and Spain will gain the most seats at five each, increasing from 74 to 79 and 54 to 59 respectively. Italy and the Netherlands will each gain three seats, from 73 to 76 and 26 to 29, and Ireland will gain two seats. Austria, Croatia, Denmark, Estonia, Finland, Poland, Romania, Slovakia, and Sweden will all be allocated one additional seat. The remaining 13 countries will keep their current allocation.

If a vacancy occurs due to the resignation or death of an MEP, it is filled by the next available person on that party's list. If an independent MEP resigns or dies, a by-election is held. Where an MEP leaves a party on whose list he/she was elected, there is no requirement to resign the post of MEP.

Nationals of member states of the European Union are eligible for election to the European parliament provided they are aged 18 or over and not subject to disqualification. Since 1994, eligible citizens have had the right to vote in elections to the European parliament in the UK as long as they were entered on the electoral register.

In July 2009 an MEP statute introduced a uniform salary for all MEPs, set at a rate of 38.5 per cent of the basic salary of a European court of justice judge. This currently equates to an annual pre-tax salary of €101,808.60 (approximately £90,422, depending on the monthly exchange rate). The salary comes from European parliament's budget and is subject to EU tax and insurance contributions. Member states can also subject the salary to national taxes. In the UK the salary is taxed by HM Revenue and Customs in order to bring the total tax paid up to the level of taxation payable by a UK resident.

For further information visit the UK's European parliament website (W www.europarl.europa.eu/unitedkingdom).

UK MEMBERS *as at 18 June 2018*

KEY
* Denotes membership of the last European parliament
† Previously sat as a member of the Conservative Party
‡ Previously sat as a member of UKIP
§ Previously sat as a member of UCUNF

*Agnew, Stuart (*b.* 1949), *UKIP, Eastern*
Aker, Tim (*b.* 1985), *UKIP, Eastern*
Anderson, Lucy, *Lab., London*
*Anderson, Martina (*b.* 1962), *SF, Northern Ireland*
Arnott, Jonathan (*b.* 1981), *UKIP, North East*
*Ashworth, Richard (*b.* 1947), *C., South East*
Atkinson, Janice (*b.* 1962), *Ind., South East*
‡Bashir, Amjad (*b.* 1952), *C., Yorkshire and the Humber*
*Batten, Gerard (*b.* 1954), *UKIP, London*
*Bearder, Catherine (*b.* 1949), *LD, South East*
Bours, Louise (*b.* 1968), *UKIP, North West*
Brannen, Paul (*b.* 1962), *Lab., North East*
Bullock, Jonathan (*b.* 1963), *UKIP, East Midlands*
*‡Campbell Bannerman, David (*b.* 1960), *C., Eastern*
‡Carver, James (*b.* 1969), *Ind., West Midlands*
Coburn, David (*b.* 1958), *UKIP, Scotland*
Collins, Jane (*b.* 1962), *UKIP, Yorkshire and the Humber*
Corbett, Richard (*b.* 1955), *Lab., Yorkshire and the Humber*
Dalton, Daniel (*b.* 1974), *C., West Midlands*
Dance, Seb (*b.* 1981), *Lab., London*
*Dartmouth, Earl of (*b.* 1949), *UKIP, South West*
*Deva, Nirj (*b.* 1948), *C., South East*
*Dodds, Diane (*b.* 1958), *DUP, Northern Ireland*
Etheridge, Bill (*b.* 1970), *UKIP, West Midlands*
*Evans, Jill (*b.* 1959), *PC, Wales*
*Farage, Nigel (*b.* 1964), *UKIP, South East*
Finch, Ray (*b.* 1963), *UKIP, South East*
Flack, John (*b.* 1957) *C., Eastern*
*Foster, Jacqueline (*b.* 1947), *C., North West*
*Fox, Ashley (*b.* 1969), *C., South West*
Gill, Nathan (*b.* 1973), *UKIP, Wales*
Gill, Neena, CBE (*b.* 1957), *Lab., West Midlands*
*Girling, Julie (*b.* 1956), *C., South West*
Griffin, Theresa (*b.* 1962), *Lab., North West*
*Hannan, Daniel (*b.* 1971), *C., South East*
*Honeyball, Mary (*b.* 1952), *Lab., London*
Hookem, Mike (*b.* 1953), *UKIP, Yorkshire and the Humber*
Howarth, John (*b.* 1958), *Lab., South East*
*Hudghton, Ian (*b.* 1951), *SNP, Scotland*
‡James, Diane (*b.* 1959), *Ind., South East*
*Kamall, Dr Syed (*b.* 1967), *C., London*
*Karim, Sajjad (*b.* 1970), *C., North West*
Khan, Wajid (*b.* 1978) *Lab., North West*
Kirton-Darling, Judith (*b.* 1977), *Lab., North East*
*Lambert, Jean (*b.* 1950), *Green, London*
*Martin, David (*b.* 1954), *Lab., Scotland*
Matthews, Rupert (*b.* 1961), *C., East Midlands*
Mayer, Alex (*b.* 1981), *Lab., Eastern*
*McAvan, Linda (*b.* 1962), *Lab., Yorkshire and the Humber*
*McClarkin, Emma (*b.* 1978), *C., East Midlands*

*McIntyre, Anthea (b. 1954), C., West Midlands
Mobarik, Baroness, CBE (b. 1975), C., Scotland
Moody, Clare (b. 1965), Lab., South West
*Moraes, Claude (b. 1965), Lab., London
*§Nicholson, James (b. 1945), UUP, Northern Ireland
*Nuttall, Paul (b. 1976), UKIP, North West
O'Flynn, Patrick (b. 1965), UKIP, Eastern
Parker, Margot (b. 1943), UKIP, East Midlands
Palmer, Rory (b. 1981), Lab, East Midlands
Procter, John, (b. 1966), C., Yorkshire and the Humber
Reid, Julia (b. 1952), UKIP, South West
Scott Cato, Molly (b. 1963), Green, South West
Seymour, Jill (b. 1958), UKIP, West Midlands
Simon, Siôn (b. 1968), Lab., West Midlands
*Smith, Alyn (b. 1973), SNP, Scotland
*Stihler, Catherine (b. 1973), Lab., Scotland
*Swinburne, Dr Kay (b. 1967), C., Wales
*Tannock, Dr Charles (b. 1957), C., London

*Taylor, Keith (b. 1953), Green, South East
*Van Orden, Geoffrey (b. 1945), C., Eastern
*Vaughan, Derek (b. 1961), Lab., Wales
Ward, Julie (b. 1957), Lab., North West
‡Woolfe, Steven (b. 1967), Ind., North West

STATE OF THE PARTIES as at June 2018

Party	No. of Seats
Labour (Lab.)	20
Conservative (C.)	20
UK Independence Party (UKIP)	19
Independent (Ind.)	4
Green Party (Green)	3
Scottish National Party (SNP)	2
Others*	5
Total	73

* The Democratic Unionist Party (DUP), Liberal Democrats (LD), Plaid Cymru (PC), Ulster Unionist Party (UUP), and Sinn Fein (SF) have one seat each.

UK REGIONS AS AT 22 MAY 2014 ELECTION

Abbreviations

4FP	4 Freedoms Party (UK EPP)
AIFE	An Independence from Europe
AW	Animal Welfare
BF	Britain First
CPA	Christian Peoples Alliance
CUP	Communities United Party
EP	Europeans Party
Harmony	Harmony Party
Liberty	Liberty GB
NLP	National Liberal Party
NI21	NI21
No2EU	No2EU Yes to Democracy
Peace	Peace Party
Roman	Roman Party
SGB	Socialist Party of Great Britain
SLP	Socialist Labour Party
TUV	Traditional Unionist Voice (NI)
WDR	We Demand a Referendum
Your	YOURvoice
YF	Yorkshire First

For other abbreviations, *see* UK General Election Results.

E. 46,437,794 T.35.32%

EASTERN

(Bedfordshire, Cambridgeshire, Essex, Hertfordshire, Luton, Norfolk, Peterborough, Southend-on-Sea, Suffolk, Thurrock)
E. 4,369,382 T. 36.19%

UKIP	542,812 (34.5%)
C.	446,569 (28.4%)
Lab.	271,601 (17.2%)
Green	133,331 (8.5%)
LD	108,010 (6.9%)
AIFE	26,564 (1.7%)
Eng. Dem.	16,497 (1.0%)
BNP	12,465 (0.8%)
CPA	11,627 (0.7%)
No2EU	4,870 (0.3%)
UKIP majority	96,243

(June 2009, C. maj. 186,410)

MEMBERS ELECTED
1. P. O'Flynn, UKIP 2. *V. Ford, C. 3. *R. Howitt, Lab. 4. *S. Agnew, UKIP 5. *G. Van Orden, C. 6. T. Aker, UKIP 7. *‡ D. Campbell Bannerman, C.

EAST MIDLANDS

(Derby, Derbyshire, Leicester, Leicestershire, Lincolnshire, Northamptonshire, Nottingham, Nottinghamshire, Rutland)
E 3,437,794 T. 32.6%

UKIP	368,734 (32.9%)
C.	291,270 (26.0%)
Lab.	279,363 (24.9%)
Green	67,066 (6.0%)
LD	60,773 (5.4%)
AIFE	21,384 (1.9%)
BNP	18,326 (1.6%)
Eng. Dem.	11,612 (1.0%)
Harmony	2,194 (0.2%)
UKIP majority	77,464

(June 2009, C. maj. 163,330)

MEMBERS ELECTED
1. *†R. Helmer, UKIP 2.*E. McClarkin, C. 3. *G. Willmott, Lab. 4. M. Parker, UKIP 5. A. Lewer, C.

LONDON

E. 5,490,248 T. 40.5%

Lab.	806,959 (36.7%)
C.	495,639 (22.5%)
UKIP	371,133 (16.9%)
Green	196,419 (8.9%)
LD	148,013 (6.7%)
4FP	28,014 (1.3%)
AIFE	26,675 (1.2%)
CPA	23,702 (1.1%)
NHAP	23,253 (1.1%)
AW	21,092 (1.0%)
BNP	19,246 (0.9%)
EP	10,712 (0.5%)
Eng. Dem.	10,142 (0.5%)
CUP	6,951 (0.3%)
NLP	6,736 (0.3%)
No2EU	3,804 (0.2%)
Harmony	1,985 (0.1%)
Lab. majority	311,320

(June 2009, C. maj. 106,447)

MEMBERS ELECTED
1. *C. Moraes, Lab. 2. *S. Kamall, C. 3. *M. Honeyball, Lab. 4. *G. Batten, UKIP 5. L. Anderson, Lab. 6. *C. Tannock, C. 7. S. Dance, Lab. 8. *J. Lambert, Green

NORTH EAST

(Co. Durham, Darlington, Hartlepool, Middlesbrough, Northumberland, Redcar and Cleveland, Stockton-on-Tees, Tyne and Wear)
E. 1,968,780 T. 31.0%

Lab.	221,988 (36.5%)
UKIP	177,660 (29.2%)
C.	107,733 (17.7%)
LD	36,093 (5.9%)
Green	31,605 (5.2%)
AIFE	13,934 (2.3%)
BNP	10,360 (1.7%)
Eng. Dem.	9,279 (1.5%)
Lab. majority	44,328

(June 2009, Lab. maj. 30,427)

MEMBERS ELECTED
1. J. Kirton-Darling, Lab. 2. J. Arnott, UKIP 3. P. Brannen, Lab.

NORTHERN IRELAND

(Northern Ireland forms a three-member seat with a single transferable vote system)

E. 1,225,771 T. 51.84%

		1st Pref. Votes
Martina Anderson, *SF*	159,813 (25.5%)
Diane Dodds, *DUP*	131,163 (20.9%)
Jim Nicholson, *UUP*	83,438 (13.3%)
Alex Attwood, *SDLP*	81,594 (13%)
Jim Allister, *TUV*	75,806 (12.1%)
Anna Lo, *Alliance*	44,432 (7.1%)
Henry Reilly, *UKIP*	24,584 (3.9%)
Ross Brown, *Green*	10,598 (1.7%)
Tina McKenzie, *NI21*	10,553 (1.7%)
Mark Brotherston, *C.*	4,144 (0.7%)

MEMBERS ELECTED
1. *M. Anderson, *SF* 2. *D. Dodds, *DUP* 3. *§ J. Nicholson, *UUP*

NORTH WEST

(Blackburn-with-Darwen, Blackpool, Cheshire, Cumbria, Greater Manchester, Halton, Lancashire, Merseyside, Warrington)

E. 5,207,777 T. 33.68%

Lab.	594,063 (33.9%)
UKIP	481,932 (27.5%)
C.	351,985 (20.1%)
Green	123,075 (7.0%)
LD	105,487 (6.0%)
BNP	32,826 (1.9%)
AIFE	26,731 (1.5%)
Eng. Dem.	19,522 (1.1%)
Pirate	8,597 (0.5%)
No2EU	5,402 (0.3%)
SEP	5,067 (0.3%)
Lab. majority	112,131

(June 2009, C. maj. 86,343)

MEMBERS ELECTED
1. T. Griffin, *Lab.* 2.*P. Nuttall, *UKIP* 3. *J. Foster, *C.* 4. A. Khan, *Lab.* 5. L. Bours, *UKIP* 6. J. Ward, *Lab.* 7. *S. Karim, *C.* 8. S. Woolfe, *UKIP*

SCOTLAND

E. 4,016,735 T. 33.5%

SNP	389,503 (29.0%)
Lab.	348,219 (25.9%)
C.	231,330 (17.2%)
UKIP	140,534 (10.5%)
Green	108,305 (8.7%)
LD	95,319 (7.1%)
BF	13,639 (1.0%)
BNP	10,216 (0.8%)
No2EU	6,418 (0.5%)
SNP majority	41,284

(June 2009, SNP. maj. 91,154)

MEMBERS ELECTED
1. *I. Hudghton, *SNP* 2. *D. Martin, *Lab.* 3. I. Duncan, *C.* 4. *A. Smith, *SNP* 5. *C. Stihler, *Lab.* 6. D. Coburn, *UKIP*

SOUTH EAST

(Bracknell Forest, Brighton and Hove, Buckinghamshire, East Sussex, Hampshire, Isle of Wight, Kent, Medway, Milton Keynes, Newbury, Oxfordshire, Portsmouth, Reading, Slough, Southampton, Surrey, West Sussex, Windsor and Maidenhead, Wokingham)

E. 6,441,003 T. 36.46%

UKIP	751,439 (32.1%)
C.	723,571 (31.0%)
Lab.	342,775 (14.7%)
Green	211,706 (9.1%)
LD	187,876 (8.0%)
AIFE	45,199 (1.9%)
Eng. Dem.	17,771 (0.8%)
BNP	16,909 (0.7%)
CPA	14,893 (0.6%)
Peace	10,130 (0.4%)
SGB	5,454 (0.2%)
Roman	2,997 (0.1%)
Your	2,932 (0.1%)
Liberty	2,494 (0.1%)
Harmony	1,904 (0.1%)
UKIP majority	27,868

(June 2009, C. maj. 372,286)

MEMBERS ELECTED
1. *N. Farage, *UKIP* 2. *D. Hannan, *C.* 3. J. Atkinson, *UKIP* 4. *N. Deva, *C.* 5. A. Dodds, *Lab.* 6. D. James, *UKIP* 7. *R. Ashworth, *C.* 8. *K.Taylor, *Green* 9. *C. Bearder, *LD* 10. R. Finch, *UKIP*

SOUTH WEST

(Bath and North East Somerset, Bournemouth, Bristol, Cornwall, Devon, Dorset, Gloucestershire, North Somerset, Plymouth, Poole, Somerset, South Gloucestershire, Swindon, Torbay, Wiltshire, Isles of Scilly, Gibraltar)

E. 4,059,889 T. 37.03%

UKIP	484,184 (32.3%)
C.	433,151 (28.9%)
Lab.	206,124 (13.8%)
Green	166,447 (11.1%)
LD	160,376 (10.7%)
AIFE	23,169 (1.6%)
Eng. Dem.	15,081 (1.0%)
BNP	10,910 (0.7%)
UKIP majority	51,033

(June 2009, C. maj. 126,627)

MEMBERS ELECTED
1. *W. Dartmouth, *UKIP* 2. *A. Fox, *C.* 3. J. Reid, *UKIP* 4. *J. Girling, *C.* 5. C. Moody, *Lab.* 6. M. Scott Cato, *Green*

WALES

E. 2,327,175 T. 31.50%

Lab.	206,332 (28.2%)
UKIP	201,983 (27.6%)
C.	127,742 (17.4%)
PC	111,864 (15.3%)
Green	33,275 (4.5%)
LD	28,930 (4.0%)
BNP	7,655 (1.0%)
BF	6,633 (0.9%)
SLP	4,459 (0.6%)
No2EU	2,803 (0.4%)
SGB	1,384 (0.2%)
Lab. majority	4,349

(June 2004, Lab. maj. 120,039)

MEMBERS ELECTED
1. *D. Vaughan, *Lab.* 2. N. Gill, *UKIP* 3. *K. Swinburne, *C.* 4. *J. Evans, *PC*

WEST MIDLANDS

(Herefordshire, Shropshire, Staffordshire, Stoke-on-Trent, Telford and Wrekin, Warwickshire, West Midlands Metropolitan area, Worcestershire)

E. 4,105,305 T. 33.31%

UKIP	428,010 (28.1%)
Lab.	363,033 (21.3%)
C.	330,470 (17.0%)
LD	75,648 (12.0%)
Green	71,464 (8.6%)
AIFE	27,171 (6.2%)
WDR	23,426 (2.3%)
BNP	20,643 (1.3%)
Eng. Dem.	12,832 (1.0%)
No2EU	4,653 (0.9%)
Harmony	1,857 (0.6%)
UKIP majority	64,977

(June 2009, C. maj. 96,016)

MEMBERS ELECTED
1. J Seymour, *UKIP* 2. N. Gill, *Lab.* 3. *P. Bradbourn, *C.* 4. J. Carver, *UKIP* 5. S. Simon, *Lab.* 6. *A. McIntyre, *C.* 7. B. Etheridge, *UKIP*

YORKSHIRE AND THE HUMBER

(East Riding of Yorkshire, Kingston-upon-Hull, North East Lincolnshire, North Lincolnshire, North Yorkshire, South Yorkshire, West Yorkshire, York)

E. 3,905,726 T. 33.2%

UKIP	403,630 (31.1%)
Lab.	380,189 (29.3%)
C.	248,945 (19.2%)
Green	102,282 (7.9%)
LD	81,108 (6.3%)
AIFE	24,297 (1.9%)
BNP	20,138 (1.6%)
YF	19,017 (1.5%)
Eng. Dem.	13,288 (1.0%)
No2EU	3,807 (0.3%)
UKIP majority	23,441

(June 2009, C. maj. 69,793)

MEMBERS ELECTED
1. J. Collins, *UKIP* 2. *L. McAvan, *Lab.* 3. *T. Kirkhope, *C.* 4. A. Bashir, *UKIP* 5. R. Corbett, *Lab.* 6. M. Hookem, *UKIP*

LOCAL GOVERNMENT

Major changes in local government were introduced in England and Wales in 1974 and in Scotland in 1975 by the Local Government Act 1972 and the Local Government (Scotland) Act 1973. Further significant alterations were made in England by the Local Government Acts of 1985, 1992 and 2000.

The structure in England was based on two tiers of local authorities (county councils and district councils) in the non-metropolitan areas; and a single tier of metropolitan councils in the six metropolitan areas of England and London borough councils in London.

Following reviews of the structure of local government in England by the Local Government Commission (now the Boundary Commission for England), 46 unitary (all-purpose) authorities were created between April 1995 and April 1998 to cover certain areas in the non-metropolitan counties. The remaining county areas continue to have two tiers of local authorities. The county and district councils in the Isle of Wight were replaced by a single unitary authority on 1 April 1995; the former counties of Avon, Cleveland, Humberside and Berkshire were replaced by unitary authorities; and Hereford & Worcester was replaced by a new county council for Worcestershire (with district councils) and a unitary authority for Herefordshire. On 1 April 2009 the county areas of Cornwall, Durham, Northumberland, Shropshire and Wiltshire were given unitary status and two new unitary authorities were created for Bedfordshire (Bedford and Central Bedfordshire) and Cheshire (Cheshire East and Cheshire West & Chester) replacing the two-tier county/district system in these areas.

In May 2018 parliament passed legislation for Dorset's nine councils to merge into two unitary authorities. Under the plans, due to come into effect in April 2019, Bournemouth and Poole unitary authorities will merge with Christchurch district council to become one new unitary authority, while a second unitary authority would be formed from Dorset County Council, together with East Dorset, North Dorset, Purbeck, Weymouth & Portland and West Dorset district councils.

The Local Government (Wales) Act 1994 and the Local Government etc (Scotland) Act 1994 abolished the two-tier structure in Wales and Scotland with effect from 1 April 1996, replacing it with a single tier of unitary authorities.

In Northern Ireland a reform programme to reduce the number of local authorities from 26 to 11 began in 2012 when legislation finalising the boundaries of the new 11 local government district authorities was approved by the Northern Ireland Assembly. The Local Government Act (Northern Ireland) 2014 received royal assent on 12 May 2014, providing the legislative framework for the 11 new councils. On 1 April 2015 additional functions, previously the responsibility of the Northern Ireland executive, fully transferred to the new district authorities.

ELECTIONS

Local elections are normally held on the first Thursday in May. Generally, all citizens of the UK, the Republic of Ireland, Commonwealth and other European Union citizens who are 18 years or over and resident on the qualifying date in the area for which the election is being held, are entitled to vote at local government elections. A register of electors is prepared and published annually by local electoral registration officers.

A returning officer has the overall responsibility for an election. Voting takes place at polling stations, arranged by the local authority and under the supervision of a presiding officer specially appointed for the purpose. Candidates, who are subject to various statutory qualifications and disqualifications designed to ensure that they are suitable to hold office, must be nominated by electors for the electoral area concerned.

In England, the Local Government Boundary Commission for England is responsible for carrying out periodic reviews of electoral arrangements, to consider whether the boundaries of wards or divisions within a local authority need to be altered to take account of changes in electorate; structural reviews, to consider whether a single, unitary authority should be established in an area instead of an existing two-tier system; and administrative boundary reviews of district or county authorities.

The Local Democracy and Boundary Commission for Wales, the Local Government Boundary Commission for Scotland and the local government boundary commissioner for Northern Ireland (appointed when required by the Boundary Commission for Northern Ireland) are responsible for reviewing the electoral arrangements and boundaries of local authorities within their respective regions.

The Local Government Act 2000 provided for the secretary of state to change the frequency and phasing of elections in England and Wales.

LOCAL GOVERNMENT BOUNDARY COMMISSION FOR ENGLAND, 14th Floor, Millbank Tower, London SW1P 4QP T 0330-500 1525 E reviews@lgbce.org.uk W www.lgbce.org.uk

LOCAL DEMOCRACY AND BOUNDARY COMMISSION FOR WALES, Ground Floor, Hastings House, Fitzalan Court, Cardiff CF24 0BL T 029-2046 4819 E ldbc.wales@gov.wales W www.ldbc.gov.wales

LOCAL GOVERNMENT BOUNDARY COMMISSION FOR SCOTLAND, Thistle House, 91 Haymarket Terrace, Edinburgh EH12 5HD T 0131-244 2001 E lgbcs@scottishboundaries.gov.uk W www.lgbc-scotland.gov.uk

BOUNDARY COMMISSION FOR NORTHERN IRELAND, The Bungalow, Stormont House, Stormont Estate, Belfast BT4 3SH T 028-9052 7821 E contact@boundarycommission.org.uk W www.boundarycommission.org.uk

LOCAL GOVERNMENT DEVOLUTION

Local government is a devolved matter in Scotland, Wales and Northern Ireland.

In England, under the Cities and Local Government Devolution Act 2016, multiple local authorities can combine and take on more functions, over and above those they were allowed to take on under previous legislation. In order for a combined or 'regional' authority to be given these extra powers a mayor must be elected for the region by the electorate in the combined-authority area. The first six combined authority mayoral elections took place in May 2017. The exact functions the combined authority and mayor manage varies depending on the devolution agreement reached with central government, but the directly-elected 'metro' mayor does have powers and responsibilities to make strategic decisions across whole city regions. This is in contrast to existing city mayors (which are also directly elected) or local council leaders that only make decisions for, and on behalf of, their local authority (see Internal Organisation). To date, nine combined authorities have been established, seven of which have a mayor and a devolution agreement with national government (see Combined Authorities for a complete list).

INTERNAL ORGANISATION

The council as a whole is the final decision-making body within any authority. Councils are free to a great extent to make their own internal organisational arrangements. The Local Government Act, given royal assent on 28 July 2000, allows councils to adopt one of three broad categories of constitution which include a separate executive:

- A directly elected mayor with a cabinet selected by that mayor
- A cabinet, either elected by the council or appointed by its leader
- A directly elected mayor and council manager

Normally, questions of policy are settled by the full council, while the administration of the various services is the responsibility of committees of councillors. Day-to-day decisions are delegated to the council's officers, who act within the policies laid down by the councillors.

FINANCE

Local government in England, Wales and Scotland is financed from four sources: council tax, non-domestic rates, government grants and income from fees and charges for services.

COUNCIL TAX

Council tax is a local tax levied by each local council. Liability for the council tax bill usually falls on the owner-occupier or tenant of a dwelling which is their sole or main residence. Council tax bills may be reduced because of the personal circumstances of people resident in a property and there are discounts in the case of dwellings occupied by fewer than two adults.

In England, unitary and metropolitan authorities are responsible for collecting their own council tax. In areas where there are two tiers of local authority, each county and district authority sets its own council tax rate; the district authorities collect the combined council tax and the county councils claim their share from the district councils' collection funds. In Wales and Scotland each unitary authority sets its own council tax rate and is responsible for collection.

The tax relates to the value of the dwelling. In England and Scotland each dwelling is placed in one of eight valuation bands, ranging from A to H, based on the property's estimated market value as at 1 April 1991. In Wales there are nine bands, ranging from A to I, based on the estimated market value of property as at 1 April 2003.

The valuation bands and ranges of values in England, Wales and Scotland are:

England

A	Up to £40,000	E	£88,001–£120,000
B	£40,001–£52,000	F	£120,001–£160,000
C	£52,001–£68,000	G	£160,001–£320,000
D	£68,001–£88,000	H	Over £320,001

Wales

A	Up to £44,000	F	£162,001–£223,000
B	£44,001–£65,000	G	£223,001–£324,000
C	£65,001–£91,000	H	£324,001–£424,000
D	£91,001–£123,000	I	Over £424,001
E	£123,001–£162,000		

Scotland

A	Up to £27,000	E	£58,001–£80,000
B	£27,001–£35,000	F	£80,001–£106,000
C	£35,001–£45,000	G	£106,001–£212,000
D	£45,001–£58,000	H	Over £212,001

The council tax within a local area varies between the different bands according to proportions laid down by law. The charge attributable to each band as a proportion of the Band D charge set by the council is approximately:

A	67%	F	144%
B	78%	G	167%
C	89%	H	200%
D	100%	I*	233%
E	122%		
* Wales only			

The average Band D council tax bill for each authority area is given in the complete lists of local authorities for England, London, Wales and Scotland which follow. There may be variations from the given figure within each district council area because of different parish or community precepts being levied.

NON-DOMESTIC RATES

Non-domestic (business) rates are collected by billing authorities; these are the district councils in those areas of England with two tiers of local government and unitary authorities in other parts of England, in Wales and in Scotland. In respect of England and Wales, the Local Government Finance Act 1988 provides for liability for rates to be assessed on the basis of a poundage (multiplier) tax on the rateable value of property (hereditaments). Separate multipliers are set by the Ministry for Housing, Communities and Local Government (MHCLG) in England, the Welsh government and the Scottish government. Rates are collected by the billing authority for the area where a property is located. Rate income collected by billing authorities is paid into a national non-domestic rating (NNDR) pool and redistributed to individual authorities on the basis of the adult population figure as prescribed by DCLG, the Welsh government or the Scottish government. The rates pools are maintained separately in England, Wales and Scotland. Actual payment of rates in certain cases is subject to transitional arrangements, to phase in the larger increases and reductions in rates resulting from the effects of the latest revaluation.

The most recent rating lists for England, Wales and Scotland came into effect on 1 April 2017. The rateable values on these lists are derived from the rental value of property as at 1 April 2015 and determined on certain statutory assumptions by the Valuation Office Agency in England and Wales, and by local area assessors in Scotland. New property which is added to the list, and significant changes to existing property, necessitate amendments to the rateable value on the same basis. Rating lists (valuation rolls in Scotland) remain in force until the next general revaluation, which usually takes place every five years to reflect changes in the property market.

A revaluation of non-domestic properties in Northern Ireland was completed at the start of 2015 and since 1 April 2015 the rateable value of all non-domestic properties in Northern Ireland is based on the rental value of the property as at 1 April 2013. The next revaluation is currently underway with a view to new valuation lists being available for use from April 2020.

Certain types of property are exempt from rates, eg agricultural land and buildings, buildings used for the training or welfare of disabled people and buildings registered for public religious worship. Charities and other non-profit-making organisations may receive full or partial relief and relief schemes for small businesses are available in England, Wales, Scotland and Northern Ireland. Empty commercial property in England and Wales is exempt from business rates for the first three months that the property is vacant, empty industrial property for six months and listed buildings are exempt until re-occupied; after which full business rates are normally payable. In Scotland empty commercial property is entitled to a 50 per cent discount on business rates for the first three months and a 10 per cent discount thereafter, empty industrial buildings are entitled to full relief for six months and a 10 per cent discount thereafter and empty listed buildings and properties with a rateable value of less than £1,700 are entirely exempt. In Northern Ireland all vacant non-domestic property, which has been previously occupied for at least six weeks, is entirely exempt from rates for three months, after this period, rates are billed at 50 per cent of the normal occupied amount.

COMPLAINTS

ENGLAND
In England the Local Government Ombudsman investigates complaints of injustice arising from maladministration by local authorities and certain other bodies. The Local Government Ombudsman will not usually consider a complaint unless the local authority concerned has had an opportunity to investigate and reply to a complainant.
LOCAL GOVERNMENT OMBUDSMAN, 53–55 Butts Road, Coventry CV1 3BH T 0300-061 0614 W www.lgo.org.uk
Ombudsman, Michael King

WALES
The office of Public Services Ombudsman for Wales came into force on 1 April 2006, incorporating the functions of the Local Government Ombudsman for Wales.
PUBLIC SERVICES OMBUDSMAN FOR WALES, 1 Ffordd yr Hen Gae, Pencoed CF35 5LJ T 0300-790 0203
W www.ombudsman-wales.org.uk
Ombudsman, Nick Bennett

SCOTLAND
The Scottish Public Services Ombudsman is responsible for complaints regarding the maladministration of local government in Scotland.
SCOTTISH PUBLIC SERVICES OMBUDSMAN, 4 Melville Street, Edinburgh EH3 7NS T 0800-377 7330
W www.spso.org.uk
Ombudsman, Rosemary Agnew

NORTHERN IRELAND
The Local Government Commissioner for Standards fulfils a similar function in Northern Ireland, investigating complaints about local authorities and certain public bodies. Complaints are made to the relevant local authority in the first instance but may also be made directly to the commissioner.
NORTHERN IRELAND LOCAL GOVERNMENT COMMISSIONER FOR STANDARDS, Progressive House, 33 Wellington Place, Belfast BT1 6HN T 028-9023 3821
E nipso@nipso.org.uk W www.nipso.org.uk
Local Government Commissioner for Standards, Marie Anderson

THE QUEEN'S REPRESENTATIVES

The lord-lieutenant of a county is the permanent local representative of the Crown in that county. The appointment of lord-lieutenants is now regulated by the Lieutenancies Act 1997. They are appointed by the sovereign on the recommendation of the prime minister. The retirement age is 75. The office of lord-lieutenant dates from 1551, and its holder was originally responsible for maintaining order and for local defence in the county. The duties of the post include attending on royalty during official visits to the county, performing certain duties in connection with the armed forces (and in particular the reserve forces), and making presentations of honours and awards on behalf of the Crown. In England, Wales and Northern Ireland, the lord-lieutenant usually also holds the office of *Custos Rotulorum.* As such, he or she acts as head of the county's commission of the peace (which recommends the appointment of magistrates).

The office of sheriff (from the Old English *shire-reeve*) of a county was created in the tenth century. The sheriff was the special nominee of the sovereign, and the office reached the peak of its influence under the Norman kings. The Provisions of Oxford (1258) laid down a yearly tenure of office. Since the mid-16th century the office has been purely civil, with military duties taken over by the lord-lieutenant of the county. The sheriff (commonly known as 'high sheriff') attends on royalty during official visits to the county, acts as the returning officer during parliamentary elections in county constituencies, attends the opening ceremony when a high court judge goes on circuit, executes high court writs, and appoints under-sheriffs to act as deputies. The appointments and duties of the sheriffs in England and Wales are laid down by the Sheriffs Act 1887.

The serving high sheriff submits a list of names of possible future sheriffs to a tribunal, which chooses three names to put to the sovereign. The tribunal nominates the high sheriff annually on 12 November and the sovereign picks the name of the sheriff to succeed in the following year. The term of office runs from 25 March to the following 24 March (the civil and legal year before 1752). No person may be chosen twice in three years if there is any other suitable person in the county.

CIVIC DIGNITIES

District councils in England and local councils in Wales may petition for a royal charter granting borough or 'city' status to the council.

In England and Wales the chair of a borough or county borough council may be called a mayor, and the chair of a city council may be called a lord mayor (if lord mayoralty has been conferred on that city). Parish councils in England and community councils in Wales may call themselves 'town councils', in which case their chair is the town mayor.

In Scotland the chair of a local council may be known as a convenor; a provost is the mayoral equivalent. The chair of the councils for the cities of Aberdeen, Dundee, Edinburgh and Glasgow are lord provosts.

ENGLAND

The country of England lies between 55° 46′ and 49° 57′ 30″ N. latitude (from a few miles north of the mouth of the Tweed to the Lizard), and between 1° 46′ E. and 5° 43′ W. longitude (from Lowestoft to Land's End). England is bounded on the north by the Cheviot Hills; on the south by the English Channel; on the east by the Straits of Dover (Pas de Calais) and the North Sea; and on the west by the Atlantic Ocean, Wales and the Irish Sea. It has a total area of 130,432 sq. km (50,360 sq. miles): land 130,279 sq. km (50,301 sq. miles); inland water 153 sq. km (59 sq. miles).

There are 27 counties, divided into 201 districts, 56 unitary authorities (including the Isles of Scilly), 36 metropolitan boroughs and 32 London Boroughs (including the Corporation of London). *See* Local Government, London for information on London Borough councils and the Corporation of London.

POPULATION
The population at the 2011 census was 53,012,456 (men 26,069,148; women 26,943,308). The average density of the population in 2011 was 406 persons per sq km (1,053 per sq. mile).

The populations of most of the unitary authorities are in the range of 100,000 to 300,000. The district councils have populations broadly in the range of 60,000 to 150,000; some, however, have larger populations, because of the need to avoid dividing large towns, and some in mainly rural areas have smaller populations.

The main conurbations outside Greater London – Tyne and Wear, West Midlands, Merseyside, Greater Manchester, West Yorkshire and South Yorkshire – are divided into 36 metropolitan boroughs, most of which have a population of over 200,000.

ELECTIONS
For districts, counties and for around 9,000 towns and parishes, there are elected councils, consisting of directly elected councillors. The councillors elect one of their number as chair annually.

In general, councils can have whole council elections, elections by thirds or elections by halves. However all metropolitan authorities must hold elections by thirds. The electoral cycle of any new unitary authority is specified in the appropriate statutory order under which it is established.

COMBINED AUTHORITIES
Under the Cities and Local Government Devolution Act 2016, multiple local authorities can combine and take on more functions, over and above those they were allowed to take on under previous legislation. In order for a combined or 'regional' authority to be given these extra powers a mayor must be elected for the region by the electorate in the combined-authority area. The first six combined authority mayoral elections took place in May 2017.

The exact functions the combined authority and mayor manage varies depending on the devolution agreement reached with central government, but the directly-elected 'metro' mayor does have powers and responsibilities to make strategic decisions across whole city regions. This is in contrast to existing city mayors (which are also directly elected) or local council leaders that only make decisions for, and on behalf of, their local authority. Currently, seven city regions have a devolution agreement with national government and the first six regional mayoral elections took place in May 2017. To date, nine combined authorities have

been established, seven of which have a mayor and a devolution agreement with national government.

The combined authorities comprise constituent and non-constituent councils and other local authorities. Constituent councils have full voting rights and cannot be a member of another combined authority. Non-constituent councils usually have restricted voting rights, although this decision rests with the combined authority. In addition, non-constituent councils can be a member of more than one combined authority, as long as this is also on a non-constituent basis. *See* the list of Combined Authorities for details of these devolved regions, their mayors and constituent councils.

COUNCIL FUNCTIONS
In areas with a two-tier system of local governance, functions are divided between the district and county authorities, with those functions affecting the larger area or population generally being the responsibility of the county council. A few functions continue to be exercised over the larger area by joint bodies, made up of councillors from each authority within the area.

Generally the allocation of functions is as follows:

County councils: education; strategic planning; traffic, transport and highways; fire service; consumer protection; refuse disposal; smallholdings; social care; libraries

District councils: local planning; housing; highways (maintenance of certain urban roads and off-street car parks); building regulations; environmental health; refuse collection; cemeteries and crematoria; collection of council tax and non-domestic rates

Unitary and metropolitan councils: their functions are all those listed above, except that the fire service is exercised by a joint body

Concurrently by county and district councils: recreation (parks, playing fields, swimming pools); museums; encouragement of the arts, tourism and industry

PARISH COUNCILS
Parish or town councils are the most local tier of government in England. There are currently around 10,000 parishes in England, of which around 9,000 have councils. Since 15 February 2008 local councils have been able to create new parish councils without seeking approval from the government. Around 80 per cent of parish councils represent populations of less than 2,500; parishes with no parish council can be grouped with neighbouring parishes under a common parish council. A parish council comprises at least five members, the number being fixed by the district council. Elections are held every four years, at the time of the election of the district councillor for the ward including the parish. Full parish councils must be formed for those parishes with more than 999 electors – below this number, parish meetings comprising the electors of the parish must be held at least twice a year.

Parish council functions include: allotments; encouragement of arts and crafts; community halls, recreational facilities (eg open spaces, swimming pools), cemeteries and crematoria; and many minor functions. They must also be given an opportunity to comment on planning applications. They may, like county and district councils, spend limited sums for the general benefit of the parish. They levy a precept on the district councils for their funds. Parish precepts for 2018–19 total £518m, an increase of 6.8 per cent on 2017–18.

FINANCE
Local government revenue expenditure is budgeted to be £95.9bn in 2018–19; of this £29.6bn is to be raised through

council tax, £17.1bn from the business rate retention scheme and £48.0bn from government grants. The remainder will be drawn down from local authority reserves.

Since April 2013 local authorities retain a share of business rates and keep the growth on that share (the 'rate retention scheme'). Revenue support grant is paid to local authorities to enable all authorities in the same class to broadly set the same council tax; in 2018–19 revenue support grant totals £1.4bn. In addition central government pays specific grants in support of revenue expenditure on particular services. Police grant totals £7.1bn in 2018–19. In 2018–19, local authorities with adult social care responsibilities were able to increase council tax by up to 3 per cent to fund adult social care; this is in addition to the usual funding of adult social care through council tax. Adult social care precept totals £538m in 2018–19.

In England, the average council tax per dwelling for 2018–19 is £1,258, an increase of 6.1 per cent from 2017–18. The average council tax bill for a Band D dwelling (occupied by two adults, including adult social care and parish precepts) for 2018–19 is £1,671, an increase of 5.1 per cent from 2017–18. The average Band D council tax is £1,749 in shire districts, £1,658 in metropolitan areas, £1,729 in unitary authority areas and £1,405 in London.

The non-domestic rating multiplier for England for 2018–19 is 49.3p (48.0p for small businesses). The City of London is able to set a different multiplier from the rest of England; for 2018–19 this is 49.8p (48.5p for small businesses).

Under the Local Government and Housing Act 1989, local authorities have four main ways of paying for capital expenditure: borrowing and other forms of extended credit; capital grants from central government towards some types of capital expenditure; 'usable' capital receipts from the sale of land, houses and other assets; and revenue.

The amount of capital expenditure which a local authority can finance by borrowing (or other forms of credit) is effectively limited by the credit approvals issued to it by central government. Most credit approvals can be used for any kind of local authority capital expenditure; these are known as basic credit approvals. Others (supplementary credit approvals) can be used only for the kind of expenditure specified in the approval, and so are often given to fund particular projects or services.

Local authorities can use all capital receipts from the sale of property or assets for capital spending, except in the case of sales of council houses. Generally, the 'usable' part of a local authority's capital receipts consists of 25 per cent of receipts from the sale of council houses and 50 per cent of other housing assets such as shops or vacant land. The balance has to be set aside as provision for repaying debt and meeting other credit liabilities.

EXPENDITURE

Budgeted revenue expenditure for 2018–19 is:

Service	£ million
Education	33,862
Highways and transport	4,251
Social care	24,689
Public health	3,314
Housing (excluding HRA)	1,575
Cultural, environment and planning	8,258
Police	11,374
Fire and rescue	2,081
Central	2,875
Other	319
Total Service Expenditure	92,599
*Housing benefits	19,286
Parish precepts	515
†Levies & trading account and other adjustments	(378)

Total Net Current Expenditure	112,022
Non-current Expenditure and External Receipts	
Capital expenditure charged to revenue account	1,509
Housing benefits subsidies	(19,105)
Community infrastructure levy	(129)
Capital financing and debt servicing	4,370
REVENUE EXPENDITURE	95,940

HRA = Housing Revenue Account
* Includes all mandatory and non-mandatory housing benefits
† Includes Integrated Transport Authority levy, Waste Disposal Authority levy, London Pensions Fund Authority levy and other levies

RELIEF

There is a marked division between the upland and lowland areas of England. In the extreme north the Cheviot Hills (highest point, the Cheviot, 815m/2,674ft) form a natural boundary with Scotland. Running south from the Cheviots, though divided from them by the Tyne Gap, is the Pennine range (highest point, Cross Fell, 893m/2,930ft), the main orological feature of the country. The Pennines culminate in the Peak District of Derbyshire (Kinder Scout, 636m/2,088ft). West of the Pennines are the Cumbrian mountains, which include Scafell Pike (978m/3,210ft), the highest peak in England, and to the east are the Yorkshire Moors, their highest point being Urra Moor (454m/1,490ft).

In the west, the foothills of the Welsh mountains extend into the bordering English counties of Shropshire (the Wrekin, 407m/1,334ft; Long Mynd, 516m/1,694ft) and Hereford and Worcester (the Malvern Hills – Worcestershire Beacon, 425m/1,394ft). Extensive areas of highland and moorland are also to be found in the south-western peninsula formed by Somerset, Devon and Cornwall, principally Exmoor (Dunkery Beacon, 519m/1,704ft), Dartmoor (High Willhays, 621m/2,038ft) and Bodmin Moor (Brown Willy, 420m/1,377ft). Ranges of low, undulating hills run across the south of the country, including the Cotswolds in the Midlands and south-west, the Chilterns to the north of London, and the North (Kent) and South (Sussex) Downs of the south-east coastal areas.

The lowlands of England lie in the Vale of York, East Anglia and the area around the Wash. The lowest-lying are the Cambridgeshire Fens in the valleys of the Great Ouse and the river Nene, which are below sea-level in places. Since the 17th century extensive drainage has brought much of the Fens under cultivation. The North Sea coast between the Thames and the Humber, low-lying and formed of sand and shingle for the most part, is subject to erosion and defences against further incursion have been built along many stretches.

HYDROGRAPHY

The Severn is the longest river in Great Britain, rising on the north-eastern slopes of Plynlimon (Wales) and entering England in Shropshire, with a total length of 354km (220 miles) from its source to its outflow into the Bristol Channel, where it receives the Bristol Avon on the east and the Wye on the west; its other tributaries are the Vyrnwy, Tern, Stour, Teme and Upper (or Warwickshire) Avon. The Severn is tidal below Gloucester, and a high bore or tidal wave sometimes reverses the flow as high as Tewkesbury (21.75km/13.5 miles above Gloucester). The scenery of the greater part of the river is very picturesque, and the Severn is a noted salmon river, with some of its tributaries being famous for trout. Navigation is assisted by the Gloucester and Berkeley Ship Canal (26km/16.25 miles), which admits vessels of 350 tons to Gloucester. The Severn Tunnel was begun in 1873 and completed in 1886 at a cost of £2m and after many difficulties caused by flooding. It is 7km (4 miles 628 yards) in length (of which 3.67km/2.25 miles are under the river). The Severn road bridge between Haysgate, Gwent, and Almondsbury,

Glos, with a centre span of 988m (3,240ft), was opened in 1966.

The longest river wholly in England is the Thames, with a total length of 346km (215 miles) from its source in the Cotswold hills to the Nore, and is navigable by ocean-going ships to London Bridge. The Thames is tidal to Teddington (111km/69 miles from its mouth) and forms county boundaries almost throughout its course; on its banks are situated London, Windsor Castle, Eton College and Oxford University. Of the remaining English rivers, those flowing into the North Sea are the Tyne, Wear, Tees, Ouse and Trent from the Pennine Range, the Great Ouse (257km/160 miles), which rises in Northamptonshire, and the Orwell and Stour from the hills of East Anglia. Flowing into the English Channel are the Sussex Ouse from the Weald, the Itchen from the Hampshire hills, and the Axe, Teign, Dart, Tamar and Exe from the Devonian hills. Flowing into the Irish Sea are the Mersey, Ribble and Eden from the western slopes of the Pennines and the Derwent from the Cumbrian mountains.

The English Lakes, notable for their picturesque scenery and poetic associations, lie in Cumbria's Lake District; the largest are Windermere (14.7 sq. km/5.7 sq. miles), Ullswater (8.8 sq. km/3.4 sq. miles) and Derwent Water (5.3 sq. km/2.0 sq. miles).

FLAG

The flag of England is the cross of St George, a red cross on a white field (cross gules in a field argent). The cross of St George, the patron saint of England, has been used since the 13th century.

ISLANDS

The Isle of Wight is separated from Hampshire by the Solent. The capital, Newport, stands at the head of the estuary of the Medina, and Cowes (at the mouth) is the chief port. Other centres are Ryde, Sandown, Shanklin, Ventnor, Freshwater, Yarmouth, Totland Bay, Seaview and Bembridge.

Lundy (the name is derived from the Old Norse for 'puffin island'), 18km (11 miles) north-west of Hartland Point, Devon, is around 5km (3 miles) long and almost 1km (half a mile) wide on average, with a total area of around 452 hectares (1,116 acres), and a population of 27. It became the property of the National Trust in 1969 and is now principally a bird sanctuary and the UK's first marine conservation zone.

The Isles of Scilly comprise around 140 islands and skerries (total area, 10 sq. km/6 sq. miles) situated 45 km (28 miles) south-west of Land's End in Cornwall. Only five are inhabited: St Mary's, St Agnes, Bryher, Tresco and St Martin's. The population at the 2011 census was 2,200. The entire group has been designated an Area of Outstanding Natural Beauty because of its unique flora and fauna. Tourism and the winter/spring flower trade for the home market form the basis of the economy of the islands. The island group is a recognised rural development area.

EARLY HISTORY

Archaeological evidence suggests that England has been inhabited since at least the Palaeolithic period, though the extent of the various Palaeolithic cultures was dependent upon the degree of glaciation. The succeeding Neolithic and Bronze Age cultures have left abundant remains throughout the country; the best-known of these are the henges and stone circles of Stonehenge (ten miles north of Salisbury, Wilts) and Avebury (Wilts), both of which are believed to have been of religious significance. In the latter part of the Bronze Age the Goidels, a people of the Celtic race, invaded the country and brought with them Celtic civilisation and dialects; as a result place names in England bear witness to the spread of the invasion across the whole region.

THE ROMAN CONQUEST

The Roman conquest of Gaul (57–50 BC) brought Britain into close contact with Roman civilisation, but although Julius Caesar raided the south of Britain in 55 and 54 BC, conquest was not undertaken until nearly 100 years later. In AD 43 the Emperor Claudius dispatched Aulus Plautius, with a well-equipped force of 40,000, and himself followed with reinforcements in the same year. Success was delayed by the resistance of Caratacus (Caractacus), the British leader from AD 48–51, who was finally captured and sent to Rome, and by a great revolt in AD 61 led by Boudicca (Boadicea), Queen of the Iceni, but the south of Britain was secured by AD 70, and Wales and the area north to the Tyne by about AD 80.

In AD 122, the Emperor Hadrian visited Britain and built a continuous rampart, since known as Hadrian's Wall, from Wallsend to Bowness (Tyne to Solway). The work was entrusted by the Emperor Hadrian to Aulus Platorius Nepos, legate of Britain from AD 122 to 126, and it was intended to form the northern frontier of the Roman Empire.

The Romans administered Britain as a province under a governor, with a well-defined system of local government, each Roman municipality ruling itself and its surrounding territory, while London was the centre of the road system and the seat of the financial officials of the Province of Britain. Colchester, Lincoln, York, Gloucester and St Albans stand on the sites of five Roman municipalities, and Wroxeter, Caerleon, Chester, Lincoln and York were at various times the sites of legionary fortresses. Well-preserved Roman towns have been uncovered at or near Silchester *(Calleva Atrebatum)*, ten miles south of Reading, Wroxeter *(Viroconium Cornoviorum)*, near Shrewsbury and St Albans *(Verulamium)* in Hertfordshire.

Four main groups of roads radiated from London, and a fifth (the Fosse) ran obliquely from Lincoln through Leicester, Cirencester and Bath to Exeter. Of the four groups radiating from London, one ran south-east to Canterbury and the coast of Kent, a second to Silchester and thence to parts of western Britain and south Wales, a third (later known as Watling Street) ran through St Albans to Chester, with various branches, and the fourth reached Colchester, Lincoln, York and the eastern counties.

In the fourth century Britain was subjected to raids along the east coast by Saxon pirates, which led to the establishment of a system of coastal defences from the Wash to Southampton Water, with forts at Brancaster, Burgh Castle (Yarmouth), Walton (Felixstowe), Bradwell, Reculver, Richborough, Dover, Lympne, Pevensey and Porchester (Portsmouth). The Irish (Scoti) and Picts in the north were also becoming more aggressive and from around AD 350 incursions became more frequent and more formidable. As the Roman Empire came increasingly under attack towards the end of the fourth century, many troops were removed from Britain for service in other parts of the empire. The island was eventually cut off from Rome by the Teutonic conquest of Gaul, and with the withdrawal of the last Roman garrison early in the fifth century, the Romano-British were left to themselves.

SAXON SETTLEMENT

According to legend, the British King Vortigern called in the Saxons to defend his lands against the Picts. The Saxon chieftains Hengist and Horsa landed at Ebbsfleet, Kent, and established themselves in the Isle of Thanet, but the events during the one-and-a-half centuries between the final break with Rome and the re-establishment of Christianity are unclear. However, it would appear that over the course of this period the raids turned into large-scale settlement by invaders traditionally known as Angles (England north of the Wash and East Anglia), Saxons (Essex and southern England) and Jutes (Kent and the Weald), which pushed the Romano-

British into the mountainous areas of the north and west. Celtic culture outside Wales and Cornwall survives only in topographical names. Various kingdoms established at this time attempted to claim overlordship of the whole country, hegemony finally being achieved by Wessex (with the capital at Winchester) in the ninth century. This century also saw the beginning of raids by the Vikings (Danes), which were resisted by Alfred the Great (871–899), who fixed a limit on the advance of Danish settlement by the Treaty of Wedmore (878), giving them the area north and east of Watling Street on the condition that they adopt Christianity.

In the tenth century the kings of Wessex recovered the whole of England from the Danes, but subsequent rulers were unable to resist a second wave of invaders. England paid tribute *(Danegeld)* for many years, and was invaded in 1013 by the Danes and ruled by Danish kings (including Cnut) from 1016 until 1042, when Edward the Confessor was recalled from exile in Normandy. On Edward's death in 1066 Harold Godwinson (brother-in-law of Edward and son of Earl Godwin of Wessex) was chosen to be King of England. After defeating (at Stamford Bridge, Yorkshire, 25 September 1066) an invading army under Harald Hadraada, King of Norway (aided by the outlawed Earl Tostig of Northumbria, Harold's brother), Harold was himself defeated at the Battle of Hastings on 14 October 1066, and the Norman conquest secured the throne of England for Duke William of Normandy, a cousin of Edward the Confessor.

CHRISTIANITY

Christianity reached the Roman province of Britain from Gaul in the third century (or possibly earlier). Alban, traditionally Britain's first martyr, was put to death as a Christian during the persecution of Diocletian (22 June 303) at his native town *Verulamium,* and the bishops of *Londinium, Eboracum* (York), and *Lindum* (Lincoln) attended the Council of Arles in 314. However, the Anglo-Saxon invasions submerged the Christian religion in England until the sixth century: conversion was undertaken in the north from 563 by Celtic missionaries from Ireland led by St Columba, and in the south by a mission sent from Rome in 597 which was led by St Augustine, who became the first archbishop of Canterbury. England appears to have been converted again by the end of the seventh century and followed, after the Council of Whitby in 663, the practices of the Roman Church, which brought the kingdom into the mainstream of European thought and culture.

PRINCIPAL CITIES

There are 51 cities in England and space constraints prevent us from including profiles of them all. Below is a selection of England's principal cities with the date on which city status was conferred in parentheses. Other cities are Bradford (pre-1900), Chelmsford (2012), Chichester (pre-1900), Coventry (pre-1900), Derby (1977), Ely (pre-1900), Exeter (pre-1900), Gloucester (pre-1900), Hereford (pre-1900), Kingston-upon-Hull (pre-1900), Lancaster (1937), Lichfield (pre-1900), London (pre-1900), Peterborough (pre-1900), Plymouth (1928), Portsmouth (1926), Preston (2002), Ripon (pre-1900), Salford (1926), Stoke-on-Trent (1925), Sunderland (1992), Truro (pre-1900), Wakefield (pre-1900), Wells (pre-1900), Westminster (pre-1900), Wolverhampton (2000) and Worcester (pre-1900).

Certain cities have also been granted a lord mayoralty – this grant confers no additional powers or functions and is purely honorific. Cities with lord mayors are Birmingham, Bradford, Bristol, Canterbury, Chester, Coventry, Exeter, Kingston-upon-Hull, Leeds, Leicester, Liverpool, London, Manchester, Newcastle-upon-Tyne, Norwich, Nottingham, Oxford, Plymouth, Portsmouth, Sheffield, Stoke-on-Trent, Westminster and York.

BATH (PRE-1900)

Bath stands on the river Avon between the Cotswold Hills to the north and the Mendips to the south, and was originally a small roman town *(Aquae Sulis)* with a baths and temple complex built around naturally occurring hot springs. In the early 18th century Bath became England's premier spa town where the rich and celebrated members of fashionable society gathered to 'take the waters' and enjoy the town's theatres and concert rooms. During this period the architect John Wood laid the foundations of a new Georgian city built using the honey-coloured stone for which Bath is famous today. Since 1987 the city has been listed as a UNESCO World Heritage Site.

Contemporary Bath is a thriving tourist destination and remains a leading cultural, religious and historical centre with many art galleries and historic sites including the Pump Room (1790); the Royal Crescent (1767); the Circus (1754); the 18th-century Assembly Rooms (housing the Museum of Costume); Pulteney Bridge (1771); the Guildhall and the Abbey, now over 500 years old, which is built on the site of a Saxon monastery. In 2006 the Bath Thermae Spa was completed and the hot springs reopened to the public for the first time since 1978.

BIRMINGHAM (PRE-1900)

Birmingham is Britain's second largest city, with a population of over one million. The generally accepted derivation of 'Birmingham' is the *ham* (dwelling-place) of the *ing* (family) of *Beorma,* presumed to have been Saxon. During the Industrial Revolution the town grew into a major manufacturing centre, known as the 'city of a thousand trades', and in 1889 was granted city status. By the 18th century, Birmingham was the main European producer of items such as buckles, medals and coins. Today, around 40 per cent of all the UK's handmade jewellery is produced in Birmingham's Jewellery Quarter. Another product of the Industrial Revolution are the city's 34 miles (56km) of canals.

Recent developments include Millennium Point, which houses Thinktank, the Birmingham science museum, and Brindleyplace, a development of shops, offices and leisure facilities on a former industrial site clustered around canals. In 2003 the Bullring shopping centre was officially opened as part of the city's urban regeneration programme.

The principal buildings are the Town Hall (1834–50), the Council House (1879), Victoria Law Courts (1891), the University of Birmingham (1906–9), the 13th-century church of St Martin in the Bull Ring (rebuilt 1873), the cathedral (formerly St Philip's Church) (1711), the Roman Catholic cathedral of St Chad (1839–41), the Assay Office (1773), the Rotunda (1964) and the National Exhibition Centre (1976).

BRIGHTON AND HOVE (2000)

Brighton and Hove is situated on the south coast of England, around 96km (60 miles) south of London. Originally a fishing village called Brighthelmstone, it was transformed into a fashionable seaside resort in the 18th century when Dr Richard Russell popularised the benefits of his 'sea-water cure'; as one of the closest beaches to London, Brighton began to attract wealthy visitors. One of these was the Prince Regent (the future King George IV), who first visited in 1783 and became so fond of the city that in 1807 he bought the former farmhouse he had been renting, and gradually turned it into Brighton's most recognisable building, the Royal Pavilion. The Pavilion is renowned for its Indo-Saracenic exterior, featuring minarets and an enormous central dome designed by John Nash, combined with the lavish chinoiserie of Frederick

Crace's and Robert Jones' interiors. Queen Victoria sold the Pavilion to Brighton's municipal authority in 1850.

Brighton and Hove's Regency heritage can also be seen in the numerous elegant squares and crescents designed by Amon Wilds and Augustin Busby that dominate the seafront.

BRISTOL (PRE-1900)

Bristol was a royal borough before the Norman conquest. The earliest form of the name is *Bricgstow*. Due to the city's position close to the mouth of the River Avon, it was an important location for marine trade for centuries and prospered greatly from the transatlantic slave trade during the 18th century.

The principal buildings include the 12th-century cathedral with Norman chapter house and gateway; the 14th-century church of St Mary Redcliffe; Wesley's Chapel, Broadmead; the Merchant Venturers' Almshouses; the Council House (1956); the Guildhall; the Exchange (erected from the designs of John Wood in 1743); Cabot Tower; the university and Clifton College.

The Clifton Suspension Bridge, with a span of 214m (702ft) over the Avon, was projected by Isambard Kingdom Brunel in 1836 but was not completed until 1864. Brunel's SS *Great Britain,* the first ocean-going propeller-driven ship, now forms a museum at the western dockyard, from where she was originally launched in 1843. The docks themselves have been extensively restored and redeveloped; the 19th-century two-storey former tea warehouse is now the Arnolfini Centre for Contemporary Arts, and an 18th-century sail-loft houses the Architecture Centre. On Princes Wharf, 1950s transit sheds have been renovated and converted into the museum of Bristol, M Shed, which opened in 2011.

CAMBRIDGE (1951)

Cambridge, a settlement far older than its ancient university, lies on the River Cam (or Granta). Its industries include technology research and development, and biotechnology. Among its open spaces are Jesus Green, Sheep's Green, Coe Fen, Parker's Piece, Christ's Pieces, the University Botanic Garden, and the 'Backs' – lawns and gardens through which the Cam winds behind the principal line of college buildings. Historical sites east of the Cam include King's Parade, Great St Mary's Church, Gibbs' Senate House and King's College Chapel.

University and college buildings provide the outstanding features of Cambridge's architecture but several churches (especially St Benet's, the oldest building in the city, and Holy Sepulchre or the Round Church) are also notable. The Guildhall (1937) stands on a site of which at least part has held municipal buildings since 1224. In 2009 the University of Cambridge celebrated its 800th anniversary.

CANTERBURY (PRE-1900)

Canterbury, seat of the Archbishop of Canterbury, the primate of the Church of England, dates back to prehistoric times. It was the Roman *Durovernum Cantiacorum* and the Saxon *Cant-wara-byrig* (stronghold of the men of Kent). It was here in 597 that St Augustine began the conversion of the English to Christianity, when Ethelbert, King of Kent, was baptised.

Of the Benedictine St Augustine's Abbey, burial place of the Jutish kings of Kent, only ruins remain. According to Bede, St Martin's Church, on the eastern outskirts of the city, was the place of worship of Queen Bertha, the Christian wife of King Ethelbert, before the advent of St Augustine. In 1170 rivalry of Church and State culminated in the murder of Archbishop Thomas Becket in Canterbury Cathedral, by Henry II's knights. His shrine became a great centre of pilgrimage, as described in Chaucer's *Canterbury Tales.* After the Reformation pilgrimages ceased, the prosperity of the city was strengthened by an influx of Huguenot refugees, who

introduced weaving. The poet and playwright Christopher Marlowe was born and raised in Canterbury and the city is home to the 1,200-seat Marlowe Theatre, which reopened to the public in 2011, following an extensive £25m rebuild.

The cathedral, with its architecture ranging from the 11th to the 15th centuries, is famous worldwide. Visitors are attracted particularly to the Martyrdom, the Black Prince's Tomb and the Warriors' Chapel.

The medieval city walls are built on Roman foundations and the 14th-century West Gate is one of the finest buildings of its kind in the country.

CHESTER (PRE-1900)

Chester is situated on the River Dee. Its recorded history dates from the first century when the Romans founded the fortress of *Deva.* The city's name is derived from the latin *Castra* (a camp or encampment). During the middle ages, Chester was the principal port of north-west England but declined with the silting of the Dee estuary and competition from Liverpool. The city was also an important military centre, notably during Edward I's Welsh campaigns and the Elizabethan Irish campaigns. During the Civil War, Chester supported the king and was besieged from 1643 to 1646. Chester's first charter was granted *c.*1175 and the city was incorporated in 1506. The office of sheriff is the earliest created in the country (1120s), and in 1992 the mayor, who also enjoys the title 'Admiral of the Dee', was made a lord mayor.

The city's architectural features include the city walls (an almost complete two-mile circuit), the unique 13th-century Rows (covered galleries above the street-level shops), the Victorian Gothic town hall (1869), the castle (rebuilt 1788 and 1822) and numerous half-timbered buildings. The cathedral was a Benedictine abbey until the dissolution of the monasteries. Chester racecourse is the oldest racecourse in Britain, believed to have origins in the 13th century. The first recorded horserace was in 1539 during the reign of Henry VIII. Chester also houses the ruins of a Roman amphitheatre, built in the late first century AD.

DURHAM (PRE-1900)

The city of Durham's prominent Norman cathedral and castle are set high on a wooded peninsula overlooking the River Wear. The cathedral was founded as a shrine for the body of St Cuthbert in 995. The present building dates from 1093 and among its many treasures is the tomb of the Venerable Bede (673–735). Durham's prince bishops had unique powers up to 1836, being lay rulers as well as religious leaders. As a palatinate, Durham could have its own army, nobility, coinage and courts. The castle was the main seat of the prince bishops for nearly 800 years; it is now used as a college by the University of Durham. The university, founded in the early 19th century on the initiative of Bishop William Van Mildert, is England's third oldest.

Annual events include Durham's regatta in June (claimed to be the oldest rowing event in Britain) and the annual Gala (formerly Durham Miners' Gala) in July. Durham County Cricket Club was established in 1882.

LEEDS (PRE-1900)

Leeds, situated in the lower Aire valley, was first incorporated by Charles I in 1626. The earliest forms of the name are *Loidis* or *Ledes,* the origins of which are obscure.

The principal buildings are the Civic Hall (1933), the Town Hall (1858), the Municipal Buildings and Art Gallery (1884) with the Henry Moore Gallery (1982), the Corn Exchange (1863) and the university. The parish church of St Peter was rebuilt in 1841 and granted minister status in 2012. The 17th-century St John's Church has a fine interior with a famous English Renaissance screen; the last remaining 18th-century church in the city is Holy Trinity in Boar Lane (1727). Kirkstall Abbey (about three miles from the centre of the city), founded by Henry de Lacy in 1152, is one of the most complete examples of a Cistercian house now remaining. The Royal Armouries Museum forms part of a group of museums that house the national collection of antique arms and armour. The Grand Theatre and Opera House is home to Northern Ballet and Opera North.

LEICESTER (1919)

Leicester is situated in central England. The city was an important Roman settlement and also one of the five 'burghs' or boroughs of the Danelaw. In 1485 Richard III was buried in Leicester following his death at the nearby Battle of Bosworth. In 1589 Queen Elizabeth I granted a charter to the city and the ancient title was confirmed by letters patent in 1919.

The textile industry was responsible for Leicester's early expansion and the city still maintains a strong manufacturing base. Cotton mills and factories are now undergoing extensive regeneration and are being converted into offices, apartments, bars and restaurants. The principal buildings include the two universities (the University of Leicester and De Montfort University), as well as the Town Hall, the 13th-century Guildhall, De Montfort Hall, Leicester Cathedral, the Jewry Wall (the UK's highest standing Roman wall), St Nicholas Church and St Mary de Castro church. The motte and Great Hall of Leicester can be seen from the castle gardens, situated next to the River Soar.

LINCOLN (PRE-1900)

Situated 64km (40 miles) inland on the river Witham, Lincoln derives its name from a contraction of *Lindum Colonia,* the settlement founded in AD 48 by the Romans to command the crossing of Ermine Street and Fosse Way. Sections of the third-century Roman city wall can be seen, including an extant gateway (Newport Arch). The Romans also drained the surrounding fenland and created a canal system, laying the foundations of Lincoln's agricultural prosperity and also the city's importance in the medieval wool trade as a port and staple town.

As one of the five 'burghs' or boroughs of the Danelaw, Lincoln was an important trading centre in the ninth and tenth centuries and prosperity from the wool trade lasted until the 14th century. This wealth enabled local merchants to build parish churches, of which three survive, and there are also remains of a 12th-century Jewish community. However, the removal of the staple to Boston in 1369 heralded a decline, from which the city only recovered fully in the 19th century, when improved fen drainage made Lincoln agriculturally important. Improved canal and rail links led to industrial development, mainly in the manufacture of machinery and engineering products.

The castle was built shortly after the Norman Conquest and is unusual in having two mounds; on one motte stands a keep (Lucy's Tower) added in the 12th century. It currently houses one of the four surviving copies of the Magna Carta. The cathedral was begun c.1073 but was mostly destroyed by fire and earthquake in the 12th century. Rebuilding was begun by St Hugh and completed over a century later. Other notable architectural features are the 12th-century High Bridge, the oldest in Britain still to carry buildings, and the Guildhall, situated above the 15th-century Stonebow gateway.

LIVERPOOL (PRE-1900)

Liverpool, on the north bank of the river Mersey, 5km (3 miles) from the Irish Sea, is the UK's foremost port for Atlantic trade.

There are 2,100 acres of dockland on both sides of the river and the Gladstone and Royal Seaforth Docks can accommodate tanker-sized vessels. Liverpool Free Port was opened in 1984.

Liverpool was created a free borough in 1207 and was given city status in 1880. From the early 18th century it expanded rapidly with the growth of industrialisation and the transatlantic slave trade. Surviving buildings from this period include the Bluecoat Chambers (1717, formerly the Bluecoat School), and the Town Hall (1754, rebuilt to the original design 1795). Notable from the 19th and 20th centuries are the Anglican cathedral (built from the designs of Sir Giles Gilbert Scott, it took 74 years to construct), and the Catholic Metropolitan Cathedral (designed by Sir Frederick Gibberd, consecrated 1967). Both of these cathedrals are situated on Hope Street, named after the merchant William Hope, which is the only street in the UK with a cathedral at either end. The refurbished Albert Dock (designed by Jesse Hartley) contains the Merseyside Maritime Museum, the International Slavery Museum, the Beatles Story and the Tate Liverpool art gallery. The Museum of Liverpool opened in 2011.

MANCHESTER (PRE-1900)

Manchester (the *Mamucium* of the Romans, who occupied it in AD 79) is a commercial and industrial centre connected with the sea by the Manchester Ship Canal, 57km (35.5 miles) long, opened in 1894 and accommodating ships up to 15,000 tons. During the Industrial Revolution the city had a thriving cotton industry and by 1853 there were over 100 cotton mills, which dominated the city's landscape.

The principal buildings are the Town Hall, erected in 1877 from the designs of Alfred Waterhouse, with a large extension of 1938; the Royal Exchange (1869, enlarged 1921); the Central Library (1934); Heaton Hall; the 17th-century Chetham Library; the Rylands Library (1900), which includes the Althorp collection; the university precinct; the 15th-century cathedral (formerly the parish church); the Manchester Central conference and exhibition centre and the Bridgewater Hall (1996) concert venue. Manchester is the home of the Hallé Orchestra, the Royal Northern College of Music, the Royal Exchange Theatre and numerous public art galleries.

The town received its first charter of incorporation in 1838 and was created a city in 1853.

NEWCASTLE UPON TYNE (PRE-1900)

Newcastle upon Tyne, on the north bank of the River Tyne, is 13km (8 miles) from the North Sea. A cathedral and university city, it is the administrative, commercial and cultural centre for north-east England and the principal port.

The principal buildings include the Castle Keep (12th century), Black Gate (13th century), Blackfriars (13th century), West Walls (13th century), St Nicholas Cathedral (15th century, fine lantern tower), St Andrew's Church (12th–14th century), St John's (14th–15th century), All Saints (1786 by Stephenson), St Mary's Roman Catholic Cathedral (1844), Trinity House (17th century), Sandhill (16th-century houses), Guildhall (Georgian), Grey Street (1834–9), Central Station (1846–50) and the Central Library (1969). Open spaces include the Town Moor (927 acres).

Numerous bridges span the Tyne at Newcastle, including the Tyne Bridge (1928) and the Tilting Millennium Bridge (2001) which links the city with Gateshead to the south.

The city's name is derived from the 'new castle' (1080) erected as a defence against the Scots. In 1265 defensive walls over two miles in length were built around the city as further protection; parts of these walls remain today and can be found to the west of the city centre.

NORWICH (PRE-1900)

Norwich grew from an early Anglo-Saxon settlement near the confluence of the rivers Yare and Wensum, and now serves as the provincial capital for the predominantly agricultural region of East Anglia. The name is thought to relate to the most northerly of a group of Anglo-Saxon villages or *wics.* The city's first known charter was granted in 1158 by Henry II.

Norwich serves its surrounding area as a market town and commercial centre. From the 14th century until the Industrial Revolution, Norwich was the regional centre of the woollen industry. Now the biggest single industry is financial services and principal trades are engineering, printing and shoemaking. The University of East Anglia is on the city's western boundary and admitted its first students in 1963. Norwich is accessible to seagoing vessels by means of the river Yare, entered at Great Yarmouth, 32km (20 miles) to the east.

Among many historic buildings are the cathedral (completed in the 12th century and surmounted by a 15th-century spire 96m (315ft) in height); the keep of the Norman castle (now a museum and art gallery); the 15th-century flint-walled Guildhall; some 30 medieval parish churches; St Andrew's and Blackfriars' Halls; the Tudor houses preserved in Elm Hill and the Georgian Assembly House.

NOTTINGHAM (PRE-1900)

Nottingham stands on the river Trent. *Snotingaham* or *Notingeham,* the 'homestead of the people of Snot', is the Anglo-Saxon name for the Celtic settlement of *Tigguocobauc,* or the house of caves. In 878, Nottingham became one of the five 'burghs' or boroughs of the Danelaw. William the Conqueror ordered the construction of Nottingham Castle, while the town itself developed rapidly under Norman rule. Its laws and rights were formally recognised by Henry II's charter in 1155. The castle became a favoured residence of King John. In 1642 Charles I raised his personal standard at Nottingham Castle at the start of the Civil War.

Architecturally, Nottingham has a wealth of notable buildings, particularly those designed in the Victorian era by T. C. Hine and Watson Fothergill. The city council owns the castle (of Norman origin but restored in 1878), Wollaton Hall (1580–8), Newstead Abbey (once the home of Lord Byron), the Guildhall (1888) and the Council House (1929). St Mary's, St Peter's and St Nicholas' churches are of interest, as is the Roman Catholic cathedral (Pugin, 1842–4). Nottingham was granted city status in 1897.

OXFORD (PRE-1900)

Oxford is a university city, an important industrial centre and a market town.

Oxford is known for its architecture, its oldest specimens being the reputedly Saxon tower of St Michael's Church, the remains of the Norman castle and city walls, and the Norman church at Iffley. It also has many Gothic buildings, such as the Divinity Schools, the Old Library at Merton College, William of Wykeham's New College, Magdalen and Christ Church colleges and many other college buildings. Later centuries are represented by the Laudian Quadrangle at St John's College, the Renaissance Sheldonian Theatre by Sir Christopher Wren, Trinity College Chapel, All Saints Church, Hawksmoor's mock-Gothic at All Souls College, and the 18th-century Queen's College. In addition to individual buildings, High Street and Radcliffe Square both form interesting architectural compositions. Most of the colleges have gardens, those of Magdalen, New College, St John's and Worcester being the largest.

The Oxford University Museum of Natural History, renowned for its spectacular neo-Gothic architecture, houses the university's scientific collections of zoological, entomological and geological specimens and is attached to the neighbouring Pitt Rivers Museum, which houses ethnographic and archaeological objects from around the world. The Ashmolean is the city's museum of art and archaeology and

Modern Art Oxford hosts a programme of contemporary art exhibitions.

ST ALBANS (PRE-1900)

The origins of St Albans, situated on the river Ver, stem from the Roman town of *Verulamium.* Named after the first Christian martyr in Britain, who was executed there, St Albans has developed around the Norman abbey and the cathedral church (consecrated 1115), which was built partly of materials from the old Roman city. The museums house Iron Age and Roman artefacts and the Roman theatre, unique in Britain, has a stage as opposed to an amphitheatre. Archaeological excavations in the city centre have revealed evidence of pre-Roman, Saxon and medieval occupation.

The town's significance grew to the extent that it was a signatory and venue for the drafting of the Magna Carta. It was also the scene of riots during the Peasants' Revolt, the French King John was imprisoned there after the Battle of Poitiers, and heavy fighting took place there during the Wars of the Roses.

Previously controlled by the Abbot, the town achieved a charter in 1553 and city status in 1877. The street market, first established in 1553, is still an important feature of the city, as are many hotels and inns, surviving from the days when St Albans was an important coach stop. St Albans is also noted for its clock tower, built between 1403 and 1412, the only remaining medieval town belfry in England.

SALISBURY (PRE-1900)

The history of Salisbury centres around the cathedral and cathedral close. The city evolved from an Iron Age camp a mile to the north of its current position which was strengthened by the Romans and called *Serviodunum.* The Normans built a castle and cathedral on the site and renamed it Sarum. In 1220 Bishop Richard Poore and the architect Elias de Derham decided to build a new Gothic-style cathedral. The cathedral was completed 38 years later and a community known as New Sarum, now called Salisbury, grew around it. Originally the cathedral had a squat tower; the 123m (404ft) spire that makes the cathedral the tallest medieval structure in the world was added c.1315. A walled close with houses for the clergy was built around the cathedral; the Medieval Hall still stands today, alongside buildings dating from the 13th to the 20th century, including some designed by Sir Christopher Wren.

A prosperous wool and cloth trade allowed Salisbury to flourish until the 17th century. When the wool trade declined new crafts were established, including cutlery, leather and basket work, saddlery, lacemaking, joinery and malting. By 1750 it had become an important road junction and coaching centre and in the Victorian era the railways enabled a new age of expansion and prosperity.

SHEFFIELD (PRE-1900)

Sheffield is situated at the confluence of the rivers Sheaf, Porter, Rivelin and Loxley with the river Don and was created a city in 1893.

The parish church of St Peter and St Paul, founded in the 12th century, became the cathedral church of the diocese of Sheffield in 1914. The Roman Catholic Cathedral Church of St Marie (founded 1847) was made a cathedral for the new diocese of Hallam in 1980; parts of the present building date from c.1435. The principal buildings are the Town Hall (1897), the Cutlers' Hall (1832), City Hall (1932), Graves Art Gallery (1934), Mappin Art Gallery, the Crucible Theatre and the restored Lyceum Theatre, which dates from 1897 and was reopened in 1990. Three major sporting and entertainment venues were opened between 1990 and 1991: Sheffield Arena, Pond's Forge and Don Valley Stadium – which was closed and demolished in 2013, but the site is now being redeveloped as the Olympic Legacy Park. The Millennium Galleries opened in 2001. The Leadmill, Sheffield's longest-running independent live music venue, opened in 1980.

SOUTHAMPTON (1964)

Southampton is a major seaport on the south coast of England, situated between the mouths of the Test and Itchen rivers. Southampton's natural deep-water harbour has made the area an important settlement since the Romans built the first port (known as *Clausentum*) in the first century, and Southampton's port has witnessed several important departures, including those of Henry V in 1415 for the Battle of Agincourt, the *Mayflower* in 1620, and the RMS *Titanic* in 1912.

The city's strategic importance, not only as a seaport but also as a centre for aircraft production, meant that it was heavily bombed during the Second World War. However, many historically significant structures remain, including the Wool House, dating from 1417 and now used as the Maritime Museum; parts of the Norman city walls, which are among the most complete in the UK; the Bargate, which was originally the main gateway into the city; God's House Tower, now the Museum of Archaeology; St Michael's, the city's oldest church; and the Tudor Merchants Hall.

WINCHESTER (PRE-1900)

Winchester, the ancient capital of England, is situated on the river Itchen. The city is rich in architecture of all types, and especially notable is the cathedral. Built in 1079–93 the cathedral exhibits examples of Norman, early English and Perpendicular styles and is the burial place of author Jane Austen. Winchester College, founded in 1382, is one of the country's most famous public schools, and the original building (1393) remains largely unaltered. St Cross Hospital, another great medieval foundation, lies one mile south of the city. The almshouses were founded in 1136 by Bishop Henry de Blois, and Cardinal Henry Beaufort added a new almshouse of 'Noble Poverty' in 1446. The chapel and dwellings are of great architectural interest, and visitors may still receive the 'Wayfarer's Dole' of bread and ale, a tradition now 900 years old.

Excavations have done much to clarify the origins and development of Winchester. Part of the forum and several of the streets from the Roman town have been discovered. Excavations in the cathedral close have uncovered the entire site of the Anglo-Saxon cathedral (known as the Old Minster) and parts of the New Minster which was built by Alfred the Great's son, Edward the Elder, and is the burial place of the Alfredian dynasty. The original burial place of St Swithun, before his remains were translated to a site in the present cathedral, was also uncovered.

Excavations in other parts of the city have cast much light on Norman Winchester, notably on the site of the Royal Castle (adjacent to which the new Law Courts have been built) and in the grounds of Wolvesey Castle, where the great house built by bishops Giffard and Henry de Blois in the 12th century has been uncovered. The Great Hall, built by Henry III between 1222 and 1236, survives and houses the Arthurian Round Table.

YORK (PRE-1900)

The city of York is an archiepiscopal seat. Its recorded history dates from AD 71, when the Roman Ninth Legion established a base under Petilius Cerealis that would later become the fortress of *Eburacum,* or *Eboracum.* In Anglo-Saxon times the city was the royal and ecclesiastical centre of Northumbria, and after capture by a Viking army in AD 866 it became the capital of the Viking kingdom of Jorvik. By the 14th century the city had become a great mercantile centre, mainly because of its control of the wool trade, and was used as the chief base against the Scots. Under the Tudors its fortunes declined, although Henry VIII made it the headquarters of the Council of the North. Excavations on many sites, including Coppergate, have greatly expanded knowledge of Roman, Viking and medieval urban life. The JORVIK Viking Centre (reopened in 2017) takes visitors on a journey through a reconstructed 10th century Viking-age York.

The city is rich in examples of architecture of all periods. The earliest church was built in AD 627 and, from the 12th to 15th centuries, the present Minster was built in a succession of styles.

LORD-LIEUTENANTS AND HIGH SHERIFFS

Area	Lord-Lieutenant	High Sheriff (2018–19)
Bedfordshire	Helen Nellis	Arthur Polhill
Berkshire	James Puxley	Graham Barker
Bristol	Lois Golding, OBE	Roger Opie
Buckinghamshire	Sir Henry Aubrey-Fletcher, Bt.	Prof. Ruth Farwell, CBE
Cambridgeshire	Julie Spence, OBE, QPM	Dr Andrew Harter, CBE
Cheshire	David Briggs, MBE	Alexis Redmond, MBE
Cornwall	Col. Edward Bolitho, OBE	Sarah Coryton
Cumbria	Claire Hensman	Simon Berry
Derbyshire	William Tucker	Lucy Palmer
Devon	David Fursdon	Grania Phillips
Dorset	Angus Campbell	Jacqueline Swift
Durham	Susan Snowden	Dr Stephen Cronin
East Riding of Yorkshire	Hon. Susan Cunliffe-Lister	Deborah Rosenberg
East Sussex	Peter Field	Maj.-Gen. John Moore-Bick, CBE
Essex	Jennifer Tolhurst	Bryan Burrough
Gloucestershire	Dame Janet Trotter, DBE, CVO	Charles Martell
Greater London	Kenneth Olisa, OBE	Charles Spicer
Greater Manchester	Warren Smith	Kui Yeung, OBE
Hampshire	Nigel Atkinson	Mark Thistlethwayte
Herefordshire	Countess of Darnley	Thomas Hone
Hertfordshire	Robert Voss, CBE	Suzana Harvey
Isle of Wight	Maj.-Gen. Martin White, CD, CBE	Gioia Minghella-Giddens
Kent	Viscount De L'Isle, MBE	Susan Ashton
Lancashire	Lord Shuttleworth, KG, KCVO	Robert Webb
Leicestershire	Lady Gretton, DCVO	Diana Thompson
Lincolnshire	Toby Dennis	Ian Walter
Merseyside	Mark Blundell	Stephen Burrows
Norfolk	Richard Jewson	Charles Watt
North Yorkshire	Barry Dodd, CBE	Christopher Legard
Northamptonshire	David Laing	James Watson
Northumberland	Duchess of Northumberland	Michael Orde
Nottinghamshire	Sir John Peace	Nicholas Ebbs
Oxfordshire	Tim Stevenson, OBE	Richard Venables
Rutland	Dr Sarah Furness	Margaret Jarron
Shropshire	Sir Algernon Heber-Percy, KCVO	Rhoderick Swire
Somerset	Anne Maw	Denis Burn
South Yorkshire	Andrew Coombe	Barry Eldred
Staffordshire	Ian Dudson, CBE	Phillipa Gee
Suffolk	Countess of Euston	George Vestey
Surrey	Michael More-Molyneux	William Glover
Tyne and Wear	Susan Winfield, OBE	Paul Callaghan, CBE
Warwickshire	Timothy Cox	Clare Sawdon
West Midlands	John Crabtree, OBE	Christopher Loughran
West Sussex	Susan Pyper	Caroline Nicholls
West Yorkshire	Dame Dr Ingrid Roscoe, DCVO	Charles Jackson, MBE
Wiltshire	Sarah Troughton	Nicola Alberry
Worcestershire	Lt.-Col. Patrick Holcroft, LVO, OBE	Cassian Roberts

COMBINED AUTHORITIES

Authority	Constituent Councils*	Non-constituent Councils*	Pop.†	Mayor, Political Party
Cambridgeshire & Peterborough	Cambridge, Cambridgeshire, E. Cambridgeshire, Fenland, Huntingdonshire, Peterborough, S. Cambridgeshire	–	847,151	James Palmer, *C.*
Greater Manchester	Bolton, Bury, Manchester, Oldham, Rochdale, Salford, Stockport, Tameside, Trafford, Wigan	–	2,798,799	Andy Burnham, *Lab.*
Liverpool City Region	Halton, Knowsley, Liverpool, St Helens, Sefton, Wirral	Warrington, W. Lancashire	1,544,420	Steve Rotheram, *Lab.*
North East	Durham, Gateshead, Newcastle upon Tyne, N. Tyneside, Northumberland, S. Tyneside, Sunderland	–	1,972,230	None
Sheffield City Region	Barnsley, Doncaster, Rotherham, Sheffield	Bassetlaw, Bolsover, Chesterfield, Derbyshire Dales, N. E. Derbyshire	1,393,445	Dan Jarvis, *Lab.*
Tees Valley	Darlington, Hartlepool, Middlesbrough, Redcar & Cleveland, Stockton-On-Tees	–	672,497	Ben Houchen, *C.*
West of England	Bath & N. E. Somerset, Bristol, S. Gloucestershire	–	926,957	Tim Bowles, *C.*
West Midlands	Birmingham, Coventry, Dudley, Sandwell, Solihull, Walsall, Wolverhampton	Cannock Chase, N. Warwickshire, Nuneaton & Bedworth, Redditch, Rugby, Shropshire, Stratford-on-Avon, Tamworth, Telford & Wrekin, Warwickshire	2,897,303	Andy Street, *C.*
West Yorkshire	Bradford, Calderdale, Kirklees, Leeds, Wakefield	York	2,307,035	None

COUNTY COUNCILS

Council & Administrative HQ	Telephone	Population†	Council Tax‡	Chief Executive§
Buckinghamshire, Aylesbury	01296-395000	535,918	£1,291	Rachael Shimmin, OBE
Cambridgeshire, Cambridge	0345-045 5200	648,237	£1,250	Gillian Beasley
Cumbria, Carlisle	01228-606060	498,375	£1,332	Katherine Fairclough
Derbyshire, Matlock	01629-580000	791,966	£1,272	Paul Wilson
Devon, Exeter	0345-155 1015	787,171	£1,331	Dr Phil Norrey
Dorset, Dorchester	01305-221000	424,667	£1,406	Debbie Ward
East Sussex, Lewes	0345-608 0190	552,259	£1,393	Becky Shaw
Essex, Chelmsford	0845-7430 430	1,468,177	£1,222	Gavin Jones
Gloucestershire, Gloucester	01452-425000	628,139	£1,232	Peter Bungard
Hampshire, Winchester	0300-555 1375	1,370,728	£1,201	John Coughlan, CBE
Hertfordshire, Hertford	0300-123 4040	1,180,934	£1,320	John Wood
Kent, Maidstone	0300-041 4141	1,554,636	£1,238	David Cockburn
Lancashire, Preston	0300-123 6701	1,201,855	£1,295	Angie Ridgwell *(interim)*
Leicestershire, Leicester	0116-232 3232	690,212	£1,243	John Sinnott
Lincolnshire, Lincoln	01522-552222	751,171	£1,231	Keith Ireland
Norfolk, Norwich	0344-800 8020	898,390	£1,323	Dr Wendy Thomson, CBE
North Yorkshire, Northallerton	01609-780780	611,633	£1,249	Richard Flinton
Northamptonshire, Northampton	0300-126 1000	741,209	£1,236	Theresa Grant
Nottinghamshire, Nottingham	0115-982 3823	817,851	£1,419	Anthony May
Oxfordshire, Oxford	01865-792422	682,444	£1,426	Peter Clark
Somerset, Taunton	0300-123 2224	555,195	£1,192	Patrick Flaherty
Staffordshire, Stafford	0300-111 8000	870,825	£1,211	John Henderson, CB
Suffolk, Ipswich	03456-606 6067	756,978	£1,243	Nicola Beach
Surrey, Kingston upon Thames	0345-600 9009	1,185,321	£1,411	Joanna Killian
Warwickshire, Warwick	01926-410410	564,562	£1,364	David Carter & Monica Fogarty
West Sussex, Chichester	01243-777100	852,353	£1,318	Nathan Elvery
Worcestershire, Worcester	01905-763763	588,370	£1,212	Paul Robinson

*See the following pages for information on individual constituent and non-constituent councils
† *Source:* Office for National Statistics – *Mid-2017 Population Estimates* (Crown copyright)
‡ Average 2018–19 Band D council tax in the county area inclusive of the adult social care precept, but exclusive of precepts for fire authorities and Police and Crime Commissioners. County councils claim their share of the combined council tax from the collection funds of the district authorities within their area. Band D council tax bills for the billing authority are given on the following pages
§ Or equivalent postholder

DISTRICT COUNCILS

District Council	Telephone	Pop.*	Council Tax†	Chief Executive‡
Adur	01273-263000	63,506	£1,794	Alex Bailey
Allerdale	01900-702702	97,213	£1,800	Ian Frost
Amber Valley	01773-570222	125,898	£1,750	Sylvia Delahay & Julian Townsend
Arun	01903-737500	156,997	£1,731	Nigel Lynn
Ashfield	01623-450000	126,164	£1,887	Robert Mitchell
Ashford	01233-331111	127,527	£1,675	Tracey Kerly
Aylesbury Vale	01296-585858	196,020	£1,776	Andrew Grant
Babergh	01473-822801	90,794	£1,670	Arthur Charvonia
Barrow-in-Furness	01229-876543	67,099	£1,799	Phil Huck
Basildon	01268-533333	184,479	£1,739	Scott Logan
Basingstoke and Deane	01256-844844	175,337	£1,581	Melbourne Barrett
Bassetlaw	01909-533533	116,304	£1,893	Neil Taylor
Blaby	0116-275 0555	98,977	£1,760	Jane Toman
Bolsover	01246-242424	79,098	£1,840	Daniel Swaine
Boston	01205-314200	68,488	£1,691	Phil Drury
Braintree	01376-552525	151,677	£1,675	Andy Wright
Breckland	01362-656870	138,602	£1,726	Anna Graves
Brentwood	01277-312500	76,575	£1,660	Philip Ruck
Broadland	01603-431133	128,535	£1,751	Phil Kirby
Bromsgrove	01527-881288	97,594	£1,732	Kevin Dicks
Broxbourne	01992-785555	96,762	£1,613	Jeff Stack
Broxtowe	0115-917 7777	112,618	£1,879	Ruth Hyde, OBE
Burnley	01282 425011	87,705	£1,836	Mick Cartledge
CAMBRIDGE	01223-457000	124,919	£1,709	Antoinette Jackson
Cannock Chase	01543-462621	99,126	£1,714	Tony McGovern
CANTERBURY	01227-862000	164,100	£1,702	Colin Carmichael
CARLISLE	01228-817000	108,274	£1,790	Dr Jason Gooding
Castle Point	01268-882200	89,814	£1,720	David Marchant
Charnwood	01509-263151	180,387	£1,709	Geoffrey Parker
CHELMSFORD	01245-606606	176,194	£1,688	Nick Eveleigh
Cheltenham	01242-262626	117,530	£1,668	Pat Pratley
Cherwell	01295-227001	147,602	£1,825	Yvonne Rees
Chesterfield	01246-345345	104,579	£1,714	Huw Bowen
Chichester	01243-785166	118,175	£1,698	Diane Shepherd
Chiltern	01494-729000	95,355	£1,785	Bob Smith
Chorley	01257-515151	115,772	£1,745	Gary Hall
Christchurch	01202-495000	49,481	£1,888	David McIntosh
Colchester	01206-282222	190,098	£1,674	Adrian Pritchard
Copeland	01946-598300	68,689	£1,816	Mike Starkie
Corby	01536-464000	69,540	£1,655	Norman Stronach
Cotswold	01285-623000	85,756	£1,658	Nigel Adams
Craven	01756-700600	56,604	£1,779	Paul Shevlin
Crawley	01293-438000	111,375	£1,683	Natalie Brahma-Pearl
Dacorum	01442-228000	153,316	£1,694	Sally Marshall
Dartford	01322-343434	107,516	£1,689	Graham Harris
Daventry	01327-871100	82,638	£1,691	Ian Vincent
Derbyshire Dales	01629-761100	71,849	£1,796	Paul Wilson
Dover	01304-821199	115,803	£1,727	Nadeem Aziz
East Cambridgeshire	01353-665555	88,858	£1,732	John Hill
East Devon	01395-516551	139,908	£1,805	Mark Williams
East Dorset	01202-886201	89,093	£1,963	David McIntosh
East Hampshire	01730-266551	119,392	£1,650	Sandy Hopkins
East Hertfordshire	01279-655261	147,080	£1,715	Liz Watts
East Lindsey	01507-601111	139,718	£1,641	Stuart Davy
East Northamptonshire	01832-742000	93,135	£1,705	David Oliver
East Staffordshire	01283-508000	117,552	£1,687	Andy O'Brien
Eastbourne	01323-410000	103,251	£1,890	Robert Cottrill
Eastleigh	023-8068 8000	130,498	£1,640	Nick Tustian
Eden	01768-817817	52,779	£1,806	Rose Rouse
Elmbridge	01372-474474	132,764	£1,864	Robert Moran
Epping Forest	01992-564000	130,576	£1,679	Derek Macnab (acting)
Epsom and Ewell	01372-732000	79,588	£1,840	Kathryn Beldon
Erewash	0115-907 2244	115,314	£1,731	Lorraine Poyser (acting)
EXETER	01392-277888	129,801	£1,745	Karime Hassan
Fareham	01329-236100	116,219	£1,599	Peter Grimwood
Fenland	01354-654321	100,776	£1,825	Paul Medd
Forest Heath	01638-719000	65,523	£1,668	Ian Gallin
Forest of Dean	01594-810000	,385	£1,708	Sue Pangbourne
Fylde	01253-658658	78,863	£1,774	Allan Oldfield

Gedling	0115-901 3901	117,128	£1,874	John Robinson
GLOUCESTER	01452-396396	1,488	£1,661	Peter Bungard
Gosport	023-9258 4242	85,509	£1,663	David Williams
Gravesham	01474-564422	106,121	£1,689	David Hughes
Great Yarmouth	01493-856100	99,417	£1,722	Sheila Oxtoby
Guildford	01483-505050	148,020	£1,843	James Whiteman
Hambleton	01619-779977	90,718	£1,696	Dr Justin Ives
Harborough	01858-828282	91,461	£1,721	Beverley Jolly & Norman Proudfoot
Harlow	01279-446655	86,191	£1,733	Brian Keane
Harrogate	01423-500600	1600,044	£1,800	Wallace Sampson
Hart	01252-622122	95,465	£1,688	Patricia Hughes & Daryl Phillips
Hastings	01424-451066	92,813	£1,908	Neil Taylor *(acting)*
Havant	023-9244 6019	125,065	£1,643	Sandy Hopkins
Hertsmere	020-8207 2277	104,031	£1,686	Dr Donald Graham
High Peak	0345-129 7777	92,063	£1,745	Simon Baker
Hinckley and Bosworth	01455-238141	111,370	£1,686	Bill Cullen
Horsham	01403-215100		£1,687	Glen Chip
Huntingdonshire	01480-388388	176,979	£1,753	Jo Lancaster
Hyndburn	01254-388111	80,410	£1,781	David Welsby
Ipswich	01473-432000	138,480	£1,783	Russell Williams
Kettering	01536-410333	100,252	£1,682	Graham Soulsby
King's Lynn and West Norfolk	0155-616200	151,945	£1,733	Ray Harding
LANCASTER	01524-582000	142,487	£1,775	Susan Parsonage
Lewes	01273-471600	102,257	£1,944	Robert Cottrill
Lichfield	01543-308000	103,507	£1,693	Diane Tilley
LINCOLN	01522-881188	98,438	£1,716	Angela Andrews
Maidstone	01622-602000	167,730	£1,765	Alison Broom
Maldon	01621-854477	63,975	£1,713	Fiona Marshall
Malvern Hills	01684-862151	77,165	£1,714	Jack Hegarty
Mansfield	01623-463463	108,576	£1,881	Hayley Barsby
Melton	01664-502502	50,873	£1,737	Edd de Coverly
Mendip	0300-3038588	112,545	£1,717	Stuart Brown
Mid Devon	01884-255255	79,789	£1,856	Stephen Walford
Mid Suffolk	01449-720711	101,543	£1,664	Arthur Charvonia
Mid Sussex	01444-458166	147,089	£1,714	Kathryn Hall
Mole Valley	01306-885001	86,223	£1,829	Karen Brimacombe
New Forest	023-8028 5000	179,590	£1,694	Bob Jackson
Newark and Sherwood	01636-650000	120,965	£1,936	Kirsty Cole *(acting)*
Newcastle-under-Lyme	01782-717717	128,963	£1,682	John Sellgren
North Devon	01271-327711	94,615	£1,838	Mike Mansell
North Dorset	01258-454111	71,064	£1,925	Matt Prosser
North East Derbyshire	01246-231111	100,780	£1,825	Daniel Swaine
North Hertfordshire	01462-474000	133,321	£1,730	David Scholes
North Kesteven	01529-414155	115,230	£1,694	Ian Fytche
North Norfolk	01263-513811	104,067	£1,751	Nick Baker & Steve Blatch
North Warwickshire	01827-715341	64,069	£1,823	Jerry Hutchinson
North West Leicestershire	01530-454545	100,109	£1,741	Beverley Smith
Northampton	0300-330 7000	225,656	£1,694	David Kennedy
NORWICH	0344-980 3333	140,353	£1,808	Laura McGillivray
Nuneaton and Bedworth	024-7637 6376	128,659	£1,795	Alan Franks
Oadby and Wigston	0116-288 8961	57,035	£1,725	Mark Hall
OXFORD	01865-249811	161,291	£1,912	Gordon Mitchell *(interim)*
Pendle	01282-661661	90,696	£1,872	Dean Langton & Philip Mousdale
PRESTON	01772-906900	141,346	£1,852	Lorraine Norris
Purbeck	01929-556561	46,336	£1,957	Steve Mackenzie
Redditch	01527-64252	85,204	£1,726	Kevin Dicks
Reigate and Banstead	01737-276000	145,648	£1,875	John Jory
Ribble Valley	01200-425111	59,504	£1,710	Marshal Scott
Richmondshire	01748-829100	53,699	£1,793	Tony Clark
Rochford	01702-318111	86,209	£1,731	Nick Khan & Shaun Scrutton
Rossendale	01706-217777	70,365	£1,806	Stuart Sugarman
Rother	01424-787000	94,997	£1,884	Malcolm Johnston & Dr Anthony Leonard
Rugby	01788-533533	106,350	£1,773	Adam Norburn
Runnymede	01932-838383	86,889	£1,807	Paul Turrell
Rushcliffe	0115-981 9911	115,996	£1,890	Allen Graham
Rushmoor	01252-398398	95,917	£1,643	Paul Shackley
Ryedale	01653-600666	54,311	£1,789	Janet Waggott
ST ALBANS	01727-866100	147,095	£1,700	James Blake
St Edmundsbury	01284-763233	113,725	£1,674	Ian Gallin

Scarborough	01723-232323	108,370	£1,801	Jim Dillon
Sedgemoor	0845-408 2540	121,436	£1,684	Kerry Rickards
Selby	01757-705101	87,887	£1,784	Janet Waggott
Sevenoaks	01732-227000	119,429	£1,776	Dr Pav Ramewal
Shepway	01303-853000	111,427	£1,800	Alistair Stewart
South Bucks	01895-837200	69,785	£1,769	Bob Smith
South Cambridgeshire	0345-045 0500	156,705	£1,746	Alex Colyer *(acting)*
South Derbyshire	01283-595795	1002,385	£1,722	Frank McArdle
South Hams	01803-861234	84,306	£1,822	Sophie Hosking & Steve Jorden
South Holland	01775-761161	93,295	£1,656	Anna Graves
South Kesteven	01476-406080	141,662	£1,638	Beverly Agass
South Lakeland	01539-733333	104,321	£1,791	Lawrence Conway
South Norfolk	01508-533633	135,471	£1,773	Sandra Dinneen
South Northamptonshire	01327-322322	91,074	£1,723	Yvonne Rees
South Oxfordshire	01235-520202	138,128	£1,811	David Hill
South Ribble	01772-421491	110,400	£1,765	Jean Hunter *(interim)*
South Somerset	01935-462462	165,645	£1,720	Alex Parmley
South Staffordshire	01902-696000	111,890	£1,641	Dave Heywood
Spelthorne	01784-451499	98,902	£1,845	Roberto Tambini
Stafford	01785-619000	134,764	£1,651	Ian Thompson
Staffordshire Moorlands	0345-605 3010	98,496	£1,671	Simon Baker
Stevenage	01438-242242	87,739	£1,689	Scott Crudgington
Stratford-on-Avon	01789-267575	152,202	£1,764	Dave Buckland & Dave Webb
Stroud	01453-766321	117,381	£1,744	David Hagg
Suffolk Coastal	01394-383789	129,016	£1,657	Stephen Balter
Surrey Heath	01276-707100	88,387	£1,880	Karen Whelan
Swale	01795-417850	146,694	£1,677	Mark Radford *(interim)*
Tamworth	01827-709709	76,527	£1,648	Tony Goodwin
Tandridge	01883-722000	86,665	£1,880	Louise Round
Taunton Deane	01823-356356	115,515	£1,644	Penny James
Teignbridge	01626-361101	129,856	£1,835	Phil Shears
Tendring	01255-686868	144,705	£1,660	Ian Davidson
Test Valley	01264-368000	123,957	£1,623	Roger Tetstall
Tewkesbury	01684-295010	88,589	£1,630	Michael Dawson
Thanet	01843-577000	141,337	£1,749	Madeline Homer
Three Rivers	01923-776611	92,641	£1,704	Dr Steven Halls
Tonbridge and Malling	01732-844522	128,891	£1,741	Julie Beilby
Torridge	01237-428700	66,977	£1,821	Jenny Wallace
Tunbridge Wells	01892-526121	118,061	£1,709	William Benson
Uttlesford	01799-510510	87,684	£1,695	Dawn French
Vale of White Horse	01235-520202	128,738	£1,811	David Hill
Warwick	01926-410410	140,282	£1,758	Chris Elliott
Watford	01923-226400	96,7675	£1,747	Manny Lewis
Waveney	01502-562111	117,897	£1,664	Stephen Baker
Waverley	01483-523333	123,768	£1,883	Paul Wenham
Wealden	01323-443322	158,941	£1,935	Charles Lant
Wellingborough	01933-229777	78,194	£1,626	Liz Elliott *(interim)*
Welwyn & Hatfield	01707-357000	122,274	£1,730	Rob Bridge
West Devon	01822-813600	54,582	£1,896	Sophie Hosking & Steve Jorden
West Dorset	01305-251010	101,382	£1,926	Matt Prosser
West Lancashire	01695-577177	113,881	£1,755	Kim Webber
West Lindsey	01427-676676	94,340	£1,722	Manjeet Gill
West Oxfordshire	01993-861000	108,674	£1,786	Christine Gore & Frank Wilson
West Somerset	01643-703704	34,306	£1,699	Penny James
Weymouth and Portland	01305-838000	65,371	£1,991	Matt Prosser
WINCHESTER	01962-840222	123,879	£1,665	Laura Taylor
Woking	01483-755855	99,695	£1,881	Ray Morgan, OBE
WORCESTER	01905-722233	102,314	£1,676	David Blake
Worthing	01903-239999	108,605	£1,715	Alex Bailey
Wychavon	01386-565000	125,378	£1,658	Jack Hegarty
Wycombe	01494-461000	174,758	£1,718	Karen Satterford
Wyre	01253-891000	110,426	£1,752	Garry Payne
Wyre Forest	01562-732928	100,715	£1,732	Ian Miller

* *Source*: Office for National Statistics – *Mid-2017 Population Estimates* (Crown copyright)
† Band D council tax bill for 2018–19 inclusive of adult social care and parish precepts
‡ Or equivalent postholder
Councils in CAPITAL LETTERS have city status

METROPOLITAN BOROUGH COUNCILS

Metropolitan Borough Council	Telephone	Pop.*	Council Tax†	Chief Executive‡
Barnsley	01226-770770	243,341	£1,667	Diana Terris
BIRMINGHAM	0121-303 1111	1,137,123	£1,510	Dawn Baxendale
Bolton	01204-333333	284,813	£1,701	Tony Oakman
BRADFORD	01274-432001	534,800	£1,573	Kersten England
Bury	0161-253 5000	189,628	£1,749	Geoff Little
Calderdale	01422-288001	209,454	£1,681	Robin Tuddenham
COVENTRY	0500-834 333	360,149	£1,762	Dr Martin Reeves
Doncaster	01302-736000	308,940	£1,556	Jo Miller
Dudley	0300-555 2345	319,419	£1,459	Sarah Norman
Gateshead	0191-433 3000	202,419	£1,877	Sheena Ramsey
Kirklees	01484-221000	437,145	£1,698	Jacqui Gedman
Knowsley	0151-489 6000	148,560	£1,729	Mike Harden
LEEDS	0113-222 4444	784,846	£1,574	Tom Riordan
LIVERPOOL	0151-233 3000	491,549	£1,857	vacant
MANCHESTER	0161-234 5000	545,501	£1,567	Joanne Roney, OBE
NEWCASTLE UPON TYNE	0191-278 7878	295,842	£1,772	Pat Ritchie
North Tyneside	0191-643 5991	204,473	£1,713	Patrick Melia
Oldham	0161-770 3000	233,759	£1,809	Dr Carolyn Wilkins, OBE
Rochdale	01706-647474	218,459	£1,764	Steve Rumbelow
Rotherham	01709-382121	263,375	£1,759	Sharon Kemp
St Helens	01744-676789	179,331	£1,665	Mike Palin
SALFORD	0161-794 4711	251,332	£1,759	Jim Taylor
Sandwell	0121-569 2200	325,460	£1,535	Jan Britton
Sefton	0345 140 0845	274,589	£1,792	Margaret Carney
SHEFFIELD	0114-273 4567	577,789	£1,759	John Mothersole
Solihull	0121-704 8001	213,933	£1,525	Nick Page
South Tyneside	0191-427 7000	149,555	£1,698	Martin Swales
Stockport	0161-480 4949	291,045	£1,840	Pam Smith
SUNDERLAND	0191-520 5555	277,249	£1,550	Irene Lucas, CBE
Tameside	0161-342 8355	224,119	£1,656	Steven Pleasant
Trafford	0161-912 2000	235,493	£1,489	Theresa Grant
WAKEFIELD	0845-850 6506	340,790	£1,590	Merran McRae
Walsall	01922-650000	281,293	£1,836	Dr Helen Paterson
Wigan	01942-244991	324,650	£1,533	Donna Hall
Wirral	0151-606 2000	322,796	£1,734	Eric Robinson
WOLVERHAMPTON	01902-551155	259,926	£1,728	Keith Ireland

* Source: Office for National Statistics – Mid-2017 Population Estimates (Crown copyright)
† Band D council tax bill for 2018–19 inclusive of adult social care and parish precepts
‡ Or equivalent postholder
Councils in CAPITAL LETTERS have city status

UNITARY COUNCILS

Unitary Council	Telephone	Pop.*	Council Tax†	Chief Executive‡
Bath and North East Somerset	01225-477000	187,751	£1,652	Ashley Ayre
Bedford	01234-267422	168,751	£1,773	Philip Simpkins
Blackburn with Darwen	01254-585585	147,049	£1,715	Harry Catherall
Blackpool	01253-477477	139,195	£1,756	Neil Jack
Bournemouth	01202-451451	197,657	£1,718	Jane Portman
Bracknell Forest	01344-352000	119,447	£1,584	Timothy Wheadon
BRIGHTON AND HOVE	01273-290000	289,229	£1,807	Geoff Raw
BRISTOL	0117-922 2000	454,213	£1,891	vacant
Central Bedfordshire	0300-300 8000	278,937	£1,876	Richard Carr
Cheshire East	0300-123 5500	376,695	£1,706	Mike Suarez
Cheshire West and Chester	0300-123 8123	335,680	£1,729	Gerald Meehan
Cornwall	0300-123 4100	553,687	£1,772	Kate Kennally
Darlington	01325-380651	105,646	£1,749	Paul Wildsmith
DERBY	01332-293111	256,233	£1,643	Carole Mills
DURHAM	0300-026000	522,143	£1,887	Terry Collins
East Riding of Yorkshire	01482-393939	337,696	£1,737	Caroline Lacey
Halton	0303-333 4300	126,903	£1,633	David Parr
Hartlepool	01429-266522	92,817	£1,925	Gill Alexander
Herefordshire	01432-260000	183,309	£1,785	Alistair Neill
Isle of Wight	01983-821000	139,798	£1,807	John Metcalfe
Isles of Scilly§	01720-424000	2,308	£1,428	Theo Leijser
KINGSTON-UPON-HULL	01482-609100	260,240	£1,613	Matt Jukes
LEICESTER	0116 254 1000	348,343	£1,771	Andy Keeling
Luton	01582-546000	216,791	£1,709	Trevor Holden
Medway	01634-333333	278,542	£1,624	Neil Davies
Middlesbrough	01642-245432	140,398	£1,869	Tony Parkinson
Milton Keynes	01908-691691	264,479	£1,673	Carole Mills
North East Lincolnshire	01472-313131	159,144	£1,783	Rob Walsh
North Lincolnshire	01724-296296	170,786	£1,742	Denise Hyde
North Somerset	01934-888888	211,681	£1,667	Mike Jackson
Northumberland	0345-600 6400	316,002	£1,827	Daljit Lally
NOTTINGHAM	0115-915 5555	325,282	£1,961	Ian Curryer
PETERBOROUGH	01733-747474	197,095	£1,583	Gillian Beasley
PLYMOUTH	01752-668000	264,199	£1,743	Tracey Lee
Poole	01202-633633	151,500	£1,679	Andrew Flockhart
PORTSMOUTH	023-9282 2251	214,832	£1,580	David Williams
Reading	0118-937 3787	162,666	£1,827	Peter Sloman
Redcar and Cleveland	0164-277 4774	135,404	£1,834	Amanda Skelton, CBE
Rutland	01572-722577	38,606	£1,936	Helen Briggs
Shropshire	0345-678 9000	313,373	£1,700	Clive Wright
Slough	01753-475111	147,181	£1,583	Nigel Pallace *(interim)*
South Gloucestershire	01454-868009	277,623	£1,783	Amanda Deeks
SOUTHAMPTON	023-8083 3000	254,275	£1,734	Richard Crouch *(interim)*
Southend-on-Sea	01702-215000	179,799	£1,569	Alison Griffin
Stockton-on-Tees	01642-393939	195,681	£1,861	Neil Schneider
STOKE-ON-TRENT	01782-234567	253,226	£1,534	shared between six directors
Swindon	01793-463000	217,905	£1,672	John Gilbert
Telford and Wrekin	01952-380000	172,976	£1,640	Richard Partington
Thurrock	01375-652652	167,025	£1,527	Lyn Carpenter
Torbay	01803-201201	133,833	£1,738	Steve Parrock
Warrington	01925-443322	208,809	£1,675	Prof. Steven Broomhead
West Berkshire	01635-42400	156,837	£1,773	Nick Carter
Wiltshire	0300-456 0100	488,409	£1,778	C. Brand; T. Herbert; A. Cunningham
Windsor and Maidenhead	01628-683800	148,814	£1,275	Alison Alexander
Wokingham	0118-974 6000	161,878	£1,741	Manjeet Gill
YORK	01904-551550	208,367	£1,601	Mary Weastell

* *Source*: Office for National Statistics – *Mid-2016 Population Estimates* (Crown copyright)
† Band D council tax bill for 2018–19 inclusive of adult social care and parish precepts
‡ Or equivalent postholder
§ Under the Isles of Scilly Clause the council has additional functions to other unitary authorities

Councils in CAPITAL LETTERS have city status

MAP OF COUNTY, METROPOLITAN, UNITARY AND LONDON BOROUGH COUNCILS IN ENGLAND

1 Stockton-on-Tees
2 Middlesbrough
3 Blackpool
4 Blackburn with Darwen
5 Bolton
6 Bury
7 Rochdale
8 Salford
9 Oldham
10 Liverpool
11 Knowsley
12 St Helens
13 Halton
14 Warrington
15 Trafford
16 Manchester
17 Tameside
18 Stockport
19 Nottingham
20 Telford and Wrekin
21 Wolverhampton
22 Walsall
23 Sandwell
24 Dudley
25 Birmingham
26 Solihull
27 Coventry
28 Peterborough
29 South Glos
30 Bristol
31 Bath and NE Somerset
32 Windsor and Maidenhead
33 Slough
34 Reading
35 Wokingham
36 Bracknell Forest
37 Thurrock
38 Southend
39 Medway
40 Plymouth
41 Torbay
42 Bournemouth

LONDON

1 Hillingdon
2 Harrow
3 Barnet
4 Enfield
5 Waltham Forest
6 Redbridge
7 Barking and Dagenham
8 Havering
9 Ealing
10 Brent
11 Camden
12 Haringey
13 Islington
14 Hackney
15 Newham
16 Hounslow
17 Hammersmith and Fulham
18 Kensington and Chelsea
19 City of Westminster
20 City of London
21 Tower Hamlets
22 Richmond upon Thames
23 Wandsworth
24 Lambeth
25 Southwark
26 Lewisham
27 Greenwich
28 Bexley
29 Kingston upon Thames
30 Merton
31 Sutton
32 Croydon
33 Bromley

LONDON

The Greater London Council was abolished in 1986 and London was divided into 32 borough councils, which have a status similar to the metropolitan borough councils in the rest of England, and the City of London Corporation.

In March 1998 the government announced proposals for a Greater London Authority (GLA) covering the area of the 32 London boroughs and the City of London, which would comprise a directly elected mayor and a 25-member assembly. A referendum was held in London on 7 May 1998 and 72 per cent of voters balloted in favour of the GLA. A London mayor was elected on 4 May 2000 and the authority assumed its responsibilities on 3 July 2000 (*see also* Regional Government).

LONDON BOROUGH COUNCILS

The London boroughs have whole council elections every four years, in the year immediately following the county council election year. The most recent elections took place on 3 May 2018.

The borough councils have responsibility for the following functions: building regulations, cemeteries and crematoria, consumer protection, education, youth employment, environmental health, electoral registration, food, drugs, housing, leisure services, libraries, local planning, local roads, museums, parking, recreation (parks, playing fields, swimming pools), refuse collection and street cleaning, social services, town planning and traffic management.

LONDON BOROUGH COUNCILS

Council	Telephone	Pop.*	Council Tax†	Chief Executive‡
Barking and Dagenham	020-8592 4500	210,711	£1,494	Chris Naylor
Barnet	020-8359 2000	387,803	£1,484	John Hooton
Bexley	020-8303 7777	246,124	£1,588	Gill Steward
Brent	020-8937 1234	329,102	£1,497	Carolyn Downs
Bromley	020-8464 3333	329,391	£1,453	Doug Patterson
Camden	020-7974 4444	253,361	£1,489	Mike Cooke
CITY OF LONDON CORPORATION	020-7606 3030	7,654	£933	John Barradell, OBE
Croydon	020-8726 6000	384,837	£1,637	Jo Negrini
Ealing	020-8825 5000	342,736	£1,440	Paul Najsarek
Enfield	020-8379 1000	332,705	£1,555	Ian Davies
Greenwich	020-8854 8888	282,849	£1,429	Debbie Warren
Hackney	020-8356 5000	275,929	£1,375	Tim Shields
Hammersmith and Fulham	020-8748 3020	182,998	£1,022	Kim Dero
Haringey	020-8489 0000	271,224	£1,576	Zina Etheridge
Harrow	020-8863 5611	248,880	£1,689	Michael Lockwood
Havering	01708-434343	256,039	£1,658	Andrew Blake-Herbert
Hillingdon	01895-250111	302,343	£1,407	Fran Beasley
Hounslow	020-8583 2000	269,100	£1,462	Mary Harpley
Islington	020-7527 2000	235,000	£1,429	Lesley Seary
Kensington and Chelsea	020-7361 3000	155,741	£1,139	Barry Quirk, CBE
Kingston upon Thames	020-8547 5000	174,609	£1,772	Roy Thompson (interim)
Lambeth	020-7926 1000	324,048	£1,386	Andrew Travers (interim)
Lewisham	020-8314 6000	301,307	£1,498	Ian Thomas
Merton	020-8274 4901	206,052	£1,468	Ged Curran
Newham	020-8430 2000	347,996	£1,259	Kim Bromley-Derry, CBE
Redbridge	020-8554 5000	301,785	£1,550	Andy Donald
Richmond upon Thames	020-8891 1411	195,680	£1,707	Paul Martin
Southwark	020-7525 5000	314,232	£1,330	Eleanor Kelly
Sutton	020-8770 5000	203,243	£1,603	Niall Bolger
Tower Hamlets	020-7364 5000	307,964	£1,280	Will Tuckley
Waltham Forest	020-8496 3000	275,505	£1,615	Martin Esom
Wandsworth	020-8871 6000	323,257	£723	Paul Martin
WESTMINSTER	020-7641 6000	244,796	£711	Stuart Love

* *Source:* Office for National Statistics – *Mid-2017 Population Estimates* (Crown copyright)
† Band D council tax bill for 2018–19 inclusive of adult social care and parish precepts
‡ Or equivalent postholder
Councils in CAPITAL LETTERS have city status

CITY OF LONDON CORPORATION

The City of London Corporation is the local authority for the City of London. Its legal definition is the 'Mayor and Commonalty and Citizens of the City of London'. It is governed by the court of common council, which consists of the lord mayor, 24 other aldermen and 100 common councilmen. The lord mayor and two sheriffs are nominated annually by the City guilds (the livery companies) and elected by the court of aldermen. Aldermen and councilmen are elected from the 25 wards into which the City is divided; councilmen must stand for re-election every four years. The council is a legislative assembly, and there are no political parties.

The corporation has the same functions as the London borough councils. In addition, it runs the City of London Police; is the health authority for the Port of London; has health control of animal imports throughout Greater London, including at Heathrow airport; owns and manages public open spaces throughout Greater London; runs the central criminal court; and runs Billingsgate, New Spitalfields and Smithfield markets.

The City of London is the historic centre at the heart of London known as 'the square mile', around which the vast metropolis has grown over the centuries. The City's residential population was 7,400 at the 2011 census and in addition, around 400,000 people work in the City. The City is an international financial and business centre, generating about £30bn a year for the British economy. It includes the head offices of the principal banks, insurance companies and mercantile houses, in addition to buildings ranging from the historic Roman Wall and the 15th-century Guildhall, to the massive splendour of St Paul's Cathedral and the architectural beauty of Wren's spires.

The City of London was described by Tacitus in AD 62 as 'a busy emporium for trade and traders'. Under the Romans it became an important administration centre and hub of the road system. Little is known of London in Saxon times, when it formed part of the kingdom of the East Saxons. In 886 Alfred recovered London from the Danes and reconstituted it a burgh under his son-in-law. In 1066 the citizens submitted to William the Conqueror who in 1067 granted them a charter, which is still preserved, establishing them in the rights and privileges they had hitherto enjoyed.

THE MAYORALTY

The mayoralty was probably established about 1189, the first mayor being Henry Fitz Ailwyn who filled the office for 23 years and was succeeded by Fitz Alan (1212–14). A new charter was granted by King John in 1215, directing the mayor to be chosen annually, which has been done ever since, though in early times the same individual often held the office more than once. A familiar instance is that of 'Whittington, thrice Lord Mayor of London' (in reality four times: 1397, 1398, 1406 and 1419); and many modern cases have occurred. The earliest instance of the phrase 'lord mayor' in English is in 1414. It was used more generally in the latter part of the 15th century and became invariable from 1535 onwards. At Michaelmas the liverymen in Common Hall choose two aldermen who have served the office of sheriff for presentation to the Court of Aldermen, and one is chosen to be lord mayor for the following mayoral year.

LORD MAYOR'S DAY

The lord mayor of London was previously elected on the feast of St Simon and St Jude (28 October), and from the time of Edward I, at least, was presented to the King or to the Barons of the Exchequer on the following day, unless that day was a Sunday. The day of election was altered to 16 October in 1346, and after some further changes was fixed for

Michaelmas Day in 1546, but the ceremonies of admittance and swearing-in of the lord mayor continued to take place on 28 and 29 October respectively until 1751. In 1752, at the reform of the calendar, the lord mayor was continued in office until 8 November, the 'new style' equivalent of 28 October. The lord mayor is now presented to the lord chief justice at the royal courts of justice on the second Saturday in November to make the final declaration of office, having been sworn in at Guildhall on the preceding day. The procession to the royal courts of justice is popularly known as the Lord Mayor's Show.

REPRESENTATIVES

Aldermen are mentioned in the 11th century and their office is of Saxon origin. They were elected annually between 1377 and 1394, when an act of parliament of Richard II directed them to be chosen for life. Aldermen now serve a six-year term of office before submitting themselves for re-election.

The Common Council was, at an early date, substituted for a popular assembly called the *Folkmote*. At first only two representatives were sent from each ward, but now each of the City's 25 wards is represented by an alderman and at least two Common Councilmen (the number depending on the size of the ward). Common Councilmen are elected every four years at all-out ward elections.

OFFICERS

Sheriffs were Saxon officers; their predecessors were the *wic-reeves* and *portreeves* of London and Middlesex. At first they were officers of the Crown, and were named by the Barons of the Exchequer; but Henry I (in 1132) gave the citizens permission to choose their own sheriffs, and the annual election of sheriffs became fully operative under King John's charter of 1199. The citizens lost this privilege, as far as the election of the sheriff of Middlesex was concerned, by the Local Government Act 1888; but the liverymen continue to choose two sheriffs of the City of London, who are appointed on Midsummer Day and take office at Michaelmas.

The office of chamberlain is an ancient one, the first contemporary record of which is 1237. The town clerk (or common clerk) is first mentioned in 1274.

ACTIVITIES

The work of the City of London Corporation is assigned to a number of committees which make decisions on behalf of the Court of Common Council or which make recommendations for decisions by the court. The committees are extensive given the diverse services delivered by the city corporation and include: Audit and Risk Management; Barbican Centre; Barbican Residential; Board of Governors of the City of London Freeman's School, the City of London School, the City of London School for Girls and the Guildhall School of Music and Drama; the City Bridge Trust; Community and Children's Services; Culture, Heritage and Libraries; Education; Epping Forest and Commons; Establishment; Finance; Freedom Applications; Gresham (City Side); Hampstead Heath, Highgate Wood and Queen's Park; Health and Wellbeing; Investment; Licensing; Markets; Open Spaces and City Gardens; Pensions Board; Planning and Transportation; Police; Policy and Resources; Port Health and Environmental Services; Standards; and West Ham Park. There are numerous other sub-committees which report to the city corporation's committees.

The City's estate, in the possession of which the City of London Corporation differs from other municipalities, is largely managed by the property investment board.

The Honourable the Irish Society, which manages the City Corporation's estates in Ulster, consists of a governor, two other aldermen and 12 common councilmen.

THE LORD MAYOR 2018–19

The Rt. Hon. the Lord Mayor, Peter Estlin*
Executive Director of Mansion House and the Central Criminal Court, Vic Annells

* Provisional

THE SHERIFFS 2018–19

Alderman Vincent Keaveny (Farringdon Wn.); Elizabeth Green

OFFICERS, ETC

Town Clerk, John Barradell
Chamberlain, Peter Kane
Chief Commoner (2018), John Scott
Clerk, The Honourable the Irish Society, H. E. J. Montgomery, MBE

THE ALDERMEN

with office held and date of appointment to that office

Name and Ward	Common Councilman	Alderman	Sheriff	Lord Mayor
Ian Luder, *Castle Baynard*	1998	2005	2007	2008
Nicholas Anstee, *Aldersgate*	1987	1996	2003	2009
Sir David Wootton, *Langbourn*	2002	2005	2009	2011
Sir Roger Gifford, *Cordwainer*	–	2004	2008	2012
Sir Alan Yarrow, *Bridge & Bridge Wt.*	–	2007	2011	2014
Dr Sir Andrew Parmley, *Vintry*	1992	2001	2014	2016
Charles Bowman, *Lime Street*	–	2013	2015	2017
Peter Estlin, *Coleman Street*	–	2013	2016	2018

All the above have passed the Civic Chair

	Common Councilman	Alderman	Sheriff
Alison Gowman, *Dowgate*	1991	2002	–
David Graves, *Cripplegate*	–	2008	–
John Garbutt, *Walbrook*	–	2009	–
Peter Hewitt, *Aldgate*	–	2012	–
Matthew Richardson, *Billingsgate*	2009	2012	–
William Russell, *Bread Street*	–	2013	2016
Timothy Hailes, *Bassishaw*	–	2013	2017
Prof. Michael Mainelli, *Broad Street*	–	2013	–
Vincent Keaveny, *Farringdon Wn.*	–	2013	2018
Baroness Scotland of Asthal, QC, *Bishopsgate*	–	2015	–
Robert Howard, *Cornhill*	2011	2015	–
Alistair King, *Queenhithe*	–	2016	–
Gregory Jones, QC, *Farringdon Wt.*	2013	2017	–
Prem Goyal, *Portsoken*	2017	2017	–
Nicholas Lyons, *Tower*	2017	2017	–
Emma Edhem, *Candlewick*	2018	2018	–
Robert Hughes-Penney, *Cheap*	2018	2018	–

THE COMMON COUNCIL

Deputy: each common councilman so described serves as deputy to the alderman of her/his ward.

Abrahams, G. C. (2000)	*Farringdon Wt.*
Absalom, *Deputy* J. D. (1994)	*Farringdon Wt.*
Addy, C. K. (2017)	*Farringdon Wt.*
Ali, M. (2017)	*Portsoken*
Ameer, R. B. (2017)	*Vintry*
Anderson, R. K. (2013)	*Aldersgate*
Anderson, T. A. (2017)	*Farringdon Wn.*
Barr, A. R. M. (2017)	*Cordwainer*
Barrow, *Deputy* D. G. F. (2007)	*Aldgate*
Bastow, A. M. (2017)	*Aldersgate*
Bell, M. (2017)	*Farringdon Wn.*
Bennett, *Deputy* J. A. (2005)	*Broad Street*
Bennett, P. G. (2016)	*Walbrook*
Bensted-Smith, N. M. (2014)	*Cheap*
Boden, C. P. (2013)	*Castle Baynard*
Boleat, Sir Mark (2002)	*Cordwainer*
Bostock, R. M. (2017)	*Cripplegate*
Bottomley, *Deputy* K. D. F. (2015)	*Bridge & Bridge Wt.*
Bradshaw, *Deputy* D. J. (1991)	*Cripplegate Wn.*
Broeke, T. (2017)	*Cheap*
Cassidy, *Deputy* M. J., CBE (1980)	*Coleman Street*
Chadwick, *Deputy* R. A. H., OBE (1994)	*Tower*
Chapman, *Deputy* J. D. (2006)	*Langbourn*
Christian, D. G. (2016)	*Lime Street*
Clementi, T. C. (2017)	*Lime Street*
Colthurst, H. N. A. (2013)	*Lime Street*
Crossan, R. P. (2017)	*Aldersgate*
Dostalova, K. H. (2013)	*Farringdon Wn.*
Duckworth, S. D., OBE (2000)	*Bishopsgate Wn.*
Dunphy, P. G. (2009)	*Cornhill*
Durcan, J. M. (2017)	*Cripplegate*
Everett, *Deputy* K. M. (1984)	*Candlewick*
Fairweather, A. H. (2016)	*Tower*
Fernandes, S. A. (2009)	*Coleman Street*
Fletcher, J. W. (2011)	*Portsoken*
Fraser, S. J., CBE (1993)	*Coleman Street*
Fredericks, M. B. (2008)	*Tower*
Haines, C. W. (2017)	*Queenhithe*
Haines, *Deputy* Revd S. D. (2005)	*Cornhill*
Harrower, G. G. (2015)	*Bassishaw*
Hayward, C. M. (2013)	*Broad Street*
Hill, C. (2017)	*Farringdon Wn.*
Hoffman, *Deputy* T. D. D. (2002)	*Vintry*
Holmes, A. (2013)	*Farringdon Wn.*
Hudson, M. (2007)	*Castle Baynard*
Hyde, *Deputy* W. (2011)	*Bishopsgate Wt.*
Ingham Clark, *Deputy* J. (2013)	*Billingsgate*
James, *Deputy* C. (2008)	*Farringdon Wn.*
Jones, *Deputy* H. L. M. (2004)	*Portsoken*
Joshi, S. J. (2018)	*Bishopsgate*
Knowles-Cutler, A. (2017)	*Castle Baynard*
Lawrence, G. A. (2002)	*Farringdon Wt.*
Levene, T. C. (2017)	*Bridge and Bridge Wt.*
Littlechild, V. (2009)	*Cripplegate Wn.*
Lodge, O. A. W., TD (2009)	*Bread Street*
Lord, *Deputy* C. E., OBE (2001)	*Farringdon Wt.*
Martinelli, P. N. (2013)	*Farringdon Wt.*
Mayer, A. P. (2017)	*Bishopsgate*
Mayhew, J. P. (1996)	*Aldersgate*
McGuinness, *Deputy* C. S. (1997)	*Castle Baynard*
McMurtie, A. S. (2013)	*Coleman Street*
Mead, W., OBE (1997)	*Farringdon Wt.*
Merrett, *Deputy* R. A. (2009)	*Bassishaw*
Meyers, A. G. D. (2017)	*Aldgate*
Mooney, *Deputy* B. D. F. (1998)	*Queenhithe*
Morris, H. F. (2008)	*Aldgate*
Moss, *Deputy* A. M. (2013)	*Cheap*
Moys, S. D. (2001)	*Aldgate*
Murphy, B. D. (2017)	*Bishopsgate*
Nash, *Deputy* J. C., OBE (1983)	*Aldersgate*
Newman, B. P., CBE (1989)	*Aldersgate*
Packham, G. D. (2013)	*Castle Baynard*
Patel, D. (2013)	*Aldgate*
Pearson, S. J. (2017)	*Cripplegate*
Petrie, J. (2018)	*Billingsgate*
Pimlott, W. (2017)	*Cripplegate*
Pleasance, J. L. (2013)	*Langbourn*
Pollard, *Deputy* J. H. G. (2002)	*Dowgate*
Priest, H. J. S. (2009)	*Castle Baynard*

Pritchard, J. P. (2017)	*Portsoken*
Quilter, S. D. (1998)	*Cripplegate Wt.*
Regan, *Deputy* R. D., OBE (1998)	*Farringdon Wn.*
Rogula, *Deputy* E. (2008)	*Lime Street*
de Sausmarez, H. J. (2015)	*Candlewick*
Sayed, R. (2017)	*Farringdon Wt.*
Scott, (Chief Commoner) J. G. S. (1999)	*Broad Street*
Seaton, I. C. N. (2009)	*Cornhill*
Sells, O. M., QC (2017)	*Farringdon Wt.*
Shilson, *Deputy*, G. R. E. (2009)	*Bread Street*
Simons, J. L. (2004)	*Castle Baynard*
Sleigh, *Deputy* T. C. C. (2013)	*Bishopsgate Wt.*
Smith, G. M. (2013)	*Farringdon Wn.*
Snyder, *Deputy* Sir Michael (1986)	*Cordwainer*
Thompson, D. J. (2004)	*Aldgate*
Tomlinson, *Deputy* J. (2004)	*Cripplegate Wt.*
Tumbridge, J. R. (2009)	*Tower*
Upton, J. W. D. (2017)	*Farringdon Wt.*
Wheatley, M. R. P. H. D. (2013)	*Dowgate*
Woodhouse, *Deputy* P. J. (2013)	*Langbourn*

THE CITY GUILDS (LIVERY COMPANIES)

The livery companies of the City of London grew out of early medieval religious fraternities and began to emerge as trade and craft guilds, retaining their religious aspect, in the 12th century. From the early 14th century, only members of the trade and craft guilds could call themselves citizens of the City of London. The guilds began to be called livery companies, because of the distinctive livery worn by the most prosperous guild members on ceremonial occasions, in the late 15th century.

By the early 19th century the power of the companies within their trades had begun to wane, but those wearing the livery of a company continued to play an important role in the government of the City of London. Liverymen still have the right to nominate the Lord Mayor and sheriffs, and most members of the Court of Common Council are liverymen.

The constitution of the livery companies has been unchanged for centuries. There are three ranks of membership: freemen, liverymen and assistants. A person can become a freeman by patrimony (through a parent having been a freeman); by servitude (through having served an apprenticeship to a freeman); or by redemption (by purchase).

Election to the livery is the prerogative of the company, who can elect any of its freemen as liverymen. Assistants are usually elected from the livery and form a court of assistants which is the governing body of the company. The master (in some companies called the prime warden) is elected annually from the assistants.

The register for 2018–19 lists 26,281 liverymen of the guilds entitled to vote at elections at common hall.

The order of precedence, omitting extinct companies, is given in parentheses after the name of each company in the list below. In certain companies the election of master or prime warden for the year does not take place until the autumn. In such cases the master or prime warden for 2017–18, rather than 2018–19, is given.

The Twelve Great Companies are given in order of civic precedence and appear first in the list below; the remaining guilds are listed in alphabetical order. Parish clerks and watermen and lightermen have requested to remain with no livery and are marked with a '*'

MERCERS (1). *Hall*, Mercers' Hall, 6 Frederick's Place, London EC2R 8AB *Livery*, 247.
  Clerk, Rob Abernethy *Master*, Xenia Dennen

GROCERS (2). *Hall*, Grocers' Hall, Princes Street, London EC2R 8AD *Livery*, 361.
  Clerk, Brig. Greville Bibby, CBE *Master*, James Whitmore

DRAPERS (3). *Hall*, Drapers' Hall, Throgmorton Avenue, London EC2N 2DQ *Livery*, 320.
  Clerk, Col. Richard Winstanley, OBE
  Master, Prof. Philip Ogden

FISHMONGERS (4). *Hall*, Fishmongers' Hall, London Bridge, London EC4R 9EL *Livery*, 369.
  Clerk, Cdre Toby Williamson, MVO, RN
  Prime Warden, David Robertson

GOLDSMITHS (5). *Hall*, Goldsmiths' Hall, Foster Lane, London EC2V 6BN *Livery*, 285.
  Clerk, Sir David Reddaway, KCMG, MBE
  Prime Warden, Michael Prideaux

MERCHANT TAYLORS (6/7). *Hall*, Merchant Taylors' Hall, 30 Threadneedle Street, London EC2R 8JB *Livery*, 325.
  Clerk, Rear-Adm. J. Clink, CBE *Master*, D. Eggar

SKINNERS (6/7). *Hall*, Skinners' Hall, 8 Dowgate Hill, London EC4R 2SP *Livery*, 400.
  Clerk, Maj.-Gen. Andrew Kennett, CB, CBE
  Master, Lord Lisvane, KCB

HABERDASHERS (8). *Hall*, Haberdashers' Hall, 18 West Smithfield, London EC1A 9HQ *Livery*, 325.
  Clerk, Cdre Philip Thicknesse, RN *Master*, James Kininmonth

SALTERS (9). *Hall*, Salters' Hall, 4 London Wall Place, London EC2Y 5DE *Livery*, 176.
  Clerk, Capt. David Morris, RN
  Master, Hon. Philip Remnant, CBE

IRONMONGERS (10). *Hall*, Ironmongers' Hall, Shaftesbury Place, London EC2Y 8AA *Livery*, 150.
  Clerk, Col. Charlie Knaggs, OBE *Master*, Lord Garvagh

VINTNERS (11). *Hall*, Vintners' Hall, Upper Thames Street, London EC4V 3BG *Livery*, 360.
  Clerk, Brig. Jonathan Bourne-May *Master*, Sir Andrew Parmley

CLOTHWORKERS (12). *Hall*, Clothworkers' Hall, Dunster Court, London EC3R 7AH *Livery*, 255.
  Clerk, Jocelyn Stuart-Grumbar *Master*, John Coombe-Tennant

ACTUARIES (91). 2nd Floor, 2 London Wall Place, London EC2Y 5AU *Livery*, 220.
  Clerk, Lyndon Jones *Master*, Nick Salter

AIR PILOTS AND AIR NAVIGATORS (81). *Hall*, Dowgate Hill House, 14–16 Dowgate Hill, London EC4R 2SU *Livery*, 600.
  Clerk, Paul Tacon *Master*, Capt. Colin Cox
  Grand Master, HRH the Duke of York, KG, GCVO, ADC(P)

APOTHECARIES (58). *Hall*, Apothecaries' Hall, 14 Black Friars Lane, London EC4V 6EJ *Livery*, 1,215.
  Clerk, Nick Royle *Master*, Prof. Martin Rossor

ARBITRATORS (93). 28 The Meadway, Cuffley EN6 4ES *Livery*, 180.
  Clerk, Biagio Fraulo *Master*, Eur Ing David Wilson

ARMOURERS AND BRASIERS (22). *Hall*, Armourers' Hall, 81 Coleman Street, London EC2R 5BJ *Livery*, 135.
  Clerk, Peter Bateman *Master*, Christopher Weston-Simons

ARTS SCHOLARS (110). 5 Queen Anne's Gate, White House Walk, Farnham GU9 9AN *Livery*, 85.
  Clerk, Lt.-Col. Chris Booth *Master*, Paul Viney

BAKERS (19). *Hall*, Bakers' Hall, 9 Harp Lane, London EC3R 6DP *Livery*, 240.
  Clerk, Lance Whitehouse *Master*, Paul Morrow

BARBERS (17). *Hall*, Barber-Surgeons' Hall, Monkwell Square, London EC2Y 5BL *Livery*, 230.
  Clerk, Malachy Doran *Master*, Malachy Doran

BASKETMAKERS (52). 30 Cadgwith Place, Port Solent, Portsmouth PO6 4TD *Livery*, 300.
  Clerk, Fiona Janczur *Prime Warden*, Stephen Gee

BLACKSMITHS (40). Painters' Hall, 9 Little Trinity Lane, London EC4V 2AD *Livery*, 246.
  Clerk, Jill Moffatt *Prime Warden*, Robin McNeill Love

BOWYERS (38). Fosters Lodge, Duck Street, Warminster BA12 7AL *Livery*, 99.
  Clerk, Lt.-Col. Tony Marinos *Master*, Ian Spring

BREWERS (14). *Hall*, Brewers' Hall, Aldermanbury Square, London EC2V 7HR *Livery*, 200.
  Clerk, Col. Michael O'Dwyer, OBE
  Master, Stephen Spencer-Jones

BRODERERS (48). Orchard House, Vicarage Lane, Steeple Ashton BA14 6HH *Livery*, 119.
Clerk, Brig. Bill Aldridge, CBE
Master, Sir Christopher Bellamy, QC

BUILDERS MERCHANTS (88). 4 College Hill, London EC4R 2RB *Livery*, 206.
Clerk, Virginia Rounding *Master*, Pippa Latham

BUTCHERS (24). 4th Floor, 14 Charterhouse Square, London EC1M 6AX *Livery*, 635.
Clerk, Maj.-Gen. Jeff Mason, MBE, RM *Master*, Graham Baker

CARMEN (77). Plaisterers' Hall, 1 London Wall, London EC2Y 5JU *Livery*, 500.
Clerk, Walter Gill *Master*, Stephen Britt

CARPENTERS (26). *Hall*, Carpenters' Hall, 1 Throgmorton Avenue, London EC2N 2JJ *Livery*, 150.
Clerk, Brig. Tim Gregson, MBE
Master, His Hon. Peter Birts, QC

CHARTERED ACCOUNTANTS (86). 35 Ascot Way, Bicester OX26 1AG *Livery*, 365.
Clerk, Jonathan Grosvenor *Master*, Clive Parritt

CHARTERED ARCHITECTS (98). The Old Vicarage, Anchor Road, Calne SN11 8DR *Livery*, 159.
Clerk, Jonathan Soar *Master*, Barry Munday

CHARTERED SECRETARIES AND ADMINISTRATORS (87). 3rd Floor, Saddlers' Hall, 40 Gutter Lane, London EC2V 6BR *Livery*, 220.
Clerk, Keith Povey *Master*, Christina Parry, OBE

CHARTERED SURVEYORS (85). 75 Meadway Drive, Woking GU21 4TF *Livery*, 335.
Clerk, Amanda Jackson *Master*, Allan Flower

CLOCKMAKERS (61). 1 Throgmorton Avenue, London EC2N 2BY *Livery*, 280.
Clerk, Oliver Bartrum *Master*, Andrew James

COACHMAKERS AND COACH-HARNESS MAKERS (72). The Old Barn, Church Lane, Glentham LN8 2EL *Livery*, 500.
Clerk, Cdr Mark Leaning, RN *Master*, Tony Edwards

CONSTRUCTORS (99). 5 Delft Close, Southampton S031 7TQ *Livery*, 170.
Clerk, Kim Tyrrell *Master*, Anthony Ward

COOKS (35). *Livery*, 71.
Clerk, Vice-Adm. Peter Wilkinson, CB, CVO
Master, Lt.-Col. Marcus Appleton

COOPERS (36). *Hall*, Coopers' Hall, 13 Devonshire Square, London EC2M 4TH *Livery*, 260.
Clerk, Lt.-Col. Adrian Carroll *Master*, Anthony Behrens

CORDWAINERS (27). Clothworkers' Hall, Dunster Court, London EC3R 7AH *Livery*, 188.
Clerk, John Miller *Master*, Jonathan Hooper

CURRIERS (29). Oak Lodge, 4 Greenhill Lane, BH21 2RN *Livery*, 108.
Clerk, Adrian Rafferty *Master*, Jeremy Kean

CUTLERS (18). *Hall*, Cutlers' Hall, Warwick Lane, London EC4M 7BR *Livery*, 100.
Clerk, Rupert Meacher *Master*, Dr Tim Osborn-Jones

DISTILLERS (69). 1 The Sanctuary, London SW1P 3JT *Livery*, 260.
Clerk, Edward Macey-Dare *Master*, Bryan Burrough

DYERS (13). *Hall*, Dyers' Hall, 10 Dowgate Hill, London EC4R 2ST *Livery*, 140.
Clerk, Russell Vaizey *Prime Warden*, Nigel Back

EDUCATORS (109). 8 Little Trinity Lane, London EC4V 2AN *Livery*, 200.
Clerk, Christian Jensen *Master*, Dr Elisabeth Goodwin, OBE

ENGINEERS (94). Ironmongers' Hall, 1 Shaftesbury Place, London EC2Y 8AA *Livery*, 310.
Clerk, Col. David Swann, CBE *Master*, Prof. David Johnson

ENVIRONMENTAL CLEANERS (97). 92 Stondon Park, Forest Hill SE23 1JS *Livery*, 189.
Clerk, Matthew Johnson *Master*, Maureen Marden

FAN MAKERS (76). Skinners' Hall, 8 Dowgate Hill, London EC4R 2SP *Livery*, 180.
Clerk, Martin Davies *Master*, Dr Michael Smith

FARMERS (80). *Hall*, The Farmers' and Fletchers' Hall, 3 Cloth Street, London EC1A 7LD *Livery*, 350.
Clerk, Graham Bamford *Master*, Julian Sayers

FARRIERS (55). 19 Queen Street, WD4 9BT *Livery*, 330.
Clerk, Charlotte Clifford *Master*, David Buckton

FELTMAKERS (63). Post Cottage, Hook RG29 1DA *Livery*, 190.
Clerk, Maj. Jollyon Coombs
Master, His Hon. Judge Nicholas Hilliard, QC

FIREFIGHTERS (103). 3rd Floor, Wax Chandlers' Hall, 6 Gresham Street, London EC2V 7AD *Livery*, 100.
Clerk, Steven Tamcken *Master*, Andrew Mayes

FLETCHERS (39). *Hall*, The Farmers' and Fletchers' Hall, 3 Cloth Street, London EC1A 7LD *Livery*, 150.
Clerk, Kate Pink *Master*, Dr Roger Watson

FOUNDERS (33). *Hall*, Founders' Hall, 1 Cloth Fair, London EC1A 7JQ *Livery*, 170.
Clerk, Andrew Bell *Master*, Matthew Farrant

FRAMEWORK KNITTERS (64). The Grange, Walton Road, Lutterworth LE17 5RU *Livery*, 185.
Clerk, Shaun Mackaness *Master*, Sheila Turner

FRUITERERS (45). 3 Parsonage Vale, Marlborough SN8 3SZ *Livery*, 283.
Clerk, Lt.-Col. Philip Brown *Master*, John Warner

FUELLERS (95). Skinners' Hall, 8 Dowgate Hill, London EC4R 2SP *Livery*, 164.
Clerk, Bill Walworth, CBE *Master*, Shravan Joshi

FURNITURE MAKERS (83). *Hall*, Furniture Makers' Hall, 12 Austin Friars, London EC2N 2HE *Livery*, 230.
Clerk, Jonny Westbrooke *Master*, Hayden Davies

GARDENERS (66). Ingrams, Ingram's Green, Midhurst GU29 0LJ *Livery*, 287.
Clerk, Maj. Jeremy Herrtage *Master*, Margaret Holland Prior

GIRDLERS (23). *Hall*, Girdlers' Hall, Basinghall Avenue, London EC2V 5DD *Livery*, 80.
Clerk, Brig. Murray Whiteside, OBE
Master, Charlie Crowther-Smith

GLASS SELLERS (71). PO Box 241, *Livery*, 142.
Clerk, Lance Whitehouse *Master*, Mr Leigh Baildham

GLAZIERS AND PAINTERS OF GLASS (53). *Hall*, Glaziers' Hall, 9 Montague Close, London SE1 9DD *Livery*, 168.
Clerk, Alison Evans *Master*, Andrew Lane

GLOVERS (62). Seniors Farmhouse, Shaftesbury SP7 9AX *Livery*, 250.
Clerk, Mark Butler *Master*, Rodney Jagelman

GOLD AND SILVER WYRE DRAWERS (74). Lye Green Forge, Lye Green, Crowborough TN6 1UU *Livery*, 280.
Clerk, Mark Dickens *Master*, John Walsham

GUNMAKERS (73). The Proof House, 48–50 Commercial Road, London E1 1LP *Livery*, 350.
Clerk, Adrian Mundin, MVO *Master*, Diana Berry

HACKNEY CARRIAGE DRIVERS (104). 25 The Grove, Latimer HP5 1UE *Livery*, 105.
Clerk, Mary Whitworth *Master*, David Cannell

HORNERS (54). 12 Coltsfoot Close, Ixworth IP31 2NJ *Livery*, 225.
Clerk, Jonathan Mead *Master*, Gordon Haines, MBE

INFORMATION TECHNOLOGISTS (100). *Hall*, Information Technologists' Hall, 39A Bartholomew Close, London EC1A 7JN *Livery*, 365.
Clerk (interim), Philip Grant *Master*, Dr Stefan Fafinski

INNHOLDERS (32). *Hall*, Innholders' Hall, 30 College Street, London EC4R 2RH *Livery*, 180.
Clerk, Charles Henty *Master*, Nicholas Rettie

INSURERS (92). First Floor, 21 Lombard Street, London EC3V 9AH *Livery*, 360.
Clerk, Sarah Clark *Master*, Terry Masters

INTERNATIONAL BANKERS (106). 12 Austin Friars, London EC2N 2HE *Livery*, 210.
Clerk, Nicholas Westgarth *Master*, Peter Estlin

JOINERS AND CEILERS (41). 75 Meadway Drive, Woking GU21 4TF *Livery*, 150.
Clerk, Amanda Jackson *Master*, Clive Capel

LAUNDERERS (89). *Hall*, Launderers' Hall, 9 Montague Close, London SE1 9DD *Livery*, 175.
Clerk, Margaret Campbell *Master*, Forbes MacDougall

LEATHERSELLERS (15). 7 St Helen's Place, London EC3A 6AB *Livery*, 150.
Clerk, David Santa-Olalla, DSO, MC
Master, Michael Bradley Russell

LIGHTMONGERS (96). 1 Manor House Garden, E11 2RU *Livery*, 148.
Clerk, Phillip Hyde *Master*, Stephen Thomas

LORINERS (57). 30 Elm Park, Royal Wootton Bassett SN4 7TA *Livery*, 400.
Clerk, Honor Page *Master*, Judge Patrick Clyne

MAKERS OF PLAYING CARDS (75). 256 St David's Square, London E14 3WE *Livery*, 147.
Clerk, David Barrett *Master*, Anthony Komedera

MANAGEMENT CONSULTANTS (105). Skinners' Hall, 8 Dowgate Hill, London EC4R 2SP *Livery*, 180.
Clerk, Julie Fox *Master*, David Johnson

MARKETORS (90). Plaisterers' Hall, One London Wall, London EC2Y 5JU *Livery*, 257.
Clerk, John Hammond *Master*, Richard Christou

MASONS (30). 8 Little Trinity Lane, London EC4V 2AN *Livery*, 163.
Clerk, Maj. Giles Clapp *Master*, Andrew Bowles

MASTER MARINERS (78). *Hall*, HQS Wellington, Temple Stairs, London WC2R 2PN *Livery*, 188.
Clerk, Cdre Angus Menzies, RN *Master*, Capt. Robert Booth

MUSICIANS (50). 1 Speed Highwalk, Barbican EC2Y BDX *Livery*, 420.
Clerk, Hugh Lloyd *Master*, Lady Brewer, OBE

NEEDLEMAKERS (65). PO Box 73635, London SW14 9BY *Livery*, 200.
Clerk, Fiona Sedgwick *Master*, Colin Tiffin

PAINTER-STAINERS (28). *Hall*, Painters' Hall, 9 Little Trinity Lane, London EC4V 2AD *Livery*, 250.
Clerk, Christopher Twyman *Master*, Julian Briant

PATTENMAKERS (70). 3 The High Street, Sutton Valence ME17 3AG *Livery*, 203.
Clerk, Col. R. W. Murfin, TD *Master*, Alastair Watson-Gandy

PAVIORS (56). Paviors' House, Charterhouse, London EC1M 6AN *Livery*, 285.
Clerk, John Freestone *Master*, Dyfrig James

PEWTERERS (16). *Hall*, Pewterers' Hall, Oat Lane, London EC2V 7DE *Livery*, 140.
Clerk, Capt. Paddy Watson, RN *Master*, Ann Buxton

PLAISTERERS (46). *Hall*, Plaisterers' Hall, 1 London Wall, London EC2Y 5JU *Livery*, 233.
Clerk, Nigel Bamping *Master*, Timothy Cooke, OBE

PLUMBERS (31). Carpenters' Hall, 1 Throgmorton Avenue, London EC2N 2JJ *Livery*, 350.
Clerk, Air Cdre Paul Nash *Master*, Dame Fiona Woolf, DBE

POULTERS (34). 20 Waltham Road, Woodford Green 1GB 8DN *Livery*, 306.
Clerk, Julie Pearce *Master*, Robert Haynes

SADDLERS (25). *Hall*, Saddlers' Hall, 40 Gutter Lane, London EC2V 6BR *Livery*, 83.
Clerk, Brig. Philip Napier, OBE *Master*, James Welch

SCIENTIFIC INSTRUMENT MAKERS (84). Glaziers' Hall, 9 Montague Close, London SE1 9DD *Livery*, 185.
Clerk, Neville Watson *Master*, Prof. Ron Summers

SCRIVENERS (44). HQS Wellington, Temple Stairs, London WC2R 2PN *Livery*, 191.
Clerk, Giles Cole *Master*, Edward Gardiner

SECURITY PROFESSIONALS (108). 34 Tye Green, Sudbury CO10 7RG *Livery*, 185.
Clerk, Patricia Boswell *Master*, Phillip Hagon, QPM

SHIPWRIGHTS (59). Ironmongers Hall, Shaftesbury Place, London EC2Y 8AA *Livery*, 436.
Clerk, Lt.-Col. Richard Cole-Mackintosh
Prime Warden, Anthony Vlasto
Grand Master, HRH the Prince of Wales, KG, KT, GCB

SOLICITORS (79). 4 College Hill, London EC4R 2RB *Livery*, 350.
Clerk, Linzi James *Master*, David Graves

SPECTACLE MAKERS (60). Apothecaries' Hall, Black Friars Lane, London EC4V 6EL *Livery*, 390.
Clerk, Helen Perkins *Master*, John McGregor, OBE

STATIONERS AND NEWSPAPER MAKERS (47). *Hall*, Stationers' Hall, Ave Maria Lane, London EC4M 7DD *Livery*, 540.
Clerk, William Alden, MBE *Master*, David Allan

TALLOW CHANDLERS (21). *Hall*, Tallow Chandlers' Hall, 4 Dowgate Hill, London EC4R 2SH *Livery*, 180.
Clerk, David Homer *Master*, John Baxter, CBE

TAX ADVISERS (107). 10 Deena Close, Queen's Drive W3 OHR *Livery*, 158.
Clerk, Stephen Henderson *Master*, Marcus Fincham

TIN PLATE WORKERS (ALIAS WIRE WORKERS) (67). PO Box 71002, London W4 9FH *Livery*, 180.
Clerk, Dr Piers Baker *Master*, Peter Wilinson

TOBACCO PIPE MAKERS AND TOBACCO BLENDERS (82). 14 Montpelier Road, Sutton SM1 4QE *Livery*, 133.
Clerk, Sandra Stocker *Master*, Roger Brookes

TURNERS (51). Skinner's Hall, 8 Dowgate Hill, London EC4R 2SP *Livery*, 185.
Clerk, Alex Robertson *Master*, David Batchelor

TYLERS AND BRICKLAYERS (37). 3 Farmers' Way, Seer Green HP9 2YY *Livery*, 160.
Clerk, John Brooks *Master*, Lesley Day

UPHOLDERS (49). Pembroke Lodge, 162 Tonbridge Road, Hildenborough TN11 9HP *Livery*, 160.
Clerk, Susan Nevard *Master*, Tim Solway

WATER CONSERVATORS (102). The Lark, Bell Lane, Bury St Edmunds IP28 8SE *Livery*, 201.
Clerk, Ralph Riley *Master*, Simon Catford

WAX CHANDLERS (20). *Hall*, Wax Chandlers' Hall, 6 Gresham Street, London EC2V 7AD *Livery*, 115.
Clerk, Richard Moule *Master*, Joan Beavington

WEAVERS (42). Saddlers' House, Gutter Lane, London EC2V 6BR *Livery*, 128.
Clerk, John Snowdon *Upper Bailiff*, John Garbutt

WHEELWRIGHTS (68). 90 Fernside Road, London SW12 8LJ *Livery*, 218.
Clerk, Susie Morris *Master*, Bert Wiegman

WOOLMEN (43). 153 Leathwaite Road, SW11 6RW *Livery*, 160.
Clerk, Duncan Crole *Master*, Andrew Dawson

WORLD TRADERS (101). 13 Hall Gardens, St. Albans AL4 0QF *Livery*, 216.
Clerk, Gaye Duffy *Master*, Dr Edwina Moreton, OBE

PARISH CLERKS (No Livery*). Acreholt, 33 Medstead Road, Alton GU34 4AD *Members*, 89.
Clerk, Alana Coombes *Master*, Lynette Stone, CBE

WATERMEN AND LIGHTERMEN (No Livery*). *Hall*, Watermen's Hall, 16–18 St Mary at Hill, London EC3R 8EF *Craft Owning Freemen*, 376.
Clerk, Colin Middlemiss *Master*, Iain Reid

WALES

Cymru

The principality of Wales (Cymru) occupies the extreme west of the central southern portion of the island of Great Britain, with a total area of 20,778 sq. km (8,022 sq. miles): land 20,733 sq. km (8,005 sq. miles); inland water 45 sq. km (17 sq. miles). It is bordered in the north by the Irish Sea, in the south by the Bristol Channel, in the east by the English counties of Cheshire West and Chester, Shropshire, Herefordshire and Gloucestershire, and in the west by St George's Channel.

Across the Menai Straits is Ynys Mon (Isle of Anglesey) (715 sq. km/276 sq. miles), communication with which is facilitated by the Menai Suspension Bridge (305m/1,000ft long) built by Telford in 1826, and by the Britannia Bridge (351m/1,151ft), a two-tier road and rail truss arch design, rebuilt in 1972 after a fire destroyed the original tubular railway bridge built by Stephenson in 1850. Holyhead harbour, on Holy Isle (north-west of Anglesey), provides ferry services to Dublin (113km/70 miles).

The Local Government (Wales) Act 1994 abolished the two-tier structure of eight county and 37 district councils which had existed since 1974, and replaced it, from 1 April 1996, with 22 unitary authorities. The new authorities were elected in May 1995. Each unitary authority inherited all the functions of the previous county and district councils, except fire services (which are provided by three combined fire authorities, composed of representatives from the unitary authorities) and national parks (which are the responsibility of three independent national park authorities).

POPULATION
The population at the 2011 census was 3,063,456 (men 1,504,228; women 1,559,228). The average density of population in 2011 was 147 persons per sq. km (382 per sq. mile).

COMMUNITY COUNCILS
In Wales communities are the equivalent of parishes in England. Unlike England, where many areas are not in any parish, communities have been established for the whole of Wales, approximately 865 communities in all. Community meetings may be convened as and when desired.

Community or town councils exist in around 730 of the communities and further councils may be established at the request of a community meeting. Community councils have broadly the same range of powers as English parish councils. Community councillors are elected for a term of four years.

ELECTIONS
Elections usually take place every four years; the last elections took place on 4 May 2017.

FINANCE
Total budgeted revenue expenditure for 2018–19 is £8.1bn, an increase of 2 per cent on 2017–18. Total budget requirement, which excludes expenditure financed by specific and special government grants and any use of reserves, is £6.4bn. This comprises revenue support grant of £3.3bn, support from the national non-domestic rate pool of £1.1bn, police grant of £209m and £1.8bn to be raised through council tax. The non-domestic rating multiplier for Wales for 2018–19 is 51.4p. The average Band D council tax levied in Wales for 2018–19 is £1,492, comprising unitary authorities £1,219, police and crime commissioners £239 and community councils £34.

EXPENDITURE
Local authority budgeted revenue expenditure for 2018–19 is:

Service	£ million
Education	2,625.8
Social services	1,839.8
Council fund housing	1,125.8
Local environmental services	376.6
Roads and transport	273.0
Libraries, culture, heritage, sport and recreation	198.4
Planning, economic and community development	70.7
Council tax collection	27.3
Debt financing	298.3
Central administrative and other revenue expenditure	381.5
Police	721.9
Fire	157.0
National parks	14.8
Gross revenue expenditure	8,110.8
Less specific and special government grants	(1,851.4)
Net revenue expenditure	6,259.4
Less appropriations from reserves	(147.3)
Council tax reduction scheme	261.7
BUDGET REQUIREMENT	6,373.8

RELIEF
Wales is a country of extensive tracts of high plateau and shorter stretches of mountain ranges deeply dissected by river valleys. Lower-lying ground is largely confined to the coastal belt and the lower parts of the valleys. The highest mountains are those of Snowdonia in the north-west (Snowdon, 1,085m/3,559ft and Aran Fawddwy, 906m/2,971ft). Snowdonia is also home to Cader Idris (Pen y Gadair, 892m/2,928ft). Other high peaks are to be found in the Cambrian range (Plynlimon, 752m/2,467ft), and the Black Mountains, Brecon Beacons and Black Forest ranges in the south-east (Pen y Fan, 886m/2,906ft; Waun Fâch, 811m/2,660ft; Carmarthen Van, 802m/2,630ft).

HYDROGRAPHY
The principal river in Wales is the Severn, which flows from the slopes of Plynlimon to the English border. The Wye (209km/130 miles) also rises on the slopes of Plynlimon. The Usk (90km/56 miles) flows into the Bristol Channel through Gwent. The Dee (113km/70 miles) rises in Bala Lake and flows through the Vale of Llangollen, where an aqueduct (built by Telford in 1805) carries the Pontcysyllte branch of the Shropshire Union Canal across the valley. The estuary of the Dee is the navigable portion; it is 23km (14 miles) in length and about 8km (5 miles) in breadth. The Towy (109km/68 miles), Teifi (80km/50 miles), Taff (64km/40 miles), Dovey (48km/30 miles), Taf (40km/25 miles) and Conway (39km/24 miles) are wholly Welsh rivers.

The largest natural lake is Bala (Llyn Tegid) in Gwynedd, nearly 7km (4 miles) long and 1.6km (1 mile) wide. Lake Vyrnwy is an artificial reservoir, about the size of Bala, and forms the water supply of Liverpool; Birmingham's water is supplied from reservoirs in the Elan and Claerwen valleys.

WELSH LANGUAGE

According to the 2011 census results, the percentage of people aged three years and over who are able to speak Welsh is:

Blaenau Gwent	7.8	Neath Port Talbot	15.3
Bridgend	9.7	Newport	9.3
Caerphilly	11.2	Pembrokeshire	19.2
Cardiff	11.1	Powys	18.6
Carmarthenshire	43.9	Rhondda Cynon Taf	12.3
Ceredigion	47.3	Swansea	11.4
Conwy	27.4	Torfaen	9.8
Denbighshire	24.6	Vale of Glamorgan	10.8
Flintshire	13.2	Wrexham	12.9
Gwynedd	65.4	Ynys Mon	
Merthyr Tydfil	8.9	(Isle of Anglesey)	57.2
Monmouthshire	9.9	*Total in Wales*	19.0

FLAG

The flag of Wales, the Red Dragon *(Y Ddraig Goch),* is a red dragon on a field divided by white over green *(per fess argent and vert a dragon passant gules).* The flag was augmented in 1953 by a royal badge on a shield encircled with a riband bearing the words *Ddraig Goch Ddyry Cychwyn* and imperially crowned, but this augmented flag is rarely used.

EARLY HISTORY

The earliest inhabitants of whom there is any record appear to have been subdued or exterminated by the Goidels (a people of Celtic race) in the Bronze Age. A further invasion of Celtic Brythons and Belgae followed in the ensuing Iron Age. The Roman conquest of southern Britain and Wales was for some time successfully opposed by Caratacus (Caractacus or Caradog), chieftain of the Catuvellauni and son of Cunobelinus (Cymbeline). South-east Wales was subjugated and the legionary fortress at Caerleon-on-Usk established by around AD 75–7; the conquest of Wales was completed by Agricola around AD 78. Communications were opened up by the construction of military roads from Chester to Caerleon-on-Usk and Caerwent, and from Chester to Conwy (and thence to Carmarthen and Neath). Christianity was introduced in the fourth century, during the Roman occupation.

ANGLO-SAXON ATTACKS

The Anglo-Saxon invaders of southern Britain drove the Celts into the mountain stronghold of Wales, and into Strathclyde (Cumberland and south-west Scotland) and Cornwall, giving them the name of *Waelisc* (Welsh), meaning 'foreign'. The West Saxons' victory of Deorham (AD 577) isolated Wales from Cornwall and the battle of Chester (AD 613) cut off communication with Strathclyde and northern Britain. In the eighth century the boundaries of the Welsh were further restricted by the annexations of Offa, King of Mercia, and counter-attacks were largely prevented by the construction of an artificial boundary from the Dee to the Wye (Offa's Dyke).

In the ninth century Rhodri Mawr (844–878) united the country and successfully resisted further incursions of the Saxons by land and raids of Norse and Danish pirates by sea, but at his death his three provinces of Gwynedd (north), Powys (central) and Deheubarth (south) were divided among his three sons, Anarawd, Mervyn and Cadell. Cadell's son Hywel Dda ruled a large part of Wales and codified its laws but the provinces were not united again until the rule of Llewelyn ap Seisyllt (husband of the heiress of Gwynedd) from 1018 to 1023.

THE NORMAN CONQUEST

After the Norman conquest of England, William I created palatine counties along the Welsh frontier, and the Norman barons began to make encroachments into Welsh territory. The Welsh princes recovered many of their losses during the civil wars of Stephen's reign (1135–54), and in the early 13th century Owen Gruffydd, prince of Gwynedd, was the dominant figure in Wales. Under Llewelyn ap Iorwerth (1194–1240) the Welsh united in powerful resistance to English incursions and Llywelyn's privileges and *de facto* independence were recognised in the Magna Carta. His grandson, Llywelyn ap Gruffydd, was the last native prince; he was killed in 1282 during hostilities between the Welsh and English, allowing Edward I of England to establish his authority over the country. On 7 February 1301, Edward of Caernarvon, son of Edward I, was created Prince of Wales, a title subsequently borne by the eldest son of the sovereign.

Strong Welsh national feeling continued, expressed in the early 15th century in the rising led by Owain Glyndwr, but the situation was altered by the accession to the English throne in 1485 of Henry VII of the Welsh House of Tudor. Wales was politically annexed by England under the Act of Union of 1535, which extended English laws to the principality and gave it parliamentary representation for the first time.

EISTEDDFOD

The Welsh are a distinct nation, with a language and literature of their own; the national bardic festival (Eisteddfod), instituted by Prince Rhys ap Griffith in 1176, is still held annually.

PRINCIPAL CITIES

There are six cities in Wales (with date city status conferred): Bangor (pre-1900), Cardiff (1905), Newport (2002), St Asaph (2012), St David's (1994) and Swansea (1969).

Cardiff and Swansea have also been granted lord mayoralities.

CARDIFF

Cardiff *(Caerdydd),* at the mouth of the rivers Taff, Rhymney and Ely, is the capital city of Wales. The city has changed dramatically in recent years following the regeneration of Cardiff Bay and construction of a barrage, which has created a permanent freshwater lake and waterfront for the city. As the capital city, Cardiff is home to the National Assembly for Wales and is a major administrative, retail, business and cultural centre.

The city is home to many fine buildings, including the City Hall, Cardiff Castle, Llandaff Cathedral, the National Museum of Wales, university buildings, law courts and the Temple of Peace and Health. The Millennium Stadium opened in 1999 and has hosted high-profile events since 2001.

SWANSEA

Swansea *(Abertawe)* is a seaport with a population of 239,023 at the 2011 census. The Gower peninsula was brought within the city boundary under local government reform in 1974.

The principal buildings are the Norman castle (rebuilt *c.*1330), the Royal Institution of South Wales, founded in 1835 (including library), the University of Swansea at Singleton and the Guildhall, containing Frank Brangwyn's British Empire panels. The Dylan Thomas Centre, formerly the old Guildhall, was restored in 1995. More recent buildings include the County Hall, the Maritime Quarter Marina, the Wales National Pool and the National Waterfront Museum.

Swansea was chartered by the Earl of Warwick (1158–84), and further charters were granted by King John, Henry III, Edward II, Edward III and James II, Oliver Cromwell and the Marcher Lord William de Breos. It was formally invested with city status in 1969.

LORD-LIEUTENANTS AND HIGH SHERIFFS

Area	Lord-Lieutenant	High Sheriff (2018–19)
Clwyd	Henry Fetherstonhaugh, OBE	Lady Hanmer
Dyfed	Sara Edwards	Stephen Davies
Gwent	Brig. Robert Aiken, CBE	Sharon Linnard
Gwynedd	Edmund Bailey	Kathryn Ellis
Mid Glamorgan	Dame Kate Thomas, DCVO	Jonathan Wall
Powys	Hon. Dame Elizabeth Legge-Bourke, DCVO	David Price
S. Glamorgan	Morfudd Ann Meredith	Brian Lakin
W. Glamorgan	D. Byron Lewis	Henry Gilbert

LOCAL COUNCILS

Council	Administrative HQ	Telephone	Pop.*	Council Tax†	Chief Executive
Blaenau Gwent	Ebbw Vale	01495-311556	69,609	£1,828	Nigel Daniels
Bridgend	Bridgend	01656-643643	144,288	£1,676	Darren Mepham
Caerphilly	Hengoed	01443-815588	180,795	£1,309	Christina Harrhy
CARDIFF	Cardiff	029-2087 2087	362,756	£1,391	Paul Orders
Carmarthenshire	Carmarthen	01267-234567	186,452	£1,500	Mark James, CBE
Ceredigion	Aberaeron	01545-570881	73,076	£1,484	Eifion Evans
Conwy	Conwy	01492-574000	116,863	£1,496	Iwan Davies
Denbighshire	Ruthin	01824-706101	95,159	£1,555	Judith Greenhalgh
Flintshire	Mold	01352-752121	155,155	£1,480	Colin Everett
Gwynedd	Caernarfon	01766-771000	123,742	£1,601	Dilwyn Williams
Merthyr Tydfil	Merthyr Tydfil	01685-725000	59,953	£1,735	Gareth Chapman
Monmouthshire	Cwmbran	01633-644644	93,590	£1,539	Paul Matthews
Neath Port Talbot	Port Talbot	01639-686868	142,090	£1,772	Stephen Phillips
NEWPORT	Newport	01633-656656	151,485	£1,301	Will Godfrey
Pembrokeshire	Haverfordwest	01437-764551	124,711	£1,252	Ian Westley
Powys	Llandrindod Wells	01597-827460	132,515	£1,471	Dr Mohammed Mehet
Rhondda Cynon Taff	Tonypandy	01443-425005	239,127	£1,666	Chris Bradshaw
SWANSEA	Swansea	01792-636000	245,480	£1,518	Phil Roberts
Torfaen	Pontypool	01495-762200	92,264	£1,526	Alison Ward
Vale of Glamorgan	Barry	01446-700111	130,690	£1,466	Rob Thomas
Wrexham	Wrexham	01978-292000	135,571	£1,398	Ian Barncroft
Ynys Mon (Isle of Anglesey)	Ynys Mon	01248-750057	69,794	£1,441	Dr Gwynne Jones

* Source: Office for National Statistics – Mid-2017 Population Estimates (Crown copyright)
† Average Band D council tax bill 2018–19
Councils in CAPITAL LETTERS have city status

Key	Council	Key	Council
1	Anglesey (Ynys Mon)	12	Merthyr Tydfil
2	Blaenau Gwent	13	Monmouthshire
3	Bridgend	14	Neath Port Talbot
4	Caerphilly	15	NEWPORT
5	CARDIFF	16	Pembrokeshire
6	Carmarthenshire	17	Powys
7	Ceredigion	18	Rhondda Cynon Taff
8	Conwy	19	SWANSEA
9	Denbighshire	20	Torfaen
10	Flintshire	21	Vale of Glamorgan
11	Gwynedd	22	Wrexham

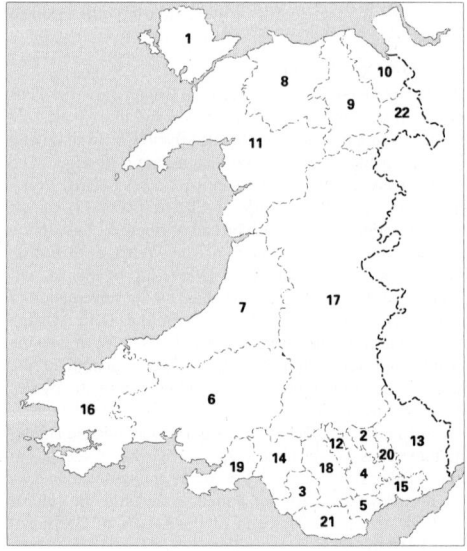

SCOTLAND

Scotland occupies the northern portion of the main island of Great Britain and includes the Inner and Outer Hebrides, Orkney, Shetland and many other islands. It lies between 60° 51′ 30″ and 54° 38′ N. latitude and between 1° 45′ 32″ and 6° 14′ W. longitude, with England to the south-east, the North Channel and the Irish Sea to the south-west, the Atlantic Ocean on the north and west, and the North Sea on the east.

The greatest length of the mainland (Cape Wrath to the Mull of Galloway) is 441km (274 miles), and the greatest breadth (Buchan Ness to Applecross) is 248km (154 miles). The customary measurement of the island of Great Britain is from the site of John o' Groats house, near Duncansby Head, Caithness, to Land's End, Cornwall, a total distance of 970km (603 miles) in a straight line and approximately 1,448km (900 miles) by road.

The Local Government etc (Scotland) Act 1994 abolished the two-tier structure of nine regional and 53 district councils which had existed since 1975 and replaced it, from 1 April 1996, with 29 unitary authorities on the mainland; the three islands councils remained. The new authorities were elected in April 1995.

In July 1999 the Scottish parliament assumed responsibility for legislation on local government.

The total area of Scotland is 78,807 sq. km (30,427 sq. miles): land 77,907 sq. km (30,080 sq. miles), inland water 900 sq. km (347 sq. miles).

POPULATION
The population at the 2011 census was 5,295,403 (men 2,567,444; women 2,727,959). The average density of the population in 2011 was 67 persons per sq. km (174 per sq. mile).

ELECTIONS
The unitary authorities consist of directly elected councillors. The Scottish Local Government (Elections) Act 2002 moved elections from a three-year to a four-year cycle. The last local authority elections took place in May 2017.

FUNCTIONS
The functions of the councils and islands councils are: education; social work; strategic planning; the provision of infrastructure such as roads; consumer protection; flood prevention; coast protection; valuation and rating; the police and fire services; civil defence; electoral registration; public transport; registration of births, deaths and marriages; housing; leisure and recreation; development and building control; environmental health; licensing; allotments; public conveniences; and the administration of district courts.

COMMUNITY COUNCILS
Scottish community councils differ from those in England and Wales. Their purpose as defined in statute is to ascertain and express the views of the communities they represent, and to take in the interests of their communities such action as appears to be expedient or practicable. Around 1,200 community councils have been established under schemes drawn up by local authorities in Scotland.

FINANCE
For 2018–19 Scotland's local authorities set a net revenue expenditure budget of £12.1bn for spending on all services; education accounted for 43 per cent of the total budget and social work 27.3 per cent.

Budgeted total revenue income for 2018–19 is £12bn, comprising government grants (£7.1bn), non-domestic rates

(£2.6bn) and council tax (£2.3bn). The remaining £113m will be funded from local authority reserves.

The non-domestic rate multiplier or poundage for 2018–19 is 48p. Larger businesses in 2018–19 (rateable value in excess of £51,000) pay a poundage supplement of 2.6p, which contributes towards the cost of the small business bonus scheme. Non-domestic properties with a rateable value of £15,000 or less do not have to pay business rates in 2018–19. The average Band D council tax for 2018–19 is £1,208.

EXPENDITURE
Local authority budgeted net revenue expenditure for 2018–19 is:

Service	£ million
Education	5,159.0
Cultural and related services	537.5
Social work	3,260.0
Roads and transport	388.5
Environmental services	679.0
Planning and development services	241.3
Other services	716.8
Non-service costs	1,155.2
TOTAL	12,137.3

RELIEF
There are three natural orographic divisions of Scotland. The southern uplands have their highest points in Merrick (843m/2,766ft), Rhinns of Kells (814m/2,669ft) and Cairnsmuir of Carsphairn (797m/2,614ft), in the west; and the Tweedsmuir Hills in the east (Broad Law 840m/2,756ft; Dollar Law 817m/2,682ft; Hartfell 808m/2,651ft).

The central lowlands, formed by the valleys of the Clyde, Forth and Tay, divide the southern uplands from the Highlands, which extend from close to the extreme north of the mainland to the central lowlands, and are divided into a northern and a southern system by the Great Glen.

The Grampian Mountains, the southern Highland system, include in the west Ben Nevis (1,345m/4,412ft), the highest point in the British Isles, and in the east the Cairngorm Mountains (Ben Macdui 1,309m/4,296ft; Braeriach 1,295m/4,248ft; Cairn Gorm 1,245m/4,084ft). The north-west Highlands contain the mountains of Wester and Easter Ross (Carn Eige 1,183m/3,880ft; Sgurr na Lapaich 1,151m/3,775ft).

Created, like the central lowlands, by a major geological fault, the Great Glen (97km/60 miles long) runs between Inverness and Fort William, and contains Loch Ness, Loch Oich and Loch Lochy. These are linked to each other and to the north-east and south-west coasts of Scotland by the Caledonian Canal, providing a navigable passage between the Moray Firth and the Inner Hebrides.

HYDROGRAPHY
The western coast is fragmented by peninsulas and islands, and indented by fjords (sea-lochs), the longest of which is Loch Fyne (68km/42 miles long) in Argyll. Although the east coast tends to be less fractured and lower, there are several great drowned inlets (firths), including the Firth of Forth, Firth of Tay and the Moray Firth, as well as the Firth of Clyde in the west.

The lochs are the principal hydrographic feature. The largest in Scotland and in Britain is Loch Lomond (70 sq. km/27 sq. miles), in the Grampian valleys, and the longest and deepest is Loch Ness (39km/24 miles long and 244m/800ft deep), in the Great Glen.

The longest river is the Tay (188km/117 miles), noted for its salmon. It flows into the North Sea, with Dundee on the estuary, which is spanned by the Tay Bridge (3,136m/

10,289ft) opened in 1887 and the Tay Road Bridge (2,245m/7,365ft) opened in 1966. Other noted salmon rivers are the Dee (145km/90 miles) which flows into the North Sea at Aberdeen, and the Spey (177km/110 miles), the swiftest flowing river in the British Isles, which flows into the Moray Firth. The Tweed, which gave its name to the woollen cloth produced along its banks, marks in the lower stretches of its 154km (96 mile) course the border between Scotland and England.

The most important river commercially is the Clyde (171km/106 miles), formed by the junction of the Daer and Portrail water, which flows through the city of Glasgow to the Firth of Clyde. During its course it passes over the picturesque Falls of Clyde, Bonnington Linn (9m/30ft), Corra Linn (26m/84ft), Dundaff Linn (3m/10ft) and Stonebyres Linn (24m/80ft), above and below Lanark. The Forth (106km/66 miles), upon which stands Edinburgh, the capital, is spanned by the Forth Railway Bridge (1890), which is 1,625m (5,330ft) long, and the Forth Road Bridge (1964), which has a total length of 1,876m (6,156ft) (over water) and a single span of 914m (3,000ft).

The highest waterfall in Scotland, and the British Isles, is Eas a'Chùal Aluinn with a total height of 201m (658ft), which falls from Glas Bheinn in Sutherland. The Falls of Glomach, on a head-stream of the Elchaig in Wester Ross, have a drop of 113m (370ft).

GAELIC LANGUAGE
According to the 2011 census, 1.1 per cent (58,000 people) of the population of Scotland aged three and over were able to speak the Scottish form of Gaelic. This was a slight decrease from the 1.2 per cent recorded at the 2001 census.

LOWLAND SCOTTISH LANGUAGE
Several regional lowland Scottish dialects, known variously as Scots, Lallans or Doric, are widely spoken. According to the 2011 census, 43 per cent of the population of Scotland aged three and over stated they could do one or a combination of read, write, speak or understand Scots. A question on Scots was not included in the 2001 census.

FLAG
The flag of Scotland is known as the Saltire. It is a white diagonal cross on a blue field (saltire argent in a field azure) and represents St Andrew, the patron saint of Scotland.

THE SCOTTISH ISLANDS

ORKNEY
The Orkney Islands (total area 972 sq. km/376 sq. miles) lie about 10km (six miles) north of the mainland, separated from it by the Pentland Firth. Of the 90 islands and islets (holms and skerries) in the group, about one-third are inhabited.

The total population at the 2011 census was 21,349; the 2011 populations of the islands shown here include those of smaller islands forming part of the same council district.

Mainland, 17,162	Inner Holm, 1
Auskerry, 4	Norh Ronaldsay, 72
Burray, 409	Papa Westray, 90
Eday, 160	Rousay, 216
Egilsay, 26	Sanday, 494
Flotta, 8	Shapinsay, 307
Gairsay, 3	South Ronaldsay, 909
Graemsay, 28	Stronsay, 349
Holm of Grimbister, 3	Westray, 588
Hoy, 419	Wyre, 29

The islands are rich in prehistoric and Scandinavian remains, the most notable being the Stone Age village of Skara Brae, the burial chamber of Maes Howe, the many brochs (towers) and the 12th-century St Magnus Cathedral. Scapa Flow,

between the Mainland and Hoy, was the war station of the British Grand Fleet from 1914 to 1919 and the scene of the scuttling of the surrendered German High Seas Fleet (21 June 1919).

Most of the islands are low-lying and fertile, and farming (principally beef cattle) is the main industry. Flotta, to the south of Scapa Flow, is the site of the oil terminal for the Piper, Claymore and Tartan fields in the North Sea.

The capital is Kirkwall (population 7,045) situated on Mainland.

SHETLAND
The Shetland Islands have a total area of 1,427 sq. km (551 sq. miles) and had a population at the 2011 census of 23,167. They lie about 80km (50 miles) north of the Orkneys, with Fair Isle about half way between the two groups. Out Stack, off Muckle Flugga, 1.6km (one mile) north of Unst, is the most northerly part of the British Isles (60° 51′ 30″ N. lat.).

There are over 100 islands, of which 16 are inhabited. Populations at the 2011 census were:

Mainland, 18,765	Muckle Roe, 130
Bressay, 368	Papa Stour, 15
Bruray, 24	Trondra, 135
East Burra, 76	Unst, 632
Fair Isle, 68	Vaila, 2
Fotlar, 61	West Burra, 776
Foula, 38	Whalsay, 1,061
Housay, 50	Yell, 966

Shetland's many archaeological sites include Jarlshof, Mousa and Clickhimin, and its long connection with Scandinavia has resulted in a strong Norse influence on its place names and dialect.

Industries include fishing, knitwear and farming. In addition to the fishing fleet there are fish processing factories, and the traditional handknitting of Fair Isle and Unst is now supplemented with machine-knitted garments. Farming is mainly crofting, with sheep being raised on the moorland and hills of the islands. Latterly the islands have become a centre of the North Sea oil industry, with pipelines from the Brent and Ninian fields running to the terminal at Sullom Voe, the largest of its kind in Europe.

The capital is Lerwick (population 6,958) situated on Mainland. Lerwick is the main centre for supply services for offshore oil exploration and development.

THE HEBRIDES
Until the late 13th century the Hebrides included other Scottish islands in the Firth of Clyde, the peninsula of Kintyre (Argyll), the Isle of Man and the (Irish) Isle of Rathlin. The origin of the name is probably the Greek *Eboudai,* latinised as *Hebudes* by Pliny, and corrupted to its present form. The Norwegian name *Sudreyjar* (Southern Islands) was latinised as *Sodorenses,* a name that survives in the Anglican bishopric of Sodor and Man.

There are over 500 islands and islets, of which about 100 are inhabited, though mountainous terrain and extensive peat bogs mean that only a fraction of the total area is under cultivation. Stone, Bronze and Iron Age settlement has left many remains, including those at Callanish on Lewis, and Norse colonisation influenced language, customs and place names. Occupations include farming (mostly crofting and stock-raising), fishing and the manufacture of tweeds and other woollens. Tourism is also an important part of the economy.

The Inner Hebrides lie off the west coast of Scotland and are relatively close to the mainland. The largest and best-known is Skye (area 1,665 sq. km/643 sq. miles; pop. 10,008; chief town, Portree), which contains the Cuillin Hills (Sgurr Alasdair, 993m/3,257ft), Bla Bheinn (928m/3,046ft), the

Storr (719m/2,358ft) and the Red Hills (Beinn na Caillich, 732m/2,403ft). Other islands in the Highland council area include Raasay (pop. 161), Eigg (pop. 83), Muck (pop. 27) and Rhum (pop. 22).

Further south the Inner Hebridean islands include Arran (pop. 4,629), containing Goat Fell (874m/2,868ft); Coll (pop. 195) and Tiree (pop. 653); Colonsay (pop. 124) and Oronsay (pop. 8); Easdale (pop. 59); Gigha (pop. 163); Islay (area 608 sq. km/235 sq. miles; pop. 3,228); Jura (area 414 sq. km/160 sq. miles; pop. 196), with a range of hills culminating in the Paps of Jura (Beinn-an-Oir, 785m/2,576ft, and Beinn Chaolais, 755m/2,477ft); Lismore (pop. 192); Luing (pop. 195); and Mull (area 950 sq. km/367 sq. miles; pop. 2,800; chief town Tobermory), containing Ben More (967m/3,171ft).

The Outer Hebrides, separated from the mainland by the Minch, now form the Eilean Siar (Western Isles) council (area 2,897 sq. km/1,119 sq. miles; pop. 27,684). The main islands are Lewis with Harris (area 1,994 sq. km/770 sq. miles, pop. 21,031), whose chief town, Stornoway, is the administrative seat; North Uist (pop. 1,254); South Uist (pop. 1,754); Benbecula (pop. 1,303) and Barra (pop. 1,174). Other inhabited islands include Great Bernera (252), Berneray (138), Eriskay (143), Grimsay (169), Scalpay (291) and Vatersay (90).

EARLY HISTORY

There is evidence of human settlement in Scotland dating from the third millennium BC, the earliest settlers being Mesolithic hunters and fishermen. Early in the second millennium BC, Neolithic farmers began to cultivate crops and rear livestock; their settlements were on the west coast and in the north, and included Skara Brae and Maeshowe (Orkney). Settlement by the early Bronze Age 'Beaker Folk', so-called from the shape of their drinking vessels, in eastern Scotland dates from about 1800 BC. Further settlement is believed to have occurred from 700 BC onwards, as tribes were displaced from further south by new incursions from the Continent and the Roman invasions from AD 43.

Julius Agricola, the Roman governor of Britain AD 77–84, extended the Roman conquests in Britain by advancing into Caledonia, culminating with a victory at Mons Graupius, probably in AD 84; he was recalled to Rome shortly after and his forward policy was not pursued. Hadrian's Wall, mostly completed by AD 30, marked the northern frontier of the Roman empire except for the period between about AD 144 and 190 when the frontier moved north to the Forth-Clyde isthmus and a turf wall, the Antonine Wall, was manned.

After the Roman withdrawal from Britain, there were centuries of warfare between the Picts, Scots, Britons, Angles and Vikings. The Picts, generally accepted to be descended from the indigenous Iron Age people of northern Scotland, occupied the area north of the Forth. The Scots, a Gaelic-speaking people of northern Ireland, colonised the area of Argyll and Bute (the kingdom of Dalriada) in the fifth century AD and then expanded eastwards and northwards. The Britons, speaking a Brythonic Celtic language, colonised Scotland from the south from the first century BC; they lost control of south-eastern Scotland (incorporated into the kingdom of Northumbria) to the Angles in the early seventh century but retained Strathclyde (south-western Scotland and Cumbria). Viking raids from the late eighth century were followed by Norse settlement in the western and northern isles, Argyll, Caithness and Sutherland from the mid-ninth century onwards.

UNIFICATION

The union of the areas which now comprise Scotland began in AD 843 when Kenneth MacAlpin, king of the Scots from c.834, also became king of the Picts, joining the two lands to form the kingdom of Alba (comprising Scotland north of a line between the Forth and Clyde rivers). Lothian, the eastern part of the area between the Forth and the Tweed, seems to have been leased to Kenneth II of Alba (reigned 971–995) by Edgar of England c.973, and Scottish possession was confirmed by Malcolm II's victory over a Northumbrian army at Carham c.1016. At about this time Malcolm II (reigned 1005–34) placed his grandson Duncan on the throne of the British kingdom of Strathclyde, bringing under Scots rule virtually all of what is now Scotland.

The Norse possessions were incorporated into the kingdom of Scotland from the 12th century onwards. An uprising in the mid-12th century drove the Norse from most of mainland Argyll. The Hebrides were ceded to Scotland by the Treaty of Perth in 1266 after a Norwegian expedition in 1263 failed to maintain Norse authority over the islands. Orkney and Shetland fell to Scotland in 1468–9 as a pledge for the unpaid dowry of Margaret of Denmark, wife of James III, although Danish claims of suzerainty were relinquished only with the marriage of Anne of Denmark to James VI in 1590.

From the 11th century, there were frequent wars between Scotland and England over territory and the extent of England's political influence. The failure of the Scottish royal line with the death of Margaret of Norway in 1290 led to disputes over the throne which were resolved by the adjudication of Edward I of England. He awarded the throne to John Balliol in 1292 but Balliol's refusal to be a puppet king led to war. Balliol surrendered to Edward I in 1296 and Edward attempted to rule Scotland himself. Resistance to Scotland's loss of independence was led by William Wallace, who defeated the English at Stirling Bridge (1297), and Robert Bruce, crowned in 1306, who held most of Scotland by 1311 and routed Edward II's army at Bannockburn (1314). England recognised the independence of Scotland in the Treaty of Northampton in 1328. Subsequent clashes include the disastrous battle of Flodden (1513) in which James IV and many of his nobles fell.

THE UNION

In 1603 James VI of Scotland succeeded Elizabeth I on the throne of England (his mother, Mary Queen of Scots, was the great-granddaughter of Henry VII), his successors reigning as sovereigns of Great Britain. Political union of the two countries did not occur until 1707.

THE JACOBITE REVOLTS

After the abdication (by flight) in 1688 of James VII and II, the crown devolved upon William III (grandson of Charles I) and Mary II (elder daughter of James VII and II). In 1689 Graham of Claverhouse roused the Highlands on behalf of James VII and II, but died after a military success at Killiecrankie.

After the death of Anne (younger daughter of James VII and II), the throne devolved upon George I (great-grandson of James VI and I). In 1715, armed risings on behalf of James Stuart (the Old Pretender, son of James VII and II) led to the indecisive battle of Sheriffmuir, and the Jacobite movement died down until 1745, when Charles Stuart (the Young Pretender) defeated the Royalist troops at Prestonpans and advanced to Derby (1746). From Derby, the adherents of 'James VIII and III' (the title claimed for his father by Charles Stuart) fell back on the defensive and were finally crushed at Culloden (16 April 1746) by an army led by the Duke of Cumberland, son of George II.

PRINCIPAL CITIES

ABERDEEN

Aberdeen, 209km (130 miles) north-east of Edinburgh, received its charter as a Royal Burgh in 1124. Scotland's third largest city, Aberdeen lies between two rivers, the Dee and the Don, facing the North Sea; the city has a strong maritime history and is today a major centre for offshore oil exploration and production. It is also an ancient university town and distinguished research centre. Other industries include engineering, food processing, textiles, paper manufacturing and chemicals.

Places of interest include King's College, St Machar's Cathedral, Brig o' Balgownie, Duthie Park and Winter Gardens, Hazlehead Park, Kirk of St Nicholas, Mercat Cross, Marischal College and Marischal Museum, Provost Skene's House, Aberdeen Art Gallery, Gordon Highlanders Museum, Satrosphere Science Centre, and Aberdeen Maritime Museum.

DUNDEE

The Royal Burgh of Dundee is situated on the north bank of the Tay estuary. The city's port and dock installations are important to the offshore oil industry and the airport also provides servicing facilities. Principal industries include textiles, biotechnology and digital media, lasers, printing, tyre manufacture, food processing, engineering and tourism.

The unique City Churches – three churches under one roof, together with the 15th-century St Mary's Tower – are the most prominent architectural feature. Dundee is home to two historic ships: the Dundee-built RRS *Discovery* which took Capt. Scott to the Antarctic lies alongside Discovery Quay, and the frigate *Unicorn*, the only British-built wooden warship still afloat, is moored in Victoria Dock. Places of interest include Mills Public Observatory, the Tay road and rail bridges, Dundee Contemporary Arts centre, McManus Galleries, Claypotts Castle, Broughty Castle, Verdant Works (textile heritage centre) and the Sensation Science Centre.

EDINBURGH

Edinburgh is the capital city and seat of government in Scotland. The new Scottish parliament building designed by Enric Miralles was completed in 2004 and is open to visitors. The city is built on a group of hills and both the Old and New Towns are inscribed on the UNESCO World Cultural and Natural Heritage List for their cultural significance.

Other places of interest include the castle, which houses the Stone of Scone and also includes St Margaret's Chapel, the oldest building in Edinburgh, and near it, the Scottish National War Memorial; the Palace of Holyroodhouse, the Queen's official residence in Scotland; Parliament House, the present seat of the judicature; Princes Street; three universities (Edinburgh, Heriot-Watt, Napier); St Giles' Cathedral; St Mary's (Scottish Episcopal) Cathedral (Sir George Gilbert Scott); General Register House (Robert Adam); the National and Signet libraries; the National Gallery of Scotland; the Royal Scottish Academy and the Scottish National Portrait Gallery.

GLASGOW

Glasgow, a Royal Burgh, is Scotland's largest city and its principal commercial and industrial centre. The city occupies the north and south banks of the Clyde, formerly one of the chief commercial estuaries in the world. The main industries include engineering, electronics, finance, chemicals and printing.

The chief buildings are the 13th-century Gothic cathedral, the university (Sir George Gilbert Scott), the City Chambers, the Royal Concert Hall, St Mungo Museum of Religious Life and Art, Pollok House, the School of Art (Charles Rennie Mackintosh), Kelvingrove Art Gallery and Museum, the Gallery of Modern Art, the Riverside Museum: Scotland's Museum of Transport and Travel (Zaha Hadid), the Burrell Collection museum and the Mitchell Library. The city is home to the Royal Scottish National Orchestra, Scottish Opera, Scottish Ballet, BBC Scotland and Scottish Television (STV).

INVERNESS

Inverness was granted city status in 2000. The city's name is derived from the Gaelic for 'the mouth of the Ness', referring to the river on which it lies. Inverness is recorded as being at the junction of trade routes since AD 565. Known as the capital of the Highlands it is the main administrative centre for the north of Scotland.

Among the city's most notable buildings is Abertarff House, built in 1593 and the oldest secular building remaining in Inverness. Balnain House, built as a town house in 1726, is a fine example of early Georgian architecture. The Old High Church, on St Michael's Mount, is the original parish church of Inverness and is built on the site of the earliest Christian church in the city. Parts of the church date back to the 14th century.

Stirling was granted city status in 2002 and Perth in 2012. Aberdeen, Dundee, Edinburgh and Glasgow have also been granted lord mayoralty/lord provostship.

LORD-LIEUTENANTS

Title	Name
Aberdeen City*	Lord Provost Barney Crockett
Aberdeenshire	James Ingleby
Angus	Georgiana Osborne, CVO
Argyll and Bute	Patrick Stewart, MBE
Ayrshire and Arran	Iona McDonald
Banffshire	Clare Russell, CVO
Berwickshire	Jeannna Swan
Caithness	Viscount Thurso, PC
Clackmannanshire	Lt.-Col. Johnny Stewart
Dumfries	Lady Fiona MacGregor of MacGregor (Fiona Armstrong)
Dunbartonshire	Rear-Adm. Michael Gregory, OBE
Dundee City*	Lord Provost Ian Borthwick
East Lothian	Maj. Michael Williams, MBE
Edinburgh City*	Rt. Hon. Lord Provost Frank Ross
Eilean Siar (Western Isles)	Donald Martin
Fife	Robert Balfour
Glasgow City*	Rt. Hon. Lord Provost Eva Bolander
Inverness-shire	Donald Cameron of Lochiel, CVO
Kincardineshire	Carol Kinghorn
Lanarkshire	Lady Susan Haughey, CBE
Midlothian	Sir Robert Clerk, Bt., OBE
Moray	Lt.-Col. Grenville Johnston, CVO, OBE, TD
Nairn	George Asher
Orkney	William Spence
Perth and Kinross	Brig. Sir Melville Jameson, KCVO, CBE
Renfrewshire	Guy Clark, CVO
Ross and Cromarty	Janet Bowen, CVO
Roxburgh, Ettrick and Lauderdale	Duke of Buccleuch and Queensberry, KT, KBE, FRSE
Shetland	Robert Hunter
Stirling and Falkirk	Alan Simpson, OBE
Sutherland	Dr Monica Main
The Stewartry of Kirkcudbright	Lt.-Col. Sir Malcolm Ross, GCVO, OBE
Tweeddale	Prof. Sir Hew Strachan
West Lothian	Moira Niven, MBE
Wigtown	John Ross, CBE

* The Lord Provosts of the four cities of Aberdeen, Dundee, Edinburgh and Glasgow are Lord-Lieutenants *ex officio* for those districts

LOCAL COUNCILS

Council	Administrative Headquarters	Telephone	Pop.*	Council Tax†	Chief Executive
ABERDEEN	Aberdeen	01224-522000	228,800	£1,267	Angela Scott
Aberdeenshire	Aberdeen	08456-081207	261,800	£1,205	Jim Savege
Angus	Forfar	0845-277 7778	116,280	£1,137	Margo Williamson
Argyll and Bute	Lochgilphead	01546-602127	86,810	£1,249	Cleland Sneddon
Clackmannanshire	Alloa	01259-450000	51,450	£1,271	Nikki Bridle (acting)
Dumfries and Galloway	Dumfries	030-3333 3000	149,200	£1,113	Gavin Stevenson
DUNDEE	Dundee	01382-434000	148,710	£1,278	David Martin
East Ayrshire	Kilmarnock	01563-576000	121,940	£1,261	Fiona Lees
East Dunbartonshire	Kirkintilloch	0300-123 4510	108,130	£1,211	Gerry Cornes
East Lothian	Haddington	01620-827827	104,840	£1,186	Angela Leitch
East Renfrewshire	Giffnock	0141-577 3000	94,760	£1,195	Lorraine McMillan
EDINBURGH	Edinburgh	0131-200 2000	513,210	£1,240	Andrew Kerr
Eilean Siar (Western Isles)	Stornoway	01851-703773	26,950	£1,086	Malcolm Burr
Falkirk	Falkirk	01324-506070	160,130	£1,135	Kenneth Lawrie
Fife	Glenrothes	0345-155 0000	371,410	£1,186	Steve Grimmond
GLASGOW	Glasgow	0141-287 2000	621,020	£1,286	Annemarie O'Donnell
Highland	Inverness	01349-886606	235,180	£1,234	Steve Barron
Inverclyde	Greenock	01475-717171	78,760	£1,234	Aubrey Fawcett
Midlothian	Dalkeith	0131-270 7500	90,090	£1,283	Dr Grace Vickers
Moray	Elgin	01343-543451	95,780	£1,204	Roddy Burns
North Ayrshire	Irvine	0845-603 0590	135,790	£1,222	Elma Murray
North Lanarkshire	Motherwell	01698-403200	339,960	£1,131	Paul Jukes
Orkney	Kirkwall	01856-873535	22,000	£1,100	Alistair Buchan
Perth and Kinross	Perth	01738-475000	151,100	£1,216	Karen Reid
Renfrewshire	Paisley	0300-300 0300	176,830	£1,200	Sandra Black
Scottish Borders	Melrose	01835-824000	115,020	£1,150	Tracey Logan
Shetland	Lerwick	01595-693535	23,080	£1,117	Maggie Sandison
South Ayrshire	Ayr	0300-123 0900	112,680	£1,224	Eileen Howat
South Lanarkshire	Hamilton	0303-123 1015	318,170	£1,134	Lindsay Freeland
STIRLING	Stirling	0845-277 7000	94,000	£1,233	Stewart Carruth
West Dunbartonshire	Dumbarton	01389-737000	89,610	£1,198	Joyce White
West Lothian	Livingston	01506-280000	181,310	£1,162	Graham Hope

* Source: Office for National Statistics – Mid-2017 Population Estimates (Crown copyright)
† Average Band D council tax bill 2018–19.
Councils in CAPITAL LETTERS have city status

Key	Council	Key	Council
1	Aberdeen City	17	Inverclyde
2	Aberdeenshire	18	Midlothian
3	Angus	19	Moray
4	Argyll and Bute	20	North Ayrshire
5	City of Edinburgh	21	North Lanarkshire
6	Clackmannanshire	22	Orkney
7	Dumfries and Galloway	23	Perth and Kinross
8	Dundee City	24	Renfrewshire
9	East Ayrshire	25	Scottish Borders
10	East Dunbartonshire	26	Shetland
11	East Lothian	27	South Ayrshire
12	East Renfrewshire	28	South Lanarkshire
13	Falkirk	29	Stirling
14	Fife	30	West Dunbartonshire
15	Glasgow City	31	Western Isles (Eilean Siar)
16	Highland	32	West Lothian

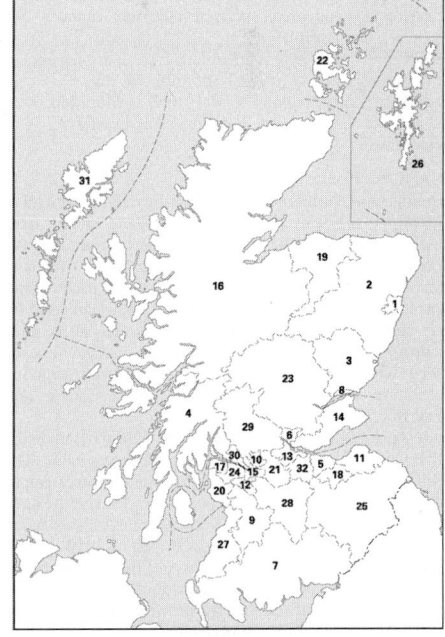

NORTHERN IRELAND

Northern Ireland has a total area of 14,149 sq. km (5,463 sq. miles): land, 13,576 sq. km (5,242 sq. miles); inland water, 573 sq. km (221 sq. miles).

In 2012 a reform programme began to reduce the number of district councils from 26 to 11. The Local Government Act (Northern Ireland) received royal assent on 12 May 2014 providing new governance arrangements for local councils and made transitional provisions for the transfer of staff, assets and liabilities etc to the new 11 councils. On 1 April 2015 additional functions, that were previously the responsibility of the Northern Ireland executive, fully transferred to the new district authorities.

POPULATION
The population of Northern Ireland at the 2011 census was 1,810,863 (men 887,323; women 923,540). The average density of population in 2011 was 128 persons per sq. km (331 per sq. mile).

ELECTIONS
Elections to the 11 councils took place on 22 May 2014.

FUNCTIONS
The councils are responsible for approving business and financial plans, setting domestic and non-domestic rates. Since April 2016 councils have also been responsible for urban regeneration and community development.

The district councils are responsible for:

Direct Service Provision of a wide range of local services, including: building control-inspection and the regulation of new buildings; byelaw enforcement; cemeteries; community centres; cultural facilities; dog control; environmental health; food safety; health and safety; local economic development; local planning; off-street parking (except park and ride schemes); parks, open spaces and playgrounds; public conveniences; recycling and waste management; registration of births, deaths and marriages; sport, leisure and recreational facilities; and street cleaning. District councils also have a role in community development and safety; sports development; summer schemes; and tourism.

Representation: nominating representatives to sit as members of the various statutory bodies responsible for the administration of regional services such as education, health and social services, libraries and road safety committees

FINANCE
Government in Northern Ireland is part-funded by a system of rates, which supplement the Northern Ireland budget from the UK government. The ratepayer receives a combined tax bill consisting of the regional rate, set by the Northern Ireland executive, and the district rate, which is set by each district council. The regional and district rates are both collected by Land and Property Services (part of the Department of Finance). The product of the district rates is paid over to each council while the product of the regional rate supports expenditure by the departments of the executive and assembly.

Since April 2007 domestic rates bills have been based on the capital value of a property, rather than the rental value. The capital value is defined as the price the property might reasonably be expected to realise had it been sold on the open market on 1 January 2005. Non-domestic rates bills are based on the rental value of the property as at 1 April 2013.

Rate bills are calculated by multiplying the property's net annual rental value (in the case of non-domestic property), or capital value (in the case of domestic property), by the regional and district rate poundages respectively.

For 2018–19 the overall average domestic poundage is 0.8016p compared to 0.7735p in 2017–18. The overall average non-domestic rate poundage in 2018–19 is 58.40p compared to 57.28p in 2017–18.

FLAG
The official national flag of Northern Ireland is the Union Flag.

PRINCIPAL CITIES
In addition to Belfast and Londonderry, three other places in Northern Ireland have been granted city status: Armagh (1994), Lisburn (2002) and Newry (2002).

BELFAST
Belfast, the administrative centre of Northern Ireland, is situated at the mouth of the River Lagan at its entrance to Belfast Lough. The city grew to be a great industrial centre, owing to its easy access by sea to Scottish coal and iron.

The principal buildings are of a relatively young age and include the parliament buildings at Stormont, the City Hall, Waterfront Hall, the Law Courts, the Public Library and the Museum and Art Gallery. In March 2012, a new museum, Titanic Belfast, opened on the banks of the Lagan River – the site where RMS *Titanic* was built and launched. The museum forms the centrepiece of a new mixed-use maritime quarter.

Belfast received its first charter of incorporation in 1613 and was created a city in 1888; the title of lord mayor was conferred in 1892.

LONDONDERRY
Londonderry (originally Derry) is situated on the River Foyle, and has important associations with the City of London. The Irish Society was created by the City of London in 1610, and under its royal charter of 1613 it fortified the city and was for a long time closely associated with its administration. Because of this connection the city was incorporated in 1613 under the new name of Londonderry.

The city is famous for the great siege of 1688–9, when for 105 days the town held out against the forces of James II. The city walls are still intact and form a circuit of 1.6 km (one mile) around the old city.

Interesting buildings are the Protestant cathedral of St Columb's (1633) and the Guildhall, reconstructed in 1912 and containing a number of beautiful stained glass windows, many of which were presented by the livery companies of London.

CONSTITUTIONAL HISTORY
Northern Ireland is subject to the same fundamental constitutional provisions which apply to the rest of the UK. It had its own parliament and government from 1921 to 1972, but after increasing civil unrest the Northern Ireland (Temporary Provisions) Act 1972 transferred the legislative and executive powers of the Northern Ireland parliament and government to the UK parliament and a secretary of state. The Northern Ireland Constitution Act 1973 provided for devolution in Northern Ireland through an assembly and executive, but a power-sharing executive formed by the Northern Ireland political parties in January 1974 collapsed in May 1974. Following the collapse Northern Ireland returned to direct rule governance under the provisions of the Northern Ireland Act 1974, placing the Northern Ireland department under the direction and control of the Northern Ireland secretary.

In December 1993 the British and Irish governments published the Joint Declaration, complementing their political talks and making clear that any settlement would need to be founded on principles of democracy and consent.

On 12 January 1998 the British and Irish governments issued a joint document, *Propositions on Heads of Agreement,* proposing the establishment of various new cross-border bodies; further proposals were presented on 27 January. A draft peace settlement was issued by the talks' chairman, US Senator George Mitchell, on 6 April 1998 but was rejected by the Unionists the following day. On 10 April agreement was reached between the British and Irish governments and the eight Northern Ireland political parties still involved in the talks (the Good Friday Agreement). The agreement provided for an elected Northern Ireland Assembly, a North/South Ministerial Council, and a British-Irish Council comprising representatives of the British, Irish, Channel Islands and Isle of Man governments and members of the new assemblies for Scotland, Wales and Northern Ireland. Further points included the abandonment of the Republic of Ireland's constitutional claim to Northern Ireland, the decommissioning of weapons, the release of paramilitary prisoners and changes in policing.

The agreement was ratified in referendums held in Northern Ireland and the Republic of Ireland on 22 May 1998. In the UK, the Northern Ireland Act received royal assent in November 1998.

On 28 April 2003 the secretary of state again assumed responsibility for the direction of the Northern Ireland departments on the dissolution of the Northern Ireland Assembly, following its initial suspension from midnight on 14 October 2002. In 2006, following the passing of the Northern Ireland Act, the secretary of state created a non-legislative fixed-term assembly which would cease to operate either when the political parties agreed to restore devolution, or on 24 November 2006 (whichever occurred first). In October 2006 a timetable to restore devolution was drawn up (St Andrews Agreement) and a transitional Northern Ireland Assembly was formed on 24 November. The transitional assembly was dissolved in January 2007 in preparation for elections to be held on 7 March; following the elections a power-sharing executive was formed and the new 108-member Northern Ireland Assembly became operational on 8 May 2007.

For further developments *see* Devolved Government.

LORD-LIEUTENANTS AND HIGH SHERIFFS

County	Lord-Lieutenant	High Sheriff (2018)
Antrim	Joan Christie, CVO, OBE	Gillian Bingham
Armagh	Earl of Caledon, KCVO	Catherine Adams
Belfast City	Fionnuala Mary Jay-O'Boyle, CBE	Carole Howard
Down	David Lindsay	Susan Cunningham
Fermanagh	Viscount Brookeborough, KG	John Maguire
Londonderry	Alison Millar	Anna Clyde, MBE
Londonderry City	Dr Angela Josepha Garvey	Agnes Gavin
Tyrone	Robert Scott, OBE	Barry McGonigle

LOCAL COUNCILS

Council	Telephone	Population*	Chief Executive
Antrim & Newtownabbey	028-9448 1311	141,697	Jacqui Dixon
Armagh, Banbridge & Craigavon	0300-030 0900	211,898	Roger Wilson
Belfast	028-9027 0549	340,220	Suzanne Wylie
Causeway Coast & Glens	028-7034 7034	143,920	David Jackson, MBE
Derry & Strabane	028-7138 2204	150,497	John Kelpie
Fermanagh & Omagh	0300-303 1777	116,289	Brendan Hegarty
Lisburn & Castlereagh	028-9250 9250	142,640	Dr Theresa Donaldson
Mid & East Antrim	028-9335 8000	138,152	Anne Donaghy
Mid Ulster	0300-013 2132	146,427	Anthony Tohill
Newry, Mourne & Down	028-3031 3037	178,996	Liam Hannaway
North Down & Ards	0300-013 3333	160,098	Stephen Reid

* *Source:* Office for National Statistics – *Mid-2017 Population Estimates* (Crown copyright)

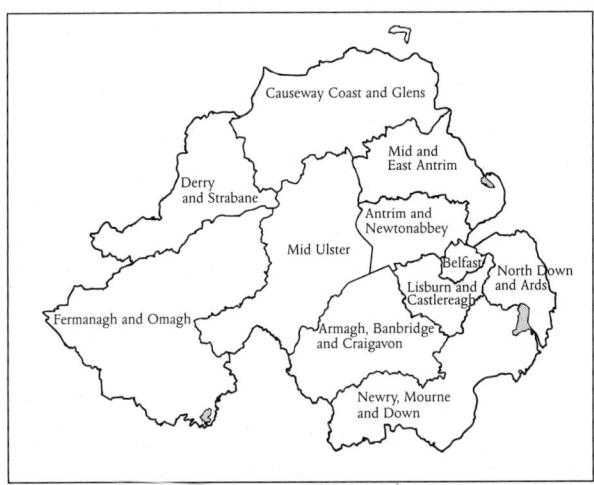

POLITICAL COMPOSITION OF LOCAL COUNCILS

Following the local elections held on 4 May 2018

Abbreviations

All.	Alliance
BNP	British National Party
C.	Conservative
DUP	Democratic Unionist Party
Green	Green
Ind.	Independent
Ind. Un.	Independent Unionist
Lab.	Labour
LD	Liberal Democrat
Lib.	Liberal
O.	Other
PC	Plaid Cymru
PUP	Progressive Unionist Party of Northern Ireland
R.	Residents Associations/Ratepayers
SD	Social Democrat
SDLP	Social Democratic and Labour Party
SF	Sinn Féin
SNP	Scottish National Party
Soc.	Socialist
TUV	Traditional Unionist Voice
UKIP	UK Independence Party
UUP	Ulster Unionist Party
v.	vacant

Total number of seats is given in parentheses after the council name.

ENGLAND

COUNTY COUNCILS

Buckinghamshire (49)   C. 41; LD 4; Ind. 3; Lab. 1
Cambridgeshire (61)   C. 36; LD 15; Lab. 7; Ind. 3
Cumbria (84)   C. 37; Lab. 26; LD 16; Ind. 5
Derbyshire (64)   C. 37; Lab. 24; LD 3
Devon (60)   C. 42; Lab. 7; LD 7; Ind. 3; Green 1
Dorset (46)   C. 32; LD 11; Green 2; Lab. 1
East Sussex (50)   C. 30; LD 11; Ind. 5; Lab. 4
Essex (75)   C. 56; LD 7; Lab. 6; Ind. 4; R 1; Green 1
Gloucestershire (53)   C. 31; LD 14; Lab. 5; Green 2; Ind. 1
Hampshire (78)   C. 56; LD 19; Lab. 2; Ind. 1
Hertfordshire (78)   C. 51; LD 18; Lab. 9
Kent (81)   C. 67; LD 7; Lab. 5; Green 1; R 1
Lancashire (84)   C. 46; Lab. 30; LD 4; Ind. 2; Green 1; UKIP 1
Leicestershire (55)   C. 36; LD 13; Lab. 6
Lincolnshire (70)   C. 58; Lab. 6; Ind. 5; LD 1
Norfolk (84)   C. 55; Lab. 17; LD 11; Ind. 1
North Yorkshire (72)   C. 55; Ind. 10; Lab. 4; LD 3
Northamptonshire (57)   C. 43; Lab. 12; LD 2
Nottinghamshire (66)   C. 31; Lab. 23; Ind. 11; LD 1
Oxfordshire (63)   C. 31; Lab. 14; LD 13; Ind. 4; R 1
Somerset (55)   C. 35; LD 12; Ind. 3; Lab. 3; Green 2
Staffordshire (62)   C. 51; Lab. 10; Ind. 1
Suffolk (75)   C. 52; Lab. 11; LD 5; Ind. 4; Green 3
Surrey (81)   C. 60; LD 9; R 8; Ind. 2; Lab. 1; Green 1
Warwickshire (57)   C. 36; Lab. 10; LD 7; Ind. 2; Green 2
West Sussex (70)   C. 56; LD 9; Lab. 5
Worcestershire (57)   C. 40; Lab. 10; LD 3; Green 2; Ind. 1; O. 1

DISTRICT COUNCILS

Adur (29)   C. 16; Lab. 7; UKIP 4; Ind. 2
Allerdale (56)   Lab. 28; C. 17; Ind. 4; O. 4; UKIP 3
Amber Valley (45)   C. 25; Lab. 20
Arun (54)   C. 42; LD 5; UKIP 4; Ind. 2; Lab. 1
Ashfield (35)   Lab. 22; LD 5; C. 4; Ind. 3; O. 1
Ashford (43)   C. 34; Lab. 4; Ind. 3; LD 1; UKIP 1
Aylesbury Vale (59)   C. 43; LD 9; UKIP 4; Lab. 2; Ind. 1
Babergh (43)   C. 31; Ind. 8; LD 3; Lab. 1
Barrow-in-Furness (36)   Lab. 27; C. 9
Basildon (42)   C. 23; Lab. 12; UKIP 5; Ind. 2
Basingstoke and Deane (60)   C. 33; Lab. 21; LD 5; Ind. 1
Bassetlaw (48)   Lab. 33; C. 12; Ind. 3
Blaby (39)   C. 29; Lab. 6; LD 4
Bolsover (37)   Lab. 32; Ind. 4; O. 1
Boston (30)   C. 13; UKIP 12; Ind. 2; Lab. 2; O. 1
Braintree (49)   C. 44; Lab. 2; R. 2; Green 1
Breckland (49)   C. 42; UKIP 4; Lab. 2; Ind. 1
Brentwood (37)   C. 25; LD 9; Lab. 2; Ind. 1
Broadland (47)   C. 43; LD 4
Bromsgrove (31)   C. 18; Lab. 7; Ind. 3; R. 3
Broxbourne (30)   C. 28; Lab. 2
Broxtowe (44)   C. 27; Lab. 12; LD 4; Ind. 1
Burnley (45)   Lab. 25; Ind. 7; C. 5; LD 5; UKIP 2; Green 1
Cambridge (42)   Lab. 26; LD 14; Green 1; Ind. 1
Cannock Chase (41)   Lab. 21; C. 15; Green 3; Ind. 1; LD 1
Canterbury (39)   C. 31; Lab. 3; LD 3; UKIP 2
Carlisle (52)   Lab. 25; C. 22; Ind. 4; LD 1
Castle Point (41)   C. 27; Ind. 14
Charnwood (52)   C. 41; Lab. 9; Ind. 1; LD 1
Chelmsford (57)   C. 52; LD 5
Cheltenham (40)   LD 32; C. 6; Ind. 2
Cherwell (48)   C. 36; Lab. 9; Ind. 1; LD 1; v. 1
Chesterfield (48)   Lab. 34; LD 11; Ind. 2; UKIP 1
Chichester (48)   C. 42; Ind. 3; LD 3
Chiltern (40)   C. 35; LD 3; Ind. 2
Chorley (47)   Lab. 32; C. 13; Ind. 2
Christchurch (24)   C. 21; Ind. 2; UKIP 1
Colchester (51)   C. 25; LD 12; Lab. 11; Ind. 3
Copeland (51)   Lab. 29; C. 17; Ind. 5
Corby (29)   Lab. 24; C. 5
Cotswolds (34)   C. 24; LD 10
Craven (30)   C. 17; Ind. 7; Lab. 3; Green 1; LD 1; UKIP 1
Crawley (37)   Lab. 20; C. 17
Dacorum (51)   C. 46; LD 3; Lab. 2
Dartford (44)   C. 34; Lab. 7; R. 3
Daventry (36)   C. 30; Lab. 5; LD 1
Derbyshire Dales (39)   C. 29; Lab. 5; LD 3; Ind. 1; O. 1
Dover (45)   C. 25; Lab. 17; UKIP 3
East Cambridgeshire (39)   C. 36; LD 2; Ind. 1
East Devon (59)   C. 37; Ind. 15; LD 6; O. 1
East Dorset (29)   C. 25; LD 3; Ind. 1
East Hampshire (44)   C. 42; LD 2
East Hertfordshire (50)   C. 50

East Lindsey (55) — C. 33; UKIP 8; Ind. 6; Lab. 4; O. 3; LD 1

East Northamptonshire (40) — C. 37; Ind. 2; LD 1

East Staffordshire (39) — C. 25; Lab. 12; LD 1; UKIP 1

Eastbourne (27) — LD 18; C. 9

Eastleigh (39) — LD 32; C. 4; Ind. 3

Eden (38) — C. 21; Ind. 10; LD 7

Elmbridge (48) — C. 24; R 15; LD 9

Epping Forest (58) — C. 39; R 13; Green 2; Ind. 2; LD 2

Epsom and Ewell (38) — R. 31; C. 4; Lab. 3

Erewash (47) — C. 30; Lab. 17

Exeter (39) — Lab. 29; C. 8; Green 1; LD 1

Fareham (31) — C. 24; LD 5; Ind. 1; UKIP 1

Fenland (39) — C. 34; Ind. 3; LD 2

Forest Heath (27) — C. 20; Ind. 7

Forest of Dean (48) — C. 21; Lab. 13; UKIP 7; Ind. 5; Green 2

Fylde (51) — C. 32; Ind. 12; LD 2; O. 2; R. 2; Lab. 1

Gedling (41) — Lab. 25; C. 15; LD 1

Gloucester (39) — C. 22; Lab. 10; LD 7

Gosport (34) — C. 18; LD 14; Lab. 2

Gravesham (44) — C. 23; Lab. 21

Great Yarmouth (39) — C. 23; Lab. 15; UKIP 1

Guildford (48) — C. 35; LD 9; O. 3; Lab. 1

Hambleton (28) — C. 27; UKIP 1

Harborough (37) — C. 29; LD 8

Harlow (33) — Lab. 20; C. 13

Harrogate (40) — C. 31; LD 7; Ind. 2

Hart (38) — C. 15; R 10; LD 8

Hastings (32) — Lab. 24; C. 8

Havant (38) — C. 31; Lab. 2; Ind. 2; UKIP 2; LD 1

Hertsmere (39) — C. 37; Lab. 2

High Peak (43) — C. 23; Lab. 17; LD 2; Ind. 1

Hinckley and Bosworth (34) — C. 21; LD 12; Lab. 1

Horsham (44) — C. 39; LD 4; Ind. 1

Huntingdonshire (52) — C. 30; Ind. 11; LD 7; Lab. 4

Hyndburn (35) — Lab. 26; C. 9

Ipswich (48) — Lab. 34; C. 12; LD 2

Kettering (36) — C. 25; Lab. 7; Ind. 1; v. 3

King's Lynn and West Norfolk (62) — C. 50; Lab. 10; Ind. 2

Lancaster (60) — Lab. 29; C. 19; Green 9; Ind. 2; O. 1

Lewes (41) — C. 24; LD 11; Green 3; Ind. 2; UKIP 1

Lichfield (47) — C. 41; Lab. 4; LD 1; UKIP 1

Lincoln City (33) — Lab. 24; C. 9

Maidstone (55) — C. 25; LD 20; Ind. 7; Lab. 3

Maldon (31) — C. 28; Ind. 2; UKIP 1

Malvern Hills (38) — C. 23; Ind. 7; LD 5; Green 3

Mansfield (36) — Lab. 18; Ind. 16; UKIP 2

Melton (28) — C. 26; Ind. 2

Mendip (47) — C. 32; LD 11; Green 3; Ind. 1

Mid Devon (42) — C. 28; Ind. 6; LD 5; UKIP 2; LD 1

Mid Suffolk (40) — C. 29; Green 5; LD 4; Ind. 2

Mid Sussex (54) — C. 54

Mole Valley (41) — C. 20; LD 14; Ind. 7

New Forest (60) — C. 58; LD 2

Newark and Sherwood (39) — C. 24; Lab. 12; Ind. 3

Newcastle-under-Lyme (44) — Lab. 20; C. 18; Ind. 3; LD 3

North Devon (43) — C. 19; LD 12; Ind. 10; O. 1; UKIP 1

North Dorset (33) — C. 27; LD 4; Ind. 2

North East Derbyshire (53) — Lab. 34; C. 18; Ind. 1

North Hertfordshire (49) — C. 29; Lab. 14; LD 6

North Kesteven (43) — C. 28; O. 15

North Norfolk (48) — C. 33; LD 15

North Warwickshire (35) — C. 22; Lab. 13

North West Leicestershire (38) — C. 25; Lab. 10; Ind. 2; LD 1

Northampton (45) — C. 26; Lab. 17; LD 2

Norwich (39) — Lab. 31; Green 5; LD 3

Nuneaton and Bedworth (34) — Lab. 17; C. 16; Green 1

Oadby and Wigston (26) — LD 19; C. 6; Lab. 1

Oxford (48) — Lab. 36; LD 9; Green 2; Ind. 1

Pendle (49) — C. 24; Lab. 15; LD 9; Ind. 1

Preston (57) — Lab. 35; C. 17; LD 5

Purbeck (25) — C. 20; LD 4; Ind. 1

Redditch (29) — C. 17; Lab. 12

Reigate and Banstead (51) — C. 40; R 7; Green 3; LD 1

Ribble Valley (40) — C. 35; LD 4; Lab. 1

Richmondshire (34) — C. 21; Ind. 11; LD 2

Rochford (39) — C. 25; Ind. 4; R 4; Green 3; LD 3

Rossendale (36) — Lab. 20; C. 14; Ind. 2

Rother (38) — C. 31; O. 3; LD 2; Ind. 1; Lab. 1

Rugby (42) — C. 24; Lab. 9; LD 9

Runnymede (42) — C. 32; Ind. 9; Lab. 1

Rushcliffe (44) — C. 34; Lab. 4; Green 2; Ind. 2; LD 2

Rushmoor (39) — C. 26; Lab. 11; Ind. 1; LD 1

Ryedale (30) — C. 20; Ind. 5; LD 3; LD 2

Scarborough (50) — C. 26; Lab. 14; UKIP 5; Ind. 3; Green 2

Sedgemoor (48) — C. 35; Lab. 10; UKIP 2; LD 1

Selby (31) — C. 22; Lab. 8; Ind. 1

Sevenoaks (54) — C. 49; LD 2; Ind. 1; Lab. 1; UKIP 1

Shepway (30) — C. 22; UKIP 7; Lab. 1

South Bucks (28) — C. 27; Ind. 1

South Cambridgeshire (45) — LD 30; C. 11; Ind. 2; Lab. 2

South Derbyshire (36) — C. 24; Lab. 12

South Hams (31) — C. 25; Green 3; LD 2; Lab. 1

South Holland (37) — C. 28; Ind. 7; UKIP 2

South Kesteven (58) — C. 45; Ind. 5; Lab. 3; O. 2; UKIP 1; v. 2

South Lakeland (51) — LD 29; C. 19; Lab. 3

South Norfolk (46) — C. 40; LD 6

South Northamptonshire (42) — C. 35; Lab. 4; LD 3

South Oxfordshire (36) — C. 33; Lab. 1; LD 1; R 1

South Ribble (50) — C. 29; Lab. 19; LD 2

South Somerset (60) — LD 29; C. 28; Ind. 3

South Staffordshire (49) — C. 43; Ind. 4; Lab. 1; UKIP 1

Spelthorne (39) — C. 35; LD 3; Lab. 1

St Albans (58) — C. 30; LD 19; Lab. 6; Ind. 2; Green 1

St Edmundsbury (45) — C. 34; Ind. 5; Lab. 2; O. 2; Green 1; UKIP 1

Stafford (40) — C. 29; Lab. 9; Ind. 2

Staffordshire Moorlands (56) — C. 41; Lab. 7; O. 6; LD 2

Stevenage (39) — Lab. 26; C. 9; LD 4

Stratford-on-Avon (36) — C. 31; LD 3; Ind. 1; Lab. 1

Stroud (51) — C. 23; Lab. 18; Green 8; LD 2

Suffolk Coastal (42) — C. 37; Ind. 2; LD 2; Lab. 1

Surrey Heath (40) — C. 36; Ind. 2; Lab. 1; LD 1

Swale (47) — C. 32; UKIP 9; Lab. 4; Ind. 2

Tamworth (30)   C. 22; Lab. 5; Ind. 1; UKIP 1; v. 1
Tandridge (42)   C. 22; LD 9; Ind. 7; R 4
Taunton Deane (56)   C. 36; LD 14; Ind. 3; Lab. 2; UKIP 1
Teignbridge (46)   C. 30; LD 11; Ind. 5
Tendring (60)   C. 23; UKIP 16; Ind. 11; Lab. 4; R. 3; LD 1; O. 1; v. 1
Test Valley (48)   C. 38; LD 9; Ind. 1
Tewkesbury (38)   C. 33; Ind. 2; LD 2; O. 1
Thanet (56)   UKIP 33; C. 18; Lab. 4; Ind. 1
Three Rivers (39)   LD 20; C. 16; Lab. 3
Tonbridge and   C. 48; LD 4; Ind. 2
Malling (54)
Torridge (36)   C. 19; O. 10; UKIP 7
Tunbridge Wells (48) C. 41; LD 4; Lab. 2; Ind. 1
Uttlesford (39)   C. 23; O. 9; LD 6; Ind. 1
Vale of White Horse   C. 29; LD 9
(38)
Warwick (46)   C. 31; Lab. 9; R. 3; LD 2; Green 1
Watford (36)   LD 26; Lab. 10
Waveney (48)   C. 27; Lab. 20; Green 1
Waverley (57)   C. 53; R. 3; Ind. 1
Wealden (55)   C. 50; Ind. 5
Wellingborough (36)   C. 27; Lab. 9
Welwyn and Hatfield   C. 25; Lab. 15; LD 8
(48)
West Devon (31)   C. 21; Ind. 9; LD 1
West Dorset (42)   C. 30; LD 12
West Lancashire (54) Lab. 33; C. 19; Ind. 2
West Lindsey (36)   C. 24; LD 7; Lab. 3; Ind. 2
West Oxfordshire   C. 35; LD 8; Lab. 6
(49)
West Somerset (28)   C. 21; Ind. 3; UKIP 3; Lab. 1
Weymouth and   C. 14; Lab. 12; LD 6; Ind. 2; Green 1;
Portland (36)   UKIP 1
Winchester (45)   C. 23; LD 22
Woking (30)   C. 16; LD 8; Ind. 3; Lab. 3
Worcester (35)   C. 17; Lab. 15; Green 3
Worthing (37)   C. 28; Lab. 5; LD 2; Ind. 1; UKIP 1
Wychavon (45)   C. 38; LD 5; UKIP 1; v. 1
Wycombe (60)   C. 47; Lab. 6; O. 3; Ind. 2; LD 1; UKIP 1
Wyre (50)   C. 36; Lab. 14
Wyre Forest (33)   C. 21; Lab. 4; Ind. 3; LD 3; O. 2

LONDON BOROUGH COUNCILS

Barking and   Lab. 51
Dagenham (51)
Barnet (63)   C. 38; Lab. 25
Bexley (45)   C. 34; Lab. 11
Brent (63)   Lab. 57; C. 3; v. 3
Bromley (60)   C. 50; Lab. 8; Ind. 2
Camden (54)   Lab. 43; C. 7; LD 3; Green 1
Croydon (70)   Lab. 41; C. 29
Ealing (69)   Lab. 57; C. 8; LD 4
Enfield (63)   Lab. 46; C. 17
Greenwich (51)   Lab. 42; C. 9
Hackney (57)   Lab. 52; C. 5
Hammersmith and   Lab. 35; C. 11
Fulham (46)
Haringey (57)   Lab. 42; LD 15
Harrow (63)   Lab. 35; C. 28
Havering (54)   C. 25; R 23; Lab. 5; Ind. 1
Hillingdon (65)   C. 44; Lab. 21
Hounslow (60)   Lab. 51; C. 9
Islington (48)   Lab. 47; Green 1
Kensington and   C. 36; Lab. 13; LD 1
Chelsea (50)
Kingston upon   C. 28; LD 18; Lab. 2
Thames (48)
Lambeth (63)   Lab. 57; Green 5; C. 1
Lewisham (54)   Lab. 54

Merton (60)   Lab. 34; C. 17; LD 6; R 3
Newham (60)   Lab. 60
Redbridge (63)   Lab. 51; C. 12
Richmond upon   C. 39; LD 15
Thames (54)
Southwark (63)   Lab. 49; LD 11; v. 3
Sutton (54)   LD 33; C. 18; Ind. 3
Tower Hamlets (45)   Lab. 42; C. 2; Ind. 1
Waltham Forest (60)   Lab. 46; C. 14
Wandsworth (60)   C. 33; Lab. 26; Ind. 1
Westminster (60)   C. 41; Lab. 19

METROPOLITAN BOROUGHS

Barnsley (63)   Lab. 56; C. 4; Ind. 2; LD 1
Birmingham (101)   Lab. 67; C. 25; LD 8; Green 1
Bolton (60)   Lab. 31; C. 19; Ind. 4; LD 3; UKIP 3
Bradford (90)   Lab. 52; C. 22; Ind. 7; LD 7; Green 2
Bury (51)   Lab. 31; C. 17; LD 3
Calderdale (51)   Lab. 24; C. 19; LD 6; Ind. 2
Coventry (54)   Lab. 40; C. 13; Ind. 1
Doncaster (55)   Lab. 43; C. 7; Ind. 5
Dudley (72)   Lab. 35; C. 35; UKIP 1; Ind. 1
Gateshead (66)   Lab. 54; LD 12
Kirklees (69)   Lab. 36; C. 20; LD 7; Green 3; Ind. 3
Knowsley (45)   Lab. 40; LD 3; Green 1; Ind. 1
Leeds (99)   Lab. 61; C. 22; Ind. 0; LD 0; Green 2
Liverpool (90)   Lab. 76; LD 7; Green 4; Lib. 2; Ind. 1
Manchester (96)   Lab. 94; LD 2
Newcastle-upon-Tyne   Lab. 56; LD 19; Ind. 3
(78)
North Tyneside (60)   Lab. 53; C. 6; LD 1
Oldham (60)   Lab. 47; LD 8; C. 4; Ind. 1
Rochdale (60)   Lab. 46; C. 10; LD 3; Ind. 1
Rotherham (63)   Lab. 48; UKIP 14; Ind. 1
St Helens (48)   Lab. 41; LD 3; C. 3; Ind. 1
Salford (60)   Lab. 50; C. 9; Ind. 1
Sandwell (72)   Lab. 70; Ind. 2
Sefton (66)   Lab. 43; LD 12; C. 8; Ind. 3
Sheffield (84)   Lab. 53; LD 22; Green 6; UKIP 3
Solihull (51)   C. 32; Green 11; LD 4; Lab. 2; UKIP 1; Ind. 1
South Tyneside (54)   Lab. 53; C. 1
Stockport (63)   Lab. 23; LD 21; C. 13; Ind. 3; R 2; v. 1
Sunderland (75)   Lab. 61; C. 8; LD 6
Tameside (57)   Lab. 51; C. 6
Trafford (63)   Lab. 30; C. 29; LD 2; Green 2
Wakefield (63)   Lab. 52; C. 11
Walsall (60)   C. 30; Lab. 26; LD 2; Ind. 2
Wigan (75)   Lab. 60; Ind. 8; C. 7
Wirral (66)   Lab. 39; C. 21; LD 5; Green 1
Wolverhampton (60)   Lab. 51; C. 9

UNITARY COUNCILS

Bath and North East   C. 37; LD 15; Lab. 6; Ind. 5; Green 2
Somerset (65)
Bedford (40)   C. 15; Lab. 14; LD 9; Ind. 2
Blackburn with   Lab. 37; C. 13; LD 1
Darwen (51)
Blackpool (42)   Lab. 29; C. 13; LD 1; v. 1
Bournemouth (54)   C. 51; Green 1; Ind. 1; UKIP 1
Bracknell Forest (42) C. 41; Lab. 1
Brighton and Hove   Lab. 23; C. 20; Green 11
(54)
Bristol (70)   Lab. 37; C. 14; Green 11; LD 8
Central Bedfordshire C. 53; Ind. 3; Lab. 2; LD 1
(59)
Cheshire East (82)   C. 53; Lab. 16; O. 7; R. 3; LD 2; Ind. 1
Cheshire West and   Lab. 38; C. 36; Ind. 1
Chester (75)

Cornwall (123)	C. 46; LD 37; Ind. 30; Lab. 5; O. 4; v. 1
Darlington (50)	Lab. 29; C. 17; LD 3; Ind. 1
Derby (51)	Lab. 23; C. 20; LD 5; UKIP 3
Durham (126)	Lab. 74; Ind. 28; LD. 14; C. 10
East Riding of Yorkshire (67)	C. 51; Lab. 6; Ind. 5; UKIP 3; LD 2
Halton (56)	Lab. 52; C. 2; LD 2
Hartlepool (33)	Lab. 19; Ind. 11; C. 3
Herefordshire (58)	C. 27; Ind. 13; O. 13; LD 3; Green 2
Isle of Wight (40)	C. 25; Ind. 11; LD 2; Green 1; Lab. 1
*Isles of Scilly (16)	Ind. 9; O. 7
Kingston-upon-Hull (57)	Lab. 31; LD 24; C. 2
Leicester (54)	Lab. 52; C. 1; LD 1
Luton (48)	Lab. 35; LD 8; C. 5
Medway (55)	C. 36; Lab. 15; UKIP 3; Ind. 1
Middlesbrough (47)	Lab. 34; O. 6; C. 4; Ind. 3
Milton Keynes (57)	C. 24; Lab. 21; LD 12
North East Lincolnshire (42)	Lab. 19; C. 18; LD 4; Ind. 1
North Lincolnshire (43)	C. 26; Lab. 17
North Somerset (50)	C. 36; Ind. 7; LD 4; Lab. 3
Northumberland (67)	C. 33; Lab. 24; Ind. 7; LD. 3
Nottingham (55)	Lab. 52; C. 3
Peterborough (60)	C. 31; Lab. 14; LD 6; Ind. 5; Lib. 2; UKIP 1; Green 1
Plymouth (57)	Lab. 31; C. 26
Poole (42)	C. 32; LD 6; O. 3; UKIP 1
Portsmouth (42)	C. 19; LD 16; Lab. 6; Ind. 1
Reading (46)	Lab. 30; C. 12; Green 3; LD 1
Redcar and Cleveland (59)	Lab. 29; LD 11; C. 10; Ind. 8; UKIP 1
Rutland (26)	C. 17; Ind. 7; LD 2
Shropshire (74)	C. 49; LD. 12; Lab. 8; Ind. 3; Green 1, O. 1
Slough (42)	Lab. 34; C. 7; Ind. 1
South Gloucestershire (70)	C. 40; LD 16; Lab. 14
Southampton (48)	Lab. 25; C. 19; Ind. 4
Southend-on-Sea (51)	C. 29; Lab. 11; Ind. 9; LD 2
Stockton-on-Tees (56)	Lab. 32; C. 13; O. 10; LD 1
Stoke-on-Trent (44)	Lab. 21; Ind. 14; C. 7; UKIP 2
Swindon (57)	C. 29; Lab. 26; LD 2
Telford and Wrekin (54)	Lab. 27; C. 22; LD 3; Ind. 2
Thurrock (49)	C. 20; Lab. 17; Ind. 12
Torbay (37)	C. 26; LD 7; Ind. 3; UKIP 1
Warrington (58)	Lab. 45; LD 11; C. 2
West Berkshire (52)	C. 48; LD 4
Wiltshire (98)	C. 69; LD. 19; Ind. 7; Lab. 3
Windsor and Maidenhead (57)	C. 54; R. 2; LD 1
Wokingham (54)	C. 42; LD 8; Lab. 3; Ind. 1
York (47)	Lab. 15; C. 14; LD 12; Green 4; Ind. 2

* Twelve councillors are elected by the residents of the isle of St Mary's and one councillor each are elected by the residents of the four other islands (Bryher, St Agnes, St Martins and Tresco)

WALES

Blaenau Gwent (42)	Ind. 28; Lab. 13; PC 1
Bridgend (54)	Lab. 26; Ind. 13; C. 11; PC 3; LD 1
Caerphilly (73)	Lab. 50; PC 18; Ind. 5
Cardiff (75)	Lab. 40; C. 20; LD 11; PC 3; Ind. 1
Carmarthenshire (74)	PC 36; Lab. 22; Ind. 16
Ceredigion (42)	PC 19; Ind. 13; LD 8; v. 1; Lab. 1
Conwy (59)	Ind. 21; C. 16; PC 10; Lab. 8; LD 4
Denbighshire (47)	C. 16; Lab. 13; PC 9; Ind. 8; LD 1
Flintshire (70)	Lab. 34; Ind. 25; C. 6; LD 5
Gwynedd (75)	PC 41; Ind. 26; O. 6; Lab. 1; LD 1
Merthyr Tydfil (33)	Ind. 16; Lab. 14; v. 3
Monmouthshire (43)	C. 25; Lab. 10; Ind. 5; LD 3
Neath Port Talbot (64)	Lab. 43; PC 15; Ind. 5; LD 1
Newport (50)	Lab. 31; C. 12; Ind. 5; LD 2
Pembrokeshire (60)	Ind. 35; C. 11; Lab. 7; PC 6; LD 1
Powys (73)	Ind. 30; C. 19; LD 13; Lab. 7; PC 2; v. 1, Green 1
Rhondda Cynon Taff (75)	Lab. 47; PC 18; Ind. 5; C. 4; LD 1
Swansea (72)	Lab. 48; Ind. 9; C. 8; LD 7
Torfaen (44)	Lab. 29; Ind. 11; C. 4
Vale of Glamorgan (47)	C. 23; Lab. 14; Ind. 6; PC 4
Wrexham (52)	Ind. 26; Lab. 12; C. 9; PC 3; LD 2
Ynys Mon (Isle of Anglesey) (30)	PC 14; Ind. 13; Lab. 2; LD 1

SCOTLAND

Aberdeen (45)	SNP 19; C. 11; Lab. 9; LD 4; Ind. 2
Aberdeenshire (70)	C. 23; SNP 21; LD 14; Ind. 10; Green 1; Lab. 1
Angus (28)	Ind. 9; SNP 9; C. 8; LD 2
Argyll and Bute (36)	SNP 11; Ind. 10; C. 9; LD 6
Clackmannanshire (18)	SNP 8; Lab. 5; C. 5
Dumfries and Galloway (43)	C. 16; Lab. 11; SNP 11; Ind. 4; LD 1
Dundee (29)	SNP 14; Lab. 9; C. 3; LD 2; Ind. 1
East Ayrshire (32)	SNP 14; Lab. 9; C. 6; Ind. 3
East Dunbartonshire (22)	SNP 7; C. 6; LD 6; Lab. 2; Ind. 1
East Lothian (22)	Lab. 9; C. 7; SNP 6
East Renfrewshire (18)	C. 7; SNP 5; Lab. 4; Ind. 2
Edinburgh (63)	SNP 19; C. 18; Lab. 12; Green 8; LD 6
Eilean Siar (Western Isles) (31)	Ind. 23; SNP 7; C. 1
Falkirk (30)	SNP 12; Lab. 9; C. 7; Ind. 2
Fife (75)	SNP 29; Lab. 24; C. 15; LD 7
Glasgow (85)	SNP 39; Lab. 31; C. 8; Green 7
Highland (74)	Ind. 28; SNP 22; LD 10; C. 10; Lab. 3; Green 1
Inverclyde (22)	Lab. 8; SNP 7; Ind. 4; C. 2; LD 1
Midlothian (18)	Lab. 7; SNP 6; C. 5
Moray (26)	SNP 9; Ind. 8; C. 8; Lab. 1
North Ayrshire (32)	Lab. 11; SNP 11; C. 7; Ind. 4
North Lanarkshire (77)	SNP 33; Lab. 32; C. 10; Ind. 2
Orkney Islands (21)	Ind. 20; Green 1
Perth and Kinross (40)	C. 17; SNP 15; LD 4; Ind. 3; Lab. 1
Renfrewshire (43)	SNP 19; Lab. 13; C. 8; Ind. 2; LD 1
Scottish Borders (34)	C. 15; SNP 9; Ind. 8; LD 2
Shetland Islands (22)	Ind. 21; SNP 1

South Ayrshire (28)	C. 12; SNP 9; Lab. 5; Ind. 2
South Lanarkshire (64)	SNP 27; Lab. 22; C. 14; LD 1
Stirling (23)	C. 9; SNP 9; Lab. 4; Green 1
West Dunbartonshire (22)	SNP 10; Lab. 8; Ind. 2; C. 2
West Lothian (33)	SNP 13; Lab. 12; C. 7; Ind. 1

NORTHERN IRELAND

Antrim and Newtownabbey (40)	DUP 15; UUP 11; All. 4; SDLP 4; SF 3; TUV 2; v. 1
Armagh, Banbridge and Craigavon (41)	DUP 13; UUP 12; SF 8; SDLP 6; Ind. 1; UKIP 1
Belfast (60)	SF 19; DUP 13; All. 8; SDLP 7; UUP 7; PUP 3; Green 1; O. 1; TUV 1
Causeway Coast and Glens (40)	DUP 11; UUP 9; SF 7; SDLP 6; TUV 3; All. 1; Ind. 1; Ind. Un. 1; PUP 1
Derry and Strabane (40)	SF 16; SDLP 10; DUP 8; Ind. 4; UUP 2
Fermanagh and Omagh (40)	SF 17; UUP 9; SDLP 8; DUP 5; Ind. 1
Lisburn and Castlereagh (40)	DUP 18; UUP 10; All. 7; SDLP 3; O. 1; TUV 1
Mid and East Antrim (40)	DUP 16; UUP 9; TUV 5; All. 3; SF 3; Ind. 2; SDLP 1; UKIP 1
Mid Ulster (40)	SF 18; DUP 8; UUP 7; SDLP 6; Ind. 1
Newry, Mourne and Down (41)	SF 14; SDLP 13; Ind. 5; DUP 4; UUP 3; All. 1; UKIP 1
North Down and Ards (40)	DUP 17; UUP 9; All. 7; Ind. 3; Green 2; SDLP 1; TUV 1

THE ISLE OF MAN

Ellan Vannin

The Isle of Man is an island situated in the Irish Sea, at latitude 54° 3′–54° 25′ N. and longitude 4° 18′–4° 47′ W., nearly equidistant from England, Scotland and Ireland. Although the early inhabitants were of Celtic origin, the Isle of Man was part of the Norwegian Kingdom of the Hebrides until 1266, when this was ceded to Scotland. Subsequently granted to the Stanleys (Earls of Derby) in the 15th century and later to the Dukes of Atholl, it was brought under the administration of the Crown in 1765. The island forms the bishopric of Sodor and Man.

The total land area is 572 sq. km (221 sq. miles). The 2016 census showed a resident population of 83,314 (men, 41,269; women, 42,045). The main language in use is English. Around 1,660 people are able to speak the Manx Gaelic language.

CAPITAL – ΨDouglas; population, 26,997 (2016). ΨCastletown (3,216) is the ancient capital; the other towns are ΨPeel (5,374) and ΨRamsey (7,845)

FLAG – A red flag charged with three conjoined armoured legs in white and gold

NATIONAL DAY – 5 July (Tynwald Day)

GOVERNMENT

The Isle of Man is a self-governing Crown dependency, with its own parliamentary, legal and administrative system. The British government is responsible for international relations and defence. Under the UK Act of Accession, Protocol 3, the island's relationship with the European Union is limited to trade alone and does not extend to financial aid. The Lieutenant-Governor is the Queen's personal representative on the island.

The legislature, Tynwald, is the oldest parliament in the world in continuous existence. It has two branches: the Legislative Council and the House of Keys. The council consists of the President of Tynwald, the Bishop of Sodor and Man, the Attorney-General (who does not have a vote) and eight members elected by the House of Keys. The House of Keys has 24 members, elected by universal adult suffrage. The branches sit separately to consider legislation and sit together, as Tynwald Court, for most other parliamentary purposes.

The presiding officer of Tynwald Court is the President of Tynwald, elected by the members, who also presides over sittings of the Legislative Council. The presiding officer of the House of Keys is the Speaker, who is elected by members of the house.

The principal members of the Manx government are the chief minister and eight departmental ministers, who comprise the Council of Ministers.

Lieutenant-Governor, HE Sir Richard Gozney, KCMG, CVO

President of Tynwald, Hon. Steve Rodan
Speaker, House of Keys, Hon. Juan Paul Watterson, SHK
Deputy Speaker, House of Keys, Chris Robertshaw, MHK
The First Deemster and Clerk of the Rolls, His Hon. Andrew Corlett
Clerk of Tynwald, Secretary to the House of Keys and Counsel to the Speaker, Roger Phillips
Clerk of the Legislative Council and Deputy Clerk of Tynwald, Jonathan King
Attorney-General, John Quinn
Chief Minister, Hon. Howard Quayle, MHK
Chief Secretary, Will Greenhow

ECONOMY

Much of the income generated in the island is earned in the services sector with financial and professional services accounting for 42.6 per cent of the national income. Two other significant sectors are e-gaming and ICT, contributing 18.4 per cent and 10 per cent respectively, to the national income. Under the terms of protocol 3, the island has tariff-free access to EU markets for the products of its engineering, farming and fishing industries.

In July 2018 the island's unemployment rate was 0.8 per cent and the rate of inflation for CPI was 1.6 per cent.

FINANCE

The budget for 2018–19 provides for gross revenue expenditure of £1,062m. The principal sources of government revenue are direct and indirect taxes. Income tax is payable at a rate of 10 per cent on the first £6,500 of taxable income for single resident individuals and 20 per cent on the balance, after personal allowances of £13,250. These bands are doubled for married couples. The rate of income tax for trading companies is zero per cent except for income from banking and major retail operations which is taxed at 10 per cent, and income from land and property which is taxed at 20 per cent. By agreement with the British government, the island keeps most of its rates of indirect taxation (VAT and duties) the same as those in the UK. However, VAT on tourist accommodation, property, repairs and renovations is charged at 5 per cent. Taxes are also charged on property (rates), but these are comparatively low.

The major government expenditure items are social security payments, health and education. The island makes an annual contribution to the UK for defence and other external services.

The island has a special relationship with the European Union and neither contributes money to nor receives funds from the EU budget.

Ψ = sea port

THE CHANNEL ISLANDS

The Channel Islands, situated off the north-west coast of France (at a distance of 16km (10 miles) at their closest point), are the only portions of the Dukedom of Normandy still belonging to the Crown, to which they have been attached since the Norman Conquest of 1066. They were the only British territory to come under German occupation during the Second World War, following invasion on 30 June and 1 July 1940. Guernsey and Jersey were relieved by British forces on 9 May 1945, Sark on 10 May 1945 and Alderney on 16 May 1945; 9 May (Liberation Day) is now observed as a bank and public holiday in Guernsey and Jersey.

The islands consist of Jersey (11,630ha/28,717 acres), Guernsey (6,340ha/15,654 acres), and the dependencies of Guernsey: Alderney (795ha/1,962 acres), Brecqhou (30ha/74 acres), Great Sark (419ha/1,035 acres), Little Sark (97ha/239 acres), Herm (130ha/320 acres), Jethou (18ha/44 acres) and Lihou (15ha/38 acres) – a total of 19,474ha/48,083 acres, or 195 sq. km/75 sq. miles.

The 2011 census (taken in March) showed the population of Jersey as 97,857. Guernsey uses a rolling electronic census system and the most recent figures (June 2017) showed the populations of Guernsey and Alderney to be 62,514 and 1,985 respectively. Sark's population is estimated to be around 600. The official language is English but French is often used for ceremonial purposes. A Norman-French *patois* is also spoken by a few in Jersey, Guernsey and Sark.

GOVERNMENT
The islands are Crown dependencies with their own legislative assemblies (the States of Jersey,the States of Alderney, the States of Deliberation in Guernsey and the Chief Pleas in Sark), systems of local administration and law, and their own courts. *Projets de Loi* (Acts) passed by the States require the sanction of the Queen-in-council. The UK government is responsible for defence and international relations, although the islands are increasingly entering into agreements with other countries in their own right. The Channel Islands are not members of the European Union but, under protocol 3 of the UK's Treaty of Accession, have trading rights with the free movement of goods within the EU. A common customs tariff, levies and agricultural and import measures apply to trade between the islands and non-member countries.

In both Jersey and Guernsey bailiwicks the Lieutenant-Governor and Commander-in-Chief, who is appointed by the Crown, is the personal representative of the Queen and the official channel of communication between the Crown (via the Privy Council) and the islands' governments.

The head of government in both Jersey and Guernsey is the Chief Minister. Jersey has a ministerial system of government; the executive comprises the Council of Ministers and consists of a chief minister and ten other ministers. The ministers are assisted by up to ten assistant ministers. Members of the States who are not in the executive are able to sit on a number of scrutiny panels and the Public Accounts Committee to examine the policy of the executive and hold ministers to account. Guernsey is administered by a number of committees. The Policy and Resources committee is the senior committee responsible for leadership and coordination of the work of the States and is presided over by the Chief Minister, in addition there are six principal committees with mandated responsibilities. The States of Deliberation is the island's parliamentary assembly. Alderney has a legislature comprising a President and ten members elected by universal suffrage. Sark has a directly elected legislature of 28 members *(conseillers)* who serve on a number of committees.

Justice is administered by the royal courts of Jersey and Guernsey, each consisting of the bailiff and 12 elected jurats. The bailiffs of Jersey and Guernsey, appointed by the Crown, are presidents of the royal courts of their respective islands. Each bailiff is the *ex-officio* presiding officer in their respective parliaments and, by convention, the civic head.

The Church of England in each bailiwick is under the jurisdiction of the Dean of Jersey and the Dean of Guernsey respectively. The Bishop of Dover (Diocese of Canterbury) has episcopal oversight of the Channel Islands.

ECONOMY
A mild climate and good soil have led to the development of intensive systems of agriculture and horticulture, which form a significant part of the economy. Equally important are earnings from tourism and banking and finance: the low rates of income and corporation tax and the absence of death duties make the islands an important offshore financial centre. The financial services sector contributes over 50 per cent of GDP in Jersey and around 33 per cent in Guernsey. In addition, there is no VAT or equivalent tax in Guernsey and only small goods and services tax in Jersey (5 per cent since 1 June 2011). The international stock exchange is located in Guernsey, which also has a thriving e-gaming sector.

Principal exports are agricultural produce and flowers; imports are chiefly machinery, manufactured goods, food, fuel and chemicals. Trade with the UK is regarded as internal.

British currency is legal tender in the Channel Islands but each bailiwick issues its own coins and notes (*see* Currency section). They also issue their own postage stamps; UK stamps are not valid.

JERSEY
Lieutenant-Governor and Commander-in-Chief of Jersey, HE Air Chief Marshal Sir Stephen Dalton, GCB, *from* 2017
Chief of Staff, Maj. Justin Oldridge
Bailiff of Jersey, Sir William J. Bailhache
Deputy Bailiff, Timothy J. Le Cocq
Attorney-General, Robert J. MacRae, QC
Receiver-General, David Pett
Solicitor-General, Mark Temple, QC
Greffier of the States, Mark Egan
States Treasurer, Richard Bell
Chief Minister, Senator John Le Fondré

FINANCE
	2016	2017
Revenue income	£736,800,000	£767,300,000
Revenue expenditure	£698,500,000	£703.800,000
Capital expenditure	£40,856,000	£47,600,000

CHIEF TOWN – ΨSt Helier, on the south coast
FLAG – A white field charged with a red saltire cross, and the arms of Jersey in the upper centre

GUERNSEY AND DEPENDENCIES
Lieutenant-Governor and Commander-in-Chief of the Bailiwick of Guernsey and its Dependencies, Vice-Adm. Sir Ian Corder, KBE, CB
Presiding Officer of the Royal Court and of the States of Deliberation, Bailiff Sir Richard Collas
Deputy Presiding Officer of the Royal Court and States of Deliberation, Deputy Bailiff Richard McMahon, QC

HM Procureur and Receiver-General (Attorney-General), Megan
   Pullum, QC
HM Comptroller (Solicitor-General), Robert Titterington, QC

GUERNSEY
Chief Minister, Deputy Gavin St Pier
Chief Executive, Paul Whitfield

FINANCE

	2016	2017
Revenue income	£477,163,000	£500,010,000
Revenue expenditure	£451,658,000	£450,419,000
Capital expenditure	£14,282,000	£15,103,000

CHIEF TOWNS – ΨSt Peter Port, on the east coast of
   Guernsey; St Anne on Alderney
FLAG – White, bearing a red cross of St George, with a gold
   cross of Normandy overall in the centre

ALDERNEY
President of the States, Stuart Trought
Chief Executive, Andrew Muter
Greffier, Jonathan Anderson

SARK
Sark was the last European territory to abolish feudal
parliamentary representation. Elections for a democratic
legislative assembly took place in December 2008, with the
conseillers taking their seats in the newly constituted Chief
Pleas in January 2009.
Seigneur of Sark, Maj. Christopher Beaumont
Seneschal, Jeremy la Trobe-Bateman
President, Arthur Rolfe
Greffier, Trevor Hamon

OTHER DEPENDENCIES
Herm and Lihou are owned by the States of Guernsey; Herm
is leased, Lihou is uninhabited. Jethou is leased by the Crown
to the States of Guernsey and is sub-let by the States.
Brecqhou is within the legislative and judicial territory of
Sark.

Ψ = seaport

LAW COURTS AND OFFICES

SUPREME COURT OF THE UNITED KINGDOM

The Supreme Court of the United Kingdom is the highest domestic judicial authority; it replaced the appellate committee of the House of Lords (the house functioning in its judicial capacity) on 1 October 2009. It is the final court of appeal for cases heard in Great Britain and Northern Ireland (except for criminal cases from Scotland). Cases concerning the interpretation and application of European Union law, including preliminary rulings requested by British courts and tribunals, which are decided by the Court of Justice of the European Union (CJEU) (*see* European Union), and the supreme court can make a reference to the CJEU in appropriate cases. Additionally, in giving effect to rights contained in the European Convention on Human Rights, the supreme court must take account of any decision of the European Court of Human Rights.

The supreme court also assumed jurisdiction in relation to devolution matters under the Scotland Act 1998 (now partly superseded by the Scotland Act 2012), the Northern Ireland Act 1988 and the Government of Wales Act 2006; these powers were transferred from the Judicial Committee of the Privy Council. Ten of the 12 Lords of Appeal in Ordinary (Law Lords) from the House of Lords transferred to the 12-member supreme court when it came into operation (at the same time one law lord retired and another was appointed Master of the Rolls). All new justices of the supreme court are now appointed by an independent selection commission, and, although styled *Rt. Hon. Lord,* are not members of the House of Lords. Peers who are members of the judiciary are disqualified from sitting or voting in the House of Lords until they retire from their judicial office. *See* Life Peers for a list of such peers (§).

President of the Supreme Court (£225,091), Rt. Hon. Baroness Hale of Richmond, DBE *born* 1945, *apptd* 2017
Deputy President of the Supreme Court (£217,409), Rt. Hon. Lord Reed, *born* 1956, *apptd* 2018

HIERARCHY OF ENGLISH AND WELSH COURTS

JUSTICES OF THE SUPREME COURT *as at September 2018*
(each £217,409)
Style, The Rt. Hon. Lord/Lady–

Rt. Hon. Lord Kerr of Tonaghmore, *born* 1948, *apptd* 2009
Rt. Hon. Lord Wilson of Culworth, *born* 1945, *apptd* 2011
Rt. Hon. Lord Sumption, *born* 1948, *apptd* 2012
Rt. Hon. Lord Carnwath of Notting Hill, CVO, *born* 1945, *apptd* 2012
Rt. Hon. Lord Hodge, *born* 1953, *apptd* 2013
Rt. Hon. Lady Black of Derwent, DBE *born* 1954, *apptd* 2017
Rt. Hon. Lord Lloyd-Jones, *born* 1952, *apptd* 2017
Rt. Hon. Lord Briggs of Westbourne, *born* 1954, *apptd* 2017

UNITED KINGDOM SUPREME COURT
Parliament Square, London SW1P 3BD T 020-7960 1900
Chief Executive, Mark Ormerod, CB

JUDICATURE OF ENGLAND AND WALES

The legal system in England and Wales is divided into criminal law and civil law. Criminal law is concerned with acts harmful to the community and the rules laid down by the state for the benefit of citizens, whereas civil law governs the relationships and transactions between individuals. Administrative law is a kind of civil law usually concerning the interaction of individuals and the state, and most cases are heard in tribunals specific to the subject (*see* Tribunals section). Scotland and Northern Ireland possess legal systems that differ from the system in England and Wales in law, judicial procedure and court structure, but retain the distinction between criminal and civil law.

Under the provisions of the Criminal Appeal Act 1995, a commission was set up to direct and supervise investigations into possible miscarriages of justice and to refer cases to the appeal courts on the grounds of conviction and sentence; these functions were formerly the responsibility of the home secretary.

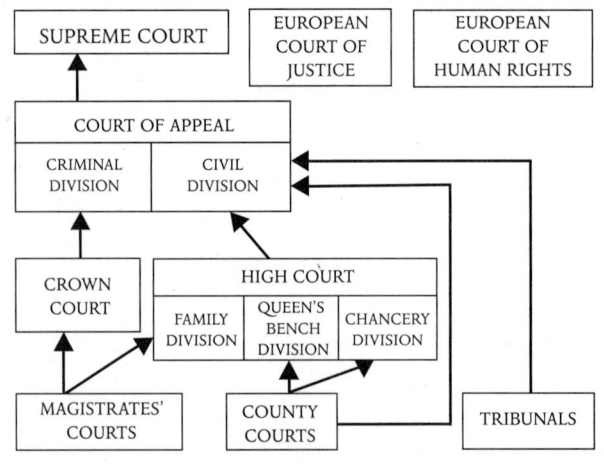

SENIOR COURTS OF ENGLAND AND WALES

The senior courts of England and Wales (until September 2009 known as the supreme court of judicature of England and Wales) comprise the high court, the crown court and the court of appeal. The President of the Courts of England and Wales, a new title given to the Lord Chief Justice under the Constitutional Reform Act 2005, is the head of the judiciary.

The high court was created in 1875 and combined many previously separate courts. Sittings are held at the royal courts of justice in London or at around 120 district registries outside the capital. It is the superior civil court and is split into three divisions – the chancery division, the Queen's bench division and the family division – each of which is further divided. The chancery division is headed by the Chancellor of the High Court and is concerned mainly with equity, trusts, tax and bankruptcy, while also including two specialist courts, the patents court and the companies court. The Queen's bench division (QBD) is the largest of the three divisions, and is headed by its own president. It deals with common law (ie tort, contract, debt and personal injuries), some tax law, eg VAT tribunal appeals, and encompasses the admiralty court and the commercial court. The QBD also administers the technology and construction court. The family division was created in 1970 and is headed by its own president, who is also Head of Family Justice, and hears cases concerning divorce, access to and custody of children, and other family matters. The divisional court of the high court sits in the family and chancery divisions, and hears appeals from the magistrates' courts and county courts.

The crown court was set up in 1972 and sits at 77 centres throughout England and Wales. It deals with more serious (indictable) criminal offences, which are triable before a judge and jury, including treason, murder, rape, kidnapping, armed robbery and Official Secrets Act offences. It also handles cases transferred from the magistrates' courts where the magistrate decides his or her own power of sentence is inadequate, or where someone appeals against a magistrate's decision, or in a case that is triable 'either way' where the accused has chosen a jury trial. The crown court centres are divided into three tiers: high court judges, circuit judges and sometimes recorders (part-time circuit judges), sit in first-tier centres, hearing the most serious criminal offences (eg murder, treason, rape, manslaughter) and some civil high court cases. The second-tier centres are presided over by high court judges, circuit judges or recorders and also deal with the most serious criminal cases. Third-tier courts deal with the remaining criminal offences, with circuit judges or recorders presiding.

The court of appeal hears appeals against both fact and law, and was last restructured in 1966 when it replaced the court of criminal appeal. It is split into the civil division (which hears appeals from the high court, tribunals and in certain cases, the county courts) and the criminal division (which hears appeals from the crown court). Cases are heard by Lords Justices of Appeal and high court judges if deemed suitable for reconsideration.

The Constitutional Reform Act 2005 instigated several key changes to the judiciary in England and Wales. These included the establishment of the independent supreme court, which opened in October 2009; the reform of the post of Lord Chancellor, transferring its judicial functions to the President of the Courts of England and Wales; a duty on government ministers to uphold the independence of the judiciary by barring them from trying to influence judicial decisions through any special access to judges; the formation of a fully transparent and independent Judicial Appointments Commission that is responsible for selecting candidates to recommend for judicial appointment to the Lord Chancellor and Secretary of State for Justice; and the creation of the post of Judicial Appointments and Conduct Ombudsman.

CRIMINAL CASES

In criminal matters the decision to prosecute (in the majority of cases) rests with the Crown Prosecution Service (CPS), which is the independent prosecuting body in England and Wales. The CPS is headed by the director of public prosecutions, who works under the superintendence of the Attorney-General. Certain categories of offence continue to require the Attorney-General's consent for prosecution.

Most minor criminal cases (summary offences) are dealt with in magistrates' courts, usually by a bench of three unpaid lay magistrates (justices of the peace) sitting without a jury and assisted on points of law and procedure by a legally trained clerk. There are approximately 23,000 justices of the peace. In some courts a full-time, salaried and legally qualified district judge (magistrates' court) – formerly known as a stipendiary judge – presides alone. There are 140 district judges and 170 deputy district judges operating in around 330 magistrates' courts in England and Wales. Magistrates' courts deal with 95 per cent of all criminal cases. Magistrates' courts also house some family proceedings courts (which deal with relationship breakdown and childcare cases) and youth courts. Cases of medium seriousness (known as 'offences triable either way') where the defendant pleads not guilty can be heard in the crown court for a trial by jury, if the defendant so chooses. Preliminary proceedings in a serious case to decide whether there is evidence to justify committal for trial in the crown court are dealt with in the magistrates' courts.

The 77 centres that the crown court sits in are divided into seven regions. There are over 600 circuit judges and 1,000 recorders (part-time circuit judges); expected to sit for 30 days a year. A jury is present in all trials that are contested.

Appeals from magistrates' courts against sentence or conviction are made to the crown court, and appeals upon a point of law are made to the high court, which may ultimately be appealed to the supreme court. Appeals from the crown court, either against sentence or conviction, are made to the court of appeal (criminal division). Again, these appeals may be brought to the supreme court if a point of law is contested, and if the house considers it is of sufficient importance.

CIVIL CASES

Most minor civil cases – including contract, tort (especially personal injuries), property, divorce and other family matters, bankruptcy etc – are dealt with by the county courts, of which there are around 200 (see W www.justice.gov.uk for further details). Cases are heard by circuit judges, recorders or district judges. For cases involving small claims (with certain exceptions, where the amount claimed is £5,000 or less) there are informal and simplified procedures designed to enable parties to present their cases themselves without recourse to lawyers. Where there are financial limits on county court jurisdiction, claims that exceed those limits may be tried in county courts with the consent of the parties, subject to the court's agreement, or in certain circumstances on transfer from the high court. Outside London, bankruptcy proceedings can be heard in designated county courts. Magistrates' courts also deal with certain classes of civil case, and committees of magistrates license public houses, clubs and betting shops. For the implementation of the Children Act 1989, a new structure of hearing centres was set up in 1991 for family proceedings cases, involving magistrates' courts (family proceedings courts), divorce county courts, family hearing centres and care centres.

Appeals in certain family matters heard in the family proceedings courts go to the family division of the high court. Appeals from county courts may be heard in the court of appeal (civil division) or the high court, and may go on to the supreme court.

CORONERS' COURTS

Unlike the unified courts system, administered by HM Courts and Tribunals Service, there are 92 separate coroners' jurisdictions in England and Wales. Each jurisdiction is locally funded and resourced by local authorities. Coroners are barristers, solicitors or medical practitioners of not less than five years standing, who continue in their legal or medical practices when not sitting as coroners. Some 30 coroners are 'full-time' coroners and are paid an annual salary regardless of their caseload. The remainder are paid according to the number of cases referred to them. The coroner's jurisdiction is territorial – it is the location of the dead body which dictates which coroner has jurisdiction in any particular case.

The coroners' courts investigate violent and unnatural deaths or sudden deaths where the cause is unknown. Doctors, the police, various public authorities or members of the public may bring cases before a coroner. Where a death is sudden and the cause is unknown, the coroner may order a post-mortem examination to determine the cause of death rather than hold an inquest in court. An inquest must be held, however, if a person died in a violent or unnatural way, or died in prison or other unusual circumstances. If the coroner suspects murder, manslaughter or infanticide, then they must summon a jury.

Coroners are required to appoint a deputy or assistant deputy to act in their stead if they are out of the district or otherwise unable to act. Deputies and assistant deputies have the same professional qualifications as the coroner. In exceptionally high-profile or complex cases, a serving judge may be appointed as a deputy coroner.

SENIOR JUDICIARY OF ENGLAND AND WALES

Lord Chief Justice of England and Wales and Head of Criminal Justice (£252,079), Rt. Hon. Lord Burnett of Maldon, *born* 1958, *apptd* 2017

Master of the Rolls and Head of Civil Justice (£225,091), Rt. Hon. Sir Terence Etherton, *born* 1951, *apptd* 2016

President of the Queen's Bench Division and Head of Criminal Justice (£217,409), Rt. Hon. Sir Brian Leveson, *born* 1949, *apptd* 2013

President of the Family Division and Head of Family Justice (£217,409), Rt. Hon. Sir Andrew McFarlane, *born* 1954, *apptd* 2018

Chancellor of the High Court (£217,409), Rt. Hon. Sir Geoffrey Vos, *born* 1955, *apptd* 2016

SENIOR COURTS OF ENGLAND AND WALES

COURT OF APPEAL

Presiding Judge, Criminal Division, Lord Chief Justice of England and Wales
Presiding Judge, Civil Division, Master of the Rolls
Vice-President, Civil Division (£206,742), Rt. Hon. Sir Nicholas Underhill *born* 1952, *apptd* 2018
Vice-President, Criminal Division (£206,742), Rt. Hon. Dame Heather Hallett, DBE, *born* 1949, *apptd* 2013

LORD JUSTICES OF APPEAL *as at September 2018* (each £206,742)
Style, The Rt. Hon. Lord/Lady Justice [surname]

Rt. Hon. Dame Mary Arden, DBE, *born* 1947, *apptd* 2000
Rt. Hon. Sir Andrew Longmore, *born* 1944, *apptd* 2001
Rt. Hon. Dame Heather Hallett, DBE, *born* 1949, *apptd* 2005
Rt. Hon. Sir Nicholas Patten, *born* 1950, *apptd* 2009
Rt. Hon. Sir Peter Gross, *born* 1952, *apptd* 2010
Rt. Hon. Dame Anne Rafferty, DBE, *born* 1950, *apptd* 2011
Rt. Hon. Sir Nigel Davis, *born* 1951, *apptd* 2011
Rt. Hon. Sir Kim Lewison, *born* 1952, *apptd* 2011

Rt. Hon. Sir David Kitchin, *born* 1955, *apptd* 2011
Rt. Hon. Sir Colman Treacy, *born* 1949, *apptd* 2012
Rt. Hon. Sir Richard McCombe, *born* 1952, *apptd* 2012
Rt. Hon. Sir Ernest Ryder, TD, *born* 1957, *apptd* 2013
Rt. Hon. Sir Nicholas Underhill, *born* 1952, *apptd* 2013
Rt. Hon. Sir Christopher Floyd, *born* 1951, *apptd* 2013
Rt. Hon. Sir Adrian Fulford, *born* 1953, *apptd* 2013
Rt. Hon. Dame Julia Macur, DBE, *born* 1957, *apptd* 2013
Rt. Hon. Dame Victoria Sharp, DBE, *born* 1956, *apptd* 2013
Rt. Hon. Sir David Bean, *born* 1954, *apptd* 2014
Rt. Hon. Dame Eleanor King, DBE, *born* 1957, *apptd* 2014
Rt. Hon. Sir Philip Sales, *born* 1962, *apptd* 2014
Rt. Hon. Sir Peregrine Simon, *born* 1950, *apptd* 2015
Rt. Hon. Sir Keith Lindblom, *born* 1956, *apptd* 2015
Rt. Hon. Sir David Richards, *born* 1951, *apptd* 2015
Rt. Hon. Sir Nicholas Hamblen, *born* 1957, *apptd* 2016
Rt. Hon. Sir Stephen Irwin, *born* 1953, *apptd* 2016
Rt. Hon. Sir Launcelot Henderson, *born* 1951, *apptd* 2016
Rt. Hon. Sir Julian Flaux, *born* 1955, *apptd* 2016
Rt. Hon. Dame Kathryn Thirlwall, DBE, *born* 1957, *apptd* 2017
Rt. Hon. Sir Gary Hickinbottom, *born* 1955, *apptd* 2017
Rt. Hon. Sir Andrew Moylan, *born* 1953, *apptd* 2017
Rt. Hon. Sir Timothy Holroyde, *born* 1955, *apptd* 2017
Rt. Hon. Sir Peter Jackson, *born* 1955, *apptd* 2017
Rt. Hon. Sir Guy Newey, *born* 1959, *apptd* 2017
Rt. Hon Sir Rabinder Singh, *born* 1964, *apptd* 2017
Rt. Hon. Dame Sarah Asplin, DBE, *born* 1959, *apptd* 2017
Rt. Hon. Sir George Leggatt, *born* 1957, *apptd* 2018
Rt. Hon. Sir Peter Coulson, *born* 1958, *apptd* 2018
Rt. Hon. Sir Jonathan Baker, *born* 1955, *apptd* 2018
Rt. Hon. Dame Nicola Davies, DBE, *born* 1953, *apptd* 2018
Rt. Hon. Sir Nicholas Green, *born* 1958, *apptd* 2018
Rt. Hon. Sir Charles Haddon-Cave, *born* 1956, *apptd* 2018
Rt. Hon. Sir Stephen Males, *born* 1955, *apptd* 2018
Rt. Hon. Dame Vivien Rose, DBE, *born* 1960, *apptd* 2018
Rt. Hon. Dame Ingrid Simler, DBE, *born* 1963, *apptd* 2018

Ex Officio Judges, Lord Chief Justice of England and Wales; Master of the Rolls; President of the Queen's Bench Division; President of the Family Division; Chancellor of the High Court

COURTS-MARTIAL APPEAL COURT

Judges, Lord Chief Justice of England and Wales; Master of the Rolls; Lord Justices of Appeal; Judges of the High Court of Justice

HIGH COURT

CHANCERY DIVISION

Chancellor of the High Court (£217,409), Rt. Hon. Sir Geoffrey Vos, *born* 1955, *apptd* 2016
Clerk, Jessie Davidson
Legal Secretary, Vannina Ettori

JUDGES *as at September 2018* (each £181,566)
Style, The Hon. Mr/Mrs/Ms Justice [surname]

Hon. Sir George Mann, *born* 1951, *apptd* 2004

Hon. Sir Paul Morgan, *born* 1952, *apptd* 2007
Hon. Sir Alastair Norris, *born* 1950, *apptd* 2007
Hon. Sir Gerald Barling, *born* 1949, *apptd* 2007
Hon. Sir Richard Arnold, *born* 1961, *apptd* 2008
Hon. Sir Peter Roth, *born* 1952, *apptd* 2009
Hon. Sir Robert Hildyard, *born* 1952, *apptd* 2011
Hon. Sir Colin Birss, *born* 1964, *apptd* 2013
Hon. Sir Christopher Nugee, *born* 1959, *apptd* 2013
Hon. Sir Richard Snowden, *born* 1962, *apptd* 2015
Hon. Sir Henry Carr, *born* 1958, *apptd* 2015

Hon. Sir Marcus Smith, *born* 1967, *apptd* 2017
Hon. Sir Antony Zacaroli, *born* 1963, *apptd* 2017
Hon. Sir Timothy Fancourt, *born* 1964, *apptd* 2018
Hon. Dame Sarah Falk, DBE, *born* 1962, *apptd* 2018
The Chancery Division also includes three specialist courts: the Companies Court, the Patents Court and the Bankruptcy Court.

QUEEN'S BENCH DIVISION
President (£217,409), Rt. Hon. Sir Brian Leveson, *born* 1949, *apptd* 2013
Vice-President (£206,742), Rt. Hon. Dame Victoria Sharp, DBE, *born* 1956, *apptd* 2016

JUDGES *as at September 2018* (each £181,566)
Style, The Hon. Mr/Mrs/Ms Justice [surname]

Hon. Sir Duncan Ouseley, *born* 1950, *apptd* 2000
Hon. Sir Paul Walker, *born* 1954, *apptd* 2004
Hon. Sir Nigel Teare, *born* 1952, *apptd* 2006
Hon. Sir Timothy King, *born* 1949, *apptd* 2007
Hon. Sir David Foskett, *born* 1949, *apptd* 2007
Hon. Sir Nigel Sweeney, *born* 1954, *apptd* 2008
Hon. Dame Elizabeth Slade, DBE, *born* 1949, *apptd* 2008
Hon. Sir Andrew Nicol, *born* 1951, *apptd* 2009
Hon. Sir Michael Supperstone, *born* 1950, *apptd* 2010
Hon. Sir Robin Spencer, *born* 1955, *apptd* 2010
Hon. Sir Andrew Popplewell, *born* 1959, *apptd* 2011
Hon. Dame Beverley Lang, DBE, *born* 1955, *apptd* 2011
Hon. Sir Jeremy Stuart-Smith, *born* 1955, *apptd* 2012
Hon. Sir Mark Turner, *born* 1959, *apptd* 2013
Hon. Sir Jeremy Baker, *born* 1958, *apptd* 2013
Hon. Sir Stephen Stewart, *born* 1953, *apptd* 2013
Hon. Sir Robert Jay, *born* 1959, *apptd* 2013
Hon. Sir James Dingemans, *born* 1964, *apptd* 2013
Hon. Sir Clive Lewis, *born* 1960, *apptd* 2013
Hon. Dame Sue Carr, DBE, *born* 1964, *apptd* 2013
Hon. Sir Stephen Phillips, *born* 1961, *apptd* 2013
Hon. Dame Geraldine Andrews, DBE, *born* 1959, *apptd* 2013
Hon. Dame Elisabeth Laing, DBE, *born* 1956, *apptd* 2014
Hon. Sir William Davis, *born* 1954, *apptd* 2014
Hon. Sir Mark Warby, *born* 1958, *apptd* 2014
Hon. Sir Andrew Edis, *born* 1957, *apptd* 2014
Hon. Sir James Goss, *born* 1953, *apptd* 2014
Hon. Dame Maura McGowan, DBE, *born* 1957, *apptd* 2014
Hon. Sir Robin Knowles, *born* 1960, *apptd* 2014
Hon. Sir Ian Dove, *born* 1963, *apptd* 2014
Hon. Sir David Holgate, *born* 1956, *apptd* 2014
Hon. Sir Timothy Kerr, *born* 1958, *apptd* 2015
Hon. Sir Simon Picken, *born* 1966, *apptd* 2015
Hon. Dame Philippa Whipple, DBE, *born* 1966, *apptd* 2015
Hon. Sir Peter Fraser, *born* 1963, *apptd* 2015
Hon. Sir Neil Garnham, *born* 1959, *apptd* 2015
Hon. Dame Bobbie Cheema-Grubb, DBE *born* 1966, *apptd* 2015
Hon. Sir Michael Soole, *born* 1954, *apptd* 2015
Hon. Dame Juliet May, DBE, *born* 1961, *apptd* 2015
Hon. Sir Stephen Morris, *born* 1957, *apptd* 2016
Hon. Dame Nerys Jefford, DBE, *born* 1962, *apptd* 2016
Hon. Sir Nicholas Lavender, *born* 1964, *apptd* 2016
Hon. Dame Finola O'Farrell, DBE, *born* 1960, *apptd* 2016
Hon. Sir Andrew Baker, *born* 1965, *apptd* 2016
Hon. Sir Julian Goose, *born* 1961, *apptd* 2017
Hon. Sir Peter Lane, *born* 1953, *apptd* 2017
Hon. Sir Simon Bryan, *born* 1965, *apptd* 2017
Hon. Dame Jane Moulder, DBE, *born* 1960, *apptd* 2017
Hon. Sir Martin Spencer, *born* 1956, *apptd* 2017
Hon. Sir Julian Knowles, *born* 1969, *apptd* 2017
Hon Dame Amanda Yip, DBE, *born* 1969, *apptd* 2017

Hon. Sir Matthew Nicklin, *born* 1970, *apptd* 2017
Hon. Sir Akhlaq Choudhury, *born* 1967, *apptd* 2017
Hon. Dame Sara Cockerill, DBE, *born* 1968, *apptd* 2017
Hon. Dame Christina Lambert, DBE, *born* 1963, *apptd* 2018
Hon. Sir Christopher Butcher, *born* 1962, *apptd* 2018
Hon. Sir Richard Jacobs, *born* 1956, *apptd* 2018
Hon. Dame Judith Farbey, DBE, *born* 1965, *apptd* 2018
Hon. Sir Edward Murray, *born* 1958, *apptd* 2018
Hon. Dame Johannah Cutts, *born* 1964, *apptd* 2018
Hon. Sir David Waksman, *born* 1957, *apptd* 2018
The Queen's Bench Division also includes the Divisional Court, the Admiralty Court, Commercial Court and Technology and Construction Court.

FAMILY DIVISION
President (£217,409), Rt. Hon. Sir Andrew McFarlane, *born* 1954, *apptd* 2018

JUDGES *as at September 2018* (each £181,566)
Style, The Hon. Mr/Mrs/Ms Justice [surname]

Hon. Sir Edward Holman, *born* 1947, *apptd* 1995
Hon. Dame Judith Parker, DBE *born* 1950, *apptd* 2008
Hon. Sir Nicholas Mostyn, *born* 1957, *apptd* 2010
Hon. Dame Lucy Theis, DBE, *born* 1960, *apptd* 2010
Hon. Sir Philip Moor, *born* 1959, *apptd* 2011
Hon. Sir Stephen Cobb, *born* 1962, *apptd* 2013
Hon. Sir Michael Keehan, *born* 1960, *apptd* 2013
Hon. Sir Anthony Hayden, *born* 1961, *apptd* 2013
Hon. Dame Alison Russell, DBE, *born* 1958, *apptd* 2014
Hon. Roderick Newton, *born* 1958, *apptd* 2014
Hon. Dame Jennifer Roberts, DBE, *born* 1953, *apptd* 2014
Hon. Sir Alistair MacDonald, *born* 1970, *apptd* 2015
Hon. Sir Peter Francis, *born* 1958, *apptd* 2016
Hon. Dame Gwynneth Knowles, DBE *born* 1962, *apptd* 2017
Hon. Sir Jonathan Cohen, *born* 1951, *apptd* 2017
Hon. Sir David Williams, *born* 1961, *apptd* 2017

COURTS, DIVISIONS AND OFFICES OF THE HIGH COURT OF ENGLAND AND WALES

ADMINISTRATIVE COURT
Royal Courts of Justice, London WC2A 2LL
T 020-7947 6655
Judge in charge of the Administrative Court (£181,566), Hon. Mr Justice Supperstone
Registrar of Criminal Appeals, Master of the Crown Office and Queen's Coroner and Attorney (£134,841), vacant

ADMIRALTY COURT
Ground Floor, 7 Rolls Building, Fetter Lane, London EC4A 1NL
T 020-7947 6112
Registrar (£108,171), Jervis Kay, QC
Admiralty Judge (£181,566), Hon. Mr Justice Teare
Clerk, Paul Doerr

CIRCUIT COMMERCIAL COURT (formerly Mercantile Court)
Ground Floor, 7 Rolls Building, Fetter Lane, London EC4A 1NL
T 020-7947 6112

CHANCERY DIVISION
7 Rolls Building, Fetter Lane, London EC4A 1NL T 020-7947 7391
Chief Chancery Master (£134,841), Chief Master Marsh *apptd* 2014
Masters of Chancery (£108,171), Master Bowles *apptd* 1999; Master Clark *apptd* 2015; Master Matthews *apptd* 2015; Master Price *apptd* 1999; Master Shuman *apptd* 2017; Master Teverson *apptd* 2005

COMMERCIAL COURT

Ground Floor, 7 Rolls Building, Fetter Lane, London EC4A 1NL
T 020-7947 7501
Judge in charge of the Commercial Court (£181,566), Hon. Mr
Justice Popplewell
Clerk, Quincey Boachie-Wiredu

COURT OF APPEAL CIVIL DIVISION

Royal Courts of Justice, London WC2A 2LL T 020-7947 6916

COURT OF APPEAL CRIMINAL DIVISION

Royal Courts of Justice, London WC2A 2LL T 020-7947 6011

COURT OF PROTECTION

First Avenue House, 42–49 High Holborn, London WC1V 6NP
T 0300-456 4600
Senior Judge and Master of the Court of Protection (£134,841),
Her Hon. Judge Hilder, *apptd* 2017

FAMILY DIVISION

Royal Courts of Justice, London WC2A 2LL T 020-7947 6000

INSOLVENCY AND COMPANIES LIST

7 Rolls Building, Fetter Lane, London EC4A 1NL
T 020-7947 6294
Chief Registrar (134,841), Nicholas Briggs *apptd* 2017
Insolvency and Companies Court Judges (£108,171), Judge
Barber *apptd* 2009; Judge Jones *apptd* 2012

INTELLECTUAL PROPERTY ENTERPRISE COURT

7 Rolls Building, Fetter Lane, London EC4A 1NL
T 020-7947 7783 E ipec@hmcts.gsi.gov.uk
Judge in Charge, His Hon. Judge Hacon
Clerk, Adam Wilcox

PATENTS COURT

7 Rolls Building, Fetter Lane, London EC4A 1NL
T 020-7073 1789
Judge in Charge, Hon. Sir Richard Arnold
Clerk, Pauline Drewett

PLANNING COURT

Royal Courts of Justice, London WC2A 2LL
T 020-7947 6655

QUEEN'S BENCH DIVISION

Senior Master and Queen's Remembrancer (£134,841), Senior
Master Fontaine *apptd* 2014
Masters of the Queen's Bench Division (£108,171), Master Cook
apptd 2011; Master Davison *apptd* 2016; Master Eastman
apptd 2009; Master Gidden *apptd* 2012; Master Kay, QC;
apptd 2009; Master McCloud *apptd* 2010; Master
Thornett *apptd* 2016; Master Yoxall *apptd* 2002

SENIOR COURT COSTS OFFICE

Thomas More Building, Royal Courts of Justice, London WC2A 2LL
T 020-7947 6000
Senior Costs Judge (Chief Taxing Master) (£134,841), Chief
Master Gordon-Saker *apptd* 2014
Cost Judges (Taxing Masters) (£108,171), Master Brown *apptd*
2016; Master Haworth *apptd* 2006; Master James *apptd*
2015; Master Leonard *apptd* 2010; Master Nagalingam
apptd 2017; Master Rowley *apptd* 2013; Master Whalan
apptd 2015

TECHNOLOGY AND CONSTRUCTION COURT (TCC)

Ground Floor, 7 Rolls Building, Fetter Lane, London EC4A 1NL
T 020-7947 7156
Judge in charge of the TCC (£181,566), Hon. Mr Justice Fraser

COURT FUNDS OFFICE

Sunderland SR43 3AB T 0300-020 0199 E enquiries@cfo.gsi.gov.uk

The Court Funds Office (CFO), established in 1726, provides
a banking and administration service for the civil courts
throughout England and Wales, including the High Court.

ELECTION PETITIONS OFFICE

Room E113, Royal Courts of Justice, Strand, London WC2A 2LL
T 020-7947 6877

The office accepts petitions and deals with all matters relating
to the questioning of parliamentary, European parliament,
local government and parish elections, and with applications
for relief under the 'representation of the people' legislation.

Prescribed Officer, The Senior Master and Senior Remembrancer
(£134,841), B. Fontaine

EXAMINERS OF THE COURT

A panel of 18 advocates and solicitor advocates, of at least three
years standing, is empowered to take examination of witnesses
in all divisions of the High Court.

Examiners, Tony Baumgartner; Naomi Candlin; Angharad
Davies; Judy Dawson; Alison Green; Nicholas Hill; Mathias
Kelly; John Leslie; Simon Lewis; Josh Lewison; Susan Lindsey;
Andrew McLoughlin; Christopher McNall; Michael Salter;
Ashley Serr; Frederico Singarajah; Lara Spencer; John
Hamilton

OFFICIAL SOLICITOR AND PUBLIC TRUSTEE

Victory House, 30–34 Kingsway, London WC2B 6EX
E enquiries@offsol.gsi.gov.uk

The Official Solicitor and the Public Trustee are independent
statutory office holders. Their office (OSPT) is an arms-length
body of the Ministry of Justice that exists to support their work.
The Official Solicitor provides access to the justice system to
those who are vulnerable by virtue of minority or lack of mental
capacity. The Public Trustee acts as executor or administrator
of estates and as the appointed trustee of settlements, providing
an effective executor and trustee service of last resort.

Official Solicitor to the Senior Courts and the Public Trustee, vacant
Deputy Public Trustee, Janet Peel
Deputy Official Solicitors, Brid Breathnach; Elaine Brown; Janet
Ilett

PROBATE REGISTRIES

London Probate Department, 7th Floor, First Avenue House, 42–49
High Holborn, London WC1V 6NP T 020-7421 8509

Probate registries issue grants of probate and grants of letters
of administration. The principal probate registry is situated in
central London and there are 11 district probate registries in
Birmingham, Brighton, Bristol, Cardiff, Ipswich, Leeds,
Liverpool, Manchester, Newcastle, Oxford and Winchester,
and a further 18 probate sub-registries. Probate registries are
administered by HM Courts and Tribunals Service.

JUDGE ADVOCATES GENERAL

The Judge Advocate General is the judicial head of the Service
justice system, and the leader of the judges who preside over
trials in the court martial and other Service courts. The
defendants are service personnel from the Royal Navy, the
army and the Royal Air Force, and civilians accompanying
them overseas.

JUDGE ADVOCATE GENERAL OF THE FORCES
9th Floor, Thomas More Building, Royal Courts of Justice, Strand, London WC2A 2LL **T** 020-7218 8089

Judge Advocate General (£145,614), His Hon. Judge Blackett
Vice-Judge Advocate General (£126,946), Judge Hunter
Assistant Judge Advocates General (£108,171), J. P. Camp; R. D. Hill; A. M. Large; A. J. B. McGrigor
Style, Judge [surname]

CROWN COURT CENTRES
The crown court sits in 77 court centres across England and Wales. It deals with serious criminal cases which include:
* cases sent for trial by magistrates' courts because the offences are 'indictable only' (ie those which can only be heard by the crown court)
* 'either way' offences (which can be heard in a magistrates' court, but can also be sent to the crown court if the defendant chooses a jury trial)
* defendants convicted in magistrates' courts, but sent to the Crown Court for sentencing due to the seriousness of the offence
* appeals against decisions of magistrates' courts
First-tier centres deal with both civil and criminal cases and are served by high court and circuit judges. Second-tier centres deal with criminal cases only and are served by high court and circuit judges. Third-tier centres deal with criminal cases only and are served only by circuit judges.
   In London, the high court acts as the first-tier centre, sitting at the Royal Courts of Justice, and the second-tier is the Central Criminal Court.

CIRCUIT JUDGES
Circuit judges are barristers of at least seven years' standing or recorders of at least five years' standing. Circuit judges serve in the county courts and the crown court.

Style, His/Her Hon. Judge [surname]
Senior Presiding Judge, Rt. Hon. Lady Justice Macur
Deputy Senior Presiding Judge, vacant
Senior Circuit Judges, each £145,614
Circuit Judges at the Central Criminal Court, London (Old Bailey Judges), each £145,614
Circuit Judges, each £134,841

MIDLAND CIRCUIT
Presiding Judges, Hon. Mrs Justice Carr; Hon. Mr Justice Jeremy Baker
NORTH-EASTERN CIRCUIT
Presiding Judges, Hon. Mr Justice Males; Hon. Mr Justice Goss
NORTHERN CIRCUIT
Presiding Judges, Hon. Mr Justice William Davis; Hon. Mr Justice Dove
SOUTH-EASTERN CIRCUIT
Presiding Judges, Hon. Mr Justice Stuart-Smith; Hon. Mrs Justice McGowan; Hon. Mr Justice Edis; Hon. Mr Justice Whipple
WALES CIRCUIT
Presiding Judges, Hon. Mr Justice Lewis; Hon. Mr Justice Picken
WESTERN CIRCUIT
Presiding Judges, Hon. Mr Justice Dingemans; Hon. Mrs Justice May

DISTRICT JUDGES
District judges, formerly known as registrars of the court, are solicitors of at least seven years' standing and serve in county courts.
District Judges, each £108,171

DISTRICT JUDGES (MAGISTRATES' COURTS)
District judges (magistrates' courts), formerly known as stipendiary magistrates, serve in magistrates courts where they hear criminal cases, youth cases and some civil proceedings. Many also hear family cases in the single family court. Some may be authorised to handle extradition proceedings and terrorist cases. District judges (magistrates' courts) are appointed following competition conducted by the Judicial Appointments Commission.
District Judges (Magistrates' Courts), each £108,171

OFFICE OF THE CHIEF MAGISTRATE
181 Marylebone Road, London NW1 5BR
T 020-3126 3100

The Chief Magistrate (senior district judge) is responsible for hearing many of the sensitive or complex cases – extradition and special jurisdiction cases in particular – in the magistrates' courts. The Chief Magistrate also supports and guides district judges (magistrates' courts), and liaises with the senior judiciary and presiding judges on matters pertaining to magistrates' courts.
   The Office of the Chief Magistrate provides administration support to both the Chief Magistrate and to all the district judges sitting at magistrates' courts in England and Wales.

Chief Magistrate, Emma Arbuthnot
Deputy Chief Magistrate, Tanweer Ikram

CROWN PROSECUTION SERVICE
102 Petty France, London SW1H 9EA
T 020-3357 0899 **E** enquiries@cps.gov.uk **W** www.cps.gov.uk

The Crown Prosecution Service (CPS) is responsible for prosecuting cases investigated by the police in England and Wales, with the exception of cases conducted by the Serious Fraud Office and certain minor offences.
   The CPS is headed by the director of public prosecutions (DPP), who works under the superintendence of the attorney-general. The service is divided into 14 regional teams across England and Wales, with each area led by a chief crown prosecutor.

Director of Public Prosecutions, Alison Saunders, CB
Interim Chief Executive, Paul Staff
Directors, Jean Ashton, OBE *(Business Services);* Gregor McGill *(Legal Services);* Paul Staff *(Corporate Services)*

CPS AREAS
EAST MIDLANDS, 2 King Edward Court, King Edward Street, Nottingham NG1 1EL **T** 0115-852 3300
Chief Crown Prosecutor, Janine Smith
EAST OF ENGLAND, County House, 100 New London Road, Chelmsford, Essex CM2 0RG **T** 01245-455800
Chief Crown Prosecutor, Jenny Hopkins
LONDON, 1st Floor, Zone A, 102 Petty France, London SW1H 9EA **T** 020-3357 7000
Chief Crown Prosecutor London North, Ed Beltrami, CBE
   Chief Crown Prosecutor London South, Claire Lindley
MERSEY–CHESHIRE, 2nd Floor, Walker House, Exchange Flags, Liverpool L2 3YL **T** 0151-239 6400
Chief Crown Prosecutor, Siobhan Blake
NORTH EAST, St Ann's Quay, 112 Quayside, Newcastle Upon Tyne, NE1 3BD **T** 0191-260 4200
Chief Crown Prosecutor, Andrew Penhale
NORTH WEST, 1st Floor, Stocklund House, Castle Street, Carlisle CA3 8SY **T** 01228-882900
Chief Crown Prosecutor, Martin Goldman
SOUTH EAST, Riding Gate House, 37 Old Dover Road, Canterbury, Kent CT1 3JG **T** 01227-866000
Chief Crown Prosecutor, Jaswant Kaur Narwal

SOUTH WEST, 5th Floor, Kite Wing, Temple Quay House, 2 The
Square, Bristol BS1 6PN **T** 0117-930 2800
Chief Crown Prosecutor, Chris Long
THAMES AND CHILTERN, Eaton Court, 112 Oxford Road,
Reading, Berks RG1 7LL **T** 01727-798700
Chief Crown Prosecutor, Adrian Foster
WALES, 20th Floor, Capital Tower, Greyfriars Road, Cardiff CF10
3PL **T** 029-2080 3800
Chief Crown Prosecutor, Barry Hughes
WESSEX, 3rd Floor, Black Horse House, 8–10 Leigh Road,
Eastleigh, Hants SO50 9FH **T** 0238-067 3800
Chief Crown Prosecutor, Joanne Jakymec
WEST MIDLANDS, Colmore Gate, 2 Colmore Row, Birmingham
B3 2QA **T** 0121-262 1300
Chief Crown Prosecutor, Grace Ononiwu, OBE
YORKSHIRE AND HUMBERSIDE, 27 Park Place, Leeds LS1
2SZ **T** 0113-290 2700
Chief Crown Prosecutor, Gerry Wareham

HER MAJESTY'S COURTS AND TRIBUNALS SERVICE

1st Floor, 102 Petty France, London SW1H 9AJ
W www.gov.uk/government/organisations/
hm-courts-and-tribunals-service

Her Majesty's Courts Service and the Tribunals Service merged
on 1 April 2011 to form HM Courts and Tribunals Service. It
is an agency of the Ministry of Justice, operating as a
partnership between the Lord Chancellor, the Lord Chief
Justice and the Senior President of Tribunals. It is responsible
for administering the criminal, civil and family courts and
tribunals in England and Wales and non-devolved tribunals in
Scotland and Northern Ireland.

Chief Executive, Susan Acland-Hood

JUDICIAL APPOINTMENTS COMMISSION

5th Floor, Clive House, 70 Petty France, London SW1H 9EX
T 020-3334 0123 **E** jaas@judicialappointments.gov.uk
W www.judicialappointments.gov.uk

The Judicial Appointments Commission was established as an
independent non-departmental public body in April 2006 by
the Constitutional Reform Act 2005. Its role is to select judicial
office holders independently of government (a responsibility
previously held by the Lord Chancellor) for courts and
tribunals in England and Wales, and for some tribunals whose
jurisdiction extends to Scotland or Northern Ireland. It has a
statutory duty to encourage diversity in the range of persons
available for selection and is sponsored by the Ministry of
Justice and accountable to parliament through the Lord
Chancellor. It is made up of 15 commissioners, including a
chair.

Chair, Rt. Hon. Prof. Lord Kakkar
Vice-Chair, Rt. Hon. Dame Anne Rafferty, DBE
Commissioners, Judge Mathu Asokan; Her Hon. Judge Anuja
Dhir; Emir Khan Feisal; Jane Furness, CBE; Andrew
Kennon; Sarah Lee; Prof. Noel Lloyd, CBE; Judge Fiona
Monk; Brie Stevens-Hoare; Dame Valerie Strachan, DCB;
His Hon. Judge Phillip Sycamore; Sir Simon Wessely;
Dame Philippa Whipple, DBE
Chief Executive, Richard Jarvis

JUDICIAL OFFICE

The Judicial Office was established in April 2006 to support
the judiciary in discharging its responsibilities under the
Constitutional Reform Act 2005. It is led by a chief executive,
who reports to the Lord Chief Justice and Senior President of
Tribunals rather than to ministers, and its work is directed by
the judiciary rather than by the administration of the day. The

Judicial Office incorporates the Judicial College, sponsorship
of the Family and Civil Justice Councils, the Office for Judicial
Complaints and Office of the Chief Coroner.

Chief Executive, Andrew Key

JUDICIAL COMMITTEE OF THE PRIVY COUNCIL

The Judicial Committee of the Privy Council is the final court
of appeal for the United Kingdom overseas territories (*see* UK
Overseas Territories section), crown dependencies and those
independent Commonwealth countries which have retained
this avenue of appeal and the sovereign base areas of Akrotiri
and Dhekelia in Cyprus. The committee also hears appeals
against pastoral schemes under the Pastoral Measure 1983, and
deals with appeals from veterinary disciplinary bodies.

Until October 2009, the Judicial Committee of the Privy
Council was the final arbiter in disputes as to the legal
competence of matters done or proposed by the devolved
legislative and executive authorities in Scotland, Wales and
Northern Ireland. This is now the responsibility of the UK
Supreme Court.

The members of the Judicial Committee are the justices of the
supreme court, and Privy Counsellors who hold or have held
high judicial office in the United Kingdom or in certain
designated courts of Commonwealth countries from which
appeals are taken to committee.

JUDICIAL COMMITTEE OF THE PRIVY COUNCIL
Parliament Square, London SW1P 3BD **T** 020-7960 1500
W www.jcpc.uk
Chief Executive, Mark Ormerod
Registrar of the Privy Council, Louise di Mambro

SCOTTISH JUDICATURE

Scotland has a legal system separate from, and differing greatly
from, the English legal system in enacted law, judicial
procedure and the structure of courts.

In Scotland the system of public prosecution is headed by the
Lord Advocate and is independent of the police, who have no
say in the decision to prosecute. The Lord Advocate,
discharging his functions through the Crown Office in
Edinburgh, is responsible for prosecutions in the high court,
sheriff courts and justice of the peace courts. Prosecutions in
the high court are prepared by the Crown Office and
conducted in court by one of the law officers, by an advocate-
depute, or by a solicitor advocate. In the inferior courts the
decision to prosecute is made and prosecution is preferred by
procurators fiscal, who are lawyers and full-time civil servants
subject to the directions of the Crown Office. A permanent
legally qualified civil servant, known as the crown agent, is
responsible for the running of the Crown Office and the
organisation of the Procurator Fiscal Service, of which he or
she is the head.

Scotland is divided into six sheriffdoms, each with a full-time
sheriff principal. The sheriffdoms are further divided into
sheriff court districts, each of which has a legally qualified
resident sheriff or sheriffs, who are the judges of the court.

In criminal cases sheriffs principal and sheriffs have the same
powers; sitting with a jury of 15 members, they may try more
serious cases on indictment, or, sitting alone, may try lesser
cases under summary procedure. Minor summary offences are
dealt with in justice of the peace courts, which replaced district
courts formerly operated by local authorities, and presided over
by lay justices of the peace (of whom some 500 regularly sit in
court) and, in Glasgow only, by stipendiary magistrates.
Juvenile offenders (children under 16) may be brought before
an informal children's hearing comprising three local lay

people. The superior criminal court is the high court of justiciary which is both a trial and an appeal court. Cases on indictment are tried by a high court judge, sitting with a jury of 15, in Edinburgh and on circuit in other towns. Appeals from the lower courts against conviction or sentence are also heard by the high court, which sits as an appeal court only in Edinburgh. There is no further appeal to the UK supreme court in criminal cases.

In civil cases the jurisdiction of the sheriff court extends to most kinds of action. Appeals against decisions of the sheriff may be made to the sheriff principal and thence to the court of session, or direct to the court of session, which sits only in Edinburgh. The court of session is divided into the inner and the outer house. The outer house is a court of first instance in which cases are heard by judges sitting singly, sometimes with a jury of 12. The inner house, itself subdivided into two divisions of equal status, is mainly an appeal court. Appeals may be made to the inner house from the outer house as well as from the sheriff court. An appeal may be made from the inner house to the UK supreme court.

The judges of the court of session are the same as those of the high court of justiciary, with the Lord President of the court of session also holding the office of Lord Justice General in the high court. Senators of the College of Justice are Lords Commissioners of Justiciary as well as judges of the court of session. On appointment, a senator takes a judicial title, which is retained for life. Although styled The Hon./Rt. Hon. Lord, the senator is not a peer, although some judges are peers in their own right.

The office of coroner does not exist in Scotland. The local procurator fiscal inquires privately into sudden or suspicious deaths and may report findings to the crown agent. In some cases a fatal accident inquiry may be held before the sheriff.

COURT OF SESSION AND HIGH COURT OF JUSTICIARY

The Lord President and Lord Justice General (£225,091), Rt. Hon. Lord Carloway, *born* 1954, *apptd* 2015
Private Secretary, Paul Gilmour

INNER HOUSE
Lords of Session (each £206,742)

FIRST DIVISION
The Lord President

Rt. Hon. Lord Menzies (Duncan Menzies), *born* 1953, *apptd* 2012
Rt. Hon. Lady Smith (Anne Smith), *born* 1955, *apptd* 2012
Rt. Hon. Lord Brodie (Philip Brodie), *born* 1950, *apptd* 2012
Rt. Hon. Lady Clark of Calton (Lynda Clark), *born* 1949, *apptd* 2013
Rt. Hon. Lord Glennie (Angus Glennie), *born* 1950, *apptd* 2016

SECOND DIVISION
Lord Justice Clerk (£217,409), Rt. Hon. Lady Dorrian (Leeona Dorrian), *born* 1957, *apptd* 2016

Rt. Hon. Lady Paton (Ann Paton), *born* 1952, *apptd* 2007
Rt. Hon. Lord Drummond Young (James Drummond Young), *born* 1950, *apptd* 2013
Rt. Hon. Lord Malcolm (Colin M. Campbell), *born* 1953, *apptd* 2015
Hon. Lord Turnbull (Alan Turnbull), *born* 1958, *apptd* 2016

OUTER HOUSE
Lords of Session (each £181,566)

Hon. Lord Kinclaven (Alexander F. Wylie, OBE), *born* 1951, *apptd* 2005

Hon. Lord Brailsford (S. Neil Brailsford), *born* 1954, *apptd* 2006
Hon. Lord Uist (Roderick Macdonald), *born* 1951, *apptd* 2006
Hon. Lord Matthews (Hugh Matthews), *born* 1953, *apptd* 2007
Hon. Lord Woolman (Stephen Woolman), *born* 1953, *apptd* 2008
Hon. Lord Pentland (Paul Cullen), *born* 1957, *apptd* 2008
Hon. Lord Bannatyne (Iain Peebles, QC), *born* 1954, *apptd* 2008
Hon. Lady Stacey (Valerie E. Stacey), *born* 1954, *apptd* 2009
Hon. Lord Tyre (Colin Tyre, CBE), *born* 1956, *apptd* 2010
Hon. Lord Doherty (J. Raymond Doherty), *born* 1958, *apptd* 2010
Rt. Hon. Lord Boyd of Duncansby (Colin Boyd), *born* 1953, *apptd* 2012
Hon. Lord Burns (David Burns), *born* 1952, *apptd* 2012
Hon. Lady Scott (Margaret Scott), *born* 1960, *apptd* 2012
Hon. Lady Wise (Morag Wise), *born* 1963, *apptd* 2013
Hon. Lord Armstrong (Iain Armstrong), *born* 1956, *apptd* 2013
Hon. Lady Rae (Rita Rae), *born* 1950, *apptd* 2014
Hon. Lady Wolffe (Sarah Wolffe, QC), *apptd* 2014
Hon. Lord Beckett (John Beckett, QC), *apptd* 2016
Hon. Lord Clark (Alistair Clark, QC), *born* 1955, *apptd* 2016
Hon. Lord Ericht (Andrew Stewart, QC), *born* 1963, *apptd* 2016
Hon. Lady Carmichael (Ailsa Carmichael, QC), *born* 1969, *apptd* 2016
Rt. Hon. Lord Mulholland (Frank Mulholland, QC), *born* 1959, *apptd* 2016
Hon. Lord Summers (Alan Summers, QC), *born* 1964, *apptd* 2017
Hon. Lord Arthurson (Paul Arthurson, QC), *born* 1964, *apptd* 2017

COURT OF SESSION AND HIGH COURT OF JUSTICIARY
Parliament House, Parliament Square, Edinburgh EH1 1RQ
T 0131-225 2595

Director and Principal Clerk of Session and Justiciary, Gillian Prentice
Deputy Principal Clerk of Session, Diane Machin
Deputy Principal Clerk of Justiciary, Joe Moyes
Depute in Charge of the Court of Session Office, Christina Bardsley
Officer in Charge of the Justiciary Office, Ross Martin
Keeper of the Rolls, Trish Fiddes
Assistant Keeper of the Rolls, Grahame Simpson
Appeals Manager, Alex McKay
Clerking Services Manager, Chris Fyffe
Court Manager, Nicola Boyle

JUDICIAL APPOINTMENTS BOARD FOR SCOTLAND
Thistle House, 91 Haymarket Terrace, Edinburgh EH12 5HE
T 0131-528 5101 W www.judicialappointments.scot

The board's remit is to provide the first minister with the names of candidates recommended for appointment to the court posts of senator of the college of justice, chair of the Scottish Land Court, sheriff principal, sheriff and part-time sheriff. It is also responsible for recommending individuals to the office of vice-president of the Upper Tribunal; chamber and deputy chamber presidents of the First-tier Tribunal; and members of the Upper Tribunal and First-tier Tribunal.

Chair, Nicola Gordon
Chief Executive, Erica Clarkson

JUDICIAL OFFICE FOR SCOTLAND
Parliament House, Edinburgh EH1 1RQ
T 0131-240 6677 W www.scotland-judiciary.org.uk

The Judicial Office for Scotland came into being on 1 April 2010 as part of the changes introduced by the Judiciary and Courts (Scotland) Act 2008. It provides support for the Lord President in his role as head of the Scottish judiciary with responsibility for the training, welfare, deployment and conduct of judges and the efficient disposal of business in the courts.

Executive Director, Tim Barraclough

SCOTTISH COURTS AND TRIBUNALS SERVICE
Saughton House, Broomhouse Drive, Edinburgh EH11 3XD
T 0131-444 3300 W www.scotcourts.gov.uk

The Scottish Courts and Tribunals Service (SCTS) is an independent body which was established on 1 April 2010 under the Judiciary and Courts (Scotland) Act 2008. Its function is to provide administrative support to Scottish courts and tribunals and to the judiciary of courts, including the High Court of Justiciary, Court of Session, sheriff courts and justice of the peace courts, and to the Office of the Public Guardian and Accountant of Court.

Chief Executive, Eric McQueen

SCOTTISH GOVERNMENT JUSTICE DIRECTORATE
St Andrew's House, Edinburgh EH1 3DG
T 0131-244 4000

The Justice Directorate is responsible for the appointment of judges and sheriffs to meet the needs of the business of the supreme and sheriffs court in Scotland. It is also responsible for providing resources for the efficient administration of certain specialist courts and tribunals.

Director (Justice), Neil Rennick

SCOTTISH LAND COURT
126 George Street, Edinburgh EH2 4HH
T 0131-271 4360 W www.scottish-land-court.org.uk

The court deals with disputes relating to agricultural and crofting land in Scotland.

Chair (£145,614), Hon. Lord Miningish (Roderick John MacLeod, QC)
Deputy Chair, Iain Maclean
Members, Tom Campbell; John Smith
Principal Clerk, Barbara Brown

SHERIFF COURTS
The majority of cases in Scotland are handled by one of the 39 sheriff courts. Criminal cases are heard by a sheriff and a jury (solemn procedure) but can be heard by a sheriff alone (summary procedure). Civil cases are heard by a single sheriff. Scotland is split into six sheriffdoms, each headed by a sheriff principal.

SALARIES
Sheriff Principal, £145,614
Sheriff, £134,841

SHERIFFDOMS

GLASGOW AND STRATHKELVIN
Sheriff Principal, Craig Turnbull
GRAMPIAN, HIGHLAND AND ISLANDS
Sheriff Principal, Derek Pyle
LOTHIAN AND BORDERS
Sheriff Principal, Mhairi Stephen, QC
NORTH STRATHCLYDE
Sheriff Principal, Duncan Murray

SOUTH STRATHCLYDE, DUMFRIES AND GALLOWAY
Sheriff Principal, Ian Abercrombie, QC
TAYSIDE, CENTRAL AND FIFE
Sheriff Principal, Marysia Lewis

JUSTICE OF THE PEACE COURTS
Justice of the peace courts replaced district courts and are a unique feature of Scotland's judicial system. Justices of the peace are lay magistrates who either sit alone, or in a bench of three, and deal with summary crimes such as speeding and careless driving. In court, justices have access to solicitors, who fulfil the role of legal advisers or clerks of court.

A justice of the peace court can be presided over by a stipendiary magistrate – a legally qualified solicitor or advocate who sits alone. They deal with more serious summary business similar to sheriffs, such as drink driving and assault. All sheriffs principal have powers to appoint stipendiary magistrates, but at present there are no justice of the peace courts in the sheriff court districts of Lerwick, Kirkwall, Wick, Stornoway, Lochmaddy and Portree.

CROWN OFFICE AND PROCURATOR FISCAL SERVICE
25 Chambers Street, Edinburgh EH1 1LA
T 0300-020 3000 W www.copfs.gov.uk

The Crown Office and Procurator Fiscal Service (COPFS) is Scotland's prosecution service. COPFS receive reports about crimes from the police and other reporting agencies and then decide what action to take, including whether to prosecute someone. It is also responsible for looking into deaths that need further explanation and investigating allegations of criminal conduct against police officers.

Lord Advocate, James Wolffe, QC
Solicitor-General, Alison Di Rollo
Crown Agent, David Harvie

COURT OF THE LORD LYON
HM New Register House, Edinburgh EH1 3YT
T 0131-556 7255 W www.courtofthelordlyon.scot

The Court of the Lord Lyon is the Scottish Court of Chivalry (including the genealogical jurisdiction of the *Ri-Sennachie* of Scotland's Celtic kings). The Lord Lyon King of Arms has jurisdiction, subject to appeal to the Court of Session and the House of Lords, in questions of heraldry and the right to bear arms. The court also administers the Public Register of All Arms and Bearings and the Public Register of All Genealogies in Scotland. Pedigrees are established by decrees of Lyon Court and by letters patent. As Royal Commissioner in Armory, the Lord Lyon grants patents of arms to virtuous and well-deserving Scots and to petitioners (personal or corporate) in the Queen's overseas realms of Scottish connection, and also issues birthbrieves. For information on Her Majesty's Officers of Arms in Scotland, *see* the Court of the Lord Lyon in the Public Bodies section.

Lord Lyon King of Arms, Dr Joseph Morrow, QC
Lyon Clerk and Keeper of the Records, Russell Hunter
Procurator Fiscal, Alexander Green

NORTHERN IRELAND JUDICATURE

In Northern Ireland the legal system and the structure of courts closely resemble those of England and Wales; there are, however, often differences in enacted law.

The court of judicature of Northern Ireland comprises the court of appeal, the high court of justice and the crown court. The practice and procedure of these courts is similar to that in England. The superior civil court is the high court of justice, from which an appeal lies to the Northern Ireland court of appeal; the UK supreme court is the final civil appeal court.

The crown court, served by high court and county court judges, deals with criminal trials on indictment. Cases are heard before a judge and, except those certified by the Director of Public Prosecutions under the Justice and Security Act 2007, a jury. Appeals from the crown court against conviction or sentence are heard by the Northern Ireland court of appeal; the UK supreme court is the final court of appeal.

The decision to prosecute in criminal cases in Northern Ireland rests with the Director of Public Prosecutions.

Minor criminal offences are dealt with in magistrates' courts by a legally qualified district judge (magistrates' courts) and, where an offender is under the age of 18, by youth courts each consisting of a district judge (magistrates' courts) and two lay magistrates (at least one of whom must be a woman). There are approximately 200 lay magistrates in Northern Ireland. Appeals from magistrates' courts are heard by the county court, or by the court of appeal on a point of law or an issue as to jurisdiction.

Magistrates' courts in Northern Ireland can deal with certain classes of civil case but most minor civil cases are dealt with in county courts. Judgments of all civil courts are enforceable through a centralised procedure administered by the Enforcement of Judgments Office.

COURT OF JUDICATURE
The Royal Courts of Justice, Chichester Street, Belfast BT1 3JF
T 0300-200 7812 W www.courtsni.gov.uk

Lord Chief Justice of Northern Ireland (£225,091), Rt. Hon. Sir Declan Morgan, *born* 1952, *apptd* 2009

LORDS JUSTICES OF APPEAL (£206,742)
Style, The Rt. Hon. Lord/Lady Justice [surname]

Rt. Hon. Sir Benjamin Stephens, *born* 1954, *apptd* 2017
Rt. Hon. Sir Donnell Deeny, *born* 1950, *apptd* 2017
Hon. Sir Seamus Treacy, *born* 1956, *apptd* 2017

HIGH COURT JUDGES (£181,566)
Style, The Hon. Mr/Mrs/Ms Justice [surname]

Hon. Sir Bernard McCloskey, *born* 1956, *apptd* 2008
Hon. Sir Paul Maguire, *born* 1952, *apptd* 2012
Hon. Sir Mark Horner, *born* 1956, *apptd* 2012
Hon. Sir John O'Hara, *born* 1956, *apptd* 2013
Hon. Sir Adrian Colton, *born* 1959, *apptd* 2015
Hon. Dame Denise McBride, DBE, *apptd* 2015
Hon. Dame Siobhan Keegan, DBE, *apptd* 2015
Hon. Sir Gerry McAlinden, *apptd* 2018

MASTERS OF THE HIGH COURT (£108,171)
Presiding Master, Master McCorry, *apptd* 2001
Masters, Master Bell *apptd* 2006; Master Hardstaff, *apptd* 2014; Master Kelly, *apptd* 2005; Master McGivern *apptd* 2015; Master Sweeney, *apptd* 2015; Master Wells, *apptd* 2005

COUNTY COURTS

JUDGES (£145,614†)
Style, His/Her Hon. Judge [surname]

Judge Babington *apptd* 2004; Judge Crawford *apptd* 2015; Judge Devlin *apptd* 2011; Judge Fowler, QC *apptd* 2011; Judge

Grant *apptd* 2005; Judge Kerr, QC *apptd* 2012; Judge Kinney *apptd* 2012; Judge Lynch, QC *apptd* 2004; Judge McCaffrey *apptd* 2016; Judge McColgan, QC *apptd* 2013; Judge McFarland *apptd* 1998; Judge McReynolds *apptd* 2004; Judge Miller, QC *apptd* 2009; Judge Rafferty, QC *apptd* 2016; Judge Ramsay, QC *apptd* 2014; Judge Sherrard *apptd* 2012; Judge Smyth *apptd* 2010

† County court judges are paid £145,614 so long as they are required to carry out significantly different work from their counterparts elsewhere in the UK

RECORDERS
Belfast (£157,263), Judge McFarland
Londonderry (£145,614), Judge Babington

DISTRICT JUDGES (£108,171)
Only barristers and solicitors with ten years' standing are eligible to become district judges. There are four district judges in Northern Ireland:

Presiding District Judge Brownlie *apptd* 1997; District Judge Collins *apptd* 2000; District Judge Duncan *apptd* 2014; District Judge Gilpin *apptd* 2014

MAGISTRATES' COURTS

DISTRICT JUDGES (MAGISTRATES' COURTS) (£108,171)
There are usually 21 district judges (magistrates' courts) in Northern Ireland:

Presiding District Judge Bagnall *apptd* 2003; District Judge Brady *apptd* 2016; District Judge Broderick *apptd* 2013; District Judge Conner *apptd* 1999; District Judge Copeland *apptd* 1993; District Judge Hamill *apptd* 1999; District Judge Henderson *apptd* 2005; District Judge Kelly *apptd* 1997; District Judge E. King *apptd* 2005; District Judge P. King *apptd* 2013; District Judge McElholm *apptd* 1998; District Judge McKibbin *apptd* 1995; District Judge McNally *apptd* 2003; District Judge Meehan *apptd* 2002; District Judge Mullan *apptd* 2016; District Judge Prytherch *apptd* 2005; District Judge Ranaghan *apptd* 2017; District Judge Watters *apptd* 1998

NORTHERN IRELAND COURTS AND TRIBUNALS SERVICE
23–27 Oxford Street, Belfast BT1 3LA
T 0300-200 7812 W www.justice-ni.gov.uk/topics/courts-and-tribunals
Chief Executive (acting), Peter Luney

CROWN SOLICITOR'S OFFICE
Royal Courts of Justice, Chichester Street, Belfast BT1 3JE
T 028-9054 2555
Crown Solicitor, Fiona Chamberlain

PUBLIC PROSECUTION SERVICE
Belfast Chambers, 93 Chichester Street, Belfast BT1 3JR
T 028-9089 7100 W www.ppsni.gov.uk
Director of Public Prosecutions, Stephen Herron

TRIBUNALS

Information on all the tribunals listed here, with the exception of the independent tribunals and the tribunals based in Scotland, Wales and Northern Ireland, can be found on the Ministry of Justice website (W www.justice.gov.uk/tribunals).

HM COURTS AND TRIBUNALS SERVICE

102 Petty France, London SW1H 9AJ
W www.gov.uk/government/organisations/
hm-courts-and-tribunals-service
W www.gov.uk/find-court-tribunal

HM Courts Service and the Tribunals Service merged on 1 April 2011 to form HM Courts and Tribunals Service, an integrated agency providing support for the administration of justice in courts and tribunals. It is an agency within the Ministry of Justice, operating as a partnership between the Lord Chancellor, the Lord Chief Justice and the Senior President of Tribunals. It is responsible for the administration of the criminal, civil and family courts and tribunals in England and Wales and non-devolved tribunals in Scotland and Northern

Ireland. The agency's work is overseen by a board headed by an independent chair working with non-executive, executive and judicial members.

A two-tier tribunal system, comprising the First-tier Tribunal and Upper Tribunal, was established on 3 November 2008 as a result of radical reform under the Tribunals, Courts and Enforcement Act 2007. Both of these tiers are split into a number of separate chambers. These chambers group together individual tribunals (also known as 'jurisdictions') which deal with similar work or require similar skills. Cases start in the First-tier Tribunal and there is a right of appeal to the Upper Tribunal. Some tribunals transferred to the new two-tier system immediately, with more transferring between 2009 and 2011. The exception is employment tribunals, which remain outside this structure. The Act also allowed legally qualified tribunal chairs and adjudicators to swear the judicial oath and become judges.

Senior President, Rt. Hon. Sir Ernest Ryder, TD
Vice-President of the Unified Tribunals, Hon. Sir Keith Lindblom
Chief Executive, Susan Acland-Hood

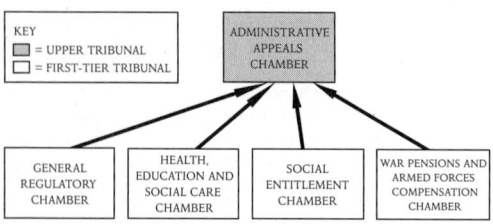

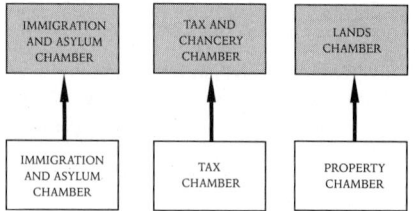

FIRST-TIER TRIBUNAL

The main function of the First-tier Tribunal is to hear appeals by citizens against decisions of the government. In most cases appeals are heard by a panel made up of one judge and two specialists in their relevant field, known as 'members'. Both judges and members are appointed through the Independent Judicial Appointments Commission. Most of the tribunals administered by central government are part of the First-tier Tribunal, which is split into seven separate chambers.

GENERAL REGULATORY CHAMBER

For all jurisdictions: General Regulatory Chamber, HMCTS, PO Box 9300, Leicester LE1 8DJ T 0300-123 4504 E grc@hmcts.gsi.gov.uk
Chamber President, Judge McKenna

CHARITY

Under the Charities Act 2011 (only applicable to England and Wales), First-tier Tribunal (Charity) hears appeals against the decisions of the Charity Commission, applications for the review of decisions made by the Charity Commission and considers references from the Attorney-General or the Charity Commission on points of law.

CLAIMS MANAGEMENT SERVICES

Under section 13 of the Compensation Act 2006, Claims Management Services hears appeals pertaining to decisions made by the claims regulator, such as the regulator's decision to cancel or suspend a claims management licence, refuse authorisation for claims management services or add

conditions to a claims management licence. Claims management services include all companies and individuals that offer a service for people hoping to claim compensation for personal injury, mis-sold financial products and services, redundancy, criminal or industrial injury and housing disrepair.

COMMUNITY RIGHT TO BID

The Community Right to Bid jurisdiction of the General Regulatory Chamber was established in January 2013 and hears appeals against review decisions made by local authorities to list your property as a community asset and give local communities the right to bid for it if you decide to sell. Individuals have the right to appeal against a listing decision under the Localism Act 2011 and the assets of community value (England) regulations 2012.

CONSULTANT LOBBYISTS

First-tier Tribunal (Consultant Lobbyists) hears appeals against penalties imposed for an offence under section 12 of the Transparency of Lobbying, Non-Party Campaigning and Trade Union Administration Act 2014 by the Office of the Registrar of Consultant Lobbyists.

CONVEYANCING

The professional regulation jurisdiction hears appeals against decisions made by the Council for Licensed Conveyancers under the Legal Services Act 2007.

COPYRIGHT LICENSING
Under the copyright (regulation of relevant licensing bodies) regulations 2014 a copyright licensing body may appeal to a First-tier Tribunal (Copyright Licensing) against a government decision to fine or impose a code of conduct on their organisation.

DRIVING INSTRUCTORS
First-tier Tribunal (Driving Instructors) hears appeals against decisions made by the Registrar of Approved Driving Instructors under the Road Traffic Act 1988, Transport Act 2000 and the Motor Cars (Driving Instruction) Regulations 2005. Its jurisdiction covers England, Scotland and Wales.

ELECTRONIC COMMUNICATIONS AND POSTAL SERVICES
Hears appeals against decisions made by the Interception of Communications Commissioner under the Regulation of Investigatory Powers (Monetary Penalty Notices and Consents for Interceptions) Regulations 2011.

ENVIRONMENT
First-tier Tribunal (Environment) was created to decide appeals regarding civil sanctions made by environmental regulators. Established in April 2010, the jurisdiction of the tribunal extends to England and Wales.

ESTATE AGENTS
First-tier Tribunal (Estate Agents) hears appeals, under the Estate Agents Act 1979, against decisions made by the Office of Fair Trading pertaining to orders prohibiting a person from being employed as an estate agent when that person has been, for example, convicted of fraud or another offence involving dishonesty. The tribunal also hears appeals relating to decisions refusing to revoke or vary a prohibition order or warning order, as well as appeals regarding the issuing of a warning order when a person has not fulfilled their obligations under the Act.

EXAM BOARDS
Under the Education Act 1997 regulated awarding organisations can appeal to the Exam Board tribunal if they disagree with a decision by OFQUAL or the Welsh government to impose a fine, the amount of the fine, or to recover the costs of taking enforcement action. The board is an independent tribunal and hears appeals across England and Wales.

FOOD
The food jurisdiction of the General Regulatory Chamber was established in January 2013 and hears appeals against some of the decisions taken by the Food Standards Agency, Department for Environment, Food and Rural Affairs and local authority trading standards departments. It also deals with appeals against decisions under the Fish Labelling (England) Regulations.

GAMBLING
First-tier Tribunal (Gambling) hears and decides appeals against decisions made by the Gambling Commission under the Gambling Act 2005.

IMMIGRATION SERVICES
First-tier Tribunal (Immigration Services) is an independent judicial body established in 2000. It hears appeals against decisions made by the Office of the Immigration Services Commissioner and considers disciplinary charges brought against immigration advisers by the Commissioner. The tribunal does not deal with immigration and asylum cases.

INFORMATION RIGHTS
First-tier Tribunal (Information Rights) determines appeals against notices issued by the Information Commissioner under the Freedom of Information Act 2000 and other regulations.

When a minister of the crown issues a certificate on the grounds of national security, the appeal must be transferred to the Administrative Appeals Chamber of the Upper Tribunal on receipt.

LETTING AND MANAGING AGENTS
First-tier Tribunal (Letting and Managing Agents) hears appeals against a decision by a local authority or the Trading Standards Office to impose a fine on an agent for not being a member of an approved complaints scheme or for not clearly publicising fees under The Redress Schemes for Lettings Agency Work and Property Management Work (Requirements to Belong to a Scheme etc) (England) Order 2014 and schedule 9 of the Consumer Rights Act 2015.

MICROCHIPPING DOGS
Established under the Microchipping of Dogs (England) Regulations 2015, appeals can be made to First-Tier Tribunal (Microchipping Dogs) against a decision by the Department for the Environment and Rural Affairs to ban or stop an individual from microchipping dogs or from running a database on microchipped dogs. Dog owners can also appeal against a notice to microchip their dog served by the police or local authority.

PENSIONS REGULATION
First-tier Tribunal (Pensions) hears appeals against decisions made by the Pensions Regulator under section 44 of the Pensions Act 2008. Appeals under section 102 of the Act are heard by the Tax and Chancery Chamber of the Upper Tribunal.

HEALTH, EDUCATION AND SOCIAL CARE CHAMBER
Chamber President, His Hon. Judge Sycamore

CARE STANDARDS
First-tier Tribunal (Care Standards), 1st Floor Darlington Magistrates' Court, Parkgate DL1 1RU
T 01325-289350 E cst@hmcts.gsi.gov.uk

First-tier Tribunal (Care Standards) was established under the Protection of Children Act 1999 and considers appeals in relation to decisions made by the Secretary of State for Education, the Secretary of State for Health, the Care Quality Commission, Ofsted or the Care Council for Wales about the inclusion of individuals' names on the list of those considered unsuitable to work with children or vulnerable adults, restrictions from teaching and employment in schools/further education institutions, and the registration of independent schools. It also deals with general registration decisions made about care homes, children's homes, childcare providers, nurses' agencies, social workers, residential family centres, independent hospitals and fostering agencies.

MENTAL HEALTH
PO Box 8793, 5th Floor, Leicester LE1 8BN
T 0300-123 2201 E mhrtenquiries@hmcts.gsi.gov.uk

The First-tier Tribunal (Mental Health) hears applications and references for people detained under the Mental Health Act 1983 (as amended by the Mental Health Act 2007). There are separate mental health tribunals for Wales and Scotland.

PRIMARY HEALTH LISTS
First-tier Tribunal (Primary Health Lists), 1st Floor Darlington Magistrates' Court, Parkgate DL1 1RU T 01325-289350

First-tier Tribunal (Primary Health Lists) hears appeals against decisions made by the NHS Commissioning Board to not include, to remove or to change the conditions of inclusion for medical practitioners and providers on the NHS medical, dental, ophthalmic or pharmaceutical lists.

SPECIAL EDUCATIONAL NEEDS AND DISABILITY
First-tier Tribunal (SEND), 1st Floor Darlington Magistrates' Court, Parkgate DL1 1RU
T 01325-289350 E sendistqueries@hmcts.gsi.gov.uk

First-tier Tribunal (Special Educational Needs and Disability) considers parents' appeals against the decisions of local authorities about children's special educational needs if parents cannot reach agreement with the local authority. It also considers claims of disability discrimination in schools.

IMMIGRATION AND ASYLUM CHAMBER
Chamber President, Judge Clements
PO Box 6987, Leicester LE1 6ZX
T 0300-123 1711 E customer.service@hmcts.gsi.gov.uk

The Immigration and Asylum Chamber is an independent tribunal dealing with appeals against decisions made by the Home Office concerning immigration, asylum and nationality matters.

PROPERTY CHAMBER
Chamber President, Judge McGrath
10 Alfred Place, London WC1E 7LR
T 020-7291 7250 E landregistration@hmcts.gsi.gov.uk

The First-tier Tribunal (Property Chamber) handles applications, appeals and references relating to disputes over property and land. It serves the private-rented and leasehold property market in England regarding rent increases, leasehold disputes, improvement notices under the Housing Act 2004, land registration matters and agricultural land and drainage matters.

SOCIAL ENTITLEMENT CHAMBER
Chamber President, His Hon. Judge Aitken

ASYLUM SUPPORT
2nd Floor, Anchorage House, 2 Clove Crescent, London E14 2BE
T 0800-681 6509

First-tier Tribunal (Asylum Support) deals with appeals against decisions made by the Home Office. The Home Office decides whether asylum seekers, failed asylum seekers and/or their dependants are entitled to support and accommodation on the grounds of destitution, as provided by the Immigration and Asylum Act 1999. The tribunal can only consider appeals against a refusal or termination of support. It can, if appropriate, require the Secretary of State for the Home Department to reconsider the original decision, substitute the original decision with the tribunal's own decision or dismiss the appeal.

CRIMINAL INJURIES COMPENSATION
20 York Street, Glasgow G2 8GT T 0300-790 6234
E cic.enquiries@justice.gov.uk

First-tier Tribunal (Criminal Injuries Compensation) determines appeals against review decisions made by the Criminal Injuries Compensation Authority on applications for compensation made by victims of violent crime.

SOCIAL SECURITY AND CHILD SUPPORT
England and Wales T 0300-123 1142
Scotland T 0300-790 6234

First-tier Tribunal (Social Security and Child Support) arranges and hears appeals against decisions made by the Department for Work and Pensions and HM Revenue and Customs regarding social security benefits. Appeals considered include those concerned with: attendance, bereavement and carer's allowances; child benefit; child support; the compensation recovery scheme (including NHS recovery claims); diffuse mesotheliomia and the industrial injuries disablement benefit payment schemes; income support; jobseeker's allowance; tax credits; universal credit; and vaccine damage payment.

TAX CHAMBER
Chamber President, Judge Sinfield
PO Box 16972, Birmingham B16 6TZ
T 0300-123 1024 E taxappeals@justice.gov.uk

First-tier Tribunal Tax Chamber hears most appeals against decisions made by HM Revenue and Customs in relation to income tax, corporation tax, capital gains tax, inheritance tax, stamp duty land tax, statutory sick and maternity pay, national insurance contributions and VAT or duties. The tribunal also hears some appeals relating to goods seized by HM Revenue and Customs or Border Force and against some decisions made by the National Crime Agency. Appeals can be made by individuals or organisations, single taxpayers or large multinational companies. First-tier Tribunal (Tax) also hears appeals against certain decisions made by a compliance officer, an independent office holder appointed by the Independent Parliamentary Standards Authority, the organisation responsible for determining and paying MP expenses. Appeals can be made by current or former MPs under the Parliamentary Standards Act 2009. The jurisdiction is UK-wide.

WAR PENSIONS AND ARMED FORCES COMPENSATION CHAMBER
Acting Chamber President, Judge Sehba Storey
5th Floor, Fox Court, 14 Gray's Inn Road, London WC1X 8HN
T 020-3206 0701 E armedforces.chamber@hmcts.gsi.gov.uk

The War Pensions and Armed Forces Compensation Chamber of the First-tier Tribunal hears appeals brought by ex-servicemen and women against decisions by Veterans UK regarding pensions, compensation and other amounts under the war pensions legislation for injuries sustained before 5 April 2005, and under the armed forces compensation scheme for injuries after that date.

UPPER TRIBUNAL

Comprising four separate chambers, the Upper Tribunal deals mostly with appeals from, and enforcement of, decisions taken by the First-tier Tribunal, but it also handles some cases that do not go through the First-tier Tribunal. Additionally, it has assumed some of the supervisory powers of the courts to deal with the actions of tribunals, government departments and some other public authorities. All the decision-makers of the Upper Tribunal are judges or expert members sitting in a panel chaired by a judge, and are specialists in the areas of law they handle. Over time their decisions are expected to build comprehensive case law for each area covered by the tribunals.

ADMINISTRATIVE APPEALS CHAMBER
Acting Chamber President, Hon. Sir Keith Lindblom
England and Wales, 5th Floor, 7 Rolls Building, Fetter Lane, London EC4A 1NL T 020-7071 5662
E adminappeals@hmcts.gsi.gov.uk
Scotland, George House, 126 George Street, Edinburgh EH2 4HH
T 0131-271 4310 E UTAAmailbox@scotland.gsi.gov.uk

Northern Ireland, Tribunal Hearing Centre, 2nd Floor Royal Courts of Justice, Chichester Street, Belfast BT1 3JF **T** 028-9072 4883 **E** tribunalsunit@courtsni.gov.uk

The Administrative Appeals Chamber appeals against decisions made by certain lower tribunals and organisations including: social security and child support, war pensions and armed forces compensation, mental health, special education needs or disabilities, disputes heard by the General Regulatory Chamber, decisions made by the Disclosure and Barring Service, decisions made by the Traffic Commissioner (or the Transport Regulation Unit in Northern Ireland), Special Education Needs Tribunal for Wales, Mental Health Review Tribunal for Wales and the Pensions Appeal Tribunal in Northern Ireland (only for assessment appeals under the War Pensions Scheme). It also handles applications for judicial review of decisions made by: First-tier Tribunal (Criminal Injuries Compensation) and other first-tier tribunals where there is no right of appeal.

IMMIGRATION AND ASYLUM CHAMBER

Chamber President, Hon. Sir Peter Lane
1A Field House, 15–25 Bream's Buildings, London EC4A 1DZ
T 0300-123 1711 **E** fieldhousecorrespondence@hmcts.gsi.gov.uk

The Immigration and Asylum Chamber hears appeals against decisions made by the First-tier Tribunal (Immigration and Asylum) relating to visa and asylum applications and the right to enter or stay in the UK. The chamber also deals with applications for judicial review of certain decisions made by the Home Office relating to immigration, asylum and human rights claims.

LANDS CHAMBER

Chamber President, Hon. Sir David Holgate
5th Floor, 7 Rolls Buildings, London EC4A 1NL
T 020-7612 9710 **E** lands@hmcts.gsi.gov.uk

The Lands Chamber is responsible for handling appeals against decisions made by the First-tier Tribunal (Property Chamber) (except decisions about land registration), the Residential Property Tribunal in Wales and the Leasehold Valuation Tribunal in Wales, It is also responsible for handling applications for cases regarding decisions about rates made by the Valuation Tribunal in England or Wales, compensation for the compulsory purchase of land, discharge or modification of land affected by a 'restrictive covenant', compensation for the effect on land affected by public works, a tree preservation order, compensation for damage to land damaged by subsidence from mining, the valuation of land or buildings for Capital Gains Tax or Inheritance Tax purposes and compensation for blighted land.

TAX AND CHANCERY CHAMBER

Chamber President, Hon. Sir Antony Zacaroli
5th Floor, 7 Rolls Buildings, London EC4A 1NL
T 020-7612 9730 **E** uttc@hmcts.gsi.gov.uk

The Tax and Chancery Chamber hears appeals against decisions made by the First-tier Tribunal (Tax), the land registration division of the First-tier Tribunal (Property Chamber) and the General Regulatory Chamber in cases relating to charities. The chamber also hears appeals against decisions issued by the Financial Conduct Authority, the Prudential Regulation Authority, the Pensions Regulator, the Bank of England, HM Treasury and OFGEM.

SPECIAL IMMIGRATION APPEALS COMMISSION

15–25 Bream's Buildings, London EC4A 1DZ
T 0300-123 1711

The commission was set up under the Special Immigration Appeals Commission Act 1997. It remains separate from the First-tier and Upper Tribunal structure but is part of HM Courts and Tribunals Service. Its main function is to consider appeals against orders for deportation or exclusion, or orders withdrawing or refusing British nationality, in cases which involve considerations of national security.
Chair, Hon. Dame Elisabeth Laing, DBE

EMPLOYMENT TRIBUNALS

Employment Tribunal Central Office England and Wales, PO Box 10218, Leicester LE1 8EG **T** 0300-123 1024
Employment Tribunal Central Office Scotland, PO Box 27105, Glasgow G2 9JR **T** 0141-354 8574

Employment tribunals hear claims regarding matters of employment law, redundancy, dismissal, contract disputes, sexual, racial and disability discrimination and related areas of dispute which may arise in the workplace.

President (England and Wales), Judge Doyle
President (Scotland), Judge Simon

EMPLOYMENT APPEAL TRIBUNAL

Employment Appeal Tribunal England and Wales, 2nd Floor, Fleetbank House, 2–6 Salisbury Square, London EC4Y 8AE
T 020-7273 1041 **E** londoneat@hmcts.gsi.gov.uk
Employment Appeal Tribunal Scotland, 52 Melville Street, Edinburgh EH3 7HF **T** 0131-225 3963
E edinburgheat@justice.gov.uk

The Employment Appeal Tribunal hears appeals (on points of law only) arising from decisions made by employment tribunals.

President, Hon. Dame Ingrid Simler, DBE

SCOTTISH COURTS AND TRIBUNALS SERVICE

Saughton House, Broomhouse Drive, Edinburgh EH11 3XD
T 0131-444 3300
W www.scotcourts.gov.uk
E enquiries@scotcourts.gov.uk

The Tribunals (Scotland) Act 2014 created a new, simplified statutory framework for tribunals in Scotland, bringing existing jurisdictions together and providing a structure for new ones. The Act created two new tribunals, the First-tier Tribunal for Scotland and the Upper Tribunal for Scotland.

The Lord President is the head of the Scottish Courts and Tribunals Service and has delegated various functions to the President of Scottish Tribunals.

President of Scottish Tribunals, Rt. Hon. Lady Smith (Anne Smith)

THE UPPER TRIBUNAL FOR SCOTLAND

4th Floor, 1 Atlantic Quay, 45 Robertson Street, Glasgow G2 8JB
T 0141-302 5880
E uppertribunalforscotland@scotcourtstribunals.gov.uk

The Upper Tribunal hears appeals on decisions of the chambers of the First-tier Tribunal.

FIRST-TIER TRIBUNAL

The First-tier Tribunal is organised into four chambers.

GENERAL REGULATORY CHAMBER
George House, 126 George Street, Edinburgh EH2 4HH
T 0131-271 4340

HEALTH AND EDUCATION CHAMBER
20 York Street, Glasgow G2 8GT
T 0141-302 5860

HOUSING AND PROPERTY CHAMBER
20 York Street, Glasgow G2 8GT
T 0141-302 5900

TAX CHAMBER
George House, 126 George Street, Edinburgh EH2 4HH
T 0131-271 4385 E taxchamber@scotcourtstribunals.gov.uk

The Scottish Courts and Tribunals Service currently provides administrative support for the following Scottish tribunals:

COUNCIL TAX REDUCTION REVIEW PANEL, 20 York Street, Glasgow G2 8GT T 0141-302 5840
E ctrrpadmin@scotcourtstribunals.gov.uk
W www.counciltaxreductionreview.gov.uk
THE LANDS TRIBUNAL FOR SCOTLAND, George House, 126 George Street, Edinburgh EH2 4HH T 0131-271 4350
E LTS_mailbox@scotcourtstribunals.gov.uk
W www.lands-tribunal-scotland.org.uk
President, Hon. Lord Minginish (Roderick MacLeod)
THE MENTAL HEALTH TRIBUNAL FOR SCOTLAND, Bothwell House, First Floor, Hamilton Business Park, Caird Park, Hamilton ML3 0QA T 0800-345 7060
E mhtsTeam1@scotcourtstribunals.gov.uk
W www.mhtscotland.gov.uk
President, Dr Joe Morrow, CBE
THE PENSIONS APPEAL TRIBUNAL SCOTLAND, 126 George Street, Edinburgh EH2 4HH T 0131-271 4340
E PAT_Info_Mailbox@scotcourtstribunals.gov.uk
W www.patscotland.org.uk
President, Marion Caldwell, QC

NORTHERN IRELAND COURTS AND TRIBUNALS SERVICE

Laganside House, 23–27 Oxford Street, Belfast BT1 3LA
T 028-9032 8594 W www.courtsni.gov.uk
Lord Chief Justice of Northern Ireland, Rt. Hon. Sir Declan Morgan

The Northern Ireland Courts and Tribunals Service currently provides administrative support for the following Northern Ireland tribunals. All the tribunals below, unless otherwise specified, can be contacted at: 2nd Floor, Royal Courts of Justice, Chichester Street, Belfast BT1 3JF T 0300-200 7812
E tribunalsunit@courtsni.gov.uk

THE APPEALS SERVICE, 6th Floor, Oyster House, 12 Wellington Place, Belfast BT1 6GE T 028-9054 4000
E appeals.service.belfast@dsdni.gov.uk
THE CARE TRIBUNAL
Chairs, Diane Drennan, Stephen Quinn
THE CHARITY TRIBUNAL
CRIMINAL INJURIES COMPENSATION APPEALS PANEL NORTHERN IRELAND,
E cicapnicustomer@courtsni.gov.uk
Chair, Patricia McKaigue
LANDS TRIBUNAL, E landstribunal@courtsni.gov.uk
MENTAL HEALTH REVIEW TRIBUNAL
NORTHERN IRELAND HEALTH AND SAFETY TRIBUNAL

NORTHERN IRELAND TRAFFIC PENALTY TRIBUNAL
NORTHERN IRELAND VALUATION TRIBUNAL
OFFICE OF SOCIAL SECURITY COMMISSIONERS AND CHILD SUPPORT COMMISSIONERS
Chief Commissioner, His Hon. Judge Martin, QC
PAROLE COMMISSIONERS FOR NORTHERN IRELAND, Laganside Court, Mezzanine 1st Floor, Oxford Street, Befast BT1 3LL T 028-9041 2969
E info@parolecomni.org.uk
Chief Commissioner, Christine Glenn
PENSIONS APPEAL COMMISSIONERS
PENSIONS APPEAL TRIBUNALS
RENT ASSESSMENT PANEL, Cleaver House, 3 Donegall Square North, Belfast BT1 5GA T 028-9051 8518
E appeals.service.belfast@dsdni.gov.uk
SPECIAL EDUCATIONAL NEEDS AND DISABILITY TRIBUNAL

INDEPENDENT TRIBUNALS

The following represents a selection of tribunals not administered by HM Courts and Tribunals Service.

CIVIL AVIATION AUTHORITY
CAA House, 45–59 Kingsway, London WC2B 6TE
T 0330-022 1500 E infoservices@caa.co.uk
W www.caa.co.uk

The Civil Aviation Authority (CAA) does not have a separate tribunal department as such, but for certain purposes the CAA must conform to tribunal requirements, for example, to deal with appeals against the refusal or revocation of aviation licences and certificates issued by the CAA, and the allocation of routes outside of the EU to airlines.

The chair and five non-executive members who may sit on panels for tribunal purposes are appointed by the Secretary of State for Transport.

Chair, Dame Deirdre Hutton, DBE

COMPETITION APPEAL TRIBUNAL
Victoria House, Bloomsbury Place, London WC1A 2EB
T 020-7979 7979 E info@catribunal.org.uk
W www.catribunal.org.uk

The Competition Appeal Tribunal (CAT) is a specialist tribunal established to hear certain cases in the sphere of UK competition and economic regulatory law. It hears appeals against decisions of the Competition and Markets Authority (CMA) and the sectoral regulators in respect of infringements of competition law and with respect to mergers and markets. The CAT also has jurisdiction to award damages in respect of infringements of EU or UK competition law and to hear appeals against decisions of the Office of Communications (OFCOM) in telecommunications matters.

President, Hon. Sir Peter Roth

COPYRIGHT TRIBUNAL
4 Abbey Orchard Street, London SW1P 2HT
T 020-7034 2836 E copyright.tribunal@ipo.gov.uk
W www.gov.uk/government/organisations/copyright-tribunal

The Copyright Tribunal resolves disputes over the terms and conditions of licences offered by, or licensing schemes operated by, collective management organisations in the copyright and related rights area. Its decisions are appealable to the high court on points of law only.

Chair, His Hon. Judge Hacon

INDUSTRIAL TRIBUNALS AND THE FAIR EMPLOYMENT TRIBUNAL (NORTHERN IRELAND)
Killymeal House, 2 Cromac Quay, Ormeau Road, Belfast BT7 2JD
T 028-9032 7666 E mail@employmenttribunalsni.org
W www.employmenttribunalsni.org

The industrial tribunal system in Northern Ireland was set up in 1965 and has a similar remit to the employment tribunals in the rest of the UK. There is also a Fair Employment Tribunal, which hears and determines individual cases of alleged religious or political discrimination in employment. Employers can appeal to the Fair Employment Tribunal if they consider the directions of the Equality Commission to be unreasonable, inappropriate or unnecessary, and the Equality Commission can make application to the tribunal for the enforcement of undertakings or directions with which an employer has not complied.

President, Eileen McBride, CBE

INVESTIGATORY POWERS TRIBUNAL
PO Box 33220, London SW1H 9ZQ
T 020-7035 3711 E info@ipt-uk.com W www.ipt-uk.com

The Investigatory Powers Tribunal replaced the Interception of Communications Tribunal, the Intelligence Services Tribunal, the Security Services Tribunal and the complaints function of the commissioner appointed under the Police Act 1997.

The Regulation of Investigatory Powers Act 2000 (RIPA) provides for a tribunal made up of senior members of the legal profession, independent of the government and appointed by the Queen, to consider all complaints against the intelligence services and those against public authorities in respect of powers covered by RIPA; and to consider proceedings brought under section 7 of the Human Rights Act 1998 against the intelligence services and law enforcement agencies in respect of these powers.

President, vacant

NATIONAL HEALTH SERVICE TRIBUNAL (SCOTLAND)
Anderson Strathern LLP, Lomond House, 9 George Square, Glasgow G2 1DY
T 0141-242 7974 E nhstribunal@nhs.net
W www.nhstribunal.scot.nhs.uk

The Scottish National Health Service Tribunal considers representations that the continued inclusion of a family health service practitioner (eg a doctor, dentist, optometrist or pharmacist) on a health board's list would be prejudicial to the efficiency of the service concerned, by virtue either of fraudulent practices or unsatisfactory personal or professional conduct. If this is established, the tribunal has the power to disqualify practitioners from working in the NHS family health services.

Chair, Michael Graham

SOLICITORS' DISCIPLINARY TRIBUNAL
3rd Floor, Gate House, 1 Farringdon Street, London EC4M 7LG
T 020-7329 4808 E enquiries@solicitorsdt.com
W www.solicitorstribunal.org.uk

The Solicitors' Disciplinary Tribunal is an independent statutory body whose members are appointed by the Master of the Rolls. The tribunal adjudicates upon alleged breaches of the rules and regulations applicable to solicitors and their firms, including the Solicitors' Code of Conduct 2007. It also decides applications by former solicitors for restoration to the Roll.

Chair, Edward Nally

SCOTTISH SOLICITORS' DISCIPLINE TRIBUNAL
Unit 3.5, The Granary Business Centre, Coal Road, Cupar, Fife KY15 5YQ
T 01334-659088 E enquiries@ssdt.org.uk W www.ssdt.org.uk

The Scottish Solicitors' Discipline Tribunal is an independent statutory body with a panel of 24 members, 12 of whom are solicitors appointed by the Lord President of the Court of Session. Its principal function is to consider complaints of misconduct against solicitors in Scotland.

Chair, Nicholas Whyte

TRAFFIC PENALTY TRIBUNAL
Springfield House, Water Lane, Wilmslow, Cheshire SK9 5BG
T 0800-160 1999 E help@trafficpenaltytribunal.gov.uk
W www.trafficpenaltytribunal.gov.uk

The Traffic Penalty Tribunal adjudicators consider appeals in relation to penalty charge notices issued by local authorities in England (outside London) and Wales for parking and bus lane contraventions and, additionally in Wales, moving traffic contraventions. The tribunal also considers appeals in relation to penalties issued by the Secretary of State for Transport for failing to pay a charge at the Dartford river crossing, the Durham peninsular congestion charging zone and the Mersey Gateway bridge crossings.

Chief Adjudicator, Caroline Sheppard, OBE

VALUATION TRIBUNAL FOR ENGLAND
2nd Floor, 120 Leman Street, London E1 8EU
T 020-7246 3900 W www.valuationtribunal.gov.uk

The Valuation Tribunal for England (VTE) came into being on 1 October 2009, replacing 56 valuation tribunals in England. Provision for the VTE was made in the Local Government and Public Involvement in Health Act 2007. The VTE hears appeals concerning council tax and non-domestic (business) rates, as well as a small number of appeals against drainage boards' assessments of drainage rates. A separate panel is constituted for each hearing, and consists of a chair and usually one or two other members.

The Valuation Tribunal Service (VTS) was created as a corporate body by the Local Government Act 2003, and is responsible for providing or arranging the services required for the operation of the Valuation Tribunal for England. The VTS board consists of a chair and members appointed by the secretary of state. The VTS is sponsored by the Ministry of Housing, Communities and Local Government.

President (VTE), Gary Garland
Chair (VTS), Robin Evans

VALUATION TRIBUNAL FOR WALES
Government Buildings, Block A (L1), Sarn Mynach, Llandudno Junction LL31 9RZ
T 0300-062 5350 E VTWalesnorth@vtw.gsi.gov.uk
W www.valuation-tribunals-wales.org.uk

The Valuation Tribunal for Wales (VTW) was established by the Valuation Tribunal for Wales Regulations 2010, and hears and determines appeals concerning council tax, non-domestic rating and drainage rates in Wales. The governing council, comprising the president, four regional representatives and one member who is appointed by the Welsh government, performs the management functions on behalf of the tribunal.

President, Carol Cobert

OMBUDSMAN SERVICES

The following section is a listing of selected ombudsman services. Ombudsmen are a free, independent and impartial means of resolving certain disputes outside of the courts. These disputes are, in the majority of cases, concerned with whether something has been badly or unfairly handled (for example owing to delay, neglect, inefficiency or failure to follow proper procedures). Most ombudsman schemes are established by statute; they cover various public and private bodies and generally examine matters only after the relevant body has been given a reasonable opportunity to deal with the complaint.

After conducting an investigation an ombudsman will usually issue a written report, which normally suggests a resolution to the dispute and often includes recommendations concerning the improvement of procedures.

OMBUDSMAN ASSOCIATION

PO Box 343, Carshalton, Surrey SM5 9BX
E secretary@ombudsmanassociation.org
W www.ombudsmanassociation.org

The Ombudsman Association was established in 1994 and exists to provide information to the government, public bodies and the public about ombudsmen and other complaint-handling services in the UK and Ireland. An ombudsman scheme must meet four criteria in order to attain full Ombudsman Association membership: independence from the organisations the ombudsman has the power to investigate, fairness, effectiveness and public accountability. Complaint Handler membership is open to complaint-handling bodies that do not meet these criteria in full. Ombudsmen schemes from the UK, Ireland, British crown dependencies and overseas territories may apply to the Ombudsman Association for membership. The Ombudsman Association publishes a triannual newsletter containing news about ombudsmen and complaint-handling services in the UK, Ireland and overseas, along with topical articles of interest to members of the Association.

Chair, Nick Bennett

The following is a selection of organisations that are members of the Ombudsman Association.

FINANCIAL OMBUDSMAN SERVICE

Exchange Tower, London E14 9SR
T 020-7964 1000 E complaint.info@financial-ombudsman.org.uk
W www.financial-ombudsman.org.uk

The Financial Ombudsman Service settles individual disputes between businesses providing financial services and their customers. The service answers around a million enquiries every year and deals with over 250,000 disputes. The service examines complaints about most financial matters, including banking, insurance, mortgages, pensions, savings, loans and credit cards. *See also* Banking and Finance.

Chief Ombudsman and Chief Executive, Caroline Wayman

HOUSING OMBUDSMAN SERVICE

Exchange Tower, London E14 9GE
T 0300-111 3000 E info@housing-ombudsman.org.uk
W www.housing-ombudsman.org.uk

The Housing Ombudsman Service was established in 1997 to deal with complaints and disputes involving tenants and housing associations and social landlords, certain private-

sector landlords and managing agents. The ombudsman has a statutory jurisdiction over all registered social landlords in England. Private and other landlords can join the service on a voluntary basis. On 1 April 2013 a new Housing Ombudsman Service was launched with an extended jurisdiction covering all housing associations and local authorities.

Ombudsman, Denise Fowler

INDEPENDENT OFFICE FOR POLICE CONDUCT

90 High Holborn, London WC1V 6BH
T 0300-020 0096 E enquiries@policeconduct.gov.uk
W www.policeconduct.gov.uk

Established under the Policing and Crime Act 2017, the Independent Office for Police Conduct (IOPC) succeeded the Independent Police Complaints Commission (IPCC) in January 2018. The IOPC is responsible for carrying out independent investigations into serious incidents or allegations of misconduct by those serving with the police forces in England and Wales, as well as Police and Crime Commissioners in England and Wales and the London Mayor's Office for Policing and Crime (MOPAC). The IOPC's director-general and its regional directors must not have worked for the police in any capacity prior to their appointment. It has the power to initiate, undertake and oversee investigations and is also responsible for the way in which complaints are handled by local police forces. The IOPC is also responsible for serious complaints and conduct matters relating to staff at the National Crime Agency (NCA), Her Majesty's Revenue and Customs (HMRC), and the Gangmasters and Labour Abuse Authority.

Director-General, Michael Lockwood

LEGAL OMBUDSMAN

Edward House, Quay Place, Birmingham B1 2RA
T 0300-555 0333 E enquiries@legalombudsman.org.uk
W www.legalombudsman.org.uk

The Legal Ombudsman was set up by the Office for Legal Complaints under the Legal Services Act 2007 and is the single body for all consumer legal complaints in England and Wales. It replaced the Office of the Legal Services Ombudsman in 2010. The Legal Ombudsman aims to resolve disputes between individuals and authorised legal practitioners, including barristers, law cost draftsmen, legal executives, licensed conveyancers, notaries, patent attorneys, probate practitioners, registered European lawyers, solicitors and trade mark attorneys. The Legal Ombudsman is an independent and impartial organisation and deals with various types of complaints against legal services, such as wills, family issues, personal injury and buying or selling a house.

Chief Ombudsman, Rebecca Marsh

LOCAL GOVERNMENT AND SOCIAL CARE OMBUDSMAN

PO Box 4771, Coventry CV4 OEH
T 0300-061 0614 W www.lgo.org.uk

The Local Government and Social Care Ombudsman deals with complaints about councils and service failure by local authorities, schools and social care providers.

There are two ombudsmen in England, each with responsibility for different regions; they aim to provide satisfactory redress for complainants and better administration by the authorities. The ombudsmen investigate complaints about most council matters, including housing, planning, education, social care, housing benefit, transport and highways, environment and waste, and council tax. *See also* Local Government.

Local Government and Social Care Ombudsman, Michael King

NORTHERN IRELAND PUBLIC SERVICES OMBUDSMAN

33 Wellington Place, Belfast BT1 6HN
T 028-9023 3821 E nipso@nipso.org.uk
W www.nipso.org.uk

The Office of Northern Ireland Public Services Ombudsman (NIPSO) was established in April 2016, replacing and expanding the functions of the Northern Ireland Assembly Ombudsman and Commissioner for Complaints. NIPSO provides an independent review of complaints of members of the public, where they believe they have sustained an injustice or hardship as a result or inaction of a public service provider. NIPSO additionally ensures that public services improve as a result of the complaints brought to them by the public. The professional, independent and impartial service is provided free of charge to the citizens of Northern Ireland.

Ombudsman, Marie Anderson

OFFICE OF THE PENSIONS OMBUDSMAN

11 Belgrave Road, London SW1V 1RB
T 020-7630 2200 E enquiries@pensions-ombudsman.org.uk
W www.pensions-ombudsman.org.uk

The Pensions Ombudsman is appointed by the Secretary of State for Work and Pensions, under the Pension Schemes Act 1993 as amended by the Pensions Act 1995. He investigates and decides complaints and disputes about the way that personal and occupational pension schemes are run and between members of pensions schemes and their beneficiaries, employers, trustees, managers and scheme administrators. As the ombudsman for the Board of the Pension Protection Fund, he can deal with disputes about the decisions made by the board or the actions of their staff. He also deals with appeals against decisions made by the scheme manager under the Financial Assistance Scheme.

Pensions Ombudsman, Anthony Arter
Deputy Pensions Ombudsman, Karen Johnston

OMBUDSMAN SERVICES

3300 Daresbury Park, Warrington WA4 4HS
W www.ombudsman-services.org

Ombudsman Services was founded in 2002 and provides independent dispute resolution for the communications, copyright licensing and energy sectors. Ombudsman Services ceased dealing with complaints concerning the property sector in 2018.

Ombudsman Services: Communications investigates complaints from consumers about companies which provide communication services to the public.

Ombudsman Services: Copyright Licensing helps to resolve complaints about bodies that either own or administer, on behalf of third parties, the licensing of copyright materials.

Ombudsman Services: Energy helps to resolve complaints from consumers about energy (gas and electricity companies). This service is also responsible for handling investigations concerning the government's Green Deal policy, which launched in 2013, and offers long-term loans towards energy-saving home improvements.

Chair, Lord Tim Clement-Jones, CBE
Chief Ombudsman, Lewis Shand Smith

OMBUDSMAN SERVICES: COMMUNICATIONS
PO Box 730, Warrington WA4 6WU
T 0330-440 1614

OMBUDSMAN SERVICES: COPYRIGHT LICENSING
PO Box 1124, Warrington WA4 9GH
T 0330-440 1601

OMBUDSMAN SERVICES: ENERGY
PO Box 966, Warrington WA4 9DF
T 0330-440 1624

PARLIAMENTARY AND HEALTH SERVICE OMBUDSMAN

Millbank Tower, Millbank, London SW1P 4QP
T 0345-015 4033
W www.ombudsman.org.uk

The Parliamentary Commissioner for Administration (commonly known as the Parliamentary Ombudsman) is independent of government and is an officer of Parliament. He is responsible for investigating complaints referred to him by MPs from members of the public who claim to have sustained injustice in consequence of maladministration by or on behalf of government departments and certain non-departmental public bodies in the UK. Certain types of action by government departments or bodies are excluded from investigation.

The Health Service Ombudsman is responsible for investigating complaints about services funded by the National Health Service in England that have not been dealt with by the service providers to the satisfaction of the complainant. This includes complaints about doctors, dentists, pharmacists and opticians. Complaints can be referred directly by the member of the public who claims to have sustained injustice or hardship in consequence of the failure in a service provided by a relevant organisation.

The two offices of the Parliamentary and Health Service Ombudsman are traditionally held by the same person.

Parliamentary Ombudsman and Health Service Ombudsman, Robert Behrens, CBE

PRISONS AND PROBATION OMBUDSMAN

PO Box 70769, London SE1P 4XY
T 020-7633 4100 E mail@ppo.gsi.gov.uk
W www.ppo.gov.uk

The Prisons and Probation Ombudsman investigates complaints from prisoners, people on probation and immigration detainees, deaths of prisoners, residents of probation-service approved premises and those held in immigration removal centres. The ombudsman is appointed by the Secretary of State for Justice and works closely with the Ministry of Justice. All deaths that occur in prison are investigated and an anonymised fatal incident report is written after each investigation.

Acting Ombudsman, Elizabeth Moody

PROPERTY OMBUDSMAN

Milford House, 43–55 Milford Street, Salisbury SP1 2BP
T 01722-333306
W www.tpos.co.uk

The Property Ombudsman (TPO) scheme was established in 1998 and provides a free, impartial and independent service for dealing with unresolved disputes between property agents and buyers, sellers, tenants and landlords of property in the UK.

The ombudsman's role is to consider complaints against the agents' obligation to act in accordance with the TPO codes of practice and to propose a full and final resolution to the dispute. Consumers are not bound by the Ombudsman's decision, but registered agents are.

With over 12,800 estate agent offices and 11,500 lettings offices registered, TPO is the primary dispute-resolution service for the property industry.

Ombudsman, Katrine Sporle, CBE

PUBLIC SERVICES OMBUDSMAN FOR WALES

1 Ffordd yr Hen Gae, Pencoed CF35 5LJ
T 0300-790 0203
W www.ombudsman-wales.org.uk

The office of Public Services Ombudsman for Wales was established, with effect from 1 April 2006, by the Public Services Ombudsman (Wales) Act 2005. The ombudsman, who is appointed by the Queen, investigates complaints of injustice caused by maladministration or service failure by public services such as the Assembly Commission (and public bodies sponsored by the assembly); Welsh government; National Health Service bodies, including GPs, family health service providers and hospitals; registered social landlords; local authorities, including community councils; fire and rescue authorities; police authorities; the Arts Council of Wales; national park authorities; and countryside and environmental organisations.

Ombudsman, Nick Bennett

REMOVALS INDUSTRY OMBUDSMAN SCHEME

PO Box 1535, High Wycombe HP12 9EE
T 020-8144 3790 E ombudsman@removalsombudsman.co.uk
W www.removalsombudsman.co.uk

The Removals Industry Ombudsman Scheme was established to resolve disputes between removal companies that are members of the scheme and their clients, both domestic and commercial. It comprises a board of four members, only one of whom has any connection with the removals industry. The ombudsman investigates complaints such as breaches of contract, unprofessional conduct, delays, excessive charges or breaches in the code of practice. The National Guild of Removers and Storers is currently the principal member.

Ombudsman, Tony Kaye

SCOTTISH PUBLIC SERVICES OMBUDSMAN

4 Melville Street, Edinburgh EH3 7NS
T 0800-377 7330
W www.spso.org.uk

The Scottish Public Services Ombudsman (SPSO) was established in 2002. The SPSO is the final stage for complaints about public services in Scotland. Its service is free and independent. SPSO investigates complaints about the Scottish government, its agencies and departments; the Scottish Parliamentary Corporate Body; colleges and universities; councils; housing associations; NHS Scotland; prisons; some water and sewerage service providers; and most other Scottish public bodies. The ombudsman looks at complaints regarding poor service or administrative failure and can usually only look at those that have been through the formal complaints process of the organisation concerned. It also has a statutory function in improving complaints handling in public services, which it carries out through its Complaints Standards Authority.

Scottish Public Services Ombudsman, Rosemary Agnew

WATERWAYS OMBUDSMAN

PO Box 854, Altrincham WA15 5JS
T 0161-980 4858 E enquiries@waterways-ombudsman.org
W www.waterways-ombudsman.org

Since July 2012, the Waterways Ombudsman has investigated complaints about the Canal and River Trust and its subsidiaries (such as British Waterways Marinas Limited). The ombudsman does not consider complaints about canals in Scotland, which are the responsibility of the Scottish Public Services Ombudsman.

Ombudsman, Andrew Walker

THE POLICE SERVICE

There are 45 police forces in the United Kingdom: 43 in England and Wales, including the Metropolitan Police and the City of London Police, Police Scotland and the Police Service of Northern Ireland. The Isle of Man, Jersey and Guernsey have their own forces responsible for policing in their respective islands and bailiwicks. The National Crime Agency, which became operational in October 2013, is responsible for preventing organised crime and strengthening UK borders.

Since 1964, police authorities – separate independent bodies for each police force – were responsible for the supervision of local policing in England and Wales. Following the government's white paper *Policing in the 21st Century* it was concluded that, in order to make the police more accountable, police authorities should be replaced with a directly elected commissioner for each force, supported by a police and crime panel made up of representatives from each local authority in a police force area. In November 2012, following the enactment of the Police Reform and Social Responsibility Act 2011, the first elections to install police and crime commissioners (PCCs) were held in November 2012 across England and Wales; the most recent elections took place in May 2016. The PCCs are responsible for appointing the chief constable of their force, establishing local priorities and setting budgets. The PCCs are not in place to run their local force but rather to hold them to account. The Mayor of London, through the Deputy Mayor for Policing and Crime and supported by the Mayor's Office for Policing and Crime (MOPAC), acts as the PCC for the Metropolitan Police. Since 2017 the Mayor of Greater Manchester fulfils the PCC responsibilities for this area's force. The City of London Corporation acts as the police authority for the City of London Police.

Under the Police and Fire Reform (Scotland) Act 2012, Police Scotland was established on 1 April 2013, merging the eight separate territorial police forces, the Scottish Crime and Drug Enforcement Agency and the Association of Chief Police Officers in Scotland. Responsible for policing the whole of Scotland, Police Scotland is the second largest force in the UK after the Metropolitan Police. The service is led by a chief constable who is supported by a team of four deputy constables, assistant chief constables and three directors. The Scottish Police Authority, established in October 2012, is responsible for maintaining policing, promoting policing principles, the continuous improvement of policing and holds the Chief Constable to account. In Northern Ireland, the Northern Ireland Policing Board, an independent public body consisting of 19 political and independent members, fulfils a similar role.

Police forces in England, Scotland and Wales are financed by central and local government grants and a precept on the council tax. The Police Service of Northern Ireland is wholly funded by central government.

The home secretary, the Scottish government and the Northern Ireland Minister of Justice are responsible for the organisation, administration and operation of the police service. They regulate police ranks, discipline, hours of duty and pay and allowances. All police forces are subject to inspection by HM Inspectorate of Constabulary, which reports to the home secretary and the Northern Ireland Minister of Justice. Police forces in Scotland are inspected by HM Inspectorate of Constabulary for Scotland which operates independently of the Scottish government.

COMPLAINTS

Established under the Policing and Crime Act 2017, the Independent Office for Police Conduct (IOPC) succeeded the Independent Police Complaints Commission (IPCC) in January 2018. The IOPC is responsible for carrying out independent investigations into serious incidents or allegations of misconduct by those serving with the police forces in England and Wales, as well as Police and Crime Commissioners in England and Wales and the London Mayor's Office for Policing and Crime (MOPAC). The IOPC's director-general and its regional directors must not have worked for the police in any capacity prior to their appointment. It has the power to initiate, undertake and oversee investigations and is also responsible for the way in which complaints are handled by local police forces. The IOPC is also responsible for serious complaints and conduct matters relating to staff at the National Crime Agency (NCA).

Complaints about the police must first be recorded with the relevant police force and the local force will attempt to resolve the matter internally. Certain serious complaints are automatically referred to the IOPC. The IOPC or police force may refer the case to the Crown Prosecution Service, which will decide whether to bring criminal charges against the officer/s involved.

On 1 April 2013, under the Police and Fire Reform (Scotland) Act 2012 which brought together Scotland's eight police services into the single Police Service of Scotland, the remit of the Police Complaints Commissioner for Scotland (PCCS) was expanded to include investigations into the most serious incidents concerning the police. To reflect this change, the PCCS was renamed the Police Investigations and Review Commissioner (PIRC).

The Police Ombudsman for Northern Ireland provides an independent police complaints system for Northern Ireland, dealing with all stages of the complaints procedure. Complaints that cannot be resolved informally are investigated and the ombudsman recommends a suitable course of action to the Chief Constable of the Police Service of Northern Ireland or the Northern Ireland Policing Board based on the investigation's findings. The ombudsman may recommend that a police officer be prosecuted, but the decision to prosecute a police officer rests with the Director of Public Prosecutions.

INDEPENDENT OFFICE FOR POLICE CONDUCT, PO Box 473, Sale M33 0BW T 0300-020 0096
E enquiries@policeconduct.gov.uk
W www.policeconduct.gov.uk
Director-General, Michael Lockwood

POLICE INVESTIGATIONS AND REVIEW COMMISSIONER, Hamilton House, Hamilton Business Park, Caird Park, Hamilton ML3 0QA T 01698-542900
E enquiries@pirc.gsi.gov.uk W www.pirc.scotland.gov.uk
Police Investigations and Review Commissioner, Kate Frame

POLICE OMBUDSMAN FOR NORTHERN IRELAND, New Cathedral Buildings, Writers' Square, 11 Church Street, Belfast BT1 1PG T 028-9082 8600 E info@policeombudsman.org
W www.policeombudsman.org
Police Ombudsman, Dr Michael Maguire

POLICE SERVICES

COLLEGE OF POLICING

Leamington Road, Ryton-on-Dunsmore, Coventry CV8 3EN
T 0800-496 3322 E contactus@college.pnn.police.uk
W www.college.police.uk

The College of Policing was established in December 2012 as the first professional body set up for policing. It works on behalf of the public to raise professional standards in policing and to assist forces to reduce crime and protect the public. It engages with the public through the Police and Crime Commissioners to ensure that it is responsive to the issues of greatest concern.

The government has designated the college as a centre for reviewing and testing practices and interventions to identify which are effective in reducing crime. It makes this information accessible for all in policing, particularly frontline practitioners. The college also supports continuous professional development and sets national standards for promotion and progression.

Chief Executive, Mike Cunningham
Chair, Millie Banerjee, CBE

NATIONAL CRIME AGENCY

Units 1–6 Citadel Place, Tinworth Street, London SE11 5EF
T 0370-496 7622
E communication@nca.x.gsi.gov.uk
W www.nationalcrimeagency.gov.uk

Established under the Crime and Courts Act 2013 the National Crime Agency (NCA) became fully operational in October 2013. The NCA is a non-ministerial government department.

The NCA's remit is to fight organised crime, including child sexual exploitation, modern slavery and human trafficking, illegal firearms, cyber crime and money laundering.

The director-general has independent operational direction and control over the NCA's activities and, through the home secretary, is accountable to parliament.

Director-General, Lynne Owens, CBE, QPM

UK MISSING PERSONS UNIT

PO Box 58358, London NW1W 9LA T 0845-234 6034
E ukmpu@nca.x.gsi.gov.uk
W www.missingpersons.police.uk

The UK Missing Persons Unit, part of the National Crime Agency, acts as the centre for the exchange of information connected with the search for missing persons nationally and internationally alongside the police and other related organisations. The unit focuses on cross-matching missing persons with unidentified persons or bodies by maintaining records, including a dental index of ante-mortem chartings of long-term missing persons and post-mortem chartings from unidentified bodies.

Information is supplied and collected for all persons who have been missing in the UK for over 72 hours (or fewer where police deem appropriate), foreign nationals reported missing in the UK, UK nationals reported missing abroad and all unidentified bodies and persons found within the UK.

SPECIALIST FORCES

BRITISH TRANSPORT POLICE

25 Camden Road, London NW1 9LN T 0800-405040
W www.btp.police.uk
Strength (March 2017), 2,679

British Transport Police is the national police force for the railways in England, Wales and Scotland, including the London Underground system, Docklands Light Railway, Glasgow Subway, Midland Metro tram system, Sunderland Metro, London Tramlink and the Emirates Air Line cable car.

The chief constable reports to the British Transport Police Authority. The members of the authority are appointed by the transport secretary and include representatives from the rail industry as well as independent members. Officers are paid the same salary as those in other police forces.

Chief Constable, Paul Crowther, OBE

CIVIL NUCLEAR CONSTABULARY

Building F6, Culham Science Centre, Abingdon,
Oxfordshire OX14 3DB T 0330-135 5400
W www.gov.uk/government/organisations/
civil-nuclear-constabulary
*Strength, c.*1,500

The Civil Nuclear Constabulary (CNC) is overseen by the Civil Nuclear Police Authority, an executive non-departmental public body sponsored by the Department for Business, Energy and Industrial Strategy. The CNC is a specialised armed force that protects civil nuclear sites and nuclear materials. The constabulary is responsible for policing UK civil nuclear industry facilities and for escorting nuclear material between establishments within the UK and worldwide.

Chief Constable, Michael Griffiths, CBE
Deputy Chief Constable, Simon Chesterton, QPM

MINISTRY OF DEFENCE POLICE

Ministry of Defence Police HQ, Wethersfield, Braintree, Essex
CM7 4AZ T 01371-854000
W www.mod.police.uk
*Strength, c.*2,600

Part of the Ministry of Defence Police and Guarding Agency, the Ministry of Defence Police is a statutory civil police force with particular responsibility for the security and policing of the MoD environment. It contributes to the physical protection of property and personnel within its jurisdiction and provides a comprehensive police service to the MoD as a whole.

Chief Constable, Andy Adams
Deputy Chief Constable, Peter Terry, QPM

THE SPECIAL CONSTABULARY

W www.policespecials.com
Strength (September 2017) 12,601

The Special Constabulary is a force of trained volunteers who support and work with their local police force, usually for a minimum of 16 hours a month. Special constables are thoroughly grounded in the basic aspects of police work, such as self-defence, powers of arrest, common crimes and preparing evidence for court, before they can begin to carry out any police duties. Once they have completed their training, they have the same powers as a regular officer and wear a similar uniform.

POLICE FORCES

The telephone number for each local police force in England, Wales, Scotland and Northern Ireland is T 101

Force	Strength†	Chief Constable	Police and Crime Commissioner
ENGLAND			
Avon and Somerset	2,601	Andy Marsh, QPM	Sue Mountstevens
Bedfordshire	1,056	Jon Boutcher, QPM	Kathryn Holloway
Cambridgeshire	1,308	Alec Wood	Jason Ablewhite
Cheshire	1,919	Janette McCormick *(acting)*	David Keane
Cleveland	1,226	Mike Veale	Barry Coppinger
Cumbria	1,076	Michelle Skeer, QPM	Peter McCall
Derbyshire	1,643	Peter Goodman	Hardyal Dhindsa
Devon and Cornwall	2,840	Shaun Sawyer	Alison Hernandez
Dorset	1,205	James Vaughan	Martyn Underhill
Durham	1,113	Mike Barton, QPM	Ron Hogg
Essex	2,724	Stephen Kavanagh, QPM	Roger Hirst
Gloucestershire	1,053	Rod Hansen	Martin Surl
Greater Manchester	5,971	Ian Hopkins, QPM	Mayor of Greater Manchester
Hampshire	2,754	Olivia Pinkney	Michael Lane
Hertfordshire	1,850	Charlie Hall, QPM	David Lloyd
Humberside	1,591	Lee Freeman	Keith Hunter
Kent	3,180	Alan Pughsley, QPM	Matthew Scott
Lancashire	2,708	Andy Rhodes	Clive Grunshaw
Leicestershire	1,715	Simon Cole, QPM	Lord Bach
Lincolnshire	1,062	Bill Skelly	Marc Jones
Merseyside	3,374	Andy Cooke, QPM	Jane Kennedy
Norfolk	1,464	Simon Bailey, QPM	Lorne Green
North Yorkshire	3,201	Lisa Winward	Julia Mulligan
Northamptonshire	1,135	Nick Adderley	Stephen Mold
Northumbria	1,309	Winton Keenen	Dame Vera Baird, DBE
Nottinghamshire	1,764	Craig Guilford	Paddy Tipping
South Yorkshire	2,362	Stephen Watson	Dr Alan Billings
Staffordshire	1,585	Gareth Morgan	Matthew Ellis
Suffolk	1,066	Gareth Wilson	Tim Passmore
Surrey	1,884	Nick Ephgrave	David Munro
Sussex	2,470	Giles York, QPM	Katy Bourne
Thames Valley	3,940	Francis Habgood, QPM	Anthony Stansfeld
Warwickshire	786	Martin Jelley, QPM	Philip Seccombe
West Mercia	1,968	Anthony Bangham	John-Paul Campion
West Midlands	6,565	Dave Thompson, QPM	David Jamieson
West Yorkshire	4,539	Dee Collins, CBE, QPM	Mark Burns-Williamson, OBE
Wiltshire	951	Kier Pritchard *(interim)*	Angus Macpherson
WALES			
Dyfed-Powys	1,115	Mark Collins	Dafydd Llywelyn
Gwent	1,117	Julian Williams	Jeff Cuthbert
North Wales	1,403	Carl Foulkes	Arfon Jones
South Wales	2,729	Matt Jukes	Rt. Hon. Alun Michael
POLICE SCOTLAND	17,256	Iain Livingstone, QPM	–
POLICE SERVICE OF NORTHERN IRELAND	6,840	George Hamilton, QPM	–

ISLANDS	Strength†	Chief Constable	Telephone
Isle of Man	207	Gary Roberts	01624-631212
States of Jersey	214	James Wileman *(acting)*	01534-612612
Guernsey	147	Patrick Rice	01481-725111

† Size of force (full-time equivalent; excluding long-term absentees) as at 31 March 2017

LONDON FORCES

CITY OF LONDON POLICE

Guildhall Yard East, London EC2V 5AE T 020-7601 2222
W www.cityoflondon.police.uk
Strength (March 2017), 673

The City of London has one of the most important financial centres in the world and the force has particular expertise in fraud investigation. The force concentrates on: economic crime, counter terrorism and community policing. It has a wholly elected police authority, the police committee of the City of London Corporation, which appoints the commissioner.

Commissioner, Ian Dyson, QPM
Assistant Commissioner, Alistair Sutherland, QPM
Commanders, Jane Gyford *(Operations);* Karen Baxter *(Economic Crime)*

METROPOLITAN POLICE SERVICE

New Scotland Yard, Broadway, London SW1H 0BG
T 020-7230 1212 W www.met.police.uk
Strength (March 2017), 30,083

Commissioner, Cressida Dick, CBE, QPM
Deputy Commissioner, Sir Craig Mackey, QPM

The Metropolitan Police Service (MPS) is divided into four main areas for operational purposes:

FRONTLINE POLICING
Most of the day-to-day policing of London is carried out by 32 borough operational command units operating within the same boundaries as the London borough councils.

Assistant Commissioner, Martin Hewitt

SPECIALIST OPERATIONS
Counter Terrorism Command is responsible for the prevention and disruption of terrorist activity, domestic extremism and related offences within London and nationally. It provides an explosives disposal and chemical, biological, radiological and nuclear capability in London, assists the security services in fulfilling their roles and provides a point of contact for international partners.
Protection Command is responsible for the protection and security of high-profile persons, such as the royal family, prime minister and visiting heads of state.
Security Command works with authorities at the Houses of Parliament to provide security for peers, MPs, employees and visitors to the Palace of Westminster.

Assistant Commissioner & National Coordinator for Counter Terrorism Policing, Neil Basu

MET OPERATIONS
Met Operations provides two main services: reducing the harm caused by serious crime and criminal networks and providing specialist policing services across London.

Assistant Commissioner, Sir Stephen House, QPM

PROFESSIONALISM
The Directorate of Professionalism's key aims are to uphold and improve professional standards across the MPS. It works with the IOPC to establish good practice, reduce bureaucracy and review decision making. It also works with the CPS to ensure timely investigations of complaints and conduct matters.

Assistant Commissioner, Helen Ball

STAFF ASSOCIATIONS

Police officers are not permitted to join a trade union or to take strike action. All ranks have their own staff associations.
NATIONAL POLICE CHIEFS' COUNCIL (NPCC), 10 Victoria Street, London SW1H 0NN T 020-3276 3795
W www.npcc.police.uk
Chair, Sara Thornton, CBE, QPM

ENGLAND AND WALES
POLICE FEDERATION OF ENGLAND AND WALES, Federation House, Highbury Drive, Leatherhead, Surrey KT22 7UY T 01372-352000 W www.polfed.org
General Secretary, Andy Fittes
POLICE SUPERINTENDENTS' ASSOCIATION OF ENGLAND AND WALES, 67A Reading Road, Pangbourne, Reading RG8 7JD T 0118-984 4005 W www.policesupers.com
National Secretary, Chief Supt. Dan Murphy

SCOTLAND
ASSOCIATION OF SCOTTISH POLICE SUPERINTENDENTS, Scottish Police College, Kincardine, Fife FK10 4BE T 01259-732122
W www.scottishpolicesupers.org.uk
General Secretary, Craig Suttie
SCOTTISH POLICE FEDERATION, 5 Woodside Place, Glasgow G3 7QF T 0300-303 0027 W www.spf.org.uk
General Secretary, Calum Steele

NORTHERN IRELAND
POLICE FEDERATION FOR NORTHERN IRELAND, 77–79 Garnerville Road, Belfast BT4 2NX T 028-9076 4200
W www.policefed-ni.org.uk
Secretary, Colin McCrum
SUPERINTENDENTS' ASSOCIATION OF NORTHERN IRELAND, T 028-9092 2201
E SuptAssociation@psni.pnn.police.uk

RATES OF PAY

As at 1 September 2018

Chief Constable of Greater Manchester or W. Midlands*	£190,710
Chief Constable	£136,677–£177,999
Deputy Chief Constable	£114,429–£146,217
Assistant Chief Constable/ Commander	£98,538–£111,249
Chief Superintendent	£81,156–£85,614
Superintendent	
in rank on or after 1 April 2014	£65,478–£77,340
in rank before 1 April 2014	£65,478–£76,287
Chief Inspector†	£54,432 (£56,601)–£57,597 (£59,751)
Inspector†	£49,176 (£51,330)–£53,340 (£55,512)
Sergeant	£39,693–£43,134
Constable	
apptd on or after 1 April 2013	£19,971–£38,382
apptd before 1 April 2013	£24,447–£38,382
Metropolitan Police	
Commissioner	£273,354
Deputy Commissioner	£225,675
City of London Police	
Commissioner	£169,110
Assistant Commissioner	£139,482
Police Scotland	
Chief Constable	£214,404
Deputy Chief Constable	£174,741
Assistant Chief Constable	£118,485
Police Service of Northern Ireland	
Chief Constable	£203,422
Deputy Chief Constable	£165,277

* Also applicable to the four Assistant Commissioners of the MPS
† London salary in parentheses. All other officers (not MPS or City of London Commissioners) working in London receive an additional payment of £2,445 per annum

THE PRISON SERVICE

The prison services in the UK are the responsibility of the Secretary of State for Justice, the Scottish Secretary for Justice and the Minister of Justice in Northern Ireland. The chief executive (director-general in Northern Ireland), officers of HM Prison and Probation Service (HMPPS), the Scottish Prison Service (SPS) and the Northern Ireland Prison Service are responsible for the day-to-day running of the system.

There are 120 prison establishments in England and Wales, 15 in Scotland and three in Northern Ireland. Convicted prisoners are classified according to their assessed security risk and are housed in establishments appropriate to that level of security. There are no open prisons in Northern Ireland. Female prisoners are housed in women's establishments or in separate wings of mixed prisons. Remand prisoners are, where possible, housed separately from convicted prisoners. Offenders under the age of 21 are usually detained in a Young Offender Institution, which may be a separate establishment or part of a prison. Appellant and failed asylum seekers are held in Immigration Removal Centres, or in separate units of other prisons.

Thirteen prisons are now run by the private sector in England and Wales, and in England, Wales and Scotland all escort services have been contracted out to private companies. In Scotland, two prisons (Kilmarnock and Addiewell) were built and financed by the private sector and are being operated by private contractors.

There are independent prison inspectorates in England, Wales and Scotland which report annually on conditions and the treatment of prisoners. The Chief Inspector of Criminal Justice in Northern Ireland and HM Inspectorate of Prisons for England and Wales perform an inspectorate role for prisons in Northern Ireland. Every prison establishment also has an independent monitoring board made up of local volunteers.

Any prisoner whose complaint is not satisfied by the internal complaints procedures may complain to the prisons and probation ombudsman for England and Wales, the Scottish public services ombudsman or the prisoner ombudsman for Northern Ireland. The prisons and probation inspectors, the prisons ombudsman and the independent monitoring boards report to the home secretary and to the Minister of Justice in Northern Ireland.

PRISON STATISTICS

The projected 'high scenario' prison population for 2020 in England and Wales is 98,900; the 'low scenario' is 81,400.

PRISON POPULATION (UK) *as at June 2018*

	Remand	Sentenced	Other
ENGLAND AND WALES	9,285	72,619	869
Male	8,752	69,370	848
Female	533	3,249	021
SCOTLAND*	1,543	6,206	–
Male	1,452	5,908	–
Female	091	298	–
N. IRELAND	462	1,059	–
Male	433	1,015	–
Female	029	044	–
UK TOTAL	11,290	79,884	869

* Figures from August 2018
Sources: MoJ; Scottish Prison Service; NI Prison Service

PRISON CAPACITY (ENGLAND AND WALES) *as at August 2018*

Male prisoners	79,263
Female prisoners	3,801
Total	83,064
Useable operational capacity	85,854
Under home detention curfew supervision	3,290

Source: MoJ – *Prisons and Probation Statistics*

SENTENCED PRISON POPULATION BY SEX AND OFFENCE (ENGLAND AND WALES) *as at 30 June 2018*

	Male	Female
Violence against the person	17,779	934
Sexual offences	13,452	128
Robbery	6,845	311
Theft offences	8,731	620
Criminal damage and arson	971	101
Drugs offences	10,476	441
Possession of weapons	2,502	077
Public order offences	1,218	048
Miscellaneous crimes against society	3,023	198
Fraud offences	1,138	155
Summary non-motoring	1,573	190
Summary motoring	344	007
Offence not recorded	255	029
Total	68,307	3,294

Source: MoJ – *Prisons and Probation Statistics*

SENTENCED POPULATION BY LENGTH OF SENTENCE (ENGLAND AND WALES) *as at 30 June 2018*

	British	Other Nationalities or Not Recorded
Less than 12 months	4,752	538
12 months to less than 4 years	14,641	1,677
4 years to less than life	30,636	3,479
Indeterminate	8,958	904
*Total**	58,987	6,598

* Figures do not include civil (non-criminal) prisoners or fine defaulters
Source: MoJ – *Prisons and Probation Statistics*

AVERAGE DAILY POPULATION BY TYPE OF CUSTODY 2017–18 (SCOTLAND)

Remand	1,358
Persons under sentence: sub total	6,103
Under 4 years	3,221
4 years and over	2,882
Total	7,461

Source: SPS – *Annual Report and Accounts 2017–18*

SUICIDES IN PRISON, 2017–18 (ENGLAND AND WALES)

Total	77

Source: MoJ

THE PRISON SERVICES

HM PRISON AND PROBATION SERVICE

102 Petty France, London SW1H 9EX
T 0203-193 5921 E public.enquiries@noms.gsi.gov.uk
W www.gov.uk/government/organisations/
her-majestys-prison-and-probation-service

HM Prison and Probation Service (HMPPS) was formed on 1 April 2017, incorporating the National Offender Management Service (NOMS) and HM Prisons. HMPPS is responsible for implementing government policy concerning the welfare of prison populations and local communities, working closely with HM Prison Service to oversee the management of public sector prisons in England and Wales.

SALARIES (ENGLAND AND WALES)
from 1 April 2018

All salary ranges given are for the average across England and Wales (includes inner and outer London salaries) and are based on a 37-hour-week inclusive of the required hours allowance (Governors, Deputy Governors and Heads of Function) or the additional 17 per cent unsocial hours payment for all other grades.

Governor	£67,620–£91,789
Deputy Governor	£47,958–£73,715
Head of Function	£41,129–£49,358
Custodial Manager	£31,161–£35,075
Supervising/Specialist Officer	£27,699–£31,031
Prison Officer	£21,803–£24,829
Operational Support Grade	£18,864–£19,807

HM PRISON AND PROBATION SERVICE BOARD
Chief Executive, Michael Spurr
Executive Directors, Martin Beecroft *(Human Resources);* Simon Boddis *(Estate Transformation);* Phil Copple *(Prisons);* Sonia Crozier *(Probation and Women Offenders);* Andrew Emmett *(Finance);* Digby Griffith *(Rehabilitation and Assurance);* Ian Porée *(Community Interventions);* Amy Rees *(HMPPS Wales and Strategy);* Sara Robinson *(Youth Custody);* Adrian Scott *(Electronic Monitoring Programme and Procurement);* Claudia Sturt *(Security, Order and Counter Terrorism)*

OPERATING COSTS OF HM PRISON AND PROBATION SERVICE 2017–18

Staff costs	£1,951,586,000
Operating income	(£254,809,000)
Total operating expenditure	£4,640,644,000
Net operating expenditure	£4,385,835,000

Source: HM Prison and Probation Service – *Annual Report 2017–18*

SCOTTISH PRISON SERVICE (SPS)

Calton House, 5 Redheughs Rigg, Edinburgh EH12 9HW
T 0131-330 3500 E gaolinfo@sps.pnn.gov.uk
W www.sps.gov.uk

SALARIES

Governor in Charge	£62,160–£70,509
Deputy Governor	£50,323–£58,424
Head of Operations	£40,654–£48,579
Unit Manager	£32,778–£41,269
First Line Manager	£26,717–£34,430
Residential Officer	£22,427–£28,891
Operations Officer	£17,521–£22,245

SPS BOARD
Chief Executive, Colin McConnell
Directors, James Kerr *(Operations);* Teresa Medhurst *(Strategy and Innovation);* Eric Murch *(Corporate Change);* Ruth Sutherland *(Corporate Services, acting)*
Non-Executive Directors, K. Hampton; R. Molan; H. Monro; G. Scott; G. Stillie

OPERATING COSTS OF SPS 2017–18

Staff costs	£170,437,000
Total income	(£7,389,000)
Total operating expenditure	£331,518,000
Net operating expenditure	£324,129,000

Source: SPS – *Annual Report and Accounts 2017–18*

NORTHERN IRELAND PRISON SERVICE

Dundonald House, Upper Newtownards Road, Belfast BT4 3SU
T 028-9052 2922 E niprisonservice@nics.gov.uk
W www.justice-ni.gov.uk/topics/prisons

SALARIES

Governing Governor	£75,120–£82,170
Governor in Charge	£65,900–£73,629
Head of Function	£53,300–£57,621
Head of Unit	£47,810–£51,566
Senior Prison Officer	£34,050–£38,380
Main Grade Prison Officer	£30,710–£38,116
Operational Support Grade	£20,500
Custody Prison Officer	£20,000–£26,005

MANAGEMENT BOARD
Chair, Ronnie Armour
Directors, Austin Treacy, OBE *(Prisons, acting);* Louise Cooper *(Rehabilitation, acting)*

OPERATING COSTS OF NORTHERN IRELAND PRISON SERVICE 2016–17

Staff costs	£61,639,000
Operating income	(£2,559,000)
Total operating expenditure	£119,450,000
Net operating expenditure	£116,891,000

Source: NI Prison Service – *Annual Report and Accounts 2016–17*

PRISON ESTABLISHMENTS

ENGLAND AND WALES *AS AT JULY 2018*

Prison	*Address*	*Capacity*	*Prisoners*	*Governor/Director*
ALTCOURSE (private prison)	Liverpool L9 7LH	1,184	1,176	Steve Williams
ASHFIELD (private prison)	Bristol BS16 9QJ	412	410	Vicky Pails
*‡ASKHAM GRANGE	York YO23 3FT	128	100	Susan Howard
‡AYLESBURY	Bucks HP20 1EH	434	398	Laura Sapwell
BEDFORD	Bedford MK40 1HG	466	421	Helen Clayton-Hoar
BELMARSH	London SE28 0EB	906	837	Rob Davis
BIRMINGHAM	Birmingham B18 4AS	1,334	1,269	Peter Small
BLANTYRE HOUSE	Kent TN17 2NH	122	–	James Bourke
†‡BRINSFORD	Wolverhampton WV10 7PY	577	520	Heather Whithead
‡BRISTOL	Bristol BS7 8PS	602	505	Steve Cross
‡BRIXTON	London SW2 5XF	798	742	Dave Bamford
*BRONZEFIELD (private prison)	Middlesex TW15 3JZ	557	534	Ian Whiteside
BUCKLEY HALL	Lancs OL12 9DP	399	387	Rob Knight
BULLINGDON	Oxon OX25 1PZ	1,114	1,097	Ian Blakeman
BURE	Norfolk NR10 5GB	656	647	Simon Rhoden
†CARDIFF	Cardiff CF24 0UG	799	703	Danny Khan
CHANNINGS WOOD	Devon TQ12 6DW	724	688	Richard Luscombe
‡CHELMSFORD	Essex CM2 6LQ	665	635	Penny Bartlett (*acting*)
COLDINGLEY	Surrey GU24 9EX	411	409	Jo Sims
‡COOKHAM WOOD	Kent ME1 3LU	188	174	Paul Durham
DARTMOOR	Devon PL20 6RR	640	631	Bridie Oakes-Richards
‡DEERBOLT	Co. Durham DL12 9BG	447	420	Gavin O'Malley
‡DONCASTER (private prison)	Doncaster DN5 8UX	1,145	1,087	Jerry Spencer
DOVEGATE (private prison)	Staffs ST14 8XR	1,160	1,147	John Hewitson
*DOWNVIEW	Surrey SM2 5PD	340	315	Robin Eldridge
*‡DRAKE HALL	Staffs ST21 6LQ	340	322	Carl Hardwick
DURHAM	Durham DH1 3HU	996	902	Phil Husband (*acting*)
*‡EAST SUTTON PARK	Kent ME17 3DF	101	099	Robin Eldridge
*EASTWOOD PARK	Glos GL12 8DB	430	354	Suzy Dymond-White
ELMLEY	Kent ME12 4DZ	1,252	1,234	Sara Pennington
ERLESTOKE	Wilts SN10 5TU	524	510	Tim Knight
†‡EXETER	Devon EX4 4EX	561	426	Pete Elbourn
FEATHERSTONE	Wolverhampton WV10 7PU	687	632	Babafemi Dada
†‡FELTHAM	Middx TW13 4ND	568	515	Glenn Knight
FORD	W. Sussex BN18 0BX	544	538	Stephen Fradley
‡FOREST BANK (private prison)	Salford M27 8FB	1,460	1,437	Matt Spencer
*FOSTON HALL	Derby DE65 5DN	342	324	Andrea Black
FRANKLAND	Durham DH1 5YD	844	832	Norman Griffin
FULL SUTTON	York YO41 1PS	558	524	Mark Allen
GARTH	Preston PR26 8NE	845	818	Steve Pearson
GARTREE	Leics LE16 7RP	708	693	Ali Barker
GRENDON/SPRING HILL	Bucks HP18 0TL	559	546	Jamie Bennett
‡GUYS MARSH	Dorset SP7 0AH	477	456	Paul Millett
HAVERIGG	Cumbria LA18 4NA	309	266	Tony Corcoran
HEWELL	Worcs B97 6QS	1,262	1,027	Gareth Sands
HIGH DOWN	Surrey SM2 5PJ	1,203	1,108	Louise Spencer
HIGHPOINT	Suffolk CB8 9YG	1,325	1,281	Nigel Smith
†‡HINDLEY	Lancs WN2 5TH	606	513	Mark Livingston
‡HOLLESLEY BAY	Suffolk IP12 3JW	480	470	Declan Moore
HOLME HOUSE	Stockton-on-Tees TS18 2QU	1,210	1,197	Chris Dyer
‡HULL	Hull HU9 5LS	1,030	973	Rick Stuart
HUMBER	E. Yorks HU15	1,062	1,003	Marcella Goligher
‡HUNTERCOMBE	Oxon RG9 5SB	480	479	David Redhouse
ISIS	Thamesmead SE28 0NZ	628	617	Emily Thomas
ISLE OF WIGHT	Isle of Wight PO30 5RS	1,096	1,085	Doug Graham
KIRKHAM	Lancs PR4 2RN	654	584	Graham Beck
KIRKLEVINGTON GRANGE	Cleveland TS15 9PA	283	261	Angie Petit
†‡LANCASTER FARMS	Lancaster LA1 3QZ	560	545	Derek Harrison
LEEDS	Leeds LS12 2TJ	1,212	1,022	Steven Robson
LEICESTER	Leicester LE2 7AJ	411	286	Philip Novis
‡LEWES	E. Sussex BN7 1EA	692	631	Paul Woods
LEYHILL	Glos GL12 8BT	515	510	Helen Ryder
LINCOLN	Lincoln LN2 4BD	729	532	Paul Yates
LINDHOLME	Doncaster DN7 6EE	970	925	Simon Walters
LITTLEHEY	Cambs PE28 0SR	1,220	1,208	Susan Doolan
LIVERPOOL	Liverpool L9 3DF	700	672	Pia Sinha
LONG LARTIN	Worcs WR11 8TZ	535	489	Clare Pearson
*‡LOW NEWTON	Durham DH1 5YA	352	322	Gabrielle Lee
LOWDHAM GRANGE (private prison)	Notts NG14 7DA	920	918	Trudy McCaffery
MAIDSTONE	Kent ME14 1UZ	600	591	Dave Atkinson

MANCHESTER	Manchester M60 9AH	1,136	968	Rob Young
‡MOORLAND/HATFIELD	Doncaster DN7 6BW	1,384	1,315	Tim Beeston
§MORTON HALL	Lincoln LN6 9PT	392	239	Karen Head
MOUNT	Herts HP3 0NZ	1,024	998	Kevin Leggett
*‡NEW HALL	W. Yorks WF4 4XX	425	355	Susan Howard
NORTH SEA CAMP	Lincs PE22 0QX	420	411	Paul Yates
‡NORTHUMBERLAND	Northumberland NE65 9XG	1,348	1,337	Nick Leader
(private prison)				
‡NORWICH	Norfolk NR1 4LU	759	718	Bev Beven
NOTTINGHAM	Notts NG5 3AG	1,060	926	Tom Wheatley
OAKWOOD (private prison)	W. Midlands WV10 7QD	2,106	2,052	John McLaughlin
ONLEY	Warks CV23 8AP	742	726	Matthew Tilt
†‡PARC (private prison)	Bridgend CF35 6AP	1,719	1,593	Janet Wallsgrove
‡PENTONVILLE	London N7 8TT	1,294	1,215	Dean Gardiner (acting)
*†PETERBOROUGH (private prison)	Peterborough PE3 7PD	1,252	1,220	Damian Evans
‡PORTLAND	Dorset DT5 1DL	530	496	Steve Hodson
PRESTON	Lancs PR1 5AB	811	656	Steve Lawrence
RANBY	Notts DN22 8EU	1,038	963	Nigel Hirst
RISLEY	Cheshire WA3 6BP	1,096	1,071	Jerry Spencer
‡ROCHESTER	Kent ME1 3QS	695	679	Dawn Mauldon (acting)
RYE HILL (private prison)	Warks CV23 8SZ	664	660	Pete Small
*SEND	Surrey GU23 7LJ	282	272	Carlene Dixon
STAFFORD	Stafford ST16 3AW	751	740	Ralph Lubkowski
STANDFORD HILL	Kent ME12 4AA	464	459	James Padley
STOCKEN	Rutland LE15 7RD	853	790	Neil Thomas
‡STOKE HEATH	Shropshire TF9 2JL	782	724	John Huntington
*‡STYAL	Cheshire SK9 4HR	486	460	Mahala McGuffie
SUDBURY	Derbys DE6 5HW	581	570	Adrian Turner
SWALESIDE	Kent ME12 4AX	1,112	1,069	Paul Newton
†‡SWANSEA	Swansea SA1 3SR	497	403	Graham Barrett
‡SWINFEN HALL	Staffs WS14 9QS	594	538	Ian West
THAMESIDE (private prison)	London SE28 0FJ	1,232	1,195	Craig Thomson
‡THORN CROSS	Cheshire WA4 4RL	387	379	Mick Povall
USK/PRESCOED	Monmouthshire NP15 1XP	536	526	Steve Cross
§VERNE	Dorset DT5 1EQ	40	15	David Bourne
WAKEFIELD	W. Yorks WF2 9AG	750	715	David Harding
WANDSWORTH	London SW18 3HU	1,512	1,376	Jeanne Bryant
‡WARREN HILL	Suffolk IP12 3BF	258	248	Sonia Walsh
WAYLAND	Norfolk IP25 6RL	934	910	Paul Cawkwell
WEALSTUN	W. Yorks LS23 7AZ	832	786	Diane Lewis
‡WERRINGTON	Stoke-on-Trent ST9 0DX	128	107	Pete Gormley
‡WETHERBY	W. Yorks LS22 5ED	336	265	Andrew Dickinson
WHATTON	Nottingham NG13 9FQ	841	830	Lynn Saunders, OBE
WHITEMOOR	Cambs PE15 0PR	458	432	Will Styles
WINCHESTER	Winchester SO22 5DF	655	607	Stephanie Roberts-Bibby
WOODHILL	Bucks MK4 4DA	637	609	Nicola Marfleet
WORMWOOD SCRUBS	London W12 0AE	1,195	1,133	Steve Bradford
WYMOTT	Preston PR26 8LW	1,169	1,146	John Illingsworth

SCOTLAND *AS AT JULY 2018*

Prison	Address	Average Daily	Max. Number	Governor/Director
ADDIEWELL (private prison)	West Lothian EH55 8QA	696	702	Ian Whitehead
†‡BARLINNIE	Glasgow G33 2QX	1,127	1,195	Michael Stoney
*†‡CORNTON VALE	Stirling FK9 5NU	86	96	Caroline Johnston
†DUMFRIES	Dumfries DG2 9AX	172	180	Karen Smith
*†EDINBURGH	Edinburgh EH11 3LN	872	913	David Abernethy
GLENOCHIL	Tullibody FK10 3AD	641	667	Nigel Ironside
*‡GRAMPIAN	Peterhead AB42 2YY	449	474	Allister Purdie
†GREENOCK	Greenock PA16 9AH	248	257	Rhona Hotchkiss
†INVERNESS	Inverness IV2 3HH	98	104	Stephen Coyle
†KILMARNOCK (private prison)	Kilmarnock KA1 5AA	499	509	Michael Guy
LOW MOSS	Glasgow G64 2PZ	757	778	Sharanne Findlay
OPEN ESTATE – CASTLE HUNTLY	Dundee DD2 5HL	189	220	Gary Law
†PERTH	Perth PH2 8AT	617	654	Fraser Munro
*†‡POLMONT	Falkirk FK2 0AB	470	478	Brenda Stewart
SHOTTS	Lanarkshire ML7 4LE	531	540	Jacqueline Clinton

NORTHERN IRELAND *AS AT AUGUST 2018*

Prison	Address	Prisoners	Governor/Director
*†‡HYDEBANK WOOD	Belfast BT8 8NA	144	Richard Taylor
†§MAGHABERRY	Co. Antrim BT28 2NF	827	David Kennedy
MAGILLIGAN	Co. Londonderry BT49 0LR	429	Gary Milling

* Women's establishment or establishment with units for women
† Remand Centre or establishment with units for remand prisoners
‡ Young Offender Institution or establishment with units for young offenders
§ Immigration Removal Centre or establishment with units for immigration detainees

DEFENCE

The armed forces of the UK comprise the Royal Navy, the Army and the Royal Air Force (RAF). The Queen is Commander-in-Chief of all the armed forces. The Secretary of State for Defence is responsible for the formulation and content of defence policy and for providing the means by which it is conducted. The formal legal basis for the conduct of defence in the UK rests on a range of powers vested by statute and letters patent in the Defence Council, chaired by the Secretary of State for Defence. Beneath the ministers lies the top management of the Ministry of Defence (MoD), headed jointly by the Permanent Secretary and the Chief of Defence Staff. The Permanent Secretary is the government's principal civilian adviser on defence and has the primary responsibility for policy, finance, management and administration. The Permanent Secretary is also personally accountable to parliament for the expenditure of all public money allocated to defence purposes. The Chief of the Defence Staff is the professional head of the armed forces in the UK and the principal military adviser to the secretary of state and the government.

The Defence Board is the executive of the Defence Council. Chaired by the Permanent Secretary, it acts as the main executive board of the Ministry of Defence, providing senior level leadership and strategic management of defence.

The Central Staff, headed by the Vice-Chief of the Defence Staff and the Second Permanent Under-Secretary of State, is the policy core of the department. Defence Equipment and Support, headed by the Chief of Defence Materiel, is responsible for purchasing defence equipment and providing logistical support to the armed forces.

A permanent Joint Headquarters for the conduct of joint operations was set up at Northwood in 1996. The Joint Headquarters connects the policy and strategic functions of the MoD head office with the conduct of operations and is intended to strengthen the policy/executive division.

The UK pursues its defence and security policies through its membership of NATO (to which most of its armed forces are committed), the European Union, the Organisation for Security and Cooperation in Europe and the UN (see International Organisations section).

STRENGTH OF THE REGULAR ARMED FORCES

	Royal Navy	Army	RAF	All Services
1975 strength	76,200	167,100	95,000	338,300
2000 strength	42,850	110,050	54,720	207,620
2005 strength	39,940	109,290	51,870	201,100
2010 strength	38,730	108,920	44,050	191,700
2011 strength	37,660	106,240	42,460	186,360
2012 strength	35,540	104,250	40,000	179,800
2013 strength	33,960	99,730	37,030	170,710
2014 strength	33,330	91,070	35,230	159,630
2015 strength	32,740	87,060	33,930	153,720
2016 strength	32,500	85,040	33,460	151,000
2017 strength	32,540	83,560	33,260	149,370
2018 strength	32,480	81,120	32,960	146,560

Source: MoD – Defence Statistics (Tri-Service)

UK REGULAR ARMED FORCES BY RANK 2018

Officers	27,260
Other Ranks	119,300

Source: MoD – Defence Statistics (Tri-Service)

UK regular forces include trained and untrained personnel and nursing services, but exclude Gurkhas, full-time reserve service personnel, mobilised reservists and naval activated reservists. As at 1 April 2018 these groups numbered:

All Gurkhas	3,150
Full-time reserve service	5,012
Mobilised reservists	294
Army	140
RAF	114
Royal Navy	40

Source: MoD – Defence Statistics (Tri-Service)

CIVILIAN PERSONNEL

2000 level	121,300
2005 level	107,680
2006 level	102,970
2007 level	95,790
2008 level	89,499
2009 level	86,621
2010 level	85,850
2011 level	83,063
2012 level	71,008
2013 level	65,400
2014 level	62,501
2015 level	58,161
2016 level	56,243
2017 level	56,675
2018 level	56,865

Source: MoD – Defence Statistics (Tri-Service)

UK REGULAR FORCES: DEATHS

In 2017 there were a total of 63 deaths among the UK regular armed forces, of which 12 were serving in the Royal Navy and Royal Marines, 40 in the Army and 11 in the RAF. The largest single cause of death was cancers, which accounted for 14 deaths (22 per cent of the total) in 2017. Land transport accidents accounted for 13 deaths (21 per cent) and other accidents accounted for a further 19 deaths (30 per cent). There were no deaths as a result of hostile action. Suicides and open verdicts accounted for four deaths.

NUMBER OF DEATHS AND MORTALITY RATES

	2013	2014	2015	2016	2017
Total number	86	68	60	72	63
Royal Navy	13	12	11	17	12
Army	63	40	39	41	40
RAF	10	16	10	14	11
Mortality rates per thousand					
Tri-service rate	0.50	0.42	0.39	0.47	0.42
Navy	0.42	0.35	0.32	0.52	0.36
Army	0.65	0.42	0.45	0.47	0.49
RAF	0.23	0.40	0.28	0.36	0.27

Source: MoD National Statistics

NUCLEAR FORCES

The Vanguard Class SSBN (ship submersible ballistic nuclear) provides the UK's strategic nuclear deterrent. Each Vanguard Class submarine is capable of carrying 16 Trident D5 missiles equipped with nuclear warheads.

There is a ballistic missile early warning system station at RAF Fylingdales in North Yorkshire.

ARMS CONTROL

The 1990 Conventional Armed Forces in Europe (CFE) Treaty, which commits all NATO and former Warsaw Pact members to limiting their holdings of five major classes of conventional weapons, has been adapted to reflect the changed geo-strategic environment and negotiations continue for its implementation. The Open Skies Treaty, which the UK signed in 1992 and entered into force in 2002, allows for the overflight of states parties by other states parties using unarmed observation aircraft.

The UN Convention on Certain Conventional Weapons (as amended 2001), which bans or restricts the use of specific types of weapons that are considered to cause unnecessary or unjustifiable suffering to combatants, or to affect civilians indiscriminately, was ratified by the UK in 1995. In 1968 the UK signed and ratified the Nuclear Non-Proliferation Treaty, which came into force in 1970 and was indefinitely and unconditionally extended in 1995. In 1996 the UK signed the Comprehensive Nuclear Test Ban Treaty and ratified it in 1998. The UK is a party to the 1972 Biological and Toxin Weapons Convention, which provides for a worldwide ban on biological weapons, and the 1993 Chemical Weapons Convention, which came into force in 1997 and provides for a verifiable worldwide ban on chemical weapons.

DEFENCE BUDGET

DEPARTMENTAL EXPENDITURE LIMITS
£ billion

	2018–19
Resource DEL	28.2
Capital DEL	8.7
Total	36.9

Source: HM Treasury – Autumn Budget 2017 (Crown copyright)

MINISTRY OF DEFENCE

Main Building, Whitehall, London SW1A 2HB
T 020-7218 9000
W www.gov.uk/government/organisations/ministry-of-defence

Secretary of State for Defence, Rt. Hon. Gavin Williamson, CBE, MP
Parliamentary Private Secretary, Will Quince, MP
Special Advisers, Eleanor Lyons; Robert Golledge
Minister of State, Rt. Hon. Earl Howe (Lords)
Minister of State, Rt. Hon. Mark Lancaster, TD, MP (Armed Forces)
Parliamentary Private Secretaries, Jack Lopresti, MP; Anne-Marie Trevelyan, MP
Parliamentary Under-Secretary of State and Minister for Defence People and Veterans, Rt. Hon. Tobias Ellwood, MP
Parliamentary Under-Secretary of State and Minister for Defence Procurement, Stuart Andrew, MP

CHIEFS OF STAFF

Chief of the Defence Staff, Gen. Sir Nick Carter, KCB, CBE, DSO, ADC
Vice-Chief of the Defence Staff, Gen. Sir Gordon Messenger, KCB, DSO*, OBE, ADC
Chief of the Naval Staff and First Sea Lord, Adm. Sir Philip Jones, KCB, ADC

Second Sea Lord and Deputy Chief of Naval Staff, Vice-Adm. Antony Radakin, CB
Chief of the General Staff, Gen. Mark Carleton-Smith, CBE
Assistant Chief of the General Staff, Maj.-Gen. Rupert Jones, CBE
Chief of the Air Staff, Air Chief Marshal Sir Stephen Hillier, KCB, CBE, DFC, ADC
Assistant Chief of the Air Staff, Air Vice-Marshal Gerard Mayhew, CBE

SENIOR OFFICIALS

Permanent Secretary, Stephen Lovegrove
Chief Scientific Adviser, Prof. Hugh Durrant-Whyte
Chief Scientific Adviser (Nuclear), Prof. Robin Grimes
Director-General Finance, Cat Little

THE DEFENCE COUNCIL

The Defence Council is chaired by the Secretary of State, and comprises the other ministers, the Permanent Under-Secretary, the Chief of Defence Staff and senior service officers and officials who head the armed services and the department's major corporate functions. It provides the formal legal basis for the conduct of UK defence through a range of powers vested in it by statute and letters patent.

THE DEFENCE BOARD

The Defence Board is the main corporate board of the MoD, providing senior level leadership and strategic management of defence. The Defence Board is the highest committee in the MoD, responsible for the full range of defence business, other than the conduct of operations.

Permanent Secretary, Stephen Lovegrove
Members, Lt.-Gen. Doug Chalmers (Deputy Chief of Defence Staff (Military Strategy and Operations)); Prof. Hugh Durrant-Whyte (Chief Scientific Adviser); Charlie Forte (Chief Information Officer); Prof. Robin Grimes (Chief Scientific Adviser (Nuclear)); Julian Kelly (Nuclear); Cat Little (Finance); Lt.-Gen. Richard Nugee, CVO, CBE (Chief of Defence People); Lt.-Gen. Mark Poffley, KCB, OBE (Deputy Chief of Defence Staff (Financial and Military Capability)); Peter Watkins, CBE (Strategy and International)
Non-Executive Members, Sir Gerry Grimstone (Lead); Simon Henry; Danuta Gray; Paul Skinner, CBE

CENTRAL STAFF

Vice-Chief of the Defence Staff, Gen. Sir Gordon Messenger, KCB, DSO*, OBE, ADC

JOINT FORCES COMMAND

Commander of Joint Forces Command, Gen. Sir Chris Deverell, KCB, MBE, ADC
Chief of Joint Operations, Vice-Adm. Timothy Fraser, CB
Chief of Staff, Air Vice-Marshal Johnny Stringer, CBE

FLEET COMMAND

First Sea Lord, Adm. Sir Philip Jones, KCB, ADC
Fleet Commander and Chief Naval Warfare Officer, Vice-Adm. Benjamin Key, CBE

NAVAL HOME COMMAND

Second Sea Lord, Vice-Adm. Antony Radakin, CB

LAND FORCES

Commander Field Army, Lt.-Gen. Patrick Saunders, CBE, DSO
Deputy Commander Field Army, Maj.-Gen. William O'Leary, QVRM, TD, VR

AIR COMMAND

Deputy Commander Operations and Air Member for Operations, Air Marshal Stuart Atha, CB, DSO
Deputy Commander Capability and Air Member for Personnel and Capability, Air Marshal Michael Wigston, CBE

DEFENCE EQUIPMENT AND SUPPORT

Chief Executive, Sir Simon Bollom
Chief of Materiel (Fleet), vacant
Chief of Materiel (Land), Lt.-Gen. Paul Jacques, CBE
Chief of Materiel (Air), Air Marshal Julian Young, CB, OBE

EXECUTIVE AGENCIES

DEFENCE ELECTRONICS AND COMPONENTS AGENCY

Welsh Road, Deeside, Flintshire CH5 2LS **T** 01244-847694
E decainfo@deca.mod.uk
W www.gov.uk/government/organisations/
defence-electronics-and-components-agency

The Defence Electronics and Components Agency (DECA) provides maintenance, repair, overhaul, upgrade and procurement in avionics, electronics and components fields to support the MoD. As a 'trading' executive agency DECA is run along commercial lines with funding for DECA's activities being generated entirely by payments for delivery of services provided to the MoD and other private sector customers. DECA currently has an annual turnover of around £25m and employs approximately 430 staff across its head office and main operating centre in North Wales, a site in Stafford and various deployed locations across the UK.

Chief Executive, Geraint Spearing

DEFENCE SCIENCE AND TECHNOLOGY LABORATORY

Porton Down, Salisbury, Wiltshire SP4 0JQ **T** 01980-950000
E centralenquiries@dstl.gov.uk
W www.gov.uk/government/organisations/
defence-science-and-technology-laboratory

The Defence Science and Technology Laboratory (DSTL) supplies specialist science and technology services to the MoD and wider government.

Chief Executive, Gary Aitkenhead

UK HYDROGRAPHIC OFFICE

Admiralty Way, Taunton, Somerset TA1 2DN
T 01823-484444
E customerservices@ukho.gov.uk
W www.gov.uk/government/organisations/uk-hydrographic-office

The UK Hydrographic Office (UKHO) collects and supplies hydrographic and geospatial data for the Royal Navy and merchant shipping, to protect lives at sea. Working with other national hydrographic offices, UKHO sets and raises global standards of hydrography, cartography and navigation.

Chief Executive, John Humphrey

ARMED FORCES TRAINING AND RECRUITMENT

From Naval Bases at Plymouth, the Clyde in Scotland and a small team at Northwood in Middlesex, Flag Officer Sea Training (FOST) provides Operational Sea Training for all surface ships, submarines and Royal Fleet Auxiliaries of the Royal Navy. All aspects of naval training are offered by FOST including new entry, officer, Royal Marine, submarine, surface and aviation training. FOST also offers specialist training in a number of areas including hydrography, meteorology, oceanography, marine engineering and diving.

The Army Recruiting and Training Division (ARTD) is responsible for the four key areas of army training: soldier initial training, at the School of Infantry or at one of the army's four other facilities; officer initial training at the Royal Military Academy Sandhurst; trade training at one of the army's specialist facilities; and resettlement training for those about to leave the army. Trade training facilities include: the Armour Centre; the Infantry Battle School; the Infantry Training Centre, Catterick; the Royal School of Military Engineering and the Army Aviation Centre.

The Royal Air Force No. 22 (Training) Group is responsible for the recruitment, selection, initial and professional training of RAF personnel as well as providing trained specialist personnel to the armed forces as a whole, such as providing the army air corps with trained helicopter pilots. The group is split into five areas: RAF College Cranwell; the Air Cadet Organisation (ACO); the Directorate of Flying Training (DFT); the Directorate of Ground Training; and the Defence College of Technical Training.

The Defence College of Technical Training provides technical training to all three services and includes the Defence School of Communications Information Systems (DSCIS); the Defence School of Electronic and Mechanical Engineering (DSEME); and the Defence School of Marine Engineering (DSMarE).

USEFUL WEBSITES

W www.royalnavy.mod.uk
W www.army.mod.uk
W www.raf.mod.uk

THE ROYAL NAVY

In Order of Seniority as at November 2018

LORD HIGH ADMIRAL OF THE UNITED KINGDOM
HRH The Prince Philip, Duke of Edinburgh, KG, KT, OM, GBE, AK, QSO, PC, *apptd* 2011

ADMIRALS OF THE FLEET
HRH The Prince Philip, Duke of Edinburgh, KG, KT, OM, GBE, AC, QSO, PC, *apptd* 1953
Sir Benjamin Bathurst, GCB, *apptd* 1995
HRH The Prince of Wales, KG, KT, GCB, OM, AK, QSO, PC, ADC, *apptd* 2012
Lord Boyce, KG, GCB, OBE, *apptd* 2014

ADMIRALS
(Former Chiefs or Vice Chiefs of Defence Staff and First Sea Lords who remain on the active list)
Slater, Sir Jock, GCB, LVO, *apptd* 1991
Essenhigh, Sir Nigel, GCB, *apptd* 1998
West of Spithead, Lord, GCB, DSC, PC, *apptd* 2000
Band, Sir Jonathon, GCB, *apptd* 2002
Stanhope, Sir Mark, GCB, OBE, *apptd* 2004
Zambellas, Sir George, GCB, DSC, *apptd* 2012

ADMIRALS
HRH The Princess Royal, KG, KT, GCVO, QSO *(Cdre-in-Chief Portsmouth)*
Jones, Sir Philip, KCB, ADC *(First Sea Lord and Chief of Naval Staff)*

VICE-ADMIRALS
HRH The Duke of York, KG, GCVO, ADC *(Adm. of the Sea Cadet Corps and Cdre-in-Chief Fleet Air Arm)*
Lister, Sir Simon, KCB, OBE *(career intermission)*
Johnstone, Clive, CB, CBE *(Cdr Maritime Command)*
Key, Benjamin, CBE *(Fleet Cdr and Chief Naval Warfare Officer)*
Fraser, Timothy, CB *(Chief of Joint Operations)*
Radakin, Antony, CB *(Second Sea Lord and Deputy Chief of Naval Staff)*
Bennett, Paul, CB, OBE *(Chief of Staff, Supreme Allied Cdr Transformation)*

REAR-ADMIRALS
Lowe, Timothy, CBE *(National Hydrographer and Deputy Chief Executive (Hydrography))*
Kingwell, John, CBE *(Deputy Commandant Royal College of Defence Studies)*
Beckett, Keith, CBE *(Chief Strategic Systems Executive)*
Weale, John, OBE *(Flag Officer Scotland & Northern Ireland, Assistant Chief of Naval Staff (Submarines) and Rear-Adm. Submarines (Head of Fighting Arm))*
Blount, Keith, CB, OBE *(Assistant Chief of Naval Staff (Aviation, Amphibious Capability and Carriers) and Rear-Adm. Fleet Air Arm (Head of Fighting Arm))*
Hine, Nicholas, CB *(Assistant Chief of Naval Staff (Policy))*
Gardner, Christopher, CBE *(Assistant Chief of Naval Staff (Ships))*
Chivers, Paul, OBE *(Director Military Aviation Authority)*
Hodgson, Timothy, MBE *(Director Submarine Capability)*
Thompson, Richard, CBE *(secondment)*
Methven, Paul *(Director Submarines Acquisition)*
Entwisle, William, OBE, MVO *(Senior British Military Adviser, US Central Command)*
Pentreath, Jonathan, OBE *(Cdr Joint Helicopter Command)*

Halton, Paul, OBE *(Cdr Operations)*
Robinson, Guy, OBE *(Deputy Cdr Strike Force NATO)*
Briers, Matthew *(Director Carrier Strike)*
Morley, James *(Director Capability Joint Forces Command)*
Warrender, William, CBE *(Flag Officer Sea Training and Assistant Chief of the Naval Staff (Training))*
Bath, Michael *(Naval Secretary, Assistant Chief of the Naval Staff (Personnel) and Flag Officer Reserves)*
Toy, Malcolm *(Director (Technical) Military Aviation Authority)*
Kyd, Jeremy *(Cdr UK Maritime Forces and Rear-Adm. Surface Ships (Head of Fighting Arm))*
Kyte, Andrew *(Assistant Chief of Defence Staff (Logistics Operations) and Chief Naval Logistics Officer)*

MEDICAL
Walker, Alasdair, CB, OBE, QHS *(Surgeon Vice-Adm.)*

ROYAL MARINES

CAPTAIN-GENERAL
HRH the Duke of Sussex, KCVO

GENERAL
Messenger, Sir Gordon, KCB, DSO*, OBE, ADC *(Vice-Chief of the Defence Staff)*

MAJOR-GENERALS
Bevis, Timothy, CBE *(Director Operations and Plans, International Military Staff)*
Magowan, Robert, CB, CBE *(Assistant Chief of Naval Staff (Capability) and Chief of Staff Navy Command HQ)*
Stickland, Charles, OBE *(Cdr UK Amphibious Forces and Commandant-General Royal Marines)*
Holmes, Matthew, DSO *(Deputy Adviser, Ministry of the Interior)*

The Royal Marines were formed in 1664 and are part of the Naval Service. Their primary purpose is to conduct amphibious and land warfare. The principal operational units are:

- Three Commando Brigade, an amphibious all-arms brigade trained to operate in arduous environments (a core element of the UK's Joint Rapid Reaction Force). The commando units, 40 Commando, 42 Commando and 45 Commando each have a strength of around 700 and are based in Taunton, Plymouth and Arbroath, respectively. 43 Commando Fleet Protection Group is around 550 strong and is based at HM Naval Base Clyde on the west coast of Scotland.
- 1 Assault Group, which has its headquarters located in Devonport, Plymouth is responsible for ten landing craft training squadron at Poole, Dorset and 11 amphibious trials and training squadron at Instow, Devon

The Royal Marines also provide detachments for warships and land-based naval parties as required.

ROYAL MARINES RESERVES (RMR)
The Royal Marines Reserve is a commando-trained volunteer force with the principal role, when mobilised, of supporting the Royal Marines. The RMR consists of approximately 600 trained ranks who are distributed between the four RMR centres in the UK. Approximately 10 per cent of the RMR are working with the regular corps on long-term attachments within all of the Royal Marines regular units.

THE ROYAL AIR FORCE

In Order of Seniority as at November 2018

THE QUEEN

MARSHALS OF THE ROYAL AIR FORCE
HRH The Prince Philip, Duke of Edinburgh, KG, KT, OM, GBE, AK, QSO, PC, *apptd* 1953
HRH The Prince of Wales, KG, KT, GCB, OM, AK, QSO, PC, ADC, *apptd* 2012

FORMER CHIEFS OF THE AIR STAFF

MARSHALS OF THE ROYAL AIR FORCE
Lord Craig of Radley, GCB, OBE, *apptd* 1988
Lord Stirrup, KG, GCB, AFC, *apptd* 2014

AIR CHIEF MARSHALS
Sir Michael Graydon, GCB, CBE, *apptd* 1991
Sir Richard Johns, GCB, KCVO, OBE, *apptd* 1994
Sir Glenn Torpy, GCB, CBE, DSO, *apptd* 2006
Sir Stephen Dalton, GCB, *apptd* 2009
Sir Andrew Pulford, GCB, CBE, *apptd* 2013

AIR RANK LIST

AIR CHIEF MARSHALS
Peach, Sir Stuart, GBE, KCB, ADC *(Chair of the Military Committee, NATO)*
Hillier, Sir Stephen, KCB, CBE, DFC, ADC *(Chief of the Air Staff)*

AIR MARSHALS
Stacey, Sir Graham, KBE, CB *(pending assignment)*
Osborne, P., CBE *(Chief of Defence Intelligence)*
Young, J., CB, OBE *(Chief of Materiel (Air) and Air Member for Materiel)*
Atha, S., CB, DSO *(Deputy Cdr Operations and Air Member for Operations)*
Evans, S., CBE *(Deputy Cdr NATO Air Command, Ramstein)*
Stringer, E., CB, CBE *(Director-General Joint Force Development)*
Wigston, M., CBE *(Deputy Cdr Capability and Air Member for Personnel and Capability)*

AIR VICE-MARSHALS
Gray, S., CB, OBE *(Air Officer Commanding No. 38 Group)*
Turner, A., CBE *(Assistant Chief of the Defence Staff (Operations))*
Waterfall, G., CBE *(Chief of Staff (Operations), Permanent Joint HQ)*
Knighton, R. CB *(Assistant Chief of Defence Staff (Capability and Force Design))*
Parker, G., OBE *(Head of British Forces (USA) and Defence Attaché, Washington)*
Mayhew, G., CBE *(Assistant Chief of the Air Staff)*
Hedley, B., MBE *(Director Joint Warfare, Joint Forces Command)*
Tunnicliffe, G. *(Assistant Chief of the Defence Staff (Personnel Capability) and Defence Services Secretary)*
Bethell, K., CBE *(Director Combat Air, Defence Equipment and Support)*

Elliot, C., CBE *(Chief of Staff Personnel and Air Secretary)*
Russell, G., CB *(Director Helicopters, Defence Equipment and Support)*
Shell, S., OBE *(Director Military Aviation Authority (designate))*
Luck, C., MBE, DFC *(Chief Executive Defence Academy and Commandant Joint Services Command and Staff College)*
Rochelle, S., OBE, DFC *(Chief of Staff Capability, Air Command)*
James, W., CBE *(Air Officer Commanding No. 22 (Training) Group and Chief of Staff Training)*
Cooper, D., CBE *(Air Officer Commanding No 2. Group)*
Hart, M. *(Head of Joint Terrorism Analysis Centre)*
Sampson, M., CBE, DSO *(Director Saudi Armed Forces Project)*
Vallely, I., OBE *(Cdr Cyber and Intelligence and Reconnaissance, Joint Forces Command)*
Moore, C. *(Director Service Operations, Information Services and Solutions)*
Stringer, J., CBE *(Chief of Staff, Joint Forces Command)*
Reid, A. *(Defence Medical Director, Joint Forces Command)*
Smyth, H., OBE, DFC *(Air Officer Commanding No. 1 Group)*
Ellis, J., *(Chaplain-in-Chief and Director-General Chaplaincy Service (RAF))*
Jennings, T., OBE *(Director Legal Services (RAF))*
Duguid, I., OBE *(Chief of Staff Operations, Air Command)*

CONSTITUTION OF THE RAF
The RAF consists of a single command, Air Command, based at RAF High Wycombe. RAF Air Command was formed on 1 April 2007 from the amalgamation of Strike Command and Personnel and Training Command.

Air Command consists of three groups, each organised around specific operational duties. No. 1 Group is the coordinating organisation for the tactical fast-jet forces responsible for attack, offensive support and air defence operations. No. 2 Group provides air combat support including air transport and air-to-air refuelling; intelligence surveillance; targeting and reconnaissance; and force protection. No. 22 (Training) Group recruits personnel and provides trained specialist personnel to the RAF, as well as to the Royal Navy and the Army (*see also* Armed Forces Training and Recruitment).

RAF EQUIPMENT

AIRCRAFT

Combat Aircraft	Lightening II, Tornado GR4, Typhoon FGR4
Training Aircraft	Embraer Phenom 100, Hawk T1, Hawk T2, 120TP Prefect, Texan T, Tucano T1, Tutor T1, Viking T1
Surveillance Aircraft	MQ-9 Reaper, RC-135W Rivet Joint, Sentinel R1, E-3D Sentry AEW1, Shadow R1

HELICOPTERS

Helicopters	Chinook, Griffin HAR2, Puma HC2
Training Helicopters	Airbus H135 Juno, Airbus H145 Jupiter

ROYAL AUXILIARY AIR FORCE

The Auxiliary Air Force was formed in 1924 to train an elite corps of civilians to serve their country in flying squadrons in their spare time. In 1947 the force was awarded the prefix 'royal' in recognition of its distinguished war service and the Sovereign's Colour for the RAuxAF was presented in 1989. The RAuxAF continues to recruit civilians who undertake military training in their spare time, with a standard minimum commitment of 27 days a year. With the amendments to the reserve service made under the Defence Reform Act 2014, reservists can now be employed to support the RAF across the full spectrum of military tasks. There are currently 27 squadrons with the RAuxAF, with a total establishment of just under 3,200 posts, with reservist posts being available in the majority of trades.

Air Commodore-in-Chief, HM The Queen
Commandant General, Air Vice-Marshal Lord Beaverbrook, ADC
Inspector, Gp Capt. Gavin Hellard, ADC

PRINCESS MARY'S ROYAL AIR FORCE NURSING SERVICE

The Princess Mary's Royal Air Force Nursing Service (PMRAFNS) was formed on 1 June 1918 as the Royal Air Force Nursing Service. In June 1923, His Majesty King George V gave his royal assent for the Royal Air Force Nursing Service to be known as the Princess Mary's Royal Air Force Nursing Service. The Princess Mary's Royal Air Force Nursing Service (PMRAFNS) is committed to providing a skilled, knowledgeable and able nursing workforce to deliver high quality care, whilst being responsive to the dynamic nature of RAF Nursing in peacetime and on operations.

Patron and Air Chief Commandant, HRH Princess Alexandra, The Hon. Lady Ogilvy, KG, GCVO
Matron-in-Chief, Gp Capt. Michael Priestley

SERVICE SALARIES

Pay16 was introduced on 1 April 2016, replacing the previous Pay 2000 scheme for all regular and reserve personnel on the main pay spines up to and including the rank of Commodore/ Brigadier/ Air Commodore (*see* following page for table of relative rank). Compared with Pay 2000 the total number of increments has been reduced and personnel, with the exception of Lieutenants, remain on the same salary for the first two years in rank.

The following rates of pay apply from 1 April 2018 and are rounded to the nearest pound.

The pay rates shown are for army personnel. The rates also apply to personnel of equivalent rank and pay band in the other services.

Rank	Annual Salary
Second Lieutenant	£26,738

LIEUTENANT

On appointment	£32,138
After 1 year in rank	£33,266
After 2 years in rank	£34,394
After 3 years in rank	£35,523

CAPTAIN

On appointment	£41,186
After 2 years in rank	£42,485
After 3 years in rank	£43,784
After 4 years in rank	£45,082
After 5 years in rank	£46,381
After 6 years in rank	£47,680
After 7 years in rank	£48,979

MAJOR

On appointment	£51,879
After 2 years in rank	£53,588
After 3 years in rank	£55,297
After 4 years in rank	£57,006
After 5 years in rank	£58,715
After 6 years in rank	£60,423
After 7 years in rank	£62,132

LIEUTENANT-COLONEL

On appointment	£72,812
After 2 years in rank	£74,734
After 3 years in rank	£76,645
After 4 years in rank	£78,561
After 5 years in rank	£80,478
After 6 years in rank	£82,394
After 7 years in rank	£84,310

COLONEL

On appointment	£88,212
After 2 years in rank	£89,672
After 3 years in rank	£91,132
After 4 years in rank	£92,592
After 5 years in rank	£94,051
After 6 years in rank	£95,511
After 7 years in rank	£96,970

BRIGADIER

On appointment	£105,121
After 2 years in rank	£106,185
After 3 years in rank	£107,248
After 4 years in rank	£108,312
After 5 years in rank	£109,375

PAY SYSTEM FOR SENIOR MILITARY OFFICERS

Pay rates effective as at 1 April 2018 for all military officers of 2* rank and above (excluding medical and dental officers). All pay rates are rounded to the nearest pound.

Rank	Annual Salary
MAJOR-GENERAL (2*)	
Scale 1	£113,810
Scale 2	£116,034
Scale 3	£118,303
Scale 4	£120,617
Scale 5	£122,979
Scale 6	£125,385
LIEUTENANT-GENERAL (3*)	
Scale 1	£132,420
Scale 2	£138,911
Scale 3	£145,727
Scale 4	£151,452
Scale 5	£155,917
Scale 6	£160,518
GENERAL (4*)	
Scale 1	£173,715
Scale 2	£178,058
Scale 3	£182,510
Scale 4	£187,072
Scale 5	£190,814
Scale 6	£194,630

Field Marshal – appointments to this rank will not usually be made in peacetime. The salary for holders of the rank is equivalent to the salary of a 5-star General, a salary created only in times of war. In peacetime, the equivalent rank to Field Marshal is the Chief of the Defence Staff. As at 1 April 2018, the annual salary range for the Chief of the Defence Staff is £250,270–£265,588.

OFFICERS COMMISSIONED FROM THE SENIOR RANKS

Rank	Annual salary
Level 15	£55,051
Level 14	£54,690
Level 13	£54,312
Level 12	£53,578
Level 11	£52,849
Level 10	£52,110
Level 9	£51,376
Level 8	£50,642
Level 7*	£49,726
Level 6	£49,161
Level 5	£48,587
Level 4†	£47,453
Level 3	£46,888
Level 2	£46,310
Level 1‡	£45,180

* Officers commissioned from the ranks with more than 15 years' service enter on level 7
† Officers commissioned from the ranks with between 12 and 15 years' service enter on level 4
‡ Officers commissioned from the ranks with less than 12 years' service enter on level 1

SOLDIERS' SALARIES

Pay16 was introduced on 1 April 2016, replacing the previous Pay 2000 scheme for all regular and reserve personnel on the main pay spines up to and including the rank of Commodore/ Brigadier/ Air Commodore (*see* below for table of relative rank). Rank remains the key determinant of pay, but the 'high' and 'low' bands under the Pay 2000 scheme were removed and replaced with 4 supplements *(Supp.)* under which trades are allocated. All ranks in a particular trade are treated the same for pay supplement purposes. Compared with Pay 2000 the total number of increments has been reduced and personnel remain on increment Level 1 for the first two years in rank, with the exception of Privates who remain on increment Level 2 for two years.

Rates of pay effective from 1 April 2018 (rounded to the nearest pound) are:

Rank	Supp. 1	Supp. 2	Supp. 3	Supp 4
PRIVATE				
Level 1	19,025	–	–	–
Level 2	20,406	–	–	–
Level 3	21,761	22,018	22,285	22,285
Level 4	22,900	23,156	23,601	23,873
Level 5	24,011	24,356	24,788	25,110
Level 6	25,122	25,621	26,146	26,480
LANCE CORPORAL				
(levels 7 to 9 also applicable to Privates)				
Level 7	26,265	26,875	27,400	27,877
Level 8	27,482	28,203	28,754	29,263
Level 9	28,759	29,554	30,178	30,766

CORPORAL				
Level 1	30,632	31,523	32,390	33,194
Level 2	31,451	32,361	33,253	34,056
Level 3	31,917	33,004	34,001	34,855
Level 4	32,352	33,456	34,717	35,691
Level 5	32,813	33,915	35,347	36,404
SERGEANT				
Level 1	34,462	35,622	37,128	38,347
Level 2	35,320	36,566	38,076	39,455
Level 3	36,209	37,554	39,012	40,496
Level 4	37,110	38,639	39,986	41,549
Level 5	38,020	39,620	41,009	42,642
STAFF SERGEANT				
Level 1	38,791	40,423	41,889	43,580
Level 2	39,402	41,128	42,638	44,288
Level 3	40,035	41,762	43,389	45,038
Level 4	40,646	42,373	44,159	45,508
Level 5	41,285	43,011	45,046	46,527
WARRANT OFFICER CLASS II				
(also applicable to Staff Sergeants)				
Level 1	42,191	44,147	46,320	47,830
Level 2	43,095	45,050	46,982	48,336
Level 3	43,949	45,675	47,319	48,697
Level 4	44,694	46,295	47,621	49,000
Level 5	45,457	46,898	47,906	49,284
WARRANT OFFICER CLASS I				
Level 1	48,865	–	–	50,282
Level 2	49,147	–	–	50,712
Level 3	49,709	–	–	51,198
Level 4	50,271	–	–	51,691
Level 5	50,785	–	–	52,155

RELATIVE RANK – ARMED FORCES

Royal Navy
1 Admiral of the Fleet
2 Admiral (Adm.)
3 Vice-Admiral (Vice-Adm.)
4 Rear-Admiral (Rear-Adm.)
5 Commodore (Cdre)
6 Captain (Capt.)
7 Commander (Cdr)
8 Lieutenant-Commander (Lt.-Cdr)
9 Lieutenant (Lt.)
10 Sub-Lieutenant (Sub-Lt.)
11 Midshipman

Army
1 Field Marshal
2 General (Gen.)
3 Lieutenant-General (Lt.-Gen.)
4 Major-General (Maj.-Gen.)
5 Brigadier (Brig.)
6 Colonel (Col.)
7 Lieutenant-Colonel (Lt.-Col.)
8 Major (Maj.)
9 Captain (Capt.)
10 Lieutenant (Lt.)
11 Second Lieutenant (2nd Lt.)

Royal Air Force
1 Marshal of the RAF
2 Air Chief Marshal
3 Air Marshal
4 Air Vice-Marshal
5 Air Commodore (Air Cdre)
6 Group Captain (Gp Capt.)
7 Wing Commander (Wg Cdr)
8 Squadron Leader (Sqn Ldr)
9 Flight Lieutenant (Flt Lt)
10 Flying Officer (FO)
11 Pilot Officer (PO)

EDUCATION

THE UK EDUCATION SYSTEM

The structure of the education system in the UK is a devolved matter with each of the countries of the UK having separate systems under separate governments. There are differences between the school systems in terms of the curriculum, examinations and final qualifications and, at university level, in terms of the nature of some degrees and in the matter of tuition fees. The systems in England, Wales and Northern Ireland are similar and have more in common with one another than the Scottish system, which differs significantly.

Education in England is overseen by the Department for Education (DfE).

Responsibility for education in Wales lies with the Department for Education and Skills (DfES) within the Welsh government. Ministers in the Scottish government are responsible for education in Scotland, led by the directorates of Learning and Lifelong Learning, while in Northern Ireland responsibility lies with the Department of Education (DfE) and the Department for the Economy (DE) within the Northern Ireland government.

DEPARTMENT FOR EDUCATION T 0370-000 2288
W www.gov.uk/government/organisations/
department-for-education
DEPARTMENT FOR EDUCATION AND SKILLS (DFES)
T 0300-060 4400 W www.gov.wales/topics/educationandskills
SCOTTISH GOVERNMENT – EDUCATION
T 0300-244 4000 W www.gov.scot/Topics/Education
DEPARTMENT OF EDUCATION (NI) T 028-9127 9279
W www.education-ni.gov.uk
DEPARTMENT FOR THE ECONOMY T 028-9052 9900
W www.economy-ni.gov.uk

RECENT DEVELOPMENTS

The Conservative government continued to implement pledges to ensure good, fairly funded schools for all children and a major reform of technical education, and to carry through significant changes to higher education and research arrangements in England.

ENGLAND
- The government announced a new national funding formula for schools, increasing funding per pupil. The formula includes a minimum cash increase for every school of 1 per cent per pupil by 2019–20, rises for the most underfunded schools of 3 per cent per pupil in 2018–19 and 2019–20, a £110,000 lump sum for every school to help with fixed costs and an additional £26m for rural and isolated schools
- A new baseline assessment is to come into force from 2020 for children in their first (reception) year at school. Once the baseline is established, the 20 minute teacher-recorded assessment of children's communication, language, literacy and early mathematics skills will replace the statutory tests pupils currently take in Year 2, aged 6–7. A new multiplication tables check to be taken by pupils in Year 4, aged 8–9, was announced in February 2018; it will be voluntary from June 2019 but become mandatory in June 2020
- A new Institute of Teaching was launched in December 2017 and a Centre of Excellence for Literacy Teaching in January 2018, as part of the government's plan *Unlocking Talent, Fulfilling Potential*. Backed with £26m, the Centre will set up a national network of 35 English hubs across the country to work with schools in challenging circumstances and help raise standards. A new £7.7m curriculum fund will develop high-quality teaching resources
- In further education, the government announced £15m of Strategic College Improvement Funding, available until 2020, to enable strong colleges to partner with those in need of improvement, share best practice and drive up standards. Seven college principals were appointed as National Leaders of Further Education (NLFE), to support the sector and help improve education and training quality
- The government launched a £170m fund to enable employers and education and training providers to establish new Institutes of Technology, to deliver the higher-level technical skills that employers need. As part of plans to reform technical education, 54 colleges have been chosen to teach new T-level courses. T-levels will be on a par with A-levels, giving young people a choice between technical and academic education post-16. Courses in digital, construction and education and childcare will be first taught from September 2020, with a further 22 courses in subjects from finance to engineering available from 2021
- The Higher Education Funding Council for England closed in March 2018, transferring its functions to two new organisations. The Office for Students (OfS), which opened in January 2018, has statutory responsibility for higher education quality and standards, approving new entrants to the HE sector, managing the Register of Higher Education Providers and conferring university title and degree awarding powers. HE institutions in England cannot access public funding for teaching or student support, or recruit international students, unless they are registered with the OfS. UK Research and Innovation (UKRI), a new single funding body opened in April 2018, brings together the seven existing Research Councils, Innovate UK and the research and knowledge exchange functions of the former Higher Education Funding Council for England. Quality-related research funding is administered through UKRI's Council, Research England
- In October 2017 the government announced that, in the academic year 2018–19, maximum tuition fees for full-time undergraduate courses will continue to be frozen at £9,250 and the amount borrowers can earn before they need to repay their loans will increase from £21,000 to £25,000. A major review of post-18 education and funding – focusing on choice, value for money, access and skills provision – was also announced: it is due to conclude in early 2019
- The Teaching Excellence Framework (TEF), which rates teaching quality in English universities, is being extended to subject level. The TEF will rate universities gold, silver or bronze by subject, holding them to account for the quality of their teaching, learning environment and graduate outcomes. There will be a pilot scheme in 2017–18 and 2018–19; full subject-level rating is expected to start in 2019–20
- A new Institute of Coding, announced in January 2018, will be set up to tackle the UK's digital skills gap. This consortium of 60 universities, businesses and industry experts will receive £20m of government funding, to be matched by a further £20m from industry. The government also urged universities to open new maths schools and allocated £15m to a new higher education provider – New Model in Technology & Engineering (NMiTE) – to train up engineers

- In June 2018, the government announced £1.3bn of investment for British universities and businesses to develop the next generation of entrepreneurs, innovators and scientific leaders. The inaugural UKRI Future Leaders Fellowship Scheme will receive £900m over the next 11 years, with six funding competitions and at least 550 fellowships awarded over the next three years

WALES
- In September 2017 the Welsh government set out plans to improve its school system, including: reducing class sizes, reforming teacher training, supporting those with additional learning needs, establishing a national approach to long-term career development for teachers and a new National Academy for Educational Leadership, reducing unnecessary bureaucracy for teachers and investing £1.1bn to upgrade the quality of school buildings. It also revised the timeline for introducing the new Curriculum for Wales; roll out will begin in 2022
- Relationships and Sexuality Education will be reformed after a review of the subject by an expert panel, becoming a statutory part of Wales' curriculum for 5–16-year-olds
- A new National Academy for Educational Leadership launched in May 2018 will work with partners across the education system to support school leaders, encouraging and inspiring future leaders
- £100m is to be invested over the next three years, to speed up delivery of the 21st Century Schools and Education programme to modernise education infrastructure and to help reach the government's goal of a million Welsh speakers by 2050, announced in December 2017
- The Additional Learning Needs and Education Tribunal (Wales) Act 2018, which focuses on the needs of children and young people aged 0 to 25, replaces the terms 'special educational needs' and 'learning difficulties/disabilities' with 'additional learning needs'. It creates a single statutory plan – the Individual Development Plan (IDP) – for every learner.
- From 2019, only a pupil's first entry to a GCSE examination will count in their school's performance measures
- In November 2017, £50m was announced for further and higher education capital projects and £260m for apprenticeships in an effort to boost skills across Wales
- A new Tertiary Education and Research Commission for Wales (TERCW) was proposed in June 2017's consultation paper Public Good and a Prosperous Wales. TERCW is to develop, with the help of an expert panel, a public annual performance monitoring and management system that assesses post-16 institutions' contributions to achieving national goals in six areas: widening access, economic impact, innovation and research, institutional sustainability, learning value added and promotion of Welsh language and culture
- A new student finance package for 2018–19 undergraduate entrants gives all full-time students a minimum non-repayable grant of £1,000 and gives part-time students equivalent support. Tuition fees will be capped at £9,000 and the repayment earning threshold will rise to £25,000

SCOTLAND
- The 2018 National Improvement Framework and Improvement Plan set out improvement activity the Scottish government and partners intend to take, including the establishment of Regional Improvement Collaboratives to complement delivery of Getting It Right For Every Child, Curriculum for Excellence and Developing the Young Workforce. School improvement planning and reporting will be based on self-evaluation against four priorities: improving attainment, particularly in literacy and numeracy; closing the attainment gap; improving the health and wellbeing of children and young people; improving employability skills and sustained, positive school-leaver destinations for all young people
- A new Scottish Education Council, established in November 2017, will meet every two months to oversee work to improve education
- Reforms to make schools responsible for raising attainment and closing poverty-related gaps, choosing staff and management structure and deciding curriculum content will start to be implemented by agreement with stakeholders, ahead of planned legislation
- In 2018–19, 2,387 schools will receive around £120m in Pupil Equity Funding to help close poverty-related attainment gaps. An additional £50m will go to nine local authorities and another 74 schools, to help primary and secondary schoolchildren in communities affected by high levels of deprivation. Further improvement funding, totalling £46m, includes £10m in 2018–19 to support schools through regional improvement collaboratives, £32m over three years to support children who have been in local authority care and £4m over three years for an enhanced leadership development programme
- As part of the fifth phase of the £1.8bn Schools for the Future programme, £28m will be invested in four new schools
- The government announced £1.8bn of public funding to individual universities and colleges for 2018–19. Universities will share over £1.1bn. For colleges, the revenue budget will increase by 8.3 per cent to nearly £600m; the capital budget will increase by nearly £30m to £76.7m. Core student support funding increasing by £3.6m, with an extra £5.2m allocated to implementing the Independent Review of Student Support
- Scottish universities will also get a boost of £11.6m in 2018–19, to help them and their industry partners compete for UK-wide funding for research projects. This brings total grant funding for university research and innovation to £296.2m
- Student finance reforms announced in June 2018 will increase the Care Experienced FE bursary from £4,185 to £8,100 and the Care Experienced HE bursary from £7,625 to £8,100 in 2018–19. Other bursaries for further and higher education students will be increased from 2019–20 and the repayment threshold for student loans will be raised to £25,000 from April 2021. Tuition fee loans of £5,500 are to be made available to distance learning students on taught postgraduate courses from 2018–19, and full-time distance learning postgraduate students will also be able to access a £4,500 living cost loan for the first time

NORTHERN IRELAND
- After a successful pilot, a further Teaching Workforce Scheme was launched, which will allow up to 200 teachers aged 55+ to retire in 2018–19, so that recently qualified teachers can fill their posts
- A £21m state-of-the-art new special school opened in Ballymena. The School Enhancement Programme gave a total of £12.5m to schools in Ballymoney, Belfast and Dungannon
- Statistics released in June 2018 showed that the number of applicants to Northern Ireland higher education institutions increased by 34.6 per cent between 2008–9 and 2017–18, from 18,070 to 24,330
- The Department for the Economy has appointed 43 organisations based throughout Northern Ireland to deliver Training for Success and ApprenticeshipsNI programmes, offering training across a wide range of industry sectors and occupations.

• Statistics from the pilot phase of the Higher Level Apprenticeship programme from 2015–16 to 2016–17 showed 853 enrolments (592 individuals) in further education colleges and 115 in higher education institutions (20 in 2015–16, 95 in 2016–17)

STATE SCHOOL SYSTEM

PRE-SCHOOL

Pre-school education is not compulsory. In England, a free place is available for every 3- and 4-year-old whose parents want one, although parents may use as little or as much of their entitlement as they choose. All 3- and 4-year-olds, and disadvantaged 2-year-olds, are entitled to 15 hours a week of free early education over 38 weeks of the year until they reach compulsory school age (the term following their fifth birthday). From September 2017, working parents of 3- and 4-year-old children may be eligible for up to 30 hours free childcare. Free places are funded by local authorities and are delivered by a range of approved providers in the maintained and non-maintained sectors: nursery schools, nursery classes in primary schools, private schools, private day nurseries, voluntary playgroups, pre-schools and registered childminders. In order to receive funding, providers must be working towards the early learning goals and the Early Years Foundation Stage curriculum, must be inspected on a regular basis by Ofsted and must meet any conditions set by the local authority.

In Wales, every child is entitled to receive free Foundation Phase education for a minimum of two hours a day from the term following their third birthday. The Flying Start scheme allows disadvantaged 2- to 3-year-olds 2.5 hours childcare a week for 39 weeks. The government is testing offering 30 hours free childcare to working parents of 3- to 4-year-olds in seven local authorities, before extending the offer across Wales by 2020. All children in Wales are entitled to a minimum of 10 hours of free, part-time Foundation Phase education in a school or funded nursery, in the term following their third birthday.

In Scotland, councils have a duty to provide a pre-school education for all 3- and 4-year-olds, and some disadvantaged 2- to 3-year-olds, whose parents request one. Education authorities must offer each child at least 600 hours of free pre-school education a year, although they may provide more if they choose.

In Northern Ireland, the Department of Education aims to provide a funded place for all 3- and 4-year-old children in their final pre-school year. All places offer 2.5 hours a day, five days a week for at least 38 weeks a year.

PRIMARY AND SECONDARY SCHOOLS

By law, full-time education starts at the age of five for children in England, Scotland and Wales and at the age of four in Northern Ireland. In practice, most children in the UK start school before their fifth birthday: in England all children are entitled to a primary school place from the September after their fourth birthday.

Children in England are required to stay in education or training until the end of the academic year in which they turn 18. In all other parts of the UK, compulsory schooling ends at age 16, but children born between certain dates may leave school before their 16th birthday; most young people stay in some form of education until 17 or 18.

Primary education consists mainly of infant schools for children aged 5 to 7, junior schools for those aged 7 to 11, and combined infant and junior schools for both age groups. Scotland has only primary schools with no infant/junior division.

In a few parts of England there are schools catering for ages 5 to 10 as the first stage of a three-tier system of first (lower), middle and secondary (upper) schools.

Children usually leave primary school and move on to secondary school at the age of 11 (or 12 in Scotland). In the few areas of England that have a three-tier system, middle schools cater for children for three to four years between the ages of 8 and 14, depending on the local authority.

Secondary schools cater for children aged 11 to 16 and, if they have a sixth form, for those who choose to stay on to the age of 18. From the age of 16, students may move instead to further education colleges or work-based training.

Most UK secondary schools are co-educational. The largest secondary schools have more than 1,500 pupils and around 60 per cent of secondary pupils in the UK are in schools that take more than 1,000 pupils.

Most state-maintained secondary schools in England, Wales and Scotland are comprehensive schools, which admit pupils without reference to ability. In England there remain some areas with grammar schools, catering for pupils aged 11 to 18, which select pupils on the basis of high academic ability. Nearly two-thirds of state secondary schools in England (2,250) are now academies: academies are funded directly by the state rather than being maintained by local authorities. Northern Ireland still has 66 grammar schools; the 11-plus has been officially discontinued but schools, or consortia of schools, use their own unregulated entry tests.

More than 90 per cent of pupils in the UK attend publicly funded schools and receive free education. The rest (6.5 per cent) attend privately funded 'independent' schools which charge fees, or are educated at home.

The bulk of the UK government's expenditure on school education is through local authorities (Education and Library Boards (ELBs) in Northern Ireland), which pass on state funding to schools and other educational institutions.

SPECIAL EDUCATION

Schools and local authorities in England and Wales, Education and Library Boards (ELBs) in Northern Ireland and education authorities in Scotland are required to identify and secure provision for children with special educational needs and to involve parents in decisions. The majority of children with special educational needs are educated in ordinary mainstream schools, sometimes with supplementary help from outside specialists. Parents of children with special educational needs (referred to as additional support needs in Scotland and additional learning needs in Wales) have a right of appeal to independent tribunals if their wishes are not met.

Special educational needs provision may be made in maintained special schools, special units attached to mainstream schools or in mainstream classes themselves, all funded by local authorities. There are also non-maintained special schools run by voluntary bodies, mainly charities, who may receive grants from central government for capital expenditure and equipment but whose other costs are met primarily from the fees charged to local authorities for pupils placed in the schools. Some independent schools also provide education wholly or mainly for children with special educational needs.

ADDITIONAL SUPPORT NEEDS TRIBUNALS FOR
  SCOTLAND T 0141-302 5860
  W www.healthandeducationchamber.scot
FIRST-TIER TRIBUNAL (SPECIAL EDUCATIONAL
  NEEDS AND DISABILITY) T 01325-289350
  W www.gov.uk/special-educational-needs-disability-tribunal
INFORMATION ADVICE AND SUPPORT SERVICES
  NETWORK FOR SEND E iassn@ncb.org.uk W https://
  councilfordisabledchildren.org.uk/
  information-advice-and-support-services-network
SPECIAL EDUCATIONAL NEEDS TRIBUNAL FOR
  WALES T 01597-829800 W www.sentw.gov.uk

HOME EDUCATION

In England and Wales parents have the right to educate their children at home and do not have to be qualified teachers to do so. Home-educated children do not have to follow the National Curriculum or take national tests. Nor do they need a fixed timetable, formal lessons or to observe school hours, days or terms. However, by law parents must ensure that the home education provided is full-time and suitable for the child's age, ability and aptitude and, if appropriate, for any special educational needs. Parents have no legal obligation to notify the local authority that a child is being educated at home, but if they take a child out of school, they must notify the school in writing and the school must report this to the local authority. Local authorities can make informal enquiries of parents to establish that a suitable education is being provided. For children in special schools, parents must seek the consent of the local authority before taking steps to educate them at home.

In Northern Ireland, ELBs monitor the quality of home provision and provide general guidance on appropriate materials and exam types through regular home visits.

The home schooling law in Scotland is similar to that of England. One difference, however, is that if parents wish to take a child out of school they must have permission from the local education authority.

HOME EDUCATION ADVISORY SERVICE
T 01707-371854 W www.heas.org.uk
HOME EDUCATION IN NORTHERN IRELAND
W www.hedni.org
SCHOOLHOUSE HOME EDUCATION ASSOCIATION
(SCOTLAND) T 01307-463120
E contact@schoolhouse.org.uk W www.schoolhouse.org.uk
EDUCATION OTHERWISE T 0845-4786345
W www.educationotherwise.org

FURTHER EDUCATION

In the UK, further education (FE) is generally understood as post-secondary education, ie any education undertaken after an individual leaves school that is below higher education level. FE therefore embraces a wide range of general and vocational study, full-time or part-time, undertaken by people of all ages from 16 upwards who may be self-funded, employer-funded or state-funded.

There are three types of technical and applied qualifications for 16- to 19-year-olds: level 3 tech levels which equip people to specialise in specific technical jobs; level 2 technical certificates to help them get employment or progress to another tech level; and applied general qualifications which prepare them to continue general education at advanced level through applied learning.

FE in the UK is often undertaken at further education colleges, although some takes place on employers' premises. Many of these colleges offer some courses at higher education level; some FE colleges teach certain subjects to 14- to 16-year-olds under collaborative arrangements with schools. Colleges' income comes from public funding, student fees and work for and with employers.

HIGHER EDUCATION

Higher education (HE) in the UK describes courses of study, provided in universities, specialist colleges of higher education and in some FE colleges, where the level of instruction is above that of A-level or equivalent exams.

All UK universities and colleges that provide HE are autonomous bodies with their own internal systems of governance. They are not owned by the state. However, most receive a portion of their income from state funds distributed by the Office for Students in England (*see* Recent Developments), the Higher Education Funding Council for Wales, the Scottish Funding Council or the Department for the Economy in Northern Ireland. The rest of their income comes from a number of sources including fees from home and overseas students, government funding for research, endowments and work with or for business.

EXPENDITURE

TOTAL-MANAGED EXPENDITURE ON EDUCATION
(Real terms adjusted to 2017–18 price levels) £bn

2013–14	87.4
2014–15	92.3
2015–16	84.8
2016–17	91.0
2017–18	96.1
2018–19 (est)	98.0

Source: HM Treasury – *Public Expenditure Statistical Analyses (PESA)* July 2018

SCHOOLS

ENGLAND AND WALES

In England and Wales, publicly funded schools are referred to as 'state schools'. Local authorities have a duty to ensure there is a suitable place for every school-age child resident in their area. Local authorities maintain four categories of state school – Community, Foundation, Voluntary-aided and Voluntary-controlled. Each school has a governing body – made up of volunteers elected or appointed by parents, staff, the community and the local authority – which is responsible for strategic management, ensuring accountability, monitoring school performance, setting budgets and appointing the headteacher and senior staff. The headteacher is responsible for the school's day-to-day management and operations and for decisions requiring professional teaching expertise.

In *Community schools,* which are non-denominational, local authorities are the employers of the staff, own the land and buildings and set the admissions criteria.

In *Foundation schools,* the governing body employs the staff and sets the admissions criteria. The land and buildings are usually owned by the governing body or a charitable foundation. A Foundation school may have a religious character, although most do not. A *Trust school* is a distinct type of foundation school that forms a charitable trust with an outside partner – for example a business, a university, an educational charity or simply another school – that shares the school's aspirations.

Most *Voluntary-aided schools* are religious schools founded by Christian denominations or other faiths. As with Foundation schools, the governing body employs the staff and sets the admissions criteria, which may include priority for members of the faith or denomination. The school buildings and land are normally owned and provided by a charitable foundation, often a religious organisation, which appoints a majority of the school's governors and makes a small contribution to major building costs.

Voluntary-controlled schools are similar to Voluntary-aided schools in that they often have a particular religious ethos, commonly Church of England, and the school land and buildings are normally owned by a charity. However, as with Community schools, the local authority employs the school's staff, sets the admissions criteria and bears all the costs.

Among the local authority-maintained schools are some with particular characteristics:

- *Community and Foundation Special schools* cater for children with specific special educational needs, which may include physical disabilities or learning difficulties
- *Grammar schools* are secondary schools catering for pupils aged 11 to 18 that select all of their pupils based on academic ability. In England there are 164 grammar schools, concentrated in certain local authority areas. Wales has none
- *Maintained boarding schools* are state-funded and offer free tuition but charge fees for board and lodging

In Wales, Welsh-medium primary and secondary schools were first established in the 1950s and 1960s, originally in response to the wishes of Welsh-speaking parents who wanted their children to be educated through the medium of the Welsh language. Now, many children who are not from Welsh-speaking homes also attend Welsh-medium and bilingual schools throughout Wales. There are 420 Welsh-medium primary schools where instruction is mainly or solely in the Welsh language, six Welsh-medium middle schools and 49 Welsh-medium secondary schools, where more than half of foundation subjects (other than English and Welsh) and religious education are taught wholly or partly in Welsh.

England now has increasing numbers of *Academies.* Those set up before the Academies Act 2010 were sponsored by business, faith or voluntary groups who contributed to funding their land and buildings, while the government covered the running costs at a level comparable to other local schools. The Academies Act 2010 streamlined the process of becoming an academy, enabled high-performing schools to convert without a sponsor and allowed primary and special schools to become academies. All academies now receive funding from central government at the level they would have received if still maintained by their local authority, with extra funding only to cover those services the local authority no longer provides. Academies have greater freedoms over how they use their budgets, set staff pay and conditions and deliver the curriculum. As at March 2018 there were 7,317 open academies, of which 4,721 were primary schools.

SCOTLAND

Most schools in Scotland, known as 'publicly funded' schools, are state-funded and charge no fees. Funding is met from resources raised by the Scottish local authorities and from an annual grant from the Scottish government. Scotland does not have school governing bodies like the rest of the UK: local authorities retain greater responsibility for the management and performance of publicly funded schools. Headteachers manage at least 80 per cent of a school's budget, covering staffing, furnishings, repairs, supplies, services and energy costs. Spending on new buildings, modernisation projects and equipment is financed by the local authority within the limits set by the Scottish government.

Scotland has 370 state-funded *faith schools,* the majority of which are Catholic. It has no grammar schools.

Integrated community schools form part of the Scottish government's strategy to promote social inclusion and to raise educational standards. They encourage closer and better joint working among education, health and social work agencies and professionals, greater pupil and parental involvement in schools, and improved support and service provision for vulnerable children and young people.

Scotland has eight *grant-aided schools* that are independent of local authorities but supported financially by the Scottish government. These schools are managed by boards and most of them provide education for children and young people with special educational needs.

NORTHERN IRELAND

Most schools in Northern Ireland are maintained by the state and generally charge no fees, though fees may be charged in preparatory departments of some grammar schools. There are different types of state-funded schools, each under the control of management committees, which also employ the teachers.

Controlled schools (nursery, primary, special, secondary and grammar schools) are managed by Northern Ireland's five ELBs through boards of governors consisting of teachers, parents, members of the ELB and transferor representatives (mainly from the Protestant churches).

Catholic maintained schools (nursery, primary, special and secondary) are under the management of boards of governors consisting of teachers, parents and members nominated by the employing authority, the Council for Catholic Maintained Schools (CCMS).

Other maintained schools (primary, special and secondary) are, in the main, Irish-medium schools that provide education in an Irish-speaking environment. The Department of Education has a duty to encourage and facilitate the development of Irish-medium education. Northern Ireland has 29 standalone Irish-medium schools, most of them primary schools, and 11 Irish-medium units attached to English-medium host schools.

Voluntary schools are mainly grammar schools (66 in 2017–18), which select most pupils according to academic ability. They are managed by boards of governors consisting of teachers, parents and, in most cases, representatives from the Department of Education and the ELB.

Integrated schools (primary and secondary) educate pupils from both the Protestant and Catholic communities as well as those of other faiths and no faith; each school is managed by a board of governors. There are at present 65 integrated schools maintained by the state, 27 of which are controlled schools.

Since 2013 all pupils are guaranteed access to a wide range of courses, with a minimum of 24 courses at Key Stage 4, and 27 at post-16. At least one-third of the courses on offer will be academic and another third will be vocational. Schools work with other schools, FE colleges and other providers to widen the range of courses on offer.

INDEPENDENT SCHOOLS

Around 6 per cent of UK schoolchildren are educated by privately funded 'independent' schools that charge fees and set their own admissions policies. Independent schools are required to meet certain minimum standards but need not teach the National Curriculum. *See also* Independent Schools.

UK SCHOOLS BY CATEGORY (2016–17)

	England	Wales
*Maintained nursery schools	402	11
†Maintained primary and secondary schools	14,118	1,497
Community	7,840	–
Voluntary-aided	3,298	–
Voluntary-controlled	2,095	–
Foundation	885	–
Pupil Referral Units	351	–
Maintained Special schools	973	39
‡Non-maintained Special schools	64	–
‡Academies	6,076	–
Independent schools	2,297	70
Total	24,281	1,617

* Includes one direct grant school in England
† Includes seven middle schools in Wales
‡ Includes City Technology Colleges, University Technology Colleges, studio schools and free schools; excludes voluntary and private pre-school education centres and academies and free schools alternative provision
Source: Department for Education; Welsh government

SCOTLAND

Publicly funded schools	2,515
Primary	2,025
Secondary	358
Special	132
Independent schools	99
Total	2,614

Source: Scottish government

NORTHERN IRELAND

State-maintained nursery schools	95
State-maintained primary and secondary schools	1,022
Controlled	432
Voluntary	61
Catholic maintained	434
Other maintained	30
Integrated	65
*Special schools	40
Independent schools	14
Total	1,171

* Includes one hospital school

Source: DENI

INSPECTION

ENGLAND

The Office for Standards in Education, Children's Services and Skills (Ofsted) is the main body responsible for inspecting education in English schools. As well as inspecting all publicly funded and some independent schools, Ofsted inspects a range of other services in England, including childcare, children's homes, pupil referral units, local authority children's services, further education, initial teacher training and publicly funded adult skills training. Inspection reports, recommendations and statistical information are published on Ofsted's website.

Ofsted is an independent, non-ministerial government department that reports directly to parliament, headed by Her Majesty's Chief Inspector (HMCI). Ofsted is required to promote improvement in the public services that it inspects; ensure that these services focus on the interests of their users – children, parents, learners and employers; and see that these services are efficient, effective and promote value for money. A new 'common inspection regime' came into effect in September 2015 to make inspections of different settings with similar age groups more coherent.

From October 2017, Ofsted changed the current system of giving all schools previously judged 'good' short (one-day) inspections. Where it is clear on the day that a full inspection is needed, the full inspection will be completed within 15 working days rather than 48 hours. Ofsted will also select around one in five good schools for full inspections in advance.

OFFICE FOR STANDARDS IN EDUCATION, CHILDREN'S SERVICES AND SKILLS **T** 0300-123 1231
W www.gov.uk/government/organisations/ofsted

WALES

Estyn is the office of Her Majesty's Inspectorate for Education and Training in Wales. It is independent of, but funded by, the Welsh government and is led by Her Majesty's Chief Inspector of Education and Training in Wales.

Estyn's role is to inspect quality and standards in education and training in Wales, including in primary, secondary, special and independent schools, pupil referral units, publicly funded nursery schools and settings, further education, adult community-based and work-based learning, local authorities and teacher education and training.

Estyn also provides advice on quality and standards in education and training to the Welsh government and others and its remit includes making public good practice based on inspection evidence. Estyn publishes on its website the findings of its inspection reports, its recommendations and statistical information.

From September 2017, the inspection regime changed to focus on: standards; wellbeing and attitudes to learning; teaching and learning experiences; care, support and guidance; leadership and management; and a thematic area.

Reports are now shorter and no longer feature an overall judgement on current performance or prospects for improvement. Many aspects previously covered in reports are only included by exception, in particularly strong or weak cases. The notice period for inspections has been reduced to 15 days, with inspections typically taking four days rather than five. Follow-up work will be more supportive.

HER MAJESTY'S INSPECTORATE FOR EDUCATION AND TRAINING IN WALES **T** 029-2044 6446
W www.estyn.gov.uk

SCOTLAND

HM Inspectorate of Education (HMIE) merged with Learning and Teaching Scotland in July 2011 to become Education Scotland, an executive agency of the Scottish government. Education Scotland operates independently and impartially while being directly accountable to Scottish ministers for the standards of its work. The agency's core business is inspection and review. It is responsible for delivering measurable year-on-year improvements, with maximum efficiency, by promoting excellence, building on strengths, and identifying and addressing underperformance. Since August 2015, inspections take account of national expectations of progress in implementing Curriculum for Excellence.

Inspection reports and reviews, recommendations, examples of good practice and statistical information are published on Education Scotland's website.

EDUCATION SCOTLAND **T** 0131-244 4330 **W** https://education.gov.scot

NORTHERN IRELAND

The Education and Training Inspectorate (ETINI) provides inspection services for the Department of Education and the Department for the Economy in Northern Ireland.

ETINI carries out inspections of all schools, pre-school services, special education, further education colleges, initial teacher training, training organisations, and curriculum advisory and support services. Since September 2013 regional colleges of further education have received four weeks' notice of inspection, while all other organisations have received two weeks' notice.

The inspectorate's role is to improve services and provide ministers with evidence-based advice to assist in policy formulation. It publishes the findings of its inspection reports, its recommendations and statistical information on its website.

EDUCATION AND TRAINING INSPECTORATE **T** 028-9127 9726 **W** www.etini.gov.uk

THE NATIONAL CURRICULUM

ENGLAND

The National Curriculum, first introduced in 1988, is mandatory in all state schools for children from age five onwards.

Until age five, or the end of Reception Year in primary school, children are in the Early Years Foundation Stage

(EYFS), which has its own learning and development requirements for children in nursery and primary schools. Changes to the EYFS came into effect in 2012, 2014 and 2017. These included simplifying the statutory assessment of children's development at age five; reducing the number of early learning goals from 69 to 17; focusing on seven areas of learning and development (communication and language; physical development; personal, social and emotional development; literacy; mathematics; understanding the world; and expressive arts and design) and, for parents, a new progress check on their child's development between the ages of two and three.

After the Foundation Stage the National Curriculum is organised into 'Key Stages', and sets out the core subjects that must be taught and the standards or attainment targets for each subject at each Key Stage.

- Key Stage 1 covers Years 1 and 2 of primary school, for children aged 5–7
- Key Stage 2 covers Years 3 to 6 of primary school, for children aged 7–11
- Key Stage 3 covers Years 7 to 9 of secondary school, for children aged 11–14
- Key Stage 4 covers Years 10 and 11 of secondary school, for children aged 14–16

Within the framework of the National Curriculum, schools may plan and organise teaching and learning in the way that best meets the needs of their pupils, but maintained schools are expected to follow the programmes of study associated with particular subjects. The programmes of study describe the subject knowledge, skills and understanding that pupils are expected to have developed by the end of each Key Stage.

The government brought in a new National Curriculum for England for maintained primary and secondary schools from September 2014. From September 2017 schools have taught the new programmes of study to all pupils in all Key Stages.

COMPULSORY SUBJECTS IN KEY STAGES 1 AND 2	
English	Design and technology
Mathematics	Geography
Science	History
Art and design	Music
Computing	Physical education (incl. swimming)

Foreign languages are compulsory in Key Stage 2, but not Key Stage 1: schools can choose from French, German, Italian, Mandarin, Spanish, Latin and Ancient Greek.

In Key Stage 3, compulsory subjects include those compulsory for Key Stage 2 (though the language taught should be a modern foreign language) plus citizenship.

Pupils in Key Stage 4 study a mix of compulsory and optional subjects in preparation for national examinations such as GCSEs. The compulsory subjects are English, mathematics, science, citizenship, computing and physical education. Key Stage 4 pupils also have to undertake careers education and work-related learning. In addition, schools must offer at least one subject from each of four 'entitlement' areas: arts (art and design, music, dance, drama and media arts); design and technology; humanities (history and geography); and modern foreign languages. To meet the entitlement requirements, schools must ensure that courses in these areas lead to approved qualifications, and must allow pupils to take courses in all four areas if they wish to do so.

Schools must teach religious education (RE) at all key stages, although parents have the right to withdraw children from all or part of the subject. Secondary schools must provide sex and relationship education.

ASSESSMENT

Statutory assessment must be undertaken for all pupils in publicly funded schools in the relevant years. It first takes place towards the end of the Early Years Foundation Stage, when children's level of development is compared to and recorded against a Foundation Stage Profile. This will continue to be statutory until the end of the 2017–18 academic year. Pupils receive a phonics screening check at the end of the first year in Key Stage 1, repeated the following year if necessary. Teacher assessments in English, mathematics and science take place at the end of Key Stage 1 (Year 2) and Key Stage 2 (Year 6); at the end of Key Stage 3 (Year 9) teachers assess progress in all subjects being studied. National tests in English and mathematics take place in Year 6. At Key Stage 4, national examinations are the main form of assessment.

The assessment process for English at the end of Key Stage 2 now involves three elements: English reading; English grammar, punctuation and spelling.

Key stage 2 results no longer use the previous system of levels. Instead, test results are converted into 'scaled scores', with a score of 100 being the expected standard. Any score below 100 means the pupil is working 'towards the expected standard'; any score above 100 means the pupil is working 'above the expected standard'. Previously the expected standard was a level 4.

Each year the Department for Education publishes on its website performance tables covering every school, college and local authority. The primary school tables are based mainly on the results of the tests taken by children at the end of Key Stage 2 when they are usually aged 11; since 2010 teacher assessment results are also included.

Headline indicators in the secondary school tables are: pupils' average progress and attainment across eight specified subjects; percentages of pupils achieving passes and strong passes (grades 5 and above) in English and maths; percentages of pupils entering and achieving strong passes in the English Baccalaureate (the EBacc is made up of English, maths, two sciences, a language and history or geography); and the percentage of pupils staying in education or employment for at least two terms after Key Stage 4.

DEPARTMENT FOR EDUCATION T 0370-000 2288
W www.gov.uk/government/organisations/
department-for-education

WALES

A new curriculum for 3- to 16-year-olds in Wales is expected to be available for feedback by April 2019 and in use by 2022 (*see* below). For now a Foundation Phase curriculum for 3- to 7-year-olds, introduced in September 2008, places emphasis on learning by doing. Children's skills and knowledge are planned across seven areas of learning. They are:

- Personal and social development, well-being and cultural diversity
- Language, literacy and communication skills
- Mathematical development
- Welsh language development
- Knowledge and understanding of the world
- Physical development
- Creative development

Full details of the Foundation Phase can be found in *Framework for Children's Learning for 3- to 7-year-olds in Wales*, available on the Welsh government website (*see* below).

Currently the National Curriculum is for 7- to 16-year-olds. Originally it was broadly similar to that of England, with distinctive characteristics for Wales reflected in the programmes of study. From September 2008 a revised school curriculum was implemented, consisting of the National Curriculum subjects together with non-statutory frameworks for personal and social education, the world of work, religious education and skills.

The National Curriculum in Wales includes the following subjects:

- *Key Stage 2* – English, Welsh, mathematics, science, design and technology, ICT, history, geography, art and design, music, and physical education
- *Key Stage 3* – as Key Stage 2, plus a modern foreign language
- *Key Stage 4* – English, Welsh, mathematics, science and physical education

Welsh is compulsory for pupils at all key stages, either as a first or as a second language. In 2010, 16.5 per cent of pupils were taught Welsh as a first language. In April 2012, the Minister for Education and Skills approved an action plan to raise standards and attainment in Welsh second language education.

Qualified for Life, the new curriculum for Wales from age 3 to 16, is being developed and was tested in 106 Pioneer schools in 2016 with the aim of making it available to all settings and schools, originally by September 2018, now by 2019. The purpose of the curriculum in Wales is to develop children and young people as:

- Ambitious, capable learners, ready to learn throughout their lives
- Enterprising, creative contributors, ready to play a full part in life and work
- Ethical, informed citizens of Wales and the world
- Healthy, confident individuals, ready to lead fulfilling lives as valued members of society

The new curriculum will include:

- Six areas of learning and experience from 3 to 16 years old
- Three cross-curriculum responsibilities: literacy, numeracy and digital competence
- Progression reference points at ages 5, 8, 11, 14 and 16
- Achievement outcomes which describe expected achievements at each progression reference point

The six Areas of Learning and Experience will be:

- Expressive arts
- Health and well-being
- Humanities (including RE which should remain compulsory to age 16)
- Languages, literacy and communication (including Welsh, which should remain compulsory to age 16, and modern foreign languages)
- Mathematics and numeracy
- Science and technology (including computer science)

All teachers should be responsible for developing literacy, numeracy and digital competence across the curriculum.

The Pioneer schools had developed individual action plans and the Digital Competence Framework was available from September 2016. From 2017 to 2021 the Welsh Assembly will help schools and teachers to prepare for the new curriculum. Final curriculum and assessment arrangements will be available by January 2020. First teaching of all year groups from primary school to Year 7 will begin in September 2022 and the new curriculum will roll out from this point.

ASSESSMENT

Statutory testing at the end of Key Stage 2 was removed for pupils in Wales from 2004–5, leaving only statutory teacher assessment which takes place at the end of Key Stage 1 (the Foundation Phase) and Key Stage 3, and is being strengthened by moderation and accreditation arrangements.

A National Literacy and Numeracy Framework (LNF), outlining the skills 5- to 15-year-olds are expected to acquire, became statutory from September 2013. For literacy, this means children should become accomplished in reading for information, writing for information and expressing themselves fluently and grammatically in speech. In numeracy, children are expected to develop numerical reasoning and use number skills, measuring skills and data skills.

National reading and numeracy tests for pupils in Years 2 to 9 started in Wales in May 2013. The tests are designed to give teachers a clearer insight into a learner's development and progress, to allow them to intervene at an earlier stage if learners are falling behind.

The reading test includes a statutory 'core' test, and a set of optional test materials to help teachers to investigate learners' strengths and development needs in more depth.

The numeracy test is split into two papers: numerical procedures and numerical reasoning. The procedural paper consists of a set of questions designed to assess the basic, essential numeracy skills such as addition, multiplication and division.

A numerical reasoning paper was introduced in May 2014. It assesses learners' ability to find the most effective ways to solve everyday numeracy problems.

Learners in Welsh-medium schools take a reading test in Welsh only in Years 2 and 3, but in both English and Welsh from Year 4 onwards. Schools have the option to use both tests in Year 3. Learners take the numeracy test in either English or Welsh.

THE WELSH GOVERNMENT – EDUCATION AND SKILLS W https://curriculumforwales.gov.wales
W www.learning.wales.gov.uk

SCOTLAND

The curriculum in Scotland is not prescribed by statute but is the responsibility of education authorities and individual schools. However, schools and authorities are expected to follow the Scottish government's guidance on management and delivery of the curriculum, which is primarily through Education Scotland.

Scotland is now implementing *Curriculum for Excellence,* which aims to provide more autonomy for teachers, greater choice and opportunity for pupils and a single coherent curriculum for all children and young people aged 3 to 18.

The purpose of Curriculum for Excellence is encapsulated in 'the four capacities': to enable each child or young person to be a successful learner, a confident individual, a responsible citizen and an effective contributor. It focuses on providing a broad curriculum that develops skills for learning, skills for life and skills for work, with a sustained focus on literacy and numeracy. The period of education from pre-school through to the end of secondary stage 3, when pupils reach 14, aims to provide every young person in Scotland with this broad general education.

Curriculum for Excellence sets out 'experiences and outcomes', which describe broad areas of learning and what is to be achieved within them. They are:

- Expressive arts (including art and design, dance, drama, music)
- Health and well-being (including physical education, food and health, relationships and sexual health and mental, physical and social well-being)
- Languages
- Mathematics
- Religious and moral education
- Sciences
- Social studies (including history, geography, society and economy)
- Technologies (including business, computing, food and textiles, craft, design, engineering and graphics)

The experiences and outcomes are written at five levels with progression to examinations and qualifications during the senior phase, which covers secondary stages 4 to 6 when students are generally aged 14 to 17. The framework is designed to be flexible so that pupils can progress at their own pace.

Level	Stage
Early	The pre-school years and primary 1 (ages 3–5), or later for some
First	To the end of primary 4 (age 8), but earlier or later for some
Second	To the end of primary 7 (age 11), but earlier or later for some
Third and Fourth	Secondary 1 to secondary 3 (ages 12–14), but earlier for some. The fourth level experiences and outcomes are intended to allow choice, and young people's programmes will not include all of the fourth level outcomes
Senior phase	Secondary 4 to secondary 6 (ages 15–18), and college or other studies

Under the new curriculum, assessment of students' progress and achievements from ages 3 to 15 is carried out by teachers who base their assessment judgments on a range of evidence rather than single assessment instruments such as tests. Teachers have access to an online National Assessment Resource, which provides a range of assessment material and national exemplars across the curriculum areas.

In the senior phase, young people aged 16 to 18, including those studying outside school, build up a portfolio of national qualifications, awarded by the Scottish Qualifications Authority (SQA).

Provision is made for teaching in Gaelic in many parts of Scotland and the number of pupils in Gaelic-medium education, from nursery to secondary, is growing.

EDUCATION SCOTLAND T 0113-1244 4330 W https://education.gov.scot

SCOTTISH QUALIFICATIONS AUTHORITY
    T 0345-279 1000 W www.sqa.org.uk

NORTHERN IRELAND

Children aged four to 16 in all grant-aided schools in Northern Ireland must be taught the curriculum put in place in September 2009. The statutory curriculum for Years 1 to 12 places greater emphasis on developing skills and preparing young people for life and work.

This curriculum includes a Foundation Stage to cover Years 1 and 2 of primary school, to allow a more appropriate learning style for the youngest pupils and to ease the transition from pre-school. Key Stage 1 covers primary Years 3 and 4, until children are 8, and Key Stage 2 covers primary Years 5, 6 and 7, until children are 11. Post-primary, Key Stage 3 covers Years 8, 9 and 10 and Key Stage 4 covers Years 11 and 12.

The primary curriculum is made up of the following areas of learning:

- Language and literacy
- Mathematics and numeracy
- The arts
- The world around us
- Personal development and mutual understanding
- Physical education
- Religious education

The post-primary curriculum includes a new area of learning for life and work, made up of employability, personal development, local and global citizenship and home economics (at Key Stage 3). It is also made up of RE and the following areas of learning:

- Language and literacy
- Mathematics and numeracy
- Modern languages
- The arts
- Environment and society
- Physical education
- Science and technology

At Key Stage 4, there are nine areas of learning, but statutory requirements are reduced to learning for life and work, physical education and RE. The aim is to provide greater choice and flexibility for pupils and allow them access to a wider range of academic and vocational courses provided under the revised curriculum's 'Entitlement Framework' (EF).

Since September 2013, schools have been required to provide pupils with access to at least 18 courses at Key Stage 4 and 21 courses at post-16. This increased to 24 and 27 courses respectively in September 2015. At least one third of the courses must be 'general' with one third 'applied'. The remaining third is at the discretion of each school. Individual pupils decide on the number and mix of courses they wish to follow.

RE is a compulsory part of the Northern Ireland curriculum, although parents have the right to withdraw their children from part or all of RE or collective worship. Schools have to provide RE in accordance with a core syllabus drawn up by the province's four main churches (Church of Ireland, Presbyterian, Methodist and Roman Catholic) and specified by the Department of Education.

Revised assessment and reporting arrangements were introduced when the curriculum was revised. The focus from Foundation to Key Stage 3 is on 'Assessment for Learning'. This programme includes classroom-based teacher assessment, computer-based assessment of literacy and numeracy and pupils deciding on their strengths and weaknesses and how they might progress to achieve their potential. Assessment information is given to parents in an annual report. Pupils at Key Stage 4 and beyond continue to be assessed through public examinations.

The Council for the Curriculum, Examinations and Assessment (CCEA), a non-departmental public body reporting to the Department of Education in Northern Ireland, is unique in the UK in combining the functions of a curriculum advisory body, an awarding body and a qualifications regulatory body. It advises the government on what should be taught in Northern Ireland's schools and colleges, ensures that the qualifications and examinations offered by awarding bodies in Northern Ireland are of an appropriate quality and standard and, as the leading awarding body itself, offers a range of qualifications including GCSEs, A-levels and AS-levels.

The CCEA hosts a dedicated curriculum website covering all aspects of the revised curriculum, assessment and reporting.

COUNCIL FOR THE CURRICULUM, EXAMINATIONS
    AND ASSESSMENT T 028-9026 1200 W www.ccea.org.uk

QUALIFICATIONS

ENGLAND, WALES AND NORTHERN IRELAND

There is a very wide range of public examinations and qualifications available, accredited by the Office of Qualifications and Examinations Regulation (OFQUAL) in England, Qualifications Wales in Wales and the Council for the Curriculum, Examinations and Assessment (CCEA) in Northern Ireland. Up-to-date information on all accredited qualifications and awarding bodies is available online at the Register of Regulated Qualifications website.

The qualifications frameworks group all accredited qualifications into levels. All the qualifications within a level place similar demands on individuals as learners. Entry level, for example, covers basic knowledge and skills in English, maths and ICT not geared towards specific occupations, level

3 includes qualifications such as A-levels which are appropriate for those wishing to go on to higher education, level 7 covers Master's degrees and vocational qualifications appropriate for senior professionals and managers and level 8 is equivalent to a doctorate.

Young people aged 14 to 19 in schools or (post-16) colleges or apprenticeships may gain academic qualifications such as GCSEs, AS-levels and A-levels; qualifications linked to particular career fields, like diplomas; vocational qualifications such as BTECs and NVQs; and functional key or basic skills qualifications.

In October 2015, both the National Qualifications Framework (NQF) formerly used in England, Wales and Northern Ireland and its successor the Qualifications and Credit Framework (QCF) for England and Northern Ireland were replaced by the Regulated Qualifications Framework (RQF) for England and the Credit and Qualifications Framework for Wales (CQFW). In Northern Ireland the Council for the Curriculum, Examinations and Assessment (CCEA) regulates qualifications. There is also a Framework for Higher Education Qualifications (FHEQ) for England, Wales and Northern Ireland.

In England, Wales and Northern Ireland there are nine qualification levels:

Entry level – each entry-level qualification is available at three sub-levels: 1, 2 and 3, with level 3 the most difficult.

Entry-level qualifications are: entry-level award; entry-level certificate (ELC); entry-level diploma; entry-level English for speakers of other languages (ESOL); entry-level essential skills; entry-level functional skills; Skills for Life.

Level 1 qualifications are: first certificate; GCSE – grade D, E, F or G (3, 2 or 1 in the new grading structure); level 1 award; level 1 certificate; level 1 diploma; level 1 ESOL; level 1 essential skills; level 1 functional skills; level 1 national vocational qualification (NVQ); music grades 1, 2 and 3.

Level 2 qualifications are: CSE – grade 1; GCSE – grade A*, A, B or C (4 or above in the new grading structure); intermediate apprenticeship; level 2 award; level 2 certificate; level 2 diploma; level 2 ESOL; level 2 essential skills; level 2 functional skills; level 2 national certificate; level 2 national diploma; level 2 NVQ; music grades 4 and 5; O level – grade A, B or C.

Level 3 qualifications are: A level – grade A, B, C, D or E; access to higher education; diploma; advanced apprenticeship; applied general; AS level; international Baccalaureate diploma; level 3 award; level 3 certificate; level 3 diploma; level 3 ESOL; level 3 national certificate; level 3 national diploma; level 3 NVQ; music grades 6, 7 and 8; tech level.

Level 4 qualifications are: certificate of higher education (CertHE); higher apprenticeship; higher national certificate (HNC); level 4 award; level 4 certificate; level 4 diploma; level 4 NVQ.

Level 5 qualifications are: diploma of higher education (DipHE); foundation degree; higher national diploma (HND); level 5 award; level 5 certificate; level 5 diploma; level 5 NVQ.

Level 6 qualifications are: degree apprenticeship; degree with honours – for example bachelor of arts (BA) with honours, bachelor of science (BSc) with honours; graduate certificate; graduate diploma; level 6 award; level 6 certificate; level 6 diploma; level 6 NVQ; ordinary degree without honours.

Level 7 qualifications are: integrated master's degree, for example master of engineering (MEng); level 7 award; level 7 certificate; level 7 diploma; level 7 NVQ; master's degree, for example master of arts (MA), master of science (MSc); postgraduate certificate; postgraduate certificate in education (PGCE); postgraduate diploma.

Level 8 qualifications are: doctorate, for example doctor of philosophy (PHD or DPHIL); level 8 award; level 8 certificate; level 8 diploma.

FRAMEWORK FOR HIGHER EDUCATION QUALIFICATIONS (FHEQ)

This framework applies to degrees, diplomas, certificates and other academic awards (other than honorary degrees and higher doctorates) granted by a higher education provider in the exercise of its degree awarding powers. It starts at RQF level 4 and goes up to level 8 and includes the following qualifications: Certificate of Higher Education; Diploma of Higher Education; Bachelor's degrees; Master's degrees; and Doctoral degrees.

COUNCIL FOR THE CURRICULUM, EXAMINATIONS
   AND ASSESSMENT (NORTHERN IRELAND)
   T 028-9026 1200 W www.ccea.org.uk
QUALIFICATIONS WALES T 01633-373222
   W www.qualificationswales.org
REGISTER OF REGULATED QUALIFICATIONS W http://
   register.ofqual.gov.uk
OFFICE OF QUALIFICATIONS AND EXAMINATIONS
   REGULATION (OFQUAL) T 0300-303 3344
   W www.ofqual.gov.uk

GCSE

The vast majority of pupils in their last year of compulsory schooling in England, Wales and Northern Ireland take at least one General Certificate of Secondary Education (GCSE) exam, though GCSEs may be taken at any age. GCSEs assess the performance of pupils on a subject-specific basis and are mostly taken after a two-year course. They are available in more than 50 subjects, most of them academic subjects, though some, known as vocational or applied GCSEs, involve the study of a particular area of employment and the development of work-related skills. Some subjects are also offered as short-course qualifications, equivalent to half a standard GCSE, or as double awards, equivalent to two GCSEs.

For many years GCSEs were assessed on coursework completed by students during the course as well as exams at the end, and GCSE certificates were awarded on an eight-point scale from A* to G. In most subjects two different papers, higher tier and foundation tier, were provided for different ranges of ability, with grades A*–D available to students taking the higher paper and grades C–G available from the foundation paper.

In England, all traditional GCSEs are being replaced by new GCSEs or, in some subjects, withdrawn. The new GCSEs no longer involve modules and coursework, just exam assessment at the end of the two-year course; a very few subjects (such as music technology) may include an element of non-exam assessment. Only maths, science and foreign language GCSEs will be tiered. New GCSEs are graded 9 to 1, rather than A* to G.

The changeover to new GCSEs is being phased in. In September 2015 schools began teaching revised GCSEs in English language, English literature and mathematics, for exams in 2017. Teaching of revised GCSEs in ancient and modern foreign languages, art and design, biology, chemistry, citizenship, computer science, double science, dance, drama, food preparation and nutrition, geography, history, music, physics, physical education and religious studies started in September 2016 for exams in 2018. Teaching in 14 other subjects started in September 2017 for exams in 2019.

In 2017 English language, English literature and maths were the first subjects to be graded from 9 to 1. Another 20 subjects were graded 9 to 1 in 2018, with most others following in 2019. During this transition, students will receive a mixture of letter and number grades. It will take until summer 2020 for all reformed GCSEs to be graded on the new scale.

In Northern Ireland, new CCEA GCSEs will be introduced for first teaching in 2017, with first awards in 2019 (W www.gov.uk/government/collections/gcse-subject-content). They will be graded on a 9 grade system from A*-G with a new C* grade.

All GCSE specifications, assessments and grading procedures are monitored by OFQUAL, QW and the CCEA.

Since September 2010 state schools have been allowed to offer pupils International GCSE (iGCSE) qualifications in key subjects including English, mathematics, science and ICT. Though iGCSEs were considered more rigorous than traditional GCSEs, the government regards the new GCSEs in these subjects as superior, and has announced that iGCSE results will no longer count in school performance tables from 2017, or later, depending on the subject.

GCE A-LEVEL AND AS-LEVEL

GCE (General Certificate of Education) Advanced levels (A-levels) are the qualifications used by most young people in England, Wales and Northern Ireland to gain entry to university.

A-levels are subject-based qualifications. They are mostly taken by UK students aged 16 to 19 over a two-year course in school sixth forms or at college, but can be taken at any age. They are available in more than 45, mostly academic, subjects, though there are some A-levels in vocational areas, often termed 'applied A-levels'.

Traditionally, A-level qualifications consisted of two parts: advanced subsidiary (AS) and A2 units. The AS was a qualification assessed at the standard expected of a learner half way through an A-level course, normally consisting of two units that together contributed 50 per cent towards the full A-level. The A2 was the second half of a full A-level qualification. It was assessed at the standard expected of a learner at the end of a full A-level course, and normally consisted of two units that together made up the remaining 50 per cent of the full A-level qualification. Each unit was graded A–E, with an A* grade available to exceptional candidates since 2010.

An extended project was introduced in September 2008 as a separate qualification. It is a single piece of work on a topic of the student's own choosing that requires a high degree of planning, preparation, research and autonomous working. Awards are graded A–E and the extended project is accredited as half an A-level.

Since September 2013, students in England in their first or second year of A-level studies have not been allowed to sit A-level exams in January. A-levels are still examined unit by unit, but all exams are taken in the summer.

Revised AS and A-levels were introduced in phases from 2015 to 2017. All assessment of the new A-levels now takes place at the end of the two-year course and the AS has become a standalone qualification rather than contributing to a full A-level qualification.

Since September 2015, students have been taught the new-style AS-levels and A-levels in art and design, biology, business, chemistry, computer science, economics, English language, English language and literature, English literature, history, physics, psychology and sociology. New AS and A-levels in ancient languages, dance, drama and theatre, geography, modern foreign languages (French, German and Spanish), music, physical education and religious studies started to be taught in September 2016.

From September 2017, new-style A-levels were introduced in: accounting, ancient history, archaeology, classical civilisation, design and technology, electronics, film studies, geology, government and politics, history of art, law, maths and further maths, media studies, music technology, philosophy and statistics.
W www.gov.uk/government/collections/gce-as-and-a-level-subject-content

INTERNATIONAL BACCALAUREATE

The International Baccalaureate (IB) offers four educational programmes for students aged 3 to 19: IB primary years programme, IB middle years programme, IB diploma programme, IB career-related certificate.

Some 155 'IB World Schools' in the UK offer at least one IB programme.

The IB diploma programme for students aged 16 to 19 is based around detailed academic study of a wide range of subjects, including languages, the arts, science, maths, history and geography, leading to a single qualification recognised by UK universities.

The IB diploma is made up of a compulsory 'core' plus six separate subjects where individuals have some choice over what they study. The compulsory core contains three elements: theory of knowledge; creativity, action and service; and a 4,000-word extended essay.

The IB diploma normally takes two years to complete and most of the assessment is done through externally marked examinations. Candidates are awarded points for each part of the programme, up to a maximum of 45. A candidate must score 24 points or more to achieve a full diploma.

Successfully completing the diploma earns points on the 'UCAS tariff', the UK system for allocating points to qualifications used for entry to higher education. An IB diploma total of 24 points is worth 260 UCAS points – the same as a B and two C grades at A-level. The maximum of 45 points earns 720 UCAS points – equivalent to six A-levels at grade A.

WELSH BACCALAUREATE

The Welsh Baccalaureate Qualification (WBQ), available for 14- to 19-year-olds in Wales, combines a compulsory core, which incorporates personal development skills, with options from existing academic and vocational qualifications, such as A-levels, GCSEs and NVQs, to make one broader award. The WBQ can be studied in English or Welsh, or a combination of the two. Candidates who meet the requirements of the compulsory core and options relevant to each level of the qualification are awarded the Welsh Baccalaureate Foundation, Intermediate or Advanced Diploma as appropriate.

WJEC (Welsh Joint Education Committee), which administers the WBQ, has also developed two new WBQs at level 1 and level 2 suitable for delivery over one year and with a particular focus on employability.

A revised and more rigorous Welsh Baccalaureate has been taught since September 2015. It is based on a graded Skills Challenge Certificate and supporting qualifications. The aim is to enable learners to develop and demonstrate an understanding of, and proficiency in, essential and employability skills: communication, numeracy, digital literacy, planning and organisation, creativity and innovation, critical thinking and problem solving, and personal effectiveness. The emphasis is on applied and purposeful learning and opportunities for assessment in a range of real life contexts through three 'challenge briefs' and an individual project.

APPLIED GENERAL AND TECH LEVEL QUALIFICATIONS

Tech levels, first taught in schools from September 2014, are a new advanced qualification for students aged 16-19 who wish to specialise in a technical occupation. They take as long to complete as A-levels and, like A-levels, are at level 3; they lead to recognised occupations in, for example, engineering, IT, accounting or hospitality. They must be recognised by a relevant trade or professional body or at least five employers representative of the industry sector or occupation. Many higher education institutions have pledged support for Tech levels.

Tech levels count towards the TechBacc (Technical Baccalaureate) performance measure in the post-16 school and college performance tables from 2016. To achieve the TechBacc, students need an approved level 3 Tech level qualification, an approved level 3 mathematics qualification and the extended project qualification. Additional funding is provided for students who successfully complete a large TechBacc programme (960 guided learning hours or more).

From 2017, post-16 performance tables have also recognised Applied General Qualifications, which take the same time to complete as AS-levels and focus on broader study of a technical area. These are advanced (level 3) qualifications that allow 16 to 19 year old students to develop transferable knowledge and skills. They allow entry to a range of higher education courses, either by meeting the entry requirements in their own right or by adding value to other qualifications such as A-levels.

New 'T-level' qualifications in Digital, Construction and Education and Childcare are due to be taught from 2020 (see also Recent Developments).

BTECS, OCR NATIONALS AND OTHER VOCATIONAL QUALIFICATIONS

Vocational qualifications can range from general qualifications where a person learns skills relevant to a variety of jobs, to specialist qualifications designed for a particular sector. They are available from several awarding bodies, such as City & Guilds, Edexcel and OCR, and can be taken at many different levels. All vocational and work-related qualifications fit into the Regulated Qualifications Framework (RQF).

BTEC qualifications and OCR Nationals are particular types of work-related qualifications, available in a wide range of subjects, including: art and design, business, health and social care, information technology, media, public services, science and sport. The qualifications offer a mix of theory and practice, can include work experience and can be part of an Apprenticeship. They can be studied full-time at college or school, or part-time at college.

Learners complete a range of assignments, case studies and practical activities, as well as a portfolio of evidence that shows what work has been completed.

Since 2016, the quality and assessment of all vocational courses offered by schools and colleges for 14- to 19-year-olds has been strengthened. The standards of reformed BTECs, along with Cambridge OCR National Certificates and Vocational Certificates (V-Certs), equal those of GCSE A*–C grades. All vocational qualifications are graded (previously many were simply pass/fail) and all have a 25 per cent externally examined component. New Substantial Vocational Qualifications at level 2 provide 16- to 19-year-old students seeking entry at a more basic level to a skilled trade or occupation with qualifications that are valued by employers.

NVQs

A National Vocational Qualification (NVQ) is a 'competence-based' qualification that is recognised by employers. Individuals learn practical, work-related tasks designed to help them develop the skills and knowledge to do a particular job effectively. NVQs can be taken in school, at college or by people already in work. There are more than 1,300 different NVQs available from the vast majority of business sectors. NVQs exist at levels 1 to 5 on the RQF. An NVQ qualification at level 2 or 3 can also be taken as part of an Apprenticeship.

Functional Skills

Functional skills qualifications were launched during 2010, for all learners aged 14 and above. They test practical skills that allow people to work confidently, effectively and independently in life, and are available only in England. Wales and Northern Ireland have literacy and numeracy qualifications known as 'Essential Skills'.

In England, the government is reforming functional skills qualifications in English and mathematics. The reformed qualifications will be available for first teaching from September 2019.

Apprenticeships

Apprenticeships combine on-the-job training with nationally recognised qualifications, allowing individuals to gain skills and qualifications while working and earning a wage. More than 200 different types of apprenticeships are available, offering over 1,500 job roles; they take between one and five years to complete. There are four levels available:
- Intermediate Apprenticeships – at level 2 on the Regulated Qualifications Framework (RQF), they are equivalent to five good GCSE passes (9–4)
- Advanced Apprenticeships – at level 3 on the RQF, they are equivalent to two A-level passes/Level 3 Diploma/ International Baccalaureate
- Higher Apprenticeships – levels 4, 5, 6 and 7 equivalent to Foundation degree and above
- Degree Apprenticeships – added in 2015 (RQF level 6 and 7) equivalent to a bachelor's or master's degree

In England, the National Apprenticeship Service (NAS), launched in 2009, is responsible for the delivery of apprenticeships and provides an online vacancy matching system. The way in which the government funds the training and assessment costs of apprenticeships was revised in May 2017, when the apprenticeship levy was introduced. In 2016–17, there were 491,300 apprenticeship starts in England, while 912,200 were participating in an apprenticeship. Some 18 groups of universities have developed new degree apprenticeships, which began in September 2017. The Welsh government and the Department for the Economy are responsible for the apprenticeship programmes in Wales and Northern Ireland respectively.

NATIONAL APPRENTICESHIP SERVICE (NAS)
 T 0800-015 0400 W www.gov.uk/apply-apprenticeship
REGISTER OF APPRENTICESHIP TRAINING
 PROVIDERS W www.gov.uk/guidance/
 register-of-apprenticeship-training-providers

SCOTLAND

Scotland has its own system of public examinations and qualifications. The Scottish Qualifications Authority (SQA) is Scotland's national body for qualifications, responsible for developing, accrediting, assessing and certificating all Scottish qualifications apart from university degrees and some professional body qualifications.

There are qualifications at all levels of attainment. Almost all school candidates gain SQA qualifications in the fourth year of secondary school and most obtain further qualifications in the fifth or sixth year or in further education colleges. Increasingly, people also take qualifications in the workplace.

SQA, with partners such as Universities Scotland, has introduced the Scottish Credit and Qualifications Framework (SCQF) as a way of comparing and understanding Scottish qualifications. It includes qualifications across academic and vocational sectors and compares them by giving a level and credit points. There are 12 levels in the SCQF, level 1 being the least difficult and level 12 the most difficult. The number of SCQF credit points shows how much learning has to be done to achieve the qualification. For instance, one SCQF credit point equals about 10 hours of learning including assessment.

Since reforms introduced in 2013, qualifications in Scotland are divided into academic National Qualifications and more practical-based Qualifications for Work.

National Qualifications
- National 1 units are assessed as a pass or fail by a teacher or lecturer. They could lead to National 2 courses or awards at SCQF level 1 or 2
- National 2 courses are made up of units assessed as pass or fail by a teacher or lecturer. Learners need to pass all units to achieve the qualification. They could lead to National 3 courses or awards at SCQF level 2 or 3
- National 3 courses comprise three National Units assessed as pass or fail by a teacher or lecturer. They could lead to related courses at National 4, awards at SQCF level 3 or 4, National Certificates or National Progression Awards or employment opportunities
- National 4 courses are made up of units, including an added value unit, which assesses learners' performance across the course. They could lead to National 5 courses, units or awards at SCQF level 4 or 5, National Certificate or National Progression Awards, or Modern Apprenticeships or other employment opportunities
- National 5 courses are assessed through exams, coursework or both, most of which is marked by the Scottish Qualifications Authority. Courses are graded 1 to D or 'no award'. They could lead to Higher courses, units or awards at SCQF level 5 or 6, National Certificate or National Progression Awards, Foundation Apprenticeships or a Modern Apprenticeship at SCQF level 6
- Higher courses are made up of exams or coursework (units will be removed from 2018–19) or both, marked by the SQA, or teachers or lecturers in some cases. They could lead to Advanced Higher courses, units or awards at SCQF level 6 or 7, National Certificate or National Progression Awards, Higher National Certificate or Higher National Diplomas, or Modern Apprenticeships at SCQF level 7
- Advanced Higher courses are made up of exams or coursework (units will be removed from 2019–20) or both, marked by the SQA, or teachers or lecturers in some cases. They could lead to a Higher National Diploma, undergraduate degree or a Technical Apprenticeship at SCQF level 8
- Skills for Work courses encourage learners to become familiar with the world of work. They are available in a variety of areas such as construction, hairdressing and hospitality (W www.sqa.org.uk/skillsforwork)
- Scottish Baccalaureates are qualifications at SCQF level 7, and are available for learners in S5 and S6. They exist in Expressive Arts, Languages, Science, and Social Sciences and are awarded as a pass or distinction. Learners undertake an interdisciplinary project, which allows them to develop and show evidence of initiative, responsibility, and independent working – skills of value in the world of higher education (W www.sqa.org.uk/baccalaureates)

Qualifications For Work
- Introduction to Work Place Skills qualification is designed to help 'can do' learners to develop core and employability skills. It comprises an employer-assessed work experience placement of a minimum of 150 hours. Successful completion allows learners to go to Certificate of Work Readiness, further training, education or employment (W www.sqa.org.uk/introtowork)
- Certificate of Work Readiness award includes an employer-assessed work experience placement and is available

through colleges and training providers working in partnership with employers (W www.sqa.org.uk/workready).
- Foundation Apprenticeships are new, work-based learning qualifications for secondary school pupils and allow pupils in S4 to S6 to complete elements of a Modern Apprenticeship while still at school. Depending on their subject, pupils study towards Foundation Apprenticeships alongside their other subjects and spend part of their school week at college or with a local employer. By December 2017, some 18,700 young people had started apprenticeships. (W www.apprenticeships.scot/foundation-apprenticeships).
- Modern Apprenticeships offer anyone aged over 16 paid employment combined with the opportunity to train for jobs at craft, technician and management level. They are developed by the industry or sector in which they will be implemented. (W www.sqa.org.uk/modernapprenticeships or W www.apprenticeships.scot)
- SQA Awards are flexible and nationally recognised. They provide learners with opportunities to acquire skills, recognise achievement and promote confidence
- Wider Achievement qualifications provide young people with the opportunity to have learning and skills formally recognised, whether developed in or outside the classroom. Available at a number of levels in subjects including Employability, Leadership and Enterprise, these qualifications help schools deliver skills for learning, life and work
- Scottish Vocational Qualifications are based on national standards drawn up by people from industry, commerce and education covering a wide range of occupations
- Professional Development Awards develop the skills of those already in professional employment and can be embedded within another qualification such as a Higher National Certificate or Diploma
- National Certificates prepare people for employment, development or progression to advanced study. They are aimed at 16-18 year olds and are at SCQF levels 2 to 6
- National Progression Awards assess a defined set of skills and knowledge in specialist vocational areas, linking to National Occupational Standards, which are the basis of SVQs
- Higher National qualifications are offered by colleges, universities and other training centres. Higher National Certificates, Higher National Diplomas and Professional Development Awards are designed to meet employers' needs and can give candidates access to second or third year entry at university

As part of the Curriculum for Excellence programme SQA developed these revised National qualifications that became available in schools from August 2013, replacing Standard Grade, Intermediate and Access qualifications at all levels. New Higher qualifications became available from August 2014 and Advanced Higher qualifications from August 2015:

SCQF level	New national qualifications	Replaces
1 & 2	National 1 & 2	Access 1 and Access 2
3	National 3	Access 3 Standard Grade (Foundation Level)
4	National 4	Standard Grade (General Level) Intermediate 1
5	National 5	Standard Grade (Credit Level) Intermediate 2
6	Higher (new)	Higher
7	Advanced Higher (new)	Advanced Higher

Revised qualifications were available alongside existing qualifications until 2015–16. Final results for existing Access,

Intermediate, Higher and Advanced Higher qualifications were issued in August 2015.

Since 2017–18 mandatory unit assessments have been removed from the National 5 qualification to reduce teacher and pupil workload. Course assessments for National 5 – a combination of exam and coursework – were strengthened to maintain their integrity, breadth and standards.

Mandatory unit assessment will be removed for Higher courses from 2018–19 and from Advanced Higher courses from 2019–20.

THE SCOTTISH QUALIFICATIONS AUTHORITY (SQA)
   T 0345-279 1000 W www.sqa.org.uk
SCOTTISH CREDIT AND QUALIFICATIONS
   FRAMEWORK (SCQF) T 0845-270 7371
   W www.scqf.org.uk
SKILLS DEVELOPMENT SCOTLAND (SDS)
   T 0800-917 8000 W www.skillsdevelopmentscotland.co.uk

FURTHER EDUCATION AND LIFELONG LEARNING

ENGLAND

The further education (FE) system in England provides a wide range of education and training opportunities for young people and adults. From the age of 16, young people who wish to remain in education, but not in a school setting, can undertake further education (including skills training) in an FE college. There are two main types of college in the FE sector: sixth form colleges and general further education (GFE) colleges. Some FE colleges focus on a particular area, such as art and design or agriculture and horticulture. Each institution decides its own range of subjects and courses. Students at FE colleges can study for a wide and growing range of academic and/or work-related qualifications, from entry level to higher education level.

The Department for Business, Innovation and Skills was responsible for the FE sector and for funding adult FE until July 2016, when these responsibilities passed to the Department for Education, which already funded all education and training for 16- to 18-year-olds.

The proportion of 16- to 18-year-olds in education or training has risen steadily over recent years, driven by increases in state-funded schools and in higher education. The 'September Guarantee', introduced in 2007, offers a place in post-16 education or training to all 16- and 17-year-olds who want one. The latest statistics for 2017, show 81 per cent of young people in full-time education and apprenticeships, and 86 per cent in education and training.

The Education and Skills Funding Agency (ESFA) replaced the Skills Funding Agency and the Education Funding Agency in April 2017. The ESFA is accountable for £63bn of funding for the education and training sector, regulating academies, FE colleges, employers and training providers, intervening where there is risk of failure or where there is evidence of mismanagement of public funds, and delivering major projects in the education and skills sector, such as school capital programmes, the National Careers Service, the digital Apprenticeship Service and National Apprenticeship Service.

In November 2010, the government announced a new strategy for FE, including more adult apprenticeships; fully-funded training for 19- to 24-year-olds undertaking their first full level 2 (GCSE equivalent) or first level 3 qualification; and fully-funded basic skills training for people who left school without basic skills in reading, writing and mathematics. 'Train to Gain', the programme that funded trainees sponsored by employers, was replaced in July 2011 by a programme focused on helping small employers to train low-skilled staff. In April 2012 the National Careers Service was created.

In April 2013, the government announced plans to make the skills system more responsive and to create new traineeships.

There are currently 12 centres of training excellence called National Skills Academies, led, funded and designed by employers, in various stages of development. Each academy offers specialist training in a key sector of the economy, working in partnership with colleges, schools and independent training providers.

Among the many voluntary bodies providing adult education, the Workers' Educational Association (WEA) is the UK's largest, operating throughout England and Scotland. It provides part-time courses to adults in response to local need in community centres, village halls, schools, pubs or workplaces. Similar but separate WEA organisations operate in Wales and Northern Ireland.

In 2016, the National Institute of Adult Continuing Education (NIACE), a charitable non-governmental organisation, merged with the Centre for Economic and Social Inclusion to form the Learning and Work Institute, which promotes lifelong learning opportunities for adults in England and Wales.

LEARNING AND WORK INSTITUTE T 0116-204 4200
   W www.learningandwork.org.uk
THE EDUCATION AND SKILLS FUNDING AGENCY
   W www.gov.uk/government/organisations/
   education-and-skills-funding-agency
WORKERS' EDUCATIONAL ASSOCIATION (WEA)
   T 0300-303346 W www.wea.org.uk
EDUCATION AND TRAINING FOUNDATION
   T 020-3740 8280 W www.et-foundation.co.uk

WALES

In Wales, the aims and makeup of the FE system are similar to those outlined for England. The Welsh government funds a wide range of learning programmes for young people through its 15 FE colleges, local authorities and private organisations. The Welsh government has set out plans to improve learning opportunities for all post-16 learners in the shortest possible time, to increase the engagement of disadvantaged young people in the learning process, and to transform the learning network to increase learner choice, reduce duplication of provision and encourage higher-quality learning and teaching in all post-16 provision.

Responsibility for adult and continuing education lies with the Department for Education and Skills (DfES) within the Welsh government. Wales operates a range of programmes to support skills development, including subsidised work-based training courses for employees and the Workforce Development Programme, where employers can use the free services of experienced skills advisers to develop staff training plans.

COLLEGES WALES T 029-2052 2500
   W www.collegeswales.ac.uk
ADULT LEARNING WALES T 029-2023 5277
   W www.adultlearning.wales
LEARNING AND WORK INSTITUTE T 029-2037 0900
   W www.learningandwork.wales
WEA SOUTH WALES T 029-2023 5277
   W www.swales.wea.org.uk

SCOTLAND

Following a series of mergers, Scotland now has 27 FE colleges (known simply as colleges), which are at the forefront of lifelong learning, education, training and skills in Scotland. Colleges cater for the needs of learners both in and out of employment, at all stages in their lives from middle secondary school and earlier to retirement. Colleges' courses span much of the range of learning needs, from specialised vocational education and training through to general educational programmes. The level of provision ranges from essential life skills and provision for students with learning difficulties to HNCs and HNDs. Some colleges, notably those in the Highlands and Islands, also deliver degrees and postgraduate qualifications.

A shift in study patterns is taking place within the college sector as colleges concentrate on full-time courses aimed at helping people gain employment and no longer fund short courses lasting less than ten hours. Overall figures are stable but this change has led to a decline in part-time study and an increase in full-time study.

The Scottish Funding Council (SFC) is the statutory body responsible for funding teaching and learning provision, research and other activities in Scotland's colleges. Overall strategic direction for the sector is provided by the Lifelong Learning Directorate of the Scottish government, which provides annual guidance to the SFC and liaises closely with bodies such as Colleges Scotland, the Scottish Qualifications Authority and the FE colleges themselves to ensure that policies remain relevant and practical.

The Scottish government takes responsibility for community learning and development in Scotland while Skills Development Scotland, a non-departmental public body, is charged with improving Scotland's skills performance by linking skills supply and demand and helping people and organisations to learn, develop and make use of these skills to greater effect.

ILA SCOTLAND T 0800-917 8000
  W www.myworldofwork.co.uk/learn-and-train/funding
COLLEGES SCOTLAND T 01786-892100
  W www.collegesscotland.ac.uk
SCOTTISH FUNDING COUNCIL T 0131-313 6500
  W www.sfc.ac.uk
SKILLS DEVELOPMENT SCOTLAND T 0800-917 8000
  W www.skillsdevelopmentscotland.co.uk

NORTHERN IRELAND

FE in Northern Ireland is provided through six regional multi-campus colleges and the College of Agriculture, Food and Rural Affairs. Most secondary schools also have a sixth form which students may attend for two additional years to complete their AS-levels and A-levels.

Colleges Northern Ireland acts as the representative body for the six FE colleges which, like their counterparts in the rest of the UK, are independent corporate bodies each managed by their own governing body. The range of courses that they offer spans essential skills, a wide choice of vocational and academic programmes and higher education programmes. Most full-time students in the six colleges are aged 16 to 19, while most part-time students are over 19.

The Department for the Economy is responsible for the policy, strategic development and financing of the statutory FE sector and for lifelong learning, and also provides support to a small number of non-statutory FE providers. The Educational Guidance Service for Adults, an independent, not-for-profit organisation, has a network of local offices based across Northern Ireland that provide services to adult learners, learning advisers, providers, employers and others interested in improving access to learning for adults.

THE EDUCATIONAL GUIDANCE SERVICE FOR ADULTS E info@egsa.org.uk W www.egsa.org.uk
NI DIRECT FE COLLEGES W www.nidirect.gov.uk/contacts/further-education-fe-colleges

FINANCIAL SUPPORT

England has a bursary scheme of up to £1,200 a year for full-time 16- to 19-year-old students facing financial hardship. Two types of bursary exist: vulnerable student bursary and discretionary bursary. Help with transport costs is also possible for some students. This scheme replaced the Education Maintenance Allowance (EMA), which gave 16- to 19-year-olds from low-income families a weekly allowance to continue in education.

There are EMA schemes in Scotland, Wales and Northern Ireland, but with slightly different eligibility conditions. Students must apply to the EMA scheme for the part of the UK where they intend to study. In Northern Ireland 16- to 19-year-old students who meet the relevant criteria and live in a household that has an annual income of £20,500 or less a year (£22,500 if more than one young person in the household qualifies for child benefit) automatically get £30 a week in 2018–19. There is a possibility of two £200 bonus payments too.

Colleges and learning providers award learner support funds directly to new students aged 19 and over.

Care to Learn is available in England to help young parents under the age of 20, who are caring for their own child or children while they are in some form of publicly funded learning (below higher education level), with the costs of childcare and travel. The scheme is not income-assessed and pays up to £160 a week (£175 in London) to cover costs.

Dance and Drama Awards (DaDA) are state-funded scholarships for students aged 16 to 23 enrolled at one of 19 private dance and drama schools in England, who are taking specified courses at National Certificate or National Diploma level. Awards, based on household income, cover some of students' tuition fees and from £1,350 to £5,185 of maintenance in 2018–19.

Young people studying away from home because their chosen course is not available locally may qualify for the *Residential Support Scheme* (up to £3,458 outside London and £4,079 in London for household incomes of less than £21,000).

Information and advice on funding support and applications are available from the Learner Support helpline (T 0800-121 8989) or on the GOV.UK website (*see* below).

Discretionary Support Funds (DSF) are available in colleges and school sixth forms to help students who have trouble meeting the costs of participating in further education.

In Wales, students aged 19 or over on FE courses may be eligible for the *Welsh Government Learning Grant FE* (previously the Assembly Learning Grant for Further Education). This is a means-tested payment of up to £1,500 for full-time students and up to £750 for those studying part-time. *Discretionary Assistance Funds* are also available to all students in Wales suffering hardship.

In Scotland, FE students can apply to their college for discretionary support in the form of *Further Education Bursaries,* which can include allowances for maintenance, travel, study, childcare and additional support needs. *Individual Training Accounts,* which replaced *Individual Learning Accounts* from October 2017, allow eligible students up to £200 a year towards one course a year geared to getting a job.

In Northern Ireland, FE students with annual household incomes below £21,330 may be eligible for *Further Education Awards,* of up to £2,092, non-refundable assistance administered on behalf of the five Education and Library Boards by the Western Education and Library Board.

UK FE students over 18 whose costs are not fully met from the grants described above may also be eligible for *Professional and Career Development Loans*. These loans – also available to HE students – cover up to 80 per cent of course fees (up to 100 per cent for those unemployed for three months); other course costs, such as books, travel and childcare; and living expenses, such as rent, food and clothing (for those who are unemployed or working fewer than 30 hours a week). The loans, of between £300 and £10,000, are available from participating high street banks; but the scheme is due to close, with final applications by 25 January 2019.

EDUCATION AUTHORITY W www.eani.org.uk
GOV.UK W www.gov.uk/further-education-courses/financial-help
MY WORLD OF WORK W www.myworldofwork.co.uk
STUDENT FINANCE WALES T 0300-200 4050
    W www.studentfinancewales.co.uk

HIGHER EDUCATION

Publicly funded higher education (HE) in the UK is provided in universities, higher education colleges and other specialist HE institutions, and in a significant number of FE colleges offering higher education courses.

Since the closure of the Higher Education Funding Council for England (HEFCE) in March 2018, universities and university colleges are funded through UKRI (*see* Recent Developments).

The Higher Education Funding Council for Wales (HEFCW) distributes funding for HE in Wales through Wales' 8 HEIs, the Open University in Wales and some FE colleges.

The Scottish Funding Council (SFC) – which is also responsible for FE in Scotland – is the national strategic body responsible for funding HE teaching and research in Scotland's 19 HEIs and 26 colleges.

In Northern Ireland, HE is provided by two universities, two university colleges, six regional institutes of further and higher education and the Open University (OU), which operates UK-wide. Northern Ireland has no higher education funding body; the Department for the Economy fulfils that role.

All UK universities and a number of HE colleges award their own degrees and other HE qualifications. HE providers who do not have their own degree-awarding powers offer degrees under 'validation arrangements' with other institutions that do have those powers. The OU, for example, runs a validation service which enables a number of other institutions to award OU degrees, after the OU has assured itself that the academic standards of their courses are as high as the OU's own standards.

Each HE institution is responsible for the standards of the awards it makes and the quality of the education it provides to its students, and each has its own internal quality assurance procedures. External quality assurance for HE institutions throughout the UK is provided by the Quality Assurance Agency for Higher Education (QAA).

The QAA is independent of government, funded by subscriptions from all publicly funded UK universities and colleges of HE. Its main role is to safeguard the standards of HE qualifications. It does this by defining standards for HE through a framework known as the academic infrastructure. QAA carries out reviews of the quality of UK HE institutions via a system known as 'institutional audits', advises on a range of HE quality issues and publishes reports on its website.

DEPARTMENT FOR THE ECONOMY (NI)
    T 028-9052 9900 W www.economy-ni.gov.uk
HIGHER EDUCATION FUNDING COUNCIL FOR
    WALES T 029-2085 9698 W www.hefcw.ac.uk
RESEARCH ENGLAND T 0117-905 7600 W https://re.ukri.org
SCOTTISH FUNDING COUNCIL T 0131-313 6500
    W www.sfc.ac.uk

THE QUALITY ASSURANCE AGENCY FOR HIGHER
    EDUCATION T 01452-557000 W www.qaa.ac.uk
See also Universities for information on the Research Excellence Framework and listings of universities in the UK.

STUDENTS APPLYING TO UNIVERSITY			
	2017	2018	*Difference*
Total applicants by 15 Jan*	564,190	559,030	−1%
* Deadline for 2018 cycle			
Source: UCAS			

STUDENTS IN HIGHER EDUCATION 2016–17*		
	Full-time	*Part-time*
HE students	1,798,055	519,825
Postgraduate students	321,220	230,380
Undergraduate students	1,476,835	289,445
* Includes UK, EU and non-EU students		
Source: Higher Education Statistics Authority (HESA) 2018		

UK HIGHER EDUCATION QUALIFICATIONS AWARDED 2016 17		
	Full-time	*Part-time*
First degrees	382,620	31,720
Other undergraduate qualifications	46,340	30,490
Postgraduate Certificate in Education	18,655	795
Other postgraduate research and taught qualifications	171,930	74,745
Total qualifications awarded	619,545	137,750
Source: HESA 2018		

COURSES

HE institutions in the UK mainly offer courses leading to the following qualifications. These qualifications go from levels 4 to 8 on England's Regulated Qualifications Framework, levels 7 to 12 on Scotland's Credit and Qualifications Framework. Individual HEIs may not offer all of these.

Certificates of Higher Education (CertHE) are awarded after one year's full-time study (or equivalent). If available to students on longer courses, they certify that students have reached a minimum standard in their first year.

Diplomas of Higher Education (DipHE) and other *Higher Diplomas* are awarded after two to three years' full-time study (or equivalent). They certify that a student has achieved a minimum standard in first- and second-year courses and, in the case of nursing, third-year courses. They can often be used for entry to the third year of a related degree course.

Foundation degrees are awarded after two years of full-time study (or equivalent). These degrees combine academic study with work-based learning, and have been designed jointly by universities, colleges and employers with a particular area of work in mind. They are usually accepted as a basis for entry to the third year of a related degree course.

Bachelor's degrees, also referred to as *first degrees,* have different titles, Bachelor of Arts (BA) and Bachelor of Science (BSc) being the most common. In England, Wales and Northern Ireland most Bachelor's degree courses are 'with Honours' and awarded after three years of full-time study, although in some subjects the courses last longer. In Scotland, where young people may leave school and go to university a year younger, HE institutions typically offer Ordinary Bachelor's degrees after three years' study and Bachelor's degrees with Honours after four years. Honours degrees are graded as first, upper second (2:1), lower second (2:2), or third. HEIs in England, Wales and Northern Ireland may allow students who fail the first year of an Honours degree by a small margin to transfer to an Ordinary degree course, if they have one. Ordinary degrees may also be awarded to Honours degree students who do not finish an Honours degree course but complete enough of it to earn a pass.

Postgraduate or *Higher degrees.* Graduates may go on to take *Master's degrees,* which involve one or two years' work and can be taught or research-based. They may also take one-year postgraduate diplomas and certificates, often linked to a specific profession, such as the *Postgraduate Certificate in Education* (PGCE) required to become a state school teacher. A *doctorate,* leading to a qualification such as Doctor of Philosophy – a PHD or DPHIL – usually involves at least three years of full-time research.

The framework for HE qualifications in England, Wales and Northern Ireland (FHEQ) and the framework for qualifications of HE institutions in Scotland can both be found on the QAA website, which describes the achievement represented by HE qualifications.

ADMISSIONS

When preparing to apply to a university or other HE college, individuals can compare facts and figures on institutions and courses using the government's Unistats website. This includes details of students' views from the annual National Student Survey. They can also consult the results of the Teaching Excellence Framework, which is an official survey of teaching quality in universities listed on the Office for Students' website (*see also* Recent Developments).

For the vast majority of full-time undergraduate courses, individuals need to apply online through UCAS, the organisation responsible for managing applications to HE courses in the UK. More than half a million people wanting to study at a university or college each year use this UCAS service, which has useful online tools to help students find the right course.

UCAS also provides two specialist applications services used by more than 50,000 people each year: the Conservatoires UK Admissions Service (CUKAS), for those applying to UK music conservatoires, and the Graduate Teacher Training Registry (GTTR), for postgraduate applications for initial teacher training courses in England and Wales and some in Scotland. Details of initial teacher training courses in Scotland can also be obtained from Universities Scotland and from Teach in Scotland, the website created by the Scottish government to promote teaching.

Each university or college sets its own entry requirements. These can be in terms of particular exam grades or total points on the 'UCAS tariff' (UCAS's system for allocating points to different qualifications on a common basis), or be non-academic, like having a health check. HE institutions will make 'firm offers' to candidates who have already gained the qualifications they present for entry, and 'conditional offers' to those who have yet to take their exams or obtain their results. Conditional offers often require a minimum level of achievement in a specified subject, for example '300 points to include grade A at A-level Chemistry'. If candidates' achievements are lower than specified in their conditional offers, the university or college may not accept them; then, if they still wish to go into HE, they need to find another institution through the UCAS 'clearing' process.

The Open University conducts its own admissions. It is the UK's only university dedicated to distance learning and the UK's largest for part-time HE. Because it is designed to be 'open' to all, no qualifications are needed for entry to the majority of its courses.

Individuals can search thousands of UK postgraduate courses and research opportunities on UK graduate careers website Prospects. The application process for postgraduate places can vary between institutions. Most universities and colleges accept direct applications and many accept applications through UKPASS, a free, centralised online service run by UCAS that allows individuals to submit up to ten different applications, track their progress and attach supporting material, such as references.

UNISTATS **W** http://unistats.direct.gov.uk
TEACHING EXCELLENCE FRAMEWORK
   W www.officeforstudents.org.uk/advice-and-guidance/teaching
UCAS **T** 0371-468 0468 **W** www.ucas.com
UNIVERSITIES SCOTLAND **T** 0131-226 1111
   W www.universities-scotland.ac.uk
TEACH IN SCOTLAND **T** 0845-345 4745 **W** https://
   teachinscotland.scot
PROSPECTS **T** 0161-277 5200 **W** www.prospects.ac.uk
UKPASS **T** 0371-334 4447 **W** http://ukpass.ac.uk

TUITION FEES AND STUDENT SUPPORT

TUITION FEES

HE institutions (HEIs) in England, Wales and Northern Ireland charge tuition fees for full-time HE courses. Although students from outside the EU can be charged the full cost of their courses, the tuition fees that HEIs may charge undergraduate degree students from the UK and other EU countries are capped. The maximum fee was set at £9,000 a year in September 2012, but increased to £9,250 in September 2017, where it will remain during 2018–19.

Under the Higher Education and Research Act 2017 the government plans to link higher fees to better teaching, allowing those HEIs with high quality teaching to increase tuition fees in line with inflation in subsequent years. The exact fee depends on the course studied and the institution attended.

Full-time students do not have to pay their fees themselves before or during their course, as tuition fee loans are available to cover the full cost; these do not have to be repaid until the student is working and earning more than a specified amount (*see* below).

In recent years, Scottish HE institutions have charged flat rate fees, set by the Scottish government, to undergraduate students classed as being ordinarily resident in England, Wales or Northern Ireland; though, as explained above, students can get repayable tuition fee loans to cover the cost. Since 2012 universities can set their own fees, up to £9,250 a year, for undergraduates starting courses. Undergraduate students classed as being ordinarily resident in Scotland or another EU country do not have to pay tuition fees at Scottish HE institutions. All tuition fees are paid on their behalf by the Scottish government through the Student Awards Agency for Scotland (SAAS); students must apply for this funding every year. In Wales, maximum tuition fees are £9,000, while in Northern Ireland they are £4,160 for resident and EU students, otherwise £9,250.

STUDENT LOANS, GRANTS AND BURSARIES
England

Students starting their first full-time HE course in 2018–19 can apply through Student Finance England for financial support. Two student loans are available from the government: a *tuition fee loan* of up to £9,250 for 2018–19, or up to £6,165 for a private university or college; and a *maintenance loan* (for students aged under 60) to help with living expenses of up to £8,700 for those living away from home (£11,354 if studying away from home in London), or up to £7,324 for those living with their parents during term time, or up to £9,963 if living and studying abroad for a year.

The tuition fee loan is not affected by household income and is paid directly to the relevant HE institution. A proportion (currently 65 per cent) of the maximum maintenance loan is available irrespective of household income while the rest depends on an income assessment. Student Finance England usually pays the money into the student's own bank account in three instalments, one at the start of each term.

Repayment of both loans does not start until the April after the student has left university or college, or before they are earning over £25,000 a year (£21,000 for postgraduate loans).

At this point the individual's employer will deduct 9 per cent of any salary above the starting limit through the Pay As You Earn (PAYE) system. The self-employed make repayments through their tax returns. Student loans accrue interest from the date they are paid out, until they are repaid in full. Generally, the interest rate for student loans is set in September each year. The latest rate can be found online (W www.studentloanrepayment.co.uk).

For all new full-time students starting HE from September 2016, maintenance grants are replaced by loans. Students whose family income is up to £42,620 will be able to apply in 2018–19 for maintenance grants of up to £8,700 a year (£11,354 in London) – the maximum amount applying only to students with a household income of less than £25,000 a year. Special support grants will also be replaced by maintenance loans.

Students needing extra help may also be entitled to receive disabled students' allowance, adult dependants' grant, childcare grant or parents' learning allowance.

Part-time Higher Education Students are entitled to tuition fee loans (which replaced grants) of up to £6,935 in 2018–19. Part-time students who earn over £21,000 a year have to start paying back their loans after four years even if their course has not finished.

Details are available on the Student Finance England website (W www.gov.uk/student-finance/loans-and-grants). There is a student finance calculator on the website to work out what financial support is available.

Universities and other higher education providers offer their own grants and bursaries, with differing criteria. Bursaries do not have to be repaid. Students should always check with the institution they are planning to attend to find out what extra financial support may be available.

If the student's chosen HE institution runs the *additional fee support scheme*, it could provide extra financial help if the student is on a low income and in certain other circumstances. For students in financial difficulty help may also be available through the institution's *access to learning fund*.

Wales

Welsh students starting a full-time HE course in 2018–19 can apply through Student Finance Wales for the forms of financial support described below.

The system of tuition fee and maintenance loans and grants in Wales is similar to England's, particularly for new students, but continuing Welsh students can also receive a substantial tuition *fee grant*. Maximum maintenance loans are: up to £9,000 for students living away from home (£11,250 if studying away from home in London) and up to £7,650 for those living with their parents during term time.

Welsh-domiciled students may apply for a *Welsh government learning grant* of up to £10,124 to help meet general living costs. This is paid in three instalments, one at the start of each term, like the student maintenance loan. The amount that a student gets depends on household income. The maximum grant is available to those with a household income of £18,370 or under. Those with an income of £59,200 or over will receive £1,000.

There is also a *special support grant* for single parents, student parents or those with disabilities, which is worth up to £5,161 a year in 2018–19. It is paid directly to students and is not offset against student loan borrowing.

Students can use the student finance calculator on the Student Finance Wales website to work out what financial support they may be entitled to.

Welsh HE institutions also hold financial contingency funds to provide discretionary assistance to students experiencing financial difficulties.

For 2018–19 part-time undergraduate higher education students and continuing students studying at least 25 per cent of an equivalent full-time course are entitled to receive a fee loan of £2,625 (£6,935 for a course at a publicly funded university or college elsewhere in the UK, or £4,625 at a private university or college). The maximum amount of grants and loans available is £4,987.50 depending on household income and course intensity.

Childcare Grants, Parents' Learning Allowance, Adult Dependants' Grant, and Disabled Students' Allowances are also available.

STUDENT FINANCE WALES T 0300-200 4050
    W www.studentfinancewales.co.uk

Scotland

Students starting a full-time HE course in 2018–19 can apply through the Student Awards Agency for Scotland for financial support. In 2018–19 students can receive tuition fee help of £1,285 for a HND/HNC, £1,820 for a degree or equivalent or £1,205 at a private university. Living cost support is mainly provided through a *student loan*, the majority of which is income-assessed. The maximum loan for 2018–19 is £7,625.

The *young students' bursary* (YSB) is available to young students from low-income backgrounds and is non-repayable. Eligible students receive this bursary instead of part of the student loan, thus reducing their level of repayable debt. In 2018–19 the maximum annual support provided through YSB is £1,875 if household income is £18,999 or less a year.

The *independent students' bursary* (ISB) similarly replaces part of the loan and reduces repayable debt for low-income students independent of parental support. The maximum paid is £875 a year to those whose household income is £18,999 or less a year.

In 2018–19, students who have come from a care setting will be eligible to apply for a non-means-tested bursary of £7,625 and a grant of £105 a week for accommodation costs. This new bursary replaces the current income-assessed living cost loan and bursary (ISB/YSB) package.

Travel expenses are included within the student loan. There are *supplementary grants* available to certain categories of students such as lone parents (£1,305) and those with dependants (£2,640). Extra help is also available to those who have a disability, learning difficulty or mental health problem.

STUDENT AWARDS AGENCY FOR SCOTLAND
    T 0300-555 0505 W www.saas.gov.uk/forms/funding_guide.pdf

Northern Ireland

Students starting a full-time HE course in 2018–19 can apply through Student Finance Northern Ireland for financial support. The arrangements for both full-time and part-time students are similar to those for England. The main difference is that the income-assessed *maintenance grant* (or *special support grant* for students on certain income-assessed benefits) for new full-time students studying at UK universities and colleges is worth up to £3,475 (for household incomes of £19,203 or less).

Universities and colleges in Northern Ireland can charge up to £4,160 for tuition fees in academic year 2018–19, and students can get a loan for up to this amount. There are tuition fee loans of up to £9,250 for students studying in England, Scotland and Wales.

Loans are available for living costs: £3,750 for study in Northern Ireland, £4,840 for study elsewhere in the UK

(£6,780 in London), £4,840 for study in the Republic of Ireland or £5,770 for study overseas.

STUDENT FINANCE NORTHERN IRELAND
T 0300-100 0077 W www.studentfinanceni.co.uk

Disabled Students' Allowances
Disabled Students' Allowances (DSAs) are grants available throughout the UK to help meet the extra course costs that full-time, part-time and postgraduate (taught or research) students can face as a direct result of a disability, ongoing health condition, mental health condition or specific learning difficulty. They help disabled people to study in HE on an equal basis with other students. They are paid on top of the standard student finance package and do not have to be repaid. The amount that an individual gets depends on the type of extra help needed, not on household income.

In all parts of the UK, the following three allowances are available: a specialist equipment or large items allowance for the entire course (2018–19 maximum rates vary from £5,529 in England to £5,226 in Northern Ireland); an annual non-medical helper allowance (2018–19 maximum rates for full-time students vary from £21,987 in England to £20,938 in Northern Ireland); and an annual general or basic allowance (2018–19 maximum rates for full-time students vary from £1,847 in England to £1,759 in Northern Ireland). Reasonable spending on extra disability-related travel costs can also be reimbursed. Eligible individuals should apply as early as possible to the relevant UK awarding authority.

POSTGRADUATE AWARDS
In England, postgraduate loans for a master's course of £10,609 and doctoral loans of up to £25,000 are available to cover tuition and living costs for the duration of study, dependent on course, age and nationality or residency as well as other factors. Some courses such as a Postgraduate Certificate in Education (PGCE) allow students to qualify for the finance package usually available only to undergraduates. There are also bursaries available for social work and some medical students.

In Wales, master's loans of up to £13,000 and doctoral loans of up to £25,000 are available, while in Northern Ireland up to £5,500 is available to cover course fees only. Eligible full-time and part-time postgraduate students from Scotland aged under 60 can get £5,500 towards tuition fees and living cost loans of £4,500.

There is heavy competition for other postgraduate funding available. Individuals can search for postgraduate awards and scholarships on two websites: Hot Courses and Prospects. They can also search for grants available from educational trusts, often reserved for students from poorer backgrounds or for those who have achieved academic excellence, on W www.gov.uk/grant-bursary-adult-learners or the Family Action website.

In Scotland, student support reforms now enable eligible students to receive a loan of up to £10,000 in any taught postgraduate course up to full Master's level, at any Scottish higher education institute.

DEPARTMENT FOR THE ECONOMY (DE),
NORTHERN IRELAND T 028-9052 9900
W www.nidirect.gov.uk/articles/postgraduate-awards
FAMILY ACTION T 020-7254 6251
W www.family-action.org.uk
HOT COURSES W www.hotcourses.com
POSTGRADUATE SEARCH W www.postgraduatesearch.com
PROSPECTS W www.prospects.ac.uk
STUDENT AWARDS AGENCY FOR SCOTLAND (SAAS)
T 0300-555 0505 W www.saas.gov.uk

TEACHER TRAINING

See Professional Education/Teaching.

EMPLOYEES AND SALARIES

EMPLOYEES

QUALIFIED TEACHERS IN MAINTAINED SCHOOLS
November 2016–17, Full-time equivalent, thousands

	England	Wales	Scotland	NI	UK
Nursery and primary schools	*214.7	12.6	24.5	8.4	260.2
Secondary schools	*193.1	10.6	23.2	9.2	236.1
Special schools	†23.0	0.7	1.8	0.8	26.3
Total	430.8	23.9	49.5	18.4	522.6

* Includes academies and city technology colleges in England
† Includes all centrally employed teachers

SUPPORT STAFF IN MAINTAINED SCHOOLS, ENGLAND AND WALES (2016–17)
Full-time equivalent, thousands

	England	Wales
Teaching assistants	262.8	–
Other support staff	*145.3	–
Total	*408.1	23.6

* Includes academies and city technology colleges in England

ACADEMIC STAFF IN UK HIGHER EDUCATION INSTITUTIONS (2016–17)

	Full-time	Part-time	Total
Professors	16,295	4,255	20,550
Non-professors	122,110	64,210	186,320
Teaching only	15,540	40,590	56,130
Teaching and research	81,515	18,650	100,165
Research only	40,350	8,735	49,085
Neither teaching nor research	1,000	490	1,490

Source: HESA 2017

SALARIES

State school teachers in England and Wales are employed by local authorities or the governing bodies of their schools. All teachers are eligible for membership of the Teachers' Pension Scheme.

There are teaching and learning responsibility payments for specific posts, special needs work and recruitment and retention factors which may be awarded at the discretion of the school governing body or the local authority. There are separate pay ranges for Headteachers and other school leaders. Academies are free to set their own salaries.

In 2013 every school was required to revise its pay and appraisal policies, setting out how pay progression would, in future, be linked to a teacher's performance. From September 2014, school governing bodies were given more flexibility, within the national pay ranges, to determine the pay of headteachers and other school leaders. In July 2018 the Secretary of State for Education announced a pay award from September 2018 of 3.5 per cent for teachers on the main scale, 2 per cent for those on the upper scale and 1.5 per cent for school leaders. From September 2018 the pay of school leaders ranges from £39,965 to £111,006 (Headteachers £45,212 to £111,006) a year outside London and from £47,516 to £118,489 (Headteachers £52,771 to £118,489) a year in Inner London.

After completing initial teacher training and achieving qualified teacher status (QTS), newly qualified teachers

(NQTs) in maintained schools can expect to start on a salary of £23,719 a year in England and Wales (or £29,663 in Inner London). The pay ranges for teachers in England and Wales from September 2018 are:

Main pay range (including NQTs)	
London fringe	£24,859–£36,157
Outer London	£27,595–£38,963
Inner London	£29,663–£40,371
Rest of England and Wales	£23,719–£35,008
Upper pay range	
London fringe	£37,757–£40,520
Outer London	£40,309–£43,348
Inner London	£44,488–£48,244
Rest of England and Wales	£36,646–£39,406

Teachers in Scotland are paid on a seven-point scale where the entry point is for newly qualified teachers undertaking their probationary year. Experienced, ambitious teachers who reach the top of the main pay scale are eligible to become chartered teachers and earn more on a separate pay spine. However, to do so they must study for further professional qualifications. Headteachers and deputies have a separate pay spine as do 'principals' or heads of department. Additional allowances are payable to teachers in circumstances such as working in distant islands and remote schools. Teaching salaries in Scotland were increased by 1 per cent in April 2017 and by a further 1 per cent in January 2018.

Salary scales for teachers in Scotland as at 1 January 2018:

Headteacher/deputy headteacher	£45,111–£88,056
Principal teacher	£39,774–£51,330
Chartered teacher	£37,611–£44,727
Main grade	£22,866–£36,480

Teachers in Northern Ireland have broadly similar pay scales to teachers in England and Wales. Classroom teachers who take on teaching and learning responsibilities outside their normal classroom duties may be awarded one of five teaching allowances. In July 2015 a 1 per cent increase to salary scales was announced; this increase was backdated to September 2014. A further 1 per cent pay increase was awarded from September 2016. As at 1 September 2018, salary scales in Northern Ireland were:

Principal (headteacher)	£43,664–£108,282
School leaders	£38,597–£42,596
Classroom teacher (upper pay scale)	£35,217–£37,870
Classroom teacher (main pay scale)	£22,243–£32,509
Unqualified teacher	£14,151
Teaching allowances	£1,903–£12,272

Since 2007, most academic staff in HE across the UK are paid on a single national pay scale as a result of a national framework agreement negotiated by the HE unions and HE institutions. Staff are paid according to rates on a 51-point national pay spine and academic and academic-related staff are graded according to a national grading structure. As HE institutions are autonomous employers, precise job grades and salaries may vary but the following table outlines salaries that typically tally with certain job roles in HE. In July 2018, higher education unions rejected a 2 per cent pay rise offered by the government and proceeded to a statutory ballot of members in autumn 2018.

The current pay spine is as follows:

Principal lecturer	£47,801–£55,389
Senior lecturer	£37,768–£46,414
Lecturer	£31,655–£36,672
Junior researcher	£25,023–£30,738

UNIVERSITIES

The following is a list of universities, which are those institutions that have been granted degree-awarding powers by either a royal charter or an act of parliament, or have been permitted to use the word 'university' (or 'university college') by the Privy Council. There are other recognised bodies in the UK with degree-awarding powers, as well as institutions offering courses leading to a degree from a recognised body. Further information is available at W www.gov.uk/recognised-uk-degrees

Student figures represent the number of undergraduate (UG) and postgraduate (PG) students based on information available at July 2018.

For information on tuition fees and student loans, *see* Education, Higher Education.

RESEARCH EXCELLENCE FRAMEWORK
The research excellence framework (REF) was the system for assessing the quality of research in UK higher education institutions. The 2014 REF was conducted jointly by the former Higher Education Funding Council for England (HEFCE), the Scottish Funding Council (SFC), the Higher Education Funding Council for Wales (HEFCW) and the Department for Employment and Learning (DEL), Northern Ireland. The primary purpose of REF 2014 was to assess the quality of research and produce outcomes for each submission made by institutions. The table below shows the top five universities or specialist colleges for each discipline based on the mean average ranking of the overall quality of their research.

The teaching excellence framework (TEF) will replace the REF. The TEF will rate universities gold, silver or bronze by subject, holding them to account for the quality of their teaching, learning environment and graduate outcomes. There will be a pilot scheme in 2017–18 and 2018–19; full subject-level rating is expected to start in 2019–20.

Subject	Universities or university colleges
Agriculture, Veterinary & Food Science	Aberdeen (1), Warwick (2), Glasgow (3), Stirling (4), Queen's Belfast (5)
Anthropology	Oxford (1), Manchester: Anthropology (2), Manchester: Development Studies (3), UEA (4), LSE (5)
Architecture	Bath (1), Glasgow (1), Cambridge (3), Sheffield (4), Loughborough (5)
Area Studies	LSE(1), Birmingham (2), Exeter (3), London Met (4), UEA (5), Aston (5)
Art & Design	Reading (1), Courtauld (2), Westminster (3), St Andrews (4), York (5)
Biological Sciences	Institute of Cancer Research (1), Dundee (2), Edinburgh (3), Imperial (4), Oxford (5), Sheffield (5), Newcastle (5)
Business & Management	LSE (1), Cambridge (2), Imperial (3), Oxford (4), London Business School (5)
Chemistry	Cambridge (1), Liverpool (2), Oxford (3), Bristol (4), Durham (5)
Classics	Cambridge (1), Durham (2), St Andrews (2), Oxford (4), Birmingham (5)
Clinical Medicine	Oxford (1), Cambridge (2), King's (3), Imperial (4), Institute of Cancer Research (4)
Computer Science	UCL (1), Warwick (2), Imperial (3), Manchester (4), Sheffield (5)
Dentistry, Nursing & Pharmacy	Sheffield (1), Swansea (2), Southampton (3), Cardiff (4), Nottingham (4)
Earth Systems & Environmental Sciences	Oxford (1), Bristol (2), Cambridge (3), Southampton (4), Leeds (5)
Economics	UCL (1), LSE (2), Oxford (3), Cambridge (4), Warwick (5)
Education	Oxford (1), King's (2), Nottingham (3), Sheffield (4), Cambridge (5), Durham (5), Cardiff (5)
Engineering (Civil & Construction)	Cardiff (1), Imperial (2), Dundee (3), Sheffield (4), Manchester (5)
Engineering (Electronic)	Cambridge (1), Oxford (2), Imperial: Electrical and Electronic (3), Imperial: Metallurgy & Materials (4), Leeds (5)
Engineering (General)	Cambridge (1), Imperial (2), Manchester (3), Birmingham (4), Leeds (4)
English	Warwick (1), York (2), Newcastle (3), Durham (4), Queen Mary (5)
Geography, Environment & Archaeology	Bristol (1), Cambridge (2), Royal Holloway (2), LSE (4), St Andrews (5)
History	Birmingham (1), York (2), Southampton (3), Sheffield (3), King's (5), Hertfordshire (5)
Law	King's (1), LSE (2), Durham (3), Ulster (4), UCL (5), York (5)
Maths	Oxford (1), Cambridge (2), Warwick (3), Imperial (4), Bristol (5), Lancaster (5)
Modern Languages	Queen Mary (1), Edinburgh (2), Kent (3), Queen Margaret (3), Southampton (5), Queen's Belfast (5)
Philosophy	Oxford (1), Birmingham (2), King's (3), Warwick (4), St Andrew's (5), LSE (5)
Physics	Strathclyde (1), Oxford (2), Edinburgh (3), Nottingham (3), St Andrews (3)
Politics & International Studies	Essex (1), LSE (2), Sheffield (3), Oxford (4), UCL (5)
Psychology, Psychiatry & Neuroscience	Oxford (1), Cardiff (1), Cambridge (3), York (4), Birkbeck (5)
Public Health, Health Services & Primary Care	Oxford (1), Imperial (2), Cambridge (3), Bristol (4), Queen Mary (5)
Social Work and Social Policy	Oxford (1), LSE (2), York (3), UEA (4), Kent (5)
Sociology	York (1), Manchester (2), Cardiff (3), Lancaster (4), Oxford (5)
Sports-related subjects	Bristol (1), Liverpool John Moores (2), Leeds (3), Birmingham (4), Bath (5)
Theology & Religious Studies	Durham (1), Birmingham (2), Lancaster (3), Leeds (3), UCL (3)

UNIVERSITY OF ABERDEEN (1495)
King's College, Aberdeen AB24 3FX T 01224-272000
W www.abdn.ac.uk
Fee: £9,250 *Students:* 10,210 UG; 3,940 PG
Chancellor, HRH the Duchess of Rothesay, GCVO, PC
Vice-Chancellor, Prof. George Boyne
University Secretary, Caroline Inglis

UNIVERSITY OF ABERTAY DUNDEE (1994)
Bell Street, Dundee DD1 1HG T 01382-308000
E enquiries@abertay.ac.uk W www.abertay.ac.uk
Fee: £9,250 *Students:* 3,460 UG; 390 PG
Chancellor, Lord Cullen of Whitekirk, KT, PC, FRSE
Vice-Chancellor, Prof. Nigel Seaton, FRENG
University Secretary, Sheena Stewart

ABERYSTWYTH UNIVERSITY (1872)
Penglais, Aberystwyth SY23 3FL **T** 01970-62311 1
W www.aber.ac.uk
Fee: £9,000 *Students:* 7,325 UG; 1,130 PG
Chancellor, Lord Thomas of Cwmgiedd, PC, QC
Vice-Chancellor, Prof. Elizabeth Treasure
University Secretary, Geraint Pugh

ANGLIA RUSKIN UNIVERSITY (1992)
Chelmsford Campus, Bishop Hall Lane, Chelmsford CM1 1SQ
T 0845-271 3333 **E** answers@anglia.ac.uk **W** www.anglia.ac.uk
Fee: £9,250 *Students:* 18,125 UG; 4,115 PG
Chancellor, Lord Ashcroft, KCMG, PC
Vice-Chancellor, Prof. Iain Martin
Secretary and Clerk, Paul Bogle

ARTS UNIVERSITY BOURNEMOUTH (2012)
Wallisdown BH12 5HH **T** 01202-533011 **W** www.aub.ac.uk
Fee: £9,250 *Students:* 3,195 UG; 120 PG
Chancellor, Prof. Sir Christopher Frayling
Vice-Chancellor, Prof. Stuart Bartholomew, CBE
University Secretary, Jon Reynard

UNIVERSITY OF THE ARTS LONDON (2003 (Formerly
The London Institute (1986), renamed 2004))
272 High Holborn, London WC1V 7EY **T** 020-7514 6000
E admissions@arts.ac.uk **W** www.arts.ac.uk
Fee: £9,250 *Students:* 14,523 UG; 2,475 PG
Chancellor, Grayson Perry, CBE
Vice-Chancellor, Nigel Carrington
Secretary and Registrar, Stephen Marshall

COLLEGES
CAMBERWELL COLLEGE OF ARTS (1898)
45–65 Peckham Road, London SE5 8UF
T 020-7514 6301
W www.arts.ac.uk/camberwell
Head of College, Prof. David Crow
CENTRAL SAINT MARTINS COLLEGE OF ART AND
DESIGN (1854)
Granary Building, 1 Granary Square, London N1C 4AA
T 020-7514 7444
W www.arts.ac.uk/csm
Head of College, Prof. Jeremy Till
CHELSEA COLLEGE OF ARTS (1895)
16 John Islip Street, London SW1P 4JU
T 020-7514 7751
W www.arts.ac.uk/chelsea
Head of College, Prof. David Crow
LONDON COLLEGE OF COMMUNICATION (1894)
Elephant and Castle, London SE1 6SB
T 020-7514 6500
W www.arts.ac.uk/cc
Head of College, Natalie Brett
LONDON COLLEGE OF FASHION (1963)
20 John Prince's Street, London W1G 0BJ
T 020-7514 7400
W www.arts.ac.uk/fashion
Head of College, Prof. Frances Corner, OBE
WIMBLEDON COLLEGE OF ART (1930)
Merton Hall Road, London SW19 3QA
T 020-7514 9641
W www.arts.ac.uk/wimbledon
Head of College, Prof. David Crow

ASTON UNIVERSITY (1966)
Aston Triangle, Birmingham B4 7ET **T** 0121-204 3000
W www.aston.ac.uk
Fee: £9,250 *Students:* 11,035 UG; 2,570 PG
Chancellor, Sir John Sunderland
Vice-Chancellor, Prof. Alec Cameron
Chief Operating Officer, Neil Scott

BANGOR UNIVERSITY (1884)
Gwynedd LL57 2DG **T** 01248-3511 51 **W** www.bangor.ac.uk
Fee: £9,000 *Students:* 8,615 UG; 2,650 PG
Chancellor, Sir George Meyrick
Vice-Chancellor, Prof. John G. Hughes
University Secretary, Dr Kevin Mundy

UNIVERSITY OF BATH (1966)
Bath BA2 7AY **T** 01225-388388 **W** www.bath.ac.uk
Fee: £9,250 *Students:* 12,875 UG; 4,035 PG
Chancellor, HRH the Earl of Wessex, KG, GCVO
Vice-Chancellor, Prof. Dame Glynis Breakwell, DBE, FRSA
University Secretary, Mark Humphriss

BATH SPA UNIVERSITY (2005)
Newton Park, Bath BA2 9BN **T** 01225-875875
E enquiries@bathspa.ac.uk **W** www.bathspa.ac.uk
Fee: £9,250 *Students:* 6,250 UG; 1,730 PG
Chancellor, Jeremy Irons
Vice-Chancellor, Prof. Sue Rigby
Registrar, Christopher Ellicott

UNIVERSITY OF BEDFORDSHIRE (1993)
University Square, Luton LU1 3JU **T** 01234-400400
W www.beds.ac.uk
Fee: £9,250 *Students:* 10,860 UG; 3,140 PG
Chancellor, Rt. Hon. John Bercow, MP
Vice-Chancellor, Bill Rammell
Registrar, Jenny Jenkin

UNIVERSITY OF BIRMINGHAM (1900)
Edgbaston, Birmingham B15 2TT **T** 0121-414 3344
W www.birmingham.ac.uk
Fee: £9,250 *Students:* 22,440 UG; 12,395 PG
Chancellor, Lord Bilimoria, CBE
Vice-Chancellor and Principal, Prof. Sir David Eastwood
Registrar and Secretary, Lee Sanders

BIRMINGHAM CITY UNIVERSITY (1992)
City North Campus, Birmingham B42 2SU **T** 0121-331 5000
W www.bcu.ac.uk
Fee: £9,250 *Students:* 19,640 UG; 4,490 PG
Chancellor, Sir Lenny Henry, CBE
Vice-Chancellor, Prof. Philip Plowden
University Secretary, Karen Stephenson

UNIVERSITY COLLEGE BIRMINGHAM (2012)
Summer Rowe, Birmingham B3 1JB **T** 0121-604 1000
E admissions@ucb.ac.uk **W** www.ucb.ac.uk
Fee: £9,250 *Students:* 4,475 UG; 460 PG
Vice-Chancellor and Principal, Prof. Ray Linforth

BISHOP GROSSETESTE UNIVERSITY (2013)
Longdales Road, Lincoln LN1 3DY **T** 01522-527347
E admissions@bton.ac.uk **W** www.bishopg.ac.uk
Fee: £9,250 *Students:* 1,760 UG; 465 PG
Chancellor, Dame Judith Mayhew-Jonas, DBE
Vice-Chancellor, Revd. Canon Prof. Peter Neil
Registrar and University Secretary, Dr Anne Craven

UNIVERSITY OF BOLTON (2005)
Deane Road, Bolton BL3 5AB **T** 01204-900600
E enquiries@bolton.ac.uk **W** www.bolton.ac.uk
Fee: £9,250 *Students:* 5,225 UG; 1,195 PG
Chancellor, Earl of St Andrews
Vice-Chancellor, Prof. George E. Holmes, DL
Registrar and Secretary, Sue Duncan, LLD

BOURNEMOUTH UNIVERSITY (1992)
Fern Barrow, Poole BH12 5BB **T** 01202-52411 1
E askbu@bournemouth.ac.uk **W** www1.bournemouth.ac.uk
Fee: £9,250 *Students:* 16,140 UG; 4,060 PG
Chancellor, Lord Phillips of Worth Matravers, KG, PC
Vice-Chancellor, Prof. John Vinney
Chief Operating Officer, Jim Andrews

UNIVERSITY OF BRADFORD (1966)
Richmond Road, Bradford BD7 1DP T 01274-232323
E enquiries@bradford.ac.uk W www.bradford.ac.uk
Fee: £9,250 *Students:* 8,045 UG; 2,915 PG
Chancellor, Kate Swann
Vice-Chancellor and Principal, Prof. Brian Cantor, CBE
University Secretary, Alison Jones
UNIVERSITY OF BRIGHTON (1992)
Mithras House, Lewes Road, Brighton BN2 4AT T 01273-600900
E postmaster@bton.ac.uk W www.brighton.ac.uk
Fee: £9,250 *Students:* 17,615 UG; 4,035 PG
Vice-Chancellor, Prof. Debra Humphris
Secretary and Registrar, Stephen Dudderidge
UNIVERSITY OF BRISTOL (1909)
Senate House, Tyndall Avenue, Bristol BS8 1TH T 0117-928 9000
W www.bristol.ac.uk
Fee: £9,250 *Students:* 16,630 UG; 5,960 PG
Chancellor, Sir Paul Nurse, FRS, FMEDSCI
Vice-Chancellor, Prof. Hugh Brady
Registrar, Robin Geller
BRUNEL UNIVERSITY LONDON (1966)
Kingston Lane, Uxbridge UB8 3PH T 01895-274000
E admissions@brunel.ac.uk W www.brunel.ac.uk
Fee: £9,250 *Students:* 9,840 UG; 4,905 PG
Chancellor, Sir Richard Sykes
Vice-Chancellor, Prof. Julia Buckingham, CBE, PHD, DSC, FRSA
Chief Operating Officer, Paul Thomas, CBE
UNIVERSITY OF BUCKINGHAM (1983)
Buckingham MK18 1EG T 01280-814080
E info@buckingham.ac.uk W www.buckingham.ac.uk
Fee: £12,600 *Students:* 1,315 UG; 1,205 PG
Chancellor, The Hon. Lady Keswick
Vice-Chancellor, Sir Anthony Seldon, PHD, FRSA
Registrar, Anne Miller
BUCKS NEW UNIVERSITY (2007)
High Wycombe Campus, Queen Alexandra Road, High Wycombe HP11 2JZ T 01494-522141 E advice@bucks.ac.uk
W www.bucks.ac.uk
Fee: £9,250 *Students:* 7,850 UG; 1,020 PG
Vice-Chancellor, Prof. Rebecca Bunting
UNIVERSITY OF CAMBRIDGE (1209)
The Old Schools, Trinity Lane, Cambridge CB2 1TN
T 01223-337733 W www.cam.ac.uk
Fee: £9,250 *Students:* 12,220 UG; 7,440 PG
Chancellor, Lord Sainsbury of Turville, FRS (King's)
Vice-Chancellor, Prof. Stephen J. Toope (Clare Hall)
High Steward, Lord Watson of Richmond, CBE (Jesus)
Deputy High Steward, Mrs A. Lonsdale, CBE (Murray Edwards)
Commissary, Lord Judge, PC (Magdalene)
Pro-Vice-Chancellors, Prof. G. J. Virgo, QC (Downing); Prof. E. L. Ferran, FBA (St Catharine's); Prof. C. Abell, FRS, FMEDSCI (Christ's); Prof. A. Neely (Sidney Sussex); Prof. D. A. Cardwell, FRENG (Fitzwilliam)
Proctors (2018–19), J. H. Xuereb (St Catherine's); Dr K. Otwell (Lucy Cavendish)
Deputy Proctors (2018–19), T. N. Milner (Darwin); Dr G. L. Burgess (Newnham)
Orator, Dr R. J. E. Thompson (Selwyn)
Registrar, E. M. C. Rampton (Sidney Sussex)
Librarian, Dr J. Gardner (Selwyn)
Director of the Fitzwilliam Museum, vacant
Interim Academic Secretary, Dr. R. H. Coupe
Director of Finance, J. D. Hughes (Wolfson)
Executive Director of Development, Ms A. Traub
Esquire Bedells, Mrs N. Hardy (Jesus); Ms S. V. Scarlett (Lucy Cavendish)
University Advocate, R. E. Thornton (Emmanuel)
Deputy University Advocate, Dr J. K. Seymour (Sidney Sussex)

COLLEGES AND HALLS
(with dates of foundation)
CHRIST'S (1505)
Master, Prof. J. Stapleton, FBA
CHURCHILL (1960)
Master, Prof. Dame Athene Donald, DBE, FRS
CLARE (1326)
Master, Lord Grabiner, QC
CLARE HALL (1966)
President, Prof. D. J. Ibbetson, FBA
CORPUS CHRISTI (1352)
Master, Prof. C. Kelly
DARWIN (1964)
Master, C. M. R. Fowler
DOWNING (1800)
Master, A. Bookbinder
EMMANUEL (1584)
Master, Dame Fiona Reynolds, DBE
FITZWILLIAM (1966)
Master, Mrs N. M. Padfield
GIRTON (1869)
Mistress, Prof. S. J. Smith, FBA
GONVILLE AND CAIUS (1348)
Master, Dr. P. Rogerson
HOMERTON (1976)
Principal, Prof. G. Ward
HUGHES HALL (1885)
President, Dr Anthony Freeling
JESUS (1496)
Master, Prof. I. H. White
KING'S (1441)
Provost, Prof. M. R. E. Proctor, FRS
LUCY CAVENDISH (1965)
President, Prof. M. Atkins, CBE
MAGDALENE (1542)
Master, Rt. Revd Lord Williams of Oystermouth, PC, FBA
MURRAY EDWARDS (1954)
President, Dame Barbara Stocking, DBE
NEWNHAM (1871)
Principal, Prof. Dame Carol Black, DBE, FRCP
PEMBROKE (1347)
Master, Lord Smith of Finsbury, PC
PETERHOUSE (1284)
Master, Ms Bridget Kendall, MBE
QUEENS' (1448)
President, Prof. Lord Eatwell of Stratton St Margaret
ROBINSON (1977)
Warden, Prof. A. D. Yates
ST CATHARINE'S (1473)
Master, Prof. Sir Mark Welland, FRS, FRENG
ST EDMUND'S (1896)
Master, Hon. Matthew Bullock
ST JOHN'S (1511)
Master, Prof. Sir C. M. Dobson, FRS
SELWYN (1882)
Master, Roger Mosey
SIDNEY SUSSEX (1596)
Master, Prof. R. V. Penty, FRENG
TRINITY (1546)
Master, Sir Gregory Winter, CBE, FRS
TRINITY HALL (1350)
Master, Revd. Dr Jeremy Morris
WOLFSON (1965)
President, Prof. Jane Clarke, FRS, FMEDSCI

CANTERBURY CHRIST CHURCH UNIVERSITY (2005)
North Holmes Road, Canterbury CT1 1QU T 01227-767700
E admissions@canterbury.ac.uk W www.canterbury.ac.uk
Fee: £9,250 *Students:* 12,395 UG; 2,805 PG
Chancellor, Most Revd and Rt. Hon. Archbishop of
  Canterbury
Vice-Chancellor, Prof. Rama Thirunamachandran
Director of Academic Administration, Cathy Lambert

CARDIFF UNIVERSITY (1883)
Cardiff CF10 3XQ T 029-2087 4000 W www.cardiff.ac.uk
Fee: £9,000 *Students:* 23,085 UG; 8,510 PG
Vice-Chancellor, Prof. Colin Riordan
Chief Operating Officer, Jayne Sadgrove

CARDIFF METROPOLITAN UNIVERSITY (1865)
Western Avenue, Cardiff CF5 2YB T 029-2041 6070
W www.cardiffmet.ac.uk
Fee: £9,000 *Students:* 8,790 UG; 2,200 PG
President and Vice-Chancellor, Prof. Cara Carmichael Aitchison,
  FACSS, FRGS, FHEA
Chief Operating Officer, John Cappock

UNIVERSITY OF CENTRAL LANCASHIRE (1992)
Preston PR1 2HE T 01772-201201 E cenquiries@uclan.ac.uk
W www.uclan.ac.uk
Fee: £9,250 *Students:* 19,450 UG; 4,710 PG
Chancellor, Ranvir Singh
Vice-Chancellor, Prof. Mike Thomas
University Secretary, Ian Fisher

UNIVERSITY OF CHESTER (Founded in 1839 as Chester
Diocesan Training College; gained University status in
2005)
Parkgate Road, Chester CH1 4BJ T 01244-511000
E enquiries@chester.ac.uk W www.chester.ac.uk
Fee: £9,250 *Students:* 11,160 UG; 4,165 PG
Chancellor, Gyles Brandreth
Vice-Chancellor, Canon Prof. Tim Wheeler
University Secretary, Adrian Lee

UNIVERSITY OF CHICHESTER (2005)
College Lane, Chichester PO19 6PE T 01243-816000
E help@chi.ac.uk W www.chi.ac.uk
Fee: £9,250 *Students:* 4,650 UG; 890 PG
Vice-Chancellor, Prof. Jane Longmore

COVENTRY UNIVERSITY (1992)
Priory Street, Coventry CV1 5FB T 024-7688 7688
W www.coventry.ac.uk
Fee: £9,250 *Students:* 25,705 UG; 5,985 PG
Chancellor, Margaret Casely-Hayford
Vice-Chancellor, Prof. John Latham
Academic Registrar, Kate Quantrell

CRANFIELD UNIVERSITY (1969)
Cranfield MK43 0AL T 01234-750111 E info@cranfield.ac.uk
W www.cranfield.ac.uk
Students: 3,935 PG (postgraduate only)
Chancellor, Baroness Young of Old Scone
Vice-Chancellor, Prof. Sir Peter Gregson
University Secretary, Gregor Douglas

UNIVERSITY FOR THE CREATIVE ARTS (2008)
Falkner Road, Farnham GU9 7DS T 01252-722441
W www.ucreative.ac.uk
Fee: £9,250 *Students:* 5,840 UG; 340 PG
Chancellor, Prof. Magdalene Odundo, OBE
Vice-Chancellor, Prof. Bashir Makhoul
University Secretary, Marion Wilks

UNIVERSITY OF CUMBRIA (2007)
Fusehill Street, Carlisle CA1 2HH T 01228-616234
W www.cumbria.ac.uk
Fee: £9,250 *Students:* 6,890 UG; 1,745 PG
Chancellor, Most Revd and Rt. Hon. Archbishop of York
Vice-Chancellor, Prof. Julie Mennell
Registrar and Secretary, Jean Brown

DE MONTFORT UNIVERSITY (1992)
The Gateway, Leicester LE1 9BH T 0116-255 1551
E enquiry@dmu.ac.uk W www.dmu.ac.uk
Fee: £9,250 *Students:* 19,125 UG; 4,075 PG
Chancellor, Baroness Lawrence of Clarendon, OBE
Vice-Chancellor, Prof. Dominic Shellard

UNIVERSITY OF DERBY (1992)
Kedleston Road, Derby DE22 1GB T 01332-590500
E askadmissions@derby.ac.uk W www.derby.ac.uk
Fee: £9,250 *Students:* 14,180 UG; 3,400 PG
Chancellor, William Cavendish, Earl of Burlington
Vice-Chancellor and Principal, Prof. Kathryn Mitchell
Registrar, June Hughes

UNIVERSITY OF DUNDEE (1967)
Nethergate, Dundee DD1 4HN T 01382-383000
E university@dundee.ac.uk W www.dundee.ac.uk
Fee: £9,250 *Students:* 10,585 UG; 4,800 PG
Chancellor, Dame Jocelyn Bell Burnell, DBE, FRS, FRSE,
  FRAS
Vice-Chancellor and Principal, Prof. Sir Pete Downes, OBE,
  FRSE
University Secretary, Dr James McGeorge

DURHAM UNIVERSITY (1832)
The Palatine Centre, Stockton Road, Durham DH1 3LE
T 0191-334 2000 W www.dur.ac.uk
Fee: £9,250 *Students:* 13,668 UG; 4,345 PG
Chancellor, Sir Thomas Allen, CBE
Vice-Chancellor, Prof. Stuart Corbridge
University Secretary, Jennifer Sewel

COLLEGES
COLLINGWOOD (1972)
Principal, Prof. J. Elliott
GREY (1959)
Master, Prof. T. Allen
HATFIELD (1846)
Master, Prof. A. M. MacLarnon
JOHN SNOW (2001)
Principal, Prof. C. Summerbell
JOSEPHINE BUTLER (2006)
Principal, A. Simpson
ST AIDAN'S (1947)
Principal, S. F. Frenk
ST CHAD'S (1904)
Principal, M. Masson
ST CUTHBERT'S SOCIETY (1888)
Principal, Prof. E. Archibald
ST HILD AND ST BEDE (1839)
Principal, Prof. J. Clarke
ST JOHN'S (1909)
Principal, Revd Dr D. Wilkinson
ST MARY'S (1899)
Principal, Prof. S. Hackett
STEPHENSON (2001)
Principal, Prof. J. Ashworth
TREVELYAN (1966)
Principal, Prof. H. M. Evans
UNIVERSITY (1832)
Master, Prof. D. Held

USTINOV (2003)
Principal, Prof. G. McGregor

VAN MILDERT (1965)
Principal, Prof. D. Harper

UNIVERSITY OF EAST ANGLIA (1963)
Norwich Research Park, Norwich NR4 7TJ T 01603-456161
E admissions@uea.ac.uk W www.uea.ac.uk
Fee: £9,250 *Students:* 12,260 UG; 4,935 PG
Chancellor, Karen Jones, CBE
Vice-Chancellor, Prof. David Richardson
Registrar and Secretary (Interim), Ian Callaghan

UNIVERSITY OF EAST LONDON (1898)
University Way, London E16 2RD T 020-8223 3000
E study@uel.ac.uk W www.uel.ac.uk
Fee: £9,250 *Students:* 9,710 UG; 3,510 PG
Chancellor, Shabir Randeree, CBE
Vice-Chancellor, Prof. Amanda Broderick
University Secretary (Interim), Tristan Foote

EDGE HILL UNIVERSITY (2006)
St Helens Road, Ormskirk L39 4QP T 01695-575171
W www.edgehill.ac.uk
Fee: £9,250 *Students:* 11,615 UG; 3,605 PG
Chancellor, Prof. Tanya Byron
Vice-Chancellor, Dr John Cater, CBE
University Secretary, Lynda Brady

UNIVERSITY OF EDINBURGH (1583)
Old College, South Bridge, Edinburgh EH8 9YL T 0131-650 1000
E communications.office@ed.ac.uk W www.ed.ac.uk
Fee: £9,250 *Students:* 21,640 UG; 10,265 PG
Chancellor, HRH the Princess Royal, KG, KT, GCVO
Vice-Chancellor and Principal, Prof. Peter Mathieson, FRCP, FRCPE
University Secretary, Sarah Smith

EDINBURGH NAPIER UNIVERSITY (1992)
Sighthill Campus, Edinburgh EH11 4BN T 0333-900 6040
W www.napier.ac.uk
Fee: £9,000 *Students:* 10,525 UG; 2,390 PG
Chancellor, David Eustace
Vice-Chancellor, Prof. Andrea Nolan, OBE
Secretary, David Cloy

UNIVERSITY OF ESSEX (1965)
Wivenhoe Park, Colchester CO4 3SQ T 01206-873333
E enquiries@essex.ac.uk W www.essex.ac.uk
Fee: £9,250 *Students:* 11,285 UG; 3,295 PG
Chancellor, Rt. Hon. John Bercow, MP
Vice-Chancellor, Prof. Anthony Forster, DPHIL
Registrar, Bryn Morris

UNIVERSITY OF EXETER (1955)
Stocker Road, Exeter EX4 4PY T 01392-661000
W www.exeter.ac.uk
Fee: £9,250 *Students:* 18,260 UG; 4,915 PG
Chancellor, Lord Myners of Truro, CBE
Vice-Chancellor, Prof. Sir Steve Smith, FACSS
Registrar and Secretary, Mike Shore-Nye

FALMOUTH UNIVERSITY (2012)
Falmouth Campus, Woodlane, Falmouth TR11 4RH
T 01326-211077 W www.falmouth.ac.uk
Fee: £9,250 *Students:* 5,085 UG; 300 PG
Chancellor, Dawn French
Vice-Chancellor, Prof. Anne Carlisle

UNIVERSITY OF GLASGOW (1451)
University Avenue, Glasgow G12 8QQ T 0141-330 2000
E student.recruitment@glasgow.ac.uk W www.gla.ac.uk
Fee: £9,250 *Students:* 20,420 UG; 8,195 PG
Chancellor, Prof. Sir Kenneth Calman, KCB, FRCS, FRSE
Vice-Chancellor, Prof. Sir Anton Muscatelli, FRSE, FACSS
Registrar, David Bennion

GLASGOW CALEDONIAN UNIVERSITY (1993)
City Campus, Cowcaddens Road, Glasgow G4 0BA
T 0141-331 3000 E ukroenquiries@gcu.ac.uk W www.gcu.ac.uk
Fee: £9,250 *Students:* 13,510 UG; 2,910 PG
Chancellor, Annie Lennox, OBE
Vice-Chancellor, Prof. Pamela Gillies, CBE, FRSE
University Secretary, Jan Hulme

UNIVERSITY OF GLOUCESTERSHIRE (2001)
The Park, Cheltenham GL50 2RH T 0844-801 0001
E admissions@glos.ac.uk W www.glos.ac.uk
Fee: £9,250 *Students:* 6,965 UG; 1,540 PG
Chancellor, Baroness Fritchie, DBE
Vice-Chancellor, Stephen Marston
Secretary and Registrar, Dr Matthew Andrews

UNIVERSITY OF GREENWICH (1992)
Old Royal Naval College, Park Row, London SE10 9LS
T 020-8331 8000 E courseinfo@gre.ac.uk W www.gre.ac.uk
Fee: £9,250 *Students:* 15,545 UG; 4,370 PG
Chancellor, Baroness Scotland of Asthal, PC, QC
Vice-Chancellor, Prof. David Maguire
Secretary, Peter Garrod

HARPER ADAMS UNIVERSITY (2012)
Newport TF10 8NB T 01952-820280
E admissions@harper-adams.ac.uk W www.harper-adams.ac.uk
Fee: £9,250 *Students:* 4,960 UG; 455 PG
Chancellor, HRH the Princess Royal, KG, KT, GCVO
Vice-Chancellor, David Llewellyn
University Secretary, Dr Catherine Baxter

HERIOT-WATT UNIVERSITY (1966)
Edinburgh EH14 4AS T 0131-449 5111 E enquiries@hw.ac.uk
W www.hw.ac.uk
Fee: £9,250 *Students:* 7,415 UG; 3,090 PG
Chancellor, Dr Robert Buchan
Vice-Chancellor, Prof. Richard A. Williams, OBE
University Secretary, Ann Marie Dalton-Pillay

UNIVERSITY OF HERTFORDSHIRE (1992)
Hatfield AL10 9AB T 01707-284000 W www.herts.ac.uk
Fee: £9,250 *Students:* 18,915 UG; 5,660 PG
Chancellor, Marquess of Salisbury, KCVO, PC
Vice-Chancellor, Prof. Quintin McKellar, CBE
Secretary and Registrar, Sue Grant

UNIVERSITY OF THE HIGHLANDS AND ISLANDS (2011)
Ness Walk, Inverness IV3 5SQ T 01463-279000 W www.uhi.ac.uk
Fee: £9,000 *Students:* 8,055 UG; 665 PG
Chancellor, HRH the Princess Royal, KG, KT, GCVO
Vice-Chancellor, Prof. Clive Mulholland
Chief Operating Officer, Fiona Larg

UNIVERSITY OF HUDDERSFIELD (1992)
Queensgate, Huddersfield HD1 3DH T 01484-422288
W www.hud.ac.uk
Fee: £9,250 *Students:* 14,180 UG; 4,100 PG
Chancellor, HRH the Duke Of York, KG, GCVO, ADC(P)
Vice-Chancellor, Prof. Bob Cryan, CBE, DL, FRENG
University Secretary, Michaela Boryslawskyj

UNIVERSITY OF HULL (1927)
Cottingham Road, Hull HU6 7RX T 01482-346311
W www.hull.ac.uk
Fee: £9,250 *Students:* 13,600 UG; 2,930 PG
Chancellor, Baroness Bottomley of Nettlestone, PC
Vice-Chancellor, Prof. Susan Lea, PHD
Registrar, Jeanette Strachan

IMPERIAL COLLEGE LONDON (1907)
South Kensington SW7 2AZ T 020-7589 5111
W www.imperial.ac.uk
Fee: £9,250 *Students:* 9,520 UG; 8,170 PG
President, Prof. Alice Gast
Provost, Prof. Ian Walmsley, FRS
Secretary and Registrar, David Ashton

KEELE UNIVERSITY (1962)
Keele ST5 5BG T 01782-732000 E admissions.ukeu@keele.ac.uk
W www.keele.ac.uk
Fee: £9,250 *Students:* 8,400 UG; 2,200 PG
Chancellor, Sir Jonathon Porritt, CBE
Vice-Chancellor, Prof. Trevor McMillan
Academic Registrar, Dr Helen Galbraith

UNIVERSITY OF KENT (1965)
Canterbury CT2 7NZ T 01227-764000 E information@kent.ac.uk
W www.kent.ac.uk
Fee: £9,250 *Students:* 15,730 UG; PG 4,485
Chancellor, Gavin Esler
Vice-Chancellor & Principal, Prof. Karen Cox
Provost, David Nightingale

KINGSTON UNIVERSITY (1992)
River House, 53–57 High Street, Kingston upon Thames KT1 1LQ
T 020-841 / 9000 E aps@kingston.ac.uk W www.kingston.ac.uk
Fee: £9,250 *Students:* 14,930 UG; 4,540 PG
Chancellor, Bonnie Greer, OBE
Vice-Chancellor, Prof. Stephen Spier
University Secretary, Keith Brennan

UNIVERSITY OF LANCASTER (1964)
Bailrigg, Lancaster LA1 4YW T 01524-65201
W www.lancaster.ac.uk
Fee: £9,250 *Students:* 9,690 UG; 3,925 PG
Chancellor, Rt. Hon. Alan Milburn
Vice-Chancellor, Prof. Mark E. Smith, PHD
University Secretary, Fiona Aiken

UNIVERSITY OF LEEDS (1904)
Leeds LS2 9JT T 0113-243 1751 W www.leeds.ac.uk
Fee: £9,250 *Students:* 23,565 UG; 8,225 PG
Chancellor, Prof. Dame Jane Francis, DCMG
Vice-Chancellor, Sir Alan Langlands
University Secretary, Roger Gair

LEEDS ARTS UNIVERSITY (2017)
Blenheim Walk, Leeds LS2 9AQ T 0113-202 8000
W www.leeds-art.ac.uk
Fee: £9,250 *Students:* 1,390 UG; 35 PG
Vice-Chancellor, Prof. Simone Wonnacott

LEEDS BECKETT UNIVERSITY (1992)
City Campus, Leeds LS1 3HE T 0113-812 0000
W www.leedsbeckett.ac.uk
Fee: £9,250 *Students:* 21,465 UG; 4,455 PG
Chancellor, Sir Bob Murray, CBE
Vice-Chancellor, Prof. Peter Slee
Secretary and Registrar, Jenny Share

LEEDS TRINITY UNIVERSITY (2012)
Brownberrie Lane, Leeds LS18 5HD T 0113-283 7100
E enquiries@leedstrinity.ac.uk W www.leedstrinity.ac.uk
Fee: £9,250 *Students:* 2,865 UG; 850 PG
Chancellor, Gabby Logan
Vice-Chancellor, Prof. Margaret House, OBE
Chief Operating Officer, Denise McConnell

UNIVERSITY OF LEICESTER (1957)
University Road, Leicester LE1 7RH T 0116-252 2522
W www.le.ac.uk
Fee: £9,250 *Students:* 11,505 UG; 6,315 PG
Chancellor, Lord Grocott, PC
Vice-Chancellor, Prof. Paul Boyle, CBE, FBA, FRSE
Registrar, David Hall

UNIVERSITY OF LINCOLN (1992)
Brayford Pool, Lincoln LN6 7TS T 01522-882000
E enquiries@lincoln.ac.uk W www.lincoln.ac.uk
Fee: £9,250 *Students:* 12,500 UG; 2,500 PG
Chancellor, Lord Adebowale, CBE
Vice-Chancellor, Prof. Mary Stuart
Registrar, Chris Spendlove

UNIVERSITY OF LIVERPOOL (1903)
Brownlow Hill, Liverpool L69 7ZX T 0151-794 2000
W www.liverpool.ac.uk
Fee: £9,250 *Students:* 19,595 UG; 5,185 PG
Chancellor, Colm Tóibín
Vice-Chancellor, Prof. Dame Janet Beer, DBE

LIVERPOOL HOPE UNIVERSITY (2005)
Hope Park, Liverpool L16 9JD T 0151-291 3000
E enquiry@hope.ac.uk W www.hope.ac.uk
Fee: £9,250 *Students:* 3,935 UG; 1,005 PG
Chancellor, Lord Guthrie of Craigiebank, GCB, LVO, OBE
Vice-Chancellor and Rector, Prof. Gerald Pillay
University Secretary, Graham Donelan

LIVERPOOL JOHN MOORES UNIVERSITY (1992)
Kingsway House, 2nd Floor, Hatton Garden, Liverpool L3 2AJ
T 0151-231 2121 E courses@ljmu.ac.uk W www.ljmu.ac.uk
Fee: £9,250 *Students:* 18,375 UG; 3,500 PG
Chancellor, Rt. Hon. Sir Brian Leveson
Vice-Chancellor, Prof. Nigel Weatherill, DSC, FRENG
Registrar, Mark Power

UNIVERSITY OF LONDON (1836)
Senate House, Malet Street, London WC1E 7HU T 020-7862 8000
W www.london.ac.uk
Fee: £9,250
Chancellor, HRH the Princess Royal, KG, KT, GCVO
Interim Vice-Chancellor, Prof. Peter Kopelman, FRCP
University Secretary, Chris Cobb

COLLEGES
BIRKBECK
Malet Street, London WC1E 7HX
Students: 8,010 UG; 4,905 PG
President, Baroness Bakewell, DBE
Master, Prof. David Latchman, CBE
CITY
Northampton Square, London EC1V 0HB
Students: 10,075 UG; 9,330 PG
President, Prof. Sir Paul Curran
COURTAULD INSTITUTE OF ART
Somerset House, Strand, London WC2R 0RN
Students: 200 UG; 295 PG
Director, Prof. Deborah Swallow
GOLDSMITHS
New Cross, London SE14 6NW
Students, 6,190 UG; 3,155 PG
Warden, Patrick Loughrey
INSTITUTE OF CANCER RESEARCH
15 Cotswold Road, Sutton, Surrey SM2 5NG
Students: 275 PG (postgraduate only)
Chief Executive, Prof. Paul Workman
KING'S COLLEGE LONDON
(includes Guy's, King's and St Thomas's Schools of
Medicine, Dentistry and Biomedical Sciences)
Strand, London WC2R 2LS
Students: 18,255 UG; 12,315 PG
Principal, Prof. Edward Byrne
LONDON BUSINESS SCHOOL
Regent's Park, London NW1 4SA
Students: 2,060 PG (postgraduate only)
Dean, François Ortalo-Magné

LONDON SCHOOL OF ECONOMICS AND POLITICAL
SCIENCE
Houghton Street, London WC2A 2AE
Students: 4,810 UG; 6,395 PG
Director, Dame Minouche Shafik
LONDON SCHOOL OF HYGIENE AND TROPICAL
MEDICINE
Keppel Street, London WC1E 7HT
Students: 1,345 PG (postgraduate only)
Director, Prof. Peter Piot, CMG, MD, PHD
QUEEN MARY'S
(incorporating St Bartholomew's and the London School of
Medicine and Dentistry)
Mile End Road, London E1 4NS
Students: 13,625 UG; 5,260 PG
Principal, Prof. Colin Bailey
ROYAL ACADEMY OF MUSIC
Marylebone Road, London NW1 5HT
Students: 400 UG; 420 PG
Principal, Prof. Jonathan Freeman-Attwood, CBE
ROYAL CENTRAL SCHOOL OF SPEECH AND DRAMA
Eton Avenue, London NW3 3HY
Students: 675 UG; 420 PG
Principal, Prof. Gavin Henderson, CBE
ROYAL HOLLOWAY
Egham Hill, Egham, Surrey TW20 0EX
Students: 7,640 UG; 2,690 PG
Principal, Prof. Paul Layzell
ROYAL VETERINARY COLLEGE
Royal College Street, London NW1 0TU
Students: 1,870 UG; 500 PG
Principal, Prof. Stuart Reid
ST GEORGE'S
Cranmer Terrace, London SW17 0RE
Students: 3,905 UG; 945 PG
Principal, Prof. Jenny Higham
SOAS
Thornhaugh Street, Russell Square, London WC1H 0XG
Students: 3,275 UG; 3,085 PG
Director, Baroness Amos, CH
UNIVERSITY COLLEGE LONDON
(including the Institute of Neurology, Eastman Dental
Institute, School of Pharmacy and Institute of Education)
Gower Street, London WC1E 6BT
Students: 18,610 UG; 19,295 PG
Provost and President, Prof. Michael Arthur, FRCP, FMEDSCI
UNIVERSITY OF LONDON INSTITUTE IN PARIS
9–11 rue de Constantine, 75340 Paris Cedex 07, France
Chief Executive, Dr Tim Gore, OBE

INSTITUTES
SCHOOL OF ADVANCED STUDY
Senate House, Malet Street, London WC1H 0XG
Dean and Chief Executive, Prof. Rick Rylance
The school consists of nine institutes:
INSTITUTE OF ADVANCED LEGAL STUDIES
Charles Clore House, 17 Russell Square, London WC1B 5DR
Director, Prof. Carl Stychin
INSTITUTE OF CLASSICAL STUDIES
Senate House, Malet Street, London WC1E 7HU
Director, Prof. Greg Woolf, FSA
INSTITUTE OF COMMONWEALTH STUDIES
Senate House, Malet Street, London WC1E 7HU
Director, Prof. Philip Murphy
INSTITUTE OF ENGLISH STUDIES
Senate House, Malet Street, London WC1E 7HU
Director, Prof. Clare A. Lees

INSTITUTE OF HISTORICAL RESEARCH
Senate House, Malet Street, London WC1E 7HU
Director, Prof. Jo Fox
INSTITUTE OF LATIN AMERICAN STUDIES
Senate House, Malet Street, London WC1E 7HU
Director, Prof. Linda Newson
INSTITUTE OF MODERN LANGUAGES RESEARCH
Senate House, Malet Street, London WC1E 7HU
Director, Prof. Catherine Davies
INSTITUTE OF PHILOSOPHY
Senate House, Malet Street, London WC1E 7HU
Director, Prof. Barry Smith
THE WARBURG INSTITUTE
Woburn Square, London WC1H 0AB
Director, Prof. Bill Sherman

LONDON METROPOLITAN UNIVERSITY (2002)
166–220 Holloway Road, London N7 8DB **T** 020-7423 0000
W www.londonmet.ac.uk
Fee: £9,250 *Students:* 9,945 UG; 2,915 PG
Patron, HRH the Duke of York, KG, GCVO, ADC(P)
Vice-Chancellor, Prof. John Raftery
University Secretary, Peter Garrod

LONDON SOUTH BANK UNIVERSITY (1992)
103 Borough Road, London SE1 0AA **T** 020-7815 7815
E course.enquiry@lsbu.ac.uk **W** www.lsbu.ac.uk
Fee: £9,250 *Students:* 12,620 UG; 4,985 PG
Chancellor, Richard Farleigh
Vice-Chancellor, Prof. David Phoenix
University Secretary, James Stevenson

LOUGHBOROUGH UNIVERSITY (1966)
Epinal Way, Loughborough LE11 3TU **T** 01509-222222
W www.lboro.ac.uk
Fee: £9,250 *Students:* 12,725 UG; 4,225 PG
Chancellor, Lord Coe, CH, OBE, MBE
Vice-Chancellor, Prof. Robert Allison
Chief Operating Officer, Richard Taylor

UNIVERSITY OF MANCHESTER (2004. Formed by the
amalgamation of Victoria University of Manchester (1851;
reorganised 1880 and 1903) and the University of
Manchester Institute of Science and Technology (1824))
Oxford Road, Manchester M13 9PL **T** 0161-306 6000
W www.manchester.ac.uk
Fee: £9,250 *Students:* 27,635 UG; 12,065 PG
Chancellor, Lemn Sissay, MBE
Vice-Chancellor, Prof. Dame Nancy Rothwell, DBE, FRS
Secretary and Registrar, Will Spinks

MANCHESTER METROPOLITAN UNIVERSITY (1992)
All Saints, Manchester M15 6BH **T** 0161-247 2000
W www.mmu.ac.uk
Fee: £9,250 *Students:* 26,835 UG; 5,650 PG
Chancellor, Rt. Hon. Lord Mandelson
Vice-Chancellor, Prof. Malcolm Press
Registrar, Prof. Karen Moore

MIDDLESEX UNIVERSITY (1992)
Hendon Campus, London NW4 4BT **T** 020-8411 5555
W www.mdx.ac.uk
Fee: £9,250 *Students:* 14,435 UG; 4,670 PG
Chancellor, Dame Janet Ritterman, DBE
Vice-Chancellor, Prof. Tim Blackman
Chief Operating Officer, Sophie Bowen, PHD

NEWCASTLE UNIVERSITY (1963)
Newcastle upon Tyne NE1 7RU **T** 0191-208 6000
W www.ncl.ac.uk
Fee: £9,250 *Students:* 17,720 UG; 6,070 PG
Chancellor, Prof. Sir Liam Donaldson
Vice-Chancellor, Prof. Chris Day, FRS, DPHIL
Registrar, Dr. John Hogan

NEWMAN UNIVERSITY, BIRMINGHAM (2013)
Genners Lane, Birmingham B32 3NT **T** 0121-476 1181
E admissions@newman.ac.uk **W** www.newman.ac.uk
Fee: £9,250 *Students:* 2,250 UG; 560 PG
Chancellor, vacant
Vice-Chancellor, Prof. Scott Davidson
Secretary and Registrar, Andrea Bolshaw

UNIVERSITY OF NORTHAMPTON (2005)
Park Campus, Boughton Green Road, Northampton NN2 7AL
T 01604-735500 **E** study@northampton.ac.uk
W www.northampton.ac.uk
Fee: £9,250 *Students:* 10,670 UG; 2,315 PG
Chancellor, Revd Richard Coles
Vice-Chancellor, Prof. Nick Petford, PHD, DSC
Chief Operating Officer, Terry Neville

NORTHUMBRIA UNIVERSITY AT NEWCASTLE (1992)
Ellison Building, Ellison Place, Newcastle upon Tyne NE1 8ST
T 0191-232 6002 **E** course.enquiries@northumbria.ac.uk
W www.northumbria.ac.uk
Fee: £9,250 *Students:* 22,415 UG; 4,750 PG
Chancellor, Baroness Grey-Thompson, DBE
Vice-Chancellor, Prof. Andrew Wathey, CBE, DPHIL
Chief Operating Officer, Chris Reilly

NORWICH UNIVERSITY OF THE ARTS (2012)
Francis House, 3–7 Redwell Street, Norwich NR2 4SN
T 01603-610561 **E** info@nua.ac.uk **W** www.nua.ac.uk
Fee: £9,250 *Students:* 1,920 UG; 75 PG
Chancellor, vacant
Vice-Chancellor, Prof. John Last
Academic Registrar, Angela Tubb

UNIVERSITY OF NOTTINGHAM (1948)
University Park, Nottingham NG7 2RD **T** 0115-951 5151
E undergraduate-enquiries@nottingham.ac.uk
W www.nottingham.ac.uk
Fee: £9,250 *Students:* 23,935 UG; 8,185 PG
Chancellor, Sir Andrew Witty
Vice-Chancellor, Prof. Shearer West
Registrar, Paul Greatrix

NOTTINGHAM TRENT UNIVERSITY (1992)
Burton Street, Nottingham NG1 4BU **T** 0115-941 8418
E ask.ntu@ntu.ac.uk **W** www.ntu.ac.uk
Fee: £9,250 *Students:* 22,840 UG; 5,080 PG
Chancellor, Kevin Cahill, CBE
Vice-Chancellor, Prof. Edward Peck
Chief Operating Officer, Steve Denton

OPEN UNIVERSITY (1969)
Walton Hall, Milton Keynes MK7 6AA **T** 01908-274066
W www.open.ac.uk
Fee: £5,856 *Students:* 119,115 UG; 7,465 PG
Chancellor, Baroness Lane-Fox of Soho, CBE
Acting Vice-Chancellor, Mary Kellett
University Secretary, Dr Jonathan Nicholls

UNIVERSITY OF OXFORD (c.12th century)
University Offices, Wellington Square, Oxford OX1 2JD
T 01865-270000 **E** information.office@admin.ox.ac.uk
W www.ox.ac.uk
Fee: £9,250 *Students:* 14,265 UG; 10,385 PG
Chancellor, Lord Patten of Barnes, CH, PC (BALLIOL, ST ANTONY'S)
Vice-Chancellor, Prof. Louise Richardson, FRSE
Pro-Vice-Chancellors, Dr D. Prout, CB (Queen's); Prof. M. Williams (New College); Dr R. Easton (New College); Prof. A. Trefethen (St Cross); Prof. I. A. Walmsley (St Hugh's); Prof. A. Buchan (Corpus Christi); Dr R. Surender (Green Templeton)
Registrar, Prof. E McKendrick (Lady Margaret Hall)
Academic Registrar, Emma Potts (Kellogg)
Public Orator, Dr J. Katz (All Souls)
Director of University Library Services and Bodley's Librarian, R. Ovenden (Balliol)
Director of the Ashmolean Museum, Dr A. Sturgis (Worcester)
Director of the Museum of the History of Science, Dr Silke Ackermann (Linacre)
Director of the Pitt Rivers Museum, Dr Laura Van Broekhoven (Linacre)
Director of the University Museum of Natural History, Prof. Paul Smith (Kellogg)
Keeper of Archives, S. Bailey (Linacre)
Director of Estates, P. Goffin
Director of Finance, G. F. B. Kerr (Keble)

COLLEGES AND HALLS *(with dates of foundation)*
ALL SOULS (1438)
Warden, Prof. Sir John Vickers, FBA
BALLIOL (1263)
Master, Dame Helen Ghosh, DCB
BLACKFRIARS (1221)
Regent, Very Revd Dr Simon Gaine
BRASENOSE (1509)
Principal, John Bowers, QC
CAMPION HALL (1896)
Master, Revd James Hanvey
CHRIST CHURCH (1546)
Dean, Very Revd Prof. Martyn Percy
CORPUS CHRISTI (1517)
President, Prof. Stephen Cowley, FRS, FREng
EXETER (1314)
Rector, Prof. Sir Rick Trainor, KBE
GREEN TEMPLETON (2008)
Principal, Prof. Denise Lievesley, CBE
HARRIS MANCHESTER (1889)
Principal, Revd Prof. Jane Shaw
HERTFORD (1740)
Principal, Will Hutton
JESUS (1571)
Principal, Prof. Sir Nigel Shadbolt, FRS, FREng
KEBLE (1870)
Warden, Sir Jonathan Phillips, KCB
KELLOGG (1990)
President, Prof. Jonathan M. Michie
LADY MARGARET HALL (1878)
Principal, Alan Rusbridger
LINACRE (1962)
Principal, Dr Nick Brown
LINCOLN (1427)
Rector, Prof. Henry Woudhuysen, FBA
MAGDALEN (1458)
President, Prof. Sir David Clary, FRS
MANSFIELD (1886)
Principal, Helen Mountfield, QC

MERTON (1264)
Warden, Prof. Irene Tracey, FMedSci
NEW COLLEGE (1379)
Warden, Miles Young
NUFFIELD (1958)
Warden, Sir Andrew Dilnot, CBE
ORIEL (1326)
Provost, Neil Mendoza
PEMBROKE (1624)
Master, Dame Lynne Brindley, DBE, FBA
QUEEN'S (1341)
Provost, Prof. Paul Madden, FRS, FRSE
REGENT'S PARK (1810)
Principal, Revd Dr Robert Ellis
ST ANNE'S (1878)
Principal, Helen King
ST ANTONY'S (1953)
Warden, Prof. Roger Goodman
ST BENET'S HALL (1897)
Master, Prof. Werner Jeanrond
ST CATHERINE'S (1963)
Master, Prof. Roger Ainsworth
ST CROSS (1965)
Master, Carole Souter, CBE
ST EDMUND HALL (C. 1278)
Principal, Prof. Katherine Willis, CBE
ST HILDA'S (1893)
Principal, Prof. Sir Gordon Duff, FRCP, FRSE, FMedSci
ST HUGH'S (1886)
Principal, Dame Elish Angiolini, DBE, PC, QC
ST JOHN'S (1555)
President, Prof. Margaret J. Snowling, FBA, FMedSci
ST PETER'S (1929)
Principal, Mark Damazer, CBE
ST STEPHEN'S HOUSE (1876)
Principal, Revd Dr Robin Ward
SOMERVILLE (1879)
Principal, Baroness Royall of Blaisdon, PC
TRINITY (1554)
President, Dame Hilary Boulding, DBE
UNIVERSITY (1249)
Master, Sir Ivor Crewe
WADHAM (1610)
Warden, Lord Macdonald of River Glaven, QC
WOLFSON (1981)
President, Sir Tim Hitchens, KCVO, CMG, LVO
WORCESTER (1714)
Provost, Prof. Sir Jonathan Bate, CBE, FBA, FRSL
WYCLIFFE HALL (1877)
Principal, Revd Michael Lloyd

OXFORD BROOKES UNIVERSITY (1992)
Gipsy Lane, Oxford OX3 0BP T 01865-741111
E query@brookes.ac.uk W www.brookes.ac.uk
Fee: £9,250 *Students:* 13,905 UG; 3,935 PG
Chancellor, Dame Katherine Granger, DBE
Vice-Chancellor, Prof. Alistair Fitt
Registrar, Brendan Casey

UNIVERSITY OF PLYMOUTH (1992)
Drake Circus, Plymouth PL4 8AA T 01752-600600
E prospectus@plymouth.ac.uk W www.plymouth.ac.uk
Fee: £9,250 *Students:* 20,080 UG; 3,075 PG
Chancellor, Lord Kestenbaum
Vice-Chancellor, Prof. Judith Petts, CBE
University Secretary, Gordon Stewart

UNIVERSITY OF PORTSMOUTH (1992)
University House, Winston Churchill Avenue, Portsmouth PO1 2UP
T 023-9284 8484 E info.centre@port.ac.uk W www.port.ac.uk
Fee: £9,250 *Students:* 18,745 UG; 3,315 PG
Chancellor, Karen Blackett, OBE
Vice-Chancellor, Prof. Graham Galbraith, PHD
Chief Operating Officer, Bernie Topham

QUEEN MARGARET UNIVERSITY (2007)
Edinburgh EH21 6UU T 0131-474 0000 W www.qmu.ac.uk
Fee: £7,000 *Students:* 3,665 UG; 3,075 PG
Chancellor, Prue Leith, CBE
Vice-Chancellor, Prof. Petra Wend, FRSE
Secretary, Prof. Irene Hynd

QUEEN'S UNIVERSITY BELFAST (1908)
University Road, Belfast BT7 1NN T 028-9024 5133
E comms.office@qub.ac.uk W www.qub.ac.uk
Fee: £9,250 *Students:* 18,960 UG; 4,910 PG
Chancellor, Thomas J. Moran
Vice-Chancellor, Prof. Ian Greer, FRCP, FMEDSCI
Registrar, James O'Kane

RAVENSBOURNE UNIVERSITY LONDON (2018)
Greenwich Peninsula, 6 Penrose Way, London SE10 0EW
T 020-3040 3500 W www.ravensbourne.ac.uk
Fee: £9,250 *Students:* 2,280 UG; 55 PG
Director and Chief Executive, Prof. Linda Drew

UNIVERSITY OF READING (1926)
Whiteknights, PO Box 217, Reading RG6 6AH T 0118-987 5123
W www.reading.ac.uk
Fee: £9,250 *Students:* 10,315 UG; 4,665 PG
Chancellor, Rt. Hon. Lord Waldegrave of North Hill, PC
Vice-Chancellor, Sir David Bell, KCB
University Secretary, Dr Richard Messer

ROBERT GORDON UNIVERSITY (1992)
Schoolhill, Aberdeen AB10 1FR T 01224-262000
E admissions@rgu.ac.uk W www.rgu.ac.uk
Fee: £8,500 *Students:* 8,995 UG; 3,755 PG
Chancellor, Sir Ian Wood, GBE
Vice-Chancellor, Prof. Ferdinand von Prondzynski
Academic Registrar, Hilary Douglas

ROEHAMPTON UNIVERSITY (2004)
Erasmus House, Roehampton Lane, London SW15 5PU
T 020-8392 3000 E enquiries@roehampton.ac.uk
W www.roehampton.ac.uk
Fee: £9,250 *Students:* 7,050 UG; 1,700 PG
Chancellor, Dame Jacqueline Wilson, DBE, FRSL
Vice-Chancellor, Prof. Paul O'Prey
University Secretary, Andrew Skinner

ROYAL AGRICULTURAL UNIVERSITY (2013)
Stroud Road, Cirencester GL7 6JS T 01285-652531
E admissions@rau.ac.uk W www.rau.ac.uk
Fee: £9,250 *Students:* 965 UG; 235 PG
Vice-Chancellor, Prof. Joanna Price
Academic Registrar, Nigel Warner

ROYAL COLLEGE OF ART (1967)
Kensington Gore, London SW7 2EU T 020-7590 4444
E info@rca.ac.uk W www.rca.ac.uk
Students: 1,610 PG (postgraduate only)
Chancellor, Sir Jonathan Ive, KBE
Vice-Chancellor, Dr Paul Thompson
Chief Operating Officer, Richard Benson

UNIVERSITY OF ST ANDREWS (1413)
St Andrews KY16 9AJ T 01334-476161 W www.st-andrews.ac.uk
Fee: £9,250 *Students:* 8,035 UG; 2,710 PG
Chancellor, Rt. Hon. Lord Campbell of Pittenweem, CH, CBE, QC
Vice-Chancellor, Prof. Sally Mapstone
Academic Registrar, Ester Ruskuc

UNIVERSITY OF ST MARK AND ST JOHN (2012)
Derriford Road, Plymouth PL6 8BH **T** 01752-636700
E admissions@marjon.ac.uk **W** www.marjon.ac.uk
Fee: £9,250 *Students:* 2,000 UG; 360 PG
Vice-Chancellor, Prof. Rob Warner
Registrar, Stephen Plant

ST MARY'S UNIVERSITY (2014)
Waldegrave Road, Strawberry Hill, Twickenham TW1 4SX
T 020-8240 4000 **W** www.stmarys.ac.uk
Fee: £9,250 *Students:* 4,120 UG; 1,415 PG
Chancellor, Cardinal Vincent Nichols
Vice-Chancellor, Prof. Francis Campbell
University Secretary, Simon Williams

UNIVERSITY OF SALFORD (1967)
The Crescent, Salford M5 4WT **T** 0161-295 5000
W www.salford.ac.uk
Fee: £9,250 *Students:* 15,725 UG; 4,790 PG
Chancellor, Jackie Kay, MBE
Vice-Chancellor, Prof. Helen Marshall
University Secretary, Alison Blackburn

UNIVERSITY OF SHEFFIELD (1905)
Western Bank, Sheffield S10 2TN **T** 0114-222 2000
E ask@sheffield.ac.uk **W** www.sheffield.ac.uk
Fee: £9,250 *Students:* 19,661 UG; 8,286 PG
Chancellor, Rt. Hon. Justice Rafferty, DBE
President and Vice-Chancellor, Prof. Sir Keith Burnett, CBE,
    DPHIL, FRS

SHEFFIELD HALLAM UNIVERSITY (1992)
City Campus, Howard Street, Sheffield S1 1WB **T** 011 4-225 5555
E enquiries@shu.ac.uk **W** www.shu.ac.uk
Fee: £9,250 *Students:* 24,705 UG; 6,775 PG
Chancellor, Prof. Lord Winston, FRCOG, FRCP, FMEDSCI
Vice-Chancellor, Prof. Sir Chris Husbands
Chief Operating Officer, Richard Calvert

UNIVERSITY OF SOUTHAMPTON (1952)
University Road, Southampton SO17 1BJ **T** 023-8059 5000
W www.southampton.ac.uk
Fee: £9,250 *Students:* 17,485 UG; 7,390 PG
Chancellor, vacant
Vice-Chancellor, Prof. Sir Christopher Snowden, FRS,
    FRENG
Chief Operating Officer, Ian Dunn

SOUTHAMPTON SOLENT UNIVERSITY (2005)
East Park Terrace, Southampton SO14 0YN **T** 023-8031 9039
E ask@solent.ac.uk **W** www.solent.ac.uk
Fee: £9,250 *Students:* 10,885 UG; 405 PG
Chancellor, Adm. Lord West of Spithead, GCB, DSC, PC
Vice-Chancellor, Prof. Graham Baldwin
Academic Registrar, Dave Dowland

UNIVERSITY OF SOUTH WALES (1992)
Pontypridd CF37 1DL **T** 0345-576 0101
E enquiries@southwales.ac.uk **W** www.southwales.ac.uk
Fee: £9,000 *Students:* 20,840 UG; 4,425 PG
Chancellor, Rt. Revd and Rt. Hon. Lord Williams of
    Oystermouth, PC, DPHIL
Vice-Chancellor, Prof. Julie Lydon, OBE
Academic Registrar, Mary Hulford

STAFFORDSHIRE UNIVERSITY (1992)
College Road, Stoke-on-Trent ST4 2DE **T** 01782-294000
W www.staffs.ac.uk
Fee: £9,250 *Students:* 13,600 UG; 2,260 PG
Chancellor, Lord Stafford
Vice-Chancellor, Prof. Liz Barnes
Chief Operating Officer, Ian Blachford

UNIVERSITY OF STIRLING (1967)
Stirling FK9 4LA **T** 01786-473171 **E** externalaffairs@stir.ac.uk
W www.stir.ac.uk
Fee: £6,750 *Students:* 8,585 UG; 3,255 PG
Chancellor, vacant
Vice-Chancellor, Prof. Gerry McCormac, FRSE
University Secretary, Eileen Schofield

UNIVERSITY OF STRATHCLYDE (1964)
16 Richmond Street, Glasgow G1 1XQ **T** 0141-552 4400
E corporatecomms@strath.ac.uk **W** www.strath.ac.uk
Fee: £9,250 *Students:* 14,965 UG; 6,505 PG
Chancellor, Lord Smith of Kelvin, KT, CH
Vice-Chancellor, Prof. Sir Jim McDonald, FRSE, FRENG
Academic Registrar, Dr Veena O'Halloran

UNIVERSITY OF SUFFOLK (2016)
Waterfront Building, Neptune Quay, Ipswich IP4 1QJ
T 01473-338000 **W** www.uos.ac.uk
Fee: £9,250 *Students:* 4,640 UG; 390 PG
Vice-Chancellor, Prof. Helen Langton
Secretary and Registrar, Tim Greenacre

UNIVERSITY OF SUNDERLAND (1992)
Edinburgh Building, Chester Road, Sunderland SR1 3SD
T 0191-515 2000 **E** student.helpline@sunderland.ac.uk
W www.sunderland.ac.uk
Fee: £9,250 *Students:* 10,575 UG; 2,425 PG
Chancellor, Steve Cram, MBE
Vice-Chancellor, Shirley Atkinson
Chief Operating Officer, Steve Knight

UNIVERSITY OF SURREY (1966) Guildford GU2 7XH
T 01483-300800 **E** studentdata@surrey.ac.uk **W** www.surrey.ac.uk
Fee: £9,250 *Students:* 12,114 UG; 3,605 PG
Chancellor, HRH the Duke of Kent, KG, GCMG, GCVO
Vice-Chancellor, Prof. G. Q. Max Lu
Registrar, Prof. Jane Powell

UNIVERSITY OF SUSSEX (1961)
Sussex House, Brighton BN1 9RH **T** 01273-606755
E information@sussex.ac.uk **W** www.sussex.ac.uk
Fee: £9,250 *Students:* 10,995 UG; 4,055 PG
Chancellor, Sanjeev Bhaskar, OBE
Vice-Chancellor, Prof. Adam Tickell
Academic Registrar, Sharon Jones

SWANSEA UNIVERSITY (1920)
Singleton Park, Swansea SA2 8PP **T** 01792-205678
W www.swansea.ac.uk
Fee: £9,000 *Students:* 14,680 UG; 2,765 PG
Chancellor, Prof. Dame Jean Thomas, DBE, FMEDSCI,
    FLSW, FRS
Vice-Chancellor, Prof. Richard B. Davies
Registrar, Raymond Ciborowski

TEESIDE UNIVERSITY (1992)
Middlesbrough TS1 3BA **T** 01642-218121 **E** enquiries@tees.ac.uk
W www.tees.ac.uk
Fee: £9,250 *Students:* 16,340 UG; 2,240 PG
Chancellor, Paul Drechsler, CBE
Vice-Chancellor, Prof. Paul Croney, CBE
Chief Operating Officer, Malcolm Page

UNIVERSITY OF ULSTER (1984)
Cromore Road, Coleraine BT52 1SA **T** 028-7012 3456
W www.ulster.ac.uk
Fee: £9,000 *Students:* 19,865 UG; 5,290 PG
Chancellor, James Nesbitt, OBE
Vice-Chancellor, Prof. Paddy Nixon
University Secretary, Eamon Mullan

UNIVERSITY OF WALES, TRINITY SAINT DAVID (1828)
Carmarthen Campus, SA31 3EP T 01267-676767
W www.uwtsd.ac.uk
Fee: £9,000 *Students:* 8,420 UG; 1,510 PG
Vice-Chancellor, Prof. Medwin Hughes

UNIVERSITY OF WARWICK (1965)
Coventry CV4 7AL T 024-7652 3523 W www.warwick.ac.uk
Fee: £9,250 *Students:* 15,380 UG; 9,285 PG
Chancellor, Baroness Ashton of Upholland, GCMG, PC
Vice-Chancellor, Prof. Stuart Croft
Registrar, Rachel Sandby Thomas, CB

UNIVERSITY OF WEST LONDON (1992)
St Mary's Road, London W5 5RF T 0800-036 8888
W www.uwl.ac.uk
Fee: £9,250 *Students:* 9,050 UG; 1,360 PG
Chancellor, Laurence Geller, CBE
Vice-Chancellor, Prof. Peter John
University Secretary, Marion Lowe

UNIVERSITY OF WESTMINSTER (1992)
309 Regent Street, London W1B 2HW T 020-7911 5000
E course-enquiries@westminster.ac.uk W www.westminster.ac.uk
Fee: £9,250 *Students:* 16,035 UG; 4,160 PG
Chancellor, Lady Sorrell, OBE
Vice-Chancellor and Rector, Prof. Geoffrey Petts
Registrar and Secretary, Suzanne Enright

UNIVERSITY OF THE WEST OF ENGLAND (1992)
Frenchay Campus, Coldharbour Lane, Bristol BS16 1QY
T 0117-965 6261 E infopoint@uwe.ac.uk W www.uwe.ac.uk
Fee: £9,250 *Students:* 21,070 UG; 6,650 PG
Chancellor, Sir Ian Carruthers, OBE
Vice-Chancellor, Prof. Steve West, CBE
Registrar, Rachel Cowie

UNIVERSITY OF THE WEST OF SCOTLAND (2007)
Paisley PA1 2BE T 0141-848 3000 E uni-direct@uws.ac.uk
W www.uws.ac.uk
Fee: £9,250 *Students:* 13,410 UG; 2,145 PG
Chancellor, Dame Elish Angiolini, DBE, PC, QC
Vice-Chancellor and Principal, Prof. Craig Mahoney
Chief Operating Officer, Susan Mitchell

UNIVERSITY OF WINCHESTER (2005)
Winchester SO22 4NR T 01962-841515
E course.enquiries@winchester.ac.uk W www.winchester.ac.uk
Fee: £9,250 *Students:* 6,125 UG; 1,415 PG
Chancellor, Alan Titchmarsh, MBE
Vice-Chancellor, Prof. Joy Carter, CBE
Registrar, Dee Povey

UNIVERSITY OF WOLVERHAMPTON (1992)
Wulfruna Street, Wolverhampton WV1 1LY T 01902-321000
E enquiries@wlv.ac.uk W www.wlv.ac.uk
Fee: £9,250 *Students:* 16,755 UG; 3,035 PG
Chancellor, Lord Paul of Marylebone, PC
Vice-Chancellor, Prof. Geoff Layer, OBE
Academic Registrar, Chris Twine

UNIVERSITY OF WORCESTER (1946)
Henwick Grove, Worcester WR2 6AJ T 01905-855000
E study@worc.ac.uk W www.worcester.ac.uk
Fee: £9,250 *Students:* 8,865 UG; 1,595 PG
Chancellor, HRH the Duke of Gloucester, KG, GCVO
Vice Chancellor, Prof. David Green
Registrar, Kevin Pickess

WREXHAM GLYNDWR UNIVERSITY (2008)
Mold Road, Wrexham LL11 2AW T 01978-290666
E reception@glyndwr.ac.uk W www.glyndwr.ac.uk
Fee: £9,000 *Students:* 5,825 UG; 590 PG
Chancellor, Trefor Glyn Jones, CBE, CVO
Vice-Chancellor, Maria Hinfelaar

WRITTLE UNIVERSITY COLLEGE (2015)
Lordship Road, Writtle, Chelmsford CM1 3RR T 01245-424200
E info@writtle.ac.uk W www.writtle.ac.uk
Fee: £9,250 *Students:* 657 UG; 103 PG
Chancellor, Baroness Jenkin of Kennington
Vice-Chancellor, Prof. Tim Middleton
University Secretary, Andrew Williamson

UNIVERSITY OF YORK (1963)
York YO10 5DD T 01904-320000 W www.york.ac.uk
Fee: £9,250 *Students:* 13,090 UG; 4,065 PG
Chancellor, Prof. Sir Malcolm Grant, CBE
Vice-Chancellor, Prof. Koen Lamberts, PHD
Registrar and Secretary, Jo Horsburgh, PHD

YORK ST JOHN UNIVERSITY (2006)
Lord Mayor's Walk, York YO31 7EX T 01904-624624
E admissions@yorksj.ac.uk W www.yorksj.ac.uk
Fee: £9,250 *Students:* 5,265 UG; 715 PG
Chancellor, Most Revd and Rt. Hon. Archbishop of York
Vice-Chancellor, Prof. Karen Stanton
Registrar, Alison Kennel

PROFESSIONAL EDUCATION

The organisations selected below provide specialist training, conduct examinations or are responsible for maintaining a register of those with professional qualifications in their sector, thereby controlling entry into a profession.

EU RECOGNITION

It is possible for those with professional qualifications obtained in the UK to have these recognised in other European countries. Further information can be obtained from:

UK NARIC, Suffolk House, 68–70 Suffolk Road, Cheltenham GL50 2ED **T** 01242-258614 **W** www.ecctis.co.uk/naric

ACCOUNTANCY

Salary range for chartered accountants:
Certified £25,000 (starting), rising to £26,000–£50,000+ (qualified), £40,000–£100,000+ at senior levels
Management £28,000 (starting), £61,000 (average), £46,000–£129,000+ at senior levels
Public finance £18,000–£30,000 (starting), £32,000–£65,000 (qualified), £80,000+ at senior levels

Chartered Accountancy trainees can be school-leavers or graduates. They usually undertake a three-year training contract with an approved employer culminating in professional exams provided by ICAEW, ICAS or CAI. Success in the exams and membership of one of the professional bodies - which includes continuous professional development and regulation - allows them to use the designation 'chartered accountant' and the letters ACA, FCA or CA.

The Association of Chartered Certified Accountants (ACCA) is the global body for professional accountants. The ACCA aims to offer business-relevant qualifications to students in a range of business sectors and countries seeking a career in accountancy, finance and management. The ACCA Qualification consists of up to 13 examinations, practical experiences and a professional ethics module. Chartered certified accountants can use the designatory letters ACCA.

Chartered global management accountants focus on accounting for businesses, and most do not work in accountancy practices but in industry, commerce, not-for-profit and public-sector organisations. Graduates who have not studied a business or accounting degree must complete the Chartered Institute of Management Accountants (CIMA) Certificate in Business Accounting before progressing to the CIMA Professional Qualification, which requires three years of practical experience and twelve examinations. In May 2011, CIMA and the American Institute of Certified Public Accountants (AICPA) agreed on the creation of a new professional designation, the Chartered Global Management Accountant (CGMA), which represents a worldwide standard of professional excellence in management accounting.

The Chartered Institute of Public Finance and Accountancy (CIPFA) is the professional body for people working in public finance. Chartered public finance accountants usually work for public bodies, but they can also work in the private sector. To gain chartered public finance accountant status (CPFA), trainees must complete a professional qualification in public sector accountancy. In addition, CIPFA also offers a postgraduate diploma for those already working in leadership positions.

ASSOCIATION OF CHARTERED CERTIFIED ACCOUNTANTS (ACCA), The Adelphi, 1–11 John Adam Street, London WC2N 6AU **T** 0141-582 2000
E info@accaglobal.com **W** www.accaglobal.com
Chief Executive, Helen Brand, OBE

CHARTERED ACCOUNTANTS IRELAND (CAI), 47–49 Pearse Street, Dublin 2 **T** 0353-1637 7200
W www.charteredaccountants.ie
Chief Executive, Barry Dempsey

CHARTERED INSTITUTE OF MANAGEMENT ACCOUNTANTS (CIMA), The Helicon, One South Place, London EC2M 2RB **T** 020-8849 2251
E cima.contact@cimaglobal.com **W** www.cimaglobal.com
Chief Executive, Andrew Harding

CHARTERED INSTITUTE OF PUBLIC FINANCE AND ACCOUNTANCY (CIPFA), 77 Mansell Street, London E1 8AN **T** 020-7543 5600 **E** customerservices@cipfa.org
W www.cipfa.org
Chief Executive, Rob Whiteman

INSTITUTE OF CHARTERED ACCOUNTANTS IN ENGLAND AND WALES (ICAEW), Chartered Accountants' Hall, Moorgate Place, London EC2R 6EA
T 020-7920 8100 **E** general.enquiries@icaew.com
W www.icaew.com
Chief Executive, Michael Izza

INSTITUTE OF CHARTERED ACCOUNTANTS OF SCOTLAND (ICAS), CA House, 21 Haymarket Yards, Edinburgh EH12 5BH **T** 0131-347 0100 **E** enquiries@icas.org.uk
W www.icas.com
Chief Executive, Bruce Cartwright

ACTUARIAL SCIENCE

Salary range: £25,000–£35,000 for graduate trainees; £40,000–£55,000 after qualification; £60,000–£100,000+ for senior roles; £185,000+ for senior directors

Actuaries apply financial and statistical theories to solve business problems. These problems usually involve analysing future financial events in order to assess investment risks. To qualify, graduate trainees must complete 15 exams and three years worth of actuarial work-based training; most graduate trainees take between three and six years to qualify. Students can become Associate members of the Institute and Faculty of Actuaries (IFoA) and gain the right to describe themselves as an actuary and to use the letters AIA or AFA. Members of the profession who wish to continue their studies to an advanced level, or who specialise in a particular actuarial field, may take further specialist exams to qualify as a Fellow and bear the designations FIA or FFA.

The IFoA is the UK's chartered professional body dedicated to educating, developing and regulating actuaries based both in the UK and internationally. The IFoA represent and regulate their 29,000 members and oversee their education at all stages of qualification and development throughout their careers.

The Financial Reporting Council (FRC) is the unified independent regulator for corporate reporting, auditing, actuarial practice, corporate governance and the professionalism of accountants and actuaries. In 2012, the FRC assumed responsibility for setting and maintaining technical actuarial standards independently of the profession, as well as overseeing the regulation of the accountancy and actuarial professions by their respective professional bodies.

FINANCIAL REPORTING COUNCIL (FRC), 8th Floor, 125 London Wall, London EC2Y 5AS **T** 020-7492 2300
E enquiries@frc.org.uk **W** www.frc.org.uk
Chief Executive, Stephen Haddrill

INSTITUTE AND FACULTY OF ACTUARIES (IFoA), 7th
Floor, Holborn Gate, 326–330 High Holborn, London WC1V 7PP
T 020-7632 2100 E IFoA@actuaries.org.uk
W www.actuaries.org.uk
Chief Executive, Derek Cribb

ARCHITECTURE

Salary range: architectural assistant £24,000–£31,000; fully qualified £30,000–£45,000; senior associate, partner or director £90,000

It takes a minimum of seven years to become an architect, involving three stages: a three-year first degree, a two-year second degree or diploma and two years of professional experience followed by the successful completion of a professional practice examination.

The Architects Registration Board (ARB) is the independent regulator for the profession. It was set up by an act of parliament in 1997 and is responsible for maintaining the register of UK architects, prescribing qualifications that lead to registration as an architect, investigating complaints about the conduct and competence of architects and ensuring that only those who are registered with ARB offer their services as an architect. It is only following registration with ARB that an architect can apply for chartered membership of the Royal Institute of British Architects (RIBA). RIBA, the UK body for architecture and the architectural profession, received its royal charter in 1837 and validates courses at over 80 schools of architecture in the UK; it also validates overseas courses. RIBA provides support and guidance for its members in the form of training, technical services and events and sets standards for the education of architects.

The Chartered Institute of Architectural Technologists is the international qualifying body for Chartered Architectural Technologists (MCIAT) and Architectural Technicians (TCIAT).

ARCHITECTS REGISTRATION BOARD (ARB) 8
Weymouth Street, London W1W 5BU T 020-7580 5861
E info@arb.org.uk W www.arb.org.uk
Registrar and Chief Executive, Karen Holmes
CHARTERED INSTITUTE OF ARCHITECTURAL
TECHNOLOGISTS 397 City Road, London EC1V 1NH
T 020-7278 2206 E info@ciat.org.uk W www.ciat.org.uk
Chief Executive, Francesca Berriman, MBE
ROYAL INCORPORATION OF ARCHITECTS IN
SCOTLAND 15 Rutland Square, Edinburgh EH1 2BE
T 0131-229 7545 E info@rias.org.uk W www.rias.org.uk
Secretary and Treasurer, Karen Stevenson (acting)
ROYAL INSTITUTE OF BRITISH ARCHITECTS (RIBA)
66 Portland Place, London W1B 1AD T 020-7580 5533
E info@riba.org W www.architecture.com
Chief Executive, Alan Vallance

ENGINEERING

Salary range:
Civil/structural £23,500–£30,000 (graduate); £49,793 (members of the Institution of Civil Engineers (ICE)); £81,447 (fellows of ICE)
Chemical £29,500 average (graduate); £70,000+ (chartered)
Electrical £20,000–£25,000 (graduate); £28,000–£40,000 with experience; £40,000–£60,000+ (chartered)

The Engineering Council holds the national registers of Engineering Technicians (EngTech), Incorporated Engineers (IEng), Chartered Engineers (CEng) and Information and Communication Technology Technicians (ICTTech). It also sets and maintains the internationally recognised standards of competence and ethics that govern the award and retention of these titles.

To apply for the EngTech, IEng, CEng or ICTTech titles, an individual must be a member of one of the 35 engineering institutions and societies (listed below) currently licensed by the Engineering Council to assess candidates. Applicants must demonstrate that they possess a range of technical and personal competences and are committed to keeping these up-to-date.

ENGINEERING COUNCIL, 5th Floor, Woolgate Exchange, 25
Basinghall Street, London EC2V 5HA T 020-3206 0500
W www.engc.org.uk
Chief Executive, Alasdair Coates

LICENSED MEMBERS
BCS – The Chartered Institute for IT
W www.bcs.org
British Institute of Non-Destructive Testing
W www.bindt.org
Chartered Institute of Plumbing and Heating Engineering
W www.ciphe.org.uk
Chartered Institution of Building Services Engineers
W www.cibse.org
Chartered Institution of Highways and Transportation
W www.ciht.org.uk
Chartered Institution of Water and Environmental Management
W www.ciwem.org.uk
Energy Institute
W www.energyinst.org
Institute of Acoustics
W www.ioa.org.uk
Institute of Cast Metals Engineers
W www.icme.org.uk
Institute of Healthcare Engineering and Estate Management
W www.iheem.org.uk
Institute of Highway Engineers
W www.theihe.org
Institute of Marine Engineering, Science and Technology
W www.imarest.org
Institute of Materials, Minerals and Mining
W www.iom3.org
Institute of Measurement and Control
W www.instmc.org.uk
Institute of Physics
W www.iop.org
Institute of Physics and Engineering in Medicine
W www.ipem.ac.uk
Institute of Water
W www.instituteofwater.org.uk
Institution of Agricultural Engineers
W www.iagre.org
Institution of Chemical Engineers
W www.icheme.org
Institution of Civil Engineers
W www.ice.org.uk
Institution of Engineering Designers
W www.ied.org.uk
Institution of Engineering and Technology
W www.theiet.org
Institution of Fire Engineers
W www.ife.org.uk
Institution of Gas Engineers and Managers
W www.igem.org.uk
Institution of Lighting Professionals
W www.theilp.org.uk
Institution of Mechanical Engineers
W www.imeche.org
Institution of Railway Signal Engineers
W www.irse.org
Institution of Royal Engineers
W www.instre.org

Institution of Structural Engineers
W www.istructe.org
Nuclear Institute
W www.nuclearinst.com
Royal Aeronautical Society
W www.aerosociety.com
Royal Institution of Naval Architects
W www.rina.org.uk
Society of Environmental Engineers
W www.environmental.org.uk
Society of Operations Engineers
W www.soe.org.uk
The Welding Institute
W www.theweldinginstitute.com

HEALTHCARE

CHIROPRACTIC
Salary range: £20,000–£40,000 starting salary; with own practice £50,000–£70,000

Chiropractors diagnose and treat conditions caused by problems with joints, ligaments, tendons and nerves of the body. The General Chiropractic Council (GCC) is the independent statutory regulatory body for chiropractors and its role and remit is defined in the Chiropractors Act 1994. The GCC sets the criteria for the recognition of chiropractic degrees and for standards of proficiency and conduct. Details of the institutions offering degree programmes are available on the GCC website (*see* below). It is illegal for anyone in the UK to use the title 'chiropractor' unless registered with the GCC.

The British Chiropractic Association, Scottish Chiropractic Association, McTimoney Chiropractic Association and United Chiropractic Association are the representative bodies for the profession and are sources of further information.

BRITISH CHIROPRACTIC ASSOCIATION, 59 Castle Street, Reading RG1 7SN T 0118-950 5950
E enquiries@chiropractic-uk.co.uk W www.chiropractic-uk.co.uk
Executive Director, Mark Rawden
GENERAL CHIROPRACTIC COUNCIL (GCC), Park House, 186 Kennington Park Road, London SE11 4BT
T 020-7713 5155 E enquiries@gcc-uk.org W www.gcc-uk.org
Chief Executive and Registrar, Tricia McGregor (interim)
SCOTTISH CHIROPRACTIC ASSOCIATION, The Old Barn, Houston Road, Houston, Renfrewshire PA6 7BH
T 0141-404 0260 E admin@sca-chiropractic.org
W www.sca-chiropractic.org
Administrator, Morag Cairns

DENTISTRY
Salary range: see Health: Employees and Salaries

The General Dental Council (GDC) is the organisation that regulates dental professionals in the UK. All dentists, dental hygienists, dental therapists, dental technicians, clinical dental technicians, dental nurses and orthodontic therapists must be registered with the GDC to work in the UK.

There are various different routes to qualify for registration as a dentist, including holding a degree from a UK university, completing the GDC's qualifying examination or holding a relevant European Economic Area or overseas diploma. The GDC's purpose is to protect the public through the regulation of UK dental professionals. It keeps up-to-date registers of dental professionals, works to set standards of dental practice, behaviour and education, and helps to protect patients by hearing complaints and taking action against professionals where necessary.

Founded in 1880, the British Dental Association (BDA) is the professional association and trade union for dentists in the UK. It represents dentists working in general practice, in community and hospital settings, in academia, research and the armed forces, and includes dental students.

BRITISH DENTAL ASSOCIATION (BDA), 64 Wimpole Street, London W1G 8YS T 020-7935 0875 E enquiries@bda.org
W www.bda.org
Chief Executive, Peter Ward
GENERAL DENTAL COUNCIL (GDC), 37 Wimpole Street, London W1G 8DQ T 020-7167 6000 E information@gdc-uk.org
W www.gdc-uk.org
Chief Executive, Ian Brack

MEDICINE
Salary range: see Health: Employees and Salaries

The General Medical Council (GMC) regulates medical education and training in the UK. This covers undergraduate study (usually five years), the two-year foundation programme taken by doctors directly after graduation and all subsequent postgraduate study, including specialty and GP training.

All doctors must be registered with the GMC, which is responsible for protecting the public. It does this by promoting high standards of medical education and training, fostering good medical practice, keeping a register of qualified doctors and taking action where a doctor's fitness to practise is in doubt. Doctors are eligible for full registration upon successful completion of the first year of training after graduation.

Following the foundation programme, many doctors undertake specialist training (provided by the colleges and faculties listed below) to become either a consultant or a GP. Once specialist training has been completed, doctors are awarded the Certificate of Completion of Training (CCT) and are eligible to be placed on either the GMC's specialist register or its GP register.

GENERAL MEDICAL COUNCIL (GMC), Regent's Place, 350 Euston Road, London NW1 3JN T 0161-923 6602
E gmc@gmc-uk.org W www.gmc-uk.org
Chief Executive, Charlie Massey
WORSHIPFUL SOCIETY OF APOTHECARIES OF LONDON, Black Friars Lane, London EC4V 6EJ
T 020-7236 1189 E clerksec@apothecaries.org
W www.apothecaries.org
Master, Prof. Martin Rossor

SPECIALIST TRAINING COLLEGES AND FACULTIES
College of Emergency Medicine
W www.rcem.ac.uk
Faculty of Occupational Medicine
W www.facoccmed.ac.uk
Faculty of Public Health
W www.fph.org.uk
Joint Committee on Surgical Training
W www.jcst.org
Joint Royal Colleges of Physicians Training Board
W www.jrcptb.org.uk
Royal College of Anaesthetists
W www.rcoa.ac.uk
Royal College of General Practitioners
W www.rcgp.org.uk
Royal College of Obstetricians and Gynaecologists
W www.rcog.org.uk
Royal College of Ophthalmologists
W www.rcophth.ac.uk
Royal College of Paediatrics and Child Health
W www.rcpch.ac.uk
Royal College of Pathologists
W www.rcpath.org
Royal College of Physicians, London
W www.rcplondon.ac.uk
Royal College of Psychiatrists
W www.rcpsych.ac.uk
Royal College of Radiologists
W www.rcr.ac.uk

MEDICINE, SUPPLEMENTARY PROFESSIONS

The standard of professional education for arts therapists, biomedical scientists, chiropodists and podiatrists, clinical scientists, dietitians, hearing aid dispensers, occupational therapists, operating department practitioners, orthoptists, paramedics, physiotherapists, practitioner psychologists, prosthetists and orthotists, radiographers, social workers in England and speech and language therapists are regulated by the Health and Care Professions Council (HCPC), which only registers those practitioners who meet certain standards of training, professional skills, behaviour and health. The HCPC can take action against professionals who do not meet these standards or falsely declare they are registered. Each profession regulated by the HCPC has at least one professional title that is protected by law.

HEALTH AND CARE PROFESSIONS COUNCIL (HCPC),
Park House, 184 Kennington Park Road, London SE11 4BU
T 0300-500 6184 E registration@hcpc-uk.org
W www.hcpc-uk.org
Chief Executive and Registrar, Marc Seale

ART, DRAMA AND MUSIC THERAPIES
Salary range: £26,000–£35,000 (starting); £31,000–£48,000 with experience

An art, drama or music therapist encourages people to express their feelings and emotions through art, such as painting and drawing, drama or music. A postgraduate qualification in the relevant therapy is required. Details of accredited training programmes in the UK can be obtained from the following organisations:

BRITISH ASSOCIATION FOR MUSIC THERAPY, 24–27 White Lion Street, London N1 9PD T 020-7837 6100
E info@bamt.org W www.bamt.org
Chair, Ben Saul
BRITISH ASSOCIATION OF ART THERAPISTS, 24–27 White Lion Street, London N1 9PD T 020-7686 4216
E info@baat.org W www.baat.org
Chief Executive, Val Huet
BRITISH ASSOCIATION OF DRAMATHERAPISTS, PO Box 1257, Cheltenham, Gloucestershire GL50 9YX
T 01242-235515 E info@badth.org.uk W www.badth.org.uk
Chair, Alyson Coleman

BIOMEDICAL SCIENCES
Salary range: £21,000–£28,000 (starting); £26,000–£35,000 with experience; £31,500–48,000 for senior roles

The Institute of Biomedical Science (IBMS) is the professional body for biomedical scientists in the UK. Biomedical scientists carry out investigations on tissue and body fluid samples to diagnose disease and monitor the progress of a patient's treatment. The IBMS sets quality standards for the profession through training, education, assessments, examinations and continuous professional development.

INSTITUTE OF BIOMEDICAL SCIENCE (IBMS), 12 Coldbath Square, London EC1R 5HL T 020-7713 0214
E mail@ibms.org W www.ibms.org
Chief Executive, Jill Rodney

CHIROPODY AND PODIATRY
Salary range: £22,000–£41,500

Chiropodists and podiatrists assess, diagnose and treat problems of the lower leg and foot. The Society of Chiropodists and Podiatrists is the professional body and trade union for the profession. Qualifications granted and degrees recognised by the society are approved by the HCPC. HCPC registration is required in order to use the titles chiropodist and podiatrist.

SOCIETY OF CHIROPODISTS AND PODIATRISTS,
Quartz House, 207 Providence Square, Mill Street, London SE1 2EW T 020-7234 8620 E reception@scpod.org
W www.scpod.org
Chief Executive, Steve Jamieson

CLINICAL SCIENCE
Salary range: £25,000–£99,000

Clinical scientists conduct tests in laboratories in order to diagnose and manage disease. The Association of Clinical Scientists is responsible for setting the criteria for competence of applicants to the HCPC's register and for presenting a Certificate of Attainment to candidates following a successful assessment. This certificate will allow direct registration with the HCPC.

ASSOCIATION OF CLINICAL SCIENTISTS, 130–132 Tooley Street, London SE1 2TU T 020-7940 8960
E info@assclinsci.org W www.assclinsci.org
Chair, Prof. Richard Lerski

DIETETICS
Salary range: £22,000–£41,500

Dietitians advise patients on how to improve their health and counter specific health problems through diet. The British Dietetic Association, established in 1936, is the professional association for dietitians. Full membership is open to UK-registered dietitians, who must also be registered with the HCPC.

BRITISH DIETETIC ASSOCIATION, 5th Floor, Charles House, 148–149 Great Charles Street Queensway, Birmingham B3 3HT T 0121-200 8080 E info@bda.uk.com
W www.bda.uk.com
Chief Executive, Andy Burman

MENTAL HEALTH
Salary range:
Clinical psychologist £26,000, rising to £46,000–£81,000 at senior levels
Counselling psychologist £26,000–£35,000 (starting), rising to £31,500–£41,500 (qualified) and up to £82,000 at senior levels
Educational psychologist £22,000, rising to £47,000 (fully qualified) and up to £65,000 at senior levels
Psychotherapist £21,600–£28,000 (starting), rising to £47,500 with experience

Psychologists and counsellors are mental health professionals who can work in a range of settings including prisons, schools and hospitals. The British Psychological Society (BPS) is the representative body for psychology and psychologists in the UK. The BPS is responsible for the development, promotion and application of psychology for the public good. The Association of Educational Psychologists (AEP) represents the interests of educational psychologists. The British Association for Counselling and Psychotherapy (BACP) sets educational standards and provides professional support to counsellors, psychotherapists and others working in counselling, psychotherapy or counselling-related roles. The BPS website provides more information on the different specialisations that may be pursued by psychologists.

ASSOCIATION OF EDUCATIONAL PSYCHOLOGISTS
(AEP), 4 The Riverside Centre, Frankland Lane, Durham DH1 5TA T 0191-384 9512 E enquiries@aep.org.uk W www.aep.org.uk
President, vacant

BRITISH ASSOCIATION FOR COUNSELLING AND PSYCHOTHERAPY (BACP), BACP House, 15 St John's Business Park, Lutterworth, Leicestershire LE17 4HB
T 01455-883300 E bacp@bacp.co.uk W www.bacp.co.uk
President, David Weaver

BRITISH PSYCHOLOGICAL SOCIETY (BPS), St Andrews House, 48 Princess Road East, Leicester LE1 7DR
T 0116-254 9568 E enquiries@bps.org.uk
W www.beta.bps.org.uk
President, Kate Bullen

OCCUPATIONAL THERAPY
Salary range: £22,000–£41,500; £40,000–£58,000 for consultancy roles

Occupational therapists work with people who have physical, mental and/or social problems, either from birth or as a result of accident, illness or ageing, and aim to make them as independent as possible. The professional qualification and eligibility for registration may be obtained upon successful completion of a validated course in any of the educational institutions approved by the College of Occupational Therapists, which is the professional body for occupational therapy in the UK. The courses are normally degree-level and based in higher education institutions.

COLLEGE OF OCCUPATIONAL THERAPISTS, 106–114 Borough High Street, London SE1 1LB T 020-7357 6480
E hello@rcot.co.uk W www.rcot.co.uk
Chief Executive, Julia Scott

ORTHOPTICS
Salary range: £21,500 (graduate), rising to £30,700–£81,500 in senior posts

Orthoptists undertake the diagnosis and treatment of all types of squint and other anomalies of binocular vision, working in close collaboration with ophthalmologists. The all-graduate workforce comes from three universities: the University of Liverpool, the University of Sheffield and Glasgow Caledonian University.

BRITISH AND IRISH ORTHOPTIC SOCIETY, Salisbury House, Station Road, Cambridge CB1 2LA T 07748-288238
E bios@orthoptics.org.uk W www.orthoptics.org.uk
Chair, Rowena McNamara

PARAMEDICAL SERVICES
Salary range: £22,000–£35,500; £56,000–£68,500 for consultancy roles

Paramedics deal with accidents and emergencies, assessing patients and carrying out any specialist treatment and care needed in the first instance. The body that represents ambulance professionals is the College of Paramedics.

COLLEGE OF PARAMEDICS, The Exchange, Express Park, Bristol Road, Bridgwater TA6 4RR T 01278-420014
E membership@collegeofparamedics.co.uk
W www.collegeofparamedics.co.uk
Chief Executive, Gerry Egan

PHYSIOTHERAPY
Salary range: £22,000–£41,500

Physiotherapists are concerned with movement and function and deal with problems arising from injury, illness and ageing. Full-time three- or four-year degree courses are available at around 36 higher education institutions in the UK. Information about courses leading to state registration is available from the Chartered Society of Physiotherapy.

CHARTERED SOCIETY OF PHYSIOTHERAPY, 14 Bedford Row, London WC1R 4ED T 020-7306 6666
W www.csp.org.uk
Chief Executive, Karen Middleton, CBE

PROSTHETICS AND ORTHOTICS
Salary range: £21,000 on qualification, up to £67,000 as a consultant

Prosthetists provide artificial limbs, while orthotists provide devices to support or control a part of the body. It is necessary to obtain an honours degree to become a prosthetist or orthotist. Training is centred at the University of Salford and the University of Strathclyde.

BRITISH ASSOCIATION OF PROSTHETISTS AND ORTHOTISTS, Unit 3010, Mile End Mill, Abbey Mill Business Centre, Paisley PA1 1JS T 0141-561 7217 E enquiries@bapo.com
W www.bapo.com
Chair, Lynne Rowley

RADIOGRAPHY
Salary range: £21,000–£40,000, rising to £67,800 in consultancy posts

In order to practise both diagnostic and therapeutic radiography in the UK, it is necessary to have successfully completed a course of education and training recognised by the HCPC. Such courses are offered by around 24 universities throughout the UK and lead to the award of a degree in radiography. Further information is available from the Society of Radiographers, the trade union and professional body which represents the whole of the radiographic workforce in the UK.

SOCIETY OF RADIOGRAPHERS, 207 Providence Square, Mill Street, London SE1 2EW T 020-7740 7200 W www.sor.org
Chief Executive, Richard Evans, OBE

SPEECH AND LANGUAGE THERAPY
Salary range: £21,500–£40,500

Speech and language therapists (SLTs) work with people with communication, swallowing, eating and drinking problems. The Royal College of Speech and Language Therapists is the professional body for speech and language therapists and support workers. Alongside the HCPC, it accredits education and training courses leading to qualification.

ROYAL COLLEGE OF SPEECH AND LANGUAGE THERAPISTS, 2 White Hart Yard, London SE1 1NX
T 020-7378 1200 E info@rcslt.org W www.rcslt.org
Chief Executive, Kamini Gadhok, MBE

NURSING
Salary range: see Health: Employees and Salaries

In order to practise in the UK, all nurses and midwives must be registered with the Nursing and Midwifery Council (NMC). The NMC is a statutory regulatory body that establishes and maintains standards of education, training, conduct and performance for nursing and midwifery. Courses leading to registration are currently at a minimum of degree level. All take a minimum of three years if undertaken full-time. The NMC approves programmes run jointly by higher education institutions with their healthcare service partners who offer clinical placements. The nursing part of the register has four fields of practice: adult, children's (paediatric), learning disability and mental health nursing. In most cases students must select one specific field to study before applying to an institution. Some universities run courses which offer the simultaneous study of two nursing fields. In addition, those studying to become adult nurses gain experience of nursing in relation to medicine, surgery, maternity care and nursing in the home. The NMC also sets standards for programmes leading to registration as a midwife and a range of post-registration courses including specialist practice programmes, nurse prescribing and those for teachers of nursing and midwifery. The NMC has a part of the register for specialist community public health nurses and approves programmes for health visitors, occupational health nurses and school nurses.

The Royal College of Nursing is the largest professional union for nursing in the UK, representing qualified nurses, midwives, healthcare assistants and nursing students in the NHS and the independent sector.

NURSING AND MIDWIFERY COUNCIL (NMC), 23
Portland Place, London W1B 1PZ T 020-7637 7181
E ukenquiries@nmc-uk.org W www.nmc.org.uk
Chief Executive and Registrar, Sue Killen (interim)
ROYAL COLLEGE OF NURSING, 20 Cavendish Square,
London W1G 0RN T 020-7409 3333 W www.rcn.org.uk
Chief Executive and General Secretary, Janet Davies

OPTOMETRY AND DISPENSING OPTICS
Salary range:
Optometrist £19,00–£82,000 (NHS); £14,000–£60,000+ (private)
Dispensing Optician £16,000–£35,000+

There are various routes to qualification as a dispensing optician. Qualification takes three years in total, and can be completed by combining a distance learning course or day release while working as a trainee under the supervision of a qualified and registered optician. Alternatively, students can do a two-year full-time course followed by one year of supervised practice with a qualified and registered optician. Training must be done at a training establishment approved by the regulatory body – the General Optical Council (GOC). There are six training establishments which are approved by the GOC: ABDO (Association of British Dispensing Opticians) College, Anglia Ruskin University, Bradford College, City and Islington College, City University and Glasgow Caledonian University. After the completion of training to fit contact lenses and attaining the ABDO Level 6 certificate in contact lens practice qualification, a Contact Lens Optician may apply to be included in the GOC Speciality Register. Students are also able to complete a Foundation or Undergraduate degree in Ophthalmic Dispensing, offered by ABDO in conjunction with Canterbury Christ Church University. All routes are concluded by professional qualifying examinations, successful completion of which leads to the awarding of the Level 6 Fellowship Diploma of the Association of British Dispensing Opticians (FBDO) by ABDO. FBDO holders are able to register with the GOC following the awarding of their diploma, with registration being compulsory for all practising dispensing opticians.

Continuing Education and Training (CET) is a statutory requirement for all registered dispensing opticians and contact lens opticians to retain GOC registration.

ASSOCIATION OF BRITISH DISPENSING OPTICIANS
(ABDO), Godmersham Park, Godmersham, Canterbury, Kent
CT4 7DT T 01227-733905 E general@abdo.org.uk
W www.abdo.org.uk
General Secretary, Sir Anthony Garrett, CBE
COLLEGE OF OPTOMETRISTS, 42 Craven Street, London
WC2N 5NG T 020-7839 6000 W www.college-optometrists.org
Chief Executive, Ian Humphreys
GENERAL OPTICAL COUNCIL (GOC), 10 Old Bailey,
London EC4M 7NG T 020-7580 3898 E goc@optical.org
W www.optical.org
Chief Executive and Registrar, Adam Sampson (interim)

OSTEOPATHY
Salary Range: £20,000–£100,000+

Osteopathy is a system of diagnosis and treatment for a wide range of conditions. It works with the structure and function of the body, and is based on the principle that the well-being of an individual depends on the skeleton, muscles, ligaments and connective tissues functioning smoothly together. The General Osteopathic Council (GOsC) regulates the practice of osteopathy in the UK and maintains a register of those entitled to practise. It is a criminal offence for anyone to describe themselves as an osteopath unless they are registered with the GOsC.

To gain entry to the register, applicants must hold a recognised qualification from an osteopathic education institute accredited by the GOsC; this involves a four- to five-year honours degree programme combined with clinical training.

GENERAL OSTEOPATHIC COUNCIL (GOsC), Osteopathy
House, 176 Tower Bridge Road, London SE1 3LU
T 020-7357 6655 E info@osteopathy.org.uk
W www.osteopathy.org.uk
Chief Executive and Registrar, Tim Walker

PHARMACY
Salary range: £20,000–£68,000+

Pharmacists are involved in the preparation and use of medicines, from the discovery of their active ingredients to their use by patients. Pharmacists also monitor the effects of medicines, both for patient care and for research purposes.

The General Pharmaceutical Council (GPhC) is the independent regulatory body for pharmacists in England, Scotland and Wales, having taken over the regulating function of the Royal Pharmaceutical Society in 2010. The GPhC maintains the register of pharmacists, pharmacy technicians and pharmacy premises; it also sets national standards for training, ethics, proficiency and continuing professional development. The Pharmaceutical Society of Northern Ireland (PSNI) performs the same role in Northern Ireland. In order to register, students must complete a four-year degree in pharmacy that is accredited by either the GPhC or the PSNI, followed by one year of pre-registration training at an approved pharmacy; they must then pass an entrance examination.

GENERAL PHARMACEUTICAL COUNCIL (GPhC), 25
Canada Square, London, E14 5LQ T 020-3713 8000
E info@pharmacyregulation.org
W www.pharmacyregulation.org
Chief Executive and Registrar, Duncan Rudkin
PHARMACEUTICAL SOCIETY OF NORTHERN
IRELAND (PSNI), 73 University Street, Belfast BT7 1HL
T 028-9032 6927 E info@psni.org.uk W www.psni.org.uk
Chief Executive, Trevor Patterson
ROYAL PHARMACEUTICAL SOCIETY, 66 East Smithfield,
London, E1W 1AW T 020-7572 2737 E support@rpharms.com
W www.rpharms.com
Chief Executive, Paul Bennett

INFORMATION MANAGEMENT

Salary range: Archivist £22,443 (newly qualified); £25,000–£38,000 (with experience); £55,000 in senior posts
Information Officer £17,000–£21,000 (starting); £21,000–£28,000 (newly qualified); £26,000–£50,000+ in senior and chartered posts
Librarian £19,800–£24,500 (newly qualified); £24,000–£30,000 (chartered); £32,000–£40,000 (senior); £45,000–£55,000 (head of service)

The Chartered Institute of Library and Information Professionals (CILIP) is the leading professional body for librarians, information specialists and knowledge managers. The Archives and Records Association is the professional body for archivists and record managers.

ARCHIVES AND RECORDS ASSOCIATION, Prioryfield House, 20 Canon Street, Taunton, Somerset TA1 1SW
T 01823-327077 E ara@archives.org.uk W www.archives.org.uk
Chief Executive, John Chambers
CHARTERED INSTITUTE OF LIBRARY AND INFORMATION PROFESSIONALS (CILIP), 7 Ridgmount Street, London WC1E 7AE T 020-7255 0500 E info@cilip.org.uk
W www.cilip.org.uk
Chief Executive Nick Poole

JOURNALISM

Salary range: £12,000–£15,000 (trainee); £25,000 for established journalists, rising to £35,000–£40,000 for those with over a decade's experience

The National Council for the Training of Journalists (NCTJ) accredits courses for journalists run by a number of different education providers throughout the United Kingdom; it also provides professional support to journalists.
The Broadcast Journalism Training Council (BJTC) is an association of the UK's main broadcast journalism employers and accredits courses in broadcast journalism.

BROADCAST JOURNALISM TRAINING COUNCIL (BJTC), Sterling House, 20 Station Road, Gerard's Cross, Buckinghamshire, SL9 8EL T 0845-600 8789 E sec@bjtc.org.uk
W www.bjtc.org.uk
Chief Executive, Jon Godel
NATIONAL COUNCIL FOR THE TRAINING OF JOURNALISTS (NCTJ), The New Granary, Station Road, Newport, Saffron Walden, Essex CB11 3PL T 01799-544014
E info@nctj.com W www.nctj.com
Chief Executive, Joanne Butcher

LAW

There are three types of practising lawyers: barristers, notaries and solicitors. Solicitors tend to work as a group in firms, and can be approached directly by individuals. They advise on a variety of legal issues and must decide the most appropriate course of action, if any. Notaries have all the powers of a solicitor other than the conduct of litigation. Most of them are primarily concerned with the preparation and authentication of documents for use abroad. Barristers are usually self-employed. If a solicitor believes that a barrister is required, he or she will instruct one on behalf of the client; the client will not have contact with the barrister without the solicitor being present.
When specialist expertise is needed, barristers give opinions on complex matters of law, and when clients require representation in the higher courts (crown courts, the high court, the court of appeal and the supreme court), barristers provide a specialist advocacy service. However, solicitors – who represent their clients in the lower courts such as magistrates' courts and county courts – can also apply for advocacy rights in the higher courts instead of briefing a barrister.

THE BAR

Salary range: £12,000–£65,000 (pupillage); £25,000–£300,000 (qualified); £1,000,000+ with ten years experience

The governing body of the Bar of England and Wales is the General Council of the Bar, also known as the Bar Council. Since January 2006, the regulatory functions of the Bar Council (including regulating the education and training requirements for those wishing to enter the profession) have been undertaken by the Bar Standards Board.
In the first (or 'academic') stage of training, aspiring barristers must obtain a law degree of a good standard (at least second class). Alternatively, those with a non-law degree (at least second class) may complete a one-year full-time or two-year part-time Common Professional Examination (CPE) or Graduate Diploma in Law (GDL).
The second (vocational) stage is the completion of the Bar Professional Training Course (BPTC), which is available at a number of validated institutions in the UK and must be applied for around one year in advance. All barristers must join one of the four Inns of Court prior to commencing the BPTC.
Students are 'called to the Bar' by their Inn after completion of the vocational stage, but cannot practise as a barrister until completion of the third stage, which is called 'pupillage'. Being called to the Bar does not entitle a person to practise as a barrister – successful completion of pupillage is now a prerequisite. Pupillage lasts for two six-month periods: the 'first six' and the 'second six'. The former consists of shadowing an experienced barrister, while the latter involves appearing in court as a barrister. Chambers can then offer a long term 'tenancy' to students. Students who are not given 'tenancy' may take a 'third six'.
Admission to the Bar of Northern Ireland is controlled by the Bar of Northern Ireland; admission as an Advocate to the Scottish Bar is through the Faculty of Advocates.

BAR STANDARDS BOARD address as below
E contactus@barstandardsboard.org.uk
W www.barstandardsboard.org.uk
Chair of the Bar Council, Sir Andrew Burns, KCMG
FACULTY OF ADVOCATES, Parliament Square, Edinburgh EH1 1RF T 0131-226 5071 E info@advocates.org.uk
W www.advocates.org.uk
Dean, Gordon Jackson, QC
GENERAL COUNCIL OF THE BAR (THE BAR COUNCIL), 289–293 High Holborn, London WC1V 7HZ
T 020-7242 0082 E contactus@barcouncil.org.uk
W www.barcouncil.org.uk
Chief Executive, Malcolm Cree, CBE
THE BAR OF NORTHERN IRELAND, 91 Chichester Street, Belfast BT1 3JQ T 028-9024 1523 W www.barofni.com
Chief Executive, David Mulholland

THE INNS OF COURT

HONOURABLE SOCIETY OF GRAY'S INN, 8 South Square, London WC1R 5ET T 020-7458 7800
W www.graysinn.org.uk
Under-Treasurer, Brig. Anthony Harking, OBE
HONOURABLE SOCIETY OF LINCOLN'S INN, Treasury Office, Lincoln's Inn, London WC2A 3TL T 020-7405 1393
E mail@lincolnsinn.org.uk W www.lincolnsinn.org.uk
Under-Treasurer, Mary Kerr
HONOURABLE SOCIETY OF THE INNER TEMPLE, Treasury Office, Inner Temple, London EC4Y 7HL
T 020-7797 8250 E enquiries@innertemple.org.uk
W www.innertemple.org.uk
Treasurer, Rt. Hon. Dame Elizabeth Gloster, DBE

HONOURABLE SOCIETY OF THE MIDDLE TEMPLE, Treasury Office, Ashley Building, Middle Temple Lane, London EC4Y 9BT T 020-7427 4800 E education@middletemple.org.uk W www.middletemple.org.uk
Chief Executive, Guy Perricone

NOTARIES PUBLIC

Notaries are qualified lawyers with a postgraduate diploma in notarial practice. Once a potential notary has passed the postgraduate diploma, they can petition the Court of Faculties for a 'faculty'. After the faculty is granted, the notary is able to practise; however, for the first two years this must be under the supervision of an experienced notary. The admission and regulation of notaries in England and Wales is a statutory function of the Faculty Office. This jurisdiction was confirmed by the Courts and Legal Services Act 1990. The Notaries Society of England and Wales is the representative body for practising notaries.

THE FACULTY OFFICE, 1 The Sanctuary, Westminster, London SW1P 3JT T 020-7222 5381 E faculty.office@1thesanctuary.com W www.facultyoffice.org.uk
Registrar, Howard Dellar
THE NOTARIES SOCIETY OF ENGLAND AND WALES, PO Box 1023, Ipswich IP1 9XB E admin@thenotariessociety.org.uk W www.thenotariessociety.org.uk
Secretary, Christopher Vaughan

SOLICITORS
Salary range: Trainee solicitors paid at least the national minimum wage; £25,000–£75,000 after qualification; £100,000+ (associate or partner)

Graduates from any discipline can train to be a solicitor; however, if the undergraduate degree is not in law, a one-year conversion course – either the Common Professional Examination (CPE) or the Graduate Diploma in Law (GDL) – must be completed. The next stage, and the beginning of the vocational phase, is the Legal Practice Course (LPC), which takes one year and is obligatory for both law and non-law graduates. The LPC provides professional instruction for prospective solicitors and can be completed on a full-time or part-time basis. Trainee solicitors then enter the final stage, which is a paid period of supervised work that lasts two years for full-time contracts. The employer that provides the training contract must be authorised by the Solicitors Regulation Authority (SRA) (the regulatory body of the Law Society of England and Wales), the Law Society of Scotland or the Law Society of Northern Ireland. The SRA also monitors the training contract to ensure that it provides the trainee with the expertise to qualify as a solicitor.

Conveyancers are specialist property lawyers, dealing with the legal processes involved in transferring buildings, land and associated finances from one owner to another. This was the sole responsibility of solicitors until 1987 but under current legislation it is now possible for others to train as conveyancers.

COUNCIL FOR LICENSED CONVEYANCERS (CLC), WeWork, 131 Finsbury Pavement, London EC2A 1NT T 020-3859 0904 E clc@clc-uk.org W www.clc-uk.org
Chief Executive, Sheila Kumar
THE LAW SOCIETY OF ENGLAND AND WALES, The Law Society's Hall, 113 Chancery Lane, London WC2A 1PL T 020-7242 1222 W www.lawsociety.org.uk
Chief Executive, Paul Tennant, OBE
LAW SOCIETY OF NORTHERN IRELAND, 96 Victoria Street, Belfast BT1 3GN T 028-9023 1614 E enquiry@lawsoc-ni.org W www.lawsoc-ni.org
Chief Executive, Alan Hunter

LAW SOCIETY OF SCOTLAND, Atria One, 144 Morrison Street, Edinburgh EH3 8EX T 0131-226 7411 E lawscot@lawscot.org.uk W www.lawscot.org.uk
Chief Executive, Lorna Jack
SOLICITORS REGULATION AUTHORITY (SRA), The Cube, 199 Wharfside Street, Birmingham B1 1RN T 0370-606 2555 W www.sra.org.uk
Chief Executive, Paul Philip

SOCIAL WORK
Salary range: £22,000 (newly qualified); £40,000 (with experience); £26,041–£34,876 (NHS)

Social workers tend to specialise in either adult or children's services. The HCPC obtained regulatory responsibility from the General Social Care Council in August 2012 and is responsible for setting standards of conduct and practice for social care workers and their employers, regulating the workforce and social work education and training. A degree or postgraduate qualification is needed in order to become a social worker. For more information *see* Social Welfare.

HEALTH AND CARE PROFESSIONS COUNCIL (HCPC), Park House, 184 Kennington Park Road, London SE11 4BU T 0300-500 6184 E registration@hcpc-uk.org W www.hcpc-uk.org
Chief Executive and Registrar, Marc Seale

SURVEYING
Salary range: £18,500–£22,000 (starting); £45,000 (senior); up to £100,000 (partners and directors)

The Royal Institution of Chartered Surveyors (RICS) is the professional body that represents and regulates property professionals including land surveyors, valuers, auctioneers, quantity surveyors and project managers. Entry to the institution, following completion of a RICS-accredited degree, is through completion of the Assessment of Professional Competence (APC), which involves a period of practical training concluded by a final assessment of competence. Entry as a technical surveyor requires completion of the Assessment of Technical Competence (ATC), which mirrors the format of the APC. The different levels of RICS membership are MRICS (member) or FRICS (fellow) for chartered surveyors, and AssocRICS for associate members.

Relevant courses can also be accredited by the Chartered Institute of Building (CIOB), which represents managers working in a range of construction disciplines. The CIOB offers four levels of membership to those who satisfy its requirements: FCIOB (fellow), MCIOB (member), ICIOB (incorporated) and ACIOB (associate).

CHARTERED INSTITUTE OF BUILDING (CIOB), 1 Arlington Square, Downshire Way, Bracknell RG12 1WA T 01344-630700 E reception@ciob.org W www.ciob.org
Chief Executive, Chris Blythe, OBE
ROYAL INSTITUTION OF CHARTERED SURVEYORS (RICS), Parliament Square, London SW1P 3AD T 024-7686 8555 E contactrics@rics.org W www.rics.org
Chief Executive, Sean Tompkins

TEACHING
Salary range: school teachers £23,500–£48,000; school leaders £39,500–£111,000 (for more detailed information *see* Education: Employees and Salaries)

Since 1 April 2018, the Teaching Regulation Agency, an executive agency sponsored by the Department for Education, is responsible for maintaining the register of qualified teachers in England and is the awarding body for Qualified Teacher Status (QTS). The Education Workforce Council in Wales and the General Teaching Council for Scotland fulfil this responsibility in their respective administrations. In Northern Ireland teacher registration is the responsibility of the General Teaching Council for Northern Ireland. Registration is a legal requirement in order to teach in local authority maintained schools. UCAS Teacher Training is the body through which to apply for postgraduate teacher training in the UK. To become a qualified teacher, all entrants must have a degree and gain QTS, which includes a minimum of 24 weeks in at least two different schools and academic study of teaching. Another route is through School-centred Initial Teacher Training (SCITT), where practical, hands-on teacher training is delivered by experienced, practising teachers in their own government-approved school.

Many courses also award an academic qualification known as the Postgraduate Certificate in Education (PGCE) in England and Wales and the Professional Graduate Diploma in Education (PGDE) in Scotland. Once training is completed, applicants spend a year in school as a newly qualified teacher (NQT).

Teachers in Further Education (FE) need not have QTS, though new entrants to FE may be required to work towards a specified FE qualification by employers. A range of courses are offered and usually require one year of study in addition to 100 hours of teaching experience. Similarly, academic staff in Higher Education require no formal teaching qualification, but are expected to obtain a qualification that meets standards set by the Higher Education Academy.

Details of routes to gaining QTS in England are available from the Department for Education, the Teaching Regulation Agency and UCAS. In the devolved administrations information is available from the Welsh government, Teach in Scotland and from the Department of Education in Northern Ireland.

In July 2017, the College of Teaching became the Chartered College of Teaching. Under the terms of its royal charter, it provides professional qualifications and membership to teachers and those involved in education in the UK and overseas.

CHARTERED COLLEGE OF TEACHING, 9–11 Endsleigh Gardens, London WC1H 0EH T 020-7911 5589
E hello@chartered.college W www.chartered.college
Chief Executive, Prof. Dame Alison Peacock, DBE
DEPARTMENT OF EDUCATION NORTHERN IRELAND, Rathgael House, Balloo Road, Rathgill, Bangor BT19 7PR T 028-9127 9279 E DE.DEWebMail@education-ni.gov.uk W www.education-ni.gov.uk
EDUCATION WORKFORCE COUNCIL, 9th Floor, Eastgate House, 35–43 Newport Road, Cardiff CF24 0AB
T 029-2046 0099 E information@ewc.wales W www.ewc.wales
Chief Executive, Hayden Llewellyn
GENERAL TEACHING COUNCIL FOR NORTHERN IRELAND, 3rd Floor, Albany House, 73–75 Great Victoria Street, Belfast BT2 7AF T 028-9033 3390 E info@gtcni.org.uk W www.gtcni.org.uk
Chair, David Canning, OBE

GENERAL TEACHING COUNCIL FOR SCOTLAND, Clerwood House, 96 Clermiston Road, Edinburgh EH12 6UT T 0131-314 6000 E gtcs@gtcs.org.uk W www.gtcs.org.uk
Chief Executive, Ken Muir
HIGHER EDUCATION ACADEMY, Innovation Way, York Science Park, Heslington, York YO10 5BR T 01904-717500
E enquiries@advance-he.ac.uk W www.heacademy.ac.uk
Chief Executive, Prof. Stephanie Marshall
TEACHING REGULATION AGENCY, 53–55 Butts Road, Earlsdon Park, Coventry CV1 3BH T 0207 593 5394
E qts.enquiries@education.gov.uk W www.gov.uk/government/organisations/teaching-regulation-agency
Chief Executive, Alan Meyrick
UCAS TEACHER TRAINING, Rosehill, New Barn Lane, Cheltenham GL52 3LZ T 0371-468 0469 W www.ucas.com/teaching-in-the-uk
Chief Executive, Clare Marchant

VETERINARY MEDICINE

Salary range: £31,150 (newly qualified); £41,148–£44,142 (with experience); £70,000 (twenty years experience)

The regulatory body for veterinary surgeons in the UK is the Royal College of Veterinary Surgeons (RCVS), which keeps the register of those entitled to practise veterinary medicine, the register of veterinary nurses and veterinary practice premises (on behalf of the Veterinary Medicines Directorate). Holders of recognised degrees from any of the seven UK university veterinary schools that have been approved by the RCVS or from certain EU or overseas universities are entitled to be registered, and holders of certain other degrees may take a statutory membership examination. The UK's RCVS-approved veterinary schools are located at the University of Bristol, the University of Cambridge, the University of Edinburgh, the University of Glasgow, the University of Liverpool, Middlesex University and the Royal Veterinary College in London; all veterinary degrees last for five years except that offered at Cambridge, which lasts for six.

The British Veterinary Association is the national representative body for the UK veterinary profession. The British Veterinary Nursing Association is the professional body representing veterinary nurses.

BRITISH VETERINARY ASSOCIATION, 7 Mansfield Street, London W1G 9NQ T 020-7636 6541 E bvahq@bva.co.uk W www.bva.co.uk
Chief Executive, David Calpin
BRITISH VETERINARY NURSING ASSOCIATION, 79 Greenway Business Centre, Harlow Business Park, Harlow, Essex CM19 5QE T 01279-408644 E bvna@bvna.co.uk W www.bvna.org.uk
Honorary Treasurer, Erika Feilberg
ROYAL COLLEGE OF VETERINARY SURGEONS (RCVS), Belgravia House, 62–64 Horseferry Road, London SW1P 2AF T 020-7222 2001 E info@rcvs.org.uk W www.rcvs.org.uk
Chief Executive, Lizzie Lockett

INDEPENDENT SCHOOLS

Independent schools (non-maintained mainstream schools) charge fees and are owned privately or managed under special trusts, with profits being used for the benefit of the schools concerned. In 2016–17 there were 2,480 non-maintained mainstream schools in the UK, educating around 584,000 pupils, or around 6 per cent of the total school-age population. The number of pupils at non-maintained mainstream schools as at January 2018 was approximately:

England	545,000
Wales	9,200
Scotland	29,600
Northern Ireland	490

The Independent Schools Council (ISC), formed in 1974, acts on behalf of the seven independent schools' associations which constitute it. These associations are:

Association of Governing Bodies of Independent Schools (AGBIS)
Girls' Schools Association (GSA)
Headmasters' & Headmistresses' Conference (HMC)
Independent Association of Prep Schools (IAPS)
Independent Schools Association (ISA)
Independent Schools' Bursars Association (ISBA)
The Society of Heads

In 2017 there were 529,164 pupils being educated in 1,316 schools in membership of associations within the Independent Schools Council (ISC). Most schools not in membership of an ISC association are likely to be privately owned. The

Independent Schools Inspectorate (ISI) was demerged from ISC with effect from 1 January 2008 and is legally and operationally independent of ISC. ISI works as an accredited inspectorate of schools in membership of the ISC associations under a framework agreed with the Department for Education (DfE). A school must pass an ISI accreditation inspection to qualify for membership of an association within ISC.

In 2018 at GCSE 62.6 per cent of all exams taken by candidates in ISC associations' member schools achieved either an A/7 grade or higher (compared to the national average of 20.5 per cent), and at A-level 17.7 per cent of entries were awarded an A* grade (national average, 8 per cent). In 2017 a total of 171,488 (33 per cent) pupils at schools in ISC associations received help with their fees, mainly in the form of bursaries and scholarships from the schools. ISC schools provided more than £800m of assistance with fees.

INDEPENDENT SCHOOLS COUNCIL
First Floor, 27 Queen Anne's Gate, London SW1H 9BU
T 020-7766 7070 W www.isc.co.uk

The list of schools below was compiled from the *Independent Schools Yearbook 2017–18* (ed. Judy Mott, published by Bloomsbury Publishing) which includes schools whose heads are members of one of the ISC's five Heads' Associations. Further details are available online (W www.isyb.co.uk).

The fees shown below represent the upper limit payable for the year 2018–19 (marked with an asterisk); where these are not yet known, the fees below are the upper limit payable for 2017–18.

School	Web Address	Termly Fees Day	Board	Head
ENGLAND				
Abbey Gate College, Cheshire	www.abbeygatecollege.co.uk	£4,136	–	Mrs T. Pollard
Abbots Bromley School, Staffs	www.abbotsbromleyschool.com	£5,119	£8,575	Mrs M. Shackleton
Abbot's Hill School, Herts	www.abbotshill.herts.sch.uk	£5,998	–	Mrs E. Thomas
Abbotsholme School, Derbys, Staffs	www.abbotsholme.co.uk	£7,290	£10,705	R. Barnes
Abingdon School, Oxon	www.abingdon.org.uk	£6,425	–	M. Windsor
Adcote School, Shrops	www.adcoteschool.org.uk	£4,946	£9,032	Mrs D. Browne
AKS Lytham, Lancs	www.arnoldkeqms.com	£3,778	–	M. Walton
Aldenham School, Herts	www.aldenham.com	£7,338	£10,827	J. Fowler
Alderley Edge School for Girls, Cheshire	www.aesg.co.uk	£3,990	–	Mrs H. Jeys
Alleyn's School, London, SE22	www.alleyns.org.uk	£6,284	–	Dr G. Savage
Ampleforth College, N. Yorks	www.ampleforth.org.uk/college	£7,973	£11,464	Fr W. Peterburs
Ardingly College, W. Sussex	www.ardingly.com	£7,870	£11,140	B. Figgis
Ashford School, Kent	www.ashfordschool.co.uk	£5,600	£11,999	M. Hall
Austin Friars, Cumbria	www.austinfriars.co.uk	£4,815	–	M. Harris
Bablake School, W. Midlands	www.bablake.com	£3,784	–	J. Watson
Badminton School, Bristol	www.badmintonschool.co.uk	£5,395	£12,220	Mrs R. Tear
Bancroft's School, Essex	www.bancrofts.org	£5,794	–	S. Marshall
Barnard Castle School, Durham	www.barnardcastleschool.org.uk	£4,500	£8,100	A. Jackson
*Bedales School, Hants	www.bedales.org.uk	£9,505	£12,095	M. Bashaarat
Bede's Senior School, E. Sussex	www.bedes.org	£7,150	£11,365	P. Goodyer
Bedford Girls' School, Beds	www.bedfordgirlsschool.co.uk	£4,313	–	Miss J. MacKenzie
Bedford Modern School, Beds	www.bedmod.co.uk	£4,346	–	A. Tate
Bedford School, Beds	www.bedfordschool.org.uk	£6,159	£10,417	J. Hodgson
Bedstone College, Shrops	www.bedstone.org	£4,885	£8,840	D. Gajadharsingh
Beechwood Sacred Heart School, Kent	www.beechwood.org.uk	£5,650	£9,500	Mrs H. Rowe
Benenden School, Kent	www.benenden.kent.sch.uk	–	£12,250	Mrs S. Price
Berkhamsted School, Herts	www.berkhamstedschool.org	£6,750	£11,310	R. Backhouse
Bethany School, Kent	www.bethanyschool.org.uk	£5,975	£10,195	M. Healy
Birkdale School, S. Yorks	www.birkdaleschool.org.uk	£4,210	–	N. Pietrek
Birkenhead School, Merseyside	www.birkenheadschool.co.uk	£3,900	–	P. Vicars
Bishop's Stortford College, Herts	www.bishopsstortfordcollege.org	£6,362	£9,708	J. Gladwin

School	Website			Head
Blackheath High School, London, SE3	www.blackheathhighschool.gdst.net	£5,292	–	Mrs C. Chandler-Thompson
Blundell's School, Devon	www.blundells.org	£7,250	£11,285	B. Wielenga
Bolton School Boys' Division, Lancs	www.boltonschool.org/seniorboys	£3,912	–	P. Britton
Bolton School Girls' Division, Lancs	www.boltonschool.org/seniorgirls	£3,912	–	Miss S. Hincks
Bootham School, N. Yorks	www.boothamschool.com	£5,955	£10,390	C. Jeffrey
Bournemouth Collegiate School, Dorset	www.bournemouthcollegiateschool.co.uk	£4,715	£9,465	R. Slatford
Box Hill School, Surrey	www.boxhillschool.com	£6,330	£12,800	C. Lowde
Bradfield College, Berks	www.bradfieldcollege.org.uk	£9,684	£12,105	Dr C. Stevens
Bradford Grammar School, W. Yorks	www.bradfordgrammar.com	£4,148	–	Dr S. Hinchliffe
Bredon School, Glos	www.bredonschool.org	£6,300	£10,250	D. Ward
Brentwood School, Essex	www.brentwoodschool.co.uk	£6,072	£11,900	D. Davies
Brighton & Hove High School, E. Sussex	www.bhhs.gdst.net	£4,667	–	Ms J. Smith
Brighton College, E. Sussex	www.brightoncollege.org.uk	£7,930	£14,140	R. Cairns
Bristol Grammar School, Bristol	www.bristolgrammarschool.co.uk	£4,740	–	J. Barot
Bromley High School, Kent	www.bromleyhigh.gdst.net	£5,521	–	Mrs A. Drew
Bromsgrove School, Worcs	www.bromsgrove-school.co.uk	£5,340	£11,950	P. Clague
Bruton School for Girls, Somerset	www.brutonschool.co.uk	£5,665	£9,650	Mrs N. Botterill
Bryanston School, Dorset	www.bryanston.co.uk	£10,109	£12,328	Ms S. Thomas
Burgess Hill Girls, W. Sussex	www.burgesshillgirls.com	£5,930	£10,680	Mrs L. Laybourn
Bury Grammar School Boys, Lancs	www.burygrammar.com	£3,514	–	D. Cassidy
Bury Grammar School Girls, Lancs	www.burygrammar.com	£3,514	–	Mrs J. Anderson
Caterham School, Surrey	www.caterhamschool.co.uk	£6,060	£11,610	C. Jones
Channing School, London, N6	www.channing.co.uk	£6,155	–	Mrs B. Elliott
Charterhouse, Surrey	www.charterhouse.org.uk	–	£12,687	Dr A. Peterken
Cheltenham College, Glos	www.cheltenhamcollege.org	£8,920	£11,900	Mrs N. Huggett
Cheltenham Ladies' College, Glos	www.cheltladiescollege.org	£7,970	£11,870	Ms E. Jardine-Young
Chetham's School of Music, Greater Manchester	www.chethams.com	–	–	A. Jones
Chigwell School, Essex	www.chigwell-school.org	£5,665	£9,690	M. Punt
Christ's Hospital, W. Sussex	www.christs-hospital.org.uk	£7,110	£10,930	S. Reid
Churcher's College, Hants	www.churcherscollege.com	£4,940	–	S. Williams
City of London Freemen's School, Surrey	www.freemens.org	£5,847	£9,753	R. Martin
City of London School, London, EC4	www.cityoflondonschool.org.uk	£5,577	–	A. Bird
City of London School for Girls, London, EC2	www.clsg.org.uk	£5,727	–	Mrs E. Harrop
*Claremont Fan Court School, Surrey	www.claremontfancourt.co.uk	£5,890	–	W. Brierly
Claymore School, Dorset	www.clayesmore.com	£8,740	£11,910	Mrs J. Thomson
Clifton College, Bristol	www.cliftoncollege.com	£8,000	£12,036	Dr T. Greene
Clifton High School, Bristol	www.cliftonhigh.bristol.sch.uk	£4,850	–	Dr A. Neill
Cobham Hall, Kent	www.cobhamhall.com	£7,123	£11,085	Ms M. Roberts
Cokethorpe School, Oxon	www.cokethorpe.org.uk	£6,100	–	D. Ettinger
Colfe's School, London, SE12	www.colfes.com	£5,478	–	R. Russell
Colston's, Bristol	www.colstons.org	£4,535	–	J. McCullough
Concord College, Shrops	www.concordcollegeuk.com	£4,667	£12,600	N. Hawkins
Cranford House, Oxon	www.cranfordhouse.net	£5,510	–	Dr J. Raymond
Cranleigh School, Surrey	www.cranleigh.org	£9,995	£12,205	M. Reader
Croydon High School, Surrey	www.croydonhigh.gdst.net	£5,378	–	Mrs E. Pattison
Culford School, Suffolk	www.culford.co.uk	£6,330	£10,665	J. Johnson-Munday
Dauntsey's School, Wilts	www.dauntseys.org	£6,150	£10,180	M. Lascelles
Dean Close School, Glos	www.deanclose.org.uk	£7,772	£11,485	Mrs E. Taylor
Denstone College, Staffs	www.denstonecollege.org	£5,114	£8,904	M. Norris
Derby Grammar School, Derbys	www.derbygrammar.org	£4,331	–	Dr R. Norris
Derby High School, Derbys	www.derbyhigh.derby.sch.uk	£4,140	–	Mrs A. Chapman
Dodderhill School, Worcs	www.dodderhill.co.uk	£3,750	–	Mrs C. Mawston
Dover College, Kent	www.dovercollege.org.uk	£5,200	£10,000	G. Doodes
d'Overbroeck's, Oxon	www.doverbroecks.com	£7,675	£12,075	Mrs E. Henry
Downe House, Berks	www.downehouse.net	£8,755	£12,100	Mrs E. McKendrick
Downside School, Somerset	www.downside.co.uk	£6,111	£10,905	A. Hobbs
Dulwich College, London, SE21	www.dulwich.org.uk	£6,554	£13,680	Dr J. Spence
Dunottar School, Surrey	www.dunottarschool.com	£5,164	–	M. Tottman
Durham High School for Girls, Durham	www.dhsfg.org.uk	£4,245	–	Mrs S. Niblock
Eastbourne College, E. Sussex	www.eastbourne-college.co.uk	£7,540	£11,440	T. Lawson
Edgbaston High School, W. Midlands	www.edgbastonhigh.co.uk	£4,114	–	Dr R. Weeks
Ellesmere College, Shrops	www.ellesmere.com	£5,973	£10,605	B. Wignall
Eltham College, London, SE9	www.elthamcollege.london	£5,686	–	G. Sanderson
Emanuel School, London, SW11	www.emanuel.org.uk	£5,999	–	R. Milne
Epsom College, Surrey	www.epsomcollege.org.uk	£8,059	£11,886	J. Piggot

School	Website			Head
Eton College, Berks	www.etoncollege.com	–	£12,910	S. Henderson
Ewell Castle School, Surrey	www.ewellcastle.co.uk	£5,325	–	P. Harris
Exeter School, Devon	www.exeterschool.org.uk	£4,259	–	B. Griffin
Farlington School, W. Sussex	www.farlingtonschool.com	£5,775	£9,795	Miss L. Higson
Farnborough Hill, Hants	www.farnborough-hill.org.uk	£4,747	–	Mrs A. Neil
Farringtons School, Kent	www.farringtons.org.uk	£4,870	£10,200	Mrs D. Nancekievill
Felsted School, Essex	www.felsted.org	£7,575	£11,425	C. Townsend
Forest School, London, E17	www.forest.org.uk	£5,992	–	M. Hodges
Framlingham College, Suffolk	www.framcollege.co.uk	£6,392	£9,941	P. Taylor
Francis Holland School, London, NW1	www.fhs-nw1.org.uk	£6,420	–	C. Fillingham
Francis Holland School, London, SW1	www.fhs-sw1.org.uk	£6,695	–	Mrs L. Elphinstone
Frensham Heights, Surrey	www.frensham.org	£6,220	£9,560	A. Fisher
Fulneck School, W. Yorks	www.fulneckschool.co.uk	£4,245	£8,235	P. Taylor
Gateways School, W. Yorks	www.gatewaysschool.co.uk	£4,370	–	Dr T. Johnson
Giggleswick School, N. Yorks	www.giggleswick.org.uk	£6,795	£10,920	M. Turnbull
Godolphin, Wilts	www.godolphin.org	£6,829	£10,374	Mrs E. Hattersley
*The Godolphin and Latymer School, London, W6	www.godolphinandlatymer.com	£6,978	–	Dr F. Ramsey
*The Grange School, Cheshire	www.grange.org.uk	£3,720	–	Mrs D. Leonard
Gresham's School, Norfolk	www.greshams.com	£7,900	£11,320	D. Robb
Guildford High School, Surrey	www.guildfordhigh.co.uk	£5,504	–	Mrs F. Boulton
The Haberdashers' Aske's Boys' School, Herts	www.habsboys.org.uk	£6,490	–	G. Lock
Haberdashers' Aske's School for Girls, Herts	www.habsgirls.org.uk	£5,811	–	Miss B. O'Connor
Halliford School, Middx	www.hallifordschool.co.uk	£5,095	–	J. Davies
Hampshire Collegiate School, Hants	www.hampshirecs.org.uk	£5,110	£8,700	C. Canning
Hampton School, Middx	hamptonschool.org.uk	£6,390	–	K. Knibbs
Harrogate Ladies' College, N. Yorks	www.hlc.org.uk	£7,685	£11,815	Mrs S. Brett
Harrow School, Middx	www.harrowschool.org.uk	–	£12,850	J. Hawkins
Headington School, Oxon	www.headington.org	£6,200	£12,330	Mrs C. Jordan
Heathfield School, Berks	www.heathfieldschool.net	£7,305	£11,740	Mrs M. Legge
Hereford Cathedral School, Herefords	www.herefordcs.com	£4,536	–	P. Smith
Hethersett Old Hall School, Norfolk	www.hohs.co.uk	£5,035	£9,430	S. Crump
Highclare School, W. Midlands	www.highclareschool.co.uk	£4,070	–	Dr R. Luker
Highgate School, London, N6	www.highgateschool.org.uk	£6,790	–	A. Pettitt
Hill House School, S. Yorks	www.hillhouse.doncaster.sch.uk	£4,300	–	D. Holland
Hurstpierpoint College, W. Sussex	www.hppc.org.uk	£7,720	£11,500	T. Manly
Hymers College, E. Yorks	www.hymerscollege.co.uk	£3,658	–	D. Elstone
Immanuel College, Herts	www.immanuelcollege.co.uk	£5,725	–	G. Griffin
Ipswich High School, Suffolk	www.ipswichhighschool.co.uk	£4,658	–	Ms O. Carlin
Ipswich School, Suffolk	www.ipswich.school	£4,993	£9,670	N. Weaver
James Allen's Girls' School (JAGS), London, SE22	www.jags.org.uk	£5,755	–	Mrs S. Huang
The John Lyon School, Middx	www.johnlyon.org	£5,710	–	Miss K. Haynes
Kent College, Kent	www.kentcollege.com	£5,985	£11,327	Dr D. Lamper
Kent College Pembury, Kent	www.kent-college.co.uk	£6,625	£10,577	Ms J. Lodrick
Kimbolton School, Cambs	www.kimbolton.cambs.sch.uk	£5,100	£8,485	J. Belbin
King Edward VI High School for Girls, W. Midlands	www.kehs.org.uk	£4,134	–	Mrs A. Clark
King Edward VI School, Hants	www.kes.hants.sch.uk	£5,170	–	J. Thould
King Edward's School, Bath	www.kesbath.com	£4,660	–	M. Boden
King Edward's School, Birmingham	www.kes.org.uk	£4,245	–	Dr M. Fenton
King Edward's Witley, Surrey	www.kesw.org	£6,650	£10,260	J. Attwater
King Henry VIII School, W. Midlands	www.khviii.com	£3,784	–	J. Slack
King William's College, Isle of Man	www.kwc.im	£7,200	£10,450	J. Buchanan
King's College, London, SW19	www.kcs.org.uk	£6,995	–	A. Halls
King's College, Taunton, Somerset	www.kings-taunton.co.uk	£7,210	£10,685	R. Biggs
King's Ely, Cambs	www.kingsely.org	£6,951	£10,063	Mrs S. Freestone
King's High School, Warwicks	www.kingshighwarwick.co.uk	£4,159	–	R. Nicholson
The King's School, Kent	www.kings-school.co.uk	£9,165	£12,120	P. Roberts
The King's School, Chester, Cheshire	www.kingschester.co.uk	£4,425	–	G. Hartley
The King's School, Macclesfield, Cheshire	www.kingsmac.co.uk	£4,185	–	Dr S. Hyde
King's Rochester, Kent	www.kings-rochester.co.uk	£6,235	£10,130	J. Walker
The King's School, Worcs	www.ksw.org.uk	£4,534	–	M. Armstrong
The Kingsley School, Warwicks	www.thekingsleyschool.com	£4,290	–	Ms H. Owens
Kingsley School, Devon	www.kingsleyschoolbideford.co.uk	£4,395	£8,595	P. Last
Kingston Grammar School, Surrey	www.kgs.org.uk	£6,225	–	S. Lehec
Kingswood School, Somerset	www.kingswood.bath.sch.uk	£4,938	£10,643	S. Morris
Kirkham Grammar School, Lancs	www.kirkhamgrammar.co.uk	£3,743	£6,835	D. Berry

School	Website	Fee 1	Fee 2	Contact
Lady Eleanor Holles, Middx	www.lehs.org.uk	£6,536	–	Mrs H. Hanbury
Lancing College, W. Sussex	www.lancingcollege.co.uk	£8,190	£11,645	D. Oliver
Latymer Upper School, London, W6	www.latymer-upper.org	£6,420	–	D. Goodhew
The Grammar School at Leeds, W. Yorks	www.gsal.org.uk	£4,425	–	Mrs S. Woodroofe
Leicester Grammar School, Leics	www.leicestergrammar.org.uk	£4,237	–	C. King
Leicester High School for Girls, Leics	www.leicesterhigh.co.uk	£3,945	–	A. Whelpdale
Leighton Park School, Berks	www.leightonpark.com	£7,218	£11,348	M. Judd
Leweston School, Dorset	www.leweston.co.uk	£4,950	£10,400	Mrs K. Reynolds
The Leys, Cambs	www.theleys.net	£7,130	£10,655	M. Priestley
Lichfield Cathedral School, Staffs	www.lichfieldcathedralschool.com	£5,060	–	Mrs S. Hannam
Lincoln Minster School, Lincolns	www.lincolnminsterschool.co.uk	£4,474	£9,022	M. Wallace
Lingfield College, Surrey	www.lingfieldcollege.co.uk	£4,867	–	R. Bool
Longridge Towers School, Northumberland	www.lts.org.uk	£4,411	£8,981	J. Lee
Lord Wandsworth College, Hants	www.lordwandsworth.org	£7,525	£10,700	A. Williams
Loughborough Grammar School, Leics	www.lesgrammar.org	£4,042	£9,135	D. Byrne
Loughborough High School, Leics	www.leshigh.org	£3,996	–	Mrs G. Byrom
Luckley House School, Berks	www.luckleyhouseschool.org	£5,405	£9,458	Mrs J. Tudor
LVS Ascot, Berks	www.lvs.ascot.sch.uk	£5,801	£10,192	Mrs C. Cunniffe
Magdalen College School, Oxon	www.mcsoxford.org	£5,710	–	Miss H. Pike
Malvern College, Worcs	www.malverncollege.org.uk	£8,178	£12,739	A. Clark
The Manchester Grammar School, Greater Manchester	www.mgs.org	£4,090	–	Dr M. Boulton
Manchester High School for Girls, Greater Manchester	www.manchesterhigh.co.uk	£3,824	–	Mrs C. Hewitt
Manor House School, Bookham, Surrey	www.manorhouseschool.org	£5,621	–	Ms T. Fantham
The Marist School, Berks	www.themarist.com	£4,680	–	K. McCluskey
Marlborough College, Wilts	www.marlboroughcollege.org	£10,350	£12,175	Mrs L. Moelwyn-Hughes
Marymount International School, Surrey	www.marymountlondon.com	£7,620	£12,958	Mrs M. Frazier
Mayfield School, E. Sussex	www.mayfieldgirls.org	£6,800	£10,975	Miss A. Beary
The Maynard School, Devon	www.maynard.co.uk	£4,298	–	Miss S. Dunn
Merchant Taylors' Boys' School, Merseyside	www.merchanttaylors.com	£3,723	–	D. Wickes
Merchant Taylors' Girls' School, Merseyside	www.merchanttaylors.com	£3,723	–	Mrs C. Tao
Merchant Taylors' School, Middx	www.mtsn.org.uk	£8,000	–	S. Everson
Mill Hill School, London, NW7	millhill.org.uk	£6,875	£10,964	Mrs F. King
*Millfield, Somerset	millfieldschool.com	£8,535	£12,870	G. Horgan
Milton Abbey School, Dorset	www.miltonabbey.co.uk	£6,900	£12,900	Mrs J. Fremont-Barnes
Moira House Girls School, E. Sussex	www.moirahouse.co.uk	£5,875	£10,685	Mrs E. Vallantine
Monkton Combe School, Somerset	www.monkton.org.uk	£6,800	£10,845	C. Wheeler
More House School, London, SW1	www.morehouse.org.uk	£6,310	–	Mrs A. Leach
Moreton Hall, Shrops	www.moretonhall.org	£9,250	£11,230	J. Forster
Mount House School (formerly St Martha's), Herts	www.mounthouse.org.uk	£4,760	–	M. Burke
Mount Kelly, Devon	www.mountkelly.com	£5,700	£9,940	M. Semmence
Mount St Mary's College, Derbys	www.msmcollege.com	£4,469	£9,682	Dr N. Cuddihy
New Hall School, Essex	www.newhallschool.co.uk	£6,480	£9,949	Mrs K. Jeffrey
Newcastle High School for Girls, Tyne and Wear	www.newcastlehigh.gdst.net	£4,204	–	M. Tippett
Newcastle School for Boys, Tyne and Wear	www.newcastleschool.co.uk	£4,440	–	D. Tickner
Newcastle-under-Lyme School, Staffs	www.nuls.org.uk	£3,915	–	M. Getty
North London Collegiate School, Middx	www.nlcs.org.uk	£6,545	–	Mrs S. Clark
Northwood College for Girls, Middx	www.northwoodcollege.gdst.net	£5,319	–	Mrs Z. Hubble
Norwich High School, Norfolk	www.norwichhigh.gdst.net	£4,690	–	Mrs K. Malaisé
Norwich School, Norfolk	www.norwich-school.org.uk	£5,221	–	S. Griffiths
Notre Dame School, Surrey	www.notredame.co.uk	£5,360	–	Mrs A. King
Notting Hill and Ealing High School, London, W13	www.nhehs.gdst.net	£5,978	–	M. Shoults
Nottingham Girls' High School, Notts	www.nottinghamgirlshigh.gdst.net	£4,374	–	Miss J. Keller
Nottingham High School, Notts	www.nottinghamhigh.co.uk	£4,769	–	K. Fear
Oakham School, Rutland	www.oakham.rutland.sch.uk	£6,675	£10,840	N. Lashbrook
Ockbrook School, Derbys	www.ockbrooksch.co.uk	£4,220	£8,740	T. Brooksby
Oldham Hulme Grammar School, Lancs	www.ohgs.co.uk	£3,672	–	C. Mairs
The Oratory School, Oxon	www.oratory.co.uk	£8,080	£11,100	J. Smith
Oswestry School, Shrops	www.oswestryschool.org.uk	£5,050	£9,920	J. Noad
Oundle School, Northants	www.oundleschool.org.uk	£7,595	£11,855	Mrs S. Kerr-Dineen
Our Lady's Abingdon Senior School, Oxon	www.olab.org.uk	£5,100	–	S. Oliver
Oxford High School, Oxon	www.oxfordhigh.gdst.net	£4,995	–	Dr P. Hills
Palmers Green High School, London, N21	www.pghs.co.uk	£5,100	–	Mrs W. Kempster
Pangbourne College, Berks	www.pangbourne.com	£8,012	£11,332	T. Garnier

The Perse Upper School, Cambs	www.perse.co.uk	£5,555	– E. Elliott
The Peterborough School, Cambs	www.thepeterboroughschool.co.uk	£5,018	– A. Meadows
Pipers Corner School, Bucks	www.piperscorner.co.uk	£5,850	– Mrs H. Ness-Gifford
Pitsford School, Northants	www.pitsfordschool.com	£4,759	– N. Toone
Plymouth College, Devon	www.plymouthcollege.com	£5,300 £10,225	J. Standen
Pocklington School, E. Yorks	www.pocklingtonschool.com	£4,708 £9,176	M. Ronan
Portland Place School, London, W1B	www.portland-place.co.uk	£6,840	– D. Bradbury
The Portsmouth Grammar School, Hants	www.pgs.org.uk	£5,112	– Dr A. Cotton
Portsmouth High School, Hants	www.portsmouthhigh.co.uk	£4,549	– Mrs J. Prescott
Princess Helena College, Herts	www.princesshelenacollege.co.uk	£6,545 £9,515	Mrs L. Corry
Princethorpe College, Warwicks	www.princethorpe.co.uk	£4,069	– E. Hester
Prior Park College, Somerset	www.priorparkschools.com	£5,440 £10,065	J. Murphy-O'Connor
The Purcell School, Herts	www.purcell-school.org	£8,569 £10,942	S. Yeo
Putney High School, London, SW15	www.putneyhigh.gdst.net	£6,064	– Mrs S. Longstaff
Queen Anne's School, Berks	www.qas.org.uk	£7,735 £11,405	Mrs J. Harrington
Queen Elizabeth's Hospital (QEH), Bristol	www.qehbristol.co.uk	£4,662	– S. Holliday
Queen Mary's School, N. Yorks	www.queenmarys.org	£6,140 £8,055	Mrs C. Cameron
Queen's College, London, London, W1G	www.qcl.org.uk	£6,135	– R. Tillett
Queen's College, Somerset	www.queenscollege.org.uk	£5,975 £10,160	Dr L. Earps
Queen's Gate School, London, SW7	www.queensgate.org.uk	£6,525	– Mrs R. Kamaryc
Queenswood School, Herts	www.queenswood.org	£8,275 £11,250	Mrs J. Cameron
Radley College, Oxon	www.radley.org.uk	– £12,300	J. Moule
Ratcliffe College, Leics	www.ratcliffe-college.co.uk	£5,323 £8,483	J. Reddin
The Read School, N. Yorks	www.readschool.co.uk	£4,132 £9,482	Mrs R. Ainley
Reading Blue Coat School, Berks	www.rbcs.org.uk	£5,373	– J. Elzinga
Reddam House Berkshire, Berks	www.reddamhouse.org.uk	£5,600 £10,625	Mrs T. Howard
Redmaids' High School, Bristol	www.redmaidshigh.co.uk	£4,600	– Mrs I. Tobias
Reed's School, Surrey	www.reeds.surrey.sch.uk	£7,950 £10,245	M. Hoskins
Reigate Grammar School, Surrey	www.reigategrammar.org	£6,020	– S. Fenton
Rendcomb College, Glos	www.rendcombcollege.org.uk	£7,550 £10,500	R. Jones
Repton School, Derbys	www.repton.org.uk	£8,582 £11,569	A. Land
Rishworth School, W. Yorks	www.rishworth-school.co.uk	£4,100 £9,255	P. Seery
Roedean School, E. Sussex	www.roedean.co.uk	£6,955 £12,480	O. Blond
Rossall School, Lancs	www.rossall.org.uk	£4,250 £12,150	J. Quartermain
Royal Grammar School, Guildford	www.rgsg.co.uk	£5,865	– Dr J. Cox
Royal Grammar School, Newcastle upon Tyne	www.rgs.newcastle.sch.uk	£4,219	– J. Fern
RGS Worcester, Worcs	www.rgsw.org.uk	£4,154	– J. Pitt
The Royal High School Bath, Somerset	www.royalhighbath.gdst.net	£4,542 £9,883	Mrs J. Duncan
Royal Hospital School, Suffolk	www.royalhospitalschool.org	£5,472 £10,395	S. Lockyer
The Royal Masonic School for Girls, Herts	www.rmsforgirls.org.uk	£5,625 £9,945	K. Carson
Royal Russell School, Surrey	www.royalrussell.co.uk	£5,945 £11,750	C. Hutchinson
Rugby School, Warwicks	www.rugbyschool.co.uk	£7,268 £11,584	P. Green
*Ryde School with Upper Chine, Isle of Wight	www.rydeschool.org.uk	£4,270	– M. Waldron
Rye St Antony, Oxon	www.ryestantony.co.uk	£4,845 £8,195	Mrs S. Ryan
St Albans High School for Girls, Herts	www.stahs.org.uk	£5,910	– Mrs J. Brown
St Albans School, Herts	www.st-albans.herts.sch.uk	£5,976	– J. Gillespie
St Augustine's Priory School, London, W5	www.sapriory.com	£5,054	– Mrs S. Raffray
St Bede's College, Greater Manchester	www.sbcm.co.uk	£3,665	– Mrs S. Pike
St Benedict's School, London, W5	www.stbenedicts.org.uk	£5,368	– A. Johnson
*St Catherine's School, Surrey	www.stcatherines.info	£5,965	– Mrs A. Phillips
St Catherine's School, Middx	www.stcatherineschool.co.uk	£4,839	– Mrs J. McPherson
St Christopher School, Herts	www.stchris.co.uk	£5,865 £10,250	R. Palmer
St Columba's College, Herts	www.stcolumbascollege.org	£5,041	– D. Buxton
St Dominic's Grammar School, Staffs	www.stdominicsgrammarschool.co.uk	£4,234 £7,167	P. McNabb
St Dunstan's College, London, SE6	www.stdunstans.org.uk	£5,512	– N. Hewlett
St Edmund's College, Herts	www.stedmundscollege.org	£5,735 £9,955	P. Durán
St Edmund's School Canterbury, Kent	www.stedmunds.org.uk	£6,655 £11,101	E. O'Connor
St Edward's, Oxford, Oxon	www.stedwardsoxford.org	£9,755 £12,190	S. Jones
St Edward's School, Glos	www.stedwards.co.uk	£5,645	– Mrs P. Clayfield
Saint Felix School, Suffolk	www.stfelix.co.uk	£5,295 £9,390	J. Harrison
St Gabriel's, Berks	www.stgabriels.co.uk	£5,610	– R. Smith
St George's College, Weybridge, Surrey	www.stgeorgesweybridge.com	£6,150	– Mrs R. Owens
St George's, Ascot, Berks	www.stgeorges-ascot.org.uk	£7,300 £11,450	Mrs E. Hewer
St Helen & St Katharine, Oxon	www.shsk.org.uk	£5,330	– Mrs R. Dougall
St Helen's School, Middx	www.sthelens.london	£5,539	– Dr M. Short
St James Senior Boys' School, Surrey	www.stjamesboys.co.uk	£6,040	– D. Brazier

School	Website	Fee 1	Fee 2	Contact
St James Senior Girls' School, London, W14	www.stjamesgirls.co.uk	£6,410	–	Mrs S. Labram
St John's College, Hants	www.stjohnscollege.co.uk	£3,895	£8,400	Mrs M. Maguire
St Joseph's College, Suffolk	www.stjos.co.uk	£4,845	£10,805	Mrs D. Clarke
St Lawrence College, Kent	www.slcuk.com	£6,165	£11,545	A. Spencer
St Mary's School Ascot, Berks	www.st-marys-ascot.co.uk	£8,730	£12,260	Mrs M. Breen
St Mary's Calne, Wilts	www.stmaryscalne.org	£9,350	£12,550	Dr F. Kirk
St Mary's School, Essex	www.stmaryscolchester.org.uk	£4,715	–	Mrs H. Vipond
St Mary's College, Merseyside	www.stmarys.ac	£3,629	–	M. Kennedy
St Mary's School, Bucks	www.stmarysschool.co.uk	£5,440	–	Mrs P. Adams
St Mary's School, Dorset	www.stmarys.eu	£6,875	£10,185	Mrs M. Young
St Nicholas' School, Hants	www.st-nicholas.hants.sch.uk	£4,641	–	Dr O. Wright
St Paul's Girls' School, London, W6	www.spgs.org	£7,978	–	Mrs S. Fletcher
St Paul's School, London, SW13	www.stpaulsschool.org.uk	£8,101	–	Prof. Mark Bailey
St Peter's School, York, N. Yorks	www.stpetersyork.org.uk	£5,850	£9,720	Dr A. Dunn
St Swithun's School, Hants	www.stswithuns.com	£6,721	£10,770	Ms J. Gandee
Scarborough College, N. Yorks	www.scarboroughcollege.co.uk	£4,710	£7,949	C. Ellison
Seaford College, W. Sussex	www.seaford.org	£6,925	£10,710	J. Green
Sevenoaks School, Kent	www.sevenoaksschool.org	£7,485	£11,955	Dr K. Ricks
Shebbear College, Devon	www.shebbearcollege.co.uk	£4,195	£8,350	S. Weale
Sheffield High School for Girls, S. Yorks	www.sheffieldhighschool.org.uk	£4,189	–	Mrs N. Gunson
Sherborne Girls, Dorset	www.sherborne.com	£6,820	£11,500	Dr R. Sullivan
Sherborne School, Dorset	www.sherborne.org	£9,780	£12,085	D. Luckett
*Shiplake College, Oxon	www.shiplake.org.uk	£7,410	£11,025	A. Davies
Shrewsbury School, Shrops	www.shrewsbury.org.uk	£8,130	£11,680	L. Winkley
Sibford School, Oxon	www.sibfordschool.co.uk	£4,775	£9,279	T. Spence
Solihull School, W. Midlands	www.solsch.org.uk	£4,195	–	D. Lloyd
South Hampstead High School, London, NW3	www.shhs.gdst.net	£5,951	–	Mrs V. Bingham
*Stafford Grammar School, Staffs	www.staffordgrammar.co.uk	£4,138	–	M. Darley
Stamford High School, Lincolns	www.ses.lincs.sch.uk	£4,922	£9,118	W. Phelan
Stamford School, Lincolns	www.ses.lincs.sch.uk	£4,922	£9,118	W. Phelan
The Stephen Perse Foundation, Cambs	www.stephenperse.com	£5,675	–	Miss P. Kelleher
Stockport Grammar School, Cheshire	www.stockportgrammar.co.uk	£3,798	–	Dr P. Owen
Stonar, Wilts	www.stonarschool.com	£5,330	£9,740	Dr S. Divall
Stonyhurst College, Lancs	www.stonyhurst.ac.uk	£6,520	£11,370	J. Browne
Stover School, Devon	www.stover.co.uk	£4,243	£8,692	R. Notman
Stowe School, Bucks	www.stowe.co.uk	£8,530	£11,865	Dr A. Wallersteiner
Streatham & Clapham High School, London, SW16	www.schs.gdst.net	£5,676	–	Dr M. Sachania
Sutton Valence School, Kent	www.svs.org.uk	£6,895	£10,740	B. Grindlay
Sydenham High School, London, SE26	www.sydenhamhighschool.gdst.net	£5,417	–	Mrs K. Woodcock
Talbot Heath, Dorset	www.talbotheath.org	£4,619	£8,182	Mrs A. Holloway
Tettenhall College, W. Midlands	www.tettenhallcollege.co.uk	£4,492	£10,128	D. Williams
Thetford Grammar School, Norfolk	www.thetgram.norfolk.sch.uk	£4,555	–	M. Brewer
Tonbridge School, Kent	www.tonbridge-school.co.uk	£9,743	£12,988	J. Priory
Tormead School, Surrey	www.tormeadschool.org.uk	£4,963	–	Mrs C. Foord
Tring Park School for the Performing Arts, Herts	www.tringpark.com	£6,915	£10,810	S. Anderson
Trinity School, Surrey	www.trinity-school.org	£5,552	–	A. Kennedy
Trinity School, Devon	www.trinityschool.co.uk	£3,980	£8,875	L. Coen
Truro High School for Girls, Cornwall	www.trurohigh.co.uk	£4,411	£8,779	Mrs S. Matthews
Truro School, Cornwall	www.truroschool.com	£4,540	£8,995	A. Gordon-Brown
Tudor Hall, Oxon	www.tudorhallschool.com	£7,115	£11,370	Miss W. Griffiths
University College School, London, NW3	www.ucs.org.uk	£6,525	–	M. Beard
Uppingham School, Rutland	www.uppingham.co.uk	£8,435	£12,050	Dr R. Maloney
Walthamstow Hall, Kent	www.walthamstow-hall.co.uk	£6,460	–	Miss S. Ferro
Warminster School, Wilts	www.warminsterschool.org.uk	£5,010	£10,665	M. Mortimer
Warwick School, Warwicks	www.warwickschool.org	£4,229	£9,217	Dr D. Smith
Welbeck - The Defence Sixth Form College, Leics	www.dsfc.ac.uk	£6,500	–	J. Middleton
Wellingborough School, Northants	www.wellingboroughschool.org	£4,970	–	A. Holman
Wellington College, Berks	www.wellingtoncollege.org.uk	£9,310	£12,740	J. Thomas
Wellington School, Somerset	www.wellington-school.org.uk	£4,928	£9,875	H. Price
Wells Cathedral School, Somerset	www.wells-cathedral-school.com	£6,114	£10,232	A. Tighe
West Buckland School, Devon	www.westbuckland.com	£4,850	£9,895	P. Stapleton
Westfield School, Tyne and Wear	www.westfield.newcastle.sch.uk	£4,355	–	N. Walker
*Westholme School, Lancs	www.westholmeschool.com	£3,625	–	Mrs L. Horner
Westminster School, London, SW1	www.westminster.org.uk	£8,710	£12,580	P. Derham
Westonbirt School, Glos	www.westonbirt.org	£4,995	£9,750	Mrs N. Dangerfield
Wimbledon High School, London, SW19	www.wimbledonhigh.gdst.net	£6,035	–	Mrs J. Lunnon

School	Website			Head
Winchester College, Hants	www.winchestercollege.org	–	£12,700	Dr T. Hands
Windermere School, Cumbria	www.windermereschool.co.uk	£5,770	£10,173	I. Lavender
Wisbech Grammar School, Cambs	http://wisbechgrammar.com	£4,333	–	C. Staley
Withington Girls' School, Greater Manchester	www.wgs.org	£3,973	–	Mrs S. Haslam
Woldingham School, Surrey	www.woldinghamschool.co.uk	£7,297	£11,769	Mrs A. Hutchinson
Wolverhampton Grammar School, W. Midlands	www.wgs.org.uk	£4,421	–	Mrs K. Crewe-Read
Woodbridge School, Suffolk	www.woodbridgeschool.org.uk	£5,340	£9,995	Dr R. Robson
Woodhouse Grove School, W. Yorks	www.woodhousegrove.co.uk	£4,425	£8,995	J. Lockwood
Worth School, W. Sussex	www.worthschool.org.uk	£7,570	£10,700	S. McPherson
Wrekin College, Shrops	www.wrekincollege.com	£5,825	£10,320	T. Firth
Wychwood School, Oxon	www.wychwoodschool.org	£5,075	£8,100	Mrs A. Johnson
Wycliffe College, Glos	www.wycliffe.co.uk	£6,495	£10,990	N. Gregory
Wycombe Abbey, Bucks	www.wycombeabbey.com	–	£12,600	Mrs R. Wilkinson
*The Yehudi Menuhin School, Surrey	www.menuhinschool.co.uk	–	–	Mrs K. Clanchy

WALES

School	Website			Head
The Cathedral School Llandaff, Cardiff	www.cathedral-school.co.uk	£4,115	–	Mrs C. Sherwood
Christ College, Brecon	www.christcollegebrecon.com	£5,996	£9,264	G. Pearson
Howell's School Llandaff, Cardiff	www.howells-cardiff.gdst.net	£4,563	–	Mrs S. Davis
Monmouth School for Boys, Monmouth	www.habsmonmouth.org	£5,118	£10,276	Dr A. Daniel
Monmouth School for Girls, Monmouth	www.habsmonmouth.org	£4,782	£9,940	R. James-Robbins
Myddelton College, Denbigh	www.myddeltoncollege.com	£4,000	£9,367	M. Roberts
Rougemont School, Newport	www.rougemontschool.co.uk	£4,359	–	R. Carnevale
Ruthin School, Ruthin	www.ruthinschool.co.uk	£4,500	£10,500	T. Belfield
Rydal Penrhos School, Colwyn Bay	www.rydalpenrhos.com	£5,485	£10,930	S. Smith

SCOTLAND

School	Website			Head
Dollar Academy, Dollar	www.dollaracademy.org.uk	£4,197	£9,711	D. Knapman
The High School of Dundee, Dundee	www.highschoolofdundee.org.uk	£4,166	–	Dr J. Halliday
The Edinburgh Academy, Edinburgh	www.edinburghacademy.org.uk	£4,548	–	B. Welsh
Fettes College, Edinburgh	www.fettes.com	£8,930	£11,160	G. Stanford
George Heriot's School, Edinburgh	www.george-heriots.com	£4,013	–	Mrs L. Franklin
The Glasgow Academy, Glasgow	www.theglasgowacademy.org.uk	£4,008	–	P. Brodie
The High School of Glasgow, Glasgow	www.highschoolofglasgow.co.uk	£4,112	–	J. O'Neill
Glenalmond College, Perth	www.glenalmondcollege.co.uk	£7,318	£11,060	Ms E. Logan
Gordonstoun, Elgin	www.gordonstoun.org.uk	£9,113	£12,303	Mrs L. Kerr
Kelvinside Academy, Glasgow	www.kelvinsideacademy.org.uk	£4,080	–	I. Munro
Kilgraston School, Bridge of Earn	www.kilgraston.com	£5,655	£9,660	Mrs D. MacGinty
Lomond School, Helensburgh	www.lomondschool.com	£3,850	£8,910	Mrs J. Urquhart
Loretto School, Musselburgh	www.loretto.com	£7,625	£11,200	G. Hawley
Merchiston Castle School, Edinburgh	www.merchiston.co.uk	£7,835	£10,550	J. Anderson
Morrison's Academy, Crieff	www.morrisonsacademy.org	£4,223	–	G. Warren
Robert Gordon's College, Aberdeen	www.rgc.aberdeen.sch.uk	£4,237	–	S. Mills
St Aloysius' College, Glasgow	www.staloysius.org	£3,957	–	M. Bartlett
St Columba's School, Kilmacolm	www.st-columbas.org	£3,897	–	Mrs A. Angus
St Leonards School, St Andrews	www.stleonards-fife.org	£4,532	£11,054	Dr M. Carslaw
St Margaret's School for Girls, Aberdeen	www.st-margaret.aberdeen.sch.uk	£5,040	–	Miss A. Tomlinson
Strathallan School, Perth	www.strathallan.co.uk	£7,249	£10,683	M. Lauder

NORTHERN IRELAND

School	Website			Head
Campbell College, Belfast	www.campbellcollege.co.uk	£0,877	£4,562	R. Robinson
The Royal School Dungannon, Dungannon	www.royaldungannon.com	£0,050	£3,400	D. Burnett

CHANNEL ISLANDS

School	Website			Head
Elizabeth College, Guernsey	www.elizabethcollege.gg	£3,780	–	Mrs J. Palmer
Victoria College, Jersey	www.victoriacollege.je	£1,842	–	A. Watkins

NATIONAL ACADEMIES OF SCHOLARSHIP

The national academies are self-governing bodies whose members are elected as a result of achievement and distinction in the academy's field. Within their discipline, the academies provide advice, support education and exceptional scholars, stimulate debate, promote UK research worldwide and collaborate with international counterparts.

The UK's four national academies – the Royal Society, the British Academy, the Royal Academy of Engineering and the Academy of Medical Sciences – receive funding from the Department for Business, Energy and Industrial Strategy (BEIS) for key programmes that help deliver government priorities. The total amount of resource funding allocated by BEIS to the four national academies for 2018–19 is £176m. The Royal Society of Edinburgh is aided by funds provided by the Scottish government. In addition to government funding, the national academies generate additional income from donations, membership contributions, trading and investments.

ACADEMY OF MEDICAL SCIENCES (1998)

41 Portland Place, London W1B 1QH
T 020-3141 3200 W www.acmedsci.ac.uk

Founded in 1998, the Academy of Medical Sciences is the independent body in the UK representing the diversity of medical science. The Academy seeks to improve health through research, as well as to promote medical science and its translation into benefits for society.

The academy is self-governing and receives funding from a variety of sources, including the fellowship, charitable donations, government and industry.

Fellows are elected from a broad range of medical sciences: biomedical, clinical and population based. The academy includes in its remit veterinary medicine, dentistry, nursing, medical law, economics, sociology and ethics. Elections are from nominations put forward by existing fellows.

There are around 1,200 fellows and 4 honorary fellows.

President, Prof. Sir Robert Lechler, PMEDSCI
Executive Director, Dr Helen Munn

BRITISH ACADEMY (1902)

10–11 Carlton House Terrace, London SW1Y 5AH
T 020-7969 5200 W www.britac.ac.uk

The British Academy is an independent, self-governing learned society for the promotion of the humanities and social sciences. It was founded in 1901 and granted a royal charter in 1902. The British Academy supports advanced academic research and is a channel for the government's support of research in those disciplines.

The fellows are scholars who have attained distinction in one of the branches of study that the academy exists to promote. Candidates must be nominated by existing fellows. There are just over 1,000 fellows, around 30 honorary fellows and 300 corresponding fellows overseas.

President, Prof. Sir David Cannadine
Chief Executive, Alun Evans

ROYAL ACADEMY OF ENGINEERING (1976)

3 Carlton House Terrace, London SW1Y 5DG
T 020-7766 0600 W www.raeng.org.uk

The Royal Academy of Engineering was established as the Fellowship of Engineering in 1976. It was granted a royal charter in 1983 and its present title in 1992. It is an independent, self-governing body whose object is the pursuit, encouragement and maintenance of excellence in the whole field of engineering, in order to promote the advancement of the science, art and practice of engineering for the benefit of the public.

Election to the fellowship is by invitation only, from nominations supported by the body of fellows. There are around 1,500 fellows, 40 honorary fellows and 100 international fellows. The Duke of Edinburgh is the senior fellow and the Princess Royal and the Duke of Kent are both royal fellows.

President, Dame Ann Dowling, DBE, FRENG, FRS
Chief Executive, Hayaatun Sillem, PHD

ROYAL SOCIETY (1660)

6–9 Carlton House Terrace, London SW1Y 5AG
T 020-7451 2500 W www.royalsociety.org

The Royal Society is an independent academy promoting the natural and applied sciences. Founded in 1660 and granted a royal charter in 1662, the society has three roles: as the UK academy of science, as a learned society and as a funding agency. It is an independent, self-governing body under a royal charter, promoting and advancing all fields of physical and biological sciences, of mathematics and engineering, medical and agricultural sciences and their application.

Fellows are elected for their contributions to science, both in fundamental research resulting in greater understanding, and also in leading and directing scientific and technological progress in industry and research establishments. Each year up to 52 new fellows, who must be citizens or residents of the Commonwealth or Ireland, and up to ten foreign members may be elected. In addition one honorary fellow may also be elected annually from those not eligible for election as fellows or foreign members. There are around 1,600 fellows and foreign members and seven honorary members covering all scientific disciplines. The Queen is the patron of the Royal Society, and there are also five royal fellows.

President, Sir Venki Ramakrishnan, PRS
Executive Director, Dr Julie Maxton, CBE

ROYAL SOCIETY OF EDINBURGH (1783)

22–26 George Street, Edinburgh EH2 2PQ
T 0131-240 5000 W www.rse.org.uk

The Royal Society of Edinburgh (RSE) is an educational charity and Scotland's national academy. An independent body with charitable status, its multidisciplinary membership represents a knowledge resource for the people of Scotland. Granted its royal charter in 1783 for the 'advancement of learning and useful knowledge', the society organises conferences, debates and lectures; conducts independent inquiries; facilitates international collaboration and showcases the country's research and development capabilities; provides educational activities for primary and secondary school students; and awards prizes and medals. The society also awards over £2m annually to Scotland's top researchers and entrepreneurs working in Scotland.

There are just over 1,600 fellows, including 70 honorary fellows and 74 corresponding fellows overseas.

President, Prof. Dame Anne Glover
Chief Executive, Dr Rebekah Widdowfield

PRIVATELY FUNDED ARTS ACADEMIES

The Royal Academy and the Royal Scottish Academy support the visual arts community in the UK, hold educational events and promote interest in the arts. They are entirely privately funded through contributions by 'friends' (regular donors who receive benefits such as free entry, previews and magazines), bequests, corporate donations and exhibitions.

ROYAL ACADEMY OF ARTS (1768)

Burlington House, Piccadilly, London W1J 0BD
T 020-7300 8000 W www.royalacademy.org.uk

Founded by George III in 1768, the Royal Academy of Arts is an independent, self-governing society devoted to the encouragement and promotion of the fine arts.

Membership of the academy is limited to 80 academicians, all of whom are either painters, engravers, printmakers, draughtsmen, sculptors or architects. There must always be at least 14 sculptors, 12 architects and eight printmakers among the academicians. Candidates must be professionally active in the UK and are nominated and elected by the existing academicians. The members are known as royal academicians (RAs) and are responsible for both the governance and direction of the academy. When RAs reach the age of 75, they become senior academicians and can no longer serve as officers or on the committees.

The title of honorary academician is awarded to a small number of distinguished artists who are not resident in the UK; as at September 2018, there were 33 honorary academicians. Unlike the RAs, they do not take part in the governance of the academy and are unable to vote.

President, Christopher Le Brun, PRA
Secretary and Chief Executive, vacant

ROYAL SCOTTISH ACADEMY (1838)

The Mound, Edinburgh EH2 2EL
T 0131-225 6671 W www.royalscottishacademy.org

Founded in 1826 and led by a body of academicians comprising eminent artists and architects, the Royal Scottish Academy (RSA) is an independent voice for cultural advocacy and one of the largest supporters of artists in Scotland. The Academy administers a number of scholarships, awards and residencies and has a historic collection of Scottish artworks, recognised by the Scottish government as being of national significance. The Academy is independent from local or national government funding, relying instead on bequests, legacies, sponsorship and earned income.

Academicians have to be Scots by birth or domicile, and are elected from the disciplines of art and architecture following nominations put forward by the existing membership. There are also a small number of honorary academicians – distinguished artists and architects, writers, historians and musicians – who do not have to be Scottish. As at September 2018 there were 108 academicians and 30 honorary academicians.

President, Arthur Watson, PRSA
Secretary, Marion Smith, RSA
Treasurer, Gareth Fisher, RSA

RESEARCH COUNCILS

The government funds research through nine research councils, supported by the Department for Business, Energy and Industrial Strategy (BEIS) through UK Research and Innovation (for further information *see* W www.ukri.org). The councils support research and training in universities and other higher education and research facilities.

Under the Higher Education and Research Act 2017, the existing seven research councils, Innovate UK and the research and knowledge exchange functions of the former Higher Education Funding Council for England (HEFCE) were subsumed into a new single funding body, UK Research and Innovation (UKRI), which became operational in April 2018. Research England is a new council within UKRI, taking forward the England-only responsibilities of HEFCE in relation to research and knowledge exchange. Innovate UK is a non-departmental public body which works with companies and partner organisations to facilitate scientific and technological development for the UK economy.

Quality-related research funding is administered through UKRI. Additional funds may also be provided by other government departments, devolved administrations and other international bodies. The councils also receive income for research specifically commissioned by government departments and the private sector, and income from charitable sources.

ARTS AND HUMANITIES RESEARCH COUNCIL

Polaris House, North Star Avenue, Swindon SN2 1FL
T 01793-416000 W www.ahrc.ac.uk

The AHRC is the successor organisation to the Arts and Humanities Research Board and was incorporated by royal charter and established in 2005. It provides funding for postgraduate training and research in the arts and humanities; in any one year, the AHRC makes approximately 700 research awards and around 2,000 postgraduate scholarships. Awards are made after a rigorous peer review system, which ensures the quality of applications.

Executive Chair, Prof. Andrew Thompson, DPHIL

BIOTECHNOLOGY AND BIOLOGICAL SCIENCES RESEARCH COUNCIL

Polaris House, North Star Avenue, Swindon SN2 1UH
T 01793-413200 W www.bbsrc.ac.uk

Established by royal charter in 1994, the BBSRC is the UK funding agency for research in the non-clinical life sciences. It funds research into how all living organisms function and behave, benefiting the agriculture, food, health, pharmaceutical and chemical sectors. To deliver its mission, the BBSRC supports research and training in universities and research centres throughout the UK, including providing strategic research grants to the eight institutes listed below. In June 2015, the institutes founded the National Institutes of Bioscience (NIB) partnership in order to increase the impact of bioscience research and to strengthen the UK's reputation in the field.

Chair, Prof. Melanie Welham

INSTITUTES
BABRAHAM INSTITUTE, Babraham, Cambridge CB22 3AT
 T 01223-496000
Director, Prof. Michael Wakelam

INSTITUTE FOR BIOLOGICAL, ENVIRONMENTAL AND RURAL SCIENCES (ABERYSTWYTH UNIVERSITY), Penglais, Aberystwyth SY23 3DA
 T 01970-621986
Director, Prof. Mike Gooding
EARLHAM INSTITUTE, Norwich Research Park, Colney, Norwich NR4 7UZ T 01603-450001
Director, Prof. Neil Hall
JOHN INNES CENTRE, Norwich Research Park, Colney, Norwich NR4 7UH T 01603-450000
Director, Prof. Dale Sanders
PIRBRIGHT INSTITUTE, Pirbright Laboratory, Ash Road, Pirbright, Surrey GU24 0NF T 01483-232441
Director, Dr Bryan Charleston
QUADRAM INSTITUTE, Norwich Research Park, Norwich, Norfolk NR4 7UA T 01603-255000
Director, Prof. Ian Charles
ROSLIN INSTITUTE (UNIVERSITY OF EDINBURGH), Easter Bush, Midlothian EH25 9RG T 0131-651 9100
Director, Prof. Eleanor Riley
ROTHAMSTED RESEARCH, Harpenden, Herts AL5 2JQ T 01582-763133
Director, Prof. Achim Dobermann

ECONOMIC AND SOCIAL RESEARCH COUNCIL

Polaris House, North Star Avenue, Swindon SN2 1UJ
T 01793-413000 W www.esrc.ac.uk

The ESRC was established by royal charter in 1965 as an organisation for funding and promoting research and postgraduate training in the social sciences. It supports independent research which has an impact on business, the public sector and civil society and also provides advice, disseminates knowledge and promotes public understanding in these areas.

The ESRC has a total budget of around £202m and provides funding to over 4,000 researchers and postgraduate students in academic institutions and independent research institutes.

Chair, Prof. Jennifer Rubin
Chief Executive, Prof. Jane Elliott

ENGINEERING AND PHYSICAL SCIENCES RESEARCH COUNCIL

Polaris House, North Star Avenue, Swindon SN2 1ET
T 01793-444000 W www.epsrc.ac.uk

Formed in 1994 by royal charter, the EPSRC is the UK government's main agency for funding research and training in engineering and the physical sciences in universities and other organisations throughout the UK. The EPSRC invests around £800m a year in a broad range of subjects – from mathematics to materials science, and from information technology to structural engineering. It also provides advice, disseminates knowledge and promotes public understanding in these areas.

Executive Chair, Prof. Lynn Gladden, CBE

MEDICAL RESEARCH COUNCIL

Polaris House, North Star Avenue, Swindon SN2 1FL
T 01793-416200 W www.mrc.ac.uk

The MRC is a publicly funded organisation dedicated to improving human health. The MRC supports research across the entire spectrum of medical sciences, in universities, hospitals, centres and institutes.

Chair, Prof. Fiona Watt
Chair, Infections and Immunity Board, Prof. Paul Kaye
Chair, Molecular and Cellular Medicine Board, Prof. Anne Ferguson-Smith
Chair, Neurosciences and Mental Health Board, Prof. Patrick Chinnery
Chair, Population and Systems Medicine Board, Prof. Paul Elliott

NATURAL ENVIRONMENT RESEARCH COUNCIL

Polaris House, North Star Avenue, Swindon SN2 1EU
T 01793-411500 W www.nerc.ac.uk

NERC is the leading funder of independent research, training and innovation in environmental science in the UK. Its work covers the full range of atmospheric, earth, biological, terrestrial and aquatic sciences. NERC invests around £330m a year in research exploring how we can sustainably benefit from our natural resources, predict and respond to natural hazards and understand environmental change. NERC works closely with policymakers and industry to support sustainable economic growth in the UK and around the world.
Executive Chair, Prof. Duncan Wingham

RESEARCH CENTRES
BRITISH ANTARCTIC SURVEY, High Cross, Madingley Road, Cambridge CB3 OET T 01223-221400
Director, Prof. Dame Jane Francis, DCMG
BRITISH GEOLOGICAL SURVEY, Kingsley Dunham Centre, Keyworth, Nottingham NG12 5GG T 0115-936 3100
Executive Director, Prof. John Ludden
CENTRE FOR ECOLOGY AND HYDROLOGY, Maclean Building, Benson Lane, Crowmarsh Gifford, Wallingford OX10 8BB T 01491-838800
Director, Prof. Mark Bailey
NATIONAL CENTRE FOR ATMOSPHERIC SCIENCE, NCAS Headquarters, School of Earth and Environment, University of Leeds, Leeds LS2 9JT T 0113-343 6408
Director, Prof. Stephen Mobbs

NATIONAL CENTRE FOR EARTH OBSERVATION, Michael Atiyah Building, University of Leicester, University Road, Leicester LE1 7RH T 0116-252 2016
Director, Prof. John Remedios
NATIONAL OCEANOGRAPHY CENTRE, University of Southampton Waterfront Campus, European Way, Southampton SO14 3ZH T 0238-059 6666
Director, Prof. Ed Hill, OBE

SCIENCE AND TECHNOLOGY FACILITIES COUNCIL

Polaris House, North Star Avenue, Swindon SN2 1SZ
T 01793-442000 W www.stfc.ac.uk

Formed by royal charter in 2007, through the merger of the Council for the Central Laboratory of the Research Councils and the Particle Physics and Astronomy Research Council, the STFC is a non-departmental public body reporting to BEIS.

The STFC invests in large national and international research facilities, while delivering science and technology expertise for the UK. The council is involved in research projects such as the Diamond Light Source Synchrotron and the Large Hadron Collider, and develops new areas of science and technology. The EPSRC has transferred its responsibility for nuclear physics to the STFC.

Executive Chair, Prof. Mark Thompson

RESEARCH CENTRES
BOULBY UNDERGROUND SCIENCE FACILITY, Boulby Mine, Loftus, Saltburn-by-the-Sea, Cleveland TS13 4UZ T 01287-646300
CHILBOLTON OBSERVATORY, Chilbolton, Stockbridge, Hampshire SO20 6BJ T 01264-860391
DARESBURY LABORATORY, SciTech Daresbury, Keckwick Lane, Warrington WA4 4AD T 01925-603000
RUTHERFORD APPLETON LABORATORY, Harwell Campus, Didcot OX11 0QX T 01235-445000
UK ASTRONOMY TECHNOLOGY CENTRE, Royal Observatory Edinburgh, Blackford Hill, Edinburgh EH9 3HJ T 0131-668 8100

HEALTH

NATIONAL HEALTH SERVICE

The National Health Service (NHS) came into being on 5 July 1948 under the National Health Service Act 1946, covering England and Wales and, under separate legislation, Scotland and Northern Ireland. The NHS is now administered by the Secretary of State for Health (in England), the Welsh government, the Scottish government and the Northern Ireland Executive.

The function of the NHS is to provide a comprehensive health service designed to secure improvement in the physical and mental health of the people and to prevent, diagnose and treat illness. It was founded on the principle that treatment should be provided according to clinical need rather than ability to pay, and should be free at the point of delivery.

Hospital, mental, dental, nursing, ophthalmic and ambulance services and facilities for the care of expectant and nursing mothers and young children are provided by the NHS to meet all reasonable requirements. Rehabilitation services such as occupational therapy, physiotherapy, speech therapy and surgical and medical appliances are supplied where appropriate. Specialists and consultants who work in NHS hospitals can also engage in private practice, including the treatment of their private patients in NHS hospitals.

STRUCTURE

The structure of the NHS remained relatively stable for the first 30 years of its existence. In 1974, a three-tier management structure comprising regional health authorities, area health authorities and district management teams was introduced in England, and the NHS became responsible for community health services. In 1979, area health authorities were abolished and district management teams were replaced by district health authorities.

The National Health Service and Community Care Act 1990 provided for more streamlined regional health authorities and district health authorities, and for the establishment of family health services authorities (FHSAs) and NHS trusts. The concept of the 'internal market' was introduced into health care, whereby care was provided through NHS contracts where health authorities or boards and GP fundholders (the purchasers) were responsible for buying health care from hospitals, non-fundholding GPs, community services and ambulance services (the providers). The Act also paved the way for the community care reforms, which were introduced in April 1993, and changed the way care is administered for older people, the mentally ill, the physically disabled and people with learning disabilities.

ENGLAND

Under the Health and Social Care Act 2012, which gained royal assent in March 2012, The NHS in England underwent a complete operational and budgetary restructure at a cost of approximately £1.4bn.

Hospitals were extensively affected by the overhaul, with the cap on income from private hospital patients increased from 1.5 per cent to 49 per cent. All hospitals will become foundation trusts, competing for treatment contracts from clinical commissioning groups (CCGs).

On 1 April 2013 the new commissioning board, NHS England, took on full statutory responsibilities; at the same time, strategic health authorities (SHAs) and primary care trusts (PCTs) which, alongside the Department of Health (DoH), had

been responsible for NHS planning and delivery, were abolished. NHS England is an executive non-departmental public body of the DoH with a remit to:

- provide national leadership to improve the quality of care
- oversee the operation of clinical commissioning groups
- allocate resources to clinical commissioning groups
- commission primary care and specialist services

The secretary of state has ultimate responsibility for the provision of a comprehensive health service in England and for ensuring the system works to its optimum capacity to meet the needs of its patients. The DoH is responsible for strategic leadership of the health and social care systems, but is not the headquarters of the NHS, nor does it directly manage any NHS organisations.

In October 2014, NHS England published *Five Year Forward View* which committed the organisation to further change, including additional decentralisation and a greater emphasis on out-of-hospital care and preventative medicine.

NHS ENGLAND, PO Box 16738, Redditch B97 9PT
T 0300-311 2233 W www.england.nhs.uk
Chief Executive, Simon Stevens

CLINICAL COMMISSIONING GROUPS (CCGS)

On 1 April 2013, PCTs, which controlled 80 per cent of the NHS budget and commissioned most NHS services, were abolished. They were replaced with CCGs which took on many of the functions of the PCTs in addition to some functions previously assumed by the Department of Health. All GP practices now belong to a CCG which also includes other health professionals, such as nurses. CCGs commission most services, including:

- mental health and learning disability services
- planned hospital care
- rehabilitative care
- urgent and emergency care (including out-of-hours)
- most community health services

CCGs can commission any service provider that meets NHS standards and costs. These can be NHS hospitals, social enterprises, charities, or private-sector providers. There are around 200 CCGs, which together are responsible for around two-thirds of the NHS budget, around £75.6bn in 2018–19. In April 2015, 64 CCGs were approved to take on the additional responsibility for commissioning GP services within their area.

HEALTH AND WELLBEING BOARDS

Every upper-tier local authority has established a health and wellbeing board to act as a forum for local commissioners across the NHS, social care, public health and other services. There are more than 130 health and wellbeing boards in England, which are intended to:

- encourage integrated commissioning of health and social care services
- increase democratic input into strategic decisions about health and wellbeing services
- strengthen working relationships between health and social care

PUBLIC HEALTH ENGLAND (PHE)

This new organisation was established on 1 April 2013. It provides national leadership and expert services to support public health and also works with local government and the NHS to respond to emergencies. PHE's responsibilities are to:

- coordinate a national public health service

- support the public to make healthier choices
- provide leadership to the public health delivery system
- support the development of the public health workforce

REGULATION

Since the restructuring of the NHS in England began in April 2013, some elements of the regulation system have changed. Responsibility for the regulation of particular aspects of care is shared across a number of different bodies, including the Care Quality Commission (CQC), and individual professional regulatory bodies, such as the General Medical Council, Nursing and Midwifery Council, General Dental Council and the Health and Care Professions Council.

CARE QUALITY COMMISSION (CQC)

The CQC regulates all health and social care services in England, including those provided by the NHS, local authorities, private companies or voluntary organisations. In addition it protects the interests of people detained under the Mental Health Act. The CQC ensures that all essential standards of quality and safety are met where care is provided, from hospitals to private care homes. By law all NHS providers (such as hospitals and ambulance services) must register with the CQC to show they are protecting people from the risk of infection. The CQC possesses a range of legal powers and duties and will take action if providers do not meet essential standards of quality or safety.

NHS IMPROVEMENT

NHS Improvement is responsible for overseeing NHS foundation trusts, NHS trusts and independent providers, helping them give patients consistently high quality, safe and compassionate care within local health systems that are financially sustainable.

HEALTHWATCH

Healthwatch England was established in October 2012 following the restructuring of the NHS. The organisation functions at a national and local level as an independent consumer body, gathering and representing the views of the public about health and social care services in England.

CARE QUALITY COMMISSION, 151 Buckingham Palace Road, London SW1W 9SZ T 03000-616161 W www.cqc.org.uk
Chief Executive, David Behan, CBE

NHS IMPROVEMENT, Wellington House, 133–155 Waterloo Road, London SE1 8UG T 0300-123 2257
W https://improvement.nhs.uk
Chief Executive, Ian Dalton, CBE

HEALTHWATCH, Citygate, Gallowgate, Newcastle upon Tyne NE1 4PA T 0300-068 3000 W www.healthwatch.co.uk
National Director, Imelda Redmond, CBE

AUTHORITIES AND TRUSTS

Overseen by NHS Improvements, all NHS trusts are expected to eventually become foundation trusts.

ACUTE TRUSTS

Hospitals in England are managed by acute trusts. There were 135 acute non-specialist trusts as at July 2018, of which 84 have foundation trust status and 17 acute specialist trusts, of which 16 have foundation trust status. Acute trusts ensure hospitals provide high-quality healthcare and spend money efficiently. They employ a large sector of the NHS workforce, including doctors, nurses, pharmacists, midwives and health visitors. Acute trusts also employ those in supplementary medical professions, such as physiotherapists, radiographers and podiatrists, in addition to many other non-medical staff.

AMBULANCE TRUSTS

There are 10 ambulance services (five foundation trusts) in England, providing emergency services to healthcare.

CLINICAL SENATES AND STRATEGIC CLINICAL NETWORKS

Clinical senates are advisory groups of experts from across health and social care. There are 12 senates covering England comprising clinical leaders from across the healthcare system, in addition to members from social care and public health.

There are 12 strategic clinical networks across England, comprising groups of clinical experts covering a particular disease, patient or professional group. They offer advice to CCGs and NHS England.

Neither organisation is a statutory body, and although they comment on CCG plans to NHS England, they are unable to veto them.

FOUNDATION TRUSTS

NHS foundation trusts are independent legal entities with unique governance arrangements. Each NHS foundation trust has a duty to consult and involve a board of governors in the strategic planning of its organisation. They have financial freedoms and can raise capital from both the public and private sectors within borrowing limits determined by projected cash flows and based on affordability.

MENTAL HEALTH TRUSTS

There are 69 mental health trusts in England, 42 of which have foundation trust status. They provide health and social care services for people with mental health problems.

SPECIAL HEALTH AUTHORITIES

There are 12 Special health authorities with a nationwide remit, including:
- The National Blood and Transplant Authority
- NHS Commissioning Board Authority
- NHS Trust Development Authority

WALES

The NHS Wales was reorganised according to Welsh Assembly commitments laid out in the *One Wales* strategy which came into effect in October 2009. There are now seven local health boards (LHBs) that are responsible for delivering all health care services within a geographical area, rather than the trust and local health board system that existed previously. Community health councils (CHCs) are statutory lay bodies that represent the public for the health service in their region. There are currently eight CHCs.

NHS TRUSTS

There are three NHS trusts in Wales. The Welsh Ambulance Services NHS Trust is for emergency services; the Velindre NHS Trust offers specialist services in cancer care; while Public Health Wales serves as a unified public health organisation for Wales.

LOCAL HEALTH BOARDS

The websites of the seven LHBs, and contact details for community health councils and NHS trusts, are available in the *NHS Wales Directory* on the NHS Wales website (W www.wales.nhs.uk).

ABERTAWE BRO MORGANNWG UNIVERSITY, One Talbot Gateway, Baglan Energy Park, Baglan, Port Talbot SA12 7BR T 01656-752752
Chief Executive, Tracy Myhill

ANEURIN BEVAN, Headquarters, Lodge Road, Caerleon, Newport NP18 3XQ T 01873-732732
Chief Executive, Judith Paget

BETSI CADWALADR UNIVERSITY, Ysbyty Gwynedd, Penrhosgarnedd, Bangor, Gwynedd LL57 2PW T 01248-384384
Chief Executive, Gary Doherty

CARDIFF AND VALE UNIVERSITY, Cardigan House,
University Hospital of Wales, Heath Park, Cardiff CF14 4XW
T 029-2074 7747
Chief Executive, Len Richards

CWM TAF UNIVERSITY, Ynysmeurig House, Navigation Park,
Abercynon CF45 4SN T 01443-744800
Chief Executive, Allison Williams

HYWEL DDA, Corporate Offices, Ystwyth Building, Hafan
Derwen, Jobswell Road, Carmarthen SA31 3BB T 01267-235151
Chief Executive, Steve Moore

POWYS TEACHING, Glasbury House, Bronllys Hospital,
Bronllys, Brecon, Powys LD3 0LS T 01874-771661
Chief Executive, Carol Shillabeer

SCOTLAND

The Scottish government Health and Social Care directorates
are responsible both for NHS Scotland and for the
development and implementation of health and community
care policy. The chief executive of NHS Scotland leads the
central management of the NHS, is accountable to ministers
for the efficiency and performance of the service and heads the
Health Department which oversees the work of the 14 regional
health boards. These boards provide strategic management for
the entire local NHS system and are responsible for ensuring
that services are delivered effectively and efficiently.

In addition to the 14 regional health boards there are a further
seven special boards and one public health body, which
provide national services, such as the Scottish ambulance
service and NHS Health Scotland. Healthcare Improvement
Scotland, was formed on 1 April 2011 by the Public Services
Reform Act 2010 to improve the quality of Scottish healthcare.

REGIONAL HEALTH BOARDS

AYRSHIRE AND ARRAN, Eglinton House, Ailsa Hospital,
Dalmellington Road, Ayr KA6 6AB T 0800-169 1441
W www.nhsaaa.net
Chief Executive, John Burns

BORDERS, Borders General Hospital, Melrose, Roxburghshire
TD6 9BS T 01896-826000 W www.nhsborders.scot.nhs.uk
Chief Executive, Jane Davidson

DUMFRIES AND GALLOWAY, Crichton Hall, Dumfries DG1
4TG T 01387-246246 W www.nhsdg.scot.nhs.uk
Chief Executive, Jeff Ace

EILEAN SIAR (WESTERN ISLES), 37 South Beach Street,
Stornoway, Isle of Lewis HS1 2BB T 01851-702997
W www.wihb.scot.nhs.uk
Chief Executive, Gordon Jamieson

FIFE, Hayfield House, Hayfield Road, Kirkcaldy, Fife KY2 5AH
T 01592-643355 W www.nhsfife.org
Chief Executive, Paul Hawkins

FORTH VALLEY, Carseview House, Castle Business Park, Stirling
FK9 4SW T 01786-463031 W www.nhsforthvalley.com
Chief Executive, Cathie Cowan

GRAMPIAN, Summerfield House, 2 Eday Road, Aberdeen AB15
6RE T 0345-456 6000 W www.nhsgrampian.org
Chief Executive, Malcolm Wright

GREATER GLASGOW AND CLYDE, J B Russell House,
Gartnavel Royal Hospital Campus, 1055 Great Western Road,
Glasgow G12 0XH T 0141-201 4444 W www.nhsggc.org.uk
Chief Executive, Jane Grant

HIGHLAND, Assynt House, Beechwood Park, Inverness IV2 3BW
T 01463-717123 W www.nhshighland.scot.nhs.uk
Chief Executive, Elaine Mead

LANARKSHIRE, Kirklands, Fallside Road, Bothwell G71 8BB
T 0300-3030 243 W www.nhslanarkshire.org.uk
Chief Executive, Calum Campbell

LOTHIAN, Waverley Gate, 2–4 Waterloo Place, Edinburgh EH1
3EG T 0131-536 9000 W www.nhslothian.scot.nhs.uk
Chief Executive, Tim Davison

ORKNEY, Garden House, New Scapa Road, Kirkwall, Orkney
KW15 1BQ T 01856-888000 W www.ohb.scot.nhs.uk
Chief Executive, Gerry O'Brien

SHETLAND, Upper Floor Montfield, Burgh Road, Lerwick ZE1
0LA T 01595-743060 W www.shb.scot.nhs.uk
Chief Executive, Ralph Roberts

TAYSIDE, Ninewells Hospital & Medical School, Dundee DD1 9SY
T 01382-660111 W www.nhstayside.scot.nhs.uk
Chief Executive, Malcolm Wright, OBE

NORTHERN IRELAND

On 1 April 2009 the four health and social services boards in
Northern Ireland were replaced by a single health and social
care board for the whole of Northern Ireland. The new board
together with its local commissioning groups (whose
boundaries are subject to review pending the outcome of local
government reform) are responsible for improving the health
and social wellbeing of people in the area for which they are
responsible, planning and commissioning services, and
coordinating the delivery of services in a cost-effective manner.
In March 2016, the health minister announced plans to abolish
the health and social care board, with all commissioning
powers to be transferred to the Department of Health and a
new group being established to hold the five Northern Ireland
trusts to account. As at July 2018, no further decision regarding
the future of the board had been taken and the board remains
operational.

HEALTH AND SOCIAL CARE BOARD, 12–22 Linenhall
Street, Belfast BT2 8BS T 030-0555 0115
W www.hscboard.hscni.net
Chief Executive, Valerie Watts

FINANCE

The NHS is still funded mainly through general taxation,
although in recent years more reliance has been placed on the
NHS element of national insurance contributions, patient
charges and other sources of income.

Funding for NHS England was set at £114bn for 2018–19.
Expenditure for the NHS in Wales, Scotland and Northern
Ireland is set by the devolved governments.

EMPLOYEES AND SALARIES

NHS ENGLAND HEALTH SERVICE STAFF 2018
Full-time equivalent

All hospital, community and dental staff	1,205,949
Consultants	46,297
Ambulance staff	20,536
Qualified nursing and midwifery staff	320,422
Qualified scientific, therapeutic and technical staff	136,765

Source: NHS Digital

SALARIES

Many general practitioners (GPs) are self-employed and hold
contracts, either on their own or as part of a Clinical
Commissioning Group (CCG). The profit of GPs varies
according to the services they provide for their patients and
the way they choose to provide these services. Salaried GPs
who are part of a CCG earn between £58,786 and £88,709.
Most NHS dentists are self-employed contractors. A contract

for dentists was introduced on 1 April 2006 which provides dentists with an annual income in return for carrying out an agreed amount, or units, of work. A salaried dentist employed by the NHS, who works mainly with community dental services earn between £39,638 and £84,780.

BASIC SALARIES FOR HOSPITAL MEDICAL AND DENTAL STAFF 2018–19

Consultant (2003 contract)	£78,296–£105,560
Associate specialist	£55,030–£90,585
Speciality doctor	£39,250– £73,193
Core/higher training year 3+	£47,132
Core training year 1 & 2	£37,191
Foundation doctor year 2	£31,422
Foundation doctor year 1	£27,146

NURSES
From 1 December 2004 the *Agenda for Change* pay system was introduced throughout the UK for all NHS staff with the exception of medical and dental staff, doctors in public health medicine and the community health service. Nurses' salaries are incorporated in the *Agenda for Change* nine band pay structure, which provides additional payments for flexible working such as providing out-of-hours services, working weekends and nights and being on-call. There is also additional payments for those staff who work in high-cost areas such as London.

SALARIES FOR NURSES AND MIDWIVES 2018–19

Nurse/Midwife consultant	£41,034–£71,243
Modern matron	£41,034–£49,969
Nurse advanced/team manager	£32,171–£43,041
Midwife higher level	£32,171–£43,041
Nurse specialist/team leader	£26,963–£36,644
Hospital/community midwife	£26,963–£35,644
Registered nurse/entry level midwife*	£22,460–£29,608

*The starting salary in Wales is currently the same as in England. The starting salary is £23,112 in Scotland and £22,460 in Northern Ireland.

HEALTH SERVICES

PRIMARY CARE

Primary care comprises the services provided by general practitioners, community health centres, pharmacies, dental practices and opticians. Primary nursing care includes the work carried out by practice nurses, community nurses, community midwives and health visitors.

PRIMARY MEDICAL SERVICES
In England, primary medical services (PMS) are provided by 34,435 registerd GPs, working in around 7,100 GP practices, with 59.1 million registered patients.

In Wales, responsibility for primary medical services rests with local health boards (LHBs), in Scotland with the 14 regional health boards and in Northern Ireland with the Health and Social Care Board.

Any vocationally trained doctor may provide general or personal medical services. GPs may also have private fee-paying patients, but not if that patient is already an NHS patient on that doctor's patient list.

A person who is ordinarily resident in the UK is eligible to register with a GP (or PMS provider) for free primary care treatment. Should a patient have difficulty in registering with a doctor, he or she should contact the local CCG for help. When a person is away from home he/she can still access primary care treatment from a GP if they ask to be treated as a temporary resident. In an emergency any doctor in the service will give treatment and advice.

GPs or CCGs are responsible for the care of their patients 24 hours a day, seven days a week, but can fulfil the terms of their contract by delegating or transferring responsibility for out-of-hours care to an accredited provider.

In addition, NHS walk-in centres (WICs) throughout England are usually open seven days a week, from early in the morning until late in the evening. They are nurse-led and provide treatment for minor illnesses and injuries, health information and self-help advice. Some WICs are not able to treat young children.

HEALTH COSTS
Some people are exempt from, or entitled to help with, health costs such as prescription charges, ophthalmic and dental costs, and in some cases help towards travel costs to and from hospital.

The following list is intended as a general guide to those who may be entitled to help, or who are exempt from some of the charges relating to the above:

• children under 16 and young people in full-time education who are under 19
• people aged 60 or over
• pregnant women and women who have had a baby in the last 12 months and have a valid maternity exemption certificate (MatEx)
• people, or their partners, who are in receipt of income support, income-based jobseeker's allowance and/or income-based employment and support allowance
• people in receipt of the pension credit
• diagnosed glaucoma patients, people who have been advised by an ophthalmologist that they are at risk of glaucoma and people aged 40 or over who have an immediate family member who is a diagnosed glaucoma patient
• NHS in-patients
• NHS out-patients for all prescribed contraceptives, medication given at a hospital, NHS walk-in centre, personally administered by a GP or supplied at a hospital or primary care trust clinic for the treatment of tuberculosis or a sexually transmissible infection
• out-patients of the NHS Hospital Dental Service
• people registered blind or partially sighted
• people who need complex lenses
• war pensioners whose treatment/prescription is for their accepted disablement and who have a valid exemption certificate
• people who are entitled to, or named on, a valid NHS tax credit exemption or HC2 certificate
• people who have a medical exemption (MedEx) certificate, including those with cancer or diabetes

People in other circumstances may also be eligible for help; *see* www.nhs.uk/using-the-nhs/help-with-health-costs for further information.

WALES
On 1 April 2007 all prescription charges (including those for medical supports and appliances and wigs) for people living in Wales were abolished. The above guide still applies for NHS dental and optical charges although all people aged under 25 living in Wales are also entitled to free dental examinations.

SCOTLAND
On 1 April 2011 all prescription charges in Scotland were abolished. Those entitled to free prescriptions in Scotland include patients registered with a Scottish GP and receiving a prescription from a Scottish pharmacy, and Scottish patients who have an English GP and an entitlement card.

NORTHERN IRELAND
On 1 April 2010 all prescription charges in Northern Ireland were abolished. All prescriptions dispensed in Northern

Ireland are free, even for patients visiting from England, Wales or Scotland.

PHARMACEUTICAL SERVICES

Patients may obtain medicines and appliances under the NHS from any pharmacy whose owner has entered into arrangements with the CCG to provide this service. There are also some suppliers who only provide special appliances. In rural areas, where access to a pharmacy may be difficult, patients may be able to obtain medicines, etc, from a dispensing doctor.

In England, a charge of £8.80 is payable for each item supplied (except for contraceptives for which there is no charge), unless the patient is exempt and the declaration on the back of the prescription form is completed. Prescription prepayment certificates (£29.10 valid for three months, £104.00 valid for a year) may be purchased by those patients not entitled to exemption who require frequent prescriptions.

DENTAL SERVICES

Dentists, like doctors, may take part in the NHS and also have private patients. Dentists are responsible to the local health provider in whose areas they provide services. Patients may go to any dentist who is taking part in the NHS and is willing to accept them. There is a three-tier payment system based on the individual course of treatment required.

NHS DENTAL CHARGES *from 1 April 2018*	
	England/Wales
Band 1* – Examination, diagnosis, preventive care (eg x-rays, scale and polish)	£21.60/£14.00
Band 2 – Band 1 + basic additional treatment (eg fillings and extractions)	£59.10/£45.00
Band 3 – Bands 1 and 2 + all other treatment (eg crowns, dentures and bridges)	£256.50/£195.00
* Urgent and out-of-hours treatment is also charged at this payment tier	

The cost of individual treatment plans should be known prior to treatment and some dental practices may require payment in advance. There is no charge for writing a prescription or removing stitches and only one charge is payable for each course of treatment even if more than one visit to the dentist is required. If additional treatment is required within two months of visiting the dentist and this is covered by the course of treatment most recently paid for (eg payment was made for the second tier of treatment but an additional filling is required) then this will be provided free of charge.

SCOTLAND AND NORTHERN IRELAND

Scotland and Northern Ireland have yet to simplify their charging systems. NHS dental patients pay 80 per cent of the cost of the individual items of treatment provided up to a maximum of £390. Patients in Scotland are entitled to free basic and extensive examinations.

GENERAL OPHTHALMIC SERVICES

General ophthalmic services are administered by local health providers. Testing of sight may be carried out by any ophthalmic medical practitioner or ophthalmic optician (optometrist). The optician must give the prescription to the patient, who can take this to any supplier of glasses to have them dispensed. Only registered opticians can supply glasses to children and to people registered as blind or partially sighted.

Free eyesight tests and help towards the cost are available to people in certain circumstances. Help is also available for the purchase of glasses or contact lenses (*see* Health Costs). In Scotland eye examinations, which include a sight test, are free to all UK residents. Help is also available for the purchase of glasses or contact lenses to those entitled to help with health costs in the same way it is available to those in England and Wales.

CHILD HEALTH SERVICES

Pre-school services at GP surgeries or child health clinics provide regular monitoring of children's physical, mental and emotional health and development and advise parents on their children's health and welfare.

NHS 111, NHS DIRECT AND NHS 24

NHS Direct Wales is a website and 24-hour nurse-led advice telephone service for Wales. It provides medical advice as well as directing people to the appropriate part of the NHS for treatment if necessary. (T 0845 46 47 W www.nhsdirect.wales.nhs.uk). NHS Direct had also operated in England but closed on 31 March 2014. Non-urgent 24-hour nurse-led advice in England can be accessed via the NHS 111 service (T 111).

NHS 24 provides an equivalent service for Scotland (T 111 W www.nhs24.com).

SECONDARY CARE AND OTHER SERVICES

HOSPITALS

NHS hospitals provide acute and specialist care services, treating conditions which normally cannot be dealt with by primary care specialists, and provide for medical emergencies.

NUMBER OF BEDS 2017–18

	Average daily	
	available beds	occupation of beds
England	130,232	117,209
Wales*	10,857	9,489
Scotland	13,349	11,587
Northern Ireland*	6,000	5,034

* Figures are for 2016–17
Sources: NHS England, Welsh government, ISD Scotland, Northern Ireland Executive

HOSPITAL CHARGES

Acute or foundation trusts can provide hospital accommodation in single rooms or small wards, if not required for patients who need privacy for medical reasons. The patient is still an NHS patient, but there may be a charge for these additional facilities. Acute or foundation trusts can charge for certain patient services that are considered to be additional treatments over and above the normal hospital service provision. There is no blanket policy to cover this and each case is considered in the light of the patient's clinical need. However, if an item or service is considered to be an integral part of a patient's treatment by their clinician, then a charge should not be made.

In some NHS hospitals, accommodation and services are available for the treatment of private patients where it does not interfere with care for NHS patients. Income generated by treating private patients is then put back into local NHS services. Private patients undertake to pay the full costs of medical treatment, accommodation, medication and other related services. Charges for private patients are set locally.

WAITING LISTS
England
During May 2018, 306,500 referral to treatment (RTT) patients started admitted treatment and 1,092,667 started

non-admitted treatment. Of the admitted patients, 92 per cent were waiting up to 21.5 weeks, and for patients waiting to start treatment the median waiting time was seven weeks.

Wales

In the quarter ending March 2018, 85.6 per cent of 436,478 patients were treated within 26 weeks and 96.4 per cent were treated within 36 weeks of the date the referral letter was received by the hospital.

Scotland

In the quarter ending March 2018, 81.2 per cent of patients were seen within the 18 week RTT standard. 81 per cent of patients waiting for a new outpatient appointment in the same month had waited 12 weeks or less.

Northern Ireland

From March 2018 the aim was for at least 50 per cent of patients to wait no longer than nine weeks for a first outpatient appointment, with no patient waiting longer than 52 weeks. The total number of people waiting for a first outpatient appointment at the end of March 2018 was 269,834, of these 73.5 per cent had been waiting over nine weeks, compared with 69.6 per cent at the end of March 2017. The number of people waiting to be admitted to hospital in Northern Ireland at the end of March 2018 was 80,570 – of these, 62.3 per cent had been waiting for more than 13 weeks.

AMBULANCE SERVICE

The NHS provides emergency ambulance services free of charge via the 999 emergency telephone service. Air ambulances, provided through local charities and partially funded by the NHS, are used throughout the UK. They assist with cases where access may be difficult or heavy traffic could hinder road progress. Non-emergency ambulance services are provided free to patients who are deemed to require them on medical grounds.

Since 1 April 2001 all services have had a system of call prioritisation. Since 2017, ambulances have been expected to reach Red 1 – calls requiring a defibrillator – and Red 2 emergency calls within seven minutes, at least 75 per cent of the time. Non-emergency calls are categorised as Green 1, 2, 3 or 4, with category Green 4 calls being the least serious. Green calls are generally responded to between 20 minutes and one hour.

In 2016 it was agreed that all ambulance staff were to be re-banded from a band 5 to a band 6 under the *Agenda for Change* pay scale. In 2018, the NHS employed 20,536 qualified ambulance staff in England earning between £17,460 (emergency care assistant) and £36,644 (senior paramedic).

BLOOD AND TRANSPLANT SERVICES

There are four national bodies which coordinate the blood donor programme and transplant and related services in the UK. Donors give blood at local centres on a voluntary basis.

NHS BLOOD AND TRANSPLANT, Oak House, Reeds Crescent, Watford, Herts WD24 4QN T 0300-123 2323 W www.nhsbt.nhs.uk

WELSH BLOOD SERVICE, Ely Valley Road, Talbot Green, Pontyclun CF72 9WB T 0800-252 2266 W www.welsh-blood.org.uk

SCOTTISH NATIONAL BLOOD TRANSFUSION SERVICE, The Jack Copland Centre, 52 Research Avenue North, Herriot-Watt Research Park, Edinburgh EH14 4BE T 0131-314536 5510 W www.scotblood.co.uk

NORTHERN IRELAND BLOOD TRANSFUSION SERVICE, Lisburn Road, Belfast BT9 7TS T 028-9032 1414 W www.nibts.org

HOSPICES

Hospice or palliative care may be available for patients with life-threatening illnesses. It may be provided at the patient's home in a voluntary or NHS hospice or in hospital, and is intended to ensure the best possible quality of life for the patient, and to provide help and support to both the patient and the patient's family. The National Council for Palliative Care coordinates NHS and voluntary services in England, Wales and Northern Ireland; the Scottish Partnership for Palliative Care performs the same function in Scotland.

NATIONAL COUNCIL FOR PALLIATIVE CARE, Hospice House, 34–44 Britannia Street, London WC1X 9JG T 020-7697 1520 W www.ncpc.org.uk

SCOTTISH PARTNERSHIP FOR PALLIATIVE CARE, CBC House, 24 Canning Street, Edinburgh EH3 8EG T 0131-272 2735 W www.palliativecarescotland.org.uk

COMPLAINTS

Patient advice and liaison services (PALS) have been established for every NHS and PCT in England. PALS can give advice on local complaints procedure, or resolve concerns informally. If the case is not resolved locally or the complainant is not satisfied with the way a local NHS body or practice has dealt with their complaint, they may approach the Parliamentary and Health Service Ombudsman in England, the Scottish Public Services Ombudsman, Public Services Ombudsman for Wales or the Northern Ireland Public Services Ombudsman. *See* Ombudsman Services.

HEALTH ADVICE AND MEDICAL TREATMENT ABROAD

IMMUNISATION

Country-by-country guidance is set out on the website W www.fitfortravel.nhs.uk

RECIPROCAL ARRANGEMENTS

The European Health Insurance Card (EHIC) allows UK residents access to state-provided healthcare while temporarily travelling in all European Economic Area countries and Switzerland either free or at a reduced cost. A card is free, valid for up to five years and should be obtained before travelling. Applications can be made by telephone (T 0300 330 1350) online (W www.ehic.org.uk) or by post (a form is available from the post office).

The UK also has bilateral agreements with several other countries, including Australia and New Zealand, for the free provision of urgent medical treatment.

European Economic Area nationals visiting the UK and visitors from other countries with which the UK has bilateral health care agreements are able to receive emergency health care on the NHS on the same terms as is available to UK residents.

SOCIAL WELFARE

SOCIAL SERVICES

The Secretary of State for Health (in England), the Welsh government, the Scottish government and the Secretary of State for Northern Ireland are responsible, under the Local Authority Social Services Act 1970, for the provision of social services for older people, disabled people, families and children, and those with mental disorders. Personal social services are administered by local authorities according to policies, with standards set by central and devolved government. Each authority has a director and a committee responsible for the social services functions placed upon them. Local authorities provide, enable and commission care after assessing the needs of their population. The private and voluntary sectors also play an important role in the delivery of social services, and an estimated 7 million people in the UK provide substantial regular care for a member of their family.

The Care Quality Commission (CQC) was established in April 2009, bringing together the independent regulation of health, mental health and adult social care. Prior to 1 April 2009 this work was carried out by three separate organisations: the Healthcare Commission, the Mental Health Act Commission and the Commission for Social Care Inspection. The CQC is responsible for the registration of health and social care providers, the monitoring and inspection of all health and adult social care, issuing fines, public warnings or closures if standards are not met and for undertaking regular performance reviews. Since April 2007 the Office for Standards in Education, Children's Services and Skills (Ofsted) has been responsible for inspecting and regulating all care services for children and young people in England. Both Ofsted and CQC collate information on local care services and make this information available to the public.

The Care and Social Services Inspectorate Wales (CSSIW), an operationally independent part of the Welsh government, is responsible for the regulation and inspection of all social care services in Wales. A new unified body, the Care Inspectorate, was established on 1 April 2011, replacing the Scottish Commission for the Regulation of Care (the Care Commission) and is now the independent care services regulator for Scotland.

The Department of Health is responsible for social care in Northern Ireland.

CARE QUALITY COMMISSION (CQC), Citygate,
  Gallowgate, Newcastle upon Tyne NE1 4PA T 0300-061 6161
  W www.cqc.org.uk

OFFICE FOR STANDARDS IN EDUCATION,
  CHILDREN'S SERVICES AND SKILLS (Ofsted),
  Piccadilly Gate, Store Street, Manchester M1 2WD
  T 0300-123 1231 E enquiries@ofsted.gov.uk W www.gov.uk/
  government/organisations/ofsted

CARE AND SOCIAL SERVICES INSPECTORATE WALES
  (CSSIW), Welsh Government Office, Rhydcar Business Park,
  Merthyr Tydfil CF48 1UZ T 0300-790 0126
  E cssiw@wales.gsi.gov.uk W www.cssiw.org.uk

CARE INSPECTORATE, Compass House, 11 Riverside Drive,
  Dundee DD1 4NY T 0845-600 9527
  E enquiries@careinspectorate.com
  W www.careinspectorate.com

DEPARTMENT OF HEALTH, Castle Buildings, Stormont,
  Belfast BT4 3SQ T 028-9052 0500
  E webmaster@health-ni.gov.uk W www.health-ni.gov.uk

STAFF (ENGLAND)

Total Adult Social Care Staff, by job role	1,585,000
Managerial	115,000
Regulated professional	85,000
Direct care	1,205,000
Other	180,000

Source: Skills for Care, 2017

OLDER PEOPLE

Services for older people are designed to enable them to remain living in their own homes for as long as possible. Local authority services include advice, domestic help, meals in the home, alterations to the home to aid mobility, emergency alarm systems, day and/or night attendants, laundry services and the provision of day centres and recreational facilities. Charges may be made for these services. Respite care may also be provided in order to allow carers temporary relief from their responsibilities.

Local authorities and the private sector also provide 'sheltered housing' for older people, sometimes with resident wardens.

If an older person is admitted to a residential home, charges are made according to a means test; if the person cannot afford to pay, the costs are met by the local authority.

DISABLED PEOPLE

Services for disabled people are designed to enable them to remain living in their own homes wherever possible. Local authority services include advice, adaptations to the home, meals in the home, help with personal care, occupational therapy, educational facilities and recreational facilities. Respite care may also be provided in order to allow carers temporary relief from their responsibilities.

Special housing may be available for disabled people who can live independently, and residential accommodation for those who cannot.

FAMILIES AND CHILDREN

Local authorities are required to provide services aimed at safeguarding the welfare of children in need and, wherever possible, allowing them to be brought up by their families. Services include advice, counselling, help in the home and the provision of family centres. Many authorities also provide short-term refuge accommodation for women and children.

DAY CARE

In allocating day care places to children, local authorities give priority to children with special needs, whether in terms of their health, learning abilities or social needs. Since September 2001, Ofsted has been responsible for the regulation and registration of all early years childcare and education provision in England (previously the responsibility of the local authorities). All day care and childminding services that care for children under eight years of age for more than two hours a day must register with Ofsted and are inspected at least every two years. As at 31 March 2017, there were 81,400 providers in England.

CHILD PROTECTION

Children considered to be at risk of physical injury, neglect or sexual abuse are placed on the local authority's child protection register. Local authority social services staff, schools, health visitors and other agencies work together to prevent and detect cases of abuse. As at 31 March 2016, there was a total of 58,239 children on child protection registers or subject to a child protection plan in the UK. In England, there were 50,310 children on child protection registers, of these, 23,150 were at risk of neglect, 4,200 of physical abuse, 2,370 of sexual abuse and 17,770 of emotional abuse. At 31 March (July in Scotland) 2016 there were 3,060 children on child protection registers in Wales, 2,723 in Scotland and 2,146 in Northern Ireland.

LOCAL AUTHORITY CARE

Local authorities are required to provide accommodation for children who have no parents or guardians or whose parents or guardians are unable or unwilling to care for them. A family proceedings court may also issue a care order where a child is being neglected or abused, or is not attending school; the court must be satisfied that this would positively contribute to the well-being of the child.

The welfare of children in local authority care must be properly safeguarded. Children may be placed with foster families, who receive payments to cover the expenses of caring for the child or children, or in residential care.

Children's homes may be run by the local authority or by the private or voluntary sectors; all homes are subject to inspection procedures. As at 31 March 2016, 70,440 children in the UK were in the care of local authorities, of these, 51,850 were in foster placements and 7,600 were in children's homes, hostels or secure units.

ADOPTION

Local authorities are required to provide an adoption service, either directly or via approved voluntary societies. In 2016–17, 4,350 children in local authority care were adopted.

PEOPLE WITH LEARNING DISABILITIES

Services for people with learning disabilities are designed to enable them to remain living in the community wherever possible. Local authority services include short-term care, support in the home, the provision of day care centres, and help with other activities outside the home. Residential care is provided for the severely or profoundly disabled.

MENTALLY ILL PEOPLE

Under the care programme approach, mentally ill people should be assessed by specialist services and receive a care plan. A key worker should be appointed for each patient and regular reviews of the person's progress should be conducted. Local authorities provide help and advice to mentally ill people and their families, and places in day centres and social centres. Social workers can apply for a mentally disturbed person to be compulsorily detained in hospital. Where appropriate, mentally ill people are provided with accommodation in special hospitals, local authority accommodation, or at homes run by private or voluntary organisations. Patients who have been discharged from hospitals may be placed on a supervision register.

NATIONAL INSURANCE

The National Insurance (NI) scheme operates under the Social Security Contributions and Benefits Act 1992 and the Social Security Administration Act 1992, and orders and regulations made thereunder. The scheme is financed by contributions payable by earners, employers and others (*see* below). Money collected under the scheme is used to finance the National Insurance Fund (from which contributory benefits are paid) and to contribute to the cost of the National Health Service.

NATIONAL INSURANCE FUND

Estimated receipts, payments and statement of balances of the National Insurance Fund for 2018–19:

Receipts	£ million
Net national insurance contributions	103,269
Compensation from the Consolidated Fund for statutory sick, maternity, paternity and adoption pay recoveries	2,645
Income from investments	174
State scheme premiums	43
Other receipts	0
TOTAL RECEIPTS	106,131

Payments	£ million
Benefits	
At present rates	99,175
Increase due to proposed rate changes	2,887
Administration costs	726
Redundancy fund payments	295
Transfer to Northern Ireland	612
Other payments	206
TOTAL PAYMENTS	103,901

Balances	£ million
Balance at the beginning of the year	23,957
Excess of receipts over payments	2,230
BALANCE AT END OF YEAR	26,187

CONTRIBUTIONS

There are six classes of National Insurance contributions (NICs):

Class 1	paid by employees and their employers
Class 1A	paid by employers who provide employees with certain benefits in kind for private use, such as company cars
Class 1B	paid by employers who enter into a pay as you earn (PAYE) settlement agreement (PSA) with HM Revenue and Customs
Class 2	paid by self-employed people
Class 3	voluntary contributions paid to protect entitlement to the state pension for those who do not pay enough NI contributions in another class
Class 4	paid by the self-employed on their taxable profits over a set limit. These are normally paid by self-employed people in addition to class 2 contributions. Class 4 contributions do not count towards benefits.

The lower and upper earnings limits and the percentage rates referred to below apply from April 2018 to April 2019.

CLASS 1

Class 1 primary (employee) contributions are paid where a person:
- is an employed earner (employee), office holder (eg company director) or employed under a contract of service in Great Britain or Northern Ireland
- is 16 or over and under state pension age
- earns at or above the earnings threshold of £162.00 per week (including overtime pay, bonus, commission, etc, without deduction of superannuation contributions)

Class 1 contributions are made up of primary and secondary contributions. Primary contributions are those paid by the employee and these are deducted from earnings by the employer. Since 6 April 2001 the employee's and employer's earnings thresholds have been the same. Primary contributions are not paid on earnings below the earnings threshold of £162.00 per week. However, between the lower earnings limit of £116.00 per week and the earnings threshold of £162.00 per week, NI contributions are treated as having been paid to protect the benefit entitlement position

388   Social Welfare

of lower earners. Contributions are payable at the rate of 12 per cent on earnings between the earnings threshold and the upper earnings limit of £892.00 per week. Above the upper earnings limit 2 per cent is payable.

Some married women or widows pay a reduced rate of 5.85 per cent on earnings between the earnings threshold and upper earnings limits and 2 per cent above this. It is no longer possible to elect to pay the reduced rate but those who had reduced liability before 12 May 1977 may retain it for as long as certain conditions are met.

Secondary contributions are paid by employers of employed earners at the rate of 13.8 per cent on all earnings above the earnings threshold of £162.00 per week. There is a zero rate between the earnings threshold and the upper threshold of £892 per week for employers of relevant apprentices and employed earners under the age of 21.

CLASS 2

Class 2 contributions are paid where a person is self-employed and is 16 or over and under state pension age. Contributions are paid at a flat rate of £2.95 per week regardless of the amount earned. However, those with earnings of less than £6,205 a year can apply for small earnings exception. Those granted exemption from class 2 contributions may pay class 2 or class 3 contributions voluntarily. Self-employed earners (whether or not they pay class 2 contributions) may also be liable to pay class 4 contributions based on profits. There are special rules for those who are concurrently employed and self-employed.

Married women and widows can no longer choose not to pay class 2 contributions but those who elected not to pay class 2 contributions before 12 May 1977 may retain the right for as long as certain conditions are met.

Class 2 contributions are assessed and collected annually by HM Revenue and Customs (HMRC) as part of the self-assessment tax bill. For self-employed people that do not pay tax through self-assessment, a bill is issued by HMRC by the end of October.

CLASS 3

Class 3 contributions are voluntary flat-rate contributions of £14.65 per week payable by persons over the age of 16 who would otherwise be unable to qualify for retirement pension and certain other benefits because they have an insufficient record of class 1 or class 2 contributions. This may include those who are not working, those not liable for class 1 or class 2 contributions, or those excepted from class 2 contributions. Married women and widows who on or before 11 May 1977 elected not to pay class 1 (full rate) or class 2 contributions cannot pay class 3 contributions while they retain this right. Class 3 contributions are collected by HMRC by quarterly bills or monthly direct debit. One-off payments can also be made.

CLASS 4

Self-employed people whose profits and gains are over £8,424 a year pay class 4 contributions in addition to class 2 contributions. This applies to self-employed earners over 16 and under the state pension age. Class 4 contributions are calculated at 9 per cent of annual profits or gains between £8,424 and £46,350 and 2 per cent above. Class 4 contributions are assessed and collected annually by HMRC as part of the self-assessment tax bill. It is possible, in some circumstances, to apply for exceptions from liability to pay class 4 contributions or to have the amount of contribution reduced.

PENSIONS

Many people will qualify for a state pension; however, there are further pension choices available, such as workplace, personal and stakeholder pensions. There are also other non-pension savings and investment options.

STATE PENSION

From 6 April 2016, the system of basic and additional state pension was replaced with a new scheme for people reaching state pension age after that date (ie men born on or after 6 April 1951, and women born on or after 6 April 1953).

Those that reached state pension age before this date continue to receive their state pension in line with existing rules. Information about the new state pension can be found online (www.gov.uk/new-state-pension).

The state pension does not have to be claimed at state pension age, people can delay claiming it to earn weekly state pension or a lump sum payment. For the new state pension scheme from 6 April 2016 additional qualifying years can be added to a person's national insurance record until the person reaches the full new state pension amount or the state pension age – whichever is first.

NEW STATE PENSION

The full rate of the new state pension, for people reaching state pension age on or after 6 April 2016, is £164.35 per week for a single person in 2018–19. It is set at a level that is above the basic level of means-tested support, the standard minimum guarantee in pension credit.

The amount received (starting amount) is based on the individual's NI record before 6 April 2016.

An individual's starting amount will be the higher of either:
- the amount received under the old state pension rules (including basic state pension, additional state pension and graduated retirement benefit)
- the amount received if the new state pension had been in place from the start of their working life

A deduction may be made to these amounts for periods an individual was contracted out of the additional state pension before 6 April 2016.

If the individual's starting amount is less than the full new state pension (£164.35 per week) more qualifying years can be added to their national insurance record after 5 April 2016 until the individual reaches the full rate of new state pension or reaches state pension age – whichever is first. If the individual's starting amount is more than the full new state pension of £164.35 per week, then the amount above the full new state pension (the 'protected payment') is paid on top of the full new state pension.

If an individual did not make NI contributions or get NI credits prior to 6 April 2016 than their state pension will be calculated entirely under the new state pension rules.

CATEGORY A OR B STATE PENSION

The category A or B state pension scheme is paid to individuals who reached state pension age before 6 April 2016 and is based on their own contributions or those made by a deceased spouse or civil partner. The full weekly rate in 2018–19 is £125.95.

For further information see Benefits, State Pension: Categories A and B.

WORKING LIFE

The working life is from the start of the tax year (6 April) in which a person reaches 16 to the end of the tax year (5 April) before the one in which they reach state pension age (see State Pension Age).

QUALIFYING YEARS

A 'qualifying year' is a tax year in which a person has sufficient earnings upon which they have paid, are treated as having paid, or have been credited with national insurance (NI) contributions (see National Insurance Credits).

For people reaching state pension age on or after 6 April 2016 a full new state pension (£164.35 per week in 2018–19) is payable to those individuals who have 35 qualifying years on their national insurance record. Individuals usually need at least ten qualifying years and will receive a proportion of the new state pension if they have between ten and 35 qualifying years.

For people who reached state pension age between 6 April 2010 and 5 April 2016 a full category A or B pension (£125.95 per week in 2018–19) is payable to those individuals who have 30 qualifying years on their national insurance record. Someone with less than 30 qualifying years will be entitled to a proportion of the full category A or B pension based on the number of qualifying years they have. Just one qualifying year, achieved through paid or credited contributions, will give entitlement to the basic state pension worth one-thirtieth of the full basic state pension.

For people who reached state pension age before 6 April 2010, women normally needed 39 qualifying years for a full basic state pension (£125.95 per week in 2018–19) and men normally needed 44 qualifying years. A reduced-rate basic state pension was payable if the number of qualifying years was less than 90 per cent of the individual's working life, but to receive any state pension at all, a person must have had enough qualifying years, normally ten or 11, to receive a basic state pension of at least 25 per cent of the full rate.

NATIONAL INSURANCE CREDITS

Those in receipt of carer's allowance, working tax credit (with a disability premium), jobseeker's allowance, employment and support allowance, unemployability supplement, statutory sick pay, maternity allowance, statutory maternity, paternity or statutory adoption pay may have class 1 NI contributions credited to them each week. People may also get credits if they are unemployed and looking for work or too sick to work, even if they are not in receipt of any benefit, although the credits must be applied for in these circumstances. Since April 2010, spouses and civil partners of members of HM forces may get credits if they are on an accompanied assignment outside the UK. Those who reach state pension age on or after 6 April 2016 can apply for NI credits for periods before April 2010 during which they were married to, or in a civil partnership with, a member of HM forces and accompanied them on a posting outside the UK. Persons undertaking certain training courses or jury service or who have been wrongly imprisoned for a conviction which is quashed on appeal may also get class 1 NI credits for each week they fulfil certain conditions. Class 1 credits may also be available to men approaching state pension age, born before 6 October 1953 who live in the UK for at least 183 days a year and who don't work, earn enough to make a qualifying year or are self-employed with profits of less than £6,205. Class 1 NI credits count toward all future contributory benefits.

A class 3 NI credit for basic state pension and bereavement benefit purposes is awarded, where required, for each week universal credit, working tax credit (without a disability premium) or child benefit, for a child under 12, has been received. Class 3 credits may also be awarded, on application, to approved foster carers and people caring for at least 20 hours a week. Since 6 April 2011, class 3 credits have been available to adults under state pension age who care for a family member under 12.

STATE PENSION AGE

From 6 November 2018 state pension age is 65 for both men and women and this will increase to age 66 for both men and women by October 2020. The Pensions Act 2014 makes provision for a regular review of state pension age. Reviews will take place at least once every six years and will take into account up-to-date life expectancy data and the findings of an independently led review, which will consider wider factors such as variation in life expectancy and employment opportunities for older workers. Further information can be obtained from the online state pension calculator (W www.gov.uk/state-pension-age).

USING THE NI CONTRIBUTION RECORD OF ANOTHER TO CLAIM A STATE PENSION

Married people or civil partners who reached state pension age before 6 April 2016 whose own NI record is incomplete may get a lower-rate basic state pension calculated using their partner's NI contribution record. This can be up to £75.50 a week in 2018–19.

People who reached state pension age before 6 April 2016 will continue to be able to use these provisions, even if their spouse or civil partner reaches state pension age on or after that date. However, contributions their spouse or civil partner pays, or is credited with, following implementation of the new system will only count towards their own state pension. This means that only the NI record of the spouse or civil partner up to and including 2015–16 will be used to calculate any derived entitlement.

People who reached state pension age on or after 6 April 2016 will not be able to claim state pension on their spouse's or civil partner's NI record. There will be special arrangements for women who had opted to pay the married women's and widows reduced rate contributions before May 1977.

NON-CONTRIBUTORY STATE PENSIONS

A non-contributory state pension may be payable to those aged 80 or over who live in England, Scotland or Wales, and have done so for a total of ten years or more for any continuous period in the 20 years after their 60th birthday, if they are not entitled to another category of state pension, or are entitled to one below the rate of £75.50 a week in 2018–19 (*see also* Benefits, State Pension for people aged 80 and over).

GRADUATED RETIREMENT BENEFIT

Graduated Retirement Benefit (GRB) is based on the amount of graduated NI contributions paid into the GRB scheme between April 1961 and April 1975 (*see also* Benefits, Graduated Retirement Benefit). It is normally paid as an increase to a main state pension. For those reaching state pension age under the new state pension rules, it will be included in the calculation of their basic amount.

HOME RESPONSIBILITIES PROTECTION

From 6 April 1978 until 5 April 2010, it was possible for people who had low income or were unable to work because they cared for children or a sick or disabled person at home to reduce the number of qualifying years required for basic state pension. This was called home responsibilities protection (HRP); the number of years for which HRP was given was deducted from the number of qualifying years needed. HRP could, in some cases, also qualify the recipient for additional state pension. From April 2003 to April 2010 HRP was also available to approved foster carers.

From 6 April 2010, HRP was replaced by weekly credits for parents and carers. A class 3 national insurance credit is given, where eligible, towards state pension and bereavement benefits for spouses and civil partners. An earnings factor credit towards additional state pension was also awarded. Any years of HRP accrued before 6 April 2010 have been converted into qualifying years of credits for people reaching state pension age after that date, up to a maximum of 22 years for state pension purposes.

ADDITIONAL STATE PENSION

The amount of additional state pension paid depends on the amount of earnings a person has, or is treated as having, between the lower and upper earnings limits (from April 2009, the upper accruals point replaced the upper earnings limit for additional pension) for each complete tax year between 6 April 1978 (when the scheme started) and the tax year before they reach state pension age.

From 1978 to 2002, additional state pension was called the State Earnings-Related Pension Scheme (SERPS). SERPS covered all earnings by employees from 6 April 1978 to 5 April 1997 on which standard rate class 1 NI contributions had been paid, and earnings between 6 April 1997 and 5 April 2002 if the standard rate class 1 NI contributions had been contracted-in.

In 2002, SERPS was reformed through the state second pension, by improving the pension available to low and moderate earners and extending access to certain carers and people with long-term illness or disability. If earnings on which class 1 NI contributions have been paid or can be treated as paid are above the annual NI lower earnings limit (£6,032 for 2018–19) but below the primary threshold (£8,424 for 2018–19), the state second pension regards this as earnings of £8,424 and it is treated as equivalent. Certain carers and people with long-term illness and disability will be considered as having earned at the primary threshold for each complete tax year since 2002–3 even if they do not work at all, or earn less than the annual NI lower earnings limit.

The amount of additional state pension paid also depends on when a person reaches state pension age; changes phased in from 6 April 1999 mean that pensions are calculated differently from that date.

ADDITIONAL STATE PENSION INHERITANCE

Men or women widowed before 6 October 2002 may inherit all of their late spouse's SERPS pension. Since 6 October 2002, the maximum percentage of SERPS pension that a person can inherit from a late spouse or civil partner depends on their late spouse's or civil partner's date of birth:

Maximum SERPS entitlement	d.o.b (men)	d.o.b (women)
100%	5/10/37 or earlier	5/10/42 or earlier
90%	6/10/37 to 5/10/39	6/10/42 to 5/10/44
80%	6/10/39 to 5/10/41	6/10/44 to 5/10/46
70%	6/10/41 to 5/10/43	6/10/46 to 5/10/48
60%	6/10/43 to 5/10/45	6/10/48 to 5/7/50
50%	6/10/45 or later	6/7/50 or later

The maximum state second pension a person can inherit from a spouse or civil partner is 50 per cent. If a person is bereaved before they have reached their state pension age, inherited SERPS or state second pension can be paid as part of widowed parent's allowance (in the case of a person who has dependent children) or otherwise only from state pension age. If they remarry or form a new civil partnership before state pension age they lose the right to inherit any state pension.

NEW STATE PENSION INHERITANCE

A person who reached state pension age before 6 April 2016 will still be able to inherit additional state pension under the existing rules. However, if their late spouse or civil partner reaches state pension age on or after that date, the amount they can inherit will be based on the deceased's contributions up to 5 April 2016 only.

A person reaching state pension age on or after 6 April 2016 whose deceased spouse or civil partner reached state pension age or died before that date will be able to inherit additional state pension under the current rules. If the deceased spouse or civil partner is also in the new state pension the survivor may inherit half of any 'protected payment'. A person will have a protected payment if their state pension calculated under current rules is more than the full rate of new state pension at April 2016. The protected payment is the amount of the excess.

In order for a person reaching state pension age on or after 6 April 2016 to qualify for an inherited amount the marriage

or civil partnership must have begun before that date; and, in the case of a person widowed under state pension age, they must not remarry or form a new civil partnership before state pension age.

STATE PENSION STATEMENTS

The Department for Work and Pensions provide state pension statements. These statements give an estimate of the state pension an individual may get based on their current NI contribution record.

There is also an online state pension calculator (W www.gov.uk/check-state-pension).

PRIVATE PENSIONS

CONTRACTED-OUT PENSIONS

From 6 April 2012, employees have not been able to contract-out of the state second pension through a money purchase (defined contribution) occupational pension scheme or a personal or stakeholder pension. Anyone contracted-out via these schemes, from that date, was automatically contracted back into the additional state pension. Although those rights built up before the abolition date can be used to provide pension benefits. These changes did not affect contracting-out via a salary-related occupational pension scheme (also known as contracted-out defined benefit (DB) or final salary schemes), which provide a pension related to earnings and the length of pensionable service. However, the introduction of the single-tier pension scheme in April 2016 closed the additional state pension for those reaching state pension age after this date, and contracting out on a DB basis ended.

STAKEHOLDER PENSION SCHEMES

Introduced in 2001, stakeholder pensions are available to everyone but are principally for moderate earners who do not have access to a good value company pension scheme. Stakeholder pensions must meet minimum standards to make sure they are flexible, portable and annual management charges are capped. The minimum contribution is £20.

AUTOMATIC ENROLMENT INTO WORKPLACE PENSIONS

Since October 2012, under the Pensions Act 2008, employers must automatically enrol their workers who meet the age and earnings criteria into a workplace pension. This applies to people who are not already in a qualifying workplace pension scheme and who:
• earn at least £10,000 per annum
• are aged 22 or over
• are under state pension age
• ordinarily work in the UK

Employees who meet the above requirements are entitled to opt out of the scheme, if they wish to do so, within one calendar month of enrolment. Additionally certain employees can also choose to opt in to the scheme. Currently, employees can opt in if they are:
• aged 16 to 21, or state pension age to 74
• earning above £6,032 up to and including £10,000 per annum

If they remain in the scheme, they, together with their employer, will pay into it every month. The government will also contribute through tax relief. Employees can cease active membership from their workplace pension at any time after the opt-out period. Further information is available at W www.gov.uk/workplace-pensions

COMPLAINTS

The Pensions Advisory Service provides information and guidance to members of the public, on state, company, personal and stakeholder schemes. They also help any member of the public who has a problem, complaint or dispute with their occupational or personal pensions.

There are two bodies for pension complaints. The Financial Ombudsman Service deals with complaints which predominantly concern the sale and/or marketing of occupational, stakeholder and personal pensions. The Pensions Ombudsman deals with complaints which predominantly concern the management (after sale or marketing) of occupational, stakeholder and personal pensions.

The Pensions Regulator is the UK regulator for work-based pension schemes; it concentrates its resources on schemes where there is the greatest risk to the security of members' benefits, promotes good administration practice for all work-based schemes and works with trustees, employers and professional advisers to put things right when necessary.

WAR PENSIONS AND THE ARMED FORCES COMPENSATION SCHEME

Veterans UK is part of the Ministry of Defence. It was formed on 1 April 2007 to provide services to both serving personnel and veterans.

Veterans UK is responsible for the administration of the war pensions scheme and the armed forces compensation scheme (AFCS) to members of the armed forces in respect of disablement or death due to service. There is also a scheme for civilians and civil defence workers in respect of the Second World War, and other schemes for groups such as merchant seamen and Polish armed forces who served under British command during the Second World War. They are also responsible for the administration of the armed forces pension scheme (AFPS), which provides occupational pensions for ex-service personnel.

THE WAR PENSIONS SCHEME

War disablement pension is awarded for the disabling effects of any injury, wound or disease which was the result of, or was aggravated by, service in the armed forces prior to 6 April 2005. Claims are only considered once the person has left the armed forces. The amount of pension paid depends on the severity of disablement, which is assessed by comparing the health of the claimant with that of a healthy person of the same age and sex. The person's earning capacity or occupation are not taken into account in this assessment. A pension is awarded if the person has a disablement of 20 per cent or more and a lump sum is usually payable to those with a disablement of less than 20 per cent. No award is made for noise-induced sensorineural hearing loss where the assessment of disablement is less than 20 per cent. Where an assessment of disablement is at 40 per cent or more, an age addition is automatically given when the pensioner reaches 65.

A pension is payable to war widows, widowers and surviving civil partners where the spouse's or civil partner's death was due to, or hastened by, service in the armed forces prior to 6 April 2005 or where the spouse or civil partner was in receipt of a war disablement pension constant attendance allowance (or would have been if not in hospital) at the time of death. A pension is also payable to widows, widowers or surviving civil partners if the spouse or civil partner was receiving the war disablement pension at the 80 per cent rate or higher in conjunction with unemployability supplement at the time of death. War widows, widowers and surviving civil partners receive a standard rank-related rate, but a lower weekly rate is payable to war widows, widowers and surviving civil partners of personnel of the rank of Major or below who are under the age of 40, without children and capable of maintaining themselves. This is increased to the standard rate at age 40. Allowances are paid for children and adult dependants. An age allowance is automatically given when the widow, widower or surviving civil partner reaches 65 and increased at ages 70 and 80.

Pensioners living overseas receive the same pension rates as those living in the UK. All war disablement pensions and allowances and pensions for war widows, widowers and surviving civil partners are tax-free in the UK; this does not always apply in overseas countries due to different tax laws.

SUPPLEMENTARY ALLOWANCES

A number of supplementary allowances may be awarded to a war pensioner and are intended to meet various needs. The principal supplementary allowances are unemployability supplement, allowance for lowered standard of occupation, constant attendance allowance and war pensions mobility supplement. Others include exceptionally severe disablement allowance, severe disablement occupational allowance, treatment allowance, comforts allowance, clothing allowance, age allowance and widow/widower/surviving civil partner's age allowance. Rent and children's allowances are also available with pensions for war widows, widowers and surviving civil partners.

ARMED FORCES COMPENSATION SCHEME

The armed forces compensation scheme (AFCS) became effective on 6 April 2005 and covers all regular (including Gurkhas) and reserve personnel whose injury, ill health or death is caused predominantly by service on or after 6 April 2005. There are time limits under this scheme and generally claims must be made within seven years of the injury occurring or from first seeking medical advice about an illness. There are some exceptions to this time limit, the main one being for a late-onset illness. Claims for a late-onset illness can be made, after discharge, at any time after the event to which it relates, providing the claim is made within three years of medical advice being sought.

The AFCS provides compensation where service in the armed forces is the only or predominant cause of injury, illness or death. Any other personal accident cover held by the individual is not taken into account when determining an AFCS award. Under the terms of the scheme a tax-free lump sum is payable to service or ex-service personnel based on a 15-level tariff, graduated according to the seriousness of the injury. If multiple injuries are sustained in the same incident compensation for each injury, up to the scheme maximum, is awarded. For those with the most serious injuries and illness a tax-free, index-linked monthly payment – a guaranteed income payment or GIP – is paid for life from the point of discharge. A taxable survivor's GIP (SGIP) will also be paid to surviving spouses, civil partners and unmarried partners who meet certain criteria. GIP and SGIP are calculated by multiplying the pensionable pay of the service person by a factor that depends on the age at the person's last birthday. The younger the person, the higher the factor, because there are more years to normal retirement age.

ARMED FORCES INDEPENDENCE PAYMENT

Armed forces independence payment (AFIP) is designed to provide financial support for service personnel and veterans who have been seriously injured to cover the extra costs they may incur as a result of their injury. It is administered by Veterans UK as part of AFCS although payments are made by the Department for Work and Pensions (DWP). It is non-taxable and non-means-tested.

Service personnel and veterans awarded a GIP of 50 per cent or higher under the AFCS are eligible. Those eligible for AFIP are not required to undergo an assessment and will keep the payment for as long as they are entitled to receive a GIP of 50 per cent or higher.

DEPARTMENT FOR WORK AND PENSIONS BENEFITS

Payments under the AFCS and the war pensions scheme may affect income related benefits from the DWP. In particular any supplementary allowances in payment with war pensions.

Any state pension for which a war widow, widower or surviving civil partner qualifies for on their own NI contribution record can be paid in addition to monies received under the war pensions scheme.

CLAIMS AND QUESTIONS

Further information on the war pensions scheme, the AFCS and the nearest Veterans' Welfare Office can be obtained from Veterans UK (T 0808-191 4218, if calling from the UK or, if living overseas, T (+44) (1253) 866-043).

VETERANS UK, Norcross Lane, Thornton-Cleveleys FY5 3WP
E veterans-uk@mod.gov.uk W www.gov.uk/government/
organisations/veterans-uk

TAX CREDITS

Tax credits are administered by HM Revenue and Customs (HMRC). They are based on an individual's or couple's household income and current circumstances. Adjustments can be made during the year to reflect changes in income and/or circumstances. Further information regarding the qualifying conditions for tax credits, how to claim and the rates payable is available online at (W www.gov.uk/browse/benefits/tax-credits).

WORKING TAX CREDIT

Working tax credit is a payment from the government to support people on low incomes. New claims may only be made by those, or those whose partners, qualify for pension credit or by those that do not live in a universal credit area. It may be claimed by:
• those aged 25 or over who work at least 30 hours a week
• those aged 16 or over who work at least 16 hours a week, who are responsible for a child or young person, or have a disability that puts them at a disadvantage of getting a job
• those aged 60 or over, who work at least 16 hours a week
• couples who are responsible for a child or young person, who work at least 24 hours per week between them with one partner working at least 16 hours a week

The amount received depends on individual circumstances and income. The basic amount is up to £1,960 per annum and extra 'elements' are paid on top of this:

Element	Amount per annum
Couple applying together	up to £2,010
Single parent	up to £2,010
An individual working at least 30 hours a week	up to £810
An individual with a disability	up to £3,090
An individual with a severe disability	up to £1,330*

* Usually in addition to the disability payment

Childcare Element
In families with children where a lone parent works at least 16 hours a week, or couples who work at least 24 hours a week between them with one partner working at least 16 hours a week, or where one partner works at least 16 hours a week and the other is disabled, an in-patient in hospital, or in prison, the family is entitled to the childcare element of working tax credit. Depending on circumstances this payment can contribute up to £175 a week towards childcare costs for one child and up to £300 a week for two or more children. Families can only claim if they use an approved or registered childcare provider.

CHILD TAX CREDIT

Child tax credit combines all income-related support for children and is paid direct to the main carer. The credit is made up of a main 'family' element of up to £545 a year with an additional payment of up to £2,780 a year for each child in a household born before 6 April 2017. For children born after this date, only the child element of child tax credit will apply for the first two children in a household with no 'family element', however there are exceptions to this two-child rule. An additional payment is paid for children with a disability, plus a further payment for children who are severely disabled. Child tax credit is available to households not in a universal credit area where:
• there is at least one dependant under 16
• there is at least one dependant between 16 and 20 who is in relevant education or training or is registered for work, education or training with an approved body
For those households that do live in a universal credit area, claims can only be made if either of the following apply:
• there are three or more children in the household
• the applicant or their partner have reached pension credit qualifying age

BENEFITS

The following is intended as a general guide to the benefits system. Conditions of entitlement and benefit rates change annually and all prospective claimants should check exact entitlements and rates of benefit directly with their local Jobcentre Plus office, pension centre or online (W www.gov.uk/browse/benefits). Leaflets relating to the various benefits and contribution conditions for different benefits are available from local Jobcentre Plus offices.

UNIVERSAL CREDIT

Universal credit is replacing six means tested benefits with a single monthly payment. The six benefits being replaced by universal credit are:
• Income-based jobseeker's allowance (JSA)
• Income-related employment and support allowance (ESA)
• Income support
• Child tax credit
• Working tax credit
• Housing benefit

The roll-out of universal credit to all local authority areas for new claimants is due to be completed by the end of 2018. From July 2019, eligible existing claimants of the above six benefits will be transferred onto universal credit; the transfer of existing claimants is due to be completed by March 2022. The amount of universal credit awarded is determined by the circumstances of the claimant, this includes income and number of dependants in the household. It consists of a basic 'standard allowance' and additional payments as applicable to the claimant's circumstances. Universal credit can be claimed while working, but the monthly payment will reduce gradually as the claimant earns more.

Standard monthly allowance from April 2018

Single, under 25	£251.77
Single, over 25	£317.82
Couple, both under 25	£395.20
Couple, one or both over 25	£498.89

Additional monthly payments from April 2018

Disability or health condition	£328.32
Carer allowance	£156.45
First child born before 6 April 2017	£277.08
First child born after 6 April 2017	£231.67
Second child	£231.67
Childcare for one child (max.)	£646.35
Childcare for two or more children (max.)	£1,108.04
Child with a disability	£126.11
Severely disabled child	£383.86

For more information and to check eligibility visit W www.gov.uk/universal-credit

CONTRIBUTORY BENEFITS

Entitlement to contributory benefits depends on national insurance contribution conditions being satisfied either by the claimant or by someone on the claimant's behalf (depending on the kind of benefit). The class or classes of national insurance contribution relevant to each benefit are:

Jobseeker's allowance (contribution-based)	Class 1
Employment and Support Allowance (contributory)	Class 1 or 2
Widow's benefit and bereavement benefit	Class 1, 2 or 3
State pensions, categories A and B	Class 1, 2 or 3

The system of contribution conditions relates to yearly levels of earnings on which national insurance (NI) contributions have been paid.

JOBSEEKER'S ALLOWANCE

Jobseeker's allowance (JSA) replaced unemployment benefit and income support for unemployed people under state pension age from 7 October 1996. There are two routes of entitlement. Contribution-based JSA is paid at a personal rate (ie additional benefit for dependants is not paid) to those who have made sufficient NI contributions in two particular tax years. Savings and partner's earnings are not taken into account and payment can be made for up to six months. Rates of JSA correspond to income support rates.

Claims are made through Jobcentre Plus. A person wishing to claim JSA must generally be unemployed or working on average less than 16 hours a week, capable of work and available for any work which he or she can reasonably be expected to do, usually for at least 40 hours a week. The claimant must agree and sign a 'jobseeker's agreement', which will set out his or her plans to find work, and must actively seek work. If the claimant refuses work or training the benefit may be sanctioned for between one and 26 weeks.

A person will be sanctioned from JSA for up to 26 weeks if he or she has left a job voluntarily without just cause or through misconduct. In these circumstances, it may be possible to receive hardship payments, particularly where the claimant or the claimant's family is vulnerable, eg if sick or pregnant, or with children or caring responsibilities.

Weekly Rates from April 2018	
Person aged 18–24	£57.90
Person aged 25 to state pension age*	£73.10
* Since October 2003 people aged between 60 and state pension age can choose to claim pension credits instead of JSA	

EMPLOYMENT AND SUPPORT ALLOWANCE

From 27 October 2008, employment and support allowance (ESA) replaced incapacity benefit and income support paid on the grounds of incapacity or disability. The benefit consists of two strands, contribution-based benefit and income-related benefit, so that people no longer need to make two claims for benefit in order to gain their full entitlement. Contributory ESA is available to those who have limited capability for work but cannot get statutory sick pay from their employer. Those over pensionable age are not entitled to ESA. Apart from those who qualify under the special provisions for people incapacitated in youth, entitlement to contributory ESA is based on a person's NI contribution record. In order to qualify for contributory ESA, two contribution conditions, based on the last three years before the tax year in which benefit is claimed, must be satisfied. The amount of contributory ESA payable may be reduced where the person receives more than a specified amount of occupational or personal pension. Contributory ESA is paid only in respect of the person

claiming the benefit – there are no additional amounts for dependants.

At the outset, new claimants are paid a basic allowance (the same rate as jobseeker's allowance) for 13 weeks while their medical condition is assessed and a work capability assessment is conducted. Following the completion of the assessment phase those claimants capable of engaging in work-related activities will receive a work-related activity component on top of the basic rate. The work-related activity component can be subject to sanctions if the claimant does not engage in the conditionality requirements without good reason. The maximum sanction is equal to the value of the work-related activity component of the benefit.

Those with the most severe health conditions or disabilities will receive the support component, which is more than the work-related activity component. Claimants in receipt of the support component are not required to engage in work-related activities, although they can volunteer to do so or undertake permitted work if their condition allows.

Weekly Rates from April 2018	
ESA plus work-related activity component	up to £102.15
ESA plus support component	up to £110.75

BEREAVEMENT SUPPORT PAYMENT

Bereavement support payment replaced bereavement payment, widowed parent's allowance and bereavement allowance for those whose spouse or civil partner died on or after 6 April 2017. It may be paid to those under state pension age at the time of their spouse or civil partner's death and whose spouse or civil partner had paid National Insurance contributions for at least 25 weeks or died because of an accident at work or a disease caused by work.

It consists of an initial one-off payment followed by up to 18 monthly payments. There are two rates: those in receipt of, or entitled to, child benefit or those who were pregnant when their spouse or civil partner died receive the higher rate. In order to receive the full amount claims must be made within three months of the death of the spouse or civil partner. After three months, claims can still be made up to 21 months after the spouse or civil partner's death but the payments will be less.

Weekly Rates from April 2018	
Standard rate	
lump sum	£2,500.00
monthly payment	£100.00
Higher rate	
lump sum	£3,500
monthly payment	£350.00

NEW STATE PENSION

The new state pension is payable to men and women who reach state pension age on or after 6 April 2016 (ie men born on or after 6 April 1951 or women born on or after 6 April 1953). Those that reached state pension age before this date continue to receive state pension under the old rules outlined below.

The full new state pension of £164.35 a week in 2018–19 is payable to those individuals who have 35 qualifying years on their national insurance record. Individuals usually need at least ten qualifying years and will receive a proportion of the new state pension if they have between ten and 35 qualifying years. The starting amount is the higher of the amount receivable under the old state pension rules (category A and B) and the amount the individual would receive had the new state pension been in place at the start of their working life.

The amount received includes a deduction for those who were contracted out of the additional state pension.

Each qualifying year on an individual's national insurance record after 5 April 2016 adds £4.70 a week to the new state pension. The exact amount can be calculated by dividing £164.35 by 35 and then multiplying by the number of qualifying years after 5 April 2016. Additional qualifying years can be added to a person's national insurance record until the person reaches the full new state pension amount or the state pension age – whichever is first.

Those individuals who have accrued an amount, before 5 April 2016, which is above the new full state pension – a 'protected payment' – have this paid on top of the full new state pension.

The new state pension increases each year by whichever is the highest:

• earnings – the average percentage growth in wages (in Great Britain)
• prices – the percentage growth in prices in the UK as measured by the Consumer Prices Index (CPI)
• 3 per cent

Any protected payment increases each year in line with the CPI.

The new state pension can be deferred beyond state pension age and will increase by 1 per cent for every nine weeks it is deferred, as long as you deferred for at least nine weeks. This equates to just under 5.8 per cent for every full year a new state pension is deferred.

Weekly Rate from April 2018	
Full new state pension	£164.35

STATE PENSION: CATEGORIES A AND B

Category A pension is payable for life to men and women who reach state pension age, who satisfy the contributions conditions and who claim for it. Category B pension may be payable to married women, married men and civil partners who are not entitled to a basic state pension on their own NI contributions or whose own basic state pension entitlement is less than £75.50 a week in 2018–19. It is based on their spouse or civil partner's NI contributions and is payable when both members of the couple have reached state pension age. Married men and civil partners may only be able to qualify for a category B pension if their wife or civil partner was born on or after 6 April 1950. Category B pension is also payable to widows, widowers and surviving civil partners who are bereaved before state pension age if they were previously entitled to widowed parent's allowance or bereavement allowance based on their late spouse's or civil partner's NI contributions. If they were receiving widowed parent's allowance on reaching state pension age, they could qualify for a category B pension payable at the same rate as their widowed parent's allowance comprising a basic pension, plus, if applicable, the appropriate share of their late spouse's or late civil partner's additional state pension. If their widowed parent's allowance had stopped before they reached state pension age, or they had been getting bereavement allowance at any time before state pension age, their category B pension will consist of inheritable additional state pension only. No basic state pension is included, although they may qualify for a basic state pension or have their own basic state pension improved by substituting their late spouse's or late civil partner's NI records for their own.

Widows who are bereaved when over state pension age can qualify for a category B pension regardless of the age of their husband when he died. This is payable at the same rate as the basic state pension the widow's late husband was entitled to (or would have been entitled to) at the time of his death. It can also be paid to widowers and civil partners who are bereaved when over state pension age if their wife or civil partner had reached state pension age when they died. Widowers and surviving civil partners who reached state pension age on or after 6 April 2010 and bereaved when over state pension age can qualify for a category B pension regardless of the age of their wife or civil partner when they died.

Where a person is entitled to both a category A and category B pension then they can be combined to give a composite pension, but this cannot be more than the full rate pension. Where a person is entitled to more than one category A or category B pension then only one can be paid. In such cases the person can choose which to get; if no choice is made, the most favourable one is paid.

A person may defer claiming their pension beyond state pension age. In doing so they may earn increments which will increase the weekly amount paid by 1 per cent per five weeks of deferral (equivalent to 10.4 per cent/year) when they claim their state pension. If a person delays claiming for at least 12 months they are given the option of a one-off taxable lump sum, instead of a pension increase, based on the weekly pension deferred, plus interest of at least 2 per cent above the Bank of England base rate. Since 6 April 2010, a category B pension has been treated independently of the spouse's or partner's pension. It is possible to take a category B pension even if the spouse or partner has deferred theirs.

It is no longer possible to claim an increase on a state pension for another adult (known as adult dependency increase). Those who received the increase before April 2010 can keep receiving it until the conditions are no longer met or until 5 April 2020, whichever is first.

Provision for children is made through child tax credits. An age addition of 25p a week is payable with a state pension if a pensioner is aged 80 or over.

Since 1989 pensioners have been allowed to have unlimited earnings without affecting their state pension. See also Pensions.

Weekly Rates from April 2018	
Category A or B pension for a single person	£125.95
Category B pension based on spouse or civil partner's NI contributions	£75.50

GRADUATED RETIREMENT BENEFIT

Graduated retirement benefit (GRB) is based on the amount of graduated NI contributions paid into the GRB scheme between April 1961 and April 1975; however, it is still paid in addition to any state pension to those who made the relevant contributions. A person will receive graduated retirement benefit based on their own contributions, even if not entitled to a basic state pension. Widows, widowers and surviving civil partners may inherit half of their deceased spouse's or civil partner's entitlement, but none that the deceased spouse or civil partner may have been eligible for from a former spouse or civil partner. If a person defers making a claim beyond state pension age, they may earn an increase or a one-off lump sum payment in respect of their deferred graduated retirement benefit; calculated in the same way as for category A or B state pension.

NON-CONTRIBUTORY BENEFITS

These benefits are paid from general taxation and are not dependent on NI contributions.

JOBSEEKER'S ALLOWANCE (INCOME-BASED)

Those who do not qualify for contribution-based jobseeker's allowance (JSA), those who have exhausted their entitlement to contribution-based JSA or those for whom contribution-based JSA provides insufficient income may qualify for income-based JSA. The amount paid depends on age, whether they are single or a couple and amount of income and savings. To get income-based JSA the claimant must usually be aged 18 or over but below state pension age, although there are some exceptions for 16- or 17-year-olds. Since April 2003, child dependants have been provided for through the child tax credit system.

The rules of entitlement are the same as for contribution-based JSA.

If one person in a couple was born after 28 October 1957 and neither person in the couple has responsibility for a child or children, then the couple will have to make a joint claim for JSA if they wish to receive income-based JSA.

Weekly Rates from April 2018	
Person aged 16–24	£57.90
Person aged 25 to state pension age	£73.10
Couple, both aged 18 to state pension age	£114.85

MATERNITY ALLOWANCE

Maternity allowance (MA) is a benefit available for pregnant women who cannot get statutory maternity pay (SMP) from their employer or have been employed/self-employed during or close to their pregnancy. In order to qualify for payment, a woman must have been employed and/or self-employed for at least 26 weeks in the 66-week period up to and including the week before the baby is due (test period). These weeks do not have to be in a row and any part weeks worked will count towards the 26 weeks. She must also have an average weekly earning of at least £30 (maternity allowance threshold) over any 13 weeks of the woman's choice within the test period.

Self-employed women who pay class 2 NI contributions or who hold a small earnings exception certificate are deemed to have enough earnings to qualify for MA.

A woman can choose to start receiving MA from the 11th week before the week in which the baby is due (if she stops work before then) up to the day following the day of birth. The exact date MA starts will depend on when the woman stops work to have her baby or if the baby is born before she stops work. However, where the woman is absent from work wholly or partly due to her pregnancy in the four weeks before the week the baby is due to be born, MA will start the day following the first day of absence from work. MA is paid for a maximum of 39 weeks.

Women who are not eligible for statutory maternity pay or the higher amount of MA may be eligible for a reduced rate of MA for either a 39-week or a 14-week period. For example, women who have not made enough Class 2 National Insurance contributions or who take part in the business of their self-employed spouse or civil partner, for at least 26 weeks in the 66 weeks before their baby is due, and the work they do is unpaid.

Weekly Rates from April 2018	
Standard rate	£145.18 or 90 per cent of the woman's average weekly earnings if less than £145.18
39-week reduced rate	£27.00
14-week reduced rate	£27.00

CHILD BENEFIT

A person responsible for one or more children under 16 (or under 20 if they stay in approved education or training) is entitled to claim child benefit. There's no limit to the number of children that can be claimed for, but only one person can receive child benefit for a child. Child benefit is taxable if the claimant or their partner's individual income is over £50,000. An individual can choose not to receive child benefit payments, but they should still fill in the claim form in order to get National Insurance credits and to ensure the child is registered to get a National Insurance number when they become 16-years-old

Weekly Rates from April 2018	
Eldest/only child	£20.70
Each subsequent child	£13.70

GUARDIAN'S ALLOWANCE

Guardian's allowance is payable to a person who is bringing up a child or young person because the child's parents have died, or in some circumstances, where only one parent has died. To receive the allowance the person must be in receipt of child benefit for the child or young person, although they do not have to be the child's legal guardian.

Weekly Rate (in addition to child benefit) from April 2018	
Each child	£17.20

CARER'S ALLOWANCE

Carer's allowance (CA) is a benefit payable to people who spend at least 35 hours a week caring for a severely disabled person. To qualify for CA a person must be caring for someone in receipt of one of the following benefits:
- attendance allowance
- disability living allowance
- personal independence payment
- constant attendance allowance, paid at not less than the normal maximum rate with an industrial injuries disablement payment or basic (full-day) rate, under the industrial injuries or war pension schemes.
- armed forces independence payment (AFIP)

Weekly Rate from April 2018	
Carer's allowance	£64.60

ATTENDANCE ALLOWANCE

This may be payable to people aged 65 or over who need help with personal care because they are physically or mentally disabled, and who have needed help for a period of at least six months. Attendance allowance has two rates: the lower rate is for day or night care, and the higher rate is for day and night care. People not expected to live for more than six months because of a progressive disease can receive the highest rate of attendance allowance straight away.

Weekly Rates from April 2018	
Higher rate	£85.60
Lower rate	£57.30

PERSONAL INDEPENDENCE PAYMENT (PIP)

Personal independence payment (PIP) replaced disability living allowance (DLA) for people aged 16 to 64 on 8 April 2013. PIP has two components: the daily living component and the mobility component, with each offering two different benefit rates: standard and enhanced. Whether one or both components are claimed depends on the requirements of the individual. Claimants are assessed on their ability to carry out everyday activities, with the majority of claims evaluated via an interview. Claimants with a terminal illness automatically receive the enhanced daily living component.

Weekly Rates from April 2018	
Daily living component	
Standard	£57.30
Enhanced	£85.60
Mobility component	
Standard	£22.65
Enhanced	£59.75

STATE PENSION FOR PEOPLE AGED 80 AND OVER

A state pension, also referred to as category D pension, is provided for people aged 80 and over if they are not entitled to another category of state pension or are entitled to a state pension that is less than £75.50 a week. The person must also live in Great Britain and have done so for a period of ten years or more in any continuous 20-year period since their 60th birthday.

Weekly Rate from April 2018	
Single person	£75.50
Age addition	£0.25

INCOME SUPPORT

Broadly speaking income support is a benefit for those between age 16 and the age they can receive pension credit, whose income is below a certain level, who work on average less than 16 hours a week and who are:

- bringing up children alone
- registered sick or disabled
- a student who is also a lone parent or disabled
- caring for someone who is sick or elderly

Income support is not payable if the claimant, or claimant and partner, have capital or savings in excess of £16,000 – and deductions are made for capital and savings in excess of £6,000. For people permanently in residential care and nursing homes deductions apply for capital over £10,000.

Sums payable depend on fixed allowances laid down by law for people in different circumstances. If both partners are eligible for income support, either may claim it for the couple. People receiving income support may be able to receive housing benefit, help with mortgage or home loan interest and help with healthcare. They may also be eligible for help with exceptional expenses from the Social Fund. Special rates may apply to some people living in residential care or nursing homes.

INCOME SUPPORT PREMIUMS

Income support premiums are extra weekly payments for those with additional needs. People qualifying for more than one premium will normally only receive the highest single premium for which they qualify. However, family premium, disabled child premium, severe disability premium and carer premium are payable in addition to other premiums.

Child tax credit replaced premiums for people with children for all new income support claims from 6 April 2004. People with children who were already in receipt of income support in April 2004 and have not claimed child tax credit may qualify for:

- the family premium if they have at least one child
- the disabled child premium if they have a child who receives disability living allowance or is registered blind
- the enhanced disability child premium if they have a child in receipt of the higher rate disability living allowance care component

Carers may qualify for:

- the carer premium if they or their partner are in receipt of carer's allowance

Long-term sick or disabled people may qualify for:

- the disability premium if they or their partner are receiving

certain benefits because they are disabled or cannot work; are registered blind; or if the claimant has been incapable of work or receiving statutory sick pay for at least 364 days (196 days if the person is terminally ill), including periods of incapacity separated by eight weeks or less

- the severe disability premium if the person lives alone and receives the middle or higher rate of disability living allowance care component and no one receives carer's allowance for caring for that person
- the enhanced disability premium if the person is in receipt of the higher rate disability living allowance care component

People with a partner aged over 60 may qualify for:

- the pensioner premium

WEEKLY RATES OF INCOME SUPPORT
from April 2018

Single person	
Aged under 18	£57.90
aged 25+	£73.10
Aged under 18 and a single parent	£57.90
Aged 18+ and a single parent	£73.10

Couples	
Both under 18	£57.90
Both under 18, in certain circumstances	£87.50
One under 18, one under 25	£57.90
One under 18, one aged 25+	£73.10
Both aged 18+	£114.85

Premiums	
Carer premium	£36.00
Severe disability premium	£64.30
Enhanced disability premium	
Single person	£16.40
Couples	£23.55
Pensioner premium (couple)	£133.95

PENSION CREDIT

Pension credit was introduced on 6 October 2003 and replaced income support for those aged 60 and over. Since April 2010 the pension credit qualifying age has increased from 60 to 65 alongside the increase in women's state pension age.

There are two elements to pension credit:

THE GUARANTEE CREDIT

The guarantee credit guarantees a minimum income of £163.00 for single people and £248.80 for couples, with additional elements for people who have:

- severe disabilities
- caring responsibilities

Income from state pension, private pensions, earnings, working tax credit and certain benefits are taken into account when calculating the pension credit. For savings and capital in excess of £10,000, £1 for every £500 or part of £500 held is taken into account as income when working out entitlement to pension credit.

People receiving the guarantee credit element of pension credit will be able to receive housing benefit, council tax benefit and help with healthcare costs.

Weekly Rates from April 2018	
Additional amount for severe disability	
Single person	£64.30
Couple (one qualifies)	£64.30
Couple (both qualify)	£128.60
Additional amount for carers	£36.00

THE SAVINGS CREDIT

Single people aged 65 or over (and couples where one member is 65 or over) may be entitled to a savings credit which provides additional support for pensioners who have made modest provision towards their retirement. The savings credit is calculated by taking into account any qualifying income above the savings credit threshold. For 2018–19 the threshold is £140.67 for single people and £223.82 for couples. The maximum savings credit is £13.40 a week (£14.99 a week for couples).

Income that qualifies towards the savings credit includes state pensions, earnings, second pensions and income taken into account from capital above £10,000.

Some people will be entitled to the guarantee credit, some to the savings credit and some to both.

Where only the savings credit is in payment, people need to claim standard housing benefit or council tax benefit. Although local authorities take any savings credit into account in the housing benefit or council tax benefit assessment, for people aged 65 and over housing benefit or council tax benefit is enhanced to ensure that gains in pension credit are not depleted.

HOUSING BENEFIT

Housing benefit is designed to help people with rent (including rent for accommodation in guesthouses, lodgings or hostels). It does not cover mortgage payments. The amount of benefit paid depends on:

- the income of the claimant, and partner if there is one, including earned income, unearned income (any other income including some other benefits) and savings
- number of dependants
- certain extra needs of the claimant, partner or any dependants
- number and gross income of people sharing the home who are not dependent on the claimant
- how much rent is paid

Housing benefit is not payable if the claimant, or claimant and partner, have savings in excess of £16,000. The amount of benefit is affected if savings held exceed £6,000 (£10,000 for people living in residential care and nursing homes). Housing benefit is not paid for meals, fuel or certain service charges that may be included in the rent. Deductions are also made for most non-dependants who live in the same accommodation as the claimant (and their partner). If the claimant is living with a partner or civil partner there can only be one claim.

The maximum amount of benefit (which is not necessarily the same as the amount of rent paid) may be paid where the claimant is in receipt of income support, income-based jobseeker's allowance, the guarantee element of pension credit or where the claimant's income is less than the amount allowed for their needs. Any income over that allowed for their needs will mean that their benefit is reduced.

LOCAL HOUSING ALLOWANCE

Local housing allowance (LHA), which was rolled out nationally from 7 April 2008, is a way of calculating the rent element of housing benefit based on the area in which a person lives and household size. It affects people in the deregulated private rented sector who make a new claim for housing benefit or existing recipients who move address. LHA ensures that tenants in similar circumstances in the same area receive the same amount of financial support for their housing costs. It does not affect the way a person's income or capital is taken into account. LHA is paid to the tenant rather than the landlord in most circumstances. A weekly limit on payments is now in place so LHA does not exceed:

- £268.46 for a one bedroom property
- £311.40 for a two bedroom property
- £365.09 for a three bedroom property
- £429.53 for a four bedroom property

COUNCIL TAX REDUCTION

From April 2013, council tax benefit was replaced by council tax reduction. Nearly all the rules that apply to housing benefit apply to council tax reduction, which helps people on low incomes to pay council tax bills. The amount payable depends on how much council tax is paid and who lives with the claimant. The benefit may be available to those receiving income support, income-based jobseeker's allowance, the guarantee element of pension credit or to those whose income is less than that allowed for their needs. Any income over that allowed for their needs will mean that they will receive less help with their council tax reduction. Deductions are made for non-dependants.

A full council tax bill is based on at least two adults living in a home. Residents may receive a 25 per cent reduction on their bill if they count as an adult for council tax and live on their own. If the property is the resident's main home and there is no-one who counts as an adult, the reduction is 50 per cent.

THE SOCIAL FUND

REGULATED PAYMENTS

Sure Start Maternity Grant

Sure start maternity grant (SSMG) is a one-off payment of £500 to help people on low incomes pay for essential items for new babies that are expected, born, adopted, the subject of a parental order (following a surrogate birth) or, in certain circumstances, the subject of a residency order. SSMG can be claimed any time from within 11 weeks of the expected birth and up to three months after the birth, adoption or date of parental or residency order. Those eligible are people in receipt of universal credit, income support, income-based jobseeker's allowance, pension credit, child tax credit at a rate higher than the family element or working tax credit where a disability or severe disability element is in payment. Since 11 April 2011, new rules have been applied for babies due, born or adopted on this date. These are that SSMG is only available if there are no other children under 16 in the family or in the case of a dependent child's new baby, SSMG is only available if the dependent is under the age of 20 and has no other children.

Funeral Expenses Payment

Payable to help cover the necessary cost of burial or cremation, a new burial plot with an exclusive right of burial (where burial is chosen), certain other expenses, and up to £700 for any other funeral expenses, such as the funeral director's fees, the coffin or flowers. Those eligible are people receiving universal credit, income support, income-based jobseeker's allowance, pension credit, child tax credit at a higher rate than the family element, working tax credit where a disability or severe disability element is in payment, council tax benefit or housing benefit who have good reason for taking responsibility for the funeral expenses. These payments are recoverable from any estate of the deceased.

Cold Weather Payments

A payment of £25 per seven-day period between 1 November and 31 March when the average temperature is recorded at or forecast to be 0°C or below over seven consecutive days in the qualifying person's area. Payments are made to people on universal credit, pension credit or child tax credit with a disability element, those on income support whose benefit includes a pensioner or disability premium, and those on income-based jobseeker's allowance or employment and support allowance who have a child who is disabled or under the age of five. Payments are made automatically and do not have to be repaid.

Winter Fuel Payments

For 2018–19 the winter fuel payment is £200 for households with someone born on or before 5 November 1953 and £300 for households with someone aged 80 or over. The rate paid is based on the person's age and circumstances in the 'qualifying week' between 17 and 23 September 2018. The majority of eligible people are paid automatically between November and December, although a few need to claim. Payments do not have to be repaid.

Christmas Bonus

The Christmas bonus is a one-off tax-free £10 payment made before Christmas to those people in receipt of a qualifying benefit in the qualifying week (usually the first full week of December).

DISCRETIONARY PAYMENTS

Finance Support – Northern Ireland

The Northern Ireland (Welfare Reform) Act 2016 introduced Finance Support to replace Crisis Loans and Community Care Grants on 31 October 2016. Since 31 October 2016, people suffering a financial crisis are able to apply for a discretionary support loan or short term benefit advance from the Finance Support Service (W www.nidirect.gov.uk/contacts/contacts-az/finance-support-service-times-crisis-and-need). To receive discretionary support, the applicant must have a crisis which places themselves or their family's health, safety or wellbeing at significant risk. Applicants must be a resident of Northern Ireland and be over 18-years-old (16-years-old if they do not have any parental support) and be earning less than £15,600 per annum (the national living wage). If eligibility conditions are met the applicant may be offered a discretionary support loan or grant; no more than three loans and one grant can be awarded within a 12-month period.

If the applicant is receiving one of the following benefits: jobseeker's allowance; employment and support allowance; income support; pension credit; state pension; carer's allowance, bereavement allowance, widowed parent's allowance, maternity allowance or incapacity benefit, they are able to apply for short-term benefit advance. It works on an advance of the benefit payment if they have an urgent financial need that may impact the applicant or their family's health, safety or wellbeing. The applicant must be able to afford to repay the advance within 12 weeks.

If an applicant's combined discretionary support and short-term benefit advance debt is £1,000 or more they will not be able to get further discretionary support until their debt falls below this limit.

Budgeting Loans

These are interest-free loans to people who have been receiving universal credit, income support, income-based jobseeker's allowance or income-related employment and support allowance or pension credit for the past six months, for intermittent expenses that may be difficult to budget for. The smallest amount available to borrow is £100.

SAVINGS

Savings of £1,000 (£2,000 if the applicant or their partner is aged 63 or over) are taken into account for budgeting loans. Savings are not taken into account for sure start maternity grant, funeral payments, cold weather payments, winter fuel payments or the Christmas bonus.

INDUSTRIAL INJURIES AND DISABLEMENT BENEFITS

The Industrial Injuries Scheme, administered under the Social Security Contributions and Benefits Act 1992, provides a range of benefits designed to compensate for disablement resulting from an industrial accident (ie an accident arising out of and in the course of an earner's employment) or from a prescribed disease due to the nature of a person's employment. Those who are self-employed are not covered by this scheme.

INDUSTRIAL INJURIES DISABLEMENT BENEFIT

A person may be able to claim industrial injuries disablement benefit if they are ill or disabled due to an accident or incident that happened at work or in connection with work in England, Scotland or Wales. The amount of benefit awarded depends on the person's age and the degree of disability as assessed by a doctor.

The benefit is payable whether the person works or not and those who are incapable of work are entitled to draw other benefits, such as statutory sick pay or incapacity benefit, in addition to industrial injuries disablement benefit. It may also be possible to claim the following allowances:

- reduced earnings allowance for those who are unable to return to their regular work or work of the same standard and who had their accident (or whose disease started) before 1 October 1990. At state pension age this is converted to retirement allowance
- constant attendance allowance for those with a disablement of 100 per cent who need constant care. There are four rates of allowance depending on how much care the person needs
- exceptionally severe disablement allowance can be claimed in addition to constant care attendance allowance at one of the higher rates for those who need constant care permanently

Weekly Rates from April 2018

Degree of disablement	Aged 18+ or with dependants
100 per cent	£174.80
90	£157.32
80	£139.84
70	£122.36
60	£104.88
50	£87.40
40	£69.92
30	£52.44
20	£34.96
Unemployability supplement	£108.05
Reduced earnings allowance (max)	£69.92
Retirement allowance (max)	£17.48
Constant attendance allowance (normal max rate)	£69.90
Exceptionally severe disablement allowance	£69.90

OTHER BENEFITS

People who are disabled because of an accident or disease that was the result of work that they did before 5 July 1948 are not entitled to industrial injuries disablement benefit. They may, however, be entitled to payment under the Workmen's Compensation Scheme or the Pneumoconiosis, Byssinosis and Miscellaneous Diseases Benefit Scheme. People who suffer from certain industrial diseases caused by dust can make a claim for an additional payment under the Pneumoconiosis Act 1979 if they are unable to get damages from the employer who caused or contributed to the disease.

Diffuse Mesothelioma Payments (2008 Scheme)

Since 1 October 2008 any person suffering from the asbestos-related disease, diffuse mesothelioma, who is unable to make a claim under the Pneumoconiosis Act 1979, have not received payment in respect of the disease from an employer, via a civil claim or elsewhere, and are not entitled to compensation from a MoD scheme, can claim a one-off lump sum payment. The scheme covers people whose exposure to asbestos occurred in the UK and was not as a result of their work as an employee (ie they lived near a factory using asbestos). The amount paid depends on the age of the person when the disease was diagnosed, or the date of the claim if the diagnosis date is not known. The current rate is £90,097 for those aged 37 and under to £13,998 for persons aged 77 and over. Since 1 October 2009 claims must be received within 12 months of the date of diagnosis. If the sufferer has died, their dependants may be able to claim, but must do so within 12 months of the date of death.

CLAIMS AND QUESTIONS

Entitlement to benefit and regulated Social Fund payments is determined by a decision maker on behalf of the Secretary of State for the Department for Work and Pensions. A claimant who is dissatisfied with that decision can ask for an explanation. He or she can dispute the decision by applying to have it revised or, in particular circumstances, superseded. The claimant can appeal to the First-tier Tribunal (Social Security and Child Support). There is a further right of appeal to the Administrative and Appeals Chamber of the Upper Tribunal (see Tribunals).

Decisions on claims and applications for housing benefit and council tax benefit are made by local authorities. The explanation, dispute and appeals process is the same as for other benefits.

All decisions on applications to the discretionary Social Fund are made by Jobcentre Plus Social Fund decision makers. Applicants can ask for a review of the decision within 28 days of the date on the decision letter. As above, the claimant has a right of appeal to the First-tier Tribunal (Social Security and Child Support).

EMPLOYER PAYMENTS

STATUTORY MATERNITY PAY

Employers pay statutory maternity pay (SMP) to pregnant women who have been employed by them, full or part-time, continuously for at least 26 weeks into the 15th week before the week the baby is due, and whose earnings on average at least equal the lower earnings limit applied to NI contributions (£116 a week if the end of the qualifying week is in the 2018–19 tax year). SMP can be paid for a maximum period of up to 39 weeks. If the qualifying conditions are met women will receive a payment of 90 per cent of their average earnings for the first six weeks, followed by 33 weeks at £145.18 or 90 per cent of the woman's average weekly earnings if this is less than £145.18. SMP can be paid, at the earliest, 11 weeks before the week in which the baby is due, up to the day following the birth. Women can decide when they wish their maternity leave and pay to start and can work until the baby is born. However, where the woman is absent from work wholly or partly due to her pregnancy in the four weeks before the week the baby is due to be born, SMP will start the day following the first day of absence from work.

Employers are reimbursed for 92 per cent of the SMP they pay. Small employers with annual gross NI payments of £45,000 or less recover 103 per cent of the SMP paid out.

STATUTORY PATERNITY PAY

Employers pay statutory paternity pay (SPP) to employees who are taking leave when a child is born or placed for adoption. To qualify the employee must:
- have responsibility for the child's upbringing
- be the biological father of the child (or the child's adopter), or the spouse/civil partner/partner of the mother or adopter
- have been employed by the same employer for at least 26 weeks ending with the 15th week before the baby is due

(or the week in which the adopter is notified of having been matched with a child)
- continue working for the employer up to the child's birth (or placement for adoption)
- be earning an average of at least £116 a week (before tax)

Employees who meet these conditions receive payment of £145.18 or 90 per cent of the employee's average weekly earnings if this is less than £145.18. The employee can choose to be paid for one or two consecutive weeks. The earliest SPP period can begin is the date of the child's birth or placement for adoption. The SPP period must be completed within eight weeks of that date. SPP is not payable for any week in which the employee works. Employers are reimbursed in the same way as for statutory maternity pay.

STATUTORY ADOPTION PAY

Employers pay statutory adoption pay (SAP) to employees taking adoption leave from their employers. To qualify for SAP the employee must:
- be newly matched with a child by an adoption agency
- have been employed by the same employer for at least 26 weeks ending the week in which they have been notified of being matched with a child
- be earning an average of at least £116 a week (before tax)

Employees who meet these conditions receive payment of £145.18 or 90 per cent of their average weekly earnings if this is less than £145.18 for up to 39 weeks. The earliest SAP can be paid from is two weeks before the expected date of placement; the latest it can start is the date of the child's placement. Where a couple adopt a child, only one of them may receive SAP, the other may be able to receive statutory paternity pay if they meet the eligibility criteria. Employers are reimbursed in the same way as for statutory maternity pay.

STATUTORY SHARED PARENTAL PAY

The Children and Families Act 2014 provided parents greater flexibility as to how they use their maternity and paternity provisions. Shared parental leave (SPL) provides up to 50 weeks of leave and 37 weeks of pay for couples having a baby or adopting a child. The leave and pay is shared between the couple in the first year after the birth or, in the case of adoption, placement, of the child. SPL is flexible and can be used in blocks separated by periods of work, or taken all in one go. Couples can also choose to be off work together or to stagger the leave and pay. There are different eligibility criteria for birth and adoptive parents. For further information see W www.gov.uk/shared-parental-leave-and-pay.

The current rate of statutory shared parental pay is £145.18 a week or 90 per cent of the employee's average weekly earnings if this is less than £145.18 and the earnings threshold is the same as for SMP and SPP (£116 a week (before tax)).

STATUTORY SICK PAY

Employers pay statutory sick pay (SSP) for up to a maximum of 28 weeks to any employee incapable of work for four or more consecutive days. Employees must have done some work under their contract of service and have average weekly earnings of at least £116 a week (before tax). SSP is a daily payment and is usually paid for the days that an employee would normally work. SSP is paid at £92.05 a week and is subject to PAYE and NI contributions.

THE WATER INDUSTRY

In the UK, the water industry provides clean and safe drinking water to over 60 million homes and has an annual turnover of around £10bn. It supplies around 15 billion litres of water a day to domestic and commercial customers and collects and treats more than 16 billion litres of wastewater a day. It also manages assets that include around 1,400 water treatment and 9,350 wastewater treatment works, 550 impounding reservoirs, over 6,500 service reservoirs/water towers and 800,000km of water mains and sewers.

Water services in England and Wales are provided by private companies. In Scotland and Northern Ireland there are single authorities, Scottish Water and Northern Ireland Water, that are publicly owned companies answerable to their respective governments. In drinking water quality tests carried out in 2018 by the Drinking Water Inspectorate, the water industry in England and Wales achieved 99.96 per cent compliance with the standards required by the EU Drinking Water Directive; Scotland achieved 99.92 per cent and Northern Ireland 99.88 per cent.

In 2016, the Drinking Water Inspectorate (DWI) introduced the Compliance Risk Index (CRI) to illustrate the risk arising from failing to meet water safety standards and the proportion of consumers potentially at risk. In 2017, the CRI for England and Wales was 3.56, an improvement from 4.78 the previous year.

Water UK is the industry association that represents all UK water and wastewater service suppliers at national and European level and is funded directly by its members, who are the service suppliers for England, Scotland, Wales and Northern Ireland; every member has a seat on the Water UK Council.

WATER UK, 3rd Floor, 36 Broadway, London SW1H 0BH
 T 020-7344 1844 **W** www.water.org.uk
 Chief Executive, Michael Roberts

ENGLAND AND WALES

In England and Wales, the Secretary of State for Environment, Food and Rural Affairs and the Welsh government have overall responsibility for water policy and oversee environmental standards for the water industry.

The statutory consumer representative body for water services is the Consumer Council for Water.

CONSUMER COUNCIL FOR WATER, 1st Floor, Victoria Square House, Victoria Square, Birmingham B2 4AJ
 T 0300-034 2222 **E** enquiries@ccwater.org.uk
 W www.ccwater.org.uk

REGULATORY BODIES

The Water Services Regulation Authority (OFWAT) was established in 1989 when the water and sewerage industry in England and Wales was privatised. Its statutory role and duties are laid out under the Water Industry Act 1991 and it is the independent economic regulator of the water and sewerage companies in England and Wales. OFWAT's main duties are to ensure that the companies can finance and carry out their statutory functions and to protect the interests of water customers. OFWAT is a non-ministerial government department headed by a board following a change in legislation introduced by the Water Act 2003.

Under the Competition Act 1998, from 1 March 2000 the Competition Appeal Tribunal has heard appeals against the regulator's decisions regarding anti-competitive agreements and abuse of a dominant position in the marketplace. The Water Act 2003 placed a new duty on OFWAT to contribute to the achievement of sustainable development.

The Environment Agency has statutory duties and powers in relation to water resources, pollution control, flood defence, fisheries, recreation, conservation and navigation in England and Wales. It is also responsible for issuing permits, licences, consents and registrations such as industrial licences to extract water and fishing licences.

The Drinking Water Inspectorate (DWI) is the drinking water quality regulator for England and Wales, responsible for assessing the quality of the drinking water supplied by the water companies and investigating any incidents affecting drinking water quality, initiating prosecution where necessary. The DWI science and strategy group provides scientific advice on drinking water policy issues to DEFRA and the Welsh government.

OFWAT, Centre City Tower, 7 Hill Street, Birmingham B5 4UA
 T 0121-644 7500 **E** mailbox@ofwat.gsi.gov.uk
 W www.ofwat.gov.uk
 Chair, Jonson Cox
 Chief Executive, Rachel Fletcher

METHODS OF CHARGING

In England and Wales, most domestic customers still pay for domestic water supply and sewerage services through charges based on the rateable value of their property. OFWAT estimated that the proportion of household customers in England and Wales to have metered supplies was over 50 per cent in 2016–17. Nearly all non-household customers are charged according to consumption.

Under the Water Industry Act 1999, water companies can continue basing their charges on the old rateable value of the property. Domestic customers can continue paying on an unmeasured basis unless they choose to pay according to consumption. After having a meter installed (which is free of charge), a customer can revert to unmeasured charging within 12 months. However, water companies may charge by meter for new homes, or homes where there is a high discretionary use of water. Domestic, school and hospital customers cannot be disconnected for non-payment.

In December 2014, OFWAT finalised its 2014 price review decisions for household water bills for the five-year period to 2020. With the exception of Bristol Water, all the water and sewerage, and water only companies confirmed acceptance of OFWAT's price decisions by the 12 February 2015 deadline. This means that average bills for water and wastewater customers in England and Wales will decrease by around 5 per cent, before adjustments for inflation, between 2015 and 2020; an average decrease of around £20, from £396 to £376 per annum.

AVERAGE HOUSEHOLD BILLS 2016–20 (£)
WATER AND SEWERAGE COMPANIES

	2016–17	2017–18	2019–20
	(£)	(£)	(£) estimated
Anglian	411	428	390
Dwr Cymru	438	439	416
Northumbrian	378	402	382
Severn Trent	329	348	316
South West	488	491	506
Southern	411	436	403
Thames	374	383	353
United Utilities	415	435	398
Wessex	460	475	442
Yorkshire	366	385	361

WATER ONLY COMPANIES

	2016–17	2017–18	2019–20
	(£)	(£)	(£) estimated
Affinity	185	185	163
Bristol	175	177	160
Cambridge	127	132	–
Dee Valley	145	150	149
Northumbrian	236	178	–
Portsmouth	98	100	96
Sembcorp Bournemouth	136	138	134
South East	198	206	194
South Staffordshire	142	144	135
Sutton and East Surrey	186	188	180

Source: OFWAT

SCOTLAND

In 2002 the three existing water authorities in Scotland (East of Scotland Water, North of Scotland Water and West of Scotland Water) merged to form Scottish Water. Scottish Water, which serves more than 2.4 million households and provides 1.34 billion litres of water per day while removing 847 million litres of waste water, is a public sector company, structured and managed like a private company, but remains answerable to the Scottish parliament. Scottish Water is regulated by the Water Industry Commission for Scotland (established under the Water Services (Scotland) Act 2005), the Scottish Environment Protection Agency (SEPA) and the Drinking Water Quality Regulator for Scotland. The Water Industry Commissioner is responsible for regulating all aspects of economic and customer service performance, including water and sewerage charges. SEPA, created under the Environment Act 1995, is responsible for environmental issues, including controlling pollution and promoting the cleanliness of Scotland's rivers, lochs and coastal waters. The Public Services Reform (Scotland) Act 2010 transferred the complaints handling function of Waterwatch Scotland regarding Scottish Water, to the Scottish Public Services Ombudsman. Consumer Futures represented the views and interests of Scottish Water customers but became part of Citizens Advice Scotland in 2014.

METHODS OF CHARGING

Scottish Water sets charges for domestic and non-domestic water and sewerage provision through charges schemes which are regulated by the Water Industry Commission for Scotland. In February 2004 the harmonisation of all household charges across the country was completed following the merger of the separate authorities under Scottish Water. In November 2014 the Water Industry Commission for Scotland published *The Strategic Review of Charges 2015–2021*, stating that annual price rises would not increase at a rate higher than that of consumer price inflation during this six-year period. For the year 2018–19, the combined service charge, covering the water supply and waste water collection, increased by a maximum of 1.6 per cent; resulting in an annual average household bill of £363.

CITIZENS ADVICE SCOTLAND, T 0808-800 9060
W www.cas.org.uk
DRINKING WATER QUALITY REGULATOR FOR
SCOTLAND, Area 3-J South, Victoria Quay, Edinburgh EH6
6QQ T 0131-244 0190 W www.dwqr.scot
SCOTTISH ENVIRONMENT PROTECTION AGENCY,
Third Floor, Silvan House, 231 Corstorphine Road, Edinburgh
EH12 7AT T 0300-099 6699 W www.sepa.org.uk
SCOTTISH PUBLIC SERVICES OMBUDSMAN, 4 Melville
Street, Edinburgh EH3 7NS T 0800-377 7330
W www.spso.org.uk

SCOTTISH WATER, Castle House, 6 Castle Drive, Dunfermline
KY11 8GG T 0800-077 8778 W www.scottishwater.co.uk
Chief Executive, Douglas Millican
WATER INDUSTRY COMMISSION FOR SCOTLAND,
First Floor, Moray House, Forthside Way, Stirling FK8 1QZ
T 01786-430200 W www.watercommission.co.uk

NORTHERN IRELAND

Formerly an executive agency of the Department for Regional Development, Northern Ireland Water is a government-owned company but with substantial independence from government. Northern Ireland Water was set up as a result of government reform of water and sewerage services in April 2007. It is responsible for policy and coordination with regard to the supply, distribution and cleanliness of water, and the provision and maintenance of sewerage services. It supplies 560 million litres of clean water a day to just over 1.5 million people and treats 330 million litres of waste water each day. The Northern Ireland Authority for Utility Regulation (known as the Utility Regulator) is responsible for regulating the water services provided by Northern Ireland Water. The Drinking Water Inspectorate, a unit in the Northern Ireland Environment Agency (NIEA), regulates drinking water quality. Another NIEA unit, the Water Management Unit, has responsibility for the protection of the aquatic environment. The Consumer Council for Northern Ireland is the consumer representative body for water services.

METHODS OF CHARGING

The water and sewerage used by metered domestic customers in Northern Ireland is currently paid for by the Department for Infrastructure (un-metered domestic customers pay 50 per cent of the full charge), however the future of the subsidy system is uncertain. Non-domestic customers in Northern Ireland became subject to water and sewerage charges and trade effluent charges where applicable in April 2008.

CONSUMER COUNCIL FOR NORTHERN IRELAND,
Seatem House, 28–32 Alfred Street, Belfast BT2 8EN
T 028-9025 1600 W www.consumercouncil.org.uk
NORTHERN IRELAND AUTHORITY FOR UTILITY
REGULATION, Queens House, 14 Queen Street, Belfast BT1
6ED T 028-9031 1575 W www.uregni.gov.uk
NORTHERN IRELAND WATER, Westland House, 40 Old
Westland Road, Belfast BT14 6TE T 0345-744 0088
W www.niwater.com
Chief Executive, Sara Venning

WATER SERVICE COMPANIES

WATER UK MEMBERS

AFFINITY WATER, Tamblin Way, Hatfield, Herts AL10 9EZ
T 01707-268111 W www.affinitywater.co.uk
ALBION WATER, Harpenden Hall, Southdown Road,
Harpenden, Herts AL5 1TE T 0158-276 7720
W www.albionwater.co.uk
ANGLIAN WATER SERVICES LTD, Lancaster House,
Lancaster Way, Huntington PE29 6YJ T 01480 32300
W www.anglianwater.co.uk
SEMBCORP BOURNEMOUTH WATER, George Jessel
House, Francis Avenue, Bournemouth, Dorset BH11 8NX
T 01202-591111 W www.bournemouthwater.co.uk
BRISTOL WATER PLC, Bridgwater Road, Bristol BS13 7AT
T 0345-702 3797 W www.bristolwater.co.uk
CAMBRIDGE WATER COMPANY, PO Box 7040, Green
Lane, Walsall WS1 9QG T 01223-706050
W www.cambridge-water.co.uk

DEE VALLEY WATER PLC, Packsaddle, Wrexham Road, Rhostyllen, Wrexham LL14 4EH T 01978-846946 W www.deevalleywater.co.uk

DWR CYMRU (WELSH WATER), Pentwyn Road, Nelson, Treharris, Mid Glamorgan CF46 6LY T 0800-052 0145 W www.dwrcymru.co.uk

ESSEX & SUFFOLK WATER PLC (subsidiary of Northumbrian Water Ltd), Customer Centre, PO Box 292, Durham DH1 9TX T 0845-782 0111 W www.eswater.co.uk

ICOSA WATER LTD, Sophia House, 28 Cathedral Road, Cardiff CF11 9LI T 0330-111 0780 W www.icosawater.co.uk

INDEPENDENT WATER NETWORKS, Driscoll 2, Ellen Street, Cardiff CF10 4BP T 02920-028711 W www.iwnl.co.uk

NORTHERN IRELAND WATER, PO Box 1026, Belfast BT1 9DJ T 0345-744 0088 W www.niwater.com

NORTHUMBRIAN WATER LTD, Abbey Road, Pity Me, Durham DH1 5FJ T 0845-604 7468 W www.nwl.co.uk

PEEL, Peel Dome, intu Trafford Centre, Manchester M17 8PL T 0161-629 8200 W www.peel.co.uk

PORTSMOUTH WATER PLC, PO Box 8, West Street, Havant, Hants PO9 1LG T 023-9249 9888 W www.portsmouthwater.co.uk

SCOTTISH WATER, Castle House, 6 Castle Drive, Carnegie Campus Dunfermline KY11 8GG T 0345-601 8855 W www.scottishwater.co.uk

SEVERN TRENT WATER LTD, 2 St Johns Street, Coventry CV1 2LZ T 024-7771 5000 W www.stwater.co.uk

SOUTH EAST WATER LTD, Rocfort Road, Snodland, Kent ME6 5AH T 0333-000 0001 W www.southeastwater.co.uk

SOUTH STAFFORDSHIRE WATER PLC, Green Lane, Walsall WS2 7PD T 0845-607 0456 W www.south-staffs-water.co.uk

SOUTH WEST WATER LTD, Peninsula House, Rydon Lane, Exeter EX2 7HR T 01392-443020 W www.southwestwater.co.uk

SOUTHERN WATER SERVICES LTD, PO Box 41, Worthing BN13 3NZ T 01903-264444 W www.southernwater.co.uk

SSE, T 0345-078 3200 W www.sse.co.uk

SUTTON AND EAST SURREY WATER PLC, London Road, Redhill, Surrey RH1 1LJ T 01737-772000 W www.waterplc.com

THAMES WATER UTILITIES LTD, Clearwater Court, Vastern Road, Reading RG1 8DB T 0800-980 8800 W www.thameswater.co.uk

UNITED UTILITIES WATER PLC, Haweswater House, Lingley Mere Business Park, Great Sankey, Warrington WA5 3LP T 0845-746 2200 W www.unitedutilities.com

VEOLIA WATER PROJECTS, Kings Place, 90 York Way, London, N1 9AG T 020-784 38500 W www.veoliawater.co.uk

WESSEX WATER SERVICES LTD, Claverton Down, Bath BA2 7WW T 01225-526000 W www.wessexwater.co.uk

YORKSHIRE WATER SERVICES LTD, Western House, Western Way, Bradford BD6 2LZ T 01274-691111 W www.yorkshirewater.com

ASSOCIATE MEMBERS
(not members of Water UK)

GUERNSEY WATER, PO Box 30, Brickfield House, St Andrew, Guernsey GY1 3AS T 01481-239500 W www.water.gg

IRISH WATER (UISCE EIREANN), Colvill House, 24–26 Talbot Street, Dublin 1 W www.water.ie

JERSEY WATER, PO Box 69, Mulcaster House, Westmount Road, St Helier, Jersey JE1 1DG T 01534-707300 W www.jerseywater.je

ENERGY

The main primary sources of energy in Britain are coal, oil, natural gas, renewables and nuclear power. The main secondary sources are electricity, coke and smokeless fuels and petroleum products. The UK was a net importer of fuels in the 1970s, however as a result of growth in oil and gas production from the North Sea, the UK became a net exporter of energy for most of the 1980s. Output decreased in the late 1980s following the Piper Alpha disaster until the mid-1990s, after which the UK again became a net exporter. Since 2004, the UK has reverted back to become a net importer of energy. In 2017, the UK net import gap decreased to 73 million tonnes of oil equivalent – from the 2013 peak of 104 million tonnes of oil equivalent – accounting for 36.3 per cent of the total energy used in the UK.

The Department for Business, Energy and Industrial Strategy (BEIS) is responsible for promoting energy efficiency.

INDIGENOUS PRODUCTION OF PRIMARY FUELS
Million tonnes of oil equivalent

	2016	2017
Primary oils	52.0	50.9
Natural gas	39.9	40.0
Primary electricity	20.0	20.9
Coal	2.6	1.9
Bioenergy and waste	11.8	12.9
Total	126.3	126.6
Source: DBEIS		

INLAND ENERGY CONSUMPTION BY PRIMARY FUEL
Million tonnes of oil equivalent

	2016	2017
Natural gas	76.8	75.0
Petroleum	68.6	68.9
Coal	12.4	10.1
Nuclear electricity	15.4	15.1
Bioenergy and waste	15.2	16.0
Wind and hydro electricity	4.5	5.8
Net Imports	1.5	1.3
Total	194.5	192.2
Source: DBEIS		

TRADE IN FUELS AND RELATED MATERIALS (2017)

	Quantity, million tonnes of oil equivalent	Value £m
Imports		
Crude oil	58.5	16,165
Petroleum products	36.7	13,855
Natural gas	45.1	7,565
Coal and other solid fuel	10.0	1,175
Electricity	1.6	870
Total	151.9	39,630
Exports		
Crude oil	42.0	12,835
Petroleum products	25.4	10,545
Natural gas	10.8	1,830
Coal and other solid fuel	0.8	65
Electricity	0.3	175
Total	79.3	25,450
Source: DBEIS, ONS		

OIL

Until the 1960s Britain imported almost all its oil supplies. In 1969 oil was discovered in the Arbroath field in the North Sea. The first oilfield to be brought into production was Argyll in 1975, and since the mid-1970s Britain has been a major producer of crude oil.

To date, the UK has produced around 3.7 billion tonnes of oil. It is estimated that there are around 501 million tonnes remaining to be produced. Licences for exploration and production are granted to companies by the Oil and Gas Authority. As at July 2017, 519 offshore production licences and 203 onshore petroleum exploration and development licences had been awarded and there was a total of 325 offshore oil and gas fields in production. Total UK oil production peaked in 1999 but is now declining. Production stood at 46.9 million tonnes in 2017, just under a third of the 1999 level. Profits from oil production are subject to a special tax regime with different taxes applying depending on the date of approval of each field.

DRILLING ACTIVITY (2017)
by number of wells started

	Offshore	Onshore
Exploration	14	1
Appraisal	8	0
Exploration and appraisal	22	1
Development	87	4
Source: OGA		

INDIGENOUS PRODUCTION AND REFINERY RECEIPTS
Thousand tonnes

	2016	2017
Indigenous production	47,872	46,916
Crude oil	44,306	43,050
*NGLs	3,139	3,446
Refinery receipts	60,363	60,245

* Natural Gas Liquids: condensates and petroleum gases derived at onshore treatment plants
Source: DBEIS

DELIVERIES OF PETROLEUM PRODUCTS FOR INLAND CONSUMPTION BY ENERGY USE
Thousand tonnes

	2016	2017
Transport	49,501	49,957
Industry	3,956	3,983
Domestic	2,303	2,230
Other	1,815	1,841
Total	57,575	58,011
Source: DBEIS		

COAL

Mines were in private ownership until 1947 when they were nationalised and came under the management of the National Coal Board, later the British Coal Corporation. The corporation held a near monopoly on coal production until 1994 when the industry was restructured. Under the Coal Industry Act 1994, the Coal Authority was established to take over ownership of coal reserves and to issue licences to private mining companies. The Coal Authority is also responsible for the physical legacy of mining, eg subsidence damage claims that are not the responsibility of licensees, and for holding and making available all existing records. It also publishes current data on the coal industry on its website (W www.gov.uk/government/organisations/the-coal-authority).

The mines owned by the British Coal Corporation were sold as five separate businesses in 1994 and coal production is now undertaken entirely in the private sector. Coal output was around 50 million tonnes a year in 1994 but has since declined. In 2017, coal output stood at around 3.0 million tonnes, a decrease of 27 per cent on the previous year. The decrease was mainly due to one of the large surface mines not producing coal since April 2017, as it was under 'care and maintenance', along with a lower demand. Deep mine production decreased by 8 per cent and surface production by 27 per cent. As at 31 December 2017, there were eight deep mines and 19 surface mines in production in the UK.

The main consumer of coal in the UK is the electricity supply industry. Coal supplies 9 per cent of the UK's electricity needs but as indigenous production has declined, imports have continued to make up the shortfall and now represent around 60 per cent of UK coal supply, 46 per cent of which is currently supplied from Russia.

UK government policy is to meet the long-term challenges posed by climate change while continuing to ensure secure, clean and affordable energy. Coal's availability, flexibility and reliability compared to other sources mean that it is expected to continue to play an important role in the future generating mix, but its carbon emissions will need to be managed through the introduction of abatement technologies including carbon capture and storage (CCS).

CCS attempts to mitigate the effects of global warming by capturing the carbon dioxide emissions from power stations that burn fossil fuels, preventing the gas from being released into the atmosphere, and storing it in underground geological formations. CCS is still in its infancy and only through its successful demonstration and development will it be possible for coal to remain a part of a low-carbon UK energy mix. The government is committed to public sector investment in CCS technology on four power stations and has made it clear that there can be no new coal power stations in England and Wales without CCS on a defined amount of capacity. As part of a wider package of reforms to the electricity market, the government will also be introducing an Emissions Performance Standard, which will limit the emissions from new fossil fuel power stations.

COAL PRODUCTION AND FOREIGN TRADE
Thousand tonnes

	2016	2017
Surface mining	4,156	3,021
Deep-mined	22	20
Imports	8,494	8,498
Exports	(443)	(495)
*Total supply	17,775	14,203
Total demand	17,745	14,183

* Includes stock change
Source: DBEIS

INLAND COAL USE
Thousand tonnes

	2016	2017
Fuel producers		
Electricity generators	12,056	8,724
Coke manufacture	1,821	1,888
Blast furnaces	1,364	1,301
Heat generation	6	6
Patent fuel manufacture	223	207
Final consumption		
Industry	1,667	1,468
Transport	15	15
Domestic	550	535
Public administration	33	26
Commercial	5	5
Agriculture	0	0
Miscellaneous	7	7

Source: DBEIS

GAS

From the late 18th century gas in Britain was produced from coal. In the 1960s town gas began to be produced from oil-based feedstocks using imported oil. In 1965 gas was discovered in the North Sea in the West Sole field, which became the first gasfield in production in 1967, and from the late 1960s natural gas began to replace town gas. From October 1998 Britain was connected to the continental European gas system via a pipeline from Bacton, Norfolk to Zeebrugge, Belgium. Gas is transported through 278,000km of mains pipeline including 7,600km of high-pressure gas pipelines owned and operated in the UK by National Grid Gas plc.

The gas industry in Britain was nationalised in 1949 and operated as the Gas Council. The Gas Council was replaced by the British Gas Corporation in 1972 and the industry became more centralised. The British Gas Corporation was privatised in 1986 as British Gas plc. In 1993 the Monopolies and Mergers Commission found that British Gas's integrated business in Great Britain as a gas trader and the owner of the gas transportation system could operate against the public interest. In February 1997, British Gas demerged its trading arm to become two separate companies, BG plc and Centrica plc. In February 2016, Royal Dutch Shell announced that it had acquired BG Group, whose principal business was finding and developing gas reserves and building gas markets. Its core operations are located in the UK, South America, Egypt, Trinidad and Tobago, Kazakhstan and India. Centrica runs the trading and services operations under the British Gas brand name in Great Britain. In October 2000 BG demerged its pipeline business, Transco, which became part of Lattice Group, finally merging with the National Grid Group in 2002 to become National Grid Transco plc.

In July 2005 National Grid Transco plc changed its name to National Grid plc and Transco plc became National Grid Gas plc. In the same year National Grid Gas also completed the sale of four of its eight gas distribution networks. The distribution networks transport gas at lower pressures, which eventually supply the consumers such as domestic customers. The Scotland and south-east of England networks were sold to Scotia Gas Networks. The Wales and south-west network was sold to Wales & West Utilities and the network in the north-east to Northern Gas Networks. This was the biggest change in the corporate structure of gas infrastructure since privatisation in 1986.

Competition was gradually introduced into the industrial gas market from 1986. Supply of gas to the domestic market was opened to companies other than British Gas, starting in April 1996 with a pilot project in the West Country and Wales, with the rest of the UK following soon after.

Declines in UK indigenous gas production and increasing demand led to the UK becoming a net importer of gas once more in 2004. With the depletion of the UK Continental Shelf reserves, UK gas production has seen growing rates of decline. As part of the Energy Act 2008, the government planned to strengthen regulation of the offshore gas supply infrastructure, to allow private sector investment to help maintain UK energy supplies.

In 2012, it was estimated that there could be over 200 trillion cubic feet of untapped gas underneath Lincolnshire. Trapped inside rock formations, the gas is known as shale gas and the process to release the gas is called hydraulic fracturing or fracking, whereby water, chemicals and sand are pumped into a drilled well at high pressure. A further investigation by the British Geological Survey in 2012 claimed that there could in fact be up to 1,300 trillion cubic feet of gas but opponents to the process raised concerns that fracking results in more greenhouse gas emissions than conventional gas, fracking damages the environment significantly and that it may cause seismic tremors.

CENTRICA PLC, Millstream, Maidenhead Road, Windsor,
  Berkshire SL4 5GD T 01753-494000 W www.centrica.com
  Chair, Rick Haythornthwaite
  Chief Executive, Iain Conn

NATIONAL GRID PLC, National Grid House, Warwick
  Technology Park, Gallows Hill, Warwick CV34 6DA
  T 01926-653000 W www.nationalgrid.com
  Chair, Sir Peter Gershon, CBE
  Chief Executive, John Pettigrew

UK GAS CONSUMPTION BY INDUSTRY
GWh

	2016	2017
Domestic	311,375	297,035
Industry	97,755	100,917
Public administration	37,867	36,184
Commercial	46,577	44,990
Agriculture	1,146	1,278
Non-energy use	5,109	4,956
Miscellaneous	10,041	10,070
Total gas consumption	509,870	495,430

Source: DBEIS

ELECTRICITY

The first power station in Britain generating electricity for public supply began operating in 1882. In the 1930s a national transmission grid was developed and it was reconstructed and extended in the 1950s and 1960s. Power stations were operated by the Central Electricity Generating Board.

Under the Electricity Act 1989, 12 regional electricity companies, responsible for the distribution of electricity from the national grid to consumers, were formed from the former area electricity boards in England and Wales. Four companies were formed from the Central Electricity Generating Board: three generating companies (National Power plc, Nuclear Electric plc and Powergen plc) and the National Grid Company plc, which owned and operated the transmission system in England and Wales. National Power and Powergen were floated on the stock market in 1991.

National Power was demerged in October 2000 to form two separate companies: International Power plc and Innogy plc, which manages the bulk of National Power's UK assets. Nuclear Electric was split into two parts in 1996.

The National Grid Company was floated on the stock market in 1995 and formed a new holding company, National Grid Group. National Grid Group completed a merger with Lattice in 2002 to form National Grid Transco, a public limited company (*see* Gas).

Following privatisation, generators and suppliers in England and Wales traded via the Electricity Pool. A competitive wholesale trading market known as NETA (New Electricity Trading Arrangements) replaced the Electricity Pool in March 2001, and was extended to include Scotland via the British Electricity Transmissions and Trading Arrangements (BETTA) in 2005. As part of BETTA, National Grid became the system operator for all transmission. The introduction of competition into the domestic electricity market was completed in May 1999.

In Scotland, three new companies were formed under the Electricity Act 1989: Scottish Power plc and Scottish Hydro-Electric plc, which were responsible for generation, transmission, distribution and supply; and Scottish Nuclear Ltd. Scottish Power and Scottish Hydro-Electric were floated on the stock market in 1991. Scottish Hydro-Electric merged with Southern Electric in 1998 to become Scottish and Southern Energy plc. Scottish Nuclear was incorporated into British Energy in 1996.

In Northern Ireland, Northern Ireland Electricity plc (NIE) was set up in 1993 under a 1991 Order in Council. In 1993 it was floated on the stock market and in 1998 it became part of the Viridian Group and was responsible for distribution and supply until NIE was sold to ESB Independent Energy in December 2010. In June 2010, Airtricity became the first new electricity supplier since the Northern Ireland electricity market was opened to competition in 2007.

On 12 July 2011, the government published *Planning Our Electric Future: a White Paper for Secure, Affordable and Low-carbon Electricity* in response to the challenges set by increasing electricity demands. It was agreed that extensive investment is needed to update the grid and build new power stations. Currently, 21 per cent of the UK electricity generation comes from nuclear reactors, a process by which uranium atoms are split to produce heat through a chemical process known as fission. While nuclear power stations will close gradually over the next decade, with only one expected to produce power beyond 2030, there are plans in place for a new generation of reactors to be built, the first of which is expected to be running by 2025. A significant proportion of the UK's electricity still comes from burning fossil fuels and in 2017 natural gas provided 40 per cent of electricity production, coal provided 7 per cent and 0.48 per cent was provided from oil. However, the picture is changing; renewables provided 29.3 per cent of the UK's electricity in 2017, up from 24.5 per cent in 2016.

Interconnecting cables import and export electricity to Europe, in France, the Netherlands and Ireland. In 2017, the UK was a net importer from France and the Netherlands, accounting for 4.0 per cent of electricity supplied.

On 30 September 2003 the Electricity Association, the industry's main trade association, was replaced with three separate trade bodies: the Association of Electricity Producers; the Energy Networks Association; and the Energy Retail Association. In April 2012, following a merger between the Association of Electricity Producers, the Energy Retail Association and the UK Business Council for Sustainable Energy, Energy UK – the new trade association for the gas and electricity sector – was established.

ENERGY NETWORKS ASSOCIATION, 4 More London
  Riverside, London SE1 2AU T 020-7706 5100
  W www.energynetworks.org
  Chief Executive, David Smith

ENERGY UK, 1st Floor, 26 Finsbury Square, London EC2A 1DS
T 020-7930 9390 W www.energy-uk.org.uk
Chief Executive, Lawrence Slade

ELECTRICITY PRODUCTION, SUPPLY AND CONSUMPTION

GWh

	2016	2017
Electricity produced		
Nuclear	71,726	70,336
Hydro	5,390	5,928
Wind, wave and solar photovoltaics	47,674	61,533
Coal	30,699	22,530
Oil	1,890	1,615
Gas	143,356	136,746
Other renewables	30,064	31,869
Other	5,573	5,219
Total	336,342	335,776
Electricity supplied		
Production	336,342	335,776
*Other sources	2,959	2,872
Imports	20,018	18,167
Exports	(2,273)	(3,407)
Total	357,046	353,408
Electricity consumed		
Industry	91,808	92,627
Transport	4,686	4,783
Other	207,302	203,242
Domestic	107,971	105,396
Public administration	19,827	19,726
Commercial	75,081	73,782
Agriculture	4,423	4,338
Total	303,796	300,652

* Pumped storage production
Source: DBEIS

GAS AND ELECTRICITY SUPPLIERS

With the gas and electricity markets open, most suppliers offer their customers both services. The majority of gas/electricity companies have become part of larger multi-utility companies, often operating internationally.

As part of measures to reduce the UK's carbon output, the government has outlined plans to introduce 'smart meters' to all UK homes. Smart meters perform the traditional meter function of measuring energy consumption, in addition to more advanced functions such as allowing energy suppliers to communicate directly with their customers and removing the need for meter readings and bill estimates. The meters also allow domestic customers to have direct access to energy consumption information.

The following list comprises a selection of suppliers offering gas and electricity. In England, Scotland and Wales, the 'Big Six' are the largest energy suppliers in the UK, providing gas and electricity to around 50 million homes and businesses, and owning a 90 per cent share of the domestic customer market. Organisations in italics are subsidiaries of the companies listed in capital letters directly above.

ENGLAND, SCOTLAND AND WALES

CENTRICA PLC, Millstream, Maidenhead Road, Windsor,
Berkshire SL4 5GD T 01753-494000 W www.centrica.com
British Gas, PO Box 4805, Worthing BN11 9QW T 0800-048 0202
W www.britishgas.co.uk
EDF ENERGY, Osprey House, Osprey Road, Exeter EX2 7WN
T 0345-303 3040 W www.edfenergy.com
E.ON UK, Westward Way, Coventry, CV4 8LG T 024-7619 2000
W www.eonenergy.com

NPOWER, Windmill Business Park, Whitehill Way, Swindon SN5
6PB T 0800-073 3000 W www.npower.com
SCOTTISH POWER, 330–336 St Vincent Street, Glasgow G3
8UR T 0800-027 0072 W www.scottishpower.co.uk
SSE PLC, Inveralmond House, 200 Dunkeld Road, Perth PH1 3AQ
T 0345-026 2658 W www.sse.co.uk

NORTHERN IRELAND

AIRTRICITY (a member of SSE plc), 3rd Floor, Millennium
House, 17–25 Great Victoria Street, Belfast BT2 7AQ
T 0345-266 1787 W www.sseairtricity.com/uk
ELECTRIC IRELAND, The Gasworks, 1 Cromac Place, Belfast
BT7 2JD T 0345-600 5335 W www.electricireland.com
VIRIDIAN GROUP PLC, Greenwood House, 64 Newforge
Lane, Belfast BT9 5NF T 028-9066 8416
W www.viridiangroup.co.uk
PowerNI, 120 Malone Road, Belfast BT9 5HT T 0345-745 5455
W www.powerni.co.uk

REGULATION OF THE GAS AND ELECTRICITY INDUSTRIES

The Office of Gas and Electricity Markets (OFGEM) regulates the gas and electricity industries in Great Britain. It was formed in 1999 by the merger of the Office of Gas Supply and the Office of Electricity Regulation. OFGEM's overriding aim is to protect and promote the interests of all gas and electricity customers by promoting competition and regulating monopolies. It is governed by an authority and its powers are provided for under the Gas Act 1986, the Electricity Act 1989, the Competition Act 1998, the Utilities Act 2000 and the Enterprise Act 2002.

THE OFFICE OF GAS AND ELECTRICITY MARKETS (OFGEM), 10 South Colonnade, Canary Wharf, London E14 4PU T 020-7901 7000 W www.ofgem.gov.uk

NUCLEAR POWER

Nuclear reactors began to supply electricity to the national grid in 1956. There are presently 15 reactors at eight sites which supply approximately 21 per cent of the UK's electricity generation or 20 per cent of supply. Approximately half of this capacity is due to end by 2025. In December 2015, the final magnox reactor (Wylfa 1) was shut down after 44 years of operation, which left seven advanced gas-cooled reactors (AGR) and one pressurised water reactor (PWR), Sizewell 'B' in Suffolk. The AGRs and PWR are owned by a private company, EDF Energy. Apart from Sizewell B, which first produced power in 1995, the seven other sites are expected to be shut down by 2035, however in June 2011, eight new sites across the UK were selected for locations of new nuclear power stations. The eight sites, which stemmed from the 2008 Energy bill, are: Bradwell, Hartlepool, Heysham, Hinkley Point, Oldbury, Sellafield, Sizewell and Wylfa. EDF Energy planned to construct four new European Pressurised Reactors, two of which are scheduled to be established at Hinkley Point, with the other two at Sizewell. The four new reactors could supply 10 million homes with energy by 2025. Each year, EDF Energy spends around £600 million upgrading its eight sites.

Hinkley Point, which was designated as the first new nuclear power plant to be built in 20 years, was scheduled to be given the green light in the summer of 2016, but the Secretary of State for Business, Energy and Industrial Strategy, Greg Clark, delayed the decision. The French firm EDF Energy, which is set to finance two-thirds of the £18bn site (the other £6bn being funded by China), had approved the funding but critics of the planned nuclear site warned of environmental damage, increasing costs and implications of nuclear sites being built in the UK by foreign investors. However, in September 2016, Theresa May gave the go ahead for the nuclear power station at Hinkley Point after the government imposed significant new safeguards for future projects.

In April 2005 the responsibility for the decommissioning of civil nuclear reactors and other nuclear facilities used in research and development was handed to the Nuclear Decommissioning Authority (NDA). The NDA is a non-departmental public body, funded mainly by the Department for Business, Energy and Industrial Strategy. The total planned expenditure for the NDA in 2017–18 was £3.3bn. Until April 2007, UK Nirex was responsible for the disposal of intermediate and some low-level nuclear waste. After this date Nirex was integrated into the NDA and renamed the Radioactive Waste Management directorate.

There are currently 17 nuclear sites owned by the NDA that are in various stages of decommissioning, including the world's first commercial power station at Calder Hall on the Sellafield site in Cumbria and Windscale, which produced plutonium in the 1950s to be used for military reasons. The responsibilities of the NDA include: decommissioning and cleaning up nuclear facilities; ensuring that all waste, including radioactive and non-radioactive products are safely managed; developing nationwide strategies and plans for Low Level Waste; implementing a long-term plan for the management of nuclear waste; and scrutinising EDF Energy's decommissioning plans, which includes the fleet of AGR nuclear stations.

In 2017 electricity supplied from nuclear sources accounted for 21 per cent of the total electricity generation, which equated to 70TWh of a total 339TWh produced or 20 per cent of supply, which equated to 64TWh of the total 323 supplied. A number of factors have led to government backing for nuclear power: domestic gas supplies are running low; oil and gas prices are high; and carbon emissions must be cut to comply with EU legislation and meet global climate change targets.

Nuclear power has its advantages: reactors emit virtually no carbon dioxide and uranium prices remain relatively steady. However, the advantages of low emissions are countered by the high costs of construction and difficulties in disposing of nuclear waste. Currently, the only method is to store it securely until it has slowly decayed to safe levels. Public distrust persists despite the advances in safety technology. Following the tsunami which struck Japan in March 2011 and the level 7 meltdowns of three reactors in the Fukushima Daiichi Nuclear Plant, the safety of nuclear reactors was brought further into public interest and became a government priority.

SAFETY AND REGULATION
The Office for Nuclear Regulation (ONR) is responsible for regulation of nuclear safety and security across the UK. The Civil Nuclear Constabulary, a specialised armed force created in April 2005, is responsible for policing the industry.

RENEWABLE SOURCES
Progress was made towards the UK's target of consuming 15 per cent of energy from renewable sources by 2020, introduced in the 2009 EU Renewable Directive, as 10.2 per cent of energy consumption came from renewable sources in 2017, up from 8.2 per cent in 2015. Renewable sources provided 29.3 per cent of the electricity generated in the UK in 2017, up from 24.5 per cent in 2016. This rise is attributed to a 12.8 per cent increase in capacity, as weather conditions were broadly similar to the previous year.

In 2017 onshore wind was the leading technology in terms of capacity at 31.7 per cent, overtaking solar photovoltaics

(31.5 per cent), which had been the leading technology for the past two years. The capacity of onshore wind increased by 18 per cent from 2016. Combined with higher wind speed, this led to a 39 per cent increase in onshore wind generation between 2016 and 2017. Generation from both offshore wind and hydro sources both increased, by 27 per cent and 10 per cent, respectively. Meanwhile heat generation from renewable sources increased by 3.6 per cent.

The government's principal mechanism for developing renewable energy sources is the Contracts for Difference (CfD) scheme. The CfD scheme recently replaced the Renewables Obligation (RO) which had been in place since 2002. it aims to increase the contribution of electricity from renewables in the UK by offering long-term contracts to new low carbon electricity generators. These guarantee a certain price for their generated electricity, which helps to tackle the risks and uncertainties associated with investing in renewables. The RO closed to new capacity in March 2017, but will continue to provide support to existing generators for 20 years.

The Feed-in Tariff (FIT) scheme has run alongside CfDs and the RO, providing incentives to encourage the uptake of small-scale low carbon electricity generation technologies, principally renewables such as solar photovoltaics, wind and hydro-electricity. The scheme has been hugely successful in attracting investment. An export tariff can be applied to sell any extra units not used by the owner to the local network, currently worth 5.24p per unit of electricity. However the scheme is due to close to new registrations in April 2019 and the government has announced there will be no new subsidies for renewables before 2025.

In addition to these schemes, the Renewable Heat Incentive (RHI) aims to promote the use of renewable heating systems. The RHI was originally introduced in November 2011 to provide a long-term financial incentive to support the uptake of renewable heat in the non-domestic sector. In April 2014, the RHI was extended to cover the domestic sector replacing the renewable heat premium payment scheme which closed in March 2013. Participants of the scheme receive tariff payments for the heat generated from an eligible renewable heating system which is heating a single dwelling.

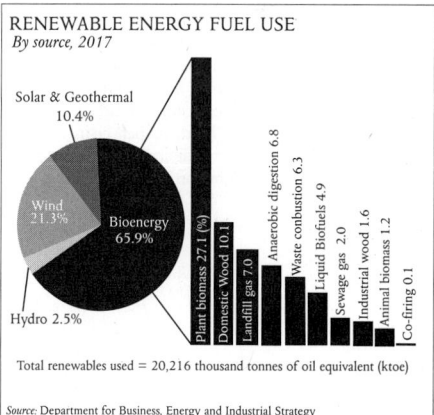

RENEWABLE ENERGY FUEL USE
By source, 2017

Solar & Geothermal 10.4%
Wind 21.3%
Bioenergy 65.9%
Hydro 2.5%

Plant biomass 27.1 (%)
Domestic Wood 10.1
Landfill gas 7.0
Anaerobic digestion 6.8
Waste combustion 6.3
Liquid Biofuels 4.9
Sewage gas 2.0
Industrial wood 1.6
Animal biomass 1.2
Co-firing 0.1

Total renewables used = 20,216 thousand tonnes of oil equivalent (ktoe)

Source: Department for Business, Energy and Industrial Strategy

TRANSPORT

CIVIL AVIATION

Since the privatisation of British Airways in 1987, UK airlines have been operated entirely by the private sector. In 2017, total capacity of British airlines amounted to 54 billion tonne-km, of which 49 billion tonne-km was on scheduled services. UK airlines carried around 162 million passengers; 151 million on scheduled services and 11 million on charter flights. Passenger traffic through UK airports increased by 6 per cent in 2017. Traffic at the six main London area airports (Gatwick, Heathrow, London City, Luton, Southend and Stansted) increased by 5 per cent over 2016 and other UK regional airports saw an increase of 9 per cent.

Leading British airlines include British Airways, EasyJet, Thomas Cook Airlines, Thomson Airways and Virgin Atlantic. Irish airline Ryanair also operates frequent flights from the UK.

There are around 140 licensed civil aerodromes in Britain, with Heathrow and Gatwick handling the highest volume of passengers.

The Civil Aviation Authority (CAA), an independent statutory body, is responsible for the regulation of UK airlines. This includes economic and airspace regulation, air safety, consumer protection and environmental research and consultancy. All commercial airline companies must be granted an air operator's certificate, which is issued by the CAA to operators meeting the required safety standards. The CAA issues airport safety licences, which must be obtained by any airport used for public transport and training flights. All British-registered aircraft must be granted an airworthiness certificate, and the CAA issues professional licences to pilots, flight crew, ground engineers and air traffic controllers. The CAA also manages the Air Travel Organiser's Licence (ATOL), the UK's principal travel protection scheme. The CAA's costs are met entirely from charges on those whom it regulates; there is no direct government funding of the CAA's work.

The Transport Act 2000 separated the CAA from its subsidiary, National Air Traffic Services (NATS), which provides air traffic control services to aircraft flying in UK airspace and over the eastern part of the North Atlantic. NATS is a public private partnership (PPP) between the Airline Group (a consortium of UK airlines), which holds 42 per cent of the shares; NATS staff, who hold 5 per cent; UK airport operator LHR Airports Limited, which holds 4 per cent, and the government, which holds 49 per cent and a golden share. In 2017 NATS handled 2.45m flights, an increase of 7.6 per cent on 2016.

AIR PASSENGERS 2017

All UK Airports: Total	284,708,287
Aberdeen	3,090,642
Barra	14,913
Belfast City	2,559,846
Belfast International	5,836,735
Benbecula	33,312
Birmingham	12,990,303
Blackpool	23,391
Bournemouth	694,660
Bristol	8,239,250
Cambridge	–
Campbeltown	8,806
Cardiff	1,465,227
City of Derry (Eglinton)	193,981
Doncaster Sheffield	1,335,599
Dundee	21,327
Durham Tees Valley	130,911
East Midlands	4,878,781
Edinburgh	13,410,343
Exeter	908,750
Gatwick	45,556,899
Glasgow	9,897,959
Gloucestershire	1,488
Heathrow	78,012,825
Humberside	190,936
Inverness	874,934
Islay	32,644
Isle of Man	797,615
Isles of Scilly (St Mary's)	91,852
Kirkwall	177,248
Lands End (St Just)	59,386
Leeds Bradford	4,076,616
Lerwick (Tingwall)	4,139
Liverpool	4,901,157
London City	4,530,439
Luton	15,990,276
Lydd	865
Manchester	27,826,054
Newcastle	5,300,274
Newquay	371,500
Norwich	528,153
Oxford (Kidlington)	90
Prestwick	696,309
Scatsta	170,847
Shoreham	–
Southampton	2,069,910
Southend	1,092,391
Stansted	25,904,450
Stornoway	134,148
Sumburgh	256,418
Tiree	12,488
Wick	17,697
Channel Islands Airports	2,535,795
Alderney	54,760
Guernsey	843,272
Jersey	1,637,763

Source: Civil Aviation Authority

CAA, CAA House, 45–59 Kingsway, London WC2B 6TE
   T 020-7379 7311 W www.caa.co.uk

Heathrow Airport	T 0844-335 1801
Gatwick Airport	T 0344-892 0322
Manchester Airport	T 0800-042 0213
Stansted Airport	T 0844-335 1803

BRITISH AIRLINES

BRITISH AIRWAYS, PO Box 365, Waterside, Harmondsworth UB7 0GB T 0344-493 0787 W www.britishairways.com

EASYJET, Hangar 89, London Luton Airport LU2 9PF
   T 0330-365 5000 W www.easyjet.com

THOMAS COOK AIRLINES, 3rd Floor, South Building, 200 Aldersgate, London, EC1A 4HD T 01733-244330
   W www.thomascookairlines.com

TUI AIRWAYS, Wigmore House, Wigmore Place, Wigmore Lane, Luton, Beds LU2 9TN T 0203-451 2688 W www.tui.co.uk/flight

VIRGIN ATLANTIC, Fleming Way, Crawley, W. Sussex RH10 9DF T 0344-874 7747 W www.virgin-atlantic.com

RAILWAYS

The railway network in Britain was developed by private companies in the 19th century. In 1948 the main railway companies were nationalised and were run by a public authority, the British Transport Commission. The commission was replaced by the British Railways Board in 1963, operating as British Rail. On 1 April 1994, responsibility for managing the track and railway infrastructure passed to a newly formed company, Railtrack plc. In October 2001 Railtrack was put into administration under the Railways Act 1993. In October 2002 Railtrack was taken out of administration and replaced by the not-for-profit company Network Rail. The British Railways Board continued as operator of all train services until 1996–7, when they were sold or franchised to the private sector.

The Strategic Rail Authority (SRA) was created to provide strategic leadership to the rail industry and formally came into being on 1 February 2001 following the passing of the Transport Act 2000. In January 2002 it published its first strategic plan, setting out the strategic priorities for Britain's railways over the next ten years. In addition to its coordinating role, the SRA was responsible for allocating government funding to the railways and awarding and monitoring the franchises for operating rail services.

On 15 July 2004 the transport secretary announced a new structure for the rail industry in the white paper *The Future of Rail*. These proposals were implemented under the Railways Act 2005, which abolished the SRA, passing most of its functions to the Department for Transport; established the Rail Passengers Council as a single national body, dissolving the regional committees; and gave devolved governments in Scotland and Wales more say in decisions at a local level. In addition, responsibility for railway safety regulation was transferred to the Office of Rail Regulation from the Health and Safety Executive.

OFFICE OF RAIL AND ROAD

The Office of Rail and Road (ORR), previously known as the Office of Rail Regulation, was established on 5 July 2004 by the Railways and Transport Safety Act 2003, replacing the Office of the Rail Regulator. In April 2015 it acquired responsibility for monitoring Highways England in addition to its existing role as the railway industry's economic and safety regulator and changed its name to better reflect its functions. The ORR regulates Network Rail's stewardship of the national network, licenses operators, approves network access agreements, and enforces domestic competition law. The ORR is led by a board appointed by the Secretary of State for Transport and chaired by Stephen Glaister.

SERVICES

For privatisation, under the Railways Act 1993, domestic passenger services were divided into 25 train operating units, which were franchised to private sector operators via a competitive tendering process. The train operators formed the Association of Train Operating Companies (ATOC) to act as the official voice of the passenger rail industry and provide its members with a range of services enabling them to comply with conditions imposed on them through their franchise agreements and operating licences.

As at September 2018 there were 32 passenger train operating companies: Arriva Trains Wales, c2c, Caledonian Sleeper, Chiltern Railways, CrossCountry, East Midlands Trains, Eurostar, Gatwick Express, Grand Central, Great Northern, Great Western Railway, Greater Anglia, Heathrow Express, Hull Trains, Island Line, London North Eastern Railway, London Northwestern Railway, London Overground, London Underground, Merseyrail, Northern, ScotRail, South Western Railway, Southeastern, Southern, Stansted Express, TfL Rail, Thameslink, TransPennine Express, Virgin Trains, West Midlands Railway and West Midlands Trains.

Network Rail publishes a national timetable which contains details of rail services operated over the UK network and sea ferry services which provide connections with Ireland, the Isle of Man, the Isle of Wight, the Channel Islands and some European destinations.

The national rail enquiries service offers information about train times and fares for any part of the country, Transport for London (TfL) provides London-specific travel information for all modes of travel and Eurostar provides information for international channel tunnel rail services:

NATIONAL RAIL ENQUIRIES
T 0345-748 4950 W www.nationalrail.co.uk

TRANSPORT FOR LONDON
T 0343-222 1234 W www.tfl.gov.uk

EUROSTAR
T 0343-186186 W www.eurostar.com

CONSUMER WATCHDOGS

Previously known as Passenger Focus, Transport Focus is the national consumer watchdog for bus, tram, coach and rail passengers in England. Under The Infrastructure Act 2015 Transport Focus's role was expanded to also represent users of the strategic road network. The entity is funded by the Department for Transport and is an executive non-departmental public body.

Established in July 2000, London TravelWatch is the operating name of the official watchdog organisation representing the interests of transport users in and around the capital. Officially known as the London Transport Users' Committee, it is sponsored and funded by the London Assembly and is independent of the transport operators. London TravelWatch represents users of buses, the Underground, river and rail services in and around London, including Eurostar and Heathrow Express, Croydon Tramlink and the Docklands Light Railway. The interests of pedestrians, cyclists and motorists are also represented, as are those of taxi users.

FREIGHT

On privatisation in 1996, British Rail's bulk freight operations were sold to North and South Railways – subsequently called English, Welsh and Scottish Railways (EWS). In 2007, EWS was bought by Deutsche Bahn and is now DB Cargo UK. The other major companies in the rail freight sector are: Colas Rail, Direct Rail Services, Freightliner and GB Railfreight (GBRf). In 2017–18 total volume of freight moved by rail amounted to 17 billion net tonne-kilometres, a 1.7 per cent decrease from 2016–17.

NETWORK RAIL

Network Rail is responsible for the tracks, bridges, tunnels, level crossings, viaducts and main stations that form Britain's rail network. In addition to providing the timetables for the passenger and freight operators, Network Rail is also responsible for all the signalling and electrical control equipment needed to operate the rail network and for monitoring and reporting performance across the industry.

In September 2014, Network Rail was reclassified as a public body after being privately run since 2002 as a commercial business which was directly accountable to its members. The members had similar rights to those of shareholders in a public company except they did not receive dividends or share capital and thereby had no financial interest in Network Rail. On 1 July 2015, the 46 public members were dismissed and the company is now accountable directly to parliament through the Secretary of State for Transport. Network Rail is regulated by the ORR and all of its profits are reinvested into maintaining and upgrading the rail infrastructure. In 2017–18 a total of 1.7 billion passenger journeys were made on the rail network.

LONDON TRAVELWATCH, 169 Union Street, London SE1 0LL T 020-3176 2999 W www.londontravelwatch.org.uk

NETWORK RAIL, 1 Eversholt Street, London NW1 2DN T 020-7557 8000 W www.networkrail.co.uk

OFFICE OF RAIL AND ROAD, 1 Kemble Street, London WC2B 4AN T 020-7282 2000 W www.orr.gov.uk

TRANSPORT FOCUS, Fleetbank House, 2–6 Salisbury Square, London EC4Y 8JX T 0300-123 2350 W www.transportfocus.org.uk

RAIL SAFETY
On 1 April 2006 responsibility for health and safety policy and enforcement on the railways transferred from the Health and Safety Executive to the Office of Rail Regulation (ORR).

In 2017–18 a total of 49 passengers, railway staff and other members of the public were fatally injured in all rail incidents (excluding suicides).

ACCIDENTS ON RAILWAYS

	2016–17	2017–18
Rail incident fatalities	40	49
Passengers	5	4
Railway employees	1	1
Public	34	44
Rail incident major injuries	466	526
Passengers	264	318
Railway employees	165	164
Public	37	44

SUICIDES AND ATTEMPTED SUICIDES 2017–18
Fatalities 242

Source: RSSB – Annual Safety Performance Report 2017–18

OTHER RAIL SYSTEMS
Responsibility for the London Underground passed from the government to the Mayor and Transport for London on 15 July 2003, with a public-private partnership already in place. Plans for a public-private partnership for London Underground were pushed through by the government in February 2002 despite opposition from the Mayor of London and a range of transport organisations. Under the PPP, long-term contracts with private companies were estimated to enable around £16bn to be invested in renewing and upgrading the London Underground's infrastructure over 15 years. In July 2007, Metronet, which was responsible for two of three PPP contracts, went into administration; TfL took over both contracts. Responsibility for stations, trains, operations, signalling and safety remains in the public sector. In 2017–18 there were 1,357 million passenger journeys on the London Underground.

In addition to Glasgow Subway (12.7 million passenger journeys in 2017–18) and Edinburgh Trams (6.8 million passenger journeys in 2017–18), Britain has eight other light rail and tram systems: Blackpool Tramway, Docklands Light Railway (DLR), London Tramlink, Manchester Metrolink, Midland Metro, Nottingham Express Transit (NET), Sheffield Supertram and Tyne and Wear Metro. These eight accounted for 267.2 million passenger journeys in 2017–18; a decrease of 0.2 per cent on 2016–17 figures.

THE CHANNEL TUNNEL
The earliest recorded scheme for a submarine transport connection between Britain and France was in 1802. Tunnelling began simultaneously on both sides of the Channel three times: in 1881, in the early 1970s, and on 1 December 1987, when construction workers bored the first of the three tunnels which form the Channel Tunnel. Engineers 'holed through' the first tunnel (the service tunnel) on 1 December 1990 and tunnelling was completed in June 1991. The tunnel was officially inaugurated by the Queen and President Mitterrand of France on 6 May 1994.

The submarine link comprises two rail tunnels, each carrying trains in one direction, which measure 7.6m (24.93ft) in diameter. Between them lies a smaller service tunnel, measuring 4.8m (15.75ft) in diameter. The service tunnel is linked to the rail tunnels by 130 cross-passages for maintenance and safety purposes. The tunnels are 50km (31 miles) long, 38km (24 miles) of which is under the seabed at an average depth of 40m (132ft). The rail terminals are situated at Folkestone and Calais, and the tunnels go underground at Shakespeare Cliff, Dover and Sangatte, west of Calais.

HIGH SPEED 1
The Channel Tunnel rail link, High Speed 1, runs from Folkestone to St Pancras station, London, with intermediate stations at Ashford and Ebbsfleet in Kent and Stratford International in east London.

Construction of the rail link was financed by the private sector with a substantial government contribution. A private sector consortium, London and Continental Railways Ltd (LCR), comprising Union Railways and the UK operator of Eurostar, owns the rail link and was responsible for its design and construction. The rail link was constructed in two phases: phase one, from the Channel Tunnel to Fawkham Junction, Kent, began in October 1998 and opened to fare-paying passengers on 28 September 2003; phase two, from Southfleet Junction to St Pancras, was completed in November 2007.

Eurostar provides direct services from the UK to Avignon (5 hours 49 minutes), Calais (1 hour 2 minutes), Disneyland Paris (2 hours 35 minutes), Lille (1 hour 20 minutes), Lyon (4 hours 41 minutes), Marseille (6 hours 27 minutes) and Paris (2 hours 15 minutes) in France; Brussels (1 hour 51 minutes) in Belgium; and Amsterdam (3 hours 41 minutes) and Rotterdam (3 hours 1 minute) in the Netherlands.

ROADS

HIGHWAY AUTHORITIES
The powers and responsibilities of highway authorities in England and Wales are set out in the Highways Act 1980; for Scotland there is separate legislation.

Responsibility for motorways and other trunk roads in Great Britain rests in England with the Secretary of State for Transport, in Scotland with the Scottish government, and in Wales with the Welsh government. The highway authority for non-trunk roads in England, Wales and Scotland is, in general, the local authority in whose area the roads lie. With the establishment of the Greater London Authority in July 2000, Transport for London became the highway authority for roads in London.

In Northern Ireland the Department for Infrastructure is responsible for public roads and their maintenance and construction.

FINANCE
In England all aspects of trunk road and motorway funding are provided directly by the government to Highways England, which operates, maintains and improves a network of motorways and trunk roads around 6,920km (4,300 miles) long, on behalf of the secretary of state. Since 2001 the length of the network that the Highways England is responsible for has been decreasing owing to a policy of de-trunking, which transfers responsibility for non-core roads to local authorities.

For the financial year 2018–19 Highways England's total capital and resource budget is £3,794m. This includes maintenance, major schemes, traffic management, technology improvements, other programmes and administration costs.

Government support for local authority capital expenditure on roads and other transport infrastructure is provided through grant and credit approvals as part of the Local Transport Plan (LTP). Local authorities bid for resources on the basis of a five-year programme built around delivering integrated transport strategies. As well as covering the structural maintenance of local roads and the construction of major new road schemes, LTP funding also includes smaller-scale safety and traffic management measures with associated improvements for public transport, cyclists and pedestrians.

Total budgeted expenditure by the Welsh government for 2016–17 to improve and maintain the motorway and trunk road network in Wales was £231.1m.

Since 1 July 1999 all decisions on Scottish transport expenditure have been devolved to the Scottish government. Total expenditure on motorways and trunk roads in Scotland during 2016–17 was £949m.

In Northern Ireland all roads, some 26,000km (16,160 miles) are managed by the Department for Infrastructure (DfI) for Northern Ireland as the sole road authority. The road network is made up of some 300km (185 miles) of motorway, 1,300km (810 miles) of trunk roads and 24,500km (15,225miles) of other roads. The department is also responsible for maintaining some 10,000km (6,210 miles) of footpaths and 5,800 bridges.

For the financial year 2017–18 DfI Roads gross expenditure, excluding depreciation, was £350m. This included maintenance, capital schemes, traffic management and technology improvements. Planned gross expenditure for 2018–19 is £398m, excluding depreciation.

The Transport Act 2000 gave English and Welsh local authorities (outside London) powers to introduce road-user charging or workplace parking levy schemes. The act requires that the net revenue raised is used to improve local transport services and facilities for at least ten years. The aim is to reduce congestion and encourage greater use of alternative modes of transport. Schemes developed by local authorities require government approval. The UK's first toll road, the M6 Toll, opened in December 2003 and runs for 43.5km (27 miles) around Birmingham from junction 3a to junction 11a on the M6.

Charging schemes in London are allowed under the 1999 Greater London Authority Act. The Central London Congestion Charge Scheme began on 17 February 2003 (see also Regional Government London).

ROAD LENGTHS 2017
Miles

	England	Wales	Scotland	Great Britain
Major Roads	22,066	2,696	6,670	31,432
Motorways	1,917	88	287	2,292
Minor Roads	166,765	18,344	30,169	215,277
Total	188,831	21,039	36,838	246,709

Source: Department for Transport

BUSES
The majority of bus services outside London are provided on a commercial basis by private operators. Local authorities have powers to subsidise services where needs are not being met by a commercial service.

Since April 2008 men and women who have attained the state pension age and disabled people who qualify under the categories listed in the Transport Act 2000 have been able to travel for free on any local bus across England between 9.30am and 11pm Monday to Friday and all day on weekends and bank holidays. Local authorities recompense operators for the reduced fare revenue. The age of eligibility for concessionary travel is state pension age. A similar scheme from age 60 operates in Wales and within London, although there is no time restriction. In Scotland, people aged 60 and over and disabled people have been able to travel for free on any local or long-distance bus since April 2006.

In London, Transport for London (TfL) has overall responsibility for setting routes, service standards and fares for the bus network. Almost all routes are competitively tendered to commercial operators.

In Northern Ireland, passenger transport services are provided by Ulsterbus and Metro (formerly Citybus), two wholly owned subsidiaries of the Northern Ireland Transport Holding Company. Along with Northern Ireland Railways, Ulsterbus and Metro operate under the brand name of Translink and are publicly owned. Ulsterbus is responsible for virtually all bus services in Northern Ireland except Belfast city services, which are operated by Metro. People living in Northern Ireland aged 60 and over can travel on buses and trains for free once they have obtained a SmartPass from Translink.

LOCAL BUS PASSENGER JOURNEYS 2016–17
No. of journeys (millions)

England	4,438
London	2,240
Scotland	393
Wales	100
Total	4,931

Source: Department for Transport

TAXIS AND PRIVATE HIRE VEHICLES
A taxi is a public transport vehicle with fewer than nine passenger seats, which is licensed to 'ply for hire'. This distinguishes taxis from private hire vehicles (PHVs) which must be booked in advance through an operator. In London, taxis and private hire vehicles are licensed by the Public Carriage Office (PCO), part of TfL. At the end of March 2017 there were 21,300 taxis and 87,400 PHVs licensed in London. Outside London, local authorities are responsible for the licensing of taxis and private hire vehicles operational in their respective administrative areas. At the end of March 2017 there were 75,500 licensed taxis and 205,500 licensed PHVs in England.

ROAD TRAFFIC BY VEHICLE TYPE (UK) 2017

	Million vehicle miles
All motor vehicles	327,100
Cars & taxis	254,400
Light goods vehicles	50,500
Heavy goods vehicles	17,000
Motorcycles	2,800
Buses & coaches	2,400

Source: Department for Transport

ROAD SAFETY
The key findings from the Department for Transport's 2017 annual road casualty report found that, despite a 2.2 per cent rise in traffic volume, the total number of reported casualties of all severities in Great Britain in 2016 was 181,384; a 3 per cent decrease from 2015. Of these a total of 1,792 people were killed in 2016; an increase of 4 per cent from 2015. Serious injuries accounted for 24,101 of the casualties and slight injuries for 155,491. Total reported child casualties (0–15 years) decreased by 1 per cent to 15,976 in 2016.

ROAD ACCIDENT CASUALTIES

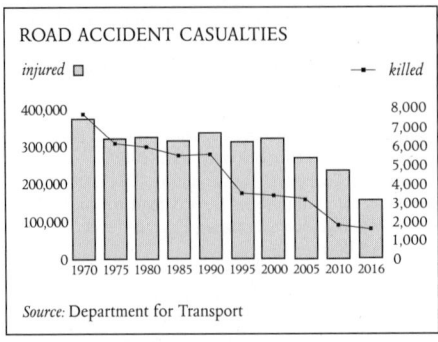

injured ☐   ▪ killed

Source: Department for Transport

DRIVING LICENCES

It is necessary to hold a valid full licence in order to drive unaccompanied on public roads in the UK. Learner drivers must obtain a provisional driving licence before starting to learn to drive and must then pass theory and practical tests to obtain a full driving licence.

There are separate tests for driving motorcycles, cars, passenger-carrying vehicles (PCVs) and large goods vehicles (LGVs). Drivers must hold full car entitlement before they can apply for PCV or LGV entitlements.

The Driver and Vehicle Licensing Agency (DVLA) ceased the issue of paper licences in March 2000, but those currently in circulation will remain valid until they expire or the details on them change. The photocard driving licence was introduced to comply with the second EC directive on driving licences. This requires a photograph of the driver to be included on all UK licences issued from July 2001. The photocard licence must be renewed every ten years, with fines of up to £1,000 for failure to do so.

To apply for a first photocard driving licence, individuals are required to either apply online or complete the form *Application for a Driving Licence* (D1) and submit by post.

The minimum age for driving motor cars, light goods vehicles up to 3.5 tonnes and motorcycles is 17 (moped, 16). Since June 1997, drivers who collect six or more penalty points within two years of qualifying lose their licence and are required to take another test. Forms and leaflets are available from post offices and online (W www.gov.uk/dvlaforms or W www.gov.uk/government/organisations/driver-and-vehicle-licensing-agency).

The DVLA is responsible for issuing driving licences, registering and licensing vehicles, and collecting excise duty in Great Britain. The Driver and Vehicle Agency (DVA), has similar responsibilities in Northern Ireland.

DRIVING LICENCE FEES *as at September 2018*

	fee* online/postal
Provisional licence	
Car, motorcycle or moped	£34/£43
Bus or lorry	Free
Changing a provisional licence to a full licence	Free
Renewal	
Renewing an expired licence (must be renewed every 10 years)	£14/£17
At age 70 and over	Free
For medical reasons	Free
Bus or lorry driver entitlement	Free
After disqualification	£65
After disqualification for some drink driving offences†	£90
After revocation (under the New Drivers Act)	£50
Replacing a lost, stolen, defaced or destroyed licence	£20/£20
Adding an entitlement to a full licence	Free
Exchanging	
a paper licence for a photocard licence‡	£20/£20
a full Northern Ireland licence for a full GB licence	Free
a full GB licence for a full EU/EEA or other designated foreign licence	Free

a full EU/EEA or other designated foreign licence for a full GB licence	£43
Changing	
name or address	Free
photo	£14/£17

* Not all services are available online; in these instances just the postal fee is shown. Licence fees differ in Northern Ireland (W www.nidirect.gov.uk/the-cost-of-a-driving-licence).
† For an alcohol-related offence where the DVLA need to arrange medical enquiries
‡ If a paper licence is exchanged for a photocard at the same time as name or address details are changed there is no charge

DRIVING TESTS

The Driver and Vehicle Standards Agency (DVSA) is responsible for improving road safety in Great Britain by setting standards for driving and motorcycling and making sure drivers, vehicle operators and MOT garages understand and follow roadworthiness standards. The agency also provides a range of licensing, testing, education and enforcement services.

DRIVING TESTS TAKEN AND PASSED
2017–2018

Practical Test	Number Taken	Percentage Passed
Car	1,718,519	46.3
Motorcycle Module 1	57,239	71.9
Motorcycle Module 2	56,110	71.3
PCV	7,682	58.9
LGV	70,619	57.8
Theory Test		
Car	1,886,218	48.7
Motorcycle	70,740	71.4
PCV		
Multiple choice	8,562	62.1
Hazard perception	6,949	82.1
Driver CPC*	6,210	47.5
LGV		
Multiple choice	53,971	62.3
Hazard perception	43,619	82.1
Driver CPC*	35,643	65.2

LGV = Large goods vehicle; PCV = Passenger-carrying vehicle
* Driver Certificate of Professional Competence – legal requirement for all professional bus, coach and lorry drivers
Source: DVSA

The theory and practical driving tests can be booked online (W www.gov.uk/book-driving-test) or by phone (T 0300-200 1122).

DRIVING TEST FEES *as at September 2018* *(Weekday/evening* and weekend)*	
Theory tests	
Car and motorcycle	£23.00/£23.00
Bus and lorry	
Multiple choice	£26.00/£26.00
Hazard perception	£11.00/£11.00
Driver CPC†	£23.00/£23.00
Practical tests	
Car	£62.00/£75.00
Tractor and other specialist vehicles	£62.00/£75.00
Motorcycle	
Module 1 (off-road)	£15.50/£15.50
Module 2 (on-road)	£75.00/£88.50
Lorry and bus	£115.00/£141.00
Driver CPC†	£55.00/£63.00
Car and trailer	£115.00/£141.00
Extended tests for disqualified drivers	
Car	£124.00/£150.00
Motorcycle Module 1 (on-road)	£150.00/£177.00

* After 4.30pm
* Driver Certificate of Professional Competence – legal requirement for all professional bus, coach and lorry drivers

VEHICLE LICENCES
Registration and first licensing of vehicles is through local offices of the DVLA in Swansea. Local facilities for relicensing are available at any post office which deals with vehicle licensing. Applicants will need to take their vehicle registration document (V55/5) or, if this is not available, the applicant must complete form V62. Forms are available at post offices and online (W www.gov.uk/dvlaforms)

MOTOR VEHICLES LICENSED (UK)
As at 31 March 2018

	Thousands
All cars	32,314
Light goods vehicles	4,045
Motorcycles	1,241
Heavy goods vehicles	521
Buses and coaches	163
Other vehicles*	774
Total	39,058

* Includes rear diggers, lift trucks, rollers, ambulances, Hackney Carriages, three-wheelers and agricultural vehicles
Source: Department for Transport

VEHICLE EXCISE DUTY
Details of the present duties chargeable on motor vehicles are available at post offices and online (W www.gov.uk/government/publications/rates-of-vehicle-tax-v149). The Vehicle Excise and Registration Act 1994 provides *inter alia* that any vehicle kept on a public road but not used on roads is chargeable to excise duty as if it were in use. All non-commercial vehicles constructed before 1 January 1973 are exempt from vehicle excise duty. Any vehicle licensed on or after 31 January 1998, not in use and not kept on public roads must be registered as SORN (Statutory Off Road Notification) to be exempted from vehicle excise duty. From 1 January 2004 the registered keeper of a vehicle remains responsible for taxing a vehicle or making a SORN declaration until that liability is formally transferred to a new keeper.

All rates of duty can also be paid by direct debit – the 6-month direct debit rate is slightly cheaper than the non-direct debit rate listed below. There is also the option to pay vehicle duty by direct debit monthly instalments.

RATES OF DUTY *from 1 April 2018*

	6 months	12 months
Cars registered on or after 1 April 2017 *†		
petrol/diesel car	£77.00	£140.00
alternative fuel car	£71.50	£130.00
Cars registered before 1 March 2001		
Under 1,549cc	£85.25	£155.00
Over 1,549cc	£140.25	£255.00
Light goods vehicles registered on or after 1 March 2001		
	£137.50	£250.00
Euro 4 light goods vehicles registered between 1 March 2003 and 31 December 2006		
	£77.00	£140.00
Euro 5 light goods vehicles registered between 1 January 2009 and 31 December 2010		
	£77.00	£140.00
Motorcycles (with or without sidecar)		
Not over 150cc	–	£19.00
151–400cc	–	£42.00
401–600cc	£32.50	£64.00
600cc+	£48.40	£88.00
Tricycles		
Not over 150cc	–	£19.00
All others	£48.40	£88.00

* Different first year licence rates based on CO_2 emissions are payable at first registration
† Cars with a list price of over £40,000 at first registration pay an additional £310 on the standard 12-month rate above for five years from the start of the second tax payment

RATES OF DUTY FOR CARS REGISTERED BETWEEN 1 MARCH 2001 AND 1 APRIL 2017
from 1 April 2018

	CO_2 Emissions	Petrol and Diesel Car		Alternative Fuel Car	
	(g/km)	6 months	12 months	6 months	12 months
A	Up to 100	–	£0.00	–	£0.00
B	101–110	–	£20.00	–	£10.00
C	111–120	–	£30.00	–	£20.00
D	121–130	£66.00	£120.00	£60.50	£110.00
E	131–140	£77.00	£140.00	£71.50	£130.00
F	141–150	£85.25	£155.00	£79.75	£145.00
G	151–165	£107.25	£195.00	£101.75	£185.00
H	166–175	£126.50	£230.00	£121.00	£220.00
I	176–185	£137.50	£250.00	£132.00	£240.00
J	186–200	£159.50	£290.00	£154.00	£280.00
K*	201–255	£173.25	£315.00	£167.75	£305.00
L	226–255	£297.00	£540.00	£291.50	£530.00
M	255+	£305.25	£555.00	£299.75	£545.00

* Includes cars that have a CO_2 emission figure over 225g/km but were registered before 23 March 2006

MOT TESTING
Cars, motorcycles, motor caravans, light goods and dual-purpose vehicles more than three years old must be covered by a current MOT test certificate. However, some vehicles (ie minibuses, ambulances and taxis) may require a certificate at one year old. All certificates must be renewed annually. Only MOT testing stations showing a blue sign with three triangles and an official 'MOT: Test: Fees and Appeals' poster may carry out an approved MOT. The MOT testing scheme is administered by the Driver and Vehicle Standards Agency (DVSA) on behalf of the Secretary of State for Transport.

A fee is payable to MOT testing stations. The current maximum fees are:

For cars, private hire and public service vehicles, motor caravans, dual purpose vehicles, ambulances and taxis (all up to eight passenger seats)	£54.85
For motorcycles	£29.65
For motorcycles with sidecar	£37.80
For three-wheeled vehicles (up to 450kg unladen weight)	£37.80
*Private passenger vehicles and ambulances with:	
9–12 passenger seats	£57.30 (£64.00)
13–16 passenger seats	£59.55 (£80.50)
16+ passenger seats	£80.65 (£124.50)
Goods vehicles (3,000–3,500kg)	£58.60

* Figures in parentheses include seatbelt installation check

SHIPPING AND PORTS

Sea trade has always played a central role in Britain's economy. By the 17th century Britain had built up a substantial merchant fleet and by the early 20th century it dominated the world shipping industry. In 2017 the UK registered trading fleet grew 7 per cent in gross tonnage (GT), to 16.2 million GT, and is now 18 per cent higher than the recent low in 2014. At the end of 2017, the number of UK registered trading vessels was 1,317, broadly unchanged since 2014 (1,327). The UK registered share of the world fleet has been broadly stable in recent years – 0.8 per cent of the world fleet on a deadweight tonnage basis and 1.2 per cent when measured using GT. The UK registered trading fleet was 18th largest in the world by deadweight tonnage at the end of 2017.

Freight is carried by liner and bulk services, almost all scheduled liner services being containerised. About 95 per cent by weight of Britain's overseas trade is carried by sea. Passengers and vehicles are carried by roll-on, roll-off ferries, hovercraft, cruise ships and high-speed catamarans. In 2017 the number of international short-sea route passengers decreased by 2 per cent to 19.5 million compared to 20 million in 2016.

Lloyd's of London provides the most comprehensive shipping intelligence service in the world. *Lloyd's List* (www.lloydslistintelligence.com) lists 120,000 ocean-going vessels and gives the latest known report of each.

PORTS

There are 51 major ports in the UK. Total freight tonnage handled by UK ports in 2017 was 481.8 million tonnes, broadly level with 2016 (484.0 million tonnes). The largest ports in terms of freight tonnage in 2017 were Grimsby and Immingham (54.0 million tonnes), London (49.9 million tonnes), Southampton (34.5 million tonnes), Liverpool (32.5 million tonnes) and Milford Haven (32.0 million tonnes). Belfast (18.2 million tonnes) is the principal freight port in Northern Ireland.

Broadly speaking, ports are owned and operated by private companies, local authorities or self-owning bodies, known as trust ports. The largest operator is Associated British Ports which owns 21 ports.

MARINE SAFETY

The Maritime and Coastguard Agency (MCA) is an executive agency of the Department for Transport responsible for implementing the government's maritime safety policy in the UK and works to prevent the loss of life on the coast and at sea.

HM Coastguard maintains a 24-hour search and rescue response and coordination capability for the whole of the UK coast and the internationally agreed search and rescue region. HM Coastguard is responsible for mobilising and organising

resources in response to people in distress at sea, or at risk of injury or death on the UK's cliffs or shoreline.

The MCA also inspects and surveys ships to ensure that they are meeting UK and international safety rules, provides certification to seafarers, registers vessels and responds to pollution from shipping and offshore installations.

Locations hazardous to shipping in coastal waters are marked by lighthouses and other lights and buoys. The lighthouse authorities are the Corporation of Trinity House (for England, Wales and the Channel Islands), the Northern Lighthouse Board (for Scotland and the Isle of Man), and the Commissioners of Irish Lights (for Northern Ireland and the Republic of Ireland). Trinity House maintains 66 lighthouses, nine light vessels/floats, 450 buoys, 21 beacons, 52 radar beacons, eight DGPS (differential global positioning system) stations* and three AIS (automatic identification system) stations. The Northern Lighthouse Board maintains 206 lighthouses, 165 buoys, 26 beacons, 29 radar beacons, 35 AIS stations, four DGPS stations and one LORAN (long-range navigation) station; and Irish Lights looks after 71 lighthouses, 117 buoys, 24 beacons, and three DGPS stations, with AIS in operation on 37 lighthouses.

Harbour authorities are responsible for pilotage within their harbour areas; and the Ports Act 1991 provides for the transfer of lights and buoys to harbour authorities where these are used mainly for local navigation.

* DGPS is a satellite-based navigation system

UK-OWNED TRADING VESSELS
500 gross tons and over, as at end 2017

Type of vessel	No.	Gross tonnage
Tankers	93	2,898,000
Fully cellular container	74	3,458,000
Dry bulk carriers	77	2,739,000
Ro-Ro (passenger & cargo)	81	1,156,000
Passenger (incl cruise)	32	1,955,000
Other general cargo	94	324,000
Specialised carriers	22	994,000
All vessels	473	13,524,000

Source: Department for Transport

UK SEA PASSENGER* MOVEMENTS 2016

Type of journey	No. of passenger movements
Short-sea routes	19,959,000
Cruises beginning or ending at a UK port*	1,985,000
Long sea journeys	59,000
Total	22,003,000

* Passengers are included at both departure and arrival if their journeys begin and end at a UK seaport
Source: Department for Transport

UK SHIPPING FORECAST AREAS

Weather bulletins for shipping are broadcast daily on BBC Radio 4 at 00h 48m, 05h 20m, 12h 01m and 17h 54m. All transmissions are broadcast on long wave at 198kHz and the 00h 48m and 05h 20m transmissions are also broadcast on FM 92–95. The bulletins consist of a gale warning summary, general synopsis, sea-area forecasts and coastal station reports. In addition, gale warnings are broadcast at the first available programme break after receipt. If this does not coincide with a news bulletin, the warning is repeated after the next news bulletin. Shipping forecasts and gale warnings are also available on the Met Office and BBC Weather websites.

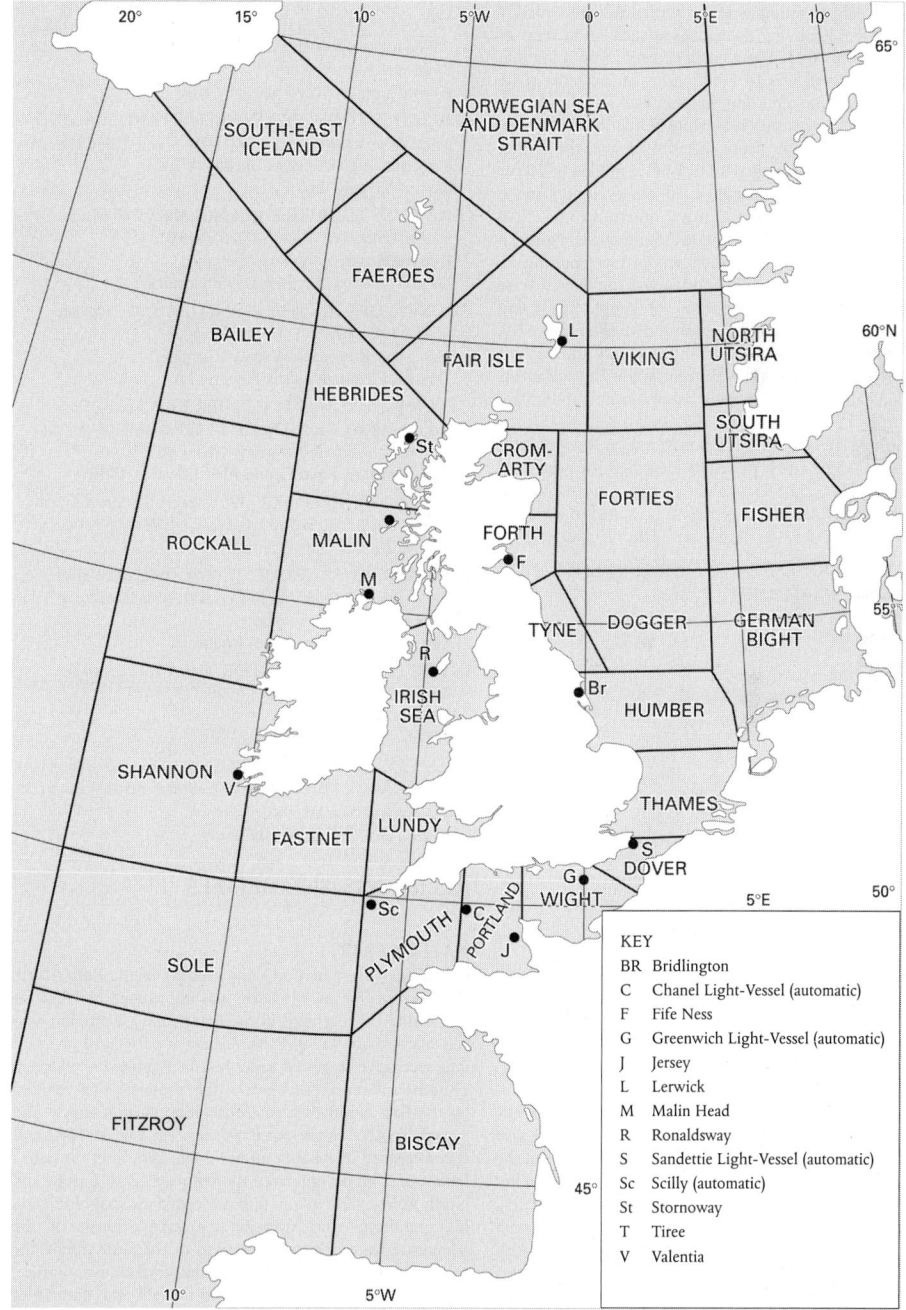

KEY
BR   Bridlington
C   Chanel Light-Vessel (automatic)
F   Fife Ness
G   Greenwich Light-Vessel (automatic)
J   Jersey
L   Lerwick
M   Malin Head
R   Ronaldsway
S   Sandettie Light-Vessel (automatic)
Sc   Scilly (automatic)
St   Stornoway
T   Tiree
V   Valentia

RELIGION IN THE UK

The 2011 census in England and Wales included a voluntary question on religion; 92.8 per cent of the population chose to answer the question. Christianity remained the largest religion, despite a decrease of 4 million people from the 2001 census, to 33.2 million adherents, or 59.3 per cent of the population. The second largest religious group were Muslims with 2.7 million people identifying themselves as such, an increase of 1.2 million since 2001. The number of people reporting that they had 'no religion' was 14.1 million, around a quarter of the population. Of those reporting that they had no religion, the majority identified themselves as white (93 per cent) and born in the UK (also 93 per cent); in terms of age, the largest demographic were those aged 20 to 24 (1.4 million or 10 per cent). More than 240,000 people listed 'other religion' on the census, which included, among many others, 176,632 Jedi Knights, 56,620 Pagans and 39,061 Spiritualists. Norwich remained the city with the highest proportion reporting no religion (42.5 per cent), while London was the most diverse region with the largest proportion of people classifying themselves as Buddhist, Hindu, Jewish and Muslim. Knowsley, in Merseyside, was the local authority with the highest proportion of Christians at 80.9 per cent, while Tower Hamlets in London had the highest population of Muslims at 34.5 per cent.

In Northern Ireland, the religion question was phrased differently; 738,033 (41 per cent) identified themselves as Roman Catholic, 752,555 (42 per cent) as 'Protestant and other Christian', 14,859 (0.8 per cent) belonged to an 'other religion' and 183,164 (10 per cent) stated they had no religion.

CENSUS 2011 RESULTS – RELIGION IN ENGLAND, WALES AND SCOTLAND*

	thousands	per cent
Christian	36,093	58.8
Buddhist	261	0.4
Hindu	833	1.4
Jewish	269	0.4
Muslim	2,783	4.5
Sikh	432	0.7
Other religion	256	0.4
All religions	40,927	66.6
No religion	16,038	26.1
Not stated	4,406	7.2
All no religion/not stated	20,444	33.3
TOTAL	61,371	100

* Figures from the 2011 census for Northern Ireland did not contain a full breakdown of each major religion
Source: Census 2011

INTER-CHURCH AND INTER-FAITH COOPERATION

The main umbrella body for the Christian churches in the UK is Churches Together in Britain and Ireland. There are also ecumenical bodies in each of the constituent countries of the UK: Churches Together in England, Action of Churches Together in Scotland, CYTUN (Churches Together in Wales), and the Irish Council of Churches. The Free Churches Group (formerly the Free Churches Council), which is closely associated with Churches Together in England, represents most of the free churches in England and Wales, and the Evangelical Alliance represents evangelical Christians.

The Inter Faith Network for the United Kingdom promotes cooperation between faiths, and the Council of Christians and Jews works to improve relations between the two religions. Churches Together in Britain and Ireland also has a commission on inter-faith relations.

ACTION OF CHURCHES TOGETHER IN SCOTLAND, Jubilee House, Forthside Way, Stirling FK8 1QZ T 01259-216980 W www.acts-scotland.org
General Secretary, Revd Matthew Ross

CHURCHES TOGETHER IN BRITAIN AND IRELAND, 39 Eccleston Square, London SW1V 1BX T 020-3794 2288 E info@ctbi.org.uk W www.ctbi.org.uk
General Secretary, Bob Fyffe

CHURCHES TOGETHER IN ENGLAND, 27 Tavistock Square, London WC1H 9HH T 020-7529 8131 E office@cte.org.uk W www.cte.org.uk
General Secretary, Revd Dr David Cornick

COUNCIL OF CHRISTIANS AND JEWS, 333 Edgware Road, London NW9 6TD T 020-3515 3003 E cjrelations@ccj.org.uk W www.ccj.org.uk
Director, Elizabeth Harris-Sawczenko

CYTUN (CHURCHES TOGETHER IN WALES), 58 Richmond Road, Cardiff CF24 3AT T 029-2046 4204 E post@cytun.org.uk W www.cytun.org.uk
Chief Executive, Revd Canon Aled Edwards, OBE

EVANGELICAL ALLIANCE, 176 Copenhagen Street, London N1 0ST T 020-7520 3830 E info@eauk.org W www.eauk.org
General Director, Steve Clifford

FREE CHURCHES GROUP, 27 Tavistock Square, London WC1H 9HH T 020-3651 8334 E info@freechurches.org.uk W www.freechurches.org.uk
General Secretary, Revd Paul Rochester

INTERFAITH NETWORK FOR THE UK, 2 Grosvenor Gardens, London SW1W 0DH T 020-7730 0410 W www.interfaith.org.uk
Director, Dr Harriet Crabtree, OBE

IRISH COUNCIL OF CHURCHES, 48 Elmwood Avenue, Belfast BT9 6AZ T 028-9066 3145 E info@churchesinireland.com W www.irishchurches.org
General Secretary, Dr Nicola Brady

RELIGIONS AND BELIEFS

BAHA'I FAITH

Baha'u'llah ('Glory of God'), the founder of the Baha'i faith, was born in Iran in 1817. He was imprisoned in 1852 for advocating the teachings of the Bab ('Gate'), a prophet who was martyred in 1850. Baha'u'llah was persecuted and sent into successive stages of exile, first to Baghdad – where in 1863 he announced that he was the 'promised one' foretold by the Bab – and then to Constantinople, Adrianople and eventually Acre, in present day Israel. He died in 1892 and was succeeded by his son, Abdu'l-Baha, as head of the Baha'i faith, under whose guidance the faith spread to Europe and North America. He was in turn succeeded by Shoghi Effendi, his grandson, who oversaw the establishment of the administrative order and the spread of the faith around the world until his death in 1957. The Universal House of Justice, an elected international governing council, was formed in 1963 in accordance with Baha'u'llah's teachings.

The Baha'i faith espouses the oneness of humanity and of religion and teaches that there is only one God, whose will has been revealed to mankind by a series of messengers, such as Zoroaster, Abraham, Moses, Buddha, Krishna, Christ, Muhammad, the Bab and Baha'u'llah, who were seen as the founders of separate religions, but whose common purpose was to bring God's message to mankind. The Baha'i faith attributes the differences in teachings between religions to humanity's changing needs. Baha'i teachings include that all races and both sexes are equal and deserving of equal opportunities and treatment, that education is a fundamental right and that extremes of wealth and poverty should be eliminated. In addition, the faith exhorts mankind to establish a world federal system to promote peace and unity.

In an effort to translate these principles into action, Baha'is have initiated an educational process across the world that seeks to raise the capacity of people of all ages and from all backgrounds to contribute towards the betterment of society. There is no clergy; each local community elects a local spiritual assembly to tend to its administrative needs. A national spiritual assembly is elected annually by locally elected delegates, and every five years the national spiritual assemblies meet together to elect the Universal House of Justice, the supreme international governing body of the Baha'i Faith. Worldwide there are over 13,000 local spiritual assemblies and nearly 7 million followers, with around 7,000 in the UK.

BAHA'I COMMUNITY OF THE UK, 27 Rutland Gate, London SW7 1PD T 020-7584 2566 E opa@bahai.org.uk W www.bahai.org.uk
Director, Office of Public Affairs, Padideh Sabeti

BUDDHISM
Buddhism originated in what is now the Bihar area of northern India in the teachings of Siddhartha Gautama, who became the *Buddha* ('Enlightened One'). In the Thai or Suriyakati calendar the beginning of the Buddhist era is dated from the death of Buddha; the year 2018 is therefore 2561 by the Thai Buddhist reckoning.

Fundamental to Buddhism is the concept of rebirth, whereby each life carries with it the consequences of the conduct of earlier lives (known as the law of *karma)* and this cycle of death and rebirth is broken only when the state of *nirvana* has been reached. Buddhism steers a middle path between belief in personal continuity and the belief that death results in total extinction.

While doctrine does not have a pivotal position in Buddhism, a statement of four 'Noble Truths' is common to all its schools and varieties. These are: suffering is inescapable in even the most fortunate of existences; craving is the root cause of suffering; abandonment of the selfish mindset is the way to end suffering; and bodily and mental discipline, accompanied by the cultivation of wisdom and compassion, provides the spiritual path ('Noble Eightfold Path') to accomplish this. Buddhists deny the idea of a creator and prefer to emphasise the practical aspects of moral and spiritual development.

The schools of Buddhism can be broadly divided into three: *Theravada,* the generally monastic-led tradition practised in Sri Lanka and South East Asia; *Mahayana,* the philosophical and popular traditions of the Far East; and *Esoteric,* the Tantric-derived traditions found in Tibet and Mongolia and, to a lesser extent, China and Japan. The extensive Theravada scriptures are contained in the *Pali Canon,* which dates in its written form from the first century BC. Mahayana and Esoteric schools have Sanskrit-derived translations of these plus many more additional scriptures as well as exegetical material.

In the East the new and full moons and the lunar quarter days were (and to a certain extent, still are) significant in determining the religious calendar. Most private homes contain a shrine where offerings, worship and other spiritual practices (such as meditation, chanting or mantra recitation) take place on a daily basis. Buddhist festivals vary according to local traditions within the different schools and there is little uniformity – even in commemorating the birth, enlightenment and death of the Buddha.

There is no governing authority for Buddhism in the UK. Communities representing all schools of Buddhism operate independently. The Buddhist Society was established in 1924; it runs courses, lectures and meditation groups, and publishes books about Buddhism. The Network of Buddhist Organisations was founded in 1993 to promote fellowship and dialogue between Buddhist organisations and to facilitate cooperation in matters of common interest.

There are estimated to be at least 490 million Buddhists worldwide. Of the 248,000 Buddhists in England and Wales (according to the 2011 census), 72,000 are white British (the majority are converts), 49,000 Chinese, 93,000 'other Asian' and 36,000 are 'other ethnic'.

THE BUDDHIST SOCIETY, 58 Eccleston Square, London SW1V 1PH T 020-7834 5858 E info@thebuddhistsociety.org W www.thebuddhistsociety.org
President, Dr Desmond Biddulph, CBE

LONDON BUDDHIST CENTRE, 51 Roman Road, London E2 0HU T 020-8981 1225 E contact@lbc.org.uk W www.lbc.org.uk
Chair, Dharmachari Jnanavaca

THE NETWORK OF BUDDHIST ORGANISATIONS, PO Box 4147, Maidenhead SL60 1DN T 0845-345 8978 E secretary@nbo.org.uk W www.nbo.org.uk
Chair, Juliet Hackney

SOKA GAKKAI UK, Taplow Court Grand Cultural Centre, Cliveden Road, Taplow, Berkshire SL6 0ER T 01628-773163 W www.sgi-uk.org
General Director, Robert Harrap

TIBET HOUSE TRUST, Tibet House, 1 Culworth Street, London NW8 7AF T 020-7722 5378 E secretary@tibet-house-trust.co.uk W http:// www.tibet-house-trust.co.uk
Secretary, Kunga Tenzin

CHRISTIANITY
Christianity is a monotheistic faith based on the person and teachings of Jesus Christ, and all Christian denominations claim his authority. Central to its teaching is the concept of God and his son Jesus Christ, who was crucified and resurrected in order to enable mankind to attain salvation.

The Jewish scriptures predicted the coming of a *Messiah,* an 'anointed one', who would bring salvation. To Christians, Jesus of Nazareth, a Jewish rabbi (teacher) who was born in Palestine, was the promised Messiah. Jesus' birth, teachings, crucifixion and subsequent resurrection are recorded in the *Gospels,* which, together with other scriptures that summarise Christian belief, form the *New Testament.* This, together with the Hebrew scriptures – entitled the *Old Testament* by Christians – makes up the Bible, the sacred texts of Christianity.

Christians believe that sin distanced mankind from God, and that Jesus was the son of God, sent to redeem mankind from sin by his death. In addition, many believe that Jesus will return again at some future date, triumph over evil and establish a kingdom on earth, thus inaugurating a new age. The Gospel assures Christians that those who believe in Jesus and obey his teachings will be forgiven their sins and will be resurrected from the dead.

The Apostles were Jesus' first converts and are recognised by Christians as the founders of the Christian community.

Early Christianity spread rapidly throughout the eastern provinces of the Roman Empire but was subjected to great persecution until AD 313, when Emperor Constantine's Edict of Toleration confirmed its right to exist. Christianity was established as the religion of the Roman Empire in AD 381.

Between AD 325 and 787 there were seven Oecumenical Councils at which bishops from the entire Christian world assembled to resolve various doctrinal disputes. The estrangement between East and West began after Constantine moved the centre of the Roman Empire from Rome to Constantinople, and it grew after the division of the Roman Empire into eastern and western halves. Linguistic and cultural differences between Greek East and Latin West served to encourage separate ecclesiastical developments which became pronounced in the tenth and early 11th centuries. Administration of the church was divided between five ancient patriarchates: Rome and all the West, Constantinople (the imperial city – the 'New Rome'), Jerusalem and all of Palestine, Antioch and all the East, and Alexandria and all of Africa. Of these, only Rome was in the Latin West and after the schism in 1054, Rome developed a structure of authority centralised on the Papacy, while the Orthodox East maintained the style of localised administration. Papal authority over the doctrine and jurisdiction of the church in Western Europe was unrivalled after the split with the Eastern Orthodox Church until the Protestant Reformation in the 16th century.

Christian practices vary widely between different Christian churches, but prayer, charity and giving (for the maintenance of the church buildings, for the work of the church, and to those in need) are common to all. In addition, certain days of observance, ie the *Sabbath, Easter* and *Christmas,* are celebrated by most Christians. The Orthodox, Roman Catholic and Anglican churches celebrate many more days of observance, based on saints and significant events in the life of Jesus. The belief in sacraments, physical signs believed to have been ordained by Jesus Christ to symbolise and convey spiritual gifts, varies greatly between Christian denominations; *baptism* and the *Eucharist* are practised by most Christians. Baptism, symbolising repentance and faith in Jesus, is an act marking entry into the Christian community; the Eucharist, the ritual re-enactment of the Last Supper, Jesus' final meal with his disciples, is also practised by most denominations. Other sacraments, such as anointing the sick, the laying on of hands to symbolise the passing on of the office of priesthood or to heal the sick, and speaking in tongues, where it is believed that the person is possessed by the Holy Spirit, are less common. In denominations where infant baptism is practised, confirmation (where the person confirms the commitments made on their behalf in infancy) is common. Matrimony and the ordination of priests are also widely believed to be sacraments. Many Protestants regard only baptism and the Eucharist to be sacraments; the Quakers and the Salvation Army reject the use of sacraments.

See Churches for contact details of the Church of England, the Roman Catholic Church and other Christian churches in the UK.

HINDUISM

Hinduism has no historical founder but had become highly developed in India by c.2500 BC. Its adherents originally called themselves Aryans; Muslim invaders first called the Aryans 'Hindus' (derived from 'Sindhu', the name of the river Indus) in the eighth century.

Most Hindus hold that *satya* (truthfulness), honesty, sincerity and devotion to God are essential for good living. They believe in one supreme spirit *(Brahman),* and in the transmigration of *atman* (the soul). Most Hindus accept the doctrine of *karma* (consequences of actions), the concept of

samsara (successive lives) and the possibility of all atmans achieving *moksha* (liberation from samsara) through *jnana* (knowledge), *yoga* (meditation), *karma* (work or action) and *bhakti* (devotion).

Most Hindus offer worship to *murtis* (images of deities) representing different incarnations or aspects of Brahman, and follow their *dharma* (religious and social duty) according to the traditions of their *varna* (social class), *ashrama* (stage in life), *jaiti* (caste) and *kula* (family).

Hinduism's sacred texts are divided into *shruti* ('that which is heard'), including the *Vedas,* and *smriti* ('that which is remembered'), including the *Ramayana,* the *Mahabharata,* the *Puranas* (ancient myths), and the sacred law books. Most Hindus recognise the authority of the *Vedas,* the oldest holy books, and accept the philosophical teachings of the *Upanishads,* the *Vedanta Sutras* and the *Bhagavad-Gita.*

Hindus believe Brahman to be omniscient, omnipotent, limitless and all-pervading. Brahman is usually worshipped in its deity form. Brahma, Vishnu and Shiva are the most important deities or aspects of Brahman worshipped by Hindus; their respective consorts are Saraswati, Lakshmi and Durga or Parvati, also known as Shakti. There are believed to have been ten *avatars* (incarnations) of Vishnu, of whom the most important are Rama and Krishna. Other popular gods are Ganesha, Hanuman and Subrahmanyam. All Hindu gods are seen as aspects of the supreme spirit (Brahman), not as competing deities.

Orthodox Hindus revere all gods and goddesses equally, but there are many denominations, including the Hare-Krishna movement (ISKCon), the Arya Samaj and the Swaminarayan Hindu mission, in which worship is concentrated on one deity. The *guru* (spiritual teacher) is seen as the source of spiritual guidance.

Hinduism does not have a centrally trained and ordained priesthood. The pronouncements of the *shankaracharyas* (heads of monasteries) of Shringeri, Puri, Dwarka and Badrinath are heeded by the orthodox but may be ignored by the various sects.

The commonest form of worship is *puja,* in which water, flowers, food, fruit, incense and light are offered to the deity. Puja may be done either in a home shrine or a *mandir* (temple). Many British Hindus celebrate *samskars* (purification rites), to name a baby, for the sacred thread (an initiation ceremony), marriage and cremation.

The largest communities of Hindus in Britain are in Leicester, London, Birmingham and Bradford, and developed as a result of immigration from India, eastern Africa and Sri Lanka.

There are an estimated 800 million Hindus worldwide; there are around 817,000 adherents, according to the 2011 census in England and Wales, and around 135 temples in the UK.

ARYA SAMAJ LONDON, 69 Argyle Road, London W13 0LY
T 020-8991 1732 E aryasamajlondon@yahoo.co.uk
W www.aryasamajlondon.org.uk
General Secretary, Amrit Lal Bhardwaj

BHARATIYA VIDYA BHAVAN, 4A Castletown Road, London
W14 9HE T 020-7381 3086 E info@bhavan.net
W www.bhavan.net
Executive Director, Dr M. N. Nandakumara

INTERNATIONAL SOCIETY FOR KRISHNA
CONSCIOUSNESS (ISKCON), Bhaktivedanta Manor,
Dharam Marg, Hilfield Lane, Aldenham, Watford, Herts
WD25 8EZ T 01923-851000 E info@krishnatemple.com
W www.krishnatemple.com
Temple President, Sruti Dharma Das

NATIONAL COUNCIL OF HINDU TEMPLES (UK), c/o
Shree Sanatan Mandir, 84 Weymouth Street, Leicester LE4 6FQ
T 0771-781 4357 E info@nchtuk.org W www.nchtuk.org
General Secretary, Satish K. Sharma
SWAMINARAYAN HINDU MISSION (SHRI
SWAMINARAYAN MANDIR), 105–119 Brentfield Road,
London NW10 8
LD T 020-8965 2651 E info@londonmandir.baps.org
W www.londonmandir.baps.org

HUMANISM

Humanism traces its roots back to ancient times, with Chinese, Greek, Indian and Roman philosophers expressing Humanist ideas some 2,500 years ago. Confucius, the Chinese philosopher who lived *c.*500 BC, believed that religious observances should be replaced with moral values as the basis of social and political order and that 'the true way' is based on reason and humanity. He also stressed the importance of benevolence and respect for others, and believed that the individual situation should be considered rather than the global application of traditional rules.

Humanists believe that there is no God or other supernatural being, that humans have only one life (Humanists do not believe in an afterlife or reincarnation) and that humans can live ethical and fulfilling lives without religious beliefs through a moral code derived from a shared history, personal experience and thought. There are no sacred Humanist texts. Particular emphasis is placed on science as the only reliable source of knowledge of the universe. Many Humanists recognise a need for ceremonies to mark important occasions in life and the British Humanist Association has a network of celebrants who are trained and accredited to conduct baby namings, weddings and funerals. The British Humanist Association's campaigns for a secular state (a state based on freedom of religious or non-religious belief with no privileges for any particular set of beliefs) are based on equality and human rights. The association also campaigns for inclusive schools that meet the needs of all parents and pupils, regardless of their religious or non-religious beliefs. According to figures from the 2011 census, there are just over 15,000 Humanists in England and Wales.

BRITISH HUMANIST ASSOCIATION, 39 Moreland Street,
London EC1V 8BB T 020-7324 3060 E info@humanism.org.uk
W www.humanism.org.uk
Chief Executive, Andrew Copson

ISLAM

Islam (which means 'peace arising from submission to the will of Allah' in Arabic) is a monotheistic religion which was taught in Arabia by the Prophet Muhammad, who was born in Mecca (Al-Makkah) in 570 AD. Islam spread to Egypt, north Africa, Spain and the borders of China in the century following the Prophet's death, and is now the predominant religion in Indonesia, the near and Middle East, northern and parts of western Africa, Pakistan, Bangladesh, Malaysia and some of the former Soviet republics. There are also large Muslim communities in other countries.

For Muslims (adherents of Islam), there is one God *(Allah)*, who holds absolute power. Muslims believe that Allah's commands were revealed to mankind through the prophets, who include Abraham, Moses and Jesus, but that Allah's message was gradually corrupted until revealed finally and in perfect form to Muhammad through the angel *Jibril* (Gabriel) over a period of 23 years. This last, incorruptible message is said to have been recorded in the *Qur'an* (Koran), which contains 114 divisions called *surahs,* each made up of *ayahs* of various lengths, and is held to be the essence of all previous scriptures. The *Ahadith* are the records of the Prophet

Muhammad's deeds and sayings (the *Sunnah*) as practised and recounted by his immediate followers. A culture and a system of law and theology gradually developed to form a distinctive Islamic civilisation. Islam makes no distinction between sacred and worldly affairs and provides rules for every aspect of human life. The *Shariah* is the sacred law of Islam based primarily upon prescriptions derived from the *Qur'an* and the *Sunnah* of the Prophet.

The 'five pillars of Islam' are *shahadah* (a declaration of faith in the oneness and supremacy of Allah and the messengership of Muhammad); *salat* (formal prayer, to be performed five times a day facing the *Ka'bah* (the most sacred shrine in the holy city of Mecca)); *zakat* (welfare due, paid annually on all savings at the rate of 2.5 per cent); *sawm* (fasting during the month of Ramadan from dawn until sunset); and *hajj* (pilgrimage to Mecca made once in a lifetime if the believer is financially and physically able). Some Muslims would add *jihad* as the sixth pillar (striving for the cause of good and resistance to evil).

Two main groups developed among Muslims. *Sunni* Muslims accept the legitimacy of Muhammad's first four *caliphs* (successors as head of the Muslim community) and of the authority of the Muslim community as a whole. About 90 per cent of Muslims are Sunni Muslims.

Shi'ites recognise only Muhammad's son-in-law Ali as his rightful successor and the *Imams* (descendants of Ali, not to be confused with *imams*, who are prayer leaders or religious teachers) as the principal legitimate religious authority. The largest group within Shi'ism is *Twelver Shi'ism,* which has been the official school of law and theology in Iran since the 16th century; other subsects include the *Ismailis,* the *Druze* and the *Alawis,* the latter two differing considerably from the main body of Muslims. The *Ibadis* of Oman are neither Sunni nor Shia, deriving from the strictly observant *Khariji* (Seceders). There is no organised priesthood, but learned men such as imams, *ulama,* and *ayatollahs* are accorded great respect. The *Sufis* are the mystics of Islam. Mosques are centres for worship and teaching and also for social and welfare activities.

Islam was first recorded in western Europe in the eighth century AD when 800 years of Muslim rule began in Spain. Later, Islam spread to eastern Europe. More recently, Muslims came to Europe from Africa, the Middle East and Asia in the late 19th century. Both the Sunni and Shia traditions are represented in Britain, but the majority of Muslims in Britain adhere to Sunni Islam. Efforts to establish a representative national body for Muslims in Britain resulted in the founding, in 1997, of the Muslim Council of Britain. In addition, there are many other Muslim organisations in the UK. There are around 1.6 billion Muslims worldwide, with around 2.8 million adherents in England, Wales and Scotland and about 1,500 mosques in the UK.

ISLAMIC CULTURAL CENTRE – THE LONDON
CENTRAL MOSQUE, 146 Park Road, London NW8 7RG
T 020-7724 3363 E info@iccuk.org W www.iccuk.org
Director-General, Dr Ahmad Al-Dubayan
MUSLIM COUNCIL OF BRITAIN, PO Box 57330, London E1
2WJ T 0845-262 6786 E admin@mcb.org.uk
W www.mcb.org.uk
Secretary-General, Harun Rashid Khan
MUSLIM LAW (SHARIAH) COUNCIL UK, 20–22 Creffield
Road, London W5 3RP T 0208-992 6636
E info@shariahcouncil.org W www.shariahcouncil.org
Chair, Dr Mohamed Benotman
MUSLIM WORLD LEAGUE LONDON, 46 Goodge Street,
London W1T 4LU T 020-7636 7568 E info@mwllo.org.uk
W www.mwllo.org.uk
Director, Dr Ahmed Makhdoom

JAINISM

Jainism traces its history to Vardhamana Jnatriputra, known as *Tirthankara Mahavira* ('the Great Hero') whose traditional dates were 599–527 BC. Jains believe he was the last of the current era in a series of 24 *Jinas* (those who overcome all passions and desires) or *Tirthankaras* (those who show a way across the ocean of life) stretching back to remote antiquity. Born to a noble family in north-eastern India (presently the state of Bihar), he renounced the world for the life of a wandering ascetic and after 12 years of austerity and meditation he attained enlightenment. He then preached his message until, at the age of 72, he left the mortal world and achieved total liberation *(moksha)* from the cycle of death and rebirth.

Jains declare that the Hindu rituals of transferring merit are not acceptable as each living being is responsible for its own actions. They recognise some of the minor deities of the Hindu pantheon, but the supreme objects of worship are the Tirthankaras. The pious Jain does not ask favours from the Tirthankaras, but seeks to emulate their example in his or her own life.

Jains believe that the universe is eternal and self-subsisting, that there is no omnipotent creator God ruling it and the destiny of the individual is in his or her own hands. *Karma,* the fruit of past actions, is believed to determine the place of every living being and rebirth may be in the heavens, on earth as a human, an animal or other lower being, or in the hells. The ultimate goal of existence for Jains is *moksha,* a state of perfect knowledge and tranquillity for each individual soul, which can be achieved only by gaining enlightenment.

The Jainist path to liberation is defined by the three jewels: *Samyak Darshan* (right perception), *Samyak Jnana* (right knowledge) and *Samyak Charitra* (right conduct). Of the five fundamental precepts of the Jains, *Ahimsa* (non-injury to any form of being, in any mode: thought, speech or action) is the first and foremost, and was popularised by Gandhi as *Ahimsa paramo dharma* (non-violence is the supreme religion).

The largest population of Jains can be found in India but there are approximately 30,000 Jains in Britain, with sizeable communities in North America, East Africa, Australia and smaller groups in many other countries.

INSTITUTE OF JAINOLOGY, Unit 18, Silicon Business Centre, 28 Wadsworth Road, Perivale, Greenford, Middx UB6 7JZ T 020-8997 2300 E info@jainology.org W www.jainology.org
Chair, Nemu Chandaria, OBE

JUDAISM

Judaism is the oldest monotheistic faith. The primary text of Judaism is the Hebrew bible or *Tanakh,* which records how the descendants of Abraham were led by Moses out of their slavery in Egypt to Mount Sinai where God's law *(Torah)* was revealed to them as the chosen people. The *Talmud,* which consists of commentaries on the *Mishnah* (the first text of rabbinical Judaism), is also held to be authoritative, and may be divided into two main categories: the *halakeh* dealing with legal and ritual matters) and the *aggadah* (dealing with theological and ethical matters not directly concerned with the regulation of conduct). The *midrash* comprises rabbinic writings containing biblical interpretations in the spirit of the aggadah. The halakah has become a source of division: orthodox Jews regard Jewish law as derived from God and therefore unalterable; progressive Jews seek to interpret it in the light of contemporary considerations; and conservative Jews aim to maintain most of the traditional rituals but to allow changes in accordance with tradition. Reconstructionist Judaism, a 20th-century movement, regards Judaism as a culture rather than a theological system and accepts all forms of Jewish practice.

The family is the basic unit of Jewish ritual, with the synagogue playing an important role as the centre for public worship and religious study. A synagogue is led by a group of laymen who are elected to office. The Rabbi is primarily a teacher and spiritual guide. The *Sabbath* is the central religious observance. Most British Jews are descendants of either the *Ashkenazim* of central and eastern Europe or the *Sephardim* of Spain, Portugal and the Middle East.

The Chief Rabbi of the United Hebrew Congregations of the Commonwealth is appointed by a Chief Rabbinate Conference, and is the rabbinical authority of the mainstream Orthodox sector of the Ashkenazi Jewish community, the largest body of which is the United Synagogue. His formal ecclesiastical authority is not recognised by the Reform Synagogues of Great Britain (the largest progressive group), the Union of Liberal and Progressive Synagogues, the Spanish and Portuguese Jews' Congregation or the Assembly of Masorti Synagogues. He is, however, generally recognised both outside the Jewish community and within it as the public religious representative of the totality of British Jewry. The Chief Rabbi is President of the London *Beth Din* (Court of Judgment), a rabbinic court. The *Dayanim* (Judges) adjudicate in disputes or on matters of Jewish law and tradition; they also oversee dietary law administration, marriage, divorce and issues of personal status.

The Board of Deputies of British Jews, established in 1760, is the representative body of British Jewry. The basis of representation is through the election of deputies by synagogues and communal organisations. It protects and promotes the interests of British Jewry, acts as the central voice of the community and seeks to counter anti-Jewish discrimination and anti-Semitic activities.

There are approximately 13.9 million Jews worldwide; in the UK there are an estimated 290,000 adherents and over 400 synagogues.

OFFICE OF THE CHIEF RABBI, 305 Ballards Lane, London N12 8GB T 020-8343 6301 E info@chiefrabbi.org
W www.chiefrabbi.org
Chief Rabbi, Ephraim Mirvis

BETH DIN (THE UNITED SYNAGOGUE), 305 Ballards Lane, London N12 8GB T 020-8343 6270 E info@bethdin.org.uk
W www.theus.org.uk
Registrar, David Frei
Dayanim, Yonason Abraham; Menachem Gelley *(Rosh Beth Din);* Ivan Binstock; Shmuel Simons

MASORTI JUDAISM, Alexander House, 3 Shakespeare Road, London N3 1XE T 020-8349 6650 E enquiries@masorti.org.uk
W www.masorti.org.uk
Executive Director, Matt Plen

BOARD OF DEPUTIES OF BRITISH JEWS, 1 Torriano Mews, London NW5 2RZ T 020-7543 5400 E info@bod.org.uk
W www.bod.org.uk
Chief Executive, Gillian Merron

FEDERATION OF SYNAGOGUES, 65 Watford Way, London NW4 3AQ T 020-8202 2263
E info@federationofsynagogues.com
W www.federationofsynagogues.com
Chief Executive, Rabbi Ari Lazarus

LIBERAL JUDAISM, The Montagu Centre, 21 Maple Street, London W1T 4BE T 020-7580 1663
E montagu@liberaljudaism.org W www.liberaljudaism.org
Chief Executive, Rabbi Danny Rich

THE MOVEMENT FOR REFORM JUDAISM, The Sternberg Centre for Judaism, 80 East End Road, London N3 2SY T 020-8349 5640 E admin@reformjudaism.org.uk
W www.reformjudaism.org.uk
Senior Rabbi, Laura Janner-Klausner

THE SEPHARDI COMMUNITY, 2 Ashworth Road, London W9 1JY T 020-7289 2573 E admin@spsyn.org.uk
W www.sephardi.org.uk
Executive Director, David Arden

UNITED SYNAGOGUE HEAD OFFICE, Adler House, 735
High Road, London N12 0US T 020-8343 8989
W www.theus.org.uk
Chief Executive, Dr Stephen Wilson

PAGANISM

Paganism draws on the ideas of the Celtic people of pre-Roman Europe and is closely linked to Druidism. The first historical record of Druidry comes from classical Greek and Roman writers of the third century BC, who noted the existence of Druids among a people called the Keltoi who inhabited central and southern Europe. The word druid may derive from the Indo-European 'dreo-vid', meaning 'one who knows the truth'. In practice it was probably understood to mean something like 'wise-one' or 'philosopher-priest'.

Paganism is a pantheistic nature-worshipping religion which incorporates beliefs and ritual practices from ancient times. Pagans place much emphasis on the natural world and the ongoing cycle of life and death is central to their beliefs. Most Pagans believe that they are part of nature and not separate from, or superior to it, and seek to live in a way that minimises harm to the natural environment (the word Pagan derives from the Latin *Paganus*, meaning 'rural'). Paganism strongly emphasises the equality of the sexes, with women playing a prominent role in the modern Pagan movement and goddess worship featuring in most ceremonies. Paganism cannot be defined by any principal beliefs because it is shaped by each individual's experiences.

The Pagan Federation was founded in 1971 to provide information on Paganism, campaigns on issues which affect Paganism and provides support to members of the Pagan community. Within the UK the Pagan Federation is divided into 12 districts each with a district manager and a regional coordinator. Local meetings are called 'moots' and take place in private homes, pubs or coffee bars. The Pagan Federation publishes a quarterly journal, *Pagan Dawn,* formerly *The Wiccan* (founded in 1968). The federation also publishes other material, arranges members-only and public events and maintains personal contact by letter with individual members and the wider Pagan community. Regional gatherings and conferences are held throughout the year.

THE PAGAN FEDERATION, Suite 1, The Werks, 45 Church
Road, Hove BN3 2BE E info@paganfederation.co.uk
W www.paganfed.org
President, Robin Taylor

SIKHISM

The Sikh religion dates from the birth of Guru Nanak in the Punjab in 1469. 'Guru' means teacher but in Sikh tradition has come to represent the divine presence of God giving inner spiritual guidance. Nanak's role as the human vessel of the divine guru was passed on to nine successors, the last of whom (Guru Gobind Singh) died in 1708. The immortal guru is now held to reside in the sacred scripture, *Guru Granth Sahib*, and so to be present in all Sikh gatherings.

Guru Nanak taught that there is one God and that different religions are like different roads leading to the same destination. He condemned religious conflict, ritualism and caste prejudices. The fifth Guru, Guru Arjan Dev, largely compiled the Sikh Holy scripture, a collection of hymns *(gurbani)* known as the *Adi Granth*. It includes the writings of the first five gurus and the ninth guru, and selected writings of Hindu and Muslim saints whose views are in accord with the gurus' teachings. Guru Arjan Dev also built the Golden Temple at Amritsar, the centre of Sikhism. The tenth guru, Guru Gobind Singh, passed on the guruship to the sacred scripture, Guru Granth Sahib, and founded the *Khalsa*, an order intended to fight against tyranny and injustice. Male initiates to the order added 'Singh' to their given names and women added 'Kaur'. Guru Gobind Singh also made the

wearing of five symbols obligatory: *kaccha* (a special undergarment), *kara* (a steel bangle), *kirpan* (a small sword), *kesh* (long unshorn hair, and consequently the wearing of a turban) and *kangha* (a comb). These practices are still compulsory for those Sikhs who are initiated into the Khalsa (the *Amritdharis*). Those who do not seek initiation are known as *Sehajdharis*.

There are no professional priests in Sikhism; anyone with a reasonable proficiency in the Punjabi language can conduct a service. Worship can be offered individually or communally, and in a private house or a *gurdwara* (temple). Sikhs are forbidden to eat meat prepared by ritual slaughter; they are also asked to abstain from smoking, alcohol and other intoxicants. Such abstention is compulsory for the Amritdharis.

There are about 24 million Sikhs worldwide and, according to the 2011 census, there are 432,000 adherents in England, Wales and Scotland. Every gurdwara manages its own affairs; there is no central body in the UK. The Sikh Missionary Society provides an information service.

SIKH MISSIONARY SOCIETY UK, 10 Featherstone Road,
Southall, Middx UB2 5AA T 020-8574 1902
E info@sikhmissionarysociety.org
W www.sikhmissionarysociety.org

ZOROASTRIANISM

Zoroastrians are followers of the Iranian prophet Spitaman Zarathushtra (or Zoroaster in its hellenised form) who lived *c.*1200–1500 BC. Zoroastrians were persecuted in Iran following the Arab invasion of Persia in the seventh century AD and a group (who are known as Parsis) migrated to India in the ninth century AD to avoid harassment and persecution. Zarathushtra's words are recorded in 17 hymns called the *Gathas,* which, together with other scriptures, form the *Avesta.* Zoroastrianism teaches that there is one God, *Ahura Mazda* ('Wise Lord'), and that all creation stems ultimately from God; the Gathas teach that human beings have free will, are responsible for their own actions and can choose between good and evil. It is believed that choosing *Asha* (truth or righteousness), with the aid of *Vohu Manah* (good mind), leads to happiness for the individual and society, whereas choosing evil leads to unhappiness and conflict. The *Gathas* also encourage hard work, good deeds and charitable acts. Zoroastrians believe that after death the immortal soul is judged by God, and is then sent to paradise or hell, where it will stay until the end of time to be resurrected for the final judgment.

In Zoroastrian places of worship, an urn containing fire is the central feature; the fire symbolises purity, light and truth and is a visible symbol of the *Fravashi* or *Farohar* (spirit), the presence of Ahura Mazda in every human being. Zoroastrians respect nature and much importance is attached to cultivating land and protecting air, earth and water.

The Zoroastrian Trust Funds of Europe is the main body for Zoroastrians in the UK. Founded in 1861 as the Religious Funds of the Zoroastrians of Europe, it disseminates information on the Zoroastrian faith, provides a place of worship and maintains separate burial grounds for Zoroastrians. It also holds religious and social functions and provides assistance to Zoroastrians as considered necessary, including the provision of loans and grants to students of Zoroastrianism, and participates in inter-faith educational activities.

There are approximately 150,000 Zoroastrians worldwide, of which around 4,000 reside in England and Wales, mainly in London and the South East.

ZOROASTRIAN TRUST FUNDS OF EUROPE, Zoroastrian
Centre, 440 Alexandra Avenue, Harrow, Middx HA2 9TL
T 020-8866 0765 E secretary@ztfe.com W www.ztfe.com
President, Malcolm Deboo

CHURCHES

There are two established (ie state) churches in the UK: the Church of England and the Church of Scotland. There are no established churches in Wales or Northern Ireland, though the Church in Wales, the Scottish Episcopal Church and the Church of Ireland are members of the Anglican Communion.

THE CHURCH OF ENGLAND

The Church of England is divided into the two provinces of Canterbury and York, each under an archbishop. The two provinces are subdivided into 42 dioceses, the newest of which came into existence on 20 April 2014. The new Diocese of Leeds was formed from the amalgamation of the former dioceses of Bradford, Ripon and Leeds and Wakefield.

Legislative provision for the Church of England is made by the General Synod, established in 1970. It also discusses and expresses opinion on any other matter of religious or public interest. The General Synod has 483 members in total, divided between three houses: the House of Bishops, the House of Clergy and the House of Laity. It is presided over jointly by the Archbishops of Canterbury and York and normally meets twice a year. The synod has the power, delegated by parliament, to frame statute law (known as a 'measure') on any matter concerning the Church of England. A measure must be laid before both houses of parliament, who may accept or reject it but cannot amend it. Once accepted the measure is submitted for royal assent and then has the full force of law. In addition to the General Synod, there are synods at diocesan level. The entire General Synod is re-elected once every five years. The tenth General Synod was inaugurated by the Queen on 23 November 2015.

THE ARCHBISHOPS' COUNCIL

The Archbishops' Council was established in January 1999. Its creation was the result of changes to the Church of England's national structure proposed in 1995 and subsequently approved by the synod and parliament. The council's purpose, set out in the National Institutions Measure 1998, is 'to coordinate, promote and further the work and mission of the Church of England'. It reports to the General Synod. The Archbishops' Council comprises the Archbishops of Canterbury and York, ex officio, the prolocutors elected by the convocations of Canterbury and York, the chair and vice-chair of the House of Laity, two bishops, two clergy and two lay persons elected by their respective houses of the General Synod, the Church Estates Commissioner, and up to six persons appointed jointly by the two archbishops.

There are also a number of national boards, councils and other bodies working on matters such as social responsibility, mission, Christian unity and education, which report to the General Synod through the Archbishops' Council.

GENERAL SYNOD OF THE CHURCH OF ENGLAND/ ARCHBISHOPS' COUNCIL, Church House, Great Smith Street, London SW1P 3AZ T 020-7898 1000
Secretary-General, William Nye

THE ORDINATION AND CONSECRATION OF WOMEN

The canon making it possible for women to be ordained to the priesthood was promulgated in the General Synod in February 1994 and the first 32 women priests were ordained on 12 March 1994.

On 14 July 2014 the General Synod approved the Bishops and Priests (Consecration and Ordination of Women) Measure which made provision for the consecration of women as bishops and for the continuation of provision for the ordination of women. The Revd Elizabeth Lane was consecrated as the first female bishop on 26 January 2015 when she became Bishop Suffragan of Stockport in the diocese of Chester. The first female diocesan bishop, Rachel Treweek, was consecrated as the 41st Bishop of Gloucester on 22 July 2015.

PORVOO DECLARATION

The Porvoo Declaration was approved by the General Synod of the Church of England in July 1995. Churches that approve the declaration regard baptised members of each other's churches as members of their own, and allow free interchange of episcopally ordained ministers within the rules of each church.

MEMBERSHIP AND MINISTRY

	Full-time Diocesan Clergy 2017		Electoral Roll Membership 2016
	Male	Female	
Bath and Wells	132	52	29,800
Birmingham	108	42	15,400
Blackburn	132	24	27,500
Bristol	70	29	14,600
Canterbury	97	27	23,400
Carlisle	72	16	17,400
Chelmsford	222	85	40,300
Chester	138	53	38,800
Chichester	217	31	46,600
Coventry	79	29	15,200
Derby	94	38	14,700
Durham	95	43	18,700
Ely	75	41	17,500
Europe	63	5	11,100
Exeter	154	33	26,600
Gloucester	77	40	21,500
Guildford	119	48	26,300
Hereford	58	25	14,500
Leeds	218	89	38,900
Leicester	79	37	15,400
Lichfield	179	56	38,800
Lincoln	102	53	20,800
Liverpool	119	60	23,800
London	427	86	73,900
Manchester	135	63	27,400
Newcastle	86	32	13,800
Norwich	125	45	17,400
Oxford	264	96	52,000
Peterborough	94	47	17,800
Portsmouth	64	27	14,200
Rochester	145	40	25,800
St Albans	163	70	31,900
St Edmundsbury and Ipswich	79	36	19,200
Salisbury	132	60	34,900
Sheffield	94	32	15,300
Sodor and Man	15	3	2,000
Southwark	231	87	42,900
Southwell and Nottingham	76	31	16,900
Truro	48	34	13,300
Winchester	119	33	28,100
Worcester	74	34	14,700
York	139	54	28,700
Channel Islands	26	4	–
Total	5,235	1,870	1,047,900

In 2016, 111,500 people were baptised, 42,700 people were married in parish churches, the Church of England had an electoral roll membership of 1.05 million, and each week an average 927,000 people attended services. There were 15,638 churches and places of worship; 383 senior clergy (including bishops, archdeacons and cathedral clergy); 7,790 full-time equivalent parochial stipendiary clergy; 117 full-time equivalent non-parochial stipendiary clergy; 3,230 self-supporting ministers; 1,113 chaplains; 5,760 readers and licensed lay ministers; and 2,910 readers with permission to officiate and active emeriti.

STIPENDS

The stipends below are for those appointed on or after 1 April 2004; transitional arrangements are in place for those appointed prior to this date. The national minimum stipend from 1 April 2018 is £24,360; under common tenure all full-time office-holders must receive stipend, or stipend together with other income related to their office, of at least this amount.

	2018–19
Archbishop of Canterbury	£81,760
Archbishop of York	£70,070
Bishop of London	£64,230
Diocesan bishops	£44,380
Suffragan bishops	£36,210
Assistant bishops (full-time)	£30,050
Deans	£36,210
Archdeacons	£35,400
Residentiary canons	*£28,020
Incumbents and clergy of similar status	*£25,950

* National stipend benchmark: adjusted regionally to reflect variations in the cost of living

CANTERBURY

105TH ARCHBISHOP AND PRIMATE OF ALL ENGLAND

Most Revd and Rt. Hon. Justin Welby, *cons.* 2011, *apptd* 2013; Lambeth Palace, London SE1 7JU
Signs Justin Cantuar:

BISHOPS SUFFRAGAN

Dover, Rt. Revd Trevor Willmott, *cons.* 2002, *apptd* 2009; Upway, St Martin's Hill, Canterbury, Kent CT1 1PR
Ebbsfleet, Rt. Revd Jonathan Goodall, *cons.* 2013, *apptd* 2013; Hill House, Treetops, The Mount, Caversham, Reading RG4 7RE
Richborough, Rt. Revd Norman Banks, *cons.* 2011, *apptd* 2011; Parkside House, Abbey Mill Lane, St Albans AL3 4HE
Maidstone, Rt. Revd Roderick Thomas, *cons.* 2015, *apptd* 2015; The Bishop's Lodge, Church Road, Worth, Crawley RH10 7RT
*responsible for episcopal oversight of the Channel Islands

DEAN

Very Revd Robert Willis, *apptd* 2001

Dean of Jersey (A Peculiar), Very Revd Mike Keirle, *apptd* 2017
Dean of Guernsey (A Peculiar), Very Revd Tim Barker, *apptd* 2015

Organist (Canterbury Cathedral), David Flood, FRCO, *apptd* 1988

ARCHDEACONS

Ashford, Ven. Darren Miller, *apptd* 2018
Canterbury, Ven. Jo Kelly Moore *apptd* 2017
Maidstone, Ven. Stephen Taylor, *apptd* 2011

Vicar-General of Province and Diocese, Chancellor Sheila Cameron, QC

Commissary-General, Morag Ellis, QC
Joint Registrars of the Province, Canon John Rees; Stephen Slack
Diocesan Registrar and Legal Adviser, Owen Carew Jones
Diocesan Secretary, Julian Hills, Diocesan House, Lady Wootton's Green, Canterbury CT1 1NQ T 01227-459401

YORK

97TH ARCHBISHOP AND PRIMATE OF ENGLAND

Most Revd and Rt. Hon. Dr John Sentamu, *cons.* 1996, *trans.* 2005; Bishopthorpe, York YO23 2GE
Signs Sentamu Ebor:

BISHOPS SUFFRAGAN

Hull, Rt. Revd Alison White, *cons.* 2015, *apptd* 2015; Hullen House, Woodfield Lane, Hessle, Hull HU13 0ES
Selby, Rt. Revd John Thomson, *cons.* 2014, *apptd* 2014; 6 Pinfold Garth, Malton YO17 7XQ
Whitby, Rt. Revd Paul Fergson, *cons.* 2014, *apptd* 2014; 21 Thornton Road, Stainton TS8 9DS

PRINCIPAL EPISCOPAL VISITOR

Beverley, Rt. Revd Glyn Webster, *cons.* 2013, *apptd* 2013; Holy Trinity Rectory, Micklegate, York YO1 6LE

DEAN

vacant

Director of Music, Robert Sharpe, *apptd* 2008

ARCHDEACONS

Cleveland, Ven. Samantha Rushton, *apptd* 2015
East Riding, Ven. Andy Broom, *apptd* 2014
York, Ven. Sarah Bullock, *apptd* 2013

Chancellor of the Diocese, His Hon. Judge Collier, QC, *apptd* 2006
Registrar and Legal Secretary, Caroline Mockford
Diocesan Secretary, Canon Peter Warry, Diocesan House, Amy Johnson Way, York YO30 4XT T 01904-699500

LONDON (CANTERBURY)

133RD BISHOP

Rt. Revd Dame Sarah Mullally, DBE, *cons.* 2015, *apptd* 2017; Bishop of London's Office, St Michael Paternoster Royal, College Hill, London EC4R 2RL
Signs Sarah Londin:

AREA BISHOPS

Edmonton, Rt. Revd Robert Wickham, *cons.* 2015, *apptd* 2015; 27 Thurlow Road, London NW3 5PP
Kensington, Rt. Revd Graham Tomlin, *cons.* 2015, *apptd* 2015; Dial House, Riverside, Twickenham TW1 3DT
Stepney, Rt. Revd Adrian Newman, *cons.* 2011, *apptd* 2011; 63 Coburn Road, London E3 2DB
Willesden, Rt. Revd Peter Broadbent, *cons.* 2001, *apptd* 2001; 173 Willesden Lane, London NW6 7YN

BISHOP SUFFRAGAN

Islington, Rt. Revd Ric Thorpe, *cons.* 2015, *apptd* 2015; St Edmund the King, Lombard Street, London, EC3V 9EA
Fulham, Rt. Revd Jonathan Baker, *cons.* 2011, *apptd* 2013; The Vicarage, 5 St Andrew Street, London EC4A 3AF

DEAN OF ST PAUL'S

Very Revd Dr David Ison, PHD, *apptd* 2012

Director of Music, Andrew Carwood, *apptd* 2007

ARCHDEACONS

Hackney, Ven. Liz Adekunle, *apptd* 2016
Hampstead, Ven. John Hawkins, *apptd* 2015

London, Ven. Luke Miller, *apptd* 2016
Middlesex, Ven. Stephan Welch, *apptd* 2006
Northolt, Ven. Duncan Green, *apptd* 2013
Two Cities, Ven. Rosemary Lain-Priestley, *apptd* 2016

Chancellor, Nigel Seed, QC, *apptd* 2002
Registrar and Legal Secretary, Paul Morris

Diocesan Secretary, Richard Gough, London Diocesan House, 36 Causton Street, London SW1P 4AU **T** 020-7932 1100

DURHAM (YORK)

74TH BISHOP

Rt. Revd Paul Butler, *cons.* 2004, *trans.* 2013; Auckland Castle, Bishop Auckland DL14 7NR
Signs Paul Dunelm:

BISHOP SUFFRAGAN

Jarrow, Rt. Revd Mark Bryant, *cons.* 2007, *apptd* 2007; Bishop's House, 25 Ivy Lane, Low Fell, Gateshead NE9 6QD

DEAN

Very Revd Andrew Tremlett, *apptd* 2015

Organist, Daniel Cook, *apptd* 2017

ARCHDEACONS

Auckland, Ven. Rick Simpson, *apptd* 2017
Durham, Ven. Ian Jagger, *apptd* 2006
Sunderland, Ven. Bob Cooper, *apptd* 2018

Chancellor, Adrian Iles, *apptd* 2017
Registrar and Legal Secretary, Philip Wills, *apptd* 2018

Diocesan Secretary, Andrew Thurston, Diocesan Office, Cuthbert House, Stonebridge, Durham DH1 3RY **T** 01388-660010

WINCHESTER (CANTERBURY)

97TH BISHOP

Rt. Revd Tim Dakin, cons. 2012, *apptd* 2011; Wolvesey, Winchester SO23 9ND
Signs Tim Winton:

BISHOPS SUFFRAGAN

Basingstoke, Rt. Revd David Williams, *cons.* 2014, *apptd* 2014; Bishop's Office, Old Alresford Place, Alresford, Hants SO24 9DH
Southampton, Rt. Revd Jonathan Frost, *cons.* 2010, *apptd* 2010; Bishop's House, St Mary's Church Close, Wessex Lane, Southampton SO18 2ST

DEAN

Very Revd Catherine Ogle, *apptd* 2017

Director of Music, Andrew Lumsden, *apptd* 2002

ARCHDEACONS

Bournemouth, Ven. Dr Peter Rouch, *apptd* 2011
Winchester, Ven. Richard Brand, *apptd* 2011
For Mission Development, Ven. Paul Moore, *apptd* 2014

Chancellor, Cain Ormondroyd, *apptd* 2017
Registrar and Legal Secretary, Sue de Candole

Chief Executive, Andrew Robinson, Old Alresford Place, Alresford, Hants SO24 9DH **T** 01962-737300

BATH AND WELLS (CANTERBURY)

79TH BISHOP

Rt. Revd Peter Hancock, *cons.* 2010, *apptd* 2014; The Bishop's Palace, Wells, Somerset BA5 2PD
Signs Peter Bath & Wells:

BISHOP SUFFRAGAN

Taunton, Rt. Revd Ruth Worsley, *cons.* 2015, *apptd* 2015; The Bishop's Palace, Market Place, Wells BA5 2PD

DEAN

Very Revd John Davies, *apptd* 2016

Organist, Matthew Owens, *apptd* 2005

ARCHDEACONS

Bath, Ven. Dr Adrian Youings, *apptd* 2017
Taunton, Ven. Simon Hill, *apptd* 2016
Wells, Ven. Anne Gell, *apptd* 2017

Chancellor, Timothy Briden, *apptd* 1993
Registrar and Legal Secretary, Roland Callaby

Diocesan Secretary, Nick May, The Old Deanery, St Andrew's Street, Wells, Somerset BA5 2UG **T** 01749-670777

BIRMINGHAM (CANTERBURY)

9TH BISHOP

Rt. Revd David Urquhart, KCMG *cons.* 2000, *apptd* 2006; Bishop's Croft, Old Church Road, Harborne, Birmingham B17 0BG
Signs David Birmingham:

BISHOP SUFFRAGAN

Aston, Anne Hollinghurst, *cons.* 2015, *apptd* 2015, Bishop's Lodge, 16 Coleshill Street, Sutton Coldfield B72 1SH

DEAN

Very Revd Matt Thompson, *apptd* 2017

Director of Music, David Hardie, *apptd* 2018

ARCHDEACONS

Aston, Ven. Simon Heathfield, *apptd* 2014
Birmingham, Ven. Hayward Osborne, *apptd* 2001

Chancellor, Mark Powell, QC, *apptd* 2012
Registrar and Legal Secretary, Vicki Simpson

Diocesan Secretary, Andrew Halstead, 1 Colmore Row, Birmingham B3 2BJ **T** 0121-426 0400

BLACKBURN (YORK)

9TH BISHOP

Rt. Revd Julian Henderson, *cons.* 2013, *apptd* 2013; Bishop's House, Ribchester Road, Blackburn BB1 9EF
Signs Julian Blackburn

BISHOPS SUFFRAGAN

Burnley, Rt. Revd Philip North, *cons.* 2015, *apptd* 2015; Dean House, 449 Padiham Road, Burnley BB12 6TE
Lancaster, Rt. Revd Dr Jill Duff, *cons.* 2018, *apptd* 2018; Shireshead Vicarage, Whinney Brow, Forton, Preston PR3 0AE

DEAN

Very Revd Peter Howell-Jones, *apptd* 2016

Organist and Director of Music, Samuel Hudson, *apptd* 2011

ARCHDEACON

Blackburn, Ven. Mark Ireland, *apptd* 2015
Lancaster, Ven. Michael Everitt, *apptd* 2011

Chancellor, His Hon. Judge Bullimore, *apptd* 1990
Registrar and Legal Secretary, Revd Paul Benfield

Diocesan Secretary, Graeme Pollard, Diocesan Office, Clayton House, Walker Office Park, Blackburn BB1 2QE **T** 01254-503070

BRISTOL (CANTERBURY)

56TH BISHOP

Rt. Revd Vivienne Faull, *cons.* 2018, *apptd* 2018; 58A High Street, Winterbourne, Bristol BS36 1JQ
Signs Vivienne Bristol

BISHOP SUFFRAGAN

Swindon, Rt. Revd Dr Lee Rayfield, *cons.* 2005, *apptd* 2005; Mark House, Field Rise, Swindon, Wiltshire SN1 4HP

DEAN

Very Revd David Hoyle, *apptd* 2010

Organist and Director of Music, Mark Lee, *apptd* 1998

ARCHDEACONS

Bristol, Revd Canon Michael Johnson *(acting),* *apptd* 2018
Malmesbury, Ven. Christine Froude, *apptd* 2011

Chancellor, Revd Justin Gau
Registrar and Legal Secretary, Roland Callaby

Diocesan Secretary, Oliver Home, First Floor, Hillside House, 1500 Parkway North, Stoke Gifford, Bristol BS34 8YU **T** 0117-9060100

CARLISLE (YORK)

67TH BISHOP

Rt. Revd James Newcome, *cons.* 2002, *apptd* 2009; Bishop's House, Ambleside Road, Keswick CA12 4DD
Signs James Carliol

BISHOP SUFFRAGAN

Penrith, Revd Dr Emma Ineson (bishop designate), *cons.* 2019, *apptd* 2018; Holm Croft, 13 Castle Road, Kendal, Cumbria LA9 7AU

DEAN

Very Revd Mark Boyling, *apptd* 2004

Director of Music, Mark Duthie, *apptd* 2017

ARCHDEACONS

Carlisle, Ven. Lee Townend, *apptd* 2017
West Cumberland, Ven. Dr Richard Pratt, *apptd* 2009
Westmorland and Furness, Ven. Vernon Ross, *apptd* 2017

Chancellor, Geoffrey Tattersall, QC, *apptd* 2003
Registrar and Legal Secretary, Jane Lowdon

Diocesan Secretary, Derek Hurton, Church House, 19–24 Friargate, Penrith, Cumbria CA11 7XR **T** 01768-807777

CHELMSFORD (CANTERBURY)

10TH BISHOP

Rt. Revd Stephen Cottrell, *cons.* 2004, *apptd* 2010; Bishopscourt, Main Road, Margaretting, Ingatestone, Essex CM4 0HD
Signs Stephen Chelmsford

BISHOPS SUFFRAGAN

Barking, Rt. Revd Peter Hill, *cons.* 2014, *apptd* 2014; Barking Lodge, Verulam Avenue, London E17 8ES
Bradwell, Rt. Revd Dr John Perumbalath, *cons.* 2018, *apptd* 2018; Bishop's House. Orsett Road, Horndon-on-the-Hill, Essex SS17 8NS
Colchester, Rt. Revd Roger Morris, *cons.* 2014, *apptd* 2014; 1 Fitzwater Road, Colchester, Essex CO3 3SS

DEAN

Very Revd Nicholas Henshall, *apptd* 2013

Director of Music, James Davy, *apptd* 2012

ARCHDEACONS

Barking, vacant
Chelmsford, Ven. Elizabeth Snowden, *apptd* 2016
Colchester, Ven. Annette Cooper, *apptd* 2004
Harlow, Ven. Vanessa Herrick, *apptd* 2017
Southend, Ven. Mike Lodge, *apptd* 2017
Stansted, Ven. Robin King, *apptd* 2013
West Ham, Ven. Elwin Cockett, *apptd* 2007

Chancellor, George Pulman, QC, *apptd* 2001
Registrar and Legal Secretary, Aiden Hargreaves-Smith

Chief Executive, vacant, 53 New Street, Chelmsford, Essex CM1 1AT **T** 01245-294400

CHESTER (YORK)

40TH BISHOP

Rt. Revd Peter Forster, PHD, *cons.* 1996, *apptd* 1996; Bishop's House, Abbey Square, Chester CH1 2JD
Signs Peter Cestr:

BISHOPS SUFFRAGAN

Birkenhead, Rt. Revd Keith Sinclair, *cons.* 2007, *apptd* 2007; Bishop's Lodge, 67 Bidston Road, Prenton CH43 6TR
Stockport, Rt. Revd Elizabeth Lane, *cons.* 2015, *apptd* 2015; Bishop's Lodge, Back Lane, Dunham, Altrincham WA14 4SG

DEAN

Very Revd Dr Timothy Stratford, *apptd* 2018

Organist and Director of Music, Philip Rushforth, FRCO, *apptd* 2008

ARCHDEACONS

Chester, Ven. Dr Michael Gilbertson, *apptd* 2010
Macclesfield, Ven. Ian Bishop, *apptd* 2011

Chancellor, His Hon. Judge Turner, QC, *apptd* 1998
Registrar and Legal Secretary, Lisa Moncur

Diocesan Secretary, George Colville, Church House, 5500 Daresbury Park, Daresbury, Warrington WA4 4GE **T** 01928-718834

CHICHESTER (CANTERBURY)

103RD BISHOP

Rt. Revd Dr Martin Warner, *cons.* 2010, *apptd* 2012; The Palace, Chichester PO19 1PY
Signs Martin Cicestr:

BISHOPS SUFFRAGAN

Horsham, Rt. Revd Mark Sowerby, *cons.* 2009, *apptd* 2009; 21 Guildford Road, Horsham, W. Sussex RH12 1LU
Lewes, Rt. Revd Richard Jackson, *cons.* 2014, *apptd* 2014; Ebenezer House, Kingston Ridge, Kingston, Lewes BN7 3JU

DEAN

Very Revd Stephen Waine, *apptd* 2015

Organist, Charles Harrison, *apptd* 2014

ARCHDEACONS

Brighton and Lewes, Ven. Martin Lloyd Williams, *apptd* 2015
Chichester, vacant
Horsham, Ven. Fiona Windsor, *apptd* 2014
Hastings, Ven. Edward Dowler, *apptd* 2016

Chancellor, Prof. Mark Hill, QC
Registrar and Legal Secretary, Matthew Chinery

Diocesan Secretary, Gabrielle Higgins, Diocesan Church House, 211 New Church Road, Hove, E. Sussex BN3 4ED **T** 01273-421021

COVENTRY (CANTERBURY)

9TH BISHOP

Rt. Revd Dr Christopher Cocksworth, *cons.* 2008, *apptd*
2008; The Bishop's House, 23 Davenport Road, Coventry
CV5 6PW

Signs Christopher Coventry

BISHOP SUFFRAGAN

Warwick, Rt. Revd John Stroyan, *cons.* 2005, *apptd* 2005;
Warwick House, School Hill, Offchurch, Leamington Spa CV33 9AL

DEAN
Very Revd John Witcombe, *apptd* 2013

Director of Music, Mr Kerry Beaumont, *apptd* 2006

ARCHDEACONS
Archdeacon Pastor, Ven. Sue Field *apptd* 2017
Archdeacon Missioner, Ven. Morris Rodham, *apptd* 2010

Chancellor, His Hon. Judge Eyre, *apptd* 2009
Registrar and Legal Secretary, Mary Allanson
Diocesan Secretary, Ruth Marlow, Cathedral & Diocesan Offices, 1
Hilltop, Coventry CV1 5AB T 024-7652 1200

DERBY (CANTERBURY)

8TH BISHOP
vacant

BISHOP SUFFRAGAN

Repton, Rt. Revd Jan McFarlane, *cons.* 2016, *apptd* 2016;
Repton House, 39 Hickton Road, Swanwick, Alfreton DE55 1AF

DEAN
Very Revd Dr Stephen Hance, *apptd* 2017

Director of Music, Hugh Morris, *apptd* 2015

ARCHDEACONS
Chesterfield, Ven. Carol Coslett, *apptd* 2018
Derby, Ven. Dr Christopher Cunliffe, *apptd* 2006

Chancellor, His Hon. Judge Bullimore, *apptd* 1981
Registrar and Legal Secretary, Nadine Waldron
Diocesan Secretary, vacant, Derby Church House, Full Street, Derby
DE1 3DR T 01332-388650

ELY (CANTERBURY)

69TH BISHOP

Rt. Revd Stephen Conway, *cons.* 2006, *apptd* 2011; The
Bishop's House, Ely CB7 4DW

Signs Stephen Ely

BISHOP SUFFRAGAN

Huntingdon, Rt. Revd David Thomson, DPHIL, *cons.* 2008,
apptd 2008; 14 Lynn Road, Ely, Cambs CB6 1DA

DEAN
Very Revd Mark Bonney, *apptd* 2012

Director of Music, Paul Trepte, FRCO, *apptd* 1991

ARCHDEACONS
Cambridge, Ven. Dr Alex Hughes, *apptd* 2014
Huntingdon and Wisbech, Ven. Hugh McCurdy, *apptd* 2005

Chancellor, His Hon. Judge Leonard, QC
Registrar, Howard Dellar

Diocesan Secretary, Canon Paul Evans, Bishop Woodford House,
Barton Road, Ely, Cambs CB7 4DX T 01353-652702

EXETER (CANTERBURY)

71ST BISHOP

Rt. Revd Robert Atwell, *cons.* 2008, *apptd* 2014; The Palace,
Exeter EX1 1HY

Signs Robert Exon:

BISHOPS SUFFRAGAN
Crediton, vacant

Plymouth, Rt. Revd Nick McKinnel, *cons.* 2012, *trans.* 2015;
108 Molesworth Road, Stoke, Plymouth PL3 4AQ

DEAN
Very Revd Jonathan Greener, *apptd* 2017

Director of Music, Timothy Noon, *apptd* 2016

ARCHDEACONS
Barnstaple, Ven. Mark Butchers, *apptd* 2015
Exeter, Ven. Christopher Futcher, *apptd* 2012
Plymouth, Ven. Ian Chandler, *apptd* 2010
Totnes, Ven. Douglas Dettmer, *apptd* 2015

Chancellor, Hon. Sir Andrew McFarlane
Registrar and Legal Secretary, Alison Stock

Diocesan Secretary, Stephen Hancock, The Old Deanery, The
Cloisters, Exeter EX1 1HS T 01392-272686

GIBRALTAR IN EUROPE (CANTERBURY)

4TH BISHOP

Rt. Revd Robert Innes, PHD, *cons.* 2014, *apptd* 2014; Office
of the Bishop in Europe, 47, rue Capitaine Crespel – boite 49,
1050 Brussels, Belgium

BISHOP SUFFRAGAN

In Europe, Rt. Revd David Hamid, *cons.* 2002, *apptd* 2002; 14
Tufton Street, London SW1P 3QZ

Dean, Cathedral Church of the Holy Trinity, Gibraltar, vacant

Chancellor, Pro-Cathedral of St Paul, Valletta, Malta, Canon
Simon Godfrey
Chancellor, Pro-Cathedral of the Holy Trinity, Brussels, Belgium,
Ven. Dr Paul Vrolijk

ARCHDEACONS
Eastern, Ven. Colin Williams
North-West Europe, Ven. Dr Paul Vrolijk
France, Ven. Meurig Williams
Gibraltar, Canon Geoffrey Johnston *(interim)*
Italy and Malta, Ven. Vickie Sims
Germany and Northern Europe, Ven. Colin Williams
Switzerland, Canon Adèle Kelham *(acting)*

Chancellor, Prof. Mark Hill, QC
Registrar and Legal Secretary, Aiden Hargreaves-Smith

Diocesan Secretary, Michael Fegan *(interim),* 14 Tufton Street,
London SW1P 3QZ T 020-7898 1155

GLOUCESTER (CANTERBURY)

41ST BISHOP

Rt. Revd Rachel Treweek, *cons.* 2015, *apptd* 2015; 2 College
Green, Gloucester GL1 2LR

Signs Rachel Gloucestr

BISHOP SUFFRAGAN

Tewkesbury, Rt. Revd Robert Springett, *cons.* 2016, *apptd*
2016; 2 College Green, Gloucester GL1 2LR

DEAN
Very Revd Stephen Lake, *apptd* 2011

Director of Music, Adrian Partington, *apptd* 2007

ARCHDEACONS
Cheltenham, Ven. Phil Andrew, *apptd* 2017
Gloucester, Ven. Jackie Searle, *apptd* 2012

Chancellor and Vicar-General, June Rodgers, *apptd* 1990
Registrar and Legal Secretary, Jos Moule

Diocesan Secretary, Ben Preece Smith, Church House, College Green, Gloucester GL1 2LY T 01452-410022

GUILDFORD (CANTERBURY)

10TH BISHOP
Rt. Revd Andrew Watson, *cons.* 2008, *apptd* 2014; Willow Grange, Woking Road, Guildford, Surrey GU4 7QS
Signs Andrew Guildford

BISHOP SUFFRAGAN
Dorking, Rt Revd Jo Wells, *cons.* 2016, *apptd* 2016; Dayspring, 13 Pilgrim's Way, Guildford, Surrey GU4 8AD

DEAN
Very Revd Dianna Gwilliams, *apptd* 2013

Organist, Katherine Dienes-Williams, *apptd* 2007

ARCHDEACONS
Dorking, Ven. Paul Bryer, *apptd* 2014
Surrey, Ven. Paul Davies, *apptd* 2017

Chancellor, Andrew Jordan
Registrar and Legal Secretary, Howard Dellar

Diocesan Secretary, Peter Coles, Church House, 20 Alan Turing Road, Guildford GU2 7YF T 01483-790300

HEREFORD (CANTERBURY)

105TH BISHOP
Rt. Revd Richard Frith, cons. 1998, apptd 2014; Bishop's House, The Palace, Hereford HR4 9BN
Signs Richard Hereford

BISHOP SUFFRAGAN
Ludlow, Rt. Revd Alistair Magowan, *cons.* 2009, *apptd* 2009; Bishop's House, Corvedale Road, Craven Arms, Shropshire SY7 9BT

DEAN
Very Revd Michael Tavinor, *apptd* 2002

Organist and Director of Music, Geraint Bowen, FRCO, *apptd* 2001

ARCHDEACONS
Hereford, Ven. Derek Chedzey, *apptd* 2018
Ludlow, Rt. Revd Alistair Magowan, *apptd* 2009

Chancellor, His Hon. Judge Kaye, QC
Registrar and Legal Secretary, Howard Dellar

Diocesan Secretary, Sam Pratley, The Palace, Hereford HR4 9BL T 01432-373300

LEEDS (YORK)

1ST BISHOP OF LEEDS
Rt. Revd Nicholas Baines, *cons.* 2003, *apptd* 2014; Hollin House, Weetwood Avenue, Leeds LS16 5NG
Signs Nicholas Leeds

AREA BISHOPS
Bradford, Rt. Revd Dr Toby Howarth, *cons.* 2014, *apptd* 2014; 47 Kirkgate, Shipley BD18 3EH
Huddersfield, Rt. Revd Jonathan Gibbs, *cons.* 2014, *apptd* 2014; University of Huddersfield, Ground Floor, Sir John Ramsden Court, Huddersfield HD1 3AQ

Ripon, Rt. Revd Dr Helen-Ann Hartley, *cons.* 2014, *apptd* 2018; The Bishop's Office, Redwood, New Road, Sharow, Ripon HG4 5BS
Wakefield, Rt. Revd Anthony Robinson, *cons.* 2002, *apptd* 2014; Pontefract House 181A Manygates Lane, Sandal, Wakefield WF2 7DR

SUFFRAGAN BISHOP
Richmond, Rt. Revd Paul Slater, *cons.* 2015, apptd 2015; Church House, 17–19 York Place, Leeds LS1 2EX

DEANS
Bradford, Very Revd Jerry Lepine, *apptd* 2013
Ripon, Very Revd John Dobson, *apptd* 2014
Wakefield, Very Revd Simon Cowling, *apptd* 2018

Directors of Music, Alexander Berry (Bradford), *apptd* 2017; Andrew Bryden (Ripon), *apptd* 2003; Thomas Moore (Wakefield), *apptd* 2010

ARCHDEACONS
Bradford, Ven. Andrew Jolley, *apptd* 2016
Halifax, Ven. Dr Anne Dawtry, *apptd* 2011
Leeds, Ven. Paul Ayers, *apptd* 2017
Richmond and Craven, Ven. Beverley Mason, *apptd* 2016
Pontefract, Ven. Peter Townley, *apptd* 2008

Chancellor, Prof. Mark Hill, QC
Registrar and Legal Secretary, Peter Foskett

Diocesan Secretary, Debbie Child; Church House, 17–19 York Place, Leeds LS1 2EX T 0113-200 0540

LEICESTER (CANTERBURY)

7TH BISHOP
Rt Revd Martyn Snow, *cons.* 2013, *apptd* 2016; Bishop's Lodge, 10 Springfield Road, Leicester LE2 3BD
Signs Martyn Leicester

SUFFRAGAN BISHOP
Loughborough, Rt. Revd Gulnar Francis-Dehqani, *cons.* 2017, *apptd* 2017; c/o Bishop's Lodge, 10 Springfield Road, Leicester LE2 3BD

DEAN
Very Revd David Monteith, *apptd* 2013

Director of Music, Dr Christopher Ouvry-Johns

ARCHDEACONS
Leicester, Ven. Timothy Stratford, *apptd* 2012
Loughborough, Ven. Claire Wood, *apptd* 2017

Chancellor, Mark Blackett-Ord
Registrar and Legal Secretary, Revd Trevor Kirkman

Diocesan Secretary, Jonathan Kerry, St Martin's House, 7 Peacock Lane, Leicester LE1 5PZ T 0116-261 5200

LICHFIELD (CANTERBURY)

99TH BISHOP
Rt. Revd Dr Michael Ipgrave, OBE, *cons.* 2012, *apptd* 2016; 22 The Close, Lichfield, WS13 7LG
Signs Michael Lich:

AREA BISHOPS
Shrewsbury, vacant

Stafford, Rt. Revd Geoffrey Annas, *cons.* 2010, *apptd* 2010; Ash Garth, Broughton Crescent, Barlaston, Stoke-on-Trent ST12 9DD
Wolverhampton, Rt. Revd Clive Gregory, *cons.* 2007, *apptd* 2007; 61 Richmond Road, Wolverhampton WV3 9JH

DEAN
Very Revd Adrian Dorber, *apptd* 2005

Director of Music, Ben Lamb, *apptd* 2010
Organist, Martyn Rawles, *apptd* 2010

ARCHDEACONS
Lichfield, Ven. Simon Baker, *apptd* 2013
Salop, Ven. Paul Thomas, *apptd* 2011
Stoke-on-Trent, Ven. Matthew Parker, *apptd* 2013
Walsall, Ven. Dr Susan Weller, *apptd* 2015

Chancellor, His Hon. Judge Eyre, *apptd* 2012
Joint Registrars and Legal Secretaries, Niall Blackie; Andrew Wynne
Diocesan Secretary, Julie Jones, St Mary's House, The Close, Lichfield, Staffs WS13 7LD **T** 01543-306030

LINCOLN (CANTERBURY)

72ND BISHOP
Rt. Revd Christopher Lowson, *cons.* 2011, *apptd* 2011; Bishop's Office, The Old Palace, Minster Yard, Lincoln LN2 1PU
Signs Christopher Lincoln

BISHOPS SUFFRAGAN
Grantham, Rt. Revd Dr Nicholas Chamberlain, *cons.* 2015, *apptd* 2015; The Old Palace, Minster Yard, Lincoln LN2 1PU
Grimsby, Rt. Revd Dr David Court, *cons.* 2014, *apptd* 2014; The Old Palace, Minster Yard, Lincoln LN2 1PU

DEAN
Very Revd Christine Wilson, *apptd* 2016

Director of Music, Aric Prentice, *apptd* 2003

ARCHDEACONS
Boston, Ven. Dr Justine Allain Chapman, *apptd* 2013
Lincoln, Ven. Gavin Kirk, *apptd* 2016
Stow and Lindsey, Ven. Mark Steadman, *apptd* 2015

Chancellor, His Hon. Judge Bishop
Registrar and Legal Secretary, Ian Blaney
Diocesan Secretary, Revd David Dadswell, Edward King House, Minster Yard, Lincoln LN2 1PU **T** 01522-504050

LIVERPOOL (YORK)

8TH BISHOP
Rt. Revd Paul Bayes, *cons.* 2010, *apptd* 2014; Bishop's Lodge, Woolton Park, Liverpool L25 6DT
Signs Paul Liverpool

BISHOP SUFFRAGAN
Warrington, vacant

DEAN
Very Revd Susan Jones, PHD, *apptd* 2018

Director of Music, Lee Ward, *apptd* 2017

ARCHDEACONS
Liverpool, Ven. Mike McGurk, *apptd* 2017
Knowsley & Sefton, Ven. Pete Spiers *apptd* 2015
St Helens & Warrington, Ven. Peter Preece, *apptd* 2015
Wigan & West Lancashire, Ven. Jennifer McKenzie, *apptd* 2015

Chancellor, Sir Mark Hedley, QC
Registrar and Legal Secretary, Howard Dellar
Diocesan Secretary, Mike Eastwood, St James House, 20 St James Street, Liverpool L1 7BY **T** 0151-709 9722

MANCHESTER (YORK)

12TH BISHOP
Rt. Revd Dr David Walker, *cons.* 2000, *apptd* 2013; Bishopscourt, Bury New Road, Salford M7 4LE
Signs David Manchester

BISHOPS SUFFRAGAN
Bolton, Rt. Revd Mark Ashcroft, *cons.* 2016, *apptd* 2016; Bishop's Lodge, Walkenden Road, Walkenden M28 2WH
Middleton, Rt. Revd Mark Davies, *cons.* 2008, *apptd* 2008; The Hollies, Manchester Road, Rochdale OL11 3QY

DEAN
Very Revd Rogers Govender, *apptd* 2006

Organist, Christopher Stokes, *apptd* 1992

ARCHDEACONS
Bolton, Ven. Jean Burgess, *apptd* 2018
Manchester, Ven. Karen Lund, *apptd* 2017
Rochdale, Ven. Cherry Vann, *apptd* 2008
Salford, Ven. David Sharples, *apptd* 2009

Chancellor, Canon Geoffrey Tattersall, QC
Registrar and Legal Secretary, Jane Monks
Diocesan Secretary, vacant, Diocesan Church House, 90 Deansgate, Manchester M3 2GH **T** 0161-828 1400

NEWCASTLE (YORK)

12TH BISHOP
Rt. Revd Christine Elizabeth Hardman, *cons.* 2015, apptd 2015; Bishop's House, 29 Moor Road South, Gosforth, Newcastle upon Tyne NE3 1PA
Signs Christine Newcastle

SUFFRAGAN BISHOP
Berwick Rt. Revd Mark Tanner, *cons.* 2016, *apptd* 2016; Berwick House, Longhirst Road, Pegswood, Morpeth NE61 6XF

DEAN
Very Revd Geoff Miller, *apptd* 2018

Director of Music, Ian Roberts, *apptd* 2016

ARCHDEACONS
Lindisfarne, Ven. Dr Peter Robinson, *apptd* 2008
Northumberland, vacant

Chancellor, Euan Duff, *apptd* 2013
Registrar and Legal Secretary, Jane Lowdon
Diocesan Secretary, Canon Shane Waddle, Church House, St John's Terrace, North Shields NE29 6HS **T** 0191-270 4100

NORWICH (CANTERBURY)

71ST BISHOP
Rt. Revd Graham R. James, *cons.* 1993, *apptd* 2000; Bishop's House, Norwich NR3 1SB
Signs Graham Norvic:

BISHOPS SUFFRAGAN
Lynn, Rt. Revd Jonathan Meyrick, *cons.* 2011, *apptd* 2011; The Old Vicarage, Castle Acre, King's Lynn PE32 2AA
Thetford, Rt. Revd Alan Winton, PHD, *cons.* 2009, *apptd* 2009; The Red House, 53 Norwich Road, Stoke Holy Cross, Norwich NR14 8AB

DEAN
Very Revd Jane Hedges, *apptd* 2014

Master of Music, Ashley Grote, *apptd* 2012

ARCHDEACONS
Lynn, Ven. Ian Bentley, *apptd* 2018
Norfolk, Ven. Steven Betts, *apptd* 2012
Norwich, Ven. Karen Hutchinson, *apptd* 2016

Chancellor, Ruth Arlow, *apptd* 2012
Registrar and Legal Secretary, Stuart Jones
Diocesan Secretary, Richard Butler, Diocesan House, 109
   Dereham Road, Easton, Norwich, Norfolk NR9 5ES **T** 01603-
   880853

OXFORD (CANTERBURY)

44TH BISHOP
Rt. Revd Steven Croft, *cons.* 2009, *apptd* 2016; Church House
   Oxford, Langford Locks, Kidlington, Oxford OX5 1GF
Signs Steven Oxon:

AREA BISHOPS
Buckingham, Rt. Revd Dr Alan Wilson, *cons.* 2003, *apptd*
   2003; Sheridan, Grimms Hill, Great Missenden, Bucks HP16 9BD
Dorchester, Rt. Revd Colin Fletcher, *cons.* 2000, *apptd* 2000;
   Arran House, Sandy Lane, Yarnton, Oxon OX5 1PB
Reading, Rt. Revd Andrew Proud, *cons.* 2011, *apptd* 2011;
   Bishop's House, Tidmarsh Lane, Tidmarsh, Reading RG8 8HA

DEAN OF CHRIST CHURCH
Very Revd Martyn Percy, PHD, *apptd* 2014

Organist, Steven Grahl, *apptd* 2018

ARCHDEACONS
Berkshire, Ven. Olivia Graham, *apptd* 2013
Buckingham, Ven. Guy Elsmore, *apptd* 2016
Dorchester, Ven. Judy French, *apptd* 2014
Oxford, Ven. Martin Gorick, *apptd* 2013

Chancellor, Revd Alex McGregor, *apptd* 2013
Registrar and Legal Secretary, Revd Canon John Rees
Diocesan Secretary, Rosemary Pearce, Church House Oxford,
   Langford Locks, Kidlington, Oxford OX5 1GF **T** 01865-208200

PETERBOROUGH (CANTERBURY)

38TH BISHOP
Rt. Revd Donald Allister, *cons.* 2010, *apptd* 2009; Bishop's
   Lodging, The Palace, Peterborough PE1 1YA
Signs Donald Petriburg:

BISHOP SUFFRAGAN
Brixworth, Rt. Revd John Holbrook, *cons.* 2011, *apptd* 2011;
   Orchard Acre, 11 North Street, Mears Ashby, Northants NN6
   0DW

DEAN
Very Revd Christopher Dalliston, *apptd* 2018

Director of Music, Tansy Castledine, *apptd* 2018

ARCHDEACONS
Northampton, Ven. Richard Ormston, *apptd* 2014
Oakham, Ven. Gordon Steele, *apptd* 2012

Chancellor, David Pittaway, QC, *apptd* 2005
Registrar and Legal Secretary, Anna Spriggs
Diocesan Secretary, Andrew Roberts, Diocesan Office, The Palace,
   Peterborough PE1 1YB **T** 01733-887000

PORTSMOUTH (CANTERBURY)

9TH BISHOP
Rt. Revd Christopher Foster, *cons.* 2010, *apptd* 2010;
   Bishopsgrove, 26 Osborn Road, Fareham, Hants PO16 7DQ
Signs Christopher Portsmouth

DEAN
vacant

Organist, David Price, *apptd* 1996

ARCHDEACONS
Isle of Wight, vacant
Portsdown, Ven. Joanne Grenfell, *apptd* 2013
The Meon, Ven. Gavin Collins, *apptd* 2011

Chancellor, His Hon. Judge Waller, CBE
Registrar and Legal Secretary, Hilary Tyler
Diocesan Secretary, Jenny Hollingsworth *(interim),* Diocesan
   Offices, 1st Floor, Peninsular House, Wharf Road, Portsmouth
   PO2 8HB **T** 023-9289 9664

ROCHESTER (CANTERBURY)

107TH BISHOP
Rt. Revd James Langstaff, *cons.* 2004, *apptd* 2010;
   Bishopscourt, 24 St Margaret's Street, Rochester ME1 1TS
Signs, James Roffen:

BISHOP SUFFRAGAN
Tonbridge, Rt. Revd Simon Burton-Jones, *cons.* 2018, *apptd*
   2018; 25 Shoesmith Lane, Kings Hill, Kent ME19 4FF

DEAN
Very Revd Dr Philip Hesketh, *apptd* 2016

Director of Music, Scott Farrell, *apptd* 2008

ARCHDEACONS
Bromley & Bexley, Ven. Dr Paul Wright, *apptd* 2003
Rochester, vacant
Tonbridge, Ven. Julie Conalty *apptd* 2017

Chancellor, The Worshipful John Gallagher
Registrar and Legal Secretary, Owen Carew-Jones
Diocesan Secretary, Geoff Marsh, St Nicholas Church, Boley Hill,
   Rochester ME1 1SL **T** 01634-560000

ST ALBANS (CANTERBURY)

10TH BISHOP
Rt. Revd Dr Alan Smith, *cons.* 2001, *apptd* 2009, *trans.* 2009;
   Abbey Gate House, St Albans AL3 4HD
Signs Alan St Albans

BISHOPS SUFFRAGAN
Bedford, Rt. Revd Richard Atkinson, OBE, *cons.* 2012, *apptd*
   2012; Bishop's Lodge, Bedford Road, Cardington, Bedford
   MK44 3SS
Hertford, Rt. Revd Dr Michael Beasley, *cons.* 2015, *apptd*
   2015; Bishopswood, 3 Stobarts Close, Knebworth SG3 6ND

DEAN
Very Revd Dr Jeffrey John, *apptd* 2004

Organist, Andrew Lucas, *apptd* 1998

ARCHDEACONS
Bedford, Ven. Paul Hughes, *apptd* 2003
Hertford, Ven. Janet Mackenzie, *apptd* 2016
St Albans, Ven. Jonathan Smith, *apptd* 2008

Chancellor, Roger Kaye, QC, *apptd* 2002
Registrar and Legal Secretary, Matthew Chinery, *apptd* 2015
Diocesan Secretary, Susan Pope, Holywell Lodge, 41 Holywell Hill,
   St Albans AL1 1HE **T** 01727-854532

ST EDMUNDSBURY AND IPSWICH (CANTERBURY)

11TH BISHOP

Rt. Revd Martin Seeley, *cons.* 2015, *apptd* 2015; The Bishop's House, 4 Park Road, Ipswich IP1 3ST
Signs Martin St Edmundsbury and Ipswich

BISHOP SUFFRAGAN

Dunwich, Rt. Revd Michael Harrison, PHD, *cons.* 2016, *apptd* 2015; Robin Hall, Chapel Lane, Mendlesham, Stowmarket IP14 55Q

DEAN

Very Revd Joe Hawes, *apptd* 2018

Director of Music, James Thomas, *apptd* 1997

ARCHDEACONS

Sudbury, Ven. Dr David Jenkins, *apptd* 2010
Suffolk, Ven. Ian Morgan, *apptd* 2012

Chancellor, David Etherington, QC
Deputy Registrar and Legal Secretary, Stuart Jones
Diocesan Secretary, Anna Hughes, Diocesan Office, St Nicholas Centre, 4 Cutler Street, Ipswich IP1 1UQ **T** 01473-298500

SALISBURY (CANTERBURY)

78TH BISHOP

Rt. Revd Nicholas Holtam, *cons.* 2011, *apptd* 2011; South Canonry, 71 The Close, Salisbury SP1 2ER
Signs Nicholas Sarum

BISHOPS SUFFRAGAN

Ramsbury, Rt. Revd Edward Condry, DPHIL, *cons.* 2012, *apptd* 2012; Bishop's Office, Southbroom House, London Road, Devizes SN10 1LT
Sherborne, Rt. Revd Karen Gorham, *cons.* 2016, *apptd* 2015; The Sherborne Office, St Nicholas' Church Centre, 30 Wareham Road, Corfe Mullen BH21 3LE

DEAN

Very Revd Nicholas Popadopulos *apptd* 2018

Director of Music, David Halls, *apptd* 2005

ARCHDEACONS

Dorset, Ven. Antony MacRow-Wood, *apptd* 2015
Sarum, Ven. Alan Jeans, *apptd* 2003
Sherborne, Ven. Paul Taylor, *apptd* 2004
Wilts, Ven. Sue Groom, *apptd* 2016

Chancellor, Canon Ruth Arlow, *apptd* 2016
Registrar and Legal Secretary, Sue de Candole
Diocesan Secretary, Lucinda Herklots, Church House, Crane Street, Salisbury SP1 2QB **T** 01722-411922

SHEFFIELD (YORK)

8TH BISHOP

Rt. Revd Dr Peter Wilcox, *cons.* 2017, *apptd* 2017; Bishopscroft, Snaithing Lane, Sheffield S10 3LG
Signs Peter Sheffield

BISHOP SUFFRAGAN

Doncaster, Rt. Revd Peter Burrows, *cons.* 2012, *apptd* 2011; Doncaster House, Church Lane, Fishlake, Doncaster DN7 5JW

DEAN

Very Revd Peter Bradley, *apptd* 2003

Director of Music, Thomas Corns, *apptd* 2017

ARCHDEACONS

Doncaster, Ven. Steve Wilcockson, *apptd* 2012
Sheffield and Rotherham, Ven. Malcolm Chamberlain, *apptd* 2013

Chancellor, Her Hon. Judge Sarah Singleton, QC, *apptd* 2014
Registrar and Legal Secretary, Andrew Vidler
Diocesan Secretary, Heidi Adcock, Church House, 95–99 Effingham Street, Rotherham S65 1BL **T** 01709-309100

SODOR AND MAN (YORK)

82ND BISHOP

Rt. Revd Peter Eagles, *cons.* 2017, *apptd* 2017; Thie yn Aspick, 4 The Falls, Douglas, Isle of Man IM4 4PZ
Signs Peter Sodor as Mannin

ARCHDEACON OF MAN

Ven. Andrew Brown, *apptd* 2011

Vicar-General and Chancellor, Geoffrey Tattersall, QC
Registrar, Louise Connacher
Diocesan Secretary, Andrew Swithinbank, c/o Thie yn Aspick, 4 The Falls, Douglas, Isle of Man IM4 4PZ **T** 07624-314590

SOUTHWARK (CANTERBURY)

10TH BISHOP

Rt. Revd Christopher Chessun, *cons.* 2005, *apptd* 2011; Trinity House, 4 Chapel Court, Borough High Street, London SE1 1HW
Signs Christopher Southwark

AREA BISHOPS

Croydon, Rt. Revd Jonathan Clark, *cons.* 2012, *apptd* 2012; St Matthew's House, 100 George Street, Croydon CR0 1PE
Kingston upon Thames, Rt. Revd Dr Richard Cheetham, *cons.* 2002, *apptd* 2002; 620 Kingston Road, Raynes Park, London SW20 8DN
Woolwich, Rt. Revd Dr Karowei Dorga, *cons,* 2017, *apptd* 2017; Trinity House, 4 Chapel Court, Borough High Street, London SE1 1HW

DEAN

Very Revd Andrew Nunn, *apptd* 2011

Organist, Peter Wright, FRCO, *apptd* 1989

ARCHDEACONS

Croydon, Ven. Christopher Skilton, *apptd* 2013
Lambeth, Ven. Simon Gates, *apptd* 2013
Lewisham & Greenwich, Ven. Alastair Cutting, *apptd* 2013
Reigate, Ven. Moira Astin, *apptd* 2016
Southwark, Ven. Dr Jane Steen, *apptd* 2013
Wandsworth, Ven. John Kiddle, *apptd* 2015

Chancellor, Philip Petchey
Registrar and Legal Secretary, Paul Morris
Diocesan Secretary, Ruth Martin, Trinity House, 4 Chapel Court, Borough High Street, London SE1 1HW **T** 020-7939 9400

SOUTHWELL AND NOTTINGHAM (YORK)

12TH BISHOP

Rt. Revd Paul Williams, *cons.* 2009, *trans.* 2015; Bishop's Manor, Southwell, Nottinghamshire NG25 0JR
Signs Paul Southwell and Nottingham

BISHOP SUFFRAGAN

Sherwood, Rt. Revd Anthony Porter, *cons.* 2006, *apptd* 2006; Jubilee House, Westgate, Southwell NG25 0JH

DEAN
Very Revd Nicola Sullivan, *apptd* 2016

Rector Chori, Paul Provost, *apptd* 2017

ARCHDEACONS
Newark, Ven. David Picken, *apptd* 2012
Nottingham, Ven. Sarah Clark, *apptd* 2014

Chancellor, His Hon. Judge Ockelton
Registrar and Legal Secretary, Amanda Redgate
Chief Executive, Nigel Spraggins, Jubilee House, Westgate, Southwell, Notts NG25 0JH **T** 01636-814331

TRURO (CANTERBURY)

16TH BISHOP
Rt. Revd Philip Mountstephen, *cons.* 2018, *apptd* 2018
Signs Philip Truro

BISHOP SUFFRAGAN
St Germans, Rt. Revd Christopher Goldsmith, DPHIL, *cons.* 2013, *apptd* 2013; Vounder, Tresillian, Truro TR2 4BW

DEAN
Very Revd Roger Bush, *apptd* 2012

Organist and Director of Music, Chris Gray, *apptd* 2008

ARCHDEACONS
Bodmin, Ven. Audrey Elkington, *apptd* 2011
Cornwall, vacant

Chancellor, Timothy Briden, *apptd* 1998
Registrar and Legal Secretary, Jos Moule

Diocesan Secretary, Esther Pollard, Church House, Woodlands Court, Truro Business Park, Threemilestone, Truro TR4 9NH **T** 01872-274351

WORCESTER (CANTERBURY)

113TH BISHOP
Rt. Revd Dr John Inge, *cons.* 2003, *apptd* 2007; The Bishop's Office, The Old Palace, Deansway, Worcester WR1 2JE
Signs John Wigorn

SUFFRAGAN BISHOP
Dudley, Rt. Revd Graham Usher, *cons.* 2014, *apptd* 2014; Bishop's House, 60 Bishop's Walk, Cradley Heath, West Midlands B64 7RH

DEAN
Very Revd Peter Atkinson, *apptd* 2006

Organist, Dr Peter Nardone, *apptd* 2012

ARCHDEACONS
Dudley, Ven. Nikki Groarke, *apptd* 2014
Worcester, Ven. Robert Jones, *apptd* 2014

Chancellor, Charles Mynors, *apptd* 1999
Registrar and Legal Secretary, Stuart Ness

Diocesan Secretary, Robert Higham, The Old Palace, Deansway, Worcester WR1 2JE **T** 01905-20537

ROYAL PECULIARS

WESTMINSTER
The Collegiate Church of St Peter

Dean, Very Revd Dr John Hall
Canon Steward, Revd Anthony Ball

Chapter Clerk, Receiver-General and Registrar, Sir Stephen Lamport, GCVO; Chapter Office, 20 Dean's Yard, London SW1P 3PA

Organist, James O'Donnell, *apptd* 2000
Legal Secretary, Christopher Vyse, *apptd* 2000

WINDSOR
The Queen's Free Chapel of St George within Her Castle of Windsor

Dean, Rt. Revd David Conner, KCVO, *apptd* 1998

Chapter Clerk, Charlotte Manley, CVO, OBE, *apptd* 2003; Chapter Office, The Cloisters, Windsor Castle, Windsor, Berks SL4 1NJ
Director of Music, James Vivian, *apptd* 2013

OTHER ANGLICAN CHURCHES

THE CHURCH IN WALES

The Anglican Church was the established church in Wales from the 16th century until 1920, when the estrangement of the majority of Welsh people from Anglicanism resulted in disestablishment. Since then the Church in Wales has been an autonomous province consisting of six sees. The bishops are elected by an electoral college comprising elected lay and clerical members, who also elect one of the diocesan bishops as Archbishop of Wales.

The legislative body of the Church in Wales is the Governing Body, which has 143 members divided between the three orders of bishops, clergy and laity. Its president is the Archbishop of Wales and it meets twice annually. Its decisions are binding upon all members of the church. The church's property and finances are the responsibility of the Representative Body. There are 46,580 members of the Church in Wales, with 417 stipendiary clergy and 690 parishes.

THE REPRESENTATIVE BODY OF THE CHURCH IN WALES, 2 Callaghan Square, Cardiff CF10 5BT **T** 029-2034 8200 *Secretary,* Simon Lloyd
13TH ARCHBISHOP OF WALES, Most Revd John Davies (Bishop of Swansea and Brecon), *elected* 2017
Signs John Cambrensis

BISHOPS
Bangor (81st), Rt. Revd Andrew John, *b.* 1964, *cons.* 2008, *elected* 2008; Ty'r Esgob, Bangor, Gwynedd LL57 2SS
Signs Andrew Bangor. *Stipendiary clergy,* 47
Llandaff (103rd), Rt. Revd June Osborne, *b.* 1953, *cons.* 2017, *elected* 2017; Llys Esgob, The Cathedral Green, Llandaff, Cardiff CF5 2YE
Signs June Landav. *Stipendiary clergy,* 106
Monmouth (10th), Rt. Revd Richard Pain, *b.* 1956, *cons.* 2013, *elected* 2013; Bishopstow, Stow Hill, Newport NP20 4EA
Signs Richard Monmouth. *Stipendiary clergy,* 43
St Asaph (76th), Rt. Revd Gregory Cameron, *b.* 1959, *cons.* 2009, *elected* 2009; Esgobty, Upper Denbigh Road, St Asaph, Denbighshire LL17 0TW
Signs Gregory Llanelwy. *Stipendiary clergy,* 76
St David's (129th), Rt. Revd Joanna Penberthy, *b.* 1960, *cons.* 2017, *elected* 2016; Llys Esgob, Abergwili, Carmarthen SA31 2JG
Signs Joanna Tyddewi. *Stipendiary clergy,* 91
Swansea and Brecon (9th), Most Revd John Davies (also Archbishop of Wales), *b.* 1953, *cons.* 2008, *trans.* 2017; Ely Tower, Castle Square, Brecon, Powys LD3 9DJ
Signs John Cambrensis. *Stipendiary clergy,* 54

The stipend for a diocesan bishop of the Church in Wales is £44,879 a year for 2018–19.

SCOTTISH EPISCOPAL CHURCH

The Scottish Episcopal Church was founded after the Act of Settlement (1690) established the presbyterian nature of the

Church of Scotland. The Scottish Episcopal Church is a member of the worldwide Anglican Communion. The governing authority is the General Synod, which consists of the Church's seven bishops, the conveners of the provincial Standing Committee, the conveners of the boards, the Church's representatives on the Anglican Consultative Council and 124 elected members (62 from the clergy and 62 from the laity). The General Synod meets once a year. The bishop who convenes and presides at meetings of the General Synod is called the 'primus' and is elected by his fellow bishops.

There are around 30,000 members of the Scottish Episcopal Church, seven bishops, around 500 serving clergy and 300 churches and places of worship.

THE GENERAL SYNOD OF THE SCOTTISH
   EPISCOPAL CHURCH, 21 Grosvenor Crescent, Edinburgh
   EH12 5EE T 0131-225 6357 W www.scotland.anglican.org
   Secretary-General, John Stuart

PRIMUS OF THE SCOTTISH EPISCOPAL CHURCH,
   Most Revd Mark Strange (Bishop of Moray, Ross and
   Caithness), *elected* 2017

BISHOPS
Aberdeen and Orkney, Rt. Revd Anne Dyer, *b.* 1957, *cons.*
   2018, *elected* 2017. *Clergy,* 50
Argyll and the Isles, Rt. Revd Kevin Pearson, *b.* 1954, *cons.*
   2011, *elected* 2010. *Clergy,* 25
Brechin, Rt. Revd Andrew Swift, *b.* 1968, *cons.* 2018, *elected*
   2018. *Clergy,* 30
Edinburgh, Rt. Revd Dr John Armes, *b.* 1955, *cons.* 2012,
   elected 2012. *Clergy,* 160
Glasgow and Galloway, Rt. Revd Dr Gregor Duncan, *b.* 1950,
   cons. 2010, *elected* 2010. *Clergy,* 110
Moray, Ross and Caithness, Most Revd Mark Strange, *b.* 1961,
   cons. 2007, *elected* 2007. *Clergy,* 60
St Andrews, Dunkeld and Dunblane, Rt. Revd Ian Paton, *elected*
   2018. *Clergy,* 75
The minimum stipend of a diocesan bishop of the Scottish Episcopal Church for 2018 is £38,925 (ie 1.5 times the standard clergy stipend of £25,950).

CHURCH OF IRELAND

The Anglican Church was the established church in Ireland from the 16th century but never secured the allegiance of the majority and was disestablished in 1871. The Church of Ireland is divided into the provinces of Armagh and Dublin, each under an archbishop. The provinces are subdivided into 12 dioceses.

The legislative body is the General Synod, which has 660 members in total, divided between the House of Bishops (12 members) and the House of Representatives (216 clergy and 432 laity). The Archbishop of Armagh is elected by the House of Bishops; other episcopal elections are made by an electoral college.

There are around 375,400 members of the Church of Ireland, 249,000 in Northern Ireland and 126,400 in the Republic of Ireland. There are two archbishops, ten bishops and 449 stipendiary clergy.

CENTRAL OFFICE, Church of Ireland House, Church Avenue,
   Rathmines, Dublin D06 CF67 T (+353) (1) 497 8422
*Chief Officer and Secretary-General of the Representative Church
   Body,* David Ritchie

PROVINCE OF ARMAGH
Archbishop of Armagh, Primate of all Ireland and Metropolitan,
   Most Revd Richard Clarke, PHD, *b.* 1949, *cons.* 1996,
   trans. 2012. *Clergy,* 42

BISHOPS
Clogher, Rt. Revd John McDowell, *b.* 1956, *cons.* 2011, *elected*
   2011. *Clergy,* 26
Connor, Rt. Revd Alan Abernethy, *b.* 1957, *cons.* 2007, *elected*
   2007. *Clergy,* 70
Derry and Raphoe, Rt. Revd Kenneth Good, *b.* 1952, *cons.*
   2002, *elected* 2002. *Clergy,* 45
Down and Dromore, Rt. Revd Harold Miller, *b.* 1950, *cons.*
   1997, *elected* 1997. *Clergy,* 82
Kilmore, Elphin and Ardagh, Rt. Revd Ferran Glenfield, PHD
   b. 1954, *cons.* 2013, *elected* 2013. *Clergy,* 21
Tuam, Killala and Achonry, Rt. Revd Patrick Rooke, *b.* 1955,
   cons. 2011, *elected* 2011. *Clergy,* 11

PROVINCE OF DUBLIN
*Archbishop of Dublin, Bishop of Glendalough, Primate of Ireland
   and Metropolitan,* Most Revd Michael Jackson, PHD,
   DPHIL, *b.* 1956, *cons.* 2002, *trans.* 2011. *Clergy,* 65

BISHOPS
Cashel, Ferns and Ossory, Rt. Revd Michael Burrows, *b.* 1961,
   cons. 2006, *elected* 2006. *Clergy,* 30
Cork, Cloyne and Ross, Rt. Revd Paul Colton, PHD, *b.* 1960,
   cons. 1999, *elected* 1999. *Clergy,* 23
Limerick, Killaloe and Ardfert, Rt. Revd Kenneth Kearon, *b.*
   1953, *cons.* 2015, *elected* 2014. *Clergy,* 18
Meath and Kildare, Most Revd Patricia Storey, *b.* 1960, *cons.*
   2013, *elected* 2013. *Clergy,* 15

OVERSEAS

PRIMATES
Primate and Archbishop of Aotearoa, New Zealand and Polynesia,
   Most Revd Winston Halapua
Primate of Australia, Most Revd Phillip Freier
Primate of Brazil, Most Revd Naudal Alves Gomes
Archbishop of the Province of Burundi, Most Revd Martin
   Nyaboho
Primate of Canada, Most Revd Frederick Hiltz
Archbishop of the Province of Central Africa, Most Revd Albert
   Chama
Primate of the Central Region of America, Rt. Revd Julio
   Thompson
Archbishop of the Province of Congo, Most Revd Zacharie
   Masimango Katanda
Archbishop of Hong Kong Sheng Kung Hui, Most Revd Paul
   Kwong
Archbishop of the Province of the Indian Ocean, Most Revd James
   Wong Yin Song
Primate of Japan (Nippon Sei Ko Kai), Most Revd Nathaniel
   Makoto Uematsu
Archbishop of Jerusalem and the Middle East, Most Revd Suheil
   Dawani
Primate and Archbishop of All Kenya, Most Revd Jackson Ole
   Sapit
Primate of Korea, Most Revd Onesimus Dongsin Park
Archbishop of Melanesia, Most Revd George Takeli
Presiding Bishop of Mexico, Most Revd Francisco Moreno
Archbishop of the Province of Myanmar (Burma), Most Revd
   Stephen Oo
Metropolitan and Primate of All Nigeria, Most Revd Nicholas
   Okoh
Archbishop of Papua New Guinea, Rt. Revd Allan Migi
Prime Bishop of the Philippines, Most Revd Joel Atiwag Pachao
Archbishop of the Province of Rwanda, Most Revd Laurent
   Mbanda
Archbishop of the Province of South East Asia, Most Revd Ng
   Moon Hing
Primate of Southern Africa, Most Revd Dr Thabo Makgoba

Presiding Bishop of South America, Most Revd Gregory
   Venables
Archbishop of the Province of South Sudan, Most Revd Justin
   Badi Arama
Archbishop of the Province of Sudan, Most Revd Ezekiel Kumir
   Kondo
Archbishop of Tanzania, Most Revd Maimbo Mndolwa
Archbishop of the Province of Uganda, Most Revd Stanley
   Ntagali
Presiding Bishop of the USA, Most Revd Michael Curry
Primate and Metropolitan of the Province of West Africa, Most
   Revd Dr Daniel Sarfo
Archbishop of the Province of the West Indies, vacant

OTHER CHURCHES AND EXTRA-PROVINCIAL
DIOCESES

Anglican Church of Bermuda, extra-provincial to Canterbury
   Bishop, Rt. Revd Nicholas Dill
Church of Ceylon, extra-provincial to Canterbury
   Bishop of Colombo, Rt. Revd Dhiloraj Canagasabey
   Bishop of Kurunegala, Rt. Revd Keerthisiri Fernando
Episcopal Church of Cuba, Rt. Revd Griselda Del Carpio
Falkland Islands, extra-provincial to Canterbury
   Bishop, Rt. Revd Timothy Thornton (Bishop to the Forces)
*Lusitanian Church (Portuguese Episcopal Church), extra-provincial
   to Canterbury*
   Bishop, Rt. Revd Jose Cabral
Reformed Episcopal Church of Spain, extra-provincial to Canterbury
   Bishop, Rt. Revd Carlos López-Lozano

MODERATION OF CHURCHES IN FULL
COMMUNION WITH THE ANGLICAN
COMMUNION

Church of Bangladesh, Most Revd Paul Sarker
Church of North India, Most Revd Dr Prem Chand Singh
Church of South India, Most Revd Thomas Oommen
Church of Pakistan, Most Revd Humphrey Peters

CHURCH OF SCOTLAND

The Church of Scotland is the national church of Scotland. The
church is reformed in doctrine, and presbyterian in
constitution; ie based on a hierarchy of courts of ministers and
elders and, since 1990, of members of a diaconate. At local
level the Kirk Session consists of the parish minister and ruling
elders. At district level the presbyteries, of which there are 44
in Britain, consist of all the ministers in the district, one ruling
elder from each congregation, and those members of the
diaconate who qualify for membership. The General Assembly
is the supreme authority, and is presided over by a Moderator
chosen annually by the Assembly. The sovereign, if not present
in person, is represented by a Lord High Commissioner who
is appointed each year by the Crown.

The Church of Scotland has around 360,000 members, 780
parish ministers and 30,000 elders. The majority of parishes
are in Scotland, but there are also churches in England, Europe
and overseas.

Lord High Commissioner (2018–19), Duke of Buccleuch and
   Queensberry, KT, KBE
Moderator of the General Assembly (2018–19), Rt. Revd Susan
   Brown
Principal Clerk, Revd Dr George Whyte
Procurator, Laura Dunlop, QC
Law Agent and Solicitor of the Church, Mary Macleod
Parliamentary Officer, Chloe Clemmons
General Treasurer, Anne Macintosh
Secretary to the Council of Assembly, Revd Dr Martin Scott
CHURCH OFFICE, 121 George Street, Edinburgh EH2 4YN
   T 0131-225 5722

PRESBYTERIES AND CLERKS
Aberdeen, Revd Dr John Ferguson
Abernethy, Revd James MacEwan
Angus, Revd Dr Ian McLean
Annandale and Eskdale, Revd Adam Dillon
Ardrossan, Jean Hunter
Argyll, Dr Christopher Brett
Ayr, Revd Kenneth Elliott
Buchan, Revd Sheila Kirk
Caithness, Revd Ronald Johnstone
Dumbarton, David Sinclair
Dumfries and Kirkcudbright, Revd Donald Campbell
Dundee, Revd James Wilson
Dunfermline, Revd Iain Greenshields
Dunkeld and Meigle, Revd John Russell
Duns, David Philp
Edinburgh, Revd Marjory McPherson
England, Revd Alistair Cumming
Europe, Revd Jim Sharp
Falkirk, Revd Andrew Sarle
Glasgow, Revd George Cowie
Gordon, Revd Euan Glen
Greenock and Paisley, Revd Dr Peter McEnhill
Hamilton, Revd Dr Gordon McCracken
Inverness, Revd Trevor Hunt
Irvine and Kilmarnock, Steuart Dey
Jedburgh, Revd Lisa-Jane Rankin
Kincardine and Deeside, Revd Hugh Conkey
Kirkcaldy, Revd Alan Kimmitt
Lanark, Revd Bryan Kerr
Lewis, John Cunningham
Lochaber, Revd Donald McCorkindale
Lochcarron-Skye, Revd John Murray
Lothian, John McCulloch
Melrose and Peebles, Revd Victoria Linford
Moray, Revd Alastair Gray
Orkney, Dr Mike Partridge
Perth, Revd Colin Caskie
Ross, Cath Chambers
St Andrews, Revd Nigel Robb
Shetland, Revd Deborah Dobby
Stirling, Revd Alan Miller
Sutherland, Revd Ian McCree
Uist, Revd Gavin Elliott
West Lothian, Revd Duncan Shaw
Wigtown and Stranraer, Sam Scobie
The stipends for ministers in the Church of Scotland in 2018
range from £27,044–£33,234, depending on length of
service.

ROMAN CATHOLIC CHURCH

The Roman Catholic Church is a worldwide Christian church
acknowledging as its head the Bishop of Rome, known as the
Pope (father). Despite its widespread usage, 'Pope' is actually
an unofficial term. The *Annuario Pontificio,* (Pontifical
Yearbook) lists eight official titles: Bishop of Rome, Vicar of
Jesus Christ, Successor of the Prince of the Apostles, Supreme
Pontiff of the Universal Church, Primate of Italy, Archbishop
and Metropolitan of the Roman Province, Sovereign of the
State of the Vatican City and Servant of the Servants of God.

The Pope leads a communion of followers of Christ, who
believe they continue His presence in the world as servants of
faith, hope and love to all society. The Pope is held to be the
successor of St Peter and thus invested with the power which
was entrusted to St Peter by Jesus Christ. A direct line of
succession is therefore claimed from the earliest Christian
communities. With the fall of the Roman Empire the Pope also
became an important political leader. His territory is now

limited to the 0.44 sq. km (0.17 sq. miles) of the Vatican City State, created to provide some independence to the Pope from Italy and other nations. The episcopal jurisdiction of the Roman Catholic Church is called the Holy See.

The Pope exercises spiritual authority over the church with the advice and assistance of the Sacred College of Cardinals, the supreme council of the church. The number of cardinals was fixed at 70 by Pope Sixtus V in 1586 but has increased steadily since the pontificate of John XXIII. On 28 February 2013, the date of Pope Benedict XVI's resignation, there were 207 cardinals.

Following the death or resignation of the Pope, the members of the College of Cardinals under the age of 80 are called to the Vatican to elect a successor. They are known as cardinal electors and form an assembly called the conclave. The conclave, which comprised 115 cardinal electors when it convened in March 2013, conducts a secret ballot in complete seclusion to elect the next Pope. A two-thirds majority is necessary before the vote can be accepted as final. When a cardinal receives the necessary number of votes, the Dean of the Sacred College formally asks him if he will accept election and the name by which he wishes to be known. On his acceptance of the office of Supreme Pontiff, the conclave is dissolved and the first Cardinal Deacon announces the election to the assembled crowd in St Peter's Square.

The Pope has full legislative, judicial and administrative power over the whole Roman Catholic Church. He is aided in his administration by the curia, which is made up of a number of departments. The Secretariat of State is the central office for carrying out the Pope's instructions and is presided over by the Cardinal Secretary of State. It maintains relations with the departments of the curia, with the episcopate, with the representatives of the Holy See in various countries, governments and private persons. The congregations and pontifical councils are the Pope's ministries and include departments such as the Congregation for the Doctrine of Faith, whose field of competence concerns faith and morals; the Congregation for the Clergy and the Congregation for the Evangelisation of Peoples, the Pontifical Council for the Family and the Pontifical Council for the Promotion of Christian Unity.

The Holy See, composed of the Pope and those who help him in his mission for the church, is recognised by the Conventions of Vienna as an international moral body. Apostolic nuncios are the Pope's diplomatic representatives; in countries where no formal diplomatic relations exist between the Holy See and that country, the papal representative is known as an apostolic delegate.

According to the 2018 Pontifical Yearbook the number of baptised Roman Catholics worldwide was 1,299 million in 2016; the number of bishops was 5,353 and there were 414,969 priests.

SUPREME PONTIFF

His Holiness Pope Francis (Jorge Mario Bergoglio), *born* Buenos Aires, Argentina, 17 December 1936; *ordained priest* 13 December 1969; *appointed Archbishop* (of Buenos Aires), 28 February 1998; *created Cardinal* 21 February 2001; *assumed pontificate* 13 March 2013

PONTIFF EMERITUS

His Holiness Pope Benedict XVI (Joseph Ratzinger), *born* Bavaria, Germany, 16 April 1927; *ordained priest* 29 June 1951; *appointed Archbishop* (of Munich), 24 March 1977; *created Cardinal* 27 June 1977; *assumed pontificate* 19 April 2005; *resigned pontificate* 28 February 2013

SECRETARIAT OF STATE

Secretary of State, His Eminence Cardinal Pietro Parolin
First Section (General Affairs), Most Revd Giovanni Angelo Becciu (Titular Archbishop of Roselle)

Second Section (Relations with Other States), Most Revd Paul Gallagher (Titular Archbishop of Hodelm)

BISHOPS' CONFERENCE

The Catholic Bishops' Conference of England and Wales is the permanent assembly of Catholic Bishops and Ordinaries in the two member countries. The membership of the Conference comprises the Archbishops, Bishops and Auxiliary Bishops of the 22 Dioceses within England and Wales, the Bishop of the Forces (Military Ordinariate), the Apostolic Eparchs of the Ukrainian Church and Syro-Malabar Catholics in Great Britain, the Ordinary of the Personal Ordinariate of Our Lady of Walsingham, and the Apostolic Prefect of the Falkland Islands. The Conference is headed by a president and vice-president. There are six departments, each with an episcopal chair: Dialogue and Unity, Education and Formation, Evangelisation and Catechesis, International Affairs, Life and Worship and Responsibility and Citizenship.

The Bishops' Conference Standing Committee is made up of two directly elected bishops in addition to the Metropolitan Archbishops and chairs from each of the above departments. The committee has general responsibility for continuity of policy between the plenary sessions of the conference, preparing the conference agenda and implementing its decisions.

The administration of the Bishops' Conference is funded by a levy on each diocese, according to income. A general secretariat in London coordinates and supervises the Bishops' Conference administration activities. There are also other agencies and consultative bodies affiliated to the conference.

The Bishops' Conference of Scotland is the permanently constituted assembly of the eight bishops of Scotland. The conference is headed by the president (Most Revd Philip Tartaglia, Archbishop of Glasgow). The conference establishes various agencies which perform advisory functions in relation to the conference. The more important of these agencies are called commissions; each one is headed by a bishop president who, with the other members of the commissions, are appointed by the conference.

The Irish Catholic Bishops' Conference (also known as the Irish Episcopal Conference) has as its president the Most Revd Eamon Martin (Archbishop of Armagh and Primate of All Ireland). Its membership comprises all the archbishops and bishops of Ireland. It appoints various commissions and agencies to assist with the work of the Catholic Church in Ireland.

The Catholic Church in the UK has over 900,000 mass attendees, 5,500 priests and 4,550 churches.

Bishops' Conferences secretariats:

ENGLAND AND WALES, 39 Eccleston Square, London SW1V 1BX **T** 020-7630 8220 **W** www.cbcew.org.uk
General Secretary, Revd Christopher Thomas
SCOTLAND, 64 Aitken Street, Airdrie ML6 6LT **T** 01236-764061 **W** www.bcos.org.uk
General Secretary, Mgr Hugh Bradley
IRELAND, Columba Centre, Maynooth, County Kildare W23 P6D3 **T** (+353) (1) 505 3000 **E** info@catholicbishops.ie **W** www.catholicbishops.ie
Episcopal Secretary, Most Revd Kieran O'Reilly (Archbishop of Cashel and Emly)
Executive Secretary, Mgr Gearóid Dullea

GREAT BRITAIN

APOSTOLIC NUNCIO TO GREAT BRITAIN

HE Most Revd Edward Joseph Adams (Titular Archbishop of Scala), *apptd* 2017. *Apostolic Nunciature,* 54 Parkside, London SW19 5NE **T** 020-8944 7189

ENGLAND AND WALES

THE MOST REVD ARCHBISHOPS

Westminster, HE Cardinal Vincent Nichols, *cons.* 1992, *apptd* 2009 *Auxiliaries,* John Sherrington, *cons.* 2011; Nicholas Hudson, *cons.* 2014; Paul McAleenan, *cons.* 2016; John Wilson, *cons.* 2016. *Clergy,* 318. *Archbishop's House,* Ambrosden Avenue, London SW1P 1QJ T 020-7798 9033

Birmingham, Bernard Longley, *cons.* 2003, *apptd* 2009 *Auxiliaries,* William Kenney, *cons.* 1987; David McGough, *cons.* 2005; Robert Byrne, *cons.* 2014. *Clergy,* 430. *Archbishop's House,* 8 Shadwell Street, Birmingham B4 6EY T 0121-236 9090

Cardiff, George Stack, *cons.* 2001, *apptd* 2011. *Clergy,* 47. *Archbishop's House,* 41–43 Cathedral Road, Cardiff CF11 9HD T 029-2022 0411

Liverpool, Malcolm McMahon, *cons.* 2000, *apptd* 2014 *Auxiliary,* Thomas Williams, *cons.* 2003. *Clergy,* 402. *Archbishop's House,* 19 Salisbury Road, Cressington Park, Liverpool L19 0PH T 0151-494 0686

Southwark, Peter Smith, *cons.* 1995, *apptd* 2010 *Auxiliaries,* Patrick Lynch, *cons.* 2006; Paul Hendricks, *cons.* 2006. *Clergy,* 366. *Archbishop's House,* 150 St George's Road, London SE1 6HX T 020-7928 2495

THE RT. REVD BISHOPS

Arundel and Brighton, Richard Moth, *cons.* 2009, *apptd* 2015. *Clergy,* 95. *Bishop's House,* High Oaks, Old Brighton Road North, Pease Pottage RH11 9AJ T 01293-526428

Brentwood, Alan Williams, *cons.* 2014, *apptd* 2014. *Clergy,* 170. *Bishop's Office,* Cathedral House, Ingrave Road, Brentwood, Essex CM15 8AT T 01277-232266

Clifton, Declan Lang, *cons.* 2001, *apptd* 2001. *Clergy,* 153. *Bishop's House,* St Ambrose, North Road, Leigh Woods, Bristol BS8 3PW T 0117-973 3072

East Anglia, Alan Hopes, *cons.* 2003, *apptd* 2013. *Clergy,* 129. *Diocesan Curia,* The White House, 21 Upgate, Poringland, Norwich NR14 7SH T 01508-492202

Hallam, Ralph Heskett, *cons.* 2010, *apptd* 2014. *Clergy,* 71. *Bishop's House,* 75 Norfolk Road, Sheffield S2 2SZ T 0114-278 7988

Hexham and Newcastle, Seamus Cunningham, *cons.* 2009, *apptd* 2009. *Clergy,* 164. *Bishop's House,* 800 West Road, Newcastle upon Tyne NE5 2BJ T 0191-228 0003

Lancaster, Paul Swarbrick, *cons.* 2018, *apptd* 2018. *Clergy,* 97. *Bishop's Office,* The Pastoral Centre, Balmoral Road, Lancaster LA1 3BT T 01524-596050

Leeds, Marcus Stock, *cons.* 2014, *apptd* 2014. *Clergy,* 193. *Diocesan Curia,* Hinsley Hall, 62 Headingley Lane, Leeds LS6 2BX T 0113-230 4533

Menevia (Wales), Tom Burns, *cons.* 2002, *apptd* 2008. *Clergy,* 60. *Diocesan Office,* 27 Convent Street, Swansea SA1 2BX T 01792-644017

Middlesbrough, Terence Drainey, *cons.* 2008, *apptd* 2007. *Clergy,* 50. *Diocesan Curia,* 16 Cambridge Road, Middlesbrough TS5 5NN T 01642-850505

Northampton, Peter Doyle, *cons.* 2005, *apptd* 2005. *Clergy,* 116. *Bishop's House,* Marriott Street, Northampton NN2 6AW T 01604-715635

Nottingham, Patrick McKinney, *cons.* 2015, *apptd* 2015. *Clergy,* 166. *Bishop's House,* 27 Cavendish Road East, The Park, Nottingham NG7 1BB T 0115-947 4786

Plymouth, Mark O'Toole, *cons.* 2014, *apptd* 2013. *Clergy,* 50. *Bishop's House,* 45 Cecil Street, Plymouth PL1 5HW T 01752-224414

Portsmouth, Philip Egan, *cons.* 2012, *apptd* 2012. *Clergy,* 214. *Bishop's House,* Bishop Crispian Way, Portsmouth, Hants PO1 3HG T 023-9282 0894

Salford, John Arnold, *cons.* 2006, *apptd* 2014. *Clergy,* 218. *Diocesan Curia,* Wardley Hall, Worsley, Manchester M28 2ND T 0161-794 2825

Shrewsbury, Mark Davies, *cons.* 2010, *apptd* 2010. *Clergy* 112. *Diocesan Curia,* 2 Park Road South, Prenton, Wirral CH43 4UX T 0151-652 9855

Wrexham (Wales), Peter Brignall, *cons.* 2012, *apptd* 2012. *Clergy,* 16. *Bishop's House,* Sontley Road, Wrexham LL13 7EW T 01978-262726

SCOTLAND

THE MOST REVD ARCHBISHOPS

St Andrews and Edinburgh, Leo Cushley, *cons.* 2013, *apptd* 2013. *Clergy,* 50. *Archdiocese Offices,* 100 Strathearn Road, Edinburgh EH9 1BB T 0131-623 8900

Glasgow, Philip Tartaglia, *cons.* 2005, *apptd* 2012. *Clergy,* 198. *Diocesan Curia,* 196 Clyde Street, Glasgow G1 4JY T 0141-226 5898

THE RT. REVD BISHOPS

Aberdeen, Hugh Gilbert, *cons.* 2011, *apptd* 2011. *Clergy,* 47. *Bishop's House,* 3 Queen's Cross, Aberdeen AB15 4XU T 01224-319154

Argyll and the Isles, Brian McGee, *cons.* 2016, *apptd* 2015. *Clergy,* 32. *Diocesan Office* Bishop's House, Esplanade, Oban, Argyll PA34 5AB T 01631-567436

Dunkeld, Stephen Robson, *cons.* 2012, *apptd* 2013. *Clergy,* 43. *Diocesan Curia,* 24–28 Lawside Road, Dundee DD3 6XY T 01382-225453

Galloway, William Nolan, *cons.* 2015, *apptd* 2014. *Clergy,* 19. *Diocesan Office,* 8 Corsehill Road, Ayr KA7 2ST T 01292-266750

Motherwell, Joseph Toal, *cons.* 2008, *trans.* 2014. *Clergy,* 123. *Diocesan Curia,* Coursington Road, Motherwell ML1 1PP T 01698-269114

Paisley, John Keenan, *cons.* 2014, *apptd* 2014. *Clergy,* 75. *Diocesan Curia,* Cathedral Precincts, Incle Street, Paisley PA1 1HR T 0141-847 6131

BISHOPRIC OF THE FORCES

Rt. Revd Paul Mason, *cons.* 2016, *apptd* 2018. *Administration,* RC Bishopric of the Forces, Wellington House, St Omer Barracks, Thornhill Road, Aldershot, Hants GU11 2BG T 01252-348234

IRELAND

There is one hierarchy for the whole of Ireland. Several of the dioceses have territory partly in the Republic of Ireland and partly in Northern Ireland.

APOSTOLIC NUNCIO TO IRELAND

Most Revd Jude Thaddeus Okolo (Titular Archbishop of Novica), *apptd* 2017. *Apostolic Nunciature,* 183 Navan Road, Dublin 7 T (+353) (1) 838 0577

THE MOST REVD ARCHBISHOPS

Armagh, Eamon Martin (*also* Primate of All Ireland), *cons.* 2013, *apptd* 2014. *Archbishop Emeritus,* HE Cardinal Seán Brady *cons.* 1995, *elevated* 2007. *Clergy,* 135. *Bishop's Residence,* Ara Coeli, Cathedral Road, Armagh BT61 7QY T 028-3752 2045

Cashel and Emly, Kieran O'Reilly, *cons.* 2010, *apptd* 2015. *Clergy,* 83. *Archbishop's House,* Thurles, Co. Tipperary T (+353) (504) 21512

Dublin, Diarmuid Martin (*also* Primate of Ireland), *cons.* 1999, *apptd Coadjutor Archbishop* 2003, *succeeded as Archbishop* 2004. *Auxiliaries,* Éamonn Walsh, *cons.* 1990; Raymond Field, *cons.* 1997. *Clergy,* 389. *Archbishop's House,* Drumcondra, Dublin 9 T (+353) (1) 837 3732

Tuam, Dr Michael Neary, *cons.* 1992, *apptd* 1995. *Clergy,* 110. *Archbishop's House,* Tuam, Co. Galway **T** (+353) (93) 24166

THE MOST REVD BISHOPS

Achonry, vacant. *Clergy,* 50. *Bishop's House,* Edmondstown, Ballaghadereen, Co. Roscommon **T** (+353) (94) 986 0021

Ardagh and Clonmacnois, Francis Duffy, *cons.* 2013, *apptd* 2013. *Clergy,* 60. *Diocesan Office,* St Mel's, Longford **T** (+353) (43) 334 6432

Clogher, vacant. *Clergy,* 74. *Bishop's House,* Monaghan **T** (+353) (47) 81019

Clonfert, John Kirby, *cons.* 1988, *apptd* 1988. *Clergy,* 37. *Bishop's House,* Coorheen, Loughrea, Co. Galway **T** (+353) (91) 841560

Cloyne, William Crean, *cons.* 2013, *apptd* 2013. *Clergy,* 126. *Diocesan Office,* Cobh, Co. Cork **T** (+353) (21) 481 1430

Cork and Ross, John Buckley, *cons.* 1984, *apptd* 1998. *Clergy,* 133. *Diocesan Office,* Cork and Ross Offices, Redemption Road, Cork **T** (+353) (21) 430 1717

Derry, Dónal McKeown, *cons.* 2001, *apptd* 2014. *Clergy,* 108. *Bishop's House.* PO Box 227, Derry BT48 9YG **T** 028-7126 2302

Down and Connor, Noël Treanor, *cons.* 2008, *apptd* 2008. *Clergy,* 199. *Bishop's Residence,* Lisbreen, 73 Somerton Road, Belfast, Co. Antrim BT15 4DE **T** 028-9077 6185

Dromore, Philip Boyce (Apostolic Administrator), *cons.* 1995, *apptd* 2018. *Clergy,* 33. *Bishop's House,* 44 Armagh Road, Newry, Co. Down BT35 6PN **T** 028-3026 2444

Elphin, Kevin Doran, *cons.* 2014, *apptd* 2014. *Clergy,* 66. *Bishop's House,* Temple St, St Mary's, Sligo **T** (+353) (71) 915 0106

Ferns, Denis Brennan, *cons.* 2006, *apptd* 2006. *Clergy,* 88. *Bishop's House,* Summerhill, Wexford **T** (+353) (53) 912 2177

Galway, Kilmacduagh and Kilfenora, Brendan Kelly, *cons.* 2008, *apptd* 2018. *Clergy,* 57. *Diocesan Office,* The Cathedral, Galway **T** (+353) (91) 563566

Kerry, Ray Browne, *cons.* 2013, *apptd* 2013. *Clergy,* 88. *Bishop's House,* Killarney, Co. Kerry **T** (+353) (64) 663 1168

Kildare and Leighlin, Denis Nulty, *cons.* 2013, *apptd* 2013. *Clergy,* 72. *Bishop's House,* Old Dublin Road, Carlow Town **T** (+353) (59) 917 6725

Killala, John Fleming, *cons.* 2002, *apptd* 2002. *Clergy,* 40. *Bishop's House,* Ballina, Co. Mayo **T** (+353) (96) 21518

Killaloe, Fintan Monahan, *cons.* 2016, *apptd* 2016. *Clergy,* 95. *Diocesan Office,* Westbourne, Ennis, Co. Clare **T** (+353) (65) 682 8638

Kilmore, Leo O'Reilly, *cons.* 1997, *apptd* 1998. *Clergy,* 67. *Bishop's House,* Cullies, Cavan, Co. Cavan **T** (+353) (49) 433 1496

Limerick, Brendan Leahy, *cons.* 2013, *apptd* 2013. *Clergy,* 109. *Diocesan Office,* Social Service Centre, Henry Street, Limerick **T** (+353) (61) 315856

Meath, Thomas Deenihan, *cons.* 2018, *apptd* 2018. *Clergy,* 120. *Bishop's House,* Dublin Road, Mullingar, Co. Westmeath **T** (+353) (44) 934 8841

Ossory, Dermot Farrell, *cons.* 2018, *apptd* 2018. *Clergy,* 81. *Diocesan Office,* James's Street, Kilkenny **T** (+353) (56) 776 2448

Raphoe, Alan McGuckian, *cons.* 2017, *apptd* 2017. *Clergy,* 80. *Bishop's House,* Ard Adhamhnáin, Letterkenny, Co. Donegal **T** (+353) (74) 912 1208

Waterford and Lismore, Alphonsus Cullinan, *cons.* 2015, *apptd* 2015. *Clergy,* 114. *Bishop's House,* John's Hill, Waterford **T** (+353) (51) 874463

OTHER CHURCHES IN THE UK

ASSOCIATED PRESBYTERIAN CHURCHES OF SCOTLAND

The Associated Presbyterian Churches came into being in 1989 as a result of a division within the Free Presbyterian Church of Scotland. The Associated Presbyterian Churches is reformed and evangelistic in nature and emphasises the importance of doctrine based primarily on the Bible and secondly on the Westminster Confession of Faith. There are an estimated 500 members, 8 ministers and 18 congregations in Scotland. There are also congregations in Canada.

ASSOCIATED PRESBYTERIAN CHURCHES OF SCOTLAND, Bruach Taibh, 2 Borve, Arnisort, Isle of Skye IV51 9PS **T** 01470-582264 **W** www.apchurches.org
Presbytery Clerk, Revd Ross Macaskill

BAPTIST CHURCH

Baptists trace their origins to John Smyth, who in 1609 in Amsterdam reinstituted the baptism of conscious believers as the basis of the fellowship of a gathered church. Members of Smyth's church established the first Baptist church in England in 1612. They came to be known as 'General' Baptists and their theology was Arminian, whereas a later group of Calvinists who adopted the baptism of believers came to be known as 'Particular' Baptists. The two sections of the Baptists were united into one body in 1891: the Baptist Union of Great Britain and Ireland (renamed the Baptist Union of Great Britain in 1988).

Baptists emphasise the complete autonomy of the local church, although individual churches are linked in various kinds of associations. There are international bodies (such as the Baptist World Alliance) and national bodies, but some Baptist churches belong to neither. However, in Great Britain the majority of churches and associations belong to the Baptist Union of Great Britain. There are also Baptist unions in Wales, Scotland and Ireland and there is some overlap of membership.

There are currently around 135,000 members, 2,500 ministers and 2,080 churches associated with the Baptist Union of Great Britain. The Baptist Union of Great Britain is one of the founder members of the European Baptist Federation (1948) and the Baptist World Alliance (1905); the latter represents 42 million members worldwide.

In the Baptist Union of Wales (Undeb Bedyddwyr Cymru) there are 11,355 members, 88 pastors and 386 churches, including those in England.

In the Baptist Union of Scotland there are 11,500 members and 161 churches.

BAPTIST UNION OF GREAT BRITAIN, Baptist House, PO Box 44, 129 Broadway, Didcot, Oxon OX11 8RT **T** 01235-517700 **W** www.baptist.org.uk
President (2018–19), Dave Gregory
General Secretary, Lynn Green

BAPTIST UNION OF WALES, Y Llwyfan, Trinity St David College, College Road, Carmarthen SA31 3EQ **T** 01267-245660 **E** mennajones@ubc.cymru **W** www.buw.org.uk
President of the Welsh Assembly (2018–19), Revd Aled Davies
President of the English Assembly (2018–19), Revd Terry Broadhurst
General Secretary of the Baptist Union of Wales, Revd Judith Morris

BAPTIST UNION OF SCOTLAND, 48 Speirs Wharf, Glasgow G4 9TH **T** 0141-423 6169 **E** admin@scottishbaptist.org.uk **W** www.scottishbaptist.com
National Team Leader, Revd Alan Donaldson

THE BRETHREN

The Brethren was founded in Dublin in 1827–8, basing itself on the structures and practices of the early church and rejecting denominationalism and clericalism. Many groups sprang up; the group at Plymouth became the best known, resulting in its designation by others as the 'Plymouth Brethren'. Early worship had a prescribed form but quickly assumed an unstructured, non-liturgical format.

There are services devoted to worship, usually involving the breaking of bread, and separate preaching meetings. There is no salaried ministry.

A theological dispute led in 1848 to schism between the Open Brethren and the Closed or Exclusive Brethren, each branch later suffering further divisions.

Open Brethren churches are run by appointed elders and are completely independent, but freely cooperate with each other. Exclusive Brethren churches believe in a universal fellowship between congregations. They do not have appointed elders, but use respected members of their congregation to perform certain administrative functions.

There are a number of publishing houses that publish Brethren-related literature. Chapter Two is the main supplier of such literature in the UK; it also has a Brethren history archive which is available for use by appointment.

CHAPTER TWO, 3 Conduit Mews, London SE18 7AP **T** 020-8316 5389 **E** info@chaptertwobooks.org.uk
W www.chaptertwobooks.org.uk

CONGREGATIONAL FEDERATION

The Congregational Federation was founded by members of Congregational churches in England and Wales who did not join the United Reformed Church in 1972. There are also churches in Scotland and France affiliated to the federation. The federation exists to encourage congregations of believers to worship in free assembly, but it has no authority over them and emphasises their right to independence and self-governance.

The federation has around 7,000 members, 187 accredited ministers and 265 churches in England, Wales and Scotland.

CONGREGATIONAL FEDERATION, 8 Castle Gate, Nottingham NG1 7AS **T** 0115-911 1460
E admin@congregational.org.uk **W** www.congregational.org.uk
President of the Federation (2018–19), Revd Martin Spain *(acting)*
General Secretary, Yvonne Campbell

FELLOWSHIP OF INDEPENDENT EVANGELICAL CHURCHES

The Fellowship of Independent Evangelical Churches (FIEC) was founded by Revd E. J. Poole-Connor (1872–1962) in 1922. In 1923 the fellowship published its first register of non-denominational pastors, evangelists and congregations who had accepted the doctrinal basis for the fellowship.

Members of the fellowship have two primary convictions: firstly to defend the evangelical faith, and secondly that evangelicalism is the bond that unites the fellowship, rather than forms of worship or church government.

The FIEC exists to promote the welfare of non-denominational Bible churches and to give expression to the fundamental doctrines of evangelical Christianity. It supports individual churches by providing resources and advising churches on current theological, moral, social and practical issues.

There are currently around 600 churches affiliated to the fellowship.

FELLOWSHIP OF INDEPENDENT EVANGELICAL CHURCHES, 39 The Point, Market Harborough, Leics LE16 7QU **T** 01858-434540 **E** admin@fiec.org.uk **W** www.fiec.org.uk
National Director, John Stevens

FREE CHURCH OF ENGLAND

The Free Church of England, otherwise called the Reformed Episcopal Church, is an independent episcopal church, constituted according to the historic faith, tradition and practice of the Church of England. Its roots lie in the 18th century, but it started to grow significantly from the 1840s onwards, as clergy and congregations joined it from the established church in protest against the Oxford Movement. The historic episcopate was conferred on the English church in 1876 through bishops of the Reformed Episcopal Church (which had broken away from the Protestant Episcopal Church in the USA in 1873). A branch of the Reformed Episcopal Church was founded in the UK and this merged with the Free Church of England in 1927 to create the present church. The Orders of the Free Church of England are recognised by the Church of England.

Worship is according to the *Book of Common Prayer* and some modern liturgy is permissible. Only men are ordained to the orders of deacon, presbyter and bishop.

The Free Church of England has two dioceses, 19 congregations and around 900 members in England. There is one congregation in St Petersburg, Russia and three congregations and six missions in Brazil.

THE FREE CHURCH OF ENGLAND, 329 Wolverhampton Road West, Willenhall, W. Midlands WV13 2RL **T** 01902-607335
W www.fcofe.org.uk
Bishop Primus, Rt. Revd Dr John Fenwick (Bishop of the Northern Diocese)
General Secretary, Rt. Revd Paul Hunt (Bishop of the Southern Diocese)

FREE CHURCH OF SCOTLAND

The Free Church of Scotland was formed in 1843 when over 400 ministers withdrew from the Church of Scotland as a result of interference in the internal affairs of the church by the civil authorities. In 1900, all but 26 ministers joined with others to form the United Free Church (most of which rejoined the Church of Scotland in 1929). In 1904 the remaining 26 ministers were recognised by the House of Lords as continuing the Free Church of Scotland.

The church maintains strict adherence to the Westminster Confession of Faith (1648) and accepts the Bible as the sole rule of faith and conduct. Its general assembly meets annually. It also has links with reformed churches overseas. The Free Church of Scotland has about 13,000 members, 90 ministers and 100 congregations.

FREE CHURCH OF SCOTLAND, 15 North Bank Street, The Mound, Edinburgh EH1 2LS **T** 0131-226 5286
E offices@freechurchofscotland.org.uk **W** www.freechurch.org
Chief Executive, Scott Matheson

FREE PRESBYTERIAN CHURCH OF SCOTLAND

The Free Presbyterian Church of Scotland was formed in 1893 by two ministers of the Free Church of Scotland who refused to accept a Declaratory Act passed by the Free Church General Assembly in 1892. The Free Presbyterian Church of Scotland is Calvinistic in doctrine and emphasises observance of the Sabbath. It adheres strictly to the Westminster Confession of Faith (1648).

The church has about 700 members in Scotland. It has 17 ministers and 40 churches in the UK.

FREE PRESBYTERIAN CHURCH OF SCOTLAND, 133 Woodlands Road, Glasgow G3 6LE **E** outreach@fpchurch.org.uk
W www.fpchurch.org.uk
Moderator (2018–19), Revd Allan MacColl
Clerk of the Synod, Revd Keith Watkins

HOLY APOSTOLIC CATHOLIC ASSYRIAN CHURCH OF THE EAST

The Holy Apostolic Catholic Assyrian Church of the East traces its beginnings to the middle of the first century. It spread from Upper Mesopotamia throughout the territories of the Persian Empire. The Assyrian Church of the East became theologically separated from the rest of the Christian community following the Council of Ephesus in 431. The church is headed by the Catholicos Patriarch and is episcopal in government. The liturgical language is Syriac (Aramaic). The Assyrian Church of the East and the Roman Catholic Church agreed a common Christological declaration in 1994, and a process of dialogue between the Assyrian Church of the East and the Chaldean Catholic Church, which is in communion with Rome but shares the Syriac liturgy, was instituted in 1996.

The church has around 325,000 members in the Middle East, India, Russia, Europe, North America and Australasia. In Great Britain there is one parish, which is situated in London. The church in Great Britain forms part of the Diocese of Europe under HG Mar Odisho Oraham.

HOLY APOSTOLIC CATHOLIC ASSYRIAN CHURCH OF THE EAST, St Mary's Church Hall, 62 Greenford Avenue, Hanwell, London W7 3QP **T** 0780-073 7112

INDEPENDENT METHODIST CHURCHES

The Independent Methodist Churches were formed in 1805 and remained independent when the Methodist Church in Great Britain was formed in 1932. They are mainly concentrated in the industrial areas of the north of England.

The churches are Methodist in doctrine but their organisation is congregational. All the churches are members of the Independent Methodist Connexion of Churches. The controlling body of the Connexion is the Annual Meeting, to which churches send delegates. The Connexional President is elected every two years. Between annual meetings the affairs of the Connexion are handled by the Connexional Committee and departmental committees. Ministers are appointed by the churches and trained through the Connexion. The ministry is open to both men and women.

There are 1,600 members, 70 ministers and 74 churches in Great Britain.

INDEPENDENT METHODIST RESOURCE CENTRE, The Resource Centre, Fleet Street, Wigan WN5 0DS **T** 01942-223526 **E** resourcecentre@imcgb.org.uk **W** www.imcgb.org.uk
President, vacant
General Secretary, Brian Rowney

LUTHERAN CHURCH

Lutheranism is based on the teachings of Martin Luther, the German leader of the Protestant Reformation. The authority of the scriptures is held to be supreme over church tradition. The teachings of Lutheranism are explained in detail in 16th-century confessional writings, particularly the Augsburg Confession. Lutheranism is one of the largest Protestant denominations and it is particularly strong in northern Europe and the USA. Some Lutheran churches are episcopal, while others have a synodal form of organisation; unity is based on doctrine rather than structure. Most Lutheran churches are members of the Lutheran World Federation, based in Geneva.

Lutheran services in Great Britain are held in 15 languages to serve members of different nationalities. Services usually follow ancient liturgies. English-language congregations are members either of the Lutheran Church in Great Britain or of the Evangelical Lutheran Church of England. The Lutheran Church in Great Britain and other Lutheran churches in Britain are members of the Lutheran Council of Great Britain, which represents them and coordinates their common work.

There are around 70 million Lutherans worldwide, with around 180,000 members in Great Britain.

THE LUTHERAN COUNCIL OF GREAT BRITAIN, 30 Thanet Street, London WC1H 9QH **T** 020-7554 9753 **E** enquiries@lutheran.org.uk **W** www.lutheran.org.uk
Chair, Revd Torbjorn Holt
General Secretary, James Laing

METHODIST CHURCH

The Methodist movement started in England in 1729 when the Revd John Wesley, an Anglican priest, and his brother Charles met with others in Oxford and resolved to conduct their lives by 'rule and method'. In 1739 the Wesleys began evangelistic preaching and the first Methodist chapel was founded in Bristol in the same year. In 1744 the first annual conference was held, at which the Articles of Religion were drawn up. Doctrinal emphases included repentance, faith, the assurance of salvation, social concern and the priesthood of all believers. After John Wesley's death in 1791 the Methodists withdrew from the established church to form the Methodist Church. Methodists gradually drifted into many groups, but in 1932 the Wesleyan Methodist Church, the United Methodist Church and the Primitive Methodist Church united to form the Methodist Church in Britain.

The governing body is the Conference. The Conference meets annually and consists of two parts: the ministerial and representative sessions. The Methodist Church is structured as a 'Connexion' of churches, circuits and districts. The local churches in a defined area form a circuit, and a number of these 368 circuits make up each of the 31 districts. The latest 2018 *Statistics for Mission* show that as at October 2017 the Methodist Church in Britain had 179,984 members, 1,600 active ministers and 4,374 local churches.

THE METHODIST CHURCH IN BRITAIN, Methodist Church House, 25 Marylebone Road, London NW1 5JR **T** 020-7486 5502 **E** enquiries@methodistchurch.org.uk **W** www.methodist.org.uk
Conference President (2018–19), Revd Michaela Youngson
Conference Vice-President (2018–19), Bala Gnanapragasam
Conference Secretary, Revd Canon Gareth Powell

THE METHODIST CHURCH IN IRELAND

The Methodist Church in Ireland is autonomous but has close links with British Methodism. As at December 2014 it had 45,828 members, 121 active ministers and 270 lay preachers.

METHODIST CHURCH IN IRELAND, 1 Fountainville Avenue, Belfast BT9 6AN **T** 028-9032 4554 **E** secretary@irishmethodist.org **W** www.irishmethodist.org
President of the Conference (2018–19), Revd Billy Davison
Lay Leader of the Conference (2018–19), Lynda Neilands
Secretary, Revd Tom McKnight

ORTHODOX CHURCHES

EASTERN ORTHODOX CHURCH

The Eastern (or Byzantine) Orthodox Church is a communion of self-governing Christian churches that recognises the honorary primacy of the Ecumenical Patriarch of Constantinople.

The position of Orthodox Christians is that the faith was fully defined during the period of the Oecumenical Councils. In doctrine it is strongly trinitarian, and stresses the mystery and importance of the sacraments. It is episcopal in government. The structure of the Orthodox Christian year differs from that of western churches.

Orthodox Christians throughout the world are estimated to number about 300 million; there are around 300,000 in the UK.

GREEK ORTHODOX CHURCH (PATRIARCHATE OF ANTIOCH)

The church is led by John X, Patriarch of Antioch, who was enthroned in February 2013. The Archdiocese of the British Isles and Ireland has 18 parishes, including St George's Cathedral in London, and 27 clergy.

ANTIOCHIAN ORTHODOX ARCHDIOCESE OF THE
BRITISH ISLES AND IRELAND, St George's Cathedral, 1A
Redhill Street, London NW1 4BG **T** 020-7383 0403
E fr.s.gholam@antiochianorth.co.uk
W www.antiochian-orthodox.co.uk
Archbishop, Metropolitan Silouan Oner

GREEK ORTHODOX CHURCH (PATRIARCHATE OF
CONSTANTINOPLE)
The presence of Greek Orthodox Christians in Britain dates
back at least to 1677 when Archbishop Joseph Geogirenes of
Samos fled from Turkish persecution and came to London. The
present Greek cathedral in Moscow Road, Bayswater, was
opened for public worship in 1879, and the Diocese of
Thyateira and Great Britain was established in 1922. There are
now around 100 parishes and one monastery in the UK, served
by one archbishop, three bishops and around 120 clergy.

THE PATRIARCHATE OF CONSTANTINOPLE IN
GREAT BRITAIN, Archdiocese of Thyateira and Great
Britain, Thyateira House, 5 Craven Hill, London W2 3EN
T 020-7723 4787 **E** mail@thyateira.org.uk
W www.thyateira.org.uk
Archbishop, Gregorios of Thyateira and Great Britain

THE RUSSIAN ORTHODOX CHURCH (PATRIARCHATE
OF MOSCOW)
The records of Russian Orthodox Church activities in Britain
date from the visit to England of Tsar Peter I in the early 18th
century. Clergy were sent from Russia to serve the chapel
established to minister to the staff of the Imperial Russian
Embassy in London.
  In 2007, after an 80-year division, the Russian Orthodox
Church Outside Russia agreed to become an autonomous part
of the Russian Orthodox Church, Patriarchate of Moscow. The
reunification agreement was signed by Patriarch Alexy II, 15th
Patriarch of Moscow and All Russia and Metropolitan Laurus,
leader of the Russian Orthodox Church Outside Russia on 17
May at a ceremony at Christ the Saviour Cathedral in Moscow.
Patriarch Alexy II died on 5 December 2008. Metropolitan
Kirill of Smolensk and Kaliningrad was enthroned as the 16th
Patriarch of Moscow and All Russia on 1 February 2009,
having been elected by a secret ballot of clergy on 27 January
2009.
  The diocese of Sourozh is the diocese of the Russian
Orthodox Church in Great Britain and Ireland and is led by
Bishop Matthew of Sourozh.

DIOCESE OF SOUROZH, Diocesan Office, Cathedral of the
Dormition of the Mother of God and All Saints, 67 Ennismore
Gardens, London SW7 1NH **T** 020-7584 0096
W www.sourozh.org
Diocesan Hierarch, Bishop Matthew of Sourozh

SERBIAN ORTHODOX CHURCH (PATRIARCHATE OF
SERBIA)
There are seven parishes in Great Britain and around 4,000
members. Great Britain is part of the Diocese of Great Britain
and Scandinavia, which is led by Bishop Dositey. The church
can be contacted via the church of St Sava in London.

SERBIAN ORTHODOX CHURCH IN GREAT BRITAIN,
Church of Saint Sava, 89 Lancaster Road, London W11 1QQ
T 020-7727 8367 **E** crkva@spclondon.org
W www.spclondon.org
Archpriest, Very Revd Goran Spaic

OTHER NATIONALITIES
The Patriarchates of Romania and Bulgaria (Diocese of
Western Europe) have memberships estimated at 20,000 and
2,000 respectively, while the Georgian Orthodox Church has
around 500 members. The Belarusian (membership estimated
at 2,400) and Latvian (membership of around 100).

ORIENTAL ORTHODOX CHURCHES
The term 'Oriental Orthodox Churches' is now generally
used to describe a group of six ancient eastern churches
(Armenian, Coptic, Eritrean, Ethiopian, Indian (Malankara)
and Syrian) which rejected the Christological definition of
the Council of Chalcedon (AD 451). There are around 50
million members worldwide of the Oriental Orthodox
Churches and over 20,000 in the UK.

ARMENIAN ORTHODOX CHURCH (CATHOLICOSATE
OF ETCHMIADZIN)
The Armenian Orthodox Church is led by HH Karekin II,
Catholicos of All Armenians. HG Bishop Hovakim Manukyan
was appointed Primate of the Armenian Church in the UK
and Ireland in 2015.

ARMENIAN CHURCH IN THE UK AND IRELAND, The
Armenian Vicarage, 27 Haven Green, London W5 2NZ
T 020-8998 9210 **W** www.armeniandiocese.org.uk
Primate, HG Bishop Hovakim Manukyan

COPTIC ORTHODOX CHURCH
The Coptic Orthodox Church is headed by Pope Tawadros
II, who was appointed in November 2012. There are three
dioceses in the UK: the Midlands, led by HG Bishop Missael;
Ireland, Scotland and north-east England, led by HG Bishop
Antony; and the Papal Diocese which is led by HG Bishop
Angaelos and covers all the remaining parishes in the UK.

CATHEDRAL OF ST GEORGE AT THE COPTIC
ORTHODOX CHURCH CENTRE, Shephalbury Manor,
Broadhall Way, Stevenage, Herts SG2 8NP **T** 020-7993 9001
W www.copticcentre.com
Bishop, HG Bishop Angaelos

BRITISH ORTHODOX CHURCH
The British Orthodox Church is a small autonomous
Orthodox jurisdiction, originally deriving from the Syrian
Orthodox Church. It was canonically part of the Coptic
Orthodox Patriarchate of Alexandria from 1994–2015. As it
ministers to British people, all of its services are in English.

THE BRITISH ORTHODOX CHURCH, 10 Heathwood
Gardens, Charlton, London SE7 8EP **T** 020-8854 3090
E info@britishorthodox.org **W** www.britishorthodox.org
Metropolitan, Abba Seraphim

ERITREAN ORTHODOX TEWAHEDO CHURCH
The Eritrean Orthodox Church was granted independence in
1994 by Pope Shenouda III, following the declaration of
Eritrea's independence from Ethiopia in 1993. In 2006, the
Eritrean government removed the third patriarch, Abune
Antonios, from office and imprisoned him; the government
replaced him with Abune Dioskoros in 2007, although the
Oriental Orthodox Churches continue to recognise Antonios
as the rightful patriarch. The diocesan bishop for North
America, Europe and the Middle East is HG Abune Makarios.

ETHIOPIAN ORTHODOX TAWAHEDO CHURCH
The Ethiopian Orthodox Church was administratively part of
the Coptic Orthodox Church of Alexandria until 1959, when
it was granted its own patriarch by the Coptic Orthodox
Pope of Alexandria and Patriarch of All Africa, Cyril VI. The
current patriarch is HH Abune Mathias. The church in
London was established in 1976.

ETHIOPIAN ORTHODOX TAWAHEDO CHURCH, St
Mary of Zion, PO Box 56856, London N13 5US **T** 020-8807 5885
E pc@tserhasion.org.uk **W** www.stmaryofzion.co.uk
Priest-in-Charge, Melake Sion Habte Mariam

INDIAN ORTHODOX CHURCH
The Indian Orthodox Church, also known as the Malankara
Orthodox Church, traces its origins to the first century. The

head of the Malankara Orthodox Church is HH Baselios Marthoma Paulose II. The mother church of all the parishes in the UK and the Republic of Ireland is St Gregorios Church in London. The London parish has around 280 families as practising members.

INDIAN ORTHODOX CHURCH, St Gregorios Indian
Orthodox Church, Cranfield Road, Brockley, London SE4 1UF
T 020-8691 9456 E ioclondon@gmail.com
W www.ioclondon.co.uk
Diocesan Metropolitan, HG Dr Mathews Mar Thimothios
Vicar, Revd Fr Dr Ninan V. George

SYRIAN ORTHODOX CHURCH
The Syrian (Syriac) Orthodox Church of Antioch is an Oriental Orthodox Church based in the Eastern Mediterranean headed by HH Moran Mor Ignatius Aphrem II. The Patriarchate Vicariate in the UK is represented by HE Archbishop Mor Athanasius Toma Dawod.

SYRIAN ORTHODOX CHURCH IN THE UK, St Thomas
Cathedral, 7–11 Armstrong Road, London W3 7JL
T 020-8749 5834 E enquiry-uk@syrianorthodoxchurch.net
W www.syrianorthodoxchurch.net
Archbishop, HE Mor Athanasius Toma Dawod

PENTECOSTAL CHURCHES

Pentecostalism is inspired by the descent of the Holy Spirit upon the apostles at Pentecost. The movement began in Los Angeles, USA, in 1906 and is characterised by baptism with the Holy Spirit, divine healing, speaking in tongues (glossolalia) and a literal interpretation of the scriptures.

The Pentecostal movement in Britain dates from 1907. Initially, groups of Pentecostalists were led by laymen and did not organise formally. However, in 1915 the Elim Foursquare Gospel Alliance (more commonly called the Elim Pentecostal Church) was founded in Ireland by George Jeffreys and currently has about 550 churches, 68,500 adherents and 650 accredited ministers. In 1924 about 70 independent assemblies formed a fellowship called Assemblies of God in Great Britain and Ireland, which now incorporates around 600 churches, around 75,000 adherents and 1,000 ministers.

The Apostolic Church grew out of the 1904–5 Christian revivals in South Wales and was established in 1916. The Apostolic Church has around 90 churches, 7,000 adherents and 100 ministers in the UK. The New Testament Church of God was established in England in 1953 and has over 130 congregations, 11,000 members and over 300 ministers across England and Wales.

There are about 105 million Pentecostalists worldwide, with over 350,000 adherents in the UK.

THE APOSTOLIC CHURCH, Suite 105, Crystal House, New
Bedford Road, Luton LU1 1HS T 020-7587 1802
E admin@apostolic-church.org W www.apostolic-church.org
National Leader, Jim Jack
ASSEMBLIES OF GOD, National Ministry Centre, Mattersey,
Doncaster DN10 5HD T 017-7781 7663 E info@aog.org.uk
W www.aog.org.uk
THE ELIM PENTECOSTAL CHURCH, Elim International
Centre, De Walden Road, Malvern WR14 4DF T 0345-302 6750
W www.elim.org.uk
General Superintendent, Chris Cartwright
THE NEW TESTAMENT CHURCH OF GOD, 3 Cheyne
Walk, Northampton NN1 5PT T 01604-824222
E mmcc@ntcg.org.uk W www.ntcg.org.uk
Administrative Bishop, Donald Bolt

PRESBYTERIAN CHURCH IN IRELAND

Irish Presbyterianism traces its origins back to the Plantation of Ulster in 1606, when English and Scottish Protestants began to settle on the land confiscated from the Irish chieftains. The first presbytery was established in Ulster in 1642 by chaplains of a Scottish army that had been sent to crush a Catholic rebellion in 1641.

The Presbyterian Church in Ireland is reformed in doctrine and belongs to the World Alliance of Reformed Churches. Structurally, the 536 congregations are grouped in 19 presbyteries under the General Assembly. This body meets annually and is presided over by a moderator who is elected for one year. The ongoing work of the church is undertaken by boards under which there are specialist committees.

There are over 225,000 members and 326 active ministers of Irish presbyterian churches in Ireland and Northern Ireland.

THE PRESBYTERIAN CHURCH IN IRELAND, Assembly
Buildings, 2–10 Fisherwick Place, Belfast BT1 6DW
T 028-9032 2284 E info@presbyterianireland.org
W www.presbyterianireland.org
Moderator (2018–19), Rt. Revd Dr Charles McMullen
Clerk of Assembly and General Secretary, Revd Trevor Gribben

PRESBYTERIAN CHURCH OF WALES

The Presbyterian Church of Wales or Calvinistic Methodist Church of Wales is Calvinistic in doctrine and presbyterian in constitution. It was formed in 1811 when Welsh Calvinists severed the relationship with the established church by ordaining their own ministers. It secured its own confession of faith in 1823 and a Constitutional Deed in 1826, and since 1864 the General Assembly has met annually, presided over by a moderator elected for a year. The doctrine and constitutional structure of the Presbyterian Church of Wales was confirmed by act of parliament in 1931–2.

The Church has 20,000 members, 55 ministers and 600 congregations.

THE PRESBYTERIAN CHURCH OF WALES, Tabernacle
Chapel, 81 Merthyr Road, Whitchurch, Cardiff CF14 1DD
T 029-2062 7465 E swyddfa.office@ebcpcw.org.uk
W www.ebcpcw.cymru
Moderator (2017–18), Revd Brian Huw Jones
General Secretary, Revd Meirion Morris

RELIGIOUS SOCIETY OF FRIENDS (QUAKERS)

Quakerism is a religious denomination which was founded in the 17th century by George Fox and others in an attempt to revive what they saw as the original 'primitive Christianity'. The movement, at first called Friends of the Truth, started in the Midlands, Yorkshire and north-west England, but there are now Quakers all over the world and in 36 countries around the world. The colony of Pennsylvania, founded by William Penn, was originally a Quaker settlement.

Quakers place an emphasis on the experience of God in daily life rather than on sacraments or religious occasions. There is no church calendar. Worship is largely silent and there are no appointed ministers; the responsibility for conducting a meeting is shared equally among those present. Religious tolerance and social reform have always been important to Quakers, together with a commitment to peace and non-violence in resolving disputes.

There are more than 23,000 'friends' or Quakers in Great Britain. There are around 475 places where Quaker meetings are held, many of them Quaker-owned Friends Meeting Houses. The Britain Yearly Meeting is the name given to the central organisation of Quakers in Britain.

THE RELIGIOUS SOCIETY OF FRIENDS (QUAKERS) IN
BRITAIN, Friends House, 173–177 Euston Road, London
NW1 2BJ T 020-7663 1000 E enquiries@quaker.org.uk
W www.quaker.org.uk
General Secretary, Helen Drewery

SALVATION ARMY

The Salvation Army is an international Christian organisation working in 126 countries worldwide. As a church and registered charity, The Salvation Army is funded through donations from its members, the general public and, where appropriate, government grants.

The Salvation Army was founded by Methodists William and Catherine Booth in the East End of London in 1865 and marked its 150th anniversary on 2 July 2015. It now has around 40,000 members and 1,067 Salvation Army Officers (full-time ministers) in the UK. There are over 700 local church and community centres, 62 residential support centres for homeless people, 16 care homes for older people and six substance-misuse centres. It also runs a clothing recycling programme, charity shops, foodbanks, a prison-visiting service and a family-tracing service. In 1878 it adopted a quasi-military command structure intended to inspire and regulate its endeavours and to reflect its view that the church was engaged in spiritual warfare.

UK TERRITORIAL HEADQUARTERS, 101 Newington Causeway, London SE1 6BN **T** 020-7367 4500 **E** info@salvationarmy.org.uk **W** www.salvationarmy.org.uk *UK Territorial Leaders,* Commissioners Anthony and Gillian Cotterill

SEVENTH-DAY ADVENTIST CHURCH
The Seventh-day Adventist Church is a worldwide Christian church marked by its observance of Saturday as the Sabbath and by its emphasis on the imminent second coming of Jesus Christ. Adventists summarise their faith in '28 fundamental beliefs'.

The church grew out of the Millerite movement in the USA during the mid-19th century and was formally established in 1863. The church has a worldwide membership of over 17 million. In the UK and Ireland there are 37,917 members worshipping in around 300 churches and companies.

SEVENTH-DAY ADVENTIST CHURCH HQ, Stanborough Park, Watford WD25 9JZ **T** 01923-672251 **E** info@adventist.org.uk **W** www.adventist.org.uk *President,* Pastor Ian Sweeney *Executive Secretary,* John Sturridge

THE (SWEDENBORGIAN) NEW CHURCH
The New Church is based on the teachings of the 18th-century Swedish scientist and theologian Emanuel Swedenborg (1688–1772), who believed that Jesus Christ appeared to him and instructed him to reveal the spiritual meaning of the Bible. He claimed to have visions of the spiritual world, including heaven and hell, and conversations with angels and spirits. He published several theological works, including descriptions of the spiritual world and a Bible commentary.

Swedenborgians believe that the second coming of Jesus Christ is taking place, being not an actual physical reappearance of Christ, but rather his return in spirit. It is also believed that concurrent with our life on earth is life in a parallel spiritual world, of which we are usually unconscious until death. There are around 30,000 Swedenborgians worldwide, with around 600 members, 18 churches and five ministers in the UK.

THE GENERAL CONFERENCE OF THE NEW CHURCH, Purley Chase Centre, Purley Chase Lane, Mancetter, Atherstone CV9 2RQ **T** 01827-712370 **W** www.generalconference.org.uk

UNDEB YR ANNIBYNWYR CYMRAEG
Undeb Yr Annibynwyr Cymraeg (the Union of Welsh Independents) was formed in 1872 and is a voluntary association of Welsh Congregational churches and personal members. It is mainly Welsh-speaking. Congregationalism in Wales dates back to 1639 when the first Welsh Congregational church was opened in Gwent.

Member churches are traditionally congregationalist in organisation and Calvinistic in doctrine, although a wide range of interpretations are permitted. Each church has complete independence in the governance and administration of its affairs.

The Union has around 24,000 members, 80 ministers and 400 member churches.

UNDEB YR ANNIBYNWYR CYMRAEG, 5 Axis Court, Riverside Business Park, Swansea Vale, Swansea SA7 0AJ **T** 01792-795888 **E** undeb@annibynwyr.org **W** www.annibynwyr.org *President of the Union (2018–20),* Revd Jill-Hailey Harries *General Secretary,* Revd Dyfrig Rees

UNITED REFORMED CHURCH
The United Reformed Church (URC) was first formed by the union of most of the Congregational churches in England and Wales with the Presbyterian Church of England in 1972. It is Calvinistic in doctrine, and its followers form independent self-governing congregations bound under God by covenant, a principle laid down in the writings of Robert Browne (1550–1633). From the late 16th century the movement was driven underground by persecution, but the cause was defended at the Westminster Assembly in 1643 and the Savoy Declaration of 1658 laid down its principles. Congregational churches formed county associations and in 1832 these associations merged to form the Congregational Union of England and Wales.

In the 1960s there was close cooperation locally and nationally between congregational and presbyterian churches. This led to union negotiations and a Scheme of Union, supported by an act of parliament in 1972. In 1981 a further unification took place, with the Reformed Association of Churches of Christ becoming part of the URC. In 2000 a third union took place, with the Congregational Union of Scotland. At its basis the URC reflects local church initiative and responsibility with a conciliar pattern of oversight.

The URC is divided into 13 synods, each with a synod moderator. There are 1,406 churches which serve 49,517 members. There are 401 stipendiary ministers.

The General Assembly is the central body, and comprises around 400 representatives, mainly appointed by the synods, of which half are lay persons and half are ministers. Since 2010 the General Assembly has met biennially to elect two moderators (one lay and one ordained), who then become the public representatives of the URC.

UNITED REFORMED CHURCH, 86 Tavistock Place, London WC1H 9RT **T** 020-7916 2020 **E** urc@urc.org.uk **W** www.urc.org.uk *Moderators of the General Assembly 2018–20,* Revd Nigel Uden; Derek Estill *General Secretary,* Revd John Proctor

WESLEYAN REFORM UNION
The Wesleyan Reform Union was founded by Methodists who left or were expelled from Wesleyan Methodism in 1849 following a period of internal conflict. Its doctrine is conservative evangelical and its organisation is congregational, each church having complete independence in the government and administration of its affairs. The union has around 1,250 members, 20 ministers and 96 churches.

THE WESLEYAN REFORM UNION, Church Street, Jump, Barnsley S74 0HZ **T** 01226-891608 **E** admin@thewru.co.uk **W** www.thewru.com *President,* Revd Colin Braithwaite

NON-TRINITARIAN CHURCHES

CHRISTADELPHIAN
Christadelphians believe that the Bible is the word of God and that it reveals both God's dealings with mankind in the past and his plans for the future. These plans centre on the work of Jesus Christ, who it is believed will return to Earth to establish God's kingdom. The Christadelphian group was founded in the USA in the 1850s by Englishman Dr John Thomas.

THE CHRISTADELPHIAN MAGAZINE AND PUBLISHING ASSOCIATION, 404 Shaftmoor Lane, Hall Green, Birmingham B28 8SZ **T** 0121-777 6328 **W** www.thechristadelphian.com

CHURCH OF CHRIST, SCIENTIST

The Church of Christ, Scientist was founded by Mary Baker Eddy in the USA in 1879 to 'reinstate primitive Christianity and its lost element of healing'. Christian Science teaches the need for spiritual regeneration and salvation from sin, but it is best known for its reliance on prayer alone in the healing of sickness. Adherents believe that such healing is the result of divine laws, or divine science, and is in direct line with that practised by Jesus Christ (revered, not as God, but as the son of God) and by the early Christian church.

The denomination consists of The First Church of Christ, Scientist, in Boston, Massachusetts, USA ('The Mother Church') and its branch churches in almost 80 countries worldwide. The Bible and Mary Baker Eddy's book, *Science and Health with Key to the Scriptures,* are used for daily spiritual guidance and healing by all members and are read at services. There are no clergy; those engaged in full-time healing are called Christian Science practitioners, of whom there are around 1,500 worldwide.

No membership figures are available, since Mary Baker Eddy felt that numbers are no measure of spiritual vitality and ruled that such statistics should not be published. There are almost 2,000 branch churches worldwide, including 100 in the UK.

CHRISTIAN SCIENCE COMMITTEE ON PUBLICATION UK AND IRELAND, 90 Long Acre, London WC2E 9RZ **T** 020-8150 0245 **E** londoncs@csps.com **W** http://ukchristianscience.com
District Manager for the UK and Ireland, Robin Harragin Hussey

CHURCH OF JESUS CHRIST OF LATTER-DAY SAINTS

The Church of Jesus Christ of Latter-day Saints ('Mormons') was founded in New York State, USA, in 1830, and came to Britain in 1837.

Mormons are Christians who claim to belong to the 'restored church' of Jesus Christ. They believe that true Christianity died when the last original apostle died, but that it was given back to the world by God and Jesus Christ through Joseph Smith, the church's founder and first president. They accept and use the Bible as scripture, but believe in continuing revelation from God; Mormons also use additional scriptures, including *The Book of Mormon: Another Testament of Jesus Christ.* The importance of the family is central to the church's beliefs and practices. Polygamy was formally discontinued in 1890.

The church has no paid ministry: local congregations are headed by a leader chosen from among their number. The world governing body, based in Utah, USA, is led by a president, believed to be the chosen prophet, and his two counsellors. There are over 15 million members worldwide, with 185,848 members and 333 congregations in the UK.

THE CHURCH OF JESUS CHRIST OF LATTER-DAY SAINTS, London Temple Visitors' Centre, West Park Road, Newchapel, Surrey RH7 6HW **T** 01342-832759 **W** www.lds.org.uk

JEHOVAH'S WITNESSES

The movement now known as Jehovah's Witnesses grew from a Bible study group formed by Charles Taze Russell in 1872 in Pennsylvania, USA. In 1896 it adopted the name of the Watch Tower Bible and Tract Society, and in 1931 its members became known as Jehovah's Witnesses.

Jehovah's Witnesses believe in the Bible as the word of God, and consider it to be inspired and historically accurate. They take the scriptures literally, except where there are obvious indications that they are figurative or symbolic, and reject the doctrine of the Trinity. Witnesses also believe that all those approved of by Jehovah will have eternal life on a cleansed and beautified earth; only 144,000 will go to heaven to rule with Jesus Christ. They believe that the second coming of Christ began in 1914, that his thousand-year reign over the earth is imminent, and that armageddon (a final battle in which evil will be defeated) will precede Christ's rule of peace. Jehovah's Witnesses refuse to take part in military service and do not accept blood transfusions.

The world governing body is based in New York, USA. There is no paid ministry, but each congregation has elders assigned to look after various duties and every Witness takes part in the public ministry in their neighbourhood. There are 8.3 million Jehovah's Witnesses worldwide, with around 136,000 Witnesses in Great Britain organised into around 1,500 congregations.

BRITISH HEADQUARTERS, The Ridgeway, London NW7 1RN **T** 020-8906 2211 **W** www.jw.org/en

UNITARIAN AND FREE CHRISTIAN CHURCHES

Unitarianism has its historical roots in the Judaeo-Christian tradition but rejects the deity of Christ and the doctrine of the Trinity. There is no fixed creed and it allows the individual to take insights from all of the world's faiths and philosophies. It is accepted that beliefs may evolve in the light of personal experience.

Unitarian communities first became established in Poland and Transylvania in the 16th century. The first avowedly Unitarian place of worship in Britain opened in London in 1774. The General Assembly of Unitarian and Free Christian Churches came into existence in 1928 as the result of the amalgamation of two earlier organisations.

There are around 3,400 Unitarians in Great Britain in 170 self-governing congregations and fellowship groups.

GENERAL ASSEMBLY OF UNITARIAN AND FREE CHRISTIAN CHURCHES, Essex Hall, 1–6 Essex Street, London WC2R 3HY **T** 020-7240 2384 **E** info@unitarian.org.uk **W** www.unitarian.org.uk
President (2018–19), Joan Cook
Chief Officer, Derek McAuley

COMMUNICATIONS

POSTAL SERVICES

Under the Postal Services Act 2011 Royal Mail was privatised on 15 October 2013 when it was listed on the London Stock Exchange. The government initially retained a 30 per cent stake in Royal Mail, however it sold its remaining shares in 2015. Royal Mail Group ltd operates Royal Mail, Parcelforce Worldwide and General Logistics Systems (GLS). Under the same 2011 Act, the Post Office became independent of Royal Mail Group on 1 April 2012. The government, through the Department for Business, Energy and Industrial Strategy (BEIS), holds a special share in Post Office ltd. The Post Office has a strategic agreement in place to continue to supply Royal Mail products and services through its network and also has the same group holding company (Royal Mail Holdings plc) which holds shares in both Post Office ltd and Royal Mail Group ltd. Neither Royal Mail Holdings plc, nor BEIS, have any involvement in the day-to-day operations of the Post Office.

Royal Mail is the sole provider of the 'universal service': postal products and associated minimum service standards that must be available to all addresses in the UK.

Following the passing of the Postal Services Act 2011, the Office of Communications (OFCOM) assumed regulatory responsibility for postal services. OFCOM's primary responsibility is to secure the provision of a universal postal service with regard to its financial sustainability.

ROYAL MAIL GROUP LTD, 100 Victoria Embankment, London EC4Y 0HQ T 0345-774 0740
   W www.royalmailgroup.com

OFCOM, Riverside House, 2A Southwark Bridge Road, London SE1 9HA T 0207-981 3000 W www.ofcom.org.uk

PRICING IN PROPORTION

Since 2006 Royal Mail has priced mail according to its size as well as its weight. The system is intended to reflect the fact that larger, bulkier items cost more to handle than smaller, lighter ones. There are five basic categories of correspondence:

LETTER: *Length* up to 240mm, *width* up to 165mm, *thickness* up to 5mm, *weight* up to 100g; eg most cards and postcards

LARGE LETTER: *Length* up to 353mm, *width* up to 250mm, *thickness* up to 25mm, *weight* up to 750g; eg most A4 documents and magazines

SMALL PARCEL: *Length* up to 450mm, *width* up to 350mm, *thickness* up to 160mm, *weight* up to 2kg; eg books, clothes and gifts

MEDIUM PARCEL: *Length* up to 610mm, *width* up to 460mm, *thickness* up to 460mm, *weight* up to 20kg; eg gifts, shoes, heavy or bulky items

ROLLED OR CYLINDER SHAPED PARCEL: The length of the item plus twice the diameter must not exceed 104cm, with the greatest dimension being no more than 90cm; eg posters and prints

Items larger than those listed above can only be sent via Parcelforce:

STANDARD PARCELFORCE: *Length* up to 150cm, with a combined length and girth of less than 300cm, *weight* up to 30kg

LARGE PARCELFORCE*: *Length* up to 250cm, with a combined length and girth of less than 500cm, *weight* up to 30kg

* Only available at selected Post Office branches

INLAND POSTAL SERVICES

Following are the details of a number of popular postal services along with prices correct as at April 2018. For a full list of prices *see* W www.royalmail.com

FIRST AND SECOND CLASS

Format	Maximum weight	First class	Second class
Letter/postcard	100g	£0.67	£0.58
Large letter	100g	£1.01	£0.79
	250g	£1.40	£1.26
	500g	£1.87	£1.64
	750g	£2.60	£2.22
Small parcel	1,000g	£3.45	£2.95
	2,000g	£5.50	£2.95
Medium parcel	1,000g	£5.75	£5.05
	2,000g	£8.95	£5.05
	5,000g	£15.85	£13.75
	10,000g	£21.90	£20.25
	20,000g	£33.40	£28.55

First class post is normally delivered on the following working day and second class within three working days. Prices are exempt from VAT.

STANDARD PARCELFORCE

Maximum weight	Lowest tariff*
2kg	£12.12
5kg	£13.14
10kg	£16.62
15kg	£23.40
20kg	£28.80
25kg	£40.08
30kg	£44.22

* The rate listed includes VAT and is for delivery within 48 hours

OVERSEAS POSTAL SERVICES

For charging purposes Royal Mail divides the world into four zones: UK, Europe, World Zone 1 and World Zone 2. There is a complete listing on the Royal Mail website (W www.royalmail.com/international-zones)

Europe: Albania, Andorra, Armenia, Austria, Azerbaijan, Azores, Balearic Islands, Belarus, Belgium, Bosnia and Hercegovina, Bulgaria, Canary Islands, Corsica, Croatia, Cyprus, Czech Rep., Denmark, Estonia, Faroe Islands, Finland, France, Georgia, Germany, Gibraltar, Greece, Greenland, Hungary, Iceland, Irish Rep., Italy, Kazakhstan, Kosovo, Kyrgyzstan, Latvia, Liechtenstein, Lithuania, Luxembourg, Macedonia, Madeira, Malta, Moldova, Monaco, Montenegro, Netherlands, Norway, Poland, Portugal, Romania, Russia, San Marino, Serbia, Slovakia, Slovenia, Spain, Sweden, Switzerland, Tajikistan, Turkey, Turkmenistan, Ukraine, Uzbekistan, Vatican City State

World Zone 1: N. America, S. America, Africa, the Middle East, the Far East and S. E. Asia

World Zone 2: Australia, British Indian Ocean Territory, Fiji, French Polynesia, Kiribati, Laos, Macau, Nauru, New Caledonia, New Zealand, Palau, Papua New Guinea, Pitcairn Islands, Singapore, Solomon Islands, Tonga, Tuvalu, Samoa

INTERNATIONAL ECONOMY MAIL RATES*

Maximum weight	Standard tariff
Letters up to 100g†	
10g	£1.10
20g	£1.10
100g	£1.45

* Formerly Surface Mail
† Can only be sent by International Economy to destinations outside of Europe

Maximum weight	Large letters	Small parcels/ printed papers
100g	£2.60	£3.90
250g	£3.80	£4.20
500g	£4.85	£6.10
750g	£5.90	£7.15
1,000g	–	£8.55
2,000g	–	£12.05

Printed papers only add £1.15 for each additional 250g, or part thereof, up to 5,000g

INTERNATIONAL STANDARD MAIL RATES*

Weight up to and including	Europe	World Zone 1	World Zone 2
Letters			
10g	£1.25	£1.25	£1.25
20g	£1.25	£1.45	£1.44
100g	£1.55	£2.25	£2.25
Large letters			
100g	£2.65	£3.30	£3.45
250g	£3.85	£4.85	£5.15
500g	£4.90	£7.10	£7.50
750g	£5.95	£9.15	£9.70
Small parcels and printed papers			
100g	£4.15	£4.85	£5.25
250g	£4.45	£5.55	£6.05
500g	£6.20	£8.50	£9.20
750g	£7.45	£10.95	£11.65
1,000g	£8.65	£13.35	£14.10
2,000g	£12.10	£18.30	£20.05

Printed papers only add £1.15 for Europe, £1.70 for World Zone 1 or £1.90 for World Zone 2 for each additional 250g, or part thereof, up to 5,000g

* Formerly Airmail

SPECIAL DELIVERY SERVICES

INTERNATIONAL TRACKED AND SIGNED FOR SERVICES

There are various services available: *International Tracked & Signed* provides full end-to-end tracking, signature on delivery and online delivery confirmation to over 60 destinations; *International Tracked* provides the same, but without a signature on delivery, to over 50 destinations; and International Signed is tracked within the UK, a signature is taken on delivery and is available to over 155 destinations. All Tracked and Signed For services deliver to Europe within 3–5 working days, and worldwide within 5–7 working days. Proof of posting and compensation up to £50 is provided as standard. Additional compensation up to £250 can be provided for an extra fee.

SAME DAY

A courier service which provides same day delivery of urgent items in most places in the UK. With collection within the hour of booking, satellite tracking, delivery confirmation and automatic compensation up to £2,500, and for an additional fee, up to £10,000, the service is charged on a loaded mile basis T 0330-088 5522

SIGNED FOR

A service which offers proof of delivery including a signature from the receiver and compensation cover up to £50. The first class service is delivered the next working day and prices vary from £1.77 to £34.40 depending on the size and weight of the item. The second class service allows two to three working days for delivery with charges of £1.68 to £29.55.

SPECIAL DELIVERY GUARANTEED

A guaranteed next working day delivery service by 9am or 1pm with a refund option guaranteed for late delivery. With many options available, Royal Mail offers a full list of prices online W www.royalmail.com/personal/uk-delivery/special-delivery

OTHER SERVICES

KEEPSAFE

Mail is held for up to two months while the addressee is away, and is delivered when the addressee returns. Prices start at £14.00 for 10 days up to £75.00 for 100 days.

PASSPORT CHECK & SEND

For a fee of £9.75 passport applications are checked to ensure they meet the requirements set by HM Passport Office and are dispatched by special delivery. For further information *see* W www.postoffice.co.uk

POST OFFICE BOX

A Post Office (PO) Box provides a short and memorable alternative address. Mail is held at a local delivery office until the addressee is ready to collect it, or delivered to a street address for an extra fee. Prices start at £152.40 for six months or £267.00 for a year or a monthly fee of £29.40.

POSTCODE FINDER

Customers can search an online database to find UK postcodes and addresses. For more information *see* Royal Mail's postcode finder W www.royalmail.com/postcode-finder

REDELIVERY

Customers can request a redelivery of an item for up to 18 days if it was unable to be delivered and the person is unable to collect from the address on the delivery notification card. A 48-hour notice period is required for redelivery. Redelivery can be arranged to the customer's house, an alternative local address or, for a fee of £0.70 payable on collection, to a local post office branch.

REDIRECTION

Customers may arrange the redirection of their mail via post, at the Post Office or online, subject to verification of their identity. The service is available for 0–3 months, 3–6 months or 6–12 months at varying prices depending on the location of delivery. A full price list is available at W www.royalmail.com/personal/receiving-mail/redirection

TRACK AND TRACE

An online service for customers to track the progress of items sent using any special delivery tracked and signed for service. It is accessible from W www.royalmail.com/track-your-item

CONTACTS

Parcelforce Worldwide T 0344-800 4466
W www.parcelforce.com
Post Office enquiries T 0345-722 3355 W www.postoffice.co.uk

TELECOMMUNICATIONS

Mobile network technology has improved dramatically since the launch in 1985 of the first-generation global system for mobile communications (GSM), which offered little or no data capability. In 1992 Vodafone launched a new GSM network, usually referred to as 2G or second generation, which used digital encoding and allowed voice and low-speed data communications. This technology was extended, via the enhanced data transfer rate of 2.5G, to 3G – a family of mobile standards that provide high bandwidth support to applications such as voice- and video-calling, high-speed data transfer, television streaming and full internet access. Most recently, a 4G superfast mobile spectrum was rolled out, which delivers speeds of up to 100 megabits per second (Mbps), allowing for faster download speeds on a range of devices.

In February 2015, OFCOM stated that 5G data connections could be available in the UK by 2020 and phone manufacturers have announced that they are working with the chip manufacturer Qualcomm to bring out 5G-ready devices in 2019. In December 2017, the organisation that governs cellular standards, The 3rd Generation Partnership Project (3GPP), signed off on a universal standard, called 5G NR. Despite these developments, it is expected to be a while before network providers are ready to roll out widespread coverage.

FOURTH GENERATION (4G) AND WI-FI

In March 2011 OFCOM announced plans for the auction of additional spectrum (the airwaves on which all communications rely) to provide the necessary capacity for 4G technology in the UK. OFCOM originally aimed to begin the auction in early 2012, but following a consultation regarding the proposals in 2011, the auction did not take place until February 2013. The spectrum was auctioned in two bands – 800 MHz and 2.6 GHz – which lie within the 'sweetspot', the frequency in greatest demand. This combination of low and high frequencies provides the potential to cope with high demand of 4G services. The auction raised £2.34bn for HM Treasury, less than the £3.5bn that was forecast by the Office for Budget Responsibility, and considerably less than the 3G auction in 2000 which raised £22bn. The winning bidders for the distribution of 4G mobile broadband were Everything Everywhere (EE), Hutchison 3G UK (3), Niche Spectrum Ventures (a BT subsidiary), Telefonica (O2) and Vodafone.

4G coverage was expected to cover 98 per cent of the UK population indoors and above that when outdoors. However, according to a survey taken by OpenSignal in conjunction with consumer watchdog Which? in April 2017, smartphone users in the UK could only access their 4G network 65 per cent of the time on average. The speeds offered by 4G are approximately four times faster than 3G networks which allows for higher quality and faster streaming of media such as TV and films. The average download speed of 4G across all four network providers is 21.3Mbps, whereas the figure for 3G is approximately 5Mbps.

EE was the first operator to launch 4G in late 2012 and by April 2013 the service was available in ten cities where the broadband speed was doubled to more than 20Mbps. O2 and Vodafone subsequently launched their 4G networks in late August 2013 while 3 began their service in December 2013. As at autumn 2017 EE provided the fastest 4G connection with an average download speed of 29Mbps, slightly slower than its previous average speed in April 2017 of 32Mbps; 3, Vodafone and O2 offered average download speeds of 22Mbps, 19Mbps and 15Mbps respectively.

The number of Wi-Fi hotspots around the world continued to increase with approximately 290 million public hotspots available worldwide as at April 2018. There is Wi-Fi access at over 260 London Underground stations, available in ticket halls, corridors and platforms. Additionally Wi-Fi is also available at 79 London Overground stations.

FIXED-LINE SERVICES

The total number of fixed-line services in the UK remained fairly static in 2016 at a total of 33.5 million connections. However, fixed voice call minutes continued to decline, from 74 billion minutes in 2015 to 65 billion minutes in 2016; part of a steady decline from the 141 billion minutes recorded in 2008. The number of business lines also fell by 7 per cent in 2016, largely due to the increasing use of voice over internet protocol (VoIP) services such as Skype.

By June 2016, 44 per cent of all fixed broadband connections were able to receive actual download speeds of 30Mbps or more, up from 38 per cent a year previously. Average data use per fixed line residential broadband connection increased by 36 per cent from June 2015 to 132G in June 2016.

MOBILE COMMUNICATIONS

At the end of 2016 the total number of mobile subscriptions in the UK had only slightly increased by 0.1 million to 92.0 million since the previous year. The volume of SMS and MMS messages sent continued to decline for the fourth year in a row, decreasing by 5.6 billion messages (5.5 per cent) to 96.4 billion messages in 2016. The decline in text messaging is likely to be a result of the increasing number of smartphones being used for communication, with social media platforms and instant messaging services such as Whatsapp and iMessenger providing alternatives to SMS. Total outgoing mobile calls increased by 8 billion minutes (5.7 per cent) in 2016. Average data use per mobile connection increased by 44 per cent to 1.3G.

By the end of 2016, 52.4 million mobile connections could access 4G, which represented an increase of 13 million (32.9 per cent) since the previous year and constituted 62 per cent of all UK mobile connections. 4G coverage improved in 2017, with 58 per cent of all indoor premises covered by all operators, up from 40 per cent in 2016. The ability to make telephone calls on a mobile continues to vary according to location; 90 per cent of urban UK premises are able to make indoor calls on all four networks, as opposed to 57 per cent in rural areas.

MOBILE PHONE USAGE

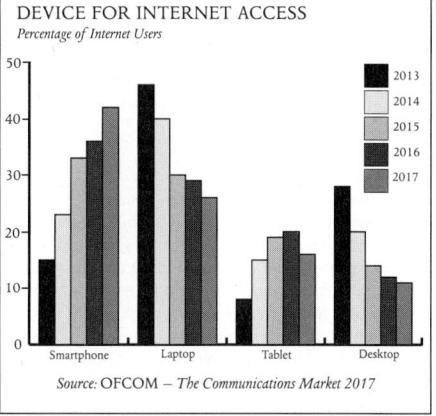

DEVICE FOR INTERNET ACCESS
Percentage of Internet Users

Source: OFCOM – *The Communications Market 2017*

In 2017 the mobile phone was considered the most important device for accessing the internet by adults aged between 16 and 54 (57 per cent). The most important device for internet access for those aged 55+ was the laptop (31 per cent). Around one in ten UK internet users considered a desktop PC their most important device for accessing the internet, and there was a decrease in the proportion of people considering a tablet to be their most important device (from 20 per cent to 16 per cent).

HEALTH

In 1999 the Independent Expert Group on Mobile Phones (IEGMP) was established to examine the possible effects on health of mobile phones, base stations and transmitters. The main findings of the IEGMP's report *Mobile Phones and Health*, published in May 2000, were:

- exposure to radio frequency radiation below guideline levels did not cause adverse health effects to the general population
- the use of mobile phones by drivers of any vehicle can increase the chance of accidents
- the widespread use of mobile phones by children for non-essential calls should be discouraged as if there are unrecognised adverse health effects children may be more vulnerable
- there is no general risk to the health of people living near to base stations on the basis that exposures are expected to be much lower than guidelines set by the International Commission on Non-Ionising Radiation Protection

The government set up the Mobile Telecommunications Health and Research (MTHR) programme in 2001 to undertake independent research into the possible health risks from mobile telephone technology. The MTHR programme published its report in September 2007 concluding that, in the short term, neither mobile phones nor base stations have been found to be associated with any biological or adverse health effects. An international cohort study into the possible long-term health effects of mobile phone use was launched by the MTHR in April 2010. The study is known as COSMOS and aims to follow the health of 250,000 mobile phone users from five countries over 20 to 30 years. Details of the study can be found on the COSMOS website (W www.ukcosmos.org).

A national measurement programme to ensure that emissions from mobile phone base stations do not exceed the ICNIRP guideline levels is overseen by OFCOM and annual audits of these levels can be found on the sitefinder part of its website. The Health Protection Agency (HPA), part of Public Health England, is responsible for providing information and advice on the health effects of electromagnetic fields, including those emitted from mobile phones and base stations. In April 2012, the HPA's independent Advisory Group on Non-ionising Radiation published a report concluding that there was no convincing evidence that mobile phone technologies cause adverse effects on human health.

SAFETY WHILE DRIVING

Under legislation that came into effect in December 2003 it is illegal for drivers to use a hand-held mobile phone while driving. Since March 2017 the fixed penalty for using a hand-held mobile device while driving is £200 and six penalty points. The same fixed penalty can also be issued to a driver for not having proper control of a vehicle while using a hands-free device. If the police or driver chooses to take the case to court rather than issue or accept a fixed penalty notice, the driver may be disqualified from driving in addition to a maximum fine of £1,000 for car drivers and £2,500 for drivers of buses, coaches or heavy goods vehicles. The only exceptions for using a mobile phone while driving are to call the emergency services, or when the driver is safely parked.

REGULATION

Under the Communications Act 2003, OFCOM is the independent regulator and competition authority for the UK communications industries, with responsibilities across television, radio, telecommunications and wireless communications services. Competition in the communications market is also regulated by the Competition and Markets Authority, although OFCOM takes the lead in competition investigations in the UK market. The Competition Appeal Tribunal hears appeals against OFCOM's decisions.

CONTACTS

OFCOM, Riverside House, 2A Southwark Bridge Road, London SE1 9HA T 020-7981 3000 W www.ofcom.org.uk

INTERNET

At the beginning of 2017, 83 per cent of UK adults (aged 16+) had broadband internet access at home. There were 25.3 million fixed broadband connections in the UK at the end of 2016, 44 per cent of which were superfast broadband. Home internet access varies significantly according to age group, with 95 per cent of those aged 16 to 24 reporting they have home internet access, as opposed only 53 per cent of those aged over 75. The most frequently cited reason for not having internet access was that they did not need it, with 90 per cent of those aged over 54 citing this. Of adults without home internet access, just over 10 per cent said they were likely to get it in the next year.

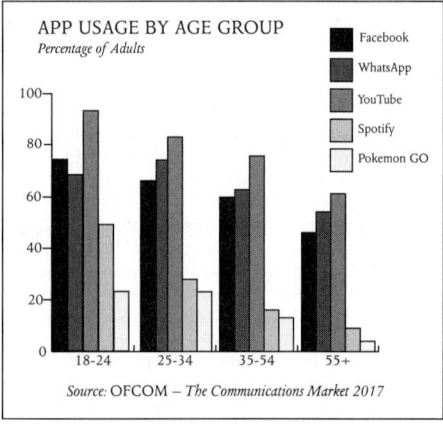

APP USAGE BY AGE GROUP
Percentage of Adults

Source: OFCOM – *The Communications Market 2017*

In 2017 the most popular internet activity was general browsing, with 80 per cent of adults having browsed the internet in the past week. Sending emails was the second most common activity, with 76 per cent of adults reporting to have done this in the last week. Just under half of adults (48 per cent) reported they had shopped online in the last week, a reduction from 67 per cent in 2016, and around half of UK adults had used online banking and social media in the last week. In 2016, 42 per cent of internet users claimed to use the same password for most, if not all websites.

Apps have become an important part of communication services. A survey of 1,200 panellists by OFCOM over December 2016 showed that:

- social network users opened their apps on average almost 13 times a day
- use of social and communications apps was high among all age groups, with 90 per cent using communications apps
- use of social media apps declines with age; 91 per cent of 18–24-year-olds used at least one app compared to 69 per cent of those aged over 54

- at least 60 per cent of all age groups used YouTube
- of total mobile phone users, 61 per cent used Facebook Messenger and 50 per cent used Whatsapp

In March 2017, the organisation with the largest online audience was Google (48.3 million visitors), closely followed by Microsoft and Facebook (41.9 million and 40.6 million visitors respectively). YouTube and Google both had similar unique visitor counts at around 40 million, 10 million more unique visitors than Google Maps (30.9 million), the third most visited site. UK visitors alone spent nearly 755 million hours browsing Google websites and apps in one month.

GLOSSARY OF TERMS

The following is a list of selected internet terms. It is by no means exhaustive but is intended to cover those that the average computer user might encounter.

BANNER AD: An advertisement on a web page that links to a corresponding website when clicked.

BLOG: Short for 'web log' – an online personal journal that is frequently updated and intended to be read by the public. Blogs are kept by 'bloggers' and are commonly available as RSS feeds.

BOOKMARKS: A method of storing links or automatic pathways within web browsers which allow a user to quickly return to a webpage. Referred to as 'Favourites' in Internet Explorer.

BROWSER: Typically refers to a 'web browser' program that allows a computer user to view web page content on their computer, eg Firefox, Internet Explorer or Safari.

CLICK-THROUGH: The number of times a web user 'clicks through' a paid advertisement link to the corresponding website.

CLOUD COMPUTING: The use of IT resources as an on-demand service across a network; through cloud computing, software, advanced computation and archived information can be accessed remotely, without the user needing local dedicated hardware.

COOKIE: A piece of information placed on a user's hard disk by a web server. Cookies contain data about the user's activity on a website, and are returned to the server whenever a browser makes further requests. They are important for remembering information such as login and registration details, 'shopping cart' data, user preferences etc, and are often set to expire after a fixed period.

DOMAIN: A set of words or letters, separated by dots, used to identify an internet server, eg www.whitakersalmanack.com, where 'www' denotes a web (http) server, 'whitakersalmanack' denotes the organisation name and 'com' denotes that the organisation is a company.

ENCRYPTION: The conversion of information or data into a code in order to prevent unauthorised access.

FIREWALL: A protection system designed to prevent unauthorised access to or from a private network.

FTP: File Transfer Protocol – a set of network rules enabling a user to exchange files with a remote server.

HACKER: A person who attempts to break or 'hack' into websites. Motives typically involve the desire to procure personal information such as addresses, passwords or credit card details. Hackers may also delete code or incorporate traces of malicious code to damage the functionality of a website.

HIT: A single request from a web browser for a single item from a web server. In order for a web browser to display a page that contains three graphics, four 'hits' would occur at the server: one for the HTML page and one for each of the three graphics. Therefore the number of hits on a website is not synonymous with the number of visitors.

HTML: HyperText Mark-up Language – a programming language used to denote or mark up how an internet page should be presented to a user from an HTTP server via a web browser.

HTTP: HyperText Transfer Protocol – an internet protocol whereby a web server sends web pages, images and files to a web browser.

HYPERLINK: A piece of specially coded text that users can click on to navigate to the web page, or element of a web page, associated with that link's code. Links are typically distinguished through the use of bold, underlined or differently coloured text.

JAVA: A programming language used widely on the internet.

MALWARE: A combination of the words 'malicious' and 'software'. Malware is software designed with the intention of infiltrating a computer and damaging its system.

OPEN-SOURCE: Describes a computer program that has its source code (the instructions that make up a program) freely available for viewing and modification.

PAGERANK: A link analysis algorithm used by search engines that assigns a numerical value based on a website's relevance and reputation. In general, a site with a higher pagerank has more traffic than a site with a lower one.

PHISHING: The fraudulent practice of sending emails to acquire personal information by masquerading as a legitimate company.

PODCAST: A form of audio and video broadcasting using the internet. Although the word is a portmanteau of 'iPod' and broadcasting, podcasting does not require the use of an iPod. A podcaster creates a list of files and makes it available in the RSS 2.0 format. The list can then be obtained using podcast 'retriever' software which makes the files available to digital devices (including iPods); users may then listen or watch at their convenience.

RSS FEED: Rich Site Summary or RDF Site Summary or Real Simple Syndication – a commonly used protocol for syndication and sharing of content, originally developed to facilitate the syndication of news articles, now widely used to share the content of blogs.

SEO: Search engine optimisation – the process of optimising the content of a web page to ensure that it is indexed by search engines.

SERVER: A node on a network that provides service to the terminals on the network. These computers have higher hardware specifications, ie more resources and greater speed, in order to handle large amounts of data.

SOCIAL NETWORKING: The practice of using a web-hosted service such as Facebook or Twitter to upload and share content and build friendship networks.

SPAM: A term used for unsolicited, generally junk, email.

TRAFFIC: The number of visitors to a website.

TWITTER: An online microblogging service that allows users to stay connected through the exchange of 140-character posts, known as 'tweets'.

URL: Uniform Resource Locator – address of a file accessible on the internet, eg http://www.whitakersalmanack.com

USER-GENERATED CONTENT (UGC): Refers to various media content produced or primarily influenced by end-users, as opposed to traditional media producers such as licensed broadcasters and production companies. These forms of media include digital video, blogging, podcasting, mobile phone photography and wikis.

WIKI: A website or database developed collaboratively by a community of users, allowing any user to add or edit content.

CONSERVATION AND HERITAGE

NATIONAL PARKS

ENGLAND AND WALES

There are nine national parks in England, and three in Wales. In addition, the Norfolk and Suffolk Broads are considered to have equivalent status to a national park. Under the National Parks and Access to the Countryside Act 1949, as clarified by the Natural Environment and Rural Communities Act 2006, the two purposes of the national parks are to conserve and enhance the parks' natural beauty, wildlife and cultural heritage, and to promote opportunities for the understanding and enjoyment of the special qualities of national parks by the public. If there is a conflict between the two purposes, then conservation takes precedence.

Natural England is the statutory body that has the power to designate national parks in England, and Natural Resources Wales (formerly Countryside Council for Wales) is responsible for national parks in Wales. Designations in England are confirmed by the Secretary of State for Environment, Food and Rural Affairs and those in Wales by the Welsh government. The designation of a national park does not affect the ownership of the land or remove the rights of the local community. The majority of the land in the national parks is owned by private landowners (around 75 per cent) or by bodies such as the National Trust and the Forestry Commission. The national park authorities own only a small percentage of the land themselves.

The Environment Act 1995 replaced the existing national park boards and committees with free-standing national park authorities (NPAs). NPAs are the sole local planning authorities for their areas and as such influence land use and development, and deal with planning applications. NPAs are responsible for carrying out the statutory purposes of national parks stated above.

In pursuing these purposes they have a statutory duty to seek to foster the economic and social well-being of the communities within national parks. The NPAs publish management plans setting out overarching policies for their area and appoint their own officers and staff.

The Broads Authority was established under the Norfolk and Suffolk Broads Act 1988 and meets the requirement for the authority to have a navigation function in addition to a regard for the needs of agriculture, forestry and the economic and social interests of those who live or work in the Broads.

MEMBERSHIP
Membership of English NPAs comprises local authority appointees, members directly appointed by the Secretary of State for Environment, Food and Rural Affairs and members appointed by the secretary after consultation with local parishes. Under the Natural Environment and Rural Communities Act 2006 every district, county or unitary authority with land in a national park is entitled to appoint at least one member unless it chooses to opt out. The total number of local authority and parish members must exceed the number of national members.

Northumberland, Pembrokeshire Coast and Snowdonia NPAs have 18 members; Dartmoor has 19; the Lake District and North York Moors have 20; the Broads has 21; Exmoor, the New Forest 22; Brecon Beacons 24; Yorkshire Dales 25; South Downs 27; and the Peak District 30.

In Wales, two-thirds of NPA members are appointed by the constituent local authorities and one-third by the Welsh government, advised by Natural Resources Wales.

FUNDING
Core funding for the English NPAs and the Broads Authority is provided by central government through the Department for Environment, Food and Rural Affairs (DEFRA) National Park Grant.

In Wales, the three national parks are funded by the Welsh government (£9.5m in 2018–19) and their constituent local authorities (£14.8m in 2018–19).

All NPAs and the Broads Authority can take advantage of grants from other bodies including lottery and European grants.

The national parks (with date that designation was confirmed) are:

BRECON BEACONS (1957), Powys (66 per cent)/
Carmarthenshire/Rhondda, Cynon and Taff/Merthyr
Tydfil/Blaenau Gwent/Monmouthshire, 1,344 sq. km/
519 sq. miles – The park is centred on the Brecon
Beacons mountain range, which includes the three highest
mountains in southern Britain (Pen y Fan, Corn Du and
Cribyn), but also includes the valleys of the rivers Usk and
Wye, the Black Mountains to the east and the Black
Mountain to the west. There are information centres at
Abergavenny and Llandovery.
National Park Authority, Plas y Ffynnon, Cambrian Way, Brecon,
Powys LD3 7HP **T** 01874-624437 **W** www.beacons-npa.gov.uk
Chief Executive, Julian Atkins
BROADS (1989), Norfolk/Suffolk, 303 sq. km/117 sq.
miles – The Broads is located between Norwich and Great

Yarmouth on the flood plains of the six rivers flowing through the area to the sea. The area is one of fens, winding waterways, woodland and marsh. The 60 or so broads are man-made, and many are connected to the rivers by dykes, providing over 200km (125 miles) of navigable waterways. There are information centres at Hoveton, Whitlingham Country Park and How Hill National Nature Reserve. There are yacht stations at Norwich, Reedham and Great Yarmouth.

Broads Authority, Yare House, 62–64 Thorpe Road, Norwich NR1 1RY **T** 01603-610734 **W** www.broads-authority.gov.uk
Chief Executive, Dr John Packman

DARTMOOR (1951), Devon, 953 sq. km/368 sq. miles – The park consists of moorland and rocky granite tors, and is rich in prehistoric remains. There are visitor centres at Haytor, Princetown (main visitor centre) and Postbridge.

National Park Authority, Parke, Bovey Tracey, Devon TQ13 9JQ **T** 01626-832093 **E** hq@dartmoor.gov.uk
W www.dartmoor.gov.uk
Chief Executive, Kevin Bishop

EXMOOR (1954), Somerset (71 per cent)/Devon, 694 sq. km/268 sq. miles – Exmoor is a moorland plateau inhabited by wild Exmoor ponies and red deer. There are many ancient remains and burial mounds. There are national park centres at Dunster, Dulverton and Lynmouth.

National Park Authority, Exmoor House, Dulverton, Somerset TA22 9HL **T** 01398-323665 **E** info@exmoor-nationalpark.gov.uk
W www.exmoor-nationalpark.gov.uk
Chief Executive, Sarah Bryan

LAKE DISTRICT (1951), Cumbria, 2,362 sq. km/912 sq. miles – The Lake District includes England's highest mountains (Scafell Pike, Helvellyn and Skiddaw) but it is most famous for its glaciated lakes. There are national park information centres at Bowness-on-Windermere, Keswick, Ullswater and a visitor centre at Brockhole, Windermere.

National Park Authority, Murley Moss, Oxenholme Road, Kendal, Cumbria LA9 7RL **T** 01539-724555
E hq@lakedistrict.gov.uk **W** www.lakedistrict.gov.uk
Chief Executive, Richard Leafe

NEW FOREST (2005), Hampshire, 570 sq. km/220 sq. miles – The forest has been protected since 1079 when it was declared a royal hunting forest. The area consists of forest, ancient woodland, heathland, farmland, coastal saltmarsh and mudflats. Much of the forest is managed by the Forestry Commission, which provides several campsites.

National Park Authority, Town Hall, Avenue Road, Lymington, Hants SO41 9ZG **T** 01590-646600
E enquiries@newforestnpa.gov.uk **W** www.newforestnpa.gov.uk
Chief Executive, Alison Barnes

NORTH YORK MOORS (1952), North Yorkshire (96 per cent)/Redcar and Cleveland, 1,434 sq. km/554 sq. miles – The park consists of dales woodland, moorland and coast, and includes the Hambleton Hills and the Cleveland Way. There are visitor centres at Danby and Sutton Bank.

National Park Authority, The Old Vicarage, Bondgate, Helmsley, York YO62 5BP **T** 01439-772700
E general@northyorkmoors.org.uk
W www.northyorkmoors.org.uk
Chief Executive, Andy Wilson

NORTHUMBERLAND (1956), Northumberland, 1,048 sq. km/404 sq. miles – The park is an area of hill country, comprising open moorland, blanket bogs and very small patches of ancient woodland, stretching from Hadrian's Wall to the Scottish border. Visitor information is available from the Sill National Landscape Discovery Centre on Hadrian's Wall.

National Park Authority, Eastburn, South Park, Hexham, Northumberland NE46 1BS **T** 01434-605555
E enquiries@nnpa.org.uk
W www.northumberlandnationalpark.org.uk
Chief Executive, Tony Gates

PEAK DISTRICT (1951), Derbyshire (64 per cent)/Staffordshire/South Yorkshire/Cheshire/West Yorkshire/Greater Manchester, 1,437 sq. km/555 sq. miles – The Peak District includes the gritstone moors of the Dark Peak, the limestone dales of the White Peak and the crags and rolling farmland of the South West Peak. There are information centres at Bakewell, Castleton, Edale and Upper Derwent.

National Park Authority, Aldern House, Baslow Road, Bakewell, Derbyshire DE45 1AE **T** 01629-816200
E customer.service@peakdistrict.gov.uk
W www.peakdistrict.gov.uk
Chief Executive, Sarah Fowler

PEMBROKESHIRE COAST (1952 and 1995), Pembrokeshire, 615 sq. km/240 sq. miles – The park includes cliffs, moorland and a number of islands, including Skomer and Ramsey, and the 186-mile Pembrokeshire Coast Path National Trail. There is a gallery and visitor centre at Oriel y Parc, St Davids. The park also manages Castell Henllys Iron Age Village and Carew Castle and Tidal Mill.

National Park Authority, Llanion Park, Pembroke Dock, Pembrokeshire SA72 6DY **T** 01646-624800
E info@pembrokeshirecoast.org.uk
W www.pembrokeshirecoast.wales
Chief Executive, Tegryn Jones

SNOWDONIA/ERYRI (1951), Gwynedd/Conwy, 2,176 sq. km/840 sq. miles – Snowdonia, which takes its name from Snowdon, is an area of deep valleys and rugged mountains. There are information centres at Aberdyfi, Beddgelert and Betws y Coed.

National Park Authority, Penrhyndeudraeth, Gwynedd LL48 6LF **T** 01766-770274 **E** parc@eyri-npa.gov.uk
W www.eyri-npa.gov.uk
Chief Executive, Emyr Williams

THE SOUTH DOWNS (2010), West Sussex/Hampshire, 1,624 sq. km/627 sq. miles – The South Downs contains a diversity of natural habitats, including flower-studded chalk grassland, ancient woodland, flood meadow, lowland heath and rare chalk heathland. There are visitor centres at Beachy Head, Queen Elizabeth Country Park in Hampshire and Seven Sisters Country Park in East Sussex.

National Park Authority, North Street, Midhurst, W. Sussex GU29 9DH **T** 01730-814810 **W** www.southdowns.gov.uk
Chief Executive, Trevor Beattie

YORKSHIRE DALES (1954), North Yorkshire (71 per cent)/Cumbria (28 per cent)/Lancashire (1 per cent), 2,179 sq. km/841 sq. miles – The Yorkshire Dales is composed primarily of limestone overlaid in places by millstone grit. The three peaks of Ingleborough, Whernside and Pen-y-ghent are within the park. There are information centres at Grassington, Hawes, Aysgarth Falls, Malham and Reeth.

National Park Authority, Yoredale, Bainbridge, Leyburn, N. Yorks DL8 3EL **T** 0300-456 0030 **E** info@yorkshiredales.org.uk
W www.yorkshiredales.org.uk
Chief Executive, David Butterworth

SCOTLAND

On 9 August 2000 the national parks (Scotland) bill received royal assent, giving parliament the ability to create national parks in Scotland. The Act gives Scottish parks wider powers than in England and Wales, including statutory responsibilities for the local economy and rural communities. The board of the Cairngorms NPA comprises 19 members; seven appointed by the Scottish ministers, a further seven nominated to the board by the five local authorities in the park area and five locally elected members. The board of Loch Lomond and the Trossachs NPA comprises 17 members; five elected by the community and 12 appointed by Scottish Ministers, six of whom are nominated by local authorities. In Scotland, the national parks are central government bodies and are wholly funded by the Scottish government. The draft budget for 2018–19 totalled £12.8m.

CAIRNGORMS (2003), North-East Scotland, 4,528 sq. km/1,748 sq. miles – The Cairngorms national park is the largest in the UK, covering around 6 per cent of Scotland. It displays a vast collection of landforms, including five of the six highest mountains in the UK and contains 25 per cent of Britain's threatened species. The near natural woodlands contain remnants of the original ancient Caledonian pine forest. There are nine visitor centres within the park.
National Park Authority, 14 The Square, Grantown-on-Spey, Morayshire PH26 3HG **T** 01479-873535
E enquiries@cairngorms.co.uk **W** www.cairngorms.co.uk
Chief Executive, Grant Moir

LOCH LOMOND AND THE TROSSACHS (2002), Argyll and Bute/Perth and Kinross/Stirling/West Dunbartonshire, 1,865 sq. km/720 sq. miles – The park boundaries encompass lochs, rivers, forests, 20 mountains above 914m (3,000ft) including Ben More and a further 20 mountains between 762m (2,500ft) and 914m (3,000ft). There is a national park centre in Balmaha and several other visitor centres across the park which are administered by VisitScotland.
National Park Authority, Carrochan, Carrochan Road, Balloch G83 8EG **T** 01389-722600 **E** info@lochlomond-trossachs.org
W www.lochlomond-trossachs.org
Chief Executive, Gordon Watson

NORTHERN IRELAND

There is a power to designate national parks in Northern Ireland under the Nature Conservation and Amenity Lands Order (Northern Ireland) 1985, but there are currently no national parks in Northern Ireland.

AREAS OF OUTSTANDING NATURAL BEAUTY

ENGLAND AND WALES

Under the National Parks and Access to the Countryside Act 1949, provision was made for the designation of areas of outstanding natural beauty (AONBs). Natural England is responsible for designating AONBs in England and Natural Resources Wales for the Welsh AONBs. Designations in England are confirmed by the Secretary of State for Environment, Food and Rural Affairs and those in Wales by the Welsh government. The Countryside and Rights of Way (CROW) Act 2000 placed greater responsibility on local authorities to protect AONBs and made it a statutory duty for relevant authorities to produce a management plan for their AONB area. The CROW Act also provided for the creation of conservation boards for larger and more complex AONBs.

The primary objective of the AONB designation is to conserve and enhance the natural beauty of the area. Where an AONB has a conservation board, it has the additional purpose of increasing public understanding and enjoyment of the special qualities of the area; the board has greater weight should there be a conflict of interests between the two. In addition, the board is also required to foster the economic and social well-being of the local communities but without incurring significant expenditure in doing so. Overall responsibility for AONBs lies with the relevant local authorities or conservation board. To coordinate planning and management responsibilities between local authorities in whose area they fall, AONBs are overseen by a joint advisory committee (or similar body) which includes representatives from the local authorities, landowners, farmers, residents and conservation and recreation groups. Core funding for AONBs is provided by central government through DEFRA, local authorities and Natural Resources Wales.

The 38 AONBs (with date designation confirmed) are:

ARNSIDE AND SILVERDALE (1972), Cumbria/ Lancashire, 75 sq. km/29 sq. miles
BLACKDOWN HILLS (1991), Devon/Somerset, 370 sq. km/143 sq. miles
CANNOCK CHASE (1958), Staffordshire, 68 sq. km/26 sq. miles
CHICHESTER HARBOUR (1964), Hampshire/West Sussex, 74 sq. km/29 sq. miles
CHILTERNS (1965; extended 1990), Bedfordshire/ Buckinghamshire/Herefordshire/Oxfordshire, 839 sq. km/324 sq. miles
CLWYDIAN RANGE AND DEE VALLEY (1985; extended 2011), Denbighshire/Flintshire, 389 sq. km/150 sq. miles
CORNWALL (1959; Camel Estuary 1983), 958 sq. km/ 370 sq. miles
COTSWOLDS (1966; extended 1990), Gloucestershire/ Oxfordshire/Warwickshire/Wiltshire/Worcestershire, 2,046 sq. km/790 sq. miles
CRANBORNE CHASE AND WEST WILTSHIRE DOWNS (1983), Dorset/Hampshire/Somerset/Wiltshire, 983 sq. km/380 sq. miles
DEDHAM VALE (1970; extended 1978, 1991), Essex/ Suffolk, 90 sq. km/35 sq. miles
DORSET (1959), Dorset/Somerset, 1,129 sq. km/436 sq. miles
EAST DEVON (1963), 268 sq. km/103 sq. miles
FOREST OF BOWLAND (1964), Lancashire/North Yorkshire, 803 sq. km/310 sq. miles
GOWER (1956), Swansea, 188 sq. km/73 sq. miles
HIGH WEALD (1983), East Sussex/Kent/Surrey/West Sussex, 1,461 sq. km/564 sq. miles
HOWARDIAN HILLS (1987), North Yorkshire, 204 sq. km/79 sq. miles
ISLE OF WIGHT (1963), 189 sq. km/73 sq. miles
ISLES OF SCILLY (1976), 16 sq. km/6 sq. miles
KENT DOWNS (1968), 878 sq. km/339 sq. miles
LINCOLNSHIRE WOLDS (1973), 558 sq. km/215 sq. miles
LLYN (1957), Gwynedd, 155 sq. km/60 sq. miles
MALVERN HILLS (1959), Gloucestershire/Worcestershire, 105 sq. km/41 sq. miles
MENDIP HILLS (1972; extended 1989), Somerset, 198 sq. km/76 sq. miles
NIDDERDALE (1994), North Yorkshire, 603 sq. km/233 sq. miles
NORFOLK COAST (1968), 451 sq. km/174 sq. miles
NORTH DEVON (1960), 171 sq. km/66 sq. miles
NORTH PENNINES (1988), Cumbria/Durham/North Yorkshire/Northumberland, 1,983 sq. km/766 sq. miles
NORTH WESSEX DOWNS (1972), Hampshire/ Oxfordshire/Wiltshire, 1,730 sq. km/668 sq. miles
NORTHUMBERLAND COAST (1958), 138 sq. km/64 sq. miles

QUANTOCK HILLS (1957), Somerset, 99 sq. km/38 sq. miles
SHROPSHIRE HILLS (1959), 804 sq. km/310 sq. miles
SOLWAY COAST (1964), Cumbria, 115 sq. km/44 sq. miles
SOUTH DEVON (1960), 337 sq. km/130 sq. miles
SUFFOLK COAST AND HEATHS (1970), 403 sq. km/156 sq. miles
SURREY HILLS (1958), 419 sq. km/162 sq. miles
TAMAR VALLEY (1995), Cornwall/Devon, 190 sq. km/73 sq. miles
WYE VALLEY (1971), Gloucestershire/Herefordshire/Monmouthshire, 326 sq. km/126 sq. miles
YNYS MON (ISLE OF ANGLESEY) (1967), 221 sq. km/85 sq. miles

NORTHERN IRELAND

The Department of Agriculture, Environment and Rural Affairs (Northern Ireland), with advice from the Council for Nature Conservation and the Countryside, designates AONBs in Northern Ireland. Dates given are those of designation.

ANTRIM COAST AND GLENS (1988), Co. Antrim, 725 sq. km/280 sq. miles
BINEVENAGH (2006), Co. Londonderry, 166 sq. km/64 sq. miles
CAUSEWAY COAST (1989), Co. Antrim, 42 sq. km/ 16 sq. miles
LAGAN VALLEY (1965), Co. Down, 39 sq. km/15 sq. miles
MOURNE (1986), Co. Down, 580 sq. km/224 sq. miles
RING OF GULLION (1991), Co. Armagh, 153 sq. km/59 sq. miles
SPERRIN (1968; extended 2008), Co. Tyrone/Co. Londonderry, 1,182 sq. km/456 sq. miles
STRANGFORD LOUGH (2010), Co. Down, 528 sq. km/ 204 sq. miles

NATIONAL SCENIC AREAS

In Scotland, national scenic areas have a broadly equivalent status to AONBs. Scottish Natural Heritage recognises areas of national scenic significance. As at June 2018, there were 40, covering a land area of 1,021,600 hectares (2,524,400 acres) and a marine area of 359,500 hectares (888,300 acres).

Development within national scenic areas is dealt with by local authorities, who are required to consult Scottish Natural Heritage concerning certain categories of development. Disagreements between Scottish Natural Heritage and local authorities are referred to the Scottish government. Land management uses can also be modified in the interest of scenic conservation.

ASSYNT-COIGACH, Highland, 90,200ha/222,884 acres
BEN NEVIS AND GLEN COE, Highland, 101,600ha/251,053 acres
CAIRNGORM MOUNTAINS, Highland/Aberdeenshire/Moray, 67,200ha/166,051 acres
CUILLIN HILLS, Highland, 21,900ha/54,115 acres
DEESIDE AND LOCHNAGAR, Aberdeenshire, 40,000ha/98,840 acres
DORNOCH FIRTH, Highland, 7,500ha/18,532 acres
EAST STEWARTRY COAST, Dumfries and Galloway, 4,500ha/11,119 acres
EILDON AND LEADERFOOT, Borders, 3,600ha/8,896 acres
FLEET VALLEY, Dumfries and Galloway, 5,300ha/13,096 acres
GLEN AFFRIC, Highland, 19,300ha/47,690 acres
GLEN STRATHFARRAR, Highland, 3,800ha/9,390 acres
HOY AND WEST MAINLAND, Orkney Islands, 14,800ha/36,571 acres
JURA, Argyll and Bute, 21,800ha/53,868 acres
KINTAIL, Highland, 15,500ha/38,300 acres
KNAPDALE, Argyll and Bute, 19,800ha/48,926 acres
KNOYDART, Highland, 39,500ha/97,604 acres
KYLE OF TONGUE, Highland, 18,500ha/45,713 acres
KYLES OF BUTE, Argyll and Bute, 4,400ha/10,872 acres
LOCH LOMOND, Argyll and Bute, 27,400ha/67,705 acres
LOCH NA KEAL, Mull, Argyll and Bute, 12,700ha/31,382 acres
LOCH RANNOCH AND GLEN LYON, Perthshire and Kinross, 48,400ha/119,596 acres
LOCH SHIEL, Highland, 13,400ha/33,111 acres
LOCH TUMMEL, Perthshire and Kinross, 9,200ha/22,733 acres
LYNN OF LORN, Argyll and Bute, 4,800ha/11,861 acres
MORAR, MOIDART AND ARDNAMURCHAN, Highland, 13,500ha/33,358 acres
NITH ESTUARY, Dumfries and Galloway, 9,300ha/22,980 acres
NORTH ARRAN, North Ayrshire, 23,800ha/58,810 acres
NORTH-WEST SUTHERLAND, Highland, 20,500ha/50,655 acres
RIVER EARN, Perthshire and Kinross, 3,000ha/7,413 acres
RIVER TAY, Perthshire and Kinross, 5,600ha/13,838 acres
ST KILDA, Eilean Siar (Western Isles), 900ha/2,224 acres
SCARBA, LUNGA AND THE GARVELLACHS, Argyll and Bute, 1,900ha/4,695 acres
SHETLAND, Shetland Isles, 11,600ha/28,664 acres
SMALL ISLANDS, Highland, 15,500ha/38,300 acres
SOUTH LEWIS, HARRIS AND NORTH UIST, Eilean Siar (Western Isles), 109,600ha/270,822 acres
SOUTH UIST MACHAIR, Eilean Siar (Western Isles), 6,100ha/15,073 acres
THE TROSSACHS, Stirling, 4,600ha/11,367 acres
TROTTERNISH, Highland, 5,000ha/12,355 acres
UPPER TWEEDDALE, Borders, 10,500ha/25,945 acres
WESTER ROSS, Highland, 145,300ha/359,036 acres

THE NATIONAL FOREST

The National Forest is one of the UK's biggest environmental projects, creating a forest across 518.5 sq. km (200.2 sq. miles) of Derbyshire, Leicestershire and Staffordshire. Since the early 1990s, more than 8.5 million trees have been planted to create over 7,000ha of new woodland landscapes. Forest cover has increased from 6 per cent to 20 per cent, with the aim of eventually covering approximately one-third of the designated area.

Since its establishment in 1995, the National Forest Company leads the project and is responsible for delivery of the government-approved National Forest Strategy, sponsored by DEFRA. Priorities include continued forest creation and management, economic development of the area for recreation and tourism, and engaging local communities in the forest to improve quality of life.

NATIONAL FOREST COMPANY, Enterprise Glade, Bath Yard, Moira, Swadlincote, Derbyshire DE12 6BA
T 01283-551211 E enquiries@nationalforest.org
W www.nationalforest.org
Chief Executive, John Everitt

SITES OF SPECIAL SCIENTIFIC INTEREST

A site of special scientific interest (SSSI) is a legal notification applied to land in England, Scotland or Wales which Natural England (NE), Scottish Natural Heritage (SNH) or Natural Resources Wales (NRW) identifies as being of special interest because of its flora, fauna, geological or physiographical features. In some cases, SSSIs are managed as nature reserves.

NE, SNH and NRW must notify the designation of an SSSI to the local planning authority, every owner/occupier of the land, and the environment secretary, the Scottish ministers or the Welsh government. The Environment Agency (in England), water companies and internal drainage authorities and a number of other interested parties are also formally notified.

Objections to the notification of an SSSI can be made and ultimately considered at a full meeting of the board of NE or, in Wales, a subgroup committee of the NRW board. In Scotland an objection will be dealt with by the main board of SNH or an appropriate subgroup.

The protection of these sites depends on the cooperation of individual landowners and occupiers. Owner/occupiers must consult NE, SNH or NRW and gain written consent before they can undertake certain listed activities on the site. Funds are available through management agreements and grants to assist owners and occupiers in conserving sites' interests. Sites can also be protected by management schemes, management notices and other enforcement mechanisms. As a last resort a site can be purchased.

SSSIs in Britain as at June 2018:

	Number	Hectares	Acres
England	4,126	1,092,779	2,700,316
Scotland	1,423	1,022,888	2,527,611
Wales	1,072	262,200	647,909

Sources: Natural England; © Natural Resources Wales and database right (all rights reserved); Scottish Natural Heritage

NORTHERN IRELAND

In Northern Ireland areas of special scientific interest (ASSIs) are designated by the Department of Agriculture, Environment and Rural Affairs (Northern Ireland).

NATIONAL NATURE RESERVES

National Nature Reserves are defined in the National Parks and Access to the Countryside Act 1949 as modified by the Natural Environment and Rural Communities Act 2006. National Nature Reserves may be managed solely for the purpose of conservation, or for both the purposes of conservation and recreation, providing this does not compromise the conservation purpose.

NE, SNH or NRW can declare as a national nature reserve land which is held and managed as a nature reserve under an agreement; land held and managed by NE, SNH or NRW; or land held and managed as a nature reserve by an approved body. NE, SNH or NRW can make by-laws to protect reserves from undesirable activities; these are subject to confirmation by the Secretary of State for Environment, Food and Rural Affairs, the Welsh government or the Scottish ministers.

National nature reserves in Britain as at June 2018:

	Number	Hectares	Acres
England	225	93,910	232,057
Scotland	43	154,262	381,190
Wales*	76	26,127	64,561

Sources: Natural England; © Natural Resources Wales and database right (all rights reserved); Scottish Natural Heritage

NORTHERN IRELAND

Nature reserves are established and managed by the Department of Agriculture, Environment and Rural Affairs (Northern Ireland), with advice from the Council for Nature Conservation and the Countryside. Nature reserves are declared under the Nature Conservation and Amenity Lands (Northern Ireland) Order 1985.

LOCAL NATURE RESERVES

Local Nature Reserves are defined in the National Parks and Access to the Countryside Act 1949 (as amended by the Natural Environment and Rural Communities Act 2006) as land designated for the study and preservation of flora and fauna, or of geological or physiographical features. Local Nature Reserves also have a statutory obligation to provide opportunities for the enjoyment of nature or open air recreation, providing this does not compromise the conservation purpose of the reserve. Local authorities in England, Scotland and Wales have the power to acquire, declare and manage reserves in consultation with NE, SNH and NRW. There is similar legislation in Northern Ireland, where the consulting organisation is the Environment Agency.

Any organisation, such as water companies, educational trusts, local amenity groups and charitable nature conservation bodies, such as wildlife trusts, may manage local nature reserves, provided that a local authority has a legal interest in the land. This means that the local authority must either own it, lease it or have a management agreement with the landowner.

Designated local nature reserves in Britain as at June 2018:

	Number	Hectares	Acres
England	1,615	41,746	103,157
Scotland	75	10,780	26,638
Wales	95	6,187	15,288

Sources: Natural England; © Natural Resources Wales and database right (all rights reserved); Scottish Natural Heritage

There are also local nature reserves in Northern Ireland.

FOREST RESERVES

The Forestry Commission is the government department responsible for forestry policy throughout Great Britain. Forestry is a devolved matter, with the separate Forestry Commissions for England, Scotland and Wales reporting directly to their appropriate minister. The equivalent body in Northern Ireland is the Forest Service, an agency of the Department of Agriculture and Rural Development for Northern Ireland. The Forestry Commission in each country is led by a director who is also a member of the GB Board of Commissioners. As at March 2018, UK woodland certified by the Forestry Commission (including Forestry Commission-managed woodland) amounted to around 1,388,000ha (3,429,823 acres): 337,000ha (832,745 acres) in England, 145,000ha (358,303 acres) in Wales, 841,000ha (2,078,156 acres) in Scotland and 65,000ha (160,619 acres) in Northern Ireland. For more information, *see* W www.forestry.gov.uk

There are forest nature reserves in Northern Ireland, designated and administered by the Forest Service.

MARINE NATURE RESERVES

Marine protected areas provide protection for marine flora and fauna, and geological and physiographical features on land covered by tidal waters or parts of the sea in or adjacent to the UK. These areas also provide opportunities for study and research.

ENGLAND AND WALES

The Marine and Coastal Access Act 2009 created a new kind of statutory protection for marine protected areas in England and Wales, marine conservation zones (MCZs), which are designed to increase the protection of species and habitats deemed to be of national importance. The Secretary of State for Environment, Food and Rural Affairs and the Welsh ministers have the power to designate MCZs. Individual MCZs can have varying levels of protection: some include specific activities that are appropriately managed, while others prohibit all damaging and disturbing activities. The act converted the waters around Lundy Island, a former marine protected area, to MCZ status in 2010 and this was formerly designated as such in 2013. Similarly, the marine nature reserve in the waters around Skomer was reclassified and designated an MCZ in 2014; forming the only MCZ solely in Welsh waters.

In 2009, Natural England and the Joint Nature Conservation Committee (JNCC) gave sea-users and stakeholders the ability to recommend potential MCZs to the UK government by establishing four regional projects. On 21 November 2013, the government announced the creation of 27 MCZs, covering an area of around 9,700 sq. km, to protect wildlife including seahorses, coral reefs and oyster beds from dredging and bottom-trawling. In January 2016, 23 additional MCZs were designated, which extended the area of protection to 20,700 sq. km. The new MCZ designations means that 20 per cent of English waters are considered protected.

The 51 MCZs in England and Wales (with date designation confirmed) are:

Inshore Sites
ALLONBY BAY (2016), Cumbria, 40 sq. km
ALN ESTUARY (2013), Northumberland, 0.39 sq. km
BEACHY HEAD WEST (2013), E. Sussex, 24 sq. km
BIDEFORD TO FORELAND POINT (2016), Devon, 104 sq. km
BLACKWATER, CROUCH, ROACH AND COLNE ESTUARIES (2013), Essex, 284 sq. km
CHESIL BEACH AND STENNIS LEDGES (2013), Dorset, 37 sq. km
COQUET TO ST. MARYS (2016), Northumberland, 192 sq. km
CROMER SHOAL CHALK BEDS (2016), Norfolk, 321 sq. km
CUMBRIA COAST (2013), Cumbria, 18 sq. km
DOVER TO DEAL (2016), Kent, 10 sq. km
DOVER TO FOLKESTONE (2016), Kent, 20 sq. km
FARNES EAST (2016), Northumberland, 945 sq. km
FOLKESTONE POMERANIA (2013), Kent, 34 sq. km
FYLDE (2013), Lancs, 260 sq. km
HARTLAND POINT TO TINTAGEL (2016), Devon/Cornwall, 304 sq. km
HOLDERNESS INSHORE (2016), Yorkshire, 309 sq. km
ISLES OF SCILLY (2013), 30 sq. km
KINGMERE (2013), Sussex, 47 sq. km
LUNDY (2010 and 2013), Bristol Channel, 31 sq. km
THE MANACLES (2013), Cornwall, 3.5 sq. km
MEDWAY ESTUARY (2013), Kent, 60 sq. km
MOUNTS BAY (2016), Cornwall, 12 sq. km
THE NEEDLES (2016), Isle of Wight, 11 sq. km
NEWQUAY AND THE GANNEL (2016), Cornwall, 9 sq. km
PADSTOW BAY AND SURROUNDS (2013), Cornwall, 90 sq. km
PAGHAM HARBOUR (2013), Sussex, 3 sq. km
POOLE ROCKS (2013), Dorset, 4 sq. km
RUNNEL STONE (2016), Cornwall, 20 sq. km
RUNSWICK BAY (2016), Yorkshire, 68 sq. km
SKERRIES BANK AND SURROUNDS (2013), Devon, 250 sq. km

SOUTH DORSET (2013), 193 sq. km
THE SWALE ESTUARY (2016), Kent, 51 sq. km
TAMAR ESTUARY (2013), Devon/Cornwall, 15 sq. km
THANET COAST (2013), Kent, 64 sq. km
TORBAY (2013), Devon, 20 sq. km
UPPER FOWEY AND PONT PILL (2013), Cornwall, 2 sq. km
UTOPIA (2016), Isle of Wight, 3 sq. km
WEST OF WALNEY (2016), Cumbria, 388 sq. km
WHITSAND AND LOOE BAY (2013), Cornwall, 52 sq. km

Offshore Sites
THE CANYONS (2013), Cornwall, 661 sq. km
EAST OF HAIG FRAS (2013), Cornwall, 400 sq. km
FULMAR (2016), Northumberland, 2,439 sq. km
GREATER HAIG FRAS (2016), Cornwall, 2,048 sq. km
NORTH EAST OF FARNES DEEP (2013), Northumberland, 492 sq. km
NORTH-WEST OF JONES BANK (2016), Cornwall, 400 sq. km
OFFSHORE BRIGHTON (2016), Sussex, 861 sq. km
OFFSHORE OVERFALLS (2016), Isle of Wight, 594 sq. km
SKOMER (2014), Pembrokeshire, 13 sq. km
SOUTH-WEST DEEPS (WEST) (2013), Cornwall, 1,800 sq. km
SWALLOW SAND (2013), Northumberland, 4,746 sq. km
WESTERN CHANNEL (2016), Cornwall, 1,614 sq. km

SCOTLAND

In July 2014, under the Marine (Scotland) Act 2010, the Scottish government designated 17 marine protected areas (MPAs) in Scottish inshore territorial waters (Clyde Sea Sill; East Caithness Cliffs; Fetlar to Haroldswick; Loch Creran; Loch Sunart; Loch Sunart to the Sound of Jura; Loch Sween; Lochs Duich, Long and Alsh; Monarch Isles; Mousa to Boddam; Noss Head; Papa Westray; Small Isles; South Arran; Upper Loch Fyne and Loch Goil; Wester Ross; and Wyre and Rousay Sounds). A further 13, also in July 2014, were designated in offshore waters under the UK Marine and Coastal Access Act 2009. These are: Central Fladen; East of Gannet and Montrose Fields; Faroe–Shetland Sponge Belt; Firth of Forth Banks Complex; Geikie Slide and Hebridean Slope; Hatton–Rockall Basin; North-east Faroe Shetland Channel; North-west Orkney; Norwegian Boundary Sediment Plain; Rosemary Bank Seamount; The Barra Fan and Hebrides Terrace Seamount; Turbot Bank; and West Shetland Shelf.

NORTHERN IRELAND

The Marine Act (Northern Ireland) 2013 includes provisions for establishing Marine Conservation Zones (MCZs), as well as a system of marine planning, fisheries management and marine licensing. MCZs may be designated for various purposes including the conservation of marine species and habitats, taking fully into account any economic, cultural or social consequences of doing so. The Act also allows the NI Department of Agriculture, Environment and Rural Affairs to make byelaws to protect MCZs from damage caused by unregulated activities such as anchoring, kite surfing or jet skiing. It is an offence to intentionally or recklessly destroy or damage a protected feature of an MCZ.

As at June 2018 there were five MCZs in Northern Ireland. Strangford Lough was Northern Ireland's only marine nature reserve, established in 1995 under the Nature Conservation and Amenity Lands Order (Northern Ireland) 1985, but it was redesignated as Northern Ireland's first MCZ on the introduction of the Marine Act (Northern Ireland) 2013. After a consultation period, the NI Department of Agriculture, Environment and Rural Affairs announced four new MCZ's in December 2016; Carlingford Lough, Outer Belfast Lough, Rathlin and Waterfoot.

INTERNATIONAL CONVENTIONS

The UK is party to a number of international conventions.

BERN CONVENTION

The 1979 Bern Convention on the Conservation of European Wildlife and Natural Habitats came into force in the UK in June 1982. There are 51 contracting parties and a number of other states attend meetings as observers.

The aims are to conserve wild flora and fauna and their habitats, especially where this requires the cooperation of several countries, and to promote such cooperation. The convention imposes legal obligations on contracting parties, protecting over 500 wild plant species and more than 1,000 wild animal species.

All parties to the convention must promote national conservation policies and take account of the conservation of wild flora and fauna when setting planning and development policies. Reports on contracting parties' conservation policies must be submitted to the standing committee every four years.

SECRETARIAT OF THE BERN CONVENTION
STANDING COMMITTEE, Council of Europe, Avenue de l'Europe, F-67075 Strasbourg Cedex, France
W www.coe.int/bernconvention

BIOLOGICAL DIVERSITY

The UK ratified the Convention on Biological Diversity (CBD) in June 1994. As at June 2018 there were 196 parties to the convention.

There are seven programmes addressing agricultural biodiversity, marine and coastal biodiversity and the biodiversity of inland waters, dry and sub-humid lands, islands, mountains and forests. On 29 January 2000 the Conference of the Parties adopted a supplementary agreement to the convention known as the Cartagena Protocol on Biosafety. The protocol seeks to protect biological diversity from potential risks that may be posed by introducing modified living organisms, resulting from biotechnology, into the environment. As at June 2018, 171 countries were party to the protocol; the UK joined on 17 February 2004. The Nagoya Protocol on Access and Benefit-sharing was adopted in October 2010 and entered into force on 12 October 2014. It provides international rules and procedure on liability and redress for damage to biodiversity resulting from living modified organisms. As at June 2018, 105 countries were party to the protocol; the UK became party on 22 May 2016. The Nagoya-Kuala Lumpur Supplementary Protocol on Liability and Redress was adopted as a supplementary agreement to the Cartagena Protocol on Biosafety and aims to contribute to the conservation and sustainable use of biodiversity by providing international rules and procedures in the field of liability and redress relating to living modified organisms; requiring that response measures are taken in the event of damage resulting from living modified organisms, or where there is sufficient likelihood that damage will result if timely response measures are not taken. The Nagoya-Kuala Lumpur Supplementary Protocol entered into force on 5 March 2018 for the 41 countries, including the UK, which were party to the protocol at this date.

The UK Biodiversity Action Plan (UKBAP), published in 1994, was the UK government's response to the CBD at the 1992 Rio Earth Summit. The UK Post-2010 Biodiversity Framework replaced UKBAP when it was published in 2012 by DEFRA and the devolved administrations. The framework covers the period 2011–20 and forms the UK government's response to the strategic plan of the CBD. It includes five internationally agreed strategic goals to be achieved by 2020: to address the underlying causes of biodiversity loss by

making biodiversity a mainstream issue across government and society; to reduce the direct pressures on biodiversity and promote sustainable use; to safeguard ecosystems, species and genetic diversity; to enhance the benefits to all from biodiversity and ecosystem services; and to enhance implementation through participatory planning, knowledge management and capacity building. The list of priority species and habitats under the biodiversity framework covers 1,150 species and 65 habitats and is administered by the Joint Nature Conservation Committee (JNCC).

SECRETARIAT OF THE CONVENTION ON
BIOLOGICAL DIVERSITY, 413, Saint Jacques Street, suite 800, Montreal, QC H2Y 1N9 Canada
T +1514-288 2220 E secretariat@cbd.int W www.cbd.int
JNCC, Monkstone House, City Road, Peterborough PE1 1JY
T 01733-562626 W www.jncc.defra.gov.uk

BONN CONVENTION

The 1979 Convention on Conservation of Migratory Species of Wild Animals (also known as the CMS or Bonn Convention) came into force in the UK in October 1985. As at June 2018, 126 countries were party to the convention. It requires the protection of listed endangered migratory species and encourages international agreements covering these and other threatened species.

Seven agreements have been concluded to date under the convention. They aim to conserve African-Eurasian migratory waterbirds; albatrosses and petrels; European bats; cetaceans of the Black Sea, Mediterranean and contiguous Atlantic area; small cetaceans in the Baltic, north-east Atlantic, Irish and North Seas; gorillas and their habitats; and seals in the Wadden Sea. A further 19 memorandums of understanding have been agreed for West-African populations of the African elephant, aquatic warbler, bukhara deer, cetaceans of the Pacific Islands, dugongs (large marine mammals), middle-European population of the great bustard, high Andean flamingos, huemuls (Andean deer). manatee and small cetaceans of Western Africa and Macaronesia, marine turtles of the Atlantic coast of Africa, Indian Ocean and South East Asia, migratory birds of prey in Africa and Eurasia, migratory grassland birds of southern South America, migratory sharks, eastern-Atlantic populations of the Mediterranean monk seal, ruddy-headed goose, saiga antelope, Siberian crane and the slender-billed curlew. In addition, there are four special species initiatives for: African carnivores, central Asian mammals, Sahelo–Saharan megafauna and the central Asian flyway.

UNEP/CMS SECRETARIAT, Platz der Vereinten Nationen 1, 53113 Bonn, Germany T (+49) (228) 815 2401
E cms.secretariat@cms.int W www.cms.int

CITES

The 1973 Convention on International Trade in Endangered Species of Wild Fauna and Flora (CITES), which entered into force in 1975, is an agreement between governments to ensure that international trade in specimens of wild animals and plants does not threaten their survival. The convention came into force in the UK in October 1976 and there are currently 183 member countries. Countries party to the convention ban commercial international trade in an agreed list of endangered species and regulate and monitor trade in other species that might become endangered. The convention accords varying degrees of protection to approximately 30,000 species of plants and 5,800 species of animals, whether they are traded as live specimens or as products derived from them.

The Conference of the Parties to CITES meets every two to three years to review the convention's implementation. The

Animal and Plant Health Agency at the Department for Environment, Food and Rural Affairs carries out the government's responsibilities under CITES.

CITES is implemented in the EU through a series of EC regulations known as the Wildlife Trade Regulations.

CITES SECRETARIAT, International Environment House, 11 Chemin des Anémones, CH-1219 Châtelaine, Geneva, Switzerland T (+41) (22) 917 8139/40 E info@cites.org W www.cites.org

INTERNATIONAL CONVENTION FOR THE REGULATION OF WHALING

The International Convention for the Regulation of Whaling was signed in Washington DC in 1946 and currently has 92 member countries.

The measures in the convention provide for the complete protection of certain species; designate specified areas as whale sanctuaries; set limits on the numbers and size of whales which may be taken; prescribe open and closed seasons and areas for whaling; and prohibit the capture of suckling calves and female whales accompanied by calves. The International Whaling Commission meets biennially to review and revise these measures.

INTERNATIONAL WHALING COMMISSION, The Red House, 135 Station Road, Impington, Cambridge CB24 9NP T 01223-233971 W www.iwc.int

OSPAR

The Convention for the Protection of the Marine Environment of the North-East Atlantic (the OSPAR Convention) was adopted in Paris, France in September 1992 and entered into force in March 1998. The OSPAR Convention replaced both the Oslo Convention (1972) and the Paris Convention (1974), with the intention of providing a comprehensive approach to addressing all sources of pollution which may affect the maritime area, and matters relating to the protection of the maritime environment. An annex on biodiversity and ecosystems was adopted in 1998 to cover non-polluting human activities that can adversely affect the sea.

Fifteen countries plus the European Union are party to the convention; the UK ratified OSPAR in 1998. The OSPAR Commission makes decisions and recommendations and sets out actions to be taken by the contracting parties. The OSPAR Secretariat administers the work under the convention, coordinates the work of the contracting parties and runs the formal meeting schedule of OSPAR.

OSPAR COMMISSION, Victoria House, 37–63 Southampton Row, London WC1B 4DA T 020-7430 5200 E secretariat@ospar.org W www.ospar.org

RAMSAR CONVENTION

The 1971 Convention on Wetlands of National Importance, called the Ramsar Convention, is an inter-governmental treaty that provides for the conservation and sustainable use of wetlands and their resources. The Convention entered into force in the UK in 1976.

Governments that are contracting parties to the convention must designate wetlands for inclusion in the List of Wetlands of International Importance (the 'Ramsar List') and include wetland conservation considerations in their land-use planning. As at June 2018, the Convention's 170 contracting parties had designated 2,312 wetland sites, covering 244,794,979 hectares. The UK currently has 174 designated sites covering 1,281,989 hectares.

The contracting parties meet every three years to assess progress. The 13th Meeting of the Conference of the Contracting Parties to the Ramsar Convention on Wetlands took place in Dubai, UAE in October 2018.

RAMSAR CONVENTION SECRETARIAT, Rue Mauverney 28, CH-1196 Gland, Switzerland T (+41) (22) 999 0170 E ramsar@ramsar.org W https://www.ramsar.org

UK LEGISLATION

The Wildlife and Countryside Act 1981 gives legal protection to a wide range of wild animals and plants. Every five years the statutory nature conservation agencies (Natural England, Natural Resources Wales and Scottish Natural Heritage), working jointly through the Joint Nature Conservation Committee, are required to review schedules 5 (animals, other than birds) and 8 (plants) of the Wildlife and Countryside Act 1981. They make recommendations to the Secretary of State for Environment, Food and Rural Affairs, the Welsh ministers and the Scottish government for changes to these schedules. The most recent variations of schedules 5 and 8 for England came into effect on 1 October 2011, following the fifth quinquennial review. The sixth review was submitted to DEFRA, the Welsh government and the Scottish government in April 2014; once these governments have considered the review, they will respond formally and publish amendments to the Wildlife and Countryside Act (1981).

Under section 9 of the act it is an offence to kill, injure, take, possess or sell (whether alive or dead) any wild animal included in schedule 5 of the act and to disturb its place of shelter and protection or to destroy that place. However certain species listed on schedule 5 are protected against some, but not all, of these activities.

Under section 13 of the act it is illegal without a licence to pick, uproot, sell or destroy plants listed in schedule 8. Since January 2001, under the Countryside and Rights of Way Act 2000, persons found guilty of an offence under part 1 of the Wildlife and Countryside Act 1981 face a maximum penalty of up to £5,000 and/or up to a six-month custodial sentence per specimen.

BIRDS

The act lays down a close season for birds (listed on Schedule 2, part 1) from 1 February to 31 August inclusive, each year. Variations to these dates are made for:

Black grouse – 10 December to 20 August (10 December – 1 September for Somerset, Devon and New Forest)
Capercaillie – 1 February to 30 September (England and Wales only)
Grey partridge – 1 February to 1 September
Pheasant – 1 February to 1 October
Ptarmigan and Red grouse – 10 December to 12 August
Red-legged partridge – 1 February to 1 September
Snipe – 1 February to 11 August
Woodcock – 1 February to 30 September (England and Wales); 1 February to 31 August (Scotland)
Birds listed on schedule 2, part 1 (below high water mark) (see below) – 21 February to 31 August
Wild duck and wild geese, in or over any area below the high-water mark of ordinary spring tides – 21 February to 31 August
Sundays and Christmas Day in Scotland, and Sundays for any area of England or Wales prescribed by the Secretary of State.

Birds listed on schedule 2, part 1, which may be killed or taken outside the close season are: capercaillie (England and Wales only); coot; certain wild duck (gadwall, goldeneye, mallard, Northern pintail, common pochard, Northern shoveler, teal, tufted duck, Eurasian wigeon); certain wild geese (Canada, greylag, pink-footed, white-fronted (in England and Wales only); golden plover; moorhen; snipe; and woodcock.

Section 16 of the 1981 act allows licences to be issued on either an individual or general basis, to allow the killing, taking and sale of certain birds for specified reasons such as public health and safety. All other wild birds are fully protected by law throughout the year.

ANIMALS PROTECTED BY SCHEDULE 5

Adder *(Vipera berus)*
Anemone, Ivell's Sea *(Edwardsia ivelli)*
Anemone, Starlet Sea *(Nematosella vectensis)*
Bat, Horseshoe, all species *(Rhinolophidae)*
Bat, Typical, all species *(Vespertilionidae)*
Beetle *(Hypebaeus flavipes)*
Beetle, Bembridge Water *(Paracymus aeneus)*
Beetle, Lesser Silver Water *(Hydrochara caraboides)*
Beetle, Mire Pill *(Curimopsis nigrita)*
Beetle, Moccas *(Hypebaeus flavipes)*
Beetle, Rainbow Leaf *(Chrysolina cerealis)*
Beetle, Spangled Water *(Graphoderus zonatus)*
Beetle, Stag *(Lucanus cervus)*
Beetle, Violet Click *(Limoniscus violaceus)*
Beetle, Water *(Paracymus aeneus)*
Burbot *(Lota lota)*
Butterfly, Adonis Blue *(Lysandra bellargus)*
Butterfly, Black Hairstreak *(Strymonidia pruni)*
Butterfly, Brown Hairstreak *(Thecla betulae)*
Butterfly, Chalkhill Blue *(Lysandra coridon)*
Butterfly, Chequered Skipper *(Carterocephalus palaemon)*
Butterfly, Duke of Burgundy Fritillary *(Hamearis lucina)*
Butterfly, Glanville Fritillary *(Melitaea cinxia)*
Butterfly, Heath Fritillary *(Mellicta athalia or Melitaea athalia)*
Butterfly, High Brown Fritillary *(Argynnis adippe)*
Butterfly, Large Blue *(Maculinea arion)*
Butterfly, Large Copper *(Lycaena dispar)*
Butterfly, Large Heath *(Coenonympha tullia)*
Butterfly, Large Tortoiseshell *(Nymphalis polychloros)*
Butterfly, Lulworth Skipper *(Thymelicus acteon)*
Butterfly, Marsh Fritillary *(Eurodryas aurinia)*
Butterfly, Mountain Ringlet *(Erebia epiphron)*
Butterfly, Northern Brown Argus *(Aricia artaxerxes)*
Butterfly, Pearl-bordered Fritillary *(Boloria euphrosyne)*
Butterfly, Purple Emperor *(Apatura iris)*
Butterfly, Silver Spotted Skipper *(Hesperia comma)*
Butterfly, Silver-studded Blue *(Plebejus argus)*
Butterfly, Small Blue *(Cupido minimus)*
Butterfly, Swallowtail *(Papilio machaon)*
Butterfly, White Letter Hairstreak *(Stymonida w-album)*
Butterfly, Wood White *(Leptidea sinapis)*
Cat, Wild *(Felis silvestris)*
Cicada, New Forest *(Cicadetta montana)*
Crayfish, Atlantic Stream *(Austropotamobius pallipes)*
Cricket, Field *(Gryllus campestris)*
Cricket, Mole *(Gryllotalpa gryllotalpa)*
Cricket, Wart-biter *(Decticus verrucivorus)*
Damselfly, Southern *(Coenagrion mercuriale)*
Dolphin, all species *(Cetacea)*
Dormouse *(Muscardinus avellanarius)*
Dragonfly, Norfolk Aeshna *(Aeshna isosceles)*
Frog, Common *(Rana temporaria)*
Frog, Pool, Northern Clade *(Pelophylax lessonae)*
Goby, Couch's *(Gobius couchii)*
Goby, Giant *(Gobius cobitis)*
Hatchet Shell, Northern *(Thyasira gouldi)*
Hydroid, Marine *(Clavopsella navis)*
Lagoon Snail, De Folin's *(Caecum armoricum)*
Lagoon Worm, Tentacled *(Alkmaria romijni)*
Leech, Medicinal *(Hirudo medicinalis)*
Lizard, Sand *(Lacerta agilis)*
Lizard, Viviparous *(Lacerta vivipara)*

Marten, Pine *(Martes martes)*
Moth, Barberry Carpet *(Pareulype berberata)*
Moth, Black-veined *(Siona lineata or Idaea lineata)*
Moth, Fiery Clearwing *(Bembecia chrysidiformis)*
Moth, Fisher's Estuarine *(Gortyna borelii)*
Moth, New Forest Burnet *(Zygaena viciae)*
Moth, Reddish Buff *(Acosmetia caliginosa)*
Moth, Slender Scotch Burnet *(Zygaena loti)*
Moth, Sussex Emerald *(Thalera fimbrialis)*
Moth, Talisker Burnet *(Zygaena lonicerae)*
Mussel, Fan *(Atrina fragilis)*
Mussel, Freshwater Pearl *(Margaritifera margaritifera)*
Newt, Great Crested (or Warty) *(Triturus cristatus)*
Newt, Palmate *(Triturus helveticus)*
Newt, Smooth *(Triturus vulgaris)*
Otter, Common *(Lutra lutra)*
Porpoise, all species *(Cetacea)*
Sandworm, Lagoon *(Armandia cirrhosa)*
Sea Fan, Pink *(Eunicella verrucosa)*
Sea Slug, Lagoon *(Tenellia adspersa)*
Sea-mat, Trembling *(Victorella pavida)*
Seahorse, Short Snouted (England only) *(Hippocampus hippocampus)*
Seahorse, Spiny (England only) *(Hippocampus guttulatus)*
Shad, Allis *(Alosa alosa)*
Shad, Twaite *(Alosa fallax)*
Shark, Angel (England only) *(Squatina squatina)*
Shark, Basking *(Cetorhinus maximus)*
Shrimp, Fairy *(Chirocephalus diaphanus)*
Shrimp, Lagoon Sand *(Gammarus insensibilis)*
Shrimp, Tadpole (Apus) *(Triops cancriformis)*
Skate, White *(Rostroraja alba)*
Slow-worm *(Anguis fragilis)*
Snail, Glutinous *(Myxas glutinosa)*
Snail, Roman (England only) *(Helix pomatia)*
Snail, Sandbowl *(Catinella arenaria)*
Snake, Grass *(Natrix natrix or Natrix helvetica)*
Snake, Smooth *(Coronella austriaca)*
Spider, Fen Raft *(Dolomedes plantarius)*
Spider, Ladybird *(Eresus niger)*
Squirrel, Red *(Sciurus vulgaris)*
Sturgeon *(Acipenser sturio)*
Toad, Common *(Bufo bufo)*
Toad, Natterjack *(Bufo calamita)*
Turtle, Flatback *(Cheloniidae/Natator Depressus)*
Turtle, Green Sea *(Chelonia mydas)*
Turtle, Hawksbill *(Eretmochelys imbricate)*
Turtle, Kemp's Ridley Sea *(Lepidochelys kempii)*
Turtle, Leatherback Sea *(Dermochelys coriacea)*
Turtle, Loggerhead Sea *(Caretta caretta)*
Turtle, Olive Ridley *(Lepidochelys olivacea)*
Vendace *(Coregonus albula)*
Vole, Water *(Arvicola terrestris)*
Walrus *(Odobenus rosmarus)*
Whale, all species *(Cetacea)*
Whitefish *(Coregonus lavaretus)*

PLANTS PROTECTED BY SCHEDULE 8

Adder's Tongue, Least *(Ophioglossum lusitanicum)*
Alison, Small *(Alyssum alyssoides)*
Anomodon, Long-leaved *(Anomodon longifolius)*
Beech-lichen, New Forest *(Enterographa elaborata)*
Blackwort *(Southbya nigrella)*
Bluebell *(Hyacinthoides non-scripta)*
Bolete, Royal *(Boletus regius)*
Broomrape, Bedstraw *(Orobanche caryophyllacea)*
Broomrape, Oxtongue *(Orobanche loricata)*
Broomrape, Thistle *(Orobanche reticulata)*
Cabbage, Lundy *(Rhynchosinapis wrightii)*

Calamint, Wood *(Calamintha sylvatica)*
Caloplaca, Snow *(Caloplaca nivalis)*
Catapyrenium, Tree *(Catapyrenium psoromoides)*
Catchfly, Alpine *(Lychnis alpina)*
Catillaria, Laurer's *(Catellaria laureri)*
Centaury, Slender *(Centaurium tenuiflorum)*
Cinquefoil, Rock *(Potentilla rupestris)*
Cladonia, Convoluted *(Cladonia convoluta)*
Cladonia, Upright Mountain *(Cladonia stricta)*
Clary, Meadow *(Salvia pratensis)*
Club-rush, Triangular *(Scirpus triquetrus)*
Colt's-foot, Purple *(Homogyne alpina)*
Cotoneaster, Wild *(Cotoneaster integerrimus)*
Cottongrass, Slender *(Eriophorum gracile)*
Cow-wheat, Field *(Melampyrum arvense)*
Crocus, Sand *(Romulea columnae)*
Crystalwort, Lizard *(Riccia bifurca)*
Cudweed, Broad-leaved *(Filago pyramidata)*
Cudweed, Jersey *(Gnaphalium luteoalbum)*
Cudweed, Red-tipped *(Filago lutescens)*
Cut-grass *(Leersia oryzoides)*
Diapensia *(Diapensia lapponica)*
Dock, Shore *(Rumex rupestris)*
Earwort, Marsh *(Jamesoniella undulifolia)*
Eryngo, Field *(Eryngium campestre)*
Fern, Dickie's Bladder *(Cystopteris dickieana)*
Fern, Killarney *(Trichomanes speciosum)*
Flapwort, Norfolk *(Leiocolea rutheana)*
Fleabane, Alpine *(Erigeron borealis)*
Fleabane, Small *(Pulicaria vulgaris)*
Fleawort, South Stack *(Tephroseris integrifolia ssp maritima)*
Frostwort, Pointed *(Gymnomitrion apiculatum)*
Fungus, Hedgehog *(Hericium erinaceum)*
Galingale, Brown *(Cyperus fuscus)*
Gentian, Alpine *(Gentiana nivalis)*
Gentian, Dune *(Gentianella uliginosa)*
Gentian, Early *(Gentianella anglica)*
Gentian, Fringed *(Gentianella ciliata)*
Gentian, Spring *(Gentiana verna)*
Germander, Cut-leaved *(Teucrium botrys)*
Germander, Water *(Teucrium scordium)*
Gladiolus, Wild *(Gladiolus illyricus)*
Goblin Lights *(Catolechia wahlenbergii)*
Goosefoot, Stinking *(Chenopodium vulvaria)*
Grass-poly *(Lythrum hyssopifolia)*
Grimmia, Blunt-leaved *(Grimmia unicolor)*
Gyalecta, Elm *(Gyalecta ulmi)*
Hare's-ear, Sickle-leaved *(Bupleurum falcatum)*
Hare's-ear, Small *(Bupleurum baldense)*
Hawk's-beard, Stinking *(Crepis foetida)*
Hawkweed, Northroe *(Hieracium northroense)*
Hawkweed, Shetland *(Hieracium zetlandicum)*
Hawkweed, Weak-leaved *(Hieracium attenuatifolium)*
Heath, Blue *(Phyllodoce caerulea)*
Helleborine, Red *(Cephalanthera rubra)*
Horsetail, Branched *(Equisetum ramosissimum)*
Hound's-tongue, Green *(Cynoglossum germanicum)*
Knawel, Perennial *(Scleranthus perennis)*
Knotgrass, Sea *(Polygonum maritimum)*
Lady's-slipper *(Cypripedium calceolus)*
Lecanora, Tarn *(Lecanora archariana)*
Lecidea, Copper *(Lecidea inops)*
Leek, Round-headed *(Allium sphaerocephalon)*
Lettuce, Least *(Lactuca saligna)*
Lichen, Arctic Kidney *(Nephroma arcticum)*
Lichen, Ciliate Strap *(Heterodermia leucomelos)*
Lichen, Coralloid Rosette *(Heterodermia propagulifera)*
Lichen, Ear-lobed Dog *(Peltigera lepidophora)*
Lichen, Forked Hair *(Bryoria furcellata)*

Lichen, Golden Hair *(Teloschistes flavicans)*
Lichen, Orange-fruited Elm *(Caloplaca luteoalba)*
Lichen, River Jelly *(Collema dichotomum)*
Lichen, Scaly Breck *(Squamarina lentigera)*
Lichen, Starry Breck *(Buellia asterella)*
Lily, Snowdon *(Lloydia serotina)*
Liverwort, Lindenberg's Leafy *(Adelanthus lindenbergianus)*
Lungwort, Tree *(Lobaria pulmonaria)*
Marsh-mallow, Rough *(Althaea hirsuta)*
Marshwort, Creeping *(Apium repens)*
Milk-parsley, Cambridge *(Selinum carvifolia)*
Moss *(Drepanocladius vernicosus)*
Moss, Alpine Copper *(Mielichoferia mielichoferi)*
Moss, Baltic Bog *(Sphagnum balticum)*
Moss, Blue Dew *(Saelania glaucescens)*
Moss, Blunt-leaved Bristle *(Orthotrichum obtusifolium)*
Moss, Bright Green Cave *(Cyclodictyon laetevirens)*
Moss, Cordate Beard *(Barbula cordata)*
Moss, Cornish Path *(Ditrichum cornubicum)*
Moss, Derbyshire Feather *(Thamnobryum angustifolium)*
Moss, Flamingo *(Desmatodon cernuus)*
Moss, Glaucous Beard *(Barbula glauca)*
Moss, Green Shield *(Buxbaumia viridis)*
Moss, Hair Silk *(Plagiothecium piliferum)*
Moss, Knothole *(Zygodon forsteri)*
Moss, Large Yellow Feather *(Scorpidium turgescens)*
Moss, Millimetre *(Micromitrium tenerum)*
Moss, Multi-fruited River *(Cryphaea lamyana)*
Moss, Nowell's Limestone *(Zygodon gracilis)*
Moss, Polar Feather *(Hygrohypnum polare)*
Moss, Rigid Apple *(Bartramia stricta)*
Moss, Round-leaved Feather *(Rhyncostegium rotundifolium)*
Moss, Schleicher's Thread *(Bryum schleicheri)*
Moss, Slender Green Feather *(Drepanocladus vernicosus)*
Moss, Triangular Pygmy *(Acaulon triquetrum)*
Moss, Vaucher's Feather *(Hypnum vaucheri)*
Mudwort, Welsh *(Limosella australis)*
Naiad, Holly-leaved *(Najas marina)*
Naiad, Slender *(Najas flexilis)*
Nail, Rock *(Calicium corynellum)*
Orache, Stalked *(Halimione pedunculata)*
Orchid, Early Spider *(Ophrys sphegodes)*
Orchid, Fen *(Liparis loeselii)*
Orchid, Ghost *(Epipogium aphyllum)*
Orchid, Lapland Marsh *(Dactylorhiza lapponica)*
Orchid, Late Spider *(Ophrys fuciflora)*
Orchid, Lizard *(Himantoglossum hircinum)*
Orchid, Military *(Orchis militaris)*
Orchid, Monkey *(Orchis simia)*
Pannaria, Caledonia *(Panneria ignobilis)*
Parmelia, New Forest *(Parmelia minarum)*
Parmentaria, Oil Stain *(Parmentaria chilensis)*
Pear, Plymouth *(Pyrus cordata)*
Penny-cress, Perfoliate *(Thlaspi perfoliatum)*
Pennyroyal *(Mentha pulegium)*
Pertusaria, Alpine Moss *(Pertusaria bryontha)*
Petalwort *(Petallophyllum ralfsi)*
Physcia, Southern Grey *(Physcia tribacioides)*
Pigmyweed *(Crassula aquatica)*
Pine, Ground *(Ajuga chamaepitys)*
Pink, Cheddar *(Dianthus gratianopolitanus)*
Pink, Childing *(Petroraghia nanteuilii)*
Pink, Deptford (England and Wales only) *(Dianthus armeria)*
Polypore, Oak *(Buglossoporus pulvinus)*
Pseudocyphellaria, Ragged *(Pseudocyphellaria lacerata)*
Psora, Rusty Alpine *(Psora rubiformis)*
Puffball, Sandy Stilt *(Battarraea phalloides)*
Ragwort, Fen *(Senecio paludosus)*
Ramping-fumitory, Martin's *(Fumaria martinii)*

Rampion, Spiked *(Phyteuma spicatum)*
Restharrow, Small *(Ononis reclinata)*
Rock-cress, Alpine *(Arabis alpina)*
Rock-cress, Bristol *(Arabis stricta)*
Rustwort, Western *(Marsupella profunda)*
Sandwort, Norwegian *(Arenaria norvegica)*
Sandwort, Teesdale *(Minuartia stricta)*
Saxifrage, Drooping *(Saxifraga cernua)*
Saxifrage, Tufted *(Saxifraga cespitosa)*
Saxifrage, Yellow Marsh *(Saxifrage hirulus)*
Solenopsora, Serpentine *(Solenopsora liparina)*
Solomon's-seal, Whorled *(Polygonatum verticillatum)*
Sow-thistle, Alpine *(Cicerbita alpina)*
Spearwort, Adder's-tongue *(Ranunculus ophioglossifolius)*
Speedwell, Fingered *(Veronica triphyllos)*
Speedwell, Spiked *(Veronica spicata)*
Spike-rush, Dwarf *(Eleocharis parvula)*
Star-of-Bethlehem, Early *(Gagea bohemica)*

Starfruit *(Damasonium alisma)*
Stonewort, Bearded *(Chara canescens)*
Stonewort, Foxtail *(Lamprothamnium papulosum)*
Strapwort *(Corrigiola litoralis)*
Sulphur-tresses, Alpine *(Alectoria ochroleuca)*
Turpswort *(Geocalyx graveolens)*
Violet, Fen *(Viola persicifolia)*
Viper's-grass *(Scorzonera humilis)*
Water-plantain, Floating *(Luronium natans)*
Water-plantain, Ribbon-leaved *(Alisma gramineum)*
Wood-sedge, Starved *(Carex depauperata)*
Woodsia, Alpine *(Woodsia alpina)*
Woodsia, Oblong *(Woodsia ilvenis)*
Wormwood, Field *(Artemisia campestris)*
Woundwort, Downy *(Stachys germanica)*
Woundwort, Limestone *(Stachys alpina)*
Yellow-rattle, Greater *(Rhinanthus serotinus)*

WORLD HERITAGE SITES

The Convention Concerning the Protection of the World Cultural and Natural Heritage was adopted by the United Nations Educational, Scientific and Cultural Organization (UNESCO) in 1972 and ratified by the UK in 1984. As at July 2018, 193 states were party to the convention. The convention provides for the identification, protection and conservation of cultural and natural sites of outstanding universal value.

Cultural sites may be:

- an extraordinary exponent of human creative genius
- sites representing architectural and technological innovation or cultural interchange
- sites of artistic, historic, aesthetic, archaeological, scientific, ethnologic or anthropologic value
- 'cultural landscapes', ie sites whose characteristics are marked by significant interactions between human populations and their natural environment
- exceptional examples of a traditional settlement or land- or sea-use, especially those threatened by irreversible changes.
- unique or exceptional examples of a cultural tradition or a civilisation either still present or extinct

Natural sites may be:

- those displaying critical periods of earth's history
- superlative examples of on-going ecological and biological processes in the evolution of ecosystems
- those exhibiting remarkable natural beauty and aesthetic significance or those where extraordinary natural phenomena are witnessed
- the habitat of threatened species and plants

Governments which are party to the convention nominate sites in their country for inclusion in the World Heritage List. Nominations are considered by the World Heritage Committee, an inter-governmental committee composed of 21 representatives of the parties to the convention. The committee is advised by the International Council on Monuments and Sites (ICOMOS), the International Centre for the Study of the Preservation and Restoration of Cultural Property (ICCROM) and the International Union for the Conservation of Nature (IUCN). ICOMOS evaluates and reports on proposed cultural and mixed sites, ICCROM provides expert advice and training on how to conserve and restore cultural property and IUCN provides technical evaluations of natural heritage sites and reports on the state of conservation of listed sites.

A prerequisite for inclusion in the World Heritage List is the existence of an effective legal protection system in the country in which the site is situated and a detailed management plan to ensure the conservation of the site. Inclusion in the list does not confer any greater degree of protection on the site than that offered by the national protection framework.

If a site is considered to be in serious danger of decay or damage, the committee may add it to the World Heritage in Danger List. Sites on this list may benefit from particular attention or emergency measures to allay threats and allow them to retain their world heritage status, or in extreme cases of damage or neglect they may lose their world heritage status completely. At the 42nd session of the World Heritage Committee in July 2018, Lake Turkana National Parks in Kenya was added to the list and, following safeguarding measures taken by the country, Belize's Barrier Reef Reserve System was removed. A total of 54 sites are currently inscribed on the World Heritage in Danger List.

Financial support for the conservation of sites on the World Heritage List is provided by the World Heritage Fund, administered by the World Heritage Committee. The fund's income is derived from compulsory and voluntary contributions from the states party to the convention and from private donations.

WORLD HERITAGE CENTRE, UNESCO, 7 Place de Fontenoy, 75352 Paris Cedex 07, France **W** https://whc.unesco.org

DESIGNATED SITES

As at 5 July 2018, following the 42nd session of the World Heritage Committee, 1,092 sites across 167 countries were on the World Heritage List. Of these, 27 are in the UK and four in UK overseas territories; 26 are listed for their cultural significance (†), four for their natural significance (*) and one for both cultural and natural significance. Liverpool's Maritime Mercantile City is the only UK site on the List of World Heritage in Danger. The year in which sites were designated appears in the first set of parentheses. The number in the second set of parentheses denotes the position of each site on the map below.

WORLD HERITAGE SITES IN THE UK

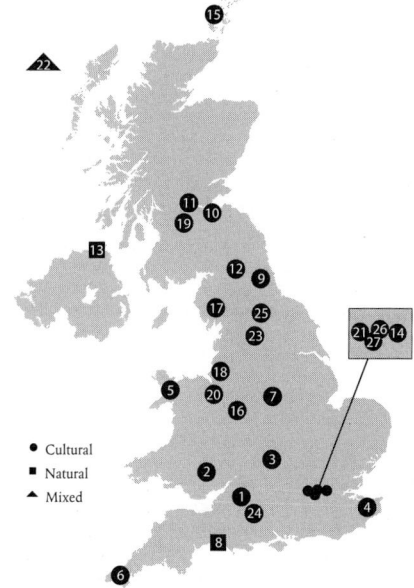

UNITED KINGDOM

†Bath – the city (1987). (1)

†Blaenarvon industrial landscape, Wales (2000). (2)

†Blenheim Palace and Park, Oxfordshire (1987). (3)

†Canterbury Cathedral, St Augustine's Abbey, St Martin's Church, Kent (1988). (4)

†Castle and town walls of King Edward I, north Wales – Beaumaris, Caernarfon Castle, Conwy Castle, Harlech Castle (1986). (5)

†Cornwall and west Devon mining landscape (2006). (6)

†Derwent Valley Mills, Derbyshire (2001). (7)

*Dorset and east Devon coast (2001). (8)

†Durham Cathedral and Castle (1986). (9)

†Edinburgh old and new towns (1995). (10)

†Forth Bridge, Firth of Forth, Scotland (2015). (11)

†Frontiers of the Roman Empire– Hadrian's Wall, northern England; Antonine Wall, central Scotland (1987, 2005, 2008). (12)

*Giant's Causeway and Causeway coast, Co. Antrim (1986). (13)

†Greenwich, London – maritime Greenwich, including the Royal Naval College, Old Royal Observatory, Queen's House, town centre (1997). (14)

†Heart of Neolithic Orkney (1999). (15)

†Ironbridge Gorge, Shropshire – the world's first iron bridge and other early industrial sites (1986). (16)

†Lake District, Cumbria (2017). (17)

†Liverpool – six areas of the maritime mercantile city (2004). (18)

†New Lanark, South Lanarkshire, Scotland (2001). (19)

†Pontcysyllte Aqueduct and Canal, Wrexham, Wales (2009). (20)

†Royal Botanic Gardens, Kew (2003). (21)

†*St Kilda, Eilean Siar (Western Isles) (1986). (22)

†Saltaire, West Yorkshire (2001). (23)

†Stonehenge, Avebury and related megalithic sites, Wiltshire (1986). (24)

†Studley Royal Park, Fountains Abbey, St Mary's Church, N. Yorkshire (1986). (25)

†Tower of London (1988). (26)

†Westminster Abbey, Palace of Westminster, St Margaret's Church, London (1987). (27)

UK OVERSEAS TERRITORIES

*Henderson Island, Pitcairn Islands, South Pacific Ocean (1988)

*Gough Island and Inaccessible Island (part of Tristan da Cunha), South Atlantic Ocean (1995)

†Historic town of St George and related fortifications, Bermuda (2000)

†Gorham's Cave Complex, Gibraltar (2016)

HISTORIC BUILDINGS AND MONUMENTS

ENGLAND

Under the Planning (Listed Buildings and Conservation Areas) Act 1990, the Secretary of State for Digital, Culture, Media and Sport has a statutory duty to approve buildings or groups of buildings in England that are of special architectural or historic interest. Since April 2015 the list of such buildings is maintained by Historic England who are also responsible for making recommendations to the secretary of state for additions, removals and amendments to the list. Under the Ancient Monuments and Archaeological Areas Act 1979 as amended by the National Heritage Act 1983, the secretary of state is also responsible for compiling a schedule of ancient monuments. Decisions are taken on the advice of Historic England. A searchable database of all nationally designated heritage assets, The National Heritage List for England (NHLE), is available online: W www.historicengland.org.uk/listing/the-list.

LISTED BUILDINGS

Listed buildings are classified into Grade I, Grade II* and Grade II. There are 378,011 listed buildings in England, of which approximately 90 per cent are Grade II listed. Almost all pre-1700 buildings are listed, as are most buildings of 1700 to 1840. Historic England surveys particular types of buildings with a view to making recommendations for listing. The main purpose of listing is to ensure that care is taken in deciding the future of a building. No changes which affect the architectural or historic character of a listed building can be made without listed building consent (in addition to planning permission where relevant). Applications for consent are normally dealt with by the local planning authority, although Historic England is always consulted about proposals affecting Grade I and Grade II* properties. It is a criminal offence to demolish a listed building, or alter it in such a way as to affect its character, without consent.

SCHEDULED MONUMENTS

There are 19,852 scheduled monuments in England. All monuments proposed for scheduling are considered to be of national importance. Where buildings are both scheduled and listed, ancient monuments legislation takes precedence. The main purpose of scheduling a monument is to preserve it for the future and to protect it from damage, destruction or any unnecessary interference. Once a monument has been scheduled, scheduled monument consent is required before any works can be carried out. The scope of the control is more extensive and more detailed than that applied to listed buildings, but certain minor works, as detailed in the Ancient Monuments (Class Consents) Order 1994, may be carried out without consent. It is a criminal offence to carry out unauthorised work to scheduled monuments.

WALES

Under the Planning (Listed Buildings and Conservation Areas) Act 1990 and the Ancient Monuments and Archaeological Areas Act 1979, the National Assembly for Wales is responsible for listing buildings and scheduling monuments in Wales on the advice of Cadw (the Welsh government's historic environment division) and the Royal Commission on the Ancient and Historical Monuments of Wales (RCAHMW). The criteria for evaluating buildings are similar to those in England and the same listing system is used. As at 31 March 2018, there were 29,997 listed buildings and 4,191 scheduled monuments in Wales.

SCOTLAND

Under the Planning (Listed Buildings and Conservation Areas) (Scotland) Act 1997 and the Ancient Monuments and Archaeological Areas Act 1979, Scottish ministers are responsible for listing buildings and scheduling monuments in Scotland on the advice of Historic Environment Scotland. The Historic Environment Scotland Act 2014 sets out Historic Environment Scotland's role and legal status. The criteria for evaluating buildings are similar to those in England but an A, B, C categorisation is used. As at 31 March 2018 there were 67,713 listed buildings and 8,120 scheduled monuments in Scotland.

NORTHERN IRELAND

Under the Planning (Northern Ireland) Act 2011 and the Historic Monuments and Archaeological Objects (Northern Ireland) Order 1995, the Historic Environment Division (part of the Department for Communities, Northern Ireland) is responsible for listing buildings and scheduling monuments. The Historic Buildings Council for Northern Ireland and the relevant district council must be consulted on listing proposals, and the Historic Monuments Council for Northern Ireland must be consulted on scheduling proposals. The criteria for evaluating buildings are similar to those in England but an A, B+, B1 and B2 categorisation is used. As at 31 March 2018 there were 10,221 listed buildings and 1,981 scheduled monuments in Northern Ireland.

ENGLAND

English Heritage cares for over 400 historic monuments, buildings and places. For more information on English Heritage properties, including those listed below, the official website is W www.english-heritage.org.uk
For more information on National Trust properties in England, including those listed below, the official website is W www.nationaltrust.org.uk

KEY
(EH) English Heritage property
(NT) National Trust property
* UNESCO World Heritage Site (see also World Heritage Sites)

A LA RONDE (NT), Exmouth, Devon EX8 5BD T 01395-265514
 Unique 16-sided house completed c.1796
ALNWICK CASTLE, Alnwick, Northumberland NE66 1NQ
 T 01665-511100 W www.alnwickcastle.com
 Seat of the Dukes of Northumberland since 1309; Italian Renaissance-style interior; gardens with spectacular water features
ALTHORP, Northants NN7 4HQ T 01604-770006
 W www.spencerofalthorp.com
 Spencer family seat built in 1508; home to the annual Althorp Literary Festival
ANGLESEY ABBEY (NT), Lode, Cambs CB25 9EJ
 T 01223-810080
 Jacobean house (c.1600) with gardens and a working watermill (Lode Mill) on the site of a 12th-century priory; fine furnishings and a unique clock collection
APSLEY HOUSE (EH), London W1J 7NT T 020-7499 5676
 Built by Robert Adam 1771–8, home of the Dukes of Wellington since 1817 and known as 'No. 1 London'; collection of fine and decorative arts
ARUNDEL CASTLE, Arundel, W. Sussex BN18 9AB
 T 01903-882173 W www.arundelcastle.org
 Castle dating from the Norman Conquest; seat of the Dukes of Norfolk

AVEBURY (EH/NT), Wilts SN8 1RF T 01672-539250
Remains of stone circles constructed 4,000 years ago
enclosing part of the later village of Avebury

BANQUETING HOUSE, Whitehall, London SW1A 2ER
T 020-3166 6000 W www.hrp.org.uk/banquetinghouse
Designed by Inigo Jones in 1619; ceiling paintings by
Rubens; site of the execution of Charles I

BASILDON PARK (NT), Reading, Berks RG8 9NR
T 01491-672382
Palladian mansion built in 1776–83 by John Carr

BATTLE ABBEY (EH), Battle, E. Sussex TN33 0AD
T 01424-775705
Remains of the abbey founded by William the Conqueror
on the site of the Battle of Hastings

BEESTON CASTLE (EH), Cheshire CW6 9TX T 01829-260464
Built in the 13th century by Ranulf, sixth Earl of Chester,
on the site of an Iron Age hillfort

BELVOIR CASTLE, Grantham, Lincs NG32 1PE
T 01476-871001 W www.belvoircastle.com
Seat of the Dukes of Rutland; 19th-century Gothic-style
castle; notable art collection

BERKELEY CASTLE, Glos GL13 9BQ T 01453-810303
W www.berkeley-castle.com
Completed late 12th century; site of the murder of
Edward II (1327)

BIRDOSWALD ROMAN FORT (EH), Brampton, Cumbria
CA8 7DD T 01697-747602
Stretch of Hadrian's Wall with Roman wall fort, turret
and milecastle

*BLENHEIM PALACE, Woodstock, Oxon OX20 1PP
T 01993-810530 W www.blenheimpalace.com
Seat of the Dukes of Marlborough and Winston
Churchill's birthplace; house designed by Vanbrugh;
landscaped parkland by Capability Brown

BLICKLING ESTATE (NT), Blickling, Norfolk NR11 6NF
T 01263-738030
Jacobean house with state rooms; extensive gardens,
temple and 18th-century orangery

BODIAM CASTLE (NT), Bodiam, E. Sussex TN32 5UA
T 01580-830196
Well-preserved medieval moated castle built in 1385

BOLSOVER CASTLE (EH), Bolsover, Derbys S44 6PR
T 01246-822844
17th-century castle on site of medieval fortress

BOSCOBEL HOUSE (EH), Bishops Wood, Shrops ST19 9AR
T 01902-850244
Timber-framed 17th-century hunting lodge; refuge of
fugitive Charles II from parliamentary troops

BOUGHTON HOUSE, Kettering, Northants NN14 1BJ
T 01536-515731 W www.boughtonhouse.org.uk
17th-century house with French-style additions; home of
the Dukes of Buccleuch and Queensbury

BOWOOD HOUSE, Calne, Wilts SN11 0LZ T 01249-812102
W www.bowood.org/bowood-house-gardens/house/
18th-century house in Capability Brown park, featuring
Robert Adam orangery and renowned pinetum and
arboretum

BUCKFAST ABBEY, Buckfastleigh, Devon TQ11 0EE
T 01364-645500 W www.buckfast.org.uk
Benedictine monastery on medieval foundations

BUCKINGHAM PALACE, London SW1A 1AA
T 030-3123 7300 W www.royalcollection.org.uk
Purchased by George III in 1761, and the Sovereign's
official London residence since 1837; 19 state rooms,
including the Throne Room, and Queen's Gallery

BUCKLAND ABBEY (NT), Yelverton, Devon PL20 6EY
T 01822-853607
13th-century Cistercian monastery; home of Sir Francis
Drake

BURGHLEY HOUSE, Stamford, Lincs PE9 3JY T 01780-752451
W www.burghley.co.uk
Late Elizabethan house built by William Cecil, first Lord
Burghley

CARISBROOKE CASTLE (EH), Newport, Isle of Wight PO30
1XY T 01983-522107
Norman castle; museum; prison of Charles I 1647–8

CARLISLE CASTLE (EH), Carlisle, Cumbria CA3 8UR
T 01228-591922
Medieval castle; prison of Mary, Queen of Scots

CASTLE ACRE PRIORY (EH), King's Lynn, Norfolk PE32 2XD
T 01760-755394
Remains include 12th-century church and prior's lodgings

CASTLE DROGO (NT), Drewsteignton, Devon EX6 6PB
T 01647-433306
Granite castle designed by Lutyens in 1911

CASTLE HOWARD, N. Yorks YO60 7DA T 01653-648333
W www.castlehoward.co.uk
Designed by Vanbrugh 1699–1726; mausoleum designed
by Hawksmoor

CASTLE RISING CASTLE (EH), King's Lynn, Norfolk PE31
6AH T 01553-631330 W www.castlerising.co.uk
12th-century keep with gatehouse and bridge, surrounded
by 20 acres of defensive earthworks

CHARLES DARWIN'S HOME (DOWN HOUSE) (EH),
Downe, Kent BR6 7JT T 01689-859119
The family home where Darwin wrote On the Origin of
Species

CHARTWELL (NT), Westerham, Kent TN16 1PS
T 01732-868381
Home and studio of Sir Winston Churchill

CHATSWORTH, Bakewell, Derbys DE45 1PP T 01246-565300
W www.chatsworth.org
Tudor mansion set in magnificent parkland; seat of the
Dukes of Devonshire

CHESTERS ROMAN FORT (EH), Chollerford,
Northumberland NE46 4EU T 01434-681379
Roman cavalry fort built to guard Hadrian's Wall

CHYSAUSTER ANCIENT VILLAGE (EH), Penzance,
Cornwall TR20 8XA T 07831-757934
Remains of nearly 2,000-year-old Celtic settlement; eight
stone-walled homesteads

CLIFFORD'S TOWER (EH), York YO1 9SA T 01904-646940
13th-century keep built on a mound; remains of a castle
built by William the Conqueror

CORBRIDGE ROMAN TOWN (EH), Corbridge,
Northumberland NE45 5NT T 01434-632349
Excavated central area of a Roman garrison town

CORFE CASTLE (NT), Wareham, Dorset BH20 5EZ
T 01929-481294
Former royal castle dating from the 11th century and
partially ruined during the English Civil War

CROFT CASTLE AND PARKLAND (NT), Yarpole,
Herefordshire HR6 9PW T 01568-780246
17th-century quadrangular manor house with Georgian-
Gothic interior; built close to ruin of pre-Conquest border
castle

DEAL CASTLE (EH), Deal, Kent CT14 7BA T 01304-372762
Largest of the coastal defence forts built by Henry VIII;
shaped like a rose with six inner and outer bastions

*DERWENT VALLEY MILLS, Belper, Derbyshire
T 01629-536831 W www.derwentvalleymills.org
Series of 18th- and 19th-century cotton mills; birthplace
of the modern factory

DOVER CASTLE (EH), Dover, Kent CT16 1HU T 01304-211067
Castle with Roman, Saxon and Norman features; tunnels
used as wartime operations rooms

DR JOHNSON'S HOUSE, Gough Square, London EC4A 3DE
T 020-7353 3745 W www.drjohnsonshouse.org
Home of Samuel Johnson 1748–59

DUNSTANBURGH CASTLE (EH/NT), Craster, nr Alnwick, Northumberland NE66 3TT T 01665-576231
14th-century castle ruins on a cliff with a substantial twin-towered gatehouse-keep

ELTHAM PALACE (EH), Eltham, London SE9 5QE
T 020-8294 2548
Art Deco house next to remains of medieval palace once occupied by Henry VIII; moated gardens

FARLEIGH HUNGERFORD CASTLE (EH), Bath, Somerset BA2 7RS T 01225-754026
Late 14th-century castle with inner and outer courts; chapel with rare medieval wall paintings

FARNHAM CASTLE KEEP (EH), Farnham, Surrey GU9 0AG
T 01252-721194 W www.farnhamcastle.com
Large 12th-century castle keep with motte and bailey wall

FISHBOURNE ROMAN PALACE, Fishbourne, Chichester, W. Sussex PO19 3QR T 01243-785859 W www.sussexpast.co.uk
Excavated Roman palace with largest collection of in-situ mosaics in Britain

*FOUNTAINS ABBEY (NT), nr Ripon, N. Yorks HG4 3DY
T 01765-608888
Ruined Cistercian monastery and corn mill; site includes Studley Royal, a Georgian water garden and deer park

FRAMLINGHAM CASTLE (EH), Framlingham, Suffolk IP13 9BP T 01728-724189
Castle (c.1200) with high curtain walls enclosing an almshouse (1639); once the refuge of Mary Tudor

FURNESS ABBEY (EH), Barrow-in-Furness, Cumbria LA13 0PJ
T 01229-823420
Remains of church and cloister buildings founded in 1124 by Stephen, later king of England

GLASTONBURY ABBEY, Glastonbury, Somerset BA6 9EL
T 01458-832267 W www.glastonburyabbey.com
12th-century abbey destroyed by fire in 1184 and later rebuilt; ruined in 1539 during dissolution of monasteries; site of an early Christian settlement

GOODRICH CASTLE (EH), Ross-on-Wye, Herefordshire HR9 6HY T 01600-890538
Remains of 12th- and 13th-century castle; contains a famous mortar that ruined the castle in 1646

GREENWAY (NT), nr Brixham, Devon TQ5 0ES T 01803-842382
Agatha Christie's holiday home which inspired several of the settings in her books, including the murder in *Dead Man's Folly*; large woodland; walled garden

*GREENWICH, London SE10 9NF T 0870-608 2000
W www.visitgreenwich.org.uk
Former Royal Observatory (founded 1675) housing the time ball and zero meridian of longitude; the Queen's House, designed for Queen Anne, wife of James I, by Inigo Jones; Painted Hall and neoclassical Chapel (Old Royal Naval College)

GRIME'S GRAVES (EH), Brandon, Norfolk IP26 5DE
T 01842-810656
Neolithic flint mines; one shaft can be descended

GUILDHALL, London EC2V 7HH T 020-7332 1313
W www.guildhall.cityoflondon.gov.uk
Centre of civic government of the City built c.1441; facade built 1788–9

HADDON HALL, Bakewell, Derbys DE45 1LA T 01629-812855
W www.haddonhall.co.uk
Well-preserved 12th-century manor house

HAILES ABBEY (EH), Cheltenham, Glos GL54 5PB
T 01242-602398
Ruins of a 13th-century Cistercian monastery

HAM HOUSE AND GARDEN (NT), Richmond-upon-Thames, Surrey TW10 7RS T 020-8940 1950
Stuart house with lavish interiors and formal gardens

HAMPTON COURT PALACE, East Molesey, Surrey KT8 9AU
T 020-3166 6000 W www.hrp.org.uk/hampton-court-palace
16th-century palace originally built for Cardinal Wolsey with 17th- and 18th-century additions by Wren; Royal Tennis Court and world-renowned maze

HARDWICK HALL (NT), Chesterfield, Derbys S44 5QJ
T 01246-850430
Elizabethan house built for Bess of Hardwick

HARDY'S COTTAGE (NT), Higher Bockhampton, Dorset DT2 8QJ T 01305-262366
Birthplace and home of Thomas Hardy

HAREWOOD HOUSE, Harewood, W. Yorks LS17 9LG
T 0113-218 1010 W www.harewood.org
18th-century house designed by John Carr and Robert Adam; park by Capability Brown

HATFIELD HOUSE, Hatfield, Herts AL9 5NQ T 01707-287010
W www.hatfield-house.co.uk
Jacobean house built by Robert Cecil; features surviving wing of Royal Palace of Hatfield (c.1485), the childhood home of Elizabeth I

HELMSLEY CASTLE (EH), Helmsley, N. Yorks YO62 5AB
T 01439-770442
12th-century keep and curtain wall with 16th-century buildings; spectacular earthwork defences

HEVER CASTLE, nr Edenbridge, Kent TN8 7NG
T 01732-865224 W www.hevercastle.co.uk
13th-century double-moated castle; childhood home of Anne Boleyn

HOLKHAM HALL, Wells-next-the-Sea, Norfolk NR23 1AB
T 01328-713111 W www.holkham.co.uk
Palladian mansion; notable fine art collection

HOUSESTEADS ROMAN FORT (EH), Hexham, Northumberland NE47 6NN T 01434-344363
Excavated Roman infantry fort on Hadrian's Wall with museum

*IRONBRIDGE GORGE, Ironbridge, Shropshire
T 01952-433424 W www.ironbridge.org.uk
Important Industrial Revolution site, featuring the world's first iron bridge

KEDLESTON HALL (NT), Derbys DE22 5JH T 01332-842191
Palladian mansion built 1759–65; complete Robert Adam interiors; museum of Asian artefacts

KELMSCOTT MANOR, nr Lechlade, Glos GL7 3HJ
T 01367-252486 W www.sal.org.uk/kelmscott-manor/
Built c.1600; summer home of William Morris, with products of Morris and Co.

KENILWORTH CASTLE (EH), Kenilworth, Warks CV8 1NE
T 01926-852078
Largest castle ruin in England; Norman keep with 13th-century outer walls

KENSINGTON PALACE, Kensington Gardens, London W8 4PX
T 020-3166 6000 W www.hrp.org.uk/kensington-palace
Built in 1605 and enlarged by Wren; birthplace of Queen Victoria

KENWOOD HOUSE (EH), Hampstead Lane, London NW3 7JR
T 020-8348 1286
Neoclassical villa housing the Iveagh bequest of paintings and furniture

KEW PALACE, Richmond-upon-Thames, Surrey TW9 3AB
T 020-3166 6000 W www.hrp.org.uk/kew-palace
Red-brick mansion (c.1631); includes Queen Charlotte's Cottage, used by King George III and family as a summerhouse

KINGSTON LACY (NT), Wimborne Minster, Dorset BH21 4EA
T 01202-883402
17th-century mansion with 19th-century alterations; important art collection

KNEBWORTH HOUSE, Knebworth, Herts SG3 6PY
T 01438-812661 W www.knebworthhouse.com
Tudor manor house concealed by 19th-century Gothic decoration; Lutyens gardens

KNOLE (NT), Sevenoaks, Kent TN15 0RP T 01732-462100
House built in 1456 set in 1,000-acre deer park; fine art and furniture collection; birthplace of Vita Sackville-West

LAMBETH PALACE, London SE1 7JU T 020-7898 1200
W www.archbishopofcanterbury.org/about-lambeth-palace
Official residence of the Archbishop of Canterbury since the 13th century

LANERCOST PRIORY (EH), Brampton, Cumbria CA8 2HQ
T 01697-73030 W www.lanercostpriory.org.uk
The nave of the Augustinian priory's church, c.1166, is still used; remains of other claustral buildings

LANHYDROCK (NT), Bodmin, Cornwall PL30 5AD
T 01208-265950
House dating from the 17th century; 50 rooms, including kitchen and nursery

LEEDS CASTLE, nr Maidstone, Kent ME17 1PL T 01622-765400
W www.leeds-castle.com
Castle dating from the 12th century, situated on two islands in a lake; used as a royal palace by Henry VIII

LEVENS HALL, Kendal, Cumbria LA8 0PD T 01539-560321
W www.levenshall.co.uk
Elizabethan house with unique topiary garden (1694); steam engine collection

LINCOLN CASTLE, Lincoln, Lincs LN1 3AA T 01522-554559
W www.lincolncastle.com
Built by William the Conqueror in 1068 on a Roman site; one of only two double-motted castles in Britain

LINDISFARNE PRIORY (EH), Holy Island, Northumberland
TD15 2RX T 01289-389200
Founded in AD 635; re-established in the 12th century as a Benedictine priory, now ruined

LITTLE MORETON HALL (NT), Congleton, Cheshire CW12
4SD T 01260-272018
Iconic timber-framed moated Tudor manor house with knot garden

LONGLEAT HOUSE, Warminster, Wilts BA12 7NW
T 01985-844400 W www.longleat.co.uk
Elizabethan house in Italian Renaissance style; Capability Brown parkland with lakes; safari park

LULLINGSTONE ROMAN VILLA (EH), Eynsford, Kent DA4
0JA T 01322-863467
Large villa occupied for much of the Roman period; fine mosaics and unique Christian paintings

MIDDLEHAM CASTLE (EH), Middleham, N. Yorks DL8 4QG
T 01969-623899
12th-century keep within later fortifications; childhood home of Richard III

MONTACUTE HOUSE (NT), Montacute, Somerset TA15 6XP
T 01935-823289
Elizabethan mansion with National Portrait Gallery collection of portraits from the period

MOUNT GRACE PRIORY (EH), Northallerton, N. Yorks DL6
3JG T 01609-883494
Carthusian priory with remains of monastic buildings

OLD SARUM (EH), Salisbury, Wilts SP1 3SD T 01722-335398
Iron Age hill fort enclosing remains of Norman castle and cathedral

ORFORD CASTLE (EH), Orford, Suffolk IP12 2ND
T 01394-450472
Polygonal tower keep of c.1170 and remains of coastal defence castle built by Henry II

OSBORNE HOUSE (EH), East Cowes, Isle of Wight PO32 6JX
T 01983-200022
Queen Victoria's seaside residence; built by Thomas Cubitt in Italian Renaissance style; summer house, Swiss Cottage and museum

OSTERLEY PARK AND HOUSE (NT), Isleworth, Middx TW7
4RB T 020-8232 5050
18th-century neoclassical mansion with Tudor stable block

PENDENNIS CASTLE (EH), Falmouth, Cornwall TR11 4LP
T 01326-316594
Well-preserved 16th-century coastal defence castle

PENSHURST PLACE, Penshurst, Kent TN11 8DG
T 01892-870307 W www.penshurstplace.com
Medieval house featuring Baron's Hall (1341) and gardens (1346); toy museum

PETWORTH HOUSE (NT), Petworth, W. Sussex GU28 0AE
T 01798-342207
Late 17th-century house set in Capability Brown landscaped deer park; fine art collection

PEVENSEY CASTLE (EH), Pevensey, E. Sussex BN24 5LE
T 01323-762604
Walls of a fourth-century Roman fort; remains of an 11th-century castle

PEVERIL CASTLE (EH), Castleton, Derbys S33 8WQ
T 01433-620613
Remains of a 12th-century castle defended on two sides by precipitous rocks

POLESDEN LACEY (NT), nr Dorking, Surrey RH5 6BD
T 01372-452048
Regency villa remodelled in the Edwardian era; fine paintings and furnishings; walled rose garden

PORTCHESTER CASTLE (EH), Portchester, Hants PO16 9QW
T 02392-378291
Walls of a late Roman fort enclosing a Norman keep and an Augustinian priory church

POWDERHAM CASTLE, Kenton, Devon EX6 8JQ
T 01626-890243 W www.powderham.co.uk
Medieval castle with 18th- and 19th-century alterations, including James Wyatt music room

RABY CASTLE, Staindrop, Co. Durham DL2 3AH
T 01833-660202 W www.rabycastle.com
14th-century castle with walled gardens

RAGLEY HALL, Alcester, Warks B49 5NJ T 01789-762090
W www.ragley.co.uk
17th-century Palladian house with gardens and lake

RICHBOROUGH ROMAN FORT (EH), Richborough, Kent
CT13 9JW T 01304-612013
Remains of a Roman Saxon Shore fortress; landing-site of the Claudian invasion in AD 43

RICHMOND CASTLE (EH), Richmond, N. Yorks DL10 4QW
T 01748-822493
12th-century keep with 11th-century curtain wall

RIEVAULX ABBEY (EH), nr Helmsley, N. Yorks YO62 5LB
T 01439-798228
Remains of a Cistercian abbey founded c.1132

ROCHESTER CASTLE (EH), Rochester, Kent ME1 1SW
T 01634-335882
11th-century castle partly on the Roman city wall, with a well-preserved square keep of c.1127

ROCKINGHAM CASTLE, Market Harborough, Leics LE16 8TH
T 01536-770240 W www.rockinghamcastle.com
Built by William the Conqueror; formal gardens and 400-year-old 'elephant' hedge

ROMAN BATHS, Pump Room, Stall Street, Bath BA1 1LZ
T 01225-477785 W www.romanbaths.co.uk
Extensive remains of a Roman temple and bathing complex which still flows with natural thermal water; museum

ROYAL PAVILION, Brighton BN1 1EE T 03000-290900
W https://brightonmuseums.org.uk/royalpavilion
Unique palace of George IV, in indo-gothic style with chinoiserie interiors and Regency gardens

ST AUGUSTINE'S ABBEY (EH), Canterbury, Kent CT1 1PF
T 01227-767345
Remains of Benedictine monastery founded in 598
ST MAWES CASTLE (EH), St Mawes, Cornwall TR2 5DE
T 01326-270526
Coastal defence castle built by Henry VIII
ST MICHAEL'S MOUNT (NT), Marazion, Cornwall TR17 0HS
T 01736-710265 W www.stmichaelsmount.co.uk
12th-century church and castle with later additions,
situated on an iconic rocky island
*SALTAIRE VILLAGE, nr Shipley, W. Yorks T 01274-437942
W www.saltairevillage.info
Victorian industrial village founded by mill owner Titus
Salt for his workers; see also World Heritage Sites
SANDRINGHAM, Norfolk PE35 6EN T 01485-545400
W www.sandringhamestate.co.uk
The Queen's private residence; neo-Jacobean house built
in 1870 with gardens and country park
SCARBOROUGH CASTLE (EH), Scarborough, N. Yorks YO11
1HY T 01723-372451
Remains of 12th-century keep and curtain walls
SHERBORNE CASTLE, Sherborne, Dorset DT9 5NR
T 01935-812072 W www.sherbornecastle.com
16th-century castle built by Sir Walter Raleigh set in
Capability Brown landscaped gardens
SHUGBOROUGH ESTATE (NT), Milford, Staffs ST17 0XB
T 01889-880160
Late 17th century house in 18th-century park with
monuments, temples and pavilions in the Greek Revival
style; seat of the Earls of Lichfield
SISSINGHURST CASTLE GARDEN (NT), Nr Cranbrook,
Kent TN17 2AB T 01580-710700
Early 14th century site, purchased by Vita Sackville-West
in the 1930s where the writer, poet and Bloomsbury
Group member created the famous gardens
SKIPTON CASTLE, Skipton, N. Yorks BD23 1AW
T 01756-792442 W www.skiptoncastle.co.uk
Well-preserved D-shaped medieval castle with six round
towers and inner courtyard
SMALLHYTHE PLACE (NT), Tenterden, Kent TN30 7NG
T 01580-762334
Half-timbered 16th-century house
*STONEHENGE (EH), nr Amesbury, Wilts SP4 7DE
T 0370-333 1181
World-famous prehistoric monument comprising
concentric stone circles surrounded by a ditch and bank
STONOR PARK, Henley-on-Thames, Oxon RG9 6HF
T 01491-638587 W www.stonor.com
Medieval house with Georgian facade; refuge for Catholic
recusants after the Reformation
STOURHEAD (NT), Stourton, Wilts BA12 6QD T 01747-841152
18th-century Palladian mansion with world-renowned
landscape gardens; King Alfred's Tower
STRATFIELD SAYE HOUSE, Hants RG7 2BT T 01256-882694
W www.wellingtonestates.co.uk/stratfield-saye-house
House built 1630–40; home of the Dukes of Wellington
since 1817
STRATFORD-UPON-AVON, Warks T 01789-868191
W www.stratford-upon-avon.co.uk
Shakespeare's Birthplace Trust with Shakespeare Centre;
Anne Hathaway's Cottage; Holy Trinity Church, where
Shakespeare is buried
STRAWBERRY HILL HOUSE, Waldegrave Road, Twickenham
TW1 4ST T 020-8744 1241 W www.strawberryhillhouse.org.uk
Early Gothic Revival villa built between 1749 and 1776
for Horace Walpole (1717–97)
SUDELEY CASTLE, Winchcombe, Glos GL54 5JD
T 01242-604244 W www.sudeleycastle.co.uk
Castle built in 1442; once owned by Richard III and
former home to Catherine Parr, sixth wife of Henry VIII;
restored in the 19th century

SULGRAVE MANOR, nr Banbury, Oxon OX17 2SD
T 01295-760205 W www.sulgravemanor.org.uk
Home of George Washington's family
SUTTON HOUSE (NT), Hackney, London E9 6JQ
T 020-8986 2264
Tudor house, built in 1535 by Sir Ralph Sadleir
SYON HOUSE, Brentford, Middx TW8 8JF T 020-8560 0882
W www.syonpark.co.uk
Built on the site of a former monastery; Robert Adam
interior; Capability Brown park
TINTAGEL CASTLE (EH), Tintagel, Cornwall PL34 0HE
T 01840-770328
13th-century cliff-top castle and 5th–6th-century Celtic
settlement; linked with Arthurian legend
TOWER OF LONDON, London EC3N 4AB T 020-3166 6000
W www.hrp.org.uk/tower-of-london
Royal palace and fortress begun by William the
Conqueror in 1078; houses the Crown Jewels
TYNEMOUTH PRIORY AND CASTLE (EH), Tyne and Wear
NE30 4BZ T 01912-571090
Remains of a Benedictine priory, founded c.1090, moated
castle-towers, a gatehouse and keep on Saxon monastic
site
UPPARK (NT), South Harting, W. Sussex GU31 5QR
T 01730-825415
17th-century house, restored after fire; Fetherstonhaugh
art collection; 18th-century dolls' house
WALMER CASTLE (EH), Walmer, Kent CT14 7LJ
T 01304-364288
One of Henry VIII's coastal defence castles, now the
residence of the Lord Warden of the Cinque Ports
WARKWORTH CASTLE (EH), Warkworth, Northumberland
NE65 0UJ T 01665-711423
14th-century keep amid earlier ruins, with hermitage
upstream
WHITBY ABBEY (EH), Whitby, N. Yorks YO22 4JT
T 01947-603568
Remains of Norman church on the site of a monastery
founded in AD 657
WILTON HOUSE, nr Salisbury, Wilts SP2 0BJ T 01722-746728
W www.wiltonhouse.com
17th-century house on the site of a Tudor house and
ninth-century nunnery; Palladian bridge
WINDSOR CASTLE, Windsor, Berks SL4 1NJ T 030-3123 7304
W www.royalcollection.org.uk
Official residence of the Queen; oldest royal residence still
in regular use; largest inhabited castle in the world. Also
St George's Chapel; Queen Mary's Dolls' House
WOBURN ABBEY, Woburn, Beds MK17 9WA T 01525-290333
W www.woburn.co.uk
Built on the site of a Cistercian abbey; seat of the Dukes
of Bedford; art collection
WROXETER ROMAN CITY (EH), nr Shrewsbury, Shropshire
SY5 6PH T 01743-761330
Second-century public baths and part of the forum of the
Roman town of Viroconium

WALES

For more information on Cadw properties, including those
listed below, the official website is W www.cadw.wales.gov.uk
For more information on National Trust properties in Wales,
including those listed below, the official website is
W www.nationaltrust.org.uk

KEY
(C) Property of Cadw: Welsh Historic Monuments
(NT) National Trust property
* UNESCO World Heritage Site (see also World Heritage Sites)

*BEAUMARIS CASTLE (C), Anglesey LL58 8AP
T 01248-810361
Concentrically planned 13th-century castle, still virtually
intact

*BLAENAVON, Church Road, Blaenavon NP4 9AS T 01495-742333 W www.visitblaenavon.co.uk

18th- and 19th-century industrial landscape associated with coal and iron production

CAERLEON ROMAN BATHS AND AMPHITHEATRE (C), Newport NP18 1AE T 01633-422518

Rare example of a legionary bath-house and late first-century arena surrounded by bank for spectators

*CAERNARFON CASTLE (C), Gwynedd LL55 2AY T 01286-677617 W www.caernarfon-castle.co.uk

Huge fortress with polygonal towers built between 1283 and 1330, initially for King Edward I of England; setting for the investiture of Prince Charles in 1969

CAERPHILLY CASTLE (C), Caerphilly CF83 1JD T 029-2088 3143

Concentrically planned castle (c.1270) notable for its scale and use of water defences

CARDIFF CASTLE, Cardiff CF10 3RB T 029-2087 8100 W www.cardiffcastle.com

Norman keep built on site of Roman fort; 'fairytale' gothic-revival mansion added in the 19th century

CASTELL COCH (C), Tongwynlais, Cardiff CF15 7JS T 029-2081 0101

'Fairytale'-style castle, rebuilt 1872–91 on medieval foundations

CHEPSTOW CASTLE (C), Monmouthshire NP16 5EY T 01291-624065

Rectangular keep amid extensive fortifications; developed throughout the Middle Ages

*CONWY CASTLE (C), Gwynedd LL32 8AY T 01492-592358

Built for Edward I in 1283–9 on narrow rocky outcrop; features eight towers and two barbicans

CRICCIETH CASTLE (C), Gwynedd LL52 0DP T 01766-522227

Native Welsh 13th-century castle, taken and altered by Edward I and Edward II

DENBIGH CASTLE (C), Denbighshire LL16 3NB T 01745-813385

Remains of the castle (begun 1282), including triple-towered gatehouses

DYFFRYN GARDENS (NT), St Nicholas, Cardiff CF5 6SU T 029-2059 3328

Edwardian gardens designed by Thomas Mawson, overlooked by a grand Edwardian mansion

*HARLECH CASTLE (C), Gwynedd LL46 2YH T 01766-780552

Well-preserved castle, constructed 1283–95, on an outcrop above the former shoreline; withstood seven-year siege 1461–8

PEMBROKE CASTLE, Pembrokeshire SA71 4LA T 01646-681510 W www.pembroke-castle.co.uk

Castle founded in 1093; Great Tower built in late 12th century; birthplace of King Henry VII

PENRHYN CASTLE (NT), Bangor, Gwynedd LL57 4HN T 01248-353084

Neo-Norman castle built in the 19th century; railway and dolls' museums; private art collection

*PONTCYSYLLTE AQUEDUCT AND CANAL, Trevor, Wrexham LL20 7TG T 01978-292015 W www.pontcysyllte-aqueduct.co.uk

Longest and highest aqueduct in Great Britain; designed by Thomas Telford and finished in 1805

POWIS CASTLE (NT), Welshpool, Powys SY21 8RF T 01938-551944

Medieval castle with interior in variety of styles; 17th-century gardens; Clive of India museum

RAGLAN CASTLE (C), Monmouthshire NP15 2BT T 01291-690228

Remains of 15th-century castle with moated hexagonal keep

ST DAVIDS BISHOP'S PALACE (C), Pembrokeshire SA62 6PE T 01437-720517

Remains of residence of Bishops of St Davids built 1328–47

TINTERN ABBEY (C), nr Chepstow, Monmouthshire NP16 6SE T 01291-689251

Remains of 13th-century church and conventual buildings of a 12th-century Cistercian monastery

TRETOWER COURT AND CASTLE (C), Nr Crickhowell, Powys NP8 1RD T 01874-730279

Medieval manor house rebuilt in the 15th century, with remains of 12th-century castle nearby

SCOTLAND

For more information on Historic Environment Scotland properties, including those listed below, the official website is W www.historicenvironment.scot

For more information on National Trust for Scotland properties, including those listed below, the official website is W www.nts.org.uk

KEY

(HES) Historic Environment Scotland property
(NTS) National Trust for Scotland property
* Part of the Heart of Neolithic Orkney UNESCO World Heritage Site

ABBOTSFORD HOUSE, Melrose, Roxburghshire TD6 9BQ T 01896-752043 W www.scottsabbotsford.co.uk

Home of Sir Walter Scott; features historic Scottish relics and formal gardens

BALMORAL CASTLE, Ballater, Aberdeenshire AB35 5TB T 01339-742534 W www.balmoralcastle.com

Baronial-style castle built for Victoria and Albert; the Queen's private residence

BLACKHOUSE, ARNOL (HES), Lewis, Western Isles HS2 9DB T 01851-710395

Traditional Lewis thatched house

BLAIR CASTLE, Blair Atholl, Perthshire PH18 5TL T 01796-481207 W www.blair-castle.co.uk

Mid-18th-century mansion with 13th-century tower; seat of the Dukes and Earls of Atholl

BOWHILL, Selkirk, Scottish Borders TD7 5ET T 01750-22204 W www.bowhillhouse.co.uk

Present house dates mainly from 1812; Seat of the Dukes of Buccleuch and Queensberry; fine collection of paintings

BROUGH OF BIRSAY (HES), Orkney KW17 2LX T 01856-841815

Remains of Norse and Pictish village on the tidal island of Birsay

CAERLAVEROCK CASTLE (HES), Glencaple, Dumfries and Galloway DG1 4RU T 01387-770244

Unique triangular 13th-century moated castle with classical Renaissance additions

CAIRNPAPPLE HILL (HES), Torphichen, West Lothian T 01506-634622

Neolithic ceremonial site and Bronze Age burial chambers

CALANAIS STANDING STONES (HES), Lewis, Western Isles HS2 9DY T 01851-621422

Standing stones in a cross-shaped setting, dating from between 2900 and 2600 BC

CATERTHUNS (BROWN AND WHITE) (HES), Menmuir, nr Brechin, Angus

Two large Iron Age hill forts

CAWDOR CASTLE, Nairn, Moray IV12 5RD T 01667-404401 W www.cawdorcastle.com

14th-century keep with 15th- and 17th-century additions

CLAVA CAIRNS (HES), nr Inverness, Inverness-shire IV2 5EU
T 0131-668 8600
Bronze Age cemetery complex of cairns and standing stones

CRATHES CASTLE (NTS), nr Banchory, Aberdeenshire AB31 5QJ T 01330-844525
16th-century baronial castle in woodland, fields and gardens

CULZEAN CASTLE (NTS), Maybole, Ayrshire KA19 8LE
T 01655-884455
18th-century Robert Adam castle with oval staircase and circular saloon

DRYBURGH ABBEY (HES), nr Melrose, Roxburghshire TD6 0RQ T 01835-822381
12th-century abbey containing the tomb of Sir Walter Scott

DUNVEGAN CASTLE, Skye IV55 8WF T 01470-521206
W www.dunvegancastle.com
13th-century castle with later additions; home of the chiefs of the Clan MacLeod

EDINBURGH CASTLE (HES), EH1 2NG T 0131-225 9846
W www.edinburghcastle.gov.uk
Fortress perched on extinct volcano; includes the Scottish Crown Jewels, Scottish National War Memorial, Scottish United Services Museum

EDZELL CASTLE (HES), nr Brechin, Angus DD9 7UE
T 01356-648631
Ruined 16th-century tower house on medieval foundations; early 17th-century walled garden

EILEAN DONAN CASTLE, Dornie, Ross and Cromarty IV40 8DX T 01599-555202 W www.eileandonancastle.com
13th-century castle situated at the meeting point of three sea lochs; Jacobite relics

ELGIN CATHEDRAL (HES), Moray IV30 1HU T 01343-547171
13th-century cathedral and octagonal chapterhouse

FLOORS CASTLE, Kelso, Roxburghshire TD5 7SF
T 01573-223333 W www.floorscastle.com
Largest inhabited castle in Scotland; seat of the Dukes of Roxburghe; built in the 1720s by William Adam

FORT GEORGE (HES), Ardersier, Inverness-shire IV2 7TD
T 01667-460232
18th-century fort; still a working army barracks

GLAMIS CASTLE, Forfar, Angus DD8 1RJ T 01307-840393
W www.glamis-castle.co.uk
Seat of the Lyon family (later Earls of Strathmore and Kinghorne) since 1372; the setting for Shakespeare's *Macbeth*

GLASGOW CATHEDRAL (HES), Lanarkshire G4 0QZ
T 0141-552 8198 W www.glasgowcathedral.org.uk
Late 12th-century cathedral with vaulted crypt

GLENELG BROCHS (HES), Glenelg, Ross and Cromarty
T 0131-668 8600
Two broch towers (Dun Telve and Dun Troddan) with well-preserved structural features

HOPETOUN HOUSE, South Queensferry, West Lothian EH30 9SL T 0131-331 2451 W www.hopetoun.co.uk
Designed by Sir William Bruce in 1699 and enlarged by William Adam 1721–48

HUNTLY CASTLE (HES), Aberdeenshire AB54 4SH
T 01466-793191
Ruin of a 16th- and 17th-century baronial residence

INVERARAY CASTLE, Argyll PA32 8XE T 01499-302203
W www.inveraray-castle.com
Gothic-style 18th-century castle designed by William Adam and Roger Morris; seat of the Dukes of Argyll

IONA ABBEY (HES), Iona, Inner Hebrides PA76 6SQ
T 01681-700512
Monastery founded by St Columba in AD 563

JARLSHOF (HES), Sumburgh Head, Shetland ZE3 9JN
T 01950-460112
Prehistoric settlement with later ninth-century Norse additions

JEDBURGH ABBEY (HES), Scottish Borders TD8 6JQ
T 01835-863925
Ruined Augustinian abbey founded c.1138

KISIMUL CASTLE (HES), Castlebay, Barra, Western Isles HS9 5UZ T 01871-810313
Medieval island home of the Clan MacNeil

LINLITHGOW PALACE (HES), Kirkgate, Linlithgow, West Lothian EH49 7AL T 01506-842896
Ruined royal palace, founded in 1424, set in park; birthplace of James V and Mary, Queen of Scots

*MAESHOWE (HES), Stenness, Orkney KW16 3HH
T 01856-851266
Neolithic chambered tomb with Viking runes

MEIGLE SCULPTURED STONES (HES), Meigle, Perthshire PH12 8SB T 01828-640612
Twenty-six carved Pictish stones dating from the late 8th to the late 10th centuries

MELROSE ABBEY (HES), Melrose, Roxburghshire TD6 9LG
T 01896-822562
Ruin of Cistercian abbey founded c.1136 by David I; museum of medieval objects

MOUSA BROCH (HES), Island of Mousa, Shetland ZE2 9HP
Finest surviving Iron Age broch tower

NEW ABBEY CORN MILL (HES), Dumfriesshire DG2 8BX
T 01387-850260
Working water-powered mill built in the late 18th century

*NEW LANARK, South Lanarkshire ML11 9DB T 01555-661345
W www.newlanark.org
18th-century village built around a cotton mill

PALACE OF HOLYROODHOUSE, Edinburgh EH8 8DX
T 0303-123 7306 W www.royalcollection.org.uk
The Queen's official Scottish residence; home to Mary, Queen of Scots; main part of the palace built 1671–9 close to ruined 12th-century Augustinian abbey

*RING OF BRODGAR (HES), Stenness, Orkney KW16
T 0131-668 8600
Neolithic circle of upright stones surrounded by circular ditch

ROSSLYN CHAPEL, Roslin, Midlothian EH25 9PU
T 0131-440 2159 W www.rosslynchapel.org.uk
Historic church built between 1446 and 1484 with unique stone carvings

ST ANDREWS CASTLE AND CATHEDRAL (HES), Fife KY16 9AR (castle); 9QL (cathedral) T 01334-477196 (castle); 01334-472563 (cathedral)
Ruins of 13th-century castle, the former residence of bishops of St Andrews, and remains of the largest cathedral in Scotland; museum

SCONE PALACE, Perth, Perthshire PH2 6BD T 01738-552300
W www.scone-palace.co.uk
Georgian-Gothic house built 1802–12

*SKARA BRAE (HES), nr Stromness, Orkney KW16 3LR
T 01856-841815
Neolithic village with adjacent replica house

SMAILHOLM TOWER (HES), nr Kelso, Roxburghshire TD5 7PG T 01573-460365
Well-preserved 15th-century tower-house

STIRLING CASTLE (HES), Stirlingshire FK8 1EJ
T 01786-450000 W www.stirlingcastle.gov.uk
Great Hall and gatehouse built for James IV c.1500; palace built for James V in 1538; site of coronations including Mary, Queen of Scots

*STONES OF STENNESS (HES), Stenness, Orkney
T 0131-668 8600
Four surviving Neolithic standing stones and the uprights
of a three-stone dolmen

TANTALLON CASTLE (HES), North Berwick, East Lothian
EH39 5PN T 01620-892727
Ruined 14th-century curtain wall with towers

THREAVE CASTLE (HES), Castle Douglas, Kirkcudbrightshire
DG7 1TJ T 07711-223101
Ruined late 14th-century tower on an island; accessible
only by boat

URQUHART CASTLE (HES), Drumnadrochit, Inverness-shire
IV63 6XJ T 01456-450551
13th-century castle remains on the banks of Loch Ness

NORTHERN IRELAND

For the Northern Ireland Department for Communities, the
official website is W www.discovernorthernireland.com
For more information on National Trust properties in Northern
Ireland, including those listed below, the official website is
W www.nationaltrust.org.uk

KEY
(NIDC) Property in the care of the Northern Ireland
Department for Communities
(NT) National Trust property

CARRICKFERGUS CASTLE (NIDC), Carrickfergus, Co.
Antrim BT38 7BG T 028-9335 1273
Castle built in 1177 and taken by King John in 1210;
garrisoned until 1928

CASTLE COOLE (NT), Enniskillen, Co. Fermanagh BT74 6JY
T 028-6632 2690
18th-century neoclassical mansion in parkland; designed
by James Wyatt

CASTLE WARD (NT), Strangford, Co. Down BT30 7LS
T 028-4488 1204
18th-century house with Classical and Gothic facades

DEVENISH MONASTIC SITE (NIDC), nr Enniskillen, Co.
Fermanagh T 028-9082 3207
Island monastery founded in the sixth century by St
Molaise; church dating from 13th century

DOWNHILL DEMESNE AND HEZLETT HOUSE (NT),
Castlerock, Co. Londonderry BT51 4RP T 028-7084 8728
Ruins of 18th-century mansion and a 17th century
cottage in landscaped estate including Mussenden Temple

DUNLUCE CASTLE (NIDC), Bushmills, Co. Antrim BT57 8UY
T 028-2073 1938
Ruins of medieval stronghold of the McDonnells

FLORENCE COURT (NT), Enniskillen, Co. Fermanagh BT92
1DB T 028-6634 8249
Mid-18th-century house with Rococo decoration

GREY ABBEY (NIDC), Greyabbey, Co. Down BT22 2NQ
T 028-9082 3207
Substantial remains of a Cistercian abbey founded in
1193 set in landscaped parkland

MOUNT STEWART (NT), Newtownards, Co. Down BT22 2AD
T 028-4278 8387
19th-century neoclassical house; octagonal Temple of the
Winds

NENDRUM MONASTIC SITE (NIDC), Mahee Island, Co.
Down T 028-9082 3207
Island monastery founded in the fifth century by St
Machaoi

PATTERSON'S SPADE MILL (NT), Templepatrick, Co. Antrim
BT39 0AP T 028-9443 3619
Last working water-driven spade mill in the UK

TULLY CASTLE (NIDC), Co. Fermanagh T 028-9082 3207
Fortified house and bawn built c.1619

MUSEUMS AND GALLERIES

There are approximately 2,500 museums and galleries in the UK. As at April 2018, 1,566 of these were fully accredited by Arts Council England. Accreditation indicates that the museum or gallery has an appropriate constitution, is soundly financed, has adequate collection management standards and public services and has access to professional curatorial advice. A further 154 museums hold provisional accreditation and another 91 have applied for, or are in the process of obtaining accreditation. These applications are assessed by either Arts Council England, the Museums, Archives and Libraries division of the Welsh government; Museums Galleries Scotland or the Northern Ireland Museums Council.

The following is a selection of museums and art galleries in the UK. Opening hours and admission charges vary. Further information about museums and galleries in the UK is available from the Museums Association (T 020-7566 7800 W www.museumsassociation.org).

W www.weareculture24.org.uk includes a database of all the museums and galleries in the UK.

ENGLAND

* England's national museums and galleries, which receive funding from a government department, such as the DCMS or MoD. These institutions are deemed to have collections of national importance, and the government is able to call upon their staff for expert advice.

ALTON
Jane Austen's House Museum, Chawton, Hants GU34 1SD
   T 01420-83262 W www.jane-austens-house-museum.org.uk
   17th-century house which tells the author's story
BARNARD CASTLE
The Bowes Museum, Co. Durham DL12 8NP T 01833-690606
   W www.bowesmuseum.org.uk
   Public gallery in a French châteaux style featuring archaeology, fashion and ceramics. Houses one of the largest collections of Spanish art in the country
BATH
American Museum, Claverton Manor BA2 7BD T 01225-460503
   W www.americanmuseum.org
   American decorative arts from the 17th to 20th centuries; American heritage exhibition
Fashion Museum, Bennett Street BA1 2QH T 01225-477789
   W www.museumofcostume.co.uk
   Fashion from the 17th century to the present day
Victoria Art Gallery, Bridge Street BA2 4AT T 01225-477233
   W www.victoriagal.org.uk
   European Old Masters and British art since the 15th century
BEAMISH
Beamish Museum, Co. Durham DH9 0RG T 0191-370 4000
   W www.beamish.org.uk
   Living working museum of a northern industrial town during Georgian, Victorian and Edwardian times
BEAULIEU
National Motor Museum, Hants SO42 7ZN T 01590-612345
   W www.beaulieu.co.uk
   Former royal estate within the New Forest national park home to Beaulieu Abbey, Palace House and the National Motor Museum
BIRMINGHAM
Aston Hall, Trinity Road B6 6JD T 0121-348 8100
   W www.birminghammuseums.org.uk/aston
   Jacobean House containing paintings, furniture and tapestries from the 17th to 19th centuries

Barber Institute of Fine Arts, University of Birmingham, Edgbaston B15 2TS T 0121-414 7333 W www.barber.org.uk
   Extensive coin collection; fine arts, including Old Masters
Birmingham Museum and Art Gallery, Chamberlain Square B3 3DH
   T 0121-348 8038 W www.birminghammuseums.org.uk/bmag
   Includes notable collection of Pre-Raphaelite art
Museum of the Jewellery Quarter, Vyse Street, B18 6HA
   T 0121-348 8140 W www.birminghammuseums.org.uk/jewellery
   Preserved jewellery workshop
Sarehole Mill, Cole Bank Road, B13 0BD T 0121-348 8160
   W www.birminghammuseums.org.uk/sarehole
   A 250 year old working mill with close associations with J.R.R. Tolkien and his writings of Middle-earth
Thinktank, Curzon Street B4 7XG T 0121-348 8000
   W www.birminghammuseums.org.uk/thinktank
   Science museum featuring over 200 hands-on displays and a Planetarium
BOURNEMOUTH
Russell-Cotes Art Gallery and Museum, East Cliff Promenade BH1 3AA T 01202-451858 W www.russellcotes.com
   Seaside villa housing 19th- and 20th-century art and sculptures from around the world
BOVINGTON
Tank Museum, Dorset BH20 6JG T 01929-405096
   W www.tankmuseum.org
   Collection of 300 tanks from their invention in 1915 to the modern conflict in Afghanistan
BRADFORD
Bradford Industrial Museum, Moorside Mills, Moorside Road, Eccleshill BD2 3HP T 01274-435900
   W www.bradfordmuseums.org
   Steam power, machinery and motor vehicle exhibits
Cartwright Hall Art Gallery, Lister Park BD9 4NS T 01274-431212
   W www.bradfordmuseums.org
   British 19th- and 20th-century fine art, contemporary prints and south Asian art
National Science and Media Museum, BD1 1NQ T 0844-856 3797
   W www.scienceandmediamuseum.org.uk
   The science and culture of image and sound technologies, film and television with interactive exhibits and experiments; features an IMAX cinema and the only permanent Cinerama screen in Europe
BRIGHTON
Booth Museum of Natural History, Dyke Road BN1 5AA
   T 03000-290900 W www.brightonmuseums.org.uk/booth
   Zoology, botany and geology collections; British birds in recreated habitats
Brighton Museum and Art Gallery, Royal Pavilion Gardens BN1 1EE
   T 03000-290900 W www.brightonmuseums.org.uk/brighton
   Includes fine art and design, fashion, world art; Sussex history
Royal Pavilion, 4/5 Pavilion Buildings BN1 1EE T 0300-029 0900
   W https://brightonmuseums.org.uk/royalpavilion
   Regency seaside pleasure palace for George IV built in the visual style of India and China; includes the Prince Regent and Indian Military Hospital galleries
BRISTOL
Arnolfini, Narrow Quay BS1 4QA T 0117-917 2300
   W www.arnolfini.org.uk
   Experimental contemporary visual arts, dance, performance, music; talks and workshops
Blaise Castle House Museum, Henbury Road BS10 7QS
   T 0117-903 9818 W www.bristolmuseums.org.uk/blaise-castle-house-museum
   18th-century mansion; social history collections

Bristol Museum and Art Gallery, Queen's Road BS8 1RL
T 0117-922 3571 W www.bristolmuseums.org.uk/
bristol-museum-and-art-gallery
Includes Victorian, Edwardian and French fine art;
archaeology, local history and natural sciencies

M Shed, Prince's Wharf BS1 4RN T 0117-352 6600
W www.bristolmuseums.org.uk/m-shed
The story of Bristol's heritage of engineering, transport,
music and industry

Red Lodge Museum, Park Row BS1 5LJ T 0117-921 1360
W www.bristolmuseums.org.uk/red-lodge-museum
House museum showcasing original historical interiors
from the Tudor to Victorian periods

CAMBRIDGE
Fitzwilliam Museum, Trumpington Street CB2 1RB
T 01223-332900 W www.fitzmuseum.cam.ac.uk
Antiquities, fine and applied arts, clocks, ceramics,
manuscripts, furniture, sculpture, coins and medals

*Imperial War Museum Duxford, Duxford CB22 4QR
T 01223-835000 W www.iwm.org.uk/visits/iwm-duxford
Displays of military and civil aircraft, tanks and naval
exhibits

Museum of Archaeology and Anthropology, Downing Street CB2
3DZ T 01223-333516 W www.maa.cam.ac.uk
Global archaeological and anthropological collections;
photography and modern art collections

Museum of Zoology, Downing Street CB2 3EJ T 01223-336650
W www.museum.zoo.cam.ac.uk
Extensive assortment of zoological specimens; includes the
collections of Charles Darwin and Alfred Russel Wallace

Sedgwick Museum of Earth Sciences, Downing Street CB2 3EQ
T 01223-333456 W www.sedgwickmuseum.org
Extensive geological collection

Whipple Museum of the History of Science, Free School Lane CB2
3RH T 01223-330906 W www.hps.cam.ac.uk/whipple
Scientific instruments from the 14th century to the present

CARLISLE
Tullie House Museum and Art Gallery, Castle Street CA3 8TP
T 01228-618718 W www.tulliehouse.co.uk
Jacobean house with fine art, local social history,
prehistoric archaeology and natural sciences including
Hadrian's Wall exhibit

CHATHAM
The Historic Dockyard, ME4 4TE T 01634-823800
W www.thedockyard.co.uk
Maritime attractions including HMS *Cavalier,* the UK's last
Second World War destroyer

Royal Engineers Museum, Prince Arthur Road, Gillingham ME4 4UG
T 01634-822839 W www.re-museum.co.uk
Regimental history, ethnography, decorative art and
photography

CHELTENHAM
The Wilson Art Gallery and Museum, Clarence Street GL50 3JT
T 01242-237431 W www.cheltenhammuseum.org.uk
Arts and crafts, local heroes, fine art and natural history

CHESTER
Grosvenor Museum, Grosvenor Street CH1 2DD T 01244-972197
W www.grosvenormuseum.co.uk
Roman collections, natural history, art, Chester silver,
local history and costume

CHICHESTER
Weald and Downland Open Air Museum, Singleton PO18 0EU
T 01243-811363 W www.wealddown.co.uk
Rebuilt vernacular buildings from south-east England;
includes medieval houses and a working watermill; craft
demonstrations, Tudor kitchen and cooking

COLCHESTER
Colchester Castle Museum, Castle Park CO1 1TJ T 01206-282939
W www.colchestercastlepark.co.uk/colchester-castle
Largest Norman keep in Europe standing on foundations
of the Roman Temple of Claudius

COVENTRY
Coventry Transport Museum, Hales Street CV1 1JD
T 024-7623 4270 W www.transport-museum.com
Extensive collection of motor vehicles and bicycles; land
speed record-holding car

Herbert Art Gallery and Museum, Jordan Well CV1 5QP
T 024-7623 7521 W www.theherbert.org
Local history, archaeology, industry and visual arts

DERBY
Derby Museum and Art Gallery, The Strand DE1 1BS
T 01332-641901 W www.derbymuseums.org/museumartgallery
Includes paintings by Joseph Wright of Derby, origins of
Derby and military history

Pickford's House Museum, Friar Gate DE1 1DA T 01332-641901
W www.derbymuseums.org/pickfords-house
Georgian town house designed by architect Joseph
Pickford; museum of Georgian life and costume

DEVIZES
Wiltshire Museum, Library and Gallery, Long Street SN10 1NS
T 01380-727369 W www.wiltshiremuseum.org.uk
Natural and local history; art gallery; archaeological finds
from prehistoric, Roman and Saxon sites

DORCHESTER
Dorset County Museum, High West Street DT1 1XA
T 01305-262735 W www.dorsetcountymuseum.org
Includes a collection of Thomas Hardy's manuscripts,
books, notebooks and drawings; local history, geology
and Roman mosaics

DOVER
Dover Museum, Market Square CT16 1PH T 01304-201066
W www.dovermuseum.co.uk
Contains the Dover Bronze Age Boat Gallery and
archaeological finds from Bronze Age, Roman and Saxon
sites

EXETER
Royal Albert Memorial Museum and Art Gallery, Queen Street EX4
3RX T 01392-265858 W www.rammuseum.org.uk
Natural history; archaeology; worldwide fine and
decorative art including Exeter silver

GATESHEAD
BALTIC Centre for Contemporary Art, NE8 3BA T 0191-478 1810
W www.baltic.art
Contemporary art exhibitions and events

Shipley Art Gallery, Prince Consort Road NE8 4JB T 0191-477 1495
W www.shipleyartgallery.org.uk
Contemporary crafts

GAYDON
British Motor Museum, Banbury Road, Warks CV35 0BJ
T 01926-641188 W www.britishmotormuseum.co.uk
The world's largest collection of British cars with nearly
300 vehicles spanning the classic, vintage and veteran eras

GLOUCESTER
Gloucester Waterways Museum, Gloucester Docks GL1 2EH
T 01452-318200 W www.canalrivertrust.org.uk/
gloucester-waterways-museum
200-year history of Britain's canals and inland waterways

GOSPORT
Royal Navy Submarine Museum, Haslar Jetty Road, Hants PO12 2AS
T 023-9251 0354 W www.submarine-museum.co.uk
Underwater warfare exhibition, including submarines
HMS *Alliance* and HMS *Holland 1* – the Royal Navy's first
submarine

GRASMERE
Dove Cottage and the *Wordsworth Museum,* Cumbria LA22 9SH
T 015394-35544 W www.wordsworth.org.uk
William Wordsworth's manuscripts, home and garden

HOVE
Hove Museum and Art Gallery, New Church Road BN3 4AB
T 03000-290900 W www.brightonmuseums.org.uk/hove
Toys, cinema, local history and fine art collections

2

HULL

Ferens Art Gallery, Queen Victoria Square HU1 3RA
T 01482-300300 W www.hcandl.co.uk/ferens-art-gallery
European Old Masters, Victorian, Edwardian and
contemporary British art

Hull and East Riding Museum of Archaeology, High Street, HU1
1NQ T 01482-613902 W www.hcandl.co.uk/
hull-and-east-riding-museum
Local history from the pre-historic to the present day

Hull Maritime Museum, Queen Victoria Square HU1 3DX
T 01482-300300 W www.hcandl.co.uk/maritime-museum
Hull's maritime heritage including whaling, fishing,
navigation and merchant trade

Wilberforce House, 23–25 High Street HU1 1NQ T 01482-300300
W www.hcandl.co.uk/wilberforce-house
Birthplace of abolitionist William Wilberforce; history of
the transatlantic slave trade

HUNTINGDON

The Cromwell Museum, Grammar School Walk PE29 3LF
T 01480-375830 W www.cromwellmuseum.org
Portraits and memorabilia relating to Oliver Cromwell

IPSWICH

Christchurch Mansion and *Wolsey Art Gallery,* Christchurch Park
IP4 2BE T 01473-433554 W www.cimuseums.org.uk
Tudor house with paintings by Gainsborough, Constable
and other Suffolk artists; furniture and 18th-century
ceramics; temporary exhibitions

KEIGHLEY

The Brontë Parsonage Museum, Haworth, W. Yorks BD22 8DR
T 01535-642323 W www.bronte.org.uk
The former home of the literary Brontë family

KESWICK

Derwent Pencil Museum, Southey Works CA12 5NG
T 01768-773626 W www.derwentart.com
500-year history of the pencil; demonstration events and
workshops throughout the year

LEEDS

Armley Mills, Leeds Industrial Museum, Canal Road, Armley
LS12 2QF T 0113-378 3173 W www.leeds.gov.uk/armleymills
Once the world's largest woollen mill, now a museum for
textiles and Leeds' industrial heritage

Leeds Art Gallery, The Headrow LS1 3AA T 0113-378 5350
W www.leeds.gov.uk/artgallery
Includes English watercolours, sculpture, contemporary
art and prints from the region's artists

Royal Armouries Museum, Armouries Drive LS10 1LT
T 0113-220 1999 W www.royalarmouries.org
National collection of over 8,500 items of arms and
armour from BC to present over five galleries: War,
Tournament, Oriental, Self Defence and Hunting

LEICESTER

New Walk Museum and Art Gallery, 53 New Walk LE1 7EA
T 0116-255 4900 W www.leicester.gov.uk/leisure-and-culture/
museums-and-galleries
Natural and cultural history; ancient Egypt gallery;
European art including works by the German
expressionists and ceramics by Picasso

LINCOLN

The Collection, Danes Terrace LN2 1LP T 01522-782040
W www.thecollectionmuseum.com
Artefacts from the Stone Age to the Roman, Viking and
Medieval eras; adjacent art gallery; collections of
contemporary art and craft, sculpture, porcelain, clocks
and watches

Museum of Lincolnshire Life, Burton Road LN1 3LY
T 01522-782040 W www.lincolnshire.gov.uk/
museumoflincolnshirelife
Social history; agricultural, industrial, military and
commercial exhibits

LIVERPOOL

International Slavery Museum, Albert Dock L3 4AX
T 0151-478 4499 W www.liverpoolmuseums.org.uk/ism
Explores historical and contemporary aspects of slavery

Lady Lever Art Gallery, Wirral CH62 5EQ T 0151-478 4136
W www.liverpoolmuseums.org.uk/ladylever
Paintings, furniture and porcelain

Merseyside Maritime Museum, Albert Dock L3 4AQ
T 0151-478 4499 W www.liverpoolmuseums.org.uk/maritime
Floating exhibits, working displays and craft
demonstrations; incorporates the *UK Border Agency
National Museum*

Museum of Liverpool, Pier Head L3 1DG T 0151-478 4545
W www.liverpoolmuseums.org.uk/mol
Explores the significance of the city's geography, history
and culture

Sudley House, Mossley Hill Road L18 8BX T 0151-478 4016
W www.liverpoolmuseums.org.uk/sudley
Late 18th- and 19th-century paintings in former
shipowner's home

Tate Liverpool, Albert Dock L3 4BB T 0151-1702 7400
W www.tate.org.uk/liverpool
20th-century paintings and sculpture

Walker Art Gallery, William Brown Street L3 8EL
T 0151-478 4199 W www.liverpoolmuseums.org.uk/walker
Paintings and decorative arts from the 13th century to the
present day

World Museum Liverpool, William Brown Street L3 8EN
T 0151-478 4393 W www.liverpoolmuseums.org.uk/wml
Includes Egyptian mummies, weapons and classical
sculpture; planetarium, aquarium, vivarium and natural
history centre

LONDON: GALLERIES

Barbican Art Gallery, Barbican Centre, Silk Street EC2Y 8DS
T 020-7638 4141 W www.barbican.org.uk
Art, music, theatre, dance and film exhibitions

Courtauld Institute of Art Gallery, Somerset House, Strand
WC2R 0RN T 020-7848 2526 W www.courtauld.ac.uk
Fine art from the early renaissance to the 20th century,
including impressionist and post-impressionist paintings

Dennis Severs' House, 18 Folgate Street E1 6BX T 020-7247 4013
W www.dennissevershouse.co.uk
Candlelit recreation of a Huguenot silk weaver's home

Dulwich Picture Gallery, Gallery Road SE21 7AD T 020-8693 5254
W www.dulwichpicturegallery.org.uk
England's first public art gallery; designed by Sir John
Soane to house 17th- and 18th-century paintings

Estorick Collection of Modern Italian Art, Canonbury Square
N1 2AN T 020-7704 9522 W www.estorickcollection.com
Early 20th-century Italian drawings, paintings, sculptures
and etchings, with an emphasis on Futurism

Hayward Gallery, Belvedere Road SE1 8XX T 020-7960 4200
W www.southbankcentre.co.uk
Temporary exhibitions

National Gallery, Trafalgar Square WC2N 5DN T 020-7747 2885
W www.nationalgallery.org.uk
Western painting from the 13th to 19th centuries; early
Renaissance collection in the Sainsbury Wing

National Portrait Gallery, St Martin's Place WC2H 0HE
T 020-7306 0055 W www.npg.org.uk
Portraits of eminent people in British history

Photographers' Gallery, Ramillies Street W1F 7LW T 020-7087 9300
W www.thephotographersgallery.org.uk
Temporary exhibitions; permanent camera obscura

The Queen's Gallery, Buckingham Palace SW1A 1AA
T 020-7766 7300 W www.royalcollection.org.uk
Art from the Royal Collection

Royal Academy of Arts, Burlington House, Piccadilly W1J 0BD
T 020-7300 8000 W www.royalacademy.org.uk
British art since 1750 and temporary exhibitions; annual
Summer Exhibition
Saatchi Gallery, Duke of York's HQ, King's Road SW3 4RY
T 020-7823 2363 W www.saatchi-gallery.co.uk
Contemporary art including paintings, photographs,
sculpture and installations
Serpentine Gallery, Kensington Gardens W2 3XA T 020-7402 6075
W www.serpentinegallery.org
Temporary exhibitions of British and international
contemporary art
* *Tate Britain*, Millbank SW1P 4RG T 020-7887 8888
W www.tate.org.uk/britain
British art from the 16th century to the present;
international modern art
* *Tate Modern*, Bankside SE1 9TG T 020-7887 8888
W www.tate.org.uk/modern
International modern art from 1900 to the present
* *Wallace Collection*, Manchester Square W1U 3BN
T 020-7563 9500 W www.wallacecollection.org
Old Masters; French 18th-century paintings, furniture,
armour, porcelain, clocks and sculpture
Whitechapel Art Gallery, Whitechapel High Street E1 7QX
T 020-7522 7888 W www.whitechapelgallery.org
Temporary exhibitions of modern art
LONDON: MUSEUMS
Bank of England Museum, Bartholomew Lane EC2R 8AH
T 020-7601 5545 W www.bankofengland.co.uk/museum
History of the Bank of England since 1694
* *British Museum*, Great Russell Street WC1B 3DG T 020-7323 8000
W www.britishmuseum.org
Collection of art and antiquities spanning 2 million years
of human history; temporary exhibitions; houses the Elgin
Marbles from the Parthenon
Brunel Museum, Rotherhithe SE16 4LF T 020-7231 3840
W www.brunel-museum.org.uk
Explores the engineering achievements of Isambard
Kingdom Brunel and his father, Marc Brunel
Cartoon Museum, Little Russell Street WC1A 2HH T 020-7580 8155
W www.cartoonmuseum.org
British cartoons, caricature and comic art from the 18th
century to the present
Charles Dickens Museum, Doughty Street WC1N 2LX
T 020-7405 2127 W www.dickensmuseum.com
Dickens's home from 1837–9; manuscripts, personal
items and paintings
* *Churchill War Rooms*, King Charles Street SW1A 2AQ
T 020-7416 5000 W www.iwm.org.uk/visits/churchill-war-rooms
Underground rooms used by Churchill and the
government during the Second World War
Cutty Sark, King William Walk SE10 9HT T 020-8858 4422
W www.rmg.co.uk/cuttysark
The world's last remaining tea clipper; re-opened in April
2012 following extensive restoration
Design Museum, Kensington High Street W8 6AG T 020-3862 5900
W www.designmuseum.org
The development of design and the mass-production of
consumer objects
Garden Museum, Lambeth Palace Road SE1 7LB T 020-7401 8865
W www.gardenmuseum.org.uk
History and development of gardens and gardening;
temporary exhibitions, symposia and events
* *HMS Belfast*, The Queen's Walk SE1 2JH T 020-7940 6300
W www.iwm.org.uk/hms-belfast
Life and work on board a Second World War cruiser

* *Horniman Museum and Gardens*, London Road SE23 3PQ
T 020-8699 1872 W www.horniman.ac.uk
Museum of anthropology, musical instruments and natural
history; aquarium; reference library; gardens
* *Imperial War Museum*, Lambeth Road SE1 6HZ T 020-7416 5000
W www.iwm.org.uk
All aspects of the two World Wars and other military
operations involving Britain and the Commonwealth since
1914
Jewish Museum, Albert Street NW1 7NB T 020-7284 7384
W www.jewishmuseum.org.uk
Jewish life, history, art and religion
London Metropolitan Archives, Northampton Road EC1R 0HB
T 020-7332 3820 W www.cityoflondon.gov.uk/lma
Material on the history of London and its people dating
from 1067 to the present day
London Museum of Water and Steam, Green Dragon Lane TW8 0EN
T 020-8568 4757 W www.waterandsteam.org.uk
Large collection of steam engines; reopened in 2014 after
refurbishment
London Transport Museum, Covent Garden Piazza WC2E 7BB
T 020-7379 6344 W www.ltmuseum.co.uk
Vehicles, photographs and graphic art relating to the
history of transport in London
MCC Museum, Lord's Cricket Ground, St John's Wood NW8 8QN
T 020-7616 8656 W www.lords.org/mcc
Cricket exhibits including the Ashes Urn, kits, paintings
and W. G. Grace exhibit
Migration Museum, Lambeth High Street SE1 7AG
E info@migrationmuseum.org W www.migrationmuseum.org
Opened in 2017, tells the story of migration through the
ages and how it has affected and transformed Britain
* *Museum of Childhood (V&A)*, Cambridge Heath Road E2 9PA
T 020-8983 5200 W www.vam.ac.uk/moc
Toys, games and exhibits relating to the social history of
childhood from the 17th century to the present
* *Museum of London*, London Wall EC2Y 5HN T 020-7001 9844
W www.museumoflondon.org.uk
History of London from prehistoric times to the present
day; Galleries of Modern London
Museum of London Docklands, West India Quay, Canary Wharf
E14 4AL T 020-7001 9844 W www.museumoflondon.org.uk/
docklands
Explores the story of London's river, port and people over
2,000 years; includes the London Sugar Slavery Gallery
National Archives Museum, Kew TW9 4DU T 020-8876 3444
W www.nationalarchives.gov.uk/museum
Displays treasures from the archives, including the
Domesday Book and Magna Carta
* *National Army Museum*, Royal Hospital Road SW3 4HT
T 020-7730 0717 W www.nam.ac.uk
Five-hundred-year history of the British soldier; exhibits
include model of the Battle of Waterloo and recreated
First World War trench
* *National Maritime Museum*, Romney Road SE10 9NF
T 020-8858 4422 W www.rmg.co.uk/
national-maritime-museum
Maritime history of Britain; collections include globes,
clocks, telescopes and paintings; comprises the main
building, the Royal Observatory and the Queen's House
* *Natural History Museum*, Cromwell Road SW7 5BD
T 020-7942 5000 W www.nhm.ac.uk
Natural history collections and interactive Darwin Centre
Petrie Museum of Egyptian Archaeology, University College London,
Malet Place WC1E 6BT T 020-7679 2884 W www.ucl.ac.uk/
museums/petrie
Egyptian and Sudanese archaeology featuring around
80,000 objects

Postal Museum, 15–20 Phoenix Place, WC1X 0DL **T** 0300-030 0700
  W www.postalmuseum.org
  British postal service and communications from Tudor
  times to the present; interactive galleries, archives and
  subterranean mail train ride
*Royal Air Force Museum, Hendon NW9 5LL **T** 020-8205 2266
  W www.rafmuseum.org.uk
  Aviation from before the Wright brothers to the present
Royal Mews, Buckingham Palace SW1W 1QH **T** 020-7766 7302
  W www.royalcollection.org.uk/visit/royalmews
  State vehicles, including the Queen's gold state coach;
  home to the Queen's horses; guided tours
* Science Museum, Exhibition Road SW7 2DD **T** 020-7942 4000
  W www.sciencemuseum.org.uk
  Science, technology, industry and medicine exhibitions;
  children's interactive gallery; IMAX cinema
Shakespeare's Globe Exhibition, New Globe Walk, Bankside SE1 9DT
  T 020-7902 1400 **W** www.shakespearesglobe.com
  Recreation of Elizabethan theatre using 16th-century
  techniques; includes a tour of the theatre
* Sir John Soane's Museum, Lincoln's Inn Fields WC2A 3BP
  T 020-7405 2107 **W** www.soane.org
  Art and antiquities collected by Soane throughout his
  lifetime; authentic Georgian and Victorian interior
Tower Bridge Exhibition, SE1 2UP **T** 020-7403 3761
  W www.towerbridge.org.uk
  History of the bridge and display of Victorian steam
  machinery; panoramic views from walkways
*Victoria and Albert Museum, Cromwell Road SW7 2RL
  T 020-7942 2000 **W** www.vam.ac.uk
  Includes the National Art Library and the Gilbert
  Collection; fine and applied art and design; furniture,
  glass, textiles, theatre and dress collections; temporary
  exhibitions
Wellcome Collection, Euston Road NW1 2BE **T** 020-7611 2222
  W www.wellcomecollection.org
  Contemporary and historic exhibitions and collections
  including the Wellcome Library
Wimbledon Lawn Tennis Museum, Church Road SW19 5AE
  T 020-8944 1066 **W** www.wimbledon.com/museum
  Tennis trophies, fashion and memorabilia; view of Centre
  Court
MALTON
Eden Camp, N. Yorks YO17 6RT **T** 01653-697777
  W www.edencamp.co.uk
  Restored POW camp and Second World War
  memorabilia
MANCHESTER
Gallery of Costume, Platt Hall, Rusholme M14 5LL **T** 0161-245 7245
  W www.manchestergalleries.org
  Exhibits from the 17th century to the present day
*Imperial War Museum North, Trafford Wharf Road M17 1TZ
  T 0161-836 4000 **W** www.iwm.org.uk/north
  History of war from the 20th century to the present
Manchester Art Gallery, Mosley Street M2 3JL **T** 0161-235 8888
  W www.manchestergalleries.org
  European fine and decorative art from the 17th to 20th
  centuries
Manchester Museum, Oxford Road M13 9PL **T** 0161-275 2648
  W www.museum.manchester.ac.uk
  Collections include decorative arts, natural history and
  zoology; three Ancient Worlds galleries
*Museum of Science and Industry, Liverpool Road M3 4FP
  T 0161-832 2244 **W** www.msimanchester.org.uk
  On site of world's oldest passenger railway station;
  galleries relating to space, energy, power, transport,
  aviation, textiles and social history

National Football Museum, Cathedral Gardens M4 3BG
  T 0161-605 8200 **W** www.nationalfootballmuseum.com
  Home to the FIFA, FA and Football League collections
  including the 1966 World Cup final ball
People's History Museum, Left Bank, Spinningfields M3 3ER
  T 0161-838 9190 **W** www.phm.org.uk
  History of British political and working life
The Whitworth, Oxford Road M15 6ER **T** 0161-275 7450
  W www.whitworth.manchester.ac.uk
  Fine and modern art, wallpapers, prints, textiles and
  sculptures
MILTON KEYNES
Bletchley Park National Codes Centre, Bucks MK3 6EB
  T 01908-640404 **W** www.bletchleypark.org.uk
  Home of British codebreaking during the Second World
  War; Enigma machine; computer museum and Alan
  Turing gallery
The National Museum of Computing Block H, Bletchley Park, MK3
  6EB **T** 01908-374708 **W** www.tnmoc.org
  Charts the development of computing from the 1940s
  onwards and houses the world's largest collection of
  functional historical computers, including the Colossus
  and the WITCH
NEWCASTLE UPON TYNE
Discovery Museum, Blandford Square NE1 4JA **T** 0191-232 6789
  W www.twmuseums.org.uk/discovery
  Science and industry, local history, fashion; Tyneside's
  maritime history; digital jukebox of 2,000 film and TV
  titles from the BFI National Archive
Great North Museum: Hancock, Barras Bridge NE2 4PT
  T 0191-222 6765 **W** www.twmuseums.org.uk/
  greatnorthmuseum
  Natural and ancient history; planetarium; Living Planet
  display incorporates live animal tanks and aquaria
Laing Art Gallery, New Bridge Street NE1 8AG **T** 0191-278 1611
  W www.twmuseums.org.uk/laing
  19th and 20th century art including local painters;
  ceramics, glass, Japanese decorative arts and prints
NEWMARKET
*Palace House: National Heritage Centre for Horseracing and
  Sporting Art,* Palace Street CB8 8EP **T** 01638-667314
  W www.palacehousenewmarket.co.uk
  Collection of horseracing memorabilia, British Sporting
  Art from around the UK and home of the retraining of
  racehorses
NORTH SHIELDS
Stephenson Railway Museum, Middle Engine Lane NE29 8DX
  T 0191-200 7146 **W** www.twmuseums.org.uk/stephenson
  Locomotive engines and rolling stock; open April through
  November and school holidays outside this period
NOTTINGHAM
Museum of Nottingham Life at Brewhouse Yard, Castle Boulevard
  NG7 1FB **T** 0115-876 1400 **W** www.nottinghamcity.gov.uk
  Social history from the 17th to 20th centuries
Natural History Museum, Wollaton Hall, Wollaton NG8 2AE
  T 0115-876 3100 **W** www.wallatonhall.org.uk
  Geology, botany and zoology specimens housed in an
  Elizabethan mansion
Nottingham Castle and Art Gallery, Lenton Road NG1 6EL
  T 0115-876 1400 **W** www.nottinghamcastle.org.uk
  Paintings, ceramics, silver, glass and jewellery; history of
  Nottingham
OXFORD
Ashmolean Museum, Beaumont Street OX1 2PH **T** 01865-278000
  W www.ashmolean.org
  Art and archaeology including Egyptian, Minoan, Anglo-
  Saxon and Chinese exhibits; largest collection of Raphael
  drawings in the world

Modern Art Oxford, Pembroke Street OX1 1BP T 01865-722733
W www.modernartoxford.org.uk
Temporary exhibitions

Museum of the History of Science, Broad Street OX1 3AZ
T 01865-277280 W www.mhs.ox.ac.uk
Displays include early scientific instruments, chemical
apparatus, clocks and watches

Oxford University Museum of Natural History, Parks Road
OX1 3PW T 01865-272950 W www.oum.ox.ac.uk
Entomology, geology, mineralogy and petrology, and
zoology

Pitt Rivers Museum, South Parks Road OX1 3PP T 01865-270927
W www.prm.ox.ac.uk
Anthropological and archaeological artefacts

PLYMOUTH

City Museum and Art Gallery, Drake Circus PL4 8AJ
T 01752-304774 W www.plymouthmuseum.gov.uk
Local and natural history; ceramics; silver; Old Masters;
world artefacts; temporary exhibitions

PORTSMOUTH

Charles Dickens Birthplace, Old Commercial Road PO1 4QL
T 023-9282 1879 W www.charlesdickensbirthplace.co.uk
Reproduction Regency house; Dickens memorabilia

The D-Day Story, Clarence Esplanade, Southsea PO5 3NT
T 023-9282 6722 W www.theddaystory.com
The evacuation of Dunkirk, the D-Day landings and the
Battle of Normandy exhibitions with over 10,000 objects
and artefacts including the Overlord embroidery

Portsmouth Historic Dockyard, HM Naval Base PO1 3LJ
T 023-9283 9766 W www.historicdockyard.co.uk
Incorporates the *National Museum of the Royal Navy*** (PO1
3NH T 023-9272 7574 W www.nmrn.org.uk), HMS *Victory*
(PO1 3NH T 023-9283 9766 W www.hms-victory.com), HMS
Warrior (PO1 3QX T 023-9277 8600 W www.hmswarrior.org),
Mary Rose (PO1 3LX T 023-9281 2931 W www.maryrose.org)
and *Action Stations* (PO1 3LJ T 023-9289 3338
W www.actionstations.org)
History of the Royal Navy and of the dockyard; warships
and technology spanning 500 years

PRESTON

Harris Museum and Art Gallery, Market Square PR1 2PP
T 01772-258248 W www.harrismuseum.org.uk
British art since the 18th century; ceramics, glass, costume
and local history; contemporary exhibitions

ST ALBANS

Verulamium Museum, St Michael's Street AL3 4SW
T 01727-751810 W www.stalbansmuseums.org.uk
Remains of Iron Age settlement and the third-largest city
in Roman Britain; moving to a new site in 2017

ST IVES

*Tate St Ives, Porthmeor Beach, Cornwall TR26 1TG
T 01736-796226 W www.tate.org.uk/stives
Modern art, much by artists associated with St Ives;
includes the Barbara Hepworth Museum and Sculpture
Garden; open after 2014 part closure

SALISBURY

Salisbury & South Wiltshire Museum, The Close SP1 2EN
T 01722-332151 W www.salisburymuseum.org.uk
Local history and archaeology; Stonehenge exhibits

SHEFFIELD

Graves Gallery, Surrey Street S1 1XZ T 0114-278 2600
W www.museums-sheffield.org.uk
Twentieth-century British art; European art spanning four
centuries

Millennium Galleries, Arundel Gate S1 2PP T 0114-278 2600
W www.museums-sheffield.org.uk
Incorporates four different galleries: the Special
Exhibition Gallery, the Craft and Design Gallery, the
Metalwork Gallery and the Ruskin Gallery, which houses
John Ruskin's collection of paintings, drawings, books
and medieval manuscripts

Weston Park Museum, Western Bank S10 2TP T 0114-278 2600
W www.museums-sheffield.org.uk
World and local history; art and temporary exhibitions

SOUTHAMPTON

City Art Gallery, Commercial Road SO14 7LP T 023-8083 3007
W www.southamptoncityartgallery.com
Western art from the Renaissance to the present

SeaCity Museum, Havelock Road SO14 7FY T 023-8083 3007
W www.seacitymuseum.co.uk
Opened in 2012, the museum tells the story of the city's
maritime past and present

SOUTH SHIELDS

Arbeia Roman Fort, Baring Street NE33 2BB T 0191-456 1369
W www.twmuseums.org.uk/arbeia
Excavated ruins; reconstructions of original buildings

South Shields Museum and Art Gallery, Ocean Road NE33 2JA
T 0191-277 1410 W www.twmuseums.org.uk/southshields
South Tyneside history; interactive art gallery

STOKE-ON-TRENT

Etruria Industrial Museum, Lower Bedford Street ST4 7AF
T 01782-233144 W www.etruriamuseum.org.uk
Britain's sole surviving steam-powered potter's mill

Gladstone Pottery Museum, Uttoxeter Road, Longton ST3 1PQ
T 01782-237777 W www.stokemuseums.org.uk/visit/gpm
The last complete Victorian pottery factory in Britain

Potteries Museum and Art Gallery, Bethesda Street ST1 3DW
T 01782-232323 W www.stokemuseums.org.uk/visit/pmag
Pottery, china and porcelain collections and a Mark XVI
Spitfire

The Wedgwood Museum, Barlaston ST12 9ER T 01782-371900
W www.wedgwoodmuseum.org.uk
The story of Josiah Wedgwood and the company he
founded

SUNDERLAND

Sunderland Museum and Winter Gardens, Burdon Road SR1 1PP
T 0191-553 2323 W www.seeitdoitsunderland.co.uk/
sunderland-museum-winter-gardens
Fine and decorative art, local history and gardens

TELFORD

Ironbridge Gorge Museums, TF8 7DQ T 01952-433424
W www.ironbridge.org.uk
Ten museums including The Museum of the Gorge; The
Iron Bridge and Tollhouse; Blists Hill (late Victorian
working town); Brosely Pipeworks; Coalbrookdale
Museum of Iron; Coalport China Museum; Jackfield Tile
Museum; Tar Tunnel; Darby Houses

WAKEFIELD

Hepworth Wakefield, Gallery Walk WF1 5AW T 01924-247360
W www.hepworthwakefield.org
Historic and modern art; temporary exhibitions of
contemporary art

National Coal Mining Museum for England, New Road, Overton
WF4 4RH T 01924-848806 W www.ncm.org.uk
Includes underground tours of one of Britain's oldest
working mines

Yorkshire Sculpture Park, West Bretton WF4 4LG T 01924-832631
W www.ysp.co.uk
Open-air sculpture gallery including works by Henry
Moore, Barbara Hepworth and others in 500 acres of
parkland

WEYBRIDGE

Brooklands Museum, Brooklands Road KT13 0QN T 01932-857381
W www.brooklandsmuseum.com
Birthplace of British motorsport; world's first purpose-
built motor racing circuit

WILMSLOW
Quarry Bank Mill and Styal Estate, Wilmslow SK9 4LA
T 01625-527468 W www.quarrybankmill.org.uk
Europe's most powerful working waterwheel owned by
the National Trust illustrating history of cotton industry;
costumed guides at restored Apprentice House

WINCHESTER
Winchester Science Centre and Planetarium, Telegraph Way, Hants
SO21 1HZ T 01962-863791
W www.winchestersciencecentre.org
Interactive science centre and planetarium

WORCESTER
City Art Gallery and Museum, Foregate Street WR1 1DT
T 01905-25371 W www.worcestershire.gov.uk/museums
Includes the Regimental museum, 19th-century chemist
shop and changing art exhibitions
Museum of Royal Worcester, Severn Street WR1 2ND
T 01905-21247 W www.museumofroyalworcester.org
Worcester porcelain from 1751 to the present day

YEOVIL
Fleet Air Arm Museum, RNAS Yeovilton, Somerset BA22 8HT
T 01935-840565 W www.fleetairarm.com
History of naval aviation; historic aircraft, including
Concorde 002

YORK
Beningbrough Hall, Beningbrough YO30 1DD T 01904-472027
W www.nationaltrust.org.uk/beningbrough-hall
18th-century house with portraits from the National
Portrait Gallery; parklands and gardens
JORVIK Viking Centre, Coppergate YO1 9WT T 01904-615505
W www.jorvik-viking-centre.co.uk
Reconstruction of Viking York based on archaeological
evidence
*National Railway Museum, Leeman Road YO26 4XJ
T 0844-815 3139 W www.nrm.org.uk
Includes locomotives, rolling stock and carriages
York Art Gallery, Exhibition Square, YO1 7EW T 01904 687687
W www.yorkartgallery.org.uk
600 years of British and European painting; ceramics and
sculpture
York Castle Museum, Eye of York YO1 9RY T 01904-687687
W www.yorkcastlemuseum.org.uk
Includes Kirkgate, a reconstructed Victorian street;
costume and military collections
Yorkshire Museum, Museum Gardens YO1 7FR T 01904-687687
W www.yorkshiremuseum.org.uk
Yorkshire life from Roman to medieval times; geology
and biology; York observatory

WALES
* Members of National Museum Wales, a public body that
receives its core funding from the Welsh government

ABERYSTWYTH
Ceredigion Museum, Terrace Road SY23 2AQ T 01970-633088
W www.ceredigion.gov.uk
Local history, housed in a restored Edwardian theatre
Silver Mountain Experience, Ponterwyd SY23 3AB T 01970-890620
W www.silvermountainexperience.co.uk
Tours of an 18th-century silver mine, with interactive
challenges and games for children

BLAENAFON
*Big Pit National Coal Museum, Torfaen NP4 9XP
T 030-0111 2333 W www.museum.wales/bigpit
Colliery with an underground tour and exhibitions of
modern mining equipment

BODELWYDDAN
Bodelwyddan Castle, Denbighshire LL18 5YA T 01745-584060
W www.bodelwyddan-castle.co.uk
Art gallery within an historic house; features temporary art
exhibits

CAERLEON
*National Roman Legion Museum, NP18 1AE T 030-0111 2333
W www.museum.wales/roman
Features the oldest recorded piece of writing in Wales;
pottery, Roman era gemstones

CARDIFF
*National Museum Cardiff, Cathays Park CF10 3NP
T 030-0111 2333 W www.museum.wales/cardiff
Houses Wales's national art, archaeology and natural
history collections
*St Fagans: National History Museum, St Fagans CF5 6XB
T 029-2057 3500 W www.museum.wales/stfagans
Open-air museum with re-erected buildings, agricultural
equipment and costume
TECHNIQUEST, Stuart Street CF10 5BW T 029-2047 5475
W www.techniquest.org
Interactive science exhibits, planetarium and science
theatre

CRICCIETH
Lloyd George Museum, Llanystumdwy LL52 0SH T 01766-522071
W www.gwynedd.llyw.cymru
Childhood home of David Lloyd George

DRE-FACH FELINDRE
*National Wool Museum, Llandysul SA44 5UP T 030-0111 2333
W www.museum.wales/wool
Exhibitions, a working woollen mill and craft workshops

LLANBERIS
*National Slate Museum, Gwynedd LL55 4TY T 030-0111 2333
W www.museum.wales/slate
Former slate quarry with original machinery and plant;
slate crafts demonstrations; working waterwheel

LLANDRINDOD WELLS
National Cycle Collection, Automobile Palace, Temple Street
LD1 5DL T 01597-825531 W www.cyclemuseum.org.uk
Approximately 250 bicycles on display, from 1819 to the
present

PRESTEIGNE
Judge's Lodging Museum, Broad Street LD8 2AD T 01544-260650
W www.judgeslodging.org.uk
Restored apartments, courtroom, cells and servants'
quarters

SWANSEA
Glynn Vivian Art Gallery, Alexandra Road SA1 5DZ
T 01792-516900 W www.swansea.gov.uk/glynnvivian
Fine art and ceramics from 1700 to the present
*National Waterfront Museum, Oystermouth Road SA1 3RD
T 030-0111 2333 W www.museum.wales/swansea
Wales during the Industrial Revolution
Swansea Museum, Victoria Road SA1 1SN T 01792-653763
W www.swansea.gov.uk/swanseamuseum
Paintings, Egyptian artifacts, transport and nautical
collections; war time Swansea

TENBY
Tenby Museum and Art Gallery, Castle Hill SA70 7BP T 01834-
842809 W www.tenbymuseum.org.uk
Local archaeology, history, geology and art

SCOTLAND
* Members of National Museums Scotland or National
Galleries of Scotland, which are non-departmental public
bodies funded by, and accountable to, the Scottish government

ABERDEEN
Aberdeen Art Gallery, Schoolhill AB10 1FQ T 0300-020 0293
W www.aagm.co.uk
Paintings, sculptures and graphics; temporary exhibitions
Aberdeen Maritime Museum, Shiprow AB11 5BY T 01224-337700
W www.aagm.co.uk
Maritime history, including shipbuilding and North Sea
oil

AYR

Robert Burns Birthplace Museum, Murdoch's Lone, Alloway
KA7 4PQ **T** 0129-244 3700 **W** www.burnsmuseum.org.uk
Comprises Burns Cottage, birthplace of the poet, gardens
and a museum

EDINBURGH

Britannia, Leith EH6 6JJ **T** 0131-555 5566
W www.royalyachtbritannia.co.uk
Former royal yacht with royal barge and royal family
picture gallery

City Art Centre, Market Street EH1 1DE **T** 0131-529 3993
W www.edinburghmuseums.org.uk
Rolling programme of exhibitions including historic and
modern photography; contemporary art, design and
architecture

Museum of Childhood, High Street EH1 1TG **T** 0131-529 4142
W www.edinburghmuseums.org.uk
Toys, games, clothes and exhibits relating to the social
history of childhood

Museum of Edinburgh, Canongate, Royal Mile EH8 8DD
T 0131-529 4143 **W** www.edinburghmuseums.org.uk
Local history, silver, glass and Scottish pottery

National Museum of Flight, East Fortune Airfield, East Lothian
EH39 5LF **T** 0300-123 6789 **W** www.nms.ac.uk/flight
Aviation from the early 20th century to the present

National Museum of Scotland, Chambers Street EH1 1JF
T 0300-123 6789 **W** www.nms.ac.uk/scotland
Scottish history; world cultures; natural world; art and
design; science and technology

National War Museum of Scotland, Edinburgh Castle EH1 2NG
T 0300-123 6789 **W** www.nms.ac.uk/war
Scotland's military history housed within Edinburgh
Castle

Scottish National Gallery, The Mound EH2 2EL **T** 0131-624 6200
W www.nationalgalleries.org
Fine art from the early Renaissance to the end of the 19th
century

Scottish National Gallery of Modern Art, Belford Road EH4 3DR
T 0131-624 6200 **W** www.nationalgalleries.org
Contemporary art featuring British, French and Russian
collections; outdoor sculpture park

Scottish National Portrait Gallery, Queen Street EH2 1JD
T 0131-624 6200 **W** www.nationalgalleries.org/portraitgallery
Portraits of eminent people in Scottish history;
Photography Gallery; Victorian Library

The Writers' Museum, Lady Stair's Close EH1 2PA
T 0131-529 4901 **W** www.edinburghmuseums.org.uk
Exhibitions relating to Robert Burns, Sir Walter Scott and
Robert Louis Stevenson

FORT WILLIAM

West Highland Museum, Cameron Square PH33 6AJ
T 01397-702169 **W** www.westhighlandmuseum.org.uk
Highland life; Military, Victorian and Jacobite collections

GLASGOW

Burrell Collection, Pollokshaws Road G43 1AT **T** 0141-287 2550
W www.glasgowlife.org.uk/museums
Paintings by major artists; medieval art, Chinese and
Islamic art

Gallery of Modern Art, Royal Exchange Square G1 3AH
T 0141-287 3005 **W** www.glasgowlife.org.uk/museums
Collection of contemporary Scottish and world art

Hunterian, University of Glasgow G12 8QQ **T** 0141-330 4221
W www.gla.ac.uk/hunterian
Rennie Mackintosh and Whistler collections; coins;
Scottish paintings; Pacific ethnographic collection;
archaeology; medicine

Kelvingrove Art Gallery & Museum, Argyle Street G3 8AG
T 0141-276 9500 **W** www.glasgowlife.org.uk/museums
Includes Old Masters; natural history; arms and armour

Museum of Piping, McPhater Street G4 0HW **T** 0141-353 0220
W www.thepipingcentre.co.uk
The history and origins of bagpiping

Museum of Rural Life, Philipshill Road, East Kilbride G76 9HR
T 0300-123 6789 **W** www.nms.ac.uk/rural
History of rural life and work

People's Palace and Winter Gardens, Glasgow Green G40 1AT
T 0141-276 0788 **W** www.glasgowlife.org.uk/museums
Social history of Glasgow since 1750

Riverside Museum, 100 Pointhouse Place G3 8RS **T** 0141-287 2720
W www.glasgowlife.org.uk/museums
Scotland's museum of transport and travel; the Tall Ship
Glenlee, a Clyde-built sailing ship, is berthed alongside

St Mungo Museum of Religious Art and Life, Castle Street G4 0RH
T 0141-276 1625 **W** www.glasgowlife.org.uk/museums
Exhibits detailing the world's major religions; oldest Zen
garden in Britain

NORTHERN IRELAND

* Members of National Museums Northern Ireland, a public
body sponsored by the Department for Communities,
Northern Ireland executive.

ARMAGH

Armagh County Museum, The Mall East BT61 9BE
T 028-3752 3070 **W** www.nimc.co.uk
Local history; fine art; archaeology; crafts

BANGOR

North Down Museum, Town Hall BT20 4BT **T** 028-9127 1200
W www.northdownmuseum.com
Local history from the Bronze age to the present

BELFAST

Titanic Belfast, Queen's Road, Titanic Quarter BT3 9EP
T 028-9076 6386 **W** www.titanicbelfast.com
The story of RMS *Titanic* from her conception to demise;
Shipyard ride and ocean exploration centre

Ulster Museum, Botanic Gardens BT9 5AB **T** 0289-044 0000
W www.nmni.com/um
Irish antiquities; natural and local history; fine and applied
arts

W5, Queen's Quay BT3 9QQ **T** 028-9046 7700
W www.w5online.co.uk
Interactive science and technology centre

HOLYWOOD

Ulster Folk and Transport Museum, Cultra BT18 0EU
T 028-9042 8428 **W** www.nmni.com/uftm
Open-air museum with original buildings from Ulster
town and rural life *c.*1900; indoor galleries including Irish
rail and road transport

LONDONDERRY

The Tower Museum, Union Hall Place BT48 6LU **T** 028-7137 2411
W www.derrystrabane.com/towermuseum
Tells the story of Ireland through the history of
Londonderry

NEWTOWNARDS

The Somme Heritage Centre, Bangor Road BT23 7PH
T 028-9182 3202 **W** www.sommeassociation.com
Commemorates the part played by Irish forces in the First
World War

OMAGH

Ulster American Folk Park, Castletown, Co. Tyrone BT78 5QU
T 028-8224 3292 **W** www.nmni.com/uafp
Open-air museum telling the story of Ulster's emigrants to
America; restored or recreated dwellings and workshops;
ship and dockside gallery

SIGHTS OF LONDON

For historic buildings, museums and galleries in London, *see* the Historic Buildings and Monuments, and Museums and Galleries sections.

BRIDGES

The bridges over the Thames in London, from east to west, are:

Tower Bridge (268m/880ft by 18m/60ft), architect: Horace Jones, engineer: John Wolfe Barry, opened 1894

London Bridge (262m/860ft by 32m/105ft), original 13th-century stone bridge rebuilt and opened 1831 (engineer: John Rennie, reconstructed in Arizona when current London Bridge opened 1973 (architect: Lord Holford, engineer: Mott, Hay and Anderson)

Cannon Street Railway Bridge (261m/855ft), engineers: John Hawkshaw and John Wolfe Barry, originally named Alexandra Bridge, opened 1866; renovated 1979–82

Southwark Bridge (244m/800ft by 17m/56ft), engineer: John Rennie, originally named Queen Street Bridge, opened 1819; rebuilt 1912–21 (architect: Ernest George, engineer: Mott, Hay and Anderson)

Millennium Bridge (325m/1,066ft by 4m/13ft), architect: Foster and Partners, engineer: Ove Arup and Partners, opened 2000; reopened after modification 2002

Blackfriars Railway Bridge (284m/933ft), engineers: John Wolfe Barry and Henri Marc Brunel, orginally named St Paul's Railway Bridge, opened 1886

Blackfriars Bridge (294m/963ft by 32m/105ft), engineer: Robert Mylne, opened 1769; rebuilt 1869 (engineer: Joseph Cubitt); widened 1909

Waterloo Bridge (366m/1,200ft by 24m/80ft), engineer: John Rennie, opened 1817; rebuilt 1945 (architect: Sir Giles Gilbert Scott, engineer: Rendel, Palmer and Triton)

Golden Jubilee Bridges (325m/1,066ft by 4.7m/15ft), architect: Lifschutz Davidson, engineer: WSP Group, opened 2002; commonly known as the Hungerford Footbridges

Hungerford Railway Bridge (366m/1,200ft), engineer: Isambard Kingdom Brunel, suspension bridge opened 1845; present railway bridge opened 1864 (engineer: John Hawkshaw); widened in 1886

Westminster Bridge (228m/748ft by 26m/85ft), engineer: Charles Labelye, opened 1750; rebuilt 1862 (architect: Charles Barry, engineer: Thomas Page)

Lambeth Bridge (237m/776ft by 18m/60ft), engineer: Peter W. Barlow, original suspension bridge opened 1862; current structure opened 1932 (architect: Reginald Blomfield, engineer: George W. Humphreys)

Vauxhall Bridge (231m/759ft by 24m/80ft), engineer: James Walker, opened 1816; redesigned and opened 1906 (architect: William Edward Riley, engineers: Alexander Binnie and Maurice Fitzmaurice)

Grosvenor Railway Bridge (213m/699ft), engineer: John Fowler, opened 1860; rebuilt 1965; also known as the Victoria Railway Bridge

Chelsea Bridge (213m/699ft by 25m/83ft), original suspension bridge opened 1858 (engineer: Thomas Page); rebuilt 1937 (architects: George Topham Forrest and E. P. Wheeler, engineer: Rendel, Palmer and Triton)

Albert Bridge (216m/710ft by 12m/40ft), engineer: Rowland M. Ordish, opened 1873; restructured 1884 (engineer: Joseph Bazalgette); strengthened 1971–3

Battersea Bridge (204m/670ft by 17m/56ft), engineer: Henry Holland, opened 1771; rebuilt 1890 (engineer: Joseph Bazalgette)

Battersea Railway Bridge (204m/670ft), engineer: William Baker, opened 1863; also known as Cremorne Bridge

Wandsworth Bridge (189m/619ft by 18m/60ft), engineer: Julian Tolmé, opened 1873; rebuilt 1940 (architect: E. P. Wheeler, engineer: T. Pierson Frank)

Putney Railway Bridge (229m/750ft), engineers: W. H. Thomas and William Jacomb, opened 1889; also known as the Fulham Railway Bridge or the Iron Bridge – it has no official name

Putney Bridge (213m/699ft by 23m/74ft), architect: Jacob Ackworth, original wooden bridge opened 1729; current granite structure completed in 1886 (engineer: Joseph Bazalgette). The starting point of the Boat Race.

Hammersmith Bridge (210m/688ft by 10m/33ft), engineer: William Tierney Clarke; the first suspension bridge in London, originally built 1827; rebuilt 1887 (engineer: Joseph Bazalgette)

Barnes Railway Bridge (also footbridge, 110m/360ft), engineer: Joseph Locke, opened 1849; rebuilt 1895 (engineers: London and South Western Railway); the original structure stands unused

Chiswick Bridge (137m/450ft by 21m/70ft), architect: Herbert Baker, engineer: Alfred Dryland, opened 1933. The bridge marks the end point of the Boat Race.

Kew Railway Bridge (175m/575ft), engineer: W. R. Galbraith, opened 1869

Kew Bridge (110m/360ft by 17m/56ft), engineer: Robert Tunstall, original timber bridge built 1759; replaced by a Portland stone structure in 1789 (engineer: James Paine); current granite bridge renamed King Edward VII Bridge in 1903, but still known as Kew Bridge (engineers: John Wolfe Barry and Cuthbert Brereton)

Richmond Lock (91m/300ft by 11m/36ft), engineer: F. G. M. Stoney, lock and footbridge opened 1894

Twickenham Bridge (85m/280ft by 21m/70ft), architect: Maxwell Ayrton, engineer: Alfred Dryland, opened 1933

Richmond Railway Bridge (91m/300ft), engineer: Joseph Locke, opened 1848; rebuilt 1906–8 (engineer: J. W. Jacomb-Hood)

Richmond Bridge (85m/280ft by 10m/33ft), architect: James Paine, engineer: Kenton Couse, built 1777; widened 1939

Teddington Lock (198m/650ft), engineer: G. Pooley, two footbridges opened 1889; marks the end of the tidal reach of the Thames

Kingston Railway Bridge architects: J. E. Errington and W. R. Galbraith, engineer: Thomas Brassey, opened 1863

Kingston Bridge (116m/382ft), engineer: Edward Lapidge, built 1825–8; widened 1911–14 (engineers: Basil Mott and David Hay) and 1999–2001

Hampton Court Bridge, engineers: Samuel Stevens and Benjamin Ludgator, built 1753; replaced by iron bridge 1865; present bridge opened 1933 (architect: Edwin Lutyens, engineer: W. P. Robinson)

CEMETERIES

In 1832, in response to the overcrowding of burial grounds in London, the government authorised the establishment of seven non-denominational cemeteries that would encircle the city. These large cemeteries, known as the 'magnificent seven', were seen by many Victorian families as places in which to demonstrate their wealth and stature, and as a result there are some highly ornate graves and tombs.

THE MAGNIFICENT SEVEN

Abney Park, Stoke Newington, N16 (13ha/32 acres), established 1840; tomb of William and Catherine Booth, founders of the Salvation Army, and memorials to many nonconformists and dissenters

Brompton, Old Brompton Road, SW10 (16.5ha/40 acres), established 1840; graves of Sir Henry Cole, Emmeline Pankhurst, John Wisden

Highgate, Swains Lane, N6 (15ha/38 acres), established 1839; graves of Douglas Adams, George Eliot, Eric Hobsbawm, Michael Faraday, Karl Marx, Ralph Miliband and Christina Rossetti

Kensal Green, Harrow Road, W10 (29ha/72 acres), established 1833; tombs of Charles Babbage, Isambard Kingdom Brunel, Wilkie Collins, George Cruikshank, Tom Hood, Leigh Hunt, Harold Pinter, William Makepeace Thackeray, Anthony Trollope

Nunhead, Linden Grove, SE15 (21ha/52 acres), established 1840; closed in 1969, restored and opened for burials

Tower Hamlets, Southern Grove, E3 (11ha/27 acres), established 1841, 350,000 interments; bombed heavily during the Second World War and closed to burials in 1966; now a nature reserve

West Norwood Cemetery and Crematorium, Norwood High Street, SE27 (17ha/42 acres), established 1837; tombs of C. W. Alcock, Mrs Beeton, Sir Henry Tate and Joseph Whitaker *(Whitaker's Almanack)*

OTHER CEMETERIES

Bunhill Fields, City Road, EC1 (1.6ha/4 acres), 17th-century nonconformist burial ground containing the graves of William Blake, John Bunyan and Daniel Defoe

City of London Cemetery and Crematorium, Aldersbrook Road, E12 (81ha/200 acres), established 1856; grave of Bobby Moore

Golders Green Crematorium, Hoop Lane, NW11 (5ha/12 acres), established 1902; retains the ashes of Kingsley Amis, Lionel Bart, Enid Blyton, Marc Bolan, Sigmund Freud, Keith Moon, Ivor Novello, Bram Stoker and H. G. Wells

Hampstead, Fortune Green Road, NW6 (10.5ha/26 acres), established 1876; graves of Alan Coren, Kate Greenaway, Joseph Lister and Marie Lloyd

MARKETS

Billingsgate, Trafalgar Way, E14 (fish), a market site for over 1,000 years, with the Lower Thames Street site dating from 1876; moved to the Isle of Dogs in 1982; owned and run by the City of London Corporation

Borough, Southwark Street, SE1 (vegetables, fruit, meat, dairy, bread), established on present site in 1756; privately owned and run

Brick Lane, E1 (jewellery, vintage clothes, bric-a-brac, food), open Saturday and Sunday

Brixton, SW9 (African-Caribbean food, music, clothing), open Monday to Saturday

Broadway, E8 (food, fashion, crafts), re-established in 2004, open Saturday

Camden Lock, NW1 (second-hand clothing, jewellery, alternative fashion, crafts), established 1973

Columbia Road, E2 (flowers), dates from 19th century; became dedicated flower market in the 20th century

Covent Garden, WC2 (antiques, handicrafts, jewellery, clothing, food), originally a fruit and vegetable market *(see* New Covent Garden market); it has been trading in its current form since 1980

Grays, Davies Street, W1K (antiques), indoor market in listed building, established 1977

Greenwich, SE10 (crafts, fashion, food), market revived in the 1980s

Leadenhall, Gracechurch Street, EC3V (meat, poultry, cheese, clothing), site of market since 14th century; present hall built 1881; owned and run by the City of London Corporation

New Covent Garden, SW8 (wholesale vegetables, fruit, flowers), established in 1670 under a charter of Charles II; relocated from central London in 1974

New Spitalfields, E10 (vegetables, fruit), established 1682, modernised 1928, moved out of the City to Leyton in 1991, open Monday to Saturday

Old Spitalfields, E1 (arts, crafts, books, clothes, organic food, antiques), continues to trade on the original Spitalfields site on Commercial Street

Petticoat Lane, Middlesex Street, E1, a market has existed on the site for over 500 years, now a Sunday morning market selling almost anything

Portobello Road, W11, originally for herbs and horse-trading from 1870; became famous for antiques after the closure of the Caledonian Market in 1948

Smithfield, EC1 (meat, poultry), built 1866–8, refurbished 1993–4; the site of St Bartholomew's Fair from 12th to 19th century; owned and run by the City of London Corporation, open Monday to Friday

MONUMENTS

CENOTAPH

Whitehall, SW1. The Cenotaph (from the Greek meaning 'empty tomb') was built to commemorate 'The Glorious Dead' and is a memorial to all ranks of the sea, land and air forces who gave their lives in the service of the Empire during the First World War. Designed by Sir Edwin Lutyens and constructed in plaster as a temporary memorial in 1919, it was replaced by a permanent structure of Portland stone and unveiled by George V on 11 November 1920, Armistice Day. An additional inscription was made in 1946 to commemorate those who gave their lives in the Second World War

FOURTH PLINTH

Trafalgar Square, WC2. The fourth plinth (1841) was designed for an equestrian statue that was never built due to lack of funds. From 1999 temporary works have been displayed on the plinth including *Ecce Homo* (Mark Wallinger), *Monument* (Rachel Whiteread), *Alison Lapper Pregnant* (Marc Quinn), *One & Other* (Antony Gormley) and *Hahn/Cock* (Katharina Fritsch). Since March 2018 *The Invisible Enemy Should Not Exist* (Michael Rakowitz), a recreation of the Lamassu, a winged bull and protective deity that stood at the entrance to the Nergal Gate of Nineveh from *c.*700 BC until it was destroyed by Islamic State in 2015, has occupied the plinth. The Lamassu is made from 10,500 empty Iraqi date syrup cans, representing a once-renowned industry now decimated by war.

LONDON MONUMENT

(Commonly called the Monument), Monument Street, EC3. Built to designs by Sir Christopher Wren and Robert Hooke between 1671 and 1677, the Monument commemorates the Great Fire of London, which broke out in Pudding Lane on 2 September 1666. The fluted Doric column is 36.6m (120ft) high, the moulded cylinder above the balcony supporting a flaming vase of gilt bronze is an additional 12.8m (42ft), and the column is based on a square plinth 12.2m (40ft) high (with fine carvings on the west face), making a total height of 61.6m (202ft) – the tallest isolated stone column in the world, with views of London from a gallery at the top (311 steps)

OTHER MONUMENTS

(sculptor's name in parentheses):

7 July Memorial (Carmody Groarke), Hyde Park

Afghanistan and Iraq War Memorial (Day), Victoria Embankment
African and Caribbean War Memorial, Windrush Square, Brixton
Viscount Alanbrooke (Roberts-Jones), Whitehall
Albert Memorial (Scott), Kensington Gore
Battle of Britain (Day), Victoria Embankment
Beatty (Wheeler), Trafalgar Square
Belgian Gratitude (setting by Blomfield, statue by Rousseau), Victoria Embankment
Boadicea (or *Boudicca*), *Queen of the Iceni* (Thornycroft), Westminster Bridge
Brunel (Marochetti), Victoria Embankment
Burghers of Calais (Rodin), Victoria Tower Gardens, Westminster
Burns (Steell), Embankment Gardens
Canada Memorial (Granche), Green Park
Carlyle (Boehm), Chelsea Embankment
Cavalry (Jones), Hyde Park
Edith Cavell (Frampton), St Martin's Place
Charles I (Le Sueur), Trafalgar Square
Charles II (Gibbons), Royal Hospital, Chelsea
Churchill (Roberts-Jones), Parliament Square
Cleopatra's Needle (20.9m/68.5ft high, *c.*1500 BC, erected in London in 1878; the sphinxes are Victorian), Thames Embankment
Clive (Tweed), King Charles Street
Captain Cook (Brock), The Mall
Oliver Cromwell (Thornycroft), outside Westminster Hall
Cunningham (Belsky), Trafalgar Square
Gen. Charles de Gaulle (Conner), Carlton Gardens
Diana, Princess of Wales Memorial Fountain (Gustafson Porter), Hyde Park
Disraeli, Earl of Beaconsfield (Raggi), Parliament Square
Duke of Cambridge (Jones), Whitehall
Duke of York (37.8m/124ft column, with statue by Westmacott), Carlton House Terrace
Edward VII (Mackennal), Waterloo Place
Elizabeth I (Kerwin, 1586, oldest outdoor statue in London; from Ludgate), Fleet Street
Eros (Shaftesbury Memorial) (Gilbert), Piccadilly Circus
Lord Dowding (Winter), Strand
Millicent Fawcett (Wearing), Parliament Square
Marechal/Marshall Foch (Mallisard, copy of one in Cassel, France), Grosvenor Gardens
Charles James Fox (Westmacott), Bloomsbury Square
Yuri Gagarin (Novikov, copy of Russian statue), The Mall
Mahatma Gandhi (Jackson), Parliament Square
George III (Cotes Wyatt), Cockspur Street
George IV (Chantrey), Trafalgar Square
George V (Reid Dick and Scott), Old Palace Yard
George VI (McMillan), Carlton Gardens
Gladstone (Thornycroft), Strand
Guards' (Crimea; Bell), Waterloo Place
Guards Division (Ledward, figures, Bradshaw, cenotaph), Horse Guards' Parade
Haig (Hardiman), Whitehall
Sir Arthur (Bomber) Harris (Winter), Strand
Gen. Henry Havelock (Behnes), Trafalgar Square
International Brigades Memorial (Spanish Civil War) (Ian Walters), Jubilee Gardens, South Bank
Irving (Brock), north side of National Portrait Gallery
Isis (Gudgeon), Hyde Park
James II (Gibbons), Trafalgar Square
Jellicoe (McMillan), Trafalgar Square
Samuel Johnson (Fitzgerald), opposite St Clement Danes
Kitchener (Tweed), Horse Guards' Parade
Abraham Lincoln (Saint-Gaudens, copy of one in Chicago), Parliament Square
Mandela (Walters), Parliament Square
Milton (Montford), St Giles, Cripplegate
Mountbatten (Belsky), Foreign Office Green

Gen. Charles James Napier (Adams), Trafalgar Square
Nelson (Railton), Trafalgar Square, with Landseer's lions (cast from guns recovered from the wreck of the *Royal George)*
Florence Nightingale (Walker), Waterloo Place
Palmerston (Woolner), Parliament Square
Sir Keith Park (Johnson), Waterloo Place
Peel (Noble), Parliament Square
Pitt (Chantrey), Hanover Square
Portal (Nemon), Embankment Gardens
Prince Albert (Bacon), Holborn Circus
Queen Elizabeth Gate (Lund and Wynne), Hyde Park Corner
Queen Mother (Jackson), Carlton Gardens
Raleigh (McMillan), Greenwich
Richard I (Coeur de Lion) (Marochetti), Old Palace Yard
Roberts (Bates), Horse Guards' Parade
Franklin D. Roosevelt (Reid Dick), Grosvenor Square
Royal Air Force (Blomfield), Victoria Embankment
Royal Air Force Bomber Command Memorial (O'Connor), Green Park
Royal Artillery (Great War) (Jagger and Pearson), Hyde Park Corner
Royal Artillery (South Africa) (Colton), The Mall
Captain Scott (Lady Scott), Waterloo Place
Shackleton (Jagger), Kensington Gore
Shakespeare (Fontana, copy of one by Scheemakers in Westminster Abbey), Leicester Square
Smuts (Epstein), Parliament Square
Sullivan (Goscombe John), Victoria Embankment
Trenchard (McMillan), Victoria Embankment
Victoria Memorial (Webb and Brock), in front of Buckingham Palace
Raoul Wallenberg (Jackson), Great Cumberland Place
George Washington (Houdon copy), Trafalgar Square
Wellington (Boehm), Hyde Park Corner
Wellington (Chantrey), outside Royal Exchange
John Wesley (Adams Acton), City Road
Westminster School (Crimea) (Scott), Broad Sanctuary
William III (Bacon), St James's Square
Wolseley (Goscombe John), Horse Guards' Parade

PARKS, GARDENS AND OPEN SPACES

CITY OF LONDON CORPORATION OPEN SPACES
W www.cityoflondon.gov.uk
Ashtead Common (202ha/500 acres), Surrey
Burnham Beeches and *Fleet Wood* (220ha/540 acres), Bucks. Acquired by the City of London for the benefit of the public in 1880, Fleet Wood (26ha/65 acres) being presented in 1921
Coulsdon Common (51ha/127 acres), Surrey
Epping Forest (2,476ha/6,118 acres), Essex. Acquired by the City of London in 1878 and opened to the public in 1882. The Queen Elizabeth Hunting Lodge, built for Henry VIII in 1543, lies at the edge of the forest. The present forest is 19.3km (12 miles) long by around 3km (2 miles) wide, approximately one-tenth of its original area
*Epping Forest Buffer Land (718ha/1,774 acres), Waltham Abbey/Epping
Farthing Downs and New Hill (95ha/235 acres), Surrey
Hampstead Heath (275ha/680 acres), NW3. Including Golders Hill (15ha/36 acres) and Parliament Hill (110ha/271 acres)
Highgate Wood (28ha/70 acres), N6/N10
Kenley Common (56ha/139 acres), Surrey
Queen's Park (12ha/30 acres), NW6
Riddlesdown (43ha/104 acres), Surrey
Spring Park (20ha/50 acres), Kent
Stoke Common (80ha/198 acres), Bucks. Ownership was transferred to the City of London in 2007

West Ham Park (31ha/77 acres), E15

West Wickham Common (10ha/26 acres), Kent
Also over 150 smaller open spaces within the City of
London, including *Finsbury Circus* and *St Dunstan-in-the-East*
* Includes Copped Hall Park, Woodredon Estate and Warlies Park

OTHER PARKS AND GARDENS

CHELSEA PHYSIC GARDEN, 66 Royal Hospital Road SW3
4HS T 020-7352 5646 W www.chelseaphysicgarden.co.uk A
garden of general botanical research and education,
maintaining a wide range of rare and unusual plants;
established in 1673 by the Society of Apothecaries

HAMPTON COURT PARK AND GARDENS (328ha/810
acres), Surrey KT8 9AU T 0844-482 7777 W www.hrp.org.uk
Also known as Home Park, the park lies beyond the
palace's formal gardens. It contains a herd of deer and a
750-year-old oak tree from the original park

HOLLAND PARK (22.5ha/54 acres), Ilchester Place W8
T 020-7361 3000 W www.rbkc.gov.uk The largest park in
the Royal Borough of Kensington and Chelsea, includes
the Kyoto Garden

KEW, ROYAL BOTANIC GARDENS (120ha/300 acres),
Richmond, Surrey TW9 3AB T 020-8332 5655 W www.kew.org
Founded in 1759 and declared a UNESCO World
Heritage Site in 2003

THAMES BARRIER PARK (9ha/22acres), North Woolwich
Road E16 2HP T 020-7476 3741 Opened in 2000,
landscaped gardens with spectacular views of the Thames
Barrier

ROYAL PARKS
W www.royalparks.org.uk

Bushy Park (450ha/1,099 acres), Middx. Adjoins Hampton
Court; contains an avenue of horse-chestnuts enclosed in a
fourfold avenue of limes planted by William III

Green Park (19ha/47 acres), W1. Between Piccadilly and St
James's Park, with Constitution Hill leading to Hyde Park
Corner

Greenwich Park (74ha/183 acres), SE10. Enclosed by
Humphrey, Duke of Gloucester, and laid out by Charles II
from the designs of Le Nôtre. On a hill in Greenwich Park
is the Royal Observatory (founded 1675). Its buildings
are now managed by the National Maritime Museum
(T 020-8858 4422 W www.rmg.co.uk) and the earliest
building is named Flamsteed House, after John Flamsteed
(1646–1719), the first astronomer royal

Hyde Park (142ha/350 acres), W1/W2. From Park Lane to
Kensington Gardens and incorporating the Serpentine
lake, Apsley House, the Achilles Statue, Rotten Row and
the Ladies' Mile; fine gateway at Hyde Park Corner. To
the north-east is Marble Arch, originally erected by
George IV at the entrance to Buckingham Palace and re-
erected in the present position in 1851. At Hyde Park
Corner stands Wellington Arch, built in 1825–7, it
opened to the public in 2012 following major renovation

Kensington Gardens (111ha/275 acres), W2/W8. From the
western boundary of Hyde Park to Kensington Palace;
contains the Albert Memorial, Serpentine Gallery, Diana,
Princess of Wales' Memorial Playground and the Peter
Pan statue

The Regent's Park and *Primrose Hill* (197ha/487 acres), NW1.
From Marylebone Road to Primrose Hill surrounded by
the Outer Circle; divided by the Broad Walk leading to
the Zoological Gardens

Richmond Park (1,000ha/2,500 acres), Surrey. Designated a
National Nature Reserve, a Site of Special Scientific
Interest and a Special Area of Conservation

St James's Park (23ha/58 acres), SW1. From Whitehall to
Buckingham Palace; ornamental lake of 4.9ha (12 acres);
the Mall leads from Admiralty Arch to Buckingham
Palace

PLACES OF HISTORICAL AND CULTURAL INTEREST

1 Canada Square
Canary Wharf E14 5AB T 020-7418 2000
W www.canarywharf.com
Also known as 'Canary Wharf', the steel and glass
skyscraper is designed to sway 35cm in the strongest
winds

20 Fenchurch Street
W www.skygarden.london
Designed by architect Rafael Viñoly the skyscraper was
completed in March 2014. The top three storeys are
home to the Sky Garden, London's highest public garden
with viewing platforms, bars, restaurants and an open air
terrace. Access to the Sky Garden is free, but tickets must
be booked in advance.

30 St Mary Axe
EC3A 8EP W www.30stmaryaxe.com
Completed in 2004 and commonly known as the
'Gherkin', each of the floors rotates five degrees from the
one below

122 Leadenhall Street
EC3V 4AB W www.theleadenhallbuilding.com
The distinctive 225m (737ft) asymmetrical Leadenhall
Building, designed by architects Rogers Stirk Harbour &
Partners, was completed in 2014.

Alexandra Palace
Alexandra Palace Way N22 7AY T 020-8365 2121
W www.alexandrapalace.com
The Victorian palace was severely damaged by fire in
1980 but was restored, and reopened in 1988. Alexandra
Palace now provides modern facilities for exhibitions,
conferences, banquets and leisure activities. There is a
winter ice rink, a boating lake and a conservation area.
Restoration of the east wing and Victorian theatre is due
for completion in late 2018.

Barbican Centre
Silk Street EC2Y 8DS T 020-7638 4141 W www.barbican.org.uk
Owned, funded and managed by the City of London
Corporation, the Barbican Centre opened in 1982 and
houses the Barbican Theatre, a studio theatre called The
Pit and the Barbican Hall; it is also home to the London
Symphony Orchestra. There are three cinemas, six
conference rooms, two art galleries, a sculpture court, a
lending library, trade and banqueting facilities and a
conservatory

British Library
St Pancras, 96 Euston Road NW1 2DB T 0330-333 1144
W www.bl.uk
The largest building constructed in the UK in the 20th
century with basements extending 24.5m underground.
Holdings include the *Magna Carta*, the Gutenburg Bible,
Shakespeare's First Folio, Beatles manuscripts and the first
edition of *The Times* from 1788. Holds temporary
exhibitions on a range of topics

Central Criminal Court
Old Bailey EC4M 7EH T 020-7192 2739
W www.cityoflondon.gov.uk
The highest criminal court in the UK, the 'Old Bailey' is
located on the site of the old Newgate Prison. Trials held
here have included those of Oscar Wilde, Dr Crippen and
the Yorkshire Ripper. The courthouse has been rebuilt
several times since 1674; Edward VII officially opened the
current neo-baroque building in 1907

Charterhouse
Charterhouse Square EC1M 6AN T 020-7253 9503
W www.thecharterhouse.org
A Carthusian monastery from 1371 to 1538, purchased in
1611 by Thomas Sutton, who endowed it as a residence
for aged men 'of gentle birth' and a school for poor
scholars (removed to Godalming in 1872)

Downing Street

SW1A 2AA **W** www.number10.gov.uk

Number 10 Downing Street is the official town residence
of the prime minister and number 11 of the Chancellor of
the Exchequer. The street was named after Sir George
Downing, Bt., soldier and diplomat, who was MP for
Morpeth 1660–84

George Inn

The George Inn Yard SE1 1NH **T** 020-7407 2056

W www.nationaltrust.org.uk/george-inn

The last galleried inn in London, built in 1677. Now
owned by the National Trust and run as an ordinary
public house

Horse Guards

Whitehall SW1

Archway and offices built about 1753. The changing of
the guard takes place daily at 11am (10am on Sundays)
and the inspection at 4pm. Only those with the Queen's
permission may drive through the gates and archway into
Horse Guards Parade, where the colour is 'trooped' on the
Queen's official birthday

HOUSES OF PARLIAMENT

T 020-7219 3000 **W** www.parliament.uk

House of Commons, Westminster SW1A 0AA

House of Lords, Westminster SW1A 0PW

The royal palace of Westminster, originally built by
Edward the Confessor, was the normal meeting place of
Parliament from about 1340. St Stephen's Chapel was
used from about 1550 for the meetings of the House of
Commons, which had previously been held in the
Chapter House or Refectory of Westminster Abbey. The
House of Lords met in an apartment of the royal palace.
The fire of 1834 destroyed much of the palace, and the
present Houses of Parliament were erected on the site
from the designs of Sir Charles Barry and Augustus Welby
Pugin between 1840 and 1867. The chamber of the
House of Commons was destroyed by bombing in 1941,
and a new chamber designed by Sir Giles Gilbert Scott
was used for the first time in 1950. *Westminster Hall and the
Crypt Chapel* was the only part of the old palace of
Westminster to survive the fire of 1834. It was built by
William II from 1097 to 1099 and altered by Richard II
between 1394 and 1399. The hammerbeam roof of
carved oak dates from 1396–8. The Hall was the scene of
the trial of Charles I. *The Victoria Tower* of the House of
Lords is 98.5m (323ft) high and *The Elizabeth Tower* of
the House of Commons is 96.3m (316ft) high and
contains 'Big Ben', the hour bell said to be named after Sir
Benjamin Hall, First Commissioner of Works when the
original bell was cast in 1856. This bell, which weighed
16 tons 11 cwt, was found to be cracked in 1857. The
present bell (13.5 tons) is a recasting of the original and
was first brought into use in 1859. The dials of the clock
are 7m (23ft) in diameter, the hands being 2.7m (9ft) and
4.3m (14ft) long (including balance piece).
During session, tours of the Houses of Parliament are only
available to UK residents who have made advance
arrangements through an MP or peer. Overseas visitors
are no longer provided with permits to tour the Houses of
Parliament during session, although they can tour on
Saturdays and during the summer opening and attend
debates for both houses in the Strangers' Galleries. During
the summer recess, tickets for tours of the Houses of
Parliament can be booked online, by telephone
(**T** 020-7219 4114) or bought on site at the ticket office
located at the front of Portcullis House SW1A 2LW. The
Strangers' Gallery of the House of Commons is open to
the public when the house is sitting. To acquire tickets in
advance, UK residents should write to their local MP and

overseas visitors should apply to their embassy or high
commission in the UK for a permit. If none of these
arrangements has been made, visitors should join the
public queue outside St Stephen's Entrance, where there is
also a queue for entry to the House of Lords Gallery

INNS OF COURT

The Inns of Court are ancient unincorporated bodies of
lawyers which for more than five centuries have had the
power to call to the Bar those of their members who have
qualified for the rank or degree of Barrister-at-Law. There
are four Inns of Court as well as many lesser inns:

Lincoln's Inn, WC2A 3TL **T** 020-7405 1393

W www.lincolnsinn.org.uk

The most ancient of the inns with records dating back to
1422. The hall and library buildings are from 1845,
although the library is first mentioned in 1474; the old
hall (late 15th century) and the chapel were rebuilt
c.1619–23

Inner Temple, King's Bench Walk EC4Y 7HL **T** 020-7797 8250

W www.innertemple.org.uk

Middle Temple, Middle Temple Lane EC4Y 9BT

T 020-7427 4800 **W** www.middletemple.org.uk

Records for the Inner and Middle Temple date back to
the beginning of the 16th century. The site was originally
occupied by the Order of Knights Templar c.1160–1312.
The two inns have separate halls thought to have been
formed c.1350. The division between the two societies
was formalised in 1732 with Temple Church and the
Masters House remaining in common. The Inner Temple
Garden is normally open to the public on weekdays
between 12.30pm and 3pm

Temple Church, EC4Y 7BB **T** 020-7353 8559

W www.templechurch.com

The nave forms one of five remaining round churches in
England

Gray's Inn, South Square WC1R 5ET **T** 020-7458 7800

W www.graysinn.info

Founded early 14th century; hall 1556–8

No other 'Inns' are active, but there are remains of *Staple
Inn*, a gabled front on Holborn (opposite Gray's Inn Road).
Clement's Inn (near St Clement Danes Church), *Clifford's Inn*,
Fleet Street, and *Thavies Inn*, Holborn Circus, are all rebuilt.
Serjeants' Inn, Fleet Street, and another (demolished 1910) of
the same name in Chancery Lane, were composed of
Serjeants-at-Law, the last of whom died in 1922

Institute of Contemporary Arts

The Mall SW1Y 5AH **T** 020-7930 3647 **W** www.ica.art

Exhibitions of modern art in the fields of film, theatre,
new media and the visual arts

Lloyd's

Lime Street EC3M 7HA **T** 020-7327 1000 **W** www.lloyds.com

International insurance market which evolved during the
17th century from Lloyd's Coffee House. The present
building was opened for business in May 1986, and
houses the Lutine Bell. Underwriting is on three floors
with a total area of 10,591 sq. m (114,000 sq. ft). The
Lloyd's building is not open to the general public

London Central Mosque and the Islamic Cultural Centre

Park Road NW8 7RG **T** 020-7724 3363 **W** www.iccuk.org

The focus for London's Muslims; established in 1944 but
not completed until 1977, the mosque can accommodate
about 5,000 worshippers; guided tours are available

London Eye

South Bank SE1 7PB **T** 0870-990 8883 **W** www.londoneye.com

Opened in March 2000 as London's millennium
landmark, this 137m (450ft) observation wheel is the
tallest cantilevered observation wheel in the world. The
wheel provides a 30-minute ride offering panoramic views
of the capital

London Zoo

Regent's Park NW1 4RY **T** 0344-225 1826 **W** www.zsl.org

Opened in 1828 by the Zoological Society of London (ZSL) to house an array of exotic and endangered animals with an emphasis on scientific research and conservation.

Madame Tussauds

Marylebone Road NW1 5LR **T** 0871-894 3000 **W** www.madametussauds.com

Waxwork exhibition

Mansion House

Cannon Street EC4N 8BH **T** 020-7626 2500 **W** www.cityoflondon.gov.uk

The official residence of the Lord Mayor. Built in the 18th century in the Palladian style. Open to groups by appointment only

Marlborough House

Pall Mall SW1Y 5HX **T** 020-7747 6500 **W** www.thecommonwealth.org

Built by Wren for the first Duke of Marlborough and completed in 1711, the house reverted to the Crown in 1835. In 1863 it became the London house of the Prince of Wales and was the London home of Queen Mary until her death in 1953. In 1959 Marlborough House was given by the Queen as the headquarters for the Commonwealth Secretariat and it was opened as such in 1965. The Queen's Chapel, Marlborough Gate, was begun in 1623 from the designs of Inigo Jones for the Infanta Maria of Spain, and completed for Queen Henrietta Maria. Marlborough House is not open to the public

Neasden Temple

BAPS Shri Swaminarayan Mandir, Brentfield Road, Neasden NW10 8LD **T** 020-8965 2651 **W** http://londonmandir.baps.org

The first and largest traditional Hindu Mandir outside of India; opened in 1995

Port of London

Port of London Authority, Royal Pier Road, Kent DA12 2BG **T** 01474-562200 **W** www.pla.co.uk

The Port of London covers the tidal section of the river Thames from Teddington to the seaward limit (the outer Tongue buoy and the Sunk light vessel), a distance of 153km (95 miles). The governing body is the Port of London Authority (PLA). Cargo is handled at privately operated riverside terminals between Fulham and Canvey Island, including the enclosed dock at Tilbury, 40km (25 miles) below London Bridge. Passenger vessels and cruise liners can be handled at moorings at Greenwich, Tower Bridge and Tilbury

Queen Elizabeth Olympic Park

Stratford E20 **T** 0203-288 1800 **W** www.queenelizabetholympicpark.co.uk

Built for the London 2012 Olympic and Paralympic Games, the park, which included the Olympic Stadium, Velodrome and Aquatics Centre has been redeveloped to provide 227ha (560 acres) of parkland with play areas, outside arts and theatre spaces, waterways and wetlands. The north of the park, which includes the Copper Box Arena sport venue, re-opened to the public in 2013. The south of the park, which re-opened in April 2014, incorporates three venues for arts and sports events and the *ArcelorMittal Orbit*, designed by Sir Anish Kapoor and Cecil Balmond; it is the UK's tallest sculpture (114.5m/376ft) and has two accessible observation floors

Roman Remains

The city wall of Roman *Londinium* was largely rebuilt during the medieval period but sections may be seen near the White Tower in the Tower of London; at Tower Hill; at Coopers' Row; at All Hallows, London Wall, its vestry being built on the remains of a semi-circular Roman

bastion; at St Alphage, London Wall, showing a succession of building repairs from the Roman until the late medieval period; and at St Giles, Cripplegate. Sections of the great forum and basilica, more than 165 sq. m (1,776 sq. ft), have been encountered during excavations in the area of Leadenhall, Gracechurch Street and Lombard Street. Traces of Roman activity along the river include a massive riverside wall built in the late Roman period, and a succession of Roman timber quays along Lower and Upper Thames Street. Finds from these sites can be seen at the Museum of London.

Other major buildings are the amphitheatre at Guildhall, remains of bath-buildings in Upper and Lower Thames Street, and the temple of Mithras in Walbrook

Royal Albert Hall

Kensington Gore SW7 2AP **T** 0845-401 5045 **W** www.royalalberthall.com

The elliptical hall, one of the largest in the world, was completed in 1871; since 1941 it has been the venue each summer for the Promenade Concerts founded in 1895 by Sir Henry Wood. Other events include pop and classical music concerts, dance, opera, sporting events, conferences and banquets

Royal Courts of Justice

Strand WC2A 2LL **T** 020-7947 7726 **W** www.justice.gov.uk

Victorian Gothic building that is home to the high court. Visitors are free to watch proceedings

Royal Hospital, Chelsea

Royal Hospital Road SW3 4SR **T** 020-7881 5200 **W** www.chelsea-pensioners.co.uk

Founded by Charles II in 1682, and built by Wren; opened in 1692 for old and disabled soldiers. The extensive grounds include the former Ranelagh Gardens and are the venue for the Chelsea Flower Show each May

Royal Naval College

Greenwich SE10 9NN **T** 020-8269 4747 **W** www.ornc.org

The building was the Greenwich Hospital until 1869. It was built by Charles II, largely from designs by John Webb, and by Queen Mary II and William III, from designs by Wren. It stands on the site of an ancient abbey, a royal house and Greenwich Palace, which was constructed by Henry VII. Henry VIII, Mary I and Elizabeth I were born in the royal palace and Edward VI died there

Royal Opera House

Covent Garden WC2E 9DD **T** 020-7240 1200 **W** www.roh.org.uk

Home of The Royal Ballet (1931) and The Royal Opera (1946). The Royal Opera House is the third theatre to be built on the site, opening 1858; the first was opened in 1732

St James's Palace

Pall Mall SW1A 1BQ **W** www.royal.gov.uk

Built by Henry VIII, only the Gatehouse and Presence Chamber remain; later alterations were made by Wren and Kent. Representatives of foreign powers are still accredited 'to the Court of St James's'. *Clarence House* (1825), the official London residence of the Prince of Wales, stands within the St James's Palace estate

St Paul's Cathedral

St Paul's Churchyard EC4M 8AD **T** 020-7246 8350 **W** www.stpauls.co.uk

Built 1675–1710. The cross on the dome is 111m (365ft) above ground level, the inner cupola 66.4m (218ft) above the floor. 'Great Paul' in the south-west tower weighs nearly 17 tons. The organ by Father Smith (enlarged by Willis and rebuilt by Mander) is in a case carved by Grinling Gibbons, who also carved the choir stalls

Shakespeare's Globe
New Globe Walk SE1 9DT T 020-7902 1400
W www.shakespearesglobe.com
Reconstructed in 1997, the open-air playhouse is a unique resource for the works of William Shakespeare through perfomance and education; a new indoor replica Jacobean theatre staged its first public performance in January 2014
Shard
London Bridge SE1 T 020-7493 5311 W www.the-shard.com
Completed in May 2012, the skyscraper stands at 310m (1,016ft) and possesses a unique facade of 11,000 glass panels and a 360-degree viewing gallery
Somerset House
Strand WC2R 1LA T 020-7845 4600
W www.somersethouse.org.uk
The river facade (183m/600ft long) was built in 1776–1801 from the designs of Sir William Chambers; the eastern extension, which houses part of King's College, was built by Smirke in 1829–35. Somerset House was the property of Lord Protector Somerset, at whose attainder in 1552 the palace passed to the Crown, and it was a royal residence until 1692. Somerset House has recently undergone extensive renovation and is home to the Embankment Galleries and the Courtauld Gallery. Open-air concerts and ice-skating (Dec–Jan) are held in the courtyard
SOUTH BANK, SE1
Arts complex on the south bank of the river Thames which consists of:
BFI Southbank T 020-7928 3232 W www.bfi.org.uk
Opened in 1952 and administered by the British Film Institute, has four auditoria of varying capacities. Venue for the annual London Film Festival.
The *Royal Festival Hall* T 020-7960 4200
W www.southbankcentre.co.uk
Opened in 1951 for the Festival of Britain, adjacent are the *Queen Elizabeth Hall,* the *Purcell Room* and the *Hayward Gallery*
The *Royal National Theatre,* T 020-7452 3000
W www.nationaltheatre.org.uk
Opened in 1976; comprises the Olivier, the Lyttelton and Dorfman theatres. The Cottesloe Theatre closed in February 2013 and, following refurbishment reopened in 2014 as the Dorfman Theatre
Southwark Cathedral
London Bridge SE1 9DA T 020-7367 6700
W www.cathedral.southwark.anglican.org
Mainly 13th century, but the nave is largely rebuilt. The tomb of John Gower (1330–1408) is between the Bunyan and Chaucer memorial windows in the north aisle; Shakespeare's effigy, backed by a view of Southwark and the Globe Theatre, is in the south aisle; the tomb of Bishop Andrewes (d.1626) is near the screen. The Lady Chapel was the scene of the consistory courts of the reign of Mary (Gardiner and Bonner) and is still used as a consistory court. John Harvard, after whom Harvard University is named, was baptised here in 1607, and the chapel by the north choir aisle is his memorial chapel

Thames Embankments
Sir Joseph Bazalgette (1819–91) constructed the *Victoria Embankment,* on the north side from Westminster to Blackfriars for the Metropolitan Board of Works, 1864–70; (the seats, of which the supports of some are a kneeling camel, laden with spicery, and of others a winged sphinx, were presented by the Grocers' Company and by W. H. Smith, MP, in 1874); the *Albert Embankment,* on the south side from Westminster Bridge to Vauxhall, 1866–9, and the Chelsea Embankment, 1871–4. The total cost exceeded £2m. Bazalgette also inaugurated the London main drainage system, 1858–65. A medallion *(Flumini vincula posuit)* has been placed on a pier of the *Victoria Embankment* to commemorate the engineer
Thames Flood Barrier
W www.environment-agency.gov.uk
Officially opened in May 1984, though first used in February 1983, the barrier consists of ten rising sector gates which span approximately 520m from bank to bank of the Thames at Woolwich Reach. When not in use the gates lie horizontally, allowing shipping to navigate the river normally; when the barrier is closed, the gates turn through 90 degrees to stand vertically more than 50 feet above the river bed. The barrier took eight years to complete and can be raised within about 90 minutes
Trafalgar Tavern
Park Row, Greenwich SE10 9NW T 020-3887 9886
W www.trafalgartavern.co.uk
Regency-period riverside public house built in 1837. Charles Dickens and William Gladstone were patrons
Wembley Stadium
Wembley HA9 0WS T 0844-980 8001
W www.wembleystadium.com
The second largest stadium in Europe; hosts major sporting events and music concerts
Westminster Abbey
SW1P 3PA T 020-7222 5152 W www.westminster-abbey.org
Founded as a Benedictine monastery over 1,000 years ago, the church was rebuilt by Edward the Confessor in 1065 and again by Henry III in the 13th century. The abbey is the resting place for monarchs including Edward I, Henry III, Henry V, Henry VII, Elizabeth I, Mary I and Mary, Queen of Scots, and has been the setting for coronations since that of William the Conqueror in 1066. In Poets' Corner there are memorials to many literary figures, and many scientists and musicians are also remembered here. The grave of the Unknown Warrior is to be found in the nave
Westminster Cathedral
Francis Street SW1P 1QW T 020-7798 9055
W www.westminstercathedral.org.uk
Roman Catholic cathedral built 1895–1903 from the designs of John Francis Bentley. The campanile is 83m (273ft) high
Wimbledon All England Lawn Tennis Club
Church Road SW19 5AE T 020-8944 1066
W www.wimbledon.com
Venue for the Wimbledon Championships. Includes the Wimbledon Lawn Tennis Museum

HALLMARKS

Hallmarks are the symbols stamped on gold, silver, palladium or platinum articles to indicate that they have been tested at an official Assay Office and that they conform to one of the legal standards. The marking of gold and silver articles to identify the maker was instituted in England in 1363 under a statute of Edward III. In 1478 the Assay Office in Goldsmiths' Hall was established and all gold and silversmiths were required to bring their wares to be date-marked by the Hall, hence the term 'hallmarked'.

With certain exceptions, all gold, silver, palladium or platinum articles are required by law to be hallmarked before they are offered for sale. Current hallmarking requirements come under the UK Hallmarking Act 1973 and subsequent amendments. The act is built around the principle of description, where it is an offence for any person to apply to an unhallmarked article a description indicating that it is wholly or partly made of gold, silver, palladium or platinum. There is an exemption by weight: compulsory hallmarks are not needed on gold and palladium under 1g, silver under 7.78g and platinum under 0.5g. Also, some descriptions, such as rolled gold and gold plate, are permissible. The British Hallmarking Council is a statutory body created as a result of the Hallmarking Act. It ensures adequate provision for assaying and hallmarking, supervises the assay offices and ensures the enforcement of hallmarking legislation. The four assay offices at London, Birmingham, Sheffield and Edinburgh operate under the act.

BRITISH HALLMARKING COUNCIL Secretariat, 1 Colmore Square, Birmingham B4 6AA T 0870-763 1455 W www.gov.uk/government/organisations/british-hallmarking-council

COMPULSORY MARKS

Since January 1999 UK hallmarks have consisted of three compulsory symbols – the sponsor's mark, the millesimal fineness (purity) mark and the assay office mark. The distinction between UK and foreign articles has been removed, and more finenesses are now legal, reflecting the more common finenesses elsewhere in Europe.

SPONSOR'S MARK

Formerly known as the maker's mark, the sponsor's mark was instituted in England in 1363. Originally a device such as a bird or fleur-de-lis, now it consists of a combination of at least two initials (usually a shortened form of the manufacturer's name) and a shield design. The London Assay Office offers 45 standard shield designs but other designs are possible by arrangement.

MILLESIMAL FINENESS MARK

The millesimal fineness (purity) mark indicates the number of parts per thousand of pure metal in the alloy. The current finenesses allowed in the UK are:

Gold	999; 990; 916 (22 carat); 750 (18 carat); 585 (14 carat); 375 (9 carat)
Silver	999; 958 (Britannia); 925 (sterling); 800
Palladium	999; 950; 500
Platinum	999; 950; 900; 850

ASSAY OFFICE MARK

This mark identifies the particular assay office at which the article was tested and marked. The British assay offices are:

 LONDON, Goldsmiths' Hall, Gutter Lane, London EC2V 8AQ T 020-7606 8971 W www.assayofficelondon.co.uk

 BIRMINGHAM, 1 Moreton Street, Birmingham B1 3AS T 0121-236 6951 W www.theassayoffice.co.uk

 SHEFFIELD, Guardians' Hall, Beulah Road, Hillsborough, Sheffield S6 2AN T 0114-231 2121 W www.assayoffice.co.uk

 EDINBURGH, Goldsmiths' Hall, 24 Broughton Street, Edinburgh EH1 3RH T 0131-556 1144 W www.edinburghassayoffice.co.uk

Assay offices formerly existed in other towns, eg Chester, Exeter, Glasgow, Newcastle, Norwich and York, each having its own distinguishing mark.

OPTIONAL MARKS

Since 1999 traditional pictorial marks such as a crown for gold, the Britannia for 958 silver, the lion passant for 925 Sterling silver (lion rampant in Scotland) and the orb for 950 platinum may be added voluntarily to the millesimal mark. In 2010 a pictorial mark of the Greek goddess Pallas Athene was introduced for 950 palladium.

 Gold – a crown

 Sterling silver (Scotland)

 Britannia silver

 Platinum – an orb

 Sterling silver (England)

 Palladium – the Greek goddess Pallas Athene

DATE LETTER

The date letter shows the year in which an article was assayed and hallmarked. Each alphabetical cycle has a distinctive style of lettering or shape of shield. The date letters were different at the various assay offices and the particular office must be established from the assay office mark before reference is made to tables of date letters. Date letter marks became voluntary from 1 January 1999.

The table which follows shows one specimen shield and letter used by the London Assay Office on silver articles for each alphabetical cycle from 1498. The same letters are found on gold articles but the surrounding shield may differ. Until 1 January 1975, each hallmark covered two calendar years as the letter changed annually in May on St Dunstan's Day (the patron saint of silversmiths). Since 1 January 1975, each date letter has indicated a calendar year from January to December and each office has used the same style of date letter and shield for all articles.

LONDON (GOLDSMITHS' HALL) DATE LETTERS

	from	to		from	to
	1498–9	1517–18		1756–7	1775–6
	1518–19	1537–8		1776–7	1795–6
	1538–9	1557–8		1796–7	1815–16
	1558–9	1577–8		1816–17	1835–6
	1578–9	1597–8		1836–7	1855–6
	1598–9	1617–18		1856–7	1875–6
	1618–19	1637–8		1876–7 (A to M square shield, N to Z as shown)	1895–6
	1638–9	1657–8		1896–7	1915–16
	1658–9	1677–8		1916–17	1935–6
	1678–9	1696–7		1936–7	1955–6
	1697 (from March, 1697 only)	1715–16		1956–7	1974
	1716–17	1735–6		1975	1999
	1736–7	1738–9		2000	
	1739–40	1755–6			

OTHER MARKS

FOREIGN GOODS

Foreign goods imported into the UK are required to be hallmarked before sale, unless they already bear a convention mark or a hallmark struck by an independent assay office in the European Economic Area which is deemed to be equivalent to a UK hallmark.

The following are the assay office marks used for gold imported articles until the end of 1998. For silver and platinum the symbols remain the same but the shields differ in shape.

𝕩	*London*	Ω	*Sheffield*
△	*Birmingham*	✕	*Edinburgh*

CONVENTION HALLMARKS

The UK has been a signatory to the International Convention on Hallmarks since 1972. A convention hallmark struck by the UK assay offices is recognised by all member countries in the convention and, similarly, convention marks from member countries are legally recognised in the UK. There are currently 19 members of the hallmarking convention: Austria, Cyprus, Czech Republic, Denmark, Finland, Hungary, Ireland, Israel, Latvia, Lithuania, the Netherlands, Norway, Poland, Portugal, Slovakia, Slovenia, Sweden, Switzerland, and the UK.

A convention hallmark comprises four marks: a sponsor's mark, a common control mark, a fineness mark, and an assay office mark.

Examples of common control marks (figures differ according to fineness, but the style of each mark remains the same for each article):

GOLD	SILVER	PALLADIUM	PLATINUM
375	800	950	850

COMMEMORATIVE MARKS

There are other marks to commemorate special events: the silver jubilee of King George V and Queen Mary in 1935, the coronation of Queen Elizabeth II in 1953, her silver jubilee in 1977, and her golden jubilee in 2002. During 1999 and 2000 there was a voluntary additional Millennium Mark. A mark to commemorate the Queen's diamond jubilee in 2012 was available from July 2011 to October 2012:

BRITISH CURRENCY

The unit of currency is the pound sterling (£) of 100 pence. The decimal system was introduced on 15 February 1971.

COIN

Gold Coins	Nickel-Brass Coins
One hundred pounds £100*	Two pounds £2 (pre-1997)℃
Fifty pounds £50*	One pound £1
Twenty-five pounds £25*	
Ten pounds £10*	*Cupro-Nickel Coins*
Five pounds £5	Crown £5 (since 1990)℃
Two pounds £2	50 pence 50p
Sovereign £1	Crown 25p (pre-1990)℃
Half-sovereign 50p	20 pence 20p
Silver Coins	*Nickel-plated Steel Coins***
(Britannia coins)*	10 pence 10p
Two pounds £2	5 pence 5p
One pound £1	
50 pence 50p	*Bronze Coins*
Twenty pence 20p	2 pence 2p
	1 penny 1p
Maundy Money†	
Fourpence 4p	*Copper-plated Steel Coins††*
Threepence 3p	2 pence 2p
Twopence 2p	1 penny 1p
Penny 1p	
Bi-colour Coins‡	
Two pounds £2	
One pound £1§	

* Britannia coins: gold bullion introduced 1987; silver, 1997
† Ceremonial money given annually by the sovereign on Maundy Thursday to as many elderly men and women as there are years in the sovereign's age
‡ Cupro-nickel centre and nickel-brass outer ring
§ The 12-sided £1 entered circulation on 28 March 2017
℃ Commemorative coins; not intended for general circulation
** Since September 1992; in 1998 the 2p was additionally struck in bronze
†† Pre-2012 the 10p and 5p coins were struck in cupro-nickel

GOLD COIN

Gold ceased to circulate during the First World War. Since then controls on buying, selling and holding gold coin have been imposed at various times but have subsequently been revoked. Under the Exchange Control (Gold Coins Exemption) Order 1979, gold coins may now be imported and exported without restriction, except gold coins which are more than 50 years old and valued at a sum in excess of £8,000.

Value Added Taxation on the sale of gold coins was revoked in 2000.

SILVER COIN

Prior to 1920 silver coins were struck from sterling silver, an alloy of which 925 parts in 1,000 were silver. In 1920 the proportion of silver was reduced to 500 parts. Since 1947 all 'silver' coins, except Maundy money, have been struck from cupro-nickel, an alloy of 75 parts copper and 25 parts nickel, except for the 20p, composed of 84 parts copper, 16 parts nickel. Maundy coins continue to be struck from sterling silver.

BRONZE COIN

Bronze, introduced in 1860 to replace copper, is an alloy consisting mainly of copper with small amounts of zinc and tin. Bronze was replaced by copper-plated steel in September 1992 with the exception of 1998 when the 2p was made in both copper-plated steel and bronze.

LEGAL TENDER *as at July 2017*

	Legal up to
Gold*	any amount
£2	any amount
£1	any amount
50p	£10
20p	£10
10p	£5
5p	£5
2p	20p
1p	20p

* Dated 1838 onwards, if not below least current weight

£5 (Crown since 1990) and 25p (Crown pre-1990) up to £10 are also legal tender under the Coinage Act 1971 but, as for all commemorative coins, are not designed for general circulation and are unlikely to be accepted by banks and shops.

The following coins have ceased to be legal tender:

Farthing	31 Dec 1960
Halfpenny (½d)	31 Jul 1969
Half-crown	31 Dec 1969
Threepence	31 Aug 1971
Penny (1d)	31 Aug 1971
Sixpence	30 Jun 1980
Halfpenny (½p)	31 Dec 1984
Old 5 pence	31 Dec 1990
Old 10 pence	30 Jun 1993
Old 50 pence	28 Feb 1998
Old £1 (nickel-brass/round)	15 Oct 2017

The Channel Islands and the Isle of Man issue their own coinage, which is legal tender only in the island of issue.

COIN STANDARDS

	Metal	Standard weight (g)	Standard diameter (mm)
1p	bronze	3.56	20.3
1p	copper-plated steel	3.56	20.3
2p	bronze	7.12	25.9
2p	copper-plated steel	7.12	25.9
5p	nickel-plated steel	3.25	18.0
10p	nickel-plated steel	6.50	24.5
20p	cupro-nickel	5.00	21.4
25p Crown	cupro-nickel	28.28	38.6
50p	cupro-nickel	8.00	27.3
£1	cupro-nickel, nickel-brass	8.75	23.4
£2	nickel-brass	15.98	28.4
£2	cupro-nickel, nickel-brass	12.00	28.4
£5 Crown	cupro-nickel	28.28	38.6

The 'remedy' is the amount of variation from standard permitted in weight and fineness of coins when first issued from the Royal Mint.

THE TRIAL OF THE PYX

The Trial of the Pyx is the examination by a jury to ascertain that coins made by the Royal Mint, which have been set aside in the pyx (or box), are of the proper weight, diameter and composition required by law. The trial is held annually, presided over by the Queen's Remembrancer, with a jury of freemen of the Company of Goldsmiths.

BANKNOTES

Bank of England notes are issued in denominations of £5, £10, £20 and £50 for the amount of the fiduciary note issue, and are legal tender in England and Wales.

LEGAL TENDER
A new-style £20 note, the first in series F, was introduced in March 2007. A £50 note, the second in the F series, and the first banknote issued by the Bank of England to feature two portraits on the reverse, was issued in November 2011. The first polymer G series banknote, a £5 note featuring Sir Winston Churchill, was issued in September 2016 and the second, a £10 polymer note featuring Jane Austen, followed in September 2017.

The historical figures portrayed in the F and G series are:

£5	Sep 2016–date	Sir Winston Churchill
£10	Sep 2017–date	Jane Austen
£20	Mar 2007–date	Adam Smith
£50	Nov 2011–date	Matthew Boulton and James Watt

NOTE CIRCULATION
Note circulation is highest at the two peak spending periods of the year: around Christmas and during the summer holiday period.

The value of notes in circulation (£ million) at the end of February 2017 and 2018 was:

	2017	2018
£5	1,912	1,910
£10	8,006	7,789
£20	43,357	42,692
£50	15,601	16,508
Other notes*	4,322	4,351
Total	73,198	73,250

* Includes higher value notes used as backing for the note issues of authorised banks in Scotland and Northern Ireland

WITHDRAWN BANKNOTES
Banknotes which are no longer legal tender are payable when presented at the head office of the Bank of England in London.

The white notes for £10, £20, £50, £100, £500 and £1,000, which were issued until April 1943, ceased to be legal tender in May 1945, and the white £5 note in March 1946.

The white £5 note issued between October 1945 and September 1956, the £5 notes issued between 1957 and 1963 (bearing a portrait of Britannia) and the first series to bear a portrait of the Queen, issued between 1963 and 1971, ceased to be legal tender in March 1961, June 1967 and September 1973 respectively.

The series of £1 notes issued during the years 1928 to 1960 and the 10 shilling notes issued from 1928 to 1961 (those without the royal portrait) ceased to be legal tender in May and October 1962 respectively. The £1 note first issued in March 1960 (bearing on the back a representation of Britannia) and the £10 note first issued in February 1964 (bearing a lion on the back), both bearing a portrait of the Queen on the front, ceased to be legal tender in June 1979.

The £1 note first issued in 1978 ceased to be legal tender on 11 March 1988. The 10 shilling note was replaced by the 50p coin in October 1969, and ceased to be legal tender on 21 November 1970.

The D series of banknotes was introduced from 1970 and ceased to be legal tender from the dates shown below. The predominant identifying feature of each note was the portrayal on the back of a prominent figure from British history:

£1	Feb 1978–Mar 1988	Sir Isaac Newton
£5	Nov 1971–Nov 1991	Duke of Wellington
£10	Feb 1975–May 1994	Florence Nightingale
£20	Jul 1970–Mar 1993	William Shakespeare
£50	Mar 1981–Sep 1996	Sir Christopher Wren

The £1 coin was introduced on 21 April 1983 to replace the £1 note. No £1 notes have been issued since 1984 and in March 1998 the outstanding notes were written off in accordance with the provision of the Currency Act 1983.

The E series of notes was introduced from June 1990, replacing the D series. E series notes were withdrawn from circulation on the dates shown below:

£5	Jun 1990–Nov 2003	George Stephenson
£5	May 2002–May 2017	Elizabeth Fry
£10	Apr 1992–Jul 2003	Charles Dickens
£10	Nov 2000–Mar 2018	Charles Darwin
£20	Jun 1991–Feb 2001	Michael Faraday
£20	Jun 1999–Jun 2010	Sir Edward Elgar
£50	Apr 1994–Apr 2014	Sir John Houblon

OTHER BANKNOTES
Scotland – Banknotes are issued by three Scottish banks. The Royal Bank of Scotland issues notes for £1, £5, £10, £20, £50 and £100. Bank of Scotland and the Clydesdale Bank issue notes for £5, £10, £20, £50 and £100. Scottish notes are not legal tender in the UK but they are an authorised currency.

Northern Ireland – Banknotes are issued by four banks in Northern Ireland. The Bank of Ireland and the Ulster Bank issue notes for £5, £10, £20, £50 and £100. The First Trust Bank issue notes for £10, £20, £50 and £100 and Danske Bank (formerly Northern Bank) issue notes for £10 and £20. Northern Ireland notes are not legal tender in the UK but they are an authorised currency.

Channel Islands – The States of Guernsey issues its own currency notes and coinage. The notes are for £1, £5, £10, £20 and £50, and the coins are for 1p, 2p, 5p, 10p, 20p, 50p, £1 and £2.

The States of Jersey issues its own currency notes and coinage. The notes are for £1, £5, £10, £20, £50 and £100, and the coins are for 1p, 2p, 5p, 10p, 20p, 50p, £1 and £2.

The Isle of Man – The Isle of Man government issues notes for £1, £5, £10, £20 and £50. Although these notes are only legal tender in the Isle of Man, they may be exchanged at face value at certain UK banks at their discretion. The Isle of Man issues coins for 1p, 2p, 5p, 10p, 20p, 50p, £1, £2 and £5.

Although none of the series of notes specified above is legal tender in the UK, they are generally accepted by banks irrespective of their place of issue. At one time banks made a commission charge for handling Scottish and Irish notes but this was abolished some years ago.

BANKING AND PERSONAL FINANCE

There are two main types of deposit-taking institutions: banks and building societies, although National Savings and Investments also provides savings products. Banks and building societies are regulated by the Prudential Regulation Authority, part of the Bank of England (*see* Financial Services Regulation), and National Savings and Investments is accountable to HM Treasury.

The main institutions within the British banking system are the Bank of England (the central bank), retail banks, investment banks and overseas banks. In its role as the central bank, the Bank of England acts as banker to the government and as a note-issuing authority; it also oversees the efficient functioning of payment and settlement systems.

Since May 1997, the Bank of England has had operational responsibility for monetary policy. At monthly meetings of its monetary policy committee the Bank sets the interest rate at which it will lend to the money markets.

OFFICIAL INTEREST RATES 2006–17	
3 August 2006	4.75%
9 November 2006	5.00%
11 January 2007	5.25%
10 May 2007	5.50%
5 July 2007	5.75%
6 December 2007	5.50%
7 February 2008	5.25%
10 April 2008	5.00%
8 October 2008	4.50%
6 November 2008	3.00%
4 December 2008	2.00%
8 January 2009	1.50%
5 February 2009	1.00%
5 March 2009	0.50%
4 August 2016	0.25%
2 November 2017	0.50%
2 August 2018	0.75%

RETAIL BANKING

Retail banks offer a wide variety of financial services to individuals and companies, including current and deposit accounts, loan and overdraft facilities, credit and debit cards, investment services, pensions, insurance and mortgages. All banks offer internet and telephone banking facilities and the majority also offer traditional branch services.

The Financial Ombudsman Service provides independent and impartial arbitration in disputes between banks and their customers (*see* Financial Services Regulation).

PAYMENT CLEARINGS

The Payment Systems Regulator (PSR), a subsidiary of the Financial Conduct Authority (*see* Financial Services Regulation), is the economic regulator for the payment systems industry in the UK. Funded by an annual levy on the firms it regulates, it was established on 1 April 2015. The PSR's statutory objectives are:

- to ensure that payment systems are operated and developed in a way that considers and promotes the interests of all the businesses and consumers that use them
- to promote effective competition in the markets for payment systems and services – between operators, payment service providers and infrastructure providers
- to promote development and innovation in payment systems, in particular the infrastructure used to operate these systems

DESIGNATED PAYMENT SYSTEMS

The PSR can only use its regulatory powers in relation to payment systems designated by HM Treasury, which regularly reviews this list. The current designated payment systems are: BACS, C&C (Cheque & Credit), CHAPS, Faster Payments Scheme (FPS), LINK, Northern Ireland Cheque Clearing (NICC), MasterCard, Visa Europe (Visa).

PSR, 25 The North Colonnade, Canary Wharf, London E14 5HS
T 020-7066 1000 E contactus@psr.org.uk W www.psr.org.uk

MAJOR RETAIL BANKS' FINANCIAL RESULTS 2017

Bank group	Profit/(loss) before taxation £ million	Profit/(loss) after taxation £ million	Total assets £ million
Barclays Bank	3,541	(894)	1,133,248
Cooperative Bank	216	233	24,490
HSBC Bank	2,370	1,842	818.868
Lloyds Banking Group	5,275	3,547	812,109
RBS Group	2,239	1,415	738,056
Santander UK	1,817	1,256	314,765
TSB Banking Group	159	115	42,537
Virgin Money Group	263	192	41,108

GLOSSARY OF FINANCIAL TERMS

AER (ANNUAL EQUIVALENT RATE) – A notional rate quoted on savings and investment products which demonstrates the return on interest, when compounded and paid annually.

APR (ANNUAL PERCENTAGE RATE) – Calculates the total amount of interest payable over the whole term of a product (such as investment or loan), allowing consumers to compare rival products on a like-for-like basis. Companies offering loans, credit cards, mortgages or overdrafts are required by law to provide the APR rate. Where typical APR is shown, it refers to the company's typical borrower and so is given as a best example; rate and costs may vary depending on individual circumstances.

ANNUITY – A type of insurance policy that provides regular income in exchange for a lump sum. The annuity can be bought from a company other than the existing pension provider.

ASU – Accident, sickness and unemployment insurance taken out by a borrower to protect against being unable to work for these reasons. The policy will usually pay a percentage of the normal monthly mortgage repayment if the borrower is unable to work.

ATM (AUTOMATED TELLER MACHINES) – Commonly referred to as cash machines. Users can access their bank accounts using a card for simple transactions such as withdrawing money and viewing an account balance. Some banks and independent ATM deployers charge for transactions.

BANKER'S DRAFT – A cheque drawn on a bank against a cash deposit. Considered to be a secure way of receiving money in instances where a cheque could 'bounce' or where it is not desirable to receive cash.

BASE RATE – The interest rate set by the Bank of England at which it will lend to financial institutions. This acts as a benchmark for all other interest rates.

BASIS POINT – Unit of measure (usually one-hundredth of a percentage point) used to express movements in interest rates, foreign rates or bond yields.

BUY-TO-LET – The purchase of a residential property for the sole purpose of letting to a tenant. Not all lenders provide mortgage finance for this purpose. Buy-to-let lenders assess projected rental income (typical expectations are between 125 and 130 per cent of the monthly interest payment) in addition to, or instead of, the borrower's income. Buy-to-let mortgages are available as either interest only or repayment.

CAPITAL GAIN/LOSS – Increase/decrease in the value of a capital asset when it is sold or transferred compared to its initial worth.

CAPPED RATE MORTGAGE – The interest rate applied to a loan is guaranteed not to rise above a certain rate for a set period of time; the rate can therefore fall but will not rise above the capped rate. The level at which the cap is fixed is usually higher than for a fixed rate mortgage for a comparable period of time. The lender normally imposes early redemption penalties within the first few years.

CASH CARD – Issued by banks and building societies for withdrawing cash from ATMs.

CHARGE CARD – Charge cards, eg American Express and Diners Club, can be used in a similar way to credit cards but the debt must be settled in full each month.

CHIP AND PIN CARD – A credit/debit card which incorporates an embedded chip containing unique owner details. When used with a PIN, such cards offer greater security as they are less prone to fraud. Since 14 February 2006, most card transactions in the UK have required the use of a chip and pin card.

CREDIT CARD – Normally issued with a credit limit, credit cards can be used for purchases until the limit is reached. There is normally an interest-free period on the outstanding balance of up to 56 days. Charges can be avoided if the balance is paid off in full within the interest-free period. Alternatively part of the balance can be paid and in most cases there is a minimum amount set by the issuer (normally a percentage of the outstanding balance) which must be paid on a monthly basis. Some card issuers charge an annual fee and most issuers belong to at least one major credit card network, eg Mastercard or Visa.

CREDIT RATING – Overall credit worthiness of a borrower based on information from a credit reference agency, such as Experian or Equifax, which holds details of credit agreements, payment records, county court judgments etc for all adults in the UK. This information is supplied to lenders who use it in their credit scoring or underwriting systems to calculate the risk of granting a loan to an individual and the probability that it will be repaid. Each lender sets their own criteria for credit worthiness and may accept or reject a credit application based on an individual's credit rating.

CRITICAL ILLNESS COVER – Insurance that covers borrowers against critical illnesses such as stroke, heart attack or cancer and is designed to protect mortgage or other loan payments.

DEBIT CARD – Debit cards were introduced on a large scale in the UK in the mid-1980s, replacing cash and cheques to purchase goods and services. They can be used to withdraw cash from ATMs in the UK and abroad and may also function as a cheque guarantee card. Funds are automatically withdrawn from an individual's bank account after making a purchase and no interest is charged.

DIRECT DEBIT – An instruction from a customer to their bank, which authorises the payee to charge costs to the customer's bank account.

DISCOUNTED MORTGAGE – Discounted mortgages guarantee an interest rate set at a margin below the standard variable rate for a period of time. The discounted rate will move up or down with the standard variable rate, but the payment rate will retain the agreed differential below the standard variable rate. The lender normally imposes early redemption penalties within the first few years.

EARLY REDEMPTION PENALTY – see Redemption Penalty

ENDOWMENT MORTGAGE – Only the interest on a property loan is paid back to the lender each month as long as an endowment life insurance policy is taken out for an agreed amount of time, typically 25 years. When the policy matures the lender will take repayment of the money owed on the property loan and any surplus goes to the policyholder. If the endowment policy shows a shortfall on projected returns, the policy holder must make further provision to pay off the mortgage.

EQUITY – When applied to real estate, equity is the difference between the value of a property and the amount outstanding on any loan secured against it. Negative equity occurs when the loan is greater than the market value of the property.

FIXED RATE MORTGAGE – A repayment mortgage where the interest rate on the loan is fixed for a set amount of time, normally a period of between one and ten years. The interest rate does not vary with changes to the base rate resulting in the monthly mortgage payment remaining the same for the duration of the fixed period. The lender normally imposes early redemption penalties within the first few years.

ISA (INDIVIDUAL SAVINGS ACCOUNT) – A means by which investors can save (in a cash ISA) and invest (in a stocks and shares ISA) without paying any tax on the proceeds. There are limits on the amount that can be invested during any given tax year (*see* Taxation).

INTEREST ONLY MORTGAGE – Only interest is paid by the borrower and capital remains constant for the term of the loan. The onus is on the borrower to make provision to repay the capital at the end of the term. This is usually achieved through an investment vehicle such as an endowment policy or pension.

LOAN TO VALUE (LTV) – This is the ratio between the size of a mortgage loan sought and the mortgage lender's valuation. On a loan of £55,000, for example, on a property valued at £100,000, the loan to value is 55 per cent. This means that there is sufficient equity in the property for the lender to be reassured that if interest or capital repayments were stopped, it could sell the property and recoup the money owed. Fewer options are available to borrowers requiring high LTV.

LONDON INTERBANK OFFERED RATE (LIBOR) – Is the interest rate that London banks charge when lending to one another on the wholesale money market. LIBOR is set by supply and demand of money as banks lend to each other in order to balance their books on a daily basis.

MIG (MORTGAGE INDEMNITY GUARANTEE) – An insurance for the lender paid by the borrower on high LTV mortgages (typically more than 90 per cent). It is a policy designed to protect the lender against loss in the event of the borrower defaulting or ceasing to repay a mortgage and is usually paid as a one-off premium or can be added to the value of the loan. It offers no protection to the borrower. Not all lenders charge MIG premiums.

OVERDRAFT – An 'authorised' overdraft is an arrangement made between customer and bank allowing the balance of the customer's account to go below zero; interest is normally charged at an agreed rate and sometimes an arrangement fee is charged. If the negative balance exceeds the agreed terms or a prior arrangement for an overdraft facility has not been made (an 'unauthorised' overdraft) then additional penalty fees may be charged and higher interest rates may apply. Interest-free overdrafts are available for customers in certain circumstances, such as full-time higher education students and recent graduates.

PERSONAL PENSION PLAN (PPP) – Designed for the self-employed or those in non-pensionable employment. Contributions made to a PPP are exempt from tax and the retirement age may be selected at any time, usually from age 55. Up to 25 per cent of the pension fund may be taken as a tax-free cash sum on retirement.

PHISHING – A fraudulent attempt to obtain bank account details and security codes through an email. The email purports to come from a *bona fide* bank or building society and attempts to steer the recipient, usually under the pretext that the banking institution is updating its security arrangements, to a website which requests personal details.

PIN (PERSONAL IDENTIFICATION NUMBER) – A PIN is issued alongside a cash card to allow the user to access a bank account via an ATM. PINs are also issued with smart, credit and debit cards and, since 14 February 2006, have been compulsory as a security measure in the majority of purchases.

PORTABLE MORTGAGE – A mortgage product that can be transferred to a different property in the event of a house move. Preferable where early redemption penalties are charged.

REDEMPTION PENALTY – A charge levied for paying off a loan, debt balance or mortgage before a date agreed with the lender.

REPAYMENT MORTGAGE – In contrast to the interest only mortgage, the monthly repayment includes an element of the capital sum borrowed in addition to the interest charged.

SHARE – A share is a divided-up unit of the value of a company. If a company is worth £100m, and there are 50 million shares in issue, then each share is worth £2 (usually listed as pence). As the overall value of the company fluctuates so does the share price.

STANDING ORDER – An instruction made by the customer to their bank, which allows the transfer of a set amount to a payee at regular intervals.

UNIT TRUST – A 'pooled' fund of assets, usually shares, owned by a number of individuals. Managed by professional, authorised fund-management groups, unit trusts have traditionally delivered better returns than average cash deposits, but do rise and fall in value as their underlying investment varies in value.

VARIABLE RATE MORTGAGE – Repayment mortgages where the interest rate set by the lender increases or decreases in relation to the base interest rate which can result in fluctuating monthly repayments.

WITH-PROFITS – Usually applies to pensions, endowments, savings schemes or bonds. The intention is to smooth out the rises and falls in the stock market for the benefit of the investor. Actuaries working for the insurance company, or fund managers, hold back some profits in good years in order to make up the difference in years when shares perform badly.

BANK FAMILY TREE

Includes the major retail banks operating in the UK as at
April 2018. For financial results for these banks *see* Banking
and Personal Finance. Building societies are only included
in instances where they demutualised to become
a bank.

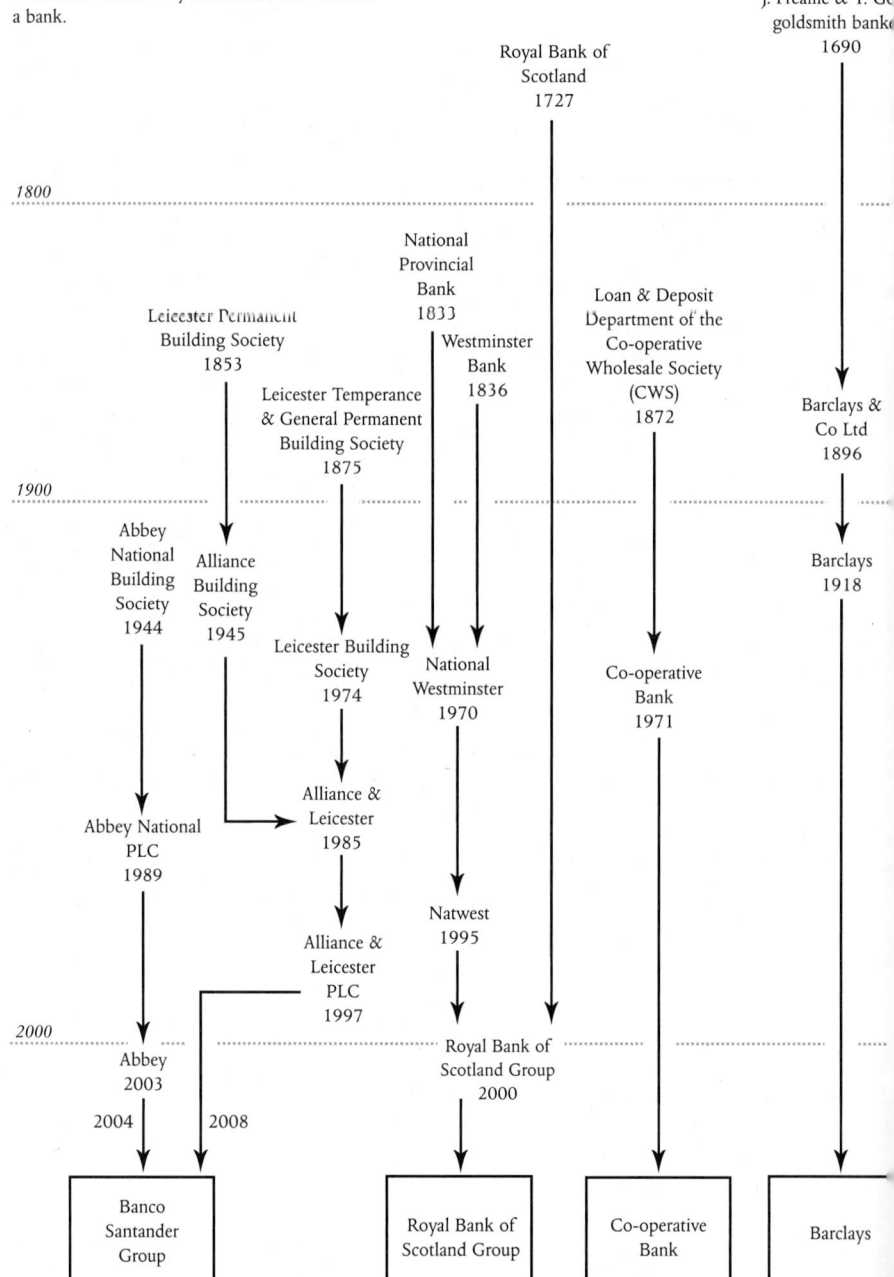

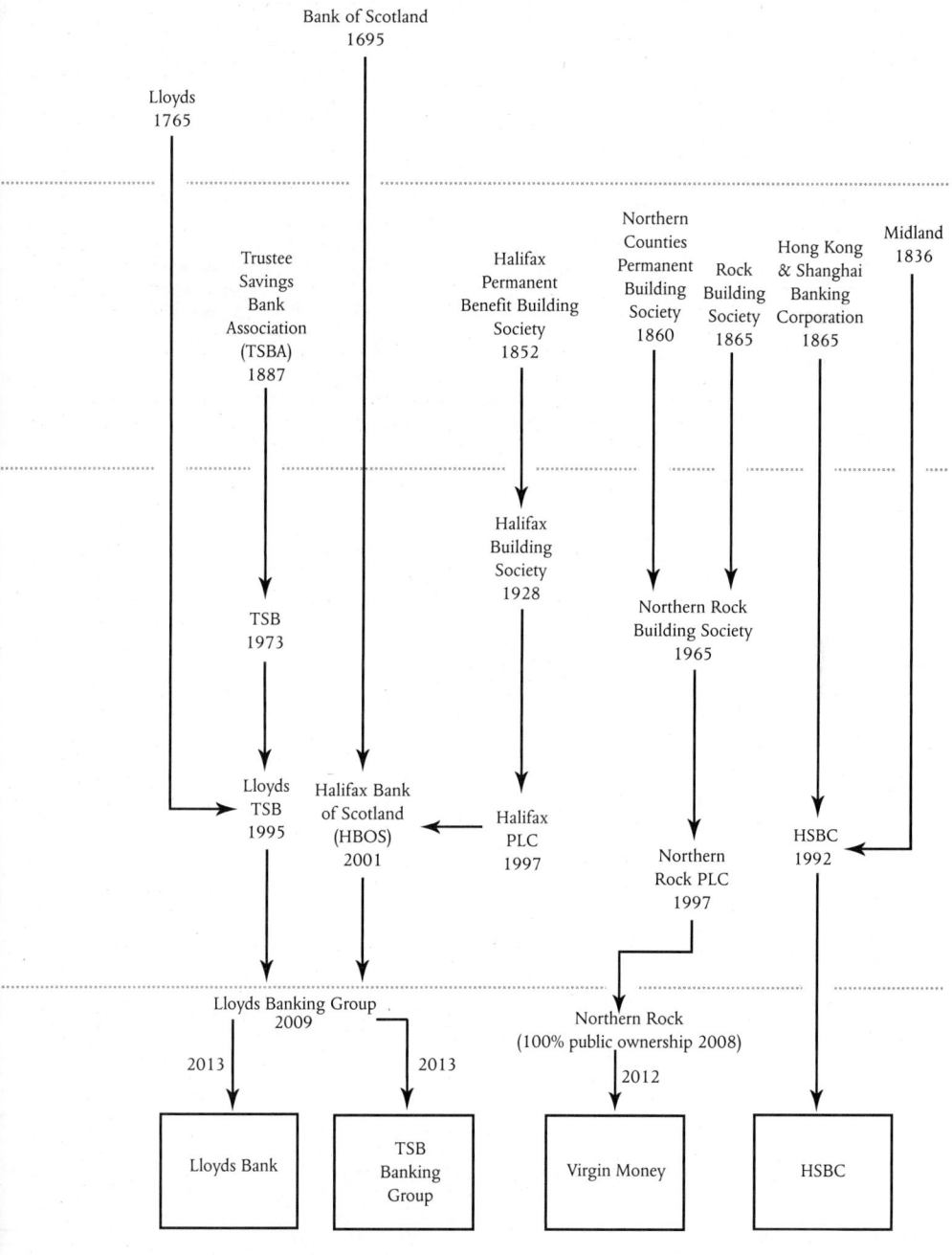

FINANCIAL SERVICES REGULATION

Under the Financial Services and Markets Act 2000, as amended by the Financial Services Act (2012), the Financial Conduct Authority and the Prudential Regulation Authority are responsible for financial regulation in the UK.

FINANCIAL CONDUCT AUTHORITY

The Financial Conduct Authority (FCA) is responsible for supervising the conduct of over 58,000 financial services firms and financial markets in the UK and for regulating the prudential standards of those firms – over 18,000 – not regulated by the Prudential Regulation authority. The FCA has three statutory objectives:
- to secure an appropriate degree of protection for consumers
- to protect and enhance the integrity of the UK financial system
- to promote effective market competition in the interests of consumers

The FCA is accountable to HM Treasury and therefore to parliament, but is operationally independent of the government and is funded entirely by the firms which it regulates. The FCA is governed by a board appointed by HM Treasury, but day-to-day decisions and staff management are the responsibility of the executive committee.

The FCA's annual budget for ongoing regulatory activity (ORA) in 2018–19 is £527.2m, a 3.8 per cent increase from 2017–18. The 2018–19 annual funding requirement totals £543.9m, an increase of 3.2 per cent due to the increase in the ORA budget and an additional £5m allocated for the costs associated with withdrawing from the European Union.

THE FINANCIAL SERVICES REGISTER

The Financial Services Register lists financial services firms and individuals in the UK who are authorised by the FCA to do business and specifies which activity each firm or individual is regulated to undertake and what products or services each is approved to provide.

FINANCIAL CONDUCT AUTHORITY, 25 The North Colonnade, Canary Wharf, London E14 5HS T 020-7066 1000 W www.fca.org.uk
Chair, Charles Randell, CBE
Chief Executive, Andrew Bailey

PRUDENTIAL REGULATION AUTHORITY

The Prudential Regulation Authority (PRA), part of the Bank of England, works alongside the FCA and is responsible for the prudential regulation and supervision of around 1,500 banks, building societies, credit unions, insurers and major investment firms. The PRA has three statutory objectives:
- to promote the safety and soundness of the firms it regulates
- to contribute to securing an appropriate degree of protection for those who are, or may become, insurance policyholders
- to facilitate effective competition

The members of the PRA's committee are: the Governor of the Bank of England (chair); four Deputy Governors; the chief executive of the FCA; a member appointed by the Governor with the approval of the chancellor; and six other external members appointed by the chancellor.

The PRA's budget for 2018–19 is £275m.

PRUDENTIAL REGULATION AUTHORITY, 20 Moorgate, London EC2R 6DA T 020-3461 4444
E enquiries@bankofengland.co.uk
W www.bankofengland.co.uk/pra
Chief Executive, Sam Woods

COMPENSATION

Created under the Financial Services and Markets Act (2000), the Financial Services Compensation Scheme (FSCS) is the UK's statutory fund of last resort for customers of authorised financial services firms. It provides compensation if a firm authorised by the FCA or PRA is unable, or likely to be unable, to pay claims against it. In general this is when a firm has stopped trading and has insufficient assets to meet claims, or is in insolvency. The FSCS protects banks and building societies, credit unions, deposits, endowments, debt management, insurance, investments, mortgages (including mortgage advice) and pensions (including retirement savings). The FSCS is independent of the UK regulators (FCA and PRA), with separate staff and premises. However, the FCA and PRA appoint the directors. The chair's appointment (and removal) is subject to Treasury approval. The FSCS is funded by annual levies on authorised firms.

The Pension Protection Fund (PPF) is a statutory fund established under the Pensions Act 2004 and became operational on 6 April 2005. The fund was set up to pay compensation to members of eligible defined benefit pension schemes, where there is a qualifying insolvency event in relation to the employer and where there are insufficient assets in the pension scheme to cover PPF levels of compensation. Compulsory annual levies are charged on all eligible schemes to help fund the PPF, in addition to investment of PPF assets. The PPF is also responsible for the Fraud Compensation Fund – a fund that will provide compensation to occupational pension schemes that suffer a loss attributable to dishonesty.

FINANCIAL SERVICES COMPENSATION SCHEME, PO Box 300, Mitcheldean GL17 1DY T 020-7741 4100/0800-678 1100 W www.fscs.org.uk
Chair, Marshall Bailey
Chief Executive, Mark Neale
PENSION PROTECTION FUND, Renaissance, 12 Dingwall Road, Croydon CR0 2NA T 0345-600 2541
E information@ppf.gsi.gov.uk
W www.pensionprotectionfund.org.uk
Chair, Arnold Wagner, OBE
Chief Executive, Oliver Morley, CBE

DESIGNATED PROFESSIONAL BODIES

Professional firms are exempt from requiring direct regulation by the FCA if they carry out only certain restricted activities that arise out of, or are complementary to, the provision of professional services, such as arranging the sale of shares on the instructions of executors or trustees, or providing services to small, private companies. These firms are, however, supervised by designated professional bodies (DPBs). There are a number of safeguards to protect consumers dealing with firms that do not require direct regulation. These arrangements include:
- the FCA's power to ban a specific firm from taking advantage of the exemption and to restrict the regulated activities permitted to the firms

- rules which require professional firms to ensure that their clients are aware that they are not authorised persons
- a requirement for the DPBs to supervise and regulate the firms and inform the FCA on how the professional firms carry on their regulated activities

See Professional Education section for contact details of the following DPBs:
Association of Chartered Certified Accountants
Council for Licensed Conveyancers
Institute of Actuaries
Institute of Chartered Accountants in England and Wales
Institute of Chartered Accountants in Ireland
Institute of Chartered Accountants of Scotland
Law Society of England and Wales
Law Society of Northern Ireland
Law Society of Scotland
Royal Institution of Chartered Surveyors

RECOGNISED INVESTMENT EXCHANGES

The FCA currently supervises six recognised investment exchanges (RIEs) in the UK; recognition confers an exemption from the need to be authorised to carry out regulated activities in the UK. The RIEs are organised markets on which member firms can trade investments such as equities and derivatives. The RIEs are listed with their year of recognition in parentheses:

CBOE EUROPE (2013), 5th Floor, 11 Monument Street, London EC3R 8AF **T** 020-7012 8900 **W** https:// markets.cboe.com
EURONEXT LONDON (2014), 10th Floor, 110 Cannon Street, London EC4N 6EU **T** 020-7076 0900 **W** www.euronext.com/en
ICE FUTURES EUROPE (2001), 5th Floor Milton Gate, 60 Chiswell Street, London EC1Y 4SA **T** 020-7065 7700 **W** www.theice.com
LONDON METAL EXCHANGE (2001), 10 Finsbury Square, London EC2A 1AJ **T** 020-7113 8888 **W** www.lme.com
LONDON STOCK EXCHANGE (2001), 10 Paternoster Square, London EC4M 7LS **T** 020-7797 1000 **W** www.londonstockexchange.com
NEX EXCHANGE (2007), 2 Broadgate, London EC2M 7UR **T** 020-7818 9774 **W** www.nexexchange.com

RECOGNISED CENTRAL COUNTERPARTIES

The Bank of England is responsible for recognising and supervising central counterparties (CCPs) and clearing houses (RCHs). CCPs and RCHs provide clearing and settlement services for transactions in foreign exchange, securities, options and derivatives on recognised investment exchanges. There are currently three UK CCPs authorised under the European Market Infrastructure regulation (EMIR) and one recognised RCH (dates of authorisation and recognition are given in parentheses):

EUROCLEAR UK AND IRELAND (RCH, 2001), 33 Cannon Street, London EC4M 5SB **T** 020-7849 0000 **W** www.euroclear.com
ICE CLEAR EUROPE (CCP, 2016), 5th Floor, Milton Gate, 60 Chiswell Street, London EC1Y 4SA **T** 020-7065 7600 **W** www.theice.com/clear_europe
LCH (LONDON CLEARING HOUSE) (CCP, 2014), Aldgate House, 33 Aldgate High Street, London EC3N 1EA **T** 020-7426 7000 **W** www.lch.com

LME (LONDON METAL EXCHANGE) CLEAR (CCP, 2014), 10 Finsbury Square, London EC2A 1AJ **T** 020-7113 8888 **W** www.lme.com/LME-Clear

OMBUDSMAN SCHEMES

The Financial Ombudsman Service was set up by the Financial Services and Markets Act 2000 to provide consumers with a free, independent service for resolving disputes with authorised financial firms. It can consider complaints about most financial matters including: banking; credit cards and store cards; financial advice; hire purchase and pawnbroking; insurance; loans and credit; money transfer; mortgages; payday lending and debt collecting; payment protection insurance; pensions; savings and investments; stocks, shares, unit trusts and bonds.

Complainants must first complain to the firm involved. They do not have to accept the ombudsman's decision and are free to go to court if they wish, but if a decision is accepted, it is binding for both the complainant and the firm.

The Pensions Ombudsman can investigate and decide complaints and disputes regarding the way occupational and personal pension schemes are administered and managed. Unless there are special circumstances, this only usually includes issues and disputes that have arisen within the past three years. The Pensions Ombudsman is also the Ombudsman for the Pension Protection Fund (PPF) and the Financial Assistance Scheme (which offers help to those who were a member of an under-funded defined benefit pension scheme that started to wind-up in specific financial circumstances between 1 January 1997 and 5 April 2005).

FINANCIAL OMBUDSMAN SERVICE, Exchange Tower, London E14 9SR **Helpline** 0800-023 4567 **T** 020-7964 1000 **E** complaint.info@financial-ombudsman.org.uk **W** www.financial-ombudsman.org.uk
Chief Ombudsman, Caroline Wayman
PENSIONS OMBUDSMAN, 10 South Colonnade, Canary Wharf, London E14 4PU **T** 0800-917 4487 **E** enquiries@pensions-ombudsman.org.uk **W** www.pensions-ombudsman.org.uk
Pensions Ombudsman, Anthony Arter
Deputy Pensions Ombudsman, Karen Johnston

THE TAKEOVER PANEL

The Panel on Takeovers and Mergers is an independent body, established in 1968, whose main functions are to issue and administer the City code and to ensure equality of treatment and opportunity for all shareholders in takeover bids and mergers. The panel's statutory functions are set out in the Companies Act 2006.

The panel comprises up to 36 members representing a spread of expertise in takeovers, securities markets, industry and commerce. The chair, deputy chair and up to 20 other members are nominated by the panel's own nomination committee. The remaining members are nominated by professional bodies representing the financial advice, insurance, investment, pension and accountancy industries; the Association for Financial Markets in Europe; the Confederation of British Industry; the Quoted Companies Alliance; and UK Finance.

THE TAKEOVER PANEL, 10 Paternoster Square, London EC4M 7DY **T** 020-7382 9026 **E** supportgroup@thetakeoverpanel.org.uk **W** www.thetakeoverpanel.org.uk
Chair, Michael Crane, QC

NATIONAL SAVINGS AND INVESTMENTS

NS&I (National Savings and Investments) is both a non-ministerial government department and an executive agency of the Chancellor of the Exchequer. It is one of the UK's largest savings organisations, with 25 million customers and £157bn invested. When people invest in NS&I they are lending money to the government which pays them interest or prizes in return. All deposits are 100 per cent financially secure because they are guaranteed by HM Treasury.

TAX-FREE PRODUCTS

PREMIUM BONDS
Introduced in 1956, premium bonds enable savers to enter a regular draw for tax-free prizes, while retaining the right to get their money back. A sum equivalent to interest on each bond is put into a prize fund and distributed by monthly prize draws. The prizes are drawn by ERNIE (electronic random number indicator equipment) and are free of all UK income tax and capital gains tax. Two £1m jackpots are drawn each month in addition to other tax-free prizes ranging in value from £25 to £100,000.

Bonds are in units of £1, with a minimum purchase of £100 (£50 by standing order or electronic transfer), up to a maximum holding limit of £50,000 per person. Bonds become eligible for prizes once they have been held for one clear calendar month following the month of purchase. Each £1 unit can win only one prize per draw, but it will be awarded the highest for which it is drawn. Bonds remain eligible for prizes until they are repaid.

The scheme offers a facility to reinvest prize wins automatically. Upon completion of an automatic prize reinvestment mandate, holders receive new bonds which are immediately eligible for future prize draws. Bonds can only be held in the name of an individual and not by organisations.

INDIVIDUAL SAVINGS ACCOUNTS
Since April 1999 NS&I has offered cash individual savings accounts (ISAs). Its Direct ISA, launched in April 2006, can be opened and managed online and by telephone with a minimum investment of £1 and a maximum investment of £20,000 in the 2018–19 tax year. Interest for the Direct ISA is calculated daily and is free of tax.

Its Junior ISA, launched in August 2017 as a successor to children's bonds, can be opened for children under 18 by those with parental responsibility or, by a young person aged 16 or 17 for themselves. There is a minimum investment of £1 and a maximum investment of £4,260 in the 2018–19 tax year. It can only be opened and managed online and there are no withdrawals allowed until the young person reaches 18. Interest is accrued daily, added to the account annually and is free of tax.

OTHER PRODUCTS

INCOME BONDS
NS&I income bonds were introduced in 1982. They are suitable for those who want to receive regular monthly payments of interest while preserving the full cash value of their capital. The minimum holding for each investment is £500 and the maximum £1m per person. A variable rate of interest is calculated on a day-to-day basis and paid monthly. Interest is taxable but is paid without deduction of tax at source.

GUARANTEED GROWTH AND GUARANTEED INCOME BONDS
Guaranteed growth and guaranteed income bonds, re-launched in December 2017, offer a lump sum investment that earns a fixed rate of interest over either a one-year term or a three-year term. The minimum holding is £500 to a maximum of £10,000 per person or trust per issue. For the guaranteed growth bond interest is calculated daily and added to the bond on each anniversary of the investment. The guaranteed income bond has interest paid monthly. Interest on both bonds is taxable but is paid without deduction of tax at source.

SAVINGS AND INVESTMENT ACCOUNTS
The direct saver account was launched in March 2010. Customers are able to invest between £1 and £2m per person. The account can be managed online or by telephone. Interest is paid without deduction of tax at source.

The investment account can be opened with a minimum balance of £20 and has a maximum limit of £1m. The interest is paid without deduction of tax at source.

FURTHER INFORMATION
Further information regarding products and their current availability can be obtained online (W www.nsandi.com), by telephone (T 080-0092 1228), by email (E adviser@nsandi.com) or via post (NS&I, Glasgow G58 1SB).

THE NATIONAL DEBT

HISTORY

The early 1700s saw the meteoric rise of the banking and financial markets in Great Britain, with the emerging stock market revolving around government funds. The ability to raise money by means of creating debt through the issue of bills and bonds heralded the beginning of the national debt.

The war years of 1914–18 saw an increase in the national debt from £650m at the start of the war to £7,500m by 1919. The Treasury developed new expertise in foreign exchange, currency, credit and price control in order to manage the post-war economy. The slump of the 1930s necessitated the restructuring of the UK economy following the Second World War (the national debt stood at £21bn by its end) and the emphasis was placed on economic planning and financial relations.

The relatively high period of inflation in the 1970s and 1980s led to the rise of the national debt in nominal terms from £36bn in 1972 to £197bn in 1987 and then to £419bn in March 1998. Although in nominal terms the national debt has risen sharply in recent years, as a percentage of GDP it has decreased dramatically since the end of the Second World War, when it stood at 250 per cent of GDP (for current figures, *see* table below).

THE UK DEBT MANAGEMENT OFFICE

The decision in 1997 to transfer monetary policy to the Bank of England, while the Treasury retained control of fiscal policy, led to the creation of the UK Debt Management Office (DMO) as an executive agency of HM Treasury in April 1998. Initially the DMO was responsible only for the management of government marketable debt and for issuing gilts. In April 2000 responsibility for exchequer cash management and for issuing Treasury bills (short-dated securities with maturities of less than one year) was transferred from the Bank of England to the DMO. The national debt also includes the (non-marketable) liabilities of National Savings and Investments and other public sector and foreign currency debt.

In 2002 the operations of the long-standing statutory functions of the Public Works Loan Board, which lends capital to local authorities, and the Commissioners for the Reduction of the National Debt, which manages the investment portfolios of certain public funds, were integrated within the DMO (*see also* Government Departments).

UK PUBLIC SECTOR NET DEBT

	£ billion	per cent of GDP
2016–17 (outturn)	1,727	85.8
2017–18 (forecast)	1,791	86.5
2018–19 (forecast)	1,840	86.4

Source: Office for Budget Responsibility – *Economic and Fiscal Outlook November 2017* (Crown copyright)

THE LONDON STOCK EXCHANGE

The London Stock Exchange Group (LSEG) serves the needs of companies by providing facilities for raising capital. It also operates marketplaces for members to trade financial instruments. including equities, bonds and derivatives, on behalf of investors and institutions such as pension funds and insurers.

LSEG's key subsidiary companies are the London Stock Exchange, Borsa Italiana, MTS (an electronic platform for the trading of European government and corporate bonds), Turquoise (a trading platform for European equities) and FTSE (a global index provider).

Headquartered in London, with significant operations in Italy, France, North America and Sri Lanka, the group employs around 4,700 people.

HISTORY

The London Stock Exchange is one of the world's oldest stock exchanges, dating back more than 300 years to its origins in the coffee houses of 17th-century London. It was formally established as a membership organisation in 1801.

MAJOR DEVELOPMENTS

'BIG BANG'

In 1986 a package of reforms which are now known as 'Big Bang' transformed the London Stock Exchange and the City of London, liberalising the way in which banks and stock-broking firms operated and facilitating greater foreign investment. The London Stock Exchange ceased granting voting rights to individual members and became a private company. The 'Big Bang' also saw the start of a move towards fully electronic trading and the closure of the trading floor.

INTRODUCTION OF SETS

In October 1997, the Exchange introduced SETS, its electronic order book. The system enhanced the efficiency and transparency of trading on the Exchange, allowing trades to be executed automatically and anonymously rather than negotiated by telephone.

DEMUTUALISATION AND LISTING

The London Stock Exchange demutualised in 2000 and listed on its own main market in 2001.

MERGER WITH BORSA ITALIANA

In October 2007 the London Stock Exchange merged with the Italian stock exchange, Borsa Italiana, creating London Stock Exchange Group (LSEG).

DIVERSIFICATION

Since 2009 LSEG has diversified its business beyond the listing and trading of UK and Italian equities:
• In 2009 LSEG purchased Sri Lankan technology company MillenniumIT which provides technology to stock exchanges, brokerages and regulators around the world. It also supplies the trading technology to LSEG's own markets
• In 2010 LSEG acquired a majority stake in Turquoise, a platform facilitating the trading of stocks listed in 19 European countries and the USA
• In 2011 LSEG became the owner of FTSE, the international business which creates and manages financial indices
• In 2013 LSEG purchased a majority stake in LCH (London Clearing House) Clearnet (*see also* Financial Services Regulation, Recognised Central Counterparties and Recognised Clearing Houses)

UK EQUITY MARKETS

LSEG offers a range of listing options for companies, according to their size, history and requirements:
• The Main Market has the highest standards of regulation and disclosure obligations and is overseen by the UK Listing Authority (UKLA), a division of the Financial Conduct Authority (FCA). A Main Market listing enables established companies to raise capital, widen their investor base and have their shares traded alongside global peers. They are also eligible for inclusion in key indices, such as the FTSE 100 and the FTSE 250
• The Alternative Investment Market (AIM), established in June 1995, is specially designed to meet the needs of small and growing companies. It enables them to raise capital and broaden their investor base in a more flexible regulatory environment, while still being traded on an internationally recognised market. AIM companies retain an experienced Nominated Adviser (or 'Nomad') firm, which is responsible for ensuring the company's suitability for the market
• The Professional Securities Market (PSM), established in July 2005, allows companies to target professional investors only, on a market that offers greater flexibility in accounting standards
• The Specialist Fund Market (SFM), established in November 2007, is a market for highly specialised investment entities, such as hedge funds or private equity funds, that wish to target institutional investors only

As at 31 May 2018 there were 5,624 companies listed on LSEG's primary markets, with a combined market value of £1,981,942m: 1,770 on the Main Market (1,390 on the UK main market and 380 on the international main market), 3,803 on the AIM, 16 on the PSM and 35 entities on the SFM.

LONDON STOCK EXCHANGE, 10 Paternoster Square, London EC4M 7LS T 020-7797 1000 W www.lseg.com
Chair, Donald Brydon, CBE
Chief Executive, David Schwimmer

ECONOMIC STATISTICS

THE AUTUMN BUDGET 2017

GOVERNMENT EXPENDITURE

DEPARTMENTAL EXPENDITURE LIMITS *(£bn)*

	Plans *2018–19*
Resource DEL	
Defence	28.2
Single Intelligence Account	1.9
Home Office	10.7
Foreign and Commonwealth Office	1.2
International Development	8.7
Health (incl. NHS)	121.9
Work and Pensions	6.0
Education	62.4
Business, Energy and Industrial Strategy	1.8
Transport	2.1
Exiting the European Union	0.1
Digital, Culture, Media and Sport	1.5
MHCLG Communities	2.3
MHCLG Local Government	4.8
Scotland	13.8
Wales	13.2
Northern Ireland	10.00
Justice	6.2
Law Officers Departments	0.5
Environment, Food and Rural Affairs	1.5
HM Revenue and Customs	3.4
HM Treasury	0.2
Cabinet Office	0.3
International Trade	0.3
Small and Independent bodies	1.3
Reserves	6.5
Adjustment for budget exchange	0.0
TOTAL RESOURCE DEL	310.9
*OBR Allowance for shortfall	(1.3)
OBR Resource DEL	309.6
Capital DEL	
Defence	8.7
Single Intelligence Account	0.6
Home Office	0.5
Foreign and Commonwealth Office	0.1
International Development	3.2
Health (incl. NHS)	6.4
Work and Pensions	0.3
Education	5.2
Business, Energy and Industrial Strategy	10.5
Transport	8.1
Exiting the European Union	0.0
Digital, Culture, Media and Sport	0.5
MHCLG Communities	8.6
MHCLG Local Government	0.0
Scotland	3.9
Wales	1.9
Northern Ireland	1.4
Justice	0.7
Law Officers Departments	0.0
Environment, Food and Rural Affairs	0.6
HM Revenue and Customs	0.2
HM Treasury	0.2
Cabinet Office	0.0
International Trade	0.0
Small and Independent bodies	0.2

Reserves	1.0
Adjustment for budget exchange	0.0
TOTAL CAPITAL DEL	62.9
*OBR Allowance for shortfall	(1.8)
OBR Capital DEL	61.1
TOTAL DEL	370.7

* OBR = Office for Budget Responsibility
Source: HM Treasury – *Autumn Budget 2017* (Crown copyright)

TOTAL MANAGED EXPENDITURE *(£bn)*

	2017–18	*2018–19*	*2019–20*
Current Expenditure			
Resource Annually Managed Expenditure (AME)	386.5	397.8	406.2
Resource DEL (excl. depreciation)	304.0	309.6	310.7
Ring-fenced depreciation	22.0	22.8	23.3
Public Sector Current Expenditure	712.5	730.2	740.1
Capital Expenditure			
Capital AME	26.0	18.0	17.7
Capital DEL	56.9	61.1	69.0
Public Sector Gross Investment	82.8	79.1	86.6
TOTAL MANAGED EXPENDITURE	795.3	809.3	826.7
Total Managed Expenditure (% GDP)	38.9	38.5	38.3

Source: HM Treasury – *Autumn Budget 2017* (Crown copyright)

GOVERNMENT RECEIPTS *(£bn)*

	Outturn *2016–17*	*Forecast* *2017–18*	*Forecast* *2018–19*
Income tax (gross of tax credits)[1]	177.2	177.2	184.7
Pay as you earn	149.7	154.5	158.0
Self assessment	28.5	25.5	29.9
National insurance contributions (NICs)	125.9	131.0	134.4
Value added tax	121.6	125.8	130.3
Corporation tax	54.1	52.8	55.4
Petroleum revenue tax	(0.7)	(0.6)	(0.5)
Fuel duties	27.9	27.9	28.0
Business rates	29.2	29.3	30.5
Council tax	30.4	32.2	33.8
VAT refunds	13.8	14.1	14.5
Capital gains tax	8.4	8.8	9.9
Inheritance tax	4.8	5.3	5.4
Stamp duty land tax[2]	11.9	13.2	13.2
Stamp taxes on shares	3.7	3.4	3.5
Tobacco duties	8.7	9.4	9.2
Spirits duties	3.3	3.5	3.5
Wine duties	4.2	4.3	4.3
Beer and cider duties	3.6	3.7	3.7
Air passenger duty	3.2	3.3	3.5
Insurance premium tax	4.9	5.8	6.0
Climate change levy	1.9	1.8	1.9
Other HMRC taxes[3]	7.4	7.3	7.3
Vehicle excise duties	5.8	6.0	6.2
Bank levy	3.0	2.6	2.6
Bank surcharge	1.6	1.8	1.7
Apprenticeship levy	0.0	2.7	2.7
Licence fee receipts	3.2	3.2	3.3
Environmental levies	5.2	8.6	10.5

EU ETS* Auction receipts	0.4	0.4	0.6
Scottish and Welsh taxes	0.6	0.7	1.0
Diverted profits tax	0.1	0.2	0.3
Soft drinks industry levy	0.0	0.0	0.3
Other taxes	7.2	7.0	6.8
Total National Accounts			
Taxes	672.7	692.8	718.6
Less own resources			
contribution to EU	(3.4)	(3.5)	(3.5)
Interest and dividends	6.5	7.1	8.1
Gross operating surplus	47.2	45.5	43.1
Other receipts	3.7	3.5	3.4
CURRENT RECEIPTS	726.7	745.4	769.8
UK oil and gas revenues[4]	0.0	0.7	0.5

* ETS = Emissions Trading System
[1] Includes PAYE and Self Assessment receipts, tax on savings income and other minor income tax components
[2] Includes stamp duty land tax for England, Wales (up to 2018–19) and Northern Ireland
[3] Consists of landfill tax (excl. Scotland and Wales from 2018–19), aggregates levy, betting and gaming duties and customs duties
[4] Consists of offshore corporation tax and petroleum revenue tax
Source: HM Treasury – *Autumn Budget 2017* (Crown copyright)

TRADE

TRADE IN GOODS
£ million

	Exports	Imports	Balance
2013	303,147	423,811	(120,664)
2014	292,894	415,469	(122,575)
2015	287,584	407,304	(119,720)
2016	302,067	437,562	(135,495)
2017	342,479	478,061	(135,582)

Source: ONS (Crown copyright)

BALANCE OF PAYMENTS, 2017

Current Account	*£ million*
Trade in goods and services	
Trade in goods	(135,582)
Trade in services	106,962
Total trade in goods and services	(28,620)
Income	
Compensation of employees	(190)
Investment income	(32,250)
Other	(840)
Total income	(33,280)
Total secondary income	(20,974)
TOTAL (CURRENT BALANCE)	(82,874)

Source: ONS (Crown copyright)

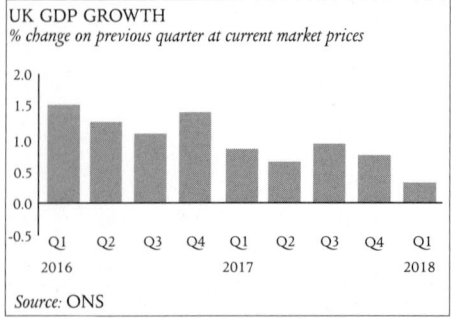

UK GDP GROWTH
% change on previous quarter at current market prices

Source: ONS

UK EMPLOYMENT

DISTRIBUTION OF THE WORKFORCE

	Mar 2017	Mar 2018*
Workforce jobs	34,988,000	35,180,000
HM forces	157,000	154,000
Self-employment jobs	4,504,000	4,498,000
Employees jobs	30,266,000	30,501,000
Government-supported trainees	62,000	28,000

* provisional data
Source: ONS – *Labour Market Statistics 2018* (Crown copyright)

EMPLOYED AND UNEMPLOYED
thousands, all aged 16+

	Feb–Apr 2017		Feb–Apr 2018	
	Number	Rate (%)	Number	Rate (%)
Employed	31,954	60.7	32,394	61.1
Unemployed	1,530	4.6	1,416	4.2

Source: ONS – *Labour Market Statistics 2018* (Crown copyright)

DURATION OF UNEMPLOYMENT, FEB–APR 2018

All unemployed	1,416,000
Less than 6 months	833,000
6 months–1 year	214,000
1 year +	369,000
2 years +	202,000

Source: ONS – *Labour Market Statistics 2018* (Crown copyright)

MEDIAN EARNINGS, 2017
full-time, £

	All	Male	Female
Gross annual earnings	28,758.00	31,103.00	25,308.00
Weekly earnings*	533.10	565.60	485.20
Hourly earnings*	13.94	14.48	13.16

* Excluding overtime
Source: ONS (Crown copyright)

LABOUR STOPPAGES BY DURATION, 2017

1 day	15
2–3 days	20
4 days	7
5–10 days	15
11+ days	22
All stoppages	79

Source: ONS (Crown copyright)

LABOUR DISPUTES BY INDUSTRY, 2017

Industry Group	Working Days Lost
Manufacturing	25,200
Sewage, waste management, water supply	2,300
Transport & storage	187,000
Information & Communication	6,300
Financial, professional, scientific, administration	19,400
Public administration & defence	2,300
Education	27,300
Human health and social work	6,400
Other	100
All industries & services	276,400

Source: ONS (Crown copyright)

TRADE UNIONS

Year	No. of unions	Total membership
2012–13	166	7,197,415
2013–14	166	7,086,116
2014–15	160	7,010,527
2015–16	160	6,948,725
2016–17	151	6,865,056

Source: Annual Report of the Certification Officer 2016–17

COST OF LIVING AND INFLATION RATES

The first cost of living index to be calculated took July 1914 as 100 and was based on the pattern of expenditure of working-class families in 1914. The cost of living index was superseded in 1947 by the general index of retail prices (RPI), although the older term is still popularly applied.

The Harmonised Index of Consumer Prices (HICP) was introduced in 1997 to enable comparisons within the European Union using an agreed methodology. In 2003 the National Statistician renamed the HICP the Consumer Prices Index (CPI) to reflect its role as the main target measure of inflation for macroeconomic purposes. In March 2013 CPIH, an additional index which includes owner-occupiers' housing costs, was introduced.

The RPI and indices based on it continue to be published alongside the CPI. Private-sector pensions and index-linked gilts continue to be calculated with reference to RPI or its derivatives.

CPI AND RPI

The CPI and RPI measure the changes month by month in the average level of prices of goods and services purchased by households in the UK. The indices are compiled using a selection of around 700 goods and services, and the prices charged for these items are collected at regular intervals at about 140 locations throughout the country, from the internet and over the phone. The Office for National Statistics (ONS) reviews the components of the indices once a year to reflect changes in consumer preferences and the establishment of new products. The table below shows changes made by the ONS to the CPI 'shopping basket' in 2018.

The CPI excludes a number of items that are included in the RPI, mainly related to housing, such as council tax, and a range of owner-occupier housing costs, such as mortgage payments. The CPI covers all private households, whereas the RPI excludes the top 4 per cent by income and pensioner households which derive at least three-quarters of their income from state benefits. The two indices use different methodologies to combine the prices of goods and services, which means that since 1996 the CPI inflation measure is less than the RPI inflation measure.

INFLATION RATE

The 12-monthly percentage change in the 'all items' index of the RPI or CPI is referred to as the rate of inflation. As the most familiar measure of inflation, the RPI is often referred to as the 'headline rate of inflation'. The CPI is the main measure of inflation for macroeconomic purposes and forms the basis of the government's inflation target, which is currently 2 per cent. The percentage change in prices between any two months/years can be obtained using this formula:

$$\frac{\text{Later date RPI/CPI} - \text{Earlier date RPI/CPI}}{\text{Earlier date RPI/CPI}} \times 100$$

For example, to find the CPI rate of inflation for 2006, using the annual averages for 2005 and 2006:

$$\frac{79.9 - 78.1}{78.1} \times 100 = 2.3$$

From 14 February 2006 the reference year for the CPI was re-based to 2005=100 to improve price comparison clarity across the EU. None of the underlying data, from which the re-referenced series was calculated, was revised. Historical rates of change (such as annual inflation figures), calculated from the re-based rounded index levels, were revised due to the effect of rounding. The CPI rate of inflation figure given in the table below may differ by plus or minus 0.1 percentage points from the figure calculated by the above equation. The change of reference period and revision due to rounding does not apply to the RPI, which remains unchanged.

The RPI and CPI figures are published around the the middle of each month in an indices bulletin on the ONS website (W www.ons.gov.uk/economy/inflationandpriceindices).

CHANGES TO THE 'SHOPPING BASKET' OF GOODS AND SERVICES IN 2018

The table below shows changes to the CPI* basket of goods and services made by the ONS in 2018 in order to reflect changes in consumer preferences and the establishment of new products.

Goods and services group	Removed items	New items
Food	pork pie; edam cheese; peaches/ nectarines	quiche; raspberries (punnet); prepared mashed potato (chilled)
Clothing	–	women's exercise leggings; girl's leggings
Furniture, furnishings & carpet	–	high chair
Audio-visual equipment & related products	digital television recorder/receiver; television 14–22"/35–55cm; television 23–32"/57.5–80cm; television 33"/ 82.5cm or larger; digital camcorder	digital media player; television 39"/ 102cm or smaller; television 40"/ 102cm or larger; action camera
Recreational items, gardens & pets	child's tricycle	child's sit and ride toy
Recreational & cultural services	–	soft play session
Catering services	pasty/savoury pie; bottle of lager in a nightclub	cooked pastry based savoury snack
Personal care	full leg wax	body moisturising lotion
Financial services	ATM charges	–

* RPI goods and services are grouped together under different classifications

PURCHASING POWER OF THE POUND

Changes in the internal purchasing power of the pound may be defined as the 'inverse' of changes in the level of prices: when prices go up, the amount which can be purchased with a given sum of money goes down. To find the purchasing power of the pound in one month or year, given that it was 100p in a previous month or year, the calculation would be:

$$100p \times \frac{\text{Earlier month/year RPI}}{\text{Later month/year RPI}}$$

Thus, if the purchasing power of the pound is taken to be 100p in 1975, the comparable purchasing power in 2000 would be:

$$100p \times \frac{34.2}{170.3} = 20.1p$$

For longer term comparisons, it has been the practice to use an index which has been constructed by linking together the RPI for the period 1962 to date; an index derived from the consumers' expenditure deflator for the period from 1938 to 1962; and the pre-war 'cost of living' index for the period 1914 to 1938. This long-term index enables the internal purchasing power of the pound to be calculated for any year from 1914 onwards. It should be noted that these figures can only be approximate.

ANNUAL INDICES

	Annual average RPI (1987 = 100)	Purchasing power of £ (1998 = 1.00)	Annual average CPI (2015 = 100)*	Annual average CPIH† (2015=100)*	Rate of inflation (RPI/CPI/CPIH)†
1914	2.8	58.18			
1915	3.5	46.54			
1920	7.0	23.27			
1925	5.0	37.58			
1930	4.5	36.20			
1935	4.0	40.72			
1938	4.4	37.02			
There are no official figures for 1939–45					
1946	7.4	22.01			
1950	9.0	18.10			
1955	11.2	14.54			
1960	12.6	12.93			
1965	14.8	11.00			
1970	18.5	8.80			
1975	34.2	4.76			
1980	66.8	2.44			
1985	94.6	1.72			
1990	126.1	1.29			9.5/7.0
1995	149.1	1.09			3.5/2.6
1998	162.9	1.00	71.2		3.4/1.6
2000	170.3	0.96	72.7		3.0/0.8
2005	192.0	0.85	78.1	79.4	2.8/2.1
2006	198.1	0.82	79.9	81.4	3.2/2.3/2.5
2007	206.6	0.79	81.8	83.3	4.3/2.3/2.4
2008	214.8	0.76	84.7	86.2	4.0/3.6/3.5
2009	213.7	0.76	86.6	87.9	−0.5/2.2/2.0
2010	223.6	0.73	89.4	90.1	4.6/3.3/2.5
2011	235.2	0.69	93.4	93.6	5.2/4.5/3.8
2012	242.7	0.67	96.1	96.0	3.2/2.8/2.6
2013	250.1	0.65	98.5	98.2	3.0/2.6/2.3
2014	256.0	0.64	100.0	99.6	2.4/1.5/1.5
2015	258.5	0.63	100.0	100.0	1.0/0.0/0.4
2016	263.1	0.62	100.7	101.0	1.8/0.7/1.0
2017	272.5	0.60	103.4	103.6	3.6/2.7/2.6

* All CPI indices were re-based to 2015=100 on 16 February 2016, replacing the 2005=100 series

INSURANCE

AUTHORISATION AND REGULATION OF INSURANCE COMPANIES

Since 1 April 2013, under the Financial Services Act 2012, the prudential supervision of banks and insurers is the responsibility of the Prudential Regulation Authority (PRA), an operationally independent subsidiary of the Bank of England. The Financial Conduct Authority (FCA) is responsible for consumer protection and markets oversight. All life insurers, general insurers, reinsurers, insurance and reinsurance brokers, financial advisers and composite firms are statutorily regulated. *See also* Financial Services Regulation.

Firms wishing to effect or carry out contracts of insurance must be granted authorisation to do so. The PRA assesses applicant insurers from a prudential perspective, using the same framework that is employed for supervision of existing insurers. The FCA then assesses applicants from a conduct perspective. Although the PRA manages the authorisation process, an insurer will be granted authorisation only where both the FCA and the PRA are satisfied that they meet their relevant requirements.

There are around 700 insurance organisations and friendly societies with authorisation to transact one or more class of insurance business in the UK. Until the UK leaves the EU, it remains part of the single European insurance market. This permits insurers authorised in any EU state automatic authorisation to transact business in all other EU countries without further formality. The number of insurers currently operating within this market is over 3,500. *See also* Brexit.

COMPLAINTS

Disputes between consumers and financial businesses can be referred to the Financial Ombudsman Service (FOS). Consumers with a complaint about any form of money matter, including bank accounts, insurance, mortgages, savings and credit, must first take the matter to the highest level within the provider. The provider has to provide a 'final response' within eight weeks. If the complaint remains unresolved consumers can refer the complaint, free of charge, to the FOS. The FOS can tell a financial business to compensate up to a maximum limit of £150,000, excluding any interest and costs (£100,000 for complaints received before 1 January 2012). If the FOS decides that fair compensation exceeds £150,000 the provider is only bound to accept the FOS decision up to the limit. Businesses falling under the EU definition of a micro enterprise (businesses with a turnover of up to €2m and fewer than ten employees) may also refer a matter to the FOS. In 2016, 52 per cent of new complaints about financial services companies related to payment protection insurance. Other types of insurance, such as motor, buildings and life insurance, accounted for just 12 per cent of the total number of complaints received. *See also* Financial Services Regulation.

ASSOCIATION OF BRITISH INSURERS

Over 80 per cent of the domestic business of UK insurance companies is transacted by the 250 members of the Association of British Insurers (ABI). The ABI is a trade association which protects and promotes the interests of all its insurance company members. Only insurers authorised in the EU are eligible for membership. Brokers, intermediaries, financial advisers and claims handlers may not join the ABI, but may have their own trade associations. Since November 2015 legal firms, consultants, price comparison websites and other firms which help insurers deliver their services can join the ABI as associate members.

ASSOCIATION OF BRITISH INSURERS (ABI), One America Square, 17 Crosswall, London EC3N 2LB
T 020-7600 3333 W www.abi.org.uk
Chair, Andy Briggs (Chief Executive AVIVA UK)
Director-General, Huw Evans

BALANCE OF PAYMENTS

The financial services industry contributes 10.7 per cent to the UK's gross domestic product (GDP). In 2016 the UK trade surplus for insurance and pensions was around £12.8bn.

WORLDWIDE MARKET

In 2017 the UK insurance industry was the largest in Europe and the fourth largest in the world behind the USA, Japan and China. China moved from eighth largest in 2006 to third in 2016.

Market	Premium income (€bn)
USA	1,352
Japan	471
China	466
UK	304

TAKEOVERS AND MERGERS

The year 2017 was not a good one for insurers, with uncertainty about Brexit, bedding in the Solvency II provisions and heavy general insurance losses due to meteorological disasters. This made insurers less attractive as takeover targets. A reduction in weather damage claims, tax reforms and softer regulation in the US may see things pick up in 2018. A number of deals were, nevertheless, completed.

One deal that failed to materialise was a European insurance mega-merger between French company AXA and Italian insurer Generali. These two companies are among the largest insurers in the world. Press reports suggested there were preliminary moves but these were denied by both parties. Its thought shareholder opposition and regulatory difficulties may have prevented any progress.

Allianz was active, firstly in August 2017 when it announced a joint venture with LV= (the trading name of Liverpool Victoria Friendly Society) to create the third largest personal insurer in the UK. The first stage saw the acquisition of a 49 percent stake in LV='s UK General Insurance businesses which was completed in December 2017. In 2019 Allianz will pay another £213m for a further 20.9 percent stake in LV= General Insurance. Allianz also increased its holdings in trade credit insurer Euler Hermes in November, bringing their stake to 94.9 per cent.

Late in 2017 Markerstudy Limited, who underwrite around 5 percent of UK motor insurance through their various brands including Markerstudy Ins. Co., Zenith Insurance, St Julians Insurance and Ultimate Insurance Co. were sold to reinsurers Qatar Re. No financial details were released.

Having de-merged from parent company esure in 2016, Price comparison website Go Compare rejected two bids from property portal Zoopla in May 2017 and again in November.

BREXIT

The Insurance and financial services sector are very important to the UK and its economy. The UK is the third largest insurance and long-term savings industry in the world and the largest in the EU. Certainly, the insurance industry made no secret of being firmly in the 'remain' camp in the Brexit debate, with the ABI, British Insurance Brokers' Association (BIBA) and Lloyd's all stressing the volatility and uncertainty they believed a 'leave' vote would create. But the result in June 2016 proved that their lobbying had not persuaded enough voters.

While leaving the EU may present opportunities to expand global markets and the demand for insurance products will certainly not reduce, the result leaves the industry with a number of concerns, not least the need for the UK government to negotiate a very complicated trade agreement, or at least interim measures, in a short space of time.

The most important issue concerning many insurers is access. At present, the UK insurance industry can offer its products to the single European insurance market covering 28 countries with some half a billion people. Authorisation in the UK automatically grants an ability to do business anywhere in the European Economic Area without any further formalities or costs. This is known as 'passporting' and, at the time of writing, this facility will end with the UK leaving the EU in March 2019. This could mean on 30 March 2019 it will be illegal for EU-based clients of UK insurers to be paid pensions or claims. Similarly, UK based clients of EU insurers will no longer be able to renew policies as they will not be UK authorised.

One option to solve this problem would be for UK insurers to set up an EU based subsidiary which would then have passporting rights. A number of insurers, including Lloyd's have already begun preparations for this with subsidiaries being incorporated and seeking authorisation in various European countries including Ireland, Malta, Belgium and Luxembourg. To date, no one country has emerged as a favourite destination.

There is also the question of over 700 EU insurers doing business with UK policyholders. On 29 March 2019, if no agreement is reached, they will be operating illegally. Here again, the solution may be to set up and seek authorisation for a UK based subsidiary but given that authorisation of a new UK insurer can often take up to 36 months, this will not prevent problems in March 2019.

There are other alternatives, for example, the UK remaining in the European Economic Area (EEA). This option is likely to be very unpopular as it would also involve the UK agreeing to the free movement of people, accepting rulings from the European Court of Justice and inevitable budget contributions – all issues cited by the 'leave' campaign as reasons to quit the EU in the first place.

GENERAL INSURANCE

In February 2017, despite strong lobbying from a wide range of organisations, the then Lord Chancellor, Liz Truss announced a reduction in the Ogden Discount Rate. This is an adjustment that is applied to a lump sum compensation payment made to people who have suffered serious personal injuries to reflect the likely return on the money when they invest it. It aims to ensure that people are not under or over-compensated. The rate was altered from 2.5 per cent to −0.75 per cent. This unexpectedly deep cut prompted a furious reaction from insurers amid claims that it will 'overcompensate' victims of car crashes or medical incompetence in hospitals. It was also suggested the armed forces would face far higher compensation bills.

The Association of British Insurers described the rate cut as 'crazy', pointing out that the −0.75% rate was the lowest in the western world and could add £6bn to the claims costs of liability and motor insurers – costs which would ultimately be passed on to policyholders.

The day after the announcement Chancellor Philip Hammond met with the chief executives of a number of major insurers and on 30 March, the government launched an open consultation, as part of the review of the framework under which the personal injury discount rate is set. The consultation closed on 11 May 2017 and the Ministry of Justice announced the conclusions on 7 September 2017. The conclusions accepted that, under the current law, the assumptions on how claimants invest are unrealistic and could produce larger awards. It was also suggested the government was looking at a discount rate of 0 to 1 per cent but that no rate change was possible without legislation.

While the −0.75 percent rate remains, it is estimated that premiums will have to rise by between 7.5 and 10 per cent on motor insurances and between 4 and 5 per cent on liability insurances solely to reflect the increased claims costs.

Despite seeing motor insurance premium increases of around 11 per cent, bringing the annual cost of an average policy to £493, there was some good news for motorists as it was confirmed that after Brexit the UK would remain in the free circulation zone. This means commercial and private drivers will not need to obtain a 'green card' every time they take their vehicle outside the UK. The same will apply for any drivers and haulage operators from Serbia, Switzerland, Andorra and all EU countries who bring their vehicles to the UK.

In the light of the tragic consequences of the fire in Grenfell Tower in West London, in June 2017 the insurance industry, through the ABI, commissioned the Fire Protection Association to provide insurer relevant information to Dame Judith Hackitt's Independent Review of Building Regulations and Fire Safety and the Grenfell Inquiry. The results exposed the utter inadequacy of the laboratory tests currently used to check the fire safety of building materials. The real-life factors overlooked by the official testing regime included:

• test fires are only made up of wood. In modern blazes, around 20 per cent of the materials involved are plastic
• cladding materials are sometimes tested as a sealed unit, whereas when fitted on a building they often include gaps, and cover a far more extensive area
• materials tested are in a 'just manufactured condition' when, during their actual use, they will often be pierced by things such as vents or ducts

The results of this research confirmed long-held concerns by many in the fire sector that the current cladding test standard needed urgent review to ensure that safety tests adequately examine the systems that are installed and the risks to which they are exposed.

TOP FIVE GENERAL INSURANCE COMPANIES BY GROSS WRITTEN PREMIUMS

Insurance Company (2015 position)	2016 (£bn)	2017 (£bn)
1. AVIVA (1)	5.1	5.3
2. AIG (2)	4.9	5.3
3. RSA Insurance Group (3)	4.6	4.7
4. AXA UK (4)	4.3	4.5
5. Direct Line Group (5)	3.3	3.4

LONDON INSURANCE MARKET

In recent years it has become increasingly difficult to define the London Insurance Market business. Many businesses operate in London as branch offices of parent companies located elsewhere in the world and may no longer separately identify as London Market premiums. What is acknowledged is that, despite the growth of other international centres, London remains the world's leading market for internationally traded insurance and reinsurance, its business comprising mainly overseas non-life large and high-exposure risks. The market is centred on the square mile of the City of London, which provides the required financial, banking, legal and other support services. Around 53 per cent of London market business is transacted at Lloyd's of London, the remainder through insurance companies and protection and indemnity clubs. In 2016 the market had a written gross premium income of around £52.6bn. Around 200 Lloyd's brokers service the market.

The trade association for the international insurers and reinsurers writing primarily non-marine insurance and all classes of reinsurance business in the London market is the International Underwriting Association (IUA).

INTERNATIONAL UNDERWRITING ASSOCIATION, 1 Minster Court, Mincing Lane, London EC3R 7AA T 020-7617 4444 W www.iua.co.uk
Chair, Malcolm Newman
Chief Executive, Dave Matcham

BRITISH INSURANCE COMPANIES

The following insurance company figures refer to members and certain non-members of the ABI.

DOMESTIC PROPERTY CLAIMS STATISTICS 2016

Type	Payment (£m)
Theft	351
Fire	433
Weather	431
Escape of water	756
Domestic subsidence	108
Accidental damage	297
other domestic claims	325
Total	2,701

WORLDWIDE GENERAL BUSINESS TRADING RESULTS (£m)

	2015	2016
Net written premiums	42,548	41,780
Underwriting results	1,131	2,812
Investment income	2,201	1,918
Overall trading profit	3,332	4,730
Profit as percentage of premium income	8%	11%

LLOYD'S OF LONDON

Lloyd's of London is an international market for almost all types of general insurance. Lloyd's currently has the capacity to accept insurance premiums of around £25bn. Much of this business comes from outside the UK and makes a valuable contribution to the balance of payments.

A policy is underwritten at Lloyd's by a mixture of private and corporate members. Specialist underwriters accept insurance risks at Lloyd's on behalf of members (referred to as 'names') grouped in syndicates. There are currently 83 syndicates of varying sizes, each managed by one of the 56 underwriting agents approved by the Council of Lloyd's.

Members divide into three categories: corporate organisations, individuals who have no limit to their liability for losses, and those who have an agreed limit (known as NameCos).

Lloyd's is incorporated by an act of parliament (Lloyd's Acts 1871 onwards) and is governed by an 18-person council, made up of six working, six external and six nominated members. The structure immediately below this changed when, in 2002, Lloyd's members voted at an extraordinary general meeting to implement a new franchise system for the market with the aim of improving profitability. The first move was the introduction of a new governance structure, replacing the Lloyd's Market Board and the Lloyd's Regulatory Board with an 11-person Lloyd's Franchise Board. Four main committees report to this board.

The corporation is a non-profit making body chiefly financed by its members' subscriptions. It provides the premises, administrative staff and services for Lloyd's underwriting syndicates. It does not, however, assume corporate liability for the risks accepted by its members. Individual members are responsible to the full extent of their personal means for their underwriting affairs unless they have converted to limited liability companies.

Lloyd's syndicates have no direct contact with the public. All business is transacted through insurance brokers accredited by the Corporation of Lloyd's. In addition, non-Lloyd's brokers in the UK, when guaranteed by Lloyd's brokers, are able to deal directly with Lloyd's motor syndicates, a facility that has made the Lloyd's market more accessible to the insuring public.

Under the Financial Services and Markets Act 2000, Lloyds is regulated by the FCA and the PRA. However, in situations where Lloyd's internal regulatory and compensation arrangements are more far-reaching – as for example with the Lloyd's Central Fund which safeguards claim payments to policyholders – the regulatory role is delegated to the Council of Lloyd's.

DEVELOPMENTS IN 2017

It was a difficult year for the Lloyd's market. For the first time in six years they reported a loss with the aggregated 2017 market result being a loss of £2bn. The result reflected the market facing one of the costliest years for natural catastrophes in the past ten years with Hurricane Irma, which devastated large parts of the Caribbean and the US Gulf States; Hurricane Harvey which caused significant wind and flood damage in Texas and Hurricane Irma which once again hit the Caribbean. There were also wildfires in northern California in October, southern California in December and in Chile; an earthquake in Mexico; monsoon flooding in Bangladesh; a mudslide in Colombia; and Cyclone Debbie which caused damage and flooding in Australia. The frequency and scale of the disasters that struck around the world resulted in major claims costing £4.5bn, more than double the previous year (£2.1bn).

Most classes of business suffered underwriting losses, with the exception of the energy market, which saw profits rise from £59m in 2016 to £105m. The most substantial losses came, unsurprisingly, in the property and reinsurance accounts, which saw a profit of £548m and a loss of £202m respectively plunge to losses of £1,757 (for property) and £1,330 (for reinsurance).

A foreign exchange loss was also reported in 2017 as sterling had marginally strengthened against the US dollar throughout the year, reversing the significant foreign exchange gain reported in 2016, when sterling weakened following the Brexit referendum result.

Premium levels overall rose by around 6 per cent during 2017 and are likely to rise again, particularly in the motor and liability markets to reflect the changes in the Ogden Discount Rate (*see* General Insurance). However the premium rises may not be as high as underwriters might wish due to continuing overcapacity.

LLOYD'S OF LONDON, One Lime Street, London EC3M 7HA T 020-7327 1000 W www.lloyds.com
Chair, Bruce Carnegie-Brown
Chief Executive, Dame Inga Beale, DBE

LLOYD'S MEMBERSHIP

	2015	2016
Individual	321	290
Corporate	1,771	1,760

LLOYD'S SEGMENTAL RESULTS 2017 (£m)

	Gross written premiums	Net earned premiums	Underwriting result
Reinsurance	10,560	7,751	(1,330)
Casualty	8,464	6,082	(189)
Property	8,965	6,367	(1,757)
Marine	2,506	2,092	(469)
Motor	1,057	843	(188)
Energy	1,253	783	105
Aviation	687	509	(11)
Life	99	71	(24)
Total from syndicate operations	33,591	24,498	(3,863)

LIFE AND LONG-TERM INSURANCE AND PENSIONS

In July 2017 The Financial Conduct Authority (FCA) published the interim findings of their Retirement Outcomes Review. Launched in July 2016, this was the first major study into how the retirement income market had changed since the pension freedoms were announced in the 2014 Budget and implemented in 2015.

The review found that an increasing number of people were accessing their pension pots early. Almost three quarters (72 per cent) of pots that had been accessed were by consumers under 65. Most were choosing to take lump sums rather than a regular income. Over half (53 per cent) of pension pots accessed had been fully withdrawn but, of these, 52 per cent were not being spent but were being moved into other savings or investments. Some of this was probably due to a lack of public trust in pensions.

The review also found that 30 per cent of drawdowns were being carried out without any form of financial advice. As this process can be complex the regulators pledged to investigate ways to encourage more support and protection for consumers.

April 2017 saw the deadline for all existing employers to set up a workplace pension for their staff. The immediate duty to set up such a scheme for new employers began in October 2017. To date, the scheme has been a success with an estimated 9 million people, who would not otherwise have had any pension provision, now saving for their retirement. Initially the employee contribution was set at 2 per cent of salary with an increase in April 2018 to 5 per cent and a further increase to 8 percent in 2019. Despite these increased contributions, insurers continued to point out that savings at this level will not provide an adequate standard of living in retirement.

In December 2017 the government launched a review of auto-enrolment, which included a proposal to reduce the eligibility age to 18.

Insurance industry payouts on protection policies topped £5bn for the first time in 2017. Over £2.7bn was paid in respect of life claims with a further £498m being paid for whole life policies. Overall, 97.8 per cent of all protection claims were paid out.

PROTECTION INSURANCE CLAIMS 2017

Type of product	No. of claims paid*	% of new claims paid	% of new claims declined	Total value paid (£ thousand)	Average claim paid (£)
Critical illness	15,962	92.20	7.80	1,166,590	73,085.47
Life	35,604	98.00	2.00	2,788,625	78,323.35
Total permanent disability	422	62.60	37.40	30,350	71,919.43
Whole of life	110,420	99.99	0.01	498,122	4,511.16
Income protection	28,398	87.20	12.80	604,748	21,295.44
All protection products	190,806	97.80	2.20	5,088,435	–

* Figures are for new claims, as well as all income protection claims in payment

UK LONG-TERM INSURANCE NET PREMIUM INCOME

Year	Life & annuities	Individual pensions	Occupational pensions	Income protection & other business	Total
2005	36,590	22,702	58,868	2,034	120,194
2006	42,058	35,874	65,071	2,048	145,050
2007	49,866	35,252	98,575	1,660	185,353
2008	36,300	30,523	62,820	1,541	131,183
2009	20,336	27,725	68,988	1,473	118,521
2010	19,241	28,218	64,033	1,482	112,975
2011	16,008	27,401	71,680	1,456	116,545
2012	14,893	33,219	71,148	1,862	121,122
2013	9,944	25,119	80,192	1,457	116,712
2014	9,985	23,721	70,826	1,290	105,822
2015	10,461	35,194	76,188	1,290	123,133
2016	12,679	29,684	75,634	1,553	119,551

TAXATION

The government raises money to pay for public services such as education, health and the social welfare system through tax. Each year the Chancellor of the Exchequer's Budget sets out how much it will cost to provide these services and how much tax is therefore needed to pay for them. The tax is collected by HM Revenue and Customs (HMRC). There are several different types of tax. Individuals may have to pay:
* income tax payable on earnings, pensions, state benefits, savings and investments
* capital gains tax (CGT) payable on the disposal of certain assets
* inheritance tax (IHT) payable on estates upon death and certain lifetime gifts
* stamp duty payable when purchasing property and shares
* value added tax (VAT) payable on goods and services
* certain other duties such as fuel duty on petrol and excise duty on alcohol and tobacco

Corporation tax raises funds from companies and small businesses.

New taxation measures and changes to the administration of the taxation system are normally announced by the incumbent Chancellor of the Exchequer in the government's annual Budget in the autumn, with a spring statement on government spending forecasts.

The government has a stated policy of investing resources into reducing tax evasion and avoidance by both individuals and companies. Information and updates on the latest measures can be found on the government's website: www.gov.uk/government/policies/tax-evasion-and-avoidance).

The government also has an ongoing drive to simplify the UK tax system via the Office of Tax Simplification (OTS). Details of the OTS and its work can also be found on the government's website (W www.gov.uk/government/organisations/office-of-tax-simplification). The OTS welcomes views from individuals and can be contacted via email (E ots@ots.gsi.gov.uk).

HELP AND INFORMATION ON TAXATION
For information and help on any aspect of personal taxation, call the HMRC helpline (T 0300-200 3300). The lines are open 8am to 8pm from Monday to Friday, 8am to 4pm on Saturday, and 9am to 5pm on Sunday. For general queries (not specific cases) you can also use Twitter, starting your query with @HMRCcustomers.

HMRC no longer has a network of enquiry centres, because visitor numbers had dropped dramatically.

The HMRC website (W www.gov.uk/government/organisations/hm-revenue-customs) provides wide-ranging information online. This includes all HMRC forms, leaflets and guides (which can be downloaded), all HMRC telephone helplines and order lines. Links to topics covered in this section are included in the text.

INCOME TAX
Income tax is assessed on different sorts of income. Not all types of income are taxable and individuals are entitled to certain reliefs and allowances which reduce or, in some cases, cancel out their income tax bill.

An individual's taxable income is assessed each tax year, starting on 6 April and ending on 5 April the following year. The information below relates specifically to the year of assessment 2018–19, ending on 5 April 2019, and has only limited application to earlier years. Changes due to come into operation at a later date are briefly mentioned where information is available. Types of income that are taxable include:

* earnings from employment or profits from self-employment
* most pensions income, including state, company and personal pensions
* interest over the savings allowance
* income (dividends) from shares
* income from property
* income received from a trust
* certain state benefits
* an individual's share of any joint income

There are certain sorts of income on which individuals never pay tax. These are ignored altogether when working out how much income tax an individual may need to pay. Types of income that are not taxable include:
* certain state benefits and tax credits, such as child benefit, working tax credit, child tax credit, pension credit, attendance allowance, personal independence payment, housing benefit and maternity allowance
* winter fuel payments
* income from National Savings and Investments savings certificates
* interest, dividends and other income from various tax-free investments, notably individual savings accounts (ISAs)
* premium bond and national lottery prizes

PERSONAL ALLOWANCE
Every individual resident in the UK has a 'personal allowance' for tax purposes. This is the amount of taxable income that an individual can earn or receive each year tax-free. This tax year (2018–19) the basic personal allowance or tax-free amount is £11,850, an increase of £350 from the 2017–18 figure of £11,500. The personal allowance is for all taxpayers regardless of age.

Income tax is only due on an individual's taxable income that is above his or her tax-free allowance. Spouses and civil partners are taxed separately, with each entitled to his or her personal allowance. Each spouse or civil partner may obtain other allowances and reliefs where the required conditions are satisfied.

The personal allowance is available for all individuals with income up to £100,000. Those individuals with an 'adjusted net income' above the £100,000 limit have their personal allowance reduced by half the excess (£1 for every £2) they have over that limit until their personal allowance is reduced to nil.

An individual's 'adjusted net income' is calculated in a series of steps. The starting point is 'net income', which is the total of the individual's income subject to income tax less specified deductions such as payments made gross to pension schemes or trading losses. This net income is then reduced by the grossed-up amount of the individual's Gift Aid contributions to charities and the grossed-up amount of the individual's pension contributions that have received tax relief at source. The final step is to add back any relief for payments to trade unions or police organisations deducted in arriving at the individual's net income. The result is the individual's adjusted net income.

MARRIAGE ALLOWANCE
Some married couples and civil partners, made up of one non-taxpayer and one basic rate taxpayer, are eligible for a marriage allowance, which allows them to share some of the non-taxpayer's unused annual income tax allowance. In the 2018–19 tax year, the allowance allows a spouse or civil partner with an income less than £11,850 to transfer up to £1,185 of their

unused personal allowance to their higher-income partner. So long as the person receiving the transfer is a basic rate taxpayer, which, in most cases, means having an income of between £11,850 and £46,350 (£43,430 in Scotland), this transferable tax allowance is worth up to £237 in 2018–19.

BLIND PERSON'S ALLOWANCE

If an individual is registered blind or is unable to perform any work for which eyesight is essential, he or she can claim blind person's allowance, an extra amount of tax-free income added to the personal allowance. In 2018–19 the blind person's allowance is £2,390. It is the same for everyone who can claim it and is not dependent on age or level of income. If an individual is married or in a civil partnership and cannot use all of his or her blind person's allowance because of insufficient income, the unused part of the allowance can be passed to the spouse or civil partner.

PROPERTY AND TRADING ALLOWANCES

These allowances benefit 'micro-entrepreneurs' who use one or more of a wide range of money-making activities to supplement their income. Individuals with property or trading income do not need to declare or pay tax on the first £1,000 they earn from each source per year. Should they earn more than that amount they will have to declare it to HMRC, but they can still take advantage of the allowance

Property income qualifying for relief under the property allowance could be any income that an individual makes from renting out a residence, home, building, property or land – even from renting out a driveway as a parking space, for example, or renting out a room to visiting tourists via websites like Airbnb.

Trading income qualifying for the allowance can be income from any sale of goods or services. An individual could do tasks such as cleaning or odd jobs, hiring out their own equipment such as power tools, or selling goods through websites like eBay or Etsy.

INCOME TAX ALLOWANCES

	2017–18	2018–19
Personal allowance	£11,500	£11,850
Income limit for personal allowance	£100,000	£100,000
Marriage allowance	£1,150	£1,185
Blind person's allowance	£2,320	£2,390
Property allowance	£1,000	£1,000
Trading allowance	£1,000	£1,000

CALCULATING INCOME TAX DUE

Individuals' liability to pay income tax is determined by establishing their level of taxable income for the year. For married couples and civil partners, income must be allocated between the couple by reference to the individual who is beneficially entitled to that income. Where income arises from jointly held assets, it is normally apportioned equally between the partners. If, however, the beneficial interests in jointly held assets are not equal, in most cases couples can make a special declaration to have income apportioned by reference to the actual interests in that income.

To work out an individual's liability for tax, his or her taxable income must be allocated between three different types:

- earned income (excluding income from savings and dividends)
- income from savings
- company dividends from shares and other equity-based investments

After the tax-free personal allowance plus any deductible allowances and reliefs have been taken into account, the amount of tax an individual pays is calculated using different tax rates and a series of tax bands. Each tax band applies to a slice of an individual's income after tax allowances and any reliefs have been taken into account.

SCOTLAND

From the tax year 2017–18, the Scottish government is able to set the rates and bands for tax on income from earnings, pensions and most other taxable income in Scotland. The tax raised is paid to the Scottish government.

Income from savings and dividends continues to be taxed at the same rate as in the rest of the UK.

UK INCOME TAX BANDS AND RATES 2018–19

	Band	Rate
Starter rate*	£0–13,850	19%
Basic rate	£0–34,500	20%
Scotland	£13,851–24,000	20%
Intermediate rate*	£24,001–44,273	21%
Higher rate	£34,501–150,000	40%
Scotland	£44,273–150,000	41%
Additional/Top* rate	£150,000+	45%/46%*
* Scotland only		

The first calculation is applied to earned income, which includes income from employment or self-employment, most pension income and rental income, plus the value of a wide range of employee 'benefits in kind' such as company cars, living accommodation and private medical insurance (for more information on benefits in kind, see later section on payment of income tax). In working out the amount of an individual's net taxable earnings, all expenses incurred 'wholly, exclusively and necessarily' in the performance of his or her employment duties, together with the cost of business travel, may be deducted. Fees and subscriptions to certain professional bodies may also be deducted. Redundancy payments and other sums paid on the termination of an employment are assessable income, but the first £30,000 is normally tax-free provided the payment is not linked with the recipient's retirement or performance.

For UK taxpayers other than Scottish residents, the first £34,500 of taxable income remaining after the tax-free allowance and any deductible allowances and reliefs have been taken into account is taxed at the basic rate of 20 per cent. Taxable income between £34,501 and £150,000 is taxed at the higher rate of 40 per cent. Taxable income above £150,001 is taxed at the additional rate of 45 per cent.

Savings and dividend income is added to an individual's other taxable income and taxed last. This means that tax on such sorts of income is based on an individual's highest income tax band.

SAVINGS INCOME

The second calculation is applied to any income from savings received by an individual. Savings income includes interest paid on bank and building society accounts, interest paid on accounts from providers like credit unions or National Savings and Investments, interest distributions (but not dividend distributions) from authorised unit trusts, open-ended investment companies and investment trusts, interest from peer-to-peer lending, government or company bonds and life annuity payments.

The appropriate rate at which savings income must be taxed is determined by adding income from savings to an individual's other taxable income (excluding dividends). Savings interest may be set against the personal allowance (if that is not used up on income from employment or pension), the starting rate for savings income and the personal savings allowance.

The starting rate of tax for savings income allows an individual to earn up to £5,000 of interest tax-free in 2018–19, provided their other income is less than £16,500. The £5,000 allowance is reduced by £1 for every £1 of their non-savings income above the personal allowance threshold.

The personal savings allowance (PSA) allows a basic rate taxpayer to earn their first £1,000 of savings income tax-free. A higher rate taxpayer may earn their first £500 of savings income tax-free. Additional rate taxpayers do not get a PSA.

With the introduction of the PSA in April 2016, banks and building societies stopped automatically deducting 20 per cent tax from savings interest before it was paid to individuals. This means that non-taxpayers no longer have to apply to have their savings interest paid gross. It is now an individual's responsibility to inform HMRC if they earn savings income above the PSA on which tax is payable; any tax owed will normally be collected via the individual's tax code.

Tax on interest over the allowance is paid at the individual's usual rate of income tax, ie for a taxpayer not resident in Scotland 20 per cent for basic rate taxpayers, 40 per cent for higher rate taxpayers and 45 per cent for additional rate taxpayers. If savings income falls on both sides of a tax band, the relevant amounts are taxed at the rates for each tax band.

DIVIDEND INCOME

The third and final income tax calculation is on UK dividends, which means income from shares in UK companies and other share-based investments.

All taxpayers now have a £2,000 tax-free dividend allowance (£5,000 in 2017/18). This means that individuals do not have to pay tax on the first £2,000 of their dividend income, no matter what non-dividend income they have. The allowance is available to anyone who has dividend income.

Dividends received that exceed the £2,000 allowance are treated as the top band of income. This means that if an individual's divided income takes them from one income tax band into the next, they will then pay the higher dividend rate on that portion of income.

TAX RATES ON DIVIDENDS OVER £2,000

Band	2018–19
Basic rate	7.5%
Higher rate	32.5%
Additional rate	38.1%

If there is significant change to an individual's savings or other income, whatever his or her current tax bracket, it is the individual's responsibility to contact the relevant tax office immediately, even if he or she does not normally complete a tax return. This enables the tax office to work out whether more tax should be paid, or if a refund is due.

TAX FREE SAVINGS

There is a small selection of savings and investment products that are tax-free. This means that there is no tax to pay on any income generated in the form of interest or dividends, nor on any increase in the value of the capital invested. Their tax-efficient status has been granted by the government in order to give people an incentive to save more. For this reason there are usually limits and restrictions on the amount of money an individual may invest in such savings and investments.

Individual savings accounts (ISAs) are the best known among tax-efficient savings and investments. There are four types: cash ISAs, stocks and shares ISAs, innovative finance ISAs (earning interest and capital gains free of tax on loans made via peer-to-peer lending platforms) and lifetime ISAs. Money may be invested in one of each type of ISA each tax year, up to an overall annual subscription limit, which is £20,000 in 2018–19. This may be paid into one ISA or split

between some or all of the other types, although no more than £4,000 may be paid into a lifetime ISA in one tax year.

To be eligible to invest in ISAs and receive all profits free of tax, individuals must be:

* aged 16 or over to hold a cash ISA
* aged 18 or over for a stocks and shares or innovative finance ISA
* aged 18 or over but under 40 for a lifetime ISA
* resident in the UK or, if not resident in the UK, a Crown servant or their spouse or civil partner

An ISA must be in an individual's name and cannot be held jointly with another person, but spouses and civil partners may inherit their partner's ISA allowance after death.

The lifetime ISA introduced in April 2017 may be opened by UK residents between the ages of 18 and 40, and allows individuals to save up to £4,000 a year between the ages of 18 and 50. Savings put into the account before their 50th birthday will qualify for a government bonus of 25 per cent, up to £1,000 a year. An individual may use their savings and bonus towards the purchase of a first-time home worth up to £450,000. Alternatively, they may choose to keep the account as retirement savings until their 60th birthday, after which date they can withdraw all the money tax-free.

There are also long-term, tax-free savings accounts for children called Junior ISAs. The investment limit for these in 2018–19 is £4,260 per child. Parents or guardians with parental responsibility can open Junior ISAs for children aged under 18 who live in the UK. However, while parents can open and manage Junior ISAs for their children, the invested money belongs to the child, who can take control of their account when they are 16 and withdraw the money when they are 18. Children aged 16 and 17 can open their own Junior ISA as well as an adult cash ISA. Junior ISAs automatically turn into an adult ISA when the child turns 18.

The Help to Buy ISA, introduced in autumn 2015, is one of a number of government measures to help individuals save towards buying their first home. Aspiring first-time buyers aged 16 or over may save up to £200 a month in a Help to Buy ISA and the government boosts their savings by 25 per cent, up to a maximum of £3,000 per person. If, therefore, an individual saves £12,000, the government bonus boosts their total savings to £15,000. Savers can start an account with a lump-sum deposit of up to £1,200. The minimum government bonus is £400, meaning that the individual must save at least £1,600 to qualify for the scheme, but there is no monthly minimum investment.

Savings held in a Help to Buy ISA can be accessed at any time, but the government payment is only added if and when the savings are used as a deposit on a first and only home in the UK. The bonus is available on home purchases of up to £450,000 in London and up to £250,000 outside London. Qualifying properties must be purchased with a mortgage and must be lived in by the purchaser and not rented out.

Individuals are able to open a Help to Buy ISA until 30 November 2019, after which they will no longer be available to new savers. Those who open an account before the cut-off date may continue saving into their account, but must claim their bonus by 1 December 2030.

Further details about ISAs are available via the HMRC's savings helpline (T 0300-200 3312).

DEDUCTIBLE ALLOWANCES AND RELIEF

Income taxpayers may be entitled to certain tax-deductible allowances and reliefs as well as their personal allowances. Examples include the married couple's allowance and maintenance payments relief, see below. Unlike the tax-free allowances, these are not amounts of income that an individual can receive tax-free but amounts by which their tax bill can be reduced.

MARRIED COUPLE'S ALLOWANCE

A married couple's allowance (MCA) is available to taxpayers who are married or are in a civil partnership where at least one partner was born before 6 April 1935 and they usually live together. Eligible couples can start to claim the MCA from the year of marriage or civil partnership registration.

The MCA is restricted to give relief at a fixed rate of 10 per cent, which means that – unlike the personal allowance – it is not income that can be received without paying tax. Instead, it reduces an individual's tax bill by up to a fixed amount of 10 per cent of the amount of the allowance to which they are entitled.

In 2018–19, the maximum MCA is £8,695 and is therefore worth £869.50 off a couple's tax bill. In 2018–19 this maximum is reduced by £1 for every £2 the highest earner's income exceeds £28,900, to a minimum MCA of £3,360. The minimum always applies, regardless of the level of the highest earner's income.

For marriages before 5 December 2005, the allowance is based on the husband's income; for marriages and civil partnerships after that date, the allowance is based on the income of the highest earner. A couple can decide to have the minimum amount of the allowance split equally between them, or transfer the whole of the minimum MCA from one to the other. If an individual does not have enough income to use all of his or her share of the MCA, the unused part of it can be transferred to his or her spouse or civil partner. A couple must inform their tax office of their decision before the start of the new tax year in which they want the decision to take effect.

MAINTENANCE PAYMENTS RELIEF

An allowance is available to reduce an individual's tax bill for maintenance payments he or she makes to his or her ex-spouse or former civil partner in certain circumstances. To be eligible:
- one or other partner must have been born before 6 April 1935
- the couple must be legally separated or divorced
- the maintenance payments being made must be under a court order
- the payments must be for the maintenance of an ex-spouse or former civil partner (provided he or she is not now remarried or in a new civil partnership) or for children who are under 21.

For the tax year 2018–19, this allowance can reduce an individual's tax bill by:
- 10 per cent of £3,360 (maximum £336) – this applies where an individual makes maintenance payments of £3,360 or more a year
- 10 per cent of the amount the individual has actually paid – this applies where an individual makes maintenance payments of less than £3,360 a year

An individual cannot claim a tax reduction for any voluntary payments he or she makes for a child, ex-spouse or former civil partner. To claim maintenance payments relief, individuals should contact their tax office.

TAX RELIEF FOR LANDLORDS

Up to April 2017 individual landlords were able to deduct all their costs, including mortgage interest, from their profits before they paid tax. Wealthier landlords received tax relief at 40 per cent and 45 per cent.

From April 2017, this calculation is changing for properties other than furnished holiday lettings. By April 2020, tax relief on financing costs will only be at the basic rate. Property profits (excluding interest costs) and other income will be assessed, and then amount of tax due will be reduced by the amount of the interest multiplied by the basic rate of income tax. The changes are being phased in between April 2017 and April 2020. This change only applies to landlords who are individuals, including where they operate through a partnership. It does not apply to companies who rent out property. See W www.gov.uk/government/news/changes-to-tax-relief-for-residential-landlords.

CHARITABLE DONATIONS

A number of charitable donations qualify for tax relief. Individuals can increase the value of regular or one-off charitable gifts of money, however small, by using the Gift Aid scheme that allows charities or community amateur sports clubs (CASCs) to reclaim 20 per cent basic rate tax relief on donations they receive. If a taxpayer gives £10 using Gift Aid, for example, the donation is worth £12.50 to the charity or CASC.

Individuals who pay 40 per cent higher rate income tax can claim back the difference between the 40 per cent and the 20 per cent basic rate of income tax on the total (gross) value of their donations. For example, a 40 per cent tax payer donates £100; the total value of this donation to the charity or CASC is £125, of which the individual can claim back 20 per cent (£25) for themselves. Similarly, those who pay 45 per cent additional rate income tax can claim back the difference between the 45 per cent and the 20 per cent basic rate on the total (gross) value of their donations. On a £100 donation, this means they can claim back £31.25. Scottish taxpayers who pay tax at rates higher than the basic 20 per cent rate can claim extra tax relief.

In order to make a Gift Aid donation, individuals need to make a Gift Aid declaration. The charity or CASC will normally ask an individual to complete a simple form. One form can cover every gift made to the same charity or CASC for whatever period chosen, including both gifts made in the past and in the future. Charities are able to claim a Gift Aid-type tax refund on small donations in various circumstances, see W www.gov.uk/claim-gift-aid/small-donations-scheme.

Individuals can use Gift Aid provided the amount of income tax and/or capital gains tax they have paid in the tax year in which their donations are made is at least equal to the amount of basic rate tax the charity or CASC is reclaiming on their gifts. It is the responsibility of the individual to make sure this is the case. If an individual makes Gift Aid donations and has not paid sufficient tax, they may have to pay the shortfall to HMRC. The Gift Aid scheme is not available for non-taxpayers.

Individuals who complete a tax return and are due a tax refund can ask HMRC to treat all or part of it as a Gift Aid donation.

For employees or those in receipt of an occupational pension, a tax-efficient way of making regular donations to charities is to use the payroll giving scheme. It allows the donations to be paid from a salary or pension before income tax is deducted. This effectively reduces the cost of giving for donors, which may allow them to give more.

For example, it costs a basic rate taxpayer only £8 in take-home pay to give £10 to charity from their pre-tax pay. Where a donor pays 40 per cent higher rate tax, that same £10 donation costs the taxpayer £6, and for donors who pay the additional 45 per cent rate tax, it costs £5.50.

Anyone who pays tax through the pay as you earn (PAYE) system (see Payment of Income Tax) can give to any charity of their choosing in this way, providing their employer or pension provider offers the payroll giving scheme. There is no limit to the amount individuals can donate.

Details of tax-efficient charitable giving methods can be found at W www.gov.uk/donating-to-charity.

TAX RELIEF ON PENSION CONTRIBUTIONS

Pensions are long-term investments designed to help ensure that people have enough income in retirement. The government encourages individuals to save towards a pension by offering tax relief on their contributions. Tax relief reduces an individual's tax bill or increases their pension fund.

The way tax relief is given on pension contributions depends on whether an individual pays into a company, public service or personal pension scheme.

For employees who pay into a company or public service pension scheme, most employers take the pension contributions from the employee's pay before deducting tax, which means that the individual – whether they pay income tax at the basic or higher rate – gets full tax relief straight away. Some employers, however, use the same method of paying pension contributions as that used by personal pension scheme payers described below.

Individuals who pay into a personal pension scheme normally make contributions from their net salary; that is, after tax has been deducted. For each pound that individuals contribute to their pension from net salary, the pension provider claims tax back from the government at the basic rate of 20 per cent and reinvests it on behalf of the individual into the scheme. In practice this means that for every £80 an individual pays into their pension, they receive £100 in their pension fund.

Subject to certain income related limits (see below) higher rate taxpayers currently get 40 per cent tax relief on money they put into a pension. On contributions made from net salary, the first 20 per cent is claimed back from HMRC by the pension scheme in the same way as for a lower rate taxpayer. It is then up to individuals to claim back the other 20 per cent from their tax office, either when they fill in their annual tax return. In a similar fashion, individuals subject to the 45 per cent additional rate of income tax can get 45 per cent tax relief on their pension contributions.

Non-taxpayers can still pay into a personal pension scheme and benefit from 20 per cent basic rate relief on the first £2,880 a year they contribute. In practice this means that the government tops up their £2,880 contribution to make it £3,600, which is the current universal pension allowance. Such pension contributions may be made on behalf of a non-taxpayer by another individual. An individual may, for example, contribute to a pension on behalf of a husband, wife, civil partner, child or grandchild. Tax relief will be added to their contribution at the basic rate, again on up to £2,880 a year benefiting the recipient, but their own tax bill will not be affected.

In any one tax year, individuals can get tax relief on pension contributions made into any number and type of registered pension schemes of up to 100 per cent of their annual earnings, irrespective of age, up to a maximum 'annual allowance'. For the tax year 2018–19 the annual allowance for most individuals is £40,000. This £40,000 annual allowance is reduced by £1 for every £2 of income between £150,000 and £210,000, so that those earning £210,000 and over have a £10,000 annual allowance.

Everyone also has a 'lifetime allowance' which defines the total amount a taxpayer can save in their pension fund and still get tax relief at their highest rate of income tax on all their contributions. The lifetime allowance is £1.03m in 2018–19, increased from £1m in 2017–18.

For information on pensions and tax relief visit W www.gov.uk/browse/working/workplace-personal-pensions. Another useful source of information and advice is the Pensions Advisory Service (TPAS), an independent voluntary organisation grant-aided by the government, at W www.pensionsadvisoryservice.org.uk; or the pensions helpline is on T 0300-123 1047.

PAYMENT OF INCOME TAX
Employees have their income tax deducted from their wages throughout the year by their employer, who sends it on to HMRC. Those in receipt of a company pension have their tax deducted in the same way by their pension provider. This system of collecting income tax is known as 'pay as you earn' (PAYE).

BENEFITS IN KIND
The PAYE system is also used to collect tax on certain employee benefits or 'benefits in kind' that employees or directors receive from their employer as part of their remuneration package. These include company cars, living accommodation, private medical insurance paid for by the employer or cheap or free loans from the employer. Some of these benefits are tax-free, including employer-paid contributions into an employee's pension fund, cheap or free canteen meals, works buses, in-house sports facilities, reasonable relocation expenses, provision of a mobile phone and workplace nursery places provided for the children of employees. Tax is paid on the 'taxable value' of any taxable benefit.

Employers submit returns for individual employees to the tax office on form P11D, with details of any benefits they have been given. Employees should get a copy of this form by 6 July following the end of the tax year and must enter the value of the benefits they have received on their tax return for the relevant year, even if tax has already been paid on them under PAYE. Benefits in kind may be taxed under PAYE by being offset against personal tax allowances in an individual's PAYE code. Otherwise tax will be collected after the end of the tax year by the issue of an assessment on the value of the benefits.

SELF ASSESSMENT
Individuals who are not on PAYE, notably the self-employed, need to complete a self assessment tax return each year, in paper form or online (W www.gov.uk/log-in-file-self-assessment-tax-return), and pay any income tax owed in twice-yearly instalments. Some individuals with more complex tax affairs, such as those who earn money from rents or investments above a certain level, may also need to fill out a self assessment return even if they are on PAYE. HMRC uses the figures supplied on the tax return to work out the individual's tax bill, or they can choose to work it out themselves. It is called self assessment because individuals are responsible for making sure the details they provide are correct.

Central to the self assessment system is the requirement for individuals to register online if they should complete a self assessment return. Individuals have six months from when the tax year ends to report any new income. The registration process is online (W www.gov.uk/log-in-file-self-assessment-tax-return), but it is important to allow enough time for the process – HMRC recommend allowing up to 20 working days extra for a first online return.

TAX RETURN FILING AND PAYMENT DEADLINES
There are also key deadlines for filing (sending in) completed tax returns and paying the tax due. Failure to do so can incur penalties, interest charges and surcharges.

KEY FILING DATES FOR SELF ASSESSMENT RETURNS
Date   *Why the date is important*
31 Oct*   Deadline for filing paper returns* for tax year ending the previous 5 April

30 Dec   Deadline for online filing where the amount owed for tax year ending the previous 5 April is less than £3,000 and the taxpayer wants HMRC to collect any tax due through their PAYE tax code

31 Jan†   Deadline for online filing of returns for tax year ending the previous 5 April

* Or three months from the date the return was requested if this was after 31 July

† Or three months from the date the return was requested if this was after 31 October

KEY SELF ASSESSMENT PAYMENT DATES

Date   *What payment is due?*

31 Jan   Deadline for paying the balance of any tax owed – the 'balancing payment' – for the tax year ending the previous 5 April. It is also the date by which a taxpayer must make any first 'payment on account' (advance payment) for the current tax year. For example, on 31 January 2019 a taxpayer may have to pay both the balancing payment for the year 2017–18 and the first payment on account for 2018–19.

31 Jul   Deadline for making a second payment on account for the current tax year

LATE FILING AND PAYMENT PENALTIES

Late filing of tax returns incurs an automatic £100 penalty, although individuals may appeal against the penalty if they have a reasonable excuse.

• Over three months late – £10 each day, up to a maximum of £900, in addition to the penalty above
• Over six months late – an additional £300 or 5 per cent of the tax due, whichever is the higher, in addition to the penalty above
• Over 12 months late – a further £300 or 5 per cent of the tax due, whichever is the higher. In serious cases HMRC reserve the right to ask for 100 per cent of the tax due instead. In both instances this is in addition to the penalty above

Late payment of tax owing incurs the following penalties:

• Over 30 days – 5 per cent of the tax unpaid at that date
• Over six months – an additional 5 per cent of the tax unpaid at that date
• Over 12 months – a further 5 per cent of the tax unpaid at that date

Interest is due on all outstanding amounts, including any unpaid penalties, until payment is received in full. Individuals may calculate the penalties they owe for late self assessment tax returns and payments online (W www.gov.uk/ estimate-self-assessment-penalties).

PERSONAL TAX ACCOUNTS

The government has announced that it intends to abolish the annual tax return for millions of individuals and small businesses through the introduction of digital tax accounts as part of its aim to modernise and simplify the taxation system. Since April 2016 all personal taxpayers have been able to access their personal tax account, which replaces annual tax returns, at W www.gov.uk/personal-tax-account. The plan is that, by 2020, the system will allow taxpayers to register, file, pay and update tax information at any time using the digital device of their choice, much like online banking. It will be mandatory for every individual taxpayer and business.

TAX CREDITS

Child tax credit, working tax credit and the new universal credit are paid to qualifying individuals. Although the titles of these credits incorporate the word 'tax', they do not affect the amount of income tax payable or repayable. They are forms of social security benefits. *See* Social Welfare.

CAPITAL GAINS TAX

Capital gains tax (CGT) is a tax on the gain or profit that an individual makes when they sell, give away or otherwise dispose of certain assets, for example shares, land or buildings. An individual potentially has to pay CGT on gains they make from any disposal of taxable assets during a tax year. There is a tax-free allowance and some additional reliefs that may reduce an individual's CGT bill. The following information relates to the tax year 2018–19 ending on 5 April 2019.

CGT is paid by individuals who are either resident or ordinarily resident in the UK for the tax year, executors or administrators – 'personal representatives' – responsible for a deceased person's financial affairs and trustees of a settlement. Non-residents are not usually liable to CGT unless they carry on a business in the UK through a branch or agency. However, from April 2015, the government introduced a CGT charge on gains made by non-residents disposing of UK residential property. Special CGT rules apply to individuals who used to live and work in the UK but have since left the country.

CAPITAL GAINS CHARGEABLE TO CGT

Typically, individuals have made a gain if they sell an asset for more than they paid for it. It is the gain that is taxed, not the amount the individual receives for the asset. For example, a man buys shares for £1,000 and later sells them for £3,000. He has made a gain of £2,000 (£3,000 less £1,000). If someone gives an asset away, the gain will be based on the difference between what the asset was worth when originally acquired and its worth at the time of disposal. The same is true when an asset is sold for less than its full worth in order to give away part of the value. For example, a woman buys a property for £120,000 and three years later, when the property's market value has risen to £180,000, she gives it to her son. The son may pay nothing for the property, or pay less than its true worth, eg £100,000. Either way, she has made a gain of £60,000 (£180,000 less £120,000).

If an individual disposes of an asset he or she received as a gift, the gain is worked out according to the market value of the asset when it was received. For example, a man gives his sister a painting worth £8,000. She pays nothing for it. Later she sells the painting for £10,000. For CGT purposes, she is treated as making a gain of £2,000 (£10,000 less £8,000). If an individual inherits an asset, the estate of the person who died does not pay CGT at the time. If the inheritor later disposes of the asset, the gain is worked out by looking at the market value at the time of the death (the probate value). For example, a woman acquires some shares for £5,000 and leaves them to her niece when she dies. No CGT is payable at the time of death when the shares are worth £8,000. Later the niece sells the shares for £10,000. She has made a gain of £2,000 (£10,000 less £8,000).

Individuals may also have to pay CGT if they dispose of part of an asset or exchange one asset for another. Similarly, CGT may be payable if an individual receives a capital sum of money from an asset without disposing of it, for example where he or she receives compensation when an asset is damaged.

Assets that may lead to a CGT charge when they are disposed of include:

• shares in a company that are not held in an ISA or PEP
• units in a unit trust
• land and buildings (though not normally an individual's main home – *see* 'Disposal of a home' section for details)
• personal possessions, including jewellery, paintings, antiques and other personal effects, individually worth £6,000 or more
• business assets

EXEMPT GAINS

Certain kinds of assets do not give rise to a chargeable gain when they are disposed of. Assets exempt from CGT include:
- a car
- an individual's main home, if certain conditions are met
- tax-free investments such as assets held in an ISA or PEP
- UK government gilts or 'bonds' (including premium bonds)
- personal belongings, including jewellery, paintings and antiques, individually worth £6,000 or less
- betting, lottery or pools winnings

DISPOSAL OF A HOME: PRIVATE RESIDENCE RELIEF

When an individual sells their own home they automatically qualify for private residence relief, which means they do not have to pay any CGT provided that:
- the property has been their only home or main residence since they bought it, and
- they have used it as their home and for no other purpose

Even if an individual has not lived in the property for all of the time that they owned it, they may still be entitled to the full relief.

Under the relief rules, the final 18 months of ownership are always treated as if the individual lived in the property even if they did not. This means that if an individual moves out of one home and into a new one, they have up to 18 months in which to sell their former home without incurring any CGT on the sale proceeds.

Full relief is granted to individuals when they sell their home if they could not live in it for periods because they were working abroad. Full relief is also granted if an individual is prevented from living in the home for periods totalling a maximum of four years because their job requires them to work elsewhere in the UK. In both cases, however, for the property to qualify for full relief, the general rule is that it must have been the individual's only or main home both before and after they worked away.

Individuals can also get full relief when they sell their home if they have lived away from it for reasons other than working away, provided all of the following apply:
- they were not living away from the home for more than three years in total during the time they owned the property
- they were not entitled to private residence relief on any other property during that time
- the property was their only or main home both before and after they lived elsewhere

There are instances when individuals may not get the full amount of private residence relief when they sell their home. These include if:
- the grounds, including all buildings, are larger than 5,000 square metres
- any part of the home has been used exclusively for business purposes
- all or part of the home has been let out (or more than one lodger has been taken in at a time). The owner may, however, be entitled to another form of CGT relief – letting relief – instead
- the main reason the property was bought was to make a profit from a quick sale

If an individual lives in – not just owns – more than one property, they can 'nominate' which should be treated as their main home for private residence relief purposes. Married couples or those in a civil partnership must make such a nomination jointly as they are only entitled to private residence relief on one house between them.

There is a calculator to help individuals work out how much private residence relief they may be entitled to when selling their main residence at **W** www.gov.uk/tax-relief-selling-home.

OTHER TRANSACTIONS NOT CHARGEABLE TO CGT

Certain other kinds of disposal similarly do not give rise to a chargeable gain. For example, individuals who are married or in a civil partnership and live together may sell or give assets to their spouse or civil partner without having to pay CGT. Individuals may not, however, give or sell assets cheaply to their children without having to consider CGT. There is no CGT to pay on assets given to a registered charity.

CALCULATING CGT

CGT is worked out for each tax year and is charged on the total of an individual's taxable gains after taking into account certain costs and reliefs that can reduce or defer chargeable gains, allowable losses made on assets to which CGT normally applies and an annual exempt (tax-free) amount that applies to every individual. If the total of an individual's net gains in a tax year is less than the annual exempt amount (AEA), the individual will not have to pay CGT. For the tax year 2018–19 the AEA is £11,700. If an individual's net gains are more than the AEA, they pay CGT on the excess. Should any part of the exemption remain unused, this cannot be carried forward to a future year.

There are certain reliefs available that may eliminate, reduce or defer CGT. Some reliefs are available to many people while others are available only in special circumstances. Some reliefs are given automatically while others are given only if they are claimed. Some of the costs of buying, selling and improving assets may be deducted from total gains when working out an individual's chargeable gain.

RATES OF TAX

The net gains remaining, if any, calculated after subtracting the AEA, deducting costs and taking into account all CGT reliefs, incur liability to capital gains tax. Individuals pay CGT at a rate of 10 per cent on gains up to the unused amount of the basic rate income tax band (if any) and at 20 per cent on gains above that amount. Rates for individuals for gains on residential property not eligible for private residence relief (*see* above) are charged at a rate of 18 per cent up to any unused amount of the basic rate income tax band and at 28 per cent on gains above that amount. The CGT rate charged to trustees and personal representatives is 28 per cent on residential property and 20 per cent on other chargeable assets.

An individual can report any CGT they need to pay (*see* below):
- straight away using the 'real time' Capital Gains Tax service
- annually in a self assessment tax return

VALUATION OF ASSETS

The disposal proceeds (the amount received as consideration for the disposal of an asset) are the sum used to establish the gain or loss once certain allowable costs have been deducted. In most cases this is straightforward because the disposal proceeds are the amount actually received for disposing of the asset. This may include cash payable now or in the future and the value of any asset received in exchange for the asset disposed of. However, in certain circumstances, the disposal proceeds may not accurately reflect the value of the asset and the individual may be treated as disposing of an asset for an amount other than the actual amount (if any) that they received. This applies, in particular, where an asset is transferred as a gift or sold for a price known to be below market value. Disposal proceeds in such transactions are deemed to be equal to the market value of the asset at the time it was disposed of rather than the actual amount (if any) received for it.

Market value represents the price that an asset might reasonably be expected to fetch upon sale in the open market. In the case of unquoted shares or securities, it is assumed that the hypothetical purchaser in the open market would have available all the information that a prudent prospective purchaser of shares or securities might reasonably require if that person were proposing to purchase them from a willing vendor by private treaty and at arm's length. The market value of unquoted shares or securities will often be established following negotiations with the specialist HMRC Shares and Assets Valuation department. The valuation of land and interests in land in the UK is dealt with by the Valuation Office Agency. Special rules apply to determine the market value of shares quoted on the London Stock Exchange.

ALLOWABLE COSTS

When working out a chargeable gain, once the actual or notional disposal proceeds have been determined, certain allowable costs may be deducted. There is a general rule that no costs that could be taken into account when working out income or losses for income tax purposes may be deducted. Subject to this, allowable costs are:

- acquisition costs – the actual amount spent on acquiring the asset or, in certain circumstances, the equivalent market value
- incidental costs of acquiring the asset, such as fees paid for professional advice, valuation costs, stamp duty and advertising costs to find a seller
- enhancement costs – incurred for the purpose of enhancing the value of the asset (not including normal maintenance and repair costs)
- expenditure on defending or establishing a person's rights over the asset
- incidental costs of disposing of the asset, such as fees paid for professional advice, valuation costs, stamp duty and advertising costs to find a buyer

If an individual disposes of part of his or her interest in an asset, or part of a holding of shares of the same class in the same company, or part of a holding of units in the same unit trust, he or she can deduct the relevant part of the allowable costs of the asset or holding when working out the chargeable gain.

ENTREPRENEURS' RELIEF

Entrepreneurs' relief allows individuals in business and some trustees to claim relief on the first £10m of gains made on the disposal of any of the following:

- all or part of a business
- the assets of a business after it has ceased
- shares in a company.

The relief is available to taxpayers as individuals if they are in business, for example as a sole trader or as a partner in a trading business, or if they hold shares in their own personal trading company. This relief is not available for companies.

Depending on the type of disposal, certain qualifying conditions need to be met throughout a qualifying one-year period. For example, if an individual is selling all or part of their business, they must have owned the business during a one-year period that ends on the date of the disposal.

Where all gains qualify for entrepreneurs' relief, CGT is charged at 10 per cent. An individual can make claims for this relief on more than one occasion as long as the lifetime total of all their claims does not exceed £10m of gains qualifying for relief.

BUSINESS ASSET ROLL-OVER RELIEF

When certain types of business asset are sold or disposed of and the proceeds are reinvested in new qualifying trading assets, business asset rollover relief makes it possible to 'rollover' or postpone the payment of any CGT that would normally be due. The gain is deducted from the base cost of the new asset and only becomes chargeable to CGT on the eventual disposal of that replacement asset, unless a further rollover situation then develops. Full relief is available if all the proceeds from the original asset are reinvested in the qualifying replacement asset.

For example, a trader sells a freehold office for £75,000 and makes a gain of £30,000. All of the proceeds are reinvested in a new freehold business premises costing £90,000. The trader can postpone the whole of the £30,000 gain made on the sale of the old office, as all of the proceeds have been reinvested. When the trader eventually sells the new business premises and the CGT bill becomes payable, the cost of the new premises will be treated as £60,000 (£90,000 less the £30,000 gain).

If only part of the proceeds from the disposal of an old asset is reinvested in a new one, different rules may apply, but it may still be possible to postpone paying tax on part of the gain until the eventual disposal of the new asset.

Relief is only available if the acquisition of the new asset takes place within a period between 12 months before and 36 months after the disposal of the old asset. However, HMRC may extend this time limit at their discretion where there is a clear intention to acquire a replacement asset. The most common types of business asset that qualify for rollover relief are land, buildings occupied and used for the purposes of trade, and fixed plant and machinery. Assets used for the commercial letting of furnished holiday accommodation qualify if certain conditions are satisfied.

GIFT HOLD-OVER RELIEF

The gift of an asset is treated as a disposal made for a consideration equal to market value, with a corresponding acquisition by the transferee at an identical value. In the case of gifts of business assets made by individuals and a limited range of trustees, a form of hold-over relief may be available. This relief, which must be claimed, in effect enables liability for CGT to be deferred and passed to the person to whom the gift is made. Relief is limited to the transfer of certain assets, including the following:

- gifts of assets used for the purposes of a business carried on by the donor or his or her personal company
- gifts of shares in trading companies that are not listed on a stock exchange
- gifts of shares or securities in the donor's personal trading company
- gifts of agricultural land and buildings that would qualify for inheritance tax agricultural property relief
- gifts that are chargeable transfers for inheritance tax purposes
- certain types of gifts that are specifically exempt from inheritance tax

Hold-over relief is automatically due on certain sorts of gifts, including gifts to charities and community amateur sports clubs, and gifts of works of art where certain undertakings have been given. There are certain rules to prevent gifts hold-over relief being used for tax-avoidance purposes. For example, restrictions may apply where an individual gifts assets to trustees administering a trust in which the individual retains an interest, or the assets transferred comprise a dwelling-house. Subject to these exceptions, the effect of a valid claim for hold-over relief is similar to a claim for roll-over relief on the disposal of business assets.

OTHER CGT RELIEFS

There are certain other CGT reliefs available on the disposal of property, shares and business assets. For detailed information on all CGT reliefs and for more general guidance on CGT, visit W www.gov.uk/personal-tax/capital-gains-tax.

REPORTING AND PAYING CGT

Individuals are responsible for telling HMRC about capital gains on which they have to pay tax, either:

- on their self assessment tax return by filling in the capital gains supplementary pages (the return explains how to obtain these pages if needed), or
- by visiting W www.gov.uk/capital-gains-tax/report-and-There is a time limit for claiming capital losses. The deadline is four years from 31 January after the end of the tax year in which the loss was made.

INHERITANCE TAX

Inheritance tax (IHT) is a tax on the value of a person's estate on death and on certain gifts made by an individual during his or her lifetime, usually payable within six months of death. Broadly speaking, a person's estate is everything he or she owned at the time of death, including property, possessions, money and investments, less his or her debts. Not everyone pays IHT. It only applies if the taxable value of an estate is above the current IHT threshold. If an estate, including any assets held in trust and gifts made within seven years of death, is less than the threshold (ie in the nil rate band), no IHT will be due.

A claim can be made to transfer any unused IHT nil-rate band on a person's death to the estate of their surviving spouse or civil partner. This applies where the IHT nil-rate band of the first deceased spouse or civil partner was not fully used in calculating the IHT liability of their estate. When the surviving spouse or civil partner dies, the unused amount may be added to their own nil-rate band (*see* below for details).

IHT used to be something only very wealthy individuals needed to consider. This is no longer the case. The fact that the IHT threshold has not kept pace with house price inflation in recent years means that the estates of some 'ordinary' taxpayers are now liable for IHT purely because of the value of their home. However, there are a number of ways that individuals – while still alive – can legally reduce the IHT bill that will apply to their estates on death. Several valuable IHT exemptions are available (explained further below) which allow individuals to pass on assets during their lifetime or in their will without any IHT being due. Detailed information on IHT is available at W www.gov.uk/inheritance-tax. Further help is also available from the probate and inheritance tax helpline (T 0300-123 1072).

DOMICILE

Liability to IHT depends on an individual's domicile at the time of any gift or on death. Domicile is a complex legal concept and what follows explains some of the main issues. An individual is domiciled in the country where he or she has a permanent home. Domicile is different from nationality or residence, and an individual can only have one domicile at any given time.

A 'domicile of origin' is normally acquired from the individual's father on birth, so this may not be the country in which the individual is born. For example, a child born in Germany to a father who is working there, but whose permanent home is in the UK, will have the UK as his or her domicile of origin. Until a person legally changes his or her domicile, it will be the same as that of the person on whom they are legally dependent.

Individuals can legally acquire a new domicile – a 'domicile of choice' – from the age of 16 by leaving the current country of domicile, settling in another country and providing strong evidence of intention to live there permanently or indefinitely. Women who were married before 1974 acquired their husband's domicile and still retain it until they legally acquire a new domicile.

For IHT purposes, there is a concept of 'deemed domicile'. This means that even if a person is not domiciled in the UK under general law, he or she is treated as domiciled in the UK

at the time of a transfer (ie at the time of a lifetime gift or on death) if he or she was:

- domiciled in the UK at any time in the three years immediately before the transfer, or
- 'resident' in the UK in at least 17 of the 20 income tax years of assessment ending with the year in which a transfer is made

Where a person is domiciled, or treated as domiciled, in the UK at the time of a gift or on death, the location of assets is immaterial and full liability to IHT arises. A non-UK domiciled individual is also liable to IHT, but only on chargeable property in the UK.

The assets of spouses and registered civil partners are not merged for IHT purposes, except that the IHT value of assets owned by one spouse or civil partner may be affected if the other also owns similar assets (eg shares in the same company or a share in their jointly owned house). Each spouse or partner is treated as a separate individual entitled to receive the benefit of his or her exemptions, reliefs and rates of tax.

IHT EXEMPTIONS

There are some important exemptions that allow individuals to legally pass assets on to others, both before and after their death – without being subject to IHT.

Exempt Beneficiaries

Assets can be given away to certain people and organisations without any IHT having to be paid. These gifts, which are exempt whether individuals make them during their lifetime or in their will, include gifts to:

- a spouse or civil partner, even if the couple is legally separated (but not if they are divorced or the civil partnership has been dissolved). Note that gifts to an unmarried partner or a partner with whom the donor has not formed a civil partnership are not exempt
- a 'qualifying' charity established in the EU or another specified country
- some national institutions, including national museums, universities and the National Trust
- UK political parties

Annual Exemption

The first £3,000 of gifts made each tax year by each individual is exempt from IHT. If this exemption is not used, or not wholly used in any year, the balance may be carried forward to the following year only. A couple, therefore, may give away a total of £6,000 per tax year between them or £12,000 if they have not used their previous year's annual exemptions.

Wedding Gifts/Civil Partnership Ceremony Gifts

Some gifts are exempt from IHT because of the type of gift or reason for making it. Wedding or civil partnership ceremony gifts made to either of the couple are exempt from IHT up to certain amounts:

- gifts by a parent or step-parent, £5,000
- gifts by a grandparent or great-grandparent, £2,500
- gifts by anyone else, £1,000

The gift must be made on or shortly before the date of the wedding or civil partnership ceremony. If the ceremony is called off but the gift is made, this exemption will not apply.

Small Gifts

An individual can make small gifts, up to the value of £250, to any number of people in any one tax year without them being liable for IHT. However, a larger sum such as £500 cannot be given and exemption claimed for the first £250. Note that this exemption cannot be used with any other exemption when giving to the same person. For example, a parent cannot combine a 'small gifts exemption' with a 'wedding/civil partnership ceremony gift exemption' to give a child £5,250 when he or she gets married or forms a civil partnership. Neither may an individual combine a 'small gifts exemption' with the 'annual exemption' to give someone £3,250. Note that it is possible to use the 'annual exemption' with any other exemption, such as the 'wedding/civil partnership ceremony gift exemption'. For example, if a child marries or forms a civil partnership, the parent who has not made any other taxable transfers in the year can give him or her a total IHT-free gift of £8,000 by combining £5,000 under the wedding/civil partnership gift exemption and £3,000 under the annual exemption.

Normal Expenditure

Any gifts made out of an individual's after-tax income (not capital) are exempt from IHT if they are part of their normal expenditure and do not result in a fall in their standard of living. These can include regular payments to someone, such as an allowance or gifts for Christmas or a birthday, and regular premiums paid on a life insurance policy for someone else.

Maintenance Gifts

An individual can make IHT-free maintenance payments to his or her spouse or registered civil partner, ex-spouse or former civil partner, relatives dependent because of old age or infirmity, and children (including adopted children and step-children) who are under 18 or in full-time education.

POTENTIALLY EXEMPT TRANSFERS

If an individual makes a gift to either another individual or a certain type of trust and it is not covered by one of the above exemptions, it is known as a 'potentially exempt transfer' (PET). A PET is only free of IHT on two strict conditions:

- the gift must be made at least seven years before the donor's death; if the donor does not survive seven years after making the gift, it will be liable for IHT
- the gift must be made as a true gift with no strings attached (technically known as a 'gift with reservation of benefit'). This means that the donor must give up all rights to the gift and stop benefiting from it in any way

If a gift is made and the donor does retain some benefit from it, then it will still count as part of the donor's estate no matter how long he or she lives after making it. For example, a father could make a lifetime gift of his home to his child, on condition that he continue to live in it. HMRC would not accept this as a true gift unless he paid his child a full commercial rent to do so, because he would be considered to still have a material interest in the gifted home. Its value, therefore, would still be liable for IHT.

In some circumstances a gift with strings attached might give rise to an income tax charge on the donor based on the value of the benefit he or she retains. In this case the donor can choose whether to pay the income tax or have the gift treated as a gift with reservation.

CHARGEABLE TRANSFERS

Any remaining lifetime gifts that are not (potentially or otherwise) exempt transfers are chargeable transfers or 'chargeable gifts', meaning that they incur liability to IHT. Chargeable transfers comprise mainly gifts to or from companies and gifts to particular types of trust. There is an immediate charge to IHT on chargeable gifts, and additional tax may be payable if the donor dies within seven years of making a chargeable gift.

DEATH

Immediately before the time of death an individual is deemed to make a transfer of value. This transfer will comprise the value of assets forming part of the deceased's estate after subtracting most liabilities. Any exempt transfers may be excluded, such as transfers for the benefit of a surviving spouse or civil partner and charities. Death may also trigger three additional liabilities:

- on a PET made within the seven years before death, which loses its potential status and becomes chargeable to IHT
- on the value of gifts made with reservation may incur liability if any benefit was enjoyed within the seven years before the death
- additional tax may become payable for chargeable lifetime transfers made within the seven years before the death

The 'personal representative' (the person nominated to handle the affairs of the deceased person) arranges to value the estate and pay any IHT that is due. One or more personal representatives can be nominated in a person's will, in which case they are known as the 'executors'. If a person dies without leaving a will a court can nominate the personal representative, who is then known as the 'administrator'. Valuing the deceased person's estate is one of the first things a personal representative needs to do. The representative will not normally be able to take over management of the estate (called 'applying for probate') until all or some of any IHT that is due has been paid.

VALUATIONS

When valuing a deceased person's estate, all assets (property, possessions and money) owned at the time of death and certain assets given away during the seven years before death must be included. The valuation must accurately reflect what those assets would reasonably fetch in the open market at the date of death. The value of all of the assets that the deceased owned should include:

- his or her share of any assets owned jointly with someone else, for example a house owned with a partner
- any assets that are held in a trust, from which the deceased had the right to benefit
- any assets given away, but in which he or she kept an interest (gifts with reservation)
- PETs given away within the last seven years

Most estate assets can be valued quite easily, for example money in bank accounts or stocks and shares. In other instances the help of a professional valuer may be needed. Advice on how to value different assets, including joint or trust assets, is available at W www.gov.uk/valuing-estate-of-someone-who-died.

When valuing an estate, special relief is made available for certain assets. The two main reliefs are agricultural property relief and business relief, outlined below. Once all assets have been valued, the next step is to deduct from the total assets everything that the deceased person owed, such as unpaid bills, outstanding mortgages, other loans and their funeral expenses.

The value of all of the assets, less the deductible debts, is their estate. IHT is only payable on any value above the threshold for the tax year. It is payable at the current rate of 40 per cent. This rate is reduced to 36 per cent where 10 per cent or more of a net estate (after deducting IHT exemptions, reliefs and the nil-rate band) is left to charity.

RELIEF FOR SELECTED ASSETS

Agricultural Property

If an individual owns agricultural property and it is part of a working farm, it is possible to pass on some of this property free of IHT, either during that individual's lifetime or on their death. Agricultural property generally includes land or pasture used in the growing of crops or intensive rearing of animals for food consumption. It can also include farmhouses and farm cottages. The agricultural property can be owner-occupied or let. Relief is only due if the transferor has owned the property and it has been occupied for agricultural purposes for a minimum period.

The chargeable value transferred, either in a lifetime gift or on death, must be determined. This value may then be reduced by a percentage. Depending on the type of property, it will normally qualify for relief of 100 per cent.

Business Relief

Business relief is available on transfers of certain types of business and of business assets if they qualify as relevant business property and the transferor has owned them for a minimum period. The relief can be claimed for transfers made during the person's lifetime or on their death. Where the chargeable value transferred is attributable to relevant business property, the business relief reduces that value by either 50 or 100 per cent, depending on the type of asset. Business relief may be claimed on relevant business property, including property and buildings or assets such as unlisted shares or machinery.

It is a general requirement that the property must have been retained for a period of two years before the transfer or death, and restrictions may be necessary if the property has not been used wholly for business purposes. The same property cannot obtain both business property relief and the relief available for agricultural property.

CALCULATION OF TAX PAYABLE

The calculation of IHT payable adopts the use of a cumulative or 'running' total. Each chargeable lifetime transfer is added to the total if it was made within seven years of the donor's death. To the running total this produces is added the total value of the estate at death. If the total exceeds the inheritance tax threshold (the 'nil-rate band') IHT becomes payable. The rate of tax that is paid is determined by the element that causes the estate to exceed the threshold; gifts use up all or part of the nil-rate band first.

Lifetime Chargeable Transfers

The value transferred by total chargeable transfers during the deceased's lifetime must be added to the seven-year running total to calculate whether any IHT is due. If the nil-rate band is exceeded, tax will be imposed on the excess at the rate of 20 per cent. However, if the donor dies within a period of seven years from the date of the chargeable lifetime transfer, additional tax is calculated by applying tax at the full rate of 40 per cent (rather than 20 per cent). The amount of tax is then reduced by applying taper relief, which is a percentage of the full rate of 40 per cent. This percentage is governed by the number of years from the date of the lifetime gift to the date of death, as follows:

TAPER RELIEF

Years between transfer and death	Taper relief %
More than 3 but not more than 4	20%
More than 4 but not more than 5	40%
More than 5 but not more than 6	60%
More than 6 but not more than 7	80%

Should this exercise produce liability greater than that previously paid at the 20 per cent rate on the lifetime transfer, the difference must be paid in additional tax. Where the calculation shows an amount falling below tax paid on the lifetime transfer, no additional liability can arise nor will the shortfall become repayable.

Taper relief is only available if the calculation discloses a liability to IHT. There is no liability if the lifetime transfer falls within the nil-rate band.

Potentially Exempt Transfers

Where a PET loses immunity from liability to IHT because the donor dies within seven years of making the transfer, the value transferred enters into the running total. Any liability to IHT will be calculated by applying the full rate of 40 per cent, reduced by taper relief if applicable. Again, liability to IHT can only arise if the nil-rate band is exceeded.

Death

On death, IHT is due on the value of the deceased's estate plus the running total of gifts made in the seven years before death if that comes to more than the nil-rate band. IHT is then charged at the full rate of 40 per cent on the amount in excess of the nil-rate band.

Settled Property and Trusts

Trusts are special legal arrangements that can be used by individuals to control how their assets are distributed to their beneficiaries and minimise their IHT liability. Complex rules apply to establish IHT liability on 'settled property' which includes property held in trust, and individuals are advised to take expert legal advice when setting up trusts.

RATES OF TAX

There are four rates:
- nil rate
- lifetime rate of 20 per cent
- full rate of 40 per cent
- reduced rate of 36 per cent applicable to taxable estates where 10 per cent of the net estate has been left to charity (*see* above)

The basic nil-rate band threshold is £325,000 for 2018–19. In 2015 the government announced that the nil-rate band would remain at this figure until April 2021. Any excess over this level is taxable at the relevant rate.

ADDITIONAL THRESHOLD (RNRB)

The additional threshold (or residence nil-rate band) was introduced from April 2017, applying where a residence the deceased owns and has lived in passes on their death to direct descendants. The additional threshold is £125,000 in 2018–19, £150,000 in 2019–20 and £175,000 in 2020–21. It will increase in line with the consumer prices index (CPI) from 2021–22 onwards. Any unused nil-rate band may be transferred to the surviving spouse or civil partner.

The RNRB will also be available when an individual downsizes or ceases to own a home and other assets of an equivalent value are passed on death to direct descendants. These changes apply for deaths on or after 6 April 2017 where the deceased downsized or disposed of a property after 7 July 2015.

There is a tapered withdrawal of the RNRB for estates with a net value of more than £2m. This will be at a rate of £1 for every £2 over the additional threshold. Guidance on the additional threshold can be found at W www.gov.uk/guidance/inheritance-tax-residence-nil-rate-band.

TRANSFER OF NIL-RATE BAND

Transfers of property between spouses or civil partners are generally exempt from IHT. This means that someone who dies leaving some or all of their property to their spouse or civil partner may not have fully used up their nil-rate band. Any nil-rate band unused on the first death can be used when the surviving spouse or civil partner dies. A transfer of unused nil-rate band from a deceased spouse or civil partner may be made to the estate of their surviving spouse or civil partner.

Where a valid claim to transfer unused nil-rate band is made, the nil-rate band that is available when the surviving spouse or civil partner dies is increased by the proportion of the nil-rate band unused on the first death. For example, if on the first death the chargeable estate is £150,000 and the nil-rate band is £300,000, 50 per cent of the nil-rate band would be unused. If the nil-rate band when the survivor dies is £329,000, then that would be increased by 50 per cent to £493,500. The amount of the nil-rate band that can be transferred does not depend on the value of the first spouse or civil partner's estate. Whatever proportion of the nil-rate band is unused on the first death is available for transfer to the survivor.

The amount of additional nil-rate band that can be accumulated by any one surviving spouse or civil partner is limited to the value of the nil-rate band in force at the time of their death. This may be relevant where a person dies having survived more than one spouse or civil partner.

Where these rules have effect, personal representatives do not have to claim for the unused nil-rate band to be transferred at the time of the first death. Any claims for transfer of unused nil-rate band amounts are made by the personal representatives of the estate of the second spouse or civil partner to die when they make an IHT return.

Guidance on how to transfer the nil-rate band can be found at W www.gov.uk/government/publications/claim-the-residence-nil-rate-band-rnrb-iht435.

PAYMENT OF TAX

IHT is normally due six months after the end of the month in which the death occurs or the chargeable transaction takes place. This is referred to as the 'due date'. Tax on some assets, such as business property, certain shares and securities and land and buildings (including the deceased person's home), can be deferred and paid in equal instalments over ten years, though interest will be charged in most cases. If IHT is due on lifetime gifts and transfers, the person who received the gift or assets (the transferee) is normally liable to pay the IHT, though any IHT already paid at the time of a transfer into a trust or company will be taken into account. If tax owed is not paid by the due date, interest is charged on any unpaid IHT, no matter what caused the delay in payment.

HMRC has developed an online service to support the administration of IHT. This does away with the need to complete paper forms and enables individuals to proceed with their application for probate and submit IHT accounts online:

- if you are dealing with the estate of someone who has died, there is some guidance about the basic processes at W www.gov.uk/valuing-estate-of-someone-who-died and this page also gives links to make the relevant return
- to get a payment reference number, go to W www.gov.uk/paying-inheritance-tax/get-a-reference-number at least three weeks before the payment is due
- forms and worksheets for calculating IHT liabilities are available at W www.gov.uk/government/publications/inheritance-tax-inheritance-tax-account-iht100

CORPORATION TAX

Corporation tax is a tax on a company's profits, including all its income and gains. This tax is payable by UK resident companies and by non-resident companies carrying on a trade in the UK through a permanent establishment. The following comments are confined to companies resident in the UK. The word 'company' is also used to include:

- members' clubs, societies and associations
- trade associations
- housing associations
- groups of individuals carrying on a business but not as a partnership (for example, cooperatives)

A company's taxable income is charged by reference to income or gains arising in its 'accounting period', which is normally 12 months long. In some circumstances accounting periods can be shorter than 12 months, but never longer. The accounting period is normally the period for which a company's accounts are drawn up, but the two periods do not have to coincide.

If a company is liable to pay corporation tax on its profits, several things must be done. HMRC must be informed that the company exists and is liable for tax. A self assessment company tax return plus full accounts and calculation of tax liability must be filed by the statutory filing date, normally 12 months after the end of the accounting period. Companies have to work out their own tax liability and have to pay their tax without prior assessment by HMRC. Records of all company expenditure and income must be kept in order to work out the tax liability correctly. Companies are liable to penalties if they fail to carry out these obligations.

There is a radically simpler way for small self-employed businesses, such as sole traders and partnerships, to calculate their tax. Such businesses with receipts of £150,000 or less are able to work out their income on a cash basis and use simplified expenses rules, rather than having to follow the rules for larger businesses. Limited companies and limited liability partnerships can not use the cash basis. If a small business uses cash basis accounting and the business grows during the tax year, it can stay in the scheme up to a total business turnover of £300,000 a year.

Corporation tax information is available at W www.gov.uk/browse/business/business-tax and companies may file their company tax returns online (W www.gov.uk/file-your-company-accounts-and-tax-return).

RATE OF TAX

The rate of corporation tax is fixed for a financial year starting on 1 April and ending on the following 31 March. If a company's accounting period does not coincide with the financial year, its profits must be apportioned between the financial years and the tax rates for each financial year applied to those profits. The corporation tax liability is the total tax for both financial years.

The rate of corporation tax has been 19 per cent since 1 April 2017.

ALLOWANCES AND RELIEFS

Businesses can claim capital allowances, on certain purchases or investments. This means that a proportion of these costs can be deducted from a business' taxable profits and reduce its tax bill. Capital allowances are currently available on plant and machinery such as equipment and business vehicles. Reliefs are also available for research and development, profits from patented inventions and certain creative industries. The amount of the allowance or relief depends on what is being claimed for.

Detailed information on allowances and reliefs is available at W www.gov.uk/corporation-tax-rates/allowances-and-reliefs.

PAYMENT OF TAX

Corporation tax liabilities are normally due and payable in a single lump sum not later than nine months and one day after the end of the accounting period. For 'large' companies – those with profits over £1.5m – there is a requirement to pay corporation tax in four quarterly instalments. Where a company is a member of a group, the profits of the entire group must be merged to establish whether the company is 'large'.

HMRC runs a Business Payment Support Service (BPSS) which allows businesses facing temporary financial difficulties more time to pay their tax bills. Traders concerned about their ability to meet corporation tax, VAT or other payments owed to HMRC can call the BPSS Line (T 0300-200 3835) seven days a week. This helpline is for new enquiries only, not for traders who have already been contacted by HMRC about an overdue payment. For details of the service, visit W www.gov.uk/government/organisations/hm-revenue-customs/contact/business-payment-support-service.

CAPITAL GAINS

Chargeable gains arising to a company are calculated in a manner similar to that used for individuals. However, companies are not entitled to the CGT annual exemption. Companies incur liability to corporation tax rather than CGT on chargeable gains. Tax is due on the full chargeable gain of an accounting period after subtracting relief for any losses.

GROUPS OF COMPANIES

Each company within a group is separately charged corporation tax on profits, gains and income. However, where one group member realises a loss for which special rules apply, other than a capital loss, a claim may be made to offset the taxable loss against profits of some other member of the same group. The transfer of capital assets from one member of a group to a fellow member will usually incur no liability to tax on chargeable gains.

SPORTS CLUBS

Though corporation tax is payable by unincorporated associations (including most sports clubs) on their profits, a substantial exemption from liability to corporation tax is available to qualifying registered community amateur sports clubs (CASCs). Sports clubs that are registered as CASCs are exempt from liability to corporation tax on:

- profits from trading where the turnover of the trade is less than £50,000 in a 12-month period
- income from letting property where the gross rental income is less than £30,000 in a 12-month period
- bank and building society interest received
- chargeable gains
- any Gift Aid donations

All of the exemptions depend upon the club having been a registered CASC for the whole of the relevant accounting period and the income or gains being used only for qualifying purposes. If the club has only been a registered CASC for part of an accounting period the exemption amounts of £50,000 (for trading) and £30,000 (for income from property) are reduced proportionally. Only interest and gains received after the club is registered are exempted. Some of the rules for CASCs changed on 1 April 2015. Full details can be found at W www.gov.uk/government/publications/community-amateur-sports-clubs-detailed-guidance-notes.

Charities do not pay corporation tax on profits from their charitable activities. To minimise their liability, they often operate their trading activities through a subsidiary company.

VALUE ADDED TAX

Value added tax (VAT) is a tax on consumption which is collected at each stage in the supply chain. It is included in the sale price of taxable goods and services and paid at the point of purchase. Each EU country has its own rates of VAT. VAT is charged on most business transactions involving the supply of goods and services by VAT registered traders in the UK and Isle of Man. It is also charged on goods and some services imported from places outside the EU and on goods and some services coming into the UK from the other EU countries. VAT is administered by HMRC. A wide range of information on VAT, including VAT forms, is available online (W www.gov.uk/topic/business-tax/vat) and HMRC also runs a VAT enquiries helpline (T 0300-200 3700).

RATES OF TAX

There are three rates of VAT in the UK:

- the standard rate, payable on most goods and services in the UK, is 20 per cent
- the reduced rate – currently 5 per cent – is payable on certain goods and services, including domestic fuel and power, children's car seats, women's sanitary products, smoking cessation products and the installation of energy-saving materials such as wall insulation and solar panels
- zero rate applies to certain items, including, children's clothes, books, newspapers, most food and drink, and drugs and aids for disabled people. There are numerous exceptions to the zero-rated categories, including: confectionery, potato crisps, alcoholic drinks, soft drinks and items sold for consumption in a restaurant or café. Takeaway cold items such as sandwiches are zero-rated, but hot foods like fish and chips are not.

REGISTRATION

All traders, including professional persons and companies, must register for VAT if they are making 'taxable supplies' of a value exceeding the registration threshold. All goods and services that are VAT rated are defined as 'taxable supplies'. This includes zero-rated items, which must be included when calculating the total value of a trader's taxable supplies – his or her 'taxable turnover'. The limits that govern mandatory registration are amended periodically.

An unregistered trader must register for VAT if:

- at the end of any month the total value of his or her taxable turnover (not just profit) for the past 12 months or less is more than the current VAT threshold of £85,000

or

- at any time he or she has reasonable grounds to expect that his or her taxable turnover will be more than the current registration threshold of £85,000 in the next 30 days alone

VAT registration must be completed within 30 days. Most businesses register online, but some need to download a form (W www.gov.uk/vat-registration/how-to-register). Traders who do not register at the correct time can be fined. Traders must charge VAT on their taxable supplies from the effective date of registration.

Traders who only supply zero-rated goods may not have to register for VAT even if their taxable turnover goes above the registration threshold. However, a trader in this position must inform HMRC first and apply to be 'exempt from registration'.

A trader whose taxable turnover does not reach the mandatory registration limit may choose to register for VAT voluntarily. This step may be thought advisable to recover input tax (*see* below) or to compete with other registered traders.

Registered traders may submit an application for deregistration if their taxable turnover subsequently falls. An application for deregistration can be made if the taxable turnover for the 12 months beginning on the application date is not expected to exceed £83,000.

INPUT TAX

Registered traders suffer input tax when buying in goods or services for the purposes of their business. It is the VAT that traders pay out to their suppliers on goods and services coming *in* to their business. Relief can usually be obtained for input tax suffered, either by setting that tax against output tax due on sales or by repayment. Most items of input tax can be relieved in this manner. Where a registered trader makes both exempt supplies and taxable supplies to his customers or clients, there may be some restriction in the amount of input tax that can be recovered.

OUTPUT TAX

When making a taxable supply of goods or services, registered traders must account for output tax on the value of that supply. Output tax is the term used to describe the VAT on the goods and services that they supply or sell, going *out* of the business. It is collected from customers on each sale by increasing the price by the VAT. Failure to make the required addition will not remove liability to pay the output tax to HMRC.

The liability to account for output tax, and also relief for input tax, may be affected where a trader is using a special secondhand goods scheme.

EXEMPT SUPPLIES

VAT is not chargeable on certain goods and services because the law deems them 'exempt' from VAT. These include:

- the provision of burial and cremation facilities
- insurance
- loans of money
- certain types of education and training
- most property transactions, unless the owner has opted to tax the property

Exempt supplies do not enter into the calculation of taxable turnover that governs liability to mandatory registration (*see* above). Such supplies made by a registered trader may limit the amount of input tax that can be relieved.

COLLECTION OF TAX

Registered traders submit VAT returns for accounting periods usually of three months in duration, but arrangements can be made to submit returns on a monthly basis. Very large traders – those whose annual VAT liability exceeds £2.3m – must make payments on account on a monthly basis, with the quarterly return used to determine the balancing payment. The return will show the output tax due for supplies made by the trader in the accounting period and the input tax for which relief is claimed. If the output tax exceeds input tax the balance must be remitted at the time of the VAT return. Where input tax suffered exceeds the output tax due, the registered trader may claim the excess from HMRC.

In this way, each trader in the supply chain collects the tax relating to the value added by their business. Where the supply is made to a person who is not a registered trader there can be no recovery of input tax and it is on this person that the final burden of VAT eventually falls.

Where goods are acquired by a UK trader from a supplier within the EU, the trader must also account for the tax due on acquisition.

There are a number of simplified arrangements to make VAT accounting easier for businesses, particularly small businesses, and there is advice on the HMRC website about how to choose the most appropriate scheme for a business:

Cash Accounting Scheme

This scheme allows businesses to only pay VAT on the basis of payments received from their customers rather than on invoice dates or time of supply. This is useful for businesses with cash flow problems. Businesses may use the cash accounting scheme if estimated taxable turnover is £1.35m or less for the next 12 months. There is no need to apply for the scheme – eligible businesses may start using it at the beginning of a new tax period. If a trader opts to use this scheme, he or she can do so until the taxable turnover reaches £1.6m. For further information *see* W www.gov.uk/vat-cash-accounting-scheme.

Annual Accounting Scheme

If estimated taxable turnover is £1.35m or less in the next 12 months, the trader may join the annual accounting scheme which allows them to make nine monthly or three quarterly instalments during the year based on an estimate of their total annual VAT bill. At the end of the year they submit a single return and any balance due. The advantages of this scheme for businesses are easier budgeting and cash flow planning,

because fixed payments are spread regularly throughout the year. Once a trader has joined the annual accounting scheme, membership may continue until the annual taxable turnover reaches £1.6m. This scheme is not helpful where businesses receive a refund of VAT, because it delays receipt of the refund. For more information *see* W www.gov.uk/vat-annual-accounting-scheme.

Flat Rate Scheme

This scheme allows small businesses with an annual taxable turnover of £150,000 or less to save on administration by paying VAT as a set flat percentage of their annual turnover instead of accounting internally for VAT on each individual 'in and out'. The percentage rate used is governed by the trade sector into which the business falls. The scheme can no longer be used once annual income exceeds £230,000.

Under this scheme, it is not possible to reclaim the VAT on purchases, except for certain assets over £2,000. For further information *see* W www.gov.uk/vat-flat-rate-scheme.

A business can not use the Flat Rate Scheme and the Cash Accounting Scheme at the same time.

Retail Schemes

There are special schemes that offer retailers an alternative if it is impractical for them to issue invoices for a large number of supplies direct to the public. These schemes include a provision to claim relief from VAT on bad debts where goods or services are supplied to a customer who does not pay for them.

VAT FACT SUMMARY *from 1 April 2018*

Standard rate	20%
Reduced rate	5%
Registration (last 12 months or next 30 days)	over £85,000
Deregistration (next 12 months)	under £83,000
Cash accounting scheme	up to £1,350,000
Annual accounting scheme	up to £1,350,000
Flat rate scheme	up to £150,000

STAMP DUTY

Stamp duty is payable by the buyer based on the purchase price of a property, stocks and shares. For the majority of people, contact with stamp duty arises when they buy a property. This section aims to provide a broad overview of stamp duty as it may affect the average person.

STAMP DUTY LAND TAX

Stamp duty land tax (SDLT) covers the purchase of houses, flats and other land, buildings and certain leases in the UK.

Buyers of property are responsible for completing a land transaction return form, SDLT1, which contains all information regarding the purchase that is relevant to HMRC and paying SDLT, though the solicitor or licensed conveyancer acting for them in a land transaction will normally complete the relevant paperwork. Once HMRC has received the completed land transaction return and the payment of any SDLT due, a certificate, SDLT5, will be issued that enables a solicitor or licensed conveyancer to register the property in the new owner's name at the land registry.

The threshold for notification of residential property is currently £40,000. This means that taxpayers entering into a transaction involving residential or non-residential property where the chargeable consideration is less than £40,000 do not need to notify HMRC about the transaction.

Since 1 April 2015 stamp duty has no longer applied to land transactions in Scotland. These are now subject to land and buildings transaction tax, details of which can be found online (W www.gov.uk/sdlt-scottish-transactions).

RATES OF SDLT

SDLT is charged at different rates and has thresholds for different types of property and different values of transaction. The tax rate and payment threshold can vary according to whether the property is in residential or non-residential use and whether it is freehold or leasehold.

SDLT on purchases of residential property is charged at increasing rates for each portion of the price.

SDLT ON RESIDENTIAL PROPERTY PURCHASES

2018–19

Portion of the transaction value	SDLT is charged at
Up to £125,000	zero
Between £125,001 and £250,000	2 per cent
Between £250,001 and £925,000	5 per cent
Between £925,001 and £1,500,000	10 per cent
Over £1,500,000	12 per cent

For example, on a property bought for £275,000, a total of £3,750 is payable in SDLT. This is made up of: nothing on the first £125,000, £2,500 (2 per cent) on the next £125,000, and £1,250 (5 per cent) on the remaining £25,000.

Higher rates of SDLT apply to purchases of additional residential properties such as second homes and buy-to-let properties. The higher rates are 3 per cent above the standard rates of SDLT. They do not apply to purchases of property under £40,000 or purchases of caravans, mobile homes and houseboats.

HIGHER RATE SDLT ON ADDITIONAL RESIDENTIAL PROPERTY PURCHASES 2018–19

Portion of the transaction value	SDLT is charged at
Up to £125,000	3 per cent
Between £125,001 and £250,000	5 per cent
Between £250,001 and £925,000	8 per cent
Between £925,001 and £1,500,000	13 per cent
Over £1,500,000	15 per cent

Each of these higher rates again applies to the portion of the consideration that falls within each rate band. For example, on a buy-to-let property bought for £300,000, a total of £14,000 is payable in higher rate SDLT. This is made up of: £3,750 (3 per cent) on the first £125,000, £6,250 (5 per cent) on the next £125,000, and £4,000 (8 per cent) on the remaining £50,000.

The SDLT on purchases of non-residential and mixed-use property is charged at increasing rates for each portion of the price (in the same way that it is charged on purchases of residential property).

SDLT ON NON-RESIDENTIAL AND MIXED USE PROPERTY PURCHASES 2018–19

Portion of the transaction value	SDLT is charged at
Up to £150,000	zero
Between £150,001 and £250,000	2 per cent
Over £250,001	5 per cent

FIRST TIME BUYERS

From November 2017, first time buyers of homes worth between £300,000 and £500,000 will not pay SDLT on the first £300,000. They will pay the normal rates of SDLT on the price above that. This will save £1,660 on the average first-time property. It is estimated that 80 per cent of people buying their first home will pay no SDLT.

This relief does not apply for those buying properties over £500,000.

CALCULATING SDLT

To work out the amount of SDLT payable on residential or non-residential property, a SDLT calculator is available online (W www.tax.service.gov.uk/calculate-stamp-duty-land-tax/#/intro).

STAMP DUTY RESERVE TAX

Stamp duty or stamp duty reserve tax (SDRT) is payable at the rate of 0.5 per cent when shares are purchased. Stamp duty is payable when the shares are transferred using a stock transfer form, whereas SDRT is payable on 'paperless' share transactions where the shares are transferred electronically without using a stock transfer form. Most share transactions nowadays are paperless and settled by stockbrokers through CREST (the electronic settlement and registration system). SDRT therefore now accounts for the majority of taxation collected on share transactions effected through the London Stock Exchange.

The flat rate of 0.5 per cent is based on the amount paid for the shares, not what they are worth. If, for example, shares are bought for £2,000, £10 SDRT is payable, whatever the value of the shares themselves. If shares are transferred for free, no SDRT is payable.

A higher rate of 1.5 per cent is payable where shares are transferred into a 'depositary receipt scheme' or a 'clearance service'. These are special arrangements where the shares are held by a third party.

CREST automatically deducts the SDRT and sends it to HMRC. A stockbroker will settle up with CREST for the cost of the shares and the SDRT and then bill the purchaser for these and the broker's fees. If shares are not purchased through CREST, the stamp duty must be paid by the purchaser to HMRC.

UK stamp duty or SDRT is not payable on the purchase of foreign shares, though there may be foreign taxes to pay. SDRT is already accounted for in the price paid for units in unit trusts or shares in open-ended investment companies.

HELP AND INFORMATION

Further information on stamp duty land tax and SDRT is available via the stamp taxes helpline on T 0300-200 3510 or the government information website (W www.gov.uk/topic/business-tax).

LEGAL NOTES

These notes outline certain aspects of the law as they might affect the average person. They are intended only as a broad guideline and are by no means definitive. The law is constantly changing so expert advice should always be taken. In some cases, sources of further information are given in these notes.

It is always advisable to consult a solicitor without delay. Anyone who does not have a solicitor can contact the following for assistance in finding one: Citizens Advice (W www.citizensadvice.org.uk), the Community Legal Service (W www.gov.uk) or the Law Society of England and Wales. For assistance in Scotland, contact Citizens Advice Scotland (W www.cas.org.uk) or the Law Society of Scotland.

Legal aid schemes exist to make the help of a lawyer available to those who would not otherwise be able to afford one. Entitlement for most types of legal aid depends on an individual's means but a solicitor or Citizens Advice will be able to advise on this.

LAW SOCIETY OF ENGLAND AND WALES, 113 Chancery Lane, London WC2A 1PL T 020-7242 1222
W www.lawsociety.org.uk

LAW SOCIETY OF SCOTLAND, Atria One, 144 Morrison Street, Edinburgh EH8 8EX T 0131-226 7411
W www.lawscot.org.uk

ABORTION

Abortion is governed by the Abortion Act 1967. Under its provisions, a legally induced abortion must be:
- performed by a registered medical practitioner
- carried out in an NHS hospital or other approved premises
- certified by two registered medical practitioners, acting in good faith, on the basis of one or more of the following grounds:
1. that the pregnancy has not exceeded its 24th week and that the continuance of the pregnancy would involve risk, greater than if the pregnancy were terminated, of injury to the physical or mental health of the pregnant woman or any existing children of her family
2. that the termination is necessary to prevent grave permanent injury to the physical or mental health of the pregnant woman
3. that the continuance of the pregnancy would involve risk to the life of the pregnant woman, greater than if the pregnancy were terminated
4. that there is a substantial risk that if the child were born it would suffer from such physical or mental abnormalities as to be seriously handicapped.

In determining whether the continuance of a pregnancy would involve such risk of injury to health as is mentioned in the first and second grounds, account may be taken of the pregnant woman's actual or reasonably foreseeable environment.

The requirements relating to the opinion of two registered medical practitioners and to the performance of the abortion at an NHS hospital or other approved place cease to apply in circumstances where a registered medical practitioner is of the opinion, formed in good faith, that a termination is immediately necessary to save the life, or to prevent grave permanent injury to the physical or mental health, of the pregnant woman.

The Abortion Act 1967 does not apply to Northern Ireland, where abortion is not legal.

FAMILY PLANNING ASSOCIATION (UK), 23–28 Penn Street, London N1 5DL T 020-7608 5240 W www.fpa.org.uk

BRITISH PREGNANCY ADVISORY SERVICE (BPAS), 20 Timothys Bridge Road, Stratford-upon-Avon CV37 9BF
T 0345-365 5050 W www.bpas.org

ADOPTION OF CHILDREN

The Adoption and Children Act 2002 reformed the framework for domestic and intercountry adoption in England and Wales and some parts of it extend to Scotland and Northern Ireland. The Children and Adoption Act 2006, recently amended by the Children and Families Act 2014, introduced further provisions for adoptions involving a foreign element.

WHO MAY APPLY FOR AN ADOPTION ORDER

A couple (whether married or two people living as partners in an enduring family relationship) may apply for an adoption order where both of them are over 21 or where one is only 18 but the natural parent and the other is 21. An adoption order may be made for one applicant where that person is 21 and: a) the court is satisfied that person is the partner of a parent of the person to be adopted; or b) they are not married and are not civil partners; or c) married or in a civil partnership but they are separated from their spouse or civil partner and living apart with the separation likely to be permanent; or d) their spouse/civil partner is either unable to be found, or their spouse/civil partner is incapable by reason of ill-health of making an application. There are certain qualifying conditions an applicant must meet, eg residency in the British Isles.

ARRANGING AN ADOPTION

Adoptions may generally only be arranged by an adoption agency or by way of an order from the high court; breach of the restrictions on who may arrange an adoption would constitute a criminal offence. When deciding whether a child should be placed for adoption, the court or adoption agency must consider all the factors set out in the 'welfare checklist' – the paramount consideration being the child's welfare, throughout his or her life. These factors include the child's wishes, needs, age, sex, background and any harm which the child has suffered or is likely to suffer. At all times, the court or adoption agency must bear in mind that delay is likely to prejudice a child's welfare.

ADOPTION ORDER

Once an adoption has been arranged, a court order is necessary to make it legal; this may be obtained from the high court, county court or magistrates' court (including the family proceedings court). An adoption order may not be given unless the court is satisfied that the consent of the child's natural parents (or guardians) has been given correctly. Consent can be dispensed with on two grounds: where the parent or guardian cannot be found or is incapable of giving consent, or where the welfare of the child so demands.

An adoption order extinguishes the parental responsibility that a person other than the adopters (or adopter) has for the child. Where an order is made on the application of the partner of the parent, that parent keeps parental responsibility. Once adopted, the child has the same status as a child born to the adoptive parents, but may lose rights to the estates of those losing their parental responsibility.

REGISTRATION AND CERTIFICATES

All adoption orders made in England and Wales are required to be registered in the Adopted Children Register which also contains particulars of children adopted under registrable foreign adoptions. The General Register Office keeps this register from which certificates may be obtained in a similar way to birth certificates. The General Register Office also has equivalents in Scotland and Northern Ireland.

TRACING NATURAL PARENTS OR CHILDREN WHO HAVE BEEN ADOPTED

An adult adopted person may apply to the Registrar-General to obtain a certified copy of his/her birth certificate. Adoption agencies and adoption support agencies should provide services to adopted persons to assist them in obtaining information about their adoption and facilitate contact with their relatives. There is an Adoption Contact Register which provides a safe and confidential way for birth parents and other relatives to assure an adopted person that contact would be welcome. CoramBAAF (*see* below) can provide addresses of organisations which offer advice, information and counselling to adopted people, adoptive parents and people who have had their children adopted.

CORAMBAAF ADOPTION AND FOSTERING

ACADEMY, 41 Brunswick Square, London WC1N 1AF
T 020-7520 0300 W https://corambaaf.org.uk

SCOTLAND

The relevant legislation is the Adoption and Children (Scotland) Act 2007 which came into force on 28 September 2009. In addition, adoptions with a foreign element are governed by the Adoptions with a Foreign Element (Scotland) Regulations 2009. Pre-2009 adoptions are governed by Part IV of the Adoption (Scotland) Act 1978. The provisions of the 2007 act are similar to those described above. In Scotland, petitions for adoption are made to the sheriff court or the court of session.

ADOPTION AND FOSTERING ALLIANCE SCOTLAND,

Foxglove Offices/GF2, 14 Links Place, Edinburgh EH6 7EZ
T 0131-322 8490 W www.afascotland.com

BIRTHS (REGISTRATION)

It is the duty of the parents of a child born in England or Wales to register the birth within 42 days of the date of birth at the register office in the district in which the baby was born. If it is inconvenient to go to the district where the birth took place, the information for the registration may be given to a registrar in another district, who will send your details to the appropriate register office. Failure to register the birth within 42 days without reasonable cause may leave the parents liable to a penalty. If a birth has not been registered within 12 months of its occurrence it is possible for the late registration of the birth to be authorised by the Registrar-General, provided documentary evidence of the precise date and place of birth are satisfactory.

Births that take place in England may only be registered in English, but births that take place in Wales may be registered bilingually in Welsh and English. In order to do this, the details must be given in Welsh and the registrar must be able to understand and write in Welsh.

If the parents of the child were married to each other at the time of the birth (or conception), either the mother or the father may register the birth alone. If the parents were not married to each other at the time of the child's birth (or conception), the father's particulars may be entered in the register only where he attends the register office with the mother and they sign the birth register together. Where an unmarried parent is unable to attend the register office, either parent may submit to the registrar a statutory declaration of acknowledgement of parentage (this form may be obtained from any registrar in England or Wales or online at W www.gro.gov.uk); alternatively a parental responsibility agreement or appropriate court order may be produced to the registrar.

If the father's details are not included in the birth register, it may be possible to re-register the birth at a later date. If the parents do not register the birth of their child the following people may do so:

- an occupier of the house or an administrative member of staff of the hospital where the child was born
- a person who was present at the birth
- a person who is responsible for the child

Upon registration of the birth a short certificate is issued for free. It may be possible to register the birth while still at hospital. Hospitals will advise individually whether this is possible.

SAME-SEX COUPLES

Male couples must get a parental order from the court before they can be registered as parents. Female couples can include both of their names on the child's birth certificate when registering the birth; however the rules differ depending on whether or not they are in a civil partnership.

In the case of female civil partners, either woman can register the birth on her own if all of the following are true:

- the mother had the child by donor insemination or fertility treatment
- she was married or in a civil partnership at the time of the treatment

When a mother is not in a civil partnership, her partner can be seen as the child's second parent if both women:

- were treated together in the UK by a licensed clinic
- have made a 'parenthood agreement'

However, for both parents' details to be recorded on the birth certificate, the parents must do one of the following:

- register the birth jointly
- complete a 'statutory declaration of acknowledgement of parentage' form and one parent takes the signed form when she registers the birth
- get a document from the court (eg a court order) giving the second female parent parental responsibility and one parent shows the document when she registers the birth

BIRTHS ABROAD

There are certain countries where birth registrations may be made for British citizens overseas (for more details on British citizenship *see* below). The British consul or high commission may register the births and issue certificates which are then sent to the General Register Office. If a birth is registered by the British consul or high commission, the registration would show the person's claim to British citizenship, British overseas territories citizenship or British overseas citizenship. All consular birth registrations are now performed at the Foreign and Commonwealth Office's facility.

SCOTLAND

In Scotland the birth of a child must be registered within 21 days at the registration office of any registration district in Scotland.

If the child is born, either in or out of Scotland, on a ship, aircraft or land vehicle that ends its journey at any place in Scotland, the child, in most cases, will be registered as if born in that place.

CERTIFICATES OF BIRTHS, DEATHS OR MARRIAGES

Certificates of births, marriages and deaths that have taken place in England and Wales since 1837 can be obtained from the General Register Office (GRO).

Marriage or death certificates may also be obtained from the minister of the church in which the marriage or funeral took place. Any register office can advise about the best way to obtain certificates.

The fees for certificates are:

Online application:
- full certificate of birth, marriage, death or adoption, £9.25
- full certificate of birth, marriage, death or adoption with GRO reference supplied, £9.25

By postal/phone/fax application:
- full certificate of birth, marriage, death or adoption, £9.25
- full certificate of birth, marriage, death or adoption with GRO reference supplied, £9.25
- extra copies of the same birth, marriage or death certificate issued at the same time, £9.25

A priority service is available for a fee of £23.40.

A complete set of the GRO indexes including births, deaths and marriages, civil partnerships, adoptions and provisional indexes for births and deaths are available at the British Library, City of Westminster Archives Centre, Manchester Central Library, Newcastle City Library, Library of Birmingham, Bridgend Reference and Information Library and Plymouth Central Library. Copies of GRO indexes may also be held at some libraries, family history societies, local records offices and The Church of Jesus Christ of Latter Day Saints family history centres. Some organisations may not hold a complete record of indexes and a small fee may be charged by some of them. GRO indexes are also available online.

The Society of Genealogists has many records of baptisms, marriages and deaths prior to 1837.

SCOTLAND

Certificates of births, deaths or marriages that have taken place in Scotland since 1855 can be obtained from the National Records of Scotland (formerly the General Register Office for Scotland) or from the appropriate local registrar.

Applicable fees – local registrar:
- each extract or abbreviated certificate of birth, death, marriage, civil partnership or adoption within a month of registration, £10.00
- each extract or abbreviated certificate of birth, death, marriage, civil partnership or adoption outwith a month of registration, £15.00

A priority service is available for an additional fee.

The National Records of Scotland also keeps the Register of Divorces (including decrees of declaration of nullity of marriage), and holds parish registers dating from before 1855.

Applicable fees – National Records of Scotland:
- personal application, or postal, telephone or fax order: £15.00

A priority service for a response within 24 hours is available for an additional fee of £15.00.

A search of birth, death and marriage records including records of Church of Scotland parishes and other statutory records can be done at the Scotland's People Centre. There are also indexes to some of the old parish registers death and burial records in the library at the centre and indexes and images of census records from 1841–1911 are available. The charges for a full or part-day search pass is £15.00.

Online searching is also available. For more information, visit W www.scotlandspeople.gov.uk

THE GENERAL REGISTER OFFICE, General Register Office, Certificate Services Section, PO Box 2, Southport PR8 2JD T 0300-123 1837 W www.gro.gov.uk/gro/content/certificates

THE NATIONAL RECORDS OF SCOTLAND, HM General Register House, 2 Princes Street, Edinburgh EH1 3YT T 0131-334 0380 W www.nrscotland.gov.uk

SCOTLAND'S PEOPLE CENTRE, General Register House, 2 Princes Street, Edinburgh EH1 3YY T 0131-314 4300 W www.scotlandspeoplehub.gov.uk

THE SOCIETY OF GENEALOGISTS, 14 Charterhouse Buildings, Goswell Road, London EC1M 7BA T 020-7251 8799 W www.sog.org.uk

BRITISH NATIONALITY

There are different types of British nationality status: British citizenship; British overseas citizenship; British national (overseas); British overseas territories citizenship; British protected persons; and British subjects. The most widely held of these is British citizenship. Everyone born in the UK before 1 January 1983 became a British citizen when the British Nationality Act 1981 came into force, with the exception of children born to certain diplomatic staff working in the UK at the time. Individuals born outside the UK before 1 January 1983 but who at that date were citizens of the UK and colonies and had a right of abode in the UK also became British citizens. British citizens have the right to live permanently in the UK and are free to leave and re-enter the UK at any time.

A person born on or after 1 January 1983 in the UK (including, for this purpose, the Channel Islands and the Isle of Man) is entitled to British citizenship if he/she falls into one of the following categories:
- he/she has a parent who is a British citizen
- he/she has a parent who is settled in the UK
- he/she is a newborn infant found abandoned in the UK
- his/her parents subsequently settle in the UK or become British citizens and an application is made before he/she is 18
- he/she lives in the UK for the first ten years of his/her life and is not absent for more than 90 days in each of those years
- he/she is adopted in the UK and one of the adopters is a British citizen
- the home secretary consents to his/her registration while he/she is a minor
- if he/she has always been stateless and lives in the UK for a period of five years before his/her 22nd birthday
- if he/she has been born on or after 13 January 2010 to a parent who is a member of the UK armed forces
- if he/she has been born on or after 13 January 2010 and a parent becomes a member of the UK armed forces, and an application is made before he/she is 18

A person born outside the UK may acquire British citizenship if he/she falls into one of the following categories:
- he/she has a parent who is a British citizen otherwise than by descent, eg a parent who was born in the UK
- he/she has a parent who is a British citizen serving the crown or a European community institution overseas and was recruited to that service in the UK (including qualifying territories for those born on or after 21 May 2002) or in the European Community (for services within an EU institution); or if the applicant himself/herself has at any time been in crown, or similar, service under the government of a British overseas territory
- if he/she has been born on or after 13 January 2010 to a parent who is a member of the UK armed forces serving outside the UK and qualifying territories, is of good

character and (if he/she is a minor at the time of application) all parents then alive consent in signed writing
- the home secretary consents to his/her registration while he/she is a minor
- he/she is a British overseas territories citizen, a British overseas citizen, a British subject or a British protected person and has been lawfully resident in the UK for five years
- he/she is a British overseas territories citizen who acquired that citizenship from a connection with Gibraltar
- he/she is adopted or naturalised

Where parents are married, the status of either may confer citizenship on their child. Since July 2006, both parents are able to pass on nationality even if they are not married, provided that there is satisfactory evidence of paternity. For children born before July 2006, it must be shown that there is parental consent and that the child would have an automatic claim to citizenship or entitlement to registration had the parents been married. Where parents are not married, the status of the mother determines the child's citizenship.

Under the 1981 act, Commonwealth citizens and citizens of the Republic of Ireland were entitled to registration as British citizens before 1 January 1983. In 1983, citizens of the Falkland Islands were granted British citizenship.

Renunciation of British citizenship must be registered with the home secretary and will be revoked if no new citizenship or nationality is acquired within six months. If the renunciation was required in order to retain or acquire another citizenship or nationality, the citizenship may be reacquired only once. If the renunciation was for another reason, the home secretary may allow reacquisition more than once, depending on the circumstances. The secretary of state may deprive a person of a citizenship status if he or she is satisfied that the person has done anything seriously prejudicial to the vital interests of the UK, or a British overseas territory, unless making the order would have the effect of rendering such a person stateless. A person may also be deprived of a citizenship status which results from his registration or naturalisation if the secretary of state is satisfied that the registration or naturalisation was obtained by fraud, false representation or concealment of a material fact.

BRITISH DEPENDENT TERRITORIES CITIZENSHIP
Since 26 February 2002, this category of nationality no longer exists and has been replaced by British overseas territory citizenship.

If a person had this class of nationality only by reason of a connection to the territory of Hong Kong, they lost it automatically when Hong Kong was returned to the People's Republic of China. However, if after 30 June 1997, they had no other nationality and would have become stateless, or were born after 30 June 1997 and would have been born stateless (but had a parent who was a British national (overseas) or a British overseas citizen), they became a British overseas citizen.

BRITISH OVERSEAS CITIZENSHIP
Under the 1981 act, as amended by the British Overseas Territories Act 2002, this type of citizenship was conferred on any UK and colonies citizens who did not become either a British citizen or a British overseas territories citizen on 1 January 1983 and as such is now, for most purposes, only acquired by persons who would otherwise be stateless.

BRITISH OVERSEAS TERRITORIES CITIZENSHIP
This category of nationality replaced British dependent territories citizenship. Most commonly, this form of nationality is acquired where, after 31 December 1982, a person was a citizen of the UK and colonies and did not become a British citizen, and that person, and their parents or grandparents,

were born, registered or naturalised in the specified British overseas territory. However, on 21 May 2002, people became British citizens if they had British overseas territories citizenship by connection with any British overseas territory, except for the sovereign base areas of Akrotiri and Dhekelia in Cyprus.

RESIDUAL CATEGORIES
British subjects, British protected persons and British nationals (overseas) may be entitled to registration as British citizens on completion of five years' legal residence in the UK.

Citizens of the Republic of Ireland who were also British subjects before 1 January 1949 can retain that status if they fulfil certain conditions.

EUROPEAN UNION CITIZENSHIP
British citizens (including Gibraltarians who are registered for this purpose) are also EU citizens and are entitled to travel freely to other EU countries to work, study, reside and set up a business. EU citizens have the same rights with respect to the UK. At the time of writing, it is not known whether the UK's decision to withdraw from the EU will affect these rights.

NATURALISATION
Naturalisation is granted at the discretion of the home secretary. The basic requirements are lawful residence in the UK in the five years immediately preceding application (three years if the applicant is married to, or is the civil partner of a British citizen), good character, adequate knowledge of the English, Welsh or Scottish Gaelic language, passing the UK citizenship test and an intention to reside permanently in the UK.

STATUS OF ALIENS
Aliens, being persons without any of the above forms of British nationality, may not hold public office or vote in Britain and they may not own a British ship or aircraft. Citizens of the Republic of Ireland and Commonwealth citizens are not deemed to be aliens. Certain provisions of the Immigration and Asylum Act 1999 make provision about immigration and asylum and about procedures in connection with marriage by superintendent registrar's certificate.

CONSUMER LAW

SALE OF GOODS
The law in this area is enacted to protect buyers who deal as 'consumers' (where the seller is selling in the course of a business, the goods are of a type ordinarily bought for private use and the goods are purchased by a buyer who is not a business buyer).

A sale of goods contract is the most common type of contract. These are governed by the Consumer Rights Act 2015 (CRA), which was designed to modernise and simplify the law in this area by codifying consumer legislation, most notably incorporating the Sale of Goods Act 1979.

The CRA provides protection for buyers by implying terms into every business-to-consumer sale of goods contract. These terms include:
- that the goods must be of a standard such that a reasonable person would deem them to be of satisfactory quality, considering, among other relevant factors, any description of the goods given by the seller and their price. The goods should be of satisfactory quality for the purpose for which they are usually intended, as well as in appearance, and they should not pose safety concerns. Should, prior to purchase, any issue affecting the quality of the goods be made clear to the consumer, then the term will not be applied. The same is true if, prior to purchase, the consumer

has the opportunity to make a reasonable examination of the goods or a sample of them which would reveal any issue affecting their quality

- that goods must be suitable for the purpose for which the consumer has, expressly or implicitly, stated that they are intended. This term is applicable regardless of whether or not goods of such a nature are usually intended for this purpose, unless the consumer is advised otherwise by the trader and ignores such advice
- that any description of the goods provided by the seller must be accurate. If the seller provides both a description and a sample, the goods must ultimately correspond with the description, irrespective of whether they mostly correspond with the sample. This term is included even when the goods have been exposed for supply prior to purchase and selected by the consumer
- that goods will match any sample or model provided by the seller before purchase. In the case of the provision of a sample or a model, the goods must match the sample or model with the exception of any difference made clear to the consumer prior to purchase. Where a sample is provided, there must be no defect to the goods that a reasonable examination of the sample would not reveal
- that, in the event that the contract includes the installation of the goods, it is the duty of the seller to install or ensure that the goods are installed correctly
- that, in the event that goods include digital content, such digital content must comply with the contract for the provision of such content, or the goods will be considered as breaching the contract; and
- that the seller has the right to sell the goods, and that the goods have and will continue to have no charge or encumbrance that has not been made clear to the consumer prior to purchase. In the case of the hire of goods, the trader must have the right to transfer the goods for such a purpose

Under the CRA, which draws together and slightly amends the pre-existing rules under the Unfair Contract Terms Act 1977 and the Unfair Terms in Consumer Contracts Regulations 1999, these terms can not be excluded from contracts by the seller.

In a sale of secondhand goods by auction (at which individuals have the opportunity of attending the sale in person), a buyer does not deal as a consumer.

HIRE-PURCHASE AGREEMENTS

Terms similar to those implied in contracts of sales of goods are implied into contracts of hire-purchase, under the CRA. The Act limits the exclusion of these implied terms as before.

SUPPLY OF GOODS AND SERVICES

Before the CRA, the Supply of Goods and Services Act 1982 regulated other types of contracts (including for services, contracts under which ownership of goods pass and contracts for hire of goods). This Act has now also been amalgamated into the CRA. Similar terms to those above are implied into such contracts, however there are additional terms including:

- that the supplier will use reasonable care and skill in carrying out the service
- that the supplier will carry out the service in a reasonable time (unless the time has been agreed)
- that the supplier will make a reasonable charge (unless the charge or mechanism for its calculation has already been agreed)

The CRA Act limits the exclusion of these implied terms in a similar manner as before.

DIGITAL CONTENT

The CRA is the first statute to address the sale and supply of digital products, defined as 'data which are produced and supplied in digital form.' The Act applies to any digital content which is purchased or that which comes free alongside purchased services or goods. As above, implied terms for quality, fitness for purpose and adherence to description will be imposed on all consumer contracts. However, there is an extra term for contracts for digital content: that the seller has the right to provide such content.

These terms also apply to any future update or modification of the content. Should such future alterations fail to meet these standards, then the breach will be treated as having occurred at the time of supply rather than the point at which it was adapted.

Where digital content causes damage to other digital content or devices, and this could have been prevented where the seller had exercised reasonable skill and care, then that seller will be required to remedy the breach.

UNFAIR TERMS

The CRA has also consolidated the provisions of the Unfair Terms in Consumer Contracts Regulations 1999 that protected consumers against the imposition of unfair consumer contract terms. Where the terms have not been individually negotiated (ie where the terms were drafted in advance so that the consumer was unable to influence those terms), a term will be deemed unfair if it operates to the detriment of the consumer (ie causes a significant imbalance in the parties' rights and obligations arising under the contract). An unfair term does not bind the consumer but the contract may continue to bind the parties if it is capable of existing without the unfair term. The CRA contains a non-exhaustive list of terms that are regarded as potentially unfair. When a term does not fall into such a category, whether it will be regarded as fair or not will depend on many factors, including the nature of the goods or services, the surrounding circumstances (such as the bargaining strength of both parties) and the other terms in the contract.

CONSUMER PROTECTION

The Consumer Protection from Unfair Trading Regulations 2008 (CPRs) replaced much previous consumer protection regulation, including the majority of the Trade Descriptions Act 1968. The CPRs prohibit 31 specific practices, including pyramid schemes. In addition the CPRs prohibit business sellers from making misleading actions and misleading omissions, which cause, or are likely to cause, the average consumer to take a different transactional decision. There is also a general duty not to trade unfairly. The CPRs were amended by the Consumer Protection (Amendment) Regulations 2014, which entered into force on 1 October 2014 and introduced a new direct civil right of redress for consumers against businesses for misleading and aggressive practices, as well as extending the CPRs to cover misleading and aggressive demands for payment.

Under the Consumer Protection Act 1987, producers of goods are liable for any injury, death or damage to any property exceeding £275 caused by a defect in their product (subject to certain defences).

Consumers are also afforded protection under the Consumer Contracts (Information, Cancellation and Additional Charges) Regulations 2013, which came into force on 13 June 2014.

CONSUMER CREDIT

In matters relating to the provision of credit (or the supply of goods on hire or hire-purchase), consumers are also protected by the Consumer Credit Act 1974 (as amended by the Consumer Credit Act 2006). The Act was most recently amended by a number of statutory instruments made under the Financial Services and Markets Act 2000. These came into force on 1 April 2014 and represent a major overhaul of the consumer credit regime which was carried out in order to implement the recent EU Consumer Credit Directive. Under the new regime, responsibility for consumer credit regulation has been transferred from the Office of Fair Trading (OFT), which has ceased to exist, to the Financial Conduct Authority (FCA). Previously, a licence issued by the OFT was required in order to conduct a consumer credit, consumer hire or an ancillary credit business, subject to certain exemptions. The requirement to obtain a licence from the OFT has been replaced by the need to obtain authorisation from the FCA to carry out a consumer credit 'regulated' activity, which is likewise subject to certain exemptions. Provisions of the 1974 Act as amended include:

- in order for a creditor to enforce a regulated agreement, the agreement must comply with certain formalities and must be properly executed. An improperly executed regulated agreement is enforceable only on an order of the court. The debtor must also be given specified information by the creditor or his/her broker or agent during the negotiations which take place before the signing of the agreement. The agreement must also state certain information to ensure that the debtor or hirer is aware of the rights and duties conferred or imposed on him/her and the protection and remedies available to him/her under the Act
- the right to withdraw from or cancel some contracts depending on the circumstances. For example, subject to certain exceptions, a borrower may withdraw from a regulated credit agreement within 14 days without giving any reason. The exceptions include agreements for credit exceeding £60,260 and agreements secured on land. The right to withdraw applies only to the credit agreement itself and not to goods or services purchased with it. The borrower must also repay the credit and any interest
- if the debtor is in breach of the agreement, the creditor must serve a default notice before taking any action such as repossessing the goods
- if the agreement is a hire purchase or conditional sale agreement, the creditor cannot repossess the goods without a court order if the debtor has paid one third of the total price of the goods
- in agreements where the relationship between the creditor and the debtor is unfair to the debtor, the court may alter or set aside some of the terms of the agreement

It is intended that the statutory basis of consumer credit regulation, under the 1974 Act, will be replaced by a rules-based approach under the new regime. The FCA will be reviewing the statutory framework over the next few years and will develop rule-based alternatives where possible.

SCOTLAND

The legislation governing the sale and supply of goods applies to Scotland as follows:

- the Consumer Rights Act 2015 (with the exception of chapter three)
- the Sale of Goods Act 1979 applies with some modifications and it has been amended by the Sale and Supply of Goods Act 1994
- the Supply of Goods (Implied Terms) Act 1973 applies
- the Supply of Goods and Services Act 1982 does not extend to Scotland but some of its provisions were introduced by the Sale and Supply of Goods Act 1994
- only Parts II and III of the Unfair Contract Terms Act 1977 apply
- the Trade Descriptions Act 1968 applies with minor modifications
- the Consumer Credit Act 1974 applies
- the Consumer Credit Act 2006 applies
- the Consumer Protection Act 1987 applies
- the General Product Safety Regulations 2005 apply

- the Unfair Terms in Consumer Contracts (Amendment) Regulations 2001 apply
- the Consumer Protection (Distance Selling) Regulations 2000 apply
- the Consumer Protection from Unfair Trading Regulations 2008 apply

PROCEEDINGS AGAINST THE CROWN

Until 1947, proceedings against the Crown were generally possible only by a procedure known as a petition of right, which put the private litigant at a considerable disadvantage. The Crown Proceedings Act 1947 placed the Crown (not the sovereign in his/her private capacity, but as the embodiment of the state) largely in the same position as a private individual and made proceedings in the high court involving the Crown subject to the same rules as any other case. The act did not, however, extinguish or limit the Crown's prerogative or statutory powers, and it continued the immunity of HM ships and aircraft. It also left certain Crown privileges unaffected. The act largely abolished the special procedures which previously applied to civil proceedings by and against the Crown. Civil proceedings may be initiated against the appropriate government department or, if there is doubt regarding which is the appropriate department, against the attorney-general.

In Scotland proceedings against the Crown founded on breach of contract could be taken before the 1947 act and no special procedures applied. The Crown could, however, claim certain special pleas. The 1947 act applies in part to Scotland and brings the practice of the two countries as closely together as the different legal systems permit. As a result of the Scotland Act 1998, actions against government departments should be raised against the Lord Advocate or the advocate-general. Actions should be raised against the Lord Advocate where the department involved administers a devolved matter. Devolved matters include agriculture, education, housing, local government, health and justice. Actions should be raised against the advocate-general where the department is dealing with a reserved matter. Reserved matters include defence, foreign affairs and social security.

DEATHS

WHEN A DEATH OCCURS

If the death (including stillbirth) was expected, the doctor who attended the deceased during their final illness should be contacted. If the death was sudden or unexpected, the family doctor (if known) and police should be contacted. If the cause of death is quite clear, the doctor will provide:

- a medical certificate that shows the cause of death
- a formal notice that states that the doctor has signed the medical certificate and that explains how to get the death registered
- if the death was known to be caused by a natural illness but the doctor wishes to know more about the cause of death, he/she may ask the relatives for permission to carry out a post-mortem examination

In England and Wales a coroner is responsible for investigating deaths occurring:

- when there is no doctor who can issue a medical certificate of cause of death
- no doctor has treated the deceased during his or her last illness or when the doctor attending the patient did not see him or her within 14 days before death, or after death
- the death occurred during an operation or before recovery from the effect of an anaesthetic
- the death was sudden and unexplained or attended by suspicious circumstances

- the death might be due to an industrial injury or disease, or to accident, violence, neglect or abortion
- the death occurred in prison or in police custody

The doctor will write on the formal notice that the death has been referred to the coroner; if the post-mortem shows that death was due to natural causes, the coroner may issue a notification which gives the cause of death so that the death can be registered. If the cause of death was violent or unnatural, is still undetermined after a post-mortem, or took place in prison or police custody, the coroner must hold an inquest. The coroner must hold an inquest in these circumstances even if the death occurred abroad (and the body has been returned to England or Wales).

In Scotland the office of coroner does not exist. The local procurator fiscal inquires into sudden or suspicious deaths. A fatal accident inquiry will be held before the sheriff where the death has resulted from an accident during the course of the employment of the person who has died, or where the person who has died was in legal custody or a child required to be kept or detained in secure accommodation, or where the Lord Advocate deems it in the public interest that an inquiry be held.

REGISTERING A DEATH

In England and Wales the death can be registered at any register office, although if it is registered by the registrar of births and deaths for the district in which it occurred, the necessary documents can be obtained on the same day. A death which occurs in Scotland can be registered in any registration district in Scotland. Information concerning a death can be given before any registrar of births and deaths in England and Wales. The registrar will pass the relevant details to the registrar for the district where the death occurred, who will then register the death.

In England and Wales the death must normally be registered within five days (unless the registrar says this period can be extended); in Scotland within eight days. If the death has been referred to the coroner/local procurator fiscal it cannot be registered until the registrar has received authority from the coroner/local procurator fiscal to do so. Failure to register a death involves a penalty in England and Wales and may lead to a court decree being granted by a sheriff in Scotland. A stillbirth normally needs to be registered within 42 days, and at the latest within three months. In many cases this can be done at the hospital or at the local register office. In Scotland this must be done within 21 days.

If the death occurred at a house or hospital, the death may be registered by:

- any relative of the deceased
- any person present at the death
- the owner or occupier of the house or hospital if he/she knew of the occurrence of the death
- any person making the funeral arrangements with the funeral director
- an administrator from the hospital
- in Scotland, the deceased's executor or legal representative

For deaths that took place elsewhere, the death may be registered by:

- any relative of the deceased
- someone present at the death
- someone who found the body
- a person in charge of the body
- any person making the funeral arrangements with the funeral director

The majority of deaths are registered by a relative of the deceased. The registrar would normally allow one of the other listed persons to register the death only if there were no relatives available.

The person registering the death should take the medical certificate of the cause of death (signed by a doctor) with them; it is also useful, though not essential, to take the deceased's birth and marriage/civil partnership certificates, council tax bill, driving licence, passport, NHS medical card, pension documentation and life assurance details. The details given to the registrar must be absolutely correct, otherwise it may be difficult to change them later. The person registering the death should check the entry carefully before it is signed. The registrar will issue a certificate for burial or cremation, and a certificate of registration of death (commonly known as a 'death certificate' which is issued for social security purposes if the deceased received a state pension or benefits) – both free of charge. A death certificate is a certified copy of the entry in the death register; copies can be provided on payment of a fee and may be required for the following purposes, in particular by the executor or administrator when sorting out the deceased's affairs:

- the will
- bank and building society accounts
- savings bank certificates and premium bonds
- insurance policies
- pension claims

If the death occurred abroad or on a foreign ship or aircraft, the death should be registered according to the local regulations of the relevant country and a death certificate should be obtained. In many countries the death can also be registered with the British consulate in that country and a record will be kept at the General Register Office. This avoids the expense of bringing the body back.

After 12 months (three months in Scotland) of death or the finding of a dead body, no death can be registered without the written authority of the registrar-general.

BURIAL AND CREMATION

In most circumstances in England and Wales a certificate for burial or cremation must be obtained from the registrar before the burial or cremation can take place. If the death has been referred to the coroner, an order for burial or a certificate for cremation must be obtained. In Scotland a death or still birth must be registered in order that the appropriate certificate can be obtained to allow burial or cremation of the body.

Funeral costs can normally be repaid out of the deceased's estate and should be given priority over any other claims. If the deceased has left a will it may contain directions concerning the funeral; however, these directions need not be followed by the executor.

The deceased's papers should also indicate whether a grave space had already been arranged. This information will be contained in a document known as a 'Deed of Grant'. Most town churchyards and many suburban churchyards are no longer open for burial because they are full. Most cemeteries are non-denominational and may be owned by local authorities or private companies; fees vary.

If the body is to be cremated, an application form, two cremation certificates (for which there is a charge) or a certificate for cremation if the death was referred to the coroner, and a certificate signed by the medical referee must be completed in addition to the certificate for burial or cremation (the form is not required if the coroner has issued a certificate for cremation). All the forms are available from the funeral director or crematorium. Most crematoria are run by local authorities; the fees can include the medical referee's fee and the use of the chapel. Ashes may be scattered, buried in a churchyard or cemetery, or kept.

The registrar must be notified of the date, place and means of disposal of the body within 96 hours (England and Wales) or three days (Scotland).

If the death occurred abroad or on a foreign ship or aircraft, a local burial or cremation may be arranged. If the body is to be brought back to England or Wales, a death certificate from the relevant country or an authorisation for the removal of the body from the country of death from the coroner or relevant authority, together with a certificate of embalming, will be required. The British consulate can help to arrange this documentation. To arrange a funeral in England or Wales, an authenticated translation of a foreign death certificate or a death certificate issued in Scotland or Northern Ireland which must show the cause of death, is needed, together with a certificate of no liability to register from the registrar in England and Wales in whose sub-district it is intended to bury or cremate the body. If it is intended to cremate the body, a cremation order will be required from the Home Office or a certificate for cremation. If the body is to be cremated in Scotland, a certificate permitting this must be obtained from the Death Certification Review Service run by Healthcare Improvement Scotland.

THE GENERAL REGISTER OFFICE, General Register Office, PO Box 2, Southport PR8 2JD **T** 0300-123 1837 **W** www.gro.gov.uk/gro/content/certificates

THE NATIONAL RECORDS OF SCOTLAND, New Register House, 3 West Register Street, Edinburgh EH1 3YT **T** 0131-334 0380 **W** www.nrscotland.gov.uk

DIVORCE, DISSOLUTION AND RELATED MATTERS

Divorce is the legal process which ends a marriage. The process is the same whether the parties are of the opposite or same sex pursuant to the Marriage (Same Sex Couples) Act 2013. Dissolution is a similar process which ends a civil partnership. Divorce and dissolution should be distinguished from judicial separation which does not legally dissolve the marriage/civil partnership but removes the legal requirement for a married couple to live together.

DIVORCE

An application for a matrimonial order for divorce may only be presented to the court after one year of marriage and it must be based on matters which occurred within that time. The spouse who lodges this document is known as the 'petitioner' throughout the divorce proceedings and the other spouse is the 'respondent'.

Whether the English court may or may not have jurisdiction to deal with any divorce will depend on where the parties spent their married life and whether or not one party has retained their residence or domicile in England (and Wales). If there is a dispute as to which of two jurisdictions should host the divorce, where the two jurisdictions likely to be relevant are EU countries then the usual rule is that the divorce takes place in the country where the petition is filed first. The exception to this rule is Denmark, which opted out of the EU regulation which determines forums in this way.

If the two countries are not within the EU, or one of them is Denmark, then the forum of divorce may be determined by which is the more appropriate or convenient. In these circumstances, an election of a country in a pre-nuptial agreement can be very important in resolving that dispute, although it cannot override the 'first in time' rule between EU countries (except Denmark) referred to above (save in the case of maintenance claims).

Some EU countries have signed up to the Convention on the Recognition of Divorces and Legal Separations which would allow a couple to elect a choice of law even in EU countries whereby one country would be required to apply the law of another. For the time being, England has not signed up to that convention and would apply English law only.

There is only one ground for divorce, namely that the marriage has broken down irretrievably. This ground must be 'proved' by one of the following facts:

- the respondent has committed adultery and the petitioner finds it intolerable to live with him/her
- the respondent has behaved in such a way that the petitioner cannot reasonably be expected to live with him/her
- the respondent has deserted the petitioner for a continuous period of at least two years immediately prior to the petition
- the two spouses have lived apart for at least two years immediately prior to the petition and the respondent agrees to a divorce
- the two spouses have lived apart for at least five years immediately prior to the petition

If the court is satisfied that the petitioner has proved one of those facts then it must grant a decree nisi (*see* below) unless it is satisfied that the marriage has not broken down.

DECREE NISI

If the judge is satisfied that the petitioner has proved the contents of the divorce petition, a date will be set for the pronouncement of the decree nisi in open court. The decree nisi is a preliminary decree of divorce; the marriage will not be legally dissolved until the decree absolute. Neither party needs to attend and all the proceedings up to this point are usually carried out on paper.

DECREE ABSOLUTE

The final step in the divorce procedure is to obtain a decree absolute which formally ends the marriage. The petitioner can apply for this six weeks and one day after the date of the decree nisi. If the petitioner does not apply the respondent can apply, but only after three months from the earliest date on which the petitioner could have applied.

A decree absolute will not usually be granted until the parties have agreed, or the court has dealt with, the parties' financial situation (*see* below for details of financial provision).

DISSOLUTION OF CIVIL PARTNERSHIPS

The legal process for dissolution of a civil partnership follows a model closely based on divorce. Irretrievable breakdown of the partnership is the sole ground for dissolution. The facts to be proved to establish this are the same as for divorce, with the exception of adultery which, due to its legal definition, can only apply to opposite sex couples. Adultery can, however, be used as an example of unreasonable behaviour.

FINANCIAL RELIEF ANCILLARY TO DIVORCE, NULLITY AND JUDICIAL SEPARATION

Following a petition for divorce, nullity or judicial separation, it is open to either spouse or former spouse to make a claim for financial provision provided they have not remarried. It is common practice for such an application to be made at the same time, or shortly after, a divorce petition has been issued. The courts have wide powers to make financial provision where a marriage breaks down. Orders can be made for:

- spousal maintenance (periodical payments) which can be capitalised into a lump sum
- lump sum payments
- adjustment or transfer of interests in property
- adjustment of interests in trusts and settlements
- orders relating to pensions

EXERCISE OF THE COURT'S POWERS TO ORDER FINANCIAL PROVISION

The court must exercise its powers so as to achieve an outcome which is fair between the parties, although it has a wide discretion in determining what is a fair financial outcome. It will consider the worldwide assets of both parties, whether liquid or illiquid. In exercising its discretion, the court has to consider a range of statutory factors including:

- the income, earning capacity, property and other financial resources which either party has or is likely to have in the foreseeable future, including, in the case of earning capacity, any increase in that capacity which it would in the opinion of the court be reasonable to expect a party to the marriage to take steps to acquire

- the financial needs, obligations and responsibilities which each of the parties to the marriage has or is likely to have in the foreseeable future
- the standard of living enjoyed by the family before the breakdown of the marriage
- the age of each party to the marriage and the duration of the marriage
- any physical or mental disability of either of the parties to the marriage
- the contribution which each of the parties has made or is likely to make in the foreseeable future to the welfare of the family, including any contribution by looking after the home or caring for the family
- the conduct of each of the parties, if that conduct is such that it would in the opinion of the court be inequitable to disregard it
- the value to each of the parties to the marriage of any benefit which, by reason of the dissolution of that marriage, that party will lose the chance of acquiring

When considering the above factors, the court must give first consideration to the welfare of any child of the family.

The court has a wide discretion in considering these factors in order to achieve an outcome it considers to be fair. The court's approach changed dramatically following the House of Lords decision of *White v White* in October 2000 where it was said that, after providing for the parties' reasonable needs, the remaining assets should be shared.

In the House of Lords cases of Miller and McFarlane the court refined the thinking in the White case to say that the court should strive to achieve a fair result by considering three strands:

- the needs of the parties going forward
- compensation for any economic disparity between the parties (such as where one party has sacrificed their career to become a full-time parent)
- sharing

In October 2010, the supreme court gave judgment in *Radmacher v Granatino* which made it clear that a person now entering into a pre-nuptial agreement will be considered to have intended to be held to that agreement. However, the court will still be able to decide as to whether the agreement is fair and whether the terms setting out the financial provision on divorce should be enforced in whole or in part. The supreme court gave some guidelines on when a pre-nuptial agreement would be considered 'fair', but ultimately it depends on the facts of the individual case.

The Law Commission's Marital Property, Needs and Agreements Report, published in February 2014, proposed the introduction of 'qualifying nuptial agreements' which would be enforceable contracts allowing couples to make binding agreements concerning the financial consequences of divorce or dissolution. The commission appended a draft Nuptial Agreements bill to the report. In order for an agreement to qualify, certain procedural safeguards would need to be met. Agreements could not be used by parties to contract out of meeting the financial needs of the other or of any children. The government acknowledged the commissions's recommendations, but as yet has not taken steps to implement any reform.

FINANCIAL PROVISION ON DISSOLUTION OF A CIVIL PARTNERSHIP

The Civil Partnership Act 2004 makes provisions for financial relief for civil partners generally and extends the same rights and responsibilities invoked by marriage. Again the court must consider a number of factors when exercising its discretion and

must take into account all of the circumstances of the case while giving first consideration to the welfare of any child of the family who is under 18. The list of statutory factors the court must consider resemble those for marriage and it is likely that the interpretation of these factors will be based on the courts' interpretation of the factors relating to marriage.

COHABITING COUPLES

There is no such thing as a common law spouse. Unmarried couples do not benefit from the same statutory protection afforded to married couples. Instead, the rights of cohabitees are based on property law and trust interests. Therefore, it is advisable to consider entering into a contract, or 'cohabitation agreement', which establishes how money, property and the care of any children should be divided in the event of a relationship breakdown.

The Cohabitation Rights bill 2017–19 seeks to introduce certain protections for cohabitees during their lifetime and on death, It received its first reading in the House of Lords on 5 July 2017, but has made no further progress. Thus, cohabitation agreements continue to be governed by the same general principles of property, trust, and contract law.

FINANCIAL PROVISION FOR CHILDREN

Under the Child Support Act 1991, all parents are under a legal obligation to support their children financially. A parent who does not have day-to-day care of a child is under a duty to pay child maintenance to the parent who does.

Parents can arrange child maintenance themselves (a so-called 'family based arrangement') or through statutory child maintenance schemes managed by the Child Maintenance Service (CMS), (formerly the Child Support Agency (CSA)).

From 31 December 2017, CMS will handle all child maintenance arrangements (save for some CSA cases opened before December 2013 with outstanding liabilities, which will continue to be managed by CSA during the 'transitional period' until 31 December 2018).

There is a £20 application fee for applying to CMS (unless the applicant is under the age of 18 or a victim of domestic abuse), which covers the costs for calculating the amount of child maintenance, the provision to both parties of a yearly updated calculation using HMRC data and provision of information about 'Direct Pay' services.

There are three different methods of calculating child support under the statutory child maintenance schemes:

- the 'old' scheme (for all applications up until 3 March 2003)
- the net income scheme (for applications from 3 March 2003)
- the gross income scheme (for all new applications since 25 November 2013)

All CMS child maintenance calculations will be dealt with under the gross income scheme. CMS uses the paying parent's gross annual income from the latest available tax year (using information obtained from HMRC) as a starting point to work out child maintenance with reference to the gross income maximum of £156,000. Once the gross income information is received, the CMS applies a specific formula to work out the level of child maintenance payable. The child maintenance calculation may only be reassessed annually, unless the income variation is 25 per cent or more or in cases involving long-term illness or redundancy. It is a criminal offence to make a false statement or representation or to withhold information from the CMS and also to fail to notify CMS of a change of address or other change of circumstances.

Under the gross income scheme, it is mandatory for parents to have a conversation with the Child Maintenance Options (CMO) team to discuss their choices and consider alternatives before they proceed with their application. The CMO will discuss the various options available to parents if they cannot agree a 'family-based arrangement' between themselves:

- 'Direct Pay' (previously known as 'Maintenance Direct' under CSA arrangements) which enables parents to keep control of making and receiving payments. The statutory service works out the payment amounts for parents but will not be involved in collection
- 'Collect and Pay' (previously known as the 'full collection service' under CSA arrangements) whereby CMS calculates how much maintenance the paying parent owes. If the Collect and Pay Service is used, parties will be required to pay a fee for use of the service. Paying parents are required to pay a 20 per cent fee on top of their regular child maintenance payment and receiving parents will have 4 per cent of their child maintenance payment deducted from the total they receive

If payments are not made on time, a range of enforcement actions can be taken by CMS. CMS will contact the paying parent to seek continuing payments. Where there is persistent non-payment, the CMS is able to take money directly from the paying parent, either from their earnings or bank account, or to take court action. There are CMS fees for pursuing enforcement action, which may affect the eventual amount of child maintenance received by the receiving party.

Provision is also made under Schedule 1 of the Children Act 1989 for unmarried parents, step-parents and guardians to apply to the court for periodical payments, lump sum and property adjustment orders.

SCOTLAND

Although some provisions are similar to those for England and Wales, there is separate legislation for Scotland covering nullity of marriage, judicial separation, divorce and ancillary matters. The principal legislation in relation to family law in Scotland is the Family Law (Scotland) Act 1985. The Family Law (Scotland) Act 2006 came in to force on 4 May 2006, and introduced reforms to various aspects of Scottish family law. The following is confined to major points on which the law in Scotland differs from that of England and Wales.

An action for judicial separation or divorce may be raised in the court of session; it may also be raised in the sheriff court if either party was resident in the sheriffdom for 40 days immediately before the date of the action or for 40 days ending not more than 40 days before the date of the action and has no known residence in Scotland at that date. The fee for starting a divorce petition in the sheriff court is £153.

The grounds for raising an action of divorce in Scotland are set down in The Divorce (Scotland) Act 1976 and have been subject to reform in terms of the 2006 act. The current grounds for divorce are:

- the defender has committed adultery. When adultery is cited as proof that the marriage has broken down irretrievably, it is not necessary in Scotland to prove that it is also intolerable for the pursuer to live with the defender
- the defender's behaviour is such that the pursuer cannot reasonably be expected to cohabit with the defender
- there has been no cohabitation between the parties for one year prior to the raising of the action for divorce, and the defender consents to the granting of decree of divorce
- there has been no cohabitation between the parties for two years prior to the raising of the action for divorce
- the marriage has broken down irretrievably
- an interim gender recognition certificate under the Gender Recognition Act 2004 has, after the date of marriage, been issued to either party to the marriage. However, as a result of changes under the Marriage and Civil Partnership (Scotland) Act 2014, this ground of divorce will sometimes not be available where a full gender recognition certificate has been issued under the 2004 Act

The previously available ground of desertion was abolished by the 2006 Act.

A simplified procedure for 'do-it-yourself divorce' was introduced in 1983 for certain divorces. If the action is based on one or two years' separation and will not be opposed or because a gender recognition certificate has been issued; there are no children under 16; no financial claims; there is no sign that the applicant's spouse is unable to manage his or her affairs through mental illness or handicap; and there are no other court proceedings underway which might result in the end of the marriage, the applicant can access the appropriate forms to enable him or her to proceed on the Scottish Courts and Tribunals' website. From 25 April 2018 the fee is £123, however the applicant may be exempt from paying the fee if they are in receipt of certain benefits; or if legal advice and assistance is being provided by a solicitor in terms of the Legal Aid (Scotland) Act 1986.

Where a divorce action has been raised, it may be put on hold for a variety of reasons. In all actions for divorce an extract decree, which brings the marriage to an end, will be made available 14 days after the divorce has been granted. Unlike in England, there is no decree nisi, only a final decree of divorce. Parties must ensure that all financial issues have been resolved prior to divorce, as it is not possible to seek further financial provision after divorce has been granted.

FINANCIAL PROVISION

In relation to financial provision on divorce, the first, and most important, principle is fair sharing of the matrimonial property. There is a presumption that fair share means an equal share of the matrimonial property, which can be departed from if justified by special circumstances. In terms of Scots law matrimonial property is defined as all property acquired by either spouse from the date of marriage up to the date of separation. Property acquired before the marriage is not deemed to be matrimonial unless it was acquired for use by the parties as a family home or as furniture for that home. Property acquired after the date of separation is not matrimonial property. Any property acquired by either of the parties by way of gift or inheritance during the marriage is excluded and does not form part of the matrimonial property.

When considering whether to make an award of financial provision a court shall also take account of any economic advantage derived by either party to the marriage as a result of contributions, financial or otherwise, by the other, and of any economic disadvantage suffered by either party for the benefit of the other party. The court must also ensure that the economic burden of caring for a child under the age of 16 is shared fairly between the parties.

A court can also consider making an order requiring one party to pay the other party a periodical allowance for a certain period of time following divorce. Such an order may be appropriate in cases where there is insufficient capital to effect a fair sharing of the matrimonial property. Orders for periodical allowance are uncommon, as courts will favour a 'clean break' where possible.

CHILDREN

The court has the power to award a residence order in respect of any children of the marriage or to make an order regulating the child's contact with the non-resident parent. The court will only make such orders if it is deemed better for the child to do so than to make no order at all, and the welfare of the children is of paramount importance. The fact that a spouse has caused the breakdown of the marriage does not in itself preclude him/her from being awarded residence.

NULLITY

An action for 'declaration of nullity' can be brought if someone with a legitimate interest is able to show that the marriage is void or voidable. Although the grounds on which a marriage may be void or voidable are similar to those on which a marriage can be declared invalid in England, there are some differences. Where a spouse is capable of sexual intercourse but refuses to consummate the marriage, this is not a ground for nullity in Scots law, though it could be a ground for divorce. Where a spouse was suffering from venereal disease at the time of marriage and the other spouse did not know, this is not a ground for nullity in Scots law, neither is the fact that a wife was pregnant by another man at the time of marriage without the knowledge of her husband.

COHABITING COUPLES
The law in Scotland now provides certain financial and property rights for cohabiting couples in terms of the Family Law (Scotland) Act 2006, or 'the 2006 Act'. The relevant 2006 Act provisions do not place cohabitants in Scotland on an equal footing with married couples or civil partners, but provide some rights for cohabitants in the event that the relationship is terminated by separation or death. The provisions relate to couples who cease to cohabit after 4 May 2006.

The legislation provides for a presumption that most contents of the home shared by the cohabitants are owned in equal shares. A former cohabitant can also seek financial provision on termination of the relationship in the form of a capital payment if they can successfully demonstrate that they have been financially disadvantaged, and that conversely the other cohabitant has been financially advantaged, as a consequence of contributions made (financial or otherwise). An order can also be made in respect of the economic burden of caring for a child of whom the cohabitants are the parents. Such a claim must be made no later than one year after the day on which the cohabitants cease to cohabit.

The 2006 Act also provides that a cohabitant may make a claim on their partner's estate in the event of that partner's death, providing that there is no will. A claim of this nature must be made no later than six months after the date of the partner's death.

THE CENTRAL FAMILY COURT, First Avenue House, 42–49 High Holborn, London WC1 6NP T 020-7421 8594

THE COURT OF SESSION, Parliament House, Parliament Square, Edinburgh EH1 1RQ T 0131-225 2595 W www.scotcourts.gov.uk

THE CHILD MAINTENANCE SERVICE, T 0800-171 2033 W www.gov.uk/child-maintenance

EMPLOYMENT LAW

EMPLOYEES
A fundamental distinction in UK employment law is that drawn between an employee and someone who is self-employed. Further, there is an important, intermediate category introduced by legislation: 'workers' covers all employees but also catches others who do not have full employment status. An 'employee' is someone who has entered into or works under a contract of employment, while a 'worker' has entered into or works under a contract whereby he undertakes to do or perform personally any work or services for another party whose status is not that of a client or customer. Whether or not someone is an employee or a worker as opposed to being genuinely self-employed is an important and complex question, for it determines that person's statutory rights and protections. For certain purposes, such as protection against discrimination, protection extends to some genuinely self-employed people as well as workers and employees.

The greater the level of control that the employer has over the work carried out, the greater the depth of integration of the employee in the employer's business, and the closer the obligations to provide and perform work between the parties, the more likely it is that the parties will be employer and employee.

PAY AND CONDITIONS
The Employment Rights Act 1996 consolidated the statutory provisions relating to employees' rights. Employers must give each employee employed for one month or more a written statement containing the following information:
- names of employer and employee
- date when employment began and the date on which the employee's period of *continuous* employment began (taking into account any employment with a previous employer which counts towards that period)
- the scale, rate or other method of calculating remuneration and intervals at which it will be paid
- job title or description of job
- hours and the permitted place(s) of work and, where there are several such places, the address of the employer
- holiday entitlement and holiday pay
- provisions concerning incapacity for work due to sickness and injury, including provisions for sick pay
- details of pension scheme(s)
- length of notice the employee is obliged to give and entitled to receive in order to terminate the contract of employment
- if the employment is not intended to be permanent, the period for which it is expected to continue or, if it is for a fixed term, the end date of the contract
- details of any collective agreement (including the parties to the agreement) which directly affects the terms of employment
- details of disciplinary and grievance procedures (including the individual to whom a complaint should be made and the process of making that complaint)
- if the employee is to work outside the UK for more than one month, the period of such work and the currency in which payment is made and any additional remuneration or benefits payable to them
- a note stating whether a contracting-out certificate is in force

This must be given to the employee within two months of the start of their employment.

If the employer does not provide the written statement within two months (or a statement of any changes to these particulars within one month of the changes being made) then the employee can complain to an employment tribunal, which can specify the information that the employer should have given. When, in the context of an employee's successful tribunal claim, the employer is also found to have been in breach of the duty to provide the written statement at the time proceedings were commenced, the tribunal must award the employee two weeks' pay, and may award four weeks' pay, subject to the statutory cap, unless it would be unjust or inequitable to do so.

The Working Time Regulations 1998, the National Minimum Wage Act 1998, Employment Relations Act 1999, the Employment Act 2002 and the Employment Act 2008 now supplement the 1996 Act.

FLEXIBLE WORKING
The Flexible Working Regulations 2014 gives all employees, from 30 June 2014, the right to apply for flexible working after continuously working for the same employer for at least 26 weeks. An employer must consider and decide upon a request within three months and must have a sound business reason for rejecting any request. If an application under the act is not dealt with in accordance with a prescribed procedure, or is rejected on other than specific grounds, the employee may complain to an employment tribunal.

SICK PAY
Employees absent from work through illness or injury are entitled to receive Statutory Sick Pay (SSP) from the employer from the fourth day of absence for a maximum period of 28 weeks. The right to SSP will cease where an employee has had linked periods of sickness that have spanned a period of three years.

MATERNITY AND PARENTAL RIGHTS

Under the Employment Relations Act 1999, the Employment Act 2002, the Maternity and Parental Leave Regulations 1999 (as amended in 2002, 2006 and 2014), the Paternity and Adoption Leave Regulations 2002 and 2003, the Additional Paternity Leave Regulations 2010 and the Shared Parental Leave Regulations 2014, both men and women are entitled to take leave when they become a parent (including by adoption). Women are protected from discrimination, detriment or dismissal by reason of their pregnancy or maternity, including discrimination by association and by perception. Men and adoptive parents are protected from suffering a detriment or dismissal for taking paternity, adoption or parental leave.

Any woman who needs to attend an antenatal appointment on the advice of a registered medical professional is entitled to paid leave from work to attend. All pregnant women are entitled to a maximum period of maternity leave of 52 weeks. This comprises 26 weeks' ordinary maternity leave, followed immediately by 26 weeks' additional maternity leave. A woman who takes ordinary maternity leave normally has the right to return to the job in which she was employed before her absence. If she takes additional maternity leave, she is entitled to return to the same job or, if that is not reasonably practicable, to another job that is suitable and appropriate for her to do. There is a two-week period of compulsory maternity leave, immediately following the birth of the child, wherein the employer is not permitted to allow the mother to work.

A woman will qualify for Statutory Maternity Pay (SMP), which is payable for up to 39 weeks, if she has been continuously employed for not less than 26 weeks prior to the 15th week before the expected week of childbirth. For further information *see* Social Welfare, Employer Payments.

Employees are entitled to adoption leave and adoption pay (at the same rates as SMP) subject to fulfilment of similar criteria to those in relation to maternity leave and pay, but note that there is a 26-week qualifying period for adoption leave. Where a couple is adopting a child, either one (but not both) of the parents may take adoption leave, and the other may take paternity leave.

Certain employees are entitled to paternity leave on the birth or adoption of a child. To be eligible, the employee must be the child's father, or the partner of the mother or adopter, and meet other conditions. These conditions are, firstly, that they must have been continuously employed for not less than 26 weeks prior to the 15th week before the expected week of childbirth (or, in the case of adoptions, 26 weeks ending with the week in which notification of the adoption match is given) and, secondly, that the employee must have or expect to have responsibility for the upbringing of the child. The employee may take either one week's leave, or two consecutive weeks' leave. This leave may be taken at any time between the date of the child's birth (or placement for adoption) and 56 days later. A statutory payment is available during this period.

For births and adoptions from 3 April 2011 but before 5 April 2015, an eligible employee has been able to take additional paternity leave at the end of the mother's or adopter's leave period provided the child is at least 20 weeks old or was placed for adoption at least 20 weeks previously. The maximum period of leave is 26 weeks and leave cannot extend beyond the child's first birthday.

For births on or after 5 April 2015, eligible parents are entitled to shared parental leave (SPL) whereby they will be able to share a pot of leave of up to 50 weeks and 27 weeks of pay, after the initial two weeks of maternity leave that is compulsory for the mother. During that 50 week period, parents can decide to be off work at the same time and/or take it in turns to have periods of leave to look after their child. To be eligible, the employee must be the child's mother, father, partner of the mother or adopter, and must have worked for the same employer for not less than 26 weeks prior to the 15th week before the expected week of childbirth (or, in case of adoptions, 26 weeks ending with the week in which notification of the adoption match is given). The amount of leave available is calculated using the mother's entitlement to maternity leave. If a mother reduces maternity leave she and/or her partner may opt to take SPL for the remaining weeks. On taking SPL, a woman will be entitled to statutory shared parental pay at the same rate as SMP.

For more information *see* Social Welfare, Employer Payments.

Any employee with one year's service who has, or expects to have, responsibility for a child may take parental leave to care for the child. Each parent is entitled to a total of 18 weeks parental leave for each child or adopted child. This leave must be taken (at the rate of no more than four weeks a year, and in blocks of whole weeks only) before the child's 18th birthday.

SUNDAY TRADING

The Sunday Trading Act 1994 allows shops to open on Sunday. The Employment Rights Act 1996 gives shop workers and betting workers the right not to be dismissed, selected for redundancy or to suffer any detriment (such as the denial of overtime, promotion or training) if they refuse to work on Sundays. This does not apply to those who, under their contracts, are employed to work on Sundays.

TERMINATION OF EMPLOYMENT

An employee may be dismissed without notice if guilty of gross misconduct but in other cases a period of notice must be given by the employer. The minimum periods of notice specified in the Employment Rights Act 1996 are:

- one week if the employee has been continuously employed for one month or more but for less than two years
- one week for each complete year of continuous employment, if the employee has been employed for two years or more, up to a maximum of 12 weeks' notice
- longer periods apply if these are specified in the contract of employment

If an employee is dismissed with less notice than he/she is entitled to by statute, or under their contract if longer, he/she will have a wrongful dismissal claim (unless the employer paid the employee in lieu of notice in accordance with a contractual provision entitling it to do so). This claim for wrongful dismissal can be brought by the employee either in the civil courts or the employment tribunal, but if brought in the tribunal the maximum amount that can be awarded is £25,000.

REDUNDANCY

An employee dismissed because of redundancy may be entitled to redundancy pay. This applies if:

- the employment commenced before 6 April 2012 and the employee has at least one year's continuous service or the employment commenced on or after 6 April 2012 and the employee has at least two years' continuous service
- the employee is dismissed by the employer by reason of redundancy (this can include cases of voluntary redundancy)

Redundancy can mean closure of the entire business, closure of a particular site of the business, or a reduction in the need for employees to carry out work of a particular kind.

An employee may not be entitled to a redundancy payment if offered a suitable alternative job by the same employer. The amount of statutory redundancy pay depends on the length of service, age, and their earnings, subject to a weekly maximum of (currently) £508. The maximum payment that can be awarded is £15,240. The redundancy payment is guaranteed by the government in cases where the employer becomes insolvent.

UNFAIR DISMISSAL

Complaints of unfair dismissal are dealt with by an employment tribunal. Any employee whose employment commenced before 6 April 2012 with at least one year's continuous service or any employee whose employment commenced on or after 6 April 2012 with at least two year's continuous service (subject to exceptions, including in relation to whistleblowers – see below) can make a complaint to the tribunal. At the tribunal, it is for the employee to show that the employer dismissed them either expressly or constructively and it is for the employer to prove that the dismissal was due to one or more potentially fair reasons: a statutory restriction preventing the continuation of the employee's contract; the employee's capability or qualifications for the job he/she was employed to do; the employee's conduct; redundancy; or some other substantial reason.

If the employer succeeds in showing this, the tribunal must then decide whether the employer acted reasonably in dismissing the employee for that reason. If the employee is found to have been unfairly dismissed, the tribunal can order that he/she be reinstated, re-engaged or compensated. Any person believing that they may have been unfairly dismissed should contact their local Citizens Advice bureau or seek legal advice. A claim must be brought within three months of the date of effective termination of employment.

The normal maximum compensatory award for unfair dismissal is £83,682 (as at April 2018). If the dismissal occurred after 6 April 2009 and the employer unreasonably failed to follow the ACAS Code of Practice on Disciplinary and Grievance Procedures in carrying out the dismissal, the tribunal may increase the employee's compensation by up to 25 per cent.

WHISTLEBLOWING
Under the whistleblowing legislation (Public Interest Disclosure Act 1998, which inserted provisions into the Employment Rights Act 1996) dismissal of an employee is automatically unfair if the reason or principal reason for the dismissal is that the employee has made a protected disclosure. The legislation also makes it unlawful to subject workers (a broad category that includes employees and certain other individuals, such as agency workers) who have made a protected disclosure to any detriment on the ground that they have done so.

For a disclosure to qualify for protection, the claimant must show that he or she has disclosed information, which in his or her reasonable belief tends to show one or more of the following six categories of wrongdoing: criminal offences; breach of any legal obligation; miscarriages of justice; danger to the health and safety of any individual; damage to the environment; or the deliberate concealing of information about any of the other categories. The malpractices can be past, present, prospective or merely alleged.

A qualifying disclosure will only be protected if the manner of the disclosure fulfils certain conditions, which varies according to the type of disclosure. With effect from 25 June 2013, there is no requirement for the disclosure to have been made in 'good faith', although where it appears to the tribunal that the protected disclosure was not made in good faith, the tribunal may reduce any compensatory award it makes by up to 25 per cent if it considers that it is just and equitable to do so in all the circumstances.

Any whistleblower claim in the employment tribunal must normally be brought within three months of the date of dismissal or other act leading to a detriment.

An individual does not need to have been working with the employer for any particular period of time to be able to bring such a claim and compensation is uncapped (and can include an amount for injury to feelings).

DISCRIMINATION
Discrimination in employment on the grounds of sex (including gender reassignment), sexual orientation, being pregnant or on maternity leave, race, colour, nationality, ethnic or national origins, religion or belief, marital or civil partnership status, age or disability is unlawful. Discrimination legislation generally covers direct discrimination, indirect discrimination, harassment and victimisation. Only in limited circumstances can such discrimination be justified (rendering it lawful).

An individual does not need to be employed for any particular period of time to be able to claim discrimination (discrimination can be alleged at the recruitment phase), and discrimination compensation is uncapped (and can include an amount for injury to feelings). These features distinguish the discrimination laws from, for example, the unfair dismissal laws.

The Equality Act 2010 was passed on 8 April 2010 and the main provisions came into force on 1 October 2010. The act unifies several pieces of discrimination legislation, providing one definition of direct discrimination, indirect discrimination, harassment and victimisation. The Equality Act applies to those employed in Great Britain but not to employees in Northern Ireland or (subject to EC exceptions) to those who work mainly abroad, and provides that:

• it is unlawful to discriminate on the grounds of sex, gender reassignment or marital/civil partner status, being pregnant or on maternity leave, including discrimination by association and by perception. This covers all aspects of employment (including advertising for jobs), but there are some limited exceptions, such as where the essential nature of the job requires it to be given to someone of a particular sex, or where decency and privacy requires it. The act entitles men and women to equality of remuneration for equivalent work or work of the same value

• individuals have the right not to be discriminated against on the grounds of race, colour, nationality, or ethnic or national origins and this applies to all aspects of employment. Employers may also take lawful positive action, including in relation to recruitment and promotion

• discrimination against a disabled person in all aspects of employment is unlawful. This includes protecting carers from discrimination by association with the disabled persons that they look after. The act also imposes a duty on employers to make 'reasonable adjustments' to the arrangements and physical features of the workplace if these place disabled people at a substantial disadvantage compared with those who are not disabled. The definition of a 'disabled person' is wide and includes people diagnosed with HIV, cancer and multiple sclerosis

• discrimination against a person on the grounds of religion or belief (or lack of belief) including discrimination by association and by perception, in all aspects of employment, is unlawful

• discrimination against an individual on the grounds of sexual orientation, including discrimination by association and by perception, in all aspects of employment, is unlawful

• age discrimination in the workplace is unlawful, and an employer may no longer dismiss an employee by reason of retirement once they have reached a certain age. However, it is lawful to discriminate because of age in relation to benefits based on length of service, redundancy pay, national minimum wage and insurance benefits

The responsibility for monitoring equality in society rests with the Equality and Human Rights Commission.

In Northern Ireland similar provisions exist to those that were in force in Great Britain prior to the coming into force of the Equality Act but are contained in separate legislation (although the Disability Discrimination Act does extend to Northern Ireland).

In Northern Ireland there is one combined body working towards equality and eliminating discrimination, the Equality Commission for Northern Ireland.

WORKING TIME

The Working Time Regulations 1998 impose rules that limit working hours and provide for rest breaks and holidays. The regulations apply to workers and so cover not only employees but also other individuals who undertake to perform personally any work or services (eg freelancers). The regulations are complex and subject to various exceptions and qualifications but the basic provisions relating to adult day workers are as follows:

- No worker is permitted to work more than an average of 48 hours per week (unless they have made a genuine voluntary opt-out of this limit – it is not sufficient to make it a term of the contract that the worker opts out), and a worker is entitled to, but is not required to take, the following breaks:
- 11 consecutive hours' uninterrupted rest in every 24-hour period
- an uninterrupted rest period of 24 hours in each 7-day period or 48 hours in each fortnight (in addition to the daily rest period)
- 20 minutes' rest break provided that the working day is longer than 6 hours
- 5.6 weeks' paid annual leave (28 days full-time). This equates to 4 weeks plus public holidays

There are specific provisions relating to night work, young workers (ie those over school leaving age but under 18) and a variety of workers in specialised sectors (such as off-shore oil rig workers).

HUMAN RIGHTS

On 2 October 2000 the Human Rights Act 1998 came into force in the UK. This act incorporates the European Convention on Human Rights into the law of the UK. The main principles of the act are as follows:

- all legislation must be interpreted and given effect by the courts as compatible with the Convention so far as it is possible to do so. Before the second reading of a new bill the minister responsible for the bill must provide a statement regarding its compatibility with the Human Rights Act
- subordinate legislation (eg statutory instruments) which is incompatible with the Convention can be struck down by the courts
- primary legislation (eg an act of parliament) which is incompatible with the Convention cannot be struck down by a court, but the higher courts can make a declaration of incompatibility which is a signal to parliament to change the law
- all public authorities (including courts and tribunals) must not act in a way which is incompatible with the Convention
- individuals whose Convention rights have been infringed by a public authority may bring proceedings against that authority, but the act is not intended to create new rights as between individuals

The main human rights protected by the Convention are the right to life (article 2); protection from torture and inhuman or degrading treatment (article 3); protection from slavery or forced labour (article 4); the right to liberty and security of the person (article 5); the right to a fair trial (article 6); the right not to be subject to retrospective criminal offences (article 7); the right to respect for private and family life (article 8); freedom of thought, conscience and religion (article 9); freedom of expression (article 10); freedom of peaceful association and assembly (article 11); the right to marry and found a family (article 12); protection from discrimination (article 14); the right to protection of property (article 1 protocol No.1); the right to education (article 2 protocol No.1); and the right to free elections (article 3 protocol No.1). Most of the Convention rights are subject to limitations which deem the breach of the right acceptable on the basis it is 'necessary in a democratic society'.

Human rights are also enshrined in the common law (of tort). Although this is of historical significance, the common law (for example the duty of confidentiality) remains especially important regarding violations of human rights that occur between private parties, where the Human Rights Act 1998 does not apply.

PARENTAL RESPONSIBILITY

The Children Act 1989 (as amended by the Children and Families Act 2014) gives both the mother and father parental responsibility for the child if the parents are married to each other at the time of the child's birth. If the parents are not married, only the mother has parental responsibility. The father may acquire it in accordance with the provisions of section 4 of the Children Act 1989. He can do this in one of several ways, including: by being registered as the father on the child's birth certificate with the consent of the mother (only for fathers of children born after 1 December 2003, following changes to the Adoption and Children Act 2002); by applying to the court for a parental responsibility order; by entering into a parental responsibility agreement with the mother which must be in the prescribed form; or by marrying the mother of the child.

Following changes to the Children Act 1989 (introduced by the Children and Families Act 2014), if a court makes a child arrangements order in favour of a father, providing that the child lives with that father, the court must make a parental responsibility order in his favour. If the child arrangements order provides that the child spend time or otherwise have contact with the father, the court must consider whether to make a parental responsibility order (residence orders were replaced by child arrangement orders under the Children and Families Act 2014, but if obtained prior to 22 April 2014 are still valid).

Where a child's parent, who has parental responsibility, marries or enters into a civil partnership with a person who is not the child's parent, the child's parent(s) with parental responsibility can agree for the step-parent to have parental responsibility, or the step-parent may acquire parental responsibility by order of the court (section 4A(1) Children Act 1989).

If a child is born to female civil partners or female same-sex spouses as a result of IVF or AID treatment received after 5 April 2009, both individuals will have parental responsibility for that child. From 1 September 2009 a female, who is not in a civil partnership or same-sex marriage with the mother at the date of the child's birth, but is the child's other parent (under the Human Fertilisation and Embryology Act 2008), can acquire parental responsibility in the same way as set out above in relation to a father. Parental responsibility will also be acquired if the mother and the child's other parent enter into a civil partnership or (from 13 March 2014) a same-sex marriage after the child's date of birth.

Where the court makes a child arrangements order and a person (who is not the parent or guardian of the child) is named in the order as a person with whom the child is to spend time or otherwise have contact (but not named as a person with whom the child is to live), the court may provide in the order for that person to have parental responsibility for the child.

An adoption order gives parental responsibility for the child to the adopters. It extinguishes parental responsibility that any person had for the child immediately before the making of the order.

In Scotland, the relevant legislation is the Children (Scotland) Act 1995, which gives the mother parental rights and responsibilities for her child whether or not she is married to the child's father. A father who is married to the mother, either at the time of the child's conception or subsequently, will also have automatic parental rights and responsibilities. Section 3 of the 2006 act provides that an unmarried father will obtain automatic parental responsibilities and rights if he is registered as the father on the child's birth certificate. For unmarried fathers who are not named on the birth certificate, or whose children were born before the 2006 act came into force, it is possible to acquire parental responsibilities and rights by applying to the court or by entering into a parental responsibilities and rights agreement with the mother. The father of any child, regardless of parental rights, has a duty to aliment that child until he/she is 18 (or under 25 if the child is still at an educational establishment or training for employment or for a trade, profession or vocation).

LEGITIMATION

Under the Legitimacy Act 1976, an illegitimate person automatically becomes legitimate when his/her parents marry. This applies even where one of the parents was married to a third person at the time of the birth. In such cases it is necessary to re-register the birth of the child. In Scotland, the status of illegitimacy has been abolished by section 21 of the 2006 act. The Family Law Reform Act 1987 reformed the law so as to remove so far as possible the legal disadvantages of illegitimacy.

JURY SERVICE

In England and Wales, the law concerning juries is largely consolidated in the Juries Act 1974 (as amended by the Criminal Justice and Courts Act 2015). In England and Wales, a person charged with a serious criminal offence is entitled to have their trial heard by a jury in a crown court, except in cases where there is a danger of jury tampering or where jury tampering has taken place.

In civil cases, there is a right to a jury in the Queen's Bench Division of the high court in cases where the person applying for a jury has been accused of fraud, as well as in cases of malicious prosecution or false imprisonment. The same applies to the county court. In all other cases in the Queen's Bench Division only the judge has discretion to order trial with a jury, though such an order is seldom made. In the chancery division of the high court a jury is never used. The same is true in the family division of the high court.

No right to a jury trial exists in Scotland, although more serious offences are heard before a jury. In England and Wales criminal cases and civil cases in the high court are generally heard by a jury of 12 members, but in the county court the jury is smaller, normally consisting of eight members. In the event that a juror is excused the trial can proceed so long as there are at least seven remaining jurors in the county court and nine in the case of the high court or crown court. At an inquest, there must be at least seven and no more than 11 members. In Scotland there are 12 members of a jury in a civil case in the court of session and certain sheriff court cases, and 15 in a criminal trial in the high court of justiciary. Jurors are normally asked to serve for ten working days, during which time they could sit on more than one case. Jurors selected for longer cases are expected to sit for the duration of the trial.

In England and Wales, every 'registered' parliamentary or local government elector between the ages of 18 and 75 who has lived in the UK (including, for this purpose, the Channel Islands and the Isle of Man) for any period of at least five years since reaching the age of 13 is qualified to serve on a jury unless he/she is disqualified.

Those disqualified from jury service include:

- those who have at any time been sentenced by a court in the UK (including, for this purpose, the Channel Islands and the Isle of Man) to a term of imprisonment or youth custody of five years or more
- those who have within the previous ten years served any part of a sentence of imprisonment, youth custody or detention, been detained in a young offenders' institution, received a suspended sentence of imprisonment or order for detention, or received a community order
- those who are on bail in criminal proceedings
- those who have been convicted of a jury misconduct offence
- those who are liable to be detained, who are under guardianship or who are under a community treatment order under the Mental Health Act 1983 or who are in resident in a hospital on account of mental disorder
- Those who lack capacity, as defined under the Mental Capacity Act 2005, to serve as a juror

The court has the discretion to excuse a juror from service, or defer the date of service, if the juror can show there is good reason why he/she should be excused from attending or good reason why his/her attendance should be deferred. It is an offence (punishable by a fine) to fail to attend when summoned, to serve knowing that you are disqualified from service, or to make false representations in an attempt to evade service. If a juror fails to turn up for service, or attends but cannot serve due to being under the influence of drink or drugs, this is punishable as contempt of court. Any party can object to any juror if he/she can show cause to the trial judge.

It may be appropriate for a judge to excuse a juror from a particular case if he is personally concerned in the facts of the particular case, or closely connected with a party to the proceedings or with a prospective witness. The judge may also discharge any juror who, from a mental or physical incapacity, temporary or permanent, or alternatively due to linguistic difficulties, cannot pay proper attention to the evidence.

An individual juror (or the entire jury) can be discharged if it is shown that they or any of their number have, among other things, separated from the rest of the jury without the leave of the court; talked to any person out of court who is not a member of the jury; determined the verdict of the trial by drawing lots; come to a compromise on the verdict; been drunk, or otherwise incapacitated, while carrying out their duties as a juror; exerted improper pressure on the other members of the jury (eg harassment or bullying); declined to take part in the jury's functions; displayed actual or apparent bias (eg racism, sexism or other discriminatory or deliberate hostility); or inadvertently possessed knowledge of the bad character of a party to the proceedings which has not been adduced as evidence in the proceedings. The factual situations that arise are many, and include falling asleep during the trial, asking friends on Facebook for help in making a decision, consulting an ouija board in the course of deliberations, making telephone calls after retirement, and lunching with a barrister not connected with the proceedings.

The Criminal Justice and Courts Act 2015 has introduced four new offences of juror misconduct with a penalty of up to two years in prison. A juror commits an offence if he: (a) intentionally seeks information during a trial where he knows, or ought to reasonably know, that the information sought is or may be relevant to the case; (b) passes on to another juror information obtained through such research; (c) engages in conduct from which it may reasonably be concluded that he intends to try the issue otherwise than on the basis of the evidence presented in the proceedings on the issue; and (d) discloses information about the jury's deliberations, subject to specified exceptions. A person who has been convicted of one of the above offences within the last ten years will be disqualified from jury duty. A judge now has a discretionary power to order members of a jury to surrender their electronic communication devices for a period of time, and a court security officer is authorised to search a juror for a device that a judge has ordered be surrendered.

In England and Wales, the jury's verdict need not be unanimous. In criminal proceedings, and civil proceedings in the high court, the agreement of ten jurors will suffice when there are not fewer than 11 people on the jury (or nine in a jury of ten). In civil proceedings in the county court the agreement of seven or eight jurors will suffice. Where a majority verdict is given, the court must be satisfied that the jury had reasonable time to consider its verdict based on the nature and complexity of the case. In criminal proceedings this must be no less than two hours and ten minutes (allowing time for the jury to settle after retiring).

A juror is immune from prosecution or civil claim in respect of anything said or done by him or her in the discharge of their office. It is an offence for a juror to disclose what happened in the jury room even after the trial is over. A juror may claim travelling expenses, a subsistence allowance and an allowance for other financial loss (eg loss of earnings or benefits, fees paid to carers or child-minders) up to a stated limit. For more information on jury service, visit W www.gov.uk/jury-service/overview

SCOTLAND

Qualification criteria for jury service in Scotland are similar to those in England and Wales, except that members of the judiciary are ineligible for ten years after ceasing to hold their post, and others concerned with the administration of justice are only eligible for service five years after ceasing to hold office. Certain persons have the right to apply to be excused – full-time members of the medical, dental, nursing, veterinary and pharmaceutical professions, full-time members of the armed forces, ministers of religion, persons who have served on a jury within the previous five years, persons who have attended court to serve on a jury but were not selected by ballot within the previous two years, members of the Scottish parliament, members of the Scottish government, junior Scottish ministers and those aged 71 years or over. Those who are incapable by reason of a mental disorder may also be excused. Such an application will be accepted if the application is made within 7 days of the person being notified that they may have to serve. For civil trials there is an age limit of 65 years. Those convicted of a crime and sentenced to a period of imprisonment of 5 years or more are automatically disqualified. The maximum fine for a person serving on a jury while knowing himself/herself to be ineligible is £1,000. The maximum fine for failing to attend without good cause in criminal trials is also £1,000, however in civil proceedings the maximum fine is £200.

HER MAJESTY'S COURTS AND TRIBUNALS SERVICE, 102 Petty France, London SW1H 9AJ T 0845-456 8770

JURY CENTRAL SUMMONING BUREAU, Freepost LON 19669, Pocock Street, London SE1 0YG T 0845-803 8003
E jurysummoning@hmcts.gsi.gov.uk

SCOTTISH COURTS AND TRIBUNALS SERVICE, Saughton House, Broomhouse Drive, Edinburgh EH11 3XD
T 0131-444 3300
W www.scotcourts.gov.uk

THE CLERK OF JUSTICIARY, Parliament House, Parliament Square, Edinburgh EH1 1RQ T 0131-225 2595

LANDLORD AND TENANT

RESIDENTIAL LETTINGS

The provisions outlined here apply only where the tenant lives in a separate dwelling from the landlord and where the dwelling is the tenant's only or main home. It does not apply to licensees such as lodgers, guests or service occupiers.

The 1996 Housing Act radically changed certain aspects of the legislation referred to below; in particular, the grant of assured and assured shorthold tenancies under the Housing Act 1988.

ASSURED SHORTHOLD TENANCIES

If a tenancy was granted on or after 15 January 1989 and before 28 February 1997, the tenant would have an assured tenancy unless the landlord served notice under section 20 in the prescribed form prior to the commencement of the tenancy, stating that the tenancy is to be an assured shorthold tenancy and the tenancy is for a minimum fixed term period of six months (see below). An assured tenancy gives that tenant greater security. The tenant could, for example, stay in possession of the dwelling for as long as the tenant observed the terms of the tenancy. The landlord cannot obtain possession from such a tenant unless the landlord can establish a specific ground for possession (set out in the Housing Act 1988) and obtains a court order. The rent payable is that agreed with the landlord at the start of the tenancy. The landlord has the right to increase the rent annually by serving a notice. If that happens the tenant can apply to have the rent fixed by the rent assessment committee of the local authority. The tenant or the landlord may request that the committee sets the rent in line with open market rents for that type of property.

Under the Housing Act 1996, all new lettings (below an annual rent threshold of £100,000 since October 2010 in England or December 2011 in Wales) entered into on or after 28 February 1997 (for whatever term) will be assured shorthold tenancies unless the landlord serves a notice stating that the tenancy is not to be an assured shorthold tenancy. This means that the landlord is entitled to possession at the end of the tenancy provided he serves a notice under section 21 Housing Act 1988 and commences the proceedings in accordance with the correct procedure. The landlord must obtain a court order, however, to obtain possession if the tenant refuses to vacate at the end of the tenancy. If the tenancy is an assured shorthold tenancy, the court must grant the order.

REGULATED TENANCIES

Before the Housing Act 1988 came into force on 15 January 1989 there were regulated tenancies; some are still in existence and are protected by the Rent Act 1977. Under this act it is possible for the landlord or the tenant to apply to the local rent officer to have a 'fair' rent registered. The fair rent is then the maximum rent payable.

SECURE TENANCIES

Secure tenancies are generally given to tenants of local authorities, housing associations (before 15 January 1989) and certain other bodies. This gives the tenant security of tenure unless the terms of the agreement are broken by the tenant and it is reasonable to make an order for possession. Those with secure tenancies may have the right to buy their property. In practice this right is generally only available to council tenants. However, the Housing and Planning Act 2016 will enable housing associations voluntarily to extend the right to buy. The 2016 act is now in force and a roll out of the extended right to buy regime has now taken place as the Department for Communities and Local Government published its guidance in April 2018.

The Prevention of Social Housing Fraud Act came into force in October 2013. It creates criminal offences for unlawful sub-letting by secure and assured tenants of social housing.

AGRICULTURAL PROPERTY

Tenancies in agricultural properties are governed by the Agricultural Holdings Act 1986, the Agricultural Tenancies Act 1995 (both amended by the Regulatory Reform (Agricultural Tenancies) (England and Wales) Order 2006), the Tribunals, Courts and Enforcement Act 2007, the Legal Services Act 2007 and the Rent (Agriculture) Act 1976, which give similar protections to those described above, eg security of tenure, right to compensation for disturbance, etc. Similar provisions are applied to Scotland by the Agricultural Holdings (Scotland) Act 2003 for those leases entered into on or after 27 November 2003. The Agricultural Holdings (Scotland) Act 1991 continues to apply to those leases in Scotland entered into prior to this date and in certain other circumstances outlined by the 2003 act. However, one distinction to note between the 1991 act and the 2003 act is that those leases governed by the former have full security of tenure, subject to certain exceptions, whereas leases under the 2003 act are fixed term arrangements of various durations.

EVICTION

The Protection from Eviction Act 1977 (as amended by the Housing Act 1988 and Nationality, Immigration and Asylum Act 2002) sets out the procedure a landlord must follow in order to obtain possession of property. It is unlawful for a landlord to evict a tenant otherwise than in accordance with the law. For common law tenancies and for Rent Act tenants a notice to quit in the prescribed form giving 28 days notice is required. For secure and assured tenancies a notice seeking possession must be served. It is unlawful for the landlord to evict a person by putting their belongings on to the street, by changing the locks and so on. It is also unlawful for a landlord to harass a tenant in any way in order to persuade him/her to give up the tenancy. The tenant may be able to obtain an injunction to restrain the actions of the landlord and get back into the property and be awarded damages.

LANDLORD RESPONSIBILITIES

Under the Landlord and Tenant Act 1985, where the term of the lease is less than seven years, the landlord is responsible for maintaining the structure and exterior of the property, for sanitation, for heating and hot water, and all installations for the supply of water, gas and electricity.

While the responsibility of maintaining the premises remains intact, since July 2012 landlords are no longer permitted to enter the rental premises for the purpose of viewing their state and condition. This power of entry was revoked by the Protection of Freedoms Act 2012.

LEASEHOLDERS

Strictly speaking, leaseholders have bought a long lease rather than a property and in certain limited circumstances the landlord can end the tenancy. Under the Leasehold Reform Act 1967 (as amended by the Housing Acts 1969, 1974, 1980 and 1985), leaseholders of houses, as opposed to flats, may have the right to buy the freehold or to take an extended lease for a term of 50 years. This applies to leases where the term of the lease is over 21 years, at a low rent, and where the leaseholder has occupied the house as his/her only or main residence for the last two years, or for a total of two years over the last ten. The tenant must give the landlord written notice of his desire to acquire the freehold or extend the leasehold.

The Leasehold Reform, Housing and Urban Development Act came into force in 1993 and allows the leaseholders of flats in certain circumstances to buy the freehold of the building in which they live. Owners of certain long leases of flats may also have the right to take an extended act of 90 years plus the unexpired residue of their current lease: although technically a grant of a new lease, these are commonly called 'lease extensions'.

Responsibility for maintenance of the structure, exterior and interior of the building should be set out in the lease. Usually the upkeep of the interior of his/her part of the property is the responsibility of the leaseholder, and responsibility for the structure, exterior and common interior areas is shared between the freeholder and the leaseholder(s).

If leaseholders are dissatisfied with charges made in respect of lease extensions, they are entitled to have their situation evaluated by the First-tier Tribunal (Property Chamber).

The Commonhold and Leasehold Reform Act 2002 makes provision for the freehold estate in land to be registered as commonhold land and for the legal interest in the land to be vested in a 'commonhold association', ie a private limited company.

BUSINESS LETTINGS

The Landlord and Tenant Acts 1927 and 1954 (as amended) give security of tenure to the tenants of most business premises. The landlord can only evict the tenant on one of the grounds laid down in the 1954 act, and in some cases where the landlord repossesses the property the tenant may be entitled to compensation. However, it is commonplace for landlords and tenants to agree that these provisions will not apply to their lease, meaning that no security or tenure is granted.

SCOTLAND

In Scotland assured and short assured tenancies exist for residential lettings entered into after 2 January 1989 and before December 2017 are similar to assured shorthold tenancies in England and Wales. The relevant legislation for these is the Housing (Scotland) Act 1988. However, under the provisions of the Private Housing (Tenancies) (Scotland) Act 2016 all new tenancies for private residential lettings from 1 December 2017 take the form of a private rental tenancy. They will provide more security for tenants as the 'no fault ground of repossession' (the equivalent of recovering possession under section 21 of the Housing Act 1988 in England) has been abolished. The act also introduced a model tenancy agreement, rent controls and move the adjudication of disputes from the sheriff court to the housing tribunal.

Most tenancies created before 2 January 1989 were regulated tenancies and the Rent (Scotland) Act 1984 still applies where these exist. The act defines, among other things, the circumstances in which a landlord can increase the rent when improvements are made to the property. It does not apply to tenancies where the landlord is the Crown, a local authority or a housing corporation.

The Antisocial Behaviour etc (Scotland) Act 2004 provides that all private landlords letting property in Scotland must register with the local authority in which the let property is situated, unless the landlord is a local authority, or a registered social landlord. Exceptions also apply to holiday lets, owner-occupied accommodation and agricultural holdings. The act applies to partnerships, trusts and companies as well as to individuals.

Tenancy Deposit Schemes (Scotland) Regulations 2011 require that a landlord must pay deposits taken from tenants into an approved scheme and ensure that the money is held by an approved scheme for the duration of the tenancy. Evidence of registration with the relevant local authority in terms of the 2004 Act must be provided when the deposit is paid over.

Landlords who provide a private residential tenancy must provide new tenants with a Tenant Information Pack. The

Tenant Information Pack includes information on the Repairing Standard, and its provision satisfies the separate obligation of a landlord to provide a tenant with written information about the landlord's duty to repair and maintain in terms of the Housing (Scotland) Act 2006.

The Housing (Scotland) Acts of 1987 and 2001 relate to local authority and registered social landlord responsibilities for housing, the right to buy, and local authority secured tenancies. The provisions are broadly similar to England and Wales. The Housing (Scotland) Act 2010 reformed right-to-buy provisions, modernised social housing regulation, introduced the Scottish social housing charter and replaced the regulatory framework established by the 2001 act.

In Scotland, business premises are not controlled by statute to the same extent as in England and Wales, although the Tenancy of Shops (Scotland) Act 1949 gives some security to tenants of shops. Tenants of shops can apply to the sheriff, within 21 days of being served a notice to quit, for a renewal of tenancy if threatened with eviction. This application may be dismissed on various grounds, including where the landlord has offered to sell the property to the tenant at an agreed price or, in the absence of agreement as to price, at a price fixed by a single arbiter appointed by the parties or the sheriff. The act extends to properties where the Crown or government departments are the landlords or the tenants.

Under the Leases Act 1449 the landlord's successors (either purchasers or creditors) are bound by the agreement made with any tenants so long as the following conditions are met:
• the lease, if for more than one year, must be in writing
• there must be a rent
• there must be a term of expiry
• the tenant must have entered into possession
• the subjects of the lease must be land
• the landlord, if owner, must be the proprietor with a recorded title, ie the title deeds recorded in the Register of Sasines or registered in the Land Register

On 28 November 2013 certain leases which were granted for more than 175 years and under which the rent does not exceed £100 a year, converted to heritable titles. Therefore the tenants under these leases will become the owners of the property. Conversion of the lease will be automatic, provided certain conditions are met, unless the tenant opts out. It is possible for the landlord to claim compensation for their loss of income.

LEGAL AID

The Access to Justice Act 1999 transformed what used to be known as the Legal Aid system. The Legal Aid Board was replaced by the Legal Services Commission, which was responsible for the development and administration of two legal funding schemes in England and Wales, namely the Criminal Defence Service and the Community Legal Service. The Criminal Defence Service assisted people who were under police investigation or facing criminal charges. The Community Legal Service was designed to increase access to legal information and advice by involving a much wider network of funders and providers in giving publicly funded legal services. In Scotland, provision of legal aid is governed by the Legal Aid (Scotland) Act 1986, the Legal Profession and Legal Aid (Scotland) Act 2007 and the Scottish Civil Justice Council and Criminal Legal Assistance Act 2013, and administered by the Scottish Legal Aid Board.

Under the Legal Aid, Sentencing and Punishment of Offenders Act 2012 (LASPO), which came into force on 1 April 2013, the Legal Services Commission was abolished and replaced by the newly created Legal Aid Agency. The act has also limited the areas of law that fall within the scope of legal aid funding, especially those related to civil legal

services. However, the act does include provisions for funding in exceptional cases, such as where failure to provide legal aid would result in a violation of an individual's human rights or where providing legal aid would serve a wider public interest. Further, the act allows for areas of law to be added or omitted from the scope of legal aid independently, without subsequent legislation.

LASPO took whole areas of law out of scope for legal aid; some areas only qualify if they meet certain criteria. Broadly, the following categories of cases are now out of such scope: (a) family cases where there is no proof of domestic violence, forced marriage or child abduction; (b) immigration cases that do not involve asylum or detention; (c) housing and debt matters unless they constitute an immediate risk to the home; (d) welfare benefit cases except appeals to the upper tribunal or high court; (e) almost all clinical negligence cases; and (f) employment cases that do not involve human trafficking or a contravention of the Equality Act 2010.

LEGAL AID AGENCY, W www.gov.uk/government/organisations/legal-aid-agency

CIVIL LEGAL AID

From 1 January 2000, only organisations (such as solicitors or Citizens Advice) with a contract with the Legal Services Commission (now Legal Aid Agency) have been able to give initial help in any civil matter. Moreover, from that date decisions about funding were devolved from the Legal Services Commission to contracted organisations in relation to any level of publicly funded service in family and immigration cases. For other types of case, applications for public funding are made through a solicitor (or other contracted legal services providers) in much the same way as the former Legal Aid.

Under the civil funding scheme there are broadly six levels of service available:
• legal help
• help at court
• family help – either family help (lower) or family help (higher)
• legal representation – either investigative help or full representation
• family mediation
• such other services as authorised by specific orders

ELIGIBILITY

Eligibility for funding from the Legal Aid Agency depends broadly on five factors:
• the level of service sought (see above)
• whether the applicant qualifies financially
• the merits of the applicant's case
• a costs-benefits analysis (if the costs are likely to outweigh any benefit that might be gained from the proceedings, funding may be refused)
• whether there is any public interest in the case being litigated (ie whether the case has a wider public interest beyond that of the parties involved, eg a human rights case)

The limits on capital and income above which a person is not entitled to public funding vary with the type of service sought. As of Spring 2017, there is a consultation on government proposals seeking to amend the legal financial eligibility system to accommodate the expansion of Universal Credit. Nothing in the consultation will affect the scope of or eligibility threshold for legal aid, but instead when claimants are passported and so would not have to undergo a full assessment of their means. The consultation closed on 11 May 2017 and the outcome is pending.

The 2012 act also amended the merits criteria so that legal aid may be refused where the case is suitable for alternative funding, such as Conditional Fee Agreements. Children, and individuals on certain welfare benefits, may be relieved from means testing and from the liability to make contributions.

CONTRIBUTIONS

Some of those who qualify for Legal Aid Agency funding will have to contribute towards their legal costs. Contributions must be paid by anyone who has a disposable income or disposable capital exceeding a prescribed amount. The rules relating to applicable contributions are complex and detailed information can be obtained from the Legal Aid Agency.

STATUTORY CHARGE

A statutory charge is made if a person keeps or gains money or property in a case for which they have received legal aid. This means that the amount paid by the Legal Aid Agency fund on their behalf is deducted from the amount that the person receives. This does not apply if the court has ordered that the costs be paid by the other party (unless the amount paid by the other party does not cover all of the costs). In certain circumstances, the Legal Aid Agency may waive or postpone payment.

CONTINGENCY OR CONDITIONAL FEES

This system was introduced by the Courts and Legal Services Act 1990. It can offer legal representation on a 'no win, no fee' basis. It provides an alternative form of assistance, especially for those cases which are ineligible for funding by the Legal Aid Agency. The main area for such work is in the field of personal injuries.

Not all solicitors offer such a scheme and different solicitors may well have different terms. The effect of the agreement is that solicitors may not make any charges, or may waive some of their charges, until the case is concluded successfully. If a case is won then the losing party will usually have to pay towards costs, with the winning party contributing around one third.

SCOTLAND

Civil legal aid is available for cases in the following:
• the sheriff courts
• the court of session
• the supreme court
• the lands valuation appeal court
• the Scottish land court
• the sheriff appeal court
• the Lands Tribunal for Scotland
• the employment appeal tribunals
• the Proscribed Organisations Appeal Commission
• the Upper Tribunal for Scotland
• certain appeals before the Social Security Commissioners
Civil legal aid is not available for election petitions, some simple procedure actions, simplified divorce procedures or petitions by a debtor for his own sequestration. In defamation actions additional criteria must be met in order for legal aid to be available.

Eligibility for civil legal aid is assessed in a similar way to that in England and Wales, though the financial limits differ in some respects. A person shall be eligible for civil legal aid if their disposable income does not exceed £26,239 a year. A person may be refused civil aid if their disposable capital exceeds £13,017 and it appears to the Legal Aid board that they can afford to pay without legal aid. Additionally:
• if disposable capital is between £7,853 and £13,017, the applicant will be required to pay a contribution which will be equal to the difference between £7,853 and their disposable capital
• if disposable income is between £3,522 and £11,540, a contribution of one third of the difference between £3,522 and the disposable income may be payable

• if disposable income is between £11,541 and £15,743, one third of the difference between £3,522 and £11,540 plus half the difference between £11,541 and the disposable income may be payable
• if disposable income is between £15,744 and £26,239, a contribution of the following: one third of the difference between £3,522 and £11,540, plus half the difference between £11,541 and £15,743, plus all the remaining disposable income between £15,744 and £26,239 – will be payable

CRIMINAL LEGAL AID

The Legal Aid Agency provides defendants facing criminal charges with free legal representation if they pass a merits test and a means test.

Criminal legal aid covers the cost of preparing a case and legal representation in criminal proceedings. It is also available for appeals against verdicts or sentences in magistrates' courts, the crown court or the court of appeal. It is not available for bringing a private prosecution in a criminal court.

If granted criminal legal aid, either the person may choose their own solicitor or the court will assign one. Contributions to the legal costs may be required. The rules relating to applicable contributions are complex and detailed information can be obtained from the Legal Aid Agency.

DUTY SOLICITORS

LASPO also provides for free initial advice and initial assistance to anyone questioned by the police (whether under arrest or helping the police with their enquiries). No means test or contributions are required for this.

SCOTLAND

Legal advice and assistance operates in a similar way in Scotland. A person is eligible:
• if disposable income does not exceed £245 a week. If disposable income is between £105 and £245 a week, contributions are payable
• if disposable capital does not exceed £1,716 (if the person has dependent relatives, the savings allowance is higher)
• if receiving income support or income-related job seeker's allowance they qualify automatically provided their disposable capital is not over the limit
The procedure for application for criminal legal aid depends on the circumstances of each case. In solemn cases (more serious cases, such as murder) heard before a jury, a person is automatically entitled to criminal legal aid until they are given bail or placed in custody. Thereafter, it is for the court to decide whether to grant legal aid. The court will do this if the person accused cannot meet the expenses of the case without undue hardship on him or his dependants. In less serious cases the procedure depends on whether the person is in custody:
• anyone taken into custody has the right to free legal aid from the duty solicitor up to and including the first court appearance
• if the person is not in custody and wishes to plead guilty, they are not entitled to criminal legal aid but may be entitled to legal advice and assistance, including assistance by way of representation
However, regardless of whether the person is in custody if they wish to plead not guilty, they can apply for criminal legal aid. This must be done within 14 days of the first court appearance at which they made the plea.

The criteria used to assess whether or not criminal legal aid should be granted is similar to the criteria for England and Wales. When meeting with your solicitor, take evidence of your financial position such as details of savings, bank statements, pay slips, pension book or benefits book.

Under the relevant provisions of the Scottish Civil Justice Council and Criminal Legal Assistance Act 2013, a person in receipt of criminal legal aid or criminal assistance by way of representation will be required, in most circumstances, to make contributions where their weekly disposable income is £82 or above or if their disposable capital is £750 or more. The Scottish government has delayed the implementation of these provisions and no timetable has yet been proposed.

THE SCOTTISH LEGAL AID BOARD, Thistle House, 91 Haymarket Terrace, Edinburgh EH12 5HE **T** 0131-226 7061 **W** www.slab.org.uk

MARRIAGE

Any two persons may marry provided that:
- they are at least 16 years old on the day of the marriage (in England and Wales persons under the age of 18 must generally obtain the consent of their parents or guardian; if consent is refused an appeal may be made to the high court or the family court)
- they are not related to one another in a way which would prevent their marrying
- they are unmarried (a person who has already been married must produce documentary evidence that the previous marriage has been ended by death, divorce or annulment)
- they are capable of understanding the nature, duties and responsibilities of a marriage
- they consent to the marriage

It is now lawful for same sex couples to marry by way of civil or religious ceremony following the passing of the Marriage (Same Sex Couples) Act 2013, which came into force in March 2014. In addition, an existing marriage will now be able to continue where one or both parties change their legal gender and both parties wish to remain married. Civil partnerships are also still available for same sex couples, although The Marriage (Same Sex Couples) Act 2013 provides that couples in civil partnerships may convert their relationship to a marriage if they wish.

The parties should check the marriage will be recognised as valid in their home country if either is not a British citizen.

DEGREES OF RELATIONSHIP

A marriage between persons within the prohibited degrees of consanguinity, affinity or adoption is void.

Neither party may marry his or her parent, child, grandparent, grandchild, sibling, parent's sibling, sibling's child, adoptive parent, former adoptive parent, adoptive child or former adoptive child. All references to siblings include half-brothers/sisters.

Under the Marriage (Prohibited Degrees of Relationship) Act 1986, some exceptions to the law permit a person to marry certain step-relatives or in-laws.

In addition to the above, a person may not marry a child of their former civil partner, a child of a former spouse, the former civil partner of a grandparent, the former civil partner of a parent, the former spouse of a grandparent, the former spouse of a parent, the grandchild of a former civil partner or the grandchild of a former spouse, unless that relationship is the only reason they cannot marry and both persons are over 21 and the younger party has not at any time before attaining the age of 18 been a child of the family in relation to the other party.

ENGLAND AND WALES

TYPES OF MARRIAGE CEREMONY

It is possible to marry by either religious or civil ceremony. A religious ceremony can take place at a church or chapel of the Church of England or the Church in Wales, or at any other place of worship which has been formally registered by the Registrar-General. Same-sex marriages can also take place in a religious building, provided that the premises have been registered for the marriage of same-sex couples and the relevant governing authority in relation to the building has provided written consent. It is not possible, however, for same-sex marriages to take place in an Anglican church (although the Church of England is currently considering proposals to give same-sex marriage blessings).

A civil ceremony can take place at a register office, a venue approved by the local authority or any religious premises where permission has been given by the relevant religious organisation and is approved by the local authority.

An application for an approved premises licence must be made by the owners or trustees of the building concerned; it cannot be made by the prospective marriage couple. Approved premises must be regularly open to the public for marriages and civil partnerships; be a seemly and dignified venue; and the venue must be deemed to be a permanent and immovable structure. Open-air ceremonies are prohibited.

Non-Anglican marriages may also be solemnised following the issue of a Registrar-General's licence in other premises where one of the parties is seriously ill, is not expected to recover, and cannot be moved to premises where the marriage could normally be solemnised. The marriage must be solemnised in the place stated on the relevant notice of marriage, which may be one of the parties' place of residence. Detained and house-bound persons may also be married at their usual place of residence on the authority of a superintendent registrar's certificates with proper notice and consents.

MARRIAGE IN THE CHURCH OF ENGLAND OR THE CHURCH IN WALES

Marriage by banns

The marriage can take place in a parish in which one of the parties lives, or in a church in another parish if it is the usual place of worship of either or both of the parties. Further to measures introduced in October 2008, marriages can also take place in a parish where one of the parties has a 'qualifying connection', ie in: a parish where one of the parties was baptised (but not if it was part of a combined rite) or confirmed (where the confirmation was entered into the register book of confirmation for a church or chapel in that parish); a parish where one of the parties lived or habitually attended worship for six months or more; a parish where one of the parents of either of the parties lived for six months or more in the child's lifetime; a parish where one of the parents of either of the parties has habitually attended public worship for six months or more in the child's lifetime; or a parish where a parent or grandparent of either of the parties was married. The banns (ie the announcement of the marriage ceremony) must be called in the parish in which the marriage is to take place on three Sundays before the day of the ceremony; if either or both of the parties lives in a different parish the banns must also be called there. After three months the banns are no longer valid. The minister will not perform the marriage unless satisfied that the banns have been properly called.

Marriage by common licence

The couple and the member of the church who is to conduct the marriage will arrange for a common licence to be issued by the local diocese; this dispenses with the necessity for banns. One of the parties must reside in the parish, must usually worship at the parish church or authorised chapel of that parish, or otherwise have a 'qualifying connection' to the parish. The party must swear that they believe there is no lawful impediment to hinder the solemnisation of the marriage in accordance with the licence. If either party is under 18 years old, evidence of consent by their parent or guardian will be required. Any further eligibility requirements vary from diocese to diocese. The licence is valid for three months.

Marriage by special licence
A special licence is granted at the discretion of the Archbishop of Canterbury where a party has a genuine connection to a particular church or chapel but does not satisfy the legal requirements to marry there. The parties are usually required to demonstrate that they have a genuine worshipping connection to the church or chapel. The special licence will usually be issued to the officiating priest approximately three weeks prior to the date of the wedding and expire three months after the date of issue. An application for the special licence must be made in hard copy to the registrar of the Faculty Office: 1 The Sanctuary, London SW1P 3JT T 020-7222 5381.

Marriage by certificate
The marriage can be conducted on the authority of a superintendent registrar's certificate, provided that the consent of the minister of the church or chapel where the celebration of the marriage is to take place is obtained. Since 2 March 2015, the marriage of non-EU nationals in the Church of England must take place by superintendent registrar's certificate (unless a special marriage licence is required or certain transitional arrangements apply to them), and will be allowed in any situation where the couple would otherwise have qualified for marriage by banns. In the case of British/ EU nationals, the certificate procedure will be only be available if one of the parties lives in the parish for at least seven days or usually worships at the church/chapel.

Registration of the Marriage
Immediately following the solemnisation of a marriage according to the rites of the Church of England, the marriage must be registered in duplicate in two marriage register books provided by the Registrar-General for England and Wales. The entry must contain the particulars of the marriage in the prescribed form and must be signed by the clergyman, the parties to the marriage and two witnesses.

MARRIAGE BY OTHER RELIGIOUS CEREMONY
The parties will need to give notice to the register office at least 28 days before the ceremony. One of the parties must normally live in the registration district where the marriage is to take place or usually worship in the building where they wish to be married. If the building where the parties wish to be married has not been registered, the couple can still have a religious ceremony there, but this will have to follow a separate civil marriage ceremony for it to be valid. If the building is registered, in addition to giving notice to the superintendent registrar it may also be necessary to book a registrar, or authorised person to be present at the ceremony.

CIVIL MARRIAGE
A marriage may be solemnised at any register office, registered building or approved premises in England and Wales, without either of the parties being resident in the same district. The superintendent registrar of the district should be contacted and given notice, and, if the marriage is to take place at approved premises, the necessary arrangements at the venue must also be made.

NOTICE OF MARRIAGE
Where a marriage is intended to take place on the authority of a superintendent registrar's certificates, a notice of the marriage must be given in person to the superintendent registrar of the relevant district.

Both parties must have lived in a registration district in England or Wales for at least seven days immediately before giving notice personally at the local register office. If they live in different registration districts, notice must be given in both districts by the respective party in person. The marriage can take place in any register office or other approved premises in England and Wales no sooner than 28 days after notice has been given, when the superintendent registrar issues a certificate. The parties must get married or register the civil partnership within one year of giving notice.

When giving notice of the marriage it is necessary to provide evidence of name and surname, date of birth, place of residence and nationality, for example, with a passport or birth certificate and a recent bank statement. It will also be necessary to produce official proof, if relevant, that any previous marriage has ended in divorce or death by producing the original decree absolute or death certificate (or a certified copy). If the divorce or annulment documents were granted outside the UK, Channel Islands or Isle of Man the registrar may need to get in touch with the General Register Office to confirm their validity, which will incur further costs of between £50–£75.

If either party is under 18 years old, evidence of consent by their parent or guardian is required. There are special procedures for those wishing to get married in the UK that are subject to immigration control; the register office will be able to advise on these.

SOLEMNISATION OF THE MARRIAGE
On the day of the wedding there must be at least two other people present who are prepared to act as witnesses and sign the marriage register. A registrar of marriages must be present at a marriage in a register office or at approved premises, but an authorised person may act in the capacity of registrar in a registered building.

If the marriage takes place at approved premises, the room must be separate from any other activity on the premises at the time of the ceremony, and no food or drink can be sold or consumed in the room during the ceremony or for one hour beforehand. In addition, proceedings conducted on approved premises cannot be religious in nature (although predominantly non-religious music and/or readings with incidental references to deities may be included).

The marriage must be solemnised with open doors. At some time during the ceremony the parties must make a declaration that they know of no legal impediment to the marriage and they must also say the contracting words; the declaratory and contracting words may vary according to the form of service. It may also be possible to embellish the marriage vows taken by the couple.

CIVIL FEES
Notice and registration of Marriage at a Register Office
By superintendent registrar's certificate, £35 per person for the notice of the marriage (which is not refundable if the marriage does not in fact take place) and £46 for the registration of the marriage.

Marriage at a Register Office/Approved Premises
Fees for marriage at a register office are set by the local authority responsible. An additional fee will also be payable for the registrar's attendance at the marriage on an approved premises. This is also set locally by the local authority responsible. A further charge is likely to be made by the owners of the building for the use of the premises.

For marriages taking place in a registered religious building, an additional fee (determined by the local authority) is payable for the registrar's attendance at the marriage unless an 'authorised person' has agreed to register the marriage. Additional fees may be charged by the trustees and/or proprietors of the building for the wedding and by the person who performs the ceremony.

ECCLESIASTICAL FEES
(Church of England and Church in Wales)

Marriage by banns
For publication of banns, £29*
For certificate of banns issued at time of publication, £14*
For marriage service, £441*
For marriage certificate at time of registration £4 and £10 thereafter
* These fees are revised from 1 January each calendar year. Some may not apply to the Church in Wales

Marriage by common licence
The fee will be specified by each individual diocese
Marriage by special licence £315*
* This fee is revised on 1 April each calendar year

SCOTLAND

REGULAR MARRIAGES
A regular marriage is one which is celebrated by a minister of religion or authorised registrar or other celebrant. Each of the parties must complete a marriage notice form and return it to the district registrar for the area in which they are to be married, irrespective of where they live, within the three month period prior to the date of the marriage and not later than 29 days prior to that date. The district registrar must then enter the date of receipt and certain details in a marriage book kept for this purpose, and must also enter the names of the parties and the proposed date of marriage in a list which is displayed in a conspicuous place at the registration office until the date of the marriage has passed. All persons wishing to enter into a regular marriage in Scotland must follow the same preliminary procedure regardless of whether they intend to have a religious or civil ceremony. Before the marriage ceremony takes place any person may submit an objection in writing to the district registrar.

A marriage schedule, which is prepared by the registrar, will be issued to one or both of the parties in person up to seven days before a religious marriage; for a civil marriage the schedule will be available at the ceremony. The schedule must be handed to the celebrant before the ceremony starts and it must be signed immediately after the wedding. For religious marriages the schedule must be sent within three days by the parties to the district registrar who must register the marriage as soon as possible thereafter. In civil marriages, the district registrar must register the marriage as soon as possible.

The authority to conduct a religious marriage is deemed to be vested in the authorised celebrant rather than the building in which it takes place; open-air religious ceremonies are therefore permissible in Scotland.

From 10 June 2002 it has been possible, under the Marriage (Scotland) Act 2002, for venues or couples to apply to the local council for a licence to allow a civil ceremony to take place at a venue other than a registration office. To obtain further information, a venue or couple should contact the district registrar in the area they wish to marry.

MARRIAGE BY COHABITATION WITH HABIT AND REPUTE
Prior to the enactment of the Family Law (Scotland) Act 2006, if two people had lived together constantly as husband and wife and were generally held to be such by the neighbourhood and among their friends and relations, a presumption could arise from which marriage could be inferred. Before such a marriage could be registered, however, a decree of declarator of marriage had to be obtained from the court of session. Section 3 of the 2006 act provides that it will no longer be possible for a marriage to be constituted by cohabitation with habit and repute, but it will still be possible for couples whose period of cohabitation began before commencement of the 2006 act to seek a declarator under the old rule of law.

SAME-SEX MARRIAGES
On 12 March 2014 the Scottish government passed the Marriage and Civil Partnership (Scotland) Act 2014. This permits same-sex couples to get married, either in a civil ceremony or a 'religious or belief' ceremony where the religious or belief body has opted-in to solemnising same-sex marriage. Also, certain same-sex couples who have entered into a civil partnership have the option under the act to change their civil partnership to a marriage.

It is still possible for same-sex couples to enter into a civil partnership and this may be a 'religious or belief' civil partnership if the religious or belief body has agreed to perform these.

CIVIL FEES
The fee for submitting a notice of marriage to the district registrar is £30.00 per person. Solemnisation of a civil marriage costs £55.00, while the extract of the entry in the register of marriages attracts a fee of £10.00. The costs of religious marriage ceremonies can vary.

THE GENERAL REGISTER OFFICE, PO Box 2, Southport PR8 2JD **T** 0300-123 1837 **W** www.gro.gov.uk/gro/content/certificates

THE NATIONAL RECORDS OF SCOTLAND, New Register House, 3 West Register Street, Edinburgh EH1 3YT **T** 0131-314 0380 **W** www.nrscotland.gov.uk

TOWN AND COUNTRY PLANNING

There are a number of acts governing the development of land and buildings in England and Wales and advice should always be sought from Citizens Advice or the local planning authority before undertaking building works on any land or property. If development takes place which requires planning permission without permission being given, enforcement action may take place and the situation may need to be rectified. Planning law in Scotland is similar but certain Scotland-specific legislation applies so advice should always be sought.

PLANNING PERMISSION
Planning permission is needed if the work involves:
* making a material change in use, such as dividing off part of the house or garden so that it can be used as a separate home or dividing off part of the house for commercial use, eg for a workshop
* going against the terms of the original planning permission, eg there may be a restriction on fences in front gardens on an open-plan estate
* building, engineering or mining, except for the permitted developments below
* new or wider access to a main road
* additions or extensions to flats or maisonettes
* work which might obstruct the view of road users

Planning permission is not needed to carry out internal alterations or work which does not affect the external appearance of the building, and are not works for making good war damage or works begun after 5 December 1968 for the alteration of a building by providing additional space in it underground.

Under regulations which came into effect on 15 April 2015, there are certain types of development for which the Secretary of State for the Environment, Food and Rural Affairs has granted general permissions (permitted development rights). These include house extensions and additions, outbuildings and garages, other ancillary garden buildings such as swimming pools or ponds, and laying patios, paths or driveways for domestic use. All developments are subject to a number of conditions.

Before carrying out any of the above permitted developments you should contact your local planning authority to find out whether the general permission has been modified in your area. For more information, visit W www.planningportal.gov.uk

OTHER RESTRICTIONS

It may be necessary to obtain other types of permissions before carrying out any development. These permissions are separate from planning permission and apply regardless of whether or not planning permission is needed, eg:

- building regulations will probably apply if a new building is to be erected, if an existing one is to be altered or extended, or if the work involves building over a drain or sewer. The building control department of the local authority will advise on this
- any alterations to a listed building or the grounds of a listed building must be approved by the local authority. Listing will include not only the main building but everything in the curtilage of the building
- local authority approval is necessary if a building (or, in some circumstances, gates, walls, fences or railings) in a conservation area is to be demolished; each local authority keeps a register of all local buildings that are in conservation areas
- many trees are protected by tree preservation orders and must not be pruned or taken down without local authority consent
- bats and many other species are protected, and Natural England, Natural Resources Wales or Scottish Natural Heritage must be notified before any work is carried out that will affect the habitat of protected species, eg timber treatment, renovation or extensions of lofts
- developments in areas with special designations, such as National Parks, Areas of Outstanding Natural Beauty, National Scenic Areas or in the Norfolk or Suffolk Broads, are subject to greater restrictions. The local planning authority will advise or refer enquirers to the relevant authority

There may also be restrictions contained in the title to the property which require you to get someone else's agreement before carrying out certain developments, and which should be considered when works are planned.

VOTERS' QUALIFICATIONS

Those entitled to vote at parliamentary and local government elections are those who, at the date of taking the poll, are:

- on the electoral roll
- aged 18 years or older (although for Scottish parliament and local government elections in Scotland those aged 16 and older can vote)
- British citizens, qualifying Commonwealth citizens or citizens of the Irish Republic who are resident in the UK
- those who suffer from no other legal bar to voting (eg prisoners). It should be noted that there is some uncertainty regarding the future of the legal bar on prisoners' voting following a decision taken by the European Court of Human Rights
- citizens of any EU member state may vote in local elections if they meet the criteria listed above (save for the nationality requirements). There is some uncertainty regarding future voting rights of EU citizens in light of Brexit. However, it should be noted that there will be no change to the voting rights of EU citizens living in the UK while the UK remains in the EU

British citizens resident abroad are entitled to vote, provided they have been registered to vote in the UK within the last 15 years, as overseas electors in domestic parliamentary elections in the constituency in which they were last resident if they are on the electoral roll of the relevant constituency. The government released a policy statement in October 2016 proposing to abolish the current 15 year time limit for British citizens registering as overseas electors although it is unclear when this proposal will be legislated for. Members of the armed forces and their spouses or civil partners, Crown servants and employees of the British Council who are overseas, along with their spouses and civil partners, are entitled to vote regardless of how long they have been abroad. British citizens who had never been registered as an elector in the UK are not eligible to register as an overseas voter unless they left the UK before they were 18, providing they left the country no more than 15 years ago. Overseas electors may opt to vote by proxy or by postal vote. Overseas voters may not vote in local government elections.

The main categories of people who are not entitled to vote at general elections are:

- sitting peers in the House of Lords
- convicted persons detained in pursuance of their sentences (though remand prisoners, unconvicted prisoners and civil prisoners can vote if on the electoral register). This is currently subject to review, as detailed above
- those convicted within the previous five years of corrupt or illegal election practices
- EU citizens (who may only vote in EU and local government elections)

Under the Representation of the People Act 2000, several new groups of people are permitted to vote for the first time. These include: people who live on barges; people in mental health hospitals (other than those with criminal convictions) and homeless people who have made a 'declaration of local connection'.

REGISTERING TO VOTE

Voters must be entered on an electoral register. The Electoral Registration Officer (ERO) for each council area is responsible for preparing and publishing the register for his area by 1 December each year. Names may be added to the register to reflect changes in people's circumstances as they occur and each month during December to August, the ERO publishes a list of alterations to the published register.

On 10 May 2012, the government introduced the electoral registration and administration bill, which received royal assent on 31 January 2013. The act replaced household registration with individual elector registration, meaning each elector must apply individually to be registered to vote. Individuals will also be asked for identifying information such as date of birth and national insurance number. The act also introduced a number of changes relating to electoral administration and the conduct of elections. Anyone failing to supply information to the ERO when requested, or supplying false information, may be fined by up to £1,000. Further, the ERO may impose a civil penalty on those who fail to make an application for registration when required to do so by the ERO. Application forms and more information are available from the Electoral Commission (W www.aboutmyvote.co.uk).

VOTING

Voting is not compulsory in the UK. Those who wish to vote do so in person at the allotted polling station. Postal votes are now available to anyone on request and you do not need to give a reason for using a postal vote.

A proxy (whereby the voter nominates someone to vote in person on their behalf) can be appointed to act in a specific election, for a specified period of time or indefinitely. For the appointment of an indefinite or long-term proxy, the voter needs to specify physical employment, study reasons or a disability to explain why they are making an application. With proxy votes where a particular election is specified, the voter needs to provide details of the circumstances by which they cannot reasonably be expected to go to the polling station. Applications for a proxy are normally available up to six working days before an election, but should the voter fall ill on election day, it is possible to appoint a proxy up until polling day.

WILLS

A will is used to appoint executors (who will administer the estate), give directions as to the disposal of the body, appoint guardians for children and determine how and to whom property is to be passed. A well-drafted will can operate to reduce the level of inheritance tax which the estate pays. It is best to have a will drawn up by a solicitor, but if a solicitor is not employed the following points must be taken into account:

- if possible the will must not be prepared on behalf of another person by someone who is to benefit from it or who is a close relative of a major beneficiary
- the language used must be clear and unambiguous and it is better to avoid the use of legal terms where the same thing can be expressed in plain language
- it is better to rewrite the whole document if a mistake is made. If necessary, alterations can be made by striking through the words with a pen, and the signature or initials of the testator and the witnesses must be put in the margin opposite the alteration. No alteration of any kind should be made after the will has been executed
- if the person later wishes to change the will or part of it, it is better to write a new will revoking the old. The use of codicils (documents written as supplements or containing modifications to the will) should be left to a solicitor
- the will should be typed or printed, or if handwritten be legible and preferably in ink

The form of a will varies to suit different cases, a solicitor will be able to advise as to wording, however, 'DIY' will-writing kits can be purchased from good stationery shops and many banks offer a will-writing service.

LAPSED LEGATEES

If a person who has been left property in a will dies before the person who made the will, the gift fails and will pass to the person entitled to everything not otherwise disposed of (the residuary estate). If the beneficiary of the residuary estate dies before the person who made the will, the gift of the residuary estate also fails and passes to the closest relative(s) of the testator in accordance with the intestacy rules.

It is always better to draw up a new will if a beneficiary predeceases the person who made the will.

EXECUTORS

It is usual to appoint two executors, although one is sufficient. No more than four persons can deal with the estate of the person who has died. The name and address of each executor should be given in full (the addresses are not essential but including them adds clarity to the document). Executors should be 18 years of age or over. An executor may be a beneficiary of the will.

WITNESSES

A person who is a beneficiary of a will, or the spouse or civil partner of a beneficiary at the time the will is signed, must not act as a witness or else he/she will be unable to take his/her gift. There is nothing preventing the spouse or civil partner of the person making the will from acting as a witness, but as it is rare for a spouse or civil partner not to benefit from the will of his/her spouse or civil partner, an independent witness is usually better.

It is also better that a person does not act as an executor and as a witness, as he/she can take no benefit (including

remuneration) under a will to which he/she is witness. In relation to deaths on or after 1 February 2001, however, a professional executor who is also a witness can receive payments due to him or her under a term in the will for services provided as executor.

The identity of the witnesses should be made as explicit as possible, such as by stating their names, addresses, and occupations.

EXECUTION OF A WILL

The person making the will should sign his/her name in the presence of the two witnesses. It is advisable to sign at the foot of the document, so as to avoid uncertainty about the testator's intention. The witnesses must then sign their names while the person making the will looks on. If this procedure is not adhered to, the will may be considered invalid. There are certain exceptional circumstances where these rules are relaxed, eg where the person may be too ill to sign.

CAPACITY TO MAKE A WILL

Anyone aged 18 or over can make a will. However, if there is any suspicion that the person making the will is not, through reasons of infirmity or age, fully in command of his/her faculties, it is advisable to arrange for a medical practitioner to examine the person making the will as near to the time that the testator gives instructions for the will and to when the will is executed (to verify his/her mental capacity and to record that medical opinion in writing), and to ask the examining practitioner to act as a witness. If a person is not mentally able to make a will, the court of protection may do this for him/her by virtue of the Mental Capacity Act 2005.

REVOCATION

A will may be revoked or cancelled in a number of ways:

- a later will revokes an earlier one if it says so; otherwise the earlier will is by implication revoked by the later one to the extent that it contradicts or repeats the earlier one
- a will is revoked if the original physical document on which it is written is destroyed by the person whose will it is. There must be an intention to revoke the will and an act of destruction. It may not be sufficient to obliterate the will with a pen
- a will is revoked by the testator making a written declaration to this effect executed in the same way as a will
- a will is also revoked when the person marries or forms a civil partnership, unless it is clear from the will that the person intended the will to stand after that particular marriage or civil partnership. A will is not revoked, however, by the conversion of a civil partnership to a marriage, or when the testator is treated as having formed a civil partnership on 5 December 2005 because he/she registered a recognised overseas relationship before that date.
- where a marriage or civil partnership ends in divorce or dissolution or is annulled or declared void, gifts to the spouse or civil partner and the appointment of the spouse or civil partner as executor fail unless the will says that this is not to happen. A former spouse or civil partner is treated as having predeceased the testator. A separation does not change the effect of a married person or civil partner's will.

PROBATE AND LETTERS OF ADMINISTRATION

The grant of probate is granted to the executors named in a will and once granted, the executors are obliged to carry out the instructions of the will. Letters of administration are granted where the deceased died intestate or did not leave a valid will. Letters of administration with will annexed are granted when the deceased did not appoint an executor in the will or the appointed executor(s) are not able or willing to act. The letters of administration give a person, often the next of kin, similar powers and duties to those of an executor.

Applications for the grant of probate or for letters of administration can be made to the Principal Registry of the Family Division, to a district probate registry or to a probate sub-registry. Applicants not using a solicitor will need to send the following documents to the main probate registry of choice: the Probate Application Form (PA1); the original will and codicils (if any) and three copies of the same; an official copy of the death certificate; and the appropriate tax form (an 'IHT 205' if no inheritance tax is owed; otherwise an 'IHT 421' stamped by HMRC confirming payment of inheritance tax), in addition to a cheque for the relevant probate fee. The applicant will then be invited to an interview at the probate registry of choice where they will swear an oath. Where an applicant is using a solicitor, the PA1 is not necessary and the appropriate oath (for executors or administrators) will be included in the documents to be sent to the probate registry; there is no interview. In both cases, where the estate of the deceased is below £5,000, there is no probate fee to pay. Certain property, up to the value of £5,000, may be disposed of without a grant of probate or letters of administration, as can assets that do not pass under the will such as jointly owned assets which pass automatically on the death of one of the joint holders to the survivor, life policies written in trust, or discretionary pension death benefits.

WHERE TO FIND A PROVED WILL

Since 1858 wills which have been proved, that is wills on which probate or letters of administration have been granted, must have been proved at the Principal Registry of the Family Division or at a district probate registry. The Lord Chancellor has power to direct where the original documents are kept but most are filed where they were proved and may be inspected there and a copy obtained. You can search for a probate record online or by post. The Principal Registry also holds copies of all wills proved at district probate registries and these may be inspected at First Avenue House, High Holborn, London. An index of all grants, both of probate and of letters of administration, is compiled by the Principal Registry and may be seen either at the Principal Registry or at a district probate registry.

It is also possible to discover when a grant of probate or letters of administration is issued by requesting a standing search. In response to a request and for a small fee, a district probate registry will supply the names and addresses of executors or administrators and the registry in which the grant was made, of any grant in the estate of a specified person made in the previous six months or following six months.

PRINCIPAL REGISTRY (FAMILY DIVISION), 7th Floor, 42–49 High Holborn, First Avenue House, London WC1V 6NP
T 020-7421 8509

INTESTACY

Intestacy occurs when someone dies without leaving a will or leaves a will which is invalid or which does not take effect for some reason. Intestacy can be partial, for instance, if there is a valid will which disposes of some but not all of the testator's property. In such cases the person's estate (property, possessions, other assets following the payment of debts) passes to certain members of the family. If a will has been written that disposes of only part of a person's property, these rules apply to the part which is undisposed of.

Some types of property do not follow the intestacy rules, for example, property held as joint tenants, insurance policies taken out for specified individuals or assigned into trust during the testator's lifetime and death benefits under a pension scheme.

Following a lengthy review by the Law Commission, the intestacy rules changed on 1 October 2014.

If the person (intestate) leaves a spouse or a civil partner who survives for 28 days and children (legitimate, illegitimate and adopted children and other descendants), the estate is divided as follows:

- if the estate is worth more than £250,000, the spouse or civil partner takes the 'personal chattels' (household articles, including cars, but nothing used for business purposes or held solely as an investment), £250,000 and half of the rest of the estate absolutely
- the rest of the estate goes to the children*

If the intestate leaves a spouse or civil partner who survives for 28 days but no children, the spouse or civil partner will take the estate in its entirety, regardless of its value.

If there is no surviving spouse or civil partner, the estate is distributed among those who survive the intestate as follows (these provisions remained unchanged at 1 October 2014):

- to surviving children*, but if none to
- parents (equally, if both alive), but if none to
- brothers and sisters of the whole blood* (including issue of deceased ones), but if none to
- brothers and sisters of the half blood* (including issue of deceased ones), but if none to
- grandparents (equally, if more than one), but if none to
- aunts and uncles of the whole blood*, but if none to
- aunts and uncles of the half blood*, but if none to
- the Crown, Duchy of Lancaster or the Duke of Cornwall (bona vacantia)

* To inherit, a member of these groups must survive the intestate and attain the age of 18, or marry under that age. If they die under the age of 18 (unless married under that age), their share goes to others, if any, in the same group. If any member of these groups predeceases the intestate leaving children, their share is divided equally among their children.

In England and Wales the provisions of the Inheritance (Provision for Family and Dependants) Act 1975 may allow other people to claim provision from the deceased's assets. This act also applies to cases where a will has been made and allows a person to apply to the court if they feel that the will or rules of intestacy (or both) do not make adequate provision for them. The court can order payment from the deceased's assets or the transfer of property from them if the applicant's claim is accepted. The application must be made within six months of the grant of probate or letters of administration and the following people can make an application:

- the spouse or civil partner
- a former spouse or civil partner who has not remarried or formed a subsequent civil partnership
- a child of the deceased
- someone treated as a child of the deceased's family where the deceased stood in the role of a parent to the applicant
- someone maintained wholly or partly by the deceased
- where the deceased died on or after 1 January 1996, someone who has cohabited for two years before the death in the same household as the deceased and was living as the husband or wife or civil partner of the deceased

SCOTLAND

In Scotland any person over 12 and of sound mind can make a will. The person making the will can only freely dispose of the heritage and what is known as the 'dead's part' of the estate because:

- the spouse or civil partner has the right to inherit one-third of the moveable estate if there are children or other descendants, and one-half of it if there are not
- children are entitled to one-third of the moveable estate if there is a surviving spouse or civil partner, and one-half of it if there is not

The remaining portion of the moveable estate is the dead's part, and legacies and bequests are payable from this. Debts are payable out of the whole estate before any division. The Scottish government has indicated that it intends to reform the law in this area to remove the distinction which currently applies in relation to the treatment of heritable and moveable property.

From August 1995, wills no longer needed to be 'holographed' and it is now only necessary to have one witness. The person making the will still needs to sign each page. It is better that the will is not witnessed by a beneficiary although the attestation would still be sound and the beneficiary would not have to relinquish the gift.

As a result of the changes brought in by the Succession (Scotland) Act 2016, from 1 November 2016 a divorce, dissolution or annulment (granted by a UK court) will revoke any provision in a will which confers a benefit or power of appointment on the former spouse or civil partner unless the will expressly provides that the benefit or appointment should still apply in the event of a divorce, dissolution or annulment. Subsequent marriage or civil partnership does not revoke a will but the birth of a child who is not provided for may do so. A will may be revoked by a subsequent will, either expressly or by implication, but in so far as the two can be read together both have effect. If a subsequent will is revoked, the earlier will may be revived provided it was not physically destroyed.

Wills may be registered in the sheriff court Books of the Sheriffdom in which the deceased lived or in the Books of Council and Session at the Registers of Scotland.

CONFIRMATION

Confirmation (the Scottish equivalent of probate) is obtained in the sheriff court of the sheriffdom in which the deceased was domiciled at the time of death. Executors are either 'nominate' (named by the deceased in the will) or 'dative' (appointed by the court in cases where no executor is named in a will or in cases of intestacy). Applicants for confirmation must first provide an inventory of the deceased's estate and a schedule of debts, with an affidavit. In estates under £36,000 gross, confirmation can be obtained under a simplified procedure at reduced fees, with no need for a solicitor. The local sheriff clerk's office can provide assistance.

PRINCIPAL REGISTRY (FAMILY DIVISION), First Avenue House, 42–49 High Holborn, London WC1 6NP
T 020-7947 6000

REGISTERS OF SCOTLAND, Meadowbank House, 153 London Road, Edinburgh EH8 7AU T 0800-169 9391

INTESTACY

The rules of distribution are contained in the Succession (Scotland) Act 1964 and are extended to include civil partners by the Civil Partnership Act 2004.

A surviving spouse or civil partner is entitled to 'prior rights'. Once the provisions of the Marriage and Civil Partnership Act 2014 come into force references to people who are or were married are to be read as referring to both opposite and same-sex marriage. Prior rights mean that if certain conditions are met the spouse or civil partner has the right to inherit:

- the matrimonial or family home up to a value of £473,000, or one matrimonial or family home if there is more than one, or, in certain circumstances, the value of the home
- the furnishings and contents of that home, up to the value of £29,000
- a cash sum of £50,000 if the deceased left children or other descendants, or £89,000 if not

These figures are increased from time to time by regulations.

Once prior rights have been satisfied legal rights are settled. Legal rights are:

- *Jus relicti(ae) and rights under the section 131 of the Civil Partnership Act 2004* – the right of a surviving spouse or civil partner to one-half of the net moveable estate, after satisfaction of prior rights, if there are no surviving children; if there are surviving children, the spouse or civil partner is entitled to one-third of the net moveable estate
- *Legitim and rights under the section 131 of the Civil Partnership Act 2004* – the right of surviving children to one-half of the net moveable estate if there is no surviving spouse or civil partner; if there is a surviving spouse or civil partner, the children are entitled to one-third of the net moveable estate after the satisfaction of prior rights

Once prior and legal rights have been satisfied, the remaining estate will be distributed in the following order:

- to descendants
- if no descendants, then to collaterals (ie brothers and sisters) and parents with each being entitled to half of the estate, or if only either parents or collaterals survive, the whole of the estate
- surviving spouse or civil partner
- if no collaterals, parents, spouse or civil partner, then to ascendants collaterals (ie aunts and uncles), and so on in an ascending scale
- if all lines of succession fail, the estate passes to the Crown

Relatives of the whole blood are preferred to relatives of the half blood. Also the right of representation, ie the right of the issue of a person who would have succeeded if he/she had survived the intestate, applies.

The Family Law (Scotland) Act 2006 makes provision to allow an unmarried cohabitant to make a financial claim against the estate of a cohabitant who dies intestate. In general a claim must be made within six months of the deceased's death. The court must take into account certain factors when considering such a claim. If the claim is successful the court has the power to order payment of a capital sum and transfer of property.

INTELLECTUAL PROPERTY

Intellectual property is a broad term covering a number of legal rights provided by the government to help people protect their creative works and encourage further innovation. By using these legal rights people can own the things they create and control the way in which others use their innovations. Intellectual property owners can take legal action to stop others using their intellectual property, they can license their intellectual property to others or they can sell it on. Different types of intellectual property utilise different forms of protection including copyright, designs, patents and trade marks, which are all covered below in more detail.

CHANGES TO INTELLECTUAL PROPERTY LAW
Reforms to the Copyright, Designs and Patents Act 1988 came into force on 1 June 2014, giving a number of sectors a legal framework suitable for the digital age, removing unnecessary regulations and enabling these sectors to better preserve and use copyright material. Under the reforms, disabled people and disability groups can make accessible copies of copyright material (eg music, film, books) when no commercial alternative exists, researchers benefit from the introduction of a new text and data mining exception for non-commercial research and schools, colleges and universities can obtain a licence to use copyright material on interactive whiteboards and in presentations without accidentally infringing copyright. An existing preservation exception was expanded to cover all types of copyright work, and now applies to museums and galleries as well as libraries and archives.

The Intellectual Property Act 2014 came into effect on 1 October 2014. The act modernised intellectual property law to help UK businesses better protect their rights. The act also implemented reforms to design legislation and introduced a number of changes to patent law, making it cheaper and easier to use and defend patents. Additional patent rule changes came into effect on 1 October 2016 and 6 April 2017. The changes streamlined the application process, made procedures more flexible and increased the legal certainty of patents that are granted.

The Intellectual Property (Unjustified Threats) Act 2017 came into effect on 1 October 2017. The act serves to protect businesses against unfair threats of legal action, when no infringement of intellectual property has actually taken place, and to help businesses negotiate fairly over intellectual property disputes and avoid costly litigation.

COPYRIGHT

Copyright protects all original literary, dramatic, musical and artistic works, as well as sound and film recordings and broadcasts. Among the works covered by copyright are novels, computer programs, newspaper articles, sculptures, technical drawings, websites, maps and photographs. Under copyright the creators of these works can control the various ways in which their material may be exploited, the rights broadly covering copying, adapting, issuing (including renting and lending) copies to the public, performing in public, and broadcasting the material. The transfer of copyright works to formats accessible to visually impaired persons without infringement of copyright was enacted in 2002.

Copyright protection in the UK is automatic and there is no official registration system. The creator of a work can help to protect it by including the copyright symbol ©, the name of the copyright owner, and the year in which the work was created. In addition, steps can be taken by the work's creator to provide evidence that they had the work at a particular time (eg by depositing a copy with a bank or solicitor). The main legislation is the Copyright, Designs and Patents Act 1988 (as amended). The term of copyright protection for literary, dramatic, musical (including song lyrics and musical compositions) and artistic works lasts for 70 years after the death of the creator. For film, copyright lasts for 70 years after the director, authors of the screenplay and dialogue, or the composer of any music specially created for the film have all died. Sound recordings are protected for 50 years after their publication (or their first performance if they are not published), and broadcasts for 50 years from the end of the year in which the broadcast/transmission was made. The typographical arrangement of published editions remains under copyright protection for 25 years from the end of the year in which the particular edition was published.

The main international treaties protecting copyright are the Berne Convention for the Protection of Literary and Artistic Works (administered by the World Intellectual Property Organization (WIPO)), the Rome Convention for the Protection of Performers, Producers of Phonograms and Broadcasting Organisations (administered by the the International Labour Organisation, UNESCO and WIPO), the Geneva Phonograms Convention (administered by WIPO), and the Universal Copyright Convention (developed by UNESCO); the UK is a signatory to these conventions. Copyright material created by UK nationals or residents is protected in the countries that have signed one of the above-named conventions by the national law of that country. A list of participating countries may be obtained from the UK Intellectual Property Office. The World Trade Organization's Trade-Related Aspects of Intellectual Property Rights (TRIPS) agreement may also provide copyright protection abroad.

In May 2001 the EU passed a new directive (which became law in the UK in 2003) aimed at harmonising copyright law throughout the EU to take account of the internet and other technologies. More information can be found online (W www.ipo.gov.uk).

LICENSING
Use of copyright material without seeking permission in each instance may be permitted under 'blanket' licences available from national copyright licensing agencies. The International Federation of Reproduction Rights Organisations facilitates agreements between its member licensing agencies and on behalf of its members with organisations such as WIPO, UNESCO, the EU and the Council of Europe. More information can be found online (W www.ifrro.org).

DESIGN PROTECTION

Design protection covers the outward appearance of an article, and in the UK it takes two forms: registered design and design right, which are not mutually exclusive. Registered design protects the aesthetic appearance of an article, including shape, configuration, pattern or ornament; artistic works such as sculptures are excluded, being generally protected by copyright. To achieve design protection the owner of the design must apply to the Intellectual Property Office. In order to qualify for protection, a design must be new and materially different from earlier UK published designs. Initial registration lasts for five years and can be extended in five-year increments to a maximum of 25 years. The current legislation is the Registered Designs Act 1949 (as amended).

UK applicants wishing to protect their designs in the EU can do so by applying for a Registered Community Design with the Office for Harmonisation in the Internal Market. Outside the EU separate applications must be made in each country in which protection is sought.

Design right is an automatic right which applies to the shape or configuration of articles and does not require registration. Unlike registered design, two-dimensional designs do not qualify for protection but designs of electronic circuits are protected by design right. Designs must be original and non-commonplace. The term of design right is ten years from first marketing of the design, or 15 years after the creation of the design, whichever is earlier. This right is effective only in the UK. After five years anyone is entitled to apply for a licence of right, which allows others to make and sell products copying the design. The current legislation is Part 3 of the Copyright, Designs and Patents Act 1988.

PATENTS

A patent is a document issued by the UK Intellectual Property Office relating to an invention. It gives the proprietor the right for a limited period to stop others from making, using, importing or selling the invention without the inventor's permission. In return the patentee pays a fee to cover the costs of processing the patent and publicly discloses details of the invention.

To qualify for a patent, an invention must be new, must be functional or technical, must exhibit an inventive step, and must be capable of industrial application. The patent is valid for a maximum of 20 years from the date on which the application was filed, subject to payment of annual fees from the end of the fifth year.

The UK Intellectual Property Office, established in 1852, is responsible for ensuring that all stages of an application comply with the Patents Act 1977, and that the invention meets the criteria for a patent. An online patent renewal service is available at: www.gov.uk/renew-patent.

WIPO is responsible for administering many of the international conventions on intellectual property. The Patent Cooperation Treaty allows inventors to file a single application for patent rights in some or all of the contracting states. This application is searched by an International Searching Authority to confirm the invention is novel and that the same concept has not already been made publicly available. The application and search report are then published by the International Bureau of WIPO. It may also be the subject of an (optional) international preliminary examination. Applicants must then deal directly with the patent offices in the countries where they are seeking patent rights. The European Patent Convention allows inventors to obtain patent rights in all the contracting states by filing a single application with the European Patent Office. More information can be found online (W www.ipo.gov.uk).

RESEARCH DISCLOSURES

Research disclosures are publicly disclosed details of inventions. Once published, an invention is considered no longer novel and becomes 'prior art'. Publishing a disclosure is significantly cheaper than applying for a patent; however, unlike a patent, it does not entitle the author to exclusive rights to use or license the invention. Instead, research disclosures are primarily published to ensure the inventor the freedom to use the invention. This works because publishing legally prevents other parties from patenting the disclosed innovation and, in the UK, patent law dictates that by disclosing details of an invention, even the inventor relinquishes their right to a patent.

In theory, publishing details of an invention anywhere should be enough to constitute a research disclosure. However, to be effective, a research disclosure needs to be published in a location which patent examiners will include in their prior art searches. To ensure global legal precedent it must be included in a publication with a recognised date stamp and made publicly available throughout the world.

Research Disclosure, established in 1960 and operated by Questel Ireland Ltd, is the primary publisher of research disclosures. It is the only disclosure service recognised by the Patent Cooperation Treaty as a mandatory search resource which must be consulted by the international search authorities. More information can be found online (W www.researchdisclosure.com).

TRADE MARKS

Trade marks are a means of identification, enabling traders to make their goods and services readily distinguishable from those supplied by others. Trade marks can take the form of words, a logo or a combination of both. Registration prevents other traders using the same or similar trade marks for similar products or services.

In the UK trade marks are registered at the UK Intellectual Property Office. In order to qualify for registration, a trade mark must be capable of distinguishing its proprietor's goods or services from those of other undertakings; it should be non-deceptive, should not describe the goods and services or any characteristics of them, should not be contrary to law or morality and should not be similar or identical to any earlier trade marks for the same or similar goods or services. The owner of a registered trade mark may include an ® symbol next to it, and must renew their registration every ten years to keep it in force. The relevant current legislation is the Trade Marks Act 1994 (as amended).

It is possible to obtain an international trade mark registration, effective in 92 countries, under the Madrid system for the international registration of marks, to which the UK is party. British companies can obtain international trade mark registration in those countries party to the system through a single application to WIPO.

EU trade mark regulation is administered by the EU Intellectual Property Office in Alicante, Spain. The office registers Community trade marks, which are valid throughout the EU. The registration of trade marks in individual member states continues in parallel with EU trade mark standards.

DOMAIN NAMES

An internet domain name (eg www.whitakersalmanack.com) has to be registered separately from a trade mark, and this can be done through a number of registrars which charge varying rates and compete for business. For each top-level domain name (eg uk.com), there is a central registry to store the unique internet names and addresses using that suffix. A list of accredited registrars can be found online (W www.icann.org).

CONTACTS

COPYRIGHT LICENSING AGENCY LTD, Barnard's Inn, 86 Fetter Lane, London EC4A 1EN **T** 020-7400 3100 **W** www.cla.co.uk
EUROPEAN PATENT OFFICE, 80298 Munich, Germany **T** (+49) 89 2399-0 **W** www.epo.org
INTELLECTUAL PROPERTY OFFICE, Concept House, Cardiff Road, Newport NP10 8QQ **T** 0300-300 2000 **W** www.ipo.gov.uk
WORLD INTELLECTUAL PROPERTY ORGANIZATION, 34 chemin des Colombettes, CH-1211 Geneva 20, Switzerland **T** (+41) 22 338 9111 **W** www.wipo.int

THE MEDIA

CROSS-MEDIA OWNERSHIP

The rules surrounding cross-media ownership were overhauled as part of the 2003 Communications Act. The act simplified and relaxed existing rules to encourage dispersion of ownership and new market entry while preventing the most influential media in any community being controlled by too narrow a range of interests. However, transfers and mergers are not solely subject to examination on competition grounds by the competition authorities. The Secretary of State for Digital, Culture, Media and Sport has a broad remit to decide if a transaction is permissible and can intervene on public interest grounds (relating both to newspapers and cross-media criteria, if broadcasting interests are also involved). The Office of Communications (OFCOM) has an advisory role in this context. Government and parliamentary assurances were given that any intervention into local newspaper transfers would be rare and exceptional. Following a request from the Secretary of State for Digital, Culture, Media and Sport in June 2010 for a removal of all restrictions from the ownership of local media, OFCOM recommended the liberalisation of local cross-media regulations to enable a single owner to control newspapers, a TV licence and radio stations in one area.

REGULATION

OFCOM is the regulator for the communication industries in the UK and has responsibility for television, radio, telecommunications and wireless communications services. OFCOM is required to report annually to parliament and exists to further the interests of consumers by balancing choice and competition with the duty to foster plurality; protect viewers and listeners and promote cultural diversity in the media; and to ensure full and fair competition between communications providers.

OFFICE OF COMMUNICATIONS (OFCOM), Riverside House, 2A Southwark Bridge Road, London SE1 9HA
T 020-7981 3000 W www.ofcom.org.uk
Chief Executive, Sharon White

COMPLAINTS

Under the Communications Act 2003 OFCOM's licensees are obliged to adhere to the provisions of its codes (including advertising, programme standards, fairness, privacy and sponsorship). Complainants should contact the broadcaster in the first instance (details can be found on OFCOM's website); however, if the complainant wishes the complaint to be considered by OFCOM, it will do so. Complaints must be submitted within 20 working days of broadcast, as broadcasters are only required to keep recordings for the following periods: radio, 42 days; television, 90 days; and cable and satellite, 60 days. OFCOM can fine a broadcaster, revoke a licence or take programmes off the air. Since November 2004 complaints relating to individual advertisements on TV or radio have been dealt with by the Advertising Standards Authority.

ADVERTISING STANDARDS AUTHORITY Mid City Place, 71 High Holborn, London WC1V 6QT T 020-7492 2222
W www.asa.org.uk
Chief Executive, Guy Parker

TELEVISION

There are six major television channel owners who are responsible for the biggest audience share. They are the British Broadcasting Corporation (BBC), Independent Television (ITV), Channel 4, Channel 5, Sky and UKTV. Overall there are around 480 channels available to viewers, through free-to-air, free-to-view and subscription-based services. Following the completion of the switchover to a digital format in October 2012, analogue transmissions ended and digital-only content was broadcast through a range of services, including terrestrial, satellite, cable and IP.

Beginning as a radio station in 1922, the BBC is the oldest broadcaster in the world. The corporation began a London-only television service from Alexandra Palace in 1936 and achieved nationwide coverage 15 years later. A second station, BBC Two, was launched in 1964. The BBC's other free-to-air channels available in the UK comprise BBC Four, BBC News, BBC Parliament, the children's channels, CBeebies and CBBC, and regional channels including BBC Alba. Many of the BBC's channels have a corresponding HD (high definition) service and there are additionally several local channels. BBC's iPlayer service was launched on Christmas Day 2007 and allows users to view and listen to content instantly, stream live television and download programmes on to a computer, tablet or mobile device for up to 30 days. An integrated service for radio was launched in June 2008. In 2009, iPlayer was extended to more than 20 devices, including mobile phones and games consoles, and an HD service was launched. The BBC services are funded by the licence fee. The corporation also has a commercial arm, BBC Worldwide, which was formed in 1994 and exists to maximise the value of the BBC's programme and publishing assets for the benefit of the licence payer. Its businesses include international programming distribution, magazines, other licensed products, live events and media monitoring.

The ITV (Independent Television) network began broadcasting in 1955 on Channel 3 in the London area, under the Television Act 1954 which made provision for commercial television in the UK. The ITV network originally comprised a number of independent licensees, the majority of which have now merged to form ITV plc. The network generates funds through broadcasting television advertisements. The ITV network channels now include ITV2, ITV3, ITV4, ITVBe, ITV Encore and CiTV, while the network also owns UTV Ireland. The majority of ITV channels have corresponding HD services. ITV Player, similar to iPlayer, was launched December 2008. ITV Network Centre is wholly owned by the ITV companies and undertakes commissioning and scheduling of programmes shown across the ITV network and, as with the other terrestrial channels, 25 per cent of programmes must come from independent producers.

Channel 4 and S4C (Sianel Pedwar Cymru – Channel Four Wales) were launched in 1982 to provide programmes with a distinctive character that appeal to interests not catered for by ITV. Channel 4 has a remit to be innovative, experimental and distinctive. Although publicly owned, Channel 4 receives no public funding and is financed predominantly through advertising, but unlike ITV, Channel 4 is not shareholder-owned. It has expanded to create the stations E4, More4, Film4, 4Music and, in July 2012, catchup channel 4seven. All 4 is Channel 4's online service which enables viewers to download and revisit programmes from the last 30 days as well as access an older archive of footage. All 4 replaced Channel 4's first online platform 4oD (launched in 2006) in March

2015. S4C, the Welsh language public service broadcaster, receives annual funding from the Department for Digital, Culture, Media and Sport (DCMS). The DCMS provided £6.7m in funding for 2017–18, around 8 per cent of its total budget of £84m. In March 2018, the government decided that S4C would be entirely funded through the TV licence from 2022, which currently fulfils 90 per cent of its budget. S4C will remain independent and be entitled to receive UK government funding and generate its own revenue. The on-demand service is called S4C Clic.

Channel 5 began broadcasting in 1997. It was rebranded Five in 2002 but reverted to its original name, Channel 5, after the station was acquired by Northern & Shell in July 2010. Digital stations 5USA and 5Star (formerly Five Life, then Fiver) were launched in October 2006. My5 (formerly Demand 5) is an online service, launched in June 2008, where viewers can watch and download content from the last 30 days on various platforms.

BSkyB was formed after the merger in 1990 of Sky Television and British Sky Broadcasting. Now known as Sky plc, the company operates across five countries: Italy, Germany, Austria, the UK and Ireland and serves 22 million customers. In addition to television services, Sky provides broadband and fixed line telephone services and is the UK's largest pay-TV broadcaster, with 12.5 million customers in 2017. In 2007, Freeview overtook Sky as the UK's most popular digital service. In 2014, BSkyB acquired Sky Italia and a 90.04 per cent majority interest in Sky Deutschland. 21st Century Fox owns a 39.14 per cent controlling stake in the company. In the UK, the company changed its operations name to Sky UK Limited but continued to trade under the name Sky. Its television service includes Sky Sports, Sky Cinema and Sky Arts.

In February 2011, a new version of OFCOM's Broadcasting Code came into force, permitting product placement for the first time in UK-produced television programmes. A large 'P' logo designed by OFCOM and broadcasters is displayed at the beginning and end of each programme containing product placement. The first instance of product placement occurred on 28 February 2011.

THE TELEVISION LICENCE
In the UK and its dependencies, a television licence is required to receive any publicly broadcast television service, regardless of its source, including commercial, satellite and cable programming. A TV licence registered to a home address allows the viewer to watch television on laptops, tablets and mobile phones outside the place of residence. From 1 September 2016, new legislation required a TV licence to be needed for viewers using services such as BBC iPlayer, even if the programme was not being watched live. The BBC hoped that the new legislation would fill a £150m gap in its finances, which had been caused by the increasing number of viewers only using the iPlayer service.

The TV licence is classified as a tax, therefore non-payment is a criminal offence. A fine of up to £1,000 can be imposed on those successfully prosecuted. The TV licence is issued on behalf of the BBC as the licensing authority under the Communications Act 2003. In 2017–18 income from licence fees totalled £3,830m, an increase from £3,787m the previous year. In 2017, the TV licence fee increased for the first time since 2010. As at 1 April 2018, an annual colour television licence costs £150.50 and a black and white licence £50.50. Concessions are available for the elderly and people with disabilities. Further details can be found at **W** www.tvlicensing.co.uk/information

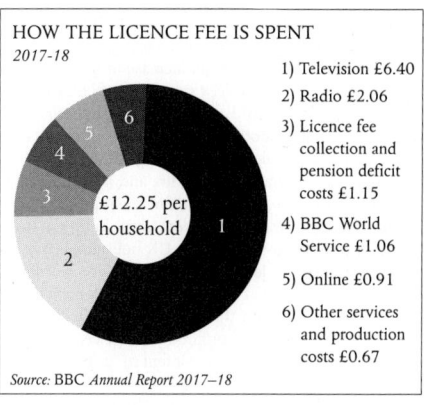

HOW THE LICENCE FEE IS SPENT
2017-18

£12.25 per household

1) Television £6.40
2) Radio £2.06
3) Licence fee collection and pension deficit costs £1.15
4) BBC World Service £1.06
5) Online £0.91
6) Other services and production costs £0.67

Source: BBC *Annual Report 2017–18*

DIGITAL TELEVISION
The Broadcasting Act 1996 provided for the licensing of 20 or more digital terrestrial television (DTT) channels (on six frequency channels or 'multiplexes'). The first digital services went on air in autumn 1998.

In June 2002, following the collapse of ITV Digital, the digital terrestrial television licence was awarded to a consortium made up of the BBC, BSkyB and transmitter company Crown Castle by the Independent Television Commission. Freeview was launched on 30 October 2002 with 25 free-to-air channels: it now offers over 70 digital channels, up to 15 HD channels and 30 radio stations and requires the one-off purchase of a set-top box, but is subsequently free of charge with no subscription. In Autumn 2005 ITV and Channel 4 officially became shareholders, each taking a 20 per cent stake. As at 2018, around 20 million homes use Freeview on at least one set, amounting to around 30 per cent of UK households. There is an additional Freeview+ service which works in a similar fashion to Sky+, allowing viewers to record programmes. Over 97 per cent of UK homes have access to digital television.

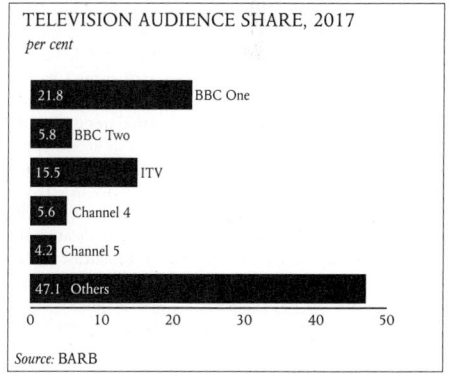

TELEVISION AUDIENCE SHARE, 2017
per cent

21.8	BBC One
5.8	BBC Two
15.5	ITV
5.6	Channel 4
4.2	Channel 5
47.1	Others

Source: BARB

RECENT DEVELOPMENTS
The internet has now firmly established itself as an alternative to live and programmed TV, particularly for those aged 16 to 34. Since the launch of 4oD in 2006 and BBC iPlayer in 2007, there has been a noticeable shift in the way viewers can watch their favourite programmes. Technological advancements have also contributed to this new phenomenon; more than half of the UK population uses a tablet, over 90 per cent of UK homes and businesses have access to superfast broadband and there are millions of public Wi-Fi hotspots across the UK. There is now a much bigger emphasis on

catch-up, and subscription video on demand (SVOD) services then ever before, with BBC iPlayer recording 285 million requests in February 2018 alone, an increase of 4 per cent on the previous year. SVOD services such as Netflix, Now TV and Amazon Prime Video have experienced a surge in popularity, with subscribers able to stream programmes through computers, mobiles, tablets and games consoles on up to four devices at a time. Both Netflix and Amazon Prime Video commission and distribute their own programmes, available exclusively to their subscribers, contributing to their popularity. As at 2018, over 9 million UK households had an active subscription to at least one SVOD service, a 24 per cent year-on-year increase. The BBC has provided exclusive content and programmes on the iPlayer since 2014 and in 2016 moved BBC Three to an online-only service, to expand the platform's offering of exclusive content to further compete with SVOD service providers.

Set-top boxes have also adapted to this viewing shift. YouView, in partnership with ITV, Channel Four, Channel Five, BT, Talk Talk and Arqiva, launched in July 2012. Subscribers are able to watch programmes (including on-demand), pause and rewind live TV and listen to digital radio via a hybrid set-top box connected to broadband. Originally envisaged as free-to-air, it has drawn criticism for tying customers into broadband services and subscriptions with BT and Talk Talk, with the one-off payment for the YouView box more expensive than the Freeview box. In June 2014, Freeview announced plans for a Freeview Connect service, which launched as Freeview Play – offering over 70 TV channels and up to 15 HD channels, allowing viewers to watch programmes broadcast over the past seven days via an internet connection.

Despite the rise in the popularity of tablets, traditional TV sets are still the most popular way to watch television. HD TV provides more vibrant colours, and greater detail and picture clarity, along with improved sound quality. An HD television screen uses 1,280 by 720 pixels up to 1,920 by 1,080 pixels. HD Ready TVs operate at 720p while full HD TVs tend to operate on 1080p or 1080i; the differences between these three settings are down to the number of lines in the resolution and the type of scanning technology. 'HD Ready' simply means the TV will only operate a higher definition once plugged into a decoder, whereas full HD has this built in. In 2017, the average screen size in the UK was 43.7 inches wide and this is expected to increase to 48.9 inches by 2020, indicating a rapidly increasing trend towards bigger screens. Sales of Smart TVs, which can access apps, browse the internet and stream video, are rising with around 42 per cent of UK households owning a Smart TV in 2018.

In April 2010, Samsung released the first consumer 3D TV; in the same month Sky launched the UK's first dedicated 3D channel. Several sporting events have been broadcast in 3D including the Wimbledon Championships. The BBC began a two-year 3D trial in 2011 but announced in July 2013 it would suspend 3D programming for an indefinite period of time due to a lack of public appetite for the technology. Of the estimated 1.5 million 3D TV sets in the UK, just 5 per cent used 3D to watch the Queen's Christmas Speech 2013 and in the past two years the number of 3D TVs sold in the UK has begun to decline leading companies like LG and Sony to announce in 2017 their intention to discontinue their lines of 3D TVs.

In September 2012, OFCOM awarded its first local TV licences after announcing plans to broadcast 21 channels in total. In November 2013, Estuary TV, based in Grimsby, was the first to be launched. The government has backed the local TV initiative and the channels broadcast on channel 7 on Freeview in England and Northern Ireland and channel 8 in Scotland and Wales. In March 2013, OFCOM stated plans for a further 30 areas to invite bids for local television services. However in April 2018, OFCOM announced its intention to halt the roll out of new local TV stations due several service providers facing financial difficulties and poor audience figures.

CONTACTS

THE BRITISH BROADCASTING CORPORATION (BBC)

BBC Broadcasting House, Portland Place, London W1A 1AA
W www.bbc.co.uk
BBC North, Media City UK, Bridge House, Salford Quays, Manchester M50 2BH
Chair, BBC Board, Sir David Clementi
Director-General, Baron Hall of Birkenhead
BBC Worldwide, 1 Television Centre, Wood Lane, London W12 7FA W www.bbcworldwide.com

INDEPENDENT TELEVISION (ITV)

London Television Centre, 72 Upper Ground, London SE1 9LT W www.itv.com
Chair, Sir Peter Bazalgette
Chief Executive, Dame Carolyn McCall, DBE

INDEPENDENT TELEVISION (ITV) REGIONS

Anglia (eastern England), W www.itv.com/anglia
Border (Borders and the Isle of Man), W www.itv.com/border
Calendar (Yorkshire), W www.itv.com/calendar
Central (east, west and south Midlands), W www.itv.com/central
Channel (Channel Islands), W www.itv.com/channel
Granada (north-west England), W www.itv.com/granada
London, W www.itv.com/london
Meridian (south and south-east England), W www.itv.com/meridian
STV (Scotland), W www.stv.tv
Tyne Tees (north-east England), W www.itv.com/tynetees
Ulster (Northern Ireland), W www.itv.com/utv
Wales, W www.itv.com/wales
West, W www.itv.com/west

OTHER TELEVISION COMPANIES

Channel 4 Television, 124 Horseferry Road, London SW1P 2TX
T 020-7396 4444 W www.channel4.com
Channel 5 Broadcasting Ltd, 10 Lower Thames Street, London EC3R 6EN T 020-8612 7700 W www.channel5.com
Independent Television Network (ITN), 200 Gray's Inn Road, London WC1X 8XZ T 020-7833 3000 W www.itn.co.uk
Provides news programming and services for ITV, Channel 4 and Channel 5. as well as content for international news.
Sianel Pedwar Cymru (S4/C), Parc Ty Glas, Llanishen, Cardiff CF14 5DU T 0870-600 4141 W www.s4c.cymru
Freeview, DTV Services Ltd, 27 Mortimer Street, London W1T 3JF
W www.freeview.co.uk

DIRECT BROADCASTING BY SATELLITE TELEVISION

Sky plc, Grant Way, Isleworth, Isleworth TW7 5QD
T 033-3100 0333 W www.sky.com
Chair, James Murdoch

RADIO

UK domestic radio services are broadcast across three wavebands: FM, medium wave and long wave (used by BBC Radio 4). In the UK the FM waveband extends in frequency from 87.5MHz to 108MHz and the medium waveband from 531kHz to 1602kHz. A number of radio stations are broadcast in both analogue and digital as well as a growing number in digital alone. As at June 2018, the BBC Radio network controlled around 51.7 per cent of the listening market (see BBC Radio section), and the independent sector (see Independent Radio section) 45.7 per cent. As at June 2018, a listener tunes into an average of 20.8 hours of radio per week.

ESTIMATED AUDIENCE SHARE

	Apr–Jun 2016	Apr–Jun 2017	Percentage Apr–Jun 2018
BBC Radio 1	5.7	6.2	5.9
BBC Radio 2	17.2	16.8	17.9
BBC Radio 3	1.2	1.2	1.1
BBC Radio 4	11.2	12.3	11.7
BBC Radio Five Live	3.9	3.4	3.1
Five Live Sports Extra	0.3	0.3	0.3
BBC 6 Music	2.1	1.9	2.4
BBC Asian Network UK	0.4	0.3	0.3
1Xtra	0.5	0.5	0.4
BBC Local/Regional	7.0	7.3	6.7
BBC World Service	0.7	0.9	0.7
All BBC	52.2	52.3	45.0
All independent	45.2	45.0	45.7
All national independent	15.8	16.7	18.1
All local independent	29.6	28.4	27.6
Other	2.6	2.8	2.5

Source: RAJAR

DIGITAL RADIO

The UK has the world's largest digital radio network, with 103 transmitters, two national Digital Audio Broadcasting (DAB) ensembles and a total of 48 local and regional DAB ensembles, which broadcast around 250 independent and 34 BBC radio stations. The BBC began test transmissions of the DAB Eureka 147 digital radio service in 1990 from the Crystal Palace transmitting station and the service was publicly launched in 1995. As well as DAB, digital televisions, car radios, games consoles, mobile devices and the internet are commonly employed as platforms to listen to radio in the UK. One of the major benefits of DAB is better sound quality than analogue radio, and the availability of a wider choice of stations, in addition to the lack of interference experienced by other broadcast media.

The UK government intends to migrate the majority of AM and FM analogue radio services to digital between 2015–19, based on certain conditions being met such as coverage, listening figures and agreements in relation to funding. In the second quarter of 2018, 50.2 per cent of all radio listening hours in the UK were through digital platforms. From this 50.2 per cent, DAB made up the majority of listenership with 72 per cent. In 2018, over 63 per cent of all UK households were believed to have access to DAB radio.

The BBC's national DAB ensemble has coverage across the UK of around 97 per cent and broadcasts on the frequency 225.648 MHz. Owned and operated by the BBC, the multiplex of broadcasts is transmitted across the UK from a number of sites. Local and regional ensembles, which cover 71.7 per cent of the UK, are transmitted through a number of DAB multiplex operators across the UK, including Digital One and Sound Digital – the two national operators – in addition to local multiplex operators.

There are two criteria that must be met for digital migration to occur:
- at least 50 per cent of radio listening is digital
- national DAB coverage is comparable to FM coverage, and local DAB reaches 90 per cent of the population and all major roads

LICENSING

The Broadcasting Act 1996 provided for the licensing of digital radio services (on multiplexes, where a number of stations share one frequency to transmit their services). To allocate the multiplexes, OFCOM advertises licences for which interested parties can bid. Once the licence has been awarded, the new owner seeks out services to broadcast on the multiplex. The BBC has a separate national multiplex for its services. There are local multiplexes around the country, each broadcasting an average of seven services, plus the local BBC station.

INNOVATIONS

The internet offers a number of advantages compared to other digital platforms such as DAB, including higher sound quality, a greater range of channel availability and flexibility in listening opportunity. Listeners can tune in to the majority of radio stations live on the internet or listen again online generally up to seven days after broadcast. DAB radio does not allow the same interactivity: the data is only able to travel one-way from broadcaster to listener whereas the internet allows a two-way flow of information.

Increases in Wi-Fi hotspots also means listening to radio, podcasts and catch-up programmes is easy to do through tablets and mobile phones; in 2018, over 50 per cent of all reported radio listening was via a digital service. The increase in music streaming services and radio-related apps has had a major effect on music discovery and sharing. In the UK in 2018 the number of streams per week averaged around 550 million. Since 6 July 2014 the UK Official Charts Company has included streaming services in its compilation, with 100 streams the equivalent to one purchase.

Since 2005 most radio stations offer all or part of their programmes as downloadable files, known as podcasts, to listen to on computers, mobiles or tablets. Podcasting technology allows listeners to subscribe in order to receive automatically the latest episodes of regularly transmitted programmes as soon as they become available.

The relationship between radio stations and their audiences is also undergoing change. The quantity and availability of music on the internet has led to the creation of shows dedicated entirely to music sent in by listeners. Another new development in internet-based radio has been personalised radio stations, such as Soundcloud and Spotify. Soundcloud allows users to upload, record, promote and share their music and sounds. Artists who upload their music are given a URL, allowing their music to be embedded anywhere, making it easier to share through social media platforms such as Twitter and Facebook. Users can also create their own playlists and link them to social media platforms. Spotify, available as an app on most smart phones and tablets as well as online, allows listeners access to the track, artist or genre of their choice, or to share and create playlists. It has seen steady growth in popularity since its launch in 2008, with 83 million paying subscribers and 180 million active users globally, as at June 2018. Spotify 'learns as you listen' and makes associated recommendations based on user choices. Radioplayer (W www.radioplayer.co.uk), a not-for-profit company backed by the BBC, Global Radio, Bauer Media and RadioCentre, allows audiences to listen to live and catch-up radio from one place. Over 6 million people per month use the Radioplayer service. There are over 400 stations available and a 'recommended' service which offers station suggestions depending on location, what is trending and the type of music the user likes. Radioplayer launched as a mobile app in 2012 and a tablet app in 2013. Through the tablet app, users sample an average of 4.6 stations a week in comparison with just 2.1 for analogue users.

BBC RADIO

BBC Radio broadcasts network services to the UK, Isle of Man and the Channel Islands, with around 34.7 million listeners each week. There is also a tier of national services in Wales, Scotland and Northern Ireland and around 40 local radio stations in England and the Channel Islands. In Wales and Scotland there are also dedicated language services in Welsh and Gaelic respectively. The frequency allocated for digital BBC broadcasts is 225.648MHz.

BBC Radio, Broadcasting House, Portland Place, London W1A 1AA
    W www.bbc.co.uk/radio

BBC NETWORK RADIO STATIONS

Radio 1 (contemporary pop music and entertainment news) – 24 hours a day, *Frequencies:* 97–99 FM and digital
Radio 2 (popular music, entertainment, comedy and the arts) – 24 hours a day, *Frequencies:* 88–91 FM and digital
Radio 3 (classical music, classic drama, documentaries and features) – 24 hours a day, *Frequencies:* 90–93 FM and digital
Radio 4 (news, documentaries, drama, entertainment and cricket on long wave in season) – 5.20am–1am daily, with BBC World Service overnight, *Frequencies:* 92–95 FM/103–105 FM and 198 LW and digital
Radio Five Live (news and sport) – 24 hours a day, *Frequencies:* 909/693 MW and digital*Five Live Sports Extra* (live sport) – schedule varies, digital only
6 Music (contemporary and classic pop and rock music) – 24 hours a day, digital only
Asian Network (news, music and sport) – 5am–1am, with Radio Five Live overnight, *Frequencies:* various MW frequencies in Midlands and digital

BBC NATIONAL RADIO STATIONS

Radio Cymru (Welsh-language), *Frequencies:* 92–105 FM and digital
Radio Foyle, Frequencies: 93.1 FM and 792 MW and digital
Radio nan Gaidheal (Gaelic service), *Frequencies:* 103–105 FM and digital
Radio Scotland, Frequencies: 92–95 FM and 810 MW and digital. Local programmes for Orkney, Shetland and Highlands and Islands
Radio Ulster, Frequencies: 1341 MW and 92–95 FM and digital. Local programmes on Radio Foyle
Radio Wales, Frequencies: 657/882 MW and 93–104 FM and digital

BBC WORLD SERVICE

The BBC World Service broadcasts to an estimated weekly audience of 1.5 million people in the UK and 280 million worldwide, in 40 languages including English, and is now available in around 150 capital cities. It no longer broadcasts in Dutch, French for Europe, German, Hebrew, Italian, Japanese or Malay because it was found that most speakers of these languages preferred to listen to the English broadcasts. In 2006 services in ten languages (Bulgarian, Croatian, Czech, Greek, Hungarian, Kazakh, Polish, Slovak, Slovene and Thai) were terminated to provide funding for a new Arabic television channel, which was launched in March 2008. In August 2008 the BBC's Romanian World Service broadcasts were discontinued after 68 years. In January 2011 the BBC announced five more language services would be terminated: Albanian, Caribbean English, Macedonian, Portuguese for Africa and Serbian. The BBC World Service website offers interactive news services in 28 languages including English, Arabic, Chinese, Hindi, Persian, Portuguese for Brazil, Russian, Spanish and Urdu with audiostreaming available.

LANGUAGES

Afaan Oromoo, Amharic, Arabic, Azeri, Bengali, Burmese, Cantonese, English, French, Gujarati, Hausa, Hindi, Igbo, Indonesian, Kinyarwanda, Kirundi, Korean, Kyrgyz, Marathi, Nepali, Nigerian, Pashto, Pidgin, Persian, Portuguese, Punjabi, Russian, Sinhala, Somali, Spanish, Swahili, Tamil, Telugu, Tigrinya, Turkish, Ukrainian, Urdu, Uzbek, Yoruba and Vietnamese.

UK frequencies: digital; overnight on BBC Radio 4.
BBC Learning English teaches English worldwide through radio, television and a wide range of published and online courses.
BBC Media Action is a registered charity established in 1999 by BBC World Service, known as the BBC World Service Trust until December 2011. It promotes development through the innovative use of the media in the developing world.
BBC Monitoring tracks the global media for the latest news reports emerging around the world.

BBC WORLD SERVICE, Broadcasting House, Portland Place, London W1A 1AA W www.bbc.co.uk/worldservice

INDEPENDENT RADIO

Until 1973, the BBC had a legal monopoly on radio broadcasting in the UK. During this time, the corporation's only competition came from pirate stations located abroad, such as Radio Luxembourg. Christopher Chataway, Minister for Post and Telecommunications, changed this by creating the first licences for commercial radio stations. The Independent Broadcasting Authority (IBA) awarded the first of these licences to the London Broadcasting Company (LBC) to provide London's news and information service. LBC was followed by Capital Radio, to offer the city's entertainment service, Radio Clyde in Glasgow and BRMB in Birmingham.

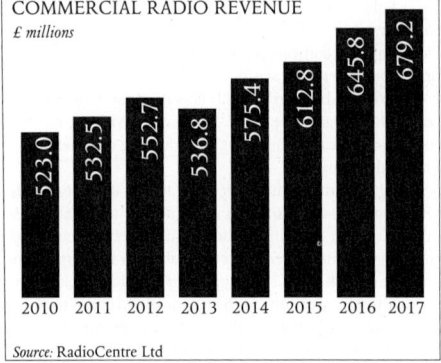

COMMERCIAL RADIO REVENUE
£ millions

2010	2011	2012	2013	2014	2015	2016	2017
523.0	532.5	552.7	536.8	575.4	612.8	645.8	679.2

Source: RadioCentre Ltd

The IBA was dissolved when the Broadcasting Act of 1990 de-regulated broadcasting, to be succeeded by the less rigid Radio Authority (RA). The RA began advertising new licences for the development of independent radio in January 1991. It awarded national and local radio, satellite and cable services licences, and long-term restricted service licences for stations serving non-commercial establishments such as hospitals and universities. The first national commercial digital multiplex licence was awarded in October 1998 and a number of local digital multiplex licences followed. At the end of 2003 the RA was replaced by OFCOM, which now carries out the licensing administration.

RadioCentre was formed in July 2006 as a result of the merger between the Radio Advertising Bureau (RAB) and the Commercial Radio Companies Association (CRCA), the former non-profit trade body for commercial radio companies in the UK, to operate essentially as a union for commercial radio stations.

RadioCentre, 6th Floor, 55 New Oxford Street, London WC1A 1BS
T 020-7010 0600 W www.radiocentre.org
Chief Executive, Siobhan Kenny

THE PRESS

The newspaper and periodical press in the UK is large and diverse, catering for a wide variety of views and interests. There is no state control or censorship of the press; however, it is subject to the laws on publication.

The press is not state-subsidised and receives few tax concessions. The income of most newspapers and periodicals is derived largely from sales and from advertising. The Advertising Association reported in July 2018 that national newspaper brands experienced their first increase in advertising spend in seven years in 2017. The UK advertising market in general grew to £22.2bn in 2017, an increase of 4.6 per cent.

LEVESON REPORT

The Leveson Inquiry, established under the Inquiries Act 2005, was announced by the prime minister on 13 July 2011 to investigate the role of press and police in the *News of the World* phone-hacking scandal. Lord Justice Leveson was appointed as chair of the inquiry. The hearings began on 14 November 2011 and ended on 24 July 2012 following the testimonies of 650 witnesses.

The Leveson Report was published in late November 2012 and featured several broad and complex recommendations as to how the press should be regulated. The report generally recommended that the press should continue to be self-regulated, with the government allowed no direct power over what is published, and that a new press standards body, with a new code of conduct, should be established by legislation in order to ensure regulation is independent and effective. Lord Justice Leveson concluded that this arrangement should give the public confidence that their complaints would be dealt with seriously and ensure the press would be protected from interference.

SELF-REGULATION

Following the publication of the Leveson Report the Press Complaints Commission (PCC), which had been established in January 1991 as a non-statutory body to operate the press's self-regulation, was closed and replaced by the Independent Press Standards Organisation (IPSO) on 8 September 2014. While the majority of newspapers have signed up to the new regulator, several have not, including *The Guardian*, the *Financial Times* and the *London Evening Standard*.

In 2013 a royal charter on press regulation was granted by the Privy Council to create a watchdog to oversee a new regulator. On 3 November 2014, a fully independent body, the Press Recognition Panel (PRP) was established to consider whether press regulators meet the criteria recommended in the Leveson Report and, if so, to afford these regulators official recognition.

IPSO has not sought recognition from the PRP, but another regulator, IMPRESS, established by a group of free speech campaigners, is aiming to become compliant with the requirements of the Leveson Report and announced in May 2015 its intention to seek recognition from the PRP.

INDEPENDENT PRESS STANDARDS ORGANISATION,
Gate House, 1 Farringdon Street, London EC4M 7LH
T 0300-123 2220 E inquiries@ipso.co.uk W www.ipso.co.uk
Chair, Rt. Hon. Sir Alan Moses

PRESS RECOGNITION PANEL, Mappin House, 4 Winsley Street, London W1W 8HF
E contact@pressrecognitionpanel.org.uk
W www.pressrecognitionpanel.org.uk
Chair, Dr David Wolfe, QC

NEWSPAPERS

Newspapers are mostly financially independent of any political party, though most adopt a political stance in their editorial comments, usually reflecting proprietorial influence. Ownership of the national and regional daily newspapers is concentrated in the hands of large corporations whose interests cover publishing and communications, although *The Guardian* and *The Observer* are owned by the Scott Trust, formed in 1936 to protect the financial and editorial independence of *The Guardian* in perpetuity. The rules on cross-media ownership, as amended by the Broadcasting Act 1996, which limited the extent to which newspaper organisations may become involved in broadcasting, have been relaxed by the Communications Act 2003: newspapers with over a 20 per cent share of national circulation may own national and/or local radio licences.

In October 2010, *The Independent* launched a concise newspaper, *i*, the first new daily newspaper since 1986 but the final editions of *The Independent* and *The Independent on Sunday* were published in March 2016 as the paper moved to digital only. In July 2011, *News of the World* was closed by its parent company, News International, following accusations of phone-hacking. In February 2012 News International printed the first edition of *The Sun on Sunday*, a Sunday format of the daily tabloid paper *The Sun*. In February 2016, Trinity Mirror launched a compact daily newspaper, *The New Day* – the first new standalone paper since *The Independent* in 1986 – but it ceased publication in May 2016 after a sharp drop in circulation. There are 11 daily and Sunday national papers and several hundred local papers that are published daily, weekly or twice-weekly. Scotland, Wales and Northern Ireland all have at least one daily and one Sunday national paper.

UK CIRCULATION

National Sunday Newspapers	June 2017	June 2018	% +/–
The Sun on Sunday	1,344,894	1,224,119	−8.98
The Mail on Sunday	1,236,839	1,056,916	−14.55
The Sunday Times	792,081	721,808	−8.87
Sunday Mirror	555,800	475,976	−14.36
The Sunday Telegraph	355,539	288,484	−18.86
Sunday Express	328,559	295,294	−10.12
Daily Star Sunday	250,248	220,684	−11.81
Sunday People	224,652	183,784	−18.19
The Observer	192,889	166,317	−13.78
Sunday Mail	153,427	131,716	−14.15
Sunday Post	135,747	115,973	−14.57

Source: Audit Bureau of Circulations Ltd

Newspapers are usually published in either broadsheet or smaller, tabloid format. The 'quality' daily papers – ie those providing detailed coverage of a wide range of public matters – have traditionally been broadsheets, the more populist newspapers tabloid. In 2004 this correlation between format and content was redefined when two traditionally broadsheet newspapers, *The Times* and *The Independent*, switched to tabloid-sized editions, while *The Guardian* launched a 'Berliner' format in September 2005. In October 2005 *The Independent on Sunday* became the first Sunday broadsheet to be published in the tabloid (or 'compact') size. *The Observer*, like its daily counterpart *The Guardian*, began publishing in the Berliner format in January 2006 and began publishing in tabloid format in January 2018.

NEWSPAPERS ONLINE

The demand to read news instantly and while on the move has increased the popularity of newspaper websites. Most newspapers now operate their own websites in line with their print editions, often including the same material as seen in daily printed editions but can also include video and audio features. Many articles and columns additionally have the option of reader contributions and debate. Certain newspapers charge a subscription fee to access their websites but the majority are free to browse.

NATIONAL PRESS WEBSITE DAILY AVERAGE BROWSERS

National Press Website	June 2017	June 2018	% +/-
MailOnline	15,053,614	12,622,077	-18.07
metro.co.uk	2,676,403	1,689,148	-36.89
Reach PLC*	10,121,154	8,976,593	-11.31
thesun.co.uk	5,281,981	5,410,691	2.44

* Formerly known as Trinity Mirror Group PLC
Source: Audit Bureau of Circulations Ltd

NATIONAL DAILY NEWSPAPERS

DAILY EXPRESS
Northern & Shell Building, 10 Lower Thames Street, London EC3R 6EN T 020-8612 7000 W www.express.co.uk
Editor, Guy Jones

DAILY MAIL
Northcliffe House, 2 Derry Street, London W8 5TT T 020-7938 6000 W www.dailymail.co.uk
Editor, Geordie Greig

DAILY MIRROR
1 Canada Square, Canary Wharf, London E14 5AP
T 020-7293 3000 W www.mirror.co.uk
Editor, Allison Phillips

DAILY RECORD
1 Central Quay, Glasgow G3 8DA T 0141-309 3000
W www.dailyrecord.co.uk
Editor, Murray Foote

DAILY STAR
Northern & Shell Building, 10 Lower Thames Street, London EC3R 6EN T 020-8612 7000 W www.dailystar.co.uk
Editor, Jon Clark

THE DAILY TELEGRAPH
111 Buckingham Palace Road, London SW1W 0DT
T 020-7931 2000 W www.telegraph.co.uk
Editor, Chris Evans

FINANCIAL TIMES
1 Southwark Bridge, London SE1 9HL T 020-7873 3000
W www.ft.com
Editor, Lionel Barber

THE GUARDIAN
Kings Place, 90 York Way, London N1 9GU T 020-3353 2000
W www.theguardian.com
Editor, Katharine Viner

THE HERALD
200 Renfield Street, Glasgow G2 3QB T 0141-302 7000
W www.heraldscotland.com
Editor, Graeme Smith

i
2 Derry Street, London W8 5HF T 020-7005 2000
W www.inews.co.uk
Editor, Oliver Duff

THE SCOTSMAN
Orchard Brae House, 30 Queensferry Road, Edinburgh EH4 2HS
T 0131-311 7311 W www.scotsman.com
Editorial Director, Frank O'Donnell

THE SUN
1 London Bridge Street, London SE1 9GF T 020-7782 4000
W www.thesun.co.uk
Editor, Tony Gallagher

THE TIMES
1 London Bridge Street, London SE1 9GF T 020-7782 5000
W www.thetimes.co.uk
Editor, John Witherow

WEEKLY NEWSPAPERS

DAILY STAR SUNDAY
Northern & Shell Building, 10 Lower Thames Street, London EC3R 6EN T 020-8612 7000 W www.dailystar.co.uk/sunday
Editor, Stuart James

MAIL ON SUNDAY
Northcliffe House, 2 Derry Street, London W8 HFT T 020-7938 6000
W www.mailonsunday.co.uk
Editor, Ted Verity

THE OBSERVER
Kings Place, 90 York Way, London N1 9GU T 020-3353 2000
W www.theguardian.com/observer
Editor, Paul Webster

THE SUNDAY PEOPLE
1 Canada Square, Canary Wharf, London E14 5AP
T 020-7293 3000 W www.people.co.uk
Editor, Peter Willis

SCOTLAND ON SUNDAY
Orchard Brae House, 30 Queensferry Road, Edinburgh EH4 2HS
T 0131-311 7311 W www.scotlandonsunday.com
Editorial Director, Frank O'Donnell

THE SUN ON SUNDAY
1 London Bridge Street, London SE1 9GF T 020-7782 4000
W www.thesun.co.uk
Editor, Victoria Newton

SUNDAY EXPRESS
Northern & Shell Building, 10 Lower Thames Street, London EC4R 6EN T 020-8612 7000 W www.sundayexpress.co.uk
Editor, Martin Townsend

SUNDAY MAIL
1 Central Quay, Glasgow G3 8DA T 0141-309 3000
W www.sundaymail.com
Editor, Jim Wilson

SUNDAY MIRROR
1 Canada Square, Canary Wharf, London E14 5AP
T 020-7293 3000 W www.sundaymirror.co.uk
Editor, Peter Willis

SUNDAY POST
2 Albert Square, Dundee, DD1 1DD T 01382-223131
W www.sundaypost.com
Editor, Richard Prest

SUNDAY TELEGRAPH
111 Buckingham Palace Road, London SW1W 0DT
T 020-7931 2000 W www.telegraph.co.uk
Editor, Allister Heath

THE SUNDAY TIMES
1 London Bridge Street, London SE1 9GF T 020-7782 5000
W www.thesundaytimes.co.uk
Editor, Martin Ivens

REGIONAL NEWSPAPERS

EAST ANGLIA

CAMBRIDGE NEWS
Winship Road, Milton, Cambs. CB24 6PP T 01223-434434
W www.cambridge-news.co.uk
Editor, David Bartlett

EAST ANGLIAN DAILY TIMES
Portman House, 120 Princes Street, Ipswich IP1 1RS
T 01473-230023 W www.eadt.co.uk
Editor, Brad Jones

EASTERN DAILY PRESS
Prospect House, Rouen Road, Norwich NR1 1RE T 01603-628311
W www.edp24.co.uk
Editor, David Powles

IPSWICH STAR
Lower Brook Street, Ipswich, Suffolk IP4 1AN **T** 01473-230023
W www.ipswichstar.co.uk
Editor, Brad Jones

NORWICH EVENING NEWS
Prospect House, Rouen Road, Norwich NR1 1RE **T** 01603-628311
W www.eveningnews24.co.uk
Editor, Kate Nelson

EAST MIDLANDS

BURTON MAIL
Milton House, Worthington Way, Burton upon Trent DE14 1BQ
T 01283-245000 **W** www.burtonmail.co.uk
Editor, Julie Crouch

DERBY TELEGRAPH
2 Siddals Road, Derby DE1 2PB **T** 01332-411888
W www.derbytelegraph.co.uk
Editor, Steve Hall

THE LEICESTER MERCURY
St George Street, Leicester LE1 9FQ **T** 0116-251 2512
W www.leicestermercury.co.uk
Editor, George Oliver

LINCOLNSHIRE ECHO
Witham Wharf, Brayford Wharf East, Lincoln LN5 7AY
T 01522-804300 **W** www.lincolnshirelive.co.uk
Editor, Robert Rowlands

NORTHAMPTON CHRONICLE & ECHO
Albert House, Victoria Street, Northants NN1 3NR **T** 01604-467000
W www.northamptonchron.co.uk
Editor, David Summers

NOTTINGHAM POST
City Gate, Tollhouse Hill, Notts NG1 5FS **T** 0115-948 2000
W www.nottinghampost.com
Editor, Mike Sassi

LONDON

EVENING STANDARD
Northcliffe House, 2 Derry Street, London W8 5TT **T** 020-3367 7000
W www.standard.co.uk
Editor, George Osborne

METRO
Northcliffe House, 2 Derry Street, London W8 5TT **T** 020-3615 3480
W www.metro.co.uk
Editor, Ted Young

NORTH EAST

EVENING CHRONICLE
Groat Market, Newcastle upon Tyne NE1 1ED **T** 0191-232 7500
W www.chroniclelive.co.uk
Editor, Neil Hodgkinson

HARTLEPOOL MAIL
9–13 Scarborough Street, Hartlepool TS24 7DA **T** 01429-235197
W www.hartlepoolmail.co.uk
Editor, Joy Yates

THE JOURNAL
Groat Market, Newcastle upon Tyne NE1 1ED **T** 0191-201 6491
W www.thejournal.co.uk
Editor, Neil Hodgkinson

THE NORTHERN ECHO
PO Box 14, Priestgate, Darlington, Co. Durham DL1 1NF
T 01325-381313 **W** www.thenorthernecho.co.uk
Editor, Hannah Chapman

THE SHIELDS GAZETTE
7 Beach Road, South Shields, Tyne & Wear NE33 2QA
T 0191-501 7436 **W** www.shieldsgazette.com
Editor, Joy Yates

THE SUNDAY SUN
Groat Market, Newcastle upon Tyne NE1 1ED **T** 0191-232 7500
W www.sundaysun.co.uk
Editor, Neil Hodgkinson

SUNDERLAND ECHO
Echo House, Pennywell, Sunderland SR4 9ER **T** 0191-501 5800
W www.sunderlandecho.com
Editor, Joy Yates

TEESIDE GAZETTE
1st Floor, Hudson Quay, The Halyard, Middlehaven, Middlesbrough
TS3 6RT **T** 01642-234262 **W** www.gazettelive.co.uk
Editor, Neil Hodgkinsons

NORTH WEST

THE BLACKPOOL GAZETTE
Avroe House, Avroe Crescent, Blackpool FY4 2DP **T** 01253-400888
W www.blackpoolgazette.co.uk
Editor, Gillian Parkinson

THE BOLTON NEWS
The Wellsprings, Victoria Square, Bolton BL1 1AR **T** 01204-522345
W www.theboltonnews.co.uk
Editor, Ian Savage

CARLISLE NEWS AND STAR
Newspaper House, Dalston Road, Carlisle CA2 5UA
T 01228-612600 **W** www.newsandstar.co.uk
Editor, Chris Story

LANCASHIRE EVENING POST
Stuart House, 89 Caxton Road, Fulwood, Preston PR2 9ZB
T 01772-254841 **W** www.lep.co.uk
Editor, Gillian Parkinson

LANCASHIRE TELEGRAPH
50–54 Church Street, Blackburn, Lancs. BB1 5AL **T** 01254 678678
W www.lancashiretelegraph.co.uk
Editor, Steven Thompson

LIVERPOOL ECHO
PO Box 48, Old Hall Street, Liverpool L69 3EB **T** 0151-227 2000
W www.liverpoolecho.co.uk
Editor, Alastair Machray

MANCHESTER EVENING NEWS
Mitchell Henry House, Hollinwood Avenue, Chadderton OL9 8EF
T 0161-832 7200 **W** www.manchestereveningnews.co.uk
Editor, Darren Thwaites

NORTH-WEST EVENING MAIL
Abbey Road, Barrow-in-Furness, Cumbria LA14 5QS
T 01229-840100 **W** www.nwemail.co.uk
Editor, Vanessa Sims

SOUTH EAST

THE ARGUS
Dolphin House, 2–5 Manchester Street, Brighton BN2 1TF
T 01273-021400 **W** www.theargus.co.uk
Editor, Aaron Hendy

ECHO
Newspaper House, Chester Hall Lane, Basildon, Essex SS14 3BL
T 01268-522792 **W** www.echo-news.co.uk
Editor, Chris Hatton

MEDWAY MESSENGER
Medway House, Ginsbury Close, Sir Thomas Longley Road, Strood,
Kent ME2 4DU **T** 01634-227800 **W** www.kentonline.co.uk/
medway
Editor, Matt Ramsden

THE NEWS, PORTSMOUTH
1000 Lakeside, North Harbour, Portsmouth PO6 3EN
T 023-9266 4488 **W** www.portsmouth.co.uk
Editor, Mark Waldron

OXFORD MAIL
Newsquest Oxfordshire & Wiltshire, Osney Mead, Oxford OX2 0EJ
T 01865-425262 **W** www.oxfordmail.co.uk
Managing Editor, Samantha Harmon

READING CHRONICLE
2–10 Bridge Street, Reading, Berks. RG1 2LU **T** 0118-955 3333
W www.readingchronicle.co.uk
Group Editor, Andrew Colley

THE SOUTHERN DAILY ECHO
Newspaper House, Test Lane, Redbridge, Southampton SO16 9JX
T 023-8042 4777 **W** www.dailyecho.co.uk
Editor, Gordon Sutter

SOUTH WEST

BRISTOL POST
Temple Way, Bristol BS2 0BY T 0117-934 3000
W www.bristolpost.co.uk
Editor, Mike Norton

BOURNEMOUTH ECHO
Richmond Hill, Bournemouth BH2 6HH T 01202-554601
W www.bournemouthecho.co.uk
Editor, Andy Martin

DORSET ECHO
Fleet House, Hampshire Road, Weymouth, Dorset DT4 9XD
T 01305-830930 W www.dorsetecho.co.uk
Editor, Diarmuid MacDonagh

EXETER EXPRESS & ECHO
Heron Road, Sowton, Exeter EX2 7NF T 01392-442220
W www.exeterexpressandecho.co.uk
Editor, Rich Booth

GLOUCESTER CITIZEN
St James's Square, Cheltenham GL50 3PR T 01242-278000
W www.gloucestershirelive.co.uk
Editor, Jenny Eastwood

GLOUCESTERSHIRE ECHO
St James's Square, Cheltenham GL50 3PR T 01242-278000
W www.gloucestershirelive.co.uk
Editor, Matt Holmes

THE HERALD
3rd Floor, Millbay Road, Plymouth PL1 3LF T 01752-293000
W www.plymouthherald.co.uk
Editor, Edd Moore

SUNDAY INDEPENDENT
Oakland Mews, Owen Sivell Close, Liskeard PL14 3UX
T 01579-556972 W www.sundayindependent.co.uk
Editor, John Collings

SWINDON ADVERTISER
100 Victoria Road, Old Town, Swindon SN1 3BE T 01793-528144
W www.swindonadvertiser.co.uk
Editor, Pete Gavan

TORQUAY HERALD EXPRESS
Barton Hill Road, Torquay, Devon TQ2 8JN T 01803-676000
W www.torquayheraldexpress.co.uk
Editor, Scott Harrison

WESTERN DAILY PRESS
Temple Way, Bristol BS99 7HD T 0117-934 3000
W www.somersetlive.co.uk
Editor, Gavin Thompson

THE WESTERN MORNING NEWS
3rd Floor, Millbay Road, Plymouth PL1 3LF T 01752-293000
W www.westernmorningnews.co.uk
Editor, Bill Martin

WEST MIDLANDS

BIRMINGHAM MAIL
6th Floor, Fort Dunlop, Fort Parkway, Birmingham B24 9FF
T 0121-234 5536 W www.birminghammail.co.uk
Editor-in-Chief, Marc Reeves

THE BIRMINGHAM POST
6th Floor, Fort Dunlop, Fort Parkway, Birmingham B24 9FF
T 0121-236 5000 W www.birminghampost.co.uk
Editor-in-Chief, Marc Reeves

COVENTRY TELEGRAPH
Corporation Street, Coventry CV1 1FP T 024-7663 3633
W www.coventrytelegraph.net
Editor, Keith Perry

EXPRESS & STAR
51–53 Queen Street, Wolverhampton WV1 1ES T 01902-313131
W www.expressandstar.com
Editor, Keith Harrison

THE SENTINEL
Sentinel House, Bethesda Street, Stoke-on-Trent ST1 3GN
T 01782-864100 W www.stokesentinel.co.uk
Editor, Martin Tideswell

SHROPSHIRE STAR
Waterloo Road, Ketley, Telford TF1 5HU T 01952-242424
W www.shropshirestar.com
Editor, Martin Wright

WORCESTER NEWS
Berrows House, Hylton Road, Worcester WR2 5JX T 01905-748200
W www.worcesternews.co.uk
Editor, Peter John

YORKSHIRE AND HUMBERSIDE

GRIMSBY TELEGRAPH
80 Cleethorpe Road, Grimsby, Lincs DN31 3EH T 01472-360360
W www.grimsbytelegraph.co.uk
Editor, Jamie Macaskill

HALIFAX COURIER
PO Box 19, King Cross Street, Halifax HX1 2SF T 01422-260200
W www.halifaxcourier.co.uk
Editor, John Kenealy

THE HUDDERSFIELD DAILY EXAMINER
Pennine Business Park, Longbow Close, Bradley Road, Huddersfield
HD2 1GQ T 01484-430000 W www.examiner.co.uk
Editor, Wayne Ankers

HULL DAILY MAIL
Blundell's Corner, Beverley Road, Hull HU3 1XS T 01482-327111
W www.hulldailymail.co.uk
Editor, Neil Hodgkinson

THE PRESS
PO Box 29, 76–86 Walmgate, York YO1 9YN T 01904-567131
W www.yorkpress.co.uk
Editor (acting), Nigel Burton

SCARBOROUGH NEWS
17–23 Aberdeen Walk, Scarborough, N. Yorks YO11 1BB
T 01723-60100 W www.thescarboroughnews.co.uk
Editor, Ed Asquith

SHEFFIELD STAR
York Street, Sheffield S1 1PU T 0114-276 7676
W www.thestar.co.uk
Editor, Nancy Fielder

TELEGRAPH & ARGUS
Hall Ings, Bradford BD1 1JR T 01274-729511
W www.thetelegraphandargus.co.uk
Editor (acting), Nigel Burton

YORKSHIRE EVENING POST
26 Whitehall Road, Leeds LS12 1BE T 0113-243 2701
W www.yorkshireeveningpost.co.uk
Editor, Hannah Thaxter

YORKSHIRE POST
26 Whitehall Road, Leeds LS12 1BE T 0113-243 2701
W www.yorkshirepost.co.uk
Editor, James Mitchinson

SCOTLAND

THE COURIER
80 Kingsway East, Dundee DD4 8SL T 01382-223131
W www.thecourier.co.uk
Editor, Richard Rooney

DUNDEE EVENING TELEGRAPH
2 Albert Square, Dundee DD1 1DD T 01382-575950
W www.eveningtelegraph.co.uk
Editor, Andrew Kellock

EDINBURGH EVENING NEWS
Orchard Brae House, 30 Queensferry Road, Edinburgh EH4 2HS
T 0131-311 7311 W www.edinburghnews.scotsman.com
Deputy Editor, Euan McGrory

EVENING EXPRESS
Aberdeen Journals Ltd, Lang Stracht, Mastrick, Aberdeen AB15 6DF
T 01224-691212 W www.eveningexpress.co.uk
Editor, Craig Walker

GLASGOW EVENING TIMES
200 Renfield Street, Glasgow G2 3QB T 0141-302 7000
W www.eveningtimes.co.uk
Editor, Donald Martin

INVERNESS COURIER
New Century House, Stadium Road, Inverness IV1 1FF
T 01463-233059 W www.inverness-courier.co.uk
Editor, David Bourn
PAISLEY DAILY EXPRESS
1 Central Quay, Glasgow G3 8DA T 0141-887 7911
W www.paisleydailyexpress.co.uk
Editor, Cheryl McEvoy
THE PRESS AND JOURNAL
Lang Stracht, Aberdeen AB15 6DF T 01224-690222
W www.pressandjournal.co.uk
Editor, Richard Neville
WALES
THE LEADER
Mold Business Park, Mold, Flintshire CH7 1XY T 01352-707707
W www.leaderlive.co.uk
Editor, Wayne Ankers
SOUTH WALES ARGUS
Cardiff Road, Maesglas, Newport NP20 3QN T 01633-810000
W www.southwalesargus.co.uk
Editor, Nicole Garnon
SOUTH WALES ECHO
6 Park Street, Cardiff CF10 1XR T 029-2024 3630
W www.walesonline.co.uk
Editor, Tryst Williams
SOUTH WALES EVENING POST
Urban Village, High Street, Swansea SA1 1NW T 01792-545500
W www.southwales-eveningpost.co.uk
Editor, Jonathan Roberts
WESTERN MAIL
6 Park Street, Cardiff CF10 1XR T 029-2024 3630
W www.walesonline.co.uk
Editor, Alan Edmunds
NORTHERN IRELAND
BELFAST TELEGRAPH
124–144 Royal Avenue, Belfast BT1 1DN T 028-9026 4000
W www.belfasttelegraph.co.uk
Editor, Gail Walker
IRISH NEWS
113–117 Donegall Street, Belfast BT1 2GE T 028-9032 2226
W www.irishnews.com
Editor, Noel Doran
NEWS LETTER
Ground Floor, Metro Building, 6–9 Donegall Sq. South, Belfast BT1 5JA T 028-3839 5577 W www.newsletter.co.uk
Editor, Alistair Bushe
SUNDAY LIFE
124–144 Royal Avenue, Belfast BT1 1EB T 028-9026 4000
W www.belfasttelegraph.co.uk/sunday-life
Editor, Martin Breen
CHANNEL ISLANDS
GUERNSEY PRESS
PO Box 57, Braye Road, Vale, Guernsey GY1 3BW T 01481-240240
W www.guernseypress.com
Editor, Shaun Green
JERSEY EVENING POST
Guiton House, Five Oaks, St Saviour, Jersey JE4 8XQ
T 01534-611611 W www.jerseyeveningpost.com
Editor, Andy Sibcy

PERIODICALS
ART
AESTHETICA
PO Box 371, York YO23 1WL T 01904-629137
W www.aestheticamagazine.com
Editor, Cherie Federico
APOLLO
22 Old Queen Street, London SW1H 9HP T 020-7961 0150
W www.apollo-magazine.com
Editor, Thomas Marks

ART MONTHLY
30 Charing Cross Road, London WC2H 0DE T 020-7240 0389
W www.artmonthly.co.uk
Editor, Patricia Bickers
ARTREVIEW
1 Honduras Street, London EC1Y 0TH T 020-7490 8138
W www.artreview.com
Editor, Mark Rappolt
TATE ETC.
Tate, Millbank, London SW1P 4RG T 020-7887 8724
W www.tate.org.uk
Editor, Simon Grant
BUSINESS AND FINANCE
THE ECONOMIST
20 Cabot Square, London E14 4QW T 020-7576 8000
W www.economist.com
Editor, Zanny Minton Beddoes
MANAGEMENT TODAY
Bridge House, 69 London Road, Twickenham TW1 3SP
T 020-8267 5000 W www.managementtoday.co.uk
Editor, Matthew Gwyther
MARKETING WEEK
79 Wells Street, London W1T 3QN T 020-7292 3711
W www.marketingweek.co.uk
Editor, Russell Parsons
MONEYWEEK
2nd Floor, Crowne House, 56–58 Southwark Street, London SE1 1UN T 020-7633 3780 W www.moneyweek.com
Editor-in-Chief, Merryn Somerset Webb
PUBLIC FINANCE
78 Chamber Street, London E1 8BL T 020-7880 6200
W www.publicfinance.co.uk
Managing Editor, Vivienne Russell
CELEBRITY
CLOSER
Endeavour House, 189 Shaftesbury Avenue, London WC2H 8JG
T 020-7859 8463 W www.closeronline.co.uk
Editor, Lisa Burrow
HEAT
Endeavour House, 189 Shaftesbury Avenue, London WC2H 8JG
T 020-7437 9011 W www.heatworld.com
Editor, Lucie Cave
HELLO!
Wellington House, 69–71 Upper Ground, London SE1 9PQ
T 020-7667 8901 W www.hellomagazine.com
Editor, Rosie Nixon
OK!
10 Lower Thames Street, London EC3R 6EN T 020-8612 7000
W www.ok.co.uk
Editor, Kirsty Tyler
CHILDREN'S AND FAMILY
THE BEANO
185 Fleet Street, London EC4A 2HS W www.beano.com
Editor, John Anderson
MOTHER & BABY
Bauer Media Group, Media House, Lynchwood, Peterborough Business Park, Peterborough PE2 6EA T 01733- 468000
W www.motherandbaby.co.uk
Editor, Sally Saunders
YOUR CAT
BPG Media, 1-6 Buckminster Yard, Main Street, Buckminster, Grantham, Lincs NG33 5SA T 0844-848-8257
W www.yourcat.co.uk
Editor-in-Chief, Sarah Wright
YOUR DOG
BPG Media, 1-6 Buckminster Yard, Main Street, Buckminster, Grantham, Lincs NG33 5SA T 0844-848 8257
W www.yourdog.co.uk
Editor, Sarah Wright

CLASSICAL MUSIC AND OPERA
BBC MUSIC
Immediate Media Company Bristol Ltd, Tower House, Fairfax Street, Bristol BS1 3BN **T** 0117-927 9009 **W** www.classical-music.com
Editor, Oliver Condy
CLASSICAL MUSIC
Rhinegold House, 20 Rugby Street, London WC1N 3QZ
T 020-7333 1729 **W** www.classicalmusicmagazine.org
Consultant Editor, Keith Clarke
GRAMOPHONE
c/o Mark Allen Group, St Jude's Church, Dulwich Road, London SE24 0PB **T** 020-7738 5454 **W** www.gramophone.co.uk
Editor, Martin Cullingford
OPERA
36 Black Lion Lane, London W6 9BE **T** 020-8563 8893
W www.opera.co.uk
Editor, John Allison

COMPUTERS AND TECHNOLOGY
PC PRO
Dennis Technology, 30 Cleveland Street, London W1T 4JD
T 020-7907 6000 **W** www.alphr.com
Editor-in-Chief, Tim Danton
STUFF
Bridge House, 69 London Road, Twickenham TW1 3SP
T 020-8267 5036 **W** www.stuff.tv
Editor, James Day
T3
T3.com, 5 Pinesway Industrial Estate, Bath BA2 3QS
W www.t3.com
Editor, Matt Bolton
WEB USER
Dennis Publishing, 30 Cleveland Street, London W1T 4JD
T 020-7907 6000 **W** www.webuser.co.uk
Group Editor, Daniel Booth
WIRED
Condé Nast, Vogue House, Hanover Square, London W1S 1JU
T 0844-848 5202 **W** www.wired.co.uk
Editor-in-Chief, Nicholas Thompson

CRAFT
CARDMAKING & PAPERCRAFT
Immediate Media, Vineyard House, 44 Brook Green, London W6 7BT **T** 0117-933 8081 **W** www.cardmakingandpapercraft.com
Deputy Editor, Jo Stenlake
SIMPLY KNITTING
Immediate Media, Vineyard House, 44 Brook Green, London W6 7BT **T** 0117-3008 253 **W** www.simplyknitting.co.uk
Commissioning Editor, Kirstie McLeod
THE WORLD OF CROSS STITCHING
Immediate Media, Vineyard House, 44 Brook Green, London W6 7BT **T** 0117-314 8351 **W** www.cross-stitching.com
Editor, Ruth Southorn

ENTERTAINMENT
EMPIRE
Endeavour House, 189 Shaftesbury Avenue, London WC2H 8JG
T 020-7437 9011 **W** www.empireonline.com
Editor-in-Chief, Terri White
RADIO TIMES
Vineyard House, 44 Brook Green, London W6 7BT
T 020-7150 5800 **W** www.radiotimes.com
Editorial Director, Mark Frith
SIGHT & SOUND
BFI, 21 Stephen Street, London W1T 1LN **T** 020-7255 1444
W www.bfi.org.uk/sightandsound
Editor, Nick James
TIME OUT LONDON
4th Floor, 125 Shaftesbury Avenue, London WC2H 8AD
T 020-7813 3000 **W** www.timeout.com
Editor, Caroline McGinn

TOTAL FILM
Future Publishing Ltd, 1–10 Praed Mews, London W2 1QY
T 020-7042 4831 **W** www.gamesradar.com/totalfilm
Editor, Jane Crowther

FASHION AND BEAUTY
COSMOPOLITAN
Hearst Magazines, 33 Broadwick Street, London W1F 0DQ
T 020-7439 5000 **W** www.cosmopolitan.co.uk
Editor, Farrah Storr
ELLE
Hearst Magazines, 72 Broadwick Street, London W1F 9EP
T 020-7150 7000 **W** www.elleuk.com
Editor-in-Chief, Anne-Marie Curtis
GLAMOUR
Condé Nast, Vogue House, Hanover Square, London W1S 1JU
T 020-7499 9080 **W** www.glamourmagazine.co.uk
Editor-in-Chief, Samantha Barry
GRAZIA
Endeavour House, 189 Shaftesbury Avenue, London WC2H 8JG
T 0845-601 1356 **W** www.graziadaily.co.uk
Editor, Hattie Brett
HARPER'S BAZAAR
Hearst Magazines, 72 Broadwick Street, London W1F 9EP
T 0844-848 5203 **W** www.harpersbazaar.co.uk
Editor-in-Chief, Justine Picardie
MARIE CLAIRE
Blue Fin Building, 110 Southwark Street, London SE1 4SU
T 020-3148 5000 **W** www.marieclaire.co.uk
Editor-in-Chief, Trish Halpin
VOGUE
Condé Nast, Vogue House, Hanover Square, London W1S 1JU
T 0844-848 5202 **W** www.vogue.co.uk
Editor, Edward Enninful

FOOD AND DRINK
FOOD AND TRAVEL
Suite 51, The Business Centre, Ingate Place, London SW8 3NS
T 020-7501 0511 **W** www.foodandtravel.com
Editor, Mark Sansom
GOOD FOOD
44 Vineyard House, Brook Green, London W6 7BT
T 020-7150 5022 **W** www.bbcgoodfood.com
Editorial Director, Gillian Carter
OLIVE
Vineyard House, 44 Brook Green, London W6 7BT
T 020-7150 5024 **W** www.olivemagazine.com
Editor, Laura Rowe
WHISKY
6 Woolgate Court, St Benedicts Street, Norwich NR2 4AP
T 01603-633 808 **W** www.whiskymag.com
Editor, Rob Allanson

GENERAL INTEREST
BBC HISTORY
Tower House, Fairfax Street, Bristol BS1 3BN **T** 0117-927 9009
W www.historyextra.com
Editor, Rob Attar
BOOKSELLER
Floor 10, Westminster Tower, 3 Albert Embankment, London SE1 7SP **T** 020-3358 0365 **W** www.thebookseller.com
Editor, Philip Jones
HISTORY TODAY
2nd Floor, 9 Staple Inn, London WC1V 7QH **T** 020-3219 7810
W www.historytoday.com
Editor, Paul Lay
LITERARY REVIEW
44 Lexington Street, London W1F 0LW **T** 020-7437 9392
W www.literaryreview.co.uk
Editor, Nancy Sladek

NEW STATESMAN
John Carpenter House, 7 Carmelite Street, Blackfriars, London EC4Y
0AN **T** 020-7936 6400 **W** www.newstatesman.com
Editor, Jason Cowley
PRIVATE EYE
6 Carlisle Street, London W1D 3BN **T** 020-7437 4017
W www.private-eye.co.uk
Editor, Ian Hislop
PROSPECT
5th Floor, 23 Savile Row, London W1S 2ET **T** 020-7255 1281
W www.prospectmagazine.co.uk
Editor, Tom Clark
READER'S DIGEST
The Maltings, West Street, Bourne BH24 9PH **T** 0330-333 2220
W www.readersdigest.co.uk
Editor, Fiona Hicks
SAGA
Saga Publishing Ltd, Enbrook Park, Folkestone, Kent CT20 3SE
T 01303-771111 **W** www.saga.co.uk
THE SPECTATOR
22 Old Queen Street, London SW1H 9HP **T** 020-7961 0200
W www.spectator.co.uk
Editor, Fraser Nelson
TLS (THE TIMES LITERARY SUPPLEMENT)
1 London Bridge Street, London SE1 9GF **T** 020-7782 5000
W www.the-tls.co.uk
Editor, Stig Abell
THE WEEK
31–32 Alfred Place, London WC1E 7DP **T** 020-3890 3890
W www.theweek.co.uk
Editor-in-Chief, Jeremy O'Grady
WHO DO YOU THINK YOU ARE?
Tower House, Fairfax Street, Bristol BS1 3BN **T** 0117-314 7400
W www.whodoyouthinkyouaremagazine.com
Editor, Sarah Williams

HEALTH AND FITNESS
MEN'S FITNESS
31–32 Alfred Place, London WC1E 7DP **T** 020-3890 3890
W www.coachmag.co.uk
Editor, Joe Warner
RUNNER'S WORLD
33 Broadwick Street, London W1F 9EP **T** 020-7339 4409
W www.runnersworld.co.uk
Editor, Betty Wong Ortiz
WEIGHT WATCHERS
The River Group, 1 Neal Street, London WC2H 9QL
T 020-7306 0304 **W** www.weightwatchers.co.uk
Deputy Editor, Andrea Leebody
WOMEN'S FITNESS
31–32 Alfred Place, London WC1E 7DP **T** 020-3890 3890
W www.womensfitness.co.uk
Editor, Jonathan Shannon

HOBBIES AND GAMES
AIRFIX MODEL WORLD
Key Publishing Ltd, PO Box 100, Stamford PE9 1XQ
T 01780-755131 **W** www.airfixmodelworld.com
Editor, Chris Clifford
ANGLING TIMES
Bauer Media Group, Media House, Lynchwood, Peterborough
Business Park, Peterborough PE2 6EA **T** 01733-395097
W www.gofishing.co.uk
Editor-in-Chief, Steve Fitzpatrick
BRITISH RAILWAY MODELLING
Warners Group Publications, The Maltings, West Street, Bourne,
Lincs PE10 9PH **T** 01778-391000 **W** www.model-railways-live.co.uk
Managing Editor, Andy McVittie
CHESS
Chess & Bridge Ltd, 44 Baker Street, London W1U 7RT
T 020-7486 7015 **W** www.chess.co.uk
Editor, Byron James

COIN NEWS
Token Publishing Ltd, 40 Southernhay East, Exeter, Devon EX1 1PE
T 01404-46972 **W** www.tokenpublishing.com
Editor, Pete Rizzo
HORNBY
Key Publishing Ltd, PO Box 100, Stamford PE9 1XQ
T 01780-755131 **W** www.hornbymagazine.com
Editor, Mike Wild

HOME AND GARDEN
GARDENERS' WORLD
Immediate Media, 5th Floor, Vineyard House, 44 Brook Green,
London W6 7BT **T** 020-7150 5700 **W** www.gardenersworld.com
Editor, Lucy Hall
GOOD HOUSEKEEPING
Hearst Magazines, 72 Broadwick Street, London W1F 9EP
T 020-7439 5000 **W** www.goodhousekeeping.co.uk
Editor-in-chief, Jane Francisco
HOUSE & GARDEN
Condé Nast Publications, Vogue House, Hanover Square, London
W1S 1JU **T** 020-7499 9080 **W** www.houseandgarden.co.uk
Editor, Hatta Byng
LIVING ETC
IPC Media, Blue Fin Building, 110 Southwark Street, London SE1
0SU **T** 020-3148 7443 **W** www.housetohome.co.uk/livingetc
Editor, Suzanne Imre

MEN'S LIFESTYLE
ESQUIRE
Hearst Magazines, 72 Broadwick Street, London W1F 9EP
T 020-7439 5000 **W** www.esquire.co.uk
Editor, Alex Bilmes
GAY TIMES
Millivres Prowler Group, Spectrum House, 32-34 Gordon House
Road, London NW5 1LP **T** 020-7424 7400 **W** www.gaytimes.co.uk
Editor, Darren Scott
GQ
Vogue House, 1 Hanover Square, London W1S 1JU
T 020-7499 9080 **W** www.gq-magazine.co.uk
Editor, Dylan Jones
LOADED
114 The Strand, London WC2R 0AG **T** 020-8900 4590
W www.loaded.co.uk
Head of Traffic, Oliver Tang

MOTORING
BIKE
Bauer Media, Media House, Lynchwood, Peterborough PE2 6EA
T 01733-468000 **W** www.bikemagazine.co.uk
Editor, Hugo Wilson
CARAVAN
Warners Group Publications, The Maltings, West Street, Bourne,
Lincs PE10 9PH **T** 01778-392450 **W** www.outandaboutlive.co.uk
Editor, John Sootheran
F1 RACING
Haymarket, Teddington Studios, Broom Road, Teddington TW11
9BE **T** 020-8267 5806 **W** www.f1racing.co.uk
Editorial Director, Anthony Rowlinson
PRACTICAL CARAVAN
Haymarket Ltd, Bridge House, 69 London Road, Twickenham TW1
3SP **T** 020-8267 5712 **W** www.practicalcaravan.com
Group Editor, Alastair Clement
TOP GEAR
Energy Centre, Media Centre, 201 Wood Lane, London W12 7TQ
T 020-7150 5558 **W** www.topgear.com
Editor, Charlie Turner

PHOTOGRAPHY
AMATEUR PHOTOGRAPHER
Pinehurst 2, Pinehurst Road, Farnborough, Hants. GU14 7BF
T 01252-555213 **W** www.amateurphotographer.co.uk
Group Editor, Nigel Atherton

DIGITAL CAMERA
Future Publishing Ltd Quay House, The Ambury, Bath BA1 1UA
W www.digitalcameraworld.com
Editor, Mark Hawkins
DIGITAL PHOTOGRAPHER
Future Publishing Ltd, Quay House, The Ambury, Bath BA1 1UA
T 01202-586200 W www.dphotographer.co.uk
Editor-in-Chief, Amy Squibb

POPULAR MUSIC
CLASH
Studio 86, Hackney Downs Studios, 17 Amhurst Terrace, London E8
2BT T 020-7628 2312 W www.clashmusic.com
Editor-in-Chief, Simon Harper
CLASSIC ROCK
Future Publishing Ltd, Quay House, The Ambury, Bath BA1 1UA
W www.classicrock.teamrock.com
Editor, Siân Llewellyn
DIY
2nd Floor, Unit 23, Tileyard Studios, Tileyard Road, London N7 9AH
W www.diymag.com
Founding Editor, Emma Swann
GUITARIST
Future Publishing Ltd, Beauford Court, 30 Monmouth Street, Bath
BA1 2BW T 01225-442244 W www.musicradar.com/guitarist
Editor, Jamie Dickson
MOJO
Endeavour House, 189 Shaftesbury Avenue, London WC2H 8JG
T 020-7208 3443 W www.mojo4music.com
Editor, Phil Alexander
Q
Endeavour House, 189 Shaftesbury Avenue, London WC2H 8JG
T 020-7295 5000 W www.qthemusic.com
Editor-in-Chief, Phil Alexander
UNCUT
Blue Fin Building, 110 Southwark Street, London SE1 0SU
T 020-3148 5000 W www.uncut.co.uk
Editor, Michael Bonnier

SCIENCE AND NATURE
BBC WILDLIFE
4th Floor, Tower House, Fairfax Street, Bristol BS1 3BN
T 0117-314 7366 W www.discoverwildlife.com
Editor, Sheena Harvey
BIRD WATCHING
Bauer Media, Media House, Lynch Wood, Peterborough PE2 6EA
T 01733-468000 W www.birdwatching.co.uk
Editor, Matthew Merritt
COUNTRYFILE
9th Floor, Tower House, Fairfax Street, Bristol BS1 3BN
T 0117-927 9009 W www.countryfile.com
Editor, Fergus Collins
FOCUS
Immediate Media, 9th Floor, Tower House, Fairfax Street, Bristol
BS1 3BN T 0117-314 7388 W www.sciencefocus.com
Editor, Daniel Bennett
HOW IT WORKS
Future Publishing Limited Quay House, The Ambury, Bath BA1 1UA
W www.howitworksdaily.com
Editor-in-Chief, Dave Harfield
NEW SCIENTIST
110 High Holborn, London WC1V 6EU T 020-7611 1206
W www.newscientist.com
Editor-in-Chief, Emily Wilson
SKY AT NIGHT
Immediate Media Co., Tower House, Fairfax Street, Bristol BS1 3BN
T 0117-314 8758 W www.skyatnightmagazine.com

Editor, Chris Bramley

SPORT
ALL OUT CRICKET
TriNorth Ltd, Unit 3.40 Canterbury Court, 1–3 Brixton Road, London
SW9 6DE T 020-3176 0187 W www.alloutcricket.com
Editor, Phil Walker
BOXING MONTHLY
Topwave Ltd, 40 Morpeth Road, London E9 7LD T 020-8986 4141
W www.boxing-monthly.co.uk
Editor, Graham Houston
THE CRICKETER
120 New Cavendish Street, London W1W 6XX T 020-3198 1359
W www.thecricketer.com
Editor, Simon Hughes
FOURFOURTWO
Haymarket Ltd, Bridge House, 69 London Road, Twickenham TW1
3SP T 020-8267 5000 W www.fourfourtwo.com
Editor, Hitesh Ratna
GOLF MONTHLY
Time Inc. (UK), Pinehurst 2, Pinehurst Road, Farnborough Business
Park, Farnborough, Hants GU14 7BF T 01252-555197
W www.golf-monthly.co.uk
Editor, Michael Harris
HORSE & HOUND
Time Inc. (UK), Pinehurst 2, Pinehurst Road, Farnborough Business
Park, Farnborough, Hants GU14 7BF T 01252-555029
W www.horseandhound.co.uk
Content Director, Sarah Jenkins
MATCH
Kelsey Media, Cudham Tithe Barn, Berrys Hill, Cudham, Kent, TN16
3AG T 01733-353358 W www.matchfootball.co.uk
Editor, Stephen Fishlock
RUGBY WORLD
Time Inc (UK) Ltd, 2nd Floor, Pinehurst 2, Pinehurst Road,
Farnborough Business Park, Farnborough, Hants GU14 7BF
T 01252-555271 W www.rugbyworld.com
Editor, Sarah Mockford
TENNISHEAD
Advantage Publishing (UK) Ltd, Suite 142, 61 Victoria Road,
Surbiton KT6 4JX T 020-8408 7148 W www.tennishead.net
Consultant Editor, Paul Newman
WORLD SOCCER
Time Inc (UK) Ltd, 2nd Floor, Pinehurst 2, Pinehurst Road,
Farnborough Business Park, Farnborough, Hants GU14 7BF
T 020-3148 4817 W www.worldsoccer.com
Editor, Gavin Hamilton

TRAVEL
CONDÉ NAST TRAVELLER
Vogue House, Hanover Square, London W1S 1JU T 0844-848 2851
W www.cntraveller.com
Editor, Pilar Guzman
FRANCE
Archant House, 3 Oriel Road, Cheltenham GL50 1BB
T 01242-216050 W www.completefrance.com
Editor, Lara Dunn
LONELY PLANET
240 Blackfriars Road, London SE1 8NW W www.lonelyplanet.com
Editor, Peter Grunert
NATIONAL GEOGRAPHIC TRAVELLER
APL Media Ltd, Unit 310 Highgate Studios, 53–79 Highgate Road,
London NW5 1TL T 020-7253 9906 W www.natgeotraveller.co.uk
Editor, Pat Riddell

TRADE AND PROFESSIONAL BODIES

The following is a list of employers' and trade associations and other professional bodies in the UK. It does not represent a comprehensive list. For further professional bodies *see* Professional Education.

ASSOCIATIONS

ABTA – THE TRAVEL ASSOCIATION 30 Park Street, London SE1 9EQ T 020-311 70500 E abta@abta.co.uk
W www.abta.com
Chief Executive, Mark Tanzer

ADVERTISING ASSOCIATION 7th Floor North, Artillery House, London SW1P 1RT T 020-7340 1100
E aa@adassoc.org.uk W www.adassoc.org.uk
Chief Executive, Stephen Woodford

AEROSPACE DEFENCE SECURITY Salamanca Square, 9 Albert Embankment, London SE1 7SP T 020-7091 4500
E enquiries@adsgroup.org.uk W www.adsgroup.org.uk
Chief Executive, Paul Everitt

AGRICULTURAL ENGINEERS ASSOCIATION Samuelson House, 62 Forder Way, Peterborough PE7 8JB T 0845-644 8748
E ab@aea.uk.com W www.aea.uk.com
Chief Executive, Ruth Bailey

ASBESTOS REMOVAL CONTRACTORS ASSOCIATION Unit 1, Stretton Business Park 2, Brunel Drive, Stretton DE13 0BY
T 01283-566467 E info@arca.org.uk W www.arca.org.uk
Chief Executive, Steve Sadley

ASSOCIATION FOR CONSULTANCY AND ENGINEERING Alliance House, 12 Caxton Street, London SW1H 0QL T 020-7222 6557 E consult@acenet.co.uk
W www.acenet.co.uk
Chief Executive, Hannah Vickers

ASSOCIATION OF ACCOUNTING TECHNICIANS 140 Aldersgate Street, London EC1A 4HY T 020-3735 2468
E aat@aat.org.uk W www.aat.org.uk
Chief Executive, Mark Farrar

ASSOCIATION OF ANAESTHETISTS OF GREAT BRITAIN AND IRELAND 21 Portland Place, London W1B 1PY T 020-7631 1650 E info@aagbi.org W www.aagbi.org
Executive Director, Karin Pappenheim

ASSOCIATION OF BRITISH INSURERS One America Square, London EC3N 2LB T 020-7600 3333 E info@abi.org.uk
W www.abi.org.uk
Director-General, Huw Evans

ASSOCIATION OF BUSINESS RECOVERY PROFESSIONALS 8th Floor, 120 Aldersgate Street, London EC1A 4JQ T 020-7566 4200 E association@r3.org.uk
W www.r3.org.uk
Interim Chief Executive, Emma Lovell

ASSOCIATION OF CONSULTING SCIENTISTS 5 Willow Heights, Cradley Heath B64 7PL T 0121-602 3515
E secretary@consultingscientists.co.uk
Secretary, Dr Stuart Guy

ASSOCIATION OF CONVENIENCE STORES LTD Federation House, 17 Farnborough Street, Farnborough GU14 8AG T 01252-515001 E acs@acs.org.uk
W www.acs.org.uk
Chief Executive, James Lowman

ASSOCIATION OF CORPORATE TREASURERS 68 King William Street, London EC4N 7DZ T 020-7847 2540
E enquiries@treasurers.org W www.treasurers.org
Chief Executive, Caroline Stockmann

ASSOCIATION OF DRAINAGE AUTHORITIES Rural Innovation Centre, Avenue H, Stoneleigh Park CV8 2LG
T 024-7699 2889 E admin@ada.org.uk W www.ada.org.uk
Chief Executive, Innes Thomson, CENG

BOOKSELLERS ASSOCIATION 6 Bell Yard, London WC2A 2JR T 020-7421 4640 E mail@booksellers.org.uk
W www.booksellers.org.uk
Chief Executive, Meryl Halls

BRITISH ANTIQUE DEALERS' ASSOCIATION 14 Dufferin Street, London EC1Y 8PD T 020-7589 4128 E info@bada.org
W www.bada.org.uk
President, Lady Borwick

BRITISH ASSOCIATION OF SOCIAL WORKERS 16 Kent Street, Birmingham B5 6RD T 0121-622 3911
E online@basw.co.uk W www.basw.co.uk
Chief Executive, Colum Conway

BRITISH BEER & PUB ASSOCIATION Ground Floor, Brewers' Hall, Aldermanbury Square, London EC2V 7HR
T 020-7627 9191 E contact@beerandpub.com
W www.beerandpub.com
Chief Executive, Brigid Simmonds, OBE

BRITISH CHAMBERS OF COMMERCE 65 Petty France, London SW1H 9EU T 020-7654 5800
W www.britishchambers.org.uk
Director-General, Adam Marshall

BRITISH ELECTROTECHNICAL AND ALLIED MANUFACTURERS ASSOCIATION (BEAMA)
Westminster Tower, 3 Albert Embankment, London SE1 7SL
T 020-7793 3000 E info@beama.org.uk W www.beama.org.uk
Chief Executive, Dr Howard Porter

BRITISH HOROLOGICAL INSTITUTE Upton Hall, Upton, Newark NG23 5TE T 01636-813795 E info@bhi.co.uk
W www.bhi.co.uk
Chairman, Stella Haward

BRITISH INSTITUTE OF PROFESSIONAL PHOTOGRAPHY The Coach House, The Firs, High Street, Aylesbury HP22 4SJ T 01296-642020 E info@bipp.com
W www.bipp.com
Chief Executive, Chris Harper

BRITISH INSURANCE BROKERS' ASSOCIATION 8th Floor, John Stow House, 18 Bevis Marks, London EC3A 7JB
T 0344-770 0266 E enquiries@biba.org.uk W www.biba.org.uk
Chief Executive, Steve White

BRITISH MARINE FEDERATION Marine House, Thorpe Lea Road, Egham TW20 8BF T 01784-473377
E info@britishmarine.co.uk W www.britishmarine.co.uk
Chief Executive, Lesley, ROBINSON

BRITISH MEDICAL ASSOCIATION BMA House, Tavistock Square, London WC1H 9JP T 020-7387 4499
W www.bma.org.uk
Chief Executive, Keith Ward

BRITISH OFFICE SUPPLIES AND SERVICES (BOSS) FEDERATION c/o British Printing Industries Federation, 2 Villiers Court, Copse Drive CV5 9RN T 01676-526030
E liz@bossfederation.co.uk W www.bossfederation.co.uk
Chief Executive, Charles Jarrold

BPI (BRITISH PHONOGRAPHIC INDUSTRY) Riverside Building, County Hall, Westminster Bridge Road, London SE1 7JA
T 020-7803 1300 E general@bpi.co.uk W www.bpi.co.uk
Chief Executive, Geoff Taylor

BRITISH PLASTICS FEDERATION 6 Bath Place, London EC2A 3JE T 020-7457 5000 E reception@bpf.co.uk
W www.bpf.co.uk
Director-General, Philip Law

BRITISH PORTS ASSOCIATION 1st Floor, 30 Park Street, London SE1 9EQ T 020-7260 1780 E info@britishports.org.uk
W www.britishports.org.uk
Chief Executive, Richard Ballantyne

BRITISH PRINTING INDUSTRIES FEDERATION Unit 2, Villiers Court, Meriden Business Park CV5 9RN **T** 01676-526030 **W** www.britishprint.com
Chief Executive, Charles Jarrold

BRITISH PROPERTY FEDERATION 5th Floor, St Albans House, 57–59 Haymarket, London SW1Y 4QX **T** 020-7828 0111 **E** info@bpf.org.uk **W** www.bpf.org.uk
Chief Executive, Melanie Leech

BRITISH RETAIL CONSORTIUM 2 London Bridge, London SE1 9RA **T** 020-7854 8900 **E** info@brc.org.uk **W** www.brc.org.uk
Director-General, Helen Dickinson, OBE

BRITISH TYRE MANUFACTURERS' ASSOCIATION LTD 5 Berewyk Hall Court, White Colne, Colchester CO6 2QB **T** 01787-226995 **E** mail@btmauk.com **W** www.btmauk.com
Chief Executive, Graham Willson

BUILDING SOCIETIES ASSOCIATION 6th Floor, York House, London WC2B 6UJ **T** 020-7520 5900 **E** simon.rex@bsa.org.uk **W** www.bsa.org.uk
Chief Executive, Robin Fieth

CHARTERED ASSOCIATION OF BUILDING ENGINEERS Lutyens House, Billing Brook Road, Northampton NN3 8NW **T** 01604-404121 **W** www.cbuilde.com
Chief Executive, Dr Gavin Dunn

CHARTERED INSTITUTE FOR ARCHAEOLOGISTS Miller Building, Reading RG6 6AB **T** 0118-378 6446 **E** admin@archaeologists.net **W** www.archaeologists.net
Chief Executive, Peter Hinton

CHARTERED INSTITUTE OF ENVIRONMENTAL HEALTH Chadwick Court, 15 Hatfields, London SE1 8DJ **T** 020-7928 6006 **E** information@cieh.org **W** www.cieh.org
Chief Executive, Anne Godfrey

CHARTERED INSTITUTE OF JOURNALISTS 2 Dock Offices, Surrey Quays Road, London SE16 2XU **T** 020-7252 1187 **E** memberservices@cioj.co.uk **W** www.cioj.co.uk
General Secretary, Dominic Cooper

CHARTERED INSTITUTE OF PURCHASING AND SUPPLY Easton House, Church Street, Stamford PE9 3NZ **T** 01780-756777 **W** www.cips.org
Chief Executive, Malcolm Harrison

CHARTERED INSTITUTE OF TAXATION 1st Floor Artillery House, 11–19 Artillery Row, London SW1P 1RT **T** 020-7340 0550 **E** comms@tax.org.uk **W** www.tax.org.uk
Chief Executive, Peter Fanning

CHARTERED INSURANCE INSTITUTE The Insurance Hall, 20 Aldermanbury, London EC2V 7HY **T** 020-8989 8464 **E** customer.serv@cii.co.uk **W** www.cii.co.uk
Chief Executive, Sian Fisher

CHARTERED MANAGEMENT INSTITUTE Management House, Cottingham Road, Corby NN17 1TT **T** 01536-207360 **E** enquiries@managers.org.uk **W** www.managers.org.uk
Chief Executive, Anne Francke

CHARTERED QUALITY INSTITUTE 2nd Floor North, Chancery Exchange, London EC4A 1AB **T** 020-7245 6722 **E** membership@quality.org **W** www.quality.org
Chief Executive, Vincent Desmond

CHARTERED TRADING STANDARDS INSTITUTE 1 Sylvan Court, Sylvan Way, Basildon SS15 6TH **T** 01268-582200 **E** institute@tsi.org.uk **W** www.tradingstandards.uk
Chief Executive, Leon Livermore

CHEMICAL INDUSTRIES ASSOCIATION Kings Buildings, Smith Square, London SW1P 3JJ **T** 020-7834 3399 **E** enquiries@cia.org.uk **W** www.cia.org.uk
Chief Executive, Steve Elliott

CONFEDERATION OF PAPER INDUSTRIES 1 Rivenhall Road, Swindon SN5 7BD **T** 01793-889600 **E** cpi@paper.org.uk **W** www.paper.org.uk
Director-General, Andrew Large

CONFEDERATION OF PASSENGER TRANSPORT UK Fifth Floor Offices (South), Chancery House, London WC2A 1QS **T** 020-7240 3131 **E** admin@cpt-uk.org **W** www.cpt-uk.org
Chief Executive, Simon Posner

CONSTRUCTION PRODUCTS ASSOCIATION The Building Centre, 26 Store Street, London WC1E 7BT **T** 020-7323 3770 **W** www.constructionproducts.org.uk
Chief Executive, Diana Montgomery

DAIRY UK 6th Floor, London WC1V 7EP **T** 020-7405 1484 **E** info@dairyuk.org **W** www.dairyuk.org
Chief Executive, Dr Judith Bryans

EEF, THE MANUFACTURERS' ORGANISATION Broadway House, Tothill Street, London SW1H 9NQ **T** 020-7222 7777 **E** enquiries@eef.org.uk **W** www.eef.org.uk
Chief Executive, Terry Scuoler

ENERGY UK Charles House, 5–11 Regent Street, London SW1Y 4LR **T** 020-7930 9390 **W** www.energy-uk.org.uk
Chief Executive, Lawrence Slade

FEDERATION OF BAKERS 6th Floor, 10 Bloomsbury Way, London WC1A 2SL **T** 020-7420 7190 **E** info@fob.uk.com **W** www.fob.uk.com
Director, Gordon Polson

FEDERATION OF MASTER BUILDERS David Croft House, 25 Ely Place, London EC1N 6TD **T** 0330-333 7777 **W** www.fmb.org.uk
Chief Executive, Brian Berry

FSPA (FEDERATION OF SPORTS AND PLAY ASSOCIATIONS) Office 8, Rural Innovation Centre, Unit 169 – Avenue H, Kenilworth CV8 2LG **T** 024-7641 4999 **E** info@sportsandplay.com **W** www.sportsandplay.com
Chair, Jack Osborne

FINANCE AND LEASING ASSOCIATION 2nd Floor, Imperial House, 15–19 Kingsway, London WC2B 6UN **T** 020-7836 6511 **E** info@fla.org.uk **W** www.fla.org.uk
Director-General, Stephen Sklaroff

FOOD AND DRINK FEDERATION 6th Floor, London WC1A 2SL **T** 020-7836 2460 **W** www.fdf.org.uk
Director-General, Ian Wright

FREIGHT TRANSPORT ASSOCIATION LTD Hermes House, St John's Road, Tunbridge Wells TN4 9UZ **T** 01892-526171 **E** enquiry@fta.co.uk **W** www.fta.co.uk
President, Leigh Pomlett

GLASGOW CHAMBER OF COMMERCE 30 George Square, Glasgow G2 1EQ **T** 0141-204 2121 **E** chamber@glasgowchamberofcommerce.com **W** www.glasgowchamberofcommerce.com
Chief Executive, Stuart Patrick

INSTITUTE OF BREWING AND DISTILLING 44A Curlew Street, London SE1 2ND **T** 020-7499 8144 **E** enquiries@ibd.org.uk **W** www.ibd.org.uk
Chief Executive, Dr Jerry Avis

INSTITUTE OF BRITISH ORGAN BUILDING 13 Ryefields, Bury St Edmunds IP31 3TD **T** 01359-233433 **E** administrator@ibo.co.uk **W** www.ibo.co.uk
President, Andrew Moyes

INSTITUTE OF CHARTERED FORESTERS 59 George Street, Edinburgh EH2 2JG **T** 0131-240 1425 **E** icf@charteredforesters.org **W** www.charteredforesters.org
Executive Director, Shireen Chambers

INSTITUTE OF CHARTERED SECRETARIES AND ADMINISTRATORS Saffron House, 6–10 Kirby Street, London EC1N 8TS **T** 020-7580 4741 **E** info@icsa.org.uk **W** www.icsa.org.uk
Chief Executive, Simon Osborne

INSTITUTE OF CHARTERED SHIPBROKERS 85 Gracechurch Street, London EC3V 0AA **T** 020-7623 1111 **E** enquiries@ics.org.uk **W** www.ics.org.uk
Director, Julie Lithgow

INSTITUTE OF DIRECTORS 116 Pall Mall, London
SW1Y 5ED T 020-7766 8888 E enquiries@iod.com
W www.iod.com
Director-General, Stephen Martin

INSTITUTE OF EXPORT AND INTERNATIONAL
TRADE Export House, Minerva Business Park, Peterborough
PE2 6FT T 01733-404400 W www.export.org.uk
Chair, Terry Scuoler, CBE

INSTITUTE OF FINANCIAL ACCOUNTANTS The Podium,
1 Eversholt Street, London NW1 2DN T 020-7554 0730
E mail@ifa.org.uk W www.ifa.org.uk
Chief Executive, Andrew Conway

INSTITUTE OF HEALTHCARE MANAGEMENT 33
Cavendish Square, London W1G 0PW T 020-7182 4066
E contact@ihm.org.uk W www.ihm.org.uk
Chief Executive, Jill de Bene

INSTITUTE OF HOSPITALITY Trinity Court, 34 West Street,
Surrey SM1 1SH T 020-8661 4900
W www.instituteofhospitality.org
Chief Executive, Peter Ducker

INSTITUTE OF INTERNAL COMMUNICATION Suite
G10, Gemini House, Sunrise Parkway, MK14 6PW
T 01908-232168 E enquiries@ioic.org.uk W www.ioic.org.uk
Chief Executive, Jennifer Sproul

INSTITUTE OF MANAGEMENT SERVICES Brooke House,
24 Dam Street, Lichfield WS13 6AA T 01543-266909
E admin@ims-productivity.com W www.ims-productivity.com
Chair, Julian Cutler

INSTITUTE OF QUARRYING McPherson House, 8A Regan
Way, Chilwell NG9 6RZ T 0115-972 9995 E mail@quarrying.org
W www.quarrying.org
Chief Executive, James Thorne

INSTITUTE OF THE MOTOR INDUSTRY Fanshaws,
Hertford SG13 8PQ T 01992-511 521 E comms@theimi.org.uk
W www.theimi.org.uk
Chief Executive, Steve Nash

INSTITUTION OF OCCUPATIONAL SAFETY AND
HEALTH The Grange, Highfield Drive, Wigston LE18 1NN
T 0116-257 3100 E reception@iosh.co.uk W www.iosh.co.uk
Chief Executive, Bev Messinger

IP FEDERATION 5th Floor, 63–66 Hatton Garden, London
EC1N 8LE T 020-7242 3923 E admin@ipfederation.com
W www.ipfederation.com
President, Belinda Gascoyne

MAGISTRATES' ASSOCIATION 28 Fitzroy Square, London
W1T 6DD T 020-7387 2353
E information@magistrates-association.org.uk
W www.magistrates-association.org.uk
Chief Executive, Jon Collins

MANAGEMENT CONSULTANCIES ASSOCIATION 5th
Floor, 36–38 Cornhill, London EC3V 3NG T 020-7645 7950
E info@mca.org.uk W www.mca.org.uk
Chief Executive, Alan Leaman, OBE

MASTER LOCKSMITHS ASSOCIATION 5D Great Central
Way, Daventry NN11 3PZ T 01327-262255
E enquiries@locksmiths.co.uk W www.locksmiths.co.uk
Director of Development, Dr Steffan George

NATIONAL ASSOCIATION OF BRITISH MARKET
AUTHORITIES The Guildhall, Shrops SY11 1PZ
T 01691-680713 E nabma@nabma.com W www.nabma.com
Chief Executive, Hilary Paxman

NATIONAL ASSOCIATION OF ESTATE AGENTS Arbon
House, 6 Tournament Court, Warwick CV34 6LG
T 01926-496800 E help@propertymark.co.uk
W www.naea.co.uk
President, David Mackie

NATIONAL FARMERS' UNION (NFU) Agriculture House,
Stoneleigh Park, Stoneleigh CV8 2LZ T 024-7685 8500
W www.nfuonline.com
Director-General, Terry Jones

NATIONAL FEDERATION OF RETAIL NEWSAGENTS
Yeoman House, Sekforde Street, London EC1R 0HF
T 020-7253 4225 E connect@nfrnonline.com
W www.nfrnonline.com
Chief Executive, Paul Baxter

NATIONAL LANDLORDS ASSOCIATION 2nd Floor, 200
Union Street, London SE1 0LX T 020-7840 8900
E info@landlords.org.uk W www.landlords.org.uk
Chief Executive, Richard Lambert

NATIONAL MARKET TRADERS FEDERATION Hampton
House, Hawshaw Lane, Barnsley S74 0HA T 01226-749021
E genoffice@nmtf.co.uk W www.nmtf.co.uk
Chief Executive, Joe Harrison

NATIONAL PHARMACY ASSOCIATION Mallinson House,
38–42 St Peter's Street, Herts AL1 3NP T 01727-858687
E npa@npa.co.uk W www.npa.co.uk
Chief Executive, Mark Lyonette

NEWS MEDIA ASSOCIATION 292 Vauxhall Bridge Road,
London SW1V 1AE T 020-7963 7480 E nma@newsmediauk.org
W www.newsmediauk.org
Chief Executive, David Newell

OIL AND GAS UK 6th Floor East, Portland House, London
SW1E 5BH T 020-7802 2400 E info@oilandgasuk.co.uk
W www.oilandgasuk.co.uk
Chief Executive, Deirdre Michie

PROPERTY CARE ASSOCIATION 11 Ramsay Court,
Kingfisher Way, Huntingdon PE29 6FY T 0844-375 4301
E pca@property-care.org W www.property-care.org
Chief Executive, Stephen Hodgson

PUBLISHERS ASSOCIATION 50 Southwark Street, London
SE1 1UN T 020-7378 0504 E mail@publishers.org.uk
W www.publishers.org.uk
Chief Executive, Stephen Lotinga

RADIOCENTRE 6th Floor, 55 New Oxford Street, London
WC1A 1BS T 020-7010 0600 E info@radiocentre.org
W www.radiocentre.org
Chief Executive, Siobhan Kenny

ROAD HAULAGE ASSOCIATION LTD Roadway House,
Bretton Way, Bretton PE3 8DD T 01274-863100
W www.rha.uk.net
Chief Executive, Richard Burnett

ROYAL ASSOCIATION OF BRITISH DAIRY FARMERS
Dairy House, Unit 31, Abbey Park, Kenilworth CV8 2LY
T 024-7663 9317 E office@rabdf.co.uk W www.rabdf.co.uk
Managing Director, Matthew Knight

ROYAL FACULTY OF PROCURATORS IN GLASGOW
12 Nelson Mandela Place, Glasgow G2 1BT T 0141-332 3593
E library@rfpg.org W www.rfpg.org
Chief Executive, John McKenzie

SHELLFISH ASSOCIATION OF GREAT BRITAIN
Fishmongers' Hall, London Bridge, London EC4R 9EL
T 020-7283 8305 E projects@shellfish.org.uk
W www.shellfish.org.uk
Director, David Jarrad

SOCIETY OF LOCAL AUTHORITY CHIEF EXECUTIVES
AND SENIOR MANAGERS (SOLACE) Suite 1.3A, 1st
Floor, Millbank Tower, London SW1P 4QP T 0845-652 4010
E info@solace.org.uk W www.solace.org.uk
Directors, Graeme McDonald; Terry McDougall

SOCIETY OF MOTOR MANUFACTURERS AND
TRADERS LTD 71 Great Peter Street, London SW1P 2BN
T 020-7235 7000 E communications@smmt.co.uk
W www.smmt.co.uk
Chief Executive, Mike Hawes

TIMBER TRADE FEDERATION The Building Centre, 26
Store Street, London WC1E 7BT T 020-3205 0067 E ttf@ttf.co.uk
W www.ttf.co.uk
Managing Director, David Hopkins

UK CHAMBER OF SHIPPING 30 Park Street, London
SE1 9EQ **T** 020-7417 2800 **E** query@ukchamberofshipping.com
W www.ukchamberofshipping.com
Chief Executive, Bob Sanguinetti

UK FASHION AND TEXTILE ASSOCIATION 3 Queen
Square, London WC1N 3AR **T** 020-7843 9460 **E** info@ukft.org
W www.ukft.org
Chief Executive, Adam Mansell

UK FINANCE 5th Floor, 1 Angel Court, London EC2R 7HJ
T 020-7706 3333 **E** membership@ukfinance.org.uk
W www.ukfinance.org.uk
Chief Executive, Stephen Jones

UKHOSPITALITY 10 Bloomsbury Way, London WC1A 2SL
T 020-7404 7744 **W** www.ukhospitality.org.uk
Chairman, Nick Varney

UK LEATHER FEDERATION Leather Trade House, Kings Park
Road, Northampton NN3 6JD **T** 01604-679999 **E** info@uklf.org
W www.ukleather.org
Director, Dr Kerry Senior

UK PETROLEUM INDUSTRY ASSOCIATION LTD
Quality House, Quality Court, London WC2A 1HP
T 020-7269 7600 **E** info@ukpia.com **W** www.ukpia.com
Director-General, Stephen Marcos Jones

ULSTER FARMERS' UNION 475 Antrim Road, Belfast
BT15 3DA **T** 028-9037 0222 **E** info@ufuhq.com
W www.ufuni.org
Chief Executive, Wesley Aston

THE WINE AND SPIRIT TRADE ASSOCIATION
International Wine and Spirit Centre, 39–45 Bermondsey Street,
London SE1 3XF **T** 020-7089 3877 **E** info@wsta.co.uk
W www.wsta.co.uk
Chief Executive, Miles Beale

CBI

Cannon Place, 78 Cannon Street, London EC4N 6HN
T 020-7379 7400 **E** enquiries@cbi.org.uk **W** www.cbi.org.uk

The CBI was founded in 1965 and is an independent non-party political body financed by industry and commerce. It works with the UK government, international legislators and policymakers to help UK businesses compete effectively. It is the recognised spokesman for the business viewpoint and is consulted as such by the government.

The CBI speaks for some 190,000 businesses that together employ approximately one-third of the private sector workforce. Member companies, which decide all policy positions, include FTSE 100 index listed companies, small- and medium-size firms, micro businesses, private and family owned businesses, start-ups and trade associations.

The CBI board is chaired by the president and meets four times a year. It is assisted by 14 expert standing committees which advise on the main aspects of policy. There are nine regional councils for England and three national councils for, Wales, Scotland and Northern Ireland. There are also offices in Beijing, Brussels, New Delhi and Washington DC.

President, Paul Drechsler, CBE
Director-General, Carolyn Fairbairn

WALES, 2 Caspian Point, Caspian Way, Cardiff Bay, Cardiff CF10
4DQ **T** 029-2097 7600 **E** wales.mail@cbi.org.uk
Regional Director, Ian Price

SCOTLAND, 160 West George Street, Glasgow G2 2HQ
T 0141-222 2184 **E** scot.mail@cbi.org.uk
Regional Director, Tracy Black

NORTHERN IRELAND, Hamilton House, 3 Joy Street, Belfast
BT2 8LE **T** 028-9010 1100 **E** ni.mail@cbi.org.uk
Regional Director, Angela McGowan

TRADE UNIONS

A trade union is an organisation of workers formed for the purpose of collective bargaining over pay and working conditions. Trade unions may also provide legal and financial advice, sickness benefits and education facilities to their members. Legally any employee has the right to join a trade union, but not all employers recognise all or any trade unions. Conversely an employee also has the right not to join a trade union, in particular since the practice of a 'closed shop' system, where all employees have to join the employer's preferred union, is no longer permitted.

THE CENTRAL ARBITRATION COMMITTEE

Fleetbank House, 2–6 Salisbury Square, London EC4Y 8JX
T 020-7904 2300 E enquiries@cac.gov.uk
W www.gov.uk/government/organisations/
central-arbitration-committee

The Central Arbitration Committee's main role is concerned with requests for trade union recognition and de-recognition under the statutory procedures of Schedule A1 of the Employment Rights Act 1999. It also determines disclosure of information complaints under the Trade Union and Labour Relations (Consolidation) Act 1992, considers applications and complaints under the Information and Consultation Regulations 2004, and performs a similar role in relation to European works councils, companies, cooperative societies and cross-border mergers.

Chair, Sir Stephen Redmond
Chief Executive, James Jacob

TRADES UNION CONGRESS (TUC)

Congress House, 23–28 Great Russell Street, London WC1B 3LS
T 020-7636 4030 E info@tuc.org.uk
W www.tuc.org.uk

The Trades Union Congress (TUC), founded in 1868, is an independent association of trade unions. The TUC promotes the rights and welfare of those in work and helps the unemployed. The TUC brings Britain's unions together to draw up common polices; lobbies the government to implement policies that will benefit people at work; campaigns on economic and social issues; represents working people on public bodies and at the UN employment body – the International Labour Organisation; carries out research on employment-related issues; runs training and education programmes for union representatives; helps unions to develop new services for their members and negotiate with each other; and builds links with other trade union bodies worldwide.

The governing body of the TUC is the annual congress which sets policy. Between congresses, business is conducted by a 55-member general council, which meets every two months to oversee the TUC's work programme and sanction new policy initiatives. Each year, at its first post-congress meeting, the general council appoints an executive committee and the TUC president for that congress year. The executive committee meets monthly to implement and develop policy, manage TUC financial affairs and deal with any urgent business. The president chairs general council and executive meetings and is consulted by the General Secretary on all major issues.

President (2017–18), Sally Hunt
General Secretary, Frances O'Grady

SCOTTISH TRADES UNION CONGRESS (STUC)

333 Woodlands Road, Glasgow G3 6NG T 0141-337 8100
E info@stuc.org.uk W www.stuc.org.uk

The congress was formed in 1897 and acts as a national centre for the trade union movement in Scotland. The STUC promotes the rights to welfare of those in work and helps the unemployed. It helps its member unions to promote membership in new areas and industries, and campaigns for rights at work for all employees, including part-time and temporary workers, whether union members or not. It also makes representations to government and employers. In 2016 the STUC had over 580,000 members from 39 affiliated unions and 20 trade union councils.

The annual congress in April elects a 36-member general council on the basis of six sections.

General Secretary, Grahame Smith

WALES TUC

Wales TUC was established in 1974 to ensure that the role of the TUC was effectively undertaken in Wales. Its structure reflects the four economic regions of Wales and matches the regional committee areas of the National Assembly of Wales. The regional committees oversee the implementation of Wales TUC policy and campaigns in the relevant regions, and liaise with local government, training organisations and regional economic development bodies. The Wales TUC seeks to reduce unemployment, increase the levels of skill and pay, and eliminate discrimination.

The governing body of Wales TUC is the conference, which meets annually in May and elects a general council (usually of around 50 people) that oversees the work of the TUC throughout the year.

There are 49 affiliated unions representing around 400,000 workers.

President (2017–18), Mike Jenkins
General Secretary, Martin Mansfield

TUC-AFFILIATED UNIONS
As at May 2018

ACCORD Simmons House, 46 Old Bath Road, Reading
RG10 9QR T 0118-934 1808 E info@accordhq.org
W www.accord-myunion.org
General Secretary, Ged Nichols
Membership: 23,927

ADVANCE 2nd Floor, 16–17 High Street, Tring HP23 5AH
T 01442-891122 E info@advance-union.org
W www.advance-union.org
General Secretary, Linda Rolph
Membership: 6,665

AEGIS THE UNION 1–3 Lochside Crescent, Edinburgh
EH12 9SE T 0131-549 5474 E members@aegistheunion.co.uk
W www.aegistheunion.co.uk
General Secretary, Brian Linn
Membership: 4,444

AEP (ASSOCIATION OF EDUCATIONAL
PSYCHOLOGISTS) 4 The Riverside Centre, Durham DH1 5TA
T 0191-384 9512 E enquiries@aep.org.uk W www.aep.org.uk
General Secretary, Kate Fallon
Membership: 3,396

AFA (ASSOCIATION OF FLIGHT ATTENDANTS) 32
Wingford Road, London SW2 4DS **T** 0789-1182947
E afalhr@unitedafa.org **W** www.afacwa.org
General Secretary, Anthony King
Membership: 440

ARTISTS' UNION ENGLAND 3 Albert Street, Oxford
OX2 6AY **T** 07931-774469 **E** info@artistsunionengland.org.uk
W www.artistsunionengland.org.uk
General Secretary, Theresa Easton
Membership: 295

**ASLEF (ASSOCIATED SOCIETY OF LOCOMOTIVE
ENGINEERS AND FIREMEN)** 77 St John Street, London
EC1M 4NN **T** 020-7324 2400 **E** info@aslef.org.uk
W www.aslef.org.uk
General Secretary, Mick Whelan
Membership: 22,078

BALPA (BRITISH AIRLINE PILOTS ASSOCIATION)
BALPA House, 5 Heathrow Boulevard, 278 Bath Road, West
Drayton UB7 0DQ **T** 020-8476 4000 **E** balpa@balpa.org
W www.balpa.org
General Secretary, Brian Strutton
Membership: 14,688

BDA (BRITISH DIETETIC ASSOCIATION) 5th Floor,
Charles House, 148–149 Great Charles Street, Birmingham
B3 3JT **T** 0121-200 0021 **E** info@bda.uk.com
W www.bda.uk.com
General Secretary, Annette Mansell-Green
Membership: 8,868

**BFAWU (BAKERS, FOOD AND ALLIED WORKERS'
UNION)** Stanborough House, Great North Road, Welwyn
Garden City AL8 7TA **T** 01707-260150 **E** info@bfawu.org
W www.bfawu.org
General Secretary, Ronnie Draper
Membership: 19,054

**BOS TU (BRITISH ORTHOPTIC SOCIETY TRADE
UNION)** Salisbury House, Station Road, Cambridge CB1 2LA
T 01353-665541 **E** bios@orthoptics.org.uk
W www.orthoptics.org.uk
Chair, Veronica Greenwood
Membership: 1,081

BSU (BRITANNIA STAFF UNION) Court Lodge, Leonard
Street, Leek ST13 5JP **T** 01538-399627 **E** bsu@themail.co.uk
W www.britanniasu.org.uk
General Secretary, John Stoddard
Membership: 1,449

COMMUNITY 465C Caledonian Road, London N7 9GX
T 020-7420 4000 **E** info@community-tu.org
W www.community-tu.org
General Secretary, Roy Rickhuss
Membership: 26,277

CSP (CHARTERED SOCIETY OF PHYSIOTHERAPY) 14
Bedford Row, London WC1R 4ED **T** 020-7306 6641
E enquiries@csp.org.uk **W** www.csp.org.uk
Chief Executive, Karen Middleton, CBE
Membership: 57,141

CWU (COMMUNICATION WORKERS UNION) 150 The
Broadway, London SW19 1RX **T** 020-8971 7200 **E** info@cwu.org
W www.cwu.org
General Secretary, Dave Ward
Membership: 191,421

EIS (EDUCATIONAL INSTITUTE OF SCOTLAND) 46
Moray Place, Edinburgh EH3 6BH **T** 0131-225 6244
E enquiries@eis.org.uk **W** www.eis.org.uk
General Secretary, Larry Flanagan
Membership: 55,879

EQUITY Guild House, Upper St Martin's Lane, London
WC2H 9EG **T** 020-7379 6000 **E** info@equity.org.uk
W www.equity.org.uk
General Secretary, Christine Payne
Membership: 43,555

FBU (FIRE BRIGADES UNION) Bradley House, 68 Coombe
Road, Kingston upon Thames KT2 7AE **T** 020-8541 1765
E office@fbu.org.uk **W** www.fbu.org.uk
General Secretary, Matthew Wrack
Membership: 33,042

FDA Elizabeth House, 39 York Road, London SE1 7NQ
T 020-7401 5555 **E** info@fda.org.uk **W** www.fda.org.uk
General Secretary, Dave Penman
Membership: 16,759

GMB 22 Stephenson Way, London NW1 2HD **T** 020-7391 6700
E info@gmb.org.uk **W** www.gmb.org.uk
General Secretary, Tim Roache
Membership: 614,494

**HCSA (HOSPITAL CONSULTANTS' AND SPECIALISTS'
ASSOCIATION)** 1 Kingsclere Road, Basingstoke RG25 3JA
T 01256-771777 **E** conspec@hcsa.com **W** www.hcsa.com
Chief Executive, Eddie Saville
Membership: 3,069

MU (MUSICIANS' UNION) 60–62 Clapham Road, London
SW9 0JJ **T** 020-7582 5566 **E** info@theMU.org
W www.musiciansunion.org.uk
General Secretary, Horace Trubridge
Membership: 30,421

**NACO (NATIONAL ASSOCIATION OF COOPERATIVE
OFFICIALS)** 6A Clarendon Place, Hyde SK14 2QZ
T 0161-351 7900 **E** info@naco.coop **W** www.naco.coop
General Secretary, Bob Lister (interim)
Membership: 1,388

**NAHT (NATIONAL ASSOCIATION OF HEAD
TEACHERS)** 1 Heath Square, Haywards Heath RH16 1BL
T 01444-472472 **E** info@naht.org.uk **W** www.naht.org.uk
General Secretary, Paul Whiteman
Membership: 41,612

**NAPO (TRADE UNION AND PROFESSIONAL
ASSOCIATION FOR FAMILY COURT AND
PROBATION STAFF)** 160 Falcon Road, London SW11 2NY
T 020-7223 4887 **E** info@napo.org.uk **W** www.napo.org.uk
General Secretary, Ian Lawrence
Membership: 4,996

NASS (NATIONAL ASSOCIATION OF STABLE STAFF)
The Racing Centre, Fred Archer Way, Newmarket CB8 8NT
T 01638-663411 **E** admin@naoss.co.uk **W** www.naoss.co.uk
Chief Executive, George McGrath
Membership: 2,137

**NASUWT (NATIONAL ASSOCIATION OF
SCHOOLMASTERS/ UNION OF WOMEN
TEACHERS)** Hillscourt Education Centre, Rose Hill, Birmingham
B45 8RS **T** 0121-453 6150 **E** nasuwt@mail.nasuwt.org.uk
W www.nasuwt.org.uk
General Secretary, Ms Chris Keates
Membership: 316,230

**NATIONAL HOUSE BUILDING COUNCIL STAFF
ASSOCIATION** NHBC House, Davey Avenue, Milton Keynes
MK5 8FP **T** 01908-746735 **E** lheritage@nhbc.co.uk
W www.nhbc.co.uk
General Secretary, Tom Howard
Membership: 686

NAUTILUS INTERNATIONAL 1–2 The Shrubberies, George
Lane, London E18 1BD **T** 020-8989 6677
E enquiries@nautilusint.org **W** www.nautilusint.org
General Secretary, Mark Dickinson
Membership: 20,797

NEU (NATIONAL EDUCATION UNION) Hamilton House,
Mabledon Place, London WC1H 9BD **T** 020-7388 6191
W www.neu.org.uk
General Secretaries, Dr Mary Bousted; Kevin Courtney
Membership: 459,519

NGSU (NATIONWIDE GROUP STAFF UNION) Middleton
Farmhouse, 37 Main Road, Middleton Cheney OX17 2QT
T 01295-710767 **E** ngsu@ngsu.org.uk **W** www.ngsu.co.uk
General Secretary, Tim Poil
Membership: 12,666

NSEAD (NATIONAL SOCIETY FOR EDUCATION IN ART AND DESIGN) 3 Mason's Wharf, Potley Lane, Corsham SN13 9FY T 01225-810134 E info@nsead.org W www.nsead.org
General Secretary, Mrs Lesley Butterworth
Membership: around 2,000

NUJ (NATIONAL UNION OF JOURNALISTS) 72 Acton Street, London WC1X 9NB T 020-7843 3700 E info@nuj.org.uk W www.nuj.org.uk
General Secretary, Michelle Stanistreet
Membership: 27,019

NUM (NATIONAL UNION OF MINEWORKERS) Miners' Offices, 2 Huddersfield Road, Barnsley S70 2LS T 01226-215555 E chris.kitchen@num.org.uk W www.num.org.uk
National Secretary, Chris Kitchen
Membership: 319

PCS (PUBLIC AND COMMERCIAL SERVICES UNION) 160 Falcon Road, London SW11 2LN T 020-7924 2727 W www.pcs.org.uk
General Secretary, Mark Serwotka
Membership: 181,063

PFA (PROFESSIONAL FOOTBALLERS' ASSOCIATION) 20 Oxford Court, Manchester M2 3WQ T 0161-236 0575 E info@thepfa.co.uk W www.thepfa.com
Chief Executive, Gordon Taylor, OBE
Membership: 4,930

POA (PROFESSIONAL TRADE UNION FOR PRISON, CORRECTIONAL AND SECURE PSYCHIATRIC WORKERS) Cronin House, 245 Church Street, London N9 9HW T 020-8803 0255 E general@poauk.org.uk W www.poauk.org.uk
General Secretary, Steve Gillan
Membership: 30,011

PROSPECT New Prospect House, 8 Leake Street, London SE1 7NN T 020-7902 6600 E enquiries@prospect.org.uk W www.prospect.org.uk
General Secretary, Mike Clancy
Membership: 142,486

RCM (ROYAL COLLEGE OF MIDWIVES) 15 Mansfield Street, London W1G 9NH T 030-0303 0444 E info@rcm.org.uk W www.rcm.org.uk
General Secretary, Gill Walton
Membership: 47,167

RMT (NATIONAL UNION OF RAIL, MARITIME AND TRANSPORT WORKERS) Unity House, 39 Chalton Street, London NW1 1JD T 020-7387 4771 E info@rmt.org.uk W www.rmt.org.uk
General Secretary, Mick Cash
Membership: 83,854

SCP (SOCIETY OF CHIROPODISTS AND PODIATRISTS) Quartz House, London SE1 2EW T 020-7234 8620 E reception@scpod.org W www.scpod.org
General Secretary (interim), Rosemary Gillespie
Membership: 9,367

SOR (SOCIETY OF RADIOGRAPHERS) 207 Providence Square, Mill Street, London SE1 2EW T 020-7740 7200 W www.sor.org
Chief Executive, Richard Evans
Membership: 26,954

STAFF UNION WEST BROMWICH BUILDING SOCIETY 2 Providence Place, West Bromwich B70 8AF T 0121-796 7720 E staffunion@westbrom.co.uk
General Secretary, vacant
Membership: 500

TSSA (TRANSPORT SALARIED STAFFS' ASSOCIATION) Walkden House, 10 Melton Street, London NW1 2EJ T 020-7387 2101 E enquiries@tssa.org.uk W www.tssa.org.uk
General Secretary, Manuel Cortes
Membership: 19,238

UCAC (UNDEB CENEDLAETHOL ATHRAWON CYMRU/ NATIONAL UNION OF THE TEACHERS OF WALES) Prif Swyddfa UCAC, Ffordd Penglais, Aberystwyth SY23 2EU T 01970-639950 E ucac@ucac.cymru W www.athrawon.com
General Secretary, Elaine Edwards
Membership: 3,600

UCU (UNIVERSITY AND COLLEGE UNION) Carlow Street, London NW1 7LH T 020-7756 2500 E hq@ucu.org.uk W www.ucu.org.uk
General Secretary, Sally Hunt
Membership: 103,985

UNISON 130 Euston Road, London NW1 2AY T 0800-085 7857 W www.unison.org.uk
General Secretary, Dave Prentis
Membership: 1,377,006

UNITE 128 Theobald's Road, London WC1X 8TN T 020-7611 2500 W www.unitetheunion.org
General Secretary, Len McCluskey
Membership: 1,340,841

URTU (UNITED ROAD TRANSPORT UNION) Almond House, Oak Green, Cheadle, Hulme SK8 6QL T 0800-526 639 E info@urtu.com W www.urtu.com
General Secretary, Robert Monks
Membership: 9,490

USDAW (UNION OF SHOP, DISTRIBUTIVE AND ALLIED WORKERS) 188 Wilmslow Road, Manchester M14 6LJ T 0161-224 2804 E enquiries@usdaw.org.uk W www.usdaw.org.uk
General Secretary, John Hannett
Membership: 433,260

WGGB (WRITERS' GUILD OF GREAT BRITAIN) 134 Tooley Street, London SE1 2TU T 020-7833 0777 E admin@writersguild.org.uk W www.writersguild.org.uk
General Secretary, Ellie Peers
Membership: 2,171

NON-AFFILIATED UNIONS
As at May 2018

ASCL (ASSOCIATION OF SCHOOL AND COLLEGE LEADERS) 130 Regent Road, Leicester LE1 7PG T 0116-299 1122 E info@ascl.org.uk W www.ascl.org.uk
General Secretary, Geoff Barton
Membership: 18,695

BDA (BRITISH DENTAL ASSOCIATION) 64 Wimpole Street, London W1G 8YS T 020-7935 0875 E enquiries@bda.org W www.bda.org
General Secretary, Michael Armstrong
Membership: 18,034

CIOJ (CHARTERED INSTITUTE OF JOURNALISTS) 2 Dock Offices, Surrey Quays Road, London SE16 2XU T 020-7252 1187 E memberservices@cioj.co.uk W www.cioj.co.uk
General Secretary, Dominic Cooper
Membership: 1,965

SOCIETY OF AUTHORS 84 Drayton Gardens, London SW10 9SB T 020-7373 6642 E info@societyofauthors.org W www.societyofauthors.org
Chief Executive, Nicola Solomon
Membership: around 9,400

SSTA (SCOTTISH SECONDARY TEACHERS' ASSOCIATION) West End House, 14 West End Place, Edinburgh EH11 2ED T 0131-313 7300 E info@ssta.org.uk W www.ssta.org.uk
General Secretary, Seamus Searson
Membership: 6,586

SPORTS BODIES

SPORTS COUNCILS

SPORT AND RECREATION ALLIANCE Burwood House, 14 Caxton Street, London SW1H 0QT **T** 020-7976 3900 **E** info@sportandrecreation.org.uk **W** www.sportandrecreation.org.uk *Chief Executive,* Emma Boggis

SPORT ENGLAND 21 Bloomsbury Street, London WC1B 3HF **T** 020-7273 1551 **E** info@sportengland.org **W** www.sportengland.org *Chief Executive,* Jennie Price

SPORT NORTHERN IRELAND House of Sport, 2A Upper Malone Road, Belfast BT9 5LA **T** 028-9038 1222 **E** info@sportni.net **W** www.sportni.net *Chief Executive,* Antoinette McKeown

SPORTSCOTLAND Doges, Templeton on the Green, 62 Templeton Street, Glasgow G40 1DA **T** 0141-534 6500 **E** website@sportscotland.org.uk **W** www.sportscotland.org.uk *Chief Executive,* Stewart Harris

SPORT WALES Sophia Gardens, Cardiff CF11 9SW **T** 0300-300 3111 **E** info@sportwales.org.uk **W** www.sport.wales *Chief Executive,* Sarah Powell

UK SPORT 21 Bloomsbury Street, London WC1B 3HF **T** 020-7211 5100 **E** info@uksport.gov.uk **W** www.uksport.gov.uk *Chief Executive,* Liz Nicholl, CBE

AMERICAN FOOTBALL

BRITISH AMERICAN FOOTBALL ASSOCIATION 1 Franchise Street, Kidderminster DY11 6RE **E** human.resources@britishamericanfootball.org **W** www.britishamericanfootball.org *Chair,* Martin Cockerill

ANGLING

ANGLING TRUST Eastwood House, 6 Rainbow Street, Herefordshire HR6 8DQ **T** 0343-507 7006 **E** admin@anglingtrust.net **W** www.anglingtrust.net *Chief Executive,* Mark Lloyd

ARCHERY

ARCHERY GB Lilleshall National Sports Centre, Newport TF10 9AT **T** 0195-267 7888 **E** enquiries@archerygb.org **W** www.archerygb.org *Chief Executive,* Neil Armitage

ASSOCIATION FOOTBALL

ENGLISH FOOTBALL LEAGUE EFL House, 10-12 West Cliff, Preston PR1 8HU **T** 01772-325800 **E** enquiries@efl.com **W** www.efl.com *Chief Executive,* Shaun Harvey

FOOTBALL ASSOCIATION Wembley Stadium, PO Box 1966, London SW1P 9EQ **T** 0800-169 1863 **E** info@thefa.com **W** www.thefa.com *Chief Executive,* Martin Glenn

FOOTBALL ASSOCIATION OF WALES 11–12 Neptune Court, Vanguard Way, Cardiff CF24 5PJ **T** 029-2043 5830 **E** info@faw.co.uk **W** www.faw.cymru *Chief Executive,* Jonathan Ford

IRISH FOOTBALL ASSOCIATION Donegal Avenue, Belfast BT12 6LU **T** 028-9066 9458 **E** info@irishfa.com **W** www.irishfa.com *Chief Executive,* Patrick Nelson

PREMIER LEAGUE 30 Gloucester Place, London W1U 8PL **T** 020-7864 9000 **E** info@premierleague.com **W** www.premierleague.com *Chief Executive,* Richard Scudamore

SCOTTISH FOOTBALL ASSOCIATION Hampden Park, Glasgow G42 9AY **T** 0141-616 6000 **E** info@scottishfa.co.uk **W** www.scottishfa.co.uk *Chief Executive,* Ian Maxwell

SCOTTISH PROFESSIONAL FOOTBALL LEAGUE Hampden Park, Glasgow G42 9DE **T** 0141-620 4140 **E** info@spfl.co.uk **W** www.spfl.co.uk *Chief Executive,* Neil Doncaster

ATHLETICS

BRITISH ATHLETICS Athletics House, Alexander Stadium, Birmingham B42 2BE **T** 0121-713 8400 **E** majorevents@britishathletics.org.uk **W** www.britishathletics.org.uk *Chief Executive,* Niels de Vos

ATHLETICS NORTHERN IRELAND Athletics House, Old Coach Road, Belfast BT9 5PR **T** 028-9060 2707 **E** info@athleticsni.org **W** www.athleticsni.org *General Secretary,* John Allen

SCOTTISH ATHLETICS Caledonia House, Edinburgh EH12 9DQ **T** 0131-539 7320 **E** admin@scottishathletics.org.uk **W** www.scottishathletics.org.uk *Chief Executive,* Mark Munro

WELSH ATHLETICS Cardiff International Sports Stadium, Leckwith Road, Cardiff CF11 8AZ **T** 029-2064 4870 **E** office@welshathletics.org **W** www.welshathletics.org *Chief Executive,* Matt Newman

BADMINTON

BADMINTON ENGLAND National Badminton Centre, Bradwell Road, Milton Keynes MK8 9LA **T** 01908-268400 **E** enquiries@badmintonengland.co.uk **W** www.badmintonengland.co.uk *Chief Executive,* Adrian Christy

BADMINTON SCOTLAND Cockburn Centre, 40 Bogmoor Place, Glasgow G51 4TQ **T** 0141-445 1218 **E** enquiries@badmintonscotland.org.uk **W** www.badmintonscotland.org.uk *Chief Executive,* Anne Smillie

BADMINTON WALES Sport Wales National Centre, Sophia Gardens, Cardiff CF11 9SW **T** 0300-300 3124 **E** info@badminton.wales **W** www.badminton.wales *General Manager,* Gareth Hall

BASEBALL

BASEBALLSOFTBALL UK Marathon House, 190 Great Dane Street, London SE1 4YB **T** 020-7453 7055 **W** www.baseballsoftballuk.com *Chief Executive,* John Boyd

BRITISH BASEBALL FEDERATION Marathon House, 190 Great Dane Street, London SE1 4YB **T** 0207-7453 7055 **W** www.britishbaseball.org *President,* Gerry Perez

BASKETBALL

BASKETBALL ENGLAND Etihad Stadium, Rowsley Street, Manchester M11 3FF **T** 0300-600 1170 **E** info@basketballengland.co.uk **W** www.basketballengland.co.uk *Chief Executive,* Stewart Kellett

BASKETBALL SCOTLAND Caledonia House, Edinburgh
EH12 9DQ **T** 0131-317 7260
E enquiries@basketball-scotland.com
W www.basketballscotland.co.uk
Chief Executive, Kevin Pringle

BILLIARDS AND SNOOKER

WORLD SNOOKER 75 Whiteladies Road, Bristol BS8 2NT
T 0117-317 8200 **E** info@worldsnooker.com
W www.worldsnooker.com
Chief Executive, Steve Dawson

BOBSLEIGH

BRITISH BOBSLEIGH & SKELETON ASSOCIATION
University of Bath, Claverton Down, Bath BA2 7AY
T 01225-384343 **E** office@thebbsa.co.uk **W** www.thebbsa.co.uk
Chair, Christopher Rodrigues

BOWLS

BOWLS ENGLAND Riverside House, Milverton Hill, Royal
Leamington Spa CV32 5HZ **T** 01926-334609
E enquiries@bowlsengland.com **W** www.bowlsengland.com
Chief Executive, Tony Allcock, MBE
BRITISH ISLES BOWLS COUNCIL
E bibcsecretary@aol.co.uk **W** www.britishislesbowls.com
President (2018), Gerard Thomas
ENGLISH INDOOR BOWLING ASSOCIATION David
Cornwell House, Bowling Green, Melton Mowbray LE13 0FA
T 01664-481900 **E** enquiries@eiba.co.uk **W** www.eiba.co.uk
Chief Executive, Peter Thompson

BOXING

BRITISH BOXING BOARD OF CONTROL 14 North Road,
Cardiff CF10 3DY **T** 029-2036 7000 **E** admin@bbbofc.com
W www.bbbofc.com
General Secretary, Robert Smith
ENGLAND BOXING English Institute of Sport, Coleridge Road,
Sheffield S9 5DA **T** 0114-223 5654
E enquiries@englandboxing.org **W** www.abae.co.uk
Chief Executive, Gethin Jenkins

CANOEING

BRITISH CANOEING National Water Sport Centre, Adbolton
Lane, Nottingham NG12 2LU **T** 0300-011 9500
E info@britishcanoeing.org.uk **W** www.britishcanoeing.org.uk
Chief Executive, David Joy

CHESS

ENGLISH CHESS FEDERATION The Watch Oak, Chain Lane,
Battle TN33 0YD **T** 01424-775222 **E** office@englishchess.org.uk
W www.englishchess.org.uk
Chief Executive, Mike Truran

CRICKET

ENGLAND AND WALES CRICKET BOARD Lord's Cricket
Ground, St John's Wood Road, London NW8 8QZ
T 020-7432 1200 **W** www.ecb.co.uk
Chief Executive, Tom Harrison
MCC Lord's Cricket Ground, London NW8 8QN **T** 020-7616 8500
E reception@mcc.org.uk **W** www.lords.org
Chief Executive and Secretary, Guy Lavender

CROQUET

CROQUET ASSOCIATION Old Bath Road, Cheltenham
GL53 7DF **T** 01242-242318 **E** caoffice@croquet.org.uk
W www.croquet.org.uk
Manager, Mark Suter

CURLING

BRITISH CURLING c/o The Royal Caledonian Curling Club,
Ochil House, Stirling FK7 7XE **E** info@britishcurling.com
W www.britishcurling.org.uk
Chief Executive, Bruce Crawford
SCOTTISH CURLING Ochil House, Stirling FK7 7XE
T 0131-333 3003 **E** office@scottishcurling.org
W www.scottishcurling.org
Chief Executive, Bruce Crawford

CYCLING

BRITISH CYCLING FEDERATION Stuart Street, Manchester
M11 4DQ **T** 0161-274 2000 **E** info@britishcycling.org.uk
W www.britishcycling.org.uk
Chief Executive, Julie Harrington

DARTS

BRITISH DARTS ORGANISATION Unit 4, Glan-y-Llyn
Industrial Estate, Cardiff CF15 7JD **T** 029-2081 1815
E contact@bdodarts.com **W** www.bdodarts.com
Chairman, Sue Williams

EQUESTRIANISM

BRITISH EQUESTRIAN FEDERATION Abbey Park,
Kenilworth CV8 2RH **T** 024-7669 8871 **E** info@bef.co.uk
W www.bef.co.uk
Chief Executive, Nick Fellows
BRITISH EVENTING Abbey Park, Kenilworth CV8 2RN
T 024-7669 8856 **E** info@britisheventing.com
W www.britisheventing.com
Chief Executive, David Holmes

ETON FIVES

ETON FIVES ASSOCIATION 45 Sandhills Crescent, Solihull
B91 3UE **T** 07833-600230 **W** www.etonfives.com
Chair, Chris Davies

FENCING

BRITISH FENCING 1 Baron's Gate, 33 Rothschild Road,
London W4 5HT **T** 020-8742 3032
E headoffice@britishfencing.com **W** www.britishfencing.com
Chief Executive, Georgina Usher

GLIDING

BRITISH GLIDING ASSOCIATION 8 Merus Court, Meridian
Business Park, Leicester LE19 1RJ **T** 0116-289 2956
E office@gliding.co.uk **W** www.gliding.co.uk
Chief Executive, Pete Stratten

GOLF

ENGLAND GOLF The National Golf Centre, Woodhall Spa
LN10 6PU **T** 01526-354500 **E** info@englandgolf.org
W www.englandgolf.org
Chief Executive, Nick Pink
THE ROYAL AND ANCIENT GOLF CLUB Golf Place, St
Andrews KY16 9JD **T** 01334-460000
E thesecretary@randagc.org **W** www.randa.org
Chief Executive and Secretary, Martin Slumbers

GYMNASTICS

BRITISH GYMNASTICS Ford Hall, Lilleshall National Sports
Centre, Newport TF10 9NB **T** 0345-129 7129
E information@british-gymnastics.org
W www.british-gymnastics.org
Chief Executive, Jane Allen

HANDBALL

ENGLAND HANDBALL The Halliwell Jones Stadium, Winwick Road, Warrington WA2 7NE **T** 01925-246482 **E** office@englandhandball.com **W** www.englandhandball.com *Chief Executive,* David Meli

HOCKEY

ENGLAND HOCKEY Bisham Abbey National Sports Centre, Marlow SL7 1RR **T** 01628-897500 **E** info@englandhockey.co.uk **W** www.englandhockey.co.uk *Chief Executive,* Sally Munday

HOCKEY WALES Sport Wales National Centre, Sophia Gardens, Cardiff CF11 9SW **T** 0300-300 3126 **E** info@hockeywales.org.uk **W** www.hockeywales.org.uk *Chief Executive,* David Phenis

SCOTTISH HOCKEY UNION Glasgow National Hockey Centre, 8 King's Drive, Glasgow G40 1HB **T** 0141-550 5999 **W** www.scottish-hockey.org.uk *Chief Executive,* David Sweetman

HORSERACING

BRITISH HORSERACING AUTHORITY 75 High Holborn, London WC1V 6LS **T** 020-7152 0000 **E** info@britishhorseracing.com **W** www.britishhorseracing.com *Chief Executive,* Nick Rust

THE JOCKEY CLUB 75 High Holborn, London WC1V 6LS **T** 020-7611 1800 **E** info@thejockeyclub.co.uk **W** www.thejockeyclub.co.uk *Chief Executive,* Simon Bazalgette

ICE SKATING

NATIONAL ICE SKATING ASSOCIATION Grains Building, High Cross Street, Nottingham NG1 3AX **T** 0115-988 8060 **E** info@iceskating.org.uk **W** www.iceskating.org.uk *Chair,* Maggie Worsfold

LACROSSE

ENGLISH LACROSSE ASSOCIATION National Squash Centre and Regional Arena, Gate 13, Manchester M11 3FF **T** 0161-231 1357 **E** info@englishlacrosse.co.uk **W** www.englishlacrosse.co.uk *Chief Executive,* Mark Coups

LAWN TENNIS

LAWN TENNIS ASSOCIATION National Tennis Centre, 100 Priory Lane, London SW15 5JQ **T** 020-8487 7000 **E** info@lta.org.uk **W** www.lta.org.uk *Chief Executive,* Scott Lloyd

MARTIAL ARTS

BRITISH JUDO ASSOCIATION Suite B, Loughborough Technology Centre, Epinal Way, Loughborough LE11 3GE **T** 01509-637680 **E** bja@britishjudo.org.uk **W** www.britishjudo.org.uk *Chief Executive,* Andrew Scoular

BRITISH JU JITSU ASSOCIATION 5 Avenue Parade, Accrington BB5 6PN **T** 03333-202039 **E** bjjagb@icloud.com **W** www.bjjagb.com *Chairman,* Prof. Martin Dixon

BRITISH TAEKWONDO The Business Place, Park Road, Mansfield Woodhouse NG19 8ER **T** 01623-665005 **E** admin@britishtaekwondo.org **W** www.britishtaekwondo.org.uk *Chair,* Jon Smith

MODERN PENTATHLON

PENTATHLON GB Sports Training Village, University of Bath, Bath BA2 7AY **T** 01225-386808 **E** admin@pentathlongb.org **W** www.pentathlongb.org *Chief Executive,* Danielle Every

MOTOR SPORTS

AUTO-CYCLE UNION ACU House, Rugby CV21 2YX **T** 01788-566400 **E** admin@acu.org.uk **W** www.acu.org.uk *General Secretary,* Gary Thompson, MBE

MOTOR SPORTS ASSOCIATION Motor Sports House, Riverside Park, Colnbrook SL3 0HG **T** 01753-765000 **W** www.msauk.org *Chief Executive,* Rob Jones

SCOTTISH AUTO CYCLE UNION 28 West Main Street, Uphall EH52 5DW **T** 01506-858354 **E** office@sacu.co.uk **W** www.sacu.co.uk *Chair,* Sandy Mack

MOUNTAINEERING

BRITISH MOUNTAINEERING COUNCIL The Old Church, 177–179 Burton Road, Manchester M20 2BB **T** 0161-445 6111 **E** office@thebmc.co.uk **W** www.thebmc.co.uk *Chief Executive,* Dave Turnbull

MULTI-SPORTS BODIES

BRITISH OLYMPIC ASSOCIATION 60 Charlotte Street, London W1T 2NU **T** 020-7842 5700 **E** club@teamgb.com **W** www.teamgb.com *Chief Executive,* Bill Sweeney

BRITISH PARALYMPIC ASSOCIATION 60 Charlotte Street, London W1T 2NU **T** 020-7842 5789 **E** info@paralympics.org.uk **W** www.paralympics.org.uk *Chief Executive,* Tim Hollingsworth, OBE

BRITISH UNIVERSITIES AND COLLEGES SPORT 20–24 Kings Bench Street, London SE1 0QX **T** 020-7633 5080 **W** www.bucs.org.uk *Chief Executive,* Vince Mayne

COMMONWEALTH GAMES ENGLAND The Dutch House, 307–308 High Holborn, London WC1V 7LL **T** 020-7831 3444 **E** info@weareengland.org **W** www.weareengland.org *Chief Executive,* Paul Blanchard

COMMONWEALTH GAMES FEDERATION Commonwealth House, 55–58 Pall Mall, London SW1Y 5JH **T** 020-7104 6427 **E** info@thecgf.com **W** www.thecgf.com *Chief Executive,* David Grevemberg, CBE

ENGLISH FEDERATION OF DISABILITY SPORT Loughborough University, 3 Oakwood Drive, LE11 3QF **T** 01509-227750 **W** www.efds.co.uk *Chief Executive,* Barry Horne

NETBALL

ENGLAND NETBALL SportPark, 3 Oakwood Drive, Loughborough LE11 3QF **T** 01509-277850 **E** info@englandnetball.co.uk **W** www.englandnetball.co.uk *Chief Executive,* Joanna Adams

NETBALL NI Unit F, Curlew Pavilion, Portside Business Park, Belfast BT3 9ED **T** 028-9073 6320 **E** bookingsandadmin@netballni.org **W** www.netballni.org *President,* Micaela Diver

NETBALL SCOTLAND Emirates Arena, 1000 London Road, Glasgow G40 3HY **T** 0141-428 3460 **E** membership@netballscotland.com **W** www.netballscotland.com *Chief Executive,* Claire Nelson

WELSH NETBALL ASSOCIATION Sport Wales National Centre, Sophia Gardens, Cardiff CF11 9SW **T** 029-2033 4950 **E** welshnetball@welshnetball.com **W** www.welshnetball.com *Chief Executive,* Sarah Jones

ORIENTEERING

BRITISH ORIENTEERING Scholes Mill, Old Coach Road, Matlock DE4 5FY **T** 01629-583037
E info@britishorienteering.org.uk
W www.britishorienteering.org.uk
Chief Executive, Peter Hart

POLO

THE HURLINGHAM POLO ASSOCIATION Manor Farm, Little Coxwell, Faringdon SN7 7LW **T** 01367-242828
E enquiries@hpa-polo.co.uk **W** www.hpa-polo.co.uk
Chief Executive, David Woodd

RACKETS AND REAL TENNIS

TENNIS AND RACKETS ASSOCIATION c/o The Queen's Club, Palliser Road, London W14 9EQ **T** 020-7835 6937
E office@tennisandrackets.com **W** www.tennisandrackets.com
Chief Executive, C. S. Davies

ROWING

BRITISH ROWING 6 Lower Mall, London W6 9DJ
T 020-8237 6700 **E** info@gbrowingteam.org.uk
W www.britishrowing.org
Chief Executive, Andy Parkinson
HENLEY ROYAL REGATTA Regatta Headquarters, Henley-on-Thames RG9 2LY **T** 01491-572153 **W** www.hrr.co.uk
Secretary, Daniel Grist

RUGBY LEAGUE

BRITISH AMATEUR RUGBY LEAGUE ASSOCIATION West Yorkshire House, 4 New North Parade, Huddersfield HD1 5JP **T** 01484-599113 **E** secretary@barla.org.uk
W www.barla.org.uk
Chair, Sue Taylor
RUGBY FOOTBALL LEAGUE Red Hall, Red Hall Lane, Leeds LS17 8NB **T** 0844-477 7113 **E** enquiries@rfl.uk.com
W www.rugby-league.com
Interim Chief Executive, Ralph Rimmer

RUGBY UNION

IRISH RUGBY FOOTBALL UNION 10–12 Lansdowne Road, Dublin 4 **T** (+353) 1647 3800 **E** info@irishrugby.ie
W www.irishrugby.ie
Chief Executive, Philip Browne
RUGBY FOOTBALL UNION Rugby House, Twickenham Stadium, 200 Whitton Road, Twickenham TW2 7BA
T 0871-222 2120 **E** enquiries@therfu.com
W www.englandrugby.com
Chief Executive, Steve Brown
RUGBY FOOTBALL UNION FOR WOMEN Rugby House, Twickenham Stadium, 200 Whitton Road, Twickenham TW2 7BA **T** 0871-222 2120 **E** enquiries@therfu.com
W www.englandrugby.com
Managing Director, Rosie Williams
SCOTTISH RUGBY UNION BT Murrayfield, Edinburgh EH12 5PJ **T** 0131-346 5000 **E** feedback@sru.org.uk
W www.scottishrugby.org
Chief Executive, Mark Dodson
SCOTTISH WOMEN'S RUGBY UNION Scottish Rugby Union, Edinburgh EH12 5PJ **T** 0131-346 5000
E feedback@sru.org.uk **W** www.scottishrugby.org
Chief Executive, Mark Dodson
WELSH RUGBY UNION Principality Stadium, Westgate Street, Cardiff CF10 1NS **T** 0844-249 1999 **E** info@wru.co.uk
W www.wru.co.uk
Chief Executive, Martyn Phillips

SHOOTING

BRITISH SHOOTING Bisham Abbey National Sports Centre, Marlow Road, Marlow SL7 1RR **T** 01628-488800
E admin@britishshooting.org.uk **W** www.britishshooting.org.uk
Chief Executive, Hamish McInnes
CLAY PIGEON SHOOTING ASSOCIATION Edmonton House, National Shooting Centre, Brookwood, Woking GU24 0NP **T** 01483-485400 **E** info@cpsa.co.uk
W www.cpsa.co.uk
Chief Executive, Nick Fellows
NATIONAL RIFLE ASSOCIATION Bisley Camp, Brookwood GU24 0PB **T** 01483-797777 **E** info@nra.org.uk
W www.nra.org.uk
Chief Executive, Andrew Mercer
NATIONAL SMALL-BORE RIFLE ASSOCIATION Lord Roberts Centre, Bisley Camp, Woking GU24 0NP
T 01483-485502 **W** www.nsra.co.uk
Chair, Robert Newman

SKIING AND SNOWBOARDING

BRITISH SKI AND SNOWBOARD 60 Charlotte Street, London W1T 2NU **T** 020-7842 5764 **E** bss@teambss.org.uk
W www.teambss.org.uk
Chief Executive, Victoria Gosling, OBE

SPEEDWAY

BRITISH SPEEDWAY ACU Headquarters, Wood Street, Rugby CV21 2YX **T** 01788-560648 **E** office@speedwaygb.co
W www.speedwaygb.co
Chair, Keith Chapman

SQUASH

ENGLAND SQUASH National Squash Centre, Manchester M11 3FF **T** 0161-231 4499 **W** www.englandsquash.com
Chief Executive, Keir Worth
SCOTTISH SQUASH Oriam, Edinburgh EH14 4AS
T 0131-451 8525 **E** info@scottishsquash.org
W www.scottishsquash.org
Chief Executive, Maggie Still
WALES SQUASH AND RACKETBALL Sport Wales National Centre, Sophia Close, Cardiff CF11 9SW **T** 0300-300 3121
W www.walessquashandracketball.co.uk
General Manager, Gareth Hall

SUB-AQUA

BRITISH SUB-AQUA CLUB Telford's Quay, South Pier Road, Ellesmere Port CH65 4FL **T** 0151-350 6200 **E** info@bsac.com
W www.bsac.com
Chief Executive, Mary Tetley

SWIMMING

SWIM ENGLAND Pavilion 3, Sport Park, Loughborough LE11 3QF **T** 01509-618700 **E** customerservices@swimming.org
W www.swimming.org
Chief Executive, Jane Nickerson
SCOTTISH SWIMMING National Swimming Academy, University of Stirling, FK9 4LA **T** 01786-466520
E info@scottishswimming.com **W** www.scottishswimming.com
Chief Executive, Forbes Dunlop
SWIM WALES WNPS, Sketty Lane, Swansea SA2 8QG
T 01792-513636 **W** www.swimwales.org
Chief Executive, Fergus Feeney

TABLE TENNIS

TABLE TENNIS ENGLAND Norfolk House, 88 Saxon Gate West, Milton Keynes MK9 2DL **T** 01908-208860
E help@tabletennisengland.co.uk
W www.tabletennisengland.co.uk
Chief Executive, Sara Sutcliffe

TABLE TENNIS SCOTLAND Caledonia House, South Gyle,
Edinburgh EH12 9DQ **T** 0131-317 8077
E info@tabletennisscotland.co.uk
W www.tabletennisscotland.co.uk
Chair, Terry McLernon, MBE
TABLE TENNIS WALES Glanrhyd, Ebbw View, Ebbw Vale
NP23 5NU **T** 01244-571335 **W** www.tabletennis.wales
Company Secretary, Neil O'Connell

TRIATHLON

BRITISH TRIATHLON PO Box 25, Loughborough LE11 3WX
T 01509-226161 **E** info@britishtriathlon.org
W www.britishtriathlon.org
Chief Executive, Andy Salmon

VOLLEYBALL

NORTHERN IRELAND VOLLEYBALL ASSOCIATION 7
Greengage Cottages, Ballymoney BT53 6GZ
W www.nivolleyball.com
General Secretary, Paddy Elder
SCOTTISH VOLLEYBALL ASSOCIATION 48 The
Pleasance, Edinburgh EH8 9TJ **T** 0131-556 4633
E info@scottishvolleyball.org **W** www.scottishvolleyball.org
Chief Executive, Margaret Ann Fleming
VOLLEYBALL ENGLAND SportPark, Loughborough University,
3 Oakwood Drive, Loughborough LE11 3QF **T** 01509-227722
E info@volleyballengland.org **W** www.volleyballengland.org
Chief Executive, Janet Inman
VOLLEYBALL WALES 13 Beckgrove Close, Cardiff CF24 2SE
T 029-2041 6537 **E** yperkins@cardiffmet.ac.uk
W www.volleyballwales.org
Chair, Yvonne Perkins

WALKING

RACE WALKING ASSOCIATION Hufflers, Heard's Lane,
Brentwood CM15 0SF **T** 01277-220687
E racewalkingassociation@btinternet.com
W www.racewalkingassociation.com
Hon. General Secretary, Colin Vesty

WATER SKIING

BRITISH WATER SKI AND WAKEBOARD The Forum,
Hanworth Lane, Chertsey KT16 9JX **T** 01932-560007
E info@bwsf.co.uk **W** www.bwsw.org.uk
Chief Executive, Patrick Donovan

WEIGHTLIFTING

BRITISH WEIGHT LIFTING St Ann's Mill, Kirkstall Road,
Leeds LS5 3AE **T** 0113-224 9402
E enquiries@britishweightlifting.org
W www.britishweightlifting.org
Chief Executive, Ashley Metcalfe

WRESTLING

BRITISH WRESTLING ASSOCIATION 41 Great Clowes St,
Salford M7 1RQ **T** 0161-835 2112 **E** admin@britishwrestling.org
W www.britishwrestling.org
Chief Executive, Colin Nicholson

YACHTING

ROYAL YACHTING ASSOCIATION RYA House, Ensign
Way, Southampton SO31 4YA **T** 023-8060 4100
E enquiries@rya.org.uk **W** www.rya.org.uk
Chief Executive, Sarah Treseder

CHARITIES AND SOCIETIES

The following is a selection of charities, societies and non-profit organisations in the UK and does not represent a comprehensive list. For professional and employment-related organisations, *see* Professional Education and Trade and Professional Bodies.

ABBEYFIELD SOCIETY (1956) St Peter's House, 2 Bricket Road, St Albans AL1 3JW **T** 01727-857536
E post@abbeyfield.com **W** www.abbeyfield.com
Chief Executive, David McCullough

ACTIONAID (1972) 33–39 Bowling Green Lane, London EC1R 0BJ **T** 020-3122 0561 **E** mail@actionaid.org
W www.actionaid.org.uk
Chief Executive, Girish Menon

ACTION FOR CHILDREN (1869) 3 The Boulevard, Watford WD18 8AG **T** 01923-361500 **E** ask.us@actionforchildren.org.uk
W www.actionforchildren.org.uk
Acting Chief Executive, Carol Iddon

ACTION MEDICAL RESEARCH (1952) Vincent House, Horsham RH12 2DP **T** 01403-210406 **E** info@action.org.uk
W www.action.org.uk
Chief Executive, Julie Buckler

ACTION ON HEARING LOSS (1911) 1–3 Highbury Station Road, London N1 1SE
T 0808-808 0123, **Textphone** 0808-808 9000
E informationline@hearingloss.org.uk
W www.actiononhearingloss.org.uk
Interim Chief Executive, Mike O'Connor

ACTORS' BENEVOLENT FUND (1882) 6 Adam Street, London WC2N 6AD **T** 020-7836 6378 **E** office@abf.org.uk
W www.actorsbenevolentfund.co.uk
General Secretary, Jonathan Ellicott

ACTORS' CHILDREN'S TRUST (1896) 58 Bloomsbury Street, London WC1B 3QT **T** 020-7636 7868
E robert@actorschildren.org **W** www.actorschildren.org
General Secretary, Robert Ashby

ADAM SMITH INSTITUTE (1977) 23 Great Smith Street, London SW1P 3DJ **T** 020-7222 4995 **W** www.adamsmith.org
Director, Dr Eamonn Butler

ADDACTION (1967) 67–69 Cowcross Street, London EC1M 6PU **T** 020-7251 5860 **E** info@addaction.org.uk
W www.addaction.org.uk
Chief Executive, Mike Dixon

ADVERTISING STANDARDS AUTHORITY (1962) Mid City Place, 71 High Holborn, London WC1V 6QT
T 020-7492 2222 **W** www.asa.org.uk
Chief Executive, Guy Parker

AFASIC (1968) 209–211 City Road, London EC1V 1JN
T 020-7490 9410 **W** www.afasic.org.uk
Chief Executive, Linda Lascelles

AGE CYMRU (2010) Ground Floor, Mariners House, East Moors Road CF24 5TD **T** 029-2043 1555 **E** advice@agecymru.org.uk
W www.ageuk.org.uk/cymru
Chief Executive, Victoria Lloyd

AGE SCOTLAND (1943) Causewayside House, 160 Causewayside, Edinburgh EH9 1PR **T** 0333-323 2400
E info@agescotland.org.uk **W** www.ageuk.org.uk/scotland
Chief Executive, Brian Sloan

AGE UK (2010) Tavis House, 1–6 Tavistock Square, London WC1H 9NA **T** 0800-169 2081 **E** contact@ageuk.org.uk
W www.ageuk.org.uk
Chief Executive, Steph Harland

ALEXANDRA ROSE CHARITIES (1912) 5 Mead Lane, Farnham GU9 7DY **T** 01252-726171 **E** info@alexandrarose.org
W www.alexandrarosecharities.org.uk
Chief Executive, Jonathan Pauling

ALZHEIMER'S SOCIETY (1979) 43–44 Crutched Friars, London EC3N 2AE **T** 0330-333 0804
E enquiries@alzheimers.org.uk **W** www.alzheimers.org.uk
Chief Executive, Jeremy Hughes

AMNESTY INTERNATIONAL UK (1961) The Human Rights Action Centre, 17–25 New Inn Yard, London EC2A 3EA
T 020-7033 1500 **E** sct@amnesty.org.uk
W www.amnesty.org.uk
UK Director, Kate Allen

AMREF UK (1957) 15–18 White Lion Street, London N1 9PD
T 020-7269 5520 **E** info@amrefuk.org **W** www.amrefuk.org
Chief Executive, Frances Longley

ANGLO-BELGIAN SOCIETY (1982) 15 Westmoreland Terrace, London SW1V 4AG
E secretary@anglobelgiansociety.co.uk
W www.anglobelgiansociety.com
Chair, Caroline Colvin, OBE

ANGLO-DANISH SOCIETY (1924) 43 Maresfield Gardens, London NW3 5TF **T** 07934-236686
E info@anglo-danishsociety.org.uk
W www.anglo-danishsociety.org.uk
Chair, Christian Williams

ANGLO-NORSE SOCIETY (1918) 25 Belgrave Square, London SW1X 8QD **T** 020-8452 4843
E secretariat@anglo-norse.org.uk **W** www.anglo-norse.org.uk
Chair, Sir Richard Dales, KCVO, CMG

ANIMAL HEALTH TRUST (1942) Lanwades Park, Newmarket CB8 7UU **T** 01638-751000 **E** info@aht.org.uk
W www.aht.org.uk
Chief Executive, Dr Mark Vaudin

ANTHONY NOLAN (1974) 2 Heathgate Place, 75–87 Agincourt Road, London NW3 2NU **T** 0303-303 0303
W www.anthonynolan.org
Chief Executive, Henny Braund

ANTI-SLAVERY INTERNATIONAL (1839) Thomas Clarkson House, The Stableyard, London SW9 9TL
T 020-7501 8920 **E** info@antislavery.org **W** www.antislavery.org
CEO, Jasmine O'Connor

ARCHITECTS BENEVOLENT SOCIETY (1850) 43 Portland Place, London W1B 1QH **T** 020-7580 2823
E help@absnet.org.uk **W** www.absnet.org.uk
CEO, Robert Ball

ARCHITECTURAL HERITAGE FUND (1976) 3 Spital Yard, London E1 6AQ **T** 020-7925 0199 **E** ahf@ahfund.org.uk
W www.ahfund.org
Chief Executive, Matthew McKeague

ARLIS/UK AND IRELAND (1969) National Art Library, Victoria & Albert Museum, London SW7 2RL **T** 020-7942 2317
E arlis@vam.ac.uk **W** www.arlis.org.uk
Chair, Carla Marchesan

ART FUND (1903) 2 Granary Square, King's Cross, London N1C 4BH **T** 020-7225 4800 **E** info@artfund.org
W www.artfund.org
Director, Dr Stephen Deuchar

ARTHRITIS CARE (1947) Saffron House, 6–10 Kirby Street, London EC1N 8TS **T** 0300-790 0400 **E** info@arthritiscare.org.uk
W www.arthritiscare.org.uk
Chief Executive, Liam O'Toole

ASSOCIATION FOR LANGUAGE LEARNING (1990) 1A Duffield Road, Derby DE21 5DR **T** 01332-227779
E info@all-languages.org.uk **W** www.all-languages.org.uk
Director, Rachel Middleton

ASSOCIATION FOR SCIENCE EDUCATION (1901)
College Lane, Hatfield AL10 9AA T 01707-283000
E info@ase.org.uk W www.ase.org.uk
Chief Executive, Shaun Reason

ASSOCIATION FOR THE PROTECTION OF RURAL
SCOTLAND (1926) Dolphin House, 4 Hunter Square,
Edinburgh EH1 1QW T 0131-225 7012 E info@aprs.scot
W www.aprs.scot
Director, John Mayhew

ASSOCIATION OF FINANCIAL MUTUALS (1995) 7
Castle Hill, Caistor LN7 6QL T 0844-879 7863
E martin@financialmutuals.org W www.financialmutuals.org
Chief Executive, Martin Shaw

ASSOCIATION OF GENEALOGISTS AND
RESEARCHERS IN ARCHIVES (1968) Box A, 14
Charterhouse Buildings, Goswell Road, London EC1M 7BA
E info@agra.org.uk W www.agra.org.uk
Chair, Sharon Grant

ASSOCIATION OF ROYAL NAVY OFFICERS (1920) 70
Porchester Terrace, London W2 3TP T 020-7402 5231
E asec@arno.org.uk W www.arno.org.uk
Director, Cdr Mike Goldthorpe

ASTHMA UK (1927) 18 Mansell Street, London E1 8AA
T 0300-??? 5800 E info@asthma.org.uk W www.asthma.org.uk
Chief Executive, Kay Boycott

AUDIT BUREAU OF CIRCULATIONS LTD (1931) Saxon
House, 211 High Street, Berkhamsted HP4 1AD T 01442-870800
E enquiries@abc.org.uk W www.abc.org.uk
Chair, Derek Morris

AUTISM INITIATIVES (1971) Petersfield, Bridle Road,
Merseyside L30 4XR T 0151-330 9500
E info@autisminitiatives.org W www.autisminitiatives.org
Chair, Brian Williams

AUTOMOBILE ASSOCIATION (1905) Fanum House, Basing
View, Basingstoke RG21 4EA T 0345-607 6727
E customersupport@theaa.com W www.theaa.com
CEO, Simon Breakwell

BALTIC EXCHANGE (1744) St Mary Axe, London EC3A 8BH
T 020-7283 9300 W www.balticexchange.com
Chief Executive, Mark Jackson

BARNARDO'S (1866) Tanners Lane, Ilford IG6 1QG
T 020-8550 8822 W www.barnardos.org.uk
Chief Executive, Javed Khan

BBC MEDIA ACTION (1999) Ibex House, 42–47 Minories,
London EC2N 1DY T 020-7481 9797 E media.action@bbc.co.uk
W www.bbc.co.uk/mediaaction
Executive Director, Caroline Nursey

BCS, THE CHARTERED INSTITUTE FOR IT (1957) 1st
Floor, Block D, North Star House, North Star Avenue SN2 1FA
T 01793-417417 W www.bcs.org
Chief Executive, Paul Fletcher

BEAT (1989) Unit 1 Chalk Hill House, 19 Rosary Road, Norwich
NR1 1SZ
T 0300-123 3355 Helpline 0808-801 0677 Youthline 0808-801
0711 E info@b-eat.co.uk W www.b-eat.co.uk
Chief Executive, Andrew Radford

BIBLE SOCIETY (1804) Stonehill Green, Swindon SN5 7DG
T 01793-418222 W www.biblesociety.org.uk
Chief Executive, Paul Williams

BIBLIOGRAPHICAL SOCIETY (1892) c/o University of
London, Institute of English Studies, Senate House, London
WC1E 7HU E admin@bibsoc.org.uk W www.bibsoc.org.uk
Hon. Secretary, Karen Limper-Herz

BIPOLAR UK (1983) 11 Belgrave Road, London SW1V 1RB
T 0333-323 3880 E info@bipolaruk.org.uk
W www.bipolaruk.org.uk
Chief Executive, Simon Kitchen

BLIND VETERANS UK (1915) 12–14 Harcourt Street, London
W1H 4HD T 020-7723 5021 E info@blindveterans.org.uk
W www.blindveterans.org.uk
Chief Executive, Maj.-Gen. Nick Caplin, CB

BLISS (1979) Fourth Floor, Maya House, London SE1 1LB
T 020-7378 1122, Helpline 0808-801 0322 E ask@bliss.org.uk
W www.bliss.org.uk
Chief Executive, Caroline Lee-Davey

BLOODWISE (1960) 39–40 Eagle Street, London WC1R 4TH
T 020-7504 2200 W bloodwise.org.uk
Chief Executive, Gemma Peters

BLUE CROSS (1897) Shilton Road, Burford OX18 4PF
T 0300-777 1897 W www.bluecross.org.uk
Chief Executive, Sally de la Bedoyere

BOOK AID INTERNATIONAL (1954) 39–41 Coldharbour
Lane, London SE5 9NR T 020-7733 3577 E info@bookaid.org
W www.bookaid.org
Director, Alison Tweed

BOOK TRADE CHARITY (BTBS) (1837) The Foyle Centre,
The Retreat, Kings Langley WD4 8LT T 01923-263128
E info@booktradecharity.org W www.btbs.org
Chief Executive, David Hicks

BOOKTRUST (1926) GR Battersea Studios, 80 Silverthorne
Road, London SW8 3HE T 020-7801 8800
E query@booktrust.org.uk W www.booktrust.org.uk
Chief Executive, Diana Gerald

BOTANICAL SOCIETY OF BRITAIN AND IRELAND
(1836) 4 High Firs Crescent, Harpenden AL5 1NA
T 07725-862957 E enquiries@bsbi.org.uk W www.bsbi.org
Chair, Ian Denholm

BOTANICAL SOCIETY OF SCOTLAND (1836) c/o Royal
Botanic Garden Edinburgh, 20A Inverleith Row, Edinburgh
EH3 5LR T 0131-552 7171
W www.botanical-society-scotland.org.uk
General Secretary, Julia Wilson, Liz Lavery

BRISTOL AND GLOUCESTERSHIRE
ARCHAEOLOGICAL SOCIETY (1876) 10 Paddock
Gardens, Gloucester GL2 0ED T 01452-414279
E secretary@bgas.org.uk W www.bgas.org.uk
Hon. General Secretary, Dr Graham Barton

BRITISH ASSOCIATION FOR EARLY CHILDHOOD
EDUCATION (1923) 54 Clarendon Road, Watford
WD17 1DU T 01923-438995 E office@early-education.org.uk
W www.early-education.org.uk
Chief Executive, Beatrice Merrick

BRITISH ASSOCIATION FOR LOCAL HISTORY (1982)
Chester House, 68 Chestergate, Macclesfield SK11 6DY
T 01625-664524 E admin@balh.org.uk W www.balh.org.uk
President, Professor Caroline Barron

BRITISH ASTRONOMICAL ASSOCIATION (1890)
Burlington House, London W1J 0DU T 020-7734 4145
W www.britastro.org
President, Callum Potter

BRITISH BOARD OF FILM CLASSIFICATION (1912) 3
Soho Square, London W1D 3HD T 020-7440 1570
E feedback@bbfc.co.uk W www.bbfc.co.uk
President, Patrick Swaffer

BRITISH CATTLE BREEDERS CLUB (1946) Underhill
Farm, Glutton Bridge, Buxton SK17 0RN T 07966-032079
E heidi.bradbury@cattlebreeders.org.uk
W www.cattlebreeders.org.uk
Chair, Anya Westland

BRITISH COPYRIGHT COUNCIL (1965) 2 Pancras Square,
London N1C 4AG T 020-3290 1444 E info@britishcopyright.org
W www.britishcopyright.org
Chairman, Trevor Cook

BRITISH DEAF ASSOCIATION (1890) 3rd Floor, 356
Holloway Road, London N7 6PA T 020-7697 4140
E bda@bda.org.uk W www.bda.org.uk
Executive Director, Damian Barry

BRITISH ECOLOGICAL SOCIETY (1913) Charles Darwin House, 12 Roger Street, London WC1N 2JU T 020-7685 2500 E hello@britishecologicalsociety.org W www.britishecologicalsociety.org *Chief Executive*, Dr Hazel Norman

BRITISH FEDERATION OF WOMEN GRADUATES (1907) 4 Mandeville Courtyard, 142 Battersea Park Road, London SW11 4NB T 020-7498 8037 E office@bfwg.org.uk W www.bfwg.org.uk *President*, Patrice Wellesley-Cole

BRITISH HEART FOUNDATION (1961) Greater London House, 180 Hampstead Road, London NW1 7AW T 020-7554 0000 W www.bhf.org.uk *Chief Executive*, Simon Gillespie

BRITISH HEDGEHOG PRESERVATION SOCIETY (1982) Hedgehog House, Dhustone, Ludlow SY8 3PL T 01584-890801 E info@britishhedgehogs.org.uk W www.britishhedgehogs.org.uk *Chief Executive*, Fay Vass

BRITISH HERPETOLOGICAL SOCIETY (1947) 11 Strathmore Place, Montrose DD10 8LQ E info@thebhs.org W www.thebhs.org *Secretary*, Trevor Rose

BRITISH HORSE SOCIETY (1947) Abbey Park, Stareton, Kenilworth CV8 2XZ T 024-7684 0500 E enquiry@bhs.org.uk W www.bhs.org.uk *Chief Executive*, Lynn Petersen

BRITISH LUNG FOUNDATION (1985) 73–75 Goswell Road, London EC1V 7ER T 020-7688 5555, Helpline 03000-030 555 W www.blf.org.uk *Chief Executive*, Dr Penny Woods

BRITISH MENSA LTD (1946) St John's House, St John's Square, Wolverhampton WV2 4AH T 01902-772771 W www.mensa.org.uk *Chief Executive*, John Stevenage

BRITISH NATURALISTS' ASSOCIATION (1905) BM 8129, London WC1N 3XX T 0844-892-1817 E info@bna-naturalists.org W www.bna-naturalists.org *Hon. Chair*, Roger Tabor

BRITISH NUTRITION FOUNDATION (1967) New Derwent House, 69–73 Theobalds Road, London WC1X 8TA T 020-7557 7930 E postbox@nutrition.org.uk W www.nutrition.org.uk *Director-General*, Prof. Judith Buttriss, PHD

BRITISH ORNITHOLOGISTS' UNION (1858) PO Box 417, Peterborough PE7 3FX T 01733-844820 E bou@bou.org.uk W www.bou.org.uk *Chief Operations Officer*, S. P. Dudley

BRITISH PHARMACOLOGICAL SOCIETY (1931) The Schild Plot, 16 Angel Gate, London EC1V 2PT T 020-7239 0171 E info@bps.ac.uk W www.bps.ac.uk *Chief Executive*, Jonathan Brüün

BRITISH POLIO FELLOWSHIP (1939) The Xchange, Wilmington Close, Watford WD18 0FQ T 0800-043 1935 E info@britishpolio.org.uk W www.britishpolio.org.uk *National Chairman*, David Mitchell

BRITISH RED CROSS (1870) 44 Moorfields, London EC2Y 9AL T 0344-871 11 11 , Textphone 020-7562 2050 E information@redcross.org.uk W www.redcross.org.uk *Chief Executive*, Mike Adamson

BRITISH REFUGEE COUNCIL PO Box 68614, London E15 9DQ T 020-7346 6700 W www.refugeecouncil.org.uk *Chief Executive*, Maurice Wren

BRITISH SAFETY COUNCIL (1957) 70 Chancellors Road, London W6 9RS T 020-3510 8355 E customer.service@britsafe.org W www.britsafe.org *Chief Executive*, Michael Robinson

BRITISH SCIENCE ASSOCIATION (1831) Wellcome Wolfson Building, London SW7 5HD T 0870-770 7101 E info@britishscienceassociation.org W www.britishscienceassociation.org *Chief Executive*, Katherine Mathieson

BRITISH SUNDIAL SOCIETY (1989) c/o The Royal Astronomical Society, London W1J 0BQ T 01438-871057 E secretary@sundialsoc.org.uk W www.sundialsoc.org.uk *Chair*, Dr Frank King

BRITISH TRUST FOR ORNITHOLOGY (1933) The Nunnery, Thetford IP24 2PU T 01842-750050 E info@bto.org W www.bto.org *Director*, Dr Andy Clements

BUCKINGHAMSHIRE ARCHAEOLOGICAL SOCIETY (1847) County Museum, Church Street, Aylesbury HP20 2QP T 01296-397200 E help@bucksas.org.uk W www.bucksas.org.uk *Chair*, Peter Marsden

BUILD AFRICA (1978) 14th Floor, Tower Building, London SE1 7NX T 01892-519619 E hello@build-africa.org.uk W www.build-africa.org *Chief Executive*, Martin Realey

CAFOD (CATHOLIC AGENCY FOR OVERSEAS DEVELOPMENT) (1962) Romero House, 55 Westminster Bridge Road, London SE1 7JB T 020-7733 7900 E cafod@cafod.org.uk W www.cafod.org.uk *Director*, Chris Bain

CALOUSTE GULBENKIAN FOUNDATION (1956) 50 Hoxton Square, London N1 6PB T 020-7012 1400 E info@gulbenkian.org.uk W gulbenkian.pt/uk-branch/ *Director*, Andrew Barnett

CAMBRIAN ARCHAEOLOGICAL ASSOCIATION (1847) Braemar, SA31 2PB T 01248-364865 E h.james443@gmail.com W www.cambrians.org.uk *General Secretary*, Heather James

CAMERON FUND (1970) BMA House, Tavistock Square, London WC1H 9JP T 020-7388 0796 E info@cameronfund.org.uk W www.cameronfund.org.uk *Chief Executive*, Adrian Mumford

CAMPAIGN FOR FREEDOM OF INFORMATION (1984) Free Word Centre, 60 Farringdon Road, London EC1R 3GA T 020-7324 2519 E admin@cfoi.demon.co.uk W www.cfoi.org.uk *Director*, Maurice Frankel

CAMPAIGN FOR NUCLEAR DISARMAMENT (1958) Mordechai Vanunu House, 162 Holloway Road, London N7 8DQ T 020-7700 2393 E enquiries@cnduk.org W www.cnduk.org *General Secretary*, Kate Hudson

CAMPAIGN FOR THE PROTECTION OF RURAL WALES (1928) Tŷ Gwyn, 31 High Street, Welshpool SY21 7YD T 01938-552525 E info@cprwmail.org.uk W www.cprw.org.uk *Chair*, Peter Alexander-Fitzgerald

CANCER RESEARCH UK (2002) Angel Building, 407 St John Street, London EC1V 4AD T 0300-123 1022 W www.cancerresearchuk.org *Chief Executive*, Michelle Mitchell

CAREERS RESEARCH AND ADVISORY CENTRE (1964) 22 Signet Court, Swanns Road, Cambridge CB5 8LA T 01223-460277 E enquiries@crac.org.uk W www.crac.org.uk *Chief Executive*, Clare Viney

CARERS TRUST (2012) 32–36 Loman Street, London SE1 0EH T 0300-772 9600 E info@carers.org W www.carers.org *Chief Executive*, Giles Meyer

CARERS UK (1965) 20 Great Dover Street, London SE1 4LX T 020-7378 4999 E info@carersuk.org W www.carersuk.org *Chief Executive*, vacant

CARNEGIE UNITED KINGDOM TRUST (1913) Andrew Carnegie House, Pittencrieff Street, Dunfermline KY12 8AW T 01383-721445 E info@carnegieuk.org W www.carnegieuktrust.org.uk *Chief Executive*, Martyn Evans

CATHEDRALS FABRIC COMMISSION FOR ENGLAND (1991) Church House, 27 Great Smith Street, London SW1P 3AZ T 020-7898 1863 E churchcare@churchofengland.org W www.churchcare.co.uk *Cathedrals Officer*, Anne Locke

CATHOLIC TRUTH SOCIETY (1868) 42–46 Harleyford Road, London SE11 5AY T 020-7640 0042 E info@ctsbooks.org W www.ctsbooks.org *General Secretary*, Fergal Martin

CATHOLIC UNION OF GREAT BRITAIN (1872) St Maximillian Kolbe House, 63 Jeddo Road, London W12 9EE T 020-8749 1321 W www.catholicunion.org.uk *President*, Sir Edward Leigh, MP

CAVELL NURSES' TRUST (1917) Grosvenor House, Prospect Hill, Redditch B97 4DL T 01527-595999 E admin@cavellnursestrust.org W www.cavellnursestrust.org *Chief Executive*, John Orchard

CENTRAL AND CECIL HOUSING TRUST (1927) Cecil House, 266 Waterloo Road, London SE1 8RQ T 020-7922 5300 E enquiries@ccht.org.uk W www.ccht.org.uk *Chief Executive*, Julia Ashley

CENTREPOINT (1969) Central House, 25 Camperdown Street, London E1 8DZ T 0845-466 3400 W www.centrepoint.org.uk *Chief Executive*, Seyi Obakin, OBE

CEREDIGION HISTORICAL SOCIETY (1909) 78 Maesceinion, Aberystwyth SY23 3QJ T 01974-261222 E ymholiadau@cymdeithashanesceredigion.org W www.ceredigionhistoricalsociety.org *Hon. Secretary*, Sian Bowyer

CHANGING FACES (1992) The Squire Centre, 33–37 University Street, London WC1E 6JN T 0345-450 0275 E info@changingfaces.org.uk W www.changingfaces.org.uk *Chief Executive*, Becky Hewitt

CHARITIES AID FOUNDATION (1924) 25 Kings Hill Avenue, West Malling ME19 4TA T 0300-012 3000 E enquiries@cafonline.org W www.cafonline.org *Chief Executive*, Sir John Low, CBE

CHARTERED INSTITUTE OF ARBITRATORS (1915) 12 Bloomsbury Square, London WC1A 2LP T 020-7421 7444 E info@ciarb.org W www.ciarb.org *Director-General*, Anthony Abrahams

CHARTERED INSTITUTE OF LINGUISTS (1910) Dunstan House (4th floor), 14a St Cross Street, London EC1N 8XA T 020-7940 3100 E info@ciol.org.uk W www.ciol.org.uk *Chief Executive*, Ann Carlisle

CHARTERED SOCIETY OF FORENSIC SCIENCES (1959) Copthall Bridge House, Station Bridge, Harrogate HG1 1SP T 01423-790391 E csofs@csofs.org W www.csofs.org *Chief Executive*, Dr Anya Hunt

CHATHAM HOUSE (1920) The Royal Institute of International Affairs, Chatham House, London SW1Y 4LE T 020-7957 5700 E contact@chathamhouse.org W www.chathamhouse.org *Director*, Dr Robin Niblett, CMG

CHILD POVERTY ACTION GROUP (1965) 30 Micawber Street, London N1 7TB T 020-7837 7979 E info@cpag.org.uk W www.cpag.org.uk *Chief Executive*, Alison Garnham

CHILDREN 1ST (1884) 83 Whitehouse Loan, Edinburgh EH9 1AT T 0131-446 2300 E cfs@children1st.org.uk W www.children1st.org.uk *Chief Executive (Interim)*, Mary Glasgow

CHILDREN'S SOCIETY (1881) Edward Rudolf House, Margery Street, London WC1X 0JL T 0300-303 7000 E supportercare@childrenssociety.org.uk W www.childrenssociety.org.uk *Chief Executive*, Matthew Reed

CHOICE SUPPORT (1987) 100 Westminster Bridge Road, London SE1 7XA T 020-7261 4100 E enquiries@choicesupport.org.uk W www.choicesupport.org.uk *Chief Executive*, Sarah Maguire

CHRISTIAN AID (1945) 35–41 Lower Marsh, London SE1 7RL T 020-7620 4444 E info@christian-aid.org W www.christianaid.org.uk *Chief Executive*, Amanda Mukwashi

CHRISTIAN AID SCOTLAND (1945) First Floor, Sycamore House, Glasgow G2 4JR T 0141-221 7475 E glasgow@christian-aid.org W www.christianaid.org.uk/scotland *Head of Christian Aid Scotland*, Sally Foster-Fulton

CHRISTIAN EDUCATION (2001) 5/6 Imperial Court, Birmingham B30 3FH T 0121-458 3313 E sales@christianeducation.org.uk W www.christianeducation.org.uk *Chief Executive*, Zoe Keens

CHURCH BUILDINGS COUNCIL (1921) Church House, 27 Great Smith Street, London SW1P 3NZ T 020-7898 1863 E churchcare@churchofengland.org W www.churchcare.co.uk *Senior Church Buildings Officer*, Dr David Knight

CHURCH LADS' AND CHURCH GIRLS' BRIGADE (1891) 2 Barnsley Road, Barnsley S63 6PY T 01709-876535 E contactus@clcgb.org.uk W www.clcgb.org.uk *Chief Executive*, Audrey Simm

CHURCH MISSION SOCIETY (1799) Watlington Road, Oxford OX4 6BZ T 01865-787400 E info@churchmissionsociety.org W www.churchmissionsociety.org *Executive Leader*, Rev. Philip Mounstephen

CHURCH MONUMENTS SOCIETY (1979) c/o The Society of Antiquaries, Burlington House, London W1V 0HS E secretaryofcms@gmail.com W www.churchmonumentssociety.org *Secretary*, Hilary Wheeler

CHURCH UNION (1859) c/o Additional Curates Society, Gordon Browning House, Birmingham B24 9PB T 0121-382 5533 E membership@churchunion.co.uk W www.churchunion.co.uk *Chair*, Father Darren Smith

CITIZENS ADVICE (1939) 3rd Floor North, 200 Aldersgate, London EC1A 4HD T 03000-231231 W www.citizensadvice.org.uk *Chief Executive*, Gillian Guy, CBE

CITY BUSINESS LIBRARY (1970) Aldermanbury, London EC2V 7HH T 020-7332 1812 E cbl@cityoflondon.gov.uk W www.cityoflondon.gov.uk/business/economic-research-and-information/city-business-library/Pages/default.aspx

CLASSICAL ASSOCIATION (1903) Park House, 15–23 Greenhill Crescent, Watford WD18 8HB T 01923-239 300 E office@classicalassociation.org W www.classicalassociation.org *Hon. Secretary*, Dr J. Robson

CLIMATE GROUP (2004) 2nd Floor, Riverside Building, County Hall, London SE1 7PB T 020-7960 2970 E info@theclimategroup.org W www.theclimategroup.org *Chief Executive*, Helen Clarkson

COMBAT STRESS (1919) Tyrwhitt House, Oaklawn Road, Leatherhead KT22 0BX T 01372-587000 E contactus@combatstress.org.uk W www.combatstress.org.uk *Chief Executive*, Sue Freeth

COMMONWEALTH SOCIETY FOR THE DEAF 'SOUND SEEKERS' (1959) c/o UCL Ear Institute, 332–336 Gray's Inn Road, London WC1X 8EE T 020-7833 0035 E help@sound-seekers.org.uk W www.sound-seekers.org.uk *Chief Executive*, Kavita Prasad

COMMUNITY INTEGRATED CARE (1988) Old Market Court, Miners Way, Widnes WA8 7SP T 0151 420 3637 E information@c-i-c.co.uk W www.c-i-c.co.uk
Chief Executive, Mark Adams

CONCERN WORLDWIDE (1968) 13–14 Calico House, Clove Hitch Quay, London SW11 3TN T 020-7801 1850
W www.concern.net
Chief Executive, Dominic MacSorley

THE CONSERVATION VOLUNTEERS (1959) Sedum House, Mallard Way, Doncaster DN4 8DB T 01302-388888 E information@tcv.org.uk W www.tcv.org.uk
Chief Executive, Darren York

CONTEMPORARY APPLIED ARTS (1948) 89 Southwark Street, London SE1 0HX T 020-7620 0086 E shop@caa.org.uk
W www.caa.org.uk
Executive Director, Christine Lalumia

CO-OPERATIVES UK (1869) Holyoake House, Hanover Street, Manchester M60 0AS T 0161-214 1750 E info@uk.coop
W www.uk.coop
Secretary-General, Ed Mayo

CORAM FAMILY (1739) Coram Campus, 41 Brunswick Square, London WC1N 1AZ T 020-7520 0300
E reception@coram.org.uk W www.coram.org.uk
Chief Executive, Dr Carol Homden, CBE

CORONERS' SOCIETY OF ENGLAND AND WALES (1846) HM Coroner's Court, Gerard Majella Courthouse, Liverpool L5 2QD T 0151-233 0135
W www.coronersociety.org.uk
Hon. Secretary, André Joseph Anthony Rebello, OBE

CORPORATION OF THE CHURCH HOUSE (1888) Church House, Great Smith Street, London SW1P 3AZ
T 020-7898 1316 E info@churchhouse.org.uk
W www.churchhouse.org.uk
Secretary, Christopher Palmer, CBE

COUNCIL FOR BRITISH ARCHAEOLOGY (1944) Beatrice de Cardi House, 66 Bootham, York YO30 7BZ
T 01904-671417 E info@archaeologyuk.org
W www.archaeologyuk.org
Director, Dr Mike Heyworth, MBE

COUNCIL FOR WORLD MISSION (1977) Ipalo House, 32–34 Great Peter Street, London SW1P 2DB T 020-7222 4214 E council@cwmission.org W www.cwmission.org
General Secretary, Revd Dr Collin Cowan

COUNCIL OF UNIVERSITY CLASSICAL DEPARTMENTS (1972) Institute of Classical Studies, Senate House, Malet Street, London WC1E 7HU T 07764-212575 E director.ics@sas.ac.uk W cucd.blogs.sas.ac.uk
Chair, Prof. G. Woolf, FSA SCOT, FSA

COUNTRY HOUSES FOUNDATION (2005) Steephouse Farm, Uley Road, Dursley GL11 5AD T 0845-402 4102
E info@countryhousesfoundation.org.uk
W www.countryhousesfoundation.org.uk
Chief Executive, David Price

COUNTRY LAND & BUSINESS ASSOCIATION (1907) 16 Belgrave Square, London SW1X 8PQ T 020-7235 0511 E mail@cla.org.uk W www.cla.org.uk
President, Tim Breitmeyer

COUNTRYSIDE ALLIANCE (1997) 1 Spring Mews, Tinworth Street, London SE11 4AN T 020-7840 9200
W www.countryside-alliance.org.uk
Chief Executive, Tim Bonner

CPRE (CAMPAIGN TO PROTECT RURAL ENGLAND) (1926) 5–11 Lavington Street, London SE1 0NZ
T 020-7981 2800 E info@cpre.org.uk W www.cpre.org.uk
Chief Executive, Crispin Truman

CRAFTS COUNCIL (1971) 44A Pentonville Road, London N1 9BY T 020-7806 2500 E reception@craftscouncil.org.uk
W www.craftscouncil.org.uk
Executive Director, Rosy Greenlees, OBE

CRANSTOUN (1969) Thames Mews, Esher KT10 9AD
T 020-8335 1830 E info@cranstoun.org.uk
W www.cranstoun.org
Chair, Richard Pertwee

CRISIS UK (1967) 66 Commercial Street, London E1 6LT
T 0300-636 1967 E enquiries@crisis.org.uk W www.crisis.org.uk
Chief Executive, Jon Sparkes

CROHN'S AND COLITIS UK (1979) 1 Bishop Square, Hatfield Business Park AL10 9NE T 01727-830038
E info@crohnsandcolitis.org.uk W www.crohnsandcolitis.org.uk
Chief Executive, David Barker

CRUELTY FREE INTERNATIONAL (1898) 16A Crane Grove, London N7 8NN T 020-7700 4888
E info@crueltyfreeinternational.org
W www.crueltyfreeinternational.org
Chief Executive, Michelle Thew

CRUSE BEREAVEMENT CARE (1959) Unit 01, One Victoria Villas, Richmond TW9 2GW
T 020-8939 9530, **Helpline** 0808-808 1677 E info@cruse.org.uk
W www.cruse.org.uk
Chief Executive, Steven Wibberley

CUMBERLAND AND WESTMORLAND ANTIQUARIAN AND ARCHAEOLOGICAL SOCIETY (1866) Westlands, Westbourne Drive, Lancaster LA1 5EE T 01524-67523
E general.secretary@cumbriapast.com W www.cwaas.org.uk
General Secretary, Marion E. M. McClintock, MBE

CYCLING UK (1878) Parklands, Railton Road, Guildford GU2 9JX T 01483-238301 E cycling@cycling.org
W www.cyclinguk.org
Chief Executive, Paul Tuohy

CYSTIC FIBROSIS TRUST (1964) One Aldgate, 2nd Floor, London EC3N 1RE T 020-3795 1555
E enquiries@cysticfibrosis.org.uk W www.cysticfibrosis.org.uk
Chief Executive, David Ramsden

DEMOS (1994) 76 Vincent Square, London SW1P 2PD
T 020-3878 3955 E hello@demos.co.uk W www.demos.co.uk
Director, Polly Mackenzie

DESIGN AND TECHNOLOGY ASSOCIATION (1989) 16 Wellesbourne House, Walton Road, Wellesbourne CV35 9JB
T 01789-470007 E info@data.org.uk W www.data.org.uk
Chief Executive, Tony Ryan

DEVON ARCHAEOLOGICAL SOCIETY (1929) Royal Albert Memorial Museum, Queen Street, Exeter EX4 3RX
E dashonsec@devonarchaeologicalsociety.org.uk
W www.devonarchaeologicalsociety.org.uk
Hon. Secretary, Debbie Griffiths

DIABETES UK (1934) Wells Lawrence House, 126 Back Church Lane, London E1 1FH T 0345-123 2399
E helpline@diabetes.org.uk W www.diabetes.org.uk
Chief Executive, Chris Askew

DISABILITY RIGHTS UK (1977) Plexal, 14 East Bay Lane, Queen Elizabeth Olympic Park E20 3BS T 0330-995 0400
E enquiries@disabilityrightsuk.org W www.disabilityrightsuk.org
Chief Executive, Kamran Mallick

DITCHLEY FOUNDATION (1958) Ditchley Park, Chipping Norton OX7 4ER T 01608-677346 E info@ditchley.co.uk
W www.ditchley.co.uk
Director, James Arroyo, OBE

DOWN'S SYNDROME ASSOCIATION (1970) Langdon Down Centre, 2A Langdon Park, Teddington TW11 9PS
T 0333-1212300 E info@downs-syndrome.org.uk
W www.downs-syndrome.org.uk
Chief Executive, Carol Boys

DUKE OF EDINBURGH'S AWARD (1956) Gulliver House, Madeira Walk, Windsor SL4 1EU T 01753-727400
E info@dofe.org W www.dofe.org
Chief Executive, Peter Westgarth

EAST OF ENGLAND AGRICULTURAL SOCIETY (1797)
East of England Showground, Peterborough PE2 6XE
T 01733-234451 E info@eastofengland.org.uk
W www.eastofengland.org.uk
Chief Executive, Jeremy Staples

ECCLESIOLOGICAL SOCIETY (1879) 68 Scholars Road,
Balham SW12 0PG E admin@ecclsoc.org W www.ecclsoc.org
Chairman, Mark Kirby

EDINBURGH CHAMBER OF COMMERCE (1785)
Chamber Business Centre, 40 George Street, Edinburgh EH2 2LE
T 0131-221 2999 E info@edinburghchamber.co.uk
W www.edinburghchamber.co.uk
Chief Executive, Liz McAreavey

EDUCATION SUPPORT PARTNERSHIP (1877) 40A
Drayton Park, London N5 1EW
T 020-7697 2750, **Helpline** 0800-056 2561
E enquiries@edsupport.org.uk
W www.educationsupportpartnership.org.uk
Chief Executive, Julian Stanley

EGYPT EXPLORATION SOCIETY (1882) 3 Doughty Mews,
London WC1N 2PG T 020-7242 1880 E contact@ees.ac.uk
W www.ees.ac.uk
Director, Dr Cédric Gobeil

ELECTORAL REFORM SOCIETY (1884) 3rd Floor, News
Building, London SE1 9SG T 020-3743 6066
E ers@electoral-reform.org.uk W www.electoral-reform.org.uk
Chief Executive, Darren Hughes

ELGAR SOCIETY (1951) 6 Carriage Close, Worcester
WR2 6AE T 01905-339371 E vice.chair@elgar.org
W elgar.org/elgarsoc/
Chairman, Steven Halls

EMERGENCY PLANNING SOCIETY (1993) The Hawkhills,
Easingwold, York YO61 3EG T 01347-821972
E info@the-eps.org W www.the-eps.org
Chair, Jacqui Semple

ENABLE SCOTLAND (1954) Inspire House, 3 Renshaw Place,
Glasgow ML1 4UF T 01698-737000
E enabledirect@enable.org.uk W www.enable.org.uk
Chief Executive, Theresa Shearer

ENERGY INSTITUTE (2003) 61 New Cavendish Street,
London W1G 7AR T 020-7467 7100 E info@energyinst.org
W www.energyinst.org
Chief Executive, Louise Kingham, OBE

ENGLISH ASSOCIATION (1906) University of Leicester,
University Road, Leicester LE1 7RH T 0116-229 7622
E engassoc@le.ac.uk W www.le.ac.uk/engassoc
Chief Executive, Helen Lucas

ENGLISH CHESS FEDERATION (1904) The Watch Oak,
Chain Lane, Battle TN33 0YD T 01424-775222
E office@englishchess.org.uk W www.englishchess.org.uk
Chief Executive, Mike Truran

ENGLISH FOLK DANCE AND SONG SOCIETY (1932)
Cecil Sharp House, 2 Regent's Park Road, London NW1 7AY
T 020-7485 2206 E info@efdss.org W www.efdss.org
Chief Executive, Katy Spicer

ENGLISH-SPEAKING UNION OF THE
COMMONWEALTH (1918) Dartmouth House, 37 Charles
Street, London W1J 5ED T 020-7529 1550 E esu@esu.org
W www.esu.org
Director-General, Jane Easton

EPILEPSY SOCIETY (1892) Chesham Lane, Chalfont St Peter
SL9 0RJ T 01494-601300, **Helpline** 01494-601400
W www.epilepsysociety.org.uk
Chief Executive, Clare Pelham

EQUINOX CARE (1986) 1 Waterloo Gardens, London N1 1TY
T 020-3668 9270 E enquiries@equinoxcare.org.uk
W www.equinoxcare.org.uk
Chief Executive, Gill Arukpe

ESPERANTO ASSOCIATION OF BRITAIN (1976)
Esperanto House, Station Road, Stoke-on-Trent ST12 9DE
T 0845-230 1887 E eab@esperanto.org.uk
W www.esperanto.org.uk
President, Ian Carter

FABIAN SOCIETY (1884) 61 Petty France, London SW1H 9EU
T 020-7227 4900 E info@fabians.org.uk W www.fabians.org.uk
General Secretary, Andrew Harrop

FAITH AND THOUGHT (VICTORIA INSTITUTE) (1865)
15 The Drive, Harlow CM20 3QD E admin@faithandthought.org
W www.faithandthought.org
President, Prof. Sir Colin J. Humphreys, CBE

FAMILY ACTION (1869) 24 Angel Gate, London EC1V 2PT
T 020-7254 6251 E info@family-action.org.uk
W www.family-action.org.uk
Chief Executive, David Holmes, CBE

FAUNA & FLORA INTERNATIONAL (1903) The David
Attenborough Building, Pembroke Street, Cambridge CB2 3QZ
T 01223-571000 E info@fauna-flora.org
W www.fauna-flora.org
Chief Executive, Mark Rose

FEDERATION OF BRITISH ARTISTS (1961) 17 Carlton
House Terrace, London SW1Y 5DD T 020-7930 6844
E info@mallgalleries.com W www.mallgalleries.org.uk
Director, Lewis McNaught

FEDERATION OF FAMILY HISTORY SOCIETIES (1974)
PO Box 62, Sheringham NR26 9AR T 0800-085 6322
E info@ffhs.org.uk W www.ffhs.org.uk
Chairman, Steve Benson

FEDERATION OF SMALL BUSINESSES (1974) Sir Frank
Whittle Way, Blackpool FY4 2FE T 0808-2020 888
E press@fsb.org.uk W www.fsb.org.uk
National Chairman, Mike Cherry, OBE

FIELDS IN TRUST (1925) Unit 2D, Woodstock Studios, 36
Woodstock Grove, London W12 8LE T 020-7427 211 0
E info@fieldsintrust.org W www.fieldsintrust.org
Chief Executive, Helen Griffiths

FIELD STUDIES COUNCIL (1943) Preston Montford,
Shrewsbury SY4 1HW T 01743-852100
E enquiries@field-studies-council.org
W www.field-studies-council.org
Chief Executive, Mark Castle, OBE

FIGHT FOR SIGHT (1965) 18 Mansell Street, London E1 8AA
T 020-7264 3900 E info@fightforsight.org.uk
W www.fightforsight.org.uk
Chief Executive, Michele Acton

FIRE FIGHTERS CHARITY (1943) Level 6, Belvedere, Basing
View, Basingstoke RG21 4HG T 01256-366566
E info@firefighterscharity.org.uk
W www.firefighterscharity.org.uk
Chief Executive, Jill Tolfrey

FIRE PROTECTION ASSOCIATION (1946) London Road,
Moreton in Marsh, Glos GL56 0RH T 01608-812500
E fpa@thefpa.co.uk W www.thefpa.co.uk
Managing Director, Jonathan O'Neill, OBE

FLAG INSTITUTE (1971) HQS Wellington, Victoria
Embankment, London WC2R 2PN E info@flaginstitute.org
W www.flaginstitute.org
President, Capt. Malcolm Farrow, OBE, FFI, RN

FLEET AIR ARM OFFICERS' ASSOCIATION (1957) 4 St
James's Square, London SW1Y 4JU T 020-7930 7722
E admin@fleetairarmoa.org W www.fleetairarmoa.org
President, Vice-Adm. Sir Adrian Johns, KCB, CBE

FOREIGN PRESS ASSOCIATION IN LONDON (1888) 8
St James's Square, London SW1Y 4JU T 020-3858 0047
W www.fpalondon.net
Director, Deborah Bonetti

FOUNDATION FOR CREDIT COUNSELLING (STEP CHANGE) (1993) Wade House, Merrion Centre, Leeds LS2 8NG T 0113-297 0107 W www.stepchange.org
Chief Executive, Phil Andrew

FPA (1930) 23–28 Penn Street, London N1 5DL T 0300-123 7123 E fpadirect@fpa.org.uk W www.fpa.org.uk
Chief Executive, Natika H Halil

FRANCO-BRITISH SOCIETY (1924) 3 Dovedale Studios, 465 Battersea Park Road, London SW11 4LR
E francobritsoc@gmail.com W www.franco-british-society.org
Executive Secretary, Isabelle Gault

FRIENDS OF CATHEDRAL MUSIC (1956) 27 Old Gloucester Street, London WC1N 3XX T 020-3637 2172
E info@fcm.org.uk W www.fcm.org.uk
Secretary, Roger Bishton

FRIENDS OF FRIENDLESS CHURCHES (1957) St Ann's Vestry Hall, 2 Church Entry, London EC4V 5HB T 020-7236 3934
E office@friendsoffriendlesschurches.org.uk
W www.friendsoffriendlesschurches.org.uk
Director, Rachel Morley

FRIENDS OF THE BODLEIAN (1925) Bodleian Library, Broad Street, Oxford OX1 3BG T 01865-277234
E fob@bodleian.ox.ac.uk
W www.bodleian.ox.ac.uk/bodley/friends
Chair, Prof. Richard McCabe

FRIENDS OF THE EARTH SCOTLAND (1978) Thorn House, 5 Rose Street, Edinburgh EH2 2PR T 0131-243 2700
W www.foe-scotland.org.uk
Director, Dr Richard Dixon

FRIENDS OF THE ELDERLY (1905) 40–42 Ebury Street, London SW1W 0LZ T 020-7730 8263 E enquiries@fote.org.uk
W www.fote.org.uk
Chief Executive, Steve Allen

FRIENDS OF THE NATIONAL LIBRARIES (1931) PO Box 4291, Reading RG8 9JA
W www.friendsofnationallibraries.org.uk
Chair, Geordie Greig

FUTURES FOR WOMEN (SPTW) (1859) 11 Church Street, Rugby CV23 9RL E futuresforwomen@btinternet.com
W futuresforwomen.org.uk
Secretary, Ms Jane Hampson

GALLIPOLI ASSOCIATION (1969) Box 630, Wey House, Weybridge KT138NA T 028-2177 2996
E secretary@gallipoli-association.org
W www.gallipoli-association.org
Hon. Secretary, Foster Summerson

GAME AND WILDLIFE CONSERVATION TRUST (1969) Burgate Manor, Fordingbridge SP6 1EF T 01425-652381
E info@gwct.org.uk W www.gwct.org.uk
Chief Executive, Teresa Dent

GARDENS TRUST (1965) 70 Cowcross Street, London EC1M 6EJ T 020-7608 2409 E enquiries@thegardenstrust.org
W thegardenstrust.org
Chairman, Dr James Bartos

GEMMOLOGICAL ASSOCIATION OF GREAT BRITAIN (GEM-A) (1931) 21 Ely Place, London EC1N 6TD
T 020-7404 3334 E information@gem-a.com
W www.gem-a.com
Chief Executive, Alan Hart

GENERAL MEDICAL COUNCIL (1858) 3 Hardman Street, Manchester M3 3AW T 0161-923 6602 E gmc@gmc-uk.org
W www.gmc-uk.org
Chief Executive, Charlie Massey

GENERAL OPTICAL COUNCIL (1958) 10 Old Bailey, London EC4M 7NG T 020-7580 3898 E goc@optical.org
W www.optical.org
Chief Executive/Registrar, Vicky McDermott

GEOGRAPHICAL ASSOCIATION (1893) 160 Solly Street, Sheffield S1 4BF T 0114-296 0088 E info@geography.org.uk
W www.geography.org.uk
Chief Executive, Alan Kinder

GEOLOGICAL SOCIETY OF LONDON (1807) Burlington House, Piccadilly, London W1J 0BG T 020-7434 9944
E enquiries@geolsoc.org.uk W www.geolsoc.org.uk
Executive Secretary, Richard Hughes

GEORGIAN GROUP (1937) 6 Fitzroy Square, W1T 5DX
T 020-7529 8920 E office@georgiangroup.org.uk
W www.georgiangroup.org.uk
Secretary, David McKinstry

GIRLGUIDING (1910) 17–19 Buckingham Palace Road, SW1W 0PT T 020-7834 6242 E info@girlguiding.org.uk
W www.girlguiding.org.uk
Chief Guide, Amanda Medler

GIRLS' FRIENDLY SOCIETY IN ENGLAND AND WALES (1875) Unit 30 Angel Gate, 326 City Road, London EC1V 2PT T 020-7837 9669 E info@girlsfriendlysociety.org.uk
W girlsfriendlysociety.org.uk
Executive Director, Paul Rompani

GLADSTONE'S LIBRARY (1894) Church Lane, Hawarden CH5 3DF T 01244-532350 E enquiries@gladlib.org
W www.gladstoneslibrary.org
Warden, Revd Peter Francis

GREENPEACE UK (1979) Canonbury Villas, N1 2PN
T 020-7865 8100 W www.greenpeace.org.uk
Executive Director, John Sauven

GUIDE DOGS (1934) Hillfields, Burghfield Common, Reading RG7 3YG T 0118-983 5555 E guidedogs@guidedogs.org.uk
W www.guidedogs.org.uk
Chief Executive, Thomas Wright

GUILD OF FREEMEN OF THE CITY OF LONDON (1908) Rooms 78/79, 65 London Wall, London EC2M 5TU
T 020-7239 9016 E clerk@guild-freemen-london.co.uk
W www.guild-freemen-london.co.uk
Clerk to the Guild, Christine Cook

GUILD OF GLASS ENGRAVERS (1975) c/o Red House Glass Cone, High Street, Stourbridge DY8 4AZ T 07834-549925
E enquiries@gge.org.uk W www.gge.org.uk
President, Tracey Sheppard

GUILD OF PASTORAL PSYCHOLOGY (1937) GPP Administration, Unit 1 Chapleton Lodge, Blackborough End PE32 1SF T 01553-849849
E administration@guildofpastoralpsychology.org.uk
W www.guildofpastoralpsychology.org.uk
Chair, Caroline Payton

GURKHA WELFARE TRUST (1969) PO Box 2170, 22 Queen Street, Salisbury SP2 2EX T 01722-323955 E info@gwt.org.uk
W www.gwt.org.uk
Director, Al Howard

GUY'S AND ST THOMAS' CHARITY (1553) Francis House, 9 King's Head Yard, SE1 1NA T 020-7089 4550
E info@gsttcharity.org.uk W www.gsttcharity.org.uk
Chief Executive, Kieron Boyle

HAEMOPHILIA SOCIETY (1950) Willcox House, 140–148 Borough High Street, London SE1 1LB T 020-7939 0780
E info@haemophilia.org.uk W www.haemophilia.org.uk
Chief Executive, Liz Carroll

HAIG HOUSING TRUST (2009) Alban Dobson House, Green Lane, Morden SM4 5NS T 020-8685 5777
E enquiries@haighousing.org.uk W www.haighousing.org.uk
Chief Executive, James Richardson

HAKLUYT SOCIETY (1846) c/o Map Library, The British Library, London NW1 2DB T 07568-468066
E office@hakluyt.com W www.hakluyt.com
President, Prof. Jim. Bennett

HANSARD SOCIETY (1944) 5th Floor, 9 King Street,
EC2V 8EA **T** 020-7710 6070 **E** contact@hansardsociety.org.uk
W www.hansardsociety.org.uk
Director, Dr Ruth Fox

HARVEIAN SOCIETY OF LONDON (1831) Lettsom House,
11 Chandos Street, W1G 9EB **T** 020-7580 1043
E harveiansoclondon@btconnect.com
W www.harveiansocietyoflondon.btck.co.uk
Executive Secretary, Cdr Mike Flynn, FCMI MCPID

HEARING LINK (1947) 23 The Waterfront, Eastbourne
BN23 5UZ **T** 07526-123255 **E** enquiries@hearinglink.org
W www.hearinglink.org
Chief Operating Officer, Dr Lorraine Gailey

HELP FOR HEROES (2007) 14 Parkers Close, Salisbury
SP5 3RB **T** 01725-513212 **W** www.helpforheroes.org.uk
Chief Executive, Melanie Waters

HELP MUSICIANS (MUSICIANS BENEVOLENT FUND)
(1921) 7–11 Britannia Street, London WC1X 9JS
T 020-7239 9100 **E** info@helpmusicians.org.uk
W www.helpmusicians.org.uk
Chief Executive (interim), James Ainscough

HERALDRY SOCIETY (1947) 53 Hitchin Street, Baldock
SG7 6AQ **E** info@theheraldrysociety.com
W www.theheraldrysociety.com
Hon. Secretary, John Tunesi of Liongam

HIGH SHERIFFS' ASSOCIATION OF ENGLAND &
WALES (1971) Heritage House, PO Box 21, Baldock SG7 5SH
T 01462-896688 **E** secretary@highsheriffs.com
W www.highsheriffs.com
Chair, Hon. Hugh Tollemache

HISPANIC AND LUSO BRAZILIAN COUNCIL
(CANNING HOUSE) (1943) Canning House, 126 Wigmore
Street, W1U 3RZ **T** 020-7811 5600
E enquiries@canninghouse.org **W** www.canninghouse.org
Chief Executive, Cristina Cortes

HISTORIC HOUSES ASSOCIATION (1973) 2 Chester
Street, London SW1X 7BB **T** 020-7259 5688 **E** info@hha.org.uk
W www.hha.org.uk
Director-General, Ben Cowell

HISTORICAL ASSOCIATION (1906) 59A Kennington Park
Road, London SE11 4JH **T** 0300-100 0223
E enquiries@history.org.uk **W** www.history.org.uk
Chief Executive, Rebecca Sullivan

HONG KONG ASSOCIATION (1961) Swire House, 59
Buckingham Gate, London SW1E 6AJ **T** 020-7963 9447
E communications@hkas.org.uk **W** www.hkas.org.uk
Executive Director, Tom Wright

HONOURABLE SOCIETY OF CYMMRODORION
(1751) 157–163, Grays Inn Road, London WC1X 8UE
E secretary@cymmrodorion.org **W** www.cymmrodorion.org
Honorary Secretary, Dr Lynn Williams, FLSW

HOSPITAL SATURDAY FUND (1873) 24 Upper Ground,
London SE1 9PD **T** 020-7202 1365 **E** charity@hsf.eu.com
W www.hospitalsaturdayfund.org
Chief Executive, Paul Jackson

HOUSING JUSTICE (2003) 256 Bermondsey Street, London
SE1 3UJ **T** 020-3544 8094 **E** info@housingjustice.org.uk
W www.housingjustice.org.uk
Chief Executive, Kathy Mohan

HR SOCIETY LTD (1970) 4 Durnford Close, Chilbolton
SO20 6AP **T** 07909-515 126 **E** gemma@hrsociety.co.uk
W www.hrsociety.co.uk
Chairman, George Blair

THE HUMANE RESEARCH TRUST (1962) Brook House, 29
Bramhall Lane South, Stockport SK7 2DN **T** 0161-439 8041
E info@humaneresearch.org.uk **W** www.humaneresearch.org.uk
Chair, L. M. Rhoades

HUMANISTS UK 39 Moreland Street, London EC1V 8BB
T 020-7324 3060 **E** info@humanism.org.uk
W www.humanism.org.uk
Chief Executive, Andrew Copson

I CAN (1888) 31 Angel Gate (Gate 5), Goswell Road, London
EC1V 2PT **T** 020-7843 2510 **E** info@ican.org.uk
W www.ican.org.uk
Chief Executive, Bob Reitemeier, CBE

INCORPORATED COUNCIL OF LAW REPORTING
FOR ENGLAND AND WALES (1865) Megarry House, 119
Chancery Lane, WC2A 1PP **T** 020-7242 6471
E enquiries@iclr.co.uk **W** www.iclr.co.uk
Chief Executive, Kevin Laws

INCORPORATED SOCIETY OF MUSICIANS (1882) 4–5
Inverness Mews, London W2 3JQ **T** 020-7221 3499
E membership@ism.org **W** www.ism.org
Chief Executive, Deborah Annetts

INDEPENDENT SCHOOLS' BURSARS ASSOCIATION
(1932) Bluett House, Unit 11 –12, Cliddesden RG25 2JB
T 01256-330369 **E** office@theisba.org.uk
W www.theisba.org.uk
Chief Executive, David Woodgate

INDEPENDENT AGE (1863) 18 Avonmore Road, W14 8RR
T 020-7605 4200 **E** charity@independentage.org
W www.independentage.org
Chief Executive, Janet Morrison

INDUSTRY AND PARLIAMENT TRUST (1977) Suite 101,
3 Whitehall Court, SW1A 2EL **T** 020-7839 9400
E enquiries@ipt.org.uk **W** www.ipt.org.uk
Chief Executive, Nick Maher

INSPIRING FUTURES (1973) The Fountain Building, Howbery
Park, Wallingford OX10 8BA **T** 01491-820381
E helpline@inspiringfutures.org.uk **W** www.inspiringfutures.org.uk/isco
Commercial and Finance Director, Graeme Smith

INSTITUTE FOR PUBLIC POLICY RESEARCH (1988)
Ground Floor, 14 Buckingham Street, London WC2N 6DF
T 020-7470 6100 **E** info@ippr.org **W** www.ippr.org
Director, Tom Kibasi

INSTITUTE OF CANCER RESEARCH (1909) 123 Old
Brompton Road, London SW7 3RP **T** 020-7352 8133
W www.icr.ac.uk
Chief Executive, Prof. Paul Workman

INSTITUTE OF ECONOMIC AFFAIRS (1955) 2 Lord North
Street, London SW1P 3LB **T** 020-7799 8900 **E** iea@iea.org.uk
W www.iea.org.uk
Director-General, Mark Littlewood

INSTITUTE OF FOOD SCIENCE AND TECHNOLOGY
(1964) 5 Cambridge Court, 210 Shepherd's Bush Road, London
W6 7NJ **T** 020-7603 6316 **E** info@ifst.org **W** www.ifst.org
Chief Executive, Jon Poole

INSTITUTE OF HEALTH PROMOTION AND
EDUCATION (1962) c/o 20 Mardley Avenue, Herts AL6 0UD
E admin@ihpe.org.uk **W** www.ihpe.org.uk
President, Sylvia Cheater

INSTITUTE OF HERALDIC AND GENEALOGICAL
STUDIES (1961) 79–82 Northgate, Canterbury CT1 1BA
T 01227-768664 **E** enquiries@ihgs.ac.uk **W** www.ihgs.ac.uk
Principal, Dr Richard Baker

INSTITUTE OF MASTERS OF WINE (1955) 6 Riverlight
Quay, London SW11 8EA **T** 020-7383 9130
E info@mastersofwine.org **W** www.mastersofwine.org
Executive Director, Penny Richards

INSTITUTE OF MATHEMATICS AND ITS
APPLICATIONS (1964) Catherine Richards House, 16 Nelson
Street, Southend-on-Sea SS1 1EF **T** 01702-354020
E post@ima.org.uk **W** www.ima.org.uk
Executive Director, David Youdan

INSTITUTE OF PHYSICS AND ENGINEERING IN MEDICINE (1997) Fairmount House, 230 Tadcaster Road, York YO24 1ES **T** 01904-610821 **E** office@ipem.ac.uk **W** www.ipem.ac.uk
Chief Executive, Rosemary Cook, CBE

INSTITUTION OF ENGINEERING AND TECHNOLOGY (1871) Michael Faraday House, Six Hills Way, Stevenage SG1 2AY **T** 01438-313311 **E** postmaster@theiet.org **W** www.theiet.org
Chief Executive & Secretary, Nigel Fine

INTERCONTINENTAL CHURCH SOCIETY (1823) Unit 11, Ensign Business Centre, Westwood Way, Coventry CV4 8JA **T** 024-7646 3940 **E** enquiries@ics-uk.org **W** www.ics-uk.org
Mission Director, Revd Richard Bromley

INTERNATIONAL AFRICAN INSTITUTE (1926) School of Oriental and African Studies, Thornhaugh Street, London WC1H 0XG **T** 020-7898 4420 **E** iai@soas.ac.uk **W** www.internationalafricaninstitute.org
Honorary Director, Prof. Philip Burnham

INTERNATIONAL CHURCHILL SOCIETY UK (1968) Churchill College, Storey's Way, Cambridge CB3 0DS **T** 01223-331646 **E** asmith@winstonchurchill.org **W** www.winstonchurchill.org
Executive Director, Andrew Smith

INTERNATIONAL INSTITUTE FOR CONSERVATION OF HISTORIC AND ARTISTIC WORKS (1950) 3 Birdcage Walk, London SW1H 9JJ **T** 020-7799 5500 **E** iic@iiconservation.org **W** www.iiconservation.org
Secretary-General, Josephine Kirby Atkinson

INTERNATIONAL RESCUE COMMITTEE UK (1997) 3 Bloomsbury Place, London WC1A 2QL **T** 020-7692 2727 **E** contactus@rescue-uk.org **W** www.rescue-uk.org
Executive Director (acting), Sanj Srikanthan

INTERNATIONAL STUDENTS HOUSE (1962) 229 Great Portland Street, London W1W 5PN **T** 020-7631 8300 **E** info@ish.org.uk **W** www.ish.org.uk
Chief Executive, Martin Chalker

INTERNATIONAL TREE FOUNDATION (1924) Mayfield House, Banbury OX2 7DE **T** 01865-318836 **E** info@internationaltreefoundation.org **W** www.internationaltreefoundation.org
Director, Andy Egan

IRAN SOCIETY (1911) 1a St Martin's House, London NW1 1QB **T** 020-7235 5122 **E** info@iransociety.org **W** www.iransociety.org
President, Sir Richard Dalton, KCMG

JAPAN SOCIETY (1891) 13–14 Cornwall Terrace, London NW1 4QP **T** 020-7935 0475 **E** info@japansociety.org.uk **W** www.japansociety.org.uk
Chief Executive, Heidi Potter

THE JERUSALEM AND THE MIDDLE EAST CHURCH ASSOCIATION (1929) 1 Hart House, The Hart, Farnham GU9 7HJ **T** 01252-726994 **E** information@jmeca.org.uk **W** www.jmeca.org.uk
Chair, John Clark

JEWISH CARE (1990) Amélie House, Maurice and Vivienne Wohl Campus, London NW11 9DQ **T** 020-8922 2000 **E** info@jcare.org **W** www.jewishcare.org
Chair, Steven Lewis

JOURNALISTS' CHARITY (1864) Dickens House, 35 Wathen Road, Dorking RH4 1JY **T** 01306-887511 **E** enquiries@journalistscharity.org.uk **W** www.journalistscharity.org.uk
Director, David Ilott

JUSTICE (1957) 59 Carter Lane, London EC4V 5AQ **T** 020-7329 5100 **E** admin@justice.org.uk **W** www.justice.org.uk
Director, Andrea Coomber

KENT ARCHAEOLOGICAL SOCIETY (1857) Maidstone Museum, St Faith's Street, Maidstone ME14 1LH **E** secretary@kentarchaeology.org.uk **W** www.kentarchaeology.org.uk
Hon. General Secretary, Dr Clive Drew

KING'S FUND (1897) 11–13 Cavendish Square, London W1G 0AN **T** 020-7307 2400 **E** enquiry@kingsfund.org.uk **W** www.kingsfund.org.uk
Chief Executive, Sir Chris Ham

LCIA (LONDON COURT OF INTERNATIONAL ARBITRATION) (1892) 70 Fleet Street, London EC4Y 1EU **T** 020-7936 6200 **E** enquiries@lcia.org **W** www.lcia.org
Director-General, Dr Jacomijn van Haersolte-van Hof

LEAGUE OF THE HELPING HAND (1908) PO Box 342, Burgess Hill RH15 5AQ **T** 01444-236099 **E** secretary@lhh.org.uk **W** www.lhh.org.uk
Chair and Director, Moira Parrott

THE LEPROSY MISSION, ENGLAND, WALES, THE CHANNEL ISLANDS AND THE ISLE OF MAN (1874) Goldhay Way, Peterborough PE2 5GZ **T** 01733-370505 **E** post@tlmew.org.uk **W** www.leprosymission.org.uk
National Director, Peter Waddup

LIBERTY (NATIONAL COUNCIL FOR CIVIL LIBERTIES) (1934) Liberty House, 26–30 Strutton Ground, London SW19 2HR **T** 020-7403 3888 **W** www.liberty-human-rights.org.uk
Director, Martha Spurrier

LINNEAN SOCIETY OF LONDON (1788) Burlington House, London W1J 0BF **T** 020-7434 4479 **E** info@linnean.org **W** www.linnean.org
Executive Secretary, Dr Elizabeth Rollinson

LISTENING BOOKS (1959) 12 Lant Street, London SE1 1QH **T** 020-7407 9417 **E** info@listening-books.org.uk **W** www.listening-books.org.uk
Director, Bill Dee

LIVABILITY (c.1840) 6 Mitre Passage, London SE10 0ER **T** 020-7452 2000 **E** info@livability.org.uk **W** www.livability.org.uk
Chief Executive, Helen England

LOCAL GOVERNMENT ASSOCIATION (1997) 18 Smith Square, London SW1P 3HZ **T** 020-7664 3000 **E** info@local.gov.uk **W** www.local.gov.uk
Chief Executive, Mark Lloyd

LOCAL SOLUTIONS (1974) Mount Vernon Green, Hall Lane, Liverpool L7 8TF **T** 0151-709 0990 **E** info@localsolutions.org.uk **W** www.localsolutions.org.uk
Chief Executive, Steve Hawkins

LONDON AND MIDDLESEX ARCHAEOLOGICAL SOCIETY (1855) c/o Museum of London, London EC2Y 5HN **T** 020-7410 2228 **W** www.lamas.org.uk
Hon. Secretary, Karen Thomas

LONDON CITY MISSION (1835) Nasmith House, 175 Tower Bridge Road, London SE1 2AH **T** 020-7407 7585 **E** enquiries@lcm.org.uk **W** www.lcm.org.uk
Chief Executive, Graham Miller

LONDON COLLEGE OF OSTEOPATHIC MEDICINE (1946) 8–10 Boston Place, London NW1 6QH **T** 020-7262 1128 **W** www.lcom.org.uk
Director, Dr Judith Neaves

LONDON CATALYST (1873) 45 Westminster Bridge Road, London SE1 7JB **T** 020-3828 4204 **E** london.catalyst@peabody.org.uk **W** www.londoncatalyst.org.uk
Director, Victor Willmott

LONDON COUNCILS (2000) 59½ Southwark Street, London SE1 0AL **T** 020-7934 9999 **E** info@londoncouncils.gov.uk **W** www.londoncouncils.gov.uk
Chief Executive, John O'Brien

LONDON INSTITUTE OF FINANCE AND BANKING (1879) 8th Floor, Peninsular House, London EC3R 8LJ T 01227-818609 E customerservices@libf.ac.uk W www.libf.ac.uk
Chief Executive, Alex Fraser

LONDON LIBRARY (1841) 14 St James's Square, London SW1Y 4LG T 020-7766 4700 E reception@londonlibrary.co.uk W www.londonlibrary.co.uk
Director, Philip Marshall

LONDON PLAYING FIELDS FOUNDATION (1890) 58 Bloomsbury Street, London WC1B 3QT T 020-7323 0331 E enquiries@lpff.org.uk W www.lpff.org.uk
Chief Executive, Alex Welsh

LONDON SOCIETY (1912) Mortimer Wheeler House, 46 Eagle Wharf Road, London N1 7ED T 020-7253 9400 E info@londonsociety.org.uk W www.londonsociety.org.uk
Chair, Peter Murray

LOTTERIES COUNCIL (1979) 66 Lincoln's Inn Fields, London WC2A 3LH T 07954-723224 E frank@lotteriescouncil.org.uk W www.lotteriescouncil.org.uk
Chair, Tony Vick

LULLABY TRUST (1971) 11 Belgrave Road, London SW1V 1RB T 020-7802 3200 E office@lullabytrust.org.uk W www.lullabytrust.co.uk
Chief Executive, Francine Bates

MACMILLAN CANCER SUPPORT (1911) 89 Albert Embankment, London SE1 7UQ T 020-7840 7840 W www.macmillan.org.uk
Chief Executive, Lynda Thomas

MAIL USERS' ASSOCIATION 70 Main Road, Emsworth PO10 8AX T 01243-370840 E jeremy.partridge@mailusers.co.uk W www.mailusers.co.uk
Chair, Ian Paterson

MAKING MUSIC, THE NATIONAL FEDERATION OF MUSIC SOCIETIES (1935) 8 Holyrood Street, London SE1 2EL T 020-7939 6030 W www.makingmusic.org.uk
Chief Executive, Barbara Eifler

MARIE CURIE CANCER CARE (1948) 89 Albert Embankment, SE1 7TP T 0800-716146 E supporter.relations@mariecurie.org.uk W www.mariecurie.org.uk
Chief Executive, Dr Jane Collins

MARINE BIOLOGICAL ASSOCIATION OF THE UK (1884) The Laboratory, Citadel Hill, Plymouth PL1 2BP T 01752-426493 E sec@mba.ac.uk W www.mba.ac.uk
President, Prof. Sir John Beddington, CMG FRS

MARINE SOCIETY AND SEA CADETS (1756) 202 Lambeth Road, London SE1 7JW T 020-7654 7000 E info@ms-sc.org W www.ms-sc.org
Chief Executive, Martin Coles

MASONIC CHARITABLE FOUNDATION (1982) 60 Great Queen Street, London WC2B 5AZ T 020-3146 3333 E info@mcf.org.uk W www.mcf.org.uk
Chief Executive, David Innes

MATERNITY ACTION (2008) 52–54 Featherstone Street, London EC1Y 8RT T 020-7253 2288 W www.maternityaction.org.uk
Director, Ros Bragg

MATHEMATICAL ASSOCIATION (1871) 259 London Road, Leicester LE2 3BE T 0116-221 0013 E office@m-a.org.uk W www.m-a.org.uk
President, Prof. Mike Askew

ME ASSOCIATION (1976) 7 Apollo Office Court, Radclive Road, Gawcott MK18 4DF T 0844-576 5326 E meconnect@meassociation.org.uk W www.meassociation.org.uk
Chair, Neil Riley

MEDIAWATCH-UK (1965) 3 Willow House, Kennington Road, Ashford TN24 0NR T 01233-633936 E info@mediawatchuk.org W www.mediawatchuk.org
Director, Vivienne Pattison

MEDICAL SOCIETY OF LONDON (1773) Lettsom House, 11 Chandos Street, London W1G 9EB T 020-7580 1043 E info@medsoclondon.org W www.medsoclondon.org
Registrar, Cdr Mike Flynn, FCMI MCPID

MEDICAL WOMEN'S FEDERATION (1917) Tavistock House North, Tavistock Square, London WC1H 9HX T 020-7387 7765 E admin@medicalwomensfederation.org.uk W www.medicalwomensfederation.org.uk
President, Dr Henrietta Bowden-Jones

MENCAP (ROYAL MENCAP SOCIETY) (1946) 123 Golden Lane, EC1Y 0RT T 020-7454 0454 E helpline@mencap.org.uk W www.mencap.org.uk
Chief Executive, Jan Tregelles

MENTAL HEALTH FOUNDATION (1972) Colechurch House, 1 London Bridge Walk, London SE1 2SX T 020-7803 1100 W www.mentalhealth.org.uk
Chief Executive, vacant

MERCHANT NAVY WELFARE BOARD (1948) 8 Cumberland Place, Southampton SO15 2DI I T 023-8033 7799 E enquiries@mnwb.org.uk W www.mnwb.org
Chief Executive, Peter Tomlin, MBE

MHA (1943) Epworth House, 3 Stuart Street, Derby DE1 2EQ T 01332-296200 E enquiries@mha.org.uk W www.mha.org.uk
Chief Executive, Sam Monaghan

MIGRAINE ACTION (1958) 27 East Street, Leicester LE1 6NB T 0845-601 1033 E info@migraine.org.uk W www.migraine.org.uk
Chief Executive, Simon Evans

MILITARY HISTORICAL SOCIETY (1948) 38 Hawthorn Way, Shipston on Stour CV36 4FD T 01252-621056 E flers99@yahoo.com W www.themilitaryhistoricalsociety.co.uk
Chair, Clive Elderton, CBE

MIND (NATIONAL ASSOCIATION FOR MENTAL HEALTH) (1946) 15–19 Broadway, London E15 4BQ T 020-8519 2122, **Infoline** 0300-123 3393 E supporterrelations@mind.org.uk W www.mind.org.uk
Chief Executive, Paul Farmer, CBE

MINERALOGICAL SOCIETY (1876) 12 Baylis Mews, Twickenham TW1 3HQ T 020-8891 6600 E info@minersoc.org W www.minersoc.org
Executive Director, Kevin Murphy

MISSING PEOPLE (1993) 284 Upper Richmond Road West, London SW14 7JE T 020-8392 4590 W www.missingpeople.org.uk
Chief Executive, Jo Youle

MISSION TO SEAFARERS (1856) St Michael Paternoster Royal, College Hill, London EC4R 2RL T 020-7248 5202 E info@missiontoseafarers.org W www.missiontoseafarers.org
Secretary General, Revd Andrew Wright

MULTIPLE SCLEROSIS SOCIETY (1953) MS National Centre, 372 Edgware Road, London NW2 6ND T 020-8438 0700 E supportercare@mssociety.org.uk W www.mssociety.org.uk
Chief Executive, vacant

MUSEUMS ASSOCIATION (1889) 42 Clerkenwell Close, London EC1R 0AZ T 020-7566 7800 E info@museumsassociation.org W www.museumsassociation.org
Director, Sharon Heal

NABS (1916) 6th Floor, 388 Oxford Street, London W1C 1JT T 020-7290 7070 W www.nabs.org.uk
Chief Executive, Diana Tickell

NACRO, THE SOCIAL JUSTICE CHARITY (1966) 1st Floor, 46 Loman Street, London SE1 0EH T 0300-123 1889 E helpline@nacro.org.uk W www.nacro.org.uk
Chief Executive, Jacob Tas

NAT (NATIONAL AIDS TRUST) (1987) Aztec House, 397–405 Archway Road, London N6 4EY **T** 020-7814 6767 **E** info@nat.org.uk **W** www.nat.org.uk
Chief Executive, Deborah Gold

NATIONAL BENEVOLENT CHARITY (1812) Peter Hervé House, Eccles Court, Tetbury GL8 8EH **T** 01666-505500 **E** office@thenbc.org.uk **W** www.thenbc.org.uk
Chief Executive, Paul Rossi

NATIONAL CAMPAIGN FOR THE ARTS LTD (1985) c/o Cog Design, 11 Greenwich Centre Business Park, London SE10 9QF **T** 020-8269 1800 **E** hello@forthearts.org.uk **W** forthearts.org.uk
Executive Chair, Michael Smith

NATIONAL CAMPAIGN FOR COURTESY (1986) Walmere, Wrigglebrook Lane, Kingsthorne HR2 8AW **T** 020-3633 4650 **E** courtesy@campaignforcourtesy.org.uk **W** www.campaignforcourtesy.org.uk
Chair, John Stokes

NATIONAL CHILDBIRTH TRUST (1956) 30 Euston Square, London NW1 2FB **T** 0300-330 0770 **E** enquiries@nct.org.uk **W** www.nct.org.uk
Chief Executive, Nick Wilkie

NATIONAL COUNCIL OF WOMEN GREAT BRITAIN (1895) 81 Bondgate, Darlington DL3 7JT **T** 01325-367375 **E** info@ncwgb.org **W** www.ncwgb.org
President, Dr Andrena Telford

NATIONAL EXTENSION COLLEGE (1963) Michael Young Centre, School House, Cambridge CB2 8EB **T** 0800-389 2839 **E** info@nec.ac.uk **W** www.nec.ac.uk
Chief Executive, Dr Ros Morpeth

NATIONAL FAMILY MEDIATION (1981) Civic Centre, Paris Street, Exeter EX1 1JN **T** 0300-400 0636 **E** general@nfm.org.uk **W** www.nfm.org.uk
Chief Executive, Jane Robey

NATIONAL FEDERATION OF WOMEN'S INSTITUTES (1915) 104 New Kings Road, London SW6 4LY **T** 020-7371 9300 **W** www.thewi.org.uk
General Secretary, Jana Osborne

NATIONAL FOUNDATION FOR EDUCATIONAL RESEARCH IN ENGLAND AND WALES (1946) The Mere, Upton Park, Slough SL1 2DQ **T** 01753-574123 **E** enquiries@nfer.ac.uk **W** www.nfer.ac.uk
Chief Executive, Carole Willis

NATIONAL GARDENS SCHEME CHARITABLE TRUST (1927) East Wing, Hatchlands Park, Guildford GU4 7RT **T** 01483-211535 **E** hello@ngs.org.uk **W** www.ngs.org.uk
Chief Executive, George Plumptre

NATIONAL OPERATIC AND DRAMATIC ASSOCIATION (NODA) (1899) 15 The Metro Centre, Peterborough PE2 7UH **T** 01733-374790 **E** info@noda.org.uk **W** www.noda.org.uk
Chief Operating Officer, Dale Freeman

NATIONAL OSTEOPOROSIS SOCIETY (1986) Bath BA2 0PJ **T** 01761-471771, **Helpline** 0808-800 0035 **E** info@nos.org.uk **W** www.nos.org.uk
Chief Executive, Claire Severgnini

NATIONAL SECULAR SOCIETY (1866) 25 Red Lion Square, London WC1R 4RL **T** 020-7404 3126 **E** enquiries@secularism.org.uk **W** www.secularism.org.uk
President, K. P. Wood

NATIONAL TRUST (1895) Heelis, Kemble Drive, Swindon SN2 2NA **T** 0344-800 1895 **E** enquiries@thenationaltrust.org.uk **W** www.nationaltrust.org.uk
Director-General, Hilary McGrady

NATIONAL TRUST FOR SCOTLAND (1931) Hermiston Quay, Edinburgh EH11 4DF **T** 0131-458 0200 **E** information@nts.org.uk **W** www.nts.org.uk
Chief Executive, Simon Skinner

NATIONAL UNION OF STUDENTS (NUS) (1922) Macadam House, 275 Gray's Inn Road, London WC1X 8QB **T** 0845-521 0262 **W** www.nus.org.uk
President, Shakira Martin

NATIONAL WOMEN'S REGISTER (1966) Unit 23, Vulcan House, Norwich NR6 6AQ **T** 01603-406767 **E** office@nwr.org.uk **W** www.nwr.org.uk
Chair of Trustees, Josephine Burt

NEWCOMEN SOCIETY (1920) The Science Museum, London SW7 2DD **T** 020-7371 4445 **E** office@newcomen.com **W** www.newcomen.com
President, Robert Taylor

NHS CONFEDERATION (1997) Floor 15, Portland House, London SW1E 5BH **T** 020-7799 6666 **E** enquiries@nhsconfed.org **W** www.nhsconfed.org
Chief Executive, Niall Dickson, CBE

NOISE ABATEMENT SOCIETY (1959) 44 Grand Parade, Brighton BN2 9QA **T** 01273-823850 **E** info@noise-abatement.org **W** www.noiseabatementsociety.com
Chief Executive, Gloria Elliott

NORFOLK AND NORWICH ARCHAEOLOGICAL SOCIETY (1846) 64 The Close, Norwich NR1 4DH **E** secretary@nnas.info **W** www.nnas.info
Hon. Secretary, Edmund Perry

NORTH OF ENGLAND ZOOLOGICAL SOCIETY (1934) Chester Zoo, Chester CH2 1LH **T** 01244-380280 **E** reception@chesterzoo.co.uk **W** www.chesterzoo.org
Chief Executive Officer, Dr Mark Pilgrim

NSPCC (1884) Weston House, 42 Curtain Road, London EC2A 3NH **T** 0808-800 5000 **E** help@nspcc.org.uk **W** www.nspcc.org.uk
Chief Executive, Peter Wanless

NUCLEAR INSTITUTE (1962) CK International House, 1–6 Yarmouth Place, London W1J 7BU **T** 020-3475 4701 **E** admin@nuclearinst.com **W** www.nuclearinst.com
President, John Clarke

NUFFIELD FOUNDATION (1943) 28 Bedford Square, London WC1B 3JS **T** 020-7631 0566 **E** info@nuffieldfoundation.org **W** www.nuffieldfoundation.org
Director, Timothy Gardam

NUFFIELD TRUST (1940) 59 New Cavendish Street, London W1G 7LP **T** 020-7631 8450 **E** info@nuffieldtrust.org.uk **W** www.nuffieldtrust.org.uk
Chief Executive, Nigel Edwards

NUTRITION SOCIETY (1941) 10 Cambridge Court, 210 Shepherds Bush Road, London W6 7NJ **T** 020-7602 0228 **E** office@nutritionsociety.org **W** www.nutritionsociety.org
Chief Executive, Mark Hollingsworth

OFFICERS' ASSOCIATION (1919) First Floor, Mountbarrow House, London SW1W 9RB **T** 020-7808 4160 **E** info@officersassociation.org.uk **W** www.officersassociation.org.uk
Chief Executive, Lee Holloway

OPEN-AIR MISSION (1853) 4 Harrier Court, Woodside Road, Luton LU1 4DQ **T** 01582-841141 **E** oamission@btinternet.com **W** www.oamission.com
General Secretary, Andy Banton

OPEN SPACES SOCIETY (1865) 25A Bell Street, Henley-on-Thames RG9 2BA **T** 01491-573535 **E** hq@oss.org.uk **W** www.oss.org.uk
General Secretary, Kate Ashbrook

OVERSEAS DEVELOPMENT INSTITUTE (1960) 203 Blackfriars Road, London SE1 8NJ **T** 020-7922 0300 **E** odi@odi.org **W** www.odi.org
Executive Director, Alex Thier

OXFAM GREAT BRITAIN (1942) Oxfam House, John Smith Drive, Oxford OX4 2JY **T** 0300-200 1292 **E** enquiries@oxfam.org.uk **W** www.oxfam.org.uk
Chief Executive, Mark Goldring

OXFORD PRESERVATION TRUST (1927) 10 Turn Again Lane, Oxford OX1 1QL T 01865-242918
E info@oxfordpreservation.org.uk
W www.oxfordpreservation.org.uk
Director, Debbie Dance

OXFORDSHIRE ARCHITECTURAL AND HISTORICAL SOCIETY (1839) 99 Wellington Street, Thame OX9 3BW
E secretary@oahs.org.uk W www.oahs.org.uk
President, Geoffrey Tyack

OXFORD UNIVERSITY SOCIETY (1932) University Alumni Office, Wellington Square, Oxford OX1 2JD T 01865-611610
E enquiries@alumni.ox.ac.uk W www.alumni.ox.ac.uk
Director of Alumni Relations, Christine Fairchild

THE PALAEONTOLOGICAL ASSOCIATION (1957)
Ainsley House, 12 Waddington Street, Durham DH1 4BG
T 0191-386 1482 W www.palass.org
Executive Officer, Dr Jo Hellawell

PARKINSON'S UK (1969) 215 Vauxhall Bridge Road, London SW1V 1EJ T 020-7931 8080 E hello@parkinsons.org.uk
W www.parkinsons.org.uk
Chief Executive, Steve Ford

PARLIAMENTARY AND SCIENTIFIC COMMITTEE (1939) 3 Birdcage Walk, London SW1H 9JJ T 020-7222 7085
E office@scienceinparliament.org.uk
W www.scienceinparliament.org.uk
Executive Secretary, Dr Isabel Spence

PATIENTS ASSOCIATION (1963) PO Box 935, Harrow HA1 3YJ T 020-8423 9111, Helpline 020-8423 8999
E helpline@patients-association.com
W www.patients-association.org.uk
Chief Executive, Rachel Power

PEABODY (1862) 45 Westminster Bridge Road, London SE1 7JB
T 020-7021 4444 E peabody.direct@peabody.org.uk
W www.peabody.org.uk
Chief Executive, Brendan Sarsfield

PEN INTERNATIONAL (1921) Unit A Koops Mill Mews, 162–164 Abbey Street, London SE1 2AN T 020-7405 0338
E info@pen-international.org W www.pen-international.org
Executive Director, Carles Torner

PENSIONS ADVISORY SERVICE (1983) 11 Belgrave Road, London SW1V 1RB T 0800-011 3797
W www.pensionsadvisoryservice.org.uk
Chief Executive, Michelle Cracknell

PERENNIAL (1839) 115–117 Kingston Road, Leatherhead KT22 7SU T 0800-093 8510 E info@perennial.org.uk
W www.perennial.org.uk
Chief Executive, Peter Newman

PHYSIOLOGICAL SOCIETY (1876) Hodgkin Huxley House, 30 Farringdon Lane, London EC1R 3AW T 020-7269 5710
E contactus@physoc.org W www.physoc.org
Chief Executive, Dariel Burdass

PILGRIM TRUST (1930) 23 Lower Belgrave Street, London SW1W 0NR T 020-7834 6510 E info@thepilgrimtrust.org.uk
W www.thepilgrimtrust.org.uk
Director, Georgina Nayler

PLAIN ENGLISH CAMPAIGN (1979) PO Box 3, New Mills, High Peak SK22 4QP T 01663-744409 E info@plainenglish.co.uk
W www.plainenglish.co.uk
Director, Ms C. Maher, OBE

POETRY SOCIETY (1909) 22 Betterton Street, London WC2H 9BX T 020-7420 9880 E info@poetrysociety.org.uk
W www.poetrysociety.org.uk
Director, Judith Palmer

POTENTIAL PLUS UK (1967) Challenge House, Sherwood Drive, Milton Keynes MK3 6DP T 01908-646433
E amazingchildren@potentialplusuk.org
W www.potentialplusuk.org
Chief Executive, Julie Taplin

PRAYER BOOK SOCIETY (1975) The Studio, Copyhold Farm, Reading RG8 7RT T 01189-842582
E pbs.admin@pbs.org.uk W www.pbs.org.uk
Chairman, Prudence Dailey

PRE-SCHOOL LEARNING ALLIANCE (1961) 50 Featherstone Street, London EC1Y 8RT T 020-7697 2500
E info@pre-school.org.uk W www.pre-school.org.uk
Chief Executive, Neil Leitch

PRINCE'S TRUST (1976) 9 Eldon Street, London EC2M 7LS
T 0800-842 842 E webinfops@princes-trust.org.uk
W www.princes-trust.org.uk
Chief Executive, Dame Martina Milburn, DCVO, CBE

PRISONERS ABROAD (1978) 89–93 Fonthill Road, London N4 3JH T 020-7561 6820 E info@prisonersabroad.org.uk
W www.prisonersabroad.org.uk
Chief Executive, Pauline Crowe, OBE

PRIVATE LIBRARIES ASSOCIATION (1956) Ravelston, South View Road, Pinner HA5 3YD E info@plabooks.org
W www.plabooks.org
Hon. Secretary, Jim Maslen

PROFESSIONAL ASSOCIATION FOR CHILDCARE AND EARLY YEARS (1971) Northside House, Third Floor, 69 Tweedy Road, Bromley BR1 3WA T 0300-003 0005
E info@pacey.org.uk W www.pacey.org.uk
Chief Executive, Liz Bayram

PROFESSIONAL PUBLISHERS ASSOCIATION (1970) Second Floor, 35–38 New Bridge Street, London EC4V 6BW
T 020-7404 4166 E info@ppa.org.uk W www.ppa.co.uk
Chief Executive, Barry McIlheney

PROSTATE CANCER UK (1996) Fourth Floor, The Counting House, 53 Tooley Street, London SE1 2QN T 020-3310 7000
E info@prostatecanceruk.org W www.prostatecanceruk.org
Chief Executive, Angela Culhane

PRS FOR MUSIC 2 Pancras Square, London N1C 4AG
T 020-7580 5544 E enquiry@prsformusic.com
W www.prsformusic.com
Chief Executive, Robert Ashcroft

QUAKER PEACE AND SOCIAL WITNESS (2000) Friends House, 173–177 Euston Road, London NW1 2BJ
T 020-7663 1071 E qpsw@quaker.org.uk
W www.quaker.org.uk
General Secretary, Helen Drewery

QUEEN ELIZABETH'S FOUNDATION FOR DISABLED PEOPLE (1934) Leatherhead Court, Woodlands Road, Leatherhead KT22 0BN T 01372-841100 E info@qef.org.uk
W www.qef.org.uk
Chief Executive, Karen Deacon

QUEEN'S NURSING INSTITUTE (1887) 1A Henrietta Place, London W1G 0LZ T 020-7549 1400 E mail@qni.org.uk
W www.qni.org.uk
Chief Executive, Dr Crystal Oldman, CBE

RAILWAY BENEFIT FUND (1858) 1st Floor, Millennium House, Crewe CW2 6AD T 0345-241 2885
E info@railwaybenefitfund.org.uk
W www.railwaybenefitfund.org.uk
Chief Executive, Jason Tetley

RAMBLERS' ASSOCIATION (1935) 2nd Floor, Camelford House, 87–90 Albert Embankment, London SE1 7TW
T 020-7339 8500 E ramblers@ramblers.org.uk
W www.ramblers.org.uk
Chief Executive, Vanessa Griffiths

RARE BREEDS SURVIVAL TRUST (1973) Stoneleigh Park, Nr. Kenilworth CV8 2LG T 024-7669 6551
E enquiries@rbst.org.uk W www.rbst.org.uk
CEO (interim), Nicole Lander

REFUGEE COUNCIL (1951) PO Box 68614, London E15 9DQ
T 020-7346 6700 E info@refugeecouncil.org.uk
W www.refugeecouncil.org.uk
Chief Executive, Maurice Wren

REGIONAL STUDIES ASSOCIATION (1965) Sussex Innovation Centre, Falmer Brighton BN1 9SB **T** 01273-698017 **E** office@regionalstudies.org **W** www.regionalstudies.org
Chief Executive, Sally Hardy

RELATE (1938) Premier House, Carolina Court, Doncaster DN4 5RA **T** 0300-100 1234 **E** relate.enquiries@relate.org.uk **W** www.relate.org.uk
Chief Executive, Chris Sherwood

RETHINK (1972) 89 Albert Embankment, London SE1 7TP **T** 0121-522 7007 **E** info@rethink.org **W** www.rethink.org
Chief Executive, Mark Winstanley

RFEA (REGULAR FORCES EMPLOYMENT ASSOCIATION LTD) (1885) 1st Floor, Mountbarrow House, 12 Elizabeth Street, London SW1W 9RB **T** 0121-236 0058 **E** info@rfea.org.uk **W** www.rfea.org.uk
Chief Executive, Brig. Stephen Gledhill

RICHARD III SOCIETY (1924) 18 Berberis Close, Milton Keynes MK7 7DZ **E** secretary@richardiii.net **W** www.richardiii.net
Chair, Dr P. T. Stone

ROYAL AERONAUTICAL SOCIETY (1866) 4 Hamilton Place, London W1J 7BQ **T** 020-7670 4300
E raes@aerosociety.com **W** www.aerosociety.com
President, Rear Adm. Simon Henley, MBE

ROYAL AGRICULTURAL BENEVOLENT INSTITUTION (1860) Shaw House, 27 West Way, Oxford OX2 0QH **T** 01865-724931 **E** info@rabi.org.uk **W** www.rabi.org.uk
Chief Executive, Paul Burrows

ROYAL AGRICULTURAL SOCIETY OF THE COMMONWEALTH (1957) c/o Royal Norfolk Agricultural Association, Norfolk Showground, Norwich NR5 0TT **T** 01603-731977 **E** info@therasc.com **W** www.therasc.com
Hon. Secretary, Michael Lambert

ROYAL AIR FORCE BENEVOLENT FUND (1919) 67 Portland Place, London W1B 1AR **T** 0800-169 2942 **E** mail@rafbf.org.uk **W** www.rafbf.org
Controller, Air Vice-Marshal Hon. David Murray, CVO, OBE

ROYAL AIR FORCES ASSOCIATION (1943) Atlas House, 41 Wembley Road, Leicester LE3 1UT **T** 0800-018 2361 **E** enquiries@rafa.org.uk **W** www.rafa.org.uk
Secretary General, Nick Bunting

ROYAL ARTILLERY ASSOCIATION (1920) Artillery House, Royal Artillery Barracks, Salisbury SP4 8QT **T** 01980-845233 **E** sarah.davies119@mod.gov.uk **W** www.theraa.co.uk
General Secretary, Lt.-Col. I. A. Vere Nicoll, MBE

ROYAL ASIATIC SOCIETY (1823) 14 Stephenson Way, London NW1 2HD **T** 020-7388 4539
E info@royalasiaticsociety.org **W** www.royalasiaticsociety.org
President, Dr. A. Stockwell

ROYAL ASSOCIATION FOR DEAF PEOPLE (1841) Century House South, Riverside Office Centre, Colchester CO1 1RE **T** 0300-688 2525 **E** info@royaldeaf.org.uk **W** www.royaldeaf.org.uk
Chief Executive, Dr Jan Sheldon

ROYAL ASTRONOMICAL SOCIETY (1820) Burlington House, London W1J 0BQ **T** 020-7734 4582 **W** www.ras.ac.uk
Executive Director, Philip Diamond

ROYAL BRITISH LEGION (1921) 199 Borough High Street, London SE1 1AA **T** 0808-802 8080 **E** info@britishlegion.org.uk **W** www.britishlegion.org.uk
Director-General, Charles Byrne

ROYAL BRITISH LEGION SCOTLAND (1921) New Haig House, Logie Green Road, Edinburgh EH7 4HQ **T** 0131-550 1586 **E** info@legionscotland.org.uk **W** www.legionscotland.org.uk
Chief Executive Officer, Kevin Gray, MM

ROYAL CAMBRIAN ACADEMY (1882) Crown Lane, Conwy LL32 8AN **T** 01492-593413 **E** rca@rcaconwy.org
W www.rcaconwy.org
President, Jeremy Yates

ROYAL CELTIC SOCIETY (1820) 25 Rutland Street, Edinburgh EH1 2RN **T** 0131-228 6449
E info@royalcelticsociety.scot **W** www.royalcelticsociety.scot
Secretary, J. Gordon Cameron, WS

ROYAL COMMISSION FOR THE EXHIBITION OF 1851 (1850) 453 Sherfield Building, Imperial College SW7 2AZ **T** 020-7594 8790 **E** royalcom1851@imperial.ac.uk **W** www.royalcommission1851.org.uk
Secretary, Nigel Williams, CENG

ROYAL GEOGRAPHICAL SOCIETY (WITH THE INSTITUTE OF BRITISH GEOGRAPHERS) (1830) 1 Kensington Gore, SW7 2AR **T** 020-7591 3000 **W** www.rgs.org
Director, Dr Rita Gardner, CBE

ROYAL HIGHLAND AND AGRICULTURAL SOCIETY OF SCOTLAND (1784) Ingliston House, Royal Highland Centre, Edinburgh EH28 8NB **T** 0131-335 6200 **E** info@rhass.org.uk **W** www.rhass.org.uk
Chief Executive, Alan Laidlaw

ROYAL HISTORICAL SOCIETY (1868) University College London, Gower Street, London WC1E 6BT **T** 020-7387 7532 **E** enquiries@royalhistsoc.org **W** www.royalhistoricalsociety.org
Executive Secretary, Dr S. E. Carr

ROYAL HORTICULTURAL SOCIETY (1804) 80 Vincent Square, London SW1P 2PE **T** 020-3176 5800 **W** www.rhs.org.uk
Director-General, Sue Biggs

ROYAL HOSPITAL FOR NEURO-DISABILITY (1854) West Hill, London SW15 3SW **T** 020-8780 4500 **E** info@rhn.org.uk **W** www.rhn.org.uk
Chief Executive, Paul Allen

ROYAL HUMANE SOCIETY (1774) 50–51 Temple Chambers, 3–7 Temple Avenue, London EC4Y 0HP **T** 020-7936 2942 **E** info@royalhumanesociety.org.uk **W** www.royalhumanesociety.org.uk
Secretary, Lt.-Col. Andrew Chapman

ROYAL INSTITUTE OF NAVIGATION (1947) 1 Kensington Gore, SW7 2AT **T** 020-7591 3134 **E** admin@rin.org.uk **W** www.rin.org.uk
Director, J R Pottle, BSC, MBA, FIET

ROYAL INSTITUTE OF OIL PAINTERS (1882) 17 Carlton House Terrace, London SW1Y 5BD **T** 020-7930 6844 **E** enquiries@theroi.org.uk **W** www.theroi.co.uk
President, Tim Benson

ROYAL INSTITUTE OF PAINTERS IN WATER COLOURS (1831) 17 Carlton House Terrace, London SW1Y 5BD **T** 020-7930 6844
W www.royalinstituteofpaintersinwatercolours.org
President, Rosa Sepple

ROYAL INSTITUTE OF PHILOSOPHY (1925) 14 Gordon Square, London WC1H 0AR **T** 020-7387 4130
W www.royalinstitutephilosophy.org
Secretary, Dr James Garvey

ROYAL INSTITUTION OF GREAT BRITAIN (1799) 21 Albemarle Street, London W1S 4BS **T** 020-7409 2992 **E** ri@ri.ac.uk **W** www.rigb.org
Director, Dr Shaun Fitzgerald

ROYAL LIFE SAVING SOCIETY UK (1891) Red Hill House, 227 London Road, Worcester WR5 2JG **T** 0300-323 0096 **E** info@rlss.org.uk **W** www.rlss.org.uk
Chief Executive Officer, Di Steer

ROYAL LITERARY FUND (1790) 3 Johnson's Court, off Fleet Street, London EC4A 3EA **T** 020-7353 7150 **W** www.rlf.org.uk
Chief Executive, Eileen Gunn

ROYAL MEDICAL BENEVOLENT FUND (1836) 24 Kings Road, London SW19 8QN **T** 020-8540 9194 **E** info@rmbf.org **W** www.rmbf.org
Chief Executive, Steve Crone

ROYAL MICROSCOPICAL SOCIETY (1839) 37–38 St Clements, Oxford OX4 1AJ **T** 01865-254760 **E** info@rms.org.uk **W** www.rms.org.uk
Chief Executive, Allison Winton

ROYAL MUSICAL ASSOCIATION (1874) 4 Chandos Road, Chorlton-cum-Hardy M21 0ST T 0161-861 7542
E exec@rma.ac.uk W www.rma.ac.uk
President, Prof. Simon McVeigh

ROYAL NATIONAL COLLEGE FOR THE BLIND (1872) Venns Lane, Hereford HR1 1DT T 01432-265725
E info@rnc.ac.uk W www.rnc.ac.uk
Principal, Mark Fisher

ROYAL NATIONAL INSTITUTE OF BLIND PEOPLE (1868) 105 Judd Street, London WC1H 9NE T 030-3123 9999
E helpline@rnib.org.uk W www.rnib.org.uk
Chief Executive (interim), Eliot Lyne

ROYAL NATIONAL LIFEBOAT INSTITUTION (1824) West Quay Road, Poole BH15 1HZ T 0300-300 9990
W www.rnli.org
Chief Executive, Paul Boissier, CB MA

ROYAL NAVAL ASSOCIATION (1949) Room 209, Royal Semaphore Tower, PP70, HM Naval Base, Portsmouth PO1 3LT
T 023-9272 3747 E admin@royalnavalassoc.com
W www.royal-naval-association.co.uk
Chief Executive, Capt. Paul Quinn, OBE, RN

ROYAL NAVAL BENEVOLENT TRUST (1922) Castaway House, 311 Twyford Avenue, Portsmouth PO2 8RN
T 023-9269 0112 E rnbt@rnbt.org.uk W www.rnbt.org.uk
Chief Executive, Cdr Rob Bosshardt, RN

ROYAL PHILATELIC SOCIETY LONDON (1869) 41 Devonshire Place, London W1G 6JY T 020-7486 1044
E secretary@rpsl.org.uk W www.rpsl.org.uk
President, Patrick Maselis

ROYAL PHILHARMONIC SOCIETY (1813) 48 Great Marlborough Street, London W1F 7BB T 020-7289 0019
E web@royalphilharmonicsociety.org.uk
W www.royalphilharmonicsociety.org.uk
Chief Executive, James Murphy

ROYAL PHOTOGRAPHIC SOCIETY (1853) Fenton House, 122 Wells Road, Bath BA2 3AH T 01225-325733
E reception@rps.org W www.rps.org
Chief Executive, Dr Michael Pritchard

ROYAL SCHOOL OF CHURCH MUSIC (1927) 19 The Close, Salisbury SP1 2EB T 01722-424848 E enquiries@rscm.com
W www.rscm.org.uk
Director, Hugh Morris

ROYAL SCHOOL OF NEEDLEWORK (1872) Apartment 12A, Hampton Court Palace KT8 9AU T 020-3166 6932
E enquiries@royal-needlework.org.uk
W www.royal-needlework.org.uk
Chief Executive, Dr Susan Kay-Williams

ROYAL SOCIETY FOR ASIAN AFFAIRS (1901) 1a St Martin's House, Polygon Road, London NW1 1QB
T 020-7235 5122 E info@rsaa.org.uk W www.rsaa.org.uk
Chair, Frank Slevin

ROYAL SOCIETY FOR BLIND CHILDREN (1838) 52–58 Arcola Street, London E8 2DJ T 020-3198 0225
E enquiries@rsbc.org.uk W www.rsbc.org.uk
Chief Executive, Dr Tom Pey

ROYAL SOCIETY FOR THE ENCOURAGEMENT OF ARTS, MANUFACTURES AND COMMERCE (RSA) (1754) 8 John Adam Street, London WC2N 6EZ
T 020-7930 5115 E general@rsa.org.uk W www.thersa.org
Chief Executive, Matthew Taylor

THE ROYAL SOCIETY FOR THE PREVENTION OF ACCIDENTS (1916/17) 28 Calthorpe Road, Birmingham B15 1RP T 0121-248 2000 E help@rospa.com
W www.rospa.com
Chief Executive, Errol Taylor

ROYAL SOCIETY FOR THE PREVENTION OF CRUELTY TO ANIMALS (1824) Wilberforce Way, Horsham RH13 9RS T 0300-123 0346 W www.rspca.org.uk
Chief Executive, Chris Sherwood

ROYAL SOCIETY FOR THE PROTECTION OF BIRDS (1889) The Lodge, Potton Road, Sandy SG19 2DL
T 01767-680551 W www.rspb.org.uk
Chief Executive, Mike Clarke

ROYAL SOCIETY OF BIOLOGY (2009) Charles Darwin House, 12 Roger Street, London WC1N 2JU T 020-7685 2400
E info@rsb.org.uk W www.rsb.org.uk
Chief Executive, Dr Mark Downs

ROYAL SOCIETY OF CHEMISTRY (1841) Burlington House, London W1J 0BA T 020-7437 8656 W www.rsc.org
Chief Executive, Dr Robert Parker

ROYAL SOCIETY OF LITERATURE (1820) Somerset House, London WC2R 1LA T 020-7845 4679
E info@rsliterature.org W www.rsliterature.org
President, Dame Marina Warner, DBE, FRSL

ROYAL SOCIETY OF MARINE ARTISTS (1939) 17 Carlton House Terrace, London SW1Y 5BD T 020-7930 6844
E rsma.contact@gmail.com W www.rsma-web.co.uk
President, Elizabeth Smith

ROYAL SOCIETY OF MEDICINE (1805) 1 Wimpole Street, London W1G 0AE T 020-7290 2900 E membership@rsm.ac.uk
W www.rsm.ac.uk
Chief Executive (acting), Nigel Collett

ROYAL SOCIETY OF MINIATURE PAINTERS, SCULPTORS AND GRAVERS (1895) 89 Roseberry Road, Dursley GL11 4PU T 01454-269268
W www.royal-miniature-society.org.uk
President, Rosalind Pierson

THE ROYAL SOCIETY OF MUSICIANS OF GREAT BRITAIN (1738) 26 Fitzroy Square, London W1T 6BT
T 020-7629 6137 E enquiries@royalsocietyofmusicians.org
W www.royalsocietyofmusicians.org
President, Judith Weir, CBE

ROYAL SOCIETY OF PAINTER-PRINTMAKERS (1880) Bankside Gallery, 48 Hopton Street, SE1 9JH T 020-7928 7521
E info@banksidegallery.com W www.re-printmakers.co.uk
President, Mychael Barratt

ROYAL SOCIETY OF PORTRAIT PAINTERS (1891) 17 Carlton House Terrace, London SW1Y 5BD T 020-7930 6844
E enquiries@therp.co.uk W www.therp.co.uk
President, Richard Foster

ROYAL SOCIETY OF ST GEORGE (1894) PO Box 397, Loughton IG10 1LA T 020-3225 5011 E info@rssg.org.uk
W http://rssg.org.uk
Chairman, Joanna M. Cadman

ROYAL SOCIETY OF TROPICAL MEDICINE AND HYGIENE (1907) Northumberland House, 303–306 High Holborn, London WC1V 7JZ T 020-7405 2628 E info@rstmh.org
W www.rstmh.org
Chief Executive, Tamar Ghosh

ROYAL STAR AND GARTER HOMES (1916) 15 Castle Mews, Hampton TW12 2NP T 020-8481 7676
E general.enquiries@starandgarter.org
W www.starandgarter.org
Chief Executive, Andy Cole, OBE

ROYAL THEATRICAL FUND (1839) 11 Garrick Street, London WC2E 9AR T 020-7836 3322 E admin@trtf.com
W www.trtf.com
President, Robert Lindsay

ROYAL UNITED SERVICES INSTITUTE FOR DEFENCE AND SECURITY STUDIES (1831) Whitehall, London SW1A 2ET T 020-7747 2600 W www.rusi.org
Director-General, Dr Karin von Hippel

ROYAL VOLUNTARY SERVICE (1938) Beck Court, Cardiff Gate Business Park, Cardiff CF23 8RP T 0845-608 0122
W www.royalvoluntaryservice.org.uk
Chief Executive, Catherine Johnstone, CBE

ROYAL WATERCOLOUR SOCIETY (1804) Bankside Gallery, 48 Hopton Street, London SE1 9JH T 020-7928 7521
E info@banksidegallery.com
W www.royalwatercoloursociety.co.uk
President, Jill Leman

ROYAL ZOOLOGICAL SOCIETY OF SCOTLAND (1909) Edinburgh Zoo, 134 Corstorphine Road, Edinburgh EH12 6TS **T** 0131-334 9171 **E** info@rzss.org.uk **W** www.edinburghzoo.org.uk *Chief Executive*, Barbara Smith

ST JOHN AMBULANCE (1877) St John's Gate, 27 St John's Lane, London EC1M 4BU **T** 0870-010 4950 **W** www.sja.org.uk *Chief Executive*, Martin Houghton-Brown

SALTIRE SOCIETY (1936) 9 Fountain Close, 22 High Street, Edinburgh EH1 1TF **T** 0131-556 1836 **E** saltire@saltiresociety.org.uk **W** www.saltiresociety.org.uk *Convener*, Prof Alan Riach

SAMARITANS (1953) The Upper Mill, Ewell KT17 2AF **T** 020-8394 8300, **Helpline** 116 123 **E** admin@samaritans.org **W** www.samaritans.org *Chief Executive*, Ruth Sutherland

SANE (1986) St Mark's Studios, 14 Chillingworth Street, London N7 8QJ **T** 020-3805 1790, **Helpline** 0300-304 7000 **E** info@sane.org.uk **W** www.sane.org.uk *Chief Executive*, Ms M. Wallace, CBE

SAVE BRITAIN'S HERITAGE (1975) 70 Cowcross Street, London EC1M 6EJ **T** 020-7253 3500 **E** office@savebritainsheritage.org **W** www.savebritainsheritage.org *President*, Marcus Binney, CBE

SAVE THE CHILDREN (1919) 1 St John's Lane, London EC1M 4AR **T** 020-7012 6400 **E** supportercare@savethechildren.org.uk **W** www.savethechildren.org.uk *Chief Executive*, Kevin Watkins

SCHOOL LIBRARY ASSOCIATION (1937) 1 Pine Court, Swindon SN2 8AD **T** 01793-530166 **E** info@sla.org.uk **W** www.sla.org.uk *Director*, Alison Tarrant

SCOPE (1952) Here East Press Centre, 14 East Bay Lane, London E15 2GW **T** 020-7619 7100, **Helpline** 0808-800 3333 **E** supportercare@scope.org.uk **W** www.scope.org.uk *Chief Executive*, Mark Atkinson

SCOTTISH ASSOCIATION FOR MARINE SCIENCE (1884) Scottish Marine Institute, Argyll PA37 1QA **T** 01631-559000 **E** info@sams.ac.uk **W** www.sams.ac.uk *Director*, Prof. Nicholas Owens

SCOTTISH ASSOCIATION FOR MENTAL HEALTH (1923) Brunswick House, 51 Wilson Street, Glasgow G1 1UZ **T** 0141-530 1000 **E** enquire@samh.org.uk **W** www.samh.org.uk *Chief Executive*, Billy Watson

SCOTTISH CHAMBERS OF COMMERCE (1948) Strathclyde Business School, 199 Cathedral Street, Glasgow G4 0QU **T** 0141-444 7500 **E** admin@scottishchambers.org.uk **W** www.scottishchambers.org.uk *Chief Executive*, Liz Cameron, OBE

SCOTTISH COUNCIL FOR VOLUNTARY ORGANISATIONS (1943) Mansfield Traquair Centre, 15 Mansfield Place, Edinburgh EH3 6BB **T** 0131-474 8000 **E** enquiries@scvo.org.uk **W** www.scvo.org.uk *Chief Executive*, Anna Fowlie

SCOTTISH LAND AND ESTATES (1906) Stuart House, Eskmills Business Park, Musselburgh EH21 7PB **T** 0131-653 5400 **E** info@scottishlandandestates.co.uk **W** www.scottishlandandestates.co.uk *Chief Executive*, Sarah-Jane Laing

SCOTTISH SOCIETY FOR THE PREVENTION OF CRUELTY TO ANIMALS (1839) Kingseat Road, Dunfermline KY11 8RY **T** 03000-999 999 **E** info@scottishspca.org **W** www.scottishspca.org *Chief Executive*, Kirsteen Campbell

SCOTTISH WILDLIFE TRUST (1964) Harbourside House, 110 Commercial Street, Edinburgh EH6 6NF **T** 0131-312 7765 **E** enquiries@scottishwildlifetrust.org.uk **W** www.scottishwildlifetrust.org.uk *Chief Executive*, Jonathan Hughes

SCOUT ASSOCIATION (1907) Gilwell Park, Chingford, London E4 7QW **T** 0345-300 1818 **E** info.centre@scouts.org.uk **W** www.scouts.org.uk *Chief Executive*, Matt Hyde

SEEABILITY (1799) Newplan House, 41 East Street, Epsom KT17 1BL **T** 01372-755000 **E** enquiries@seeability.org **W** www.seeability.org *Chief Executive*, Lisa Hopkins

SELDEN SOCIETY (1887) School of Law, Queen Mary, London E1 4NS **T** 020-7882 3968 **E** selden-society@qmul.ac.uk **W** www.selden-society.qmul.ac.uk *Secretary*, Victor Tunkel

SENSE (1955) 101 Pentonville Road, N1 9LG **T** 0300-330 9256 **E** info@sense.org.uk **W** www.sense.org.uk *Chief Executive*, Richard Kramer

SHELTER (NATIONAL CAMPAIGN FOR HOMELESS PEOPLE) (1966) 88 Old Street, London EC1V 9HU **T** 0300-330 1234, **Helpline** 0808-800 4444 **E** info@shelter.org.uk **W** www.shelter.org.uk *Chief Executive*, Polly Neate

SIGHTSAVERS (ROYAL COMMONWEALTH SOCIETY FOR THE BLIND) (1950) Bumpers Way, Bumpers Farm, Chippenham SN14 6NG **T** 01444-446600 **E** info@sightsavers.org **W** www.sightsavers.org *Chief Executive*, Dr Caroline Harper, CBE

SOCIÉTÉ JERSIAISE (1873) 7 Pier Road, St Helier JE2 4XW **T** 01534-758314 **E** info@societe-jersiaise.org **W** www.societe-jersiaise.org *Administrative Secretary*, Ms C. Cornick

SOCIETY FOR PROMOTING CHRISTIAN KNOWLEDGE (SPCK) (1698) 36 Causton Street, London SW1P 4ST **T** 020-7592 3900 **E** spck@spck.org.uk **W** www.spck.org.uk *CEO*, Sam Richardson

SOCIETY FOR THE PROMOTION OF HELLENIC STUDIES (1879) Senate House, Malet Street, WC1E 7HU **T** 020-7862 8730 **E** secretary@hellenicsociety.org.uk **W** www.hellenicsociety.org.uk *President*, Prof. Judith Mossman

SOCIETY FOR THE PROMOTION OF ROMAN STUDIES (1910) Senate House, Malet Street, London WC1E 7HU **T** 020-7862 8727 **E** office@romansociety.org **W** www.romansociety.org *Secretary*, Dr Fiona Haarer

SOCIETY FOR THE PROTECTION OF UNBORN CHILDREN (1967) 3 Whitacre Mews, London SE11 4AB **T** 020-7091 7091 **E** information@spuc.org.uk **W** www.spuc.org.uk *Chief Executive*, John Smeaton

SOCIETY OF ANTIQUARIES OF LONDON (1707) Burlington House, London W1J 0BE **T** 020-7479 7080 **E** admin@sal.org.uk **W** www.sal.org.uk *General-Secretary*, John S. C. Lewis, FSA

SOCIETY OF ANTIQUARIES OF NEWCASTLE UPON TYNE (1813) Great North Museum: Hancock, Barras Bridge, Newcastle upon Tyne NE2 4PT **T** 0191-231 2700 **E** admin@newcastle-antiquaries.org.uk **W** www.newcastle-antiquaries.org.uk *President*, Richard Pears

SOCIETY OF ANTIQUARIES OF SCOTLAND (1780) National Museums Scotland, Chambers Street, Edinburgh EH1 1JF **T** 0131-247 4133 **E** info@socantscot.org **W** www.socantscot.org *Director*, Dr Simon Gilmour, FSA, FSA SCOT, MIFA

SOCIETY OF BOTANICAL ARTISTS (1985) 1 Knapp Cottages, Gillingham SP8 4NQ **T** 01747-825718 **E** info@soc-botanical-artists.org **W** www.soc-botanical-artists.org *Executive Secretary*, Pam Henderson

SOCIETY OF EDITORS (1999) University Centre, Granta Place, Cambridge CB2 1RU T 01223-304080 E office@societyofeditors.org W www.societyofeditors.org
Executive Director, Ian Murray

SOCIETY OF GENEALOGISTS (1911) 14 Charterhouse Buildings, Goswell Road, London EC1M 7BA T 020-7251 8799 E genealogy@sog.org.uk W www.sog.org.uk
Chief Executive, June Perrin

SOCIETY OF GLASS TECHNOLOGY (1917) 9 Churchill Way, Sheffield S35 2PY T 0114-263 4455 E info@sgt.org W www.sgt.org
Managing Editor, David Moore

SOCIETY OF INDEXERS (1957) Woodbourn Business Centre, 10 Jessell Street, Sheffield S9 3HY T 0114-244 9561 E admin@indexers.org.uk W www.indexers.org.uk
Chair, Ann Kingdom

SOCIETY OF LEGAL SCHOLARS (1908) School of Law, Southampton University, Southampton SO17 1BJ T 023-8059 4039 E admin@legalscholars.ac.uk W www.legalscholars.ac.uk
Hon. Secretary, Prof. Paula Giliker

SOCIETY OF SCRIBES AND ILLUMINATORS (1921) Art Workers Guild, 6 Queen Square, London WC1N 3AT E honsec@calligraphyonline.org W www.calligraphyonline.org
Chair, Julie Chaney

SOCIETY OF SOLICITORS IN THE SUPREME COURT OF SCOTLAND (1784) SSC Library, Parliament House, Edinburgh EH1 1RF T 0131-225 6268 E enquiries@ssclibrary.co.uk W www.ssclibrary.co.uk
Secretary, Robert Shiels

SOCIETY OF WOMEN ARTISTS (1855) Foxcote Cottage, Foxcote, Cheltenham GL54 4LP T 07528-477002 E rebeccacottonswa@gmail.com W www.society-women-artists.org.uk
Executive Secretary, Rebecca Cotton

SOCIETY OF WRITERS TO HM SIGNET (1594) The Signet Library, Parliament Square, Edinburgh EH1 1RF T 0131-220 3249 E reception@wssociety.co.uk W www.wssociety.co.uk
Chief Executive, Robert Pirrie

SOIL ASSOCIATION (1946) Spear House, 51 Victoria Street, Bristol BS1 6AD T 0300-330 0100 W www.soilassociation.org
Chief Executive, Helen Browning, OBE

SOMERSET ARCHAEOLOGICAL AND NATURAL HISTORY SOCIETY (1849) Somerset Heritage Centre, Brunel Way, Taunton TA2 6SF T 01823-272429 E office@sanhs.org W www.sanhs.org
Chair, Christine Jessop

SOUND AND MUSIC (1967) 3rd Floor, South Wing, Somerset House, London WC2R 1LA T 020-7759 1800 E info@soundandmusic.org W www.soundandmusic.org
Chief Executive, Susanna Eastburn

SPURGEONS (1867) 74 Wellingborough Road, Rushden NN10 9TY T 01933-412412 E info@spurgeons.org W www.spurgeons.org
Chief Executive, Ross Hendry

STANDING COUNCIL OF THE BARONETAGE (1903) 1 Tarrel Farm Cottages, Tain IV20 1SL T 01862-870177 E secretary@baronetage.org W www.baronetage.org
Chair, Sir Nicholas Thompson, BT.

STOLL (SIR OSWALD STOLL FOUNDATION) (1916) 446 Fulham Road, London SW6 1DT T 020-7385 2110 E info@stoll.org.uk W www.stoll.org.uk
Chief Executive, Ed Tytherleigh

STRATEGIC PLANNING SOCIETY (1967) New Bond House, 124 New Bond Street, London W1S 1DX T 0845-056 3663 E members@sps.org.uk W www.sps.org.uk
Chair, Chris Hafner

SUFFOLK INSTITUTE OF ARCHAEOLOGY AND HISTORY (1848) 116 Hardwick Lane, IP33 2LE T 01284-753228 E generalsecretary@suffolkinstitute.org.uk W www.suffolkinstitute.org.uk
Hon. Secretary, Jane Carr

SURREY ARCHAEOLOGICAL SOCIETY (1854) Castle Arch, Guildford GU1 3SX T 01483-532454 E info@surreyarchaeology.org.uk W www.surreyarchaeology.org.uk
Hon. Secretary, David Calow

SUSSEX ARCHAEOLOGICAL SOCIETY (1846) Bull House, 92 High Street, Lewes BN7 1XH T 01273-486260 E adminlewes@sussexpast.co.uk W www.sussexpast.co.uk
Chief Executive, Tristan Bareham

SUSTRANS (1977) Head Office, 2 Cathedral Square, Bristol BS1 5DD T 0117 926 8893 E reception@sustrans.org.uk W www.sustrans.org.uk
Chief Executive, Xavier Brice

SUZY LAMPLUGH TRUST (1986) 17 Oval Way, London SE11 5RR T 020-7091 0014 E info@suzylamplugh.org W www.suzylamplugh.org
Chief Executive, Rachel Griffin

SWEDENBORG SOCIETY (1810) 20–21 Bloomsbury Way, London WC1A 2TH T 020-7405 7986 E admin@swedenborg.org.uk W www.swedenborg.org.uk
Executive Director, Stephen McNeilly

TAVISTOCK INSTITUTE (1947) 30 Tabernacle Street, London EC2A 4UE T 020-7417 0407 E hello@tavinstitute.org W www.tavinstitute.org
Chief Executive, Dr Eliat Aram

TERRENCE HIGGINS TRUST (1982) 314–320 Gray's Inn Road, London WC1X 8DP T 020-7812 1600 E info@tht.org.uk W www.tht.org.uk
Chief Executive, Ian Green

THEATRES TRUST (1976) 22 Charing Cross Road, London WC2H 0QL T 020-7836 8591 E info@theatrestrust.org.uk W www.theatrestrust.org.uk
Director, Jon Morgan

THORESBY SOCIETY (1889) The Leeds Library, 18 Commercial Street, Leeds LS1 6AL E secretary@thoresby.org.uk W www.thoresby.org.uk
President, Prof. J. Chartres

TOGETHER FOR MENTAL WELLBEING (1879) 52 Walnut Tree Walk, London SE11 6DN T 020-7780 7300 E contact-us@together-uk.org W www.together-uk.org
Chief Executive, Linda Bryant

TOWN AND COUNTRY PLANNING ASSOCIATION (1899) 17 Carlton House Terrace, London SW1Y 5AS T 020-7930 8903 E tcpa@tcpa.org.uk W www.tcpa.org.uk
Chief Executive, Kate Henderson

TOWNSWOMEN'S GUILDS Gee Business Centre, First Floor, Gee House, Birmingham B7 5JR T 0121-326 0400 E contact@the-tg.com W www.the-tg.com
National Chairman, Jenny Rideout

TREE COUNCIL (1974) 4 Docks Offices, Surrey Quays Road, London SE16 2XU T 020-7407 9992 E info@treecouncil.org.uk W www.treecouncil.org.uk
Chief Executive, Sarah Lom

TURN2US (1897) Hythe House, 200 Shepherds Bush Road, London W6 7NL T 020-8834 9200 W www.turn2us.org.uk
Chair, Sally O'Sullivan

UK YOUTH (1911) 483–485 Liverpool Road, London N7 8PG T 0203-137 3810 E info@ukyouth.org W www.ukyouth.org
Chief Executive (interim), Allan Carr

UNDERSTANDING ANIMAL RESEARCH (2008) Abbey House, 74–76 St John Street, London EC1M 4DZ E office@uar.org.uk W www.uar.org.uk
Chief Executive, Wendy Jarrett

UNITED GRAND LODGE OF ENGLAND (1717) Freemasons' Hall, 60 Great Queen Street, London WC2B 5AZ T 020-7831 9811 E enquiries@ugle.org.uk W www.ugle.org.uk
Grand Master, HRH the Duke of Kent, KG, GCMG, GCVO

UNITED KINGDOM RESERVE FORCES ASSOCIATION (1972) Holderness House, 51–61 Clifton Street, London EC2A 4EY T 020-7426 8358 E co-rfa@rfca.mod.uk W www.gov.uk/government/organisations/united-kingdom-reserve-forces-association
President, Maj. Gen. G. S. Smith, CB, TD, QVRM

UNITED NATIONS ASSOCIATION - UK (1945) 3 Whitehall Court, London SW1A 2EL T 020-7766 3454 E info@una.org.uk W www.una.org.uk
Executive Director, Natalie Samarasinghe

UNITED REFORMED CHURCH HISTORY SOCIETY (1972) Westminster College, Madingley Road, Cambridge CB3 0AA T 01223-330620 E mt212@cam.ac.uk W www.westminster.cam.ac.uk/rcl/about/urc-history-society
Hon. Secretary, Mrs M. Thompson

UNIVERSITIES FEDERATION FOR ANIMAL WELFARE (1926) The Old School, Brewhouse Hill, Wheathampstead AL4 8AN T 01582-831818 E ufaw@ufaw.org.uk W www.ufaw.org.uk
Chief Executive & Scientific Director, Dr R. C. Hubrecht

UNIVERSITIES UK (2000) Woburn House, 20 Tavistock Square, London WC1H 9HQ T 020-7419 4111 E info@universitiesuk.ac.uk W www.universitiesuk.ac.uk
Chief Executive, Alistair Jarvis

VEGAN SOCIETY (1944) Donald Watson House, 34–35 Ludgate Hill, Birmingham B3 1EH T 0121-523 1730 E info@vegansociety.com W www.vegansociety.com
Chief Executive, George Gill

VEGETARIAN SOCIETY OF THE UNITED KINGDOM LTD (1847) Parkdale, Dunham Road, Cheshire WA14 4QG T 0161-925 2000 E info@vegsoc.org W www.vegsoc.org
Chief Executive, Lynne Elliot

VERNACULAR ARCHITECTURE GROUP (1952) Kangaroo House, Colby, Appleby-in-Westmorland CA16 6BD E secretary@vag.org.uk W www.vag.org.uk
President, Dr Adam Menuge

VICTIM SUPPORT (1979) Hallam House, 56–60 Hallam Street, London W1W 6JL T 020-7268 0200, **Helpline** 0808-1689 111 W www.victimsupport.org.uk
Chief Officer, Diana Fawcett

VICTIM SUPPORT SCOTLAND (1985) 15–23 Hardwell Close, Edinburgh EH8 9RX T 0131-668 4486 E info@victimsupportsco.org.uk W www.victimsupportsco.org.uk
Chief Executive, Kate Wallace

VICTORIA CROSS AND GEORGE CROSS ASSOCIATION (1956) Horse Guards, Whitehall, London SW1A 2AX T 020-7930 3506 E secretary@vcandgc.org W vcgca.org
Secretary, Rebecca Maciejewska

VICTORIAN SOCIETY (1958) 1 Priory Gardens, Bedford Park, London W4 1TT T 020-8994 1019 E admin@victoriansociety.org.uk W www.victoriansociety.org.uk
Director, Christopher Costelloe

VOLUNTEERING MATTERS (1962) The Levy Centre, 18–24 Lower Clapton Road, London E5 0PD T 020-3780 5870 W www.volunteeringmatters.org.uk
Chief Executive, Oonagh Aitken

VSO (VOLUNTARY SERVICE OVERSEAS) (1958) 100 London Road, Kingston-Upon-Thames KT2 6QJ T 020-8780 7500 E enquiry@vso.org W www.vsointernational.org
Chief Executive, Dr Philip Goodwin

WAR WIDOWS ASSOCIATION OF GREAT BRITAIN (1971) 199 Borough High Street, SE1 1AA T 0845-241 2189 E info@warwidows.org.uk W www.warwidows.org.uk
Chairman, Mary Moreland

WELLBEING OF WOMEN (1965) First Floor, Fairgate House, 78 New Oxford Street, WC1A 1HB T 020-3697 7000 E hello@wellbeingofwomen.org.uk W www.wellbeingofwomen.org.uk
Chief Executive, Tina Weaver

WESTMINSTER FOUNDATION FOR DEMOCRACY (1992) Artillery House, 11 –19 Artillery Row, London SW1P 1RT T 020-7799 1311 W www.wfd.org
Chief Executive, Anthony Smith, CMG

WHICH? (1957) 2 Marylebone Road, London NW1 4DF T 020-7770 7000 W www.which.co.uk
Chair, Tim Gardam

WILDFOWL AND WETLANDS TRUST (1946) Slimbridge GL2 7BT T 01453-891900 E enquiries@wwt.org.uk W www.wwt.org.uk
Chief Executive, Martin Spray, CBE

WILLIAM MORRIS SOCIETY AND KELMSCOTT FELLOWSHIP (1955) Kelmscott House, 26 Upper Mall, London W6 9TA T 020-8741 3735 E info@williammorrissociety.org.uk W www.williammorrissociety.org.uk
Hon. Secretary, Natalia Martynenko-Hunt

WILTSHIRE ARCHAEOLOGICAL AND NATURAL HISTORY SOCIETY (1853) Wiltshire Heritage Museum, 41 Long Street, Devizes SN10 1NS T 01380-727369 E hello@wiltshiremuseum.org.uk W www.wiltshiremuseum.org.uk/society
Director, David Dawson

WOMEN'S ENGINEERING SOCIETY (1919) c/o The IET, Michael Faraday House, Stevenage SG1 2AY T 01438-765506 E info@wes.org.uk W www.wes.org.uk
Chief Executive, Kirsten Bodley

WOMEN'S ROYAL NAVAL SERVICE BENEVOLENT TRUST (1941) Castaway House, 311 Twyford Avenue, Portsmouth PO2 8RN T 023-9265 5301 E generalsecretary@wrnsbt.org.uk W www.wrnsbt.org.uk
General Secretary, Sarah Ayton

WOODLAND TRUST (1972) Kempton Way, Grantham NG31 6LL T 0330-333 3300 W www.woodlandtrust.org.uk
Chief Executive, Beccy Speight

WORKING FAMILIES (2003) Spaces, City Point, London EC2Y 9HT T 020-7153 1230 E office@workingfamilies.org.uk W www.workingfamilies.org.uk
Chief Executive, Jane van Zyl

YMCA (1844) 10–11 Charterhouse Square, London EC1M 6EH T 020-7186 9500 E enquiries@ymca.org.uk W www.ymca.org.uk
Chief Executive, Denise Hatton

YORKSHIRE ARCHAEOLOGICAL AND HISTORICAL SOCIETY (1863) Stringer House, 34 Lupton Street, Leeds LS10 2QW T 0113-245 7910 E yahs.office@gmail.com W www.yahs.org.uk
Hon. General Secretary, David Buck, MA, MBA, MRES, PHD

YOUNG WOMEN'S TRUST (1855) Unit D, 15–18 White Lion Street, London N1 9PD T 020-7837 2019 W www.youngwomenstrust.org
Chief Executive, Dr Carole Easton, OBE

YOUTH HOSTELS ASSOCIATION (ENGLAND & WALES) (1930) Trevelyan House, Dimple Road, Matlock DE4 3YH T 01629-592700 E customerservices@yha.org.uk W www.yha.org.uk
Chief Executive, James Blake

ZOOLOGICAL SOCIETY OF LONDON (1826) Outer Circle, Regent's Park, London NW1 4RY T 0344-225 1826 E generalenquiries@zsl.org W www.zsl.org
Director-General, Dominic Jermey, CVO, OBE

THE WORLD

THE WORLD IN FIGURES

THE EARTH

The shape of the Earth is that of an oblate spheroid or solid of revolution whose meridian sections are ellipses, while the sections at right angles are circles.

DIMENSIONS
Equatorial diameter = 12,742.01km (7,917.51 miles)
Polar diameter = 12,713.50km (7,899.80 miles)
Equatorial circumference = 40,030.20km (24,873.6 miles)
Polar circumference = 40,007.86km (24,859.73 miles)
Mass = 5,972,190,000,000,000,000,000,000kg
  (5.972×10^{24}kg)

The equatorial circumference is divided into 360 degrees of longitude, which is measured in degrees, minutes and seconds east or west of the Greenwich (or 'prime') meridian (0°) to 180°; the meridian 180° E coinciding with 180° W. This was internationally ratified in 1884.

Distance north and south of the equator is measured in degrees, minutes and seconds of latitude. The equator is 0°, the North Pole is 90°N. and the South Pole is 90°S. The tropics lie at 23° 27′ N. (tropic of cancer) and 23° 27′ S. (tropic of capricorn). The Arctic Circle lies at 66° 33′ N. and the Antarctic Circle at 66° 33′ S. (Note the tropics and the Arctic and Antarctic circles are affected by the slow decrease in obliquity of the ecliptic, of about 0.47 arcseconds a year. The effect of this is that the Arctic and Antarctic circles are currently moving towards their respective poles by about 14m per annum, while the tropics move towards the equator by the same amount.)

AREA ETC
The surface area of the Earth is 510,064,472km² (196,936,994 miles²), of which the water area is 70.92 per cent and the land area is 29.08 per cent.

The radial velocity on the Earth's surface at the equator is 1,669.79km per hour (1,037.56mph). The Earth's mean velocity in its orbit around the Sun is 107,218km per hour (66,622mph). The Earth's mean distance from the Sun is 149,598,262km (92,956,050 miles).

OCEANS

LARGEST BY AREA
	km²	miles²
Pacific	165,250,000	63,800,000
Atlantic	82,440,000	31,830,000
Indian	73,440,000	28,360,000
Southern	20,327,000	7,848,300
Arctic	14,090,000	5,440,000

The equator divides the Pacific into the North and South Pacific and the Atlantic into the North and South Atlantic. In 2000 the International Hydrographic Organisation approved the description of the 20,327,000km² (7,848,300 miles²) of circum-Antarctic waters up to 60°S. as the Southern Ocean.

GREATEST KNOWN OCEAN DEPTHS
Greatest depth	Location	metres	feet
Mariana Trench*	Pacific	10,994	36,070
Puerto Rico Trench	Atlantic	8,380	27,493
Diamantina Trench	Indian	8,047	26,401
South Sandwich Trench	Southern	7,235	23,737
Molloy Deep	Arctic	5,607	18,397

* On 23 January 1960, Jacques Piccard (Switzerland) and Don Walsh (USA) descended in the bathyscaphe *Trieste* to the floor of the Mariana Trench, a depth later calculated as 10,916m (35,814ft). The current depth was calculated by the Japanese remote-controlled probe *Kaiko* on 24 March 1995. On 1 June 2009, sonar mapping of the Challenger Deep in the Mariana Trench by the US oceanographic research vessel *Kilo Moana* indicated a possible depth of 10,971m (35,994ft).

SEAS

LARGEST BY AREA
	km²	miles²
South China	3,685,000	1,423,000
Caribbean	2,753,000	1,063,000
Mediterranean	2,509,900	969,100
Bering	2,304,000	890,000
Okhotsk	1,582,000	611,000
Gulf of Mexico	1,550,000	600,000
Japan	978,000	377,600
Hudson Bay	819,000	316,000
Andaman	798,000	308,000
East China	750,000	290,000
North Sea	570,000	220,000
Red Sea	453,000	174,900
Black Sea	422,000	163,000

GREATEST KNOWN SEA DEPTHS
Greatest depth	metres	feet
Caribbean (Cayman Trench)	7,686	25,216
Philippine Sea (Ryukyu Trench)	7,507	24,629
Mediterranean (Calypso Deep)	5,267	17,280
Gulf of Mexico (Sigsbee Deep)	5,203	17,070
South China	5,016	16,457
Andaman	4,400	14,500
Bering (Bowers Basin)	4,097	13,442
Japan	3,742	12,276
Okhotsk	3,372	11,063
Red Sea	3,040	9,974
Black Sea	2,212	7,257
North Sea	700	2,300

THE CONTINENTS

There are generally considered to be seven continents: Africa, North America, South America, Antarctica, Asia, Australia and Europe. Europe and Asia are sometimes considered a single continent: Eurasia, and North and South America are sometimes referred to together as the Americas.

AFRICA is surrounded by sea except for the narrow isthmus of Suez in the north-east, through which was cut the Suez Canal (opened 17 November 1869). Its extreme longitudes are 17° 20′ W. at Cabo Verde, Senegal, and 51° 24′ E. at Raas Xaafunn, Somalia. The extreme latitudes are 37° 20′ N. at Cape Blanc, Tunisia, and 34° 50′ S. at Cape Agulhas, South Africa, about 7,081km (4,400 miles) apart. The equator passes across Gabon, Republic of the Congo, Uganda, Kenya and Somalia in the middle of the continent.

NORTH AMERICA, including Mexico, is surrounded by ocean except in the south, where the isthmian states of Central America link North America with South America. Its extreme longitudes are 168° 5′ W. at Cape Prince of Wales, Alaska, and 55° 40′ W. at Cape Charles, Newfoundland. The extreme continental latitudes are the tip of the Boothia peninsula, NW Territories, Canada (71° 51′ N.) and 14° 22′ N. in southern Mexico near La Victoria, Guatemala.

SOUTH AMERICA lies mostly in the southern hemisphere, the equator passing across Ecuador, Colombia and Brazil in the north of the continent. It is surrounded by ocean except where it is joined to Central America in the north by the narrow isthmus through which was cut the Panama Canal (opened 15 August 1914). Its extreme longitudes are 34° 47′ W. at Cape Branco in Brazil and 81° 20′ W. at Punta Pariña, Peru. The extreme continental latitudes are 12° 25′ N. at Punta Gallinas, Colombia, and 53° 54′ S. at the southernmost tip of Peninsula de Brunswick, Chile. Cape Horn, on Cape Island, Chile, lies in 55° 59′ S.

ANTARCTICA lies almost entirely within the Antarctic Circle (66° 33′ S.) and is the largest of the world's glaciated areas. Ninety-eight per cent of the continent is permanently covered in ice. The ice amounts to some 29 million km³ (7 million miles³) and represents more than 70 per cent of the world's fresh water. The ice sheet is on average 2.45km (1.5 miles) thick; if it were to melt, the world's seas would rise by more than 60m (197ft). The environment is too hostile for unsupported human habitation.

ASIA is the largest continent and occupies 29.6 per cent of the world's land surface. The extreme longitudes are 26° 05′ E. at Baba Buran, Turkey, and 169° 40′ W. at Mys Dezhneva, Russia, a distance of about 9,656km (6,000 miles). Its extreme northern latitude is 77° 45′ N. at Mys Chelyuskin, Russia, and it extends over 8,046km (5,000 miles) south to Tanjong Piai, Malaysia.

AUSTRALIA is the smallest of the continents and lies in the southern hemisphere. It is entirely surrounded by ocean. Its extreme longitudes are 113° 11′ E. at Steep Point, Western Australia, and 153° 11′ E. at Cape Byron, New South Wales. The extreme latitudes are 10° 42′ S. at Cape York, Queensland, and 39°S. at South East Point, Tasmania. Australia, together with New Zealand (Australasia), Papua New Guinea and the Pacific Islands, comprises Oceania.

EUROPE, including European Russia, is the smallest continent in the northern hemisphere. Its extreme latitudes are 71° 11′ N. at Nord Kapp in Norway, and 36° 23′ N. at Akra Tainaron (Matapas) in southern Greece, a distance of about 3,862km (2,400 miles). Its breadth from Cabo Carvoeiro in Portugal (9° 34′ W.) in the west to the Kara River, north of the Urals (66° 30′ E.) in the east is about 5,310km (3,300 miles). The division between Europe and Asia is generally regarded as the watershed of the Ural Mountains; down the Ural river to Atyrau, Kazakhstan; across the Caspian Sea to Apsheronskiy Poluostrov, near Baku; along the watershed of the Caucasus Mountains to Anapa and then across the Black Sea to the Bosporus in Turkey; across the Sea of Marmara to Canakkale Bogazi (Dardanelles).

	Area km²	Area miles²
Asia	44,614,000	17,226,000
Africa	30,365,000	11,724,000
North America	24,230,000	9,355,000
South America	17,814,000	6,878,000
Antarctica	14,200,000	5,500,000
Europe*	9,699,000	3,745,000
Australia	7,702,501	2,973,952

* Includes 5,571,000km² (2,151,000 miles²) of former USSR territory, including the Baltic states, Belarus, Moldova, Ukraine and the part of Russia west of the Ural Mountains and Kazakhstan west of the Ural river. European Turkey (24,378km²/9,412 miles²) comprises territory to the west and north of the Bosporus and the Dardanelles

GLACIATED AREAS

It is estimated that around 14,800,000km² (5,712,800 miles²) or 10 per cent of the world's land surface is permanently covered with ice. Glacial retreat and thinning occurs where glaciers melt faster than they are created. The phenomenon has been observed since the mid-19th century but has accelerated since about 1980 as a result of global warming. It is most notable in the Antarctic: a 2005 report by the American Association for the Advancement of Science indicated that 87 per cent of the continent's 244 marine glaciers have retreated over the past 50 years. The largest glacier is the 515km (320 miles) long Lambert-Fisher Ice Passage, Mac Robertson Land, Eastern Antarctica.

Location	km²	miles²
South Polar regions	13,829,000	5,340,000
North Polar regions (incl. Greenland)	1,965,000	758,500

LARGEST ISLANDS

	km²	miles²
Greenland (Kalaallit Nunaat), Arctic	2,166,086	836,330
New Guinea, Pacific	785,753	303,381
Borneo, Pacific	743,330	287,000
Madagascar, Indian	587,041	226,657
Baffin Island, Arctic	507,451	195,928
Sumatra, Indian	473,606	182,860
Honshu, Pacific	227,898	87,992
Great Britain, Atlantic	218,077	84,200
Victoria Island, Arctic	217,291	83,896
Ellesmere Island, Arctic	196,236	75,767

LARGEST DESERTS

	km²	miles²
Antarctica	14,000,000	5,400,000
Sahara, N. Africa	8,600,000	3,320,000
Arabian, Middle East	2,330,000	900,000
Gobi, Mongolia/China	1,300,000	500,000
Kalahari, Botswana/Namibia/ S. Africa	930,000	360,000
Patagonian, Argentina/Chile	670,000	260,000
Syrian, Middle East	518,000	200,000
Great Basin, USA	492,000	190,000
Great Victoria, Australia	424,400	163,900
Chihuahuan, USA/Mexico	362,600	140,000

DEEPEST DEPRESSIONS

The depth given is the maximum depth below sea level.

	metres	feet
Dead Sea, Jordan/Israel	413	1,354
Lake Assal, Djibouti	157	515
Turfan Depression, Sinkiang, China	155	508
Qattara Depression, Egypt	133	435
Batyr Depression, Kazakhstan	130	425
Kobar Sink, Ethiopia	116	381
Death Valley, California, USA	86	282
Salton Sea, California, USA	69	227
Caspian Depression, Russia/Kazakhstan	27	90

The world's largest exposed depression is the Caspian Depression covering the hinterland of the northern third of the Caspian Sea, which is itself 27m (90ft) below sea level.

Western Antarctica and central Greenland largely comprise crypto-depressions under ice burdens. The Antarctic Bentley subglacial trench has a bedrock 2,538m (8,326ft) below sea level. In Greenland (lat. 73° N., long. 39° W.) the bedrock is 365m (1,197ft) below sea level.

Around 26 per cent of the area of the Netherlands lies marginally below sea level, an area of more than 10,000km² (3,860 miles²).

CAVES

DEEPEST CAVES

The world's deepest cave was discovered in January 2001 by a team of Ukrainian cave explorers in the Arabikskaya system in the western Caucasus mountains of Georgia. It is a branch of the Voronya or 'Crow's Cave'.

	metres	feet
Krubera (Voronya), Georgia	2,191	7,188
Illyuzia-Mezhonnogo-Snezhnaya, Georgia	1,753	5,751
Lamprechtsofen Vogelschacht, Austria	1,632	5,354
Gouffre Mirolda, France	1,626	5,335
Réseau Jean Bernard, France	1,602	5,256
Torca del Cerro del Cuevon/Torca de las Saxifragas, Spain	1,589	5,213
Sarma, Georgia	1,543	5,062
Shakta Vyacheslav, Georgia	1,508	4,947
Sima de la Cornisa (Torca Magali), Spain	1,507	4,944
Cehi 2, Slovenia	1,502	4,928
Sistema Cheve (Cuicateco), Mexico	1,484	4,868
Sistema Huautla, Mexico	1,475	4,839

LONGEST CAVE SYSTEMS

	km	miles
Mammoth Cave System, Kentucky, USA	643.7	400
Jewel Cave, South Dakota, USA	241.6	150
Optymistychna, Ukraine	232.0	144
Wind Cave, South Dakota, USA	218.4	136
Sistema Sac Actun, Mexico (submerged, but dry)	217.4	135
Lechuguilla Cave, New Mexico, USA	209.6	130
Hölloch, Switzerland	195.9	122
Fisher Ridge System, Kentucky, USA	183.6	114
Sistema Ox Bel Ha, Mexico (submerged)	182.2	113
Gua Air Jernih, Malaysia	175.7	109
Siebenhengste-hohgant, Switzerland	156.0	97
Schoenbergsystem, Austria	130.2	81

LONGEST MOUNTAIN RANGES

	km	miles
Cordillera de Los Andes, South America	8,900	5,500
Rocky Mountains, North America	4,800	3,000
Great Dividing Range, Australia	3,700	2,300
Transantarctic Mountains, Antarctica	3,200	2,000
West Sumatran-Javan Range, Indonesia	2,900	1,800
Serra do Mar, Brazil	2,600	1,600
Himalaya, Central Asia	2,500	1,550
Tien Shan, Central Asia	2,400	1,500
New Guinea Highlands, New Guinea	2,010	1,250

HIGHEST MOUNTAINS

Mountain (first ascent)	metres	feet
Mt Everest* [Qomolangma] (29 May 1953)	8,850	29,035
K2 [Qogir]† (31 July 1954)	8,611	28,251
Kangchenjunga (25 May 1955)	8,586	28,169
Lhotse (18 May 1956)	8,516	27,940
Makalu (15 May 1955)	8,463	27,766
Cho Oyu (19 October 1954)	8,201	26,906
Dhaulagiri I (13 May 1960)	8,167	26,795
Manaslu I [Kutang I] (9 May 1956)	8,163	26,781
Nanga Parbat [Diamir] (3 July 1953)	8,126	26,660
Annapurna I (3 June 1950)	8,091	26,545

* Named after Sir George Everest (1790–1866), Surveyor-General of India 1830–43, in 1863. He pronounced his name 'Eve-rest'.

† Formerly named after Col. Henry Haversham Godwin-Austen (1834–1923), who worked on the Trigonometrical Survey of India, which established the heights of the Himalayan peaks, including Everest

The culminating summits in the other major mountain ranges are:

	metres	feet
Victory Peak [Pik Pobedy], Tien Shan	7,439	24,406
Mt Aconcagua, Cordillera de Los Andes	6,959	22,831
Denali (S. Peak), Alaska Range	6,190	20,310
Kilimanjaro (Kibo), Tanzania	5,895	19,340
Hkakabo Razi, Myanmar	5,881	19,296
Mt Elbrus, (W. Peak), Caucasus	5,642	18,510
Citlaltépetl [Orizaba], Mexico	5,610	18,406
Jaya Peak, Central New Guinea Range	5,030	16,500
Vinson Massif, Antarctica	4,892	16,050
Mt Blanc, Alps	4,807	15,771

HIGHEST ACTIVE VOLCANOES

Although it displays fumarolic activity, emitting steam and gas, no major eruption has ever been observed of the world's highest volcano and second highest peak in the western hemisphere, the 6,893m (22,615ft) Ojos del Salado, in the Andes on the Argentina/Chile border. For comparison, Eyjafjallajokull, the Icelandic volcano which erupted in 2010 causing air transport chaos, has an elevation of 1,666m (5,466ft).

The volcanoes listed below include only those that have had activity recorded since 1960.

Volcano, location (most recent activity)	metres	feet
San Pedro, Andes, Chile (1960)	6,145	20,161
Aracar, Andes, Argentina (1993)	6,082	19,954
Volcan Guallatiri, Andes, Chile (1960)	6,071	19,918
Tupungatito, Andes, Chile (1987)	6,000	19,685
Sabancaya, Andes, Peru (ongoing)	5,967	19,577
San José, Andes, Argentina/Chile (1960)	5,856	19,213
Lascar, Andes, Chile (2015)	5,592	18,346
Popocatepetl, Mexico (ongoing)	5,426	17,802
Nevado del Ruiz, Colombia (2016)	5,321	17,457
Sangay, Andes, Ecuador (2016)	5,230	17,159
Irruputuncu, Chile (1995)	5,163	16,939
Tungurahua, Ecuador (2016)	5,023	16,479

LAKES

LARGEST LAKES

The areas of some of the lakes listed are subject to seasonal variation. The most voluminous lakes are the Caspian Sea (saline) with 78,200km³ (18,800 miles³) and Baikal (fresh water) with 23,000km³ (5,518 miles³). Baikal is also the world's deepest lake (*see* below). It is estimated that it contains as much water as the entire Great Lakes system in North America – more than 20 per cent of the world's fresh water and some 90 per cent of all the fresh water in Russia.

The Aral was once the fifth largest in the world, with an area of 68,000km² (26,255 miles²), but since the 1960s many of its feeder rivers have been diverted for irrigation, as a result of which its area shrank to 17,160km² (6,626 miles²). Its salinity was almost three times that of seawater, and pollution led to the extinction of many aquatic species. Since the construction of the Kok-Aral dam (2005), water levels are rising again, especially in the north.

Lake and location	Area		Length	
	km²	*miles²*	*km*	*miles*
Caspian Sea, Iran/ Azerbaijan/Russia/ Turkmenistan/Kazakhstan	386,400	149,200	1,200	750
Michigan–Huron, USA/ Canada*	117,610	45,300	1,010	627
Superior, Canada/USA	82,100	31,700	563	350
Victoria, Uganda/ Tanzania/Kenya	69,484	26,828	337	210
Tanganyika, Dem. Rep. of Congo/Tanzania/Zambia/ Burundi	32,900	12,700	660	410
Baikal, Russia	31,500	12,200	636	395
Great Bear, Canada	31,328	12,096	320	200
Malawi [Nyasa], Tanzania/ Malawi/Mozambique	29,604	11,430	584	363
Great Slave, Canada	28,568	11,030	480	298
Erie, Canada/USA	25,670	9,910	388	241

* Lakes Michigan and Huron may be regarded as lobes of the same lake. The Michigan lobe has an area of 57,750km² (22,300 miles²) and the Huron lobe an area of 59,570km² (23,000 miles²)

UNITED KINGDOM (BY COUNTRY)

Lake and location	*km²*	*miles²*	*km*	*miles*
Lough Neagh, Northern Ireland	396.00	153.00	28.90	18.00
Loch Lomond, Scotland	71.12	27.46	36.44	22.64
Windermere, England	14.74	5.69	16.90	10.50
Lake Vyrnwy, Wales (artificial)	4.53	1.75	7.56	4.70
Llyn Tegid [Bala], Wales	4.38	1.69	5.80	3.65

LARGEST MANMADE LAKES

by volume

Dam/lake* (year of completion)	*km³*	*miles³*
Nalubaale dam [Owen Falls], Uganda/ Kenya/Tanzania (1954)	204.80	49.13
Kariba, Zimbabwe/Zambia (1959)	180.60	43.33
Bratsk, Russia (1967)	169.27	40.61
Nasser, Egypt (1970)	168.90	40.52
Volta, Ghana (1965)	153.00	36.71
Manicouagan [Daniel Johnson dam], Canada (1968)	141.85	34.03
Guri [Raul Leoni], Venezuela (1986)	138.00	33.11
Krasnoyarskoye, Russia (1967)	73.30	17.58
Wadi-Tatar, Iraq (1967)	72.80	17.46
Williston (W. A. C. Bennett dam), Canada (1967)	70.31	16.87

* Formed as a result of dam construction

The UK's largest reservoir is Kielder Water, Northumberland (1982) with a volume of 0.2km³ (0.048 miles³)

DEEPEST LAKES

Lake, location	*metres*	*feet*
Baikal, Russia	1,637	5,371
Tanganyika, Burundi/Tanzania/Dem. Rep. of Congo/Zambia	1,470	4,823
Caspian Sea, Azerbaijan/Iran/Kazakhstan/ Russia/Turkmenistan	1,025	3,363
O'Higgins [San Martin], Chile/Argentina	836	2,743
Malawi [Nyasa], Malawi/Mozambique/ Tanzania	706	2,316
Ysyk, Kyrgyzstan	668	2,192
Great Slave, Canada	614	2,015
Quesnel, Canada	610	2,001
Crater, Oregon, USA	594	1,949
Matano, South Sulawesi, Indonesia	590	1,936
Buenos Aires [General Carrera], Argentina/ Chile	586	1,923
Hornindalsvatnet, Norway	514	1,686
Sarez, Tajikistan	505	1,657
Toba, Sumatra, Indonesia	505	1,657
Argentino, Argentina	500	1,640
Tahoe, California/Nevada, USA	500	1,640

Loch Morar, Highland, Scotland is the UK's deepest lake at 310m (1,017ft).

LONGEST RIVERS

River, source–outflow	*km*	*miles*
Nile [Bahr-el-Nil], R. Luvironza, Burundi–E. Mediterranean Sea	6,650	4,132
Amazon [Amazonas], Lago Villafro, Peru–S. Atlantic Ocean	6,448	4,007
Yangtze [Chang Jiang], Kunlun Mts, W. China–Yellow Sea	6,300	3,915
Mississippi-Missouri-Red Rock, Montana– Gulf of Mexico	5,971	3,710
Yenisey-Selenga, W. Mongolia–Kara Sea	5,539	3,442
Huang He [Yellow River], Bayan Har Shan range, Central China–Yellow Sea	5,464	3,395
Ob-Irtysh, W. Mongolia–Kara Sea	5,410	3,362
Congo [Zambia], R. Lualaba, Dem. Rep. of Congo-Zambia–S. Atlantic Ocean	4,665	2,900
Amur-Argun, R. Argun, Khingan Mts, N. China–Sea of Okhotsk	4,416	2,744
Lena, R. Kirenga, W. of Lake Baikal–Laptev Sea, Arctic Ocean	4,400	2,734

BRITISH ISLES

River, source–outflow	*km*	*miles*
Shannon, Co. Cavan, Rep. of Ireland–Atlantic Ocean	372	231
Severn, Powys, Wales–Bristol Channel	354	220
Thames, Gloucestershire, England–North Sea	346	215
Tay, Perthshire, Scotland–North Sea	193	120
Clyde, Lanarkshire, Scotland–Firth of Clyde	170	106
Tweed, Scottish Borders–North Sea	155	97
Bann (Upper and Lower), Co. Down, N. Ireland–Atlantic Ocean	129	80

WATERFALLS

GREATEST BY HEIGHT

	Total drop		Greatest single leap	
	metres	feet	metres	feet
Angel, Carrao Auyan Tepui, Venezuela	979	3,212	807	2,648
Tugela, Tugela, S. Africa (5 leaps)	947	3,110	411	1,350
Ramnefjellsfossen, Jostedal Glacier, Norway	800	2,625	600	1,970
Mongefossen, Monge, Norway	773	2,535	–	–
Gocta, Cocahuayco, Peru	771	2,531	–	–
Mutarazi, Mutarazi, Zimbabwe	762	2,499	479	1,572
Yosemite, Yosemite Creek, USA	740	2,425	436	1,430
Ostre Mardola Foss, Mardals, Norway*	655	2,149	296	974
Tyssestrengene, Tysso, Norway*	646	2,120	289	948
Kukenaam, Arabopo, Venezuela	610	2,000	–	–

* Volume much affected by hydroelectric harnessing

POPULATIONS

MOST POPULOUS COUNTRIES IN THE WORLD

Country	Population*	Area (sq. km)	Area: world comparison†
China	1,379,302,771	9,596,961	4
India	1,281,935,911	3,287,263	7
USA	326,625,791	9,826,675	3
Indonesia	260,580,739	1,904,569	15
Brazil	207,353,391	8,514,877	5
Pakistan	204,924,861	796,095	36
Nigeria	190,632,261	923,768	32
Bangladesh	157,826,578	143,998	95
Russia	142,257,519	17,098,242	1
Japan	126,451,398	377,915	62

* July 2018 estimate
† Country's position in terms of area when compared against all the countries of the world, with '1' (Russia) having the largest land area

POPULATION GROWTH RATE

Top 10		Bottom 10	
Country	Growth Rate (%)*	Country	Growth Rate (%)*
South Sudan	3.83	Cook Islands	−2.70
Angola	3.52	Puerto Rico	−1.74
Malawi	3.31	American Samoa	−1.30
Burundi	3.25	Lebanon	−1.10
Uganda	3.20	Lithuania	−1.08
Niger	3.19	Latvia	−1.08
Mali	3.02	Moldova	−1.05
Burkina Faso	3.00	Bulgaria	−0.61
Zambia	2.93	Estonia	−0.57
Ethiopia	2.85	Micronesia	−0.52

* 2018 estimate

DAMS

TALLEST DAMS

Dam, location (year of completion)	metres	feet
Jinping-I, China (2014)	305	1,001
Nurek, Tajikistan (1980)	300	984
Xiaowan, China (2010)	292	958
Grande Dixence, Switzerland (1961)	285	935
Xiluodu, China (2014)	278	912
Enguri, Georgia (1980)	272	892
Vajont, Italy (1961)	262	859
Nuozhadu, China (2013)	262	858
Manuel Moreno Torres, Mexico (1981)	261	856

TALLEST

All heights are in accordance with the Council on Tall Buildings and Urban Habitat's regulations, which measure from the ground level of the main entrance to the architectural tip of the building and include spires but not antennae, signage or flag poles.

INHABITED BUILDINGS

Building and location (year of completion)	metres	feet
Burj Khalifa, Dubai, UAE (2010)	828	2,717
Wuhan Greenland Center, China (2018*)	636	2,087
Shanghai Tower, Shanghai, China (2015)	632	2,073
Makkah Royal Clock Tower, Mecca, Saudi Arabia (2012)	601	1,972
Ping An Finance Center, Shenzhen, China (2016)	599	1,965
Lotte World Tower, Seoul South Korea (2016)	555	1,819
One World Trade Centre, New York, USA (2014)	541	1,776
Guangzhou CTF Finance Centre, Guangzhou, China (2016)	530	1,739
TAIPEI 101, Taipei, Taiwan (2004)	508	1,667
Shanghai World Financial Center, Shanghai, China (2008)	492	1,614
International Commerce Centre, Hong Kong, China (2010)	484	1,588
Petronas Towers I and II, Kuala Lumpur, Malaysia (1998)	452	1,483
Zifeng Tower, Nanjing, China (2010)	450	1,476
Willis Tower, Chicago, USA (1974)	442	1,451
KK100, Shenzhen, China (2011)	441	1,449
Guangzhao International Finance Center, Guangzhou, China (2010)	438	1,439
432 Park Avenue, New York, USA (2015)	425	1,396

* Scheduled completion date

TWIN TOWERS

Structure, location (year of completion)	Floors	metres	feet
Petronas Towers, Kuala Lumpur, Malaysia (1998)	88	452	1,483
JW Marriott Marquis Dubai, Dubai, UAE (2012)	82	355	1,166
SPG Global Twin Towers, Suzhou, China (2010)	54	282	925
The Cullinan, Hong Kong, China (2008)	68	270	886
Al Kazim Towers, Dubai, UAE (2008)	53	265	869
Grand Gateway, Shanghai, China (2005)	54	262	859
Dual Towers, Manama, Bahrain (2007)	53	260	853
The Imperial, Mumbai, India (2009)	60	256	840
Al Fattan Towers, Dubai, UAE (2006)	51	245	804
Abraj Al Bait Towers, Mecca, Saudi Arabia (2012)	42	240	787
Destroyed 2001			
World Trade Center One New York City (1972)	110	417	1,368
World Trade Center Two New York City (1973)	110	415	1,362

STRUCTURES

Structure, location (year of completion)	metres	feet
Tokyo Skytree, Tokyo, Japan (2012)	634	2,080
KVLY (formerly KTHI)-TV Mast, North Dakota (guyed), USA (1963)*	629	2,063
Canton, Guangzhou, China (2010)	600	1,968
CN Tower, Toronto, Canada (1976)	553	1,815
Ostankino Tower, Moscow, Russia (1967)	540	1,772

* The USA has numerous other guyed TV towers above 600m (1,969ft)

CHURCHES

Structure, location (year of completion)	metres	feet
Sagrada Família, Barcelona, Spain (2026*)	170	560
Ulm Minster, Ulm, Germany (1890)	162	530
Our Lady of Peace Basilica, Yamoussoukro, Côte d'Ivoire (1990)	158	518
Cologne Cathedral, Cologne, Germany (1880)	157	515
Notre-Dame Cathedral, Rouen, France (1876)	151	495
St Nicholas Church, Hamburg, Germany (1874)	148	485
Notre-Dame Cathedral, Strasbourg, France (1439)	144	472
Queen of Peace Shrine and Basilica, Lichen, Poland (2004)	140	459
Basilica of St Peter, Rome, Italy (1626)	138	452
St Stephen's Cathedral, Vienna, Austria (1433)	137	448

* Scheduled completion date, the 100th anniversary of the death of its architect, Antoni Gaudí; open for worship following its consecration by Pope Benedict XVI in 2010

The Chicago Methodist Temple, Chicago, USA (completed 1924) is 173m (568ft) high, but is sited atop a 25-storey, 100m (328ft) building. Salisbury Cathedral (1521), at 123m (404ft), is the UK's tallest religious building. St Paul's Cathedral, London, and Liverpool Anglican Cathedral are the only others in the UK over 100m (328ft) tall. At 94m (309ft) the Church of St Walburge, Preston, Lancashire is the tallest church in Britain that is not a cathedral.

TALLEST STRUCTURES – A CHRONOLOGY

Structure and location	Year	metres	feet
Djoser's Step Pyramid, Saqqara, Egypt	c.2650 BC	62	204
Pyramid of Meidum, Egypt	c.2600 BC	92	302
Snefru's Bent Pyramid, Dahshur, Egypt	c.2600 BC	102	336
Red Pyramid, Dahshur, Egypt	c.2590 BC	104	341
Great Pyramid, Giza, Egypt*	c.2580 BC	147	481
Liuhe (Six Harmonies) Pagoda, Hangzhou, China†	AD 970	150	492
Lincoln Cathedral, Lincoln, England‡	1311–1400	160	525
St Paul's Cathedral, London, England§	1315	149	489
St Mary's Church, Stralsund, Germany	1384–1478	151	495
St Olaf's Church, Tallinn, Estonia⟪	1438–1519	159	522
Notre-Dame Cathedral, Strasbourg, France	1439	142	466
St Nicholas Church, Hamburg, Germany	1874	147	482
Notre-Dame Cathedral, Rouen, France	1876	151	495
Cologne Cathedral, Cologne, Germany	1880	157	515
Washington Monument, Washington DC, USA	1884	169	555
Eiffel Tower, Paris, France	1889	300	984
Chrysler Building, New York, USA	1930	319	1,046
Empire State Building, New York, USA	1931	381	1,250
KWTV Mast, Oklahoma City, USA	1954	481	1,577
KOBR-TV Tower, Caprock, USA	1960	490	1,608
KFVS TV Mast, Egypt Mills, USA	1960	511	1,677
KVLY (formerly KTHI)-TV Mast, Blanchard, USA	1963	629	2,063
Warszawa Radio Mast, Konstantynow, Poland**	1974	646	2,120
Burj Khalifa, Dubai, UAE	2010	828	2,717

* Later reduced through loss of topstone to 137m (449ft)
† Destroyed in 1121
‡ Destroyed in 1549
§ Destroyed in 1561
⟪ Spire burned down in 1625; renovated in 1931 to present height of 123m (403ft)
** Collapsed in 1991 during renovation

BRIDGES

The longest stretch of bridging of any kind is the Danyang–Kunshan Grand Bridge (2010) in China at 164km (102 miles).

LONGEST SUSPENSION SPANS

Bridge, location (year of completion)	metres	feet
Akashi-Kaikyo, Japan (1998)	1,991	6,532
Xihoumen, China (2009)	1,650	5,413
Great Belt Bridge, Denmark (1998)	1,624	5,328
Osman Gazi, Turkey (2016)	1,550	5,085
Yi Sun-sin, South Korea (2012)	1,545	5,069
Runyang, China (2005)	1,490	4,888
Nanjing Fourth Yangtze, China (2012)	1,418	4,652
Humber, England (1981)	1,410	4,626
Yavuz Sultan Selim, Turkey (2016)	1,408	4,619
Jiangyin, China (1999)	1,385	4,544

LONGEST CANTILEVER SPANS

Bridge, location (year of completion)	metres	feet
Pont de Québec, St Lawrence, Canada (1917)	548.6	1,800
Forth, Scotland (two spans of 1,710ft each) (1890)	521.2	1,710
Minato, Japan (1974)	510.0	1,673
Commodore Barry, New Jersey/Pennsylvania, USA (1974)	501.1	1,644
Crescent City Connection, Louisiana, USA (I 1958, II 1988)	480.0	1,575
Howrah, India (1943)	457.2	1,500
Veterans Memorial, Louisiana, USA (1995)	445.0	1,460
Tokyo Gate, Japan (2012)	440.0	1,443
San Francisco Oakland Bay, California, USA (1936)	426.7	1,400
J. C. Van Home, New Brunswick, Canada (1961)	380.0	1,247

LONGEST ARCH SPANS

Bridge, location (year of completion)	metres	feet
Chaotianmen, China (2009)	552.0	1,811
Lupu, China (2003)	550.0	1,804
Bosideng, China (2012)	530.0	1,740
New River Gorge, West Virginia, USA (1977)	518.0	1,700
Bayonne, New Jersey/New York, USA (1931)	510.0	1,675
Sydney Harbour, Australia (1932)	502.9	1,650
Chenab, India (2019*)	467.0	1,532
Wushan, China (2005)	460.0	1,509
Mingzhou, China (2011)	450	1,476
Zhaoqing, China (2014)	450	1,476

* Scheduled completion date

LONGEST SHIP CANALS

Canal	Length		Min. depth	
	km	miles	metres	feet
White Sea–Baltic [formerly Stalin] (1933), of which canalised river 51.5km (32 miles)	227	141.00	5.0	16.5
Rhine–Main–Danube, Germany (1992)	171	106.25	4.0	13.1
*Suez (1869), links Red and Mediterranean Seas	162	100.60	12.9	42.3
V. I. Lenin Volga–Don, Russia (1952), links Black and Caspian Seas	100	62.20	3.6	11.8
Kiel (or North Sea), Germany (1895), links North and Baltic Seas	98	60.90	11.0	37.0
Alphonse XIII, Spain (1926), gives Seville access to Atlantic Ocean	85	53.00	7.6	25.0
Panama (1914), links Pacific Ocean and Caribbean Sea; lake chain, 78.9km (49 miles) dug	82	50.71	13.0	43.0
*Houston, USA (1940), links inland city with Gulf of Mexico	81	50.50	11.0	36.0
Danube–Black Sea, Romania (1984)	64.4	40.02	7.0	23.0
Manchester Ship, UK (1894), links city with Irish Channel	58	36.00	8.5	28.0

* Has no locks

The first section of China's Grand Canal, running 1,782km (1,107 miles) from Beijing to Hangzhou, was opened in AD 610 and completed in 1283. Today it is limited to 2,000-tonne vessels.

The St Lawrence Seaway comprises the Beauharnois, Welland and Welland Bypass and Seaway 54–59 canals, and allows access to Duluth, Minnesota, USA via the Great Lakes from the Atlantic end of Canada's Gulf of St Lawrence, a distance of 3,769km (2,342 miles). The St Lawrence Canal, completed in 1959, is 293km (182 miles) long.

AIR DISTANCES

	London (LHR)	Paris (CDG)	Madrid (MAD)	Rome (FCO)	Moscow (DME)	Dubai (DXB)	New York (JFK)	Delhi (DEL)	Beijing (PEK)	Los Angeles (LAX)	Durban (DUR)	Bangkok (BKK)	Tokyo (HND)	Hong Kong (HKG)	Singapore (SIN)	Buenos Aires (BHI)	Sydney (SYD)
London (LHR)		216 / 348km	773 / 1,244km	899 / 1,446km	1,587 / 2,553km	3,421 / 5,505km	3,452 / 5,554km	4,191 / 6,744km	5,081 / 8,175km	5,457 / 8,780km	5,904 / 9,499km	5,959 / 9,588km	5,975 / 9,614km	5,996 / 9,647km	6,767 / 10,888km	7,241 / 11,651km	10,575 / 17,016km
Paris (CDG)	216 / 348km		660 / 1,063km	685 / 1,102km	1,547 / 2,489km	3,260 / 5,245km	3,635 / 5,849km	4,088 / 6,578km	5,103 / 8,211km	5,671 / 9,124km	5,692 / 9,159km	5,879 / 9,459km	6,047 / 9,730km	5,971 / 9,607km	6,668 / 10,729km	7,220 / 11,617km	10,529 / 16,941km
Madrid (MAD)	773 / 1,244km	660 / 1,063km		829 / 1,334km	2,140 / 3,444km	3,517 / 5,659km	3,589 / 5,775km	4,518 / 7,269km	5,734 / 9,226km	5,846 / 9,406km	5,312 / 8,546km	6,343 / 10,206km	6,706 / 10,790km	6,541 / 10,524km	7,079 / 11,390km	6,589 / 10,602km	10,986 / 17,676km
Rome (FCO)	899 / 1,446km	685 / 1,102km	829 / 1,334km		1,491 / 2,398km	2,703 / 4,349km	4,278 / 6,884km	3,694 / 5,944km	5,076 / 8,167km	6,356 / 10,226km	5,059 / 8,140km	5,523 / 8,886km	6,162 / 9,915km	5,779 / 9,298km	6,250 / 10,057km	7,252 / 11,668km	10,157 / 16,342km
Moscow (DME)	1,587 / 2,553km	1,547 / 2,489km	2,140 / 3,444km	1,491 / 2,398km		2,262 / 3,639km	4,702 / 7,566km	2,679 / 4,311km	3,605 / 5,800km	6,122 / 9,851km	5,868 / 9,441km	4,388 / 7,060km	4,672 / 7,518km	4,424 / 7,118km	5,218 / 8,396km	8,720 / 14,031km	8,992 / 14,468km
Dubai (DXB)	3,421 / 5,505km	3,260 / 5,245km	3,517 / 5,659km	2,703 / 4,349km	2,262 / 3,639km		6,850 / 11,022km	1,359 / 2,187km	3,639 / 5,855km	8,340 / 13,420km	4,102 / 6,600km	3,051 / 4,909km	4,941 / 7,949km	3,685 / 5,929km	3,634 / 5,847km	8,733 / 14,051km	7,482 / 12,039km
New York (JFK)	3,452 / 5,554km	3,635 / 5,849km	3,589 / 5,775km	4,278 / 6,884km	4,702 / 7,566km	6,850 / 11,022km		7,319 / 11,777km	6,839 / 11,004km	2,475 / 3,983km	8,249 / 13,273km	8,678 / 13,963km	6,774 / 10,899km	8,074 / 12,990km	9,539 / 15,349km	5,511 / 8,868km	9,952 / 16,013km
Delhi (DEL)	4,191 / 6,744km	4,088 / 6,578km	4,518 / 7,269km	3,694 / 5,944km	2,679 / 4,311km	1,359 / 2,187km	7,319 / 11,777km		2,371 / 3,815km	8,015 / 12,896km	5,024 / 8,083km	1,831 / 2,947km	3,649 / 5,871km	2,332 / 3,752km	2,580 / 4,152km	10,017 / 16,117km	6,477 / 10,422km
Beijing (PEK)	5,081 / 8,175km	5,103 / 8,211km	5,734 / 9,226km	5,076 / 8,167km	3,605 / 5,800km	3,639 / 5,855km	6,839 / 11,004km	2,371 / 3,815km		6,252 / 10,059km	7,276 / 11,707km	2,057 / 3,309km	1,303 / 2,097km	1,235 / 1,987km	2,781 / 4,474km	12,321 / 19,825km	5,553 / 8,934km
Los Angeles (LAX)	5,457 / 8,780km	5,671 / 9,124km	5,846 / 9,406km	6,356 / 10,226km	6,122 / 9,851km	8,340 / 13,420km	2,475 / 3,983km	8,015 / 12,896km	6,252 / 10,059km		10,635 / 17,111km	8,271 / 13,308km	5,489 / 8,831km	7,261 / 11,684km	8,772 / 14,114km	6,164 / 9,918km	7,490 / 12,051km
Durban (DUR)	5,904 / 9,499km	5,692 / 9,159km	5,312 / 8,546km	5,059 / 8,140km	5,868 / 9,441km	4,102 / 6,600km	8,249 / 13,273km	5,024 / 8,083km	7,276 / 11,707km	10,635 / 17,111km		5,511 / 8,868km	8,353 / 13,440km	6,560 / 10,555km	5,244 / 8,438km	5,147 / 8,282km	6,571 / 10,573km
Bangkok (BKK)	5,959 / 9,588km	5,879 / 9,459km	6,343 / 10,206km	5,523 / 8,886km	4,388 / 7,060km	3,051 / 4,909km	8,678 / 13,963km	1,831 / 2,947km	2,057 / 3,309km	8,271 / 13,308km	5,511 / 8,868km		2,853 / 4,590km	1,049 / 1,688km	877 / 1,411km	10,420 / 16,766km	4,663 / 7,503km
Tokyo (HND)	5,975 / 9,614km	6,047 / 9,730km	6,706 / 10,790km	6,162 / 9,915km	4,672 / 7,518km	4,941 / 7,949km	6,774 / 10,899km	3,649 / 5,871km	1,303 / 2,097km	5,489 / 8,831km	8,353 / 13,440km	2,853 / 4,590km		1,805 / 2,904km	3,289 / 5,292km	11,217 / 18,048km	4,838 / 7,785km
Hong Kong (HKG)	5,996 / 9,647km	5,971 / 9,607km	6,541 / 10,524km	5,779 / 9,298km	4,424 / 7,118km	3,685 / 5,929km	8,074 / 12,990km	2,332 / 3,752km	1,235 / 1,987km	7,261 / 11,684km	6,560 / 10,555km	1,049 / 1,688km	1,805 / 2,904km		1,588 / 2,555km	11,278 / 18,147km	4,582 / 7,372km
Singapore (SIN)	6,767 / 10,888km	6,668 / 10,729km	7,079 / 11,390km	6,250 / 10,057km	5,218 / 8,396km	3,634 / 5,847km	9,539 / 15,349km	2,580 / 4,152km	2,781 / 4,474km	8,772 / 14,114km	5,244 / 8,438km	877 / 1,411km	3,289 / 5,292km	1,588 / 2,555km		9,717 / 15,634km	3,908 / 6,288km
Buenos Aires (BHI)	7,241 / 11,651km	7,220 / 11,617km	6,589 / 10,602km	7,252 / 11,668km	8,720 / 14,031km	8,733 / 14,051km	5,511 / 8,868km	10,017 / 16,117km	12,321 / 19,825km	6,164 / 9,918km	5,147 / 8,282km	10,420 / 16,766km	11,217 / 18,048km	11,278 / 18,147km	9,717 / 15,634km		6,996 / 11,257km
Sydney (SYD)	10,575 / 17,016km	10,529 / 16,941km	10,986 / 17,676km	10,157 / 16,342km	8,992 / 14,468km	7,482 / 12,039km	9,952 / 16,013km	6,477 / 10,422km	5,553 / 8,934km	7,490 / 12,051km	6,571 / 10,573km	4,663 / 7,503km	4,838 / 7,785km	4,582 / 7,372km	3,908 / 6,288km	6,996 / 11,257km	

Figures are in miles, and represent the great circle distance (the shortest distance between two points on the surface of the earth)

TRAVEL OVERSEAS

PASSPORT REGULATIONS

Application forms for UK passports can be obtained from Her Majesty's Passport Office's telephone advice line or website, regional passport offices or from main post offices.

HM PASSPORT OFFICE, T 0300-222 0000 W www.gov.uk/government/organisations/hm-passport-office

Regional Passport Offices

BELFAST, Law Society House, Ground Floor, 90–106 Victoria Street, Belfast BT1 3GN

DURHAM, Freeman's Reach, Durham DH1 1SL

GLASGOW, 3 Northgate, 96 Milton Street, Cowcaddens, Glasgow G4 0BT

LIVERPOOL, 101 Old Hall Street, Liverpool L3 9BD

LONDON, Globe House, 89 Eccleston Square, London SW1V 1PN

NEWPORT, Nexus House, Mission Court, Newport NP20 2DW

PETERBOROUGH, Aragon Court, Northminster Road, Peterborough PE1 1QG

Passport offices are open Monday to Saturday on an appointment-only basis (appointments should be arranged by calling the central telephone number listed above). For an additional fee, passport offices provide either a premium one-day service (not available for a first adult or child passport, extending a limited passport, replacing a lost, stolen or damaged passport or for complex amendments) or a one-week fast track service (except for first adult passports).

Standard postal applications take at least three weeks to be processed. Application forms are provided by post offices. The completed application form should be posted, with the appropriate supporting documents and fee, to the regional passport office indicated on the addressed envelope which is provided with each application form. Accompanying cheques should be made payable to 'Her Majesty's Passport Office', or to 'Post Office Ltd' when using the Check & Send service.

Applications can also be submitted through Check & Send outlets at selected main post offices, who, for a handling charge of £9.75, will forward the application form to the relevant regional passport office after having checked that it has been completed correctly and has the appropriate documents attached. These applications take a minimum of two weeks (first adult passport applications may take six weeks including a passport interview).

Online applications can be made (W www.gov.uk/apply-renew-passport). The applicant must be over 26, reside in the UK, already possess a passport which must expire after 2012 and have only British nationality. No changes to the applicant's name can be made through this service.

A passport cannot be issued or extended on behalf of a person already abroad; such persons should apply online (W https://passportapplication.service.gov.uk) or to the nearest local embassy, British High Commission or Consulate.

UK passports are granted to British citizens, British nationals (overseas), British overseas territories citizens, British overseas citizens, British subjects and British protected persons, and are generally available for travel to all countries. The possession of a passport does not exempt the holder from compliance with any immigration regulations in force in British or foreign countries, or from the necessity of obtaining a visa where required (*see* below for a list of countries for which UK citizens do not require a visa).

Biometric passports were introduced in 2006. The design and security features, including a chip containing the biometrics (the facial image and biographical data of the holder), render the passport more secure against forgery and aid border controls.

ADULTS

A passport granted to a person over 16 will normally be valid for ten years. Thereafter, or if at any time the passport contains no further space for visas, a new passport must be obtained.

British nationals born on or before 2 September 1929 are eligible for a free standard passport.

CHILDREN

Since 5 October 1998 all children under the age of 16 travelling abroad are required to have their own passport. This is primarily to help prevent child abductions. The passports are initially valid for five years, but can be renewed for a further five years at the end of this period.

COUNTERSIGNATURES

A countersignature is needed if the application is for a first passport, to replace a lost, stolen or damaged passport, or to renew a passport for a child aged 11 or under. A countersignature is also needed for renewals if the applicant's appearance has significantly changed and the photograph in their previous passport is unrecognisable. The signatory must be willing to enter their own passport number on to the form. The list of acceptable countersignatories includes: MP; justice of the peace; minister of religion; a professionally qualified person (eg engineer, lawyer, teacher); bank officer; military officer; airline pilot; police officer; or a person of similar standing who has known the applicant for at least two years, who lives in the UK and who holds a British or Irish passport. A doctor is only acceptable if they know the applicant well. A relative or partner, someone living at the same address as the applicant, or an employee of HM Passport Office must not countersign the application.

PHOTOGRAPHS

Two identical, unmounted, recent colour photographs of the applicant must be sent. These photographs should measure 45mm by 35mm, be printed on plain white photographic paper and should be taken full face against a plain cream or light grey background. The photo must show the applicant's full face, looking straight at the camera, with a neutral expression and with their mouth closed. If a countersignature is required for the application, the person who countersigned the form should also certify one photograph as a true likeness of the applicant.

DOCUMENTATION

In addition to two photographs, the applicant's current or previous British passport, and other documents in support of the statements made in the application, must be produced at the time of applying. Details of which documents are required are set out in the notes accompanying the application form.

If the passport applicant is a British national by naturalisation or registration, the certificate proving this must be produced with the application, unless the applicant holds a previous British passport issued after registration or naturalisation.

INTERVIEWS

Interviews for adults applying for their first passport (not including those who held their own passport as a child) were introduced on 1 June 2007 to combat passport fraud and forgery. After applying for a passport, applicants will be sent a letter asking them to book an interview at one of the offices in the UK. Interviews last for approximately 30 minutes and applicants are asked to confirm facts about themselves that someone attempting to steal their identity would not know. HM Passport Office recommends that new applicants now allow six weeks to receive their passport. There is no one-week fast-track service for first adult passports.

48-PAGE PASSPORTS

The 48-page 'jumbo' passport is intended to meet the needs of frequent travellers who fill standard passports well before the validity has expired. It is valid for ten years but is not available for children.

PASSPORT FEES*

Adult passport†	£72.50
Child passport†	£46.00
48-page passport	£85.50
People born on or before 2 Sep 1929	Free

* Standard postal applications only. Applications made at UK regional offices have a higher fee

† New passports and renewal or amendment of a passport are priced at the same rate

HEALTH ADVICE

The NHS Choices website provides health advice for those travelling abroad, including information on immunisations and reciprocal health agreements with other countries. *See* W www.nhs.uk/livewell/travelhealth

See also National Health Service, Health Advice and Medical Treatment Abroad.

VISA REQUIREMENTS

It is advisable to check specific visa requirements with the appropriate embassy before making final travel arrangements (*see* Countries of the World section for foreign embassy contact details or W www.gov.uk/browse/abroad).The lists below are intended as a guide.

The countries listed below do not require British citizens to hold a valid visa or tourist card before arrival on short visits:

All EU member states and their overseas territories (*see* The European Union) except Ascension Island and Tristan da Cunha; Albania, Andorra, Antigua and Barbuda, Argentina, Armenia, Bahamas, Barbados, Belize, Bolivia, Bosnia and Hercegovina, Botswana, Brazil, Brunei, Canada, Chile, Colombia, Costa Rica, Dominica, Ecuador, El Salvador, Fiji, Gambia, Georgia, Grenada, Guatemala, Guyana, Haiti, Honduras*, Hong Kong, Iceland, Indonesia, Israel, Jamaica, Japan, Kazakhstan, Kiribati, Kosovo, Kuwait‡, Republic of Korea (South Korea), Kyrgyzstan, Lebanon*, Lesotho*, Liechtenstein, Macau, Macedonia, Malaysia, Maldives*, Mauritius, Mexico*, Micronesia (Federated States of)*, Moldova, Monaco, Montenegro, Morocco, Namibia, New Zealand, Nicaragua, Norway, Palau, Panama‡, Paraguay, Peru, the Philippines, Samoa, San Marino, Senegal, Serbia, Seychelles, Singapore, Solomon Islands, South Africa, St Kitts and Nevis, St Lucia, St Vincent and the Grenadines, Swaziland, Switzerland, Taiwan, Thailand, Tonga, Trinidad and Tobago, Tunisia, Tuvalu, Ukraine, United Arab Emirates*, Uruguay, USA†, Vanuatu, Venezuela‡, Vietnam, Western Sahara.

* Upon entry to these countries a visa or tourist card will be issued at no extra charge

† Those travelling to the USA under the Visa Waiver Programme must provide details online (the Electronic System for Travel Authorisation) at least 72 hours in advance of travel

‡ Only applicable when arriving by air, those arriving at overland crossings or by sea should arrange documentation in advance

Brunei, Iraq, Solomon Islands, Sudan and Yemen bar entry to travellers with HIV/AIDS. Jordan, Papua New Guinea, Qatar, Russia and UAE have some entry restrictions for visitors with HIV/AIDS.

Residents of the following countries must hold a valid visa for every entry to the UK:

Afghanistan, Albania, Algeria, Angola, Armenia, Azerbaijan, Bahrain, Bangladesh, Belarus, Benin, Bhutan, Bolivia, Bosnia and Hercegovina, Burkina Faso, Burundi, Cabo Verde, Cambodia, Cameroon, Central African Republic, Chad, China, Colombia, Comoros, Dem. Rep. of Congo, Rep. of Congo, Côte d'Ivoire, Cuba, Djibouti, Dominican Republic, Ecuador, Egypt, Equatorial Guinea, Eritrea, Ethiopia, Fiji, Gabon, Gambia, Georgia, Ghana, Guinea, Guinea-Bissau, Guyana, Haiti, India, Indonesia, Iran, Iraq, Jamaica, Jordan, Kazakhstan, Kenya, Dem. People's Republic of Korea (North Korea), Kosovo, Kuwait, Kyrgyzstan, Laos, Lebanon, Lesotho, Liberia, Libya, Macedonia, Madagascar, Malawi, Mali, Mauritania, Moldova, Mongolia, Montenegro, Morocco, Mozambique, Myanmar, Nepal, Niger, Nigeria, Oman*, Pakistan, Palestinian Authority, Peru, Philippines, Qatar*, Russian Federation, Rwanda, Sao Tome and Príncipe, Saudi Arabia, Senegal, Serbia, Sierra Leone, Somalia, South Africa, South Sudan, Sri Lanka, Sudan, Suriname, Swaziland, Syria, Taiwan†, Tajikistan, Tanzania, Thailand, Togo, Tunisia, Turkey, Turkmenistan, Uganda, Ukraine, United Arab Emirates*, Uzbekistan, Venezuela, Vietnam, Yemen, Zambia, Zimbabwe.

* An electronic visa waiver should be obtained online prior to travel

† Passports containing personal ID numbers do not require visas

BAGGAGE RESTRICTIONS

Individual airlines may set their own limits for hand luggage sizes, and travellers should check these before arriving at the airport: oversized baggage may have to be checked in as hold luggage, which often incurs a fee. Since January 2008, some airports have allowed passengers to take more than one item into the aircraft cabin. Other airports in the UK still have a one-bag restriction in place, and individual airlines may operate their own policies.

Passengers are allowed to carry small amounts of liquids as cabin luggage. These must be in containers not greater than 100ml, and placed in a single, transparent resealable bag which must not exceed 1 litre in capacity. Liquids are classified as drinks, make-up such as mascara or lipstick, sprays, pastes and gels. Medicines that are larger than 100ml must be accompanied by relevant documentation, such as a doctor's letter, and prior approval should be sought from the airline and departure airport. When travelling with a baby, enough liquid baby food, milk and sterilised water for the journey can be taken on board but containers may be opened and screened by security. One lighter is permitted as cabin luggage; this must be carried separately in a clear bag for the duration of the flight and not placed in the main hand luggage bag.

Sharp items must not be carried in hand luggage; any essential items should be placed in a bag in the hold. Prohibited sharp items include knives, large scissors, razor blades, tools, hiking poles and corkscrews. Other prohibited items include ammunition, chemical and toxic substances, work tools, sporting equipment, fireworks, party poppers, cork screws and non-safety matches.

Electrical equipment such as charged laptops, mobile phones and cameras are allowed in hand luggage but they must be removed and screened separately prior to boarding. Some electronic equipment is prohibited from use at certain times during a flight. Electrical equipment taken on flights to the UK from Egypt, Jordan, Lebanon, Saudi Arabia and Turkey must be put in the hold if larger than 16cm by 9.3cm by 1.5cm.

The amount passengers can check-in to the hold is determined by each airline. The airline will usually set a 'free baggage allowance' according to the number of items and the weight of each item; if this is exceeded there is normally an excess charge.

W www.gov.uk/hand-luggage-restrictions

THE EUROPEAN UNION

MEMBER STATE	ACCESSION DATE	POPULATION*	COUNCIL VOTES	EP SEATS
Austria	1 Jan 1995	8,754,413	10	18
Belgium	1 Jan 1958	11,491,346	12	21
Bulgaria	1 Jan 2007	7,101,510	10	17
Croatia	1 July 2013	4,292,095	7	11
Cyprus	1 May 2004	1,221,549	4	6
Czech Republic	1 May 2004	10,647,723	12	21
Denmark	1 Jan 1973	5,605,948	7	13
Estonia	1 May 2004	1,251,581	4	6
Finland	1 Jan 1995	5,518,371	7	13
France	1 Jan 1958	67,106,161	29	74
Germany	1 Jan 1958	80,549,017	29	96
Greece	1 Jan 1981	10,768,477	12	21
Hungary	1 May 2004	9,850,845	12	21
Ireland	1 Jan 1973	5,011,102	7	11
Italy	1 Jan 1958	62,137,802	29	73
Latvia	1 May 2004	1,944,643	4	8
Lithuania	1 May 2004	2,823,859	7	11
Luxembourg	1 Jan 1958	582,291	4	6
Malta	1 May 2004	416,338	3	6
The Netherlands	1 Jan 1958	17,084,719	13	26
Poland	1 May 2004	38,746,269	27	51
Portugal	1 Jan 1986	10,839,514	12	21
Romania	1 Jan 2007	21,529,967	14	32
Slovakia	1 May 2004	5,445,829	7	13
Slovenia	1 May 2004	1,972,126	4	8
Spain	1 Jan 1986	48,958,159	27	54
Sweden	1 Jan 1995	9,960,487	10	20
United Kingdom	1 Jan 1973	64,769,452	29	73

* July 2017 estimate

† Under the Lisbon Treaty the total number of MEPs was set at 751 from the 2014 election. Following the UK's withdrawal from the EU, the total number of seats will be reduced to 705, with 27 of the current 73 UK seats redistributed among the remaining member states.

Sources: CIA World Factbook; www.europa.eu

LEGISLATION

The core of the European Union (EU) policy-making process is a dialogue between the European Commission (EC), which initiates and implements policy, and the Council of the European Union and the European Parliament, which take policy decisions.

The original legislative process is known as the consultation procedure. The commission drafts a proposal which it submits to the council and to the parliament. The council then consults the Economic and Social Committee, the parliament and the Committee of the Regions; the parliament may request that amendments are made. With or without these amendments, the proposal is then adopted by the council and becomes law. The consultation procedure now only applies to cases not specifically subject to one of the other procedures.

The Single European Act introduced the assent procedure (now the consent procedure), whereby an absolute majority of the parliament must vote to approve laws in certain fields before they are passed. Issues covered by the procedure include uniform procedure for elections, some international agreements, violation of human rights and the accession of new member states.

The Maastricht Treaty introduced the co-decision procedure as an extension of the cooperation procedure; if, after the parliament's second reading of a proposal, the council and parliament fail to agree, a conciliation committee of the two will aim to reach a compromise. If a compromise is not reached, the parliament can reject the legislation by the vote of an absolute majority of its members. The Amsterdam Treaty extended the co-decision procedure to all areas covered by qualified majority voting, with the exception of measures related to the European Monetary Union.

The Lisbon Treaty extended the use of the co-decision procedure to several new fields, and renamed it the ordinary legislative procedure. The treaty strengthens the role of the European parliament so that it is involved in almost all new legislation. The changes give the European parliament equal powers in areas such as legal immigration, crime prevention and police cooperation. As a result of the Lisbon Treaty, the Council of the European Union must now vote in public on any new legislation, and if one-third of national parliaments disagree with a proposal then it can be sent back to be reviewed.

The council, commission and parliament can issue the following legislation:

- regulations, which are binding in their entirety and directly applicable to all member states; they do not need to be incorporated into national law to come into effect
- directives, which are less specific, binding as to the result to be achieved but leaving the method of implementation open to member states; a directive thus has no force until it is incorporated into national law
- decisions, which are also binding but are addressed solely to one or more member states or individuals in a member state
- recommendations or opinions, which are merely persuasive.

The council and parliament also have certain budgetary powers and determine all expenditure together. The final decision on whether the budget should be adopted or rejected lies with the parliament.

The European Central Bank (ECB) has legislative powers within its field of competence. The commission also has limited legislative powers, where it has been delegated the power to implement or revise legislation by the council.

SCHENGEN AGREEMENT

The Schengen agreement was signed by France, Germany, Belgium, Luxembourg and the Netherlands in 1985. The agreement committed the five states to abolishing internal border controls, erecting external frontiers against illegal immigrants, drug traffickers, terrorists and organised crime, and it implemented the Schengen Information System which enables national border control, customs and police authorities from Schengen member states to share and access data on specific individuals, such as a person who may have been involved in a serious crime, or vehicles, documents or objects which may have been stolen, lost or misappropriated. The second-generation Schengen Information System (SIS II) entered into operation in April 2013. SIS II has improved functionalities such as new types of alerts and the potential to enter biometrics. It also contains copies of European arrest warrants, facilitating the detention of persons wanted for arrest, surrender or extradition.

Subsequently signed by Portugal and Spain, the agreement was ratified by the seven signatory states and entered into force in March 1995 with the removal of internal frontier, passport, customs and immigration controls. Austria and Italy became full members of the agreement in 1997; Greece in 2000; and Denmark, Finland and Sweden in 2001. The Czech Republic, Estonia, Hungary, Latvia, Lithuania, Malta, Poland, Slovakia and Slovenia joined in 2007. Although not members of the EU, Iceland and Norway joined the agreement in 2001 and Switzerland in 2008. The European Council granted Liechtenstein membership in 2011. There is no date set for Bulgaria, Croatia, Cyprus or Romania to join. The UK and the Republic of Ireland have not signed the agreement and are only partial participants, since their border controls have been maintained.

The Schengen agreement originated as an intergovernmental agreement and was adopted by the EU following the signing of the Amsterdam Treaty.

MAASTRICHT TREATY

Agreed in Maastricht, the Netherlands, in 1991, the treaty came into effect in November 1993 following ratification by the member states. Three pillars formed its basis:

- the European Community (removing Economic from its name) with its established institutions and decision-making processes
- a common foreign and security policy charged with providing a forum for member states and EU institutions to consult on foreign affairs
- cooperation in justice and home affairs, with the Council of the European Union coordinating policies on asylum, immigration, conditions of entry, cross-border crime, drug trafficking and terrorism

The treaty established a common European citizenship for nationals of all member states and introduced the principle of subsidiarity, whereby decisions are taken at the most appropriate level (national, regional or local). It extended European Community competency into the areas of

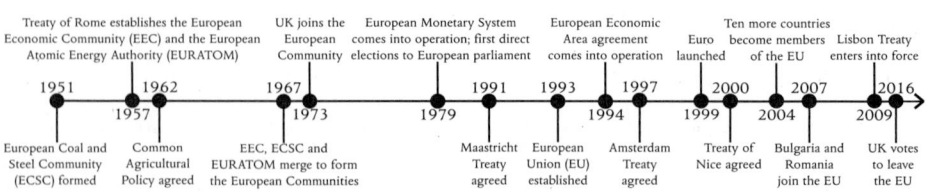

Treaty of Rome establishes the European Economic Community (EEC) and the European Atomic Energy Authority (EURATOM)	UK joins the European Community	European Monetary System comes into operation; first direct elections to European parliament	European Economic Area agreement comes into operation		Ten more countries Euro become members launched of the EU	Lisbon Treaty enters into force
1951	1967	1991	1993	1997	2000	2007	2016
1957	1973	1979	1994	1999	2004	2009	
European Coal and Steel Community (ECSC) formed	Common Agricultural Policy agreed	EEC, ECSC and EURATOM merge to form the European Communities	Maastricht Treaty agreed	European Union (EU) established	Amsterdam Treaty agreed	Treaty of Nice agreed	Bulgaria and Romania join the EU	UK votes to leave the EU

environmental and industrial policies, consumer affairs, health, and education and training, and extended qualified majority voting in the Council of the European Union to some areas which had previously required a unanimous vote. The powers of the European parliament over the budget and over the EC were also enhanced, and a co-decision procedure enabled the parliament to override decisions made by the council in certain policy areas. A separate protocol to the Maastricht Treaty on social policy was agreed by 11 states and was incorporated into the Amsterdam Treaty in 1997 following adoption by the UK.

AMSTERDAM TREATY
The treaties of Rome and Maastricht were amended through the Amsterdam Treaty, which was signed in 1997 and came into effect on 1 May 1999. It extended the scope of qualified majority voting and the powers of the European parliament. It also included a formal commitment to fundamental human rights, gave additional powers to the European Court of Justice and provided for the reform of common foreign and security policy.

LISBON TREATY
The Lisbon Treaty was drawn up to replace the original European constitution, which was rejected in referendums in France and the Netherlands in 2005. It amends, rather than replaces, existing EU and European Community treaties. Ireland, the only country to hold a referendum on the Lisbon Treaty, voted against ratification on 12 June 2008. It held a second referendum on 2 October 2009 in which 67 per cent voted in favour, and – as a result of all EU countries approving the treaty – it came into force on 1 December 2009.

The Lisbon Treaty granted 'legal personality' (the right under international law to adopt laws and treaties) to the EU. The three pillars created by the Maastricht Treaty (*see* above) merged to make the EU a single legal entity, replacing the European Community. The Lisbon Treaty introduced a number of changes to the EU: a new president was appointed to the European Council for a two-and-a-half year term to replace the previous system of a six-month rotating presidency (this still exists in a reduced capacity for the Council of the European Union). The position of High Representative of the Union for Foreign Affairs and Security Policy was created, to enhance the EU's relations with other countries. The European parliament was strengthened and given more legislative and budgetary powers, and the number of MEPs was set at 751* from the 2014 election. The system of qualified majority voting was extended to new policy areas and since 2014 has been based on a double majority of member states and people; a decision must be agreed by 55 per cent of member states representing at least 65 per cent of the EU population. The treaty establishes the principle of 'mutual recognition', whereby each member state acknowledges that legal decisions by other member states are valid; the UK has an opt-out clause with regard to some policies, such as external borders, asylum and immigration.

* Following the UK's withdrawal from the EU, the total number of seats in the European parliament will be reduced to 705, with 27 of the current 73 UK seats redistributed among the remaining member states. France and Spain will gain the most seats at five each, increasing from 74 to 79 and 54 to 59 respectively. Italy and the Netherlands will each gain three seats, from 73 to 76 and 26 to 29, and Ireland will gain two seats. Austria, Croatia, Denmark, Estonia, Finland, Poland, Romania, Slovakia, and Sweden will all be allocated one additional seat. The remaining 13 countries will keep their current allocation.

MEMBERSHIP AND EXTERNAL RELATIONS

ACCESSION
The procedure for accession to the EU is laid down in the Treaty of Rome; states must be stable European democracies

governed by the rule of law with free-market economies. A membership application is studied by the EC, which produces an 'opinion'. If the opinion is positive, negotiations may be opened leading to an accession treaty that must be approved by all member state governments and parliaments, the European parliament, and the applicant state's government and parliament.

Cyprus, the Czech Republic, Estonia, Hungary, Latvia, Lithuania, Malta, Poland, Slovakia and Slovenia became full members of the EU on 1 May 2004. Bulgaria and Romania joined the EU on 1 January 2007, and Croatia on 1 July 2013. The Council of the EU recalled the offer of an accession partnership to Turkey in 2002, following the commission's conclusion that Turkey did not yet fully meet the required political criteria. However, at its December 2004 meeting in Brussels, the council decided that Turkey sufficiently met the Copenhagen political criteria, and accession negotiations began in October 2005. However, in November 2016, negotiations again stalled after a non-binding vote in the EU parliament resulted overwhelmingly in favour of a motion to suspend negotiations with Turkey due to concerns over human rights and rule of law abuses in the country. Montenegro was granted candidate status in December 2005 and accession negotiations began on 29 June 2012. Macedonia was granted candidate status in December 2005, but accession negotiations have not yet begun. Iceland applied for membership in July 2009 and accession negotiations started in June 2010, but were put on hold by the Icelandic government in May 2013. Serbia applied for membership in December 2009 and accession negotiations commenced in January 2014 while Albania was granted candidate status in June 2014. There are currently two potential candidates for membership of the EU: Bosnia and Hercegovina, and Kosovo.

UK WITHDRAWAL FROM THE EU
A referendum was held in the UK on 23 June 2016 in which the UK electorate (turnout 72 per cent) voted to leave the EU (52 per cent).

The UK government invoked Article 50 of the Lisbon Treaty on 29 March 2017 therefore setting the country on course to leave the EU by 29 March 2019. Official negotiations between the EU and the UK to decide the terms of the UK's withdrawal from the EU began on 19 June 2017. A draft withdrawal agreement was published on 19 March 2018 and the EU and UK negotiators aim to finalise the agreement in October 2018 so that it can be ratified before 30 March 2019.

If the agreement is ratified before 30 March 2019 there will be a transition period of 21 months, so that most of the legal effects of Brexit will apply as at 1 January 2021. The terms of the transition period are set out in the draft withdrawal agreement. In the absence of a withdrawal agreement, there will be no transition period, and EU law will cease to apply to and in the UK as at 30 March 2019. EU law still stands in the UK until it ceases being a member and the future relationship between the EU and the UK can only be negotiated after the UK has left the EU.

EU AGREEMENTS WITH OTHER STATES
The EU has several types of agreements with other European and non-European states. Association agreements (AAs), which must be ratified by all EU member states, can include commitments to reforming the country's trade, human rights, economy or political system in exchange for financial assistance or trade agreements. Partnership and cooperation agreements (PCAs) are legal frameworks, based on respect for democratic principles and human rights, setting out the political, economic and trade relationship between the EU and

its partner countries. Each PCA is a ten-year bilateral treaty signed and ratified by the EU and the individual state. After the ten-year period expires the agreements are automatically renewed annually unless one of the parties objects. Agreements have been implemented (date when PCA entered into force in parentheses) with Russia (1997), Moldova and Ukraine (1998), Armenia, Azerbaijan, Georgia, Kazakhstan, Kyrgyzstan and Uzbekistan (1999), Tajikistan (2010), Indonesia (2014) and the Philippines and Vietnam (2015). In 2003 the PCA council summit strengthened EU cooperation with the Russian Federation by establishing a permanent partnership council (PPC). Negotiations for a new agreement to replace and update the existing PCA between the EU and Russia began in 2008 but have since been suspended. There are PCAs under ratification with Iraq (2012), Belarus (1995), Kazakhstan (Enhanced) (2015), and Turkmenistan (1998), and in negotiations with Malaysia, Singapore, and Thailand.

Trade and cooperation agreements are intended to foster trade and economic relations, and include a commitment to respect the human rights and democratic principles of both parties. The EC has negotiated around 120 agreements worldwide.

While the EU has agreements with over 60 trade partners, it does not have current agreements with some of the largest economies such as China, India, Japan, and the USA. There are ongoing trade negotiations with Australia, Chile, Japan, Mexico, MERCOSUR and New Zealand. Trade negotiations with the USA through the Transatlantic Trade and Investment Partnership (TTIP) are uncertain due to US President Trump's reversion of trade terms in 2017. The Comprehensive Economic and Trade Agreement between the EU and Canada was signed in 2016.

The European neighbourhood policy was developed in 2004 and applies to the enlarged EU's immediate neighbours. It aims to strengthen stability and security through economic integration and deeper political relationships based on a mutual commitment to European common values (democracy, human rights, rule of law, good governance and market economy).

A stabilisation and association agreement (SAA) – which is tailored to the western Balkan states – provides the contractual framework for relations to enable accession to the EU. Candidate or potential candidate countries with SAAs in force are Macedonia (2004), Albania (2009), Montenegro (2010), Serbia (2013), Bosnia and Hercegovina (2015) and most recently Kosovo (1 April 2016).

TREATY OF NICE
The Treaty of Nice was signed in 2001 and came into effect in 2003. It enabled the EU to accommodate up to 13 new member states, and extended qualified majority voting to 30 further articles of the treaties that previously required unanimity. The weighting of votes in the European Council was altered from 1 January 2005 for the new member states. To obtain a qualified majority, a decision requires a specified number of votes (to be reviewed following each accession); the decision has to be approved by a majority of member states and represent at least 62 per cent of the total population of the EU. The treaty also set the number of MEPs that both existing and new member states would have following enlargement.

The Maastricht Treaty established the right of groups of member states to work together without requiring the participation of all members (enhanced cooperation); the Treaty of Nice removed the right of individual member states to veto the launch of enhanced cooperation.

ECONOMY

BUDGET OF THE EUROPEAN UNION
The principles of funding the European Union budget (formerly known as the European Community budget) were established by the Treaty of Rome and remain, with modifications, to this day. There is a legally binding limit on the overall level of resources (known as 'own resources') that the EU can raise from its member states; this limit is defined as a percentage of gross national income (GNI). Budget revenue and expenditure must balance, and there is therefore no deficit financing. The 'own resources' decision, which came into effect in 1975 and has been regularly updated, states that there are four sources of funding under which each member state makes contributions:
- duties charged on agricultural imports into the EU from non-member states
- customs duties on imports from non-member states
- contributions based on member states' shares of a notional EU-harmonised VAT base
- contributions based on member states' shares of total GNI

The latter source above is the budget-balancing item and covers the difference between total expenditure and the revenue from the other three sources. On 3 July 2013 the European parliament voted in favour of a budget for 2014–20; the budget was officially adopted following a vote on the legislation in November 2013. The overall budget for the seven-year period is €963bn in commitments and €908bn in payments (at 2011 prices).

The EU's multi annual financial framework (MFF) for 2014–20 is 3.5 per cent less than the commitment appropriations under the MFF 2007–13 and 3.7 per cent less than the payment appropriations for the same period. In line with the political priorities of the EU, a strong emphasis was put on expenditure aimed at boosting growth and creating jobs, with an increase of 37 per cent over the 2007–13 model dedicated to 'competitiveness for growth and jobs'.

In 2017, an extra €6bn in commitments was pledged to help member states tackle the refugee crisis. Measures include, the creation of reception centres, resettlement and integration programmes for those refugees with the right to remain, counter terrorism activities and border control enhancement.

In February 2018 the EU adopted legislation enabling the European Investment Bank (EIB) to lend an additional €5.3bn to projects outside the EU with €3.7bn of this allocated for projects addressing migration issues. The EU provides a maximum budgetary guarantee to the EIB of €30bn (€27bn plus €3bn in reserve) for the 2014–20 period. The new rules release the €3bn kept in reserve, of which €1.4bn is for public sector projects addressing the root causes of migration, plus an additional €2.3bn for private sector lending for migration-related projects; increasing the EU's guarantee to the EIB to €32.3bn.

EU BUDGET 2018

	CA	PA
Smart and inclusive growth*	77,534	66,624
Sustainable growth	59,285	56,084
Security and citizenship	3,493	2,981
Global Europe	9,569	8,906
Administration	9,666	9,666
Special Instruments	567	420
Total	€160,114m	€144,681m

(1 euro = £0.89 as at 1 July 2018)

* Includes 'competitiveness for growth and jobs' and 'economic, social and territorial cohesion'

CA = commitment appropriations (maximum value of commitments to pay future bills)

PA = payment appropriations (actual amounts to pay for previous commitments)

Source: www.consilium.europa.eu

SINGLE MARKET

Even after the removal of tariffs and quotas between member states in the 1970s and 1980s, the European Community was still separated into a number of national markets by a series of non-tariff barriers. It was to overcome these internal barriers to trade that the concept of the single market was developed. The measures to be undertaken were codified in the commission's 1985 white paper on completing the internal market.

The white paper included articles removing obstacles distorting the internal market: the elimination of frontier controls; the mutual recognition of professional qualifications; the harmonisation of product specifications, largely by the mutual recognition of national standards; open tendering for public procurement contracts; the free movement of capital; the harmonisation of VAT and excise duties; and the reduction of state aid to particular industries. The Single European Act (SEA) aided the completion of the single market by changing the legislative process within the European Community, particularly with the introduction of qualified majority voting in the Council of the European Union for some policy areas, and the introduction of the assent procedure in the European parliament. The Single European Act also extended European Community competence into the fields of technology, the environment, regional policy, monetary policy and external policy. The single market came into effect on 1 January 1993, though full implementation of the elimination of frontier controls and the harmonisation of taxes have been repeatedly delayed. A fundamental review of the single market was completed in 2007, which resulted in an operational set of initiatives intended to modernise single market policy. Following the abolition of the European Community in 2009 as a result of the Lisbon Treaty, the single market policy now applies to the EU.

EUROPEAN ECONOMIC AREA

The single market programme spurred European non-member states to open negotiations with the European Community on preferential access for their goods, services, labour and capital to the single market. Principal among these states were European Free Trade Association (EFTA) members who opened negotiations on extending the single market to EFTA by the formation of the European Economic Area (EEA), encompassing all 19 European Community and EFTA states. Agreement was reached in 1992, but the operation of the EEA was delayed by its rejection in a Swiss referendum, necessitating an additional protocol agreed by the remaining 18 states. The EEA came into effect in 1994 after ratification by 17 member states (Liechtenstein joined in 1995 after adapting its customs union with Switzerland).

Austria, Finland and Sweden joined the EU on 1 January 1995, leaving only Iceland, Liechtenstein and Norway as the non-EU EEA members. Under the EEA agreement, the three states are to adopt the EU's *acquis communautaire,* apart from in the fields of agriculture, fisheries, and coal and steel.

The EEA is controlled by regular ministerial meetings and by a joint EU-EFTA committee which extends relevant EU legislation to EEA states. Apart from single market measures, there is cooperation in several areas, including education, civil protection, research and development, consumer policy and tourism. An EFTA court has been established in Luxembourg and an EFTA surveillance authority in Brussels to supervise the implementation of the EEA Agreement.

The EEA Enlargement Agreement came into force on 1 May 2004, which allowed the simultaneous expansion of both the EU and the EEA without disruption of the internal market. A similar process took place to ensure that Bulgaria and Romania could become contracting parties to the EEA upon joining the EU in 2007 and Croatia in 2013.

EUROPEAN MONETARY SYSTEM AND THE SINGLE CURRENCY

The European Monetary System (EMS) began operation in March 1979 with three main purposes. The first was to establish monetary stability in Europe, initially in exchange rates between European Community member state currencies through the Exchange Rate Mechanism (ERM), and in the longer term as part of a wider stabilisation process, overcoming inflation and budget and trade deficits. The second purpose was to overcome the constraints resulting from the interdependence of European Community economies, and the third was to aid the long-term process of European monetary integration.

The Maastricht Treaty set in motion timetables for achieving economic and monetary union (EMU) and a single currency (the euro). In May 1998, 11 member states were judged to fulfil or be close to fulfilling the necessary convergence criteria for participation in the first stage of EMU: Austria, Belgium, Finland, France, Germany, Ireland, Italy, Luxembourg, the Netherlands, Portugal and Spain. The criteria were that:

- the budget deficit should be 3 per cent or less of gross domestic product (GDP)
- total national debt must not exceed 60 per cent of GDP
- inflation should be no more than 1.5 per cent above the average rate of the three best performing economies in the EU
- long-term interest rates should be no more than 2 per cent above the average of the three best-performing economies in the EU in the previous 12 months
- applicants must have been members of the ERM for two years without having realigned or devalued their currency

Under the terms of a stability and growth pact agreed in December 1996 and revised in 2005, penalties may be imposed on EMU members with high budget deficits. Governments with deficits exceeding 3 per cent of GDP will receive a warning and will be obliged to pay up to 0.5 per cent of their GDP into a fund after ten months. This will become a fine if the budget deficit is not rectified within two years. A member state with negative growth will be allowed to apply for an exemption from the fine by referring to a number of relevant factors outlined in the pact.

As a result of the global economic downturn, by May 2010, 24 out of 27 countries in the EU had a deficit exceeding 3 per cent of GDP. The EC revised its existing recommendations in November 2009 and proposed extended deadlines for each country to correct its budget deficit. In the case of the UK, a deadline of 2014–15 was proposed, the longest deadline given to any of the EMU nations.

On 1 January 1999 the 11 qualifying member states adopted the euro at irrevocably fixed exchange rates, the European Central Bank (ECB) took charge of the single monetary policy, and the euro replaced the ECU (an artificial currency adopted by European Community member states in 1979 as an internal accounting unit for the EMS) on a one-for-one basis.

Subsequent member states who have fulfilled the criteria for participation and adopted the euro includes Greece on 1 January 2001, Slovenia on 1 January 2007, Cyprus and Malta on 1 January 2008, Slovakia on 1 January 2009, Estonia on 1 January 2011, Latvia on 1 January 2014 and Lithuania on 1 January 2015. Referendums on the adoption of the euro have been held in Denmark and Sweden, but participation was rejected. In June 2003 the UK announced that the euro would not be adopted on the grounds that the country was not economically ready to join the single currency.

The euro is now the legal currency in 19 participating states and is used by around 337.5 million people. Euro notes and coins were introduced on 1 January 2002 and circulated alongside national currencies for a period of up to two months, after which time national notes and coins ceased to be legal tender.

The ECB meets twice a month in Frankfurt to set the following month's monetary policy applicable to the countries participating in the euro. Its governing council has 25 members: the six members of the ECB's executive board and the 19 governors of the national central banks of the participating states.

THE EURO CRISIS
Greece
Early in 2010, Greece's soaring budget deficit and the escalating cost of servicing the country's debt brought it to the verge of economic meltdown. In May 2010 the EC, ECB and IMF agreed a rescue package totalling €110bn (£95bn) and in February 2012 provided a further bailout package worth €130bn (£110bn). In November 2012, faced with the possibility of defaulting on its repayments, the Greek parliament passed a number of austerity measures. In June–July 2015 Greece defaulted on an IMF repayment, the ECB withdrew emergency funding and the government had to impose capital controls and close banks. International creditors offered a further bailout plan on the basis of the introduction of additional austerity measures; the rescue package was rejected by 60 per cent of the population in a referendum held on 5 July. Subsequently, a third bailout package totalling €86bn (£62bn), with different, but equally stringent, austerity measures was secured in August 2015, essentially to avoid Greece's departure from the eurozone.
Other Countries
In November 2010 the near collapse of the banking system in Ireland led to the approval of an €85bn (£72bn) rescue package by the EU and the IMF. In April 2011 Portugal requested financial assistance from the EU after rising borrowing costs left the government unable to pay its debts, and in May 2011 European finance ministers finalised the terms of a three-year bailout agreement worth €78bn (£69bn). The Spanish government requested a eurozone rescue loan of around €100bn (£77bn) on 10 June 2012; eurozone finance ministers approved the loan on the same day. On 25 June, Cyprus became the fifth eurozone member to ask for financial assistance, citing significant exposure to the crippled Greek economy. A €10bn support package was agreed on 25 March 2013.

COMMON AGRICULTURAL POLICY
The Common Agricultural Policy (CAP) was established to increase agricultural production, provide a fair standard of living for farmers and ensure the availability of food at reasonable prices. This aim was achieved by a number of mechanisms, including import levies, intervention purchase and export subsidies.

These measures stimulated production but also placed increasing demands on the budget, which was exacerbated by the increase in EC members and yields enlarged by technological innovation; the CAP now accounts for over 40 per cent of EU expenditure. To surmount these problems reforms were agreed in 1984, 1988, 1992, 1997, 1999, 2003, 2008 and 2013.

REFORMS
The 1984 reforms created the system of co-responsibility levies: farm payments to the EC by volume of product sold. This system was supplemented by national quotas for particular products, such as milk. The 1988 reforms emphasised 'set-aside', whereby farmers are given direct grants to take land out of production as a means of reducing surpluses. The set-aside reforms were extended in 1993 for another five years and to every farm in the EC. The 1999 reforms further reduced surpluses of cereals, beef and milk by cutting the intervention prices by up to 20 per cent and compensating producers by making area payments. Under the reforms, CAP rules were also simplified, eliminating inconsistencies between policies.

In 2003, EU farm ministers adopted a fundamental reform of the CAP, which included the following provisions:
- a single farm payment for EU farmers, independent of production (begun in 2005)
- payment to be linked to meeting environmental, food safety, animal and plant health and animal welfare standards, and the requirement to keep all farmland in good condition
- a strengthened rural development policy with more EU money to help farmers meet EU production standards (begun in 2005)
- a reduction in direct payments for bigger farms
- a mechanism for financial discipline to ensure that the farm budget fixed until 2013 is not exceeded

The ten EU members that joined in 2004 were also given access to a special €5.8bn (£3.9bn) three-year funding package.

A CAP 'health check' was carried out in 2008 and resulted in proposals intended to further modernise and streamline EU agricultural policy, and to allow farmers to follow market signals by breaking the link between direct payments and production. These include abolishing the requirement for farmers to leave 10 per cent of their arable land fallow, a gradual increase in milk quotas before their abolition in 2015 and a general reduction in market intervention.

On 13 March 2013, MEPs voted to adopt a controversial package of legislation, including approving both the extension of quotas and the rural development programme that involves shared financing with national governments. The stated aim of the CAP reform was to strengthen the competitiveness and sustainability of agriculture and maintain its presence in all regions, to guarantee European citizens healthy and quality food production, and to preserve the environment and develop rural areas. On 26 June 2013, a political agreement on the CAP 2014–20 reforms was reached between the European Commission, parliament and council and on 16 December 2013, the council of EU agriculture ministers formally adopted the four basic regulations for the reformed CAP in addition to the transition rules for 2014. The CAP 2014–20 reforms saw an investment of almost €28bn in the UK farming sector and rural areas.

INSTITUTIONS

EUROPEAN PARLIAMENT
E eplondon@europarl.europa.eu W www.europarl.europa.eu;
www.europarl.org.uk

The European parliament (EP) originated as the common
assembly of the ECSC, acquiring its present name in 1962.
The parliament now comprises 751 seats representing citizens
of the 28 countries in the EU. Members (MEPs), initially
appointed from the membership of national parliaments, have
been directly elected at five-year intervals since 1979.
Elections to the parliament are held on differing bases
throughout the EU; British MEPs have been elected by a
regional list system of proportional representation since June
1999. The most recent elections were held in May 2014.

MEPs serve on committees which scrutinise draft EU
legislation and the activities of the EC. A minimum of 12
plenary sessions a year are held in Strasbourg and six
additional shorter plenary sessions a year are held in Brussels;
committees meet in Brussels, and the secretariat's headquarters
is in Luxembourg.

The influence of the EP has gradually expanded within the
EU since the Single European Act 1985, which introduced the
cooperation procedure; the Maastricht Treaty, which
extended the cooperation procedure and introduced the co-
decision (now ordinary legislative) procedure (see Legislation);
the Amsterdam Treaty, which effectively extended the
ordinary legislative procedure to all areas except economic
and monetary union, and taxation; and the Lisbon Treaty,
which gave parliament legislative powers comparable with
the Council of the European Union. The EP has general
powers of supervision over the EC, and powers of
consultation and co-decision with the Council of the
European Union; it votes to approve a newly appointed
commission and can dismiss it at any time by a two-thirds
majority. Under the Maastricht Treaty it has the right to be
consulted on the appointment of the new commission, and can
also veto its appointment. Under the Lisbon Treaty, the
parliament elects the president of the commission on the
proposal of the European Council. The EP has an equal right
to decide on budgetary matters as the Council of the European
Union, and they work together to approve and adopt the
entire annual budget. In accordance with the Maastricht
Treaty, the EP appoints the European Ombudsman to provide
citizens with redress against maladministration by EU
institutions.

The EP's organisation is deliberately biased in favour of
multinational political groupings; recognition of a political
grouping in the parliament entitles it to offices, funding,
representation on committees and influence in debates and
legislation. A political group must be composed of a minimum
of 25 MEPs elected in at least seven member states. For a list
of UK MEPs, see European Parliament.

President, Antonio Tajani (Italy)

PARLIAMENT, allée du Printemps, F-67070 Strasbourg Cedex,
France
Wiertzstraat 60, B-1047 Brussels, Belgium
SECRETARIAT, Centre Européen, Plateau du Kirchberg, BP
1601, L-2929 Luxembourg T (+352) 43001
OMBUDSMAN, 1 avenue du Président Robert Schuman, CS
30403, F-67001 Strasbourg Cedex, France
W www.ombudsman.europa.eu
Ombudsman, Emily O'Reilly (Ireland)

EUROPEAN PARLIAMENT UK OFFICE
Europe House, 32 Smith Square, London SW1P 3EU
E eplondon@europarl.europa.eu W www.europarl.org.uk

EUROPEAN PARLIAMENT OFFICE IN SCOTLAND
The Tun, 4 Jackson's Entry, Holyrood Road, Edinburgh EH8 8PJ
E epedinburgh@europarl.europa.eu W www.europarl.org.uk

COUNCIL OF THE EUROPEAN UNION
Wetstraat 175, Rue de la Loi, B-1048 Brussels, Belgium
W www.consilium.europa.eu

The Council of the European Union (Council of Ministers) is
the main decision-making body of the EU, and formally
comprises the ministers of the member states. Depending on
the issue on the agenda, each country will be represented by
the minister responsible for that subject. It passes laws, usually
legislating jointly with the European parliament; coordinates
the broad economic policies of the member states; approves
the EU's budget jointly with the European parliament; defines
and implements the EU's common foreign and security policy;
concludes agreements between the EU and other states or
international organisations; and coordinates the actions of
member states and adopts measures in the area of police and
judicial cooperation.

Council decisions are taken using one of three methods: by
qualified majority vote, by a simple majority, or by unanimity.
The treaties define which one of the three methods should be
used in each subject area. Unanimity votes are taken on
sensitive issues such as taxation and defence, but the qualified
majority vote (QMV) is now used for the majority of council
decisions. Under the provisions of the Lisbon Treaty, a new
system of QMV began on 1 November 2014, under which a
qualified majority is achieved if:

- at least 55 per cent of member states approve (72 per cent
  where the council does not act on a proposal from the
  commission) *and*
- these member states represent at least 65 per cent of the
  EU's population

This system therefore assigns a vote to each member state
while taking account of their demographic weight.

The presidency of the Council of the European Union is held
in rotation for six-month periods, setting the agenda for and
chairing council meetings in all policy areas except foreign
affairs. The holders of the presidency for the years 2019–20
are:

2019 Jan–Jun, Romania   2019 Jul–Dec, Finland
2020 Jan–Jun Croatia   2020 Jul–Dec Germany

In the area of foreign affairs, council meetings are chaired by
the High Representative of the Union for Foreign Affairs and
Security Policy.

*High Representative of the Union for Foreign Affairs and Security
Policy,* Federica Mogherini (Italy)

GENERAL SECRETARIAT OF THE COUNCIL OF THE
EUROPEAN UNION
Wetstraat 175, rue de la Loi, B-1048 Brussels, Belgium
W www.consilium.europa.eu
Secretary-General of the Council of the European Union (2015–20),
Jeppe Tranholm-Mikkelsen (Denmark)

EUROPEAN COUNCIL
The European Council, formed in 1974, was given formal
recognition by the Single European Act in 1987; on 1
December 2009, under the Lisbon Treaty it has become a
fully fledged institution of the EU with a permanent president.
It normally meets four times a year, unless a special meeting is
convened by the president, and comprises the heads of state
or government of each EU member state and the president of
the EC. Meetings are chaired by the president of the council.

The primary function of the European Council is to give
political guidance in all areas of EU activity at both European
and national levels. The European Council can issue
declarations and resolutions expressing the opinions of the

heads of state and governments, but its decisions are not legally binding.

President of the European Council, Donald Tusk (Poland)

EUROPEAN COMMISSION

Wetstraat 200, rue de la Loi, B-1049 Brussels, Belgium

The European Commission (EC) consists of 28 commissioners, one per member state. The UK's commissioner, Jonathan Hill (Financial Stability, Financial Services and Capital Markets Union) resigned following the outcome of the UK's June 2016 referendum in which the UK electorate voted to leave the EU; a new UK commissioner will be appointed. The members of the commission are appointed for five-year renewable terms by the agreement of the member states; the terms run concurrently with the terms of the European parliament. The president and the other commissioners are nominated by the governments of the member states, and, under the terms of the Lisbon Treaty, appointments are approved by the European parliament. The commissioners pledge sole allegiance to the EU. The commission initiates and implements EU legislation and is the guardian of the EU treaties. It is the exponent of community-wide interests rather than the national preoccupations of the council. Each commissioner is supported by advisers and oversees the departments assigned to them, known as directorates-general and services.

President Jean-Claude Juncker was elected for a first mandate by the European parliament on 15 July 2014. He received 422 votes from a total of 729 and he took office in November 2014.

The commission has a total staff of around 33,000 permanent civil servants and temporary agents.

COMMISSIONERS *as at June 2018*
President, Jean-Claude Juncker (Luxembourg)
First Vice-President, Better Regulation, Inter-Institutional Relations, the Rule of Law and the Charter of Fundamental Rights, Frans Timmermans (Netherlands)
Vice-President, High Representative of the Union for Foreign Affairs and Security Policy, Federica Mogherini (Italy)
Vice-President, Budget and Human Resources, Gunther Oettinger (Germany)
Vice-President, Digital Single Market, Andrus Ansip (Estonia)
Vice-President, Energy Union, Maros Sefcovic (Slovakia)
Vice-President, Euro and Social Dialogue, and Financial Stability, Financial Services and Capital Markets Union, Valdis Dombrovskis (Latvia)
Vice-President, Jobs, Growth, Investment and Competitiveness, Jyrki Katainen (Finland)
Transport, Violeta Bulc (Slovenia)
Digital Economy and Society, Mariya Gabriel (Bulgaria)
European Neighbourhood Policy and Enlargement Negotiations, Johannes Hahn (Austria)
Trade, Cecilia Malmstrom (Sweden)
International Cooperation and Development, Neven Mimica (Croatia)
Climate Action and Energy, Miguel Arias Canete (Spain)
Environment, Maritime Affairs and Fisheries, Karmenu Vella (Malta)
Health and Food Safety, Vytenis Andriukaitis (Lithuania)
Migration and Home Affairs, Dimitris Avramopoulos (Greece)
Employment, Social Affairs, Skills and Labour Mobility, Marianne Thyssen (Belgium)
Economic and Financial Affairs, Taxation and Customs, Pierre Moscovici (France)
Humanitarian Aid and Crisis Management, Christos Stylianides (Cyprus)
Agriculture and Rural Development, Phil Hogan (Ireland)
Internal Market, Industry, Entrepreneurship and SMEs, Elzbieta Bienkowska (Poland)

Justice, Consumers and Gender Equality, Vera Jourova (Czech Republic)
Education, Culture, Youth and Sport, Tibor Navracsics (Hungary)
Regional Policy, Corina Cretu (Romania)
Competition, Margrethe Vestager (Denmark)
Research, Science and Innovation, Carlos Moedas (Portugal)
Security Union, Sir Julian King, KCVO, CMG (UK)

EC REPRESENTATION OFFICES

UK, Europe House, 32 Smith Square, London SW1P 3EU
　T 020-7973 1992
WALES, 2 Caspian Point, Caspian Way, Cardiff CF10 4QQ
　T 029-2089 5020
SCOTLAND, 9 Alva Street, Edinburgh EH2 4PH T 0131-225 2058
NORTHERN IRELAND, 74–76 Dublin Road, Belfast BT2 7HP
　T 028-9024 0708

COURT OF JUSTICE OF THE EUROPEAN UNION

Palais de la Cour de Justice, boulevard Konrad Adenauer, Kirchberg, L-2925 Luxembourg
W www.curia.europa.eu

The Lisbon Treaty gave a new framework to the EU court system. The court of justice of the European Union is now composed of two courts: the court of justice and the general court.

COURT OF JUSTICE

The court of justice exists to safeguard the law in the interpretation and application of EU treaties, to decide on the legality of EU legislation, and to determine infringements of the treaties. Cases may be brought to it directly by the member states and EU institutions. Questions on EU law may be referred to the court of justice by national courts. The decisions of the court are directly binding in the member states. The court's powers were extended by the Maastricht Treaty, allowing it to impose fines on member states who breach EU law. The court comprises 28 judges – one from each member state – and 11 advocates-general. These positions are appointed for renewable six-year terms by the member governments.

President, Koen Lenaerts (Belgium)

GENERAL COURT

Established under powers conferred by the Single European Act, the general court has jurisdiction to hear and determine direct actions brought by individuals, companies and, in some cases, EU governments against any of the institutions, bodies, agencies or offices of the EU, except those cases reserved for the court of justice. Additionally, the general court hears actions seeking compensation for damage caused by the institutions of the EU or their staff. It also has jurisdiction to hear actions brought by member states against the EC and actions relating to community trade marks. The court is composed of at least one judge from each member state (47 judges in 2017), increasing to 56 judges, or two from each member state, in 2019. Judges are appointed for renewable six-year terms by the individual national governments.

President, Marc Jaeger (Luxembourg)

EUROPEAN COURT OF AUDITORS

12 rue Alcide de Gasperi, L-1615 Luxembourg
E eca-info@eca.europa.eu W www.eca.europa.eu

The European Court of Auditors, established in 1977, examines the accounts of all revenue and expenditure of the EU. It evaluates whether all revenue has been received and all expenditure incurred in a lawful and regular manner and in accordance with the principles of sound financial management. The court issues an annual report and a statement of assurance as to the reliability of the accounts and the legality and regularity of the underlying transactions. It also publishes special reports on specific topics and delivers opinions on financial matters. The court has one member from each member state, appointed for a renewable six-year term by the Council of the European Union following consultation with the European parliament. The President is elected for a renewable term of three years.

President, Klaus-Heiner Lehne (Germany)

FINANCIAL BODIES

EUROPEAN CENTRAL BANK
Kaiserstrasse 29, D-60311 Frankfurt am Main, Germany
E info@ecb.europa.eu W www.ecb.europa.eu

The ECB, which superseded the European Monetary Institute, became fully operational on 1 January 1999 and defines and implements the single monetary policy for the euro area. The ECB's main task is to maintain the euro's purchasing power and price stability in the 19 EU countries that have introduced the currency since 1999. Its decision-making bodies are the executive board, the governing council and the general council. The executive board consists of the president, the vice-president and four other members. All members are appointed by the governments of the states participating in the single currency, at the level of heads of state and government. The governing council, the main decision-making body of the ECB, comprises the six members of the executive board and the governors of the national central banks of the 19 euro area states. The general council comprises the president and vice-president and the 28 governors of the national central banks of all the member states of the EU, the other members of the executive board being entitled to participate but not to vote. The ECB is independent of national governments and of all other EU institutions.

President, Mario Draghi (Italy)
Vice-President, Luis de Guindos (Spain)

EUROPEAN INVESTMENT BANK
100 boulevard Konrad Adenauer, L-2950 Luxembourg
E info@eib.org W www.eib.org

The European Investment Bank (EIB) was set up in 1958 under the terms of the Treaty of Rome and is the financing arm of the EU. The EIB's main activity is to provide long-term loans in support of investments undertaken by private or public promoters, for projects furthering European integration.

The EIB also operates outside the EU, in support of EU development and cooperation policies in partner countries including the enlargement area of Europe (both candidate and potential candidate countries), the Mediterranean, Russia and the southern Caucasus, Africa, the Caribbean, the Pacific, Asia and Latin America.

The bank is not dependent on the EU budget, and raises its own resources on the capital markets. It is one of the biggest supranational bond issuers and lenders in the world with an AAA credit rating. In 2017 the EIB lent a total of €69.9bn and invested €2.1bn in the UK.

The UK-EU withdrawal draft agreed that the EIB will reimburse the UK's paid-in capital in 12 annual installments, starting in 2019, in return the UK will guarantee its paid-in and callable capital and retain EIB board privileges and immunities until EIB lending undertaken while a member is recovered. The EIB will not reimburse the UK a share of the EIBs accumulated profits and, after withdrawal, UK projects will not be eligible for EIB operations reserved for member states.

The shareholders of the EIB are the 28 member states, whose ministers of economy and finance constitute its board of governors. This body lays down general directives on the credit policy of the bank and appoints members to the board of directors. The board of directors consists of 28 members nominated by the member states, and one by the European Commission. It takes decisions on the granting and raising of loans and the fixing of interest rates. The management committee, composed of the bank's president and eight vice-presidents and also appointed by the board of governors, is responsible for the day-to-day operations of the bank.

President, Werner Hoyer (Germany)

ADVISORY BODIES

COMMITTEE OF THE REGIONS
Bâtiment Jacques Delors, rue Belliard 99–101, B-1040 Brussels, Belgium
W www.cor.europa.eu

The Committee of the Regions (CoR) was established in 1994 and is the political assembly which provides local and regional authorities with a voice within the EU. The Lisbon Treaty obliges the EC, the Council of the European Union and the European parliament to consult the CoR whenever new legislative proposals are made in areas which have repercussions at regional or local level. The CoR then issues opinions on these proposals for EU laws, and also has the right to comment on any amendments to proposed legislation by MEPs. The CoR has the right to challenge new EU laws in the European court of justice if it believes it has not been correctly consulted by the commission, parliament or council or for any infringement of the subsidiarity principle.

The committee has 350 full members; the proportion of members from each of the 28 member states of the EU approximately reflects the size of the individual country's population. Committee members are proposed by the member states to the Council of the European Union, which appoints them for a five-year renewable term of office. Members must hold a regional or local authority electoral mandate or be politically accountable to an elected assembly. They participate in the work of seven specialist commissions which are responsible for drafting the CoR's opinions and resolutions on a wide range of topics.

President, Karl-Heinz Lambertz (Belgium)
Secretary-General, Jiri Burianek (Czech Republic/Germany)

EUROPEAN ECONOMIC AND SOCIAL COMMITTEE
rue Belliard 99, B-1040 Brussels, Belgium W www.eesc.europa.eu

The European Economic and Social Committee (EESC) is a consultative body of the EU. It comprises 350 members drawn from economic and social interest groups in Europe; these members are appointed by the governments of the 28 member states for a five-year renewable term. The last renewal occurred in October 2015 for the 2015–20 mandate. The EESC is divided into three groups: employers, workers, and other interest groups such as consumers, farmers and the self-employed. Every two-and-a-half years the EESC elects a bureau made up of 40 members, including a president and two vice-presidents chosen from each of the three groups in rotation. The EESC issues opinions on draft EU legislation, which are forwarded to the commission, council and parliament. The EESC's competencies have increased as a result of revisions to the Treaty of Rome, and the Lisbon Treaty strengthens the committee's role.

President, Luca Jahier (Italy)
Interim Secretary-General, María Echevarría (Spain)

AGENCIES

EUROPEAN ENVIRONMENT AGENCY
Kongens Nytorv 6, DK-1050 Copenhagen K, Denmark
T (+45) 3336 7100 W www.eea.europa.eu

The European Environment Agency (EEA) aims to support sustainable development and to help achieve significant and measurable improvement in Europe's environment, through the provision of information to policy-making agents and the public. The EEA has been operational since 1994, and now has 33 member countries. It is an EU body but is open to non-EU countries that share its objectives. The management board consists of representatives of the member countries, two representatives of the EC and two representatives designated by the European parliament.

Executive Director, Hans Bruyninckx (Belgium)

EUROPEAN JUDICIAL COOPERATION UNIT (EUROJUST)
Johan de Wittlaan 9, 2517 JR The Hague, The Netherlands
E info@eurojust.europa.eu W www.eurojust.europa.eu

The European Union's Judicial Cooperation Unit (Eurojust) was established in 2002 with the aim of developing Europe wide cooperation in cases involving serious crime committed across more than one member state's jurisdiction. Eurojust also facilitates the provision of international mutual legal assistance and helps to implement extradition requests. It is a key interlocutor with the European parliament, the Council of the European Union and the EC.

The college of Eurojust is composed of 28 national members, one nominated by each member state. These members are experienced prosecutors, judges or police officers.

President, Ladislav Hamran (Slovakia)
Director, Nick Panagiotopoulos (Greece)

EUROPEAN POLICE OFFICE (EUROPOL)
Eisenhowelaan 73, 2517 KK The Hague, The Netherlands
W www.europol.europa.eu

The European Police Office (Europol) came into being on 1 October 1998 and assumed its full powers on 1 July 1999. It superseded the Europol Drugs Unit and exists to improve police cooperation between member states and to combat terrorism, illicit traffic in drugs and other serious forms of organised international crime. It is ultimately responsible to the Council of the European Union. Each member state has a national unit to liaise with Europol, and the units send at least one liaison officer to represent its interests at Europol headquarters. Europol employs over 1,000 staff at its headquarters, with around 100 criminal analysts, handling around 40,000 international investigations each year. It works closely with law enforcement agencies in the 28 EU member states and non-EU partner states, including Australia, the USA and Canada.

Executive Director, Catherine De Bolle (Belgium)

EUROPEAN PARLIAMENT POLITICAL GROUPINGS

as at 31 July 2018

	EPP	S&D	ALDE	Greens/EFA	ECR	GUE/NGL	EFD	ENF	Others	Total
Austria	5	5	1	3	–	–	–	4	–	18
Belgium	4	4	6	2	4	–	–	1	–	21
Bulgaria	7	4	4	–	2	–	–	–	–	17
Croatia	5	2	2	1	1	–	–	–	–	11
Cyprus	1	2	–	–	1	2	–	–	–	6
Czech Republic	7	4	4	–	2	3	1	–	–	21
Denmark	1	3	3	1	3	1	–	–	1	13
Estonia	1	1	3	1	–	–	–	–	–	6
Finland	3	2	4	1	2	1	–	–	–	13
France	20	13	7	6	–	4	6	16	2	74
Germany	34	27	4	13	6	8	1	1	2	96
Greece	5	4	–	–	1	6	–	–	5	21
Hungary	12	4	–	2	–	–	–	–	3	21
Ireland	4	1	1	–	1	4	–	–	–	11
Italy	14	31	–	1	2	3	14	6	1	*72
Latvia	4	1	1	1	1	–	–	–	–	8
Lithuania	3	2	3	1	1	–	1	–	–	11
Luxembourg	3	1	1	1	–	–	–	–	–	6
Malta	3	3	–	–	–	–	–	–	–	6
The Netherlands	5	3	7	2	2	3	–	4	–	26
Poland	22	5	–	–	18	–	1	2	3	51
Portugal	8	8	1	–	–	4	–	–	–	21
Romania	13	14	3	–	2	–	–	–	–	32
Slovakia	6	4	–	–	3	–	–	–	–	13
Slovenia	5	1	1	1	–	–	–	–	–	8
Spain	17	14	8	5	–	10	–	–	–	54
Sweden	4	6	3	4	2	1	–	–	–	20
UK	2	20	1	6	19	1	19	1	4	73
Total	218	189	68	52	73	51	43	35	21	*750

* Italy has one vacant seat

EPP – European People's Party (Christian Democrats)
W www.eppgroup.eu
S&D – Progressive Alliance of Socialists and Democrats in the European Parliament
W www.socialistsanddemocrats.eu
ALDE – Alliance of Liberals and Democrats for Europe
W www.alde.eu
Greens/EFA – Greens/European Free Alliance
W www.greens-efa.eu

ECR – European Conservatives and Reformists
W www.ecrgroup.eu
GUE/NGL – European United Left/Nordic Green Left
W www.guengl.eu
EFD – Europe of Freedom and Democracy Group
W www.efdgroup.eu
ENF – Europe of Nations and Freedom Group
W www.enfgroup-ep.eu

INTERNATIONAL ORGANISATIONS

International organisations are intergovernmental organisations, whose membership can only include either sovereign states or other international organisations. They are subject to international law and are capable of entering into agreements among themselves or with states. They do not include private non-governmental organisations with an international scope. International organisations are usually established by a treaty providing them with legal recognition, which distinguishes them from collections of states such as the G7.

AFRICAN UNION

PO Box 3243, Addis Ababa, Ethiopia
T (+251) (1) 1551 7700 E DIC@africa-union.org W www.au.int

The African Union (AU) was launched in 2002 as a successor to the amalgamated Organisation of African Unity (OAU) and the African Economic Community. It currently has 54 members, representing every African country. The AU aims to further African unity, solidarity and democracy, to coordinate political, economic, social and defence policies, and to intervene in regional conflicts on a humanitarian basis.

Chief AU governing organs include the assembly of heads of state or government, the ultimate decision-making body; the executive council, composed of foreign ministers from member states and which advises the assembly; the African Commission, which is the AU secretariat and consists of one chair, one deputy chair and eight commissioners, each with a separate portfolio, who elect a chair to a four-year term; the peace and security council, modelled on that of the UN and capable of military intervention; and the pan-African parliament, established in 2004 to advise heads of state.

Substantial budgetary arrears due to delays in the payment of national contributions have presented the AU with difficulties in achieving its objectives. Currently the AU has a joint peace keeping force with the United Nations (UNAMID) that has been deployed in the Darfur region of Sudan since 2007 (*see also* United Nations, Peacekeeping Forces). The AU mission in Somalia, AMISOM, was mandated in 2007 by a UN Security Council resolution. The UN Security Council decided in August 2017 to authorise the African Union to maintain the deployment of AMISOM, reducing its uniformed personnel from 22,126 to a maximum deployment of 20,626 by October 2018.

Chair 2018, Paul Kagame (Rwanda)
Chair of the Commission, Moussa Faki Mahamat

ANDEAN COMMUNITY

General Secretariat, Av. Paseo de la República 3895, San Isidro, Lima 27, Peru
T (+51) (1) 710 6400 E correspondencia@comunidadandina.org
W www.comunidadandina.org

The Andean Community (CAN), known as the Andean Pact until 1996, began operating formally on 21 November 1969 when its commission was established. It comprises four member states – Bolivia, Colombia, Ecuador and Peru – and the organisations and institutions of the Andean Integration System (AIS). Argentina, Brazil, Chile, Paraguay and Uruguay are associated states.

The community's objectives are to facilitate economic growth, create jobs and facilitate regional integration towards the goal of a Latin American common market. It also aims to reduce the inequalities in development between member states.

It pursues its objectives through a programme of trade liberalisation, a common external tariff, the relaxation of border controls, coordination between national legislatures and the promotion of industrial, agricultural and technological development. The community also promotes democratic practices, respect for human rights and environmental sustainability. Additionally, CAN supports cultural integration by providing media platforms for sharing documentaries, news and other cultural programming.

The general secretariat of the Andean Community is its executive body, responsible for administration and dispute resolution. The general secretariat operates under the direction of the secretary-general, who is elected by the Andean Council of Foreign Ministers (ACFM). It can propose decisions or suggestions to the ACFM; it also manages the integration process, ensures that community commitments are fulfilled and maintains relations with the member countries and the executive bodies of other international organisations.

The Andean presidential council is the highest-level body of the AIS and comprises the presidents of the member states. Its responsibilities include setting new policies, evaluating the integration process and communicating with other bodies. The chairmanship is rotated among the members of the council each calendar year.

Since 2005, a policy of free flow of persons has enabled citizens to travel, work and study throughout the area without a visa.

Secretary-General, Walker San Miguel Rodríguez (Bolivia)

ARAB MAGHREB UNION

73 rue Tensift, Agdal, Rabat, Morocco
T (+212) (5) 376 81371 E sg.uma@maghrebarabe.org
W www.maghrebarabe.org

The Treaty establishing the Arab Maghreb Union (AMU) was signed on 17 February 1989 by the heads of state of the five member states: Algeria, Libya, Mauritania, Morocco and Tunisia. The AMU aims to strengthen ties between the member countries by developing agriculture and commerce, working towards a customs union and economic common market.

Decisions must be unanimous and are made by a council of heads of state, which is briefed by a council of foreign affairs ministers. The council of heads of state has not assembled since 1994 because of a dispute over the status of Western Sahara. A consultative assembly – consisting of 30 representatives from each member state – is based in Algiers; the secretariat is in Rabat; and the court of justice, with two judges from each country, operates in Nouakchott, Mauritania.

Secretary-General, Taieb Baccouche (Tunisia)

ARCTIC COUNCIL

Fram Centre, Postboks 6606 Langnes, 9296 Tromsø, Norway
T (+47) 7775 0140 E acs@arctic-council.org
W www.arctic-council.org

The Arctic Council was founded in 1996 in Ottawa, Canada, and is a regional forum for socio-economic development and scientific research within the Arctic region, with particular emphasis on environmental conservation and sustainable developments. It comprises eight states: Canada, Denmark (including Greenland and the Faroe Islands), Finland, Iceland, Norway, Russia, Sweden and the USA. A further six organisations representing indigenous peoples are granted permanent participatory status and include the Saami Council,

Inuit Circumpolar Conference and the Arctic Athabaskan Council. Thirteen states (China, France, Germany, India, Italy, Japan, the Netherlands, Poland, Singapore, South Korea, Spain, Switzerland and the UK) have observer status.

Decisions within the Arctic Council are made at biennial ministerial meetings attended by foreign ministers or designates of the member states. The chairmanship of the council and secretariat also rotate on a biennial basis. Between these meetings, the operation of the council is administered by the Committee of Senior Arctic Officials, which meets biannually.

Arctic Council initiatives are carried out by six working groups, each focusing on specific issues such as the monitoring and prevention of pollution; climate change; biodiversity; and public health.

Chair 2017–19, Aleksi Harkonen (Finland)
Director of the Secretariat, Magnus Johannesson (Iceland)

ASIA COOPERATION DIALOGUE
Al Salam, Block 7, Street 27, House 14, Kuwait City, Kuwait
E acd.secretariat@gmail.com W www.acd-dialogue.org

The Asia Cooperation Dialogue (ACD) was initiated by the former prime minister of Thailand, Thaksin Shinawatra, and inaugurated in June 2002. It currently has 34 members, with Morocco granted development partner status.

Its purpose is to provide a continent-wide forum to assist development in countries in Asia, with the ultimate goal of creating a consolidated Asian trade community to enhance competitiveness in the global market and to reduce poverty. It aims to achieve these objectives through promoting interdependence among Asian countries, improving quality of life and expanding the continent's trade and financial markets.

Representatives from each of the member states (typically foreign ministers) meet annually to discuss ACD developments, issues of regional cooperation and methods of enhancing Asian unity. In addition, ministers also meet during the annual UN general assembly to discuss the implementation of policy and a common approach to international issues.

Secretary-General, Bundit Limschoon

ASIAN-AFRICAN LEGAL CONSULTATIVE ORGANIZATION
29 C, Rizal Marg, Diplomatic Enclave, Chanakyapuri, New Delhi 110021, India
T (+91) (11) 2419 7000 E mail@aalco.int W www.aalco.int

The Asian-African Legal Consultative Organization (AALCO), founded as a result of the Bandung Conference of 1955, was previously known as both the Asian Legal Consultative Committee and the Asian-African Legal Consultative Committee before its name was changed again in 2001. It was initially established as a non-permanent committee for a five-year term which was repeatedly extended until 1981, when it was granted permanent status. It has 47 member states.

The functions of the AALCO include serving as an advisory body to its member states in the field of international law, operating as a forum for common concerns among its members and making recommendations to governments and other international organisations.

Representatives from member states meet for the annual session which is hosted on a rotational basis and is attended by members of government, observers from other organisations and members of the International Court of Justice and International Law Commission.

The secretariat is located in New Delhi and is responsible for the day-to-day functioning of the organisation. It is headed by a secretary-general, who is elected to a four-year term that can be renewed once. Other infrastructure includes four regional arbitration centres, located in Egypt, Iran, Malaysia and Nigeria.

Secretary-General, Prof. Kennedy Gastorn (Tanzania)

ASIAN DEVELOPMENT BANK
6 ADB Avenue, Mandaluyong City 1550, Metro Manila, The Philippines
T (+63) (2)632 4444 W www.adb.org

The Asian Development Bank (ADB), founded in 1966, is a multilateral financial institution dedicated to reducing poverty in Asia and the Pacific. It has 67 member countries from across the world. The ADB extends loans, equity investments and technical assistance to governments and public and private enterprises in its member countries, and promotes the investment of public and private capital for development. The bank's programmes prioritise economic growth, human development, good governance, environmental protection, private sector growth and regional cooperation.

The ADB is controlled by its board of governors, which meets annually and consists of a representative from each of the member states. It elects and delegates its powers to a board of directors which is responsible for administration and policy review.

The ADB raises funds through members' contributions and issuing bonds on the world's capital markets.

President, Takehiko Nakao (Japan)

ASIA-PACIFIC ECONOMIC COOPERATION
35 Heng Mui Keng Terrace, Singapore 119616
T (+65) 6891 9600 E info@apec.org W www.apec.org

The Asia-Pacific Economic Cooperation (APEC) is an economic forum for Pacific Rim countries to discuss regional economy, cooperation, trade and investment. APEC was founded in 1989 in response to the growing interdependence among Asia-Pacific economies. The 1994 Declaration of Common Resolve envisaged free and open trade between member states with industrialised economies by 2010, extending to members with developing economies by 2020. At the 2016 summit in Lima, Peru, APEC leaders issued the twenty-fourth APEC economic leaders' declaration in which they committed to increased regional economic integration and quality growth, enhancing the regional food market, working towards modernising small- and medium-sized businesses in the region, and developing human capital. Its 21 members define and fund work programmes for APEC's four committees, 15 working groups and other special task groups.

APEC's chairmanship rotates annually among member states and the chair is responsible for hosting the annual leaders' meeting, as well as meetings of foreign affairs and trade ministers. The permanent secretariat, based in Singapore, is responsible for implementing policy, and is headed by an executive director selected by member states to serve a three-year term.

Executive Director, Dr Alan Bollard (New Zealand)

ASSOCIATION OF SOUTH-EAST ASIAN NATIONS
Jalan Sisingamangaraja 70a, Jakarta 12110, Indonesia
T (+62) (21) 726 2991/724 3372 E public@aseansec.org
W www.asean.org

The Association of South-East Asian Nations (ASEAN) is a geo-political and economic organisation formed in 1967 with the aim of accelerating economic growth, social progress and cultural development, and ensuring regional stability. It currently has ten member states.

The ASEAN summit, a biannual meeting of the heads of government, is the organisation's highest authority. The biannual ASEAN foreign ministers' meeting (ASEAN Coordinating Council) is responsible for preparing summit meetings, implementing their policies, and coordinating ASEAN's activities. The ASEAN economic ministers meet annually to coordinate economic policy.

An ASEAN free trade area was implemented in 2003, while a common preferential tariff was introduced in 1993. At the ASEAN summit in 1995, a South East Asia nuclear-weapon-free zone was declared. In December 2008 a new charter came into force which gave ASEAN legal status and a new institutional framework, committed it to the promotion of democracy, and provided for the establishment of the intergovernmental commission on human rights. The ASEAN Economic Community was formed at the end of 2015 with the aim of establishing a common market and therefore regional economic integration.

The secretary-general of ASEAN is appointed by rotation and can initiate, advise on, coordinate and implement ASEAN activities. In addition to the ASEAN secretariat based in Jakarta, each member state has a national secretariat in its foreign ministry which organises and implements activities at a national level.

Secretary-General 2018–22, Dato Lim Jock Hoi (Brunei)

BALTIC ASSEMBLY
Citadeles Street 2 – 616, Riga, LV-1010, Latvia
T (+371) 6722 5178 E baltasam@baltasam.org
W www.baltasam.org

Established in November 1991, the Baltic Assembly (BA) is an international organisation for cooperation between the parliaments of Estonia, Latvia and Lithuania. Each member state appoints between 12 and 16 parliamentarians to the assembly, including a chair and vice-chair of the national delegation. The political allegiances of the appointees reflect party proportions in each of the domestic parliaments. The BA holds an annual session in each of the member states in rotation. Several permanent and *ad hoc* committees also meet up to three times a year. The Baltic council of ministers, which comprises the heads of government and ministers of the member states, meets with the BA once a year and promotes intergovernmental and regional cooperation between the Baltic states; the joint sessions are known as the Baltic council.

President 2018, Valerijus Simulik (Lithuania)

CAB INTERNATIONAL
Nosworthy Way, Wallingford, Oxon OX10 8DE
T 01491-832111 W www.cabi.org

Founded in 1910, CAB International (CABI) (formerly the Commonwealth Agricultural Bureau) is a non-profit organisation that provides scientific expertise to assist sustainable development and environmental protection. The organisation consists of 42 countries, five British overseas territories and one associate member (the Netherlands); each is represented on both the executive council, which meets biannually, and the review conference, held every five years to appraise policy and set future goals. A governing board provides guidance on policy issues.

CABI has three divisions: publishing, development projects and research, and microbial services. Each division undertakes research and provides consultancy aimed at raising agricultural productivity, conserving biological resources, protecting the environment and controlling disease. Any country is eligible to apply for membership.

Chief Executive, Dr Trevor Nicholls (UK)

CARIBBEAN COMMUNITY
Turkeyen, Greater Georgetown, Guyana
T (+592) 222 0001/0075 E communications@caricom.org
W www.caricom.org

The Caribbean Community (CARICOM) was established as the Caribbean Community and Common Market in 1973 with the signing of the Treaty of Chaguaramas. The objectives of CARICOM is to improve member states' working and living standards, boost employment levels, promote economic development and competitiveness, coordinate foreign and economic policies and enhance cooperation in the delivery of services such as health and education.

The supreme organ is the Conference of Heads of Government, which determines policy and resolves conflict. The Community Council of Ministers consists of ministers of government assigned to CARICOM affairs and is responsible for economic and strategic planning. The principal administrative arm is the secretariat, based in Guyana. The Bureau of the Conference of Heads of Government is the executive body; it comprises the chair of the conference, the outgoing chair and the secretary-general, who are all authorised to initiate proposals and to secure the implementation of decisions. In addition, there are five ministerial councils dealing with trade and economic development, foreign and community relations, human and social development, finance and planning, and national security and law enforcement.

There are 15 member states of CARICOM plus five associate members, 13 of which are party to the Revised Treaty of Chaguaramas, which established the Caribbean Community including the CARICOM single market and economy (CSME) in 2006.

Secretary-General, Irwin LaRocque (Dominica)

THE COMMONWEALTH

The Commonwealth is a voluntary association of 52 sovereign and independent states together with their associated states and dependencies. All of the states were formerly parts of the British Empire or League of Nations (later the UN) mandated territories, except for Mozambique and Rwanda which were admitted because of their history of cooperation with neighbouring Commonwealth nations.

The status and relationship of member nations were first defined by the inter-imperial relations committee of the 1926 Imperial Conference, when the six existing dominions (Australia, Canada, the Irish Free State, Newfoundland, New Zealand and South Africa) were described as 'autonomous communities within the British Empire, equal in status, in no way subordinate one to another in any aspect of their domestic or external affairs, though united by a common allegiance to the Crown and freely associated as members of the British Commonwealth of Nations'. This formula was given legal substance by the statute of Westminster in 1931.

This concept of a group of countries owing allegiance to a single crown changed in 1949 when India became a republic. India's continued membership of the Commonwealth was agreed by the other members on the basis of its 'acceptance of the monarch as the symbol of the free association of its independent member nations and as such the head of the Commonwealth'. This enabled subsequent new republics to join the association. Member nations agreed at the time of the accession of Queen Elizabeth II to recognise Her Majesty as the new head of the Commonwealth. However, the position is not vested in the British Crown.

THE MODERN COMMONWEALTH
As the UK's former colonies joined, after India and Pakistan in 1947, the Commonwealth was transformed into a multiracial

association of equal nations, increasingly focused on promoting development and racial equality. South Africa withdrew in 1961 when it became clear that its reapplication for membership on becoming a republic would be rejected over its policy of apartheid.

The new goals of advocating democracy, the rule of law, good government and social justice were enshrined in the Harare Commonwealth Declaration (1991), which formed the basis of new membership guidelines agreed in Cyprus in 1993. Following the adoption of measures at the New Zealand summit in 1995 against serious or persistent violations of these principles, Nigeria was suspended in 1995 and Sierra Leone was suspended in 1997 for anti-democratic behaviour. Sierra Leone's suspension was revoked the following year when a legitimate government was returned to power. Similarly, Nigeria's suspension was lifted in 1999, the day a newly elected civilian president took office. The Edinburgh Commonwealth Economic Declaration (1997) established a set of economic principles for the Commonwealth, promoting economic growth while protecting smaller member states from the negative effects of globalisation. Zimbabwe was suspended from the councils of the Commonwealth in March 2002, and in 2003 the Zimbabwean government officially confirmed its departure from the association. Following the bloodless coup led by General Pervez Musharraf in 1999, Pakistan faced its first suspension from the Commonwealth. It was readmitted in 2004 only to be suspended again in 2007 after the imposition of emergency rule. The suspension was lifted after successful democratic elections in February 2008. Fiji's Commonwealth membership was suspended in September 2009 after its military government refused to commit to elections in 2010, but was reinstated in September 2014 following democratically held elections that took place earlier in the same month. In February 2018 The Gambia rejoined the Commonwealth after a near five-year absence in an attempt by the government to end international isolation; Yahya Jammeh, president 1996 to 2017, had pulled the country out of the Commonwealth in 2013.

MEMBERSHIP
Membership of the Commonwealth involves acceptance of the association's basic principles and is subject to the approval of existing members. There are 53 members at present, of which 16 have Queen Elizabeth II as head of state, 32 are republics and five have national monarchies. (The date of joining the Commonwealth is shown in parentheses.)

COUNTRIES THAT HAVE LEFT THE COMMONWEALTH
Republic of Ireland (1949)
South Africa (1961, rejoined 1994)
Pakistan (1972, rejoined 1989; suspended 1999, suspension lifted 2004; suspended 2007, suspension lifted 2008)
Zimbabwe (2003)
The Gambia (2013, rejoined 2018)
The Maldives (2016)

In each of the realms where Queen Elizabeth II is head of state (except for the UK), she is personally represented by a governor-general, who holds in all essential respects the same position in relation to the administration of public affairs in the realm as is held by Her Majesty in the UK. The governor-general is appointed by the Queen on the advice of the government of the state concerned.

INTERGOVERNMENTAL AND OTHER LINKS
The main forum for consultation is the Commonwealth Heads of Government Meetings, held biennially to discuss international developments and to consider cooperation among members. Decisions are reached by consensus and the

*Antigua and Barbuda (1981)	Mozambique (1995)
*Australia (1931)	Namibia (1990)
*The Bahamas (1973)	Nauru (1968)
Bangladesh (1972)	*New Zealand (1931)
*Barbados (1966)	Nigeria (1960)
Belize (1981)	Pakistan (1947)
Botswana (1966)	*Papua New Guinea (1975)
Brunei (1984)	Rwanda (2009)
Cameroon (1995)	*St Kitts and Nevis (1983)
*Canada (1931)	*St Lucia (1979)
Cyprus (1961)	*St Vincent and the
Dominica (1978)	Grenadines (1979)
†eSwatini (1968)	Samoa (1970)
Fiji (1970)	Seychelles (1976)
The Gambia (1965)	Sierra Leone (1961)
Ghana (1957)	Singapore (1965)
*Grenada (1974)	*Solomon Islands (1978)
Guyana (1966)	South Africa (1931)
India (1947)	Sri Lanka (1948)
*Jamaica (1962)	Tanzania (1961)
Kenya (1963)	Tonga (1970)
Kiribati (1979)	Trinidad and Tobago (1962)
Lesotho (1966)	*Tuvalu (1978)
Malawi (1964)	Uganda (1962)
Malaysia (1957)	*United Kingdom (1931)
Malta (1964)	Vanuatu (1980)
Mauritius (1968)	Zambia (1964)

* Realms of Queen Elizabeth II
† Formerly Swaziland

views of the meeting are set out in a communiqué. There are also annual meetings of finance ministers and frequent meetings of ministers and officials in other fields, such as education, health, gender and youth affairs. Intergovernmental links are complemented by the activities of some 80 Commonwealth non-governmental organisations linking professionals, sportsmen and sportswomen, and interest groups. The Commonwealth Games take place every four years.

COMMONWEALTH SECRETARIAT
The Commonwealth has a secretariat, established in 1965 in London, which is funded by member governments. This is the main agency for multilateral communication between member governments on issues relating to the Commonwealth as a whole. It promotes consultation and cooperation, disseminates information on matters of common concern, organises meetings including the biennial summits, coordinates Commonwealth activities and provides technical assistance for economic and social development through the Commonwealth fund for technical cooperation.

The Commonwealth Foundation was established by Commonwealth governments in 1965 as an autonomous body with a board of governors representing Commonwealth governments that fund the foundation. It promotes and funds exchanges and other activities aimed at strengthening the skills and effectiveness of professionals and non-governmental organisations. It also promotes culture, rural development, social welfare, human rights and gender equality.

COMMONWEALTH SECRETARIAT, Marlborough House, Pall Mall, London SW1Y 5HX
T 020-7747 6500 E info@commonwealth.int
W www.thecommonwealth.org
Secretary-General, Rt. Hon. Baroness Scotland of Asthal, QC (Dominica)

COMMONWEALTH FOUNDATION, Marlborough House, Pall Mall, London SW1Y 5HY T 020-7930 3783
E foundation@commonwealth.int
W www.commonwealthfoundation.com
Chair, Shree Baboo Chekitan Servansing (Mauritius)

COMMONWEALTH EDUCATION TRUST, 2nd Floor, 11/
12 Tokenhouse Yard, London EC2R 7AS T 020-7487 8341
E info@cet1886.org W www.cet1886.org
Chair (acting), Jeff Twentyman (UK)

COMMONWEALTH OF INDEPENDENT STATES

Ulitsa Kirova 17, Minsk 220030, Belarus
T (+375) (17) 222 35 17 E cr@cis.minsk.by W www.cis.minsk.by

The Commonwealth of Independent States (CIS) is a multilateral grouping of 11 former Soviet republics, including nine full members; Ukraine, a participating member; and Turkmenistan, an associate member. It was formed in 1991 and its charter was signed by ten states in 1993–4. The CIS acts as a coordinating mechanism for foreign, defence and economic policies and as a forum for addressing problems common to former members of the USSR. These matters are addressed in more than 70 inter-state, intergovernmental coordinating and consultative statutory bodies.

The two supreme CIS organs are the council of heads of state, which meets twice a year, and the council of heads of government. The executive committee, based in Minsk and Moscow, provides administrative support. There are also numerous ministerial, parliamentary, economic and security councils.

On becoming members of the CIS, the member states agreed to recognise their existing borders, respect one another's territorial integrity and reject the use of military force or coercion to settle disputes. A treaty on collective security was signed in 1992 by six states, and a joint peacemaking force, to intervene in CIS conflicts, was agreed upon by nine states. Russia concluded bilateral and multilateral agreements with other CIS states under the supervision of the council of heads of collective security (established 1993). These agreements became the Collective Security Treaty, enabling Russia to station troops in eight of the CIS states, and giving Russian forces *de facto* control of virtually all of the former USSR's external borders. Only Ukraine and Moldova remained outside the defence cooperation framework and did not sign the treaty. In 1999, Azerbaijan, Georgia and Uzbekistan withdrew from the treaty and formed a new defensive (GUAM) with Moldova and Ukraine. Georgia withdrew from the organisation entirely in August 2009, following the country's war with Russia in 2008. In May 2014, Ukraine announced that it would begin the process of withdrawing from the CIS. However, in September 2015 Ukraine confirmed that it would not withdraw completely from the CIS but would instead participate on a selective basis.

In 1991, 11 republics signed a treaty forming an economic community. Members agreed to refrain from economic actions that would damage each other and to coordinate economic and monetary policies. A coordinating consultative committee, an economic arbitration court and an inter-state bank were established. Members also affirmed the principles of private ownership, free enterprise and competition as the basis for economic recovery.

The 11 CIS members who signed the Establishment of an Economic Union Treaty in September 1993 committed themselves to a common economic space with free movement of goods, services, capital and labour. In 2000 the presidents of the five countries approved a treaty establishing the Eurasian Economic Community, and in 2010 Russia, Belarus and Kazakhstan formed a customs union, which Kyrgyzstan and Armenia joined in 2015. In April 2011 the economic council approved a draft agreement for the development of a free trade zone that would include all of the CIS member states: the agreement was signed by the CIS states with the exception of Azerbaijan, Uzbekistan and Turkmenistan in October 2011.

On 1 January 2012 the customs union of Russia, Belarus and Kazakhstan transformed into an single economic space (SES), a higher form of economic integration, ensuring freedom of movement of goods, services, capital, labour, and equal treatment of economic entities within the three countries. Russia assumed the presidency of the Commonwealth on 1 January 2017.

Executive Secretary, Sergei Lebedev (Russia)

COUNCIL OF EUROPE

Avenue de l'Europe, F-67075 Strasbourg-Cedex, France
T (+33) (3) 8841 2000 W www.coe.int

The Council of Europe was founded in 1949. Its aim is to achieve greater unity between its members, to safeguard their European heritage and to facilitate their progress in economic, social, cultural, educational, scientific, legal and administrative matters, and to further pluralist democracy, human rights and fundamental freedoms. It has 47 member states, including the 28 members of the European Union.

The organs are the committee of ministers, consisting of the foreign ministers of member countries, and the parliamentary assembly of 324 members (and 324 substitutes), elected or chosen by the national parliaments of member countries in proportion to the relative strength of political parties.

The committee of ministers is the executive organ. The majority of its conclusions take the form of international agreements (known as European conventions) or recommendations to governments. Decisions of the ministers may also be embodied in partial agreements to which a limited number of member governments are party.

One of the principal achievements of the Council of Europe is the European Convention on Human Rights (1950), which entered into force on 3 September 1953, and under which the European Court of Human Rights was established in 1959. The court oversees the implementation of the convention in the member states. It sits in chambers of seven judges or, exceptionally, as a grand chamber of 17 judges. Litigants must exhaust legal processes in their own country prior to bringing cases before the court.

Among other conventions and agreements are the European Convention for the Prevention of Torture, the European Social Charter, the Framework Convention for the protection of national minorities, the Istanbul Convention which combats violence against women, the Lanzarote Convention to protect children against sexual abuse and the Convention on Cyber Crime.

In 1990 the Venice Commission, an independent legal advisory body, was set up to assist in developing legislative, administrative and constitutional reforms in both European and non-European countries; it currently has 61 member states (47 Council of Europe members and 14 other countries), five observers and one associate member.

Non-member states take part in certain Council of Europe activities, such as educational, cultural and sports activities on a regular or *ad hoc* basis.

The council's ordinary budget for 2018 totals €466m (£407m).

President, Michele Nicoletti (Italy)
Secretary-General, Thorbjorn Jagland (Norway)

COUNCIL OF THE BALTIC SEA STATES

Slussplan 9, PO Box 2010, 103 11 Stockholm, Sweden
T (+46) 8440 1920 E cbss@cbss.org W www.cbss.org

The Council of the Baltic Sea States was established in 1992 with the aim of creating a regional forum to increase cooperation and coordination among the countries that border the Baltic Sea. The organisation focuses mainly on the environment, economic development, energy, education and culture, civil security and humanitarian issues. It currently has 12 members (the 11 countries of the Baltic Sea region and the European Union) while a further 11 countries (including the UK and the USA) hold observer status.

The council consists of the foreign ministers of each member state and a member of the European Commission. The presidency of the council rotates among the member states on an annual basis, and the annual session is held in the presiding country. The foreign minister of the presiding country is responsible for coordinating the council's activities and is assisted by the committee of senior officials; a permanent international secretariat established in Stockholm, Sweden in 1998 and financed jointly by the member states. The council does not have a general budget or project fund; member countries are responsible for funding common activities and/ or for seeking and coordinating financing from other sources.

Presidency 2017–18, Sweden

ECONOMIC COMMUNITY OF WEST AFRICAN STATES

101 Yakubu Gowon Crescent, Asokoro District, PMB 401, Abuja, Nigeria
T (+234) (9) 314 76479 W www.ecowas.int

The Economic Community of West African States (ECOWAS) was founded in 1975 and came into operation in 1977. It aims to promote the economic, social and cultural development of West Africa through mutual cooperation, and to prevent and control regional conflicts.

The supreme authority of ECOWAS is vested in the annual summit of heads of government of all 15 member states. A council of ministers meets biannually to monitor the organisation and make recommendations to the summit. Since restructuring in 2007, ECOWAS has been managed by a commission, headed by the president. The ECOWAS parliament was inaugurated in November 2000 and judges for the court of justice were appointed in January 2001. Chad currently holds observer status.

An ECOWAS travel certificate is issued allowing free movement within the community, and nine of the 15 member states have a common passport.

An ECOWAS peacekeeping force has been involved in attempts to restore peace in Liberia (1990–6), Sierra Leone (1997–9) and in Guinea-Bissau (1998–9). In December 2010 the Côte d'Ivoire was suspended from ECOWAS following the failure of its *de facto* president, Laurent Gbagbo, to step down after a presidential election; the country was reinstated the following year following Mr Gbagbo's arrest. In March 2011 both Guinea and Niger were reinstated to the organisation; their memberships had been suspended, for failure to hold satisfactory democratic elections in 2009. ECOWAS suspended Mali in March 2012 and, a few weeks later, in April, Guinea-Bissau, demanding the immediate restoration of constitutional order in both states following military coups in both countries. Both countries were subsequently reinstated.

President (2018–22), Jean-Claude Brou (Côte d'Ivoire)

EUROPEAN BANK FOR RECONSTRUCTION AND DEVELOPMENT

One Exchange Square, London EC2A 2JN
T 020-7338 6000 W www.ebrd.com

Since its establishment in 1991, the European Bank for Reconstruction and Development (EBRD) has become the largest financial investor in a region that stretches from central Europe and the Western Balkans to central Asia. Since 2011 the Bank – owned by 66 countries, the EU and the European Investment Bank – has been laying the foundations for the

expansion of its operations to the southern and eastern Mediterranean region.

The main forms of EBRD financing are loans, equity investments and guarantees. EBRD's charter stipulates that at least 60 per cent of lending must go to the private sector, reflecting its particular interest in strengthening the financial sector and to promoting small and medium-sized businesses. It works in cooperation with national governments, private companies and international organisations such as the OECD, the IMF, the World Bank and the UN specialised agencies. The EBRD is also able to borrow on world capital markets.

The EBRD's highest authority is the board of governors; each member appoints one governor and one alternate. The governors delegate most powers to a 23-member board of directors; the directors are responsible for the EBRD's operations and budget, and are elected by the governors for three-year terms. The governors also elect the president of the board of directors, who acts as the bank's president for a four-year term.

In 2017 it delivered a record annual investment of €9.7bn (£8.5bn) across 412 projects.

President, Sir Suma Chakrabarti (India)

EUROPEAN FREE TRADE ASSOCIATION

9–11 rue de Varembé, CH-1211 Geneva 20, Switzerland
T (+41) (22) 332 2600 E mail.gva@efta.int W www.efta.int

The European Free Trade Association (EFTA) was founded in 1960 on the premise of free trade as a means of achieving growth and prosperity among its member states as well as promoting closer economic cooperation between the Western European countries. The immediate aim of the Association was to provide a framework for the liberalisation of trade in goods among its member states.

EFTA was founded by seven countries: Austria, Denmark, Norway, Portugal, Sweden, Switzerland and the UK. Finland joined in 1961, Iceland in 1970 and Liechtenstein in 1991. In 1973, the UK and Denmark left EFTA to join the European Community. They were followed by Portugal in 1986 and by Austria, Finland and Sweden in 1995. Today the four EFTA member states are Iceland, Liechtenstein, Norway and Switzerland.

The Agreement on the European Economic Area (EEA) was signed in 1992 and entered into force in January 1994. The agreement brings together the 28 EU (European Union) member states and the three EEA EFTA states – Iceland, Liechtenstein and Norway – in a single market, referred to as the 'internal market'. Switzerland is not a member of the EEA, but has a series of bilateral agreements with the EU. The secretariat in Brussels provides support for the management of the EEA agreement, including the preparation of new legislation.

Currently, the EFTA states have free trade agreements with the following partners: Albania; Bosnia and Hercegovina; Canada; Central American States (Costa Rica, Guatemala and Panama); Chile; Colombia; Egypt; Georgia, Hong Kong, China; Gulf Cooperation Council (GCC); Israel; Jordan; the Rep. of Korea; Lebanon; Macedonia; Mexico; Montenegro; Morocco; the Palestinian Authority; Peru; the Philippines; Serbia; Singapore; Southern African Customs Union; Tunisia; Turkey; and Ukraine. Negotiations on free trade agreements are ongoing with Ecuador; India; Indonesia; Malaysia; and Vietnam.

The EFTA Council is the highest governing body in the EFTA. Member states usually meet eight times a year at ambassadorial level in Geneva.

Secretary-General, Kristinn Arnason (Iceland)

EUROPEAN ORGANISATION FOR NUCLEAR RESEARCH (CERN)

CH-1211 Geneva 23, Switzerland
T (+41) (22) 767 8484 E cern.reception@cern.ch W www.cern.ch

The convention establishing the European Organisation for Nuclear Research (CERN) came into force in 1954. CERN promotes European collaboration in high-energy physics with scientific goals and no military implication. It has 22 member states, three associate member states in the pre-stage to membership, five associate member states, and six members with observer status, including the European Commission and UNESCO.

The council, which is the highest policy-making body, comprises two delegates from each member state and is chaired by the president, who is elected by the council in session. The council also appoints a director-general, who is responsible for the internal organisation of CERN. The director-general heads a workforce of approximately 2,500 civil servants from the 22 member states. At present more than 11,000 scientists from all over the world use CERN's facilities.

Tim Berners-Lee developed the World Wide Web while working at CERN in 1989, and in 2008 CERN completed construction work on the Large Hadron Collider, the world's largest and most powerful particle accelerator.

Director-General, Dr Fabiola Gianotti (Italy)

EUROPEAN SPACE AGENCY

8–10 rue Mario Nikis, 75738 Paris Cedex 15, France
T (+33) (1) 5369 7654 E contactesa@esa.int W www.esa.int

The European Space Agency (ESA) was created in 1975 by the merger of the European Space Research Organisation and the European Launcher Development Organisation. Its aims include the advancement of space research and technology and the implementation of European space policy. ESA has 22 member states, one associate member and one cooperating state. ESA's mandatory activities are funded by contributions from all member states and calculated in accordance with each country's gross national income. In 2018, ESA's budget amounted to €5.60bn (£4.90bn).

The agency is directed by a council composed of the representatives of its member states; its chief officer is the director-general who is appointed by the council. ESA has liaison offices in Belgium (for the EU), the USA and Russia, while a launch base is stationed in French Guiana.

Director-General, Johann-Dietrich Wörner (Germany)

EUROPEAN UNION

See European Union section

FOOD AND AGRICULTURE ORGANIZATION OF THE UNITED NATIONS

Viale delle Terme di Caracalla, 00153 Rome, Italy
T (+39) (06) 57051 E fao-hq@fao.org W www.fao.org

The Food and Agriculture Organization (FAO) is a specialised UN agency, established in 1945. It assists rural populations by raising levels of nutrition and living standards, and by encouraging greater efficiency in food production and distribution. It analyses and publishes information on agriculture and natural resources. The FAO also advises governments on national agricultural policy and planning through its investment centre and collaboration with the World Bank and other financial institutions. The FAO's field programme covers a range of activities, including strengthening crop yields, rural development and livestock heath and productivity.

The FAO's priorities are sustainable agriculture, rural development and food security. The organisation monitors potential famine areas, channels emergency aid from governments and other agencies, assists in rehabilitation and responds to urgent or unforeseen requests for technical assistance.

The FAO has 195 members (194 states plus the European Union), and two associate members (the Faroe Islands and Tokelau). It is governed by a biennial conference of its members which sets a programme and budget. The budget for 2018–19 is US$2.6bn (£2bn) funded by member countries in proportion to their gross national income. The FAO is also funded by donor governments and other institutions.

The conference elects a director-general and a 49-member council which governs between conferences. The regular and field programmes are administered by a secretariat, headed by the director-general. Five regional, ten sub-regional and numerous national offices help administer the field programme.

Director-General, Jose Graziano da Silva (Brazil)

GULF COOPERATION COUNCIL

PO Box 7153, Riyadh 11-462, Saudi Arabia
T (+966) (11) 482 7777 W www.gcc-sg.org

The Gulf Cooperation Council (GCC), or the Cooperation Council for the Arab States of the Gulf, was established on 25 May 1981. Its main objectives are increasing coordination and integration, harmonising economic, commercial, educational and social policies and promoting scientific and technical innovation among its member states. It established a common market in 2008, and set up a customs union in 2003 which became fully operational in 2015. The GCC has six members: Bahrain, Kuwait, Oman, Qatar, Saudi Arabia and the United Arab Emirates.

The highest authority of the GCC is the supreme council, whose presidency rotates among members' heads of states. It holds one regular session every year, but extraordinary sessions may be convened if necessary.

The ministerial council, which ordinarily meets every three months, consists of the foreign ministers of the member states or other delegated ministers. It is authorised to propose policies and recommendations.

Secretary-General, Abdul Latif bin Rashid Al Zayani (Bahrain)

INTERNATIONAL ATOMIC ENERGY AGENCY

Vienna International Centre, PO Box 100,1400 Vienna, Austria
T (+43) (1) 26000 W www.iaea.org

The International Atomic Energy Agency (IAEA) was established in 1957. It is an intergovernmental organisation that reports to, but is not a specialised agency of, the UN.

The IAEA aims to enhance the contribution of atomic energy to peace, health and prosperity. It does not advocate the use of atomic energy for military purposes. It establishes atomic energy safety standards and offers services to its member states to upgrade safety and security measures for their nuclear installations and material, and for radioactive sources, material and waste. It is the focal point for international conventions on the early notification of a nuclear accident, accident assistance, civil liability for nuclear damage, physical protection of nuclear material and the safety of spent fuel and radioactive waste management. The IAEA also encourages research and training in nuclear power. It is additionally charged with drawing up safeguards and verifying their enforcement in accordance with several international nuclear weapons treaties.

The IAEA has 170 members that meet annually in a general conference. The conference decides policy, a programme and a budget as well as electing a director-general and a 35-member board of governors. The board meets five times a year to review and formulate policy, address budgetary concerns and consider applications for membership. Project and policy changes are implemented by the secretariat.

Director-General, Yukiya Amano (Japan)

INTERNATIONAL CIVIL AVIATION ORGANISATION

999 Robert-Bourassa Boulevard, Montréal, Québec H3C 5H7, Canada

T (+1) (514) 954 8219 E icaohq@icao.int W www.icao.int

The International Civil Aviation Organisation (ICAO) was founded with the signing of the Chicago Convention on International Civil Aviation in 1944 and became a specialised agency of the UN in 1947. It sets international technical standards and regulations for aviation safety, security and efficiency, as well as environmental protection.

ICAO has 192 members and is governed by an assembly, which convenes triennially. A council of 36 members is elected, which represents leading air transport nations as well as less developed countries. The council elects the president, appoints the secretary-general and supervises the organisation through subsidiary committees, serviced by a secretariat.

President of the Council, Dr Olumuyiwa Bernard Aliu (Nigeria)
Secretary-General, Dr Fang Liu

INTERNATIONAL CRIMINAL POLICE ORGANISATION (INTERPOL)

200 quai Charles de Gaulle, F-69006 Lyon, France

T (+33) (4) 7244 7163 W www.interpol.int

Interpol was set up in 1923 to establish an international criminal records office and to harmonise extradition procedures. The organisation has a global membership of 192 countries. Interpol's aims are to promote cooperation between criminal police authorities and to support government agencies concerned with combating crime, while respecting national sovereignty. It is financed largely by annual contributions from the governments of the member countries and supplementary funding from private and commercial sources.

Interpol policy is formulated by the general assembly which meets annually and is composed of delegates appointed by the member countries. The 13-member executive committee is elected by the general assembly from the member countries' delegates and is chaired by the president, who serves a four-year term of office. The permanent administrative organ is the general secretariat, headed by the secretary-general, who is appointed by the general assembly.

The UK Interpol National Central Bureau is operated by the National Crime Agency (NCA).

Secretary-General, Jürgen Stock (Germany)

INTERNATIONAL ENERGY AGENCY

31–35 rue de la Fédération, 75739 Paris Cedex 15, France

T (+33) (1) 4057 6500 E info@iea.org W www.iea.org

The International Energy Agency (IEA), founded in 1974, is an autonomous agency within the framework of the Organisation for Economic Cooperation and Development (OECD). The IEA's objectives include the improvement of energy cooperation worldwide, development of alternative energy sources and the promotion of relations between oil-producing and oil-consuming countries. The IEA also maintains an emergency system to alleviate the effects of severe oil supply disruptions.

The main decision-making body is the governing board, composed of senior energy officials from member countries. The IEA secretariat, with a staff of energy experts, carries out the work of the governing board and its subordinate bodies. The executive director is appointed by the board. The IEA has 30 member states; the European Union also participates in its work.

Executive Director, Fatih Birol (Turkey)

INTERNATIONAL FRANCOPHONE ORGANISATION

Cabinet du Secrétaire général, 19–21 avenue Bosquet, 75007 Paris, France

T (+33) (1) 4437 3300 W www.francophonie.org

The International Francophone Organisation *(International Organisation of La Francophonie* – IOF) is an intergovernmental organisation founded in 1970 by 21 French-speaking countries. Its 84 member states and governments, 58 members and 26 observers, together represent over 900 million people; 274 million of which speak French regularly, with varying degrees of fluency. The IOF organises political activities and actions multilateral cooperation that benefits French-speaking populations. It represents its member states internationally, promotes French language and francophone cultural industries with the aim of preventing conflict and promoting development.

The conference of heads of state and government of countries with French as a common language – also known as La Francophonie summit – takes place biennially. Other institutions include the permanent ministerial conference and the permanent council.

Secretary-General, Michaëlle Jean (Canada)

INTERNATIONAL FUND FOR AGRICULTURAL DEVELOPMENT

44 Via Paolo di Dono, 00142 Rome, Italy

T (+39) (06) 54591 E ifad@ifad.org W www.ifad.org

The International Fund for Agricultural Development (IFAD) began operations as a UN specialised agency in 1977. It develops and finances agricultural and rural projects in developing countries and aims to promote employment and additional income for poor farmers, reduce malnutrition and improve food security systems.

IFAD has 176 member states divided into three lists: List A (primarily OECD countries), List B (primarily OPEC countries), and List C (developing countries) which is subdivided into C1 (Africa), C2 (Europe, Asia and the Pacific) and C3 (Latin America and the Caribbean). All powers are vested in a governing council of all member states, which meets annually. It elects an executive board which is composed of 18 members and 18 alternate members and is chaired by the president of the IFAD. The president serves a four-year term that can be renewed once.

President, Gilbert F. Houngbo (Togo)

INTERNATIONAL HYDROGRAPHIC ORGANIZATION

4b quai Antoine 1er, B.P. 445, MC 98011, Monaco

T (+377) 9310 8100 E info@iho.int W www.iho.int

The International Hydrographic Organization (IHO) began operating in 1921 with 19 member states and headquarters in the Principality of Monaco. In 1970 its name was changed from the International Hydrographic Bureau. The IHO is an intergovernmental organisation that has a purely consultative role and aims to support safety in international navigation, set policy for marine conservation and improve coordination between national hydrographic institutions. The IHO has a membership of 85 states that meet at triennial assemblies to set policy, approve budget, review progress and adopt programmes of work. Each member is represented at these conferences by their most senior hydrographer. All member states have an opportunity to initiate new proposals for IHO consideration. Outside of its membership, the IHO acts to promote hydrography and facilitate the exchange of technology with developing countries. It is also the source that defines the boundaries between seas and oceans.

Secretary-General, Dr Mathias Jonas (Germany)

INTERNATIONAL LABOUR ORGANIZATION
4 route des Morillons, CH-1211, Geneva 22, Switzerland
T (+41) (22) 799 6111 E ilo@ilo.org W www.ilo.org

The International Labour Organization (ILO) was established in 1919 as an autonomous body of the League of Nations and became the UN's first specialised agency in 1946. The ILO aims to promote employment, improve working conditions, extend social protection and promote dialogue between government, workers' and employers' organisations.

It sets minimum international labour standards through the drafting of international conventions. Member countries are obliged to submit these to their domestic authorities for ratification, and thus undertake to bring their domestic legislation in line with the conventions. Members must report to the ILO periodically on how these regulations are being implemented. The ILO is also a principal resource centre for information, analysis and guidance on labour and employment.

The ILO has 187 member states and is composed of the International Labour Conference, the governing body and the International Labour Office. The conference of members meets annually and is attended by national delegations. It adopts international labour conventions and recommendations, provides a forum for discussion of economic and social issues and approves the ILO's programme and budget.

The 56-member governing body is composed of 28 government, 14 worker and 14 employer members and acts as the ILO's executive council. It convenes three times a year. Ten governments, including the UK, hold permanent seats on the governing body because of their industrial importance. There are also various regional conferences and advisory committees. The ILO acts as a secretariat and as a centre for operations, publishing and research.

Director-General, Guy Ryder (UK)

INTERNATIONAL MARITIME ORGANIZATION
4 Albert Embankment, London SE1 7SR
T 020-7735 7611 E info@imo.org W www.imo.org

Originally named the Inter-Governmental Maritime Consultative Organisation, the International Maritime Organisation (IMO) was established as a UN specialised agency in 1948. Owing to delays in treaty ratification it did not commence operations until 1958.

The IMO fosters intergovernmental cooperation in technical matters relating to international shipping, particularly regarding safety and security at sea, efficiency in navigation and protecting the marine environment from pollution caused by shipping. The IMO is responsible for convening maritime conferences and drafting marine conventions. It also provides technical aid to countries wishing to develop their activities at sea.

The IMO has 172 members and three associate members. It is governed by an assembly comprising delegates of all its members. It meets biennially to formulate policy, set a budget, to vote on specific recommendations on pollution, maritime safety and security, and to elect the council. The council, which meets twice a year, fulfils the functions of the assembly between sessions and appoints a secretary-general. It consists of 40 members: ten from the world's largest shipping nations, ten from the nations most dependent on seaborne trade and 20 other members to ensure a fair geographical representation. The IMO acts as the secretariat for the London Convention (1972) and its 1996 protocol which regulates the disposal of land-generated waste at sea.

Secretary-General, Kitack Lim (Republic of Korea)

INTERNATIONAL MONETARY FUND
700 19th Street NW, Washington DC 20431, USA
T (+1) (202) 623 7000 E publicaffairs@imf.org W www.imf.org

The International Monetary Fund (IMF) was established at the UN Monetary and Financial Conference at Bretton Woods, New Hampshire, in 1944. Its articles of agreement entered into force in 1945 and it began operations in 1947.

The IMF exists to promote international monetary cooperation and the expansion of world trade to ensure international economic stability. It advises members on their economic and financial policies; promotes policy coordination among the major industrial countries; gives technical assistance in central banking, balance of payments accounting, taxation and other financial matters; and provides loans to states with weak economies. The IMF serves as a forum for members to discuss monetary policy issues and seeks the balanced growth of international trade. It has 189 members; Tuvalu joined in June 2010, South Sudan in April 2012 and Nauru in April 2016.

Upon joining the IMF, a member is assigned a quota based on that member's relative standing in the world economy and its balance of payments. The quota determines the maximum size of the member's capital subscription to the fund, access to IMF resources, voting power and share in the allocation of special drawing rights (SDRs). Quotas are reviewed at regular intervals (usually every five years) and adjusted accordingly. After the 13th general review in 2008 the IMF board of governors adopted a reform package which would grant *ad hoc* quota increases to 54 countries found to be under-represented, and triple the number of basic votes to all members, thereby enhancing the representation of emerging and low-income countries. These reforms became effective in March 2011. In December 2010 the board of governors approved recommendations of the 14th general review – namely the doubling of all available quotas, a shift in 6 per cent of quotas from over- to under-represented countries, and an overall realignment in quota shares to reflect emerging markets and developing countries (EDMCs). Under these reforms, China will become the third largest member country and three further EDMCs (Brazil, India and Russia) will be among the top ten shareholders. These reforms will become effective upon their acceptance by three-fifths of members having 85 per cent of total voting power. Work on the 15th general review has been delayed, pending implementation of the 2010 reforms. In February 2015, the board of governors adopted a resolution calling for the completion of the 15th review by 15 December 2015. The deadline has now been extended until the commencement of the 2019 annual meeting.

The SDR (special drawing rights), the reserve currency created by the IMF in 1969, is calculated daily on a basket of usable currencies and is the IMF's unit of account; as at 29 June 2018, 1 SDR equalled US\$1.41 (£1.07). SDRs are allocated at intervals to supplement members' reserves and thereby improve international financial liquidity. Total quotas currently stand at SDR477bn, a doubling of quotas from 2015, following the implementation of the reforms of the 14th general review on 26 January 2016.

The IMF is not a bank and does not lend money; it provides temporary financial assistance by selling a member's SDRs or other members' currencies in exchange for the member's own currency. The member can then use the purchased currency to alleviate its balance of payments difficulties. IMF financial resources derive primarily from members' capital subscriptions, which are proportionally related to their quotas. In addition, the IMF is authorised to borrow from official lenders. It may also draw on a line of credit from 38 member countries and institutions under the new arrangements to borrow (NAB). Once activated, NAB can provide supplementary resources of up to SDR182.4bn to the IMF. In limited cases the IMF can also access a potential amount totalling SDR17bn from 11 countries under the so-called general arrangements to borrow (GAB), with an additional SDR1.5bn available under an associated arrangement with Saudi Arabia.

Benign market conditions between 2004 and 2008 prompted many countries to start repaying their outstanding loans and demand for the fund's resources dropped dramatically; however, in 2008 the IMF increased its lending in response to the global financial crisis. In March 2009 the IMF announced a number of reforms to its lending framework, intended to provide greater speed and flexibility in lending arrangements, doubled access limits on loans and more closely tailor the conditionality of loans to fit the recipient state's requirements. In February 2010 a defined poverty line was introduced under which countries would qualify to access low-cost concessional loans under the poverty reduction and growth trust. In 2011 the IMF further refined its lending options to better meet the needs of its member countries as global growth continued to weaken in response to the ongoing crisis in the euro area. The 2011 measures included the introduction of a precautionary credit line to enable the IMF to provide upfront liquidity, including for countries with sound policies that had been affected by economic shocks beyond their control, and a rapid financing instrument for emergency assistance to support member countries experiencing a range of urgent balance of payments needs, without the need for a fully fledged programme. As at 29 June 2018 total outstanding IMF credits amounted to SDR56.04bn.

The IMF supports long-term efforts at economic reform and transformation as well as medium-term programmes under the extended fund facility, which runs for three to four years and is aimed at overcoming balance of payments difficulties stemming from macroeconomic and structural problems. Typically, measures are introduced to reform taxation and the financial sector, to privatise state-owned enterprises and to make labour markets more flexible.

The IMF is headed by a board of governors, comprising one representative and one alternate representative of each member state, which meets annually. The governors delegate powers to 24 executive directors, who are appointed or elected by member countries. The executive directors are responsible for the daily operation of the fund and the election of the managing director.

Managing Director, Christine Lagarde (France)

INTERNATIONAL ORGANIZATION FOR MIGRATION

17 Route des Morillons, PO Box 17, CH-1211 Geneva 19, Switzerland
T (+41) (22) 717 9111 E hq@iom.int W www.iom.int

The International Organization for Migration (IOM) was founded in 1951 to resettle European displaced persons and refugees. During the 1960s and 1970s the IOM developed links with the United Nations High Commissioner for Refugees and began a programme of assistance and reintegration outside of Europe.

The role of the IOM is to help ensure the orderly and humane management of migration; its remit includes migration health services, international migration law, counter-trafficking measures, emergency and post-crisis management and assisted voluntary returns. More than 9,000 staff are employed almost entirely in over 480 field locations. There are 169 member states and eight states with observer status.

The IOM is led by a director-general who is elected for a five-year term. The director-general's office has the constitutional authority to manage the organisation, carry out the activities within its mandate and develop current policies, procedures and strategies.

Director-General, William Lacy Swing (USA)

INTERNATIONAL RED CROSS AND RED CRESCENT MOVEMENT

International Committee of the Red Cross, 19 Avenue de la paix, 1202 Geneva, Switzerland
T (+41) (22) 734 6001 W www.icrc.org

The International Red Cross and Red Crescent Movement is composed of three elements – the International Committee of the Red Cross, the International Federation of Red Cross and Red Crescent Societies, and the National Red Cross and Red Crescent Societies.

The International Committee of the Red Cross (ICRC), the organisation's founding body, was formed in 1863. It aims to protect and assist victims of armed conflict. It also seeks to ensure the application of the Geneva Conventions regarding prisoners of war and detainees.

The International Federation of Red Cross and Red Crescent Societies (IFRC) was founded in 1919 to assist the humanitarian activities of national societies, coordinate their relief operations for victims of natural disasters and care for refugees outside areas of conflict. There are Red Cross and Red Crescent societies in 190 countries and it has more than 60 field delegations internationally.

The international conference of the Red Cross and Red Crescent meets every four years, bringing together delegates of the ICRC, the International Federation and the national societies, as well as representatives of all states party to the Geneva Conventions.

Director-General of the ICRC, Yves Daccord (Switzerland)
President of the IFRC, Francesco Rocca (Italy)

INTERNATIONAL TELECOMMUNICATION UNION

Place des Nations, 1211 Geneva 20, Switzerland
T (+41) (22) 730 5111 E itumail@itu.int W www.itu.int

The International Telecommunication Union (ITU) was founded in Paris in 1865 as the International Telegraph Union and became a UN specialised agency in 1947.

ITU is an intergovernmental organisation for information and communication technologies. It comprises 193 member states, almost 800 sector members and associates who represent public and private organisations involved in telecommunications. Its mission is to promote the development of information and communication technologies and to offer assistance to developing countries.

For nearly 150 years, ITU has coordinated the shared global use of the radio spectrum, promoted international cooperation in assigning satellite orbits, worked to improve communication infrastructure in the developing world and established the worldwide standards for the interconnection of a vast range of communications systems: from broadband networks to new-generation wireless technologies, aeronautical and maritime navigation, radio astronomy, satellite-based meteorology and converging fixed-line and mobile telephone, internet and broadcasting technologies.

Secretary-General, Houlin Zhao (China)

INTERNATIONAL TRADE UNION CONFEDERATION

Boulevard du Roi Albert II, 5 B 1, B-1210 Brussels, Belgium
T (+32) (2) 224 0211 E info@ituc-csi.org W www.ituc-csi.org

The International Trade Union Confederation (ITUC) was created in 2006 by the merger between the International Confederation of Free Trade Unions (ICFTU), the World Confederation of Labour (WCL) and other independent unions. Through public and industrial advocacy work it seeks to assert and defend the rights and interests of workers, and to foster international cooperation between trade unions. In November 2017 the ITUC represented 207 million workers in 163 countries and territories and had 331 national affiliates.

The congress, the supreme authority of the ITUC, meets once every four years to review and propose policy and to elect the 78-member general council. Council members are elected according to population-weighted geographical regions, with six seats reserved for nomination by the women's committee, and two by the youth committee. The council, and the general secretary elected at each congress, govern the organisation. It also elects a 25-member executive bureau from among its members which deals with urgent issues and those delegated to it by the council; it also makes decisions on finances and formulates the annual budget for council approval.

The ITUC has regional organisations for Africa (ITUC-AF), the Americas (TUCA), Asia-Pacific (ITUC-AP), and Europe (the pan-European regional council, or PERC), along with the Arab Trade Union Confederation (ATUC). It also cooperates closely with the Global Union Federations, the Trade Union Advisory Committee to the Organisation for Economic Cooperation and Development (OECD), the European Trade Union Confederation, the International Labour Organisation, a number of other UN specialised agencies and national and regional unions and organisations.

General Secretary, Sharan Burrow (Australia)

INTERNATIONAL WHALING COMMISSION

The Red House, 135 Station Road, Impington, Cambridge CB24 9NP
T 01223-233971 W www.iwc.int

The International Whaling Commission (IWC) was set up under the International Convention for the Regulation of Whaling, signed in Washington DC in 1946. It has 92 member states. The purpose of the IWC is to provide for the conservation of whale stocks, enabling the development of the whaling industry. The measures in the convention provide for the complete protection of certain species; designate specified areas as whale sanctuaries; set limits on the numbers and size of whales which may be taken; prescribe open and closed seasons and areas for whaling; and prohibit the capture of suckling calves and female whales accompanied by calves. The IWC meets biennially to review and revise these measures.

The IWC has three main committees, responsible for scientific, finance and administration, and conservation matters. There are further sub-committees and working groups concerned with subjects including aboriginal subsistence whaling, infractions, small cetaceans, whalewatching, whale-killing methods and animal welfare.

Executive Secretary, Dr Rebecca Lent (USA)

LEAGUE OF ARAB STATES

Al-Tahrir Square, PO Box 11642, Cairo, Egypt
T (+20) (2) 2575 0511 W www.lasportal.org

The League of Arab States was founded in 1945 to protect the independence and sovereignty of its member states, supervise the affairs and interests of Arab countries and promote coordination among them. The organisation has 22 members, including Palestine. The League itself has observer status at the United Nations.

The heads of member states meet annually at the Arab League summit, while foreign ministers convene every six months as part of the Arab League council. Member states participate in various specialised agencies which develop specific areas of cooperation between Arab states. These include the Arab Monetary Fund; the Arab Satellite Communications Organisation; the Arab Academy for Science, Technology and Maritime Transport; the Arab Bank for Economic Development in Africa; the Arab League Educational, Cultural and Scientific Organisation; and the Council of Arab Economic Unity.

Secretary-General, Ahmed Ali Aboul Gheit (Egypt)

MERCOSUR

Dr. Luis Piera 1992, Piso 1, 11200-Montevideo, Uruguay
T (+598) (2) 412 9024 W www.mercosur.int

MERCOSUR (the Southern Common Market) was created by the Treaty of Asunción, signed by Argentina, Brazil, Paraguay and Uruguay on 26 March 1991. Venezuela signed an adhesion protocol in 2006 and became a full member in 2012, but was suspended indefinitely as a member in August 2017. Bolivia, which had been an associate member since 1997, became a full member on 17 July 2015. Six other countries (Chile, Colombia, Ecuador, Guyana, Peru and Suriname) have associate member status. New Zealand and Mexico are observer states.

The Common Market Council (CMC) is the highest-level agency of MERCOSUR, with authority to formulate policy and enforce member states' compliance with the Treaty of Asunción. The CMC comprises ministers of foreign affairs and economic ministers of the member states; it meets at least once a year.

The Common Market Group is the executive body of MERCOSUR and is coordinated by the foreign ministries of the member states. Its function is to implement decisions made by the CMC and resolve disputes, and if necessary, establish subgroups to work on particular issues. Other bodies include a joint parliamentary committee, a trade commission and a socio-economic advisory forum. The presidency of MERCOSUR rotates between member states every six months.

In 2005, Argentina, Brazil, Paraguay and Uruguay became associate members of the Andean Community, reciprocating MERCOSUR's action to grant associate membership to all Andean Community nations. In December 2005, the Colombian president ratified a free trade agreement (FTA) with MERCOSUR giving Colombian products preferential access to MERCOSUR countries. MERCOSUR signed an FTA with Israel in December 2007, the bloc's first such agreement outside Latin America. After stalling in 2004, negotiations with the EU over a possible FTA were relaunched in May 2010 before being paused in 2012. In May 2016 negotiations with the EU were once again relaunched and offers exchanged, this was followed by a round of negotiations in the October of the same year.

Presidency (Jan–Jun 2018), Horacio Cartes (Paraguay)
Presidency (Jul–Dec 2018), Tabaré Vázquez (Uruguay)

NORDIC COUNCIL
Ved Stranden 18, 1061 Copenhagen K, Denmark
T (+45) 3396 0400 E nordisk-rad@norden.org W www.norden.org

The Nordic Council was established in March 1952 as an advisory body on economic and social cooperation, comprising parliamentary delegates from Denmark, Iceland, Norway and Sweden. It was subsequently joined by Finland (1955), and representatives from the Faroes (1970), the Aland Islands (1970) and Greenland (1984).

Cooperation is regulated by the Helsinki Treaty, signed in 1962. This was amended in 1971 to create a Nordic council of ministers, which discusses all matters except defence and foreign affairs. Decisions of the council of ministers, which are taken by consensus, are binding, although if ratification by member parliaments is required, decisions only become effective following parliamentary approval. The council of ministers is advised by the Nordic Council, to which it reports annually. There are ministers for Nordic cooperation in every member government.

The Nordic Council comprises 87 elected members. Denmark, Finland, Norway, and Sweden each have 20 members and Iceland has seven members. Of these, two of the Danish representatives are from the Faroe Islands and two are from Greenland, while Finland has two representatives from Aland. The council comprises members of the national parliaments nominated by their party groups. The council meets biannually – the ordinary session in the autumn and the theme session in the spring, at which decisions are made on issues that are then implemented by the national governments. The president, vice-president, and the 15 members of the presidium for the forthcoming year are elected at the ordinary session. The presidency of the Nordic Council rotates between the five countries, and the presiding country hosts the council sessions.

The on-going political work of the council is conducted through committees and party groups. The council is served by a secretariat that shares its premises with the secretariat to the council of ministers in Copenhagen. There is also a national secretariat in each of the Nordic parliaments.

President 2018, Michael Tetzschner (Norway)

NORTH AMERICAN FREE TRADE AGREEMENT

NAFTA SECRETARIAT, CANADIAN SECTION, 111 Sussex Drive, 5th Floor, Ottawa, Ontario K1A 0G2, Canada
T (+1) (343) 203 4274 E canada@nafta-sec-alena.org

NAFTA SECRETARIAT, MEXICAN SECTION, Avenida Paseo de la Reforma 296, 25 Piso, Colonia Juárez, Delegación Cuauhtémoc, Código Postal 06600, Ciudad de México D. F, México
T (+52) (55) 5729 9100 E naftamexico@nafta-sec-alena.org

NAFTA SECRETARIAT, US SECTION, Room 2061, 1401 Constitution Avenue NW, Washington DC 20230, USA
T (+1) (202) 482 5438 E usa@nafta-sec-alena.org
W www.nafta-sec-alena.org

The leaders of Canada, Mexico and the USA signed the North American Free Trade Agreement (NAFTA) on 17 December 1992 in their respective capitals; it came into force in January 1994 after being ratified by the legislatures of the three member states.

NAFTA aims to eliminate barriers to trade in goods and services, promote fair competition within the free trade area, protect and enforce intellectual property rights and create a framework for further cooperation. To achieve these aims, import tariffs, quotas and limits on cross-border investment have been removed.

The NAFTA secretariat is composed of Canadian, Mexican and US sections. It is responsible for administering the dispute-settlement provisions of the agreement, providing assistance to the Free Trade Commission and support for various committees and working groups, and facilitating the operation of the agreement.

NORTH ATLANTIC TREATY ORGANISATION
Blvd Leopold III, Brussels B-1110, Belgium
T (+32) (2) 707 4111 E natodoc@hq.nato.int W www.nato.int

The North Atlantic Treaty Organisation (NATO) is a political and military alliance designed to provide common security for its members through cooperation and consultation in political, military and economic as well as scientific and other non-military fields.

The North Atlantic Treaty (Treaty of Washington) was signed in 1949 by Belgium, Canada, Denmark, France, Iceland, Italy, Luxembourg, the Netherlands, Norway, Portugal, the UK and the USA. Greece and Turkey acceded to the treaty in 1952, the Federal Republic of Germany in 1955 (the reunited Germany acceded in October 1990), Spain in 1982, and the Czech Republic, Hungary and Poland in 1999. Bulgaria, Estonia, Latvia, Lithuania, Romania, Slovakia and Slovenia signed membership protocols in March 2003 and officially joined NATO in March 2004. Albania and Croatia became official members in April 2009, having signed membership accords in September 2008, while Montenegro joined in 2017.

STRUCTURE

The North Atlantic council (NAC), chaired by the secretary-general, is the highest authority of the alliance and is composed of permanent representatives of the 29 member countries. It meets weekly, but also holds meetings at higher levels involving foreign and defence ministers and heads of government. The permanent representatives (ambassadors) head national delegations of advisers and experts. The nuclear planning group (NPG) is composed of all member countries, with the exception of France, and meets at ministerial level at least once a year. The NATO secretary-general chairs the council and the NPG. Much of the NAC policy is prepared and drafted by the senior political committee, a group of deputy permanent representatives and policy advisers.

The senior military authority in NATO, which advises the council, is the military committee, composed of the chief of defence staffs of each member country except Iceland, which has no military forces and is represented by a civilian. The military committee, which is assisted by an integrated international military staff, also meets in permanent session with permanent military representatives and is responsible for making recommendations to the council on measures considered necessary for the common defence of the NATO area and for supplying guidance on military matters to the NATO strategic commanders. The chair of the military committee, elected for a period of two to three years, represents the committee on the council.

The alliance's military command structure is divided between two functional strategic commands: Allied Command Operations (ACO) is responsible for all NATO military operations, whereas Allied Command Transformation (ACT) is charged with training and restructuring NATO military forces and capabilities. The headquarters of ACO is at the Supreme Headquarters of the Allied Powers Europe (SHAPE) at Mons, Belgium, and comes under the command of the Supreme Allied Commander Europe (SACEUR). The headquarters of ACT is at Norfolk, Virginia, USA, and is under the command of the Supreme Allied Commander

Transformation (SACT). There is also a regional planning group for Canada and the USA.

POST COLD WAR DEVELOPMENTS
The Euro-Atlantic Partnership Council (EAPC) was established in 1997 to develop closer security links with Eastern European and former Soviet states. Replacing the North Atlantic Cooperation Council (NACC) as the first institutional framework for cooperation between NATO member countries and former adversaries from Central and Eastern Europe, the EAPC focuses on defence planning, defence industry conversion, defence management and force structuring. Its membership comprises the 29 NATO members and Armenia, Austria, Azerbaijan, Belarus, Bosnia and Hercegovina, Finland, Georgia, Ireland, Kazakhstan, Kyrgyzstan, Macedonia, Malta, Moldova, Russia, Serbia, Sweden, Switzerland, Tajikistan, Turkmenistan, Ukraine and Uzbekistan. The EAPC provides the multilateral, political framework for the Partnership for Peace programme (PFP). The PFP is the basis for practical, bilateral security cooperation between NATO and all partner countries in the fields of defence planning and budgeting, military exercises and civil emergency operations. It also works to improve the interoperability between the forces of partner and member countries to enable them to undertake joint operations and has provided the context for cooperation by many of the partner countries in NATO-led peacekeeping and peace-support operations in Bosnia and Hercegovina, Kosovo and Afghanistan.

NATO and Russia committed themselves to helping build a stable and secure partnership based on mutual interest when they signed the 1997 Founding Act on mutual relations, cooperation and security, which provided for the creation of a NATO-Russia Permanent Joint Council (PJC). In 2002 it was replaced by the NATO-Russia Council (NRC). In April 2014, following Russia's military intervention in Ukraine, NATO suspended all practical cooperation with Russia, including the NRC, save for high level communications at ambassadorial level and above, but meetings of the council resumed in 2016. Three meetings of the NRC took place in 2016 and three in 2017. The first meeting in 2018 took place on 31 May. NATO remains open to a periodic, focused and meaningful political dialogue with Russia on the basis of reciprocity, as agreed at the NATO Summit in Warsaw in July 2016.

The establishment of the NATO-Ukraine Commission (NUC) in 1997 committed both parties to developing their relationship under a programme of consultation and cooperation on political and security issues, and cooperation has been intensified since Russia's intervention in 2014. The NATO-Georgia Commission (NGC), created in 2008, is pursuing political dialogue between NATO and Georgia, and helping to supervise Georgia's progress towards membership of NATO. The NGC is also co-ordinating support to help the country recover from the summer 2008 conflict.

NATO's Mediterranean dialogue, launched in 1994, aims to improve trust and understanding of NATO's goals and objectives among the countries of the southern Mediterranean area: Algeria, Egypt, Israel, Jordan, Mauritania, Morocco and Tunisia.

At its summit meeting in 2004, the alliance launched the Istanbul Cooperation Initiative (ICI), promoting practical cooperation with the Gulf Cooperation Council (GCC) and other interested countries in the Middle East. To date Bahrain, Qatar, Kuwait and the United Arab Emirates have joined the ICI.

The development of a European security and defence identity, which would strengthen NATO's European pillar, was agreed at the 1999 NATO summit meeting in Washington. Subsequent developments have served to strengthen cooperation between NATO and the European Union and to establish a strategic partnership.

At the 2002 Prague summit, further measures to improve defence capabilities were taken on the basis of a new capabilities commitment, in which member countries agreed to specific targets and time frames for improvements. A military concept for defence against terrorism was also agreed, and additional initiatives taken in the areas of nuclear, biological and chemical weapons defence and protection against cyber attacks. The NATO response force (NRF), a rapid-reaction unit comprising land, sea and air special forces, was officially launched at the Prague summit and became fully operational in 2006. The Lisbon summit in 2010 saw the publication of NATO's strategic concept, a statement of core principles that emphasized the importance of international cooperation in defence, security and crisis management, with particular reference to strengthening NATO's relationships with the EU and UN. At the 2014 Wales summit, it was decided to enhance the NATO response force by establishing a very high readiness joint task force (VJTF) to deploy within just a few days to challenges that arise. The VJTF was deployed for exercises for the first time in June 2015 and has been on active standby since that time.

AFGHANISTAN
From January 2001, following the establishment of the Afghan Transitional Authority, an international security assistance force (ISAF) was created on the basis of a UN mandate to provide the security required to allow infrastructure reconstruction and create a stable democratic government. In 2002, NATO began providing support for ISAF at the request of the lead nations and, in August 2003, assumed full responsibility for the leadership of ISAF. In accordance with an October 2003 UN security council mandate, ISAF gradually extended its authority from the capital, Kabul, to assume responsibility for the security, reconstruction and development of the entire country in October 2006. The gradual transition of security responsibility from ISAF to the Afghan national security forces commenced in 2010 and was completed at the end of 2014. In January 2015, a new non-combat resolute support mission was launched to train, assist and advise Afghan security forces. It was agreed in May 2016 that this mission would extend beyond the end of the year and that a civilian-led presence would remain in Afghanistan following the end of the mission in order to help Afghan security forces become self-sufficient. NATO and its partners have committed to providing financial support to sustain the Afghan forces until the end of 2020.

KOSOVO
NATO has been leading a peace-support operation in Kosovo since June 1999 in support of wider international efforts to build peace and stability in the area. Approximately 4,000 troops from the NATO-led Kosovo Force (KFOR), provided by 29 countries, are currently deployed in the region.

TURKEY
In December 2012, the Turkish government requested support for its air defence system in the wake of the escalating conflict in Syria. The request was prompted by several incidents of cross-border fire and resulting civilian casualties. Germany, The Netherlands and the USA agreed to provide patriot air defence systems for purely defensive deployment in Adana, Gaziantep and Kahramanmaras. All defence systems have been operational under NATO command and control since February 2013. In January 2015, Spanish troops replaced the Dutch unit stationed in Adana.

AFRICA
NATO counter-piracy operations were active between October and December 2008, and again between March and

July 2009, in response to the growing threat presented by piracy in the Horn of Africa region. Operation Ocean Shield – approved by the North Atlantic Council in August 2009 and ended in November 2016 – focused on at-sea operations, but also offered assistance to regional states in developing their capacity to combat piracy.

Since June 2007, NATO has assisted the African Union Mission in Somalia (AMISOM) by providing airlift support. Following renewed African Union requests, the alliance agreed to extend its support by periods of six to twelve months and has done this on several occasions. NATO also continues to work with the African Union in identifying further areas where NATO could support the African Standby Force, a continental on-call security force. At the 2016 Warsaw Summit heads of state and government agreed to further strengthen and expand NATO's political and practical partnership with the African Union.

Secretary-General and Chair of the North Atlantic Council, of the DPC and of the NPG, Jens Stoltenberg (Norway)

ORGANISATION FOR ECONOMIC COOPERATION AND DEVELOPMENT

2 rue André Pascal, 75775 Paris Cedex 16, France
T (+33) 1 4524 8200 W www.oecd.org

The Organisation for Economic Cooperation and Development (OECD) was formed in 1961 to replace the Organisation for European Economic Cooperation. It is the instrument for international cooperation among industrialised member countries on economic and social policies. Its objectives are to assist its member governments in creating policies designed to achieve high, sustained economic growth and maintain financial stability, to contribute to world trade on a multilateral basis and to stimulate members' aid to developing countries. The OECD has 35 member countries, most of which have developed, high-income economies. The European Commission is involved in the work of the OECD but is not a member of the organisation.

The council is the supreme body of the organisation. It is composed of one representative for each member country plus one representative of the European Commission (the European Commission does not have the right to vote) and meets at permanent representative level under the chairmanship of the secretary-general, and at ministerial level (usually once a year) under the chair of a minister. Decisions and recommendations are adopted by consensus. Most of the OECD's work is undertaken by around 250 specialised committees and working parties. These are serviced by an international secretariat headed by a secretary-general.

In 2007 the OECD council opened accession discussions with Chile, Estonia, Israel, Russia and Slovenia: Chile, Estonia, Israel and Slovenia became members in 2010. In 2013 the council launched accession discussions with Colombia and Latvia and, in April 2015, also invited Costa Rica and Lithuania to open formal talks. Latvia became a member in 2016. Following its meeting in March 2014, the council postponed accession negotiations with Russia.

The funding of the OECD is divided according to a member state's economy and population size; the USA, the largest contributor, supplies almost 21 per cent of the organisation's budget (€374m (£331m) in 2017).

Secretary-General, Angel Gurría (Mexico)

ORGANIZATION FOR SECURITY AND COOPERATION IN EUROPE

6 Wallnerstrasse, 1010 Vienna, Austria
T (+43) 1 514360 E pm@osce.org W www.osce.org

The Organization for Security and Cooperation in Europe (OSCE) was launched in 1975 as the Conference on Security and Cooperation in Europe (CSCE) under the Helsinki Final Act. This established agreements between NATO members, Warsaw Pact members, and neutral and non-aligned European countries covering security, cooperation and human rights. It was renamed in 1994.

The Charter of Paris for a New Europe, signed in November 1990, committed members to support multiparty democracy, free-market economics, the rule of law and human rights. The signatories also agreed to regular meetings of heads of government, ministers and officials. The first CSCE summit was held in Helsinki in July 1992, at which the Helsinki Document was adopted. This declared the CSCE to be a regional organisation under the UN charter and defined the structures of the organisation.

Three structures have been established: the ministerial council, which comprises the foreign ministers of participating states and meets at least once a year; the permanent council, which is the main regular body for political consultation, meeting weekly in Vienna; and the forum for security cooperation, also meeting weekly. The chair of the OSCE rotates annually and the post of chair-in-office is held by the foreign minister of a participating state.

The OSCE has 16 field operations in Europe, the Caucasus and Central Asia. The OSCE observes elections throughout its 57 participating states. It also provides technical assistance to improve the legislative and administrative framework for elections in specific countries. In 1999, the charter on European security committed the OSCE to cooperating with other organisations and institutions concerned with the promotion of security within the OSCE area. In 2018 its budget was €138m (£122m).

Chair, Enzo Moavero Milanesi (Italy)

ORGANIZATION OF AMERICAN STATES

17th Street and Constitution Avenue, NW, Washington DC 20006–4499, USA
T (+1) (202) 370 5000 W www.oas.org

Originally founded in 1890 for largely commercial purposes, the Organization of American States (OAS) adopted its present name and charter in 1948. The charter entered into force in 1951 and was amended in 1970, 1988, 1996 and 1997. OAS has 35 member states, though the membership of Honduras was suspended in July 2009 following a coup against President Jose Zelaya; its suspension was lifted in June 2011. The European Union and 69 non-American states have permanent observer status.

The OAS aims to strengthen the peace and security of the Americas; to promote and consolidate representative democracy; to prevent or resolve any political, judicial or economic issues which may arise among member states; to promote their economic, social and cultural development; and to achieve an effective limitation of conventional weapons.

Policy is determined by the annual general assembly, the organisation's supreme authority, which elects the secretary-general for a five-year term. The meeting of consultation of ministers of foreign affairs considers urgent problems on an *ad hoc* basis. The permanent council, comprising one ambassador from each member state, implements the policies approved by the general assembly, acts as an intermediary in cases of disputes arising between states and oversees the general secretariat, the main administrative body. The inter-American council for integral development was created in 1996 by the ratification of the protocol of Managua to promote sustainable development and eliminate poverty.

Secretary-General, Luis Almagro (Uruguay)

ORGANIZATION OF ARAB PETROLEUM EXPORTING COUNTRIES

PO Box 20501, Safat 13066, Kuwait
T (+965) 2495 9000 E oapec@oapecorg.org W www.oapecorg.org

The Organization of Arab Petroleum Exporting Countries (OAPEC) was founded in 1968. Its objectives are to promote cooperation in economic activities, unite efforts to ensure the flow of oil to consumer markets and create a favourable climate for capital investment and the development of the petroleum industry. OAPEC has 11 member states, although Tunisia's membership has been inactive since 1986.

The ministerial council is composed of oil ministers from the member countries and meets twice a year to determine policy and approve the budgets and accounts of the general secretariat and the judicial tribunal. The judicial tribunal is composed of between seven and 11 judges who rule on disputes between member countries and between countries and oil companies. The executive organ of OAPEC is the general secretariat.

The active members are Algeria, Bahrain, Egypt, Iraq, Kuwait, Libya, Qatar, Saudi Arabia, Syria and the United Arab Emirates.

Secretary-General, Abbas Ali Naqi (Kuwait)

ORGANIZATION OF THE BLACK SEA ECONOMIC COOPERATION

Darüşşafaka Cad. Seba Center İş Merkezi, No:45 Kat 3, Istinye, 34460 Sarıyer-Istanbul, Turkey
T (+90) (212) 229 6330/6335 E info@bsec-organization.org W www.bsec-organization.org

The Black Sea Economic Cooperation (BSEC) resulted from the Istanbul Summit Declaration and the adoption of the Bosphorus statement on 25 June 1992; it acquired a permanent secretariat in 1994. A charter was inaugurated to found the Organization of the Black Sea Economic Cooperation in May 1999 following the Yalta Summit of the heads of state or government in June 1998. It has 12 member states.

The organisation aims to promote closer political and economic cooperation between the countries in the Black Sea region and to foster greater security, foreign investment and good governance.

The council of the ministers of foreign affairs is the highest decision-making authority; it elects the organisation's secretary-general and meets twice-yearly. The meetings rotate among the member states and the chair is the foreign minister of the state in which the meeting is held. There is also a committee of senior officials, and a number of working groups which deal with specific areas of cooperation. BSEC has a permanent secretariat based in Istanbul.

Secretary-General, Michael B. Christides (Greece)

ORGANISATION OF ISLAMIC COOPERATION

PO Box 178, Jeddah 21411, Saudi Arabia
T (+966) (12) 651 5222 W www.oic-oci.org

The Organisation of Islamic Cooperation (OIC) was established in 1969 with the purpose of promoting solidarity and cooperation between its member states. It also has the specific aims of supporting the formation of a Palestinian state, coordinating the views of member states in international forums such as the UN, and improving cooperation in the fields of economics, culture and science.

The OIC has three main bodies: the Islamic summit, the organisation's supreme authority composed of the heads of member states, which meets triennially; the annual conference of foreign ministers; and the general secretariat, which implements policy and is headed by a secretary-general elected by the conference of foreign ministers for a once-renewable five-year term.

In addition to this structure, the OIC has several subsidiary bodies, institutions and standing committees. These include the Islamic Solidarity Fund, to aid Islamic institutions in member countries; the Islamic Development Bank, to finance development projects in member states and the Islamic Educational, Scientific and Cultural Organisation.

Since 1991, the OIC has spoken out in protest of violence against Muslims in India, the Occupied Territories and Bosnia-Hercegovina. From 1993 to 1995 the OIC coordinated the offering of troops to the UN by Muslim states to protect Muslim areas of Bosnia-Hercegovina.

The organisation has 57 members (27 states in Africa; 24 in the Middle East, central and South East Asia plus the Palestinian Authority; three in Europe, and two in South America) and five observer states.

Secretary-General, Dr. Yousef bin Ahmad Al-Othaimeen (Saudi Arabia)

ORGANIZATION OF THE PETROLEUM EXPORTING COUNTRIES

Helferstorferstrasse 17, A-1010 Vienna, Austria
T (+43) (1) 2111 20 W www.opec.org

The Organization of the Petroleum Exporting Countries (OPEC) was created in 1960 as a permanent intergovernmental organisation with the principal aims of unifying and coordinating the petroleum policies of its 15 member countries, and stabilising prices and supply in international oil markets.

The supreme authority is the conference of ministers, which generally comprises the oil and energy ministers of the member countries. The conference meets in formal session twice a year to discuss oil policy, energy and administrative matters. The board of governors implements conference resolutions and oversees the running of the OPEC secretariat located in Vienna, Austria.

According to the *OPEC Annual Statistical Bulletin 2018* OPEC's 15 member countries held 81.89 per cent of the world's proven oil reserves at the end of 2017.

Secretary-General, Mohammad Sanusi Barkindo (Nigeria)

PACIFIC COMMUNITY

95 Promenade Roger Laroque, BP D5, 98848 Noumea, New Caledonia
T (+687) 262 000 E spc@spc.int W www.spc.int

The Secretariat of the Pacific Community (SPC) (formerly the South Pacific Commission) was established in 1947 by Australia, France, the Netherlands, New Zealand, the UK and the USA with the aim of promoting the economic and social stability of the islands in the region. The community now numbers 26 member states and territories: the four remaining founder states (the Netherlands and the UK have withdrawn) and the other 22 states and territories of Melanesia, Micronesia and Polynesia.

The SPC is a technical assistance agency with programmes in marine and land development and health and social policy. The governing body is the conference of the Pacific community, which meets every two years.

Director-General, Dr Colin Tukuitonga (Niue)

PACIFIC ISLANDS FORUM

Secretariat, Private Mail Bag, Suva, Fiji
T (+679) 331 2600 E info@forumsec.org W www.forumsec.org

The Pacific Islands Forum (PIF), formerly the South Pacific Forum, was established in 1971 and represents heads of governments of 18 independent and self-governing Pacific island countries. It aims to foster cooperation between its governments and to represent the interests of the region in international organisations. The PIF meets annually, after which a dialogue is conducted at ministerial level with 17 forum dialogue partner states and the European Union.

The PIF secretariat is governed by the forum officials committee (FOC), composed of senior figures from each member country. It comprises divisions dealing with development and economic policy, trade and investment, political and international affairs and services, and is responsible for implementing the forum's decisions.

Tokelau became an associate member in 2014. The African, Caribbean and Pacific Group of States, American Samoa, the Asian Development Bank, the Commonwealth, Commonwealth of the Northern Marianas, Guam, the International Organization for Migration, Timor-Leste, the United Nations, Wallis and Futuna, Western and Central Pacific Fisheries Commission and the World Bank currently hold observer status.

Secretary-General, Dame Meg Taylor, DBE (Papua New Guinea)

PARTNERS IN POPULATION AND DEVELOPMENT

Block-+, Plot 1 //B&C, Sher-E-Bangla Nagar, Administrative Zone, Agargaon, Dhaka-1207, Bangladesh
T (+88) (2) 911 7842 E partners@ppdsec.org
W www.partners-popdev.org

Partners in Population and Development (PPD) is an intergovernmental organisation launched at the UN International Conference on Population and Development in Cairo in 1994. It has 26 member states. PPD was created specifically for the purpose of expanding and improving South-to-South collaboration in the fields of reproductive health, population, and development and is dedicated to forming partnerships between and among individuals, organisations and the governments of developing countries.

PPD is controlled by a board of directors consisting of ministers or other high-ranking officials in the field of population and development from member countries. The responsibilities of the board include setting policy, promoting cooperation among members and providing advice to the secretariat. The secretariat is based in Dhaka, Bangladesh, and is mandated to serve as the administrative centre of the organisation. It ensures policies are implemented and identifies new areas for collaboration. PPD also has an international programme advisory committee consisting of specialists who advise the board and secretariat on current trends in population, development and reproductive health.

PPD is a permanent observer at the United Nations.

Chair, Dr Li Bin (China)

SHANGHAI COOPERATION ORGANISATION

7 Ritan Road, Chaoyang District, 100600 Beijing, China
T (+86) (10) 6532 9807 E sco@sectsco.org W http://eng.sectsco.org

The Shanghai Cooperation Organisation (SCO) is a permanent intergovernmental organisation. It was established in 1996 as the Shanghai Five, when China, Kazakhstan, Kyrgyzstan, Russia and Tajikistan signed an agreement on cooperating to resolve disputes along the former Sino-Soviet border. It was renamed in 2001 when Uzbekistan became an official member. India and Pakistan joined the organisation in June 2017, while Afghanistan, Belarus, Iran and Mongolia have observer status.

The main principle of the SCO is strengthening cooperation among member states across a range of fields, including politics, economics, science, culture, energy, transport, environmental protection and tourism.

The heads of state council is the organisation's supreme body and meets annually to formulate SCO policy. The heads of government council also holds annual meetings to discuss cooperation strategies and approve budgets. The SCO has two permanent bodies: a secretariat based in Beijing and a regional anti-terrorist structure in Tashkent. The secretary-general and the director of the executive committee are appointed by the council of heads of state for a period of three years.

Secretary-General, Rashid Alimov (Tajikistan)

SOUTH ASIAN ASSOCIATION FOR REGIONAL COOPERATION

PO Box 4222, Tridevi Marg, Kathmandu, Nepal
T (+977) (1) 422 1785/ 6350 E saarc@saarc-sec.org
W www.saarc-sec.org

The South Asian Association for Regional Cooperation (SAARC) was established in 1985 by Bangladesh, Bhutan, India, the Maldives, Nepal, Pakistan and Sri Lanka; Afghanistan was admitted as its eighth member in 2007. Its primary objective is the acceleration of economic and social development in member states through collective action in agreed areas of cooperation. These include agricultural development, climate change, science and technology, health, education, transport, energy and communications.

A SAARC preferential trading arrangement, designed to reduce tariffs on trade between SAARC member states, was signed in 1993 and entered into force in 1995. The South Asian free trade area (SAFTA) was agreed in 2004 and came into effect in 2006.

The highest authority rests with the heads of state or government of each member state. The council of ministers, which meets twice a year, is made up of the foreign ministers of the member states and is responsible for formulating policy. The standing committee is composed of the foreign secretaries of the member states and monitors and coordinates SAARC programmes; it meets as often as is necessary. Technical committees are assigned to individual areas of SAARC's activities. Its secretariat monitors, facilitates and promotes SAARC's activities and serves as a channel of communication between the association and other regional and intergovernmental institutions.

In 2005, as the only country in South Asia not to be a member of SAARC, Iran declared its wish to join and has since become an observer member, along with seven other states and the European Union.

Secretary-General, Amjad Hussain B. Sial (Pakistan)

SOUTHERN AFRICAN DEVELOPMENT COMMUNITY

Plot No. 54385, Central Business District, Private Bag 0095, Gaborone, Botswana
T (+267) 395 1863 E registry@sadc.int W www.sadc.int

The Southern African Development Community (SADC) was formed in 1992 by the members of its predecessor, the Southern African Development Coordination Conference. The latter was founded in 1980 to harmonise economic development among southern Africa's 'majority ruled' countries and reduce their dependence on then apartheid South Africa. The SADC now comprises 15 countries, including South Africa. Madagascar's membership was reactivated in January 2014 after years of suspension following a coup in March 2009.

The SADC aims to evolve common political values, promote economic growth, regional security, sustainable development and the interdependence of member states. An annual summit attended by members' heads of state is the SADC's supreme authority, and its policies are implemented by a secretariat.

Executive Secretary, Dr Stergomena Lawrence Tax (Tanzania)

UNITED NATIONS

Headquarters, 405 East 42nd Street, New York, NY 10017, USA
T (+1) (212) 963 1234 W www.un.org
Regional Information Centre, rue de la Loi 155, Block C2, 7th Floor,
   Brussels 1040, Belgium T (+32) (2) 788 8484 E info@unric.org
   W www.unric.org

The United Nations (UN) is an intergovernmental organisation dedicated, through signature of the UN charter, to the maintenance of international peace and security and the solution of economic, social and political problems through international cooperation.

The UN was founded as a successor to the League of Nations and inherited many of its procedures and institutions. The name United Nations was first used in the Washington Declaration of 1942 to describe the 26 states that had allied to fight the Axis powers. The UN charter developed from discussions at the Moscow conference of the foreign ministers of China, the Soviet Union, the UK and the USA in 1943. Further progress was made at Dumbarton Oaks, Washington, in 1944 during talks involving the same states. The role of the security council was formulated at the Yalta conference in 1945. The charter was formally drawn up by 50 allied nations at the San Francisco conference between April and June 1945, when it was signed. Following ratification, the UN came into effect on 24 October 1945, which is celebrated annually as United Nations Day. The UN flag is light blue with the UN emblem centred in white.

The principal organs of the UN are the general assembly, the security council, trusteeship council, the economic and social council, the secretariat and the international court of justice. The economic and social council is an auxiliary, charged with assisting and advising the general assembly, security council and member states, and coordinating the economic and social aspects of the work of UN agencies and commissions. The official languages used are Arabic, Chinese, English, French, Russian and Spanish; the working languages of the secretariat and the international court of justice are English and French.

OBSERVERS

Permanent observer status is held by the Holy See and the State of Palestine.

THE GENERAL ASSEMBLY

UN Plaza, New York, NY 10017, USA

The general assembly is the main deliberative organ of the UN. It consists of all members, each entitled to five representatives but having only one vote. The annual session begins on the third Tuesday of September, when the president is elected, and usually continues until mid-December. Special sessions are held on specific issues and emergency special sessions can be called within 24 hours.

The assembly is empowered to discuss any matter within the scope of the charter – except when it is under consideration by the security council – and to make recommendations. Under the peace resolution, adopted in 1950, the assembly may also take action to maintain international peace and security when the security council fails to do so because of a lack of unanimity of its permanent members. Important decisions (such as those on peace and security, the election of officers, the budget, etc) need a two-thirds majority. Others need a simple majority. The assembly has effective power only over the internal operations of the UN itself; external recommendations are not legally binding.

The work of the general assembly is divided among a number of committees, on each of which every member has the right to be represented. Subjects include human rights, the use of torture, peacekeeping, assistance to developing countries and discrimination. In addition, the general assembly appoints *ad*

hoc committees to consider more specific issues. All committees consider items referred to them by the assembly and recommend draft resolutions to its plenary meeting.

The assembly is assisted by a number of functional committees. The general committee coordinates its proceedings and operations, while the credentials committee verifies the representatives.

President of the General Assembly, Miroslav Lajcak (Slovakia)

SPECIALISED BODIES

The assembly has created a large number of specialised bodies, some of which are supervised jointly with the economic and social council. They are supported by UN and voluntary contributions from governments, non-governmental organisations and individuals. These organisations include:

CONFERENCE ON DISARMAMENT

Palais des Nations, CH-1211 Geneva 10, Switzerland

The Conference on Disarmament (CD) was established in 1979 as the international community's multilateral disarmament negotiating forum. Originally comprising 40 member states, the CD has expanded to 65 members. The Non-Proliferation of Nuclear Weapons Treaty entered into force on 5 March 1970 and has so far been ratified by 191 states. The Biological Weapons Convention, the first multilateral disarmament treaty banning the development, production and stockpiling of an entire category of weapons of mass destruction, was opened for signature on 10 April 1972 and entered into force on 26 March 1975. A chemical weapons convention was agreed in Paris in 1993 and came into force in April 1997 after being ratified by 87 countries. Currently 189 states participate in the convention, which bans the use, production, stockpiling and transfer of all chemical weapons. A convention prohibiting the use of cluster munitions, agreed in Dublin in 2008 and currently ratified by 92 states, entered into force on 1 August 2010.

The CD and its predecessors have negotiated such major multilateral arms limitation and disarmament agreements as the Treaty on the Non-Proliferation of Nuclear Weapons, the Convention on the Prohibition of Military or Any Other Hostile Use of Environmental Modification Techniques, the Treaty on the Prohibition of the Emplacement of Nuclear Weapons and Other Weapons of Mass Destruction on the Sea-Bed and the Ocean Floor and in the Subsoil thereof, the Convention on the Prohibition of the Development, Production and Stockpiling of Bacteriological (Biological) and Toxin Weapons and on their Destruction, the Convention on the Prohibition of the Development, Production, Stockpiling and Use of Chemical Weapons and on Their Destruction and Comprehensive Nuclear-Test-Ban Treaty.

UNITED NATIONS CHILDREN'S FUND (UNICEF)

3 UN Plaza, New York, NY 10017, USA T (+1) 212 326 7000
W www.unicef.org
UNICEF House, 30A Great Sutton St, London EC1V 0DU
T 020-7490 2388

Established in 1946 to assist children and mothers in the immediate post-war period, UNICEF now concentrates on developing countries. It provides primary healthcare and health education, and conducts programmes in oral hydration, immunisation against common diseases, HIV/AIDS treatment and prevention and child growth monitoring. It also works to provide children with equal access to quality education.

UNITED NATIONS DEVELOPMENT PROGRAMME (UNDP)

1 UN Plaza, New York, NY 10017, USA T (+1) 212 906 5000
W www.undp.org

MEMBERSHIP

Membership is open to all countries that accept the charter and its principle of peaceful co-existence. New members are admitted by the general assembly on the recommendation of the security council. The original membership of 51 states has grown to 193 (*see* below).

Members of the UN

Afghanistan	Dominican Republic	Libya	St Vincent and the Grenadines
Albania	Ecuador*	Liechtenstein	Samoa
Algeria	Egypt*	Lithuania	San Marino
Andorra	El Salvador*	Luxembourg*	São Tomé and Principe
Angola	Equatorial Guinea	Macedonia	Saudi Arabia*
Antigua and Barbuda	Eritrea	Madagascar	Senegal
Argentina*	Estonia	Malawi	Serbia
Armenia	eSwatini†	Malaysia	Seychelles
Australia	Ethiopia*	Maldives	Sierra Leone
Austria	Fiji	Mali	Singapore
Azerbaijan	Finland	Malta	Slovakia
Bahamas	France	Marshall Islands	Slovenia
Bahrain	Gabon	Mauritania	Solomon Islands
Bangladesh	The Gambia	Mauritius	Somalia
Barbados	Georgia	Mexico*	South Africa
Belarus	Germany	Micronesia, Fed. States of	South Sudan
Belgium*	Ghana	Moldova	Spain
Belize	Greece	Monaco	Sri Lanka
Benin	Grenada	Mongolia	Sudan
Bhutan	Guatemala*	Montenegro	Suriname
Bolivia	Guinea	Morocco	Sweden
Bosnia and Hercegovina	Guinea-Bissau	Mozambique	Switzerland
Botswana	Guyana	Myanmar	Syria*
Brazil*	Haiti*	Namibia	Tajikistan
Brunei	Honduras*	Nauru	Tanzania
Bulgaria	Hungary	Nepal	Thailand
Burkina Faso	Iceland	The Netherlands*	Timor-Leste
Burundi	India*	New Zealand*	Togo
Cabo Verde	Indonesia	Nicaragua*	Tonga
Cambodia	Iran*	Niger	Trinidad and Tobago
Cameroon	Iraq*	Nigeria	Tunisia
Canada*	Ireland	Norway*	Turkey*
Central African Republic	Israel	Oman	Turkmenistan
Chad	Italy	Pakistan	Tuvalu
Chile*	Jamaica	Palau	Uganda
China*	Japan	Panama*	Ukraine*
Colombia*	Jordan	Papua New Guinea	United Arab Emirates
Comoros	Kazakhstan	Paraguay*	United Kingdom*
Congo, Dem. Rep. of	Kenya	Peru*	United States of America
Congo, Republic of the	Kiribati	The Philippines*	Uruguay*
Costa Rica*	Korea, D.P.R.	Poland*	Uzbekistan
Côte d'Ivoire	Korea, Rep. of	Portugal	Vanuatu
Croatia	Kuwait	Qatar	Venezuela*
Cuba*	Kyrgyzstan	Romania	Vietnam
Cyprus	Laos	Russian Federation*	Yemen
Czech Republic	Latvia	Rwanda	Zambia
Denmark*	Lebanon*	St Kitts and Nevis	Zimbabwe
Djibouti	Lesotho	St Lucia	
Dominica	Liberia		

* Original member (ie from 1945). Czechoslovakia, Yugoslavia and the USSR were all original members until their dissolution.
† Formerly Swaziland

Established in 1965 from the merger of the UN expanded programme of technical assistance and the UN special fund, UNDP is the central funding agency for economic and social development projects around the world. Much of its annual expenditure is channelled through UN specialised agencies, governments and non-governmental organisations.

UNITED NATIONS HIGH COMMISSIONER FOR REFUGEES (UNHCR)
Case Postale 2500, CH-1211 Geneva 2 Depot, Switzerland
T (+41) 22 739 8111 W www.unhcr.org

Established in 1950 to protect the rights and interests of refugees, UNHCR organises emergency relief and longer-term solutions, such as voluntary repatriation, local integration or resettlement. UNHCR is also mandated to assist stateless people.

UNITED NATIONS RELIEF AND WORKS AGENCY FOR PALESTINE REFUGEES IN THE NEAR EAST (UNRWA)
HQ Gaza, PO Box 338, Gaza City
T (+972) 8 288 7701 W www.unrwa.org

The UNRWA was established in 1949 to bring relief to the Palestinians displaced by the Arab-Israeli conflict. The UN general assembly has repeatedly voted every three years to extend its mandate, most recently until June 2020.

UNITED NATIONS HUMAN RIGHTS COUNCIL (UNHRC)
Palais des Nations, CH-1211 Geneva 10, Switzerland
T (+41) (22) 917 9220 E infodesk@ohchr.org W www.ohchr.org

The UNHRC is a 47-member council, established in 2006, replacing the United Nations Commission on Human Rights (UNCHR). The UNHRC has a mandate to promote (and prevent violations of) human rights by engaging in dialogue with governments and international organisations. It is also responsible for the coordination of all UN human rights activities and reports to, and is directly elected by, the general assembly.

THE SECURITY COUNCIL
UN Plaza, New York, NY 10017, USA
W www.un.org/en/sc

The security council is the senior arm of the UN and has the primary responsibility for maintaining world peace and security. It consists of 15 members, each with one representative and one vote. There are five permanent members – China, France, Russia, the UK and the USA – and ten non-permanent members. Each of the non-permanent members is elected for a two-year term by a two-thirds majority of the general assembly and is ineligible for immediate re-election. Five of the elective seats are allocated to Africa and Asia, one to eastern Europe, two to Latin America and two to western Europe and remaining countries. Decisions on procedural matters require affirmative votes from at least nine of the 15 members. Other matters require the same, but must include the affirmative votes of the permanent members; they thus have a right of veto. The abstention of a permanent member does not constitute a veto. The presidency rotates each month by state in (English) alphabetical order. Parties in a dispute, other non-members and individuals can be invited to participate in security council debates but are not permitted to vote.

The security council is empowered to settle or adjudicate in disputes or situations which threaten international peace and security. It can adopt political, economic and military measures to achieve this end. Any matter considered to be a threat to or breach of the peace or an act of aggression can be brought to the security council's attention by any member state or by the secretary-general. The charter envisaged members placing at the disposal of the security council armed forces and other facilities which would be coordinated by the military staff committee, composed of military representatives of the five permanent members. The security council is also supported by a committee of experts, to advise on procedural and technical matters, and a committee on admission of new members.

Owing to superpower disunity, the security council has rarely played the decisive role set out in the charter; the military staff committee was effectively suspended from 1948 until 1990, when a meeting was convened during the Gulf crisis on the formation and control of UN-supervised armed forces. In 1992, heads of government laid plans to transform the UN in light of the changed post-Cold War world. The secretary-general produced *An Agenda for Peace,* a report which centred on the establishment of a UN army composed of national contingents on permanent standby, as envisaged at the time of the UN's formation. However, enthusiasm for UN intervention waned during the rest of the decade after a problematic mission in Somalia during which 42 UN personnel were killed. The security council has since been criticised for its failure to intervene in subsequent conflicts, including the genocide in Rwanda and the ongoing situation in Darfur. More recently it has applied sanctions to Iran, North Korea, the Pakistani militant group Lashkar-e-Taiba, and figures within Libya, the Côte d'Ivoire and South Sudan.

The security council also has the power to elect judges to the international court of justice and to recommend to the general assembly the election of a secretary-general.

PEACEKEEPING FORCES
The security council has established a number of peacekeeping forces since its foundation, comprising contingents provided mainly by neutral and non-aligned UN members. As at April 2018, current operations were:

Continent	UN Code	Year implemented	Uniformed personnel deployed
Western Sahara	MINURSO	1991	468
Darfur, Sudan	UNAMID	2007	15,126
Dem. Rep. of the Congo	MONUSCO	2010	20,600
South Sudan	UNMISS	2011	18,013
Sudan	UNISFA	2011	4,803
Mali	MINUSMA	2013	15,425
Central African Rep.	MINUSCA	2014	14,110
The Americas			
Haiti	MINUJUSTH	2017	1,180
Asia			
India and Pakistan	UNMOGIP	1949	114
Europe			
Cyprus	UNFICYP	1964	1,021
Kosovo	UNMIK	1999	355
Middle East			
Syria	UNTSO	1948	373
Syria	UNDOF	1974	1,112
Lebanon	UNIFIL	1978	11,343

TOP FIVE CONTRIBUTORS TO UN PEACEKEEPING MISSIONS *as at* 30 April 2018

Country	Number of Troops
Ethiopia	8,122
Bangladesh	6,090
India	5,994
Pakistan	5,692
Rwanda	5,346

Source: www.un.org/en/peacekeeping

MECHANISM FOR INTERNATIONAL CRIMINAL TRIBUNALS
AICC Complex, PO Box 6016, Arusha, Tanzania
T (+31) (07) 0512 5691 E mict-press@un.org W www.unmict.org

On 22 December 2010, the United Nations Mechanism for International Criminal Tribunals (MICT) was established to oversee the outstanding work of the ICTY (see above) and the International Tribunal for Rwanda (ICTR). There was an overlap as these organisations completed their respective mandates before the MICT took over the ICTR in July 2012 and the ICTY in July 2013. The MICT carries out the same essential functions as the ICTR and ICTY and will continue the tribunals' work of tracking and prosecuting fugitives; protecting victims and witnesses; and supervising the enforcement of sentences. The progress of the MICT was reviewed in 2018 and will continue to be reviewed every two years.

President, Theodor Meron (USA)

THE ECONOMIC AND SOCIAL COUNCIL
UN Plaza, New York, NY 10017, USA
W www.un.org/ecosoc

The economic and social council is responsible under the general assembly for the economic and social work of the UN and for the coordination of the activities of the specialised agencies and other UN bodies. It makes reports and recommendations on economic, social, cultural, educational, health and related matters, often in consultation with non-governmental organisations, passing the reports to the general assembly and other UN bodies. It also drafts conventions for submission to the assembly and calls conferences on matters within its remit.

The council consists of 54 members, who are elected by the general assembly for overlapping three-year terms. Each member has one vote and can be immediately re-elected. The council elects a president and four vice-presidents each year: this five-member bureau proposes the council's agenda, draws up a programme of work and organises the substantive session. This session is held each July, and decisions are reached by a simple majority vote of those present.

The council has established a number of functional commissions and standing committees on particular issues. These include commissions on social development, sustainable development, population and development, the status of women, crime prevention and criminal justice, narcotic drugs, and science and technology for development, as well as five regional economic commissions.

President, Marie Chatardová (Czech Republic)

THE SECRETARIAT
UN Plaza, New York, NY 10017, USA

The secretariat services the other principal UN organs and administers their programmes and policies. It is headed by a secretary-general elected by a majority vote of the general assembly on the recommendation of the security council. He is assisted by some 44,000 staff worldwide. The secretary-general is charged with bringing to the attention of the security council any matter which he considers poses a threat to international peace and security. He may also bring other matters to the attention of the general assembly and other UN bodies and may be entrusted by them with additional duties. As chief administrator to the UN, the secretary-general is present in person or via representatives at all meetings of the other five main organs of the UN. He may also act as a mediator in disputes between member states.

The power and influence of the secretary-general has been determined largely by the character of the office-holder and by the state of relations between the superpowers. The improvement of these relations since the mid-1980s has increased the effectiveness of the UN, particularly in its attempts to intervene in international disputes.

Secretary-General, António Guterres (Portugal)
Deputy Secretary-General, Amina J. Mohammed (Nigeria)

FORMER SECRETARIES-GENERAL	
1946–52	Trygve Lie (Norway)
1953–61	Dag Hammarskjold (Sweden)
1961–71	U Thant (Myanmar)
1972–81	Kurt Waldheim (Austria)
1982–91	Javier Pérez de Cuéllar (Peru)
1992–96	Boutros Boutros-Ghali (Egypt)
1997–2006	Kofi Annan (Ghana)
2007–16	Ban Ki-moon (South Korea)

UK MISSION TO THE UN
1 Dag Hammarskjold Plaza, 885 Second Avenue, New York, NY 10017, USA
T (+1) (212) 745 9200 W www.ukun.fco.gov.uk

Permanent Representative to the UN and Representative on the Security Council, HE Karen Pierce, CMG, *apptd* 2018

UK MISSION TO THE UN AND OTHER INTERNATIONAL ORGANISATIONS IN GENEVA
58 Avenue Louis Casaï, Case Postale 6, 1216 Cointrin, Geneva, Switzerland
T (+41) (22) 918 2300

Permanent UK Representative, HE Julian Braithwaite, *apptd* 2015

UK MISSION TO THE UN IN VIENNA
Jaurésgasse 12, A-1030 Vienna, Austria
T (+43) (1) 716 130 W www.ukinaustria.fco.gov.uk

Permanent UK Representative, HE Leigh Turner, CMG, *apptd* 2015

REGIONAL UN INFORMATION CENTRE
Residence Palace, 155 rue de la Loi, Brussels 1040, Belgium
T (+32) 2788 8484 E info@unric.org W www.unric.org

THE INTERNATIONAL COURT OF JUSTICE
Peace Palace, Carnegieplein 2, 2517 KJ, The Hague, The Netherlands
T (+31) (70) 302 2323 W www.icj-cij.org

The international court of justice is the principal judicial organ in the UN, and its statute is an integral part of the UN charter; all members of the UN are *ipso facto* parties to it. The court is composed of 15 judges, elected by both the general assembly and the security council for nine-year terms, which are renewable. Judges may deliberate over cases in which their country is involved. If no judge on the bench is from a country that is party to a dispute under consideration, that party may designate a judge to participate *ad hoc* in that particular deliberation. If any party to a case fails to adhere to the judgment of the court, the other party may have recourse to the security council.

President, Abdulqawi Ahmed Yusuf (Somalia)
Vice-President, Xue Hanqin (China)
Judges, James Crawford (Australia); Philippe Couvreur (Belgium); Antonio A. Cancado Trindade (Brazil); Xue Hanqin (China); Ronny Abraham (France); Dalveer Bhandari (India); Giorgio Gaja (Italy); Patrick Robinson (Jamaica); Hisashi Owada (Japan); Nawaf Salam (Lebanon); Mohamed Bennouna (Morocco); Kirill Gevorgian (Russia); Peter Tomka (Slovakia); Abdulqawi Ahmed Yusuf (Somalia); Julia Sebutinde (Uganda); Joan Donoghue (USA)

UNITED NATIONS EDUCATIONAL, SCIENTIFIC AND CULTURAL ORGANIZATION

7 place de Fontenoy, F-75007 Paris, France
T (+33) (01) 4568 1000 W www.unesco.org

The United Nations Educational, Scientific and Cultural Organization (UNESCO) was established in 1945. It promotes collaboration among its member states in education, science, culture and communication. It aims to promote a universal respect for human rights, justice and the rule of law, without distinction of race, sex, language or religion, in accordance with the UN charter.

UNESCO runs a number of programmes to improve education and extend access to it. It provides assistance to ensure the free flow of information and its wider dissemination without any barriers to freedom of expression, to safeguard cultural heritages and encourage sustainable development. It fosters research and study in the social and environmental sciences. The UNESCO world heritage list, decided upon by a 21-member committee of state representatives, includes 1,092 cultural and natural sites of 'outstanding universal value'.

UNESCO has 195 member states and 11 associate members. The general conference, consisting of representatives of all the members, meets biennially to decide the programme and the budget. It elects the 58-member executive board, which supervises operations, and appoints a director-general who heads a secretariat responsible for carrying out the organisation's programmes. In most member states national commissions liaise with UNESCO to execute its policies.

Director-General, Audrey Azoulay (France)

UNITED NATIONS INDUSTRIAL DEVELOPMENT ORGANIZATION

Vienna International Centre, Wagramerstrasse 5, PO Box 300, A-1400 Vienna, Austria
T (+43) (1) 260 260 E unido@unido.org W www.unido.org

The United Nations Industrial Development Organization (UNIDO) was established in 1966 by the UN general assembly to act as the central coordinating body for industrial activities within the UN. It became a UN specialised agency in 1979. UNIDO aims to help countries with developing and transitional economies by increasing the productivity and competitiveness of their agricultural, technological and energy industries.

As at May 2018, 168 states were members of UNIDO. It is funded by regular and operational budgets, together with contributions for technical cooperation activities. The regular budget is derived from member states' contributions. Technical cooperation is funded mainly through voluntary contributions from donor countries and institutions and by intergovernmental and non-governmental organisations. A general conference of all the members meets biennially to discuss strategy and policy, approve the budget – €175.4m (£155.4m) for the biennium 2018–19 – and elect the director-general. The industrial development board is composed of representatives from 53 member states and reviews the work programme and the budget, which is prepared by the programme and budget committee of 27 member states.

Director-General, Li Yong (China)

UNIVERSAL POSTAL UNION

PO Box 312, CH-3000 Bern 15, Switzerland
T (+41) (31) 350 3111 W www.upu.int

The Universal Postal Union (UPU) was established by the Treaty of Bern 1874, taking effect from 1875, and became a UN specialised agency in 1948. The UPU exists to form and regulate a single postal territory of all member countries for the reciprocal exchange of correspondence without discrimination. With a total of 192 members, it also assists and advises on the improvement of postal services.

The universal postal congress is the UPU's supreme authority and meets every four years. The council of administration meets annually to supervise the union's work between congresses, to investigate regulatory developments and policy issues, to approve the budget and to examine proposed treaty changes. The postal operations council, first convened in 2013, is responsible for assessing operational, commercial, technical, and economic issues affecting members. The four UPU bodies are served by the international bureau, a secretariat headed by a director-general.

Funding is provided by members according to a scale of contributions drawn up by the congress. The council of administration sets the annual budget.

Director-General, Bishar Abdirahman Hussein (Kenya)

UNREPRESENTED NATIONS AND PEOPLES ORGANIZATION

Rue du Pépin 54, Brussels, B-1000, Belgium
T (+32) (0) 251 31459 E unpo.brussels@unpo.org
W www.unpo.org

The Unrepresented Nations and Peoples Organization (UNPO) was founded in 1991 to offer an international forum for occupied nations, indigenous peoples and national minorities who are not represented in other international organisations.

The UNPO does not aim to represent these nations and peoples, but rather to assist and empower them to represent themselves more effectively, and provides professional services and facilities as well as education and training in the fields of diplomacy, international and human rights law, democratic processes, institution building, conflict management and resolution, and environmental protection.

Participation is open to all nations and peoples who are inadequately represented at the UN and who declare allegiance to five principles relating to the right of self-determination of all peoples: human rights, democracy, tolerance, non-violence and respect for the rights of minorities. Applicants must show that they constitute a nation or people and that the organisation applying for membership is representative of that nation or people.

As at July 2018, UNPO had 44 members.

General Secretary, Marino Busdachin (Italy)

WORLD BANK GROUP

1818 H Street NW, Washington, DC 20433, USA
T (+1) (202) 473 1000 W www.worldbank.org

The World Bank Group was founded in 1944 from the consolidation of five major development organisations and is one of the world's largest sources of development assistance. It has 189 member states. Originally directed towards post-war reconstruction in Europe, the bank subsequently turned towards assisting less-developed countries worldwide, and in

2017 provided US$61.8bn (£46bn) for projects across the developing world. It works with government agencies, non-governmental organisations and the private sector to formulate assistance strategies. Its local offices implement the bank's programme in each country.

The World Bank is owned by the governments of member countries and its capital is subscribed by its members. It finances its lending primarily from borrowing in world capital markets, and derives a substantial contribution to its resources from its retained earnings and the repayment of loans.

The World Bank Group consists of two institutions and three affiliates. The International Bank for Reconstruction and Development (IBRD) provides loans and development assistance to middle-income countries and credit-worthy poorer countries (total loans for 2017 US$22.6bn (£16.8bn)). The International Development Association (IDA) performs the same function as the IBRD but primarily to less-developed countries and on terms that bear less heavily on their balance of payments than IBRD loans (total loans for 2017 US$19.5bn (£14.6bn)).

The three affiliates are the International Finance Corporation (IFC), which has 184 members and promotes private sector investment in developing countries by mobilising domestic and foreign capital, the Multilateral Investment Guarantee Agency (MIGA), which has 181 members and promotes foreign direct investment in developing states by insuring investors against political risk and helping member countries to improve their investment climates; and the International Centre for Settlement of Investment Disputes (ICSID), which has 153 full members (known as contracting states) and provides facilities for resolving disputes between foreign investors and their host countries.

The IBRD, IDA and the affiliates are financially and legally distinct but share headquarters. The IBRD is headed by a board of governors, which meets annually and consists of one governor and one alternate governor appointed by each member country; most IBRD governors also serve on the separate boards of the IDA, IFC and MIGA. Twenty-five executive directors exercise all powers of the World Bank (except those reserved to the board of governors). The president, elected by the board of executive directors, conducts the business of the bank, assisted by an international staff. Membership in both the IFC and the IDA is open to all IBRD countries. The IDA is administered by the same staff as the bank; the IFC has its own personnel but can draw on the IBRD for administrative and other support. All share the same president.

President, Jim Yong Kim (USA)

WORLD CUSTOMS ORGANIZATION
30 rue de Marché, B-1210, Brussels, Belgium
T (+32) 2209 9211 W www.wcoomd.org

Established in 1952 as the Customs Cooperation Council, the World Customs Organization (WCO) is an independent intergovernmental organisation whose primary mission is to enhance the effectiveness and efficiency of customs administrations worldwide. It is the only international body specialising in customs matters, and is recognised as the voice of the global customs community and a centre of customs expertise.

Comprising 182 member customs administrations that process approximately 98 per cent of international trade, the WCO is governed by a council which meets annually and in which each member has one vote. The council is supported by a policy commission, a finance committee, an audit committee, various technical committees, and a permanent secretariat charged with implementing council decisions.

Secretary-General, Kunio Mikuriya (Japan)

WORLD HEALTH ORGANIZATION
Avenue Appia 20, 1211 Geneva 27, Switzerland
T (+41) (22) 791 2111 W www.who.int

The UN International Health Conference, held in 1946, established the World Health Organization (WHO) as a UN specialised agency, with effect from 1948. It is dedicated to attaining the highest possible level of health for all. It collaborates with member governments, UN agencies and other bodies to improve health standards, control communicable diseases and promote all aspects of family and environmental health. It seeks to raise the standards of health teaching and training, and promotes research through collaboration with research centres worldwide.

WHO has 194 members and is governed by an annual assembly of members. This sets policy, approves the budget, appoints a director-general, and adopts health conventions and regulations. It also elects 34 member states to designate one expert each to serve on the executive board. The board sets the assembly's agenda and implements its policies, suggests initiatives, and is empowered to deal with emergencies. A secretariat, headed by the director-general, supervises the activities of six regional offices.

Director-General, Dr Tedros Adhanom Ghebreyesus (Ethiopia)

WORLD INTELLECTUAL PROPERTY ORGANIZATION
34 chemin des Colombettes, CH-1211, Geneva 20, Switzerland
T (+41) (22) 338 9111 W www.wipo.int

The World Intellectual Property Organization (WIPO) was established in Stockholm in 1967 by the signing of the WIPO Convention, which entered into force in 1970. WIPO administers 26 treaties that deal with different legal and administrative aspects of intellectual property, notably the Paris Convention for the protection of industrial property and the Bern Convention for the protection of literary and artistic works. WIPO became a UN specialised agency in 1974.

Intellectual property falls into two main branches: industrial property (inventions, trademarks, industrial designs and geographical indications) and copyright (literary, musical, photographic, audiovisual and artistic works, etc). WIPO helps ensure that creative intellectual activity is rewarded, and facilitates technology transfer, particularly to developing countries.

WIPO's mission is to promote the protection of intellectual property rights worldwide. The organisation's activities fall into three broad categories: the progressive development of international intellectual property law, assistance to developing countries, and the provision of services which facilitate the process of obtaining intellectual property rights in multiple countries.

WIPO had 191 members as at June 2018. The biennial session of the general assembly, the conference and the coordination committee set policy, a programme and a budget. A separate agency, the International Union for the Protection of New Varieties of Plants (UPOV), established by convention in 1961, is linked to WIPO and has 75 members.

Director-General, Francis Gurry (Australia)

WORLD METEOROLOGICAL ORGANIZATION
7 bis, avenue de la Paix, PO Box 2300, CH-1211 Geneva 2, Switzerland
T (+41) (22) 730 8111 W http://public.wmo.int/en

The World Meteorological Organization (WMO) was established in 1950 and became a UN specialised agency in 1951, succeeding the International Meteorological

Organization founded in 1873. It facilitates cooperation in the establishment of networks for making, processing and exchanging meteorological, climatological, hydrological and geophysical observations. It also fosters collaboration between meteorological and hydrological services, and furthers the application of meteorology to aviation, shipping, environment, water problems, agriculture and the mitigation of natural disasters.

In June 2018, the WMO had 185 member states and six member territories. Six regional associations are responsible for the coordination of activities within their own regions. There are also eight technical commissions, which study meteorological and hydrological problems, establish methodology and procedures, and make recommendations to the executive council and the congress. The supreme authority is the world meteorological congress, which meets every four years to determine general policy and set the budget (SFr266.2m (£179.9m) for the four-year period 2016–19). It also elects 31 members of the 37-member executive council which supervises the implementation of congress decisions, initiates studies and makes recommendations on matters requiring international action. The secretariat is headed by a secretary-general, appointed by the congress.

Secretary-General (2016–19), Petteri Taalas (Finland)

WORLD TOURISM ORGANISATION
Poeta Joan Maragall 42, 28020 Madrid, Spain
T (+34) 9156 78100 E omt@unwto.org W www2.unwto.org

The World Tourism Organisation (UNWTO) was officially launched in 1975 to act as an executing agency of the United Nations Development Programme. Primarily concerned with developing public and private sector partnerships, the UNWTO also promotes the global code of ethics for tourism, a framework of policy aimed at tour operators, governments, labour organisations and travellers. There are 156 member states and six associate member states.

The general assembly is the principal gathering of the UNWTO and meets every two years in order to approve policy and budget. Every four years, the assembly elects a secretary-general. The executive council is UNWTO's governing board and meets at least twice a year to ensure the organisation adheres to policy and budget. It is composed of 32 members of the general assembly. As host country of UNWTO's headquarters, Spain has a permanent seat on the executive council.

Secretary-General (2018–21), Zurab Pololikashvili (Georgia)

WORLD TRADE ORGANIZATION
Centre William Rappard, 154 rue de Lausanne, CH-1211 Geneva 21, Switzerland
T (+41) (22) 739 5111 E enquiries@wto.org W www.wto.org

The World Trade Organization was established on 1 January 1995 as the successor to the General Agreement on Tariffs and Trade (GATT).

The GATT was dedicated to the expansion of non-discriminatory international trade and progressively extended free trade via 'rounds' of multilateral negotiations. The final act of the comprehensive Uruguay round of negotiations was signed by trade ministers from the 123 GATT negotiating states and the EU in Marrakesh, Morocco, in 1994. New talks on agriculture and services began in 2000 and were incorporated into a broader agenda launched at the 2001 ministerial conference in Doha, Qatar.

The WTO is the legal and institutional foundation of the multilateral trading system. It provides the contractual obligations determining how governments frame and implement trade policy, and provides the forum for the debate, negotiation and adjudication of trade issues. The WTO's principal aims are to liberalise world trade and place it on a secure basis; it seeks to achieve this through the combination of an agreed set of trade rules and market-access agreements and further trade liberalisation negotiations. The WTO also administers and implements multilateral agreements in fields such as agriculture, industrial goods, services, government procurement, rules of origin and intellectual property.

The highest authority of the WTO is the ministerial conference composed of all members, which usually meets once every two years. The general council meets as required and acts on behalf of the ministerial conference in regard to the regular working of the WTO. The general council also convenes in two particular forms: as the dispute-settlement body, dealing with disagreements between members arising from WTO agreements or commitments; and as the trade policy review body, conducting regular reviews of the trade policies of members. A secretariat of 634 staff, headed by a director-general, services WTO bodies and provides trade performance and trade policy analysis.

As at July 2018, the WTO has 164 members and 23 observer governments. The most recent member – Afghanistan – joined the WTO in 2016. The WTO budget for 2017 is SFr197.2m (£133.5m), with members' contributions calculated on the basis of their share of international trade. The official languages of the WTO are English, French and Spanish.

Director-General, Roberto Azevedo (Brazil)

COUNTRIES OF THE WORLD A–Z

DEFINITIONS, ABBREVIATIONS AND SOURCES

est = estimate

IDD = International direct dialling

AIRPORTS – figures reference airports with paved runways only, unless otherwise specified

BIRTH RATE – figures are per 1,000 population

CORRUPTION PERCEPTIONS INDEX (CPI) SCORE – the perception of the degree of public sector corruption as seen by business people and country analysts; ranging from 0 (highly corrupt) to 100 (very clean). Overall position given in parentheses. *Corruption Perceptions Index* © 2018 by Transparency International. (W www.transparency.org).

DEATH PENALTY:

Retained (not used) – countries that retain the death penalty for ordinary crimes such as murder but can be considered to have abolished it in practice

Retained for certain crimes – countries whose laws provide for the death penalty only for exceptional crimes ('Last used' = date of last execution)

Retained – countries that retain the death penalty for ordinary crimes

Abolitionist and Retentionist Countries © 2018 Amnesty International (W www.amnesty.org).

GROSS ENROLMENT RATIO – the ratio of total enrolment, regardless of age, to the total population of the relevant age group expressed as a percentage; this figure can be above 100 per cent where, for example, a greater number of children are attending classes designed for six-year-olds than there are six-year-olds in the country, owing to some children starting school late or skipping a year

GROSS NATIONAL INCOME (GNI) – the total income earned by a country's residents; the second figure is GNI divided by the population to give a per capita figure

HIV/AIDS ADULT PREVALENCE – estimate of the percentage of the total adult population (aged 15–49) infected with HIV/AIDS

INFANT MORTALITY RATE – averages for male and female infants under one year old and per 1,000 live birth

LIFE EXPECTANCY – averages, at birth, for males and females

LITERACY (ADULT) – the World Bank defines literacy as the percentage of the population aged 15 and above that can read and write a short statement on their everyday life. Where the World Bank figure is not available the statistic provided is that given by the government of that country. This figure is not always comparable due to differing definitions of what constitutes adult literacy. *World Development Indicators 2017* published by The World Bank.

MILITARY EXPENDITURE – figures are the most recent available at current 2017 prices and exchange rates. © Stockholm International Peace Research Institute (SIPRI) (W www.sipri.org).

MORTALITY RATE – figures are per 1,000 population. This indicator is significantly affected by age distribution, and most countries will eventually show a rise in the overall death rate, in spite of continued decline in mortality at all ages, as declining fertility results in an ageing population

POPULATION BELOW POVERTY LINE – although strict definitions of poverty vary considerably between nations, this figure most commonly represents the percentage of the adult population whose income is less than US$1 per day

TOTAL EXTERNAL DEBT – the total public and private debt owed to non-residents repayable in foreign currency, goods or services

WORLD PRESS FREEDOM INDEX (WPFI) SCORE – the perception of press freedom based on assessments carried out by journalists and human rights activists; two scores ranging between 0 (low censorship) and 100 (high censorship) are given. The first is based on six criteria – pluralism, media independence, environment and self-censorship, legislative framework, transparency and infrastructure – the second score measures the treatment of journalists. The overall position is given in parentheses. *Press Freedom Score 2017* © Reporters Without Borders (W https://rsf.org/en/world-press-freedom-index).

Sources (in addition to those already indicated): *Human Development Indicators 2017* published by the UN Development Programme and *UN Statistics* published by UN Data; *World Economic Outlook Database 2017* © International Monetary Fund; UNESCO Institute for Statistics (UIS) (W www.uis.unesco.org/datacentre).

Government cabinet lists are sourced from *People in Power* © Cambridge International Reference on Current Affairs Ltd (W www.circaworld.com). People in Power provides a constantly updated service at www.peopleinpower.com

AFGHANISTAN

Jamhuri-ye Eslami-ye Afghanestan – Islamic Republic of Afghanistan

Area – 652,230 sq. km

Capital – Kabul; population, 4,012,000 (2018 est)

Major cities – Herat, Jalalabad, Kandahar, Mazar-e-Sharif

Currency – Afghani (Af) of 100 puls

Population – 34,124,811 rising at 2.36 per cent a year (2017 est); Pashtun (42 per cent), Tajik (27 per cent), Hazara (9 per cent), Uzbek (9 per cent), Aimak (4 per cent), Turkmen (3 per cent), Baloch (2 per cent) (est)

Religion – Muslim (Sunni 80 per cent, Shia 19 per cent) (est); Islam is the state religion

Language – Dari (a dialect of Persian), Pashto (both official); Balochi, Nuristani, Pamiri, Pashai, Turkmen and Uzbek are official in some areas

Population density – 54 per sq. km (2017)

Urban population – 25.5 per cent (2018 est)

Median age (years) – 18.8 (2017 est)

National anthem – 'Milli Surud' 'National Anthem'

National day – 19 August (Independence Day)

Death penalty – Retained

CPI score – 15 (177)

Military expenditure – US$191m (2017)

CLIMATE AND TERRAIN

Mountains, chief among which are the Hindu Kush, cover three-quarters of the country, with plains in the north and south-west. Elevation extremes range from 7,485m (Noshak, a peak in the Hindu Kush) to 258m (Amu Darya). There are three great river basins: the Amu Dar'ya (Oxus), Helmand and Kabul. Natural hazards are flooding, drought and earthquakes. Average annual rainfall is around 247mm per year. Temperatures in Afghanistan average 0.7°C in January and 25.7°C in July.

POLITICS

Under the 2004 constitution, the executive president, who is directly elected for a five-year term, appoints the government, subject to the approval of the lower house of the legislature. The bicameral National Assembly, the *Jirga*, comprises the House of the People *(Wolesi Jirga)*, the lower house and the House of Elders *(Meshrano Jirga)*. The House of the People has 249 members directly elected for a five-year term; ten seats are reserved for the Kuchi ethnic group and at least 65 seats for women. The House of Elders has 102 members: 34 elected by provincial councils for a three-year term, 34 elected by district councils for a four-year term and 34 appointed by the president for a five-year term.

Hamid Karzai was elected president in 2004, and was re-elected in 2009; he stepped down when his second term concluded in 2014, after NATO handed control to the Afghan state. Following the disputed June 2014 presidential elections, it was declared on 21 September that Ashraf Ghani would become president, ending months of political deadlock. The Taliban, ousted in the US-led 2001 invasion, have increasingly grown in strength in recent years, contributing to rising political instability and violence.

HEAD OF STATE

President, Ashraf Ghani Ahmadzai, *sworn in* 29 September 2014
First Vice-President, Abdul Rashid Dustom
Second Vice-President, Sarwar Danish

SELECTED GOVERNMENT MEMBERS *AS AT JULY 2018*
Chief Executive, Abdullah Abdullah
Defence, Tariq Shah Bahrami
Finance, Dr Mohammad Qayoumi
Foreign Affairs, Salahuddin Rabbani

EMBASSY OF THE ISLAMIC REPUBLIC OF AFGHANISTAN
31 Princes Gate, London SW7 1QQ
T 020-7225 4743 E consulate@afganistanembassy.org.uk
W www.afghanistanembassy.org.uk/english
Ambassador Extraordinary and Plenipotentiary, HE Said Tayeb Jawad, *apptd* 2017

BRITISH EMBASSY
PO Box 334, 15th Street, Roundabout Wazir Akbar Khan, Kabul
T (+93) (0) 700 102 000 E britishembassy.kabul@fco.gov.uk
W www.gov.uk/government/world/afghanistan
Ambassador Extraordinary and Plenipotentiary, HE Sir Nicholas Kay, KCMG, *apptd* 2017

ECONOMY AND TRADE

The economy, devastated by almost 40 years of conflict, has improved significantly since 2001. Economic growth has been sustained over the decade, although security problems, weak governance, poor infrastructure and corruption continue to hamper reconstruction. Poverty is being reduced through substantial civilian aid donations, including an additional US$16bn (£10.5bn) pledged in July 2012, and US$3.8bn (£2.9bn) annual development aid pledge between 2016 and 2020. Eradication of the opium trade (which constituted as much as 60 per cent of the economy but has been reduced to about 15 per cent), and exploration for oil and gas in the north are two major long-term policy objectives. Since 2011, the Afghan and US governments have pursued a policy of turning Afghanistan into a regional trade hub for central Asian commodities, such as gas and cotton, although there has been a rise in both IS and Taliban activity since mid-2016.

Around 44 per cent of the workforce is engaged in agriculture, both subsistence and commercial, which accounts for some 23 per cent of GDP. The main agricultural products are opium, wheat, fruit, nuts, wool, meat, sheepskins and lambskins. Natural gas, coal, copper and semi-gemstones are extracted. The withdrawal of nearly 100,000 troops since 2014 has negatively impacted growth, especially the services sector. The main trading partners are Pakistan and India. Principal exports are agricultural products, handwoven carpets and gemstones. Imports are chiefly machinery and other capital goods, food, textiles and petroleum products.

GNI – US$20.2bn; US$570 per capita (2017)
Annual average growth of GDP – 2.6 per cent (2017 est)
Inflation rate – 6.0 per cent (2017 est)
Population below poverty line – 35.8 per cent (2011 est)
Imports – US$4,703m (2014 est)
Exports – US$714.3m (2014 est)

BALANCE OF PAYMENTS
Trade – US$4,900m deficit (2013)
Current Account – US$5,216m deficit (2015)

Trade with UK	2016	2017
Imports from UK	£15,952,013	£21,016,017
Exports to UK	£2,896,824	£2,697,554

COMMUNICATIONS

Airports – 43; two international: Kabul and Kandahar
Waterways – The Amu Dar'ya river makes up most of the 1,200km of inland waterways; the main river ports are Kheyrabad and Shir Khan
Roadways – Much of the road system is in disrepair, although major highways between Kabul, Kandahar and Herat have been reconstructed; there are 12,350km of paved roadways
Telecommunications – 114,192 fixed lines and 21.6 million mobile subscriptions (2016); there were 3.5 million internet users in 2016
Internet code and IDD – af; 93 (from UK), 44 (to UK)
Major broadcasters – The principal and state-owned broadcaster is National Radio Television Afghanistan (RTA),

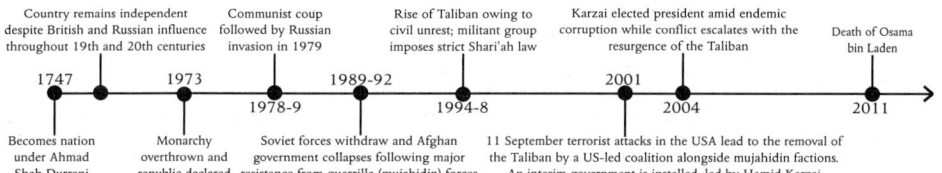

| Country remains independent despite British and Russian influence throughout 19th and 20th centuries | Communist coup followed by Russian invasion in 1979 | Rise of Taliban owing to civil unrest; militant group imposes strict Shari'ah law | Karzai elected president amid endemic corruption while conflict escalates with the resurgence of the Taliban | Death of Osama bin Laden |

1747 — 1973 — 1978-9 — 1989-92 — 1994-8 — 2001 — 2004 — 2011

Becomes nation under Ahmad Shah Durrani

Monarchy overthrown and republic declared

Soviet forces withdraw and Afghan government collapses following major resistance from guerrilla (mujahidin) forces

11 September terrorist attacks in the USA lead to the removal of the Taliban by a US-led coalition alongside mujahidin factions. An interim government is installed, led by Hamid Karzai

alongside 150 private radio stations and 50 television stations (2018)
Press – There are nine daily newspapers, including the privately owned *Hasht-e Sobh* and *Mandegar*, and the government sponsored *Hewad*
WPFI score – 37,28 (118)

EDUCATION AND HEALTH
Education is free and nominally compulsory; elementary schools having been established in most centres.
Literacy rate – 38.2 per cent (2015 est)
Gross enrolment ratio (percentage of relevant age group – primary 111.9 per cent, secondary 55.6 per cent (2015 est); tertiary 8.7 per cent (2014 est)
Health expenditure (per capita) – US$57 (2014)
Hospital beds (per 1,000 people) – 0.5 (2014)
Life expectancy (years) – 51.7 (2017 est)
Mortality rate – 13.4 (2017 est)
Birth rate – 37.9 (2017 est)
Infant mortality rate – 110.6 (2017 est)
HIV/AIDS adult prevalence – 0.1 per cent (2016 est)

ALBANIA

Republika e Shqiperise – Republic of Albania

Area – 28,748 sq. km
Capital – Tirana; population, 476,000 (2018 est)
Major towns – Durres, Elbasan, Shkoder, Vlore
Currency – Lek (Lk) of 100 qindarka
Population – 3,047,987 rising at 0.31 per cent a year (2017 est); Albanian (82.6 per cent), Greek (0.9 per cent) (est)
Religion – Muslim 56.7 per cent (Sunni, and Bektashi form of Shia Sufism), Christian (Roman Catholic 10 per cent, Orthodox 6.8 per cent) (est). Religious observance was banned in 1967; private religious practice has been permitted since 1990
Language – Albanian (official), Macedonian, Greek, Vlach, Romani, Turkish, Italian, Serbo-Croatian
Population density – 105 per sq. km (2016)
Urban population – 60.3 per cent (2018 est)
Median age (years) – 32.9 (2017 est)
National anthem – 'Himni i Flamurit' 'Hymn to the Flag'
National day – 28 November (Independence Day)
Death penalty – Abolished for all crimes (since 2007)
CPI score – 38 (91)
Military expenditure – US$163m (2017)

CLIMATE AND TERRAIN
About two-thirds of the country is mountainous, and 36 per cent is covered by forest. Elevation extremes range from 2,764m (Maja e Korabit, a peak on the Macedonian border) to 0m (Adriatic Sea). The climate is Mediterranean on the coast and continental in the interior. The average daily temperature ranges between 2.1°C in January and 21.8°C in July and August.

POLITICS
Under the 1998 constitution, the president is elected by the legislature for a five-year term, renewable once. The unicameral legislature, the People's Assembly, has 140 members directly elected for four-year terms. The president appoints the prime minister, who must be approved by the People's Assembly. The assembly elects the council of ministers.
Ilir Meta, of the Socialist Movement for Integration (LSI), was elected president in 2017 in the fourth round of voting. Legislative elections were held in June 2017 and won by the incumbent prime minister Edi Rama and his Socialist Party of Albania (PS), which increased its share of seats to 74.
Albania applied to join the EU in 2009 and obtained candidate status in 2014.

HEAD OF STATE
President, Ilir Meta, *elected* 28 April 2017

SELECTED GOVERNMENT MEMBERS *AS AT JULY 2018*
Prime Minister, Edi Rama
Deputy Prime Minister, Senida Nesi
Defence, Olta Xhacka
Finance, Arben Ahmetaj

EMBASSY OF THE REPUBLIC OF ALBANIA
33 St George's Drive, London SW1V 4DG
T 020-7828 8897 E embassy.london@mfa.gov.al
W www.ambasadat.gov.al/united-kingdom/en
Ambassador Extraordinary and Plenipotentiary, HE Qirjako Qirko, *apptd* 2016

BRITISH EMBASSY
Rruga Skenderbeg 12, Tirana
T (+355) (4) 223 4973 W www.gov.uk/government/world/albania
Ambassador Extraordinary and Plenipotentiary, HE Duncan Norman, MBE, *apptd* 2016

ECONOMY AND TRADE
Albania is one of the poorest countries in Europe, although liberalisation measures have resulted in gradual growth since 1993. Trade and banking sector ties with the fragile economies of Greece and Italy, high levels of public debt, corruption and organised crime remain significant economic challenges. The economy is increasingly able to cope with a decline in remittances from expatriate workers, which has fallen from between 12 and 15 per cent of GDP before 2008 to less than 6 per cent in 2015. The inefficient energy and transport sectors have been improved by investment, although they remain underdeveloped by European standards.
Agriculture accounts for 41.4 per cent of employment but only 22.6 per cent of GDP. The main crops are wheat, corn, vegetables, fruit, olives and livestock products. The principal industries are food processing, perfumes and cosmetic products, textiles and clothing, timber, oil, cement, chemicals, mining (base metals) and hydroelectric power.
Trade is mainly with Italy, Turkey, Spain, Greece and Kosovo. Exports include textiles and footwear, asphalt, metals and metal ores, crude oil, tobacco, fruit and vegetables. Imports include machinery and equipment, foodstuffs, textiles and chemicals.
GNI – US$12.4bn; US$4,320 per capita (2017)
Annual average growth of GDP – 3.8 per cent (2017 est)
Inflation rate – 2.1 per cent (2017 est)
Population below poverty line – 14.3 per cent (2012 est)
Unemployment – 14 per cent (2017 est)
Total external debt – US$8.579bn (2017 est)
Imports – US$4,669m (2016)
Exports – US$1,962m (2016)

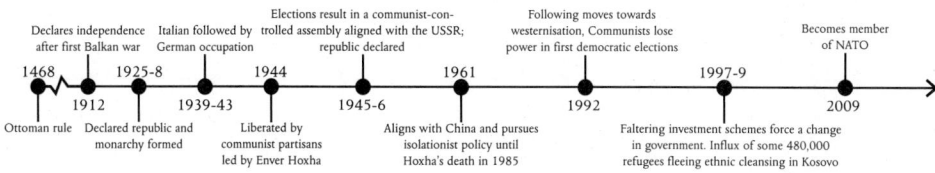

Declares independence after first Balkan war | 1468 | 1925-8 | Italian followed by German occupation | Elections result in a communist-controlled assembly aligned with the USSR; republic declared | 1944 | 1961 | Following moves towards westernisation, Communists lose power in first democratic elections | 1997-9 | Becomes member of NATO

1912 | 1939-43 | 1945-6 | 1992 | 2009

Ottoman rule | Declared republic and monarchy formed | Liberated by communist partisans led by Enver Hoxha | Aligns with China and pursues isolationist policy until Hoxha's death in 1985 | Faltering investment schemes force a change in government. Influx of some 480,000 refugees fleeing ethnic cleansing in Kosovo

BALANCE OF PAYMENTS
Trade – US$2,707m deficit (2016)
Current Account – US$909.3m deficit (2016)

Trade with UK	2016	2017
Imports from UK	£17,573,248	£18,778,901
Exports to UK	£3,354,674	£3,673,503

COMMUNICATIONS
Airports – 4; three international: Kukes, Tirana, Vlore
Roadways and railways – 7,020km; 677km
Telecommunications – 250,000 fixed lines and 3.4 million mobile subscriptions (2016); there were 2 million internet users in 2016
Internet code and IDD – al; 355 (from UK), 44 (to UK)
Major broadcasters – Albanian Radio and TV (RTSh), Top Channel and TV Klan
Press – There are 25 daily newspapers, including *Shekulli, Gazeta Shqiptare* and the *Tirana Times*
WPFI score – 29,49 (75)

EDUCATION AND HEALTH
Literacy rate – 97.6 per cent (2015 est)
Gross enrolment ratio (percentage of relevant age group) – primary 109.8 per cent, secondary 95 per cent, tertiary 61.2 per cent (2016 est)
Health expenditure (per capita) – US$272 (2014)
Hospital beds (per 1,000 people) – 2.9 (2013)
Life expectancy (years) – 78.5 (2017 est)
Mortality rate – 6.8 (2017 est)
Birth rate – 13.2 (2017 est)
Infant mortality rate – 11.9 (2017 est)
HIV/AIDS adult prevalence – 0.1 per cent (2016 est)

ALGERIA
Al-Jumhuriyah al-Jaza'iriyah ad Dimuqratiyah ash Sha'biyah –
People's Democratic Republic of Algeria

Area – 2,381,741 sq. km
Capital – Algiers (El Djazair, Al Jaza'ir); population, 2,694,000 (2018 est)

Major cities – Annaba, Blida, Constantine (Qacentina), Oran (Wahran)
Currency – Algerian dinar (DA) of 100 centimes
Population – 40,969,443 rising at 1.7 per cent a year (2017 est); Arab-Berber (99 per cent) (est)
Religion – Muslim (Sunni 99 per cent), Christian and Jewish (less than 1 per cent) (est)
Language – Arabic (official), French, Berber dialects
Population density – 17 per sq. km (2016)
Urban population – 72.6 per cent (2018 est)
Median age (years) – 28.1 (2017 est)
National anthem – 'Kassaman' 'We Pledge'
National day – 1 November (Revolution Day)
Death penalty – Retained (last used 1993)
CPI score – 33 (112)
Military expenditure – US$10,217m (2016)
Conscription – 19–30 years of age; 18 months

CLIMATE AND TERRAIN
Algeria, the largest country in Africa, is dominated by the Sahara desert, which covers more than 80 per cent of its territory. Elevation extremes range from 3,003m (Mt Tahat) to −40m (Chott Melrhir, a salt lake). The mountains are subject to earthquakes, and to flooding during the rainy season (November–March). The temperate northern coastal areas receive the greatest and most frequent rainfall, whereas the interior plateaux are drier and experience cold winters and hot summers.

POLITICS
Algeria's 1976 constitution was amended in 1989 to reintroduce political pluralism. It was revised in 2008, most notably to remove the limit on presidential terms, but a two-term limit was reinstated in February 2016. The president is directly elected for a five-year term. The bicameral *Barlaman* comprises the National People's Assembly, the lower house and Council of the Nation. The assembly has 462 members, including eight seats for Algerians living abroad, directly elected for a five-year term. The National Council has 144 members; 48 are appointed by the president, and 96 are indirectly elected for a six-year term by electoral colleges formed by local councils; half of these elected members are re-elected every three years. Although Algeria is no longer a one-party state, parties based on religion or on race, language, gender or region are banned under the constitution.
    In the 2017 legislative election, the ruling National Liberation Front-led coalition won the most seats and retained control in the assembly. In April 2014, President Bouteflika was re-elected for a fourth term despite not campaigning due to ill health.

HEAD OF STATE
President, Defence, Abdelaziz Bouteflika, *elected* 15 April 1999, *re-elected* 2004, 2009, 2014

SELECTED GOVERNMENT MEMBERS *AS AT JULY 2018*
Prime Minister, Ahmed Ouyahia
Finance, Abderrahmane Raouia

Gains independence following
guerrilla war with socialist
Front de Libération Nationale

Elected president Abdelaziz
Bouteflika's 'civil concord' with
Islamists approved by referendum

Second amnesty between militants approved
but broken by bombings carried out by a
group aligning itself with al-Qaida

Conquered by the
Ottoman Empire

*c.*600   1830   1989-92   2005   2011

*c.*1525   1962   1999   2006

A Berber-populated Roman
province, Algeria is conquered
by Arabs and converted to Islam

Annexed by
France

A ban on the Islamic Salvation
Front triggers civil unrest and
a state of emergency

Agreement reached with Berber-populated
Kabylie for increased investment in the region
and greater recognition of the Berber language

Major demonstrations cause
government to cut food prices and
lift the 19-year state of emergency

Foreign Affairs, Abdelkader Messahel

ALGERIAN EMBASSY
6 Hyde Park G, London SW7 5EW
T 020-7589 6885 **E** info@algerianembassy.org.uk
W www.algerianembassy.org.uk
Ambassador Extraordinary and Plenipotentiary, HE Amar Abba,
apptd 2010

BRITISH EMBASSY
3 Chemin Capitaine Hocine Slimane, Hydra, Algiers
T (+213) (770) 085 000 **E** britishembassy.algiers@fco.gov.uk
W www.gov.uk/government/world/algeria
Ambassador Extraordinary and Plenipotentiary, HE Barry Lowen,
apptd 2017

ECONOMY AND TRADE
After independence, Algeria's economy was dominated by the
state until a privatisation programme was introduced in 1997.
Reform, combined with high oil prices, resulted in trade
surpluses, record foreign exchange reserves and the reduction
of foreign debt, despite recent blocks on the privatisation
process. Low oil prices have dented the economy, while
diversification away from the energy sector and development
of the financial system has been hampered by a lack of foreign
investment. Annual growth is expected to average over 2 per
cent between 2017 and 2021.

Algeria has substantial oil and gas reserves, and the
hydrocarbon industry accounts for 30 per cent of GDP, nearly
60 per cent of government revenue and over 95 per cent of
export earnings. Services provide 50.7 per cent of GDP,
industry 36.1 per cent and agriculture 13.2 per cent.
Industries other than oil and gas production include mining,
electrical goods, food processing and light industries.

Algeria's main trading partners are China, France, Italy,
other EU countries and the USA. The chief imports are capital
goods, foodstuffs and consumer goods.

GNI – US$163.5bn; US$3,960 per capita (2017)
Annual average growth of GDP – 1.7 per cent (2017 est)
Inflation rate – 5.5 per cent (2017 est)
Population below poverty line – 23 per cent (2006 est)
Unemployment – 11.7 per cent (2017 est)
Total external debt – US$8.163bn (2017 est)
Imports – US$46,734m (2016)
Exports – US$29,637m (2016)

BALANCE OF PAYMENTS
Trade – US$17,097m deficit (2016)
Current Account – US$22,058m deficit (2017)

Trade with UK	2016	2017
Imports from UK	£414,247,114	£333,679,013
Exports to UK	£676,277,073	£1,372,429,704

COMMUNICATIONS
Airports and waterways – 64, including Algiers and
Constantine; major ports are at Algiers and Bejaia
Roadways and railways – 87,605km, including 645km of
motorways; 3,973km
Telecommunications – 3.4 million fixed lines and 47 million
mobile subscriptions (2016); there were 17.3 million internet
users in 2016
Internet code and IDD – dz; 213 (from UK), 44 (to UK)
Major broadcaster – Enterprise Nationale de Télévision (ENTV)
is the state broadcaster
Press – There are more than 80 newspapers available in
Algiers, including *El Khabar, Ech Chourouk* and *Le Quotidien
d'Oran*
WPFI score – 43,13 (136)

EDUCATION AND HEALTH
Literacy rate – 80.2 per cent (2015 est)
Gross enrolment ratio (percentage of relevant age group) – primary
113.6 per cent (2016 est); secondary 95 per cent (2016
est); tertiary 42.7 per cent (2016 est)
Health expenditure (per capita) – US$362 (2014)
Hospital beds (per 1,000 people) – 1.9 (2015)
Life expectancy (years) – 77 (2017 est)
Mortality rate – 4.3 (2017 est)
Birth rate – 22.2 (2017 est)
Infant mortality rate – 19.6 (2017 est)
HIV/AIDS adult prevalence – 0.1 per cent (2016 est)

ANDORRA

Principat d'Andorra – Principality of Andorra

Area – 468 sq. km
Capital – Andorra la Vella; population, 23,000 (2018 est)
Major cities – Encamp, Les Escaldes-Engordany, Sant Julià de
Lòria
Currency – Euro (€) of 100 cents
Population – 76,965 rising at 0.03 per cent a year (2017 est);
Andorran (46.2 per cent), Spanish (26.4 per cent),
Portuguese (12.8 per cent), French (5 per cent) (2016 est)
Religion – Christian (predominantly Roman Catholic)
Language – Catalan (official), French, Spanish (Castilian),
Portuguese

Population density – 164 per sq. km (2016)
Urban population – 84.1 per cent (2017 est)
Median age (years) – 44.3 (2017 est)
National anthem – 'El Gran Carlemany' 'The Great Charlemagne'
National day – 8 September (Our Lady of Meritxell Day)
Death penalty – Abolished for all crimes (since 1990)
Health expenditure (per capita) – US$3,746 (2014)
Life expectancy (years) – 82.9 (2017 est)
Mortality rate – 7.3 (2017 est)
Birth rate – 7.5 (2017 est)
Infant mortality rate – 3.6 (2017 est)

CLIMATE AND TERRAIN

Andorra is a country of dramatic mountains interspersed by narrow valleys; over a third of the country is forested. Elevation extremes range from 2,946m (Pic de Coma Pedrosa) to 840m (Riu Runer). The climate is alpine, with heavy snowfall in winter and warm summers. Average temperature ranges from 1.6°C in January to 18.3°C in August.

HISTORY AND POLITICS

Liberated from Moorish rule by Charlemagne in 803, Andorra is a neutral principality that was formed by a *paréage* (a type of feudal treaty) in 1278 and since then has owed dual allegiance to two co-princes, the Spanish Bishop of Urgell and the head of state of France. Andorra became an independent democratic parliamentary co-principality in 1993. The country subsequently formalised its links with the EU, and joined the UN and the Council of Europe.

Andorra has a unicameral legislature, the General Council of the Valleys *(Consell General de las Valls)*, whose 28 members are directly elected for a four-year term by proportional representation. The council appoints the president of the executive council, who nominates government members.

Under the 1993 constitution, the heads of state are two co-princes, the President of France and the Bishop of Urgell, Spain. They are represented in Andorra by the permanent delegates (the Spanish vicar-general of the diocese of Urgell and the French prefect of the Pyrenees Orientales department), but their powers now relate solely to relations with France and Spain. The constitution established an independent judiciary and allows Andorra to conduct its own foreign policy, while its people may now join political parties and trade unions.

In the March 2015 legislative election, the Democrats for Andorra party remained in power despite losing five seats, winning 15 of the 28 seats in the general council.

HEADS OF STATE
The President of France, Emmanuel Macron
The Bishop of Urgell, Joan Enric Vives i Sicilia
Permanent French Delegate, Patrick Strzoda
Permanent Episcopal Delegate, Josep Maria Mauri i Prior

SELECTED GOVERNMENT MEMBERS *AS AT JUNE 2018*
President of the Executive Council, Antoni Marti Petit
Finance, Jordi Cinca Mateos
Foreign Affairs, Maria Ubach Font
Interior and Justice, Xavier Espot Zamora

BRITISH CONSULATE-GENERAL
Ambassador, HE Simon Manley, CMG, *apptd* 2013, resident at Madrid, Spain

ECONOMY AND TRADE

The economy is largely based on tourism, banking and retail sales, which together account for over 75 per cent of GDP. Following pressure from the EU, controversial bank secrecy laws were reformed in 2009 and the country's low tax economy modified by the introduction of corporation tax in 2012 and the nation's first income tax in 2015, a flat rate of 10 per cent. The country has actively sought foreign investment and businesses to diversity its economy since 2008. Other activities include manufacturing tobacco products, forestry, furniture-making and sheep-farming. Andorra is a member of the EU Customs Union and is treated as an EU member for trade in manufactured goods and as a non-EU member for agricultural products.

GNI – US$3,284bn (2015 est); US$43,270 per capita (2013)
Annual average growth of GDP – 1.9 per cent (2017 est)
Inflation rate – –0.9 per cent (2015 est)
Population below poverty line – 3.7 (2016 est)
Imports – US$1,355m (2016)
Exports – US$100m (2016)

BALANCE OF PAYMENTS
Trade – US$1,255m deficit (2016)

Trade with UK	2016	2017
Imports from UK	£8,365,619	£7,790,374
Exports to UK	£245,303	£286,069

COMMUNICATIONS

Roadways – 320km
Telecommunications – 38,690 fixed lines and 71,132 mobile subscriptions (2014); there were 83,887 internet users in 2016
Internet code and IDD – ad; 376 (from UK), 44 (to UK)
Major broadcaster – Radio i Televisio d'Andorra
Press – Major newspapers include *Diari d'Andorra* and *El Periodic d'Andorra*
WPFI score – 22,21 (37)

ANGOLA

Republica de Angola – Republic of Angola

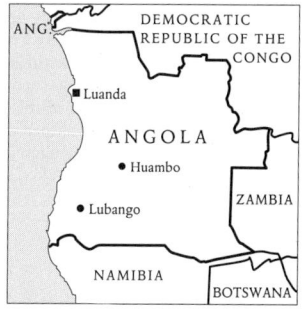

Area – 1,246,700 sq. km; includes the exclave of Cabinda
Capital – Luanda; population, 7,774,000 (2018 est)
Major cities – Benguela, Huambo, Lubango
Currency – Kwanza (Kzrl) of 100 centimos
Population – 29,310,273 rising at 3.52 per cent a year (2017 est); Ovimbundu (37 per cent), Kimbundu (25 per cent), Bakongo (13 per cent), Mestizo (2 per cent), other

African, including Lunda-Chokwe and Ngangela (22 per cent) (est)
Religion – Christian (Roman Catholic 41.1 per cent, Protestant 38.1 per cent); a small portion of the rural population practises indigenous beliefs (est)
Language – Portuguese (official), Bantu
Population density – 23 per sq. km (2016)
Urban population – 45.6 per cent (2017 est)
Median age (years) – 15.9 (2017 est)
National anthem – 'Angola Avante' 'Forward Angola'
National day – 11 November (Independence Day)
Death penalty – Abolished for all crimes (since 1992)
CPI score – 19 (167)
Military expenditure – US$3,063m (2017)
Conscription – 20–45 years of age for compulsory male service, mandatory registration at 18; 20–45 years of age for voluntary female service, 2 year obligation (2013)
Literacy rate – 71.1 per cent (2015 est)
Gross enrolment ratio (percentage of relevant age group) – primary 140 per cent, secondary 32 per cent (2011 est); tertiary 9.9 per cent (2013 est)
Health expenditure (per capita) – US$179 (2014)
Hospital beds (per 1,000 people) – 0.8 (2005)
Life expectancy (years) – 60.2 (2017 est)
Mortality rate – 9.2 (2017 est)
Birth rate – 44.2 (2017 est)
Infant mortality rate – 67.6 (2017 est)
HIV/AIDS adult prevalence – 1.9 per cent (2016 est)

CLIMATE AND TERRAIN
The land rises from a narrow coastal plain to a vast interior plateau, with desert to the south. The highest point of elevation is 2,620m (Morro do Moco) and the lowest is 0m (Atlantic Ocean). The climate is tropical in the north – with a cool, dry season from April to September and a hot, rainy season from October to March – and subtropical in the south and along the coast to Luanda.

POLITICS
Under the 2010 constitution, the president is the head of the party with the largest number of seats in the legislature. The unicameral National Assembly has 220 members, elected by proportional representation for a five-year term.

Political pluralism was introduced under the 1991 peace agreement and multiparty elections were held in 1992, though the National Union for Total Independence of Angola (UNITA) refused to accept the results. The first legislative elections since 1992, held in 2008, were won by the People's Movement for the Liberation of Angola (MPLA); it retained its majority in the 2012 and 2017 legislative elections, the latter with 150 seats to UNITA's 51. The new constitution, introduced in 2010, ended direct election of the president, created the office of vice-president and abolished the post of prime minister. After legislative elections in August 2017, Jose Eduardo dos Santos stood down as president after 38 years in power and was replaced by Joao Lourenco.

HEAD OF STATE
President, Joao Lourenco, *took office* 26 September 2017
Vice-President, Bornito De Sousa

SELECTED GOVERNMENT MEMBERS *AS AT JULY 2018*
Defence, Gen. Salviano de Jesus Sequeira
Finance, Augusto Archer de Sousa Mangueira
Foreign Affairs, Manuel Domingos Augusto
Interior, Angelo de Barros Veiga Tavares

EMBASSY OF THE REPUBLIC OF ANGOLA
22 Dorset Street, London W1U 6QY
T 020-7299 9850 **E** embassy@angola.org.uk **W** www.angola.org.uk
Ambassador Extraordinary and Plenipotentiary, HE Rui Mangueira, *apptd* 2018

BRITISH EMBASSY
Rua 17 de Setembro 4, Caixa, Luanda 1244
T (+244) (22) 233 4583 **E** postmaster.luand@fco.gov.uk
W www.gov.uk/government/world/angola
Ambassador Extraordinary and Plenipotentiary, HE Jessica Hand, *apptd* 2018

SECESSION
In the oil-rich northern exclave of Cabinda, separatists have conducted a low-level guerrilla war since the mid-1970s. The government has been unable to end the fighting either through negotiation or by military means. A ceasefire and peace agreement reached in 2006 has not been observed by all parties.

ECONOMY AND TRADE
The economy is still recovering from decades of corruption, mismanagement and civil war, but liberalisation and stabilisation are being achieved. Post-war increases in oil, diamond and agricultural production have driven strong economic growth, although the economy contracted in 2009 as the global downturn reduced demand for exports. The extractive industries and infrastructure projects have attracted foreign investment despite the corruption and stifling bureaucracy that have deterred investors in other sectors.

Angola, especially Cabinda, is rich in natural resources. The main industries involve extracting and processing oil (Angola is Africa's largest producer of oil, above Nigeria, with production and related activities accounting for around 50 per cent of GDP and 90 per cent of exports), diamonds, metals and other minerals, forestry, fishing, food processing and the manufacture of cement, metal products, tobacco products and textiles, and ship repair. Angola has large areas of good farmland, but the prevalence of unexploded landmines has reduced the area under cultivation and forced many areas back to subsistence agriculture, although coffee, sisal and cotton are produced for export. A dependence on imported consumable goods (Angola imports around 50 per cent of its food), poor infrastructure and high property prices have caused Luanda to become the world's most expensive city.

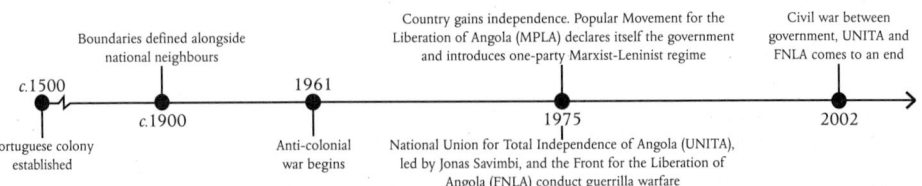

Boundaries defined alongside national neighbours

Country gains independence. Popular Movement for the Liberation of Angola (MPLA) declares itself the government and introduces one-party Marxist-Leninist regime

Civil war between government, UNITA and FNLA comes to an end

*c.*1500

*c.*1900

1961

1975

2002

Portuguese colony established

Anti-colonial war begins

National Union for Total Independence of Angola (UNITA), led by Jonas Savimbi, and the Front for the Liberation of Angola (FNLA) conduct guerrilla warfare

The main trading partners are China, the USA, India and Portugal. The principal exports are crude oil, diamonds, refined petroleum products, coffee, sisal, fish, timber and cotton. The main imports are machinery and electrical equipment, vehicles and spare parts, medicines, food, textiles and military goods.

GNI – US$99bn; US$3,330 per capita (2017)
Annual average growth of GDP – 0.7 per cent (2017 est)
Inflation rate – 30.9 per cent (2017 est)
Population below poverty line – 40.5 per cent (2008 est)
Unemployment – 6.6 per cent (2016 est)
Total external debt – US$27.34bn (2017 est)
Imports – US$20,095m (2015)
Exports – US$33,165m (2015)

BALANCE OF PAYMENTS
Trade – US$13,070m surplus (2015)
Current Account – US$3,071m deficit (2016)

Trade with UK	2016	2017
Imports from UK	£369,208,751	£381,355,553
Exports to UK	£306,923,246	£130,657,844

COMMUNICATIONS
Airports and waterways – 31; main ports include Cabinda, Lobito, Luanda and Namibe
Roadways and railways – 5,349km; 2,764km
Telecommunications – 304,493 fixed lines and 13 million mobile subscriptions; there were 2.6 million internet users in 2016
Internet code and IDD – ao; 244 (from UK), 44 (to UK)
Major broadcasters – Only the government-owned Televisao Publica de Angola (TPA) and Radio National de Angola (RNA) have national coverage
Press – The government owned *Jornal de Angola* is the only daily newspaper
WPFI score – 38,35 (121)

ANTIGUA AND BARBUDA

Antigua and Barbuda

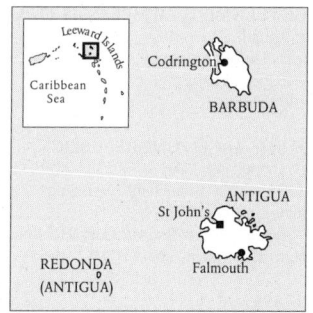

Area – 442.6 sq. km: Antigua 280 sq. km; Barbuda 161 sq. km; Redonda 1.6 sq. km
Capital – St John's; population, 21,000 (2018 est)
Currency – East Caribbean dollar (EC$) of 100 cents
Population – 94,731 rising at 1.21 per cent a year (2017 est)
Religion – Christian (Protestant 68.3 per cent, Roman Catholic 6.8 per cent), other 8.6 per cent (est)
Language – English (official), local dialects
Population density – 229 per sq. km (2016)
Urban population – 24.6 per cent (2018 est)

Median age (years) – 31.6 (2016 est)
National anthem – 'Fair Antigua, We Salute Thee'
National day – 1 November (Independence Day)
Death penalty – Retained (last used 1991)
Literacy rate – 99 per cent (2012 est)
Gross enrolment ratio (percentage of relevant age group) – primary 97.1 per cent, secondary 102.7 per cent (2015 est); tertiary 23 per cent (2012 est)
Health expenditure (per capita) – US$774 (2014)
Life expectancy (years) – 76.7 (2017 est)
Mortality rate – 5.7 (2017 est)
Birth rate – 15.7 (2017 est)
Infant mortality rate – 12.1 (2017 est)

CLIMATE AND TERRAIN
Unlike most other Leeward Islands, Antigua has few high hills and little forest cover. Its elevation extremes range from 402m (Boggy Peak) to 0m (Caribbean Sea). Barbuda, 48km north of Antigua, is a flat coral island with a large lagoon. Both islands are tropical, but drier than most of the West Indies. They lie within the hurricane belt and are subject to tropical storms and hurricanes between August and October.

HISTORY AND POLITICS
Prehistoric settlers were succeeded by the Arawaks, then the Caribs. Although the islands were discovered by Columbus in 1493, the European (English) settlement of Antigua began only in 1632. Barbuda was colonised from Antigua in 1661. Administered as part of the Leeward Islands Federation from 1871 to 1956, it became internally self-governing in 1967 and fully independent on 1 November 1981.

The head of state is Queen Elizabeth II, represented by the governor-general. The bicameral parliament comprises a senate of 17 members, appointed by the governor-general on the advice of the prime minister and opposition leader, and a House of Representatives of 17 directly elected members; both chambers serve a five-year term.

The Antigua Labour Party won the 2018 legislative elections claiming 15 seats.
Governor-General, HE Dr Sir Rodney Williams, GCMG, *apptd* 2014

SELECTED GOVERNMENT MEMBERS *AS AT JULY 2018*
Prime Minister, Gaston Browne
Foreign Affairs, Paul Green
Tourism, Charles Fernandez

HIGH COMMISSION FOR ANTIGUA AND BARBUDA
2nd Floor, 45 Crawford Place, London W1H 4LP
T 020-7258 0070 E enquiries@antigua-barbuda.com
W www.antigua-barbuda.com
High Commissioner, HE Karen-Mae Hill, *apptd* 2016

BRITISH HIGH COMMISSION
High Commissioner, HE Janet Douglas, CMG, *apptd* 2017, resident at Bridgetown, Barbados

ECONOMY AND TRADE
The economy is largely based on tourism and related services (contributing nearly 60 per cent of GDP), with petroleum products and light manufacturing (bedding, handicrafts, electronic components) for export, and agriculture (livestock, sea island cotton, market gardening, fishing) for local consumption. Economic growth and fiscal reform between 2004 and 2007 enabled the government to reduce public debt. However, from 2009, a severe decline in tourism caused by the global economic downturn and the collapse of Allen Stanford's Antigua-based financial group (which included Antigua's

major financial institution) hit the economy badly. The bleak economic outlook was exacerbated in September 2017 by Hurricane Irma, which left Barbuda uninhabitable and the government struggling to pay a reconstruction bill estimated at US$200 million.

GNI – US$1.4bn; US$14,170 per capita (2017)
Annual average growth of GDP – 2.7 per cent (2017 est)
Inflation rate – 2.4 per cent (2017 est)
Unemployment – 11 per cent (2014 est)
Total external debt – US$441.2m (2012 est)
Imports – US$494m (2016)
Exports – US$61m (2016)

BALANCE OF PAYMENTS
Trade – US$433m deficit (2016)
Current Account – US$2.2m surplus (2016)

Trade with UK	2016	2017
Imports from UK	£15,986,168	£16,739,212
Exports to UK	£27,910,435	£3,831,135

COMMUNICATIONS
Airports and waterways – Two; the main port is at St John's
Roadways – 386km
Telecommunications – 22,504 fixed lines and 180,000 mobile subscriptions (2016); there were 60,000 internet users in 2016
Internet code and IDD – ag; 1 268 (from UK), 011 44 (to UK)
Major broadcasters – The Antigua and Barbuda Broadcasting Service (ABS) is the state broadcaster; private and public TV and radio stations are affiliated with political parties
Press – *Antigua Sun* is the only daily newspaper

ARGENTINA

República Argentina – Argentine Republic

Area – 2,780,400 sq. km
Capital – Buenos Aires; population, 14,967,000 (2018 est)
Major cities – Córdoba, La Plata, Mar del Plata, Mendoza, Rosario, Salta, San Miguel de Tucumán, Santa Fé
Currency – Argentine Peso of 100 centavos
Population – 44,293,293 rising at 0.91 per cent a year (2017 est)
Religion – Christian (Roman Catholic 92 per cent, Protestant 2 per cent), Jewish (2 per cent) (est)
Language – Spanish (official), Italian, English, German, French; Mapudungun and Quechua (both indigenous)
Population density – 16 per sq. km (2016)
Urban population – 91.9 per cent (2018 est)
Median age (years) – 31.7 (2017 est)
National anthem – 'Himno Nacional Argentina' 'Argentine National Anthem'

National day – 25 May (Revolution Day)
Death penalty – Abolished for all crimes (since 2008)
CPI score – 39 (85)
Military expenditure – US$5,681m (2017)

CLIMATE AND TERRAIN
The Andes mountain range runs the full length of the country, along its western border with Chile, and the area is prone to earthquakes. East of the Andes, the north is mostly subtropical rainforest, the centre contains the vast grasslands of the pampas, and the southern Patagonian plateau is arid and desolate, with glaciers in the far south. The highest point of elevation is 6,960m (Cerro Aconcagua) and the lowest is −105m (Laguna del Carbon). Temperatures range from subtropical in the north to subantarctic in the south. Average temperatures range from 20.5°C in January to 7.3°C in July.

POLITICS
Following constitutional amendments agreed in 1994, the executive president is directly elected for a four-year term, renewable once. The bicameral National Congress consists of a 72-member senate (three members for each province and three for Buenos Aires) and a 257-member Chamber of Deputies. Deputies are directly elected for a four-year term, with half of the seats renewable every two years. Senators are directly elected for a six-year term, with one-third of seats renewable every two years.

The Argentine Republic is a federation of 23 provinces, each with an elected governor and legislature, plus the federal district of Buenos Aires, which has an elected mayor and autonomous government.

The October 2015 presidential election was won in the second round by Mauricio Macri, the former mayor of Buenos Aires and leader of the centre-right Cambiemos coalition. Following long-term acrimony between the pair, Macri's inauguration was not attended by the outgoing Cristina Fernandez de Kirchner, contrary to custom. Simultaneous legislative elections saw the centre-right 'Let's Change' coalition make gains which were strengthened in both houses in October 2017.

HEAD OF STATE
President, Mauricio Macri, *elected* 22 November 2015, *sworn in* 10 December 2015
Vice-President, Marta Gabriela Michetti

SELECTED GOVERNMENT MEMBERS *AS AT JULY 2018*
Defence, Oscar Aguad
Finance, Nicholas Dujovne
Foreign Relations, Jorge Faurie
Interior, Rogelio Frigerio

EMBASSY OF THE ARGENTINE REPUBLIC
65 Brook Street, London W1K 4AH
T 020-7318 1300 E info@argentine-embassy-uk.org
W www.argentine-embassy-uk.org
Ambassador Extraordinary and Plenipotentiary, HE Renato Carlos Sersale di Cerisano, *apptd* 2016

BRITISH EMBASSY
Dr Luis Agote 2412, 1425 Buenos Aires
T (+54) (11) 4808 2200 W www.gov.uk/government/world/argentina
Ambassador Extraordinary and Plenipotentiary, HE Mark Kent, *apptd* 2016

ECONOMY AND TRADE
The economy recovered rapidly from the economic collapse of 2001–2, experiencing strong growth from 2003. Argentina restructured its defaulted debt in 2005 and repaid its IMF loan in 2006, but experienced a recession in 2008–9 caused by the global downturn. Following a US court ruling in July 2014 in favour of bond holders who had not accepted

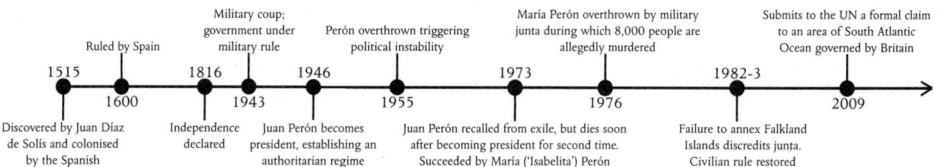

Ruled by Spain	Military coup; government under military rule
	Perón overthrown triggering political instability
	María Perón overthrown by military junta during which 8,000 people are allegedly murdered
	Submits to the UN a formal claim to an area of South Atlantic Ocean governed by Britain

1515 — 1816 — 1946 — 1973 — 1982-3

1600 — 1943 — 1955 — 1976 — 2009

Discovered by Juan Díaz de Solís and colonised by the Spanish

Independence declared

Juan Perón becomes president, establishing an authoritarian regime

Juan Perón recalled from exile, but dies soon after becoming president for second time. Succeeded by María ('Isabelita') Perón

Failure to annex Falkland Islands discredits junta. Civilian rule restored

previous debt restructuring – mainly US hedge funds – the government chose to default on its debt for the eighth time in Argentinian history. Despite high levels of inflation and the devaluing of the peso, which in January 2014 saw its sharpest one-day fall against the dollar since the 2002 crisis, the economy has slightly rebounded since 2010, initially by increased state intervention and, since 2015, through President Macri's liberalisation policies. Nonetheless, inflation nearly reached 30 per cent in 2017, and a sharp fall in the value of the peso meant President Macri asked for the early release of a US$50bn (£37.2bn) loan from the IMF to tackle the crisis in August 2018.

The country is rich in natural resources, particularly lead, zinc, tin, copper, iron ore, manganese, uranium, oil and coal. The fertile pampas supports a strong and export-orientated agricultural sector; the main crops are cereals, oil-bearing seeds, fruit, tea, tobacco and livestock products, especially beef, mutton and wool.

The main industrial activities are food processing (meat-packing, flour-milling, sugar-refining, wine production) and the production of motor vehicles, consumer durables, textiles, chemicals, petrochemicals, printing, metallurgy and steel.

The main trading partners are Brazil, China and the USA. The principal exports include soya beans and derivatives, petroleum and gas, motor vehicles and cereals. The major imports are machinery, motor vehicles, petroleum and natural gas, organic chemicals and plastics.

GNI – US$577bn; US$13,040 per capita (2017)
Annual average growth of GDP – 2.9 per cent (2017 est)
Inflation rate – 26.9 per cent (2017 est)
Population below poverty line – 32.2 per cent (2016 est)
Unemployment – 8.1 per cent (2017 est)
Total external debt – US$208.6bn (2017 est)
Imports – US$55,608m (2016)
Exports – US$57,732m (2016)

BALANCE OF PAYMENTS
Trade – US$2,124m surplus (2016)
Current Account – US$31,324m deficit (2017)

Trade with UK	2016	2017
Imports from UK	£300,227,090	£347,863,905
Exports to UK	£650,467,023	£703,073,350

COMMUNICATIONS
Airports and waterways – 161, major airports include Buenos Aires, Córdoba, Rio Gallegos and Salta; 11,000km of waterways
Roadways and railways – 69,412km, including 734km of motorways; 36,966km
Telecommunications – 9.9 million fixed lines and 63.7 million mobile subscriptions (2016); there were 30.8 million internet subscribers in 2016
Internet code and IDD – ar; 54 (from UK), 44 (to UK)

Major broadcasters – The privately owned Telefe and Canal 13 are the leading television broadcasters; Radio Nacional is the state-run radio broadcaster
Press – There are over 150 daily newspapers, including *Clarín*, *La Nación* and *Cronica*
WPFI score – 26,05 (52)

EDUCATION AND HEALTH
Education is compulsory until the age of 14.
Literacy rate – 98.1 per cent (2015 est)
Gross enrolment ratio (percentage of relevant age group) – primary 109 per cent, secondary 107.1 per cent, tertiary 85.7 per cent (2015 est)
Health expenditure (per capita) – US$605
Hospital beds (per 1,000 people) – 5 (2014)
Life expectancy (years) – 77.3 (2017 est)
Mortality rate – 7.5 (2017 est)
Birth rate – 16.7 (2017 est)
Infant mortality rate – 9.8 (2017 est)
HIV/AIDS adult prevalence – 0.4 per cent (2016 est)

ARGENTINE ANTARCTIC TERRITORY
The Argentine Antarctic Territory consists of the Antarctic Peninsula and a triangular section extending to the South Pole, defined as the area between 25°W. and 74°W. and 60°S. This overlaps with both Britain's and Chile's claimed areas (*see also* The North and South Poles). Administratively, the territory is a department of the province of Tierra del Fuego, Antarctica and South Atlantic Islands. The population varies seasonally between approximately 150 and 660 people, all of whom are scientific researchers and their dependants.

ARMENIA
Hayastani Hanrapetut'yun – Republic of Armenia

Area – 29,743 sq. km
Capital – Yerevan; population, 1,080,000 (2018 est)
Major cities – Gyumri, Vanadzor
Currency – Dram of 100 luma
Population – 3,045,191 falling at 0.21 per cent a year (2017 est); Armenian (98.1 per cent), Yezidi (1.1 per cent)

(2011). The Armenian diaspora numbers at least 4,700,000

Religion – Christian (Armenian Apostolic 92.6 per cent, other Christian 3.4 per cent) (est). The kingdom of Armenia was the first state to adopt Christianity as its official religion, in AD 301

Language – Armenian, Kurdish
Population density – 103 per sq. km (2016)
Urban population – 63.1 per cent (2018 est)
Median age (years) – 35.1 (2017 est)
National anthem – 'Mer Hayrenik' 'Our Fatherland'
National day – 21 September (Independence Day)
Death penalty – Abolished for all crimes (since 2003)
CPI score – 35 (107)
Military expenditure – US$444m (2017)
Conscription – 18–27 years of age; 2 years

CLIMATE AND TERRAIN

Landlocked Armenia is situated in the south-western part of the Caucasus region. It lies at a high altitude and consists of vast plateaux surrounded by mountain ranges. The elevation extremes range from 4,090m (Mt Aragats) to 400m (Debed river). The climate is continental, with hot summers, cold winters and low rainfall. Armenia experiences occasional droughts and severe earthquakes.

POLITICS

The 1995 constitution has been amended by referendums multiple times, most recently in 2015. The unicameral National Assembly *(Azgayin Joghov)* has 105 members who are directly elected for a five-year term. Changes to the constitution adopted in December 2015 aimed to transform the government to a parliamentary system: the prime minister is nominated by the ruling party for approval by assembly, and the president is elected by assembly for a non-renewable, seven-year term.

In the 2017 legislative election, the Republican Party of Armenia (RPA) remained the largest party in the legislature, with 58 seats, and its leader, Serzh Sargsyan, continued in office at the head of a coalition government. The March 2018 election was the first where the National Assembly elected its president; Armen Sarkisyan was elected and outgoing president Serzh Sargsyan was appointed prime minister, but popular protests forced him to resign six days after taking office. Opposition leader Nikol Pashinyan replaced him, but his Armenian National Congress party held no parliamentary majority.

HEAD OF STATE
President, Armen Sarkisyan, *elected* 9 April 2018

SELECTED GOVERNMENT MEMBERS *AS AT MAY 2018*
Prime Minister, Nikol Pashinyan, *sworn in* 8 May 2018
First Deputy Prime Minister, Ararat Mirzoyan
Defence, Davit Tonoyan
Finance, Atom Janjughazyan

EMBASSY OF THE REPUBLIC OF ARMENIA
25A Cheniston Gardens, London W8 6TG
T 020-7938 5435 E armembassyuk@mfa.am
W http://uk.mfa.am/en
Ambassador Extraordinary and Plenipotentiary, vacant

BRITISH EMBASSY
34 Baghramyan Avenue, Yerevan 0019
T (+374) (10) 264 301 E enquiries.yerevan@fco.gov.uk
W www.gov.uk/government/world/armenia
Ambassador Extraordinary and Plenipotentiary, HE Judith Farnworth, *apptd* 2015

FOREIGN RELATIONS
There is a longstanding dispute with Azerbaijan over the predominantly Armenian-populated Azeri region of Nagorny-Karabakh; Armenia claims this territory as historically native land arbitrarily granted to Soviet Azerbaijan by Stalin in 1921–2. The territory's government voted to transfer to Armenia in 1988 but this was rejected by the USSR. When the USSR collapsed in 1991, the territory declared independence. Azeri attempts to reassert control were met with resistance, which escalated into a war that lasted from 1992 until a ceasefire was agreed between Armenia, Azerbaijan and Nagorny-Karabakh in 1994. By this time, Nagorno-Karabakh forces, supported by Armenia, had captured all of Nagorny-Karabakh, all Azeri territory that separated Nagorny-Karabakh from Armenia and all mountainous Azeri territory around the enclave. Talks mediated by the Organisation for Security and Cooperation in Europe failed to make any progress towards a peaceful resolution until 2008, when Armenia and Azerbaijan agreed to intensify efforts, although recent years have seen stalled negotiations and regular ceasefire breaches – including the deaths in July 2014 of 14 Azeri soldiers and further clashes in April 2016 that left at least 30 dead. The region, renamed the Republic of Artsakh in 2017, has limited international recognition.

ECONOMY AND TRADE
The economy experienced a severe decline following the break-up of the USSR in 1991, adding to existing problems arising from the 1988 earthquake and subsequently exacerbated by the Nagorny-Karabakh conflict and the consequent trade embargos imposed by Azerbaijan and Turkey, both of which are still in place. Economic liberalisation from 1994 brought sustained high growth and falls in inflation and poverty levels until the global economic crisis. Although a recovery began in 2010, the poor performance of the eurozone and Russian economies remains a long-term threat to growth. Armenia became a founding member of the Eurasian Economic Union (EEU) on 1 January 2015.

The agricultural sector produces fruit, vegetables and livestock as cash crops, and grain; it contributes 17.7 per cent of GDP and employs 36.3 per cent of the workforce. There are large mineral deposits, including iron and copper ore, and

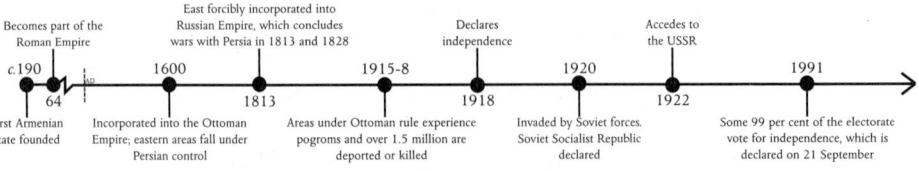

Becomes part of the Roman Empire	East forcibly incorporated into Russian Empire, which concludes wars with Persia in 1813 and 1828		Declares independence		Accedes to the USSR	
*c.*190	1600	1915-8		1920		1991
64	1813		1918		1922	
First Armenian state founded	Incorporated into the Ottoman Empire; eastern areas fall under Persian control	Areas under Ottoman rule experience pogroms and over 1.5 million are deported or killed		Invaded by Soviet forces. Soviet Socialist Republic declared		Some 99 per cent of the electorate vote for independence, which is declared on 21 September

non-ferrous metals. Industry, which contributes 27.8 per cent of GDP, is diversified and most small- and medium-sized enterprises are now privatised. The main activities are diamond-processing, the production of industrial machinery, vehicles and parts, textiles and clothing, chemicals, instruments, microelectronics, jewellery, software development and food processing. Remittances from expatriates working in Russia contribute 12 to 14 per cent of GDP.

The main trading partners are Russia, EU countries, Iran, other former Soviet bloc states, China and Iraq. Principal exports are pig iron, copper, non-ferrous metals, diamonds, mineral products, food and energy. The main imports are natural gas, petrol, tobacco products, foodstuffs and diamonds.

GNI – US$11.7bn; US$4,000 per capita (2017)
Annual average growth of GDP – 3.5 per cent (2017 est)
Inflation rate – 1.9 per cent (2017 est)
Population below poverty line – 32 per cent (2013 est)
Unemployment – 18.9 per cent (2017 est)
Total external debt – US$9.17bn (2017 est)
Imports – US$3,283m (2016)
Exports – US$1,781m (2016)

BALANCE OF PAYMENTS
Trade – US$1,502m deficit (2016)
Current Account – US$328.5m deficit (2017)

Trade with UK	2016	2017
Imports from UK	£12,622,192	£10,892,386
Exports to UK	£558,150	£1,289,815

COMMUNICATIONS
Airports – Ten
Roadways and railways – 7,705km; 869km
Telecommunications – 531,624 fixed lines and 3.4 million mobile subscriptions (2016); there were 1.9 million internet users in 2016
Internet code and IDD – am; 374 (from UK), 44 (to UK)
Major broadcasters – Public TV of Armenia (state-run) and Armenia TV (commercial), alongside 24 private television stations
Press – Daily newspapers include *Aravot, Aykakan Zhanamak* and the state-operated *Ayastani Anrapetutyun*
WPFI score – 29,99 (80)

EDUCATION AND HEALTH
State education is free and compulsory for all children aged seven to 14. Senior secondary school may be attended from the ages of 14 to 16.
Literacy rate – 99.7 per cent (2015 est)
Gross enrolment ratio (percentage of relevant age group) – primary 94.3 per cent (2016 est), secondary 88.5 per cent (2015 est), tertiary 51.5 per cent (2016 est)
Health expenditure (per capita) – US$162 (2014)
Hospital beds (per 1,000 people) – 4.2 (2015)
Life expectancy (years) – 74.9 (2017 est)
Mortality rate – 9.4 (2017 est)
Birth rate – 12.9 (2017 est)
Infant mortality rate – 12.7 (2017 est)
HIV/AIDS adult prevalence – 0.2 per cent (2016 est)

AUSTRALIA
Commonwealth of Australia

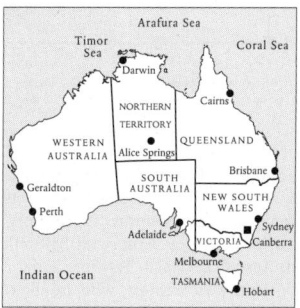

Area – 7,741,220 sq. km (excluding overseas territories)
Capital – Canberra; population, 423,000 (2018 est)
Major cities – Adelaide, Brisbane, Melbourne, Perth, Sydney
Currency – Australian dollar ($A) of 100 cents
Population – 23,232,413 rising at 1.03 per cent a year (2017 est)
Religion – Christian (Protestant 30.1 per cent, Roman Catholic 25.1 per cent), Buddhist 2.5 per cent, Muslim 2.2 per cent, Hindu 1.3 per cent (est)
Language – English, Mandarin, Italian, Arabic, Greek, Cantonese, Vietnamese, Aboriginal languages
Population density – 3 per sq. km (2016)
Urban population – 89.7 per cent (2018 est)
Median age (years) – 38.7 (2017 est)
National anthem – 'Advance Australia Fair'
National day – 26 January (Australia Day)
Death penalty – Abolished for all crimes (since 1985)
CPI score – 77 (13)
Military expenditure – US$27,462m (2017)

CLIMATE AND TERRAIN
The majority of Australia is a plateau, with hills, low mountain ranges and sparsely populated deserts in the interior, and tropical wetlands and rainforest in the north-east. Mountain ranges running down the east coast are the source of the Murray and Darling river systems, which flow across the densely populated fertile plain in the south-east. Off the north-east coast is the Great Barrier Reef, the world's largest coral reef. Elevation ranges from 2,229m (Mt Kosciuszko) to −15m (Lake Eyre). The climate is arid or semi-arid in the interior, tropical in the north and temperate in the south and east.

POLITICS
Under the 1901 constitution, the Commonwealth of Australia is a federation of six states. The constitution defines the powers of the federal government, and residuary legislative power remains with the states.

The head of state is Queen Elizabeth II, represented by the governor-general, who is appointed on the advice of the Australian prime minister. The bicameral parliament consists of the senate and the House of Representatives. The constitution provides that the number of members of the House of Representatives shall be proportionate to the population of each state, with a minimum of five members for each state, and that the number of senators shall be, as nearly as is practicable, half the number of representatives. There are currently 150 members, including two members for the

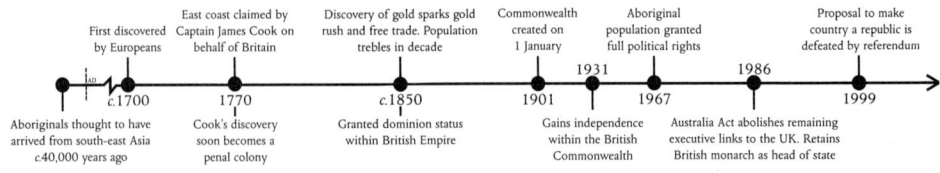

	East coast claimed by	Discovery of gold sparks gold	Commonwealth	Aboriginal	Proposal to make
First discovered	Captain James Cook on	rush and free trade. Population	created on	population granted	country a republic is
by Europeans	behalf of Britain	trebles in decade	1 January	full political rights	defeated by referendum

1931   1986

AD
  *c.*1700   1770   *c.*1850   1901   1967   1999

Aboriginals thought to have	Cook's discovery	Granted dominion status	Gains independence	Australia Act abolishes remaining	
arrived from south-east Asia	soon becomes a	within British Empire	within the British	executive links to the UK. Retains	
*c.*40,000 years ago	penal colony		Commonwealth	British monarch as head of state	

Northern Territory and two for the Australian Capital Territory; they are directly elected for a three-year term. There are 76 senators; each state returns 12 senators, who are directly elected for a six-year term, with half retiring every third year. The Australian Capital Territory and the Northern Territory each return two senators, who are directly elected for a three-year term.

Each of the six states has its own constitution, executive, legislature and judicature. Executive authority is vested in a governor (appointed by the Crown), assisted by a council of ministers or executive council headed by a state premier. There are ten territories, and two – the Northern Territory and Australian Capital Territory – have limited self-government. Northern Territory has an executive authority headed by an administrator (appointed by the governor-general), and legislative assembly led by a chief minister; authority over Australian Capital Territory rests with the governor-general acting on the advice of the federal government. The other territories are directly administered by the federal government.

The Liberal–National Coalition, led by Tony Abbott of the Liberal Party of Australia, defeated the incumbent Australian Labor Party (ALP) in the September 2013 federal elections, winning a significant overall majority in the House of Representatives, but not in the Senate. His victory ended seven years of government by the ALP and followed a divisive leadership battle within the party that saw deputy prime minister Julia Gillard challenge Kevin Rudd and become Australia's first female prime minister in June 2010 and then relinquish the premiership back to him exactly three years later. In September 2015, Malcolm Turnbull replaced Tony Abbott as prime minister after the Liberal Party carried out a leadership ballot following plummeting opinion polls. Turnbull claimed victory in the closely fought July 2016 federal elections, but was replaced by the socially-conservative Scott Morrison in August 2018 following a leadership contest.

Governor-General, HE Sir Peter Cosgrove, *apptd* 2014

SELECTED GOVERNMENT MEMBERS *AS AT SEPTEMBER 2018*
Prime Minister, Scott Morrison *sworn in* 24 August 2018
Deputy Prime Minister, Infrastructure and Transport, Michael McCormack
Defence, Christopher Pyne
Finance, Mathias Cormann
Foreign Affairs, Marise Payne

AUSTRALIAN HIGH COMMISSION
Australia House, Strand, London WC2B 4LA
T 020-7379 4334 W www.uk.embassy.gov.au
High Commissioner, HE George Brandis, QC, *apptd* 2018

BRITISH HIGH COMMISSION
Commonwealth Avenue, Yarralumla, Canberra, ACT 2600
T (+61) (2) 6270 6666 E canberra.enquiries@fconet.fco.gov.uk
W www.gov.uk/government/world/australia
High Commissioner, HE Menna Rawlings, CMG, *apptd* 2015

ECONOMY AND TRADE

Australia has a highly diversified and internationally competitive market economy that saw sustained strong growth from 1992 to 2016. It weathered the global downturn better than most developed countries, avoiding recession through a government fiscal stimulus package and low interest rates. Recent problems have been climate-related, with floods, droughts and extensive bush fires all affecting agriculture, mining and infrastructure, while the economy faces falls in key export commodity prices coupled with reduced demand from Asia and China. The service sector contributes 70.3 per cent of GDP and employs 75.3 per cent of the workforce, industry accounts for 26.1 per cent of GDP and 21.1 per cent of labour, and agriculture contributes 3.6 per cent of GDP and employs 3.6 per cent of the workforce.

The diversity of Australia's climate and soil conditions means that a wide range of crops can be grown, although most are confined to specific regions. Scant or erratic rainfall, limited scope for irrigation and unsuitable soils or topography have restricted intensive agriculture, although wheat is a major export, and sugar cane and fruit are important crops. Cattle and sheep ranching is widespread, providing meat, meat derivatives, wool and dairy products.

Significant natural resources include bauxite, coal, copper, diamonds, gold, iron ore, lead, mineral salts, nickel, silver, tin, tungsten, uranium, zinc, oil and natural gas. The main industrial activities are mining, the production of industrial and transport equipment, chemicals and steel, and food processing. Production and processing of hydrocarbons are expected to increase once the oil and gas fields in the Timor Sea begin full production.

Over the past 20 years, the focus of Australia's trade, like its foreign policy, has shifted from Europe to Asia and the Pacific region. It is a leading member of the Asia-Pacific Economic Cooperation forum, and a free-trade agreement (FTA) between Australia and the Association of Southeast Asian Nations (ASEAN) countries entered into force in 2010; it also has FTAs with China (since 2015), Japan, Chile, South Korea and Malaysia. Major trading partners include China, Japan, South Korea, India, the USA, Thailand and Germany. The chief exports are coal, iron ore, gold, meat, wool, alumina, wheat, natural gas and alcohol. The main imports are machinery and transport equipment, computers, office and telecoms equipment, crude oil and petroleum products.

GNI – US$1,263bn; US$51,630 per capita (2017)
Annual average growth of GDP – 2.2 per cent (2017 est)
Inflation rate – 2.0 per cent (2017 est)
Unemployment – 5.6 per cent (2017 est)
Total external debt – US$1.67 trillion (2017 est)
Imports – US$188,950m (2016)
Exports – US$191,089m (2016)

BALANCE OF PAYMENTS
Trade – US$2,139m surplus (2016)
Current Account – US$34,341m deficit (2017)

Trade with UK	2016	2017
Imports from UK	£3,922,917,102	£4,472,287,525
Exports to UK	£5,587,909,852	£3,924,075,979

STATES AND TERRITORIES

	Capital	Premier	Area (sq. km)	Pop. (2014 est)
Australian Capital Territory (ACT)	Canberra	Andrew Barr*	2,358	386,000
New South Wales (NSW)	Sydney	Gladys Berejiklian	800,642	7,518,500
Northern Territory (NT)	Darwin†	Michael Gunner*	1,349,129	245,100
Queensland (Qld)	Brisbane	Annastacia Palaszczuk	1,730,648	4,722,400
South Australia (SA)	Adelaide	Steven Marshall	983,482	1,685,700
Tasmania (Tas.)	Hobart	William Hodgman	68,401	514,800
Victoria (Vic.)	Melbourne	Daniel Andrews	227,416	5,841,700
Western Australia (WA)	Perth	Mark McGowan	2,529,875	2,573,400

* Chief Minister
† Seat of Administration

COMMUNICATIONS

Airports – 349; there are international airports in each of the eight territories

Waterways – 2,000km; major ports in all of the state capitals except Hobart

Roadways and railways – 356,343km; 38,445km

Telecommunications – 8.18 million fixed lines and 26.5 million mobile subscriptions (2016); there were 20.3 million internet subscribers in 2016

Internet country code and IDD – au; 61 (from UK), 11 41 (to UK)

Major broadcasters – The Australian Broadcasting Corporation (ABC) and Special Broadcasting Service (SBS), both public, provide radio and TV coverage; other major television networks include Australia Network and Foxtel (owned by News Corporation)

Press – Two major media groups – News Corp Australia and Fairfax Media – account for 85 per cent of newspaper sales; major titles include *The Sydney Morning Herald*, *The Australian* and *The Daily Telegraph*

WPFI score – 15,46 (19)

EDUCATION AND HEALTH

Education is administered by each state and territory, and is compulsory between the ages of five and 17.

Gross enrolment ratio (percentage of relevant age group) – primary 101.3 per cent, secondary 153.8 per cent, tertiary 121.9 per cent (2016 est)

Health expenditure (per capita) – US$6,031 (2014)

Hospital beds (per 1,000 people) – 3.8 (2014)

Life expectancy (years) – 82.3 (2017 est)

Mortality rate – 7.3 (2017 est)

Birth rate – 12.1 (2017 est)

Infant mortality rate – 4.3 (2017 est)

HIV/AIDS adult prevalence – 0.1 per cent (2016 est)

EXTERNAL TERRITORIES

Most of the territories are administered by the federal government through the Department of Regional Australia, Regional Development and Local Government; the Australian Antarctic Territory and the Territory of Heard Island and McDonald Islands are administered through the Australian Antarctic Division of the Department of Sustainability, Environment, Water, Population and Communities.

ASHMORE AND CARTIER ISLANDS

The Ashmore Islands (comprising Middle, East and West Islands) and Cartier Island are situated in the Indian Ocean 320km off Australia's north-west coast. The islands became an Australian territory in 1933. A nature reserve was established on Ashmore Reef in 1983 and a marine reserve around Cartier Island in 2000.

AUSTRALIAN ANTARCTIC TERRITORY

The Australian Antarctic Territory was established in 1933 and is 5,896,500 sq. km. It comprises all the islands and territories, other than Adélie Land, that are situated south of latitude 60°S. and lying between 160°E. longitude and 45°E. longitude. (*See also* The North and South Poles.)

CHRISTMAS ISLAND

Area – 135 sq. km

Population – 2,205 (2016 est) rising at 1.11 per cent a year (2014 est); Chinese (70 per cent), European (20 per cent), Malay (10 per cent) (2001 est)

Religion – Buddhist 16.9 per cent, Christian 16.4 per cent, Muslim 14.8 per cent (2011 est)

Christmas Island is situated in the Indian Ocean about 1,565km north-west of Northwest Cape in Western Australia. The island was annexed by Britain in 1888. Sovereignty was transferred to Australia in 1958. The Shire of Christmas Island (SOCI) is responsible for local government services on the island; its council has nine members directly elected for a four-year term. The main activities are phosphate mining, tourism and the government sector.

Administrator, Natasha Griggs, *apptd* 2018

COCOS (KEELING) ISLANDS

Area – 14 sq. km

Population – 596 (2014 est)

Religion – Muslim 80 per cent (2002 est)

The Cocos (Keeling) Islands are two separate atolls (North Keeling Island and, 24km to the south, the main atoll) comprising 27 small coral islands, situated in the Indian Ocean, about 2,950km north-west of Perth. The two inhabited islands of the southern atoll are West Island and Home Island, where around 80 per cent of the population lives, including most of the Cocos Malay community.

The islands were declared a British possession in 1857. In 1886 Queen Victoria granted all land in the islands to George Clunies-Ross and his heirs, who established coconut plantations worked by imported Malay labour. Sovereignty was transferred to Australia in 1955, and the government purchased the Clunies-Ross land and property in 1978, 1984 and 1993. The land is held in trust for the residents, with the local government body, the Shire of the Cocos (Keeling) Islands, as trustee. In 1984 the Cocos community, in a UN-supervised Act of Self-Determination, voted to integrate with Australia. The seven-member Shire Council of Cocos (Keeling) Islands is responsible for local government services. The public sector is the main employer and there is a little tourism; coconuts are the only cash crop.

Administrator, Natasha Griggs, *apptd* 2018

CORAL SEA ISLANDS TERRITORY

The Coral Sea Islands Territory lies east of Queensland between the Great Barrier Reef and longitude 156° 06′ E., and between latitudes 12°S. and 24°S. It comprises scattered islands, spread over a sea area of 780,000 sq. km. There is a manned meteorological station on Willis Island but otherwise the islands are uninhabited. Established in 1969, the territory is now a nature reserve, administered jointly by the Department of Sustainability, Environment, Water, Population and Communities, and the Department of Agriculture, Fisheries and Forestry.

HEARD ISLAND AND MCDONALD ISLANDS
The Territory of Heard Island and the McDonald Islands, about 4,100km south-west of Perth, comprises all the islands and rocks lying between 52° 30′ and 53° 30′ S. latitude and 72° and 74° 30′ E. longitude. The subantarctic islands, which have active volcanoes, were discovered in the 1850s and sovereignty was transferred from Britain to Australia in 1947. The islands are now part of a marine reserve established in 2002.

JERVIS BAY TERRITORY
Area – 76 sq. km
Population – 377 (2011 census)
The territory consists of 66 sq. km of land on the southern shore of Jervis Bay, 9 sq. km of marine waters and Bowen Island (0.5 sq. km), and lies about 200km south of Sydney. Originally part of New South Wales, the territory was acquired by the federal government in 1915 to provide Canberra with access to the sea. Much of the land and water now comprises Booderee National Park, leased from the Wreck Bay Aboriginal Community, who since the 1980s have been granted 90 per cent of the land. The main economic activity is tourism.

NORFOLK ISLAND
Area – 36 sq. km
Population – 1,748 (2016 est) rising at 0.01 per cent a year (2014 est); Australian (79.5 per cent), New Zealander (13.3 per cent), Fijian (2.5 per cent) (2011 est)
Religion – Christian (Protestant 49.6 per cent, Roman Catholic 11.7 per cent) (2011 est)
Seat of government – Kingston
National day – 8 June (Bounty Day)
Discovered by Captain Cook in 1774, Norfolk Island is situated in the South Pacific Ocean, about 1,600km north-east of Sydney. In 1856, 194 descendants of the *Bounty* mutineers accepted an invitation to leave Pitcairn and settle on Norfolk Island, which had served as a penal colony.
   The island became a territory in 1914 and internally self-governing in 1979, but after financial difficulties it was absorbed into the state of New South Wales in 2016. A regional council is responsible for planning and managing public services. The economy is dependent on tourism; other economic activities include the sale of postage stamps and pine and palm seeds, livestock-rearing and agriculture.
Administrator, Eric Hutchinson, *apptd* 2017

AUSTRIA
Republik Österreich – Republic of Austria

Area – 83,871 sq. km
Capital – Vienna (Wien); population, 1,901,000 (2018 est)
Major cities – Graz, Innsbruck, Klagenfurt, Linz, Salzburg
Currency – Euro (€) of 100 cents
Population – 8,754,413 rising at 0.47 per cent a year (2017 est); Austrian (91.1 per cent), former Yugoslav (4 per cent), Turkish (1.6 per cent) (2001 est)
Religion – Christian (Roman Catholic 73.6 per cent, Protestant 4.9 per cent, Eastern Orthodox 2.2 per cent), Muslim 4.2 per cent (est)
Language – German (official), Croatian and Hungarian (official in Burgenland), Slovene (official in Carinthia), Turkish, Serbian
Population density – 106 per sq. km (2016)
Urban population – 66.1 per cent (2017 est)
Median age (years) – 44 (2017 est)
National anthem – 'Land der Berge, Land am Strome' 'Land of Mountains, Land on the River'
National day – 26 October (date law of neutrality passed, 1955)
Death penalty – Abolished for all crimes (since 1968)
CPI score – 75 (16)
Military expenditure – US$2,970m (2017)
Conscription – 18–35 years of age, male only; 6 months

CLIMATE AND TERRAIN
The north and east of the country feature rolling hills in the river Danube basin, while the west and south contain the eastern Alps, which cover nearly two-thirds of the country. The highest point of elevation is 3,798m (Grossglockner) and the lowest is 115m (Neusiedler See). The climate is continental in the lowlands and alpine in the mountains, with average temperatures in Vienna ranging from −2.1°C in January to 16.4°C in July and August.

POLITICS
Under the 1955 constitution, the federal president is directly elected for a six-year term, renewable once. There is a bicameral legislature, the *Parlament,* consisting of the National Council *(Nationalrat),* which has 183 members directly elected for a four-year term, and the Federal Council *(Bundesrat),* which has 62 members elected for terms of five to six years by the provincial assemblies. Some powers may only be exercised by both houses acting together as the Federal Assembly *(Bundesversammlung).* The executive is headed by the federal chancellor, who is appointed by the president.
   In the 2013 legislative election, the Social Democrats (SPÖ) and the Austrian People's Party (ÖVP) remained the largest parties but both lost ground to the right-wing Freedom Party of Austria (FPÖ). The SPÖ–ÖVP coalition continued under SPÖ leader Werner Faymann, but Faymann resigned as

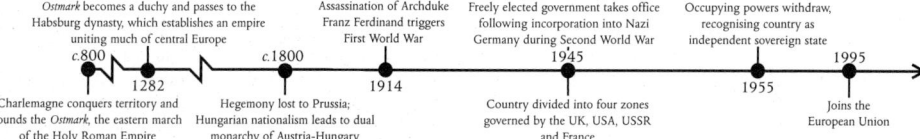

Ostmark becomes a duchy and passes to the Habsburg dynasty, which establishes an empire uniting much of central Europe *c.*800

*c.*1800

Assassination of Archduke Franz Ferdinand triggers First World War

Freely elected government takes office following incorporation into Nazi Germany during Second World War 1945

Occupying powers withdraw, recognising country as independent sovereign state 1995

1282

1914

1955

Charlemagne conquers territory and founds the *Ostmark*, the eastern march of the Holy Roman Empire

Hegemony lost to Prussia; Hungarian nationalism leads to dual monarchy of Austria-Hungary

Country divided into four zones governed by the UK, USA, USSR and France

Joins the European Union

chancellor in May 2016 and was replaced by Christian Kern. In the October 2017 legislative election, the ÖVP, led by 31-year-old Sebastian Kurz, emerged as the largest party. The independent Alexander Van der Bellen won the December 2016 presidential elections, defeating far-right candidate Norbert Hofer.

HEAD OF STATE
Federal President, Alexander Van der Bellen, *elected* 4 December 2016, *sworn in* 26 January 2017

SELECTED GOVERNMENT MEMBERS *AS AT JULY 2018*
Chancellor, Sebastian Kurz
Vice-Chancellor, Heinz-Christian Strache
Defence and Sports, Mario Kunasek
Finance, Hartwig Löger

EMBASSY OF AUSTRIA
18 Belgrave Mews West, London SW1X 8HU
T 020-7344 3250 E london-ob@bmeia.gv.at
W www.bmeia.gv.at/london
Ambassador Extraordinary and Plenipotentiary, vacant

BRITISH EMBASSY
Jaurèsgasse 12, 1030 Vienna
T (+43) (1) 716 130 E viennaconsularenquiries@fco.gov.uk
W www.gov.uk/government/world/austria
Ambassador Extraordinary and Plenipotentiary, HE Leigh Turner, CMG, *apptd* 2016

FEDERAL STRUCTURE
There are nine provinces *(Bundesländer):* Burgenland, Carinthia, Lower Austria, Salzburg, Styria, Tyrol, Upper Austria, Vienna and Vorarlberg. Each has its own assembly and government.

ECONOMY AND TRADE
Austria has a well-developed market economy, which is closely linked to other EU states. Its strong commercial links with central, eastern and south-eastern Europe, an attraction for foreign investors in the past, increased its vulnerability in the global economic downturn, and its financial sector required state support. A combination of austerity policies since 2012 and the pro-business government elected in 2017 has strengthened the economy, with growth in 2017 reaching 2.9 per cent, but unemployment remains much higher than before 2007.

The services sector contributes most to GDP (70.4 per cent in 2017), followed by industry (28.4 per cent) and the small but highly developed agricultural sector (1.2 per cent). The main industries include tourism, construction, manufacturing of machinery, vehicles and parts, food processing, timber and wood processing, production of metals and metal goods, chemicals, paper and cardboard, and communications equipment.

Austria's main trading partners are Germany, the USA, Italy and Switzerland. Principal exports include the goods produced by the main industries, iron and steel, and textiles. The main imports are machinery and equipment, vehicles, chemical products, metal goods, oil and oil products, and foodstuffs.
GNI – US$400bn; US$45,440 per capita (2017)
Annual average growth of GDP – 2.9 per cent (2017 est)
Inflation rate – 1.6 per cent (2017 est)
Population below poverty line – 4 per cent (2014 est)
Unemployment – 5.4 per cent (2017 est)
Total external debt – US$689.1bn (2016 est)
Imports – US$149,299m (2016)
Exports – US$145,503m (2016)

BALANCE OF PAYMENTS
Trade – US$3,795m deficit (2016)
Current Account – US$7,706m surplus (2017)

Trade with UK	2016	2017
Imports from UK	£1,801,953,573	£1,872,220,835
Exports to UK	£3,230,041,960	£3,314,132,742

COMMUNICATIONS
Airports – 24; principal airports include Vienna, Salzburg and Innsbruck
Waterways – 358km of navigable waterways; considerable trade through Danube ports (Vienna, Krems, Enns, Linz)
Roadways and railways – 124,508km, including 1,719km of motorways; 6,399km
Telecommunications – 3.6 million fixed lines and 14.3 million mobile subscriptions (2016); there were 7.3 million internet subscribers in 2016
Internet code and IDD – at; 43 (from UK), 44 (to UK)
Major broadcasters – Österreichischer Rundfunk (ÖRF) (public) and ATV (commercial)
Press – Regional newspapers compete effectively against national publications. Leading titles include *Die Presse, Kleine Zeitung* (Graz), *Wiener Zeitung* (Vienna), *Der Standard* and *Der Kurier*
WPFI score – 14,04 (11)

EDUCATION AND HEALTH
Education is free and compulsory from six to 15.
Gross enrolment ratio (percentage of relevant age group) – primary 102.3 per cent, secondary 101.1 per cent, tertiary 83.5 per cent (2016 est)
Health expenditure (per capita) – US$5,580 (2014)
Hospital beds (per 1,000 people) – 7.6 (2013)
Life expectancy (years) – 81.6 (2017 est)
Mortality rate – 9.6 (2017 est)
Birth rate – 9.5 (2017 est)
Infant mortality rate – 3.4 (2017 est)

AZERBAIJAN

Azarbaycan Respublikasi – Republic of Azerbaijan

Area – 86,600 sq. km
Capital – Baku (Baki); population, 2,286,000 (2018 est)
Major cities – Ganca, Sumqayit
Currency – New Manat of 100 gopik
Population – 9,961,396 rising at 0.87 per cent a year (2017 est); Azeri (91.6 per cent), Lezgian (2 per cent), Armenian (1.3 per cent), Russian (1.3 per cent), Talysh (1.3 per cent) (2009). There are more Azeris in Iran than in Azerbaijan. Almost all of the Armenian population lives in the Nagorny-Karabakh enclave
Religion – Muslim 96.9 per cent (Shia 65 per cent, Sunni 35 per cent) (est)
Language – Azeri (official), Russian, Armenian
Population density – 118 per sq. km (2016)
Urban population – 55.7 per cent (2018 est)
Median age (years) – 31.3 (2017 est)
National anthem – 'Azerbaijan Marsi' 'March of Azerbaijan'
National day – 28 May (founding of the republic, 1918)
Death penalty – Abolished for all crimes (since 1998)
CPI score – 31 (122)
Military expenditure – US$1,529m (2017)
Conscription – 18–25 years of age, male only; 18 months, or 12 months for university graduates

CLIMATE AND TERRAIN

Azerbaijan lies on the western shore of the Caspian Sea, in the eastern part of the Caucasus region. It includes the exclave of Nakhichevana, separated from it by Armenia. The north-east of Azerbaijan rises to the south-eastern end of the main Great Caucasus mountain range; to the country's south-west lie the lower Caucasus hills, and in its south-eastern corner the spurs of the Talysh Ridge. Central Azerbaijan lies in a low plain irrigated by the river Kura and the lower reaches of its tributary the Araks. Elevation ranges from 4,485m (Bazarduzu Dagi) to −28m (Caspian Sea). Climate and landscape vary greatly, but rainfall is generally low.

POLITICS

The 1995 constitution was amended in 2002 when the limit on presidential terms was restricted to two terms, but this was subsequently abolished in 2009 and presidential terms extended from five to seven years in 2016. The executive president is directly elected, as is the unicameral National Assembly *(Milli Majlis)*, which has 125 members serving five-year terms. The president appoints the prime minister and the cabinet.

Ilham Aliyev was re-elected for a fourth term in 2018. The New Azerbaijan Party, which is aligned with President Aliyev, retained its majority in the November 2015 legislative election, which was boycotted by the mainstream opposition. For dispute with Armenia over the Nagorny-Karabakh region *see* Armenia, Foreign Relations.

HEAD OF STATE

President, Ilham Aliyev, *sworn in* 31 October 2003, *re-elected* 2008, 2013, 2018

SELECTED GOVERNMENT MEMBERS *AS AT JULY 2018*
Prime Minister, Novruz Ismayil Mammadov
First Deputy Prime Minister, Yagub Abdulla Eyyubov
Deputy Prime Ministers, Ali Ahmadov; Ali Hasanov; Hajibala Abutalibov
Defence, Col.-Gen. Zakir Hasanov

EMBASSY OF THE REPUBLIC OF AZERBAIJAN
4 Kensington Court, London W8 5DL
T 020-7938 3412 E london@mission.mfa.gov.az
W www.azembassy.org.uk
Ambassador Extraordinary and Plenipotentiary, HE Tahir Taghizade, *apptd* 2014

BRITISH EMBASSY
45 Khagani Street, Baku AZ 1010
T (+994) (12) 437 7878 E generalenquiries.baku@fco.gov.uk
W www.gov.uk/government/world/azerbaijan
Ambassador Extraordinary and Plenipotentiary, HE Dr Carole Crofts, *apptd* 2016

ECONOMY AND TRADE

Despite high economic growth in recent years, Azerbaijan's transition from a command to a market economy is slow. This has been exacerbated by its failure to attract foreign investment in sectors other than energy, widespread corruption and systemic inefficiencies. The economy is dominated by oil and natural gas extraction and related industries, centred in Baku and Sumqayit, and exploited through co-production deals with foreign companies. Oil pipelines (1,424km) link the Azeri oilfields to Black Sea ports in Russia, Georgia and Turkey. Diversifying the economy is a long-term goal, but efforts have been hindered by a struggling state-owned financial sector. Although low global oil prices led to a currency devaluation in 2015 and a 3.1 per cent GDP contraction in 2016, this has slowed and the country's sovereign oil fund remains one of the wealthiest in the world at US$34.8bn.

Although agriculture contributes only 6.2 per cent of GDP, it employs 37 per cent of the workforce. The main crops are cotton, cereals, rice, fruit, vegetables, tea, tobacco and livestock. Industry, which contributes 49.1 per cent of GDP, produces oil, natural gas, petroleum products, oilfield equipment, steel, iron ore, cement, chemicals, petrochemicals and textiles.

Russia and other former Soviet republics are increasingly being replaced as trade partners by Turkey, Indonesia, the USA and various European countries. Oil and gas constitute

Turkic Azeri people form an independent state — c.100 AD
c.600
Invaded by Muslim Arabs
Invaded by Persia — c.600
Divided into the Russian north and the Persian, and subsequently Iranian, south — c.1500
1828
Newly formed Azerbaijani republic overthrown by Soviet Red Army invasion — 1920
1922
Accedes to the USSR
Azeri Popular Front takes power from the local Communist Party — 1990
1991
Declares independence from Soviet Union
Former communist leader Heydar Aliyev becomes president and is re-elected in 1998 — 1993
Heydar Aliyev's son Ilham is elected president — 2003

around 90 per cent of exports, which also include machinery, cotton and foodstuffs. Principal imports are machinery and equipment, oil products, foodstuffs, metals and chemicals.
GNI – US$40.2bn; US$4,080 per capita (2017)
Annual average growth of GDP – –1.0 per cent (2017 est)
Inflation rate – 12.0 per cent (2017 est)
Population below poverty line – 4.9 per cent (2015 est)
Unemployment – 6 per cent (2017 est)
Total external debt – US$16.62bn (2017 est)
Imports – US$8,532m (2016)
Exports – US$9,143m (2016)

BALANCE OF PAYMENTS
Trade – US$611m surplus (2016)
Current Account – US$1,684m deficit (2017)

Trade with UK	2016	2017
Imports from UK	£386,937,372	£223,058,403
Exports to UK	£136,858,084	£101,283,616

COMMUNICATIONS
Airports – 30; international airports at Baku, Ganca, Lankaran and Nakhichevan
Waterways – The Baku International Sea Trade port provides links to Turkmenistan and other trade and passenger routes
Roadways and railways – 26,789km; 2,918km
Telecommunications – 1.7 million fixed lines and 10.2 million mobile telephone subscriptions (2016); there were 7.7 million internet users in 2016
Internet – az; 994 (from UK), 44 (to UK)
Major broadcasters – AzTV, Azerbaijan Radio (state-run), iTV and ANS TV
Press – Printing presses are generally reserved for pro-government titles such as *Azarbaycan;* opposition newspapers include *Azadliq* and *Yeni Musavat*
WPFI score – 59,73 (163)

EDUCATION AND HEALTH
Education up to university level is free.
Literacy rate – 99.8 per cent (2016 est)
Gross enrolment ratio (percentage of relevant age group) – primary 106.4 per cent (2016 est); secondary 100 per cent (2012 est); tertiary 27.2 per cent (2016 est)
Health expenditure (per capita) – US$471 (2014)
Hospital beds (per 1,000 people) – 4.7 (2013)
Life expectancy – 72.8 (2017 est)
Mortality rate – 7.1 (2017 est)
Birth rate – 15.8 (2017 est)
Infant mortality rate – 23.8 (2017 est)
HIV/AIDS adult prevalence – 0.2 per cent (2015 est)

THE BAHAMAS

Commonwealth of the Bahamas

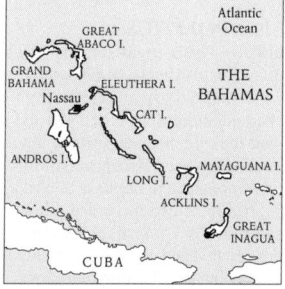

Area – 13,880 sq. km
Capital – Nassau, on New Providence; population, 280,000 (2018 est)
Major city – Freeport, on Grand Bahama
Currency – Bahamian dollar (B$) of 100 cents
Population – 329,988 rising at 0.81 per cent a year (2017 est)
Religion – Christian (Protestant 69.9 per cent, Roman Catholic 12 per cent, other 13 per cent) (est)
Language – English (official), Creole
Population density – 39 per sq. km (2016)
Urban population – 83 per cent (2018 est)
Median age (years) – 32 (2017 est)
National anthem – 'March on, Bahamaland'
National day – 10 July (Independence Day)
Death penalty – Retained (last used 2000)
CPI score – 65 (28)
Health expenditure (per capita) – US$1,720 (2014)
Life expectancy (years) – 72.6 (2017 est)
Mortality rate – 7.2 (2017 est)
Birth rate – 15.3 (2017 est)
Infant mortality rate – 11.3 (2017 est)
HIV/AIDS adult prevalence – 3.2 per cent (2015 est)

CLIMATE AND TERRAIN
The Bahamas consist of more than 700 islands and 2,400 cays, all low-lying. The highest point is 63m (Mt Alvernia, on Cat Island) and the lowest 0m (Atlantic Ocean). The principal islands include: Abaco Islands, Acklins, Andros, Berry Islands, Bimini, Cat Island, Crooked Island, Eleuthera, Exuma, Grand Bahama, Great Inagua, Harbour Island, Long Island, Mayaguana, New Providence, Ragged Island, Rum Cay, San Salvador and Spanish Wells. The 14 major islands are inhabited, as are a few of the smaller islands. The climate is semitropical. The hurricane season is June to November.

HISTORY AND POLITICS
The islands were discovered by Columbus in 1492, settled by the British from the 17th century and became a crown colony in 1717. The Bahamas became internally self-governing in 1964 and gained independence on 10 July 1973.
   The Progressive Liberal Party (PLP) held power for 25 years until the Free National Movement (FNM) won an absolute majority in the 1992 general election. Power has subsequently alternated between the two parties. The FNM, led by Hubert Minnis, overturned the PLP's majority in legislative elections in May 2017.
   The head of state is Queen Elizabeth II, who is represented by a governor-general. The bicameral parliament has a senate of 16 appointed members and a House of Assembly of 39 members; both chambers serve a five-year term.
Governor-General, HE Dame Marguerite Pindling, GCMG, apptd 2014

SELECTED GOVERNMENT MEMBERS *AS AT MAY 2018*
Prime Minister, Hubert Minnis
Deputy Prime Minister, Finance, Peter Turnquest
Foreign Affairs, Darren Henfield

HIGH COMMISSION OF THE COMMONWEALTH OF THE BAHAMAS
10 Chesterfield Street, London W1J 5JL
T 020-7408 4488 **E** information@bahamashclondon.net
W www.bahamashclondon.net
High Commissioner, HE Ellison Greenslade, apptd 2017

BRITISH HIGH COMMISSION
High Commissioner, HE Asif Ahmad, apptd 2017, resident in Kingston, Jamaica

ECONOMY AND TRADE

The economy, one of the wealthiest in the Caribbean, is dominated by tourism and offshore financial services, which together contribute around 65 per cent of GDP. The economy entered recession in 2007–11 when the service industry was disrupted by the global financial crisis and the number of tourists from the USA (about 80 per cent of all visitors) declined. The economy contracted slightly, but returned to growth in 2017. The country remains a low-tax state, charging neither corporation or income tax, though a sales tax was introduced for the first time in January 2015.

Manufacturing and agriculture account for 10 per cent of GDP and 14 per cent of employment. Agriculture centres mainly on fresh vegetables, fruit, meat and eggs. Mineral reserves produce aragonite and salt for export. Other industries include cement, rum, pharmaceuticals and steel pipe production, and the provision of oil trans-shipment services.

The main trading partners are the USA, Poland, South Korea, Côte d'Ivoire and China. The chief exports are mineral products and salt, animal products, fruit and vegetables, and polystyrene products. Imports are chiefly machinery and transport equipment, manufactured articles, chemicals, fuel, foodstuffs and livestock.

GNI – US$11.5bn, US$29,170 per capita (2016)
Annual average growth of GDP – 1.8 per cent (2017 est)
Inflation rate – 2.4 per cent (2017 est)
Population below poverty line – 9.3 per cent (2010 est)
Unemployment – 10 per cent (2017 est)
Total external debt – US$17.56bn (2013 est)
Imports – US$3,162m (2015)
Exports – US$449m (2015)

BALANCE OF PAYMENTS

Trade – US$2,713m deficit (2015)
Current Account – US$1,106m deficit (2016)

Trade with UK	2016	2017
Imports from UK	£24,110,105	£28,741,953
Exports to UK	£8,321,395	£6,155,945

COMMUNICATIONS

Airports – 24; international airports are operated from Andros, Chubb Cay, Eleuthera, Exuma, Grand Bahama and New Providence
Waterways – The main ports are Nassau (New Providence), Freeport and South Riding Point (Grand Bahama); the Bahamas is a major ship registry, and 1,063 of the 1,160 ships registered in 2010 were foreign-owned
Roadways – 1,620km
Telecommunications – 121,088 fixed lines and 360,020 mobile phone subscriptions (2016); there were 261,853 internet users in 2016
Internet code and IDD – bs; 1 242 (from UK), 011 44 (to UK)
Major broadcasters – The public Broadcasting Corporation of the Bahamas (BCB) operates ZNS TV and ZNS Bahamas (radio)
Press – Daily newspapers include *The Nassau Guardian*, *The Tribune* and *The Freeport News*

BAHRAIN

Mamlakat al-Bahrayn – Kingdom of Bahrain

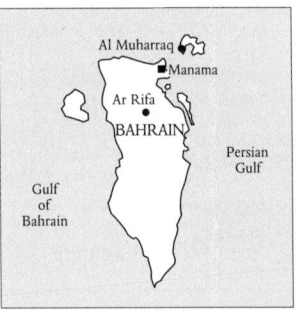

Area – 760 sq. km
Capital – Manama; population, 565,000 (2018 est)
Major towns – Al Muharraq, Ar Rifa, Madinat Hamad
Currency – Bahraini dinar (BD) of 1,000 fils
Population – 1,410,942 rising at 2.26 per cent a year (2017 est); the non-Bahraini population includes large numbers of Europeans and South Asians (almost 55 per cent of the population)
Religion – Muslim 70.3 per cent, Christian 14.5 per cent, Hindu 9.8 per cent (est); Islam is the state religion
Language – Arabic (official), English, Farsi, Urdu
Population density – 1,848 per sq. km (2016)
Urban population – 89.3 per cent (2018 est)
Median age (years) – 32.3 (2017 est)
National anthem – 'Bahrainona' 'Our Bahrain'
National day – 16 December (date of independence from British protection, 1971)
Death penalty – Retained
CPI score – 36 (103)
Military expenditure – US$1,397m (2017)
Literacy rate – 95.7 per cent (2015 est)
Gross enrolment ratio (percentage of relevant age group) – tertiary 46.6 per cent (2016 est)
Health expenditure (per capita) – US$1,243 (2014)
Life expectancy (years) – 79 (2017 est)
Mortality rate – 2.8 (2017 est)
Birth rate – 13.3 (2017 est)
Infant mortality rate – 8.9 (2017 est)

CLIMATE AND TERRAIN

Bahrain consists of an archipelago of 36 low-lying islands situated approximately halfway down the Persian Gulf, some 32km off the east coast of Saudi Arabia. The largest of these, Bahrain Island, is about 48km long and 16km wide at its broadest. Elevation extremes range from 122m (Jabal ad Dukhan) to 0m at sea level. The climate is arid, hot and humid, with average maximum temperatures ranging from 16°C in January to 37.1°C in July.

HISTORY AND POLITICS

Bahrain was ruled by Persia (Iran) from 1602 until it was ousted in 1783 by the al-Khalifa family, which remains in power. The emirate was a British protectorate from 1820 until 1971, when it became independent. In 1975 the legislature was suspended and the emir assumed virtually absolute power after clashes between Sunni and Shia factions. Moves to return to democratic rule were made in response to civil agitation in the 1990s, until Sheikh Hamad succeeded to the throne and initiated the transition to a constitutional monarchy. The 2002 constitution established Bahrain as a kingdom and a constitutional monarchy, and legalised elections. There has been ongoing agitation for further democratisation, particularly by the Shia majority against the predominantly Sunni authorities.

In February 2011 this flared up into mass demonstrations that the government repressed brutally from March, when martial law was declared and the Pearl monument, the focal point of the demonstrations in Manama, was demolished. A report into the unrest, commissioned by Sheikh Hamad, was released in November 2011 and confirmed the practice of torture and infringements of human rights; in response, the ruler vowed to 'learn lessons' from the unrest and promised to reform the country's laws to make them compatible with international standards. Despite national talks beginning in February 2013 and the appointment of the moderate Sheikh Salman bin Hamad al-Khalifa as First Deputy Prime Minister in March of that year, there has yet to be a resolution to the unrest. In October 2014, one month before legislative elections, al-Wefaq, the main Shia political organisation, was banned from operating for three months, although it had previously announced it would boycott the vote, maintaining that the current electoral system fails to represent the country's Shia majority.

In the 2014 legislative elections, independents won 37 of the 40 contested seats; al-Wefaq lost all 18 of the seats it had won in 2011. The number of seats held by Sunni Islamist groups declined by two. Voter turnout was poor – the government estimated that around 51.5 per cent of the population voted, while opposition parties claimed turnout was as low as 30 per cent.

Under the 2002 constitution, the country is a hereditary constitutional monarchy with the king as head of state. The king appoints the cabinet. The bicameral National Assembly consists of a lower house, the Council of Representatives, and an upper house, the Consultative Council. The lower house has 40 members directly elected for a four-year term, and the upper house has 40 members appointed by the king for a four-year term. The 2002 constitution granted women the right to vote and to stand for election.

HEAD OF STATE
HH The King of Bahrain, Sheikh Hamad bin Isa al-Khalifa, KCMG, *C-in-C of the Armed Forces, succeeded as emir* 6 March 1999, *proclaimed king* 14 February 2002
Crown Prince, First Deputy Prime Minister, Chair of the Economic Development Board, HRH Sheikh Salman bin Hamad al-Khalifa

SELECTED GOVERNMENT MEMBERS *AS AT MAY 2018*
Prime Minister, HH Sheikh Khalifa bin Salman al-Khalifa
Deputy Prime Ministers, Sheikh Khalid bin Abdulla al-Khalifa; Sheikh Ali bin Khalifa al-Khalifa; Sheikh Mohammad bin Mubarak al-Khalifa; Sheikh Jawad bin Salim al-Arrayedh
Defence, Lt.-Gen. Yusuf bin Ahmed bin Hussain al-Jalahma
Finance, Sheikh Ahmed bin Mohammed al-Khalifa
Foreign Affairs, Sheikh Khalid bin Ahmed bin Mohammed al-Khalifa

EMBASSY OF THE KINGDOM OF BAHRAIN
30 Belgrave Square, London SW1X 8QB
T 020-7201 9170 E information@bahrainembassy.co.uk
W www.bahrainembassy.co.uk
Ambassador Extraordinary and Plenipotentiary, HE Sheikh Fawaz bin Mohammad al-Khalifa, *apptd* 2015

BRITISH EMBASSY
PO Box 114, 21 Government Avenue, Manama 306
T (+973) 1757 4100 W www.gov.uk/government/world/bahrain
Ambassador Extraordinary and Plenipotentiary, HE Simon Martin, CMG, *apptd* 2015

ECONOMY AND TRADE

Bahrain was one of the first Gulf states to discover oil, in the 1930s, but reserves and production are lower than in neighbouring countries. Despite diversifying its economy, particularly as a regional financial and business centre, low oil prices resulted in a budget deficit of nearly 10 per cent of GDP in 2017, adding to its mounting debt. Petroleum production and refining still accounts for 85 per cent of government revenue and around 70 per cent of total export receipts. Other industries include petrochemicals, aluminium smelting, and shipbuilding and repair. Bahrain's main trading partners are Saudi Arabia, the EU, Far Eastern countries and the USA, with whom a Free Trade Agreement was agreed in 2006.

GNI – US$30.2bn; US$20,240 per capita (2017)
Annual average growth of GDP – 2.5 per cent (2017 est)
Inflation rate – 0.9 per cent (2017 est)
Unemployment – 3.8 per cent (2017 est)
Total external debt – US$42.39bn (2017 est)
Imports – US$9,700m (2015)
Exports – US$11,200m (2015)

BALANCE OF PAYMENTS
Trade – US$1,500m surplus (2015)
Current Account – US$1,599m surplus (2017)

Trade with UK	2016	2017
Imports from UK	£366,116,508	£492,933,976
Exports to UK	£118,777,953	£234,756,383

COMMUNICATIONS

Airports – Four; Bahrain International Airport is a major air traffic centre in the Gulf
Waterways – The main ports are Khalifa bin Salman and Mina Salman
Roadways – There are 3,392km of paved roadways; the four main islands are connected by causeways, and a 25km causeway links Bahrain to Saudi Arabia
Telecommunications – 279,864 main lines and 2.9 million mobile phone subscriptions (2016); there were 1.35 million internet users in 2016
Internet code and IDD – bh; 973 (from UK), 44 (to UK)
Major broadcasters – State-run Bahrain Radio and Television Corporation (BRTC) operates radio networks and five terrestrial TV networks. Bahrain suspended the Saudi-financed al-Arab satellite news TV channel from operating in February 2015
Press – Six daily newspapers are published, including *Akhbar al-Khaleej, Al-Ayam* and *Al-Wasat*
WPFI score – 60,85 (166)

BANGLADESH

Gana Prajatantri Bangladesh – People's Republic of Bangladesh

Area – 148,460 sq. km
Capital – Dhaka; population, 19,578,000 (2018 est)
Major cities – Chittagong, Gazipur, Khulna, Narayanganj
Currency – Taka (Tk) of 100 paisa
Population – 157,826,578 rising at 1.04 per cent a year
   (2017 est); Bengali (98 per cent) (1998 est)
Religion – Muslim 89.1 per cent (the vast majority are Sunni),
   Hindu 10 per cent (est); Islam is the state religion
Language – Bangla (official), English
Population density – 1,252 per sq. km (2016)
Urban population – 36.6 per cent (2018 est)
Median age (years) – 26.7 (2017 est)
National anthem – 'Amar Shonar Bangla' 'My Golden Bengal'
National day – 26 March (Independence Day)
Death penalty – Retained
CPI score – 28 (143)
Military expenditure – US$3,594m (2017)

CLIMATE AND TERRAIN
Although hilly in the south-east and north-east, over 75 per
cent of the country is less than 3m above sea level, situated on
the alluvial plain and delta of the Ganges (Padma)–
Brahmaputra (Jamuna)–Meghna river system, which empties
into the Bay of Bengal, the largest estuarine delta in the world.
The highest elevation is 1,230m (Keokradong) and the lowest
0m at the Indian Ocean. The climate is tropical, with a
monsoon season (June–September) during which heavy
rainfall causes flooding in around one-third of the country
each year; annual average rainfall is up to 2,339mm.

HISTORY AND POLITICS
Bangladesh consists of what was the eastern part of Bengal
province and the Sylhet district of Assam province in British
India. On independence in 1947, these territories acceded to
Pakistan, forming the province of East Bengal (renamed East
Pakistan in 1955). Tensions between East and West Pakistan
(separated by over 1,600km) caused the East to secede in
1971. After months of civil war, and following the
intervention of India, Bangladesh achieved independence
from Pakistan on 16 December 1971.

   Since independence, Bangladesh has experienced periods of
political instability, with a number of coups and attempted
coups, the assassinations of President Mujibar Rahman (1975)
and President Zia (1981), and periods of government under
martial law (1975–8, 1982–6) or a state of emergency
(1987–8, 2007–8). Since 2014 the country has faced a
campaign of high-profile violence by Islamists against atheists
and secular intellectuals.

   Parliamentary government has remained in place since
1991, despite occasional boycotts of parliament.
Governments have been formed, or coalition governments
led, by one of the two main parties: the Bangladesh

Nationalist Party (BNP), led by Khaleda Zia (widow of
President Zia), in 1991–6 and 2001–6; and the Awami
League, led by Sheikh Hasina Wajed (daughter of President
Rahman), in 1996–2001 and since January 2009.

   A boycott of the 2014 legislative election by the BNP
resulted in a default win and overwhelming majority for the
Awami League, with the party gaining 234 seats to the BNP's
34. Abdul Hamid was elected president unopposed in 2013.

   In January 2015 Khaleda Zia called for a general strike in
order to bring about early elections; at least 50 people died
and 1,000 were injured in the ensuing violence, with the BNP
leader herself charged with instigating an arson attack that
killed seven people.

   The head of state is the president, elected by the legislature
for a five-year term, renewable once. The unicameral
parliament, *Jatiya Sangsad,* has 300 directly elected members
and 50 women members indirectly elected, all serving five-
year terms. The president appoints the prime minister, and the
cabinet on the advice of the prime minister.

HEAD OF STATE
President, Abdul Hamid, *elected* 22 April 2013, *re-elected* 7
   February 2018

SELECTED GOVERNMENT MEMBERS *AS AT MAY 2018*
Prime Minister, Defence, Sheikh Hasina Wajed
Finance, Abul Maal Abdul Muhith
Foreign Affairs, Abul Hasan Mahmood Ali

HIGH COMMISSION FOR THE PEOPLE'S REPUBLIC OF
BANGLADESH
28 Queen's Gate, London SW7 5JA
T 020-7584 0081 E info@bhclondon.org.uk
W www.bhclondon.org.uk
High Commissioner, HE Mohammed Nazmul Quaunine, *apptd*
   2016

BRITISH HIGH COMMISSION
PO Box 6079, United Nations Road, Baridhara, Dhaka 1212
T (+880) (2) 882 2705 E press.dhaka@fco.gov.uk W www.gov.uk/
government/world/bangladesh
High Commissioner, HE Alison Blake, CMG, *apptd* 2016

ECONOMY AND TRADE
Bangladesh is a poor country, highly dependent on foreign
aid. Nearly a quarter of the population lives below the poverty
line. Many migrate to the Gulf states and South East Asia to
find work, and their remittances, which totalled US$13bn in
2016-17, and garment manufacturing are the mainstay of the
economy. These fuelled steady growth of 6 per cent a year
from the mid-1990s, which continued throughout the global
downturn. However, inefficient state-owned enterprises, slow
implementation of economic reforms, corruption, inflation
and unreliable power supplies are obstacles to greater growth.

   The service and industrial sectors account for 56.5 per cent
and 29.2 per cent of GDP respectively. Although the smallest
contributor to GDP (14.2 per cent), agriculture is the primary
occupation of 42.7 per cent of the workforce. The chief
industries are based on processing agricultural and fisheries
products such as cotton, jute, tea, sugar, fish and seafood, the
manufacture of textiles, garments, newsprint, cement and
fertiliser, and light engineering. Most exports are to the USA
and EU countries; imports come mainly from China, India and
Singapore.
GNI – US$242.8bn; US$1,470 per capita (2017)
Annual average growth of GDP – 7.1 per cent (2016 est)
Inflation rate – 5.7 per cent (2017 est)
Population below poverty line – 31.5 per cent (2010 est)
Unemployment – 4.1 per cent (2017 est)
Total external debt – US$45.07bn (2017 est)

Imports – US$52,624m (2016)
Exports – US$36,031m (2016)

BALANCE OF PAYMENTS
Trade – US$16,593m deficit (2016)
Current Account – US$6,364m surplus (2017)

Trade with UK	2016	2017
Imports from UK	£207,000,024	£235,657,613
Exports to UK	£2,216,430,965	£2,728,537,309

COMMUNICATIONS
Airports – 16, including international airports at Dhaka, Chittagong and Sylhet
Waterways – Principal seaports are Chittagong and Mongla, and there are smaller ports in Chalna and Khulna; the 8,370km of waterways are a key element of the transport infrastructure, although reduced to 5,200km in dry season
Roadways and railways – 1,063km; 2,622km
Telecommunications – 766,183 million fixed lines and 1.36 million mobile phone subscriptions (2016); there were 28.5 million internet users in 2016
Internet country code and IDD – bd; 880 (from UK), 44 (to UK)
Major broadcasters – The government-run Bangladesh Television (BTV) and Radio Bangladesh are the principal channels; private broadcasters include ATN Bangla, Channel i and NTV
Press – Leading titles include English-language dailies *New Age, The New Nation* and *The Independent,* and the Bangla *Daily Prothom Alo, Dainik Ittefaq* and *Dainik Jugantor*
WPFI score – 48,62 (146)

EDUCATION AND HEALTH
Education is compulsory and free for children aged six to ten, but drop-out rates are high.
Literacy rate – 72.8 per cent (2016 est)
Gross enrolment ratio (percentage of relevant age group) – primary 118.6 per cent, secondary 69 per cent, tertiary 17.3 per cent (2016 est)
Health expenditure (per capita) – US$31 (2014)
Hospital beds (per 1,000 people) – 0.8 (2015)
Life expectancy (years) – 73.4 (2017 est)
Mortality rate – 5.4 (2017 est)
Birth rate – 18.8 (2017 est)
Infant mortality rate – 31.7 (2017 est)
HIV/AIDS adult prevalence – 0.1 per cent (2015 est)

BARBADOS

Area – 430 sq. km
Capital – Bridgetown, in the parish of St Michael; population, 89,000 (2018 est)
Currency – Barbados dollar (BD$) of 100 cents
Population – 292,336 rising at 0.28 per cent a year (2017 est)

Religion – Christian 75.6 per cent (Protestant 66.4 per cent, of which the largest denomination is Anglican), Rastafarian 1 per cent (est)
Language – English (official), Bajan
Population density – 663 per sq. km (2016)
Urban population – 31.1 per cent (2018 est)
Median age (years) – 38.6 (2017 est)
National anthem – 'In Plenty and in Time of Need'
National day – 30 November (Independence Day)
Death penalty – Retained (last used 1984)
CPI score – 68 (25)

CLIMATE AND TERRAIN
Barbados is the most easterly of the Caribbean islands. The land rises gently to central highlands, and elevation extremes range from 336m (Mt Hillaby) to 0m (Atlantic Ocean). The climate is tropical with a wet season from July to November, when the island is subject to occasional hurricanes.

HISTORY AND POLITICS
Early settlers were succeeded by the Arawaks and then the Caribs. The island was uninhabited when settled by the English in 1627 and was a crown colony from 1652, achieving self-government in 1961. It became an independent state on 30 November 1966.

Since independence, power has alternated between the two main political parties, the Barbados Labour Party (BLP) and the Democratic Labour Party (DLP). In the 2008 general election the DLP defeated the BLP and took office under David Thompson. He died in October 2010 and was succeeded as prime minister by his deputy, Freundel Stuart. The DLP narrowly retained power in 2013, before the BLP won every parliamentary seat in the May 2018 elections. Mia Mottley was named prime minister, the first woman to hold the position.

The head of state is Queen Elizabeth II, represented by the governor-general. The bicameral parliament consists of a senate of 21 appointed members and a House of Assembly of 30 directly elected members; both chambers serve a five-year term.

There are 11 administrative areas (parishes): Christ Church, St Andrew, St George, St James, St John, St Joseph, St Lucy, St Michael, St Peter, St Philip and St Thomas.
Governor-General, HE Dame Sandra Mason, DCMG *apptd* 2018

SELECTED GOVERNMENT MEMBERS *AS AT JULY 2018*
Prime Minister, Mia Mottley
Finance, Ryan Straughn
Foreign Affairs, Jerome Walcott
Home Affairs, Edmund Hinkson

BARBADOS HIGH COMMISSION
1 Great Russell Street, London WC1B 3ND
T 020-7631 4975 E london@foreign.gov.bb
High Commissioner, HE Guy Arlington Hewitt, *apptd* 2014

BRITISH HIGH COMMISSION
PO Box 676, Lower Collymore Rock, Bridgetown
T (+1) (246) 430 7800 E ukinbarbados@fco.gov.uk
W www.gov.uk/government/world/barbados
High Commissioner, HE Janet Douglas, CMG, *apptd* 2017

ECONOMY AND TRADE
The wealthiest country in the Eastern Caribbean, historically Barbados' chief products were sugar, rum and molasses. Since independence, tourism, offshore finance and information services, and light industry have become more significant. The global economic downturn affected tourism in particular, causing the economy to enter recession in 2009. GDP growth

rose above 1 per cent for the first time in nine years in 2016, largely thanks to rising tourism.

The main trading partners are Trinidad and Tobago, the USA and Guyana. Chief exports are manufactured goods, sugar and molasses, rum, other food and beverages, chemicals and electronic components.

GNI – US$4.4bn; US$15,540 per capita (2017)
Annual average growth of GDP – 0.9 per cent (2017 est)
Inflation rate – 5.0 per cent (2017 est)
Unemployment – 9.8 per cent (2017 est)
Imports – US$1,622m (2016)
Exports – US$517m (2016)

BALANCE OF PAYMENTS
Trade – US$1,105m deficit (2016)
Current Account – US$248m deficit (2013)

Trade with UK	2016	2017
Imports from UK	£46,906,483	£43,878,007
Exports to UK	£8,774,105	£6,863,553

COMMUNICATIONS
Airports – The Grantley Adams International near Bridgetown is the only international airport on the island
Waterways – Bridgetown, the only port of entry, has a deep-water harbour
Roadways – There are 1,600km of roadways, all of which are surfaced
Telecommunications – 139,715 fixed lines and 332,208 mobile phone subscriptions (2016); there were 231,883 internet users in 2016
Internet country code and IDD – bb; 1 246 (from UK), 011 44 (to UK)
Major broadcasters – Caribbean Broadcasting Corporation (CBC) is the sole TV station and operates a number of public and commercial channels
Press – Major newspapers include *The Barbados Advocate* and *The Nation*

EDUCATION AND HEALTH
Education is free in government schools at primary (ages four to 11), secondary (ages 11 to 18) and tertiary levels, and is compulsory until the age of 16.
Literacy rate – 99.7 per cent (2004 est)
Gross enrolment ratio (percentage of relevant age group) – primary 92.6 per cent, secondary 107.1 per cent (2016 est); tertiary 61 per cent (2011 est)
Health expenditure (per capita) – US$1,146 (2014)
Hospital beds (per 1,000 people) – 5.8 (2014)
Life expectancy (years) – 75.5 (2017 est)
Mortality rate – 8.8 (2017 est)
Birth rate – 11.7 (2017 est)
Infant mortality rate – 10.2 (2017 est)
HIV/AIDS adult prevalence – 1.3 per cent (2016 est)

BELARUS
Respublika Byelarus' – Republic of Belarus

Area – 207,600 sq. km
Capital – Minsk (the administrative centre of the CIS); population, 2,005,000 (2018 est)
Major cities – Brest, Homyel, Hrodna, Mahilyow, Vitsyebsk
Currency – Belarusian rouble (Br) of 100 kopeks
Population – 9,549,747 falling at 0.22 per cent a year (2017 est); Belarusian (83.7 per cent), Russian (8.3 per cent), Polish (3.1 per cent), Ukrainian (1.7 per cent) (2009)
Religion – Christian (Belarusian Orthodox 48.3 per cent, Roman Catholic 7.1 per cent) (est)
Language – Belarusian, Russian (both official), Polish, Ukrainian
Population density – 47 per sq. km (2016)
Urban population – 78.6 per cent (2018 est)
Median age (years) – 40 (2017 est)
National anthem – 'My Belarusy' 'We, the Belarusians'
National day – 3 July (Independence Day)
Death penalty – Retained
CPI score – 44 (68)
Military expenditure – US$631m (2017)
Conscription – 18–27 years of age; 12–18 months dependent on level of education

CLIMATE AND TERRAIN
Much of Belarus is a plain, with many lakes, swamps and marshes, and forest cover is around 43 per cent. Its main rivers are the upper reaches of the Dnieper, the Nyoman and the Western Dvina. Elevation extremes range from 346m (Dzyarzhynskaya Hara) to 90m (Nyoman river). The climate is continental, with cold winters and warm, humid summers.

HISTORY AND POLITICS
In the 13th century the area was absorbed into the grand duchy of Lithuania, which entered into the Polish Commonwealth from the 16th until the 18th centuries. Following the partitions of Poland in the late 18th century it became part of the expanding Russian Empire. It was the site of fierce fighting during the First World War, but its brief period of independence in 1918 ended, after a war over the territory, in partition between Poland and the USSR. The Polish territory was largely regained by the USSR after the Second World War, which devastated Belarus; over a quarter of the population was killed.

Belarus declared its independence from the USSR after a failed coup in Moscow in 1991. Stanislav Shuskevich became Belarusian leader at the head of a coalition of communists and democrats, but he was forced to resign in 1994. He was replaced by Gen. Mecheslav Grib, who pursued closer political, economic and trade relations with Russia.

Alexander Lukashenko was elected to the newly created post of president in 1994. Since coming to power, President

Lukashenko has opposed privatisation and economic liberalisation (precipitating economic collapse), subverted political processes and repressed opposition and the media, creating what Condoleezza Rice, the former US Secretary of State, referred to in 2005 as the 'last dictatorship in Europe'. The EU and USA have imposed sanctions several times because of the regime's poor human rights record and obstructiveness towards international election monitors.

In the 2015 presidential election, President Lukashenko was returned for a fifth time with 83.5 per cent of the vote, his biggest mandate yet. In the 2012 legislative elections, all the seats were won by the president's supporters following a boycott by the two main opposition parties. In December 2014, President Lukashenko dismissed Prime Minister Mikhail Myasnikovich and instigated the biggest cabinet reshuffle since 2010 after the government failed to meet economic targets, appointing Andrey Kabyakow as the new prime minister. Opposition candidates won two seats in the 2016 parliamentary elections.

Under the 1994 constitution, the president is directly elected for a five-year term; this was renewable only once until a 2004 constitutional amendment removed the two-term limit. The legislature is the bicameral National Assembly, comprising a 110-member House of Representatives (lower chamber), directly elected for a four-year term, and a Council of the Republic, with 56 members elected by regional *soviets* (councils) and eight members appointed by the president, for a four-year term.

The president may appoint half the members of the constitutional court and the electoral commission.

HEAD OF STATE

President, Alexander Lukashenko, *elected* 10 July 1994,
   re-elected 2001, 2006, 2010, 2015

SELECTED GOVERNMENT MEMBERS *AS AT MAY 2018*
Prime Minister, Andrey Kabyakow
First Deputy Prime Minister, Vasily Matyushevsky
Deputy Prime Ministers, Mikhail Rusyi *(Agriculture);* Anatoly
   Kalinin *(Building);* Vladimir Semashko *(Fuel and Energy);*
   Vasily Zharko *(Social Sector)*
Foreign Affairs, Vladimir Makey

EMBASSY OF THE REPUBLIC OF BELARUS
6 Kensington Court, London W8 5DL
T 020-7937 3288 E uk.london@mfa.gov.by
W http://uk.mfa.gov.by/en
Ambassador Extraordinary and Plenipotentiary, HE Sergei
   Aleinik, *apptd* 2013

BRITISH EMBASSY
37 Karl Marx Street, 220030 Minsk
T (+375) (172) 298 200 E ukin.belarus@fconet.fco.gov.uk
W www.gov.uk/government/world/belarus
Ambassador Extraordinary and Plenipotentiary, HE Fionna Gibb,
   apptd 2016

FOREIGN RELATIONS
Belarus was a founder member of the Commonwealth of Independent States (CIS) in 1991. President Lukashenko, who opposed the break-up of the Soviet Union, has sought closer relations with Russia. In 1997 a treaty was signed with Russia providing for closer political and economic integration, and in 1999 the two countries signed a treaty that committed them to becoming a confederal state. In 2011 Belarus formed an economic union with Kazakhstan and Russia, removing tariffs and customs control along their shared borders. In January 2015, Belarus and Russia became founding members of the Eurasian Economic Union (EEU),

establishing a common market, commission, bank and supranational court between the two countries, and Armenia and Kazakhstan.

ECONOMY AND TRADE
Although prosperous under the Soviet regime, the country experienced a dramatic decline after independence. Since 1994 President Lukashenko has resisted structural reform of the economy and reimposed state control of prices and currency exchange rates. Some privatised businesses have been renationalised, and the small private sector is subject to pressure and intervention by the state, circumstances that continue to discourage foreign investment. The country is highly dependent on Russia for its energy needs, and economic growth in recent years was largely based on the re-export at market prices of heavily discounted oil and natural gas from Russia. Russian economic dominance over Belarus further increased in November 2011 in a deal that agreed the sale of oil to Belarus at a discount of 60 per cent below other European states in exchange for Russian ownership of Belarusian oil pipeline firm Beltransgaz, and again in January 2013 when a US$2bn loan was announced. After years of stagnation, the ruble was sharply devalued in 2014 and the nation went into recession in 2015–16, but returned to modest growth in 2017.

The main economic activities are oil-refining and the manufacture of heavy machinery and equipment, vehicles, domestic appliances, chemicals and textiles. These commodities, along with oil, mineral products, metals and foodstuffs, constitute the main exports and the main imports. The main trading partner is Russia.
GNI – US$50.2bn; US$5,280 per capita (2017)
Average annual growth of GDP – 0.7 per cent (2017 est)
Inflation rate – 8 per cent (2017 est)
Population below poverty line – 5.7 per cent (2016 est)
Unemployment – 1 per cent (2017 est)
Total external debt – US$38.75bn (2017 est)
Imports – US$27,570m (2016)
Exports – US$23,416m (2016)

BALANCE OF PAYMENTS
Trade – US$4,154m deficit (2016)
Current Account – US$931.4m deficit (2017)

Trade with UK	2016	2017
Imports from UK	£53,312,126	£127,673,097
Exports to UK	£34,438,893	£51,719,637

COMMUNICATIONS
Airports – 33, including an international airport in Minsk plus six other major domestic airports
Waterways – Belarus has an extensive 2,500km canal and river system, but its use is limited by shallowness or remoteness
Roadways and railways – 74,651km; 5,537km
Telecommunications – 4.5 million fixed lines and 11.4 million mobile phone subscriptions (2016); there were 6.8 million internet users in 2016
Internet code and IDD – by; 375 (from UK), 810 44 (to UK)
Major broadcasters – The four national TV channels, including Belarusian TV, are state-run; the government-owned Belarusian Radio is the principal radio broadcaster. Exile groups operate radio stations and TV channels from Poland, such as Belsat (TV) and Radio Racja
Press – Major government newspapers include *Sovetskaya Belorussiya* (Russian-language daily) and *Zvyazda* (Belarusian-language daily); independent titles, such as *Narodnaya Volya,* operate but face harassment
WPFI score – 52,59 (155)

EDUCATION AND HEALTH

Education is compulsory between the ages of six and 15.
Literacy rate – 99.7 per cent (2015 est)
Gross enrolment ratio (percentage of relevant age group) – primary
101.9 per cent, secondary 107.1 per cent, tertiary 87 per
cent (2016 est)
Health expenditure (per capita) – US$450 (2014)
Hospital beds (per 1,000 people) – 11 (2013)
Life expectancy (years) – 73 (2017 est)
Mortality rate – 13.2 (2017 est)
Birth rate – 10.3 (2017 est)
Infant mortality rate – 3.6 (2017 est)
HIV / AIDS adult prevalence – 1.3 per cent (2016 est)

BELGIUM

*Koninkrijk Belgie / Royaume de Belgique / Königreich Belgien –
Kingdom of Belgium*

Area – 30,528 sq. km
Capital – Brussels; population, 2,050,000 (2018 est)
Major cities – Antwerp, Bruges, Charleroi, Ghent, Liège
Currency – Euro (€) of 100 cents
Population – 11,491,346 rising at 0.7 per cent a year (2016
est); Belgian (75 per cent), Italian (4.1 per cent), Moroccan
(3.7 per cent) (2017 est)
Religion – Christian (Roman Catholic 75 per cent) (est)
Language – Dutch (Flemish), French, German (all official)
Population density – 374 per sq. km (2016)
Urban population – 98 per cent (2018 est)
Median age (years) – 41.4 (2017 est)
National anthem – 'La Brabançonne' 'The Song of Brabant'
National day – 21 July (Accession of King Leopold I, 1831)
Death penalty – Abolished for all crimes (since 1996)
CPI score – 75 (16)
Military expenditure – US$4,449m (2017)

CLIMATE AND TERRAIN

There are two distinct regions: the west is generally low-lying
and fertile, while in the east the forested hills of the Ardennes
are more rugged with poorer soil. Elevation extremes range
from 694m (Signal de Botrange) to 0m on the North Sea coast.
The polders near the coast, which are protected against floods
by dykes, cover an area of around 500 sq. km. Average
temperatures range from 3.2°C in January to 18.3°C in July
and August.

POLITICS

Belgium is a constitutional monarchy with a hereditary
monarch as head of state. Amendments to the constitution since
1968 have devolved power to the regions. The national
government retains competence only in foreign and defence
policies, the national budget and monetary policy, social
security, and the judicial, legal and penal systems. The
bicameral legislature, the Federal Chambers, consists of a
senate and a Chamber of Representatives. The latter has 150
members, directly elected by proportional representation for a
five-year term. From 2014 the senate had 60 members,
indirectly elected by parliament and the regions.

There are three language communities: Flemish,
Francophone and Germanophone. Each community has its
own assembly, which elects the community government. At
this level, Flanders is covered by the Flemish community
assembly; most of Wallonia is covered by the Francophone
community assembly, and areas of Wallonia lying in the
German-speaking communities of Eupen and Malmédy are
covered by the Germanophone community assembly; Brussels
is covered by a joint community commission of the Flemish and
Francophone community assemblies.

At regional level, Belgium is divided into three: the Brussels
capital region, the Flemish region and Walloon region. Each
region has its own directly elected assembly and government.
The ten provinces of Belgium are: Antwerp, East Flanders,
Flemish Brabant, Hainaut, Liège, Limburg, Luxembourg,
Namur, Walloon Brabant and West Flanders. In addition, 589
communes form the lowest level of local government.

Prince Philippe ascended the throne in July 2013 following
the abdication of his father, King Albert, due to ill health. In
the May 2014 legislative elections, the New Flemish Alliance
emerged as the largest party, as it had done in the 2010
elections, and was nominated to form a ruling coalition. In
October, following months of negotiations, Charles Michel of
the centre-right Francophone Reform Movement party formed
a coalition government with the Flemish nationalist New
Flemish Alliance.

Minister-President of the Brussels Capital Government, Rudi
Vervoort
Minister-President of the Flemish Community and Flemish Region,
Geert Bourgeois
Minister-President of the French Community and Walloon Region,
Willy Borsus
Minister-President of the German-speaking Community, Oliver
Paasch

HEAD OF STATE
HM The King of the Belgians, King Philippe, *born* 15 April
1960, *acceded* 21 July 2013
Heir, HRH Princess Elisabeth, *born* 25 October 2001

SELECTED GOVERNMENT MEMBERS *AS AT MAY 2018*
Prime Minister, Charles Michel
Deputy Prime Ministers, Alexander De Croo *(Development);* Kris
Peeters *(Economy);* Didier Reynders *(Foreign Affairs);* Jan
Jambon *(Interior)*

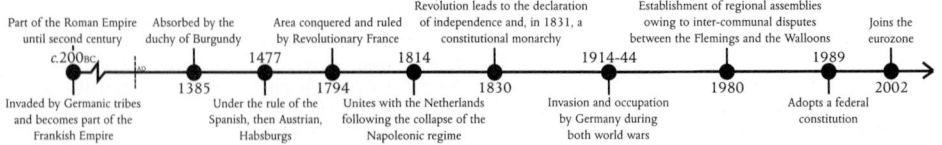

Part of the Roman Empire | Absorbed by the | Area conquered and ruled | Revolution leads to the declaration of independence and, in 1831, a constitutional monarchy | Establishment of regional assemblies owing to inter-communal disputes between the Flemings and the Walloons | Joins the eurozone
until second century | duchy of Burgundy | by Revolutionary France | | |
c.200BC | | 1477 | 1814 | 1914-44 | 1989 | 2002
| 1385 | 1794 | 1830 | 1980 |
Invaded by Germanic tribes and becomes part of the Frankish Empire | Under the rule of the Spanish, then Austrian, Habsburgs | Unites with the Netherlands following the collapse of the Napoleonic regime | Invasion and occupation by Germany during both world wars | Adopts a federal constitution |

EMBASSY OF BELGIUM
17 Grosvenor Crescent, London SW1X 7EE
T 020-7470 3700 E london@diplobel.fed.be
W www.unitedkingdom.diplomatie.belgium.be
Ambassador Extraordinary and Plenipotentiary, HE Rudolf
Huygelen, *apptd* 2017

BRITISH EMBASSY
Avenue d'Auderghem 10, 1040 Brussels
T (+32) (2) 287 6211 E public.brussels@fco.gov.uk
W www.gov.uk/government/world/belgium
Ambassador Extraordinary and Plenipotentiary, HE Alison Rose,
apptd 2014

ECONOMY AND TRADE
Belgium has a free-market economy with highly diversified
industrial and commercial sectors. With few natural resources,
industry is based largely on processing imported raw materials
for export, which makes the economy dependent on the state
of world markets. Belgium's high level of integration into the
struggling eurozone, spiralling labour costs and high public
debt are restraints to growth, but its tourism and hospitality
industries have largely recovered from the March 2016
terrorist attacks. The country's regional and political divide is
reflected in the Belgian economy. Flanders, including the
major ports of Antwerp, Brussels and Ghent, has higher levels
of employment and productivity. Wallonia, the richer portion
of the country in the 19th century, has become poorer due to
the declining importance of its heavy industry, although Liège
and Charleroi remain important industrial centres.

Principal industries are engineering and metal products,
vehicle assembly, transport equipment, scientific instruments,
food processing and beverages, chemicals, base metals, textiles,
glass, petroleum and diamonds. Industry accounts for 21.8 per
cent of GDP and 18.6 per cent of employment. There is a large
service sector, partly owing to the location in Brussels of EU
institutions, NATO headquarters and a number of other
international organisations. The service sector accounts for
77.5 per cent of GDP and 80.1 per cent of employment. There
is a small agricultural sector (0.7 per cent of GDP).

Around three-quarters of trade is with other EU states,
especially Germany, France and the Netherlands. External
trade statistics relate to Luxembourg as well as Belgium, as the
two countries formed an economic union in 1921.
GNI – US$475.2bn; US$41,790 per capita (2017)
Annual average growth of GDP – 1.6 per cent (2017 est)
Inflation rate – 2.2 per cent (2017 est)
Population below poverty line – 15.1 per cent (2013 est)
Unemployment – 7.5 per cent (2017 est)
Total external debt – US$1.281 trillion (2016 est)
Imports – US$372,812m (2016)
Exports – US$399,500m (2016)

BALANCE OF PAYMENTS
Trade – US$26,687m surplus (2016)
Current Account – US$791.6 deficit (2017)

Trade with UK	2016	2017
Imports from UK	£11,628,699,474	£13,784,918,149
Exports to UK	£23,240,174,852	£24,856,188,515

COMMUNICATIONS
Airports – 26; the main airports are at Antwerp, Brussels, Liège
and Ostend-Bruges
Waterways – There are 2,043km of inland waterways, of
which 1,528km are in regular commercial use; ship canals and
the Meuse (Maas), Sambre and Schelde rivers form an integral
part of the network. The major inland ports are located in
Brussels, Ghent and Antwerp

Roadways – 120,514km, including 1,756km of motorways
Railways – The rail system is run by Belgian National Railways
(NMBS/SNCB) and, at 3,233km, the network is one of the
densest in the world
Telecommunications – 4.4 million main lines and 12.6 million
mobile phone subscriptions (2016); there were 9.9 million
internet users in 2016
Internet code and IDD – be; 32 (from UK), 44 (to UK)
Major broadcasters – Television and radio broadcasters include
French-language RTBF and Dutch-language VRT
Press – Major newspapers include Dutch-language daily *Het
Nieuwsblad* and French-language daily *Le Soir*
WPFI score – 13,16 (7)

EDUCATION AND HEALTH
Nursery schools provide free education for children from two-
and-a-half to six years of age. The official school-leaving age
is 18.
Gross enrolment ratio (percentage of relevant age group) – primary
103.5 per cent, secondary 163.9 per cent, tertiary 74.6
per cent (2015 est)
Health expenditure (per capita) – US$4,884 (2014)
Hospital beds (per 1,000 people) – 6.2 (2014)
Life expectancy (years) – 81.1 (2017 est)
Mortality rate – 9.7 (2017 est)
Birth rate – 11.3 (2017 est)
Infant mortality rate – 3.4 (2017 est)

BELIZE

Area – 22,966 sq. km
Capital – Belmopan; population, 23,000 (2018 est)
Major towns – Belize City (the former capital), Orange Walk,
San Ignacio
Currency – Belize dollar (BZ$) of 100 cents; the Belize dollar
is tied to the US dollar
Population – 360,346 rising at 1.8 per cent a year (2017 est);
mestizo (52.9 per cent), Creole (25.9 per cent), Maya
(11.3 per cent), Garifuna (6.1 per cent) (est)
Religion – Christian 73.3 per cent (of which Roman Catholic
40.1 per cent) (est)
Language – English (official), Spanish, Creole, Mayan dialects,
Garifuna, German
Population density – 16 per sq. km (2016)
Urban population – 43.7 per cent (2017 est)
Median age (years) – 22.7 (2017 est)
National anthem – 'Land of the Free'
National day – 21 September (Independence Day)
Death penalty – Retained (last used 1985)
Military expenditure – US$22.8m (2017)

CLIMATE AND TERRAIN
Belize comprises a large coastal plain, swamps in the north, fertile land in the south and the Maya mountains in the south-west. The highest point of elevation is 1,160m (Doyle's Delight), the lowest is 0m (Caribbean Sea). Part of the Mesoamerican barrier reef system, the western hemisphere's longest, runs nearly the entire length of the coastline. The climate is subtropical but is cooled by trade winds. The hurricane season is from May to November.

HISTORY AND POLITICS
Numerous ruins in the area indicate that Belize was heavily populated by the Maya. The first British settlement was established in 1638 but was subject to repeated attacks by the Spanish, who claimed sovereignty until their defeat by the British navy and settlers in 1798. In 1862 the settlement was given colonial status as British Honduras. The colony became self-governing in 1964. In 1973 it was renamed Belize and it was granted independence on 21 September 1981.

Since independence, power has alternated between the two main political parties, the People's United Party (PUP) and the United Democratic Party (UDP). The UDP gained seats from the PUP in the November 2015 legislative elections, and retained its overall majority for a record third term under Prime Minister Dean Barrow.

Under the 1981 constitution, the head of state is Queen Elizabeth II, represented by a governor-general. There is a bicameral National Assembly, comprising a House of Representatives with 31 members directly elected for a five-year term, and a senate of 12 members appointed by the governor-general, including six on the advice of the prime minister, three on the advice of the opposition leader and three representing various sectors of society; a referendum in 2008 approved the reform of the senate into an elected chamber, effective from the next elections. The prime minister is appointed by the governor-general and is responsible to the legislature.

Governor-General, HE Sir Colville Young, GCMG, *apptd* 17 November 1993

SELECTED GOVERNMENT MEMBERS *AS AT MAY 2018*
Prime Minister, Finance, Dean Barrow
Deputy Prime Minister, Patrick Faber
Foreign Affairs, Wilfred Elrington

BELIZE HIGH COMMISSION
3rd Floor, 45 Crawford Place, London W1H 4LP
T 020-7723 3603 E info@belizehighcommission.co.uk
W www.belizehighcommission.co.uk
High Commissioner, HE Perla Maria Perdomo, *apptd* 2012

BRITISH HIGH COMMISSION
North Ring Road, Melhado Parade PO Box 91, Belmopan
T (+501) 822 2981 E brithicom@btl.net
W www.gov.uk/government/world/belize
High Commissioner, HE Peter Hughes, OBE, *apptd* 2013

FOREIGN RELATIONS
There is a longstanding territorial dispute with Guatemala, which claims the southern part of Belize. In February 2015, 37 Belizeans were arrested by Guatemalan authorities after they took part in an excursion into the disputed territory. After years of discussion, a referendum in Guatemala in April 2018 resulted in public support for mediation through the International Court of Justice.

ECONOMY AND TRADE
The economy grew steadily from 1999 to 2007, bolstered from 2006 by commercial exploitation of oil reserves. It contracted sharply in 2009 owing to the global downturn, natural disasters and the drop in international oil prices, but started to recover in 2010, and GDP grew by 2.5 per cent in 2017. In January 2013 the government announced the restructure of its US$544m commercial external debt, or 'superbond', on which it defaulted in 2012. Crime and corruption, inequality, high unemployment and a growing trade deficit remain concerns.

The services sector has grown as tourism has developed, and accounts for around 62.2 per cent of GDP; industry contributes around 13.8 per cent, and agriculture and fisheries around 9.7 per cent. The main industries apart from tourism are garment manufacturing, food processing, construction and oil production. The chief trading partners are the USA, the UK, Mexico and China. The major exports are sugar, bananas, citrus fruits and juice, garments, shrimp, fish products, molasses, timber and crude oil. Imports are primarily machinery and transport equipment, manufactured goods, fuel, chemicals, pharmaceuticals, food, beverages and tobacco.
GNI – US$1.6bn; US$4,390 per capita (2017)
Annual average growth of GDP – 2.5 per cent (2017 est)
Inflation rate – 1.8 per cent (2017 est)
Population below poverty line – 41 per cent (2013 est)
Unemployment – 10.1 per cent (2017 est)
Total external debt – US$1.326bn (2017 est)
Imports – US$1,020m (2015)
Exports – US$268m (2015)

BALANCE OF PAYMENTS
Trade – US$752m deficit (2015)
Current Account – US$130m deficit (2017)

Trade with UK	2016	2017
Imports from UK	£14,193,319	£15,394,997
Exports to UK	£54,029,153	£54,106,438

COMMUNICATIONS
Airports – Six, including the international airport at Belize City
Waterways – Although there are 825km of waterways, these are only accessible by small craft
Roadways – There are 488km of surfaced roads
Telecommunications – 23,000 fixed lines and 227,000 mobile phone subscriptions (2016); there were 157,735 internet users in 2016
Internet code and IDD – bz; 501 (from UK), 44 (to UK)
Major broadcasters – Commercial broadcasters include Channels 5 and 7 (TV), Love FM and Krem FM (radio); in 2014, a court approved the nationalisation of Belize Telemedia, the country's largest telecoms provider
Press – The country has no daily newspapers
WPFI score – 24,55 (47)

EDUCATION AND HEALTH
Education is free and compulsory for eight years.
Gross enrolment ratio (percentage of relevant age group) – primary 114.7 per cent, secondary 87.2 per cent, tertiary 24.3 per cent (2016 est)
Health expenditure (per capita) – US$279 (2014)
Hospital beds (per 1,000 people) – 1.3 (2014)
Life expectancy (years) – 68.9 (2017 est)
Mortality rate – 6 (2017 est)
Birth rate – 24 (2017 est)
Infant mortality rate – 18.9 (2017 est)
HIV/AIDS adult prevalence rate – 1.8 per cent (2016 est)

BENIN

République du Bénin – Republic of Benin

Area – 112,622 sq. km
Capital – Porto-Novo; population, 285,000 (2018 est); Cotonou, the seat of government, population, 685,000 (2018 est),
Major cities – Abomey-Calavi, Bohicon, Djougou, Parakou
Currency – Franc CFA of 100 centimes
Population – 11,038,805 rising at 2.71 per cent a year (2016 est); Fon (38.4 per cent), Adja (15.1 per cent), Yoruba (12 per cent), Bariba (9.6 per cent), Fulani (8.6 per cent), Ottamari (6.1 per cent), Yoa-Lokpa (4.3 per cent), Dendi (2.9 per cent) (2013 est)
Religion – Christian 48.5 per cent (Roman Catholic 25.5 per cent, Protestant 13.5 per cent, other Christian 9.5 per cent), Muslim 27.7 per cent (predominantly Sunni), Vodun (voodoo) 11.6 per cent (2013 est); many Christians and Muslims also practise voodoo, which originated in this region of Africa, or other indigenous religions
Language – French (official), Fon, Yoruba and other African languages
Population density – 96 per sq. km (2016)
Urban population – 47.3 per cent (2018 est)
Median age (years) – 18.2 (2017 est)
National anthem – 'L'Aube Nouvelle' 'The Dawn of a New Day'
National day – 1 August (Independence Day)
Death penalty – Abolished for all crimes (since 2016)
CPI score – 39 (95)
Military expenditure – US$116m (2017)
Conscription – 18–35 years of age; 18 months (selective)
Literacy rate – 38.4 per cent (2015 est)
Gross enrolment ratio (percentage of relevant age group) – primary 129 per cent, secondary 56.8 per cent (2015 est); tertiary 15.4 per cent (2013 est)
Health expenditure (per capita) – US$38 (2014)
Hospital beds (per 1,000 people) – 0.5 (2010)
Life expectancy (years) – 62.3 (2017 est)
Mortality rate – 7.9 (2017 est)
Birth rate – 35 (2017 est)
Infant mortality rate – 52.8 (2017 est)
HIV/AIDS adult prevalence – 1.1 per cent (2015 est)

CLIMATE AND TERRAIN

Benin has a short coastline of 121km on the Gulf of Guinea, but extends northwards inland for over 700km. The coast is a sandbar backed by lagoons that are fed by rivers. The land rises to a central plateau with the Atacora massif in the north-west, and falls to plains in the Niger basin in the north-east. Elevation extremes range from 658m (Mt Sokbaro) to 0m (Atlantic Ocean) at the lowest. The climate is tropical in the south and semi-arid in the north.

POLITICS

Under the 1990 constitution, the executive president is directly elected for a five-year term, renewable only once. The unicameral National Assembly has 83 members, directly elected for a four-year term. The president appoints and chairs the council of ministers.

The March 2016 presidential election was won in the second round by businessman Patrice Talon, an independent candidate, after Thomas Yayi Boni served his maximum two five-year terms. In the 2015 legislative election, the Cauri Forces for an Emerging Benin (FCBE) remained the largest group in the National Assembly, although it dropped seats from 41 to 33.

HEAD OF STATE
President, Defence, Patrice Talon, *elected* 20 March 2016

SELECTED GOVERNMENT MEMBERS *AS AT MAY 2018*
Economy, Finance, Romuald Wadagni
Foreign Affairs, Aurélien Agbénonci
Interior, Security, Sacca Lafia

EMBASSY OF THE REPUBLIC OF BENIN
87 Avenue Victor Hugo, 75116 Paris, France
T (+33) 1 4500 9882 E ambassade.benin@gofornet.com
Ambassador Extraordinary and Plenipotentiary, HE Jules-Armand Aniambossou, *apptd* 2014

BRITISH HIGH COMMISSION
High Commissioner, HE Iain Walker, *apptd* 2017, resident in Accra, Ghana

ECONOMY AND TRADE

Although the economy is underdeveloped and still burdened by foreign debt, Benin has benefited from increased competitiveness and debt reduction or relief since its economic restructuring commenced. Privatisation of industries, including utilities, began in 2001 and economic growth has been steady since 2000. However, this has been outweighed by rapid population growth, and over a third of the population remains below the poverty line. The economy is based on agriculture, particularly cotton production, and re-export trade with neighbouring countries; customs receipts provide over 40 per cent of government revenue, but much of the re-export trade operates outside the official economy and is unrecorded. With the economy deflating and growth slowing in 2017, efforts to attract foreign investment and tourism by improving the nation's infrastructure were given IMF support.

Agriculture is mostly at subsistence level and contributes 25.6 per cent to GDP, while industry contributes 23.1 per cent and services 51.3 per cent. The main cash crops are cotton, cashew nuts, shea butter, palm products and seafood, and the principal industrial activities are textiles and food processing. The main trading partners are Bangladesh, India, and China.

GNI – US$9.0bn; US$800 per capita (2017)
Annual average growth of GDP – 5.4 per cent (2017 est)
Inflation rate – 0.1 per cent (2017 est)
Population below poverty line – 36.2 per cent (2011 est)
Total external debt – US$2.716bn (2017 est)
Imports – US$2,369m (2015)
Exports – US$624m (2015)

BALANCE OF PAYMENTS
Trade – US$1,745m deficit (2015)
Current Account – US$808m deficit (2016)

Portuguese become first Europeans
to visit country; slavery becomes
region's primary trade
*c.*1100

1472
West African
kingdom of
Dahomey founded

1893

French establish protectorate
over the south following war
with Dahomey kingdom
1898

French protectorate
extends to the north

1904

Dahomey
incorporated into
French West Africa
1958

Becomes a self-governing
republic within French
Community

1960

Independence
declared followed by
political instability
1972

A military coup brings
to power Lt.-Col.
Mathieu Kérékou

Lt.-Col. Mathieu Kérékou
declares a Marxist-Leninist state
and changes its name to Benin
1975

Marxist-Leninism abandoned for
economic liberalisation and a
pluralistic constitution adopted

1989-90

1991
Transition to fully
democratic government

Trade with UK	2016	2017
Imports from UK	£20,558,008	£17,774,030
Exports to UK	£1,214,841	£618,309

COMMUNICATIONS
Airports and waterways – One, serving Cotonou, which is also the major seaport
Roadways and railways – 1,400km; 438km
Telecommunications – 124,883 fixed lines and 9.5 million mobile telephones in use (2016); there were 1.3 million internet users in 2016
Internet code and IDD – bj; 229 (from UK), 44 (to UK)
Major broadcasters – Télévision Nationale and Radio Nationale are the official state broadcasters
Press – Dozens of newspapers and periodicals are published, including *Le Matinal, Fraternité* and *La Nation;* the International Press Institute rates Benin as having one of West Africa's most vibrant media landscapes
WPFI score – 30,16 (84)

BHUTAN

Druk Gyalkhap – Kingdom of Bhutan

Area – 38,394 sq. km
Capital – Thimphu; population, 203,000 (2018 est)
Major towns – Geylegphug, Paro, Phodrang, Phuentsholing, Tashigang, Wangdue
Currency – Ngultrum (Nu) of 100 chetrum (Indian currency is also legal tender)
Population – 758,288 rising at 1.07 per cent a year (2017 est); Ngalop (Bhote) (50 per cent), ethnic Nepalese (35 per cent), indigenous or migrant tribes (15 per cent) (est)
Religion – Lamaistic Buddhist 75.3 per cent, Hindu 22.1 per cent (2005 est)
Language – Dzongkha (official), Sharchhopka, Lhotshamkha
Population density – 21 per sq. km (2016)
Urban population – 40.9 per cent (2018 est)
Median age (years) – 27.6 (2017 est)
National anthem – 'Druk Tsendhen' 'The Thunder Dragon Kingdom'
National day – 17 December (inauguration of first hereditary monarch, 1907)

Death penalty – Abolished for all crimes (since 2004)
CPI score – 67 (28)
Literacy rate – 64.9 per cent (2015 est)
Gross enrolment ratio (percentage of relevant age group) – primary 95 per cent, secondary 84 per cent (2016 est), tertiary 10.9 per cent (2013 est)
Health expenditure (per capita) – US$89 (2014)
Life expectancy (years) – 70.6 (2017 est)
Mortality rate – 6.5 (2017 est)
Birth rate – 17.3 (2017 est)
Infant mortality rate – 32.1 (2017 est)
HIV/AIDS adult prevalence – 0.13 per cent (2013 est)

CLIMATE AND TERRAIN
Bhutan is crossed by numerous rivers, and most of the population and cultivated land is found in the deep, fertile valleys of the highlands. There is a mountainous northern region that is infertile and sparsely populated, central highlands and densely forested foothills in the south, which are mainly inhabited by Nepalese settlers and indigenous tribespeople. Extremes of elevation range from 7,570m (Gangkar Puensum) to 97m (Drangeme Chhu). The climate is determined by altitude, varying from subtropical in the south to alpine in the north. There is heavy annual rainfall of up to 1,000mm in the central valleys and 5,000mm in the south, which experiences monsoons from June to September.

HISTORY AND POLITICS
Bhutan's external relations were under the guidance of Britain from the 19th century until 1947, and of India from 1947 until 2007; a 2007 revision of the friendship treaty between the two countries left Bhutan free to manage its external relations without India's advice.

Although the country has opened up since the 1970s, the monarchy has taken measures to preserve its indigenous culture and the environment, including the compulsory wearing of national dress and restrictions on tourism. The emphasis on the majority culture has caused tension with the sizeable Nepali minority. Many were denied citizenship in the 1990s and obliged to leave, which resulted in over 100,000 becoming refugees in Nepal, where most remain, living in refugee camps.

Bhutan's transition from an absolute monarchy to a democracy began in the 1950s, with the establishment of an elected legislature in 1953, and the transfer of powers from the king to the legislature in 1969 and 1989. The 2008 constitution formally established Bhutan as a parliamentary democracy with a constitutional monarchy, and provided for universal suffrage. King Jigme Singye Wangchuk abdicated in 2006 in favour of the Crown Prince.

In July 2013, elections to the National Assembly resulted in an unexpected win for the People's Democratic Party (PDP), which overtook the ruling Bhutan Peace and Prosperity Party (DPT) with a total of 32 seats to the DPT's 15. Tshering Tobgay, leader of the PDP, was appointed prime minister and formed a government.

Under the 2008 constitution, the head of state is a hereditary constitutional monarch, who must retire at the age of 65 and who may be required to abdicate by a two-thirds majority of the legislature. The bicameral parliament comprises a National Assembly with 47 directly elected members and a National Council with 25 members: 20 directly elected and five appointed by the king. Both chambers serve a fixed five-year term. The cabinet is appointed by the king on the recommendation of the prime minister, who may serve two parliamentary terms. In April 2018 a new National Council was elected.

HEAD OF STATE
HM The King of Bhutan, Jigme Khesar Namgyal Wangchuk,
   born 21 February 1980, *acceded* 14 December 2006,
   crowned 6 November 2008

SELECTED GOVERNMENT MEMBERS *AS AT MAY 2018*
Prime Minister, Tshering Tobgay
Finance, Namgay Dorji
Foreign Affairs, Damcho Dorji
Home and Cultural Affairs, Dawa Gyeltshen

BRITISH DEPUTY HIGH COMMISSION
British Deputy High Commissioner, Bruce Bucknell, *apptd* 2016, resident at Kolkata, India

ECONOMY AND TRADE
The growing economy is being cautiously modernised but is still based on agriculture (15.7 per cent of GDP in 2017) in what is largely a self-sufficient rural society. Industry (42.6 per cent of GDP) is on a small scale, and the growing services sector (41.7 per cent of GDP) is mostly the result of increased tourism. Agriculture and animal husbandry, much at subsistence level, engage over 58 per cent of the workforce, although the mountainous terrain and heavy forest cover limit the area under cultivation. The further construction of hydropower dams designed to export electricity to India, which already accounts for 40 per cent of total exports and 25 per cent of government revenue, should ensure future sustainable growth. The principal food crops are rice, cereals, vegetables and fruit, especially oranges. Industries include forestry, mining (limestone, gypsum, dolomite, graphite, coal), cement and calcium carbide production, food processing, distilling, hydroelectric power generation and tourism.

The main trading partner is India, which accounts for 89.5 per cent of imports and 95.3 per cent of exports. The principal exports are electricity, ferrosilicon, cement, calcium carbide, copper wire, manganese and vegetable oil. The main imports are fuel and lubricants, passenger vehicles, machinery and parts, fabrics and rice.

GNI – US$2.2bn; US$2,720 per capita (2017)
Annual average growth of GDP – 5.9 per cent (2017 est)
Inflation rate – 3.5 per cent (2016 est)
Population below poverty line – 13.3 per cent (2012 est)
Unemployment – 3.2 per cent (2017 est)
Total external debt – US$2.71bn (2017 est)
Imports – US$1,170m (2015)
Exports – US$555m (2014)

BALANCE OF PAYMENTS
Trade – US$255m deficit (2014)
Current Account – US$354m deficit (2017)

Trade with UK	2016	2017
Imports from UK	£1,303,347	£1,478,750
Exports to UK	£232,276	£82,054

COMMUNICATIONS
Airports – Two, including an international airport in Paro
Roadways – 4,991km, including 622km of motorways
Telecommunications – 21,081 fixed lines and 698,373 mobile subscriptions (2016); there were 313,347 internet users in 2016
Internet code and IDD – bt; 975 (from UK), 44 (to UK)
Major broadcasters – Fear that outside influences would undermine Bhutanese culture meant that radio broadcasting began only in 1973, and television broadcasting and internet access in 1999; radio and television services are provided by the state-owned Bhutan Broadcasting Services (BBS)
Press – The country's two daily newspapers are *Kuensel* and *Bhutan Today,* which was launched in English in 2008
WPFI score – 30,73 (94)

BOLIVIA

Estado Plurinacional de Bolivia – Plurinational State of Bolivia

Area – 1,098,581 sq. km
Capital – La Paz, the seat of government; population, 1,814,000 (2015 est); Sucre, the legal capital and seat of the judiciary; population, 278,000 (2018 est)
Major cities – Cochabamba, El Alto, Oruro, Santa Cruz
Currency – Boliviano ($b) of 100 centavos
Population – 11,138,234 rising at 1.51 per cent a year (2017 est); mestizo (68 per cent), indigenous (20 per cent) (2009 est)
Religion – Christian (Roman Catholic 76.8 per cent, Evangelical and Pentecostal 8.1 per cent, Protestant 7.9 per cent) (est)
Language – Spanish, 36 indigenous languages (all official); Quechua and Aymara are the main indigenous languages
Population density – 10 per sq. km (2016)
Urban population – 69.3 per cent (2017 est)
Median age (years) – 24.3 (2017 est)
National anthem – 'Himno Nacional de Bolivia' 'National Anthem of Bolivia'
National day – 6 August (Independence Day)
Death penalty – Abolished for all crimes (since 2013)
CPI score – 33 (112)
Military expenditure – US$657m (2017)
Conscription – 14–49 years of age; 12 months

CLIMATE AND TERRAIN
Landlocked Bolivia's main topographical feature is its great central plateau, the Altiplano. Over 800km in length and at an average altitude of 3,750m above sea level, this plateau lies between two great chains of the Andes that traverse the country from north to south. Lake Titicaca, shared with Peru, lies on the Altiplano. Elevation extremes range from 6,542m (Nevado Sajama) to 90m (Rio Paraguay). The low-lying north and eastern plains are drained by the principal rivers, the Beni,

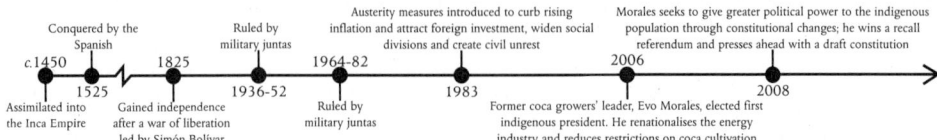

Itenez, Madre de Dios and Mamoré. The climate varies dramatically between regions: on the lowlands of the Amazon basin, temperatures average around 25°C; above 500m on the Altiplano, conditions are subpolar. The south is prone to droughts. The wet season is October to April.

POLITICS

The 1967 constitution was revised in 1994 and 2009. It provides for an executive president who is directly elected for a five-year term. The bicameral Plurinational Legislative Assembly, or National Congress, consists of a 36-member Chamber of Senators and a 130-member Chamber of Deputies; members of both chambers are directly elected for a five-year term.

President Morales, leader of the Movement Towards Socialism (MAS), won the 2005 presidential elections, and was re-elected in 2009. After the Constitutional Court ruled that Morales could stand for a third term, the president ran in and subsequently won the October 2014 presidential elections. In the simultaneous legislative elections, MAS won large majorities in both houses, winning 88 seats in the Chamber of Deputies and 25 seats in the Chamber of Senators. In February 2016 President Morales lost a referendum in which he sought support to change the constitution to allow the president and vice-president to run for re-election in 2019; however in November 2017, the constitutional court removed all limits on presidential terms of office.

HEAD OF STATE

President, Juan Evo Morales Ayma, *elected* 18 December 2005, *sworn in* 22 January 2006, *re-elected* 2009, 2014
President of the Senate, Vice-President, Alvaro Garcia Linera

SELECTED GOVERNMENT MEMBERS *AS AT MAY 2018*

Defence, Javier Zavaleta
Economy and Public Finance, Mario Alberto Guillen (acting)
Foreign Affairs, Fernando Huanacuni

BOLIVIAN EMBASSY

106 Eaton Square, London SW1W 9AD
T 020-7235 4248 E embol@bolivianembassy.co.uk
W www.bolivianembassy.co.uk
Ambassador Extraordinary and Plenipotentiary, vacant

BRITISH EMBASSY

Avenida Arce 2732, La Paz
T (+591) (2) 243 3424 E BELaPaz@fco.gov.uk
W www.gov.uk/government/world/bolivia
Ambassador Extraordinary and Plenipotentiary, HE James Thornton, *apptd* 2015

ECONOMY AND TRADE

The country is one of the most underdeveloped and least affluent in South America, although steady growth since the 1990s has lowered the proportion of the population living below the poverty line to less than 40 per cent. The government of Evo Morales has implemented a wide-reaching socialist agenda since gaining power, including nationalising the oil and gas sectors. The state energy company YPFB has a

$30bn (£21bn) investment programme for 2015–25 with an emphasis on maintaining and expanding the gas supplies on which the country is largely reliant. While the economy grew annually by around 5 per cent for a decade from 2006, it remains vulnerable to falling commodity prices and integration with the struggling Argentinian and Brazilian economies. In 2015 President Morales vowed not to nationalise additional industries in a bid to redress a shortage in international investment.

Mining (principally for zinc, tin and gold) and smelting, natural gas and oil production, agriculture and textiles are the principal industries. Industry contributes 37.4 per cent of GDP, agriculture 13 per cent and services 54.1 per cent.

The main trading partners are Brazil, the USA, Argentina and Chile. Principal exports are natural gas, soya beans and soya products, crude oil, zinc ore and tin. The main imports are petroleum products, machinery, aircraft and aircraft parts, iron and steel, and plastics.

GNI – US$34.6bn; US$3,130 per capita (2017)
Annual average growth of GDP – 4.2 per cent (2017 est)
Inflation rate – 3.2 per cent (2017 est)
Population below poverty line – 38.6 per cent (2011 est)
Unemployment – 4 per cent (2017 est)
Total external debt – US$14.81bn (2017 est)
Imports – US$8,374m (2016)
Exports – US$6,969m (2016)

BALANCE OF PAYMENTS

Trade – US$1,405m deficit (2016)
Current Account – US$2,376m deficit (2017)

Trade with UK	2016	2017
Imports from UK	£17,473,075	£18,911,796
Exports to UK	£18,771,590	£21,510,480

COMMUNICATIONS

Airports – 21, including four international airports serving the major cities
Waterways – There are 10,000km of commercially navigable waterways, with an inland port on the river Paraguay at the border with Brazil; Bolivia has free port privileges at seaports in Argentina, Brazil, Chile and Paraguay, and a lease on a free-trade zone at the Peruvian port of Ilo
Roadways and railways – 11,993km; the 3,652km of railways form an eastern network and an Andean network
Telecommunications – 867,346 fixed lines and 10.1 million mobile subscriptions (2016); there were 4.4 million internet users in 2016
Internet code and IDD – bo; 591 (from UK), 10/11/12/13 44 (to UK; depends on area and/or carrier)
Major broadcasters – Since the election of Evo Morales, the government has acquired a growing number of media outlets; the leading state-run broadcasters are Bolivia TV and Radio Patria Nueva. In 2013, a law was passed requiring that private media companies publish government messages, damaging the finances of many by limiting commercial advertising space
Press – Daily newspapers are published on a regional basis; leading titles include *La Razon* (La Paz), *Los Tiempos* (Cochabamba) and *El Deber* (Santa Cruz)
WPFI score – 32,45 (110)

EDUCATION AND HEALTH

Elementary education is free and officially, though often not in practice, compulsory from the ages of six to 13.

Literacy rate – 92.5 per cent (2015 est)

Gross enrolment ratio (percentage of relevant age group) – primary 97.7 per cent, secondary 86.5 per cent (2016 est)

Health expenditure (per capita) – US$209 (2014)

Hospital beds (per 1,000 people) – 1.1 (2014)

Life expectancy (years) – 69.5 (2017 est)

Mortality rate – 6.4 (2017 est)

Birth rate – 22 (2017 est)

Infant mortality rate – 35.3 (2017 est)

HIV/AIDS adult prevalence – 0.3 per cent (2015 est)

BOSNIA AND HERCEGOVINA

Bosna i Hercegovina – Bosnia and Hercegovina

Area – 51,197 sq. km

Capital – Sarajevo; population, 343,000 (2018 est)

Major towns – Banja Luka, Bijeljina, Mostar, Tuzla, Zenica

Currency – Convertible mark (KM) of 100 fenings

Population – 3,856,181 falling at 0.16 per cent a year (2017 est); Bosniak (50.1 per cent), Serb (30.8 per cent), Croat (15.4 per cent) (2013 est)

Religion – Muslim 50.7 per cent (predominantly Sunni), Christian (Serb Orthodox 30.7 per cent, Roman Catholic 15.2 per cent) (est)

Language – Bosnian, Croatian, Serbian (all official)

Population density – 69 per sq. km (2016)

Urban population – 48.2 per cent (2018 est)

Median age (years) – 42.1 (2017 est)

National anthem – 'Drzavna Himna Bosne i Hercegovine' 'National Anthem of Bosnia and Hercegovina'

National day – 25 November (formation of the anti-fascist resistance council, 1943)

Death penalty – Abolished for all crimes (since 2001)

CPI score – 38 (91)

Military expenditure – US$165m (2017)

Literacy rate – 98.5 per cent (2015 est)

Gross enrolment ratio (percentage of relevant age group) – primary 88 per cent, secondary 90 per cent (2010 est), tertiary 38 per cent (2012 est)

Health expenditure (per capita) – US$464 (2014)

Hospital beds (per 1,000 people) – 3.5 (2013)

Life expectancy (years) – 76.9 (2017 est)

Mortality rate – 10 (2017 est)

Birth rate – 8.8 (2017 est)

Infant mortality rate – 5.5 (2017 est)

CLIMATE AND TERRAIN

The mountainous centre of the country is split by deep valleys, while the north is lower-lying, falling to the basin of the river Sava, which forms the northern border with Croatia. The Dinaric Alps lie along the western border. The highest point of elevation is 2,386m (Maglic), the lowest point is 0m (Adriatic Sea). Average temperatures range from 0°C in January to 20.3°C in July and August.

POLITICS

Under the Dayton Peace Accord, the Bosnian republican (national) government is responsible for foreign affairs, currency, citizenship and immigration. The head of state is a collective presidency comprising a representative from each of the three main ethnic groups, all directly elected for a four-year term; the chair of the presidency rotates among its members every eight months. Legislative authority is vested in the bicameral Parliamentary Assembly, comprising a House of Peoples and a House of Representatives. Both houses have four-year terms. The House of Peoples has 15 members – ten from the Federation and five from the Republika Srpska – who are appointed from the House of Representatives. The House of Representatives has 42 members who are directly elected to the two constituent chambers: the Chamber of Deputies of the Federation, which has 28 members, and the Chamber of Deputies of the Republika Srpska, which has 14 members.

In the Bosniak–Croat Federation, the president and vice-president are elected by the Bosniak and Croat members of the House of Peoples for a four-year term; a second vice-president is elected to represent the Serb population. There is a bicameral Assembly comprising a 58-member House of Peoples elected on an ethnic basis and a House of Representatives with 98 directly elected members.

In the Republika Srpska, the president is directly elected for a four-year term. There is a unicameral People's Assembly with 83 members directly elected for a four-year term.

There is a national council of ministers and each of the entities also has its own executive. All appointments to the executives are in consultation with the UN High Representative, who has the power of veto.

The last legislative elections were held in October 2014. The Bosniak-dominated Party of Democratic Action (SDA) won the largest number of seats in the state-level House of Representatives and in the House of Representatives of the Federation of Bosnia and Hercegovina, at the expense of the mixed Social Democratic Party (SDP). In the Republika Srpska, the Alliance of Independent Social Democrats under its president Milorad Dodik won the largest number of seats.

In the simultaneous presidential elections, Mladen Ivanic (Serb) and Dragan Covic (Croat) were elected to the collective federal presidency, and Bakir Izetbegovic was re-elected as the Bosniak member. Milorad Dodik was re-elected president of Republika Srpska. The presidential election in the Bosniak–Croat Federation in February 2015 was won by Marinko Cavara.

REPUBLIC OF BOSNIA AND HERCEGOVINA

HEADS OF STATE

Presidency Members, Dragan Covic *(Croat),* Mladen Ivanic *(Serb),* Bakir Izetbegovic *(Bosniak)*

SELECTED GOVERNMENT MEMBERS *AS AT MAY 2018*

Chair of the Council of Ministers, Denis Zvizdic

Defence, Marina Pendes

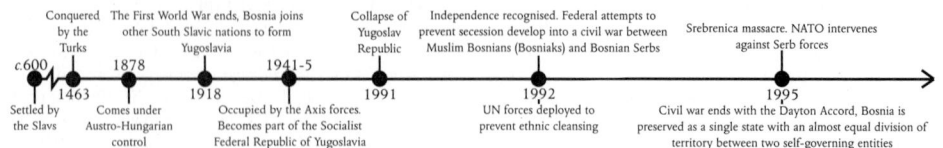

Conquered by the Turks *c.*600

1463 Settled by the Slavs

1878 The First World War ends, Bosnia joins other South Slavic nations to form Yugoslavia / Comes under Austro-Hungarian control

1918

1941-5 Occupied by the Axis forces. Becomes part of the Socialist Federal Republic of Yugoslavia

1991 Collapse of Yugoslav Republic

1992 Independence recognised. Federal attempts to prevent secession develop into a civil war between Muslim Bosnians (Bosniaks) and Bosnian Serbs / UN forces deployed to prevent ethnic cleansing

1995 Srebrenica massacre. NATO intervenes against Serb forces / Civil war ends with the Dayton Accord, Bosnia is preserved as a single state with an almost equal division of territory between two self-governing entities

Finance, Vjekoslav Bevanda
Foreign Affairs, Igor Crnadak

FEDERATION OF BOSNIA AND HERCEGOVINA
President, Marinko Cavara
Vice-Presidents, Milan Dunovic; Melika Mahmutbegovic

SELECTED GOVERNMENT MEMBERS *AS AT MAY 2017*
Prime Minister, Fadil Novalic
Deputy Prime Ministers, Jelka Milicevic; Aleksander Remetic
Interior, Aljosa Campara

REPUBLIKA SRPSKA
President, Milorad Dodik
Vice-Presidents, Josip Jerkovic; Ramiz Salkic

SELECTED GOVERNMENT MEMBERS *AS AT MAY 2018*
Prime Minister, Zeljka Cvijanovic
Finance, Zoran Tegeltija
Internal Affairs, Dragan Lukac

OFFICE OF THE UN HIGH REPRESENTATIVE/EU
SPECIAL REPRESENTATIVE
UN High Representative, Dr Valentin Inzko, *apptd* 2009
EU Special Representative, Lars-Gunnar Wigemark, *apptd* 2015

EMBASSY OF BOSNIA AND HERCEGOVINA
5–7 Lexham Gardens, London W8 5JJ
T 020-7373 0867 **E** embassy@bhembassy.co.uk
W www.bhembassy.co.uk
Ambassador Extraordinary and Plenipotentiary, HE Branko
  Neskovic, *apptd* 2015

BRITISH EMBASSY
39a Hamdije Cemerlica Street, 71000 Sarajevo
T (+387) (0) 33 282 200 **E** britemb@bih.net.ba
W www.gov.uk/government/world/bosnia-and-herzegovina
Ambassador Extraordinary and Plenipotentiary, HE Matthew
  Field, *apptd* 2018

ECONOMY AND TRADE
When the civil war broke out, the structure of the economy – dominated by state-owned industries, mainly of a military nature – still reflected the central planning of the communist era. Economic restructuring, such as privatisation, has been slow and uneven, although the financial sector is now largely privatised and stable. There has been political deadlock, however, on the reforms needed to pave the way for EU accession. The difficulties inherent in tackling problems such as the large public sector, large deficits and high unemployment are exacerbated by the duplication of administrative functions and reluctant cooperation between the different national and local political and administrative entities. There is a large unofficial economy, but undeclared activity has declined since the introduction of VAT in 2006. In 2016, an IMF loan program was agreed with Bosnia but it has struggled to meet the economic benchmarks needed to ensure all funding instalments.

Most agricultural products are for domestic consumption and foodstuffs also have to be imported. The main industrial activities include mining (metals, minerals and coal), production of steel, textiles, tobacco products, wooden furniture, ammunition and domestic appliances, assembly of vehicles, tanks and aircraft, and oil refining. The country produces enough hydroelectric power for its needs and exports electricity. The main trading partners are Croatia, Serbia, Germany, Austria and Italy. Principal exports are metals, clothing and wood products, and the main imports are machinery and equipment, chemicals, fuels and foodstuffs.

GNI – US$17.3bn; US$4,940 per capita (2017)
Annual average growth of GDP – 2.5 per cent (2017 est)
Inflation rate – 1.8 per cent (2017 est)
Population below poverty line – 17.2 per cent (2015 est)
Unemployment – 20.5 per cent (2017 est)
Total external debt – US$10.45bn (2017 est)
Imports – US$9,126m (2016)
Exports – US$5,267m (2016)

BALANCE OF PAYMENTS
Trade – US$3,859m deficit (2016)
Current Account – US$875m deficit (2017)

Trade with UK	2016	2017
Imports from UK	£21,980,279	£26,614,755
Exports to UK	£18,671,199	£21,107,127

COMMUNICATIONS
Airports – Seven, including international airports in Sarajevo, Banja Luka, Mostar and Tuzla
Waterways – Although the country has 20km of coastline on the Adriatic Sea, there are no seaports
Roadways and railways – 19,426km, including 4,652km of motorways; 601km
Telecommunications – 744,991 fixed lines and 3.4 million mobile subscriptions (2016); there were 2.7 million internet users in 2016
Internet code and IDD – ba; 387 (from UK), 44 (to UK)
Major broadcasters – More than 200 commercial TV and radio stations are on the air in Bosnia; national broadcaster BHTV1 operates alongside two separate-entity broadcasters. Major radio broadcasters include the Bosniak-Croat Radio FBiH and the Bosnian Serb station RTRS
Press – There are five major daily newspapers, including *Oslobodjenje, Nezavisne Novine* and *Dnevni List*
WPFI score – 27,37 (62)

BOTSWANA

Republic of Botswana

Area – 581,730 sq. km
Capital – Gaborone; population, 269,000 (2018 est)
Major cities – Francistown, Maun, Molepolole, Selebi-Phikwe
Currency – Pula (P) of 100 thebe
Population – 2,214,858 rising at 1.55 per cent a year (2017 est); Tswana (79 per cent), Kalanga (11 per cent), Basarwa (3 per cent) (est)
Religion – Christian 79.1 per cent (predominantly Protestant), Badimo 4.1 per cent (2010 est)
Language – English (official), Setswana, Kalanga, Sekgalagadi
Population density – 4 per sq. km (2016)
Urban population – 58 per cent (2017 est)
Median age (years) – 24.5 (2017 est)
National anthem – 'Fatshe Leno La Rona' 'Blessed Be This Noble Land'
National day – 30 September (Botswana Day)
Death penalty – Retained
CPI score – 61 (34)
Military expenditure – US$531m (2017)

CLIMATE AND TERRAIN
Botswana lies on an undulating plateau and is covered by the Kalahari desert in the south and west. To the east, streams run into the Marico, Notwani and Limpopo rivers. In the north lies a flat region comprising the Makgadikgadi salt pans and the swampland of the Okavango delta. Elevation extremes range from 1,489m (Tsodilo Hills) to 513m (junction of the Limpopo and Shashe rivers). The climate is subtropical in the north, arid in the south and west, and more temperate in the east, which has regular rain. Average temperatures range from 15°C in July to 26.7°C in January.

HISTORY AND POLITICS
The Tswana people were predominant in the area from the 17th century. In 1885, at the request of indigenous chiefs fearing invasion by the Boers, Britain formally took control of Bechuanaland, and the northern part of the territory was declared the Bechuanaland Protectorate, while land to the south of the Molopo river became British Bechuanaland, which was later incorporated into the Cape Colony and eventually South Africa. In 1964, the Bechuanaland Protectorate became self-governing, and on 30 September 1966 it became an independent republic under the name Botswana. Since independence, Botswana has been stable and relatively prosperous, owing to the diamond mining industry. There is a high level of HIV/AIDS among the population, and although an advanced treatment programme in place since 2001 is reducing the level of infection, the country faces serious demographic and social problems.

President Festus Mogae stood down in 2008, having completed two terms of office, and was succeeded by the vice-president, Lt.-Gen. Ian Khama, son of the country's first president. Khama stepped down in April 2018 having completed the constitutionally-mandated ten year term limit, and was replaced by vice-president Mokgweetsi Masisi. The Botswana Democratic Party (BDP) was re-elected to power in the October 2014 legislative elections, winning 33 of 57 seats. President Khama was re-elected by parliament on 26 October 2014.

Under the 1966 constitution, the executive president is elected by the legislature for a five-year term, renewable once. He appoints the vice-president and the cabinet. The unicameral National Assembly has 57 members directly elected for a five-year term, plus a variable number of members (currently six) nominated by the president and elected by the assembly, and two *ex officio* members. A 35-member House of Chiefs advises on tribal matters and constitutional changes.

HEAD OF STATE
President, Mokgweetsi Masisi, *sworn in* 1 April 2018
Vice-President, Slumber Tsogwane

SELECTED GOVERNMENT MEMBERS *AS AT MAY 2018*
Defence, Shaw Kgathi
Finance and Development Planning, Ontefetse Kenneth Matambo
International Affairs, Vincent Seretse

BOTSWANA HIGH COMMISSION
6 Stratford Place, London W1C 1AY
T 020-7499 0031 E bohico@govbw.com
High Commissioner, HE Roy Blackbeard, *apptd* 1998

BRITISH HIGH COMMISSION
Plot 1079–1084, Main Mall, off Queens Road, Gaborone
T (+267) 395 2841 E bhc@botsnet.bw
W www.gov.uk/government/world/botswana
High Commissioner, HE Katharine Ransome, *apptd* 2016

ECONOMY AND TRADE
Botswana has been relatively prosperous since independence because of its mining industry, political stability and sound economic management. Despite this, around 20 per cent of the population lives below the poverty line and even more are unemployed. Longer-term problems are the impact of the high levels of HIV/AIDS among the workforce and the levelling off of diamond production, which accounts for 85 per cent of export earnings; diamond exports declined owing to the global downturn, causing the economy to contract sharply in 2009. The government has sought to reduce the economy's dependence on the diamond industry by diversifying. A major drought and power shortages restricted economic growth in 2012 and 2013, but since 2010 GDP has grown steadily. Safari tourism and financial services have increased in recent years, and the services sector contributes 69.1 per cent of GDP. The industrial sector contributes 29.2 per cent of GDP, mainly from mining diamonds, copper, nickel, salt, soda ash, potash, coal, iron ore and silver. Agriculture is mostly pastoral and accounts for 1.7 per cent of GDP.

The main trading partners are the EU, southern African countries and Israel. Principal exports are diamonds, copper, nickel, soda ash, meat and textiles. The main imports are foodstuffs, machinery, electrical goods, transport equipment, textiles, fuel and petroleum products.
GNI – US$15.6bn; US$6,820 per capita (2017)
Annual average growth of GDP – 4.5 per cent (2017 est)
Inflation rate – 3.7 per cent (2017 est)
Population below poverty line – 19.3 per cent (2009 est)

Unemployment – 20 per cent (2013 est)
Total external debt – US$2.461bn (2017 est)
Imports – US$7,238m (2016)
Exports – US$6,317m (2016)

BALANCE OF PAYMENTS
Trade – US$921m deficit (2015)
Current Account – US$2,148m surplus (2017)

Trade with UK	2016	2017
Imports from UK	£49,743,779	£29,448,367
Exports to UK	£19,363,366	£19,971,927

COMMUNICATIONS
Airports – Ten, including the international airport in Gaborone
Roadways – 17,916km, of which 6,116km are paved
Railways – The only railway is the 888km line from Zimbabwe to South Africa, which passes through eastern Botswana
Telecommunications – 142,122 fixed lines and 3.3 million mobile subscriptions (2016); there were 869,610 internet users in 2016
Internet code and IDD – bw, 267 (from UK), 44 (to UK)
Major broadcasters – State-run television broadcaster Botswana TV was established in 2000 and a private station is hosted by eBotswana; state-run Radio Botswana operates a commercial FM station from Gaborone, while other stations such as Yarona FM operate a private service
Press – Major daily newspapers include the state-run *Daily News* and the privately owned *Mmegi*
WPFI score – 25,29 (48)

EDUCATION AND HEALTH
Botswana does not have a compulsory education policy, although many children receive 12 years of education (seven years of primary education, three years of junior secondary and two years of senior secondary). In 2006 fees were reintroduced for state secondary schools, which had been free of charge for over 20 years.
Literacy rate – 88.5 per cent (2015 est)
Gross enrolment ratio (percentage of relevant age group) – primary 108.6 per cent (2013 est); secondary 80 per cent (2011 est); tertiary 23.4 per cent (2017 est)
Health expenditure (per capita) – US$385 (2014)
Hospital beds (per 1,000 people) – 1.8 (2010)
Life expectancy (years) – 63.3 (2017 est)
Mortality rate – 9.6 (2017 est)
Birth rate – 22.1 (2017 est)
Infant mortality rate – 29.6 (2017 est)
HIV/AIDS adult prevalence – 22.2 per cent (2015 est)

BRAZIL

Republica Federativa do Brasil – Federative Republic of Brazil

Area – 8,515,770 sq. km
Capital – Brasilia; population, 4,470,000 (2018 est)
Major cities – Belo Horizonte, Fortaleza, Porto Alegre, Recife, Rio de Janeiro (the former capital), Salvador, Sao Paulo
Currency – Real (R$) of 100 centavos
Population – 207,353,391 rising at 0.73 per cent a year (2017 est)
Religion – Christian (Roman Catholic 64.6 per cent, Protestant 22.2 per cent), Spiritist 2.2 per cent (2010 est)
Language – Portuguese (official), Spanish, German, Italian, Japanese, English, Amerindian languages
Population density – 25 per sq. km (2016)
Urban population – 86.2 per cent (2017 est)
Median age (years) – 32 (2017 est)
National anthem – 'Hino Nacional Brasileiro' 'Brazilian National Anthem'
National day – 7 September (Independence Day)
Death penalty – Retained for certain crimes (last used 1855)
CPI score – 37 (96)
Military expenditure – US$29,284m (2017)
Conscription – 18–45 years of age; 9–12 months

CLIMATE AND TERRAIN
Brazil has six distinct topographical areas: the Amazon basin (north and west of the country), the Parana-Paraguay river basin (south; the Parana drains the Pantanal, the world's largest freshwater wetland), the Guiana Highlands (north of the Amazon), the Mato Grosso plateau (centre), the Brazilian Highlands (south of the Amazon) and the coastal strip. Elevation extremes range from 2,994m (Pico da Neblina) to 0m (Atlantic Ocean). Brazil has the world's largest rainforest, as well as large expanses of savannah *(cerrado)*. The climate is mostly tropical, with the equator passing through the north and the Tropic of Capricorn through the south-east. The Amazon basin sees annual rainfall of up to 2,300mm a year and there is no dry season. The north-east is the driest area of the country and can experience long periods of drought. The southern states have a seasonal temperate climate.

POLITICS
The Federative Republic of Brazil is composed of the Federal District of Brasilia, in which the capital lies, and 26 states: Acre, Alagoas, Amapa, Amazonas, Bahia, Ceara, Espirito Santo, Goias, Maranhao, Mato Grosso, Mato Grosso do Sul, Minas Gerais, Para, Paraiba, Parana, Pernambuco, Piaui, Rio de Janeiro, Rio Grande do Norte, Rio Grande do Sul, Rondonia, Roraima, Santa Catarina, Sao Paulo, Sergipe and Tocantins. Each state has its own governor and legislative assembly.

Under the 1988 constitution (amended in 1997), the executive president is directly elected for a four-year term, which is renewable once. The National Congress consists of an 81-member federal senate (three senators per state, directly elected for an eight-year term) and a 513-member Chamber of Deputies, which is directly elected every four years; the number of deputies per state depends upon the state's population.

In the October 2014 presidential election Dilma Rousseff of the Workers' Party (PT) was re-elected following a second round of voting. In the simultaneous legislative election, With the Strength of the People, a centre-left grouping led by the PT, won a majority in both houses of Congress. President Rousseff's government was dogged by allegations of corruption, and in August 2016 Rousseff was impeached for illegally manipulating government accounts, and Michel Temer was sworn in as president.

HEAD OF STATE
President, Michel Temer, *sworn in* 31 August 2016

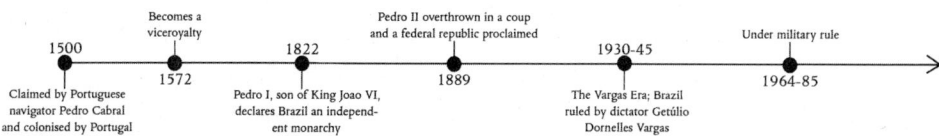

Becomes a viceroyalty — 1572

1500 — Claimed by Portuguese navigator Pedro Cabral and colonised by Portugal

1822 — Pedro I, son of King Joao VI, declares Brazil an independent monarchy

Pedro II overthrown in a coup and a federal republic proclaimed — 1889

1930-45 — The Vargas Era; Brazil ruled by dictator Getúlio Dornelles Vargas

Under military rule — 1964-85

SELECTED GOVERNMENT MEMBERS *AS AT MAY 2018*
Attorney-General, Grace Maria Fernandes Mendonca
Defence, Joaquim Silva e Luna (acting)
Finance, Eduardo Guardia
Foreign Affairs, Aloysio Nunes

EMBASSY OF BRAZIL
14/16 Cockspur Street, London SW1Y 5BL
T 020-7747 4500 **E** info.london@itamaraty.gov.br
W www.brazil.org.uk
Ambassador Extraordinary and Plenipotentiary, HE Eduardo dos Santos, *apptd* 2015

BRITISH EMBASSY
Setor de Embaixadas Sul, Quadra 801, Lote 8, CEP 70408-900, Brasilia DF
T (+55) (61) 3329 2300 **W** www.gov.uk/government/world/brazil
Ambassador Extraordinary and Plenipotentiary, HE Dr Vijay Rangarajan, CMG, *apptd* 2017

ECONOMY AND TRADE

Historically subject to boom and bust cycles, the economy was stabilised by reforms in the 1990s. Tight fiscal management, IMF programmes, a growth in output and an expanding export base produced steady growth from 2003. Brazil's economy is based on well-developed agriculture, mining, manufacturing and service sectors. Unemployment and income inequality have decreased steadily in the past 15 years, although poverty is still widespread. GDP growth has slowed since 2011 and, in 2015, the nation experienced the worst recession in its history, due to rising inflation and decreasing demand from China. The economy has since begun to recover, with decreasing inflation and a return to growth (1 per cent) in 2017.

The country is rich in mineral deposits, including iron ore (haematite), bauxite, gold, manganese, nickel, platinum and uranium. It produces oil, gas and hydroelectricity, and is close to self-sufficiency in oil. Brazil is the world's largest producer of coffee; the other main agricultural products are soya beans, wheat, rice, maize, sugar cane, cocoa, citrus fruit and beef. The expansion of agriculture and forestry threaten the rainforest, although recent governments' attempts to prevent further depredations by loggers and farmers have slowed the rate of deforestation considerably. Tourism is a growing industry. In 2017, services generated 72.8 per cent of GDP, industry 21 per cent and agriculture 6.2 per cent.

Brazil's main trading partners are the USA, China, Argentina and Germany. Principal exports are transport equipment, iron ore, soya beans, footwear, coffee and vehicles. The main imports are machinery, electrical and transport equipment, chemical products, vehicle parts and electronics.
GNI – US$1,796bn; US$8,580 per capita (2017)

Annual average growth of GDP – 0.7 per cent (2017 est)
Inflation rate – 3.7 per cent (2017 est)
Population below poverty line – 3.7 per cent (2016 est)
Unemployment – 13.1 per cent (2017 est)
Total external debt – US$544.5bn (2017 est)
Imports – US$143,632m (2016)
Exports – US$185,280m (2016)

BALANCE OF PAYMENTS
Trade – US$41,648m surplus (2016)
Current Account – US$9,761m deficit (2017)

Trade with UK	2016	2017
Imports from UK	£1,886,968,853	£1,800,842,927
Exports to UK	£2,538,734,948	£2,385,981,721

COMMUNICATIONS

Airports – 698; international flights operate to the major cities
Waterways – In remote regions, transport is primarily by air or water, utilising the 50,000km of navigable waterways
Roadways and railways – 212,798km; the Trans-Amazonian Highway connects the Amazon region with the rest of the country, although it is mostly unpaved and often becomes impassable in the rainy season; 28,538km
Telecommunications – 41.8 million fixed lines and 244 million mobile subscriptions (2016); there were 122.8 million internet users in 2016
Internet code and IDD – br; 55 (from UK), 14/15/21/23/31 44 (to UK, varies depending on area and/or carrier)
Major broadcasters – Domestic conglomerates – most notably Globo – dominate the market and run television and radio networks, newspapers and subscription television stations
Press – There are six major daily newspapers, including *O Dia, O Correio Brazilinese* and *Jornal do Brasil*
WPFI score – 31,20 (48)

EDUCATION AND HEALTH

Public education is free at all levels, and is compulsory between the ages of seven and 14.
Literacy rate – 92.6 per cent (2015 est)
Gross enrolment ratio (percentage of relevant age group) – primary 115.3 per cent, secondary 99.7 per cent, tertiary 50.6 per cent (2015 est)
Health expenditure (per capita) – US$947 (2014)
Hospital beds (per 1,000 people) – 2.2 (2014)
Life expectancy (years) – 74 (2017 est)
Mortality rate – 6.7 (2017 est)
Birth rate – 14.1 (2017 est)
Infant mortality rate – 17.5 (2017 est)
HIV/AIDS adult prevalence – 0.6 per cent (2015 est)

BRUNEI

Negara Brunei Darussalam – Brunei Darussalam

Area – 5,765 sq. km
Capital – Bandar Seri Begawan; population, 241,000 (2011 est)
Major towns – Kampong Ayer, Kuala Belait, Seria, Tutong
Currency – Brunei dollar (B$) of 100 sen (fully interchangeable with Singapore currency)
Population – 443,593 rising at 1.57 per cent a year (2017 est); Malay (65.7 per cent), Chinese (10.3 per cent), indigenous (3.4 per cent) (2011 est)
Religion – Muslim 78.8 per cent (predominantly Sunni), Christian 8.7 per cent, Buddhist 7.8 per cent (2011 est); Islam is the state religion
Language – Malay (official), English, Chinese languages
Population density – 80 per sq. km (2016)
Urban population – 77.6 per cent (2018 est)
Median age (years) – 30.2 (2017 est)
National anthem – 'Allah Peliharakan Sultan' 'God Bless the Sultan'
National day – 23 February (date of independence from British protection, 1984)
Death penalty – Retained (no known use since 1957)
CPI score – 62 (32)
Military expenditure – US$347m (2017)

CLIMATE AND TERRAIN
The country lies on the north-west coast of the island of Borneo. It is surrounded and divided in two by the Malaysian state of Sarawak. The terrain is estimated to be around 70 per cent rainforest, with extensive mangrove swamps along the coastal plain. There are mountains on the border with Sarawak. Elevation extremes range from 1,850m (Bukit Pagon) to 0m (South China Sea). The climate is tropical, with high humidity, and an annual average daily temperature of 26.3°C.

HISTORY AND POLITICS
Formerly a powerful Muslim sultanate that controlled Borneo and parts of the Philippines, Brunei was reduced to its present size by the mid-19th century and came under British protection in 1889. It chose to remain a British dependency in 1963 rather than joining the Federation of Malaysia. Internally self-governing from 1959, Brunei gained full independence on 1 January 1984.
In 1962 the legislative election was annulled after it was won by a party that sought to remove the sultan; a state of emergency was declared and the sultan has ruled by decree ever since. A ministerial system of government was introduced in 1984. Some political liberalisation and modernisation has taken place since 2004, when the legislature was reconvened after 20 years. In April 2014 Brunei became the first East

Asian country to adopt sharia law despite widespread international condemnation.
Parts of the 1959 constitution have been suspended since the state of emergency began in 1962. Supreme executive authority is vested in the sultan, a hereditary monarch who presides over and is advised by a privy council, a religious council and the council of cabinet ministers. The legislative council was reconvened in 2004 with 21 members appointed by the sultan; it has passed constitutional amendments to increase its size to 36 members.

HM The Sultan of Brunei, Prime Minister, Defence, Finance, Foreign Affairs, HM Hassanal Bolkiah, GCB, *acceded* 5 October 1967, *crowned* 1 August 1968
Heir, Senior Minister in the Prime Minister's Office, HM Crown Prince Al-Muhtadee Billah

SELECTED GOVERNMENT MEMBERS *AS AT MAY 2018*
Energy, Mat Suny bin Haji Mohammad Yusof
Home Affairs, Abu Bakar bin Haji Apong

BRUNEI DARUSSALAM HIGH COMMISSION
19–20 Belgrave Square, London SW1X 8PG
T 020-7581 0521 **E** info@bdhcl.co.uk
High Commissioner, vacant

BRITISH HIGH COMMISSION
2.01, 2nd Floor, Block D, Kompleks Yayasan Sultan Haji Hassanal Bolkiah, Jalan Pretty, PO Box 2197, Brunei
T (+673) (2) 222 231 **E** ukinbrunei@fco.gov.uk
W www.gov.uk/government/world/brunei
High Commissioner, HE Richard Lindsay, *apptd* 2017

ECONOMY AND TRADE
The economy is based on the production of oil and natural gas and the income from overseas investments. Royalties and taxes from these operations form the bulk of government revenue and have enabled the construction of free health, education and welfare services; Brunei's GDP per capita is one of the highest in the world, however, oil and gas reserves, which make up 65 per cent of GDP, are declining and Brunei is now trying to diversify its economy, developing Islamic financial services and tourism. Trade has increased in the past few years following regional economic integration with the ASEAN economic community.
Agriculture accounts for 1.2 per cent of GDP, industry 56.5 per cent and services 42.3 per cent. The main trading partners are Japan, Singapore, Indonesia, China and Malaysia. Principal exports are crude oil and organic chemicals. The main imports are machinery and transport equipment, manufactured goods, food (over 80 per cent of domestic requirements are imported) and chemicals.
GNI – US$12.7bn; US$29,600 per capita (2017)
Annual average growth of GDP – –1.3 per cent (2017 est)
Inflation rate – –0.2 per cent (2017 est)
Unemployment – 6.9 per cent (2017 est)
Imports – US$3,235m (2015)
Exports – US$6,353m (2015)

BALANCE OF PAYMENTS
Trade – US$3,118m surplus (2015)
Current Account – US$2,020m surplus (2017)

Trade with UK	2016	2017
Imports from UK	£94,260,594	£64,343,513
Exports to UK	£43,757,741	£12,520,042

COMMUNICATIONS

Airports and waterways – There is one international airport; the largest port is at Muara and the 209km of internal waterways are navigable only by shallow craft
Roadways – 2,425km
Telecommunications – 74,213 fixed lines and 523,453 mobile subscriptions (2016); there were 306,000 internet users in 2016
Internet code and IDD – bn; 673 (from UK), 44 (to UK)
Major broadcasters – The only broadcast media organisation, Radio Television Brunei (RTB), is state-owned; it broadcasts in Malay and English
Press – Daily newspapers include the English-language *Borneo Bulletin* and *Brunei Times,* and Malay *Media Permata*
WPFI score – 51,48 (153)

EDUCATION AND HEALTH

All levels of education are free but not compulsory; most children receive a minimum of 12 years of schooling.
Literacy rate – 96 per cent (2015 est)
Gross enrolment ratio (percentage of relevant age group) – primary 106.6 per cent, secondary 93.4 per cent, tertiary 30.9 per cent (2016 est)
Health expenditure (per capita) – US$958 (2014)
Hospital beds (per 1,000 people) – 2.7 (2015)
Life expectancy (years) – 77.3 (2017 est)
Mortality rate – 3.6 (2017 est)
Birth rate – 17 (2017 est)
Infant mortality rate – 9.6 (2017 est)

BULGARIA

Republika Balgariya – Republic of Bulgaria

Area – 110,879 sq. km
Capital – Sofia; population, 1,272,000 (2018 est)
Major cities – Burgas, Plovdiv, Varna
Currency – Lev of 100 stotinki
Population – 7,101,510 falling at 0.61 per cent a year (2017 est); Bulgarian (76.9 per cent), Turkish (8 per cent), Roma (4.4 per cent) (2011)
Religion – Eastern Orthodox 59.4 per cent, Muslim 7.8 per cent (predominantly Sunni) (est)
Language – Bulgarian (official), Turkish, Romani
Population density – 66 per sq. km (2016)
Urban population – 75 per cent (2018 est)
Median age (years) – 42.7 (2017 est)
National anthem – 'Mila Rodino' 'Dear Motherland'
National day – 3 March (Liberation Day)
Death penalty – Abolished for all crimes (since 1998)
CPI score – 43 (71)
Military expenditure – US$867m (2017)

CLIMATE AND TERRAIN

The Balkan mountains cross the country from west to east, averaging 2,000m in height, and the Rhodope mountains in the south-west climb to almost 3,000m. Elevation extremes range from 2,925m (Musala) to 0m (Black Sea). The lowland plains of the north and south-east are in the basins of the main rivers: the Danube in the north, which forms much of the border with Romania, and the Maritsa, which divides the Balkan and Rhodope ranges. The climate is temperate, with cold, damp winters and hot, dry summers. Average temperatures in Sofia range from 0°C in January to 22.3°C in July.

POLITICS

Under the 1991 constitution, the president is directly elected for a five-year term, renewable once. The head of government is the prime minister, who is elected by the National Assembly, and is usually the leader of the largest party in the legislature. There is a unicameral National Assembly of 240 members who are directly elected for a four-year term.

Early legislative elections arranged for October 2014 saw eight parties win seats in an election with a turnout as low as 50 per cent. In November, former prime minister Boyko Borissov of the centre-right Citizens for European Development of Bulgaria (GERB) party formed a minority government in coalition with three other parties. However, Prime Minister Borissov resigned in December 2016 after voters rejected his party in presidential elections, when socialist candidate Rumen Radev was declared the victor. Nevertheless, the GERB emerged once again as the largest party in new legislative elections in March 2017.

HEAD OF STATE
President, Rumen Radev, *elected* 13 November 2016, *sworn in* 19 January 2017
Vice-President, Iliana Yotova

SELECTED GOVERNMENT MEMBERS *AS AT MAY 2018*
Prime Minister, Boyko Borissov
Deputy Prime Ministers, Tomislav Donchev; Ekaterina Gecheva-Zaharieva; Krasimir Karakachanov; Valeri Simeonov
Finance, Vladislav Goranov

EMBASSY OF THE REPUBLIC OF BULGARIA
186–188 Queen's Gate, London SW7 5HL
T 020-7584 9400 E info@bulgarianembassy.org.uk
W www.bulgarianembassy-london.org
Ambassador Extraordinary and Plenipotentiary, HE Konstantin Stefanov Dimitrov, *apptd* 2012

BRITISH EMBASSY
9 Moskovska Street, Sofia 1000
T (+359) (2) 933 9222 E britishembassysofia@fco.gov.uk
W www.gov.uk/government/world/bulgaria
Ambassador Extraordinary and Plenipotentiary, HE Emma Hopkins, *apptd* 2015

ECONOMY AND TRADE

The government adopted radical economic reforms in 1996 and the economy achieved stability and attracted significant foreign investment, although administrative corruption, a weak judiciary and organised crime remain potential deterrents. Despite EU entry in 2007, steady economic growth in 2004–8 and responsible fiscal management, the economy contracted in the global economic downturn as industrial production and exports declined. After a slow recovery, strong domestic demand, low energy imports and rising tourism have

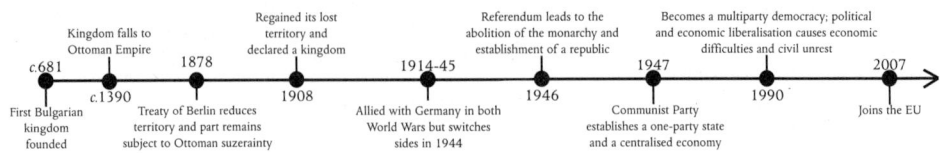

Kingdom falls to Ottoman Empire — c.681 — First Bulgarian kingdom founded — c.1390 — Treaty of Berlin reduces territory and part remains subject to Ottoman suzerainty — 1878 — Regained its lost territory and declared a kingdom — 1908 — 1914-45 — Allied with Germany in both World Wars but switches sides in 1944 — 1946 — Referendum leads to the abolition of the monarchy and establishment of a republic — 1947 — Communist Party establishes a one-party state and a centralised economy — 1990 — Becomes a multiparty democracy; political and economic liberalisation causes economic difficulties and civil unrest — 2007 — Joins the EU

boosted GDP growth to nearly 4 per cent annually in recent years.

Natural resources include copper, lead, zinc, other minerals, coal and timber. Fertile arable land produces vegetables, fruit, tobacco, wine, wheat, barley, sunflowers and livestock. Agriculture employs 6.8 per cent of the workforce and accounts for 4.3 per cent of GDP. Industries include energy generation, food processing, beverages, tobacco, machinery and equipment, base metals, chemicals, mining and oil refining.

The main trading partners are EU countries, Russia and Turkey. Principal exports are clothing and footwear, iron and steel, machinery and equipment, and fuels. The main imports are predominantly machinery and raw materials for the industrial sector.

GNI – US$54.9bn, US$7,760 per capita (2017)
Annual average growth of GDP – 3.6 per cent (2017 est)
Inflation rate – 1.1 per cent (2017 est)
Population below poverty line – 22 per cent (2015 est)
Unemployment – 6.6 per cent (2017 est)
Total external debt – US$36.51bn (2017 est)
Imports – US$28,792m (2015)
Exports – US$26,075m (2015)

BALANCE OF PAYMENTS
Trade – US$2,718m deficit (2016)
Current Account – US$2,628m surplus (2017)

Trade with UK	2016	2017
Imports from UK	£495,487,489	£455,466,796
Exports to UK	£411,505,848	£448,581,049

COMMUNICATIONS
Airports and waterways – 57, the main airports are at Sofia, Plovdiv, Burgas and Varna; the main ports are Burgas and Varna on the Black Sea, and there are 470km of waterways
Roadways and railways – 19,235km, including 458km of motorways; 4,152km
Telecommunications – 1.5 million fixed lines and 8.9 million mobile telephone subscriptions (2016); there were 4.3 million internet users in 2016
Internet code and IDD – bg; 359 (from UK), 44 (to UK)
Major broadcasters – Public service broadcasters Bulgarian National Radio and Bulgarian National Television share the radio and TV markets with a vigorous commercial sector that provides national and regional broadcasting
Press – Major daily newspapers include *Dnevnik*, *Trud* and *24 Chasa*
WPFI score – 35,22 (111)

EDUCATION AND HEALTH
Education is free and compulsory from seven to 16 years.
Literacy rate – 98.4 per cent (2015 est)
Gross enrolment ratio (percentage of relevant age group) – primary 94.8 per cent, secondary 99.9 per cent, tertiary 71.2 per cent (2016 est)
Health expenditure (per capita) – US$662 (2014)
Hospital beds (per 1,000 people) – 6.8 (2013)
Life expectancy (years) – 74.7 (2017 est)

Mortality rate – 14.5 (2017 est)
Birth rate – 8.7 (2017 est)
Infant mortality rate – 8.4 (2017 est)

BURKINA FASO

Area – 274,200 sq. km
Capital – Ouagadougou; population, 2,531,000 (2018 est)
Major city – Bobo-Dioulasso
Currency – Franc CFA of 100 centimes
Population – 20,107,509 rising at 3.0 per cent a year (2017 est); 63 ethnic groups, of which Mossi (52.5 per cent) (2010 est) is the largest
Religion – Muslim 61.6 per cent (predominantly Sunni), Christian (Roman Catholic 23.2 per cent, Protestant denominations 6.7 per cent) (2010 est)
Language – French (official), various African languages (spoken by 90 per cent of the population)
Population density – 68 per sq. km (2016)
Urban population – 31.5 per cent (2017 est)
Median age (years) – 17.3 (2017 est)
National anthem – 'Ditanye' 'Anthem of Victory'
National day – 11 December (Republic Day)
Death penalty – Retained (not used since 1988)
CPI score – 42 (74)
Military expenditure – US$191m (2017)

CLIMATE AND TERRAIN
The landlocked state occupies a plateau dissected by the White, Black and Red Volta rivers. There are tropical savannahs in the south and the north is semi-desert. Elevation extremes range from 749m (Tena Kourou) to 200m (Mouhoun, or Black Volta, river). The climate is tropical, with a wet season from May to September; there are recurring droughts. Average temperatures range from 25.2°C in January to 32.7°C in April.

HISTORY AND POLITICS
Burkina Faso (Upper Volta until 1983) was part of the Mossi Empire in the 18th and 19th centuries. It was administered as part of other French colonies between 1932 and 1947, and in 1958 it became autonomous within the French Community; independence was achieved on 5 August 1960.

In the three decades after independence there was a succession of military regimes; the last military coup, in 1987, brought to power Captain Blaise Compaoré. Military rule ended in 1991 when a new constitution was adopted and multiparty elections were held in 1992. Despite the constitutional restriction on the number of terms that a president may serve, President Compaoré was re-elected for a fourth term in 2010. In January 2014, protests took place across the country after President Compaoré announced that he would look to alter the constitution in order to stand in the 2015 elections. In October, demonstrators stormed the presidential palace, causing the president to resign and flee to the Côte d'Ivoire after 27 years in power. In simultaneous presidential and legislative elections in November 2015, Roch Marc Kaboré was elected president and his People's Movement for Progress (MPP) won 55 seats. In October 2016 it was reported that a coup by forces loyal to Compaoré had been thwarted. In recent years the government has been battling Islamist extremists in the Sahel region.

The 1991 constitution was amended in 2000 to reduce the presidential term from seven years. The president is directly elected for a five-year term, renewable once. The unicameral National Assembly has 127 members who are directly elected for a five-year term. Executive power is vested jointly in the president and the council of ministers, both responsible to the legislature.

HEAD OF STATE
President, Roch Marc Christian Kaboré, *elected* 29 November 2015, *sworn in* 29 December 2015

SELECTED GOVERNMENT MEMBERS *AS AT MAY 2018*
Prime Minister, Paul Kaba Thiéba
Economy and Finance, Hadizatou Rosine Coulibaly
Foreign Affairs, Alpha Barry

EMBASSY OF THE REPUBLIC OF BURKINA FASO
16 Place Guy d'Arezzo, 1180 Brussels, Belgium
T (00) (+32) (2) 345 9912 E ambassade.burkina@skynet.be
W www.ambassadeduburkina.be
Ambassador Extraordinary and Plenipotentiary, vacant

BRITISH AMBASSADOR
Ambassador Extraordinary and Plenipotentiary, HE Iain Walker, *apptd* 2017, resident in Accra, Ghana

ECONOMY AND TRADE
The country is one of the poorest in the world, with around 90 per cent of the population engaged in subsistence agriculture and animal husbandry, which are vulnerable to periodic droughts. The economy is heavily dependent on cotton and gold exports and therefore also exposed to the vagaries of global price fluctuations. Civil war in neighbouring Côte d'Ivoire harmed trade by cutting off transport routes, and caused many expatriate Burkinabes to return home, adding to the unemployment problem and depriving the economy of their remittances. During 2013, unrest in Mali caused similar problems and a number of public protests were held about socio-economic issues; the government reduced income taxes and price controls to alleviate discontent. Despite these difficulties, the economy continued to grow rapidly, achieving growth of 6 per cent in 2013–15, although a major terror attack in January 2016 by al-Qaida on Ouagadougou's Splendid Hotel raised security fears. Major infrastructure projects begun in 2014 include road building and the construction of a new airport in Ouagadougou, while a three-year IMF programme agreed in 2018 will also facilitate increased public investment.

Agriculture contributes 31.9 per cent of GDP; the main product apart from cotton is livestock. Although there are few natural resources, a growing quantity of gold is mined and exploration for other minerals has begun. The processing of cotton and other agricultural products, gold mining and the manufacturing of beverages, soap, cigarettes and textiles are the main industries, contributing 22 per cent to GDP. Services account for 46.1 per cent of GDP.

The main export markets are Switzerland and India. Principal exports are cotton, livestock and gold. The chief import providers are China, Côte d'Ivoire and the USA, supplying capital goods, foodstuffs and fuel.

GNI – US$11.7bn; US$610 per capita (2017)
Annual average growth of GDP – 6.4 per cent (2017 est)
Inflation rate – 1.5 per cent (2017 est)
Population below poverty line – 40.1 per cent (2009 est)
Total external debt – US$3.075bn (2017 est)
Imports – US$2,976m (2015)
Exports – US$2,177m (2015)

BALANCE OF PAYMENTS
Trade – US$799m deficit (2015)
Current Account – US$779m deficit (2014)

Trade with UK	2016	2017
Imports from UK	£9,052,437	£10,056,551
Exports to UK	£1,617,944	£4,104,438

COMMUNICATIONS
Airports – Two; the main international airport is at Ouagadougou
Roadways and railways – 15,272km; 622km
Telecommunications – 75,727 fixed lines and 5.3 million mobile subscriptions (2016); there were 574,236 internet users in 2016
Internet code and IDD – bf; 226 (to UK), 44 (from UK)
Major broadcasters – Radio is the most popular medium with the state-run Radio Burkina the largest broadcaster; state-run Television Nationale du Burkina is one of the largest television broadcasters
Press – There are five daily national newspapers, including the government-run *Sidwaya*, *L'Observateur Paalga* and *Le Pays*
WPFI score – 23,33 (41)

EDUCATION AND HEALTH
Education is nominally compulsory from ages six to 16 but the prohibitive cost of school supplies and a lack of resources prevent many children from attending.
Literacy rate – 36 per cent (2015)
Gross enrolment ratio (percentage of relevant age group) – primary 91.1 per cent, secondary 35.8 per cent, tertiary 5.6 per cent (2016 est)
Health expenditure (per capita) – US$35 (2014)
Hospital beds (per 1,000 people) – 0.4 (2010)
Life expectancy (years) – 55.9 (2017 est)
Mortality rate – 11.2 (2017 est)
Birth rate – 41.2 (2017 est)
Infant mortality rate – 72.2 (2017 est)
HIV/AIDS adult prevalence – 0.8 per cent (2015 est)

BURUNDI

Republika y'u Burundi/République du Burundi – Republic of Burundi

Area – 27,830 sq. km
Capital – Bujumbura; population, 899,000 (2018 est)
Major towns – Bubanza, Gitega, Muyinga, Ngozi, Ruyigi
Currency – Burundi franc (FBu) of 100 centimes
Population – 11,466,756 rising at 3.25 per cent a year (2017 est); Hutu (85 per cent), Tutsi (14 per cent), Twa (1 per cent) (est)
Religion – Christian (Roman Catholic 62.1 per cent, Protestant denominations 23.9 per cent), Muslim 2.5 per cent (2008 est)
Language – Kirundi, French (both official), Swahili, English
Population density – 410 per sq. km (2016)
Urban population – 12.7 per cent (2017 est)
Median age (years) – 17 (2017 est)
National anthem – 'Burundi Bwacu' 'Our Burundi'
National day – 1 July (Independence Day)
Death penalty – Abolished for all crimes (since 2009)
CPI score – 22 (157)
Military expenditure – US$66.5m (2016)
Literacy rate – 85.6 per cent (2015 est)
Gross enrolment ratio (percentage of relevant age group) – primary 130.9 per cent, secondary 48.4 per cent, tertiary 5.6 per cent (2016 est)
Health expenditure (per capita) – US$22 (2014)
Hospital beds (per 1,000 people) – 0.8 (2014)
Life expectancy (years) – 60.9 (2017 est)
Mortality rate – 8.8 (2017 est)
Birth rate – 41.3 (2017 est)
Infant mortality rate – 58.8 (2017 est)
HIV/AIDS adult prevalence – 1 per cent (2015 est)

CLIMATE AND TERRAIN

Burundi lies across the Nile–Congo watershed in central Africa. A hilly interior rises from an average altitude of 1,700m to the country's highest point at 2,670m (Heha) and falls to a plateau in the east. The river Ruzizi forms part of the north-western border with the Democratic Republic of the Congo, along with Lake Tanganyika (the lowest elevation in the country at 772m) in the south-west. The climate is equatorial, moderated by altitude; the average temperature in the lower regions is 29°C, and in the higher regions is 20°C.

There are two rainy seasons: February to April and October to December.

POLITICS

Under the 2005 constitution, amended following a referendum in 2018, the executive president is directly elected for a seven-year term, renewable once. The bicameral *Parlement* comprises the National Assembly and the senate; members of both serve a five-year term. The National Assembly has 100 directly elected members, three co-opted members from the Twa ethnic group, and up to 21 members (currently 15) co-opted to ensure a 60 per cent Hutu and 40 per cent Tutsi split and that 30 per cent of the total are women. The senate has 43 members: 36 indirectly elected by an electoral college of provincial councils; three co-opted Twa members; four former presidents; and enough women to make the number of women senators up to 30 per cent of the total. The constitution also specifies the proportion of Hutu, Tutsi and female members of the council of ministers.

Pierre Nkurunziza of the National Council for the Defence of Democracy-Forces for the Defence of Democracy (CNDD-FDD), a Hutu party, was elected president by the newly elected legislature in 2005 and by direct presidential elections in June 2010 and July 2015. The CNDD-FDD retained large majorities in both houses following the 2015 legislative elections; both polls were boycotted by a number of opposition groups.

In May 2015, Burundi's constitutional court ruled that President Nkurunziza could stand for a third term of office, notwithstanding the constitution limiting incumbents to two terms. The decision sparked protests across Burundi, which killed dozens of people and caused over 150,000 to flee to neighbouring states. The 2018 referendum extended presidential terms from five to seven years and allowed him to stand for re-election again, potentially staying in power until 2034, despite having already served three terms.

HEAD OF STATE
President, Pierre Nkurunziza, *sworn in* 26 August 2005, *re-elected* 2010, 2015

First Vice-President, Gaston Sindimwo
Second Vice-President, Joseph Butore

SELECTED GOVERNMENT MEMBERS *AS AT JUNE 2018*
Defence, Emmanuel Ntahonvukiye
Finance, Domitien Ndihokubwayo
Interior, Pascal Barandagiye

EMBASSY OF THE REPUBLIC OF BURUNDI
Uganda House, 2nd Floor, 58–59 Trafalgar Square, London WC2N 5DX
T 020-7930 4958 E info@burundiembassy.org.uk
W www.burundiembassy.org.uk
Ambassador Extraordinary and Plenipotentiary, HE Ernest Ndabashinze, *apptd* 2017

BRITISH AMBASSADOR
HE Joanne Lomas, *apptd* 2018, resident at Kigali, Rwanda

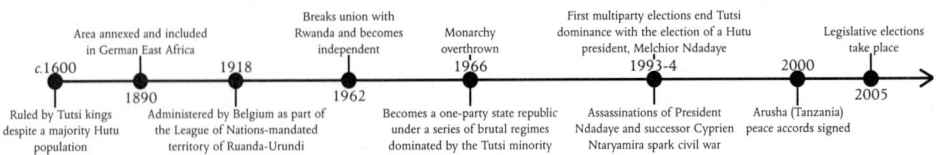

ECONOMY AND TRADE

Economic activity has increased since the civil war ended, but reform and reconstruction are hampered by a lack of administrative capacity, a poorly educated workforce, corruption and poor law enforcement. Agriculture is the mainstay of the economy, contributing 40 per cent of GDP. Subsistence agriculture has contracted recently owing to continued insecurity, population growth and soil erosion. Exports of coffee and tea account for over half of foreign exchange earnings, leaving the economy vulnerable to the effects of global price fluctuations and weather conditions. Industry is relatively small-scale and employs around 2.3 per cent of the workforce but contributes 16 per cent of GDP. The main activities are light manufacturing, food processing, the assembly of imported components and public sector construction. Since 2013 there has been major investment in infrastructure projects, but economic growth was dented by political turmoil in 2015–16 that led to a violent government clampdown. The nation is heavily reliant upon foreign aid, which constituted over one third of national income in 2016.

Most trade is with India, China, Switzerland and Kenya, but it is constrained by the poor transport infrastructure and landlocked location. The main exports are coffee, tea, sugar, cotton and hides. The principal imports are capital goods, petroleum products and food.

GNI – US$3.1bn; US$290 per capita (2017)
Annual average growth of GDP – 0.0 per cent (2017 est)
Inflation rate – 18.0 per cent (2017 est)
Population below poverty line – 64.6 per cent (2014 est)
Total external debt – US$619.8m (2017 est)
Imports – US$734m (2016)
Exports – US$111m (2016)

BALANCE OF PAYMENTS

Trade – US$623m deficit (2016)
Current Account – US$354m deficit (2016)

Trade with UK	2016	2017
Imports from UK	£2,043,070	£2,846,918
Exports to UK	£644,597	£341,849

COMMUNICATIONS

Airports and waterways – Bujumbura has the only airport with a surfaced runway and the only port, while movement around Lake Tanganyika is by water
Roadways – A limited road network, of which only 1,286km is paved, is concentrated around Bujumbura
Railways – There are no railways at present but the East African railways master plan, a project designed to expand the rail network in this region of Africa, is in its planning stage
Telecommunications – 19,540 fixed lines and 5.3 million mobile subscriptions (2016); there were 574,236 internet users in 2016
Internet code and IDD – bi; 257 (from UK), 44 (to UK)
Major broadcasters – The government-controlled Radio Télévision Nationale du Burundi (RTNB) runs the main national television and radio stations
Press – The only regularly published newspaper is the government-owned *Le Renouveau*
WPFI score – 55,26 (159)

CABO VERDE

Republica de Cabo Verde – Republic of Cabo Verde

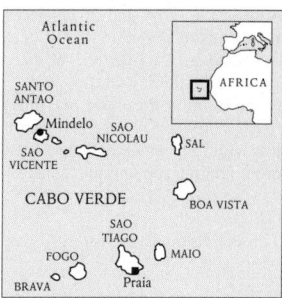

Area – 4,033 sq. km; comprises the Windward Islands (Boa Vista, Sal, Santa Luzia, Santa Antao, Sao Nicolau, Sao Vicente) and Leeward Islands (Brava, Fogo, Maio and Sao Tiago)
Capital – Praia, on Sao Tiago; population, 168,000 (2018 est)
Major town – Mindelo
Currency – Escudo Caboverdiano ($) of 100 centavos
Population – 560,899 rising at 1.33 per cent a year (2017 est)
Religion – Christian (Roman Catholic 77.3 per cent, Protestant 4.6 per cent), Muslim 1.8 per cent (2010 est)
Language – Portuguese (official), Creole
Population density – 134 per sq. km (2016)
Urban population – 66.8 per cent (2017 est)
Median age (years) – 25.4 (2017 est)
National anthem – 'Cantico da Liberdade' 'Song of Freedom'
National day – 5 July (Independence Day)
Death penalty – Abolished for all crimes (since 1981)
CPI score – 55 (48)
Military expenditure – US$9.4m (2017)
Conscription – 18–35 years of age; 24 months (selective)
Literacy rate – 86.8 per cent (2016 est)
Gross enrolment ratio (percentage of relevant age group) – primary 96.7 per cent, secondary 84.6 per cent, tertiary 21.7 per cent (2016 est)
Health expenditure (per capita) – US$173 (2014)
Life expectancy (years) – 72.4 (2017 est)
Mortality rate – 6 (2017 est)
Birth rate – 20 (2017 est)
Infant mortality rate – 21.9 (2017 est)
HIV/AIDS adult prevalence – 1 per cent (2015 est)

CLIMATE AND TERRAIN

The archipelago of ten islands of volcanic origin lies 600km off the west African coast. Elevation extremes range from 2,829m (Mt Fogo, an active volcano on Fogo island) to 0m (Atlantic Ocean). The climate is hot and dry, with periodic droughts.

HISTORY AND POLITICS

The islands were first discovered and colonised *c*.1460 by Portugal. Administered with Portuguese Guinea until 1879, they became an overseas province in 1951. The country achieved independence on 5 July 1975 after a campaign by the African Party for the Independence of Guinea Bissau and Cape Verde (PAIGC).

The republic was a one-party state under the African Party for the Independence of Cape Verde (PAICV) until 1990.

Multiparty elections in 1991 were won by the opposition Movement for Democracy (MPD), but 2001 legislative elections returned the PAICV to power and the party retained its overall majority in the 2006 and 2011 elections. MPD leader Jorge Fonseca was re-elected in the 2016 presidential election, and the MPD won 54.5 per cent of the vote in the March 2016 legislative elections.

Under the 1992 constitution, the president is directly elected for a five-year term, renewable once. There is a unicameral National Assembly with 72 members directly elected for a five-year term. The prime minister appoints the council of ministers.

HEAD OF STATE
President, Jorge Fonseca, *elected* 21 August 2011, *re-elected* 2 October 2016

SELECTED GOVERNMENT MEMBERS *AS AT MAY 2018*
Prime Minister, Ulisses Correia e Silva
Defence, Foreign Affairs, Luis Filipe Tavares
Finance, Olavo Correia
Internal Affairs, Paulo Costa Rocha

EMBASSY OF THE REPUBLIC OF CABO VERDE
Avenue Jeanne 29, 1050 Brussels, Belgium
T (+32) (2) 643 6270
Ambassador Extraordinary and Plenipotentiary, HE José Filomeno Monteiro, *apptd* 2016

BRITISH AMBASSADOR
HE Kirsty Hayes, *apptd* 2014, resident at Lisbon, Portugal

ECONOMY AND TRADE
The islands have few natural resources, little fresh water and are subject to periods of prolonged drought. A well-managed economy has produced steady growth nevertheless, and further reforms are intended to attract foreign investment to aid diversification and development of the private sector. The government is dependent on foreign aid and remittances; owing to large-scale emigration the expatriate population is larger than the resident one, and remittances are equivalent to around 10 per cent of GDP. The service sector dominates, with commerce, tourism, transport and public services accounting for 74.2 per cent of GDP. Industry contributes 17.9 per cent and agriculture 7.9 per cent; fishing resources are not fully exploited. The main industries are the production of food, beverages, garments and footwear, fishing and fish processing, salt mining and ship repair.

The main trading partners are Portugal, Spain and the Netherlands. Exports are fuel, footwear, garments, fish and hides. Imports include foodstuffs (over 80 per cent of food is imported), industrial products, transport equipment and fuel.
GNI – US$1.6bn; US$2,990 per capita (2017)
Annual average growth of GDP – 4.0 per cent (2017 est)
Inflation rate – 1.0 per cent (2017 est)
Population below poverty line – 30 per cent (2000 est)
Total external debt – US$1.808bn (2017 est)
Unemployment – 9 per cent (2017 est)
Imports – US$563m (2015)
Exports – US$58m (2015)

BALANCE OF PAYMENTS
Trade – US$505m deficit (2015)
Current Account – US$120m deficit (2017)

Trade with UK	2016	2017
Imports from UK	£3,868,209	£2,075,067
Exports to UK	£49,341	£170,152

COMMUNICATIONS
Airports and waterways – Nine, including airports at Praia and on Sal; the main ports are Praia and Mindelo
Roadways – 932km
Telecommunications – 64,724 fixed lines and 601,956 mobile subscriptions (2016); there were 266,562 internet users in 2016
Internet code and IDD – cv; 238 (from UK), 44 (to UK)
Major broadcasters – Radio and television services are operated by the state-run Radiotelevisao Caboverdiana
WPFI score – 20,39 (29)

CAMBODIA

Preahreacheanachakr Kampuchea – Kingdom of Cambodia

Area – 181,035 sq. km
Capital – Phnom Penh; population, 1,952,000 (2018 est)
Major towns – Battambang, Poipet, Siem Reap, Sihanoukville
Currency – Riel of 100 sen; the US dollar is widely used
Population – 16,204,486 rising at 1.52 per cent a year (2017 est); Khmer (97.6 per cent), Cham (1.2 per cent) (2013 est)
Religion – Buddhist (Theravada) 96.9 per cent, Muslim 1.9 per cent (predominantly Sunni) (2008 est)
Language – Khmer (official)
Population density – 89 per sq. km (2016)
Urban population – 21.2 per cent (2017 est)
Median age (years) – 25.3 (2017 est)
National anthem – 'Nokoreach' 'Royal Kingdom'
National day – 9 November (Independence Day)
Death penalty – Abolished for all crimes (since 1989)
CPI score – 21 (161)
Military expenditure – US$370m (2016)
Literacy rate – 77.2 per cent (2015 est)
Gross enrolment ratio (percentage of relevant age group) – primary 110.2 per cent (2016 est); secondary 34 per cent (2011 est); tertiary 13.1 per cent (2015 est)
Health expenditure (per capita) – US$61 (2014)
Hospital beds (per 1,000 people) – 0.8 (2015)
Life expectancy (years) – 64.9 (2017 est)
Mortality rate – 7.5 (2017 est)
Birth rate – 23 (2017 est)
Infant mortality rate – 47.4 (2017 est)
HIV/AIDS adult prevalence – 0.6 per cent (2015 est)

CLIMATE AND TERRAIN
Cambodia is a mostly flat country, apart from the Cardamom mountains in the south-west and the uplands of the north-east. The fertile central plains are drained by rivers that run into Tonle Sap, the largest lake in South East Asia, and into the Mekong river, which flows through the country from north to south. The highest point of elevation is 1,810m (Phnum Aoral) while the lowest is 0m (Gulf of Thailand). The

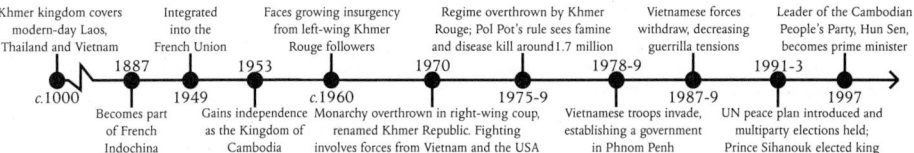

Khmer kingdom covers modern-day Laos, Thailand and Vietnam	Integrated into the French Union	Faces growing insurgency from left-wing Khmer Rouge followers	Regime overthrown by Khmer Rouge; Pol Pot's rule sees famine and disease kill around 1.7 million	Vietnamese forces withdraw, decreasing guerrilla tensions	Leader of the Cambodian People's Party, Hun Sen, becomes prime minister	
*c.*1000	1887	1949	1953	*c.*1960	1970	1975–9	1978–9	1987–9	1991–3	1997
	Becomes part of French Indochina	Gains independence as the Kingdom of Cambodia	Monarchy overthrown in right-wing coup, renamed Khmer Republic. Fighting involves forces from Vietnam and the USA	Vietnamese troops invade, establishing a government in Phnom Penh	UN peace plan introduced and multiparty elections held; Prince Sihanouk elected king	

climate is tropical, with a monsoon season from May to November.

POLITICS

Under the 1993 constitution, Cambodia is a pluralist liberal democracy with a constitutional monarchy. The monarch is chosen from eligible royal males by a Council of the Throne elected by parliament. Executive power rests with the government, which is responsible to parliament. The bicameral parliament comprises the National Assembly, which has 125 members directly elected for a five-year term, and the senate, which has 62 members, 58 of whom are elected for a six-year term by the National Assembly and commune councils, with two members appointed by the king and two appointed by the National Assembly.

King Sihanouk abdicated in 2004 and was succeeded by his son, Prince Norodom Sihamoni. In the 2013 election the Cambodian People's Party (CPP) won 68 seats in the National Assembly – losing the large majority that, in the 2008 elections, had allowed them to form a government without a coalition for the first time. In the 2018 elections, the CPP overwhelmingly extended their mandate, claiming 114 seats amid a crackdown on the press and suppression of the leading opposition party. Long-serving Prime Minister Hun Sen (CPP) was subsequently sworn in for a further five-year term, having ruled since 1985.

HEAD OF STATE

HM The King of Cambodia, Norodom Sihamoni, *crowned* 29 October 2004
President of the National Assembly, Heng Samrin

SELECTED GOVERNMENT MEMBERS *AS AT AUGUST 2018*

Prime Minister, Hun Sen
Deputy Prime Ministers, Gen. Tea Banh *(Defence);* Sar Kheng *(Interior);* Men Sam An; Yim Chhai Ly; Bin Chhin; Hor Namhong; Ke Kim Yan

ROYAL EMBASSY OF CAMBODIA

64 Brondesbury Park, London NW6 7AT
T 020-8451 7997 E cambodianembassy@btconnect.com
W www.cambodianembassy.org.uk
Ambassador Extraordinary and Plenipotentiary, HE Soeung Rathchavy, *apptd* 2017

BRITISH EMBASSY

27–29 Street 75, Sangat Srah Chak, Khan Daun Penh, Phnom Penh 12201
T (+855) (0) 23 427 124
W www.gov.uk/government/world/cambodia
Ambassador Extraordinary and Plenipotentiary, HE Tina Redshaw, *apptd* 2018

SECURITY PROBLEMS

The Khmer Rouge continued to fight a guerrilla war until 1996, when it was weakened by internal divisions. Pol Pot was tried by the Khmer Rouge in 1997 and died in captivity in 1998. The remaining Khmer Rouge soldiers surrendered in 1999. A UN-backed tribunal was established in 2007 to try former leaders of the Khmer Rouge regime for atrocities committed during its rule.

Relations with Thailand deteriorated after 2008 because of a long-running dispute over the border in the area of the Preah Vihear temple, with sporadic exchanges of fire and occasional fighting between the two countries' forces. In November 2013 the International Court of Justice ruled that Thailand must withdraw its troops from the temple and granted most of the territory to Cambodia.

ECONOMY AND TRADE

Since 1999 the government has made progress with economic reform and development but the country remains very poor. The demographic imbalance (over half the population is around 25), lack of education and skills, deeply ingrained corruption and an absence of basic infrastructure also pose serious problems. Nevertheless, the economy grew at an average rate of 8 per cent between 2000 and 2010, and around 7 per cent since 2011. Economic growth has been driven by the expansion of garment manufacturing, construction, agriculture, tourism (visitors have more than doubled in the past decade) and mining, which is attracting foreign investment, but the benefits are largely limited to urban areas. The discovery of oil and gas deposits in territorial waters promises additional revenue once exploitation begins. Around 180,000 migrants returned from Thailand in 2014, following fears that they would be persecuted by Thailand's military government.

The service sector contributes 41.9 per cent of GDP, agriculture 25.3 per cent and industry 32.8 per cent. Agriculture engages 48.7 per cent of the workforce; the main crops are rice, rubber, maize, vegetables, cashew nuts and tapioca. The main industrial activities are tourism, garment and textiles manufacturing, processing of agricultural and forestry products, fishing and mining gemstones. The main trading partners are the USA (21.5 per cent of exports), China (34.1 per cent of imports), the UK, Singapore and Thailand.
GNI – US$19.7bn; US$1,230 per capita (2017)
Annual average growth of GDP – 6.9 per cent (2017 est)
Inflation rate – 3.7 per cent (2017 est)
Population below poverty line – 17.7 per cent (2012 est)
Unemployment – 0.3 per cent (2017 est)
Total external debt – US$11.34bn (2017 est)
Imports – US$14,400m (2015)
Exports – US$11,960m (2015)

BALANCE OF PAYMENTS

Trade – US$2,440m deficit (2015)
Current Account – US$1,775m deficit (2016)

Trade with UK	2016	2017
Imports from UK	£17,370,220	£36,870,865
Exports to UK	£851,329,351	£894,342,958

COMMUNICATIONS
Airports – Six; the main airports are at Phnom Penh, Siem Reap and Sihanoukville
Waterways – There are 3,700km of navigable waterways, mostly on the Mekong river, and ships of up to 2,500 tonnes can sail as far as Phnom Penh all year round
Roadways and railways – 2,492km; 690km
Telecommunications – 227,261 fixed lines and 19.9 million mobile phone subscriptions (2016); there were 4 million internet users in 2016
Internet code and IDD – kh; 855 (from UK), 1 44 (to UK)
Major broadcasters – There are 11 TV broadcasters, including the government-run National Television of Cambodia (TVK); there are roughly 160 radio broadcasters
Press – Daily newspapers include the pro-government *Reaksmei Kampuchea* (Khmer), and the English-language *Cambodia Daily* and *Phnom Penh Post*
WPFI score – 45,90 (142)

CAMEROON

République du Cameroun – Republic of Cameroon

Area – 475,440 sq. km
Capital – Yaoundé; population, 3,412,000 (2018 est)
Major cities – Bafoussam, Bamenda, Douala, Garoua
Currency – Franc CFA of 100 centimes
Population – 24,994,885 rising at 2.56 per cent a year (2017 est); Cameroon Highlanders (31 per cent), Equatorial Bantu (19 per cent), Kirdi (11 per cent), Fulani (10 per cent), Northwestern Bantu (8 per cent), Eastern Nigritic (7 per cent) (est)
Religion – Christian 69.2 per cent (Roman Catholic 38.4 per cent, Protestant 26.3 per cent, other Christian 4.5 per cent), Muslim 20.9 per cent, indigenous beliefs 5.6 per cent (2005 est)
Language – English, French (both official), about 24 African languages
Population density – 50 per sq. km (2016)
Urban population – 55.5 per cent (2017 est)
Median age (years) – 18.5 (2017 est)
National anthem – 'O Cameroun, Berceau de nos Ancetres' 'O Cameroon, Cradle of Our Forefathers'
National day – 20 May (Republic Day)
Death penalty – Retained (last used 1997)
CPI score – 25 (153)
Military expenditure – US$408m (2017)
Literacy rate – 75 per cent (2015 est)
Gross enrolment ratio (percentage of relevant age group) – primary 119.2 per cent, secondary 61.8 per cent (2016 est), tertiary 17.5 per cent (2015 est)
Health expenditure (per capita) – US$59 (2014)
Hospital beds (per 1,000 people) – 1.3 (2010)
Life expectancy (years) – 59 (2017 est)

Mortality rate – 9.6 (2017 est)
Birth rate – 35.4 (2017 est)
Infant mortality rate – 51 (2017 est)
HIV/AIDS adult prevalence – 4.5 per cent (2015 est)

CLIMATE AND TERRAIN
There are three main geographic zones: desert plains and savannah in the north (the Lake Chad basin), mountains and plateaux in the central region and tropical rainforests in the south and east. Elevation extremes range from 4,095m (Fako on Mt Cameroon, an active volcano) to 0m (Atlantic Ocean). The climate varies from tropical in the south to arid in the north. There is a wet season from April to September in the north, while there is low rain from March to June and heavy rain from September to November in the south.

POLITICS
The 1972 constitution was amended in 1990 to enable a return to multiparty rule, in 1996 to extend the presidential term and to provide for the establishment of a second legislative chamber (not implemented until 2013), and in 2008 to remove the limit on the number of presidential terms.
The president is directly elected for a seven-year term and appoints the prime minister and cabinet. The bicameral Parliament consists of the National Assembly (lower house) with 180 directly-elected members, and the Senate with 100 members, 70 indirectly elected by regional councils and 30 appointed by the president. All members serve five-year terms.
In the 2013 election, the Cameroon People's Democratic Movement (RDPC) retained its overwhelming majority in the National Assembly, winning 148 of the available 180 seats. The RDPC also won 63 of the 70 seats available in the Senate in the 2018 elections. Incumbent president Paul Biya retained the presidency in 2011, picking up 78 per cent of the vote.
Cameroon has experienced an increasing number of cross-border raids by the Nigeria-based Islamist group Boko Haram since 2014. In response, a multinational task force consisting of troops from Cameroon and Chad has carried out attacks on Boko Haram bases in northern Nigeria. Separatist campaigns in the anglophone Southwest region in 2016–7 were violently repressed, killing dozens of peaceful protesters.

HEAD OF STATE
President, Paul Biya, *took power* 6 November 1982, *elected* 14 January 1984, *re-elected* 1988, 1992, 1997, 2004, 2011

SELECTED GOVERNMENT MEMBERS *AS AT MAY 2018*
Prime Minister, Philemon Yang
Deputy Prime Minister, Amadou Ali
Economy, Alamine Ousmane Mey
External Relations, Lejeune Mbella Mbella

HIGH COMMISSION FOR THE REPUBLIC OF CAMEROON
84 Holland Park, London W11 3SB
T 020-7727 0771 **E** info@cameroonhighcommission.co.uk
W www.cameroonhighcommission.co.uk
High Commissioner, vacant

BRITISH HIGH COMMISSION
PO Box 547, Avenue Winston Churchill, Yaoundé, Centre Region 547
T (+237) 2222 0796 **E** bhc.yaounde@fco.gov.uk
W www.gov.uk/government/world/cameroon
High Commissioner, HE Rowan Laxton, *apptd* 2017

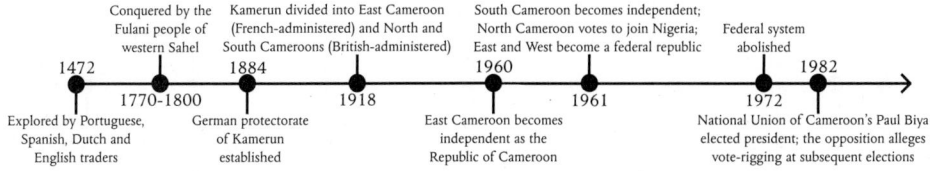

	Conquered by the Fulani people of western Sahel	Kamerun divided into East Cameroon (French-administered) and North and South Cameroons (British-administered)	South Cameroon becomes independent; North Cameroon votes to join Nigeria; East and West become a federal republic	Federal system abolished		
1472	1884	1960	1982
1770-1800	1918	1961	1972
Explored by Portuguese, Spanish, Dutch and English traders	German protectorate of Kamerun established	East Cameroon becomes independent as the Republic of Cameroon	National Union of Cameroon's Paul Biya elected president; the opposition alleges vote-rigging at subsequent elections

ECONOMY AND TRADE
Political stability and natural resources such as oil and timber have enabled agricultural, industrial and infrastructure development. Coupled with the growth of domestic demand and implementation of large-scale infrastructure projects, this has helped to counteract the effects of the global downturn. Cameroon also has a large and top-heavy public sector and endemic corruption, and recent IMF funding and debt relief have been conditional on progress towards privatisation and greater financial transparency. The emergence of Boko Haram in Nigeria presents a long-term threat to tourist revenue and international investment.

Industry contributes 28 per cent to GDP, agriculture 23.1 per cent and services 48.9 per cent. Around 70 per cent of the workforce is engaged in agriculture. The main industrial activity is oil production and refining. Revenue is also earned from the oil pipeline passing through the country from Chad. Despite starting several large-scale energy projects, Cameroon struggles to appeal to foreign investors due to the structure of its public sector and corruption.

The main trading partners are EU countries, China and Thailand. Principal exports are crude oil and petroleum products, timber, cocoa, aluminium, coffee and cotton. Imports are chiefly machinery, electrical and transport equipment, fuel and food.
GNI – US$32.7bn; US$1,360 per capita (2017)
Annual average growth of GDP – 4.0 per cent (2017 est)
Inflation rate – 0.7 per cent (2017 est)
Population below poverty line – 30 per cent (2001 est)
Total external debt – US$8.238bn (2017 est)
Imports – US$6,661m (2016)
Exports – US$3,670m (2016)

BALANCE OF PAYMENTS
Trade – US$2,901m deficit (2016)
Current Account – US$1,037m deficit (2016)

Trade with UK	2016	2017
Imports from UK	£42,201,321	£43,256,305
Exports to UK	£68,364,238	£53,310,596

COMMUNICATIONS
Airports – 11; the main airports are at Douala, Garoua and Yaoundé
Waterways – The main seaports are at Douala and the Limboh terminal; the river Benue is navigable up to Garoua in the rainy season
Roadways and railways – 4,108km; 1,245km
Telecommunications – There are 1.05 million fixed lines and 18.7 million mobile subscriptions (2016); there were 6.1 million internet users in 2016
Internet code and IDD – cm; 237 (from UK), 44 (to UK)
Major broadcasters – The state-run Cameroon Radio-Television Corporation (CRTV) held a monopoly on broadcast media until liberalisation in 2001 allowed commercial television and radio stations to be established; other major broadcasters include Canal 2 and Radio Siantou

Press – The government-owned *Cameroon Tribune* is the main daily national newspaper
WPFI score – 40,92 (129)

CANADA

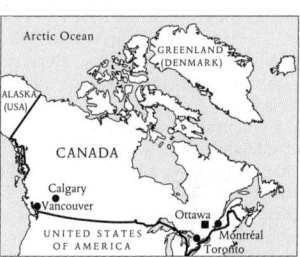

Area – 9,984,670 sq. km
Capital – Ottawa; population, 1,363,000 (2018 est)
Major cities – Calgary, Edmonton, Hamilton, Montréal, Québec, Toronto, Vancouver, Winnipeg
Currency – Canadian dollar (C$) of 100 cents
Population – 35,623,680 rising at 0.73 per cent a year (2017 est)
Religion – Christian 67 per cent (Catholic 38.8 per cent, Protestant 20.3 per cent, other Christian 7.9 per cent), Muslim 3.2 per cent, Hindu 1.5 per cent, Sikh 1.4 per cent, Buddhist 1.1 per cent, Jewish 1 per cent (2011 est)
Language – English, French (both official), Punjabi, Italian, Spanish, German, Cantonese, Tagalog, Arabic
Population density – 4 per sq. km (2016)
Urban population – 82.2 per cent (2017 est)
Median age (years) – 42.2 (2017 est)
National anthem – 'O Canada'
National day – 1 July (Canada Day)
Death penalty – Abolished for all crimes (since 1998)
CPI score – 82 (8)
Military expenditure – US$20,567m (2017)

CLIMATE AND TERRAIN
The six main geographic divisions of Canada are: the Appalachian–Acadian region; the Canadian Shield, which comprises more than half the country; the St Lawrence–Great Lakes lowland; the interior plains; the Cordilleran region; and the Arctic archipelago, which lies under continuous permafrost. The most southerly point is Middle Island in Lake Erie. Elevation extremes range from 5,959m (Mt Logan) to 0m (Atlantic Ocean). The climate varies from temperate in the south to subarctic and arctic in the north. The east and centre experience greater extremes than in corresponding latitudes in Europe, but the climate is milder in the south-western part of the prairie region and the southern parts of the Pacific slope. The tornado season is April to September, peaking in June and early July in southern Ontario, Alberta, Québec, Saskatchewan and Manitoba through to Thunder Bay. The interior of British Columbia and western New Brunswick are also tornado zones.

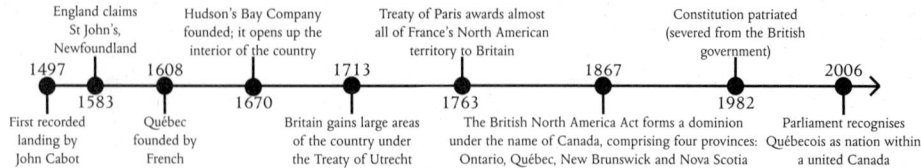

England claims St John's, Newfoundland — 1497
First recorded landing by John Cabot — 1583
Québec founded by French — 1608
Hudson's Bay Company founded; it opens up the interior of the country — 1670
Britain gains large areas of the country under the Treaty of Utrecht — 1713
Treaty of Paris awards almost all of France's North American territory to Britain — 1763
The British North America Act forms a dominion under the name of Canada, comprising four provinces: Ontario, Québec, New Brunswick and Nova Scotia — 1867
Constitution patriated (severed from the British government) — 1982
Parliament recognises Québecois as nation within a united Canada — 2006

POLITICS

Under the 1982 constitution, the head of state is Queen Elizabeth II, represented by a governor-general appointed on the advice of the Canadian prime minister.

The bicameral parliament consists of a senate and a House of Commons. The senate comprises 105 members, who serve until the age of 75, appointed by the governor-general on the recommendation of the prime minister; seats are assigned on a regional basis. The House of Commons has 338 members, directly elected for a four-year term. Representation is proportional to the population of each province. Each province is largely self-governing, with its own lieutenant-governor and unicameral legislative assembly. The territories are administered by the federal government.

A parliamentary vote of no confidence ended 12 years of Liberal government in 2005. In snap general elections in 2006 and 2008, the Conservative Party won the most seats, but not a majority, and formed minority governments under Stephen Harper. His government won a snap general election in May 2011, increasing its seats to achieve an overall majority, however in October 2015, the Liberal Party won 184 seats in federal elections, allowing it to form a majority government in which Justin Trudeau became prime minister.

GOVERNOR-GENERAL
Governor-General, HE Julie Payette, OC *apptd* 2017

SELECTED GOVERNMENT MEMBERS *AS AT MAY 2018*
Prime Minister, Justin Trudeau, *elected* 19 October 2015, *sworn in* 4 November 2015
Defence, Harjit Sajjan
Finance, Bill Morneau
Foreign Affairs, Chrystia Freeland

CANADIAN HIGH COMMISSION
Canada House, Trafalgar Square, London SW1Y 5BJ
T 020-7004 6000 W www.unitedkingdom.gc.ca
High Commissioner, HE Janice Charette, *apptd* 2016

BRITISH HIGH COMMISSION
80 Elgin Street, Ottawa, Ontario K1P 5K7
T (+1) (613) 237 1530 E ukincanada@fco.gov.uk
W www.gov.uk/government/world/canada
High Commissioner, HE Susan le Jeune d'Allegeersheceque, CMG, *apptd* 2017

ECONOMY AND TRADE

Canada has a highly developed, industrialised and diversified market economy, which was transformed from a predominantly rural to an industrial economy in the second half of the 20th century by the growth of mining, manufacturing and services. Tight management of government finances resulted in balanced budgets from the late 1990s until 2007, and free-trade agreements with the USA in 1989 and 1994 (NAFTA) stimulated trade. The economy went into recession in 2008 owing to the global downturn; recovery began in 2010 and marginal growth was achieved in 2012–16 despite the global decline in crude oil prices. Exports continue to be helped by the low value of the Canadian dollar.

Canada's wealth of natural resources make it the world's largest exporter of timber, pulp and newsprint (over half the land is tree-covered), and it is one of the world's largest exporters of minerals, particularly uranium (of which it is the world's second largest single producer) and diamonds. In 2012 around 7.2 per cent of the land area was farmed, of which 4.6 per cent was under cultivation, mostly in the prairie region of western Canada. The country is one of the world's leading food producers, particularly of wheat, barley, oilseed, fruit, vegetables and dairy products. The fishing industry is also significant but has declined in recent years because of restrictions introduced to protect stocks after decades of overfishing. Oil, natural gas and hydroelectricity production is high enough for Canada to be a net exporter of energy; oil production, in particular, has become a significant economic driver, and Canada's oil reserves are ranked third in the world behind Saudi Arabia and Venezuela. The government has plans to develop the oil and gas-rich Arctic area but the assertion of its sovereignty has attracted criticism from other Arctic countries and is complicated by the lack of international agreement on countries' territorial claims.

In 2017, the services sector contributed 70.2 per cent of GDP, industry 28.1 per cent and agriculture 1.7 per cent.

While the USA and Canada's enjoy the world's most comprehensive trade and economic partnership, Canada taking 76.4 per cent of exports and providing 53.1 per cent of imports, retaliatory tariffs on US products introduced in 2018 threatens to reduce this. The main exports are motor vehicles and parts, industrial machinery, aircraft, telecommunications equipment, chemicals, plastics, fertilisers, forestry products, energy products (including crude oil, natural gas and electricity) and aluminium.

GNI – US$1,573.5bn; US$42,870 per capita (2017)
Annual average growth of GDP – 3.0 per cent (2017 est)
Inflation rate – 1.6 per cent (2017 est)
Population below poverty line – 9.4 per cent (2008 est)
Unemployment – 6.5 per cent (2017 est)
Total external debt – US$1.608 trillion (2016 est)
Imports – US$404,433m (2016)
Exports – US$389,397m (2016)

BALANCE OF PAYMENTS
Trade – US$15,036m deficit (2016)
Current Account – US$48,779m deficit (2017)

Trade with UK	2016	2017
Imports from UK	£4,602,228,913	£4,835,495,975
Exports to UK	£10,924,310,126	£12,658,198,756

COMMUNICATIONS

Airports – There are 523 paved airports and airstrips, of which 26 serve major cities
Waterways – There are 636km of waterways and over 300 ports, the most significant of which are Vancouver and Prince Rupert on the Pacific coast and Montréal, Halifax, Port Cartier, Sept-Iles/Pointe Noire, Saint John and Québec in the east. Most deep-water ports are open all year, and Churchill, on Hudson's Bay, is ice-free for longer periods as a result of climate change. In addition, the Great Lakes/St Lawrence

FEDERAL STRUCTURE

Provinces or Territories (with official contractions)	Capital	Premier	Area (sq. km)	Pop. (2016)
Alberta (AB)	Edmonton	Rachel Notley	661,848	4,067,175
British Columbia (BC)	Victoria	John Horgan	944,735	4,648,055
Manitoba (MB)	Winnipeg	Brian Pallister	647,797	1,278,365
New Brunswick (NB)	Fredericton	Brian Gallant	72,908	747,101
Newfoundland and Labrador (NL)	St John's	Dwight Ball	405,212	519,716
Northwest Territories (NT)	Yellowknife	Bob McLeod	1,346,106	41,786
Nova Scotia (NS)	Halifax	Stephen McNeil	55,284	923,598
Nunavut (NU)	Iqaluit	Paul Quassa	2,093,190	35,944
Ontario (ON)	Toronto	Kathleen Wynne	1,076,395	13,448,494
Prince Edward Island (PE)	Charlottetown	Wade MacLauchlan	5,660	142,907
Québec (QC)	Québec City	Philippe Couillard	1,542,056	8,164,361
Saskatchewan (SK)	Regina	Scott Moe	651,036	1,098,352
Yukon Territory (YT)	Whitehorse	Sandy Silver	482,443	35,874

Seaway system, the world's longest inland waterway for ocean-going shipping, provides access to the North American interior
Roadways and railways – 415,600km, including 17,000km of motorways; the 46,552km railway network transports more than 340 million tonnes of freight each year
Telecommunications – There are 15 million fixed lines and 30.7 million mobile telephones subscriptions (2016); there were 31.7 million internet users in 2016
Internet code and IDD – ca; 1 (from UK), 011 44 (to UK)
Major broadcasters – The public broadcaster, the Canadian Broadcasting Corporation (CBC), transmits programmes in English and French, and provides services for indigenous peoples in the north of the country. Société Radio-Canada is the French-language public broadcasting service
Press – Major newspapers include *The Toronto Sun, National Post* and *Le Journal de Montréal* (French-language)
WPFI score – 15,28 (18)

EDUCATION AND HEALTH
Education is compulsory from ages six to 16 (18 in Ontario and New Brunswick).
Gross enrolment ratio (percentage of relevant age group) – primary 101.4 per cent, secondary 113 per cent (2016 est)
Health expenditure (per capita) – US$5,292 (2014)
Hospital beds (per 1,000 people) – 2.7 (2012)
Life expectancy (years) – 81.9 (2017 est)
Mortality rate – 8.7 (2017 est)
Birth rate – 10.3 (2017 est)
Infant mortality rate – 4.5 (2017 est)

CENTRAL AFRICAN REPUBLIC
République Centrafricaine – Central African Republic

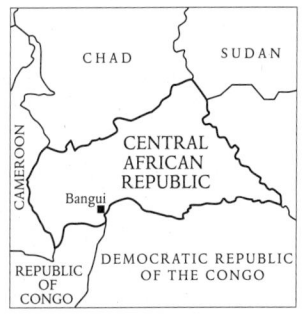

Area – 622,984 sq. km
Capital – Bangui; population, 851,000 (2018 est)
Major cities – Berbérati, Bimbo, Carnot
Currency – Franc CFA of 100 centimes

Population – 5,625,118 rising at 2.12 per cent a year (2017 est); Baya (33 per cent), Banda (27 per cent), Mandja (13 per cent), Sara (10 per cent), Mboum (7 per cent), M'Baka (4 per cent), Yakoma (4 per cent) (est)
Religion – Indigenous beliefs (35 per cent), Christian (Protestant denominations 25 per cent, Roman Catholic 25 per cent), Muslim 15 per cent (est). Some also practise animism, although these beliefs are often integrated into Christian and Muslim worship
Language – French (official), Sangho, other African languages
Population density – 7 per sq. km (2016)
Urban population – 40.6 per cent (2017 est)
Median age (years) – 19.7 (2017 est)
National anthem – 'La Renaissance' 'The Rebirth'
National day – 1 December (Republic Day)
Death penalty – Retained (last used 1981)
CPI score – 23 (156)
Military expenditure – US$27.5m (2017)
Literacy rate – 36.8 per cent (2015 est)
Gross enrolment ratio (percentage of relevant age group) – primary 105.7 per cent, secondary 15.4 per cent (2016 est), tertiary 3 per cent (2012 est)
Health expenditure (per capita) – US$16 (2014)
Hospital beds (per 1,000 people) – 1 (2011)
Life expectancy (years) – 52.8 (2017 est)
Mortality rate – 13.2 (2017 est)
Birth rate – 34.3 (2017 est)
Infant mortality rate – 86.3 (2017 est)
HIV/AIDS adult prevalence – 3.7 per cent (2015 est)

CLIMATE AND TERRAIN
This landlocked state lies on a plateau between the Chad and Congo river basins, with mostly savannah in the north and rainforest in the south. The main river is the Oubangui, which is the lowest point of elevation (335m). The highest point is Mt Ngaoui (1,420m). The climate is tropical, with a wet season in the north from May to September and in the south from May to October. The north can experience average temperatures of up to 34°C between January and April, and the humidity can be extreme. Seasonal temperatures vary slightly, ranging from 24.3°C in August to 27.7°C in March.

POLITICS
Under the 2004 constitution, the president is elected for a five-year term, renewable once. The unicameral National Assembly has 131 members, directly elected for a five-year term. The prime minister is appointed by the president and appoints the ministers.
    François Bozizé seized power in 2003 and won presidential elections in 2005 and 2011. Legislative elections in January and March 2011 were won by the Kwa Na Kwa (KNK)

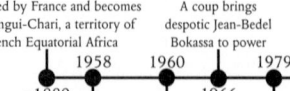

Annexed by France and becomes Oubangui-Chari, a territory of French Equatorial Africa	A coup brings despotic Jean-Bedel Bokassa to power	Military rule	Governed as a one-party state

Timeline:

- 1958 — Annexed by France and becomes Oubangui-Chari, a territory of French Equatorial Africa
- 1960 — A coup brings despotic Jean-Bedel Bokassa to power
- 1979 — Military rule
- 1981-5 — Governed as a one-party state
- 1993 — Government overthrown in a coup led by Gen. François Bozizé
- 2005 — Peace agreement brings national unity, although south-east remains vulnerable to attacks from the Lord's Resistance Army

- c.1880 — Adopts title Central African Republic
- 1966 — Becomes fully independent
- 1986-93 — Bokassa deposed in a bloodless coup
- 2003 — Civilian government and political pluralism restored. Government battles mutinies and financial crises
- 2008 — Bozizé's government faced with lawlessness and an insurgency in the north

coalition, a group loyal to the president. In March 2013 the New Seleka rebel coalition took the capital by force, forcing President Bozizé to flee; the rebel leader Michel Djotodia suspended the constitution and dissolved parliament. Djotodia was forced to resign in January 2014 after he failed to stop sectarian violence between Seleka and Christian militias. On 20 January Catherine Samba Panza was elected interim president and she remained in post as continued violence in 2015 delayed fresh elections. One-time prime minister Faustin-Archange Touadéra, a former maths professor, won a presidential run-off in February 2016, while the National Union for Democracy and Progress (UNDP) and the Union for Central African Renewal (URCA) emerged as the two largest parties in legislative elections in the same month.

HEAD OF STATE
President, Faustin-Archange Touadéra, *elected* February 2016

SELECTED GOVERNMENT MEMBERS *AS AT MAY 2018*
Prime Minister, Simplice Sarandji
Defence, Marie-Noelle Koyara
Finance, Henri-Marie Dondra
Foreign Affairs, Charles Armel Doubane

EMBASSY OF THE CENTRAL AFRICAN REPUBLIC
30 Rue des Perchamps, 75016 Paris, France
T (+33) (1) 4525 3974
Ambassador Extraordinary and Plenipotentiary, vacant

BRITISH AMBASSADOR
HE Rowan Laxton, *apptd* 2017, resident at Yaoundé, Cameroon

ECONOMY AND TRADE
The economy is largely undeveloped owing to decades of instability and misrule. Development is still hindered by political factionalism, a landlocked position and poor transport infrastructure, an unskilled workforce, massively unequal income distribution, and corruption. The country is dependent on international aid and the amount received only partially meets humanitarian needs. Despite working closely with the IMF since 2009, including receiving infrastructure funding in 2012 and extended credit in 2016, the economy has struggled to match pre-2013 levels when sectarian fighting caused a 34.2 per cent drop in GDP growth.

Natural resources include diamonds, gold, uranium and timber; diamond and gold mining, and forestry are among the main industrial activities but the economy still depends mostly on agriculture, which accounts for 42.9 per cent of GDP. Most production is at subsistence level but cotton, coffee and tobacco form the main exports along with diamonds and timber. The main imports are food, textiles, fuels and machinery. Trade is mainly with France, Cameroon and China.
GNI – US$1.8bn; US$390 per capita (2017)
Annual average growth of GDP – 4.7 per cent (2017 est)
Inflation rate – 3.8 per cent (2017 est)
Unemployment – 8 per cent (2016 est)
Total external debt – US$767.1m (2016 est)
Imports – US$220m (2014)

Exports – US$170m (2014)

BALANCE OF PAYMENTS
Trade – US$111m deficit (2013)

Trade with UK	2016	2017
Imports from UK	£2,037,632	£1,291,217
Exports to UK	£81,593	£110,307

COMMUNICATIONS
Airports – Two; the principal airport is at Bangui
Waterways – There are 2,800km of waterways, mostly on the Oubangui and Sangha rivers, that are navigable all year and are important passenger and freight transport routes
Roadways – 20,278km
Telecommunications – There are 1,964 fixed lines and 1.25 million mobile telephone subscriptions (2016); there were 246,000 internet users in 2016
Internet code and IDD – cf; 236 (from UK), 44 (to UK)
Major broadcasters – Major broadcasters include the state-run Télévision Centrafricaine and Radio Centrafique; Radio Ndeke Luka operates nationally and is funded by the UN and foreign NGOs
Press – There are five privately owned daily newspapers, including *Le Citoyen, Le Confident* and *L'Hirondelle*
WPFI score – 35,25 (112)

CHAD
République du Tchad/Jumhuriyat Tshad – Republic of Chad

Area – 1,284,000 sq. km
Capital – N'Djamena; population, 1,323,000 (2018 est)
Major cities – Abéché, Moundou, Sarh
Currency – Franc CFA of 100 centimes
Population – 12,075,985 rising at 1.86 per cent a year (2017 est); the population is made up of around 200 ethnic groups of which Sara, Mayo-Kebbi, Kanem-Bornou, Ouaddai, Hadjarai and Arab are the largest
Religion – Muslim 58.4 per cent, Christian (Roman Catholic 18.5 per cent, Protestant 16.1 per cent) (2009 est); indigenous beliefs are practised in the south
Language – French, Arabic (both official), Sara (in the south)

Population density – 11 per sq. km (2016)
Urban population – 23.1 per cent (2018 est)
Median age (years) – 17.8 (2017 est)
National anthem – 'La Tchadienne' 'People of Chad'
National day – 11 August (Independence Day)
Death penalty – Retained (last used 2003)
CPI score – 20 (165)
Military expenditure – US$210m (2017)
Conscription – 20 years of age, male only; 36 months (women are subject to 12 months of military or civic service at age 21)
Literacy rate – 22.3 per cent (2016 est)
Gross enrolment ratio (percentage of relevant age group) – primary 88 per cent, secondary 23 per cent (2016 est), tertiary 3.4 per cent (2014 est)
Health expenditure (per capita) – US$37 (2014)
Life expectancy (years) – 50.6 (2017 est)
Mortality rate – 13.8 (2017 est)
Birth rate – 35.6 (2017 est)
Infant mortality rate – 85.4 (2017 est)
HIV/AIDS adult prevalence – 2 per cent (2015 est)

CLIMATE AND TERRAIN
The population is concentrated in the fertile lowlands of the south, away from the arid central and northern desert areas. The highest point of elevation is 3,415m (Emi Koussi) and the lowest is 160m (the Djourab depression). The climate is desert in the north and tropical in the south, with a wet season from July to September.

HISTORY AND POLITICS
Chad was colonised by France from the 1890s, becoming part of French Equatorial Africa. It became self-governing after the Second World War and independent on 11 August 1960. A one-party state was declared in 1963 by the president, a southerner, which in 1965 prompted a rebellion in the north against a perceived pro-southern bias in the government. Regional and ethnic tensions, most notably between the Muslim Arab north and the Christian and animist African south have made the country politically unstable since independence. Chad's instability was exacerbated from the 1970s to the 1990s by Libya's support for some rebels and its annexation of territory in northern Chad, and since 2004 by the overspill of the Darfur conflict in Sudan.

Idriss Déby seized power in 1990 after leading a rebellion in eastern Chad, and initiated a transition to democracy. A new constitution was introduced in 1996, and the first multiparty elections were held.

Déby won the first multiparty presidential election in 1996 and was re-elected in 2001, 2006, 2011 and 2016, amid opposition boycotts and doubts over the integrity of the polls. The 2011 legislative election was won by Déby's Patriotic Salvation Movement (MPS) and its allies. That parliamentary term was due to end in June 2015 but was extended by constitutional law; the next elections are set for November 2018. In May 2018, Albert Pahimi Padacké resigned as prime minister along with his government, in protest over constitutional changes which further extended Déby's powers. The amendments were subsequently passed, allowing Déby to rule without a prime minister.

The 1996 constitution was amended in 2005 to remove the limit on the number of terms a president may serve. The president is directly elected for a six-year term. The unicameral National Assembly of 188 members is directly elected for a four-year term.

HEAD OF STATE
President, Idriss Déby, *took power* December 1990, *elected* 3 July 1996, *re-elected* 2001, 2006, 2011, 2016
First Vice President, Foreign Affairs, Epsy Campbell Barr

SELECTED GOVERNMENT MEMBERS *AS AT JULY 2018*
Economy, Edna Camacho Mejia
Finance, Rocio Aguilar Montoya
Foreign Affairs, Mahamat Zéne Chérif

EMBASSY OF THE REPUBLIC OF CHAD
Boulevard Lambermont 52, 1030 Brussels, Belgium
T (+32) (2) 215 1975 E ambassade.tchad@chello.be
W www.ambassadedutchad.be
Ambassador Extraordinary and Plenipotentiary, HE Ammo Aziza Baroud, *apptd* 2016

BRITISH AMBASSADOR
HE Rowan Laxton, *apptd* 2017, resident at Yaoundé, Cameroon

INSURGENCIES
The series of insurgencies over the decades since independence means that no government has ever controlled the whole of the country. Rebel offensives reached the capital in 2006 and 2008 before being repulsed. In 2009, eight rebel groups united to form the Union of Resistance Forces alliance.

From 2004, the east and south-east were further destabilised by the overspill of fighting from Sudan's Darfur region. The EU/UN mission deployed in 2008 to protect Sudanese refugees in Chad was withdrawn in 2010, and relations with Sudan have now been normalised and the border reopened. In 2012, the leader of rebel group the Popular Front for Recovery (FPR), Abdel Kader Baba Ladde, surrendered to military forces in the Central African Republic and returned to Chad. In 2013, following a coup in the Central African Republic, a regional summit in Chad agreed that neighbouring countries should send troops to restore security to the region.

In July 2014, France announced it would set up a new military operation in the Sahel region in an effort to stop the emergence of militant Islamist groups. The operation, based in the Chadian capital N'Djamena, involved around 3,000 French troops, along with troops from Burkina Faso, Chad, Mali and Mauritania.

ECONOMY AND TRADE
Economic development has been limited by political instability, corruption, the landlocked location and poor transport infrastructure. About 80 per cent of the workforce is occupied in subsistence agriculture, herding and fishing, which contributes 59 per cent of GDP, and the remaining 20 per cent are practically all employed in services, which contribute 27 per cent of GDP. Nearly 40 per cent of the population live below the poverty line. The main focus of development, funded by foreign investment and international aid, is to further exploit oil deposits in the Doba basin in the south, which came into production in 2003; the oil is exported via a pipeline through Cameroon. Efforts to repair public finances resulted in the restructuring of a US$1.45bn oil-backed loan in February 2018, but the ensuing cuts to public spending prompted strikes and protests. Other industries include processing cotton (the main industry before oil) and other agricultural products, and light manufacturing. Industry generates 14 per cent of GDP.

An oil refinery was constructed in N'Djamena in 2011 and production from new oil wells allowed growth to reach double digits in 2014. In October 2014, the government also received compensation from the China National Petroleum Corporation (CNPC) after the company was found to have dumped crude oil in the Koudalwa region in 2013; the decision was expected to improve economic ties with China.

Chad's main trading partners are the USA, France, China and India. Principal exports are oil, cattle, cotton and gum arabic.

The main imports are machinery and transport equipment, industrial goods, food and textiles.
GNI – US$9.4bn; US$630 per capita (2017)
Annual average growth of GDP – 0.6 per cent (2017 est)
Inflation rate – 0.2 per cent (2017 est)
Population below poverty line – 46.7 per cent (2011 est)
Total external debt – US$1.268bn (2017 est)
Imports – US$2,200m (2015)
Exports – US$2,900m (2015)

BALANCE OF PAYMENTS
Trade – US$700m surplus (2015)

Trade with UK	2016	2017
Imports from UK	£2,589,067	£7,327,869
Exports to UK	£843,733	£788,149

COMMUNICATIONS
Airports and waterways – Nine, the principal airport is at N'Djamena; the Chari and Legone rivers are navigable only in the wet season
Roadways – Only 206km are surfaced
Telecommunications – There are 14,000 fixed lines and 6.2 million mobile subscriptions (2016); there were 592,623 internet users in 2016
Internet code and IDD – td; 235 (from UK), 15 44 (to UK)
Major broadcasters – Al-Nassour and the state-owned Télé-Tchad are the only two TV stations; Radiodiffusion Nationale Tchadienne is the state-controlled radio station
Press – *Le Progres* is the country's only daily newspaper; other privately owned periodicals include *N'Djamena Bi-Hebdo*
WPFI score – 38,45 (123)

CHILE

República de Chile – Republic of Chile

Area – 756,102 sq. km
Capital – Santiago; population, 6,680,000 (2018 est)
Major cities – Antofagasta, Concepción, Puente Alto, San Bernardo, Temuco, Valparaíso, Viña del Mar
Currency – Chilean peso ($) of 100 centavos
Population – 17,789,267 rising at 0.77 per cent a year (2017 est)
Religion – Christian (Roman Catholic 66.7 per cent, Protestant 16.4 per cent) (2012 est)
Language – Spanish (official), English, Mapudungun and other indigenous languages
Population density – 24 per sq. km (2016)
Urban population – 89.9 per cent (2017 est)
Median age (years) – 34.4 (2017 est)

National anthem – 'Himno Nacional de Chile' 'National Anthem of Chile'
National day – 18 September (Independence Day)
Death penalty – Retained for certain crimes (last used 1985)
CPI score – 67 (26)
Military expenditure – US$5,135m (2017)

CLIMATE AND TERRAIN
Chile extends over 4,600km from the arid north around Arica to Cape Horn, with an average breadth of 180km. The Atacama desert lies in the north. In the central zone there is a fertile valley between the Andes and the low coastal range of mountains, with a Mediterranean climate; two-thirds of the population live here. Chilean Patagonia, in the south, extends into subantarctic terrain, with glaciers and icefields; the climate is cool with high precipitation. Elevation extremes range from 6,880m (Nevado Ojos del Salado) to 0m (Pacific Ocean). Its Pacific island possessions include the Juan Fernández group and Easter Island, and the Chilean Antarctic Territory covers the Antarctic peninsula and an area of the landmass that extends from 53°W. to 90°W. along a latitude of 60°S.

HISTORY AND POLITICS
Chile was conquered in the 16th century by the Spanish, who subjugated the indigenous population. It remained under Spanish rule until 1810, when the first autonomous government was established. Independence was achieved in 1818 after a revolutionary war.

A military coup in 1973 overthrew the Marxist president Salvador Allende. General Augusto Pinochet, the coup leader, assumed the presidency and retained the office until elections were held in 1989, beginning the transition to full democracy. Between 1998 and his death in 2006, a number of unsuccessful attempts were made to bring Gen. Pinochet to trial for human rights atrocities committed during his time in office.

In the 2017 legislative elections, the centre-left New Majority Coalition extended its mandate by winning 68 seats in the lower chamber, and 19 of the 38 seats in the senate. Conservative business tycoon Sebastián Piñera, the former president who led the country from 2010–14, returned to power in 2018.

The 1981 constitution was amended in 1989 and 2005. The executive president is directly elected for a four-year term that is not renewable. The bicameral National Congress comprises a senate of 38 members elected for an eight-year term (half renewed every four years) and a Chamber of Deputies of 118 members directly elected for a four-year term. On 15 January 2015, the senate voted to abolish Chile's unique binomial electoral system, in which two MPs were elected to each constituency, introducing a system of proportional representation.

HEAD OF STATE
President, Sebastián Piñera, *elected* 17 December 2017, *sworn in* 11 March 2018

SELECTED GOVERNMENT MEMBERS *AS AT MAY 2018*
Defence, Alberto Espina
Economy, Jorge Ramon Valente
Finance, Filipe Larrain
Foreign Affairs, Roberto Ampuero

EMBASSY OF CHILE
37–41 Old Queen Street, London SW1H 9JA
T 020-7222 2361 **E** embachile@embachile.co.uk
W www.chileabroad.gov.cl/reino-unido
Ambassador Extraordinary and Plenipotentiary, HE Rolando Drago, *apptd* 2014

BRITISH EMBASSY
Avda. El Bosque Norte 0125, Las Condes, Santiago
T (+56) (2) 370 4100 **E** embsan@britemb.cl
W www.gov.uk/government/world/chile
Ambassador Extraordinary and Plenipotentiary, HE James
   Bowden, *apptd* 2018

ECONOMY AND TRADE
Economic reforms in the late 1970s and the 1980s, and sound
financial management, have made Chile one of the most
successful economies in Latin America; in 2010 it became the
first South American country to join the OECD, and by 2018
had trade agreements covering 60 countries. Growth is based
on high copper prices, a strong export base and growing
domestic demand. In 2012, foreign investment reached a
record US$28.2bn, a 63 per cent increase on the previous
record in 2011. But the falling price of copper has slowed
growth, and in 2015 the government announced the
introduction of a US$5.5bn (£3.68bn) economic stimulus
package. A further fall in copper prices meant in 2017 the
nation experienced a third year of slow growth.
   Chile is the world's largest producer of copper, and the
world's only commercial producer of nitrate of soda (Chile
saltpetre) from natural resources. The chief industries are
mining, forestry, fishing, food and fish processing, and
winemaking.
   The main trading partners are the USA, China, Brazil and
Japan. Principal exports are copper, fruit, fish products, paper
and pulp, chemicals and wine. The main imports are petrol
and petroleum products, chemicals, electrical and
telecommunications equipment, industrial machinery, vehicles
and natural gas.
GNI – US$245.7bn; US$13,610 per capita (2017)
Annual average growth of GDP – 1.4 per cent (2017 est)
Inflation rate – 2.3 per cent (2017 est)
Population living below poverty line – 14.4 per cent (2013 est)
Unemployment – 7 per cent (2017 est)
Total external debt – US$167.9bn (2017 est)
Imports – US$58,892m (2016)
Exports – US$59,869m (2016)

BALANCE OF PAYMENTS
Trade – US$977m surplus (2016)
Current Account – US$4,146m deficit (2017)

Trade with UK	2016	2017
Imports from UK	£450,744,761	£599,540,451
Exports to UK	£648,942,360	£709,612,037

COMMUNICATIONS
Airports and waterways – 90, the principal airport is at Santiago;
the main ports are Arica, Antofagasta, Coquimbo, San
Antonio, Talcahuano and Valparaíso
Roadways and railways – 18,119km, including 2,387km of
motorways; 7,082km of railways
Telecommunications – 3.4 million fixed lines and 23.3 million
mobile subscriptions (2016); there were around 11.6 million
internet users in 2016
Internet code and IDD – cl; 56 (from UK), 44 (to UK)
Major broadcasters – The National Television of Chile is state-
owned but not under direct government control; Radio
Cooperativa is a news-based private network that broadcasts
alongside numerous other private radio stations
Press – Major newspaper publications include *El Mercurio* and
La Tercera; the government-owned *La Nación* was privatised in
January 2014
WPFI score – 22,69 (38)

EDUCATION AND HEALTH
Education is free and compulsory from ages six to 17,
although the education system has suffered from
underinvestment and mismanagement, resulting in ongoing
student protests.
Literacy rate – 97.5 per cent (2015 est)
Gross enrolment ratio (percentage of relevant age group) – primary
   99.8 per cent, secondary 99.6 per cent, tertiary 90.3 per
   cent (2016 est)
Health expenditure (per capita) – US$1,137 (2014)
Hospital beds (per 1,000 people) – 2.2 (2013)
Life expectancy (years) – 78.9 (2017 est)
Mortality rate – 6.2 (2017 est)
Birth rate – 13.6 (2017 est)
Infant mortality rate – 6.6 (2017 est)
HIV/AIDS adult prevalence – 0.3 per cent (2015 est)

CHINA

Zhonghua Renmin Gongheguo – People's Republic of China

Area – 9,596,960 sq. km
Capital – Beijing; population, 19,618,000 (2018 est)
Major cities – Chengdu, Chongqing, Dongguan, Foshan,
   Guangzhou, Nanjing, Shanghai, Shenyang, Shenzhen,
   Tianjin, Wuhan, Xi'an
Currency – Renminbi (RMB) or yuan (¥) of ten jiao or
   100 fen
Population – 1,379,302,771 rising at 0.41 per cent a year
   (2017 est); Han Chinese (91.6 per cent), around 55 ethnic
   minorities (8.4 per cent) (2010 est)
Religion – officially atheist, but permits four state-registered
   religions: Buddhism, Taoism, Islam, and Catholic and
   Protestant Christianity. It is difficult to estimate numbers,
   as many congregations worship in private; Mahayana
   Buddhism and Taoism are the predominant faiths but
   Christianity is growing rapidly
Language – Mandarin (official), Cantonese, Shanghainese,
   Fuzhou, Xiang, Gan, Taiwanese; common speech, or
   putonghua (often referred to as Mandarin), is based on the
   northern dialect and is promoted throughout the country
Population density – 147 per sq. km (2016)
Urban population – 57.9 per cent (2017 est)
Median age (years) – 37.4 (2017 est)
National anthem – 'Yiyongjun Jinxingqu' 'The March of the
   Volunteers'
National day – 1 October (Founding of People's Republic)
Death penalty – Retained
CPI score – 41 (77)

Military expenditure – US$228,231m (2017 est)
Conscription – 18–24 years of age; 24 months (selective)

CLIMATE AND TERRAIN

China is twice the size of western Europe and contains a vast range of landscapes and climates. The highest mountains are on the Tibetan plateau, in the west of the country, where the highest elevation is 8,850m (Mt Everest). To the north of the Tibetan plateau, the land drops to the arid, semi-desert steppes bisected by the Tian Shan mountains; the country's lowest elevation is −154m at Turpan Pendi. The southern plains and east coast have the most fertile land, irrigated by the Huang He (Yellow), Chang Jiang (Yangtze) and Xi Jiang (West) rivers, and are the most heavily populated areas.

There are seven climate zones. The north-east has cold winters, fierce winds, warm and humid summers, and erratic rainfall. The mountainous south-west has mild winters and warm summers. Inner Mongolia has cold winters and hot summers. Central China has warm and humid summers with occasional tropical cyclones. South China is partly tropical with heavy rainfall. The high Tibet plateau is subject to harsh winters. Xinjiang and the west have a desert climate, with cold winters and little rain.

POLITICS

The Communist Party of China is the dominant political party, and all elements of the political system are subordinate to it. A party congress is held every five years and elects the Politburo and its standing committee. This standing committee is the policy- and decision-making body and the *de facto* government.

Under the 1982 constitution, the National People's Congress (NPC) is the highest organ of state power. It has 2,987 members, indirectly elected for a five-year term, and holds only one full session a year; between sessions, its work is delegated to its standing committee. The congress elects the premier and, on his nomination, the State Council. The head of state is the president, also elected by the congress. In 2018, a constitutional amendment abolished presidential two-term limits, allowing Xi Jinping to rule indefinitely and marking a return to lifelong dictatorial rule.

Deputies to people's congresses at the primary level are directly elected by the voters from a list of approved candidates. These congresses elect the deputies to the congress at the next highest level. Deputies to the NPC are elected by the provincial and municipal people's congresses, and by the armed forces.

Local government is conducted through people's governments at provincial/municipal, prefecture/city, county/district, township and village levels. There are 22 provinces (Taiwan is claimed as a 23rd province), four municipalities directly under the central government, five autonomous regions, and two special administrative areas; provinces may contain autonomous counties or towns for ethnic minorities.

In 2012 Xi Jinping took over as General Secretary of the Communist Party of China, becoming president in 2013. He stated that he aimed to make corruption-free governance and economic growth key elements of his administration, the former of which has resulted in several high-profile purges of senior officials. Li Keqiang was elected premier by the 12th National People's Congress in 2013.

HEAD OF STATE
President, Xi Jinping, *elected* 14 March 2013
Vice-President, Wang Qishan

STATE COUNCIL *AS AT AUGUST 2018*
Premier, Li Keqiang
Vice-Premiers, Han Zheng; Sun Chunlan; Hu Chunhua; Liu He
State Councillors, Xiao Jie; Wei Fenghe; Zhao Kazhi; Wang Yong

SELECTED GOVERNMENT MEMBERS *AS AT AUGUST 2018*
Civil Affairs, Huang Shuxian
Finance, Liu Kun
Foreign Affairs, Wang Yi

EMBASSY OF THE PEOPLE'S REPUBLIC OF CHINA
49–51 Portland Place, London W1B 1JL
T 020-7299 4049 W www.chinese-embassy.org.uk
Ambassador Extraordinary and Plenipotentiary, HE Liu Xiaoming, *apptd* 2010

BRITISH EMBASSY
11 Guang Hua Lu, Jian Guo Men Wai, 100600, Beijing, China
T (+86) 0(10) 5192 4000 W www.gov.uk/government/world/china
Ambassador Extraordinary and Plenipotentiary, HE Dame Barbara Woodward, DCMG, OBE, *apptd* 2015

HUMAN RIGHTS
China's political system has become more liberal since 1978, when economic reforms allowing for greater amounts of personal freedom were introduced, with further liberalisation taking place during the regime of Deng Xiaoping from 1981 to 1987. The constitution was amended to officially recognise human rights in 2004, and National Human Rights Action Plans, issued by the State Council, were released in 2009 and 2012. The practice of sending prisoners to labour camps for 're-education' was officially abolished in 2007; the majority of camps were independently confirmed to have been closed in 2014. Despite reform, the state continues to tightly control freedom of expression, religion, association and reproduction rights. Ethnic minorities in Tibet, Inner Mongolia and Xinjiang, home to the Uygur Muslim separatist movement, experience widespread discrimination. The country is thought to have executed approximately 4,000 people in 2014, more than every other country in the world combined, and applies the death sentence to a variety of non-violent crimes, including corruption. Prominent critics of the regime are frequently subjected to house arrest and torture. Notable dissidents include: Chen Guangcheng, a blind human rights lawyer who fled to the USA in 2012; Liu Xiaobo, winner of the Nobel Peace prize in 2010, who died of cancer in custody in July 2017; and the artist Ai Weiwei. In April 2014,

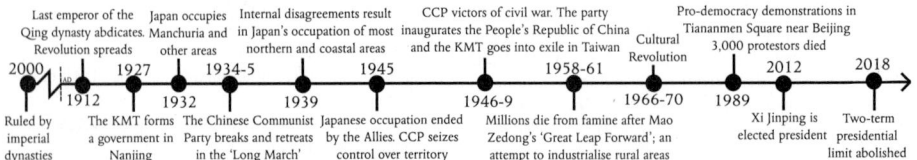

Ruled by imperial dynasties | 2000 | 1912 | 1927 | The KMT forms a government in Nanjing | 1932 | 1934-5 | The Chinese Communist Party breaks and retreats in the 'Long March' | 1939 | 1945 | Japanese occupation ended by the Allies. CCP seizes control over territory | 1946-9 | CCP victors of civil war. The party inaugurates the People's Republic of China and the KMT goes into exile in Taiwan | 1958-61 | Millions die from famine after Mao Zedong's 'Great Leap Forward'; an attempt to industrialise rural areas | 1966-70 | Cultural Revolution | 1989 | 2012 | Xi Jinping is elected president | 2018 | Two-term presidential limit abolished

Last emperor of the Qing dynasty abdicates. Revolution spreads

Japan occupies Manchuria and other areas

Internal disagreements result in Japan's occupation of most northern and coastal areas

Pro-democracy demonstrations in Tiananmen Square near Beijing 3,000 protestors died

President Xi Jinping stated that China would never develop into a pluralist, Western-style democracy.

ECONOMY AND TRADE

Liberalisation since the 1980s has transformed the economy, developing a more autonomous state sector, a rapidly growing private sector and a leading presence in global trade and investment. A massive industrial base and transport infrastructure have been constructed, especially in the coastal regions, and the economy has become a free market in all but name, with several stock markets and Shanghai's emergence as a financial centre. China attracts considerable foreign investment and has become a major investor overseas. GDP has grown more than ten-fold since 1978, and China's economy is now the largest in the world when measured on a purchasing power parity.

Although some 500 million people who migrated to urban areas in the past 35 years have been lifted out of poverty, the effects of the rapid transformation have been unevenly distributed. In 2012, it was reported that China's city dwellers outnumber China's rural population for the first time; there are wide income differences between urban and rural areas, poor healthcare provision, lack of access to public services for migrant workers, rampant official corruption and environmental degradation of land, water and air. The government is also keen to increase domestic consumption (a priority of the 2011–16 five-year plan), and so reduce the economy's reliance on exports for growth. The economy grew by 6.7 per cent in 2016, the slowest growth rate since 1990, and but slightly improved in 2017. Growth is expected to remain relatively modest as China gradually transitions from a heavy manufacturing focus to a service economy, but fears over a potential trade war with the US after China imposed retaliatory tariffs in 2018 may reduce growth further still.

China's expansion boosted its need for oil and coal, met initially by imports but increasingly by domestic production. However, to achieve its aim of reducing environmental degradation, China is looking to nuclear power and alternative energy generation, such as hydroelectric power from the Three Gorges Dam.

Although rural areas have seen few benefits from the economic transformation and are suffering the effects of rural depopulation and pollution, agriculture remains important; it contributes 8.3 per cent of GDP but employs 27.7 per cent of the workforce. The main crops are rice, cereals, vegetables, peanuts, tea, fruit, cotton and oilseed crops. Livestock is raised in large numbers. Silk farming is one of the oldest industries. Cotton, woollen and silk textiles are manufactured in large quantities.

The highly diversified industrial sector, encompassing heavy industry, manufacturing and construction, contributes 39.5 per cent of GDP and employs 28.8 per cent of the workforce. The services sector accounts for 52.2 per cent of GDP and 43.5 per cent of employment. Tourism is now a major industry.

China is the world's largest importer and exporter of goods. Exports include machinery, electrical equipment, data processing equipment, garments, textiles, iron and steel, and optical and medical equipment. The principal imports are electrical and other machinery, oil and mineral fuels, optical and medical equipment, metal ores, plastics and organic chemicals. The main trading partners are the USA, Hong Kong, Japan, Germany and South Korea, although trade with Latin America and Africa is growing.

GNI – US$12,042.9bn; US$8,690 per capita (2017)
Annual average growth of GDP – 6.8 per cent (2017 est)
Inflation rate – 1.8 per cent (2017 est)
Population below poverty line – 3.3 per cent (2016 est)
Unemployment – 4 per cent (2017 est)

Total external debt – US$1.649 trillion (2017 est)
Imports – US$1,589,900m (2016)
Exports – US$2,134,520m (2016)

BALANCE OF PAYMENTS
Trade – US$544,620m surplus (2016)
Current Account – US$320,602m surplus (2015)

Trade with UK	2016	2017
Imports from UK	£13,424,027,468	£16,675,281,933
Exports to UK	£39,250,474,199	£41,641,036,936

COMMUNICATIONS

Airports – There are 463 airports and airfields and several national air carriers
Waterways – The main seaports are Shanghai and Dalian in the north, and Guangzhou in the south; there are 110,000km of navigable waterways, Nanjing is the largest river port, and the Huang He (Yellow), Chang Jiang (Yangtze) and Xi Jiang (West) are the most significant river routes
Roadways – The 3,453,890km road network allows access to all towns and villages, and the major cities are linked by 84,946km of modern highways
Railways – The rail system has 86,000km of track, although only 36,000km is electrified; the extension of the Qinghai–Tibet railway has opened up the remote western province
Telecommunications – 206 million fixed lines and 1.36 million mobile subscriptions (2016); there were 730 million internet users in 2016
Internet code and IDD – cn; 86 (from UK), 44 (to UK)
Major broadcasters – The Communist Party maintains a firm grip on media and the internet. Television, provided by Chinese Central TV (CCTV), is the most popular medium; there are around 3,300 channels and 418 million households have access to television. All of China's 2,600 radio stations are state-owned
Press – Every city has its own newspaper – approximately 1,900 newspapers are published every week; national dailies include *Renmin Ribao* (Communist Party newspaper), *Zhongguo Qingnian Bao* and *China Daily* (English-language)
WPFI score – 78,29 (176)

EDUCATION AND HEALTH

Primary education lasts six years and secondary education six years (three years in junior middle school and three optional years in senior middle school).
Literacy rate – 96.4 per cent (2015 est)
Gross enrolment ratio (percentage of relevant age group) – primary 100.9 per cent (2016 est), secondary 94.3 per cent (2014 est), tertiary 48.4 per cent (2016 est)
Health expenditure (per capita) – US$420 (2014)
Hospital beds (per 1,000 people) – 4.2 (2012)
Life expectancy (years) – 75.7 (2017 est)
Mortality rate – 7.8 (2017 est)
Birth rate – 12.3 (2017 est)
Infant mortality rate – 12 (2017 est)
HIV/AIDS adult prevalence – 0.1 per cent (2012 est)

TIBET

Area – 1,199,164 sq. km
Population – 3,002,166 (2011 est)
Capital – Lhasa
Tibet is a plateau, seldom lower than 3,000m, in south-west China. It forms the frontier with India (boundary imperfectly demarcated), from which it is separated by the Himalayas from Kashmir to Myanmar; Nepal and Bhutan also border it

to the south. The Indus, Brahmaputra, Mekong and Yangtze rivers all rise on the Tibet plateau.

Tibet was under Mongol rule almost continuously from the 13th to the 17th centuries. Chinese control grew from the 18th century and direct rule began in 1910, but with the collapse of the Chinese Empire in 1911, Tibet declared its independence and the Dalai Lama ruled undisturbed until Communist rule was established in China. In 1950, Chinese Communist forces invaded Tibet, and in 1951 the Tibetan authorities signed a treaty agreeing joint Chinese–Tibetan rule. A series of revolts against Chinese rule culminated in a 1959 uprising in the capital, which was crushed following several days of fighting, after which military rule was imposed. The Dalai Lama fled to India, where he and his followers were granted political asylum, and established a government in exile. Tibet became an Autonomous Region of China in 1965. Martial law was declared in Tibet in 1989.

The Panchen Lama, the second-highest Lama, remained in Lhasa after 1959; when he died in 1989, China rejected the Dalai Lama's choice of successor and enthroned its own candidate. Subsequent appointments have been handled in a similar manner. Despite occasional talks between the Chinese government and representatives of the Dalai Lama, relations remain poor. In March 2011, the Dalai Lama announced his intention to withdraw from political life, transferring leadership to Lobsang Sangay, prime minister of the Tibetan parliament. In September 2012 his title was amended to political leader (Sikyong).

Another source of tension is the large number of Chinese migrants who have settled in Tibet since the 1970s, a development that the Tibetan government-in-exile regards as an attempt to eradicate the culture of the Tibetan people. Chinese now considerably outnumber Tibetans and have benefited disproportionately from the economic development of recent years.

Peaceful anti-Chinese demonstrations in Tibet increased in early 2008 as the imminence of the Beijing Olympics put China's human rights record under greater international scrutiny. The violence of the Chinese crackdown was condemned worldwide, and pro-Tibet activists abroad disrupted the Olympic torch relay in several countries. Resistance and unrest continue: in 2009, in a show of passive resistance, farmers in Tibet and neighbouring provinces refused to till the fields or plant crops; in 2011, demonstrations sparked by the self-immolation of a Tibetan monk in the Sechuan province led to hundreds of arrests. More than 130 other self-immolations have taken place since.

SPECIAL ADMINISTRATIVE REGIONS

HONG KONG
Xianggang Tebie Xingzhengqu – Hong Kong Special Administrative Region

Area – 1,108 sq. km
Currency – Hong Kong dollar (HK$) of 100 cents
Population – 7,191,503 rising at 0.32 per cent a year (2017 est)
Population density – 7,040 per sq. km (2017)
Median age – 44.4 (2017 est)
Flag – Red, with a white bauhinia flower of five petals each containing a red star
National day – 1 July (Establishment Day)
Death penalty – Abolished for all crimes (since 2003)
CPI score – 77 (13)

CLIMATE AND TERRAIN
Hong Kong consists of Hong Kong Island, Kowloon and the New Territories (on a peninsula of the mainland in Guangdong province) and over 260 islands, including Lantau Island. Hong Kong Island is about 18km long and 3–8km wide. It is separated from the mainland by a narrow strait. The highest point is Tai Mo Shan (958m). The climate is subtropical, with hot, wet summers and cool, dry winters. Mean monthly temperatures range from 16°C to 29°C. Tropical cyclones occur between May and November, and over 75 per cent of the average annual rainfall of 2,180mm falls between May and September.

HISTORY AND POLITICS
Hong Kong developed as a major regional trading port because of its location on the main Far Eastern trade routes. Hong Kong Island was first occupied by Britain in 1841 and formally ceded to Britain in 1842. Kowloon was acquired in 1860, and the New Territories by a 99-year lease signed in 1898.

In 1984, the UK and China agreed that China would resume sovereignty over Hong Kong in 1997, and on 1 July 1997, Hong Kong became a Special Administrative Region (SAR) of the People's Republic of China. The 1984 joint declaration and the Basic Law (1990) guarantee that the SAR's social and economic systems will remain unchanged for 50 years and grant it a high degree of autonomy.

Although the Basic Law provides for the development of democratic processes, political reform has been slow, prompting frequent demonstrations to demand full democracy or to oppose measures perceived to be repressive. In 2007 the Chinese government said that the chief executive could be directly elected from 2017 and the legislature members from 2020. In a rare 'inspection tour' in 2017 to coincide with the 20th anniversary of Hong Kong's return to China, China's president Xi Jinping vowed to bring 'new glory' to Hong Kong amid what is seen as a tightening of individual freedoms to match the mainland. China's foreign ministry simultaneously announced that China viewed the Sino-British joint declaration of 1984 as a 'historical document' to which it no longer felt bound.

The Basic Law, approved in 1990, has served as Hong Kong's constitution since 1997. Its government is headed by the chief executive, who is elected by a 1,200-member electoral committee and serves a five-year term. The chief executive is aided by an executive council consisting of 15 principal officials, who are the heads of administrative departments, and 14 non-official members. The legislative council consists of 70 members, 35 directly elected by geographic constituencies, five directly elected by all voters in 'super seats', and 30 elected by functional, occupation-based constituencies; they serve a four-year term.

Carrie Lam was elected chief executive in March 2017, replacing Leung Chun-ying. In the 2016 legislative elections, pro-China parties won 40 seats while pro-democracy parties won 29.

Chief Executive, Carrie Lam, *elected* 26 March 2017, *sworn in* 1 July 2017

SELECTED GOVERNMENT MEMBERS *AS AT AUGUST 2018*
Chief Secretary for Administration, Matthew Cheung
Financial Secretary, Paul Chan Mo-po
Secretary for Justice, Teresa Cheng Yeuk-wah

BRITISH CONSULATE-GENERAL
PO Box 528, 1 Supreme Court Road, Central Hong Kong
T (+852) 2901 3000 E hongkong.consular@fco.gov.uk
W www.gov.uk/government/world/hong-kong
Consul-General, Andrew Heyn, OBE, *apptd* 2016

ECONOMY AND TRADE
The economy has moved away from manufacturing (which has mostly relocated to mainland China) and is service-based, with

a high reliance on international trade and re-exports. It has developed into a regional corporate and banking centre, and has benefited in recent years from closer integration with China through increased trade, tourism and financial links. Although badly affected by the global economic downturn in 2008–9, and vulnerable to future volatility, the strength of the Chinese economy helped it to recover quickly. In 2014, Hong Kong signed the Closer Economic Partnership Arrangement with China, which aims to eliminate trade barriers and liberalise trade between the two economies.

The economy is dominated by the service sector, which accounted for 92.7 per cent of GDP in 2017. The main contributors to this are tourism, financial services and shipping. Industry contributes 7.2 per cent of GDP. Principal products are textiles, clothing, electronics, plastics, toys, clocks and watches.

The principal export markets are China (54.1 per cent), and the USA. China is also Hong Kong's principal supplier of imported goods (44.6 per cent).

GNI – US$342.3bn; US$46,310 per capita (2017)
Annual average growth of GDP – 2.9 per cent (2015 est)
Inflation rate – 3 per cent (2015 est)
Population below poverty line – 19.6 per cent (2012 est)
Unemployment – 2.6 per cent (2017 est)
Total external debt – US$494.5bn (2017 est)
Imports – US$516,411m (2016)
Exports – US$462,284m (2016)

BALANCE OF PAYMENTS
Trade – US$54,127m deficit (2016)
Current Account – US$14,736m surplus (2016)

Trade with UK	2016	2017
Imports from UK	£6,650,156,805	£7,223,029,866
Exports to UK	£9,995,039,244	£8,792,500,572

COMMUNICATIONS
Airports – There are two airports, one accommodating international flights
Waterways – Hong Kong has one of the world's finest natural harbours, and is the third-busiest container port in the world
Roadways – 2,090km (2012)
Telecommunications – 4.32 million fixed lines and 17.6 million mobile subscriptions (2016); there were 6.1 million internet users in 2016
Internet code and IDD – hk; 852 (from UK), 1 44 (to UK)
WPFI score – 29,45 (73)

EDUCATION AND HEALTH
Education is free and compulsory for children up to age 15.
Literacy rate – 99.2 per cent (2012 est)
Gross enrolment ratio (percentage of age group) – primary 98 per cent (2011 est), secondary 103 per cent (2016 est), tertiary 68.5 per cent (2016 est)
Life expectancy (years) – 83 (2017 est)
Mortality rate – 7.2 (2016 est)
Birth rate – 9.1 (2016 est)
Infant mortality rate – 2.7 (2016 est)

MACAU (AOMEN)
Aomen Tebie Xingzhengqu – Macau Special Administrative Region
Area – 28.2 sq. km
Currency – Pataca (MOP$) of 100 avos
Population – 601,969 rising at 0.74 per cent a year (2017 est)
Religion – Buddhist 50 per cent, Roman Catholic 15 per cent (1997 est)

Population density – 19,393 per sq. km (2015)
Median age (years) – 38.7 (2016 est)
Flag – Green, with a white lotus flower above a white stylised bridge and water, under a large gold five-point star and four gold stars in crescent
National day – 20 December (Establishment Day)
Internet code and IDD – mo; 853 (from UK), 44 (to UK)

CLIMATE AND TERRAIN
Macau consists of the Macau peninsula and the islands of Coloane and Taipa. It is situated at the western side of the mouth of the Pearl river, bordering Guangdong province in south-east China. It is 64km from Hong Kong. Its area has nearly doubled since the 19th century due to land reclamation. The highest point is Coloane Alto (172m). The climate is subtropical.

HISTORY AND POLITICS
The first Portuguese ship arrived at Macau in 1513 and trade with China commenced in 1553. Macau became a Portuguese colony in 1557; China recognised Portugal's sovereignty over Macau by treaty in 1887. An agreement to transfer the administration of Macau to China was signed in 1987, and Macau became the Macau Special Administrative Region (MSAR) of China on 20 December 1999. Fernando Chui was elected unopposed as chief executive in 2009 and was re-elected in 2014. The most recent legislative election was held in September 2017, returning a solid pro-government majority.

The Basic Law (1993) has served as Macao's constitution since 1999. The chief executive is elected by a 400-member election committee and serves a five-year term of office, which may be renewed once. The chief executive is assisted by the ten-member executive council. The legislative assembly has 33 members, who serve for four years; 14 are directly elected in proportional representation, 12 are indirectly elected by an electoral college of commercial and professional interest groups, and seven are appointed by the chief executive.
Chief Executive, Fernando Chui Sai On, *elected* July 2009, *sworn in* 20 December 2009

SELECTED GOVERNMENT MEMBERS *AS AT AUGUST 2018*
Economy and Finance, Leong Vai Tac
Secretary for Administration and Justice, Sonia Chan Hoi Fan

CONSUL-GENERAL
Andrew Heyn, *apptd* 2016, resident at Hong Kong

ECONOMY AND TRADE
The economy is based on tourism and gambling, which have grown rapidly since 2001, and garment and textile manufacturing, which is in decline. Visitors totalled 30.95 million in 2016, the majority coming from mainland China, where gambling is illegal. The service sector contributes about 88.7 per cent of GDP and industry 11.4 per cent. The principal products and exports are clothing, textiles, footwear, toys, electronics, machinery and parts. The main trading partners are Hong Kong, China – with whom a Comprehensive Economic Partnership Agreement was signed in 2013 – and EU nations.
GNI – US$39.9bn; US$65,130 per capita (2017)
Annual average growth of GDP – −0.9 per cent (2014 est)
Inflation rate – 4.6 per cent (2015 est)
Unemployment – 1.7 per cent (2014 est)
Imports – US$8,925m (2016)
Exports – US$1,257m (2016)

BALANCE OF PAYMENTS
Trade – US$7,668m deficit (2016)
Current Account – US$12,215m surplus (2017)

Trade with UK	2016	2017
Imports from UK	£41,611,242	£53,483,392
Exports to UK	£7,788,556	£7,630,645

COLOMBIA

República de Colombia – Republic of Colombia

Area – 1,138,910 sq. km
Capital – Bogotá; population, 10,574,000 (2018 est)
Major cities – Barranquilla, Cali, Cartagena, Medellín
Currency – Colombian peso ($) of 100 centavos
Population – 47,698,524 rising at 0.99 per cent a year (2017 est)
Religion – Christian (Roman Catholic 90 per cent) (est)
Language – Spanish (official)
Population density – 44 per sq. km (2016)
Urban population – 80.8 per cent (2018 est)
Median age (years) – 30 (2017 est)
National anthem – 'Himno Nacional de la República de Colombia' 'National Anthem of the Republic of Colombia'
National day – 20 July (Independence Day)
Death penalty – Abolished for all crimes (since 1910)
CPI score – 37 (96)
Military expenditure – US$9,714m (2017)
Conscription – 18–24 years of age; 18 months

CLIMATE AND TERRAIN

The western, central and eastern ranges of the Andes run from the south-west to north-east of Colombia, separating the arid north-eastern peninsula and the tropical coastal regions in the north and west from the densely forested south-eastern lowlands and the vast tablelands in the east. This last region, having a temperate climate, is the most densely populated part of the country. Elevation extremes range from 5,775m (Pico Simon Bolívar and Picó Cristóbal Colón) to 0m (Pacific Ocean). The principal rivers are the Magdalena, which flows into the Caribbean; the Guaviare and Meta, tributaries of the Orinoco; and the Caquetá and Putumayo, which drain into the Amazon basin. The predominantly tropical climate is moderated by altitude in the interior.

HISTORY AND POLITICS

Spanish settlement of the region began in 1525, and Colombia was ruled as part of a viceroyalty until 1810, when independence was declared. In 1819, Simón Bolivar established the Republic of Gran Colombia, consisting of the territories now known as Colombia, Panama, Venezuela and Ecuador, after finally defeating the Spanish. In 1829–30

Venezuela and Ecuador withdrew, and in 1831 the remaining territories formed a separate state, which adopted the name of Colombia in 1866; Panama seceded in 1903.

Power alternated between the Conservative and Liberal parties from the mid-19th century. In 1949, a civil war broke out that lasted until 1957, when the Conservative and Liberal parties formed a coalition government known as the National Front. This arrangement continued until 1974 and was revived in 1978 in an attempt to maintain the rule of law in the face of violence by drug cartels, a left-wing insurgency and counter-attacks by right-wing paramilitaries. In 2016, the government agreed a fragile and controversial peace deal with the left-wing guerilla group the Revolutionary Armed Forces of Columbia (FARC). Despite foreign assistance and increased military spending, drug trafficking continues to be widespread, although it has become less of a threat to civil order.

The 2018 presidential election, the first peacetime election in 52 years, was won by conservative candidate Iván Duque, who replaced Juan Manuel Santos Calderón after he reached his two-term limit. In the 2018 legislative elections, right-wing parties opposed to the 2016 peace deal won the most votes in both chambers but fell short of an overall majority.

The 1991 constitution, amended in 2005, allowed for the directly elected president to govern for two four-year terms, but an amendment in 2015 reduced this to a single term. The bicameral congress comprises the 171-member Chamber of Representatives and the 108-member senate. All members are elected for a four-year term. Two senate seats are reserved for representatives of indigenous people, and five for FARC members as per the 2016 peace deal.

HEAD OF STATE
President, Iván Duque, *elected* 17 June 2018, *sworn in* 7 August 2018
Vice-President, Martha Lucia Ramirez

SELECTED GOVERNMENT MEMBERS *AS AT AUGUST 2018*
Defence, Guillermo Botero
Finance, Carlos Alberto Carrasquilla
Foreign Affairs, Carlos Holmes Trujillo
Justice, Gloria Maria Borrero

EMBASSY OF COLOMBIA
3 Hans Crescent, London SW1X 0LN
T 020-7589 9177 E egranbretana@cancilleria.gov.co
W www.colombianembassy.co.uk
Ambassador Extraordinary and Plenipotentiary, HE Nestor Osorio, *apptd* 2014

BRITISH EMBASSY
Carrera 9, No 76–49, Piso 8, Edificio ING Barings, Bogotá
T (+57) (1) 326 8300 E embajadabritanica.bogota@fco.gov.uk
W www.gov.uk/government/world/colombia
Ambassador Extraordinary and Plenipotentiary, HE Peter Tibber, *apptd* 2015

INSURGENCIES
Colombia has been dogged by violence since the 1960s, initially from insurgency by left-wing guerrilla groups, mainly the FARC and the National Liberation Army (ELN), countered by right-wing paramilitaries affiliated with the United Self-Defence Forces of Colombia (AUC), which was suspected of having links with the security forces. In the 1980s, lawlessness increased with the rise of drug-producing and drug-trafficking cartels. An estimated 220,000 people, mainly civilians, were killed during the conflict.

Action against the insurgents and drug cartels since 2002 has extended state control to the extent that the government now has a presence in every municipality. Talks with the AUC from 2004 led to the demobilisation of most units in 2006, and in November 2012 FARC rebels declared a two-month ceasefire and began talks in Havana, Cuba. President Santos suspended negotiations in November 2014 after FARC kidnapped a Colombian general. Talks resumed in January 2015 after FARC declared an indefinite ceasefire and a final peace settlement was reached on 23 June 2016. After the deal was rejected by voters in a referendum in October 2016, a revised version was ratified by Congress on 1 December 2016.

ECONOMY AND TRADE

An improving security situation, economic liberalisation and international investment aided economic growth from 2002 to 2008 until the economy contracted in 2009 owing to the global downturn. GDP growth soon returned to an average rate of over 4 per cent while high global coffee prices allowed the government to abolish expensive farming subsidies in 2014. The economy is hindered by its vulnerability to commodity price fluctuations, an inadequate transport infrastructure, poverty and drug trafficking. The economy slowed in 2016 and GDP growth was lower than expected in 2017, at 1.8 per cent, due to low oil prices and insurgent attacks on pipelines.

Services account for around 61.4 per cent of GDP, industry 31.3 per cent and agriculture 7.4 per cent. Coal, oil, natural gas and hydroelectricity resources are exploited, and coal accounts for the majority of mining output; iron ore, nickel, gold, emeralds, copper and other minerals account for the remainder. Major cash crops are coffee, bananas and cut flowers. Cattle are raised in large numbers, and forestry is also important.

The principal trading partners are the USA, China, Mexico and the EU. Main exports are oil, coffee, coal, nickel, emeralds, garments, bananas and cut flowers. Imports include industrial and transport equipment, consumer goods, chemicals, paper products and fuels.

GNI – US$286.1bn; US$5,830 per capita (2017)
Annual average growth of GDP – 1.8 per cent (2017 est)
Inflation rate – 4.3 per cent (2017 est)
Population below poverty line – 27.8 per cent (2017 est)
Unemployment – 9.3 per cent (2017 est)
Total external debt – US$120.4bn (2017 est)
Imports – US$44,890m (2016)
Exports – US$30,985m (2016)

BALANCE OF PAYMENTS

Trade – US$13,905m deficit (2016)
Current Account – US$10,437m deficit (2017)

Trade with UK	2016	2017
Imports from UK	£263,476,411	£456,394,833
Exports to UK	£480,612,207	£470,818,681

COMMUNICATIONS

Airports – 121; the principal airports are at Bogotá, Barranquilla and Cali
Waterways – 18,300km of navigable waterways; the main seaports are Barranquilla and Cartagena on the Caribbean Sea and Buenaventura on the Pacific coast
Roadways and railways – 141,374km; 874km
Telecommunications – 7.2 million fixed lines and 58.7 million mobile subscriptions (2016); there were 27.5 million internet users in 2016

Internet code and IDD – co; 57 (from UK), 5/7/9 44 (to UK)
Major broadcasters – The state-run Senal Colombia is one of the largest television broadcasters in the country; Caracol runs several radio networks across the country alongside the state-run Radio Nacional de Colombia
Press – Daily newspapers include *El Tiempo*, *El Nuevo Siglo* and *El Espacio*
WPFI score – 41,03 (130)

EDUCATION AND HEALTH

Elementary education is free and compulsory from age six to 15. Healthcare is provided through a mixture of contributory and subsidised health schemes by both the private and the public sector.

Literacy rate – 98.7 per cent (2015 est)
Gross enrolment ratio (percentage of relevant age group) – primary 114 per cent, secondary 98.1 per cent, tertiary 58.7 per cent (2016 est)
Health expenditure (per capita) – US$569 (2014)
Hospital beds (per 1,000 people) – 1.5 (2014)
Life expectancy (years) – 75.9 (2017 est)
Mortality rate – 5.5 (2017 est)
Birth rate – 16.1 (2017 est)
Infant mortality rate – 13.6 (2017 est)
HIV/AIDS adult prevalence – 0.5 per cent (2015 est)

THE COMOROS

Udzima wa Komori/Jumhuriyat al-Qamar al-Muttahidah/Union des Comores – Union of the Comoros

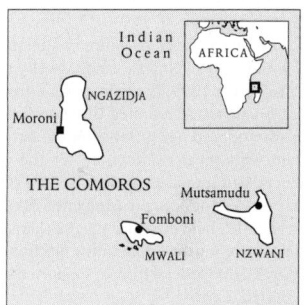

Area – 2,235 sq. km (excluding Mayotte). The Comoros includes the islands of Ngazidja (formerly Grande Comore), Nzwani (Anjouan), Mwali (Moheli) and certain islets in the Indian Ocean. Mayotte, the easternmost island of the archipelago, is a French dependency
Capital – Moroni, on Ngazidja; population, 56,000 (2015 est)
Major towns – Domoni, Fomboni, Mutsamudu
Currency – Comoran franc (KMF) of 100 centimes. The Franc CFA of 100 centimes is also used
Population – 808,080 rising at 1.64 per cent a year (2017 est)
Religion – Muslim (Sunni 98 per cent), Christian (Roman Catholic 2 per cent) (est); Islam is the state religion
Language – Arabic, French (both official), Shikomoro (a blend of Swahili and Arabic)
Population density – 53 per sq. km (2016)
Urban population – 29 per cent (2018 est)
Median age (years) – 19.9 (2017 est)
National anthem – 'Udzima wa ya Masiwa' 'The Union of the Great Islands'
National day – 6 July (Independence Day)
Death penalty – Retained (last used 1997)

CPI score – 27 (148)
Literacy rate – 77.8 per cent (2015 est)
Gross enrolment ratio (percentage of relevant age group) – primary 103.2 per cent, secondary 60.4 per cent, tertiary 8.9 per cent (2014 est)
Health expenditure (per capita) – US$57 (2014)
Life expectancy (years) – 64.6 (2017 est)
Mortality rate – 7.2 (2017 est)
Birth rate – 26.1 (2017 est)
Infant mortality rate – 60 (2017 est)
HIV / AIDS adult prevalence – 0.2 per cent (2013 est)

CLIMATE AND TERRAIN

Located in the Mozambique Channel between Africa and Madagascar, Ngazidja, Nzwani and Mwali are mountainous volcanic islands in the Comoros archipelago. The highest point is Karthala (2,360m) on Ngazidja, an active volcano that last erupted in 2007, and the lowest is 0m (Indian Ocean). The climate is tropical, with a hot, rainy season from October to April; the islands are prone to cyclones during the rainy season.

HISTORY AND POLITICS

The islands were settled by a variety of peoples before becoming part of the trading empire of the Shirazis of Persia, who established sultanates in the 15th to 16th centuries. In 1886, France established protectorates over the islands, making them a colony in 1912. They achieved internal self-government in 1961. In a 1974 referendum, the residents of three of the main islands voted in favour of independence, which was declared on 6 July 1975; Mayotte voted to remain part of France.

The republic experienced over 20 coups or attempted coups between 1975 and 1999. Nzwani and Mwali seceded in 1997 but after a coup in 1999, the military took control of all the islands' governments and reunited the state. Talks on the secessionist crisis produced a new constitution, introducing a federal structure with greater autonomy for the individual islands. Another constitutional crisis arose in June 2007 when the incumbent president of Nzwani, Mohamed Bacar, refused to stand down and then held elections that he claimed to have won. The federal government declared the elections null and void, and in March 2008 federal troops, supported by African Union forces, ousted Bacar.

The April 2016 federal presidency election was rerun in May following violence and irregularities, and was won by Azali Assoumani, a one-time coup leader. In the 2015 legislative elections, the Union for the Development of the Comoros (UPDC) became the largest party, winning eight of the 24 directly elected seats.

The 2002 constitution created a federal structure. Constitutional amendments approved in 2009 downgraded the islands' presidents to governors and harmonised presidential and legislative terms by extending those of the president and governors. In 2018, the nation overwhelmingly voted to extend presidential term limits to two consecutive five-year terms, and ended the policy of rotating the office of the president among the three islands.

The executive president appoints the union ministers. The unicameral Assembly of the Union has 33 members; three are appointed by each of the three island assemblies and 24 are directly elected for a five-year term.

Each island has its own governor and legislative assembly, and each governor may appoint eight ministers to form a government. Governors serve a five-year term. The islands' governments deal with local issues; foreign affairs, finance, defence, judicial and religious matters remain the responsibility of the union government. There are still areas of dispute, principally over security, budget control and customs revenue.

HEAD OF STATE
President of the Union, Azali Assoumani, *elected* 15 May 2016, *sworn in* 26 May 2016

SELECTED GOVERNMENT MEMBERS *AS AT AUGUST 2018*
Vice-President, Economy, Djaffar Ahmed Said Hassani
Foreign Affairs, Souef Mohamed El Amine
Interior, Mohamed Daoudou

BRITISH AMBASSADOR
Ambassador Extraordinary and Plenipotentiary, HE Dr Philip Boyle, *apptd* 2018, resident at Antananarivo, Madagascar

ECONOMY AND TRADE

The Comoros is very poor and heavily dependent on foreign aid and technical assistance. It has few natural resources, an uneducated workforce and poor transport infrastructure. Unemployment is high and remittances from 300,000 Comorans living abroad contribute around 25 per cent of the nation's GDP. In December 2012 the IMF and World Bank supported US$176m in debt relief for the Comoros, allowing a 59 per cent decrease in future external debt over a period of 40 years. Since 2011 growth has been driven by increasing external investment, particularly from Arab nations, and the country has been able to run a fiscal surplus. Agriculture, fishing and forestry account for 50 per cent of GDP and employ around 80 per cent of the population; service industries account for about 38.7 per cent and the manufacturing industry 11.8 per cent. The main industries are fishing, tourism and perfume distillation. The main trading partners are India, France, China, Pakistan and Germany. Principal exports are vanilla, perfume essence and cloves; coconuts, bananas and cassava are also cultivated.

GNI – US$0.6bn (2016 est); US$760 per capita (2017)
Annual average growth of GDP – 3.3 per cent (2017 est)
Inflation rate – 2.0 per cent (2017 est)
Population below poverty line – 44.8 per cent (2004 est)
Unemployment – 6.5 per cent (2014 est)
Total external debt – US$131.1m (2017 est)
Imports – US$263m (2014)
Exports – US$24m (2014)

BALANCE OF PAYMENTS
Trade – US$260m deficit (2013)
Current Account – US$43.7m deficit (2012)

Trade with UK	2016	2017
Imports from UK	£979,926	£1,198,252
Exports to UK	£89,117	£84,101

COMMUNICATIONS

Airports and waterways – Four; the main international airport is based on Moroni; the principal ports are based at Moroni and Mutsamudu
Roadways – 673km
Telecommunications – 13,049 fixed lines and 454,389 mobile subscriptions (2016); there were 63,084 internet users in 2016
Internet code and IDD – km; 269 (from UK), 44 (to UK)
Major broadcasters – National radio and television broadcasting is provided by state-run networks, and some island governments run radio and television stations

Press – No daily newspapers are published; the state-owned *Al-Watwan* is published weekly
WPFI score – 25,30 (49)

DEMOCRATIC REPUBLIC OF THE CONGO

République Démocratique du Congo – Democratic Republic of the Congo

Area – 2,344,858 sq. km
Capital – Kinshasa; population, 13,171,000 (2018 est)
Major cities – Bukavu, Kananga, Kisangani, Kolwezi, Likasi, Lubumbashi, Mbuji-Mayi
Currency – Congolese franc (FC) of 100 centimes
Population – 83,301,151 rising at 2.37 per cent a year (2017 est). The population is composed of over 200 ethnic groups, including Bantu, Hamitic, Nilotic, Sudanese and Pygmoid; the four largest tribes, Mongo, Luba, Kongo (all Bantu) and Mangbtu-Azande (Hamitic), make up around 45 per cent of the population
Religion – Christian (Roman Catholic 50 per cent, Protestant 20 per cent), Kimbanguist 10 per cent, Muslim 10 per cent (est)
Language – French (official), Lingala, Kingwana (a Swahili dialect), Kikongo, Tshiluba
Population density – 35 per sq. km (2016)
Urban population – 44.5 per cent (2018 est)
Median age (years) – 18.6 (2017 est)
National anthem – 'Debout Congolais' 'Arise, Congolese'
National day – 30 June (Independence Day)
Death penalty – Retained
CPI score – 21 (161)
Military expenditure – US$295m (2017)
Conscription – 18–45 years of age
Literacy rate – 77 per cent (2015 est)
Gross enrolment ratio (percentage of relevant age group) – primary 107 per cent, secondary 43.5 per cent (2014 est), tertiary 6.6 per cent (2013 est)
Health expenditure (per capita) – US$19 (2014)
Life expectancy (years) – 57.7 (2017 est)
Mortality rate – 9.6 (2017 est)
Birth rate – 33.5 (2017 est)
Infant mortality rate – 68.2 (2017 est)
HIV/AIDS adult prevalence – 0.8 per cent (2015 est)

CLIMATE AND TERRAIN

Africa's second-largest country lies on the equator, most of it in the basin of the river Congo and its principal tributaries, the Lualaba and the Kasai. A chain of mountains and lakes (Albert, Edward, Kivu and Tanganyika) runs along the eastern border. Elevation extremes range from 5,110m (Mt Ngaliema, also known as Mt Stanley) to 0m (Atlantic Ocean). The climate is tropical, though cooler in the eastern and southern highlands. There are different climatic cycles either side of the equator, which passes through the north of the country, with a wet season in the north from April to November and in the south from October to May.

POLITICS

Under the 2006 constitution, the executive president is directly elected for a five-year term, renewable once. The bicameral *Parlement* consists of the National Assembly, which has 500 members directly elected for a five-year term, and the senate, which has 108 members elected by the provincial assemblies to serve a five-year term, plus former elected presidents, who are senators for life.

Joseph Kabila succeeded his father Laurent (assassinated in 2001) as president. After a period of transitional government, a new constitution came into effect in 2006 and presidential and legislative elections were held. The presidential election was won in the second round by President Kabila, who went on to win re-election in November 2011, picking up nearly 49 per cent of the vote; his People's Party for Reconstruction and Development lost a large number of seats in the 2011 legislative election. Violent protests broke out in Kinshasa in January 2015 after President Kabila suggested he would consider changing the constitution in order to allow him to seek a third term of office; in December 2016 politician Moise Katumbi called on President Kabila to quit office to avoid further violent protests. Political instability and violence continued into 2018, with thousands killed and an estimated 4 million people displaced in the country. New legislative elections due in 2016 have been postponed by the government until December 2018.

HEAD OF STATE

President, Maj.-Gen. Joseph Kabila, *sworn in* 26 January 2001, *sworn in as president of the transitional government* 7 April 2003, *elected* 29 October 2006, *re-elected* 2011

SELECTED GOVERNMENT MEMBERS *AS AT MAY 2018*
Prime Minister, Bruno Tshibala
Deputy Prime Ministers, Léonard She Okitunda *(Foreign Affairs);* Henri Mova Sakanyi *(Interior);* José Makila Sumanda *(Transport)*
Defence, Crispin Atama Thabe
Economy, Joseph Kapika

EMBASSY OF THE DEMOCRATIC REPUBLIC OF THE CONGO
45–49 Great Portland Street, London W1W 7LD
T 020-7580 3931 E missionrdclondres@gmail.com
W http://ambardc-londres.gouv.cd
Ambassador Extraordinary and Plenipotentiary, HE Marie Ndjeka Opombo, *apptd* 2017

BRITISH EMBASSY
83 Avenue du Roi Baudouin, Gombe, Kinshasa
T (+243) 81 556 6200 E ambassade.britannique@fco.gov.uk
W www.gov.uk/government/world/democratic-republic-of-congo
Ambassador Extraordinary and Plenipotentiary, HE Dr John Murton, *apptd* 2017

ECONOMY AND TRADE

A decade of civil war left the country with huge external debt, little infrastructure, widespread corruption, a significant informal economy and an environment that discourages foreign investment. Improved stability since 2003 has allowed some economic growth, although the global downturn caused the economy to contract in 2008–9. Growth returned in 2010–11, and government reforms,

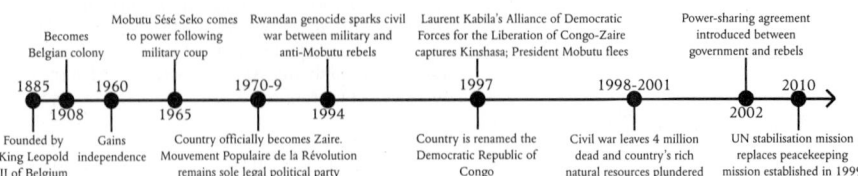

Becomes Belgian colony — 1885 · Founded by King Leopold II of Belgium · 1908 · Gains independence 1960 · Mobutu Sésé Seko comes to power following military coup 1965 · Country officially becomes Zaire. Mouvement Populaire de la Révolution remains sole legal political party · Rwandan genocide sparks civil war between military and anti-Mobutu rebels 1970-9 · 1994 · Laurent Kabila's Alliance of Democratic Forces for the Liberation of Congo-Zaire captures Kinshasa; President Mobutu flees 1997 · Country is renamed the Democratic Republic of Congo · 1998–2001 · Civil war leaves 4 million dead and country's rich natural resources plundered · Power-sharing agreement introduced between government and rebels 2010 · 2002 · UN stabilisation mission replaces peacekeeping mission established in 1999

international aid and debt relief continue to help the economy recover. The economy averaged strong growth of 8 per cent between 2012 and 2015, but wages have not grown and poverty remains high, with just under half of all children suffering from malnutrition. A subsequent fall in copper prices since 2015 has coincided with considerable inflation which peaked at nearly 50 per cent in mid-2017 and sporadic outbreaks of ebola. The east of the country was disproportionately affected by the civil war and remains particularly underdeveloped.

The country has great potential wealth in the form of immense natural resources, including copper, cobalt, diamonds, gold, silver, uranium, other minerals, coal, oil, timber and hydroelectric power; mining is the largest source of export income. Agriculture contributes 21.1 per cent of GDP, the services sector 45.9 per cent and industry 33 per cent. Apart from mining and mineral processing, the main industrial activities are the production of textiles, plastics, footwear, cigarettes, metal products, processed food, beverages, timber and cement, and ship repair. Oil deposits are exploited off the Congo estuary, and hydroelectric schemes on the river Congo supply power to the major cities.

The main trading partners are China, South Africa, Belgium, Zambia and Zimbabwe. Principal exports are diamonds, gold, copper, cobalt, wood products, crude oil and coffee. The main imports are foodstuffs, industrial machinery, transport equipment and fuels.

GNI – US$36.5bn; US$450 per capita (2017)
Annual average growth of GDP – 2.8 per cent (2017 est)
Inflation rate – 41.7 per cent (2017 est)
Population below poverty line – 63 per cent (2014 est)
Total external debt – US$5.324bn (2017 est)
Imports – US$6,200m (2015 est)
Exports – US$5,800m (2015 est)

BALANCE OF PAYMENTS
Trade – US$400m deficit (2015)
Current Account – US$1,334m deficit (2015)

Trade with UK	2016	2017
Imports from UK	£19,765,773	£22,754,782
Exports to UK	£2,848,109	£3,357,667

COMMUNICATIONS
Airport – 26, the principal airports being at Kinshasa, Kananga, Goma, Gemena and Mbandaka
Waterways – The river Congo and its main tributaries provide 15,000km of waterways, with the principal ports in Banana, Boma and Matadi
Roadways and railways – There are 2,794km of surfaced roads; the 4,007km rail system links the interior to the rivers and to the great lakes in the east
Telecommunications – 58,200 fixed lines (2012) in use and 29 million mobile subscriptions (2016); there were 3 million internet users in 2016
Internet code and IDD – cd; 243 (from UK), 44 (to UK)

Major broadcasters – The state-controlled Radio-Télévision Nationale Congolaise (RTNC) and the popular radio station La Voix du Congo approach national coverage; the UN and foreign NGOs sponsor Radio Okapi
Press – Major dailies include *Le Potentiel, La Reference Plus* and *L'Avenir*
WPFI score – 51,60 (154)

REPUBLIC OF THE CONGO

République du Congo – Republic of the Congo

Area – 342,000 sq. km
Capital – Brazzaville; population, 2,230,000 (2018 est)
Major cities – Loubomo, Pointe-Noire
Currency – Franc CFA of 100 centimes
Population – 4,954,674 rising at 2.11 per cent a year (2017 est); Kongo (48 per cent), Sangha (20 per cent), Teke (17 per cent) and M'Bochi (12 per cent) (est) are the largest of the 15 main Bantu groups
Religion – Christian (Roman Catholic 33.1 per cent, Awakening Churches 22.3 per cent, Protestant 19.9 per cent), Muslim 1.6 per cent, Kimbanguist 1.5 per cent (est)
Language – French (official), Lingala, Monokutuba, Kikongo
Population density – 15 per sq. km (2016)
Urban population – 66.9 per cent (2018 est)
Median age (years) – 19.7 (2017 est)
National anthem – 'La Congolaise' 'The Congolese'
National day – 15 August (Independence Day)
Death penalty – Abolished for all crimes (since 2015)
CPI score – 21 (161)
Military expenditure – US$484m (2017)

CLIMATE AND TERRAIN

The republic, which lies on the equator, is covered by grassland, mangrove and dense rainforest. The land rises from the narrow Atlantic coastal plain to a central plateau; in the north and east it falls to the northern part of the basin of the river Congo, which forms part of the border with the Democratic Republic of the Congo, and to the valleys of the Sangha and Alima rivers in the north. Elevation extremes range from 903m (Mt Berongou) to 0m (Atlantic Ocean). The climate is tropical. Average temperatures range from 23.5°C in July to 26°C in March. Outside the main dry season between June and September, the country is prone to flooding.

HISTORY AND POLITICS

The first European visitors to the area were the Portuguese, who established slave trading in the 16th century. The French established a colonial presence in the area in the 1880s and, as Middle Congo, it was part of French Equatorial Africa from 1910. It became independent as the Republic of the Congo on 17 August 1960.

One-party socialism was introduced in 1964; the Congolese Labour Party (PCT) was set up shortly after a military coup in 1968 and continued to rule until 1990, when Marxism was renounced and the PCT abandoned its monopoly of power. Elections in 1993 left the PCT a minority party, and the power shift destabilised the country, with factional fighting after the 1993 election, a civil war between 1997 and 1999 following Denis Sassou-Nguesso's deposition of the elected president, and a renewed insurgency by opponents of the PCT over the manipulation of the 2002 elections. A peace accord ended the insurgency in 2003 but the peace remains fragile and remnants of the rebel militias are still active in the south of the country.

Sassou-Nguesso was elected president in 2002 and was re-elected in 2009 and 2016; the legitimacy of all three victories was suspect after the barring or withdrawal of opponents, fraud and other irregularities. In 2015, President Sassou-Nguesso pushed through reforms to the country's constitution that allowed him to be elected for a third term. In the 2017 legislative election the PCT maintained its large majority, taking 89 of the 151 seats available.

Under the 2002 constitution, parties organised on regional, ethnic or religious lines are banned. The executive president is directly elected for a five-year term and appoints the cabinet. The bicameral *Parlement* comprises the National Assembly, with 151 members directly elected for a five-year term, and the senate, which has 72 members indirectly elected for a six-year term, half of the members retiring every three years.

HEAD OF STATE
President, Denis Sassou-Nguesso, *took power* October 1997, *elected* 10 March 2002, *re-elected* 2009, 2016

SELECTED GOVERNMENT MEMBERS *AS AT MAY 2018*
Prime Minister, Clément Mouamba
Defence, Charles Richard Mondjo
Economy, Gilbert Ondongo
Foreign Affairs, Jean-Claude Gakosso

EMBASSY OF THE REPUBLIC OF THE CONGO
37 bis Rue Paul Valéry, 75116 Paris, France
T (+33) (1) 4500 6057
Ambassador Extraordinary and Plenipotentiary, vacant

BRITISH AMBASSADOR
HE Dr John Murton, *apptd* 2017, resident at Kinshasa, DR of the Congo

ECONOMY AND TRADE

A decade of civil conflict left the country with a high external debt, a devastated infrastructure and widespread poverty. Since 2003 the government has made efforts to address these problems and has benefited from debt relief in 2006, 2007 and 2010. High unemployment, a contracting economy and public sector strikes continue to be a problem.

Oil production is the backbone of the economy and declining production and falling global commodity prices represent a major threat to the economy. Mining (particularly of diamonds), forestry, brewing, agricultural processing and cement production are the other main industries; new projects, notably the mining of iron ore, are expected to add around US$1bn to annual revenue. Industry accounts for 50.8 per cent of GDP, services for 40.3 per cent and agriculture, which is mostly at subsistence level, for 8.9 per cent.

The main trading partners are China, France and Belgium. Principal exports are oil, timber, plywood, sugar, cocoa, coffee and diamonds. Imports are mainly capital equipment, construction materials and foodstuffs.
GNI – US$7.2bn; US$1,360 per capita (2017)
Annual average growth of GDP – –3.6 per cent (2017 est)
Inflation rate – –0.4 per cent (2017 est)
Population below poverty line – 46.5 per cent (2011 est)
Total external debt – US$5.197bn (2017 est)
Imports – US$6,200m (2015)
Exports – US$5,800m (2015)

BALANCE OF PAYMENTS
Trade – US$400m deficit (2015)

Trade with UK	2016	2017
Imports from UK	£127,304,337	£57,945,418
Exports to UK	£25,689,796	£14,855,080

COMMUNICATIONS

Airports – Eight, including an international airport at Brazzaville
Waterways – Pointe-Noire is the main seaport and also the centre of the offshore oil industry. Brazzaville is the main river port, lying on the river Congo which, with the river Oubangui, provides 1,120km of commercially navigable waterways
Roadways and railways – 864km; 886km
Telecommunications – 17,000 fixed lines and 5.4 million mobile subscriptions (2016); there were 362,000 internet users in 2016
Internet code and IDD – cg; 242 (from UK), 44 (to UK)
Major broadcasters – TV Congo is the only television station and is controlled by the state. Two government radio stations, Radio Congo and Radio Brazzaville, exist alongside commercial and community stations
Press – The government-run *La Nouvelle République* is the country's only daily newspaper
WPFI score – 35,42 (114)

EDUCATION AND HEALTH

Schooling is free and compulsory between ages six and 16.
Literacy rate – 79.3 per cent (2015 est)
Gross enrolment ratio (percentage of relevant age group) – primary 105.7 per cent (2016 est), secondary 54 per cent (2012 est), tertiary 9.7 per cent (2013 est)
Health expenditure (per capita) – US$162 (2014)
Life expectancy (years) – 57.7 (2017 est)
Mortality rate – 9.5 (2017 est)
Birth rate – 33.5 (2017 est)
Infant mortality rate – 68.2 (2017 est)
HIV/AIDS adult prevalence – 2.75 per cent (2014 est)

COSTA RICA

República de Costa Rica – Republic of Costa Rica

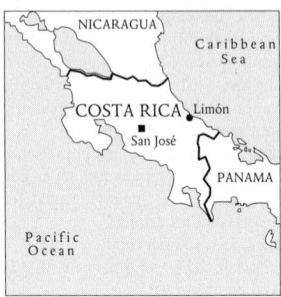

Area – 51,100 sq. km
Capital – San José; population, 1,358,000 (2018 est)
Major towns – Alajuela, Liberia, Limón, Paraíso, San
    Francisco
Currency – Costa Rican colón of 100 céntimos
Population – 4,930,258 rising at 1.16 per cent a year
    (2017 est)
Religion – Christian (Roman Catholic 76.3 per cent,
    Evangelical 13.7 per cent) (est)
Language – Spanish (official), English
Population density – 95 per sq. km (2016)
Urban population – 79.3 per cent (2018 est)
Median age (years) – 31.3 (2017 est)
National anthem – 'Noble Patria, Tu Hermosa Bandera' 'Noble
    Fatherland, Your Beautiful Flag'
National day – 15 September (Independence Day)
Death penalty – Abolished for all crimes (since 1877)
CPI score – 59 (38)
Literacy rate – 97.8 per cent (2015 est)
Gross enrolment ratio (percentage of relevant age group) – primary
    110 per cent, secondary 126.1 per cent, tertiary 54 per
    cent (2016 est)
Health expenditure (per capita) – US$970 (2014)
Hospital beds (per 1,000 people) – 1.1 (2014)
Life expectancy (years) – 78.7 (2017 est)
Mortality rate – 4.7 (2017 est)
Birth rate – 15.5 (2017 est)
Infant mortality rate – 8 (2017 est)
HIV/AIDS adult prevalence – 0.3 per cent (2015 est)

CLIMATE AND TERRAIN

The Cordillera de Guanacaste (north-west), Cordillera de
Talamanca and Cordillera Central (south-east) form a chain of
volcanic mountain ranges that traverse the country from north
to south. A central valley lies between the ranges, and the land
slopes to plains on the Pacific and Caribbean coasts. Elevation
extremes range from 3,810m (Cerro Chirripó Grande) to 0m
(Pacific Ocean). The climate is tropical, with average
temperatures ranging from 24.3°C in November to 26.8°C in
April, and a wet season from May to November. The area is
subject to occasional earthquakes, hurricanes, flooding and
landslides.

HISTORY AND POLITICS

Visited by Columbus in 1502, Costa Rica was colonised by
the Spanish from the 1560s and remained under Spanish rule
until Central America gained its independence in 1821. Costa
Rica was part of a Central American federation of former
Spanish provinces from 1823 until its secession in 1838.
Political unrest in the mid-20th century led to a brief civil war
in 1948, after which the army was abolished and replaced

with a national guard. Subsequently power alternated
between the two main political parties, the National
Liberation Party (PLN) and the Social Christian Unity Party
(PUSC), but in recent years the scandal-ridden PUSC has lost
ground to emerging new parties.

In the 2018 legislative elections the PLN remained the
largest party, despite losing votes for a third consecutive
election. The simultaneous presidential election was won by
the centre-left Citizens' Action party candidate Carlos
Alvarado Quesada.

Under the 1949 constitution, the executive president is
directly elected for a four-year term. The unicameral
legislative assembly has 57 members directly elected for a
four-year term.

HEAD OF STATE
President, Carlos Alvarado Quesada, *elected* 2 April 2018,
    sworn in 8 May 2018
First Vice-President, Foreign Affairs, Epsy Campbell Barr
Second Vice-President, Marvin Rodriquez Cordero

SELECTED GOVERNMENT MEMBERS *AS AT JULY 2018*
Economy, Victoria Hernandez Mora
Finance, Rocio Aguilar Montoya

EMBASSY OF COSTA RICA
14 Lancaster Gate, London W2 3LH
T 020-7706 8844 **E** info@costaricanembassy.co.uk
W www.costaricanembassy.co.uk
Ambassador Extraordinary and Plenipotentiary, HE José Enrique
    Castillo Barrantes, *apptd* 2015

BRITISH EMBASSY
Edificio Centro Colón, Paseo Colón and Streets 38 and 40, San Jose,
Apartado 815–1007
T (+506) 2258 2025 **E** ukin.costarica@fco.gov.uk
W www.gov.uk/government/world/costa-rica
Ambassador Extraordinary and Plenipotentiary, HE Ross Denny,
    apptd 2015

ECONOMY AND TRADE

Sixty years of political stability have allowed steady economic
growth, the creation of a social welfare system, one of the
highest levels of foreign direct investment in Latin America
and a reduction in poverty to less than 25 per cent of the
population, though the social benefit system is becoming
increasingly strained due to restrictions on government
spending and increased immigration. Costa Rica introduced a
floating exchange rate regime for the Costa Rican colón on 2
February 2015 in order to create more flexible exchange rates
and to manage inflation. GDP grew by 3.8 per cent in 2017
and is expected to remain stable.

Tourism is the largest single industry, and with one-third of
the country now national parkland or nature reserve, eco-
tourism is on the increase. Services account for about 73.5 per
cent of GDP while the manufacturing industry accounts for
21 per cent, the principal products being microprocessors,
foodstuffs, medical equipment, textiles, clothing, construction
materials, fertiliser and plastic goods. The agricultural sector
contributes 5.5 per cent of GDP; the principal products are
tropical fruit, coffee, ornamental plants, sugar, rice, vegetables,
meat and timber.

The main trading partners are the USA, China and Mexico.
The chief exports are tropical fruit, coffee, plants, sugar, beef,
seafood, electrical components and medical equipment. The
chief imports are raw materials, consumer goods, capital
equipment, petrol and construction materials.
GNI – US$54.1bn; US$11,040 per capita (2017)
Annual average growth of GDP – 3.8 per cent (2017 est)

Inflation rate – 1.7 per cent (2017 est)
Population below poverty line – 21.7 per cent (2014 est)
Unemployment – 8.1 per cent (2017 est)
Total external debt – US$25.83bn (2017 est)
Imports – US$15,343m (2016)
Exports – US$9,862m (2016)

BALANCE OF PAYMENTS
Trade – US$5,841m deficit (2016)
Current Account – US$1,691m deficit (2017)

Trade with UK	2016	2017
Imports from UK	£64,882,113	£67,403,853
Exports to UK	£210,970,327	£243,303,021

COMMUNICATIONS
Airports and waterways – 47; the principal airports are at San José and Limón; the chief seaports are Limón on the Atlantic coast, and Puntarenas and de Caldera on the Pacific coast
Roadways and railways – There are 10,133km of paved roads; 278km of railways, although the entire rail network fell into disrepair and out of use at the end of the 20th century, since 2005, certain sections of rail have been rehabilitated (2014)
Telecommunications – 849,826 fixed lines and 8.33 million mobile subscriptions (2016); there were 3.22 million internet users in 2016
Major broadcasters – Public broadcasting is provided by Canal 13 (TV) and Radio Nacional; cable television is widely available
Press – Media are generally free from state interference; daily newspapers include *Al Día, Diario Extra* and *La Nación*
Internet code and IDD – cr; 506 (from UK), 44 (to UK)
WPFI score – 14,01 (10)

CÔTE D'IVOIRE

République de Côte d'Ivoire – Republic of Côte d'Ivoire

Area – 322,463 sq. km
Capital – Yamoussoukro (since 1983); population, 231,000 (2018 est); slow progress in transferring functions means that the former capital, Abidjan (population, 4,921,000; 2018 est), remains the seat of government at present
Major cities – Abidjan, Bouaké, Daloa, Korhogo
Currency – Franc CFA of 100 centimes
Population – 24,184,810 rising at 1.84 per cent a year (2017 est); over 60 ethnic groups, including the Akan (28.8 per cent), Voltaiques or Gur (16.1 per cent), Northern Mandes (14.5 per cent), Kru (8.5 per cent), Southern Mandes (6.9 per cent) (2014 est)
Religion – Christian 45.7 per cent, Muslim 40.2 per cent, indigenous religions 12.8 per cent (est); many Christians

and Muslims incorporate indigenous beliefs into their worship
Language – French (official), around 60 native dialects of which Dioula is the most widely spoken
Population density – 75 per sq. km (2016)
Urban population – 50.5 per cent (2018 est)
Median age (years) – 20.9 (2017 est)
National anthem – 'L'Abidjanaise' 'Song of Abidjan'
National day – 7 August (Independence Day)
Death penalty – Abolished for all crimes (since 2000)
CPI score – 36 (103)
Military expenditure – US$295m (2017)
Literacy rate – 43.1 per cent (2015 est)
Gross enrolment ratio (percentage of relevant age group) – primary 96.7 per cent, secondary 46.1 per cent, tertiary 9.2 per cent (2015 est)
Health expenditure (per capita) – US$88 (2014)
Life expectancy (years) – 59 (2017 est)
Mortality rate – 9.4 (2017 est)
Birth rate – 27.7 (2017 est)
Infant mortality rate – 55.8 (2017 est)
HIV/AIDS adult prevalence – 2.8 per cent (2017 est)

CLIMATE AND TERRAIN
The land rises from a coastal plain to a large interior plateau with mountains in the north and west. Coastal lagoons give way to tropical rainforest in the centre and savannah in the north; deforestation means that the area of savannah is increasing. The country is dissected by the Sassandra, Bandama and Komoé rivers, the first two forming large central lakes. Elevation extremes range from 1,752m (Mt Nimba) to 0m (Gulf of Guinea). The climate is tropical in the south and semi-arid in the north. The south has two rainy seasons (May to July, October to November) and the north has one (June to September). The average annual temperature is 26.8°C.

POLITICS
Since the turn of the century Côte d'Ivoire has seen increased civil unrest and ethnic tensions. Following an election in 2010 the incumbent president Laurent Gbagbo refused to concede to the internationally acknowledged victor, Alassane Ouattara; after a four-month stalemate Ouattara took office by force. In the 2011 parliamentary elections, President Ouattara and his allies obtained a majority and the president was re-elected in October 2015 with 83.66 per cent of the vote.

Under the 2000 constitution, the executive president is directly elected for a five-year term. An amendment to the constitution in 2016 limited presidents to two terms beginning in 2020. The president appoints the prime minister and the other ministers, who are nominated by the prime minister. The unicameral National Assembly has 255 members, directly elected for a five-year term. Ouattara's Rally of the Republicans party won 167 seats in the December 2016 parliamentary elections. In recent years the country has been the target of attacks by Islamist militants on hotels and beach resorts.

HEAD OF STATE
President, Defence, Alassane Ouattara, *elected* 28 November 2010, *sworn in* 6 May 2011, *re-elected* 28 October 2015

SELECTED GOVERNMENT MEMBERS *AS AT MAY 2018*
Prime Minister, Amadou Gon Coulibaly
Economy and Finance, Adama Kone
Foreign Affairs, Marcel Amon-Tanoh
Interior, Sidiki Diakite

Area comes under French influence — 1460-1600
First Europeans introduce the ivory and slave trades — 1842
Gains independence as a one-party state under Felix Houphoët-Boigny — 1889-93
Côte d'Ivoire becomes French protectorate and colony — 1960
1990 — Multiparty system introduced
Death of President Houphoët-Boigny — 1993
Factional violence mars the presidential election won by Laurent Gbagbo — 2000
Country plunged into civil war after reconciliation talks break down — 2002
Civil war ends. Country divided into government-controlled south and rebel-held north — 2003
Government of national unity formed; rebel leader Guillaume Soro becomes prime minister — 2007
President Gbagbo and Alassane Ouattara both claim victory in presidential election — 2010
Ouattara's militia takes control of country and captures Gbagbo — 2011

EMBASSY OF THE REPUBLIC OF CÔTE D'IVOIRE

2 Upper Belgrave Street, London SW1X 8BJ
T 020-7235 6991
Ambassador Extraordinary and Plenipotentiary, HE Georges
  Aboua, *apptd* 2015

BRITISH EMBASSY

Cocody, Quartier Ambassades, Rue l'Impasse du Belier, Rue A 58,
01 BP 2581, Abidjan 01
T (+225) 2244 2669 E uk_abidjan@yahoo.fr
W www.gov.uk/government/world/cote-d-ivoire
Ambassador Extraordinary and Plenipotentiary, HE Josephine
  Gauld, *apptd* 2016

ECONOMY AND TRADE

The country was one of the most prosperous in the region, attracting large numbers of migrant workers from neighbouring countries, until the political turbulence of the late 1990s caused many to return home. The civil war particularly damaged the economy in the cotton-growing north, although recovery is beginning, and continuing political instability has hampered diversification away from agriculture, which makes the economy vulnerable to price fluctuations in its key exports. However, since 2006, revenue from oil, gas and refined products has outstripped earnings from cocoa, and offshore exploration for other deposits continues. The economy grew steadily in 2013–17, enjoying one of the highest growth rates in the world, and is expected to remain strong despite the threat of Islamist militant attacks. In March 2016, an attack on the Grand-Bassam beach resort left 18 dead.

In 2014 the UN overturned a ban on the export of the country's diamonds, which had been put in place in 2005 in order to stop the trade funding armed rebel groups. Improved political stability allowed the African Development Bank to return to Abidjan in 2014, having relocated to Tunisia for 11 years during the civil war. Poor infrastructure and business practices are a barrier to future growth, with Côte d'Ivoire having one of the most complex tax codes in Africa. Over 45 per cent live below the poverty line.

Services account for 53.8 per cent of GDP, agriculture for 17.4 per cent and industry for 28.8 per cent. Agriculture employs around 68 per cent of the workforce, producing cocoa (of which Côte d'Ivoire is the world's largest producer and exporter), coffee, cotton, bananas, pineapples and palm oil for export. The principal industries are food processing, forestry, oil refining, vehicle assembly, gold mining, textiles, building materials, fertiliser and hydroelectric power; the country is a net exporter of electricity. The main trading partners are Nigeria, France, other EU and west African states, and China.

GNI – US$37.5bn; US$1,540 per capita (2017)
Annual average growth of GDP – 7.6 per cent (2017 est)
Inflation rate – 1.0 per cent (2017 est)
Population below poverty line – 46.3 per cent (2015 est)
Total external debt – US$12.83bn (2017 est)
Imports – US$8,380m (2016)
Exports – US$10,661m (2016)

BALANCE OF PAYMENTS

Trade – US$2,281m surplus (2016)
Current Account – US$414m deficit (2016)

Trade	2016	2017
Imports from UK	£84,659,237	£111,294,795
Exports to UK	£241,322,545	£258,956,232

COMMUNICATIONS

Airports – Seven, the principal international airport being at Abidjan
Waterways – There are 980km of navigable rivers, canals and lagoons; the main seaports are Abidjan and San Pedro
Roadways and railways – 6,502km; 660km
Telecommunications – 289,108 fixed lines and 27 million mobile telephone subscriptions (2016); there were 6.3 million internet users in 2016
Internet code and IDD – ci; 225 (from UK), 44 (to UK)
Major broadcasters – The state broadcaster, Radiodiffusion Télévision Ivoirienne (RTI), operates two national radio stations and two television channels; in 2012 the government allowed private companies to enter the radio and TV markets for the first time
Press – Nine newspapers are published daily, including the state-owned *Fraternité Matin* and the privately owned *Le Nouveau Reveil*
WPFI score – 30,08 (82)

CROATIA

Republika Hrvatska – Republic of Croatia

Area – 56,594 sq. km
Capital – Zagreb; population, 686,000 (2018 est)
Major cities – Osijek, Rijeka (Fiume), Split, Zadar
Currency – Kuna of 100 lipa
Population – 4,292,095 falling at 0.5 per cent a year (2017 est); Croat (90.4 per cent), Serb (4.4 per cent) (2011)
Religion – Christian (Roman Catholic 86.3 per cent, Serbian Orthodox 4.4 per cent), Muslim 1.5 per cent (2011 est)
Language – Croatian (official), Serbian
Population density – 75 per sq. km (2016)

Urban population – 59.6 per cent (2018 est)
Median age (years) – 43 (2017 est)
National anthem – 'Lijepa Nasa Domovino' 'Our Beautiful Homeland'
National day – 8 October (Independence Day)
Death penalty – Abolished for all crimes (since 1990)
CPI score – 49 (57)
Military expenditure – US$772m (2017 est)

CLIMATE AND TERRAIN

There are three major geographic areas: the plains of the Pannonian region in the north, the central mountain belt, and the Adriatic coast region of Istria and Dalmatia, which has 1,185 islands and islets and 1,777km of coastline. Elevation extremes range from 1,831m (Dinara) to 0m (Adriatic Sea). The climate varies significantly between the Dalmatian coast, where the winters are mild and the summers hot, and inland areas, which have colder temperatures and rain in the summer. Average temperatures range from 1.8°C in January to 28°C in July.

POLITICS

The 1990 constitution was amended in 2000 to increase the powers of the legislature, making the presidency a largely ceremonial role, and in 2001 to abolish the upper house of the legislature. The head of state is a president, who is directly elected for a five-year term. The legislature, the Croatian Assembly, has one chamber, the House of Representatives, which has 151 members directly elected for a four-year term. The prime minister is appointed by the legislature and appoints the cabinet.

Following a vote of no confidence in Prime Minister Tihomir Oreskovic and his governing coalition in June 2016, the Croatian Democratic Union's (HDZ) Andrei Plenkovic was elected prime minister in legislative elections in September 2016. The HDZ won 61 parliamentary seats to the People's Coalition's 54. The 2015 presidential elections were narrowly won by Kolinda Grabar-Kitarovic of the HDZ after a second round of voting. Croatia became a member of the EU in July 2013.

HEAD OF STATE
President, Kolinda Grabar-Kitarovic, *elected* 12 January 2015, *sworn in* 18 February 2015

SELECTED GOVERNMENT MEMBERS *AS AT MAY 2018*
Prime Minister, Andrej Plenkovic
Deputy Prime Ministers, Damir Krsticevic *(Defence)*; Marija Pejcinovic Buric *(Foreign Affairs)*; Predrag Stromar
Finance, Zdravko Maric
Interior, Davor Bozinovic

EMBASSY OF THE REPUBLIC OF CROATIA
21 Conway Street, London W1T 6BN
T 020-7387 2022 **E** vrhlon@mvep.hr **W** http://uk.mvp.hr
Ambassador Extraordinary and Plenipotentiary, HE Igor Pokaz, *apptd* 2017

BRITISH EMBASSY
Ivana Lucica 4, 10000 Zagreb
T (+385) 600 9100 **E** british.embassyzagreb@fco.gov.uk
W www.gov.uk/government/world/croatia
Ambassador Extraordinary and Plenipotentiary, HE Andrew Dalgleish, *apptd* 2016

ECONOMY AND TRADE

As part of Yugoslavia, Croatia was a prosperous and industrialised area, but the conflict in 1991–5 damaged its infrastructure, large areas of farmland, industrial productivity and the tourist industry. From 2000 to 2007 there was steady economic growth, led by a recovery in tourism, banking and public investment. However, a growing trade deficit, high unemployment, the size of the public sector and the economy's over-reliance on tourism are longer-term problems that left the economy vulnerable in the global economic downturn in 2008. The country joined the EU in 2013 but does not yet qualify to join the Economic and Monetary Union. Following six years of recession, Croatia entered the EU's excessive-deficit procedure in 2014 but recovered enough to exit it in 2017. Reductions in tax and economic reforms since 2017 were designed to stimulate domestic consumption and foreign investment following a sharp fall in public debt.

The service sector accounts for 62.9 per cent of GDP, industry for 34.3 per cent and agriculture for 3.3 per cent. Tourism is a major economic contributor, at 19.6 per cent of GDP. Industry produces chemicals and plastics, machine tools, metals and metal products, electronics, wood products, construction materials and textiles, and includes food processing, shipbuilding and oil refining. Agricultural production includes cereals, pulses, fruit and vegetables, livestock and dairy products. Most trade is with EU and neighbouring countries.

GNI – US$51.3bn; US$12,430 per capita (2017)
Annual average growth of GDP – 2.9 per cent (2017 est)
Inflation rate – 1.1 per cent (2017 est)
Population below poverty line – 19.5 per cent (2015 est)
Unemployment – 13.9 per cent (2017 est)
Total external debt – US$44.53bn (2017 est)
Imports – US$21,802m (2016)
Exports – US$13,652m (2016)

BALANCE OF PAYMENTS
Trade – US$8,151m deficit (2016)
Current Account – US$2,363m surplus (2017)

Trade with UK	2016	2017
Imports from UK	£164,933,368	£190,102,968
Exports to UK	£99,503,748	£117,078,449

COMMUNICATIONS

Airports and waterways – 24; there are 785km of inland waterways and frequent ferry services to the many Adriatic islands
Roadways and railways – 29,410km, including 1,254km of motorways; 2,722km
Telecommunications – 1.4 million fixed lines and 4.4 million mobile subscriptions (2016); there were 3.1 million internet users in 2016

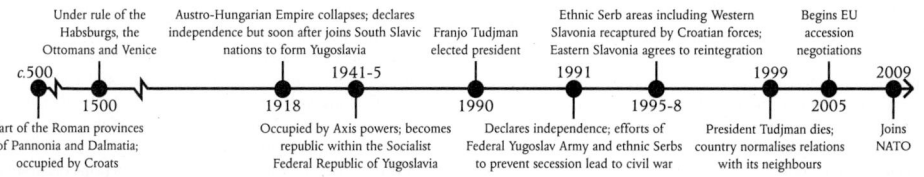

| Under rule of the Habsburgs, the Ottomans and Venice | Austro-Hungarian Empire collapses; declares independence but soon joins South Slavic nations to form Yugoslavia | Franjo Tudjman elected president | Ethnic Serb areas including Western Slavonia recaptured by Croatian forces; Eastern Slavonia agrees to reintegration | Begins EU accession negotiations |

c.500 — 1941-5 — 1991 — 1999 — 2009

1500 — 1918 — 1990 — 1995-8 — 2005

Part of the Roman provinces of Pannonia and Dalmatia; occupied by Croats — Occupied by Axis powers; becomes republic within the Socialist Federal Republic of Yugoslavia — Declares independence; efforts of Federal Yugoslav Army and ethnic Serbs to prevent secession lead to civil war — President Tudjman dies; country normalises relations with its neighbours — Joins NATO

Internet code and IDD – hr; 385 (from UK), 44 (to UK)
Major broadcasters – Croatian Radio-Television (HRT) is the national state-owned public service broadcaster
Press – Leading daily newspapers include *Vecernji List, Jutarnji List* and *Slobodna Dalmacija*
WPFI score – 28,94 (69)

EDUCATION AND HEALTH
Education is free and compulsory for all children from ages six to 15.
Literacy rate – 99.3 per cent (2015 est)
Gross enrolment ratio (percentage of relevant age group) – primary 95.4 per cent, secondary 97.8 per cent, tertiary 67.5 per cent (2016 est)
Health expenditure (per capita) – US$1,050 (2014)
Hospital beds (per 1,000 people) – 5.6 (2015)
Life expectancy (years) – 76.1 (2017 est)
Mortality rate – 12.2 (2017 est)
Birth rate – 8.9 (2017 est)
Infant mortality rate – 9.3 (2017 est)

CUBA

República de Cuba – Republic of Cuba

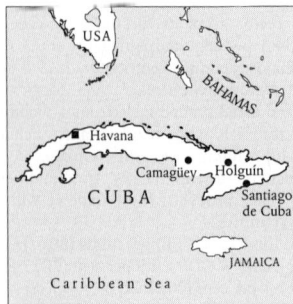

Area – 110,860 sq. km
Capital – Havana; population, 2,136,000 (2018 est)
Major cities – Camagüey, Guantánamo, Holguín, Santa Clara, Santiago de Cuba
Currency – Cuban peso ($) of 100 centavos
Population – 11,147,407 falling at 0.29 per cent a year (2017 est)
Religion – Christian (Roman Catholic 85 per cent) (est); many practise Santería (African religions syncretised with Christianity). Religious activity is tightly controlled; house churches must be state-registered
Language – Spanish (official)
Population density – 110 per sq. km (2016)
Urban population – 77 per cent (2018 est)
Median age (years) – 41.5 (2017 est)
National anthem – 'El Himno de Bayamo' 'The Anthem of Bayamo'
National day – 1 January (Triumph of the Revolution)
Death penalty – Retained
CPI score – 47 (62)
Military expenditure – US$126m (2014)
Conscription – 17–28 years of age; 24 months for men, optional for women

CLIMATE AND TERRAIN
The largest island in the Caribbean, Cuba is part of an archipelago that also includes Isla de la Juventud and around 1,600 other islets and cays. The island of Cuba has three mountainous ranges running from east to west. Elevation extremes range from 2,005m (Pico Turquino) to 0m (Caribbean Sea). The climate is subtropical, with an average annual temperature of 25.5°C.

POLITICS
The Communist Party of Cuba (PCC) is the only authorised political party. The 1976 constitution was amended in 1991 to allow direct election of the National Assembly by secret ballot, and in 2002 to enshrine socialism in the constitution. The president is elected by the legislature for a five-year term. The unicameral National Assembly of the People's Power has 605 members directly elected for a five-year term; all candidates are approved by the PCC and stand unopposed. Between its sessions, the assembly is represented by the Council of State, whose members are elected by the assembly.

A referendum on a new constitution, approved by the National Assembly in July 2018, is due to take place in early 2019. The draft constitution officially abandons communism and recognises capitalist market forces and private property.

Fidel Castro (1926–2016), who had been president since 1959, announced in February 2008 that he would not accept another term in office due to ill health. His brother, Raúl Castro, who had been acting president since July 2006, was elected head of state and head of government later that month by the National Assembly; he stepped down in April 2018 and was replaced by Miguel Díaz-Canel, ending almost 60 years of Castro rule.

HEAD OF STATE
President of Council of State and Council of Ministers, Miguel Díaz-Canel, *elected* 18 April 2018
First Vice-President of Council of State, Salvador Valdés Mesa

SELECTED GOVERNMENT MEMBERS *AS AT MAY 2018*
Vice-Presidents of Council of Ministers, Ricardo Cabrisas Ruiz *(Economy)*; Antonio Enrique Lusson Battle; Marino Murillo Jorge; Ramiro Valdes Menendez; Ulises Rosales del Toro; Jose Ramon Machado Ventura
Finance and Prices, Lina Pedraza Rodriguez
Foreign Relations, Bruno Rodriguez Parrilla

EMBASSY OF THE REPUBLIC OF CUBA
167 High Holborn, London WC1 6PA
T 020-7240 2488 E secembajador@uk.embacuba.cu
W misiones.minrex.gob.cu/en/united-kingdom/embassy-cuba-united-kingdom
Ambassador Extraordinary and Plenipotentiary, HE Teresita Vicente Sotolongo, *apptd* 2015

BRITISH EMBASSY
Calle 34, No 702, Miramar, Playa, Havana
T (+53) (0) 7214 2200 E embrit@enet.cu
W www.gov.uk/government/world/cuba
Ambassador Extraordinary and Plenipotentiary, HE Dr Antony Stokes, LVO, *apptd* 2016

ECONOMY AND TRADE
After the revolution, virtually all land and industrial and commercial enterprises were nationalised. With the collapse of communism in Europe in 1989–91, the economy deteriorated sharply, necessitating rationing of energy, food and consumer goods, and obliging the government to introduce reforms. Since 1993, liberalisation has gradually opened up the economy to limited private enterprise and foreign ownership of property and business enterprises, and introduced price rises for some goods and services and income tax. The reforms resulted in steady growth, in particular stimulating tourism and the oil and mining industries, but the standard of living for most Cubans is still below the pre-1991 level. Further economic difficulties arising from the global economic downturn, which precipitated a marked fall in tourism and nickel prices, led to a further easing of restrictions on private

			Communist state established,		Collapse of the USSR;	After 53 years Cuba
Settled by	Becomes independent; USA		allied with USSR; USA begins		Cuban government relaxes	and the USA restore
Spanish	retains naval bases on the island		economic and trade embargo		state economic controls	diplomatic relations

1492 · 1898 · 1959 · 1962 · 2008

1600 · 1902 · 1961 · 1991 · 2014

Visited by Columbus | War of independence won; Spain cedes Cuba to the USA | Dictator Gen. Fulgencio Batista overthrown by Fidel Castro | Cuban missile crisis; the USA and USSR almost engage in nuclear conflict due to missile site construction on Cuba | Fidel Castro steps down as president owing to ill-health; he is replaced by his brother Raúl

enterprise and consumption since 2011, as well as a reduction in public sector jobs.

In 2014, the Obama administration announced that it would re-establish communications with Cuba, paving the way for greater foreign travel and business interaction between the two countries. In January 2015, the two governments began talks to remove the embargo entirely and President Obama made a historic visit to Cuba in March 2016, but in June 2017 the Trump administration announced that it would reverse many aspects of the rapprochement, including tightening trade and travel rules.

Agriculture contributes 3.9 per cent of GDP and employs around 18 per cent of the workforce. Industrial activities include sugar refining, oil production, tobacco processing, construction, nickel mining and the production of steel, cement, agricultural machinery and pharmaceuticals. Industry contributes 21.5 per cent of GDP, and the service sector 74.2 per cent. As of December 2015, roughly 500,000 Cubans were self-employed.

The main trading partners are China, Spain, Venezuela and Russia; Venezuela provides Cuba with 100,000 subsidised barrels of oil a day, although economic problems in Venezuela has led to some supply issues. Principal exports are petroleum, sugar, nickel, tobacco, fish, medical products, citrus fruits and coffee. The main imports are oil, food, machinery and equipment, and chemicals.

GNI – US$66,397m; US$5,890 per capita (2011)
Annual average growth of GDP – –0.9 per cent (2016 est)
Inflation rate – 4.8 per cent (2017 est)
Unemployment – 2.2 per cent (2017 est)
Total external debt – US$20.55bn (2017 est)
Imports – US$6,415m (2014 est)
Export – US$11,703m (2014 est)

BALANCE OF PAYMENTS
Trade – US$6,573m deficit (2010)
Current Account – US$145.7m (2015 est)

Trade with UK	2016	2017
Imports from UK	£25,362,467	£24,839,852
Exports to UK	£11,068,197	£11,107,075

COMMUNICATIONS

Airports – 64; the main international airport is at Havana
Waterways – There are 240km of navigable waterways; the main ports are Havana, Cienfuegos and Matanzas
Roadways and railways – 29,820km; 8,203km, 4,533km of which are used exclusively by sugar plantations
Telecommunications – 1.3 million fixed line users and 3.9 million mobile subscriptions (2016); there were 4 million internet users in 2016
Internet code and IDD – cu; 53 (from UK), 44 (to UK)
Major broadcasters – The government operates four television channels and six radio stations including Cubavision (TV) and Radio Rebelde; Radio-TV Marti, a US government-backed station, transmits from Florida

Press – Cuba is the only country in the Americas not to have an independent press; the official Communist Party newspaper is *Granma*
WPFI score – 68,90 (172)

EDUCATION AND HEALTH
Education is free of charge and compulsory between ages six and 15. Healthcare is free.
Literacy rate – 100 per cent (2015 est)
Gross enrolment ratio (percentage of relevant age group) – primary 97.6 per cent, secondary 100.4 per cent, tertiary 36.3 per cent (2015 est)
Health expenditure (per capita) – US$817 (2014)
Hospital beds (per 1,000 people) – 5.2 (2014)
Life expectancy (years) – 78.8 (2017 est)
Mortality rate – 8.7 (2017 est)
Birth rate – 10.7 (2017 est)
Infant mortality rate – 4.4 (2017 est)
HIV/AIDS adult prevalence – 0.3 per cent (2015 est)

CYPRUS

Kypriaki Dimokratia/Kibris Cumhuriyeti – Republic of Cyprus

Area – 9,251 sq. km, of which 3,355 sq. km are in the Turkish Cypriot-administered area
Capital – Nicosia; population, 269,000 (2018 est)
Major cities – Larnaca, Limassol, Strovolos (south of the partition); Famagusta, Kyrenia (north)
Currency – Euro (€) of 100 cents (south), Turkish lira (north)
Population – 1,221,549 rising at 1.32 per cent a year (2017 est); Greek (98.8 per cent) (2011 est)
Religion – Christian (Greek Orthodox 89.1 per cent, Roman Catholic 2.9 per cent) south of the partition (2011 est); Muslim 98 per cent (mainly Sunni) in the north (est)
Language – Greek, Turkish (both official), English, Romanian, Russian, Bulgarian, Arabic, Filipino
Population density – 127 per sq. km (2016)
Urban population – 66.8 per cent (2018 est)
Median age (years) – 36.8 (2017 est)
National anthem – 'Ymnos eis tin Eleutherian' 'Hymn to Liberty'
National day – 1 October (Independence Day); Turkish Cypriots celebrate on 15 November

Death penalty – Abolished for all crimes (since 2002)
CPI score – 57 (42)
Military expenditure – US$395m (2017)
Conscription – 18–50 years of age, Greek Cypriot males only;
   14 months
Literacy rate – 99.9 per cent (2015 est)
Gross enrolment ratio (percentage of relevant age group) – primary
   99.3 per cent, secondary 99.8 per cent, tertiary 60.1 per
   cent (2015 est)
Health expenditure (per capita) – US$1,819 (2014)
Life expectancy (years) – 78.8 (2017 est)
Mortality rate – 6.8 (2017 est)
Birth rate – 11.3 (2017 est)
Infant mortality rate – 7.9 (2017 est)
HIV / AIDS adult prevalence – 0.06 per cent (2013 est)

CLIMATE AND TERRAIN

Cyprus is the third-largest island in the Mediterranean. It has
two mountain ranges, the Pentadaktylos along the north coast,
and the Troodos in the centre and west. Plains lie between the
two ranges and on parts of the south coast. Elevation extremes
range from 1,951m (Mt Olympus, Troodos range) to 0m
(Mediterranean Sea). The climate is Mediterranean, with very
warm summers.

POLITICS

The 1960 constitution provides for power-sharing between
the Greek and Turkish Cypriots but some of these provisions
have been in abeyance since 1963, when the Turkish Cypriots
withdrew from the power-sharing arrangements. The
executive president is directly elected for a five-year term. The
unicameral legislature, the House of Representatives, has 80
members, directly elected for a five-year term; elections to the
24 seats reserved for Turkish Cypriots have not taken place
since 1963.

In legislative elections held in May 2016, the right-wing
Democratic Rally (DISY) party consolidated its position
following a drop in support for all the major parties, including
the second-placed Progressive Party of the Working People
(AKEL) and the Democratic Party (DIKO). DISY's Nikos
Anastasiades was re-elected president in February 2018. Peace
talks with Northern Cyprus resumed in May 2015 after they
had been suspended in October 2014, when Cyprus claimed
it had been prevented by Turkey from exploring for potential
gas fields off the south coast of the island. However, UN-
backed talks in 2017 closed without reaching an agreement,
and Turkey continued to disrupt drilling in the disputed region
into 2018.

HEAD OF STATE
President, Nikos Anastasiades, *elected* 24 February 2013, *sworn
   in* 28 February 2013, *re-elected* 4 February 2018

SELECTED GOVERNMENT MEMBERS *AS AT MAY 2018*
Defence, Savvis Angelides
Finance, Haris Georgiades
Foreign Affairs, Nikos Christodoulides

HIGH COMMISSION FOR THE REPUBLIC OF CYPRUS
13 St James's Square, London SW1Y 4LB
T 020-7321 4100 E cyphclondon@btconnect.com
W www.mfa.gov.cy/highcomlondon/london.nsf
High Commissioner, HE Euripides L. Evriviades, *apptd* 2013

BRITISH HIGH COMMISSION
PO Box 21978, Alexander Pallis Street, 1587 Nicosia
T (+357) 2286 1100 E brithc.2@cytanet.com.cy
W www.gov.uk/government/world/cyprus
High Commissioner, HE Stephen Lillie, CMG, *apptd* 2018

BRITISH SOVEREIGN BASE AREAS
The Sovereign Base Areas (SBAs) of Akrotiri and Dhekelia are
those parts of Cyprus that remained under British sovereignty
and jurisdiction after independence, and have the status of a
UK overseas territory. They are around 231 sq. km in size.
There are approximately 15,700 residents: 7,700 Cypriots,
and 8,000 military and UK-based civilian personnel and their
dependants.
Administrator of the British Sovereign Base Areas, Air Vice-
   Marshal Michael Wigston, *apptd* 2015

TURKISH REPUBLIC OF NORTHERN CYPRUS

In 1974, a Greece-backed coup against the Cypriot
government led Turkey, fearing the coup was a precursor to
the union of Cyprus with Greece, to invade northern Cyprus
and occupy over a third of the island. The following year, a
Turkish Federated State of Cyprus was declared, and in 1983
a declaration of statehood was issued, which purported to
establish the Turkish Republic of Northern Cyprus. This was
condemned by the UN Security Council and only Turkey has
recognised the republic. A constitution was adopted in 1985,
and elections have been held at regular intervals since.

Reunification talks were unsuccessful in the 1980s and
1990s, and although Turkish Cypriots approved a UN-
sponsored reunification plan put to simultaneous referendums
in 2004, it was rejected by Greek Cypriots. Since 2004, the
EU has given aid to the area to promote and ease reunification,
and UN-facilitated talks began in 2008.

Following the 2018 legislative election, a coalition was
formed between four parties led by the left-wing Republican
Turkish Party. Mustafa Akinci won the 2015 presidential
election, replacing Dervis Eroglu.

DE FACTO HEAD OF STATE
President, Mustafa Akinci, *elected* 24 April 2015, *sworn in* 30
   April 2015
Prime Minister, Tufan Erhurman

ECONOMY AND TRADE

The Greek Cypriot economy is dominated by the service
sector, which accounted for 86.8 per cent of GDP; this was
derived mainly from tourism and financial services. Tourism
represents a major part of the total GDP, making the economy
vulnerable to fluctuations. Shipping services are also important;
about 20 per cent of the world's shipping is Cypriot-registered.

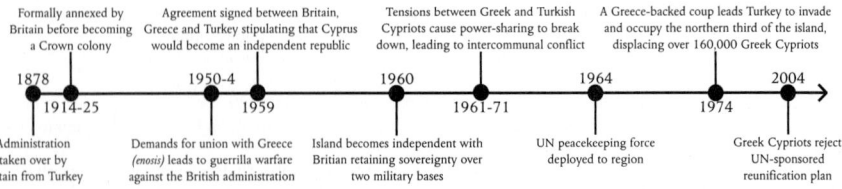

1878	1950-4	1960	1964	2004

Formally annexed by Britain before becoming a Crown colony *(1878)*

Agreement signed between Britain, Greece and Turkey stipulating that Cyprus would become an independent republic *(1950-4)*

Tensions between Greek and Turkish Cypriots cause power-sharing to break down, leading to intercommunal conflict *(1960)*

A Greece-backed coup leads Turkey to invade and occupy the northern third of the island, displacing over 160,000 Greek Cypriots *(2004)*

| 1914-25 | 1959 | 1961-71 | 1974 |

Administration taken over by Britain from Turkey *(1914-25)*

Demands for union with Greece *(enosis)* leads to guerrilla warfare against the British administration *(1959)*

Island becomes independent with Britian retaining sovereignty over two military bases *(1961-71)*

UN peacekeeping force deployed to region *(1974)*

Greek Cypriots reject UN-sponsored reunification plan

Industry contributes 11 per cent of GDP and agriculture 2.3 per cent. The main products for export are citrus fruits, potatoes, pharmaceuticals, cement and garments. Imports are primarily consumer goods, fuel and lubricants, machinery and transport equipment. Over half of trade is with other EU countries.

Between 2009 and 2013, the economy contracted by a total of 8.2 per cent following a banking crisis triggered by excessive exposure to the damaged Greek economy. In 2013, Cyprus received a US$13bn (£7.6bn) economic bailout from the European Commission, the European Central Bank and the International Monetary Fund (the 'Troika'). Conditions included the privatisation of state-owned enterprises and the downsizing and restructuring of the banking sector. In March 2016 Cyprus exited the EU/IMF bailout programme. The economy returned to real GDP growth in 2015 and grew steadily over the past few years, while unemployment has fallen. Exploitation of hydrocarbon deposits in Cypriot waters remains a long-term goal, but disagreements with Turkey over ownership have caused the project to stall.

The Turkish Cypriot economy suffers from a small domestic market, international isolation and a bloated public sector. It is heavily dependent on financial support from the Turkish government. Services accounted for about 58.7 per cent of GDP in 2012 (the latest year for which data is available), industry for 35.1 per cent and agriculture for 6.2 per cent. The main products for export are citrus fruits, dairy products, potatoes and textiles. The main imports are vehicles, fuel, cigarettes, food, minerals, chemicals and machinery.

GNI – US$20.4bn; US$23,719 per capita (2017)
Annual average growth of GDP – 3.4 per cent (2017 est)
Inflation rate – 0.8 per cent (2016 est)
Unemployment – 11.8 per cent (2017 est)
Total external debt – US$95.280m (2013 est)
Imports – US$6,604m (2016)
Exports – US$1,921m (2016)

BALANCE OF PAYMENTS
Trade – US$4,683m deficit (2016)
Current Account – US$1,452m deficit (2017)

Trade with UK	2016	2017
Imports from UK	£321,960,286	£380,302,815
Exports to UK	£171,532,805	£148,890,884

COMMUNICATIONS
Airports and waterways – 13, including Larnaca and Paphos (Greek area); flight connections to Turkish area are via Turkey; principal ports are Limassol, Larnaca and Vasilikos (Greek area), and Famagusta and Kyrenia (Turkish area)
Roadways – The road network (8,564km in the Greek part of the island and 7,000km in the Turkish part) serves the main population centres
Telecommunications – 320,573 fixed lines and 1.1 million mobile subscriptions (2016); there were 915,036 internet users in 2016
Internet code and IDD – cy; 357 (from UK), 44 (to UK)
Major broadcasters – The state-run Cyprus Broadcasting Corporation competes with a number of privately owned television and radio stations; the Turkish north has its own public broadcaster, Bayrak Radio-TV
Press – Major daily newspapers include *Cyprus Mail* (English-language), *Politis* (Greek-language) and *Kibris Gazete* (Turkish-language)
WPFI score – 19,85 (25) (Greek area); 29,59 (77) (Turkish area)

CZECHIA
Ceska Republika – Czech Republic

Area – 78,867 sq. km
Capital – Prague (Praha); population, 1,292,000 (2018 est)
Major cities – Brno (Brünn), Ostrava, Plzen (Pilsen)
Currency – Koruna (Kc) of 100 haleru
Population – 10,674,723 rising at 0.12 per cent a year (2017 est); Czech (64.3 per cent), Moravian (5 per cent), Slovak (1.4 per cent) (2011)
Religion – Christian (Roman Catholic 10.4 per cent, Protestant 1.1 per cent) (2011 est)
Language – Czech (official), Slovak
Population density – 137 per sq. km (2016)
Urban population – 73.8 per cent (2018 est)
Median age (years) – 42.1 (2017 est)
National anthem – 'Kde Domov Muj?' 'Where is My Homeland?'
National day – 28 October (Founding Day)
Death penalty – Abolished for all crimes (since 1990)
CPI score – 57 (42)
Military expenditure – US$2,233m (2017)

CLIMATE AND TERRAIN
The landlocked republic is composed of Bohemia (the west and centre) and Moravia (the east). Bohemia contains the fertile plains of the river Elbe and the surrounding low mountains, while the hilly region of Moravia extends towards the basin of the river Danube. Roughly a third of the country is covered by forest. Elevation extremes range from 1,602m (Snezka) to 115m (river Elbe). The climate is continental, with warm, humid summers and cold, dry winters. The average temperature in Prague ranges from −1.4°C in January to 18.2°C in July and August.

POLITICS
The 1992 constitution provided for the separation of the Czech Republic and Slovakia; federal laws remain in place unless superseded by Czech ones. The president is elected by popular vote for a five-year term, renewable once; prior to 2012 the president was elected by a joint session of both chambers of the legislature. The bicameral *Parlament* comprises a 200-member Chamber of Deputies, directly elected for a four-year term, and an 81-member senate directly elected for a six-year term, one-third being elected every two years. The council of ministers is appointed by the president on the recommendation of the prime minister. In April 2016 the country changed its official short geographic name to Czechia.

Early legislative elections in October 2013 gave a combined majority to three centre-left parties – the Czech Social Democratic Party (CSSD), the Christian Democratic Union/ Czech People's Party (KDU–CSL) and the Movement of Dissatisfied Citizens (ANO) – which formed a coalition

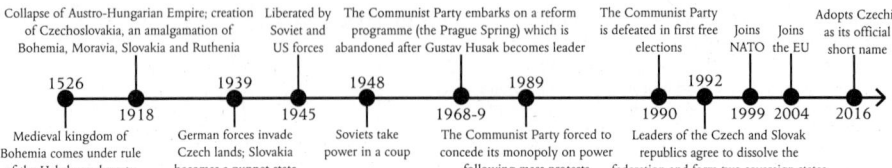

Collapse of Austro-Hungarian Empire; creation of Czechoslovakia, an amalgamation of Bohemia, Moravia, Slovakia and Ruthenia

Liberated by Soviet and US forces

The Communist Party embarks on a reform programme (the Prague Spring) which is abandoned after Gustav Husak becomes leader

The Communist Party is defeated in first free elections

Joins NATO

Joins the EU

Adopts Czechia as its official short name

1526   1939   1948   1989   1992

1918   1945   1968-9   1990   1999 2004   2016

Medieval kingdom of Bohemia comes under rule of the Habsburg dynasty

German forces invade Czech lands; Slovakia becomes a puppet state

Soviets take power in a coup

The Communist Party forced to concede its monopoly on power following mass protests

Leaders of the Czech and Slovak republics agree to dissolve the federation and form two sovereign states

government under CSSD chairman Bohuslav Sobotka. The CSSD retained its position as the largest party in the senate in October 2016 elections. The ANO, led by billionaire Andrej Babis, won legislative elections in October 2017, but the minority government resigned in January 2018 over corruption allegations regarding Babis, initiating over eight months of coalition talks. Prime Minister Babis maintained his position with the help of the CSSD. Milos Zeman (CCSD) was elected president in January 2013 and was narrowly re-elected in January 2018.

HEAD OF STATE
President, Milos Zeman, *elected* 25 January 2013, *sworn in* 8 March 2013, *re-elected* 25 January 2018

SELECTED GOVERNMENT MEMBERS *AS AT AUGUST 2018*
Prime Minister, Andrej Babis
Deputy Prime Ministers, Richard Brabec *(Environment)*; Jan Hamacek *(Interior)*
Defence, Lobomir Metnar

EMBASSY OF THE CZECH REPUBLIC
26–30 Kensington Palace Gardens, London W8 4QY
T 020-7243 1115 E london@embassy.mzv.cz
W www.mzv.cz/london
Ambassador Extraordinary and Plenipotentiary, HE Libor Secka, *apptd* 2016

BRITISH EMBASSY
Thunovska 14, 11800 Prague 1
T (+420) (2) 5740 2111 E ukinczechrepublic@fco.gov.uk
W www.gov.uk/government/world/czech-republic
Ambassador Extraordinary and Plenipotentiary, HE Nicholas Archer, MVO, *apptd* 2018

ECONOMY AND TRADE
Economic reforms and accession to the EU have produced a stable and successful market economy, as well as contributing to steady growth by expanding export markets and encouraging foreign investment. The global economic downturn caused the economy to contract in 2009, largely because of a reduced demand for the country's major exports which constitutes some 80 per cent of GDP. The economy came out of two years of recession in 2014 thanks to the manufacturing sector, internal consumption, tourism and international investment. In 2017, it had one of the highest growth rates and lowest levels of unemployment in the EU.
Services account for 59.7 per cent of GDP, industry for 37.8 per cent and agriculture for 2.5 per cent. The principal agricultural products are cereal crops, sugar beet and potatoes; the timber industry is also important. The country has been industrialised since the 19th century, and motor vehicles, metals, machinery, glass and armaments are major products. Electricity is also exported. The principal trading partners are EU countries – especially Germany – and China.
GNI – US$192.3bn; US$18,160 per capita (2017)
Annual average growth of GDP – 3.5 per cent (2017 est)
Inflation rate – 2.3 per cent (2017 est)

Population below poverty line – 9.7 per cent (2015 est)
Unemployment – 2.8 per cent (2017 est)
Total external debt – US$145.8bn (2017 est)
Imports – US$142,782m (2016)
Exports – US$162,772m (2016)

BALANCE OF PAYMENTS
Trade – US$19,990m surplus (2016)
Current Account – US$1,918m surplus (2017)

Trade with UK	2016	2017
Imports from UK	£2,140,584,181	£2,131,202,241
Exports to UK	£5,362,557,763	£5,636,718,110

COMMUNICATIONS
Airports and waterways – There are 41 airports, with the principal airport at Prague; the 664km of waterways include the Elbe, Vltava and Oder rivers
Roadways and railways – Extensive road (130,671km) and rail (9,469km) networks link the main population centres
Telecommunications – 1.76 million fixed lines and 12.5 million mobile subscriptions (2016); there were 8.1 million internet users in 2016
Internet code and IDD – cz; 420 (from UK), 44 (to UK)
Major broadcasters – The public broadcaster Ceska Televize (CT) runs two networks and a 24-hour news channel alongside two major private television stations; Czech public radio, Cesky Rozhlas (CRo), operates three national networks and local services
Press – Major daily newspapers include *Lidove Noviny, Mlada Fronta Dnes* and *Pravo*
WPFI score – 16,91 (23)

EDUCATION AND HEALTH
Education is free and compulsory for all children from the age of six to 15.
Gross enrolment ratio (percentage of relevant age group) – primary 105 per cent, secondary 97 per cent, tertiary 64.5 per cent (2015 est)
Health expenditure (per capita) – US$1,379 (2014)
Hospital beds (per 1,000 people) – 6.5 (2015)
Life expectancy (years) – 78.8 (2017 est)
Mortality rate – 10.5 (2017 est)
Birth rate – 9.3 (2017 est)
Infant mortality rate – 2.6 (2017 est)

DENMARK

Kongeriget Danmark – Kingdom of Denmark

Area – 43,094 sq. km (excluding the Faroe Islands and
    Greenland)
Capital – Copenhagen; population, 1,321,000 (2018)
Major cities – Aalborg, Aarhus, Esbjerg, Odense
Currency – Danish krone (DKr) of 100 ore
Population – 5,605,948 rising at 0.22 per cent a year (2017
    est)
Religion – Christian (Lutheran 80 per cent, Roman Catholic
    1 per cent, Muslim 4 per cent (2012 est); the Evangelical
    Lutheran Church is the state church
Language – Danish (official), Faroese, Greenlandic, German;
    English is widely spoken as a second language
Population density – 136 per sq. km (2016)
Urban population – 87.9 per cent (2018 est)
Median age (years) – 42.2 (2017 est)
National anthem – 'Det er et Yndigt Land' 'There is a Lovely
    Land'
National day – 5 June (Constitution Day)
Death penalty – Abolished for all crimes (since 1978)
CPI score – 88 (2)
Military expenditure – US$3,795m (2017)
Conscription – 18 years of age; 4–12 months

CLIMATE AND TERRAIN

Denmark consists of most of the Jutland peninsula and 406
islands, mainly in the Baltic Sea or among the northern Frisian
Islands in the North Sea. The largest islands are Sjaelland
(Zealand), Fyn, Lolland, Faister and Bornholm. It is a low-
lying country, indented by fjords on its east coast and with
lagoons and sand dunes along the west coast; Lim Fjord nearly
bisects the north of Jutland. Elevation extremes range from
171m (Mollehoj) to −7m (Lammefjord). The climate is
temperate, with cold winters and warm summers. Average
temperatures range from 1.1°C in January to 17.4°C in July.

HISTORY AND POLITICS

The Danes were at the forefront of Viking expansionism from
the eighth century. Denmark was unified in the tenth century
and was the centre of a short-lived empire, also including
Norway and England, created by Cnut (Canute) in the 11th
century. The Union of Kalmar (1397) brought Norway and
Sweden (including Finland) under Danish rule. Danish power
waned during the 16th century, enabling Sweden to re-
establish its independence in 1523, and Norway was ceded to
Sweden under the Treaty of Kiel in 1814. Denmark was
neutral during the First World War, but in the Second World
War it was invaded and occupied by Germany until May
1945.

Denmark joined the European Community in 1973. In a
2000 referendum, it rejected adopting the euro.

In the 2011 legislative election, the Liberal Party remained
the largest party in parliament, but a surge of support for the

Red Bloc (a political alliance consisting of centre-left parties)
gave them an overall majority with 97 seats. Helle Thorning-
Schmidt, leader of the Social Democrats, formed a coalition
with other member parties of the Red Bloc, and took office in
October 2011. In January 2015, the withdrawal of the
Socialist People's party caused the remaining members of the
ruling coalition to form a minority government. After the June
2015 legislative election, negotiations within the centre-right
Blue Bloc coalition proved unsuccessful despite a one-seat
majority, and the Liberal Party formed a minority
government. In November 2016 two Blue Bloc parties
entered into coalition with the government, although it still
does not hold a parliamentary majority.

The country is a constitutional monarchy, with a hereditary
monarch as head of state. The head of government is the
prime minister, who appoints the cabinet. The unicameral
legislature, the *Folketing,* has 179 members, including two for
the Faroes and two for Greenland; members are elected for a
four-year term by proportional representation.

HEAD OF STATE
HM The Queen of Denmark, Queen Margrethe II, KG, *born*
    16 April 1940, *acceded* 14 January 1972
Heir, HRH Crown Prince Frederik, *born* 26 May 1968

SELECTED GOVERNMENT MEMBERS *AS AT MAY 2018*
Prime Minister, Lars Rasmussen
Defence, Claus Frederiksen
Finance, Kristian Jensen
Foreign Affairs, Anders Samuelsen

ROYAL DANISH EMBASSY
55 Sloane Street, London SW1X 9SR
T 020-7333 0200 E lonamb@um.dk W www.storbrittanien.um.dk
Ambassador Extraordinary and Plenipotentiary, HE Lars Thuesen,
    apptd 2017

BRITISH EMBASSY
Kastelsvej 36–40, DK-2100 Copenhagen
T (+45) 3544 5200 E enquiry.copenhagen@fco.gov.uk
W www.gov.uk/government/world/denmark
Ambassador Extraordinary and Plenipotentiary, HE Dominic
    Schroeder, *apptd* 2016

ECONOMY AND TRADE

Denmark has a diversified and industrialised market economy
with a high dependence on exports. It is a net exporter of food
and energy (oil and natural gas). Slowing growth from 2007
and then the global downturn pushed the economy into
recession in 2009; a modest recovery began in 2010 but the
economy re-entered a technical recession at the beginning of
2011. The economy has recovered since 2014 and achieved
modest growth of 2 per cent in 2016 and 2.1 per cent in
2017, but this is expected to slow in 2018. The service sector
contributes 75.2 per cent of GDP, industry 23.7 per cent and
the highly efficient agricultural sector 1.1 per cent. Metals,
pharmaceuticals, shipping and renewable energy are key
industries.

The main trading partners are other EU countries, especially
Germany and Sweden. Principal exports are machinery and
instruments, meat and meat products, dairy products, fish,
pharmaceuticals, furniture and windmills. The main imports
are machinery and equipment, industrial raw materials and
semi-manufactures, chemicals, grain and foodstuffs, and
consumer goods.
GNI – US$318.6bn; US$55,220 per capita (2017)
Annual average growth of GDP – 1.9 per cent (2017 est)
Inflation rate – 1.0 per cent (2017 est)
Population below poverty line – 13.4 per cent (2011)

Unemployment – 5.8 per cent (2017 est)
Total external debt – US$484.8bn (2016 est)
Imports – US$85,001m (2016)
Exports – US$94,194m (2016)

BALANCE OF PAYMENTS
Trade – US$9,192m surplus (2016)
Current Account – US$25,342m surplus (2017)

Trade with UK	2016	2017
Imports from UK	£2,486,889,177	£2,739,539,462
Exports to UK	£3,931,585,050	£4,974,951,422

COMMUNICATIONS
Airports and waterways – The principal airports are at Copenhagen, Aarhus, Aalborg and near Vejle; the main ports are Aarhus, Odense, Copenhagen, Aalborg and Esbjerg
Roadways and railways – 73,929km of roadways, including 1,143km of motorways; 2,667km of railways, of which 640km are electrified
Telecommunications – 1.56 million fixed lines and 7 million mobile subscriptions (2016); there were 5.4 million internet users in 2016
Internet code and IDD – dk; 45 (from UK), 44 (to UK)
Major broadcasters – The public broadcaster is Danmarks Radio, which operates two television networks, and national and regional radio stations
Press – There are six major daily newspapers, including *Morgenavisen Jyllands-Posten* (English-language pages), *Berlingske Tidende* and *Ekstra Bladet*
WPFI score – 13,99 (9)

EDUCATION AND HEALTH
Education is free and compulsory for nine years.
Gross enrolment ratio (percentage of relevant age group) – primary 129 per cent, secondary 129.1 per cent, tertiary 81.1 per cent (2016 est)
Health expenditure (per capita) – US$6,463 (2014)
Hospital beds (per 1,000 people) – 2.5 (2015)
Life expectancy (years) – 79.5 (2017 est)
Mortality rate – 10.3 (2017 est)
Birth rate – 10.5 (2016 est)
Infant mortality rate – 4 (2017 est)
HIV/AIDS adult prevalence – 0.16 per cent (2014 est)

THE FAROE ISLANDS
Area – 1,393 sq. km
Capital – Torshavn; population, 21,000 (2018 est)
Population – 50,730 rising at 0.55 per cent a year (2017 est)
Religion – Christian 89.3 per cent (2011 est)
Population density – 35 per sq. km (2016)
Urban population – 42.1 per cent (2018 est)
Median age (years) – 37.6 (2017 est)
National day – 29 July (Olaifest)
Internet code and IDD – fo; 298 (from UK), 44 (to UK)
The Faroe (Sheep) Islands are a group of 18 rugged islands (17 inhabited) and a few islets in the North Atlantic Ocean, between the Shetland Islands and Iceland. First settled in the ninth century, the islands were a Norwegian province and, with Norway, came under Danish rule in the 14th century. Since 1948 the Faroes have been self-governing and are not part of the EU.
The sovereign is represented in the islands by a high commissioner, and the islands elect two representatives to the Danish legislature. The Faroese government *(Landsstyri)* is responsible for internal affairs. The parliament *(Loegting)* has 33 members, elected for a four-year term. Following the 2015

election, the Social Democrat, Republic and Progress parties formed a government under Prime Minister Aksel V. Johannesen.
Prime Minister, Aksel V. Johannesen, *sworn in* 15 September 2015

ECONOMY AND TRADE
The economy has grown steadily in recent years, although it slowed during the global downturn. It remains highly dependent on fishing and fish processing; fish and fish products account for 95 per cent of exports. Offshore oil discoveries raise the possibility of future diversification and less dependence on Danish government subsidies.
Imports – US$980m (2016)
Exports – US$1,192m (2016)

BALANCE OF PAYMENTS
Trade – US$212m surplus (2016)
Current Account – US$194m deficit (2011)

Trade with UK	2016	2017
Imports from UK	£9,655,088	£20,744,704
Exports to UK	£221,510,243	£213,078,335

BRITISH CONSULATE
P/F Damfar, PO Box 1154, Niels Finsengota 5, FR-110 Torshavn
T (+298) 35 00 77
Honorary Consul, Joannes Hansen

GREENLAND KALAALLIT NUNAAT
Area – 2,166,086 sq. km
Capital – Nuuk (Godthab); population, 18,000 (2018)
Population – 57,713 falling at 0.03 per cent a year (2017 est); Inuit (88 per cent) (2010 est)
Urban population – 86.8 per cent (2018 est)
Median age (years) – 33.9 (2017 est)
National day – 21 June (longest day)
Internet code and IDD – gl; 299 (from UK), 44 (to UK)
Greenland, the world's largest island, lies between the Atlantic and Arctic oceans, to the east of Canada and to the west of Iceland. Most of Greenland is within the Arctic Circle, with permafrost covering about 80 per cent of the island, although this ice cap is beginning to melt *(see also* The North and South Poles). Elevation extremes range from 3,700m (Gunnbjorn) to 0m (Atlantic Ocean).
Greenland was first discovered by small groups of hunters and nomadic groups who migrated from Canada *c.*500 BC. In the late tenth century Icelanders established settlements along the south-eastern coast, but these colonies had died out by the 16th century. Danish colonisation began in the 18th century. Greenland was integrated into Denmark in 1953 and was granted internal autonomy in 1979; greater autonomy was granted in 2009. Greenland negotiated its withdrawal from the EU, without discontinuing relations with Denmark, and left in 1985. The USA maintains air bases on the island.
The sovereign is represented by a high commissioner, and Greenland elects two representatives to the Danish legislature. The Greenlandic government *(Landsstyri)* is elected by the parliament *(Landsting),* which has 31 members, elected for a four-year term. Aleqa Hammond became the country's first female prime minister in 2013. Snap elections in December 2014, called after Hammond resigned following a corruption scandal and fears over the economy, were won by the governing centre-left Siumut party. In the 2018 election to the *Landsting,* the Siumut (Forward) party lost two seats but remained the largest party.
Prime Minister, Kim Kielsen, *sworn in* 10 December 2014

ECONOMY AND TRADE

The economy is dependent on Danish subsidies (56 per cent of government revenue) and fishing; fish and fish products comprise 89 per cent of exports. Natural resources include zinc, iron ore, lead, coal, molybdenum, gold, platinum and uranium, some of which are mined. Mineral exploration and mining operations are being extended as the ice cap shrinks. This is also benefiting offshore oil exploration, and global warming is extending the growing season. Tourism is being encouraged.

Imports – US$631m (2016)
Exports – US$551m (2016)

Trade with UK	2016	2017
Imports from UK	£2,322,430	£3,331,237
Exports to UK	£2,403,666	£3,417,266

DJIBOUTI

Jumhuriyat Jibuti/République de Djibouti – Republic of Djibouti

Area – 23,200 sq. km
Capital – Djibouti; population, 562,000 (2018 est)
Currency – Djibouti franc (DJF) of 100 centimes
Major cities – Ali Sabin, Danan, Tadjoura
Population – 865,267 rising at 2.16 per cent a year (2017 est); Somali (Issa) 60 per cent, Afar 35 per cent (est)
Religion – Muslim 94 per cent, Christian 6 per cent
Language – French, Arabic (both official), Somali, Afar
Population density – 41 per sq. km (2016)
Urban population – 77.8 per cent (2018 est)
Median age (years) – 23.9 (2017 est)
National anthem – 'Jabuuti' 'Djibouti'
National day – 27 June (Independence Day)
Death penalty – Abolished for all crimes (since 1995)
CPI score – 31 (122)
Military expenditure – US$36.3m (2008)
Gross enrolment ratio (percentage of relevant age group) – primary 44.1 per cent, secondary 44.1 per cent (2017 est)
Health expenditure (per capita) – US$191 (2014)
Life expectancy (years) – 63.6 (2017 est)
Mortality rate – 7.5 (2017 est)
Birth rate – 23.4 (2017 est)
Infant mortality rate – 45.8 (2017 est)
HIV/AIDS adult prevalence – 1.6 per cent (2015 est)

CLIMATE AND TERRAIN

Djibouti is situated on the strait linking the Gulf of Aden with the Red Sea, close to busy shipping lanes. The coastal plain is separated from an inland plateau by the central mountains. Elevation extremes range from 2,028m (Moussa Ali) to −155m (Lake Assal). Although the climate is semi-arid with a hot season between April and October, occasional heavy rains can cause flash floods. The country is also prone to cyclones,

drought and earthquakes. Djibouti experienced a ninth consecutive year of drought in 2016.

POLITICS

Under the 1992 constitution, amended in 2010, the president is directly elected for a five-year term, with no term limits. The president appoints the council of ministers. The unicameral National Assembly has 65 members, directly elected for a five-year term. The 2010 constitutional amendments provided for the establishment of a senate.

In the 2008 legislative elections, which were boycotted by the opposition, the Union for a Presidential Majority (UMP) retained all 65 seats in the legislature. Though opposition parties took part in the February 2013 parliamentary elections, the ruling party took 49 of 65 seats; the Union of National Salvation issued a statement claiming the vote was rigged. The major opposition parties again boycotted the 2018 elections, with UMP winning 58 seats. The 2011 presidential election was also boycotted, and in 2016 President Guelleh won a fourth term in office.

HEAD OF STATE
President, Ismail Omar Guelleh, *elected* 9 April 1999, *re-elected* 2005, 2011, 2016

SELECTED GOVERNMENT MEMBERS *AS AT MAY 2018*
Prime Minister, Abdoulkader Kamil Mohamed
Defence, Ali Hassan Bahdon
Economy and Finance, Ilyas Moussa Dawaleh
Foreign Affairs, Mahamoud Ali Youssouf
Interior, Hassan Omar Mohamed Bourhan

EMBASSY OF THE REPUBLIC OF DJIBOUTI
26 Rue Emile Ménier, 75116 Paris, France
T (+33) (1) 4727 4922 **E** webmaster@amb-djibouti.org
Ambassador Extraordinary and Plenipotentiary, HE Ayeid Mousseid Yahya, *apptd* 2015

BRITISH AMBASSADOR
HE Susanna Moorehead, *apptd* 2016, resident at Addis Ababa, Ethiopia

ECONOMY AND TRADE

A barren country with few natural resources and little industry, Djibouti's chief asset is its location on major shipping lanes. It is a transit port for neighbouring landlocked countries, especially Ethiopia, an international trans-shipment and refuelling centre, and a military base for US and EU forces because of its strategic position. The country is dependent on foreign aid, has around 40 per cent unemployment and has to import nearly all its food. The service sector accounts for 76.1 per cent of GDP, industry for 21 per cent and agriculture for 2.8 per cent. In recent years it has started to modernise with large infrastructure projects, partly with the help of China, which includes a significant port extension (Port of Doraleh) and the Djibouti-Addis Ababa Railway.

The main trading partners are Ethiopia, Somalia, France and the UAE. Principal exports are re-exports (mainly coffee), hides and skins, and scrap metal. The main imports are food, beverages, transport equipment, chemicals and petroleum products.

GNI – US$1.8m; US$1,880 per capita (2017)
Annual average growth of GDP – 7.0 per cent (2017 est)
Inflation rate – 3.0 per cent (2017 est)
Population below poverty line – 23 per cent (2015 est)
Unemployment – 40 per cent (2017 est)
Total external debt – US$1.554bn (2017 est)
Imports – US$890m (2015)
Exports – US$132m (2015)

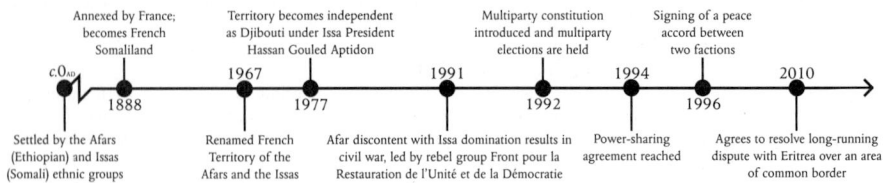

Annexed by France; becomes French Somaliland — 1888

Settled by the Afars (Ethiopian) and Issas (Somali) ethnic groups

Territory becomes independent as Djibouti under Issa President Hassan Gouled Aptidon — 1967

1977 — Renamed French Territory of the Afars and the Issas

Multiparty constitution introduced and multiparty elections are held — 1991

1992 — Afar discontent with Issa domination results in civil war, led by rebel group Front pour la Restauration de l'Unité et de la Démocratie

Signing of a peace accord between two factions — 1994

1996 — Power-sharing agreement reached

2010 — Agrees to resolve long-running dispute with Eritrea over an area of common border

BALANCE OF PAYMENTS

Trade – US$758m deficit (2015)
Current Account – US$170m deficit (2016)

Trade with UK	2016	2017
Imports from UK	£9,064,407	£10,544,725
Exports to UK	£5,524,575	£19,012,378

COMMUNICATIONS

Airports and waterways – The main port and principal airport are located in Djibouti
Roadways and railways – 1,226km; the 100km Djibouti section of the Addis Ababa–Djibouti railway is controlled by both Djibouti and Ethiopia but is largely inoperable
Telecommunications – 24,925 fixed lines and 345,246 mobile telephones in use (2016); there were 111,212 internet users in 2016
Internet code and IDD – dj; 253 (from UK), 44 (to UK)
Press – The government owns the two major newspapers: *La Nation* (French-language) and *Al-Qarn* (Arabic-language)
Major broadcasters – Radiodiffusion-Télévision de Djibouti (RTD) is the national broadcaster and operates a radio station (Radio Djibouti) and television channel (Télé Djibouti 1). Opposition parties operate media outlets from overseas, including La Voix de Djibouti radio
WPFI score – 70,77 (173)

DOMINICA

Commonwealth of Dominica

Area – 751 sq. km
Capital – Roseau; population, 15,000 (2018 est)
Currency – East Caribbean dollar (EC$) of 100 cents
Population – 73,897 rising at 0.18 per cent a year (2017 est)
Religion – Christian (Roman Catholic 61.4 per cent, Protestant 28.6 per cent) (est)
Language – English (official), Creole
Population density – 98 per sq. km (2016)
Urban population – 70.5 per cent (2018 est)
Median age (years) – 33.5 (2017 est)

National anthem – 'Isle of Beauty, Isle of Splendour'
National day – 3 November (Independence Day)
Death penalty – Retained (last used 1986)
CPI score – 57 (42)
Gross enrolment ratio (percentage of relevant age group) – primary 116 per cent, secondary 100.5 per cent (2015 est)
Health expenditure (per capita) – US$408 (2014)
Life expectancy (years) – 77.2 (2017 est)
Mortality rate – 7.9 (2017 est)
Birth rate – 15.2 (2016 est)
Infant mortality rate – 10.6 (2017 est)

CLIMATE AND TERRAIN

Dominica, the most northerly of the Windward Islands, is 46km long and 25km wide, with a mountainous and forested centre. Its peaks include volcanic craters, one of which contains Boiling Lake, the world's second-largest thermally active lake. Elevation extremes range from 1,447m (Morne Diablotins) to 0m (Caribbean Sea). The climate is tropical, with an average temperature of 23.3°C. The island is located within the hurricane zone.

HISTORY AND POLITICS

Dominica was discovered by Columbus in 1493, when it was a stronghold of the Caribs, the sole inhabitants of the island until the French founded settlements in the 18th century. It was ceded to the British in 1763 but passed back and forth between France and Britain until 1805, after which British possession was unchallenged. From 1871 until the 1960s Dominica was administered by Britain as part of various federations of West Indian islands. Internal self-government from 1967 was followed on 3 November 1978 by independence as a republic.

The Dominica Labour Party (DLP) won the legislative election in 2014, the party's fourth general election victory in a row. Charles Savarin was elected president in 2013; the main opposition United Workers Party boycotted this election, claiming the process was unconstitutional.

Under the 1978 constitution, the president is elected by the legislature for a five-year term, renewable once. The unicameral House of Assembly has 32 members, 21 directly elected, two *ex-officio* and nine appointed senators; all members serve a five-year term.

HEAD OF STATE

President, Charles Savarin, *elected* September 2013

SELECTED GOVERNMENT MEMBERS *AS AT JUNE 2018*

Prime Minister, Finance, Roosevelt Skerrit
Foreign Affairs, Francine Baron
Justice, National Security, Rayburn Blackmoore

OFFICE OF THE HIGH COMMISSIONER FOR THE COMMONWEALTH OF DOMINICA

1 Collingham Gardens, London SW5 0HW
T 020-7370 5194 E info@dominicahighcommission.co.uk
W www.dominicahighcommission.co.uk
High Commissioner, vacant

BRITISH HIGH COMMISSIONER
HE Janet Douglas, CMG, *apptd* 2017, resident at
   Bridgetown, Barbados

ECONOMY AND TRADE
The economy, traditionally dependent on banana exports,
struggled in the early 2000s as EU preferential access for the
fruit was phased out; the industry also suffered serious
hurricane damage in 2007 and 2017. Economic restructuring
from 2003 led to steady growth, with an emphasis on eco-
agriculture and eco-tourism, until the global downturn caused
the economy to contract in 2009, and again in 2013.
Diversification into offshore financial services, medical
education and light industry is also being encouraged,
alongside exploitation of geothermal energy, fishing and
forestry resources. However, following the destruction caused
by Hurricane Maria in September 2017, the government's
short-term priorities has been reconstruction and managing
mounting public debt.
   Agriculture is the principal occupation, employing 40 per
cent of the workforce but producing only 15.3 per cent of
GDP. Services contribute 71.1 per cent of GDP and industry
13.6 per cent. The main trading partners are the USA, other
Caribbean countries and Saudi Arabia. Principal exports are
bananas, soap, bay oil, vegetables and citrus fruits. The main
imports are manufactured goods, machinery and equipment,
food and chemicals.

GNI – US$0.5bn; US$6,990 per capita (2017)
Annual average growth of GDP – 3.9 per cent (2017 est)
Inflation rate – 0.6 per cent (2016 est)
Population below poverty line – 29 per cent (2009 est)
Total external debt – US$288.6m (2016 est)
Imports – US$214m (2016)
Exports – US$23m (2016)

BALANCE OF PAYMENTS
Trade – US$191m deficit (2016)
Current Account – US$4.8m surplus (2016 est)

Trade with UK	2016	2017
Imports from UK	£8,762,369	£8,287,922
Exports to UK	£606,985	£891,164

COMMUNICATIONS
Airports and waterways – The principal airports are Melville
Hall on the north-east tip of the island and Canefield, just
outside Roseau; the main seaports are located at Portsmouth
and Roseau
Roadways – 762km
Telecommunications – 13,328 fixed lines and 78,444 mobile
subscriptions (2016); there were 49,439 internet users in
2016
Internet code and IDD – dm; 1 767 (from UK), 011 44 (to UK)
Press – There are no daily newspapers
Major broadcasters – There is no national television on the
island, but cable television provider Marpim Telecom and
Broadcasting covers parts of the island; DBS Radio is
operated by the state broadcaster

DOMINICAN REPUBLIC
República Dominicana – Dominican Republic

Area – 48,670 sq. km
Capital – Santo Domingo; population, 3,172,000 (2018)
Major cities – La Romana, Los Alcarrizos, San Pedro de
   Macorís, Santiago de los Caballeros
Currency – Dominican Republic peso (RD$) of 100 centavos
Population – 10,734,247 rising at 1.18 per cent a year
   (2017 est)
Religion – Christian (Roman Catholic 95 per cent), other
   5 per cent (est)
Language – Spanish (official)
Population density – 220 per sq. km (2016)
Urban population – 80.6 per cent (2017)
Median age (years) – 28.1 (2017 est)
National anthem – 'Himno Nacional' 'National Anthem'
National day – 27 February (Independence Day)
Death penalty – Abolished for all crimes (since 1966)
CPI score – 29 (153)
Military expenditure – US$496m (2017)
Literacy rate – 97.9 per cent (2015)
Gross enrolment ratio (percentage of relevant age group) – primary
   102 per cent, secondary 77 per cent, tertiary 53 per cent
   (2016 est)
Health expenditure (per capita) – US$269 (2014)
Hospital beds (per 1,000 people) – 1.62 (2014)
Life expectancy (years) – 78.3 (2017 est)
Mortality rate – 4.7 (2017 est)
Birth rate – 18.4 (2017 est)
Infant mortality rate – 17.5 (2017 est)
HIV/AIDS adult prevalence – 1 per cent (2015 est)

CLIMATE AND TERRAIN
The republic forms the eastern two-thirds of the island of
Hispaniola and is crossed from the north-west to the south-
east by the Cordillera Central mountain range, which has a
number of peaks over 3,000m. Elevation extremes range from
3,175m (Pico Duarte) to −46m (Lake Enriquillo). The climate
is maritime tropical, with an average temperature of 24.8°C.

HISTORY AND POLITICS
The island was discovered by Columbus in 1492, and a
Spanish colony was established in 1496. The eastern province
of Santo Domingo remained under Spanish rule after the
partition of Hispaniola in 1697, but was ceded to France in
1795. It was restored to Spain in 1809, but rebelled in 1821
and achieved independence briefly before being annexed by
Haiti in 1822. Haitian rule ended in 1844 when
independence was declared as the Dominican Republic,
although the country was voluntarily under Spanish rule again
from 1861 to 1865. A long dictatorship at the end of the 19th
century was followed by revolution and bankruptcy, which
led to occupation by US forces from 1916 until 1924. A

military coup in 1930 established the dictatorship of Gen. Rafael Trujillo, whose corrupt rule continued until his assassination in 1961. After a period of political instability, a new constitution was adopted in 1966 and democracy was restored.

The May 2016 presidential election was won by incumbent Danilo Medina of the Dominican Liberation Party (PLD); in simultaneous legislative elections the ruling PLD retained its majority in both houses, although polling was marked by irregularities and violence.

In 2015, the 2010 constitution was changed to allow the president to run for a second term. The bicameral National Congress comprises the House of Representatives, which has 190 members, and the senate, with 32 members, one for each province and one for Santo Domingo; both chambers are directly elected for a four-year term.

HEAD OF STATE
President, Danilo Medina, *elected* 2012, *sworn in* August 2012, re-elected 2016
Vice-President, Margarita Cedeno de Fernández

SELECTED GOVERNMENT MEMBERS *AS AT JUNE 2018*
Defence, Ruben Dario Paulino Sem
Finance, Donald Guerrero
Foreign Affairs, Miguel Vargas Maldonado
Interior, Jose Ramon Fadul

EMBASSY OF THE DOMINICAN REPUBLIC
139 Inverness Terrace, London W2 6JF
T 020-7727 7091 E info@dominicanembassy.org.uk
W www.dominicanembassy.org.uk
Ambassador Extraordinary and Plenipotentiary, HE Federico Alberto Cuello Camilo, *apptd* 2011

BRITISH EMBASSY
Edificio Corominas Pepín, 7th–8th Floor, Ave 27 de Febrero No 233, Santo Domingo
T (+1) (829) 472 7111
W www.gov.uk/government/world/dominican-republic
Ambassador Extraordinary and Plenipotentiary, HE Christopher Campbell, *apptd* 2015

ECONOMY AND TRADE
In recent years, tourism and the free trade zones have overtaken agriculture as the mainstay of the economy, and services now account for over 60 per cent of GDP. Industry accounts for 33.8 per cent and agriculture for 5.5 per cent. The main crops are sugar, coffee, cotton, cocoa, tobacco, rice, vegetables and bananas, and the main industrial activities are sugar processing, mining and the production of textiles, cement and tobacco products. Remittances from expatriate workers are equivalent to roughly two thirds of tourism receipts. The economy returned to growth from 2010 after the global recession and the country's budget deficit was halved from 2012 to 2014. Despite being one of the fastest growing economies in Latin America, poverty and unemployment rates remain high.

The main trading partner is the USA, which claims over half of all exports and provides 41.4 per cent of imports. Principal exports are sugar, gold, silver, coffee, cocoa, tobacco, meats and consumer goods. The chief imports are foodstuffs, fuel, cotton and fabrics, chemicals and pharmaceuticals.
GNI – US$71.4bn; US$6,630 per capita (2016)
Annual average growth of GDP – 4.8 per cent (2017 est)
Inflation rate – 3.0 per cent (2017 est)
Population below poverty line – 30.5 per cent (2016 est)
Unemployment – 5.5 per cent (2017 est)
Total external debt – US$26.69bn (2017 est)

Imports – US$16,865m (2015)
Exports – US$4,011m (2015)

BALANCE OF PAYMENTS
Trade – US$12,854m deficit (2015)
Current Account – US$1,650m deficit (2017)

Trade with UK	2016	2017
Imports from UK	£103,146,585	£100,389,102
Exports to UK	£161,440,520	£128,434,458

COMMUNICATIONS
Airports and waterways – 16, the principal airport is at Santo Domingo; Santo Domingo, Rio Haina and Caucedo are the main seaports
Roadways and railways – There are 9,872km of surfaced roads, and 142km of railways
Telecommunications – 1.34 million fixed lines and 8.7 million mobile subscriptions (2016); there were 6.5 million internet users in 2016
Internet code and IDD – do; 1 809/829 (from UK), 011 44 (to UK)
Major broadcasters – Combination of state-owned and privately owned broadcast media, including over 300 radio stations. The state-owned broadcaster is Corporacion Estatal de Radio y Television (CERTV)
Press – Five main daily newspapers are published in Spanish
WPFI score – 26,79 (59)

ECUADOR
República del Ecuador – Republic of Ecuador

Area – 283,561 sq. km
Capital – Quito; population, 1,822,000 (2018 est)
Major cities – Cuenca, Guayaquil, Machala, Manta, Santo Domingo de los Colorados
Currency – US dollar (US$) of 100 cents
Population – 16,290,913 rising at 1.28 per cent a year (2017 est)
Religion – Christian (Roman Catholic 74 per cent, Evangelical 10.4 per cent) (2012 est)
Language – Spanish (official), Quechua, other Amerindian languages
Population density – 66 per sq. km (2016)
Urban population – 63.8 per cent (2018 est)
Median age (years) – 27.7 (2017 est)
National anthem – 'Salve, Oh Patria' 'We Salute You, Our Homeland'
National day – 10 August (Independence Day)
Death penalty – Abolished for all crimes (since 1906)
CPI score – 32 (117)

Military expenditure – US$2,427m (2017)
Conscription – 18 years of age; 12 months (selective), currently suspended

CLIMATE AND TERRAIN
The Andes run north to south through the centre of Ecuador, dividing the coastal plain in the west from the low-lying rainforest in the east, and between two local Andean chains lie the central highlands. Elevation extremes range from 6,267m (Chimborazo) to 0m (Pacific Ocean). Other Andean peaks include Cotopaxi (5,896m) and Cayambe (5,790m) in the Eastern Cordillera. Ecuador is located in an earthquake zone and five of its volcanoes have erupted since 2000 – most recently Tungurahua in April 2014. The country has four different climatic zones and is one of the most biodiverse countries on earth; its territory includes the Galápagos Islands in the Pacific Ocean. The average temperature is 21.9°C.

HISTORY AND POLITICS
The kingdom of the Caras, around Quito, was conquered by the Incas in the 15th century. After the Spanish defeated the Incas in Peru, Ecuador was conquered in 1534 and added to the Spanish viceroyalty of Peru. Independence from Spain was achieved in a revolutionary war that culminated in the battle of Mt Pichincha (1822). Ecuador then formed part of Gran Colombia with Colombia, Panama and Venezuela, but left this union to become a fully independent state in 1830. After independence, the country experienced periods of political instability interspersed with dictatorships and military rule. Democratic rule under civilian government was restored in 1979.

The exploitation of oil reserves funded economic and social transformation from the 1970s onwards but also caused rapid inflation and increased foreign debt. In recent years, these problems have worsened because of economic recession, leading to strikes and demonstrations. Civil unrest forced three presidents from office between 1997 and 2003.

Presidential and legislative elections were held in 2009 after a new constitution was approved by a national referendum in 2008, and in 2013 President Correa was elected for a third term – and his second four-year term. He did not contest presidential elections in February 2017, which resulted in a narrow victory for his vice president Lenín Moreno over right-wing candidate Guillermo Lasso. In the simultaneous legislative elections, the left-wing PAIS Alliance won 39 per cent of the vote. Moreno's running partner and vice president, Jorge Glas, was jailed for six years in December 2017 for bribery.

The 2008 constitution provides for an executive president who is directly elected for a four-year term, renewable once. The unicameral National Assembly has 137 members elected on a party-list proportional representation basis for a four-year term. The republic is divided into 24 provinces.

HEAD OF STATE
President, Lenín Moreno, *elected* 2 April 2017
Vice-President, Maria Alejandra Vicuña

SELECTED GOVERNMENT MEMBERS *AS AT JUNE 2018*
Defence, vacant
Economy and Finance, Richard Martinez
Foreign Affairs, Maria Fernanda Espinosa

EMBASSY OF ECUADOR
Flat 3B, 3 Hans Crescent, London SW1X 0LS
T 020-7584 1367 E eecugranbretania@mmrree.gob.ec
W www.consuladoecuador.org.uk
Ambassador Extraordinary and Plenipotentiary, HE Carlos Abad Ortiz, *apptd* 2015

BRITISH EMBASSY
PO Box 17-17-830, Citiplaza Building, Av. Naciones Unidas y Republica de El Salvador, Piso 14, Quito
T (+593) (2) 2970 800 E quito.consular@fco.gov.uk
W www.gov.uk/government/world/ecuador
Ambassador Extraordinary and Plenipotentiary, HE Katherine Ward, *apptd* 2016

ECONOMY AND TRADE
Structural reforms in 2000, including the adoption of the US dollar in response to the severe economic crisis of 1999, paved the way for strong growth from 2002 to 2006. Growth has slowed since owing to the uncertainty created by windfall taxes imposed on foreign oil companies, a fall in oil production since 2007, the government defaulting on 30 per cent of public external debt in 2008, and the cancellation of a number of bilateral investment treaties in 2009. The economy struggled after April 2016's 7.8-magnitude earthquake, which killed more than 650 people and caused up to US$3bn (£2bn) of damage. Ecuador introduced a number of non-tariff trade barriers in 2013 and terminated 13 bilateral investment treaties in 2017, but the Moreno government has since attempted to re-invigorate the private sector and tackle unemployment.

Oil is Ecuador's principal export, accounting for around a third of export earnings. After oil, agriculture, fishing and forestry are the most important activities, providing products both for export and for the food- and wood-processing industries. The main exports are oil, bananas, cut flowers, fish, cacao, coffee, hemp and timber. The main imports are industrial materials, fuels and lubricants, and consumer goods. Principal trading partners are the USA and China.
GNI – US$97.8bn; US$5,890 per capita (2017)
Annual average growth of GDP – 0.2 per cent (2017 est)
Inflation rate – 0.7 per cent (2017 est)
Population below poverty line – 25.6 per cent (2013 est)
Unemployment – 5.1 per cent (2017 est)
Total external debt – US$37.75bn (2017 est)
Imports – US$16,219m (2016)
Exports – US$16,798m (2016)

BALANCE OF PAYMENTS
Trade – US$579m surplus (2016)
Current Account – US$348m deficit (2017)

Trade with UK	2016	2017
Imports from UK	£40,276,594	£97,952,097
Exports to UK	£111,132,917	£163,977,647

COMMUNICATIONS
Airports and waterways – 104, with international flights operating to Quito and Guayaquil; the main ports are Guayaquil and Esmeraldas
Roadways and railways – There are 43,670km of roadways, 6,472km of which are surfaced, and 965km of railways
Telecommunications – 2.45 million fixed lines and 13.8 million mobile subscriptions (2016); there were 8.7 million internet users in 2016
Internet code and IDD – ec; 593 (from UK), 44 (to UK)
Major broadcasters – Combination of privately owned and nationally-owned outlets; 60 media outlets are recognised as national, with the Ecuadorian government controlling 12 national outlets and multiple radio stations. There are multiple television stations and over 300 radio channels (2018).
Press – Six newspapers are published daily, including *El Comercio, El Tiempo* and the Guayaquil-based daily *El Universo*
WPFI score – 30,56 (92)

EDUCATION AND HEALTH
Elementary education is free and compulsory until age 14.
Literacy rate – 98.8 per cent (2015 est)
Gross enrolment ratio (percentage of relevant age group) – primary 104 per cent, secondary 107 per cent (2017 est), tertiary 40.5 per cent (2013 est)
Health expenditure (per capita) – US\$579 (2014)
Hospital beds (per 1,000 people) – 1.5 (2012)
Life expectancy (years) – 77 (2017 est)
Mortality rate – 5.1 (2017 est)
Birth rate – 17.9 (2017 est)
Infant mortality rate – 16.4 (2017 est)
HIV/AIDS adult prevalence – 0.3 per cent (2015 est)

GALÁPAGOS ISLANDS

The Galápagos (Giant Tortoise) Islands, about 960km from the mainland, were annexed by Ecuador in 1832. The 12 large and several hundred smaller islands lie on the equator, and most form part of a national park where unique marine birds, iguanas and giant tortoises are conserved. This wildlife provided naturalist Charles Darwin (1809–82) with inspiration and research material for his theory of evolution by natural selection, expounded in *On the Origin of Species* (1859). The islands were declared a UNESCO World Heritage site in 1978.

EGYPT

Jumhuriyat Misr al-Arabiyah – Arab Republic of Egypt

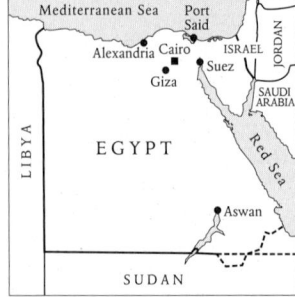

Area – 1,001,450 sq. km
Capital – Cairo; population, 20,076,000 (2018 est); stands on the Nile about 22km from the head of the delta
Major cities – Alexandria (founded 332 BC by Alexander the Great; the capital for over 1,000 years), Giza, Port Said, Shubra al-Khema, Suez
Currency – Egyptian pound (£E) of 100 piastres
Population – 97,041,072 rising at 2.45 per cent a year (2017 est); Egyptian (including Berber and Bedouin) 99.6 per cent (2006)
Religion – Muslim 90 per cent (almost all Sunni), Christian 10 per cent (mostly Coptic) (2012 est)
Language – Arabic (official), English, French
Population density – 96 per sq. km (2016)
Urban population – 42.7 per cent (2018 est)
Median age (years) – 23.9 (2017 est)
National anthem – 'Biladi, Biladi, Biladi' 'My Homeland, My Homeland, My Homeland'
National day – 23 July (Revolution Day)
Death penalty – Retained
CPI score – 32 (117)
Military expenditure – US\$2,774m (2017)
Conscription – 18–30 years of age, male only; 18–36 months

CLIMATE AND TERRAIN
There are four broad regions: the Western Desert, which covers nearly two-thirds of the country to the west of the Nile valley; the Eastern Desert, which lies between the Nile and the mountains along the Red Sea coast; the fertile Nile valley and delta, where most of the population lives; and the Sinai peninsula, where a coastal plain on the Mediterranean rises to mountains in the south. The deserts are arid plateaux, with depressions in the Western Desert whose springs irrigate oases, while the Eastern Desert is dissected by wadis (dry watercourses). Elevation extremes range from 2,629m (Mt Catherine, Sinai) to −133m (Qattara depression). The country has a desert climate, with hot, dry summers and mild winters. Temperatures increase further south, and rainfall increases nearer the coast. Average daily temperatures range from 13°C in January to 30.4°C in August.

POLITICS
The 1971 constitution was suspended after President Mubarak's resignation in 2011 and substantial changes to it were approved by referendum in March 2011. A new constitution was approved in January 2014, which provides the army with greater political powers, established Sharia as the basis of the country's laws and provides for an executive president who is directly elected for a four-year term, which is renewable once.

Under the 2014 constitution the legislature is unicameral, with 448 of the 596 members of the House of Representatives directly elected by an individual candidacy system, 120 members elected in constituencies by majority vote, and 28 appointed by the president. All members serve five-year terms.

The first legislative election since President Mubarak's departure from office was held in November 2011 and saw the Freedom and Justice Party (FJP, founded by the Muslim Brotherhood) win the most seats but fail to win a majority. The People's Assembly was suspended in July 2013 and legislative elections under the new 2014 constitution were held in July 2014.

In the first presidential election in the country's history, FJP candidate Mohammed Mursi narrowly defeated the National Democratic Party candidate Ahmed Shafiq and was inaugurated in June 2012. Following mass demonstrations, Mohammed Mursi was deposed by the army in July 2013; in April 2015, Mursi and 12 others were sentenced to 20 years in jail for the arrest and torture of protestors and incitement to violence, and in June 2015 a court confirmed a death sentence handed to Mursi and 105 others for their role in the 2011 Wadi al-Natrun prison break. In 2014, amid boycotts from opposition parties and claims that rivals had been intimidated, independent candidate and Commander-in-Chief of the Egyptian armed forces Abdel al-Sisi won the presidential election with 90 per cent of the vote. He was re-elected in March 2018 with 97 per cent of the vote following an election with no public debates or legitimate opposition.

HEAD OF STATE
President, C-in-C of the Armed Forces, Abdel Fattah al-Sisi, *elected* 29 May 2014, *sworn in* 8 June 2014, *re-elected* 2 April 2018
Head of the Supreme Council of the Armed Forces, Defence, Sedki Sobhi

SELECTED GOVERNMENT MEMBERS *AS AT JUNE 2018*
Prime Minister (Acting) Moustafa Kamal Madbouli
Finance, Amr Ali al-Garhy
Foreign Affairs, Sameh Hassan Shokri
Interior, Magdy Abdel Ghafar

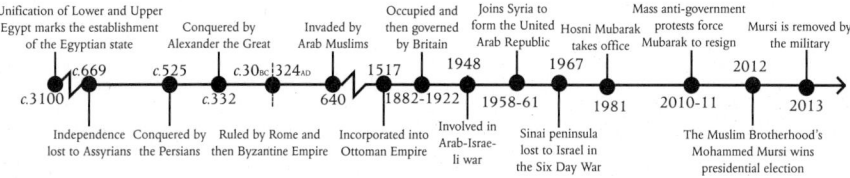

Unification of Lower and Upper Egypt marks the establishment of the Egyptian state — *c.*3100

*c.*669 — Independence lost to Assyrians

*c.*525 — Conquered by the Persians

Conquered by Alexander the Great — *c.*332

*c.*30ᴮᶜ‡324ᴀᴅ

Invaded by Arab Muslims — 640 — Ruled by Rome and then Byzantine Empire

1517 — Incorporated into Ottoman Empire

Occupied and then governed by Britain — 1882–1922

1948 — Involved in Arab-Israe-li war

Joins Syria to form the United Arab Republic — 1958-61 — Sinai peninsula lost to Israel in the Six Day War

1967

Hosni Mubarak takes office — 1981

Mass anti-government protests force Mubarak to resign — 2010-11 — The Muslim Brotherhood's Mohammed Mursi wins presidential election

2012 — Mursi is removed by the military

2013

EMBASSY OF THE ARAB REPUBLIC OF EGYPT
26 South Street, London W1K 1DW
T 020-7499 3304 E eg.emb_london@mfa.gov.eg
Ambassador Extraordinary and Plenipotentiary, HE Nasser Ahmed Kamel, *apptd* 2014

BRITISH EMBASSY
7 Ahmed Ragheb Street, Garden City, Cairo
T (+20) (2) 2791 6000 E consular.cairo@fco.gov.uk
W www.gov.uk/government/world/egypt
Ambassador Extraordinary and Plenipotentiary, HE John Casson, CMG, *apptd* 2014

ECONOMY AND TRADE
Economic liberalisation in recent years has attracted foreign investment and promoted exports, producing strong growth in GDP, but political uncertainty· significantly reduced government revenues in 2012, and Egypt's attempts to obtain a multi-billion dollar loan from the IMF in 2012–13 failed. In 2011 and 2012, the government drew down foreign exchange reserves by 50 per cent. Although the dams on the Nile have expanded the area of land under cultivation, other factors, such as population growth, put a greater strain on resources, while terrorist attacks have affected tourism. In November 2016, Egypt devalued its currency by 48 per cent and announced that its value would be allowed to float, in order to meet a key IMF demand ahead of securing a US$12bn loan. This resulted in high levels of inflation, above 30 per cent for most of 2017, but also significant levels of foreign investment. Political uncertainty, security issues and internal repression continue to hamper growth.

The services sector contributes 55.7 per cent to GDP and employs 49.1 per cent of the workforce. Tourism is the largest component of this sector (estimated to have contributed 7.5 per cent of GDP in 2014), along with Suez Canal revenues and expatriate remittances. Industry accounts for 33.1 per cent of GDP and 25.1 per cent of employment, but despite increasing industrialisation, agriculture still employs 25.8 per cent of the workforce, contributing 11.9 per cent of GDP. Egypt is a net importer of foodstuffs, especially grain, and a food security programme has been set up with the aim of achieving self-sufficiency.

The main cash crop is cotton, of which Egypt is one of the world's main producers. Other important crops are rice, maize, wheat, vegetables, fruit and livestock. Industry is centred on oil and gas extraction, processing hydrocarbons, cotton and other agricultural products, producing textiles, chemicals and pharmaceuticals. Oil is the backbone of the economy and helps, alongside considerable reserves of natural gas and the hydroelectric power produced by the Aswan High dam, to make Egypt self-sufficient in energy.

The main trading partners are the Chine, the UAE, the USA, and Italy. Principal exports are crude oil and petroleum products, cotton, textiles, metal products, chemicals and processed food. The main imports are machinery and equipment, foodstuffs, chemicals, wood products and fuels.
GNI – US$293.4bn; US$5,890 per capita (2017)
Annual average growth of GDP – 4.1 per cent (2017 est)
Inflation rate – 23.5 per cent (2017 est)

Population below poverty line – 25.2 per cent (2016 est)
Unemployment – 12.2 per cent (2017 est)
Total external debt – US$76.31bn (2017 est)
Imports – US$57,318m (2016)
Exports – US$21,863m (2016)

BALANCE OF PAYMENTS
Trade – US$35,455m deficit (2016)
Current Account – US$9,336m deficit (2017)

Trade with UK	2016	2017
Imports from UK	£1,220,323,263	£1,210,024,295
Exports to UK	£655,474,717	£648,665,283

COMMUNICATIONS
Airports – 83; the principal airports are at Cairo, Sharm el-Sheikh, Luxor, Alexandria and Hurghada (2013)
Waterways – Egypt has 3,500km of waterways, including the Nile river and Lake Nasser, the Alexandria–Cairo waterway, numerous small canals in the Nile delta and the Suez Canal (opened 1869; closed 1967–75); the main seaports are Alexandria, Damietta and Port Said on the Mediterranean Sea and Suez on the Red Sea
Roadways and railways – A road network of 126,742km and a rail network of 5,083km link the Nile valley and delta with the main development areas east and west of the river, but there are few routes in the interior
Telecommunications – 6.2 million fixed lines and 97.8 million mobile subscriptions (2016); there were 37 million internet users in 2016
Internet code and IDD – eg; 20 (from UK), 44 (to UK)
Major broadcasters – Combination of state-run and privately owned media broadcasting outlets. State-run national television channels and regional channels compete with the country's thriving satellite television industry, which is watched throughout the Arab-speaking world. State-run media operates 2 national and 6 regional television networks and approximately 30 radio outlets across 8 networks (2018)
Press – A number of daily newspapers are published, including *Al-Ahram*, the oldest newspaper in the Arab world. Mixture of publications in different languages, including Arabic, Armenian, English, and French; includes state-run newspapers
WPFI score – 56,72 (161)

EDUCATION AND HEALTH
Education is free between the ages of six and 15.
Literacy rate – 91.1 per cent (2015 est)
Gross enrolment ratio (percentage of relevant age group) – primary 104 per cent, secondary 86 per cent, tertiary 34 per cent (2016 est)
Health expenditure (per capita) – US$178 (2014)
Hospital beds (per 1,000 people) – 1.6 (2015)
Life expectancy (years) – 73 (2017 est)
Mortality rate – 4.6 (2017 est)
Birth rate – 29.6 (2017 est)
Infant mortality rate – 19 (2017 est)
HIV/AIDS adult prevalence – 0.1 per cent (2015 est)

EL SALVADOR

República de El Salvador – Republic of El Salvador

Area – 21,041 sq. km
Capital – San Salvador; population, 1,107,000 (2018 est)
Major cities – San Miguel, Santa Ana, Soyapango
Currency – US dollar (US$) of 100 cents
Population – 6,172,011 rising at 0.25 per cent a year (2017 est)
Religion – Christian (Roman Catholic 57.1 per cent, Protestant 21.2 per cent) (2003 est)
Language – Spanish (official), Nahua
Population density – 306 per sq. km (2016)
Urban population – 72 per cent (2018 est)
Median age (years) – 27.1 (2017 est)
National anthem – 'Himno Nacional de El Salvador' 'National Anthem of El Salvador'
National day – 15 September (Independence Day)
Death penalty – Retained for certain crimes (last used 1973)
CPI score – 33 (112)
Military expenditure – US$247m (2017 est)
Conscription – 18 years of age; 12 months (selective)

CLIMATE AND TERRAIN

El Salvador is mountainous, with narrow coastal plains and a central plateau. Many of its peaks are volcanoes; most are extinct, but Ilamatepec (or Santa Ana) erupted in 2005. There are also numerous volcanic lakes. Elevation extremes range from 2,730m (Cerro El Pital) to 0m (Pacific Ocean). The climate is tropical on the coast but more temperate at higher altitudes. The average annual temperature in San Salvador is 25.4°C. Earthquakes and volcanic activity are common, and the country is also susceptible to hurricanes and tropical storms.

HISTORY AND POLITICS

El Salvador was part of the Aztec kingdom conquered in 1524 by Pedro de Alvarado, and formed part of the Spanish viceroyalty of Guatemala until 1821. It was part of a Central American federation of former Spanish provinces from 1823 until the federation's dissolution in 1838, becoming fully independent in 1840.

There was political unrest in the 1970s, and guerrilla activity by the left-wing Farabundo Martí National Liberation Front (FMLN), which intensified from 1977 amid reports of human rights abuses by government troops and right-wing death squads. Decades of military rule ended in 1979, but elections in 1982 were boycotted by left-wing parties and the right-wing Nationalist Republican Alliance (ARENA) took office. The civil war between the FMLN and the US-backed government lasted throughout the 1980s, until a UN-sponsored peace agreement was signed in 1992. The FMLN was recognised as a political party, and it won seats in the 1994 election.

In March 2014 the FMLN candidate and former guerrilla fighter Salvador Sanchez Ceren was elected president. The conservative Nationalist Republican Alliance (ARENA) continued as the largest single party after the March 2018 elections, though the FMLN continued to govern as part of a coalition.

Under the 1983 constitution, the executive president is directly elected for a five-year term, which is not renewable. The unicameral legislative assembly has 84 members, who are directly elected for a three-year term. The president appoints the Council of State. The country is divided into 14 departments.

HEAD OF STATE

President, Salvador Sanchez Ceren, *elected* 13 March 2014, *took office* 1 June 2014
Vice-President, Oscar Ortiz

SELECTED GOVERNMENT MEMBERS *AS AT JUNE 2018*

Defence, David Munguia Payes
Economy, Luz Rodriguez
Foreign Affairs (Acting), Carlos Castaneda

EMBASSY OF EL SALVADOR

8 Dorset Square, 1st & 2nd Floors, London NW1 6PU
T 020-7224 9800 E embajadalondres@rree.gob.sv
Ambassador Extraordinary and Plenipotentiary, HE Lidia Hayek-Weinmann, *apptd* 2016

BRITISH EMBASSY

Edificio Torre Futura, 14th Floor, Colonia Escalon, San Salvador
T (+503) 2511 5757 E britishembassy.elsalvador@fco.gov.uk
W www.gov.uk/government/world/el-salvador
Ambassador Extraordinary and Plenipotentiary, HE Bernhard Garside, *apptd* 2015

ECONOMY AND TRADE

The country is one of the most industrialised in Central America and has the region's fourth-largest economy despite being its smallest country and having few natural resources. Recovery after the civil war was set back by a series of natural disasters, but the economy has been transformed from a mainly agricultural to a service-based economy with a growing manufacturing sector. Government diversification efforts have promoted textile production, international port services and tourism. In September 2014, El Salvador was awarded US$277m by US government agency the Millennium Challenge Corporation with the aim of stimulating economic growth and reducing poverty. Though El Salvador has struggled to attract foreign investment, not least because it is the world's most violent country that isn't at war. Expatriate remittances are received by about a third of households.

Services, through tourism, commerce and financial services, contribute 64.9 per cent of GDP. Industry contributes 24.6 per cent of GDP, mostly through assembly for re-export, food processing, beverages, oil, chemicals, fertiliser, textiles, furniture and light metals. Agriculture contributes 10.6 per cent to GDP and employs 21 per cent of the workforce. The principal agricultural products are coffee, sugar, maize, rice, beans, oilseed, cotton, sorghum, beef and dairy products.

The main trading partners are the USA and other Central American states. Principal exports are offshore assembly products, coffee, sugar, textiles, garments, gold, ethanol, chemicals and electricity. The chief imports are raw materials, consumer goods, capital goods, fuels, foodstuffs, oil and electricity.

GNI – US$22.7bn; US$3,560 per capita (2017)
Annual average growth of GDP – 2.3 per cent (2017 est)
Inflation rate – 0.8 per cent (2017 est)

Population below poverty line – 34.9 per cent (2015 est)
Unemployment – 7 per cent (2017 est)
Total external debt – US$16.29bn (2017 est)
Imports – US$9,855m (2016)
Exports – US$5,335m (2016)

BALANCE OF PAYMENTS
Trade – US$4,519m deficit (2016)
Current Account – US$501m deficit (2017)

Trade with UK	2016	2017
Imports from UK	£19,214,384	£21,492,333
Exports to UK	£19,815,417	£12,087,395

COMMUNICATIONS
Airports and waterways – Five; the principal ports are Cutuco and Acajutla, and ports in Honduras and Guatemala are also used
Roadways and railways – There are 3,247km of surfaced roads; the 283km rail network has not been in operation since 2005 due to lack of maintenance
Telecommunications – 950,000 million fixed lines and 9.2 million mobile subscriptions (2014); there were 1.7 million internet users in 2014
Internet code and IDD – sv; 503 (from UK), 44 (to UK)
Major broadcasters – Digital transition to begin in 2018, adding to hundreds of private television and radio outlets, including Teledos and Canal Cuatro; there are hundreds of radio broadcasters, including the state-run Radio Nacional de El Salvador (2017)
Press – There are five main daily newspapers: Diario Co Latino, La Prensa Grafica, El Mundo, El Diario de Hoy and El Diario Co Latino
WPFI score – 27,78 (66)

EDUCATION AND HEALTH
Primary education is state-run, compulsory and free.
Literacy rate – 88 per cent (2015 est)
Gross enrolment ratio (percentage of relevant age group) – primary 100 per cent, secondary 74 per cent, tertiary 28 per cent (2016 est)
Health expenditure (per capita) – US$280 (2014)
Hospital beds (per 1,000 people) – 1.3 (2014)
Life expectancy (years) – 74.9 (2017 est)
Mortality rate – 5.8 (2017 est)
Birth rate – 16.2 (2017 est)
Infant mortality rate – 16.8 (2017 est)
HIV/AIDS adult prevalence – 0.5 per cent (2015 est)

EQUATORIAL GUINEA
República de Guinea Ecuatorial/République de Guinée Equatoriale – Republic of Equatorial Guinea

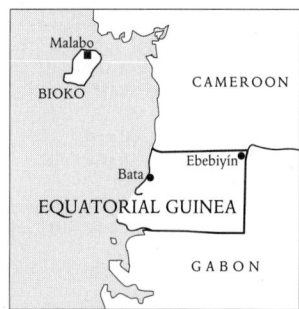

Area – 28,051 sq. km
Capital – Malabo, on Bioko; population, 297,000 (2018 est)
Major towns – Bata, the principal town and port of Río Muni; Ebebiyín

Currency – Central African CFA franc of 100 centimes
Population – 778,358 rising at 2.44 per cent a year (2017 est); predominantly Fang; indigenous Bubi now a minority on Bioko
Religion – Christian (Roman Catholic 87 per cent, other denominations 6 per cent), traditional indigenous religions 5 per cent (est); many Catholics also follow traditional beliefs
Language – Spanish, French (both official), Fang, Bubi
Population density – 44 per sq. km (2016)
Urban population – 72.1 per cent (2017 est)
Median age (years) – 19.8 (2017 est)
National anthem – 'Caminemos pisando las sendas de nuestra inmensa felicidad' 'Let Us Tread the Path of our Immense Happiness'
National day – 12 October (Independence Day)
Death penalty – Retained
Military expenditure – US$182m (2016 est)
Conscription – 18 years of age; 24 months, although conscription is rarely enforced
Literacy rate – 95.3 per cent (2015 est)
Gross enrolment ratio (percentage of relevant age group) – primary 79.1 per cent (2015 est)
Health expenditure (per capita) – US$633 (2014)
Life expectancy (years) – 64.6 (2017 est)
Mortality rate – 7.8 (2017 est)
Birth rate – 32.2 (2017 est)
Infant mortality rate – 65.2 (2017 est)
HIV/AIDS adult prevalence – 4.9 per cent (2015 est)

CLIMATE AND TERRAIN
The country consists of several islands off the Cameroon coast and a small area on the mainland, Río Muni, where 80 per cent of the population lives. The islands, of which Bioko is the largest, are of volcanic origin. The mainland rises from a narrow coastal plain to a mountainous interior plateau, and is covered in dense vegetation. Elevation extremes range from 3,008m (Pico Basile) to 0m (Atlantic Ocean). The climate is tropical, with a rainy season from July to January on Bioko, and from April to May and October to December on the mainland.

HISTORY AND POLITICS
The island of Fernando Po (Bioko) was claimed by the Portuguese in 1494 and held until 1777, when it was ceded to Spain. The mainland territory of Río Muni came under Spanish rule in 1844, and the two territories became one colony, subsequently known as Spanish Guinea, in 1904. The colony became autonomous in 1963, and independent in 1968 under its present name.
The first president, Francisco Macías Nguema, established a one-party state in 1970. His brutal regime was overthrown in 1979 in a military coup led by his nephew, Col. Obiang Nguema. A military regime was established after the coup, and only presidential nominees were allowed to stand in the 1983 and 1988 elections. Constitutional amendments were introduced in 1991 to allow multiparty elections, but President Nguema and the Democratic Party of Equatorial Guinea (PDGE) have retained power since 1992; most elections have been boycotted by the opposition parties because of election irregularities and intimidation. The regime has been accused of human rights abuses and the suppression of political opposition, and in 2003 opposition leaders set up a 'government-in-exile' in Spain. There is also a separatist movement on Bioko.
In the 2017 legislative election, the PDGE retained total control over the senate and claimed 99 of the 100 seats in the Chamber of Deputies. President Nguema was re-elected in April 2016 with 94 per cent of the vote in his first term since 2011's constitutional referendum.

The 1991 constitution introduced a multiparty system. The president is directly elected for a seven-year term; constitutional amendments approved by referendum in November 2011 introduced a two-term limit. Constitutional amendments in 2012 created a bicameral system with a lower chamber, the Chamber of Deputies, with 100 members, and an upper chamber, the senate, containing 55 elected officials and 15 presidential appointments.

HEAD OF STATE
President, Brig.-Gen. Teodoro Obiang Nguema Mbasogo, *took power* August 1979, *re-elected* 1989, 1996, 2002, 2009, 2016
Vice-President, Defence, Teodoro Nguema Obiang Mangue

SELECTED GOVERNMENT MEMBERS *AS AT JUNE 2018*
Prime Minister, Francisco Pascual Obama Asue
Deputy Prime Ministers, Clemente Engonga Nguema Onguene; Angel Mesie Mibuy; Alfonso Nsue Mokuy
Economy, Lucas Abaga Nchama
Foreign Affairs, Simeon Oyono Esono

EMBASSY OF THE REPUBLIC OF EQUATORIAL GUINEA
13 Park Place, St James's, London SW1A 1LP
T 020-7499 6867 E embarege-londres@embarege-londres.org
W www.embarege-londres.org
Ambassador Extraordinary and Plenipotentiary, HE Mari-Cruz Evuna Andeme, *apptd* 2012

BRITISH HIGH COMMISSION
High Commissioner, HE Rowan Laxton, *apptd* 2017, resident at Yaounde, Cameroon

ECONOMY AND TRADE
Large oil and natural gas deposits discovered off Bioko in the 1990s have transformed the economy, which has grown dramatically since production began in 1996. The country has the reputation of being one of the most corrupt in the world; oil exploitation has not benefited much of the population as most businesses are owned by government officials or their families. The economy entered recession in 2013 and has continued to decline with the fall in oil prices. Major economic concerns remain an undiversified economy, falling public investment and corruption.

Industry contributes 56.5 per cent of GDP, services 41 per cent and agriculture 2.2 per cent. The oil-driven growth in the GDP masks stagnation in other sectors; agriculture, once the mainstay of the economy, has declined to subsistence level owing to neglect and lack of investment. The main crops are coffee, cocoa, rice, fruit, nuts, livestock and timber. Industrial activities other than oil and natural gas production include fishing and timber processing.

The main trading partners are Spain, China and India. Principal exports are petroleum and timber. The main imports are oil-industry and other industrial equipment.
GNI – US$8.9bn; US$7,060 per capita (2017)
Annual average growth of GDP – –7.4 per cent (2017 est)
Inflation rate – 1.7 per cent (2017 est)
Population below poverty line – 44 per cent (2011)
Total external debt – US$1.181bn (2017 est)
Imports – US$6,492m (2014)
Exports – US$11,586m (2014)

BALANCE OF PAYMENTS
Trade – US$5,094m surplus (2014)

Trade with UK	2016	2017
Imports from UK	£20,862,185	£25,246,756
Exports to UK	£121,499,039	£59,983,613

COMMUNICATIONS
Airports – 7 airports, the principal airport is based in Malabo
Roadways – 2,880km
Telecommunications – 10,989 fixed lines and 575,650 mobile subscriptions (2016); there were 180,597 internet users in 2016
Internet code and IDD – gq; 240 (from UK), 44 (to UK)
Broadcasters – Television and radio broadcasts are state-controlled
Press – *Ebano* is the government-run newspaper; privately owned newspapers are unable to publish regularly due to financial and political pressure
WPFI score – 66,47 (171)

ERITREA

Hagere Ertra – State of Eritrea

Area – 117,600 sq. km
Capital – Asmara; population, 896,000 (2018 est)
Major towns – Assab, Keren, Massawa
Currency – Nakfa (Nfk) of 100 cents
Population – 5,918,919 rising at 0.85 per cent a year (2017 est); Tigrinya (55 per cent), Tigre (30 per cent), Saho (4 per cent), Bilen (2 per cent), Kunama (2 per cent), Rashaida (2 per cent) (2010 est)
Religion – Muslim (Sunni) 50 per cent, Christian 40 per cent (Eritrean Orthodox 24 per cent, Roman Catholic 10 per cent), animist 2 per cent; only Christians of the Eritrean Orthodox, Catholic and Lutheran churches, and Muslims may meet freely
Language – Arabic, English, Tigrinya (all official), Tigre, Afar, Kunama
Population density – 51 per sq. km (2014)
Urban population – 40.1 per cent (2018 est)
Median age (years) – 19.7 (2017 est)
National anthem – 'Ertra, Ertra, Ertra' 'Eritrea, Eritrea, Eritrea'
National day – 24 May (Independence Day)
Death penalty – Retained (last used 1989)
CPI score – 20 (165)
Military expenditure – US$182m (2003 est)
Conscription – 18–40 years of age; 16 months
Literacy rate – 93.2 per cent (2015 est)
Gross enrolment ratio (percentage of relevant age group) – primary 49.6 per cent, secondary 30.5 per cent (2015 est), tertiary 2 per cent (2016 est)
Health expenditure (per capita) – US$25 (2014)
Hospital beds (per 1,000 people) – 0.7 (2011)
Life expectancy (years) – 65.2 (2017 est)
Mortality rate – 7.2 (2017 est)
Birth rate – 29.6 (2017 est)
Infant mortality rate – 45 (2017 est)
HIV/AIDS adult prevalence – 0.6 per cent (2015 est)

CLIMATE AND TERRAIN

The northern end of the Ethiopian Highlands extends into central Eritrea, where the average altitude is over 2,000m. The mountains fall in the west to a plateau, which then rises to the hills on the Sudanese border. To the east of the mountains, the land falls to the narrow coastal plain. The coastal strip extending to the Djibouti border is low-lying, while the border with Ethiopia runs along the edge of the Danakil desert. Elevation extremes range from 3,018m (Soira) to −75m (Danakil depression). Average temperatures range from 23°C in January to 30.6°C in June.

HISTORY AND POLITICS

Part of the Axum empire from the first century AD, the area came under the control of the Ottoman Empire in the mid-16th century. It was occupied by Italy in the late 19th century and was the base for Italy's 1936 invasion of Abyssinia (now Ethiopia). After the Italian defeat in North Africa in 1941, Eritrea became a British protectorate until 15 September 1952, when a federation with Ethiopia was established by the UN. In 1962, Ethiopia annexed Eritrea outright.

The Eritrean Liberation Front (ELF) fought a guerrilla war for independence from 1961, and the Eritrean People's Liberation Front (EPLF) – a breakaway faction of the ELF – emerged in the 1970s, becoming the dominant rebel group in the 1980s. The EPLF joined with Ethiopian resistance groups to fight the Mengistu regime, which was overthrown in 1991. The EPLF secured the whole of Eritrea and formed an autonomous provisional government. The new Ethiopian government agreed to an Eritrean referendum on independence, held in April 1993, which recorded a 99.89 per cent vote in favour. Independence was declared on 24 May 1993.

Following independence, a transitional government for a four-year period was formed under Isaias Afewerki, and the EPLF became the ruling political party, renaming itself the People's Front for Democracy and Justice (PFDJ) in 1994. The post-independence regime has become increasingly authoritarian, and since 2001 has dealt harshly with anyone openly critical of the government. In 2015, the UN reported that Eritreans are routinely subjected to a number of abuses by the government, including torture, sexual abuse and indefinite service in the country's military.

Few of the provisions outlined in the 1997 constitution have been enacted and no presidential or legislative elections have been held, so the transitional president, state council (cabinet) and legislature remain in place. Under the constitution, the president is elected for a five-year term by the legislature, and the 150-member unicameral National Assembly is directly elected for a four-year term. The People's Front for Democracy and Justice (PFDJ) is the only legal political party.

HEAD OF STATE

President, Chairman of the State Council and of the National Assembly, C-in-C of the Armed Forces, Isaias Afewerki, *elected by the National Assembly* 22 May 1993

SELECTED GOVERNMENT MEMBERS *AS AT JULY 2018*
Defence, vacant
Finance, Berhane Habtemariam
Foreign Affairs, Osman Saleh

EMBASSY OF THE STATE OF ERITREA

96 White Lion Street, London N1 9PF
T 020-7713 0096 E eriemba@eriembauk.com
Ambassador Extraordinary and Plenipotentiary, HE Estifanos Habtemariam Ghebreyesus, *apptd* 2014

BRITISH EMBASSY

PO Box 5584, 66–68 Mariam Ghimbi Street, Asmara
T (+291) (1) 120 145 E asmara.enquiries@fco.gov.uk
W www.gov.uk/government/world/eritrea
Ambassador Extraordinary and Plenipotentiary, HE Ian Richards, *apptd* 2016

FOREIGN RELATIONS

Since independence, Eritrea has been involved in disputes with Yemen, Ethiopia and Djibouti over territory, while Sudan has accused Eritrea of supporting rebels in eastern Sudan. The dispute with Yemen was over the Hanish and Mohabaka islands in the Red Sea; possession was divided between Yemen and Eritrea by international arbitration.

There has been fighting with Ethiopia in disputes over border territory, especially in the Tigray region, since 1998. Fighting escalated in 1999–2000 into a war that left thousands of people dead. An independent boundary commission defined the international border between the two countries in 2002, but both countries failed to abide by successive rulings.

Fighting broke out on the part of the border disputed with Djibouti in 2008. Following border disputes in early 2011, Ethiopia announced that it would support Eritrean rebels fighting President Afewerki.

In July 2011, a UN report accused Eritrea of planning to attack an African Union Summit in Ethiopia and further tightened sanctions soon after, owing to Eritrea's alleged support for Islamist insurgents in Somalia. In March 2012 Ethiopia attacked three military camps in Eritrea, claiming the country was supporting Ethiopian rebels who mounted attacks on western tourists. Following a change of government in Ethiopia, a peace deal was agreed between the two countries in July 2018.

Political repression and human rights abuses have increasingly led to Eritreans seeking political asylum abroad. As many as 110,000 Eritreans are thought to have sought asylum in the EU from 2012 to 2016; nearly a quarter of refugees attempting to enter Europe via boat in 2015 were Eritrean.

ECONOMY AND TRADE

Over 30 years of conflict left the country's economy devastated, and the restrictive policies of the post-independent regime have hampered recovery. The command economy has concentrated business ownership in military and party hands. Agricultural output is restricted by lack of labour owing to the failure to demobilise the large army, the conflict with Ethiopia, which officially ended 2018, and the frequent droughts and ensuing famines. Nevertheless, agriculture and herding are the means of subsistence for around 80 per cent of the population. The industrial sector has contracted since trade with Ethiopia halted in 1998, and the principal ports have suffered from the loss of this transit trade. The Zara mining project, a new gold mine in the centre of the country, began production in early 2016.

Mineral reserves include zinc, potash, gold, copper and possibly oil; these are not fully exploited at present, although mining production began in 2010. Industries include food processing, beverages, clothing and textiles, salt, cement and light manufacturing. A free trade zone opened at Massawa in 2008 with the aim of boosting revenues, which are heavily dependent on remittances from expatriates.

Principal exports are gold and other minerals, livestock, sorghum, textiles, food and light manufactures. The main imports are machinery, petroleum products, food and manufactured goods.
GNI – US$3,063m; US$490 per capita (2013)
Annual average growth of GDP – 3.3 per cent (2017 est)

Inflation rate – 11.8 per cent (2016 est)
Population below poverty line – 50 per cent (2004 est)
Unemployment – 8.6 per cent (2013 est)
Total external debt – US$869.9m (2017 est)
Imports – US$2,359m (2014)
Exports – US$15m (2014)

BALANCE OF PAYMENTS
Trade – US$418m deficit (2010)
Current Account – US$69m deficit (2015 est)

Trade with UK	2016	2017
Imports from UK	£1,844,517	£1,050,529
Exports to UK	£26,269	£9,171

COMMUNICATIONS
Airports and waterways – Four, with the main international airport at Asmara; the principal seaports are at Assab and Massawa
Roadways and railways – There are 4,101km of roadways, of which 874km are surfaced, and 306km of railways, which link Massawa to Sudan via Asmara
Telecommunications – There are 66,086 fixed lines and 506,000 mobile subscriptions (2016); there were 69,095 internet users in 2016
Internet code and IDD – er; 291 (from UK), 44 (to UK)
Broadcasters – Eritrea is the only country in Africa without any privately owned broadcasting media; Eri TV, Voice of the Broad Masses of Eritrea and Radio Zara are state-run. There are three radio stations, including educational radio available in 9 languages
Press – *Hadas Eritrea* (Tigrinya language) and *Al-Hadisa* (Arabic) are the government-owned newspaper publications, along with two additional weekly papers
WPFI score – 84,24 (179)

ESTONIA
Eesti Vabariik – Republic of Estonia

Area – 45,228 sq. km
Capital – Tallinn; population, 437,000 (2018 est)
Major towns – Kohtla-Jarve, Narva, Parnu, Tartu
Currency – Euro (€) of 100 cents
Population – 1,251,581 falling at 0.57 per cent a year (2017 est); Estonian (68.7 per cent), Russian (24.8 per cent), Ukrainian (1.7 per cent), Belarusian (1 per cent), Finn (0.6 per cent) (2011 est)
Religion – Christian (Orthodox 16.2 per cent, Lutheran 9.9 per cent) (2011 est)
Language – Estonian (official), Russian
Population density – 31 per sq. km (2016)

Urban population – 68.9 per cent (2018 est)
Median age (years) – 42.7 (2017 est)
National anthem – 'Mu Isamaa, Mu Onn Ja Room' 'My Fatherland, My Pride and Joy'
National day – 24 February (Independence Day)
Death penalty – Abolished for all crimes (since 1998)
CPI score – 71 (21)
Military expenditure – US$536m (2017)
Conscription – 18–27 years of age; 8–11 months, depending on education

CLIMATE AND TERRAIN
The country is mostly a plain of lakes, marshes and forests, with a range of low hills in the south-east. Elevation extremes range from 318m (Suur Munamagi) to 0m (Baltic Sea). Part of the border with Russia runs through the large Lake Peipsi. The climate is maritime, with average temperatures ranging from −3.9°C in February to 17.7°C in July.

HISTORY AND POLITICS
The area came under Swedish control between 1561 and 1629, and was ceded to the Russian Empire in 1721. An Estonian nationalist movement developed in the late 19th century and fought against occupying German forces during the First World War. Estonia declared its independence in February 1918 and defended it against Soviet forces until 1920, when independence was recognised by the USSR. However, the USSR annexed Estonia in 1940, and the country was subsequently occupied by German forces when they invaded the USSR in 1941. In 1944 the USSR expelled the Germans and reannexed the country, beginning a process of 'Sovietisation'.

There was a resurgence of nationalist sentiment in the 1980s, and in 1989 the Estonian Supreme Soviet declared the republic to be sovereign and its 1940 annexation by the USSR to be illegal. In 1990, the Communist Party's monopoly on power was abolished and, following multiparty elections in which pro-independence candidates won the majority of seats, a period of transition to independence was inaugurated, culminating in its declaration on 20 August 1991. The last Russian troops withdrew in 1994. Since independence, Estonia has pursued pro-Western policies. It joined NATO and the EU in 2004.

In the 2015 legislative election, the Reform Party (ER), the main partner in the coalition government since 2005, remained the largest party and formed a coalition with the Social Democratic Party of Estonia (SDE) and Res Publica (IRL). In November 2016 Prime Minister Taavi Roivas lost a confidence vote in parliament and Center Party chairman Juri Rutas was sworn in as his replacement. In October 2016, parliament selected the country's first female president, Kersti Kaljulaid.

Under the 1992 constitution, the president is elected for a five-year term by the legislature by a two-thirds majority or, if no candidate receives this majority after three rounds of voting, by an electoral assembly composed of the legislature members and 266 local government representatives. The unicameral legislature, the *Riigikogu*, has 101 members, directly elected for a four-year term. The prime minister is appointed by the president and nominates the government.

HEAD OF STATE
President, Kersti Kaljulaid, *elected by electoral assembly*
    3 October 2016, *sworn in* 10 October 2016

SELECTED GOVERNMENT MEMBERS *AS AT JUNE 2018*
Prime Minister, Juri Rutas
Defence, Juri Luik

Finance, Toomas Toniste
Foreign Affairs, Sven Mikser
Interior, Andres Anvelt

EMBASSY OF THE REPUBLIC OF ESTONIA
16 Hyde Park Gate, London SW7 5DG
T 020-7589 3428 E london@mfa.ee W www.estonia.gov.uk
Ambassador Extraordinary and Plenipotentiary, HE Tiina
   Intelmann, *apptd* 2017

BRITISH EMBASSY
Wismari 6, Tallinn 10136
T (+372) 667 4700 E infotallinn@fco.gov.uk
W www.gov.uk/government/world/estonia
Ambassador Extraordinary and Plenipotentiary, HE Theresa
   Bubbear, *apptd* 2016

ECONOMY AND TRADE
Economic reforms and restructuring since 1992 have resulted in a market economy, the growth of which was boosted by the country's accession to the EU in 2004. Estonia entered recession in 2008 after an investment and consumption slump, and a drop in demand for exports. Prudent financial management has enabled the economy to recover slowly, and it met the accession criteria for the eurozone, which Estonia joined in January 2011; it has since garnered one of the highest GDP growth rates and lowest debt-to-GDP ratios in Europe. Strong growth and increased labour productivity in 2017 has meant the economy is in its best position since the financial crisis.

Agriculture engages 2.7 per cent of the workforce and accounts for 3.4 per cent of GDP, the main products being cereals, vegetables, livestock, dairy products and fish. Industry accounts for 20.5 per cent of employment and 27.8 per cent of GDP, concentrating on engineering, electronics, wood and wood products, textiles, information technology and telecommunications; electronics and telecommunications are particularly strong. The growing services sector accounts for 76.8 per cent of employment and 68.8 per cent of GDP.

The main trading partners are other EU countries, particularly Finland, Sweden and Germany. Principal exports are machinery and electrical equipment, food products, wood and wood products, metals, furniture, vehicles and parts and textiles. The main imports are machinery and electrical equipment, fuels, foodstuffs, vehicles and chemicals. Estonia remains dependent on Russian natural gas supplies.

GNI – US$23.9bn; US$18,190 per capita (2017)
Annual average growth of GDP – 4.0 per cent (2017 est)
Inflation rate – 3.8 per cent (2017 est)
Population below poverty line – 21.3 per cent (2015)
Unemployment – 8.4 per cent (2017 est)
Total external debt – US$19.05bn (2016 est)
Imports – US$14,951m (2016)
Exports – US$13,158m (2016)

BALANCE OF PAYMENTS
Trade – US$1,793m deficit (2016)
Current Account – US$824m deficit (2017)

Trade with UK	2016	2017
Imports from UK	£232,562,305	£252,223,770
Exports to UK	£239,389,449	£229,826,438

COMMUNICATIONS
Airports and waterways – 18, with the principal international airport in Tallinn; there are 335km of year-round navigable waterways, and the main seaports are at Talinn, Parnu Reid and Haapsalu Jahtklubi
Roadways and railways – 10,427km, including 115km of motorways; 1,196km
Telecommunications – 410,000 fixed lines and 2.1 million mobile subscriptions (2014); there were 1 million internet users in 2014
Internet code and IDD – ee; 372 (from UK), 44 (to UK)
Major broadcasters – Publicly-owned broadcaster Eesti Rahvusringhaaling (EER) operates 3 television and 5 radio channels; growing number of privately-owned broadcasting outlets regionally and nationally
Press – Major newspapers include *Postimees* (Estonian and Russian editions) and *Eesti Paevaleht*
WPFI score – 14,08 (12)

EDUCATION AND HEALTH
Primary and secondary level education is compulsory between the ages of seven and 15.
Literacy rate – 100 per cent (2015 est)
Gross enrolment ratio (percentage of relevant age group) – primary 98.4 per cent, secondary 115.2 per cent, tertiary 69.6 per cent (2015 est)
Health expenditure (per capita) – US$1,248 (2014)
Hospital beds (per 1,000 people) – 5 (2015)
Life expectancy (years) – 76.9 (2017 est)
Mortality rate – 12.6 (2017 est)
Birth rate – 10.1 (2017 est)
Infant mortality rate – 3.8 (2017 est)
HIV/AIDS adult prevalence – 1.3 per cent (2013 est)

ESWATINI

Umbuso weSwatini – Kingdom of eSwatini

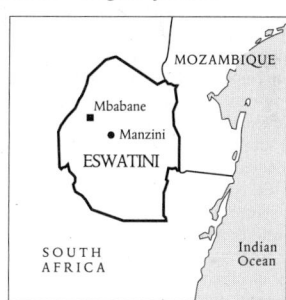

Area – 17,364 sq. km
Capital – Mbabane; population, 68,000 (2018). Lobamba is the legislative capital
Major town – Manzini
Currency – Lilangeni (E; plural *Emalangeni)* of 100 cents; the Lilangeni has a par value with the South African rand, which is also in circulation
Population – 1,468,152 rising at 1.08 per cent a year (2017 est)
Religion – Christian (Zionist 40 per cent, Roman Catholic 20 per cent), Muslim 10 per cent
Language – English, siSwati (both official)
Population density – 78 per sq. km (2016)
Urban population – 23.8 per cent (2018 est)
Median age (years) – 21.4 (2016 est)
National anthem – 'Nkulunkulu Mnikati wetibusiso temaSwati' 'Oh God, Bestower of Blessings on the Swazi'

National day – 6 September (Independence Day)
Death penalty – Retained (last used 1983)
Military expenditure – US$67.3m (2016)
Literacy rate – 94.8 per cent (2015 est)
Gross enrolment ratio (percentage of relevant age group) – primary
112.8 per cent, secondary 66 per cent (2014 est) tertiary
5.3 per cent (2013 est)
Health expenditure (per capita) – US$248 (2014)
Hospital beds (per 1,000 people) – 2.1 (2011)
Life expectancy (years) – 52.1 (2017 est)
Mortality rate – 13.2 (2017 est)
Birth rate – 24 (2017 est)
Infant mortality rate – 48.4 (2017 est)
HIV/AIDS adult prevalence – 27.2 per cent (2016 est)

CLIMATE AND TERRAIN

The main regions of the landlocked country are: the densely forested and mountainous Highveld along the western border, with an average altitude of 1,219m; the Middleveld, a mixed farming area, which averages about 609m in altitude, and the Lowveld, which was mainly scrubland until the introduction of sugar cane plantations, in the centre; and the Lubombo ridge, along the eastern edge of the Lowveld. Elevation extremes range from 1,862m (Emlembe) to 21m (Great Usutu river). Four rivers, the Komati, Usutu, Mbuluzi and Ngwavuma, flow from west to east.

The climate varies; the Highveld is humid and temperate, the Middleveld and Lubombo are subtropical, and the Lowveld is tropical and semi-arid. Average temperatures in Mbabane, in the Highveld, range from 15.8°C in July to 24°C in February.

HISTORY AND POLITICS

The Swazi people are believed to have arrived in the area in the 16th century, and by the mid-17th century had developed a strong kingdom three times the size of the present country. This became a protectorate of the Boer republic of the Transvaal in 1884, and subsequently of Britain. The Kingdom of Swaziland became independent in 1968, and was renamed the Kingdom of eSwatini in 2018 – its 'ancient name' – to mark 50 years of independence.

In 1973 King Sobhuza II suspended the constitution, banned political parties and assumed absolute power. The parliamentary system was replaced by traditional tribal communities *(tinkhundla)*. Sobhuza II died in 1982, and was succeeded by a son who was a minor. The regency between 1982 and 1986 led to power struggles within the royal family, but the real power passed to the Dlamini clan, which continues to dominate the government.

The 2005 constitution retains the executive powers of the king; it appears to permit political parties while maintaining the ban on their members standing for election. The head of state is a hereditary king who is effectively an absolute monarch who rules by decree. There is a bicameral parliament comprising a 30-member senate and a 65-member House of Assembly; members of both serve a five-year term. Each of the country's 55 administrative districts *(tinkhundla)* directly elects one member to the House of Assembly and the king appoints ten members; there is also a provision for four female members to be regionally elected if the total percentage of women is less than 30 per cent. The members of the House of Assembly elect ten of their own number to the senate and a further 20 senators are appointed by the king.

HEAD OF STATE

HM The King of eSwatini, King Mswati III, *crowned* 25 April
1986

SELECTED GOVERNMENT MEMBERS *AS AT JUNE 2018*

Prime Minister, Sibusiso Barnabas Dlamini
Deputy Prime Minister, Paul Dlamini

Finance, Martin Dlamini
Foreign Affairs, Mgwagwa Gamedze

KINGDOM OF ESWATINI HIGH COMMISSION

20 Buckingham Gate, London SW1E 6LB
T 020-7630 6611 E enquiries@swaziland.org.uk
High Commissioner, HE Christian Muzie Nkambule, *apptd*
2017

BRITISH HIGH COMMISSIONER

HE Nigel Casey, CMG, MVO, *apptd* 2017, resident at
Pretoria (Tshwane), South Africa

ECONOMY AND TRADE

The country is very poor, with 63 per cent of the population living below the poverty line and a 28 per cent unemployment rate. Customs dues from the South African Customs Union and remittances from expatriates working in South Africa are a vital supplement to the domestic economy; customs revenue dropped sharply in the global downturn and the government applied for international financial assistance. Overgrazing, soil depletion, drought and floods are potential future problems.

This country has the highest levels of HIV/AIDS infection in the world, more than a quarter of the adult population, and consequently faces serious demographic, economic and social problems.

Subsistence agriculture occupies 10.7 per cent of the population and contributes 6.5 per cent of GDP. Sugar cane, cotton, citrus fruits and pineapples are the main cash crops and the basis of industries producing sugar, canned fruit and soft drink concentrates. Coal mining has become less important since the 1980s with diversification into gold and diamond mining, alongside manufacturing products such as textiles, clothing, wood pulp and refrigerators. Industry contributes 45 per cent of GDP and services 48.6 per cent.

South Africa accounts for 94 per cent of exports and over 80 per cent of imports. Principal exports are the products of agriculture and manufacturing. The main imports are vehicles, machinery, transport equipment, foodstuffs, petroleum products and chemicals.

GNI – US$4.1bn; US$2,960 per capita (2017)
Annual average growth of GDP – 0.3 per cent (2017 est)
Inflation rate – 7 per cent (2017 est)
Population below poverty line – 63 per cent (2010)
Total external debt – US$548.2m (2017 est)
Imports – US$1,525m (2013)
Exports – US$1,894m (2013)

BALANCE OF PAYMENTS

Trade – US$370m surplus (2013)
Current Account – US$639m surplus (2016)

Trade with UK	2016	2017
Imports from UK	£3,014,949	£2,849,718
Exports to UK	£21,237,047	£3,407,254

COMMUNICATIONS

Airports – 14 airports; the international airports are in Manzini: Matsapha and Mswati III International Airport
Roadways and railways – There are 1,078km of roads; 301km of railway connect with the Mozambique port of Maputo and the South African railway to Richards Bay and Durban
Telecommunications – 42,000 fixed lines and 995,000 mobile subscriptions (2016); there were 414,724 internet users in 2016
Internet code and IDD – sz; 268 (from UK), 44 (to UK)

Media – 1 state-owned television channel, 3 radio channels; 1 private radio channel (2017). Swaziland Broadcasting and Information Service (radio) and Swazi TV are the state broadcasters; the only daily newspapers are *The Times of Swaziland* and *The Swazi Observer*
WPFI score – 51,46 (152)

ETHIOPIA

Ityop'iya Federalawi Demokrasiyawi Ripeblik – Federal Democratic Republic of Ethiopia

Area – 1,104,300 sq. km
Capital – Addis Ababa; population, 4,400,000 (2018 est)
Major cities – Bahir Dar, Dese, Dire Dawa, Gonder, Mek'ele, Nazret
Currency – Birr (EB) of 100 cents
Population – 105,350,020 rising at 2.85 per cent a year (2017 est); Oromo (34.4 per cent), Amhara (27 per cent), Somali (6.2 per cent), Tigray (6.1 per cent), Sidama (4 per cent), Guragie (2.5 per cent), Welaita (2.3 per cent) (2007 est)
Religion – Christian (Ethiopian Orthodox 43.7 per cent, Protestant 18.5 per cent, Muslim 33.9 per cent (mostly Sunni) (2007 est)
Language – Amharic, English, Arabic (all official), Oromo Tigrinya, Somali, Guaragigna, Sidamo
Population density – 102 per sq. km (2016)
Urban population – 20.8 per cent (2018 est)
Median age (years) – 17.9 (2017 est)
National anthem – 'Wodefit Gesgeshi Widd Innat Ityopp'ya' 'March Forward, Dear Mother Ethiopia']
National day – 28 May (defeat of Mengistu government, 1991)
Death penalty – Retained (last used 2007)
CPI score – 35 (107)
Military expenditure – US$469m (2016)

CLIMATE AND TERRAIN
Ethiopia is dominated by a central plateau, rising to the mountains of the Ethiopian Highlands, which are divided by the Great Rift Valley. The western mountains are the source of the Blue Nile. The land drops to desert plains in the east (Ogaden) and north-east (Danakil desert). Elevation extremes range from 4,533m (Ras Dejen) to −125m (Danakil depression). There is a tropical monsoon climate, with variations according to altitude. The wet season is from April to September.

POLITICS
The 1994 constitution provides for a federal government responsible for foreign affairs, defence and economic policy, and nine ethnically based states. The president is elected by both houses of the legislature for a six-year term, renewable once. The prime minister is appointed by the lower chamber of the legislature and appoints the government. The Federal Parliamentary Assembly is bicameral. The lower chamber, the House of People's Representatives, has 547 members, directly elected for a five-year term. The House of the Federation has 153 members, elected for a five-year term by the government councils of the nine states in the federation. These regional administrations have considerable autonomy and the right to secede.

In the 2015 legislative elections, the ruling Ethiopian People's Revolutionary Democratic Front and its allies won all seats in the House of People's Representatives; observers and opposition groups claimed the polls were not fair due to government restrictions on free speech. In 2018, Prime Minister Hailemariam Desalegn resigned after months of protests for democratic change, following an initially violent response from the government. He was replaced by Abiy Ahmed. Mulatu Teshome was elected president in 2013.

HEAD OF STATE
President, Mulatu Teshome, *elected* 7 October 2013

SELECTED GOVERNMENT MEMBERS *AS AT JULY 2018*
Prime Minister, Abiy Ahmed Ali
Deputy Prime Minister, Demeke Mekonnen
Finance, Abraham Tekeste
Foreign Affairs, Workneh Gebeyehu

EMBASSY OF THE FEDERAL DEMOCRATIC REPUBLIC OF ETHIOPIA
17 Princes Gate, London SW7 1PZ
T 020-7589 7212 E info@ethioembassy.org.uk
W www.ethioembassy.org.uk
Ambassador Extraordinary and Plenipotentiary, HE Dr Hailemichael Aberra Afework, *apptd* 2016

BRITISH EMBASSY
Comoros Street, Addis Ababa 858
T (+251) (11) 61 70100 E britishembassy.addisababa@fco.gov.uk
W www.gov.uk/government/world/ethiopia
Ambassador Extraordinary and Plenipotentiary, HE Susanna Moorehead, *apptd* 2016

FOREIGN RELATIONS
Ethiopia intervened in Somalia in 2006 in support of the Somali transitional government. It formally withdrew its forces in January 2009, in accordance with a 2008 peace agreement between the Somali government and rebels. In January 2014, 4,000 Ethiopian troops reinforced African Union soldiers

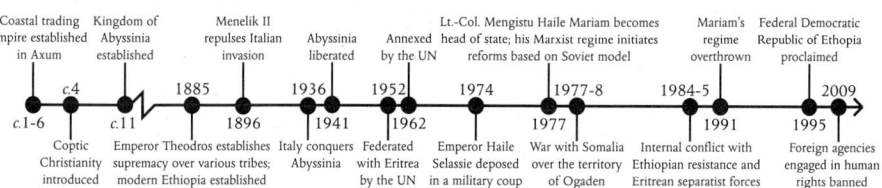

fighting the al-Qaida-aligned al-Shabab group in northern Somalia.

For border disputes with Eritrea, *see* Eritrea.

ECONOMY AND TRADE

The economy is highly dependent on agriculture, and therefore reliant on the rains; recurring droughts led to famine conditions in 1984–5, 1992, 1997, 2000, 2002, 2009, 2011 and 2015–16. Although most foreign debt was cancelled in 2005, emergency IMF funding was needed to cushion the country from the effects of the global downturn. Ethiopia has experienced more than a decade of strong growth, with GDP growing by 93 per cent between 2007 and 2013, and the government has invested revenue in improving the country's infrastructure.

Agriculture and herding account for 35.8 per cent of GDP, and 72.7 per cent of the population is dependent upon the land for a living. The main crops are cereals, pulses, coffee, oilseed, cotton, sugar, potatoes, qat (or khat, a flowering plant chewed for its stimulant properties), cut flowers, livestock products and fish. Natural resources, including gold, platinum, copper, potash, oil and natural gas, are largely unexploited; most industrial activity involves the processing of agricultural products, gold mining and metalworking, and textiles. Work continues on three major dams, which is intended to generate electricity for domestic consumption and export, despite protests from the Egyptian government that the Grand Ethiopian Renaissance Dam could threaten Egypt's water supply. Completion of this dam has been delayed.

The main trade partners are China, Saudi Arabia, Sudan, Switzerland and India. Principal exports are coffee, vegetables, gold, leather products, livestock and oilseeds. The main imports are petroleum products, chemicals, machinery, vehicles, metal and metal products.

GNI – US$77.3bn; US$740 per capita (2017)
Annual average growth of GDP – 8.5 per cent (2017 est)
Inflation rate – 8.1 per cent (2017 est)
Population below poverty line – 29.6 per cent (2014 est)
Unemployment – 17.5 per cent (2012 est)
Total external debt – US$29.09bn (2017 est)
Imports – US$19,063m (2015)
Exports – US$3,825m (2015)

BALANCE OF PAYMENTS
Trade – US$15,238m deficit (2015)
Current Account – US$8,269m deficit (2017)

Trade with UK	2016	2017
Imports from UK	£181,652,547	£240,829,178
Exports to UK	£165,431,454	£345,252,661

COMMUNICATIONS

Airports and waterways – 17; this landlocked country uses ports in Djibouti city and Berbera in Somalia
Roadways and railways – There are 6,064km of surfaced roads; the only railway line links Addis Ababa and Djibouti over 681km but is largely inoperable
Telecommunications – 1.1 million fixed lines and 51.2 million mobile subscriptions (2016); there were 15.7 million internet users in 2016
Internet country code and IDD – et; 251 (from UK), 44 (to UK)
Major broadcasters – The state-owned Ethiopian Television and Radio Ethiopia operate national and regional stations
Press – There are 6 public television outlets and 10 public radio channels alongside 7 private and 19 commercial radio stations. *Addis Zemen* and *Ethiopian Herald* are the state-owned

dailies, *The Daily Monitor* and *Addis Admass* are privately owned publications (2017)
WPFI score – 50,17 (150)

EDUCATION AND HEALTH

Non-compulsory elementary and secondary education is provided by government schools in the major population centres; there are also mission schools.
Literacy rate – 69.5 per cent (2015 est)
Gross enrolment ratio (percentage of relevant age group) – primary 100.1 per cent (2014 est); secondary 36 per cent (2011 est); tertiary 8.1 per cent (2014 est)
Health expenditure (per capita) – US$27 (2014)
Hospital beds (per 1,000 people) – 0.3 (2015)
Life expectancy (years) – 62.6 (2017 est)
Mortality rate – 7.7 (2017 est)
Birth rate – 36.5 (2017 est)
Infant mortality rate – 49.6 (2017 est)
HIV/AIDS adult prevalence – 1.1 per cent (2016 est)

FIJI

Matanitu ko Viti – Republic of Fiji

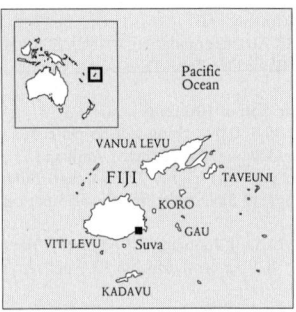

Area – 18,274 sq. km
Capital – Suva, on Viti Levu; population, 178,000 (2018)
Major towns – Lautoka, Nasinu, Nausori
Currency – Fijian dollar (F$) of 100 cents
Population – 920,938 rising at 0.60 per cent a year (2017 est); Fijian (56.8 per cent), Indian (37.5 per cent), Rotuman (1.2 per cent) (2007 est)
Religion – Christian 64.5 per cent (predominantly Methodist), Hindu 27.9 per cent, Muslim 6.3 per cent (predominantly Sunni) (2007 est)
Language – English, Fijian (official), Hindustani
Population density – 49 per sq. km (2015)
Urban population – 56.2 per cent (2018 est)
Median age (years) – 28.9 (2017 est)
National anthem – 'Meda Dau Doka' 'God Bless Fiji'
National day – Second Monday of October (Independence Day)
Death penalty – Abolished for all crimes since 2015
Military expenditure – US$45.9m (2017)
Gross enrolment ratio (percentage of relevant age group) – primary 105.5 per cent (2015 est), secondary 88 per cent (2012 est)
Health expenditure (per capita) – US$204 (2014)
Life expectancy (years) – 73 (2017 est)
Mortality rate – 6.1 (2017 est)
Birth rate – 18.6 (2017 est)
Infant mortality rate – 9.5 (2017 est)
HIV/AIDS adult prevalence – 0.1 per cent (2016 est)

CLIMATE AND TERRAIN
Fiji comprises a group of about 330 islands (around 110 are permanently inhabited) and over 500 islets in the South Pacific, about 1,770km north of New Zealand. The group extends 480km from east to west and 480km north to south. The international date line has been diverted to the east of the island group. The largest islands are Viti Levu and Vanua Levu. The terrain is mountainous and volcanic, with tropical rainforest and grassland, and most islands are surrounded by coral reefs. Elevation extremes range from 1,324m (Tomanivi, on Viti Levu) to 0m (Pacific Ocean). Fiji has a tropical maritime climate with high humidity and an average annual temperature of 24.3°C.

HISTORY AND POLITICS
The islands were settled by Melanesian peoples. European contact began with the visit of the Dutch explorer Abel Tasman in 1643; later visitors included Captain Cook in 1774. The islands became a British colony in 1874, and sugar plantations, employing more than 60,000 indentured Indian labourers, were established. Fiji became independent as a constitutional monarchy on 10 October 1970, and became a republic after the 1987 coups.

The growing size and political strength of the ethnic Indian population caused political instability in the late 1980s. There were two coups in 1987 and one in 2000 as indigenous Fijians attempted to reassert their political dominance and entrench this in the constitution. A fourth coup occurred in 2006 over the government's proposed amnesty for those involved in the 2000 coup.

In 2007 President Ratu Josefa Iloilo was reinstated and 2006 coup leader Commodore 'Frank' Bainimarama became prime minister. In response to a court of appeal ruling in April 2009 stating that the military government was illegal, President Iloilo suspended the constitution, dismissed the judiciary, reappointed Bainimarama as interim prime minister and declared a state of emergency. President Iloilo retired in July 2009.

Political instability and failure to hold elections caused Fiji to be suspended from the Commonwealth of Nations between 1987 and 1997, from 2000 to 2001 and from 2009 to 2014. The first legislative elections in eight years were held on 21 September 2014; the Fiji First Party emerged as the largest single party, winning 32 of the 50 seats in the legislature, in elections deemed credible by many international observers. Frank Bainimarama remained prime minister. Jioji Konusi Konrote was elected president in October 2015.

In September 2013, Fiji's fourth constitution was signed into law, the first to abolish race-based electoral rolls and seat quotas. It vests sole legislative authority in the single-chamber, 50-seat parliament. The president is elected by parliament for a three-year term, renewable once, and members serve four-year terms.

HEAD OF STATE
President, Jioji Konusi Konrote, *elected* 12 October 2015, *sworn in* 12 November 2015

SELECTED GOVERNMENT MEMBERS *AS AT JUNE 2018*
Prime Minister, Foreign Affairs, Josaia Voreqe ('Frank') Bainimarama
Attorney-General, Economy, Aiyaz Sayed-Khaiyum
Defence, Inoke Kubuabola

HIGH COMMISSION OF THE REPUBLIC OF FIJI
34 Hyde Park Gate, London SW7 5DN
T 020-7584 3661 E mail@fijihighcommission.org.uk
W www.fijihighcommission.org.uk
High Commissioner, HE Jitoko Tikovelu, *apptd* 2016

BRITISH HIGH COMMISSION
47 Gladstone Road, Suva
T (+679) 322 9100 E publicdiplomacy@fco.gov.uk
W www.gov.uk/government/world/fiji
High Commissioner, HE Melanie Hopkins, *apptd* 2016

ECONOMY AND TRADE
Fiji has abundant natural resources and one of the more developed economies in the region. However, the economy suffered after the 1987 coups because of the mass emigration of Indian Fijians, and was contracting until recently owing to structural problems, inefficiency and political instability. Tourism, the mainstay of the economy, has declined since the 2006 coup but has recovered following the country's return to democracy, notwithstanding the damage wrought by Cyclone Winston in February 2016. Private investment has risen sharply in recent years.

Agriculture, much of it at subsistence level, accounts for 10.6 per cent of GDP and employs 44.2 per cent of the workforce. The principal cash crop is sugar cane, but revenue has been affected by cuts in EU subsidies. The other main agricultural products are coconuts, cassava, rice, sweet potatoes, bananas, livestock and fish. The main industries are tourism, sugar processing, garment manufacturing, copra production, gold and silver mining, forestry and small cottage industries. Expatriate remittances are also an important economic contributor. The main trade partners are Australia, New Zealand, China, the USA and Singapore. Principal exports are fuel, sugar, garments, gold, timber, fish, molasses and coconut oil. The chief imports are manufactured goods, machinery and transport equipment, petroleum products, food and chemicals.
GNI – US$4.5bn; US$4,970 per capita (2017)
Annual average growth of GDP – 3.8 per cent (2017 est)
Inflation rate – 3.8 per cent (2017 est)
Unemployment – 5.5 per cent (2017 est)
Total external debt – US$750.4m (2017 est)
Imports – US$2,316m (2016)
Exports – US$926m (2016)

BALANCE OF PAYMENTS
Trade – US$1,391m deficit (2016)
Current Account – US$314m deficit (2017)

Trade with UK	2016	2017
Imports from UK	£9,988,657	£14,026,071
Exports to UK	£23,262,323	£28,785,274

COMMUNICATIONS
Airports and waterways – Four, including international airports at Suva and Nadi; the main seaports are Suva and Lautoka
Roadways and railways – There are 1,686km of surfaced roads, and 597km of railway track, principally used by the sugar industry
Telecommunications – 74,700 fixed lines and 876,200 mobile subscriptions (2014); there were 331,700 internet users in 2014
Internet code and IDD – fj; 679 (from UK), 44 (to UK)
Major broadcasters – There are two main television networks: national Fiji TV Ltd and the commercial Mai TV; Fiji Broadcasting Corporation is the state-owned radio broadcaster; 6 radio stations, 2 public broadcasters and 4 commercial broadcasters are operated by Fiji Broadcasting (2017)
Press – Newspapers include the daily *Fiji Times* (English language), and Hindi weeklies *Sartaj* and *Shanti Dut*
WPFI score – 26,55 (57)

FINLAND

Suomen tasavalta / Republiken Finland – Republic of Finland

Area – 338,145 sq. km
Capital – Helsinki (Helsingfors); population, 1,279,000 (2018 est)
Major cities – Espoo (Esbo), Oulu (Uleaborg), Tampere (Tammerfors), Turku (Aabo), Vantaa (Vanda)
Currency – Euro (€) of 100 cents
Population – 5,518,371 rising at 0.36 per cent a year (2017 est); Finnish (93.4 per cent), Swedish (5.6 per cent), Russian (0.5 per cent), Estonian (0.3 per cent), Roma (0.1 per cent), Sami (0.1 per cent) (2006 est)
Religion – Christian (Lutheran 73.8 per cent, Orthodox 1.1 per cent), none 25.1 per cent (2014 est)
Language – Finnish, Swedish (both official)
Population density – 18 per sq. km (2016)
Urban population – 84.5 per cent (2017 est)
Median age (years) – 42.5 (2017 est)
National anthem – 'Maamme' / 'Vart Land' 'Our Land'
National day – 6 December (Independence Day)
Death penalty – Abolished for all crimes (since 1972)
CPI score – 85 (3)
Military expenditure – US$3,597m (2017)
Conscription – 18 years of age, male only; 6–12 months

CLIMATE AND TERRAIN

Much of the centre of the country is a glaciated plateau of forests and lakes, with low hills along the eastern border with Russia and in the far north. Forests cover around 70 per cent of the country, including those of the coastal peatlands in the south-west. There are over 60,000 lakes, with an average depth of 7m. Elevation extremes range from 1,328m (Haltiatunturi, or Halti) to 0m (Baltic Sea). A quarter of the country lies north of the Arctic Circle; temperatures there can range from −9.4°C in February to 15.6°C in July. Average temperatures in Helsinki range from −6°C in February to 16°C in July.

Owing to isostatic uplift (the rise of landmass no longer depressed by the weight of glaciers), the surface area of Finland is growing by around 7 sq. km a year.

HISTORY AND POLITICS

Finland was part of the Swedish Empire from the 12th century until it was ceded to Russia in 1809, when it became an autonomous grand duchy of the Russian Empire. After the Russian Revolution in 1917, Finland declared its independence. An attempted coup by Finnish Bolsheviks led to a short civil war that ended in their defeat in 1918, and in 1919 a republic was established. It resisted the 1939 invasion by the USSR but was defeated in 1940 and forced to cede territory; in the hope of recovering this territory it joined Germany's attack on the USSR in 1941. After agreeing an armistice with the USSR in 1944, Finland concluded a peace treaty in 1947 that conceded further territory to the USSR and obliged it to pay reparations. A Soviet-Finnish cooperation treaty in 1948 forced Finland to demilitarise its Soviet border and to adopt a stance of neutrality; these terms lasted until the demise of the USSR in 1991.

Finland joined the EU in 1995 and the European Monetary Union in 1998.

In the 2015 legislative election, the Centre Party (KESK) emerged as the largest party, winning 49 of 200 parliamentary seats. The government includes the far-right Eurosceptic Finns party (PS) and the centre-right National Coalition Party (NCP). Sauli Niinisto of the NCP was re-elected president in January 2018.

Under the 2000 constitution, the president is directly elected for a six-year term. There is a unicameral legislature, the *Eduskunta,* with 200 members directly elected for a four-year term. The prime minister is elected by the *Eduskunta* and appointed by the president.

HEAD OF STATE
President, Sauli Niinisto, *elected* 5 February 2012, *inaugurated* 1 March 2012, *re-elected* 28 January 2018

SELECTED GOVERNMENT MEMBERS *AS AT JUNE 2018*
Prime Minister, Juha Sipila
Deputy Prime Minister, Foreign Affairs, Timo Soini
Defence, Jussi Niinisto
Finance, Petteri Orpo
Interior, Kai Mykkanen

EMBASSY OF FINLAND
38 Chesham Place, London SW1X 8HW
T 020-7838 6200 E sanomat.lon@formin.fi W www.finemb.org.uk
Ambassador Extraordinary and Plenipotentiary, HE Paivi Luostarinen, *apptd* 2015

BRITISH EMBASSY
Itainen Puistotie 17, 00140 Helsinki
T (+358) (9) 2286 5100 E info.helsinki@fco.gov.uk
W www.gov.uk/government/world/finland
Ambassador Extraordinary and Plenipotentiary, HE Thomas Dodd, *apptd* 2018

ECONOMY AND TRADE

The country has a highly industrialised market economy that has thrived as a result of its telecommunications and electronics industries, particularly the manufacture of mobile phones, as well as its traditional timber and metals industries. The economy entered recession in 2012, due to a lack of economic competitiveness, high wages and an ageing population. The economy is vulnerable to fluctuations in trade with Russia, particularly due to the economic sanctions imposed on the country in 2014, although exports have benefited from an appreciation in the rouble. Growth returned in 2016 and accelerated in 2017 thanks to rising investment, which is actively pursued.

The main trade partners are Germany, Sweden and Russia. Principal exports are electrical and optical equipment, machinery, transport equipment, paper and pulp, chemicals, base metals and timber. The main imports are foodstuffs (especially grain), petroleum and petroleum products, chemicals, transport equipment, iron and steel, machinery, textile yarn and fabrics, and components for manufactured goods. Finland is a net importer of energy.

GNI – US$245.7bn; US$44,580 per capita (2017)
Annual average growth of GDP – 2.8 per cent (2017 est)
Inflation rate – 0.8 per cent (2017 est)
Unemployment – 8.7 per cent (2017 est)
Total external debt – US$544.7bn (2016 est)

Imports – US$60,478m (2016)
Exports – US$57,314m (2016)

BALANCE OF PAYMENTS
Trade – US$3,164m deficit (2016)
Current Account – US$1,918m deficit (2017)

Trade with UK	2016	2017
Imports from UK	£1,335,749,303	£1,367,324,431
Exports to UK	£2,182,977,951	£2,476,214,587

COMMUNICATIONS
Airports and waterways – 148 airports; the principal airports are at Helsinki, Turku and Tampere; the main seaports are Helsinki, Kotka, Rauma and Turku
Roadways and railways – The 50,000km road network and 5,944km rail network are concentrated in the southern half of the country, where most of the population and industry are located
Telecommunications – 457,300 fixed lines and 7.4 million mobile telephone subscriptions (2016); there were 4.8 million internet users in 2016
Internet code and IDD – fi; 358 (from UK), 44 (to UK)
Major broadcasters – There are both commercial and state-owned broadcasters; the state broadcaster, Yleisradio Oy (YLE), is funded by licence fees and provides radio and television services in Swedish and Finnish, with radio in Sami (Lappish)
Press – Major publications include *Helsingin Sanomat* (Finnish), *Hufvudstadsbladet* (Swedish) and the English-language *Helsinki Times*
WPFI score – 10,26 (4)

EDUCATION AND HEALTH
Basic education is free and compulsory for children from seven to 16 years.
Gross enrolment ratio (percentage of relevant age group) – primary 100 per cent, secondary 152 per cent, tertiary 87 per cent (2016 est)
Health expenditure (per capita) – US$4,612 (2014)
Hospital beds (per 1,000 people) – 4.4 (2015)
Life expectancy (years) – 81 (2017 est)
Mortality rate – 10 (2016 est)
Birth rate – 10.7 (2017 est)
Infant mortality rate – 2.5 (2017 est)

FRANCE
République française – French Republic

Area – 551,500 sq. km (excluding overseas territories)
Capital – Paris; population, 10,901,000 (2018 est)
Major cities – Bordeaux, Lille, Lyon, Marseille, Montpellier, Nantes, Nice, Reims, Rennes, Strasbourg, Toulouse. The chief towns of Corsica are Ajaccio and Bastia

Currency – Euro (€) of 100 cents
Population – 62,814,233 (excluding overseas territories), rising at 0.39 per cent a year (2017 est)
Religion – Christian 63–66 per cent (mainly Roman Catholic), Muslim 7–9 per cent, Buddhist 0.5–0.75 per cent, Jewish 0.5–0.75 per cent (2015 est)
Language – French (official)
Population density – 122 per sq. km (2015) (excluding overseas territories)
Urban population – 80 per cent (2017 est)
Median age (years) – 41.4 (2017 est)
National anthem – 'La Marseillaise' 'The Song of Marseille'
National day – 14 July (Fête de la Fédération/Fête Nationale)
Death penalty – Abolished for all crimes (since 1981)
CPI score – 70 (23)
Military expenditure – US$57,770m (2017)

CLIMATE AND TERRAIN
The north and west consist of flat plains, particularly in the basins of the Somme, Seine, Loire and Garonne rivers, with some low hills. The centre of the south is occupied by the Massif Central plateau, which is divided by the valley of the Rhone and Soane rivers from the mountains – the French Alps, the Jura and the Vosges – on the eastern border. The Pyrenees range lies along the southern border with Spain. Elevation extremes range from 4,807m (Mt Blanc, Alps) to −2m (Rhône delta). The climate is generally temperate, though the south has a Mediterranean climate and the east a continental climate.

POLITICS
Under the 1958 constitution, the head of state is a president directly elected for a five-year term, which is renewable once. The legislature, the *Parlement,* consists of the National Assembly and the senate. The National Assembly has 577 deputies, 556 for metropolitan France and 21 for the overseas departments and territories; members are directly elected for a five-year term. The senate has been enlarged gradually over the past decade; since the September 2011 elections there are 348 senators (328 for metropolitan France and the overseas departments, eight for overseas collectivities and territories, and 12 for French nationals abroad) elected by an electoral college to serve a six-year term, with half elected every three years.

The prime minister is nominated by the National Assembly and appointed by the president, as is the council of ministers. They are responsible to the legislature, but as the executive is constitutionally separate from the legislature, ministers may not sit in the legislature and must hand over their seats to a substitute.

The constitution was amended in 2003 to pave the way for the devolution to the 13 metropolitan regions and 96 metropolitan departments of powers over economic development, transport, tourism, culture and further education.

In the 2012 legislative elections, the Socialist Party (PS) won an overall majority, defeating Nicolas Sarkozy's Union for a Popular Movement party by 86 seats. Following poor local election results for the PS, Manuel Valls replaced Jean-Marc Ayrault as prime minister on 1 April 2014. Valls formally declared he would stand as the PS candidate in the 2017 presidential elections and resigned as prime minister on 5 December 2016; he was replaced by Bernard Cazeneuve on the 6th. Emmanuel Macron, leader of the independent La République En Marche party, won the May 2017 presidential elections, beating the Front National's Marine Le Pen in the second round by more than 32 per cent of the vote. Édouard Philippe became prime minister on 15 May 2017. En Marche

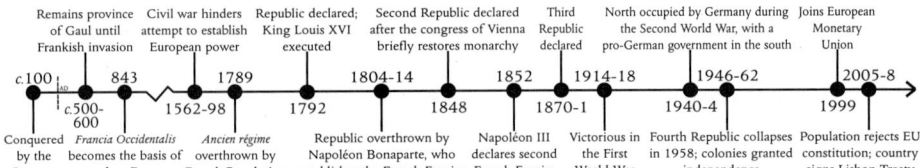

| Remains province of Gaul until Frankish invasion | Civil war hinders attempt to establish European power | Republic declared; King Louis XVI executed | Second Republic declared after the congress of Vienna briefly restores monarchy | Third Republic declared | North occupied by Germany during the Second World War, with a pro-German government in the south | Joins European Monetary Union |

*c.*100 — 843 — 1789 — 1804-14 — 1852 — 1914-18 — 1946-62 — 2005-8

*c.*500-600 — 1562-98 — 1792 — 1848 — 1870-1 — 1940-4 — 1999

| Conquered by the Romans | *Francia Occidentalis* becomes the basis of modern France | *Ancien régime* overthrown by French Revolution | Republic overthrown by Napoléon Bonaparte, who establishes the French Empire | Napoléon III declares second French Empire | Victorious in the First World War | Fourth Republic collapses in 1958; colonies granted independence | Population rejects EU constitution; country signs Lisbon Treaty |

took 350 seats in the National Assembly in legislative elections in June 2017.

HEAD OF STATE
President of the French Republic, Emmanuel Macron, *elected* 7 May 2017, *took office* 14 May 2017

SELECTED GOVERNMENT MEMBERS *AS AT JUNE 2018*
Prime Minister, Édouard Philippe
Economy, Bruno Le Maire
Europe, Foreign Affairs, Jean-Yves Le Drian
Interior, Gérard Collomb

EMBASSY OF FRANCE
58 Knightsbridge, London SW1X 7JT
T 020-7073 1000 W www.ambafrance-uk.org
Ambassador Extraordinary and Plenipotentiary, HE Jean-Pierre Jouyet, *apptd* 2017

BRITISH EMBASSY
35 rue du Faubourg St Honoré, 75383 Paris Cédex 08
T (+33) (1) 4451 3100 W www.gov.uk/government/world/france
Ambassador Extraordinary and Plenipotentiary, HE the Rt Hon. Lord Llewellyn of Steep, OBE, *apptd* 2016

INSURGENCIES
Except for a ceasefire in 2003–5, Corsican separatists pursued a campaign of bombings and shootings from the 1970s until 2016, when the main separatist faction announced it was ceasing military operations. The National Liberation Front of Corsica (FNLC) said it did not want to interfere with the work of the island's assembly, which has been led by nationalists since regional elections in 2015. The French government's proposals to combine the island's two departments and to give the Corsican regional parliament greater autonomy were narrowly rejected in a 2003 referendum.

ECONOMY AND TRADE
The economy is in transition from extensive government ownership and intervention to a more liberal and market-oriented form with many large, state-run companies becoming privatised; reform was initiated in response to poor economic growth and high unemployment. Implementation has been slow because of the constraints of eurozone membership, and strong resistance to the government's plans for privatisation and reform of labour, pensions and welfare. Since 2017, President Macron has pursued policies designed to weaken labour laws, decrease public spending and reduce corporation tax in order to increase competitiveness, causing widespread protests and strikes. Nevertheless, the economic recovery remains weak and a state of emergency was put in place following the terrorist attacks of November 2015. Growth has accelerated but unemployment, particularly in youths, remains high.

Over one-third of the land area of metropolitan France is utilised for agricultural production and a further quarter is covered by forests. Viniculture is extensive, although France has lost market share to other countries in recent years. Cognac, liqueurs and cider are also produced. Other important agricultural products include cereals, sugar beet, potatoes, beef, dairy products and fish. Agriculture employs 2.8 per cent of the workforce and contributes 2 per cent of GDP.

Oil is produced from fields in the Landes area, but France is a net importer of crude oil, for processing by its oil-refining industry. Natural gas is produced in the foothills of the Pyrenees.

Industry contributes 20.1 per cent of GDP, employing 20 per cent of the workforce. The sector is highly diversified and includes the production of machinery, iron, steel, aluminium, chemicals, vehicles, aircraft, electronic goods, textiles and processed food. The service sector contributes 77.9 per cent of GDP and employs 77.2 per cent of the workforce. Tourism is an important contributor to GDP; France is the most-visited country in the world.

The main trading partners are other EU countries, especially Germany. Principal exports are machinery, vehicles, aircraft, plastics, chemicals, pharmaceutical products, iron and steel, and beverages. The main imports are raw materials for industry (eg crude oil, chemicals, plastics), machinery, vehicles and aircraft.

GNI – US$2,548.3bn; US$37,970 per capita (2017)
Annual average growth of GDP – 1.6 per cent (2017 est)
Inflation rate – 1.2 per cent (2017 est)
Population below poverty line – 14 per cent (2013 est)
Unemployment – 9.5 per cent (2017 est)
Total external debt – US$5.36 trillion (2016 est)
Imports – US$560,752m (2016)
Exports – US$488,797m (2016)

BALANCE OF PAYMENTS
Trade – US$71,956m deficit (2016)
Current Account – US$13,306m deficit (2017)

Trade with UK	2016	2017
Imports from UK	£19,580,484,711	£23,598,442,542
Exports to UK	£24,771,675,586	£26,894,259,440

COMMUNICATIONS
Airports – 464; there are two international airports serving Paris, and many regional airports capable of accepting international flights (2013)
Waterways – The principal seaports are Marseille on the Mediterranean Sea, Bordeaux and Nantes on the Atlantic coast, and Le Havre, Calais and Dunkirk on the Channel coast; there are 8,501km of navigable inland waterways, 1,621km navigable by large vessels, and Paris, Rouen and Strasbourg are significant river ports. The French mercantile marine consisted in 2011 of 162 ships of 1,000 gross tonnage or over, 151 of which are registered overseas
Roadways and railways – There are 1,028,446km of roadways, including 11,416km of motorways, and 29,640km of railways
Telecommunications – 39 million fixed lines and 67.6 million mobile subscriptions (2016); there were 57.2 million internet users in 2016
Internet code and IDD – fr; 33 (from UK), 44 (to UK)

Major broadcasters – TV5 is an international French-language television channel co-financed by Belgium, Canada, France and Switzerland. The main domestic channel, TF1, was privatised in 1987. A global news channel, France 24, was launched in 2006 and broadcasts in French, English and Arabic

Press – France has more than 100 daily newspapers, including *Le Monde, Le Figaro* and *Libération*

WPFI score – 21,87 (33)

EDUCATION AND HEALTH

Education is compulsory and free between the ages of six and 16. There are three types of *lycée – général, technique* and *professionel* – and each leads to its own *baccalauréat* qualification. Specialist schools are numerous.

Gross enrolment ratio (percentage of relevant age group) – primary 105.4 per cent, secondary 110.6 per cent, tertiary 64.4 per cent (2014 est)

Health expenditure (per capita) – US$4,959

Hospital beds (per 1,000 people) – 6.5 (2013)

Life expectancy (years) – 81.9 (2017 est)

Mortality rate – 9.3 (2017 est)

Birth rate – 12.2 (2017 est)

Infant mortality rate – 3.2 (2017 est)

HIV/AIDS adult prevalence – 0.4 (2016 est)

OVERSEAS DEPARTMENTS/REGIONS

French Guiana, Guadeloupe, Martinique and Réunion have had departmental status since 1946. They were given regional status with greater powers of self-government and elected assemblies in 1982, and were redesignated as Overseas Regions in 2003. Their regional and departmental status is identical to that of regions and departments of metropolitan France, and they can choose to replace these with a single structure by merging their regional and departmental assemblies. The French government is represented by a *prefect* in each. In referendums in 2010, French Guiana and Martinique rejected proposals for granting greater autonomy to their local governments.

FRENCH GUIANA

Area – 83,534 sq. km

Capital – Cayenne; population, 57,229 (2011 est)

Population – 250,109 (2013 est)

Situated on the north-eastern coast of South America, French Guiana is flanked by Suriname to the west and by Brazil to the south and east. Under the administration of French Guiana are the Îles du Salut group of islands (St Joseph, Île Royal and Île du Diable). The European Space Agency rocket launch site is situated at Kourou and accounts for 25 per cent of GDP. Fishing, forestry and mining are the main activities, and the economy is dependent on government subsidies. The main exports are timber, shrimp and gold. Tourism is restricted by the lack of infrastructure, as much of the interior is only accessible by river.

Prefect, Martin Jaeger, *apptd* 2016

GUADELOUPE

Area – 1,705 sq. km

Capital – Basse-Terre; population, 11,730 (2011 est), on Guadeloupe

Population – 405,739 (2013)

The Guadeloupe archipelago consists of a number of islands in the Leeward Islands group in the West Indies, including Guadeloupe (or Basse-Terre), Grande-Terre, Marie-Galante, La Désirade and the Îles des Saintes. The main towns are Les Abymes, Pointe-à-Pitre (Grande-Terre) and Grand Bourg (Marie-Galante). The main industries are tourism, agriculture,

sugar refining and rum distilling. Bananas, sugar, rum and vanilla are the main exports.

Prefect, Phillipe Gustin, *apptd* 2018

MARTINIQUE

Area – 1,100 sq. km

Capital – Fort-de-France; population, 86,753 (2011 est)

Population – 386,486 (2013)

An island in the Windward Islands group in the West Indies, Martinique lies between Dominica in the north and St Lucia in the south. It is dominated by Mt Pelée (1,397m), an active volcano that last erupted in 1902. Tourism is a major industry. The main exports are bananas, rum and petroleum products.

Prefect, Franck Robine, *apptd* 2017

MAYOTTE

Area – 374 sq. km

Capital – Mamoudzou; population, 58,197 (2012 est)

Population – 217,091 (2012 est)

Part of the Comoros archipelago, Mayotte remained a French dependency when the other three islands became independent as the Comoros Republic in 1975. It became a *collectivité territoriale* in 1976, and an Overseas Department/Region in 2011. The main products are vanilla, ylang-ylang (perfume essence), coffee, copra, lobster and shrimp. The economy is dependent on French subsidies.

Prefect, Dominique Sorain, *apptd* 2018

RÉUNION

Area – 2,507 sq. km

Capital – St-Denis; population, 201,366 (2012 est)

Population – 840,974 (2013 est)

A French possession since 1638, Réunion lies in the Indian Ocean, about 650km east of Madagascar and 180km south-west of Mauritius. The main industries are tourism and sugar, and rum production.

Prefect, Amaury de Saint-Quentin, *apptd* 2017

TERRITORIAL COLLECTIVITIES

Overseas *collectivités* are administrative divisions with a degree of autonomy but without the status of a similar administrative division in metropolitan France; each has its own laws and an elected assembly and president. The French government is represented by a *prefect* or high commissioner in each. Constitutional changes in 2003 redesignated most of the former overseas territories as *collectivités;* New Caledonia is treated in this category because this is its *de facto* status at present, but its official designation depends upon the outcome of independence referendums to be held no later than November 2018.

FRENCH POLYNESIA

Area – 4,167 sq. km

Capital – Papeete, on Tahiti; population, 133,000 (2014 est)

Population – 287,881 rising at 0.88 per cent a year (2017 est); Polynesian (78 per cent), Chinese (12 per cent), French (10 per cent) (est)

Religion – Christian (Protestant 54 per cent, Roman Catholic 30 per cent) (est)

Population density – 77 per sq. km (2015)

Urban population – 55.9 per cent (2015 est)

Median age (years) – 31. (2016 est)

French Polynesia consists of over 118 volcanic or coral islands and atolls in the South Pacific. There are five archipelagos: the Society Islands (Windward Islands group includes Makatea, Mehetia, Moorea, Tahiti, Tetiaroa, Tubuai Manu; Leeward Islands group includes Bora-Bora, Huahine, Maupiti, Raiatea, Tahaa); the Tuamotu Islands (Hao, Rangiroa, Turéia, etc); the Gambier Islands (Mangareva etc); the Tubuai Islands

(Raivavae, Rapa, Rimatara, Rurutu, Tubuai, etc); and the Marquesas Islands (Fatu-Hiva, Hiva-Oa, Nuku-Hiva, Tahuata, Ua Huka, etc). Some of the atolls were used by France for testing nuclear weapons between 1966 and 1996. The main industries are tourism, pearl-farming, deep-sea fishing, coconut products and vanilla production.

High Commissioner, René Bidal, *apptd* 2016

NEW CALEDONIA
Area – 18,575 sq. km
Capital – Nouméa; population, 181,000 (2014 est)
Population – 275,355 rising at 1.35 per cent a year (2016 est); Kanak (40.3 per cent), European (29.2 per cent), Wallisian, Futunian (8.7 per cent) (2009 est)
Religion – Christian (Roman Catholic 60 per cent, Protestant 30 per cent) (est)
Population density – 15 per sq. km (2015)
Urban population – 70.2 per cent (2015 est)
Median age (years) – 31.7 (2016 est)
New Caledonia is a large island in the western Pacific, 1,120km off the eastern coast of Australia. Its dependencies are the Isle of Pines, the Loyalty Islands (Mahé, Lifou, Urea, etc), the Bélep Archipelago, the Chesterfield Islands, the Huon Islands and Walpole. New Caledonia was discovered in 1774 and annexed by France in 1853. Agitation for independence from the 1980s ended with the Nouméa accord in 1998, under which an increasing degree of autonomy will be transferred to the territory up to 2018, with a referendum on independence to be held by 2018. The territory is divided into three provinces, each with a provincial assembly; these combine to form the territorial assembly.

Over one tenth of the world's nickel deposits are found in the territory, and nickel mining and smelting are the main industries, along with tourism and fishing. Ferronickel, nickel ore and fish are the main exports. About 20 per cent of food has to be imported.

High Commissioner, Thierry Lataste, *apptd* 2016

ST BARTHÉLEMY
Area – 21 sq. km
Capital – Gustavia
Population – 7,267 (2014 est)
Median age (years) – 43.6 (2016 est)
The island lies in the Caribbean Sea about 240km north-west of Guadeloupe. It was settled by the French from 1648. France sold the island to Sweden in 1784 but bought it back again in 1878 and it was under the administration of Guadeloupe until 2007, when it became a *collectivité territoriale.* The economy is based on luxury tourism and duty-free commerce in luxury goods. Freshwater sources are limited, so all food and energy and most manufactured goods are imported.
Prefect, Anne Laubies, *apptd* 2015

ST MARTIN
Area – 54.4 sq. km
Capital – Marigot
Population – 31,949 (2016 est)
Population density – 584 per sq. km (2015)
Median age (years) – 32.3 (2016 est)
The territory occupies the northern part of the island of St Martin, 250km to the north-west of Guadeloupe; the southern part (Sint Maarten) is a territory of the Netherlands. The island was claimed for Spain by Columbus in 1493 but the Spanish relinquished it in 1648 to the Dutch and French, who divided the island between them. The French part was administered from Guadeloupe until it was made a *collectivité territoriale* in 2007. The economy is dependent on tourism, which employs 85 per cent of the workforce. Nearly all food, energy and manufactured goods are imported.
Prefect, Anne Laubies, *apptd* 2015

ST PIERRE AND MIQUELON
Area – 242 sq. km
Capital – St-Pierre; population, 5,000 (2014 est)
Population – 5,595 falling at 1.09 per cent a year (2016 est)
Religion – Roman Catholic 99 per cent (est)
Urban population – 90.4 per cent (2015 est)
Median age (years) – 45.9 (2016 est)
These two small groups of eight islands off the south coast of Newfoundland became a *collectivité territoriale* in 1985. The main industry of fishing and servicing fishing fleets has declined in step with the decline in cod stocks, and fish farming, crab fishing and agriculture are being developed. Tourism is of growing importance, but the economy is dependent on government subsidies.
Prefect, Thierry Devimeux, *apptd* 2018

WALLIS AND FUTUNA ISLANDS
Area – 142 sq. km
Capital – Mata-Utu, on Uvea, the main island of the Wallis group; population, 1,000 (2014 est)
Population – 15,714 rising at 0.32 per cent a year (2017 est)
Religion – Roman Catholic 99 per cent (est)
Median age (years) – 31.6 (2016 est)
The two groups of islands (the Wallis Archipelago and the Îles de Horne) lie in the South Pacific, north-east of Fiji. They became a French protectorate from the 1840s and were administered from New Caledonia until 1961. The main products are copra, vegetables, bananas, livestock products, fish and timber.
High Administrator, Jean-Francis Treffel, *apptd* 2017

OVERSEAS TERRITORIES

TERRITORY OF THE FRENCH SOUTHERN AND ANTARCTIC LANDS
Created in 1955 from former Réunion dependencies, the territory comprises the islands of Amsterdam (55 sq. km) and St Paul (7 sq. km), the Kerguelen Islands (7,215 sq. km) and Crozet Islands (352 sq. km) archipelagos, Adélie Land (about 500,000 sq. km) in the Antarctic continent and, since 2007, the islands of Bassas da India (80 sq. km), Europa (28 sq. km), les Glorieuses (5 sq. km), Juan de Nova (4.4 sq. km) and Tromelin (1 sq. km). The population consists only of staff of the meteorological and scientific research stations.
Administrator, Cécile Pozzo Di Borgo, *apptd* 2014

THE FRENCH COMMUNITY OF STATES
The 1958 constitution envisaged the establishment of a French Community of States. A number of former French colonies in Africa have seceded from the community but for all practical purposes continue to enjoy the same close links with France as do those that remain formal members. Most former French African colonies are closely linked to France by financial, technical and economic agreements.

GABON

République Gabonaise – Gabonese Republic

Area – 267,667 sq. km
Capital – Libreville; population, 813,000 (2018 est)
Major towns – Franceville (Masuku), Moanda, Oyem, Port-Gentil
Currency – Central African CFA franc of 100 centimes
Population – 1,772,255 rising at 1.92 per cent a year (2017 est); over 40 predominantly Bantu tribes, of which the Bapounou, Fang, Nzebi and Obamba are the largest tribal groupings
Religion – Christian (Catholic 41.9 per cent, other Christian 32.4 per cent, Protestant 13.7 per cent), Muslim 6.4 per cent (2012 est); many people combine elements of Christian and indigenous beliefs
Language – French (official), Fang, Myene, Nzebi, Bapounou, Bandjabi
Population density – 8 per sq. km (2016)
Urban population – 89.4 per cent (2018 est)
Median age (years) – 18.6 (2017 est)
National anthem – 'La Concorde' 'The Concord'
National day – 17 August (Independence Day)
Death penalty – Abolished for all crimes (since 2010)
CPI score – 32 (117)
Military expenditure – US$299m (2017 est)
Literacy rate – 83.2 per cent (2015 est)
Health expenditure (per capita) – US$321 (2014)
Hospital beds (per 1,000 people) – 6.3 (2010)
Life expectancy (years) – 52.1 (2017 est)
Mortality rate – 13 (2018 est)
Birth rate – 34.2 (2017 est)
Infant mortality rate – 44.1 (2017 est)
HIV/AIDS adult prevalence – 3.6 per cent (2016 est)

CLIMATE AND TERRAIN
The country lies on the equator. It rises from a narrow coastal plain to a hilly interior; approximately 85 per cent of the land is rainforest, with savannah in the east and south, although by 2006 as much as half of the country's forest was being leased for timber. In 2002, 10 per cent of the country was designated as national park. Elevation extremes range from 1,575m (Mt Iboundji) to 0m (Atlantic Ocean). The climate is tropical, with an average temperature of 25.2°C. There are two wet seasons each year, from January to June and September to December.

HISTORY AND POLITICS
The first Europeans to visit the region were the Portuguese in the 15th century; Dutch, French and English traders arrived soon after. Sovereignty was signed over to the French in 1839 by a local Mpongwe ruler. In 1849, slaves freed by the French formed a settlement, which they called Libreville, now the capital. The country was occupied by the French in 1885 and became part of French Equatorial Africa in 1910. Gabon became autonomous within the French Community in 1958 and gained independence on 17 August 1960.

Omar Bongo succeeded to the presidency in 1967 after the death of the first president, and in 1968 he established a one-party state with the *Parti Démocratique Gabonais* (PDG) as the only party. By the late 1980s, the deteriorating economy was provoking unrest and demands for greater democracy, and in 1991 a multiparty system was reintroduced.

Under the multiparty system, the PDG has remained in power (amid allegations of electoral fraud) although it has included opposition party members in coalition governments since 1994. The PDG and its coalition partners retained the majority in the 2011 legislative election, which was boycotted by the main opposition party. President Bongo was re-elected for a sixth term of office in 2005; he died in June 2009, and was succeeded by his son, Ali Bongo Ondimba, who was elected president in August 2009 amid allegations of vote-rigging. He was narrowly re-elected in August 2016 and Emmanuel Issoze-Ngondet was named prime minister in September, but was forced to resign in May 2018 after the deadline to hold legislative elections lapsed.

The 1991 constitution, amended in 1995, 1997, 2003, and 2011, provides for a president who is directly elected for a seven-year term; since 2003, there has been no limit on the number of terms a president may serve. The president appoints the prime minister, who then appoints the council of ministers. There is a bicameral *Parlement*, comprising the 120-member National Assembly, directly elected for five-year terms, and the senate, which does not fix the number of members elected for a six-year term by municipal and regional councillors.

HEAD OF STATE
President, Ali Bongo Ondimba, *elected* 30 August 2009, *sworn in* 16 October 2009, *re-elected* August 2016

SELECTED GOVERNMENT MEMBERS *AS AT JUNE 2018*
Prime Minister, vacant
Defence, Etienne Massard Kabinda Makaga
Economy, Jean-Marie Ogandaga
Foreign Affairs, Regis Immongault Tatagani

EMBASSY OF THE GABONESE REPUBLIC
27 Elvaston Place, London SW7 5NL
T 020-7823 9986
Ambassador Extraordinary and Plenipotentiary, HE Aichatou Sanni Aoudou, *apptd* 2015

BRITISH HIGH COMMISSION
HE Rowan Laxton, *apptd* 2017, resident at Yaoundé, Cameroon

ECONOMY AND TRADE
Gabon is one of the most prosperous countries in Africa, largely owing to its small population and abundance of oil and mineral resources. The economy is heavily dependent on oil (which contributes 45 per cent of GDP) and other mineral resources, including manganese and uranium, and timber, but the government is investing in diversification to reduce vulnerability to fluctuating commodity prices and the gradual decline in oil production as reserves become exhausted. Despite the country's wealth, a large proportion of the population remains poor, and weak fiscal management has resulted in a high foreign debt, which has had to be rescheduled several times. Following poor growth due to low oil prices, in June 2017 Gabon signed a three-year agreement with the IMF.

Industry contributes 44 per cent of GDP and employs 12 per cent of the workforce, mainly in oil and mineral extraction, oil refining, chemicals, ship repair, textiles, and processing agricultural and forestry products. Agriculture is largely at subsistence level, employing 64 per cent of the workforce but contributing only 4.5 per cent of GDP. It is restricted by the forest cover and lack of suitable land. The main products include cocoa, coffee, sugar, palm oil, rubber, cattle, timber and fish.

The main trading partners are France, Belgium and China. Principal exports are crude oil (80 per cent), timber, manganese and uranium. The main imports are machinery and equipment, food, chemicals and construction materials.

GNI – US$13.4bn; US$6,610 per capita (2017)
Annual average growth of GDP – 1.0 per cent (2017 est)
Inflation rate – 2.5 per cent (2017 est)
Total external debt – US$5.599bn (2017 est)
Imports – US$3,033m (2015)
Exports – US$5,074m (2015)

BALANCE OF PAYMENTS
Trade – US$2,040m surplus (2015)

Trade with UK	2016	2017
Imports from UK	£23,355,725	£41,534,511
Exports to UK	£82,388,109	£28,297,678

COMMUNICATIONS
Airports and waterways – 14, including international airports in Libreville and Port-Gentil; there are 1,600km of navigable waterways and the principal seaport is in Port-Gentil
Roadways and railways – 1,097km; 649km
Telecommunications – 18,946 fixed lines and 2.96 million mobile subscriptions (2016); there were 835,408 internet users in 2016
Internet code and IDD – ga; 241 (from UK), 44 (to UK)
Broadcasters – State-controlled broadcaster Radiodiffusion-Télévision Gabonaise operates two television channels and two radio networks; pan-African radio broadcaster Africa No. 1 is based in Gabon
Press – The only two daily newspapers, *L'Union* and *Gabon Matin,* are operated by the government
WPFI score – 32,37 (108)

THE GAMBIA

Republic of The Gambia

Area – 11,300 sq. km
Capital – Banjul; population, 437,000 (2018 est)
Major towns – Bakau, Brikama, Farafenni, Serekunda
Currency – Dalasi (D) of 100 butut
Population – 2,051,363 rising at 2.05 per cent a year (2017 est); Mandinka (33.8 per cent), Fulani (22.1 per cent),

Wolof (12.2 per cent), Jola (10.9 per cent), Serahuli (Soninke) (3.2 per cent) (2013 est)
Religion – Sunni Muslim 95.7 per cent (majority Malikite Sufi), Christian 4.2 per cent (predominantly Roman Catholic) (2013 est)
Language – English (official), Mandinka, Wolof, Fula
Population density – 201 per sq. km (2016)
Urban population – 61.3 per cent (2018 est)
Median age (years) – 21 (2017 est)
National anthem – 'For The Gambia, Our Homeland'
National day – 18 February (Independence Day)
Death penalty – Retained
CPI score – 30 (130)
Military expenditure – US$12.5m (2015)

CLIMATE AND TERRAIN
The Gambia consists of a narrow strip of land along the river Gambia, mostly comprising the basin and flood plain of the river, flanked by savannah and low hills. Elevation extremes range from 53m to 0m (Atlantic Ocean). The climate is tropical, with a wet season from June to November.

HISTORY AND POLITICS
The Gambia river basin was part of an area dominated from the 10th to 16th centuries by the Mali and Songhai kingdoms. The Portuguese reached the river Gambia in 1447 and established trading posts along the river. In 1816 a British garrison was stationed on an island at the river mouth; this became the capital of a small British colony, and a crown colony in 1843. The boundaries of the country were agreed by France and Britain in 1889; British territory would extend 10km from the upper river on either bank. The Gambia became independent on 18 February 1965 and a republic in 1970. The country withdrew from the Commonwealth in 2013, but rejoined in February 2018 in an attempt by the government to end international isolation.

The post-independence prime minister, Sir Dawda Jawara, was president from 1970 until 1994, when he was overthrown in a military coup. The coup leader, Lt. (later Col.) Yahya Jammeh, assumed the presidency and a civilian-military government was formed to govern in conjunction with the ruling military council. Civilian government was restored after elections in 1996 and 1997, following the approval of a new constitution. Jammeh was elected president and his Alliance for Patriotic Reorientation and Construction (APRC) won an overall majority of the legislative seats.

The 2012 legislative election was won by the APRC, with 43 of the 48 elected seats. Property developer Adama Barrow won the December 2016 presidential election, but incumbent president Jammeh refused to step down after 22 years in power. In January 2017, troops from neighbouring Senegal entered the country and Jammeh fled, allowing Barrow to be installed as president.

Under the 1997 constitution, the executive president is directly elected for a five-year term; there is no limit on re-election. The unicameral National Assembly has 58 members, of whom 53 are directly elected and five are appointed by the president, for a five-year term.

HEAD OF STATE
President, Defence, C-in-C of the Armed Forces, Adama Barrow, elected 2 December 2016, *sworn in* 19 January 2017
Vice-President, Women's Affairs, Aja Fatouma Jallow Tambajang

SELECTED GOVERNMENT MEMBERS *AS AT JUNE 2018*
Finance and Economic Affairs, Amadou Sanneh
Foreign Affairs, Ousainou Darboe

Interior, Ebrima Mballow
Justice, Attorney-General, Ba Tambadou

THE GAMBIA HIGH COMMISSION
92 Ledbury Road, London W11 2AH
T 020-7229 8066 E gambiahighcomuk@btconnect.com
W www.gambiaembassy.org.uk
High Commissioner, HE Francis Blain, *apptd* 2017

BRITISH HIGH COMMISSION
PO Box 507, 48 Atlantic Road, Fajara, Banjul
T (+220) 449 5133 E ukinthegambia@fco.gov.uk
W www.gov.uk/government/world/gambia
High Commissioner, HE Sharon Wardle, *apptd* 2017

ECONOMY AND TRADE

The country has limited natural resources and agricultural land. Historically, the mainstay of the economy was re-export trade with neighbouring countries, but this has declined since the late 1990s, owing to the vagaries of government policies and trade and transport disputes with Senegal. There are high levels of public and foreign debt and the country is dependent on financial and technical aid from foreign donors. Remittances from Gambians working abroad and tourism are vital revenue sources. The economy has slowed following the ebola outbreak of 2014, affecting the previously flourishing tourism sector, but following President Jammeh's departure in January 2017 the new regime is negotiating financial support deals with multiple international organisations.

The services sector employs only 6 per cent of the workforce but contributes 65.4 per cent of GDP. About 75 per cent of the population is dependent on subsistence agriculture, which contributes 20.4 per cent of GDP. The chief product, peanuts, is also the main export and the basis of the main industrial activity, leaving the economy vulnerable to market fluctuations and the weather. Industry contributes 14.2 per cent to GDP, chiefly through processing peanuts, fish and hides, assembling agricultural machinery, metalworking, woodworking and the production of beverages and clothing.

The main trade partners are China, Guinea-Bissau, Brazil, EU countries and Senegal. Principal exports (80 per cent are re-exports) are peanut products, fish, cotton lint and palm kernels. The main imports are foodstuffs, manufactures, fuel, machinery and transport equipment.

GNI – US$0.9bn; US$450 per capita (2017)
Annual average growth of GDP – 3.0 per cent (2016 est)
Inflation rate – 8.3 per cent (2017 est)
Population below poverty line – 48.4 per cent (2010 est)
Total external debt – US$619.7m (2017 est)
Imports – US$385m (2014)
Exports – US$16m (2014)

BALANCE OF PAYMENTS
Trade – US$369m deficit (2014)
Current Account – US$95m deficit (2016)

Trade with UK	2016	2017
Imports from UK	£20,231,844	£26,913,914
Exports to UK	£4,224,667	£3,203,787

COMMUNICATIONS

Airports and waterways – There is an international airport at Banjul; there are 390km of navigable waterways on the Gambia river
Roadways – 711km
Telecommunications – 37,969 fixed lines and 2.83 million mobile subscriptions (2016); there were 371,785 internet users in 2016

Internet code and IDD – gm; 220 (from UK), 44 (to UK)
Major broadcasters – Gambia Television (GRTS TV) and Radio Gambia are the state broadcasters; private television stations are banned while independent radio stations self-censor content; 1 state-run TV-channel; 1 privately-owned TV-station; 1 state-owned radio station and 15 privately owned radio stations; 6 community radio stations; transmissions of multiple international broadcasters are available (2018)
Press – Major publications include the *Daily Observer, The Standard* and *The Daily News*
WPFI score – 38,36 (122)

EDUCATION AND HEALTH

Education is compulsory between the ages of seven and 12.
Literacy rate – 55.5 per cent (2015 est)
Gross enrolment ratio (percentage of relevant age group) – primary 97 per cent (2017 est), secondary 57 per cent (2010 est), tertiary 3 per cent (2011 est)
Health expenditure (per capita) – US$31 (2014)
Hospital beds (per 1,000 people) – 1.1 (2011)
Life expectancy (years) – 65.1 (2017 est)
Mortality rate – 7 (2017 est)
Birth rate – 29.4 (2017 est)
Infant mortality rate – 60.2 (2017 est)
HIV/AIDS adult prevalence – 1.7 per cent (2016 est)

GEORGIA

Sak'art'velo – Georgia

Area – 69,700 sq. km
Capital – Tbilisi; population, 1,077,000 (2018 est)
Major cities – Batumi, Kutaisi, Poti, Rustavi, Zugdidi
Currency – Lari of 100 tetri
Population – 4,926,330 falling at 0.02 per cent a year (2017 est); Georgian (86.8 per cent), Azeri (6.3 per cent), Armenian (4.5 per cent) (2014 est)
Religion – Christian (Orthodox 83.4 per cent, Armenian Apostolic 2.9 per cent), Muslim 10.7 per cent (2014 est)
Language – Georgian (official), Russian, Armenian, Azeri, Abkhaz (official in Abkhazia)
Population density – 65 per sq. km (2016)
Urban population – 54.6 per cent (2018 est)
Median age (years) – 38.1 (2017 est)
National anthem – 'Tavisupleba' 'Freedom'
National day – 26 May (Independence Day, 1918)
Death penalty – Abolished for all crimes (since 1997)
CPI score – 56 (46)
Military expenditure – US$333m (2017 est)
Conscription – 18–27 years of age; 12 months
Literacy rate – 100 per cent (2015 est)
Gross enrolment ratio (percentage of relevant age group) – primary 103 per cent, secondary 104 per cent, tertiary 52 per cent (2016 est)
Health expenditure (per capita) – US$303 (2014)
Hospital beds (per 1,000 people) – 2.6 (2013)

Life expectancy (years) – 76.4 (2017 est)
Mortality rate – 10.9 (2017 est)
Birth rate – 12.3 (2017 est)
Infant mortality rate – 15.2 (2017 est)
HIV / AIDS adult prevalence – 0.4 per cent (2015 est)

CLIMATE AND TERRAIN

Georgia lies in the western part of the Caucasus region, on the eastern shore of the Black Sea. It is mountainous, with the Great Caucasus mountain range along the northern border with Russia, and the Lesser Caucasus in the south. These are divided by the Kolkhida lowland in the west and the Mtkvari (Kura) river basin in the east, between which runs the valley of the Mtkvari river. Elevation extremes range from 5,201m (Mt Shkhara) to 0m (Black Sea). The climate is almost tropical in summer, while cold winters affect both the mountains and valleys. Average temperatures range from −6.4°C in January to 18.6°C in August.

POLITICS

The 1995 constitution provides for a federal republic with a unicameral legislature, to become bicameral 'following the creation of appropriate conditions'. It was amended in 2010 to transfer some of the president's powers to the legislature and prime minister. The president is directly elected for a five-year term, renewable once. The unicameral parliament has 150 members, 73 elected in single-member constituencies and 77 by proportional representation, who serve for a four-year term.

In November 2013, Irakli Garibashvili, aged 31, of the Georgian Dream party became the country's prime minister and the world's youngest elected leader at the time, but he resigned in December 2015 amid increasing public dissatisfaction with the government. He was replaced by the Georgian Dream's Giorgi Kvirikashvili, who resigned in June 2018 after anti-government protests, and replaced by finance minister Mamuka Bakhtadze. The Georgian Dream won the October 2016 legislative elections with an increased majority. The October 2013 presidential election was won by Giorgi Margvelashvili, marking an end to a decade in power for outgoing president Mikheil Saakashvili.

HEAD OF STATE
President, Giorgi Margvelashvili, *sworn in* 17 November 2013

SELECTED GOVERNMENT MEMBERS *AS AT JUNE 2018*
Prime Minister, Mamuka Bakhtadze
First Deputy Prime Minister, Economy, Dimitri Kumsishvili
Vice-Prime Minister, Internal Affairs, Giorgi Gakharia
Vice-Prime Minister Foreign Affairs, Mikheil Janelidze
Defence, Levan Izoria

EMBASSY OF GEORGIA
4 Russell Gardens, London W14 8EZ
T 020-7348 1941 E embassy@geoemb.plus.com
W www.uk.mfa.gov.ge
Ambassador Extraordinary and Plenipotentiary, HE Tamar Beruchashvili, *apptd* 2016

BRITISH EMBASSY
51 Krtsanisi Street, 0144 Tbilisi
T (+995) (32) 227 47 47 E british.embassy.tbilisi@fco.gov.uk
W www.gov.uk/government/world/georgia
Ambassador Extraordinary and Plenipotentiary, HE Justin McKenzie Smith, *apptd* 2016

SECESSION

Fears that Georgian independence would deprive them of their own autonomy led to unilateral declarations of independence by the central region of South Ossetia (1991) and the north-western region of Abkhazia (1992) followed by a year of conflict in both separatist areas. In August 2008, clashes between Georgian troops and South Ossetian separatists escalated into a brief war between Georgia and Russia, in which Georgian forces were expelled from South Ossetia and Abkhazia. Russia has not fully complied with an EU-brokered ceasefire, maintaining a military presence in the areas and a 'buffer zone' around them; only Russia, Venezuela, Nicaragua and Nauru recognise their unilateral declarations of independence. Russia signed integration treaties with Abkhazia in 2014 and South Ossetia in 2015, paving the way for greater Russian involvement in the breakaway regions.

Relations between Georgia and Ajaria, a semi-autonomous region in the south-west and a key trade hub, deteriorated briefly in 2004 when Aslan Abashidze, Ajaria's leader since 1991, refused to recognise the authority of the newly elected President Saakashvili, and accused Georgia of planning to invade Ajaria. Public demonstrations against Abashidze forced him to resign. The Georgian parliament granted the Ajarian assembly powers over local affairs but the Georgian president retains the power to nominate the region's head of government and to dissolve its government and assembly.

ECONOMY AND TRADE

The economy grew rapidly from 2003, making good progress towards recovery following near-collapse in the 1990s. Reform of the tax system nearly quadrupled government revenue, while added impetus in privatisation and anti-corruption programmes attracted foreign investment. However, the economy slowed in 2008 following the war with Russia and contracted in 2009 as the global economic downturn affected the regional economy and led to a decline in foreign investment and expatriates' remittances. The fuel crises in 2005–6 prompted the renovation of hydroelectric power plants and the repair of a pipeline from Azerbaijan; the country now meets the majority of its energy needs. In 2014, Georgia signed an association agreement with the EU that provided Georgian firms with greater access to European markets, and in 2017 agreed a free trade agreement with China. Economic growth has been depressed by the poorly performing Russian economy, which has reduced the value of remittances, but is improving.

Agriculture employs 55.6 per cent of the workforce and generates 9.6 per cent of GDP, with a concentration on grapes for winemaking, tea, citrus fruits and hazelnuts. Industry, which contributes 23.4 per cent of GDP, produces steel, machine tools, electrical appliances, manganese, copper, chemicals, wood products and wine.

		Ottoman and Persian	Russia invades; Georgia joins	Communist Party's	Declares	Leaves COIS to join
Converted to	Invaded by	empires compete for	USSR as part of the Transcaucasian	monopoly on	independence	the EU-initiated
Christianity	Moguls	influence	Soviet Socialist Republic	power abolished	from USSR	Eastern Partnership

*c.*100 — *c.*1000 — 1801-4 — 1917 — 1936 — 1992-3
*c.*400 — 1236 — 1500-1700 — 1921-2 — 1990 — 1991 — 2009

| Kingdom of Georgia comes under Roman influence | Independence established following domination by Persian, Arabs and Turks | Absorbed into Russian Empire | Independent nationalist government comes to power | Country becomes separate republic | Authoritarian president Zviad Gamsakhurdia overthrown; an uprising forces the country to join Commonwealth of Independent States (COIS) |

The main trading partners are Turkey, Azerbaijan and Russia. Principal exports are vehicles, ferro-alloys, fertilisers, scrap metal, fruit and nuts. The main imports are fuels, vehicles, machinery and parts, food (especially grain) and pharmaceuticals.

GNI – US$14.1bn; US$3,790 per capita (2017)
Annual average growth of GDP – 4.0 per cent (2017 est)
Inflation rate – 6 per cent (2017 est)
Population below poverty line – 14.8 per cent (2012)
Unemployment – 11.5 per cent (2017 est)
Total external debt – US$14.15bn (2017 est)
Imports – US$9,865m (2015)
Exports – US$2,114m (2015)

BALANCE OF PAYMENTS
Trade – US$7,751m deficit (2016)
Current Account – US$1,459m deficit (2017)

Trade with UK	2016	2017
Imports from UK	£102,787,274	£98,260,716
Exports to UK	£9,590,797	£27,242,278

COMMUNICATIONS
Airports – 22, including an international terminal in Tbilisi
Roadways and railways – 19,109km, including 69km of motorways; 1,612km
Telecommunications – 1.1 million fixed lines and 5.4 million mobile subscriptions (2014); there were 2.5 million internet users in 2014
Internet code and IDD – ge; 995 (from UK), 810 44 with no extra zeros (to UK)
Major broadcasters – Government-funded Georgian Public Broadcasting provides two television and two radio networks, alongside a host of private cable operators and major commercial stations
Press – Daily titles include *Rezonansi* and *The Messenger* (English language)
WPFI score – 27,34 (61)

GERMANY

Bundesrepublik Deutschland – *Federal Republic of Germany*

Area – 357,022 sq. km
Capital – Berlin; population, 3,563,000 (2018 est)
Major cities – Bremen, Cologne, Dortmund, Dresden, Düsseldorf, Essen, Frankfurt, Hamburg, Hannover, Leipzig, Munich, Nuremberg, Stuttgart
Currency – Euro (€) of 100 cents
Population – 80,594,017 falling at 0.16 per cent a year (2017 est); German (91.5 per cent), Turkish (2.4 per cent) (est)

Religion – Christian (Protestant 34 per cent, Roman Catholic 34 per cent), Muslim 3.7 per cent, unaffiliated or other 28.3 per cent
Language – German (official)
Population density – 236 per sq. km (2016)
Urban population – 77.3 per cent (2018 est)
Median age (years) – 47.1 (2017 est)
National anthem – 'Das Deutschlandlied' 'Song of Germany'
National day – 3 October (Unity Day)
Death penalty – Abolished for all crimes (since 1949 in FRG and 1987 in GDR)
CPI score – 81 (12)
Military expenditure – US$44,329m (2017)

CLIMATE AND TERRAIN
The north of the country is low-lying, rising in the centre to uplands and Alpine foothills, then to the Bavarian Alps in the south. Elevation extremes range from 2,963m (Zugspitze, Bavaria) to −3.54m (Neuendorf bei Wilster). The Rhine, Weser and Elbe rivers flow from the south to the North Sea, the Oder and Neisse rivers flow north to the Baltic Sea, and the Danube flows east from its source in the south of the country to the Austrian border. Nearly a third of the land is covered by forest or woodland. The climate is temperate, with average temperatures ranging from 0.9°C in January to 18.2°C in July.

POLITICS
The Basic Law was adopted in 1949 as the constitution of West Germany; at unification in 1990, Berlin and the five reformed *Länder* (states) of East Germany acceded to the Federal Republic. The president is elected for a five-year term by the *Bundesversammlung*, an electoral college comprising the members of the *Bundestag* (*see* below) and an equal number of representatives elected by the state legislatures. The bicameral legislature comprises a lower house, the Federal Assembly *(Bundestag)*, with 709 members elected by a mixed constituency and proportional representation system for a four-year term. The Federal Council *(Bundesrat)* has 69 members appointed by the governments of the *Länder* in proportion to their populations; their term of office is determined by their *Land's* constitution. The head of government is the chancellor, who is proposed by the president and elected by the *Bundestag*.

Angela Merkel, leader of the Christian Democratic Union of Germany and the Christian Social Union of Bavaria (CDU/CSU), became Germany's first female chancellor in 2005 at the head of a CDU/CSU and Social Democratic Party (SPD) coalition, governing without the latter following re-election in 2009. In 2013 the CDU again formed a 'grand coalition' with the SPD after the CDU fell five seats short of claiming a historic majority in the *Bundestag* with 41.5 per cent of the vote. In the 2017 legislative election, the arrival of the far-right party Alternative for Germany (AFD) significantly cut the support of both the CDU and SPD, resulting in political stalemate for almost six months before another 'grand coalition' was negotiated between the CDU/CSU and SPD, with Merkel remaining as chancellor. It was the longest the country had been without a government in its postwar history.

Former foreign minister Frank-Walter Steinmeier of the SPD won the 2017 presidential election, picking up 931 of 1,239 valid votes.

HEAD OF STATE
Federal President, Frank-Walter Steinmeier, *elected* 12 February 2017, *sworn in* 22 March 2017

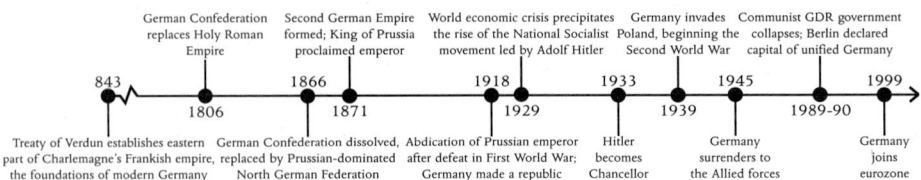

| 843 | 1866 | 1918 | 1933 | 1945 | 1999 |

German Confederation replaces Holy Roman Empire

Second German Empire formed; King of Prussia proclaimed emperor

World economic crisis precipitates the rise of the National Socialist movement led by Adolf Hitler

Germany invades Poland, beginning the Second World War

Communist GDR government collapses; Berlin declared capital of unified Germany

1806   1871   1929   1939   1989-90

Treaty of Verdun establishes eastern part of Charlemagne's Frankish empire, the foundations of modern Germany

German Confederation dissolved, replaced by Prussian-dominated North German Federation

Abdication of Prussian emperor after defeat in First World War; Germany made a republic

Hitler becomes Chancellor

Germany surrenders to the Allied forces

Germany joins eurozone

SELECTED GOVERNMENT MEMBERS *AS AT JUNE 2018*
Federal Chancellor, Angela Merkel
Defence, Ursula von der Leyen
Finance, Olaf Scholz
Foreign Affairs, Heiko Maas

EMBASSY OF THE FEDERAL REPUBLIC OF GERMANY
23 Belgrave Square, London SW1X 8PZ
T 020-7824 1300 W www.london.diplo.de
Ambassador Extraordinary and Plenipotentiary, vacant

BRITISH EMBASSY
Wilhelmstrasse 70/71, 10117 Berlin
T (+49) (30) 204 570 E ukingermany@fco.gov.uk
W www.gov.uk/government/world/germany
Ambassador Extraordinary and Plenipotentiary, HE Sir Sebastian Wood, KCMG, *apptd* 2015

FEDERAL STRUCTURE
Germany is a federal republic composed of 16 states *(Länder)* (ten from the former Federal Republic of Germany (FRG), five from the former German Democratic Republic (GDR), and Berlin). Each *Land* has its own directly elected legislature and government led by a minister-president (prime minister) or equivalent. The 1949 Basic Law vests executive power in the *Länder* governments except in those areas reserved for the federal government.

State	Population (millions)
(Capital, where name differs)	(2015 est)
Baden-Württemberg (Stuttgart)	10.90
Bavaria (Munich)	12.84
Berlin	3.52
Brandenburg (Potsdam)	2.48
Bremen	0.67
Hamburg	1.79
Hesse (Wiesbaden)	6.18
Lower Saxony (Hannover)	7.93
Mecklenburg-West Pomerania (Schwerin)	1.61
North Rhine-Westphalia (Düsseldorf)	17.87
Rhineland-Palitanate (Mainz)	4.05
Saarland (Saarbrücken)	0.96
Saxony (Dresden)	4.08
Saxony-Anhalt (Magdeburg)	2.25
Schleswig-Holstein (Kiel)	2.86
Thuringia (Erfurt)	2.17

ECONOMY AND TRADE
Germany has the world's fifth largest economy and the largest in Europe, but decades of strong economic performance gave way in the 1990s to a severe recession, largely an aftermath of reunification and of macroeconomic stagnation. Although the economy as a whole began to grow again in 2006, in the east it remains weak despite costly modernisation and integration measures. However, the revival was largely export-led and a decline in demand due to the global economic downturn caused a recession in 2008–9. The government's economic stimulus measures pushed the budget deficit slightly beyond the eurozone's 3 per cent threshold in 2010, although it remained at 1.7 per cent in 2011. The country achieved a budget surplus of 0.1 per cent in 2012. While unemployment

and government debt remains low, and the county suffers from a lack of internal investment, it is hoped €15bn of infrastructure spending between 2016 and 2018 will spur private investment. The country is the world's third largest exporter and Germany's reliance on exports means the economy has been hampered by slowdowns in the eurozone, and Russian and Chinese economies.

The country has a modern, diverse, highly industrialised and technologically advanced market economy. The services sector contributes 69.3 per cent of GDP, industry 30.1 per cent and agriculture 0.6 per cent. The industrial sector is among the world's largest producers of iron, steel, coal, cement, chemicals, machinery, vehicles, machine tools, electronics, food and beverages, ships and textiles. Germany depends on imports to meet its oil and natural gas needs, but it remains a net exporter of electricity; in the wake of Japan's Fukushima crisis in 2011, the German government committed itself to closing all 17 nuclear reactors by 2022, and replacing them with renewable energy which accounted for 29.5 per cent of consumption in 2016.

The main trading partners are EU nations, the USA and China. Machinery, vehicles, chemicals, metals and manufactures, foodstuffs and textiles are the principal imports and exports.
GNI – US$3,596.6bn; US$43,490 per capita (2017)
Annual average growth of GDP – 2.1 per cent (2016 est)
Inflation rate – 1.6 per cent (2017 est)
Population below poverty line – 16.7 per cent (2015 est)
Unemployment – 3.8 per cent (2017 est)
Total external debt – US$5.326 trillion (2016 est)
Imports – US$1,056,336m (2016)
Exports – US$1,335,897m (2016)

BALANCE OF PAYMENTS
Trade – US$279,561m surplus (2016)
Current Account – US$296,827 surplus (2017)

Trade with UK	2016	2017
Imports from UK	£32,338,643,658	£36,195,612,166
Exports to UK	£64,235,812,475	£68,717,937,376

COMMUNICATIONS
Airports – 539; the busiest airport is at Frankfurt, other major airports include Berlin, Munich and Bonn
Waterways – Around 20 per cent of domestic freight is carried on 7,467km of inland waterways. The Rhine and the Danube are linked by the Rhine–Maine–Danube (RMD) canal, creating a through route from the North Sea to the Black Sea. The Kiel canal links the North Sea and the Baltic Sea. The main river ports are Duisburg, Frankfurt, Karlsruhe and Mainz; the main seaports are Hamburg, Bremen, Bremerhaven, Lübeck, Rostock and Wilhelmshaven
Roadways and railways – There is an extensive 645,000km road network, including 12,800km of motorways; there are 41,981km of railways
Telecommunications – 44.1 million fixed lines and 103.47 million mobile subscriptions (2016); there were 72 million internet users in 2016

Internet code and IDD – de; 49 (from UK), 44 (to UK)
Major broadcasters – National and regional public television competes with a large private sector, with about 90 per cent of households having access to cable or satellite stations; broadcasters include ARD (which operates Das Erste, the main national public TV channel) and ZDF
Press – Major newspapers include *Frankfurter Allgemeine Zeitung, Süddeustche Zeitung* and *Die Welt*
WPFI score – 14,39 (15)

EDUCATION AND HEALTH
Education is free and compulsory between the ages of six and 18.
The largest universities are in Munich, Berlin, Hamburg, Bonn, Frankfurt and Cologne. Germany's oldest university is Heidelberg, founded in 1386.
Gross enrolment ratio (percentage of relevant age group) – primary 105 per cent, secondary 102.7 per cent, tertiary 68.3 per cent (2015 est)
Health expenditure (per capita) – US$5,411 (2014)
Hospital beds (per 1,000 people) – 8.3 (2013)
Life expectancy (years) – 80.8 (2017 est)
Mortality rate – 11.7 (2017 est)
Birth rate – 8.6 (2017 est)
Infant mortality rate – 3.4 (2017 est)
HIV/AIDS adult prevalence – 0.15 per cent (2013 est)

GHANA

Republic of Ghana

Area – 238,533 sq. km
Capital – Accra; population, 2,439,000 (2018 est)
Major cities – Kumasi, Sekondi-Takoradi, Tamale
Currency – Cedi of 100 pesewas
Population – 27,499,924 rising at 2.17 per cent a year (2017 est); Akan (47.5 per cent), Mole-Dagbon (16.6 per cent), Ewe (13.9 per cent), Ga-Dangme (7.4 per cent), Gurma (5.7 per cent), Guan (3.7 per cent), Grusi (2.5 per cent) (2010 est)
Religion – Christian 71.2 per cent, Muslim 17.6 per cent (predominantly Sunni), indigenous and other religions 6 per cent (2010 est)
Language – English (official), Asante, Ewe, Fante, Boron, Dagomba, Dangme, Dagarte, Akyem, Ga, Akuapem
Population density – 124 per sq. km (2016)
Urban population – 56.1 per cent (2018 est)
Median age (years) – 21.1 (2017 est)
National anthem – 'God Bless Our Homeland Ghana'
National day – 6 March (Independence Day)
Death penalty – Retained (last used 1993)
CPI score – 40 (81)
Military expenditure – US$189m (2017)

CLIMATE AND TERRAIN
Ghana consists mostly of plains dissected by the Volta river basin and the great central Lake Volta, rising to the Ashanti plateau in the west. There is dense rainforest in the south and west and forested hills in the north, with savannah in the east and far north. Elevation extremes range from 885m (Mt Afadjato) to 0m (Atlantic Ocean). The climate is tropical but with cooler temperatures on the south-east coast, and less rainfall in the south-east and north. Average temperatures range between 25.6°C in August and 29.94°C in March.

HISTORY AND POLITICS
First reached by Europeans in the 15th century, after which it became a centre for gold and slave trading, the constituent parts of Ghana came under British administration at various times. The original Gold Coast colony was constituted in 1874 and Ashanti and the Northern Territories Protectorate in 1901. Trans-Volta-Togoland, part of the former German colony of Togo, was mandated to Britain by the League of Nations after the First World War and was integrated with the Gold Coast colony in 1956 following a plebiscite. The colony became independent as Ghana on 6 March 1957. It was proclaimed a republic in 1960.
Ghana became a one-party state in 1964 and from 1966 experienced long periods of military rule (1966–9, 1972–9, 1981–91) interspersed with short-lived civilian governments (1969–72, 1979–81). Flt. Lt. Jerry Rawlings, who had ousted the military regime in 1979 and deposed the civilian government in 1981, was elected president in 1992 when the country returned to multiparty politics after a referendum approved a new constitution.
Since the mid-1990s there have been intermittent clashes over land ownership between ethnic groups in the north; a state of emergency was in place there for two years after the last major outbreak of ethnic violence in 2002.
In the 2008 elections, John Atta Mills, the candidate of the National Democratic Congress (NDC), was elected president, and the NDC became the largest party in the legislature, winning half the seats. Vice-president John Dramani Mahama took over the presidency following the death of John Atta Mills in July 2012 and was re-elected president in December. Elections in December 2016 were won by Nana Akufo-Addo and the New Patriotic party.
Under the 1993 constitution, the executive president is directly elected for a four-year term, renewable once. The president appoints members of the council of ministers subject to approval by the legislature. The unicameral parliament has 275 members who are directly elected for a four-year term.

HEAD OF STATE
President, Nana Akufo-Addo, *apptd* 7 January 2017
Vice-President, Mahamadu Bawumia

SELECTED GOVERNMENT MEMBERS *AS AT JUNE 2018*
Defence, Dominic Nittiwul
Finance, Ken Offori-Atta
Foreign Affairs, Shirley Ayorkor Botchway
Interior, Ambrose Dery

OFFICE OF THE HIGH COMMISSIONER FOR GHANA
13 Belgrave Square, London SW1X 8PN
T 020-7201 5900 W www.ghanahighcommissionuk.com
High Commissioner, HE Papa Owusu-Ankomah, *apptd* 2017

BRITISH HIGH COMMISSION
PO Box 296, Osu Link, off Gamel Abdul Nasser Avenue, Accra
T (+233) (302) 213 250 E high.commission.accra@fco.gov.uk
W www.gov.uk/government/world/ghana
High Commissioner, HE Iain Walker, *apptd* 2017

ECONOMY AND TRADE

Ghana has abundant natural resources, but high foreign debt and budget and trade deficits make it dependent on international financial and technical aid to fund its economic and social development programmes. It has benefited from tighter government management of the economy since 2001, and from debt relief in 2002 and 2006. Ghana was re-categorised as a lower middle-income country in 2010. Between 2008 and 2014, the economy grew by an average of 6 per cent, with growth driven by the service sector and industry, but it has since been dented by poor export commodity performance. In 2015, Ghana received a US$918m loan from the IMF to provide financial stability and aid job creation.

Agriculture, mostly at subsistence level, forms the basis of the economy, along with forestry and fishing. The sector employs over half the workforce and generates 18.3 per cent of GDP. The main cash crops are cocoa, timber and tuna. Industry employs 14.4 per cent of the workforce and contributes 24.5 per cent of GDP, mainly from mining (gold, manganese, bauxite, diamonds), forestry, light manufacturing, aluminium smelting, food processing and shipbuilding. Services employ 40.9 per cent of the workforce and account for 57.2 per cent of GDP. Hydroelectric power is generated at dams on Lake Volta and is transmitted to most of Ghana, and to Togo and Benin. Oil was discovered offshore in 2007 and production began in 2010. New oil and gas lines are expected to continue to improve the economy; it is believed to have oil reserves totalling 700 million barrels.

The main export markets are India, the UAE and China. Principal exports are gold, oil, cocoa, timber, tuna, metals, minerals and diamonds. Imports are provided mainly by China, the USA and the UK. The main imports are capital equipment, fuel and foodstuffs.

GNI – US$42.9bn; US$1,490 per capita (2017)
Annual average growth of GDP – 5.9 per cent (2017 est)
Inflation rate – 11.8 per cent (2017 est)
Population below poverty line – 24.2 per cent (2013 est)
Unemployment – 11.9 per cent (2015 est)
Total external debt – US$23.1bn (2017 est)
Imports – US$13,290m (2015)
Exports – US$9,550m (2015)

BALANCE OF PAYMENTS

Trade – US$3,740 deficit (2015)
Current Account – US$2,000m deficit (2017)

Trade with UK	2016	2017
Imports from UK	£554,714,801	£379,503,576
Exports to UK	£241,330,291	£205,924,489

COMMUNICATIONS

Airports and waterways – 10, including an international terminal in Accra; there are 1,293km of navigable waterways
Roadways and railways – 13,787km of surfaced roads; 947km
Telecommunications – 251,490 fixed lines and 38.3 million mobile subscriptions (2016); there were 9 million internet users in 2016
Broadcasters – Ghana has a diverse media environment with state-run and private media outlets, though journalists face occasional harassment from the government. Ghana Broadcasting Corporation (GBC) operates TV and 2 radio stations, and competes with a number of private companies
Press – Major daily titles include *The Ghanaian Chronicle, Daily Guide* and *The Ghanaian Times*
Internet code and IDD – gh; 233 (from UK), 44 (to UK)
WPFI score – 18,41 (23)

EDUCATION AND HEALTH

The government provides ten years of compulsory basic education for all children free of charge. Ghana has one of Africa's oldest universities, at Legon in Accra (established in 1948).

Literacy rate – 90.6 per cent (2015 est)
Gross enrolment ratio (percentage of relevant age group) – primary 105 per cent, secondary 60 per cent (2017 est); tertiary 16 per cent (2016 est)
Health expenditure (per capita) – US$58 (2014)
Hospital beds (per 1,000 people) – 0.9 (2011)
Life expectancy (years) – 67 (2017 est)
Mortality rate – 7 (2017 est)
Birth rate – 30.5 (2017 est)
Infant mortality rate – 35.2 (2017 est)
HIV/AIDS adult prevalence – 1.6 per cent (2016 est)

GREECE

Elliniki Dhimokratia – Hellenic Republic

Area – 131,957 sq. km
Capital – Athens; population, 3,156,000 (2018 est)
Major cities – Iraklion (Heraklion) on Crete, Larisa, Patrai (Patras), Piraeus, Rhodes on Rhodes, Thessaloniki (Salonika)
Currency – Euro (€) of 100 cents
Population – 10,768,477 falling at 0.06 per cent a year (2016 est)
Religion – Christian (Greek Orthodox 98 per cent), Muslim 1.3 per cent (est)
Language – Greek (official)
Population density – 84 per sq. km (2016)
Urban population – 79.1 per cent (2018 est)
Median age (years) – 44.5 (2017 est)
National anthem – 'Ymnos eis tin Eleutherian' 'Hymn to Liberty'
National day – 25 March (Independence Day)
Death penalty – Abolished for all crimes (since 2004)
CPI score – 48 (59)
Military expenditure – US$5,093m (2017)
Conscription – 19–45 years of age, male only; 9–12 months

CLIMATE AND TERRAIN

The main areas of Greece are: Macedonia, Thrace, Epirus, Thessaly, Continental Greece, the Peloponnese and Attica on the mainland and the island of Crete. The main island groups are the Sporades, the Dodecanese (or Southern Sporades) and the Cyclades in the Aegean Sea, and the Ionian islands, including Corfu, to the west of the mainland. Low-lying coastal areas rise to a hilly or mountainous interior on the mainland and the islands. The Pindos mountains form a spine down the centre of the mainland, continuing down the Peloponnese, which is divided from the mainland by the Gulf

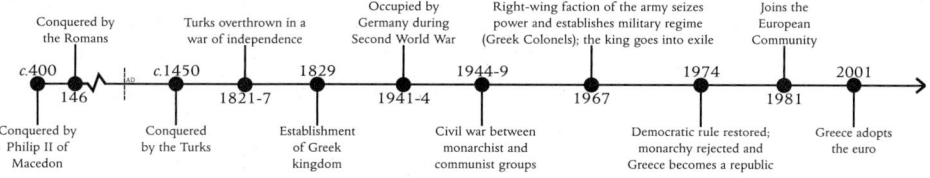

Conquered by
the Romans

Turks overthrown in a
war of independence

Occupied by
Germany during
Second World War

Right-wing faction of the army seizes
power and establishes military regime
(Greek Colonels); the king goes into exile

Joins the
European
Community

*c.*400

*c.*1450

1829

1944-9

1974

2001

146

1821-7

1941-4

1967

1981

Conquered by
Philip II of
Macedon

Conquered
by the Turks

Establishment
of Greek
kingdom

Civil war between
monarchist and
communist groups

Democratic rule restored;
monarchy rejected and
Greece becomes a republic

Greece adopts
the euro

of Corinth, the largest of the gulfs and bays indenting the coast. Elevation extremes range from 2,917m (Mt Olympus) to 0m (Mediterranean Sea). The climate is temperate; the coastline and islands have a Mediterranean climate but the weather is cooler at higher altitudes. The average temperature ranges from 6.4°C in January to 25°C in July.

POLITICS

Under the 1975 constitution, the head of state is the president, elected by the legislature for a five-year term, renewable once. The unicameral legislature, the *Vouli,* has 300 members directly elected for a four-year term.

The New Democracy party (ND) won the most seats in the 2012 legislative elections but was unable to form a coalition government; the party increased its number of seats in the subsequent election and ND leader Antonis Samaras was sworn into office on 20 June 2012. After three rounds of voting finishing in February 2015, Prokopis Pavlopoulos of the ND was elected president. In the early 2015 legislative elections, called after parliament failed to initially elect a president in 2014, Syriza became the largest party in the *Vouli,* and formed a coalition with the far-right, anti-austerity Independent Greeks (ANEL). In July 2015, voters rejected the terms of a proposed EU bailout by 61.3 per cent to 38.7 per cent in a national referendum. On 20 September, the ruling coalition was re-elected following snap legislative elections in which Syriza won 145 seats.

HEAD OF STATE
President of the Hellenic Republic, Prokopis Pavlopoulos *elected* 18 February 2015, *sworn in* 13 March 2015

SELECTED GOVERNMENT MEMBERS *AS AT JUNE 2018*
Prime Minister, Alexis Tsipras
Deputy Prime Minister, Yiannis Dragasakis
Finance, Euclid Tsakalotos
Foreign Affairs, Nikos Kotzias
Interior, Panos Skourletis

EMBASSY OF GREECE
1A Holland Park, London W11 3TP
T 020-7229 3850 E gremb.lon@mfa.gr W www.mfa.gr/uk
Ambassador Extraordinary and Plenipotentiary, HE Dimitris Caramitzos-Tziras, *apptd* 2016

BRITISH EMBASSY
1 Ploutarchou Street, 106 75 Athens
T (+30) (210) 727 2600 E consular.athens@fco.gov.uk
W www.gov.uk/government/world/greece
Ambassador Extraordinary and Plenipotentiary, HE Katherine Lucy Smith, CMG *apptd* 2017

ECONOMY AND TRADE
Greece experienced rapid economic growth in the final quarter of the 20th century, owing largely to increased tourism and its accession to the European Community. But in the 2000s, high government spending, low fiscal revenue and recession contributed to a growing budget deficit, which soared to over 15 per cent of GDP in 2009 and left the country particularly vulnerable in the global economic downturn. The New Democracy government's persistent failure to address the public finance crisis contributed to Greece's international debt rating being downgraded in late 2009. The following Panhellenic Socialist Movement (Pasok) government's austerity measures, and financial assistance from the IMF and other EU countries, saw the budget deficit reduced to 9 per cent of GDP in 2011, but unemployment rose by over 5 per cent, causing many economists to doubt the effectiveness of the government's fiscal policies.

Against a backdrop of protests, in spring 2012 the government agreed new austerity measures and a 'debt swap' deal with private-sector lenders – all conditions of an EU bailout. Further austerity measures were agreed in April 2013 in order to pave the way for more bailout funds. In 2014, the government balanced the 2013 budget (excluding debt repayments) and the economy recorded the first quarter of growth since 2008. The EU agreed to extend elements of Greece's bailout for four months in March 2015. A third bailout worth €86bn (£60bn) was negotiated with EU partners and passed by parliament on 14 August 2015. In the same month, the Syriza government approved its first privatisation, granting a 40-year concession in more than a dozen key regional airports to a German consortium. In July 2017, the EU Commission recommended that the excessive debt procedure for Greece be closed. The economy grew slightly in 2016 and performed better in 2017 as both unemployment and the deficit fell, but there remain concerns the country may leave the eurozone by 2021.

The service sector employs 72.4 per cent of the workforce and generates 80 per cent of GDP; much of this is derived from tourism, which accounts for about 18 per cent of GDP, and shipping. Greece is a net importer of energy, including oil for refining and re-export. Industrial activities, which contribute 16 per cent of GDP, include food and tobacco processing, textiles, chemicals, metal products, mining and petroleum production. Despite substantial industrialisation in the 20th century, agriculture still employs 12.6 per cent of the workforce, contributing 4 per cent of GDP. The most important agricultural products are cereals, vegetables, fruit, tobacco, beef and dairy products.

The main trading partners are Germany, Russia, Italy and Turkey. Principal exports are food and drink, manufactured goods, petroleum products, chemicals and textiles. The main imports are machinery, transport equipment, fuels and chemicals.

GNI – US$194.7bn; US$18,090 per capita (2017)
Annual average growth of GDP – 1.8 per cent (2016 est)
Inflation rate – 1.2 per cent (2017 est)
Population below poverty line – 36.0 per cent (2014 est)
Unemployment – 22.3 per cent (2017 est)
Total external debt – US$506.6bn (2016 est)
Imports – US$48,225m (2016)
Exports – US$28,055m (2016)

BALANCE OF PAYMENTS
Trade – US$20,170m deficit (2016)
Current Account – US$1,331m deficit (2017)

Trade with UK	2016	2017
Imports from UK	£908,688,381	£988,724,606
Exports to UK	£795,012,697	£883,225,309

COMMUNICATIONS

Airports – 77, the largest of which are at Athens, Thessaloniki, Iraklion (Crete) and Corfu town (Corfu)

Waterways – The main seaports are Piraeus, Thessaloniki and Patrai on the mainland, and Iraklion on Crete. An extensive ferry system connects the islands to one another and to the mainland. The 6km Corinth canal across the Corinth isthmus shortens the sea journey by 325km

Roadways and railways – There are 41,357km of surfaced roads, including 1,091km of motorways; 2,548km of railways are state-owned (with the exception of the Athens–Piraeus Electric Railway)

Telecommunications – 5.2 million fixed lines and 12.5 million mobile subscriptions (2016); there were 7.4 million internet users in 2016

Internet code and IDD – gr; 30 (from UK), 44 (to UK)

Major broadcasters – In 2013 state broadcaster ERT was closed as part of the country's ongoing austerity measures. A new public broadcaster, New Hellenic Radio, Internet and TV (NERIT), was established in 2014; private broadcasters include Mega TV and Athena 984 (radio)

Press – There are three major daily news publications: *Eleftherotypia, Ta Nea* and *Kathimerini*

WPFI score – 29,19 (74)

EDUCATION AND HEALTH

Education is free and compulsory between the ages of six and 14, and is maintained by state grants.

Literacy rate – 97.7 per cent (2015 est)

Gross enrolment ratio (percentage of relevant age group) – primary 97.6 per cent, secondary 106.5 per cent, tertiary 113.9 per cent (2014 est)

Health expenditure (per capita) – US$1,743 (2014)

Hospital beds (per 1,000 people) – 4.3 (2015)

Life expectancy (years) – 80.7 (2017 est)

Mortality rate – 11.3 (2017 est)

Birth rate – 8.4 (2017 est)

Infant mortality rate – 4.6 (2017 est)

HIV/AIDS adult prevalence – 0.3 per cent (2015 est)

GRENADA

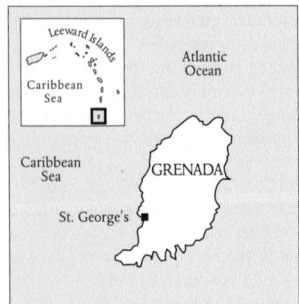

Area – 344 sq. km

Capital – St George's; population, 39,000 (2018 est)

Currency – East Caribbean dollar (EC$) of 100 cents

Population – 111,724 rising at 0.44 per cent a year (2017 est)

Religion – Christian (Roman Catholic 44.6 per cent, Anglican 11.5 per cent, other Protestant 32.1 per cent)

Language – English (official), Creole (small minority)

Population density – 316 per sq. km (2016)

Urban population – 36.3 per cent (2018 est)

Median age (years) – 31.5 (2017 est)

National anthem – 'Hail Grenada'

National day – 7 February (Independence Day)

Death penalty – Retained (last used 1978)

CPI score – 52 (52)

Literacy rate – 97.3 per cent (2008 est)

Gross enrolment ratio (percentage of relevant age group) – primary 101 per cent, secondary 101 per cent, tertiary 91 per cent (2016 est)

Health expenditure (per capita) – US$506 (2014)

Life expectancy (years) – 74.5 (2017 est)

Mortality rate – 8.1 (2016 est)

Birth rate – 15.5 (2017 est)

Infant mortality rate – 9.7 (2017 est)

CLIMATE AND TERRAIN

The most southerly of the Windward Islands, Grenada comprises three islands: Grenada (the largest at 18km in length and 34km in width), Carriacou and Petite Martinique. Elevation extremes range from 840m (Mt St Catherine) to 0m (Caribbean Sea). The climate is subtropical, with the wettest weather from July to November. Grenada lies in a hurricane zone.

HISTORY AND POLITICS

Discovered by Columbus in 1498 and named Concepción, Grenada was colonised from the mid-17th century by the French, who subdued the native Caribs; the island was ceded to Britain in 1763. It became a crown colony in 1877, a self-governing associated state in 1967 and an independent nation on 7 February 1974.

The government was overthrown in 1979 by the New Jewel Movement led by Maurice Bishop, and the People's Revolutionary Government (PRG) was set up, with Bishop as prime minister. In 1983, disagreements within the PRG led to the deposition and execution of Bishop, whose government was replaced by a revolutionary military council. These events prompted the intervention of Caribbean and US forces. After a period of interim government, democracy was restored and a general election held in 1984. Since the restoration of democracy, power has alternated between the New National Party (NNP) and the National Democratic Congress (NDC).

In 2018 the NNP won all 15 seats in parliamentary elections; Keith Mitchell returned as prime minister.

Under the 1974 constitution, reinstated in 1984, the head of state is Queen Elizabeth II, represented locally by a governor-general. The bicameral parliament consists of the House of Representatives, with 15 directly elected members, and a senate with 13 appointed members, ten of whom are appointed by the government and three by the opposition; both chambers serve a five-year term.

Governor-General, HE Dame Cécile La Grenade, GCMG, OBE apptd 2013

SELECTED GOVERNMENT MEMBERS *AS AT JUNE 2018*
Prime Minister, Finance, Home Affairs, Keith Mitchell
Foreign Affairs, Peter David

HIGH COMMISSION FOR GRENADA
The Chapel, Archel Road, London W14 9QH
T 020-7385 4415 E office@grenada-highcommission.co.uk
W www.grenada-highcommission.co.uk
Chargé d'affaires, Samuel Sandy

BRITISH HIGH COMMISSIONER
HE Janet Douglas, CMG, *apptd* 2017, resident at
   Bridgetown, Barbados

ECONOMY AND TRADE

The economy has grown considerably in recent decades
owing to diversification into tourism, offshore financial
services and other service industries. Tourism and agriculture
have recovered from severe hurricane damage in 2004 and
2005, and the global downturn's effect on tourism and
remittances caused the economy to contract in 2009 and
stagnate in 2010–14. Since then, debt has been reduced, GDP
has steadily grown and the government has pushed through
legislative reforms to lock in fiscal discipline.

Agriculture now employs only 11 per cent of the workforce
and produces 9.1 per cent of GDP. Industry consists of
processing agricultural products, textile manufacturing, light
assembly operations and construction, and contributes 14.2
per cent of GDP. The service sector, including tourism and
offshore financial services, accounts for 69 per cent of
employment and 76.7 per cent of GDP.

The main trading partners are the USA, Trinidad and
Tobago, and other Caribbean countries. Principal exports are
bananas, cocoa, nutmeg, fruit, vegetables, clothing and mace.
Imports include food, manufactured goods, machinery,
chemicals and fuels.

GNI – US$1bn; US$9,650 per capita (2017)
Annual average growth of GDP – 2.5 per cent (2017 est)
Inflation rate – 2.6 per cent (2017 est)
Unemployment – 33.5 per cent (2013)
Total external debt – US$679m (2013 est)
Imports – US$350m (2016)
Exports – US$30m (2016)

BALANCE OF PAYMENTS
Trade – US$320m deficit (2016)
Current Account – US$33m deficit (2016)

Trade with UK	2016	2017
Imports from UK	£8,089,592	£10,088,463
Exports to UK	£628,692	£554,096

COMMUNICATIONS

Airports and waterways – The main airport and port are based at
St George's
Roadways – 687km of surfaced roads
Telecommunications – 26,776 fixed lines and 118,973 mobile
subscriptions (2016); there were 62,123 internet users in
2016
Internet code and IDD – gd; 1 473 (from UK), 011 44 (to UK)
Major broadcasters and press – The Grenada Broadcasting
Network is jointly owned by the government and the
Caribbean Communications Network; there are no daily
newspapers but several weeklies, including *Grenada Today* and
The Grenada Informer

GUATEMALA

República de Guatemala – Republic of Guatemala

Area – 108,889 sq. km
Capital – Guatemala City; population, 2,851,000 (2018 est)
Major cities – Mixco, Quezaltenango, Santo Tomás de
   Castilla, Villa Nueva
Currency – Quetzal (Q) of 100 centavos
Population – 15,460,732 rising at 1.75 per cent a year (2017
   est); mestizo and European (59.4 per cent), Mayan (40.3
   per cent), indigenous non-Mayan (0.2 per cent) (2001)
Religion – Christian (Roman Catholic 65 per cent,
   Evangelical Protestant 43 per cent) (est)
Language – Spanish, 23 Amerindian languages (all official)
Population density – 155 per sq. km (2016)
Urban population – 51.1 per cent (2018 est)
Median age (years) – 22.1 (2017 est)
National anthem – 'Himno Nacional de Guatemala' 'National
   Anthem of Guatemala'
National day – 15 September (Independence Day)
Death penalty – Retained (last used 2000)
CPI score – 28 (143)
Military expenditure – US$284m (2017)
Conscription – 18–50 years of age, male only; 12–24 months
   (selective)

CLIMATE AND TERRAIN

Narrow tropical plains on both the north (Caribbean) and
south (Pacific) coasts rise to a mountainous interior in the
centre and south. The mountains fall in the north to lowlands
covered in tropical jungle. Elevation extremes range from
4,211m (Tajumulco volcano) to 0m (Pacific Ocean). There are
37 volcanoes, three active, in the central plateau. The climate
is tropical but is cooler in the highlands. The wet season runs
from May to September, when mudslides and hurricanes can
occur. There are also frequent minor earth tremors and some
earthquakes.

HISTORY AND POLITICS

Mayan and Aztec civilisations flourished in the area until the
Spanish conquest in 1523–4, after which the area became a
Spanish colony. It gained independence in 1821, and formed
part of a Central American federation of former Spanish
provinces from 1823 to 1839. After independence, the
country was ruled by a series of dictatorships and military
regimes, interspersed with periods of democratic government.
In 1960 a civil war between military governments, right-wing
vigilantes and left-wing guerrillas began, lasting 36 years and
during which over 200,000 people died or disappeared.

In 1996 the democratically elected civilian government
concluded a peace agreement with the left-wing Guatemalan
Revolutionary National Unity guerrillas that ended the civil
war. In 1999, an independent commission found that 93 per
cent of human rights abuses during the war had been

instigated by the security forces, and in 2000 and 2004 the state formally admitted guilt in several human rights cases, paying damages to the victims. At present, only a small number of the military personnel found to be responsible for the atrocities have been prosecuted.

In the 2015 legislative election, the centre-right Renewed Democratic Liberty (LIDER) became the largest party in Congress with 44 seats. After President Otto Perez Molina resigned in September 2015 following a bribery scandal, former TV comic 'Jimmy' Ernesto Morales won the October presidential election with 67.4 per cent of the vote in the second round. Following the results of a referendum in April 2018, the nation filed a claim with the International Court of Justice demanding sovereignty over 53 per cent of neighbouring Belize.

Under the 1986 constitution, the executive president is directly elected for a four-year term, which is not renewable. He or she is responsible to the congress and appoints the cabinet. The unicameral Congress of the Republic has 158 members, who are directly elected for a four-year term.

HEAD OF STATE
President, James Ernesto Morales, *elected* 25 October 2015, *sworn in* 14 January 2016
Vice-President, Jateth Cabrera Franco

SELECTED GOVERNMENT MEMBERS *AS AT JUNE 2018*
Defence, Brig.-Gen. Luis Miguel Ralda Moreno
Economy, Acisclo Valladares Urruela
Foreign Affairs, Sandra Erica Jovel Polenco

EMBASSY OF GUATEMALA
105 Westbourne Grove, London W2 4UW
T 020-7221 1525 E inglaterra@minex.gob.gt
Ambassador Extraordinary and Plenipotentiary, HE Acisclo Valladares Molina, *apptd* 2010

BRITISH EMBASSY
Edificio Torre Internacional, Nivel 11, 16 Calle 0–55, Zona 10, Guatemala City
T (+502) 2380 7300 E embassy@intelnett.com
W www.gov.uk/government/world/guatemala
Ambassador Extraordinary and Plenipotentiary, HE Carolyn Davidson, *apptd* 2017

ECONOMY AND TRADE
IMF funding and foreign aid have underpinned the government's economic reforms and stabilisation programmes, but the trade deficit, poor infrastructure, volcanic eruptions, security problems and high levels of corruption still deter foreign investment. The country suffers from a huge imbalance in wealth, and over half the population lives below the poverty line. Despite potential for tourism and increased regional integration and trade, economic growth is predicted to continue slowing into 2019 due to slow export demand.

Nearly one-third of the population is dependent on agriculture, which contributes 13.2 per cent of GDP and accounts for a high proportion of exports. Industry accounts for 23.6 per cent of GDP, and the services sector, which includes tourism, for 63.2 per cent of GDP.

The main trading partners are the USA, El Salvador, Honduras and China. The principal exports are coffee, sugar, petroleum, garments, bananas, other fruit, vegetables and cardamom. The chief imports are fuels, machinery and transport equipment, construction materials, grain, fertilisers and electricity.

GNI – US$68.6bn; US$4,060 per capita (2017)
Annual average growth of GDP – 3.2 per cent (2017 est)

Inflation rate – 4.4 per cent (2017 est)
Population below poverty line – 59.3 per cent (2014 est)
Unemployment – 2.4 per cent (2016 est)
Total external debt – US$23.54bn (2017 est)
Imports – US$16,987m (2016)
Exports – US$10,572m (2016)

BALANCE OF PAYMENTS
Trade – US$6,415m deficit (2016)
Current Account – US$1,133m deficit (2017)

Trade with UK	2016	2017
Imports from UK	£28,714,848	£35,208,502
Exports to UK	£87,826,447	£90,117,407

COMMUNICATIONS
Airports – 16; the principal international airport is based in Guatemala City
Waterways – There are 990km of navigable waterways, of which only 260km are navigable all year round; the main seaports are at Quetzal on the Pacific Ocean and Santo Tomás de Castilla on the Gulf of Honduras
Roadways and railways – 6,797km of surfaced roads; 332km
Telecommunications – 2.45 million fixed lines and 18.26 million mobile subscriptions (2016); there were 5.24 million internet users in 2016
Internet code and IDD – gt; 502 (from UK), 44 (to UK)
Major broadcasters – Private broadcasters dominate the media; four national television stations, including Canal 3, share the same owner
Press – There are four main daily newspapers, including *Prensa Libre* and *El Periodico*
WPFI score – 36,17 (116)

EDUCATION AND HEALTH
There are nine years of compulsory education.
Literacy rate – 95.4 per cent (2015 est)
Gross enrolment ratio (percentage of relevant age group) – primary 101 per cent, secondary 64 per cent (2016 est); tertiary 18.3 per cent (2013)
Health expenditure (per capita) – US$233 (2014)
Hospital beds (per 1,000 people) – 0.6 (2014)
Life expectancy (years) – 72.6 (2017 est)
Mortality rate – 4.7 (2017 est)
Birth rate – 24.1 (2017 est)
Infant mortality rate – 21.3 (2017 est)
HIV/AIDS adult prevalence – 0.5 per cent (2016 est)

GUINEA

République de Guinée – Republic of Guinea

Area – 245,857 sq. km
Capital – Conakry; population, 1,843,000 (2018 est)
Major cities – Guéckédou, Kankan, Nzérékoré
Currency – Guinea franc (GNF) of 100 centimes

Population – 12,413,867 rising at 2.61 per cent a year (2017 est); Fulani (33.9 per cent), Malinke (31.1 per cent), Susu (19.1 per cent), Guerze (6 per cent) (2012 est)
Religion – Muslim 86.7 per cent (predominantly Sunni), Christian 8.9 per cent, traditional indigenous religions 4.4 per cent (est); some combine Islam or Christianity with indigenous beliefs (2012 est)
Language – French (official), Eastern Maninkakan, Guinea Kpelle, Northern Kissi, Pular, Susu, Toma
Population density – 50 per sq. km (2016)
Urban population – 36.1 per cent (2018 est)
Median age (years) – 18.9 (2017 est)
National anthem – 'Liberté' 'Freedom'
National day – 2 October (Independence Day)
Death penalty – Retained for certain crimes (last used 2001)
CPI score – 27 (148)
Military expenditure – US$172m (2017)
Literacy rate – 30.4 per cent (2015 est)
Gross enrolment ratio (percentage of relevant age group) – primary 91.3 per cent, secondary 38.8 per cent, tertiary 10.8 per cent (2014 est)
Health expenditure (per capita) – US$30 (2014)
Hospital beds (per 1,000 people) – 0.3 (2011)
Life expectancy (years) – 61 (2017 est)
Mortality rate – 9 (2017 est)
Birth rate – 35.1 (2017 est)
Infant mortality rate – 50 (2017 est)
HIV/AIDS adult prevalence – 1.5 per cent (2016)

CLIMATE AND TERRAIN

Guinea has a flat coastal plain that rises to the hilly Fouta Djallon plateau in the north-west, where the Gambia and Senegal rivers rise. East of the plateau is the central savannah, the source of the Niger river, with rainforest in the south-east. Elevation extremes range from 1,752m (Mt Nimba) to 0m (Atlantic Ocean). The climate is tropical, with a wet season from April to November; the average daily temperature is 26.1°C.

POLITICS

Under the 2010 constitution, the executive president is directly elected for a five-year term, renewable once. The unicameral National Assembly has 114 members, who are directly elected for a five-year term. The president appoints the council of ministers.

The presidential election in 2010, the first democratic election since independence, was won by Alpha Condé; the second round of voting was delayed by allegations of fraud in the first round, and his victory sparked off several weeks of intercommunal violence. Delayed 2013 legislative elections resulted in Alpha Condé's ruling Rally of the Guinean People party (RPG) winning 53 seats and forming a coalition with smaller parties. The opposition Union of Democratic Forces in Guinea declared the result invalid and violent demonstrations occurred in the capital. In 2015, violent protests again broke out in Conakry following the announcement that overdue local elections would not take place until 2016. Condé was re-elected president by 58 per cent of the vote in October, although the opposition alleged fraud and vote-rigging in the election.

HEAD OF STATE
President, Alpha Condé, *elected* 7 November 2010, *sworn in* 21 December, *re-elected* 17 October 2015

SELECTED GOVERNMENT MEMBERS *AS AT JUNE 2018*
Prime Minister, Ibrahima Kassory Fofana
Economy and Finance, Mamady Camara
Foreign Affairs, Mamadi Touré
Defence, Mohamed Diane

EMBASSY OF THE REPUBLIC OF GUINEA
239 Old Marylebone Road, London NW1 5QT
T 020-7258 9640 E embassyofguinea@gmail.com
Ambassador Extraordinary and Plenipotentiary, HE Paul Goa Zoumanigui, *apptd* 2013

BRITISH EMBASSY
Villa 1, Residence 2000, Corniche Sud Conakry
T (+224) 6335 5329 E britembconakry@hotmail.com
W www.gov.uk/government/world/guinea
Ambassador Extraordinary and Plenipotentiary, HE Catherine Inglehearn, *apptd* 2015

ECONOMY AND TRADE

Although Guinea is the second largest producer of bauxite in the world and despite an abundance of natural resources, decades of mismanagement and corruption have left the economy undeveloped. Foreign aid was suspended following the 2008 coup and resumed in 2012 following democratic elections in 2010. The 2014–15 Ebola outbreak is thought to have cost the economy US$540m (£348m), due to the disruption caused to trade and a reduction in investor confidence; nevertheless, GDP growth was 6.6 per cent in 2016 and 6.7 per cent in 2017 due to increased mining.

Mining attracts foreign investment and a new mining code introduced in 2011 and amended in 2013 includes provisions to combat corruption. Agriculture, much of it at subsistence level, employs 76 per cent of the population and contributes 19.5 per cent of GDP. Industry accounts for 38.4 per cent of GDP, mostly through mining and the processing of minerals and agricultural produce.

The main trading partners are China, India and EU countries, especially the Netherlands. Principal exports are bauxite, gold, diamonds, coffee, fish and other agricultural products. The main imports are petroleum products, metals, machinery, transport equipment, textiles, grain and other foodstuffs.

GNI – US$10.4bn; US$820 per capita (2017)
Annual average growth of GDP – 6.7 per cent (2017 est)
Inflation rate – 8.5 per cent (2017 est)
Population below poverty line – 55.2 per cent (2012 est)
Unemployment rate – 2.8 per cent (2017 est)
Total external debt – US$1.53bn (2017 est)
Imports – US$2,115m (2014)
Exports – US$1,428m (2014)

BALANCE OF PAYMENTS
Trade – US$687m deficit (2014)
Current Account – US$2,744m deficit (2016)

Portuguese establish ivory and slave trade; north-east areas part of the Mali Empire	Country renamed French Guinea	Becomes part of French West Africa	Death of Touré; successor Lansana Conté introduces greater economic liberalisation	Civil wars in neighbouring countries cause an influx of refugees, leading to strikes and violent protests		A massacre of pro-democracy demonstrators ends in Sékouba Konaté becoming acting president
c.1200	1849		1958		1991	2008
c.1500	1891	1904	1984	2006-8		2009-10
Susi kingdoms established	French establish protectorate over coastal areas	Becomes independent under President Ahmed Sekou Touré, who establishes a one-party state	Conté introduces a multiparty election system and is successful in all subsequent elections amid allegations of electoral fraud	Military junta seizes power the day after Conté's death		The first presidential elections take place under power-sharing government

Trade with UK	2016	2017
Imports from UK	£21,486,392	£21,978,430
Exports to UK	£395,603	£148,156

COMMUNICATIONS

Airports – Four with surfaced runways; the principal airport is at Conakry
Waterways – The major seaports are Conakry and Kamsar; there are 1,300km of waterways
Roadways and railways – 4,342km of surfaced roadways, and 1,185km of railways
Telecommunications – 18,000 fixed lines (2012) and 10.8 million mobile telephone lines in use (2016); there were 1.18 million internet users in 2016
Internet code and IDD – gn; 224 (from UK), 44 (to UK)
Major broadcasters – Radiodiffusion-Télévision Guinéenne is the principal, state-run broadcaster
Press – *Horoya* is the main government-owned daily
WPFI score – 31,90 (104)

GUINEA-BISSAU

Republica da Guine-Bissau – Republic of Guinea-Bissau

Area – 36,125 sq. km
Capital – Bissau; population, 558,000 (2018 est)
Major cities – Bolama, Gabú
Currency – West African CFA franc of 100 centimes
Population – 1,792,338 rising at 1.86 per cent a year (2017 est); Fulani (28.5 per cent), Balanta (22.5 per cent), Mandinga (14.7 per cent), Papel (9.1 per cent), Manjaco (8.3 per cent) (2008 est)
Religion – Muslim 45.1 per cent, Christian 22.1 per cent, indigenous beliefs 14.9 per cent (2008 est)
Language – Portuguese (official), Creole
Population density – 65 per sq. km (2016)
Urban population – 43.4 per cent (2018 est)
Median age (years) – 20.1 (2017 est)
National anthem – 'Esta e a Nossa Patria Bem Amada' 'This is Our Beloved Country'
National day – 24 September (Independence Day)
Death penalty – Abolished for all crimes (since 1993)
CPI score – 17 (171)
Military expenditure – US$18.6m (2015)
Conscription – 18–25 years of age (selective)
Literacy rate – 77.3 per cent (2015 est)
Gross enrolment ratio (percentage of relevant age group) – primary 116 per cent (2010 est)
Health expenditure (per capita) – US$37 (2014)
Hospital beds (per 1,000 people) – 1 (2009)
Life expectancy (years) – 51 (2017 est)
Mortality rate – 13.9 (2017 est)
Birth rate – 32.5 (2017 est)

Infant mortality rate – 85.7 (2017 est)
HIV/AIDS adult prevalence – 3.1 per cent (2016 est)

CLIMATE AND TERRAIN

Guinea-Bissau has a low coastal plain that rises to savannah in the east. The coast is heavily indented and covered with mangrove swamps. Elevation extremes range from 300m (in the north-east) to 0m (Atlantic Ocean). The climate is tropical, with a wet season from July to September.

HISTORY AND POLITICS

A part of the ancient African empire of Mali, Guinea-Bissau was once the kingdom of Gabu, which became independent of the empire in 1546 and survived until 1867. In 1446, Portuguese traders discovered the coast and established slave trading there, subsequently administering Guinea-Bissau with the Cape Verde islands; it became a separate colony in 1879. After a guerrilla war led by the left-wing African Party for the Independence of Guinea and Cape Verde (PAIGC), Guinea-Bissau declared independence unilaterally in 1973 and Portugal recognised this in 1974.

After independence Guinea-Bissau became a one-party socialist state under the PAIGC, led by Luis Cabral. He was deposed in 1980, in a military coup led by General Joao Vieira, and the country was under military rule until 1994. A multiparty system was introduced in 1991 after popular agitation, but the following 15 years saw a short civil war (1998–9) and two more military coups (1999, 2003); democratic government was restored in 2004–5.

Following a military coup in April 2012, Guinea-Bissau was ruled by the Transitional National Council. The April 2014 legislative election was won by the PAIGC, whose candidate, Jose Mario Vaz, was elected president in May 2014. However, President Vaz dismissed his government in August 2015 due to a rift with Prime Minister Domingos Pereira, and a new cabinet was installed. Since then internal political instability has led to a series of new governments and prime ministers.

Under the 1999 constitution, the executive president is directly elected for a five-year term, with no term limits. The president appoints the council of ministers. The unicameral National People's Assembly has 102 members, who are directly elected for a four-year term.

HEAD OF STATE

President, Jose Mario Vaz, *elected* 20 May 2014, *sworn in* 23 June 2014

SELECTED GOVERNMENT MEMBERS *AS AT JUNE 2018*
Prime Minister, Economy and Finance, Aristides Gomes
Defence, Eduardo da Costa Sanha
Foreign Affairs, Joao Ribeiro Butiam Co

EMBASSY OF THE REPUBLIC OF GUINEA-BISSAU
94 rue St Lazare, 75009 Paris, France
T (+33) (1) 4874 3639
Ambassador Extraordinary and Plenipotentiary, vacant

BRITISH CONSULATE
Ambassador Extraordinary and Plenipotentiary, HE George Hodgson, *apptd* 2015, resident at Dakar, Senegal

ECONOMY AND TRADE

The economy is in a poor state owing to decades of mismanagement and corruption, the devastating effects of the 1998–9 civil war and ongoing political instability. Successful elections in 2014 allowed the country to resume receiving international aid, although political tensions remain. Over two thirds of the country live below the absolute poverty line.

Although Guinea-Bissau has mineral resources, including oil, the high cost of exploiting these inhibits development and the economy is based almost exclusively on agriculture (mainly cashew nuts) and fishing; drug trafficking is the most lucrative industry in the country. The agricultural sector employs 82 per cent of the population and contributes 44.1 per cent of GDP. The industrial sector generates 12.9 per cent of GDP, mainly through processing agricultural products, and beer and soft drink production.

The main trading partners are India (67.1 per cent of exports), Portugal and Vietnam. Principal exports include fish, cashew nuts, peanuts, palm kernels and timber. The main imports are foodstuffs, machinery and transport equipment, and fuels.

GNI – US$1.2bn; US$660 per capita (2017)
Annual average growth of GDP – 5.0 per cent (2017 est)
Inflation rate – 2.8 per cent (2017 est)
Population below poverty line – 67 per cent (2015 est)
Imports – US$230m (2014)
Exports – US$339m (2014)

BALANCE OF PAYMENTS
Trade – US$30m deficit (2013)
Current Account – US$10m deficit (2016)

Trade with UK	2016	2017
Imports from UK	£952,477	£722,514
Exports to UK	£82,416	£292,840

COMMUNICATIONS
Airports – Two; the principal airport is at Bissau
Waterways – The main rivers are navigable for part of their lengths, and shallow-draught craft can access much of the interior via creeks and inlets; Bissau is the main seaport
Roadways – There are 965km of surfaced roads
Telecommunications – 5,000 fixed lines (2014) and 1.3 million mobile subscriptions (2016); there were 66,169 internet users in 2016
Internet code and IDD – gw; 245 (from UK), 44 (to UK)
Major broadcasters – The state-run Radio Televisao de Guinea-Bissau is the main broadcaster
Press – Major newspapers include state-run weekly *No Pintcha* and the privately run *Gazeta de Noticias*
WPFI score – 30,09 (77)

GUYANA

Cooperative Republic of Guyana

Area – 214,969 sq. km
Capital – Georgetown; population, 110,000 (2018 est)
Major towns – Linden, New Amsterdam
Currency – Guyana dollar (G$) of 100 cents

Population – 737,718 rising at 0.32 per cent a year (2017 est); East Indian (39.8 per cent), Black African (29.3 per cent), Mixed (19.9 per cent), Amerindian (10.5 per cent) (2011 est)
Religion – Christian (Protestant 30.5 per cent, other Christian 17.7 per cent, Roman Catholic 8.1 per cent), Hindu 28.4 per cent, Muslim 7.2 per cent (2002 est)
Language – English (official), Amerindian dialects, Creole, Caribbean Hindustani (a dialect of Hindi), Urdu
Population density – 4 per sq. km (2016)
Urban population – 26.6 per cent (2018 est)
Median age (years) – 26.2 (2017 est)
National anthem – 'Dear Land of Guyana, of Rivers and Plains'
National day – 23 February (Republic Day)
Death penalty – Retained (last used 1993)
CPI score – 38 (91)
Military expenditure – US$57.3m (2017)
Literacy rate – 94.4 per cent (2015 est)
Gross enrolment ratio (percentage of relevant age group) – primary 85 per cent, secondary 89 per cent, tertiary 12 per cent (2012 est)
Health expenditure (per capita) – US$222 (2014)
Life expectancy (years) – 68.6 (2017 est)
Mortality rate – 7.4 (2017 est)
Birth rate – 15.4 (2017 est)
Infant mortality rate – 30.4 (2017 est)
HIV/AIDS adult prevalence – 1.6 per cent (2016 est)

CLIMATE AND TERRAIN
The land rises from a narrow coastal plain to forested highlands in the west and savannah on the southern border; about 90 per cent of the population lives on the coastal plain, which constitutes 5 per cent of the land area. Around 79 per cent of the country is covered by rainforest. Elevation extremes range from 2,835m (Mt Roraima) to 0m (Atlantic Ocean). The climate is tropical, with an average daily temperature of 26°C, and two wet seasons, from April to July and from November to January.

HISTORY AND POLITICS
Carib and Arawak peoples inhabited the coastal region of Guyana when Dutch merchants founded the first European settlement in the late 16th century. Guyana became an important producer of sugar, grown on plantations worked first by African slaves and then, after the abolition of slavery in 1834, by indentured labourers, mostly from India. Several areas were ceded to Britain in 1815, and consolidated as British Guiana in 1831. The country became independent, as Guyana, on 26 May 1966, and became a republic in 1970.

Guyana's first political party, the People's Progressive Party (PPP), split along ethnic lines in the 1950s; the PPP continued as a predominantly Indian party under Cheddi Jagan, while those of African descent formed the People's National Congress (PNC), led by Forbes Burnham. Burnham dominated political life after independence, first as prime minister (1966–80) and then as executive president until his death in 1985. Under his autocratic rule, politics became characterised by suspect elections and a disregard for civil liberties and human rights. The PPP's electoral victory in 1992 ended the PNC's monopoly of power but persistent ethnic tensions continue to destabilise politics.

The 2011 legislative election was won by the PPP, securing its fifth consecutive term of office but without an overall majority; Donald Ramotar (PPP) became president, replacing Bharrat Jagdeo (also PPP). In the May 2015 legislative elections, the Partnership for National Unity and Alliance for Change coalition (APNU-AFC) emerged as the single largest party, and APNU's leader, David Granger, was sworn in as president.

Under the 1980 constitution, the executive president is nominated by the majority party in the legislature after each legislative election, and serves a five-year term with no term limits. The unicameral National Assembly has 65 members serving five-year terms.

HEAD OF STATE
President, David Granger, *sworn in* 16 May 2015

SELECTED GOVERNMENT MEMBERS *AS AT JUNE 2018*
Prime Minister, First Vice-President, Moses Nagamootoo
Finance, Winston Jordan
Attorney-General, Basil Williams

HIGH COMMISSION FOR GUYANA
3 Palace Court, Bayswater Road, London W2 4LP
T 020-7229 7684 E info@guyanahclondon.co.uk
W www.guyanahclondon.co.uk
High Commissioner, HE Frederick Hamley Case, *apptd* 2016

BRITISH HIGH COMMISSION
PO Box 10849, 44 Main Street, Georgetown
T (+1592) 226 5881 W www.gov.uk/government/world/guyana
High Commissioner, HE Gregory Quinn, *apptd* 2015

ECONOMY AND TRADE
The economy grew from 2001 to 2008 owing to expansion in agriculture and mining, the cancellation of over one-third of Guyana's external debt, and increases in foreign direct investment and remittances from expatriate workers. Growth slowed in 2014, but the slowly-developing exploitation of large offshore oil deposits and increased gold mining have contributed to a moderate rise in GDP since. Attempts to develop tourism, hindered by poor infrastructure and skills shortages, are also likely to be offset by new investment in gold mining.
Agriculture accounts for 17.5 per cent of GDP and provides the raw materials for the major industries of sugar processing and rice milling. Non-agricultural activities are growing in importance, and include bauxite and gold mining, forestry, fishing and textile manufacturing; industry accounts for 37.8 per cent of GDP.
The main trading partners are the USA, Trinidad and Tobago, Canada and China. Principal exports include sugar, gold, bauxite, alumina, rice, shrimp, molasses, rum and timber. The main imports are manufactured goods, machinery, fuel and food.
GNI – US$3.5bn; US$4,460 per capita (2017)
Annual average growth of GDP – 3.5 per cent (2017 est)
Inflation rate – 2.3 per cent (2016 est)
Unemployment – 11.1 per cent (2013 est)
Total external debt – US$1.726bn (2017 est)
Imports – US$1,550m (2015)
Exports – US$1,100m (2015)

BALANCE OF PAYMENTS
Trade – US$450m deficit (2015)
Current Account – US$127m deficit (2016)

Trade with UK	2016	2017
Imports from UK	£32,512,835	£31,731,161
Exports to UK	£29,551,407	£54,487,567

COMMUNICATIONS
Airports and waterways – 11; 330km of navigable waterways (principally the Berbice, Demerara and Essequibo rivers) form the main arteries of communication
Roadways – There are 590km of surfaced roads
Telecommunications – 141,595 fixed lines and 584,659 mobile subscriptions (2016); there were 262,425 internet users in 2016

Internet code and IDD – gy; 592 (from UK), 1 44 (to UK)
Major broadcasters – The state-owned National Communications Network operates national television and radio networks
Press – There are three major daily newspapers: the government-owned *Guyana Chronicle, Stabroek News* and *Kaieteur News*
WPFI score – 26,25 (55)

HAITI
République d'Haïti / Repiblik d'Ayiti – Republic of Haiti

Area – 27,750 sq. km
Capital – Port-au-Prince; population, 2,637,000 (2018 est)
Major cities – Cap-Haïtien, Gonaïves, Pétionville
Currency – Gourde (G) of 100 centimes
Population – 10,646,714 rising at 1.34 per cent a year (2017 est)
Religion – Christian (Roman Catholic 54.7 per cent, Baptist 15.4 per cent, Pentecostal 7.9 per cent, Seventh-day Adventist 3 per cent); many Christians also practise Voodoo, recognised as an official religion in 2003
Language – French, Creole (both official)
Population density – 394 per sq. km (2016)
Urban population – 55.3 per cent (2018 est)
Median age (years) – 23 (2017 est)
National anthem – 'La Dessalinienne' 'The Song of Dessalines'
National day – 1 January (Independence Day)
Death penalty – Abolished for all crimes (since 1987)
CPI score – 22 (157)
Literacy rate – 82.1 per cent (2015 est)
Health expenditure (per capita) – US$61 (2014)
Hospital beds (per 1,000 people) – 0.3 (2011)
Life expectancy (years) – 64.2 (2017 est)
Mortality rate – 9 (2017 est)
Birth rate – 23 (2017 est)
Infant mortality rate – 46.8 (2017 est)
HIV / AIDS adult prevalence – 1.5 per cent (2016 est)

CLIMATE AND TERRAIN
The country occupies the western third of the island of Hispaniola. The terrain is mountainous, with coastal plains and a large central plateau. Elevation extremes range from 2,680m (Chaîne de la Selle) to 0m (Caribbean Sea). The climate is tropical, and semi-arid where the eastern mountains block the trade winds, with two wet seasons (April–June, August–November) and a hurricane season from June to November.

POLITICS
Under the 1987 constitution, the president is directly elected for a five-year term that may be renewed once but not consecutively. The bicameral National Assembly comprises a lower house, the Chamber of Deputies, with 118 members directly elected for a four-year term, and the senate, with 30 members directly elected for a six-year term; one-third of the

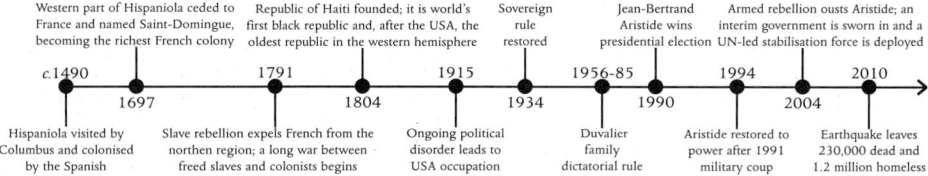

Western part of Hispaniola ceded to France and named Saint-Domingue, becoming the richest French colony	Republic of Haiti founded; it is world's first black republic and, after the USA, the oldest republic in the western hemisphere	Sovereign rule restored	Jean-Bertrand Aristide wins presidential election	Armed rebellion ousts Aristide; an interim government is sworn in and a UN-led stabilisation force is deployed

*c.*1490 — 1697 — 1791 — 1804 — 1915 — 1934 — 1956-85 — 1990 — 1994 — 2004 — 2010

Hispaniola visited by Columbus and colonised by the Spanish | Slave rebellion expels French from the northen region; a long war between freed slaves and colonists begins | Ongoing political disorder leads to USA occupation | Duvalier family dictatorial rule | Aristide restored to power after 1991 military coup | Earthquake leaves 230,000 dead and 1.2 million homeless

senators are elected every two years. The president appoints the prime minister, who must be approved by the legislature.

After a delay of more than three years legislative elections were held in late 2015, with the Haitian Tet Kale Party (PHTK) winning the largest number of seats in the Chamber of Deputies (13). In January 2017, the country's electoral commission confirmed that Jovenel Moïse of the PHTK had won November 2016's presidential election with 55.6 per cent of the vote. Violent protests against Prime Minister Jack Guy Lafontant's plans to raise fuel prices forced him from power in July 2018. He was replaced by Jean-Henry Céant.

HEAD OF STATE
President, Jovenel Moïse, *elected* 20 November 2016, *sworn in* 7 February 2017

SELECTED GOVERNMENT MEMBERS *AS AT AUGUST 2018*
Prime Minister, Jean-Henry Céant
Economy and Finance, Jude Alix Patrick Salomon
Foreign Affairs, Antonio Rodrigue
Interior, Jean-Marie Reynaldo Brunet

EMBASSY OF THE REPUBLIC OF HAITI
14 Cavendish Place, London W1G 9DJ

T 020-7637 8985
Ambassador Extraordinary and Plenipotentiary, vacant

BRITISH AMBASSADOR
HE Sharon Campbell, *apptd* 2015, resident at Santo Domingo, Dominican Republic

ECONOMY AND TRADE
The country is the poorest in the Americas with most of the population living below the poverty line and more than half in abject poverty. Its economy, damaged by years of political instability, violence and corruption as well as the natural disasters to which it is vulnerable, experienced moderate growth from 2005 and Haiti had its foreign debt written off in 2009 and 2010. But the 2010 earthquake and Hurricane Matthew in October 2016 reversed these gains, devastating infrastructure and continuing the government's complete dependence on foreign aid. Remittances from the estimated one in six Haitians who live abroad, principally in the USA, are the main source of foreign revenue, worth around 25 per cent of GDP. Two-fifths of the population depend on agriculture – predominantly small-scale subsistence farming – which contributes 21.9 per cent of GDP. Industrial activities include production of textiles and garments, sugar refining, flour milling and assembly of goods, especially vehicle parts, for re-export.

The main trading partners are the USA (which takes 80.6 per cent of exports) and China. Principal exports are garments (90 per cent of exports), manufactured goods, essential oils, cocoa, mangoes and coffee. The main imports are food, manufactured goods, machinery and transport equipment, fuels and raw materials.
GNI – US$8.4bn; US$760 per capita (2017)
Annual average growth of GDP – 1 per cent (2017 est)

Inflation rate – 14.7 per cent (2017 est)
Population below poverty line – 58.5 per cent (2012 est)
Total external debt – US$2.607bn (2017 est)
Imports – US$3,523m (2015)
Exports – US$1,018m (2015)

BALANCE OF PAYMENTS
Trade – US$2,505m deficit (2015)
Current Account – US$443m deficit (2016)

Trade with UK	2016	2017
Imports from UK	£12,295,807	£16,256,589
Exports to UK	£3,191,789	£6,024,840

COMMUNICATIONS
Airports and waterways – Four; the international airports and main ports are at Port-au-Prince and Cap-Haitien
Roadways – Only 768km of the country's roads are surfaced
Telecommunications – 5,692 fixed lines and 6.5 million mobile subscriptions (2016); there were 1.28 million internet users in 2016
Internet code and IDD – ht; 509 (from UK), 44 (to UK)
Major broadcasters – The government-owned Television Nationale d'Haiti broadcasts in Creole, French and Spanish
Press – There are two daily newspapers, *Le Matin* and *Le Nouvelliste*
WPFI score – 26,82 (60)

HONDURAS

República de Honduras – Republic of Honduras

Area – 112,090 sq. km
Capital – Tegucigalpa; population, 1,363,000 (2018 est)
Major cities – Choloma, El Progreso, La Ceiba, San Pedro Sula
Currency – Lempira of 100 centavos
Population – 9,038,741 rising at 1.60 per cent a year (2017 est); mainly mestizo, with Amerindian and black minorities
Religion – Christian (Roman Catholic 97 per cent, Protestant 3 per cent)
Language – Spanish (official), Amerindian dialects

Population density – 81 per sq. km (2016)
Urban population – 57.1 per cent (2018 est)
Median age (years) – 23 (2017 est)
National anthem – 'Himno Nacional de Honduras' 'National Anthem of Honduras'
National day – 15 September (Independence Day)
Death penalty – Abolished for all crimes (since 1956)
CPI score – 29 (135)
Military expenditure – US$364m (2017 est)

CLIMATE AND TERRAIN

Honduras has a mountainous interior, falling to narrow coastal plains. Elevation extremes range from 2,870m (Cerro Las Minas) to 0m (Caribbean Sea). The climate is subtropical in the lowlands and temperate in the mountains. The average temperature is 24.4°C.

HISTORY AND POLITICS

Honduras was home to part of the Mayan civilisation between the fourth and ninth centuries AD. Christopher Columbus first set foot on the American mainland at Trujillo in Honduras in 1502, but it was 1525 before Spanish colonisation began. In 1821, the country gained independence from Spain, and it was part of a Central American federation of former Spanish colonies from 1823 until it became fully independent in 1839. Thereafter the country underwent periods of political instability interspersed with military rule until 1982, when a civilian government took office. During the civil wars in Nicaragua and El Salvador, Honduras acted as a base for US forces and anti-Sandinista Contras, and there was a marked decline in its respect for human rights. The end of the civil wars led to a decline in the power of the army, which was brought under civilian control in 1999, but there are still very high levels of violent crime. In 2011 congress voted to allow troops to take on police responsibilities in an attempt to curb the high murder rate.

In November 2013, Juan Orlando Hernández was declared the winner of the presidential election, and was re-elected in November 2017. Hernández claimed a 2016 court ruling allowed him to stand for re-election despite a prohibition in the constitution. His National Party remained the largest party in Congress in simultaneous legislative elections, despite international pressure for a fresh vote over allegations of corruption, fraud and state-sponsored killings.

Under the 1982 constitution, the executive president is directly elected for a four-year term, which is not renewable, and appoints the government. The unicameral National Congress has 128 members, directly elected for a four-year term.

HEAD OF STATE

President, Juan Orlando Hernández, *elected* 24 November 2013, *took office* 27 January 2014, *re-elected* 26 November 2017
First Vice-President, Ricardo Antonio Alvarez Arias

SELECTED GOVERNMENT MEMBERS *AS AT JUNE 2018*

Economy and Finance, Rocio Tabora
Foreign Relations, Maria Dolores Aguero

EMBASSY OF HONDURAS

4th Floor, 136 Baker Street, London W1U 6UD
T 020-7486 4880 E hondurasuk@lineone.net
W www.honduras.embassyhomepage.com/
Ambassador Extraordinary and Plenipotentiary, HE Ivan Romero-Martinez, *apptd* 2008

BRITISH AMBASSADOR

HE Thomas Carter, *apptd* 2017, resident at Guatemala City, Guatemala

ECONOMY AND TRADE

The country has a huge imbalance in wealth and high levels of corruption and violent crime, often connected with drug-trafficking. Nearly 65 per cent live in poverty and remittances from expatriate workers are equivalent to nearly one-fifth of GDP. Economic activity is heavily dependent on the USA; a drop in exports and remittances due to the global economic downturn contributed to the economy's contraction in 2009. Economic difficulties led to government workers and suppliers going without pay in the winter of 2012. In 2014, the IMF agreed to provide the government with loans totalling US$189m (£120.7m) in order to pay off increasing government debt.

Although still dependent on agriculture, fishing and forestry, whose products form the basis of industrial activity and are the main exports, the economy is gradually diversifying into offshore assembly for re-export and tourism. Agriculture employs 39.2 per cent of the workforce and contributes 13.8 per cent of GDP. Industry accounts for 28.4 per cent of GDP and 20.9 per cent of employment, and the services sector for 57.8 per cent of GDP and 39.8 per cent of employment.

The main trading partner is the USA, which takes 34.5 per cent of exports and provides 40.3 per cent of imports. Principal exports are garments, coffee, shrimp, wire harnessing, cigars, bananas, gold, palm oil, fruit, lobster and timber. The main imports are machinery and transport equipment, industrial raw materials, chemical products, fuels and foodstuffs.
GNI – US$20.8bn; US$2,250 per capita (2017)
Annual average growth of GDP – 4.0 per cent (2017 est)
Inflation rate – 4.0 per cent (2017 est)
Unemployment – 5.9 per cent (2017 est)
Population below poverty line – 29.6 per cent (2014 est)
Total external debt – US$9.025bn (2017 est)
Imports – US$9,424m (2015)
Exports – US$3,911m (2015)

BALANCE OF PAYMENTS

Trade – US$5,513m deficit (2015)
Current Account – US$380m deficit (2017)

Trade with UK	2016	2017
Imports from UK	£11,333,938	£10,980,581
Exports to UK	£125,666,319	£128,167,993

COMMUNICATIONS

Airports – 13; the principal airports are at Tegucigalpa, La Ceiba and San Pedro Sula
Waterways – Honduras has ports on its Caribbean (Puerto Castilla, Puerto Cortes, Tela) and Pacific (San Lorenzo) coasts, and 465km of navigable waterways (mostly by small boats)
Roadways and railways – There are 3,367km of surfaced roads, and 44km of railways
Telecommunications – 442,929 fixed lines and 7.8 million mobile subscriptions (2016); there were 2.7 million internet users in 2016
Internet code and IDD – hn; 504 (from UK), 44 (to UK)
Major broadcasters – Televicentro operates several channels throughout the country; CBC Canal 6, Vica TV and Sotel Canal 11 are all private broadcasters; private radio stations include Radio America and Radio HRN
Press – There are four private daily newspapers, including *El Heraldo* and *La Prensa*
WPFI score – 45,23 (141)

EDUCATION AND HEALTH
Primary and secondary education is free of charge and primary education is compulsory between the ages of six and 11.

Literacy rate – 97.2 per cent (2015 est)
Gross enrolment ratio (percentage of relevant age group) – primary 96 per cent, secondary 65 per cent (2016 est); tertiary 21.2 per cent (2014 est)
Health expenditure (per capita) – US$212 (2014)
Hospital beds (per 1,000 people) – 0.7 (2014)
Life expectancy (years) – 71.2 (2017 est)
Mortality rate – 5.3 (2017 est)
Birth rate – 22.4 (2017 est)
Infant mortality rate – 17.2 (2017 est)
HIV/AIDS adult prevalence – 0.4 per cent (2016 est)

HUNGARY

Magyarország – Republic of Hungary

Area – 93,028 sq. km
Capital – Budapest; population, 1,759,000 (2018 est)
Major cities – Debrecen, Gyor, Miskolc, Pecs, Szeged
Currency – Forint of 100 filler
Population – 9,850,845 falling at 0.25 per cent a year (2017 est); Hungarian (85.6 per cent), Roma (3.2 per cent) (2011 est). There are also smaller groups of ethnic Germans, Serbs, Romanians and Slovaks
Religion – Christian (Roman Catholic 37.2 per cent, Calvinist 11.6 per cent) (2011 est)
Language – Hungarian (official)
Population density – 108 per sq. km (2016)
Urban population – 71.4 per cent (2018 est)
Median age (years) – 42.3 (2017 est)
National anthem – 'Himnusz' 'Hymn'
National day – 20 August (St Stephen's Day)
Death penalty – Abolished for all crimes (since 1990)
CPI score – 45 (66)
Military expenditure – US$1,415m (2017)

CLIMATE AND TERRAIN
Hungary lies mostly on the vast plain created by the Danube and Tisza rivers, with hills and mountains along the northern border. Elevation extremes range from 1,014m (Mt Kekes) to 78m (river Tisza). Lake Balaton lies in the west. Average temperatures range from –0.6°C in January to 21.1°C in July.

POLITICS
The 1949 constitution was superseded in 2012 by a new constitution approved by the legislature in April 2011. Parliament has since acted to limit the powers of the constitutional court following clashes, notably on electoral law. The president is elected by the legislature for a five-year term, renewable once; under the new constitution, he or she nominates the prime minister who is then elected by parliament. The unicameral National Assembly has 199 members directly elected for a four-year term.

The 2010 legislative election was won by the opposition Fidesz and Christian Democratic People's Party bloc and it formed a government under Viktor Orban (prime minister 1998–2002), who was re-elected in 2014 and 2018 on an anti-immigration platform. Fidesz regained its two-thirds 'super majority' in the April 2018 elections, the first time since 2015, which allowed the party to pass laws without the support of other parties. The 2010 presidential election was won outright at the first vote by Pal Schmitt of the Fidesz party, who subsequently resigned from office in April 2012 after admitting he had plagiarised much of his doctoral thesis; the Fidesz party elected Janos Ader as his replacement, and Ader was re-elected in 2017.

HEAD OF STATE
President, Janos Ader, *elected* 2 May 2012, *sworn in* 10 May 2012, *re-elected* 13 March 2017

SELECTED GOVERNMENT MEMBERS *AS AT JUNE 2018*
Prime Minister, Viktor Orban
Deputy Prime Minister, Zsolt Semjen
Defence, Tibor Benko
Economy, Mihaly Varga
Foreign Affairs, Peter Szijjarto

EMBASSY OF THE REPUBLIC OF HUNGARY
35 Eaton Place, London SW1X 8BY
T 020-7201 3440 E mission.lon@mfa.gov.hu W www.london.gov.hu
Ambassador Extraordinary and Plenipotentiary, HE Kristof Szalay-Bobrovniczky, *apptd* 2016

BRITISH EMBASSY
Harmincad Utca 6, 1051 Budapest
T (+36) (1) 266 2888 W www.gov.uk/government/world/hungary
Ambassador Extraordinary and Plenipotentiary, HE Iain Lindsay, OBE, *apptd* 2016

ECONOMY AND TRADE
Hungary made a successful transition to a market economy after 1989, attracting high levels of foreign direct investment. Largely dependent on the export market, since 2010 the government has increased its management of the economy. Strong economic growth started to slow in 2006–7, partly as a result of a government austerity programme intended to reduce the budget deficit and public debt. The global economic downturn left Hungary struggling to service both state and private debt in the face of rising interest rates and falling export demand, and the government had to obtain

Most of kingdom conquered by Ottoman Turks	Dual monarchy created between Austrian and Hungarian crowns; period of economic success	Austro-Hungarian Empire defeated in the First World War	Joins Axis powers in the Second World War		Opens border with Austria, indirectly triggering the fall of communism throughout eastern Europe; communist rule ends soon after		
c.1000	1699		1920	1944	1949	1999	2004
1526	1867	1918		1941		1989	
Settled by Magyar tribes, becomes a Christian kingdom under St Stephen	Turks expelled by Habsburgs; country becomes a province in dynasty's central European empire	Becomes a kingdom with Admiral Horthy as regent	Horthy deposed after seeking armistice with USSR	Becomes a communist state aligned with the Soviet Union	Joins NATO	Joins the EU	

international assistance in 2008. By 2013, Hungary had cut its deficit to under 3 per cent of GDP, allowing the country to exit the EU's Excessive Deficit Procedure. Increases in tourism, household spending and car manufacturing have contributed to real GDP growth in the last few years, aided by EU funding.

Nearly half the land is under cultivation, but agriculture accounts for only 4.4 per cent of GDP; the main crops are cereals, sunflower seeds, vegetables, livestock and dairy products. Industry contributes 30.9 per cent of GDP; the main activities include mining, metallurgy, food processing, and the production of construction materials, textiles, chemicals (especially pharmaceuticals) and motor vehicles. The main trading partners are Germany, Austria, Slovakia and Romania. Machinery and manufactured goods account for 88.5 per cent of exports and 79.8 per cent of imports. The country is a net importer of fuels and electricity.

GNI – US$125.9bn; US$12,870 per capita (2017)
Annual average growth of GDP – 3.2 per cent (2017 est)
Inflation rate – 2.5 per cent (2017 est)
Unemployment – 4.4 per cent (2017 est)
Population below poverty line – 14.9 per cent (2015)
Total external debt – US$131.8bn (2017 est)
Imports – US$92,016m (2016)
Exports – US$103,040m (2016)

BALANCE OF PAYMENTS
Trade – US$11,023m surplus (2016)
Current Account – US$4,053m surplus (2017)

Trade with UK	2016	2017
Imports from UK	£1,351,221,529	£1,449,025,796
Exports to UK	£2,682,075,325	£2,764,326,320

COMMUNICATIONS
Airports and waterways – 20, with the principal airport at Budapest; there are 1,622km of permanently navigable waterways, mainly on the river Danube, which has several major river ports and harbours including Budapest
Roadways and railways – There are 76,075km of surfaced roads, and 8,057km of railways (including a cross-border line to Austria jointly managed by the two countries)
Telecommunications – 3.1 million fixed lines and 11.8 million mobile subscriptions (2016); there were 7.8 million internet users in 2016
Internet code and IDD – hu; 36 (from UK), 44 (to UK)
Major broadcasters – Mixed system of state-supported public service broadcast media and private broadcasters; Magyar Televizio operates two public channels alongside private channels TV2 and RTL Klub; Duna TV operates satellite channels for Hungarian minorities living in neighbouring states
Press – There are four daily newspapers, including *Nepszabadsag, Magyar Hirlap* and *Magyar Nemzet*
WPFI score – 29,11 (73)

EDUCATION AND HEALTH
Hungarians have ten years of compulsory education until age 16; a further two years at secondary level is optional.
Literacy rate – 98.8 per cent (2015 est)
Gross enrolment ratio (percentage of relevant age group) – primary 101.6 per cent, secondary 105.2 per cent, tertiary 50.9 per cent (2015 est)
Health expenditure (per capita) – US$1,037 (2014)
Hospital beds (per 1,000 people) – 7 (2013)
Life expectancy (years) – 76.1 (2017 est)
Mortality rate – 12.8 (2017 est)

Birth rate – 9 (2017 est)
Infant mortality rate – 4.9 (2017 est)

ICELAND

Lydveldid Island – Republic of Iceland

Area – 103,000 sq. km
Capital – Reykjavik; population, 216,000 (2018 est)
Major towns – Hafnarfjordur, Kopavogur
Currency – Icelandic kronur (Kr) of 100 aurar
Population – 339,747 rising at 1.13 per cent a year (2017 est)
Religion – Christian (Lutheran 73.8 per cent, Roman Catholic 3.6 per cent) (2015 est)
Language – Icelandic (official), English, German
Population density – 3 per sq. km (2016)
Urban population – 93.8 per cent (2018 est)
Median age (years) – 36.5 (2017 est)
National anthem – 'Lofsongur' 'Hymn'
National day – 17 June (Independence Day)
Death penalty – Abolished for all crimes (since 1928)
CPI score – 77 (13)
Military expenditure – US$17.4m (2012)
Gross enrolment ratio (percentage of relevant age group) – primary 99.1 per cent, secondary 118.6 per cent, tertiary 81.3 per cent (2013 est)
Health expenditure (per capita) – US$4,662 (2014)
Life expectancy (years) – 83.1 (2017 est)
Mortality rate – 6.4 (2017 est)
Birth rate – 13.7 (2017 est)
Infant mortality rate – 2.1 (2017 est)

CLIMATE AND TERRAIN
Iceland is a volcanic island in the North Atlantic Ocean, to the east of Greenland and to the west of Norway, and its northernmost point reaches the Arctic Circle. Some parts of the coastline have narrow strips of low-lying land; others are sheer cliffs. An inland plateau of glaciers, lakes and lava fields covers most of the interior, with mountainous areas in the north and at the four glaciers in the centre and south. Elevation extremes range from 2,110m (Hvannadalshnukur, on the Oraefajokull volcano) to 0m (North Atlantic Ocean). There are geysers and hot springs owing to the numerous active volcanoes, which can create new islands, such as Surtsey in 1963; the volcano under the Eyjafjallajokull glacier has been active since March 2010 after nearly 190 years of inactivity. It is estimated that over the past 500 years, Iceland has emitted one-third of the Earth's total lava flow. The climate is influenced by the Gulf Stream; average temperatures range from −1.7°C in January to 9.3°C in July.

HISTORY AND POLITICS

The first major settlement occurred from around AD 870 onwards, as turmoil in Scandinavia drove migrants to seek new homelands. Iceland hosted a flourishing Viking culture in the ninth and tenth centuries, becoming a fully Christian country in 1000. Iceland recognised Norwegian sovereignty in 1263 and, with Norway, came under Danish rule in 1397. When Norway was ceded to Sweden in 1814, Iceland remained Danish territory, achieving autonomy in domestic affairs in 1874. Although it became an independent state with the same sovereign as Denmark in 1918, Copenhagen continued to control its foreign policy and defence. The treaty of union with Denmark expired in 1943, while Denmark was under German occupation, and in a referendum Icelanders voted to become a fully independent republic, proclaimed on 17 June 1944.

The country's dependence on the fishing industry has led occasionally to fraught foreign relations. The introduction and extensions of an exclusive fishing limit around Iceland in 1958, 1972 and 1975 caused the so-called 'Cod War' disputes with the UK.

Post-independence politics was dominated by the conservative Independence Party (SSF) until January 2009, when the country's economic crisis forced the government first to call an early election, then to resign with immediate effect. The Progressive and Independence parties won the April 2013 parliamentary elections with 19 seats each and formed a coalition government in May. In 2015, Iceland announced that it would withdraw its EU accession bid, having been a candidate country since 2010. Following snap elections in October 2016 in which no single party gained a majority, it took three months to form a government of the Independence, Bright Future and Reform parties but this collapsed within the year. Following elections in October 2017, Katrin Jakobsdottir, the leader of the Left-Green Movement, was asked to form a new government, at the head of another three-party coalition. In June 2016, history professor Gudni Johannesson was elected president.

Under the 1944 constitution, the head of state is the president, who is directly elected for a four-year term, which is renewable. The unicameral legislature, the *Althing*, has 63 members, who are directly elected for a four-year term. Founded in AD 930, the *Althing* is the world's oldest functioning parliament.

HEAD OF STATE

President, Gudni Johannesson, *elected* 26 June 2016, *sworn in* 1 August 2016

SELECTED GOVERNMENT MEMBERS *AS AT JUNE 2018*

Prime Minister, Katrin Jakobsdottir
Finance, Bjarni Benediktsson
Foreign Affairs, Gudlaugur Thor Thordarson

EMBASSY OF ICELAND

2A Hans Street, London SW1X 0JE
T 020-7259 3999 E emb.london@mfa.is W www.iceland.is/uk
Ambassador Extraordinary and Plenipotentiary, HE Stefan Haukur Johannesson, *apptd* 2017

BRITISH EMBASSY

Laufasvegur 31, 101 Reykjavík
T (+354) 550 5100 E info@britishembassy.is
W www.gov.uk/government/world/iceland
Ambassador Extraordinary and Plenipotentiary, HE Michael Nevin, *apptd* 2016

ECONOMY AND TRADE

Iceland has a market economy with an extensive welfare system. While it remains heavily dependent on the fishing industry, tourism is now its major industry accounting for 8.6 per cent of GDP in 2016 and 39 per cent of total exports of merchandise and services. There has also been a recent diversification into aluminium smelting, ferrosilicon production, software production, biotechnology and tourism, encouraged by the plentiful supply of geothermal power. A major area of diversification was banking, but aggressive expansion in the 2000s led to over-exposure in foreign markets. In the 2008 global financial crisis, the three largest banks collapsed and the government required over US$10bn (£6.3bn) in loans to stabilise its currency and financial system. The economy contracted sharply, causing widespread unemployment and rapid inflation; GDP, however, rose steadily in 2011 and 2012 and the country has begun compensation payments to international claimants of failed Icelandic banks. In January 2013, Iceland awarded licences for oil and gas exploration and production in the waters off its north-east coast to Faroe Petroleum and Valiant Petroleum; Norway took a 25 per cent stake in both. EU accession negotiations started in 2010 but were suspended in 2013 amid concerns about loss of control of the fishing industry and the eurozone's ongoing financial troubles. In March 2017 capital controls were lifted, opening up new opportunities for foreign investment, and the economy has now largely returned to pre-crisis levels.

The main trading partners are the Netherlands, Germany and the UK. Principal exports are fish and fish products, aluminium, medicines and ferrosilicon. The main imports are machinery, petroleum products, foodstuffs and textiles.

GNI – US$20.8bn; US$60,830 per capita (2017)
Annual average growth of GDP – 5.5 per cent (2017 est)
Inflation rate – 1.8 per cent (2017 est)
Unemployment – 2.8 per cent (2017 est)
Total external debt – US$27.14bn (2017 est)
Imports – US$5,600m (2016)
Exports – US$4,500m (2016)

BALANCE OF PAYMENTS

Trade – US$1,099m deficit (2016)
Current Account – US$879m surplus (2017)

Trade with UK	2016	2017
Imports from UK	£558,109,776	£396,490,970
Exports to UK	£461,639,907	£515,878,286

COMMUNICATIONS

Airports – Seven, with the principal airports at Keflavik, near Reykjavik, in the south, and Akureyri in the north
Roadways – There are 4,782km of paved and oiled gravel roads
Telecommunications – 164,566 fixed lines and 401,613 mobile subscriptions (2016); there were 329,967 internet users in 2016
Internet code and IDD – is; 354 (from UK), 44 (to UK)
Major broadcasters – Icelandic National Broadcasting Service operates radio and television services across the country
Press – There are three major daily newspapers: *Frettabladid, Morgunbladid* and *DV*
WPFI score – 14,10 (13)

INDIA

Bharatiya Ganarajya – Republic of India

Area – 3,287,263 sq. km

Capital – New Delhi; population, 28,514,000 (2015 est)

Major cities – Ahmadabad, Bengaluru (Bangalore), Chennai (Madras), Hyderabad, Jaipur, Kanpur, Kolkata (Calcutta), Mumbai (Bombay), Pune, Surat

Currency – Indian rupee (Rs) of 100 paise

Population – 1,281,935,911 rising at 1.17 per cent a year (2017 est); Indo-Aryan (72 per cent), Dravidian (25 per cent) (2000 est)

Religion – Hindu 79.8 per cent, Muslim 14.2 per cent, Christian 2.3 per cent, Sikh 1.7 per cent (2011 est)

Language – Hindi (official national language), English, Assamese, Bengali, Bodo, Dogri, Gujarati, Kannada, Kashmiri, Konkani, Maithili, Malayalam, Manipuri, Marathi, Nepali, Oriya, Punjabi, Sanskrit, Santhali, Sindhi, Tamil, Telugu, Urdu (all official)

Population density – 445 per sq. km (2016)

Urban population – 34 per cent (2018 est)

Median age (years) – 27.9 (2017 est)

National anthem – 'Jana Gana Mana' 'Thou Art the Ruler of the Minds of all People'

National day – 26 January (Republic Day)

Death penalty – Retained

CPI score – 40 (81)

Military expenditure – US$63,924m (2017)

CLIMATE AND TERRAIN

India has three well-defined regions: the mountain range of the Himalayas, the Indo-Gangetic plain and the southern peninsula. The Himalayas along the northern border reach 8,598m (Kangchenjunga), then drop to the northern plains formed by the basins of the Indus, Ganges and Brahmaputra rivers before rising to low hills running east to west that mark the division with the southern Deccan peninsula. The peninsula has narrow coastal plains rising to a central plateau, with the Western Ghats and Eastern Ghats ranges of hills lying along the west and east coasts respectively. The Thar Desert lies in the north-west. The climate varies from tropical in the south to temperate in the north. It is influenced by the south-west monsoon; the main rainy season is June to October. During the drier season from December to May, the weather is cooler until February and then becomes increasingly hot until the monsoon breaks. The average temperature in New Delhi ranges from 13.8°C in January to 34°C in June.

POLITICS

Under the 1950 constitution, the president is elected for a five-year term by an electoral college consisting of members of both chambers of the legislature, with no term limits. The president appoints the prime minister, who is responsible to the legislature. The vice-president, who is elected by both chambers for a five-year term, is *ex-officio* chair of the upper chamber. The legislature, the *Sansad,* consists of two chambers. The upper chamber, the Council of States *(Rajya Sabha),* has up to 245 members, who serve a six-year term; up to 233 members are elected by the state legislative assemblies as individual terms expire, and 12 are nominated by the president. The House of the People *(Lok Sabha)* has 545 members; 543 are directly elected for a five-year term, and two representatives of the Anglo-Indian community are nominated by the president.

There are 28 states and seven union territories (including the national capital territory). Each state has its own executive, comprising a governor, who is appointed by the president for a five-year term, and a council of ministers. All states have a legislative assembly, and some also have a legislative council, elected directly for a maximum period of five years. The states have considerable autonomy, although the union government controls such matters as foreign policy, defence and external trade. The union territories are administered, except where otherwise provided by parliament, by a lieutenant-governor or an administrator appointed by the president.

In the legislative elections held in May 2014, the Bharatiya Janata Party (BJP) won a landslide victory against the incumbent India National Congress (INC) and its coalition partners, establishing India's first majority government since 1984 with 282 seats in the *Lok Sabha.* The 2014 legislative election saw the largest turnout in history with 551 million votes cast. The 2017 presidential election was won by Ram Nath Kovind, who was backed by the ruling BJP.

HEAD OF STATE

President, Ram Nath Kovind, *elected* 17 July 2017, *took office* 25 July 2017

Vice-President, M. Venkaiah Naidu

SELECTED GOVERNMENT MEMBERS *AS AT JUNE 2018*

Prime Minister, Narendra Modi

Defence, Nirmala Sitharaman

Finance, Arun Jaitley

Home Affairs, Kiren Rijiju

OFFICE OF THE HIGH COMMISSIONER FOR INDIA

India House, Aldwych, London WC2B 4NA

T 020-7836 8484 E info.london@hcilondon.in W www.hcilondon.in

High Commissioner, HE Y. K. Sinha, *apptd* 2017

BRITISH HIGH COMMISSION

Shantipath, Chanakyapuri, New Delhi 110021

T (+91) (11) 2419 2100 E web.newdelhi@fco.gov.uk

W www.gov.uk/government/world/india

High Commissioner, Sir Dominic Asquith, KCMG, *apptd* 2016

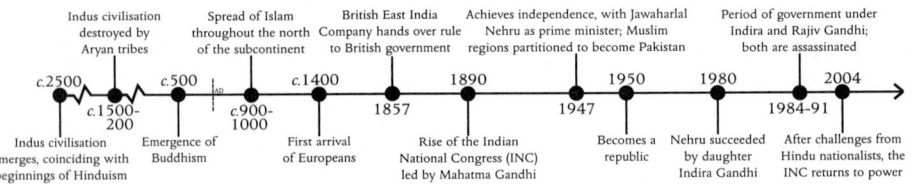

FOREIGN RELATIONS

Since partition, India and Pakistan have disputed sovereignty over the predominantly Muslim state of Jammu and Kashmir. A short war in 1947–8 resulted in the state being partitioned between the two countries; its status remains unresolved, despite further outbreaks of war in 1965 and 1971, low-level conflict for control of the Siachen glacier since 1985 and occasional increases in military exchanges, most recently in 1999–2002 and 2003. Tension was exacerbated by Pakistan's support of the Muslim insurgency in the Indian part of the state, which began in the late 1980s and has included terrorist attacks in Indian cities, and by both countries' acquisition of nuclear weapons. Moves towards a peaceful settlement began in 2003, when diplomatic missions were reopened and the resumption of transport links was initiated. Formal diplomatic talks began in 2004 and have achieved several accords intended to reduce tension between the two countries, although the status of Kashmir has yet to be addressed. Talks were temporarily suspended by the Indian government after the 2008 terrorist attacks on Mumbai, but were resumed in 2010 despite heightened tensions along Kashmir's Line of Control in late 2016 to 2017.

In the Sino-Indian war in 1962, India lost territory to China. In addition, China claims Arunachal Pradesh and does not recognise Indian sovereignty over Sikkim. Talks between India and China in 2003 resulted in India's formal recognition of the Tibetan Autonomous Region as a part of China and a cross-border trade agreement on Sikkim.

ECONOMY AND TRADE

The economy was closed for several decades after independence, with high import tariffs and limits on foreign investment intended to stimulate domestic growth. Since 1991, economic liberalisation and increased foreign investment have generated rapid expansion, with GDP growing by an average 7 per cent a year since 1997. Following a brief contraction in 2008–9 during the global economic downturn, growth exceeded 8 per cent in 2010, but slowed to a ten-year low in 2013 due to the economy performing poorly in a number of key areas. The economy continues to grow despite increasingly erratic monsoon seasons, which damage the agricultural sector.

India's large skilled workforce has enabled it to develop knowledge-based industries and become a global centre for manufacturing and services. Other areas of growth are pharmaceuticals, tourism and the provision of services to the burgeoning urban middle class. The rapidly-growing service sector now accounts for 61.5 per cent of GDP and industry for 23 per cent, employing 31 per cent and 22 per cent of the workforce respectively.

Although about 1 per cent of the population has been lifted out of poverty each year since 1997, rural areas have benefited disproportionately little from the economic growth. Agriculture, forestry and fishing support 47 per cent of the population and contribute 15.4 per cent of GDP. The main food crops are rice, cereals (principally wheat) and pulses. The major cash crops include cotton, jute, tea and sugar cane. Agriculture and forestry are threatened by deforestation, soil erosion, over-grazing and desertification.

Despite recent advances, the economy faces a number of problems, chiefly underinvestment in infrastructure and discrimination against women and girls. Economic constraints also include shortfalls in energy generation, excessive regulation, the pressures of rapid urbanisation and corruption.

The main trading partners are the USA, the UAE and China. Principal exports include petroleum products, precious stones, machinery, iron and steel, chemicals, vehicles and pharmaceuticals. Its main imports are crude oil, precious stones, machinery, fertiliser, iron and steel, and chemicals.

GNI – US$2,430.8bn; US$1,820 per capita (2017)
Annual average growth of GDP – 6.7 per cent (2017 est)
Inflation rate – 3.8 per cent (2017 est)
Population below poverty line – 21.9 per cent (2011 est)
Unemployment – 8.8 per cent (2017 est)
Total external debt – US$483.4bn (2017 est)
Imports – US$361,044m (2016)
Exports – US$264,616m (2016)

BALANCE OF PAYMENTS

Trade – US$96,428m deficit (2016)
Current Account – US$39,072m deficit (2017)

Trade with UK	2016	2017
Imports from UK	£3,274,444,955	£4,074,270,636
Exports to UK	£6,171,323,675	£7,229,284,203

COMMUNICATIONS

Airports – There are 253 airports and airfields, principally at Delhi, Mumbai, Chennai and Kolkata

Waterways – The chief seaports are Mumbai, Kolkata, Haldia, Chennai, Cochin, Visakhapatnam, Mangalore and Tuticorin; there are 340 ships of over 1,000 tonnes in the merchant fleet. There are 485km of canals and the great rivers provide around 5,200km of navigable waterways

Roadways and railways – 79,116km of motorways and 155,716km of state highways; 64,600km

Telecommunications – 24.4 million fixed lines and 1,127 million mobile subscriptions (2016); there were 374 million internet users in 2016

Internet code and IDD – in; 91 (from UK), 44 (to UK)

Major broadcasters – The public-owned Doordarshan network operates several national, regional and local services, and All India Radio is the country's largest radio broadcaster

Press – Eight major daily newspapers make up a lively press sector; these include *The Times of India, The Hindu* and *India Today*

WPFI score – 43,24 (138)

EDUCATION AND HEALTH

Education is free and became compulsory for children aged six to 14 years in April 2010.

Literacy rate – 90.2 per cent (2015 est)
Gross enrolment ratio (percentage of relevant age group) – primary 115 per cent, secondary 75 per cent, tertiary 27 per cent (2016 est)
Health expenditure (per capita) – US$75 (2014)
Hospital beds (per 1,000 people) – 0.7 (2011)
Life expectancy (years) – 68.8 (2017 est)
Mortality rate – 7.3 (2017 est)
Birth rate – 19 (2017 est)
Infant mortality rate – 39.1 (2017 est)
HIV/AIDS adult prevalence – 0.3 per cent (2016 est)

INDONESIA

Republik Indonesia – Republic of Indonesia
Area – 1,904,569 sq. km
Capital – Jakarta; population, 10,517,000 (2018 est)
Major cities – Bandung, Bekasi, Depok, Makasar, Medan, Palembang, Semarang, Surabaya, Tangerang
Currency – Rupiah (Rp) of 100 sen
Population – 260,580,739 rising at 0.86 per cent a year (2017 est); Javanese (40.1 per cent), Sundanese (15.5 per cent), Malay (3.7 per cent), Batak (3.6 per cent), Madurese (3 per cent), Belawi (2.9 per cent), Minangkabau (2.7 per cent) (2010 est)

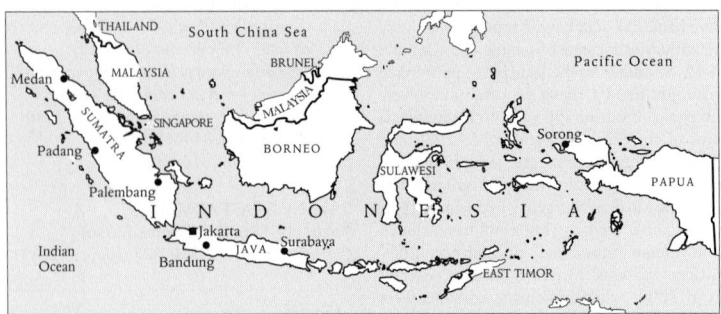

Religion – Muslim 87.2 per cent (predominantly Sunni), Christian 7 per cent, Hindu 1.7 per cent (2010 est)
Language – Bahasa Indonesia (official), English, Dutch, Javanese, over 580 languages and dialects
Population density – 144 per sq. km (2016)
Urban population – 55.3 per cent (2018 est)
Median age (years) – 30.2 (2017 est)
National anthem – 'Indonesia Raya' 'Great Indonesia'
National day – 17 August (Independence Day)
Death penalty – Retained
CPI score – 37 (96)
Military expenditure – US$8,178m (2017)
Conscription – 18–45 years of age; 24 months (selective)
Literacy rate – 99 per cent (2015 est)
Gross enrolment ratio (percentage of relevant age group) – primary 103 per cent, secondary 86 per cent, tertiary 28 per cent (2016 est)
Health expenditure (per capita) – US$99 (2014)
Hospital beds (per 1,000 people) – 1.2 (2015)
Life expectancy (years) – 73 (2017 est)
Mortality rate – 6.5 (2017 est)
Birth rate – 16.2 (2017 est)
Infant mortality rate – 22.7 (2017 est)
HIV/AIDS adult prevalence – 0.4 per cent (2016 est)

CLIMATE AND TERRAIN

Indonesia is an archipelago of over 17,500 islands, of which about 6,000 are inhabited. They include the islands of Sumatra, Java, Madura, Bali, Lombok, Sumbawa, Sumba, Flores, the Riouw-Lingga archipelago, Bangka and Billiton, part of the island of Borneo (Kalimantan), Sulawesi (formerly Celebes), the Maluku (formerly Moluccas) archipelago and others comprising the provinces of East and West Nusa Tenggara, and the western halves of the islands of New Guinea (Papua; formerly Irian Jaya) and Timor. Many of the islands have narrow coastal plains with hilly or mountainous interiors, and around half of the country is covered by tropical rainforest. Elevation extremes range from 4,884m (Puncak Jaya, in Papua) to 0m (Indian Ocean). The climate is tropical; the average temperature is 26.2°C and rainfall peaks in January and February, and is lowest in August.

The country is located near to an intersection of tectonic plates, making it susceptible to seismic activity such as earthquakes and volcanic eruptions; in January 2014 the eruption of Mt Kelud caused mass evacuations in East Java. Indonesia's weather patterns are being affected by climate change. In November 2017, Mount Agung volcano on the island of Bali erupted five times, causing thousands to evacuate, disrupting travel and causing significant environmental damage.

HISTORY AND POLITICS

Hindu and Buddhist kingdoms existed in some parts of the Indonesian islands until the 14th century. Islam was introduced in the 13th century and spread over the next three centuries. Trading by the Portuguese began in the 16th century, but the Portuguese were displaced by the Dutch who, lured by the rich spice trade, came to dominate Indonesia by the early 20th century. Opposition to Dutch rule grew in the 1920s and the Japanese occupation of Indonesia during the Second World War strengthened nationalism, leading to a declaration of independence after liberation in 1945. This was not recognised by the Dutch, but after four years of guerrilla warfare they granted independence to the Netherlands Indies in 1949. Irian Jaya (now Papua) was annexed in 1963. Timor–Leste was invaded and annexed in 1975 but gained its independence in 2002.

Achmed Soekarno, the foremost proponent of self-rule since the 1920s, became president in 1949 but was deposed in 1966 in a military coup suppressed by General Suharto, who subsequently became president. Suharto remained in power until 1998 when, amid economic and social upheaval, he was succeeded by his deputy B. J. Habibie. Habibie was defeated in 1999 by Abdurrahman Wahid, in the first democratic elections for 44 years. President Wahid was impeached for alleged financial corruption and in 2001 the legislature appointed Megawati Soekarnoputri (daughter of Achmed Soekarno) to replace him.

The April 2014 legislative elections were won by the ruling Democratic Party and the July 2014 presidential election by their candidate, Joko Widodo. The results were subsequently challenged by his opponent Prabowo Subianto who alleged that widespread electoral fraud had taken place. In August, the Constitutional Court rejected the claims, allowing Widodo to form a cabinet in October 2014.

The 1959 constitution was amended in 2001 to provide for the establishment of the upper chamber of the legislature, and in 2002 to provide for the direct election of the president and the abolition of parliamentary seats reserved for the armed forces.

The executive president is directly elected for a five-year term, renewable once, and appoints the cabinet. The bicameral People's Consultative Assembly comprises the House of Representatives, which has 560 members directly elected for a five-year term, and the Regional Representative Council, which has 132 members, four for each province, directly elected on a non-partisan basis for a five-year term.

HEAD OF STATE
President, Joko Widodo, *elected* 22 July 2014
Vice-President, Jusuf Kalla

SELECTED GOVERNMENT MEMBERS *AS AT JUNE 2018*
Defence, Ryamizard Ryacudu
Finance, Sri Mulyani Indrawati
Foreign Affairs, Retno Lestari Priansari Marsudi

EMBASSY OF THE REPUBLIC OF INDONESIA
30 Great Peter Street, London SW1P 2BU
T 020-7499 7661 E kbri@btconnect.com
W www.indonesianembassy.org.uk
Ambassador Extraordinary and Plenipotentiary, HE Dr Rizal
Sukma, *apptd* 2016

BRITISH EMBASSY
Jl Patra Kuningan Raya Blok L5-6, Jakarta 12950
T (+62) (21) 2356 5200 E jakarta.mcs@fco.gov.uk
W http://ukinindonesia.fco.gov.uk
Ambassador Extraordinary and Plenipotentiary, HE Moazzam
Malik, *apptd* 2014

INSURGENCIES
Separatist movements developed in several parts of Indonesia
after independence, including Maluku, which fought an
unsuccessful separatist war in the 1950s; Irian Jaya (now
Papua), which was granted greater autonomy in 2002,
although separatist agitation continues; Timor–Leste, from its
annexation in 1975 until independence in 2002; and Aceh
province in Sumatra, which was granted a degree of
autonomy in 2005.

Since the fall of Suharto in 1998, tensions between different
ethnic and religious groups have surfaced, and there has been
intercommunal violence in Kalimantan (1996–7, 1999,
2001), Sulawesi (1998–2000, 2001, 2005) and Maluku
(1999–2002, 2004).

Muslim extremist groups that claim links with al-Qaida have
been held responsible for bombings in Bali in 2002 and
2005, and Jakarta in 2003, 2004 and 2009, while groups
with links to IS have been blamed for attacks in Jakarta in
2016–17 and Surabaya in 2018.

ECONOMY AND TRADE
The largest economy in Southeast Asia, it struggled from the
late 1990s until recent years as it was hit in succession by the
Asian financial crisis, the political turmoil following the fall of
Suharto, and a downturn in tourism following the Bali and
Jakarta bombings. A number of natural disasters since 2004
have also disrupted the economy, including widespread
damage caused by an earthquake in August 2018. Significant
economic reforms in 2004–8 reduced debt, unemployment
and inflation, and boosted growth. Although growth slowed
in 2008, government stimulus measures countered the effect
of the global downturn in 2009 and by 2011 Indonesia's
credit rating was raised to investment grade due mainly to its
low rates of inflation and small current account surplus. The
economy slowed for a fourth consecutive year in 2014, but
has since improved and is expected to continue growing
partly due to investment in infrastructure and the reform of
expensive government fuel subsidies. Indonesia became a
member of the Asian Economic Community on 31 December
2015.

Natural resources include oil, tin, natural gas, nickel, timber,
bauxite, copper, coal, gold and silver. However, a lack of
investment in prospecting for new sources has led to a decline
in oil production and Indonesia has been a net importer since
2004. The exploitation and processing of mineral assets,
production of textiles, clothing, cement, fertilisers, plywood
and rubber, and tourism are the main industrial activities;
industry accounts for 40.3 per cent of GDP and services 45.9
per cent, employing 21 per cent and 47 per cent of the
workforce respectively. Agriculture contributes 13.9 per cent
of GDP but employs 32 per cent of the workforce. The main
crops are rice, cassava, peanuts, rubber, cocoa, coffee, palm oil,
copra and livestock products.

The main trading partners are Singapore, Japan, China, the
USA, South Korea and India. Principal exports are oil and

natural gas, animal and vegetable fats, electrical appliances,
plywood, rubber and machinery. The main imports are fuel,
machinery, and foodstuffs.

GNI – US$934.4bn; US$3,540 per capita (2017)
Annual average growth of GDP – 5.2 per cent (2017 est)
Inflation rate – 4.0 per cent (2017 est)
Population below poverty line – 10.9 per cent (2016)
Unemployment – 5.4 per cent (2017 est)
Total external debt – US$322.6bn (2017 est)
Imports – US$135,549m (2016)
Exports – US$144,291m (2016)

BALANCE OF PAYMENTS
Trade – US$8,742m surplus (2016)
Current Account – US$17,527m deficit (2017)

Trade with UK	2016	2017
Imports from UK	£530,432,374	£777,318,480
Exports to UK	£1,226,399,348	£1,128,221,729

COMMUNICATIONS
Airports – 186; each of the main islands has a major airport,
with most capable of accepting international flights
Waterways – There are nine major ports, usually the chief
towns of the major islands, and the merchant fleet contains
1,340 ships of over 1,000 tonnes
Roadways and railways – 283,102km; 5,042km
Telecommunications – 10.7 million fixed lines and 385 million
mobile subscriptions (2016); there were 65 million internet
users in 2016
Internet code and IDD – id; 62 (from UK), 1 44/8 44 (to UK)
Major broadcasters – Radio and Televisi Republik Indonesia,
the country's principal broadcaster, operates six television and
two radio networks
Press – *The Jakarta Post* and *The Jakarta Globe* dominate a
competitive market that includes eight other dailies
WPFI score – 39,68 (124)

IRAN

Jomhuri-ye Eslami-ye Iran – Islamic Republic of Iran

Area – 1,648,195 sq. km
Capital – Tehran; population, 8,896,000 (2018 est)
Major cities – Ahvaz, Esfahan, Karaj, Mashhad, Qom, Shiraz,
Tabriz
Currency – Iranian rial of 100 dinar
Population – 82,021,564 rising at 1.24 per cent a year (2017
est); Persian (61 per cent), Azeri (16 per cent), Kurdish (10
per cent), Lur (6 per cent), Arab (2 per cent), Baloch (2 per
cent), Turkmen (2 per cent) (est)

Religion – Muslim (official) 99.4 per cent (Shia 90–5 per cent, Sunni 5–10 per cent) (est); small Zoroastrian, Jewish, Christian and Baha'i minorities
Language – Persian (official), Turkic, Kurdish, Luri, Balochi, Arabic, Turkish
Population density – 49 per sq. km (2016)
Urban population – 74.9 per cent (2018 est)
Median age (years) – 30.3 (2017 est)
National anthem – 'Sorud-e Melli-e Jomhouri-ye Eslami-ye Iran' 'National Anthem of the Islamic Republic of Iran'
National day – 1 April (Republic Day)
Death penalty – Retained
CPI score – 30 (130)
Military expenditure – US$14,548m (2017)
Conscription – 18 years of age, male only; 18 months

CLIMATE AND TERRAIN

Apart from narrow coastal plains on the Gulf coasts and the shores of the Caspian Sea, the interior is a plateau consisting of barren desert in the centre and east. This is enclosed by high mountains in the west and north, with smaller ranges on the eastern border and the southern coast. Elevation extremes range from 5,671m (Kuh-e Damavand) to −28m (Caspian Sea). Earthquakes are frequent. The climate is arid or semi-arid in the interior, and subtropical on the Caspian shores. Average temperatures are 5.2°C in January and 29.8°C in July.

POLITICS

Under the 1979 constitution, overall authority rests with the spiritual leader of the republic, who is appointed for life by the Assembly of Experts; this consists of 83 clerics who are directly elected and decide religious and spiritual matters. The executive president is directly elected for a four-year term, renewable once. Ministers are nominated by the president but must be approved by the legislature. The unicameral Consultative Council *(Majlis al-Shoura)* has 290 members who are directly elected for a four-year term on a non-party basis; five seats are reserved for religious minorities. Laws passed by the legislature must be approved by the Council of Guardians of the Constitution, six theologians appointed by the spiritual leader and six jurists nominated by the judiciary and approved by the legislature; it also has a supervisory role in elections. In 1997, the Constitutional Surveillance Council, a five-member body, was established to supervise the proper application of constitutional laws.

Mahmoud Ahmadinejad won the presidential elections in 2005 and 2009. The results of the 2009 election were challenged by the other candidates, who alleged electoral fraud. Following massive protest rallies, the Council of Guardians confirmed Ahmadinejad's victory and ruled out an annulment; further popular protests were suppressed. After the protests in summer 2009, Ahmadinejad's government ruthlessly suppressed the opposition (the Green Movement) and purged liberals from official positions. In the June 2013 presidential elections, moderate candidate Hassan Rouhani defeated the conservative mayor of Tehran, Mohammed Baqer Qaliaf, gaining 50 per cent of the vote. Legislative elections in February 2016 appeared to consolidate President Rouhani's position, with wins for moderate and reformist

candidates, particularly in Tehran, plus notable successes for female candidates; he was re-elected president in May 2017, winning 59 per cent of the vote.
Spiritual Leader of the Islamic Republic and C.-in-C. of Armed Forces, Ayatollah Seyed Ali Khamenei, *apptd* June 1989
President, Hassan Rouhani, *elected* 15 June 2013, *re-elected* 19 May 2017
First Vice-President, Es'haq Jahangiri

SELECTED GOVERNMENT MEMBERS *AS AT JUNE 2018*
Defence, Brig.-Gen. Amir Hatami
Economy and Finance, Masoud Karbasian
Foreign Affairs, Mohammad Javad Zarif

EMBASSY OF THE ISLAMIC REPUBLIC OF IRAN
16 Prince's Gate, London SW7 1PT
T 020-7225 4208 W london.mfa.ir
Ambassador Extraordinary and Plenipotentiary, HE Hamid Baeidinejad, *apptd* 2016

BRITISH EMBASSY
198 Ferdowsi Avenue, 11316–91144, Tehran
T (+44) 19 0851 6666 W www.gov.uk/government/world/iran
Ambassador Extraordinary and Plenipotentiary, HE Robert Macaire, CMG, *apptd* 2018

FOREIGN RELATIONS
Between 1980 and 1988, Iran was engaged in a bitter war with Iraq over the Shatt-al-Arab waterway. Iran remained neutral in the Gulf War (1991) and the Iraq War (2003), but it has been accused since of subverting reconstruction in Iraq by arming Shia insurgents.

Since the 1978 revolution, Iran's relations with the West, and especially the USA and the UK, have been strained. It has not cooperated with international efforts to achieve peace in the Middle East, and has long been suspected of sponsoring terrorism by Islamic fundamentalists, especially in Lebanon and Palestine, as well as supporting the regime in Syria.

Since 2002 international relations deteriorated further because of concerns over Iran's nuclear and ballistic missile programmes, especially its acquisition of the ability to enrich uranium. The UN passed six resolutions from 2006 to 2010 calling on Iran to suspend uranium enrichment and reprocessing, and to comply with its IAEA obligations and responsibilities; four of the resolutions imposed or extended sanctions on trade and travel. In an escalation of the nuclear row, the EU imposed an oil embargo on Iran in January 2012, after the country reportedly began to enrich uranium at its underground plant in Fordo. In July 2015, Iran accepted strict limits on its nuclear programme in exchange for the lifting of sanctions. The country pledged to reduce the number of gas centrifuges by two-thirds, engage solely in non-military research at Fordo and reduce its stockpile of enriched uranium by 98 per cent. However, the deal was undermined following the withdrawal of United States in May 2018, and international efforts to salvage the agreement look uncertain.

Following an attack on the British embassy in November 2011, Britain closed its embassy in Tehran and expelled all Iranian diplomats from London, but the embassy reopened in August 2015.

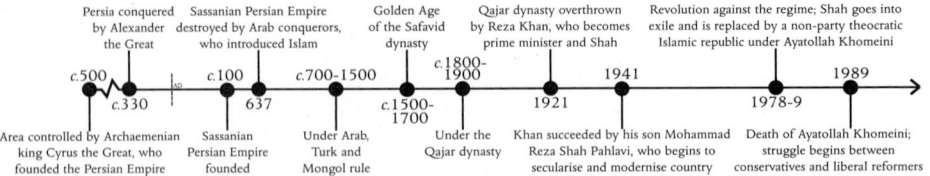

| Persia conquered by Alexander the Great | Sassanian Persian Empire destroyed by Arab conquerors, who introduced Islam | Golden Age of the Safavid dynasty | Qajar dynasty overthrown by Reza Khan, who becomes prime minister and Shah | Revolution against the regime; Shah goes into exile and is replaced by a non-party theocratic Islamic republic under Ayatollah Khomeini |

c.500   c.100   c.700–1500   c.1800–1900   1941   1989
c.330   637   c.1500–1700   1921   1978-9

Area controlled by Archaemenian king Cyrus the Great, who founded the Persian Empire | Sassanian Persian Empire founded | Under Arab, Turk and Mongol rule | Under the Qajar dynasty | Khan succeeded by his son Mohammad Reza Shah Pahlavi, who begins to secularise and modernise country | Death of Ayatollah Khomeini; struggle begins between conservatives and liberal reformers

ECONOMY AND TRADE

Iran was one of the best-performing economies in the Middle East owing to its vast reserves of oil and natural gas, but its performance has been deteriorating; the predominantly state-controlled economy is inefficient, with little diversification and only a limited, small-scale private sector. Unemployment and underemployment are serious problems, and there is a flourishing unofficial economy. Falling oil prices in 2008–10 and UN sanctions exacerbated Iran's economic problems. The election of the reformer Hassan Rouhani coincided with a strengthened national currency and an increase in the value of the Tehran stock exchange. The economy left recession in 2014 and benefited from opportunities for foreign investment since the 2015 nuclear deal, but fresh US sanctions imposed in 2018 has coincided with public protests over the economy, and the poor economic performance is likely to continue.

Oil and gas extraction and processing dominate the economy, but other industries include petrochemicals, textiles, construction materials, food processing, metal fabrication and armaments. Agricultural production includes wheat, rice, other grains, sugar beet and sugar cane, fruit, nuts, cotton, dairy products, wool and caviar.

The main trading partners are China, the UAE, Turkey, India and South Korea. Principal exports are petroleum (60 per cent), chemical and petrochemical products, fruit and nuts, carpets and cement. The main imports are industrial raw materials and intermediate goods, capital goods, foodstuffs, consumer goods and technical services.

GNI – US$438.4bn; US$5,400 per capita (2017)
Annual average growth of GDP – 3.5 per cent (2017 est)
Inflation rate – 10.5 per cent (2017 est)
Population below poverty line – 18.7 per cent (2007 est)
Unemployment – 12.4 per cent (2017 est)
Total external debt – US$10.56bn (2017 est)
Imports – US$42,500m (2015)
Exports – US$63,000m (2015)

BALANCE OF PAYMENTS

Trade – US$20,500m surplus (2015)
Current Account – US$3,063m surplus (2015 est)

Trade with UK	2016	2017
Imports from UK	£143,983,254	£226,335,760
Exports to UK	£40,257,098	£25,854,927

COMMUNICATIONS

Airports and waterways – 140; the principal airports are at Tehran and Shiraz; Iran's seaports include Asaluyeh, Bushehr and Abadan on the Persian Gulf, and Bandar Abbas on the Strait of Hormuz
Roadways and railways – There are 160,366km of roadways, including 1,948km of motorways, and 8,442km of railways
Telecommunications – 30.7 million fixed lines and 80.5 million mobile subscriptions (2016); there were 36.1 million internet users in 2016
Internet code and IDD – ir; 98 (from UK), 44 (to UK)
Major broadcasters – Islamic Republic of Iran Broadcasting is the state-run broadcast media with approximately 50 channels, including news, and 16 radio channels; no private, independent broadcasters
Press – Major daily newspapers include the English-language daily *Tehran Times,* the conservative *Kayhan* and reformist *Sharq*
WPFI score – 60,71 (164)

EDUCATION AND HEALTH

Primary education, between age six and 14, is compulsory and free.
Literacy rate – 98.4 per cent (2015 est)
Gross enrolment ratio (percentage of relevant age group) – primary 108.9 per cent, secondary 89.2 per cent (2016 est), tertiary 69 per cent (2017 est)
Health expenditure (per capita) – US$351 (2014)
Hospital beds (per 1,000 people) – 0.2 (2014)
Life expectancy (years) – 74 (2017 est)
Mortality rate – 5.3 (2017 est)
Birth rate – 17.9 (2017 est)
Infant mortality rate – 15.9 (2017 est)
HIV/AIDS adult prevalence – 0.1 per cent (2016 est)

IRAQ

Jumhuriyat al-Iraq / Komar-i Eraq – Republic of Iraq

Area – 438,317 sq. km
Capital – Baghdad; population, 6,643,000 (2018 est)
Major cities – Arbil, Basra, Karbala, Kirkuk, Mosul, Najaf, Sulaymaniyah
Currency – Iraqi dinar (NID) of 1,000 fils
Population – 39,192,111 rising at 2.55 per cent a year (2017 est); Arab (75–80 per cent), Kurdish (15–20 per cent) (est)
Religion – Muslim (official) 99 per cent (of which Shia 60–5 per cent, Sunni 32–7 per cent), Christian 0.8 per cent (predominantly Chaldean Catholic) (est)
Language – Arabic (official), Kurdish (official in Kurdish Autonomous Region), Turkoman, Assyrian, Armenian
Population density – 86 per sq. km (2016 est)
Urban population – 70.5 per cent (2018 est)
Median age (years) – 20 (2017 est)
National anthem – 'Mawtini' 'My Homeland'
National day – 14 July (Republic Day)
Death penalty – Retained
CPI score – 18 (169)
Military expenditure – US$6,233m (2016)

CLIMATE AND TERRAIN

The north-west and south of Iraq consist of an almost barren desert plain. The area between the Euphrates and Tigris rivers, which run across the country from north-west to south-east, is fertile, irrigated and heavily cultivated. The rivers run through marshland to their outflow in the Persian Gulf, on which Iraq has a 58km coastline. In the north-east the land rises to the Kurdistan mountains. Elevation extremes range from 3,611m (Cheekha Dar) to 0m (Persian Gulf). The climate is mostly desert, though colder and wetter in the mountains. Average temperatures range from 8.9°C in January to 33.9°C in July and August.

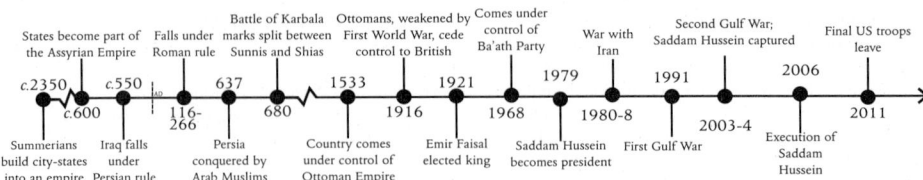

States become part of the Assyrian Empire | Falls under Roman rule | Battle of Karbala marks split between Sunnis and Shias | Ottomans, weakened by First World War, cede control to British | Comes under control of Ba'ath Party | War with Iran | Second Gulf War; Saddam Hussein captured | Final US troops leave

c.2350 | c.550 | 637 | 1533 | 1921 | 1979 | 1991 | 2006

c.600 | 116–266 | 680 | 1916 | 1968 | 1980-8 | 2003-4 | 2011

Summerians build city-states into an empire | Iraq falls under Persian rule | Persia conquered by Arab Muslims | Country comes under control of Ottoman Empire | Emir Faisal elected king | Saddam Hussein becomes president | First Gulf War | Execution of Saddam Hussein

POLITICS

Under the 2005 constitution, the president is elected by the legislature for a four-year term, renewable once. The president nominates the prime minister, subject to the approval of the legislature. The unicameral Council of Representatives *(Majlis al-Nuwab)* has 329 members, with nine seats reserved for minority groups; members are directly elected for a four-year term.

After several months of negotiations following the March 2010 elections, the Iraqi National Movement (al-Iraqiya), SL and Kurdistan Alliance (KA) blocs agreed to form a coalition government under Nouri al-Maliki, and this was sworn in on 21 December. Jalal Talabani (1933–2017), the Kurdish president of the interim government in 2005 and re-elected to the office in 2006, was re-elected for a second term in November 2010. In the April 2014 legislative elections al-Maliki's coalition remained the largest political grouping and Fouad Massoum was elected president in July. The military victories of Islamic State (IS) in the north of the country resulted in al-Maliki's resignation as prime minister in August in favour an inclusive government headed by Haider al-Abadi. Legislative elections in May 2018 was followed by a lengthy recount and months of political deadlock as competing blocs claimed victory, amid violent protests over unemployment and poor public services. As at September 2018 no government had been formed.

HEAD OF STATE
President, Fouad Massoum, *elected* 24 July 2014

SELECTED GOVERNMENT MEMBERS *AS AT SEPTEMBER 2018*
Prime Minister, Haider al-Abadi
Finance, vacant
Foreign Affairs, Ibrahim al-Jaafari

EMBASSY OF THE REPUBLIC OF IRAQ
21 Queens Gate, London SW7 5JE
T 020-7590 7650 E lonemb@mofaml.gov.iq
W www.iraqembassy.org.uk
Ambassador Extraordinary and Plenipotentiary, HE Dr Salih Husain Ali, *apptd* 2015

BRITISH EMBASSY
International Zone, Baghdad
T (+964) 790 192 6280 E baghdad.consularenquiries@fco.gov.uk
W www.gov.uk/government/world/iraq
Ambassador Extraordinary and Plenipotentiary, HE Jon Wilks, CMG, *apptd* 2017

INTERNAL UNREST
There are about 4 million Kurds in north-east Iraq, in areas adjoining the predominantly Kurdish areas in Iran and Turkey. Iraq's Kurdish nationalists have demanded an autonomous homeland, Kurdistan, since the 1960s, and turned to militant tactics in the 1970s. Their demands were opposed by Saddam Hussein's regime with great brutality. An uprising after the Gulf War (1991) was suppressed by Iraqi troops, prompting the creation of UN safe havens, which enabled the Kurds to set up a semi-autonomous region in the north. An air exclusion zone was also established, but there was further conflict with Iraqi forces and between the two main Kurdish parties in the 1990s. During the war in 2003, Kurdish fighters fought alongside US troops in the north, taking control of the northern cities and establishing an administration in the area, which is now autonomous.

The Shias in southern Iraq also rebelled after the Gulf War and were brutally suppressed. The UN established an air exclusion zone over southern Iraq in 1992 to protect the population, but persecution continued until 2003.

After May 2003, there was insurgent activity throughout the country, particularly in the Baghdad area, the predominantly Sunni-populated towns in the centre and west of the country, and in and around Mosul. The level of violence dropped after 2007 because of the US military 'surge', a ceasefire by one of the main militias, the Mahdi Army, from August 2007, and a key Sunni militia, the Awakening movement, turning against al-Qaida. There was an upsurge of violence in 2008 as the government mounted offensives against militias in Basra, Mosul and parts of Baghdad, and another upsurge in 2009–10 in the run-up to the legislative election and in the months following its inconclusive result. The approximate number of deaths as at December 2010 was: Iraqi civilians 99,000–108,000; US troops 4,400; and other coalition troops 318. Sectarian violence has continued following the withdrawal of coalition troops; in 2012 Shia areas were targeted with numerous bomb and gun attacks. In 2013 a series of deadly bomb attacks marked the ten-year anniversary of the US-led invasion.

In January 2014, after seizing territory in the east of Syria, IS captured the Iraqi cities of Fallujah and Ramadi. Mosul, Iraq's second largest city, Tikrit and the Kurdish city of Kirkuk were captured in June. Iraqi forces reclaimed Ramadi with US support in December 2015 but the local Anbar government warned civilians not to return to the city due to unexploded munitions. In June 2016 government forces entered the centre of Fallujah while Mosul was recaptured in July 2017. The government declared victory over IS in Decemeber 2017.

ECONOMY AND TRADE
The economy suffered three decades of state intervention, mismanagement, corruption, militarisation, war and international sanctions as well as the looting, insurgency and sabotage that followed the 2003 Allied invasion. With the improvement in the security situation, economic activity had increased and a debt-reduction programme had been arranged. However, civil conflict, political upheaval and low oil prices caused the economy to contract in 2014–17, with corruption and a lack of economic and legal reforms further deterring foreign investment. Prospects have since improved following the decline of IS and, in late 2017, receiving an international loan of US$1.4bn for reconstruction.

Oil is the main resource and export, providing more than 80 per cent of foreign exchange earnings. Other industries include chemicals, textiles, construction materials, food processing and metal fabrication.

The main trading partners are Turkey (27.8 per cent of imports), China, India and the USA. Principal exports are crude

oil (99 per cent), other crude materials, food and livestock. The main imports are food, medicine and manufactured goods.
GNI – US$182.6bn; US$4,700 per capita (2017)
Annual average growth of GDP – -0.4 per cent (2017 est)
Inflation rate – 2.0 per cent (2016 est)
Population below poverty line – 23 per cent (2014 est)
Unemployment – 16 per cent (2012 est)
Total external debt – US$73.43bn (2017 est)
Imports – US$52,000m (2015)
Exports – US$49,320m (2015)

BALANCE OF PAYMENTS
Trade – US$2,680m deficit (2015)
Current Account – US$3,843m surplus (2016)

Trade with UK	2016	2017
Imports from UK	£223,458,800	£325,775,204
Exports to UK	£7,548,326	£6,085,996

COMMUNICATIONS
Airports and waterways – 72; the main international airport is at Baghdad; the 5,279km of waterways are primarily on the Tigris and Euphrates rivers
Roadways and railways – 59,623km; 2,370km
Telecommunications – 2 million fixed lines and 30 million mobile subscriptions (2016); there were 8 million internet users in 2016
Internet code and IDD – iq; 964 (from UK), 44 (to UK)
Major broadcasters – State-run services include Al-Iraqiya (TV) and Republic of Iraq Radio; there are several private radio and television broadcasters
Press – There are more than 100 newspapers and periodicals, many with an ethnic or religious affiliation; publications include the state-run *Al-Sabah*, the private *Al-Mada* and the London-based *Al-Zaman*
WPFI score – 56,56 (160)

EDUCATION AND HEALTH
Since 2003 the country's education system has been reviewed and over 2,500 schools have been refurbished. Primary education is compulsory.
Literacy rate – 79.7 per cent (2015 est)
Health expenditure (per capita) – US$292 (2014)
Hospital beds (per 1,000 people) – 1.4 (2014)
Life expectancy (years) – 74.9 (2017 est)
Mortality rate – 3.8 (2017 est)
Birth rate – 30.4 (2017 est)
Infant mortality rate – 37.5 (2017 est)

IRELAND

Eire – Ireland

Area – 70,273 sq. km
Capital – Dublin *(Baile Atha Cliath);* population, 1,201,000 (2018 est)

Major cities – Cork (Corcaigh), Donegal (Dun na nGall), Galway (Gaillimh), Limerick (Liumneach), Swords (Sord Cholm Cille), Waterford (Port Lairge)
Currency – Euro (€) of 100 cents
Population – 5,011,102 rising at 1.15 per cent a year (2017 est)
Religion – Christian (Roman Catholic 84.7 per cent, Church of Ireland 2.7 per cent), Muslim 1.1 per cent (2011 est)
Language – English, Irish (Gaelic) (both official)
Population density – 70 per sq. km (2016)
Urban population – 63.2 per cent (2018 est)
Median age (years) – 36.8 (2017 est)
National anthem – 'Amhran na bhFiann' 'The Soldier's Song'
National day – 17 March (St Patrick's Day)
Death penalty – Abolished for all crimes (since 1990)
CPI score – 74 (19)
Military expenditure – US$11,117m (2017)

CLIMATE AND TERRAIN
The greatest length of the island of Ireland is 486km, from Torr Head in the north-east to Mizen Head in the south-west, and the greatest breadth is 280km, from Dundrum Bay in the east to Annagh Head in the west. Northern Ireland, in the north-east, is part of the UK. The republic has a central plain broken by hills and numerous lakes and bogs. It is surrounded by low mountains, including the Wicklow, Knockmealdown, Galty and Boggeragh mountains, and drained by the principal river, the Shannon (386km), which flows into the Atlantic Ocean. On the north coast of Achill Island (Co. Mayo) are the highest cliffs in the British Isles, 609m above sea level. Elevation extremes range from 1,041m (Carrauntoohil, Co. Kerry) to 0m (Atlantic Ocean).

POLITICS
Under the 1937 constitution, the president *(Uachtaran na Eireann)* is directly elected for a seven-year term, renewable once. The bicameral National Parliament *(Oireachtas)* consists of the House of Representatives *(Dail Eireann)* and the senate *(Seanad Eireann)*. The *Dail* has 158 members, elected for a five-year term by proportional representation. The *Seanad* has 60 members, who serve a five-year term; of these, 11 are nominated by the prime minister *(Taoiseach)* and 49 are elected, six by the universities and 43 from panels of candidates representing various sectoral interests.
  The *Taoiseach* is appointed by the president on the nomination of the *Dail,* while other members of the government are appointed by the president on the nomination of the *Taoiseach* with the previous approval of the *Dail.* The *Taoiseach* appoints a member of the government to be the deputy prime minister *(Tanaiste).*
  Support for the Labour-Fine Gail (FG) government slumped at the February 2016 election despite a strong economy. In late April, FG leader Enda Kenny formed a minority government after the opposition, Fianna Fail, pledged its support for two years in an unprecedented deal. Leo Varadkar was elected FG leader in June 2017 following Kenny's retirement and formally elected *Taoiseach* by parliament on the 14th. Following the relaxation of same-sex marriage in 2015, a referendum in May 2018 on the nation's strict abortion laws resulted overwhelmingly in support for their relaxation. Labour Party candidate Michael D. Higgins won the 2011 presidential election.

HEAD OF STATE
President, Michael D. Higgins, *elected* 27 October 2011, *confirmed in office* 11 November 2011

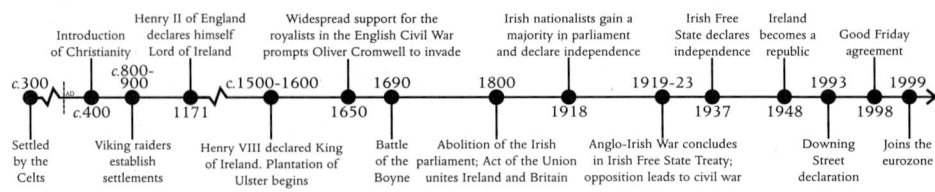

Introduction of Christianity *c.*300

Henry II of England declares himself Lord of Ireland *c.*800-900

Widespread support for the royalists in the English Civil War prompts Oliver Cromwell to invade *c.*1500-1600

1690

Irish nationalists gain a majority in parliament and declare independence 1800

Irish Free State declares independence 1919-23

Ireland becomes a republic 1993

Good Friday agreement 1999

*c.*400   1171   1650   1918   1937   1948   1998

Settled by the Celts

Viking raiders establish settlements

Henry VIII declared King of Ireland. Plantation of Ulster begins

Battle of the Boyne

Abolition of the Irish parliament; Act of the Union unites Ireland and Britain

Anglo-Irish War concludes in Irish Free State Treaty; opposition leads to civil war

Downing Street declaration

Joins the eurozone

SELECTED GOVERNMENT MEMBERS *AS AT JULY 2018*
Taoiseach (Prime Minister), Leo Varadkar
Tanaiste (Deputy Prime Minister), Foreign Affairs, Trade, Simon Coveney
Finance, Paschal Donohoe

EMBASSY OF IRELAND
17 Grosvenor Place, London SW1X 7HR
T 020-7235 2171 **E** londonembassymail@dfa.ie
W www.embassyofireland.co.uk
Ambassador Extraordinary and Plenipotentiary, HE Adrian O'Neill, *apptd* 2017

BRITISH EMBASSY
29 Merrion Road, Ballsbridge, Dublin 4
T (+353) (1) 205 3700 **W** www.gov.uk/government/world/ireland
Ambassador Extraordinary and Plenipotentiary, HE Robin Barnett, CMG, *apptd* 2016

GNI – US$266.2bn; US$55,920 per capita (2017)
Annual average growth of GDP – 4.1 per cent (2017 est)
Inflation rate – 0.4 per cent (2016 est)
Population below poverty line – 8.2 per cent (2013 est)
Unemployment – 6.4 per cent (2017 est)
Total external debt – US$2.47 trillion (2016 est)
Imports – US$71,424m (2016)
Exports – US$127,210m (2016)

BALANCE OF PAYMENTS
Trade – US$55,786m surplus (2016)
Current Account – US$42,719m surplus (2017)

Trade with UK	2016	2017
Imports from UK	£16,945,550,477	£19,391,101,999
Exports to UK	£13,137,770,099	£14,532,315,687

ECONOMY AND TRADE
Since the 1980s Ireland's economy has been transformed from a mainly agricultural to a modern, export-led economy that experienced strong growth from the mid-1990s. But an over-inflated property sector and high levels of personal debt left the economy exposed in the 2008 global financial crisis, causing it to go into a deep recession. Despite passing austerity budgets in 2009 and 2010, in November 2010 the government agreed loan packages with the IMF and EU to avoid defaulting on its sovereign debt. After Enda Kenny took office in March 2011, austerity measures increased in order to reach Ireland's EU-IMF deficit targets; Ireland achieved growth of 1.4 per cent in 2011 and in 2012 the budget deficit was cut to 8.5 per cent of GDP. Towards the end of 2013, Ireland exited its EU-IMF bailout program after meeting deficit reduction targets and reducing banking debt. Ireland was the fastest growing economy in the eurozone in 2014 and has continued to grow in real terms, which is set to continue through 2019.

Agriculture now accounts for 1 per cent of GDP and 5 per cent of employment; services contribute 60.7 per cent and industry 38.2 per cent of GDP, and these sectors account for 84 per cent and 11 per cent of employment respectively. Major industries include mining, pharmaceuticals, chemicals, computer hardware and software, food and drink production, and tourism. The Kinsale gas field off the south coast meets some of Ireland's gas needs, and hydroelectric power is generated from the Shannon barrage and other schemes; as of 2017 the country was a net exporter of energy. The introduction of charges for domestic water in 2014, a measure that was part of Ireland's bailout agreement with EU and IMF, was met with protests.

The main trading partners are the UK, other EU countries and the USA. Principal exports are machinery, computers, chemicals, pharmaceuticals, livestock and livestock products. The main imports are data processing equipment, other machinery, chemicals, petroleum and petroleum products, textiles and clothing.

COMMUNICATIONS
Airports – The principal airport is at Dublin, with others at Shannon, Waterford, Cork, Killarney, Galway and Knock
Waterways – There are 956km of waterways, although these are used only by leisure craft; the main ports are Cork, Dun Laoghaire, Galway, Limerick and Waterford
Roadways and railways – 96,036km, including 1,244km of motorways; 3,237km
Telecommunications – 1.9 million fixed lines and 4.9 million mobile subscriptions (2016); there were 4 million internet users in 2016
Internet code and IDD – ie; 353 (from UK), 44 or 048 for Northern Ireland (to UK)
Major broadcasters – The main radio and television broadcaster is the state-run Raidio Telefis Eireann (RTE), whose competitors include a handful of Irish commercial stations and British terrestrial and satellite services
Press – There are three national newspapers: *The Irish Times, Irish Independent* and *Irish Examiner*
WPFI score – 14,59 (16)

EDUCATION AND HEALTH
Primary education is directed by the state and education is compulsory until age 16.
Gross enrolment ratio (percentage of relevant age group) – primary 101 per cent, secondary 126 per cent (2016 est), tertiary 77.6 per cent (2014 est)
Health expenditure (per capita) – US$4,239 (2014)
Hospital beds (per 1,000 people) – 2.8 (2013)
Life expectancy (years) – 80.9 (2017 est)
Mortality rate – 6.6 (2017 est)
Birth rate – 14.1 (2017 est)
Infant mortality rate – 3.6 (2017 est)
HIV/AIDS adult prevalence – 0.2 per cent (2016 est)

ISRAEL AND PALESTINIAN TERRITORIES

Medinat Yisra'el / Dawlat Isra'il – State of Israel

Area – 20,770 sq. km (includes Jerusalem and the Golan Heights)

Capital – The legislature and most government departments are in Jerusalem; population, 907,000 (2018 est). A resolution proclaiming Jerusalem as the capital of Israel was adopted by the *Knesset* in 1950. It is not, however, recognised as the capital by the UN because East Jerusalem is part of the Occupied Territories captured in 1967; the UN and international law consider Tel Aviv (2018 population, 4,011,000) to be the capital

Major cities – Eilat, Haifa, Rishon Le'Zion

Currency – New Israeli Shekel (NIS) of 100 agora

Population – 8,299,706 rising at 1.51 per cent a year (2017 est); includes about 531,129 (est) settlers in the occupied areas. Since independence, Israel has had a policy of granting an immigration visa to every Jew who expresses a desire to settle in the country; between 1948 and 2009, over 3 million immigrants entered Israel from over 100 different countries

Religion – Jewish 74.8 per cent, Muslim 17.6 per cent (predominantly Sunni, Druze 2 per cent), Christian 2 per cent (predominantly Eastern Orthodox) (est)

Language – Hebrew, Arabic (both official), English

Population density – 403 per sq. km (2016)

Urban population – 92.4 per cent (2018 est)

Median age (years) – 29.7 (2017 est)

National anthem – 'Hatikvah' 'The Hope'

National day – Fifth day of Jewish month of Iyar (anniversary of Independence Day, 1948)

Death penalty – Retained for certain crimes (last used 1962)

CPI score – 62 (32)

Military expenditure – US$16,489m (2016)

Conscription – 18 years of age (Jews and Druze only; Christians, Circassians and Muslims may volunteer); 24–48 months

CLIMATE AND TERRAIN

Israel comprises the partly forested hill country of Galilee and parts of Judea and Samaria, the coastal plain from the Gaza Strip to north of Acre (including the plain of Esdraelon running from Haifa Bay to the south-east); the Negev, a triangular rocky desert in the south; and parts of the Jordan valley, including the Hula region, Lake Tiberias and the south-western part of the Dead Sea. Elevation extremes range from 1,208m (Har Meron) to −408m (Dead Sea), which is the Earth's deepest depression. The climate is temperate, with hotter, drier conditions in the south and east. Average temperatures range from 11.8°C in January to 27.8°C in August.

POLITICS

Israel has no written constitution; most constitutional provision is set out in the basic law on government. The head of state is the president, elected by the legislature for a seven-year term, which is not renewable. The unicameral *Knesset* has 120 members elected by proportional representation for a four-year term. The prime minister is responsible to the *Knesset,* and appoints the cabinet, subject to the approval of the *Knesset.*

In the March 2015 parliamentary elections the Likud party won 30 seats and Prime Minister Benjamin Netanyahu formed a coalition government with the centre-right Kulanu (10 seats), the pro-settler Habayit Hayehudi (8), the ultra-orthodox Shas (7) and Yahadut Hatorah (6) parties. The 2014 presidential election was won by Reuven Rivlin.

HEAD OF STATE

President, Reuven Rivlin, *elected* 10 June 2014, *sworn in* 27 July 2014

SELECTED GOVERNMENT MEMBERS *AS AT JUNE 2018*
Prime Minister, Foreign Affairs, Benjamin Netanyahu
Defence, Avigdor Lieberman
Finance, Moshe Kahlon
Internal Affairs, Aryeh Deri

EMBASSY OF ISRAEL

2 Palace Green, London W8 4QB
T 020-7957 9500 E info@london.mfa.gov.il
W http://embassies.gov.il/london/Pages/default.aspx
Ambassador Extraordinary and Plenipotentiary, HE Mark Regev, *apptd* 2016

BRITISH EMBASSY

192 Hayarkon Street, Tel Aviv 6340502
T (+972) (3) 725 1222 E webmaster.telaviv@fco.gov.uk
W www.gov.uk/government/world/israel
Ambassador Extraordinary and Plenipotentiary, HE David Quarrey, *apptd* 2015

ECONOMY AND TRADE

Israel has a technically advanced market economy, having developed its agriculture and industry intensively since the 1970s despite limited natural resources. After a short recession in the early 2000s, structural reforms and tighter fiscal control were implemented, resulting in steady growth from 2003 to 2007, increased foreign investment and a rising demand for exports. Despite the high level of external debt, the economy proved resilient in the global downturn, although it contracted slightly in 2008–9. Its debt and deficits are covered by foreign aid and loans; the USA is the main source of economic and military aid and is Israel's main creditor, owed about half of its external debt. Israel's income inequality and poverty rates are among the highest of any developed nation. Israel is increasingly able to produce natural gas, with production adding to the country's GDP. Low inflation and a strong currency are expected to stimulate growth in 2018 through domestic consumption.

Israel has developed a strong technology sector, central to which are the aviation, electronics, biotechnology, communications and software industries. Other important industries include timber and paper, mineral and metal products, cement, chemicals, plastics, textiles, diamond cutting and tourism, which is reviving. The country is also an important producer of citrus fruits, vegetables, cotton, beef, poultry and dairy products. Service industries account for around 70 per cent of GDP, industry for 26.6 per cent and agriculture for 2.3 per cent.

Conquered by Muslim Arabs — Part of the Ottoman Empire — Zionist settlement begins — British Mandate withdraws; UN's partitioned state rejected by Arabs; State of Israel created — The Palestine Liberation Organisation begins terrorist campaign against Israel — Yom Kippur War — Signing of the Oslo Accords ends *intifada* — UN proposes two-state 'road map' for peace

c.500-100 — c.1000-1300 — 1917 — 1956 — 1967 — 1987-93 — 2000-2 — 2014

c.600 — c.1500 — c.1880 — 1948 — c.1960 — 1973 — 1993 — 2003

Conquered by Babylon, Greece and Rome — Contested by Muslims during Crusades — British capture region from Ottomans; establish Palestine — Ten-Month War against Arab states — Suez War between Israel and Egypt — Israel gains control of Gaza Strip in Six-Day War — Uprising (*intifada*) begins in West Bank and Gaza Strip — Breakdown of Oslo Accords — Seven-week conflict in Gaza against Hamas

The main trading partners are the USA (28.8 per cent of exports), Hong Kong, the UK and other EU states. Principal exports are high-technology machinery and equipment, software, cut diamonds, agricultural products, chemicals, textiles and clothing. The main imports are raw materials, military equipment, investment goods, rough diamonds, fuels, grain and consumer goods.

GNI – US$324.7bn; US$37,270 per capita (2017)
Annual average growth of GDP – 3.1 per cent (2017 est)
Inflation rate – −0.2 per cent (2017 est)
Population below poverty line – 22 per cent (2014)
Unemployment – 4.3 per cent (2017 est)
Total external debt – US$93.02bn (2017 est)
Imports – US$68,879m (2016)
Exports – US$60,174m (2016)

BALANCE OF PAYMENTS
Trade – US$8,705m deficit (2016)
Current Account – US$10,391m surplus (2017)

Trade with UK	2016	2017
Imports from UK	£1,097,019,735	£1,193,811,090
Exports to UK	£1,036,444,753	£1,123,107,888

COMMUNICATIONS
Airports and waterways – 29, with the chief international airport Ben Gurion, between Tel Aviv and Jerusalem; the chief seaports are Haifa and Ashdod on the Mediterranean, and Eilat on the Red Sea
Roadways and railways – There are 18,566km of roadways, including 449km of motorway, and Israel State Railways operates a network of 975km
Telecommunications – 3.3 million fixed lines and 10.6 million mobile subscriptions; there were 6.5 million internet users in 2016
Internet code and IDD – il; 972 (from UK), 44/012/013/014 (to UK)
Major broadcasters – The Israel Broadcasting Authority, which operated public television and radio services across the country, was abruptly dissolved in May 2017 after nearly 70 years and replaced by the Israeli Public Broadcasting Corporation, known as KAN; Galei Zahal Israel Defence Force (IDF) radio broadcasts to a mostly civilian audience
Press – Daily newspapers include *Yediot Aharonot, Ha'aretz* and *Jerusalem Post*
WPFI score – 30,26 (87)

EDUCATION AND HEALTH
Education is compulsory between the ages of five and 16 and is free.
Literacy rate – 97.8 per cent (2011 est)
Gross enrolment ratio (percentage of relevant age group) – primary 104 per cent, secondary 104 per cent, tertiary 64 per cent (2016 est)
Health expenditure (per capita) – US$2,910 (2014)
Hospital beds (per 1,000 people) – 3.4 (2012)
Life expectancy (years) – 82.5 (2017 est)

Mortality rate – 5.2 (2017 est)
Birth rate – 18.1 (2017 est)
Infant mortality rate – 3.4 (2017 est)

PALESTINIAN AUTONOMOUS AREAS
Area – The total area is 6,231 sq. km. The area which is fully autonomous is 412 sq. km, of which the Gaza Strip is 360 sq. km
Capital – Although Palestinians claim East Jerusalem as their capital, the administrative capital was established in 1994 in Gaza City; population, 479,400 (2005 est); since 2007 the president and transitional government have been located in Ramallah, on the West Bank; population, 69,479 (2009 est)
Major towns – Jabalia, Khan Yunis, Rafah in the Gaza Strip; Hebron, Jericho, Nablus and Ramallah on the West Bank
Population – 4,451,025 (2016 est) (Gaza Strip – 1,795,183 rising at 2.33 per cent; West Bank – 2,747,943 rising at 1.186 per cent)
Religion – Muslim 98 per cent (Sunni); small Jewish and Christian minorities (est)
Population density – 735 per sq. km (2015)
Urban population – 75.3 per cent (2015 est)
Median age (years) – West Bank 20.8; Gaza Strip 16.9 (2016 est)
National anthem – 'Fidai, Fidai' 'Freedom Fighter, Freedom Fighter'
Death penalty – Retained
Literacy rate – 94.9 per cent (2010 est)

POLITICS
The Interim Agreement of 1995 invested the Palestinian Authority with executive, legislative and judicial authority, but not sovereignty, in the autonomous areas.

The executive president is directly elected for a five-year term. The unicameral Palestinian Legislative Council (*Majlis al-Tashri'i*) has one seat reserved for the president and 132 seats for members elected from party lists for a five-year term. The president appoints the prime minister, who appoints the council of ministers, which must be approved by the legislature. In August 2013 Rami Hamdallah was appointed prime minister having served briefly in office in June 2013.

SELECTED GOVERNMENT MEMBERS *AS AT JUNE 2018*
President, Mahmoud Abbas, *elected* 9 January 2005
Prime Minister, Interior, Rami Hamdallah
Foreign Affairs, Riyad Najib Abd-al-Rahman al-Maliki

PALESTINIAN GENERAL DELEGATION
5 Galena Road, London W6 0LT
T 020-8563 0008 W http://palmissionuk.org/
General Delegate, Prof. Manuel Hassassian

BRITISH CONSULATE-GENERAL
PO Box 19690, 15 Nashashibi Street, Sheikh Jarrah Quarter, East Jerusalem 97200
T (+972) (2) 541 4100
W www.gov.uk/government/world/the-occupied-palestinian-territories
Consul-General, Philip Hall, OBE, *apptd* 2017

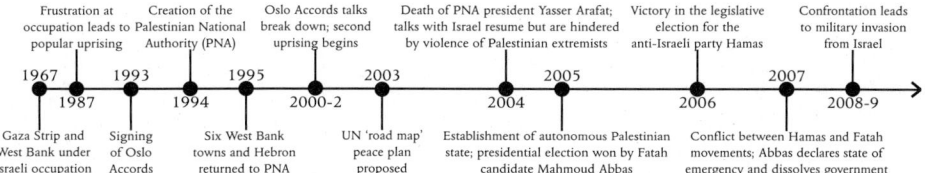

| Frustration at occupation leads to popular uprising | Creation of the Palestinian National Authority (PNA) | Oslo Accords talks break down; second uprising begins | Death of PNA president Yasser Arafat; talks with Israel resume but are hindered by violence of Palestinian extremists | Victory in the legislative election for the anti-Israeli party Hamas | Confrontation leads to military invasion from Israel |

1967	1993	1995	2003	2005	2007
1987	1994	2000-2	2004	2006	2008-9

| Gaza Strip and West Bank under Israeli occupation | Signing of Oslo Accords | Six West Bank towns and Hebron returned to PNA | UN 'road map' peace plan proposed | Establishment of autonomous Palestinian state; presidential election won by Fatah candidate Mahmoud Abbas | Conflict between Hamas and Fatah movements; Abbas declares state of emergency and dissolves government |

ECONOMY AND TRADE

The *intifada*, and Israeli security restrictions in response to it, have damaged infrastructure and severely constrained economic activity in the Palestinian areas and external trade since 2000. Incomes had dropped and poverty risen sharply even before 2006, when the policies of the new Hamas government led to an embargo by international funding providers, and Israel stopped remitting customs dues collected on behalf of the Palestinian Authority. Emergency aid, provided through channels that bypass the Hamas government, was resumed in late 2006. The effects were most severe in Gaza, where the population is dependent on food aid. Public sector salary cuts and the failure of aid to be delivered in 2017, coupled with Egypt's ongoing crackdown on smuggling networks, have exacerbated shortages and tensions with Israel. On the West Bank, some Israeli restrictions have been eased since 2007 and economic reforms made since 2008, underpinned by foreign aid donors, have stimulated economic development. Nonetheless, unemployment stood at 19 per cent in 2017. The 2014 conflict in Gaza caused an estimated US$2.8bn (£1.8bn) worth of damage.

Most economic activity consists of small family businesses engaged in farming, quarrying and small-scale manufacturing of construction materials and textiles, metal goods, handicrafts and agricultural processing. The main exports are stone, fruit, olives, vegetables and flowers, and the main trading partners are Israel, Jordan and Egypt.

GNI – US$15.7bn; US$3,180 per capita (2017)

Annual average growth of GDP – West Bank 5.3 per cent; Gaza Strip 15.2 per cent (2014 est)

Inflation rate – West Bank 1.2 per cent; Gaza Strip 0.1 per cent (2016 est)

Population below poverty line – West Bank 18 per cent; Gaza Strip 30 per cent (2011 est)

Unemployment – West Bank 17.7 per cent; Gaza Strip 43.9 per cent (2014 est)

Imports – US$5,058m (2016)

Exports – US$929m (2016)

BALANCE OF PAYMENTS

Trade – US$4,128m deficit (2016)

Current Account – US$1,563m deficit (2017)

Trade with UK	2016	2017
Imports from UK	£7,496,929	£5,635,012
Exports to UK	£1,179,430	£1,246,795

ITALY

Repubblica Italiana – Italian Republic

Area – 301,340 sq. km

Capital – Rome; population, 4,210,000 (2018 est)

Major cities – Bari, Bologna, Florence, Genoa, Milan, Naples, Turin, Venice, Verona. The chief towns of Sicily and Sardinia are Palermo and Cagliari respectively

Currency – Euro (€) of 100 cents

Population – 62,137,802 rising at 0.19 per cent a year (2017 est)

Religion – Christian (Roman Catholic 80 per cent) (est); unaffiliated 20 per cent

Language – Italian (official), German, French, Slovene

Population density – 206 per sq. km (2016)

Urban population – 70.4 per cent (2018 est)

Median age (years) – 45.5 (2017 est)

National anthem – 'Il Canto degli Italiani' 'The Song of the Italians'

National day – 2 June (Republic Day)

Death penalty – Abolished for all crimes (since 1994)

CPI score – 50 (54)

Military expenditure – US$29,236m (2017)

CLIMATE AND TERRAIN

Italy consists of a peninsula, the islands of Sicily, Sardinia, Elba and about 70 smaller islands. The smaller islands include Pantelleria, the Pelagian islands, the Aeolian islands, Capri, the Flegrean islands, the Pontine archipelago, the Tremiti islands and the Tuscan archipelago. Most of the islands are mountainous.

The peninsula is also largely mountainous, but between the spine of the Apennines and the eastern coastline are two large fertile plains: Emilia-Romagna in the north and Apulia in the south. Italy is divided from France and Switzerland by the Alps, and from Austria and Slovenia by both the Alps and the Dolomites. Three volcanoes, Vesuvius, Etna and Stromboli, are still active. Elevation extremes range from 4,748m (Mt Bianco di Courmayeur) to 0m (Mediterranean Sea). At the foot of the Alps lie the great lakes of Como, Maggiore and Garda. The chief rivers are the Po (651km) and the Adige, flowing through the northern plain to the Adriatic Sea, and the Arno (Florentine plain) and the Tiber (flowing through Rome to Ostia), which flow to the west coast. The climate is Mediterranean, with warm dry summers and mild winters.

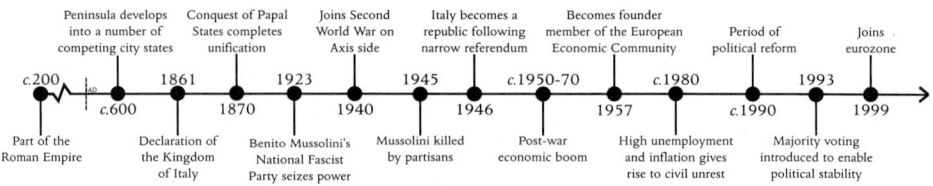

Peninsula develops into a number of competing city states

Conquest of Papal States completes unification

Joins Second World War on Axis side

Italy becomes a republic following narrow referendum

Becomes founder member of the European Economic Community

Period of political reform

Joins eurozone

c.200 | 1861 | 1923 | 1945 | c.1950-70 | c.1980 | 1993
AD c.600 | 1870 | 1940 | 1946 | 1957 | c.1990 | 1999

Part of the Roman Empire

Declaration of the Kingdom of Italy

Benito Mussolini's National Fascist Party seizes power

Mussolini killed by partisans

Post-war economic boom

High unemployment and inflation gives rise to civil unrest

Majority voting introduced to enable political stability

POLITICS

The 1948 constitution has been amended several times, notably in 2001 to provide for greater autonomy for the 20 regions in tax, education and environment matters. The president, who must be over 50 years of age, is elected for a seven-year term by an electoral college consisting of both chambers of the legislature and 58 regional representatives, with no term limits. The bicameral *Parlamento* comprises a 630-member Chamber of Deputies and a senate with 315 members directly elected on a regional basis and a variable number of life senators, who are past presidents and senators appointed by incumbent presidents. Elected members of both chambers serve a five-year term. In 2015, parliament passed new legislation to ensure that the party that wins the most votes in a legislative election will be allocated a majority of seats. Any party that wins more than 40 per cent of the national vote will be awarded 340 seats. If no party reaches the threshold, there is a second-place run-off between the two parties with the most votes.

Having been elected the leader of the Democratic Party (PD) in December 2013, Matteo Renzi succeeded Enrico Letta as prime minister in February 2014. Renzi resigned in December 2016, following defeat in a referendum to change the constitution, and was replaced by Paolo Gentiloni. Legislative elections in March 2018 were marked by the success of two populist parties which formed a coalition government in June, the anti-establishment 5-Star Movement and anti-immigration Northern League. They appointed compromise candidate and political novice Giuseppe Conte as prime minister, the country's fifth unelected head of government in a row. In January 2015, PD's Sergio Mattarella was elected president by parliament following the resignation of Georgio Napolitano due to ill health.

HEAD OF STATE
President, Sergio Mattarella, *elected* 31 January 2015, *sworn in* 4 February 2015

SELECTED GOVERNMENT MEMBERS *AS AT JULY 2018*
Prime Minister, Giuseppe Conte
Defence, Elisabetta Trenta
Foreign Affairs, Enzo Moavero Milanesi
Interior, Matteo Salvini

ITALIAN EMBASSY
14 Three Kings Yard, Davies Street, London W1K 4EH
T 020-7312 2200 E ambasciata.londra@esteri.it
W www.amblondra.esteri.it
Ambassador Extraordinary and Plenipotentiary, HE Raffaele Trombetta, *apptd* 2018

BRITISH EMBASSY
Via XX Settembre 80A, 00187 Rome
T (+39) (06) 4220 0001 W www.gov.uk/government/world/italy
Ambassador Extraordinary and Plenipotentiary, HE Jill Morris, CMG, *apptd* 2016

ECONOMY AND TRADE

Economically, Italy is divided between a prosperous and industrially developed north and a largely agricultural and welfare-dependent south that has high unemployment levels. There is a large unofficial economy that is estimated to be worth 17 per cent of GDP, but measures to tackle this and wider structural reforms have made slow progress because of political opposition and sluggish economic performance. A large budget deficit and public debt led to a −1.8 per cent contraction in 2013. Unemployment reached 12.4 per cent, with youth unemployment increasing to 40 per cent, and by 2017 this had only slightly fallen. The economy grew in 2015 for the first time in four years but post-election stasis and steadily increasing public debt, at 131 per cent of GDP in 2017, have dissuaded investment.

Tourism is the largest industry. Other major industries include precision machinery, iron and steel, chemicals, food processing, textiles, motor vehicles, fashion clothing, footwear, and ceramics. The services sector contributes 73.9 per cent of GDP, industry 24 per cent and agriculture 2.1 per cent. The main trading partners are other EU states, especially Germany and France. Principal exports are the products of the main industries, plus food, beverages, minerals and non-ferrous metals. The main imports are engineering and energy products, industrial raw materials and transport equipment.
GNI – US$1,878.3bn; US$31,020 per capita (2017)
Annual average growth of GDP – 1.5 per cent (2017 est)
Inflation rate – 1.4 per cent (2017 est)
Population below poverty line – 29.9 per cent (2012 est)
Unemployment – 11.4 per cent (2017 est)
Total external debt – US$2.444 trillion (2016 est)
Imports – US$401,622m (2016)
Exports – US$455,796m (2016)

BALANCE OF PAYMENTS
Trade – US$54,174m surplus (2016)
Current Account – US$5,293m surplus (2017)

Trade with UK	2016	2017
Imports from UK	£9,707,984,265	£10,244,653,132
Exports to UK	£17,226,725,298	£18,772,696,747

COMMUNICATIONS

Airports and waterways – 98, including major airports at Rome, Milan, Naples and Venice, Palermo and Catania (Sicily), and Cagliari (Sardinia); the main seaports are Naples, Genoa, Livorno, Trieste, Venice, Palermo and Catania
Roadways – A 6,700km network of motorways *(autostrade)* covers the country but there are 487,700km of roads in total
Railways – There are 20,255km of railways; the main railway system is run by the state-owned *Ferrovia dello Stato.* In February 2015 it was agreed a new high-speed rail link between Lyon and Turin worth €26bn (£18bn) would be built by 2020, including a 57km tunnel through the Alps

Telecommunications – 20.26 million fixed lines and 90.9 million mobile subscriptions; there were 38 million internet users in 2016

Internet code and IDD – it; 39 (from UK), 44 (to UK)

Major broadcasters – Rai is Italy's public radio and television broadcaster and competes with a number of private television broadcasters, the leading one being Mediaset, part of the media empire of former prime minister Silvio Berlusconi

Press – The press is highly regionalised; daily newspapers include *La Stampa* (Turin-based), *La Repubblica* (Rome) and *Corriere della Sera* (Milan)

WPFI score – 24,12 (46)

EDUCATION AND HEALTH

Education is free and compulsory between the ages of six and 16.

Literacy rate – 99.9 per cent (2015 est)

Gross enrolment ratio (percentage of relevant age group) – primary 101.5 per cent, secondary 102.6 per cent, tertiary 63.1 per cent (2014 est)

Health expenditure (per capita) – US$3,258 (2014)

Hospital beds (per 1,000 people) – 3.4 (2012)

Life expectancy (years) – 82.3 (2017 est)

Mortality rate – 10.4 (2017 est)

Birth rate – 8.6 (2017 est)

Infant mortality rate – 3.3 (2017 est)

HIV/AIDS adult prevalence – 0.3 per cent (2016 est)

JAMAICA

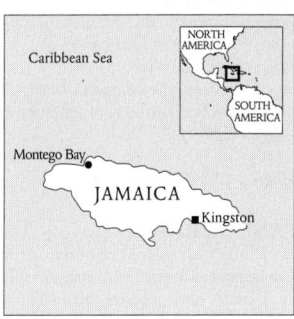

Area – 10,991 sq. km

Capital – Kingston; population, 589,000 (2018)

Major towns – Montego Bay, Portmore, Spanish Town

Currency – Jamaican dollar (J$) of 100 cents

Population – 2,990,561 rising at 0.68 per cent a year (2017 est)

Religion – Christian (Protestant 64.8 per cent, Roman Catholic 2.2 per cent), Rastafarian 1.1 per cent (2011 est)

Language – English (official), Jamaican patois

Population density – 267 per sq. km (2016)

Urban population – 55.7 per cent (2018 est)

Median age (years) – 26 (2017 est)

National anthem – 'Jamaica, Land We Love'

National day – 6 August (Independence Day)

Death penalty – Retained (last used 1988)

CPI score – 44 (68)

Military expenditure – US$131m (2017)

CLIMATE AND TERRAIN

An island in the Caribbean Sea, south of Cuba and west of Hispaniola, Jamaica is mostly mountainous and forested, with a narrow coastal plain. Elevation extremes range from 2,256m (Blue Mountain Peak) to 0m (Caribbean Sea). The climate is tropical, although more temperate inland. The average temperature in Jamaica is 25.6°C.

HISTORY AND POLITICS

Jamaica was visited by Columbus in 1494 and settled by the Spanish from 1509. Captured by the British in 1655, it became a crown colony in 1865. Jamaica became internally self-governing in 1959 and independent in 1962.

Post-independence politics has been dominated by the conservative Jamaican Labour Party (JLP) and social-democratic People's National Party (PNP). Relations between the two parties, often fraught, degenerated in the 1970s into violence that marred elections and political life for some years. Despite the current political stability, there is still widespread lawlessness often connected to drug-trafficking.

In the February 2016 legislative election, the JLP narrowly defeated the PNP to secure a 32–31 seat majority. The JLP formed a government under Andrew Holness.

Under the 1962 constitution, the head of state is Queen Elizabeth II, represented locally by a governor-general. The bicameral parliament consists of the House of Representatives, with 63 directly elected members, and the senate of 21 appointed members, 13 nominated by the prime minister and eight by the leader of the opposition; both chambers serve five-year terms. The prime minister is the leader of the majority party in the elected chamber.

Governor-General, HE Sir Patrick Allen, GCMG, *apptd* 2009

SELECTED GOVERNMENT MEMBERS *AS AT JUNE 2018*
Prime Minister, Defence, Andrew Holness
Finance, Nigel Clarke
Foreign Affairs, Kamina Johnson-Smith
National Security, Horace Chang

JAMAICAN HIGH COMMISSION
1–2 Prince Consort Road, London SW7 2BZ
T 020-7823 9911 E jamhigh@jhcuk.com W www.jhcuk.org
High Commissioner, HE Seth George Ramocan, *apptd* 2016

BRITISH HIGH COMMISSION
PO Box 575, 28 Trafalgar Road, Kingston 10
T (+1) (876) 936 0700 E ppa.kingston@fco.gov.uk
W www.gov.uk/government/world/jamaica
High Commissioner, HE Asif Ahmad, *apptd* 2017

ECONOMY AND TRADE

The economy is struggling owing to increased foreign competition, high unemployment and crime rates, internal and external debt, and hurricane and storm damage in 2004, 2007 and 2008. Following the global financial crisis, Jamaica turned to the IMF for support in 2010 and again in 2013; to secure about US$1bn in funds, the government pledged to reduce its debt below 100 per cent of GDP by 2020. In 2014 the figure stood at 132.7 per cent, but in 2017 had fallen to less than 110 per cent. Tourism and remittances from expatriates each account for 34 per cent of GDP. Economic growth is hampered by weak domestic demand, and growth has been sluggish for several years.

The economy is dominated by the service sector, which makes up 69.2 per cent of GDP; industry accounts for 23.2 per cent, and agriculture for 7.6 per cent. Industries include alumina and bauxite extraction, processing agricultural produce and light manufacturing.

The main trading partners are the USA (39.1 per cent of exports and 40.6 per cent of imports), the Netherlands and Canada. Principal exports are alumina, bauxite, sugar, coffee, yams, beverages, clothing and scrap metal. The main imports are food, consumer goods, industrial supplies, fuel, and parts and accessories for capital goods.

GNI – US$13.7bn; US$4,750 per capita (2017)

Annual average growth of GDP – 0.5 per cent (2017 est)

Inflation rate – 3.4 per cent (2017 est)
Population below poverty line – 17.1 per cent (2016 est)
Unemployment – 12.2 per cent (2017 est)
Total external debt – US$14.9bn (2017 est)
Imports – US$4,995m (2016)
Exports – US$1,265m (2016)

BALANCE OF PAYMENTS
Trade – US$3,730m deficit (2016)
Current Account – US$103m deficit (2016)

Trade with UK	2016	2017
Imports from UK	£52,739,853	£74,163,461
Exports to UK	£40,263,251	£63,157,891

COMMUNICATIONS
Airports and waterways – The principal airports are at Kingston and Montego Bay; there are several harbours, Kingston being the main seaport
Roadways and railways – The island has 16,148km of roadways; the rail network is no longer in use
Telecommunications – 310,213 fixed lines and 3.3 million mobile telephone subscriptions; there were 1.3 million internet users in 2016
Internet code and IDD – jm; 1 876 (from UK), 011 44 (to UK)
Major broadcasters – The state broadcaster was privatised in 1997 and now operates as Television Jamaica Ltd; Radio Jamaica Ltd (RJR) operates a number of stations
Press – There are three main daily newspapers: *The Jamaica Gleaner*, *The Jamaica Star* and the *Jamaica Observer*
WPFI score – 11,33 (6)

EDUCATION AND HEALTH
In 2010 the Inter-American Development Bank provided US$45m in funding to enable the government to make improvements to the education system and expand compulsory schooling from age 16 to 18.
Literacy rate – 88.7 per cent (2015 est)
Gross enrolment ratio (percentage of relevant age group) – primary 92 per cent (2013 est), secondary 84 per cent (2016 est), tertiary 27.2 per cent (2015 est)
Health expenditure (per capita) – US$266 (2014)
Hospital beds (per 1,000 people) – 1.7 (2013)
Life expectancy (years) – 73.7 (2017 est)
Mortality rate – 6.8 (2017 est)
Birth rate – 17.9 (2017 est)
Infant mortality rate – 12.8 (2017 est)
HIV/AIDS adult prevalence – 1.7 per cent (2016 est)

JAPAN
Nihon-koku/Nippon-koku – Japan

Area – 377,915 sq. km
Capital – Tokyo; population, 37,468,000 (2018 est)
Major cities – Fukuoka, Hiroshima, Kawasaki, Kobe, Kyoto (the ancient capital), Nagoya, Osaka, Saitama, Sapporo, Yokohama
Currency – Yen of 100 sen
Population – 126,451,398 falling at 0.21 per cent a year (2017 est)
Religion – Shinto 79.2 per cent, Buddhist 66.8 per cent, Christian 1.5 per cent (est); much of the population adheres to more than one religion, most commonly combining Shinto and Buddhist beliefs
Language – Japanese (official)
Population density – 348 per sq. km (2016)
Urban population – 94.3 per cent (2017 est)
Median age (years) – 46.9 (2016 est)
National anthem – 'Kimigayo' 'The Emperor's Reign'
National day – 23 December (Birthday of Emperor Akihito)
Death penalty – Retained
CPI score – 73 (20)
Military expenditure – US$45,387m (2017)

CLIMATE AND TERRAIN
Japan consists of four large islands: Honshu (or Mainland), Shikoku, Kyushu and Hokkaido, and many smaller islands. Typically, the islands have coastal plains and wooded, mountainous interiors; 67 per cent of Japan's land area is forested. The mountains running across the mainland from the Sea of Japan to the Pacific Ocean include a number of volcanoes, mainly extinct or dormant. Elevation extremes range from 3,776m (Mt Fuji) to −4m (Hachiro-gata). The climate varies from temperate in the north to tropical in the south. Average temperatures range from 1°C in January to 23.7°C in August.
    The islands are located at the intersection of three tectonic plates and are prone to seismic activity; 20 per cent of the world's major earthquakes occur in this area. A magnitude-9 earthquake and the ensuing tsunami devastated the north-east of Honshu in March 2011.

POLITICS
The 1947 constitution established Japan as a constitutional monarchy with a hereditary emperor as head of state. The bicameral Diet comprises the House of Representatives (the lower house) and the House of Councillors. The House of Representatives has 475 members directly elected for a four-year term, including 180 by proportional representation. The House of Councillors has 242 members, including 96 elected by proportional representation, who serve six-year terms, with half elected every three years; unlike the lower house, it cannot be dissolved by the prime minister. The prime minister

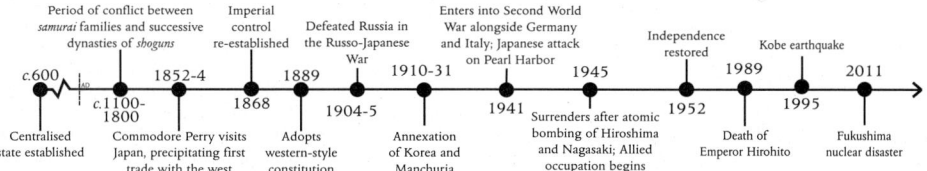

Period of conflict between *samurai* families and successive dynasties of *shoguns* — c.600 — *c.*1100-1800 — 1852-4 — 1868 — 1889 — 1904-5 — 1910-31 — 1941 — 1945 — 1952 — 1989 — 1995 — 2011

Centralised state established
Commodore Perry visits Japan, precipitating first trade with the west
Adopts western-style constitution
Imperial control re-established
Defeated Russia in the Russo-Japanese War
Annexation of Korea and Manchuria
Enters into Second World War alongside Germany and Italy; Japanese attack on Pearl Harbor
Surrenders after atomic bombing of Hiroshima and Nagasaki; Allied occupation begins
Independence restored
Death of Emperor Hirohito
Kobe earthquake
Fukushima nuclear disaster

is formally elected by the House of Representatives and appoints the cabinet.

The Liberal Democrat Party (LDP) has dominated post-war politics, holding power continuously from 1955 to 1993, and then – usually as the main party in coalition governments – from 1994 to 2009. In 2010, it regained control of the upper house of the legislature from the Democratic Party of Japan (DPJ). The LDP returned to power in the 2012 parliamentary election and Shinzo Abe once again took the position of prime minister. Following snap legislative elections in December 2014, the LDP remained in power, in coalition with the Komeito (NKP). Prime Minister Abe's ruling coalition won snap legislative elections in October 2017, gaining a two-thirds majority in the upper house.

HEAD OF STATE
HIM The Emperor of Japan, Akihito, *born* 23 December 1933, *succeeded* 8 January 1989, *enthroned* 12 November 1990
Heir, HRH Crown Prince Naruhito Hironomiya, *born* 23 February 1960

SELECTED GOVERNMENT MEMBERS *AS AT JUNE 2018*
Prime Minister, Shinzo Abe
Deputy Prime Minister, Finance, Taro Aso
Defence, Itsunori Onodera
Foreign Affairs, Taro Kono

EMBASSY OF JAPAN
101–104 Piccadilly, London W1J 7JT
T 020-7465 6500 **E** info@ld.mofa.go.jp **W** www.uk.emb-japan.go.jp
Ambassador Extraordinary and Plenipotentiary, HE Koji Tsuruoka, *apptd* 2016

BRITISH EMBASSY
No. 1 Ichiban-cho, Chiyoda-ku, Tokyo 102–8381
T (+81) (3) 5211 1100 **E** public-enquiries.tokyo@fco.gov.uk
W www.gov.uk/government/world/japan
Ambassador Extraordinary and Plenipotentiary, HE Paul Madden, CMG, *apptd* 2017

ECONOMY AND TRADE
Japan has the fourth-largest economy in the world after China, the USA and India. Its rapid post-war economic growth, based largely on car and consumer electronics manufacturing, experienced a marked contraction from 1990. Exacerbated by the 1997 Asian economic crisis, the recession lasted 14 years. Reforms introduced from 2001, particularly to the corporate and public sectors, improved economic growth from 2002 to 2007, but the economy has fallen into recession four times since 2008 owing to the global downturn. Government stimulus packages and an increase in global demand spurred the start of a recovery from late 2009.

Following the 2011 earthquake and tsunami there was a drop in production; the economy largely recovered in the following two years, but was less complete in the Tohoku region. Though the economy has benefitted from declining oil prices and a weak yen, a series of tax rises and a large public debt, which reached 240 per cent of GDP in 2014 and is still the highest debt-to-GDP ratio in the world, have limited growth. In 2018, Japan and the EU signed an Economic Partnership Agreement, allowing for reduced trade barriers likely to improve Japan's economic outlook.

High-technology industries remain the mainstay of the economy, producing vehicles, electronic equipment, machine tools, steel and other metals, ships, chemicals, textiles and processed food. Financial services are also a major sector, supplying a global market. Agriculture is constrained by the mountainous terrain but intensive cultivation produces high yields, and there is a large fishing industry. The service sector contributes 69.3 per cent of GDP, industry 29.7 per cent and agriculture 1 per cent.

The main trading partners are China, the USA and other Pacific Rim countries. Principal exports include transport vehicles, semiconductors, and electrical machinery. The main imports are machinery and equipment, fuels, clothing, chemicals and raw materials.

GNI – US$4,888.1bn; US$38,550 per capita (2017)
Annual average growth of GDP – 1.5 per cent (2017 est)
Inflation rate – 0.4 per cent (2017 est)
Population below poverty line – 16.1 per cent (2013 est)
Unemployment – 2.9 per cent (2017 est)
Total external debt – US$3.24 trillion (2016 est)
Imports – US$606,959m (2016)
Exports – US$644,899m (2016)

BALANCE OF PAYMENTS
Trade – US$37,940m surplus (2016)
Current Account – US$195,800m surplus (2017)

Trade with UK	2016	2017
Imports from UK	£4,737,649,139	£5,708,667,657
Exports to UK	£9,849,227,173	£10,409,223,861

COMMUNICATIONS
Airports – 142; the principal airports include Haneda (Tokyo), Narita, Kansai and Chubu
Waterways – Japan has a large merchant fleet, with 684 ships of over 1,000 tonnes in 2011; the main seaports are Tokyo, Osaka, Nagoya, Yokohama, Kobe and Kawasaki
Roadways and railways – There are 973,234km of roadways, including 7,803km of motorways, and 27,182km of railways
Telecommunications – 64 million fixed lines and 167 million mobile subscriptions (2016); there were 116.5 million internet users in 2016
Internet code and IDD – jp; 81 (from UK), 1 44/010 44/41 44/61 44 (to UK)
Major broadcasters – A public broadcaster, NHK, provides radio and television services; satellite and cable television is widespread and digital broadcasting is expanding
Press – Around 80 per cent of the population reads a daily newspaper, creating huge markets for publications such as *Asahi Shimbun* and English-language title *The Japan Times*
WPFI score – 28,64 (67)

EDUCATION AND HEALTH
Elementary education is free and compulsory at elementary level (six-year course) and lower secondary (three-year course).
Gross enrolment ratio (percentage of relevant age group) – primary 101.2 per cent, secondary 101.7 per cent, tertiary 63.4 per cent (2014 est)

Health expenditure (per capita) – US$3,703 (2014)
Hospital beds (per 1,000 people) – 13.4 (2012)
Life expectancy (years) – 85.3 (2017 est)
Mortality rate – 9.8 (2017 est)
Birth rate – 7.7 (2017 est)
Infant mortality rate – 2 (2017 est)

JORDAN

Al-Mamlakah al-Urduniyah al-Hashimiyah – Hashemite Kingdom of Jordan

Area – 89,342 sq. km
Capital – Amman; population, 2,065,000 (2018 est)
Major cities – Aqaba, Az Zarqa, Irbid
Currency – Jordanian dinar (JD) of 10 dirhams
Population – 10,248,069 rising at 2.05 per cent a year (2017 est); Arab (98 per cent), Armenian (1 per cent), Circassian (1 per cent) (est)
Religion – Muslim (Sunni) 97.2 per cent, Christian 2.2 per cent (est)
Language – Arabic (official), English
Population density – 109 per sq. km (2016)
Urban population – 84.1 per cent (2017 est)
Median age (years) – 22.3 (2016 est)
National anthem – 'As-Salam al-Malaki al-Urdoni' 'Long Live the King of Jordan'
National day – 25 May (Independence Day)
Death penalty – Retained
CPI score – 48 (59)
Military expenditure – US$1,940m (2017)

CLIMATE AND TERRAIN
Most of the country is a desert plateau, with the valley of the Jordan river and the Dead Sea in the west marking the border with Israel. The Jordan Valley and its extension from the Dead Sea to the Gulf of Aqaba are part of the Great Rift Valley in Africa. The only hills lie in the south, along the edge of the Great Rift Valley, although there is a hilly outcrop in the centre of the desert. Elevation extremes range from 1,854m (Jabal Umm ad Dami) to −408m (Dead Sea). The climate is arid, but with a rainy season in the west from November to April. Average daily temperatures range from 8.8°C in January to 28.3°C in August. Winters can be cold, with frost and snow on the plateau.

POLITICS
The 1952 constitution provides for a monarchy with a hereditary king as head of state. The bicameral National Assembly comprises a House of Deputies and a senate or House of Notables. The House of Deputies has 130 members, directly elected for a four-year term; 15 seats are reserved for women and 12 to represent minorities. The senate has 65 members, who are appointed by the king for a four-year term. The king appoints the prime minister, who chooses the council of ministers.

After the 2010 legislative election, over 85 per cent of seats were won by pro-government candidates; the announcement of this result led to rioting. From January 2011, Jordan experienced demonstrations similar to those elsewhere in the Arab world, with protestors demanding political reform, lower food prices and measures to tackle unemployment. This led to the king dismissing the government in February 2011 and to the appointment of four prime ministers in 14 months. Interim prime minister Hani Mulki was appointed to the post following legislative elections in September 2016, when voter turnout was just 37 per cent, but resigned in July 2018 following mass protests over plans to raise taxes. He was replaced by former World Bank economist Omar Razzaz.

HEAD OF STATE
HM The King of Jordan, Abdullah II bin al-Hussein, *born* 30 January 1962, *succeeded* 7 February 1999
Heir, HRH Crown Prince Hussein bin al-Abdullah, *born* 29 March 1982

SELECTED GOVERNMENT MEMBERS *AS AT JULY 2018*
Prime Minister, Defence, Omar Razzaz
Deputy Prime Minister, Rajai Muasher
Finance, Izzidine Kanakrieh
Interior, Samir Mubaidin

EMBASSY OF THE HASHEMITE KINGDOM OF JORDAN
6 Upper Phillimore Gardens, London W8 7HA
T 020-7937 3685 E london@fm.gov.jo
W www.jordanembassy.org.uk
Ambassador Extraordinary and Plenipotentiary, HE Omar B. Al-Nahar, *apptd* 2017

BRITISH EMBASSY
PO Box 87, Abdoun, Amman 11118
T (+962) (6) 590 9200 E amman.enquiries@fco.gov.uk
W www.gov.uk/government/world/jordan
Ambassador Extraordinary and Plenipotentiary, HE Edward Oakden, CMG, *apptd* 2015

ECONOMY AND TRADE
Jordan's economic development has been hindered by its lack of natural resources, influxes of refugees from the West Bank in 1967, Iraq since 2003, and Syria since 2013, and the impact of conflict on its trade with Israel and Iraq. High levels of poverty, unemployment and government debt are long-term problems. Since 1999, King Abdullah has implemented economic reforms, and these measures have increased productivity and exports, begun to attract foreign direct

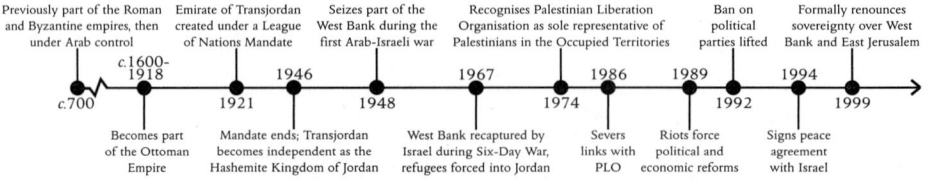

investment, and won agreement to debt rescheduling from international donors. Even so, the economy is still dependent on foreign aid, of which the USA is the largest provider, and in 2011 the government agreed two economic relief packages to improve the living conditions for the middle and poor classes. The arrival of more than 1.3 million refugees from the conflict in Syria has put an additional strain on government finances. Between 2010 and 2017 GDP has grown slowly, at an average of 2.5 per cent per year.

Jordan has no oil reserves of its own and few water resources. Shale reserves and renewable energy sources are being explored by the government. The country also imports natural gas, but aims to become a net exporter of electricity via its national grid's links with those of Syria and Egypt. It is currently considering nuclear power generation to ensure an adequate future supply. Jordan has also begun joint ventures with Israel and Syria to guarantee water supplies.

The service sector, including tourism, accounts for 66.8 per cent of GDP. Industry generates 28.9 per cent, from activities that include information technology, garment manufacturing, fertilisers, potash and phosphate mining, pharmaceuticals, oil refining, cement, inorganic chemicals and light manufacturing. Agriculture, which accounts for 4.3 per cent of GDP, produces citrus and stone fruits, tomatoes, cucumbers, olives, sheep, poultry and dairy products.

The main trade partners are the USA, Iraq, India, China and Saudi Arabia. Principal exports are clothing, fertilisers, potash, phosphates, vegetables and pharmaceuticals. The main imports are crude oil, machinery, transport equipment, iron and cereals.

GNI – US$38.7bn; US$3,980 per capita (2017)
Annual average growth of GDP – 2.3 per cent (2017 est)
Inflation rate – 3.3 per cent (2017 est)
Unemployment – 16.5 per cent (2017 est)
Total external debt – US$27.72bn (2017 est)
Imports – US$19,479m (2016)
Exports – US$7,503m (2016)

BALANCE OF PAYMENTS
Trade – US$11,970m deficit (2016)
Current Account – US$4,251m deficit (2017)

Trade with UK	2016	2017
Imports from UK	£261,619,287	£345,374,535
Exports to UK	£54,804,385	£198,520,993

COMMUNICATIONS
Airports – 16; the largest airports are at Amman and Aqaba
Waterways – Amman is linked to Jordan's seaport at Aqaba, the Saudi Arabian port of Jeddah and the Syrian and Iraqi capitals by roads which are of considerable importance in the overland trade of the Middle East
Roadways and railways – 7,203km; 507km
Telecommunications – 404,112 fixed lines and 9.8 million mobile subscriptions (2016); there were 5.1 million internet users in 2016
Internet code and IDD – jo; 962 (from UK), 44 (to UK)
Major broadcasters – Jordan Radio and Television, the state-run broadcaster, operates three terrestrial television channels and a satellite channel as well as radio services in Arabic, English and French
Press – Major daily newspapers include *Ad Dustour*, *Al Ra'y* and *Al Ghadd*
WPFI score – 41,71 (132)

EDUCATION AND HEALTH
Literacy rate – 99.2 per cent (2015 est)
Gross enrolment ratio (percentage of relevant age group) – primary 97.3 per cent, secondary 82.4 per cent (2014 est), tertiary 36 per cent (2016 est)
Health expenditure (per capita) – US$359 (2014)
Hospital beds (per 1,000 people) – 1.4 (2015)
Life expectancy (years) – 74.8 (2017 est)
Mortality rate – 3.4 (2017 est)
Birth rate – 23.9 (2017 est)
Infant mortality rate – 14.2 (2017 est)

KAZAKHSTAN

Qazaqstan Respublikasy – Republic of Kazakhstan

Area – 2,724,900 sq. km
Capital – Astana (previously known as Akmola and Tselinograd); population, 1,806,000 (2018 est)
Major cities – Almaty (the former capital), Oskemen, Pavlodar, Qaraghandy, Semey, Shymkent, Taraz
Currency – Tenge of 100 tiyn
Population – 18,556,698 rising at 1.04 per cent a year (2017 est); Kazakh (63.1 per cent), Russian (23.7 per cent), Uzbek (2.9 per cent), Ukrainian (2.1 per cent), Uygur (1.4 per cent), Tatar (1.3 per cent), German (1.1 per cent) (2009). The Russian population is concentrated in the north of the country, where it forms a significant majority, and in Almaty
Religion – Muslim 70.2 per cent (predominantly Sunni), Christian 26.2 per cent (mostly Russian Orthodox) (est)
Language – Kazakh, Russian (both official)
Population density – 7 per sq. km (2016)
Urban population – 53.2 per cent (2017 est)
Median age (years) – 30.3 (2016 est)
National anthem – 'Menin Qazaqstanim' 'My Kazakhstan'
National day – 16 December (Independence Day)
Death penalty – Retained for certain crimes
CPI score – 31 (122)
Military expenditure – US$1,337m (2017)
Conscription – 18 years of age; 24 months
Literacy rate – 99.8 per cent (2015 est)
Gross enrolment ratio (percentage of relevant age group) – primary 110.6 per cent, secondary 109.1 per cent, tertiary 46 per cent (2016 est)
Health expenditure (per capita) – US$539 (2014)
Hospital beds (per 1,000 people) – 6.7 (2013)
Life expectancy (years) – 71.1 (2017 est)
Mortality rate – 8.1 (2017 est)
Birth rate – 18.1 (2017 est)
Infant mortality rate – 19.6 (2017 est)
HIV/AIDS adult prevalence – 0.2 per cent (2016 est)

CLIMATE AND TERRAIN
Kazakhstan stretches from the basin of the river Volga and the Caspian Sea in the west to the Altai and Tien Shan mountains in the east. The terrain consists of arid steppes and semi-deserts; it is flat in the west, hilly in the east and mountainous in the south-east. Elevation extremes range from 6,995m (Khan Tangiri Shyngy) to −132m (Vpadina Kaundy). The country contains the northern part of the Aral Sea in the south-west, and Lake Balkhash and Lake Zaysan in the east. The Aral Sea has suffered significant pollution and desertification since the 1960s, creating the Aralkum desert. The climate is continental, and while arid in much of the country, it can be Siberian in the north. Average yearly temperatures in Astana range from −11.3°C in January to 23.1°C in July.

HISTORY AND POLITICS
Kazakhstan was inhabited by nomadic tribes before being invaded by Genghis Khan and incorporated into his empire in 1218. After this empire disintegrated, feudal towns emerged based on large oases and the nomadic tribes formed federations led by khans. The towns affiliated in the late 15th century and established a Kazakh state, which engaged in almost continuous warfare with the marauding khanates on its southern border. After turning to Russia for protection in the 1730s, the Kazakh khanates were formally incorporated into the Russian Empire in the early 19th century.

The 1917 Bolshevik revolution in Russia was followed by civil war in Kazakhstan, which became an autonomous republic within the USSR in 1920 and a full union republic in 1936. Kazakhstan suffered severely under Stalin's policies of agricultural collectivisation and 'sedentarisation', which forced nomadic tribes to become farmers; around 1.5 million people died of famine or disease. Later Soviet rule saw the country used as a test site for nuclear weapons.

Growing nationalism in the 1980s and a reformist leader led to economic and cultural reforms in 1989 and a declaration of sovereignty in 1990. Kazakhstan declared its independence in December 1991, and became a founding member of the Commonwealth of Independent States (CIS). It entered an economic, social and military union with Kyrgyzstan and Uzbekistan in 1994, and an economic and military pact with Russia in 1995, when it achieved nuclear-free status.

Nursultan Nazarbayev, the reformist communist leader of 1989, became head of state in 1990 and was re-elected in 1991, 1999, 2005 and 2011; the April 2011 election, in which he received 95 per cent of the vote, was criticised by international observers. A 2007 constitutional reform allows him to serve for an unlimited number of terms.

In 2006, three pro-government parties merged with Nazarbayev's Fatherland Republican Party (Otan), which subsequently changed its name to Nur-Otan. Nur-Otan won every seat in the lower legislative chamber in the 2007 legislative elections and retained 83 seats in the 2012 elections; in March 2016 legislative elections, the party won 82 per cent of the vote. Bakytzhan Sagintayev was named prime minister in September 2016, replacing Karim Massimov. President Nazarbayev was re-elected in the April 2015 presidential election and claimed to have won over 97 per cent of the popular vote, easily defeating his pro-government opponents. The elections were judged to be unsound by a number of human rights groups.

The president is directly elected; in 2007 the constitution was amended to reduce the presidential term from seven to five years, renewable once, although President Nazarbayev is exempt from this restriction. The bicameral parliament is composed of the assembly *(Majlis)* and the senate. The assembly has 107 members, 98 directly elected on a single constituency basis and nine seats reserved for ethnic groups; all serve a five-year term. The senate has 47 members, of whom 32 are indirectly elected and 15 are appointed for a six-year term, with half elected every three years. The president appoints the prime minister and other senior ministers.

HEAD OF STATE
President, C-in-C of the Armed Forces, Nursultan Nazarbayev, *elected* 1 December 1991, *confirmed in office by referendum* 1995, *re-elected* 1999, 2005, 2011, 2015

SELECTED GOVERNMENT MEMBERS *AS AT JUNE 2018*
Prime Minister, Bakytzhan Sagintayev
First Deputy Prime Minister, Askar Mamin
Defence, Saken Zhasuzakov
Foreign Affairs, Kayrat Abdrakhmanov
Internal Affairs, Maj.-Gen. Kalmukhanbet Kassymov

EMBASSY OF THE REPUBLIC OF KAZAKHSTAN
125 Pall Mall, London SW1Y 5EA
T 020-7925 1757 E london@mfa.kz W www.kazembassy.org.uk
Ambassador Extraordinary and Plenipotentiary, HE Erlan Idrissov, *apptd* 2017

BRITISH EMBASSY
62 Kosmonavtov Street, Astana
T (+7) (717) 255 6200 E ukinkz@fco.gov.uk
W www.gov.uk/government/world/kazakhstan
Ambassador Extraordinary and Plenipotentiary, HE Michael Gifford *apptd* 2018

ECONOMY AND TRADE
Economic reforms and privatisation in the 1990s enabled GDP to grow by at least 8 per cent a year from 2002 to 2007, although lower commodity prices and banking sector problems caused the economy to contract briefly in 2008–9. Growth has largely been achieved through exploitation of vast oil and natural gas reserves, particularly since the opening of export pipelines to Black Sea ports (in 2001) and China (2005), Kazakhstan's use of the Azerbaijan–Turkey pipeline (from 2008), and the exploitation of the giant Kashagan field since October 2016. The nation's oil production rose by 10.5 per cent in 2017, and significant further extraction in the Tengiz field is due for completion in 2022. As a result of the boom, the government has eliminated the budget deficit, but it is also trying to stimulate growth in other industries, especially mining, to reduce dependency on oil. The economy has been badly affected by weaknesses in the Russian economy and by falling commodity prices, with a stimulus package consequently introduced in December 2014.

Other mineral resources are considerable and there is a significant mining industry exploiting coal, iron ore, manganese, chrome, lead, zinc, copper, titanium, bauxite, silver, gold, phosphate and uranium deposits. A large and well-developed agricultural sector produces grain, wool, cotton and livestock as cash crops. The main industries are mineral extraction and processing, and machine building, especially agricultural machinery and electric motors. Services contribute 60.8 per cent of GDP, industry 34.4 per cent and agriculture 4.8 per cent.

The main trading partners are China, Russia and EU states. Principal exports are oil and oil products, natural gas, ferrous metals, chemicals, machinery, grain, wool, meat and coal. The main imports are machinery and equipment, metal products and foodstuffs. Kazakhstan became a founding member of the Eurasian Economic Union (EEU) in 2015, a customs union with Russia and Belarus which has stimulated sharp increases in trade between these nations.

GNI – US$142.3bn; US$7,890 per capita (2017)

Annual average growth of GDP – 3.3 per cent (2017 est)
Inflation rate – 7.3 per cent (2017 est)
Population below poverty line – 2.7 per cent (2015 est)
Unemployment – 5 per cent (2017 est)
Total external debt – US$159.2bn (2017 est)
Imports – US$25,175m (2016)
Exports – US$35,776m (2016)

BALANCE OF PAYMENTS
Trade – US$10,601m surplus (2016)
Current Account – US$5,352m deficit (2017)

Trade with UK	2016	2017
Imports from UK	£248,068,865	£229,941,671
Exports to UK	£540,809,974	£419,255,953

COMMUNICATIONS

Airports – 63; the largest airports are at Astana, Almaty and Atyrau
Waterways – There are important ports on the Caspian and Aral seas, which permit international trade, while the Syr Darya and Irtysh rivers provide 4,000km of navigable waterways
Roadways and railways – 87,140km; 15,333km
Telecommunications – 3.9 million fixed lines and 25.5 million mobile subscriptions (2016); there were 14 million internet users in 2016
Internet code and IDD – kz; 7 (from UK), 810 44 (to UK)
Major broadcasters – There are 250 television and radio stations according to official statistics; the influential Khabar Agency, founded by the president's eldest daughter, Dariga Nazarbayeva, operates channels in both Russian and Kazakh
Press – Major newspapers include the government-backed Russian-language *Kazakhstanskaya Pravda* and the Kazakh-language *Yegemen Qazaqstan*
WPFI score – 54,41 (158)

KENYA

Jamhuri ya Kenya – Republic of Kenya

Area – 580,367 sq. km
Capital – Nairobi; population, 4,386,000 (2018 est)
Major cities – Eldoret, Kisumu, Mombasa, Nakuru
Currency – Kenyan shilling (Ksh) of 100 cents
Population – 47,615,739 rising at 1.69 per cent a year (2017 est); Kikuyu (22 per cent), Luhya (14 per cent), Luo (13 per cent), Kalenjin (12 per cent), Kamba (11 per cent), Kisii (6 per cent), Meru (6 per cent) (2009)
Religion – Christian 83 per cent (Protestant 47.7 per cent, Roman Catholic 23.4 per cent, other 11.9 per cent), Muslim 11.2 per cent (2009 est)

Language – English, Swahili (both official), indigenous languages
Population density – 87 per sq. km (2016)
Urban population – 27 per cent (2018 est)
Median age (years) – 19.5 (2016 est)
National anthem – 'Ee Mungu Nguvu Yetu' 'Oh God of All Creation'
National day – 12 December (Independence Day)
Death penalty – Retained (last used 1987)
CPI score – 28 (143)
Military expenditure – US$964m (2017)

CLIMATE AND TERRAIN

The coastal plain and semi-desert plains in the east rise to mountainous highlands in the centre and west that are divided by the Great Rift Valley. Elevation extremes range from 5,199m (Mt Kenya) to 0m (Indian Ocean). The country includes part of Lake Victoria in the south-west and most of Lake Turkana (Rudolph) in the north. Kenya is an equatorial country; the climate is tropical on the coast and arid in the interior, tempered by altitude. The average temperature is 25°C.

HISTORY AND POLITICS

Fossils of early hominids found in the Lake Turkana region suggest that the area was inhabited some 2.6 million years ago. Arabs and Persians settled on the Kenyan coast from the eighth century AD. The Portuguese gained control of coastal areas in the 16th century but Arab overlordship was reasserted in the 18th century.

European exploration of the interior began in the 19th century and in 1895, Kenya became part of Britain's East African Protectorate, becoming a colony in 1920. Demands for internal self-government by white settlers were rejected in 1923, but from 1944 a nationalist group, the Kenya African Union (KAU), was founded to campaign for African rights. The Mau Mau rebellion of 1952–6, intended to drive white settlers from African tribal lands, resulted in a state of emergency that lasted until 1960, when preparations for majority African rule began. Kenya became independent in 1963, and a republic in 1964. President Jomo Kenyatta's death in 1978 brought Daniel arap Moi to power, and he remained president until 2002, when he was barred from standing for re-election.

Kenya was a one-party state ruled by the Kenya African National Union (KANU) between 1964 and 1991. A multiparty system was reintroduced after violent agitation and international pressure in the early 1990s but KANU maintained its grip on power until the 2002 elections, which were won by the National Rainbow Coalition (NARC). Despite the NARC's anti-corruption electoral platform, once in government it made little headway against endemic corruption, and government ministers were implicated in corruption scandals in 2005 and 2006. It is estimated that up to US$1,000m (£650m) of official funds were misappropriated in 2002–7.

After decades of stability, intercommunal violence and conflict over land and water rights have become more frequent since the 1990s, exacerbated by a rural food crisis since 2004 following persistent drought and crop failures. In 2018, the Patel Dam burst causing widespread devastation and displacing over 220,000 people.

The 2007 legislative elections were won by the Orange Democratic Movement (ODM), led by Raila Odinga. The announcement that President Kibaki had won the simultaneous presidential election triggered weeks of serious rioting; this developed into ethnic violence that left over 1,000 dead and 600,000 displaced. After international mediation, a power-sharing agreement was signed in February 2008; under this, Kibaki remained president and the post of prime minister was created for Raila Odinga, although this post was abolished in 2013.

In March 2013 Uhuru Kenyatta, the son of Kenya's first president, was elected president with 50.5 per cent of the vote; his Jubilee coalition became the largest bloc in both houses in the legislative elections. In March 2015 International Criminal Court judges terminated charges against Uhuru Kenyatta relating to 2007's post-election violence, citing lack of adequate evidence. President Kenyatta was re-elected in August 2017, although the result was contested by opposition leader Raila Odinga and was nullified in September 2017. In October, President Kenyatta won fresh elections that had been boycotted by the opposition.

In recent years Kenya has suffered a number of terrorist attacks linked to Islamism, with the Somalian group al-Shabab attacking US, Israeli and Kenyan targets within the country. In September 2013, al-Shabab gunmen killed at least 62 people in the Westgate shopping mall in Nairobi and, in April 2015, 148 people in the Garissa University College attack.

The president is directly elected for a five-year term, renewable once. The bicameral parliament as defined in the 2010 constitution was first elected in 2013; members of both houses serve five-year terms. The lower chamber, the National Assembly, has 350 members, of whom 290 are directly elected; 47 seats are reserved for women, directly elected from each county, 12 members are nominated pro rata by political parties to represent special interests including youth, persons with disabilities and workers, and the speaker is a member *ex officio*. The upper chamber, the senate, has 68 members: 47 are directly elected from each county, 16 seats are reserved for women, nominated pro rata by political parties, and four members are nominated to represent youth and persons with disabilities; the speaker is a member *ex officio*.

HEAD OF STATE
President, C-in-C of the Armed Forces, Uhuru Kenyatta, *elected* 4 March 2013, *took office* 9 April 2013, re-elected 2017
Vice-President, William Ruto

SELECTED GOVERNMENT MEMBERS *AS AT JUNE 2018*
Defence, Raychelle Omamo
Treasury and Planning, Henry Rotich
Foreign Affairs, Monica Juma

KENYA HIGH COMMISSION
45 Portland Place, London W1B 1AS
T 020-7636 2371 E info@kenyahighcom.org.uk
W www.kenyahighcom.org.uk
High Commissioner, HE Lazarus Ombai Amayo, *apptd* 2015

BRITISH HIGH COMMISSION
PO Box 30465, Upper Hill Road, 00100 Nairobi
T (+254) (20) 284 4000 E nairobi.enquiries@fco.gov.uk
W www.gov.uk/government/world/kenya
High Commissioner, HE Nic Hailey, *apptd* 2015

ECONOMY AND TRADE
Kenya acts as a regional trade and finance hub for its landlocked neighbours. However, its own economy is weak owing to endemic corruption, low commodity prices, low investor confidence and the frequent suspension of international aid because of successive governments' failure to tackle corruption. These problems are exacerbated by terrorist attacks, political instability, unemployment and the occasional severe drought. The lengthy election campaign of 2017 drained government resources and combined with drought-like conditions to slow growth; nonetheless, peaceful elections, infrastructure investment and rising tourism mean economic growth is expected to continue its decade-long 5–6 per cent GDP growth rate.

The country is overwhelmingly agricultural, with about 75 per cent of the population engaged in agricultural and horticultural production; this sector contributes 35.3 per cent of GDP. The world's third largest producer of tea, Kenya also grows coffee, maize, wheat, sugar cane, fruit and vegetables. Natural resources include gold, limestone, soda ash, salt, rubies, garnets and hydroelectric power, which makes it self-sufficient in energy.

The industrial sector has grown over the past two decades, developing a manufacturing base in consumer goods (such as textiles) and agricultural products (such as dehydrated vegetables), as well as oil refining, commercial ship repair and the production of steel, aluminium, lead and cement. Tourism is an important source of income, though it is threatened by terrorism. Industry contributes 17.2 per cent to GDP and the service sector 47.9 per cent.

The main export markets are Uganda, the USA and Pakistan, while imports come mainly from India, China, and the UAE. Principal exports are tea, horticultural products, coffee, petroleum products, fish and cement. The main imports are machinery and transport equipment, petroleum products, iron and steel, resins and plastics.

GNI – US$71.4bn; US$1,440 per capita (2017)
Annual average growth of GDP – 5.0 per cent (2017 est)
Inflation rate – 8.0 per cent (2017 est)
Population below poverty line – 43.4 per cent (2012 est)
Unemployment – 40 per cent (2013 est)
Total external debt – US$24.99bn (2017 est)
Imports – US$14,122m (2016)
Exports – US$5,700m (2016)

BALANCE OF PAYMENTS
Trade – US$8,422m deficit (2016)
Current Account – US$4,754m deficit (2017)

Trade with UK	2016	2017
Imports from UK	£309,746,727	£342,610,660
Exports to UK	£332,356,294	£455,766,057

COMMUNICATIONS
Airports – 16; the largest airports are at Nairobi, Mombasa and Eldoret
Waterways – The only significant inland waterway is the Kenyan portion of Lake Victoria; Kisumu is the main port
Roadways and railways – There are 11,189km of roadways; the Kenya Railways Corporation operates 2,066km of railways. In 2014, a Chinese company agreed to begin the construction of a new railway between Mombasa and Nairobi; the 610km line was completed in May 2017
Telecommunications – 72,801 fixed lines and 38.9 million mobile subscriptions (2016); there were 12.1 million internet users in 2016
Internet code and IDD – ke; 254 (from UK), 0 44 (to UK)
Major broadcasters – The state-run Kenya Broadcasting Corporation (KBC) competes with a range of commercial television and radio stations
Press – Daily newspapers include the English-language *Daily Nation* and *The Standard,* and *Taifa Leo* (Swahili)
WPFI score – 30,82 (96)

EDUCATION AND HEALTH

The state provides eight years of free primary education.

Literacy rate – 78 per cent (2015 est)
Gross enrolment ratio (percentage of relevant age group) – primary 105 per cent (2016 est); secondary 68 per cent (2012 est)
Health expenditure (per capita) – US$78 (2014)
Hospital beds (per 1,000 people) – 1.4 (2010)
Life expectancy (years) – 64.3 (2017 est)
Mortality rate – 6.7 (2017 est)
Birth rate – 23.9 (2017 est)
Infant mortality rate – 37.1 (2017 est)
HIV/AIDS adult prevalence – 5.4 per cent (2016 est)

KIRIBATI

Republic of Kiribati

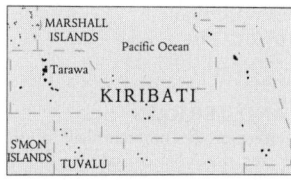

Area – 811 sq. km
Capital – Tarawa, on Bairiki; population, 64,000 (2018)
Currency – Australian dollar ($A) of 100 cents
Population – 108,145 rising at 1.13 per cent a year (2017 est); Kiribati (96.2 per cent), Kiribati/mixed (1.8 per cent), (2015 est)
Religion – Christian (Roman Catholic 55.8 per cent, Presbyterian 33.5 per cent, Mormon 4.7 per cent), Baha'i 2.3 per cent (2010 est)
Language – English, Kiribati (Gilbertese) (both official)
Population density – 144 per sq. km (2016)
Urban population – 54.1 per cent (2018 est)
Median age (years) – 24.3 (2016 est)
National anthem – 'Teirake Kaini Kiribati' 'Stand up, Kiribati'
National day – 12 July (Independence Day)
Death penalty – Abolished for all crimes (since 1979)
Gross enrolment ratio (percentage of relevant age group) – primary 104.5 per cent (2015 est), secondary 86 per cent (2011 est)
Health expenditure (per capita) – US$154 (2014)
Life expectancy (years) – 66.5 (2017 est)
Mortality rate – 7 (2017 est)
Birth rate – 21.2 (2017 est)
Infant mortality rate – 32.1 (2017 est)

CLIMATE AND TERRAIN

Kiribati (pronounced Kiri-bas) comprises 32 atolls and one island. About 20 are inhabited: Banaba island; the Kiribati (Gilbert) group (17); the Rawaki (Phoenix) Islands (8); and some of the Line Islands (11), including Kiritimati (Christmas Island). They are situated in the southern central Pacific Ocean, crossed by the equator; the area was also crossed by the international date line until 1995, when the government unilaterally moved the date line eastwards so that the whole country shared the same day. Few of the atolls are more than 800m wide or more than 3m high, making the country particularly vulnerable to rising sea levels. The highest point is 81m (on Banaba) and the lowest is 0m (Pacific Ocean). The climate is tropical.

HISTORY AND POLITICS

The islands were settled by Austronesian-speaking peoples in the first millennium BC, and Samoans, Fijians and Tongans migrated there in the 11th to 14th centuries. British settlers arrived in the islands in the early 19th century. In 1892, the Gilbert (Kiribati) and Ellice (Tuvalu) islands were proclaimed a British protectorate and in 1916 became a British colony that subsequently incorporated the Line Islands and Phoenix Islands. During the Second World War, Banaba and the Gilbert islands were occupied by the Japanese and were the scene of fierce fighting between Japanese and US troops. Some of the Line Islands were used for British nuclear weapons tests in the 1950s and 1960s. In 1975, the territories separated and the Gilbert, Phoenix and Line Islands became independent as the Republic of Kiribati in 1979.

Open-cast phosphate mining left Banaba unfit for human habitation and the population was evacuated in 1945, to be relocated to a northern island of Fiji. Overcrowding and lack of infrastructure have caused more general environmental degradation, especially in urban areas. However, the main problem is the rise in the sea level due to global warming; salination is already contaminating water supplies and agricultural land, causing villages to be relocated, and Kiribati is expected to be the first state to lose territory. The government is seeking permanent refugee status for its citizens in neighbouring countries.

In the 2015 legislative elections, the Pillars of Truth party won 26 seats while the Maurin Kiribati Party and United Coalition Party together won 19 seats. President Anote Tong stepped down in March 2016 having reached his three-term limit and Taneti Maamau was elected president in the subsequent election.

Under the 1979 constitution, the executive president is directly elected for a four-year term, with a maximum of three terms; presidential candidates are selected by and from members of the legislature. The unicameral legislature, the House of Assembly, has 46 members: 44 members directly elected for a four-year term, an appointed representative of the Banaban community in Fiji and the attorney-general. There are no formal political parties, but since the 1980s some associations of politicians formed for elections have proved durable enough to be given names.

HEAD OF STATE
President, Taneti Maamau, *elected* 9 March 2016, *sworn in* 11 March 2016
Vice-President, Kourabi Nenem

SELECTED GOVERNMENT MEMBERS *AS AT JUNE 2018*
Commerce, Industry and Co-Operatives, Tauanei Marea
Finance and Economic Development, Teuea Toatu

KIRIBATI HONORARY CONSULATE
The Great House, Llanddewi Rhydderich, Monmouthshire NP7 9UY
Honorary Consul, Michael Walsh

BRITISH HIGH COMMISSIONER
HE Melanie Hopkins, *apptd* 2016, resident at Suva, Fiji

ECONOMY AND TRADE

Since the phosphate deposits on Banaba ran out in 1979, the economy has been weak and has few natural resources. The country is dependent on coconuts, fish and tourism as the main economic activities; development is hampered by remoteness, poor transport connections and the lack of funding, infrastructure and skills. A large portion of GDP comes from international aid (around 32.7 per cent of government revenue in 2016), the sale of fishing licences,

remittances from expatriates and monies from the trust fund established with phosphate mining revenues. A financial sector is being developed. The main trading partners are Pacific Rim countries. The principal exports are coconuts and fish. The principal imports are foodstuffs, machinery and transport equipment, manufactured goods and fuel.
GNI – US$0.3bn; US$2,780 per capita (2017)
Annual average growth of GDP – 2.8 per cent (2017 est)
Inflation rate – 2.2 per cent (2017 est)
Total external debt – US$13.6m (2013 est)
Imports – US$100m (2016)
Exports – US$9m (2016)

BALANCE OF PAYMENTS
Trade – US$91m deficit (2016)
Current Account – US$35.9m surplus (2016)

Trade with UK	2016	2017
Imports from UK	£10,498	£159,957
Exports to UK	£14,016	£1,215

COMMUNICATIONS
Airports and waterways – Four, with the main international airport on Tarawa, while another on Kiritimati operates regular services to Fiji and Hawaii; the main seaport is Betio, on Tarawa
Roadways – 670km
Telecommunications – 657 fixed lines and 52,000 mobile subscriptions (2016); there were 14,649 internet users in 2016
Internet code and IDD – ki; 686 (from UK), 44 (to UK)
Media – The government-run newspaper and radio stations offer a diverse range of views; *Te Uekera* is the principal weekly newspaper

DEMOCRATIC PEOPLE'S REPUBLIC OF KOREA

Choson-minjujuui-inmin-konghwaguk – Democratic People's Republic of Korea

Area – 120,538 sq. km
Capital – Pyongyang; population, 3,038,000 (2018 est)
Major cities – Chongjin, Hamhung, Hungnam, Kaesong, Nampo, Wonsan
Currency – North Korean won of 100 chon
Population – 25,248,140 rising at 0.53 per cent a year (2017 est)
Religion – Religious activity is almost non-existent outside government-sponsored religious groups, although many believers are thought to worship in private. Historically, the main religions were Buddhism and Confucianism;

Buddhism, Christianity and Chondo (a syncretic religion) are officially recognised
Language – Korean (official)
Population density – 212 per sq. km (2016)
Urban population – 61.9 per cent (2018 est)
Median age (years) – 33.8 (2016 est)
National anthem – 'Aegukka' 'Patriotic Song'
National day – 9 September (Founding of the Democratic People's Republic of Korea, 1948)
Death penalty – Retained
CPI score – 17 (171)
Conscription – 17 years of age; 10 years for men, to age 23 for women
Literacy rate – 100 per cent (2015 est)
Gross enrolment ratio (percentage of relevant age group) – primary 76.8 per cent, secondary 93.4 per cent, tertiary 28.1 per cent (2015 est)
Health expenditure (per capita) – $22 (2007)
Life expectancy (years) – 70.7 (2017 est)
Mortality rate – 9.3 (2017 est)
Birth rate – 14.6 (2017 est)
Infant mortality rate – 22.1 (2017 est)

CLIMATE AND TERRAIN
The republic occupies the northern half of the Korean peninsula. The land rises from coastal plains in the west to mountains and hills that occupy 80 per cent of the land area. Elevation extremes range from 2,744m (Paektu-san) to 0m (Sea of Japan). The climate is temperate, though more extreme than in South Korea. Average temperatures range from −10.5°C in January to 21.3°C in July and August.

POLITICS
After the Korean war ended in 1953, Kim Il-sung continued the process of Soviet-style reform begun in 1946. He also developed *Juche* (self-reliance), an ideology demanding total economic independence. North Korea pursued an isolationist foreign policy for several decades, only signing a mutual assistance treaty with China in 1961 and improving relations with the USSR in 1985. It established diplomatic contacts with South Korea and Japan in 1990, raising hopes that it was abandoning its isolationism, but it remains a secretive, closed country under rigid state control.

Kim Il-sung died in 1994. His son Kim Jong-il became chairman of the National Defence Commission, designated as the highest post of the state, and general secretary of the Korean Workers' Party in 1997. In September 2010 the Korean Workers' Party congress (the first for 44 years) renewed the top party leadership; Kim Jong-il's third son, Kim Jong-un, was appointed to senior political and military posts, before ascending to supreme leader following the death of Kim Jong-il in December 2012. In December 2013 Kim Jong-un's uncle Chang Song-thaek, a senior political figure within North Korea, was executed in a move seen by observers as an attempt to consolidate Kim's regime.

The communist Korean Workers' Party, founded in 1946 by Kim Il-sung, is the only permitted political party. However, political control and leadership is maintained by the cult of personality created by Kim Il-sung and continued by his successors Kim Jong-il and Kim Jong-un. Elections to the Supreme People's Assembly last took place in March 2014.

The 1972 constitution was amended in 1998 to designate leading state posts; it made Kim Il-sung the Eternal President and the chairmanship of the National Defence Commission (NDC), held by Kim Jong-il, the highest post in the state, while providing that the chairman of the Presidium of the Supreme People's Assembly would represent the state on formal occasions. A further amendment in 2009 named the

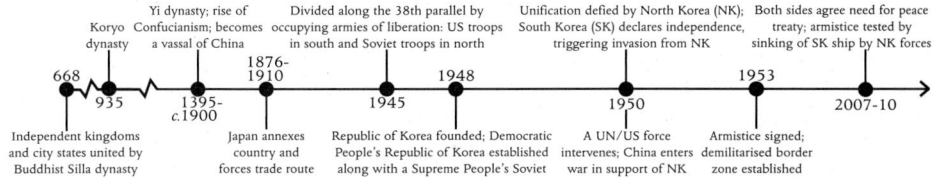

Independent kingdoms and city states united by Buddhist Silla dynasty — 668 / 935

Koryo dynasty — 1395-c.1900

Yi dynasty; rise of Confucianism; becomes a vassal of China — Japan annexes country and forces trade route

1876-1910 — Divided along the 38th parallel by occupying armies of liberation: US troops in south and Soviet troops in north

1945 — Republic of Korea founded; Democratic People's Republic of Korea established along with a Supreme People's Soviet

1948

1950 — A UN/US force intervenes; China enters war in support of NK — Unification defied by North Korea (NK); South Korea (SK) declares independence, triggering invasion from NK

1953 — Armistice signed; demilitarised border zone established — Both sides agree need for peace treaty; armistice tested by sinking of SK ship by NK forces

2007-10

NDC chairman as the 'supreme leader of the state'; it also removed all references to communism, and established the *songun* principle of military responsibility for all internal affairs.

There is a unicameral legislature, the Supreme People's Assembly, which has 687 members directly elected from a single list of candidates for a five-year term. The assembly elects a presidium and the premier, appointing the government on the recommendation of the premier. The Central People's Committee, which is also elected by the assembly, directs the administrative council (government), which implements the policy formulated by the committee.

HEAD OF STATE
Eternal President, Kim Il-sung (deceased)
Eternal General Secretary, Kim Jong-il (deceased)
Supreme Leader, Kim Jong-un
President of the Presidium of the Supreme People's Assembly, Kim Yong-nam

SELECTED GOVERNMENT MEMBERS *AS AT JUNE 2018*
Premier, Pak Pong-ju
Deputy Premiers, Ri Chol-man; Rim Chol-ung; Ri Mu-yong; Ro Tu-chol; Kim Yong-jin
Finance, Choe Kwang-jin
Foreign Affairs, Ri Yong-ho

EMBASSY OF THE DEMOCRATIC PEOPLE'S REPUBLIC OF KOREA
73 Gunnersbury Avenue, London W5 4LP
T 020-8992 4965 E prkinfo@yahoo.com
Ambassador Extraordinary and Plenipotentiary, HE Il Choe, *apptd* 2016

BRITISH EMBASSY
Munsu Dong compound, Pyongyang
T (+850) (2) 381 7980 E pyongyang.enquiries@fco.gov.uk
W www.gov.uk/government/world/north-korea
Ambassador Extraordinary and Plenipotentiary, HE Alastair Morgan, *apptd* 2015

INTERNATIONAL RELATIONS
The D. P. R. K's relations with other countries have been erratic over the past 20 years, largely owing to its nuclear ambitions and international reaction to these. It first agreed to freeze its nuclear development programme in return for fuel and development aid in 1994, only to restart the programme in 2002, claiming that other parties to the agreement had reneged on it. This pattern has been repeated several times, with the regime using the discontinuation of its nuclear and missile development programmes to bargain for aid from international agencies and regional powers. Six-nation talks to resolve the nuclear issues began in 2003 after North Korea withdrew from the Nuclear Non-Proliferation Treaty, but North Korea has never fully complied with any of the agreements concluded at the talks. The consequent suspension of aid by other nations, and UN censure and sanctions after North Korea test-fired ballistic missiles and nuclear devices in 2006, 2009, 2012, 2013 and 2015–17, had been interpreted

as acts of aggression by North Korea and was met with a bellicose response from the regime. Tensions with the USA and its allies heightened in August 2017, including the threat of sanctions from China. Renewed demilitarisation and denuclearisation talks were held with China and South Korea in early 2018, culminating in a summit between Kim Jong-un and US President Donald Trump in June 2018, the first meeting between leaders of the two nations.

ECONOMY AND TRADE
Although North Korea is rich in natural resources and had developed a heavy industry base in the first half of the 20th century, the economy is stagnant after decades of mismanagement, underinvestment, low export levels and the diversion of resources to military expenditure. Its long decline was compounded by the loss of Soviet support from 1991.

A series of natural disasters in the 1990s caused severe famine, obliging the government to request international aid. It is estimated that 3 million people have died since the 1990s as a result of the acute food shortages, which continue despite international food and fuel aid.

A redenomination of North Korea's currency in 2009 wiped out many people's savings, disrupted the nascent private sector, triggered rapid inflation and was met with unprecedented public protests that lasted some weeks. The country continues to develop special economic zones with China and South Korea.

Industrial output is centred on mining, metallurgy, chemicals, machine building and military products, but antiquated machinery and fuel shortages have limited output to a fraction of pre-1990 levels. Agriculture is in an equally parlous state, as collective farming, lack of arable land and chronic shortages of fertilisers and agricultural machinery prevent the country from producing enough to feed its population. It has been dependent on massive amounts of food aid since the mid-1990s to avert a repeat of the 1995 famine, but chronic malnutrition is widespread. A relaxation of restrictions on private farming and markets in 2003 was partially rescinded in 2005 and a centralised rationing system was reinstated. South Korean assistance in developing infrastructure, industry, the Kaesong Industrial Zone (closed in 2016 after nuclear tests) and tourism has been limited by South Korean sanctions imposed on the North in 2010, and following further missile tests the strengthening of UN sanctions in 2016 and 2017.

The main imports are petroleum, coal, machinery and equipment, textiles and grain. Principal exports are minerals, metallurgical products, armaments, textiles, and agricultural and fish products. However, in March 2016, China promised to uphold the latest sweeping sanctions on North Korea that ban the export of coal, iron and other minerals, income which is vital to the state's depleted economy.
Annual average growth of GDP – –1.1 per cent (2015 est)
Unemployment – 25.6 per cent (2013 est)
Total external debt – US$5bn (2013 est)
Imports – US$2,460m (2014)
Exports – US$965m (2014)

Trade with UK	2016	2017
Imports from UK	£52,121	£217,493
Exports to UK	£166,606	£55,111

COMMUNICATIONS

Airports and waterways – There are 39 airports, the largest of which is at Pyongyang. There are some 2,250km of waterways but these are navigable only by small craft; the main seaports are Chongjin, Nampo and Wonsan
Roadways and railways – There are 724km of paved roadways, and 5,242km of railways
Telecommunications – 1.18 million fixed lines and 3.6 million mobile subscriptions (2016)
Internet code and IDD – kp; 850 (from UK), 44 (to UK)
Media – There are no independent media outlets in North Korea; all television, radios and national newspapers are government organs. There are 12 principal newspapers and 20 major periodicals, some of which are published in English
WPFI score – 88,87 (180)

REPUBLIC OF KOREA

Taehan-min'guk – Republic of Korea

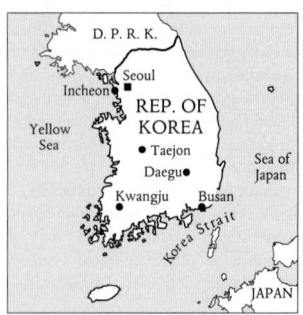

Area – 99,720 sq. km
Capital – Seoul; population, 9,963,000 (2018 est)
Major cities – Busan, Changwon, Daegu, Daejon, Gwangju, Incheon, Kwangju, Suwon, Taejon, Urusan
Currency – South Korean won of 100 jeon
Population – 51,181,299 rising at 0.48 per cent a year (2017 est)
Religion – Christian (Protestant 24 per cent, Roman Catholic 7.6 per cent), Buddhist 24.2 per cent (predominantly the Jogye order of the Seon (Zen) school), none 43.3 per cent (2010 est)
Language – Korean (official), English
Population density – 528 per sq. km (2016)
Urban population – 82.7 per cent (2017 est)
Median age (years) – 41.2 (2016 est)
National anthem – 'Aegukga' 'Patriotic Song'
National day – 15 August (Liberation Day)
Death penalty – Retained (last used 1997)
CPI score – 54 (51)
Military expenditure – US$39,153m (2017)
Conscription – 20–30 years of age; 21–24 months (selective)

CLIMATE AND TERRAIN

The country occupies the southern part of the mountainous Korean peninsula, with highlands and mountains accounting for around 70 per cent of the land area. Elevation extremes range from 1,950m (Halla-san) to 0m (Sea of Japan). The climate is temperate, although winters are very cold for the latitude. Average temperatures range from −2.5°C in January to 24.3°C in August. The rainy season lasts from June to September.

HISTORY AND POLITICS

From 1948, South Korea experienced over 40 years of mostly authoritarian, often military, rule and great industrial development. Syngman Rhee, president from 1948, resigned in 1960 in the face of popular protests at corruption and electoral fraud. A military coup in 1961 brought General Park Chung-hee to power and he instigated a programme of industrial development; by the time of his assassination in 1979, Korea was a leading shipbuilding nation and producer of electronic goods.

Following riots against the interim government, General Chun Do-hwan assumed power in 1980 after martial law was declared. Pro-democracy agitation in the mid-1980s led to constitutional changes in 1987 and the first multiparty legislative elections in 1988, but despite subsequent anti-corruption campaigns, politics has continued to be plagued by allegations of corruption and fraud, and has been subject to military influence. The first civilian president and the first wholly civilian government since 1961 were appointed in 1993.

In December 2012, Park Geun-hye was elected South Korea's first female president and assumed office in February 2013. In April 2016 legislative elections, Park's ruling, centre-right party Saenuri (formerly the Grand National Party) lost the majority it had held for 16 years by one seat to the newly formed Minjoo opposition. In March 2017, Park became the country's first democratically elected leader to be forced from office for corruption when the constitutional court upheld her impeachment, and was sentenced to 24 years in prison in April 2018. Moon Jae-in of the Democratic Party won the May 2017 presidential election with 41 per cent of the vote; he named Lee Nak-yon prime minister. President Moon has promised rapprochement with North Korea, and despite heightened tensions in late 2017, demilitarisation and denuclearisation talks initially appeared successful in the first half of 2018.

A new constitution was adopted when the Sixth Republic was inaugurated in 1988. Under this, the president is directly elected for a five-year term, which is not renewable. The president appoints the prime minister with the approval of the legislature, and members of the state council (cabinet) on the recommendation of the prime minister. The president is also empowered to take wide-ranging measures in an emergency, but must obtain the agreement of the legislature. The unicameral National Assembly has 300 members who are directly elected for a four-year term.

HEAD OF STATE
President, Moon Jae-in, *elected* 9 May 2017

SELECTED GOVERNMENT MEMBERS *AS AT JUNE 2018*
Prime Minister, Lee Nak-yon
Deputy Prime Minister, Finance, Kim Dong-yeon
Defence, Adm. (retd) Song Young-moo
Foreign Affairs, Kang Kyung-wha

EMBASSY OF THE REPUBLIC OF KOREA
60 Buckingham Gate, London SW1E 6AJ
T 020-7227 5500 E koreanembinuk@mofat.go.kr
W www.gbr.mofat.go.kr
Ambassador Extraordinary and Plenipotentiary, Park Enna

BRITISH EMBASSY
Sejong-daero 19-gil 24, Jung-gu, Seoul 100–120
T (+82) (2) 3210 5500 E enquiry.seoul@fco.gov.uk
W www.gov.uk/government/world/south-korea
Ambassador Extraordinary and Plenipotentiary, HE Simon Smith, CMG, *apptd* 2018

ECONOMY AND TRADE

Industrialisation from the 1960s transformed South Korea from a predominantly agrarian country into one of the Asian 'miracle' economies by the 1980s. Initially based on shipbuilding and electrical goods, production shifted towards electronics and IT goods in the 1980s. By 1997 South Korea was the world's 11th-largest economy, with an annual GDP growth rate of 8 per cent. However, the dominating conglomerates *(chaebols)* were experiencing difficulties which, exacerbated by the Asian financial crisis in 1997, caused a number to collapse in the late 1990s and the economy to contract sharply. Corporate and financial reforms were introduced and GDP growth resumed from the early 2000s. Slow growth in Europe, the USA and China has reduced growth in recent years, which is set to continue. Long-term challenges include an ageing population, reliance on a small number of large companies and a dependence on exports.

Services contribute 58.3 per cent to GDP, industry 39.3 per cent and agriculture 2.2 per cent. Major manufacturing industries include electronics, telecommunications, motor vehicles, chemicals, shipbuilding and steel. Tourism is of growing importance.

The main trading partners are China, Japan and the USA (the US–South Korea Trade Agreement was first signed in 2007 and ratified in 2011). Principal exports are semiconductors, petrochemicals, telecommunications equipment, motor vehicles, electronics, steel, and ships. The main imports are oil, gas, electronics and electronic equipment, steel, transport equipment, organic chemicals and textiles.

GNI – US$1,460.5bn; US$28,380 per capita (2017)
Annual average growth of GDP – 3.0 per cent (2017 est)
Inflation rate – 1.9 per cent (2017 est)
Population below poverty line – 12.5 per cent (2015 est)
Unemployment – 3.8 per cent (2017 est)
Total external debt – US$376.9bn (2017 est)
Imports – US$443,695m (2016)
Exports – US$535,739m (2016)

BALANCE OF PAYMENTS

Trade – US$92,044m surplus (2016)
Current Account – US$78,460m surplus (2017)

Trade with UK	2016	2017
Imports from UK	£4,408,641,732	£5,817,316,705
Exports to UK	£4,670,475,571	£4,434,830,130

COMMUNICATIONS

Airports and waterways – 71, including international airports at Seoul (Kimpo), Kimhae (near Busan), Daegu, Cheju city and Incheon; Busan, Incheon and Pohang are the major ports, although development and operations at Incheon are hampered by tidal variations of 9–10m
Roadways and railways – There are 83,199km of roadways, of which 3,779km are motorways; 3,381km of railway is in commercial operation, of which 1,843km is electrified
Telecommunications – 28 million fixed lines and 61 million mobile telephone subscriptions (2016); there were 44.2 million internet users in 2016
Internet code and IDD – kr; 82 (from UK), 1 44/2 44 (to UK)
Major broadcasters – Korea has a number of public radio and television broadcasters, including Korea Broadcasting System (KBS) and Munhwa Broadcasting Corporation (MBC), as well as a diversified commercial sector

Press – Major newspapers include *Chosun Ilbo, Korea Daily* and English-language daily *Korea Herald*
WPFI score – 23,51 (43)

EDUCATION AND HEALTH

Primary education is free and compulsory for nine years from the age of six.

Gross enrolment ratio (percentage of relevant age group) – primary 99 per cent, secondary 97.7 per cent, tertiary 95.3 per cent (2013 est)
Health expenditure (per capita) – US$2,060 (2014)
Hospital beds (per 1,000 people) – 11.5 (2015)
Life expectancy (years) – 82.5 (2017 est)
Mortality rate – 6 (2017 est)
Birth rate – 8.3 (2017 est)
Infant mortality rate – 3 (2017 est)

KOSOVO

Republika e Kosoves – Republic of Kosovo

Area – 10,887 sq. km
Capital – Pristina; population, 207,062 (2014 est)
Major towns – Mitrovica, Pec, Prizren
Currency – Euro (€) of 100 cents; the Serbian dinar is also in circulation
Population – 1,895,250 (2017 est); Albanian (92.2 per cent), Serb, Bosniak, Turk, Ashkali, Egyptian, Roma and Gorani (6.9 per cent) (2011)
Religion – Muslim 95.6 per cent, Roman Catholic 2.2 per cent, Serbian Orthodox 1.5 per cent (2011 est)
Language – Albanian, Serbian (both official), Bosnian, Turkish, Romani
Population density – 168 per sq. km (2016)
Median age (years) – 28.7 (2016 est)
National anthem – 'Europe'
National day – 17 February (Independence Day)
Death penalty – Not since independence
CPI score – 36 (85)
Military expenditure – US$57.3m (2017)

CLIMATE AND TERRAIN

Kosovo has a hilly central region that divides plains in the east and west. Mountains lie along the borders with Albania, Macedonia and Montenegro, and along much of the border with Serbia. Elevation extremes range from 2,656m (Gjeravica) to 297m (Drini i Bardhe river). The main rivers are the Drini i Bardhe in the west and the Iberi in the north. The climate is continental.

Serbia regains control after First Balkan War; becomes province of Serbia, then part of Yugoslavia — **1389** / **1913**

Battle of Kosovo; Serbian principalities become part of the Ottoman Empire

Stripped of its autonomy by Serbian government and Albanian majority; gradually excluded from public life — **1945** / **1989**

Becomes an autonomous republic within Serbia

Insurgency by the Kosovan Liberation Army provokes Serbian military reprisals — **1991** / **c.1995**

Vote of independence declared illegal by Serbian government

NATO intervention; Serbia signs peace plan and withdraws forces — **1998** / **1999**

Serbia begins systematic ethnic cleansing of country

International Court of Justice rules declaration legal; it is accepted by UN but refused by Serbia — **2008** / **2010**

Kosovan government declares independence; it goes unrecognised by the UN

POLITICS

Under the 2008 constitution, the president is elected by the legislature for a five-year term and can be re-elected once. The unicameral legislature, the Assembly of Kosovo, has 120 members, elected for a four-year term; 100 seats have directly elected members, ten seats are reserved for Serbs and ten for other minorities. The majority party or coalition nominates the prime minister, who is appointed by the president. Both the prime minister and the government must be approved by the legislature.

In the June 2017 legislative elections, the ruling Democratic Party of Kosovo-led coalition lost seats and was initially unable to form a government until the New Kosovo Alliance also joined the coalition. Hashim Thaci was elected president in the third round of voting, in February 2016, succeeding Atifete Jahjaga.

HEAD OF STATE
President, Hashim Thaci, *elected* 26 February 2016

SELECTED GOVERNMENT MEMBERS *AS AT JUNE 2018*
Prime Minister, Rumush Haradinaj
Finance, Bendri Hamza
Foreign Affairs, Behgjet Pacolli
Internal Affairs, Bejtush Gashi

EMBASSY OF THE REPUBLIC OF KOSOVO
8 John Street, London WC1N 2ES
T 020-3585 4167 E embassy.uk@rks-gov.net
W www.kosovoembassy.org.uk
Ambassador Extraordinary and Plenipotentiary, HE Lirim Greicevci, *apptd* 2012

BRITISH EMBASSY
Ismail Qemali 6, Arberi, Dragodan, Pristina
T (+381) 3825 4700 E britishembassy.pristina@fco.gov.uk
W www.gov.uk/government/world/kosovo
Ambassador Extraordinary and Plenipotentiary, HE Ruairí O'Connell, *apptd* 2015

ECONOMY AND TRADE

Under UN administration Kosovo began the transition to a market economy, and over half of state-owned businesses have been privatised. However, income levels are the second lowest in Europe, and the economy is dependent on international and foreign aid and the remittances of expatriates, worth about 10 per cent and 17 per cent of GDP respectively. Agriculture is close to subsistence level and inefficient; industrial output has declined because of insufficient investment and an unemployment level of over 30 per cent encourages emigration. International agencies and foreign governments are working with the Kosovan government to stimulate economic growth, attract investment and reduce unemployment.

Kosovo joined the Central Europe Free Trade Area (CEFTA) in 2006, and its members are the main markets for exports of minerals and processed metal products, scrap metals, leather goods, machinery and appliances. Imports of foodstuffs, wood, fuels, chemicals, machinery and textiles come mainly from EU and neighbouring countries. In 2011 Serbia and Bosnia resumed trade with Kosovo, while a free trade agreement was signed with Turkey in 2013. The country continues to negotiate trade liberalisation with the EU.

GNI – US$7.1bn; US$3,890 per capita (2017)
Annual average growth of GDP – 3.5 per cent (2017 est)
Inflation rate – 1.4 per cent (2017 est)
Population below poverty line – 30 per cent (2013 est)
Unemployment – 34.8 per cent (2016 est)
Total external debt – US$1.4bn (2016 est)
Imports – US$2,687m (2014 est)
Exports – US$349m (2014 est)

BALANCE OF PAYMENTS
Current Account – US$448m deficit (2017)

Trade with UK	2016	2017
Imports from UK	£4,269,629	£5,206,763
Exports to UK	£672,276	£759,254

COMMUNICATIONS

Airports – Three; the principal international terminal is at Pristina
Roadways and railways – 1,843km, including 38km of motorways; 430km
Telecommunications – 831,470 fixed lines and 562,000 mobile telephone subscriptions (2016)
Internet code and IDD – kv; 381 (from UK), 44 (to UK)
Major broadcasters – Kosovo Radio-Television is the country's public broadcaster
Press – Leading dailies include *Koha Ditore, Bota Sot* and *Kosova Sot*
WPFI score – 29,51 (43)

KUWAIT

Dawlat al-Kuwayt – State of Kuwait

Area – 17,818 sq. km
Capital – Kuwait City (al-Kuwayt); population, 2,989,000 (2018 est)
Major cities – Al-Ahmadi, As Salimiyah, Hawalli
Currency – Kuwaiti dinar (KD) of 1,000 fils
Population – 2,875,422 rising at 1.46 per cent a year (2017 est); Kuwaiti (31.3 per cent), other Arab (27.9 per cent), Asian (37.8 per cent) (2013 est)

Religion – Muslim (official) (Sunni 76.7 per cent, the remainder predominantly Shia), Christian (17.3 per cent) (est); Hindu and Parsi minorities, mostly expatriates
Language – Arabic (official), English
Population density – 232 per sq. km (2016)
Urban population – 100 per cent (2018 est)
Median age (years) – 29.2 (2016 est)
National anthem – 'Al-Nasheed al-Watani' 'National Anthem'
National day – 25 February
Death penalty – Retained
CPI score – 39 (85)
Military expenditure – US$6,831m (2017)

CLIMATE AND TERRAIN
Kuwait is an almost entirely flat desert plain, with elevation extremes ranging from 306m to 0m (Persian Gulf). Its territory includes the island of Bubiyan and others at the head of the Persian Gulf. The climate is arid, with little rainfall but high levels of humidity. Average temperatures range from 12.5°C in January to 37°C in July and August.

HISTORY AND POLITICS
The area was under the nominal control of the Ottoman Empire from the late 16th century, but in 1756 an autonomous sheikhdom was founded that has been ruled by the al-Sabah family ever since. Kuwait entered into a treaty of friendship with Britain in 1899, in order to protect itself from Ottoman and Saudi domination, and it became a British protectorate in 1914. The borders with Saudi Arabia and Iraq were agreed between 1922 and 1933. Full independence was achieved in 1961, although Britain retained a military presence in the country until 1971.

An attempted Iraqi invasion shortly after independence in 1961 was discouraged by British troops in the Gulf. However, in August 1990 Iraq invaded and occupied Kuwait, proclaiming it a province of Iraq. In 1991, a short military campaign by a US-led alliance expelled the Iraqi forces, although there were further Iraqi incursions in 1993 before Iraq renounced its claim and recognised the new UN-demarcated border in 1994. Extensive damage was caused to the country's infrastructure and environment during the Iraqi occupation and reconstruction was a priority throughout the 1990s; in 2003, Kuwait was a base for forces involved in the Iraq War.

In recent years, there have been clashes between security forces and militant Islamists, some of whom are alleged to have links to al-Qaida.

Although Kuwait was the first Arab country in the Gulf to have an elected legislature, this was suspended from 1977–81, 1986–92, and in 1999, 2012 and 2013. The political system is subject to instability, with electoral boycotts by Islamist and liberal parties common; two elections were held in 12 months in 2008–9 owing to the legislature's efforts to subject the government to parliamentary scrutiny. Pro-reform demonstrations took place in spring 2011, forcing Sheikh Nasser al-Muhammad al-Ahmad al-Sabeh's government to resign from office; the cabinet was replaced by a new government headed by Sheikh Jaber al-Mubarak al-Hamad al-Sabah who has retained power since. The last legislative elections took place in 2016.

The 1962 constitution was amended in 2005 to extend the franchise to women. The head of state is the emir, chosen from among the ruling family. He exercises executive power through the council of ministers; in 2003, the post of prime minister was separated from the role of heir to the throne for the first time. The unicameral National Assembly has 65 members who serve four-year terms; 50 are directly elected and 15 *ex-officio* members are appointed by the prime minister to serve in the cabinet. There are no political parties.

The country is divided into six governorates: Capital, Hawalli, al-Ahmadi, al-Jahrah, al-Farwaniya and Mubarak al-Kabeer.

HEAD OF STATE
HH The Emir of Kuwait, Sheikh Sabah al-Ahmad al-Jaber al-Sabah, *born* 1929, *acceded* 29 January 2006
Crown Prince, HH Sheikh Nawaf al-Ahmad al-Jaber al-Sabah

SELECTED GOVERNMENT MEMBERS *AS AT JUNE 2018*
Prime Minister, Sheikh Jaber al-Mubarak al-Hamad al-Sabah
First Deputy Prime Minister, Defence, Sheikh Nasser al-Sabah al-Ahmad al-Sabah
Deputy Prime Minister, Foreign Affairs, Sheikh Mohammad al-Khaled al-Hamad al-Sabah
Deputy Prime Minister, Interior, Sheikh Khaled al-Jarrah al-Sabah

EMBASSY OF THE STATE OF KUWAIT
2 Albert Gate, London SW1X 7JU
T 020-7590 3400 E kuwait@dircon.co.uk
Ambassador Extraordinary and Plenipotentiary, HE Khaled al-Duwaisan, GCVO, *apptd* 1993

BRITISH EMBASSY
PO Box 2, Arabian Gulf Street, Safat 13001
T (+965) 2259 4320 E kuwait.generalenquiries@fco.gov.uk
W www.gov.uk/government/world/kuwait
Ambassador Extraordinary and Plenipotentiary, HE Michael Davenport, MBE, *apptd* 2017

ECONOMY AND TRADE
Oil was discovered in 1938 and the development of the oil industry after 1945 transformed the country from one of the poorest in the world to one of the richest. Petroleum accounts for 92 per cent of export revenues and 90 per cent of government income, and extraction is set to increase. Income from foreign reserves and investment is also high, cushioning the economy from the effects of dependency on oil. Economic reform is slow owing to the tensions between the government and legislature; a diversification fund worth US$130bn was established in 2010, though much of this money has yet to be spent. Kuwait has a rich sovereign wealth fund, worth as much as US$600bn (£417bn) according to some estimates, but in 2016 it ran its first current-account deficit since 1992 due to falling oil prices and an undiversified economy.

The climate and terrain limit agriculture and, with the exception of fish, all food is imported; the agriculture sector contributes only 0.4 per cent of GDP. Services account for 40.9 per cent of GDP and industry for 58.7 per cent. Apart from the oil and petrochemical industries, activities include the production of cement and construction materials, shipbuilding and repair, water desalination and food processing.

The main export markets are South Korea, China, Japan, India and Singapore, and the main sources of imports are China, the USA, the UAE, Saudi Arabia and Germany. Principal exports are oil and refined products, and fertilisers. The main imports are food, construction materials, vehicles and vehicle parts, and clothing.
GNI – US$130bn; US$31,430 per capita (2017)
Annual average growth of GDP – –2.1 per cent (2017 est)
Inflation rate – 2.5 per cent (2017 est)
Unemployment – 2.1 per cent (2017 est)
Total external debt – US$48.91bn (2017 est)
Imports – US$30,825m (2016)
Exports – US$46,238m (2016)

BALANCE OF PAYMENTS
Trade – US$15,413m surplus (2016)
Current Account – US$7,591m surplus (2017)

Trade with UK	2016	2017
Imports from UK	£505,609,010	£617,426,755
Exports to UK	£645,204,005	£766,543,138

COMMUNICATIONS

Airports and waterways – Four, with an international airport at Kuwait City; the main seaports are Ash Shu'aybah and Ash Shuwaykh
Roadways – There are 6,608km of roadways
Telecommunications – 403,234 fixed lines and 5.4 million mobile subscriptions (2016); there were 2.2 million internet users in 2016
Internet code and IDD – kw; 965 (from UK), 44 (to UK)
Major broadcasters – Kuwaiti TV and Radio Kuwait are the public broadcasters and compete with commercial stations; satellite television is also widely watched
Press – Major dailies include *Al-Watan, Al-Qabas* and the *Kuwait Times*
WPFI score – 31,91 (105)

EDUCATION AND HEALTH

Education is free and compulsory from six to 14 years
Literacy rate – 95.6 per cent (2017 est)
Gross enrolment ratio (percentage of relevant age group) – primary 101 per cent (2016 est), secondary 95 per cent (2015 est), tertiary 27 per cent (2013 est)
Health expenditure (per capita) – US$1,386 (2014)
Hospital beds (per 1,000 people) – 2 (2014)
Life expectancy (years) – 78.2 (2017 est)
Mortality rate – 2.2 (2017 est)
Birth rate – 19.2 (2017 est)
Infant mortality rate – 7 (2017 est)

KYRGYZSTAN

Kyrgyz Respublikasy – Kyrgyz Republic

Area – 199,951 sq. km
Capital – Bishkek; population, 996,000 (2018 est)
Major city – Osh
Currency – Som of 100 tyiyn
Population – 5,789,122 rising at 1.05 per cent a year (2017 est); Kyrgyz (73.2 per cent), Uzbek (14.6 per cent), Russian (5.8 per cent), Dungan (1.1 per cent) (2017 est)
Religion – Muslim 75 per cent (predominantly Sunni), Christian (Russian Orthodox) 20 per cent, other 5 per cent
Language – Kyrgyz, Russian (both official), Uzbek, Dungan
Population density – 32 per sq. km (2016)
Urban population – 36.4 per cent (2018 est)
Median age (years) – 26.2 (2016 est)

National anthem – 'Kyrgyz Respublikasynyn Mamlekettik Gimni' 'National Anthem of the Kyrgyz Republic'
National day – 31 August (Independence Day)
Death penalty – Abolished for all crimes (since 2007)
CPI score – 29 (135)
Military expenditure – US$223m (2017 est)
Conscription – 18–27 years of age, male only; 12 months
Literacy rate – 99.5 per cent (2015 est)
Gross enrolment ratio (percentage of relevant age group) – primary 106 per cent, secondary 98 per cent, tertiary 46 per cent (2016 est)
Health expenditure (per capita) – US$82 (2014)
Hospital beds (per 1,000 people) – 4.5 (2013)
Life expectancy (years) – 70.9 (2017 est)
Mortality rate – 6.5 (2017 est)
Birth rate – 22.1 (2017 est)
Infant mortality rate – 25.9 (2017 est)
HIV/AIDS adult prevalence – 0.2 per cent (2016 est)

CLIMATE AND TERRAIN

Kyrgyzstan is a landlocked and mountainous country lying in the Tien Shan mountain range, with the Pamir mountains in the extreme south. Elevations range from 7,439m (Jengish Chokusu) to 132m (Kara-Darya), though most of the country lies at over 1,000m. The principal rivers are the Naryn and the Chu, and the vast Issyk-Kul lake lies in the north-east. The climate is continental but with temperatures and humidity moderated by the altitude; typical temperatures range from −12.6°C in January to 15.2°C in July. Rainfall is low for the altitude, owing to Kyrgyzstan's distance from the sea and the rain-shadow effect of the Himalayan and Pamir ranges.

HISTORY AND POLITICS

After centuries of Turkic, Mongol and Chinese rule, the Kyrgyz became part of the Russian Empire in the 1860s and 1870s. After the October 1917 revolution in Russia, the area became part of the Turkestan autonomous republic within the USSR until 1924, when the Kirgiz Autonomous Region was formed. Soviet rule brought land reforms in the 1920s that resulted in the settlement of many of the nomadic Kyrgyz. Kyrgyzstan became an autonomous republic in 1926 and a constituent republic of the USSR in 1936.

Reform in the USSR in the 1980s provoked an upsurge in nationalism in Kyrgyzstan and agitation for independence. Following the attempted coup in Moscow in 1991, Kyrgyzstan became an independent republic and joined the Commonwealth of Independent States.

Since independence, there has been tension between the Kyrgyz and ethnic Uzbeks, concentrated around Osh, and between the Kyrgyz and Dungans (ethnic Chinese) near Bishkek. There have also been clashes between security forces and militant Islamists, active near the border with Tajikistan.

Askar Akayev, a pro-reform Communist, was president from 1990 until he was deposed in March 2005 in a popular uprising over alleged electoral fraud; the uprising was also fuelled by years of unrest over the dire economic situation, corruption, nepotism and crime. The opposition leader Kurmanbek Bakiyev was elected president in July 2005 and re-elected in 2009, but forced from office in April 2010 after attempts to suppress anti-government demonstrations left over 80 protestors dead.

An interim government was formed, but intercommunal violence between Kyrgyz and Uzbeks erupted in June 2010, spreading to Jalalabad; a referendum held in the same month approved a draft constitution granting greater powers to parliament at the expense of the president.

In the 2015 legislative elections the Social Democratic Party (SDPK) won 27.4 per cent of the vote and received 38 seats in parliament, while the merged Respublika-Ata-Jurt party won 20.1 per cent and 28 seats, and the new Kyrgyzstan Party 12.9 per cent and 18 seats; in April 2018, Muhammetkaliy Abulgaziyez was elected prime minister by the SDPK-led ruling coalition, becoming the 20th person to fill the role since independence.

Under the 2010 constitution, the president is directly elected for a six-year term, which is not renewable. The unicameral Supreme Council has 120 members directly elected for a five-year term. The largest party in the legislature nominates the prime minister, and the president appoints the cabinet; the appointments are subject to the approval of the Supreme Council.

HEAD OF STATE
President, Sooronbai Jeenbekov, *elected* 15 October 2017, *sworn in* 24 November 2017

SELECTED GOVERNMENT MEMBERS *AS AT JUNE 2018*
Prime Minister, Muhammetkaliy Abulgaziyez
First Deputy Prime Minister, Kubatbek Boronov
Foreign Affairs, Erlan Abdyldaev
Internal Affairs, Kashkar Dzhunushaliev

EMBASSY OF THE KYRGYZ REPUBLIC
Ascot House, 119 Crawford Street, London W1U 6BJ
T 020-7935 1462 E mail@kyrgyz-embassy.org.uk
W www.kyrgyz-embassy.org.uk
Ambassador Extraordinary and Plenipotentiary, HE Gulnara
   Iskakova, *apptd* 2015

BRITISH EMBASSY
21 Erkindik Boulevard, Office 404, Bishkek, 720040, Kyrgyzstan
T (+996) 312 303 637 E ukinkyrgyzrepublic@fco.gov.uk
W www.gov.uk/government/world/kyrgyzstan
Ambassador Extraordinary and Plenipotentiary, HE Robin Ord-
   Smith, MVO, *apptd* 2015

ECONOMY AND TRADE
Economic reforms in the early 1990s caused severe hardship, and although productivity and exports have grown since the late 1990s, poverty is widespread. The economy, which is heavily dependent on gold exports, contracted in 2009 owing to the global downturn, and production and trade were reduced further by the political violence and disruption of 2010. Despite such damage to the infrastructure, the economy grew to 17.4 per cent in 2013, and has experienced steady growth since. The government, with international support, is pursuing poverty-reduction and economic-growth programmes, but the greater foreign direct investment that these require may be deterred by political volatility, lack of transparency and the high level of organised crime. Kyrgyzstan became the fifth member of the Eurasian Economic Union (EEU) in May 2015 and while membership was expected to boost trade, economic growth was expected to be hit by slowing economies in Russia and China, coupled with low commodity prices. Remittances from migrant workers located mainly in Russia are equal over 25 per cent of GDP.

The economy is predominantly agrarian, with agriculture accounting for 14.3 per cent of GDP and employing 48 per cent of the workforce. There are deposits of gold, uranium, mercury and natural gas. Apart from mining, industry consists of hydroelectric power generation and light manufacturing, contributing 32.5 per cent of GDP; services contribute 53.2 per cent.

The main trading partners are Switzerland (59.1 per cent of exports), Kazakhstan, Russia and China. Principal exports are gold, cotton, wool, meat, tobacco, mercury, uranium,

electricity, machinery and shoes. The main imports are oil, gas, machinery and equipment, chemicals and foodstuffs.
GNI – US$7bn; US$1,130 per capita (2017)
Annual average growth of GDP – 3.5 per cent (2017 est)
Inflation rate – 3.8 per cent (2017 est)
Population below poverty line – 32.1 per cent (2015 est)
Unemployment – 7.4 per cent (2017 est)
Total external debt – US$8.679bn (2017 est)
Imports – US$3,919m (2016)
Exports – US$1,545m (2016)

BALANCE OF PAYMENTS
Trade – US$2,374m deficit (2016)
Current Account – US$347m deficit (2017)

Trade with UK	2016	2017
Imports from UK	£3,801,419	£6,307,849
Exports to UK	£23,143,480	£141,526,786

COMMUNICATIONS
Airports and waterways – 18, with an international airport outside Bishkek; there are 600km of waterways
Roadways and railways – 34,000km; 470km
Telecommunications – 382,149 fixed lines and 7.6 million mobile subscriptions (2016); there were 1.9 million internet users in 2016
Internet code and IDD – kg; 996 (from UK), 44 (to UK)
Major broadcasters – Kyrgyz National TV and Radio Broadcasting Corporation runs various networks alongside a number of private broadcasters
Press – Major newspapers include the government-owned *Slovo Kyrgyzstana Plus* and the private *Vecherniy Bishkek*
WPFI score – 31 (98)

LAOS

Sathalanalat Paxathipatai Paxaxon Lao – Lao People's Democratic Republic

Area – 236,800 sq. km
Capital – Vientiane; population, 665,000 (2018 est)
Major towns – Luang Prabang, Pakse, Savannakhet
Currency – Kip (K) of 100 att
Population – 7,126,706 rising at 1.51 per cent a year (2017 est); there are (officially) 49 ethnic groups, including Lao (53.2 per cent), Khmou (11.0 per cent), Hmong (9.2 per cent) (2017)
Religion – Buddhist 66.8 per cent (predominantly Theravada), Christian 1.5 per cent (2005 est); most of the remainder practise animist beliefs
Language – Lao (official), French, English, ethnic languages
Population density – 30 per sq. km (2016)

Urban population – 35 per cent (2018 est)
Median age (years) – 22.7 (2016 est)
National anthem – 'Pheng Xat Lao' 'Hymn of the Lao People'
National day – 2 December (Republic Day)
Death penalty – Retained (last used 1989)
CPI score – 29 (135)
Military expenditure – US$22.7m (2013)
Conscription – 18 years of age; 18 months
Literacy rate – 90.2 per cent (2015 est)
Gross enrolment ratio (percentage of age group) – primary 110 per
   cent, secondary 67 per cent, tertiary 17 per cent (2016
   est)
Health expenditure (per capita) – US$33 (2014)
Hospital beds (per 1,000 people) – 1.5 (2012)
Life expectancy (years) – 64.6 (2017 est)
Mortality rate – 7.4 (2017 est)
Birth rate – 23.6 (2017 est)
Infant mortality rate – 49.9 (2017 est)
HIV/AIDS adult prevalence – 0.3 per cent (2016 est)

CLIMATE AND TERRAIN
Laos is mostly mountainous, the land rising from the Mekong river basin in the west to mountains in the north and east. Elevation extremes range from 2,817m (Phou Bia) to 70m (Mekong river). Much of the land is covered by rainforest. The climate is tropical, with a wet season from May to October, during which humidity levels are very high. Average temperatures in Vientiane range from 19.9°C in January to 26.3°C in June.

HISTORY AND POLITICS
From the ninth to the 13th centuries, Laos was part of the Khmer Empire centred on Angkor in Cambodia. Small principalities developed from the 12th century and were united in the 14th century into the Lao kingdom of Lan Xang ('the land of a million elephants'), which dominated until 1713, when it split into the separate kingdoms of Luang Prabang, Vientiane and Champassac, which became tributaries of Siam (Thailand) in the late 18th century and then a protectorate of France from 1893.

Japanese occupation during the Second World War inspired a Lao nationalist movement, which proclaimed independence in 1945, but the French regained control of the country in 1946. Independence as a constitutional monarchy was granted in 1953, but much of the following 20 years was spent in civil war between the Communist Pathet Lao movement, backed first by China and then by North Vietnam, and royalists, who attracted US and Thai support from the early 1960s. A ceasefire in 1973 partitioned the country between the two sides, but in 1975 the Pathet Lao seized power in the rest of the country and proclaimed a republic, introducing a one-party state and initiating socialist policies. Greater economic liberalisation was introduced from the mid-1980s, and the first legislative elections since 1975 were held in 1989.

Ethnic Hmong minority groups have maintained a low-level insurgency against the communist regime since 1975. In 2000 and 2004, Laos suffered serious civil disturbances, including bombings and armed attacks on buses. These were variously attributed to Hmong insurgents and anti-government groups based abroad.

In the March 2016 legislative election, Lao People's Revolutionary Party (LPRP) candidates won all but five of the seats, the remaining seats being taken by approved independent candidates. The legislature elected former vice-president Bounnhang Vorachit as president in April and approved a reshuffled council of ministers.

Under the 1991 constitution, the head of state is a president elected by the legislature for a five-year term, with no term limits. The unicameral National Assembly has 149 members, who are party-approved candidates directly elected for a five-year term. The LPRP is the only legal political party, although it has given approval to non-partisan candidates for legislative seats. Party congresses are held every five years.

HEAD OF STATE
President, Bounnhang Vorachit, *elected* 20 April 2016
Vice-President, Phankham Viphavanh

SELECTED GOVERNMENT MEMBERS *AS AT JUNE 2018*
Prime Minister, Thongloun Sisoulith
Deputy Prime Ministers, Somdy Douangdy *(Finance);* Bounpone
   Bouttanavong; Bounthong Chitmany; Sonexay
   Siphandone
Foreign Affairs, Saleumxay Kommasith
National Defence, Lt.-Gen. Chansamone Chanyalath

EMBASSY OF THE LAO PEOPLE'S DEMOCRATIC
REPUBLIC
49 Porchester Terrace, London W2 3TS
T 020-7402 3770 E laosemblondon@gmail.com
Ambassador Extraordinary and Plenipotentiary, HE Sayakane
   Sisouvong, *apptd* 2014

BRITISH EMBASSY
Rue J. Nehru, Phonexay, Saysettha District, Vientiane
T (+856) 030 770 0000 E britishembassy.vientiane@fco.gov.uk
W www.gov.uk/government/world/organisations/
british-embassy-vientiane
Ambassador Extraordinary and Plenipotentiary, HE Hugh Evans,
   apptd 2015

ECONOMY AND TRADE
Economic liberalisation and a measure of private enterprise were introduced from 1986, producing growth averaging over 6 per cent a year since 1988 except during the 1997 Asian financial crisis, and is one of the fastest growing economies in Asia. Recent economic growth has been driven by foreign investment in dam and transport construction projects, hydroelectric power and mining. The country remains very poor, with only a rudimentary infrastructure, and is dependent on international aid and investment. Laos was admitted to the World Trade Organization in 2013.

Subsistence agriculture, principally rice, accounts for 20.9 per cent of GDP and 73.1 per cent of employment. Deposits of copper, tin, gold and gypsum are exploited, as is the abundance of timber in the rainforests. Other activities include food processing, rubber production, and tourism. A hydroelectric dam on the Mekong river exports electricity to Thailand.

The main trading partners are Thailand (42.6 per cent of exports; 59.1 per cent of imports), Vietnam and China. Principal exports are timber products, coffee, electricity, tin, copper and gold. The main imports are machinery and equipment, vehicles, fuel and consumer goods.
GNI – US$15.6bn; US$2,270 per capita (2017)
Annual average growth of GDP – 6.9 per cent (2017 est)
Inflation rate – 2.3 per cent (2017 est)
Population below poverty line – 22 per cent (2013 est)
Unemployment – 1.5 per cent (2016 est)
Total external debt – US$13.64bn (2017 est)
Imports – US$3,860m (2015)
Exports – US$2,340m (2015)

BALANCE OF PAYMENTS
Trade – US$1,520m deficit (2015)
Current Account – US$1,233m deficit (2016)

Trade with UK	2016	2017
Imports from UK	£5,742,136	£9,184,532
Exports to UK	£30,483,392	£10,897,813

COMMUNICATIONS
Airports and waterways – Eight, with the largest airports at Vientiane and Luang Prabang; there are around 4,600km of navigable waterways, principally on the Mekong and its tributaries, although some are not passable in the dry season
Roadways and railways – There are 530km of paved roadways; the Friendship Bridge over the Mekong river connects with Thailand, and links up road routes from Singapore to China. A rail track across the bridge links the Thai and Laotian rail systems
Telecommunications – 1.26 million fixed lines and 3.9 million mobile subscriptions (2016); there were 1.25 million internet users in 2016
Internet code and IDD – la; 856 (from UK), 44 (to UK)
Major broadcasters – The state-run Lao National TV is the country's principal broadcaster
Press – There are three state-run news publications, including the *Vientiane Mai*
WPFI score – 66,41 (170)

LATVIA

Latvijas Republika – Republic of Latvia

Area – 64,589 sq. km
Capital – Riga; population, 637,000 (2018 est)
Major cities – Daugavpils, Jelgava, Liepaja
Currency – Euro (€) of 100 cents
Population – 1,944,643 falling at 1.08 per cent a year (2017 est); Latvian (61.8 per cent), Russian (25.6 per cent), Belarusian (3.4 per cent), Ukrainian (2.3 per cent), Polish (2.1 per cent), Lithuanian (1.2 per cent) (2016 est)
Religion – Christian (Lutheran 19.6 per cent, Orthodox 15.3 per cent, other 0.4 per cent), unspecified 63.7 per cent (2006)
Language – Latvian (official), Russian
Population density – 31 per sq. km (2016)
Urban population – 68.1 per cent (2018 est)
Median age (years) – 43.3 (2016 est)
National anthem – 'Dievs, Sveti Latviju' 'God Bless Latvia'
National day – 18 November (Independence Day)
Death penalty – Abolished for all crimes (since 2012)
CPI score – 58 (40)
Military expenditure – US$407m (2016)

CLIMATE AND TERRAIN
Latvia is a flat, low-lying country on the eastern shore of the Baltic Sea, with low hills and many lakes in the south-east. Elevation extremes range from 312m (Gaizinkalns) to 0m (Baltic Sea). The climate is temperate, and average temperatures range from −3.2°C in February to 17.9°C in July.

HISTORY AND POLITICS
Conquered and Christianised in the 13th century by the Teutonic Knights, Latvia was successively under Polish, Lithuanian and Swedish rule in the 16th and 17th centuries until it was incorporated into the Russian Empire in 1721. Under partial German occupation during the First World War, it declared its independence in 1918 and successfully defended this against the Bolsheviks in 1918–20. A dictatorship was established in 1934 following a period of political instability and economic depression. The USSR invaded and annexed Latvia in 1940, and regained control in 1944 after ousting the German forces that had invaded in 1941. Latvia suffered huge civilian losses during the Second World War, including the destruction of its large Jewish community. Many more Latvians died after the war in purges and deportations ordered by Stalin.

Agitation by nationalist groups grew from the mid-1980s. In May 1990 the legislature declared independence. The last Russian troops left in 1994 but a large Russian minority remains and there are intercommunal tensions. Latvia joined NATO and the EU in 2004.

In January 2014, Laimdota Straujuma was appointed prime minister following the resignation of Valdis Dombrovskis. In the October 2014 legislative election, the ruling coalition, led by the centre-right Unity party, retained its majority, despite the pro-Russian Harmony Centre remaining the largest single party. However, Prime Minister Straujuma resigned in December 2015 following disputes within the coalition and in February 2016 she was replaced by Maris Kucinskis. Raimonds Vejonis of the Green and Farmers' Union (ZZS) was elected president in June 2015 after winning the fifth round of voting.

The 1922 constitution was restored in 1993. The head of state is a president, who is elected by the legislature for a four-year term which may be renewed once. The president appoints the prime minister, who appoints the cabinet subject to approval by the legislature. The unicameral *Saeima* has 100 deputies who are directly elected for a four-year term.

HEAD OF STATE
President, Raimonds Vejonis, *elected* 3 June 2015, *sworn in* 8 July 2015

SELECTED GOVERNMENT MEMBERS *AS AT JUNE 2018*
Prime Minister, Maris Kucinskis
Deputy Prime Minister, Economics, Arvils Aseradens
Finance, Dana Reizniece-Ozola
Foreign Affairs, Edgars Rinkevics

EMBASSY OF THE REPUBLIC OF LATVIA
45 Nottingham Place, London W1U 5LY
T 020-7312 0041 E embassy.uk@mfa.gov.lv
W www.mfa.gov.lv/london
Ambassador Extraordinary and Plenipotentiary, HE Baiba Braze, *apptd* 2016

BRITISH EMBASSY
5 J. Alunana lela, Riga LV1010
T (+371) 6777 4700 E britishembassy.riga@fco.gov.uk
W www.gov.uk/government/world/latvia
Ambassador Extraordinary and Plenipotentiary, HE Keith Shannon, *apptd* 2017

ECONOMY AND TRADE

The country made the transition from a planned to a market economy in the decade after independence, although a few large enterprises remain in state ownership. The economy grew rapidly from 2004 to 2007, but was severely affected by the global economic downturn because of its large current account deficit and private-sector debt. The economy contracted by 14 per cent in 2009 and was slow to return to growth. The IMF, the World Bank and the EU provided aid in 2008–9 to avoid devaluation in return for a 40 per cent cut in public spending. The IMF programme was successfully concluded in December 2011 and Latvia joined the eurozone on 1 January 2014. The poor performance of the eurozone and Russian economies has contributed to a slowdown in growth since 2015, but in 2017 Latvia returned to pre-crisis levels of growth. Long-term impediments include corruption and a decreasing population.

The economy has shifted towards service industries since independence. Services, especially transit services and banking, is the largest sector, contributing 75.2 per cent of GDP. Industry contributes 21.6 per cent of GDP and includes food processing and the manufacture of processed wood products, textiles, processed metals, pharmaceuticals, rail transport vehicles, synthetic fibres and electronics. The agricultural sector accounts for 3.2 per cent of GDP, employs 7.7 per cent of the workforce and specialises in rearing livestock, dairy farming and crops including grain, rapeseed, potatoes and other vegetables.

The main trading partners are other EU states and Russia, with exports contributing nearly a third of GDP. Principal exports are food products, timber and wood products, metals, machinery and equipment, and textiles. The main imports are machinery and equipment, consumer goods, chemicals, fuel and vehicles.

GNI – US$28.6bn; US$14,470 per capita (2017)
Annual average growth of GDP – 3.8 per cent (2017 est)
Inflation rate – 3.0 per cent (2017 est)
Population below poverty line – 25.5 per cent (2015 est)
Unemployment – 9 per cent (2017 est)
Total external debt – US$40.02bn (2016 est)
Imports – US$13,631m (2016)
Exports – US$11,426m (2016)

BALANCE OF PAYMENTS

Trade – US$2,205m deficit (2016)
Current Account – US$245m deficit (2017)

Trade with UK	2016	2017
Imports from UK	£236,956,932	£354,151,419
Exports to UK	£670,541,647	£607,303,231

COMMUNICATIONS

Airports and waterways – There are 18 airports with the largest at Riga, Ventspils and Liepaja; there are major ports at Riga and Ventspils
Roadways and railways – 14,707km; 2,239km
Telecommunications – 362,940 fixed lines and 2.65 million mobile subscriptions (2016); there were 1.57 million internet users in 2016
Internet code and IDD – lv; 371 (from UK), 44 (to UK)
Major broadcasters – Latvian Television (LTV) and Latvian Radio are the state broadcasters
Press – Prominent daily newspapers include *Diena, Neatkariga Rita Avize* (both Latvian language) and *Telegraf* (mainly Russian)
WPFI score – 19,63 (24)

EDUCATION AND HEALTH

Education is compulsory from the age of seven until 16 years, after which there is the option for a further three years of either secondary or vocational study.
Literacy rate – 100 per cent (2015 est)
Gross enrolment ratio (percentage of relevant age group) – primary 100.4 per cent, secondary 115.4 per cent, tertiary 67 per cent (2014 est)
Health expenditure (per capita) – US$921 (2014)
Hospital beds (per 1,000 people) – 5.8 (2013)
Life expectancy (years) – 74.7 (2017 est)
Mortality rate – 14.5 (2017 est)
Birth rate – 9.7 (2017 est)
Infant mortality rate – 5.2 (2017 est)
HIV/AIDS adult prevalence – 0.7 per cent (2016 est)

LEBANON

Al-Jumhuriyah al-Lubnaniyah – Lebanese Republic

Area – 10,400 sq. km
Capital – Beirut (Bayrut); population, 2,385,000 (2018 est)
Major cities – Sidon, Tripoli (Tarabulus)
Currency – Lebanese pound (L£) of 100 piastres
Population – 6,229,794 falling at 1.10 per cent a year (2017 est); Arab (95 per cent), Armenian (4 per cent) (est)
Religion – Muslim 54 per cent (27 per cent Shia, 27 per cent Sunni), Christian 40.5 per cent (includes 21 per cent Maronite Catholic), Druze 5.6 per cent, small numbers of Jews, Baha'is, Buddhists, Hindus and Mormons
Language – Arabic (official), French, English, Armenian
Population density – 595 per sq. km (2016)
Urban population – 88.6 per cent (2018 est)
Median age (years) – 29.9 (2016 est)
National anthem – 'Kulluna lil-watan' 'All of Us, For Our Country'
National day – 22 November (Independence Day)
Death penalty – Retained
CPI score – 28 (143)
Military expenditure – US$2,441m (2017)

CLIMATE AND TERRAIN

A narrow plain along the Mediterranean Sea coast is backed by the Lebanon mountains, along which the Anti-Lebanon range runs parallel, forming the border with Syria. Between the two ranges lies the fertile Bekaa valley, the northern extremity of Africa's Great Rift valley. Elevations range from 3,088m (Qurnat as Sawda') to 0m (Mediterranean Sea). The climate is Mediterranean, although the mountains usually receive snow in winter. Average temperatures in Beirut are 7.4°C in January and 25.3°C in August.

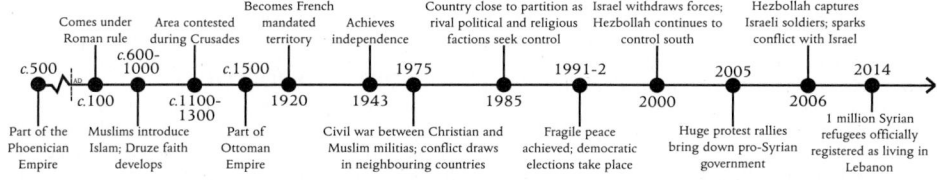

POLITICS

The constitution dates from 1926 but has been heavily amended, most significantly in 1943, when the National Covenant set out the division of power between the religious communities, and in 1990 to incorporate the provisions of the Ta'if accord. By convention, the presidency is held by a Maronite Christian, the prime minister is a Sunni Muslim and the speaker is a Shia Muslim.

The president is elected by the legislature for a six-year term, which is not renewable. The unicameral National Assembly has 128 members, directly elected for a four-year term by proportional representation; seats are divided equally between Christians and Muslims, whose quotas are subdivided by religious 'confession' according to the distribution formalised in the 2008 election law. The prime minister is appointed by the president following consultation with the legislature.

In May 2008, a neutral candidate, General Michel Suleiman, the head of the armed forces, was elected president. After months of negotiation following the 2009 legislative election, the '14 March' leader Saad al-Hariri formed a national unity government, which took office in November 2009. This government collapsed in January 2011 with the withdrawal of pro-Syria parties, and Najib Mikati was elected prime minister-designate later that month. In April 2013 Sunni politician Tamam Salam was nominated prime minister; Saad al-Hariri became prime minister for a second time in December 2016. New legislative elections, originally due to take place in 2014, were first delayed until June 2017 due to security concerns related to the conflict in Syria and then to May 2018 after politicians approved a new draft electoral law. Pro-Iran parties performed well but the elections resulted in no change in the country's political leadership. In October 2016, Michel Aoun was confirmed as president after two years of political deadlock.

HEAD OF STATE
President, Michel Aoun, *apptd* 31 October 2016

SELECTED GOVERNMENT MEMBERS *AS AT JUNE 2018*
Prime Minister, Saad al-Hariri
Deputy Prime Minister, Health, Ghassan Hasbani
Finance, Ali Hassan Khalil

EMBASSY OF LEBANON
15 Palace Gardens Mews, London W8 4RB
T 020-7229 7265 E lebanonconsulate@btconnect.com W http:// london.mfa.gov.lb/britain/english/home
Ambassador Extraordinary and Plenipotentiary, HE Rami Mortada, *apptd* 2017

BRITISH EMBASSY
PO Box 11–471, Serail Hill, Beirut Central District, Beirut
T (+961) (1) 960 800 E www.gov.uk/government/world/lebanon
Ambassador Extraordinary and Plenipotentiary, HE Christopher Rampling, MBE, *apptd* 2018

ECONOMY AND TRADE

The civil war seriously damaged Lebanon's strong commercial economy and infrastructure, as well as its role as an entrepôt and financial services centre for the region. Reconstruction was almost complete when the Israeli attacks in 2006 caused an estimated US$3.6bn (£2.1bn) of infrastructure damage. Recovery was hindered by internal instability, which also postponed the introduction of the economic reforms that were a condition of international funding for reconstruction. The mass migration of refugees from Syria since 2011 has seriously increased income inequality, social tensions and unemployment, with anywhere up to 2 million refugees estimated to be in the country. Oil exploration is expected to begin in 2019.

The service sector contributes 73.3 per cent of GDP, largely through banking and tourism, which are the two main economic activities. Industry accounts for 21 per cent, through food processing, wine production and the manufacture of jewellery, cement, textiles, mineral and chemical products, timber and furniture, oil refining and metal fabrication. Agriculture contributes 5.7 per cent of GDP, producing fruit, vegetables, tobacco and livestock.

The main export markets are China, the UAE, South Africa and Saudi Arabia, while imports come mainly from China, Italy, Greece and Germany. Principal exports include jewellery, base metals, chemicals, consumer goods, fruit, vegetables, tobacco and construction materials. The main imports are petroleum products, vehicles, medicines, clothing, meat, livestock and consumer goods.

GNI – US$50.5bn; US$8,310 per capita (2017)
Annual average growth of GDP – 1.5 per cent (2017 est)
Inflation rate – 3.1 per cent (2017 est)
Total external debt – US$39.46bn (2017 est)
Imports – US$18,439m (2015)
Exports – US$3,982m (2015)

BALANCE OF PAYMENTS
Trade – US$14,458m deficit (2015)
Current Account – US$10,555m deficit (2016)

Trade with UK	2016	2017
Imports from UK	£336,021,713	£369,434,773
Exports to UK	£29,987,447	£30,389,829

COMMUNICATIONS

Airports and waterways – There are five airports, including the international airport at Beirut; the principal seaports are Beirut and Tripoli
Roadways and railways – 170km of motorways; 401km
Telecommunications – 1.86 million fixed lines and 4.9 million mobile subscriptions (2016); there were 4.7 million internet users in 2016
Internet code and IDD – lb; 961 (from UK), 44 (to UK)

Major broadcasters – Télé-Liban is the state-run broadcaster and competes with several commercial stations, including pro-Hezbollah al-Manar TV and the market-leading Lebanese Broadcasting Corporation and Future TV
Press – Leading dailies include *An-Nahar, Al-Safir* (both Arabic language) and *L'Orient-Le Jour* (French)
WPFI score – 31,15 (100)

EDUCATION AND HEALTH

There are nine years of compulsory education.
Literacy rate – 99.1 per cent (2015 est)
Gross enrolment ratio (percentage of relevant age group) – primary 89 per cent, secondary 60 per cent, tertiary 38 per cent (2016 est)
Health expenditure (per capita) – US$569 (2014)
Hospital beds (per 1,000 people) – 2.9 (2014)
Life expectancy (years) – 77.8 (2017 est)
Mortality rate – 5 (2017 est)
Birth rate – 14.3 (2017 est)
Infant mortality rate – 7.4 (2017 est)
HIV / AIDS adult prevalence – 0.1 per cent (2016 est)

LESOTHO

Kingdom of Lesotho

Area – 30,355 sq. km
Capital – Maseru; population, 202,000 (2018)
Major cities – Leribe, Mafeteng, Quthing
Currency – Loti (M) of 100 lisente; the South African rand is also legal tender
Population – 1,958,042 rising at 0.28 per cent a year (2017 est); Sotho (99.7 per cent) (est)
Religion – Christian 80 per cent, indigenous beliefs 20 per cent (est)
Language – English, Sesotho (both official), Zulu, Xhosa
Population density – 74 per sq. km (2016)
Urban population – 28.2 per cent (2016 est)
Median age (years) – 24 (2016 est)
National anthem – 'Lesotho Fatse la Bo Ntat'a Rona' 'Lesotho, Land of Our Fathers'
National day – 4 October (Independence Day)
Death penalty – Retained
CPI score – 42 (74)
Military expenditure – US$52.6m (2017)

CLIMATE AND TERRAIN

Lesotho consists of a highland plateau with mountains in the east. The lower land in the west contains most of the arable land and 70 per cent of the population. Elevation extremes range from 3,482m (Thabana Ntlenyana) to 1,400m (the junction of the Orange and Makhaleng rivers). As 80 per cent of the country lies above 1,800m, the climate is temperate, with snow in the highlands in winter. Temperatures average 18.3°C in January and 7°C in June.

HISTORY AND POLITICS

The area was organised into a single territory by Moshoeshoe the Great from the 1820s as the Sotho people came under pressure from both the expanding Zulu nation and the Boers. In 1868, after fighting two wars with the Boers, Moshoeshoe sought protection from the British government, and Basutoland became first a British territory (1868) and then a crown colony (1884).

The country gained independence in 1966 as the kingdom of Lesotho, under Moshoeshoe II and with Chief Lebua Jonathan as prime minister. Chief Jonathan was overthrown in a military coup in 1986; military rule ended with multiparty elections in 1993 and democratic rule was restored in 1994. The 1998 elections were also followed by severe disturbances, which were quelled by an intervention force from neighbouring countries. King Moshoeshoe II, deposed in 1990, was reinstated in 1995 but died in 1996; he was succeeded by King Letsie III, who had been king during his father's exile.

In the 2012 legislative election, the Democratic Congress (DC) party won the largest number of seats but did not gain a majority, and Motsoahae Tom Thabane of the All Basotho Convention (ABC) party was appointed prime minister. In August 2014, an attempted military coup caused Thabane to briefly flee to South Africa. After the coup attempt, early elections were held in February 2015 in an attempt to create a stable government. The DC, under Bethuel Pakalitha Mosisili, emerged again as the largest single party and was able to form a governing coalition. However, in February 2017 Mosisili lost a parliamentary vote of no confidence and the ABC's Tom Thabane was re-elected prime minister following new elections in June.

Under the 1993 constitution, subsequently amended, the head of state is a hereditary monarch, with ceremonial duties but no executive or legislative powers. The bicameral parliament comprises the National Assembly, with 120 members elected for a five-year term, one-third by proportional representation, and the senate, whose 33 members comprise 22 principal chiefs and 11 members nominated by the king. The prime minister is the leader of the majority party in the legislature and appoints the council of ministers.

HEAD OF STATE
HM The King of Lesotho, King Letsie III, *acceded* 7 February 1996, *crowned* 31 October 1997
Heir, HRH Crown Prince Lerothi Seeiso

SELECTED GOVERNMENT MEMBERS *AS AT JUNE 2018*
Prime Minister, Tom Thabane
Deputy Prime Minister, Monyane Moleleke
Finance, Moeketsi Majoro

HIGH COMMISSION OF THE KINGDOM OF LESOTHO
7 Chesham Place, London SW1X 8HN
T 020-7235 5686 **E** hicom@lesotholondon.org.uk
W www.lesotholondon.org.uk
High Commissioner, HE John Oliphant, *apptd* 2017

BRITISH HIGH COMMISSION
HE Nigel Casey, CMG, MVO, *apptd* 2017, resident at Pretoria (Tshwane), South Africa

ECONOMY AND TRADE

The country is one of the poorest in the world, with around 57 per cent of the population living below the poverty line. With few natural resources apart from water, the main sources of government revenue are customs dues from the South African customs union and, since 1998, the export of water and electricity to South Africa from the hydroelectric facilities created by the Lesotho Highlands Water Project. The economic situation worsened in the early 2000s due to a series of severe droughts and declining demand for mineworkers in South Africa.

This decline has been partially compensated for by the resumption of diamond mining in 2003, and the development of a small manufacturing base processing agricultural products, producing textiles and assembling garments, coupled with tourism, especially in the highlands. Lesotho's economy recovered well from the global economic crisis in 2008–9 with growth averaging nearly 5 per cent between 2010–14, but has since slowed. The economy is heavily reliant on government consumption, which accounts for 26 per cent of GDP; diamond mining, which accounts for almost 35 per cent of total exports; and remittances supplied by migrants to South Africa. Unemployment remains high, at over 25 per cent, and industry has been in decline since 2004.

Subsistence agriculture is the major employer and engages 86 per cent of the population, although the nation produces less than one fifth of food demand. Productivity has declined in recent years because of drought, soil erosion and loss of labour due to HIV/AIDS.

Principal exports are clothing, footwear, wool and mohair, food and livestock. The main imports are food, construction materials, vehicles, machinery, medicines and petroleum products.

GNI – US$2.8bn; US$1,280 per capita (2017)
Annual average growth of GDP – 4.6 per cent (2017 est)
Inflation rate – 6.6 per cent (2017 est)
Population below poverty line – 57 per cent (2016 est)
Unemployment – 28.1 per cent (2014)
Total external debt – US$952.5m (2017 est)
Imports – US$1,949m (2016)
Exports – US$773m (2016)

BALANCE OF PAYMENTS
Trade – US$1,177m deficit (2015)
Current Account – US$165m deficit (2017)

Trade with UK	2016	2017
Imports from UK	£2,035,761	£959,456
Exports to UK	£243,635	£289,669

COMMUNICATIONS

Airports – There are three airports; the international airport is at Maseru
Roadways – There are 1,069km of surfaced roads
Telecommunications – 51,200 fixed lines and 2.1 million mobile subscriptions (2014); there were 102,000 internet users in 2014
Internet code and IDD – ls; 266 (from UK), 44 (to UK)
Major broadcasters – Radio is the most important medium, although only the state-run Radio Lesotho has national coverage; Lesotho Television, also state-run, is the only television station, but South African broadcasts can be received
Press – A number of weekly newspapers are published in English and Sesotho
WPFI score – 28,78 (68)

EDUCATION AND HEALTH

Literacy rate – 85.1 per cent (2015)
Gross enrolment ratio (percentage of relevant age group) – primary 104 per cent, secondary 52 per cent (2016 est), tertiary 9.8 per cent (2014 est)
Health expenditure (per capita) – US$105 (2014)
Life expectancy (years) – 53 (2017 est)
Mortality rate – 15 (2017 est)
Birth rate – 24.6 (2017 est)
Infant mortality rate – 46.1 (2017 est)
HIV/AIDS adult prevalence – 25 per cent (2016 est)

LIBERIA

Republic of Liberia

Area – 111,369 sq. km
Capital – Monrovia; population, 1,418,000 (2018 est)
Currency – Liberian dollar (L$) of 100 cents
Population – 4,689,021 rising at 2.50 per cent a year (2017 est); Kpelle (20.3 per cent), Bassa (13.4 per cent), Grebo (10 per cent), Gio (8 per cent), Mano (7.9 per cent), Kru (6 per cent), Loma (5.1 per cent), Kissi (4.8 per cent), Gola (4.4 per cent) (2008)
Religion – Christian 85.6 per cent, Muslim 12.2 per cent, traditional/other 0.8 per cent (2008 est)
Language – English (official), about 20 ethnic languages
Population density – 49 per sq. km (2016)
Urban population – 51.2 per cent (2018 est)
Median age (years) – 18.3 (2016 est)
National anthem – 'All Hail, Liberia, Hail!'
National day – 26 July (Independence Day)
Death penalty – Retained (last used 2000)
CPI score – 31 (122)
Military expenditure – US$13.7m (2017)
Literacy rate – 47.6 per cent (2015 est)
Gross enrolment ratio (percentage of relevant age group) – primary 93.9 per cent, secondary 37.3 per cent (2015 est), tertiary 12 per cent (2012 est)
Health expenditure (per capita) – US$46 (2014)
Hospital beds (per 1,000 people) – 0.8 (2010)
Life expectancy (years) – 63.3 (2017 est)
Mortality rate – 7.6 (2017 est)
Birth rate – 38.3 (2017 est)
Infant mortality rate – 52.2 (2017 est)
HIV/AIDS adult prevalence – 1.6 per cent (2016 est)

CLIMATE AND TERRAIN

Liberia lies on the west African coast, just north of the equator. There are forested highlands and grassy plateaux in the interior and swampy plains on the coast, where several rivers enter the ocean. Elevation extremes range from 1,380m (Mt Wuteve) to 0m (Atlantic Ocean). The climate is tropical, with very high rainfall.

HISTORY AND POLITICS

The land was purchased by the American Colonisation Society in 1821 and turned into a settlement for liberated black slaves from the USA, gaining recognition as an independent state in 1847.

In the first century of statehood, politics was dominated by the True Whig Party of the Americo-Liberian minority. Political stability ended in 1980 when a coup installed a military government under Samuel Doe. When civilian rule was restored in 1985, Doe became president, but his regime's arbitrary, corrupt rule combined with an economic collapse led to a revolt in 1989 by Charles Taylor's National Patriotic Forces of Liberia (NPFL) and the Armed Forces of Liberia (AFL). The country descended into a civil war that, apart from a respite in 1996–9, lasted until 2003. Around 250,000 people were killed and thousands were displaced. Following mediation by a number of African and European countries, all factions in the conflict signed a peace agreement in 2003 and a UN peacekeeping force was deployed. The disarming of militias was completed in 2005, and a truth and reconciliation commission was set up in 2006 and reported in 2009. In 2012 Taylor was found guilty of war crimes and sentenced to 50 years in jail to be served in a British prison.

After a period of transitional government, presidential and legislative elections were held in late 2005. In the legislative election, the Congress for Democratic Change (CDC) won the most seats but without an overall majority. The Unity Party leader, Ellen Johnson Sirleaf, was elected president in the second round of voting and took office in January 2006. Sirleaf regained the presidential nomination in the 2011 election, picking up 43.9 per cent of the overall vote. The Unity Party gained the most votes in the 2011 and 2014 legislative elections but lost control of the senate. After irregularities were alleged to have taken place in the October 2017 presidential elections, former footballer George Weah won a run-off vote in December 2017 on an anti-corruption platform.

Under the 1986 constitution, the head of state is an executive president who is directly elected for a six-year term, renewable once. There is a bicameral National Assembly, consisting of the House of Representatives, with 73 members directly elected for a six-year term, and a senate, with 30 members (two from each of the 15 counties) elected for nine-year staggered terms. The president appoints the cabinet, which must be approved by the legislature.

HEAD OF STATE
President, George Weah, *elected* 26 December 2017, *sworn in* 22 January 2018
Vice-President, Joseph N. Boakai

SELECTED GOVERNMENT MEMBERS, *AS AT JUNE 2018*
National Defence, Maj.-Gen. (retd) Daniel Dee Ziankahn
Finance, Samuel Tweah
Foreign Affairs, Gbezohngar Findley

EMBASSY OF THE REPUBLIC OF LIBERIA
23 Fitzroy Square, London W1 6EW
T 020-7388 5489 E info@embassyofliberia.org.uk
W www.embassyofliberia.org.uk
Ambassador Extraordinary and Plenipotentiary, vacant

BRITISH AMBASSADOR
Leone Compound, 12th Street Beach-side, Sinkor, Monrovia
T (+231) (0)77530320 E monrovia.generalenquiries@fco.gov.uk
W www.gov.uk/government/world/liberia
Ambassador Extraordinary and Plenipotentiary, HE David Belgrove, OBE, *apptd* 2015

ECONOMY AND TRADE

The civil war devastated an economy already weakened by government mismanagement and corruption, and drove those with expertise and capital into exile. Since the war ended, foreign aid has been received to finance reconstruction, conditional on the adoption of anti-corruption measures, and economic activity has revived. Growth since 2006 has been driven by donor aid and exports, particularly of rubber and, since UN sanctions were lifted in 2006 and 2007 respectively, timber and diamonds. The country also benefited from substantial debt relief in 2010, and in 2011 the African Development Bank approved a grant of US$48m to support economic governance and competitiveness. Economic growth has partially recovered since the 2014 Ebola outbreak, with the opening of new gold and iron ore mines.

Agriculture was the main economic activity during the civil war but its contribution to GDP and its share of the labour market has declined as the industrial and service sectors have revived. Industry centres on the processing of rubber and palm oil, forestry and mining (diamonds, gold and iron ore).

The main export markets are the USA and EU countries, while imports come mainly from Singapore, South Korea, China and Japan. Principal exports are rubber, timber, iron, diamonds, cocoa and coffee. The main imports are fuels, chemicals, machinery, transport equipment, manufactured goods and foodstuffs.

GNI – US$1.8bn; US$380 per capita (2017)
Annual average growth of GDP – 2.6 per cent (2017 est)
Inflation rate – 12.8 per cent (2017 est)
Population below poverty line – 54.1 per cent (2014 est)
Total external debt – US$1.049bn (2017 est)
Import – US$1,046m (2014)
Export – US$583m (2014)

BALANCE OF PAYMENTS
Trade – US$463m deficit (2014)
Current Account – US$565m deficit (2017)

Trade with UK	2016	2017
Imports from UK	£13,429,659	£14,685,708
Exports to UK	£33,798,478	£1,440,804

COMMUNICATIONS

Airports and waterways – There are two international airports, Robertsfield and Spriggs Payne, in Monrovia; the main seaports are Monrovia and Buchanan, and there is a merchant fleet of 2,771 ships of over 1,000 tonnes, including 2,581 foreign-owned ships registered in Liberia
Roadways and railways – There are 657km of surfaced roadways; owing to war damage, little of the 429km of railway track is operational, although reconstruction is underway
Telecommunications – 8,000 fixed lines and 3.1 million mobile subscriptions (2016); there were 314,717 internet users in 2016
Internet code and IDD – lr; 231 (from UK), 44 (to UK)
Major broadcasters – Media are largely privately owned, although the state-run Liberian Broadcasting System operates Radio Liberia; television broadcasters include Clar TV and Power TV
Press – There are two major daily newspapers, *The Inquirer* and *The New Dawn,* both privately owned
WPFI score – 30,33 (89)

LIBYA

Dawlat Libya – State of Libya

Area – 1,759,540 sq. km
Capital – Tripoli (Tarabulus); population, 1,158,000 (2018)
Major cities – al-Hums, az-Zawiyah, Benghazi, Misratah,
   Tarhunah, Zuwarah
Currency – Libyan dinar (LD) of 1,000 dirhams
Population – 6,653,210 rising at 1.58 per cent a year (2017
   est); Arab–Berber (97 per cent), with some Tuareg in the
   south-west
Religion – Muslim 96.6 per cent (vast majority Sunni),
   Christian 2.7 per cent, other 0.5 per cent (2010 est)
Language – Arabic (official), Berber dialects
Population density – 4 per sq. km (2016)
Urban population – 80.1 per cent (2018 est)
Median age (years) – 28.5 (2016 est)
National anthem – 'Libya, Libya, Libya'
National day – 23 October (Liberation Day)
Death penalty – Retained
CPI score – 17 (171)
Military expenditure – US$3,289m (2014)
Conscription – 18 years of age for mandatory or voluntary
   service

CLIMATE AND TERRAIN

Apart from hills on the north-west and north-east coasts and
in the far south, the country is made up of plains and plateaux,
with some depressions; 90 per cent is desert or semi-desert.
Elevation extremes range from 2,267m (Bikku Bitti) to −47m
(Sabkhat Ghuzayyil). The climate is Mediterranean on the
coast, and arid desert in the interior. Average temperatures in
Tripoli range from 12.9°C in January to 30.4°C in July.

POLITICS

Following the overthrow of the 'Leader of the Revolution',
Col. Muammar al-Gaddafi, the National Transitional Council
(NTC) set out plans for a 'political democratic regime to be
based upon the political multitude and multi-party system'.

In July 2012 the General National Congress was elected and
power was handed over from the transitional government in
August; Mohammed Magarief was elected interim head of
state. In October 2012, prime minister-elect Mustafa Abu

Shagur failed in two attempts to gain parliamentary approval
for his government; the national congress elected Ali Zidan
prime minister in his place. In May 2014 businessman Ahmed
Maiteg was elected prime minister but stood down one month
later, when the Supreme Court ruled his election
unconstitutional.

Abdullah al-Thinni was appointed Libya's acting prime
minister in June 2014. In August, the House of
Representatives replaced the General National Congress as
the legislative body and its president, Akila Issa, became the
new head of state. Continuing political chaos saw the former
legislative body, the General National Congress, appoint their
own prime minister, Islamist Omar al-Hassi, on 25 August,
resulting in two rival governments. Al-Thinni's government
resigned on 29 August in order to allow for the formation of
a national unity government; however, al-Thinni was
reappointed in September after Tripoli was captured by rebel
groups, forcing the government to relocate to Tobruk. Talks
between the two rival administrations, held in Morocco in
June 2015, failed to result in the formation of a new national
unity government. A new UN-backed government was
announced in January 2016, led by Prime Minister Fayez
Sarraj. While this government has maintained power, ongoing
fighting with Islamist militants has contributed to a refugee
crisis, which has seen tens of thousands attempting to cross
the Mediterranean Sea every year. Following a summit in
Paris, leaders agreed to hold fair elections in December 2018.

HEAD OF STATE
Chair of the House of Representatives, Akila Issa

SELECTED GOVERNMENT MEMBERS *AS AT JUNE 2018*
Prime Minister-designate, Chair of Presidential Council, Fayez
   Sarraj
Prime Minister, House of Representatives, Abdallah al-Thinni
First Deputy Prime Minister, Almahdi Hassan Muftah Allabad
Second Deputy Prime Minister, Abdulsalam al-Badri
Third Deputy Prime Minister, Abdulrahman al-Taher
Economy, Muneer Ali Assr

EMBASSY OF LIBYA
15 Knightsbridge, London SW1X 7LY
T 020-7201 8280 **W** http://english.libyanembassy.org
Ambassador Extraordinary and Plenipotentiary, vacant

BRITISH AMBASSADOR
24th Floor, Tripoli Towers, PO Box 4206, Tripoli

T (+218) 21335108 **E** tripoliconsular@fco.gov.uk
W www.gov.uk/government/world/libya
Ambassador Extraordinary and Plenipotentiary, HE Francis Baker,
   CMG, OBE, *apptd* 2018

ECONOMY AND TRADE

The state-controlled oil industry dominates the economy,
although production has become erratic since the start of the
civil war in 2011, and many oil wells are now controlled by
anti-government militias or IS. The end of unilateral US
sanctions in 2006 dramatically increased foreign investment
in the energy and banking sectors. Although oil production

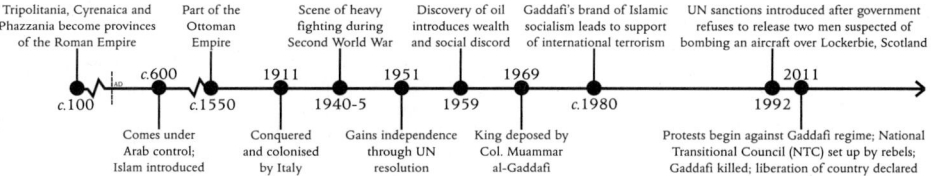

Tripolitania, Cyrenaica and Phazzania become provinces of the Roman Empire	Part of the Ottoman Empire	Scene of heavy fighting during Second World War	Discovery of oil introduces wealth and social discord	Gaddafi's brand of Islamic socialism leads to support of international terrorism	UN sanctions introduced after government refuses to release two men suspected of bombing an aircraft over Lockerbie, Scotland	

*c.*600   1911   1951   1969   2011

*c.*100   *c.*1550   1940-5   1959   *c.*1980   1992

| Comes under Arab control; Islam introduced | Conquered and colonised by Italy | Gains independence through UN resolution | King deposed by Col. Muammar al-Gaddafi | Protests begin against Gaddafi regime; National Transitional Council (NTC) set up by rebels; Gaddafi killed; liberation of country declared |

reached a five-year high in 2017, it still remains well below pre-2011 levels. Attempts to diversify the economy have led to expansion of the service and construction sectors within the past six years, which include the production of petrochemicals, iron, steel and aluminium in addition to food processing. Owing to the terrain and climate, agriculture is a small sector, contributing only 1.3 per cent of GDP. Instability and lack of security continue to restrict growth.

The main trading partners are Italy, other EU countries, China and Turkey. Principal exports are crude oil, refined petroleum products, natural gas and chemicals. The main imports are machinery, semi-finished goods, food, transport equipment and consumer products.

GNI – US$41.7bn; US$6,540 per capita (2016)
Annual average growth of GDP – 55.1 per cent (2017 est)
Inflation rate – 32.8 per cent (2017 est)
Total external debt – US$2.927bn (2017 est)
Imports – US$13,000m (2015)
Exports – US$10,200m (2015)

BALANCE OF PAYMENTS
Trade – US$2,800m deficit (2015)
Current Account – US$4,705m deficit (2016)

Trade with UK	2016	2017
Imports from UK	£154,477,268	£186,685,390
Exports to UK	£244,869,234	£847,987,510

COMMUNICATIONS
Airports and waterways – There are 68 airports; the principal airports are at Tripoli, Benghazi and Sebha, while the main seaports are Benghazi, Tripoli and Tobruk
Roadways – There are 57,214km of paved roads
Telecommunications – 1.37 million fixed lines and 7.7 million mobile subscriptions (2016); there were 1.3 million internet users in 2016
Internet code and IDD – ly; 218 (from UK), 44 (to UK)
Major broadcasters – Launched in April 2011 following the uprising, Libyan Radio and TV (LRT) has been joined by more than 20, mainly privately owned, TV and radio stations
Press – Major dailies include *February* and *New Quryna* (Arabic language), and *The Tripoli Post* (English language)
WPFI score – 56,79 (162)

EDUCATION AND HEALTH
There are six years of primary education and six of secondary, nine of which are compulsory.
Literacy rate – 100 per cent (2015 est)
Health expenditure (per capita) – US$372 (2014)
Hospital beds (per 1,000 people) – 3.7 (2014)
Life expectancy (years) – 76.7 (2017 est)
Mortality rate – 3.6 (2017 est)
Birth rate – 17.5 (2017 est)
Infant mortality rate – 10.8 (2017 est)

LIECHTENSTEIN
Fürstentum Liechtenstein – Principality of Liechtenstein

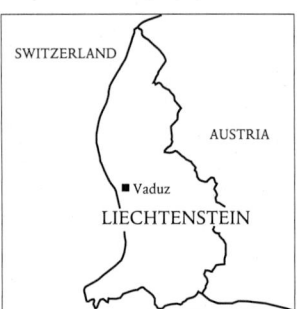

Area – 160 sq. km
Capital – Vaduz; population, 5,000 (2018)
Major town – Schaan
Currency – Swiss franc of 100 rappen (or centimes)
Population – 38,244 rising at 0.80 per cent a year (2017 est); Liechtensteiner (66.0 per cent), Other (34.0 per cent) (2013 est)
Religion – Christian (Roman Catholic 75.9 per cent, Protestant Reformed 6.5 per cent, Lutheran 1.3 per cent), Muslim (5.4 per cent) (2010 est)
Language – German (official); Alemannic is the main dialect
Population density – 237 per sq. km (2016)
Urban population – 14.3 per cent (2018 est)
Median age (years) – 42.9 (2016 est)
National anthem – 'Oben am Jungen Rhein' 'High Above the Young Rhine'
National day – 15 August (Feast of the Assumption)
Death penalty – Abolished for all crimes (since 1987)
Gross enrolment ratio (percentage of relevant age group) – primary 105 per cent, secondary 116 per cent, tertiary 35 per cent (2016 est)
Life expectancy (years) – 81.9 (2017 est)
Mortality rate – 7.4 (2017 est)
Birth rate – 10.4 (2017 est)
Infant mortality rate – 4.2 (2017 est)

CLIMATE AND TERRAIN
Liechtenstein is a small, mountainous landlocked principality in the Alps. The land falls in the west, in the valley of the river Rhine, which forms the western border. Elevation extremes range from 2,599m (Grauspitz) to 430m (Ruggeller Riet). The climate is continental, with heavy snowfall in winter; average temperatures range from −0.8°C in January to 16.2°C in July and August.

HISTORY AND POLITICS
Although there was a sovereign state within the present boundaries from the 14th century, the present state of Liechtenstein was formed from the lordships of Schellenberg and Vaduz in 1719. Part of the Holy Roman Empire, the principality became a member of the Confederation of the Rhine that succeeded the Empire in 1806, and then of the German Confederation from 1815 until 1866. It was the only German principality to remain outside the German Empire formed in 1871. The country abolished its armed forces and declared permanent neutrality in 1868. This was maintained in both world wars.

Economic decline in the years following the First World War led Liechtenstein to adopt the Swiss currency in 1921 and to enter into a Swiss customs union in 1923. The country became extremely prosperous as an international finance centre after the Second World War. Since 2000 it has tightened its laws to prevent money laundering, and since 2008 it has started to meet international financial transparency standards.

Governments in the 20th and 21st centuries have been formed by the two main parties, the northern-based Progressive Citizens' Party (FBP) and the southern-based Fatherland Union (VU). Usually they have formed a coalition government, although the FBP formed a single-party government from 2001 to 2005. However, the government's power is limited by that of the monarchy, whose authority over the government and judiciary was increased by a 2003 referendum. Prince Hans Adam II remains head of state but in 2004 he handed over day-to-day responsibility for government to his son, Prince Alois.

The VU won an overall majority in the 2009 election. The coalition government formed with the FBP in 2005 continued, although the premiership passed from the FBP to the VU. After the 2013 legislative elections the FBP became the dominant coalition partner, and this continued following the 2017 elections.

Under the 1921 constitution, Liechtenstein is a constitutional monarchy, with the hereditary prince as head of state. The unicameral legislature, the *Landtag*, has 25 members directly elected for a four-year term. The cabinet is appointed by the prince on the advice of the *Landtag* and consists of the head of government and four ministers.

HEAD OF STATE
HSH The Prince of Liechtenstein, Hans Adam II, *born* 14 February 1945, *succeeded* 13 November 1989
Heir, HSH Crown Prince Alois, *born* 11 June 1968

SELECTED GOVERNMENT MEMBERS *AS AT JUNE 2018*
Head of Government, Finance, Adrian Hasler
Deputy Head of Government, Home Affairs, Justice, Economy, Dominique Gantenbein
Foreign Affairs, Aurelia Frick

BRITISH AMBASSADOR
HE Jane Owen, *apptd* 2018, resident at Bern, Switzerland

ECONOMY AND TRADE

Liechtenstein has a prosperous, highly industrialised and diversified economy, boasting the highest GDP per capital in the world. Its mainstay is the financial services sector, which, with other service industries such as tourism, employs over half the workforce. A light industrial base produces electronics, metal manufactures, dental products, ceramics, pharmaceuticals, food products, precision and optical instruments, and employs 36.9 per cent of the workforce. Over half the workforce commutes daily from Austria, Switzerland and Germany.

Liechtenstein became a member of the European Free Trade Association in 1991, and of the European Economic Area in 1995. After completing 12 bilateral information-sharing agreements in 2008, Liechtenstein was removed from the OECD's 'grey list' of countries that have not implemented the organisation's model tax convention. In 2011, Liechtenstein joined the Schengen area. Most of its trade is with EU countries and Switzerland. In 2015 the nation agreed to held tackle international tax fraud and evasion. The principal exports are its industrial products. The main imports are agricultural and energy products, raw materials, machinery, metal goods, textiles, foodstuffs and vehicles.
GNI – US$4,816m; US$136,770 per capita (2009)
Annual average growth of GDP – 1.8 per cent (2012)
Inflation rate – −0.4 per cent (2016 est)
Unemployment – 3.4 per cent (2014)

Trade with UK	2016	2017
Imports from UK	£5,754,062	£14,888,873
Exports to UK	£7,605,090	£2,589,035

COMMUNICATIONS

Transport – Liechtenstein has no airports and only 380km of roads, 28km of waterways and 9km of rail track, which is part of the Austrian system connecting Austria and Switzerland
Telecommunications – 16,385 fixed lines and 44,298 mobile subscriptions (2016); there were 37,214 internet users in 2016
Internet code and IDD – li; 423 (from UK), 44 (to UK)
Media – The country has a very small media sector; its citizens rely on foreign broadcasters for most television and radio services. News publications include *Liechtensteiner Vaterland* and *Liechtensteiner Volksblatt*
WPFI score – 20,49 (30)

LITHUANIA

Lietuvos Respublika – Republic of Lithuania

Area – 65,300 sq. km
Capital – Vilnius; population, 536,000 (2018 est)
Major cities – Kaunas, Klaipeda, Siauliai
Currency – Euro (€) of 100 cents
Population – 2,823,859 falling at 1.08 per cent a year (2017 est); Lithuanian (84.1 per cent), Polish (6.6 per cent), Russian (5.8 per cent), Belarusian (1.2 per cent) (2011 est)
Religion – Christian (Roman Catholic 77.2 per cent, Orthodox 4.1 per cent), none 6.1 per cent (2011 est)
Language – Lithuanian (official), Russian, Polish
Population density – 45 per sq. km (2016)
Urban population – 66.7 per cent (2018 est)
Median age (years) – 43.4 (2016 est)
National anthem – 'Tautiska Giesme' 'The National Song'
National day – 16 February (Independence Day)
Death penalty – Abolished for all crimes (since 1998)
CPI score – 59 (38)
Military expenditure – US$812m (2017)
Conscription – 18 years of age; 9 months

CLIMATE AND TERRAIN

Lithuania is a low-lying country with low hills in the west and south-east. It contains around 6,000 lakes and lagoons – over 2,800 of them sizeable – mostly lying in the east, although the Courland lagoon on the west coast is a major feature. Elevation extremes range from 294m (Aukstojas Hill) to 0m (Baltic Sea). The climate is mainly continental, and average temperatures range from −2.6°C in January to 18.1°C in July.

HISTORY AND POLITICS

Lithuania became a nation in the 13th century. It remained pagan for far longer than the rest of Europe, only becoming fully Christian in the 15th century when the Samogitians and the Aukstaitiai, the two main ethnic groups in the region, were converted. In the 14th century, a grand duchy was formed that stretched from the Baltic to the Black Sea and eastwards almost as far as Moscow. It confederated with Poland in the 16th century, before coming under Russian rule in 1795. The country joined Poland in rebelling against Russian domination twice in the 19th century.

Occupied by Germany during the First World War, Lithuania declared its independence in 1918 and successfully defended its autonomy against the Bolsheviks in 1918–19. However, the province and city of Vilnius were occupied by the newly independent Poland from 1920 until 1939. The USSR invaded and annexed Lithuania in 1940, but the country revolted in 1941 and briefly established its own government before being invaded and occupied by the Germans in their 1941 offensive against the USSR. Around 210,000 Lithuanians, mainly Jews, were killed during the German occupation. Soviet troops ousted the Germans in 1944 and re-established Soviet control, against which Lithuanians carried on a guerrilla war until 1952.

Growing nationalist sentiment led to the formation of the pro-democracy *Sajudis* ('The Movement') in 1988 to campaign for greater autonomy. A unilateral declaration of independence in 1990 was blocked by the USSR but following the failed coup in Moscow in 1991, Lithuania declared its independence a second time, and this was internationally recognised. The last Russian troops left the country in 1993. Lithuania joined NATO and the EU in 2004.

In October 2016 legislative elections, the centrist, anti-emigration Lithuanian Peasants and Green party gained the largest mandate, winning 54 parliamentary seats. It formed a coalition government with Saulius Skvernelis appointed prime minister. Dalia Grybauskaite was re-elected in the 2014 presidential election.

Under the 1992 constitution, the head of state is a president, who is directly elected for a five-year term, renewable once. The unicameral *Seimas* has 141 members who are directly elected for a four-year term; 71 members are elected in first-past-the-post constituencies and 70 by proportional representation. The prime minister is appointed by the president with the approval of the *Seimas,* and ministers are appointed upon the recommendation of the prime minister.

HEAD OF STATE

President, Dalia Grybauskaite, *elected* 17 May 2009, *sworn in* 12 July 2009, *re-elected* 25 May 2014

SELECTED GOVERNMENT MEMBERS *AS AT JUNE 2018*

Prime Minister, Saulius Skvernelis
Defence, Raimundas Karoblis
Foreign Affairs, Linas Antanas Linkevicius
Interior, Eimutis Misiunas

EMBASSY OF THE REPUBLIC OF LITHUANIA

Lithuania House, 2 Bessborough Gardens, London SW1V 2JE
T 020-7592 2840 E amb.uk@urm.lt
W www.lithuanianembassy.co.uk/
Ambassador Extraordinary and Plenipotentiary, HE Renatas Norkus, *apptd* 2017

BRITISH EMBASSY

2 Antakalnio, Vilnius LT-10308
T (+370) (5) 246 2900 E consular.vilnius@fco.gov.uk
W www.gov.uk/government/world/lithuania
Ambassador Extraordinary and Plenipotentiary, HE Claire Lawrence, *apptd* 2015

ECONOMY AND TRADE

Lithuania's transition to a market economy is nearly complete, with the private sector now accounting for about 80 per cent of GDP. The transition initially caused a recession, but the economy recovered and grew steadily from 2004 to 2008 before being plunged into a deep recession, along with the other Baltic states, by the global economic downturn. Drastic government cuts in public spending and the halving of imports in 2009 restored the current account deficit, which had soared to 15 per cent of GDP in 2007–8, to a surplus. Despite high unemployment, successive governments dramatically increased the minimum wage in 2011 and 2013. The economy returned to growth in 2010 and increased exports, investment and wages have ensured steady advances and falling unemployment. The country joined the eurozone on 1 January 2015. The poor performance of the Russian and eurozone economies continue to restrict growth.

The economy is diverse, and industries include metal-cutting machine tools, electric motors, domestic appliances, oil refining, shipbuilding, furniture making, textiles and amber extraction and jewellery making. Industry contributes 28.5 per cent to GDP, services 68.3 per cent and agriculture 3.3 per cent.

The main trading partners are Russia and other EU countries. Principal exports are refined fuel, machinery and equipment, chemicals, textiles, foodstuffs and plastics. The main imports are oil, gas, machinery, transport equipment, chemicals, textiles, clothing and metals.

GNI – US$43bn; US$15,200 per capita (2017)
Annual average growth of GDP – 3.5 per cent (2017 est)
Inflation rate – 3.5 per cent (2017 est)
Population below poverty line – 22.5 per cent (2015 est)
Unemployment – 7 per cent (2017 est)
Total external debt – US$34.48bn (2016 est)
Imports – US$27,485m (2016)
Exports – US$25,012m (2016)

BALANCE OF PAYMENTS

Trade – US$2,473m deficit (2016)
Current Account – US$417m deficit (2017)

Trade with UK	2016	2017
Imports from UK	£326,852,901	£554,067,437
Exports to UK	£776,829,858	£736,081,562

COMMUNICATIONS

Airports and waterways – There are 22 airports, with the largest at Vilnius, Kaunas and Palanga; the main seaport is at Klaipeda
Roadways and railways – There are 72,297m of paved roadways, including 312km of motorways; a railway system of 1,767km links the major towns with Vilnius and Klaipeda
Telecommunications – 530,871 fixed lines and 4.2 million mobile subscriptions (2016); there were 2.1 million internet users in 2016
Internet code and IDD – lt; 370 (from UK), 44 (to UK)
Major broadcasters – Lithuania Radio and TV is the public broadcaster
Press – Major dailies include *Lietuvos Rytas, Respublika* and *Vakaro Zinios*
WPFI score – 22,20 (36)

EDUCATION AND HEALTH

Education is free and compulsory from seven to 16 years, with the system comprising primary school (four years), lower secondary school (six years) and upper secondary education (two years).

Literacy rate – 99.9 per cent (2015 est)
Gross enrolment ratio (percentage of relevant age group) – primary 101 per cent, secondary 103 per cent, tertiary 66 per cent (2016 est)
Health expenditure (per capita) – US$1,063 (2014)
Hospital beds (per 1,000 people) – 7.3 (2013)
Life expectancy (years) – 75 (2017 est)
Mortality rate – 14.6 (2017 est)
Birth rate – 9.9 (2017 est)
Infant mortality rate – 3.8 (2017 est)

LUXEMBOURG

Groussherzogtom Lëtzebuerg/Grand-Duché de Luxembourg/ Großherzogtum Luxembourg – Grand Duchy of Luxembourg

Area – 2,586 sq. km
Capital – Luxembourg; population, 120,000 (2018)
Major towns – Dudelange, Esch-sur-Alzette
Currency – Euro (€) of 100 cents
Population – 594,130 rising at 1.98 per cent a year (2017 est); Luxembourger (53.3 per cent), Portuguese (16.2 per cent), French (7.2 per cent), Italian (3.5 per cent), Belgian (3.4 per cent), German (2.2 per cent) (2016 est)
Religion – Roman Catholic 87 per cent, other 13 per cent (2000)
Language – Luxembourgish, French, German (all official)
Population density – 231 per sq. km (2016)
Urban population – 91 per cent (2018 est)
Median age (years) – 39.2 (2016 est)
National anthem – 'Ons Heemecht' 'Our Homeland'
National day – 23 June (official birthday of Grand Duchess Charlotte)
Death penalty – Abolished for all crimes (since 1979)
CPI score – 82 (8)
Military expenditure – US$318m (2017 est)
Gross enrolment ratio (percentage of relevant age group) – primary 97.1 per cent, secondary 102.3 per cent (2014 est); tertiary 19 per cent (2012 est)
Health expenditure (per capita) – US$8,138 (2014)
Hospital beds (per 1,000 people) – 4.9 (2014)
Life expectancy (years) – 82.3 (2017 est)
Mortality rate – 7.3 (2017 est)
Birth rate – 11.5 (2017 est)
Infant mortality ate – 3.4 (2017 est)

CLIMATE AND TERRAIN

Luxembourg has the forested plateau of the Ardennes in the north, forming part of the Natural Germano-Luxembourg Park, which extends east into Germany. The south of the country is mainly fertile farmland, and in the east is the wine-growing region of the Moselle valley. Elevation extremes range from 559m (Buurgplaatz) to 133m (Moselle river). The climate is modified continental, and average temperatures range from 2°C in January to 18.6°C in July.

HISTORY AND POLITICS

The area was part of the Roman Empire and then became part of the Frankish Empire in the fifth century AD. It became autonomous within the Holy Roman Empire under Siegfried, Count of Ardennes, and was given the status of a duchy in 1354. Controlled by a succession of European powers after 1437 (when the House of Luxembourg died out), it was made a grand duchy under Dutch rule after the Napoleonic wars.

Much of Luxembourg joined the Belgians in their revolt against the Netherlands in 1830; in 1838 the western, French-speaking region was assigned to Belgium, and the remainder became an independent grand duchy in 1839. The Treaty of London in 1867 confirmed its independence and neutrality. Occupation by Germany in both world wars prompted Luxembourg to give up its neutrality and it was a founding member of NATO in 1949.

Luxembourg entered into economic union with Belgium in 1921 and joined the Benelux economic union in 1948. It was a founder member of the EEC in 1958 and joined the eurozone in 1999.

Following a snap election in October 2013, the Democratic Party (DP) formed a small majority in the legislature. The elections were called after prime minister Jean-Claude Juncker of the Christian Social Party (CSV) stood down following revelations that his administration failed to prevent corruption within the security services.

Under the 1868 constitution, the head of state is a hereditary grand duke, whose role is now largely ceremonial. The unicameral legislature, the Chamber of Deputies, has 60 members directly elected for a five-year term. There is also a Council of State, which has 21 members nominated by the grand duke; this acts as the supreme administrative tribunal and has some legislative functions. The prime minister is appointed by the grand duke on the basis of the election results and appoints the cabinet.

HEAD OF STATE
HRH The Grand Duke of Luxembourg, Grand Duke Henri, *born* 16 April 1955; *succeeded* 7 October 2000
Heir, HRH Prince Guillaume, *born* 11 November 1981

SELECTED GOVERNMENT MEMBERS *AS AT JUNE 2018*
Prime Minister, Xavier Bettel
Deputy Prime Minister, Defence, Etienne Schneider
Finance, Pierre Gramegna
Interior, Dan Kersch

EMBASSY OF LUXEMBOURG
27 Wilton Crescent, London SW1X 8SD
T 020-7235 6961 E londres.amb@mae.etat.lu
W http://londres.mae.lu
Ambassador Extraordinary and Plenipotentiary, HE Jean Olinger, *apptd* 2017

BRITISH EMBASSY
5 Boulevard Joseph II, L-1840, Luxembourg
T (+352) 229 864 E britemb@internet.lu
W www.gov.uk/government/world/luxembourg
Ambassador Extraordinary and Plenipotentiary, HE John
   Marshall, *apptd* 2016

ECONOMY AND TRADE
The economy is stable, with steady growth, low
unemployment and low inflation providing an exceptionally
high standard of living and the fifth highest GDP per capita in
the world. The government offset the contraction in the
economy in 2008–9 with economic stimulus measures, which
led to a budget deficit in 2009, but growth resumed in 2010.
Banking and financial services are the dominant sector,
contributing over 35 per cent of GDP. Steel production used
to dominate the industrial sector, but this has diversified to
include IT, telecommunications, freight transport, food
processing, chemicals, metal products and construction. The
small agricultural sector consists mainly of family-owned
farms. Services account for 87.9 per cent of GDP, industry for
11.9 per cent and agriculture for 0.2 per cent. Over half of the
workforce commutes daily from France, Belgium and
Germany. Banking sector reform in 2015 ended
Luxembourg's culture of financial secrecy.
   The main trading partners are other EU countries. Principal
exports are the products of industrial activities. The main
imports are commercial aircraft, minerals, metals, foodstuffs
and luxury consumer goods.
GNI – US$42.1bn; US$70,260 per capita (2017)
Annual average growth of GDP – 3.9 per cent (2017 est)
Inflation rate – 1.2 per cent (2017 est)
Unemployment – 5.9 per cent (2017 est)
Total external debt – US$3.781 trillion (2016 est)
Imports – US$19,171m (2016)
Exports – US$13,161m (2016)

BALANCE OF PAYMENTS
Trade – US$6,010m deficit (2016)
Current Account – US$3.324m surplus (2017)

Trade with UK	2016	2017
Imports from UK	£209,541,776	£265,378,876
Exports to UK	£426,789,042	£396,401,266

COMMUNICATIONS
Transport – Luxembourg has one airport with paved runways;
there are 2,899km of road (including 152km of motorways),
and 275km of railway. The Moselle river provides 37km of
navigable waterway
Telecommunications – 276,400 fixed lines and 764,000 mobile
subscriptions (2016); there were 567,698 internet users in
2016
Internet code and IDD – lu; 352 (from UK), 44 (to UK)
Major broadcasters – Luxembourg is the headquarters of the
Société Européenne des Satellites (SES), which operates
Europe's largest satellite operation; RTL Tele Letzebuerg and
RTL Radio Letzebuerg are the public broadcasters
Press – Leading dailies include *Letzebuerger Journal, Luxemburger
Wort* and *Tageblatt* (all German language)
WPFI score – 14,72 (17)

MACEDONIA
Republika Makedonija – Republic of Macedonia

Area – 25,713 sq. km
Capital – Skopje; population, 584,000 (2018 est)
Major cities – Bitola, Kumanovo
Currency – Denar of 100 deni
Population – 2,103,721 rising at 0.17 per cent a year (2017
   est); Macedonian (64.2 per cent), Albanian (25.2 per cent),
   Turkish (3.9 per cent), Roma (2.7 per cent), Serb (1.8 per
   cent) (2002 est)
Religion – Christian (Orthodox 64.8 per cent), Muslim 33.3
   per cent (2010 est)
Language – Macedonian, Albanian (both official), Turkish,
   Romani, Serbian (each official in different regions)
Population density – 83 per sq. km (2016)
Urban population – 58 per cent (2018 est)
Median age (years) – 37.5 (2016 est)
National anthem – 'Denes Nad Makedonija' 'Today Over
   Macedonia'
National day – 8 September (Independence Day)
Death penalty – Abolished for all crimes (since 1991)
CPI score – 35 (107)
Military expenditure – US$112m (2017)
Literacy rate – 97 per cent (2011 est)
Gross enrolment ratio (percentage of relevant age group) – primary
   90.4 per cent, secondary 78.6 per cent, tertiary 39.6 per
   cent (2014 est)
Health expenditure (per capita) – US$354 (2014)
Hospital beds (per 1,000 people) – 4.4 (2013)
Life expectancy (years) – 76.2 (2016 est)
Mortality rate – 9.2 (2017 est)
Birth rate – 11.4 (2017 est)
Infant mortality rate – 7.4 (2017 est)

CLIMATE AND TERRAIN
The landlocked country is a mountainous plateau divided by
deep river valleys and basins, including the valleys of the
Vardar river and its tributaries. Elevation extremes range from
2,764m (Golem Korab) to 50m (Vardar river). Lakes Ohrid and
Prespa straddle the border with Albania, and Lake Doiran the
border with Greece. The climate is continental, with average
temperatures ranging from −0.7°C in January to 20.6°C in
July and August.

HISTORY AND POLITICS
The area of present-day Macedonia was part of the ancient
Macedonian kingdom, which also included northern Greece
and south-west Bulgaria, in the fourth century BC. Macedonia
became a province of the Roman Empire in the second century
BC, coming under the control of the Byzantine Empire from
the fourth century AD. Slav peoples settled the area in the
seventh century and mixed with the Greek, Illyrian, Thracian,
Scythian and Turkish peoples.

From the ninth to the 14th centuries the area was under the rule successively of the Bulgars, Byzantium and the Serbs, and became part of the Ottoman Empire in the late 14th century. Following the Balkan wars of 1912 and 1913 the region was divided between Bulgaria, Serbia and Greece. After the First World War, the Serbian part was awarded to the newly created state that became Yugoslavia. During the Second World War, this area was occupied by Bulgaria from 1941 to 1944, and after liberation became a republic within the communist Federal Republic of Yugoslavia.

Nationalist sentiment grew throughout the 1980s, and in 1991 Macedonia declared its independence, which Yugoslavia recognised in 1992. International recognition was initially delayed by Greece's objections to the republic's name (Greece claims that its region of Macedonia is the only one entitled to the name), but the country joined the UN in 1993 as the Former Yugoslav Republic of Macedonia; Greece recognised it under this name and lifted its trade blockade in 1995, but in 2008 blocked the republic's membership of NATO. In June 2018, the government agreed to rename the nation 'Republic of North Macedonia', paving the way for NATO and EU membership, but the change will need to be approved via a public referendum planned to take place on 30 September 2018.

Throughout the 1990s there was tension and sporadic violence with the large ethnic Albanian minority, aggrieved at their lack of civil rights. Instability in neighbouring Kosovo spilled over into Macedonia in 2001, sparking a two-month uprising by ethnic Albanian separatists. Peace talks facilitated by international bodies resulted in the Ohrid framework agreement, giving Albanians greater recognition within Macedonia and making Albanian an official language.

The 2009 presidential election was won in the second round by the VMRO-DPMNE candidate, Gjorge Ivanov. President Ivanov was re-elected in July 2014. In the legislative election in December 2016, the VMRO-DPMNE gained two more seats than the opposition Social Democrats but was unable to form a coalition. In May 2017, Zoran Zaev was narrowly elected prime minister by parliament, heading a coalition of the Social Democrats and ethnic Albanian parties.

Macedonia experienced instability in 2015, following allegations that the government had illegally tapped the phones of 20,000 people, including politicians, journalists and judges. The accusations led to large protests both against and for the government, and the resignation of two ministers and a number of intelligence officers. Ethnic Albanian groups were targeted in anti-terrorism raids.

The 1991 constitution was amended in 2001 to incorporate provisions of the Ohrid agreement relating to ethnic Albanian rights, and several times since, most notably in 2004 to give ethnic Albanians greater local autonomy in areas where they predominate.

The head of state is a president, who is directly elected for a five-year term, renewable once. The unicameral legislature, the *Sobranie,* has between 120 and 140 members directly elected for a four-year term. The prime minister is appointed by the president. Government ministers are elected by the assembly but are not members of it.

HEAD OF STATE
President, Gjorge Ivanov, *elected* 5 April 2009, *sworn in* 12 May 2009, *re-elected* 2 July 2014

SELECTED GOVERNMENT MEMBERS *AS AT JULY 2018*
Prime Minister, Zoran Zaev
Deputy Prime Ministers, Hazbi Lika; Bujar Osmani
Finance, Dragan Tevdovski
Foreign Affairs, Nikola Dimitrov
Interior, Oliver Spasovski

EMBASSY OF THE REPUBLIC OF MACEDONIA
Suites 2.1/2.2, Buckingham Court, 75–83 Buckingham Gate, London SW1E 6PE
T 020-7976 0535 E london@mfa.gov.mk
W www.missions.gov.mk/london
Ambassador Extraordinary and Plenipotentiary, vacant

BRITISH EMBASSY
Todor Aleksandrov 165, Skopje 1000
T (+389) (2) 329 9299 E britishembassyskopje@fco.gov.uk
W www.gov.uk/government/world/macedonia
Ambassador Extraordinary and Plenipotentiary, HE Rachel Galloway, *apptd* 2018

ECONOMY AND TRADE

Macedonia was the least developed republic in the former Yugoslavia before 1991, and economic growth was initially hindered by the trade embargo by Greece (1993–5) and the 2001 ethnic Albanian uprising. Liberalisation has since brought foreign investment, and economic growth was steady from 2003 to 2008, although the economy contracted briefly in 2009 owing to the global downturn. Poverty and joblessness remains high (officially the highest in Europe), although figures may be overstated because of the size of the grey economy, estimated to be between 20 and 45 per cent of GDP.

Services contribute roughly 60 per cent of GDP, industry 30 per cent and agriculture 10 per cent. Food processing and winemaking are major industries, along with textiles, chemicals, iron, steel, cement, energy and pharmaceuticals. The main trading partners are Germany, the UK, Greece and other Balkan states. Principal exports are food, wine, tobacco, textiles, manufactured goods, iron and steel. The main imports are machinery and equipment, vehicles, chemicals, fuels and food.

GNI – US$10.2bn; US$4,880 per capita (2017)
Annual average growth of GDP – 2.5 per cent (2017)
Inflation rate – 0.3 per cent (2017 est)
Population below poverty line – 21.5 per cent (2015 est)
Unemployment – 23.4 per cent (2017 est)
Total external debt – US$8.07bn (2017 est)
Imports – US$6,749m (2016)
Exports – US$4,765m (2016)

BALANCE OF PAYMENTS
Trade – US$1,984m deficit (2016)
Current Account – US$128m deficit (2017)

Trade with UK	2016	2017
Imports from UK	£662,481,507	£795,155,573
Exports to UK	£42,468,096	£59,185,280

COMMUNICATIONS

Airports – The principal airports are at Skopje and Ohrid, and there are a further six airports around the country
Roadways and railways – There are 9,489km of paved roadways, including 259km of motorways; there are 699km of railways, of which 234km are electrified
Telecommunications – 368,370 fixed lines and 2.1 million mobile subscriptions (2016); there were 1.5 million internet users in 2016
Internet code and IDD – mk; 389 (from UK), 44 (to UK)
Major broadcasters – MTV and Macedonian Radio are the public broadcasters
Media – Leading dailies include *Nova Makedonija* (state subsidised), *Utrinski Vesnik* and *Dnevnik*
WPFI score – 32,43 (109)

MADAGASCAR

Repoblikan'i Madagasikara/République de Madagascar – Republic of Madagascar

Area – 587,041 sq. km
Capital – Antananarivo; population, 3,058,000 (2018 est)
Major cities – Antsirabe, Antsiranana, Fianarantsoa, Mahajanga, Toamasina
Currency – Ariary (MGA) of five iraimbilanja
Population – 25,054,246 rising at 2.5 per cent a year (2017 est); the people are of mixed Malayo-Indonesian, Arab and African origin. There are sizeable French, Chinese and Indian communities
Religion – Indigenous beliefs 52 per cent, Christian 41 per cent, Muslim 7 per cent
Language – Malagasy, French (both official), English
Population density – 83 per sq. km (2016)
Urban population – 37.2 per cent (2018 est)
Median age (years) – 19.5 (2016 est)
National anthem – 'Ry Tanindrazanay malala ô' 'Oh, Beloved Land of our Ancestors'
National day – 26 June (Independence Day)
Death penalty – Abolished for all crimes (since 2014)
CPI score – 24 (155)
Military expenditure – US$67.3m (2017)

CLIMATE AND TERRAIN

Madagascar, the fourth-largest island in the world, lies 386km off the south-east coast of Africa, from which it is separated by the Mozambique Channel. Coastal plains rise to a central plateau and mountains indented with river valleys. Elevation extremes range from 2,876m (Maromokotro) to 0m (Indian Ocean).

The climate is tropical on the coast, temperate in the interior and arid in the south; average temperatures range from 19.6°C in July to 24.9°C in December. Madagascar is subject to tropical cyclones, which cause flooding and wind damage, particularly on the coast.

HISTORY AND POLITICS

The island was settled by peoples from South East Asia and East Africa from around the first century AD. Although first visited by Europeans c.1500, local kingdoms ruled until the early 19th century, when the Merina kingdom conquered the island. France made the island a protectorate in 1895 after the last indigenous resistance was defeated. During the Second World War, the British invaded in order to replace the pro-Vichy government with a Free French government. At the end of the war Madagascar was returned to France, which suppressed a nationalist uprising in 1947–8. Nationalist agitation continued throughout the 1950s and resulted in independence in 1960.

The military took control in 1972 following civil disturbances, and in 1975 martial law was imposed after a coup. A Marxist one-party state was created with Lt.-Cdr. Didier Ratsiraka as president. Marxism was abandoned in 1980 and a new constitution introduced parliamentary democracy in 1992.

Didier Ratsiraka was defeated in the 1993 presidential elections but returned to office in 1997 after winning the 1996 election. He refused to accept his defeat in the 2001 presidential election and the six-month struggle between his supporters and those of Marc Ravalomanana, the successful candidate, brought the country close to civil war until, in July 2002, Ratsiraka went into exile and his supporters surrendered. President Ravalomanana was re-elected in 2006 and his I Love Madagascar party (TIM) retained its large majority in the 2007 legislative election.

A power struggle between President Ravalomanana and opposition leader Andry Rajoelina began in December 2008. Following an army mutiny and Ravalomanana's resignation, Rajoelina assumed power in March 2009 with the backing of the military and the high court, but the takeover provoked continued demonstrations and widespread international condemnation. The December 2013 presidential election was won by Hery Rajaonarimampianina, while Miaraka Amin'ny Prézidà Andry Rajoelina (MAPAR) emerged as the single largest party in the simultaneous legislative elections. In May 2015, parliament voted to impeach President Rajaonarimampianina amid claims that he had failed to enact promised political reforms; the supreme court annulled the decision on legal grounds in June. Olivier Solonandrasana was replaced as prime minister by independent Christian Ntsay in June 2018 after widespread violent protests over proposed electoral changes.

Under the 2010 constitution, since amended, the president is directly elected and serves a five-year term, renewable once; the minimum age requirement for presidential candidates was lowered in 2010 to 35. The legislature is bicameral, comprising the National Assembly, which has 151 members directly elected for a four-year term, and the senate, which has 63 members, of whom two-thirds are appointed by the regional assemblies and one-third by the president; they serve a six-year term. The senate had been dissolved following the 2009 coup and re-established in December 2015.

HEAD OF STATE
President, Hery Rajaonarimampianina, *took office* 25 January 2014

SELECTED GOVERNMENT MEMBERS *AS AT JUNE 2018*
Prime Minister, Christian Ntsay
Finance, Vonintsalama Sehensosoa Andriambololona
Foreign Affairs, Henry Rabary-Njaka

EMBASSY OF THE REPUBLIC OF MADAGASCAR
Avenue de Tervuren 276,1150 Brussels, Belgium
T (+32) (0) 2770 1726 E info@madagascar-embassy.eu
W www.madagascar-embassy.eu
Ambassador Extraordinary and Plenipotentiary, vacant

BRITISH EMBASSY
Ninth Floor, Tour Zital, Ravoninahitriniarivo Street, Antananarivo 101
T (+261) (20) 223 3053 E BEAntananarivo@moov.mg
W www.gov.uk/government/world/madagascar
Ambassador Extraordinary and Plenipotentiary, HE Dr Philip Boyle, *apptd* 2017

ECONOMY AND TRADE

Economic liberalisation and privatisation since the mid-1990s have resulted in slow but steady growth, although recent political disturbances and cyclone devastation in 2000 and 2004 have been serious setbacks. While the nation has an abundance of natural resources, most remain unexploited and it is heavily reliant on vanilla exports which are vulnerable to price fluctuations. President Ravalomanana's reforms and anti-corruption measures attracted increased international aid, and in 2004 half of the country's foreign debt was written off. International aid was suspended in 2010 following the 2009 coup; the country began to receive limited amounts of aid after a new government was appointed in 2014.

Agriculture, fishing and forestry are the mainstays of the economy, accounting for 23.7 per cent of GDP and employing around 80 per cent of the workforce. The main cash crops include coffee, vanilla, fish, sugar cane, cocoa, cloves and cotton. The industrial sector contributes 16 per cent of GDP, through processing meat, fish and other agricultural products, manufacturing (textiles, paper, cement, chemicals), car assembly and mining (chromite, graphite, sapphires). Tourism is of growing importance.

The main trading partners are France, China, the USA and India. Principal exports are agricultural products, textiles, chromite and mining products. The main imports are capital goods, petroleum, consumer goods and food.

GNI – US$10.3bn; US$400 per capita (2017)
Annual average growth of GDP – 4.3 per cent (2017 est)
Inflation rate – 7.8 per cent (2017 est)
Population below poverty line – 70.7 per cent (2012 est)
Unemployment – 2.1 per cent (2016 est)
Total external debt – US$3.914bn (2017 est)
Imports – US$3,164m (2016)
Exports – US$2,251m (2016)

BALANCE OF PAYMENTS

Trade – US$913m deficit (2016)
Current Account – US$37m deficit (2016)

Trade with UK	2016	2017
Imports from UK	£14,869,948	£26,329,229
Exports to UK	£31,833,445	£33,772,309

COMMUNICATIONS

Airports and waterways – There are 26 airports, with the largest at Antananarivo and Mahajanga; there are 432km of navigable waterways
Roadways and railways – 5,613km; 854km
Telecommunications – 148,585 fixed lines and 8 million mobile subscriptions (2016); there were 1.15 million internet users in 2016
Internet code and IDD – mg; 261 (from UK), 44 (to UK)
Major broadcasters – Television Malagasy (TVM) and Malagasy National Radio (RNM) are the state broadcasters and have a monopoly on national broadcasting; there are hundreds of private local radio and TV stations
Press – Daily titles include *Midi-Madagasikara*, *Madagascar-Tribune* and *La Gazette de la Grande Ile* (all French language)
WPFI score – 26,20 (54)

EDUCATION AND HEALTH

Education is free and compulsory for nine years, but attendance is variable.
Literacy rate – 66.1 per cent (2015)
Gross enrolment ratio (percentage of relevant age group) – primary 144 per cent, secondary 38 per cent (2016), tertiary 4.8 per cent (2014 est)

Health expenditure (per capita) – US$14 (2014)
Life expectancy (years) – 66.3 (2017 est)
Mortality rate – 6.5 (2017 est)
Birth rate – 31.6 (2017 est)
Infant mortality rate – 41.2 (2017 est)
HIV/AIDS adult prevalence – 0.2 per cent (2016 est)

MALAWI

Dziko la Malawi – Republic of Malawi

Area – 118,484 sq. km
Capital – Lilongwe; population, 1,030,000 (2018 est)
Major cities – Blantyre, the commercial and industrial centre; Mzuzu; Zomba, the former capital
Currency – Kwacha (K) of 100 tambala
Population – 19,196,246 rising at 3.31 per cent a year (2017 est); about nine ethnic groups, of which the largest are Chewa (35.1 per cent), Lomwe (18.9 per cent), Yao (13.1 per cent) and Angoni (Nguni) (12 per cent) (2015–2016 est)
Religion – Christian 82.6 per cent, Muslim 13 per cent, none 2.5 per cent, other 1.9 per cent (2008 est)
Language – English (official), Chichewa, Chinyanja, Chiyao, Chitumbuka
Population density – 198 per sq. km (2016)
Urban population – 16.9 per cent (2018 est)
Median age (years) – 16.5 (2016 est)
National anthem – 'Mulungu dalitsa Malawi' 'Oh God Bless Malawi'
National day – 6 July (Independence Day)
Death penalty – Retained (last used 1992)
CPI score – 31 (122)
Military expenditure – US$47.2m (2017)

CLIMATE AND TERRAIN

The landlocked state lies along the western and southern shores of Lake Malawi (Nyasa). The northern and central regions are plateaux with rolling terrain, while the south is mainly hills and mountains. Elevation extremes range from 3,002m (Sapitwa) to 37m (junction of Shire river and Mozambique border). The climate is subtropical, with a wet season from November to April; average temperatures in Lilongwe range from 18.1°C in July to 25.2°C in November.

HISTORY AND POLITICS

Until contact was made with European missionaries in the 19th century, Malawi was dominated by a succession of powerful tribes that included the Maravi, the Yao and the Nguni. The missionaries campaigned for official intervention to end the east-coast slave trade, which had begun in the early 19th century, and in 1891 Britain established the Nyasaland and District Protectorate over the area. Renamed the British Central Africa Protectorate in 1893, it became the British colony of Nyasaland in 1907. The country was joined with Northern and Southern Rhodesia (now Zambia and Zimbabwe) between 1953 and 1963. It became independent, as Malawi, in 1964, with Dr Hastings Banda as prime minister.

In 1966, the country became a one-party state ruled by the Malawi Congress Party (MCP) and Dr Banda became president, declaring himself president for life in 1971. In the early 1990s, increasing pro-democracy agitation and international pressure forced Banda to introduce multiparty democracy in 1994.

In the 2004 legislative election, the MCP became the largest party with 60 seats, but without an overall majority. The simultaneous presidential election was won by the United Democratic Front (UDF) candidate Bingu wa Mutharika, who appointed a coalition government made up of the UDF and smaller parties.

In 2005, President Mutharika resigned from the UDF over the hostility of the party and his predecessor, Bakili Muluzi, to his anti-corruption campaign and founded a new party, the Democratic Progressive Party (DPP). The 2009 legislative election was won by the DPP and President Mutharika was re-elected; Joyce Banda was appointed interim president following his death in April 2012. The DPP returned to power in the May 2014 legislative elections. Opposition parties claimed widespread electoral fraud occurred but the results were upheld by Malawi's electoral commission on 30 May. Peter Mutharika, Bingu wa's younger brother, was elected president soon after.

Under the 1995 constitution, the executive president is directly elected for a five-year term, renewable once. The unicameral National Assembly consists of 193 members, who are directly elected for a five-year term.

HEAD OF STATE
President, Defence, C-in-C of the Armed Forces, Peter Mutharika
  elected 30 May 2014
Vice-President, Saulos Chilima

SELECTED GOVERNMENT MEMBERS *AS AT JUNE 2018*
Finance, Goodall Gondwe
Foreign Affairs, Emmanuel Fabiano
Home Affairs, Cecilia Chazama

HIGH COMMISSION OF THE REPUBLIC OF MALAWI
36 John Street, London WC1N 2AT
T 020-7421 6010 E malawihighcommission@btconnect.com
W www.malawihighcommission.co.uk
High Commissioner, HE Kenna Mphonda, *apptd* 2015

BRITISH HIGH COMMISSION
Off Convention Drive, PO Box 30042, Lilongwe 3
T (+265) (1) 772 400 E bhclilongwe@fco.gov.uk
W www.gov.uk/government/world/malawi
High Commissioner, HE Holly Tett, *apptd* 2017

ECONOMY AND TRADE
Malawi is one of the poorest countries in Africa. It has few natural resources and its agricultural land is under pressure because of population growth. It also experienced years of mismanagement under earlier governments, and corruption remains a problem despite the government's determination to eliminate it. These factors, high HIV/AIDS rates and the vulnerability of agricultural production to both drought and severe flooding, make the country heavily dependent on food and economic aid from international agencies and donor nations, although international aid was suspended from 2013 until May 2017 following a major corruption scandal. Agricultural output was very badly affected by major flooding

in January 2015, followed by severe drought from April 2016. Diversification away from agricultural exports is being pursued.

The economy is primarily agricultural, with 76.9 per cent of the workforce engaged in agriculture, which accounts for 28.1 per cent of GDP and 80 per cent of export revenue. Tobacco is the most important cash crop, along with dried legumes, tea, sugar, cotton, coffee and peanuts, all of which are the nation's main exports. The chief industrial activities are agricultural processing, sawmill products, cement and consumer goods, now supplemented by mining uranium, of which exports began in 2009.

The main export markets are Zimbabwe, Mozambique, Belgium and South Africa; imports come mainly from South Africa, China, India and the UAE. The main imports are food, fuels, semi-manufactures, consumer goods and transport equipment.

GNI – US$6bn; US$320 per capita (2017)
Annual average growth of GDP – 4.5 per cent (2017 est)
Inflation rate – 13.0 per cent (2017 est)
Population below poverty line – 50.7 per cent (2014 est)
Total external debt – US$2.184bn (2017 est)
Imports – US$2,960m (2014)
Exports – US$1,370m (2014)

BALANCE OF PAYMENTS
Trade – US$1,590m deficit (2014)
Current Account – US$1,021m deficit (2017)

Trade with UK	2016	2017
Imports from UK	£13,368,546	£13,824,231
Exports to UK	£12,184,487	£14,582,543

COMMUNICATIONS
Airports and waterways – The main airports are at Blantyre and Lilongwe, with five smaller airports around the country; there are 700km of navigable waterways on Lake Malawi (Nyasa) and the Shire river
Roadways and railways – There are 6,951km of roadways, and 797km of railways, including a line linking the Zambian town of Chipata to the Indian Ocean coast at Nacala in Mozambique
Telecommunications – 11,234 fixed lines and 7.2 million mobile subscriptions (2016); there were 1.7 million internet users in 2016
Internet code and IDD – mw; 265 (from UK), 44 (to UK)
Major broadcasters – Television Malawi (TVM) and Malawi Broadcasting Corporation (radio) are the state broadcasters
Press – *The Nation* and *The Daily Times* are the only daily national newspapers
WPFI score – 27,43 (64)

EDUCATION AND HEALTH
The government is responsible for primary and secondary schools, technical education and primary teacher training.
Literacy rate – 75.1 per cent (2010 est)
Gross enrolment ratio (percentage of relevant age group) – primary 139 per cent, secondary 37 per cent (2016 est), tertiary 1 per cent (2011 est)
Health expenditure (per capita) – US$29 (2014)
Hospital beds (per 1,000 people) – 1.3 (2011)
Life expectancy (years) – 61.7 (2017 est)
Mortality rate – 7.9 (2017 est)
Birth rate – 41 (2017 est)
Infant mortality rate – 43.4 (2017 est)
HIV/AIDS adult prevalence – 9.2 per cent (2016 est)

United Kingdom & Ireland

10°W   5°W   0°

60°N

Shetland Islands
Lerwick

© *Fair Isle*

Orkney Islands
Kirkwall

Pentland Firth
Thurso   Duncansby Head
Cape Wrath   Wick

ATLANTIC OCEAN

Outer Hebrides
Lewis   Stornoway
Harris
N. Uist
S. Uist   Ullapool   Dornoch
Portree   Kyle of Lochalsh
Skye   Dingwall   **Inverness**   Elgin
Mallaig   *Loch Ness*   *Spey*   Fraserburgh
Peterhead
North West Highlands   *Cairngorms*   **Aberdeen**
Ben Nevis   Ben Macdhui   Stonehaven
1345   1309   *Grampian Mts.*
Fort William   **SCOTLAND**
Mull   *Grampian*

North

Sea

Oban   Perth   **Dundee**
St. Andrews
Loch Lomond   Stirling   *Fife Ness*
Greenock   **Dunfermline**   Kirkcaldy
Falkirk   *Firth of Forth*
Paisley   **Glasgow**   **Edinburgh**
Islay   Kilmarnock   Peebles   Galashiels   Berwick-upon-Tweed
Arran   Ayr   *Southern Uplands*   *Tweed*   Jedburgh   Alnwick
Kintyre   *Nith*   Cheviot Hills
Blyth

55°N

Malin Head   *Southern Uplands*
Bloody   **Londonderry**   Coleraine   Dumfries   *Tyne*   **Newcastle upon Tyne**
Foreland   Ballymena   Larne   Stranraer   Kirkcudbright   Carlisle   Consett   **Sunderland**
Malinmore   Strabane   Wigtown   **Durham**   Hartlepool
Head   Donegal   Omagh   **NORTHERN**   **Belfast**   Penrith   **Darlington**   **Middlesbrough**
Donegal   Enniskillen   *Lough*   **Bangor**   Workington   Keswick   *Swale*
Bay   *Erne*   **IRELAND**   Lurgan   *Strangford*   *Lake*   Scarborough
Ballina   Sligo   Armagh   *Lough*   Downpatrick   Isle of   *District*   Kendal   Bridlington
L. Conn   Carrick on   Cavan   *Mourne*   Man   **Barrow-in-**   *Windermere*   **York**   **Kingston**
Castlebar   Shannon   *Mts.*   Douglas   **Furness**   **Harrogate**   **upon Hull**
Clew Bay   Westport   **REPUBLIC**   Dundalk   **Blackpool**   Lancaster   Spurn Head
L. Mask   Longford   Drogheda   *Irish*   **Preston**   **Leeds**   Grimsby
Clifden   *L. Corrib*   Roscommon   Navan   **Liverpool**   **Bradford**
Galway   Athlone   Mullingar   *Sea*   **Manchester**   **Sheffield**
Galway   **OF**   Tullamore   **Dublin**   Birkenhead   *Peak*   Lincoln
Bay   Milltown Malbay   *Lough*   Dun Laoghaire   Anglesey   Chester   *District*   **Chesterfield**   Skegness   Cromer
Ennis   *Derg*   Port Laoise   Bray   Holyhead   Llandudno   Denbigh   Crewe   **Nottingham**   Boston   Norfolk   Great
Kilrush   **IRELAND**   Kildare   **Wicklow**   Caernarfon   **Stoke-on**   **Derby**   *The Wash*   *Broads*   Yarmouth
Limerick   Kilkenny   *Mts.*   Snowdon   Wrexham   **-Trent**   Grantham   Kings
Tralee   Tipperary   Carlow   Arklow   1085   Dolgellau   Shrewsbury   **Leicester**   **Peterborough**   Lynn   **Norwich**   *Waveney*
Dingle   Clonmel   Wexford   *Cardigan*   Aberystwyth   Montgomery   **ENGLAND**   *Nene*
Killarney   *Suir*   Rosslare   *Bay*   Llandrindod   **Wolverhampton**   Coventry   **Northampton**   Cambridge   **Ipswich**
Valentia   Mallow   Waterford   Wells   **Birmingham**   **Rugby**   Harwich
Kenmare   Dungarvan   Fishguard   Cardigan   Worcester   Bedford   **Luton**   *The Naze*
Bantry   **Cork**   Youghal   *Mine Head*   St. David's   Carmarthen   *Teifi*   Gloucester   **Oxford**   Colchester
Cape Clear   *Head*   Llanelli   *Wye*   Ebbw Vale   *Cotswolds*   Swindon   *Chiltern Hills*   **LONDON**   Southend-on-Sea
Milford Haven   **Newport**   Reading   Margate
St. George's Channel   **Swansea**   Port Talbot   **Bristol**   Bath   Canterbury
Cardiff   *Avon*   *Salisbury*   Guildford   Maidstone   Dover
Bristol Channel   *Plain*   Salisbury   Winchester   *The Weald*   Folkestone   Calais
Hartland Point   Barnstaple   *Exmoor*   Taunton   **Southampton**   Hastings
Bude   Yeovil   **Poole**   Isle of   **Portsmouth**   **Brighton**   Le Touquet
Exeter   *Dartmoor*   Weymouth   Wight   **Bournemouth**   Boulogne
Bodmin   Tavistock   *Tamar*   Portland Bill
Truro   **Plymouth**   Torquay   *English Channel*
Penzance   *Land's End*   Start Point   Abbeville
Isles of Scilly   Falmouth   Lizard Point   Dieppe

50°N

Alderney   Cherbourg   *Baie de la Seine*   **FRANCE**
Guernsey   Sark   Le Havre   Rouen
Jersey   Caen
Collines de Normandie
Seine

| 0 | 25 | 50 | 75 | 100 Miles |

| 0 | 50 | 100 | 150 Kms |

Conical Orthomorphic Projection

© Oxford Cartographers, 98415
+44 (0)1993 705 394
E & OE

10°W   5°W   0°

55°N

50°N

Europe

ATLANTIC OCEAN

Arctic Circle

ICELAND
Reykjavik

Norwegian Sea

0 100 200 300 400 Miles
0 100 200 300 400 500 600 Kms

Conical Orthomorphic Projection

© Oxford Cartographers, 98415
+44 (0)1993 705 394
E & OE

Faroe Is.
(Denmark)

Shetland Is.

Tromso
Bodo

N O R W A Y
S W E D E N

Trondheim

Bergen

Trondheim

Hebrides

Orkney Is.

Th.Ness
Aberdeen
Dundee

Glasgow
Edinburgh

Stavanger

Kristiansand

Oslo
Orebro

Gavle
Uppsala
Vasteras
Stockholm
Norrkoping
Linkoping
Jonkoping
Gothenburg

North Sea

Skagerrak

Alborg

Arhus Helsingborg
DENMARK Copenhagen
Odense Malmo

Bornholm
(Den.)

Londonderry
Belfast
UNITED
KINGDOM
Newcastle
upon Tyne

Galway Dublin
REP. OF
IRELAND
Cork

Liverpool
Manchester
Sheffield
Leeds

Stoke-
on-Trent

Swansea Cardiff
Bristol

Plymouth Southampton

Norwich
Birmingham

Amsterdam
London NETHERLANDS
Rotterdam
Antwerp
Brussels
BELGIUM
LUX.
Luxembourg

Kiel Rostock Koszalin

Hamburg Szczecin

Bremen Hanover Berlin P O
Osnabrück Pozna
Essen Munster Wroclaw
Dortmund Leipzig Dresden
Düsseldorf Chemnitz
Cologne
GERMANY
Frankfurt Plzen Prague
Nuremberg CZECH REP
Mannheim Regensburg Brno
Stuttgart Bratislava
Munich Danube Vienna
Salzburg AUSTRIA
Innsbruck Graz

English Channel
Cherbourg
Brest
Le Havre Amiens
Caen Rouen
Rennes Seine Paris Reims
Nantes Loire Orléans
Tours
Dijon
FRANCE

Bay of
Biscay

Bordeaux

La Coruña
Vigo
Oporto
Coimbra Douro

León
Valladolid Burgos
Salamanca
Badajoz

PORTUGAL
Amadora
Lisbon
Setúbal
Tagus

Bilbao
Pamplona
San Sebastian
Zaragoza
Pyrenees ANDORRA
Lérida
Madrid
Barcelona

SPAIN

Montpellier
Toulouse
Nimes

Limoges
Clermont-
Ferrand
Lyon
Grenoble

Geneva
SWITZERLAND
Zurich
Mt. Blanc
4808
LIECH.
Bern

Milan Po
Turin Verona
Genoa Parma Venice
Bologna
La Spezia SAN
Livorno MARINO
Florence
Ancona

Trento
Ljubljana SLOV.
Trieste Zagreb
Rijeka
Banja
Luka B
CROATIA
Adriatic
Split

Maribor
Graz

Nice MONACO
Marseille

Córdoba
Seville
Granada Murcia
Málaga Almeria
Cartagena

Cadiz
Gibraltar(U.K.)
Ceuta(Sp.)
Tetouan
Melilla(Sp.)

Tangier

Faro
Huelva

Casablanca
Rabat
Fes
Meknes
Oujda

MOROCCO Mountains
Atlas

Balearic Is.
(Sp.)
Valencia Palma
Mallorca

Corsica
(Fr.)
Ajaccio

Rome

Sardinia
(It.)
Sassari

Cagliari

Pescara
ITALY
Apennines

Foggia
Bari

Naples Salerno

Palermo Messina
Sicily Reggio
Calabria
Syracuse

M e d i t e r r a n e a n

Algiers
Blida
Skikda Annaba
Bejaia Constantine Ariana Tunis

Oran
Sidi Bel Abbes

ALGERIA

TUNISIA
Sousse

Valletta
MALTA

Sfax

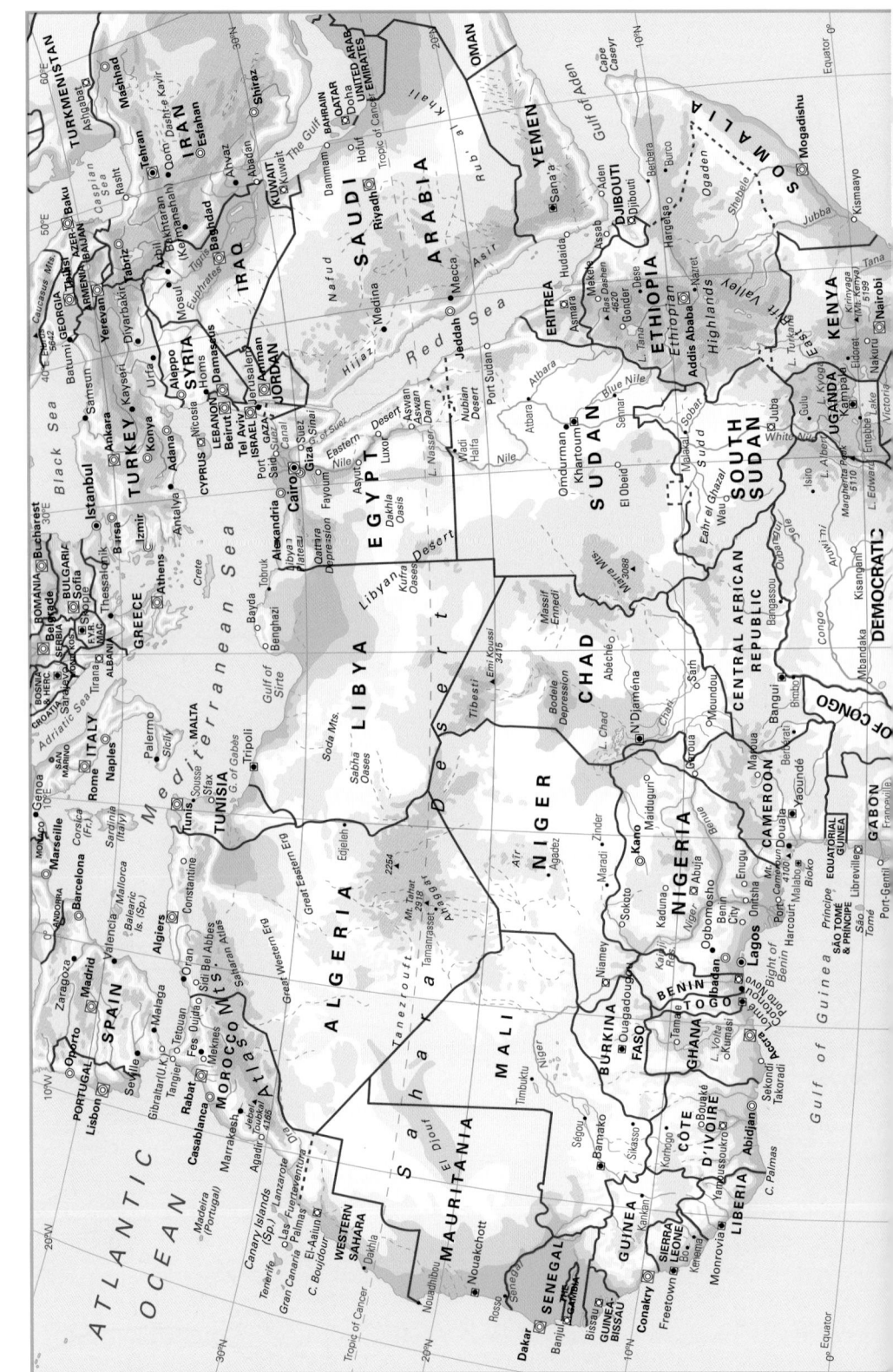

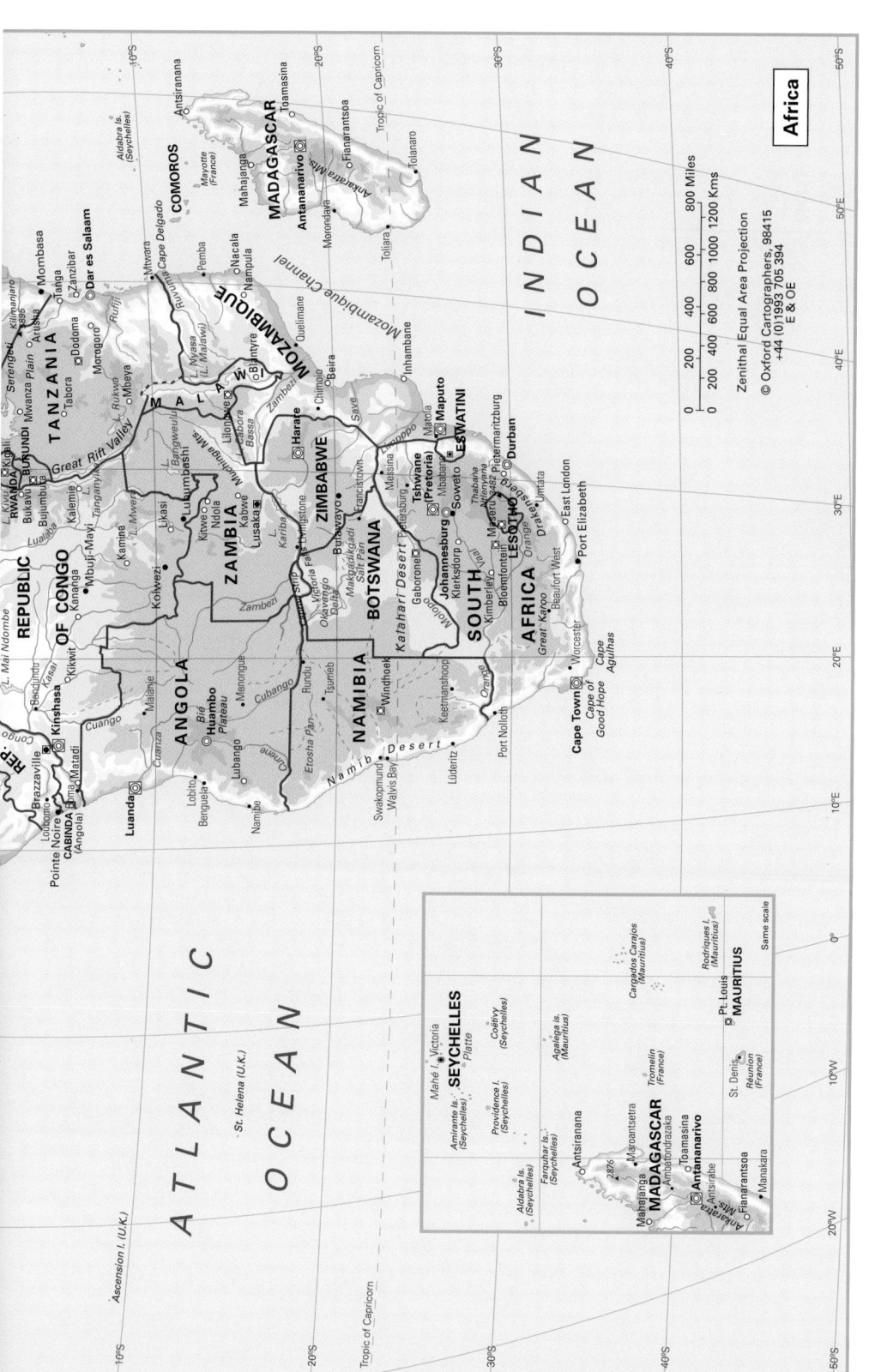

Africa

ATLANTIC OCEAN

INDIAN OCEAN

Ascension I. (U.K.)

St. Helena (U.K.)

REP. OF CONGO
Brazzaville
Pointe Noire
Loubomo
CABINDA (Angola)
Kinshasa
Boma Matadi
L. Mai Ndombe
Bandundu
Kasai
Kikwit
Kwango
Congo
Kananga
Mbuji-Mayi
Kamina
Kananga
Kikwit

REPUBLIC OF CONGO
Kalemie
L. Tanganyika
L. Mweru
Kamina
Likasi
Lubumbashi
Kolwezi

ANGOLA
Luanda
Lobito
Benguela
Namibe
Malanje
Lubango
Huambo
Bié Plateau
Cuanza
Cuango
Cubango
Cunene
Menongue

BURUNDI
RWANDA
Kigali
Bukavu
Bujumbura
L. Kivu

TANZANIA
Kilimanjaro 5895
Serengeti
Arusha
Mwanza Plain
Dodoma
Tabora
Mbeya
Morogoro
Rufiji
Great Rift Valley
Rukwa
L. Rukwa
Mombasa
Tanga
Zanzibar
Dar es Salaam

COMOROS
Aldabra Is. (Seychelles)
Antsiranana
Mayotte (France)

MADAGASCAR
Antananarivo
Mahajanga
Morondava
Antsirabe
Fianarantsoa
Toamasina
Toliara
Tolanaro
Ankaratra Mts.

MOZAMBIQUE
Mtwara
Cape Delgado
Pemba
Nacala
Nampula
Quelimane
Beira
Inhambane
Maputo
Mozambique Channel

MALAWI
L. Nyasa (L. Malawi)
Lilongwe
Blantyre

ZAMBIA
Lusaka
Ndola
Kitwe
Kabwe
Kariba
L. Kariba
Cahora Bassa
Luangwa
Zambezi

ZIMBABWE
Harare
Bulawayo
Gweru
Mutare
Masvingo
Limpopo

BOTSWANA
Gaborone
Francistown
Makgadikgadi Salt Pan
Kalahari Desert
Okavango Delta
Maun

NAMIBIA
Windhoek
Swakopmund
Walvis Bay
Lüderitz
Keetmanshoop
Namib Desert
Etosha Pan
Rundu
Tsumeb
Oranje

SOUTH AFRICA
Pretoria (Tshwane)
Johannesburg
Soweto
Klerksdorp
Kimberley
Bloemfontein
Cape Town
Cape of Good Hope
Cape Agulhas
Worcester
Beaufort West
Port Nolloth
Port Elizabeth
East London
Durban
Pietermaritzburg
Great Karoo
Drakensberg
Vaal
Orange
Matola

ESWATINI
Mbabane

LESOTHO
Maseru
Thabana Ntlenyana

SEYCHELLES
Victoria
Mahé I.
Amirante Is. (Seychelles)
Aldabra Is. (Seychelles)
Farquhar Is. (Seychelles)
Providence I. (Seychelles)
Coëtivy (Seychelles)
Platte

MAURITIUS
Pt. Louis
Agalega Is. (Mauritius)
Cargados Carajos (Mauritius)
Rodrigues I. (Mauritius)
Tromelin (France)
St. Denis
Réunion (France)

MADAGASCAR
Antananarivo
Mahajanga
Marantsetra
Ambatondrazaka
Antsiranana
Antsirabe
Toamasina
Fianarantsoa
Manakara
Ankaratra Mts.

Same scale

Zenithal Equal Area Projection

© Oxford Cartographers, 98415
+44 (0)1993 705 394
E & OE

0   200   400   600   800 Miles
0 200 400 600 800 1000 1200 Kms

Tropic of Capricorn

Tropic of Capricorn

10°S
20°S
30°S
40°S
50°S

20°W
10°W
0°
10°E
20°E
30°E
40°E
50°E

North America

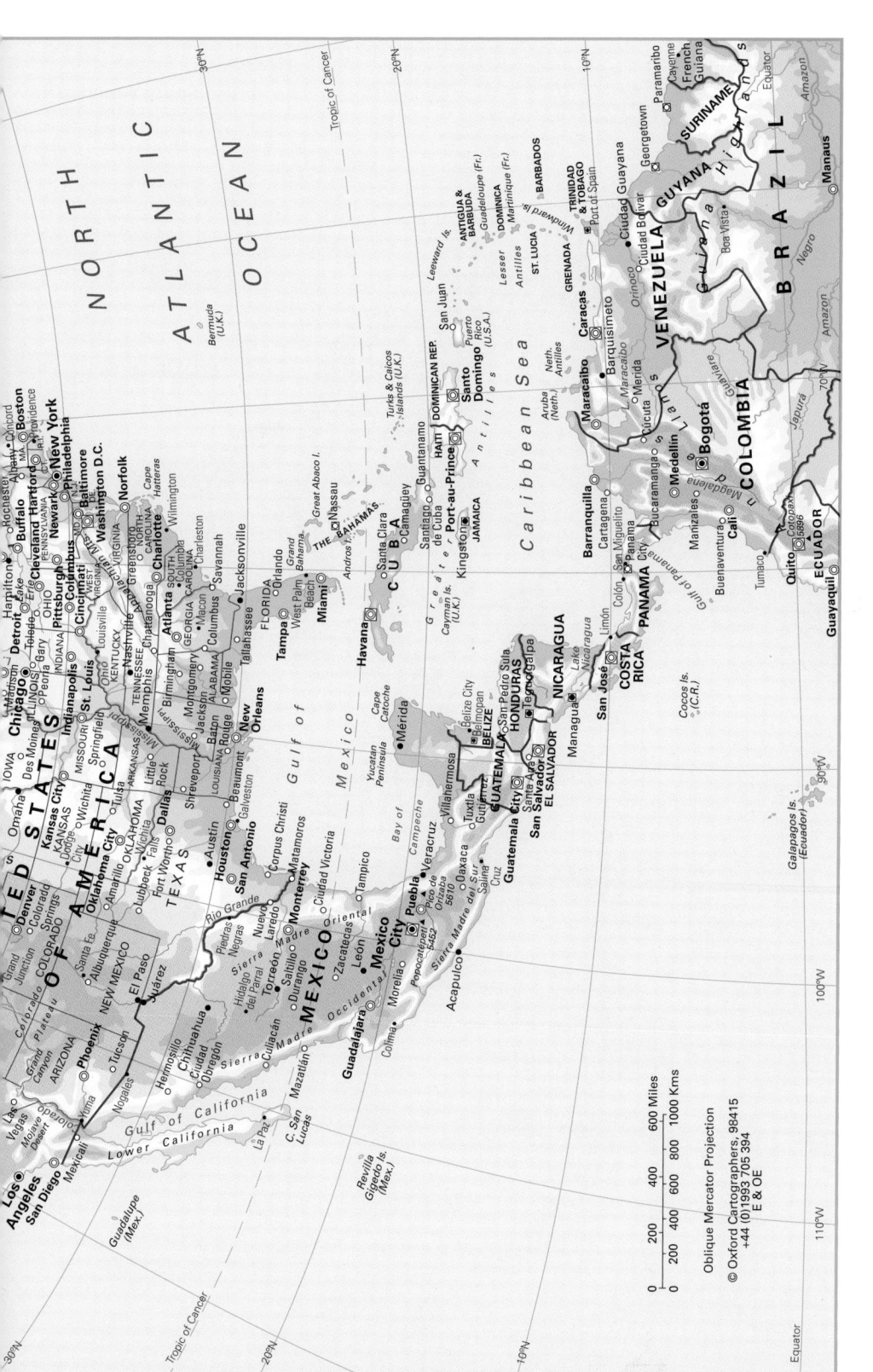

South America

CUBA
Camagüey
Santiago de Cuba
Guantanamo
Cayman Is. (U.K.)
HONDURAS
Kingston
JAMAICA
HAITI
Port-au-Prince
DOMINICAN REP.
Santo Domingo
Turks & Caicos Islands (U.K.)
San Juan
Puerto Rico (U.S.A.)
Leeward Is.
ANTIGUA & BARBUDA
Guadeloupe (Fr.)
DOMINICA
Martinique (Fr.)
ST. LUCIA
BARBADOS
GRENADA
TRINIDAD & TOBAGO
Port of Spain
Lesser Antilles
Windward Is.
Neth. Antilles
Antilles

NICARAGUA
Lake Nicaragua
COSTA RICA
Colón
Limón
San Miguelito
Panama City
PANAMA
Gulf of Panama
Buenaventura

Barranquilla
Cartagena
Maracaibo
L. Maracaibo
Merida
Cúcuta
Bucaramanga
Medellín
Manizales
Cali
COLOMBIA
Bogotá
Caracas
Barquisimeto
VENEZUELA
Ciudad Guayana
Ciudad Bolívar
Orinoco
Llanos
Guaviare
Boa Vista
Georgetown
GUYANA
Paramaribo
SURINAME
Cayenne
French Guiana
Guiana Highlands

Caribbean Sea

NORTH
ATLANTIC
OCEAN

10°N

Equator
Quito
Cotopaxi 5896
ECUADOR
Guayaquil
Chimborazo 6310
Cuenca
Tumaco
Japurá
Negro
Amazon
Marajó I.
Belem
Sao Luis
Fernando de Noronha (Brazil)

Equator

Sullana
Chiclayo
Cajamarca
Trujillo
Chimbote
Huánuco
Iquitos
Leticia
Marañón
Cruzeiro do Sul
Putumayo
Pucallpa
Porto Velho
Río Branco
Selvas
Jurua
Purus
Madeira
Tapajós
Manaus
Santarem
Amazon
Xingu
Bacabal
Teresina
Floriano
Juazeiro do Norte
Parnaiba
Fortaleza
Mossoro
Natal
Camnina Grande
Juazeiro Paulo Alfonso
Recife
João Pessoa

B R A Z I L

10°S

Callao
Lima
Huancayo
Cuzco
Titicaca
El Alto
BOLIVIA
La Paz
Cochabamba
Santa Cruz
Oruro
L. Poopó
Potosí
Sucre
Arica
Tarija
Iquique
Puno
Arequipa
Mollendo
Trinidad
Mamoré
Serra dos Parecis
Mato Grosso
Ciuaba
Plateau
Corumba
Campo Grande
Goiania
Brasília
Barreiras
São Francisco
Feira de Santana
Salvador
Olheus
Montes Claros
Governador Valadares
Caratinga
Vitoria

B r a z i l i a n
H i g h l a n d s

Brazilian
Plateau

Uberaba
Uberlandia
Belo Horizonte
Ribeirao Preto
Marilia
Londrina
Campinas
Sorocaba
Sao Paulo
Rio de Janeiro
Campos
Santos

20°S

Antofagasta
San Pedro de Atacama
Salta
Tucumán
Copiapó
Catamarca
La Rioja
La Serena
Atacama Desert
Altiplano
Pilcomayo
Gran Chaco
San Salvador de Jujuy
Santiago del Estero
Formosa
Asunción
Ciudad del Este
PARAGUAY
Paraná
Corrientes
Posadas
Resistencia
Santa Maria
Passo Fundo
Florianopolis
Porto Alegre
Pelotas
Tacuarembó
Curitiba
Paraná
Cascavel

Tropic of Capricorn

Juan Fernández Is. (Chile)
San Félix (Chile)
San Ambrosio (Chile)
Cerro Aconcagua 6960
San Juan
Mendoza
San Luis
Córdoba
Rosario
Santa Fé
Paraná
Uruguay
URUGUAY
Salto
Paysandu
Durazno
Montevideo
Buenos Aires
La Plata
Río de la Plata
Viña del Mar
Valparaíso
Santiago
Rancagua
Puente Alto
Talca
Pampas

30°S

SOUTH

PACIFIC

OCEAN

Concepción
Chillán
Temuco
Valdivia
Osorno
Puerto Montt
Chiloé Island
Neuquén
Viedma
Bahía Blanca
Mar del Plata
Negro
Colorado

A R G E N T I N A

P a t a g o n i a

40°S

SOUTH
ATLANTIC
OCEAN

Taitao Peninsula
Coihaique
Chubut
Valdés Peninsula
Trelew
Comodoro Rivadavia
G. of S. George
Deseado

50°S

Punta Arenas
Magellan Strait
Tierra del Fuego
Ushuaia
Cape Horn
Buenos Aires
Río Gallegos
Stanley
Falkland Islands (U.K.)
South Georgia (U.K.)
South Shetland Islands (U.K.)
South Orkney Islands (U.K.)
South Sandwich Islands (U.K.)

| 0 | 200 | 400 | 600 Miles |
| 0 | 200 400 600 800 | 1000 Kms |

Oblique Mercator Projection

© Oxford Cartographers, 98415
+44 (0)1993 705 394
E & OE

100°W 90°W 80°W 70°W 60°W 50°W 40°W 30°W 20°W 10°W

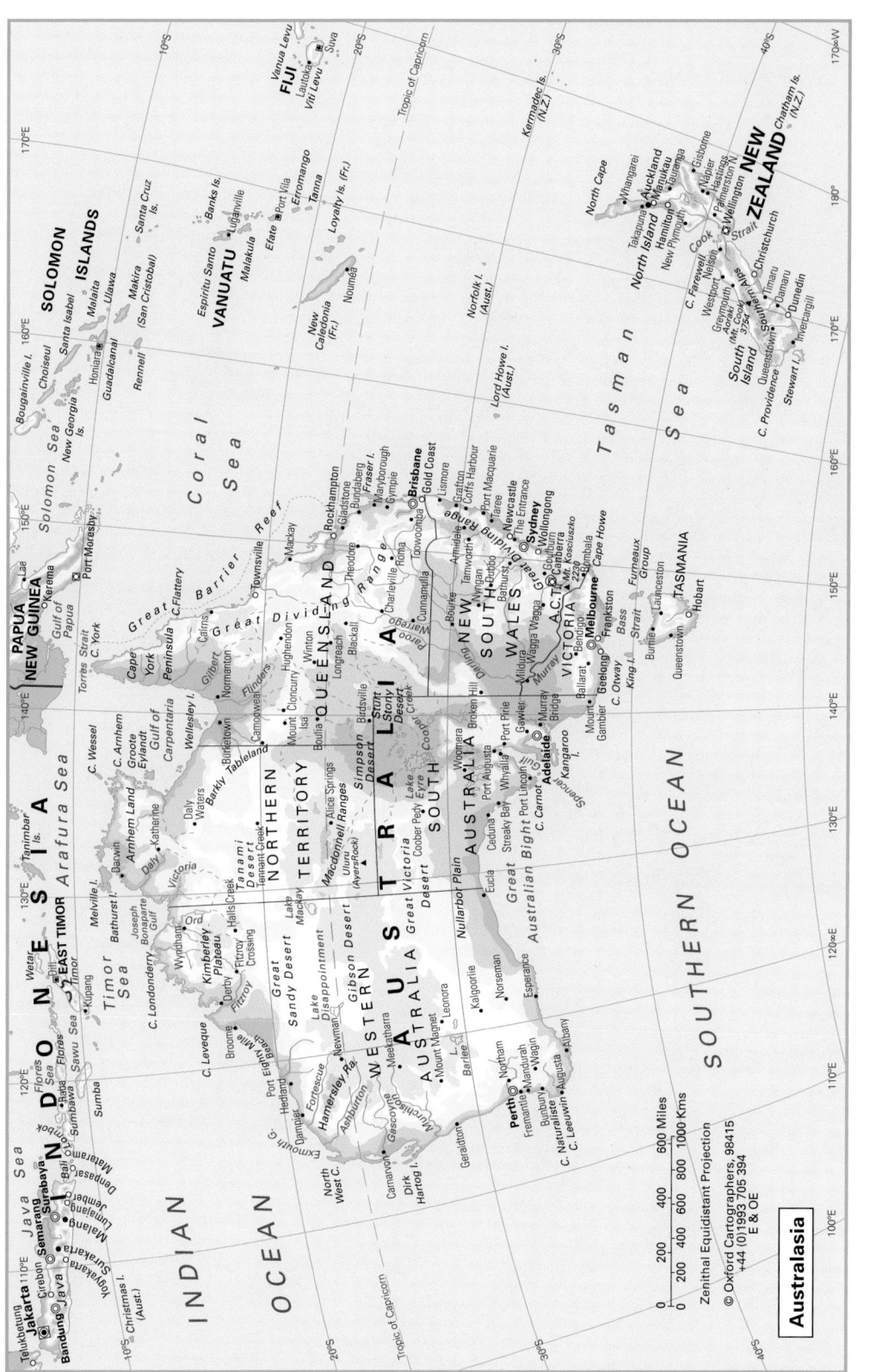

Australasia

Northern Asia

70°N   0°   10°E   20°E   30°E   40°E   60°E   80°E   60°N

Farroe Is.
(Denmark)

Spitsbergen

Svalbard
(Norway)

Franz Josef Land

A R C T I C

Arctic Circle

Trondheim
N O R W A Y
Bergen
Oslo
Stockholm
Uppsala

S W E D E N

Tromsø
North
Cape

Murmansk

Kola
Peninsula

Novaya Zemlya

Kara
Sea

Barents Sea

Umeå
Luleå
Lapland

Karelaksha

F I N L A N D

Gulf of Bothnia
Helsinki Tampere
Espoo Vaasa
Baltic Sea
Gulf of Finland
Tallinn

White
Sea

Sverodvinsk

Arkhangelsk

Pechora

Gulf of Ob

Dudinka

Vorkuta

ESTONIA
Tartu
Pskov
LATVIA
Riga
LITH.
Vilnius
Daugavpils
Velikiye-
Luki

St. Petersburg
L. Ladoga
L. Onega
Petrozavodsk
Novgorod
Tver
Cherepovets
Vologda

N. Dvina
Konosha

Syktyvkar

Ukhta
Pechora

Khanty-
Mansiysk

West
Siberian
Plain

Ob

Nadym

Surgut

Nizhnevartovsk

BELARUS
Minsk
Gomel
Vitebsk

Smolensk
Moscow
Kaluga
Tula

Yaroslavl
Volga
Ivanovo
Kostroma
Nizhniy
Novgorod
Cheboksary
Arzamas

Kirov
(Vyatka)
Glazov
Berezniki

R
U
S
S

Serov

Tyumen

Tomsk
Anzhero-Sudzhensk

Chernigov
Bryansk
Orel
Kursk
Belgorod
Voronezh

UKRAINE
Kharkiv
50°N

Lipetsk
Tambov
Ryazan
Vladimir
Saransk
Penza
Syzran
Tolyatti
Samara
Balakhovo
Saratov
Orenburg
Engels
Kamyshin

Kazan
Simbirsk
Naberezhnyye
Chelny

Perm
Izhevsk
Sarapul
Kungur

Nizhniy
Tagil
Yekaterinburg

Ufa

Zlatoust
Magnitogorsk

Tobolsk

Ishim

Kamensk-
Uralskiy
Kurgan

Chelyabinsk
Troitsk

Kostanay
Rudnyy

Petropavlovsk

Omsk

U
r
a
l

M
o
u
n
t
a
i
n
s

Irtysh

Ob

Leninsk-
Kuybyshev
Kuznetskiy

Novosibirsk
Kemerovo

Novokuznetsk

Barnaul
Biysk

Luhansk
Donetsk
Rostov

Volgograd

Volga
Ural
Uralsk
Orsk

Aqtobe

Kokshetau
Pavlodar
Irtysh

Rubtsovsk

Semey

Oskemen

Stavropol
Armavir

Elista

Caspian Lowlands
Atyrau

Astana

L. Tengiz

Qaraghandy

Kazakh
Uplands

Altay

Vladikavkaz
Grozny
Makhachkala

Astrakhan

Caucasus Mts.
GEO
Tbilisi
Rioni
AZERBAIJAN
40°N
Baku

Ardabil

C a s p i a n   S e a

Kara
Bogaz
Gol
Turkmenbashi

Sumqayit

Aksu

Ust-Urt
Plateau

Aral
Sea
Aralsk

Kirghiz   Steppe

K A Z A K H S T A N

Zhezkazgan

Balkhash

Lake
Balkhash

L. Zaysan

Tacheng

Karamay

Dzungarian Basin
(Junggar Pendi)
Yining
Kuytun
Shihezi

Urumqi

Rasht
Qazvin
Karaj
Elburz Mts.
Gorgan
Semnan
Tehran
Qom
Esfahan
IRAN
60°E

TURKMENISTAN

Dashhowuz

UZBEKISTAN

Nukus

Kyzyl-Orda
Syr Darya
Kyzylkum
Desert

Muyunkum
Desert

Shymkent
Taraz

Taldy-Kurgan

Bishkek
Pik Pobedy
7439

Almaty

KYRGYZSTAN

Issyk
Kul

Korla

Bosten
Hu

Ashgabat
Mary

Karakum   Desert

Bukhara
Navoi
Dzhizak
Samarkand

Turkmenabat
(Charjou)

Khujand
Namangan
Fergana

T i e n   S h a n

Aksu

Tarim He

Kashi
80°E

Amu Darya
Dushanbe
70°N

TAJIKISTAN

TASHKENT
Tashkent

100°E   120°E   140°E   150°E   160°E   170°E   70°N   180°   Bering Sea

0   100   200   300   400   500 Miles
0   100 200 300 400 500 600 700 800 Kms

Conical Orthomorphic Projection

© Oxford Cartographers, 98415
+44 (0)1993 705 394
E & OE

East Siberian Sea

Wrangel I.

Perek

Anadyr

Anadyr Range

Arctic Circle

Koryak Range

New Siberia Is.

O C E A N

Severnaya Zemlya

Laptev Sea

Lyakhov Is.

Indigirka

Kolyma

Kolyma Mts.

60°N

Taymyr Pen.

L. Taymyr

Tiksi

Olenek

Yana

Cherskogo Range

Magadan

Sea of Okhotsk

• Norilsk

Central

Lena

Verkhoyansk   Range

Okhotsk

Siberian

Vilyuy

Yakutsk

Aldan

Dzhugdzhur Range

Sakhalin

Lower Tunguska

Plateau

Lensk

A

Djekminsk

S

SIA

Lena

Neryungri

Aleksandrovsk-
Sakhalinskiy

• Angara

Ust Ilimsk

Yablonovyy Mts.

Stanovoy Mts.

Tynda

Komsomolsk
Na-Amure

Amur

50°N

Lesnsibirsk •

Ust-Kut

Severobaikalsk

Skovorodino

Khabarovsk

• Achinsk   Kansk Tayshek
Krasnoyarsk

Bratsk

Chita

Sretensk

Amur

Skovorodino

Belogorsk

Blagoveshchensk

Birobidzhan

Sikhote-Alin Mts.

Tulun

Hailar

Bei'an

Yichun

Shuangyashan

Sayan Mts.

Usolye-
Sibirskoye-
Angarsk

Ulan-
Ude

Manzhouli

Da Hinggan Ling

Qiqihar

Hegang

Jiamusi

Quitaihe

Jixi

Mudanjiang

Abakan

Irkutsk

Lake Baikal

Daqing

Harbin

Ussuriysk

• Kyzyl

Baicheng

Jilin

Vladivostok

Yanji

Chongjin

Hovsgol
Nuur

Darhan •

Ulanhot

Changchun

Liaoyuan

Uvs Nuur

• Ulaanbaatar

Ondorhaan

INNER MONGOLIA

Tongliao

Siping

Fushun

DEM. PEOPLE'S
REP. OF KOREA

Hangayan Mts.

Saynshand

Chifeng

Shenyang

Anshan

Pyongyang

Altai • Hovd

• Altay

M O N G O L I A

Fuxin
Jinzhou

Korea
Bay

Seoul

Altai Range

Gobi   Desert

Jining

Zhang-
jiakou

Chengde •

Tangshan

Dalian

Inchon

REP. OF
KOREA

• Turpan   Hami •

Turpan Depression

Linhe •

Baotou

A

Hohhot

Beijing
(Peking)

Tianjin

Yantai

Weihai

Kwangju

C

H

Wuhai •

Huang He (Yellow)

Datong

Baoding •

Cangzhou Bo Hai

Weifang

Qingdao

Yellow
Sea

90°E Lop Nur

N

Shizuishan •

Taiyuan

100°E

Yuci •

Dezhou •

Handan •

Shijiazhuang

110°E

Zibo

Jinan

120°E

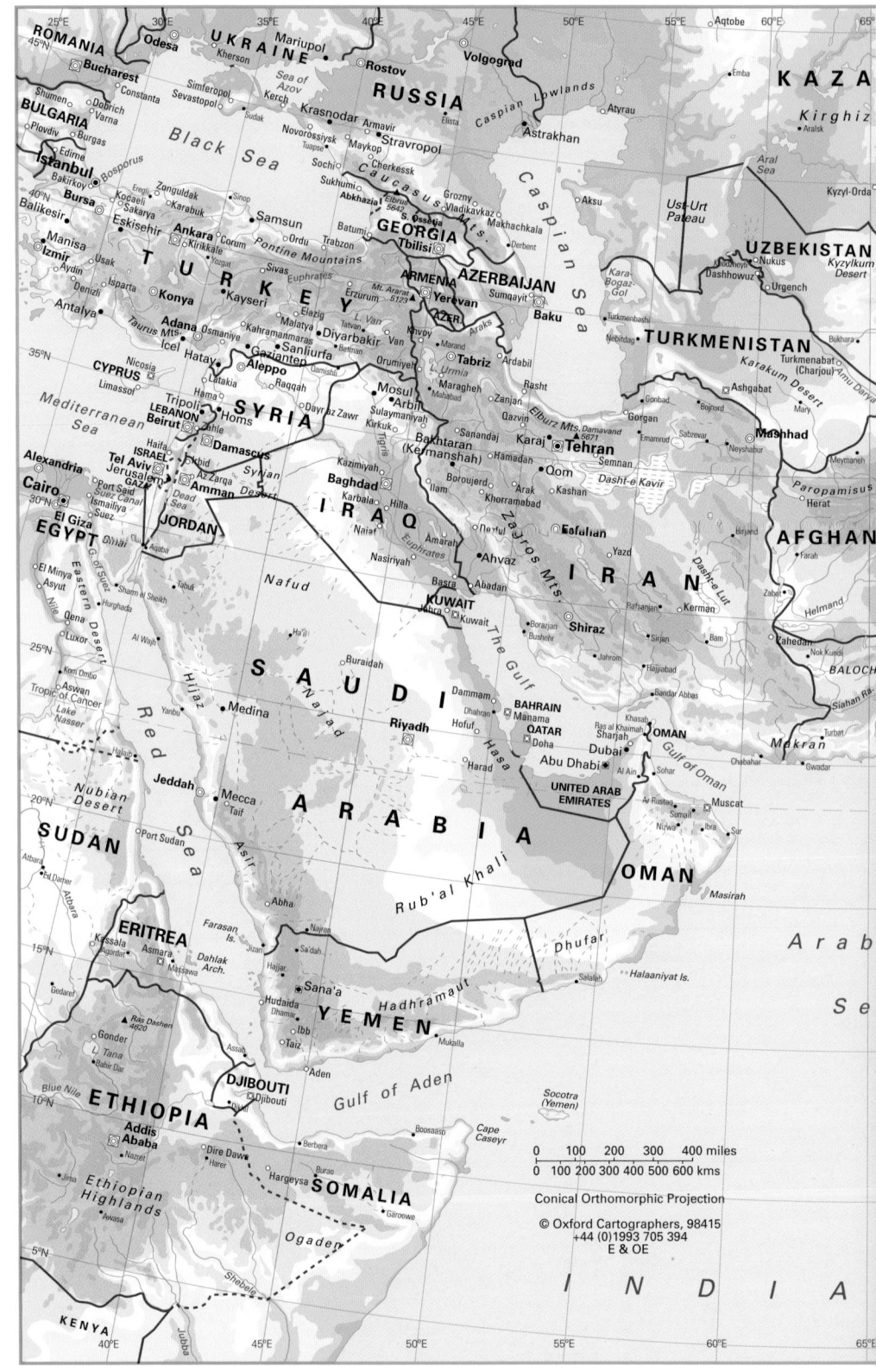

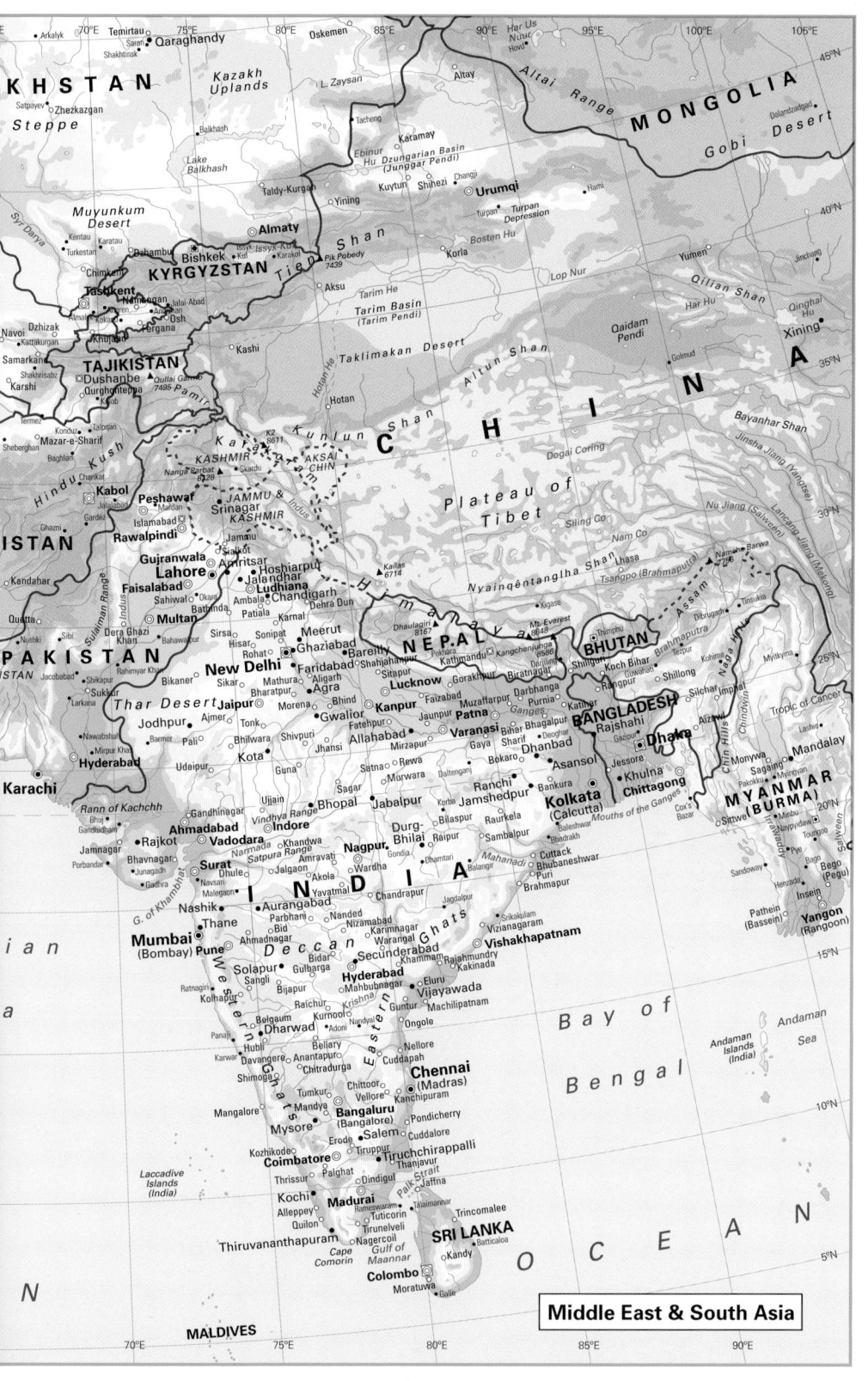

Middle East & South Asia

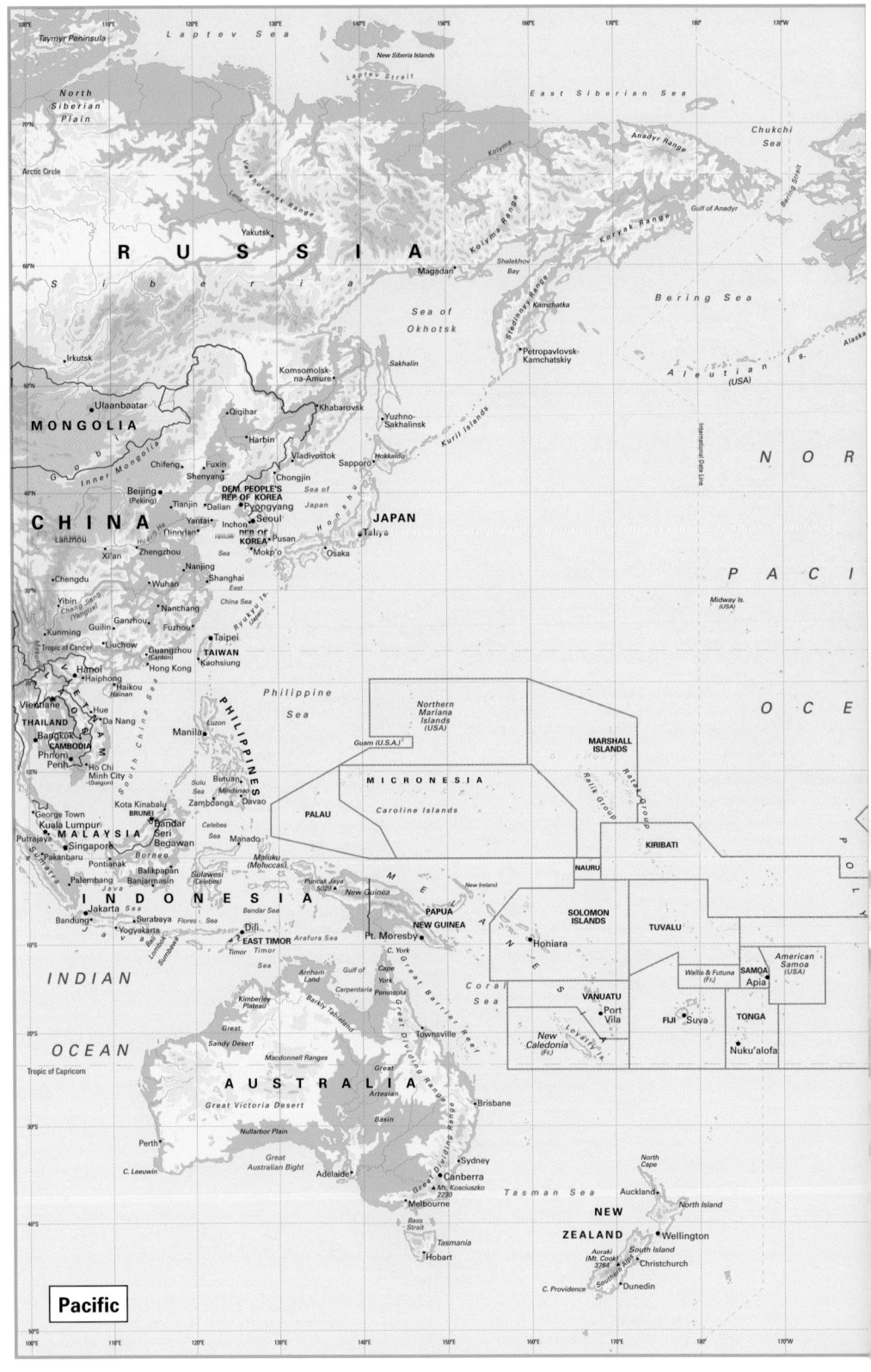

Pacific

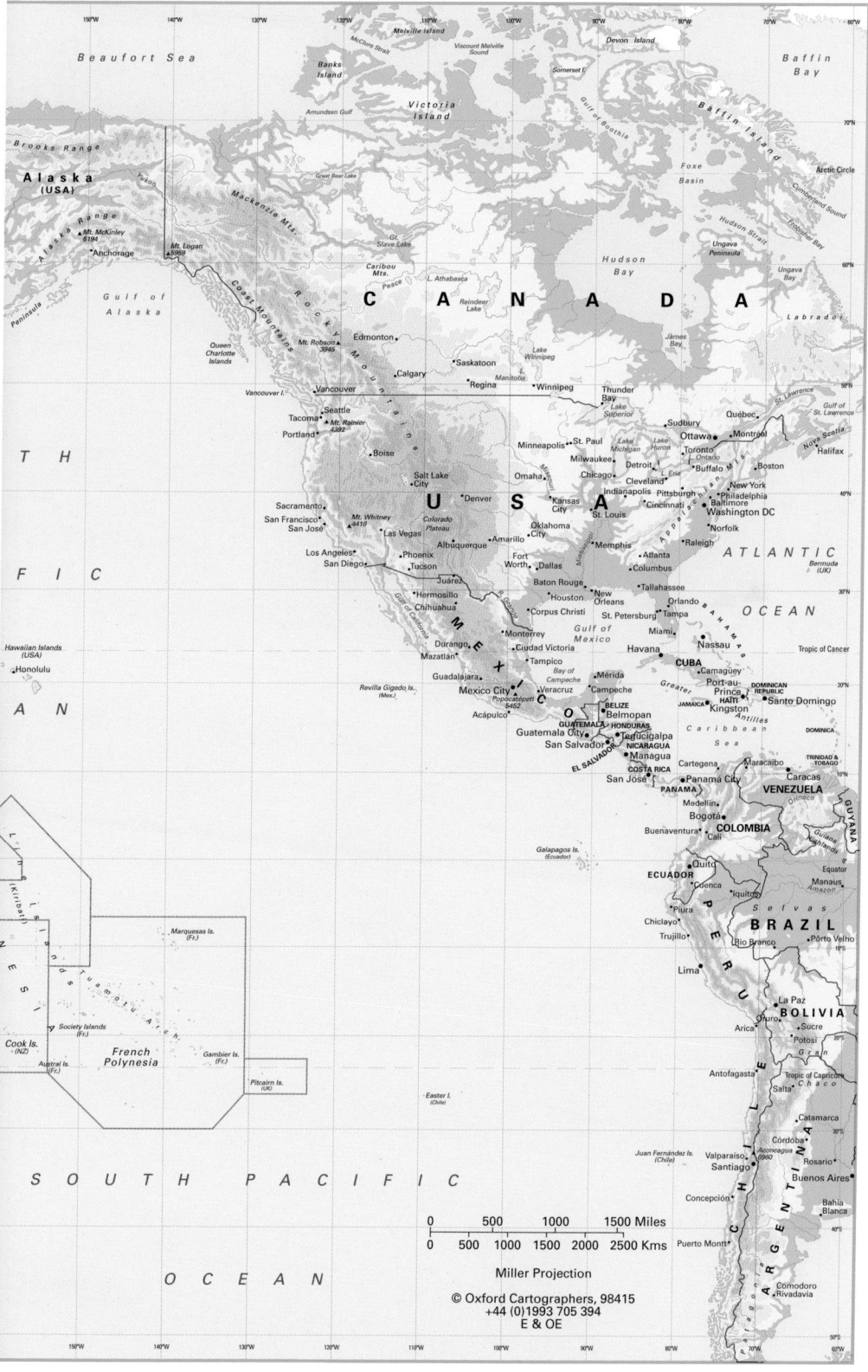

Beaufort Sea

Melville Island
Banks Island
McClure Strait
Viscount Melville Sound
Devon Island
Baffin Bay

Amundsen Gulf

Victoria Island

Somerset I.

Baffin Island

Brooks Range

Alaska (USA)

Mt. McKinley 6194
Anchorage
Mt. Logan 5959

Great Bear Lake

Gulf of Boothia

Foxe Basin

Cumberland Sound

Arctic Circle

70°N

Gulf of Alaska

Yukon

Mackenzie Mts.

Caribou Mts.

L. Athabasca

Hudson Strait

Ungava Peninsula

60°N

Peninsula

Queen Charlotte Islands

Coast Mountains

Mt. Robson 3945

Edmonton

Peace

Great Slave Lake

Reindeer Lake

Hudson Bay

James Bay

Ungava Bay

Labrador

C A N A D A

Vancouver I.
Vancouver
Seattle
Tacoma
Mt. Rainier 4392
Portland
Boise

Calgary

Saskatoon

Regina

Lake Winnipeg

Winnipeg

Manitoba

Thunder Bay
Lake Superior

Sudbury

Québec

St. Lawrence

Gulf of St. Lawrence

Nova Scotia

50°N

Sacramento
San Francisco
San Jose
Mt. Whitney 4418
Las Vegas
Los Angeles
San Diego
Phoenix
Tucson
Juárez

Salt Lake City
Denver
Colorado Plateau

U S A

Minneapolis St. Paul
Milwaukee
Omaha
Chicago
Lake Michigan
Lake Huron
Detroit
Lake Erie
Ottawa
Toronto
Ontario
Montréal
Buffalo
Cleveland
New York
Boston
Halifax

Kansas City
Oklahoma City
Amarillo
Albuquerque

Indianapolis Pittsburgh
St. Louis
Cincinnati
Appalachian Mts.
Philadelphia
Baltimore
Washington DC
Norfolk

Memphis
Atlanta
Columbus
Raleigh

ATLANTIC

Bermuda (UK)

40°N

OCEAN

Hermosillo
Chihuahua

M
E
X
I
C
O

Fort Worth
Dallas
Baton Rouge
New Orleans
Houston
Corpus Christi

Tallahassee
Orlando
St. Petersburg Tampa
Miami

30°N

Hawaiian Islands (USA)
Honolulu

T
H
E

P
A
C
I
F
I
C

O
C
E
A
N

Durango
Mazatlán
Guadalajara

Monterrey
Ciudad Victoria
Tampico

Gulf of Mexico

Havana

Nassau

CUBA

Camagüey

Tropic of Cancer

Revilla Gigedo Is. (Mex.)

Mexico City
Popocatépetl 5452
Acápulco

Veracruz
Campeche
Mérida
Bay of Campeche

BELIZE
Belmopan

Greater

Port-au-Prince
JAMAICA Kingston
HAITI
DOMINICAN REPUBLIC
Santo Domingo

Antilles

20°N

GUATEMALA HONDURAS
Guatemala City Tegucigalpa
San Salvador
NICARAGUA
EL SALVADOR
Managua
COSTA RICA
San José
PANAMA
Panama City

Cartagena
Maracaibo
Caracas

DOMINICA

Caribbean Sea

TRINIDAD & TOBAGO

Hawaiian Islands

Medellín
Bogotá
Cali
Buenaventura
COLOMBIA

VENEZUELA

GUYANA

Orinoco

Guiana Highlands

L I N E
(Kiribati)
I S L A N D S

Galapagos Is. (Ecuador)

Quito
ECUADOR
Cuenca

Equator

Manaus
Amazon

BRAZIL

Marquesas Is. (Fr.)

Tuamotu Arch.

Piura
Chiclayo
Trujillo

Selvas

Río Branco
Pôrto Velho

P O L Y N E S I A

Society Islands (Fr.)

Lima

P
E
R
U

Cook Is. (NZ)

French Polynesia

Gambier Is. (Fr.)

Austral Is. (Fr.)

Pitcairn Is. (UK)

La Paz
Oruro
Arica
BOLIVIA
Sucre
Potosí

Gran

Easter I. (Chile)

Antofagasta

Tropic of Capricorn

Salta
Catamarca

Chaco

C
H
I
L
E

Juan Fernández Is. (Chile)

Córdoba
Aconcagua 6960
Valparaíso
Santiago
Rosario
Buenos Aires

A
R
G
E
N
T
I
N
A

30°S

S O U T H   P A C I F I C

Concepción

Bahía Blanca

0		500		1000		1500 Miles
0	500	1000	1500	2000	2500 Kms

Puerto Montt

O C E A N

Miller Projection

© Oxford Cartographers, 98415
+44 (0)1993 705 394
E & OE

Comodoro Rivadavia

50°S

World Physical

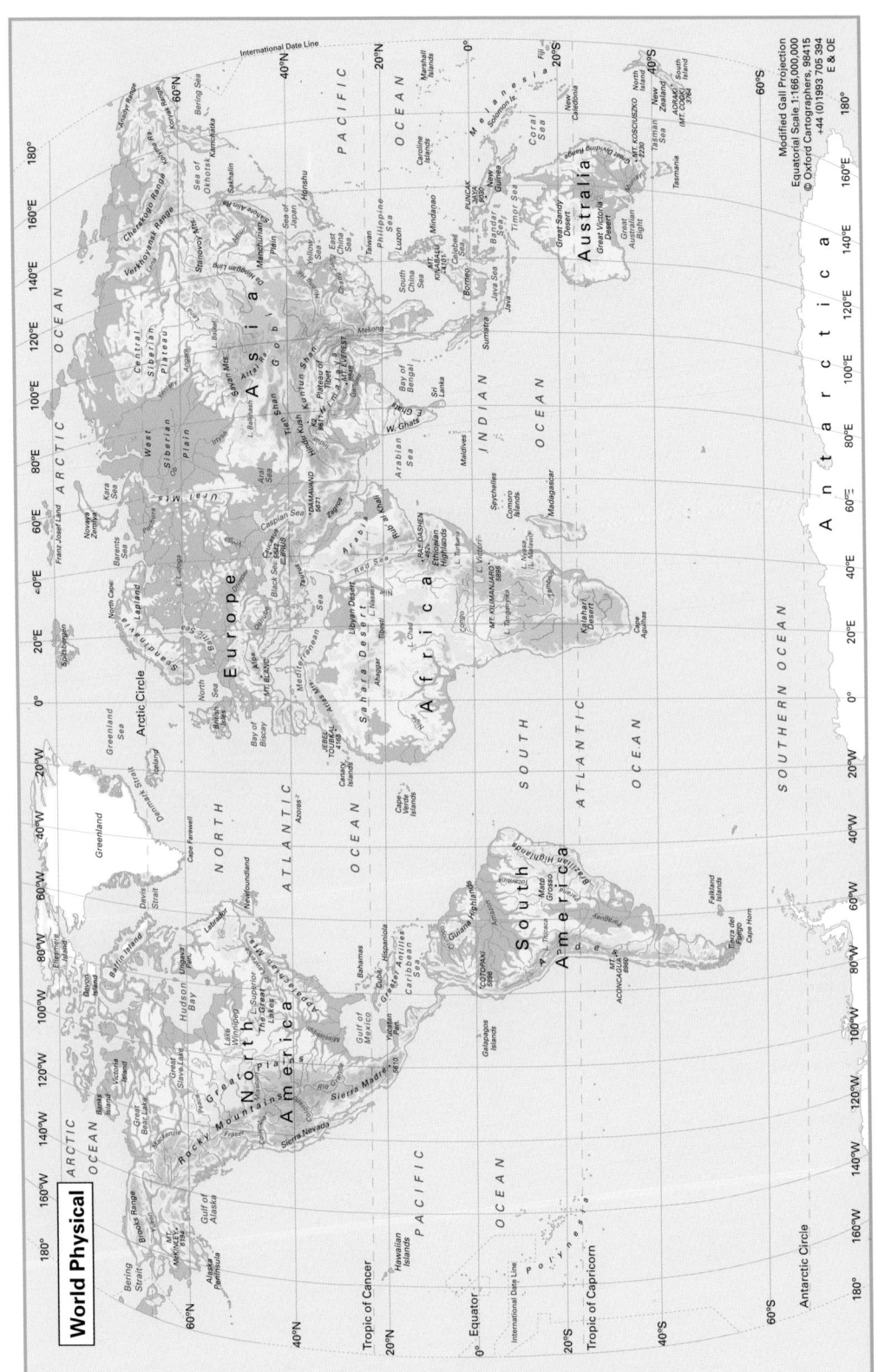

Modified Gall Projection
Equatorial Scale 1:166,000,000
© Oxford Cartographers, 98415
+44 (0)1993 705 394
E & OE

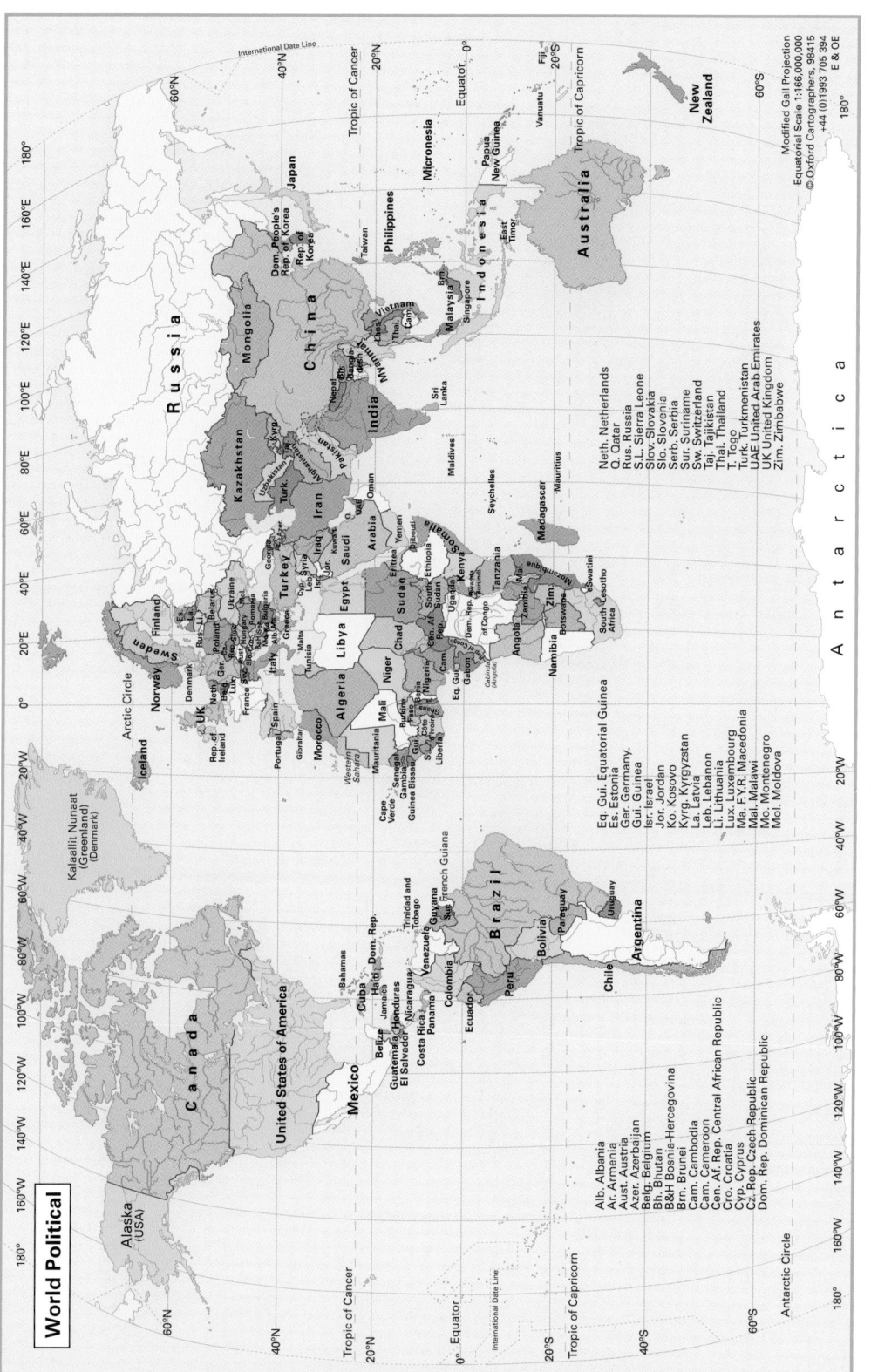

World Political

International Date Line

60°N

Alaska
(USA)

Kalaallit Nunaat
(Greenland)
(Denmark)

Iceland

Canada

United States of America

Mexico

Bahamas
Cuba
Haiti Dom. Rep.
Jamaica
Belize
Guatemala Honduras
El Salvador Nicaragua
Costa Rica Panama
Trinidad and Tobago
Venezuela Guyana
Colombia Sur. French Guiana
Ecuador

Peru

Brazil

Bolivia

Chile
Paraguay

Argentina
Uruguay

Norway
Sweden
Finland
Denmark
UK
Rep. of Ireland
Portugal/Spain
Gibraltar

Morocco
Western Sahara
Mauritania
Mali
Algeria
Niger
Libya
Chad
Cape Verde
Senegal
Gambia
Guinea Bissau
Gui.
S.L. Lbr.
Liberia
Burkina
Cote
Benin
Ghana
Togo
Nigeria
Cam.
Eq. Gui.
Gabon
Cabinda (Angola)

Egypt
Eritrea
Sudan
South Sudan
Ethiopia
Cen. Afr. Rep.
Uganda
Dem. Rep. of Congo
Angola
Rep. of Congo
Zambia
Namibia
Botswana
South Africa
Lesotho
Swatini
Zim.
Moz.
Madagascar
Mauritius
Seychelles
Tanzania
Malawi
Rwanda
Burundi
Kenya
Somalia
Djibouti
Turkey
Cyp. Syria Leb. Isr. Jor.
Georgia Azer. Arm.
Iran
Iraq
Kuwait
Saudi Arabia
Qatar
UAE
Oman
Yemen
Maldives

Russia

Kazakhstan
Turk.
Uzbekistan
Kyrg.
Taj.
Afghanistan
Pakistan
Nepal
Bhutan
India
Bangladesh
Myanmar
Sri Lanka

Mongolia

China

Dem. People's Rep. of Korea
Rep. of Korea
Japan

Laos
Thai.
Camb.
Vietnam
Phil.
Philippines
Taiwan

Indonesia
Malaysia
Singapore
Brunei
East Timor

Micronesia

Papua New Guinea

Vanuatu
Fiji

Australia

New Zealand

Antarctica

Alb. Albania
Ar. Armenia
Aust. Austria
Azer. Azerbaijan
Belg. Belgium
Bh. Bhutan
B&H Bosnia-Hercegovina
Brn. Brunei
Cam. Cambodia
Cam. Cameroon
Cen. Af. Rep. Central African Republic
Cro. Croatia
Cyp. Cyprus
Cz. Rep. Czech Republic
Dom. Rep. Dominican Republic

Eq. Gui. Equatorial Guinea
Es. Estonia
Ger. Germany.
Gui. Guinea
Isr. Israel
Jor. Jordan
Ko. Kosovo
Kyrg. Kyrgyzstan
La. Latvia
Leb. Lebanon
Li. Lithuania
Lux. Luxembourg
Ma. F.Y.R. Macedonia
Mal. Malawi
Mo. Montenegro
Mol. Moldova

Neth. Netherlands
Q. Qatar
Rus. Russia
S.L. Sierra Leone
Slov. Slovakia
Slo. Slovenia
Serb. Serbia
Sur. Suriname
Sw. Switzerland
Taj. Tajikistan
Thai. Thailand
T. Togo
Turk. Turkmenistan
UAE United Arab Emirates
UK United Kingdom
Zim. Zimbabwe

Tropic of Cancer
Tropic of Capricorn
Arctic Circle
Antarctic Circle
Equator 0°
International Date Line

Modified Gall Projection
Equatorial Scale 1:166,000,000
© Oxford Cartographers, 98415
+44 (0)1993 705 394
E & OE

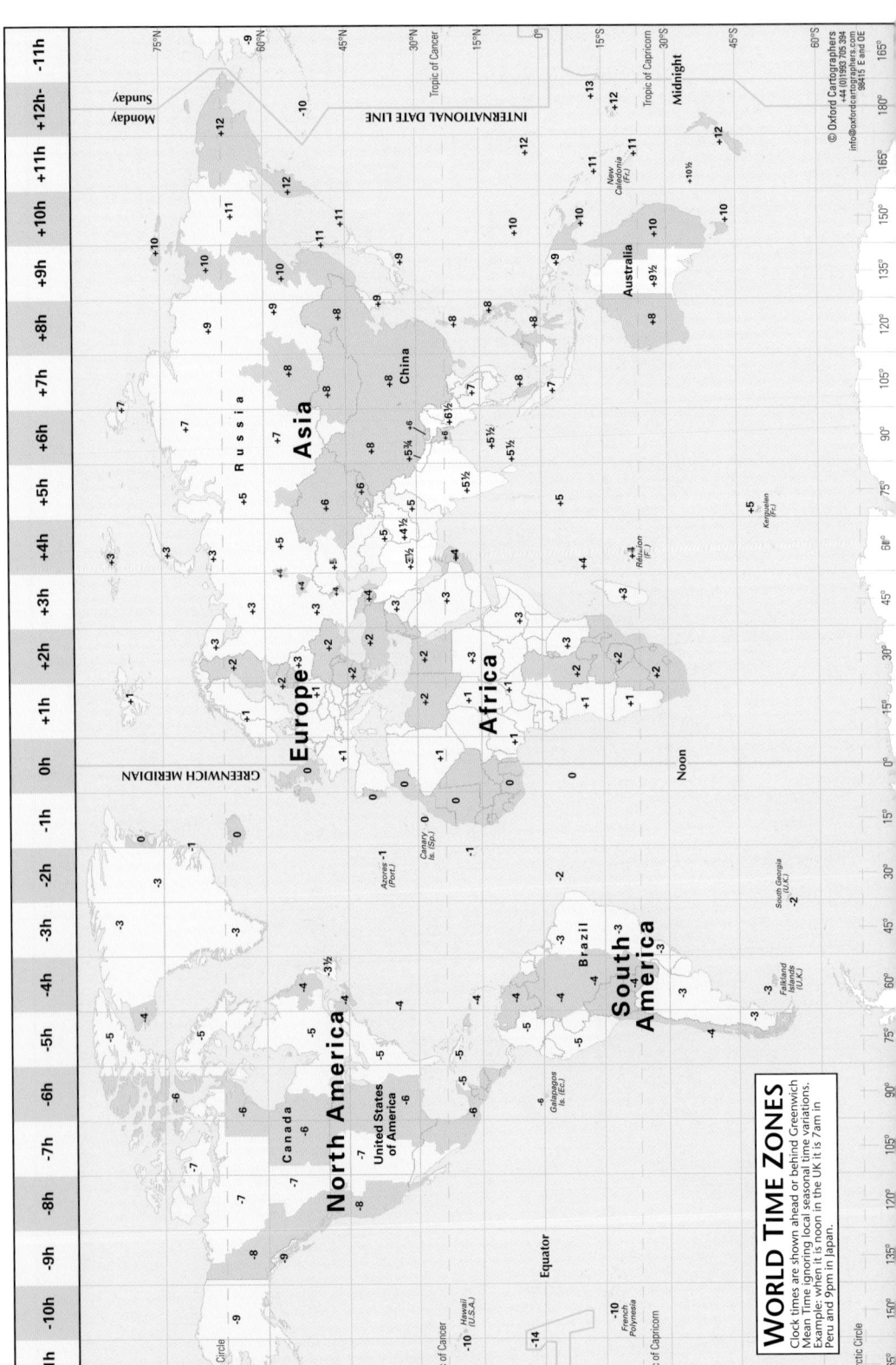

WORLD TIME ZONES

Clock times are shown ahead or behind Greenwich Mean Time ignoring local seasonal time variations. Example: when it is noon in the UK it is 7am in Peru and 9pm in Japan.

© Oxford Cartographers
+44 (0)1993 705 394
info@oxfordcartographers.com
98415 E and OE

FLAGS OF THE WORLD

The following four pages show the national flag of each country, as it is used for international purposes. In some cases this means that the state flag is shown. Where this is the case the country name is marked (†).

AFGHANISTAN

ALBANIA

ALGERIA

ANDORRA

ANGOLA

ANTIGUA AND BARBUDA

ARGENTINA

ARMENIA

AUSTRALIA

AUSTRIA

AZERBAIJAN

THE BAHAMAS

BAHRAIN

BANGLADESH

BARBADOS

BELARUS

BELGIUM

BELIZE

BENIN

BHUTAN

BOLIVIA†

BOSNIA AND HERCEGOVINA

BOTSWANA

BRAZIL

BRUNEI

BULGARIA

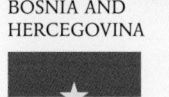
BURKINA FASO

BURUNDI

CAMBODIA

CAMEROON

CANADA

CAPE VERDE

CENTRAL AFRICAN REPUBLIC

CHAD

CHILE

CHINA

COLOMBIA

THE COMOROS

DEM. REPUBLIC OF THE CONGO

REPUBLIC OF THE CONGO

COSTA RICA

CÔTE D'IVOIRE

CROATIA

CUBA

CYPRUS

CZECH REPUBLIC

DENMARK

DJIBOUTI

DOMINICA

DOMINICAN REPUBLIC

 EAST TIMOR

 ECUADOR

 EGYPT

 EL SALVADOR

 EQUATORIAL GUINEA

 ERITREA

 ESTONIA

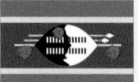 ESWATINI

 ETHIOPIA

 FIJI

 FINLAND

 FRANCE

 GABON

 THE GAMBIA

 GEORGIA

 GERMANY

 GHANA

 GREECE

 GRENADA

 GUATEMALA

 GUINEA

 GUINEA-BISSAU

 GUYANA

 HAITI†

 HONDURAS

 HUNGARY

 ICELAND

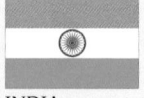 INDIA

 INDONESIA

 IRAN

 IRAQ

 IRELAND

 ISRAEL

 ITALY

 JAMAICA

 JAPAN

 JORDAN

 KAZAKHSTAN

 KENYA

 KIRIBATI

 DEM. PEOPLE'S REPUBLIC OF KOREA

 REPUBLIC OF KOREA

 KOSOVO

 KUWAIT

 KYRGYZSTAN

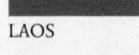 LAOS

 LATVIA

LEBANON

LESOTHO

LIBERIA

LIBYA

LIECHTENSTEIN

LITHUANIA

LUXEMBOURG

MACEDONIA

MADAGASCAR

MALAWI

MALAYSIA

MALDIVES

MALI

MALTA

MARSHALL
ISLANDS

MAURITANIA

MAURITIUS

MEXICO

FEDERATED STATES
OF MICRONESIA

MOLDOVA

MONACO

MONGOLIA

MONTENEGRO

MOROCCO

MOZAMBIQUE

MYANMAR

NAMIBIA

NAURU

NEPAL

THE
NETHERLANDS

NEW ZEALAND

NICARAGUA

NIGER

NIGERIA

NORWAY

OMAN

PAKISTAN

PALAU

PANAMA

PAPUA NEW
GUINEA

PARAGUAY

PERU

THE PHILIPPINES

POLAND

PORTUGAL

QATAR

ROMANIA

RUSSIAN
FEDERATION

RWANDA

ST CHRISTOPHER
AND NEVIS

ST LUCIA

ST VINCENT AND
THE GRENADINES

SAMOA

SAN MARINO†

SAO TOME AND PRINCIPE

SAUDI ARABIA

SENEGAL

SERBIA†

SEYCHELLES

SIERRA LEONE

SINGAPORE

SLOVAKIA

SLOVENIA

SOLOMON ISLANDS

SOMALIA

SOUTH AFRICA

SOUTH SUDAN

SPAIN

SRI LANKA

SUDAN

SURINAME

SWEDEN

SWITZERLAND

SYRIA

TAIWAN

TAJIKISTAN

TANZANIA

THAILAND

TOGO

TONGA

TRINIDAD AND TOBAGO

TUNISIA

TURKEY

TURKMENISTAN

TUVALU

UGANDA

UKRAINE

UNITED ARAB EMIRATES

UNITED KINGDOM

UNITED STATES OF AMERICA

URUGUAY

UZBEKISTAN

VANUATU

VATICAN CITY STATE

VENEZUELA

VIETNAM

YEMEN

ZAMBIA

ZIMBABWE

UK GENERAL ELECTION STATISTICS

STATE OF THE PARTIES AFTER THE 2017 GENERAL ELECTION

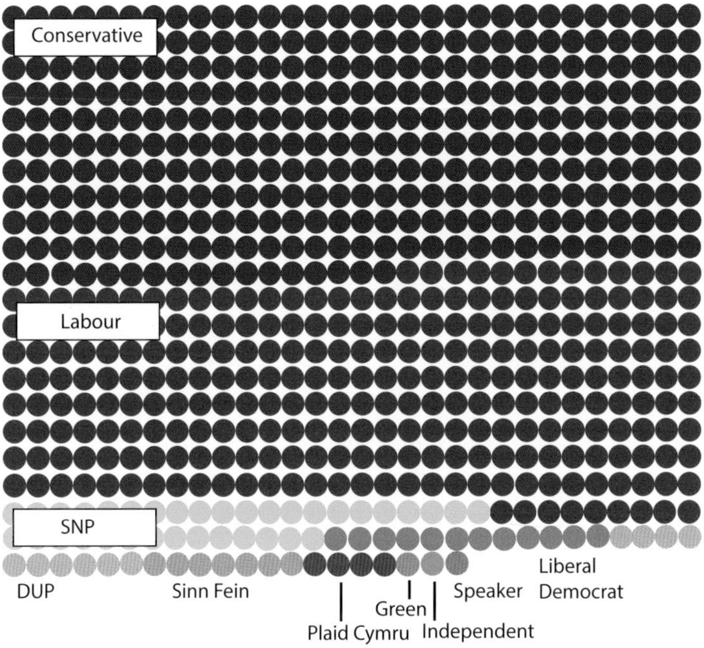

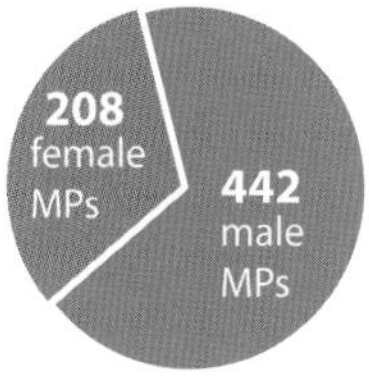

Conservative

Labour

SNP

DUP   Sinn Fein   Speaker   Liberal
                                      Democrat
                    Green
          Plaid Cymru Independent

87
new MPs

208
female
MPs

442
male
MPs

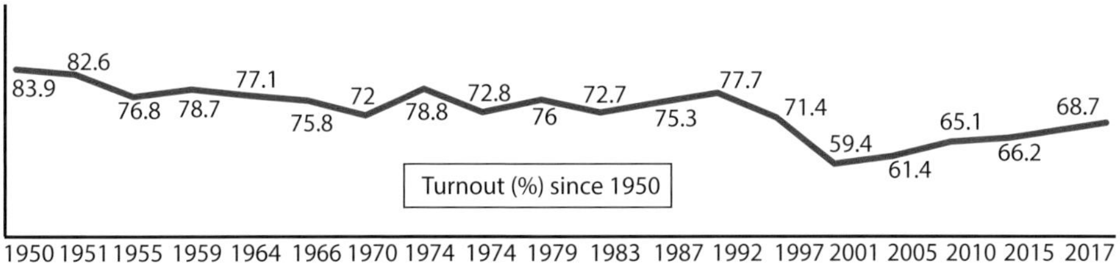

Turnout (%) since 1950

83.9 82.6 77.1 72 78.8 72.8 72.7 77.7 71.4 65.1 68.7
      76.8 78.7 75.8   76   75.3   59.4   66.2
                                                61.4

1950 1951 1955 1959 1964 1966 1970 1974 1974 1979 1983 1987 1992 1997 2001 2005 2010 2015 2017

Seats won by the top three parties
in the last five general elections

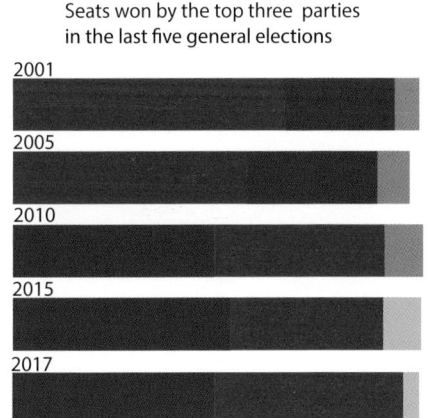

2001

2005

2010

2015

2017

Share of votes, by party (%)

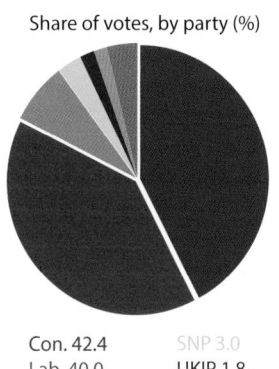

Con. 42.4   SNP 3.0
Lab. 40.0   UKIP 1.8
Lib. Dem. 7.4   Green 1.6
                 Others 3.8

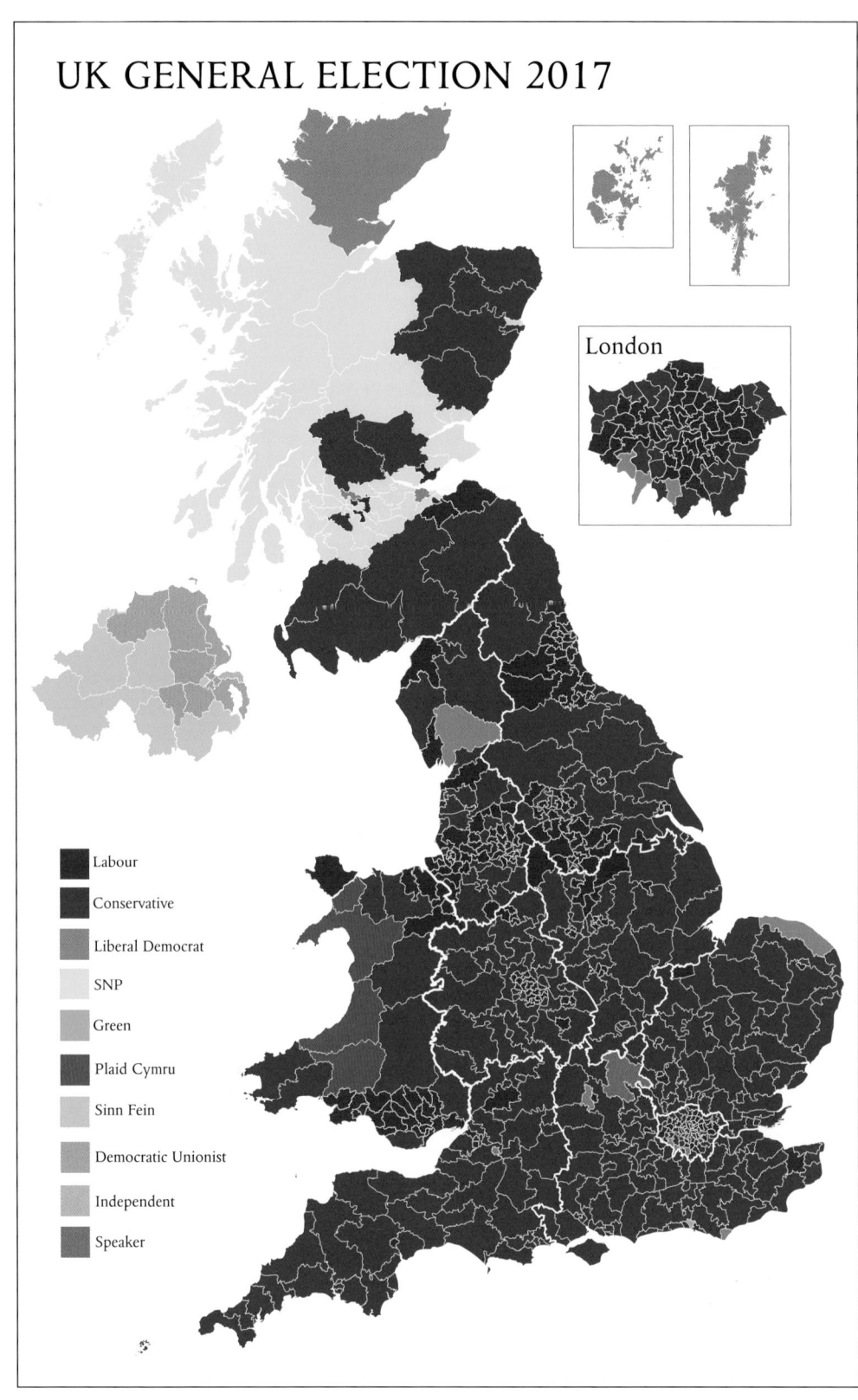

UK GENERAL ELECTION 2017

London

Labour
Conservative
Liberal Democrat
SNP
Green
Plaid Cymru
Sinn Fein
Democratic Unionist
Independent
Speaker

MALAYSIA

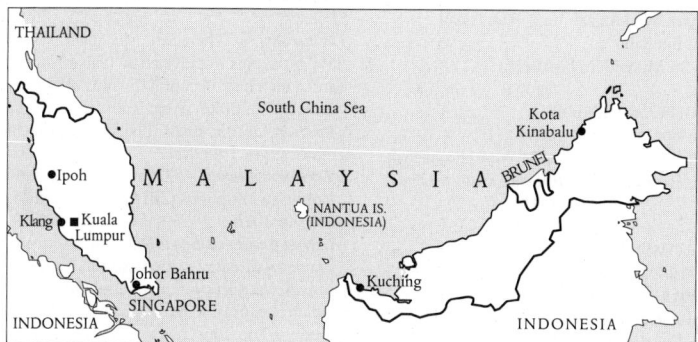

Area – 329,847 sq. km

Capital – Kuala Lumpur; population, 7,564,000 (2018 est); Putrajaya is the administrative capital

Major cities – Ampang Jaya, George Town, Ipoh, Johor Bahru, Klang, Kota Kinabalu, Kuantan, Kuching, Petaling Jaya, Shah Alam

Currency – Malaysian ringgit (RM) of 100 sen; also known as Malaysian dollar

Population – 31,381,992 rising at 1.37 per cent a year (2017 est); Bumiputera (Malay and indigenous peoples) (61.7 per cent), Chinese (20.8 per cent), Indian (6.2 per cent) (2017 est)

Religion – Muslim 61.3 per cent, Buddhist 19.8 per cent, Christian 9.2 per cent, Hindu 6.3 per cent, Chinese traditional religions 1.3 per cent (2010 est)

Language – Bahasa Malaysia (Malay) (official), English, Cantonese, Mandarin, Tamil, Telugu, Malayalam, Punjabi, Thai, Iban, Kadazan

Population density – 96 per sq. km (2016)

Urban population – 76 per cent (2018 est)

Median age (years) – 28.2 (2016 est)

National anthem – 'Negaraku' 'My Country'

National day – 31 August (Independence Day)

Death penalty – Retained

CPI score – 47 (62)

Military expenditure – US$3,495m (2017)

CLIMATE AND TERRAIN

Malaysia comprises the 11 states of peninsular Malaya plus the states of Sabah and Sarawak on the island of Borneo. The Malay peninsula, which extends from the isthmus of Kra to the Singapore Strait, is a plain with two highland areas in the north. The Malaysian part of Borneo is mostly high plateau, rising to mountains in western Sabah and eastern Sarawak, while Sarawak also has lower-lying land along the coast and in the Rajang valley; both states are densely forested. Elevation extremes range from 4,100m (Gunung Kinabalu, Sabah) to 0m (Indian Ocean). The climate is tropical, experiencing the south-west monsoon from May to September and the north-east monsoon from November to March. The average daily temperature is 25.9°C.

POLITICS

The federal *Parlimen* has two houses, the House of Representatives and the senate. The former is the lower house and has 222 members, directly elected for a five-year term. The senate has 70 members who serve a three-year term; the legislative assembly of each state elects two members, and 44 are nominated by the head of state.

The 1957 constitution provides for a federal government and a degree of autonomy for the state governments. Each of the 13 states has its own constitution, which must not be inconsistent with the federal constitution. The Malay rulers are either chosen or succeed to their position in accordance with the custom of their particular state; in other states of Malaysia, choice of the head of state is at the discretion of the *Yang di-Pertuan Agong* after consultation with the chief minister of the state. The ruler or governor acts on the advice of an executive council appointed on the advice of the chief minister and a single-chamber legislative assembly. The legislative assemblies are elected on the same basis as the lower chamber of the federal legislature.

The Barisan Nasional (BN) coalition maintained power for 60 years before being replaced in the 2018 legislative elections by the centre-left People's Alliance, led by 92-year-old former prime minister Mahathir Mohamad. Mohamad replaced former protégé and long-term ally Najib Razak as prime minister, amid embezzlement and money-laundering allegations surrounding Razak.

The supreme head of state (Abdul Halim al-Marhum Badlishah) is elected by the nine hereditary rulers of the peninsular states from among their number and serves a five-year term.

HEAD OF STATE
Supreme Head of State, HM Sultan Muhammad V, *sworn in* 13 December 2016
Deputy Head of State, HM Sultan Nazrin Muizzuddin Shah

c.800–1300	c.1500	1867	1941–5	1946	1948	1957	1963	1965	1971	1981–2003
		Portuguese, Dutch and British vie for control in the region	Occupied by Japan		Nine peninsular states federated as the Federation of Malaya		Forms Federation of Malaysia with Singapore, Sarawak and Sabah			UMNO becomes dominant partner in *Barisan Nasional* (National Front) government
Part of the Srivijaya Empire		Singapore, Penang and Malacca become crown colony		United Malays National Organisation (UMNO) founded to oppose post-war political settlement		Federation becomes independent		Singapore withdraws from federation		Mahathir bin Muhammad becomes prime minister and imposes authoritarian rule

SELECTED GOVERNMENT MEMBERS *AS AT JUNE 2018*
Prime Minister, Mahathir bin Mohamad, *sworn in* 10 May
2018
Deputy Prime Minister, Wan Azizah binti Wan Ismail
Defence, Mohamad bin Sabu
Home Affairs, Tan Sri Muhyiddin bin Yassin

MALAYSIAN HIGH COMMISSION
52 Bedford Row, London WC1R 4LR
T 020-3931 6189 E asst1@btconnect.com W www.jimlondon.net
High Commissioner, HE Dato' Ahmad Rasidi Hazizi, *apptd*
2014

BRITISH HIGH COMMISSION
Level 27 Menara Binjai, 2 Jalan Binjai, Kuala Lumpur 50450
T (+60) (3) 2170 2200 E consular.kualalumpur@fco.gov.uk
W www.gov.uk/government/world/malaysia
High Commissioner, HE Victoria Treadell, CMG, MVO, *apptd*
2014

ECONOMY AND TRADE
The economy has grown vigorously since the 1970s,
transforming the country into a diversified emerging
economy. The government's goal is to achieve developed
nation status by 2020. To this end, it has encouraged
investment in high-technology industries, medical technology
and pharmaceuticals, and growth as a regional financial hub,
especially for Islamic finance. Despite falling oil prices, high
domestic consumption and an increasing range of exports
have continued to fuel growth, which was over 5 per cent in
2017. Malaysia formed a common market with the other
members of the Association of Southeast Asian Nations
(ASEAN) in 2015.
  The agricultural sector produces the raw materials for its
highly developed industries. Industrial production includes
rubber   manufacturing,   palm   oil   processing,   light
manufacturing, electronics, natural gas, and timber processing;
in addition, oil is produced in Sabah and Sarawak, and refined
in Sarawak. Tourism is a major industry. The services sector
contributes 54.7 per cent of GDP, industry 36.9 per cent and
agriculture 8.4 per cent.
  The main trading partners are China, Singapore, Japan, the
USA and other South East Asian countries. Principal exports
are electronic equipment, petroleum and liquefied natural gas,
timber and wood products, palm oil, rubber, textiles and
chemicals. The main imports are electronics, machinery,
petroleum products, plastics, vehicles, iron and steel products,
and chemicals.
GNI – US$305bn; US$9,650 per capita (2017)
Annual average growth of GDP – 5.4 per cent (2017)
Inflation rate – 3.8 per cent (2017 est)
Unemployment – 3.4 per cent (2017 est)
Total external debt – US$213bn (2017 est)
Imports – US$168,392m (2016)
Exports – US$189,414m (2016)

BALANCE OF PAYMENTS
Trade – US$21,022m surplus (2016)
Current Account – US$9,450m surplus (2017)

Trade with UK	2016	2017
Imports from UK	£1,299,777,351	£1,414,503,998
Exports to UK	£1,797,967,160	£1,854,788,305

COMMUNICATIONS
Airports – There are 39 airports; the main international
airports are at Kuala Lumpur, Kota Kinabalu, Kuching and
Penang
Waterways – There are six main seaports in peninsular
Malaysia, plus Kota Kinabalu (Sabah) and Kuching (Sarawak),
and a merchant fleet of 315 ships of more than 1,000 tonnes;
there are 7,200km of navigable waterways
Roadways and railways – 116,1691km (including 1,821km of
motorways); 1,849km
Telecommunications – 4.8 million fixed lines and 43.9 million
mobile subscriptions (2016); there were 24.8 million internet
users in 2016
Internet country code and IDD – my; 60 (from UK), 44 (to UK)
Major broadcasters – The state-run Radio Television Malaysia
provides services in competition with commercial operators,
which broadcast in Malay, Tamil, Chinese and English
Press – The four main national daily newspapers are in
English: *The Star, The Sun, New Straits Times* and *The Malay
Mail*
WPFI score – 47,41 (145)

EDUCATION AND HEALTH
There are six years of compulsory education.
Literacy rate – 98.4 per cent (2015 est)
Gross enrolment ratio (percentage of relevant age group) – primary
  103 per cent, secondary 85 per cent, tertiary 44 per cent
  (2016 est)
Health expenditure (per capita) – US$456 (2014)
Hospital beds (per 1,000 people) – 1.9 (2015)
Life expectancy (years) – 75.2 (2017 est)
Mortality rate – 5.1 (2017 est)
Birth rate – 19.1 (2017 est)
Infant mortality rate – 12.5 (2017 est)
HIV/AIDS adult prevalence – 0.4 per cent (2016 est)

MALDIVES

Dhivehi Raajjeyge Jumhooriyyaa – Republic of Maldives

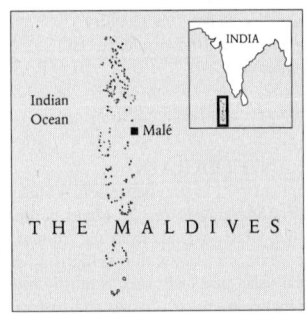

Area – 298 sq. km
Capital – Malé; population, 177,000 (2018)
Currency – Rufiyaa of 100 laarees
Population – 392,709 falling at 0.06 per cent a year (2017
  est)
Religion – Sunni Muslim; public practice of other religions is
  illegal
Language – Dhivehi (official), English
Population density – 1,454 per sq. km (2016)
Urban population – 39.8 per cent (2018 est)
Median age (years) – 27.8 (2016 est)
National anthem – 'Gaumii Salaam' 'National Salute'
National day – 26 July (Independence Day)
Death penalty – Retained (no known use since 1952)

CPI score – 33 (112)
Literacy rate – 99.8 per cent (2015 est)
Gross enrolment ratio (percentage of relevant age group) – primary
   102 per cent (2016 est), tertiary 16.2 per cent (2014 est)
Health expenditure (per capita) – US$1,165 (2014)
Life expectancy (years) – 75.8 (2017 est)
Mortality rate – 4 (2017 est)
Birth rate – 16.1 (2017 est)
Infant mortality rate – 22 (2017 est)

CLIMATE AND TERRAIN
The republic is an archipelago of atolls in the Indian Ocean, 643km to the south-west of Sri Lanka. There are about 1,190 coral islands grouped into 26 clusters of atolls, about 200 of which are inhabited. The islands are all flat and low-lying; none is more than 2.4m above sea level, making them vulnerable to rising sea levels caused by climate change. The climate is tropical, affected by the dry north-east monsoon (January–March) and the wet south-west monsoon (May–November).

HISTORY AND POLITICS
The Maldives were an independent sultanate from the mid-12th century. The sultan was overthrown by the Portuguese in 1558 but they were driven out in 1573 and the sultanate was re-established. In 1645, the islands became a dependency of Ceylon, which was under Dutch and then British rule. In 1887 they became an internally self-governing British protectorate. Independence was achieved in 1965, and in 1968 the Maldives became a republic under President Ibrahim Nasir.

The autocratic Nasir retired in 1978 and was succeeded by Maumoon Abdul Gayoom. His 30-year tenure, although equally autocratic, maintained political stability and economic development. However, unprecedented violence during anti-government demonstrations in 2003 and 2004 led to the legalising of political parties in 2005.

In the first multi-party legislative elections in 2009, the People's Party, led by Gayoom, won control of the legislature through alliances with smaller parties. In the presidential elections of November 2013 Abdulla Gayoom of the Progressive Party of Maldives (PPM) and half brother of former dictator Maumoon Abdul Gayoom, defeated Mohamed Nasheed, the country's first democratically elected president from 2008 to 2012. The March 2014 legislative elections were won by the PPM. In March 2015, Mohamed Nasheed was jailed for 13 years for illegally ordering the arrest of a senior judge during his time as president. A state of emergency was declared in February 2018 after the government refused to release political opponents, and subsequently many opposition MPs were arrested on corruption charges. Elections took place in September 2018.

Under the 2008 constitution, the executive president is directly elected for a five-year term, renewable once. The unicameral People's Assembly *(Majlis)* has 77 members, who are directly elected for a five-year term.

HEAD OF STATE
President, Abdulla Yameen Abdul Gayoom, *sworn in*
   17 November 2013
Vice-President, Abdulla Jihad

SELECTED GOVERNMENT MEMBERS *AS AT*
SEPTEMBER 2018
Defence, Adam Shareef
Finance, Ahmed Munawwar
Foreign Affairs, Mohamed Asim

EMBASSY OF THE REPUBLIC OF MALDIVES
22 Nottingham Place, London W1U 5NJ
T 020-7224 2135 E info@maldivesembassy.uk
W www.maldivesembassy.uk
Ambassador, HE Ahmed Shiaan, *apptd* 2015

BRITISH AMBASSADOR
HE James Dauris, *apptd* 2014, resident at Colombo,
   Sri Lanka

ECONOMY AND TRADE
Political stability and economic liberalisation have produced steady economic growth since the 1980s, except in 2005 owing to the devastation caused by the 2004 tsunami, and 2009, when tourist numbers and exports fell owing to the global economic downturn. Balance of payments difficulties forced the government to seek IMF standby funding in 2009; after the first two disbursements the IMF halted further funds due to the Maldives' growing budget deficit. While the economy is heavily dependent on tourism and benefits from increasing numbers of Chinese visitors, the government has created a number of special economic zones to increase foreign investment. Agriculture and manufacturing are constrained by a shortage of cultivable land and domestic labour, so most food is imported. Industry is concentrated on fish processing, boat-building and shipping. Political violence in 2018 significantly curtailed tourism, which will likely exacerbate the nation's widening fiscal deficit.

The main export markets are Thailand, Sri Lanka and Bangladesh. The only significant export is fish. Imports include petroleum products, clothing and capital goods, and are provided mainly by the UAE, India, Singapore, and China.
GNI – US$4.2bn; US$9,570 per capita (2017)
Annual average growth of GDP – 4.6 per cent (2017)
Inflation rate – 2.5 per cent (2017 est)
Population below poverty line – 16 per cent (2009 est)
Unemployment – 11.6 per cent (2017 est)
Total external debt – US$693.7m (2017 est)
Imports – US$1,896m (2015)
Exports – US$144m (2015)

BALANCE OF PAYMENTS
Trade – US$1,752m deficit (2015)
Current Account – US$876m deficit (2017)

Trade with UK	2016	2017
Imports from UK	£13,940,826	£14,020,953
Exports to UK	£6,409,215	£10,216,205

COMMUNICATIONS
Transport – The country has seven airports, two of which handle international traffic; the main port is Malé and there are 88km of roads
Telecommunications – 21,136 fixed lines and 812,128 mobile subscriptions (2016); there were 232,210 internet users in 2016
Internet code and IDD – mv; 960 (from UK), to UK (44)
Major broadcasters – The state broadcaster Maldives National Broadcasting Corporation operates radio and TV stations; a small number of private broadcasters are permitted to operate
Press – Daily newspapers include *Miadhu News* and *Haveeru Daily*
WPFI score – 37,95 (120)

MALI

République de Mali – Republic of Mali

Area – 1,240,192 sq. km
Capital – Bamako; population, 2,447,000 (2018 est)
Major cities – Kayes, Koutiala, Mopti, Ségou, Sikasso, Timbuktu
Currency – Franc CFA of 100 centimes
Population – 17,885,245 rising at 3.02 per cent a year (2017 est); Bambara (34.1 per cent), Fulani (14.7 per cent), Sarakole (10.8 per cent), Senufo (10.5 per cent), Dogon (8.9 per cent), Malinke (8.7 per cent) (2012–13 est); about 10 per cent are nomadic
Religion – Muslim 94.8 per cent, Christian 2.4 per cent, animist 2 per cent (2009 est)
Language – French (official), Bambara, other African languages
Population density – 15 per sq. km (2016)
Urban population – 42.4 per cent (2018 est)
Median age (years) – 16.2 (2016 est)
National anthem – 'Le Mali' 'Mali'
National day – 22 September (Independence Day)
Death penalty – Retained (last used 1980)
CPI score – 31 (122)
Military expenditure – US$461m (2017)
Conscription – 18 years; 24 months (selective)

CLIMATE AND TERRAIN
The west African state is mainly savannah in the south and desert plains in the north, with some hills in the north-east; over 60 per cent is desert or semi-desert. The centre is drained by the Niger river and the south-west by the Senegal river. Elevation extremes range from 1,155m (Hombori Tondo) to 23m (Senegal river). The climate is subtropical in the south with a rainy season from June to November, and arid in the north. Average temperatures range from 21.4°C in January to 33.9°C in June.

HISTORY AND POLITICS
Mali was successively part of the empire of the Malinke people from the 13th to 15th centuries, and of the Songhai Empire in the 15th to 16th centuries. With the fall of the Songhai Empire, it was divided between the Tuareg and the Fulani and Bambara kingdoms, and then the Tukolor and Samori kingdoms. It was conquered by the French in 1880–95 and became a French colony. In 1959, it formed the Federation of Mali with Senegal before becoming a separate independent state in 1960 under a one-party socialist regime.

In 1968, a military coup led by Lt. Moussa Traoré resulted in 23 years of oppressive military rule. Traoré was ousted as president in 1991 in a military coup led by Gen. Amadou Toumani Touré. Multiparty elections were held in 1992, returning the country to civilian government.

A degree of decentralisation was introduced in 1999, partly in response to rebellions in the north by the Tuareg over land

and cultural rights. Another rebellion in 2006 by Tuareg seeking greater autonomy for their region was settled within a few months, but a more militant faction carried on an insurrection from 2007 to 2009. In May 2014 Tuareg separatists occupied the northern towns Menaka, Agelhok, Anefis and Tessalit.

Amadou Toumani Touré, standing as an independent candidate, won the 2002 presidential elections, and was re-elected in 2007. In the 2007 legislative elections, the Alliance for Democracy in Mali (ADEMA), which had dominated government coalitions since 1992, won the largest number of seats and formed another coalition government. A military coup overthrew Touré's government in March 2012, claiming that the government had not supported the country's army against the advancing Tuareg-led rebellion. Cissé Mariam Kaidama Sidibé, the country's first female prime minister, was arrested shortly after the coup. In the subsequent 2013 presidential elections, former prime minister Ibrahim Boubacar Keita comfortably defeated rival candidate Soumaila Cissé. Keita was comfortably re-elected in August 2018. Following the resignations of prime ministers Oumar Tatam Ly in April 2014, Moussa Mara in January 2015 and Modibo Keita in March 2017, Abdoulaye Idrissa Maïga was appointed to the post in March 2017.

Under the 1992 constitution, the president is directly elected for a five-year term, which is renewable once. The unicameral National Assembly has 147 members directly elected for a maximum of two terms, with 13 reserved to represent Malians abroad; all serve a five-year term. The president appoints the prime minister, who appoints the cabinet.

HEAD OF STATE
President, Ibrahim Boubacar Keita, *apptd* 4 September 2013, *re-elected* 16 August 2018

SELECTED GOVERNMENT MEMBERS *AS AT AUGUST 2018*
Prime Minister, Abdoulaye Idrissa Maïga
Economy and Finance, Boubou Cissé
Foreign Affairs, Tiéman Hubert Coulibaly

EMBASSY OF THE REPUBLIC OF MALI
Avenue Molière 487, 1050 Brussels, Belgium
T (+32) (2) 345 7432 E info@amba-mali.be W www.amba-mali.be
Ambassador Extraordinary and Plenipotentiary, HE Sékou Gaoussou Cissé, *apptd* 2016

BRITISH AMBASSADOR
Immeuble Semega, Route de Koulikoro, Hippodrome, BP 2069, Bamako
T (+223) 2021 3412 W www.gov.uk/government/world/mali
Ambassador Extraordinary and Plenipotentiary, HE Cat Evans, *apptd* 2018

ECONOMY AND TRADE
Economic reform since the mid-1990s has produced steady growth, but Mali is heavily dependent on foreign aid and remittances from expatriates. The administration's purchase of a presidential jet for US$40m (£26.9m) and misappropriation of defence budget funds led the IMF to temporarily suspend aid in 2014. Good harvests and the performance of the service sector allowed the economy to grow above 5 per cent in 2014–17, and that is expected to be sustained with public investment in 2017 although security concerns, political instability and corruption constraints development.

The economy is based primarily on subsistence farming and animal husbandry, which contribute 40.9 per cent of GDP, 80 per cent of the population and 80 per cent of export earnings. Gold, phosphate and iron-ore mining, and cotton and food processing are the main activities in Mali's industrial sector, which accounts for 18.9 per cent of GDP. Export of hydroelectric power is expected to contribute to future earnings.

The main export markets are Switzerland, the UAE and Burkina Faso; imports come mainly from Senegal, China and Côte d'Ivoire. Principal exports are cotton, gold and livestock. The main imports are fuel, machinery and equipment, construction materials, foodstuffs and textiles.

GNI – US$14.3bn; US$770 per capita (2017)
Annual average growth of GDP – 5.3 per cent (2017 est)
Inflation rate – 0.2 per cent (2017 est)
Population below poverty line – 36.1 per cent (2005 est)
Unemployment – 8.1 per cent (2016 est)
Total external debt – US$4.296bn (2017 est)
Imports – US$3,167m (2015)
Exports – US$2,532m (2015)

BALANCE OF PAYMENTS
Trade – US$635m deficit (2015)
Current Account – US$375m deficit (2013)

Trade with UK	2016	2017
Imports from UK	£20,669,241	£40,222,561
Exports to UK	£1,197,679	£1,164,873

COMMUNICATIONS
Airports and waterways – There are eight airports, with the largest at Bamako; the main port is Koulikoro on the Niger river
Roadways and railways – 5,522km; 593km
Telecommunications – 200,812 fixed lines and 20.2 million mobile subscriptions (2016); there were 1.9 million internet users in 2016
Internet code and IDD – ml; 223 (from UK), 44 (to UK)
Major broadcasters – The public Office de la Radiodiffusion Télévision du Mali operates a number of radio and television channels in French and local vernacular languages
Press – There are five main daily newspapers, including *L'Essor*, the state-owned national daily
WPFI score – 36,15 (115)

EDUCATION AND HEALTH
There are nine years of free, compulsory education beginning at age seven.
Literacy rate – 54.1 per cent (2015 est)
Gross enrolment ratio (percentage of relevant age group) – primary 77 per cent, secondary 43 per cent (2016 est), tertiary 7 per cent (2012 est)
Health expenditure (per capita) – US$48 (2014)
Hospital beds (per 1,000 people) – 0.1 (2010)
Life expectancy (years) – 60.3 (2016 est)
Mortality rate – 9.8 (2017 est)
Birth rate – 43.9 (2017 est)
Infant mortality rate – 69.5 (2017 est)
HIV/AIDS adult prevalence – 1 per cent (2016 est)

MALTA

Repubblika ta' Malta – Republic of Malta

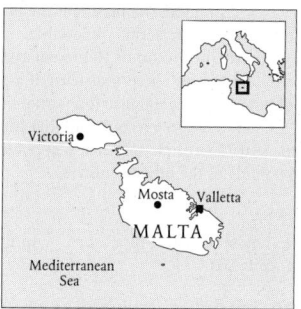

Area – 316 sq. km
Capital – Valletta; population, 213,000 (2018)
Major towns – Birkirkara, Mosta, Qormi, Saint Paul's Bay (San Pawl il-Bahar), Victoria
Currency – Euro (€) of 100 cents
Population – 416,338 rising at 0.26 per cent a year (2017 est)
Religion – Christian (Roman Catholic 90 per cent) (2011 est)
Language – Maltese, English (both official)
Population density – 1,454 per sq. km (2016)
Urban population – 94.6 per cent (2018 est)
Median age (years) – 41.5 (2016 est)
National anthem – 'L-Innu Malti' 'Hymn of Malta'
National day – 21 September (Independence Day)
Death penalty – Abolished for all crimes (since 2000)
CPI score – 56 (46)
Military expenditure – US$63.5m (2017)

CLIMATE AND TERRAIN
Malta is an archipelago of six islands in the Mediterranean Sea; Malta, Gozo and Comino are the largest. The island of Malta has a coastal plain in the north-east, rising to low hills in the south-west. Elevation extremes range from 253m (Ta'Dmejrek) to 0m (Mediterranean Sea). Average temperatures range from 12.7°C in February to 27.2°C in August.

HISTORY AND POLITICS
The islands were ruled successively by the Phoenicians, Greeks, Carthaginians, Romans, Arabs, Spanish and the Sovereign Military Order of Malta (known as the Knights of St John), which held them from 1530 until a French invasion in 1798. Liberated from French rule with British naval support in 1800, the island of Malta became a British colony in 1814, and was developed into a substantial naval base and dockyard. Malta was strategically important in both world wars, but particularly the second, when it was blockaded and subjected to aerial bombardment for five months. Its resistance led to the people of Malta being awarded the George Cross, the UK's highest award for civilian bravery, in 1942.

Malta gained its independence in 1964 and became a republic in 1974. In the 1970s it developed close links with communist and Arab states, but more pro-European and pro-US policies were adopted after the election of the Nationalist Party in 1987. Malta became a member of the EU in 2004, and adopted the euro in 2008. Since joining the EU, Malta has experienced a marked increase in illegal immigration from northern Africa. The murder of investigative journalist Daphne Caruana Galizia in October 2017 attracted international attention over alleged corruption in the country.

The Labour Party was returned to power in legislative elections in 2013 and 2017. Party leader Marie-Louise Coleiro Preca was confirmed as president in April 2014.

Under the 1974 constitution, the president is elected by the legislature for a five-year term, renewable once. The unicameral legislature, the House of Representatives, has 69 members directly elected for a five-year term; if a party wins the majority of votes in a general election without winning a majority of seats, new seats are created until that party holds a majority of one seat. The prime minister is appointed by the president and nominates the other ministers.

HEAD OF STATE
President, Marie-Louise Coleiro Preca, *elected* 1 April 2014, *took office* 4 April 2014

SELECTED GOVERNMENT MEMBERS *AS AT JUNE 2018*
Prime Minister, Joseph Muscat
Economy, Christian Cardona
Finance, Edward Scicluna
Foreign Affairs, Carmelo Abela

MALTA HIGH COMMISSION
Malta House, 36–38 Piccadilly, London W1J 0LE
T 020-7292 4800 E maltahighcommission.london@gov.mt
W www.foreign.gov.mt/uk
High Commissioner, HE Norman Hamilton, *apptd* 2013

BRITISH HIGH COMMISSION
Whitehall Mansions, Ta' Xbiex Seafront, Ta' Xbiex XBX 1026
T (+356) 2323 0000 E bhcvalletta@fco.gov.uk
W www.gov.uk/government/world/malta
High Commissioner, HE Stuart Gill, OBE, *apptd* 2016

ECONOMY AND TRADE

The mainstay of the economy for over a century was the dockyard, and shipbuilding and ship repairs remain significant industries, but since the 1980s Malta has developed into a tourist destination, financial services centre and freight trans-shipment point. Tourism is now the main source of income, followed by foreign trade and manufacturing, especially of electronics and pharmaceuticals. All were adversely affected by the global downturn in 2009, and new fiscal measures contributed further to a deterioration in public finances in 2011. The economy has since performed strongly, recording high levels of growth and employment. An excessive deficit procedure against Malta was opened by the EU in 2013, and the deficit decreased by 0.5 per cent in 2017. The service sector accounts for 88.1 per cent of GDP, industry for 10.6 per cent and agriculture for 1.3 per cent.

The main trading partners are other EU states. Principal exports are electrical machinery, mechanical appliances, mineral fuels, oil and petroleum products, and pharmaceuticals. The main imports are mineral fuels and oil, machinery, aircraft and other transport equipment, and food.
GNI – US$11.1bn; US$23,810 per capita (2017)
Annual average growth of GDP – 5.1 per cent (2017 est)
Inflation rate – 1.3 per cent (2017 est)
Population below poverty line – 16.3 per cent (2015 est)
Unemployment – 4.4 per cent (2017 est)
Total external debt – US$90.98bn (2017 est)
Imports – US$7,029m (2016)
Exports – US$3,915m (2016)

BALANCE OF PAYMENTS
Trade – US$3,114m deficit (2016)
Current Account – US$1,720m surplus (2017)

Trade with UK	2016	2017
Imports from UK	£392,159,535	£511,169,014
Exports to UK	£197,865,443	£138,296,825

COMMUNICATIONS

Airports and waterways – The international airport is at Luqa, south-west of Valletta; the main ports are Marsaxlokk (Malta's freeport) and Valletta, and there is a large merchant fleet of 1,650 ships of over 1,000 tonnes
Roadways – 2,704km
Telecommunications – 234,368 fixed lines and 532,136 mobile subscriptions (2016); there were 320,902 internet users in 2016
Internet code and IDD – mt; 356 (from UK), 44 (to UK)
Major broadcasters – Television Malta (TVM) and Radio Malta are the public broadcasters
Press – Daily national newspapers include *Times of Malta, Malta Independent* (both English language) and *L-Orizzont* (Maltese)
WPFI score – 27,44 (65)

EDUCATION AND HEALTH

Education is free at all levels and compulsory between the ages of five and 16.
Literacy rate – 99.0 per cent (2015 est)
Gross enrolment ratio (percentage of relevant age group) – primary 105 per cent, secondary 96 per cent (2016 est), tertiary 47 per cent (2015 est)
Health expenditure (per capita) – US$2,471 (2014)
Life expectancy (years) – 80.4 (2017 est)
Mortality rate – 9.4 (2017 est)
Birth rate – 10.1 (2017 est)
Infant mortality rate – 3.5 (2017 est)

MARSHALL ISLANDS

Republic of the Marshall Islands
Area – 181 sq. km (plus 11,673 sq. km of lagoon waters)
Capital – Majuro; population, 31,000 (2018)
Major towns – Ebeye, Rita
Currency – US dollar (US$) of 100 cents
Population – 74,539 rising at 1.55 per cent a year (2017 est); Marshallese (92.1 per cent), mixed Marshallese (5.9 per cent) (2006 est)
Religion – Christian (Protestant 54.8 per cent, Assembly of God 25.8 per cent, Roman Catholic 8.4 per cent) (1999 est)
Language – Marshallese, English (both official)
Population density – 295 per sq. km (2016)
Urban population – 77 per cent (2018 est)
Median age (years) – 22.7 (2016 est)
National anthem – 'Forever Marshall Islands'
National day – 1 May (Constitution Day)
Death penalty – Abolished for all crimes (since 1986)
Gross enrolment ratio (percentage of relevant age group) – primary 89 per cent, secondary 73 per cent (2016 est), tertiary 43 per cent (2012 est)
Health expenditure (per capita) – US$625 (2014)
Life expectancy (years) – 73.4 (2017 est)
Mortality rate – 4.2 (2017 est)
Birth rate – 24.4 (2017 est)
Infant mortality rate – 19.3 (2017 est)

CLIMATE AND TERRAIN

The republic consists of two chains of 29 atolls, five islands and over 1,000 islets in the western Pacific Ocean. All of the islands are low-lying (the highest point is 10m) and vulnerable to rising sea levels, which could submerge them by the mid-21st century. The climate is tropical, with a wet season from June to November.

HISTORY AND POLITICS

The Marshall Islands were first claimed by Spain in 1592 but were left largely undisturbed. Subsequently they were seized by Germany and formally became a protectorate in 1886. Japan took control of the islands in 1914 on behalf of the Allied powers and administered them from 1920 until 1944, when they were captured by US forces. In 1947 the islands became part of the UN Trust Territory of the Pacific Islands, administered by the USA. Between 1946 and 1958, US nuclear weapons were tested on Bikini and Enewetak atolls. Enewetak has been partially decontaminated but Bikini is uninhabitable; the USA paid compensation to the test victims in the 1980s but the government is seeking further compensation to cover the medical care of radiation victims and rectify environmental damage.

The islands became internally self-governing in 1979, and US administration ended in 1986, when a compact of free association between the Republic of the Marshall Islands and the USA came into effect. Under this agreement, the USA recognised the republic as a sovereign and independent state but retained responsibility for external security and defence as well as giving financial help. UN trust territory status was terminated in 1990 and full independence was granted in December 1990. A renegotiated compact with the USA was signed in 2003. The USA retains control of the Kwajalein atoll, where it has a military base and missile tracking station.

Candidates in the legislative elections, last held in November 2015, are not listed by party but by name alone. Dr Hilda Heine was elected president in the 2016 presidential election and became the country's first woman president, winning 24 of the 30 votes cast.

Under the 1979 constitution, the executive president is elected by the legislature from among its members to serve a four-year term, with no term limits. The bicameral legislature if formed of the directly elected 33-member *Nitijela,* which serves four-year terms, and the 12-member Council of Iroij made up of tribal chiefs as an advisory body. There are no formal political parties, although groupings of like-minded independents have emerged in recent years.

HEAD OF STATE
President, Dr Hilda C. Heine, *elected* 27 January 2016, *sworn in* 28 January 2016

SELECTED GOVERNMENT MEMBERS *AS AT JUNE 2018*
Finance, Brenson S. Wase
Foreign Affairs, John M. Silk
Internal and Outer Island Affairs, Amenta Matthew

BRITISH AMBASSADOR
Ambassador, HE Melanie Hopkins, *apptd* 2016, resident at Suva, Fiji

ECONOMY AND TRADE

The islands have few natural resources, apart from possible seabed mineral deposits, and the economy is dependent on aid from the USA, supplemented by ship registration fees and the sale of fishing licences. Most islanders live by subsistence farming and fishing, with coconuts, tomatoes and fish the main commercial crops. A small-scale industrial sector produces copra and handicrafts and processes tuna. Tourism is being encouraged but has declined recently which, with a similar decline in fishing licence sales, has limited economic growth. The government is the largest employer. The main trading partners are Japan, the USA, New Zealand, Australia, China and Taiwan. Principal exports are copra and coconut products, handicrafts and fish. Main imports include food and fuel.

GNI – US$0.3bn; US$4,800 per capita (2017)
Annual average growth of GDP – 1.9 per cent (2017 est)
Inflation rate – 0.7 per cent (2017 est)
Total external debt – US$97.96m (2013 est)
Imports – US$82,829m (2014)
Exports – US$23,373m (2014)

BALANCE OF PAYMENTS
Current Account – US$16.2m deficit (2016)

Trade with UK	2016	2017
Imports from UK	£432,768	£898,523
Exports to UK	£696,489	£411,078

COMMUNICATIONS

Airports and waterways – There are four airports throughout the islands; Majuro is the main airport as well as the main port, with a merchant fleet of 1,593 ships of over 1,000 tonnes, 1,468 of which are foreign-owned
Roadways – There are 2,028km of surfaced roads
Telecommunications – 2,361 fixed lines and 16,000 mobile subscriptions (2016); there were 21,857 internet users in 2016
Internet code and IDD – mh; 692 (from UK), 011 44 (to UK)
Media – MBC TV is the state-run broadcaster; the English and Marshallese-language *Marshall Islands Journal* is published on a weekly basis

MAURITANIA

Al-Jumhuriyah al-Islamiyah al-Muritaniyah – Islamic Republic of Mauritania

Area – 1,030,700 sq. km
Capital – Nouakchott; population, 1,205,000 (2018 est)
Major towns – Kaedi, Kiffa, Nouadhibou, Rosso, Zuwarat
Currency – Ouguiya (UM) of 5 khoums
Population – 3,758,571 rising at 2.17 per cent a year (2017 est)
Religion – Muslim 100 per cent (official, almost entirely Sunni) (est)
Language – Arabic (official), Pulaar, Soninke, Wolof, French
Population density – 4 per sq. km (2016)
Urban population – 53.7 per cent (2017 est)
Median age (years) – 20.3 (2016 est)
National anthem – 'National Anthem of Mauritania'
National day – 28 November (Independence Day)
Death penalty – Retained (last used 1987)
CPI score – 28 (143)
Military expenditure – US$136m (2015)
Literacy rate – 62.6 per cent (2015 est)
Gross enrolment ratio (percentage of relevant age group) – primary 94 per cent, secondary 32 per cent, tertiary 5 per cent (2016 est)

Health expenditure (per capita) – US$49 (2014)
Life expectancy (years) – 63.4 (2017 est)
Mortality rate – 7.9 (2017 est)
Birth rate – 30.4 (2017 est)
Infant mortality rate – 51.9 (2017 est)
HIV/AIDS adult prevalence – 0.5 per cent (2016 est)

CLIMATE AND TERRAIN
About 60 per cent of the country is covered by the plains of the Sahara Desert, with some hills in the centre. The terrain is arid, apart from in the Senegal river valley on the southern border; most of the population lives there or on the coast at Nouakchott and Nouadhibou. Elevation extremes range from Kediet Ijill (915m) to −5m (Sebkhet Te-n-Dghamcha). There is a desert climate; the north of the country is virtually rainless, while the south receives some unreliable rainfall between June and October. Humidity can be high in the wet season, especially on the coast. Average temperatures range from 20.3°C in January to 33.9°C in June.

HISTORY AND POLITICS
Eastern Mauritania was part of the Ghana Empire and then the Muslim Almoravid and Almohad empires from the 11th to the 13th century. The area became part of the French West Africa protectorate in 1903 and then a colony in 1920. The country became independent as the Islamic Republic of Mauritania on 28 November 1960.

Mauritania has experienced several military coups and periods of military rule since independence. The 1984 coup brought to power Col. Maaouya ould Sid Ahmed Taya, who restored civilian rule in 1992 with multiparty elections in which he was elected president. President Taya was deposed in a military coup in 2005 and after a period of transitional government, elections were held in late 2006 and early 2007.

The 2007 presidential election was won by Sidi ould Cheikh Abdallahi who was subsequently overthrown in a military coup after attempting to sack four military leaders. Democracy was restored with the 2009 presidential election, which was won by General Mohamed ould Abdelaziz, who had led the 2008 coup, but the 2011 legislative elections were postponed. In December 2013 Abdelaziz's Union for the Republic party won a majority in the first legislative elections since 2006, although the polls were widely boycotted by opposition parties. Peaceful legislative elections took place in September 2018 with broad participation from opposition parties. President Abdelaziz was elected for a further five-year term on 30 June 2014.

The 1991 constitution was amended in 2007 to reduce the term of the president, who is directly elected, to five years, renewable once. A referendum in August 2017 approved a constitutional amendment which altered the parliamentary structure from bicameral to unicameral by abolishing the senate and establishing regional councils. The National Assembly has 147 members who are directly elected for a five-year term, 107 in single- or two-seat constituencies by absolute majority and 40 by proportional representation in constituencies with three or more seats.

HEAD OF STATE
President, Gen. Mohamed ould Abdel Aziz, *elected* 18 July 2009, *sworn in* 5 August 2009, *re-elected* 30 June 2014

SELECTED GOVERNMENT MEMBERS *AS AT SEPTEMBER 2018*
Prime Minister, Yahya ould Hademine
Finance, Mokhtar ould Djay
Foreign Affairs, Smael ould Cheikh Ahmed
Interior, Amedou ould Abdella

EMBASSY OF THE ISLAMIC REPUBLIC OF MAURITANIA
Carlyle House, 235 Vauxhall Bridge Road, London SW1V 1EJ
T 020-7233 6158 E info@mauritanianembassy.org.uk
W www.mauritanianembassy.org.uk
Chargé d'Affaires, Mohamed Yahya ould Sidi Haiba

BRITISH AMBASSADOR
Ambassador Extraordinary and Plenipotentiary, HE Samuel Thomas, *apptd* 2018

ECONOMY AND TRADE
Mauritania is one of the poorer countries in the region, with 31 per cent of the population living below the poverty line and unemployment at 11.7 per cent. Past economic mismanagement and droughts created a huge foreign debt, although the country has benefited from debt cancellation since 2000. Despite a drought in 2017, GDP growth of 3.8 per cent was achieved thanks to external investment in the oil and mining sectors. In December 2017, Mauritania and the IMF agreed a three-year Extended Credit Facility to encourage infrastructure investment and economic stability.

Natural resources include iron ore, copper, gold, gypsum, oil and rich fishing waters, although the latter are threatened by over-exploitation. Potential deposits of natural gas and rare metals are also being explored. Agriculture and animal husbandry, mainly at subsistence level, are the mainstay of the economy, accounting for 22.5 per cent of GDP and engaging 50 per cent of the population. The main industries are fish processing, oil production and refining, and mining.

The main trading partners are China, the UAE, Switzerland and EU countries. Principal exports are iron ore, fish and fish products, livestock, gold, copper and oil. The main imports are machinery, petroleum products, capital goods, food and consumer goods.

GNI – US$4.9bn; US$1,100 per capita (2017)
Annual average growth of GDP – 3.8 per cent (2017 est)
Inflation rate – 2.1 per cent (2017 est)
Population below poverty line – 31 per cent (2014 est)
Unemployment – 11.7 per cent (2016 est)
Total external debt – $4.117bn (2017 est)
Imports – US$2,163m (2016)
Exports – US$1,680m (2016)

BALANCE OF PAYMENTS
Trade – US$483m deficit (2016)
Current Account – US$956m surplus (2015)

Trade with UK	2016	2017
Imports from UK	£9,366,362	£14,594,729
Exports to UK	£6,556,430	£3,515,515

COMMUNICATIONS
Transport – There are nine airports; the main seaports are Nouakchott and Nouadhibou; there are 3,158km of roadways and 728km of railways
Telecommunications – 53,191 fixed lines and 3.6 million mobile subscriptions (2016); there were 661,913 internet users in 2016
Internet code and IDD – mr; 222 (from UK), 44 (to UK)
Major broadcasters – Télévision de Mauritanie and Radio Mauritanie are the public broadcasters and offer programmes in Arabic and French; private broadcast media have been allowed to operate since 2011
Press – Major daily newspapers include the Arabic-language *Al-Sha'b* and the French-language *Horizons* (both state-run)
WPFI score – 29,09 (72)

MAURITIUS

Republic of Mauritius

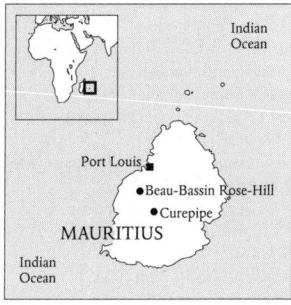

Area – 2,040 sq. km (includes Rodrigues and other islands)
Capital – Port Louis; population, 149,000 (2018)
Major towns – Beau-Bassin Rose-Hill, Curepipe, Quatre Bornes, Vacoas-Phoenix
Currency – Mauritius rupee of 100 cents
Population – 1,356,388 rising at 0.59 per cent a year (2017 est); Indo-Mauritian (68 per cent), Creole (27 per cent), Sino-Mauritian (3 per cent), Franco-Mauritian (2 per cent) (est)
Religion – Hindu 48.5 per cent, Christian (Roman Catholic 26.3 per cent), Muslim 17.3 per cent (2011 est)
Language – English (official), Creole, French, Bhojpuri
Population density – 623 per sq. km (2016)
Urban population – 40.8 per cent (2018 est)
Median age (years) – 34.8 (2015 est)
National anthem – 'Motherland'
National day – 12 March (Independence Day)
Death penalty – Abolished for all crimes (since 1995)
CPI score – 50 (54)
Military expenditure – US$24m (2017)

CLIMATE AND TERRAIN

The republic is an island group in the Indian Ocean, approximately 885km east of Madagascar. The volcanic island of Mauritius rises from narrow coastal plains to a central plateau ringed by mountains. Elevation extremes range from 828m (Mt Piton) to 0m (Indian Ocean). The island of Rodrigues, formerly a dependency but now part of Mauritius, is about 563km east of Mauritius, with an area of 109 sq. km; the population is 37,922 (2011). The islands of Agalega and St Brandon are dependencies of Mauritius; their total population is about 350 (2011).

There is a tropical climate, modified by south-east trade winds, and little variation in temperature throughout the year. The cyclone season (December–April) brings rain but cyclones usually miss the islands.

HISTORY AND POLITICS

The islands were first visited in the tenth century, but were settled only after 1638 by the Dutch, who introduced sugar cane cultivation. The colonists withdrew in 1710. A decade later they were replaced by the French, who established plantations that were worked by African slaves. In 1814 Mauritius was ceded to the British, who had occupied it in 1810. The British abolished slavery in 1834 and imported indentured Indian and Chinese labourers to work on the plantations. Independence was achieved on 12 March 1968 and the state became a republic in 1992.

The Militant Socialist Movement (MSM) under Sir Anerood Jugnauth held power from 1983 until 1995, and then returned to power in 2000 in coalition with the Mauritian Militant Movement (MMM). Jugnauth stood down as party leader and prime minister in 2003; he was elected president later that year and again in 2008. The MSM-MMM coalition lost the 2005 election to the opposition Socialist Alliance, but the MSM returned to power in 2010 in the Alliance of the Future, led by the Mauritius Labour Party (MPT). President Rajkeswur Purryag resigned from office in May 2015 and, in June, scientist Ameenah Gurib-Fakim was elected in his place, becoming the country's first woman president. However she was forced to resign from the largely ceremonial position in March 2018 following a financial scandal.

The December 2014 legislative elections were won by the Alliance Lepep, consisting of the MSM, Mauritian Social Democratic Party (PMSD) and the Mouvement Libérateur (ML); Sir Anerood Jugnauth of the MSM formed a new government and became prime minister for a third term. In January 2017 he resigned in favour of his son Pravind.

The 1968 constitution was amended in 1992 to introduce a republican form of government, and in 2001 to give the island of Rodrigues a degree of autonomy.

The president is elected by the legislature for a five-year term, renewable once. The unicameral National Assembly has 62 elected members (including two representing Rodrigues) and eight appointed members, all of whom serve a five-year term; the electoral commission allocates the appointed seats on a 'best loser' basis to give more equitable representation to ethnic minorities. The prime minister is the leader of the majority party in the legislature.

Rodrigues has had an 18-member regional assembly, a chief commissioner and a chief executive since 2002.

HEAD OF STATE
President, Paramasivum Vyapoory (acting)

SELECTED GOVERNMENT MEMBERS *AS AT AUGUST 2018*
Prime Minister, Finance, Home Affairs, Pravind Jugnauth
Deputy Prime Minister, Ivan Collendavelloo
Vice-Prime Minister, Showkutally Soodhun
Foreign Affairs, Vishnu Lutchmeenaraidoo

MAURITIUS HIGH COMMISSION
32–33 Elvaston Place, London SW7 5NW
T 020-7581 0294 E londonhc@govmu.org
W london.mauritius.gov.mu
High Commissioner, HE Girish Nunkoo, *apptd* 2015

BRITISH HIGH COMMISSION
7th floor, Cascades Building, Edith Cavell Street, PO Box 1063, Port Louis
T (+230) 202 9400 E bhc@intnet.mu
W www.gov.uk/government/world/mauritius
High Commissioner, HE Keith Allan, *apptd* 2017

ECONOMY AND TRADE

Since independence Mauritius has developed from an economy dependent on agriculture to one with prospering tourist, manufacturing (primarily of textiles and garments) and financial sectors. Although sugar remains an important commodity (sugar cane is grown on 90 per cent of cultivated land), both the sugar and textile industries are beginning to decline. Diversification into fish processing, information and communications technology, banking, hospitality and property development is being encouraged. The growing services sector accounts for 74.2 per cent of GDP, industry for 21.8 per cent and agriculture for 4 per cent.

The main trading partners are India, the UK, the USA and France. Principal exports are clothing, textiles, sugar, cut

flowers, molasses and fish. The main imports are manufactured goods, capital equipment, food, fuels and chemicals.
GNI – US$12.8bn; US$10,140 per capita (2017)
Annual average growth of GDP – 3.9 per cent (2017 est)
Inflation rate – 4.2 per cent (2017 est)
Unemployment – 6.9 per cent (2017 est)
Total external debt – US$14.67bn (2017 est)
Imports – US$4,794m (2015)
Exports – US$2,686m (2015)

BALANCE OF PAYMENTS
Trade – US$2,108m deficit (2015)
Current Account – US$878m deficit (2017)

Trade with UK	2016	2017
Imports from UK	£67,718,563	£80,444,221
Exports to UK	£167,705,354	£166,756,628

COMMUNICATIONS
Airports and waterways – The international airport and the main port are at Port Louis
Roadways – 2,149km, including 75km of motorways
Telecommunications – 389,500 fixed lines and 1.8 million mobile subscriptions (2016); there were 717,618 internet users in 2016
Internet code and IDD – mu; 230 (from UK), 44 (to UK)
Major broadcasters – The state-owned Mauritius Broadcasting Corporation runs television and radio services funded through advertising and a licence fee
Press – Leading dailies include *L'Express, Le Mauricien* and *Le Matinal*
WPFI score – 26,45 (56)

EDUCATION AND HEALTH
Twelve years of education are free and compulsory.
Literacy rate – 98.7 per cent (2015 est)
Gross enrolment ratio (percentage of relevant age group) – primary 102 per cent, secondary 93 per cent (2016 est), tertiary 36.7 per cent (2015 est)
Health expenditure (per capita) – US$482 (2014)
Hospital beds (per 1,000 people) – 3.59 (2016)
Life expectancy (years) – 75.8 (2017 est)
Mortality rate – 7.1 (2017 est)
Birth rate – 13 (2017 est)
Infant mortality rate – 9.8 (2017 est)
HIV/AIDS adult prevalence – 0.9 per cent (2015 est)

MEXICO

Estados Unidos Mexicanos – United Mexican States

Area – 1,964,375 sq. km
Capital – Mexico City; population, 21,581,000 (2018 est)
Major cities – Ciudad Juárez, Ecatepec, Guadalajara, León, Monterrey, Puebla, Tijuana

Currency – Peso of 100 centavos
Population – 124,574,795 rising at 1.12 per cent a year (2017 est)
Religion – Christian (Roman Catholic 82.7 per cent, Evangelical 8 per cent), none 4.7 per cent (2010 est)
Language – Spanish (official) indigenous languages including dialects of Mayan and Nahuatl
Population density – 66 per sq. km (2016)
Urban population – 80.2 per cent (2016 est)
Median age (years) – 28 (2016 est)
National anthem – 'Himno Nacional Mexicano' 'Mexican National Anthem'
National day – 16 September (Independence Day)
Death penalty – Abolished for all crimes (since 2005)
CPI score – 29 (135)
Military expenditure – US$5,781m (2017)
Conscription – 18 years of age; 12 months

CLIMATE AND TERRAIN
The Rio Grande river forms the eastern part of the border with the USA. South of this, coastal plains rise to a central plateau which lies between two spines of high mountains, the Western and the Eastern Sierra Madre, running from the north-west to south-east. The mountains include volcanoes such as Popocatepetl, and in the south are covered with dense jungle. The Yucatán peninsula in the south-east is low-lying, and marshy on the coast. The narrow Baja California peninsula, separated from the rest of the country by the Gulf of California, has a range of hills running along it. Elevation extremes range from 5,700m (Volcan Pico de Orizaba) to −10m (Laguna Salada). The north has a desert climate, while the south is tropical. The average temperature ranges from 16.1°C in January to 25.9°C in June and July.

POLITICS
Under the 1917 constitution, the federal republic consists of 31 states and the federal capital. The head of state is an executive president, directly elected for a single six-year term. The bicameral legislature is the Congress of the Union: the lower house, the Chamber of Deputies, has 500 members, directly elected for a three-year term, and the senate has 128 members, directly elected for a six-year term. The president appoints the cabinet.
    Each of the states has its own constitution and is administered by a governor, elected for a six-year term, and a state chamber of deputies, elected for a three-year term.
    The Institutional Revolutionary Party's (PRI) political dominance ended at the 1997 election, when it lost its absolute majority in the lower house of the legislature, although it continued in government until 2000 and was again in power from 2003 until 2006. The presidential elections were won by Felipe Calderón of the Partido Accion Nacional (PAN) in 2006 and by the PRI's Enrique Peña Nieto in 2012. The PRI became the largest party in the Chamber of Deputies in the 2012 legislative election, and along with its allies the Green Party and New Alliance Party, increased their majority in the 2015 elections. The three-party *Juntos Haremos Historia* coalition, led by the left-wing National Regeneration Movement party (MORENA), won large majorities in both houses in the July 2018 election. MORENA was founded in 2014 by populist veteran Andrés López Obrador, who won the simultaneous presidential elections on an anti-corruption platform.

HEAD OF STATE
President, Andrés López Obrador, *elected* 1 July 2018, *to be sworn in* 1 December 2018

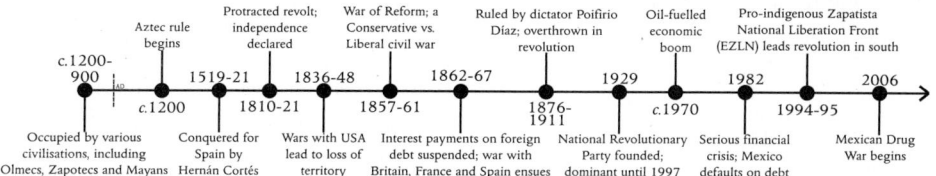

SELECTED GOVERNMENT MEMBERS *AS AT JULY 2018*
Defence, Gen. Salvador Cienfuegos Zepeda
Economy, Ildefonso Guajardo Villareal
Foreign Affairs, Luis Videgaray Caso
Interior, Alfonso Navarrete Prida

EMBASSY OF MEXICO
16 St George Street, London W1S 1FD
T 020-7499 8586 E mexuk@sre.gob.mx
W www.sre.gob.mx/reinounido
Ambassador Extraordinary and Plenipotentiary, HE Julian Ventura
Valero, *apptd* 2017

BRITISH EMBASSY
Río Lerma 71, Col. Cuauhtémoc, 06500 Mexico City
T (+52) (55) 1670 3200 E ukinmexico@fco.gov.uk
W www.gov.uk/government/world/mexico
Ambassador Extraordinary and Plenipotentiary, HE Duncan
Taylor, CBE, *apptd* 2013

ECONOMY AND TRADE
Mexico had a relatively closed economy until the mid-1980s, but increased trade and domestic liberalisation in the 1990s stimulated economic growth and development, particularly in the industrial sector. However, although it has free trade agreements with 46 countries, covering 90 per cent of its trade, its economy is still closely tied to that of the USA and experienced a deep recession in 2009 as the global downturn affected its main export market. Since 2013, GDP has underperformed at 2 per cent average annual growth, partly due to low global oil prices and the persistence of structural issues such as high inequality. The election of President Trump in the USA has adversely affected the value of the peso and the Mexican economy, but a new trade deal between the two countries was agreed in August 2018, contingent on congressional approval.

Agriculture is diverse and productive; major crops include maize, wheat, soya beans, rice, beans, cotton, coffee, fruit, tomatoes, beef, poultry and dairy products. Agriculture accounts for 3.9 per cent of GDP and 13.4 per cent of employment. The main industries include production of food, beverages, tobacco, chemicals, iron and steel, textiles, clothing, motor vehicles, consumer durables, oil production, mining and tourism. Tourism is now the fourth-largest revenue earner. The services sector accounts for 63.2 per cent of GDP and industry for 31.6 per cent.

The main trading partner is the USA (79.9 per cent of exports; 46.4 per cent of imports). Canada is the other main export market, and China and Japan the other main source of imports. Principal exports include manufactured goods, electronics, oil and oil products, silver, vehicles, and agricultural products. The main imports include metalworking machines, steel mill products, agricultural machinery, electronics, car parts for assembly, vehicle repair parts, aircraft and aircraft parts.
GNI – US$1,112.5bn; US$8,610 per capita (2017)

Annual average growth of GDP – 2.1 per cent (2017 est)
Inflation rate – 5.9 per cent (2017 est)
Population below poverty line – 46.2 per cent (2014 est)
Unemployment – 3.6 per cent (2017 est)
Total external debt – US$480.5bn (2017 est)
Imports – US$387,065m (2016)
Exports – US$374,904m (2016)

BALANCE OF PAYMENTS
Trade – US$13,161m deficit (2016)
Current Account – US$19,354m deficit (2017)

Trade with UK	*2016*	*2017*
Imports from UK	£1,265,498,273	£1,545,325,577
Exports to UK	£1,090,667,088	£1,560,862,427

COMMUNICATIONS
Airports – The main international airport is at Mexico City, with 242 others around the country
Waterways – Veracruz, Tampico and Coatzacoalcos are the chief seaports on the east coast, and Guaymas, Mazatlán, Lázaro Cárdenas and Salina Cruz on the Pacific; there are 2,900km of navigable rivers and coastal canals
Roadways and railways – There are 137,544km of paved roadways, including 7,176km of motorways; there are 17,166km of railways
Telecommunications – 20.4 million fixed lines and 111.7 million mobile subscriptions (2016); there were 73 million internet users in 2016
Internet code and IDD – mx; 52 (from UK), 44 (to UK)
Major broadcasters – The Televisa group used to dominate broadcasting but now competes with other television channels and a huge number of independent radio stations
Press – Leading dailies include *Excelsior, La Jornada* and *Reforma*
WPFI score – 48,91 (147)

EDUCATION AND HEALTH
Education is compulsory in Mexico for ten years from age six, although attainment varies among states.
Literacy rate – 99.0 per cent (2015 est)
Gross enrolment ratio (percentage of relevant age group) – primary 104 per cent, secondary 97 per cent, tertiary 37 per cent (2016 est)
Health expenditure (per capita) – US$677 (2014)
Hospital beds (per 1,000 people) – 1.5 (2015)
Life expectancy (years) – 76.1 (2017 est)
Mortality rate – 5.3 (2017 est)
Birth rate – 18.3 (2017 est)
Infant mortality rate – 11.6 (2017 est)
HIV/AIDS adult prevalence – 0.3 per cent (2016 est)

FEDERATED STATES OF MICRONESIA

Area – 702 sq. km
Capital – Palikir, on Pohnpei; population, 7,000 (2018)
Major towns – Kolonia, Weno
Currency – US dollar (US$) of 100 cents
Population – 104,196 falling at 0.52 per cent a year (2017 est); Chuukese (49.3 per cent), Pohnpeian (29.8 per cent), Kosraen (6.3 per cent), Yapese (5.7 per cent), Yap outer islanders (5.1 per cent), Polynesian (1.6 per cent) (2010 est)
Religion – Christian (Roman Catholic 54.7 per cent, Protestant 41.1 per cent, Mormon 1.5 per cent) (2010 est)
Language – English (official), Chuukese, Kosraen, Pohnpeian, Yapese, Ulithian, Woleaian, Nukuoro, Kapingamarangi
Population density – 151 per sq. km (2016)
Urban population – 22.7 per cent (2018 est)
Median age (years) – 24.7 (2017 est)
National anthem – 'Patriots of Micronesia'
National day – 10 May (Constitution Day)
Death penalty – Abolished for all crimes (since 1986)
Gross enrolment ratio (percentage of relevant age group) – primary 95.5 per cent (2015 est)
Health expenditure (per capita) – US$415 (2014 est)
Life expectancy (years) – 73.1 (2017 est)
Mortality rate – 4.2 (2017 est)
Birth rate – 20 (2017 est)
Infant mortality rate – 19.8 (2017 est)

CLIMATE AND TERRAIN
The republic consists of four major island groups totalling over 600 mountainous volcanic islands and low-lying atolls, extending over 2,900 sq. km of the western Pacific Ocean. Elevation extremes range from 791m (Dolohmwar) to 0m (Pacific Ocean). The climate is tropical, with only slight seasonal variations in temperatures; there is a stormy season between July and November. The islands are vulnerable to the effects of global warming, particularly an increase in the frequency and intensity of cyclones in the region.

HISTORY AND POLITICS
Inhabited since around 4,000 BC by migrants from the Philippines and Indonesia, Micronesia experienced contact with Europeans from the 1520s, and the islands were colonised by Spain from the 16th century. German encroachment in the 1870s and 1880s was resisted until 1899, when Germany purchased the islands from Spain. The islands were occupied by Japan on behalf of the Allies during the First World War, and administered as a League of Nations mandated territory by Japan from 1920 until the Japanese defeat in the Second World War. In 1947 the islands became part of the UN Trust Territory of the Pacific, administered by the USA.

A constitution was adopted in 1979 and the islands became independent in 1986 under a compact of free association with the USA, by which the USA retains responsibility for defence and provides substantial financial aid; a renegotiated agreement came into force in 2004. The UN trusteeship was formally terminated in 1990.

Following simultaneous legislative and presidential elections in May 2015, Peter Christian was elected president.

The 1979 constitution established a federal republic of four states: Chuuk, Kosrae, Pohnpei and Yap. The federal head of state is an executive president, who is elected by the federal legislature for a four-year term, renewable once. The unicameral congress has 14 members, ten senators directly elected for a two-year term and four senators 'at large' (one from each state) elected for a four-year term; the president and vice-president must be selected from among the 'at large' senators. The federal cabinet is appointed by the president and approved by the congress. There are no formal political parties.

Each state has its own constitution, legislature and government.

HEAD OF STATE
President, Peter Christian, *elected and sworn in* 11 May 2015
Vice-President, Yosiwo George

SELECTED GOVERNMENT MEMBERS *AS AT JUNE 2018*
Finance, Sihna Lawrence
Foreign Affairs, Lorin S, Robert
Justice, Joses Gallen

BRITISH AMBASSADOR
HE Melanie Hopkins, *apptd* 2016, resident at Suva, Fiji

ECONOMY AND TRADE
Micronesia has few natural resources apart from phosphate, which is not exploited, and is highly dependent on aid from the USA, which constitutes over half of government revenue. The main economic activities are subsistence farming and fishing, which account for 26.3 per cent of GDP, but both are threatened by climate change and over-fishing. The islands' remoteness and lack of facilities has constrained the development of tourism, the main industry; other industries include construction, fish processing, specialised aquaculture and handicrafts. Two-thirds of the workforce is employed by the government. The main trading partners are the USA and Japan. Principal exports are fish, kava, betel nuts and black pepper. The main imports are food, manufactured goods and clothing.
GNI – US$0.4bn; US$3,590 per capita (2017)
Annual average growth of GDP – 2.0 per cent (2017 est)
Inflation rate – 0.9 per cent (2017 est)
Total external debt – US$93.6m (2013 est)
Imports – US$117m (2014)
Exports – US$19m (2014)

BALANCE OF PAYMENTS
Current Account – US$22m surplus (2015)

Trade with UK	2016	2017
Imports from UK	£34,709	£305,840
Exports to UK	–	£2,439

COMMUNICATIONS
Transport – There are six airports, including major airports on the four main islands; the main seaports are Colonia (Yap), Kolonia (Pohnpei), Lele and Moen; there are 42km of paved roads
Telecommunications – 6,883 fixed lines and 23,412 mobile subscriptions (2016); there were 33,000 internet users in 2016

Internet code and IDD – fm; 691 (from UK), 011 44 (to UK)
Media – The federal government produces a fortnightly information bulletin and state governments produce weekly news publications; the majority of television programming is imported

MOLDOVA

Republica Moldova – Republic of Moldova

Area – 33,851 sq. km
Capital – Chisinau; population, 510,000 (2018 est)
Major towns – Balti, Tighina, Tiraspol
Currency – Moldovan leu (plural lei) of 100 bani
Population – 3,474,121 falling at 1.05 per cent a year (2017 est); Moldovan (75.1 per cent), Romanian (7.0 per cent), Ukrainian (6.6 per cent), Gagauz (4.6 per cent), Russian (4.1 per cent), Bulgarian (1.9 per cent) (2014 est)
Religion – Christian (Orthodox 97 per cent) (2013)
Language – Moldovan (official; linguistically identical to Romanian), Russian, Gagauz
Population density – 124 per sq. km (2016)
Urban population – 42.6 per cent (2018 est)
Median age (years) – 36.3 (2016 est)
National anthem – 'Limba Noastra' 'Our Language'
National day – 27 August (Independence Day)
Death penalty – Abolished for all crimes (since 1995)
CPI score – 31 (122)
Military expenditure – US$29.7m (2017)
Conscription – 18 years of age; 12 months

CLIMATE AND TERRAIN
The landlocked country consists of rolling steppe lying mostly between the Prut and Dniester rivers. Elevation extremes range from 430m (Dealul Balanesti) at the highest point to 2m (river Dniester) at the lowest. The climate is continental, and average temperatures range from −1.5°C in January to 22.4°C in July.

POLITICS
The 1997 constitution was amended in 2000 to increase the powers of the legislature and the executive. The head of state is the president who, following a ruling in 2016, is now directly elected for a four-year term, renewable once. The unicameral legislature, the *Parlamentul,* has 101 members, who are directly elected for a four-year term. The prime minister is nominated by the president.

The governments in the first decade after independence were made up of moderate reformists, but there was a resurgence in support for the Communist Party of Moldova (PCM), which won the majority of seats in the 1998, 2001, 2005, 2009 (April and July) and 2010 legislative elections, forming the government from 2005 to 2009. Pro-Western parties formed coalition governments after legislative elections in 2010 and 2014, despite the PCM emerging as the single largest party in both elections. In July 2015, Valeriu Strelet was appointed prime minister after the previous incumbent, Chiril Gaburici, was accused of faking academic qualifications. Strelet was dismissed in a no-confidence vote in October to be replaced in January 2016 by Pavel Filip, who immediately faced protests over political corruption and bank fraud to the tune of £700m in the country. Pro-Moscow candidate Igor Dodon was elected president in November 2016, and has since been temporarily suspended three times after clashing with the Moldovan Constitutional Court after rejecting ministerial appointments and refusing to sign laws.

HEAD OF STATE
President, Igor Dodon, *sworn in* 23 December 2016

SELECTED GOVERNMENT MEMBERS *AS AT JUNE 2018*
Prime Minister, Pavel Filip
Deputy Prime Ministers, Chiril Gaburici *(Economy);* Iurie Leanca; Cristina Lesnic
Defence, Eugen Sturza
Finance, Octavian Armasu

EMBASSY OF THE REPUBLIC OF MOLDOVA
5 Dolphin Square, Edensor Road, London W4 2ST
T 020-8995 6818 E embassy.london@mfa.md
W www.britania.mfa.gov.md
Ambassador Extraordinary and Plenipotentiary, vacant

BRITISH EMBASSY
18/1 Nicolae Iorga Str., Chisinau, MD-2012
T (+373) 222 225902 E enquiries.chisinau@fco.gov.uk
W www.gov.uk/government/world/moldova
Ambassador Extraordinary and Plenipotentiary, HE Lucy Joyce, OBE, *apptd* 2016

SECESSION
Moldovan nationalism in the late 1980s and possible reunification with Romania alarmed the republic's Russian and Ukrainian ethnic minorities in the Transdniestria region (east of the Dniester) and the Gagauz (Turkish-speaking Christians) in the south-west. Both areas declared independence unilaterally in 1990, though this was not recognised. The regions were granted a special status by the 1994 constitution, and the Gagauz have since exercised a degree of autonomy over their political, economic and cultural affairs.

In response to the Russian takeover of Crimea, in March 2014 then-president Nicolae Timofti warned Russia against trying to annex Transdniestria while also calling on the EU to fast-track Moldova's entry into the organisation in order to deter invasion.

ECONOMY AND TRADE

Moldova is one of the poorest countries in Europe, despite moves towards a market economy since independence. With few natural resources and most industry lying in the breakaway Transdniestria region, the economy is dependent on agriculture and remittances from expatriate workers (roughly 15 per cent of GDP), and the country remains one of the poorest in Europe despite declining poverty levels. Following the global downturn, the economy recovered in 2011, but a £700m bank heist in November 2014 robbed the country of one-eighth of its GDP and had ongoing political and economic repercussions, pushing the economy into recession from mid-2015. An IMF loan was approved in November 2016, easing public finances and contributed to better-than-expected growth in 2017, aided by increasing integration with the EU.

The agricultural sector accounts for 12.2 per cent of GDP. Principal crops include vegetables, fruit, wine, grain, sugar beet, sunflower seeds, tobacco, beef and milk. Major industrial activities include food processing and production of sugar, vegetable oil, agricultural machinery, foundry equipment, domestic appliances, footwear and textiles. Industry accounts for 14.6 per cent of GDP and services for 73.2 per cent.

The main trading partners are Russia, Romania and EU nations. Principal exports are foodstuffs, textiles and machinery. The main imports are mineral products and fuel, machinery and equipment, chemicals and textiles.

GNI – US$7.8bn; US$2,180 per capita (2017)
Annual average growth of GDP – 4.0 per cent (2017 est)
Inflation rate – 6.5 per cent (2017 est)
Population below poverty line – 20.8 per cent (2013 est)
Unemployment – 4.3 per cent (2017 est)
Total external debt – US$6.503bn (2017 est)
Imports – US$4,021m (2016)
Exports – US$2,045m (2016)

BALANCE OF PAYMENTS
Trade – US$1,976m deficit (2016)
Current Account – US$660m deficit (2017)

Trade with UK	2016	2017
Imports from UK	£42,502,106	£41,672,409
Exports to UK	£45,296,697	£50,789,037

COMMUNICATIONS

Airports and waterways – There are five airports, including the principal airport at Chisinau; there are 558km of navigable waterways on the Prut, Dniester and Danube rivers
Roadways and railways – 8,835m; 1,190km
Telecommunications – 1.2 million fixed lines and 3.8 million mobile subscriptions (2016); there were 2.5 million internet users in 2016
Internet code and IDD – md; 373 (from UK), 44 (to UK)
Major broadcasters – Public networks Moldova One (TV) and Radio Moldova broadcasts nationally alongside Russian and Romanian stations
Press – Major daily newspapers include *Timpul, Flux* (both in Moldovan) and *Kommersant Moldoviy* (Russian language)
WPFI score – 30,01 (81)

EDUCATION AND HEALTH

Literacy rate – 100 per cent (2015 est)
Gross enrolment ratio (percentage of relevant age group) – primary 92.4 per cent, secondary 86.1 per cent, tertiary 41.2 per cent (2015 est)
Health expenditure (per capita) – US$229 (2014)
Hospital beds (per 1,000 people) – 5.8 (2013)

Life expectancy (years) – 71 (2017 est)
Mortality rate – 12.6 (2017 est)
Birth rate – 11.5 (2017 est)
Infant mortality rate – 12 (2017 est)
HIV/AIDS adult prevalence – 0.6 per cent (2016 est)

MONACO

Principauté de Monaco – *Principality of Monaco*

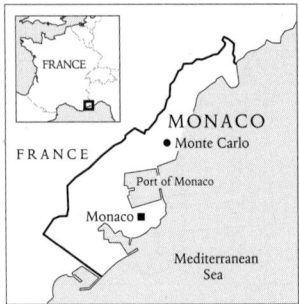

Area – 2 sq. km
Capital – Monaco; population, 39,000 (2018 est)
Major town – Monte Carlo
Currency – Euro (€) of 100 cents
Population – 30,645 growing at 0.24 per cent a year (2017 est); Monegasque (32.1 per cent), French (19.9 per cent), Italian (15.3 per cent), British (5.0 per cent), Belgian (2.3 per cent), Swiss (2.0 per cent) (2016 est)
Religion – Christian (Roman Catholic 90 per cent)
Language – French (official), English, Italian, Monegasque
Population density – 19,348 per sq. km (2016)
Urban population – 100 per cent (2018 est)
Median age (years) – 52.4 (2016 est)
National anthem – 'Hymne Monegasque' 'Hymn of Monaco'
National day – 19 November (St Rainier's Day)
Death penalty – Abolished for all crimes (since 1962)
Health expenditure (per capita) – US$8,149 (2014)
Life expectancy (years) – 89.4 (2017 est)
Mortality rate – 9.8 (2017 est)
Birth rate – 6.6 (2017 est)
Infant mortality rate – 1.8 (2017 est)

CLIMATE AND TERRAIN

Monaco lies on 4km of steep, rugged coastline. It has been expanded by 0.3 sq. km with land reclaimed from the sea by infilling. Elevation extremes range from 140m (Mt Agel) to 0m (Mediterranean Sea). The climate is Mediterranean, with average temperatures ranging from 6.6°C in January to 22°C in August.

HISTORY AND POLITICS

Monaco has been ruled by the Grimaldi family since the 13th century. Monarchical France recognised Monaco's independence in the 15th century, but Revolutionary France annexed it in 1793. Although the prince was restored to power in 1814, Monaco did not regain its independence until 1861. It was occupied by the Italians and subsequently by the Germans in the Second World War. The principality's foreign relations and security have been aligned to those of France since 1861 by various treaties; the terms were changed in 2005 to allow Monaco greater control over its foreign relations and internal administration.

The 1962 constitution was amended in 2002 to allow the throne to pass through the female line in the absence of male heirs. Legislative power is held jointly by the prince and a 24-member National Council, which is directly elected for a five-year term. Executive power is exercised by the prince and a six-member Council of Government, headed by a minister of state who is nominated by the prince and approved by the French government. The judicial code is based on that of France.

In the 2018 legislative election, the Priority Party won 21 seats and reduced the previously dominant Horizon Monaco Party's 20 seats to just two. Serge Telle replaced Michel Roger as head of the government in February 2016.

HEAD OF STATE
HSH The Prince of Monaco, Prince Albert II (Alexandre Louis Pierre), *born* 14 March 1958, *succeeded* 6 April 2005
Heir, HSH Prince Jaques (Crown Prince) *born* 10 December 2014

SELECTED GOVERNMENT MEMBERS *AS AT AUGUST 2018*
Minister of State, Serge Telle
Finance and Economy, Jean Castellini
Foreign Affairs, Gilles Tonelli
Interior, Patrice Cellario

EMBASSY OF THE PRINCIPALITY OF MONACO
7 Upper Grosvenor Street, London W1K 2LX
T 020-7318 1078 E embassy.uk@gouv.mc
W www.monaco-embassy-uk.gouv.mc
Ambassador Extraordinary and Plenipotentiary, HE Evelyne Genta, *apptd* 2010

BRITISH HONORARY CONSULATE
Contact British Consulate Marseille, 24 Avenue du Prado, 13006 Marseille
T (+33) (0) 4 9115 7210

ECONOMY AND TRADE
The economy has diversified away from its historic dependence on tourism and gambling, and over half its revenue now comes from financial services, retail, real estate, construction and light industry (chemicals, pharmaceuticals, cosmetics, medical devices, plastics, electronics).

As the state collects no taxes from individuals and little from businesses, it has become a tax haven for wealthy expatriates and foreign companies. However, as of 2014 the nation agreed to join the OECD's multilateral efforts to tackle tax avoidance and evasion. The state retains monopolies in a number of sectors, including tobacco, the telephone network and the postal service. Since 1963 Monaco has been in a customs union with France, and through this it participates in the EU market. Over half its trade is with EU countries, particularly France and Italy.
GNI – US$6,075m; US$167,021 per capita (2011)
Annual average growth of GDP – 5.4 per cent (2015 est)
Unemployment – 2 per cent (2012)

COMMUNICATIONS
Transport – The nearest international airport is the Côte d'Azur airport in Nice, France; the installation of a large floating jetty in 2002 doubled the port of Monaco's capacity to handle cruise ships; there are 77km of roads and a single railway station, Monaco-Monte Carlo
Telecommunications – 46,575 fixed lines and 33,297 mobile subscriptions (2016); there were 29,116 internet users in 2016
Internet code and IDD – mc; 377 (from UK), 44 (to UK)
Media – Monaco has one television station and the principality's news is covered by the French press

MONGOLIA
Mongol Uls – Mongolia

Area – 1,564,116 sq. km
Capital – Ulaanbaatar; population, 1,520,000 (2018 est)
Major towns – Darhan, Erdenet
Currency – Tugrik of 100 mongo
Population – 3,068,243 rising at 1.18 per cent a year (2017 est); Khalkh (81.9 per cent), Kazak (3.8 per cent), Dorvod (2.7 per cent) and several others (2010 est)
Religion – Buddhist 53 per cent, none 38.6 per cent, Muslim 3 per cent, Shamanist 2.9 per cent, Christian 2.2 per cent (2010 est)
Language – Khalkha Mongol (official), Turkic, Russian
Population density – 2 per sq. km (2016)
Urban population – 68.4 per cent (2018 est)
Median age (years) – 27.9 (2016 est)
National anthem – 'Mongol ulsyn toriin duulal' 'National Anthem of Mongolia'
National day – 11 July (Revolution Day)
Death penalty – Abolished for all crimes (since 2017)
CPI score – 36 (103)
Military expenditure – US$82.8m (2017)
Conscription – 18–27 years of age, male only; 12 months
Literacy rate – 98.5 per cent (2015 est)
Gross enrolment ratio (percentage of relevant age group) – primary 100.9 per cent, secondary 91.5 per cent, tertiary 68.6 per cent (2015 est)
Health expenditure (per capita) – US$195 (2014)
Hospital beds (per 1,000 people) – 7 (2012)
Life expectancy (years) – 69.9 (2017 est)
Mortality rate – 6.3 (2017 est)
Birth rate – 18.9 (2017 est)
Infant mortality rate – 21.1 (2017 est)
HIV / AIDS adult prevalence – 0.1 per cent (2016 est)

CLIMATE AND TERRAIN
The eastern part of Mongolia lies on a semi-desert plateau, with steppes rising to the Mongolian Altai and Hangai mountain ranges in the west. The Gobi desert covers the southern third of the country. Elevation extremes range from 4,374m (Nayramadlin Orgil) to 560m (Hoh Nuur). The country has long, cold winters, which quickly turn into short and warm summers. The wet season runs from June to September. Average temperatures range from −20.1°C in January to 18.5°C in July.

POLITICS
The 1992 constitution was amended in 2000 to give the president the right to dissolve the legislature if it is unable to reach agreement on appointing a prime minister. The president is directly elected for a four-year term, which is renewable once. The unicameral State Great Hural has 76 members who are directly elected for a four-year term. The

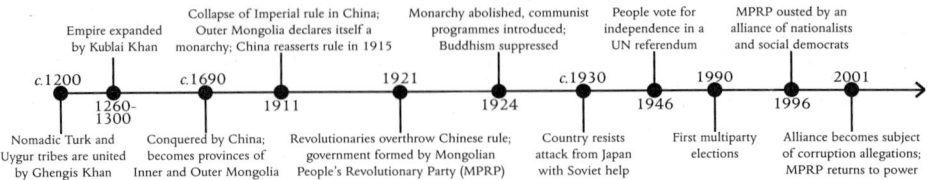

Empire expanded by Kublai Khan — Collapse of Imperial rule in China; Outer Mongolia declares itself a monarchy; China reasserts rule in 1915 — Monarchy abolished, communist programmes introduced; Buddhism suppressed — People vote for independence in a UN referendum — MPRP ousted by an alliance of nationalists and social democrats

*c.*1200 — *c.*1690 — 1921 — *c.*1930 — 1990 — 2001

1260–1300 — 1911 — 1924 — 1946 — 1996

Nomadic Turk and Uygur tribes are united by Ghengis Khan — Conquered by China; becomes provinces of Inner and Outer Mongolia — Revolutionaries overthrow Chinese rule; government formed by Mongolian People's Revolutionary Party (MPRP) — Country resists attack from Japan with Soviet help — First multiparty elections — Alliance becomes subject of corruption allegations; MPRP returns to power

prime minister is elected by the legislature and appoints the cabinet.

The opposition Mongolian People's Party (MPP) swept back to power with a landslide in legislative elections in June 2016, winning 65 seats in parliament. Jargaltulga Erdenebat was appointed prime minister in July but was voted out of office over allegations of corruption in September 2017, being replaced by Ukhnaa Khurelsukh. The 2017 presidential election was won in the second round by Khaltmaa Battulga, who replaced Tsakhiagiin Elbegdorj (prime minister 1998, 2004–6; president 2009–17).

HEAD OF STATE
President, Khaltmaa Battulga, *elected* 7 July 2017, *sworn in* 10 July 2017

SELECTED GOVERNMENT MEMBERS *AS AT JUNE 2018*
Prime Minister, Ukhnaa Khurelsukh
Deputy Prime Minister, Olziisaikhany Enkhtuvshin
Defence, Nyamaagiin Enkhbold
Justice, Tsendiin Nyamdorj

EMBASSY OF MONGOLIA
7–8 Kensington Court, London W8 5DL
T 020-7937 0150 **E** office@embassyofmongolia.co.uk
W www.embassyofmongolia.co.uk
Ambassador Extraordinary and Plenipotentiary, HE Sanjaa Bayar, *apptd* 2017

BRITISH EMBASSY
Peace Avenue 30, Bayanzurkh District, Ulaanbaatar 13381
T (+976) (11) 458 133 **E** enquiries.mongolia@fco.gov.uk
W www.gov.uk/government/world/mongolia
Ambassador Extraordinary and Plenipotentiary, HE Philip Malone, LVO, *apptd* 2018

ECONOMY AND TRADE
The economy suffered during the transition to a market economy but recovered before the global economic downturn in 2008. Declining commodity prices and export demand and soaring inflation caused difficulties that forced the government to seek an IMF loan in spring 2009. Mongolia has attracted foreign investment, particularly in mining, agricultural processing and infrastructure, but administrative corruption, dependency on imported energy supplies (mostly from Russia) and the vulnerability of the agrarian sector to climate extremes continue to hinder growth. In 2017 the IMF agreed a US$440m loan as part of a US$5.5bn bailout package that, alongside expansion of the Oyu Tolgoi copper and gold mine in the Gobi desert and rising commodity prices, significantly boosted GDP growth in 2017 to 5.1 per cent and improved economic stability.

Deposits of copper, coal, molybdenum, fluorspar, tin, tungsten, uranium, gold and oil are being exploited; copper and gold sales are major drivers of recent economic growth. The agrarian sector, which makes up 13.2 per cent of GDP, engages 31.1 per cent of the workforce in agriculture and herding. The main products are grains, vegetables, forage crops, sheep, goats and other livestock. The main industries are construction, mining, processing animal products, and the production of oil, food and beverages, cashmere and natural yarns.

The main export market is China (85 per cent) and the UK; the main import providers are China (32.6 per cent) and Russia (28.1 per cent). Principal exports are copper, clothing, livestock, animal products, cashmere, wool, hides, fluorspar, metals and coal. The main imports are machinery and equipment, fuels, cars, foodstuffs, industrial consumer goods, chemicals and construction materials.
GNI – US$10.1bn; US$3,290 per capita (2017)
Annual average growth of GDP – 2.0 per cent (2017 est)
Inflation rate – 4.4 per cent (2017 est)
Population below poverty line – 21.6 per cent (2014 est)
Unemployment – 8 per cent (2017 est)
Total external debt – US$22.28bn (2017 est)
Imports – US$3,358m (2016)
Exports – US$4,917m (2016)

BALANCE OF PAYMENTS
Trade – US$1,559m surplus (2016)
Current Account – US$1,155m deficit (2017)

Trade with UK	2016	2017
Imports from UK	£5,625,515	£26,387,433
Exports to UK	£4,078,280	£5,195,093

COMMUNICATIONS
Airports and waterways – The main airport is at Ulaanbaatar – there are 14 other airports around the country; the 580km of waterways are navigable in the summer months although Lake Hovsgol near the Russian border is the only waterway in commercial operation
Roadways and railways – 4,800km; 1,908km
Telecommunications – 225,287 fixed lines and 3.4 million mobile subscriptions (2016); there were 674,949 internet users in 2016
Internet code and IDD – mn; 976 (from UK), 1 44 (to UK)
Major broadcasters – Mongolian National Broadcaster (MNB) is the state-owned national television broadcaster; the publicly owned Mongolian Radio is the only radio station with national coverage
Press – Major national dailies include *Onoodor,* which has the biggest circulation, and *Unen* (Truth), the organ of the MPRP and the country's oldest newspaper
WPFI score – 29,05 (71)

MONTENEGRO

Crna Gora – Montenegro

Area – 13,812 sq. km
Capital – Podgorica; population, 177,000 (2018)
Major cities – Cetinje (historic and cultural capital), Niksic, Pljevlja
Currency – Euro (€) of 100 cents
Population – 642,550 falling at 0.28 per cent a year (2017 est); Montenegrin (45 per cent), Serbian (28.7 per cent), Bosniak (8.7 per cent), Albanian (4.9 per cent) (2011 est)
Religion – Christian (Orthodox 72.1 per cent, Roman Catholic 3.4 per cent), Muslim 19.1 per cent
Language – Montenegrin (a version of Serbo-Croat) (official), Serbian, Bosnian, Albanian, Croatian
Population density – 46 per sq. km (2016)
Urban population – 66.8 per cent (2018 est)
Median age (years) – 40.2 (2016 est)
National anthem – 'Oj, Svijetla Majska Zoro' 'O, Bright Dawn of May'
National day – 13 July (Statehood Day)
Death penalty – Abolished for all crimes (since 2002)
CPI score – 46 (64)
Military expenditure – US$74.3m (2017)
Literacy rate – 99.2 per cent (2015 est)
Gross enrolment ratio (percentage of relevant age group) – primary 94.3 per cent, secondary 90.3 per cent (2015 est)
Health expenditure (per capita) – US$458 (2014)
Mortality rate – 9.7 (2017 est)
Birth rate – 10 (2017 est)

CLIMATE AND TERRAIN

The terrain is mountainous in the north and centre of the country, intersected by deep canyons and river valleys, and falls to a narrow plain on the highly indented Adriatic coast. About 40 per cent of the country is forested. Elevation extremes range from 2,522m (Bobotov Kuk) to 0m (Adriatic Sea). The main rivers are the Piva (Drina), the Tara and the Lim. Lake Skadarsko straddles the border with Albania. The climate is Mediterranean on the coast, but more continental inland. Average temperatures in Podgorica range from 0.1°C in January to 20.2°C in July and August.

HISTORY AND POLITICS

The area was part of the Roman province of Illyria, and then was settled by Slavs in the seventh century. In the late 12th century it was incorporated into the medieval kingdom of Serbia and so became part of the Ottoman Empire after Serbia's defeat by the Turks in 1389. When Serbia became independent in 1878, Montenegro followed and remained an independent monarchy until the end of the First World War. In 1918, Montenegro joined with Serbia and the former Austro-Hungarian provinces of Slovenia, Croatia and Bosnia-Hercegovina to form the Kingdom of Serbs, Croats and Slovenes, which was renamed Yugoslavia in 1929. Yugoslavia was occupied by Axis forces in 1941, and after liberation it reformed as a communist federal republic in 1945. When the federation disintegrated in 1991, Serbia and Montenegro formed the Federal Republic of Yugoslavia, declared on 27 April 1992.

Montenegro's desire for independence led in 2002 to an EU-brokered agreement between the leaders of Serbia, Montenegro and the Federal Republic of Yugoslavia that restructured the republic into a union of two semi-independent states, named Serbia and Montenegro, with effect from March 2003. The agreement provided for the two republics to hold referendums on whether to retain or end the union after a minimum of three years. In a referendum held in Montenegro on 21 May 2006, 55.5 per cent voted in favour of independence, which was declared on 3 June and acknowledged by Serbia on 5 June. Montenegro joined the UN in June 2006, and formally applied for EU membership in 2008.

In December 2012, Milo Djukanovic became prime minister for the seventh time. He claimed victory in the October 2016 legislative elections but resigned nine days later, alleging a foreign power had been involved in a plot to seize power on election day. He was replaced by his deputy, Dusko Markovic. Djukanovic returned to win the 2018 presidential elections on a pro-EU platform, replacing Filip Vujanovic.

Under the 2007 constitution, the president is directly elected for a five-year term, which is renewable once. The unicameral Assembly of the Republic of Montenegro has 81 members directly elected for a four-year term; five members are elected from the ethnic Albanian community. The prime minister appoints the cabinet, subject to the approval of the assembly.

HEAD OF STATE
President, Milo Djukanovic, *elected* 15 April 2018, *sworn in* 20 May 2018

SELECTED GOVERNMENT MEMBERS *AS AT JUNE 2018*
Prime Minister, Dusko Markovic
Deputy Prime Ministers, Zoran Pazin *(Justice);* Rafet Husovic; Milutin Simovic
Defence, Predrag Boskovic
Foreign Affairs, Srdan Darmanovic

EMBASSY OF MONTENEGRO
47 De Vere Gardens, London W8 5AW
T 020-3302 7227 E unitedkingdom@mfa.gov.me
Ambassador Extraordinary and Plenipotentiary, HE Borislav Banovic, *apptd* 2016

BRITISH EMBASSY
Ulcinjska 8, Gorica C, 81000 Podgorica
T (+382) (20) 618 010 E podgorica@fco.gov.uk
W www.gov.uk/government/world/montenegro
Ambassador Extraordinary and Plenipotentiary, HE Alison Kemp, *apptd* 2017

ECONOMY AND TRADE

Montenegro achieved fiscal autonomy from the Yugoslav federation in the 1990s. However, it faced the same problems as Serbia – slow growth, foreign debt, lack of foreign investment, high unemployment, corruption and organised crime – as well as having more limited health and education facilities, and a poor administrative capacity. Since independence, it has pursued international integration and privatisation, prioritising in particular its bid for EU membership. Negotiations for membership began in 2012, and although it uses the euro as its domestic currency, it is not officially a member of the euro zone. It has privatised roughly

90 per cent of state-owned companies, and plans to better utilise its abundance of hydropower with the aim of becoming a net exporter of energy. Infrastructure spending has added to high public debt, but significant foreign investment in tourism, which accounts for 20 per cent of GDP, is set to strengthen the economy following the completion of several luxury complexes.

The main agricultural products are tobacco, citrus fruits and olives. Major industrial activities include production of steel, aluminium and consumer goods, processing of agricultural products and tourism. The main trading partners are EU and other Balkan countries.

GNI – US$4.6bn; US$7,350 per capita (2017)
Annual average growth of GDP – 3.0 per cent (2017 est)
Inflation rate – 2.1 per cent (2017 est)
Population below poverty line – 8.6 per cent (2013 est)
Unemployment – 17.1 per cent (2016 est)
Total external debt – US$1.576bn (2014 est)
Imports – US$2,283m (2016)
Exports – US$361m (2016)

BALANCE OF PAYMENTS
Trade – US$1,922m deficit (2016)
Current Account – US$881m deficit (2017)

Trade with UK	2016	2017
Imports from UK	£16,184,992	£13,633,974
Exports to UK	£3,776,189	£10,663,550

COMMUNICATIONS
Airports and waterways – There are five airports, including international airports at Podgorica and Tivat; the major seaport is located at Bar
Roadways and railways – 5,365km of roadways; 250km of railway track linking the Adriatic port of Bar with Belgrade, via Podgorica
Telecommunications – 148,015 fixed lines and 1 million mobile subscriptions (2016); there were 450,422 internet users in 2016
Internet code and IDD – me; 382 (from UK), 44 (to UK)
Major broadcasters – The state-funded TV Montenegro and Radio Montenegro operate national stations
Press – Leading national papers include *Vijesti, Pobjeda, Republika* and *Dan*
WPFI score – 31,21 (103)

MOROCCO

Al-Mamlakah al-Maghribiyah – Kingdom of Morocco

Area – 446,550 sq. km
Capital – Rabat; population, 1,847,000 (2018 est)
Major cities – Agadir, Casablanca, Fez, Marrakesh, Meknes, Tangier

Currency – Dirham (DH) of 100 centimes
Population – 33,986,655 rising at 0.45 per cent a year (2017 est); Arab–Berber (99 per cent) (est)
Religion – Muslim 99 per cent (predominantly Sunni) (2001 est)
Language – Arabic (official), French, Berber dialects
Population density – 80 per sq. km (2016)
Urban population – 62.5 per cent (2018 est)
Median age (years) – 28.9 (2016 est)
National anthem – 'Hymne Chérifien' 'Hymn of the Sharif'
National day – 30 July (Throne Day)
Death penalty – Retained (last used 1993)
CPI score – 40 (81)
Military expenditure – US$3,461m (2017)

CLIMATE AND TERRAIN
Fertile coastal plains in the west rise to a mountainous centre, with ranges, including the Atlas range, running north-east to south-west. The Rif mountains lie along the northern, Mediterranean coast. Elevation extremes range from 4,165m (Jebel Toubkal) to −55m (Sebkha Tah). The climate is Mediterranean, becoming more extreme in the interior. Average temperatures range from 9.9°C in January to 26.8°C in July, although summer temperatures in the desert can reach over 40°C.

HISTORY AND POLITICS
From the tenth century BC, the northern coast was settled by the Phoenicians. Morocco was part of the Roman Empire from the first century AD until it was invaded by first the Vandals and then the Visigoths in the fifth and sixth centuries. Arab conquest of the area began in the seventh century but Morocco was independent from about the ninth century, successfully resisting inclusion in the Ottoman Empire in the 16th century. The current Alawite dynasty was founded in the mid-17th century. Morocco remained isolated until the mid-19th century, when the country opened up to European trade. The subsequent growth in Spanish and French influence resulted in its partition into two protectorates from 1912. In the Second World War, Morocco was a base for the Allied offensives that drove German forces out of North Africa.

Nationalist campaigning for independence began in the 1940s. French and Spanish forces withdrew in 1956, leaving Morocco independent under Sultan Mohammed V, who adopted the title of king in 1957; the coastal towns of Ceuta and Melilla remain under Spanish control. King Hassan II, who ruled from 1961 to 1999, annexed the mineral-rich Western Sahara region in 1975.

Since the accession of King Mohammed VI in 1999, Morocco has been moving away from absolute monarchy, increasing civil liberties and addressing human rights issues. Pro-reform demonstrations in spring 2011 led to a referendum in July in which an overwhelming majority voted in favour of constitutional changes that would make the prime minister, rather than the king, the head of government.

In the October 2016 legislative election the Justice and Development Party (PJD) remained the largest party in the House of Representatives, but was unable to secure a ruling coalition with other parties. In March 2017 after five months of deadlock, the king replaced Prime Minister Abdelilah Benkirane and asked Saad-Eddine El Othmani, also of the PJD, to form a government.

The head of state is a hereditary constitutional monarch. The king appoints the prime minister, who appoints the members of the council of ministers. There is a bicameral legislature; the lower house, the House of Representatives *(Majlis al-Nuwab)* has 395 members who are directly elected for a five-year term. The House of Councillors *(Majlis al-Mustasharin)* has 120 members, elected by local councils, professional organisations and labour unions to serve a six-year term.

HEAD OF STATE
HM The King of Morocco, King Mohammed VI (Sidi Mohammed Ben Hassan), *born* 21 August 1963, *acceded* 23 July 1999, *crowned* 30 July 1999
Heir, HRH Crown Prince Moulay Hassan, *born* 2003

SELECTED GOVERNMENT MEMBERS *AS AT JUNE 2018*
Prime Minister, Saad-Eddine El Othmani
Economy and Finance, Mohamed Boussaid
Foreign Affairs, Nasser Bourita
Interior, Abdelouafi Laftit

EMBASSY OF THE KINGDOM OF MOROCCO
49 Queen's Gate Gardens, London SW7 5NE
T 020-7581 5001 E ambalondres@maec.gov.ma
W www.moroccanembassylondon.org.uk
Ambassador Extraordinary and Plenipotentiary, HE Abdesselam Aboudrar, *apptd* 2016

BRITISH EMBASSY
28 Avenue SAR Sidi Mohammed, Souissi 10105 (BP45), Rabat
T (+212) (0) 537 633 333 E rabat.consular@fco.gov.uk
W www.gov.uk/government/world/morocco
Ambassador Extraordinary and Plenipotentiary, HE Thomas Reilly, *apptd* 2017

ECONOMY AND TRADE
Economic liberalisation since 1999 has attracted foreign direct investment, and the industrial and service sectors are being developed. Despite steady growth, Morocco remains a poor country, with unemployment at around 10 per cent despite poverty-alleviation programmes. The remittances of expatriate workers are crucial to the domestic economy but these, along with tourism and export demand, declined in 2008–9 owing to the global downturn. Unemployment, poverty and illiteracy remain high in rural areas. The government has stabilised the country's finances by decreasing debt and reducing fuel subsidies. Investment in new ports and industrial infrastructure are improving the nation's competitiveness, while expanding renewable energy production is a government priority.

The large agrarian sector generates 14.8 per cent of GDP and engages 39.1 per cent of the workforce, producing cereals, citrus fruits, vegetables, wine, olives and livestock. It faces environmental problems such as desertification and soil erosion. Another major sector is the exploitation of mineral reserves, especially phosphate. Other industries include food processing, automotive parts, textiles, leather goods and tourism. Industry accounts for 29.1 per cent of GDP and services for 56 per cent.

The main trading partners are EU countries, especially France and Spain. Principal exports are textiles, automobiles, electrical components, inorganic chemicals, transistors, crude minerals, fertilisers, petroleum products, fruit and vegetables. The main imports are crude petroleum, fabrics, telecommunications equipment, wheat, gas and electricity.
GNI – US$103.9bn; US$2,863 per capita (2017; includes Western Sahara)
Annual average growth of GDP – 4.8 per cent (2017 est)
Inflation rate – 0.9 per cent (2017 est)
Population below poverty line – 15 per cent (2007 est)
Unemployment – 9.3 per cent (2017 est)
Total external debt – US$45.72bn (2017 est)
Imports – US$37,513m (2015)
Exports – US$21,886m (2015)

BALANCE OF PAYMENTS
Trade – US$15,627m deficit (2015)
Current Account – US$3,850m deficit (2017)

Trade with UK	2016	2017
Imports from UK	£838,982,840	£771,293,838
Exports to UK	£970,982,538	£683,821,041

COMMUNICATIONS
Airports and waterways – The principal airports are at Rabat, Agadir, Casablanca and Marrakesh; the main ports are Tangier, Casablanca and Agadir, on the Atlantic coast
Roadways and railways – There are 41,116km of roadways, including 1,080km of motorways, and 2,067km of railways
Telecommunications – 2 million fixed lines and 41.5 million mobile subscriptions (2016); there were 19.6 million internet users in 2016
Internet code and IDD – ma; 212 (from UK), 44 (to UK)
Major broadcasters – The government owns Radio-Télévision Marocaine and has a stake in 2M, the other main television network
Press – There are a number of daily newspapers, including the semi-official *Le Matin* (French language), *Al-Massae* and *Assabah* (both Arabic language)
WPFI score – 43,13 (135)

EDUCATION AND HEALTH
Education is compulsory between the ages of six and 15.
Literacy rate – 83.2 per cent (2015 est)
Gross enrolment ratio (percentage of relevant age group) – primary 114.7 per cent (2015 est), secondary 69 per cent (2012 est), tertiary 32 per cent (2016 est)
Health expenditure (per capita) – US$190 (2014)
Hospital beds (per 1,000 people) – 1.1 (2014)
Life expectancy (years) – 77.1 (2017 est)
Mortality rate – 4.9 (2017 est)
Birth rate – 17.7 (2017 est)
Infant mortality rate – 21.9 (2017 est)
HIV/AIDS adult prevalence – 0.1 per cent (2016 est)

WESTERN SAHARA
Al-Jumhuriyya al-'Arabiyya as-Sahrawiyya ad-Dimuqratiyya – *Sahrawi Arab Democratic Republic*
Area – 266,000 sq. km. Neighbours: Morocco (north), Algeria (north-east), Mauritania (east and south)
Administrative centre – El-Aaiun (Laayoune); population, 232,000 (2018)
Population – 603,253 rising at 2.70 per cent a year (2017 est)
Religion – Muslim (99 per cent) (est)
Language – Hassaniyya Arabic, Moroccan Arabic
Urban population – 80.9 per cent (2015 est)
Median age (years) – 21.1 (2016 est)
Flag – Three horizontal stripes of black, white and green with a red crescent and a five-pointed star in the centre and a red triangle based on the hoist
Western Sahara came under Spanish rule in 1884, and became a province in 1934. Following Spain's withdrawal in 1976, Morocco and Mauritania annexed the territory and divided it between them. The Polisario Front declared Western Sahara's independence as the Sahrawi Arab Democratic Republic in 1976, and began a guerrilla war to win the territory, setting up a government in exile. In 1979, Mauritania withdrew from its part of the territory, which was annexed by Morocco.

A ceasefire was established in 1991 following both sides' agreement in 1988 to UN proposals for a peace settlement, which included holding a referendum on the future status of

Western Sahara. But the precise terms of the referendum have proved a sticking point and an impasse was reached that has still not been overcome, despite further negotiations in 2001–4; Polisario agreed to a referendum offering the options of independence, semi-autonomy or integration for Western Sahara, but Morocco is only prepared to accept semi-autonomy or integration. Talks have taken place intermittently since 2007 but have made no progress; in March 2017, UN Secretary-General António Guterres called for a restart to talks.

MOZAMBIQUE

Republica de Mocambique – Republic of Mozambique

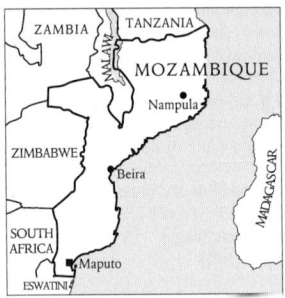

Area – 799,380 sq. km
Capital – Maputo; population, 1,102,000 (2018 est)
Major cities – Beira, Chimoio, Matola, Nampula
Currency – New metical (MT) of 100 centavos
Population – 26,573,706 rising at 2.46 per cent a year (2017 est)
Religion – Christian (Roman Catholic 28.4 per cent, Zionist Christian 15.5 per cent, Protestant 12.2 per cent), Muslim 17.9 per cent (2007 est)
Language – Portuguese (official), Emakhuwa, Xichangana, Elomwe, Cisena, Echuwabo
Population density – 38 per sq. km (2016)
Urban population – 36 per cent (2018 est)
Median age (years) – 17.1 (2016)
National anthem – 'Patria Amada' 'Beloved Fatherland'
National day – 25 June (Independence Day)
Death penalty – Abolished for all crimes (since 1990)
CPI score – 25 (153)
Military expenditure – US$102.6m (2017)
Conscription – 18–35 years of age; 24 months (selective)
Literacy rate – 76.7 per cent (2015 est)
Gross enrolment ratio (percentage of relevant age group) – primary 105.8 per cent, secondary 32.4 per cent (2015 est), tertiary 7 per cent (2016 est)
Health expenditure (per capita) – US$42 (2014)
Hospital beds (per 1,000 people) – 0.7 (2011)
Life expectancy (years) – 53.7 (2017 est)
Mortality rate – 11.6 (2017 est)
Birth rate – 38.1 (2017 est)
Infant mortality rate – 65.9 (2017 est)
HIV/AIDS adult prevalence – 12.3 per cent (2016 est)

CLIMATE AND TERRAIN

Coastal plains rise to plateaus in the centre and west, with mountains on the western borders. Elevation extremes range from 2,436m (Mt Binga) to 0m (Indian Ocean). A number of rivers run from the western highlands to the Indian Ocean coast, including the Zambezi, Limpopo, Save and Ruvuma. The climate is tropical, with average temperatures in Maputo ranging from 19.9°C in July to 26.6°C in November.

HISTORY AND POLITICS

Between the first and fourth centuries Mozambique was settled by Bantu peoples. Trade with India and the Arabian peninsula grew and migrants from both these regions settled in the coastal areas. From the 16th century the Portuguese established settlements on the coast and along the Zambezi, trading in gold, ivory, spices and slaves, and in the late 19th century they succeeded in conquering the interior. The area was administered as part of Portuguese India from 1751, becoming a separate colony in the late 19th century and an overseas province of Portugal in 1951. Concessions to private companies that had operated as *de facto* rulers over much of the country were ended in 1930.

The *Frente de Libertacao de Mocambique* (Frelimo) was founded in 1962 to fight for independence, and a ten-year guerrilla war against Portuguese forces began in 1964. Independence was achieved in 1975, when a one-party socialist republic was set up. Opposition to this was led from 1977 by the *Resistencia Nacional de Mocambique* (Renamo) and a brutal civil war broke out that lasted until 1992. Mozambique joined the Commonwealth in 1995; although it had never been under British rule, it has close relationships and a shared experience with its neighbours, all former British colonies. Reconstruction of the economy and infrastructure progressed quickly after the civil war, although a series of natural catastrophes since 2000, high HIV/AIDS infection rates and remaining civil war landmines have slowed progress.

In 1990 Frelimo abandoned Marxist-Leninism and ended one-party rule, introducing a multiparty system. The first elections under the new constitution were held in 1994 and won by Frelimo. Frelimo retained power in the 1999, 2004 and 2009 elections, prompting allegations of vote-rigging by Renamo. The October 2014 presidential elections were won by Filipe Nyusi of the Frelimo party; Frelimo also won the simultaneous legislative election, retaining an overall majority despite losing seats.

Under the 2004 constitution, the executive president is directly elected for a five-year term, renewable once. The unicameral Assembly of the Republic has 250 members, who are directly elected for a five-year term. The president appoints the prime minister and the council of ministers.

HEAD OF STATE
President, C-in-C of the Armed Forces, Filipe Jacinto Nyusi, *elected* 24 October 2014; *sworn in* 15 January 2015

SELECTED GOVERNMENT MEMBERS *AS AT JUNE 2018*
Prime Minister, Carlos Agostinho Do Rosario
Economy and Finance, Adriano Afonso Maleiane
Foreign Affairs, Jose Condugua Antonio Pacheco
Interior, Jaime Basilio Monteiro

HIGH COMMISSION FOR THE REPUBLIC OF MOZAMBIQUE
21 Fitzroy Square, London W1T 6EL
T 020-7383 3800 E sectorconsular@mozambiquehc.co.uk
W www.mozambiquehighcommission.org.uk
High Commissioner, HE Filipe Chidumo, *apptd* 2015

BRITISH HIGH COMMISSION
Avenida Vladmir Lenine, 310 Maputo City, Maputo, PO Box 55
T (+258) (21) 356 000 E maputo.consularenquiries@fco.gov.uk
W www.gov.uk/government/world/mozambique
High Commissioner, HE Joanna Kuenssberg, *apptd* 2014

ECONOMY AND TRADE

Political stability and economic liberalisation have attracted foreign direct investment and donor support, and achieved economic growth despite setbacks from devastating flooding (2000, 2001, 2007, 2008, 2010, 2015), droughts (2002, 2003, 2009, 2010, 2016) and an earthquake (2006). But the country remains dependent on foreign aid, with almost half of the population living below the poverty line. The huge foreign debt has been reduced to a more manageable size by debt cancellation and rescheduling, but there is a substantial ongoing trade imbalance. Growth slowed in 2016 and Mozambique defaulted on its sovereign bond repayment in January 2017, reflecting the country's major liquidity risks.

Agriculture and forestry are the mainstays of the economy, accounting for 22.3 per cent of GDP and engaging about 74.4 per cent of the workforce; shellfish, cashew nuts, cotton, sugar, citrus fruits and timber are important exports. There are considerable oil, gas, mineral and hydroelectric power resources, which are increasingly being exploited. Industries include aluminium, titanium, petroleum products, natural gas extraction, chemicals, food processing, cement, glass and textiles. Exploitation of natural gas reserves by international consortiums is expected to generate billions for government revenue after 2022. Industry generates 23 per cent of GDP and services 54.7 per cent.

The main trading partners are South Africa, India and China. The country also benefits from trade with its landlocked neighbours. Principal exports are aluminium, agricultural products, timber and electricity. The main imports are machinery, vehicles, fuel, chemicals, metal products, foodstuffs and textiles.

GNI – US$12.3bn; US$420 per capita (2017)
Annual average growth of GDP – 4.7 per cent (2017 est)
Inflation rate – 17.5 per cent (2017 est)
Population below poverty line – 46.1 per cent (2015 est)
Total external debt – US$10.27bn (2017 est)
Imports – US$5,295m (2016)
Exports – US$3,355m (2016)

BALANCE OF PAYMENTS

Trade – US$1,940m deficit (2016)
Current Account – US$2,557m deficit (2017)

Trade with UK	2016	2017
Imports from UK	£13,397,861	£21,996,928
Exports to UK	£69,255,687	£82,057,425

COMMUNICATIONS

Airports and waterways – The principal airports are at Maputo and Beira, with 19 other airports around the country; the main seaports are Maputo, Beira and Nacala, which also handle trade for neighbouring countries
Roadways and railways – There are 6,303km of roadways and 4,787km of railways
Telecommunications – 82,421 fixed lines and 15 million mobile subscriptions (2016); there were 4.5 million internet users in 2016
Internet code and IDD – mz; 258 (from UK), 44 (to UK)
Major broadcasters – Televisao de Mozambique (TVM) is the state-run television broadcaster; Radio Mozambique and Radio Cidade are the public radio broadcasters
Press – Leading national dailies include *Diario de Mocambique, O Pais* and *Noticias* (partly state owned)
WPFI score – 31,12 (99)

MYANMAR

Pyidaungzu Thammada Myanma Naingngandaw – Republic of the Union of Myanmar

Area – 676,578 sq. km
Capital – Yangon (Rangoon); population, 5,157,000 (2018 est)
Major cities – Bago, Mandalay, Mawlamyine (Moulmein), Pathein (Bassein)
Currency – Kyat (K) of 100 pyas
Population – 56,890,418 rising at 1 per cent a year (2016 est); Burman (68 per cent), Shan (9 per cent), Karen (7 per cent), Rakhine (4 per cent), Chinese (3 per cent), Indian (2 per cent), Mon (2 per cent) (est)
Religion – Buddhist 87.9 per cent, Christian 6.2 per cent, Muslim 4.3 per cent (2014 est)
Language – Burmese (official), numerous ethnic languages
Population density – 82 per sq. km (2016)
Urban population – 30.6 per cent (2018 est)
Median age (years) – 28.2 (2017 est)
National anthem – 'Kaba Ma Kyei' 'Till the End of the World, Myanmar'
National day – 4 January (Independence Day)
Death penalty – Retained (last used in the 1980s)
CPI score – 30 (130)
Military expenditure – US$2,193m (2015 est)

CLIMATE AND TERRAIN

Central lowlands are ringed by mountains in the west, north (part of the foothills of the Himalayas) and east. The eastern range extends down the Kra isthmus that Myanmar shares with Thailand, forming a natural border. Elevation extremes range from 5,870m (Gamlang Razi) to 0m (Andaman Sea). The lowlands are drained by the Irrawaddy river and its chief tributary, the Chindwin, and the eastern mountains by the Salween. The Irrawaddy has a large delta on the Andaman coast. The climate is tropical, with a wet season from May to September. Average temperatures in Mandalay, representative of the interior lowlands, range from 18.4°C in January to 25.2°C in April and May, although temperatures in the interior can reach 44°C in May.

POLITICS

Under the 2010 constitution, the head of state is a president elected by the legislature for a five-year term, renewable once. The president is also head of government and appoints ministers with the approval of the legislature. The bicameral People's Assembly comprises the 440-member House of Representatives, the lower chamber, and the 224-member House of Nationalities. In each chamber, 25 per cent of seats are reserved for the military and the rest are directly elected; both chambers serve a five-year term. Constitutional changes require approval by a 75 per cent majority.

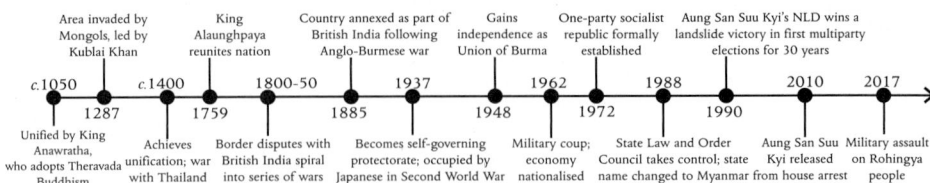

Area invaded by Mongols, led by Kublai Khan — King Alaungphaya reunites nation — Country annexed as part of British India following Anglo-Burmese war — Gains independence as Union of Burma — One-party socialist republic formally established — Aung San Suu Kyi's NLD wins a landslide victory in first multiparty elections for 30 years

c.1050   c.1400   1800-50   1937   1962   1988   2010   2017

1287   1759   1885   1948   1972   1990

Unified by King Anawratha, who adopts Theravada Buddhism — Achieves unification; war with Thailand — Border disputes with British India spiral into series of wars — Becomes self-governing protectorate; occupied by Japanese in Second World War — Military coup; economy nationalised — State Law and Order Council takes control; state name changed to Myanmar — Aung San Suu Kyi released from house arrest — Military assault on Rohingya people

In preparation for legislative elections in late 2010, several electoral laws were introduced in March 2010; these excluded many political activists, such as Aung San Suu Kyi, from participation in the elections, set restrictive conditions for party registration, and tightly regulated campaigning and funding; the National League for Democracy (NLD) announced a boycott of the elections. Several members of the government resigned their military commissions to contest the elections as civilians, registering a new political party, the Union Solidarity and Development Party (USDP).

In November 2010, the USDP won 259 of the seats in the lower chamber and 129 of the seats in the upper chamber in elections that opposition groups claimed were fraudulent and were condemned internationally as a sham. The new legislature convened in January 2011, electing prime minister Thein Sein as president in February 2011. A new, nominally civilian government was sworn in on 30 March, and the dissolution of the State Peace and Development Council was announced. In April 2012, the NLD, led by Aung San Suu Kyi, contested 44 of the 46 seats in the lower house by-elections, winning 43 of them. In November 2015 general elections, the NLD won a landslide 135 seats in the upper house and 255 seats in the lower house. Suu Kyi was ineligible to run for the presidency as both her sons have British nationality; Htin Kyaw was elected president in March 2016, and was replaced by Suu Kyi ally Win Myint in March 2018. In April 2018, Suu Kyi freed 113 political prisoners in her first act as 'state counsellor', a position comparable to prime minister, but her subsequent refusal to condemn the violence against the Rohingya alienated most of her western supporters.

HEAD OF STATE

President, Chair of National Defence and Security Council, Win Myint *sworn in* 30 March 2018
First Vice-President, Myint Swe
Second Vice-President, Henry Van Thio

SELECTED GOVERNMENT MEMBERS *AS AT SEPTEMBER 2018*
Defence, Lt. Gen. Sein Win
Home Affairs, Kyaw Swe
State Counsellor, Foreign Affairs, Aung San Suu Kyi

EMBASSY OF THE REPUBLIC OF THE UNION OF MYANMAR
19A Charles Street, London W1J 5DX
T 020-7499 4340
E ambassadoroffice@myanmarembassylondon.com
W www.myanmarembassylondon.com
Ambassador Extraordinary and Plenipotentiary, HE U. Kyaw Zwar Minn, *apptd* 2013

BRITISH EMBASSY
80 Strand Road (Box 638), Rangoon
T (+95) (1) 370 865 E be.rangoon@fco.gov.uk
W www.gov.uk/government/world/burma
Ambassador Extraordinary and Plenipotentiary, HE Daniel Chugg, *apptd* 2018

INSURGENCIES
Since independence in 1948 there have been various insurgencies, mostly by ethnic groups. These have included the Kachin, Kayin (Karen), Karenni, Wa, Shan, Mon, Arakan Chin and Kokang ethnic minorities. Since 1992, 18 ethnic groups have signed ceasefire agreements; the government is accused of breaking four of these since the November 2010 election. Some groups have achieved a degree of autonomy in their region; others have splintered, creating intra-ethnic tension. In October 2015 the government signed a ceasefire agreement with eight rebel groups, though seven other major insurgent groups refused to sign. The country's ethnic minorities are believed to bear the brunt of the government's human rights abuses, with the Muslim Rohingya of western Burma considered one of the most oppressed peoples in the world. Since August 2017, nearly 700,000 Rohingya have fled Rakhine province and an estimated 25,000 people have been killed, in what the UN described as a 'genocide' and 'a textbook example of ethnic cleansing'.

ECONOMY AND TRADE
Myanmar has fertile soil, occupies strategic trade routes between India, China and South East Asia, and has an abundance of natural resources such as natural gas (Asia's largest exporter), timber (the world's largest exporter of teak), precious gems (jade, pearls, rubies and sapphires) and oil, but the economy is characterised by mismanagement and corruption. The country became increasingly poverty-stricken under military rule and over a quarter of people live below the poverty line. The economy suffers from unpredictable policies, market distortions, insurgencies and ethnic violence, and inadequate commercial, transport and energy infrastructure. The regime's repressiveness lost it development aid and attracted economic and trade sanctions, but since the transition to a civil-led government in 2011 the nation has sought global economic reintegration. Myanmar formed a common market with the other members of the Association of Southeast Asian Nations (ASEAN) in 2015. Sanctions imposed by the US were lifted in 2016 and subsequent reforms have intended to make foreign investment easier, while Aung San Suu Kyi has attempted to modernise the nation's agriculture, banking and energy. There is a large grey economy and considerable unofficial cross-border trade. The impact of military operations which caused over 671,000 Rohingya to flee the country is yet unclear.

Agriculture is the dominant economic activity, accounting for 24.8 per cent of GDP and engaging roughly 70 per cent of the workforce; the most important export crops are rice, pulses, beans and fish. The main industries are forestry, mining and oil and gas extraction, and these have attracted some foreign investment; manufacturing and services are struggling, but the growing tourist industry failed decline despite the Rohingya humanitarian crisis in 2017–8. Industry contributes 35.4 per cent of GDP and services 39.9 per cent.

The main trading partners are China (36.5 per cent of exports; 31.4 per cent of imports), Thailand, Singapore and India. Principal exports are natural gas, wood products, agricultural produce, clothing and gems. The main imports are fabric, petroleum products, fertiliser, plastics, machinery, transport equipment, construction materials and food.

GNI – US$63.5bn; US$1,190 per capita (2017)
Annual average growth of GDP – 8.1 per cent (2016)
Inflation rate – 7 per cent (2016 est)
Population below poverty line – 32.7 per cent (2007 est)
Unemployment – 4.8 per cent (2016 est)
Total external debt – US$9.041bn (2016 est)
Imports – US$16,844m (2016)
Exports – US$11,432m (2016)

BALANCE OF PAYMENTS
Trade – US$5,412m deficit (2016)
Current Account – US$3,945m deficit (2017)

Trade with UK	2016	2017
Imports from UK	£32,298,603	£30,099,172
Exports to UK	£147,175,607	£217,278,563

COMMUNICATIONS
Airports and waterways – The main airports are at Yangon and Mandalay; the 12,800km of navigable waterways include the Irrawaddy and Chindwin rivers, and the chief seaports are Yangon (Rangoon), Mawlamyine (Moulmein) and Akyab (Sittwe)
Roadways and railways – 34,377km; 5,031km
Telecommunications – 514,385 fixed lines and 50.6 million mobile subscriptions (2016); there were 14.3 million internet users in 2016
Internet code and IDD – mm; 95 (from UK), 44 (to UK)
Major broadcasters – Democratic Voice of Burma, an opposition radio station broadcasting via short-wave from Norway, and foreign services such as the BBC and Voice of America, are key sources of information for the population; TV Myanmar is the state-run national broadcaster
Press – Leading dailies include the state-run *Kyehmon* and *Myanmar Alin;* legislation increasing journalistic freedom was passed in 2014
WPFI score – 43,15 (137)

EDUCATION AND HEALTH
Literacy rate – 96.3 per cent (2015 est)
Gross enrolment ratio (percentage of relevant age group) – primary 112 per cent, secondary 61 per cent, tertiary 16 per cent (2017 est)
Health expenditure (per capita) – US$20 (2014)
Hospital beds (per 1,000 people) – 0.9 (2012)
Life expectancy (years) – 68.2 (2017 est)
Mortality rate – 7.4 (2017 est)
Birth rate – 18.1 (2017 est)
Infant mortality rate – 35.8 (2017 est)
HIV/AIDS adult prevalence – 0.8 per cent (2016 est)

NAMIBIA

Republic of Namibia

Area – 824,292 sq. km
Capital – Windhoek; population, 404,000 (2018 est)
Major towns – Oshakati, Rundu, Walvis Bay
Currency – Namibian dollar of 100 cents, at parity with South African rand
Population – 2,484,780 rising at 1.95 per cent a year (2017 est); Ovambo (50 per cent), Kavangos (9 per cent), Damara (7 per cent), Herero (7 per cent) Nama (5 per cent), Caprivian (4 per cent), San (Bushmen) (3 per cent), Baster (2 per cent) (est)
Religion – Christian 80–90 per cent (at least 50 per cent Lutheran), indigenous beliefs 10–20 per cent
Language – English (official), Afrikaans (lingua franca), Oshiwambo, Herero, Nama, other indigenous languages
Population density – 3 per sq. km (2016)
Urban population – 50 per cent (2018 est)
Median age (years) – 21 (2016 est)
National anthem – 'Namibia, Land of the Brave'
National day – 21 March (Independence Day)
Death penalty – Abolished for all crimes (since 1990)
CPI score – 51 (53)
Military expenditure – US$434m (2017 est)
Literacy rate – 89.9 per cent (2015 est)
Gross enrolment ratio (percentage of relevant age group) – primary 111.4 per cent (2013 est)
Health expenditure (per capita) – US$499 (2014)
Hospital beds (per 1,000 people) – 2.7 (2009)
Life expectancy (years) – 64 (2017 est)
Mortality rate – 7.9 (2017 est)
Birth rate – 27.3 (2017 est)
Infant mortality rate – 35.1 (2017 est)
HIV/AIDS adult prevalence – 13.8 per cent (2016)

CLIMATE AND TERRAIN
The Namib desert runs along the Atlantic coast and is separated by a line of hills and high veldt from the Kalahari desert in the interior. Elevation extremes range from 2,606m (Konigstein) to 0m (Atlantic Ocean). Major rivers include the Orange, which forms the southern border with South Africa, and the Zambezi, which runs through the Caprivi Strip in the extreme north-east of the country. The climate is arid in the west and semi-arid in the centre and north-east; rainfall is sparse and droughts are frequent. The coast is cooler and frequently foggy. Average temperatures range from 14.9°C in July to 24.4°C in January.

HISTORY AND POLITICS
Pre-colonial Namibia was inhabited by San and then by Bantu tribes. It was annexed by Germany in 1884 and named South West Africa. Indigenous uprisings against colonial settlement in the early 20th century were brutally suppressed, with some tribes suffering severe losses; the Herero and Nama were nearly wiped out. The territory was occupied by South Africa on

behalf of the Allies in 1915 and after the First World War it became a League of Nations mandated territory, administered by South Africa.

The arrangement continued under the UN after the Second World War, but South Africa exceeded its mandate by effectively annexing the country, extending representation in the South African parliament to the white population in 1949, and applying apartheid in 1966. These actions were taken despite the UN's refusal to permit the country's incorporation into South Africa in 1946 and its termination of the mandate in 1966. In 1968, the UN changed the country's name to Namibia, and the South West Africa People's Organisation (SWAPO), which had campaigned for racial equality and independence since 1960, began a guerrilla war against South Africa.

South Africa's peace talks with Angola in 1988 led to agreement on independence for Namibia, and this was achieved on 21 March 1990; South Africa's Walvis Bay enclave was returned to Namibia in 1994.

The country has enjoyed stability since independence, apart from a brief period of secessionist violence in the Caprivi Strip in the late 1990s, and has been recognised by observers as having one of the freest media industries in Africa. Following agitation for an acceleration of land reform, the government programme moved from voluntary sales to expropriation of white-owned farms in 2005. The country's main problems arise from the demographic, economic and social impact of the high level of HIV/AIDS infection among the population.

SWAPO has been the dominant party since independence, holding the presidency and commanding a parliamentary majority without interruption. The November 2014 presidential election was won by Hage Geingob of SWAPO, who collected 86.7 per cent of the vote; SWAPO retained its large majority in the simultaneous legislative election.

Under the 1990 constitution, the executive president is directly elected for a five-year term, renewable once. There is a bicameral parliament consisting of a National Assembly, with 96 members directly elected for a five-year term and eight additional non-voting members appointed by the president, and a National Council, whose 42 members are elected by the regional councils from among their own members for a five-year term; the latter's main function is to review and consider legislation from the lower chamber. The president appoints the prime minister and the other ministers.

HEAD OF STATE
President, Hage Geingob, *elected* 28 November 2014, *sworn in* 21 March 2015
Vice-President, Nangolo Mbumba

SELECTED GOVERNMENT MEMBERS *AS AT JUNE 2018*
Prime Minister, Saara Kuugongelwa-Amadhila
Deputy Prime Minister, Netumbo Nandi-Ndaitwah
Defence, Penda Ya Ndakolo
Finance, Calle Schlettwein

HIGH COMMISSION FOR THE REPUBLIC OF NAMIBIA
6 Chandos Street, London W1G 9LU
T 020-7636 6244 E info@namibiahc.org.uk
W www.namibiahc.org.uk
High Commissioner, HE Steve Vemunavi Katjiuanjo, *apptd* 2013

BRITISH HIGH COMMISSION
116 Robert Mugabe Avenue, PO Box 22202, Windhoek
T (+264) (61) 274 800 E general.windhoek@fco.gov.uk
W www.gov.uk/government/world/namibia
High Commissioner, HE Kate Airey, OBE, *apptd* 2018

ECONOMY AND TRADE

Despite a high GDP per capita, Namibia has high levels of poverty and inequality, and very high unemployment. Its arid terrain limits agriculture, but the emphasis on environmental protection (enshrined in the constitution) is helping the development of tourism. The country has rich mineral deposits; extraction of these is the main industrial activity and minerals account for over 50 per cent of foreign exchange earnings. One of the world's largest producers of uranium, extraction at the Chinese-owned Husab mine is expected to reach full capacity in late 2018. This leaves the economy vulnerable to global price fluctuations, and the government is encouraging foreign investment to help diversification. Other industries process the products of the farming and fisheries sectors. Agriculture operates mostly at subsistence level, accounting for 6.6 per cent of GDP and engages 31 per cent of the workforce.

The main trading partners are South Africa (27.1 per cent of exports and 61.4 per cent of imports), Botswana and Switzerland. Principal exports are diamonds, copper, gold, zinc, lead, uranium and fish. The main imports are foodstuffs (particularly grain), petroleum products and fuel, machinery and equipment, and chemicals.

GNI – US$11.6bn; US$4,600 per capita (2017)
Annual average growth of GDP – −0.8 per cent (2017 est)
Inflation rate – 6.0 per cent (2017 est)
Population below poverty line – 28.7 per cent (2010 est)
Unemployment – 28.1 per cent (2016 est)
Total external debt – US$7.489bn (2017 est)
Imports – US$6,776m (2016)
Exports – US$4,809m (2016)

BALANCE OF PAYMENTS
Trade – US$1,967m deficit (2016)
Current Account – US$435m deficit (2017)

Trade with UK	2016	2017
Imports from UK	£30,460,603	£42,736,965
Exports to UK	£28,897,148	£29,846,503

COMMUNICATIONS

Airports and waterways – The main airports are at Windhoek and Odangwa, with 17 smaller airports around the country; the two main seaports are Walvis Bay and Luderitz
Roadways and railways – 6,387km; 2,626km
Telecommunications – 187,853 fixed lines and 2.7 million mobile subscriptions (2016); there were 756,118 internet users in 2016
Internet code and IDD – na; 264 (from UK), 44 (to UK)
Major broadcasters – The Namibian Broadcasting Corporation (NBC) is publicly owned and operates television and radio stations
Press – There are five national daily newspapers including *The Namibian* (English and Oshiwambo language), *Die Republikein* (Afrikaans) and the state-owned *New Era*
WPFI score – 20,24 (26)

NAURU

Republic of Nauru

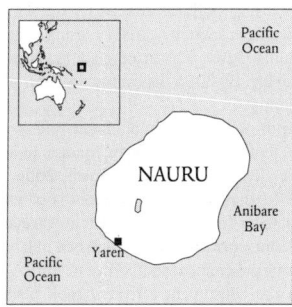

Area – 21 sq. km
Capital – Yaren (unofficial)
Currency – Australian dollar (A$) of 100 cents
Population – 11,359 rising at 0.53 per cent a year (2017 est);
  Nauruan (58 per cent), other Pacific Islander (26 per cent),
  Chinese (8 per cent), European (8 per cent) (est)
Religion – Christian (Protestant 60.4 per cent, Roman
  Catholic 33 per cent)
Language – Nauruan (official), English
Population density – 682 per sq. km (2016)
Urban population – 100 per cent (2018 est)
Median age (years) – 26.1 (2016 est)
National anthem – 'Nauru Bwiema' 'Song of Nauru'
National day – 31 January (Independence Day)
Death penalty – Abolished for all crimes (since 2016)
Life expectancy (years) – 67.4 (2017 est)
Mortality rate – 5.9 (2017 est)
Birth rate – 24 (2017 est)
Infant mortality rate – 7.8 (2017 est)

CLIMATE AND TERRAIN

Nauru is a low-lying island in the southern Pacific Ocean,
42km south of the equator and 4,000km north-east of
Sydney, Australia. There is a fertile coastal plain but about 60
per cent of the land area consists of the central plateau, formed
of phosphate, which has been extensively mined. The plateau
rim is the highest point, at 61m; the lowest is 0m at sea level.
The climate is tropical, with a rainy season from November to
February.

HISTORY AND POLITICS

Nauru was first settled by Polynesian and Melanesian groups.
The first Europeans to visit the island were British whalers in
1798, and by 1888 Nauru was annexed by Germany. At the
outbreak of the First World War, Nauru was occupied by
Australia, which continued to administer the island under a
League of Nations mandate from 1920. The island was
occupied by the Japanese in 1942–3, but in 1947 UN
trusteeship status superseded the mandate and Nauru
continued to be administered by Australia until it became
independent on 31 January 1968. A detention centre,
established in partnership with Australia to house asylum
seekers headed towards that country, has attracted
controversy for its allegedly harsh conditions.

A financial crisis in 2003 caused some political instability,
though a more stable period during Ludwig Scotty's second
presidency (2004–7) saw the introduction of austerity
measures and public sector reform. Scotty lost a vote of
confidence in December 2007 and was replaced by Marcus
Stephen. President Stephen resigned in 2011 amid allegations
of corruption and was replaced first by Frederick Pitcherr and

then former transport minister Sprent Dabwido. Baron Waqa
won the 2013 presidential election and was re-elected in
2016.

Under the 1968 constitution, the executive president is
elected by the legislature from among its members for a three-
year term, renewable once. The unicameral parliament has 19
members, who are directly elected for a three-year term. The
president appoints the cabinet. Although there are active
political parties, most parliamentary candidates stand as
independents.

HEAD OF STATE

President, Foreign Affairs, Baron Waqa, *elected* 11 June 2013,
  re-elected 11 June 2016

SELECTED GOVERNMENT MEMBERS *AS AT JUNE 2018*

Education, Home Affairs, Charmaine Scotty
Finance, Justice, David Adeang

HONORARY CONSULATE

Romshed Courtyard, Underriver, Sevenoaks, Kent TN15 0SD
T 01732-746061 **E** nauru@weald.co.uk
Honorary Consul, Martin Weston

BRITISH HIGH COMMISSIONER

HE David Ward, *apptd* 2016, resident at Honiara, Solomon
  Islands

ECONOMY AND TRADE

Phosphate is the only resource and its extraction is the
dominant industry, but reserves will be exhausted in 30 years.
Profits derived from the mining industry were invested in trust
funds to provide for the post-mining future, but heavy
spending from the funds has left the country virtually
bankrupt, causing it to default on loans and have assets seized
in 2004. The economy is dependent on international aid
(principally from Australia) and revenue from the sale of
fishing licences, but diversification efforts include offshore
banking, small-scale tourism, and the Australian Regional
Processing Centre opened in 2012.

The main trading partners are Australia and Nigeria. The
only export is phosphate. All food, fuel, manufactured goods,
machinery and construction materials are imported.

GNI – US$0.1bn; US$10,220 per capita (2017)
Annual average growth of GDP – 4.0 per cent (2017 est)
Inflation rate – 5.1 per cent (2017 est)
Imports – US$40m (2014)
Exports – US$34m (2014)

Trade with UK	2016	2017
Imports from UK	£133,846	£28,370
Exports to UK	£1,998	£1,267

COMMUNICATION

Transport – The island has one international airport and 24km
of roadways
Telecommunications – 1,900 fixed lines and 9,900 mobile
phone subscriptions (2016); there were 5,100 internet users
in 2016
Internet code and IDD – nr; 674 (from UK), 44 (to UK)
Media – The government-owned Nauru Television and Radio
Nauru are the island's principal broadcasters; there are no
daily newspapers

NEPAL

Sanghiya Loktantrik Ganatantra Nepal – Federal Democratic Republic of Nepal

Area – 147,181 sq. km
Capital – Kathmandu; population, 1,133,000 (2018 est)
Major cities – Biratnagar, Lalitpur, Lumbini, Pokhara
Currency – Nepalese rupee (Rs) of 100 paisa
Population – 29,384,297 rising at 1.16 per cent a year (2017 est); Chhetri (16.6 per cent), Brahman-Hill (12.2 per cent), Magar (7.1 per cent), Tharu (6.6 per cent), Tamang (5.8 per cent), Newar (5 per cent), Kami (4.8 per cent), Yadav (4 per cent) (2011 est)
Religion – Hindu 81.3 per cent, Buddhist 9 per cent, Muslim 4.4 per cent, Kirant 3 per cent (practised by a large proportion of Nepal's Kirati population) (2011 est)
Language – Nepali (official), English, Maithali, Bhojpuri, Tharu, Tamang, Newar, Magar, Awadhi
Population density – 204 per sq. km (2016)
Urban population – 19.7 per cent (2018 est)
Median age (years) – 23.6 (2016 est)
National anthem – 'Sayaun Thunga Phool Ka' 'Hundreds of Flowers'
National day – 29 May (Republic Day)
Death penalty – Abolished for all crimes (since 1997)
CPI score – 31 (122)
Military expenditure – US$386m (2017)

CLIMATE AND TERRAIN
The north of Nepal lies in the Himalayas, with the snowline at about 4,880m. The terrain descends from the mountains through a hilly central region with fertile valleys to the southern plains, the Terai, that lie in the valley of the Ganges. Elevation extremes range from 8,850m (Mt Everest) to 70m (Kanchan Kalan). The climate varies from subtropical in the south to much cooler with severe winters in the north. Average temperatures range from 4.8°C in January to 19.1°C in June and July. The rainy season lasts from June to September.

HISTORY AND POLITICS
Modern Nepal was formed from a number of small states that were conquered and unified in the 18th century by the Gurkha ruler Prithvi Naryan Shah. After war with the British in 1815–16, Nepal became a British-dependent buffer state; its independence was formally recognised in 1923.

Power was seized by Jung Bahdur in 1846. He assumed the title Rana and his family became hereditary chief ministers, reducing the monarchy to a purely ceremonial role and keeping the country isolated. In 1950–1, the Ranas were overthrown and the monarchy was restored to power. Apart from 1959–60, when a parliamentary system of government was in place, the kings ruled as absolute monarchs until 1990, when a new constitution was introduced that made the country a constitutional monarchy and multiparty parliamentary democracy.

However, factionalism led to frequent changes of government, causing political and social instability, which was exacerbated from 1996 by a Maoist insurgency led by the Nepal Communist Party. The insurgency began in the west and spread quickly. By 2006 the insurgents controlled 80 per cent of the country.

King Gyanendra's assumption of direct rule in 2005 led politicians to ally themselves with the Maoists to achieve the restoration of democracy, and in April 2006 the king reinstated the legislature after three months of violent pro-democracy protests. In November 2006 a peace accord was signed, an interim legislature was established in January 2007 and a multiparty government took office in April.

Elections to the constituent assembly took place in April 2008; the Communist Party of Nepal–Maoists (CPN-M) won the most seats and abolished the monarchy on 28 May 2008. The assembly elected Ram Baran Yadav of the Nepali Congress party as the country's first president in July. In legislative elections in November 2013, the Nepali Congress party became the largest party; its leader Sushil Koirala was elected prime minister by parliament but had to step down in October 2015 under the new constitution. K. P. Sharma Oli of the Communist Party of Nepal (Unified Marxist Leninist) was then elected prime minister and women's rights campaigner Bidha Devi Bhandari, vice-chair of the same political party, became the country's second president and its first woman president. Oli resigned in July 2016 just hours before a vote of no confidence in parliament and was replaced by former rebel leader Pushpa Kamal Dahal in August, but was reinstated in February 2018.

The monarchy was abolished in May 2008 and the country declared a republic; on 20 September 2015 a new constitution was adopted that divided the country into seven federal provinces. The head of state is the president, who is elected by the constituent assembly. The bicameral Federal Parliament consists of 275 directly elected members and 59 National Assembly members, 56 indirectly elected by an electoral college of state and municipal government leaders, and three appointed by the president. The first parliamentary general elections since the civil war took place between November 2017 and February 2018.

The prime minister is appointed by consensus among the political parties or elected by a two-thirds majority of the assembly. The council of ministers is appointed by the prime minister.

HEAD OF STATE
President, Bidha Devi Bhandari, *elected* 28 October 2015, *sworn in* 29 October 2015
Vice-President, Nanda Kishor Pun

SELECTED GOVERNMENT MEMBERS *AS AT JUNE 2018*
Prime Minister, Khadga Prasad Sharma Oli
Deputy Prime Ministers, Ishwor Pokharel *(Defence),* Upendra Yadav
Finance, Yuvaraj Khatiwada
Foreign Affairs, Pradeep Kumar Gyawali

EMBASSY OF NEPAL
12A Kensington Palace Gardens, London W8 4QU
T 020-7229 1594 E eon@nepembassy.org.uk
W www.nepembassy.org.uk
Ambassador Extraordinary and Plenipotentiary, HE Dr Durga Bahadur Subedi, *apptd* 2016

BRITISH EMBASSY
PO Box 106, Lainchaur, Kathmandu
T (+977) (1) 441 0583 E bekathmandu@fco.gov.uk
W www.gov.uk/government/world/nepal
Ambassador Extraordinary and Plenipotentiary, HE Richard
Morris, *apptd* 2015

ECONOMY AND TRADE

The country is one of the poorest in Asia, and the economy is
dependent on foreign aid, remittances and trade with India.
Tourism and hydroelectric power have potential for
development, although this might compound growing
environmental problems. Investment agreements have been
signed with India, China and the US, focusing on electricity
generation and infrastructure.

Agriculture is the main economic sector, generating 27 per
cent of GDP and engaging about 69 per cent of the
workforce; principal crops are pulses, rice, maize, wheat, sugar
cane, jute, root crops, milk and meat. Industries other than
tourism include carpets, textiles, cigarettes, cement and bricks,
and the processing agricultural products. Industry accounts
for 13.5 per cent of GDP and services for 51.5 per cent. The
April 2015 earthquake severely damaged the economy, with
reconstruction costs estimated to be roughly US$10bn
(£6.5bn), around 50 per cent of Nepal's GDP.

The main export market is India (53.1 per cent); the main
import providers are India (70.2 per cent) and China.
Principal exports are clothing, pulses, carpets, textiles, juice
and jute goods. The main imports are petroleum products,
machinery, gold, electrical goods and medicine.
GNI – US$23.3bn; US$790 per capita (2017)
Annual average growth of GDP – 7.5 per cent (2017 est)
Inflation rate – 4.5 per cent (2017 est)
Population below poverty line – 25.2 per cent (2011)
Unemployment rate – 3.3 per cent (2017 est)
Total external debt – US$5.948bn (2017 est)
Imports – US$6,074m (2014)
Exports – US$854m (2014)

BALANCE OF PAYMENTS
Trade – US$5,502m deficit (2013)
Current Account – US$815m deficit (2017)

Trade with UK	2016	2017
Imports from UK	£10,288,204	£10,248,671
Exports to UK	£18,647,403	£20,451,372

COMMUNICATIONS

Airports – The principal airport is at Kathmandu, and there are
ten smaller airports around the country
Roadways and railways – 4,952km; 59km
Telecommunications – 858,237 fixed lines and 32 million
mobile subscriptions (2016); there were 5.7 million internet
users in 2016
Internet code and IDD – np; 977 (from UK), 44 (to UK)
Major broadcasters – The state-run Nepal Television
Corporation operates various channels across the country
alongside numerous private operators
Press – Dailies include the semi-official *Gorkhapatra,* Nepal's
oldest newspaper, and *The Rising Nepal,* plus the private *The
Kathmandu Post*
WPFI score – 33,02 (100)

EDUCATION AND HEALTH

Literacy rate – 86.9 per cent (2015 est)
Gross enrolment ratio (percentage of relevant age group) – primary
134 per cent, secondary 71 per cent (2017 est), tertiary
21 per cent (2016 est)
Health expenditure (per capita) – US$40 (2014)
Hospital beds (per 1,000 people) – 3 (2012)
Life expectancy (years) – 71 (2017 est)
Mortality rate – 5.6 (2017 est)
Birth rate – 19.5 (2017 est)
Infant mortality rate – 27.9 (2017 est)
HIV/AIDS adult prevalence – 0.2 per cent (2016 est)

THE NETHERLANDS

Koninkrijk der Nederlanden – Kingdom of the Netherlands

Area – 41,543 sq. km
Capital – Amsterdam; population, 1,132,000 (2018 est)
Seat of government – The Hague (Den Haag or, in full,
's-Gravenhage); population, 629,000 (2009 est)
Major cities – Almere, Eindhoven, Haarlem, Groningen,
Rotterdam, Tilburg, Utrecht
Currency – Euro (€) of 100 cents
Population – 17,084,719 rising at 0.39 per cent a year (2017
est); Dutch (77.4 per cent), Turkish (2.3 per cent),
Moroccan (2.3 per cent)
Religion – Christian (Roman Catholic 28 per cent, Protestant
19 per cent, Muslim 5 per cent (2009 est)
Language – Dutch (official), Frisian, Low Saxon, and
Limburgish (official regional languages); English is widely
spoken
Population density – 509 per sq. km (2016)
Urban population – 91.5 per cent (2018 est)
Median age (years) – 42.5 (2016 est)
National anthem – 'Het Wilhelmus' 'The William'
National day – 27 April (King's Day)
Death penalty – Abolished for all crimes (since 1982)
CPI score – 82 (8)
Military expenditure – US$10,049m (2017)

CLIMATE AND TERRAIN

The Netherlands is a low-lying country; about a quarter is
below sea level, making it susceptible to flooding despite the
coastal defences and a network of dykes and canals. Its land
area has been extended over the centuries by land reclamation
(polders), found especially in the west around the huge
freshwater lake of Yssel, created in the 1930s by damming the
Zuider Zee. The country is crossed by three major European
rivers, the Rhine, Maas (Meuse) and Scheldt, whose estuaries
are in the south-west. Mount Scenery (862m), on the
Caribbean island of Saba, is considered the highest point of
the Kingdom of the Netherlands. Elevation extremes in the
Netherlands itself range from 322m (Vaalserberg) to −7m

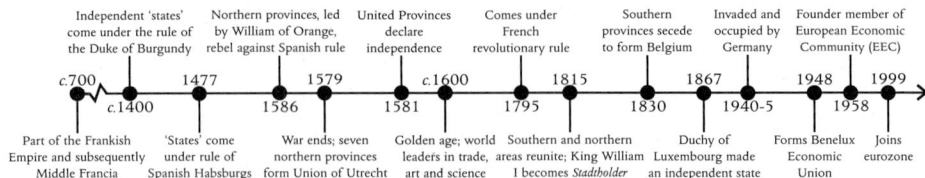

| Independent 'states' come under the rule of the Duke of Burgundy | Northern provinces, led by William of Orange, rebel against Spanish rule | United Provinces declare independence | Comes under French revolutionary rule | Southern provinces secede to form Belgium | Invaded and occupied by Germany | Founder member of European Economic Community (EEC) |

Timeline: c.700 — c.1400 — 1477 — 1586 — 1579 — 1581 — c.1600 — 1795 — 1815 — 1830 — 1867 — 1940-5 — 1948 — 1958 — 1999

| Part of the Frankish Empire and subsequently Middle Francia | 'States' come under rule of Spanish Habsburgs | War ends; seven northern provinces form Union of Utrecht | Golden age; world leaders in trade, art and science | Southern and northern areas reunite; King William I becomes *Stadtholder* | Duchy of Luxembourg made an independent state | Forms Benelux Economic Union | Joins eurozone |

(Zuidplaspolder). The climate is temperate, with average temperatures ranging from 3.5°C in January to 18°C in August.

POLITICS

Under the 1983 constitution, the head of state is a hereditary constitutional monarch. The States-General *(Staten-Generaal)* consists of the First Chamber *(Eerste Kamer)* of 75 members, elected for a four-year term by the Provincial States; and the Second Chamber *(Tweede Kamer)* of 150 members, directly elected for a four-year term. The head of government is the prime minister, who is responsible to the legislature.

Although it is a stable democracy, one party has rarely commanded a sufficient parliamentary majority to govern alone in the post-war period; governments have usually been coalitions of two or more parties. In the May 2015 election to the First Chamber, the People's Party for Freedom and Democracy (VVD) led by Mark Rutte retained its position as the largest party; since 2012 the VVD has been the largest party in the Second Chamber, elections for which were held most recently in March 2017. Following those elections, it took Prime Minister Mark Rutte 225 days to form a new government – the longest coalition talks in the Netherlands' history. In April 2013, Queen Beatrix abdicated in favour of Willem-Alexander, her eldest son.

HEAD OF STATE

The King of the Netherlands, HM King Willem-Alexander, *born* 27 April 1967, *succeeded* 30 April 2013
Heir, Princess of Orange (Crown Princess), HRH Catharina-Amalia, *born* 7 December 2003

SELECTED GOVERNMENT MEMBERS *AS AT JUNE 2018*
Prime Minister, Mark Rutte
Deputy Prime Ministers, Hugo de Jonge; Kaisa Ollongren; Carola Schouten
Defence, Ank Bijleveld-Schouten
Foreign Affairs, Stefan Blok

EMBASSY OF THE KINGDOM OF THE NETHERLANDS
38 Hyde Park Gate, London SW7 5DP
T 020-7590 3200 E lon@minbuza.nl W www.dutchembassyuk.org
Ambassador Extraordinary and Plenipotentiary, HE Simon Smits, *apptd* 2015

BRITISH EMBASSY
Lange Voorhout 10, The Hague, 2514 ED
T (+31) (70) 427 0427 E ukinnl@fco.gov.uk
W www.gov.uk/government/world/netherlands
Ambassador Extraordinary and Plenipotentiary, HE Peter Wilson, CMG, *apptd* 2017

ECONOMY AND TRADE
The Netherlands has a highly industrialised and diversified market economy, and is a major European transportation hub. The economy depends heavily on foreign trade and financial services, and contracted sharply in 2009 as exports fell by almost 25 per cent in the global economic downturn. The government nationalised two banks to stabilise the financial sector and introduced stimulus measures and austerity measures. The economy started growing again in 2014, and in 2017 the government recorded its first budget surplus since the crisis as GDP per capita also overtook pre-2008 levels. Unemployment, which doubled between 2009–13 to 7.4 per cent, has declined and is forecasted to continue falling.

The highly mechanised agricultural sector employs only 1.2 per cent of the workforce but output supplies the food processing industries and the export as well as the domestic market. Flower bulbs and cut flowers are a major contributor to this sector, as is the fishing and livestock. The industrial sector contributes 17.9 per cent of GDP; major industries include food processing, and the manufacture of metal and engineering products, electrical machinery and equipment, chemicals, oil refining, construction and micro-electronics. The service industries represent 70.2 per cent of the economy. Other EU countries, China and the USA account for most overseas trade. Principal exports are machinery and equipment, chemicals, fuels and foodstuffs. The main imports are machinery and transport equipment, chemicals, fuels, foodstuffs and clothing.

GNI – US$791.3bn; US$46,180 per capita (2017)
Annual average growth of GDP – 1.7 per cent (2015)
Inflation rate – 0.2 per cent (2016 est)
Population below poverty line – 8.8 per cent (2015 est)
Unemployment – 5.1 per cent (2017 est)
Total external debt – US$4.063 trillion (2016 est)
Imports – US$420,969m (2016)
Exports – US$511,714m (2016)

BALANCE OF PAYMENTS
Trade – US$90,745m surplus (2016)
Current Account – US$84,830m surplus (2017)

Trade with UK	2016	2017
Imports from UK	£18,853,312,085	£21,378,847,833
Exports to UK	£34,804,434,018	£39,945,035,615

COMMUNICATIONS
Airports – The principal airports are at Amsterdam, Rotterdam, Eindhoven and Maastricht, with a further 25 airports around the country
Waterways – The main seaport is Rotterdam, although there are a number of other ports on river estuaries or linked to the coast by the canals; 6,237km of inland waterways are navigable by ships of up to 50 tonnes. The large merchant fleet includes 744 ships of over 1,000 tonnes
Roadways and railways – There are 139,295km of roads, including 2,758km of motorways, and 3,013km of railways, of which 2,195km are electrified
Telecommunications – 6.7 million fixed lines and 20.1 million mobile subscriptions (2016); there were 15.4 million internet users in 2016
Internet code and IDD – nl; 31 (from UK), 44 (to UK)
Major broadcasters – A competitive broadcasting sector includes Nederlandse Omroep Stichting (NOS), which operates public radio and television stations

Press – Leading dailies include *Algemeen Dagblad, NRC Handelsblad* and *De Telegraaf*
WPFI score – 10,01 (3)

EDUCATION AND HEALTH
Education is free and compulsory for 13 years.
Gross enrolment ratio (percentage of relevant age group) – primary 103 per cent, secondary 133 per cent, tertiary 80 per cent (2016 est)
Health expenditure (per capita) – US$5,694 (2014)
Hospital beds (per 1,000 people) – 4.7 (2009)
Life expectancy (years) – 81.4 (2017 est)
Mortality rate – 8.9 (2017 est)
Birth rate – 10.9 (2017 est)
Infant mortality rate – 3.6 (2017 est)

OVERSEAS TERRITORIES
The Kingdom of the Netherlands consists of four autonomous elements: the Netherlands (European and Caribbean Netherlands), Aruba, Curacao and St Maarten; the latter two were part of the Netherlands Antilles until its dissolution on 10 October 2010. The other three islands of the Netherlands Antilles, the 'Caribbean Netherlands', comprising Bonaire, St Eustatius and Saba, are now autonomous special municipalities of the Netherlands.

ARUBA
Area – 180 sq. km
Capital – Oranjestad; population, 29,000 (2014)
Currency – Aruban florin of 100 cents
Population – 115,120 rising at 1.27 per cent a year (2017 est)
Religion – Christian (Roman Catholic 75.3 per cent, Protestant 4.9 per cent) (2010 est)
Language – Dutch (official), Papiamento, Spanish, English
Population density – 577 per sq. km (2015)
Urban population – 41.5 per cent (2015 est)
Median age (years) – 39.3 (2017 est)
National Day – 18 March (Flag Day)
The Caribbean island was colonised by the Dutch in the 17th century. It was part of the Netherlands Antilles until 1986, when it became a separate, autonomous territory. The Dutch government is responsible for external affairs and represented by a resident governor. Internal government is in the hands of the prime minister and council of ministers, who are responsible to the 21-member unicameral legislature *(Staten)*, directly elected for a four-year term.
The principal economic activities are tourism and offshore financial services.
Governor, Alfonso Boekhoudt, *apptd* 2017
Prime Minister, Evelyn Wever-Croes, *elected* 2017

CURACAO
Area – 444 sq. km
Capital – Willemstad; population, 149,035 (2016)
Currency – Caribbean guilder of 100 cents
Population – 149,648 rising at 0.40 per cent a year (2017 est)
Religion – Christian (Roman Catholic 89.1 per cent, Pentecostal 6.6 per cent, Protestant 3.2 per cent) (2011 est)
Language – Dutch (official), Papiamento, English, Spanish
Population density – 356 per sq. km (2015)
Urban population – 89.3 per cent (2015 est)
Median age (years) – 36 (2016 est)
The island was colonised by the Dutch in the 17th century and was part of the Netherlands Antilles from 1954 until 10 October 2010, when it became a separate, autonomous

territory. The Dutch government is responsible for external affairs and represented by a resident governor. Internal affairs are in the hands of a prime minister and council of ministers, who are responsible to the 21-member directly elected unicameral legislature *(Staten)*, which serves a four-year term.
The principal economic activities are tourism, oil refining and offshore financial services.
Governor, Lucille George-Wout, *apptd* 2013
Prime Minister, Eugene Rhuggenaath, *took office* 2017

ST MAARTEN
Area – 34 sq. km
Capital – Philipsburg; population, 1,327 (2011)
Currency – Caribbean guilder of 100 cents
Population – 41,486 rising at 1.44 per cent (2016 est)
Religion – Christian (Protestant 41.9 per cent, Roman Catholic 33.1 per cent), Hindu 5.2 per cent (2011 est)
Language – Dutch, English (official), Spanish, Creole
Population density – 1,142 per sq. km (2015)
Median age (years) – 40.7 (2016 est)
The territory forms the southern part of the island of St Martin in the Caribbean; the north is French territory. Possession of the island was disputed between the Dutch and the Spanish until 1648, when the Spanish relinquished it to the Dutch and French, who divided it between them. The Dutch territory was part of the Netherlands Antilles from 1954 until 10 October 2010, when it became a separate, autonomous territory. The Dutch government is responsible for external affairs and represented by a governor. Internal affairs are in the hands of a prime minister and council of ministers, who are responsible to the directly elected 15-member unicameral legislature *(Staten)*, which serves a four-year term.
The principal economic activities are tourism and sugar production.
Governor, Eugene Holiday, *apptd* 2010
Prime Minister, Leona Marlin-Romeo, *apptd* 2018

NEW ZEALAND

Aotearoa – New Zealand

Area – 268,838 sq. km (includes outlying islands)
Capital – Wellington; population, 411,000 (2018 est)
Major cities – Auckland, Christchurch, Dunedin, Hamilton, Manakau, North Shore, Tauranga, Waitakere
Currency – New Zealand dollar (NZ$) of 100 cents
Population – 4,510,327 rising at 0.79 per cent a year (2017 est); European (71.2 per cent), Maori (14.1 per cent), Asian (11.3 per cent), Pacific Islander (7.6 per cent) (2013)
Religion – Christian (Protestant 22.8 per cent, Roman Catholic 11.6 per cent, Anglican 10.8 per cent), Hindu 2.1 per cent
Language – English, Maori (both official)

Population density – 18 per sq. km (2016)
Urban population – 86.5 per cent (2018 est)
Median age (years) – 37.8 (2016 est)
National anthem – 'God Defend New Zealand', 'God Save the Queen'
National day – 6 February (Waitangi Day)
Death penalty – Abolished for all crimes (since 1989)
CPI score – 89 (1)
Military expenditure – US$2,328m (2017)

CLIMATE AND TERRAIN

New Zealand consists of North Island, South Island and neighbouring coastal islands such as Stewart Island, and outlying islands that include the Chatham, Kermadec, Three Kings, Bounty, Antipodes, Snares, Auckland and Campbell groups in the South Pacific Ocean. The two larger islands, North Island and South Island, are separated by the relatively narrow Cook Strait. The island groups are much smaller and more widely dispersed.

Much of the North and South Islands is mountainous. The North Island mountains include several volcanoes, three of which are active. The principal range is the Southern Alps, extending the entire length of South Island to the west of the Canterbury Plains. There are geysers and hot springs in the Rotorua district and glaciers in the Southern Alps. Elevation extremes range from 3,754m (Aoraki/Mt Cook) to 0m (Pacific Ocean). The climate is temperate, though with marked regional variations; average temperatures range from 5.5°C in July to 15.5°C in February. The country is subject to seismic activity; a major earthquake devastated Christchurch in February 2011.

HISTORY AND POLITICS

Settled by Polynesian tribes, the ancestors of the Maori, from about the tenth century, New Zealand was sighted by the Dutch navigator Abel Tasman in 1642 but he did not land. The British explorer James Cook surveyed the coastline in 1769, the year in which the islands were claimed by the British. The Maori accepted British sovereignty in 1840, under the Treaty of Waitangi, in return for land rights and the rights of British subjects. Large-scale European immigration and the 1860s gold rush led to encroachment by settlers and 'land wars' with the Maori in 1860 and 1872; Maori resistance was defeated but concessions such as parliamentary representation were won. A tribunal was set up in 1975 to consider grievances caused by breaches of the Waitangi Treaty, and in the 1990s the Maori were compensated for land lost to European settlers.

New Zealand was administered as part of Britain's New South Wales colony until 1841, when it became a separate colony. In 1907 it was granted dominion status; in 1931 the Statute of Westminster tacitly acknowledged its independence, which was formally confirmed in 1947.

New Zealand forces took part in the Boer War, both world wars, the Korean War and the Vietnam War. Since the UK's entry into the EEC in 1973, the focus of New Zealand's foreign and trade policies has shifted to Asia and the Pacific region.

Post-war politics has been dominated by the National Party and the Labour Party, either forming governments on their own or in coalition with smaller parties; coalitions have been the norm since a proportional representation voting system was introduced in 1993. After inconclusive legislative elections in September 2017, the Labour Party, led by Jacinda Ardern, 37, formed a government with the New Zealand First Party in October; in the process, Ardern became the country's youngest prime minister since 1856. A March 2016 referendum voted by a margin of more than 10 per cent to retain the country's flag, which features the Union Jack, as opposed to a design bearing a silver fern.

There is no written constitution. The head of state is Queen Elizabeth II, represented by the governor-general, who is appointed on the advice of the New Zealand government. The unicameral House of Representatives currently has 122 members (usually 120), elected for a three-year term; there are 70 members from single-member constituencies, which include seven Maori constituencies, and 52 (usually 50) allocated from party lists; if a party wins a significantly larger proportion of constituency seats relative to their party list vote, this can result in an 'overhang' of extra seats. The prime minister and cabinet are appointed by the governor-general on the advice of the legislature.

GOVERNOR-GENERAL
Governor-General, HE Dame Patricia Reddy, DNZM, *sworn in* September 2016

SELECTED GOVERNMENT MEMBERS *AS AT JUNE 2018*
Prime Minister, Jacinda Ardern
Deputy Prime Minister, Foreign Affairs, Winston Peters
Finance, Grant Robertson
Justice, Andrew Little

NEW ZEALAND HIGH COMMISSION
New Zealand House, 80 Haymarket, London SW1Y 4TQ
T 020-7930 8422 E aboutnz@newzealandhc.org.uk
W www.nzembassy.com/uk
High Commissioner, HE Sir Jerry Mateparae, *apptd* 2017

BRITISH HIGH COMMISSION
44 Hill Street, Thorndon, Wellington 6011
T (+64) (4) 924 2888 E consularmail.wellington@fco.gov.uk
W www.gov.uk/government/world/new-zealand
High Commissioner, HE Laura Clarke, *apptd* 2018

ECONOMY AND TRADE

Since the 1980s industrial and service sectors have superseded the large, efficient agricultural sector. Growth has been driven by trade, particularly in agricultural products, but various factors had pushed the economy into recession in 2008 before the global downturn. The government managed to return a surplus in 2014–15, and have prioritised free trade agreements with many nations in recent years, especially China. Rising house prices and rents led to a ban on the sale of homes to foreign buyers in 2018.

The agricultural sector contributes 3.9 per cent of GDP and employs 6.6 per cent of the workforce. The main products are dairy products, meat, cereals, pulses, fruit, vegetables, wool and fish. The major industries are food processing, wood and paper products, manufacturing, transport equipment, financial services, mining, and tourism, which is overtaking agriculture as the main source of foreign exchange revenue. Non-metallic minerals such as coal, limestone and dolomite are heavily exploited, and gold and iron production is economically important. Natural gas deposits in offshore and onshore fields are used for electricity generation, though a significant amount of the country's energy is derived from sustainable sources such as hydroelectric power. Industry contributes 26.2 per cent of GDP and services 69.9 per cent.

The main trading partners are China, Australia, the USA and Japan. Principal exports are dairy products, meat, wood, fruit, fish and crude oil. The main imports are machinery and equipment, vehicles and aircraft, petroleum, electronics and textiles.

GNI – US$186.8bn; US$38,970 per capita (2017)
Annual average growth of GDP – 3.5 per cent (2017 est)
Inflation rate – 2.2 per cent (2017 est)
Unemployment – 4.9 per cent (2017 est)
Total external debt – US$88.08bn (2017 est)

Imports – US$36,064m (2016)
Exports – US$33,717m (2016)

BALANCE OF PAYMENTS
Trade – US$2,348m deficit (2016)
Current Account – US$5,521m deficit (2017)

Trade with UK	2016*	2017**
Imports from UK	£704,574,226	£865,578,589
Exports to UK	£858,771,305	£903,672,009

* Includes Tokelau, Cook Islands and Niue
** Includes Cook Islands and Niue

COMMUNICATIONS
Airports and waterways – The principal airports are at Auckland, Wellington (North Island), Christchurch and Dunedin (South Island) and there are 35 smaller airports around the country; Tauranga, Christchurch, New Plymouth, Auckland and Napier are the main seaports
Roadways and railways – There are 62,759km of roadways, including 199km of motorways, and 4,128km of railways
Telecommunications – 1.76 million fixed lines and 5.8 million mobile subscriptions (2016); there were 4 million internet users in 2016
Internet code and IDD – nz; 64 (from UK), 44 (to UK)
Major broadcasters – The state-owned Television New Zealand and Radio New Zealand operate nationally; Niu FM is the national government-funded station for the Pacific island communities
Press – The Auckland-based *New Zealand Herald* has the largest circulation, alongside Wellington-based *Dominion Post* and Christchurch-based *The Press*
WPFI score – 13,62 (8)

EDUCATION AND HEALTH
Education is free of charge and compulsory between the ages of 5 and 16.
Gross enrolment ratio (percentage of relevant age group) – primary 99 per cent, secondary 114 per cent, tertiary 82 per cent (2016 est)
Health expenditure (per capita) – US$4,896 (2014)
Hospital beds (per 1,000 people) – 2.8 (2013)
Life expectancy (years) – 81.3 (2017 est)
Mortality rate – 7.5 (2017 est)
Birth rate – 13.2 (2017 est)
Infant mortality rate – 4.4 (2017 est)

TERRITORIES

TOKELAU
Area – 12 sq. km
Population – 1,285 (2016 est) falling at 0.01 per cent a year (2014 est)
Tokelau consists of three atolls, Fakaofo, Nukunonu and Atafu, in the southern Pacific Ocean. Formerly part of Britain's Gilbert and Ellice Islands colony, Tokelau was transferred to New Zealand administration in 1926 and proclaimed part of New Zealand in 1949.

The territory is self-administering, but has rejected greater autonomy in two referendums (2006 and 2007). The Council for the Ongoing Government (cabinet) comprises three *Faipule* (village leaders) and three *Pulenuku* (village mayors), one from each atoll; the position of *Ulu-o-Tokelau* (leader) is rotated among the three *Faipule* members annually. The *General Fono*, which has 20 members elected for a three-year term, has legislative powers. Each atoll has a *Taupulega* (council of elders).

The economy is dependent on New Zealand budgetary aid, with some revenue derived from remittances and the sale of fishing rights, stamps, coins and the use of its internet suffix. The main activities are subsistence farming, copra production and handicrafts. In 2011 Tokelau changed its position within the international dateline in order to improve trade links with Australia and New Zealand.
Administrator, Jonathan Kings, *apptd* 2017

THE ROSS DEPENDENCY
New Zealand has administrative responsibility for the Ross Dependency. This is defined as all the Antarctic islands and territories between 160° E. and 150° W. longitude that are situated south of the 60° S. parallel, including Edward VII Land and portions of Victoria Land (*see also* The North and South Poles).

ASSOCIATED STATES

COOK ISLANDS
Area – 236 sq. km
Population – 9,290 falling at 2.79 per cent a year (2017 est)
Capital – Avarua, on Rarotonga
Religion – Christian (Protestant 62.8 per cent, Roman Catholic 17 per cent, Mormon 4.4 per cent) (2011 est)
Urban population – 75.1 per cent (2018 est)
The Cook Islands consist of 15 volcanic islands and coral atolls in the southern Pacific Ocean. A former British protectorate, since 1965 the islands have been self-governing in free association with New Zealand.

Queen Elizabeth II has a representative on the islands, and the New Zealand government is represented by a high commissioner. There is a 24-member legislative assembly, and the House of Ariki, made up of 15 traditional leaders who advise on traditional matters. Executive power is exercised by a prime minister and a cabinet responsible to the legislature.

The main economic activities are tourism, agriculture (especially tropical fruits), fruit processing, fishing, garment manufacturing, handicrafts and pearl-farming; black pearls are the main export.
HM Representative, HE Sir Tom Marsters, KBE *apptd* 2013
Prime Minister, Henry Puna, *apptd* 2010

NIUE
Area – 260 sq. km
Population – 1,618 (2017 est) falling at 0.03 per cent a year (2014 est)
Capital – Alofi; population 1,000 falling at 0.03 per cent a year (2014 est)
Religion – Christian (Ekalesia Niue 67 per cent, Mormon 10 per cent, Roman Catholic 10 per cent) (2011 est)
Urban population – 42.5 per cent (2015 est)
Although part of the Cook Islands group, Niue was administered separately after 1903. Since 1974 the island has been self-governing in free association with New Zealand.

A New Zealand high commissioner represents both the Queen and the New Zealand government. There is a 20-member legislative assembly; executive power is exercised by a prime minister and a three-member cabinet drawn from the assembly's members.

The principal economic activities are agriculture, fishing, tourism, handicrafts, food processing and the sale of postage stamps and the use of its internet suffix.
New Zealand High Commissioner, Ross Ardern, *apptd* 2014
Premier, Toke Talagi, *apptd* 2008

NICARAGUA

República de Nicaragua – Republic of Nicaragua

Area – 130,370 sq. km
Capital – Managua; population, 1,048,000 (2018 est)
Major cities – Chinandega, León, Masaya, Tipitapa
Currency – Córdoba (C$) of 100 centavos
Population – 6,025,951 rising at 0.98 per cent a year (2017 est)
Religion – Christian (Roman Catholic 58.5 per cent, Protestant 23.2 per cent), none 15.7 per cent (2005 est)
Language – Spanish (official), English, Miskito
Population density – 52 per sq. km (2016)
Urban population – 58.5 per cent (2018 est)
Median age (years) – 25.2 (2016 est)
National anthem – 'Salve a ti, Nicaragua' 'Hail to Thee, Nicaragua'
National day – 15 September (Independence Day)
Death penalty – Abolished for all crimes (since 1979)
CPI score – 26 (151)
Military expenditure – US$84m (2017)

CLIMATE AND TERRAIN

The narrow Pacific coastal plain is broken by active volcanoes and lakes Managua and Nicaragua. A mountainous central region separates it from the broad Atlantic coastal plain, which constitutes 60 per cent of the country and is covered by tropical rainforest. Elevation extremes range from 2,438m (Mogoton) to 0m (Pacific Ocean). The climate is generally tropical on the plains but cooler at altitude; the average temperature is 25.6°C. The country is subject to frequent earthquakes.

HISTORY AND POLITICS

Nicaragua was originally populated by tribes related to the Aztec, Maya and other indigenous people. Fossilised footprints, the oldest in South America, indicate a human presence in Nicaragua dating back 6,000 years. Spanish colonisation began in 1523 but in the 17th and 18th centuries the British were the dominant presence on the Caribbean coast, with the Spanish controlling the Pacific plain. Independence from Spain was achieved in 1821 and the area was initially incorporated into Mexico. In 1823 it became part of a Central American federation of former Spanish provinces but seceded and became fully independent in 1838. British control of the Caribbean coast was ceded to Nicaragua in 1860.

In 1893, General José Santos Zelaya established a dictatorship that lasted until 1909, when he was overthrown by US troops. General Anastasio Somoza established a dictatorship in 1938 and ruled until his assassination in 1956, when he was succeeded as president by his sons Luis (1956–67) and Anastasio (1967–79). After 44 years in power, the family was overthrown in 1979 in a popular revolt led by the Frente Sandinista de Liberación Nacional (FSLN), popularly known as the Sandinistas.

The Sandinistas' socialist government redistributed land and promoted education and health services, but was opposed by US-backed right-wing guerrillas (the Contras). The civil war lasted from 1982 until 1990 (although there was a ceasefire from 1988), when the Sandinistas were unexpectedly defeated in elections by a coalition of opposition parties.

From 1990 to 2006, governments were liberal or liberal-dominated coalitions, keeping the FSLN from power even though it was often the largest party in the legislature. However, in the 2006 presidential and legislative elections, the FSLN candidate, Daniel Ortega (president 1984–90), was elected president and the FSLN was returned to government. In 2009 the Supreme Court lifted the ban on a president serving two consecutive terms and in 2014 the National Assembly eliminated constitutional term limits for the presidency altogether, allowing President Ortega to run for re-election in 2011 and again in November 2016. Opposition parties called the changes undemocratic and labelled as flawed the 2016 election, which President Ortega won with a landslide. His FSLN party also won over 65 per cent of the 2016 vote for the National Assembly. Months of violent anti-government protests began in April 2018 against Ortega's rule, resulting in hundreds of deaths.

The unicameral National Assembly has 90 members directly elected for a five-year term, plus unsuccessful presidential and vice-presidential candidates may be awarded a seat if they receive more than the average percentage of the vote in each electoral district. The cabinet is appointed by the president.

HEAD OF STATE
President, Daniel Ortega, *elected* 5 November 2006, *sworn in* 10 January 2007, *re-elected* 2011, 2016
Vice-President, Rosaria Murillo

SELECTED GOVERNMENT MEMBERS *AS AT JULY 2018*
Defence, Martha Elena Ruiz Sevilla
Finance, Ivan Acosta Montalvan
Foreign Affairs, Dennis Moncada Colindres
Interior, Maria Amelia Coronel Kinloch

EMBASSY OF NICARAGUA
Suite 31, Vicarage House, 58–60 Kensington Church Street, London W8 4DP
T 020-7938 2373
Ambassador Extraordinary and Plenipotentiary, HE Guisell Morales-Echaverry, *apptd* 2015

BRITISH AMBASSADOR
HE Ross Denny, *apptd* 2015, resident at San José, Costa Rica

ECONOMY AND TRADE

Progress towards economic recovery and reconstruction after the civil war has been slow and the country remains the poorest in Central America. The economy contracted in 2009 as the global downturn reduced key commodity prices, export demand and remittances. Although almost 80 per cent of debt was cancelled in 2004 and 2006, the government is dependent on foreign aid and 29.6 per cent of the population lives below the poverty line. A Chinese-led US$50bn inter-oceanic canal project agreed in 2013 has yet to begin construction.

Agriculture is the mainstay of the economy, accounting for 15.5 per cent of GDP and roughly 31 per cent of employment. The main commercial crops are coffee, bananas, sugar cane, beef, shellfish, tobacco and peanuts. Industry includes food and timber processing, mining, the manufacture of chemicals, machinery, metal products, textiles, clothing and footwear, oil refining and wood. Industry contributes 24.4 per cent of GDP and services 50.8 per cent.

The main trading partners are the USA, and other Central and South American countries. Principal exports are the main commercial crops and gold. The main imports are consumer goods, machinery and equipment, raw materials and petroleum products.

GNI – US$13.2bn; US$2,130 per capita (2017)
Annual average growth of GDP – 4.5 per cent (2017 est)
Inflation rate – 4.0 per cent (2017 est)
Population below poverty line – 29.6 per cent (2015 est)
Unemployment – 6.5 per cent (2017 est)
Total external debt – US$11.36bn (2017 est)
Imports – US$5,972m (2016)
Exports – US$2,225m (2016)

BALANCE OF PAYMENTS
Trade – US$3,703m deficit (2016)
Current Account – US$694m deficit (2017)

Trade with UK	2016	2017
Imports from UK	£7,204,837	£6,689,430
Exports to UK	£30,234,870	£50,392,793

COMMUNICATIONS
Airports – The main airport is at Managua, and there are a further 11 airports around the country
Waterways – The chief ports are Corinto (Pacific) and Bluefields and El Bluff (Caribbean); there are 2,220km of inland waterways, mostly on lakes Managua and Nicaragua
Roadways – There are 3,282km of roadways; the Inter-American Highway runs between Nicaragua's Honduran and Costa Rican borders, and the Inter-Oceanic Highway runs from Corinto on the Pacific coast via Managua to Rama, where there is a natural waterway to Bluefields on the Caribbean
Telecommunications – 366,636 fixed lines and 7.7 million mobile subscriptions (2016); there were 1.5 million internet users in 2016
Internet code and IDD – ni; 505 (from UK), 44 (to UK)
Major broadcasters – There are several commercial television and radio broadcasters, including Nicavision Canal 12; Radio Nicaragua is publicly owned
Press – *La Prensa* and *El Nuevo Diario* are the country's two principal daily newspapers
WPFI score – 30,41 (90)

EDUCATION AND HEALTH
Literacy rate – 91.6 per cent (2015 est)
Gross enrolment ratio (percentage of relevant age group) – primary 117 per cent, secondary 69 per cent (2010 est)
Health expenditure (per capita) – US$177 (2014)
Hospital beds (per 1,000 people) – 0.9 (2014)
Life expectancy (years) – 73.5 (2017 est)
Mortality rate – 5.1 (2017 est)
Birth rate – 17.7 (2017 est)
Infant mortality rate – 18.3 (2017 est)
HIV/AIDS adult prevalence – 0.2 per cent (2016 est)

NIGER

République du Niger – Republic of Niger

Area – 1,267,000 sq. km
Capital – Niamey; population, 1,214,000 (2018 est)
Major cities – Agadez, Maradi, Zinder
Currency – Franc CFA of 100 centimes
Population – 19,245,344 rising at 3.19 per cent a year (2017 est); Hausa (53.1 per cent), Zarma/Songhai (21.2 per cent), Tuareg (11 per cent), Fulani (6.5 per cent), Kanouri (5.9 per cent) (2006 est)
Religion – Muslim 80 per cent, other (includes indigenous beliefs and Christian) 20 per cent
Language – French (official), Arabic, Hausa, Djerma
Population density – 17 per sq. km (2016)
Urban population – 16.4 per cent (2018 est)
Median age (years) – 15.3 (2016 est)
National anthem – 'La Nigérienne' 'The Nigerian'
National day – 18 December (Republic Day)
Death penalty – Retained (no known use since 1976)
CPI score – 33 (112)
Military expenditure – US$200m (2017 est)
Conscription – 18 years of age; 24 months (selective)
Literacy rate – 26.6 per cent (2015 est)
Gross enrolment ratio (percentage of relevant age group) – primary 74 per cent, secondary 24 per cent (2016 est), tertiary 2 per cent (2012 est)
Health expenditure (per capita) – US$24 (2014)
Life expectancy (years) – 55.9 (2017 est)
Mortality rate – 11.8 (2017 est)
Birth rate – 44.2 (2017 est)
Infant mortality rate – 81.1 (2017 est)
HIV/AIDS adult prevalence – 0.4 per cent (2016 est)

CLIMATE AND TERRAIN
Niger is mostly desert, with low hills in the north and savannah in the south. Elevation extremes range from 2,022m (Mt Idoukal-n-Taghes/Bagzane) to 200m (Niger river). The Niger valley in the south-west is the only well-watered area. There is a desert climate, except in the extreme south, which is subtropical. Average temperatures range from 19.3°C in January to 33.3°C in June.

HISTORY AND POLITICS
The area was divided between several kingdoms formed by different tribes (Tuareg, Songhai, Hausa, Fulani) from the tenth to 19th centuries. French colonial expansion from the 1880s brought the whole area under its control in 1898 and in 1904 it became part of French West Africa. The country became autonomous in 1958 and achieved full independence in 1960.

The first president introduced a one-party regime, which continued under the military government installed after a coup in 1974. Following popular agitation, civilian government was reintroduced in 1989, other parties were legalised in 1990, and multi-party elections held in 1993. This political liberalisation was reversed following a military coup in 1996 led by Brig. Ibrahim Barre Mainassara. He was assassinated in 1999 by the military, who restored political pluralism.

From 1990 there was a rebellion in the north by Tuareg seeking greater social equality and political representation. Peace agreements with rebel groups in 1995 and 1997 brought calm until 2007, when a new rebel group emerged, seeking greater autonomy and access to mining revenue; this group signed a ceasefire with the government in 2009.

After seeking to increase his powers in 2009, President Mamadou Tandja (first elected in 1999) was deposed in February 2010 by the military. A referendum on a new constitution was held in October 2010, and presidential and legislative elections were held in January 2011. The Nigerien Party for Democracy and Socialism (PNDS-Tarayya) won the most seats, but without a majority; in August 2013 a unity government was declared under Prime Minister Brigi Rafini. The PNDS-Tarayya leader Mahamadou Issoufou was elected president in the second round of voting in March 2011 and re-elected in March 2016.

The 2010 constitution, amended in 2016, reduced the president's powers and restored the limit on presidential terms. The executive president is directly elected for a five-year term, renewable once. The unicameral National Assembly has 171 members directly elected for a five-year term; eight seats are reserved for minorities and five for Nigeriens living abroad. The prime minister is appointed by the president.

HEAD OF STATE
President, Mahamadou Issoufou, *elected* 12 March 2011, *took office* 7 April 2011, *re-elected* 2016

SELECTED GOVERNMENT MEMBERS *AS AT JUNE 2018*
Prime Minister, Brigi Rafini
Finance, Massaoudou Hassoumi
Foreign Affairs, Kalla Hankouraou
Interior, Bazoum Mohamed

HONORARY CONSULATE
MPC House, 15 Maple Mews, London NW6 5UZ
T 020-7328 8180 E consulate@nigerconsulateuk.org
W www.nigerconsulateuk.org
Honorary Consul, Muhammadu Dikko Ladan

BRITISH AMBASSADOR
HE Cat Evans, *apptd* 2018, resident at Bamako, Mali

ECONOMY AND TRADE
Niger is considered the second least developed country in the world, with almost half of the population living below the poverty line. Economic progress has been hampered by terrorist activity, political instability, food insecurity caused by recurrent droughts, desertification and over-grazing, and rapid population growth. The country is dependent on foreign aid, which makes up a large proportion of government revenue. Its huge foreign debt burden was much reduced by debt relief and cancellation in 2000 and 2005, but public debt has been growing since 2011 as spending on infrastructure and security has increased. While the country negotiated an extended credit facility agreement with the IMF in 2012–16 and for 2017–20, and in June 2017 agreed a three-year $1bn grant with the World Bank to boost agricultural production and alleviate poverty, Niger suffers from fluctuations in the price of its exports and has struggled to diversify its economy.

The mainstay of the economy is currently subsistence agriculture and herding, which accounts for 41.5 per cent of GDP and engages 79.2 per cent of the population; the main cash crops are cowpeas, cotton, vegetables, peanuts and livestock. The most significant export is uranium, making the economy vulnerable to fluctuations in global prices; efforts are being made to diversify into exploitation of other mineral resources, including gold and oil. The other industries include processing agricultural products and manufacturing cement, bricks, soap, textiles and chemicals. Industry contributes 18.1 per cent of GDP and services 40.4 per cent.

The main trading partners are France, Thailand and Malaysia. Principal exports are uranium ore, livestock, cowpeas and onions. The main imports are foodstuffs, machinery, vehicles and parts, petroleum and cereals.

GNI – US$7.7bn; US$360 per capita (2017)
Annual average growth of GDP – 4.2 per cent (2017 est)
Inflation rate – 1.0 per cent (2017 est)
Population below poverty line – 45.4 per cent (2014 est)
Unemployment – 2.6 per cent (2016 est)
Total external debt – US$3.09bn (2017 est)
Imports – US$1,990m (2015)
Exports – US$1,050m (2015)

BALANCE OF PAYMENTS
Trade – US$940m deficit (2015)
Current Account – US$1,180m deficit (2016)

Trade with UK	2016	2017
Imports from UK	£3,804,091	£6,583,090
Exports to UK	£160,270	£850,249

COMMUNICATIONS
Airports and waterways – The principal airport is at Niamey and there are a further nine airports; the river Niger is navigable between September and March for 300km from Niamey to the Benin frontier
Roadways – There are 3,912km of roadways
Telecommunications – 160,848 fixed lines and 8.7 million mobile subscriptions (2016); there were 805,702 internet users in 2016
Internet code and IDD – ne; 227 (from UK), 44 (to UK)
Major broadcasters – The government-owned Télé-Sahel (TV) competes with a number of commercial stations; state-run La Voix du Sahel is the only radio station offering national coverage
Press – The state-run *Le Sahel* is the only national daily
WPFI score – 27,40 (63)

NIGERIA

Federal Republic of Nigeria

Area – 923,768 sq. km
Capital – Abuja (since 1991); population, 2,919,000 (2018 est)
Major cities – Aba, Benin City, Ibadan, Ilorin, Kaduna, Kano, Lagos (the former capital), Port Harcourt, Warri, Zaria
Currency – Naira (N) of 100 kobo
Population – 190,632,261 rising at 2.43 per cent a year (2017 est); Hausa and Fulani (29 per cent), Yoruba (21 per cent), Igbo (18 per cent), Ijaw (10 per cent), Kanuri (4 per cent), Ibibio (3.5 per cent), Tiv (2.5 per cent) (est)
Religion – Muslim 50 per cent, Christian 40 per cent, indigenous beliefs 10 per cent
Language – English (official), Hausa, Yoruba, Igbo, Fula, over 500 other languages
Population density – 210 per sq. km (2016)
Urban population – 50.3 per cent (2018 est)
Median age (years) – 18.3 (2016 est)
National anthem – 'Arise O Compatriots, Nigeria's Call Obey'
National day – 1 October (Independence Day)
Death penalty – Retained
CPI score – 27 (148)
Military expenditure – US$1,621m (2016)

CLIMATE AND TERRAIN
The north is arid savannah and semi-desert plains, which rise to central hills and plateaux. There are mountains along the south-eastern border, but the south is generally low-lying and covered in tropical rainforest, with mangrove swamps along the coast and hills in the south-east. Elevation extremes range from 2,419m (Chappal Waddi) to 0m (Atlantic Ocean). The river Niger flows across the country from the north-west to the south coast, where it forms a broad delta on the Gulf of Guinea. The climate is equatorial in the south, tropical in the centre and arid in the north. The north has one rainy season (June to September), while the south has two (March–July, September–October); average national temperatures range from 24.9°C in January to 30.4°C in April.

POLITICS
The country is a federal democratic republic. Under the 1999 constitution, the executive president is directly elected for a four-year term, renewable once. The president appoints the federal executive council, which must be approved by the senate. The bicameral National Assembly comprises the 360-member House of Representatives and the 109-member senate, both elected for a four-year term.

The March 2015 presidential election was won by former military ruler Muhammadu Buhari of the All Progressives Congress (APC) – the first time an opposition candidate has unseated the incumbent at the ballot box. The APC also secured a majority in both houses during the simultaneous legislative elections. Despite some allegations of fraud, the elections were described as largely fair by the majority of observers. However, ethnic and religious violence is still commonplace. As of May 2018, the country is estimated to contain the largest concentration of people living in extreme poverty in the world, at 87 million.

HEAD OF STATE
President, C-in-C of the Armed Forces, Muhammadu Buhari, *elected* 31 March 2015, *sworn in* 5 May 2015
Vice-President, Yemi Osinbajo

SELECTED GOVERNMENT MEMBERS *AS AT JUNE 2018*
Finance, Kemi Adeosun
Foreign Affairs, Geoffrey Onyeama
Interior, Abdulrahman Dambazzau

HIGH COMMISSION FOR THE FEDERAL REPUBLIC OF NIGERIA
Nigeria House, 9 Northumberland Avenue, London WC2N 5BX
T 020-7839 1244 E information@nigeriahc.org.uk
W www.nigeriahc.org.uk
High Commissioner, HE George Oguntade, *apptd* 2017

BRITISH HIGH COMMISSION
19 Torrens Close, Mississippi, Maitama, Abuja
T (+234) (9) 462 2200 E ppainformation.abuja@fco.gov.uk
W www.gov.uk/government/world/nigeria
High Commissioner, HE Paul Arkwright, *apptd* 2015

FEDERAL STRUCTURE
The federal republic is divided into 36 states and the Federal Capital Territory: Abia, Adamawa, Akwa Ibom, Anambra, Bauchi, Bayelsa, Benue, Borno, Cross River, Delta, Ebonyi, Edo, Ekiti, Enugu, Gombe, Imo, Jigawa, Kaduna, Kano, Katsina, Kebbi, Kogi, Kwara, Lagos, Nassarawa, Niger, Ogun, Ondo, Osun, Oyo, Plateau, Rivers, Sokoto, Taraba, Yobe and Zamfara. Each state has an elected governor and legislature.

ECONOMY AND TRADE
In April 2014 a statistical 'revaluation' of the economy by the Nigerian government increased the size of the its economy by 89 per cent overnight, and Nigeria has now emerged as Sub-Saharan Africa's largest economy. Nonetheless, over 62 per cent of the nation (almost 120 million people) live in extreme poverty. The country is the largest sub-Saharan oil producer, enjoying an oil boom in the 1970s, however, mismanagement and corruption mean the majority of the population has yet to derive much benefit. Since 2008 economic reforms have been introduced to improve fiscal and monetary management, curb inflation and address regional agitation for wider distribution of oil revenues. Factors such as security and inadequate infrastructure, especially electricity supply and roads, remain obstacles to growth. Low oil prices coupled with the impact of foreign-exchange controls mean the country entered recession of 2016, but returned to growth in 2017. As a result of Boko Haram's terror campaign, internal displacement, underinvestment and difficulties in supplying aid, Nigeria faces one of the world's largest humanitarian crises with an estimated 8.5 million people in need of urgent assistance.

Agriculture, mostly at subsistence level, generates 21.6 per cent of GDP and engages about 70 per cent of the labour force. The main crops include cocoa, peanuts, cotton, palm oil, maize, rice, sorghum, millet and rubber. However, agricultural output has failed to keep pace with rapid population growth, changing Nigeria from a net food exporter to a food importer. Industrial activities include oil and natural gas production, mining (coal, tin, columbite), processing agricultural products, textiles, cement and other construction materials and

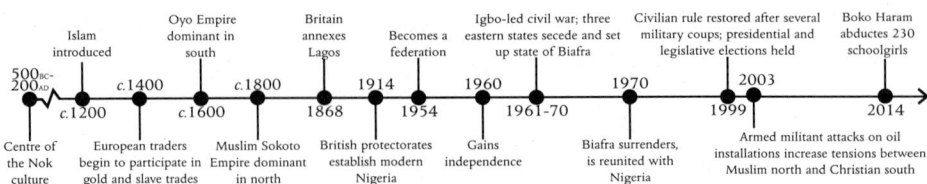

footwear. Industry contributes 18.3 per cent of GDP and services 60.1 per cent.

The main trading partners are China, India, the USA, and EU nations. Exports are almost entirely oil and oil products. The main imports are machinery, chemicals, transport equipment, manufactured goods, food and live animals.

GNI – US$397.5bn; US$2,080 per capita (2017)
Annual average growth of GDP – 0.8 per cent (2017 est)
Inflation rate – 16.3 per cent (2017 est)
Population below poverty line – 70 per cent (2010 est)
Unemployment – 13.4 per cent (2017 est)
Total external debt – US$35.23bn (2017 est)
Imports – US$34,981m (2015)
Exports – US$108,929m (2014)

BALANCE OF PAYMENTS

Trade – US$78,297m surplus (2012)
Current Account – US$10,301m deficit (2017)

Trade with UK	2016	2017
Imports from UK	£951,110,804	£1,121,999,642
Exports to UK	£908,376,730	£1,313,648,772

COMMUNICATIONS

Airports and waterways – There are 40 airports, including the principal airports at Lagos, Abuja, Kano and Port Harcourt; there are 8,600km of waterways, mostly on the Niger and Benue rivers; the main seaports are Lagos, Port Harcourt, Warri and Calabar
Roadways and railways – There are 28,980km of roadways; the Nigerian railway network, which is controlled by the Nigerian Railway Corporation, has 3,505km of track
Telecommunications – 154,513 fixed lines and 154 million mobile subscriptions (2016); there were 47.7 million internet users in 2016
Internet code and IDD – ng; 234 (from UK), 9 44 (to UK)
Major broadcasters – The Nigerian Television Authority (NTA) and Federal Radio Corporation of Nigeria (FRCN) are the public broadcasters
Press – The Guardian is one of the most influential news publications in the country
WPFI score – 37,41 (11)

EDUCATION AND HEALTH

Literacy rate – 72.8 per cent (2015 est)
Gross enrolment ratio (percentage of relevant age group) – primary 93.7 per cent, secondary 55.7 per cent (2013 est)
Health expenditure (per capita) – US$118 (2014)
Hospital beds (per 1,000 people) – 0.5 (2004–9)
Life expectancy (years) – 53.8 (2017 est)
Mortality rate – 12.4 (2017 est)
Birth rate – 36.9 (2017 est)
Infant mortality rate – 69.8 (2017 est)
HIV/AIDS adult prevalence – 2.9 per cent (2016 est)

NORWAY

Kongeriket Norge – Kingdom of Norway

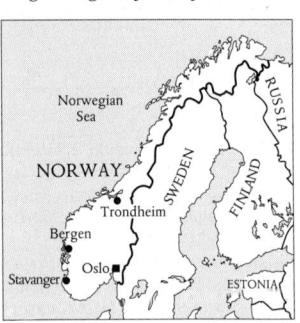

Area – 323,802 sq. km
Capital – Oslo; population, 1,012,000 (2018 est)
Major cities – Bergen, Stavanger, Trondheim
Currency – Krone of 100 ore
Population – 5,320,045 rising at 1.01 per cent a year (2017 est)
Religion – Christian (Lutheran 82.1 per cent, other 3.9 per cent), Muslim 2.3 per cent
Language – Bokmal and Nynorsk Norwegian (both official), Finnish, Sami (official in six municipalities)
Population density – 14 per sq. km (2016)
Urban population – 82.2 per cent (2018 est)
Median age (years) – 39.1 (2016 est)
National anthem – 'Ja, Vi Elsker Dette Landet' 'Yes, We Love This Country'
National day – 17 May (Constitution Day)
Death penalty – Abolished for all crimes (since 1979)
CPI score – 85 (3)
Military expenditure – US$6,567m (2017)
Conscription – 19–35 years of age; 12 months

CLIMATE AND TERRAIN

The terrain is mostly mountainous, with elevated, barren plateaux separated by deep, narrow valleys; the north is arctic tundra. The coastline is deeply indented with numerous fjords and fringed with thousands of rocky islands and islets; Geirangerfjord and Naeroyfjord are UNESCO World Heritage Sites. Elevation extremes range from 2,469m (Galdhopiggen) to 0m (Norwegian Sea).

Nearly half of the country lies north of the Arctic Circle, and at North Cape the sun does not appear to set between about 14 May and 29 July, causing the phenomenon known as the midnight sun; conversely, there is no apparent sunrise from about 18 November to 24 January. The climate is temperate on the coast but colder and wetter inland; average temperatures range from −6.6°C in January to 12.6°C in July, but winter temperatures in parts of the north can drop to −40°C.

HISTORY AND POLITICS

Norway became a unified country under the rule of King Harald Fairhair in c.900 but dissolved after his death and was reunified by Olav II in c.1016–28. Canute brought Norway under Danish rule in 1028 but the throne reverted on his death to Magnus I. When the royal house died out in the 14th century, the Danish monarch was the nearest heir and in 1397 Norway, Denmark and Sweden were united under a single monarch in the Kalmar Union. Sweden seceded from the union in 1523, but Norway continued to be ruled by the Danish crown until 1814, when it was ceded to Sweden.

Although internal self-government was established in 1814, growing tension over constraints on the Norwegian government led to the union being dissolved, and Norway became independent in 1905. The first king of the newly independent country was a Danish prince, who took the throne as King Haakon VII.

The country was neutral in the First World War, but in the Second World War Norway was invaded and occupied by Germany from 1940 until 1945. Norway joined NATO in 1949 and was a founder member of the European Free Trade Association in 1960. Membership of the EU was rejected in referendums in 1972 and 1994.

After 1945, governments pursued policies of economic planning and an extensive welfare state. The Labour Party dominated politics from the 1930s to the early 1980s, governing either on its own or in coalition with smaller parties. It was returned to power in 2005. After legislative elections in 2013 and 2017, the Conservative Party formed a minority government with the right-wing Progress Party, despite the Labour Party remaining the largest single party in the legislature.

Norway is a constitutional monarchy with a hereditary monarch as head of state. Under the 1814 constitution, the unicameral *Storting* has 169 members who are directly elected for a four-year term; a 2007 constitutional amendment abolished a bicameral division within the *Storting*, which took effect from the 2009 election. The prime minister, who is responsible to parliament, appoints the cabinet.

HEAD OF STATE

HM The King of Norway, King Harald V, KG, GCVO, *born* 21 February 1937, *succeeded* 17 January 1991
Heir, HRH Crown Prince Haakon Magnus, *born* 20 July 1973

SELECTED GOVERNMENT MEMBERS *AS AT JUNE 2018*

Prime Minister, Erna Solberg
Defence, Frank Bakke-Jensen
Finance, Siv Jensen
Foreign Affairs, Ine Marie Eriksen Soreide

ROYAL NORWEGIAN EMBASSY

25 Belgrave Square, London SW1X 8QD
T 020-7591 5500 **E** emb.london@mfa.no **W** www.norway.org.uk
Ambassador Extraordinary and Plenipotentiary, HE Mona Juul, *apptd* 2014

BRITISH EMBASSY

Thomas Heftyes Gate 8, 0244 Oslo
T (+47) 2313 2700 **E** britemb@online.no
W www.gov.uk/government/world/norway
Ambassador Extraordinary and Plenipotentiary, HE Richard Wood, *apptd* 2018

ECONOMY AND TRADE

Norway's prosperity depends primarily upon oil and gas extraction, which accounts for nearly half of exports, and its fisheries. Oil production is declining, but oil and gas deposits in the Barents Sea and other areas are becoming more accessible as the Arctic ice cap retreats. Norway has planned for the time when reserves are exhausted by investing revenue from this sector in the world's largest sovereign wealth fund, valued at over US$1 trillion in 2017. The state retains a majority share in key enterprises, including the oil industry. While the economy contracted in 2009, it has grown modestly ever since despite low oil and gas prices, and in 2017 labour force participation and employment also rose.

The nature of the terrain restricts agriculture, which generates 2.4 per cent of GDP. The main industries apart from oil and gas are fishing (the world's second largest exporter), forestry, food processing, shipbuilding, pulp and paper products, metals, chemicals, mining and textiles. Shipping freight services are also significant, with Norway ranked as the fifth largest shipping nation by fleet value. Industry contributes 31.1 per cent of GDP and services 66.5 per cent.

The main trading partners are the UK (21.1 per cent of exports), other EU countries, the USA and China. Principal exports are oil and petroleum products, machinery and equipment, metals, chemicals, ships and fish. The main imports are machinery and equipment, chemicals, metals and foodstuffs.

GNI – US$401.4bn; US$75,990 per capita (2017)
Annual average growth of GDP – 1.4 per cent (2017 est)
Inflation rate – 2.1 per cent (2017 est)
Unemployment – 4 per cent (2017 est)
Total external debt – US$642.3bn (2016 est)
Imports – US$72,013m (2016)
Exports – US$88,033m (2016)

BALANCE OF PAYMENTS

Trade – US$16,020m surplus (2016)
Current Account – US$21,842m surplus (2017)

Trade with UK	2016	2017
Imports from UK	£3,065,275,732	£2,994,085,023
Exports to UK	£13,568,498,550	£19,200,850,061

COMMUNICATIONS

Airports and waterways – There are 67 airports, including the principal airports at Oslo, Bergen, Stavanger and Trondheim; the main ports are Oslo, Bergen, Kristiansand, Tonsberg, Stavanger and Narvik, and there is a large merchant fleet, with 585 ships of over 1,000 tonnes registered in Norway and 974 registered abroad
Roadways and railways – 18,116km; 4,237km
Telecommunications – 806,264 million fixed lines and 5.7 million mobile subscriptions (2016); there were 5.1 million internet users in 2016
Internet code and IDD – no; 47 (from UK), 44 20 (to UK)
Major broadcasters – The public broadcaster NRK operates radio and television channels, in competition with a number of commercial rivals
Press – *VG* has the largest circulation among the country's daily news publications; other newspapers include *The Norway Post* and *Dagbladet*
WPFI score – 7,63 (1)

EDUCATION AND HEALTH

Education from six to 16 is free and compulsory in the basic schools, and free from 16 to 19 years.

Gross enrolment ratio (percentage of relevant age group) – primary 100 per cent, secondary 114 per cent, tertiary 81 per cent (2016 est)
Health expenditure (per capita) – US$9,522 (2014)
Hospital beds (per 1,000 people) – 3.8 (2015)
Life expectancy (years) – 81.9 (2017 est)
Mortality rate – 8.1 (2017 est)
Birth rate – 12.2 (2017 est)
Infant mortality rate – 2.5 (2017 est)
HIV/AIDS adult prevalence – 0.15 per cent (2014 est)

TERRITORIES

JAN MAYEN ISLAND
Area – 377 sq. km
Population – The only residents are the staff of the radio and meteorological stations
The island is barren, volcanic and partially covered by glaciers, with no exploitable natural resources. It lies in the North Atlantic Ocean about 950km west of Norway and is home to the Beerenberg volcano, the northernmost active volcano on Earth. It was annexed by Norway in 1922 and integrated into the kingdom in 1930; since 1995 it has been administered by the governor of Nordland county.

SVALBARD
Area – 62,045 sq. km
Population – 2,583 (2017 est) falling at 0.03 per cent a year (2014 est); Norwegian 55.4 per cent, Russian and Ukrainian 44.3 per cent
The Svalbard archipelago consists of Spitsbergen, North East Land, the Wiche Islands, Barents Island, Edge Island, Prince Charles Foreland, Hope Island and Bear Island. It lies north of the Arctic Circle, and glaciers and snow cover around 60 per cent of the area, although the west coast is ice-free for about half the year. Some 65 per cent of the Svalbard archipelago is protected to ensure biodiversity; there are seven national parks, six large nature reserves, 15 bird sanctuaries and one geotopic protected area. A global seed repository has been established on Spitsbergen. Norway's sovereignty was recognised by treaty in 1920 but the other signatories were granted equal rights to exploit mineral deposits, although this right is now only exercised by Russia. The territory is administered by a governor, who is responsible to the Ministry of Justice and Police. The main economic activities are coal mining, tourism, and research and education.

NORWEGIAN ANTARCTIC TERRITORY

The Norwegian Antarctic Territory consists of Queen Maud Land, Bouvet Island and Peter the First Island. Claimed in 1938, Queen Maud Land is a sector of the Antarctic continent that extends from 45° E. to 20° E. Peter the First Island was formally claimed in 1931 and is the only claimed area covered under the Antarctic Treaty that is not part of the main landmass. Bouvet Island was claimed in 1930 (*see also* The North and South Poles).

OMAN

Saltanat Uman – Sultanate of Oman

Area – 309,500 sq. km
Capital – Muscat (Masqat); population, 1,447,000 (2018 est)
Major cities – Ibri, Salalah, Suhar, as-Suwayq
Currency – Omani Rial (OR) of 1,000 baisas
Population – 4,613,241 rising at 2.03 per cent a year (2017 est)
Religion – Muslim 85.9 per cent (majority are Ibadhi, lesser numbers of Sunni and Shia), Christian 6.5 per cent, Hindu 5.5 per cent (2010 est)
Language – Arabic (official), English, Baluchi, Urdu
Population density – 15 per sq. km (2016)
Urban population – 84.5 per cent (2018 est)
Median age (years) – 25.4 (2016 est)
National anthem – 'Nashid as-Salaam as-Sultani' 'The Sultan's Anthem'
National day – 18 November (Birthday of Sultan Qaboos, 1940)
Death penalty – Retained
CPI score – 44 (68)
Military expenditure – US$9,103m (2016)

CLIMATE AND TERRAIN

Oman lies at the south-eastern corner of the Arabian peninsula and includes territory at the tip of the Musandam peninsula, which is separated from the rest of the country by the UAE. There are mountains in the north and the south-west of the country, divided by a high desert plateau; over 80 per cent of the country is desert. The plateau descends to a fertile plain on the Arabian Sea coast. Elevation extremes range from 2,980m (Jabal Shams) to 0m (Arabian Sea). The climate is arid, with high temperatures and humidity throughout the year; temperatures are lower on the coast, but the high humidity often makes coastal areas the most inhospitable. Average temperatures range from 20.4°C in January to 30.4°C in June.

HISTORY AND POLITICS

Oman began to build an empire in the Middle East from the eighth century AD and remained largely unchallenged until the arrival in 1506 of the Portuguese, who were ousted in 1650. An independent sultanate was established in 1749 by the founder of the dynasty that still rules the country. By the early 19th century, Omani rule extended to the east African coast and parts of Persia and Balochistan (in modern Pakistan). The kingdom came under British influence from the late 19th century until 1951.

The country was divided from 1913, with religious leaders in control of the interior and the sultan of the coastal regions. The interior's attempts to assert its independence led to clashes in the 1950s, but by 1959 the sultan had established control over the whole country. An insurrection in the south by left-wing rebels supported by South Yemen began in 1965 and was defeated with British military assistance in 1975. The discovery and subsequent exploitation of oil in the mid-1960s led to the steady economic transformation of Oman, and in 1970 the sultan was overthrown in a bloodless coup by his son, Sultan Qaboos bin Said al-Said, who initiated a modernisation programme.

The country is still essentially an absolute monarchy, although a degree of political liberalisation has occurred in the past 20 years. In 1996 the sultan issued a Basic Statute that is in effect a constitution; it established a succession mechanism, codified the system of government and set up a bicameral legislature. The first direct election to the consultative council was held in 2000 and the first by universal adult suffrage in 2003. In the 2017 election, all the candidates were independents. Pro-reform demonstrations occurred prior to the October 2011 elections.

At present, legislation is proposed by the sultan and passed by decree. The sultan is advised by the bicameral Council of Oman, comprising the Consultative Council *(Majlis al-Shura)*, which has 85 members directly elected for a four-year term, and the Council of State *(Majlis al-Dawlah)*, which has 85 members appointed by the sultan for a four-year term. The Consultative Council has the right to review legislation, question ministers and make policy proposals. The Council of State is intended to facilitate 'constructive cooperation between the government and the citizens'. Political parties are illegal.

HEAD OF STATE
HM The Sultan of Oman, Prime Minister, C-in-C of the Armed Forces, Sultan Qaboos bin Said al-Said, *succeeded following a coup,* 23 July 1970

SELECTED GOVERNMENT MEMBERS *AS AT JUNE 2018*
Deputy Prime Minister, Fahd bin Mamud al-Said
Defence, Badr bin Saud bin Hareb al-Busaidi
Foreign Affairs, Yusuf bin Alawi bin Abdullah
Interior, Hamoud bin Faisal al-Busaidi

EMBASSY OF THE SULTANATE OF OMAN
167 Queen's Gate, London SW7 5HE
T 020-7225 0001
Ambassador Extraordinary and Plenipotentiary, HE Abdul Aziz al-Hinai, *apptd* 2009

BRITISH EMBASSY
PO Box 185, Mina al-Fahal, 116 Muscat
T (+968) (24) 609 000 E muscat.enquiries@fco.gov.uk
W www.gov.uk/government/world/oman
Ambassador Extraordinary and Plenipotentiary, HE Hamish Cowell, CMG, *apptd* 2017

ECONOMY AND TRADE
Although its production is more modest than other Gulf states, oil and gas are the mainstay of Oman's economy and provide the majority of government revenue. Oil reserves are dwindling and development plans centre on diversification, industrialisation and privatisation, with the aim of reducing the oil sector's contribution to GDP to 9 per cent by 2020. Industrial development is focused on natural gas production,

metal manufacturing, petrochemicals and trans-shipment ports, with plans also to develop tourism and communication technology industries. Improved training, especially in IT and business skills, is intended to enable the local population to replace expatriate workers. In 2016, the budget deficit was estimated at roughly 20 per cent of GDP and while it has declined remains high given low oil prices.

Agriculture and fishing account for 1.7 per cent of GDP, producing dates, limes, bananas, alfalfa and vegetables as well as fish. The main industries apart from oil and natural gas extraction are oil refining, liquefied natural gas production, construction and production of cement, copper, steel, chemicals and optic fibre. Industry accounts for 45.2 per cent of GDP and services for 53 per cent.

The main trading partners are China, the UAE, the USA and South Korea. Principal exports are petroleum, re-exports, fish, metals and textiles. The main imports are machinery, transport equipment, manufactured goods, food and livestock.
GNI – US$66.9bn; US$14,440 per capita (2017)
Annual average growth of GDP – –0.3 per cent (2017 est)
Inflation rate – 3.2 per cent (2017 est)
Total external debt – US$39.17bn (2017 est)
Imports – US$29,007m (2015)
Exports – US$34,734m (2015)

BALANCE OF PAYMENTS
Trade – US$5,727m surplus (2015)
Current Account – US$12,319m deficit (2016)

Trade with UK	2016	2017
Imports from UK	£485,745,302	£1,849,888,045
Exports to UK	£104,102,664	£280,095,361

COMMUNICATIONS
Airports and waterways – The main airports are at Muscat and Salalah; the main ports are Salalah and Port Qaboos at Mutrah, which has eight deep-water berths
Roadways – There are 29,685km of roadways, including 1,943km of motorways
Telecommunications – 422,518 fixed lines and 6.8 million mobile telephone subscriptions (2016); there were 2.3 million internet users in 2016
Internet code and IDD – om; 968 (from UK), 44 (to UK)
Media – Oman TV and Radio Oman are the state-run broadcasters; *Al-Watan* and the *Oman Daily* are the principal daily newspapers
WPFI score – 40,67 (127)

EDUCATION AND HEALTH
Literacy rate – 99.2 per cent (2015 est)
Gross enrolment ratio (percentage of relevant age group) – primary 109 per cent, secondary 107 per cent, tertiary 45 per cent (2016 est)
Health expenditure (per capita) – US$675 (2014)
Hospital beds (per 1,000 people) – 1.6 (2014)
Life expectancy (years) – 75.7 (2017 est)
Mortality rate – 3.3 (2017 est)
Birth rate – 24 (2017 est)
Infant mortality rate – 12.8 (2017 est)
HIV/AIDS adult prevalence – 0.16 per cent (2014 est)

PAKISTAN

Jamhuryat Islami Pakistan – Islamic Republic of Pakistan

Area – 796,095 sq. km
Capital – Islamabad; population, 1,061,000 (2018 est)
Major cities – Faisalabad, Gujranwala, Hyderabad, Karachi, Lahore, Multan, Peshawar, Quetta, Rawalpindi
Currency – Pakistan rupee of 100 paisa
Population – 204,924,861 rising at 1.43 per cent a year (2017 est); Punjabi (44.7 per cent), Pashtun (15.4 per cent), Sindhi (14.1 per cent), Sariaki (8.4 per cent), Muhajirs (7.6 per cent), Balochi (3.6 per cent) (est)
Religion – Muslim 96.4 per cent (predominantly Sunni), other (includes Christian and Hindu) 3.6 per cent; Islam is the state religion
Language – English, Urdu (both official), Balochi, Brahui, Burushaski, Hindko, Pashto, Punjabi, Sindhi, Siraiki
Population density – 256 per sq. km (2016)
Urban population – 36.7 per cent (2018 est)
Median age (years) – 23.4 (2016 est)
National anthem – 'Qaumi Tarana' 'The Sacred Land'
National day – 23 March (Republic Day)
Death penalty – Retained
CPI score – 32 (117)
Military expenditure – US$10,775m (2017)

CLIMATE AND TERRAIN

The arid Thar desert in the east gives way to the fertile Indus valley in the centre of the country. The terrain then rises to the Makran, Kirthar and Sulaiman mountain ranges in the west and the Karakoram and Himalayan ranges in the north. Elevation extremes range from 8,611m (K2) to 0m (Indian Ocean). The climate varies greatly across the country. For most areas, the rainy season runs from July to September and is accompanied by very high humidity. Average temperatures range from 8.8°C in January to 28.6°C in June. Pakistan is prone to earthquakes – the most recent major occurrences were in 2008, 2013 and 2015 – and flooding; following heavy monsoon rains in 2010 the entire length of the Indus valley was flooded, displacing millions of people.

POLITICS

Pakistan is a federal republic. The 1973 constitution has been suspended, restored and amended several times, and in 2010 was reinstated in its original form, returning some of the president's powers to the prime minister.

The president is elected by the legislature for a five-year term, renewable once. The parliament *(Majlis as-Shura)* comprises a lower house, the National Assembly and the senate. The National Assembly has 342 seats, of which 60 are reserved for women and ten are elected by non-Muslim minorities; members serve a five-year term. The senate has 104 members indirectly elected by provincial assemblies; they serve a six-year term, with half elected every three years. The prime minister is nominated by and is responsible to the legislature.

There are four provinces: Balochistan, Khyber Pukhtoonkhwa (formerly North-West Frontier Province), Punjab and Sindh. Each has a provincial assembly and government. In addition, there are the Federally Administered Tribal Areas and the Islamabad Capital Territory.

The legislative elections originally scheduled for January 2008 were postponed to February after the assassination of Benazir Bhutto in December 2007. The two main opposition parties, Bhutto's Pakistan People's Party (PPP) and the Pakistan Muslim League–Nawaz Sharif (PML-N), won the most seats and formed a coalition government with two smaller parties; the PML-N withdrew from the coalition government in August 2008. The presidential election in July 2013 was won by Mamnoon Hussain, the first instance in Pakistan's history in which one elected civilian president was replaced by another. Nawaz Sharif was elected prime minister in June 2013, but in July 2017 was removed from office by the supreme court over corruption allegations and was later sentenced to ten years in prison. The PML-N lost the 2018 elections to the centrist Pakistan Movement for Justice (PTI), founded by former cricketer Imran Kahn in 1996, in an election marred by violent IS attacks. Kahn was later named prime minister, and PTI's Arif Alvi elected president.

HEAD OF STATE
President, Arif Alvi *elected* 4 September 2018, *sworn in* 9 September 2018

SELECTED GOVERNMENT MEMBERS *AS AT SEPTEMBER 2018*
Prime Minister, Imran Kahn
Defence, Pervez Khattak
Finance, Asad Umar
Foreign Affairs, Makhdoom Shad Mahmood Qureshi

HIGH COMMISSION FOR THE ISLAMIC REPUBLIC OF PAKISTAN
34–36 Lowndes Square, London SW1X 9JN
T 020-7664 924 E poldiv@phclondon.org W www.phclondon.org
High Commissioner, HE Syed Ibne Abbas, *apptd* 2014

BRITISH HIGH COMMISSION
Diplomatic Enclave, Ramna 5, PO Box 1122, Islamabad
T (+92) (51) 201 2000 E islamabad-general.enquiries@fco.gov.uk
W www.gov.uk/government/world/pakistan
High Commissioner, HE Thomas Drew, CMG, *apptd* 2016

INSURGENCIES
Balochistan, Punjab and Sindh provinces have all been affected since the 1980s by conflict between Shia and Sunni fundamentalists. Balochistan and, since the early 1990s, Sindh (especially Karachi) have experienced violence by armed militants seeking greater autonomy for each province.

Civil order has always been harder to maintain in Pukhtoonkhwa and the federally administered tribal areas than in the rest of the country. These areas became havens for the Taliban and al-Qaida fleeing Afghanistan after 2001, radicalising and destabilising increasingly wide areas. Government military and security forces are struggling to maintain control in over half of these areas. The government conceded the imposition of Sharia law in the Swat valley as part of a ceasefire agreement with the Taliban in early 2009, but when the Taliban attempted to extend its influence further into the country, the army began a counter-insurgency offensive to retake the area in April 2009, subsequently moving against the Taliban in other strongholds such as South Waziristan. An increase in militant attacks in the major cities

| c.700 | c.1100 | c.1850 | 1940 | 1947 | 1956 | 1971 | 1977 | 1988-99 | 1999 | 2001 | 2008 | 2014 |

Part of several empires covering northern India, including Delhi Sultanate and Mughal Empire — c.700

Islam introduced to the area — c.1100

Becomes part of British India — c.1850

All-India Muslim League endorses the Lahore resolution, which calls for a separate Muslim state — 1940

Independence gained, Muslim areas are partitioned to form Pakistan — 1947

Becomes a republic — 1956

Zulfiqar Ali Bhutto overthrown by General Zia ul-Haq — 1971

East Pakistan becomes the independent state of Bangladesh — 1977

Military coup brings General Pervez Musharraf to power — 1988-99

Unstable civilian governments under Benazir Bhutto and Nawaz Sharif — 1999

Musharraf resigns from presidency — 2001

Western alliances anger Islamic militants and provoke terrorism — 2008

Musharraf treason trial begins — 2014

led to the resumption of peace talks with the Taliban in March 2014. Nevertheless, attacks on civilian targets continue: in October 2014 Malala Yousafzai was shot in the head in an attack on a school bus in Swat; in December 2015, 150 people, predominantly children, were killed in a Taliban attack on an army-run school in Peshawar; and in March 2016, more than 70 people were killed when suicide bombers targeted Christian families celebrating Easter at a park in Lahore. A moratorium on the death penalty was lifted following the attack in Peshawar.

FOREIGN RELATIONS

Since partition, sovereignty over the predominantly Muslim state of Jammu and Kashmir has been disputed between Pakistan and India. A short war in 1947–8 resulted in the state being partitioned between the two countries; its status remains unresolved, despite further outbreaks of war in 1965 and 1971, low-level conflict for control of the Siachen glacier since 1985 and occasional increases in military exchanges, most recently in 1999–2002 and 2003. Tension was exacerbated by Pakistan's support of the Muslim insurgency in the Indian part of the state, which began in the 1980s, and by both countries' acquisition of nuclear weapons. Moves towards a peaceful settlement began in 2003, when diplomatic missions were reopened and the resumption of transport links was initiated. Formal diplomatic talks began in 2004 and have achieved several accords intended to reduce tension between the two countries. Talks were temporarily suspended by the Indian government after the Mumbai terrorist attacks in 2008, but resumed in 2010. Clashes along the Kashmiri border have intensified in recent years, with notable clashes in late 2016–17.

ECONOMY AND TRADE

Decades of political instability, inefficiency, corruption and high military expenditure have left Pakistan an underdeveloped country, averaging poor economic growth between 2008 and 2015, although this is gradually improving. In the 2000s economic reforms, international aid and greater foreign investment produced steady growth of 5–8 per cent a year until 2008, notably in the industrial and service sectors, and reduced poverty levels by 10 per cent between 2001 and 2007. However, slower growth in 2008 caused budget and fiscal deficits that forced Pakistan to seek IMF assistance. These problems have been exacerbated by the 2010 floods, which left millions homeless, destroyed crops and damaged infrastructure. A large proportion of the country's labour force works abroad, especially in the Middle East, providing valuable remittances but also causing the use of child labour within Pakistan. The informal economy is widespread and underemployment is high. The Sharif government (2013–17) implemented fiscal and energy reforms, bolstered by implementation of the China–Pakistan Economic Corridor. Nevertheless, security and political instability remain significant threats to further development, as well as underinvestment in eduction, sanitation and healthcare.

Agriculture employs 42.3 per cent of the workforce, producing cotton, wheat, rice, sugar cane, fruits, vegetables, milk, meat and eggs, and contributes 24.7 per cent of GDP.

Significant manufacturing industries include textiles and clothing, food processing, pharmaceuticals, construction materials, paper products, fertiliser and seafood. Industry accounts for 19.1 per cent of GDP and services for 56.3 per cent.

The main trading partners are China, the USA, the UAE, the UK and Germany. Principal exports are textiles (clothing, bed linen, cotton cloth and yarn), rice, leather goods, sports goods, chemicals, surgical equipment, carpets and rugs. The main imports are petroleum, machinery, plastics, transport equipment, edible oils, paper, iron, steel and tea.

GNI – US$311.7bn; US$1,580 per capita (2017)
Annual average growth of GDP – 5.3 per cent (2017 est)
Inflation rate – 4.1 per cent (2017 est)
Population below poverty line – 29.5 per cent (2013 est)
Unemployment – 6 per cent (2017 est)
Total external debt – US$75.66bn (2017 est)
Imports – US$46,827m (2016)
Exports – US$20,524m (2016)

BALANCE OF PAYMENTS

Trade – US$26,303m deficit (2016)
Current Account – US$15,818m deficit (2017)

Trade with UK	2016	2017
Imports from UK	£624,254,201	£685,689,867
Exports to UK	£1,157,821,433	£1,246,997,271

COMMUNICATIONS

Airports and waterways – The principal airports are at Karachi, Islamabad, Lahore, Peshawar and Sialkot, and 103 other airports; the main seaports are Karachi and Port Muhammad bin Qasim, and there is a deep-water port at Gwadar
Roadways and railways – 189,218km, including 708km of motorways; 7,791km
Telecommunications – 3.1 million fixed lines and 136.4 million mobile subscriptions (2016); there were 31.3 million internet users in 2016
Internet code and IDD – pk; 92 (from UK), 44 (to UK)
Major broadcasters – Radio Pakistan and Pakistan Television Corporation Ltd are the principal state broadcasters
Press – Leading dailies include *Daily Jang* (Urdu language), *Dawn* and *The Nation* (both English language)
WPFI score – 43,24 (139)

EDUCATION AND HEALTH

Education is free to upper secondary level.
Literacy rate – 74.8 per cent (2015)
Gross enrolment ratio (percentage of relevant age group) – primary 98 per cent, secondary 46 per cent, tertiary 10 per cent (2016 est)
Health expenditure (per capita) – US$36 (2014)
Hospital beds (per 1,000 people) – 0.6 (2014)
Life expectancy (years) – 68.1 (2017 est)
Mortality rate – 6.3 (2017 est)
Birth rate – 21.9 (2017 est)
Infant mortality rate – 52.1 (2017 est)
HIV / AIDS adult prevalence – 0.1 per cent (2016 est)

PALAU

Beluu er a Belau – Republic of Palau

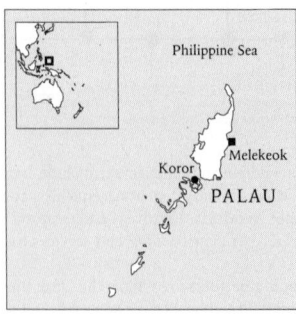

Area – 459 sq. km
Capital – Melekeok, on Babeldaob; population, 299 (2018)
Major town – Koror
Currency – US dollar (US$) of 100 cents
Population – 21,431 rising at 0.39 per cent a year (2017 est);
  Palauan (73 per cent), Carolinian (2.0 per cent), Asian
  (21.7 per cent) (2015 est)
Religion – Christian (Roman Catholic 49.4 per cent,
  Protestant 30.9 per cent), Modekngei 8.7 per cent
  (indigenous to Palau; combines Animism and Christianity)
  (2005 est)
Language – Palauan (official in most islands), English (official
  in all islands), Tobi, Sonsoralese, Angaur (official in
  respective islands), Japanese (official in Angaur), Filipino,
  Chinese
Population density – 47 per sq. km (2016)
Urban population – 79.9 per cent (2018 est)
Median age (years) – 33.3 (2016 est)
National anthem – 'Belau rekid' 'Our Palau'
National day – 9 July (Constitution Day)
Death penalty – Abolished for all crimes (since 1994)
Literacy rate – 99.8 per cent (2015 est)
Gross enrolment ratio (percentage of relevant age group) – primary
  114.3 per cent, secondary 113.6 per cent (2014 est),
  tertiary 61.9 (2013 est)
Health expenditure (per capita) – US$1,150 (2014)
Life expectancy (years) – 73.4 (2017 est)
Mortality rate – 8.1 (2017 est)
Birth rate – 11.3 (2017 est)
Infant mortality rate – 10.6 (2017 est)

CLIMATE AND TERRAIN

The republic consists of six island groups in the western
Pacific Ocean; these comprise eight large islands and over 300
smaller islands or islets that are either volcanic and
mountainous or coral and low-lying. Elevation extremes range
from 242m (Mt Ngerchelchuus) to 0m (Pacific Ocean). The
climate is tropical, with a wet season from May to November.
The average temperature is 27.8°C.

HISTORY AND POLITICS

Palau has been inhabited since the first millennium BC. In the
19th century, Spain and Germany vied for possession until
1889, when Spain sold the islands to Germany, which
exploited the phosphate deposits and developed coconut
plantations. Japan occupied the islands on behalf of the Allies
in 1914 and administered them after the First World War
under a League of Nations mandate. Japanese forces were
ousted by US troops during the Second World War.
  In 1947 the islands became part of the UN Trust Territory
of the Pacific, administered by the USA. In 1982 a compact of
free association was signed with the USA under which the
USA retained responsibility for defence and foreign policy in
return for providing economic aid; the compact was ratified in
1993 and entered into force when Palau became independent
on 1 October 1994.
  The latest presidential and legislative elections were held in
2016; Tommy Remengesau Jr was re-elected president.
  Under the 1981 constitution, the executive president is
directly elected for a four-year term, renewable once. The
president appoints the cabinet. The bicameral National
Congress comprises the House of Delegates, which has 16
members (one from each state), and the 13-member senate;
members of both chambers stand for election as independents
and serve a four-year term. A council of indigenous chiefs,
composed of the paramount chief from each of the 16 states,
acts as an advisory body to the president on matters
concerning traditional law and customs.
  Each of the 16 constituent states has its own governor and
legislature.

HEAD OF STATE

President, Tommy Remengesau Jr, *elected* 6 November 2012,
  inaugurated 17 January 2013, *re-elected* 2016
Vice-President, Justice, Raynold Oiluch

SELECTED GOVERNMENT MEMBERS *AS AT JUNE 2018*
Finance, Elbuchel Sadang
Minister of State, Billy Kuartei

HONORARY CONSULATE OF THE REPUBLIC OF
PALAU
Bankfoot Square, Bankfoot Street, Batley WF17 5LH
T 01924-470 786 W www.palauconsulate.org.uk

BRITISH AMBASSADOR
HE Daniel Pruce, *apptd* 2017, resident at Manila, Philippines

ECONOMY AND TRADE

The economy is reliant on economic aid from the USA and the
government is keen to diversify. Tourism is now the main
industry, catering for over 130,000 people a year and set to
increase with rising prosperity in East Asia. The other main
industry is fishing, which it the nation's only significant
export. Subsistence agriculture engages 1.2 per cent of the
workforce and producing crops such as coconuts, copra,
cassava and sweet potatoes. Revenue is also derived from the
sale of licences to foreign fishing fleets.
  The main trading partners are Japan (over half of all exports),
the USA, India, China and Guam. The main imports are
machinery and equipment, fuels, metals and foodstuffs.
GNI – US$0.3bn; US$12,530 per capita (2017)
Annual average growth of GDP – 1.0 per cent (2017 est)
Inflation rate – 1.5 per cent (2017 est)
Total external debt – US$18.38m (2014 est)
Imports – US$177m (2015)
Exports – US$15m (2015)

BALANCE OF PAYMENTS
Trade – US$162m deficit (2015)
Current Account – US$46.2m deficit (2016)

Trade with UK	2016	2017
Imports from UK	£258,074	£126,670
Exports to UK	£5,898	£3,208

COMMUNICATIONS

Airports and waterways – There are three airports, on Koror, Peleliu and Angaur, which receive international flights from Guam, Japan, the Philippines and Taiwan; Koror is also the main seaport

Roadways – 36km

Telecommunications – 7,204 fixed lines and 24,000 mobile subscriptions (2016); there were 7,650 internet users in 2016

Internet code and IDD – pw; 680 (from UK), 0 11 44 (to UK)

Media – T8AA Eco Paradise (radio) is the public broadcaster; there are no TV stations based in Palau or daily newspapers

PANAMA

República de Panamá – Republic of Panama

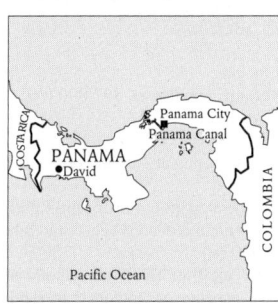

Area – 75,420 sq. km

Capital – Panama City; population, 1,783,000 (2018 est)

Major cities – Colón, David, San Miguelito

Currency – Balboa of 100 centésimos; at parity with the US dollar, which is used as paper currency. Both Panamanian and US coins are used

Population – 3,753,142 rising at 1.27 per cent a year (2017 est)

Religion – Christian (Roman Catholic 85 per cent, Protestant 15 per cent) (est)

Language – Spanish (official), English

Population density – 55 per sq. km (2015)

Urban population – 66.7 per cent (2018 est)

Median age (years) – 28.9 (2016 est)

National anthem – 'Himno Istmeño' 'Hymn of the Isthmus'

National day – 3 November (Independence Day)

Death penalty – Abolished for all crimes (since 1922)

CPI score – 37 (96)

CLIMATE AND TERRAIN

Panama lies on the isthmus connecting North and South America. A mountain range runs along the centre, falling to coastal plains on both coasts. There is dense tropical rainforest in the east. Elevation extremes range from 3,475m (Volcan Baru) to 0m (Pacific Ocean). The climate is tropical, with a prolonged wet season from May to January. The average temperature is 23.8°C.

HISTORY AND POLITICS

Panama was visited by Spanish explorers from 1502, and in 1519 became part of the Viceroyalty of New Andalucia, later New Grenada. When it gained its independence from Spain in 1821, Panama joined the confederacy of Gran Colombia (comprising Colombia, Venezuela, Ecuador, Peru and Bolivia). The confederacy split up in 1830 and Panama became part of Colombia until 1903, when it achieved its independence.

In the 1880s, the French attempted to construct a canal across Panama to link the Atlantic and Pacific oceans. In 1903 the USA bought the rights to build the canal, which was completed in 1914 and opened in 1919. The USA was also given control of the canal and land to either side of it, known as the Canal Zone, in perpetuity but, under a 1977 agreement, sovereignty over the Canal Zone was transferred to Panama on 31 December 1999.

Panama was under the military rule of General Omar Torrijos from 1968 until his death in 1981. In 1983, General Manuel Noriega seized power and instigated a period of military rule, supported by the USA until 1987. An internal coup to unseat Noriega was unsuccessful in 1988, but in 1989 US forces invaded and deposed him. Noriega surrendered in 1990 and in 1992 was tried and sentenced in the USA on drug-trafficking and money-laundering charges. He was extradited to Panama in 2011 where he was imprisoned until he died in May 2017.

The May 2014 presidential election was won by Juan Carlos Varela of the Panamenista party. In the simultaneous legislative election the four-party Alliance for Change coalition won the most seats.

Under the 1972 constitution, as amended in 1983, the executive president is directly elected for a five-year term, which is not renewable. The unicameral National Assembly has 71 members, who are directly elected for a five-year term. The president, who is responsible to the legislature, appoints the cabinet.

HEAD OF STATE

President, Juan Carlos Varela, *elected* 4 May 2014, *sworn in* 1 July 2014

Vice-President, Foreign Affairs, Isabel St Malo de Alvarado

SELECTED GOVERNMENT MEMBERS *AS AT JUNE 2018*

Economy and Finance, Dulcidio de la Guardia

Interior, Carlos Rubio

EMBASSY OF PANAMA

40 Hertford Street, London W1J 7SH

T 020-7493 4646 E panama1@btconnect.com

W www.panamaconsul.co.uk

Ambassador Extraordinary and Plenipotentiary, HE Daniel Fabrega, *apptd* 2014

BRITISH EMBASSY

Humboldt Tower, 4th Floor, Calle 53, Marbella, PO Box 0816-07946, Panama City

T (+507) 297 6550 W www.gov.uk/government/world/panama

Ambassador Extraordinary and Plenipotentiary, HE Damion Potter, *apptd* 2017

ECONOMY AND TRADE

The economy is based on a large service sector and has experienced steady growth in recent years, although this slowed in 2009 because of the global economic downturn. However, the distribution of wealth is uneven: around one-quarter of the population lives below the poverty line although unemployment is low. The economy has grown quickly since 2009, and has been boosted by the completion of the expanded Panama Canal in 2016, which has doubled the canal's capacity but significantly added to public debt.

The service sector accounts for 82 per cent of GDP, derived from the operation of the Panama Canal and the Colón free trade zone, offshore banking and financial services, container ports, ship registry and tourism. Industry, which contributes 15.7 per cent of GDP, includes construction, brewing, sugar refining and the manufacture of cement and other construction materials. Agriculture, which accounts for 2.4

per cent of GDP, is centred on bananas, rice, maize, coffee, sugar cane, vegetables, livestock and shrimp.

The main trading partners are the USA, China, the Netherlands and Mexico. Principal exports are fish, fruit, nuts, iron and steel waste, and wood. The main imports are fuel products, medicines, vehicles, iron and steel rods, and pharmaceuticals.

GNI – US$53.7bn; US$13,100 per capita (2017)
Annual average growth of GDP – 5.3 per cent (2017 est)
Inflation rate – 1.6 per cent (2017 est)
Population below poverty line – 23 per cent (2015 est)
Unemployment – 5.5 per cent (2017 est)
Total external debt – US$86.55bn (2017 est)
Imports – US$11,697m (2016)
Exports – US$636m (2016)

BALANCE OF PAYMENTS
Trade – US$11,061m deficit (2016)
Current Account – US$3,036m deficit (2017)

Trade with UK	2016	2017
Imports from UK	£128,906,719	£136,061,959
Exports to UK	£34,392,230	£31,891,467

COMMUNICATIONS

Airports – There are 57 airports; the principal airport is at Panama City
Waterways – The Panama Canal connects the Pacific and Atlantic oceans. Each year the canal handles about 5 per cent of world trade and over 40 per cent of trade between Asia and the east coast of the USA. The chief ports are Colón, Cristóbal and Balboa, at either end of the canal. Because of its role as a ship registry, there were 6,413 Panamanian- and 5,162 foreign-owned ships of over 1,000 tonnes registered under its flag in 2011
Roadways and railways – 6,351km; 76km
Telecommunications – 641,688 fixed lines and 5.1 million mobile subscriptions (2016); there were 2 million internet users in 2016
Internet code and IDD – pa; 507 (from UK), 44 (to UK)
Major broadcasters – The sector is dominated by private firms, including Telemetro (TV) and RPC Radio
Press – La Prensa, The Panama News and El Siglo are among the leading daily newspapers
WPFI score – 30,56 (91)

EDUCATION AND HEALTH

There are nine years of compulsory education.
Literacy rate – 98.1 per cent (2015 est)
Gross enrolment ratio (percentage of relevant age group) – primary 105.3 per cent, secondary 75.5 per cent, tertiary 38.7 per cent (2013 est)
Health expenditure (per capita) – US$959 (2014)
Hospital beds (per 1,000 people) – 2.3 (2013)
Life expectancy (years) – 78.8 (2017 est)
Mortality rate – 4.9 (2017 est)
Birth rate – 17.9 (2017 est)
Infant mortality rate – 9.9 (2017 est)
HIV/AIDS adult prevalence – 0.8 per cent (2016 est)

PAPUA NEW GUINEA

Gau Hedinarai ai Papua-Matamata Guinea – Independent State of Papua New Guinea

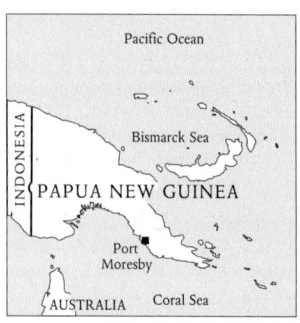

Area – 462,840 sq. km
Capital – Port Moresby; population, 367,000 (2018 est)
Major town – Arawa, Lae
Currency – Kina (K) of 100 toea
Population – 6,909,701 rising at 1.71 per cent a year (2017 est)
Religion – Christian (Protestant 69.4 per cent, Roman Catholic 27 per cent), indigenous beliefs and other 3.3 per cent (2000 est)
Language – English, Tok Pisin, Hiri Motu (all official), Motu; 836 indigenous languages are spoken, representing over 12 per cent of the world total
Population density – 18 per sq. km (2016)
Urban population – 13.2 per cent (2018 est)
Median age (years) – 22.9 (2016 est)
National anthem – 'O Arise, All You Sons'
National day – 16 September (Independence Day)
Death penalty – Retained (last used 1950)
CPI score – 29 (135)
Military expenditure – US$71.9m (2017)

CLIMATE AND TERRAIN

Papua New Guinea lies in the south-western Pacific Ocean and consists of the eastern half of the island of New Guinea, the islands of Bougainville, New Britain and New Ireland, the Admiralty Islands, the D'Entrecasteaux Islands and the Louisiade archipelago. A range of densely forested mountains runs across the centre of the Papuan part of New Guinea, descending to coastal plains and swamps, and coral reefs. Elevation extremes range from 4,509m (Mt Wilhelm) to 0m (Pacific Ocean). There are a number of active volcanoes and the country is subject to frequent eruptions and earthquakes. Over 50 per cent of the country is forested, and 20 per cent is permanently or seasonally flooded. The climate is tropical and subject to the north-west monsoon (December–March) and south-east monsoon (May–October).

POLITICS

The 1975 constitution was amended in 1998 to grant greater autonomy to Bougainville, and in March 2010 to expand the maximum number of cabinet ministers from 28 to 31. The head of state is Queen Elizabeth II, represented by a governor-general who is elected by the legislature for a six-year term. The unicameral National Parliament has a maximum of 126 members (currently 111), 20 from provincial electorates and the remainder from open electorates, who are directly elected for a five-year term. The

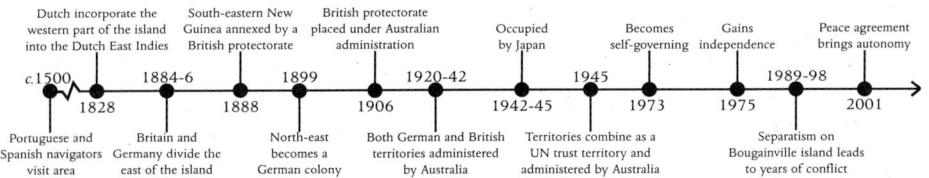

Dutch incorporate the western part of the island into the Dutch East Indies — c.1500

South-eastern New Guinea annexed by a British protectorate — 1884-6

British protectorate placed under Australian administration — 1899

Occupied by Japan — 1920-42

Becomes self-governing — 1945

Gains independence — 1989-98

Peace agreement brings autonomy

1828 — Portuguese and Spanish navigators visit area

1888 — Britain and Germany divide the east of the island

1906 — North-east becomes a German colony

1942-45 — Both German and British territories administered by Australia

1973 — Territories combine as a UN trust territory and administered by Australia

1975 — Separatism on Bougainville island leads to years of conflict

2001

prime minister is nominated by the legislature and appointed by the governor-general.

Factionalism and shifting alliances have caused political instability since independence, and a proportional representation element was introduced into the voting system in 2007 to try to increase the stability of governments. Following the 2007 legislative election, the National Alliance Party (NAP) leader, Sir Michael Somare, was elected prime minister for the fourth time, forming a new coalition government. Somare was convicted of financial irregularities in March 2011 and suspended for 14 days; former transport minister Peter O'Neill was elected as prime minister in August 2011. Legislative elections in 2012 saw the People's National Congress Party (PNC) gain the most seats but without a majority; following this, O'Neill announced that he would lead the government. The 2017 legislative elections were held over a two-week period from June to July but were marked by official irregularities, apparent voter intimidation, and illicit, stolen or destroyed ballots. The PNC again gained the most seats but did not win a majority.

Governor-General, HE Sir Robert Dadae, *sworn in* 28 February 2017

SELECTED GOVERNMENT MEMBERS *AS AT JUNE 2018*
Prime Minister, Peter O'Neill, CMG
Deputy Prime Minister, Charles Abel
Foreign Affairs, Rimbink Pato, OBE

PAPUA NEW GUINEA HIGH COMMISSION
3rd Floor, 14 Waterloo Place, London SW1Y 4AR
T 020-7930 0922 E info@pnghighcomm.org.uk
W www.pnghighcomm.org.uk
High Commissioner, HE Winnie Kiap, *apptd* 2011

BRITISH HIGH COMMISSION
Sec 411 Lot 1 & 2, Kiroki Street, Waigani, National Capital District, Port Moresby
T (+675) 325 1677 E uk.inpng@fco.gov.uk
W www.gov.uk/government/world/papua-new-guinea
High Commissioner, HE Keith Scott, *apptd* 2018

ECONOMY AND TRADE
Political instability, corruption, a weak economy and high unemployment and crime levels had brought the country to the brink of economic and social collapse in 2004. The economy has grown since, achieving 13 years of continuous growth as of 2017, owing to higher commodity prices and tight control of the national budget, but prices have recently fallen and the country remains poor and underdeveloped. Foreign investment in oil and liquid natural gas extraction since 2004 has boosted economic growth; the export of liquefied natural gas to Asian economies began in March 2014, and its success has raised the possibility of similar projects as the government seeks further investment and trade.

About 85 per cent of the population practises subsistence farming, including some tribes in the interior so isolated that their economy is not monetised. Mineral deposits, including copper, gold, silver, nickel, oil and natural gas, are abundant and constitute the main sources of revenue, although exploitation is forced to overcome difficult terrain and poor infrastructure. This has been addressed by the government, which passed legislation in 2011 for an offshore sovereign wealth fund to manage government surpluses from mineral, oil and natural gas projects. The main industries are mining, oil extraction and refining, forestry, processing of agricultural and forestry products, construction and tourism. Industry contributes 42.9 per cent of GDP and services 35 per cent.

The main trading partners are Australia, China and Singapore. Principal exports are liquefied natural gas, oil, gold, copper ore, nickel, palm oil, coffee, cocoa and shellfish. The main imports are machinery and transport equipment, manufactured goods, food, fuels and chemicals.
GNI – US$19.8bn; US$2,410 per capita (2017)
Annual average growth of GDP – 3.1 per cent (2017 est)
Inflation rate – 5.8 per cent (2017 est)
Population below poverty line – 37 per cent (2002 est)
Unemployment – 2.5 per cent (2017 est)
Total external debt – US$17.09bn (2017 est)
Imports – US$7,343m (2014)
Exports – US$9,487m (2015)

BALANCE OF PAYMENTS
Trade – US$828m surplus (2012)
Current Account – US$4,859m surplus (2016)

Trade with UK	2016	2017
Imports from UK	£47,727,465	£22,700,510
Exports to UK	£104,152,948	£116,987,076

COMMUNICATIONS
Airports and waterways – 21, the principal airports being at Port Moresby, Lae and Rabaul; there are 11,000km of navigable waterways
Roadways – 3,000km
Telecommunications – 154,000 fixed lines and 3.8 million mobile subscriptions (2016); there were 652,071 internet users in 2016
Internet code and IDD – pg; 675 (from UK), 44 (to UK)
Major broadcasters – The National Television Service and National Broadcasting Corporation (radio) are the public broadcasters
Press – There are two foreign-owned daily newspapers: *The National* (Australia) and *The Post-Courier* (Malaysia)
WPFI score – 26,19 (53)

EDUCATION AND HEALTH
Literacy rate – 72.4 per cent (2015 est)
Health expenditure (per capita) – US$92 (2014)
Life expectancy (years) – 67.3 (2017 est)
Mortality rate – 6.6 (2017 est)
Birth rate – 23.7 (2017 est)
Infant mortality rate – 36.3 (2017 est)
HIV/AIDS adult prevalence rate – 0.9 per cent (2016 est)

PARAGUAY

República del Paraguay – Republic of Paraguay

Area – 406,752 sq. km
Capital – Asunción; population, 3,222,000 (2018 est)
Major cities – Ciudad del Este, Concepción, Lambaré, Limpio, San Lorenzo
Currency – Guaraní (Gs) of 100 céntimos
Population – 6,943,739 rising at 1.18 per cent a year (2017 est)
Religion – Christian (Roman Catholic 89.6 per cent, Protestant 6.2 per cent) (2002 est)
Language – Spanish, Guaraní (both official)
Population density – 17 per sq. km (2016)
Urban population – 61.6 per cent (2018 est)
Median age (years) – 27.8 (2016 est)
National anthem – 'Paraguayos, República o Muerte' 'Paraguayans, the Republic or Death'
National day – 15 May (Independence Day)
Death penalty – Abolished for all crimes (since 1992)
CPI score – 29 (135)
Military expenditure – US$348m (2017)
Conscription – 18 years of age; 12–24 months (selective)

CLIMATE AND TERRAIN

The country is divided by the river Paraguay into two distinct regions. The area east of the Paraguay is a fertile, grassy plateau where most of the population lives. The area to the west, the Gran Chaco, consists of a grassy and occasionally marshy plain that extends into neighbouring countries. Elevation extremes range from 842m (Cerro Pero) to 46m (the junction of the Paraguay and Paraná rivers). The climate varies from subtropical to temperate, with higher rainfall in the east and semi-arid conditions in the west. Average temperatures range from 18.2°C in July to 27.6°C in January.

HISTORY AND POLITICS

Spanish colonisation of Paraguay began in the early 16th century and Asunción was founded in 1537. Paraguay became independent from Spain in 1811 under the dictator José Gaspar Rodriguez de Francia, who ruled until his death in 1840. His successors instigated a period of reform and modernisation, which ended in 1865–70 with the catastrophic War of the Triple Alliance against Brazil, Uruguay and Argentina over access to the sea. The war resulted in the loss of over half the population as well as 150,000 sq. km of territory, and initiated a period of political instability that lasted until 1912. In the Chaco War of 1932–5, Paraguay gained territory in the west from Bolivia in a conflict that killed 100,000 people.

Political instability and conflict in the late 1940s ended with a coup in 1954 in which General Alfredo Stroessner seized power. His rule was autocratic and increasingly repressive, marked by corruption and human rights abuses. He was ousted in a coup in 1989 that paved the way for free multiparty elections to the presidency and legislature in 1993. These were won by the National Republican Association-Colorado Party (ANR-PC) and its presidential candidate, and the ANR-PC won all subsequent elections until 2008. Instability has prevailed since the 1990s, however, with the assassination of a vice-president, an attempted coup, widespread corruption and the growth of drug-trafficking, money-laundering and organised crime.

The 2008 presidential election was won by Fernando Lugo of the Patriotic Alliance for Change coalition (APC), the first president from outside the ANR-PC in 61 years; Lugo, however, was removed from office by impeachment of the senate in June 2012 for failing to manage fatal clashes over land evictions. The 2013 presidential and legislative elections were both won by the ANR-RC. Horacio Cartes of the ANR-PC, elected president and in March 2017, attempted to amend the constitution to allow him to stand for re-election in 2018, provoking violent protests. The 2018 presidential election was won by ANR-RC candidate Mario Abdo Benítez. The ARN-RC lost ground but remained the largest party in both houses.

Under the 1992 constitution, the executive president is directly elected for a five-year term, which is not renewable. The bicameral Congress consists of a 45-member senate and an 80-member Chamber of Deputies, both directly elected for a five-year term. The president, who is responsible to the legislature, appoints the council of ministers.

HEAD OF STATE

President, Mario Abdo Benítez, *elected* 23 April 2018, *sworn in* 16 August 2018
Vice-President, Hugo Velazquez

SELECTED GOVERNMENT MEMBERS *AS AT SEPTEMBER 2018*

Defence, Gen. (retd) Bernardino Soto Estigarribia
Foreign Affairs, Luiz Alberto Castiglioni
Interior, Juan Ernesto Villamayor

EMBASSY OF THE REPUBLIC OF PARAGUAY

3rd Floor, 344 Kensington High Street, London W14 8NS
T 020-7610 4180 E embapar@btconnect.com
W www.paraguayembassy.co.uk
Ambassador Extraordinary and Plenipotentiary, HE Genaro Vicente Pappalardo Ayala, *apptd* 2017

BRITISH EMBASSY

Edificio Citicenter, Piso 5, Av. Mariscal López y Cruz del Chaco, Asunción
T (595) (21) 614 588 E BE-Asuncion.Enquiries@fco.gov.uk
W www.gov.uk/government/world/paraguay
Ambassador Extraordinary and Plenipotentiary, HE Matthew Hedges, *apptd* 2017

ECONOMY AND TRADE

Paraguay's economy features a large informal sector and benefits from the proceeds of re-exporting to neighbouring countries. The economy started to slow in 2008, when drought reduced production of key exports, and went into recession in 2009, when the global downturn reduced export demand and commodity prices. Although growth resumed in 2014 and has averaged 4 per cent annually, although in the longer term the economy is hampered by political instability, corruption, national and foreign debt, inadequate infrastructure and high crime levels. Almost one-quarter of the population lives below the poverty line, although this rate is higher in the cities because of migration from the countryside of families made landless by the commercialisation of agriculture and forest clearances. Real incomes are steadily growing, however, as demand for Paraguay's highly-priced commodities continue to rise, and low labour costs have helped triple the number of factories in the country since 2014.

The country has few mineral resources although exploration for oil and gas is underway. The economy is largely agricultural, much of it at subsistence level. Agricultural production, which accounts for 17.9 per cent of GDP and engages roughly a quarter of the workforce, is centred on cotton, sugar cane, soya beans, maize, wheat, tobacco, cassava, fruit, vegetables and livestock products. The main industries are sugar refining, forestry, manufacturing (cement, textiles, beverages, wood products, steel) and hydroelectric power generation. Industry accounts for 27.7 per cent of GDP and services for 54.5 per cent.

The main trading partners are Brazil, China, Argentina, Chile and the USA. Principal exports are soya beans, feed, cotton, meat, edible oils, timber. gold and leather. The main imports are road vehicles, consumer goods, tobacco and petroleum products.

GNI – US$26.7bn; US$3,920 per capita (2017)
Annual average growth of GDP – 3.9 per cent (2017 est)
Inflation rate – 3.5 per cent (2017 est)
Population below poverty line – 22.2 per cent (2015 est)
Unemployment – 6.5 per cent (2017 est)
Total external debt – US$17.35bn (2017 est)
Imports – US$9,753m (2016)
Exports – US$11,148m (2016)

BALANCE OF PAYMENTS
Trade – US$1,395m surplus (2016)
Current Account – US$298.4m deficit (2017)

Trade with UK	2016	2017
Imports from UK	£29,335,039	£33,253,488
Exports to UK	£31,023,728	£12,978,422

COMMUNICATIONS
Airports and waterways – 15, including the principal airport at Asunción; and around 3,100km of navigable waterways around the country
Roadways and railways – There are 4,860km of roadways and a small railway system of around 36km
Telecommunications – 356,455 fixed lines and 7.5 million mobile subscriptions (2016); there were 3.5 million internet users in 2016
Internet code and IDD – py; 595 (from UK), 44 (to UK)
Major broadcasters – The state-owned Radio Nacional del Paraguay and TV Publica operate alongside a wealth of private broadcasters
Press – Major daily newspapers include *ABC Color, La Nación* and *Ultima Hora*
WPFI score – 32,32 (107)

EDUCATION AND HEALTH
Basic education is free and compulsory for nine years.
Literacy rate – 99 per cent (2015 est)
Gross enrolment ratio (percentage of relevant age group) – primary 95 per cent, secondary 70 per cent (2011 est), tertiary 35 per cent (2010 est)
Health expenditure (per capita) – US$464 (2014)
Hospital beds (per 1,000 people) – 1.3 (2011)
Life expectancy (years) – 77.4 (2017 est)
Mortality rate – 4.8 (2017 est)
Birth rate – 16.6 (2017 est)
Infant mortality rate – 18.7 (2017 est)
HIV/AIDS adult prevalence – 0.5 (2016 est)

PERU

República del Perú – Republic of Peru

Area – 1,285,216 sq. km
Capital – Lima; population, 10,391,000 (2018 est)
Major cities – Arequipa, Chiclayo, Cuzco, Iquitos, Piura, Trujillo
Currency – Nuevo sol of 100 centimos
Population – 31,036,656 rising at 0.95 per cent a year (2017 est); Amerindian (45.0 per cent), Mestizo (37.0 per cent), white (15.0 per cent) (est)
Religion – Christian (Roman Catholic 81.3 per cent, Protestant 12.5 per cent) (2007 est)
Language – Spanish, Quechua, Aymara (all official), other Amerindian languages
Population density – 25 per sq. km (2016)
Urban population – 77.9 per cent (2018 est)
Median age (years) – 27.7 (2016 est)
National anthem – 'Himno Nacional del Perú' 'National Anthem of Peru'
National day – 28 July (Independence Day)
Death penalty – Retained for certain crimes (last used 1979)
CPI score – 37 (96)
Military expenditure – US$2,085m (2017)

CLIMATE AND TERRAIN
Peru has three main regions: the Costa, the coastal desert plain west of the Andes; the Sierra (mountain range) of the Andes, which runs parallel to the Pacific coast; and the Montaña (or Selva), a vast area of jungle stretching from the eastern foothills of the Andes to the country's eastern and north-eastern borders. Elevation extremes range from 6,768m (Nevado Huascaran) to 0m (Pacific Ocean). The climate is arid in the west, temperate in the mountains and tropical in the east. Occasionally, due to the El Niño weather system, the northern districts experience a period of higher temperatures accompanied by torrential rain. The average temperature is 19.9°C.

HISTORY AND POLITICS
The Inca Empire centred on Cuzco superseded earlier civilisations in Peru and flourished from the 13th to the 15th century, when the empire reached its zenith before falling to Spanish conquistadores led by Francisco Pizarro in 1532–3. The territory formed the Viceroyalty of Peru and its gold and silver mines made Peru the principal source of wealth in Spain's American empire. After 1810, Peru became the centre of Spanish colonial government as its other colonies rebelled. Although Peru declared its independence in 1821, this was achieved only with the final defeat of Spanish forces in 1824.

Peru entered into several border disputes with its neighbours in the 19th and 20th centuries, including the Pacific War (1879–83) in which it lost three southern coastal provinces to Chile. A border dispute with Ecuador was renewed in 1981, leading to a short, inconclusive war in 1995, but was resolved in 1998 following adjudication. A border dispute with Chile ended in 1999 with the implementation of accords first agreed in 1929.

Following independence, Peru alternated between periods of military dictatorship and democratic rule. Two left-wing insurgencies, by the Maoist *Sendero Luminoso* (Shining Path) and the *Movimento Revolucionario Tupac Amaru* (MRTA), began in the 1980s. The conflict caused about 69,000 deaths and saw human rights abuses by both the security forces and the guerrillas. By the late 1990s both insurgencies had been overcome, although a few Maoists remain active. The conflict has left a legacy of criminal violence, much of it related to drug production and trafficking.

Alberto Fujimori, elected president in 1990 on a platform of economic reform, subverted democratic institutions in Peru during his decade in power, suspending the legislature for three years, sacking judges and imposing order through an 'emergency national reconstruction government'. He fled to Japan in 2000 to escape corruption charges, but was extradited and convicted in 2007 of abuse of power and in 2009 of human rights abuses.

In the June 2016 legislative election, presidential candidate Keiko Fujimori's Popular Force party won 71 parliamentary seats, and Fernando Zavala became the country's eighth prime minister in five years. Former World Bank economist Pedro Pablo Kuczynski narrowly won the simultaneous presidential election, but was forced to resign in March 2018 following a corruption scandal, one day before an impeachment vote was scheduled. He was replaced by Vice President Martín Vizcarra Cornejo.

Under the 1993 constitution, the executive president is directly elected for a five-year term, renewable once. The unicameral legislature, the Congress of the Republic, has 130 members, directly elected for a five-year term. The president, who is responsible to the legislature, appoints the council of ministers.

HEAD OF STATE
President, Martín Vizcarra Cornejo, *sworn in* 23 March 2018

SELECTED GOVERNMENT MEMBERS *AS AT JUNE 2018*
President of Council of Ministers, César Villanueva Arévalo
Defence, José Modesto Huerta Torres
Economy and Finance, Carlos Augusto Oliva Neyra
Foreign Affairs, Néstor Popolizio Bardale

EMBASSY OF PERU
52 Sloane Street, London SW1X 9SP
T 020-7235 3802 E postmaster@peruembassy-uk.com
W www.peruembassy-uk.com
Ambassador Extraordinary and Plenipotentiary, HE Susana de la
   Puente-Weise, *apptd* 2017

BRITISH EMBASSY
Torre Parque Mar, Avenida José Larco 1301, Lima
T (+51) (1) 617 3000 E belima@fco.gov.uk
W www.gov.uk/government/world/peru
Ambassador Extraordinary and Plenipotentiary, HE Kate
   Harrisson, *apptd* 2018

ECONOMY AND TRADE

The Peruvian economy grew by an average of 5.6 per cent from 2009 to 2013 and has continued to perform well, driven by exports of silver, copper, agricultural produce and fish. Tourism has also driven growth. Poverty remains widespread, but the benefits of economic growth are starting to be felt in the poorer regions and the poverty rate has declined by 35 per cent since 2002. The dependence on metal exports and imported foodstuffs makes the economy vulnerable to fluctuations in world prices. Successive governments' free trade policies have contributed to greater international investment and mining output, but development has been hindered by corruption scandals, flooding and project delays in recent years.

Mineral resources, including copper, gold, silver, zinc, oil and natural gas, are abundant, and extracting and refining these is the mainstay of the economy. Other industries include steel and metal fabrication, fishing and fish processing, textiles and clothes manufacture and food processing. Agriculture is centred on asparagus, avocado, coffee, cocoa, cotton, sugar cane, rice, cereals, vegetables, fruit, coca, medicinal plants, meat and dairy products. Services contribute 56.1 per cent to GDP, industry 36.3 per cent and agriculture 7.5 per cent.

The main trading partners are China, the USA, Brazil, Switzerland and Mexico. Principal exports are copper, gold, zinc, tin, iron ore, crude oil and petroleum products, natural gas, coffee, vegetables and fruit. The main imports are oil and petroleum products, chemicals, plastics, machinery, vehicles, telecommunications equipment, iron and steel, and food.
GNI – US$191.9bn; US$5,970 per capita (2017)
Annual average growth of GDP – 2.7 per cent (2017 est)
Inflation rate – 3.2 per cent (2017 est)
Population below poverty line – 22.7 per cent (2014 est)
Unemployment – 6.7 per cent (2017 est)
Total external debt – US$70.09bn (2017 est)
Imports – US$37,014m (2015)
Exports – US$34,236m (2016)

BALANCE OF PAYMENTS
Trade – US$2,778m deficit (2015)
Current Account – US$2,719m deficit (2017)

Trade with UK	2016	2017
Imports from UK	£159,104,556	£178,646,464
Exports to UK	£305,635,660	£344,405,361

COMMUNICATIONS

Airports and waterways – There are 59 airports, including the international airport at Lima; there are 8,808km of inland waterways, and the main seaports are Callao and Matarani
Roadways and railways – There are 18,698km of roadways, including sections of the east–west Andean Highway, linking the Pacific and Atlantic coasts, and the north–south Pan-American Highway running along the Pacific coast; the state-run railways have 1,907km of track
Telecommunications – 3.1 million fixed lines and 36 million mobile subscriptions (2016); there were 13.9 million internet users in 2016
Internet code and IDD – pe; 51 (from UK), 44 (to UK)
Major broadcasters – The state-owned TV Peru and Radio Nacional operate alongside a number of private broadcasters
Press – Major daily newspapers include *El Bocón, La República* and *Ojo*
WPFI score – 30,27 (88)

EDUCATION AND HEALTH

Education is free and compulsory for 11 years.
Literacy rate – 98.9 per cent (2015 est)
Gross enrolment ratio (percentage of relevant age group) – primary 103 per cent, secondary 98 per cent (2016 est), tertiary 41 per cent (2010 est)
Health expenditure (per capita) – US$359 (2014)
Hospital beds (per 1,000 people) – 1.6 (2014)
Life expectancy (years) – 74 (2017 est)
Mortality rate – 6.1 (2017 est)

Birth rate – 17.8 (2017 est)
Infant mortality rate – 18.4 (2017 est)
HIV/AIDS adult prevalence – 0.3 per cent (2016 est)

THE PHILIPPINES

Republika ng Pilipinas – Republic of the Philippines

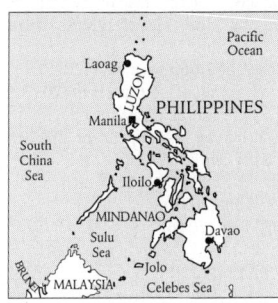

Area – 300,000 sq. km
Capital – Manila; population (Metro Manila, including Quezon City), 13,482,000 (2018 est)
Major cities – Bacolod, Cagayan de Oro, Cebu, Davao, General Santos (Dadiangas), Iloilo, Laoag, Zamboanga
Currency – Philippine peso (P) of 100 centavos
Population – 104,246,076 rising at 1.57 per cent a year (2017 est); Tagalog (28.1 per cent), Cebuano (13.1 per cent), Ilocano (9 per cent), Bisaya (7.6 per cent), Hiligaynon Ilonggo (7.5 per cent), Bikol (6 per cent), Waray (3.4 per cent) (2000)
Religion – Christian (Roman Catholic 82.9 per cent, Evangelical 2.8 per cent), Muslim 5 per cent (2000 est)
Language – Filipino, English (both official), Tagalog, Cebuano, Ilocano, Hiligaynon, Bicol, Waray, Pampango, Pangasinan
Population density – 352 per sq. km (2016)
Urban population – 46.9 per cent (2018 est)
Median age (years) – 23.4 (2016 est)
National anthem – 'Lupang Hinirang' 'Chosen Land']
National day – 12 June (Independence Day)
Death penalty – Abolished for all crimes (since 2006)
CPI score – 34 (111)
Military expenditure – US$4,378m (2017 est)

CLIMATE AND TERRAIN
The Philippines comprises over 7,100 islands in the western Pacific Ocean. The principal islands are Luzon, Mindanao, Mindoro, Samar, Negros, Palawan, Panay and Leyte; other groups include the Sulu islands, Babuyanes and Batanes, Calamian and Kalayaan islands. The islands mostly have mountainous interiors and narrow coastal plains. The mountain ranges are volcanic, and some volcanoes are still active. Elevation extremes range from 2,954m (Mt Apo) to 0m (Philippine Sea). The climate is tropical; the average temperature is 26.2°C, and relative humidity is high. The country is affected by the monsoons, which cause the rainy season between July and October. During this period the country is also susceptible to typhoons, which frequently cause widespread damage and loss of life.

HISTORY AND POLITICS
The Philippine islands were settled first by Malays, then by Chinese, Indonesian and Arab traders. Islam was introduced in the 14th century and became the dominant religion in the south. The islands were discovered by Spain and then settled from 1565 by the Spanish, who introduced Roman Catholicism. Colonial rule lasted until 1898, when Spain

ceded the colony to the USA following the Spanish-American War. The country became internally self-governing in 1935, was occupied by Japan from 1942 to 1944, and achieved independence from the USA in 1946.

Ferdinand Marcos was elected president in 1965, imposing martial law in 1972. His regime became increasingly repressive, corrupt and violent, and when he falsified election results in 1986 to prevent Corazon Aquino from taking office as president, a popular uprising forced him to flee the country. Aquino survived political unrest and ten attempted military coups to introduce a new constitution and entrench democratic politics.

Fidel Ramos, Aquino's successor in 1992, built on her work, raised the country's international profile and instigated peace talks with insurgents (*see* below). Joseph Estrada, elected president in 1998, was overthrown in 2001 in a popular uprising; his term was completed by Vice-President Gloria Arroyo. President Arroyo retained the presidency in the 2004 presidential election, but her popularity plummeted and her anti-corruption measures and economic reforms were undermined by corruption scandals and impeachment attempts.

In the May 2013 legislative elections, the Liberal Party (LP) won the most seats in the house of representatives but without a majority. The 2016 presidential election was won by Rodrigo Duterte, the former mayor of Davao City, known as 'Duterte Harry' for his support of capital punishment and backing of extrajudicial killings. He initiated a brutal crackdown on drug cartels, which Human Rights Watch claimed to have resulted in over 12,000 deaths by January 2018.

Under the 1987 constitution, the executive president is directly elected for a six-year term, which is not renewable. There is a bicameral Congress. The lower house, the House of Representatives, has up to 238 directly elected members, plus 59 members appointed from party and minority group lists; all serve a three-year term. The senate has 24 members directly elected for a six-year term, with half re-elected every three years.

The Autonomous Region of Muslim Mindanao comprises the provinces of Lanao del Sur and Maguindanao on Mindanao and the island provinces of Sulu, Tawi-Tawi and Basilan. It has a 24-member regional assembly and a governor.

HEAD OF STATE
President, Rodrigo Duterte, *elected* 9 May 2016, *sworn in* 30 June 2016
Vice-President, Leni Robredo

SELECTED GOVERNMENT MEMBERS *AS AT JUNE 2018*
Defence, Delfin Lorenzana
Finance, Carlos Dominguez
Foreign Affairs, Alan Peter Cayetano
Trade and Industry, Ramon Lopez

EMBASSY OF THE REPUBLIC OF THE PHILIPPINES
6–11 Suffolk Street, London SW1Y 4HG
T 020-7451 1780 E embassy@philemb.co.uk
W www.philembassy-uk.org
Ambassador Extraordinary and Plenipotentiary, HE Antonio Manuel Lagdameo, *apptd* 2017

BRITISH EMBASSY
120 Upper McKinley Road, McKinley Hill, Taguig City 1634, Manila
T (+63) (2) 858 2200 E ukinthephilippines@fco.gov.uk
W www.gov.uk/government/world/philippines
Ambassador Extraordinary and Plenipotentiary, HE Daniel Pruce, *apptd* 2017

INSURGENCIES

A communist insurgency by the New People's Army (NPA) began in the late 1960s. The NPA is based in Mindanao but has groups in rural areas throughout the country. Peace talks between the government and the NPA's political front, the National Democratic Front, stalled in 2004 and were resumed in early 2011, but were abandoned following the election of the belligerent President Duterte in 2016.

There has been a Muslim (Moro) insurgency in the southern islands, particularly Mindanao, since the 1970s. The Moro National Liberation Front (MNLF) concluded a peace agreement with the government in 1996 that ended its insurgency and established the Autonomous Region of Muslim Mindanao (ARMM). The Moro Islamic Liberation Front (MILF) agreed a ceasefire with the government in 2003, but negotiations over a Muslim 'homeland' broke down in 2008; a resumption of violence in 2009 displaced over 300,000 people until another ceasefire was agreed and peace talks resumed in late 2009. Talks broke down in October 2011, however, after air strikes on MILF areas in Zamboanga left 35 people dead. In January 2014, the government agreed to create a new Muslim autonomous area called Bangsamoro in the south of the Philippines by 2016 in return for the disbanding of the MILF. Despite the agreement, MILF members are believed to have been involved in an attack that killed more than 40 Filipino police officers in January 2015; the proposed Bangsamoro Basic Law that would have led to the creation of the autonomous region has since been shelved. Any development is likely to come as part of President Duterte's plans for federalism.

The radical Muslim separatist group Abu Sayyaf, based on Jolo and Basilan, is viewed as a terrorist organisation and the government refuses to negotiate with it. It pledged allegiance to Islamic State (IS) in October 2014. In May 2017, the radical Islamist Maute group took control of Marawi, in the southern Philippines, apparently after the government launched a raid to capture Abu Sayyaf leader Isnilon Hapilon, who was rumoured to be in the city; as a result, martial law was declared on the island of Mindanao amid fierce fighting.

ECONOMY AND TRADE

The economy has survived the 2009 recession better than other Asian economies thanks to low dependence on exports, robust domestic consumption and remittances from roughly 10 million overseas workers. Despite this, poverty remains high, especially in rural areas, as economic expansion struggles to offset the high rate of population growth, and nearly a fifth of the population lives below the poverty line. Growth averaging over 6 per cent annually during 2011–17 largely thanks to strong domestic demand. During 2017, significant infrastructure spending was coupled with record levels of foreign investment, but underemployment, inequality and a significant informal sector continue to limit economic potential. The Philippines formed a common market with the other members of the Association of Southeast Asian Nations (ASEAN) in 2015.

Major industries include electronics assembly, manufacture of clothing, business process outsourcing, pharmaceuticals, chemicals and wood products, food processing and fishing. The large agricultural sector employs 25.4 per cent of the workforce, producing sugar cane, coconuts, rice, maize,

tropical fruits and livestock products. Agriculture accounts for 9.6 per cent of GDP, industry for 30.6 per cent and services for 59.8 per cent.

The main trading partners are Japan, the USA, China, South Korea and other Asian states. Principal exports are semiconductors and electronic products, machinery, clothing, chemicals, coconut oil and fruit. The main imports are electronic products, fuels, machinery and transport equipment, iron and steel, fabrics, grains, chemicals and plastics.

GNI – US$383bn; US$3,660 per capita (2017)
Annual average growth of GDP – 6.6 per cent (2017 est)
Inflation rate – 3.1 per cent (2017 est)
Population below poverty line – 21.6 per cent (2017 est)
Unemployment – 6 per cent (2017 est)
Total external debt – US$80.88bn (2017 est)
Imports – US$85,938m (2016)
Exports – US$56,313m (2016)

BALANCE OF PAYMENTS

Trade – US$29,626m deficit (2016)
Current Account – US$2,517m surplus (2017)

Trade with UK	2016	2017
Imports from UK	£399,909,598	£530,036,368
Exports to UK	£478,389,317	£336,693,784

COMMUNICATIONS

Airports and waterways – There are 89 airports; the main ports are Manila (Luzon), Cebu, Davao, Subic Bay, Batangas and Iloilo, and there are 3,219km of waterways
Roadways and railways – There are 54,481km of roadways and Philippine National Railway operates 995km of railways
Telecommunications – 3.8 million fixed lines and 113 million mobile subscriptions (2016); there were 56.9 million internet users in 2016
Internet code and IDD – ph; 63 (from UK), 44 (to UK)
Major broadcasters – The government-owned People's Television and Philippine Broadcasting Service (radio) compete with two major commercial broadcasters and over 600 radio stations
Press – Daily newspapers include the *Daily Tribune*, *Malaya* and *Philippine Star*
WPFI score – 42,53 (133)

EDUCATION AND HEALTH

There are seven years of free and compulsory primary education, followed by three years of free but non-compulsory secondary education.

Literacy rate – 97.9 per cent (2015 est)
Gross enrolment ratio (percentage of relevant age group) – primary 116.8 per cent, secondary 88.4 per cent (2013 est), tertiary 35 per cent (2017 est)
Health expenditure (per capita) – US$135 (2014)
Hospital beds (per 1,000 people) – 1 (2011)
Life expectancy (years) – 69.4 (2017 est)
Mortality rate – 6.1 (2017 est)
Birth rate – 23.7 (2017 est)
Infant mortality rate – 21.4 (2017 est)
HIV / AIDS adult prevalence – 0.1 per cent (2016 est)

POLAND

Rzeczpospolita Polska – Republic of Poland

Area – 312,685 sq. km
Capital – Warsaw; population, 1,768,000 (2018 est)
Major cities – Bydgoszcz, Gdansk, Katowice, Krakow, Lodz, Lublin, Poznan, Szczecin, Wroclaw
Currency – Zloty of 100 groszy
Population – 38,476,269 falling at 0.13 per cent a year (2017 est)
Religion – Christian (Roman Catholic 87.2 per cent, Orthodox 1.3 per cent, Protestant 0.4 per cent) (2012 est)
Language – Polish (official)
Population density – 124 per sq. km (2016)
Urban population – 60.1 per cent (2018 est)
Median age (years) – 40.3 (2016 est)
National anthem – 'Mazurek Dabrowskiego' 'Dabrowski's Mazurka'
National day – 3 May (Constitution Day)
Death penalty – Abolished for all crimes (since 1997)
CPI score – 60 (36)
Military expenditure – US$10,010m (2017)

CLIMATE AND TERRAIN

Poland lies mostly in a great plain crossed by the Oder, Neisse and Vistula rivers. The land rises to the Carpathian, Tatra and Sudeten mountains along the southern border. Elevation extremes range from 2,499m (Rysy) to −2m (Raczki Elblaskie). The climate is continental, and average temperatures range from −1.3°C in January to 18.5°C in July.

POLITICS

Under the 1997 constitution, the head of state is the president, who is directly elected for a five-year term, renewable once. The president nominates the prime minister and has the right to be consulted over the appointment of the foreign, defence and interior ministers. The National Assembly is bicameral; the lower house, the Diet *(Sejm)*, has 460 members elected by proportional representation for a four-year term. The senate has 100 members elected on a provincial basis for a four-year term.

In the 2011 legislative elections, Donald Tusk of the Civil Platform (PO) became the first Polish prime minister to be appointed for a second term since the fall of communism, continuing in coalition with the Polish People's Party (PSL). Prime Minister Tusk stood down in September 2014 to become President of the European Council and was succeeded by Ewa Kopacz. The conservative opposition Law and Justice party (PiS) won the legislative elections in October 2015 securing more than one-third of the vote, and the party's Beata Szydlo was elected prime minister one month later. Andrzej Duda of the PiS was elected after a second round of voting in the May 2015 presidential elections. In July 2017, the PiS provoked international condemnation when it pushed through legal reforms that critics said threatened the independence of the judiciary; the ruling party has also attracted criticism for changes that undermine women's rights and for criminalising accusations of national complicity in crimes committed by Nazi Germany.

HEAD OF STATE

President, Andrzej Duda, *elected* 26 May 2015, *sworn in* 6 August 2015

SELECTED GOVERNMENT MEMBERS *AS AT JUNE 2018*
Prime Minister, Mateusz Morawiecki
Deputy Prime Ministers, Beata Szydlo; Piotr Glinski *(Culture);* Jaroslaw Gowin *(Science and Higher Education)*
Defence, Antoni Macierewicz
Foreign Affairs, Witold Waszczykowski

EMBASSY OF THE REPUBLIC OF POLAND
47 Portland Place, London W1B 1JH
T 020-7291 3520 **E** london@msz.gov.pl **W** www.london.polemb.net
Ambassador Extraordinary and Plenipotentiary, HE Prof. Arkady Rzegocki, *apptd* 2016

BRITISH EMBASSY
Ul. Kawalerii 12, 00-468 Warsaw
T (+48) (22) 311 0000 **E** info@britishembassy.pl
W www.gov.uk/government/world/poland
Ambassador Extraordinary and Plenipotentiary, HE Jonathan Knott, *apptd* 2016

ECONOMY AND TRADE

Poland's successful transition to a market economy in the 1990s came at the cost of high levels of public debt, unemployment and inflation, which were reduced by subsequent governments. The economy has grown steadily since 1992 and particularly since accession to the EU in 2004, and was the only EU nation to avoid recession in 2008–9. The largest recipient of EU development funds, GDP has grown by over 3 per cent annually between 2014–7 thanks to rising domestic consumption and is set to continue performing well.

Poland has vast mineral resources, especially coal, and nearly half its area is fertile arable land. The large agricultural sector has been modernised but remains inefficient; it employs 11.5 per cent of the workforce but contributes only 2.4 per cent of GDP. The agricultural products are vegetables, fruit, wheat, meat, eggs and dairy products. The main industries are machine building, iron and steel production, coal mining,

Foundation of Jagiellon dynasty brings greater power to the region	Semi-independent Congress Kingdom of Poland created, swiftly incorporated into the Russian Empire	Invaded by Germany and USSR	Eastern Poland ceded to USSR	Mass movement for civil rights emerges following popular discontent	Civil unrest forces multiparty elections and transition to market economy
c.800	1772-95	1918	1944-5	1947	1981	2004
1386	1814-5	1939	1945	1980	1989
Emerges as independent kingdom	Territory partitioned by Russia, Prussia and Austria	Regains independence under the Treaty of Versailles	Liberated by Soviet forces	Soviet-influenced government declares a communist republic	Government declares martial law, forcing movement underground	Joins EU

chemicals, shipbuilding, food processing, glass, beverages and textiles. Industry accounts for 40.2 per cent of GDP.

The main trading partners are other EU countries (especially Germany), China and Russia. Principal exports include machinery and vehicles, manufactured and semi-manufactured goods, food and livestock. The main imports are machinery and vehicles, semi-manufactured goods, chemicals, minerals, fuels and lubricants.

GNI – US$482.5bn; US$12,710 per capita (2017)
Annual average growth of GDP – 3.8 per cent (2017 est)
Inflation rate – 1.9 per cent (2017 est)
Population below poverty line – 17.6 per cent (2016 est)
Unemployment – 4.8 per cent (2017 est)
Total external debt – US$362bn (2017 est)
Imports – US$197,394m (2016)
Exports – US$202,635m (2016)

BALANCE OF PAYMENTS
Trade – US$5,240m deficit (2016)
Current Account – US$874m deficit (2017)

Trade with UK	2016	2017
Imports from UK	£4,208,724,615	£4,985,866,090
Exports to UK	£9,226,037,474	£10,527,026,453

COMMUNICATIONS
Airports and waterways – The principal airports are at Warsaw, Krakow, Katowice and Wroclaw, and there are 83 smaller airports; the principal seaports are Gdansk, Gdynia, Swinoujscie and Szczecin, and there are 3,997km of navigable rivers and canals
Roadways and railways – 280,719km, including 2,418km of motorways; 19,428km
Telecommunications – 8.4 million fixed lines and 53 million mobile subscriptions (2016); there were 28.2 million internet users in 2016
Internet code and IDD – pl; 48 (from UK), 44 (to UK)
Major broadcasters – Telewizja Polska (TVP) and Polish Radio are the principal state broadcasters
Press – *Gazeta Wyborcza, Fakt* and *Rzeczpospolita* are the principal mass-circulation dailies
WPFI score – 26,59 (58)

EDUCATION AND HEALTH
Elementary education (ages seven to 15) is free and compulsory. Secondary education is also free, but optional.
Literacy rate – 100 per cent (2015 est)
Gross enrolment ratio (percentage of relevant age group) – primary 110 per cent, secondary 107 per cent, tertiary 67 per cent (2016 est)
Health expenditure (per capita) – US$910 (2014)
Hospital beds (per 1,000 people) – 6.5 (2011)
Life expectancy (years) – 77.8 (2017 est)
Mortality rate – 10.4 (2017 est)
Birth rate – 9.5 (2017 est)
Infant mortality rate – 4.4 (2017 est)

PORTUGAL
República Portuguesa – Portuguese Republic

Area – 92,090 sq. km
Capital – Lisbon; population, 2,927,000 (2018 est)
Major cities – Coimbra, Faro, Oporto, Setubal
Currency – Euro (€) of 100 cents
Population – 10,839,514 rising at 0.04 per cent a year (2017 est)
Religion – Christian (Roman Catholic 81 per cent, other 3.3 per cent) (2011 est)
Language – Portuguese, Mirandese (both official)
Population density – 112 per sq. km (2016)
Urban population – 65.2 per cent (2018 est)
Median age (years) – 41.8 (2016 est)
National anthem – 'A Portuguesa' 'The Portuguese'
National day – 10 June (Portugal Day)
Death penalty – Abolished for all crimes (since 1976)
CPI score – 63 (29)
Military expenditure – US$3,774m (2017)

CLIMATE AND TERRAIN
The terrain is mountainous north of the river Tagus, with rolling hills and plains in the south. Elevation extremes range from 2,351m (Ponta do Pico, Azores) to 0m (Atlantic Ocean). Forests of pine, cork oak and eucalyptus cover about 38 per cent of the country. The climate is temperate, with average temperatures ranging from 9.7°C in January to 22.5°C in August.

HISTORY AND POLITICS
Part of the Roman Empire from the second century BC, the country was overrun by Vandals and Visigoths in the fifth century AD. The Visigoths were ousted by Muslims from north Africa in the eighth century, but Christian reconquest began in the tenth century and an independent Christian kingdom was established in the 12th century.

Portuguese navigators led the 15th-century European age of exploration and the country soon became a major commercial and colonial power, its empire expanding to include Brazil, parts of China and large areas of Africa. In 1807 Portugal was invaded by Napoleonic France and then became the base from which Allied forces liberated Portugal and Spain in the Peninsular War. The 19th century was politically turbulent, with power struggles between conservative and liberal politicians, and within different factions of the royal family. In 1910 an armed uprising in Lisbon drove King Manuel II into exile and a republic was declared.

A period of political instability ensued until the military intervened in 1926. The constitution of 1933 gave formal expression to the authoritarian *Estado Novo* (New State) introduced by Dr Antonio Salazar, prime minister from 1932 until 1968. Marcello Caetano succeeded Salazar in 1968 but the regime's failure to liberalise at home or to conclude wars in the African colonies resulted in the government's overthrow in a military coup in 1974. Great political turmoil followed in 1974–5, a period in which most of the country's colonies gained their independence. Elections in 1976 stabilised the situation and full civilian government was restored in 1982. Portugal joined the EEC in 1986 and adopted the euro in 2002.

The centre-right Portugal Ahead coalition won the most seats in legislative elections in October 2015 but lost the majority it had held since 2011. However, Socialist leader Antonio Costa became prime minister in November following an alliance with Communist, Green and Left Bloc parties, which toppled conservative Pedro Passos Coelho's 11-day-old government in a parliamentary vote – the shortest administration in Portuguese history. The centre-right candidate Marcelo Rebelo de Sousa won the presidential election in January 2016 with 52 per cent of the vote.

Under the 1976 constitution, amended in 1982 and 1989, the head of state is a president who is directly elected for a five-year term, renewable once. The unicameral Assembly of the Republic has 230 members, directly elected by proportional representation for a four-year term. The prime minister, appointed by the president, is usually the leader of the largest party in the assembly.

HEAD OF STATE

President of the Republic, Marcelo Rebelo de Sousa, *elected* 24 January 2016, *sworn in* 9 March 2016

SELECTED GOVERNMENT MEMBERS *AS AT JUNE 2018*
Prime Minister, Antonio Costa
Finance, Mario Centeno
Internal Administration, Eduardo Cabrita

EMBASSY OF PORTUGAL
11 Belgrave Square, London SW1X 8PP
T 020-7235 5331 E londres@mne.pt
W www.portuguese-embassy.co.uk
Ambassador Extraordinary and Plenipotentiary, HE Manuel Lobo Antunes, *apptd* 2016

BRITISH EMBASSY
Rua de Sao Bernardo 33, 1249-082 Lisbon
T (+351) (21) 392 4000 E portugal.consulate@fco.gov.uk
W www.gov.uk/government/world/portugal
Ambassador Extraordinary and Plenipotentiary, HE Christopher Sainty, *apptd* 2018

ECONOMY AND TRADE

Portugal's economy was transformed after it joined the EU in 1986 into a diversified and increasingly service-based economy. The rapid growth of the 1990s slowed in 2001–8, and the global downturn pushed the economy into recession in 2009. Despite government austerity measures, a budget deficit treble the eurozone limit led to the country's credit rating being downgraded in 2010; in April 2011 the government obtained EU financial support. GDP fell in 2012 and 2013, as the government cut spending and increased tax to comply with the conditions of an EU–IMF financial rescue package. Portugal's economic recovery has quickened since 2014 and exited the EU's excessive deficit programme in 2017. Unemployment has steadily fallen but nevertheless remains high at 9.7 per cent, down from a peak of 18 per cent in 2013. The country's budget deficit was reduced from 11.2 per cent of GDP in 2010 to 1.8 per cent in 2017 in order to comply with eurozone targets. The government has promised a socialist programme allowing for a 'sustainable reduction in deficits and debt', and has boosted confidence by repaying its IMF loan ahead of schedule.

Around 8.6 per cent of the workforce is engaged in agriculture, contributing 2.2 per cent of GDP. The chief products are grain, fruit and vegetables, livestock, fish, dairy products, timber and cork. The main industries are tourism, manufacturing (textiles, footwear, cork, pulp and paper, chemicals, motor vehicle components), metalworking, winemaking, oil refining, and shipbuilding and repair. Natural resources are being exploited to generate electricity from hydroelectric and solar sources to reduce dependence on imported fuel and energy. Industry accounts for 22.1 per cent of GDP and services for 75.7 per cent.

The main trading partners are other EU countries, particularly Spain. Principal exports are agricultural products, food, wine, oil products, wood products, other industrial products, machinery and tools. The main imports include agricultural products, chemicals, vehicles, optical and precision instruments, and computer and IT components.

GNI – US$204bn; US$19,820 per capita (2017)
Annual average growth of GDP – 2.5 per cent (2017 est)
Inflation rate – 1.6 per cent (2017 est)
Population below poverty line – 19 per cent (2015)
Unemployment – 9.7 per cent (2017 est)
Total external debt – US$449bn (2016 est)
Imports – US$67,473m (2016)
Exports – US$55,662m (2016)

BALANCE OF PAYMENTS
Trade – US$11,811m deficit (2016)
Current Account – US$1,170m surplus (2017)

Trade with UK	2016	2017
Imports from UK	£1,431,275,252	£1,573,669,076
Exports to UK	£2,662,575,795	£3,009,808,221

COMMUNICATIONS

Airports and waterways – There are 43 airports, including international airports at Lisbon, Oporto, Faro, Santa Maria (Azores) and Funchal (Madeira); the main ports are Aveiro, Figueira da Foz, Leixoes, Lisbon, Setubal and Sines
Roadways and railways – 71,294km, including 2,613km of motorways; 3,319km
Telecommunications – 4.7 million fixed lines and 11.5 million mobile subscriptions (2016); there were 7.6 million internet users in 2016
Internet code and IDD – pt; 351 (from UK), 44 (to UK)
Major broadcasters – The monopoly of the public broadcaster RTP (TV) and RDP (radio) ended in 1992, and commercial stations now dominate the market
Press – Principal national newspapers include the daily titles *Diario de Noticias, Correio da Manha* and *Jornal de Noticias*
WPFI score – 14,17 (14)

EDUCATION AND HEALTH

Education is free and compulsory for nine years from the age of six. The university at Coimbra was founded in 1290.
Literacy rate – 99.6 per cent (2015 est)
Gross enrolment ratio (percentage of relevant age group) – primary 105 per cent, secondary 118 per cent, tertiary 63 per cent (2016 est)
Health expenditure (per capita) – US$2,097 (2014)
Hospital beds (per 1,000 people) – 3.4 (2013)
Life expectancy (years) – 79.4 (2017 est)
Mortality rate – 11.1 (2017 est)
Birth rate – 9 (2017 est)
Infant mortality rate – 4.3 (2017 est)

AUTONOMOUS REGIONS

Madeira and the Azores are both autonomous regions, each with its own locally elected assembly and government.

MADEIRA is a group of islands in the Atlantic Ocean about 990km south-west of Lisbon, and consists of Madeira, Porto Santo and three uninhabited islands. Total area is 801 sq. km; population, 256,424 (2015). Funchal on Madeira, the largest island, is the capital.

THE AZORES is an archipelago of nine islands in the Atlantic Ocean 1,400–1,800km west of Lisbon, and consists of Flores, Corvo, Terceira, Sao Jorge, Pico, Faial, Graciosa, Sao Miguel and Santa Maria. Total area is 2,322 sq. km; population, 245,746 (2011). Ponta Delgada, on Sao Miguel, is the capital.

QATAR

Dawlat Qatar – State of Qatar

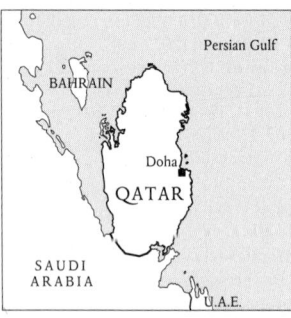

Area – 11,586 sq. km
Capital – Doha; population, 633,000 (2018 est)
Major cities – Ar Rayyan, al-Wakrah
Currency – Qatar riyal of 100 dirhams
Population – 2,314,307 rising at 2.27 per cent a year (2017 est); Arab (40 per cent), Indian (18 per cent), Pakistani (18 per cent), Iranian (10 per cent) (est)
Religion – Muslim 77.5 per cent (predominantly Sunni), Christian 8.5 per cent, other 14 per cent (2004 est)
Language – Arabic (official), English
Population density – 227 per sq. km (2016)
Urban population – 99.1 per cent (2018 est)
Median age (years) – 33 (2016 est)
National anthem – 'As-Salam al-Amiri' 'Peace to the Amir'
National day – 18 December
Death penalty – Retained
CPI score – 63 (29)
Military expenditure – US$1,877m (2010)
Conscription – Men aged 18–35
Literacy rate – 99.5 per cent (2015 est)
Gross enrolment ratio (percentage of relevant age group) – primary 104 per cent, secondary 93 per cent, tertiary 15 per cent (2016 est)
Health expenditure (per capita) – US$2,106 (2014)
Life expectancy (years) – 78.9 (2017 est)
Mortality rate – 1.5 (2017 est)
Birth rate – 9.6 (2017 est)
Infant mortality rate – 6.2 (2017 est)

CLIMATE AND TERRAIN

Qatar occupies a peninsula in the Persian Gulf and is mostly a low-lying desert plain, with sand dunes in the south. Elevation extremes range from 103m (Tuwayyir al-Hamir) to 0m (Persian Gulf). The country has a desert climate, with low rainfall and average temperatures ranging from 17.1°C in January to 36.6°C in July. Humidity along the coast often reaches 90 per cent in summer.

HISTORY AND POLITICS

Towns on the Qatari coast developed into important trading centres from the 18th century. Persian rule of the area ended in the mid-18th century and after a period of conflict, the peninsula became a dependency of Bahrain in the 1850s. A revolt against Bahraini rule in the 1860s was suppressed, but Britain intervened in 1867, recognising the dependency as a separate entity. Nominally under the rule of the Ottoman Empire from 1871 until the outbreak of the First World War, Qatar became a British protectorate in 1916, when the al-Thani family was recognised as the ruling house. It became independent in 1971.

In 1972 Sheikh Ahmad was overthrown by the crown prince and prime minister, Sheikh Khalifa. Sheikh Khalifa was overthrown in 1995 by his son and heir, Sheikh Hamad, who has since introduced liberal reforms. Municipal elections, the first democratic polls since independence, were held in 1999. A referendum in 2003 approved a new constitution, which came into force in 2005. Elections to the partially elected consultative council established by the constitution have yet to take place. In June 2013 Sheikh Tamim bin Hamad al-Thani took over as emir after his father abdicated.

In June 2017, the state was isolated by other Arab nations, including Saudi Arabia, Egypt, Bahrain and the UAE, apparently over its links with Iran and Islamist groups such as the Muslim Brotherhood. An economic blockade was put in place, alongside a denial of air space, severing of diplomatic ties and the expulsion of Qatari nationals from neighbouring countries at short notice. The blockade remained in place a year later as the nation pursued a legal resolution through the International Court of Justice.

A new constitution came into force in 2005. The head of state is a hereditary absolute monarch, the emir. There is no legislature at present, although the 2005 constitution provides for a legislative council with 45 members, 30 directly elected and 15 appointed by the emir. Elections were planned for 2007 but have been extended several times. At present there is an advisory council with 35 members appointed by the emir. There are no political parties. Women have been permitted to vote and stand for election since 1999.

HEAD OF STATE

HH Emir of Qatar, Defence, Sheikh Tamim bin Hamad al-Thani, *assumed power* 25 June 2013
Crown Prince, HH Sheikh Abdullah bin Hamad al-Thani

SELECTED GOVERNMENT MEMBERS *AS AT JUNE 2018*
Prime Minister, Interior, HH Sheikh Abdullah bin Nasser bin Khalifa al-Thani
Deputy Prime Minister, Ahmed bin Abdullah bin Zaid al-Mahmoud
Economy and Commerce, Ahmed bin Jassim bin Mohamed al-Thani
Finance, Ali Sherif al-Emadi

EMBASSY OF THE STATE OF QATAR
1 South Audley Street, London W1K 1NB
T 020-7493 2200 E amb@qatarembassy.org.uk
W www.qatarembassy.info
Ambassador Extraordinary and Plenipotentiary, HE Yousef Ali al-Khater, *apptd* 2014

BRITISH EMBASSY
West Bay, PO Box 3, Off Wahda Street near Rainbow Roundabout, Doha
T (+974) 4496 2000 E embassy.qatar@fco.gov.uk
W www.gov.uk/government/world/qatar
Ambassador Extraordinary and Plenipotentiary, HE Ajay Sharma, CMG, *apptd* 2015

ECONOMY AND TRADE

The economy is based largely on the production of oil and gas, which accounts for more than 50 per cent of GDP, and has made Qatar the world's second highest per-capita income country. The state-owned Qatar General Petroleum Corporation controls the industry, and is responsible for oil production onshore and offshore. There has been substantial foreign investment in exploitation of Qatar's gas fields, and the country is now the third largest exporter of natural gas, equal to 13 per cent of the world's production. Trade restrictions imposed in 2017 by neighbouring countries, low oil prices and construction costs (particularly for the FIFA World Cup in 2022) have resulted in efforts to curtail its budget deficit.

Other industries include oil refining, production of ammonia, fertilisers, petrochemicals, steel and cement, and ship repairing. Industry contributes 50.3 per cent of GDP and services 49.5 per cent.

The main export markets are Japan, South Korea and India; the chief sources of imports are China, the USA, and EU states. Principal exports are liquefied natural gas, petroleum products, fertilisers and steel. The main imports are machinery and transport equipment, food and chemicals.

GNI – US$161.2m; US$61,070 per capita (2017)
Annual average growth of GDP – 2.5 per cent (2017 est)
Inflation rate – 0.9 per cent (2017 est)
Unemployment – 0.6 per cent (2017 est)
Total external debt – US$168bn (2017 est)
Imports – US$32,058m (2016)
Exports – US$57,264m (2016)

BALANCE OF PAYMENTS

Trade – US$25,196m surplus (2016)
Current Account – US$6,425m surplus (2017)

Trade with UK	2016	2017
Imports from UK	£1,901,543,108	£2,419,418,134
Exports to UK	£1,973,825,729	£2,442,925,332

COMMUNICATIONS

Airports and waterways – Doha is the principal airport and also the main seaport
Roadways – 9,830km
Telecommunications – 467,148 fixed lines and 3.6 million mobile subscriptions (2016); there were 2.1 million internet users in 2016
Internet code and IDD – qa; 974 (from UK), 44 (to UK)
Major broadcasters – The country hosts the government-owned Al-Jazeera (TV), which broadcasts internationally in English and Arabic; Qatar TV and Qatar Broadcasting Service (QBS) are also public broadcasters
Press – *Al-Watan, Al-Rayah* and *Al-Sharq* are leading daily newspapers
WPFI score – 40,16 (125)

ROMANIA

Area – 238,391 sq. km
Capital – Bucharest; population, 1,821,000 (2018 est)
Major cities – Brasov, Cluj-Napoca, Constanta, Craiova, Galati, Iasi, Timisoara
Currency – New leu (plural lei) of 100 bani
Population – 21,529,967 falling at 0.33 per cent a year (2017 est); Romanian (83.4 per cent), Hungarian (6.1 per cent), Roma (3.1 per cent) (2011); small minority of Sasi (Transylvanian Saxons)
Religion – Christian (Orthodox 81.9 per cent, Protestant 6.4 per cent, Roman Catholic 4.3 per cent) (2011 est)
Language – Romanian (official), Hungarian, Romani
Population density – 85 per sq. km (2016)
Urban population – 54 per cent (2018 est)
Median age (years) – 40.7 (2016 est)
National anthem – 'Desteapta-te, Romane' 'Wake Up, Romanian'
National day – 1 December (Unification Day)
Death penalty – Abolished for all crimes (since 1989)
CPI score – 48 (59)
Military expenditure – US$4,004m (2017)

CLIMATE AND TERRAIN

The Carpathian mountain range runs south from the Ukrainian border into the centre of the country and then turns west (the Transylvanian Alps) and north. The mountains enclose the central Transylvanian plateau and divide it from the southern Wallachian plain, part of the basin of the river Danube, which runs along most of the southern border, and the eastern Moldavian plateau, through which the river Siret flows, and the Black Sea coast. The mountains are thickly forested. Elevation extremes range from 2,544m (Moldoveanu) to 0m (Black Sea). The climate is continental, with average temperatures ranging from −1.9°C in January to 20.9°C in July.

POLITICS

The 1991 constitution was amended in 2003 to bring it into line with EU requirements. The president is directly elected for a five-year term, renewable once. The bicameral parliament comprises the Chamber of Deputies with 329 seats, of which 17 are reserved for ethnic minorities, and the senate with 136 seats. Both houses are directly elected for a four-year term by proportional representation. The prime minister is appointed by the president.

In the 2012 legislative elections, the four-party Social Liberal Union won a significant majority in both chambers and the leader of the Social Democratic Party (PSD), Victor Ponta, was reappointed prime minister, but his government resigned in November 2015 following anti-corruption protests prompted by a nightclub fire in Bucharest in October 2015 that left 48 people dead. The Social Democrats clinched

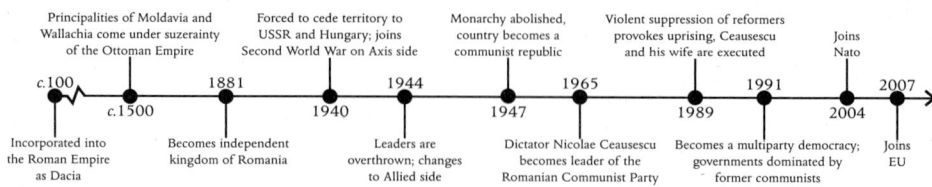

Principalities of Moldavia and Wallachia come under suzerainty of the Ottoman Empire

Forced to cede territory to USSR and Hungary; joins Second World War on Axis side

Monarchy abolished, country becomes a communist republic

Violent suppression of reformers provokes uprising, Ceausescu and his wife are executed

Joins Nato

*c.*100   1881   1944   1965   1991   2007

*c.*1500   1940   1947   1989   2004

Incorporated into the Roman Empire as Dacia

Becomes independent kingdom of Romania

Leaders are overthrown; changes to Allied side

Dictator Nicolae Ceausescu becomes leader of the Romanian Communist Party

Becomes a multiparty democracy; governments dominated by former communists

Joins EU

the December 2016 legislative elections with 46 per cent of the vote, and Sorin Grindeanu was appointed prime minister. In June 2017, the prime minister lost a vote of no confidence and was replaced by Mihai Tudose, who resigned in January 2018 following an internal dispute. Vasilica-Viorica Dancila was appointed the nation's third head of government in a year and its first woman premier shortly after. The 2014 presidential election was won by National Liberal Party (PNL) candidate Klaus Iohannis after a second round of voting.

HEAD OF STATE
President of the Republic, Klaus Iohannis, *elected* 16 November 2014, *sworn in* 21 December 2014

SELECTED GOVERNMENT MEMBERS *AS AT JUNE 2018*
Prime Minister, Vasilica-Viorica Dancila
Deputy Prime Ministers, Paul Stanescu; Gratiela Gravilescu; Viorel Stefan; Ana Birchall
Economy, Danut Andrusca
Foreign Affairs, Teodor-Viorel Melescanu

EMBASSY OF ROMANIA
Arundel House, 4 Palace Green, London W8 4QD
T 020-7937 9666 E londra@mae.ro W www.londra.mae.ro
Ambassador Extraordinary and Plenipotentiary, HE Sorin-Dan Mihalache, *apptd* 2016

BRITISH EMBASSY
24 Strada Jules Michelet, 010463 Bucharest
T (+40) (21) 201 7200 E Press.Bucharest@fco.gov.uk
W www.gov.uk/government/world/romania
Ambassador Extraordinary and Plenipotentiary, HE Andrew Noble, CVO, *apptd* 2018

ECONOMY AND TRADE
Transition to a market economy made sluggish progress until 2000, accelerating after 2004 in order to meet the requirements for EU accession. Although the economy grew steadily from 2000 to 2008, it was from a low base and poverty remains high, afflicting almost a quarter of the population. The economy contracted sharply in 2009 owing to the global downturn, and the government sought IMF and EU funding in spring 2009. Following austerity measures the economy returned to positive growth in 2011 and performed strongly between 2013–7, driven by strong industrial exports, healthy agricultural harvests and rising domestic demand. Corruption, an aging population and considerable tax evasion are long-term issues.

Agriculture remains inefficient, employing 28.3 per cent of the workforce but contributing only 4.2 per cent of GDP. The principal crops are grains, sugar beet, sunflower seeds, vegetables and livestock products. Vines and fruit are grown, and extensive forests support an important timber industry. There are reserves of natural gas and oil, but Romania is a net importer of fossil fuels, although it exports electricity. Mineral deposits, including coal, iron ore, bauxite, chromium and uranium support a mining industry. Other industries include manufacturing, electrical and light machinery and car assembly, metallurgy, food processing and textiles.

The main trading partners are EU states (especially Italy and Germany) and China. Principal exports include machinery and equipment, textiles, footwear, metals and metal products, minerals and fuels, chemicals and agricultural products. The main imports are machines and equipment, fuels, minerals, chemicals, base metals and agricultural products.
GNI – US$195.2bn; US$9,970 per capita (2017)
Annual average growth of GDP – 5.5 per cent (2017 est)
Inflation rate – 1.1 per cent (2017 est)
Population below poverty line – 22.4 per cent (2012 est)
Unemployment – 5.3 per cent (2017 est)
Total external debt – US$94.17bn (2017 est)
Imports – US$74,605m (2016)
Exports – US$63,582m (2016)

BALANCE OF PAYMENTS
Trade – US$11,023m deficit (2016)
Current Account – US$7,110m deficit (2017)

Trade with UK	2016	2017
Imports from UK	£1,036,584,798	£1,240,879,713
Exports to UK	£1,725,482,109	£1,993,074,340

COMMUNICATIONS
Airports and waterways – The main airports are at Bucharest and Timisoara; the main ports are Braila, Constanta, Galati and Tulcea, with 1,599km of navigable waterways on the river Danube and its tributaries and 132km of canals
Roadways and railways – There are 49,873km of surfaced roadways, of which 337km are motorway; there are 10,777km of railways, over one-third of which are electrified
Telecommunications – 4.1 million fixed lines and 22.9 million mobile subscriptions (2016); there were 12.8 million internet users in 2016
Internet code and IDD – ro; 40 (from UK), 44 (to UK)
Major broadcasters – The state-owned Televiziunea (TVR) and Radio Romania are the country's principal broadcasters
Press – There are several daily newspapers, including *Adevarul, Libertatea* and *Evenimentul Zilei*
WPFI score – 24,46 (46)

EDUCATION AND HEALTH
Primary and secondary education is free and compulsory for ten years.
Literacy rate – 99.3 per cent (2015 est)
Gross enrolment ratio (percentage of relevant age group) – primary 89 per cent, secondary 89 per cent, tertiary 48 per cent (2016 est)
Health expenditure (per capita) – US$557 (2014)
Hospital beds (per 1,000 people) – 6.3 (2013)
Life expectancy (years) – 75.4 (2017 est)
Mortality rate – 12 (2017 est)
Birth rate – 8.9 (2017 est)
Infant mortality rate – 9.4 (2017 est)
HIV/AIDS adult prevalence – 0.1 per cent (2016 est)

RUSSIA

Rossiyskaya Federatsiya – Russian Federation

Area – 17,098,242 sq. km. Includes the Kaliningrad exclave, between Lithuania and Poland. Neighbours: Norway, Finland, Estonia, Latvia, Belarus, Ukraine (west), Georgia, Azerbaijan, Kazakhstan, China, Mongolia, North Korea (south)

Capital – Moscow; population, 12,410,000 (2018 est). Founded in around 1147, it became the centre of the rising Moscow principality and in the 15th century the capital of the whole of Russia (Muscovy). In 1703 Peter the Great transferred the capital to St Petersburg, but Moscow became the capital again in 1918

Major cities – Chelyabinsk, Kazan, Nizhniy Novgorod (Gorky 1932–90), Novosibirsk (Novonikolayevsk until 1926), Omsk, Perm, Rostov, St Petersburg (Petrograd 1914–24; Leningrad 1924–91), Samara (Kuibyshev 1935–90), Ufa, Vladivostok, Volgograd (Stalingrad 1925–61), Yekaterinburg (Sverdlovsk 1924–91)

Currency – Rouble of 100 kopeks

Population – 142,257,519 falling at 0.08 per cent a year (2017 est); Russian (77.7 per cent), Tatar (3.7 per cent), Ukrainian (1.4 per cent), Bashkir (1.1 per cent), Chuvash (1.1 per cent), and a further 150 nationalities (2010)

Religion – Russian Orthodox 15–20 per cent, Muslim 10–15 per cent; other groups include Buddhists, Hindus and Jews

Language – Russian (official); many minority languages

Population density – 9 per sq. km (2016)

Urban population – 74.4 per cent (2018 est)

Median age (years) – 39.3 (2016 est)

National anthem – 'Gosudarstvenny Gimn Rossiyskoy Federatsii' 'State Anthem of the Russian Federation'

National day – 12 June (Russia Day)

Death penalty – Retained (last used 1999)

CPI score – 29 (135)

Military expenditure – US$66,355m (2017)

Conscription – 18–27 years of age; 12 months

CLIMATE AND TERRAIN

Russia includes the easternmost area of Europe and the whole of northern Asia. It lies mostly on plains which extend eastwards to the Ural mountains and then from the Urals to the Yenesei river. To the east of the Yenesei are plateaux, with lowlands in northern Siberia. Mountainous areas lie along the southern borders, in eastern Siberia and the Kamchatka

peninsula. The terrain varies from the tundra of the Arctic region, through the taiga (the largest zone) of the north and centre, to the grassy plains (steppe) between the forests and the mountains. Elevation extremes range from 5,633m (Mt Elbrus, Caucasus) to −28m (Caspian Sea). Russia has the longest Arctic coastline in the world (over 27,000km); it also has Baltic, Black Sea and Pacific coastlines.

The most important rivers are the Volga, the Northern Dvina, the Neva, the Don and the Kuban in the European part, and in the Asiatic part the Ob, the Irtysh, the Yenisei, the Lena, the Amur and, further north, the Khatanga, Olenek, Yana, Indigirka and Kolyma. Lake Baikal in eastern Siberia is the deepest lake in the world. Part of the Caspian Sea lies within Russia.

The climate is mostly continental, but varies with latitude and terrain, from arctic conditions in the north to subtropical in the far east and on the Black Sea coast. Average national temperatures range from −25.2°C in January to 14.9°C in July. Rainfall is low to moderate in most of the country.

POLITICS

The 1993 constitution introduced multiparty democracy and enshrines various human rights and civil liberties; amendments in 2008 extended the terms of office for the presidency and the State *Duma* from the 2012 elections. The head of state is a president, who is directly elected for a six-year term, renewable once consecutively. The bicameral Federal Assembly comprises the State *Duma* (lower house) of 450 members, all elected by proportional representation for a five-year term, and the Council of the Federation, which has 170 members (two from each member of the federation and two from Ukraine's autonomous Republic of Crimea, which Russia annexed in 2014), appointed for four-year terms. The president appoints the chairman of the council of ministers (prime minister), subject to the approval of the legislature, but is also entitled to chair sessions of the council.

In the September 2016 legislative elections, the pro-Vladimir Putin United Russia party retained its majority in the *Duma* winning 76.7 per cent of the vote. Putin (president between 2000 and 2008) was elected president once more in March 2012 and re-elected in 2018, picking up 76.7 per cent

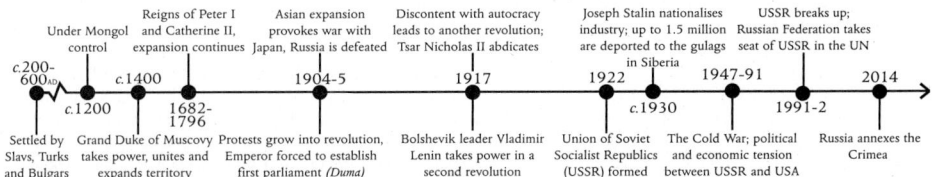

Under Mongol control — c.200–600AD

Reigns of Peter I and Catherine II, expansion continues — c.1400

Asian expansion provokes war with Japan, Russia is defeated — 1904–5

Discontent with autocracy leads to another revolution; Tsar Nicholas II abdicates — 1917

Joseph Stalin nationalises industry; up to 1.5 million are deported to the gulags in Siberia — 1922

USSR breaks up; Russian Federation takes seat of USSR in the UN — 1947–91

2014

c.1200 — Settled by Slavs, Turks and Bulgars

1682–1796 — Grand Duke of Muscovy takes power, unites and expands territory

Protests grow into revolution, Emperor forced to establish first parliament (*Duma*)

Bolshevik leader Vladimir Lenin takes power in a second revolution

c.1930 — Union of Soviet Socialist Republics (USSR) formed

1991–2 — The Cold War; political and economic tension between USSR and USA

Russia annexes the Crimea

of the overall vote amid allegations of ballot stuffing. He was inaugurated as president in May 2012 and duly appointed former president Dmitry Medvedev as Chair of the Council of Ministers.

HEAD OF STATE
President, Vladimir Putin, *elected* 4 March 2012, *took office* 7 May 2012, *re-elected* 18 March 2018

SELECTED GOVERNMENT MEMBERS *AS AT JUNE 2018*
Chair of the Council of Ministers, Dmitry Medvedev
First Deputy Prime Minister, Finance, Anton Siluanov
Deputy Prime Ministers, Maxim Akimov; Yury Borisov; Konstantin Chuichenko; Tatyana Golikova; Olga Golodets; Alexei Gordeyev; Dmitry Kozak; Vitaly Mutko; Yury Trutnev
Foreign Affairs, Sergei Lavrov

EMBASSY OF THE RUSSIAN FEDERATION
6–7 Kensington Palace Gardens, London W8 4QP
T 020-7229 6412 E info@rusemb.org.uk W www.rusemb.org.uk
Ambassador Extraordinary and Plenipotentiary, HE Alexander Yakovenko, *apptd* 2011

BRITISH EMBASSY
Smolenskaya Naberezhnaya 10, 121099 Moscow
T (+7) (495) 956 7200 E enquiriesukinrussia@fco.gov.uk
W www.gov.uk/government/world/russia
Ambassador Extraordinary and Plenipotentiary, HE Dr Laurence Bristow, CMG, *apptd* 2016

INSURGENCIES
Chechnya occupies an area that is strategically important to Russia because routes from central Russia to the Black Sea and Caspian Sea, and oil and gas pipelines from neighbouring countries, pass through it. The republic declared itself independent in 1991 but its attempts to assert its independence led to two wars with the federal government. The first of these, in 1994–6, resulted in the signing of the Khasavyurt accords. After the peace broke down and Russia invaded Chechnya again in 1999, President Putin refused negotiations and imposed direct rule from Moscow in 2000. Rebels continued with terrorist attacks, although these have decreased since 2007. Russia announced the end of counter-terrorism operations in Chechnya in 2009, but has had to reinstate these in some areas where rebels remain active.

The conflict in Chechnya has destabilised the whole of the northern Caucasus, especially Ingushetia and Dagestan, where violence has increased in recent years. The violence has also affected other parts of Russia, where extremists linked to Chechen separatists have carried out suicide bombings and attacks such as the Moscow theatre siege in 2002, the Beslan school siege in 2004 and the bombing of Moscow's metro system in 2010. A suicide-bomb attack on St Petersburg's underground in April 2017 killed 14 people; a group affiliated to al-Qaeda later claimed responsibility.

FEDERAL STRUCTURE
Following the break-up of the USSR in 1991, a new federal treaty was signed in 1992 between the central government and the autonomous republics of the Russian Federation. Tatarstan and Bashkortostan signed the treaty in 1994 after securing considerable legislative and economic autonomy.

The Russian Federation comprises 46 *oblasti* (regions), nine *krai* (autonomous territories), 21 *respubliki* (autonomous republics), four *okrugi* (autonomous areas), two cities with federal status (Moscow and St Petersburg) and one autonomous Jewish *oblast*, Yevrey. The *oblasti* are Amur, Arkhangelsk, Astrakhan, Belgorod, Bryansk, Chelyabinsk,

Irkutsk, Ivanovo, Kaliningrad, Kaluga, Kemerovo, Kirov, Kostroma, Kurgan, Kursk, Leningrad, Lipetsk, Magadan, Moscow, Murmansk, Nizhny Novgorod, Novgorod, Novosibirsk, Omsk, Orel, Orenburg, Penza, Pskov, Rostov, Ryazan, Sakhalin, Samara, Saratov, Smolensk, Sverdlovsk, Tambov, Tomsk, Tula, Tver, Tyumen, Ulyanovsk, Vladimir, Volgograd, Vologda, Voronezh and Yaroslavl. The *krai* are Altai, Kamchatka, Khabarovsk, Krasnodar, Krasnoyarsk, Perm, Primorski, Stavropol and Zabaykalsk. The *respubliki* are Adygeia, Altai, Bashkortostan, Buryatia, Chechnya, Chuvashia, Dagestan, Ingushetia, Kabardino-Balkaria, Kalmykiya, Karachayevo-Cherkessia, Karelia, Khakassia, Komi, Mari-El, Mordovia, North Ossetia, Sakha, Tatarstan, Tuva and Udmurtia. The *okrugi* are Chukotka, Khanty-Mansi, Nenets and Yamalo-Nenets. In April 2014, Russia recognised Crimea as a *respublika* and Sevastopol as a federal city, following the annexation of the territory from Ukraine. The United States and The European Union does not recognise the region as part of Russia.

ECONOMY AND TRADE
Under the Soviet regime, an essentially agrarian economy in 1917 was transformed by the early 1960s into the second-greatest industrial power in the world. However, by the early 1970s the concentration of resources on the military-industrial complex had caused stagnation in the civilian economy. Economic reforms were introduced by President Gorbachev, including the legalisation of small private businesses, the reduction of state control over the economy, and denationalisation and privatisation. Mass privatisation of state industries began in 1992, and 80 per cent of the economy had been privatised by 1996. The largest and most economically significant industries, oil and gas, were partially renationalised from 2004.

The transition to a market economy caused severe economic crises in 1993 and 1998, but from 1999 to 2008 the economy sustained growth averaging 7 per cent a year. Political and economic uncertainties, corruption, excessive red tape and a lack of trust in institutions continue to inhibit growth however. Other problems include the economy's vulnerability to fluctuations in global prices of key commodities, a dilapidated infrastructure and international sanctions. Some of these factors exacerbated the impact on Russia of the global financial crisis in autumn 2008, when a sharp fall in oil prices coincided with turmoil in the banking system and a 70 per cent drop in the stock market. Credit problems, a severe drop in production and rising unemployment caused a sharp contraction in the economy until late 2009, before high oil prices boosted economic growth in 2011–12. Russia joined the World Trade Organization in 2012, providing greater access to foreign markets. Russia's involvement in the Ukraine crisis caused a number of nations to impose economic sanctions, including the US, the EU and Japan. Sanctions since 2014 have primarily targeted the energy, financial and military sectors of the economy and contributed to a deep recession in 2015–6. Real growth returned in 2017, to 1.8 per cent as demand for Russian exports increased, but sanctions remain in place as the government looks to diversify the economy away from mineral and fossil fuel exports.

Russia has some of the world's richest natural resources, especially mineral deposits and timber. Growth in the economy reliant on the exploitation and export of its oil and natural gas reserves. Russia is the world's third largest oil producer (recently surpassed by the USA and Saudi Arabia) and leading exporter of hydrocarbons, and a leading supplier to European countries and China, a position that has led the country into disputes with some of its neighbours; Ukraine, Georgia, Lithuania, Czechia, Armenia, Azerbaijan, Poland and

Belarus have all had gas or oil supplies cut for short periods during price negotiations.

Mining (coal, iron ore, aluminium and other non-ferrous metals) and oil and natural gas extraction are concentrated in the region south of Moscow, the Volga valley, the northern Caucasus, the Urals, Siberia and the far east and north. Russia is also keen to exploit the shrinking of the Arctic ice cap to prospect for previously inaccessible deposits under the Arctic Sea. The main industries are extracting and processing oil, gas and minerals, forestry, all forms of machine building (including transport, communications, agricultural, construction, and power generating and transmitting equipment), defence industries, shipbuilding, medical and scientific instruments, consumer durables, textiles and food processing.

The vast area and the great variety in climatic conditions are reflected in the structure of agriculture. In the far north, only reindeer breeding, hunting and fishing are possible; further south, forestry is combined with grain growing. In the southern half of the forest zone and in the adjacent forest-steppe zone, the acreage under grain crops is larger and agriculture more complex. The southern part of the Western Siberian plain is an important grain-growing and stock-breeding area. In the extreme south, cotton is cultivated. Vine, tobacco and other southern crops are grown on the Black Sea shore of the Caucasus.

The service sector is the largest, accounting for 62.3 per cent of GDP and employing 63 per cent of the workforce; industry contributes 32.4 per cent of GDP and employs 27.6 per cent of the workforce; and agriculture accounts for 4.7 per cent of GDP and 9.4 per cent of employment.

Russia's main trading partners are China, EU countries (especially Germany) and the USA. Principal exports are oil and petroleum products, natural gas, metals, timber and wood products, chemicals, manufactured goods, military vehicles and defence equipment. The main imports are machinery, vehicles, pharmaceuticals, plastics, semi-finished metal products, meat, fruits and nuts, optical and medical equipment, iron and steel.

GNI – US$1,355.6bn; US$9,232 per capita (2017)
Annual average growth of GDP – 1.8 per cent (2017 est)
Inflation rate – 4.2 per cent (2017 est)
Population below poverty line – 13.3 per cent (2015)
Unemployment – 5.5 per cent (2017 est)
Total external debt – US$451.5bn (2017 est)
Imports – US$182,265m (2016)
Exports – US$285,491m (2016)

BALANCE OF PAYMENTS
Trade – US$103,226m surplus (2016)
Current Account – US$35,436m surplus (2017)

Trade with UK	2016	2017
Imports from UK	£2,574,627,758	£2,868,931,741
Exports to UK	£4,138,919,763	£5,582,997,600

COMMUNICATIONS
Airports – There are 594 airports; the principal international airports are at Moscow, St Petersburg and Novosibirsk
Waterways – Major ports include Kaliningrad on the Baltic Sea and Novorossiysk on the Black Sea. Two of the three northern ports, St Petersburg and Arkhangelsk, are icebound during winter; only Murmansk is accessible. There is a large merchant fleet of 1,143 ships of 1,000 tonnes and over, with a further 439 ships registered in other countries. There are 102,000km of waterways, supplemented by a 72,000km system of canals, which provides a through route between the White Sea and Baltic Sea in the north and the Black Sea, Caspian Sea and the Sea of Azov in the south
Roadways – There are 927,721km of roadways, 39,143km of which are motorways
Railways – The railways are state-run, with 87,157km of the network used for passenger transport plus 30,000km by industry
Telecommunications – 32.2 million fixed lines and 229 million mobile subscriptions (2016); there were 108.7 million internet users in 2016
Internet code and IDD – ru; 7 (from UK), 810 44 (to UK)
Major broadcasters – Broadcasting is dominated by the Russian State Television and Radio Broadcasting Company (VGTRK) and stations part-owned by the government or whose owners have close ties to it
Press – There are over 400 major newspapers printed every week, including *Komsomolskaya Pravda, Moskovsky Komsomolets* and *Izvestia*
WPFI score – 49,96 (148)

EDUCATION AND HEALTH
There are 11 years of compulsory education: nine at basic school level and a further two at senior secondary level.
Literacy rate – 100 per cent (2010 est)
Gross enrolment ratio (percentage of relevant age group) – primary 102 per cent, secondary 105 per cent, tertiary 82 per cent (2016 est)
Health expenditure (per capita) – US$839 (2014)
Hospital beds (per 1,000 people) – 8.2 (2013)
Life expectancy (years) – 71 (2016 est)
Mortality rate – 13.5 (2017 est)
Birth rate – 11 (2017 est)
Infant mortality rate – 6.8 (2017 est)
HIV/AIDS adult prevalence – 1 per cent (2009 est)

RWANDA

Republika y'u Rwanda/République du Rwanda – Republic of Rwanda

Area – 26,338 sq. km
Capital – Kigali; population, 1,058,000 (2018 est)
Major towns – Butare, Gisenyi, Gitarama, Ruhengeri
Currency – Rwanda franc of 100 centimes
Population – 11,901,484 rising at 2.45 per cent a year (2017 est); Hutu (84 per cent), Tutsi (15 per cent), Twa (1 per cent) (est)
Religion – Christian (Roman Catholic 49.5 per cent, Protestant 39.4 per cent, other 4.5 per cent) (2002 est)
Language – Kinyarwanda, French, English (all official), Swahili
Population density – 495 per sq. km (2016)
Urban population – 17.2 per cent (2018 est)
Median age (years) – 19 (2016 est)

National anthem – 'Rwanda Nziza' 'Rwanda, Our Beautiful Country'
National day – 1 July (Independence Day)
Death penalty – Abolished for all crimes (since 2007)
CPI score – 55 (48)
Military expenditure – US$111m (2017)
Literacy rate – 80.4 per cent (2015 est)
Gross enrolment ratio (percentage of relevant age group) – primary 137 per cent, secondary 37 per cent, tertiary 8 per cent (2016 est)
Health expenditure (per capita) – US$52 (2014)
Hospital beds (per 1,000 people) – 1.6 (2007)
Life expectancy (years) – 64.3 (2017 est)
Mortality rate – 6.4 (2017 est)
Birth rate – 30.7 (2017 est)
Infant mortality rate – 29.7 (2017 est)
HIV/AIDS adult prevalence – 3.1 per cent (2016 est)

CLIMATE AND TERRAIN

Landlocked Rwanda's terrain is mostly savannah uplands and mountains, including the volcanic Virunga range in the north-west. Elevation extremes range from 4,519m (Volcan Karisimbi) to 950m (Rusizi River). Rwanda's western border runs through Lake Kivu. The climate is temperate, with a wet season from October to May. The average temperature in Rwanda is 19.4°C.

POLITICS

The Rwandan Patriotic Front (FPR) won the 2003 legislative elections and has retained power since, aided by a number of small independent coalition partners. The coalition won roughly three-quarters of votes in the September 2018 legislative elections. FPR leader Paul Kagame became president in 2000; he was elected president under a new constitution in 2003, and re-elected in 2010 and 2017. Edouard Ngirente became prime minister in August 2017, replacing Anastase Murekezi who held the position for three years.

Under the 2003 constitution, amended multiple times, the president is directly elected for a five-year term, renewable once. In December 2016 a constitutional amendment reduced this term from seven to five years but included an exception that allowed Kagame to serve another seven-year term in 2017. The bicameral parliament consists of the Chamber of Deputies (the lower house) and the senate. The Chamber of Deputies has 80 members, of whom 53 are directly elected, 24 are women members elected by the provinces, two represent youth organisations and one represents organisations of disabled people; all serve a five-year term. The senate has 26 members indirectly elected for an eight-year term. Political parties are barred from organising on an ethnic, regional or religious basis.

In 2006 the 12 provinces were replaced by five provinces: North, East, South, West and Kigali, with the aim of creating more ethnically diverse administrative areas.

HEAD OF STATE

President, Maj.-Gen. Paul Kagame, *apptd* 17 April 2000, *sworn in* 22 April 2000, *elected* 25 August 2003, *re-elected* 2010, 2017

SELECTED GOVERNMENT MEMBERS *AS AT SEPTEMBER 2018*
Prime Minister, Edouard Ngirente
Defence, Gen. James Kabarebe
Finance and Economic Planning, Uzziel Ndagijmana
Foreign Affairs, Louise Mushikiwabo

HIGH COMMISSION OF THE REPUBLIC OF RWANDA
120–122 Seymour Place, London W1H 1NR
T 020-7224 9832 E uk@rwandahc.org W www.rwandahc.org
High Commissioner, HE Yamina Karitanyi, *apptd* 2016

BRITISH HIGH COMMISSION
Parcelle No. 1131, Blvd de l'Umuganda, Kacyira-Sud, BP 576 Kigali
T (+250) 252 556 000 E BHC.Kigali@fco.gov.uk
W www.gov.uk/government/world/rwanda
High Commissioner, HE Joanne Lomas, *apptd* 2018

ECONOMY AND TRADE

Rwanda is the most densely populated country in Africa, with few natural resources and minimal industry. Nearly 40 per cent of the population lives below the poverty line, although this is declining, and economic growth, especially in food production, struggles to keep up with population growth. It is dependent on international aid but the demands of its high foreign debt have been reduced by debt relief. Regional instability, inadequate transport links with other countries and energy shortages hamper development, although electricity supply is expected to become more reliable when methane from Lake Kivu starts to be tapped. Rwanda has actively sought foreign investment and diversification, increasingly by using accessible online systems, and plans to become a regional leader in communication technologies by 2020.

The economic base of the country has significantly improved since the genocide in 1994, which alienated private and external investment and impoverished the population, and has experienced annual average growth of 6–8 per cent since 2003 with inflation reduced to single digits.

Around 75.3 per cent of the population is engaged in agriculture, which is mainly at subsistence level and contributes 30.9 per cent of GDP. The main industries are mining, processing agricultural products and small-scale manufacturing, cement and tourism.

The main trading partners are China, Uganda and the UAE. The main exports are coffee, tea, hides and tin ore. The principal imports are foodstuffs, machinery and equipment, steel, petroleum products and construction materials.
GNI – US$8.8bn; US$720 per capita (2017)
Annual average growth of GDP – 6.2 per cent (2017 est)
Inflation rate – 7.1 per cent (2016 est)

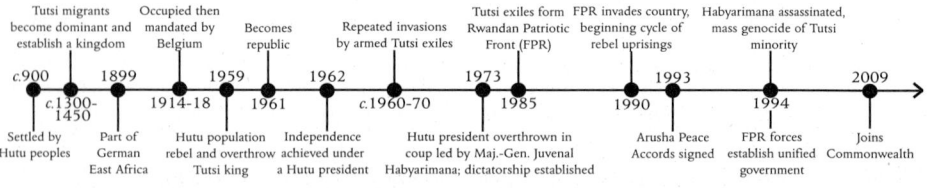

Population below poverty line – 39.1 per cent (2015 est)
Total external debt – US$2.966bn (2017 est)
Imports – US$2,457m (2014)
Exports – US$736m (2014)

BALANCE OF PAYMENTS
Trade – US$1,721m deficit (2014)
Current Account – US$621m deficit (2017)

Trade with UK	2016	2017
Imports from UK	£7,298,002	£9,147,980
Exports to UK	£4,817,851	£3,802,257

COMMUNICATIONS
Airports and waterways – The principal airport is at Kigali; Lake Kivu is navigable by shallow boats and provides access to the Democratic Republic of the Congo
Roadways – There are 1,207km of paved roads that link with those of neighbouring countries to provide access to Kenyan and Tanzanian ports
Telecommunications – 13,403 fixed lines and 8.9 million mobile subscriptions (2016); there were 2.6 million internet users in 2016
Internet code and IDD – rw; 250 (from UK), 44 (to UK)
Major broadcasters – The state-owned Rwanda Broadcasting Agency operates Rwanda TV and Radio Rwanda, which broadcasts in English, French, Kinyarwanda and Swahili
Press – Leading newspapers include The New Times and Rwanda Herald
WPFI score – 52,90 (156)

ST KITTS AND NEVIS

Federation of St Christopher and Nevis (Federation of St Kitts and Nevis)

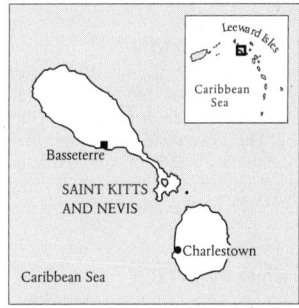

Area – 261 sq. km
Capital – Basseterre; population, 14,000 (2018)
Major town – Charlestown, the chief town of Nevis
Currency – East Caribbean dollar (EC$) of 100 cents
Population – 52,715 rising at 0.73 per cent a year (2017 est)
Religion – Christian (Anglican 50 per cent, Roman Catholic 25 per cent) (est)
Language – English (official)
Population density – 214 per sq. km (2015)
Urban population – 30.8 per cent (2018 est)
Median age (years) – 34.5 (2016 est)
National anthem – 'Oh Land of Beauty!'
National day – 19 September (Independence Day)
Death penalty – Retained (last used 2008)

Gross enrolment ratio (percentage of relevant age group) – primary 82.5 per cent, secondary 90.4 per cent, tertiary 79.6 per cent (2015 est)
Health expenditure (per capita) – US$771 (2014)
Life expectancy (years) – 75.9 (2017 est)
Mortality rate – 7.1 (2017 est)
Birth rate – 13.2 (2017 est)
Infant mortality rate – 8.4 (2017 est)

CLIMATE AND TERRAIN
The volcanic islands of St Kitts (St Christopher) (168 sq. km) and Nevis (93 sq. km) are part of the Leeward group in the eastern Caribbean Sea. The centre of St Kitts is forest-clad and mountainous, with the Great Salt Pond occupying the tip of its southern peninsula; elevation extremes range from 1,156m (Mt Liamuiga) to 0m (Caribbean Sea). Nevis, separated from the southern tip of St Kitts by a strait 3km wide, is dominated by Nevis Peak (985m). The climate is tropical, moderated by north-east trade winds, and a wet season occurs from May to September. The islands are in the hurricane belt.

HISTORY AND POLITICS
The islands were inhabited by Carib, or Kalinago, people when discovered in 1493 by Christopher Columbus, who gave St Christopher its name. Colonisation by the British began in 1623–4, when St Kitts became the first British colony in the West Indies, and French settlement began shortly after. The island was held jointly from 1628 to 1713, although there were skirmishes between the British and French settlers in the 17th century; France dropped its claims after 1783. Nevis was settled by the British from 1628. The two islands were part of the Leeward Islands colony from 1871 to 1956, and then of the West Indies Federation from 1958 to 1962. They achieved internal self-government in 1967 and became independent in September 1983.

The Labour Party, which had been in power since 1995, lost the 2015 National Assembly elections to the Team Unity coalition, which won seven of the 11 elected seats. Timothy Harris of the People's Labour Party was appointed prime minister.

Under the 1983 constitution, the head of state is Queen Elizabeth II, represented by a governor-general appointed on the advice of the prime minister. The unicameral National Assembly has 15 members: 11 directly elected for a five-year term, a speaker, and three appointed by the governor-general on the advice of the prime minister and the leader of the opposition. The prime minister, who is responsible to the legislature, and the cabinet are appointed by the governor-general.

Nevis is responsible for its own internal affairs. It has an eight-member Nevis Island assembly and is governed by the Nevis Island administration, headed by the premier.
Governor-General, HE Sir Samuel Seaton, GCMG, CVO, apptd 2015

SELECTED GOVERNMENT MEMBERS AS AT JUNE 2018
Prime Minister, Finance, Timothy Harris
Deputy Prime Minister, Shawn Richards
Foreign Affairs, Mark Brantley

HIGH COMMISSION FOR ST KITTS AND NEVIS
10 Kensington Court, London W8 5DL
T 020-7937 9718 E info@sknhc.co.uk W www.stkittsnevisuk.com/
High Commissioner, HE Kevin Isaac, apptd 2011

BRITISH HIGH COMMISSIONER
HE Janet Douglas, CMG, apptd 2017, resident at Bridgetown, Barbados

ECONOMY AND TRADE

The sugar industry was the mainstay of the economy for over 300 years but was closed down in 2005 after decades of operating at a loss. Tourism (the chief source of foreign exchange revenue), offshore financial services and manufacturing, especially distilling, food processing, clothing and electronics, are being developed. Services now account for 68.9 per cent of GDP, industry for 30 per cent and agriculture for 1.1 per cent. The economy of Nevis relies on farming, but a sea-island cotton industry is being developed for export. The economy was restricted by one of the world's highest public debt burdens, but after peaking at 154 per cent of GDP in 2011 debt has steadily fallen, and stood at 65.8 per cent of GDP in 2016. The global downturn impacted negatively on tourism and the economy contracted between 2009–13. The country remains vulnerable to costly damage from natural disasters and shifts in demand from tourism.

The main trading partners are the USA, Bangladesh, and Trinidad and Tobago. Principal exports are machinery, food, electronics, beverages and tobacco. The main imports are machinery, manufactured goods, food and fuels.

GNI – US$0.9bn; US$16,030 per capita (2017)
Annual average growth of GDP – 2.7 per cent (2017 est)
Inflation rate – 1.2 per cent (2017 est)
Total external debt – US$198m (2017 est)
Imports – US$332m (2016)
Exports – US$51m (2016)

BALANCE OF PAYMENTS

Trade – US$280m deficit (2016)
Current Account – US$102m deficit (2016)

Trade with UK	2016	2017
Imports from UK	£5,971,505	£7,271,708
Exports to UK	£195,288	£250,950

COMMUNICATIONS

Airports – There are two airports; the one on St Kitts can take most large jet aircraft
Waterways – Basseterre is a port of registry and has deep-water harbour facilities; there are regular ferries between Basseterre and Charlestown
Roadways and railways – The islands have 163km of surfaced roadways, and 50km of narrow-gauge railways on St Kitts
Telecommunications – 17,433 fixed lines and 76,583 mobile subscriptions (2016); there were 39,000 internet users in 2016
Internet code and IDD – kn; 1 869 (from UK), 011 44 (to UK)
Media – The government-owned broadcaster ZIZ operates national television and radio networks; *The Sun* is the sole daily newspaper

ST LUCIA

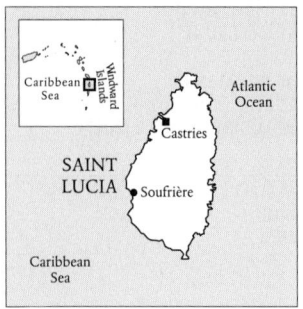

Area – 616 sq. km
Capital – Castries; population, 22,000 (2018)
Major town – Soufière
Currency – East Caribbean dollar (EC$) of 100 cents
Population – 164,994 rising at 0.32 per cent a year (2017 est)
Religion – Christian (Roman Catholic 61.5 per cent, Seventh-day Adventists 10.4 per cent, Pentecostals 8.9 per cent, Baptists 2.2 per cent), Rastafarian 1.9 per cent (2010 est)
Language – English (official), French patois
Population density – 303 per sq. km (2015)
Urban population – 18.7 per cent (2018 est)
Median age (years) – 34.2 (2016 est)
National anthem – 'Sons and Daughters of Saint Lucia'
National day – 22 February (Independence Day)
Death penalty – Retained (last used 1996)
CPI score – 55 (48)
Gross enrolment ratio (percentage of relevant age group) – secondary 88 per cent, tertiary 19 per cent (2016 est)
Health expenditure (per capita) – US$500 (2014)
Life expectancy (years) – 77.9 (2017 est)
Mortality rate – 7.7 (2017 est)
Birth rate – 13.3 (2017 est)
Infant mortality rate – 10.9 (2017 est)

CLIMATE AND TERRAIN

St Lucia is the second-largest island in the Windward group. The interior is mountainous and densely forested, with elevation extremes ranging from 950m (Mt Gimie) to 0m (Caribbean Sea). The area around the volcanic peaks of Gros Piton and Petit Piton is a UNESCO World Heritage Site. The climate is tropical, moderated by trade winds and with a wet season from July to November. The island is in the hurricane belt.

HISTORY AND POLITICS

The original Arawak settlers were superseded by Caribs by AD 800. The island was sighted by Columbus in 1502 and European settlement began in the 1550s. Control was disputed between France and Britain from the mid-17th century until 1814, when the island was ceded to Britain. It achieved internal self-government in 1967 and became independent in 1979.

The United Workers' Party (UWP) won the 2016 legislative election, defeating the incumbent St Lucia Labour Party, winning 11 assembly seats to the latter's six. Allen Chastanet of the UWP was sworn in as prime minister in June.

Under the 1979 constitution, the head of state is Queen Elizabeth II, represented by a governor-general appointed on the advice of the prime minister. The bicameral parliament consists of the house of assembly and the senate. The senate has 11 members, six nominated by the government, three by the opposition and two by the governor-general. The House of Assembly has 17 elected members and an appointed speaker who serve a five-year term. The prime minister, who is responsible to the legislature, and the cabinet are appointed by the governor-general.

Governor-General, HE Sir Neville Cenac, GCMG, *apptd* 2018

SELECTED GOVERNMENT MEMBERS *AS AT JUNE 2018*
Prime Minister, Finance, External Affairs, Finance, Allen
    Chastanet
Agriculture, Fisheries, Ezechiel Joseph
Home Affairs, Hermangild Francis

HIGH COMMISSION FOR ST LUCIA
1 Collingham Gardens, London SW5 0HW
T 020-7370 7123 E enquiries@stluciahcuk.org
W www.stluciahcuk.org
High Commissioner, HE Guy Mayers, *apptd* 2016

BRITISH HIGH COMMISSIONER
HE Janet Douglas, CMG, *apptd* 2017, resident at
    Bridgetown, Barbados

ECONOMY AND TRADE
The economy was dependent on bananas, but has diversified since preferential access to EU markets ended in 1999. Tourism is the main source of jobs, foreign exchange earnings and GDP, but has struggled since airlines cut services in 2012 and growth has since been minimal. Offshore financial services have also been developed, and the manufacturing sector is the most diverse in the Caribbean, processing agricultural products, assembling electronic components and producing clothing, beverages and corrugated cardboard boxes. Services account for 82.8 per cent of GDP, industry for 14.2 per cent and agriculture for 2.9 per cent.

The main trading partners are the USA (67.6 per cent of exports and 53.3 per cent of imports), the UK and Trinidad and Tobago. Principal exports are bananas, clothing, cocoa, fruit and coconut oil. The main imports are food, manufactured goods, machinery and transport equipment, chemicals and fuels.

GNI – US$1.6bn; US$8,780 per capita (2017)
Annual average growth of GDP – 1.6 per cent (2017 est)
Inflation rate – 0.2 per cent (2017 est)
Total external debt – US$523.2m (2016 est)
Imports – US$654m (2016)
Exports – US$120m (2016)

BALANCE OF PAYMENTS
Trade – US$535m deficit (2016)
Current Account – US$31m deficit (2016)

Trade with UK	2016	2017
Imports from UK	£19,144,604	£19,768,601
Exports to UK	£5,397,590	£6,349,274

COMMUNICATIONS
Airports and waterways – There are two airports in Castries and Vieux Fort; Castries also has a deep-water harbour
Roadways – 847km are surfaced
Telecommunications – 35,545 fixed lines and 176,648 mobile subscriptions (2016); there were 86,000 internet users in 2016
Internet code and IDD – lc; 1-758 (from UK), 011 44 (to UK)
Media – Television stations are privately owned and Radio Saint Lucia (RSL) is the state broadcaster; there are several newspapers but none daily

ST VINCENT AND THE GRENADINES

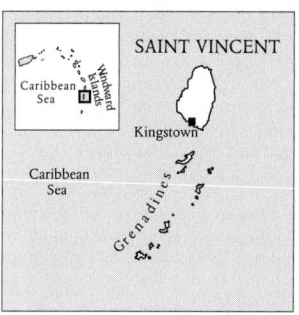

Area – 389 sq. km
Capital – Kingstown; population, 27,000 (2018)
Currency – East Caribbean dollar (EC$) of 100 cents
Population – 102,089 falling at 0.25 per cent a year (2017 est)
Religion – Christian (Anglican 47 per cent, Methodist 28 per cent and Roman Catholic 13 per cent), Hindu, Seventh-day Adventist
Language – English (official), French patois
Population density – 282 per sq. km (2016)
Urban population – 52.2 per cent (2016 est)
Median age (years) – 33 (2016)
National anthem – 'St Vincent! Land So Beautiful'
National day – 27 October (Independence Day)
Death penalty – Retained (last used 1995)
CPI score – 58 (40)
Gross enrolment ratio (percentage of relevant age group) – primary 103 per cent, secondary 107 per cent (2016 est)
Health expenditure (per capita) – US$575 (2014)
Life expectancy (years) – 75.5 (2017 est)
Mortality rate – 7.3 (2017 est)
Birth rate – 13.2 (2017 est)
Infant mortality rate – 12 (2017 est)

CLIMATE AND TERRAIN
The state, which lies in the Windward group, consists of St Vincent and the 32 small islands and cays of the northern Grenadines, a chain stretching 64km across the eastern Caribbean Sea between St Vincent and Grenada. St Vincent itself is a mountainous and densely forested volcanic island. The Grenadines, of which the largest are Bequia, Canouan, Mayreau, Mustique and Union Island, are low-lying coral islands. Elevation extremes range from 1,234m (La Soufriére volcano, St Vincent) to 0m (Caribbean Sea). The climate is tropical, with a rainy season from May to November. The islands lie in the hurricane belt.

HISTORY AND POLITICS
Settled successively by the Ciboney people, the Arawaks and the Caribs, St Vincent was sighted by Christopher Columbus in 1498. Although granted by Charles I to the Earl of Carlisle in 1627, control was disputed between the British and the French until the islands were ceded to Britain in 1783. Internal self-government was granted in 1969, and independence as St Vincent and the Grenadines was achieved in 1979.

An early election in 2001 was won decisively by the opposition Unity Labour Party, which was returned for additional terms in 2005, 2010 and 2015. A referendum in 2009 rejected a draft constitution which proposed to replace the monarchy with a republic.

Under the 1979 constitution, the head of state is Queen Elizabeth II, represented by a governor-general appointed on the advice of the prime minister. The unicameral House of Assembly has 23 members: 15 directly elected for a five-year term, six senators appointed by the governor-general and two *ex officio* members in the speaker and attorney general. The prime minister, who is responsible to the legislature, and the cabinet are appointed by the governor-general.

Governor-General, Sir Frederick Ballantyne, GCMG, *apptd* 2002

SELECTED GOVERNMENT MEMBERS *AS AT JUNE 2018*
Prime Minister, National Security, Ralph Gonsalves
Deputy Prime Minister, Foreign Affairs, Sir Louis Straker, KCMG
Attorney-General, Judith Jones-Morgan

HIGH COMMISSION FOR ST VINCENT AND THE GRENADINES
10 Kensington Court, London W8 5DL
T 020-7565 2874 E info@svghighcom.co.uk
W www.svghighcom.co.uk
High Commissioner, HE Cenio E. Lewis, *apptd* 2001

BRITISH HIGH COMMISSIONER
HE Janet Douglas, CMG, *apptd* 2017, resident at Bridgetown, Barbados

ECONOMY AND TRADE
Tourism, the development of which has been hampered by drug-related crime, is increasing and has been boosted by the construction of an international airport, which opened in 2017. Manufacturing and offshore banking services have all expanded, and while the economy contracted in 2009 it has showed signs of recovery despite a high public debt burden. Services now account for 75.5 per cent of GDP, industry for 17.4 per cent and agriculture for 7.1 per cent. Floods and mudslides caused by heavy rainfall in 2013 resulted in US$112m worth of damage.

The main export markets are Jordan, France and neighbouring island nations. Imports come mostly from the USA, Trinidad and Tobago, and the UK. Principal exports are bananas, vegetables, starch and tennis racquets. The main imports are foodstuffs, machinery and equipment, chemicals, fertilisers, minerals and fuel.

GNI – US$0.8bn; US$6,990 per capita (2017)
Annual average growth of GDP – 2.2 per cent (2017 est)
Inflation rate – 1.7 per cent (2017 est)
Total external debt – US$324.4m (2017 est)
Imports – US$335m (2016)
Exports – US$47m (2016)

BALANCE OF PAYMENTS
Trade – US$288m deficit (2016)
Current Account – US$121m deficit (2016)

Trade with UK	2016	2017
Imports from UK	£10,802,237	£12,444,771
Exports to UK	£658,413	£933,919

COMMUNICATIONS
Airports and waterways – There are five airports; one, Argyle, close to the capital Kingstown, can handle international flights and was completed in February 2017.
Roadways – 580km are surfaced
Telecommunications – 20,550 fixed lines and 112,649 mobile subscriptions (2016); there were 53,000 internet users in 2016

Internet code and IDD – vc; 1 784 (from UK), 011 44 (to UK)
Media – Television broadcasting is operated by the St Vincent and the Grenadines Broadcasting Corporation, and NBC Radio is partly government funded; there is one daily newspaper, *The Herald*

SAMOA

Malo Sa'oloto Tuto'atasi o Samoa – Independent State of Samoa

Area – 2,831 sq. km
Capital – Apia, on Upolu; population, 36,000 (2018)
Major town – Fagamalo, on Savai'i
Currency – Tala (S$) of 100 sene
Population – 200,108 rising at 0.60 per cent a year (2017 est); Samoan (Polynesian) (92.6 per cent) (2001); the population also includes Euronesians, Chinese and Europeans
Religion – Christian (Congregational 31.8 per cent, Roman Catholic 19.4 per cent, Mormon 15.2 per cent, Methodist 13.7 per cent, Assemblies of God 8 per cent, Seventh-day Adventist 3.9 per cent) (2011 est)
Language – Samoan (official), English
Population density – 69 per sq. km (2016)
Urban population – 18.2 per cent (2018 est)
Median age (years) – 23.9 (2016 est)
National anthem – 'O le Fu'a o le Sa'olotoga o Samoa' 'The Banner of Freedom'
National day – 1 June (Independence Day celebration; independence was achieved on 1 January 1962)
Death penalty – Abolished for all crimes (since 2004)
Literacy rate – 99.6 per cent (2015 est)
Gross enrolment ratio (percentage of relevant age group) – primary 108 per cent, secondary 84 per cent (2016 est)
Health expenditure (per capita) – US$301 (2014)
Life expectancy (years) – 74 (2017 est)
Mortality rate – 5.3 (2017 est)
Birth rate – 20.4 (2017 est)
Infant mortality rate – 18.6 (2017 est)

CLIMATE AND TERRAIN
Samoa consists of the islands of Savai'i, Upolu, Apolima, Manono, Fanuatapu, Namua, Nu'utele, Nu'ulua and Nu'usafe'e in the south Pacific Ocean. All the islands are volcanic in origin, with narrow coastal plains and mountainous, densely forested interiors. Elevation extremes range from 1,857m (Mauga Silisili, Savai'i) to 0m (Pacific Ocean). The climate is tropical, with a wet season from November to April; the average temperature is 27.6°C. The islands are vulnerable to cyclones and tsunamis.

HISTORY AND POLITICS

Inhabited since c.1000 BC, Samoa was visited by European traders, explorers and missionaries from the 18th century. Germany, the UK and the USA disputed control of the islands until 1899, when the nine western islands (Western Samoa) became a German colony and the eastern islands American Samoa. Western Samoa was occupied by New Zealand on the outbreak of the First World War and became a mandated territory administered by New Zealand from 1920. Internal self-government was granted in 1959, and Western Samoa became independent on 1 June 1962. The state was treated as a member country of the Commonwealth until its formal admission in 1970. In 1997 the state dropped 'Western' from its name.

Former prime minister Tuiatua Tupua Tamasese Efi was elected head of state in June 2007 and re-elected unopposed in July 2012. He was replaced by independent Tuimaleali'ifano Va'aletoa Sualauvi II in July 2017 after deciding to step down. The Human Rights Protection Party, which has been in power since 1981, remained by far the largest party in the legislature after the March 2016 election, which it won with a landslide.

Under the 1962 constitution, the head of state is elected and has functions analogous to those of a constitutional monarch. Initially an office held for life, but is now elected by the legislature for a five-year term, with no term limits. The unicameral legislative assembly *(Fono)* has 49 members elected for a five-year term; only members of the *Matai* (elected clan leaders) may stand for election. The prime minister is appointed by the head of state on the recommendation of the legislature and appoints the cabinet.

HEAD OF STATE

Head of State, Tuimaleali'ifano Va'aletoa Sualauvi II, *elected* 7 July 2017

SELECTED GOVERNMENT MEMBERS *AS AT JUNE 2018*
Prime Minister, Foreign Affairs, Tuilaepa Sailele Malielegaoi
Deputy Prime Minister, Flame Naomi Mata'afa
Finance, Sili Epa Tuioti

EMBASSY OF SAMOA
20 avenue de l'Oree, 1000 Brussels, Belgium
T (+32) (2) 660 8454 E samoanembassy@skynet.be
W www.samoaembassybelgium.com
High Commissioner, HE Dr Fatumanava Pa'olelei Luteru, *apptd* 2013

BRITISH HIGH COMMISSIONER
HE Laura Clarke, *apptd* 2018, resident at Wellington, New Zealand

ECONOMY AND TRADE
The economy is underdeveloped (until 2014, considered the least developed in the world) but has grown steadily in the past decade, diversifying away from its traditional dependence on fishing, agriculture, remittances from migrant workers and international aid. Economic strengths include a flexible labour market, stable external debt and low inflation. Agriculture and fishing generate 10.4 per cent of GDP, employing almost two-thirds of the labour force and supplying about 90 per cent of exports. Manufacturing is branching out from small-scale processing of agricultural products into light manufacturing (particularly of motor vehicle components) and building materials, and offshore financial services are being developed. Tourism has grown rapidly and accounts for about 25 per cent of GDP. Public finances were weakened by a tsunami in 2009 and a tropical cyclone in 2012, both of which caused severe damage.

The main trading partners are American Samoa, New Zealand, the USA, Australia and China. Principal exports are fish, coconut oil and cream, copra, taro, vehicle parts, garments and beer. The main imports are machinery and equipment, industrial supplies and foodstuffs.
GNI – US$0.8bn; US$4,100 per capita (2017)
Annual average growth of GDP – 2.1 per cent (2017 est)
Inflation rate – 1.8 per cent (2017 est)
Total external debt – US$447.2m (2013 est)
Imports – US$334m (2016)
Exports – US$53m (2016)

BALANCE OF PAYMENTS
Trade – US$281m deficit (2016)
Current Account – US$31.9m deficit (2016)

Trade with UK	2015	2016
Imports from UK	£165,341	£172,329
Exports to UK	£711,609	£1,028,109

COMMUNICATIONS
Airports and waterways – There is one international airport on Upolu; the southern island also contains the harbours of Apia and Mulifanua, and Salelologa, the harbour of Savai'i
Roadways – 332km are surfaced
Telecommunications – 9,679 fixed lines and 151,008 mobile subscriptions (2016); there were 58,508 internet users in 2016
Internet code and IDD – ws; 685 (from UK), 044 (to UK)
Media – The Samoa Broadcasting Corporation (TV) and National Radio 2AP are the state broadcasters; the *Samoa Observer* and *Samoa Times* are the only daily newspapers
WPFI score – 16,69 (22)

SAN MARINO

Repubblica di San Marino – Republic of San Marino

Area – 61 sq. km
Capital – San Marino; population, 4,000 (2018 est)
Currency – Euro (€) of 100 cents
Population – 33,537 rising at 0.74 per cent a year (2017 est)
Religion – Christian (Roman Catholic 97 per cent) (est)
Language – Italian (official)
Population density – 557 per sq. km (2016)
Urban population – 97.2 per cent (2018 est)
Median age (years) – 44.2 (2016 est)
National anthem – 'Inno Nazionale della Repubblica' 'National Anthem of the Republic'
National day – 3 September (Republic Day)
Death penalty – Abolished for all crimes (since 1865)

Health expenditure (per capita) – US$3,459 (2014)
Life expectancy (years) – 83.3 (2017 est)
Mortality rate – 8.6 (2016 est)
Birth rate – 8.7 (2017 est)
Infant mortality rate – 4.3 (2017 est)

CLIMATE AND TERRAIN
A landlocked enclave in central Italy, the republic lies in the foothills of the Apennines, 20km from the Adriatic Sea. Elevation extremes range from 755m (Mt Titano) to 55m (Torrente Ausa). The climate is Mediterranean, with an average annual rainfall of 836mm.

HISTORY AND POLITICS
The republic is said to have been founded in the fourth century by a Christian stonecutter seeking refuge from religious persecution. By the 12th century a self-governing commune was established, and a parliamentary constitution was adopted in 1600. The republic resisted papal claims and those of neighbouring dukedoms from the 15th to 18th centuries, and the papacy recognised its independence in 1631. In 1862 it signed a treaty with the newly united kingdom of Italy, which recognised its integrity and sovereignty and accorded it the protection of Italy. San Marino became a member of the UN in 1992. A 2013 poll supported moves to join the EU, but the number of voters did not exceed the minimum 32 per cent of the electorate needed to enact the measure.

The November 2016 legislative election did not result in a majority for any of the three main coalitions; the opposition Adesso.sm group won the second round in December, securing 35 seats.

The 1600 constitution has been amended several times. The joint heads of state are two captains-regent who are elected at six-monthly intervals (March and September) by the legislature, taking office the month after the election. Executive power is vested in the captains-regent and the Congress of State (cabinet), which is also elected by the legislature. The unicameral legislature, the Great and General Council, has 60 members, who are directly elected for a five-year term.

HEADS OF STATE
Captains-Regent, Stefano Palmieri; Matteo Ciacci

SELECTED GOVERNMENT MEMBERS *AS AT JUNE 2018*
Finance, Simone Celli
Foreign Affairs, Nicola Renzi
Internal Affairs, Guerrino Zanotti

EMBASSY OF THE REPUBLIC OF SAN MARINO
c/o Department of Foreign Affairs, Palazzo Begni – Contrado Ormerelli, 47890 San Marino
T 378 (0549) 88 2422 E dipartimentoaffariesteri@pa.sm
Ambassador Extraordinary and Plenipotentiary, HE Federica Bigi, apptd 2012

BRITISH AMBASSADOR
HE Jill Morris, CMG, *apptd* 2016, resident at Rome, Italy

ECONOMY AND TRADE
Tourism and banking are the basis of the economy, and the service sector contributes 60.7 per cent of GDP. In 2009, investment outflows following Italy's tax amnesty, a money-laundering scandal at its largest bank and the global downturn contributed to a deep recession and growing budget deficit. The government is working to improve standards of financial transparency.

The principal agricultural products are grains, grapes, olives, livestock and hides. The main industries, apart from tourism and banking, are winemaking, clothing, cement, electronics and ceramics. Sales of postage stamps and coins also generate significant revenue. San Marino is in a customs union with the EU but is not a full member.
GNI – US$1,572m; US$51,470 per capita (2008)
Annual average growth of GDP – 1.2 per cent (2017 est)
Inflation rate – 0.9 per cent (2017 est)
Unemployment – 8 per cent (2017 est)

Trade with UK	*2016*	*2017*
Imports from UK	£3,534,023	£5,734,323
Exports to UK	£4,429,288	£4,918,186

COMMUNICATIONS
Roadways – 292km
Telecommunications – 16,000 fixed lines and 36,570 mobile subscriptions (2016); there were 17,200 internet users in 2016
Internet code and IDD – sm; 378 (from UK), 44 (to UK)
Media – Broadcasting services are state-run; daily newspapers include *La Tribuna Sammarinese*

SAO TOME AND PRINCIPE
Republica Democratica de Sao Tome e Principe – *Democratic Republic of Sao Tome and Principe*

Area – 964 sq. km
Capital – Sao Tome; population, 80,000 (2018)
Major Town – Santo Antonio, on Principe
Currency – Dobra of 100 centimos
Population – 201,025 rising at 1.72 per cent a year (2017 est)
Religion – Christian (Roman Catholic 55.7 per cent, Adventist 4.1 per cent) (2012 est)
Language – Portuguese (official), Creole dialects
Population density – 213 per sq. km (2016)
Urban population – 72.8 per cent (2018 est)
Median age (years) – 18.2 (2016 est)
National anthem – 'Independencia total' 'Total Independence'
National day – 12 July (Independence Day)
Death penalty – Abolished for all crimes (since 1990)
CPI score – 46 (64)
Conscription – 18 years of age
Literacy rate – 83.2 per cent (2015 est)
Gross enrolment ratio (percentage of relevant age group) – primary 110 per cent, secondary 90 per cent (2016 est), tertiary 13.4 per cent (2015 est)
Health expenditure (per capita) – US$166 (2014)
Life expectancy (years) – 65.3 (2017 est)

Mortality rate – 6.8 (2017 est)
Birth rate – 32.4 (2017 est)
Infant mortality rate – 45.3 (2017 est)
HIV/AIDS adult prevalence – 0.79 per cent (2014 est)

CLIMATE AND TERRAIN
The republic consists of the islands of Sao Tome, Principe and several uninhabited islets off the west coast of Africa. The islands, which are volcanic in origin, are mountainous and thickly forested. Elevation extremes range from 2,024m (Pico de Sao Tome) to 0m (Atlantic Ocean). The climate is tropical, with a wet season from October to May. The average temperature is 24.1°C.

HISTORY AND POLITICS
The uninhabited islands were discovered by the Portuguese between 1469 and 1472, and settlement began in 1493. Agitation against Portuguese rule began in the late 1950s. The islands gained independence from Portugal in 1975 and became a one-party state under the rule of the Movement for the Liberation of Sao Tome and Principe (MLSTP). Close links with the communist bloc were scaled down in the 1980s as the economy deteriorated, and in 1990 the MLSTP abandoned Marxism and introduced political pluralism and economic liberalisation. The first multiparty elections were held in 1991.

The Independent Democratic Action (ADI) party secured a majority in the legislature at the 2014 elections and Patrice Trovoada was appointed prime minister in November, having previously served in the role during 2008–10. Evaristo Carvalho of the ADI was elected president in August 2016, defeating incumbent Manuel Pinto da Costa, who had been the country's first post-independence president. Da Costa pulled out of the second round of voting citing electoral fraud, so Carvalho was elected unopposed.

Under the 1990 constitution, the president is directly elected for a five-year term, renewable once. The unicameral National Assembly has 55 members, directly elected for a four-year term. The prime minister is appointed by the president and nominates the cabinet.

Since 1995 Principe has been internally self-governing, with an eight-member regional council.

HEAD OF STATE
President, C-in-C of the Armed Forces, Evaristo Carvalho, *elected* 7 August 2011, *sworn in* 3 September 2011, *re-elected* 7 August 2016

SELECTED GOVERNMENT MEMBERS *AS AT JUNE 2018*
Prime Minister, Patrice Trovoada
Defence, Arlindo Ramos
Finance, Americo d'Oliveira Ramos
Foreign Affairs, Urbino Jose Goncalves Botelho

EMBASSY OF SAO TOME AND PRINCIPE
175 avenue de Tervuren, 1150 Brussels, Belgium
T (+32) (2) 734 8966 E ambassade@saotomeprincipe.be
Ambassador Extraordinary and Plenipotentiary, vacant

BRITISH AMBASSADOR
HE Jessica Hand, *apptd* 2018, resident at Luanda, Angola

ECONOMY AND TRADE
The economy has benefited from cancellation of about 90 per cent of the country's external debt over the past decade. It is largely dependent on cocoa, which has declined in recent years due to mismanagement and drought, but tourism is being encouraged in an attempt to diversify. A major economic shift will begin with the start of oil production from offshore reserves in the Gulf of Guinea, which are being developed jointly with Nigeria and Sao Tome and Principe will receive 40 per cent of the revenue. Most of the population is engaged in subsistence farming and fishing. Chinese investment is set to significantly increase following a mutual cooperation agreement signed in 2017, lasting over five years.

The principal export markets are Guyana (43.7 per cent) and Germany (23.6 per cent), and the main source of imports is Portugal (54.7 per cent). Principal exports are cocoa (68 per cent), copra, coffee and palm oil. The main imports are machinery and electrical equipment, foodstuffs and petroleum products.

GNI – US$0.4bn; US$1,770 per capita (2017)
Annual average growth of GDP – 5 per cent (2017 est)
Inflation rate – 4.5 per cent (2017 est)
Population below poverty line – 66.2 per cent (2009 est)
Unemployment – 12.2 per cent (2017 est)
Total external debt – US$343.4m (2017 est)
Imports – US$150m (2016)
Exports – US$15m (2016)

BALANCE OF PAYMENTS
Trade – US$135m deficit (2016)
Current Account – US$73m deficit (2017)

Trade with UK	2016	2017
Imports from UK	£146,891	£2,682,787
Exports to UK	£20,039	£25,906

COMMUNICATIONS
Airports and waterways – There are two airports; the ports are Santo Antonio, on Principe, and Sao Tome
Roadways – 218km are surfaced but in poor condition
Telecommunications – 5,733 fixed lines and 178,047 mobile subscriptions (2016); there were 50,000 internet users in 2016
Internet code and IDD – st; 239 (from UK), 44 (to UK)
Media – Televisao Saotomense and Radio Nacional de Sao Tome e Principe are the state broadcasters; *Téla Nón Diario de Sao Tome e Principe* is the only daily newspaper

SAUDI ARABIA

Al-Mamlakah al-Arabiyah as-Suudiyah – Kingdom of Saudi Arabia

Area – 2,149,690 sq. km
Capital – Riyadh; population, 6,907,000 (2018 est)
Major cities – At Taif, Dammam, Jeddah, Mecca, Medina, Tabuk
Currency – Saudi riyal (SR) of 100 halalas
Population – 28,571,770 rising at 1.45 per cent a year (2017 est); includes some 5,576,076 non-nationals (2013 est)

Religion – Muslim (Sunni 85–90 per cent, predominantly Wahhabi; Shia 10–15 per cent) (2012 est); public practice of other religions is forbidden
Language – Arabic (official)
Population density – 15 per sq. km (2016)
Urban population – 83.8 per cent (2018 est)
Median age (years) – 27.2 (2016)
National anthem – 'As-Salaam al-Malaki' 'The Royal Salute'
National day – 23 September (Unification Day)
Death penalty – Retained
CPI score – 49 (57)
Military expenditure – US$69,413m (2017)

CLIMATE AND TERRAIN

Saudi Arabia comprises about 80 per cent of the Arabian peninsula. The Hejaz region (north-west) runs along the northern Red Sea coast to the Asir and contains the holy cities of Mecca and Medina. The mountainous Asir (south-west) and the coastal plain of the Tihama lie along the southern Red Sea coast from the Hejaz to the border with Yemen. The Nejd plateau extends over the centre, including the Nafud and Dahna deserts. The Hasa (east) is low-lying and largely desert. The Empty Quarter (south) is the world's largest sand desert. Elevation extremes range from 3,133m (Jabal Sawda) to 0m (Persian Gulf). There is a desert climate, with extremes of temperature in the interior; coastal areas are more temperate but extremely humid. Average temperatures range from 15.7°C in January to 32.9°C in August.

HISTORY AND POLITICS

The Arabian peninsula was the birthplace of the Muslim faith in the seventh century and the base from which the religion and four Islamic Caliphates, the Rashidun, Umayyad, Abbasid and Fatimid, emerged. When the Fatimid empire declined in the 12th century, Arabia became isolated and internally divided. The rise of the al-Saud family began in the 18th century, when it united the Nejd in support of the Wahhabi religious movement. The modern state was the culmination of a 30-year campaign by Abd-al Aziz al-Saud (often known as Ibn Saud) to unite the four tribal regions of the Hejaz, Asir, Najd and Hasa; the Kingdom of Saudi Arabia was proclaimed on 23 September 1932.

The ruling family preserved stability for many years by suppressing dissent and resisting calls for greater democracy. Since 2003 demand for political reform has grown and become more militant. In 2005, the country's first nationwide elections were held for half the seats on municipal councils, with voting by universal male suffrage. Women's rights have slowly advanced in recent years with municipal voting rights introduced (2011) and, in June 2018, the right to drive a vehicle.

King Abdullah acceded to the throne after the death of his half-brother King Fahd in 2005. Following the death of King Abdullah in January 2015, his half-brother, King Salman, acceded to the throne. In June 2017, his son Mohammed bin Salman was appointed crown prince.

There is no written constitution; constitutional practice is provided for by articles of government based on the Qur'an and the teachings and sayings of the Prophet Muhammad *(Sunnah)* and issued by royal decree.

Saudi Arabia is a hereditary monarchy. The king is head of government and appoints the council of ministers (established in 1953), whose term of office was fixed in 1993 at four years.

There is no legislature; the Consultative Council *(Majlis-al-Shura)* debates policy, proposes legislation in certain areas and makes recommendations to the king. The council's 150 members are appointed by the king and serve a four-year term. As of 2013, 30 seats are reserved for women. Its decisions are taken by majority vote, and there are no political parties.

Each of the 13 provinces has a governor appointed by the king and a council of prominent local citizens to advise the governor on local government, budgetary and planning issues.

HEAD OF STATE

The King of Saudi Arabia, Custodian of the Two Holy Mosques, Prime Minister, King Salman bin Abdul Aziz al-Saud, *born* 31 December 1935, *succeeded* 23 January 2015
Crown Prince, Deputy Prime Minister, Defence, HRH Mohammed bin Salman bin Abdul Aziz al-Saud

SELECTED GOVERNMENT MEMBERS *AS AT JUNE 2018*

Economy, Mohammed al-Tuwaijri
Finance, Mohammed bin Abdullah bin Abdulaziz al-Jadaan
Foreign Affairs, Adel bin Ahmed al-Jubeir

ROYAL EMBASSY OF SAUDI ARABIA

30 Charles Street, London W1J 5DZ
T 020-7917 3000 E ukemb@mofa.gov.sa
W www.saudiembassy.org.uk
Ambassador Extraordinary and Plenipotentiary, HE HRH Prince Mohamed bin Nawaf bin Abdul Aziz al-Saud, *apptd* 2005

BRITISH EMBASSY

PO Box 94351, Diplomatic Quarter, Riyadh 11693
T (+966) (0) 11 4819 100 E consular.riyadh@fco.gov.uk
W www.gov.uk/government/world/saudi-arabia
Ambassador Extraordinary and Plenipotentiary, HE Simon Collis, CMG, *apptd* 2015

ECONOMY AND TRADE

The economy is based on oil extraction and processing, but since 1970 the government has used five-year development plans to encourage diversification, and the growing non-oil sector accounted for about 55.7 per cent of GDP in 2016. Recent developments plan aimed to increase natural gas production and to promote the growth of small- and medium-sized businesses, partly through further privatisation; it also partially opened the Saudi stock market to foreign investors. The government announced in 2016 plans to sell some shares in Saudi Aramco to further investment, the state-owned oil company which is reported to be the most profitable business in the world.

Oil extraction since the 1940s has brought great wealth. Saudi Arabia has the second-largest proven reserves of oil in the world (about 16 per cent of the world total) and the fifth-largest reserves of recoverable gas. The oil industry contributes around 90 per cent of export earnings and 87 per cent of budget revenues.

The main industries, apart from oil extraction and refining, include production of petrochemicals, ammonia, industrial gases, caustic soda, cement, fertiliser, plastics and metals, commercial ship and aircraft repair and construction. Industry accounts for 44.2 per cent of GDP and the service sector for 53.2 per cent. Agriculture contributes 2.6 per cent but is limited by the terrain, although productivity has been increased by extensive irrigation, desalination and the use of aquifers. The main products are grains, fruit, meat and dairy.

The main trading partners are China, the USA, Japan, India and South Korea. Oil and petroleum products constitute 90 per cent of exports. The principal imports are machinery and equipment, foodstuffs, chemicals, motor vehicles and textiles.
GNI – US$661.5bn; US$20,080 per capita (2017)
Annual average growth of GDP – 0.1 per cent (2017 est)
Inflation rate – −0.2 per cent (2017 est)
Unemployment – 5.6 per cent (2017 est)
Total external debt – US$212.9bn (2017 est)
Imports – US$135,904m (2016)
Exports – US$182,329m (2016)

BALANCE OF PAYMENTS
Trade – US$46,426m surplus (2016)
Current Account – US$15,229m surplus (2017)

Trade with UK	2016	2017
Imports from UK	£4,895,231,932	£4,197,597,612
Exports to UK	£1,542,814,892	£2,016,078,780

COMMUNICATIONS
Airports – There are 82 airports; the three international airports are at Riyadh, Jeddah (serving Mecca) and Dammam
Waterways – The main cargo ports are Jeddah on the Red Sea coast and Dammam on the Gulf coast; the main oil port (the world's largest) is Ras Tanura
Roadways and railways – The surfaced network totals 47,529km, including a 3,891km motorway system, and 1,378km of railways, operated by the state-run Saudi Railway Organisation
Telecommunications – 3.6 million fixed lines and 47.9 million mobile subscriptions (2016); there were 20.7 million internet users in 2016
Internet code and IDD – sa; 966 (from UK), 44 (to UK)
Major broadcasters – Saudi TV and Saudi Radio are the state-run broadcasters
Press – Leading daily newspapers include *Al-Riyadh, Al-Watan* and the English-language *Arab News*
WPFI score – 63,13 (169)

EDUCATION AND HEALTH
With the exception of a few schools for expatriate children, all schools are segregated and supervised by the government.
Literacy rate – 99.3 per cent (2015 est)
Gross enrolment ratio (percentage of relevant age group) – primary 116 per cent (2016 est), secondary 108.3 per cent (2014 est), tertiary 67 per cent (2016 est)
Health expenditure (per capita) – US$1,147 (2014)
Hospital beds (per 1,000 people) – 2.7 (2014)
Life expectancy (years) – 75.5 (2017 est)
Mortality rate – 3.4 (2017 est)
Birth rate – 18.3 (2017 est)
Infant mortality rate – 13.2 (2017 est)

SENEGAL

République du Sénégal – Republic of Senegal

Area – 196,722 sq. km
Capital – Dakar; population, 2,978,000 (2018 est)
Major cities – Kaolack, Mbour, Saint-Louis, Thiès, Touba, Ziguinchor
Currency – Franc CFA of 100 centimes

Population – 14,668,522 rising at 2.39 per cent a year (2017 est); Wolof (41.6 per cent), Pular (28.1 per cent), Serer (15.3 per cent), Mandinka (5.4 per cent) (2016 est)
Religion – Muslim 95.4 per cent, Christian 4.2 per cent (est); most incorporate indigenous beliefs into their worship
Language – French (official), Fulani, Jola, Mandinka, Wolof
Population density – 82 per sq. km (2016)
Urban population – 47.2 per cent (2018 est)
Median age (years) – 18.7 (2016 est)
National anthem – 'Pincez Tous vos Koras, Frappez les Balafons' 'All Pluck Your Koras, Strike the Balafons'
National day – 4 April (Independence Day)
Death penalty – Abolished for all crimes (since 2004)
CPI score – 45 (66)
Military expenditure – US$305m (2017)
Conscription – 20 years of age; 24 months (selective)

CLIMATE AND TERRAIN
The terrain is generally low and rolling, with plains rising to hills in the south-east. There is desert in the north, savannah in the centre and tropical forest in the south. Elevation extremes range from 581m (near Nepen Diakha) to 0m (Atlantic Ocean). There are three rivers: the Senegal on the northern border, and the Gambia and the Casamance in the south. The climate is tropical, with a wet season from June to September; the average temperature is 28.4°C.

HISTORY AND POLITICS
Senegal was part of the Mali Empire in the 14th to 15th centuries. The first European visitors were the Portuguese in 1445. The interior was colonised by the French in the mid-19th century and the territory became part of French West Africa in 1902. It became an autonomous state in 1958 and achieved independence as part of the Federation of Mali in June 1960, seceding to form the Republic of Senegal in August 1960. From 1966 to 1978, the country was a one-party state under the rule of the Senegalese Progressive Union (UPS), which changed its name to the Socialist Party (PS) in 1976.

In the early 1980s a separatist insurgency led by the Movement of Democratic Forces of Casamance (MFDC) began in the impoverished Casamance region south of the river Gambia. Splits and leadership changes among the separatists have prevented the implementation of peace agreements in 2001 and 2004, and clashes continue between government troops and rebels.

The Socialist Party's 40 years of political domination ended in 2000 with the election of Abdoulaye Wade, leader of the Senegalese Democratic Party (PDS), as president. President Wade lost the 2012 presidential election to the Alliance for the Republic–Yakaar (BBY) leader Macky Sall, who picked up 65 per cent of the overall vote in the second round. The BBY claimed a large parliamentary majority in the 2017 elections.

The 2001 constitution was amended in 2007 to re-establish the senate as the upper chamber of a bicameral legislature, but this was abolished in 2012 by the National Assembly. The National Assembly has 165 members, directly elected for a five-year term; 105 are elected by majority in single member constituencies and 60 are elected by proportional representation. A referendum in 2016 cut presidential terms from seven to five years, renewable once, which will be introduced from 2019. The president is directly elected and appoints the prime minister, who nominates the other ministers.

HEAD OF STATE
President, C-in-C of the Armed Forces, Macky Sall, *elected* 18 March 2012, *sworn in* 2 April 2012

SELECTED GOVERNMENT MEMBERS *AS AT JUNE 2018*
Prime Minister, Mohammed Dionne
Economy and Finance, Amadou Ba
Foreign Affairs, Sidiki Kaba
Interior, Aly Ngouille Ndiaye

EMBASSY OF THE REPUBLIC OF SENEGAL
39 Marloes Road, London W8 6LA
T 020-7938 4048
Ambassador Extraordinary and Plenipotentiary, HE Cheikh
    Ahmadou Dieng, *apptd* 2015

BRITISH EMBASSY
PO Box 6025, 20 rue du Docteur Guillet, Dakar
T (+221) 823 7392 E dakar.consularenquiries@fco.gov.uk
W www.gov.uk/government/world/senegal
Ambassador Extraordinary and Plenipotentiary, HE George
    Hodgson, *apptd* 2015

ECONOMY AND TRADE

Despite steady growth since the mid-1990s and the cancellation of two-thirds of its foreign debt in recent years, Senegal remains poor. The country is heavily dependent on foreign aid and remittances from expatriate workers, but infrastructure projects and the development of the textiles, information technology, telecommunications services and tourism industries are government priorities. The government has announced a set of economic policies known as the Emerging Senegal Plan (ESP), which aims to turn Senegal into an emerging economy by 2035. Financial markets have shown increasing confidence in the economy in recent years, and 2017 was marked by the opening of a new international airport and a strong real growth rate of 6.8 per cent of GDP.

Agriculture and fishing are the mainstays of the economy, engaging around three quarters of the workforce and contributing 16.9 per cent of GDP. The main industries are food and fish processing, mining (phosphate, iron, zircon, gold), oil refining, the production of fertiliser and construction materials, ship construction and tourism. Industry accounts for 24.3 per cent of GDP and services for 58.8 per cent.

The main trading partners are France, Mali, Nigeria, China and Switzerland. The principal exports are fish, peanuts, petroleum products, phosphates and cotton. Principal imports are food, beverages, capital goods and fuels.
GNI – US$15.1bn; US$950 per capita (2017)
Annual average growth of GDP – 6.8 per cent (2017 est)
Inflation rate – 2.1 per cent (2017 est)
Population below poverty line – 46.7 per cent (2011 est)
Total external debt – US$6.745bn (2017 est)
Imports – US$5,028m (2016)
Exports – US$2,318m (2016)

BALANCE OF PAYMENTS
Trade – US$2,710m deficit (2016)
Current Account – US$1,143m deficit (2015 est)

Trade with UK	2016	2017
Imports from UK	£89,660,343	£198,564,115
Exports to UK	£40,249,266	£37,436,305

COMMUNICATIONS

Airports and waterways – Dakar is the main port and the location of the principal airport (there are nine airports in total); seaport facilities are being modernised and there are 1,000km of navigable waterways, mainly on the Senegal, Saloum and Casamance rivers
Roadways and railways – 4,099km; 906km

Telecommunications – 285,933 fixed lines and 15.2 million mobile subscriptions (2016); there were 3.7 million internet users in 2016
Internet code and IDD – sn; 221 (from UK), 44 (to UK)
Major broadcasters – State-run Radiodiffusion Television Senegalaise operates the only free television channels and the main national and regional radio networks
Press – Leading daily newspapers include the French-language *Le Quotidien, L'Observateur* and *Sud Quotidien*
WPFI score – 25,61 (50)

EDUCATION AND HEALTH

Literacy rate – 73.1 per cent (2015)
Gross enrolment ratio (percentage of relevant age group) – primary 83 per cent, secondary 48 per cent, tertiary 11 per cent (2016 est)
Health expenditure (per capita) – US$50 (2014)
Hospital beds (per 1,000 people) – 0.3 (2009)
Life expectancy (years) – 62.1 (2017 est)
Mortality rate – 8.1 (2017 est)
Birth rate – 33.4 (2017 est)
Infant mortality rate – 49.1 (2017 est)
HIV/AIDS adult prevalence – 0.4 per cent (2016 est)

SERBIA

Republika Srbija – Republic of Serbia

Area – 77,474 sq. km
Capital – Belgrade; population, 1,389,000 (2018 est)
Major cities – Kragujevac, Nis, Novi Sad
Currency – Serbian dinar of 100 paras
Population – 7,111,024 falling at 0.46 per year (2017 est); Serb (83.3 per cent), Hungarian (3.5 per cent), Romany (2.1 per cent), Bosniak (2 per cent) (2011 est)
Religion – Christian (Serbian Orthodox 84.6 per cent, Roman Catholic 5 per cent, Protestant 1 per cent), Muslim 3.1 per cent (2011 est)
Language – Serbian (official), Hungarian, Romanian, Slovak, Ukrainian, Croatian (all official in different regions), Bosnian, Romani
Population density – 80 per sq. km (2016)
Urban population – 56.1 per cent (2018 est)
Median age (years) – 42.3 (2016 est)
National anthem – 'Boze Pravde' 'God of Justice'
National day – 15 February (Constitution Day)
Death penalty – Abolished for all crimes (since 2002)
CPI score – 41 (77)
Military expenditure – US$731m (2017 est)
Literacy rate – 98.5 per cent (2015 est)
Gross enrolment ratio (percentage of relevant age group) – primary 101 per cent, secondary 96 per cent, tertiary 62 per cent (2016 est)
Health expenditure (per capita) – US$633 (2014)

Hospital beds (per 1,000 people) – 5.7 (2012)
Life expectancy (years) – 75.7 (2017 est)
Mortality rate – 13.6 (2017 est)
Birth rate – 9 (2017 est)
Infant mortality rate – 5.8 (2017 est)

CLIMATE AND TERRAIN

The landlocked country is mountainous in the south, while the north is dominated by the low-lying plains of the Danube and its major tributaries, the Sava, the Tisa and the Morava. Its highest point is 2,169m (Midzor) and its lowest is 35m (the confluence of the Danube and Timok rivers). The climate is continental; average temperatures range from –0.5°C in January to 21.5°C in July and August.

POLITICS

Under the 2006 constitution, the president is directly elected for a five-year term, renewable once. The unicameral National Assembly has 250 members, directly elected for a four-year term. The prime minister is appointed by the president.

A coalition led by the Serbian Progressive Party (SNS) won a majority in the 2014 legislative election, but required support from a bloc led by the Socialist Party of Serbia (SPS) to govern. Prime Minister Aleksander Vucic then brought forward elections due to be held in 2018 to April 2016, citing the need for stability ahead of EU accession, and his SNS-led coalition retained its majority. In April 2017, Vucic ran in and won the presidential election with 55 per cent of the vote, easily passing the 50 per cent threshold required for a run-off, and he nominated Ana Brnabic as the country's first woman prime minister.

HEAD OF STATE
President, Aleksandar Vucic, *elected* 2 April 2017, *sworn in* 31 May 2017

SELECTED GOVERNMENT MEMBERS *AS AT JUNE 2018*
Prime Minister, Ana Brnabic
First Deputy Prime Minister, Foreign Affairs, Ivaca Dacic
Deputy Prime Ministers, Rasim Ljajic; Zorana Mihajlovic; Neboisa Stefanovic
Economy, Goran Knezevic
Finance, Sinisa Mali

EMBASSY OF THE REPUBLIC OF SERBIA
28 Belgrave Square, London SW1X 8QB
T 020-7235 9049 E london@serbianembassy.org.uk
W www.serbianembassy.org.uk
Ambassador Extraordinary and Plenipotentiary, vacant

BRITISH EMBASSY
Resavska 46, 11000 Belgrade
T (+381) (11) 306 0900 E belgrade.PPD@fco.gov.uk
W www.gov.uk/government/world/serbia
Ambassador Extraordinary and Plenipotentiary, HE Denis Keefe, CMG, *apptd* 2014

ECONOMY AND TRADE

Economic mismanagement, UN sanctions in the 1990s along with damage to infrastructure and industry from NATO bombing in 1999 reduced the economy by about 50 per cent between 1990 and 1999. Since 2000, governments have pursued economic reforms and international reintegration, obtained overseas support for economic restructuring, rescheduled payments and received debt relief on much of its foreign debt. Progress has been intermittent, but most of the economy is now privatised. Economic liberalisation policies continue to be a priority, but Serbia's GDP is still sizably smaller than it was three decades ago.

Economic growth averaged 6 per cent until 2008 when it was severely affected by the global economic downturn. The government sought external fiscal support in 2008 and signed a standby agreement with the IMF in 2011–12 which was frozen after the country's 2012 budget deviated from the programme framework. Serbia gained EU candidate status in March 2012 and began accession negotiations in January 2014. After GDP contracted in 2014, the government accepted a €1.2bn (£85m) loan from the IMF in February 2015 after agreeing to implement a programme of spending cuts. Public debt, which peaked in 2015, continues to fall, but unemployment remains high at 16 per cent.

Agriculture accounts for 9.8 per cent of GDP and employs 19.4 per cent of the workforce. The main agricultural products are wheat, maize, sugar beet, sunflowers, fruit, meat and milk. Industry includes food processing and production of base metals, vehicles, furniture, machinery, chemicals, sugar, tyres, clothing and pharmaceuticals. Industry contributes 41.1 per cent of GDP and services 49.1 per cent.

The main trading partners are the EU, Russia and Bosnia and Hercegovina. Principal exports are vehicles, iron and steel, rubber, clothing, wheat, fruit, vegetables and non-ferrous metals.

GNI – US$36.4bn; US$5,180 per capita (2017)
Annual average growth of GDP – 3 per cent (2017 est)
Inflation rate – 3.4 per cent (2017 est)
Population below poverty line – 8.9 per cent (2014 est)
Unemployment – 16 per cent (2017 est)
Total external debt – US$30.6bn (2017 est)
Imports – US$19,234m (2016)
Exports – US$14,855m (2016)

BALANCE OF PAYMENTS
Trade – US$4,379m deficit (2016)
Current Account – US$2,818m deficit (2017)

Trade with UK	2016	2017
Imports from UK	£127,477,327	£144,303,659
Exports to UK	£209,562,382	£242,413,641

COMMUNICATIONS

Airports and waterways – The main international airport is at Belgrade (there are ten airports in total); there are 587km of navigable waterways, and principal ports include Belgrade and Novi Sad on the Danube

Roadways and railways – 28,000km; 3,809km

Telecommunications – 2.6 million fixed lines and 9 million mobile subscriptions (2016); there were 4.8 million internet users in 2016

Internet code and IDD – rs; 381 (from UK), 44 (to UK)

Major broadcasters – Radio-Television Serbia (RTS) is the state-operated broadcaster

Press – National daily newspapers include *Blic, Danas* and *Politika*

WPFI score – 29,58 (76)

SEYCHELLES

République des Seychelles / Repiblik Sesel – Republic of Seychelles

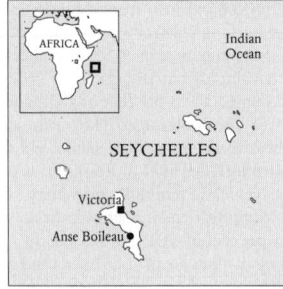

Area – 455 sq. km

Capital – Victoria, on Mahé; population, 28,000 (2018)

Major town – Anse Boileau, on Mahé

Currency – Seychelles rupee of 100 cents

Population – 93,920 rising at 0.77 per cent a year (2017 est)

Religion – Christian (Roman Catholic 76.2 per cent, Anglican 6.1 per cent), Hindu 2.4 per cent (2010 est)

Language – Seychellois Creole, English, French (all official)

Population density – 208 per sq. km (2016)

Urban population – 56.7 per cent (2018 est)

Median age (years) – 34.9 (2016 est)

National anthem – 'Koste Seselwa' 'Seychellois Unite'

National day – 18 June (Constitution Day)

Death penalty – Abolished for all crimes (since 1993)

Military expenditure – US$21.7m (2017)

Literacy rate – 99.1 per cent (2012 est)

Gross enrolment ratio (percentage of relevant age group) – primary 113 per cent, secondary 93 per cent, tertiary 21 per cent (2016 est)

Health expenditure (per capita) – US$494 (2014)

Life expectancy (years) – 74.9 (2017 est)

Mortality rate – 7 (2017 est)

Birth rate – 13.7 (2017 est)

Infant mortality rate – 10 (2017 est)

CPI score – 60 (36)

CLIMATE AND TERRAIN

Seychelles consists of 115 islands spread over 643,737 sq. km of the south-west Indian Ocean, north of Madagascar. There is a relatively compact granitic group of 32 islands, with high hills and mountains, of which Mahé is the largest and most populated (about 90 per cent of the population lives on Mahé), and an outlying coralline group, for the most part only slightly above sea level. Elevation extremes range from 905m

(Morne Seychellois) to 0m (Indian Ocean). The climate is tropical, with an average temperature of 27.3°C, and a wet season from November to March.

HISTORY AND POLITICS

The uninhabited islands were proclaimed French territory in 1756, but settlement of the Mahé group began only in 1770. The group was a dependency of Mauritius, and was ceded to Britain with Mauritius in 1814. In 1903 these islands, together with the coralline group, were formed into a colony separate from Mauritius. On 29 June 1976, the islands became an independent republic.

Following a coup d'état in 1977, when France-Albert René became president, Seychelles became a one-party state ruled by the Seychelles People's Progressive Front (SPPF) in 1979. Opposition parties were permitted from 1991 and in 1993 President René reintroduced a multiparty constitution. In 2009 the SPPF was renamed the People's Party (PL).

In the September 2016 legislative election, the PL was narrowly beaten by the opposition Linyon Demokratik Seselwa alliance (LDS); it was the first time the PL had not won a majority since 1979. Soon after President James Michel resigned and was replaced by former vice-president Danny Faure.

Under the 1993 constitution, the executive president is directly elected for a five-year term. In 2016, the country voted to reduce presidential limits from three to two consecutive terms. The unicameral National Assembly has up to 35 members: 25 directly elected by constituencies and up to ten allocated by proportional representation; members serve a five-year term. The council of ministers is appointed by the president.

HEAD OF STATE

President, Defence, Foreign Affairs, Danny Faure, *took office* 16 October 2016

Vice-President, Vincent Meriton

SELECTED GOVERNMENT MEMBERS *AS AT JUNE 2018*

Finance, Maurice Loustau-Lalanne

Home Affairs, Macsuzy Mondon

THE HIGH COMMISSION OF THE REPUBLIC OF SEYCHELLES

4th Floor, 132 Buckingham Palace Road, London SW1W 9SA

T 020-7730 2046 E seyhc.london@btconnect.com

High Commissioner, HE Derick Ally, *apptd* 2017

BRITISH HIGH COMMISSION

PO Box 161, Oliaji Trade Centre, Victoria, Mahé

T (+248) 283 666 E bhcvictoria@fco.gov.uk

W www.gov.uk/government/world/seychelles

High Commissioner, HE Caron Röhsler, *apptd* 2015

ECONOMY AND TRADE

Seychelles prospered after independence owing to the development of tuna fishing and tourism; the latter employs about 26 per cent of the workforce and accounts for over 55 per cent of GDP. The economy struggled in 2008–9 owing to external debt, high deficits, food and oil price rises and the global recession, but recovered in 2010–11. By 2013 the IMF declared that Seychelles had a successful market-based economy with full employment and a fiscal surplus, and in January 2017 gained developed country status. Growth has been strong thanks to rising tourism, but high inequality, vulnerability to changes in world markets and climate change are long-term challenges.

Agriculture, small-scale manufacturing and offshore financial services are being developed to diversify the economy. Apart from fishing and tourism, the main industries involve processing fish, coconuts and vanilla, and producing beverages.

The main trading partners are the UAE, and EU countries. The principal exports are canned tuna, frozen fish, and re-exports of petroleum products. The principal imports are machinery and equipment, foodstuffs, petroleum products, chemicals and manufactured goods.

GNI – US$1.4bn; US$14,180 per capita (2017)
Annual average growth of GDP – 4.1 per cent (2017 est)
Inflation rate – 2.8 per cent (2017 est)
Population below poverty line – 39.3 per cent (2013 est)
Unemployment – 3 per cent (2017 est)
Total external debt – US$2.729bn (2017 est)
Imports – US$990m (2015)
Exports – US$429m (2015)

BALANCE OF PAYMENTS
Trade – US$561m deficit (2015)
Current Account – US$295m deficit (2017)

Trade with UK	2016	2017
Imports from UK	£21,075,369	£23,782,663
Exports to UK	£65,068,828	£60,068,580

COMMUNICATIONS
Airports and waterways – The principal airport is at Mahé (there are seven airports in total); the main port is Victoria, and ferries run regularly between Mahé, Praslin and La Digue
Roadways – There are 490km of surfaced roads
Telecommunications – 20,836 fixed lines and 151,857 mobile subscriptions (2016); there were 52,664 internet users in 2016
Internet code and IDD – sc; 248 (from UK), 44 (to UK)
Media – The state-run Seychelles Broadcasting Corporation operates various channels across the country; daily newspapers include *The Rising Sun* and the government-owned *Seychelles Nation*
WPFI score – 30,17 (85)

SIERRA LEONE

Republic of Sierra Leone

Area – 71,740 sq. km
Capital – Freetown; population, 1,136,000 (2018 est)
Major towns – Bo, Kenema
Currency – Leone (Le) of 100 cents
Population – 6,163,195 rising at 2.38 per cent a year (2017 est); 20 ethnic groups, of which the largest are the Temne (35 per cent), Mende (31 per cent), Limba (8 per cent) and Kono (5 per cent) (2008 est)

Religion – Muslim 60 per cent, Christian 10 per cent, indigenous 30 per cent (est)
Language – English (official), Krio (Creole; lingua franca), Mende (in the south), Temne (in the north)
Population density – 105 per sq. km (2016)
Urban population – 42.1 per cent (2018 est)
Median age (years) – 19 (2016 est)
National anthem – 'High We Exalt Thee, Realm of the Free'
National day – 27 April (Independence Day)
Death penalty – Retained (last used 1998)
CPI score – 30 (130)
Military expenditure – US$28.7m (2017 est)

CLIMATE AND TERRAIN
The land rises from mangrove swamps along the coast, to low-lying wooded country, and then to a mountainous plateau in the east. Elevation extremes range from 1,948m (Loma Mansa) to 0m (Atlantic Ocean). The climate is tropical, with a rainy season from May to November; rainfall peaks in July and August, and is particularly heavy on the coast. The average temperature is 26.4°C.

HISTORY AND POLITICS
In 1787 British philanthropists and abolitionists established a settlement for repatriated former slaves from Britain and its colonies on the Freetown peninsula. In 1808 the settlement was declared a crown colony and became the main base in west Africa for enforcing the 1807 Act outlawing the slave trade. In 1896 a protectorate was declared over the hinterland. The Freetown colony and the protectorate were united in 1951, and in 1961 Sierra Leone became independent.

The country became a republic in 1971 and a one-party state in 1978. Transition to a multiparty democracy began in 1991 but was aborted by a military coup in 1992. Civilian rule was restored with the 1996 elections. Another coup in May 1997 was short-lived, and the government was reinstated in March 1998 with the assistance of Economic Community of West African States (ECOWAS) troops.

The transition to multiparty and civilian rule was complicated by the civil war with the Revolutionary United Front (RUF), which began in 1991. Fighting continued until 2001, when a lasting ceasefire was agreed, and the war was declared over in 2002. An estimated 50,000 people were killed, 30,000 mutilated and a third of the population displaced between 1991 and 2002. A truth and reconciliation commission and a UN-supported war crimes tribunal were set up in 2002.

The 2018 presidential election was won by Sierra Leone People's Party candidate and former military ruler Julius Maada Bio, following ten years of rule by Ernest Bai Koroma of the All People's Congress (APC). The APC won a majority of seats in the simultaneous legislative election.

Under the 1991 constitution, the executive president is directly elected for a five-year term, renewable once. The unicameral parliament has 144 members: 132 directly elected for a five-year term and 12 indirectly elected to represent the 12 provincial districts. The president, who is responsible to the legislature, appoints and chairs the cabinet.

HEAD OF STATE
President, Julius Maada Bio, *sworn in* 4 April 2018
Vice-President, Mohamed Juldeh Jalloh

SELECTED GOVERNMENT MEMBERS *AS AT JUNE 2018*
Finance, Jacob Jusu Saffa
Justice, Priscilla Schwartz
Internal Affairs, Edward Soluku

SIERRA LEONE HIGH COMMISSION
41 Eagle Street, London WC1R 4TL
T 020-7404 0140 E info@slhc-uk.org W www.slhc-uk.org
High Commissioner, HE Edward Turay, *apptd* 2010

BRITISH HIGH COMMISSION
6 Spur Road, Freetown
T (+232) (0) 76 541 386 E freetown.general.enquiries@fco.gov.uk
W www.gov.uk/government/world/sierra-leone
High Commissioner, HE Guy Warrington, *apptd* 2016

ECONOMY AND TRADE
The country was devastated by a decade of civil war, and unemployment increased with the demobilisation of former combatants. Economic activity has grown since the end of the war but the country remains extremely poor, dependent on foreign aid and expatriates' remittances. It benefited from having around 90 per cent of its foreign debt written off in 2006.

There are significant mineral deposits and agricultural and fishery resources, although the lack of infrastructure hampers development. Diamonds and iron ore generate most export earnings, but 60.7 per cent of GDP is generated by agriculture, much of which is at subsistence level. Industry consists mainly of mining (diamonds, rutile, iron ore, bauxite), processing agricultural products and light manufacturing for the domestic market. Economic output was severely effected by the 2014–5 Ebola outbreak and falling export prices, but growth returned in 2017 with an increase of iron ore extraction, and the nation is gradually requiring less international assistance.

The main export markets are Côte d'Ivoire, China, Belgium and the USA; the chief import suppliers are China, Belgium and the USA. Principal exports are iron ore, diamonds, rutile, cocoa, coffee and fish. The main imports are foodstuffs, machinery and equipment, fuels and lubricants, and chemicals.
GNI – US$3.8bn; US$510 per capita (2017)
Annual average growth of GDP – 6 per cent (2017 est)
Inflation rate – 16.9 per cent (2017 est)
Population below poverty line – 52.9 per cent (2011 est)
Unemployment – 9.1 per cent (2014 est)
Total external debt – US$1.707bn (2017 est)
Imports – US$1,477m (2015)
Exports – US$731m (2015)

BALANCE OF PAYMENTS
Trade – US$746m deficit (2015)
Current Account – US$405m deficit (2016)

Trade with UK	2016	2017
Imports from UK	£28,697,746	£31,218,221
Exports to UK	£606,499	£6,858,786

COMMUNICATIONS
Airports and waterways – There is an international airport at Freetown; Freetown, which has one of the world's largest natural harbours, is the main port and there are smaller ports at Pepel and Sherbro
Roadways – 904km are surfaced
Telecommunications – 17,000 fixed lines and 6.3 million mobile subscriptions (2016); there were 708,615 internet users in 2016
Internet code and IDD – sl; 232 (from UK), 44 (to UK)
Media – The Sierra Leone Broadcasting Corporation was formed in 2010 and is the country's principal TV and radio broadcaster; newspapers include *Awoko* and the *Standard Times*
WPFI score – 29,98 (79)

EDUCATION AND HEALTH
The public University of Sierra Leone incorporates several campuses in Freetown, and Njala University was established in Bo in 2005; there are a number of other technical and teacher-training institutes throughout the country.
Literacy rate – 67.6 per cent (2015 est)
Gross enrolment ratio (percentage of relevant age group) – primary 127.6 per cent, secondary 43.3 per cent (2016 est)
Health expenditure (per capita) – US$86 (2014)
Hospital beds (per 1,000 people) – 0.4 (2006)
Life expectancy (years) – 58.6 (2017 est)
Mortality rate – 10.4 (2017 est)
Birth rate – 36.3 (2017 est)
Infant mortality rate – 68.4 (2017 est)
HIV/AIDS adult prevalence – 1.7 per cent (2016 est)

SINGAPORE

Xinjiapo Gongheguo/Republik Singapura/Cinkappur Kutiyaracu – Republic of Singapore

Area – 697 sq. km
Capital – Singapore; population, 5,792,000 (2015 est)
Currency – Singapore dollar (S$) of 100 cents
Population – 5,888,926 rising at 1.82 per cent a year (2017 est); Chinese (74.3 per cent), Malay (13.4 per cent), Indian (9.1 per cent) (2016 est)
Religion – Buddhist 33.9 per cent, Muslim 14.3 per cent, Taoist 11.3 per cent, Christian (Roman Catholic 7.1 per cent, other Christian 11 per cent) (2010 est)
Language – Mandarin, English, Malay, Tamil (all official), Hokkien, Cantonese, Teochew
Population density – 7,916 per sq. km (2016)
Urban population – 100 per cent (2018 est)
Median age (years) – 34.3 (2016 est)
National anthem – 'Majulah Singapura' 'Onward, Singapore'
National day – 9 August (Independence Day)
Death penalty – Retained
CPI score – 84 (6)
Military expenditure – US$10,198m (2017)
Conscription – Men aged 18–21; 24 months
Literacy rate – 99.8 per cent (2015)
Gross enrolment ratio (percentage of relevant age group) – primary 101 per cent, secondary 108 per cent (2016 est), tertiary 69.8 per cent (2013 est)
Health expenditure (per capita) – US$2,752 (2014)
Hospital beds (per 1,000 people) – 2.4 (2015)
Life expectancy (years) – 85.2 (2017 est)
Mortality rate – 3.6 (2017 est)
Birth rate – 8.6 (2017 est)
Infant mortality rate – 2.4 (2017 est)

CLIMATE AND TERRAIN

Singapore consists of the island of Singapore and 63 islets situated off the southern extremity of the Malay peninsula, from which it is separated by the Straits of Johor. The land rises from the shore to a low, undulating central plateau. Elevation extremes range from 166m (Bukit Timah) to 0m (Singapore Strait). The state is just north of the equator and the climate is tropical, subject to monsoons in June to September and December to March. The average temperature is 27.6°C, and there is frequent rain and high humidity.

HISTORY AND POLITICS

Singapore, a trading site since the 13th century, was established as a British trading post by Sir Stamford Raffles in 1819 and was ceded to Britain in perpetuity in 1824. In 1826 it was incorporated with Penang and Malacca to form the Straits Settlements and they became a crown colony in 1867. Singapore became the commercial and financial hub of South East Asia in the 19th century, and the principal British military base in the Far East in the 1920s. In 1942, during the Second World War, it fell to Japanese forces. Liberated in 1945, it became a separate colony in 1946, and internal self-government was introduced in 1959. It became part of the Federation of Malaysia in 1963, before withdrawing to become an independent sovereign state in 1965.

Although Singapore is a multiparty state, the People's Action Party (PAP) has dominated politics since 1959; opposition candidates were elected to parliament for the first time in 1981. Independent candidate Tony Tan was elected president in August 2011, replacing PAP's Sellapan Rama Nathan. In the 2015 general election, PAP retained its large majority with 83 seats, but opposition parties won an unprecedented nine seats. Lee Hsien Loong continued in office as prime minister, a post he has held since 2004.

The 1959 constitution was amended in 1965 to end the affiliation with Malaysia and make Singapore a republic, and in 1991 to make the presidency directly elected. The president is directly elected for a single six-year term; the president appoints the prime minister and the members of the cabinet. There is a unicameral parliament with 89 directly elected members, and up to nine extra members from opposition parties (NCMPs) (currently three), depending on their share of the vote; all members serve a five-year term. Up to nine members can also be nominated by the government for a two-year term (NMPs) to bring the opposition numbers up to 18. In September 2017, Halimah Yacob was named the first female president, and was the only eligible candidate.

HEAD OF STATE
President, Halimah Yacob, *took office* 14 September 2017

SELECTED GOVERNMENT MEMBERS *AS AT JUNE 2018*
Prime Minister, Lee Hsien Loong
Deputy Prime Ministers, Tharman Shanmugaratnam *(Economy);*
    Rear-Adm. Teo Chee Hean *(National Security)*
Foreign Affairs, Vivian Balakrishnan
Home Affairs, Kasiviswanathan Shanmugam

HIGH COMMISSION FOR THE REPUBLIC OF SINGAPORE
9 Wilton Crescent, London SW1X 8SP
T 020-7235 8315 E singhc_lon@sgmfa.gov.sg
W www.mfa.gov.sg/london
High Commissioner, HE Foo Chi Hsia, *apptd* 2014

BRITISH HIGH COMMISSION
100 Tanglin Road, Singapore 247919
T (+65) 6424 4200 E consular.singapore@fco.gov.uk
W www.gov.uk/government/world/organisations/
british-high-commission-singapore
High Commissioner, HE Scott Wightman, CMG, *apptd* 2015

ECONOMY AND TRADE

Historically based on trade in raw materials from surrounding countries and on trade in finished products, the economy industrialised rapidly after independence and diversified, becoming a regional financial and technology centre, and a tourist destination. Economic growth has rarely flagged since 1965; although the global economic downturn pushed the economy into recession in 2008, it recovered strongly in 2010, before slowing in 2012–17. Singapore joined a common market with the other members of the Association of Southeast Asian Nations (ASEAN) in 2015. With low unemployment, high incomes and little corruption, Singapore enjoys one of the highest per capita GDP levels in the world.

Agriculture is limited and contributes little to GDP. Industries include manufacturing (especially consumer electronics, information technology products, biomedical sciences, pharmaceuticals and chemicals), engineering, oil refining, food processing and ship repair; industry contributes 24.8 per cent of GDP. The service sector (financial and business services, entrepôt trade, tourism) accounts for 75.2 per cent of GDP and employs 73.7 per cent of the native workforce.

The main trading partners are Malaysia, China, Hong Kong and the USA. Principal exports are machinery and equipment (especially electronic), consumer goods, pharmaceuticals and other chemicals and mineral fuels. The main imports are machinery and equipment, mineral fuels, chemicals, food and consumer goods.

GNI – US$306bn; US$54,530 per capita (2017)
Annual average growth of GDP – 2.5 per cent (2017 est)
Inflation rate – 0.9 per cent (2016 est)
Unemployment – 2.2 per cent (2017 est)
Total external debt –US$482.8bn (2017 est)
Imports – US$291,909m (2016)
Exports – US$338,082m (2016)

BALANCE OF PAYMENTS
Trade – US$46,174m surplus (2016)
Current Account – US$60,988m surplus (2017)

Trade with UK	2016	2017
Imports from UK	£4,572,616,558	£4,814,353,362
Exports to UK	£2,501,958,589	£3,062,045,082

COMMUNICATIONS

Airports and waterways – Singapore is one of the busiest seaports in the world, although there is a high risk of piracy in the South China Sea; it has a large merchant fleet of 1,599 ships of over 1,000 tonnes, with 344 registered in other countries, while 966 foreign-owned ships are registered in Singapore. There is one international airport, at Changi
Roadways and railways – There are 3,425km of roadways and an extensive light rail system on the island
Telecommunications – 1.9 million fixed lines and 8.5 million mobile subscriptions (2016); there were 4.7 million internet users in 2016
Internet code and IDD – sg; 65 (from UK), 1/2/8 44 (to UK)
Major broadcasters – TV and radio broadcasting is dominated by MediaCorp, owned by a state investment agency
Press – Singapore Press Holdings, which has close links to the ruling party, has a virtual monopoly on the newspaper industry and publishes 15 newspapers
WPFI score – 50,95 (151)

SLOVAKIA

Slovenska republika – Slovak Republic

Area – 49,035 sq. km
Capital – Bratislava; population, 430,000 (2018 est)
Major city – Kosice
Currency – Euro (€) of 100 cents
Population – 5,445,829 falling at 0.01 per cent a year (2017 est); Slovak (80.7 per cent), Hungarian (8.5 per cent), Roma (2 per cent) (2011 est)
Religion – Christian (Roman Catholic 62 per cent, Protestant 8.2 per cent), none 13.4 (2011 est)
Language – Slovak (official), Hungarian, Roma, Ukrainian
Population density – 113 per sq. km (2016)
Urban population – 53.7 per cent (2018 est)
Median age (years) – 40.1 (2016 est)
National anthem – 'Nad Tatrou sa blýska' 'Lightning Over the Tatras'
National day – 1 September (Constitution Day)
Death penalty – Abolished for all crimes (since 1990)
CPI score – 50 (54)
Military expenditure – US$1,127m (2017)
Literacy rate – 99.45 per cent (2015)
Gross enrolment ratio (percentage of relevant age group) – primary 102 per cent, secondary 89 per cent, tertiary 54.2 per cent (2011 est)
Health expenditure (per capita) – US$1,455 (2014)
Hospital beds (per 1,000 people) – 5.8 (2015)
Life expectancy (years) – 77.3 (2017 est)
Mortality rate – 9.9 (2017 est)
Birth rate – 9.7 (2017 est)
Infant mortality rate – 5.1 (2017 est)

CLIMATE AND TERRAIN

Slovakia is landlocked and mountainous, lying in the western Carpathian range, which includes the Tatra and Beskid mountains to the north. The mountains fall to plains in the south-east and south-west; the latter is the plain of the river Danube and its tributary the Vah, which rises in the Tatras. Elevation extremes range from 2,655m (Gerlachovsky stit) to 94m (Bodrog river). The climate is temperate, with warm humid summers and cold dry winters. Average temperatures range from −2.4°C in January to 18.5°C in July.

POLITICS

The 1993 constitution has been amended several times, most significantly in 1999 to allow direct elections to the presidency. The president is directly elected for a five-year term, renewable once. The unicameral National Council has 150 members, who are directly elected for a four-year term by proportional representation. The prime minister, who is appointed by the president, nominates the cabinet.

The centre-left Direction-Social Democracy (Smer-SD) remained the largest party after the March 2016 legislative election, but lost its parliamentary majority. Prime Minister Robert Fico formed a coalition government but resigned in 2018 following popular anti-corruption protests sparked by the death of a journalist, Jan Kuciak, investigating links between the mafia and his close advisers. The 2014 presidential election was won by Andrej Kiska.

HEAD OF STATE
President, Andrej Kiska, *elected* 29 March 2014

SELECTED GOVERNMENT MEMBERS *AS AT JUNE 2018*
Prime Minister, Peter Pellegrini
Deputy Prime Minister Investments, Richard Rasi
Defence, Peter Gajdos
Foreign Affairs, Miroslav Lajcak
Interior, Denisa Sakova

EMBASSY OF THE SLOVAK REPUBLIC
25 Kensington Palace Gardens, London W8 4QY
T 020-7313 6470 E emb.london@mzv.sk W www.mzv.sk/londyn
Ambassador Extraordinary and Plenipotentiary, HE Lubomir Rehak, *apptd* 2015

BRITISH EMBASSY
Panska 16, Bratislava 811 01
T (+421) (2) 5998 2000 E bebra@internet.sk
W www.gov.uk/government/world/slovakia
Ambassador Extraordinary and Plenipotentiary, HE Andrew Garth, *apptd* 2014

ECONOMY AND TRADE

Slovakia has nearly completed the transition from a centrally planned to a free-market economy, following structural reforms and privatisation begun after 1998. As a result, foreign investment has risen, especially in the vehicle and electronics industries, and GDP grew steadily between 2000–8. The economy contracted in 2009 because of the global economic downturn, recovering in 2010. In 2012 a number of pro-growth economic reforms were scaled back to shore up government finances. The economy has been affected by EU economic sanctions against Russia since 2014, but rebounded in 2017 thanks to foreign investment, rising domestic consumption and record low levels of unemployment.

Slovakia's open economy, which joined the euro zone in 2009, is fuelled by vehicle and electronic exports which account for over 80 per cent of GDP. Natural resources include brown coal and lignite, natural gas, oil, iron ore, copper and manganese. Major industries include production

of vehicles, metal and metal products, food and beverages, fuel and energy (electricity, gas, coke, oil and nuclear), chemicals and synthetic fibres, machinery, wood and paper products, ceramics, textiles and electrical and optical equipment. Slovakia's growing industrial sector accounts for 35 per cent of GDP, services 61.2 per cent and agriculture 3.8 per cent.

The main trading partners are other EU countries, especially Germany and Czechia. Principal exports are machinery and electrical equipment, vehicles, nuclear reactors and furnaces, base metals, minerals and fuels. The main imports are machinery and transport equipment, mineral products, vehicles, nuclear reactors and fuel.

GNI – US$90.3bn; US$16,610 per capita (2017)
Annual average growth of GDP – 3.3 per cent (2017 est)
Inflation rate – 1.2 per cent (2016 est)
Population below poverty line – 12.3 per cent (2015 est)
Unemployment – 8.1 per cent (2017 est)
Total external debt – US$75.04bn (2016 est)
Imports – US$77,130m (2016)
Exports – US$77,588m (2016)

BALANCE OF PAYMENTS
Trade – US$458m surplus (2016)
Current Account – US$2,044m deficit (2017)

Trade with UK	2016	2017
Imports from UK	£582,479,400	£602,501,567
Exports to UK	£2,514,871,968	£2,502,610,075

COMMUNICATIONS
Airports and waterways – The principal airport is at Bratislava and the main Danube ports are Bratislava and Komarno
Roadways and railways – 38,238km of surfaced roadways, including 417km of motorways; 3,622km of railways
Telecommunications – 823,594 fixed lines and 6.9 million mobile subscriptions (2016); there were 4.4 million internet users in 2016
Internet code and IDD – sk; 421 (from UK), 44 (to UK)
Major broadcasters – The public broadcasters Slovak TV and Slovak Radio operate national networks in competition with private companies
Press – The major daily newspapers, including *Pravda, Sme* and *Novy Cas,* are all privately owned
WPFI score – 20,26 (27)

SLOVENIA
Republika Slovenija – Republic of Slovenia

Area – 20,273 sq. km
Capital – Ljubljana; population, 286,000 (2018)
Major city – Maribor
Currency – Euro (€) of 100 cents

Population – 1,972,126 falling at 0.31 per cent a year (2017 est); Slovene (83.1 per cent), Serb (2 per cent), Croat (1.8 per cent), Bosniak (1.1 per cent) (2002)
Religion – Christian (Roman Catholic 57.8 per cent, Orthodox 2.3 per cent), Muslim 2.4 per cent (2002)
Language – Slovene (official); Serbo-Croat; Hungarian and Italian are also official in designated municipalities
Population density – 103 per sq. km (2016)
Urban population – 54.5 per cent (2018 est)
Median age (years) – 44.1 (2016 est)
National anthem – 'Zdravljica' 'A Toast'
National day – 25 June (Statehood Day)
Death penalty – Abolished for all crimes (since 1989)
CPI score – 61 (34)
Military expenditure – US$478m (2017)

CLIMATE AND TERRAIN
The Alps cover 42 per cent of the country, towards the north, and the south lies on the high Karst plateau. The only low-lying areas are the Pannonian plain in the east and north-east, and the short (47km) narrow coastal belt on the Adriatic Sea. Elevation extremes range from 2,864m (Triglav) to 0m (Adriatic Sea). The climate is continental in most of the country but Mediterranean on the coast. Average temperatures range from 0.3°C in January to 19.7°C in July.

POLITICS
Under the 1991 constitution, the president is directly elected for a five-year term, renewable once. The bicameral National Assembly consists of the 90-member National Assembly, which is directly elected for a four-year term, and the National Council which has 40 members indirectly elected for a five-year term as a largely advisory body. The prime minister, who is nominated by the president and elected by the legislature, appoints the cabinet.

The anti-immigration Slovenian Democratic Party won the largest number of seats in the June 2018 parliamentary election, but following three months of political deadlock, a centre-left minority coalition led by the newly-formed List of Marjan Sarec party (LMS) was agreed. Marjan Sarec (LMS) was elected prime minister on 17 August 2018. Borat Pahor (SD) was elected president in December 2012, defeating the incumbent Danilo Turk, and re-elected in November 2017.

HEAD OF STATE
President, Borut Pahor, *elected* 2 December 2012, *sworn in* 22 December 2012, *re-elected* 12 November 2017

SELECTED GOVERNMENT MEMBERS *AS AT SEPTEMBER 2018*
Prime Minister, Marjan Sarec
Deputy Prime Ministers, Karl Erjavek *(Foreign Affairs);* Boris Koprivnikar; Dejan Zidan
Defence, Andreja Katic
Finance, Mateja Vranicar Erman

EMBASSY OF THE REPUBLIC OF SLOVENIA
10 Little College Street, London SW1P 3SH
T 020-7222 5700 **E** vlo@gov.si
W http://london.embassy.si
Ambassador Extraordinary and Plenipotentiary, HE Tadej Rupel, *apptd* 2014

BRITISH EMBASSY
4th Floor, Trg Republike 3, 1000 Ljubljana
T (+386) (1) 200 3910 **E** info@british-embassy.si
W www.gov.uk/government/world/slovenia
Ambassador Extraordinary and Plenipotentiary, HE Sophie Honey, MBE, *apptd* 2015

ECONOMY AND TRADE

Always the most prosperous republic of the former Yugoslavia, Slovenia's transition to a market economy was smoothed by good infrastructure and a well-educated workforce. Much of the economy remains in state ownership and taxes are high, deterring foreign investment and inhibiting its international competitiveness. The economy contracted sharply in 2009 owing to the global downturn and again experienced recession in 2012 and 2013, but rebounded strongly and recorded 5 per cent real GDP growth in 2017. The government's privatisation programme is proceeding slowly, while unemployment fell in early 2018 due to rising exports and domestic consumption.

Industry contributes 33.6 per cent of GDP, the service sector 64.1 per cent and agriculture 2.3 per cent. The main agricultural products are potatoes, hops, wheat, sugar beet, maize, grapes and livestock. Industries include mining and mineral processing (iron ore, aluminium, lead, zinc), electronics (including for military purposes), vehicles, electric power equipment, wood products, textiles, chemicals and machine tools.

The main trading partners are other EU countries (particularly Germany, Austria and Italy) and China. Principal exports are manufactured goods, machinery and transport equipment, chemicals and food. These items, along with fuels and lubricants, are also the main imports.

GNI – US$45.5bn; US$22,000 per capita (2017)
Annual average growth of GDP – 4 per cent (2017 est)
Inflation rate – 1.6 per cent (2015 est)
Population below the poverty line – 14.3 per cent (2015 est)
Unemployment – 6.8 per cent (2017 est)
Total external debt – US$46.3bn (2017 est)
Imports – US$26,646m (2016)
Exports – US$27,585m (2016)

BALANCE OF PAYMENTS

Trade – US$939m surplus (2016)
Current Account – US$3,483m surplus (2017)

Trade with UK	2016	2017
Imports from UK	£243,609,288	£272,601,483
Exports to UK	£395,767,511	£416,212,273

COMMUNICATIONS

Airports and waterways – The international airports are at Ljubljana, Maribor and Portoroz; Koper is the main port
Roadways and railways – 38,985km; 1,228km
Telecommunications – 731,320 fixed lines and 2.4 million mobile subscriptions (2016); there were 1.5 million internet users in 2016
Internet code and IDD – si; 386 (from UK), 44 (to UK)
Media – The public broadcaster RTV Slovenia operates TV and radio stations; daily newspapers include *Delo, Dnevnik* and *Slovenske Novice*
WPFI score – 21,69 (32)

EDUCATION AND HEALTH

Education is free and compulsory between the ages of six and 15.
Literacy rate – 99.9 per cent (2015)
Gross enrolment ratio (percentage of relevant age group) – primary 99.3 per cent, secondary 110.7 per cent, tertiary 82.9 per cent (2014 est)
Health expenditure (per capita) – US$2,161 (2014)
Hospital beds (per 1,000 people) – 4.6 (2013)
Life expectancy (years) – 78.3 (2017 est)
Mortality rate – 11.6 (2017 est)

Birth rate – 8.2 (2017 est)
Infant mortality rate – 3.9 (2017 est)

SOLOMON ISLANDS

Area – 28,896 sq. km
Capital – Honiara, on Guadalcanal; population, 82,000 (2018)
Major town – Kirakira, on Makira
Currency – Solomon Islands dollar (SI$) of 100 cents
Population – 647,581 rising at 1.94 per cent a year (2017 est); Melanesian (95.3 per cent), Polynesian (3.1 per cent), Micronesian (1.2 per cent) (2009 est)
Religion – Christian (Church of Melanesia 31.9 per cent, Roman Catholic 19.6 per cent, Evangelical 17.1 per cent, Seventh-day Adventist 11.7 per cent) (2009 est)
Language – English (official), Melanesian Pidgin (lingua franca); around 120 indigenous languages exist
Population density – 22 per sq. km (2016)
Urban population – 22.7 per cent (2018 est)
Median age (years) – 22.2 (2016 est)
National anthem – 'God Save Our Solomon Islands'
National day – 7 July (Independence Day)
Death penalty – Abolished for all crimes (since 1966)
CPI score – 39 (85)
Gross enrolment ratio (percentage of relevant age group) – primary 115 per cent (2016 est)
Health expenditure (per capita) – US$102 (2014)
Life expectancy (years) – 75.6 (2017 est)
Mortality rate – 3.8 (2017 est)
Birth rate – 24.9 (2016 est)
Infant mortality rate – 14.7 (2017 est)

CLIMATE AND TERRAIN

Forming a scattered archipelago of mountainous islands and low-lying coral atolls in the south-west Pacific Ocean, the Solomon Islands stretch about 1,448km in a south-easterly direction from the Shortland Islands to the Santa Cruz islands. The six biggest islands are Choiseul, New Georgia, Santa Isabel, Guadalcanal, Malaita and Makira (San Cristobal). They are characterised by thickly forested mountain ranges intersected by deep, narrow valleys. Elevation extremes range from 2,310m (Mt Popomanaseu) to 0m (Pacific Ocean). The climate is tropical, with little variation in temperature, and a wet season between November and April. The islands are prone to seismic activity and tsunamis.

HISTORY AND POLITICS

The islands were colonised by Austronesian people 30,000 years ago. Spanish explorers reached the islands in 1568 and the area continued to be visited by Europeans intermittently for about 300 years. Following the arrival of missionaries and traders, Britain declared a protectorate in 1893 over the southern islands; the northern islands were ceded to Britain by

Germany in 1899. After the Second World War, campaigns began for self-government, which was achieved in 1976; independence followed in 1978.

Ethnic tension on Guadalcanal between the indigenous Isatabus and migrants from the island of Malaita escalated from 1998 into conflict between militant factions. Despite a fragile peace following a ceasefire agreement signed in October 2000, and elections in 2001, lawlessness and corruption pervaded the country. An Australian-led regional assistance mission restored public order and disarmed the militias by late 2003.

In the 2014 legislative elections, independent candidates won the majority of seats in the legislature and Prime Minister Gordon Darcy Lilo lost his seat. In November 2017 the National Parliament elected Rick Houenipwela of the Democratic Alliance Party as prime minister.

Under the 1978 constitution, the Solomon Islands is a constitutional monarchy. The head of state is Queen Elizabeth II, represented by a governor-general, who is chosen by the legislature. The unicameral National Parliament has 50 members who are directly elected for a four-year term. The prime minister is elected by the legislature from among its members, and nominates the cabinet, which is formally appointed by the governor-general.

Governor-General, Sir Frank Kabui, GCMG, *apptd* 2009

SELECTED GOVERNMENT MEMBERS *AS AT JUNE 2018*
Prime Minister, Rick Houenipwela
Deputy Prime Minister, Finance, Manasseh Sogavare
Home Affairs, Commins Mewa
Foreign Affairs, Milner Tozaka

HIGH COMMISSION FOR THE SOLOMON ISLANDS
17B Avenue Edouard Lacombe, 1040 Brussels, Belgium
T (+32) (2) 732 7085 E siembassy@compuserve.com
High Commissioner, HE Moses Kouni Mose, *apptd* 2015

BRITISH HIGH COMMISSION
PO Box 676, Tanuli Ridge, Honiara
T (+677) 21705 E bhc@solomon.com.sb
W www.gov.uk/government/world/solomon-islands
High Commissioner, HE David Ward, *apptd* 2016

ECONOMY AND TRADE
The civil unrest of 1998–2003 left the country virtually bankrupt but the restoration of law and order enabled the economy to recover until its modest but steady growth was curtailed by the global downturn and natural disasters in 2009 and 2010. The country's greater dependency since 2003 on foreign aid, principally from Australia, increased as the downturn reduced government revenues.

Agriculture, much at subsistence level, is the largest economic sector, accounting for 34.3 per cent of GDP and engaging about 75 per cent of the population. Abundant mineral resources are largely undeveloped, although there are plans to better exploit them. The main industries are fishing, mining, and forestry; industry contributes 7.6 per cent of GDP.

The main trade partners are China, Australia and Malaysia. Principal exports are timber, fish, copra, cocoa, palm and coconut oil. The main imports are food, machinery and equipment, manufactured goods, fuels and chemicals.
GNI – US$1.2bn; US$1,920 per capita (2017)
Annual average growth of GDP – 3 per cent (2017 est)
Inflation rate – –0.5 per cent (2017 est)
Total external debt – US$491.5m (2013 est)
Imports – US$467m (2015)
Exports – US$401m (2015)

BALANCE OF PAYMENTS
Trade – US$66m deficit (2015)
Current Account – US$46m deficit (2017)

Trade with UK	2016	2017
Imports from UK	£467,193	£444,882
Exports to UK	£23,059	£48,330

COMMUNICATIONS
Airports and waterways – Air Niugini flies from Papua New Guinea to Honiara; the main ports are Honiara and Viru
Roadways – 1,390km
Telecommunications – 7,405 fixed lines and 416,572 mobile subscriptions (2016); there were 69,859 internet users in 2016
Internet code and IDD – sb; 677 (from UK), 44 (to UK)
Media – The Solomon Islands Broadcasting Corporation (SIBC) operates public radio services and One Television provides television programmes; the *Solomon Star* is the single daily newspaper

SOMALIA

Jamhuuriyadda Federaalkaa Soomaaliya – Federal Republic of Somalia

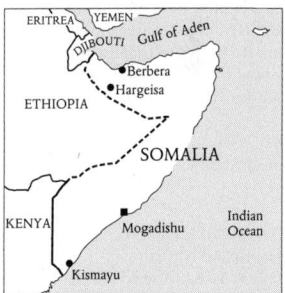

Area – 637,657 sq. km
Capital – Mogadishu; population, 2,082,000 (2018)
Major cities – Baidoa, Berbera, Burao, Hargeisa, Kismayu
Currency – Somali shilling of 100 cents; other currencies are also in circulation
Population – 11,031,386 rising at 2.0 per cent a year (2017 est); Somali (85 per cent), Bantu and other non-Somali (15 per cent), including 30,000 Arabs (est)
Religion – Muslim (predominantly Sunni, including Sunni forms of Sufism)
Language – Somali (official), Arabic, Italian, English
Population density – 24 per sq. km (2018)
Urban population – 45 per cent (2018 est)
Median age (years) – 17.9 (2016 est)
National anthem – 'Qolobaa Calankeed' 'Every Nation Has its Own Flag'
National day – 1 July (Foundation Day)
Death penalty – Retained
CPI score – 9 (180)
Military expenditure – $62.2m (2017 est)
Conscription – 18 years of age
Life expectancy (years) – 52.8 (2017 est)
Mortality rate – 13.1 (2017 est)
Birth rate – 39.6 (2017 est)
Infant mortality rate – 94.8 (2017 est)
HIV/AIDS adult prevalence – 0.4 per cent (2016 est)

CLIMATE AND TERRAIN
The country is mostly an arid and flat or undulating plateau, rising to hills in the north. Elevation extremes range from 2,416m (Shimbiris) to 0m (Indian Ocean). The climate is tropical, influenced by the north-east and south-west monsoons. Rainfall is greater in the south than the north, but is low and irregular throughout the country, leading to frequent droughts. The average temperature is 27.1°C.

POLITICS
Due to a lack of security legislative elections could not be held in 2012; initial members of the parliament were chosen by 135 clan elders, themselves selected by the outgoing constituent assembly. Nominees were approved for 215 of the seats and were sworn into office on 21 August. A new prime minister and cabinet were appointed by the president on 24 December 2014. Indirect legislative elections were held from October to November 2017, with 14,025 delegates, themselves appointed by clan elders, voting due to the ongoing civil war. Former prime minister Mohamed Abdullahi Mohamed was elected president in February 2017. It is hoped universal elections will take place in 2020.

Under the 2012 provisional constitution the president is elected by the legislature for a four-year term. The president appoints the prime minister, who names the cabinet. The bicameral parliament has 275 directly elected members in the House of the People, who serve a four-year term; the Upper House has a maximum of 54 members, serving a four-year term and directly elected from the 18 regions of Somalia. Most of Somalia's territory is under government control, but guerilla-style attacks from the Islamist militia al-Shabab are frequent, who were blamed for the killing of at least 500 people in Mogadishu in October 2017.

HEAD OF STATE
President, Mohamed Abdullahi Mohamed, *elected* 7 February 2017

SELECTED GOVERNMENT MEMBERS *AS AT JUNE 2018*
Prime Minister, Hassan Ali Khaire
Deputy Prime Minister, Mahdi Ahmed Guled
Defence, Hassan Ali Mohamed
Finance, Abdirahman Dualle Beyle
Foreign Affairs, Ahmed Isse Awad

BRITISH AMBASSADOR
Ambassador Extraordinary and Plenipotentiary, HE David Concar, *apptd* 2017, resident at Nairobi, Kenya

REPUBLIC OF SOMALILAND
In the north-east of the country, the self-declared Republic of Somaliland proclaimed independence in May 1991 from Somalia's dictator Siad Barre. While a functioning political system with its own government, currency and police force, it is not recognised by the UN or any government. The region has its own constitutional democracy, including regular municipal, parliamentary, and presidential elections; the former British protectorate has largely escaped the instability

and violence Somalia has experienced in recent decades. Muse Bihi Abdi was elected president in November 2017, succeeding incumbent Ahmed Silanyo.

ECONOMY AND TRADE
The lack of central government before 2012 prevented broad-based economic development or assistance from international donors. Natural resources are not exploited and industry is virtually non-existent, but the lack of regulation led to a thriving and relatively sophisticated informal entrepreneurial economy, especially in livestock, remittance/money transfer services (in the absence of a banking sector) and telecommunications. Infrastructure has been developed by commercial concerns, with businesses building small airfields and using natural harbours for overseas trade, and the three main telecommunications companies jointly funding internet infrastructure. The formal economy has grown in recent years, but has failed to spread beyond Mogadishu. The election of Mohamed Abdullahi Mohamed in 2017 has resulted in record levels of foreign aid and investment.

Agriculture, primarily livestock-raising by nomads or semi-nomads, is the most important economic sector. It accounts for about 60.2 per cent of GDP and over half of export earnings, but is vulnerable to drought. In March 2017, the UN warned that Somalia and three other countries face the world's largest humanitarian crisis since 1945; 2.9 million people are at risk of famine in the country.

The main export markets are the UAE, Oman and Saudi Arabia; imports come mainly from China and India. Principal exports are livestock, bananas, hides, fish, charcoal and scrap metal. The main imports are manufactured goods, petroleum products, foodstuffs, construction materials and qat.
Annual average growth of GDP – 2.4 per cent (2017 est)
Inflation rate – 1.5 per cent (2017 est)
Total external debt – US$5.3bn (2014 est)
Imports – US$519m (2014)
Exports – US$786m (2014)

Trade with UK	2016	2017
Imports from UK	£8,171,270	£11,761,157
Exports to UK	£197,783	£234,513

COMMUNICATIONS
Airports and waterways – The international airports are at Mogadishu and Hargeisa; the main ports are Mogadishu, Kismayu and Merca in the south, and Berbera in the north. Increased security has led to a significant drop in piracy and armed robbery against ships in the Gulf of Aden and Indian Ocean since 2012
Roadways – 2,608km are surfaced
Telecommunications – 48,000 fixed lines and 6.6 million mobile subscriptions (2016); there were 203,366 internet users in 2016
Internet code and IDD – so; 252 (from UK), 44 (to UK)
Broadcasters – There is one state-operated TV station and two private broadcasters, with a number of radio stations operating on a regional basis

British protectorate | Two protectorates | One-party | Siad Barre regime toppled; civil war | Federal government, with
First contact | established in the | merge to form United | socialist regime | continues between rival 'warlords'; | support from Ethiopian forces,
with Europe | north | Republic of Somalia | established | central government demolished | attempts to assert authority
c.700 | 1869 | 1889–1905 | 1969 | 1988 | 2004 | 2008
c.1500 | 1887 | 1960 | 1979 | 1991 | 2007-9
Arab settlers | Opening of Suez | Italian protectorate | Armed forces seize control | Opposition to | Two years of peace talks | Alliance against Ethiopian
begin to | Canal increases | established in the | in a coup led by Maj.-Gen. | governments leads | establish a transitional legislature | presence in country agrees
introduce Islam | interest in area | south | Muhammad Siad Barre | to civil war | and appointment of president | ceasefire with government

CLIMATE AND TERRAIN

The White Nile, flowing north out of the uplands of central Africa, is the principal feature of the country, and formed part of the Sudd, a vast swamp of more than 100,000 sq. km. Divided by the river, the terrain rises from the plains on the northern border to wet southern highlands along the Kenya–Uganda divide to a maximum height of 3,187m (Mt Kinyeti). The climate is hot with seasonal rainfall and the average annual temperature is 27.7°C.

HISTORY AND POLITICS

The history of the area is largely unrecorded until the early 19th century, as natural barriers prevented the invasions and occupations affecting northern Sudan. In the 19th century, Egypt attempted to extend its influence in the region but the south was only joined with the north with the arrival of the British in the late 19th century, becoming part of a joint Anglo-Egyptian condominium from 1899. Following the independence of Sudan in 1955, tensions between the dominant Arab, Muslim north and the black African, Christian and animist south led to civil war from 1955 to 1972, and again in 1983. A peace process began in 2000 and the parties to it – the government, the Sudan People's Liberation Army/Movement (SPLA/M) and the southern National Democratic Alliance – finalised a peace agreement in 2004. Under this, the southern parties joined a national unity government, a largely autonomous administration was set up in the south in October 2005 and a referendum on independence for the south was held after six years.

In the referendum in January 2011, the south voted overwhelmingly to separate from the north. In the run-up to independence on 9 July, disputes led to a deteriorating security situation in border areas, particularly over control of the oil-rich territory of Abyei.

In December 2013, fighting broke out between political factions after the finance minister was dismissed following corruption allegations in July. Thousands of people, including civilians, were killed and more than 1 million people were displaced by April 2014. President Kiir signed a peace treaty with rebel groups on 26 August 2015, officially ending the conflict. Legislative elections originally due to take place in 2015 were delayed by the civil war and were due to take place in 2018, when they were again delayed until 2021 after parliament voted to extent Kiir's presidential term. In July 2016 hundreds of people were killed in renewed fighting between forces loyal to President Kiir and Vice-President Riek Machar, and the latter was replaced by Taban Deng Gai.

The transitional constitution came into effect at independence and will remain in force until a permanent constitution is adopted. It provides for the current president of the government of South Sudan to become president of the independent republic, and for the National Legislative Assembly (comprising 170 members of the former South Sudan Legislative Assembly, plus 96 South Sudanese former members of the National Assembly to the Republic of Sudan; both these groups were directly elected in 2010) and the Council of States (comprising 20 former South Sudan members of the Council of States of the Republic of Sudan, plus 30 representatives appointed by the president).

HEAD OF STATE

President, C-in-C of the Armed Forces, Salva Kiir Mayardit, *sworn in under draft constitution* 9 July 2011
First Vice-President, Gen. Taban Deng Gai

SELECTED GOVERNMENT MINISTERS *AS AT AUGUST 2018*
Defence, Kuol Manyang Juuk
Finance, Salvatore Garang Mabiordit Wol
Foreign Affairs, Nhial Deng Nhial

EMBASSY OF THE REPUBLIC OF SOUTH SUDAN
16 Upper Woburn Place, London WC1H 0BS
T 020-3741 8083 E info@embrss.org.uk W www.embrss.org.uk
Ambassador Extraordinary and Plenipotentiary, vacant

BRITISH EMBASSY
EU Compound, Kololo Road, Thom Ping, Juba
T (+211) (0) 912 323 712 E ukin.southsudan@fco.gov.uk
W www.gov.uk/government/world/south-sudan
Ambassador Extraordinary and Plenipotentiary, HE Alison Blackburne, *apptd* 2017

ECONOMY AND TRADE

The troubled South Sudan economy, hindered by decades of civil war with the north, is based on subsistence agriculture, which provides a living for the majority of the population. This is of one of the richest agricultural areas in Africa with fertile soils and excellent water supplies, but a lack of industry and infrastructure has forced the reliance on imports of goods and services from the neighbouring countries. Hugely oil-dependent, the government derives 98 per cent of its budget from oil revenues and consequently economic development has been hit by falling oil prices and production cuts, as well as the country's internal conflict.

South Sudan faces tough economic challenges and has received more than US$11bn in foreign aid since 2005, mainly from the UK, the USA and the EU, while Chinese investment is rising. Annual inflation rose to 800 per cent in October 2016 and remains high, as continuing civil conflict has had a seriously deleterious effect on the economy. In March 2017, the UN warned that South Sudan is one of four countries facing the world's largest humanitarian crisis since 1945; more than 7.5 million people need aid in the country.

Subsistence crops include sorghum, maize, rice millet, wheat, sugar cane, papayas, bananas and mangoes.
GNI – US$4.8bn; US$390 per capita (2017)
*Annual average growth of GDP – –*6.3 (2017 est)
Inflation rate – 182.2 per cent (2017 est)
Population below the poverty line – 51 per cent (2010 est)
Imports – US$4,160m (2010)
Exports – US$8,229m (2010)

BALANCE OF PAYMENTS
Current Account – US$964m deficit (2017)

Trade with UK	2016	2017
Imports from UK	£1,612,808	£2,405,842
Exports to UK	£49,404	£7,031

COMMUNICATIONS

Airports – There are three airports including an international terminal in Juba
Roadways and railways – There are 7,000km of mainly unpaved roadways in poor condition and 248km of railways
Internet code and IDD – ss; 211 (from UK), 44 (to UK)
Media – The country's fledgling media network faces political, social and logistical challenges; the government-run Southern Sudan TV and Radio is the country's sole network; *The Citizen* and *Juba Monitor* (both English language), and *Al-Masir* (Arabic) are the major daily newspapers
WPFI score – 46,88 (144)

SPAIN

Reino de España – Kingdom of Spain

Area – 505,370 sq. km
Capital – Madrid; population, 6,497,000 (2018 est)
Major cities – Barcelona, Bilbao, Las Palmas (Gran Canaria), Málaga, Murcia, Palma (Majorca), Seville, Valencia, Zaragoza
Currency – Euro (€) of 100 cents
Population – 48,958,159 rising at 0.78 per cent a year (2017 est)
Religion – Christian (Roman Catholic 94 per cent) (est)
Language – Castilian (Spanish) (official), Catalan, Galician, Basque (all are official in certain regions)
Population density – 93 per sq. km (2016)
Urban population – 80.3 per cent (2018 est)
Median age (years) – 42.3 (2016 est)
National anthem – 'La Marcha Real' 'The Royal March'
National day – 12 October (marks Columbus's arrival in the Americas)
Death penalty – Abolished for all crimes (since 1995)
CPI score – 57 (42)
Military expenditure – US$16,227m (2017)

CLIMATE AND TERRAIN

Spain occupies over 80 per cent of the Iberian peninsula, and includes two archipelagos and territories on or just off the Moroccan coast. The interior consists of an elevated plateau surrounded and traversed by mountain ranges: the Pyrenees on the border with France, the Cantabrian mountains (northwest), the Sierra de Guadarrama, Sierra Morena, Montes de Toledo (centre) and the Sierra Nevada (south). Elevation extremes range from 3,718m (Pico de Teide, Tenerife, Canary Islands) to 0m (Mediterranean Sea). The principal rivers are the Duero, the Tajo (Tagus), the Guadiana, the Guadalquivir, the Ebro and the Miño. The climate is Mediterranean in the southern and eastern coastal areas, and temperate further inland and at altitude. Average temperatures range from 7°C in January to 23.1°C in July.

POLITICS

The 1978 constitution has been amended at various times to devolve powers to the 19 autonomous regions. The head of state is a hereditary constitutional monarch. There is a bicameral legislature, the *Cortes Generales,* comprising a 350-member Congress of Deputies directly elected for a four-year term, and a senate with 266 members, 208 directly elected and 58 appointed by the assemblies of the autonomous regions, for a four-year term.

There are 19 autonomous regions: Andalucía, Aragón, Asturias, Balearic Islands, the Basque Country, Canary Islands, Cantabria, Castilla-La Mancha, Castilla y León, Catalonia, Ceuta, Extremadura, Galicia, La Rioja, Madrid, Melilla, Murcia, Navarre and Valencia. Each has its own elected legislature and government.

In 2006 a referendum endorsed the *Cortes'* approval of greater autonomy for Catalonia. Unofficial independence referendums, rallies and declarations of sovereignty have augmented the independence movement since 2009, resulting in the exile of pro-independence Catalonian president Carles Puigdemont in November 2017 following a declaration of independence.

The ruling Popular Party (PP) won the December 2015 legislative elections but failed to secure a majority. In new elections in June 2016, the party increased its seat count (to 137) but again failed to gain a majority; in October, Mariano Rajoy was re-elected prime minister at the head of a minority government. In June 2018 Rajoy lost a no-confidence vote following a corruption scandal and was replaced by socialist leader Pedro Sánchez.

HEAD OF STATE
HM The King of Spain, King Felipe VI de Borbon y Grecia, *born* 30 January 1968, *acceded to the throne* 19 June 2014
Heir, HRH The Princess of the Asturias, Leonor de Borbon y Ortiz, *born* 31 October 2005

SELECTED GOVERNMENT MEMBERS *as at June 2018*
Prime Minister, Pedro Sánchez
Vice-President, María del Carmen Calvo
Finance, Maria Jesús Montero
Foreign Affairs, Josep Borrell

EMBASSY OF SPAIN
39 Chesham Place, London SW1X 8SB
T 020-7235 5555 E emb.londres@maec.es
W www.exteriores.gob.es/embajadas/londres
Ambassador Extraordinary and Plenipotentiary, HE Carlos B astarreche, *apptd* 2017

BRITISH EMBASSY
Torre Espacio, Paseo de la Castellana 259D, 28046 Madrid
T (+34) (91) 714 6300 E spain.consulate@fco.gov.uk
W www.gov.uk/government/world/spain
Ambassador Extraordinary and Plenipotentiary, HE Simon Manley, CMG, *apptd* 2013

INSURGENCIES
The Basque separatist organisation ETA (*Euzkadi ta Azkatasuna* – Basque Nation and Liberty), formed in 1959, began a terrorist campaign of bombings, shootings and kidnappings in 1961 in an attempt to gain independence for the Basque country. ETA rejected regional autonomy for the Basque country in 1979 as insufficient and continued its campaign, but was greatly weakened in the early 1990s by increased cooperation between Spanish security forces and their European counterparts. ETA announced a permanent ceasefire in January 2011; in March 2017 the group announced it was laying down its arms and handed over an inventory of weapons caches in early April.

ECONOMY AND TRADE

Economic protectionism and isolation held back economic development until the mid-20th century, but the economy improved from the 1950s with industrialisation and the development of tourism. The mixed capitalist economy showed above-average growth, stimulated by liberalisation, privatisation and deregulation from the mid-1990s until 2008, when it entered a severe recession because of the global economic crisis.

The downturn in construction and the property market left many banks struggling in 2010, and rising public-sector debt led to Spain's international credit rating being downgraded; the government introduced austerity measures in response

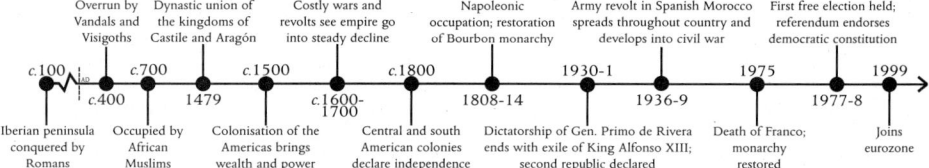

| Overrun by Vandals and Visigoths | Dynastic union of the kingdoms of Castile and Aragón | Costly wars and revolts see empire go into steady decline | Napoleonic occupation; restoration of Bourbon monarchy | Army revolt in Spanish Morocco spreads throughout country and develops into civil war | First free election held; referendum endorses democratic constitution |

*c.*100 — *c.*700 — *c.*1500 — *c.*1800 — 1930-1 — 1975 — 1999

*c.*400 — 1479 — *c.*1600-1700 — 1808-14 — 1936-9 — 1977-8

| Iberian peninsula conquered by Romans | Occupied by African Muslims | Colonisation of the Americas brings wealth and power | Central and south American colonies declare independence | Dictatorship of Gen. Primo de Rivera ends with exile of King Alfonso XIII; second republic declared | Death of Franco; monarchy restored | Joins eurozone |

alongside labour reforms. Growth returned in 2014 and while unemployment is falling it remains high, at 16.4 per cent in 2017.

Public debt remains high – growing from 60.1 per cent of GDP in 2010 to nearly 100 per cent in 2017 – but rising labour productivity, decreasing labour costs and budget deficits, and falling inflation have increased foreign investor interest. The government shored up struggling banks exposed to Spain's depressed domestic construction and real estate sectors by completing an EU-funded restructuring and recapitalisation programme in December 2013.

The generally fertile country produces grains, vegetables, olives, sugar beets, citrus and other fruits, meat and dairy products. Viticulture is widespread. Spain also has one of Europe's largest fishing industries. The agricultural sector contributes 2.6 per cent of GDP and employs 4.2 per cent of the workforce. Abundant mineral resources include coal, iron ore, copper, zinc, lead, uranium and tungsten. Metal extraction and the manufacture of metal products, including steel, are major industries. A diverse industrial sector includes manufacturing (principally textiles, clothing, footwear, beverages, chemicals, cars, machine tools, clay products, pharmaceuticals and medical equipment), food processing, shipbuilding and tourism. Industry accounts for 23.2 per cent of GDP and the service sector for 74.2 per cent.

The main trading partners are other EU countries, especially France and Germany. Principal exports include machinery, vehicles, foodstuffs, pharmaceuticals, medicines and other consumer goods. The main imports are machinery and equipment, fuels, chemicals, semi-finished goods, foodstuffs, consumer goods, and measuring and medical control instruments.

GNI – US$1,265.9bn; US$27,180 per capita (2017)
Annual average growth of GDP – 3.1 per cent (2017 est)
Inflation rate – 2 per cent (2017 est)
Population below the poverty line – 21.1 per cent (2012 est)
Unemployment – 17.1 per cent (2017 est)
Total external debt – US$2.094 trillion (2016 est)
Imports – US$310,283m (2016)
Exports – US$286,757m (2016)

BALANCE OF PAYMENTS
Trade – US$23,526m deficit (2016)
Current Account – US$25,617m surplus (2017)

Trade with UK	2016	2017
Imports from UK	£9,641,281,480	£10,459,786,707
Exports to UK	£15,669,183,123	£15,617,753,945

COMMUNICATIONS
Airports – Of the 99 airports, the principal terminals are at Madrid, Barcelona, Alicante, Málaga, Valencia and Bilbao
Waterways – The main ports are Algeciras, Alicante, Barcelona, Bilbao, Cádiz, Santander and Valencia, and Las Palmas in the Canary Islands; there are also 1,000km of navigable inland waterways

Roadways and railways – 683,175km; 15,293km
Telecommunications – 19.6 million fixed lines and 51.5 million mobile subscriptions (2016); there were 39.1 million internet users in 2016
Internet code and IDD – es; 34 (from UK), 44 (to UK)
Major broadcasters – Public radio and television services are run by Radio Television Espanola (RTVE), which is funded by advertising and state subsidies
Press – Popular newspaper titles include *El Mundo, ABC, El País* and *El Periodico de Catalunya*
WPFI score – 20,51 (31)

EDUCATION AND HEALTH
Education is free from age six to 18, and compulsory to the age of 16.
Literacy rate – 99.7 per cent (2015)
Gross enrolment ratio (percentage of relevant age group) – primary 104 per cent, secondary 128 per cent, tertiary 91 per cent (2016 est)
Health expenditure (per capita) – US$2,658 (2014)
Hospital beds (per 1,000 people) – 3 (2013)
Life expectancy (years) – 81.8 (2017 est)
Mortality rate – 9.1 (2017 est)
Birth rate – 9.2 (2017 est)
Infant mortality rate – 3.3 (2017 est)
HIV/AIDS prevalence – 0.4 per cent (2016 est)

ISLANDS AND ENCLAVES
THE BALEARIC ISLES form an archipelago off the east coast of Spain. There are four large islands (Majorca/Mallorca, Minorca, Ibiza and Formentera) and seven smaller ones (Aire, Aucanada, Botafoch, Cabrera, Dragonera, Pinto and El Rey). Area 4,992 sq. km; population 1,111,674 (2013 est). The archipelago forms a province of Spain. The capital is Palma, on Majorca.

THE CANARY ISLANDS are an archipelago in the Atlantic off the African coast, consisting of seven islands and six islets. Area 7,447 sq. km; population 2,118,679 (2013 est). The Canary Islands form two provinces of Spain: Las Palmas, comprising Gran Canaria, Lanzarote, Fuerteventura and six islets, with the seat of administration at Las Palmas, in Gran Canaria; and Santa Cruz de Tenerife, comprising Tenerife, La Palma, La Gomera and El Hierro, with the seat of administration at Santa Cruz, in Tenerife.

CEUTA is a fortified post on the Moroccan coast, opposite Gibraltar. Area 19 sq. km; population 84,180 (2013 est). Ceuta is an autonomous city of Spain.

ISLA DE FAISANES an uninhabited Franco-Spanish condominium, at the mouth of the Bidassoa in La Higuera bay.

MELILLA is a town on a rocky promontory of the Moroccan coast, connected with the mainland by a narrow isthmus. Area 13 sq. km; population 83,679 (2013 est). Melilla is an autonomous city of Spain.

OVERSEAS TERRITORIES

The following territories, which are Spanish settlements on the Moroccan seaboard, come under direct Spanish administration. They are uninhabited other than by military personnel.

PENON DE ALHUCEMAS is a bay including six islands.
PENON DE LA GOMERA (or Peñón de Velez) is a fortified rocky islet.
THE CHAFFARINAS (or Zaffarines) is a group of three islands near the Algerian frontier.

SRI LANKA

Shri Lanka Prajatantrika Samajavadi Janarajaya/Ilankai Jananayaka Choshalichak Kutiyarachu – Democratic Socialist Republic of Sri Lanka

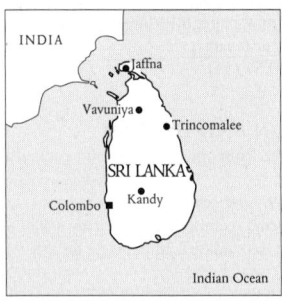

Area – 65,610 sq. km
Capital – Colombo; population, 600,000 (2018 est); the administrative capital is Sri Jayewardenepura Kotte; population, 103,000 (2018 est)
Major cities – Dehiwala-Mount Lavinia, Jaffna, Kalmunai, Kandy, Moratuwa, Negombo, Trincomalee, Vavuniya
Currency – Sri Lankan rupee of 100 cents
Population – 22,409,381 rising at 0.76 per cent a year (2017 est); Sinhalese (74.9 per cent), Sri Lankan Tamil (11.2 per cent), Sri Lankan Moor (9.2 per cent), Indian Tamil (4.2 per cent) (2012 est)
Religion – Buddhist 70.2 per cent (predominantly Theravada), Hindu 12.6 per cent, Muslim 9.7 per cent, Christian 7.4 per cent (predominantly Roman Catholic) (2012 est)
Language – Sinhala (official), Tamil, English
Population density – 342 per sq. km (2016)
Urban population – 18.5 per cent (2018 est)
Median age (years) – 32.5 (2016 est)
National anthem – 'Sri Lanka Matha' 'Mother Sri Lanka'
National day – 4 February (Independence Day)
Death penalty – Retained (last used 1976)
CPI score – 38 (91)
Military expenditure – US$1,867m (2017)
Literacy rate – 98.8 per cent (2015 est)
Gross enrolment ratio (percentage of relevant age group) – primary 102 per cent, secondary 98 per cent, tertiary 19 per cent (2015 est)
Health expenditure (per capita) – US$127 (2014)
Hospital beds (per 1,000 people) – 3.6 (2012)
Life expectancy (years) – 76.9 (2017 est)
Mortality rate – 6.2 (2017 est)
Birth rate – 15.2 (2017 est)
Infant mortality rate – 8.4 (2017 est)
HIV / AIDS adult prevalence – 0.1 per cent (2015 est)

CLIMATE AND TERRAIN

Sri Lanka (formerly Ceylon) is an island in the Indian Ocean, separated from India by the narrow Palk Strait. The land is low-lying in the north and along the coasts, rising to a central massif with hills and mountains in the south and centre. Forests, jungle and scrub cover the greater part of the island. In areas over 600m above sea level, grasslands *(patanas* or *talawas)* are found. Elevation extremes range from 2,524m (Pidurutalagala) to 0m (Indian Ocean). The climate is tropical with little seasonal variation in conditions and humidity, which often reaches around 90 per cent. The island experiences the south-west monsoon from May to September and the north-east monsoon from October to January.

POLITICS

The January 2015 presidential election was won by Maithripala Sirisena, the leader of a coalition of parties opposed to the ruling Sri Lanka Freedom Party (SLFP). After the legislative election in August 2015, the United National Front for Good Governance emerged as the single largest political grouping and formed a governing coalition with the SLFP.

The 1978 constitution was amended in 1983 to ban parties advocating separatism, in 1987 to create provincial councils, and in 2010 to remove the limit on presidential terms. The executive president is directly elected for a five-year term, which may be renewed. The unicameral parliament has 225 members directly elected by proportional representation for a five-year term. The president appoints the prime minister and cabinet.

Elected councils were set up in the nine provinces in 1987 in an attempt to defuse ethnic tensions between Sinhalese Buddhists and Muslims, but tensions still flare occasionally. The Northern and Eastern provinces were merged into one from 1988 to 2006.

HEAD OF STATE
President, Defence, Maithripala Sirisena, *elected* 8 January 2015, *sworn in* 9 January 2015

SELECTED GOVERNMENT MEMBERS *AS AT JUNE 2018*
Prime Minister, Economy, Ranil Wickremasinghe
Foreign Affairs, Tilak Marapana
Home Affairs, Vajira Abeywardena

HIGH COMMISSION OF THE DEMOCRATIC SOCIALIST REPUBLIC OF SRI LANKA
13 Hyde Park Gardens, London W2 2LU
T 020-7262 1841 E mail@slhc-london.co.uk W www.srilankahc.uk
High Commissioner, vacant

BRITISH HIGH COMMISSION
389 Bauddhaloka Mawatha, Colombo 7
T (+94) (11) 539 0639 E colombo.general@fco.gov.uk
W www.gov.uk/government/world/sri-lanka
High Commissioner, HE James Dauris, *apptd* 2015

ECONOMY AND TRADE

Despite the 26-year civil war and the 2004 Indian Ocean tsunami, which destroyed tourist resorts and the fishing industry, the economy saw sustained growth throughout the 2000s. The 2008–9 global downturn affected productivity only slightly, but high public debt and budget deficits obliged the government to seek an IMF loan in 2016. Improved trade relations with the EU and rising tourism have boosted growth in recent years, and progress has been made with international bodies on the issues of money laundering and terrorist financing. The once predominantly agricultural economy has

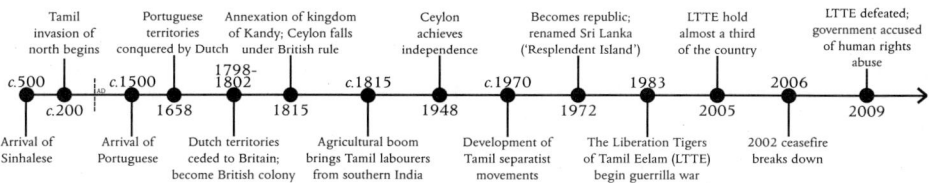

Tamil invasion of north begins	Portuguese territories conquered by Dutch	Annexation of kingdom of Kandy; Ceylon falls under British rule	Ceylon achieves independence	Becomes republic; renamed Sri Lanka ('Resplendent Island')	LTTE hold almost a third of the country	LTTE defeated; government accused of human rights abuse
c.500	c.1500	1798-1802	c.1815	c.1970	1983	2006
c.200	1658	1815	1948	1972	2005	2009
Arrival of Sinhalese	Arrival of Portuguese	Dutch territories ceded to Britain; become British colony	Agricultural boom brings Tamil labourers from southern India	Development of Tamil separatist movements	The Liberation Tigers of Tamil Eelam (LTTE) begin guerrilla war	2002 ceasefire breaks down

become increasingly industrialised and diversified. Remittances from expatriate workers are also economically significant. Government debt of around 79 per cent of GDP is among the highest of developing nations, while a large trade deficit remains a concern.

Agriculture accounts for 7.8 per cent of GDP and 27 per cent of employment. The main crops are rice, sugar cane, grains, pulses, oilseed, spices, vegetables, fruit, tea, rubber, coconuts, livestock products and fish. Manufacturing is based on processing the main cash crops of rubber, tea, coconuts, tobacco and other commodities, and production of textiles, clothing, beverages and cement; other industries include oil refining and mining gemstones. Service industries such as telecommunications, banking and insurance, information technology services and tourism are also important. The service sector accounts for 61.7 per cent of GDP and industry for 30.5 per cent.

The main trading partners are India, the USA, China, Singapore and the UK. Principal exports are textiles and clothing, tea, rubber manufactures, spices, diamonds, emeralds, rubies, coconut products and fish. The main imports are oil, textile fabrics, machinery, transport equipment, building materials, mineral products and foodstuffs.
GNI – US$82.4bn; US$3,840 per capita (2017)
Annual average growth of GDP – 4.7 per cent (2017 est)
Inflation rate – 6 per cent (2017 est)
Population below poverty line – 6.7 per cent (2012 est)
Unemployment – 4 per cent (2017 est)
Total external debt – US$47.8bn (2017 est)
Imports – US$19,039m (2015)
Exports – US$10,464m (2015)

BALANCE OF PAYMENTS
Trade – US$8,575m deficit (2015)
Current Account – US$2,309m deficit (2017)

Trade with UK	2016	2017
Imports from UK	£204,489,366	£186,548,302
Exports to UK	£1,134,996,769	£735,502,486

COMMUNICATIONS
Airports and waterways – The principal airport is Bandaranaike International, to the north of the capital; Colombo is the main port although the first phase of a deep-water container port opened in 2010 at Hambantota
Roadways and railways – 16,977km; 1,449km
Telecommunications – 2.5 million fixed lines and 25.8 million subscriptions (2016); there were 7.1 million internet users in 2016
Internet code and IDD – lk; 94 (from UK), 44 (to UK)
Media – The state-owned Sri Lanka Rupavahini Corporation operates TV and radio stations; daily newspapers include *The Island* (English language), *Dinamina* (Sinhala) and *Virakesari* (Tamil)
WPFI score – 41,37 (131)

SUDAN
Jumhuriyat as-Sudan – Republic of the Sudan

Area – 1,861,484 sq. km
Capital – Khartoum; population, 5,543,000 (2018 est)
Major cities – El Obeid, Kassala, Kusti, Nyala, Port Sudan
Currency – Sudanese pound (SDP) of 100 piastres
Population – 37,345,935 rising at 1.64 per cent a year (2017 est); Arab and Nubian peoples
Religion – Muslim 97 per cent (predominantly Sunni), Christian 3 per cent (est)
Language – Arabic, English (both official), Nubian, Ta Bedawie
Population density – 23 per sq. km (2016)
Urban population – 34.6 per cent (2018 est)
Median age (years) – 19.6 (2016 est)
National anthem – 'Nahnu Djund Allah Djund al-Watan' 'We Are the Army of God and of Our Land'
National day – 1 January (Independence Day)
Death penalty – Retained
CPI score – 16 (175)
Military expenditure – US$4,383m (2017)
Conscription – 18–33 years of age; 12–24 months

CLIMATE AND TERRAIN
Sudan is predominantly desert; the Libyan Desert in the west is separated from the rocky Nubian Desert in the east by the fertile valley of the Nile and its tributaries. There are mountains in the west and the south, and along the Red Sea coast. Elevation extremes range from 3,071m (Jabal Marrah) to 0m (Red Sea). The climate is arid on the desert plains, tropical in the south and cooler at altitude. There is a rainy season from April to October. Average temperatures range from 22.7°C in January to 31°C in May.

POLITICS
Under the 2005 constitution, the executive president is directly elected for a five-year term. The bicameral National Legislature comprises a National Assembly with 426 members, including 128 seats reserved for women, directly elected for a six-year term, and a Council of States with 32 members, two members from each state. The president appoints the cabinet.

President al-Bashir was re-elected following the April 2015 presidential election, with the president claiming to have won 95 per cent of the popular vote, while al-Bashir's National

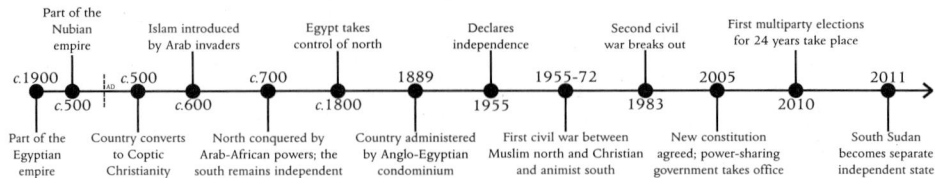

Part of the Nubian empire	Islam introduced by Arab invaders	Egypt takes control of north	Declares independence	Second civil war breaks out	First multiparty elections for 24 years take place
c.1900	c.500	c.700	1889	1955–72	2005	2011
c.500	c.600	c.1800	1955	1983	2010
Part of the Egyptian empire	Country converts to Coptic Christianity	North conquered by Arab-African powers; the south remains independent	Country administered by Anglo-Egyptian condominium	First civil war between Muslim north and Christian and animist south	New constitution agreed; power-sharing government takes office	South Sudan becomes separate independent state

Congress party won the simultaneous legislative elections. Opposition groups alleged widescale vote-rigging had taken place.

HEAD OF STATE
President, Field Marshal Omar al-Bashir, *seized power* 1989, *elected* 1996, *re-elected* 2000, *sworn in under new constitution* 9 July 2005, *re-elected* 2010, 2015
First Vice-President, Prime Minister, Bakri Hassan Salih

SELECTED GOVERNMENT MEMBERS *AS AT JUNE 2018*
Defence, Gen. Awad Mohamed Ahmed bin Auf
Finance, Lt.-Gen. Mohamed Osman Al-Rikabi
Foreign Affairs, Al-Dirdiri Mohamed Ahmed
Interior, Ibrahim Mahmoud Hamid

EMBASSY OF THE REPUBLIC OF THE SUDAN
3 Cleveland Row, London SW1A 1DD
T 020-7839 8080 **E** admin@sudanembassy.co.uk
W www.sudan-embassy.co.uk
Ambassador Extraordinary and Plenipotentiary, HE Mohammed Abdalla Ali Eltom, *apptd* 2014

BRITISH EMBASSY
PO Box 801, Off Sharia Al Baladiya, Khartoum East
T (+249) (1) 8377 7105 **E** consular.khartoum@fco.gov.uk
W www.gov.uk/government/world/sudan
Ambassador Extraordinary and Plenipotentiary, HE Irfan Siddiq, OBE, *apptd* 2018

INSURGENCIES
In the western region of Darfur, tension between nomadic Arab livestock herders and black African farmers over land and grazing rights led to a rise in intercommunal violence in the 1990s. Between 2002 and 2009 black African rebels were ruthlessly suppressed by government forces, often operating through Arab militia *(Janjaweed),* which carried out mass executions and forcible depopulation.

Two of the main rebel groups in Darfur signed peace agreements with the government, one in 2006 and the other in 2009. The International Criminal Court issued a warrant for the arrest of President al-Bashir for war crimes and crimes against humanity in 2009, and for genocide in 2010. In 2011, a related ethnic conflict broke out in the southern provinces of South Kordofan and the Blue Nile; fighting here intensified in 2015 as the government looked to make territorial gains before elections.

By 2015, 3 million people had been displaced by Sudan's conflicts, while approximately 7 million were thought to require international aid.

ECONOMY AND TRADE
Since 1997 Sudan has worked with the IMF to implement economic reforms which, despite the country's political instability and vulnerability to drought, have stabilised the economy. In 1999 Sudan began exporting oil, and the economy boomed as a result until the civil war in 2011, when it lost three quarters of production owing to the secession of South Sudan. The country has struggled to make up this lost revenue and also suffers from a poor infrastructure, high inflation, civil conflict and widespread poverty. The economy has, however, benefited from recent diversification into gold mining and the lifting of US sanctions in October 2017.

Agriculture, much at subsistence level, provides employment for around 80 per cent of the workforce and contributes 39.6 per cent of GDP. Mechanised and traditional agriculture is practised in areas with sufficient rainfall and irrigation. The principal crops include cotton, peanuts, sorghum, millet, wheat, sugar cane, tropical fruits and livestock. The country exports 75–80 per cent of the world's gum arabic. Industry consists of oil extraction and refining, cotton ginning, manufacture of textiles, cement, edible oils, sugar, soap, shoes, pharmaceuticals, armaments and vehicle assembly. Industry contributes just 2.6 per cent of GDP and services 57.8 per cent.

The main trading partners are the UAE, Egypt and Saudi Arabia. Principal exports are gold, oil and petroleum products, cotton, sesame, livestock, peanuts, gum arabic and sugar. The main imports are foodstuffs, manufactured goods, refinery and transport equipment, medicines, chemicals, textiles and wheat.
GNI – US$96.4bn; US$2,379 per capita (2017)
Annual average growth of GDP – 3.7 per cent (2017 est)
Inflation rate – 26.9 per cent (2017 est)
Population below poverty line – 15.5 per cent (2015 est)
Unemployment – 19.6 per cent (2017 est)
Total external debt – US$53.35bn (2017 est)
Imports – US$8,585m (2015)
Exports – US$2,985m (2015)

BALANCE OF PAYMENTS
Trade – US$5,600m deficit (2015)
Current Account – US$4,811m deficit (2017)

Trade with UK	2016	2017
Imports from UK	£68,335,423	£78,678,386
Exports to UK	£7,448,886	£10,167,843

COMMUNICATIONS
Airports and waterways – There are 16 airports, with the principal terminal at Khartoum; there are 4,068km of navigable waterways, including 1,723km on the White and Blue Nile rivers
Roadways and railways – 4,320km; 5,978km
Telecommunications – 136,472 fixed lines and 27.8 million mobile subscriptions (2016); there were 10.2 million internet users in 2016
Internet and IDD – sd; 249 (from UK), 44 (to UK)
Media – Sudan TV and Sudan Radio are the government-operated broadcasters; leading daily newspapers include *Al-Ra'y al-Amm, Al-Ayam* and *Al-Jareeda* (all Arabic-language)
WPFI score – 71,13 (174)

EDUCATION AND HEALTH
Education is free of charge for most children, and compulsory for eight years; six years of primary education is followed by at least two years of secondary education.
Literacy rate – 89.6 per cent (2015 est)
Gross enrolment ratio (percentage of relevant age group) – primary 70.4 per cent, secondary 42.7 per cent (2013 est), tertiary 16.3 per cent (2014 est)

Health expenditure (per capita) – US$130 (2014)
Hospital beds (per 1,000 people) – 0.8 (2013)
Life expectancy (years) – 64.4 (2017 est)
Mortality rate – 7.3 (2017 est)
Birth rate – 27.9 (2017 est)
Infant mortality rate – 48.8 (2017 est)
HIV / AIDS adult prevalence – 0.2 per cent (2016 est)

SURINAME

Republiek Suriname – Republic of Suriname

Area – 163,820 sq. km
Capital – Paramaribo; population, 239,000 (2018)
Major towns – Lelydorp, Nieuw Nickerie
Currency – Suriname dollar of 100 cents
Population – 591,919 rising at 1.02 per cent a year (2017 est); Hindustani (37 per cent), Creole (31 per cent), Javanese (15 per cent), Maroons (10 per cent), Amerindian (2 per cent), Chinese (2 per cent) (est)
Religion – Hindu 27.4 per cent, Christian (Protestant, predominantly Moravian, 25.2 per cent, Roman Catholic

HISTORY AND POLITICS
Originally settled by Arawak and Carib peoples, the area was visited by Spanish explorers in 1593. Early European settlements failed, until a British colony was founded in 1651. The colony was ceded to the Dutch in 1667. Dutch rule was interrupted by British occupation during the French Revolutionary and Napoleonic wars, but was restored in 1816. The colony, known as Dutch Guiana, became autonomous in 1954, and achieved independence in 1975 as Suriname.

The early years of independence were politically unstable, with a period of military rule under Desi Bouterse following a coup in 1980. Democratic, civilian rule was restored with elections in 1987, but the military overthrew the government in 1990 in a coup engineered by Bouterse. Democratic elections in 1991 were won by the New Front for Democracy and Development alliance, led by Ronald Venetiaan, who became president. President Venetiaan introduced an unpopular austerity programme, which improved the economy but lost him the 1996 election.

Ronald Venetiaan was re-elected president in 2000 and again in 2005. After the 2010 legislative election, the Mega Combination bloc, dominated by Desi Bouterse's National Democratic Party (NDP), held the most seats in the legislature and formed a coalition government. Bouterse was subsequently elected president by parliament. In the May 2015 legislative elections, the NDP emerged as the largest single party, retaining a majority by one seat. In July, President Bouterse was re-elected by the National Assembly.

22.8 per cent), Muslim 19.6 per cent, indigenous 5 per cent
Language – Dutch (official), English, Surinamese (Sranang Tongo), Caribbean Hindustani (a dialect of Hindi), Javanese
Population density – 4 per sq. km (2016)
Urban population – 66.1 per cent (2018 est)
Median age (years) – 29.8 (2017 est)
National anthem – 'God zij met ons Suriname' 'God Be With Our Suriname'
National day – 25 November (Independence Day)
Death penalty – Abolished for all crimes (since 2015)
CPI score – 41 (77)
Literacy rate – 95.6 per cent (2015 est)
Gross enrolment ratio (percentage of relevant age group) – primary 121 per cent (2016 est), secondary 81.1 per cent (2015 est)
Health expenditure (per capita) – US$589 (2014 est)
Life expectancy (years) – 72.5 (2017 est)
Mortality rate – 6.1 (2017 est)
Birth rate – 15.8 (2017 est)
Infant mortality rate – 24.5 (2017 est)
HIV / AIDS adult prevalence – 1.4 per cent (2016 est)

CLIMATE AND TERRAIN
The narrow, swampy coastal plain is home to about 90 per cent of the population. From the coastal belt, the land rises to a hilly interior covered by tropical rainforest and savannah; the rainforest contains a great diversity of flora and fauna. Elevation extremes range from 1,230m (Juliana Top) to −2m (coastal plain). The land is drained by several rivers, some of which have been dammed to create large artificial lakes used to generate hydroelectric power. The climate is tropical, moderated by the north-east trade winds. There are two wet seasons, from April to August and November to February.

Under the 1987 constitution, the executive president is elected for a five-year term by a two-thirds majority in the legislature or, if the required majority cannot be achieved, by a specially convened United People's Assembly including district and local council representatives. The vice-president is elected in the same way, and neither have term limits. The unicameral National Assembly has 51 members directly elected for a five-year term. The council of ministers is appointed by the president and chaired by the vice-president.

HEAD OF STATE
President, Desi Bouterse, *elected* 19 July 2010, *sworn in* 12 August 2010, *re-elected* 14 July 2015, *sworn in* 12 August 2015
Vice-President, Ashwin Adhin

SELECTED GOVERNMENT MEMBERS *AS AT JUNE 2018*
Defence, Ronni Benschop
Foreign Affairs, Yildiz Pollack-Beighle
Internal Affairs, Mike Noersaliem

HONORARY CONSULATE OF THE REPUBLIC OF SURINAME
89 Pier House, 31 Cheyne Walk, London SW3 5HG
T 07768-196 326 E ajethu@honoraryconsul.info
W www.honoraryconsul.info
Honorary consul, Amwedhkar Jethu

BRITISH AMBASSADOR
HE Gregory Quinn, *apptd* 2015, resident at Georgetown, Guyana

ECONOMY AND TRADE

Former president Venetiaan introduced policies that contained rampant inflation and other economic problems, and produced steady growth for a few years before the global downturn, which caused the economy to contract owing to reduced global prices for key commodities. The economy continued declining until 2017, partly due to the withdrawal of a US mining company and a sharp depreciation in the Suriname dollar. High inflation, government spending and debt (83 per cent of GDP in September 2017) present serious challenges to future prosperity.

The mainstays of the economy are mining, especially bauxite and gold, and oil and alumina production; these account for 85 per cent of exports and 27 per cent of government revenues, making the economy vulnerable to global price fluctuations. Bauxite reserves are declining, but oil production is increasing from existing offshore fields and onshore exploration has begun. Other industries include forestry, food processing and fishing. Industry accounts for 31.1 per cent of GDP and services for 57.4 per cent. Agriculture employs 11.2 per cent of the population and produces 11.6 per cent of GDP.

The main trading partners are the USA, Switzerland, the Netherlands and Hong Kong. Principal exports are alumina, gold, crude oil, timber, fish and shrimps, rice and bananas. The main imports are capital equipment, petroleum, foodstuffs, cotton and consumer goods.

GNI – US$3.4bn; US$6,020 per capita (2017)
Annual average growth of GDP – –1.2 per cent (2017 est)
Inflation rate – 22.3 per cent (2017 est)
Unemployment – 9.1 per cent (2017 est)
Total external debt – US$1.7bn (2017 est)
Imports – US$1,244m (2016)
Exports – US$1,437m (2016)

BALANCE OF PAYMENTS
Trade – US$193m surplus (2016)
Current Account – US$1.8m deficit (2017)

Trade with UK	2016	2017
Imports from UK	£12,062,784	£10,670,827
Exports to UK	£994,395	£340,141

COMMUNICATIONS

Airports and waterways – The principal airport and seaport is at Paramaribo
Roadways – 4,304km
Telecommunications – 89,030 fixed lines and 806,881 mobile subscriptions (2016); there were 265,964 internet users in 2016
Internet code and IDD – sr; 597 (from UK), 44 (to UK)
Media – The government operates Radio SRS Suriname and two TV stations, Algemene Televisie Verzorging and Surinaamse Televisie Stichting; there are two privately owned daily newspapers, *De West* and *De Ware Tijd*
WPFI score – 16,44 (21)

SWEDEN

Konungariket Sverige – Kingdom of Sweden

Area – 450,295 sq. km
Capital – Stockholm; population, 1,583,000 (2018 est)
Major cities – Gothenburg, Malmo, Uppsala
Currency – Swedish krona of 100 ore
Population – 9,960,487 rising at 0.81 per cent a year (2017 est)
Religion – Christian (Lutheran 87 per cent) (est)
Language – Swedish (official), Finnish, Sami
Population density – 25 per sq. km (2016)
Urban population – 87.4 per cent (2018 est)
Median age (years) – 41.2 (2017 est)
National anthem – 'Du Gamla, Du Fria' 'Thou Ancient, Thou Free'
National day – 6 June
Death penalty – Abolished for all crimes (since 1972)
CPI score – 84 (6)
Military expenditure – US$5,560m (2017)
Conscription – Abolished in practice as of 2009; retained for emergencies

CLIMATE AND TERRAIN

The terrain is mostly flat or rolling lowlands in the south and along the east coast, with mountains in the west. Elevation extremes range from 2,111m (Kebnekaise) to −2.4m (reclaimed bay of Lake Hammarsjon). There are many lakes, including Vanern, Vattern, Malaren and Hjalmaren in the south, and over 20,000 islands off the coast near Stockholm. The climate is temperate in the south and subarctic in the north; average temperatures range from −7°C in January and February to 14.5°C in July.

POLITICS

Sweden is a hereditary constitutional monarchy. The 1975 constitution was amended in 1979 to vest the succession in the monarch's eldest child irrespective of gender. The unicameral legislature, the *Riksdag*, has 349 members directly elected by proportional representation for a four-year term. The prime minister appoints the council of ministers.

Legislative elections in September 2014 saw the Social Democrats remain the largest party in the *Riksdag* and form a minority government with support from the Green Party. The government's first budget was voted down in the legislature and Prime Minister Stefan Lofven announced plans to hold early elections in March 2015 to resolve the deadlock. However, in December 2014 an agreement was reached with the opposition centre-right Alliance coalition that would allow the government to continue to operate without holding early elections. Legislative elections took place in September 2018.

Sweden is divided into 21 counties *(lan)* and 290 municipalities *(kommun)*.

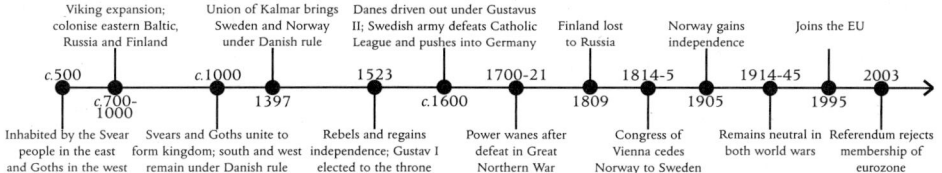

Viking expansion; colonise eastern Baltic, Russia and Finland	Union of Kalmar brings Sweden and Norway under Danish rule	Danes driven out under Gustavus II; Swedish army defeats Catholic League and pushes into Germany	Finland lost to Russia	Norway gains independence	Joins the EU	

c.500   c.1000   1523   1700-21   1814-5   1914-45   2003

c.700-1000   1397   c.1600   1809   1905   1995

Inhabited by the Svear people in the east and Goths in the west	Svears and Goths unite to form kingdom; south and west remain under Danish rule	Rebels and regains independence; Gustav I elected to the throne	Power wanes after defeat in Great Northern War	Congress of Vienna cedes Norway to Sweden	Remains neutral in both world wars	Referendum rejects membership of eurozone

HEAD OF STATE
HM The King of Sweden, King Carl XVI Gustaf, KG, *born* 30 April 1946, *succeeded* 15 September 1973
Heir, HRH Crown Princess Victoria Ingrid Alice Desiree, Duchess of Vastergotland, *born* 14 July 1977

SELECTED GOVERNMENT MEMBERS *AS AT SEPBEMBER 2018*
Prime Minister, Stefan Lofven
Deputy Prime Minister, Isabella Lovin
Defence, Peter Hultqvist
Finance, Magdalena Andersson

EMBASSY OF SWEDEN
11 Montagu Place, London W1H 2AL
T 020-7917 6400 **E** ambassaden.london@gov.se
W www.swedenabroad.com/london
Ambassador Extraordinary and Plenipotentiary, HE Torbjorn Sohlstrom, *apptd* 2016

BRITISH EMBASSY
PO Box 27819, Skarpogatan 6–8, 115 93 Stockholm
T (+46) (8) 671 3000 **E** info@britishembassy.se
W www.gov.uk/government/world/sweden
Ambassador Extraordinary and Plenipotentiary, HE David Cairns, *apptd* 2015

ECONOMY AND TRADE
Sweden developed from an agricultural to an industrial economy in the early 20th century. The prosperity that had funded the generous welfare state after 1946 ended in the early 1990s, when Sweden experienced a deep recession. It recovered to experience strong growth before briefly entering recession again in 2008–9 as a result of the global downturn. Sweden has since experienced a strong growth thanks to investment in the construction sector.

The main export-orientated industries are engineering and high-tech manufacturing, mining and forestry. Mineral resources include iron ore, copper, lead, zinc, sulphur, granite, marble, precious and heavy metals (the latter not exploited) and extensive deposits of low-grade uranium ore. The engineering sector is a key industry, particularly specialised machinery and systems such as electrical and electronic equipment and armaments, hydropower, motor vehicles and aircraft; other industries produce pharmaceuticals, plastics and chemicals.

Agriculture contributes 1.6 per cent of GDP, industry 33 per cent and services 65.4 per cent.

The main trading partners are other EU states, Norway and the USA. Principal exports include machinery, vehicles, paper products, pulp and wood, iron and steel products, and chemicals. The main imports are machinery, oil and petroleum products, chemicals, vehicles, iron and steel, foodstuffs and clothing.

GNI – US$529.5bn; US$52,590 per capita (2017)
Annual average growth of GDP – 3.1 per cent (2017 est)
Inflation rate – 1.6 per cent (2017 est)
Population below poverty line – 15 per cent (2014 est)

Unemployment – 6.6 per cent (2017 est)
Total external debt – US$939.9bn (2017 est)
Imports – US$139,798m (2016)
Exports – US$139,556m (2016)

BALANCE OF PAYMENTS
Trade – US$242m deficit (2016)
Current Account – US$17,824bn surplus (2017)

Trade with UK	2016	2017
Imports from UK	£4,586,721,084	£5,290,293,416
Exports to UK	£6,263,633,629	£6,982,169,448

COMMUNICATIONS
Airports and waterways – The principal airports are at Stockholm, Gothenburg, Lulea, Malmo and Umea; the main ports are Gothenburg, Helsingborg, Malmo and Stockholm
Roadways and railways – 135,444km; 11,633km
Telecommunications – 3.1 million fixed lines and 12.5 million mobile subscriptions (2016); there were 9 million internet users in 2016
Internet code and IDD – se; 46 (from UK), 44 (to UK)
Major broadcasters – The public broadcasters are Sveriges Television (SVT) and Sveriges Radio
Press – Major daily newspapers include *Aftonbladet, Dagens Nyheter* and *Goteborgs Posten*
WPFI score – 8,31 (2)

EDUCATION AND HEALTH
The state education system provides nine years of free and compulsory schooling from the age of seven to 16 in the comprehensive elementary schools.
Gross enrolment ratio (percentage of relevant age group) – primary 120.9 per cent, secondary 132.9 per cent, tertiary 62.4 per cent (2014 est)
Health expenditure (per capita) – US$6,808 (2014)
Hospital beds (per 1,000 people) – 2.7 (2011)
Life expectancy (years) – 82.1 (2017 est)
Mortality rate – 9.4 (2016 est)
Birth rate – 12.1 (2017 est)
Infant mortality rate – 2.6 (2017 est)
HIV/AIDS adult prevalence – 0.18 per cent (2014 est)

SWITZERLAND

Schweizerische   Eidgenossenschaft/Confédération   suisse/
Confederazione   Svizzera/Confederaziun   svizra   –   Swiss
Confederation

Area – 41,277 sq. km
Capital – Bern; population, 422,000 (2018)
Major cities – Basel, Geneva, Lausanne, Zurich
Currency – Swiss franc of 100 rappen (or centimes)
Population – 8,236,303 rising at 0.69 per cent a year (2017
   est); German (65 per cent), French (18 per cent), Italian
   (10 per cent), Romansch (1 per cent) (est)
Religion – Christian (Roman Catholic 38.2 per cent,
   Protestant 26.9 per cent, Muslim 4.9 per cent, none 21.4
   per cent (2013 est)
Language – German, French, Italian, Romansch (all official),
   Albanian, English, Portuguese, Serbo-Croatian, Spanish
Population density – 214 per sq. km (2016)
Urban population – 73.8 per cent (2018 est)
Median age (years) – 42.4 (2017 est)
National anthem – 'Schweizerpsalm'/'Cantique suisse'/'Salmo
   svizzero'/ 'Psalm svizzer' 'Swiss Psalm'
National day – 1 August (Confederation Day)
Death penalty – Abolished for all crimes (since 1992)
CPI score – 85 (3)
Military expenditure – US$4,630m (2017)
Conscription – Men aged 19–26; 18 weeks mandatory
   training, then intermittent three-week refresher courses

CLIMATE AND TERRAIN

Switzerland is the most mountainous country in Europe. The
central plateau of hills, plains and over 1,500 lakes is enclosed
by mountains. The Jura mountains lie in the north-west and
the Alps, which cover two-thirds of the country, occupy the
south and east. Elevation extremes range from 4,634m
(Dufourspitze, Alps) to 195m (Lake Maggiore). Lakes
Neuchâtel, Lucerne and Zurich lie wholly within the country,
but Lake Maggiore is shared with Italy, Lake Geneva with
France and Lake Constance with Germany and Austria. The
Rhine, Rhône and Inn rivers all rise in the Alps. The climate
is temperate, with conditions that vary with altitude. Average
temperatures range from −1.5°C in January to 15.2°C in July.

HISTORY AND POLITICS

The area was conquered by the Romans in 58 BC and then
overrun by Germanic tribes in the fourth century AD. It was a
province of the medieval Holy Roman Empire from 1033.
The Swiss confederation began in 1291 as a defensive alliance
of three cantons to protect their autonomy, and expanded
during the following centuries, becoming independent of the
Habsburgs in the 14th century. Its independence was
recognised by the Treaty of Westphalia in 1648. French
revolutionary forces captured Switzerland in 1789 and named
it the Helvetic Republic. Independence was restored in 1814,
and the congress of Vienna (1815) joined Geneva, Neuchatel
and Valais to the confederation and recognised the country's
perpetual neutrality in international affairs.

Many policy decisions are submitted to national
referendums. Although the federal government has pursued a
policy of gradual integration with the EU and applied for
membership in 1992, referendums have rejected membership
of the European Economic Area (1992), approved bilateral
trade agreements with the EU (2000) and rejected EU
membership (2001).

Proportional representation, introduced in 1919, resulted in
coalition governments throughout the 20th and into the 21st
century. Apart from a 12-month period in 2007–8, since
1959 the federal government has been a coalition of four
parties: the Swiss People's Party (SVP), the Social Democratic
Party (SP), the Christian Democratic People's Party (CVP) and
the Free Democratic Party (FDP). The SVP remained the
largest party in the National Council in the October 2015
legislative election, which was marked by a shift in voter
sentiment to the right. In a February 2015 referendum, the
electorate rejected a proposal that would have resulted in
immigrants being deported for even minor offences. In
December 2017 former vice-president Alain Berset of the SP
was elected president and took office in January 2018.

Under the 1998 constitution, the head of state is a president
elected annually (along with the vice-president) for a one-year
term by the federal legislature from the members of the
Federal Council; consecutive terms may not be served. The
bicameral legislature, the Federal Assembly, has two
chambers: the National Council has 200 members, directly
elected for a four-year term; the Council of States has 46
members (two from each canton and one from each half-
canton) directly elected within each canton for a four-year
term.

Executive power is in the hands of a Federal Council of
seven members, elected for a four-year term by the Federal
Assembly after every legislative election. The Federal Council
is chaired by the president. Not more than one person from
the same canton may be elected a member of the Council;
however, there is a tradition that Italian- and French-speaking
areas should between them be represented on the council by
at least two members.

SELECTED GOVERNMENT MEMBERS *AS AT JUNE 2018*
President of the Swiss Confederation, Home Affairs, Alain Berset,
   elected 14 December 2017, *sworn in* 1 January 2018
Vice-President, Finance, Ueli Maurer
Foreign Affairs, Ignazio Cassis

EMBASSY OF SWITZERLAND
16–18 Montagu Place, London W1H 2BQ
T 020-7616 6000 E lon.swissembassy@eda.admin.ch
W www.eda.admin.ch/london
Ambassador Extraordinary and Plenipotentiary, HE Alexandre
   Fasel, *apptd* 2017

BRITISH EMBASSY
Thunstrasse 50, 3005 Bern
T (+41) (31) 359 7700 E info.berne@fco.gsi.gov.uk
W www.gov.uk/government/world/switzerland
Ambassador Extraordinary and Plenipotentiary, HE Jane Owen,
   apptd 2018

CONFEDERAL STRUCTURE
There are 23 cantons, three of which are subdivided, making
20 cantons and six half-cantons, or 26 in all. Each canton and
half-canton has its own government and a substantial degree
of autonomy. The main language in 19 of the cantons is
German; in six others it is French and one Italian.

ECONOMY AND TRADE

Switzerland has a prosperous and stable market economy with low unemployment and a highly skilled labour force. Its prosperity is based on banking, financial services and export-orientated industrial manufacturing. The economy went into recession in 2009 owing to slower export demand and the impact on the banking sector during the 2008 global financial crisis. Growth remained slow between 2013 and 2017 due to the poor performance of the eurozone and the strength of the Swiss Franc, which made exports less competitive. Consequently, in 2015 the Swiss National Bank actively sought to weaken the currency by unpegging it to the Euro. Although not an EU member, Switzerland has brought many practices in line with the EU to maintain competitiveness, and has adopted OECD standards on tax administration and transparency owing to international pressure.

Agriculture is practised in the mountain valleys and the central plateau, where grains, fruits and vegetables are grown. Dairy farming and stock-raising are also important. The industrial sector is noted for precision, electrical and mechanical engineering, pharmaceuticals, chemicals, luxury consumer goods and textiles. Banking, insurance and tourism are the major service industries. Agriculture contributes 0.7 per cent of GDP, industry 25.6 per cent and services 73.7 per cent.

The main trading partners are EU countries (especially Germany) and the USA. Principal exports are machinery, chemicals, metals, watches and agricultural products. The main imports are machinery, chemicals, vehicles, metals, agricultural products and textiles.

GNI – US$682.1bn; US$80,560 per capita (2017)
Annual average growth of GDP – 1 per cent (2017 est)
Inflation rate – 0.5 per cent (2017 est)
Population below poverty line – 6.6 per cent (2014 est)
Unemployment – 3 per cent (2017 est)
Total external debt – US$1.664 trillion (2016 est)
Imports – US$175,908m (2016)
Exports – US$213,991m (2016)

BALANCE OF PAYMENTS

Trade – US$38,083m surplus (2016)
Current Account – US$66,558m surplus (2017)

Trade with UK	2016	2017
Imports from UK	£14,624,037,498	£15,374,060,382
Exports to UK	£22,566,394,187	£11,037,019,829

COMMUNICATIONS

Airports and waterways – The principal airports are at Zurich, Basel, Bern and Geneva; the Rhine carries commercial shipping on the 65km stretch from Basel–Rheinfelden and Schaffhausen–Bodensee, and there are 12 navigable lakes
Roadways and railways – There are 71,464km of roadways, including 1,415km of motorways, and 4,876km of railways
Telecommunications – 3.96 million fixed lines and 11.2 million mobile subscriptions (2016); there were 7.3 million internet users in 2016
Internet code and IDD – ch; 41 (from UK), 44 (to UK)
Major broadcasters – The public-service Swiss Broadcasting Corporation (SRG/SSR), which is funded mainly through licence fees, dominates broadcasting
Press – Newspapers tend to be regional, reflecting linguistic divisions: major titles include *Neue Zürcher Zeitung* (Zurich based), *Le Temps* (Geneva) and *Corriere del Ticino* (Lugano)
WPFI score – 11,27 (5)

EDUCATION AND HEALTH

Education is controlled by cantonal and communal authorities and is free and compulsory from ages seven to 16.

Gross enrolment ratio (percentage of relevant age group) – primary 104 per cent, secondary 102 per cent, tertiary 58 per cent (2016 est)
Health expenditure (per capita) – US$9,674 (2014)
Hospital beds (per 1,000 people) – 5.0 (2011)
Life expectancy (years) – 82.6 (2017 est)
Mortality rate – 8.3 (2017 est)
Birth rate – 10.5 (2017 est)
Infant mortality rate – 3.6 (2017 est)
HIV/AIDS adult prevalence – 0.35 per cent (2013 est)

SYRIA

Al-Jumhuriyah al-Arabiyah as-Suriyah – Syrian Arab Republic

Area – 185,180 sq. km
Capital – Damascus; population, 2,320,000 (2018 est)
Major cities – Aleppo (Halab), Hama (Hamah), Homs (Hims), Latakia (al-Ladhiqiyah)
Currency – Syrian pound (S£) of 100 piastres
Population – 18,028,549 (2017 est)
Religion – Muslim (Sunni 74 per cent, other 13 per cent, including Alawite, Ismaili), Christian 10 per cent (est) (of which Greek Orthodox is the largest denomination), Druze 3 per cent
Language – Arabic (official), Kurdish, Armenian, Aramaic, Circassian, French
Population density – 99 per sq. km (2016)
Urban population – 54.2 per cent (2018 est)
Median age (years) – 24.3 (2017 est)
National anthem – 'Homat al-Diyar' 'Guardians of the Homeland'
National day – 17 April (Independence Day)
Death penalty – Retained
CPI score – 14 (178)
Military expenditure – US$2,495m (2011)
Conscription – Men aged 18; 18 months

CLIMATE AND TERRAIN

There is a narrow coastal plain and ranges of mountains in the west, and the fertile basin of the river Euphrates in the north-east. The centre and south of the interior consist of semi-arid and desert plateaux. Elevation extremes range from 2,814m (Mt Hermon) to −200m (unnamed location near Lake Tiberias). There is a desert climate in much of the country, moderated by altitude in the mountains, and a Mediterranean climate on the coast. Average temperatures range from 6.4°C in January to 29.6°C in July.

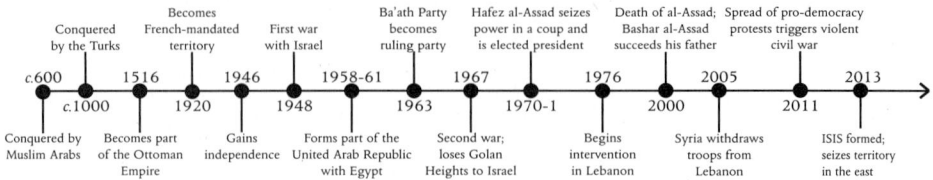

	Becomes		Ba'ath Party	Hafez al-Assad seizes	Death of al-Assad;	Spread of pro-democracy
Conquered	French-mandated	First war	becomes	power in a coup and	Bashar al-Assad	protests triggers violent
by the Turks	territory	with Israel	ruling party	is elected president	succeeds his father	civil war

c.600   1516   1946   1958-61   1967   1976   2005   2013
c.1000   1920   1948   1963   1970-1   2000   2011

Conquered by	Becomes part	Gains	Forms part of the	Second war;	Begins	Syria withdraws	ISIS formed;
Muslim Arabs	of the Ottoman	independence	United Arab Republic	loses Golan	intervention	troops from	seizes territory
	Empire		with Egypt	Heights to Israel	in Lebanon	Lebanon	in the east

POLITICS

In March 2011, protests against the ruling Assad regime broke out in a number of cities, including Damascus and Deraa. In May, the army was used to restore order in a number of towns. Many soldiers and commanders unwilling to use force against civilians broke away from the government, forming the Free Syrian Army, which began fighting against the administration. Mounting civilian casualties escalated the conflict, leading to the involvement of a number of different anti-Assad groups, including the Kurdish People's Protection Units (YPG) operating in the north-east of the country, Islamist groups and Hezbollah fighters from neighbouring Lebanon.

Following a chemical attack on the town of Ghouta by the Syrian air force in August 2013, the Syrian government came under sustained international pressure to abandon its stockpile of chemical weapons. In April 2014, 92.5 per cent of the country's chemical weapons were confirmed to have been removed or destroyed by UN observers. The government continued to cede control of its territory in 2015, losing control of Idlib province to Islamists in March, the Jordanian and Iraqi borders to secular and Islamist groups in March and June, and control of the eastern areas of the country to Kurdish fighters in June. In September, Russia entered the conflict in support of government forces; the Kremlin said its air strikes targeted IS fighters, but many Western observers and the Syrian opposition claimed the attacks hit anti-Assad rebels. In December, the Syrian Army retook Homs after four years of fighting.

A partial ceasefire between the army and major rebel forces came into effect in February 2016, although it did not include IS fighters. In March, government forces retook Palmyra with Russian air support and in May the ceasefire was extended to Aleppo. In April 2017, the government was accused of killing at least 74 people in a sarin gas attack on Khan Shaykhun, Idlib province, provoking an aerial response from the US. Following another suspected chemical attack in Douma in April 2018, chemical weapons storage facilities were targeted by US, UK and French airstrikes. In January 2018, Turkish forces attacked Kurdish militias in northern Syria, including attacking US allies. Between January 2015 and March 2018, it was estimated IS had lost 98 per cent of its territory in Syria and Iraq.

By April 2018, it was estimated 465,000 people had been killed in the conflict, more than one million had been injured and 12 million (half the country's pre-war population) had been displaced.

In February 2012, a new constitution providing for multiparty elections was approved via a referendum. The majority of countries refused to recognise the outcome of the poll; exceptions included Russia and China.

HEAD OF STATE
President, Lt.-Gen. Bashar al-Assad, elected 27 June 2000, confirmed by referendum 10 July 2000, re-elected 2007, 2014
Vice-President, Najah al-Attar

SELECTED GOVERNMENT MEMBERS AS AT JULY 2018
Prime Minister, Imad Mohammad Deeb Khamis
Deputy Prime Minister, Foreign Affairs, Walid al-Muallem
Defence, Maj.-Gen. Ali Abdullah Ayoub
Finance, Maamoun Hamdan

EMBASSY OF THE SYRIAN ARAB REPUBLIC
8 Belgrave Square, London SW1X 8PH
T 020-7245 9012 W www.syremb.com
Closed due to the conflict

ECONOMY AND TRADE

Since the start of the civil war in 2011, the economy has declined by over 70 per cent thanks to widespread disruption and damage, international sanctions, high inflation, low domestic demand, a depreciating currency and rising budgets. The humanitarian crisis continued to worsen in 2017, with more than 13 million Syrians believed to be in need of aid, 6.6 million said to be internally displaced and an estimated 5.6 million having fled to neighbouring countries.

Before the conflict, the economy was state-controlled and predominantly state-owned, but liberalising policies were being pursued. Oil and agriculture accounted for nearly half of GDP, although other activities, such as financial services, telecommunications, tourism and non-oil industry and trade, were becoming increasingly important.

GNI – US$70,501m; US$2,610 per capita (2010)
Annual average growth of GDP – –9.9 per cent (2015 est)
Inflation rate – 25.5 per cent (2017 est)
Population below poverty line – 82.5 per cent (2014 est)
Unemployment – 50 per cent (2017 est)
Total external debt – US$5.699bn (2017 est)
Imports – US$4,313m (2014)
Exports – US$2,250m (2014)

BALANCE OF PAYMENTS
Trade – US$2,800m deficit (2013)
Current Account – US$367m deficit (2010)

Trade with UK	2016	2017
Imports from UK	£5,729,831	£8,829,028
Exports to UK	£6,023,194	£7,141,748

COMMUNICATIONS

Airports and waterways – The principal airport is at Damascus; the main port is Latakia
Roadways and railways – 69,873km; 2,052km
Telecommunications – 3.5 million fixed lines and 13.3 million mobile subscriptions (2016); there were 5.5 million internet users in 2016
Internet code and IDD – sy; 963 (from UK), 44 (to UK)
Major broadcasters – Syrian Arab Republic Radio and Syrian TV are the public broadcasters; opposition groups operate TV and radio stations, including Al-Ghad (TV) and the Syrian Radio Network

Press – Only government-owned newspapers publish daily; leading titles include *Al-Baath, Al-Thawra* and *Tishrin*
WPFI score – 79,22 (177)

EDUCATION AND HEALTH

Education is under state control. Elementary education is free at state schools and is compulsory from the age of seven.
Literacy rate – 96.4 per cent (2015 est)
Gross enrolment ratio (percentage of relevant age group) – primary 80.1 per cent, secondary 50.5 per cent (2013 est), tertiary 39 per cent (2016 est)
Health expenditure (per capita) – US$66 (2014)
Hospital beds (per 1,000 people) – 1.5 (2014)
Life expectancy (years) – 75.1 (2017 est)
Mortality rate – 4 (2017 est)
Birth rate – 21.2 (2017 est)
Infant mortality rate – 14.8 (2017 est)

TAIWAN

T'ai-wan – Taiwan (Republic of China)

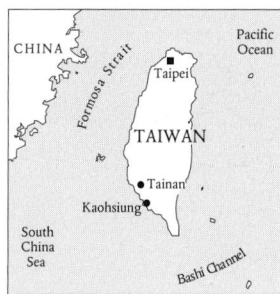

Area – 35,980 sq. km
Capital – Taipei; population, 2,706,000 (2018 est)
Major cities – Kaohsiung, Taichung, Tainan
Currency – New Taiwan dollar (NT$) of 100 cents
Population – 23,508,428 rising at 0.17 per cent a year (2017 est); Taiwanese 84 per cent, Mainland Chinese 14 per cent, indigenous 2 per cent (est)
Religion – Mixture of Buddhist and Taoist 93 per cent, Christian 4.5 per cent; many also practise Chinese folk beliefs
Language – Mandarin (official), Taiwanese (Min), Hakka dialects
Population density – 618 per sq. km (2001)
Median age (years) – 40.7 (2017 est)
National anthem – 'San Min Chu I' 'Three Principles of the People'
National day – 10 October (Republic Day)
Death penalty – Retained (last used 2011)
CPI score – 63 (29)
Military expenditure – US$10,569m (2017)
Conscription – 18–36 years of age; 4–12 months
Life expectancy (years) – 80.2 (2017 est)
Mortality rate – 7.4 (2017 est)
Birth rate – 8.3 (2017 est)
Infant mortality rate – 4.3 (2017 est)

CLIMATE AND TERRAIN

The island of Taiwan (formerly Formosa) lies 145km east of the Chinese mainland. Mountains run the length of the island, covering over half the terrain, with lowlands in the west. Elevation extremes range from 3,952m (Yu Shan) to 0m (South China Sea). Taiwan shares the tropical monsoon climate of southern China, with large seasonal variations in temperature,

dry winters and wet summers. The typhoon season lasts from May to November, with particularly high humidity between July and September. Average temperatures in Taipei range from 16°C in January and February and 29°C in July and August.

Territories include the Penghu (Pescadores) islands (80.47 sq. km), some 56km west of Taiwan, as well as Kinmen (Quemoy) (109 sq. km) and Matsu (7 sq. km), which are only a few kilometres from mainland China.

HISTORY AND POLITICS

Originally settled by Austronesian people 8,000 years ago, Chinese colonists arrived on the island from around the 12th century. The island was annexed by China in the 17th century, and ceded to Japan in 1895 at the end of the Sino-Japanese War. It was returned to China after Japan's defeat in the Second World War. The Kuomintang (KMT) government, led by Gen. Chiang Kai-shek, withdrew to Taiwan in 1949 after being defeated by the communists in mainland China. The territory remained under Chiang Kai-shek's presidency until his death in 1975. He was succeeded as president by his son, Gen. Chiang Ching-kuo, who ruled until his death in 1988. Martial law was lifted in 1987 after 38 years. In 1991 the Taiwanese government declared an end to the state of war with China, officially recognising the People's Republic of China for the first time, and ended emergency measures that had frozen political life in Taiwan since 1949.

Democratisation of the authoritarian one-party state began in the 1980s and led to the first multiparty elections in 1992. The 'Senior Parliamentarians' who had retained their seats since being elected on the mainland in 1948 were forcibly retired in 1991–2. From this point, power shifted away from the mainlanders to the native Taiwanese, and 50 years of KMT rule ended when the Democratic Progressive Party (DPP), which favours self-determination, won the presidency in 2000 and the 2001 legislative election.

The DPP retained the presidency and continued in government after the 2004 elections. However, in the 2008 elections the KMT returned to power, and the KMT candidate, Ma Ying-jeou, was elected president. The KMT retained its majority in the 2012 legislative election and Ma Ying-jeou was re-elected. The government resigned in November 2014 following poor local election results and in January 2016 Tsai Ing-wen of the DPP won the presidential election with 56 per cent of the vote, becoming the country's first woman leader, while her party won 68 seats in the simultaneous legislative election, to the KMT's 35.

Most nations acknowledge the position of the Chinese government that Taiwan is a province of the People's Republic of China, and as a result Taiwan has formal diplomatic relations with only 19 countries and no seat at the UN. China has sanctioned the use of force to prevent Taiwan declaring itself independent.

Contacts between Taiwan and China began in the 1980s and have led to a gradual relaxation of restrictions on direct economic, trade and transport links, and on travel and tourism. After the KMT returned to power in 2008, Taiwan sought greater economic cooperation and integration with the mainland, but relations have deteriorated since President Tsai's election.

The 1947 constitution (which originally applied to the whole of China) has been amended a number of times since 1991. In 2004 an amendment provided for future proposed constitutional changes to be put to a referendum instead of the National Assembly (formerly the upper house of the legislature), which was disbanded under 2005 provisions that also reduced the number of legislative seats with effect from the 2008 election.

The president is directly elected for a four-year term, renewable once. The unicameral Legislative Yuan has 113 members: 73 directly elected, 34 elected proportionally by party and six elected by indigenous peoples in two constituencies; all serve a four-year term. The president appoints the premier and, on the premier's advice, the cabinet.

HEAD OF STATE
President, Tsai Ing-wen, *elected* 17 January 2016, *sworn in* 20 May 2016
Vice-President, Chen Chien-jen

SELECTED GOVERNMENT MEMBERS *AS AT JULY 2018*
Premier, William Lai Ching-te
Defence, Gen. (retd) Yen De-fa
Finance, Su Jain-rong
Foreign Affairs, Joseph Wu Jau-shieh

ECONOMY AND TRADE
Since the 1950s Taiwan has transformed itself from a mainly agricultural country into a highly developed industrial economy. This transition was driven by exports. There has been a gradual shift away from state domination of the economy, with a reduction in government influence on investment and foreign trade, and privatisation in the financial and industrial sectors. Taiwan's export markets suffered severely in the global economic downturn and the economy contracted sharply in 2008–9. After achieving double-digit growth in 2010, the economy slowed in 2011–16 before rising to 2 per cent in 2017, thanks to a large increase in exports despite the deacceleration of the Chinese economy. The new government has shifted trade towards south and southeast Asia, and has also benefited from free-trade deals signed with New Zealand and Singapore in 2013. However, little has been done to tackle domestic concerns including youth unemployment, affordable housing, stagnant wages and pensions.

Only a quarter of the land area is suitable for agriculture but the soil is very fertile, producing rice, vegetables, fruit, tea, flowers, meat and dairy products. The industrial base includes electronics, communications and information technology products, oil refining, armaments, chemicals, textiles, iron and steel, machinery, cement, food processing, vehicles, consumer goods, pharmaceuticals and fishing. Agriculture contributes 1.8 per cent of GDP, industry 36 per cent and services 62.1 per cent.

The main trading partners are China, Japan, the USA and Hong Kong. Principal exports are electronic and computer equipment, flat panel displays, machinery, vehicles, metals, plastics, chemicals and precision instruments. The main imports are electronic and electrical equipment, machinery, crude oil and natural gas.
Average annual growth of GDP – 2 per cent (2017 est)
Inflation rate – 1 per cent (2017 est)
Population below poverty line – 1.5 per cent (2012 est)
Unemployment – 3.8 per cent (2017 est)
Total external debt – US$204.7bn (2017 est)
Imports – US$251,500m (2010)
Exports – US$274,600m (2010)

BALANCE OF PAYMENTS
Trade – US$23,100m surplus (2010)
Current Account – US$75,788m surplus (2016 est)

Trade with UK	2016	2017
Imports from UK	£1,136,555,025	£1,175,781,604
Exports to UK	£3,102,871,727	£3,374,687,440

COMMUNICATIONS
Airports and waterways – There are international airports at Taoyuan (near Taipei), Kaohsiung and Taichung; the main ports are Keelung, Kaohsiung and Taichung
Roadways and railways – 41,475km; 1,580km
Telecommunications – 13.8 million fixed lines and 29.2 million mobile subscriptions (2016); there were 20.6 million internet users in 2016
Internet code and IDD – tw; 886 (from UK), 2 44 (to UK)
Broadcasters – The government runs two non-profit public broadcasters, Public Television Service and CBS-Radio Taiwan International
Press – Major daily newspapers include *United Daily News, China Times* (both Chinese language) and *The China Post* (English)
WPFI score – 23,36 (42)

TAJIKISTAN

Jumhurii Tojikiston – Republic of Tajikistan

Area – 144,100 sq. km
Capital – Dushanbe; population, 873,000 (2018 est)
Major towns – Khujand, Kulob
Currency – Somoni of 100 dirams
Population – 8,468,555 rising at 1.62 per cent a year (2017 est); Tajik (84.3 per cent), Uzbek (13.8 per cent) (2010 est)
Religion – Muslim (Sunni 85 per cent, Shia 5 per cent) (2003 est)
Language – Tajik (official), Russian
Population density – 64 per sq. km (2016)
Urban population – 27.1 per cent (2018 est)
Median age (years) – 24.5 (2017 est)
National anthem – 'Surudi Milli' 'National Anthem'
National day – 9 September (Independence Day)
Death penalty – Retained (last used 2004)
CPI score – 21 (161)
Military expenditure – US$104m (2014)
Conscription – 18–27 years of age; 24 months
Literacy rate – 99.9 per cent (2015 est)
Gross enrolment ratio (percentage of relevant age group) – primary 99 per cent (2016 est), secondary 87.9 per cent (2013 est), tertiary 31 per cent (2016 est)
Health expenditure (per capita) – US$76 (2014)
Hospital beds (per 1,000 people) – 4.8 (2013)
Life expectancy (years) – 68.1 (2017 est)
Mortality rate – 6.1 (2017 est)
Birth rate – 23.3 (2017 est)
Infant mortality rate – 31.8 (2017 est)
HIV/AIDS adult prevalence – 0.3 per cent (2016 est)

CLIMATE AND TERRAIN

Tajikistan is mountainous, with the Pamir highlands in the east and the high ridges of the Pamir-Altai ranges in the centre. More than half of the country lies above 3,000m. Elevation extremes range from 7,495m (Qullai Ismoili Somoni) to 300m (Syr Darya river). The main rivers are the Syr Darya, flowing through the Fergana valley in the north, and the Amu Darya and its tributaries in the west and south. Most of the population lives on the fertile plains formed by these rivers. The climate is continental; average temperatures range from −8.6°C in January to 16.5°C in July.

HISTORY AND POLITICS

The area that is now Tajikistan was first settled by Iranian peoples 3,000 years ago and was conquered by Alexander the Great in the fourth century BC, remaining under Greek and Greco-Persian rule for 200 years until the kingdom of Kushan was established throughout the Bactria region.

Tajikistan was invaded by Muslim Arabs in the eighth century AD, and Islam was the prevalent religion by the time of the Samanid Persian conquest in the ninth century. In 1868, the northern part was subsumed within the Russian Empire, while the south was annexed by the Bukhara khanate. At the time of the Russian revolution in 1917 the Central Asian territories attempted to establish their independence, but Bolshevik power was consolidated in the north by April 1918, and in the rest of Tajikistan by 1920. In 1924 the Tajikistan Autonomous Soviet Socialist Republic was formed as part of the Uzbek Republic, before Tajikistan was given the status of a full republic within the USSR in 1929.

Tajikistan declared its independence on 9 September 1991. In 1992, anti-government demonstrations escalated into a five-year civil war between government forces and Islamic and pro-democracy groups. A peace accord signed in 1997 was implemented by 2000. Political assassinations and bombings occurred after the end of the civil war, but the level of violence has dropped since 2002.

Former communists have dominated politics since 1991 and power is concentrated in the president's hands. Opposition parties are weak and face harassment; a number of opposition leaders have been arrested on criminal charges, moves that their supporters claim are politically motivated.

President Rakhmon has served as head of state since 1992, and was re-elected for a fourth term in 2013. The 2010 and 2015 legislative elections were won by the incumbent (former communist) People's Democratic Party of Tajikistan with an overwhelming majority, although international observers considered both polls flawed.

The 1994 constitution has been amended multiple times, following referendums, to introduce changes to the presidential term of office and the legislative structure. The executive president is directly elected for a seven-year term, renewable once. However, the 2003 amendment permitted the current incumbent to stand for two further terms, and a 2016 referendum allowed President Rakhmon an unlimited number of terms. The bicameral parliament consists of the Assembly of Representatives *(Majlisi Namoyandogan)*, which has 63 members directly elected for a five-year term, and the Supreme Assembly *(Majlisi Milli)*, which has 33 members plus the president, 25 elected by five regional assemblies, and eight appointed by the president, to serve a five-year term. Administratively, Tajikistan is divided into two provinces and the Gorno-Badakhstan autonomous region.

HEAD OF STATE
President, Emomali Rakhmon, *elected by Supreme Soviet* 19 November 1992, *elected* 6 November 1994, *re-elected* 1999, 2006, 2013

SELECTED GOVERNMENT MEMBERS *AS AT JULY 2018*
Prime Minister, Kohir Rasulzoda
First Deputy Prime Minister, Davlatali Saidov
Deputy Prime Ministers, Murodali Alimardon; Azim Ibrohim; Marhabo Jabbarova
Defence, Col.-Gen. Mirzo Sherali

EMBASSY OF THE REPUBLIC OF TAJIKISTAN
Grove House, 26–28 Hammersmith Grove, London W6 7BA
T 020-8834 1003 **E** info@tajembassy.org.uk
W www.tajembassy.org.uk
Ambassador Extraordinary and Plenipotentiary, vacant

BRITISH EMBASSY
65 Mirzo Tursunzoda Street, Dushanbe 734002
T (+992) 372 42221 **E** dushanbe.reception@fco.gov.uk
W www.gov.uk/government/world/tajikistan
Ambassador Extraordinary and Plenipotentiary, HE Hugh Philpott, OBE, *apptd* 2015

ECONOMY AND TRADE

Since the civil war, there has been steady economic growth but the economy remains fragile owing to the inconsistent implementation of structural reforms, corruption, poor industrial and transport infrastructure, energy shortages and high foreign debt. The country has benefited from debt cancellation and is receiving substantial aid, primarily to develop industrial and transport infrastructure. The economy is dependent on remittances, with 90 per cent of the country's migrant workers residing in Russia, and is the poorest former soviet republic. A thriving informal narcotics trade, an unstable banking sector and currency devaluations are significant problems, but foreign investment in hydropower could prove a vital revenue stream once the Roghun dam is finished around 2029.

Agriculture accounts for 28.6 per cent of GDP but 43 per cent of employment. Cattle-raising and cotton-growing predominate; other crops are grain, fruit, grapes and vegetables. Abundant mineral deposits are not fully exploited. Industry consists of aluminium and hydroelectric power production, mining (mainly silver and gold) and production of cement and vegetable oil. Industry contributes 25.5 per cent of GDP and employs 10.6 per cent of the workforce. The services sector contributes the most to GDP at 45.9 per cent and employs 46.4 per cent of the workforce.

The main trading partners are China, Turkey and Russia. Principal exports are aluminium, electricity, cotton, fruit, vegetable oil and textiles. The main imports are petroleum products, aluminium oxide, machinery and equipment, and foodstuffs.

GNI – US$8.8bn; US$990 per capita (2017)
Annual average growth of GDP – 7.1 per cent (2017 est)
Inflation rate – 8.9 per cent (2017 est)
Population below poverty line – 31.5 per cent (2016 est)
Unemployment – 2.4 per cent (2016 est)
Total external debt – US$5.77bn (2017 est)
Imports – US$3,031m (2016)
Exports – US$899m (2016)

BALANCE OF PAYMENTS
Trade – US$2,132m deficit (2016)
Current Account – US$34.8m deficit (2017)

Trade with UK	2016	2017
Imports from UK	£1,711,214	£901,872
Exports to UK	£626,678	£639,851

COMMUNICATIONS
Airports and waterways – The main airport is at Dushanbe and there are 16 others around the country; 200km of the river Vakhsh is navigable
Roadways and railways – 27,767km; 680km
Telecommunications – 468,000 fixed lines and 9.4 million mobile subscriptions (2016); there were 1.7 internet users in 2016
Internet code and IDD – tj; 992 (from UK), 810 44 (to UK)
Media – The state-run Tajik TV and Tajik Radio are the state broadcasters; major newspapers include the government-owned *Jumhuriyat* (Tajik language) and *Khalq Ovozi* (Uzbek)
WPFI score – 50,06 (149)

TANZANIA

Jamhuri ya Muungano wa Tanzania – United Republic of Tanzania

Area – 947,300 sq. km
Capital – Dodoma (legislative capital); population, 262,000 (2018 est); Dar es Salaam (administrative capital); population, 6,048,000 (2018 est)
Major cities – Arusha, Mbeya, Mwanza, Zanzibar
Currency – Tanzanian shilling of 100 cents
Population – 53,950,935 rising at 2.75 per cent a year (2017 est); over 130 African ethnic groups on the mainland; Arab, African and mixed race on Zanzibar
Religion – mainland: Christian 61.4 per cent, Muslim 35.2 per cent (2010 est); Zanzibar: Muslim 99 per cent
Language – Swahili, English (both official), Arabic (especially on Zanzibar)
Population density – 65 per sq. km (2016)
Urban population – 33.8 per cent (2018 est)
Median age (years) – 17.7 (2017 est)
National anthem – 'Mungu ibariki Afrika' 'God Bless Africa'
National day – 26 April (Union Day)
Death penalty – Retained (last used 1994)
CPI score – 36 (103)
Military expenditure – US$593m (2017)

CLIMATE AND TERRAIN
Tanzania comprises the former Tanganyika, on the mainland of east Africa, and the islands of Zanzibar, Pemba and Mafia. Most of the country lies on the central African plateau, from which rise mountains that run across the centre of the country from north-east to south-west. Peaks include Mt Kilimanjaro (5,895m), the highest point on the continent of Africa; the lowest point is 0m (Indian Ocean). Large areas of lakes Victoria, Tanganyika and Malawi (Nyasa) lie on the northern and western borders, and there are smaller lakes in the north-east and south-west. The Serengeti National Park covers an area of 9,656 sq. km in the north of the country. The climate is tropical, modified by altitude, with a rainy season from November to April except in coastal regions, which get most

rain between March and May; rainfall is sporadic in the interior but more reliable and heavier on the coast.

POLITICS
The 1977 constitution was amended in 1992 to introduce multiparty elections, and in 2000 to allow the president to nominate up to ten members of parliament. The executive president is directly elected for a five-year term, renewable once. The president is always from Tanganyika and the vice-president is always from Zanzibar. The unicameral National Assembly *(Bunge)* has 393 members: 264 directly elected, 113 seats reserved for women, ten appointed by the president (including five women), five chosen by Zanzibar's legislature, and the attorney general. All serve a five-year term. The *Bunge* enacts laws that apply to the whole of Tanzania and laws that apply only to the mainland; laws that apply specifically to Zanzibar are enacted by the island's own legislature, the 82-member House of Representatives. Zanzibar also has its own directly elected president (who is a member of the Union government) and legislature.

In the October 2015 national elections, John Magufuli was elected president, while his Revolutionary Party of Tanzania (CCM) retained its overwhelming majority in the legislature. Simultaneous presidential and legislative elections in Zanzibar were annulled due to voting irregularities, although President Ali Mohamed Shein (CCM) was re-elected with 91.4 per cent of the vote in fresh presidential elections in March 2016.

HEAD OF STATE
President of the United Republic, C-in-C of the Armed Forces, John Magufuli, *elected* 25 October 2015, *took office* 4 November 2015
Vice-President, Samia Suluhu Hassan
President of Zanzibar, Ali Mohamed Shein

SELECTED GOVERNMENT MEMBERS *AS AT JULY 2018*
Prime Minister, Kassim Majaliwa Majaliwa
Defence, Hussein Mwinyi
Finance, Philip Mpango

HIGH COMMISSION OF THE UNITED REPUBLIC OF TANZANIA
3 Stratford Place, London W1C 1AS
T 020-7569 1470 E balozi@tanzania-online.gov.uk
W www.tanzania-online.gov.uk
High Commissioner, HE Asha-Rose Migiro, *apptd* 2016

BRITISH HIGH COMMISSION
PO Box 9200, Umoja House, Garden Avenue, Dar es Salaam
T (+255) (22) 229 0000 E bhc.dar@fco.gov.uk
W www.gov.uk/government/world/tanzania
High Commissioner, HE Sarah Cooke, *apptd* 2016

ECONOMY AND TRADE
State control has been dismantled gradually since the mid-1980s. Liberalisation and modernisation policies, supported by the World Bank, IMF and aid donors, have increased private-sector growth and investment. Betwwen 2009 and 2017 annual growth averaged almost 7 per cent, however 22.8 per cent of the population still live below the poverty line. The expansion of foreign banking, increased gold production, infrastructure investment and improvements in education have all strengthened the economy in recent years.

Agriculture is the mainstay of the economy, accounting for 23.4 per cent of GDP, 66.9 per cent of employment and thee majority of exports. It provides coffee, tea, cotton, pyrethrum, cashew nuts, grains, fruit and vegetables as well as the raw materials for industries producing sugar, beer, cigarettes and sisal twine. Zanzibar and Pemba produce cloves and clove oil,

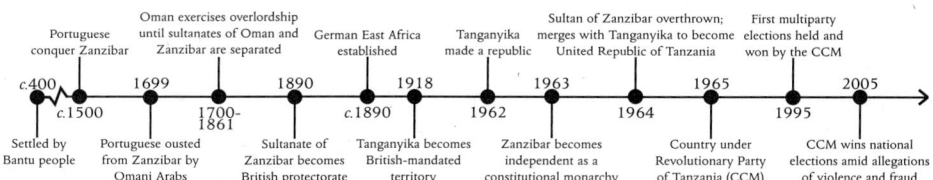

Portuguese conquer Zanzibar | *c.*400

Oman exercises overlordship until sultanates of Oman and Zanzibar are separated | 1699

German East Africa established | 1890

Tanganyika made a republic | 1918

Sultan of Zanzibar overthrown; merges with Tanganyika to become United Republic of Tanzania | 1963

First multiparty elections held and won by the CCM | 1965 | 2005

*c.*1500 | 1700–1861 | *c.*1890 | 1962 | 1964 | 1995

Settled by Bantu people | Portuguese ousted from Zanzibar by Omani Arabs | Sultanate of Zanzibar becomes British protectorate | Tanganyika becomes British-mandated territory | Zanzibar becomes independent as a constitutional monarchy | Country under Revolutionary Party of Tanzania (CCM) | CCM wins national elections amid allegations of violence and fraud

and coconuts and their derivatives. Increased output of minerals (chiefly diamonds, gold and iron) has driven recent economic growth, and salt, soda ash, cement, petroleum products, footwear, clothing, wood products and fertiliser are also produced. Tourism is a major source of revenue, especially for Zanzibar. Industry accounts for 28.6 per cent of GDP and services for 47.6 per cent.

The main trading partners are China, India, South Africa and Kenya. Principal exports are gold, coffee, cashew nuts, manufactures (especially clothing) and cotton. The main imports are consumer goods, machinery and transport equipment, industrial raw materials and crude oil.
GNI – US$50.4bn; US$905 per capita (2017; mainland Tanzania only)
Annual average growth of GDP – 6.5 per cent (2017 est)
Inflation rate – 5.4 per cent (2017 est)
Population below poverty line – 22.8 per cent (2015 est)
Total external debt – US$15.88bn (2017 est)
Imports – US$13,419m (2014)
Exports – US$6,880m (2014)

BALANCE OF PAYMENTS
Trade – US$7,191m deficit (2013)
Current Account – US$2,009m deficit (2016)

Trade with UK	2016	2017
Imports from UK	£102,235,010	£86,558,545
Exports to UK	£29,462,589	£15,747,899

COMMUNICATIONS
Airports – The principal international airports are at Dar es Salaam, Kilimanjaro and Zanzibar
Waterways – The three great lakes (Tanganyika, Victoria and Nyasa) are the principal trade routes with neighbouring countries; the main seaports are Dar es Salaam, Tanga, Mtwara, Zanzibar, Mkoani and Wete (Pemba)
Roadways and railways – 86,472km; 3,689km
Telecommunications – 129,597 fixed lines and 40 million mobile subscriptions (2016); there were 6.8 internet users in 2016
Internet code and IDD – tz; 255 (from UK), 44 (to UK)
Major broadcasters – The state-run Tanzania Broadcasting Corporation operates TV and radio stations
Press – Newspapers include the government-owned *Daily News* (English language), and Swahili *Habari Leo* and *Uhuru*
WPFI score – 30,65 (93)

EDUCATION AND HEALTH
Education is compulsory for seven years.
Literacy rate – 76.3 per cent (2015 est)
Gross enrolment ratio (percentage of relevant age group) – primary 81.7 per cent (2015 est), secondary 32.3 per cent, tertiary 3.6 per cent (2013 est)
Health expenditure (per capita) – US$52 (2014)
Hospital beds (per 1,000 people) – 0.7 (2010)
Life expectancy (years) – 62.2 (2017 est)

Mortality rate – 7.6 (2017 est)
Birth rate – 35.6 (2017 est)
Infant mortality rate – 39.9 (2017 est)
HIV/AIDS adult prevalence – 4.7 per cent (2016 est)

THAILAND

Ratcha Anachak Thai – Kingdom of Thailand

Area – 513,120 sq. km
Capital – Bangkok (Krung Thep); population, 10,156,000 (2018 est)
Major cities – Chon Buri, Nonthaburi, Samut Prakan, Udon Thani
Currency – Baht of 100 satang
Population – 68,414,135 rising at 0.30 per cent a year (2017 est), Thai (95.9 per cent), Burmese (2 per cent) (2010 est)
Religion – Buddhist 93.6 per cent, Muslim 4.9 per cent, Christian 1.2 per cent (2010 est)
Language – Thai (official), English, Burmese
Population density – 135 per sq. km (2016)
Urban population – 49.9 per cent (2018 est)
Median age (years) – 37.7 (2017 est)
National anthem – 'Phleng Chat Thai' 'National Anthem of Thailand']
National day – 5 December (Birthday of the King)
Death penalty – Retained (last used 2009)
CPI score – 37 (96)
Military expenditure – US$6,335m (2017)
Conscription – 21 years of age; 24 months

CLIMATE AND TERRAIN
Thailand is divided geographically into four regions: the north is mountainous and forested; to the north-east the semi-arid Korat plateau; the centre is a fertile plain lying in the Chao Phraya basin; and the south is the narrow, mountainous isthmus of Kra. Extremes of elevation range from 2,576m (Doi Inthanon) to 0m (Gulf of Thailand). The principal rivers are the Chao Phraya and its tributaries in the central plains and the Mekong on the northern and eastern borders. The climate is tropical, with a monsoon season from June to October and high humidity.

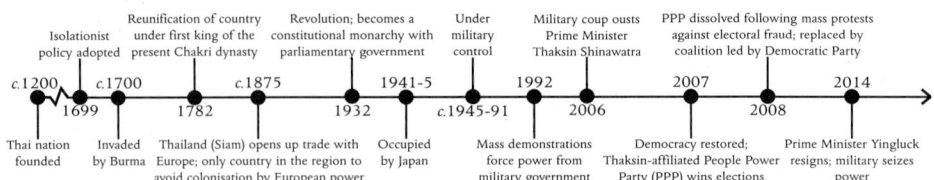

	Reunification of country	Revolution; becomes a	Under	Military coup ousts	PPP dissolved following mass protests
Isolationist	under first king of the	constitutional monarchy with	military	Prime Minister	against electoral fraud; replaced by
policy adopted	present Chakri dynasty	parliamentary government	control	Thaksin Shinawatra	coalition led by Democratic Party

c.1200 — c.1700 — c.1875 — 1941-5 — 1992 — 2007 — 2014
1699 — 1782 — 1932 — c.1945-91 — 2006 — 2008

Thai nation	Invaded	Thailand (Siam) opens up trade with	Occupied	Mass demonstrations	Democracy restored;	Prime Minister Yingluck
founded	by Burma	Europe; only country in the region to	by Japan	force power from	Thaksin-affiliated People Power	resigns; military seizes
		avoid colonisation by European power		military government	Party (PPP) wins elections	power

POLITICS

On 22 May 2014, the Royal Thai Armed Forces conducted a military coup after months of political tension between the ruling Pheu Thai Party and the opposition People's Democratic Reform Committee. Following the successful corruption proceedings filed against Prime Minister Yingluck and her subsequent removal from office on 7 May, martial law was declared by the military on 20 May before a new military government styled the National Council for Peace and Order was established. The military government announced the end of martial law in March 2015 and a new constitution backed by the military was approved in an August 2016 referendum.

Thailand is a constitutional monarchy with a hereditary monarch as head of state. The bicameral National Assembly was reestablished under the 2017 constitution, comprising a 250-member military-appointed senate, with senators serving five-year terms, and a 500-member house of representatives, elected for a four-year-term. The first elections since the coup are planned for November 2018.

HEAD OF STATE

HM The King of Thailand, King Maha Vajiralongkorn Bodindradebayavarangkun (Rama X), *born* 28 July 1952, *succeeded* 13 October 2016

SELECTED GOVERNMENT MEMBERS *AS AT JULY 2018*

Prime Minister, Prayuth Chan-ocha
Deputy Prime Ministers, Prawit Wongsuwan *(Defence);* Prajin Juntong; Chatchai Sareekalaya
Finance, Apisak Tantivorawong
Foreign Affairs, Don Pramidwani

ROYAL THAI EMBASSY

29–30 Queen's Gate, London SW7 5JB
T 020-789 2944 E csinfo@thaiembassyuk.org.uk
W www.thaiembassyuk.org.uk
Ambassador Extraordinary and Plenipotentiary, HE Pisanu Suvanajata, *apptd* 2017

BRITISH EMBASSY

14 Wireless Road, Bangkok 10330
T (+66) (0) 2 305 8333 E info.bangkok@fco.gov.uk W www.gov.uk/government/world/thailand
Ambassador Extraordinary and Plenipotentiary, HE Brian Davidson, *apptd* 2016

FOREIGN RELATIONS

Sovereignty over border territory around the Hindu temple complex at Preah Vihear has been disputed with Cambodia for over a century. Although the temple complex was awarded to Cambodia in 1962, the status of adjacent territory remains unsettled. Tensions increased in 2008, when Cambodia had the temple listed as a UNESCO World Heritage Site, and there has been frequent sporadic fighting in the area between the countries' troops. Both nations agreed to withdraw their troops from the disputed border area in 2011, and in 2013 the International Court of Justice upheld the 1962 ruling and obliged Thailand to withdraw any armed forces stationed in the area.

ECONOMY AND TRADE

Thailand was transformed from an agricultural to an export-orientated industrial economy in the last quarter of the 20th century, sustaining steady growth after its quick recovery from the 1997 economic crisis. Poverty has significantly fallen in this period, afflicting 7.2 per cent of the population in 2015. The 2008 global economic downturn caused the export-dependent economy to contract sharply, and flooding reduced growth to only 0.1 per cent in 2011. Growth increased to 5.5 per cent in 2012, but the tourism sector initially contracted following the 2014 military coup before slowly recovering, helped by greater infrastructure spending.

The agricultural sector generates 8.2 per cent of GDP and employs 31.8 per cent of the workforce. The main crops are rice, cassava, rubber, maize, sugar cane, coconuts and palm oil. In recent years fishing and livestock production have grown in importance. There are reserves of natural gas, lignite, tin, tungsten and lead.

Other industries include textiles and clothing, agricultural processing, beverages, tobacco, cement, mining and light manufacturing (jewellery, electrical appliances, computers and parts), furniture, plastics and cars, and vehicle parts. A major industry is tourism, which has been a significant foreign exchange earner since the 1980s. Industry contributes 36.2 per cent of GDP and services 55.6 per cent.

The main trading partners are Japan, China, the USA and Malaysia. Principal exports are vehicles and vehicle parts, textiles and footwear, fish products, rice, rubber, jewellery, computers and electrical appliances. The main imports are capital goods, intermediate goods and raw materials, consumer goods and fuels.

GNI – US$411.7bn; US$5,960 per capita (2017)
Annual average growth of GDP – 3.7 per cent (2017 est)
Inflation rate – 0.6 per cent (2017 est)
Population below poverty line – 7.2 per cent (2015 est)
Unemployment – 0.7 per cent (2016 est)
Total external debt – US$135.5bn (2017 est)
Imports – US$195,666m (2016)
Exports – US$213,927m (2016)

BALANCE OF PAYMENTS

Trade – US$18,260m surplus (2016)
Current Account – US$48,126m surplus (2017)

Trade with UK	2016	2017
Imports from UK	£1,096,599,753	£1,252,259,208
Exports to UK	£2,784,528,733	£3,024,553,808

COMMUNICATIONS

Airports and waterways – Bangkok is the main international airport and the main seaports are located in Bangkok and Sattahip; there are also 3,701km of navigable inland waterways (4,000km in total)
Roadways and railways – 180,053km (2006 total); 4,071km
Telecommunications – 4.7 million fixed lines and 119.7 million mobile subscriptions (2016); there were 32.4 million internet users in 2016

Internet and IDD – th; 66 (from UK), 1 44 (to UK)
Major broadcasters – The government and military both operate a number of TV and radio stations, including Thai TV3 and Radio Thailand
Press – Leading daily newspapers include the *Bangkok Post* and *The Nation* (both English language), and the *Daily News* (Thai)
WPFI score – 44,31 (140)

EDUCATION AND HEALTH

Primary and lower secondary education is compulsory and free, and upper secondary education is free in government schools.
Literacy rate – 98.2 per cent (2015 est)
Gross enrolment ratio (percentage of relevant age group) – primary 102.7 per cent, secondary 129 per cent, tertiary 48.9 per cent (2015 est)
Health expenditure (per capita) – US$360 (2014)
Life expectancy (years) – 74.9 (2017 est)
Mortality rate – 8 (2017 est)
Birth rate – 11 (2017 est)
Infant mortality rate – 9.2 (2017 est)
HIV/AIDS adult prevalence – 1.1 per cent (2016 est)

TIMOR–LESTE

Republika Demokratika Timor Lorosa'e/Republica Democratica de Timor-Leste – Democratic Republic of Timor-Leste

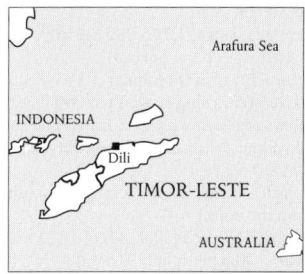

Area – 14,874 sq. km. Includes the enclave of Oecussi
Capital – Dili; population, 281,000 (2018)
Major towns – Baucau, Los Palos, Maliana, Pantemakassar (Oecussi), Same
Currency – US dollar (US$) of 100 cents
Population – 1,291,358 rising at 2.36 per cent a year (2017 est)
Religion – Christian (Roman Catholic 96.9 per cent, Protestant 2.2 per cent), Muslim 0.3 per cent (2005)
Language – Tetum, Portuguese (both official), Indonesian, English, around 16 indigenous languages
Population density – 87 per sq. km (2016)
Urban population – 30.6 per cent (2018 est)
Median age (years) – 18.9 (2017 est)
National anthem – 'Patria' 'Fatherland'
National day – 28 November (Independence Day)
Death penalty – Abolished for all crimes (since 1999)
CPI score – 38 (91)
Military expenditure – US$25.4m (2017)
Literacy rate – 82.4 per cent (2015 est)
Gross enrolment ratio (percentage of relevant age group) – primary 109 per cent (2016 est), secondary 76.8 per cent (2015 est), tertiary 16.7 per cent (2011 est)
Health expenditure (per capita) – US$57 (2014)
Life expectancy (years) – 68.4 (2017 est)
Mortality rate – 5.9 (2017 est)
Birth rate – 33.4 (2017 est)
Infant mortality rate – 35.1 (2017 est)

CLIMATE AND TERRAIN

The republic comprises the eastern half of the island of Timor, plus the enclave of Oecussi, which lies on the northern coast, separated from the rest of the country by the Indonesian province of West Timor. The island, about 296km long and 72km wide, lies at the eastern end of the Malay archipelago and is the largest of the Lesser Sunda Islands. The interior is covered in forests and mountains. Elevation extremes range from 2,963m (Mt Tatamailau) to 0m (Timor Sea). The climate is tropical.

POLITICS

The 2002 constitution established a parliamentary democracy. The president is directly elected for a five-year term, renewable once. The unicameral National Parliament has 65 members, directly elected for a five-year term. The council of ministers is nominated by the prime minister, who is appointed by the president.

The March 2017 presidential election was won in the first round by former guerilla fighter Francisco Guterres of Freitilin. In the 2012 legislative election, the National Congress for Timorese Reconstruction party (CNRT) emerged as the single largest party. The CNRT government resigned in February 2015 and was replaced by a coalition including the CNRT, Fretilin and Democratic parties. Freitlin and the CNRT won the largest share of the votes in the July 2017 legislative election, but after parliament was dissolved in January 2018 fresh elections resulted in victory for the CNRT-led coalition the Change for Progressive Alliance.

HEAD OF STATE
President, Francisco Guterres, *elected* 20 April 2017, *took office* 20 May 2017

SELECTED GOVERNMENT MEMBERS *AS AT AUGUST 2018*
Prime Minister, Taur Matan Rauk
Defence, Filomeno Tirocinado da Paixao de Jesus
Finance, vacant
Foreign Affairs, Dionisio Babo Soares

EMBASSY OF THE DEMOCRATIC REPUBLIC OF TIMOR-LESTE
4 Cavendish Square, London W1G 0PG

T 020-3440 9025
Ambassador Extraordinary and Plenipotentiary, HE Joaquim Antonio Maria Lopes da Fonseca, *apptd* 2013

BRITISH EMBASSY
HE Moazzam Malik, *apptd* 2014, resident at Jakarta, Indonesia

ECONOMY AND TRADE

An internationally funded programme in 2002–5 achieved substantial reconstruction of the infrastructure destroyed in the 1999 post-referendum violence, but civil unrest in 2006 caused further damage and disrupted economic activity. Economic growth since independence is largely down to the exploitation of offshore oil and gas deposits, which has boosted government revenue but has had little impact on unemployment levels; there are no domestic production facilities so oil and gas are piped to Australia for processing. Poverty afflicts over 40 per cent of the population, and coupled with weak civil administration, a low skills base and inadequate infrastructure, economic development has been impeded. Dependence on oil, which accounts for 90 per cent of government revenues, caused the economy to contract in 2017 due to continued low prices.

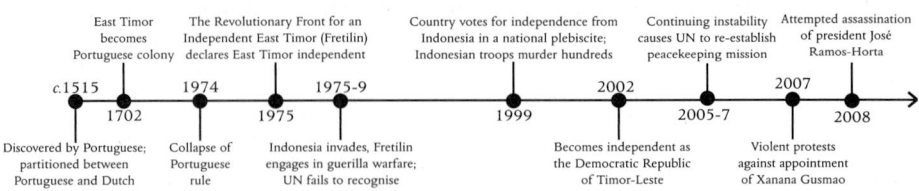

Timeline:

- *East Timor becomes Portuguese colony* — c.1515
- *Discovered by Portuguese; partitioned between Portuguese and Dutch* — 1702
- *The Revolutionary Front for an Independent East Timor (Fretilin) declares East Timor independent* — 1974
- *Collapse of Portuguese rule* — 1975
- *Indonesia invades, Fretilin engages in guerilla warfare; UN fails to recognise annexation* — 1975-9
- *Country votes for independence from Indonesia in a national plebiscite; Indonesian troops murder hundreds* — 1999
- *Becomes independent as the Democratic Republic of Timor-Leste* — 2002
- *Continuing instability causes UN to re-establish peacekeeping mission* — 2005-7
- *Violent protests against appointment of Xanana Gusmao* — 2007
- *Attempted assassination of president José Ramos-Horta* — 2008

Industry contributes 57.8 per cent of GDP, services 32.8 per cent and agriculture 9.4 per cent, although it engages 41 per cent of the population. The main commercial crops are coffee, rice, maize, vegetables, tropical fruits and vanilla. The main trading partners are Australia, Thailand, the USA and EU countries. Principal exports are coffee, oil, used clothing, sandalwood and marble. The main imports are food, fuels and machinery.

GNI – US$2.3bn; US$1,790 per capita (2017)
Annual average growth of GDP – −0.5 per cent (2017 est)
Inflation rate – 1 per cent (2017 est)
Population below poverty line – 41.8 per cent (2014 est)
Unemployment – 4.4 per cent (2014 est)
Total external debt – US$311.5m (2014 est)
Imports – US$578m (2015)
Exports – US$45m (2015)

BALANCE OF PAYMENTS
Trade – US$533 deficit (2015)
Current Account – US$339m deficit (2017)

Trade with UK	2016	2017
Imports from UK	£343,975	£226,516
Exports to UK	£27,812	£49,745

COMMUNICATIONS

Airports and waterways – The international airport and seaport are at Dili
Roadways – There are 2,600 of paved roads, including one major road linking the main townships on the northern coast
Telecommunications – 2,720 fixed lines and 1.5 mobile subscriptions (2016); there were 318,373 internet users in 2016
Internet code and IDD – tl; 670 (from UK), 44 (to UK)
Major broadcasters – Televisao de Timor-Leste and Radio Timor-Leste are the state-owned broadcasters
Press – Major daily newspapers include *Suara Timor Lorosae* (Tetum language), *Diario Nacional* (Portuguese) and the *Timor Post* (English)
WPFI score – 30,81 (95)

TOGO

République togolaise – Togolese Republic

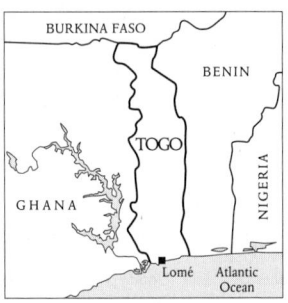

Area – 56,785 sq. km
Capital – Lomé; population, 1,746,000 (2018)
Major cities – Atakpamé, Kara, Sokodé
Currency – Franc CFA of 100 centimes
Population – 7,965,055 rising at 2.64 per cent a year (2017 est); 37 tribes, largest of which are Ewe, Mina and Kabre
Religion – Indigenous beliefs 51 per cent, Christian 29 per cent, Muslim 20 per cent
Language – French (official), Ewe, Mina (in the south), Kabye, Dagomba (in the north)
Population density – 143 per sq. km (2016)
Urban population – 30.6 per cent (2018 est)
Median age (years) – 19.8 (2017 est)
National anthem – 'Salut à toi, pays de nos aïeux' 'Hail to Thee, Land of Our Forefathers'
National day – 27 April (Independence Day)
Death penalty – Abolished for all crimes (since 2009)
CPI score – 32 (117)
Military expenditure – US$88.4m (2017)
Conscription – 18 years of age; 24 months
Literacy rate – 85.1 per cent (2015 est)
Gross enrolment ratio (percentage of relevant age group) – primary 124 per cent (2016 est), secondary 46 per cent (2011 est), tertiary 12 per cent (2016 est)
Health expenditure (per capita) – US$34 (2014)
Hospital beds (per 1,000 people) – 0.7 (2011)
Life expectancy (years) – 65.4 (2017 est)
Mortality rate – 6.9 (2017 est)
Birth rate – 33.3 (2017 est)
Infant mortality rate – 42.2 (2017 est)
HIV/AIDS adult prevalence – 2.1 per cent (2016 est)

CLIMATE AND TERRAIN

From hills in the centre of the country, the terrain declines to savannah in the north and in the south to a plateau that leads to a coastal plain with marshes and lagoons. Elevation extremes range from 986m (Mt Agou) to 0m (Atlantic Ocean). The climate in the south is tropical with two wet seasons (March to July and September to November). In the north it is semi-arid with one wet season (May to September). The average temperature is 27.4°C.

HISTORY AND POLITICS

Germany established a protectorate, Togoland, over the area in 1884, and this was occupied on the outbreak of the First World War by Britain and France. The country was divided between Britain and France as a League of Nations mandate after the war and the mandate was renewed by the UN in 1946. In 1957, following a plebiscite, British Togoland integrated with Ghana when it became independent. French Togoland achieved independence as the Republic of Togo in 1960.

There was a military coup in 1963 led by Gnassingbé Eyadéma, who installed a civilian president. In 1967 Eyadéma overthrew the government and became president himself, introducing a one-party state under his *Rassemblement du peuple togolais* (RPT). Violent demonstrations in 1990 forced the government to introduce a multiparty constitution in 1992. Eyadéma and the RPT were returned to power in the first multiparty elections in 1993 and in two subsequent elections.

After President Eyadéma's death in February 2005, the military attempted to install his son, Faure Gnassingbé, who resigned as acting president following widespread condemnation of the move, only to be elected to the presidency in April 2005. Following reconciliation talks in 2006, the government and opposition leaders signed an accord providing for the participation of opposition parties, and a national unity government was appointed until a legislative election was held in 2007. The election was nevertheless won by the RPT; the 2013 election was won by President Gnassingbé's Union for the Republic (UNIR) party following the RPT's dissolution. President Gnassingbé won the April 2015 presidential election and was re-elected for a third term.

Under the 1992 constitution, the president is directly elected for a five-year term with no term limits. The unicameral National Assembly has 91 members, who are directly elected for a five-year term. The prime minister is appointed by the president and appoints the cabinet in consultation with the president.

HEAD OF STATE

President, Defence, Faure Gnassingbé, *elected* 24 April 2005, *sworn in* 4 May 2005, *re-elected* 2010, 2015

SELECTED GOVERNMENT MEMBERS *AS AT JULY 2018*
Prime Minister, Komi Selom Klassou
Economy and Finance, Sani Yaya
Foreign Affairs, Robert Dussey

EMBASSY OF THE REPUBLIC OF TOGO
8 rue Alfred Roll, 75017 Paris, France
T (+33) (1) 4380 1213
Ambassador Extraordinary and Plenipotentiary, vacant

BRITISH AMBASSADOR
HE Iain Walker, *apptd* 2017, resident in Accra, Ghana

ECONOMY AND TRADE

Progress on economic reform, intended to attract foreign investment and balance the budget, is slow, lacking impetus on privatisation and financial transparency. Resumption of aid to Togo, mostly suspended in the 1990s because of its human rights record, has increased since the 2007 election, and the country had 95 per cent of its external debt written off in 2010. Subsequent steady growth has been assisted by infrastructure spending, including a new airport terminal, and direct foreign investment. In January 2017, the IMF agreed a further loan package worth US$238m over three years.

The economy is predominantly based on agriculture, accounting for 28.1 per cent of GDP, engaging roughly 60 per cent of the workforce and providing most of the country's exports as well as the raw materials for industry. Industrial activity centres on phosphate mining, agricultural processing and manufacture of cement, handicrafts, textiles and beverages. Industry accounts for 21.6 per cent of GDP and 5 per cent of employment. The service sector accounts for 50.3 per cent of GDP.

The main export markets are Benin, Burkina Faso, Niger and India; imports come mainly from China and EU states. Principal exports are re-exports, cotton, phosphates, coffee and cocoa. The main imports are machinery and equipment, foodstuffs and petroleum products.

GNI – US$4.7bn; US$610 per capita (2017)
Annual average growth of GDP – 5 per cent (2017 est)
Inflation rate – 0.8 per cent (2017 est)
Population below poverty line – 55.1 per cent (2015 est)
Total external debt – US$1.387bn (2017 est)
Imports – US$1,825m (2016)
Exports – US$761m (2016)

BALANCE OF PAYMENTS
Trade – US$1,064m deficit (2016)
Current Account – US$460m deficit (2015)

Trade with UK	2016	2017
Imports from UK	£123,264,137	£37,416,726
Exports to UK	£547,050	£650,257

COMMUNICATIONS
Airports – The principal airport is at Lomé
Roadways and railways – 2,447km; 568km
Telecommunications – 33,817 fixed lines in use and 5.5 million mobile subscriptions (2016); there were 877,310 internet users in 2016
Internet code and IDD – tg; 228 (from UK), 44 (to UK)
Major broadcasters – Public broadcasting is provided by Radio Togolaise, Television Togolaise and Telesports TV
Press – Major daily newspapers include *Togo-Presse, Liberté* and *Forum de la Semaine* (all French language)
WPFI score – 30,23 (86)

TONGA

Pule'anga Tonga – Kingdom of Tonga

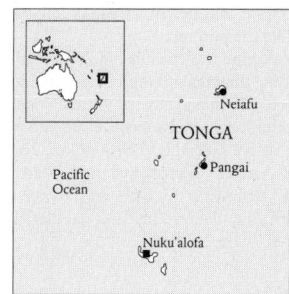

Area – 747 sq. km
Capital – Nuku'alofa, on Tongatapu; population, 23,000 (2018 est)
Major towns – Neiafu, on Vava'u, Pangai, on Lifuka
Currency – Pa'anga (T$) of 100 seniti
Population – 106,479 falling at 0.05 per cent a year (2017 est)

Religion – Christian (Free Wesleyan 37.3 per cent, Mormon 16.8 per cent, Roman Catholic 15.6 per cent, Free Church of Tonga 11.4 per cent) (2006 est)
Language – English, Tongan (both official)
Population density – 150 per sq. km (2016)
Urban population – 23.1 per cent (2018 est)
Median age (years) – 23 (2017 est)
National anthem – 'Koe Fasi Oe Tu'i Oe Otu Tonga' 'Song of the King of the Tonga Islands'
National day – 4 November (Constitution Day)
Death penalty – Retained (last used 1982)
Literacy rate – 99.4 per cent (2015 est)
Gross enrolment ratio (percentage of relevant age group) – primary 108.1 per cent, secondary 90.1 per cent (2014 est)
Health expenditure (per capita) – US$213 (2014)
Life expectancy (years) – 76.4 (2017 est)
Mortality rate – 4.9 (2017 est)
Birth rate – 22.2 (2017 est)
Infant mortality rate – 11.3 (2017 est)

CLIMATE AND TERRAIN
Tonga comprises over 170 islands in three groups, situated in the south Pacific Ocean some 724km east-south-east of Fiji. Most of the islands are of coral formation, but some are volcanic (Tofua, Kao and Niuafo'ou or 'Tin Can' Island). Elevation extremes range from 1,033m (on Kao Island) to 0m (Pacific Ocean). The climate is tropical, moderated by trade winds, with an average temperature of 25.4°C.

HISTORY AND POLITICS
The islands were settled by Polynesians from *c*.1000 AD. They were visited by European explorers from the 17th century. The country was reunited in 1845 after a civil war, and a modern constitution adopted in 1875. Tonga became a British protectorate in 1900, and regained full independence on 4 June 1970.

A pro-democracy movement began in 1992 and gathered momentum throughout the 1990s, with the first political party being established in 1994. Following consultation on political and constitutional reform in 2005 and negotiations in 2007, a commission reported in 2009, recommending reducing the monarchy to a ceremonial role and introducing a popularly elected legislature. These constitutional changes took effect with the 2010 legislative election.

In the 2017 legislative election, the Democratic Party of the Friendly Islands (DPFI) maintained power and extended its control over the Legislative Assembly. 'Akilisi Pohiva of the DPFI became prime minister in 2014, becoming the first commoner to hold the position.

The 1875 constitution was amended in 2003 to give greater powers to the king; the present king relinquished some of his executive powers in 2008 and most of the remainder in 2010, when new constitutional arrangements came into effect. The unicameral Legislative Assembly *(Fale Alea)* has 26 members: nine hereditary nobles elected by their peers, and 17 popularly elected representatives who serve a three-year term. The 14-member privy council acts as a cabinet. The prime minister is elected by the legislature.

HEAD OF STATE
HM The King of Tonga, King Tupou VI, *born* 12 July 1959, *acceded* 18 March 2012

Heir, HM Crown Prince of Tonga Tupouto'a 'Ulukalala, *born* 17 September 1985

SELECTED GOVERNMENT MEMBERS *AS AT JULY 2018*
Prime Minister, Foreign Affairs, Samiuela 'Akilisi Pohiva
Deputy Prime Minister, Semisi Sika
Finance, Pohiva Tu'i'onetoa

TONGA HIGH COMMISSION
36 Molyneux Street, London W1H 5BQ
T 020-7724 5828 E office@tongahighcom.co.uk
High Commissioner, vacant

BRITISH HIGH COMMISSIONER
HE Melanie Hopkins, *apptd* 2016, resident at Suva, Fiji

ECONOMY AND TRADE
There are few natural resources and the country is dependent on foreign aid and remittances from Tongans working abroad. The government is encouraging the development of a private sector and committing increased funds towards education and health, while deep-sea mining and renewable energy offer investment opportunities.

The main economic activities are agriculture, fishing and tourism; the latter is the second-largest source of foreign exchange revenue after remittances. The main crops are squashes, coconuts, bananas, vanilla beans, cocoa, coffee, sweet potatoes and cassava. Fish is an important staple food. A small light industry sector processes agricultural produce.

The main export markets are Hong Kong, the USA and New Zealand; imports come chiefly from Fiji, New Zealand and the USA. Principal exports are squashes, fish, vanilla beans and root crops. The main imports are foodstuffs, machinery and transport equipment, fuels and chemicals.
GNI – US$0.4bn; US$4,010 per capita (2017)
Annual average growth of GDP – 3.1 per cent (2017 est)
Inflation rate – 7.5 per cent (2017 est)
Population below poverty line – 24 per cent (2004)
Total external debt – US$233.5m (2017 est)
Imports – US$206m (2015)
Exports – US$23m (2014)

BALANCE OF PAYMENTS
Trade – US$196m deficit (2014)
Current Account – US$56.5m deficit (2015)

Trade with UK	2016	2017
Imports from UK	£396,714	£943,832
Exports to UK	£572,367	£252,149

COMMUNICATIONS
Airports and waterways – There is one airport; the principal port is Nuku'alofa
Roadways – 680km, of which 184km are paved
Telecommunications – There are 11,000 main telephone lines in use and 80,000 mobile subscriptions (2016); there were 42,552 internet users in 2016
Internet code and IDD – to; 676 (from UK), 44 (to UK)
Media – The government-run Tonga Broadcasting Commission operates TV and radio stations; there are no daily newspapers
WPFI score – 25,68 (51)

TRINIDAD AND TOBAGO

Republic of Trinidad and Tobago

Area – 5,128 sq. km
Capital – Port of Spain, on Trinidad; population, 544,000 (2018)
Major towns – Chaguanas, San Fernando, Scarborough (Tobago)
Currency – Trinidad and Tobago dollar (T$) of 100 cents
Population – 1,218,208 falling at 0.20 per cent a year (2017 est)
Religion – Christian (Protestant 32.1 per cent, Roman Catholic 21.6 per cent, other 20.5 per cent), Hindu 18.2 per cent, Muslim 5 per cent, Jehovah's Witnesses 1.5 per cent (2011 est)
Language – English (official), Caribbean Hindustani (a dialect of Hindi), French, Spanish, Chinese
Population density – 267 per sq. km (2016)
Urban population – 53.2 per cent (2018 est)
Median age (years) – 36 (2017 est)
National anthem – 'Forged from the Love of Liberty'
National day – 31 August (Independence Day)
Death penalty – Retained (last used 1999)
CPI score – 41 (77)
Military expenditure – US$202m (2017)

CLIMATE AND TERRAIN

Trinidad, the most southerly of the West Indian islands, lies 11km off the north coast of Venezuela. The island is mostly flat, with low mountains, the Northern Range, across almost its entire northern width and some low hills in the centre. Elevation extremes range from 940m (Mt Aripo) to 0m (Caribbean Sea). Pitch Lake, on the south-west coast, is the world's largest natural source of asphalt.

Tobago lies 30km north-east of Trinidad. The island has a range of hills, Main Ridge, running along its length; the highest point is 549m. Several islands, mainly, Chacachacare, Huevos, Monos and Gaspar Grande, lie west of Corozal Point, the north-west extremity of Trinidad.

The climate is tropical, with a wet season from June to December. Temperatures are constant all year round.

HISTORY AND POLITICS

Trinidad is believed to be the oldest site of human habitation in the Caribbean archipelago, with excavated human remains dating back 7,200 years. The islands were home to a number of indigenous peoples, including the Nepuyo, Yaio and Caribs.

Trinidad and Tobago were discovered by Columbus in 1498. Trinidad was colonised in 1532 by Spain, capitulated to the British in 1797 and was ceded to Britain in 1802. Tobago was colonised by the Dutch from the 1630s but subsequently changed hands numerous times until it was ceded to Britain by France in 1814. The two islands were amalgamated into a single British colony in 1889. Internal self-government was granted in 1959 and independence was attained in 1962; the country became a republic in 1976.

The People's National Movement (PNM) has dominated post-independence politics, only out of office in 1986–91, 1995–2001 and 2010–15. The PNM won the 2009 election for the Tobago legislature, but lost the early general election in 2010 to the People's Partnership coalition, which took office under Kamla Persad-Bissessar, the country's first female prime minister. The PNM reclaimed control of the House of Representatives in legislative elections in September 2015, with Keith Rowley becoming prime minister. Independent candidate Anthony Carmona was replaced by Paula-Mae Weekes in March 2018, making her the nation's first woman to take office as president.

Under the 1976 constitution, the president is elected for a five-year term by an electoral college consisting of both houses of the legislature, renewable once. The bicameral parliament comprises the House of Representatives and the senate. The former has 41 members directly elected for a five-year term. The senate has 31 members, of whom 16 are appointed on the advice of the prime minister, six on the advice of the leader of the opposition and nine at the discretion of the president, to serve a five-year term.

Since 1980 Tobago has had internal self-government through its House of Assembly, which has 16 members, 12 directly elected and four appointed, who serve a four-year term.

HEAD OF STATE
President, Paula-Mae Weekes, *took office* 19 March 2018

SELECTED GOVERNMENT MEMBERS *AS AT JULY 2018*
Prime Minister, Keith Rowley
Attorney-General, Faris al-Rawi
Finance, Colm Imbert
Foreign Affairs, Dennis Moses

HIGH COMMISSION OF THE REPUBLIC OF TRINIDAD AND TOBAGO
42 Belgrave Square, London SW1X 8NT
T 020-7245 9351 W www.tthighcommission.co.uk
High Commissioner, HE Orville London, *apptd* 2017

BRITISH HIGH COMMISSION
PO Box 778, 19 St Clair Avenue, St Clair, Port of Spain
T (+868) 350 0444
W www.gov.uk/government/world/trinidad-and-tobago
High Commissioner, HE Tim Stew, MBE, *apptd* 2015

ECONOMY AND TRADE

The country is the most prosperous in the Caribbean, owing largely to its oil and natural gas reserves, but the government has encouraged diversification into petrochemicals, aluminium, plastics, financial services and tourism to reduce its dependence on the energy sector. After years of strong growth, the economy contracted 2009–12 as export demand and oil prices fell, and fell into recession again between 2014–17. Crime and bureaucracy deter greater foreign investment.

The agricultural sector is small, accounting for 0.4 per cent of GDP; the main products are cocoa, rice, citrus fruits, coconut water, vegetables and poultry. Apart from oil and gas extraction and processing, the main industries are tourism, food processing, steel products, cement, beverages and cotton textiles.

The main trading partners are the USA, Russia, Argentina and Columbia. Principal exports are oil and petroleum products, liquefied natural gas, chemicals, steel products, beverages, cereals and cereal products, cocoa, fish, citrus fruits, cosmetics and plastic packaging. The main imports are fuels, lubricants, machinery, transport equipment, manufactured goods, food, chemicals and livestock.

GNI – US$21bn; US$15,350 per capita (2017)
Annual average growth of GDP – –3.2 per cent (2016 est)
Inflation rate – 3.2 per cent (2017 est)
Population below poverty line – 20 per cent (2014 est)
Unemployment – 4.1 per cent (2017 est)
Total external debt – US$10.07bn (2017 est)
Imports – US$6,495m (2015)
Exports – US$7,285m (2015)

BALANCE OF PAYMENTS
Trade – US$790m surplus (2015)
Current Account – US$2,325m surplus (2017 est)

Trade with UK	2016	2017
Imports from UK	£124,049,894	£107,600,048
Exports to UK	£64,348,013	£123,624,090

COMMUNICATIONS
Airports and waterways – The international airport is at Port of Spain on Trinidad, and Tobago is served by Crown Point airport; the three main ports are Scarborough (Tobago), Port of Spain and Point Lisas
Roadways – 4,252km
Telecommunications – 272,187 fixed lines and 2.16 million mobile subscriptions (2016); there were 846,000 internet users in 2016
Internet code and IDD – tt; 1 868 (from UK), 011 44 (to UK)
Media – CTV and Talk City 91.1 (radio) are the state broadcasters; leading daily newspapers include *Newsday, Trinidad Guardian* and *Trinidad and Tobago Express*
WPFI score – 22,79 (39)

EDUCATION AND HEALTH
Education is free at all state-owned and government-assisted denominational schools, and at certain faculties at the University of the West Indies.
Literacy rate – 99.6 per cent (2015 est)
Gross enrolment ratio (percentage of relevant age group) – primary 106 per cent (2010 est); secondary 90 per cent (2011 est)
Health expenditure (per capita) – US$1,136 (2014)
Hospital beds (per 1,000 people) – 3 (2014)
Life expectancy (years) – 73.1 (2017 est)
Mortality rate – 8.8 (2017 est)
Birth rate – 12.7 (2017 est)
Infant mortality rate – 22.3 (2017 est)
HIV/AIDS adult prevalence – 1.2 (2016 est)

TUNISIA
Al-Jumhuriyah at-Tunisiyah – Tunisian Republic

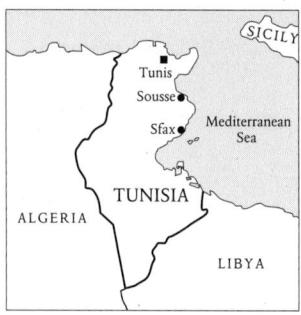

Area – 163,610 sq. km
Capital – Tunis; population, 2,291,000 (2018 est)
Major cities – Sfax, Sousse
Currency – Tunisian dinar of 1,000 millimes
Population – 11,403,800 rising at 1.01 per cent a year (2017 est)
Religion – Muslim 99.1 per cent (predominantly Sunni) (est); small minorities of Christians and Jews. Sunni Islam is the official religion
Language – Arabic (official), French, Berber
Population density – 74 per sq. km (2016)
Urban population – 68.9 per cent (2018 est)
Median age (years) – 31.6 (2017 est)
National anthem – 'Humat al-Hima' 'Defenders of the Homeland'
National day – 20 March (Independence Day)
Death penalty – Retained (last used 1991)
CPI score – 42 (74)
Military expenditure – US$835m (2017)
Conscription – 20–23 years of age; 12 months (selective)

CLIMATE AND TERRAIN
A central plain rises to mountains in the north, and in the semi-arid south merges into the Sahara desert. There are salt lakes in the west. Elevation extremes range from 1,544m (Jebel ech Chambi) to −17m (Shatt al Gharsah). The northern and coastal regions have a Mediterranean climate, while there is a desert climate in the south. Average temperatures range from 10.9°C in January to 30°C in August.

HISTORY AND POLITICS
The area was ruled successively by the Phoenicians, Carthaginians, Romans, Byzantines and Arabs before becoming a largely autonomous part of the Ottoman Empire in the 16th century. In the 19th century French influence grew and it was formally declared a French protectorate in 1883. It was briefly occupied by Germany during the Second World War (1942–3), and became independent as a monarchy under the bey, or governor, in 1956. In 1957 the bey was deposed and the country became a republic under one-party rule, with Habib Bourguiba as president.

Multiparty legislative elections were held in 1981, but the ruling party, the Constitutional Democratic Rally (RCD), retained its grip on power until 2011. Although proclaimed president for life in 1975, President Bourguiba was deposed in 1987 on the grounds of senility by the prime minister Zine el-Abidine Ben Ali. Ben Ali was subsequently elected president in unopposed elections in 1989 and 1994, and in multiparty elections in 1999, 2004 and 2009.

Nationwide protests against Ben Ali's authoritarian regime and unemployment broke out in December 2010, forcing him to leave office and flee the country in January 2011. Moncef Marzouki was elected interim president by the new Constituent Assembly in December 2011; his nomination followed legislative elections in which the former opposition party al-Nahda won the most seats but not an overall majority. Attempts to implement some Islamic reforms by the moderate Islamist government resulted in protests by supporters of secularism and more violent demonstrations from Salafi Islamists.

In July 2013, the assassination of the Arab nationalist politician Mohamed Brahmi caused a general strike and calls for the government to resign. An interim government was created in December 2013, with new electoral laws approved in May 2014. In the October 2014 legislative elections, the secular Nidaa Tounes emerged as the single largest party, winning 85 seats. A coalition government was formed in February 2015 comprising Nidaa Tounes, Afek Tunis, the Islamist al-Nahda and the Free Patriotic Union. Prime Minister Habib Essed lost a vote of no-confidence in August 2016 over the government's handling of security and the economy, and Youssef Chahed was appointed in his stead.

The new constitution was implemented on 26 January 2014. The president is directly elected by absolute majority popular vote for a five-year term, renewable once. The legislature, the Assembly of People's Representatives *(Majlis Nuwab al-Shab)*, is unicameral and directly elected for a five-year term. It has 217 seats, 18 of which are reserved for Tunisians abroad.

HEAD OF STATE
President, Beji Caid Essebsi, *elected* 22 December 2014, *sworn in* 31 December 2014

SELECTED GOVERNMENT MEMBERS *AS AT JULY 2018*
Prime Minister, Youssef Chahed
Finance, Ridha Chalghoum
Foreign Affairs, Khemaies Jhinaoui
Interior, Ghazi Jeribi (acting)

EMBASSY OF TUNISIA
29 Prince's Gate, London SW7 1QG
T 020-7584 8117 E london@tunisianembassy.co.uk
W www.at-londres.diplomatie.gov.tn
Ambassador Extraordinary and Plenipotentiary, HE Nabil Ben Khedher, *apptd* 2017

BRITISH EMBASSY
Rue du Lac Windermere, Les Berges du Lac, 1053 Tunis
T (+216) (71) 108 700 E britishembassytunis@fco.gov.uk
W www.gov.uk/government/world/tunisia
Ambassador Extraordinary and Plenipotentiary, HE Louise de Sousa, *apptd* 2016

ECONOMY AND TRADE
The economy is diverse and an increasing proportion is in private ownership, but limited by corruption, inequality and a depleted tourism industry. Growth was steady from the late 1990s until 2008, although the economy contracted in 2009 as export demand dropped. The 2011 Arab Spring led to years of economic neglect amid political instability that resulted in several downgrades of Tunisia's credit rating. The economy suffered further due to terrorist attacks on tourist sites in 2015 in which nearly 60 people were killed, coupled with unrest in 2016 provoked by high unemployment. A sizeable informal economy, high levels of joblessness especially among youth, economic disparities between the more developed coastal region and the impoverished interior,

and strikes in the phosphate sector have also slowed economic growth.

Agriculture and fisheries account for 9.9 per cent of GDP; the main products are olives, grain, tomatoes, citrus fruits, sugar beets, dates, almonds, meat and dairy products. The main industries are oil production, mining (principally phosphates and iron ore), tourism, processing agricultural products and manufacture of textiles, footwear and beverages.

The main trading partners are EU countries, especially France and Italy. Principal exports are clothing, semi-finished goods and textiles, agricultural products, mechanical goods, phosphates and chemicals, hydrocarbons and electrical equipment. The main imports are textiles, machinery and equipment, hydrocarbons, chemicals and foodstuffs.

GNI – US$40.4bn; US$3,500 per capita (2017)
Annual average growth of GDP – 2.3 per cent (2017 est)
Inflation rate – 4.5 per cent (2016 est)
Population below poverty line – 15.5 per cent (2010 est)
Unemployment – 13 per cent (2016 est)
Total external debt – US$31.05bn (2017 est)
Imports – US$19,456m (2016)
Exports – US$13,483m (2016)

BALANCE OF PAYMENTS
Trade – US$5,973m deficit (2016)
Current Account – US$3,694m deficit (2016)

Trade with UK	2016	2017
Imports from UK	£181,498,002	£150,067,601
Exports to UK	£142,848,786	£155,186,095

COMMUNICATIONS
Airports and waterways – The principal airports are at Tunis, Monastir and Djerba, and the main ports include Bizerte, Sfax and Rades
Roadways and railways – 14,756km; 2,165km
Telecommunications – 974 million fixed lines and 14.3 million mobile subscriptions (2016); there were 5.7 million internet users in 2016
Internet code and IDD – tn; 216 (from UK), 44 (to UK)
Major broadcasters – Al-Watania (TV) and Tunisian Radio are the state broadcasters
Press – Major daily newspapers include *La Presse* (French language), and *Esshafa* and *Assabah* (both Arabic)
WPFI score – 30,91 (97)

EDUCATION AND HEALTH
There are 11 years of free and compulsory education.
Literacy rate – 98.1 per cent (2015 est)
Gross enrolment ratio (percentage of relevant age group) – primary 115 per cent, secondary 93 per cent, tertiary 33 per cent (2016 est)
Health expenditure (per capita) – US$305 (2014)
Hospital beds (per 1,000 people) – 2.2 (2014)
Life expectancy (years) – 75.7 (2017 est)
Mortality rate – 6.3 (2017 est)
Birth rate – 18.2 (2017 est)
Infant mortality rate – 12.1 (2017 est)
HIV / AIDS adult prevalence – 0.1 per cent (2016 est)

TURKEY

Turkiye Cumhuriyeti – Republic of Turkey

Area – 783,562 sq. km
Capital – Ankara (Angora), in Asia; population, 4,919,000 (2018 est)
Major cities – Adana, Antalya, Bursa, Gaziantep, Istanbul, Izmir, Konya
Currency – Turkish lira (TL) of 100 kurus
Population – 80,845,215 rising at 0.52 per cent a year (2017 est); Turkish (70–5 per cent), Kurdish (19 per cent) (2016 est)
Religion – Muslim (predominantly Sunni) 99.8 per cent (est)
Language – Turkish (official), Kurdish, Dimli, Azeri, Kabardian
Population density – 105 per sq. km (2016)
Urban population – 68.9 per cent (2018 est)
Median age (years) – 30.9 (2017 est)
National anthem – 'Istiklal Marsi' 'The Independence March'
National day – 29 October (Republic Day)
Death penalty – Abolished for all crimes (since 2004)
CPI score – 40 (81)
Military expenditure – US$18,190m (2017)
Conscription – 21–41 years of age, male only; 12 months (selective)

CLIMATE AND TERRAIN

Turkey in Europe consists of the relatively low-lying area of Eastern Thrace, including the cities of Istanbul and Edirne, and is separated from Asia by the Bosporus at Istanbul and by the Sea of Marmara and the Dardanelles (a strait about 64km in length, with a width varying from 1.6km to 6.4km).

Turkey in Asia comprises the whole of Asia Minor or Anatolia. Western Anatolia consists of a high central plateau with narrow coastal plains fringed by mountains in the north and south. Eastern Anatolia is mountainous, the land falling to a plateau between the mountains and the Syrian border. Elevation extremes range from 5,166m (Mt Ararat) to 0m (Mediterranean Sea). The Euphrates and Tigris rivers rise in the eastern mountains, which also contain many lakes, including Lake Van. Anatolia is prone to earthquakes.

The climate is temperate, but more extreme in the interior. Average temperatures range from 0.2°C in January to 23.1°C in August.

POLITICS

The 1982 constitution has been amended several times, significantly in 2010 when parliamentary control over the judiciary and the military was increased. Since June 2018, the president is directly elected for a five-year term, renewable once. The unicameral Turkish Grand National Assembly has 600 members who were directly elected for a five-year term. The post of prime minister was abolished in 2018 to consolidate presidential power.

Tension between secularists and Islamists has grown in recent years, particularly since the Islamic-based Justice and Development Party (AKP), led by Recep Tayyip Erdogan, came to power in 2002. Secularists' concerns about the AKP's agenda caused a four-month political crisis in 2007, preventing the election of a new president and leading outgoing President Sezer to refuse approval of constitutional amendments. The impasse was ended by early legislative elections in July 2007, in which the AKP won a greatly increased majority; it retained its overall majority in the legislative elections in June 2018.

Legislative elections in June 2018 were won by an AKP-led coalition, who secured 344 seats. The pro-Kurdish People's Democratic Party (HDP) won 67 seats, while an alliance of three opposition parties opposed to Erdogan's presidential reforms won 189 seats. In simultaneous presidential elections President Erdogan consolidated his grip on the country following the July 2016 attempted military coup. Constitutional amendments paving the way for an executive presidency were approved by the country in April 2017, and potentially allows Erdogan to rule until 2032.

HEAD OF STATE
President, Recep Tayyip Erdogan, *elected* 10 August 2014, *sworn in* 28 August 2014, *re-elected* 24 June 2018

SELECTED GOVERNMENT MEMBERS *AS AT JULY 2018*
Defence, Hulusi Akar
Finance, Berat Albayrak
Foreign Affairs, Mevlut Cavusoglu

EMBASSY OF THE REPUBLIC OF TURKEY
43 Belgrave Square, London SW1X 8PA
T 020-7393 0202 E embassy.london@mfa.gov.tr
W www.london.emb.mfa.gov.tr
Ambassador Extraordinary and Plenipotentiary, HE Abdurrahman Bilgic, *apptd* 2014

BRITISH EMBASSY
Sehit Ersan Caddesi 46/A, Cankaya, Ankara
T (+90) (312) 455 3344 E info.officer@fco.gov.uk
W www.gov.uk/government/world/turkey
Ambassador Extraordinary and Plenipotentiary, HE Sir Dominick Chilcott, KCMG, *apptd* 2018

INSURGENCIES
Turkey's 12 million Kurds are the majority population in the south-east of the country, and have sought greater political and cultural rights for many years. The Kurdistan Workers' Party (PKK) has fought a guerrilla war for an ethnic homeland in the

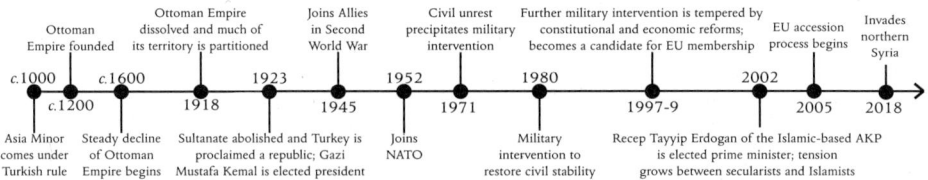

south-east since 1984 and has been blamed for bombings in other parts of Turkey. Conflict on the Turkey–Iraq border has caused tension in relations with Iraq, especially in 2008 after Turkish military incursions into the autonomous Kurdish area in northern Iraq. The government started to seek a political solution to the violence in 2009, introducing measures to increase Kurdish language rights and reduce the military presence in the south-east.

Following a statement requesting a ceasefire by jailed PKK leader Abdullah Ocalan, Kurdish fighters withdrew from Turkey in 2013. In July 2015, the Turkish Air Force bombed PKK bases in Iraq following an apparent attack by the PKK near the Turkish town of Diyarbakir that killed two soldiers. In early 2016, a hardline faction of the PKK called the Kurdistan Freedom Hawks (TAK) claimed responsibility for at least two bomb attacks in Ankara that killed 75 people in total. In January 2018, Turkish forces began an invasion of Kurdish-held territory in northern Syria, which included attacking the USA's Kurdish allies, causing hundreds of thousands to flee the region.

ECONOMY AND TRADE

The economy combines modern industry and commerce with a traditional agriculture sector. The private sector is growing steadily following large-scale privatisations of basic industry, banking, transport and communications, but recent government interference to target political opponents has shaken confidence. Financial and fiscal reforms from 2002 achieved economic growth, but continued violence – notably a terror attack on Istanbul's Ataturk airport in June 2016 – political instability and security concerns remain. Turkey's credit rating was consequently downgraded by three agencies between 2016 and 2017. Sanctions imposed by the US in 2018 over diplomatic disputes, including Turkish aggression against US allies in Syria, resulted in the lira plummeting 34 per cent against the US dollar in the first seven months of the year as fears of a trade war rose. Declining oil export revenues, rising unemployment and inflation, and a large government deficit have limited investor confidence.

The agricultural sector accounts for 6.7 per cent of GDP and employs 18.4 per cent of the workforce. The principal crops are tobacco, cotton, grain, olives, sugar beets, pulses, nuts, citrus and other fruits, and livestock products. A diverse industrial sector is dominated by textiles and clothing, but the automotive, electronics and petrochemical sectors have recently overtaken the former in exports. Food processing, mining, iron and steel, construction, timber and paper are also important industries. Turkey is also a destination and a transit route for oil and gas from central Asian countries. Tourism is a major industry and source of foreign revenue, which has strengthened in 2018 thanks for the falling lira. Industry contributes 31.8 per cent of GDP and services 61.4 per cent.

The main trading partners are EU countries (especially Germany), Russia, China and the UAE. Principal exports are clothing, foodstuffs, textiles, metal manufactures and transport equipment. The main imports are machinery, chemicals, semi-finished manufactures, fuels and transport equipment.

GNI – US$882.9bn; US$10,930 per capita (2017)
Annual average growth of GDP – 5.1 per cent (2017 est)
Inflation rate – 10.9 per cent (2017 est)
Population below poverty line – 21.9 per cent (2015 est)
Unemployment – 11.2 per cent (2017 est)
Total external debt – US$429.6bn (2017 est)
Imports – US$198,484m (2016)
Exports – US$142,790m (2016)

BALANCE OF PAYMENTS
Trade – US$55,694m deficit (2016)
Current Account – US$47,389m deficit (2017)

Trade with UK	2016	2017
Imports from UK	£4,566,979,968	£7,150,156,880
Exports to UK	£9,360,271,956	£8,016,556,674

COMMUNICATIONS

Airports and waterways – The principal airports are at Istanbul and Ankara, and the main ports are at Istanbul (Europe) and Izmir (Asia)
Roadways and railways – 352,268km; 12,008km
Telecommunications – 11.1 million fixed lines and 75 million mobile subscriptions (2016); there were 46.8 million internet users in 2016
Internet code and IDD – tr; 90 (from UK), 44 (to UK)
Major broadcasters – Turkish Radio Television (TRT) is the country's public broadcaster, and the country has over 300 private television channels and more than 1,000 private radio stations
Press – Major national daily newspapers include *Hurriyet, Milliyet* and *Cumhuriyet*
WPFI score – 53,50 (157)

EDUCATION AND HEALTH

Education is free and compulsory from the ages of six to 14.
Literacy rate – 99.2 per cent (2015 est)
Gross enrolment ratio (percentage of relevant age group) – primary 106.9 per cent, secondary 100.3 per cent (2013 est), tertiary 86.3 per cent (2014 est)
Health expenditure (per capita) – US$568 (2014)
Hospital beds (per 1,000 people) – 2.7 (2013)
Life expectancy (years) – 75 (2017 est)
Mortality rate – 6 (2017 est)
Birth rate – 15.7 (2017 est)
Infant mortality rate – 17.6 (2017 est)

TURKMENISTAN

Area – 488,100 sq. km
Capital – Ashgabat; population, 810,000 (2018)
Major cities – Dashoguz, Turkmenabat
Currency – Manat of 100 tennesi
Population – 5,351,277 rising at 1.12 per cent a year (2017 est); Turkmen (85 per cent), Uzbek (5.0 per cent), Russian (4.0 per cent) (2016 est)
Religion – Muslim 89 per cent (majority Sunni), Christian 9 per cent (mainly Eastern Orthodox) (est)
Language – Turkmen (official), Russian, Uzbek
Population density – 12 per sq. km (2016)
Urban population – 51.6 per cent (2018 est)
Median age (years) – 27.9 (2017 est)
National anthem – 'Garassyz, Bitarap Turkmenistanyn Dowlet Gimni' 'National Anthem of Independent, Neutral Turkmenistan'

National day – 27 October (Independence Day, 1991)
Death penalty – Abolished for all crimes (since 1999)
CPI score – 19 (167)
Conscription – 18–27 years of age; 24 months
Literacy rate – 100 per cent (2011 est)
Health expenditure (per capita) – US$187 (2014)
Hospital beds (per 1,000 people) – 7.4 (2013)
Life expectancy (years) – 70.4 (2017 est)
Mortality rate – 6.1 (2017 est)
Birth rate – 18.2 (2017 est)
Infant mortality rate – 34.3 (2017 est)

CLIMATE AND TERRAIN

Over 80 per cent of the country is taken up by the Kara Kum (Black Sands) desert. There are mountains in the south and along the Iranian border, and areas below sea level along the edges of the Caspian Sea. Elevation extremes range from 3,139m (Gora Ayribaba) to −81m (Vpadina Akchanaya, although Lake Sarygamysh sometimes has a lower elevation because of fluctuations in its water level). There is a subtropical desert climate. Average temperatures range from 1.8°C in January to 29.7°C in July.

HISTORY AND POLITICS

Turkmenistan was conquered successively by the Persians, Greeks (under Alexander the Great), Parthians, Arabs and Mongols from the sixth century BC. From the early 19th century Turkmenistan was gradually incorporated into the Russian Empire. A Turkmen revolt against Russian rule in 1916 brought a period of autonomy until 1921, when Soviet control over Turkmenistan was established and it became an Autonomous Soviet Socialist Republic. Turkmenistan became a full republic of the USSR in 1925. It declared its independence from the USSR on 27 October 1991.

Saparmurat Niyazov became leader of the Turkmen Communist Party in 1985, and was elected president in 1990, becoming president for life in 2004. His autocratic regime, through harassment and authoritarianism, prevented the development of any effective political opposition or press freedom, rejecting political pluralism in favour of a cult of personality. After President Niyazov's death in 2006, Gurbanguly Berdimuhammedov was elected president, and was re-elected with an overwhelming majority in 2012 and 2017. Parties supportive of the president won overwhelmingly in the 2013 and 2018 legislative elections.

The 1992 constitution was amended in 2008 to encourage multiparty politics and economic liberalisation, and abolished the People's Council and increased the powers of the enlarged legislature. It was amended again in 2016 to increase presidential term limits from five to seven years, and remove the 70-year age restriction to allow Berdimuhammedov to potentially rule for life. The unicameral parliament *(Majlis)* has 125 members directly elected for a five-year term.

The country is divided into five provinces (Ahal, Balkan, Dashhowuz, Lebap and Mary) and the city of Ashgabat.

HEAD OF STATE

President, Chair of the Council of Ministers, Gurbanguly Berdimuhammedov, *elected* 14 February 2007, *re-elected* 2012, 2017

SELECTED GOVERNMENT MEMBERS *AS AT JULY 2018*

Defence, Maj.-Gen. Begench Gundogdyev
Economy and Finance, Batyr Bazarov
Foreign Affairs, Rashid Meredov

EMBASSY OF TURKMENISTAN

131 Holland Park Avenue, London W11 4UT
T 020-7610 5239 E tkm-embassy-uk@btconnect.com

Ambassador Extraordinary and Plenipotentiary, HE Yazmurad N. Seryayev, *apptd* 2003

BRITISH EMBASSY

Third Floor Office Building, Four Points Ak Altin Hotel, 744001 Ashgabat
T (+993) (12) 363 462 E beasb@online.tm
W www.gov.uk/government/world/turkmenistan
Ambassador Extraordinary and Plenipotentiary, HE Thorda Abbott-Watt, *apptd* 2016

ECONOMY AND TRADE

Turkmenistan has large reserves of natural gas and some oil, but exports were restricted by a lack of export routes until 2009–10, when existing pipelines to Russia and Iran were supplemented by a new gas pipeline to China and a second pipeline to Iran; a trans-Caspian route to European markets and a pipeline to India are also under exploration. Attempts to privatise the primarily state-run and inefficient economy have been made since 2012, but implementation has been slow. Autocratic control and corruption have limited foreign investment opportunities, resulting in economic stagnation and currency devaluation. Falling oil prices caused the government to devalue the manat by nearly 20 per cent in 2014 in a bid to increase exports.

Agriculture is intensive around the irrigated oases, with half the irrigated land used to grow cotton. Agriculture accounts for 7.5 per cent of GDP and almost half of employment; grain and livestock are the other main products. The principal industries are gas and oil production, petroleum products, textiles (including silk) and food processing. Industry contributes 44.9 per cent of GDP.

The main trading partners are China (83.7 per cent of exports), Turkey, Algeria, Russia and the EU. Principal exports are gas, crude oil, petrochemicals, textiles and cotton fibre. The main imports are machinery and equipment, chemicals and foodstuffs.

GNI – US$38.3bn; US$6,650 per capita (2017)
Annual average growth of GDP – 6.5 per cent (2017 est)
Inflation rate – 6 per cent (2017 est)
Population below poverty line – 0.2 per cent (2012 est)
Unemployment – 11 per cent (2014 est)
Total external debt – US$443.4m (2017 est)
Imports – US$2,556m (2014)
Exports – US$3,600m (2014)

BALANCE OF PAYMENTS

Current Account – US$4,945m deficit (2015 est)

Trade with UK	2016	2017
Imports from UK	£37,792,681	£36,741,397
Exports to UK	£15,209,245	£3,486,016

COMMUNICATIONS

Airports and waterways – The main airport is at Ashgabat; there are two important waterways, the Amu Darya river in the north-east and the Niyazov (formerly Kara Kum) canal, and the main port is Turkmenbashi, on the Caspian Sea
Roadways and railways – 47,577km; 2,980km
Telecommunications – 665,000 fixed lines and 8.6 million mobile subscriptions (2016); there were 951,925 internet users in 2016
Internet code and IDD – tm; 993 (from UK), 810 44 (to UK)
Media – The country's public broadcasters are Turkmen TV and Turkmen Radio; leading daily newspapers include *Neytralnyy Turkmenistan* (Russian language), and *Turkmenistan* and *Watan* (both Turkmen)
WPFI score – 84,20 (178)

TUVALU

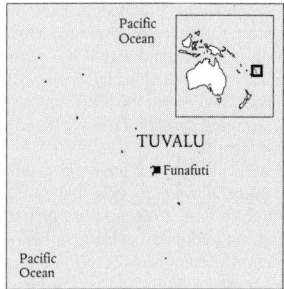

Pacific Ocean

TUVALU

Funafuti

Pacific Ocean

Area – 26 sq. km
Capital – Funafuti; population, 7,000 (2018 est)
Currency – The Australian dollar (A$) of 100 cents is legal tender; in addition there are Tuvalu dollar and cent coins in circulation
Population – 11,502 rising at 0.85 per cent a year (2017 est); Polynesian (96 per cent), Micronesian (4 per cent) (est)
Religion – Christian (Church of Tuvalu 97 per cent, Seventh-day Adventist 1.4 per cent, Baha'i 1 per cent (est)
Language – English, Tuvaluan (both official), Samoan, Kiribati (on Nui)
Population density – 373 per sq. km (2016)
Urban population – 93.1 per cent (2018 est)
Median age (years) – 25.7 (2017 est)
National anthem – 'Tuvalu mo te Atua' 'Tuvalu for the Almighty'
National day – 1 October (Independence Day)
Death penalty – Abolished for all crimes (since 1978)
Life expectancy (years) – 66.16 (2015 est)
Gross enrolment ratio (percentage of relevant age group) – primary 103.6 per cent, secondary 86.2 per cent (2015 est)
Health expenditure (per capita) – US$633 (2014)
Life expectancy (years) – 66.9 (2017 est)
Mortality rate – 8.5 (2017 est)
Birth rate – 23.7 (2017 est)
Infant mortality rate – 29 (2017 est)

CLIMATE AND TERRAIN
Tuvalu comprises nine low-lying coral islands and atolls in the south-west Pacific Ocean. The highest elevation is 5m and the lowest is 0m (Pacific Ocean). The climate is tropical, with an average temperature of 28.4°C.

HISTORY AND POLITICS
The islands were settled by Polynesians from Tonga 2,000 years ago. Europeans arrived in the 18th century and, as the Ellice Islands, Tuvalu came under the control of the British in 1877. They formed part of the Gilbert and Ellice Islands protectorate (later a colony) from 1892, but were granted separate status from the Gilbert Islands in 1975. The islands became independent as Tuvalu on 1 October 1978. The country is seriously affected by rising sea levels, which are threatening its economic viability.

There are no political parties; allegiances are influenced by personal and island loyalties. Politically stable as a democracy, there are frequent changes in government as support in parliament shifts, although incumbent Prime Minister Enele Sopoaga retained his seat in the March 2015 legislative elections.

Under the 1978 constitution, Tuvalu is a constitutional monarchy with Queen Elizabeth II as head of state, represented by a governor-general who is appointed on the advice of the prime minister. The unicameral legislature, the Parliament of Tuvalu, has 15 members who are directly elected for a four-year term. The prime minister is elected by the legislature from among its members, and appoints the cabinet, who must be members of parliament. Local government services are provided by elected island councils.
Governor-General, HE Sir Iakoba Italeli, GCMG, *apptd* 2013

SELECTED GOVERNMENT MEMBERS *AS AT JULY 2018*
Prime Minister, Enele Sopoaga
Deputy Prime Minister, Finance, Maatia Toafa
Foreign Affairs, Taukelina Finikaso

HONORARY CONSULATE OF TUVALU
Tuvalu House, 230 Worple Road, London SW20 8RH
T 020-8879 0985 E tuvaluconsulate@netscape.net
Honorary Consul, Dr Iftikhar A. Ayaz

BRITISH HIGH COMMISSIONER
HE Melanie Hopkins, *apptd* 2016, resident at Suva, Fiji

ECONOMY AND TRADE
The main economic activities are subsistence agriculture and fishing, although agricultural productivity is threatened by the increasing salinity of the soil as the sea level rises; the only cash crop is coconuts. Tourism is limited by the state's remoteness. Most employment is in the public sector or abroad, often as merchant seamen; many families rely on remittances from expatriate workers. The government receives substantial annual income from a trust fund set up in 1987, and raises revenue through the sale of fishing licences, postage stamps and coins, and the leasing of its telephone code and internet suffix.

The main trading partners are Singapore, the USA, Fiji and Australia. The only exports are copra and fish. The main imports are food, livestock, fuels, machinery and manufactured goods.
GNI – US$0.1bn; US$4,970 per capita (2017)
Annual average growth of GDP – 3.2 per cent (2017 est)
Population below poverty line – 26.3 per cent (2010 est)
Inflation rate – 2.9 per cent (2017 est)
Imports – US$12m (2014)
Exports – US$134,596 (2014)

BALANCE OF PAYMENTS
Trade – US$16m deficit (2007)
Current Account – US$7m surplus (2013)

Trade with UK	2016	2017
Imports from UK	£49,065	£4,032
Exports to UK	£93,794	£187,939

COMMUNICATIONS
Airports and waterways – Funafuti has an airfield, from which a regular service operates to Fiji and Kiribati, and it is also the main port
Roadways – 8km
Telecommunications – 2,000 fixed lines and 7,600 mobile subscriptions (2016); there were 5,042 internet users in 2016
Internet code and IDD – tv; 688 (from UK), 44 (to UK)
Media – The state-owned Tuvalu Media Corporation publishes a fortnightly newspaper and runs Radio Tuvalu, the main information source for islanders

UGANDA

Republic of Uganda

Area – 241,038 sq. km
Capital – Kampala; population, 2,986,000 (2018 est)
Major towns – Entebbe, Gulu, Lira, Mbale
Currency – Uganda shilling of 100 cents
Population – 39,570,125 rising at 3.20 per cent a year (2017 est); Baganda (16.9 per cent), Banyakole (9.6 per cent), Basoga (8.8 per cent), Bakiga (7.1 per cent), Iteso (7 per cent), Langi (6.3 per cent), Bagisu (4.9 per cent), Acholi (4.4 per cent), Lugbara (3.3 per cent); other 32.1 per cent (2014 est)
Religion – Christian 84.4 per cent (Protestant 45.1 per cent, Roman Catholic 39.3 per cent), Muslim 13.7 per cent (predominantly Sunni) (2014 est); indigenous beliefs are often blended into or observed alongside Christianity or Islam
Language – English (official), Luganda, Swahili, Arabic
Population density – 214 per sq. km (2016)
Urban population – 23.8 per cent (2018 est)
Median age (years) – 15.8 (2017 est)
National anthem – 'O Uganda, Land of Beauty!'
National day – 9 October (Independence Day)
Death penalty – Retained
CPI score – 26 (151)
Military expenditure – US$444.6m (2017 est)

CLIMATE AND TERRAIN

Uganda lies on a high plateau with mountain ranges in the west, south-west and north-east. Elevation extremes range from 5,110m (Mt Stanley) to 621m (Lake Albert). Nearly 20 per cent of the country is covered by lakes, rivers and wetlands, and it contains about half of lakes Victoria, Edward and Albert (Mobuto), as well as lakes Kyoga, Kwania, George and Bisina (formerly Salisbury) and the course of the Nile from its outlet from Lake Victoria to the South Sudan border at Nimule. The climate is tropical, moderated by the altitude. There are two rainy seasons (March–May, October–December) in the south; the north is drier, semi-arid in places, with a single, longer rainy season.

HISTORY AND POLITICS

Indigenous people had formed several kingdoms in the area by the 14th century. A British protectorate was established over the kingdom of Buganda in 1894 and gradually extended to other territory by 1914. Uganda became independent on 9 October 1962 as a federation of the kingdoms of Ankole, Buganda, Bunyoro, Busoga and Toro.

In 1963 Uganda was proclaimed a federal republic but in 1966 Prime Minister Milton Obote overthrew the president, ended the federal status and became executive president. In 1971 President Obote was deposed in an army coup led by Maj.-Gen. Idi Amin, who proclaimed himself head of state.

His brutal dictatorship was overthrown in 1979 with military assistance from Tanzania.

Milton Obote was re-elected president in 1980 but political instability and human rights abuses continued. He was ousted by a military coup in 1985 amid a civil war with the rebel National Resistance Army (NRA) led by Yoweri Museveni. A military council was installed but the NRA captured Kampala in January 1986, securing control of the rest of the country in the following few months.

Museveni's 'Movement' system of government, under which political parties were allowed to exist but not to contest elections, was in place from 1986 until a 2005 referendum resulted in a return to multiparty politics. In February 2016 elections, President Museveni was re-elected for a fifth term and the National Resistance Movement retained its majority in parliament, although domestic and international observers criticised the fairness and transparency of the electoral process.

The Lord's Resistance Army (LRA), whose stated goals have proved inconsistent, began a low-level insurgency in northern Uganda in the late 1980s. Its activities have spread into north-eastern Congo (where most of the LRA is now located), southern Sudan, the Central African Republic and Kenya, despite offensives against LRA bases by Ugandan, Sudanese and Congolese forces since 2008. In Uganda, thousands have been massacred or mutilated, an estimated 20,000 children abducted to serve in its forces and 1.7 million people displaced into camps.

Terrorist attacks by Islamic extremists have begun in recent years. Some were carried out by Somalian Islamists, as African Union peacekeepers (predominantly Ugandan) have prevented them establishing complete control of the Somalian capital, but other attacks were the work of the Allied Democratic Forces, based in the Democratic Republic of the Congo, which seeks to create an Islamic state in Uganda.

The 1995 constitution was amended in 2005 to allow multiparty elections. The president is directly elected for a five-year term; the two-term limit was abolished in 2005. The 445-seat unicameral parliament has 290 directly elected members, 137 (including 112 women) elected indirectly to represent particular groups and 18 *ex officio* members appointed by the president; all serve a five-year term. The prime minister is appointed by the president, subject to the approval of parliament.

HEAD OF STATE

President, C-in-C of the Armed Forces, Yoweri Museveni, *sworn in* 29 January 1986, *elected* 9 May 1996, *re-elected* 2001, 2006, 2011, 2016
Vice-President, Edward Kiwanuka Ssekandi

SELECTED GOVERNMENT MEMBERS *AS AT JULY 2018*
Prime Minister, Ruhakana Rugunda
First Deputy Prime Minister, Gen. Moses Ali
Defence, Adolf Mwesige
Finance, Matia Kasaija

UGANDA HIGH COMMISSION
Uganda House, 58–59 Trafalgar Square, London WC2N 5DX
T 020-7839 5783 E info@ugandahighcommission.co.uk
W www.ugandahighcommission.co.uk
High Commissioner, HE Julius Peter Moto, *apptd* 2017

BRITISH HIGH COMMISSION
PO Box 7070, 4 Windsor Loop, Kampala
T (+256) (31) 231 2000 E bhcinfo@starcom.co.ug
W www.gov.uk/government/world/uganda
High Commissioner, HE Peter West, CMG, *apptd* 2016

ECONOMY AND TRADE

Economic reforms adopted since 1986 have produced steady economic growth, which was only slightly affected by the global downturn and the conflict in South Sudan. However, there has been little industrialisation, so the economy is vulnerable to fluctuations in global commodity prices, especially that of coffee, its main export. Uganda's debt burden has been reduced by debt relief since 2000 but it is still dependent on foreign aid. Good harvests, increasing gold exports and significant foreign investment in oil production is somewhat offsetting rising government debt and the depreciation of the Uganda shilling in 2014–15.

Agriculture is the most important economic sector, contributing 25.8 per cent of GDP and engaging about 71 per cent of the workforce. The principal crops are coffee, tea, cotton, tobacco, cassava, potatoes, maize, millet, pulses, cut flowers and livestock products. Industrial activity centres on production of sugar, tobacco, cotton textiles, cement and steel, brewing and fishing. Tourism is growing, and oil has been discovered but production is years from completion.

The main export markets are neighbouring countries, the UAE and the EU; imports come chiefly from China, India, the UAE and Kenya. Principal exports are coffee, fish and fish products, tea, cotton, cut flowers, horticultural products and gold. Electricity is exported although less than a quarter of Ugandans have access to it. The main imports are capital equipment, vehicles, petroleum, medical supplies and cereals.

GNI – US$25.6bn; US$600 per capita (2017)
Annual average growth of GDP – 4.4 per cent (2017 est)
Inflation rate – 5.8 per cent (2017 est)
Population below poverty line – 19.7 per cent (2013 est)
Unemployment – 9.4 per cent (2013 est)
Total external debt – US$7.163bn (2017 est)
Imports – US$4,765m (2015)
Exports – US$2,698m (2015)

BALANCE OF PAYMENTS
Trade – US$2,067m deficit (2015)
Current Account – US$1,128m deficit (2017)

Trade with UK	2016	2017
Imports from UK	£43,959,781	£44,107,700
Exports to UK	£12,626,119	£12,828,468

COMMUNICATIONS

Airports and waterways – There is an international airport at Entebbe; some of the lakes and parts of the river Nile provide navigable routes internally
Roadways and railways – 20,000km, including 3,624 of paved roadways; 1,244km
Telecommunications – 368,243 fixed lines and 22.8 million mobile subscriptions (2016); there were 18.1 million internet users in 2016
Internet code and IDD – ug; 256 (from UK), 0 44 (to UK)
Media – The Uganda Broadcasting Company is the main public-run broadcaster; major newspapers include the state-owned *New Vision*, as well as the privately owned *The Monitor* and *The Observer*
WPFI score – 35,94 (112)

EDUCATION AND HEALTH

Education is a joint undertaking by the government, local authorities and voluntary agencies.
Literacy rate – 90.7 per cent (2015 est)
Gross enrolment ratio (percentage of relevant age group) – primary 100 per cent (2016 est); secondary 26.1 per cent (2014 est); tertiary 4 per cent (2011 est)

Health expenditure (per capita) – US$52 (2014)
Hospital beds (per 1,000 people) – 0.5 (2010)
Life expectancy (years) – 55.9 (2017 est)
Mortality rate – 10.2 (2017 est)
Birth rate – 42.9 (2017 est)
Infant mortality rate – 56.1 (2017 est)
HIV/AIDS adult prevalence – 6.5 per cent (2017 est)

UKRAINE

Ukrayina – Ukraine

Area – 603,550 sq. km
Capital – Kiev (Kyiv); population, 2,957,000 (2018 est)
Major cities – Dnipropetrovsk, Donetsk, Kharkiv, L'viv, Odesa, Sevastopol, Zaporizhzhya
Currency – Hryvnia of 100 kopiykas
Population – 44,033,874 falling at 0.41 per cent a year (2017 est); Ukrainian (77.8 per cent), Russian (17.3 per cent); small Belarusian, Moldovan, Crimean Tatar, Bulgarian, Romanian, Polish, Hungarian and Greek minorities (2001 est)
Religion – Christian (Orthodox 70.6 per cent, Greek Catholic 5.7 per cent, Roman Catholic 1.3 per cent, Protestant 0.8 per cent), Muslim 0.7 per cent (est)
Language – Ukrainian (official), Russian
Population density – 77 per sq. km (2016)
Urban population – 69.4 per cent (2018 est)
Median age (years) – 40.60 (2017 est)
National anthem – 'Shche ne vmerla, Ukraina' 'Ukraine Has Not Yet Perished'
National day – 24 August (Independence Day)
Death penalty – Abolished for all crimes (since 1999)
CPI score – 30 (130)
Military expenditure – US$3,648m (2017 est)
Conscription – 20–27 years of age; 18 months

CLIMATE AND TERRAIN

Much of the country lies in a plain (steppe), with the Carpathian mountains in the west and mountains in the south of the Crimean peninsula. Elevation extremes range from 2,061m (Hora Hoverla) to 0m (Black Sea). The main rivers are the Dnieper, which runs through the centre of the country, the Dniester in the west, the Southern Buh and the Northern Donets (a tributary of the Don). The climate is continental, and Mediterranean in the southern Crimea. Average temperatures range from −2.9°C in January to 21.2°C in July.

POLITICS

The 1996 constitution was amended in 2004 to transfer some powers from the president to the legislature *(Verkhovna Rada)*; the constitutional court returned these powers to the president in late 2010 although in February 2014 the 2004 constitutional amendments were reinstated. The president is directly elected for a five-year term, renewable once. The

Area invaded by Tatar-Mongols — Part of the Polish-Lithuanian Commonwealth — West becomes part of the Habsburg empire — Civil war partitions country between USSR and Poland — Red Army forces out German troops — Crimea transferred from Russia to Ukraine — Declares independence from USSR — Russia occupies the Crimea; separatist violence in the east

c.800   c.1300   1685   1918   1941   c.1945-9   1986   2004

c.1200   c.1500   1795   1921   1944   1954   1991   2014

The Kievan Rus' becomes the first east Slavic state — Comes under Lithuanian rule — Eastern rebellion; area becomes part of Russia — Reunified Ukraine declares independence — German occupation begins — Ukraine regains Polish controlled territory — Chernobyl nuclear disaster kills at least 10,000 people — Orange Revolution; Yulia Tymoshenko becomes PM

unicameral Supreme Council has 450 members, who are directly elected for a five-year term. The prime minister is appointed by the president, subject to the legislature's approval.

Following the decision of Viktor Yanukovych's government to abandon plans for an association agreement with the EU in November 2013, tens of thousands of pro-EU demonstrators protested in Kiev and other cities. The widespread and sometimes violent demonstrations, which left at least 77 protestors dead in Kiev, resulted in President Yanukovych leaving Ukraine and seeking asylum in Russia, causing opposition parties to form an interim government.

The speaker of the parliament, Oleksandr Turchynov, was appointed interim president on 22 February 2014. A national unity government was subsequently established, with Arseniy Yatsenyuk of the Fatherland party sworn in as prime minister on 26 February. In May 2014, Petro Poroshenko was elected president with 54.7 per cent of the popular vote. Following early elections held in October 2014, the BPP remained the largest single party, winning 132 seats, and formed a coalition government in December. In August 2015, parliament voted to provide greater autonomy to areas in the east of the country controlled by pro-Russian separatists. Prime Minister Yatsenyuk stepped down in April 2016 amid accusations of corruption levelled at his government, coupled with frustration at the slow pace of reforms, to be replaced by Volodymyr Groysman.

HEAD OF STATE
President, Petro Poroshenko, elected 25 May 2014, sworn in 7 June 2014

SELECTED GOVERNMENT MEMBERS AS AT JULY 2018
Prime Minister, Volodymyr Groysman
First Vice-Prime Minister, Trade, Stepan Kubiv
Vice Prime Ministers, Vyacheslav Kirilenko; Volodymyr Kistion; Ivanna Klympush-Tsyntsadze; Pavlo Rozenko; Dmytro Shymkiv; Hennadiy Zubko
Finance, Oksana Markarova
Foreign Affairs, Pavlo Klimkin

EMBASSY OF UKRAINE
60 Holland Park, London W11 3SJ
T 020-7727 6312 E emb_gb@mfa.gov.ua W www.ukremb.org.uk
Ambassador Extraordinary and Plenipotentiary, HE Natalia Galibarenko, apptd 2015

BRITISH EMBASSY
Desyatynna 9, Kiev 01025
T (+380) (44) 490 3660 E ukembinf@gmail.com
W www.gov.uk/government/world/ukraine
Ambassador Extraordinary and Plenipotentiary, HE Judith Gough, CMG, apptd 2015

FOREIGN RELATIONS
Following the disintegration of the USSR in 1991, relations between Ukraine and Russia were strained by disputes over the Black Sea fleet and the status of Crimea, a self-administered republic within Ukraine, which had been part of

Russia until 1954; these disputes often came to a head when Russia suspended gas supplies to Ukraine. However, in February 2014 armed pro-Russian groups seized government buildings in Crimea. The Crimea was formally annexed by the Russian government on the 18 March 2014 after a controversial independence vote in the Crimean parliament. Ukraine and a majority of UN member states do not accept the status of Crimea and Sevastopol as federal subjects of the Russian Federation.

From April, pro-Russian groups in the east of Ukraine seized government buildings and two self-proclaimed pro-Russian states were established in the east of the country: the Donetsk People's Republic and the Luhansk People's Republic. Independence referendums were held on 11 May in both territories, with administrators claiming very large wins for supporters of independence. Both republics merged on 24 May to form The Federal State of Novorossiya. The breakaway states have not been recognised by Russia, Ukraine or the wider international community.

By June 2014, at least 270 people had been killed as these groups clashed with the Ukrainian military. While political tensions eased when the Russian government advised it would be pulling troops away from the Ukrainian border, violence between the Ukrainian army and separatist militias continued to occur. A Ukraine–European Union Association Agreement was formalised by the incoming government on 27 June 2014.

Tensions were reignited by the downing of Malaysia Airlines flight MH17 over Ukrainian soil on 17 July 2014, apparently by pro-Russian separatists. In September, a ceasefire was agreed between the government and separatists, though it soon broke down and a new agreement was brokered in February 2015 after rebel forces captured the strategically important town of Debaltseve. Tensions were reignited in January–February 2017 with claims of shelling in Donetsk and Avdiyivka.

ECONOMY AND TRADE
The first decade of independence was characterised by economic mismanagement and opposition to economic restructuring. When reform began in the late 1990s, it brought economic growth, with rises in output and exports and a reduction in inflation. However, slow progress has been a drag on the economy, leaving it vulnerable to external factors such as the global economic downturn; it was heavily affected in 2009 as the economy contracted by 15 per cent. Slow economic growth between 2010–13 was marred by allegations the Yanukovych regime misappropriated billions of dollars during its time in power. A trade war with Moscow, ongoing fighting in the east and the annexation of Crimea resulted in a sharp loss of GDP and high inflation in 2014 and 2015.

After incurring debts worth US$1.9bn, with state-run Russian energy firm Gazprom, Russia ended its practice of supplying Ukraine with subsidised fossil fuels, greatly increasing domestic prices. In March 2015, the IMF approved a US$17.5bn (£11.28bn) loan to Ukraine in order to prevent the country from defaulting. Ukraine's free-trade agreement with the EU came into force at the start of 2016, deepening tensions with Russia as trade activity shifted west, but nonetheless the economy grew in 2016 and 2017.

The agricultural sector is large and productive, with over half the land under cultivation. The main crops are grain, sugar beet, sunflower seeds and vegetables; stock-raising and dairy farming are also important. Agriculture accounts for 14 per cent of GDP and 5.8 per cent of employment. There are large deposits of coal, iron ore and other minerals. The main industrial activities are mining and metal processing, manufacture of machinery and transport equipment and chemicals, electricity generation and food processing, especially sugar. Ukraine imports three-quarters of its oil and gas, principally from Russia; supplies have been suspended on occasion due to price disputes.

The main trading partners are Russia, China, Germany and Turkey. Principal exports are ferrous and non-ferrous metals (especially steel), fuel and petroleum products, chemicals, machinery and transport equipment, and foodstuffs. The main imports are energy (primarily gas), machinery and equipment, and chemicals.

GNI – US$101.5bn; US$2,338 per capita (2017)
Annual average growth of GDP – 2 per cent (2017 est)
Inflation rate – 12.8 per cent (2017 est)
Population below poverty line – 24.1 per cent (2010)
Unemployment – 9.5 per cent (2017 est)
Total external debt – US$125.3bn (2017 est)
Imports – US$39,184m (2016)
Exports – US$36,369m (2016)

BALANCE OF PAYMENTS
Trade – US$2,815m deficit (2016)
Current Account – US$2,446m deficit (2017)

Trade with UK	2016	2017
Imports from UK	£373,738,694	£407,197,790
Exports to UK	£297,794,954	£406,553,979

COMMUNICATIONS
Airports and waterways – The principal airports are at Kiev and Odesa; the main seaports are Mariupol on the Sea of Azov, and Kherson, Mykolayiv, Odesa and Sevastopol on the Black Sea
Roadways and railways – 169,095km; 21,619km
Telecommunications – 8.4 million fixed lines and 56.7 million mobile subscriptions (2016); there were 23.2 million internet users in 2016
Internet code and IDD – ua; 380 (from UK), 44 (to UK)
Major broadcasters – The National TV Company of Ukraine and the National Radio Company of Ukraine are the principal public broadcasters
Press – Major dailies include *Fakty i Kommentari,* (Ukrainian language), and *Silski Visti* and *Segodnya* (both Russian language)
WPFI score – 31,16 (102)

EDUCATION AND HEALTH
Literacy rate – 99.8 per cent (2015)
Gross enrolment ratio (percentage of relevant age group) – primary 103.9 per cent, secondary 99.2 per cent, tertiary 82.3 per cent (2014 est)
Health expenditure (per capita) – US$203 (2014)
Hospital beds (per 1,000 people) – 8.8 (2013)
Life expectancy (years) – 72.1 (2017 est)
Mortality rate – 14.4 (2017 est)
Birth rate – 10.3 (2017 est)
Infant mortality rate – 7.8 (2017 est)
HIV/AIDS adult prevalence – 0.9 per cent (2016 est)

UNITED ARAB EMIRATES
Al-Imarat al-Arabiyah al-Muttahidah – United Arab Emirates

Area – 83,600 sq. km
Capital – Abu Dhabi; population, 1,142,000 (2018 est)
Major cities – Ajman, Al-Ain, Dubai, Sharjah
Currency – UAE dirham (Dh) of 100 fils
Population – 6,072,475 rising at 2.37 per cent a year (2017 est); Emirati (19 per cent), other Arab and Iranian (23 per cent), South Asian (50 per cent) (1982)
Religion – Muslim 76 per cent, Christian 9 per cent, other (primarily Hindu and Buddhist) 15 per cent (2005 est)
Language – Arabic (official), Persian, English, Hindi, Urdu
Population density – 112 per sq. km (2016)
Urban population – 86.5 per cent (2018 est)
Median age (years) – 30.3 (2017 est)
National anthem – 'Ishy Bilady' 'Long Live My Homeland'
National day – 2 December (Independence Day)
Death penalty – Retained
CPI score – 71 (21)
Military expenditure – US$22,755m (2015)
Conscription – Men aged 18–30; 24 months (selective)

CLIMATE AND TERRAIN
The United Arab Emirates (UAE) is situated in the south-east of the Arabian peninsula. Six of the emirates lie on the shore of the Gulf, between the Musandam peninsula in the east and the Qatar peninsula in the west, while the seventh, Fujairah, lies on the Gulf of Oman. A flat coastal plain merges into the desert of the interior, and there are mountains in the east. Elevation extremes range from 1,527m (Jabal Yibir) to 0m (Persian Gulf). There is a desert climate, although it is cooler in the mountains, with high humidity on the coast. Average temperatures range from 18.5°C in January to 34.4°C in July.

HISTORY AND POLITICS
The United Arab Emirates (formerly the Trucial States) is composed of seven emirates. Six of these came together as an independent state on 2 December 1971 when they ended their individual special treaty relationships with the British government, and they were joined by Ras al-Khaimah on 10 February 1972.

Sheikh Zayed of Abu Dhabi was president from independence until his death in 2004. He was succeeded as Sultan of Abu Dhabi by his son, Sheikh Khalifa, who was also elected president of the UAE. The first national elections were held in 2006, when half the members of the Federal National Council (FNC) were elected by a small electoral college of 6,600 voters. The size of the electoral college increased significantly, to 224,279 voters (women comprised just under half of this total), in the most recent legislative election held in October 2015. President al-Nahyan has ruled since 2004.

The 1971 provisional constitution, approved in 1996, was amended in 2008 to convert the FNC from a consultative into a legislative body and to extend its original two-year term to 2011. Overall authority lies with the Supreme Council, comprising the hereditary rulers of the seven emirates, each of whom also governs in his own territory. The president is elected every five years by the Supreme Council from among its members, but is *de facto* hereditary. The president appoints the prime minister and the council of ministers. The unicameral FNC has 40 members, eight members each from Abu Dhabi and Dubai, six each from Sharjah and Ras al-Khaimah and four each for Ajman, Fujairah and Umm al-Qaiwain; half are elected by an electoral college and half are appointed by the rulers of each emirate.

HEAD OF STATE
President, HH Sheikh Khalifa bin Zayed al-Nahyan *(Abu Dhabi), elected* 3 November 2004, *re-elected* 2009, 2014
Vice-President, Prime Minister, Defence, HH Sheikh Mohammed bin Rashid al-Maktoum *(Dubai)*

SELECTED GOVERNMENT MEMBERS *AS AT JULY 2018*
Deputy Prime Ministers, Lt.-Gen. Sheikh Saif bin Zayed al-Nahyan *(Interior);* Sheikh Mansour bin Zayed al-Nahyan
Finance, HH Sheikh Hamdan bin Rashid al-Maktoum
Foreign Affairs, Sheikh Abdullah bin Zayed al-Nahyan

EMBASSY OF THE UNITED ARAB EMIRATES
30 Prince's Gate, London SW7 1PT
T 020-7581 1281 **E** informationuk@mofa.gov.ae
W www.uae-embassy.ae/uk
Ambassador Extraordinary and Plenipotentiary, HE Sulaiman Hamid Almazrou, *apptd* 2016

BRITISH EMBASSY
PO Box 248, Khalid bin al-Waleed Street (Street 22), Abu Dhabi
T (+971) (2) 610 1100 **E** consular.UAE@fco.gov.uk
W www.gov.uk/government/world/united-arab-emirates
Ambassador Extraordinary and Plenipotentiary, HE Philip Parham, CMG, *apptd* 2014

FEDERAL STRUCTURE
The emirates are: Abu Dhabi, Ajman, Dubai, Fujairah, Ras al-Khaimah, Sharjah and Umm al-Qaiwain. Each emirate has its own government, judicial system and penal code. Abu Dhabi has an executive council chaired by the crown prince.

ECONOMY AND TRADE
Exploitation of the territories' oil reserves began in the 1960s and transformed the UAE from poor rural principalities into modern states with a high standard of living. Oil and gas production dominate the economy, although diversification efforts mean that output now accounts for only 30 per cent of GDP, and it is one of the most diversified of the Gulf states. The economy is also dependent on foreign workers, but the government aims to increase opportunities for its citizens through improved education and expansion of the private sector. The economy was badly hit by the global downturn, but its debt crisis has been alleviated by loans from federal and Abu Dhabi institutions. Low oil prices have led to cuts in government expenditure and the introduction of excise taxes in 2015 and value added tax in 2018.

Agriculture is limited by the terrain but the area under cultivation has been extended by irrigation and water desalination projects. The main products are dates, vegetables, watermelons, poultry, eggs and dairy products. Non-hydrocarbon industries include fishing, aluminium, cement, petrochemicals, fertilisers, commercial ship repair, construction materials, handicrafts, textiles, boat-building, financial services and tourism. Several free-trade, zero-tax zones are attracting foreign investment.

The main export markets are India, Iran and Japan; imports come chiefly from China, the USA and India. Principal exports are crude oil (45 per cent), natural gas, re-exports, dried fish and dates. The main imports are machinery and transport equipment, chemicals and food.
GNI – US$367.8bn; US$39,130 per capita (2017)
Annual average growth of GDP – 1.3 per cent (2017 est)
Inflation rate – 2.1 per cent (2017 est)
Population below poverty line – 19.5 per cent (2003)
Total external debt – US$239.7bn (2017 est)
Imports – US$230,000m (2015)
Exports – US$265,000m (2015)

BALANCE OF PAYMENTS
Trade – US$35,000m surplus (2015)
Current Account – US$19,278m surplus (2015 est)

Trade with UK	2016	2017
Imports from UK	£6,744,184,752	£7,471,465,520
Exports to UK	£2,754,396,596	£4,087,424,905

COMMUNICATIONS
Airports and waterways – There is an international airport in every emirate except Ajman, and significant ports in Jebel Ali, Khor Fakkan, Mina Khalid, Mina Rashid, Mina Saqr, Mina Khalid and Mina Zayed
Roadways – 4,080km
Telecommunications – 2.3 million fixed lines and 19.9 million mobile subscriptions (2016); there were 5.4 million internet users in 2016
Internet code and IDD – ae; 971 (from UK), 44 (to UK)
Media – Dubai Media Incorporated (TV) is the government-owned broadcaster; major newspapers include *Al-Bayan,* the *Khaleej Times* and *Gulf News*
WPFI score – 40,86 (128)

EDUCATION AND HEALTH
Education is free in state schools and compulsory from ages six to 14.
Literacy rate – 99.4 per cent (2015 est)
Gross enrolment ratio (percentage of relevant age group) – primary 111 per cent, secondary 96 per cent, tertiary 37 per cent (2016 est)
Health expenditure (per capita) – US$1,611 (2014)
Hospital beds (per 1,000 people) – 1.2 (2013)
Life expectancy (years) – 77.7 (2017 est)
Mortality rate – 1.9 (2017 est)
Birth rate – 15.1 (2017 est)
Infant mortality rate – 10 (2017 est)

UNITED KINGDOM

United Kingdom of Great Britain and Northern Ireland

Area – 243,610 sq. km
Capital – London; population, 9,046,000 (2018 est)
Major cities – Belfast, Birmingham, Cardiff, Edinburgh, Glasgow, Leeds, Liverpool, Manchester
Currency – Pound sterling (£) of 100 pence
Population – 65,648,100 rising at 0.52 per cent a year (2017 est)
Religion – Christian 59.5 per cent, Muslim 4.4 per cent, Hindu 1.3 per cent, none 25.7 per cent (2011 est); small Jewish, Sikh and Buddhist minorities
Language – English, Welsh, Scots, Scottish Gaelic, Irish
Population density – 273 per sq. km (2016)
Urban population – 83.4 per cent (2018 est)
Median age (years) – 40.5 (2017 est)
National anthem – 'God Save the Queen'
Death penalty – Abolished for all crimes (since 1998)
CPI score – 82 (8)
Military expenditure – US$47,193m (2017)

CLIMATE AND TERRAIN

The terrain of Great Britain is higher in the north and west, with low mountains and rugged hills in Scotland, northern England and Wales; the land declines towards the south and east, with its lowest points in the south-east. Northern Ireland is more low-lying, with low mountains in the north and east. The heavily indented coastline varies in height between high cliffs and sea level. Elevation extremes range from 1,345m (Ben Nevis, Scotland) to −4m (the Fens, eastern England). Although Scotland contains numerous large lochs and northern England includes an area known as the Lake District, the largest freshwater lake is Lough Neagh in Northern Ireland. The main rivers are the Thames, the Severn and the Trent in England and Wales, and the Tay in Scotland. The climate is temperate and extremes are rare, but the convergence of Atlantic, Arctic and European weather systems produces unusually changeable weather conditions. Average temperatures range from 4.4°C in January and December to 15.1°C in August.

POLITICS

There is no written constitution. The head of state is a hereditary constitutional monarch. The bicameral parliament consists of the House of Commons, the lower house, and the House of Lords. The House of Commons has 650 seats, directly elected for a five-year term. The House of Lords is appointed and numbers vary; in May 2018 it had 780 members, comprising 26 archbishops and bishops of the Church of England, 664 life peers and 90 hereditary peers. The prime minister is the leader of the majority party or coalition in the House of Commons.

Powers over certain internal matters were devolved in 1999 to Scotland, Wales and Northern Ireland, each of which has its own legislature and government; devolution was suspended in Northern Ireland several times between 2000 and 2007 owing to the breakdown of power-sharing arrangements.

The Labour government elected in 1945 pursued socialist economic and welfare policies, nationalising key industries, setting up the National Health Service and expanding the social security system. Economic decline continued until the 1980s, when it was reversed by the Conservative government led by Margaret Thatcher, the country's first woman prime minister. Her administration privatised nationalised industries, opened up welfare services to market forces and reduced the role of local government, polarising politics and public opinion. She also established a close relationship with the USA that was supportive of its foreign policy. This has been continued by her successors, notably in the support for the US 'war on terror' and the deployment of British forces in Afghanistan from 2001, Iraq from 2003 to 2009, and in Libyan air space in 2011.

At the 2015 legislative election, the Conservative party won its first outright majority since 1996 while the Scottish Nationalist Party won 56 of the 59 seats contested in Scotland. A snap election in June 2017 intended to strengthen the Conservative mandate resulted in them losing their majority and establishing a 'confidence and supply' agreement with the Democratic Unionist Party. Following the June 2016 referendum, in which 52 per cent of voters supported UK withdrawal from the EU, David Cameron stood down as prime minister and was replaced by Theresa May in July. The formal process to exit the EU was triggered on 29 March 2017.

HEAD OF STATE
HM The Queen of the United Kingdom of Great Britain and
  Northern Ireland, Queen Elizabeth II, born 21 April 1926;
  succeeded 6 February 1952; crowned 2 June 1953
Heir, HRH The Prince of Wales (Prince Charles Philip
  Arthur George), born 14 November 1948

SELECTED GOVERNMENT MEMBERS AS AT JULY 2018
Prime Minister, First Lord of the Treasury, Civil Service, Theresa
  May
Chancellor of the Exchequer, Philip Hammond
Defence, Gavin Williamson, CBE
Foreign and Commonwealth Affairs, Jeremy Hunt

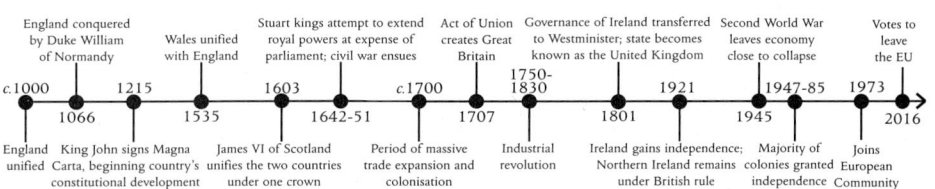

Home Affairs, Sajid Javid
Justice, Lord Chancellor, David Gauke

ECONOMY AND TRADE

The UK has a highly developed and technologically advanced economy, that is now dominated by services and trade. It was the first industrialised nation, developing an economy in the 19th century based on heavy industry, mass manufacturing and global trade. It became less predominant as industrialisation spread to other countries, and the demands of the Second World War caused a postwar industrial decline. In the 1980s, privatisation of state industries, constraints on public spending and an oil boom improved government finances, and primary industrial activities were increasingly replaced by service industries. After emerging from recession in the early 1990s, the economy experienced its longest-recorded period of expansion, outperforming the rest of the EU states, until 2008. The global economic downturn, tight credit and the end of the property boom caused the economy to go into recession from early 2008 until late 2009 and again at the start of 2012. The banking sector in particular was badly affected by the global financial crisis in 2008 and government intervention was necessary to stabilise the financial system, including nationalising or part-nationalising major banks. These measures left the government with a massive public-sector debt to service, and the new coalition government announced tight constraints on public spending from 2010. The budget deficit has fallen but remains high at 3.6 per cent and public debt has continued to increase. The first Conservative budget since 1996 was passed in 2015 and included more welfare and spending cuts, a rise in the minimum wage and further boosts to improve productivity. Since deciding to leave the EU in June 2016, growth has slowed and the pound has depreciated, resulting in lower consumer spending but no significant increase in exports due to uncertainty over the UK's future trading relations. With the UK set to leave the EU in March 2019, growth is expected to continue to slow.

The service sector, especially banking, insurance and business services, electronics, telecommunications and tourism, now contributes 80.4 per cent of GDP and employs 83.5 per cent of the workforce. Agriculture is intensive, highly mechanised and efficient, employing just 1.3 per cent of the workforce but providing about 60 per cent of food needs. The UK has large but declining reserves of oil, gas and coal, and the country became a net importer of energy in 2005. Other industrial output is mostly manufactured goods, including machine tools, electrical power equipment, automation and transport equipment, aircraft, ships, motor vehicles and parts, electronics and communications equipment, metals, chemicals, paper and paper products, food processing, textiles, clothing and other consumer goods. Manufacturing has declined in importance but still accounts for 19 per cent of GDP.

The main trading partners are other EU countries, the USA and China. The principal exports are manufactured goods, fuels, chemicals, food, beverages and tobacco. The main imports are manufactured goods, machinery, fuels and foodstuffs.

GNI – US$2,675.9bn; US$40,530 per capita (2017)
Annual average growth of GDP – 1.7 per cent (2017 est)
Inflation rate – 2.6 per cent (2017 est)
Population below poverty line – 15 per cent (2013 est)
Unemployment – 4.4 per cent (2017 est)
Total external debt – US$8.126 trillion (2016 est)
Imports – US$588,534m (2016)
Exports – US$407,329m (2016)

BALANCE OF PAYMENTS

Trade – US$181,209m deficit (2016)
Current Account – US$106,504m deficit (2017)

COMMUNICATIONS

Airports – There are 271 licensed civil airports, of which Heathrow (the world's fifth busiest international airport), Gatwick, Stansted and Manchester handle the highest volume of passengers
Waterways – Traditionally a seafaring nation, the UK has a large merchant navy, with 504 ships of over 1,000 tonnes registered in the UK and 308 ships registered overseas. The main ports are at Grimsby and Immingham, London, Milford Haven, Southampton, Tees and Hartlepool, Liverpool, Felixstowe, Forth, Dover and Belfast
Roadways – There are 394,428km of roadways, including 3,617km of motorways
Railways – The 16,454km of rail network is operated by 23 rail companies
Telecommunications – 33.5 million fixed lines and 78.9 million mobile subscriptions (2016); there were 61 million internet users in 2016
Major broadcasters – The British Broadcasting Corporation is a public service broadcaster and provides radio and television programmes, in competition with several commercial radio and television stations, including cable and satellite services
Press – The lively and occasionally controversial newspaper press publishes around ten newspapers daily, including *The Times, The Guardian* and *The Sun*
WPFI score – 23,25 (40)

EDUCATION AND HEALTH

Full-time education is compulsory between the ages of five and 16 in Wales and Scotland and four and 16 in Northern Ireland. In England, full-time education is compulsory between the age of five until the end of the academic year of the pupil's 17th birthday.
Gross enrolment ratio (percentage of relevant age group) – primary 108.2 per cent, secondary 127.8 per cent, tertiary 56.5 per cent (2014 est)
Health expenditure (per capita) – US$3,935 (2014)
Hospital beds (per 1,000 people) – 2.8 (2013)
Life expectancy (years) – 80.8 (2017 est)
Mortality rate – 9.4 (2017 est)
Birth rate – 12.1 (2017 est)
Infant mortality rate – 4.3 (2017 est)
HIV/AIDS adult prevalence – 0.33 per cent (2013 est)

OVERSEAS TERRITORIES

See UK Overseas Territories

UNITED STATES OF AMERICA

Area – 9,833,517 sq. km
Capital – Washington, District of Columbia; population, 5,207,000 (2018)
Major cities – Boston, Chicago, Dallas, Houston, Los Angeles, Miami, New York, Philadelphia, Phoenix, San Antonio, San Diego, San Francisco, San Jose
Currency – US dollar (US$) of 100 cents
Population – 326,625,791 rising at 0.81 per cent a year (2017 est); white (72.4 per cent), black (12.6 per cent), Asian (4.8 per cent), Amerindian and Alaska native (0.9 per cent), native Hawaiian and other Pacific islander (0.2 per cent) (2010 est)
Religion – Christian (Protestant 46.5 per cent, Roman Catholic 20.8 per cent, Mormon 1.6 per cent), Jewish 1.9 per cent, Muslim 0.9 per cent, Buddhist 0.7 per cent (2014 est)
Language – English, Spanish, Hawaiian (official in Hawaii)
Population density – 36 per sq. km (2016)
Urban population – 82.3 per cent (2018 est)
Median age (years) – 38.1 (2017 est)
National anthem – 'The Star-Spangled Banner'
National day – 4 July (Independence Day)
Death penalty – Abolished in 18 states, District of Columbia and US insular territories
CPI score – 75 (16)
Military expenditure – US$609,758m (2016)

CLIMATE AND TERRAIN

The coastline has a length of about 3,329km on the Atlantic Ocean, 12,268km on the Pacific, 1,705km on the Arctic and 2,624km on the Gulf of Mexico. The principal river is the Mississippi-Missouri-Red (5,970km long), traversing the whole country from Montana to its mouth in the Gulf of Mexico. The Rocky mountains range runs the length of the western portion of the country. West of this, bordering the Pacific coast, the Cascade mountains and Sierra Nevada form the outer edge of a high tableland, consisting partly of stony and sandy desert and partly of grazing land and forested mountains, and including the Great Salt Lake, which extends to the Rockies and the hills and low mountains of the eastern states, where large forests still exist, remnants of the forests that

formerly extended over the entire Atlantic slope. Elevation extremes range from 6,190m (Denali, Alaska) to −86m (Death Valley, California). The climate varies with latitude but is mostly temperate, with semi-arid conditions on the Great Plains and arid in the south-west. Average temperatures range from −4.8°C in January to 20°C in July.

Two states are detached: Alaska and Hawaii. Alaska occupies the north-western extremity of North America, separated from the rest of the USA by the Canadian province of British Columbia. The terrain is arctic tundra with mountain ranges, and the climate is arctic. The state of Hawaii is a chain of about 20 mountainous volcanic islands in the north Pacific Ocean, of which the chief islands are Hawaii, Maui, Oahu, Kauai and Molokai. The climate is tropical.

The Pacific coast and Hawaii are prone to seismic activity. The Atlantic and Gulf of Mexico coasts frequently experience hurricanes.

POLITICS

By the constitution of 17 September 1787 (which has been amended 15 times, most recently in 1992), the government of the USA is entrusted to three separate authorities: the federal executive (the president and cabinet), the legislature (Congress, which consists of a senate and a House of Representatives) and the judicature. The president is indirectly elected by an electoral college to serve a four-year term, and may serve a maximum of two consecutive terms. If a president dies in office, the vice-president serves the remainder of the term. The president appoints the cabinet officers and all the chief officials, subject to confirmation by the senate. They makes recommendations of a general nature to Congress, and when laws are passed, they can return them to Congress with a veto. But, if a measure so vetoed is again passed by both houses by a two-thirds majority in each house, it becomes law, notwithstanding the objection of the president.

Each of the 50 states has its own executive, legislature and judiciary. In theory, they are sovereign, but in practice their autonomy is increasingly circumscribed.

PRESIDENTIAL ELECTIONS
Candidates for the presidency must be at least 35 years of age and a native citizen of the USA. The electoral college for each state is directly elected by universal adult suffrage in the November preceding the January in which the presidential term expires. The number of members of the electoral college is equal to the whole number of senators and representatives to which the state is entitled in the national congress. The electoral college for each state meets in its state in December and each member votes for a presidential candidate by ballot. The ballots are sent to Washington, DC, and opened on 6 January by the president of the senate in the presence of Congress. The candidate who has received a majority of the whole number of electoral votes cast is declared president for the ensuing term. If no one has a majority, then from the highest on the list (not exceeding three) the House of Representatives elects a president, the votes being taken by states, the representation from each state having one vote. A presidential term begins at noon on 20 January.

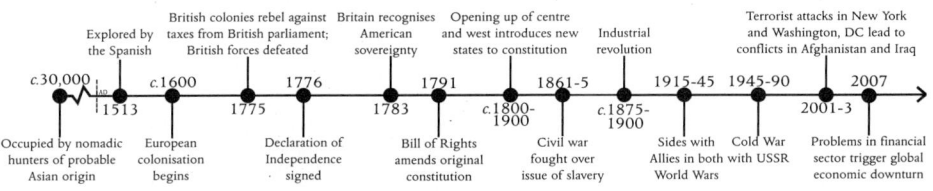

The 2008 presidential election was won by the Democrat candidate Barack Obama, the first African-American to hold the office; he was re-elected in November 2012. In the 2016 legislative elections, the Republican party retained its majority in the House of Representatives, winning 241 seats to the Democrats' 194; the Republicans also retained control of the senate. The November 2016 presidential election was won by the Republican candidate, Donald Trump.

HEAD OF STATE
President, Donald J. Trump, *elected* 2016, *sworn in* 20 January 2017
Vice-President, Mike Pence

SELECTED GOVERNMENT MEMBERS *AS AT JULY 2018*
Defence, Gen. (retd) James Mattis
Interior, Ryan Zinke
Secretary for Homeland Security, Kirstjen Nielsen
Secretary of State, Mike Pompeo
Treasury, Steven Mnuchin

THE CONGRESS
Legislative power is vested in the bicameral Congress, comprising the senate and the House of Representatives. The senate has 100 members, two from each state, elected for a six-year term, with one-third elected every two years. The House of Representatives has 435 members directly elected in each state for a two-year term; a resident commissioner from Puerto Rico and a delegate each from American Samoa, the District of Columbia, Guam, the Northern Mariana Islands and the Virgin Islands serve as non-voting members of the house.

Members of the 115th Congress were elected on 8 November 2016 and sworn into office on 3 January 2017. As at September 2018, the 115th Congress is constituted as follows:
Senate: Republicans 50; Democrats 47; Independents 2
House of Representatives: Republicans 236; Democrats 193
President of the Senate, The Vice-President
Senate majority leader, Mitch McConnell *(R), Kentucky*
Speaker of the House of Representatives, Paul Ryan *(R), Wisconsin*
House majority leader, Kevin McCarthy *(R), California*

THE JUDICATURE
The federal judiciary consists of three sets of federal courts: the Supreme Court at Washington, DC, consisting of a Chief Justice and eight Associate Justices; the US court of appeals, consisting of 179 circuit judges within 12 regional circuits and one federal circuit; and the 94 US district courts served by 678 district court judges.

THE SUPREME COURT
US Supreme Court Building, Washington, DC 20543
Chief Justice, John Roberts, *apptd* 2005

UNITED STATES EMBASSY
24 Grosvenor Square, London W1K 6AH
T 020-7499 9000 W http://london.usembassy.gov
Ambassador Extraordinary and Plenipotentiary, HE Robert Wood Johnson IV, *apptd* 2017

BRITISH EMBASSY
3100 Massachusetts Avenue NW, Washington, DC 20008
T (+1) (202) 588 6500 E washi@fco.gov.uk
W www.gov.uk/government/world/usa
Ambassador Extraordinary and Plenipotentiary, Sir Kim Darroch, KCMG, *apptd* 2016

ECONOMY AND TRADE
The USA is one of the world's leading industrial nations, with a sophisticated market economy that saw huge growth during the 20th century. Economic development was due in part to the mechanisation of the agrarian economy, the expansion of the transport infrastructure and large amounts of relatively cheap migrant labour; more recently it has been driven by rapid advances in technology. In the late 20th century, the economy shifted emphasis from industry to services, and government involvement in the economy was steadily reduced.

The US sub-prime mortgage crisis in 2007 triggered a global economic downturn, and falling property prices and tight credit pushed the domestic economy into recession by mid-2008. Following the failure of several investment banks, Congress passed a US$700bn relief programme to stabilise the financial markets in October 2008, and in spring 2009 a US$787bn fiscal stimulus package and a record US$3.6 trillion budget for 2010 were approved. Despite these measures, the economy still experienced the collapse of key industries (such as vehicle manufacturing), and rising unemployment and inflation before growth restarted in late 2009 after the USA's longest and deepest recession since the 1930s, and grew steadily during 2009–17. By 2018, the wars in Iraq and Afghanistan had cost the treasury an estimated US$1.9 trillion. Corporate and individual tax cuts introduced in January 2018 are set to increase the federal deficit, while President Trump's trade standoff with China may have long-term implications. Rising inequality, an aging population, stagnating lower-income wages, and a deteriorating infrastructure pose long-term challenges.

Agriculture is a major industry in the USA; principal crops are wheat, maize, other grains, fruit, vegetables, cotton, meat and dairy products. Agriculture, fishing and forestry contribute 0.9 per cent of GDP and employ 0.7 per cent of the workforce.

Mining and extraction are important to the economy. Large quantities of coal, iron ore, phosphate rock, copper, zinc and lead are mined. About one-half of the country's oil requirements are imported, with global prices acting as a major determinant of the health of the economy. Natural gas is also produced. Despite its domestic oil and natural gas resources and its electricity generating capacity, the USA is a net importer of energy.

The industrial sector is highly diversified and technologically advanced. The main manufacturing industries produce steel, vehicles, aircraft and aerospace equipment, telecommunications equipment, chemicals, electronic equipment and consumer goods, and process food. Industry contributes 18.9 per cent of GDP and services account for 80.2 per cent of GDP.

The main trading partners are Canada, China, Mexico, Japan and Germany. Principal exports are capital goods (chiefly transistors, aircraft, vehicle parts, computers, telecommunications equipment), industrial supplies, consumer goods (cars, medicines) and agricultural produce (soya beans, fruit, maize). The main imports are industrial goods (especially crude oil), consumer goods (cars, clothing, medicines, furniture, toys), capital goods (computers, telecommunications equipment, vehicle parts, office machines, electric power machinery) and agricultural products.

GNI – US$18,980.3bn; US$58,270 per capita (2017)
Annual average growth of GDP – 2.2 per cent (2017 est)
Inflation rate – 2.1 per cent (2017 est)
Population below poverty line – 15.1 per cent (2010 est)
Unemployment – 4.4 per cent (2017 est)
Total external debt – US$17.91 trillion (2016 est)
Imports – US$2,251,350m (2016)
Exports – US$1,453,830m (2016)

THE STATES OF THE UNION

The USA is a federal republic consisting of 50 states and the federal District of Columbia, and also of organised territories. Of the present 50 states, 13 are original states, seven were admitted without previous organisation as territories, and 30 were admitted after such organisation.

§ The 13 original states

(D) Democratic Party; (I) Independent; (R) Republican Party

State (date and order of admission)	Capital	Governor (end of term in office)	Area (sq. km)	Pop.*
Alabama (AL) (1819, 22)	Montgomery	Kay Ivey (R), Jan. 2019	135,767	4,874,747
Alaska (AK) (1959, 49)	Juneau	Bill Walker (I), Dec. 2018	1,723,337	739,795
Arizona (AZ) (1912, 48)	Phoenix	Doug Ducey (R), Nov. 2018	295,234	7,016,270
Arkansas (AR) (1836, 25)	Little Rock	Asa Hutchinson (R), Jan. 2019	137,732	3,004,279
California (CA) (1850, 31)	Sacramento	Jerry Brown (D), Jan. 2019	423,967	39,536,653
Colorado (CO) (1876, 38)	Denver	John Hickenlooper (D), Jan. 2019	269,601	5,607,154
Connecticut (CT) § (1788, 5)	Hartford	Dannel Malloy (D), Jan. 2019	14,357	3,588,184
Delaware (DE) § (1787,1)	Dover	John Carney (D), Jan. 2021	6,446	961,939
Florida (FL) (1845, 27)	Tallahassee	Rick Scott (R), Jan. 2019	170,312	20,984,400
Georgia (GA) § (1788, 4)	Atlanta	Nathan Deal (R), Jan. 2019	153,910	10,429,379
Hawaii (HI) (1959, 50)	Honolulu	David Ige (D), Jan. 2019	28,313	1,427,538
Idaho (ID) (1890, 43)	Boise	C. L. (Butch) Otter (R), Jan. 2019	216,443	1,716,943
Illinois (IL) (1818, 21)	Springfield	Bruce Rauner (R), Jan. 2019	149,995	12,802,023
Indiana (IN) (1816, 19)	Indianapolis	Eric Holcomb (R), Jan. 2021	94,326	6,666,818
Iowa (IA) (1846, 29)	Des Moines	Kim Reynolds (R), Jan. 2019	145,746	3,145,711
Kansas (KS) (1861, 34)	Topeka	Jeff Colyer (R), Jan. 2019	213,100	2,913,123
Kentucky (KY) (1792, 15)	Frankfort	Matt Bevin (R), Jun. 2019	104,656	4,454,189
Louisiana (LA) (1812, 18)	Baton Rouge	John Bel Edwards (D), Jan. 2020	135,659	4,684,333
Maine (ME) (1820, 23)	Augusta	Paul LePage (R), Jan. 2019	91,633	1,335,907
Maryland (MD) § (1788, 7)	Annapolis	Larry Hogan (R), Jan. 2019	32,131	6,052,177
Massachusetts (MA) § (1788, 6)	Boston	Charlie Baker (R), Jan. 2019	27,336	6,859,819
Michigan (MI) (1837, 26)	Lansing	Rick Snyder (R), Jan. 2019	250,487	9,962,311
Minnesota (MN) (1858, 32)	St Paul	Mark Dayton (D), Jan. 2019	225,163	5,576,606
Mississippi (MS) (1817, 20)	Jackson	Phil Bryant (R), Jan. 2019	125,438	2,984,100
Missouri (MO) (1821, 24)	Jefferson City	Mark Parson (R), Jan. 2021	180,540	6,113,532
Montana (MT) (1889, 41)	Helena	Steve Bullock (D), Jan. 2021	380,831	1,050,493
Nebraska (NE) (1867, 37)	Lincoln	Pete Ricketts (R), Jan. 2019	200,330	1,920,076
Nevada (NV) (1864, 36)	Carson City	Brian Sandoval (R), Jan. 2019	286,380	2,998,039
New Hampshire (NH) § (1788, 9)	Concord	Chris Sununu (R), Jan. 2019	24,214	1,342,795
New Jersey (NJ) § (1787, 3)	Trenton	Phil Murphy (D), Jan. 2022	22,591	9,005,644
New Mexico (NM) (1912, 47)	Santa Fe	Susana Martinez (R), Jan. 2019	314,917	2,088,070
New York (NY) § (1788, 11)	Albany	Andrew Cuomo (D), Jan. 2019	141,297	19,849,399
North Carolina (NC) § (1789, 12)	Raleigh	Roy Cooper (D), Jan. 2021	139,391	10,273,419
North Dakota (ND) (1889, 39)	Bismarck	Doug Burgum (R), Dec. 2020	183,108	755,393
Ohio (OH) (1803, 17)	Columbus	John Kasich (R), Jan. 2019	116,098	11,658,609
Oklahoma (OK) (1803, 17)	Oklahoma City	Mary Fallin (R), Jan. 2019	181,037	3,930,864
Oregon (OR) (1859, 33)	Salem	Kate Brown (D), Jan. 2019	254,799	4,142,776
Pennsylvania (PA) § (1787, 2)	Harrisburg	Tom Wolf (D), Jan. 2019	119,280	12,805,537
Rhode Island (RI) § (1790, 13)	Providence	Gina Raimondo (D), Jan. 2019	4,001	1,059,639
South Carolina (SC) § (1788, 8)	Columbia	Henry McMaster (R), Jan. 2019	82,933	5,024,369
South Dakota (SD) (1889, 40)	Pierre	Dennis Daugaard (R), Jan. 2019	199,729	869,666
Tennessee (TN) (1796, 16)	Nashville	Bill Haslam (R), Jan. 2019	109,153	6,715,984
Texas (TX) (1845, 28)	Austin	Greg Abbott (R), Jan. 2019	695,662	28,304,596
Utah (UT) (1896, 45)	Salt Lake City	Gary Herbert (R), Jan. 2021	219,882	3,101,833
Vermont (VT) (1791, 14)	Montpelier	Phil Scott (R), Jan. 2019	24,906	623,657
Virginia (VA) § (1788, 10)	Richmond	Ralph Northam (D), Jan. 2022	110,787	8,470,020
Washington (WA) (1889, 42)	Olympia	Jay Inslee (D), Jan. 2021	184,661	7,405,743
West Virginia (WV) (1863, 35)	Charleston	Jim Justice (D), Jan. 2021	62,756	1,815,857
Wisconsin (WI) (1848, 30)	Madison	Scott Walker (R), Jan. 2019	169,635	5,795,483
Wyoming (WY) (1890, 44)	Cheyenne	Matthew Mead (R), Jan. 2019	253,335	579,315
Dist. of Columbia (DC) (1791)	–	Muriel Bowser (D), Jan. 2019 (Mayor)	177	693,972

OUTLYING TERRITORIES AND POSSESSIONS

American Samoa	Pago Pago	Lolo Matalasi Moliga (I), Jan. 2021	199	51,504
Guam	Hagatna	Eddie Calvo (R), Jan. 2019	544	167,358
Northern Mariana Islands	Saipan	Ralph Torres (R), Dec. 2019	464	52,263
Puerto Rico	San Juan	Ricardo Rossello (D), Jan. 2021	13,790	3,351,827
US Virgin Islands	Charlotte Amalie	Kenneth Mapp (I), Jan. 2019	1,910	107,268

* States 2017 estimate; outlying territories 2017 estimate

BALANCE OF PAYMENTS
Trade – US$797,520m deficit (2016)
Current Account – US$449,137m deficit (2017)

Trade with UK	2016	2017
Imports from UK	£45,433,617,454	£45,805,422,567
Exports to UK	£39,618,039,106	£41,348,071,950

COMMUNICATIONS

Airports – There are 5,054 airports; nearly 200 are capable of handling international flights, the rest cater for the high domestic demand
Waterways – The main seaports are at Baton Rouge, Corpus Christi, Hampton Roads, Houston, Long Beach, Los Angeles, Miami, New Orleans, New York, Oaklands, Plaquemines, Port Canaveral, Port Everglades, Savannah, Seattle, Tampa and Texas City
Roadways and railways – 4,304,715km, including 76,334km of motorways; 224,792km
Telecommunications – 121.53 million fixed lines and 395.881 million mobile subscriptions (2016); there were 246.8 million internet users in 2016
Internet code and IDD – us; 1 (from UK), 011 44 (to UK)
Major broadcasters – The major television networks are ABC, CBS, NBC, CNN, Fox, MTV, HBO and the Public Broadcasting System, which serves around 350 local member stations and is partially funded by the government and private grants
Press – There are more than 1,500 daily newspapers, including *The Wall Street Journal, USA Today, The Washington Post* and *The New York Times*
WPFI score – 23,73 (45)

EDUCATION AND HEALTH

All the states have compulsory school attendance laws. In general, children are obliged to attend school from seven to 16 years of age.
Gross enrolment ratio (percentage of relevant age group) – primary 100.1 per cent (2015 est), secondary 97.6 per cent (2014 est), tertiary 85.8 per cent (2015 est)
Health expenditure (per capita) – US$9,403 (2014)
Hospital beds (per 1,000 people) – 2.9 (2013)
Life expectancy (years) – 80 (2017 est)
Mortality rate – 8.2 (2017 est)
Birth rate – 12.5 (2017 est)
Infant mortality rate – 5.8 (2017 est)

US TERRITORIES ETC

US insular areas are territories that are not part of one of the 50 US states or a federal district. The US Department of the Interior's Office of Insular Affairs has jurisdiction over American Samoa, Guam, the Northern Mariana Islands, the US Virgin Islands, part of Palmyra Atoll (4 sq. km) and Wake Atoll (6.4 sq. km), the latter shared with the US army's Space and Strategic Defence Command. The US Fish and Wildlife Service has jurisdiction over Baker Island (1.5 sq. km), Howland Island (2.5 sq. km), Jarvis Island (4.2 sq. km), Johnston Atoll (2.5 sq. km, shared with the Defence Threat Reduction Agency), Midway Atoll (5.2 sq. km), Navassa Island (7.8 sq. km), Kingman Reef and part of Palmyra Atoll. The Aleutian Islands (17,666 sq. km) form part of the Alaskan archipelago.

AMERICAN SAMOA
Territory of American Samoa
Area – 199 sq. km
Capital – Pago Pago; population, 48,000 (2014 est)
Population – 51,504 falling at 1.3 per cent a year (2017 est)

Population density – 278 per sq. km (2015)
Urban population – 87.2 per cent (2015 est)
Median age (years) – 25.5 (2017 est)
National day – 17 April (Flag Day)
American Samoa consists of the islands of Tutuila, Aunu'u, Ofu, Olosega, Ta'u, Rose Island and Swains Island. The islands were discovered by Europeans in the 18th century and the USA took possession in 1900. Those born in American Samoa are US non-citizen nationals, although some have acquired citizenship through service in the US armed forces or other naturalisation procedures. American Samoa is represented in Congress by a non-voting delegate, who is directly elected for a two-year term. Under the 1966 constitution, American Samoa has a measure of self-government, with certain powers reserved to the US Secretary of the Interior. The governor and deputy governor are directly elected for a four-year term. The bicameral legislative assembly comprises a 21-member House of Representatives (one appointed member and 20 members directly elected for a two-year term) and an 18-seat senate with members elected from among the traditional chiefs for a four-year term. Tuna fishing and canning are the principal economic activities.
Governor, Lolo Matalasi Moliga (D)

GUAM
Guahan – Territory of Guam
Area – 544 sq. km
Capital – Hagatna (also known as Agana); population, 143,000 (2014 est)
Population – 162,742 rising at 0.64 per cent a year (2016 est); Chamorro (37.3 per cent), Filipino (26.3 per cent), white (7.1 per cent) (2010 est). The official languages are Chamorro (a language of the Malayo-Polynesian family with admixtures of Spanish) and English; most Chamorro residents are bilingual
Religion – Roman Catholic 85 per cent (1999 est)
Population density – 315 per sq. km (2015)
Urban population – 94.5 per cent (2015 est)
Median age (years) – 30.4 (2016 est)
National day – first Monday in March (Discovery Day)
Guam is the largest of the Mariana Islands, in the north Pacific Ocean. A Spanish colony for centuries, it was ceded to the USA in 1898 after the Spanish–American War. Guam was occupied by the Japanese in 1941 but was recaptured by US forces in 1944. Any person born in Guam is a US citizen. Guam is represented in Congress by a non-voting delegate, who is directly elected for a two-year term. Under the Organic Act of Guam 1950, Guam has statutory powers of self-government. The governor and lieutenant-governor are directly elected for a four-year term. The 15-member unicameral legislature is directly elected every two years. The main sources of revenue are tourism (particularly from Japan) and US military spending; the military installation is one of the most strategically important US bases in the Pacific.
Governor, Eddie Calvo (R)
Imports – US$707m (2014)
Exports – US$41m (2014)

Trade with UK	2016	2017
Imports from UK	£2,287,502	£3,022,351
Exports to UK	£15,422,188	£87,783

NORTHERN MARIANA ISLANDS
Commonwealth of the Northern Mariana Islands
Area – 464 sq. km
Seat of government – Saipan; population, 49,000 (2014 est)
Population – 52,263 falling at 0.51 per cent a year (2017 est)

Population density – 120 per sq. km (2015)
Urban population – 89.2 per cent (2015 est)
Median age (years) – 32.7 (2016 est)
National day – 8 January (Commonwealth Day)
The USA administered the Northern Mariana Islands, a group of 14 islands in the north-west Pacific Ocean, as part of a UN trusteeship until the trusteeship agreement was terminated in 1986, when the islands became a commonwealth under US sovereignty. Those resident in 1976 or subsequently born in the islands are US citizens. The islands are represented in Congress by a non-voting representative, who is directly elected for a two-year term. Under the 1978 constitution, the islands are self-governing. The governor and lieutenant-governor are directly elected for a four-year term. The bicameral legislature comprises a 20-member House of Representatives and a nine-member senate; members are directly elected, representatives for two years and senators for four years. Tourism and manufacturing, especially of clothing, are the main industries.
Governor, Ralph Torres (R)

PUERTO RICO
Commonwealth of Puerto Rico
Area – 13,791 sq. km
Capital – San Juan; population, 2,463,000m (2015 est).
   Other major towns are Bayamón, Carolina, Poncel
Population – 3,351,827 falling at 1.74 per cent a year (2017 est); most people are of Spanish descent. The official languages are Spanish and English
Religion – Christian (Roman Catholic 85 per cent, Protestant and other 15 per cent) (est)
Population density – 392 per sq. km (2015)
Urban population – 93.6 per cent (2015 est)
Median age (years) – 39.5 (2016 est)
National day – 25 July (Constitution Day)
GNI – US$69,432 (2015 est); US$19,320 per capita (2013)
Annual average growth of GDP – –1.8 per cent (2016 est)
Puerto Rico (Rich Port) is an island of the Greater Antilles group in the Caribbean Sea and was discovered in 1493 by Columbus. It was a Spanish possession until 1898, when it was ceded to the USA after the Spanish–American War. Residents have been US citizens since 1917, and Puerto Rico is represented in Congress by a non-voting resident commissioner, who is directly elected for a four-year term. Under its 1952 constitution, Puerto Rico is a self-governing commonwealth. The governor is directly elected for a four-year term. The bicameral legislative assembly consists of a 27-member senate and a 51-member House of Representatives, whose members serve four-year terms. Tourism, pharmaceuticals, electronics, clothing and food processing are the main economic activities. In May 2017, Puerto Rico filed for the largest municipal bankruptcy in US history having accrued a US$70bn debt over ten years of recession, while an overwhelming majority of voters backed a plebiscite in June to become a fully fledged US state. Growth has been negative for each of the last 12 years. Following Hurricane Maria in September 2017, the island was declared a federal disaster zone.
Governor, Ricardo Rossello (D)

THE UNITED STATES VIRGIN ISLANDS
Area – 1,910 sq. km
Capital – Charlotte Amalie, on St Thomas; population, 52,000 (2014 est)
Population – 102,951 falling at 0.62 per cent a year (2016 est)
Religion – Christian (Protestant 59 per cent, Roman Catholic 34 per cent) (est)
Population density – 296 per sq. km (2015)

Urban population – 95.3 per cent (2015 est)
Median age (years) – 45.6 (2016 est)
National day – 31 March (Transfer Day)
There are three main islands, St Thomas, St Croix and St John, and about 50 small islets or cays. These constituted the Danish part of the Virgin Islands from the 17th century until purchased by the USA in 1917. Those born in the US Virgin Islands are US nationals. The Virgin Islands are represented in Congress by a non-voting representative, who is directly elected for a two-year term. Under the provisions of the Revised Organic Act of 1954, the islands have powers of self-government. The governor and lieutenant-governor are directly elected for a four-year term. The unicameral senate has 15 members directly elected for a two-year term. Tourism, rum and manufacturing are the main industries.
Governor, Kenneth Mapp (I)

URUGUAY

República Oriental del Uruguay – Oriental Republic of Uruguay

Area – 176,215 sq. km
Capital – Montevideo; population, 1,737,000 (2018 est)
Major towns – Ciudad de la Costa, Salto
Currency – Uruguayan peso of 100 centésimos
Population – 3,360,148 rising at 0.27 per cent a year (2017 est)
Religion – Christian 81.4 per cent (Roman Catholic 47.1 per cent) (2006 est)
Language – Spanish (official), Portunol or Brazilero (Portuguese-Spanish mix used along the northern border)
Population density – 20 per sq. km (2016)
Urban population – 95.3 per cent (2018 est)
Median age (years) – 35 (2017 est)
National anthem – 'Himno Nacional' 'National Anthem'
National day – 25 August (Independence Day)
Death penalty – Abolished for all crimes (since 1907)
CPI score – 70 (23)
Military expenditure – US$1,242m (2017)

CLIMATE AND TERRAIN
The country consists mainly of undulating grassy plains, with low hills. Elevation extremes range from 514m (Cerro Catedral) to 0m (Atlantic Ocean). The principal river is the Rio Negro (with its tributary, the Yi), flowing from north-east to south-west into the Rio Uruguay; damming of the Negro has created a reservoir that is the largest artificial lake in South America. The climate is warm temperate, with occasional cold and strong winds. Average temperatures range from 11.5°C in July to 24.1°C in January.

HISTORY AND POLITICS

The hostility of the indigenous Charrúa Amerindians when the Rio de la Plata was first explored by the Spanish in 1516 discouraged colonisation until the 17th century. Although initially settled by the Portuguese, the *Banda Oriental,* as the territory lying on the eastern bank of the river Uruguay was then called, was disputed between the Portuguese and the Spanish until the late 18th century and then between Brazil and Argentina after Spanish rule was overthrown. Uruguay's independence was recognised in 1828 and a republic was inaugurated in 1830. In the mid-19th century there was a power struggle between the conservatives *(Blancos)* and liberals *(Colorados),* which descended into civil war. From 1904 until the 1960s the country experienced political stability and prosperity.

The period from 1962 to 1973 saw economic decline and turmoil caused by the Marxist Tupamaros guerrillas. They were crushed by a military dictatorship that held power from 1973 until 1985, when a return to civilian rule was agreed after violent anti-government protests at the regime's repressive rule and the deteriorating economy.

The Colorado and National *(Blanco)* parties now both occupy the centre ground, but their dominance of politics has been eroded by left-wing parties such as New Space and coalitions such as the Progressive Encounter-Broad Front (EP-FA). The EP-FA won outright majorities in both legislative chambers in the 2004 and the 2009 elections, before losing its majority in the Chamber of Senators during the 2014 elections. The November 2014 presidential elections were won by Tabaré Vázquez of the FA.

Under the 1997 constitution, the executive president is directly elected for a five-year term, which is not consecutively renewable. The president, who appoints the council of ministers, is responsible to the legislature. The bicameral general assembly consists of a Chamber of Representatives, with 99 members directly elected for a five-year term, and the Chamber of Senators, which has 31 members, 30 directly elected for a five-year term and the vice-president as an *ex officio* member.

The republic is divided into 19 departments, each with an elected governor and legislature.

HEAD OF STATE

President, Tabaré Vázquez, *elected* 1 December 2014, *sworn in* 1 March 2015
Vice-President, Raul Sendic

SELECTED GOVERNMENT MEMBERS *AS AT JULY 2018*

Defence, Jorge Menendez
Economy and Finance, Danilo Astori
Foreign Affairs, Rodolfo Nin Novoa
Interior, Eduardo Bonomi

EMBASSY OF URUGUAY

150 Brompton Road, London SW3 1HX
T 020-7584 2947 E cdlondres@mrree.gub.uy
Ambassador Extraordinary and Plenipotentiary, HE Fernando Lopez-Fabregat, *apptd* 2014

BRITISH EMBASSY

PO Box 16024, Calle Marco Bruto 1073, 11300 Montevideo
T (+598) (2) 622 3630 E ukinuruguay@adinet.com.uy
W www.gov.uk/government/world/uruguay
Ambassador Extraordinary and Plenipotentiary, HE Ian Duddy, *apptd* 2016

ECONOMY AND TRADE

After years of steady growth, Uruguay's free market, export-oriented economy suffered a severe recession from 1998, largely owing to the economic problems of Brazil and Argentina, its main markets and sources of tourists. The recession culminated in a banking crisis in 2002; IMF loans, the rescheduling of foreign debt repayments and the government's emergency measures achieved a recovery and the economy grew strongly from 2004 to 2008. The 2008 global downturn slowed economic growth in 2009, but Uruguay avoided recession, mainly through increased public expenditure. Despite strong growth in 2010, the economy decelerated between 2012–16, before improving in 2017.

Ranching and livestock products (beef, mutton, wool) have been the mainstay of the economy since the mid-19th century, generating the prosperity that enabled Uruguay to develop an extensive welfare system in the early 20th century, although dependence on these products leaves the economy vulnerable to price fluctuations. Other crops include rice, grains, soya beans, wine grapes, linseed and sunflower seed. Agricultural produce is the basis of the food processing and beverage industries. Other industries include fishing, forestry and the manufacture of electrical machinery, transport equipment, petroleum products, textiles and chemicals. Exploited minerals include clinker, dolomite, marble and granite. Tourism and offshore financial services also contribute substantially to revenue. Agriculture contributes 6.2 per cent of GDP, industry 25 per cent and services 68.8 per cent.

The main trading partners are China, Brazil, Argentina and the USA. Principal exports are meat, soya beans, cellulose, rice, wheat, timber, dairy products and wool. The main imports are crude and refined oil, vehicles and vehicle parts, and mobile phones.

GNI – US$52.7bn; US$15,250 per capita (2017)
Annual average growth of GDP – 3.5 per cent (2017 est)
Inflation rate – 6.1 per cent (2017 est)
Population below poverty line – 9.7 per cent (2015 est)
Unemployment – 7.3 per cent (2017 est)
Total external debt – US$28.27bn (2017 est)
Imports – US$7,909m (2016)
Exports – US$7,180m (2016)

BALANCE OF PAYMENTS

Trade – US$728m deficit (2016)
Current Account – US$878.9m surplus (2017)

Trade with UK	2016	2017
Imports from UK	£120,231,700	£176,670,976
Exports to UK	£65,545,484	£57,014,153

COMMUNICATIONS

Airports and waterways – There are 11 airports, including an international airport near Montevideo; there are 1,600km of navigable waterways, mainly on the Uruguay and Negro rivers, and the main ports are located in Montevideo, Colonia, Fray Bentos and Paysandú
Roadways and railways – 7,743km; 1,641km
Telecommunications – 1.1 million fixed lines in use and 5.1 million mobile subscriptions (2016); there were 2.2 million internet users in 2016
Internet code and IDD – uy; 598 (from UK), 44 (to UK)
Major broadcasters – State-run television and radio are operated by SODRE, the official broadcasting service

Press – Major daily newspapers include *El Pais, El Observador* and *El Telegrafo*
WPFI score – 15,56 (20)

EDUCATION AND HEALTH
Primary and secondary education is compulsory and free, and technical and trade schools and evening courses for adult education are state-run.
Literacy rate – 99.0 per cent (2015 est)
Gross enrolment ratio (percentage of relevant age group) – primary 108.6 per cent, secondary 95.1 per cent (2014 est), tertiary 63 per cent (2010 est)
Health expenditure (per capita) – US$1,442 (2014)
Hospital beds (per 1,000 people) – 2.8 (2014)
Life expectancy (years) – 77.4 (2017 est)
Mortality rate – 9.4 (2017 est)
Birth rate – 13 (2017 est)
Infant mortality rate – 8.3 (2017 est)
HIV/AIDS adult prevalence – 0.6 per cent (2016 est)

UZBEKISTAN

O'zbekiston Respublikasi – Republic of Uzbekistan

Area – 447,400 sq. km
Capital – Tashkent; population, 2,464,000 (2018 est)
Major cities – Andijan, Bukhara, Karsi, Namangan, Nukus, Samarkand
Currency – Som of 100 tiyins
Population – 29,748,859 rising at 0.93 per cent a year (2017 est); Uzbek (80 per cent), Russian (5.5 per cent), Tajik (5 per cent), Kazakh (3 per cent), Karakalpak (2.5 per cent), Tatar (1.5 per cent) (1996 est)
Religion – Muslim 88 per cent (predominantly Sunni), Eastern Orthodox 9 per cent (est)
Language – Uzbek (official), Russian, Tajik
Population density – 76 per sq. km (2016)
Urban population – 50.4 per cent (2018 est)
Median age (years) – 28.6 (2017 est)
National anthem – 'O'zbekiston Respublikasining Davlat Madhiyasi' 'National Anthem of the Republic of Uzbekistan'
National day – 1 September (Independence Day, 1991)
Death penalty – Abolished for all crimes (since 2008)
CPI score – 22 (157)
Conscription – 18 years of age; 12 months (selective)

CLIMATE AND TERRAIN
Landlocked Uzbekistan has four regions: the Ustyurt plateau and Amu Darya delta in the west; the Kyzyl Kum desert east of the Aral Sea; the Tien Shan and Pamir mountains in the east and south-east; and the fertile Fergana valley in the east, crossed by the Syr Darya river. Elevation extremes range from 4,301m (Adelunga Toghi) to −12m (Sariqarnish Kuli). The

country includes the southern part of the Aral Sea. There is a semi-arid desert climate, although it is colder in the mountains. Average temperatures range from −2.6°C in January to 27.3°C in July.

HISTORY AND POLITICS
Settlements in the south developed as important transit points on the ancient 'Silk Road' in the first century BC. Bukhara and Samarkand became two of the most important cultural and academic centres in the Islamic world after the religion was introduced in the eighth century. In the 13th century the area became part of the Mongol Empire, with Samarkand as its capital during the reign of Amir Timur (Tamerlane). As the empire declined, independent principalities emerged. The three khanates in what is now Uzbekistan, Khiva, Kokand and Bukhara, were annexed by the Russian Empire in the second half of the 19th century. In 1917 a Bolshevik revolution broke out in Tashkent and by 1921 all of Uzbekistan had been absorbed into the USSR.

Uzbekistan declared its independence from the USSR on 1 September 1991 but post-independence political life has been dominated by the former communists. The main opposition parties, *Erk* (Freedom) and *Birlik* (Unity), were banned in 1992 and have since become inactive. The former communist leader Islam Karimov, who came to power in 1990, was elected president in 1991 and retained the presidency, in unopposed elections or through the extension of his term of office in referendums, until his death in September 2016. Interim leader Shavkat Mirziyoev overwhelmingly won the December 2016 presidential election and Abdulla Aripov was nominated as prime minister.

All legislative elections since independence have been won by the People's Democratic Party (the former Communist Party) or its allies. After the latest legislative election in January 2015, the largest party in the legislative chamber was the pro-Karimov Liberal Democratic Party; opposition parties were barred from contesting the election.

The Islamic Movement of Uzbekistan (IMU), founded in 1996, has carried out armed attacks and bombings sporadically since 1999, but has little support. However, its activities have provided the government with an excuse to curtail human rights and suppress political opposition and protests.

The 1992 constitution was amended in 2002 to create a bicameral legislature and extend the president's term of office. In 2011 it was amended to make the prime minister responsible to the legislature and reduce presidential terms back to five years, after they were raised to seven years in 2002. The president is directly elected and terms are renewable only once. The legislature, the Supreme Assembly, became bicameral after the 2004–5 elections. The Legislative Chamber has 150 members, 135 directly elected and 15 members of the Ecological Movement of Uzbekistan. The senate has 100 members, 16 appointed by the president and 84 elected by regional deputies to represent the regions and the capital. Members of both houses serve a five-year term. The president appoints the cabinet, which is chaired by the prime minister.

The country is divided into 12 provinces, the autonomous republic of Karakalpakstan, and the city of Tashkent.

HEAD OF STATE
President, Shavkat Mirziyoev

SELECTED GOVERNMENT MEMBERS *AS AT JULY 2018*
Prime Minister, Abdulla Aripov
First Deputy Prime Minister, Achilbay Ramatov
Deputy Prime Ministers, Jamshid Kuchkarov *(Finance)*;
   Gulomjon Ibragimov; Zoyir Mirzaev; Tanzila Narbaeva;

Nodir Otrajonov; Sukhrob Holmurodov; Aziz
Abdukhakimov
Foreign Affairs, Abdulaziz Kamilov

EMBASSY OF THE REPUBLIC OF UZBEKISTAN
41 Holland Park, London W11 3RP
T 020-7229 7679 **E** info@uzbekembassy.org
W www.uzbekembassy.org
Ambassador Extraordinary and Plenipotentiary, HE Alisher
Shaykhov, *apptd* 2017

BRITISH EMBASSY
Ul. Gulyamova 67, Tashkent 100000
T (+998) (71) 120 1500 **E** ukin.uzbekistan@fco.gov.uk
W www.gov.uk/government/world/uzbekistan
Ambassador Extraordinary and Plenipotentiary, HE Christopher
Allan, OBE, *apptd* 2015

ECONOMY AND TRADE

The economy remains centrally planned, but under President
Mirziyoev's reforms the private sector has expanded.
Economic growth and living standards are among the worst
in the former Soviet republics, with 14 per cent of the
population living below the poverty line. The 2008 global
downturn had little impact owing to the country's relative
economic isolation. Following a slowdown, the new president
is courting foreign investment by devaluing the official
currency by 50 per cent in September 2017 and loosening
currency restrictions.

The economy is based on intensive agricultural production,
particularly of cotton, made possible by extensive irrigation
schemes. Vegetables, fruit, grain and livestock are also
produced. The main industries are textile manufacture, food
processing, machine building, metallurgy, mining (especially
for gold), oil and natural gas production and chemicals. Oil
and gas exports offer potential for greater economic growth
and have attracted foreign interest, notably from Russia and
China, but exploitation is hampered by a lack of modern oil
pipelines and basic infrastructure. Agriculture contributes
18.5 per cent of GDP, industry 34.4 per cent and services 47
per cent.

The main trading partners are Russia, China, Switzerland,
Kazakhstan and South Korea. Principal exports are oil and
natural gas, cotton, gold, mineral fertilisers, metals, textiles,
food products, machinery and motor vehicles. The main
imports are machinery and equipment, foodstuffs, chemicals
and metals.

GNI – US$64.2bn; US$1,980 per capita (2017)
Annual average growth of GDP – 6 per cent (2017 est)
Inflation rate – 13 per cent (2017 est)
Population below poverty line – 14 per cent (2016 est)
Unemployment – 4.9 per cent (2017 est)
Total external debt – US$18.86bn (2017 est)
Imports – US$16,973m (2014)
Exports – US$18,529m (2014)

BALANCE OF PAYMENTS
Trade – US$1,288m surplus (2013)

Trade with UK	2016	2017
Imports from UK	£32,412,398	£29,490,928
Exports to UK	£1,415,453	£1,824,344

COMMUNICATIONS

Airports and waterways – The principal airport is at Tashkent
and there are 1,100km of waterways
Roadways and railways – 75,511km; 4,230km
Telecommunications – 3.4 million fixed lines and 23.3 million
mobile subscriptions (2016); there were 13.8 million internet
users in 2016
Major broadcasters – The National Television and Radio
Company is the state-operated broadcaster; many private
media outlets associated with President Karimov's daughter,
Gulnara Karimova, have closed since 2013
Press – Leading dailies include *Khalq Sozi* (Uzbek language),
and *Narodnoye Slovo* and *Pravda Vostoka* (both Russian
language)
WPFI score – 60,84 (165)

EDUCATION AND HEALTH

Literacy rate – 99.9 per cent (2015 est)
Gross enrolment ratio (percentage of relevant age group) – primary
103 per cent, secondary 93 per cent, tertiary 9 per cent
(2017 est)
Health expenditure (per capita) – US$124 (2014)
Hospital beds (per 1,000 people) – 4 (2013)
Life expectancy (years) – 74 (2017 est)
Mortality rate – 5.3 (2017 est)
Birth rate – 16.8 (2017 est)
Infant mortality rate – 18 (2017 est)
HIV/AIDS adult prevalence – 0.2 per cent (2015 est)

VANUATU

Ripablik blong Vanuatu/République de Vanuatu – Republic of
Vanuatu

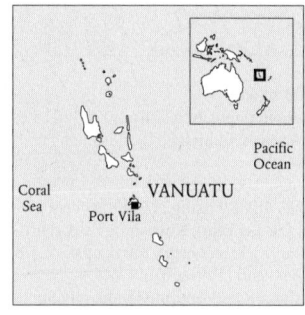

Area – 12,189 sq. km
Capital – Port Vila, on Efaté; population, 53,000 (2018 est)
Major town – Luganville, on Espiritu Santo
Currency – Vatu
Population – 282,814 rising at 1.85 per cent a year (2017
est); 98.7 per cent are Melanesian, the rest being mostly
Micronesian, Polynesian and European (2009 est)
Religion – Christian 82.4 per cent (Presbyterian 27.9 per
cent, Anglican 15.1 per cent, Seventh-day Adventist 12.5
per cent, Roman Catholic 12.4 per cent) (2009 est)
Language – Bislama, English, French (all official); over 100
local languages exist
Population density – 23 per sq. km (2016)
Urban population – 25.3 per cent (2018 est)
Median age (years) – 22 (2017 est)
National anthem – 'Yumi, Yumi, Yumi' 'We, We, We'
National day – 30 July (Independence Day)
Death penalty – Abolished for all crimes (since 1980)
Literacy rate – 95.7 per cent (2015 est)

Gross enrolment ratio (percentage of relevant age group) – primary
123.7 per cent (2013 est)
Health expenditure (per capita) – US$158 (2014)
Life expectancy (years) – 73.7 (2017 est)
Mortality rate – 4 (2017 est)
Birth rate – 24 (2017 est)
Infant mortality rate – 14.4 (2017 est)

CLIMATE AND TERRAIN

Situated in the south Pacific Ocean, Vanuatu comprises 13
large and some 70 small islands, of either coral or volcanic
origin, including the Banks Islands and Torres Islands in the
north. The principal islands are Vanua Lava, Espiritu Santo,
Maewo, Pentecost, Ambae, Malekula, Ambrym, Epi, Efaté,
Erromango, Tanna and Aneityum. Most islands are
mountainous and covered with dense rainforest. Elevation
extremes range from 1,877m (Tabwemasana) to 0m (Pacific
Ocean). The climate varies from tropical in the north of the
archipelago to subtropical in the south, and all the islands
experience cyclones. In 2018, a volcanic eruption on Ambae
island forced the evacuation of all 11,000 inhabitants.

HISTORY AND POLITICS

Some of the islands of Vanuatu have been inhabited for over
4,000 years. Europeans first visited in the early 17th century,
and Captain Cook named the islands the New Hebrides in
1774. In the 19th century, the British and the French
established plantations, and from 1906 jointly administered
the islands as the Condominium of the New Hebrides. This
became independent as the Republic of Vanuatu in 1980.

Vanuatu has a history of producing unstable governments
and three prime ministers have been deposed by
parliamentary votes of no confidence since the 2012 elections:
Sato Kilman in March 2013, Mona Kalosil in May 2014 and
Joe Natuman in June 2015. Parliament was dissolved in
November 2015 after 14 MPs were convicted of bribery. In
the January 2016 legislative elections no single party had a
parliamentary majority. After nearly two weeks of
negotiations, 11 political groupings formed the government
and Charlot Salwai of the Reunification of the Movements for
Change party was elected prime minister. Independent
candidate Baldwin Lonsdale won the presidency in 2014
following eight rounds of voting, but was replaced by Tallis
Obed Moses in July 2017 after his sudden death.

Under the 1980 constitution, the head of state is a president
who is elected for a five-year term by an electoral college
consisting of the members of the legislature and the presidents
of the six provincial governments. The unicameral parliament
has 52 members, directly elected for a four-year term. The
prime minister is elected by parliament from among its
members, and appoints the council of ministers. The National
Council of Chiefs advises on matters of custom.

HEAD OF STATE
President, Tallis Obed Moses, *elected* 6 July 2017

SELECTED GOVERNMENT MEMBERS *AS AT JULY 2018*
Prime Minister, Charlot Salwai
Deputy Prime Minister, Joe Natuman
Finance, Gaetan Pikioune
Internal Affairs, Andrew Napuat

EMBASSY OF VANUATU
Avenue de Tervueren 380, Chemin de Ronde 1150, Brussels
T (+32) (2) 771 7494 E info@vanuataembassy.be
High Commissioner, HE Roy Mickey Joy, *apptd* 2011

BRITISH HIGH COMMISSIONER
HE David Ward, *apptd* 2016, resident at Honiara, Solomon
Islands

ECONOMY AND TRADE

The economy is based on small-scale agriculture and fishing;
63.9 per cent of the population is employed on plantations or
in subsistence agriculture, although the sector was devastated
by Cyclone Pam in March 2015. Subsistence crops include
yams, taro, fruit and vegetables; the principal cash crops are
coconuts, cocoa and coffee. Cattle are kept on the plantations.
There is a small light industrial sector producing frozen food,
fish and canned meat, and processing wood. Eco-tourism and
offshore financial services are of growing importance. While
Australia and New Zealand supply revenue via aid, tourism
from those countries was hit in 2016 when three major
carriers suspended flights due to the poor runway conditions,
but tourism has since improved with 330,000 visitors in
2017.

The main export markets are the Philippines, Australia and
the USA; imports come chiefly from Russia, Australia, Japan
and New Zealand. Principal exports are copra, beef, cocoa,
timber, kava and coffee. The main imports are machinery and
equipment, foodstuffs and fuels.
GNI – US$0.8bn; US$2,920 per capita (2017)
Annual average growth of GDP – 4.5 per cent (2017 est)
Inflation rate – 2.6 per cent (2017 est)
Total external debt – US$185.4m (2017 est)
Imports – US$422m (2016)
Exports – US$50m (2016)

BALANCE OF PAYMENTS
Trade – US$372m deficit (2016)
Current Account – US$821m deficit (2015)

Trade with UK	2016	2017
Imports from UK	£380,255	£721,325
Exports to UK	£2,017,016	£250,010

COMMUNICATIONS

Airports and waterways – The main international airport is at
Port Vila and the main ports are located in Forari, Port Vila
and Santo
Roadways – 1,070km, of which 256km are unpaved
Telecommunications – 4,555 main fixed lines and 218,603
mobile subscriptions (2016); there were 66,613 internet users
in 2016
Media – Vanuatu Broadcasting and Television Corporation
operates Television Blong Vanuatu

VATICAN CITY STATE

*Status Civitatis Vaticanae or Sancta Sedes / Stato della Città del
Vaticano or Santa Sede* – *State of the Vatican City*

Area – 0.44 sq. km (enclave only)
Capital – Vatican City; population 1,000 (2018 est)
Currency – Euro (€) of 100 cents

Population – 1,000 (2017 est)
Religion – Christian (Roman Catholic)
Language – Latin (official), Italian, French
National anthem – 'Inno e Marcia Pontificale' 'Hymn and Pontifical March'
National day – 13 March (election of Pope Francis)
Death penalty – Abolished for all crimes (since 1969)

HISTORY AND POLITICS

The Vatican City State is an independent sovereign state that consists of an enclave within the city of Rome and extraterritorial areas including offices and basilicas in Rome, the pope's summer residence and the location of Vatican Radio's transmitter. The Holy See, which comprises the pope and the departments that carry out the government of the Roman Catholic Church worldwide, has sovereign authority over the Vatican City State's territory, providing its government and diplomatic representation overseas.

The head of the Roman Catholic Church became a temporal ruler in the eighth century, holding territory in central Italy. The Papal States were annexed in 1860 by the newly unified kingdom of Italy, and Rome was captured by Italian troops in 1870–1, when the pope withdrew into the Vatican palace. In the Lateran treaties (1929), Italy recognised the pope's sovereignty over the city of the Vatican, and declared the state to be neutral and inviolable territory. The Vatican City State has special observer status at the United Nations.

The pope, the Sovereign Pontiff, is the head of state of the Vatican City, which is governed as an absolute monarchy. He is elected for life by a conclave consisting of those members of the Sacred College of Cardinals who are under the age of 80. Administration of the state is carried out by the Pontifical Commission and the Secretariat of State, which are appointed by the pope. All Vatican officials vacate their offices on the death of a pope. Pope Benedict XVI confirmed in office the president of the Pontifical Commission and the members of the Secretariat of State after his election. Pope Benedict XVI resigned in February 2013 and was succeeded by Pope Francis.

Sovereign Pontiff, His Holiness Pope Francis (Jorge Mario Bergoglio), *born* 17 December 1936, *elected* 13 March 2013, *inaugurated* 19 March 2013

SECRETARIAT OF STATE *AS AT JULY 2018*
Secretary of State, Cardinal Pietro Parolin
Substitute for General Affairs, Archbishop Giovanni Becciu
Secretary for Relations with States, Archbishop Paul Gallagher

PONTIFICAL COMMISSION
President, Cardinal Giuseppe Bertello

APOSTOLIC NUNCIATURE
54 Parkside, London SW19 5NE
T 020-8944 7189
Apostolic Nuncio, HE Archbishop Edward Adams, *apptd* 2017

BRITISH EMBASSY TO THE HOLY SEE
Via XX Settembre 80/A, 00187 Rome
T (+39) (6) 4220 4000 E holysee@fco.gov.uk
W www.gov.uk/government/world/holy-see
Ambassador Extraordinary and Plenipotentiary, HE Sally Axworthy, MBE, *apptd* 2016

ECONOMY

The Vatican City budget is separate from that of the Holy See. The City's revenue is generated by museum admission charges and the sale of postage stamps, coins, medals, souvenirs and publications. The Holy See derives its income from investments, property, global banking and financial services and donations from Roman Catholics worldwide. Pope Francis

began a process of reforming the Vatican Bank in 2014 following a number of scandals. The annual collections known as Peter's Pence are used for charitable and overseas aid work and disaster relief.

VENEZUELA

República Bolivariana de Venezuela – Bolivarian Republic of Venezuela

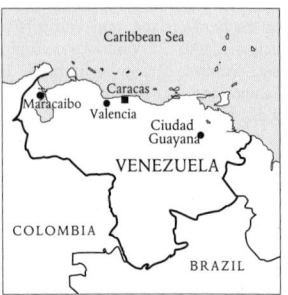

Area – 912,050 sq. km
Capital – Caracas; population, 2,935,000 (2018 est)
Major cities – Barquisimeto, Ciudad Guayana, Maracaibo, Valencia
Currency – Bolívar fuerte (Bs. F) of 100 céntimos
Population – 31,304,016 rising at 1.24 per cent a year (2017 est)
Religion – Christian (Roman Catholic 96 per cent) (est)
Language – Spanish (official), several indigenous languages
Population density – 36 per sq. km (2016)
Urban population – 88.2 per cent (2018 est)
Median age (years) – 28.3 (2017 est)
National anthem – 'Gloria al Bravo Pueblo' 'Glory to the Brave People'
National day – 5 July (Independence Day)
Death penalty – Abolished for all crimes (since 1863)
CPI score – 18 (169)
Military expenditure – US$9,222m (2016)
Conscription – 18–60 years of age; 12 months

CLIMATE AND TERRAIN

The Andean mountains, of which the main range is the Sierra Nevada de Mérida, run across the north-west of the country, separating the northern coast from the central plains *(llanos)*. The Guiana Highlands occupy the south-east of the country. Elevation extremes range from 5,007m (Pico Bolivar) to 0m (Caribbean Sea). The Orinoco flows across the centre of the country to its delta on the Atlantic coast. Its upper waters are united with those of the Rio Negro (a Brazilian tributary of the Amazon) by a natural river or canal, known as the Brazo Casiquiare. The coastal lowlands contain many lagoons and lakes, including Lake Maracaibo (area 13,351 sq. km), the largest lake in South America. The climate varies from tropical to alpine, depending on altitude, and most areas experience a wet season from May to November. The average temperature is 25.8°C.

HISTORY AND POLITICS

Columbus landed on the coast in 1498, and the first Spanish settlement was established at Cumaná in 1520. Venezuela became part of the Viceroyalty of New Granada in the early 18th century. There were several revolts against Spanish colonial rule, and a declaration of independence in 1811 was followed by several years of struggle until troops led by Simón

Bolivar defeated the Spanish at the battle of Carabobo in 1821. Venezuela became part of Gran Colombia (with Colombia, Ecuador and Panama), and then an independent republic in 1830 under the first of a series of *caudillos* (military leaders). The first truly democratic elections were held in 1947 but the government was overthrown by the military within months. An enduring civilian democracy was established in 1958.

Oil revenues supported a buoyant economy in the 1970s but a price collapse in the mid-1980s led to economic difficulties and a number of attempted coups. After he came to power in 1998, President Hugo Chávez's economic and social reforms, and his authoritarian style polarised domestic opinion, provoking strikes and demonstrations, an attempted military coup in 2002 and a recall referendum in 2004, which he won.

President Hugo Chávez was re-elected in 2006. Despite re-election in October 2012, the president was too ill to be re-inaugurated and died on 5 March 2013. Nicolas Maduro, also of the United Socialist Party of Venezuela (PSUV), was elected to succeed him in April 2013. The opposition Democratic Unity alliance (MUD) won 112 seats in the December 2015 legislative election to the PSUV's 55, threatening President Maduro's position. Calls for early presidential elections, opposition to planned constitutional changes and a failing economy have been the focus of growing demonstrations since April 2017, some of which have resulted in violence and deaths. Opposition candidates boycotted the May 2018 presidential elections amid a deteriorating economic crisis, handing Maduro a second term but claiming widespread electoral fraud.

Under the 1999 constitution, the executive president is directly elected for a six-year term; the limit on the number of successive terms was abolished in 2009. The unicameral National Assembly has 167 members, 164 directly elected and three representing indigenous people, who serve a five-year term. The president appoints the vice-president and the council of ministers.

The country is divided into 23 states, one capital district and one federal dependency composed of 11 island groups (72 individual islands). The states have considerable autonomy and each has its own legislature and elected governor.

HEAD OF STATE
President, Nicolas Maduro, *elected* 14 April 2013, *sworn in* 19 April 2013, *re-elected* 20 May 2018
Executive Vice-President, Tareck El Aissami

SELECTED GOVERNMENT MEMBERS *AS AT AUGUST 2018*
Defence, Vladimir Padrino
Economy, Simon Zerpa (acting)
Foreign Relations, Samuel Moncada

EMBASSY OF THE BOLIVARIAN REPUBLIC OF VENEZUELA
1 Cromwell Road, London SW7 2HW
T 020-7584 4206 E embavenezuk@venezlon.co.uk W http://reinounido.embajada.gob.ve
Ambassador Extraordinary and Plenipotentiary, HE Rocio Maneiro, *apptd* 2014

BRITISH EMBASSY
Edificio Torre la Castellana, Piso 11, Avenida la Principal de la Castellana, Caracas 1601
T (+58) (212) 263 8411 E ukinvenezuela@fco.gov.uk
W www.gov.uk/government/world/venezuela
Ambassador Extraordinary and Plenipotentiary, HE Andrew Soper, *apptd* 2017

ECONOMY AND TRADE

Much of industry is state-owned; after the Chávez regime came to power a large proportion of the private sector, some foreign-owned, was nationalised, including oil, electricity, financial, steel, construction and agribusiness companies. Laws passed in December 2010 aimed to increase government control of the economy, which struggled because of imbalances, high inflation and electricity shortages caused by a severe drought in 2009–10 that left hydroelectric plants inoperable. Hyperinflation, currency controls, a growing black market and low global oil prices in recent years has resulted in widespread shortages and a growing migration crisis. It is estimated over 1.5 million people have left the country between 2014–18.

Oil and gas are the mainstays of the economy; other major industries are mining (coal, iron ore, bauxite, gold), production of construction materials, medical equipment, chemicals, steel and aluminium, pharmaceuticals and food processing. Industry contributes 38.2 per cent of GDP and services 57.4 per cent.

Agriculture comprises large-scale commercial farms and subsistence farming. Land distribution is uneven, but redistribution of land to the rural poor, breaking up larger estates, has begun. Agricultural products include maize, sorghum, sugar cane, rice, bananas, vegetables and coffee. There is an extensive beef and dairy farming industry. Agriculture provides 4.4 per cent of GDP and engages 7.3 per cent of the workforce.

The main trading partners are the USA, China, Brazil, Mexico and India. Principal exports are oil, bauxite and aluminium, minerals, chemicals, and agricultural products. The main imports are agricultural products, raw materials, machinery, transport equipment and construction materials.

GNI – US$356,678m (2015 est); US$11,780 per capita (2013)
Annual average growth of GDP – –12 per cent (2017 est)
Inflation rate – 652.7 per cent (2017 est)
Population below poverty line – 19.7 per cent (2015 est)
Unemployment – 26.4 per cent (2017 est)
Total external debt – US$103.1bn (2017 est)
Imports – US$40,146m (2015)
Exports – US$37,236m (2015)

BALANCE OF PAYMENTS
Trade – US$2,910m deficit (2015)
Current Account – US$3,870m deficit (2016)

Trade with UK	2016	2017
Imports from UK	£104,675,069	£66,803,030
Exports to UK	£126,867,030	£98,293,453

COMMUNICATIONS

Airports and waterways – There are 127 airports, the principal terminals being at Caracas and Maracaibo; the main ports are Maracaibo, Puerto Cabello and Caracas-La Guaira
Roadways and railways – 32,308km; 806km
Telecommunications – 7.66 million fixed lines in use and 27.6 million mobile subscriptions (2016); there were 18.5 million internet users in 2016
Internet code and IDD – ve; 58 (from UK), 44 (to UK)
Major broadcasters – Venezolana de Television and Radio Nacional de Venezuela are the state broadcasters
Press – Major daily newspapers include *El Mundo, El Nacional* and *Ultimas Noticias*
WPFI score – 46,03 (143)

EDUCATION AND HEALTH
There are nine years of compulsory education.
Literacy rate – 98.9 per cent (2015 est)
Gross enrolment ratio (percentage of relevant age group) – primary
    97 per cent, secondary 86 per cent (2016 est), tertiary 78
    per cent (2013 est)
Health expenditure (per capita) – US$873 (2014)
Hospital beds (per 1,000 people) – 0.8 (2014)
Life expectancy (years) – 76 (2017 est)
Mortality rate – 5.3 (2017 est)
Birth rate – 18.8 (2017 est)
Infant mortality rate – 12.2 (2017 est)
HIV/AIDS adult prevalence – 0.6 per cent (2016 est)

VIETNAM

*Cong Hoa Xa Hoi Chu Nghia Viet Nam – Socialist Republic of
Vietnam*

Area – 331,210 sq. km
Capital – Hanoi; population, 1,064,000 (2018 est)
Major cities – Bien Hoa, Da Nang, Haiphong, Ho Chi Minh
    City (Saigon)
Currency – Dong of 10 ho or 100 xu
Population – 96,160,163 rising at 0.93 per cent a year (2017
    est); Kinh (85.7 per cent), Tay (1.9 per cent), Thai (1.8 per
    cent), Khmer (1.5 per cent), Muong (1.5 per cent), Hmong
    (1.2 per cent), Nung (1.1 per cent) (2009)
Religion – Buddhist 7.9 per cent, Christian (Roman Catholic,
    6.6 per cent, Protestant 0.9 per cent), Hoa Hao 1.7 per
    cent, Cao Dai 0.9 per cent, none 81.8 per cent (2009 est);
    Cao Dai is a syncretistic religion that combines elements
    of several faiths; Hoa Hao is a branch of Buddhism
Language – Vietnamese (official), English, French, Chinese,
    Khmer; Mon-Khmer and Malayo-Polynesian are spoken
    in mountain areas
Population density – 308 per sq. km (2016)
Urban population – 35.9 per cent (2018 est)
Median age (years) – 30.5 (2017 est)
National anthem – 'Tien Quan Ca' 'The Marching Song'
National day – 2 September (Independence Day)
Death penalty – Retained
CPI score – 35 (105)
Military expenditure – US$5,017m (2016)
Conscription – Men aged 18–25; 18–24 months

CLIMATE AND TERRAIN
The country is mostly mountainous, apart from the densely
populated fertile plains around the deltas of the Hong (Red
river) in the north and the Mekong in the south. Elevation
extremes range from 3,144m (Fan Si Pan) to 0m (South China
Sea). The climate is tropical and affected by the monsoon
cycle. The wet season lasts from May to September, although
the coast, being affected by typhoons and tropical storms,
receives most rain between September and January.

POLITICS
The 1992 constitution was amended in 2001 to allow small-
scale capitalism greater freedom. The president is elected by
the legislature to serve a five-year term. The unicameral
National Assembly *(Quoc-Hoi)* has 500 members, who are
directly elected for a five-year term. The head of government
is the prime minister, who is responsible to the National
Assembly, which appoints the council of ministers. However,
effective power lies with the Communist Party of Vietnam. Its
highest executive body is the Central Committee, elected by
the national party congress held every five years. The
politburo and the secretariat of the central committee, which
exercise the real power, are elected at the party congress.

After the 2006 Communist Party Congress, the president
and prime minister resigned to allow a younger leadership to
be appointed. In April 2016, Tran Dai Quang was elected
president and Nguyen Xuan Phuc became prime minister. In
the May 2016 legislative election, 496 candidates secured
enough votes to be elected to the National Assembly,
including 475 members of the Communist Party, the highest
proportion ever.

HEAD OF STATE
President, Tran Dai Quang, *elected* 2 April 2016
Vice-President, Dang Thi Ngoc Thinh

SELECTED GOVERNMENT MEMBERS *AS AT JULY 2018*
Prime Minister, Nguyen Xuan Phuc
Deputy Prime Ministers, Pham Binh Minh *(Foreign Affairs)*;
    Truong Hoa Binh; Vu Duc Dam; Trinh Dinh Dung;
    Vuong Dinh Hue
Defence, Gen. Ngo Xuan Lich
Finance, Dinh Tien Dung

EMBASSY OF THE SOCIALIST REPUBLIC OF VIETNAM
12–14 Victoria Road, London W8 5RD
T 020-7937 1912 E vanphong@vietnamembassy.org.uk
W www.vietnamembassy.org.uk
Ambassador Extraordinary and Plenipotentiary, HE An Ngoc
    Tran, *apptd* 2017

BRITISH EMBASSY
Central Building, 31 Hai Ba Trung, Hanoi
T (+84) (4) 3936 0500 E consularenquiries.vietnam@fco.gov.uk
W www.gov.uk/government/world/vietnam
Ambassador Extraordinary and Plenipotentiary, HE Gareth Ward,
    apptd 2018

ECONOMY AND TRADE
The economy struggled for a decade after 1975 owing to the
devastation of war and the imposition of a centrally planned
economy. Since economic liberalisation and international
integration were adopted in 1986, the economy has grown
substantially, albeit from a low base, and export-driven
industries are being developed. The global downturn reduced
economic growth in 2008–9, and in early 2012 the
government introduced a three-fold economic reform
programme, proposing a restructuring of the banking sector,
public spending and state-owned enterprises. Vietnam formed
a common market with the other members of the Association
of Southeast Asian Nations (ASEAN) in 2015 and in 2017
exceeded growth predictions thanks to domestic demand and
rising manufacturing exports. The country's fast-growing
economy is set to continue performing well.

Agriculture's contribution is gradually shrinking, but still
accounts for 15.3 per cent of GDP and employs 40.3 per cent
of the workforce. The main industries are food processing,
clothing and footwear, machine building, coal mining, steel,

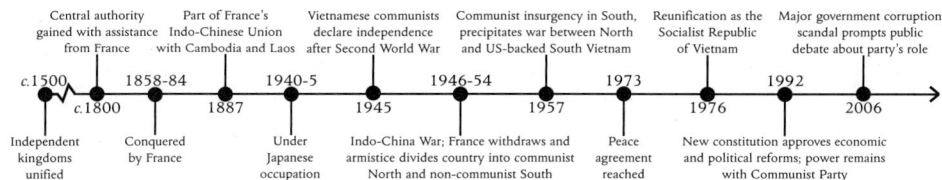

Central authority gained with assistance from France — c.1500

Part of France's Indo-Chinese Union with Cambodia and Laos — 1858-84

Vietnamese communists declare independence after Second World War — 1940-5

Communist insurgency in South, precipitates war between North and US-backed South Vietnam — 1946-54

Reunification as the Socialist Republic of Vietnam — 1973

Major government corruption scandal prompts public debate about party's role — 1992

c.1800 — Independent kingdoms unified

1887 — Conquered by France

1945 — Under Japanese occupation

1957 — Indo-China War; France withdraws and armistice divides country into communist North and non-communist South

1976 — Peace agreement reached

2006 — New constitution approves economic and political reforms; power remains with Communist Party

cement, chemical fertiliser, glass, tyres and mobile phone production, and oil and gas production from large offshore reserves. Tourism is also a growing sector. Industry contributes one-third of GDP and services 41.3 per cent.

The main trading partners are China, Japan, South Korea and the USA. Principal exports are clothing, footwear, electronics, fish and seafood, crude oil, wood products, rice and machinery. The main imports are machinery and equipment, petroleum products, steel products, raw materials, electronics, plastics and vehicles.

GNI – US$206.9bn; US$2,170 per capita (2017)
Annual average growth of GDP – 6.3 per cent (2017 est)
Inflation rate – 4.4 per cent (2017 est)
Population below poverty line – 11.3 per cent (2012 est)
Unemployment – 2.3 per cent (2017 est)
Total external debt – US$91.79bn (2017 est)
Imports – US$174,111m (2016)
Exports – US$176,632m (2016)

BALANCE OF PAYMENTS
Trade – US$2,520m surplus (2016)
Current Account – US$6,124m surplus (2017)

Trade with UK	2016	2017
Imports from UK	£482,510,392	£578,921,497
Exports to UK	£3,779,876,364	£4,173,594,011

COMMUNICATIONS
Airports and waterways – The principal airports and ports are at Ho Chi Minh City, Hanoi and Da Nang
Roadways and railways – 148,338km; 2,632km
Telecommunications – 5.6 million fixed lines and 120.6 million mobile subscriptions (2016); there were 49.7 million internet users in 2016
Internet code and IDD – vn; 84 (from UK), 44 (to UK)
Major broadcasters – Vietnam Television (VTV) and Voice of Vietnam (radio) are the state-run broadcasters
Press – Leading newspapers include the Communist Party daily *Nhan Dahn*, *Vietnam Economic Times* and *Le Courrier du Vietnam*
WPFI score – 75,05 (175)

EDUCATION AND HEALTH
Literacy rate – 98.1 per cent (2015 est)
Gross enrolment ratio (percentage of relevant age group) – primary 110 per cent (2016 est), secondary 77 per cent (2011 est), tertiary 28 per cent (2016 est)
Health expenditure (per capita) – US$142 (2014)
Hospital beds (per 1,000 people) – 2.6 (2013)
Life expectancy (years) – 73.7 (2017 est)
Mortality rate – 5.9 (2017 est)
Birth rate – 15.5 (2017 est)
Infant mortality rate – 17.3 (2017 est)
HIV/AIDS adult prevalence – 0.5 per cent (2015 est)

YEMEN

Al-Jumhuriyah al-Yamaniyah – Republic of Yemen

Area – 527,968 sq. km
Capital – Sana'a; population, 2,779,000 (2018 est)
Major cities – Aden (the former capital of South Yemen), Hudaida (al-Hudaydah), Ibb, al-Mukalla, Taiz
Currency – Riyal of 100 fils
Population – 28,036,829 rising at 2.28 per cent a year (2017 est)
Religion – Muslim (Sunni 65 per cent, Shia 35 per cent) (2010 est)
Language – Arabic (official)
Population density – 54 per sq. km (2016)
Urban population – 36.6 per cent (2018 est)
Median age (years) – 19.5 (2017 est)
National anthem – 'Al-Jumhuriyah al-Muttahida' 'United Republic'
National day – 22 May (Unification Day)
Death penalty – Retained
CPI score – 16 (175)
Military expenditure – US$1,715m (2015)

CLIMATE AND TERRAIN
A mountainous region in the west and south divides the desert plains of the interior from the narrow coastal plains. Elevation extremes range from 3,760m (Jabal an Nabi Shu'ayb) to 0m (Arabian Sea). There is a desert climate, which is particularly harsh in the east, but moderated in the western mountains by the monsoon. The coast experiences high humidity and the average temperature is 24.4°C.

The islands of Perim and Kamaran in the Red Sea, and Suqutra in the Gulf of Aden, are Yemeni territory. The border with Saudi Arabia, except for the north-west corner, is unclear and is being delineated following an agreement between the two countries.

POLITICS
The president announced in March 2011 the drafting of a new constitution transferring powers from the presidency to the legislature. Under the 1991 constitution, the president is directly elected for a seven-year term, renewable once. The bicameral parliament consists of the House of Representatives *(Majlis al-Nuwaab)* which has 301 members directly elected

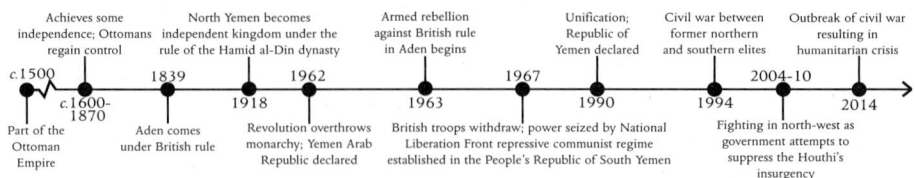

Achieves some independence; Ottomans regain control — *c.1500*

North Yemen becomes independent kingdom under the rule of the Hamid al-Din dynasty — 1839

Armed rebellion against British rule in Aden begins — 1962

Unification; Republic of Yemen declared — 1967

Civil war between former northern and southern elites — 1990

Outbreak of civil war resulting in humanitarian crisis — 2004-10

*c.*1600-1870 — Part of the Ottoman Empire

1918 — Aden comes under British rule

1963 — Revolution overthrows monarchy; Yemen Arab Republic declared

1990 — British troops withdraw; power seized by National Liberation Front repressive communist regime established in the People's Republic of South Yemen

1994 — Fighting in north-west as government attempts to suppress the Houthi's insurgency

2014

for a six-year term, and 111 members in the Shura Council *(Majilis Ashoora)*, directly appointed by the president for, who also appoints the prime minister.

In the 2003 legislative election, the ruling General People's Congress (GPC) won 238 seats and formed a coalition government with the Yemeni Alliance for Reform (YAR or al-Islah). Lt.-Gen. Ali Abdullah Saleh, president of North Yemen from 1978 and president of the united country since 1990, was forced to resign in December 2011 following sustained protests. He was replaced by former vice-president Abd-Rabbu Mansour Hadi after transitional presidential elections in 2012. Parliamentary elections scheduled for 2009 have been repeatedly postponed due to the ongoing conflict.

Following rising political tensions and violence in 2013 and 2014, in September 2014 Houthi rebels took control of most of the capital, Sana'a, after the Hadi administration failed to acquiesce to their demands for reform. In January 2015 the rebels rejected proposals for a new constitution and in February President Hadi fled to Aden. In March, the group looked to annex territory in southern Yemen and were attacked by both IS suicide bombers, who targeted Shia mosques, and Saudi Arabian air strikes. Saudi-backed forces began to recapture territory from the Houthis in September. UN-sponsored peace talks began in April 2016 but attacks have continued on the military, rebels and civilians, and Saudi Arabia and the USA continue to carry out airstrikes. In June 2018, the Saudi-led coalition launched an offensive to retake the port of Hodeidah, sparking the largest battle of the war.

A Saudi Arabian and US blockade of the country which started in 2015 contributed to a humanitarian crisis. The Red Cross estimated cholera cases in the country reached one million in December 2017, and seven million were starving.

HEAD OF STATE
President, Gen. Abd-Rabbu Mansour Hadi, *elected* 21 February 2012
Vice-President, Maj.-Gen. Ali Mohsin al-Ahmar

SELECTED GOVERNMENT MEMBERS *AS AT JULY 2018*
Prime Minister, Ahmad Obaid bin Daghr
Defence, Mahmoud Ahmed Salim al-Subaihi
Foreign Affairs, Khaled Hussein al-Yamani

EMBASSY OF THE REPUBLIC OF YEMEN
57 Cromwell Road, London SW7 2ED
T 020-7584 6607 E yemen.embassy@btconnect.com
W www.yemenembassy.co.uk
Ambassador Extraordinary and Plenipotentiary, HE Yassin Saeed Ahmed, *apptd* 2015

BRITISH EMBASSY
PO Box 1287, 938 Thaher Himiyar Street, East Ring Road (opposite Mövenpick Hotel), Sana'a
T (+967) (1) 308 114 E britishembassysanaa@fco.gov.uk
W www.gov.uk/government/world/yemen
Ambassador Extraordinary and Plenipotentiary, HE Michael Aron, *apptd* 2018

ECONOMY AND TRADE

Despite its oil industry, the mainstay of the economy, Yemen is one of the poorest countries in the Arab world. The government began an IMF restructuring programme in 2006 that aimed to diversify the economy and attract foreign investment, but the economy has been devastated by the outbreak of war in 2014 and the Saudi-led blockade from 2015 which has prevented the majority of exports. The country is in the grip of an escalating humanitarian crisis, and it is believed over 80 per cent of the population is in need of aid.

Agriculture is largely of a subsistence nature and, with herding and fishing, engages the majority of the population. Apart from oil and natural gas extraction and oil refining, industry consists of small-scale manufacturing of cotton textiles, leather goods, handicrafts, aluminium products, cement, food processing and ship repair.

The main trading partners are Egypt, the UAE, China and Thailand. Principal exports are crude oil, coffee, dried and salted fish, and liquefied natural gas. The main imports are food, livestock, machinery and equipment, and chemicals.
GNI – US$28.3 bn; US$1,030 per capita (2017)
Annual average growth of GDP – –2 per cent (2017 est)
Inflation rate – 20 per cent (2017 est)
Population below poverty line – 54 per cent (2014 est)
Unemployment – 27 per cent (2014 est)
Total external debt – US$7.252bn (2017 est)
Imports – US$13,048m (2014)
Exports – US$10,555m (2014)

BALANCE OF PAYMENTS
Trade – US$3,000m deficit (2013)
Current Account – US$3,026m deficit (2015)

Trade with UK	2016	2017
Imports from UK	£35,988,724	£36,314,832
Exports to UK	£531,640	£808,404

COMMUNICATIONS

Airports and waterways – Principal airports are at Sana'a and Aden, and the main ports are at Aden, al-Hudaydah and al-Mukalla
Roadways – 71,300km, of which 6,200km are paved
Telecommunications – 1.16 million fixed lines and 16.4 million mobile subscriptions (2016); there were 6.7 million internet users in 2016
Internet code and IDD – ye; 967 (from UK), 44 (to UK)
Media – Republic of Yemen Television and Republic of Yemen Radio are the state-run broadcasters; leading daily newspapers include *Al-Thawra* (Arabic language), and the *Yemen Post* (English language)
WPFI score – 62,23 (167)

EDUCATION AND HEALTH

Literacy rate – 90.2 per cent (2015 est)
Gross enrolment ratio (percentage of relevant age group) – primary 92 per cent, secondary 51 per cent (2016 est)
Health expenditure (per capita) – US$80 (2014)
Hospital beds (per 1,000 people) – 0.7 (2014)
Life expectancy (years) – 65.9 (2017 est)

Mortality rate – 6 (2017 est)
Birth rate – 28.4 (2017 est)
Infant mortality rate – 46 (2017 est)
HIV / AIDS adult prevalence – 0.1 per cent (2016 est)

ZAMBIA

Republic of Zambia

Area – 752,618 sq. km
Capital – Lusaka; population, 2,524,000 (2018)
Major cities – Kitwe, Ndola
Currency – Kwacha (K) of 100 ngwee
Population – 15,972,001 rising at 2.93 per cent a year (2017 est); over 70 ethnic groups, of which the Lozi, Bemba, Ngoni, Tonga, Luvale and Kaonde are the largest
Religion – Christian (Protestant 75.3 per cent, Roman Catholic 20.2 per cent) (2010 est)
Language – English (official), Bembe, Kaonde, Lozi, Lunda, Luvale, Nyanja, Tonga (national), over 70 other local languages
Population density – 23 per sq. km (2016)
Urban population – 43.5 per cent (2018 est)
Median age (years) – 16.8 (2017 est)
National anthem – 'Lumbanyeni Zambia' 'Stand and Sing of Zambia, Proud and Free'
National day – 24 October (Independence Day)
Death penalty – Retained (not used since 1997)
CPI score – 37 (96)
Military expenditure – US$340m (2017)
Conscription – National registration required at 16; 18-25 years of age for male and female voluntary military service
Literacy rate – 65.8 per cent (2015 est)
Gross enrolment ratio (percentage of relevant age group) – primary 103.7 per cent (2013 est)
Health expenditure (per capita) – US$86 (2014)
Hospital beds (per 1,000 people) – 2 (2010)
Life expectancy (years) – 52.7 (2017 est)
Mortality rate – 12.2 (2017 est)
Birth rate – 41.5 (2017 est)
Infant mortality rate – 61.1 (2017 est)
HIV/AIDS adult prevalence – 12.4 per cent (2016 est)

CLIMATE AND TERRAIN

Landlocked Zambia lies on a forested plateau cut through by river valleys and with higher land in the north and north-east. Elevation extremes range from 2,301m (in the Mafinga Hills) to 329m (Zambezi river). The Zambezi and its tributaries are the main rivers. Lake Bangweulu and parts of Lakes Tanganyika, Mweru and Kariba lie within its boundaries. The climate is tropical, moderated by altitude, with a rainy season from October to April.

HISTORY AND POLITICS

Most of the ethnic groups in Zambia migrated there between the 16th and the 18th centuries. Portuguese explorers arrived in the late 18th century and, with Arab traders, began slave-trading in the 19th century. The area came under British administration in 1889, was named Northern Rhodesia in 1911 and became a British protectorate in 1924. It was part of the Central African Federation with South Rhodesia (Zimbabwe) and Nyasaland (Malawi) from 1953 to 1963, when the federation was dissolved and Northern Rhodesia achieved internal self-government. It became an independent republic in 1964 under the name of Zambia.

Kenneth Kaunda of the United National Independence Party (UNIP) became president at independence and remained in power until 1991. Zambia was a one-party state ruled by the UNIP from 1972 until 1990, when pressure from opposition groups led to a new constitution, under which multiparty legislative and presidential elections were held in 1991.

The Patriotic Front (PF) won the 2011 legislative election, gaining enough seats for a small majority in the National Assembly, which it built on in 2016. The PF's leader, Michael Sata, won the 2011 presidential election. After the death of President Sata in October 2014 following an illness, Edgar Lungu of the PF won the January 2015 presidential elections, and was re-elected in August 2016 in polls rejected by the main opposition party.

Under the 1991 constitution, the executive president is directly elected for a five-year term, renewable once. The unicameral National Assembly has 164 members: 156 directly elected and up to eight nominated by the president; all serve a five-year term. The president appoints the cabinet.

HEAD OF STATE
President, Edgar Lungu, *elected* 24 January 2015, *sworn in* 25 January 2015, *re-elected* 2016
Vice-President, Inonge Wina

SELECTED GOVERNMENT MEMBERS *AS AT JULY 2018*
Finance, Margaret Mwanakatwe
Foreign Affairs, Joel Malanji
Home Affairs, Steven Kampyongo

HIGH COMMISSION FOR THE REPUBLIC OF ZAMBIA
Zambia House, 2 Palace Gate, London W8 5NG
T 020-7589 6655 E info@zambiahc.org.uk W www.zambiahc.org.uk
High Commissioner, HE Muyeba Shichapwa Chikonde, *apptd* 2015

BRITISH HIGH COMMISSION
PO Box 5005, 5210 Independence Avenue, 15101 Ridgeway, Lusaka
T (+260) (21) 1423 2001251 133
E lusakageneralenquiries@fco.gov.uk
W www.gov.uk/government/world/zambia
High Commissioner, HE Fergus Cochrane-Dyet, OBE, *apptd* 2016

ECONOMY AND TRADE

The transition since the 1990s from a state-controlled to a free-market economy has improved productivity, especially in the now-privatised copper industry. One of the world's fastest growing economies between 2004 and 2014, growth decelerated 2015–6 due to low copper prices and a lack of diversity, but the economy picked up in 2017. Significant international investment since 2012, including Chinese-financed infrastructure projects, has failed significantly tackle high unemployment, debt and extreme poverty.

Copper is the main source of foreign earnings and increased demand in recent years for electronics has spurred investment and greater output, although weakening global copper prices caused a rapid depreciation of the kwacha in 2014. However, 54.8 per cent of the workforce remains engaged in agriculture, mostly at subsistence level, which accounts for 5.4 per cent of GDP. The main industries are copper and cobalt mining and processing, construction, food processing, emerald mining, beverages, chemicals, textiles, fertiliser and horticulture. Hydroelectric power generation and tourism are also important sectors.

The main trading partners are South Africa, Switzerland, China and the Democratic Republic of the Congo. Principal exports are copper, cobalt, electricity, tobacco, cut flowers and cotton. The main imports are machinery, transport equipment, petroleum products, electricity, fertiliser, foodstuffs and clothing.

GNI – US$22.3bn; US$1,300 per capita (2017)
Annual average growth of GDP – 4 per cent (2017 est)
Inflation rate – 6.8 per cent (2017 est)
Population below poverty line – 60.5 per cent (2015 est)
Total external debt – US$10.79bn (2017 est)
Imports – US$7,442m (2016)
Exports – US$6,505m (2016)

BALANCE OF PAYMENTS
Trade – US$937m deficit (2016)
Current Account – US$1,006m deficit (2017)

Trade with UK	2016	2017
Imports from UK	£45,849,410	£59,930,039
Exports to UK	£20,739,243	£16,379,903

COMMUNICATIONS
Airports and waterways – There are eight airports and 2,250km of navigable waterways on Lake Tanganyika and the Zambezi and Luapula rivers
Roadways and railways – 9,403km; 2,922km
Telecommunications – 101,407 fixed lines and 12 million mobile subscriptions (2016); there were 3.9 million internet users in 2016
Internet code and IDD – zm; 260 (from UK), 44 (to UK)
Media – The state-run Zambia National Broadcasting Association operates TV and radio stations; major daily newspapers include the *Zambia Daily Mail*, *Times of Zambia* (both state-owned) and *The Post* (privately owned)
WPFI score – 35,36 (113)

ZIMBABWE

Republic of Zimbabwe

Area – 390,757 sq. km
Capital – Harare; population, 1,515,000 (2018)
Major cities – Bulawayo, Chitungwiza, Gweru, Mutare
Currency – US dollars; other currencies, including the South African rand, are in use

Population – 13,805,084 rising at 1.56 per cent a year (2017 est); Shona (82 per cent), Ndebele (14 per cent) (est)
Religion – Christian (Apostolic 38 per cent, Pentecostal 21.1 per cent, Roman Catholic 8.4 per cent) (2011 est)
Language – English (official), Shona, Ndebele, numerous tribal dialects
Population density – 43 per sq. km (2016)
Urban population – 32.3 per cent (2018 est)
Median age (years) – 20 (2017 est)
National anthem – 'Simudzai Mureza wedu WeZimbabwe' 'Blessed be the Land of Zimbabwe'
National day – 18 April (Independence Day)
Death penalty – Retained
CPI score – 22 (157)
Military expenditure – US$340m (2017)

CLIMATE AND TERRAIN
Zimbabwe lies mainly on a high plateau with a central high veld and mountains in the east. Elevation extremes range from 2,592m (Inyangani) to 162m (confluence of the Runde and Save rivers). The climate is tropical, moderated by altitude, with a wet season from November to March. Average temperatures range from 16.5°C in July to 25.4°C in November.

POLITICS
Under the 2013 constitution, the term of the executive president was reduced from six years to five and is renewable once, however this did not apply retrospectively to former-president Robert Mugabe. The bicameral parliament comprises the National Assembly and the senate. The former has 210 members directly elected for a five-year term plus 60 seats reserved for women. The senate has 80 members, who serve a five-year term: 62 elected (including six from each of the eight provinces) and 18 traditional chiefs.

The country is divided into eight provinces and two cities (Bulawayo and Harare) with provincial status. The provinces are: Manicaland, Mashonaland Central, Mashonaland East, Mashonaland West, Masvingo, Matabeleland North, Matabeleland South and Midlands.

An internationally brokered power-sharing arrangement was agreed between the Zimbabwe African National Union-Patriotic Front (ZANU-PF) and the Movement for Democratic Change (MDC) in 2008 and lasted until 2013, when Mugabe was re-elected president and ZANU-PF won the legislative election. The office of prime minister was abolished under the 2013 constitution. The army ousted President Mugabe from power in November 2017 and he was replaced by former vice-president Emmerson Mnangagwa. Mnangagwa and ZANU-PF overwhelmingly won simultaneous presidential and parliamentary elections in 2018 elections, which the MDC claimed were rigged.

HEAD OF STATE
President, C-in-C of the Armed Forces, Emmerson Mnangagwa, *sworn in* 24 November 2017, *elected* 30 July 2018
Vice-President, vacant

SELECTED GOVERNMENT MEMBERS *AS AT AUGUST 2018*
Defence, Gen. (retd) Constantino Chiwenga
Finance, Patrick Chinamasa
Foreign Affairs, Sibusiso Moyo

EMBASSY OF THE REPUBLIC OF ZIMBABWE
Zimbabwe House, 429 Strand, London WC2R 0JR
T 020-7836 7755 E zimlondon@zimfa.gov.zw
W www.zimlondon.gov.zw
Ambassador Extraordinary and Plenipotentiary, vacant

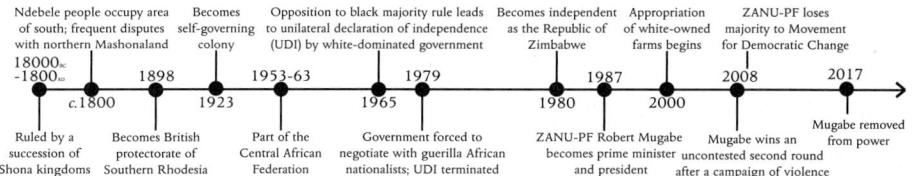

Ndebele people occupy area of south; frequent disputes with northern Mashonaland
18000ʙᴄ -1800ᴀᴅ
*c.*1800 — Ruled by a succession of Shona kingdoms

Becomes self-governing colony
1898
1923 — Becomes British protectorate of Southern Rhodesia

Opposition to black majority rule leads to unilateral declaration of independence (UDI) by white-dominated government
1953-63
1965 — Part of the Central African Federation

1979 — Government forced to negotiate with guerilla African nationalists; UDI terminated

Becomes independent as the Republic of Zimbabwe
1980 — ZANU-PF Robert Mugabe becomes prime minister and president

Appropriation of white-owned farms begins
1987

2000 — Mugabe wins an uncontested second round after a campaign of violence

ZANU-PF loses majority to Movement for Democratic Change
2008

2017 — Mugabe removed from power

BRITISH EMBASSY
PO Box 4490, 3 Norfolk Road, Mount Pleasant, Harare
T (+263) (4) 8585 5200 E ukinfo.harare@fco.gov.uk
W www.gov.uk/government/world/zimbabwe
Ambassador Extraordinary and Plenipotentiary, HE Catriona
  Laing, CMG, *apptd* 2014

Trade with UK	2016	2017
Imports from UK	£27,113,050	£29,563,145
Exports to UK	£40,462,691	£72,189,143

ECONOMY AND TRADE
Poor governance, and in particular the seizure of almost all the white-owned commercial farms, caused a rapid contraction in the agriculture-based economy in the decade from the late 1990s; agricultural output and GDP halved, international aid was suspended because of the government's outstanding arrears on past loans, and the migration of professional and skilled labour, and high levels of HIV/AIDS infection, depleted the workforce. After the national unity government took office, the US dollar was adopted in 2009 and the Zimbabwe dollar phased out by late 2015, following years of rampant hyperinflation. The Australian dollar, Chinese renminbi, Indian rupee and Japanese yen are also accepted. Almost three-quarters of the population lives below the poverty line.

  Agriculture accounts for 12.5 per cent of GDP and engages over two-thirds of the workforce. The most important crops are cotton and tobacco for export and maize for domestic consumption. Other crops include wheat, coffee, sugar cane, peanuts and livestock.

  The mining sector is important to the economy as a foreign exchange earner. Almost all mineral production is exported. Gold is the most important product; others are coal, platinum, copper, nickel, tin, diamonds, iron ore and other metal and non-metal ores. Mining is the largest industrial activity and supports a ferro-alloy industry and a steel works. Manufacturing, traditionally highly dependent on the agricultural sector for raw materials, produces wood products, cement, chemicals, fertiliser, clothing, footwear, foodstuffs and beverages; output has dropped in some industries because of transport difficulties and power rationing. Industry generates 26.9 per cent of GDP and services 60.6 per cent.

  The main trading partners are South Africa, China, Zambia and Mozambique. Principal exports are platinum, cotton, tobacco, gold, ferro-alloys, textiles and clothing. The main imports are machinery and transport equipment, other manufactures, chemicals, fuels and food.

GNI – US$15.1bn; US$910 per capita (2017)
Annual average growth of GDP – 2.8 per cent (2017 est)
Inflation rate – 2.5 per cent (2017 est)
Population below poverty line – 72.3 per cent (2012 est)
Total external debt – US$10.97m (2017 est)
Imports – US$4,000m (2015)
Exports – US$2,716m (2015)

BALANCE OF PAYMENTS
Trade – US$1,284m deficit (2015)
Current Account – US$591m deficit (2016)

COMMUNICATIONS
Airports – The main airports are at Harare and Bulawayo, and there are 15 other airports
Roadways and railways – 18,481km; 3,427km
Telecommunications – 305,720 fixed lines and 12.9 million mobile subscriptions (2016); there were 3.4 million internet users in 2016
Internet code and IDD – zw; 263 (from UK), 44 (to UK)
Major broadcasters – The Zimbabwe Broadcasting Corporation operates the only official TV and radio stations; opposition groups operate a number of illegal radio stations, such as Voice of the People and Radio Dialogue from abroad
Press – The government publishes the only daily newspapers, *The Herald* and *The Chronicle*
WPFI score – 40,53 (126)

EDUCATION AND HEALTH
Education is compulsory at primary level, and the language of instruction is English.
Literacy rate – 91.7 per cent (2015 est)
Gross enrolment ratio (percentage of relevant age group) – primary 99.9 per cent, secondary 47.6 per cent (2013 est), tertiary 8.4 per cent (2015 est)
Health expenditure (per capita) – US$58 (2014)
Hospital beds (per 1,000 people) – 1.7 (2011)
Life expectancy (years) – 60.4 (2017 est)
Mortality rate – 10.2 (2017 est)
Birth rate – 34.2 (2017 est)
Infant mortality rate – 32.7 (2017 est)
HIV/AIDS adult prevalence – 32.2 per cent (2016 est)

UK OVERSEAS TERRITORIES

ANGUILLA

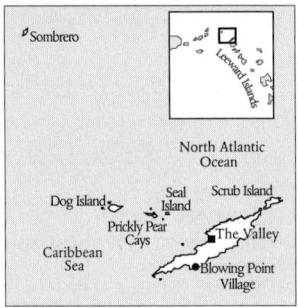

Area – 91 sq. km
Capital – The Valley; population, 1,000 (2018 est)
Currency – East Caribbean dollar (EC$) of 100 cents
Population – 17,087 rising at 1.97 per cent a year (2017 est)
Religion – Christian (Protestant 73.2 per cent, Roman
   Catholic 6.8 per cent) (2011 est)
Language – English (official)
Flag – British blue ensign with the coat of arms and three
   dolphins in the fly
National day – 30 May (Anguilla Day)
Median age (years) – 34.8 (2017 est)
Life expectancy (years) – 81.5 (2017 est)
Mortality rate – 4.6 (2017 est)
Birth rate – 12.5 (2017 est)
Infant mortality rate – 3.3 (2017 est)

CLIMATE AND TERRAIN
Anguilla is a flat coralline island in the eastern Caribbean and
one of the most northerly of the Leeward Islands. Elevation
extremes range from 65m (Crocus Hill) to 0m (Caribbean Sea).
The climate is tropical, modified by north-east trade winds,
with temperatures ranging from 24.7°C in January to 27.4°C
in August.

HISTORY AND POLITICS
Anguilla has been a British colony since 1650. For much of its
history it was linked administratively with St Kitts, but three
months after the Associated State of Saint Christopher (St
Kitts)-Nevis-Anguilla came into being in 1967, the Anguillans
repudiated government from St Kitts. Final separation from St
Kitts and Nevis was effected in December 1980 and Anguilla
reverted to a British dependency.
   The 1982 constitution (amended in 1990) provides for a
governor, an executive council comprising four of the elected
assembly members and two *ex-officio* members (the attorney-
general and deputy governor), and a 11-member House of
Assembly, consisting of a speaker, seven elected members, two
nominated members and two *ex-officio* members (the attorney-
general and deputy governor). The 2015 general election was
won by the Anguilla United Front with six seats. In September
2017 the island was badly damaged by Hurricane Irma.
Governor, Tim Foy, *apptd* 2017
Chief Minister, Hon. Victor Banks

ECONOMY
With few natural resources, the main economic activities are
luxury tourism and offshore banking. Lobster fishing and

expatriates' remittances are also important. Export earnings are
mainly from sales of lobster, fish, livestock, salt, concrete
blocks and rum.
Imports – US$158m (2015)
Exports – US$2m (2015)

BALANCE OF PAYMENTS
Trade – US$157m deficit (2015)
Current Account – US$99.2m deficit (2016)

Trade with UK	2016	2017
Imports from UK	£1,878,671	£557,991
Exports to UK	£389,154	£195,001

COMMUNICATIONS
Some 82km of the road network are paved. The main ports
are Blowing Point ferry terminal and Clayton J. Lloyd
(formerly Wallblake) airport, near The Valley.

BERMUDA

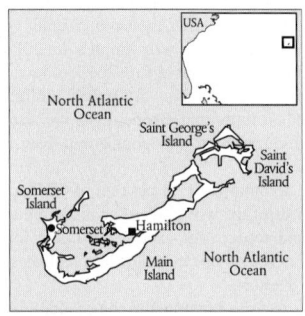

Area – 54 sq. km
Capital – Hamilton, on Main Island; population, 10,000
   (2018 est)
Currency – Bermudian dollar (BD$) of 100 cents
Population – 70,864 rising at 0.45 per cent a year (2017 est)
Religion – Christian (Protestant 46.2 per cent, Roman
   Catholic 14.5 per cent) (2010 est)
Language – English (official), Portuguese
Population density – 1,308 per sq. km (2016 est)
Flag – British red ensign with the coat of arms in the fly
National day – 24 May (Bermuda Day)
Median age (years) – 43.4 (2017 est)
Life expectancy (years) – 81.4 (2017 est)
Mortality rate – 8.6 (2017 est)
Birth rate – 11.3 (2017 est)
Infant mortality rate – 2.5 (2017 est)

CLIMATE AND TERRAIN
Bermuda is a group of over 130 small islands, of which about
20 are inhabited, in the North Atlantic Ocean. All the islands
are volcanic in origin, with hilly interiors, surrounded by coral
reefs. Elevation extremes range from 76m (Town Hill) to 0m
(Atlantic Ocean). The climate is subtropical, regulated by the
Gulf Stream, with average temperatures ranging from 16.7°C
in February to 26.3°C in August.

HISTORY AND POLITICS
Bermuda was discovered by the Spanish in 1503 but
colonised by the British from the early 17th century,

becoming a colony in 1684. Independence from the UK was rejected in a 1995 referendum.

Internal self-government was introduced in 1968. The governor is responsible for external affairs, defence, internal security and the police, although administrative matters for the police service have been delegated to the minister of labour, home affairs and public safety. The cabinet comprises the premier and six elected assembly members. The legislature consists of the senate of 11 appointed members and the House of Assembly with 36 members elected for a five-year term. At the 2012 election, centre-left opposition party One Bermuda Alliance won 19 of the 36 available seats, ousting the ruling Progressive Labour Party for the first time in 14 years. In February 2018, it became the first jurisdiction to legalise and then repeal same-sex marriage.

Governor, HE John Rankin, CMG, *apptd* 2016
Premier, Hon. David Burt

ECONOMY

The main economic activity is international financial services, accounting for about 85 per cent of GPD. Tourism claims just 5 per cent of GDP but is the largest employer. High unemployment and public debt are growing issues in recent years. Trade is dominated by re-exporting pharmaceuticals, while almost everything is imported.

GNI – US$6,778m; US$104,610 per capita (2012)
Total external debt – US$2,435m (2015 est)
Imports – US$972m (2016)
Exports – US$8m (2016)

BALANCE OF PAYMENTS
Trade – US$964m deficit (2016)
Current Account – US$766m surplus (2016)

Trade with UK	2016	2017
Imports from UK	£21,996,833	£113,815,354
Exports to UK	£25,134,324	£2,378,333

COMMUNICATIONS

The main islands are connected by a series of bridges and causeways. There are 447km of roads, all of which are paved but only around half of which are public, and one airport, near Ferry Reach on St David's Island. The main ports are at Hamilton, Freeport and St George. The telephone system is extensive, and mobile telephone distribution is widespread.

BRITISH ANTARCTIC TERRITORY

See also The North and South Poles
Area – 1,709,400 sq. km. This area is overlapped by territorial claims from Chile and Argentina. However, no claims are recognised internationally under the Antarctic Treaty of 1961
Population – There is no indigenous population. The British Antarctic Survey maintains two permanently staffed research stations, at Halley and Rothera; one part-time (summer-only) station at Signy (South Orkney Islands); and two summer-only logistics facilities, at Fossil Bluff (Alexander Island) and Sky Blu (Eastern Ellsworth Land). Several other countries maintain research stations in the territory
Flag – British white ensign, without the cross of St George, with the territory's coat of arms in the fly

CLIMATE AND TERRAIN
The British Antarctic Territory (BAT) consists of the areas south of 60°S. latitude, between longitudes 20°W. and 80°W. The territory includes the South Orkney Islands, the

South Shetland Islands, the mountainous Antarctic Peninsula and all adjacent islands, and the land mass extending to the South Pole. The highest point of the territory is 3,184m (Mt Jackson).

Only around 0.7 per cent of the territory remains ice-free, and the permanent ice-sheet that covers the remainder is, in places, nearly 5km thick. The climate is polar desert with very little precipitation, and the annual average temperature at the South Pole is −48°C.

HISTORY AND POLITICS
Britain made its first territorial claim to part of the Antarctic in 1908. Since 1943, a permanent presence has been maintained, which became the British Antarctic Survey (BAS) in 1962. In the same year, the territory, originally a Dependency of the Falkland Islands, became a UK overseas territory in its own right, although it continued to be administered from the Falkland Islands until 1989 when the role of Commissioner of the British Antarctic Territory was created.

The BAT is administered by the Foreign and Commonwealth Office, and has a full suite of laws, legal and postal administrations. All activities are governed by the Antarctic Treaty of 1961, which has the objectives of keeping Antarctica demilitarised and promoting international scientific cooperation. The territory is self-financing from income-tax revenue and the sale of postage stamps and coins.

GOVERNMENT OF THE BRITISH ANTARCTIC TERRITORY
Polar Regions Department, Overseas Territories Directorate, Room 2/135, Old Admiralty Building, London SW1A 2AH
T 020-7008 1639 E polarregions@fco.gov.uk
Commissioner (non-resident), Ben Merrick, *apptd* 2017

BRITISH INDIAN OCEAN TERRITORY

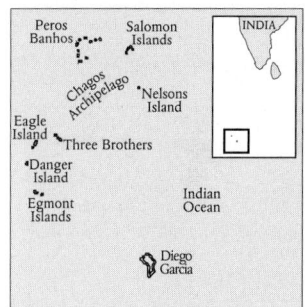

Area – 54,400 sq. km, of which 60 sq. km is land
Currency – US dollar (US$) of 100 cents
Population – No indigenous population now lives in the archipelago; around 3,000 military personnel and civilian contract employees are based at the joint UK–US naval support facility on Diego Garcia
Flag – Divided horizontally into blue and white wavy stripes, with the Union Flag in the canton and a crowned palm tree over all in the fly

CLIMATE AND TERRAIN
The British Indian Ocean Territory (BIOT) comprises the Chagos Archipelago of 55 islands in six main groups, situated on the Great Chagos Bank in the Indian Ocean. The largest and most southerly of the islands is Diego Garcia, a sand cay with an area of about 44 sq. km. The main island groups are

Peros Banhos (29 islands with a total land area of 6.5 sq. km) and Salomon (11 islands with a total land area of 3.2 sq. km). The flat and low terrain rarely rises more than 2m above sea-level, being only 15m at its highest point. The climate is hot and humid, although moderated by trade winds.

HISTORY AND POLITICS
The Chagos Archipelago, originally colonised by the French, was one of the dependencies of Mauritius ceded to Britain in 1814 and was administered from Mauritius until 1965, when the BIOT was established. The islands of Farquhar, Desroches and Aldabra became part of the Seychelles when it became independent in 1976. Since the 1980s, successive Mauritian governments have claimed sovereignty over the remaining Chagos islands, arguing that they were annexed illegally.

Diego Garcia is used as a joint naval support facility by Britain and the USA. The islands' former inhabitants were forcibly relocated between 1967 and 1973 to allow for the construction of the naval base, most being resettled in Mauritius and the Seychelles. Since the 1990s they have taken legal action to obtain the right to return to and settle in the islands. In 2006, the Chagossians won a High Court case allowing them to return to the archipelago, but not to Diego Garcia. The House of Lords overturned this ruling on appeal in 2008; a case before the European Court of Human Rights was ruled inadmissible in December 2012 as the islanders had previously accepted financial compensation. The British government unilaterally, and controversially, declared the Chagos Archipelago a marine-protected area (MPA) in April 2010, a decision that was upheld by the High Court in 2013. In March 2015, a UN tribunal declared the creation of the MPA illegal, and ordered the UK and Mauritius governments to renegotiate sovereignty of the area. In November 2016, the British Foreign Office announced that the islanders would not be allowed to return to their home. However, in June 2017, the UN general assembly ruled the sovereignty dispute should be referred to the International Court of Justice.

Commissioner (non-resident), Ben Merrick, *apptd* 2017
Deputy Commissioner (non-resident), Bryony Mathew

BRITISH VIRGIN ISLANDS

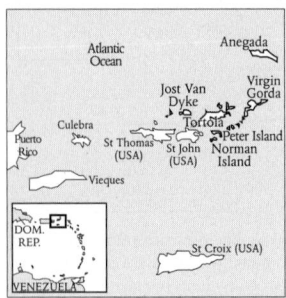

Area – 151 sq. km
Capital – Road Town, on Tortola; population, 15,000 (2018 est)
Currency – US dollar (US$) of 100 cents
Population – 35,015 rising at 2.25 per cent a year (2017 est)
Religion – Christian (Protestant 70.2 per cent, Roman Catholic 8.9 per cent) (2010 est)

Language – English (official)
Population density – 204 per sq. km (2016)
Flag – British blue ensign with the coat of arms in the fly
National day – 1 July (Territory Day)
Median age (years) – 36.5 (2017 est)
Life expectancy (years) – 78.8 (2017 est)
Mortality rate – 5.1 (2017 est)
Birth rate – 11.1 (2017 est)
Infant mortality rate – 12.1 (2017 est)

CLIMATE AND TERRAIN
The easternmost part of the Virgin Islands archipelago in the Caribbean Sea, the British Virgin Islands comprise Tortola, Anegada, Virgin Gorda, Jost Van Dyke and about 40 islets and cays; 16 of the islands are inhabited. Apart from Anegada, which is flat, the British Virgin Islands are hilly with coral reefs offshore. The highest point of elevation is 521m (Mt Sage, on Tortola). The climate is subtropical, with little variation in average temperatures, which typically range between 23.4°C in January and February and 26.4°C in August and September. The hurricane season is from June to November.

HISTORY AND POLITICS
Initially settled by Arawak Indians, the islands were named by Christopher Columbus in 1493 and colonised by the Dutch in the early 17th century. Annexed by the British in 1672, the islands were part of the Leeward Islands colony from 1872 to 1960. After a period of direct rule, a measure of self-government was introduced by the 1977 constitution and extended in 2000.

Under the 2007 constitution, the governor, appointed by the crown, retains responsibility for defence, security, external affairs and the civil service. The executive council comprises the premier, four other elected assembly members and the attorney-general. The House of Assembly consists of a speaker, one *ex-officio* member (the attorney-general) and 13 members elected for a four-year term.

The 2011 and 2015 elections were won by the National Democratic Party. In September 2017 the islands were badly damaged by Hurricane Irma.

Governor, HE Augustus Jaspert, *apptd* 2017
Premier, Hon. Orlando Smith, OBE

ECONOMY
Tourism, which generates about 45 per cent of GDP, has started to recover since the devastation caused by Hurricane Irma in September 2017. Alongside offshore financial services, other industries include construction and light manufacturing. The major exports are rum, fresh fish, fruit, livestock, gravel and sand. Chief imports are building materials, vehicles, foodstuffs and machinery.

Trade with UK	2016	2017
Imports from UK	£42,320,447	£23,384,451
Exports to UK	£9,410,952	£11,630,327

COMMUNICATIONS
The principal airport is on Beef Island, linked by bridge to Tortola, and there are also airfields on Anegada and Virgin Gorda. Road Harbour, at Road Town, is the main port, and ferry services connect the main islands. Much of the 200km of road is steep and narrow.

CAYMAN ISLANDS

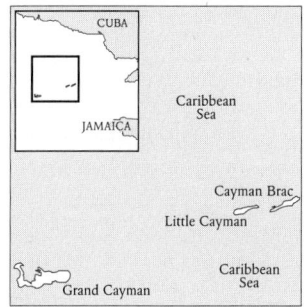

Area – 264 sq. km
Capital – George Town, on Grand Cayman; population,
   35,000 (2018 est)
Currency – Caymanian dollar (CI$) of 100 cents
Population – 58,441 rising at 2.01 per cent a year (2017 est)
Religion – Christian (Protestant 67.8 per cent, Roman
   Catholic 14.1 per cent) (2010 est)
Language – English (official), Spanish
Population density – 253 per sq. km (2016 est)
Flag – British blue ensign with the coat of arms in the fly
National day – First Monday in July (Constitution Day)
Median age (years) – 40 (2017 est)
Life expectancy (years) – 81.3 (2017 est)
Mortality rate – 5.8 (2017 est)
Birth rate – 12 (2017 est)
Infant mortality rate – 5.9 (2017 est)
Annual average growth of GDP – 2 per cent (2017)

CLIMATE AND TERRAIN

The Cayman Islands comprise Grand Cayman, Cayman Brac
and Little Cayman. Situated around 240km south of Cuba,
the low-lying islands are divided from Jamaica, 268km to the
south-east, by the Cayman Trench, the deepest part of the
Caribbean Sea. The average temperature is 27°C. Hurricane
season is from July to November.

HISTORY AND POLITICS

The territory derives its name from the Carib word *caymanas*
(crocodile). The islands were ceded to Britain by Spain in
1670, and permanent settlement began in the 1730s. A
dependency of Jamaica from 1863, the islands came under
direct rule after 1962, and a measure of self-government was
granted in 1972.

   The 1972 constitution (revised in 1994 and 2009) provides
for a governor, a legislative assembly and a cabinet. The
governor is responsible for the police, civil service, internal
security, defence, external affairs, and chairs the cabinet. The
cabinet comprises two appointed official members (the deputy
governor and attorney-general) and five of the assembly's
elected members. The Legislative Assembly has 21 members
elected for a four-year term and the two appointed official
members of the cabinet, as well as a speaker. In September
2017 the islands were badly damaged by Hurricane Irma.
Acting Governor, Franz Manderson, *apptd* 2018
Premier, Hon. Alden McLaughlin, MBE

CAYMAN ISLANDS GOVERNMENT OFFICE
6 Arlington Street, London SW1A 1RE **T** 020-7491 7772
W www.gov.ky

ECONOMY

The mainstays of the economy are offshore financial services
(largely owing to the absence of direct taxation) and tourism,
which accounts for around 70 per cent of GDP. Government
revenue is derived from fees and duties.
Imports – US$916m (2015)
Exports – US$20m (2015)

BALANCE OF PAYMENTS
Trade – US$895 deficit (2015)

Trade with UK	2016	2017
Imports from UK	£216,778,613	£35,735,081
Exports to UK	£143,978,573	£1,129,471

COMMUNICATIONS

The islands are served by airports at George Town and on
Cayman Brac and by an airfield on Little Cayman. George
Town is the main port. There are 785km of surfaced roads.

FALKLAND ISLANDS

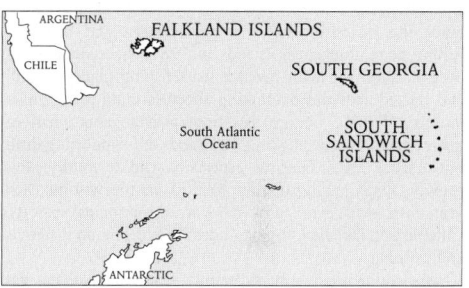

Area – 12,173 sq. km
Capital – Stanley, on East Falkland; population, 2,000 (2018
   est)
Currency – Falkland Island pound (FK£) of 100 pence
Population – 3,198 (2016 est) rising at 0.01 per cent a year
   (2014 est)
Religion – Christian 66 per cent, other 2 per cent (est)
Language – English
Urban population – 77.7 per cent (2018 est)
Flag – British blue ensign with coat of arms centred in the fly
National day – 14 June (Liberation Day)

CLIMATE AND TERRAIN

The Falkland Islands consist of East Falkland (6,759 sq. km),
West Falkland (5,413 sq. km) and around 700 small islands.
Elevation extremes range from 705m (Mt Usbourne) to 0m
(Atlantic Ocean). Average temperatures range from 1.3°C in
July to 8°C in January, and annual rainfall is low (around
543.3mm per year).

HISTORY AND POLITICS

The Falkland Islands have a long history of occupation by
European countries, including France, Spain and the UK,
which claimed sovereignty in 1765 and established its first
settlement in 1766.

   In 1820 the Falklands were claimed for the newly
independent Argentina and a settlement was founded in
1826, but this was destroyed by the USA in 1831. In 1833
occupation was resumed by the British, and the islands were
permanently colonised. Argentina continued to claim
sovereignty over the islands (known to them as *las Islas
Malvinas*), and invaded the islands on 2 April 1982. A British
naval and military task force recaptured the islands on 14 June
1982. A small naval and military garrison remains in the
islands. Argentina has reasserted its claims of sovereignty

since 2007, and political tensions with the UK remain high. In a referendum in March 2013, the islanders voted overwhelmingly to remain a UK overseas territory; on a turnout of more than 90 per cent, 1,513 votes were cast in favour, with three against.

Under the 2009 constitution, the governor chairs an executive council consisting of three of the elected members of the legislative assembly and two *ex-officio* members, the chief executive and the financial secretary. The legislative assembly consists of eight members elected for a four-year term, the same two *ex-officio* members and a speaker. The last election was held in 2017. There are no political parties and all members sit as independents.

Governor, HE Nigel Phillips, CBE *apptd* 2017
Chief Executive, Barry Rowland, *apptd* 2016

FALKLAND ISLANDS GOVERNMENT OFFICE
Falkland House, 14 Broadway, London SW1H 0BH
T 020-7222 2542 **W** www.falklands.gov.fk

ECONOMY
Since the establishment of a conservation and managed fishing zone around the islands in 1987, the economy has been transformed, with revenue from fishing (mainly squid) and related activities overtaking sheep-farming as the main industry. Fishing licence fees now provide about half of government revenue, making the islands self-supporting in all but defence costs. Tourism, especially wildlife tourism, has grown rapidly, with roughly 57,000 people visiting each year. Fish, meat, wool and hides are the principal exports. Chief imports are fuel, food and drink, construction materials and clothing.

There are believed to be substantial reserves of oil and gas offshore and the Falkland Islands government has licensed exploration for exploitable sites; in late 2015, two exploration firms announced plans to combine their efforts to commence oil production.

Imports – US$26m (2014)
Exports – US$5m (2014)

Trade with UK	2016	2017
Imports from UK	£46,995,457	£45,232,170
Exports to UK	£96,452,045	£5,415,591

COMMUNICATIONS
There is an international airport at Mt Pleasant, served by military flights to the UK and by commercial flights to Chile. The main port is Stanley Harbour and a regular shipping service operates to the UK. The road network is gradually expanding but only roads in and around Stanley are paved, and most longer internal journeys are by light aircraft. International telecommunications are possible through a satellite link, and the majority of households have internet access.

GIBRALTAR

Area – 6.5 sq. km
Capital – Gibraltar, population, 35,000 (2018)
Currency – Gibraltar pound of 100 pence
Population – 29,396 rising at 0.23 per cent a year (2017 est)
Religion – Christian (Roman Catholic 78.1 per cent, Church of England 7 per cent), Muslim 4 per cent, Jewish 2 per cent, Hindu 2 per cent (est)
Language – English (official), Spanish, Italian, Portuguese
Population density – 3,221 per sq. km (2015)
Flag – White with a red stripe along the lower edge; over all a red castle with a key hanging from its gateway
National day – 10 September
Median age (years) – 34.5 (2016 est)
Life expectancy (years) – 79.6 (2017 est)
Mortality rate – 8.5 (2017 est)
Birth rate – 14 (2017 est)
Infant mortality rate – 5.9 (2017 est)

CLIMATE AND TERRAIN
Gibraltar is a rocky promontory, 426m at its highest point, that juts southwards from the south-east coast of Spain, with which it is connected by a low isthmus. It is about 32km from the coast of Africa, across the Strait of Gibraltar.

HISTORY AND POLITICS
Gibraltar was captured in 1704, during the War of the Spanish Succession, by a combined Dutch and English force, and was ceded to Britain in the Treaty of Utrecht (1713).

Spanish claims to the territory were a source of tension for many years, but after the overwhelming rejection of a joint sovereignty arrangement in a referendum in 2002, Spain moderated its attitude and the previously bilateral Anglo-Spanish talks about the territory became tripartite with the inclusion of Gibraltar from 2006.

Gibraltar is part of the EU (with the UK government responsible for enforcing EU directives affecting Gibraltar), but is not a full member and is exempt from the common policies on customs, commerce, agriculture, fisheries and VAT. Gibraltarians have voted in EU elections since 2004.

The 1969 constitution made provision for self-government in respect of certain domestic matters, but full internal autonomy came into effect with the 2006 constitution. This limited the governor's responsibilities to external affairs, defence, internal security and public service. The House of Assembly was restyled the Gibraltar Parliament, and may determine its own size; at present, it consists of an appointed speaker and 17 members elected for a four-year term. The government is formed by the chief minister (who is the leader of the majority party) and ministers from among the elected members of parliament.

The November 2015 elections were won by Chief Minister Fabian Picardo's Gibraltar Socialist Labour Party.

Governor, HE Lt.-Gen. Edward Davis, CB, CBE, *apptd* 2016
Chief Minister, Hon. Fabian Picardo

GOVERNMENT OF GIBRALTAR
150 Strand, London WC2R 1JA **T** 020-7836 0777
W www.gibraltar.gov.uk

ECONOMY
The economy is dominated by tourism (especially retail for day visitors), offshore financial services and shipping, and these three sectors account for about 85 per cent of GDP. Diversification efforts have encouraged telecommunications in particular and Gibraltar has become a centre for internet businesses, especially online gambling and gaming. A shift from a predominantly public-sector to a private-sector economy has occurred in recent years, although government spending still has a significant impact on the local economy. The chief sources of government revenue are port dues, the rent of the Crown Estate in the town and duties on consumer items (although VAT is not applied in the territory).
Imports – US$705m (2014)
Exports – US$267m (2014)

BALANCE OF PAYMENTS
Trade – US$438m deficit (2014)

Trade with UK	2016	2017
Imports from UK	£359,299,719	£380,890,542
Exports to UK	£46,339,484	£18,542,518

COMMUNICATIONS
Gibraltar has one international airport. The 29km road network is all surfaced; road links to Spain reopened in the 1980s. The port services the large shipping industry, cruise liners and a regular ferry service to Tangiers (Morocco).

MONTSERRAT

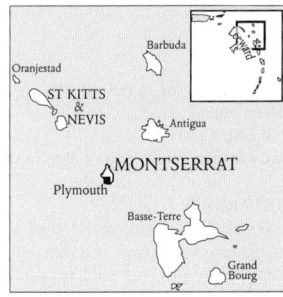

Area – 102 sq. km
Capital – Plymouth (abandoned 1997); the seat of government is now at Brades, in the north, population, 449 (2011 est); a new capital is under construction at nearby Little Bay
Currency – East Caribbean dollar (EC$) of 100 cents
Population – 5,292 rising at 0.45 per cent a year (2017 est)
Religion – Christian (Protestant 67.1 per cent, Roman Catholic 11.6 per cent)
Language – English (official)
Flag – British blue ensign with the coat of arms in the fly
National day – Second Saturday in June (birthday of Queen Elizabeth II)
Median age (years) – 33.2 (2017 est)
Life expectancy (years) – 74.6 (2017 est)
Mortality rate – 6.2 (2017 est)

Birth rate – 10.8 (2017 est)
Infant mortality rate – 12.3 (2017 est)

CLIMATE AND TERRAIN
Montserrat is a mountainous volcanic island in the Leeward group in the Caribbean Sea. Its lowest point of elevation is 0m (Caribbean Sea); its highest point was 914m (Chances Peak), although a lava dome in a crater in the Soufrière Hills volcano is estimated to be over 930m. Volcanic activity since 1995 has left over half of the island devastated by lava flows and ash. The climate is tropical and the average temperature is 25.9°C.

HISTORY AND POLITICS
Discovered by Columbus in 1493, Montserrat became a British colony in 1632. It was fought over by the French and British throughout the 17th and 18th centuries, before being finally restored to Britain in 1783.
  Continual volcanic activity by the Soufrière Hills volcano between 1995 and 2014 has left over half of the island uninhabitable, and prompted the migration of two-thirds of the population in the late 1990s. A 'special vulnerable area', to which access is restricted, covers two-thirds of the island and two maritime exclusion zones extend between 2km and 4km offshore.
  The 1990 constitution was amended in 1999 after more than half of the constituencies were made uninhabitable by volcanic activity. Following modernisation talks, a new constitution came into force in September 2011, which established a new National Advisory Council to enhance democracy and governance. Under the new constitution, the cabinet is chaired by the governor and comprises the premier, three other elected members and two *ex-officio* members (the attorney-general and the financial secretary). The legislative assembly consists of nine members elected for a five-year term and two *ex-officio* members. In the 2014 general election the People's Democratic Movement won the most seats.
Governor, HE Andrew Pearce, OBE, *apptd* 2018
Premier, Hon. Donaldson Romeo

GOVERNMENT OF MONTSERRAT
180–186 Kings Cross Road, London WC1X 9DE **T** 020-7520 2622

ECONOMY
Continuing volcanic activity has restricted economic activity to the northern third of the island and considerably impacted the agricultural sector. Activity includes mining and quarrying, construction (mostly public sector), financial and professional services, and tourism. In January 2013 the EU granted a £33.4m aid package to bolster recovery. Communications improved with the opening of Gerald's Airport in the north in 2005, allowing regular commercial air services to resume. There are port facilities at Little Bay, and a ferry service to and from Antigua.
Imports – US$36m (2016)
Exports – US$4m (2016)

BALANCE OF PAYMENTS
Trade – US$32m deficit (2016)
Current Account – US$8.8m deficit (2016)

Trade with UK	2016	2017
Imports from UK	£15,108,436	£1,559,693
Exports to UK	£26,093	£12,465

PITCAIRN ISLANDS

Pitcairn, Henderson, Ducie and Oeno Islands

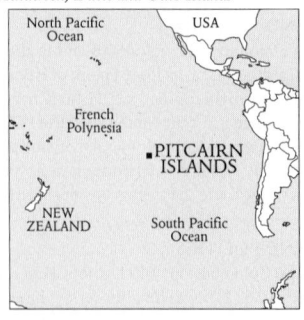

Area – 47 sq. km
Capital – Adamstown, on Pitcairn Island
Currency – New Zealand dollar (NZ$) of 100 cents
Population – 54 (2016 est)
Religion – Christian (Seventh-day Adventist)
Language – English, Pitkern (both official)
Flag – British blue ensign with the coat of arms in the fly
National day – 23 January (Bounty Day)

CLIMATE AND TERRAIN
Pitcairn is the chief of a group of rugged islands situated in the South Pacific Ocean. The other main islands of the group are Henderson, lying 168km north-east of Pitcairn; Oeno, lying 120km north-west; and Ducie, lying 470km east. These are uninhabited. Henderson Island is a UNESCO World Heritage Site. The climate is tropical with an average temperature of 20.8°C.

HISTORY AND POLITICS
Pitcairn was settled in 1790 by mutineers from the *Bounty* and their Tahitian companions. It became a British settlement under the British Settlements Act 1887.

Under the 2010 constitutional arrangements, the islands are administered by the governor (usually the British High Commissioner to New Zealand), in consultation with the island council, which manages internal affairs. The commissioner liaises between the governor and the council. The island council comprises ten members: the governor; two members appointed by the governor; one member appointed by the council itself; and six, including the mayor, who are elected. The mayor is elected every three years; elections for other council members are held every year in December.

Governor (non-resident), HE Laura Clarke, *apptd* 2017 *(British High Commissioner to New Zealand)*
Mayor, Shawn Christian

ECONOMY
The islanders live by subsistence fishing and horticulture, and the sale of honey and handicrafts, although tourism is being promoted. Apart from small fees charged for licences there are no taxes and government revenue is derived almost solely from the sale of postage stamps and .pn internet domain names, and income from investments. Since financial reserves became exhausted a few years ago the islands have received budgetary aid from the UK.

Imports – US$20m (2014)
Exports – US$12m (2014)

Trade with UK	2016	2017
Imports from UK	£148,787	£778,837
Exports to UK	£27,622	£29,326

COMMUNICATIONS
There is no airfield and the only means of access is by sea; cruise and container ships stop irregularly but a regular shipping supply route to French Polynesia was established in 2006. There are about 6km of dirt roads on the islands. A telephone system and internet access have been introduced in recent years.

ST HELENA, ASCENSION AND TRISTAN DA CUNHA

Area – 308 sq. km
Population – 7,828 rising at 0.18 per cent (2017 est); African descent (50.0 per cent), white (25.0 per cent), Chinese (25.0 per cent)
Religion – Christian (predominantly Protestant)
Language – English (official)
National day – Second Saturday in June (birthday of Queen Elizabeth II)
Median age (years) – 41.9 (2017 est)
Life expectancy (years) – 79.6 (2017 est)
Mortality rate – 7.8 (2017 est)
Birth rate – 9.6 (2017 est)
Infant mortality rate – 13.3 (2017 est)

ST HELENA

Area – 122 sq. km
Capital – Jamestown; population, 1,000 (2018 est)
Currency – St Helena pound (£) of 100 pence
Population – 4,534 (2016 est)
Flag – British blue ensign with the coat of arms in the fly

CLIMATE AND TERRAIN
St Helena is a rugged and volcanic island, with sheer cliffs rising to a central plateau. Mt Actaeon, at 818m, is the highest elevation. The climate is tropical but mild, tempered by trade winds, and the average temperature is 18.1°C.

HISTORY AND POLITICS
St Helena is believed to have been discovered by the Portuguese navigator Joao da Nova in 1502. It was used as a port of call for vessels of all nations trading to the East until the late 19th century. From 1815 to 1821 the island was lent to the British government as a place of exile for Napoléon Bonaparte, who died there on 5 May 1821, and in 1834 it was annexed to the British crown. The Zulu chief Dinizulu was exiled to the island in 1890, and up to 6,000 Boer prisoners were held there between 1900 and 1903.

Under the 2009 constitution, government is administered by a governor, advised by an executive council comprising three *ex-officio* members (the chief secretary, financial secretary and attorney-general) and five elected members of the legislative council. The legislative council consists of 12 members elected

for a four-year term, the three *ex-officio* members of the executive council and a speaker.
Governor, HE Lisa Phillips, CBE, *apptd* 2016

GOVERNMENT OF ST HELENA
16 Old Queen Street, London SW1H 9HP T 020-3170 8705

ECONOMY AND TRADE
The island has few natural resources and its economy is dependent on an annual grant from the UK. The main economic activities are agriculture, the sale of fishing licences, fish processing and tourism. The only significant exports are coffee and frozen, canned and dried fish.

Trade with UK	2016	2017
Imports from UK	£16,540,121	£15,699,045
Exports to UK	£746,121	£363,290

COMMUNICATIONS
Access is predominantly by sea to Jamestown port, provided by a regular supply ship. The first scheduled commercial flight landed at the island's £285 million airport in October 2017. Only 38km of the island's roads are paved. There are two local radio stations and two weekly newspapers.

ASCENSION ISLAND
Area – 88 sq. km
Capital – Georgetown
Currency – St Helena pound (£) of 100 pence
Population – 806 (2016 est)

CLIMATE AND TERRAIN
The island is a rocky volcanic peak that lies in the South Atlantic Ocean some 1,200km north-west of St Helena. The highest point (Green Mountain, 859m) is covered with lush vegetation. It is an important breeding place for the green turtle and a number of seabird species.

HISTORY AND POLITICS
Ascension is said to have been discovered by Joao da Nova in 1501 and two years later it was visited on Ascension Day by Alphonse d'Albuquerque, who gave the island its present name. The island was an important logistical centre in both world wars and during the Falklands conflict, and it has a continuing role as a military air base and in broadcasting, telecommunications and satellite tracking.
In 2002 new constitutional arrangements introduced a measure of self-government, and in 2009 Ascension ceased to be a dependency of St Helena. The governor, who is resident in St Helena, retains responsibility for defence, external affairs, internal security and public services. The governor, represented locally by the island administrator, chairs the island council, which consists of five elected members and two *ex-officio* members (the director of resources and the attorney-general).
Administrator, Nick Kennedy, *apptd* 2017

ECONOMY
Before 2002 the island was administered and financed by commercial operators, including the BBC and Cable and Wireless, and the military. With the change in governance in 2002, a fiscal regime was introduced to finance public services through taxation. A private sector is developing following the sale of government-owned concerns to commercial operators and the establishment of a sports fishing industry.

COMMUNICATIONS
Georgetown is the only port, but regular air links to the UK and the USA have been limited by the poor state of the runway. Ascension has 40km of roads. Telecommunication services are provided via satellite links. There is a local radio station and a weekly newspaper.

TRISTAN DA CUNHA
Area – 98 sq. km
Capital – Edinburgh of the Seven Seas
Currency – Pound sterling (£) of 100 pence
Population – 262 (2017 est)
Flag – British blue ensign with the coat of arms in the fly

CLIMATE AND TERRAIN
Tristan da Cunha is the chief of a group of islands in the South Atlantic Ocean which lie some 2,333km south-west of St Helena. All of the islands are volcanic and steep-sided with cliffs or narrow beaches. The island is home to the highest peak in the South Atlantic, Queens Mary's Peak, which rises to 2,060m above sea-level. Gough and Inaccessible Islands are UNESCO World Heritage Sites.

HISTORY AND POLITICS
Tristan da Cunha was discovered in 1506 by the Portuguese navigator Tristao da Cunha. In 1816 the group was annexed to the British crown and a garrison was placed on Tristan da Cunha. When this force was withdrawn in 1817, four adults and two children remained at their own request and formed a settlement, which was joined in 1827 by five women from St Helena and afterwards by others from Cape Colony. Owing to its position on a major sea route the colony thrived, with an economy based on trade with passing ships, until the late 19th century, when the opening of the Suez Canal led to decline.
Tristan da Cunha and Inaccessible, Nightingale and Gough Islands were dependencies of St Helena from 1938 to 2009. They are administered by the governor of St Helena through a resident administrator, who is advised by an island council. This consists of eight members elected for a three-year term, of whom one must be a woman, and three appointed members.
Administrator, Sean Burns, *apptd* 2016

ECONOMY
The island is almost financially self-sufficient; UK government aid finances training scholarships and a resident medical officer at the hospital. The main activities are crayfish fishing, fish processing, agriculture and the sale of postage stamps and coins.

COMMUNICATIONS
Communications with the outside world are by sea as there is no airport. Scheduled visits to the island are limited to about nine calls a year by fishing vessels from Cape Town and annual calls by a South African research vessel. Tristan da Cunha has 20km of roads, half of which are paved. There is a local radio station and a newspaper.

SOUTH GEORGIA AND THE SOUTH SANDWICH ISLANDS

For map *see* Falkland Islands entry.
Area – 3,903 sq. km
Capital – King Edward Point (administrative centre), on South Georgia
Currency – Pound sterling (£) of 100 pence
Population – There is no indigenous population. The British Antarctic Survey maintains two permanently staffed research stations, at King Edward Point and on Bird Island, to the north-west of South Georgia; in addition,

there are the government officers at King Edward Point; population, 268 (2015 est) and the curators of the museum at Grytviken, South Georgia
Flag – British blue ensign, with the coat of arms in the fly

CLIMATE AND TERRAIN
Over half of South Georgia is permanently ice-covered, with many large glaciers. The main mountain range is the Allardyce, and elevation extremes range from 2,934m (Mt Paget) to 0m (Atlantic Ocean). The South Sandwich Islands are a chain of 11 uninhabited volcanic islands some 350km long.

HISTORY AND POLITICS
South Georgia was used by whalers and sealers of many nationalities following its discovery by Captain Cook in 1775. Britain annexed South Georgia and the South Sandwich Islands in 1908 and since then they have been under continuous British occupation, apart from a brief period during the Falklands conflict in 1982; Argentina claims sovereignty over the territory. A small British army garrison was maintained on South Georgia until 2001, before being replaced by scientists from the British Antarctic Survey.

Under the present constitution, which came into effect in 1985, the commissioner is concurrently the governor of the Falkland Islands. A chief executive officer, also based in the Falkland Islands, is responsible for administration. Government officers are based in South Georgia.
Commissioner (non-resident), HE Nigel Phillips, CBE, *apptd* 2017
Chief Executive (non-resident), James Jansen

ECONOMY
A conservation and management fishing zone was established around the islands in 1993 and a licensing regime introduced for fishing vessels. Sale of fishing licences, passenger landing fees, harbour dues, and the sale of postage stamps and commemorative coins are the main sources of revenue. Tourism, especially wildlife tourism, is growing quickly, but prior permission to land on the islands must be sought.

TURKS AND CAICOS ISLANDS

Area – 948 sq. km
Capital – Cockburn Town, on Grand Turk; population, 5,000 (2014 est)
Currency – US dollar (US$) of 100 cents
Population – 52,570 rising at 2.16 per cent a year (2017 est)

Religion – Christian (Protestant 72.8 per cent, Roman Catholic 11.4 per cent) (est)
Language – English (official)
Population density – 37 per sq. km (2017)
Flag – British blue ensign with the coat of arms in the fly
National day – 30 August (Constitution Day)
Median age (years) – 33.3 (2017 est)
Life expectancy (years) – 80 (2017 est)
Mortality rate – 3.2 (2017 est)
Birth rate – 15.3 (2017 est)
Infant mortality rate – 10.1 (2017 est)

CLIMATE AND TERRAIN
Around 40 islands and cays make up the the Turks and Caicos Islands, of which eight are permanently inhabited. The climate is marine tropical, moderated by trade winds; the average annual temperature is 26°C. Flamingo Hill on East Caicos is the highest elevation, at 48m.

HISTORY AND POLITICS
The islands changed hands several times between the French, Spanish and British after their discovery in 1512 and before the arrival of the first settlers, a group of Bermudans, in the 1670s. They achieved separate colonial status under the administration of the Bahamas in 1848, and since 1973 the territory has had its own governor and internal self-government.

The constitution implemented in 2012 re-established home rule after the House of Assembly and 2006 constitution were suspended in 2009 following a corruption scandal. The constitution provides for a legislature consisting of 15 elected members, four members appointed by the governor and the island's attorney general. The UK remains responsible for defence, external affairs and international and offshore financial relations. The People's Democratic Movement's (PDM) won elections held in December 2016, garnering ten seats to the ruling Progressive National Party's (PNP) five, prompting the resignation of premier Rufus Ewing. In September 2017 the islands were badly damaged by Hurricane Irma and Hurricane Maria.
Governor, HE Dr John Freeman, CMG, *apptd* 2016
Premier, Hon. Sharlene Cartwright-Robinson

ECONOMY
The main industries are offshore financial services, fishing and tourism, with over one million people visiting the island in 2013. The USA is the main source of tourists.
Imports – US$389m (2016)
Exports – US$4m (2016)

BALANCE OF PAYMENTS
Trade – US$385m deficit (2016)

Trade with UK	2016	2017
Imports from UK	£2,755,118	£2,976,906
Exports to UK	£166,494	£151,402

COMMUNICATIONS
The principal airports are on the islands of Grand Turk and Providenciales and provide international air links; the main seaports are on Grand Turk and Providenciales. The islands have about 24km of surfaced roads.

THE NORTH AND SOUTH POLES

THE ARCTIC

The Arctic is the region around the Earth's north pole. It includes the ice-covered Arctic Ocean, parts of Canada, the USA, Greenland, Iceland, Finland, Norway, Sweden and Russia. The area is commonly defined as lying north of the line of latitude known as the Arctic Circle (running at 66° 34' N.) or inside the 10°C July isotherm.

The climate is harsh, particularly during winter (October–March) when the Arctic receives little sunlight; the average monthly temperature in December, January and February is around −10 to −15°C. Continental areas, including Northern Canada and Alaska, can experience lows of −60°C in winter. In summer, the interior of Greenland remains subzero, while more southerly regions such as the Siberian tundra, can rise to 30°C. Coastal areas, including Iceland and Northern Scandinavia, have a milder, maritime climate with an average yearly temperature of 10°C. The Arctic is rarely as cold as the Antarctic since there is water, not land, underneath the Arctic ice. The water is warmer than the air above it, causing heat to rise and moderate the cold.

The polar bear is the region's apex predator. Other native species include varieties of caribou, lemming, wolf, hare and fox; around 200 bird species migrate to tundra areas in summer. Until recently, vegetation was limited to Arctic tundra, a biome consisting of around 1,700 species of low-lying shrubs, grasses, sedges, lichens and mosses. However, this tundra is slowly being replaced with flora typical of more southern locations, such as trees and evergreen shrubs. In 2013, a comprehensive study of these changes, the Arctic Biodiversity Assessment (W www.arcticbiodiversity.is), concluded that climate change and the effects of collective industrial development were degrading arctic biodiversity.

ARCTIC SEA ROUTES

In 1906 Norwegian explorer Roald Amundsen first successfully navigated the Northwest passage, but the shallow waterways he encountered ensured that the route held little commercial potential until recently. Similarly, the Northern Sea route (formerly the Northeast passage) linking the Atlantic and Pacific oceans around Russia's Arctic coast, was first navigated by Finnish-Swedish explorer Adolf Erik Nordenskjold in 1878–9, but thereafter only icebreakers and Russian submarines regularly traversed it.

In summer 2007, the Northwest passage was declared open for the first time since records began in late 1978; the first commercial ship travelled through it in September 2008. In August 2008 the Northwest passage and the Northern Sea route were open simultaneously for the first time, making the Arctic circumnavigable. Two German cargo vessels became the first to navigate the Northern Sea route in September 2009 and in August 2012 *The World* became the largest passenger ship to navigate the Northwest Passage, following Amundsen's route. In February 2018 a commercial ship became the first to travel the Northern Sea route in winter without an icebreaker vessel.

CLIMATE CHANGE

The extent of ice in the Arctic has become a key measure of global climate change. The rate at which the ice melts grows exponentially: whereas the white ice reflects sunlight back into space, the darker seas absorb its heat, and the rising sea temperature melts the surrounding ice. The area of the sea ice reaches its greatest extent in March and retreats to its lowest point in September. The maximum ice extent in March 2018 was recorded as 14.48 million km² (5.59 million miles²); the second lowest in the 39-year satellite record and 1.16 million km² (448,000 miles²) below the 1981 to 2010 average maximum. The minimum ice extent in September 2017 was recorded as 4.64 million km² (1.79 million miles²); 1.25 million km² (483,000 miles²) above the record minimum extent, which occurred in September 2012, and 1.58 million km² (610,000 miles²) below the 1981 to 2010 median extent for the same day. Estimates of sea ice volume have been obtained via the University of Washington Polar Science Center's PIOMAS. For 2017, PIOMAS calculated an annual average sea ice volume of 12,900 km³ (3,095 miles³), below the 2012 annual average volume of 13,550 km³ (3,251 miles³). It was the lowest annual average volume of sea ice yet recorded; it is estimated that in 1979, the annual average was around 25,430 km³ (6,100 miles³).

NATURAL RESOURCES

The Arctic's receding ice presents opportunities for national governments to lay claim to a wealth of hydrocarbon and mineral deposits. In 2008 the US Geological Survey estimated that 20 per cent of the world's undiscovered oil and gas reserves – as much as 90 billion barrels of oil, 44 billion barrels of natural gas liquids and 1,670 trillion cubic feet of natural gas – are located within the Arctic Circle. In December 2016 the USA and Canada introduced bans on offshore drilling covering large portions of the Arctic. Under the 1982 UN Convention on the Law of the Sea, no state owns the pole or the ocean surrounding it: the five countries that border the Arctic Ocean – Canada, Denmark, Norway, Russia and the USA (a non-signatory) – are limited to an economic zone of 200 nautical miles from their coastline, unless able to prove that their continental shelf extends beyond that limit. Under the convention the countries have ten years from their date of ratification to assert a claim that their continental shelf extends into arctic territory. In August 2007, Russia planted a flag in the seabed below the pole, on the Lomonosov Ridge which spans much of the Arctic, and which Russia claims is an extension of the Eurasian continent and therefore part of its territory. However, Canadian geologists assert that Lomonosov is an extension of the North American continent, and therefore falls under their jurisdiction. In December 2014 Denmark followed Canada, Norway and Russia in submitting a claim under UNCLOS, arguing that the Lomonosov Ridge is an extension of Greenland's continental shelf. Russia resubmitted its bid in August 2015, laying claim to 1.2 million km² of the shelf.

THE ANTARCTIC

The Antarctic is generally defined as the area lying within the Antarctic Convergence, the zone where cold northward-flowing Antarctic sea water sinks below warmer southward-flowing water. This zone fluctuates unevenly between the latitudes of 48° S. and 61° S., typically extending further north in the Atlantic Ocean than in the Pacific. The continent itself lies almost entirely within the Antarctic Circle; it has an area of around 14 million km², 98 per cent of which is permanently ice-covered. In 2013 the international project Bedmap2 found that the average thickness of the grounded ice is 2,126m, but can reach 4,776m in places; it amounts to some 26.5 million km³, and represents around 90 per cent of the world's fresh water and 91 per cent of the world's glacier ice. Much of the sea freezes in winter, forming fast ice which breaks free of the coast in summer and drifts north as pack ice.

CLIMATE AND TERRAIN
Antarctica is the highest, coldest and driest continent on Earth, with average coastal temperatures ranging from just above freezing in the summer (December–February) to −30°C in winter. Conditions on the interior plateau are more severe, with katabatic (gravity-driven) winds and frequent cyclonic storms pushing average winter temperatures down to −65°C. The Vostok research station holds the record for the lowest surface temperature recorded on Earth at −89.2°C in 1983. Elevation extremes range from 4,892m (Vinson Massif) at the highest point to more than −2,540m (Bentley Subglacial Trench) at the lowest. The Transantarctic mountains bisect the continent north–south, dividing the west Antarctic ice-sheet – an ice-filled marine basin – from the significantly larger and more elevated east sheet. Precipitation levels range from less than 50mm a year inland to around 400mm in some coastal areas. With average precipitation of just 140mm a year, Antarctica is considered a desert.

CLIMATE CHANGE
While the recent decline in levels of ice in the Arctic has been clear and visible, concurrent changes in the Antarctic have been more complex. Despite reports of a recent thickening of the interior of the east ice-sheet due to increased snowfall, studies of data produced by the European Space Agency's Cryosat satellite indicate that the Antarctic ice-sheet as a whole has declined by more than 500 km³ (30 miles³) a year since 2010. However, the continent appeared to be gaining temporary sea ice in winter – which extended to a record 20.11 million km² (7.76 million miles²) in September 2014 – probably due to increased meltwater from the land ice, which re-freezes more easily than the ocean water below. This growth slowed in 2015, and on 20 and 21 February 2018 the US National Snow and Ice Data Center recorded the minimum sea ice extent for the year, the second lowest in satellite record, at 2.18 million km² (842,000 miles²), 670,000 km² (259,000 miles²) below the 1981 to 2010 average minimum. The annual sea ice extent for 2017 was a record minimum at 10.64 million km² (4.11 million miles²); 400,000 km² (154,000 miles²) less than the previous record set in 1986.

The British Antarctic Survey has found that the west coast of the Antarctic Peninsula has become one of the fastest-warming areas on the planet, with annual mean temperatures rising by around 3°C over the past 50 years. In March 2015 a record high of 17.5°C was recorded at the Esperanza research station on the western peninsula. In 2009, a group of British geophysicists found that the retreat of the Pine Island Glacier in the Western Antarctic had quadrupled between 1995 and 2006. However, the temperatures recorded by the Amundsen-Scott station at the South Pole actually show a recent cooling, as do some studies of east Antarctica. It has been determined that these falling temperatures have been caused by the thinning of Antarctica's ozone layer that has in turn cooled the stratosphere above the continent. The historical use of chlorofluorocarbons (CFCs) by humans has contributed to the destruction of Antarctica's ozone layer, as the clouds that form in the winter polar vortex – an area of very cold air above the continent – react with these CFCs to release chlorine which destroys ozone. Antarctic ozone levels are expected to recover by 2050 and this could result in warmer temperatures in the region.

HISTORY AND DISCOVERY
The idea of Antarctica is much older than proof of the continent's existence. The notion of *Terra Australis*, a vast southern continent which counterbalanced the northern lands of Europe, Asia and North Africa, originated with Aristotle, and was depicted on a world map as early as 1531. The supposed size of this land was gradually amended over the course of 16th-century exploration and further corrected after James Cook's circumnavigation of the globe in 1774. His journey from New Zealand to the Cape of Good Hope (via Tierra del Fuego), travelling at a high southern latitude (between 53° and 60°), confirmed that any land mass must be confined to the polar region.

The date of the first sighting of Antarctica is unclear. In 1820 three separate expeditions, from the UK, the USA and Russia, each claimed to have seen the continent within days of each other, and the argument has never been settled. The golden age of Antarctic exploration was prompted by the discovery of the magnetic North Pole in 1831, but it was not until the beginning of the 20th century that real progress was made. James Clark Ross was the first to identify the approximate location of the South Pole, but was unable to reach it. British explorers Robert Scott in 1901–4 and Ernest Shackleton in 1907–9 got closer, but it was not until Norwegian adventurer Roald Amundsen pioneered a new route, through the Axel Heiberg Glacier, that the pole was reached in December 1911. Scott's second attempt was also successful, but he arrived a month later and perished with his team on the return journey.

FLORA AND FAUNA
The only land animals to survive on the Antarctic continent are tiny invertebrates, including microscopic mites, lice, ticks, nematodes, rotifers and tardigrades. The largest land animal is the *Belgica antarctica*, a flightless midge just 2–6mm in size. The snow petrel, one of only three birds that breed exclusively in Antarctica, has been spotted at the South Pole. Large numbers of seals, penguins and other seabirds go ashore to breed in the summer; the emperor penguin is the only species that breeds ashore throughout the winter. Four species of albatross breed in South Georgia during the summer, but their numbers are in serious decline owing to the effects of longline fishing in the Southern Ocean region. Recent climate change has also affected the continent's wildlife, with the number of Adélie penguins falling significantly, as open-water species such as the chinstrap and gentoo penguins invade its Antarctic Peninsula habitat to take advantage of the warming temperatures.

By contrast, the Antarctic seas abound with life; recent expeditions identified over 700 previously unknown species. Krill, which congregates in large schools, is crucial to the ecosystem and provides a diet for migratory whales (including killer, humpback and blue whales), a number of species of seal, penguin, albatross and other, smaller birds. Each of these species is threatened by an 80 per cent fall in recorded levels of krill since the 1970s, thought to be caused by warmer sea water and, paradoxically, the decimation of the blue whale through hunting in the first half of the 20th century: although whales eat krill, the iron in whale excrement is essential to the algae on which the krill feed. In 2010 a group of research bodies completed the Census of Antarctic Marine Life, an inventory of over 16,000 marine species compiled from 19 expeditions; scientists estimate that 39–58 per cent of the Antarctic's marine species are yet to be described.

With almost all of the Antarctic continent permanently covered in ice, only a small number of flowering plants, ferns and club mosses survive. Most of these are found on the sub-Antarctic islands, while only two species (a grass and a pearlwort) extend south of 60° S. Antarctic vegetation is dominated by lichens and mosses, with a few liverworts, algae and fungi surviving in the cracks and pore spaces of sandstone and granite rocks.

SCIENTIFIC RESEARCH

As at December 2017 there were 20 nations with permanently manned research stations in Antarctica:

Country	Number of research stations
Russian Federation	7
Argentina	6
Chile	4
Australia	3
USA	3
China	2
France	*2
India	2
South Korea	2
UK	†2

Brazil, Germany, Italy (*shared with France), Japan, New Zealand, Norway, Poland, South Africa, Ukraine and Uruguay each have a single station.

The UK's Halley research station (†) is temporarily closed until November 2018. The Halley station was successfully relocated 14.3 miles (23km) inland at the start of February 2017 after a fissure to the west threatened to cut the base off from the mainland. A new crack was then discovered to the north of the new location and the station was shut in March 2017 to allow glaciologists to assess the stability of the area.

ANTARCTIC LAW

The Antarctic Treaty was signed on 1 December 1959 when 12 states (Argentina, Australia, Belgium, Chile, France, Japan, New Zealand, Norway, South Africa, the Soviet Union, the UK and the USA) pledged to promote scientific and technical cooperation unhampered by politics. The signatories agreed to establish free use of the Antarctic continent for peaceful scientific purposes; freeze all territorial claims and disputes in the Antarctic; ban all military activities in the area; and prohibit nuclear explosions and the disposal of radioactive waste. The Antarctic Treaty was defined as covering areas south of latitude 60° S., excluding the high seas but including the ice shelves, and came into force in 1961. The treaty provides that any member of the UN can accede to it; it has since been signed by a further 41 states. In 1998 an extension to the treaty came into effect, placing a 50-year ban on mining, oil exploration and mineral extraction in Antarctica, and stipulating that all tourists, explorers and expeditions now require permission to enter the Antarctic from a relevant national authority. However, in recent years the region's coastal states have asserted often conflicting claims to oil- and gas-rich territory on the Antarctic seabed. Under the terms of the UN Convention on the Law of the Sea, each nation's sovereignty over its continental shelf extends up to 350 nautical miles beyond its territorial coasts; the UN Commission on the Limits of the Continental Shelf is examining evidence submitted in support of these claims.

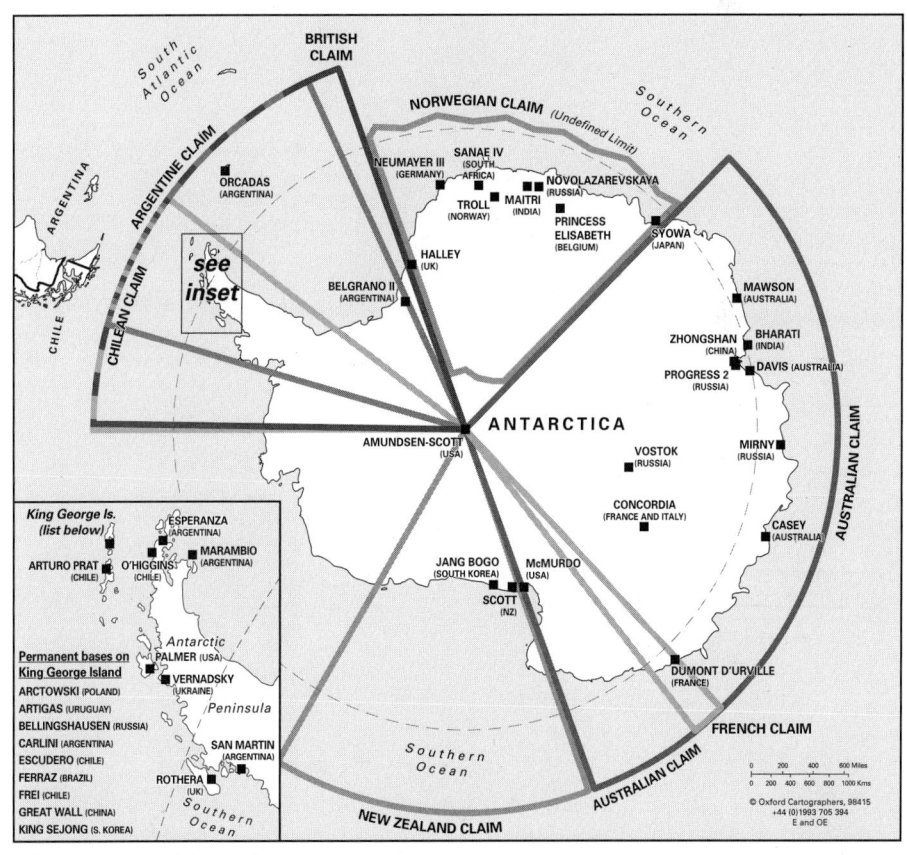

948 The North and South Poles

POPULATION AND TOURISM

Antarctica has no indigenous inhabitants, although the continent maintains a population of scientists and research workers which peaks in the summer months at over 4,400.

Antarctic tourism is a growth industry. The first *Lonely Planet* guide to Antarctica was published in 1996, and ship-borne cruises typically depart from Argentina, Chile and the Falkland Islands. The continent has also become a popular venue for extreme sports enthusiasts: it is now possible to sky-dive, ski, ride a motorbike and fly a helicopter across the continent, and the Vinson Massif and other peaks have become desirable destinations for mountaineers. The huts built by Scott and Shackleton are also popular attractions. In 1991 the International Association of Antarctica Tour Operators (IAATO) was founded with the objective of providing a self-regulating code of conduct for all operators to follow, but membership is voluntary, and fears remain regarding tourism-related environmental damage. IAATO recorded 6,704 tourists in the 1992–3 summer season, rising to more than 46,000 in 2007–8 and dipping to 45,083 in 2016–17.

THE BRITISH ANTARCTIC SURVEY

The British Antarctic Survey (BAS) is part of the Natural Environment Research Council and carries out the majority of Britain's scientific research in Antarctica. Over 500 staff are employed by BAS and the organisation supports five research stations, four of which are staffed throughout the winter months (two in South Georgia and two in Antarctica). An unmanned submersible, named Boaty McBoatface in a public competition, embarked on its first Antarctic research mission in March 2017 aboard the BAS ship RRS *James Clark Ross* as part of a seven-week expedition. *See* the BAS website (W www.antarctica.ac.uk) for further information.

THE YEAR 2017–18

The year under review covers the period from 1 August 2017 to 31 July 2018

EVENTS OF THE YEAR

OBITUARIES

ARCHAEOLOGY

ARCHITECTURE

ART

BUSINESS AND FINANCE

CLASSICAL MUSIC AND OPERA

CONSERVATION AND HERITAGE

DANCE

FILM

LITERATURE

THE MEDIA

PARLIAMENT

ACTS OF PARLIAMENT

POP MUSIC

SCIENCE AND DISCOVERY

THEATRE

SPORT

WEATHER

A CENTURY AGO IN WHITAKER'S

EVENTS OF THE YEAR 1917–18

The following constitutes selected extracts from the Events of the Year chapter as recorded in the 1918 and 1919 editions of *Whitaker's Almanack,* published a century ago. The text has been reproduced in its original form, along with its idiosyncrasies of style and archaic spellings of names. The information in parentheses following the date is the name of the sub-section the extract was taken from.

AUGUST 1917

10. (Labour) Special Conference of Labour Party in London decided, by 1,846,000 votes to 550,000, to accept the invitation to the International Socialist Conference at Stockholm, on condition that it be "consultative, and not mandatory." **11. (Diary of the War)** Liner *City of Athens* mined off Cape Town; 21 passengers and crew drowned. **13. (Imperial Politics)** Mr. Bonar Law stated in the House of Commons that the Government, in common with the Governments of the United States, France, and Italy, had decided to refuse passports to delegates to the Stockholm Conference. **14. (Diary of the War)** China declared war against Germany and Austria-Hungary. **15. (Imperial Dominions)** Publication of an important memorandum on the extension of provincial autonomy in India drawn up by Mr. Gokhale before his death. **15. (Imperial Politics)** The removal of the "Ladies Grill" was sanctioned. **18. (Labour)** Proclamation by Government prohibiting the threatened strike of the Amalgamated Society of Locomotive Engineers. **27. (Imperial Dominions)** Coalition Government formed in S. Australia, with Mr. Peake as Premier.

SEPTEMBER 1917

3. (Diary of the War) Moonlight air raid on the S.E. coast; Sheerness-Chatham district visited by 6 enemy aeroplanes, and bombs dropped in the Chatham district: 107 killed, 88 wounded. **4. (Imperial Politics)** Trades Union Congress at Blackpool, by 2,849,000 votes to 91,000, vetoed further consideration of the Stockholm Conference. **4. (Crimes)** E. D. Morel sentenced at Bow Street to 6 months' imprisonment for inciting Miss Ethel Sidgwick to smuggle out of England to Switzerland copies of pacifist literature, contrary to the Defence of the Realm Act. **13. (The King and Court)** Their Majesties presented their State portraits to the inhabitants of Windsor to be placed in the Guildhall to commemorate the King's adoption of "Windsor" as the name of the Royal House and Family. **20. (Legal)** A Divisional Court in a West Hartlepool appeal case held that no priest or minister ordained or appointed later than thirty days after the passing of the Military Service Act, 1916, could claim exemption from military service.

OCTOBER 1917

4. (Diary of the War) Passchendaele Ridge, E. of Ypres, attacked on a front of 8 miles by Sir Douglas Haig, who won a brilliant victory N. of Langemarck to the Tower Hamlets ridge on the Menin-Ypres road, gaining all objectives and winning most important positions: 3,000 prisoners taken and severe losses inflicted on the enemy; British losses light. **6. (Diary of the War)** Diplomatic relations with Germany broken off by Peru and Uruguay. **13. (Diary of the War)** Armed merchant-cruiser *Champagne* torpedoed and sunk: 5 officers and 51 men lost. **17. (Diary of the War)** The *Antilles,* a U.S. transport, torpedoed; 67 lives lost. **17. (United States)** Final call to arms of the first batch of conscripts (687,000),

bringing up the military and naval forces of the U.S. to 1,750,000 men. **19. (Diary of the War)** Raid by 10 or 12 Zeppelins over E. and N.E. counties; one airship got through to London and dropped 3 bombs; total casualties, 34 killed, 56 injured. **25. (Other Countries)** Fall of the Boselli Italian Ministry. **24. (Diary of the War)** Italians attacked by strong Austro-German forces under Mackensen on the Upper Isonzo, on either side of Tolmino.

NOVEMBER 1917

6. (Diary of the War) Pacifist motion in the House of Commons defeated by 282 votes to 33. **7. (Diary of the War)** *Coup d'état* in Petrograd by Bolshevists under Lenin: M. Kerensky and his Provisional Government deposed. **20. (Imperial Politics)** House of Commons made important changes in the Reform Bill, giving the vote to the wife of a Local Government elector, if 30 years of age, and enfranchising every sailor and soldier serving in the war who has attained the age of 19. **28. (Diary of the War)** Liner *Apapa* torpedoed and sunk; 79 lost.

DECEMBER 1917

6. (Imperial Dominions) Explosion of a munition ship in collision with another vessel in the harbour of Halifax (N.S.): one-third of the city laid in ruins, 1,226 deaths, 400 persons missing, over 3,000 houses destroyed by explosion and fire, 25,000 people rendered homeless. **8. (Diary of the War)** Ecuador broke off diplomatic relations with Germany. Armistice signed with the enemy by troops on the Romanian front. **8. (Other Countries)** Revolution in Portugal resulted in the overthrow of the Government after three days' fighting. **10. (Diary of the War)** Panama declared war on Austria-Hungary. **11. (Diary of the War)** Statement by Mr. Balfour in the House of Commons that the German Government had in Sept. made a communication to the British Government relative to peace. Entrance into Jerusalem of Gen. Allenby, accompanied by military attachés of France, Italy and the U.S. Cuba declared war on Austria-Hungary. **18. (The King and Court)** His Majesty was graciously pleased to assume the office of Ranger of Windsor Park. **23. (Diary of the War)** H.M.S. *Stephen Furness* announced by Admiralty to have been torpedoed and sunk by U-boat in the Irish Channel: six officers, 95 men lost. **29. (Other Countries)** Virtual destruction of Guatemala City in an earthquake: 1,000 reported killed, 125,000 people homeless. **30. (Imperial Dominions)** Election riots at Quebec: city placed under martial law.

JANUARY 1918

8. (United States) Pres. Wilson's message to Congress, in which he specified 14 conditions necessary for a world's peace. **9. (Other Countries)** Rapid spread of plague in China: passenger and goods traffic suspended between Pekin and Fengchen (Shansi). **10. (Diary of the War)** Russo-German peace negotiations continued at Brest-Litovsk: Ukraine Republic recognized by Petrograd delegates and enemy representatives. **11. (Imperial Politics)** Result of Australian conscription referendum: for, 1,013,000; against, 1,178,000: majority of Australian Forces voted in the affirmative. **12. (Accidents (General))** Colliery explosion at the Minnie Pit of the Podmore Hall Colliery, Halmead, Staffs, resulting in the death of 155 men. **14. (Diary of the War)** Attempted assassination of Lenin at Petrograd. **23. (Diary of the War)** New Public Meals Order establishing two meatless days a week. **24. (Diary of the War)** Reply in the Reichstag of Count

Hertling, German Imperial Chancellor, to the speeches of Pres. Wilson and Mr. Lloyd George on war aims: no cession of Alsace-Lorraine; no interference with Germany in Russian peace; Belgium to be dealt with at a Conference; Great Britain to give up Gibraltar, Malta, &c.; restoration of German Colonies demanded. **28. (Diary of the War)** Enemy air raid on London by 15 machines in three groups: five penetrated the defences: in a subsequent attack one machine reached London, and dropped bombs, killing 58, and injuring 173, including 30 killed and 91 injured in a single building used as an air raid shelter.

FEBRUARY 1918

1. (Diary of the War) Ukraine Republic recognized by Central Powers. **6. (Imperial Politics)** Royal Assent, Representation of the People Bill. **10. (Diary of the War)** Announcement by M. Trotsky that "while desisting from signing a formal treaty of peace, the state of war with the enemy Powers is ended": Russia out of the war. **14. (United States)** Death of Sir Cecil Spring Rice, Ambassador to the United States. **19. (The King and Court)** Prince of Wales took his seat in the House of Lords as a peer of the realm. **23. (Labour)** Resolution of the Inter-Allied Labour and Socialist Conference held in London adopted a statement of war aims, deciding to ask the Socialists of the Central Empires to reply without delay. **24. (Accidents (General))** Steamer *Florizel* wrecked near Cape Race with loss of 102 lives. **28. (Imperial Politics)** Sir G. Cave, in the House of Commons, explained that M. Litvinoff, the Bolshevist "Ambassador" to London, was not an Ambassador of any recognised Government.

MARCH 1918

1. (Diary of the War) H.M. armed merchant cruiser *Calgarian* torpedoed and sunk off the Irish Coast; 21 officers, 46 men lost. **2. (Diary of the War)** Peace signed at Brest-Litovsk between Russia and Central Powers: enemy demanded the detachment of Ardahan, Kars, and Batoum in the Caucasus. **13. (The King and Court)** His Majesty received at Buckingham Palace the Siamese Military Mission, and conferred the K.C.M.G. on the Chief, Maj.-Gen. Phya Bhijai Janridh. **15. (Accidents (General))** L. & N.W. ss. *Rathmore* in collision with another vessel, 26 lives lost. **20. (Imperial Politics)** Bill to enfranchise all women on equal basis with men, except those married to enemy aliens, introduced by Sir Robert Borden in Dominion House of Commons. **21. (Diary of the War)** Great German massed attack by some 40 enemy divisions on British 3rd and 4th Armies on a 50-mile front between the Scarpe and the Oise. **30. (Diary of the War)** German long-range gun bombarded Paris; a church shelled while the congregation were worshipping on Good Friday – 75 killed, 90 injured.

APRIL 1918

2. (Educational) Conference of the National Union of Teachers at Cambridge, by 42,757 votes to 26,040, decided against equal salaries for men and women. **2. (Imperial Dominions)** Inauguration of the South African University at Cape Town: Prince of Wales first Chancellor. **9. (The King and Court)** Queen assumed the position and title of Commandant-in-Chief of the Queen Mary's Women's Army Auxiliary Corps. **20. (Diary of the War)** German advance north-east of Ypres stopped by British artillery fire. At close of month of battles German thrust against British Armies held. **21. (Imperial Politics)** Irish bishops and clergy, at Mass, denounce conscription for Ireland. **23. (Diary of the War)** Guatemala declared war on Germany.

MAY 1918

5. (Imperial Politics) Gen. Lord French, K.P., appointed Lord-Lieut. of Ireland, in succession to Lord Wimborne, resigned, and Mr. E. Shortt, K.C., Chief Secretary for Ireland,

in place of Mr. Duke, resigned. **7. (Diary of the War)** "Peace of Bucharest" signed between Romania and the Central Powers. **8. (Art)** Sale at Paris of pictures by M. Degas, the famous painter, realised £224,000. **8. (Diary of the War)** Nicaragua declared war on Germany. **15. (Imperial Dominions)** Direct railway service from Cairo to Palestine by the completion of swing-bridge over Suez Canal at Kantara. **17. (Diary of the War)** Discovery of German-Irish plot: many Sinn Feiners arrested, including de Valera, Count Plunkett, Countess Markievicz, and other leaders. **18. (Imperial Politics)** Royal Assent, Military Service (No. 2) Act. **22. (Imperial Dominions)** Completion of the Katanga railway, giving direct communication from the Cape to the Congo. **19. (Diary of the War)** Group of British hospitals at Etaples, outside French battle area, bombed by German airmen: 300 casualties. **23. (Diary of the War)** Costa Rica declared war on the Central Powers. **23. (Other Countries)** Diplomatic relations between Mexico and Cuba severed. **27. (Other Countries)** Illness of King Alfonso, caused by influenza widely spread throughout Spain.

JUNE 1918

1. (Labour) Decision announced of British Workers League to form itself into a political party to be known as the National Democratic and Labour Party. **3. (Diary of the War)** Prime Ministers of Great Britain, France and Italy, at sixth session of Supreme War Council at Versailles, agreed to declaration of the creation of a united and independent Polish State with free access to the sea, and sympathy with the Czecho-Slovak and Jugo-Slav national aspirations. **10. (Other Countries)** 400 people killed by an explosion of a munitions depôt at Jassy. **21. (Imperial Politics)** Government announced the abandonment, for the present, of Home Rule and conscription for Ireland. **22. (United States)** Disastrous railway collision near Hammond, Indiana: 59 killed, 115 injured. **24. (Other Countries)** Capt. Amundsen left Christiania on a N. Polar expedition in the *Maud*. **26. (Diary of the War)** House of Lords adopted a motion approving of a League of Nations. **28. (Labour)** Series of resolutions passed at Labour Conference affecting domestic policy and the interests of workers: "equal rights for women" adopted.

JULY 1918

1. (Accidents (General)) Explosion at a national shell-filling factory in the Midlands: 100 killed, 150 injured. **5. (Crimes)** The Recorder at the Central Criminal Court, in the case of a man charged with publishing a declamatory libel of and concerning his wife, held that a man could not libel himself, and, therefore, according to old common law, he could not libel his wife. **5. (United States)** Excursion steamer *Columbia* overturned in the Illinois River: 175 drowned. **8. (Diary of the War)** House of Commons, without a division, accepted the Government Bill prolonging the life of Parliament for another six months, to Jan. 30, 1919 (the fifth extension of its life). **8. (The King and Court)** Their Majesties received at Buckingham Palace a number of deputations, who presented loyal addresses of congratulation on their Silver Wedding. **12. (Diary of the War)** Japanese battleship *Kawachi,* of the Dreadnought class, blown up in Tokuyama Bay and sunk: over 500 casualties. **15. (Diary of the War)** Third great German offensive launched on a front of 50 miles east and west of Rheims in two parts: the first against French sector on a 35 mile front between Château-Thierry and Vrigny: the other east of Rheims between Prunay and Maisons de Champagne on a front of 25 miles. Hayti declared war on Germany. **15. (Imperial Dominions)** Threatened strike of 300,000 railwaymen in Canada. **16. (Diary of the War)** Murder of Ex-Tsar Nicholas II. by Bolshevists. **19. (Diary of the War)** Honduras declared war on Germany. **27. (Diary of the War)** Spread of enemy retreat and pursuit by Allied cavalry.

EVENTS OF THE YEAR 2017–18

UK AFFAIRS

AUGUST 2017
2. After 65 years, HRH the Duke of Edinburgh undertook his last public engagement before retiring from official duties; he inspected the honour guard of the Royal Marines at Buckingham Palace to mark the finale of the 1664 Global Challenge. **13.** The Equality and Human Rights Commission called for fathers to receive a longer period of better-paid paternity leave in order to tackle the gender pay gap. **14.** The Thames Garden Bridge project was officially abandoned over fears of mounting costs to the taxpayer; the bridge had already accrued planning expenditure of £37m since 2013 and it was estimated to incur a further £9m in cancellation costs. **31.** St Olave's Grammar School in Orpington was accused of trying to alter exam results after it emerged that the high-performing school had ejected 16 students prior to sitting their A-Levels because the school felt that they would not obtain a minimum standard of 'B' grades in their upcoming examinations.

SEPTEMBER 2017
1. The Royal Air Force became the first part of the UK armed forces to open up every role to both men and women. **4.** Kensington Palace announced that the Duke and Duchess of Cambridge were expecting their third child. **10.** The 149th annual Trades Union Congress (TUC) opened at the Brighton Centre; the conference included speeches by TUC president, Mary Bousted, and general secretary, Frances O'Grady, as well as Labour leader Jeremy Corbyn. **12.** British ministers pledged to continue supplying UK troops, technology and intelligence to EU defence missions after Brexit, in an attempt to win allies among the EU 27 ahead of the following month's summit. **14.** The Office for National Statistics reported that employment surged to a record 75.3 per cent of the working-age population as 379,000 more jobs were created in the year to July 2017; nearly 70 per cent of the new jobs went to women and only 8 per cent were part-time. **20.** Prime Minister Theresa May demanded urgent reforms to the UN in a speech to world leaders at the organisation's general assembly in New York City, threatening to withhold up to £30m of the UK's £90m annual UN commitment; in the 15-minute address, the prime minister attacked Russia's behaviour on the UN security council and criticised US president Donald Trump's decision to pull out of the Paris climate deal. **22.** Theresa May promised to give residency status to EU citizens in the UK during a speech in Florence, Italy; the prime minister also agreed to pay a financial settlement totalling around £40bn to the EU, asking in return for a transition period of two years in which the UK would have single-market access and remain in the customs union. Transport for London said that it would not renew taxi company Uber's operating licence in the capital on its expiration on 30 September due to the company's lack of corporate responsibility in relation to reporting criminal offences, obtaining medical certificates and carrying out driver background checks; Uber stated that it would launch an appeal against the decision. **29.** Henry Bolton, a former army officer, was elected UK Independence Party (UKIP) leader, taking 30 per cent of the vote; he beat six other candidates, including Anne Marie Waters, the director of Sharia Watch UK, who came second with 21.3 per cent.

OCTOBER 2017
2. Theresa May announced that annual tuition fees would be frozen at £9,250 until 2019, and that the amount graduates would need to earn before repaying would be raised from £21,000 to £25,000, in a policy costing £1.2bn over four years; the policy was announced alongside a £10bn expansion of Help to Buy, which enabled first-time buyers to purchase new-build homes with a deposit of 5 per cent. Monarch Airlines went into administration and ceased operations, with 110,000 customers to be brought home on specially chartered planes and a further 750,000 told that their bookings had been cancelled; more than 1,800 employees lost their jobs. **10.** The government's race disparity audit revealed that the unemployment rate for black, Asian and minority ethnic Britons of working age was nearly double than that for white British groups (8 per cent compared with 4.6 per cent); the findings also showed that nine out of ten headteachers were white British, and that two in three white British householders owned their home, compared with two in five from any other ethnic groups. **15.** Anne Marie Waters launched a new far right party, For Britain, after quitting UKIP; she had come second in the UKIP leadership election (*see* 29 September 2017). **18.** The annual headline rate of inflation rose to 3 per cent in September 2017, up from August's 2.9 per cent, and the highest level in five years. **19.** The headmaster at St Olave's School in Orpington was suspended after it was found that he presided over a policy of 'grade exclusion'; he later resigned, as the Department for Education said that excluding pupils for non-disciplinary reasons was unlawful (*see* 31 August 2017). **25.** Jeremy Corbyn suspended Labour MP Jared O'Mara two days after it was revealed that he had used derogatory language towards women online. **30.** It was reported that a group of Westminster researchers compiled a dossier of 45 Conservative MPs who were accused of making unwanted sexual advances or behaving inappropriately towards colleagues and junior staff.

NOVEMBER 2017
1. Sir Michael Fallon resigned as defence secretary amid claims of sexual assault and inappropriate behaviour towards female journalists; chief whip Gavin Williamson was appointed as his replacement. **7.** Carl Sargeant, a member of the Welsh assembly, killed himself after being fired over allegations about his personal conduct with at least three women. **8.** Priti Patel resigned as international development secretary after it emerged that she had held 12 meetings with senior Israeli figures, including the prime minister, Binyamin Netanyahu, while on holiday in the country, without officials present. Train drivers from the ASLEF union accepted a deal with Southern rail, bringing to an end an 18-month dispute; members voted four to one to accept the resolution, which included a 28.5 per cent pay rise over five years. **13.** Prime Minister Theresa May accused Russia's President Vladimir Putin of trying to 'weaponise information' in the age of social media in order to undermine democracies. **15.** Data scientists at Swansea University and the University of California, Berkeley, revealed that more than 150,000 Twitter accounts based in Russia posted about Brexit in the days leading up to the 2016 vote. **20.** Sir Christopher Greenwood, the UK's candidate for the International Court of Justice (ICJ) who had served one nine-year term on the UN court, withdrew after being defeated in the first round of a run-off election against Dalveer Bhandari, the Indian justice; as a result, the UK lost its seat on the ICJ for the first time since the body began work in 1946. **22.** Chancellor Philip Hammond announced the 2017 autumn budget, which included abolishing stamp duty for first-time buyers of homes worth up to £300,000, pledging £2.8bn for

the NHS in England up to 2022 and setting aside £3bn for Brexit planning. **27.** The Prince of Wales announced the engagement of Prince Harry and Ms Meghan Markle, with the wedding to take place in May 2018 at Windsor Castle. **28.** Wholesaler Palmer & Harvey, one of the UK's largest private companies supplying products to more than 90,000 shops, collapsed into administration; it resulted in 2,500 immediate job losses, and a further 400 in the following weeks.

DECEMBER 2017

8. Theresa May and the EU announced that a breakthrough deal had been reached to move the Brexit talks onto future trade and a transitional period; Jean-Claude Juncker, the President of the European Commission, said 'sufficient progress' had been made on all three 'divorce issues' (the Irish border, a financial settlement and EU citizens' rights). **13.** The House of Commons voted on an amendment to the EU withdrawal bill that would give parliament the final say on any exit deal; Theresa May's government was defeated by a majority of four – 309 votes to 305 – after rebel Tories backed an amendment by former attorney-general Dominic Grieve. **20.** Theresa May asked Damian Green to resign as Cabinet Office minister after he admitted to making 'inaccurate and misleading' statements about pornography found on his parliamentary computer. **29.** Lord Adonis resigned as the government's infrastructure adviser in order to make clear his opposition to Brexit, and in protest at a rail franchise 'bailout' of Stagecoach and Virgin.

JANUARY 2018

2. Average rail ticket prices rose by 3.4 per cent across the UK, the biggest increase to fares since 2013. **8.** Education secretary Justine Greening quit the government after turning down the post of welfare secretary in the prime minister's cabinet reshuffle; Damian Hinds was named as the new education secretary. **12.** US president Donald Trump cancelled his visit to the UK after disagreeing with the new location of the US embassy, in the south London area of Nine Elms, calling it an 'off location'. **15.** Carillion, the UK's second-biggest construction company, went into liquidation after accruing debts of £1.3bn and a pension deficit estimated at up to £2.6bn; almost 1,000 jobs were lost. **18.** Prime Minister Theresa May and President Emmanuel Macron of France signed the Sandhurst Treaty at a summit in Berkshire, aimed at speeding up the processing times for the cases of migrants in Calais from six months to one month for adults, and from six months to 25 days for minors. **24.** The government appointed campaigner and charity leader Sara Khan as lead Commissioner for Countering Extremism.

FEBRUARY 2018

7. Cambridge University registered as an official apprenticeship trainer for the first time, alongside companies such as Lloyds Bank, Greggs and British Airways; other universities to register included Bath Spa and the University of Brighton. **8.** *The New York Times* reported that Alexanda Kotey and El Shafee Elsheikh, from west London, were detained by the US-backed Syrian Democratic Forces; the two remaining members of the British IS cell dubbed 'the Beatles' were later stripped of their UK citizenship. Bermuda became the first jurisdiction in the world to repeal same-sex marriage when its British governor signed into law legislation to replace same-sex marriage with domestic partnerships. The Gambia rejoined the Commonwealth after a near five-year absence in an attempt by the government to end international isolation; President Jammeh, who ruled for 22 years amid claims of human rights abuses, pulled the country out of the Commonwealth in 2013. **9.** *The Times* reported that Oxfam, which had received £300m a year in British government funds and public donations, allowed three men to resign and fired four for gross misconduct

after an inquiry into sexual exploitation, use of prostitutes, bullying and intimidation by aid workers in Haiti. **17.** Henry Bolton was ousted as UKIP leader after party members backed a motion of no confidence; the party's fourth leader in 18 months, Bolton announced the following month that he was setting up a new political party called One Nation. **20.** The International Development Committee questioned Oxfam chief executive Mark Golding regarding allegations of sexual misconduct against senior staff while they were working overseas; as a result, over 7,000 people cancelled donations to the foreign aid charity. **22.** Lecturers from over 50 universities began their protest over pensions after the University and College Union called for action, with many students demanding refunds for lost teaching.

MARCH 2018

1. Meghan Markle embarked on her first joint engagement with Prince Harry and the Duke and Duchess of Cambridge, at the Royal Foundation inaugural forum; Miss Markle said that women needed to feel empowered and use their voice in regards to the #MeToo and 'Time's Up' campaigns, defying the royal family's traditionally neutral stance on socio-political issues. **4.** Ex-Russian spy Sergei Skripal, 66, and his daughter Yulia, 33, were found unconscious on a park bench near Salisbury town centre, while DS Nick Bailey, the first police officer on the scene, was also hospitalised; officials later confirmed the pair had been poisoned with the rare nerve agent Novichok. **11.** Theresa May publicly blamed the Russian government for the poisoning incident on 4 March, declaring it a direct attack on Britain; on 14 March, the government expelled 23 Russian diplomats, while a further 100 were expelled from more than 20 western ally countries across Europe and North America. **17.** In concert with whistleblower Christopher Wylie, *The Observer* and *The Guardian* published an exposé revealing the British data analytics firm Cambridge Analytica improperly harvested over 50 million Facebook profiles in order to influence elections. The UK's Electoral Commission reopened its investigation into VoteLeave's Brexit campaign and the USA's special counsel Robert Mueller requested the firm hand over internal documents as part of its investigation into Russia's alleged role in the 2016 US presidential election. **19.** Andria Zafirakou, an art teacher at Alperton Community School in Brent, London, became the first Briton to win the Varkey Foundation's Global Teacher Prize; Ms Zafirakou beat over 30,000 entrants from around the world to the $1m (£717,000) prize, which recognised her work in one of the poorest and most ethnically diverse communities in the UK.

APRIL 2018

1. *The Times* reported more than 17,000 Labour supporters had left the party over disputes regarding anti-Semitism in the first quarter of 2018, decreasing total party membership by 3 per cent. **12.** After evidence emerged that the Syrian Army had conducted a chemical attack in Douma on 7 April, Theresa May recalled cabinet ministers from their Easter break to seek approval for UK involvement in a US-led air strike on Syrian government sites (*see* 14 April). **14.** The prime minister authorised a coordinated air strike on three chemical weapons sites in Syria without parliamentary approval; on 16 April, ministers questioned Mrs May for three hours over the decision, during which time she defended the air strike attack, stating 'we have not done this because President Trump asked us to but because it was the right thing to do'. **18.** *The Guardian* reported hundreds of members of the Windrush generation, British citizens who came to the UK from the Commonwealth after the Second World War, were denied access to healthcare, benefits and work, and faced deportation after being wrongly counted as illegal immigrants; it later emerged that an important archive of Windrush-era landing passes, used to verify migrants' right to remain, was previously destroyed, affecting 57,000 people (*see* 28 April). **21.** The Prince of Wales was approved to succeed the Queen as Head of the Commonwealth; the unanimous decision came after strong endorsement from the Queen herself and the Commonwealth chair-in-office and Maltese prime minister, Joseph Muscat. **23.** Kensington Palace announced the Duchess of Cambridge gave birth to a boy at 11:01 at London's St Mary's hospital; under the Succession to the Crown Act 2013, Princess Charlotte made history by becoming the first female royal to retain her position in the line of succession upon the birth of a younger brother. **27.** The Duke and Duchess of Cambridge announced their third child, who was fifth in line to the throne, was named Louis Arthur Charles and would be known as HRH Prince Louis of Cambridge. **28.** Amid the growing Windrush political scandal, *The Guardian* leaked an internal memo outlining the home office's target of 12,800 enforced returns of immigrants for 2017–18; Amber Rudd stepped down as home secretary on 29 April, prompting ministers to claim the move was an attempt to deflect attention from Theresa May, who had implemented the related 'hostile environment' policy during her time in the post. **30.** Sajid Javid was named home secretary while James Brokenshire, returning to the cabinet after a four-month absence for cancer treatment, replaced Mr Javid as housing and local government secretary.

MAY 2018
1. The home secretary, Sajid Javid, promised to review the 'hostile environment' policy amid claims it was causing 'significant distress' to skilled migrants; the previous week, the BMJ reported that more than 1,500 doctors with job offers in the UK were denied entry between December and March, as a result of the cap on the number of tier 2 visas issued to workers from outside the EEA. The House of Lords voted by a majority of 91 to give parliament a 'meaningful vote' over the final Brexit negotiations, including in the event of a no deal; it was the government's ninth defeat on key measures during the report stage of the EU (withdrawal) bill (see 20 June). **8.** Labour's former shadow health minister Heidi Alexander quit parliament to assume the role of Deputy Mayor for Transport, triggering a by-election for the party's safe seat in her constituency of Lewisham East. **14.** The prime minister pledged £65m in additional funding for brain cancer research in tribute to Labour minister Baroness Tessa Jowell, who died from the disease on 12 May at age 70. **20.** Prince Harry married Meghan Markle at St George's Chapel, Windsor; hours before the ceremony, the Queen bestowed on her grandson the titles Duke of Sussex, Earl of Dumbarton and Baron Kilkeel with the royal couple styled as HRH Duke and Duchess of Sussex. Doria Ragland was the only member of the Duchess of Sussex's family to attend the wedding when her father, Thomas Markle, pulled out at the last minute due to ill health; the duchess requested that the Prince of Wales accompany her down the aisle in her father's absence. **21.** The defence secretary, Gavin Williamson, announced the launch of the UK's first defence strategy in space, which was designed to protect the country against 'emerging space-based threats'; the RAF would take control of military space operations and the number of personnel in charge of defending Britain's interests beyond the Earth's atmosphere would increase to 600. The commemorative hearings, part of the ongoing public enquiry into the Grenfell Tower fire that killed 72 people on 14 June 2017, commenced with survivor testimonies; the enquiry, led by Richard Millett QC, was intended to investigate the fire's cause and its subsequent spread through the structure. **22.** After 50 years as a member of the Labour party, former London Mayor Ken Livingstone resigned, stating the issues surrounding his suspension for alleged antisemitism 'had become a distraction' to Jeremy Corbyn's bid for leadership.

31. The French government blocked Theresa May's requests for the UK to remain part of the EU security system; France claimed that Britain's refusal to submit to the European Court of Justice, the body that oversees data sharing between the bloc, would be a barrier to distributing fingerprint, DNA and vehicle data.

JUNE 2018
13. Jeremy Corbyn faced his biggest ever party rebellion when 89 MPs defied his instruction to abstain on an amendment vote that would have forced the government to negotiate remaining in the single market; one shadow minister and five aides resigned over the row (*see* 20 June). An archaic rule that permitted unwell MPs' votes to be 'nodded through' by whips if they made it onto the parliamentary estate came under scrutiny when the MP for Bradford West was forced to attend parliament in her pyjamas in order to vote on the Brexit bill; Labour's Naz Shah, who had been in hospital in Bradford after a historic hit-and-run left her with severe nerve pain, accused Conservatives of stripping her of her dignity after they insisted she leave her car and enter lobbies in a wheelchair to register her vote. **19.** Chancellor Philip Hammond warned senior ministers that a planned £25bn boost to the NHS by 2023–24 left no more money for spending on education, defence, prisons or policing. Zara Tindall gave birth to her second daughter at the NHS Stroud Maternity Unit in Gloucestershire; named Lena Elizabeth Tindall, the baby was 19th in line to succeed her great-grandmother, the Queen, to the throne. **20.** The 'Brexit bill' finally passed through parliament when Theresa May saw off a revolt from Tory MPs; after tense negotiations, MPs voted 319 to 303 in favour after accepting reassurances that they would retain power to hold the government to account over the deal. **26.** The EU (Withdrawal) Act officially became law upon receiving royal assent from the Queen; the Act repealed the 1972 European Communities Act and would enable EU law to be transferred into UK law. **29.** Mother-of-three Dawn Sturgess, 44, and her boyfriend Charlie Rowley, 45, were left critically ill after inadvertently being exposed to the nerve agent Novichok in Amesbury, Wiltshire; the same substance was found to have killed ex-Russian spy Sergei Skripal and his daughter, Yulia, in Salisbury earlier in the year (*see* 8 July).

JULY 2018
8. Brexit secretary David Davis and home secretary Boris Johnson resigned from their posts in protest of the prime minister's soft approach to Brexit negotiations; their exit triggered a cabinet re-shuffle, with Dominic Raab named as Brexit secretary and Jeremy Hunt as home secretary. Police launched a murder investigation when Dawn Sturgess died in hospital from Novichok poisoning; Neil Basu, the counter-terrorism chief heading the investigation into the incident, stated that the couple likely handled a container contaminated with the nerve agent (*see* 24 July). **9.** Eleven-week-old Prince Louis of Cambridge was baptised at the Chapel Royal in St James's Palace; the Queen and the Duke of Edinburgh were not in attendance due to a busy schedule. **24.** In his first interview since being released from hospital, poison victim Charlie Rowley revealed that the substance likely came from a perfume bottle in a sealed box, which he'd found several days earlier in Salisbury; the announcement prompted concern that there were other potential contaminants yet to be found in the city. **25.** The prime minister downgraded the Brexit department in order to take control of EU negotiations herself after weeks of hostility from government ministers over her 'soft' Brexit strategy.

ARTS AND MEDIA

AUGUST 2017

2. Media streaming provider Amazon outbid SkySports for the right to broadcast the ATP Masters 1000 and 500 other tennis tournaments from 2019. **19.** On her appointment as artistic director of the Globe Theatre, Michelle Terry revealed her plans to introduce gender blind casting, a 50:50 split in male and female roles and an emphasis on new commissions at the theatre; Terry formally began her role in April 2018. **29.** One week after it was announced that British actor Ed Skrein would play the role of Major Ben Daimio in the forthcoming film *Hellboy: Rise of the Blood Queen,* Skrein stated that he would be stepping down from the role because he felt his casting was not in line with the character's Asian-American heritage; his decision came amid media claims of the 'whitewashing' of the role.

SEPTEMBER 2017

17. *The Handmaid's Tale,* an adaptation of Margaret Atwood's classic novel about a totalitarian society that enslaves fertile women, won Outstanding Drama Series at the Primetime Emmy Awards; the Hulu drama was the first by a streaming service to claim the top award and also won seven other Emmys, including a lead actress award for Elisabeth Moss. **20.** Darren Aronofsky's film, *mother!,* became the 13th film ever to receive the lowest 'F' rating from market researchers CinemaScore; the rating was based on exit polls of thousands of viewers on the film's opening night.

OCTOBER 2017

5. Kazuo Ishiguro won the Nobel Prize in Literature; the British writer is best known for *The Remains of the Day* (1989) and *Never Let Me Go* (2005). **8.** Film producer Harvey Weinstein was dismissed from the Weinstein Company 'in light of new information about misconduct'; on 5 October the New York Times published a story detailing decades of allegations of sexual harassment against Weinstein. **15.** Hillary Clinton attended the Cheltenham Literature Festival to promote her book about the 2016 US election, *What Happened.* **17.** American author George Saunders won the Man Booker Prize, making it ten in a row for novels featuring men as the main characters; *Lincoln in the Bardo,* Saunders' prize-winning novel, focused on a single night in the life of US president Abraham Lincoln when his 11-year-old son was laid to rest in a cemetery. **26.** Condé Nast, the media company known for *Vogue, Vanity Fair* and *The New Yorker,* launched a digital magazine titled *them,* focused on everything from pop culture to politics through the lens of the LGBTQ community; it was the company's first new independent brand since 2007, with Phillip Picardi, digital editorial director of *Teen Vogue* and *Allure,* as the chief content officer. **29.** Sir David Attenborough's *Blue Planet II* aired its first of seven episodes on the BBC, a nature documentary series made over four years that highlighted the effect of plastic pollution and global warming on marine creatures and their habitats; the first episode proved to be a ratings hit, with an average of 10.3 million viewers.

NOVEMBER 2017

1. Hollywood director Brett Ratner filed a suit for libel against Melanie Kohler, who accused him of rape; following accusations of sexual assault or harassment from six other actresses against the film director, including Olivia Munn and Natasha Henstridge, Ratner stepped away from all Warner Brothers activities. **15.** *Salvator Mundi,* a 500-year-old painting widely believed to be by Leonardo da Vinci, became the world's most expensive artwork after selling for $450m at an auction in New York City. Amazon acquired the British television rights to broadcast the US Open tennis in a five-year deal worth about £30m; in August 2017 Amazon outbid Sky

to win exclusive rights to broadcast the ATP World Tour (*see* 2 August 2017). **16.** The Old Vic's investigation into Kevin Spacey's conduct during his tenure as artistic director between 2004 and 2015 revealed 20 allegations of inappropriate behaviour; the investigation was started on 30 October when actor Anthony Rapp claimed that Spacey made sexual advances towards him when he was 14 years old, an accusation that led to Spacey's removal from the Netflix series *House of Cards* and the film *All the Money in the World* (all of his scenes in the Ridley Scott film were reshot with Christopher Plummer in the role). **21.** A 17th-century portrait that had hung in a Welsh castle for nearly 150 years was established as a lost masterpiece; a Spanish art scholar confirmed that it was a genuine portrait by Murillo, depicting Don Diego Ortiz de Zúñiga.

DECEMBER 2017

5. Walt Disney announced the acquisition of 21st Century Fox's film and television studios, cable networks and international TV businesses in a deal worth $66.1bn (£49.3bn); the sale included 21st Century Fox's interest in Sky, the European satellite broadcaster. **17.** A 15th-century alchemist's scroll, said to feature instructions for the philosopher's stone (namely, turning base metals into gold) and the recipe for the elixir of life, was sold for £585,000 at Christie's in London. **21.** Apple admitted to using software releases to slow down the iPhone 6, 6S, 7 and SE when their batteries were old, cold or had a low charge; the company said that it was necessary to prevent abrupt shutdowns of the devices. **27.** Prince Harry was the guest editor for Radio 4's *Today* programme, focusing on mental health, the armed forces and the charitable sector; he interviewed former US president Barack Obama, who warned against the irresponsible use of social media.

JANUARY 2018

18. French president Emmanuel Macron announced the loan of the Bayeux Tapestry to Britain at a summit with Theresa May in Berkshire; the artwork, which had not left France since the 11th century, depicts the Norman Conquest and would most likely arrive in 2022. **24.** Sir Elton John announced the final tour of his career, called 'Farewell Yellow Brick Road', which would consist of more than 300 shows across five continents, from 8 September 2018 until 2021. **31.** Helen Dunmore's collection of poems, *Inside the Wave,* won the 2017 Costa Book of the Year; the poet, who published her final works two months before she died, became the second posthumous winner of the award.

FEBRUARY 2018

3. Uma Thurman revealed in an interview with *The New York Times* an attempted sexual assault by Harvey Weinstein at the Savoy hotel in London in the mid-1990s; Thurman also disclosed how she sustained permanent injuries to her knees and neck on the set of Kill Bill in Mexico after director Quentin Tarantino coerced her to drive a car deemed unsafe, which then crashed. **18.** The 'Time's Up' Movement against sexual harassment in the film industry dominated proceedings at the 71st British Academy Film Awards, with many guests wearing black in solidarity with the cause. **25.** Middlesbrough-born BBC broadcaster Steph McGovern stated that not enough attention is paid to the class pay-gap at the BBC; she claimed that other female presenters in a similar role to her, but from a more privileged background, are paid more and stated that one manager had said she was 'too common' to be a BBC presenter.

MARCH 2018

4. During her acceptance speech at the 90th Academy Awards, Best Actress-winner Frances McDormand asked actors to demand 'inclusion riders' in their contracts to ensure better representation of minorities in casts and crews. **9.** After 66 years in publication, the weekly music title *NME* announced that its Friday 9 March issue would be its final print edition; *NME's* publisher, Time Inc. UK, confirmed it would expand the brand's digital offerings through its website, a new music marketplace and two new radio stations. **28.** *The Invisible Enemy Should Not Exist,* by Iraqi-American artist Michael Rakowitz, was unveiled on the fourth plinth in London's Trafalgar Square; the statue, which is clad in over 10,000 Iraqi date syrup cans, recreated the 2,500-year-old lamassu statues, winged bulls with human heads, that guarded the city of Nineveh before Islamic State destroyed it in 2015.

APRIL 2018

4. The BBC admitted to a 'breach in editorial standards' after it transpired scenes in the 2011 series *Human Planet* depicting the Korowai people of West Papua living in rainforest treehouses had been faked; during filming for a new BBC Two series, *My Year with the Tribe,* a Korowai member told adventurer Will Mallard the tribe had built and moved into the treehouses at the earlier production team's request. **5.** The head of the V&A, Tristram Hunt, ruled out a comprehensive dismantling of controversial exhibits in the museum's collection in order to return artefacts looted from Ethiopia in the 19th century; Mr Hunt stated there was an ever greater need for complex and cosmopolitan collections, but he was open to discussing a long-term loan of the objects. **8.** The musical *Hamilton* won seven trophies from its record 13 Olivier nominations but was unable to beat the previous record of nine wins, which *Harry Potter and the Cursed Child* set in 2017; Jez Butterworth's *The Ferryman,* which dealt with the disappearance of a former IRA activist in 1980s Northern Ireland, won three awards including Best Play, Best Director and Best Actress. **24.** A bronze monument to leading suffragist Dame Millicent Fawcett was unveiled after a successful campaign to place the first statue of a woman in Parliament Square; the piece, produced by Turner prize-winning artist Gillian Wearing and financed from a £5m fund to celebrate the centenary of women's suffrage, also marked the first time a female artist had created a statue for the square.

MAY 2018

4. The Swedish Academy announced its intention to postpone the 2018 Nobel Prize in Literature due to its investigation into the sexual assault allegations against committee member Katarina Frostenson's husband, Jean-Claude Arnault; the head of the academy, Sara Danius, stood down from her role as a result of the scandal and ongoing issues within the academy. **7.** Author Ian McEwan expressed concerns over his books being set as A-level texts after revealing that he'd helped his son to write an essay on his novel, *Enduring Love,* only to receive a C+. **13.** Konstantin Bouki, 30, was arrested after bursting onto the stage and grabbing the microphone from singer SuRie during the UK's performance at the Eurovision Song Contest in Lisbon, Portugal. **17.** For the first time since its creation in 2000, the Bollinger Everyman Wodehouse prize for comic literature failed to pick a winner after the judges concluded that each of the short-listed books failed to make them 'laugh out loud'. **31.** A previously unknown portrait of 16th-century explorer Sir Francis Drake was due to go to auction for the first time after art historians proved its authenticity via a distinctive wart at the top of the sitter's nose; the painting, which was created in the 1570s by an unknown artist and is thought to be one of the earliest of the explorer, was expected to fetch up to £500,000 in Bonham's Old Masters sale.

JUNE 2018

5. Mayor of London Sadiq Khan unveiled plans for the rejuvenation of Queen Elizabeth Olympic Park in Stratford; the 'East Bank' would become a cultural hub for business, innovation and education, with a list of prestigious institutions,

including the University College of London, the Victoria & Albert Museum, Sadler's Wells, the BBC and the London College of Fashion, scheduled to move to the site. **6.** After 26 years in the role, Paul Dacre announced he would be stepping down as editor of the *Daily Mail* to become chair of Associated Newspapers. **12.** Queen Marie Antoinette's jewellery collection, which survived the French Revolution and was valued at £5m, was listed for auction at Sotheby's; it was the first time the jewels had been on public display in more than 200 years. **22.** A painted tile of the archangel Gabriel, dated to 1471, was revealed to be Leonardo da Vinci's earliest known work; Italian art expert Professor Ernesto Solari used infrared scanning to determine that da Vinci had left a small signature and coded message on the 20cm tile when he was 18 years old, however, Martin Kemp, the world-renowned da Vinci expert and professor of art history at Oxford University, dismissed the claim.

JULY 2018

11. ITV commissioned screenwriter Andrew Davies to adapt Jane Austen's unfinished final novel, *Sanditon,* for a new drama series to be broadcast in 2019; the author had completed 11 chapters – about 24,000 words – in the months leading up to her death in 1817. **13.** Director of the Royal Ballet Kevin O'Hare named Matthew Ball as the company's new principal dancer; Mr Ball, who joined the Royal Ballet during the 2013/14 season, was only the second British male principal dancer in the company's history.

CRIMES AND LEGAL AFFAIRS

AUGUST 2017

9. Swiss art dealer Bennet von Vertes, 32, was found guilty of killing his British friend Alex Morgan with a candlestick and was then sentenced to 12 years in jail after judges rejected his claim that he had acted in self-defence. **15.** Big Brother Watch, a civil liberties organisation, reported that body cameras for police officers had little, if any, impact on crime within the UK; of the 71 per cent of police forces that had adopted the cameras, no increase in detection or complaints rates were reported. **18.** It was reported that £10,000 compensation was awarded to a 38-year-old man with Down's syndrome after his local council issued a letter to his wife asking her to withdraw conjugal relations with her husband over fears regarding consent; a judge at the Court of Protection upheld the council's claim, deeming it to be lawful but felt the situation was mishandled, resulting in unnecessary distress to the man and his wife. **28.** Scottish conductor and violinist Finlay Ferguson was found dead in his home in Córdoba, Argentina, after being strapped to his bed and bludgeoned to death with a dumbbell; a local 19-year-old was detained in relation to the incident.

SEPTEMBER 2017

13. Emma Kelty, a British former headteacher, was robbed and murdered by a drug gang while she was kayaking solo on the Amazon river; local police arrested a 17-year-old in relation to the crime. **14.** Mark Buckley, 52, was sentenced to a minimum of 31 years in prison for the murder of 18-year-old student Ellen Higginbottom; he had pleaded guilty on 4 September to a sexually motivated, premeditated attack, which had left the victim with multiple wounds to the neck. **15.** A bomb placed on a District line train partially exploded at Parsons Green station shortly after 8am, leaving 30 people injured (experts stated that the explosive device contained triacetone triperoxide, similar to the failed bombs in the 21 July attacks on the London transport network in 2005); Ahmed Hassan, an 18-year-old Iraqi asylum seeker, was arrested in conjunction with the attack. **20.** The body of Sophie Lionnet, a French au pair, was found in the garden of the family home in southwest

London where she had worked; Ouissem Medouni and Sabrina Kouider were charged with murder on 22 September. **26.** Mehmet Aksoy, a British film-maker, journalist and prominent figure in the UK Kurdish community, was killed in an Islamic State (IS) ambush on a Kurdish base 12 miles from the frontline in Raqqa, northern Syria; Aksoy had been documenting the Kurdish forces' liberation of Raqqa.

OCTOBER 2017

2. Darren McKie, a police sergeant, was charged with the murder of his detective wife, Leanne, after her body was found in a lake in Cheshire on 29 September; the couple both worked for Greater Manchester police. **4.** Aaron Barley was jailed for life, with a minimum sentence of 30 years, for the murder of Tracey Wilkinson and her son Pierce, as well as the attempted murder of Peter Wilkinson, the victims' husband and father; his sentence was increased on 21 December to a 35-year minimum term after the Court of Appeal agreed that the initial jail term was insufficient. **12.** It was reported that Sally Jones, a British national who became a propagandist and attack plotter for IS, died in June 2017 following a US drone strike in Syria; it was confirmed in January 2018 that her son, age 12, had also been killed in the strike. **13.** Becky Reid was sentenced to life in prison, with a minimum of 20 years, for the murder of her girlfriend Lyndsey Vaux in May 2016; a post-mortem examination found that Vaux had suffered 90 separate injuries over years of abuse. **26.** Sabah Khan was jailed for life for the murder of her sister Saima at their Luton home in May 2016; she had pleaded guilty at the Central Criminal Court to stabbing her sister 68 times.

NOVEMBER 2017

1. Ryan Gibbons was handed a life sentence, with a minimum of 27 years, for the death of Mike Samwell, a former Royal Navy lieutenant, after he ran him over outside his home in Chorlton, south Manchester in April 2017; accomplice Raymond Davies was convicted of manslaughter and taking a vehicle without consent and sentenced to eight years. **6.** Matthew Scully-Hicks was found guilty of murdering his 18-month-old adopted daughter and was jailed for life, with a minimum of 18 years. **17.** Endris Mohammed was found guilty of murdering his two children in October 2016, whom he smothered with a petrol-soaked cloth, and the attempted murder of his wife; he was sentenced to 33 years in jail. **27.** Multiple reports of child sex offences at Ampleforth College, a Roman Catholic school in North Yorkshire, were disclosed at a public hearing of an inquiry into the handling of abuse allegations by the Catholic Church.

DECEMBER 2017

1. Two Romanian brothers, Ovidiu and Andrei Mamaliga, were jailed for 12 years for raping a woman in her Ealing home, with a further eight years to be served on licence; they had been released from prison in France in 2016 after serving a sentence for rape. **5.** A man was charged for an attempt to assassinate the prime minister by detonating a homemade explosive device outside 10 Downing Street and storming the building armed with a knife; it was one of nine Islamist terrorist plots that had been thwarted by the police during the past year. **11.** Four children died, and a mother was left in serious condition, after a fire in a house in Salford; police charged Zak Bolland, Courtney Brierley and David Worrall in connection with the murders. **17.** Rebecca Dykes, on secondment to the British embassy in Beirut from the Department for International Development, was found dead beside a main road in Beirut; an Uber driver confessed to attempting to rape and then killing the British diplomat.

JANUARY 2018

2. Kasim Lewis, 31, was charged with the murder of Iuliana Tudos, a 22-year-old barmaid who went missing in London on 24 December. **17.** Ashley Foster, 24, was sentenced to life in prison, with a minimum of 26 years, for the murder of 17-year-old Megan Bills in May 2017. **25.** Jeweller Ramnik Jogiya's body was found in Stoughton after a robbery at his shop; police believed that the 74-year-old was abducted after locking up the Golden Mile shop in Leicester the previous night. **29.** Cheryl Hooper, 51, was found shot dead inside a car in Newport, Shropshire; a 45-year-old man was arrested on suspicion of murder. **28.** Jaynesh Chudasama, 28, was charged in connection with a car crash at a bus stop that killed three teenage boys. **31.** A judge criticised police and prosecutors for failing to disclose crucial evidence in a trial of people trafficking, forcing a defendant to give birth in prison after spending more than a year in jail; the collapse of the trial was one in a series of cases in which prosecutors failed to hand over evidence that could have helped the defence.

FEBRUARY 2018

2. Darren Osborne, 48, was jailed for a minimum of 43 years for the murder of Makram Ali; Osborne's terrorist attack took place on 19 June 2017, when he ploughed his van into a group of Muslims who were leaving Finsbury Park mosque. **6.** Joshua Stimpson, 26, was found guilty of murdering his former girlfriend, 23-year-old Molly McLaren, by stabbing her 75 times and was jailed for 26 years. **9.** Hannah Leonard, 55, was found dead in her flat by contractors re-cladding a 23-storey tower block that was evacuated in response to safety concerns after the Grenfell Tower fire; Lucy Casey, 43, and James Whitaker, 28, were charged with murder on 12 February. **12.** The former football coach Barry Bennell, 64, was sentenced to 30 years in prison for subjecting junior players from Manchester City and Crewe Alexandra to hundreds of sexual offences between 1979 and 1991; he had served three other jail sentences for child sexual abuse.

MARCH 2018

10. Stephen Unwin, 40, and William McFall, 51, were convicted of the rape and murder of Quyen Ngoc Nguyen, 28, at Newcastle crown court; both men had previous convictions for murder but were released on licence at the time of Ms Nguyen's death. **21.** Television presenter Ant McPartlin was charged with drink driving after causing an accident in south-west London when he lost control of his car and veered into oncoming traffic. **23.** Senior police officer Darren McKie, 43, was found guilty at Chester crown court and received a life sentence for murdering his wife, detective Leanne McKie, 39, by strangling; Mrs McKie had apparently discovered that her husband had applied for multiple loans in her name to fund their lavish lifestyle.

APRIL 2018

3. In a spate of gang-related incidents in London, 17-year-old Tanesha Melbourne-Blake was killed in a drive-by shooting in Tottenham, Amaan Shakoor, 16, was fatally shot in Walthamstow and Israel Ogunsola, 18, was stabbed to death in Hackney; the attacks brought the total gang-related deaths in the capital since the start of the year to 53. **4.** Richard Osborn-Brooks, 78, was arrested on suspicion of murder after two intruders broke into his home in Hither Green, south-east London; Henry Vincent, 37, known to police for previous incidents of burglary and other crimes, sustained serious stab wounds to the chest and later died, while his accomplice fled the scene. Mr Osborn-Brooks was later cleared of all charges following pressure from MPs, who argued homeowners should have the right to use force against violent intruders. **7.** Barrister Richard Archer became, at 32, the youngest crown court judge in recent history; Mr Archer's appointment, based in chambers in Preston, came amid calls to diversify the senior judiciary, which was dominated by Oxbridge graduates from the four inns of court in London. **16.** Twenty-two-year-old Jordan

Worth was jailed for seven years at Luton crown court after a four-year campaign of abuse against her partner Alex Skeel, also 22, including stabbing, starving and withholding food from him.

MAY 2018
5. Seventeen-year-old Rhyhiem Barton was shot dead in Southwark in a suspected gang-related attack. 7. Cara Creaby, 29, a police officer from Scotland Yard's Sapphire Unit, sought £200,000 compensation after watching hundreds of hours of footage relating to child sexual abuse cases led her to develop post-traumatic stress disorder; Ms Creaby had been investigating the grooming and abuse of three young girls by Michael D'Costa, who was jailed in 2015 for 16 years. 16. Two youths aged 16 and 17 each received a 12-month referral order from Bexley magistrates' court and were forced to pay £150 after they choked 19-year-old student Will Mayrick and forced him to apologise for being gay during a homophobic attack on a London Underground train. 24. At Manchester crown court, Zak Bolland, 23, and David Worrall, 26, were given four life sentences and jailed for a minimum of 40 years and 37 years respectively, while Bolland's 20-year-old girlfriend, Courtney Brierley, was sentenced to 21 years for manslaughter for committing a petrol bomb attack that killed four siblings as they slept in their home; Greater Manchester Police was placed under investigation after it emerged the childrens' mother, Michelle Pearson, who was still in a coma at the time of sentencing, contacted police several times before the attack on 11 December to report multiple threats to the family's safety. 25. Airline pilot Andrew McIntosh, 54, received a life sentence at Warwick crown court after beating his wife to death with a saucepan. 29. The Metropolitan police force outlined new measures to tackle the sharp rise in gang-related deaths in 2018 by treating gang members in the same way as suspected terrorists; detectives were given new powers to trace and target those who promote knife and gun violence online, without being required to provide links between the posts and specific acts of violence.

JUNE 2018
1. A man was jailed for 18 months each for two counts of fraud after claiming to be a victim of the Grenfell Tower fire; Mohammad Gamoota, 31, posed as a resident of the tower block in order to receive almost £7,000 in emergency money and free accommodation in a nearby hotel. 13. As part of Operation Silk, a Thames Valley police investigation into non-recent child sexual exploitation in Oxford, eight members of a grooming ring were found guilty of raping and indecently assaulting five female teenage victims between 1998 and 2005; Assad Hussain, 37, Moinul Islam, 41, Raheem Ahmed, 40, Khalid Hussain, 38, Kameer Iqbal, 39, Haji Khan, 38, Kamran Khan, 36, and Alladitta Yousaf, 48, were given sentences ranging from life with a minimum of 12 years to seven and a half years. 15. A judge at Winchester crown court sentenced army sergeant Emile Cilliers, 38, to a life sentence with a minimum term of 18 years after he was found guilty of the attempted murder of his wife; Mr Cilliers had arranged a skydive for Victoria Cillier at the Army Parachute Association in Netheravon, Wiltshire, on 5 April 2015, but had tampered with her rig with the intended result that, were she to die, he'd use the life insurance payout to cover heavy debts. 18. The owner of several fast-food shops in Northumberland was jailed for eight and a half years for modern slavery offences committed between 2014 and 2016; Harjit Bariana, 46, forced his victims to work for free in poor conditions in return for housing them in properties he owned in Blyth.

JULY 2018
2. The body of six-year-old Alesha MacPhail was discovered in woodland hours after she was reported missing while on a family holiday to the Isle of Bute, Scotland (see 6 July). 3. George Ormond, a former coaching assistant at Newcastle United FC, was found guilty of committing 36 counts of sexual abuse against 18 victims at the club between 1973 and 1997 and was later jailed for 20 years. 20. Thomas Wyllie, 15, and Alex Bolland, also 15, were sentenced to 10 and 12 years respectively for planning a Columbine-style plot involving guns and bombs at their high school in Northallerton, Yorkshire.

ENVIRONMENT AND SCIENCE

AUGUST 2017
11. It was reported that the parakeet population within the UK increased by 12 per cent in 2016–17, to a total 15 times larger than in 1995; the bright green bird native to Africa and South East Asia is considered a danger to native bird populations and crops, and a cull was suggested however the British Trust for Ornithology and the Royal Society for the Protection of Birds opposed the idea. 25. A study by Dr Daniel Mansfield and Dr Norman Wildberger from the University of New South Wales, published in the *Historia Mathematica,* found an ancient Mesopotamian tablet called Plimpton 322 to be a ratio-based trigonometry table predating Pythagoras' theorem by 1,000 years.

SEPTEMBER 2017
4. A study found that 5.7 million-year-old footprints discovered in Crete belonged to a creature that had no claws, walked upright and featured inner toes that protruded more than its outer toes, all signs that the earliest human ancestors wandered around southern Europe at the same time that they were developing in east Africa. 5. In Shropshire, a small robot-controlled vehicle harvested the first crop in the world farmed entirely by machines; the aim behind the Hands-Free Hectare project was an attempt to automate every aspect of crop growing as a possible means to overcome Britain's shortage of agricultural labourers and near 20-year plateau in crop yields. 15. The *Cassini* spacecraft ended its 13-year mission to explore Saturn with a deliberate plunge into the planet's atmosphere. 25. The remains of a city thought to have been founded by Alexander the Great in 331 BC was discovered with the aid of drones by archaeologists from the British Museum; Qalatga Darband, the fortified settlement in northern Iraq, had gone unrecorded by history for more than 2,000 years. 29. Elon Musk, founder of SpaceX, announced plans to land cargo ships on Mars by 2022, and said that his interplanetary transport system rocket would be ready to carry crews to Mars by 2024; he also stated that the rocket would be able to take passengers anywhere on Earth within an hour.

OCTOBER 2017
4. The Nobel Prize in Physics 2017 was divided, one half awarded to Rainer Weiss, the other half jointly to Barry C. Barish and Kip S. Thorne 'for decisive contributions to the LIGO detector and the observation of gravitational waves'; Ronald Drever, a Scottish physicist who devoted his life to the experiment, died in March 2017 and was ineligible for the award. The Nobel Prize in Chemistry 2017 was awarded to Jacques Dubochet, Joachim Frank and Scottish structural biologist, Richard Henderson, for developing a new way to assemble 3D images of biological molecules like proteins, DNA and RNA; their work helped scientists to decipher processes within cells that were previously invisible, and led to better understanding of viruses like Zika. 9. The Nobel Prize in Economic Sciences was awarded to Richard H. Thaler 'for his contributions to behavioural economics'; he argued that humans were irrational, but departed from rationality in consistent ways, so that their behaviour could still be

anticipated. **16.** Storm Ophelia brought warm winds from southern Europe to break the record for the hottest 16 October, along with dust from the Sahara and debris from wildfires in southern Europe; Ophelia, which began 900 miles off the coast of the Azores a week before, was the largest hurricane ever recorded so far east in the Atlantic and the furthest north since 1939. **23.** A gene therapy that cures 'bubble baby syndrome', or adenosine deaminase deficiency, was approved by the NHS for children who inherited a defective gene which leaves them without a functioning immune system; costing £500,000, the Strimvelis treatment had previously only been offered by one hospital in Italy.

NOVEMBER 2017
3. The population of fewer than 800 Tapanuli orangutans in Sumatra was classified as one of the most endangered species of great apes in a new article in *Current Biology,* after genomic analyses showed evidence that they should be considered a separate species. **27.** Researchers at Canada's McGill University discovered that milder winters had led to physical alterations in two species of mice in southern Quebec in the past 50 years, providing an example of the consequences of climate change for small mammals.

DECEMBER 2017
11. A study published in *Environmental Science & Technology* found that 90 per cent of plastic found in oceans came from ten rivers: two from Africa and eight from Asia. **12.** University College London scientists led the first human trial of a drug that suppresses the gene behind Huntington's disease by targeting and eliminating toxic proteins; trial patients who received increasing doses of the IONIS-HTTRx drug over the course of the study exhibited lower levels of Huntington's protein concentration in their spinal fluid after they received the treatment. **18.** Researchers at the University of Tokyo developed a new type of glass made from a low-weight polymer; when pressed together by hand, breaks in the glass healed without the need for high heat to melt the material.

JANUARY 2018
3. Storm Eleanor caused power cuts, travel disruption and flooding across the UK and Ireland; winds of more than 70mph were recorded, with the strongest gusts of 100mph reported in Cumbria. Scientists in Rome unveiled the first bionic hand with a sense of touch that can be worn outside a laboratory; in 2014 the team produced the world's first feeling bionic hand, but the sensory and computer equipment it was linked to was too large to leave the laboratory. **31.** Researchers from Imperial College London at St Mary's Hospital demonstrated for the first time how surgeons could use Microsoft HoloLens headsets while operating on patients undergoing reconstructive lower limb surgery, in a study published in *European Radiology Experimental;* the HoloLens, a self-contained computer headset, immersed the wearer in 'mixed reality', enabling them to interact with holograms and to essentially 'see' inside a leg. **30.** Scientists at the University of Edinburgh announced that they had developed human egg cells in a laboratory to the point where they were ready to be fertilised, in a breakthrough advancement for fertility science.

FEBRUARY 2018
6. SpaceX launched the Falcon Heavy a $90m (£65m) rocket and the world's most powerful for 45 years, from the Kennedy Space Center in Florida; embedded in the capsule of the payload rocket was a Tesla Roadster convertible, the first car in space, moving seven miles per second towards the asteroid belt (*see* International Events, The Americas). **7.** DNA tests on the oldest complete skeleton discovered in Britain, dated to about 9,000 years ago, indicated that he had 'dark to black' skin and blue eyes; Cheddar Man's skeleton was found in a

Somerset cave in 1903. **18.** The Buttington Oak, one of the oldest trees in the UK, fell down after sustaining storm damage; originally planted in 893 to mark the Battle of Buttington where Saxon and Welsh forces defeated Viking invaders, it was used as a marker between England and Wales along Offa's Dyke. **19.** The UK failed to reduce infant mortality rates for the third consecutive year despite efforts to improve postnatal care; UNICEF found a stark north–south divide, with a baby born in the north twice as likely to die within its first month as a baby born in the south. **25.** Astrophysicists at CERN developed an experiment called PUMA (antiProton Unstable Matter Annihilation) concerning the transportation of highly volatile anti-matter in order to examine new phenomena from low-energy interactions between antiprotons and atomic nuclei and shed light on neutron stars, which contain the densest matter in the known universe.

MARCH 2018
1. Scientists at the British Museum discovered tattoos on the 5,000-year-old mummy known as the Gebelein Man, pushing back evidence of the practice by 1,000 years. **1–3.** 'The Beast from the East' continued to cause disruption, with heavy snowfall, high winds and low temperatures throughout the UK; the blizzard conditions, exacerbated by the arrival of Storm Emma, resulted in 17 deaths and forced the Met Office to issue the second red weather warning in a week – only the third time the warning had been issued – for parts of south-west England and south Wales. **12.** A team of experts led by the Zoological Society of London and the British Trust for Ornithology published a paper in *Philosophical Transactions of the Royal Society B* establishing a link between garden feeders and an increase in bird diseases. **20.** The world's last male northern white rhino died in Kenya.

APRIL 2018
9. Scientists from Harvard and MIT initiated a research project to determine whether dog breed characteristics were down to nature or nurture; the study examined the public's perception of purebreds and crossbreeds, and how this affected their interactions with and behaviour around the dogs. **10.** A study published in *Nature Ecology and Evolution* suggested that *Homo sapiens* may have left the African continent at least 25,000 years earlier than previously thought after a scrap of finger bone, dating back 85,000 years, was uncovered in Saudi Arabia's An-Nafud desert. **18.** The environment secretary, Michael Gove, announced plans to ban cotton buds, plastic stirrers and plastic straws in Britain; the move to drastically cut down on single-use plastics came amid renewed concerns regarding their role in marine pollution. **19.** A study by the University of Copenhagen's Dr Melissa Ilardo and published in *Cell* found the Bajau people, a group of extreme free divers from Indonesia, had evolved larger spleens, allowing them to retain consciousness and hold their breath under water for over five minutes.

MAY 2018
1. A study by scientists at Breast Cancer Now's research unit at the Institute of Cancer Research and Kings College London revealed that certain women with advanced triple-negative breast cancer responded better to the chemotherapy drug carboplatin rather than the standard, more expensive docetaxel; during the study, which tested 400 women around the UK, carboplatin was found to shrink tumours in females with a BRCA gene mutation by 68 per cent. **9.** The world's largest project to kill off dangerous invasive species was declared a success when South Georgia became rodent-free for the first time in 250 years; whaling ships had unwittingly unleashed a plague of rodents upon the island in the South Pacific, negatively impacting local sea bird populations for centuries and prompting the ten-year £10m campaign. **14.** A

paper published in *Nature Astronomy* concluded that NASA's Galileo spacecraft flew directly through a giant water plume blasted from the surface of Jupiter's moon Europa in 1997; the findings of researchers from the University of Michigan, who used evidence collected by the Hubble Telescope in 2016 to re-examine the original data, suggested that Europa, which has a salty ocean twice the size of Earth's, could harbour the ingredients necessary to support life.

JUNE 2018
5. Following a nine-year trial of 10,000 patients carried out by the Montefiore Medical Center, New York, a study published in the New England Journal of Medicine found that chemotherapy was not beneficial to half of breast cancer sufferers post-surgery, potentially saving thousands from the needless side effects of the treatment. **22.** The Met Office officially declared that the UK had entered a heatwave as high pressure built across the country, leading to drought, wildfires and hosepipe bans (*see* 27 June). **27.** The army was called upon to tackle a wildfire at Saddleworth Moor when fire services struggled to control the blaze; over 2,000 acres of moorland were destroyed and a line of burning peat extended almost 6.5km, causing poor visibility over much of Greater Manchester (*see* 18 July). **28.** For the first time in five years, all four countries of the UK recorded temperatures of 30°C and over; in Glasgow, the Science Centre's weatherproof roof melted after temperatures hit 31.9°C during Scotland's hottest June day in 23 years. A severe wildfire broke out at Winter Hill near Bolton; 120 fire service personnel were sent to fight the blaze, which led to the loss of 4,000 acres of moorland (*see* 18 July).

JULY 2018
5. The entire northern hemisphere continued to undergo a historic heatwave, leading to the UK experiencing its longest sustained period of hot weather in 46 years (*see* 18 July). **6.** In Northern Ireland, Charlotte Caldwell was awarded a full licence for medical marijuana and cannabis oil to treat her son's epilepsy and severe seizures. **10.** The National Infrastructure Commission published a report advising the government to stop investing in new nuclear power facilities and instead boost efforts to expand renewable energy output up to 30 per cent by 2030 in order to create a 'greener' energy system. **17.** A report regarding 'designer babies' published by the Nuffield Council on Bioethics concluded that there should not be a fundamental barrier to genetically modify embryos that prevent inheritable diseases, as long as certain criteria were met and the procedure was in the best interests of the baby. **18.** The Met Office announced that summer 2018 was the driest since modern records began 57 years ago, with only 47mm of rainfall recorded in the UK throughout June and the first half of July; wildfires on Saddleworth Moor and Winter Hill were finally extinguished after rainfall in the region.

SPORT

AUGUST 2017
5. Jamaica's Usain Bolt took bronze in the 100m final of the World Athletic Championships in London in his final international race before retirement, with the USA's Justin Gatlin taking gold. **7.** South African sprinter Wayde van Niekerk won the 400m gold at the World Athletic Championships in London after his main rival, Botswana's Isaac Makwala, was barred from competing due to a suspected sickness bug; Makwala was declared fit on 9 August, given a personal time trial and qualified in time for the 200m final later the same day. **17.** England beat West Indies at Edgbaston in their first test match by an innings and 209 runs, the first day–night test match to be played in England in a bid to appeal to

a wider audience; 40 per cent of ticket sales went to first-time spectators. **23.** Wayne Rooney retired from international football after 14 years and 119 appearances for the national team, just short of Peter Shilton's all-time record of 125 caps. **26.** England was unable to retain the Women's Rugby World Cup trophy after being beaten by New Zealand 41–32 in Belfast. **27.** In tennis, Andy Murray was forced to withdraw from the US Open due to a recurring hip injury, becoming the fifth men's singles player ranked in the top 11 to pull out of the competition.

SEPTEMBER 2017
9. James Anderson became the first England bowler to take 500 Test wickets, on day two of the final Test against West Indies at Lord's; he was only the sixth bowler, and third seamer, to reach 500. **11.** Chris Froome made history as the first rider to win La Vuelta a España and Tour de France in the same year since Bernard Hinault in 1978, additionally becoming the first Briton to win La Vuelta and the first Briton to win a major Tour other than the Tour de France. **19.** Mark Beaumont broke the record for cycling around the world, completing the 18,000 mile journey in 79 days; the previous world record was 123 days. **27.** The Football Association (FA) announced a major revamp of the women's league structure, proposing to make the top tier a fully professional league of up to 14 teams, while the second tier was rebranded as part-time and semi-professional with up to 12 teams; clubs in both tiers would be licensed if they provided contracted hours to their players. **28.** The England and Wales Cricket Board (ECB) suspended Ben Stokes and Alex Hales from international duty pending the outcome of a police investigation into an altercation that took place three days earlier in Bristol.

OCTOBER 2017
1. Enable became the first three-year-old filly trained in Britain or Ireland to win the Prix de l'Arc de Triomphe, Europe's most prestigious horse race; the winning jockey, Frankie Dettori, secured a record fifth victory. **12.** British Swimming apologised to Paralympic athletes after it was found that a former head coach 'created a climate of fear'; the Great Britain para-swimming team won 47 medals at the Paralympics in Rio 2016. **18.** An independent investigation concluded that Mark Sampson, the former manager of the England women's football team, made racially discriminatory comments to players Eni Aluko and Drew Spence; the FA apologised to both players, saying that the remarks by Sampson were 'not acceptable', but Eni Aluko accused Martin Glenn, the FA chief executive, of actions 'bordering on blackmail' after he withheld settlement money from her until she released a statement denying that the organisation was institutionally racist. **26.** Speed skater Elise Christie was named the Sunday Times sportswoman of the year; the 27-year-old Scot became a triple world champion in March 2017. **28.** England won the football Under-17 World Cup Final in Kolkata, triumphing over Spain 5–2; they joined their under-20 counterparts as champions, who won their World Cup in South Korea in June 2017. **29.** Lewis Hamilton won his fourth Formula 1 world title at the Mexican Grand Prix; he became the most successful British Formula 1 driver in history, one championship ahead of Sir Jackie Stewart.

NOVEMBER 2017
5. English golfer Justin Rose won the Turkish Airlines Open in Antalya, a week after his victory at the World Golf Championships (WGC) HSBC Champions tournament in Shanghai; he joined Tiger Woods and Rory McIlroy as the only men to have followed up a WGC title with a victory in their next tournament start. **15.** France won the right to host the 2023 Rugby World Cup after beating bids from South Africa and Ireland. **18.** Former British Cycling coach Shane Sutton admitted to manipulating therapeutic use exemptions

on banned drugs to give Team Sky riders an edge; his comments appeared in an interview with the makers of the BBC documentary, *Britain's Cycling Superheroes: The Price of Success?* **21.** In cricket, Danielle Wyatt made history after she scored 100 off 57 balls in the match against Australia, the first century for England in women's international T20s. **25.** Josephine Gordon became the second female jockey to ride 100 winners in a year in Britain, after Hayley Turner, as she guided Thunderbolt Rocks to victory at Wolverhampton. **26.** England's Eddie Jones was named World Rugby coach of the year after his team won nine victories in ten matches and a second successive Six Nations title; he became the first England coach to win the award since Sir Clive Woodward in 2003.

DECEMBER 2017

5. The International Olympic Committee announced that Russia was banned as a team from the PyeongChang Olympics in 2018 for 'systematic doping'; Russian athletes were cleared to participate under a neutral flag, and under 'strict conditions' to prove that they were clean. **7.** Cristiano Ronaldo, the Real Madrid forward, won his fifth Ballons d'Or, equalling Lionel Messi's record tally. **13.** It was reported that Team Sky cyclist Chris Froome had double the allowed level of legal asthma drug salbutamol in a urine test at the Vuelta a España, which he won in September. **14.** Hayley Turner, Britain's most successful female jockey and ITV racing presenter, received a three-month suspension for placing bets while a licensed jockey, breaking the British Horseracing Authority's rules. **17.** British distance runner Mo Farah received the BBC Sports Personality of the Year award; he won four Olympic gold medals during Rio 2016 and London 2012. **27.** In football, Virgil van Dijk became the world's most expensive defender after Liverpool signed him from Southampton for £75m.

JANUARY 2018

2. The BBC dropped the former England footballer Trevor Sinclair as a pundit after he admitted to racially abusing a police officer who arrested him for drink-driving on 12 November 2017. **6.** Philippe Coutinho moved to Barcelona from Liverpool for a reported initial fee of £106m, with a further £35.5m in bonuses, breaking the record for the highest transfer fee paid or received by a British football club. **13.** Four British rowers set a new record for crossing the Atlantic, completing the race of 3,000 miles from the Canary Islands to Antigua in 29 days and 15 hours. **15.** England opener Jason Roy scored 180 (off 151 balls) in a one-day international (ODI) against Australia at the Melbourne Cricket Ground, both the highest individual score for England in ODIs and the highest ODI score at the ground. England cricketer Ben Stokes was charged with affray over an incident outside a nightclub in Bristol in September 2017 that left a 27-year-old man with a fractured eye socket. **17.** The England and Wales Cricket Board (ECB) cleared Ben Stokes to play for England after the board had suspended him indefinitely in September 2017; the ECB had already lifted its suspension of Alex Hales on 4 December 2017 for his part in the Bristol altercation (*see* 28 September 2017). **18.** Kayaker Bren Orton set a British record by plummeting over a 128ft (39m) waterfall in Mexico; it was the highest waterfall ever navigated by a British kayaker and the second highest descent ever.

FEBRUARY 2018

2. Horse Racing Ireland accepted a £39m bid from Racing UK for exclusive satellite rights to the pictures from Ireland's 26 tracks; the five-year contract, beginning on 1 January 2019, was worth twice as much as the previous deal with the At The Races television channel. **17.** Lizzy Yarnold became the first Briton to successfully defend a Winter Olympics title by winning gold in the women's skeleton in PyeongChang, South Korea. **24.** Snowboarder Billy Morgan claimed a bronze medal

in the big air event, taking Britain's medal tally to five, making PyeongChang the country's most successful Winter Olympic Games. **26.** Boxer Scott Westgarth, 31, died after winning his fight against Dec Spelman, becoming the third boxer in five years to die after a professional bout, leading to renewed calls for the British Boxing Board of Control to make the sport safer.

MARCH 2018

1. Great Britain's Laura Muir secured the bronze medal in the women's 3,000m on the opening day of competition at the IAAF World Indoor Championships in Birmingham. **4.** At the World Indoor Championships, Great Britain's Andrew Pozzi took gold in the 60m hurdles and Laura Muir secured her second medal of the meet when she won silver in the 1500m. **24.** The Australian cricket captain, Steve Smith, and his teammate Cameron Bancroft admitted to ball tampering during the third Test match against South Africa; Smith was banned from the fourth and final Test of the series and fined his entire match fee, while Bancroft was fined 75 per cent of his fee. **28.** After an investigation, Cricket Australia announced it had stripped Steve Smith of his captaincy and issued a 12-month ban for his role in the ball-tampering incident; his vice-captain, David Warner, who was found to have masterminded the plan, was issued a 12-month suspension and banned from leadership roles in Australia for life, while Bancroft was suspended for nine months.

APRIL 2018

5. Sergio Garcia's defence of his Masters title ended in the first round after he played 13 shots at the par-five 15th hole, the joint-highest score at any hole in Master's history; Garcia finished the round second from bottom, in 85th place. **7.** At the XXI Commonwealth Games England's Adam Peaty won gold in the 100m breaststroke, but he missed out on a second gold on 9 April when South Africa's Cameron van der Burgh beat him to first place in the 50m breaststroke by just 0.10s; the race marked Peaty's first defeat in four years. **11.** Three-time Olympic gold medallist Pete Reed announced his retirement from rowing after 17 years; 36-year-old Reed was training for the Tokyo Games in 2020, but stated he 'had to be realistic' and did not want to jeopardise Great Britain's chances of winning a medal. **12.** At the Commonwealth Games, English sprinter Zharnel Hughes gave a lap of honour after winning the 200m sprint in a time of 20.12s, only to be disqualified for obstruction in the last second of the race once officials analysed race footage. **15.** England beat World Netball Champions Australia by a point after a last-minute penalty to take Commonwealth gold; it was England's best performance in the sport in 40 years of competition. **20.** Arsene Wenger resigned as Arsenal's manager after 22 years with the club, during which time he claimed seven FA Cups – the most of any manager – was voted Manager of the Year in 1998, 2002 and 2004 and became the Premier League's longest serving manager, surpassing the previous record set by Alex Ferguson.

MAY 2018

7. A study published in the *British Journal of Clinical Pharmacology* raised doubts over doping charges levelled at Chris Froome by the World Anti-Doping Agency (WADA), who discovered double the allowed level of asthma medication salbutamol in the cyclist's urine sample in September 2017; the report suggested tests for the medication were fundamentally flawed and unreliable (*see* 2 July). **8.** At 43, snooker player Mark Williams became the oldest World Champion since Ray Reardon in 1978 after he beat John Higgins 18–16 during the competition's final at the Crucible in Sheffield. **17.** Gareth Southgate finalised his squad for the FIFA World Cup in Russia, which, with an average age of 26, was one of the youngest squads in the tournament. **22.** Tottenham Hotspur striker Harry Kane, 24, was named as England captain for the World Cup, making him the youngest player ever to captain the team in the competition. **23.** Former Paris Saint-Germain manager Unai Emery was named as Arsenal's new head coach; Mr Emery replaced Arsene Wenger, who stepped down after 22 years managing the club (*see* 20 April). **27.** The International Cricket Council opened an investigation into allegations that three England cricketers were paid to 'spot-fix' runs during a 2016 Test match against India; the England Cricket Board promised full cooperation over the allegations, which were made in a documentary broadcast by Al-Jazeera. **30.** Nine months after giving birth, Serena Williams made her return to Grand Slam tennis at the French Open to beat the Czech Republic's Kristyna Pliskova 7–6 (7–4), 6–4.

JUNE 2018
3. England beat Pakistan at Lords with an innings and 55 runs, the team's first win in nine Tests. **4.** Serena Williams pulled out of the French Open minutes before her fourth-round match against Russian rival Maria Sharapova due to a pectoral injury (*see* 15 July). **5.** Italy's Marco Cecchinato, ranked 72 in the world, beat Novak Djokovic 6–3, 7–6 (7–4) 1–6, 7–6 (11–13) in the French Open semi-final; it was Djokovic's worst defeat by ranking of his career, while Cecchinato was the lowest ranked player to reach the tournament's semi-final since 1999. **13.** Spanish football coach Julen Lopetegui was dismissed on the eve of Spain's opening match against Portugal at the World Cup after he accepted an offer to manage Real Madrid without the permission of the Royal Federation of Spanish Football; Fernando Hierro, former player, captain of Real Madrid and Spain and manager of Oviedo, was named interim head coach for the remainder of the competition. **24.** England beat Panama 6–1 in what was the team's biggest ever World Cup win; captain Harry Kane scored a hat-trick alongside John Stones' brace and Jesse Lingard's goal, securing England's place in the knockout stages of the competition. **29.** Twelve-year-old Tom Goron, from Brittany, France, became the youngest person to sail a boat single-handed across the English Channel; Goron sailed from Cherbourg to the Isle of Wight in 14 hours 21 minutes.

JULY 2018
1. Andy Murray pulled out of Wimbledon after declaring he was still not physically ready to play a Grand Slam tournament. **2.** The UCI, the world governing body for cycling, dropped all charges against Chris Froome after receiving new information from WADA that Mr Froome's sample results did not constitute an Adverse Analytical Finding; the cyclist would keep his 2017 Vuelta a España title and was cleared to compete in the 2018 Tour de France (*see* 29 July). **3.** England progressed to the quarter-final after beating Colombia in their first successful World Cup penalty shootout. **7.** England beat Sweden 2–0 to reach the semi-final of the World Cup, making it the team's most successful tournament since 1990; England's goalkeeper, Jordan Pickford, was named man of the match. **11.** Croatia beat England 2–1 to secure their first ever place in a World Cup final. **14.** Novak Djokovic beat South Africa's Kevin Anderson 6–2, 6–2, 7–6 (7–3) in the men's singles final at Wimbledon to win his 13th Grand Slam title and return to a top-ten world ranking. **15.** Germany's Angelique Kerber beat 23-time Grand Slam Champion Serena Williams 6–3, 6–3 to take her third Grand Slam title in the women's singles final at Wimbledon (*see* 17 July). France beat Croatia 4–2 to win their second FIFA World Cup title; Belgium defeated England 2–0 in the competition for third place. **17.** After reaching the Wimbledon final despite being ranked outside of the top 150, Serena Williams moved up 153 spots to be placed 26th in the world rankings. **22.** Golfer Francesco Molinari became the first Italian to win a major golfing trophy when he claimed victory at the Open Championship at Carnoustie ahead of favourites

Tiger Woods, Jordan Spieth and Rory McIlroy. **29.** Welsh cyclist Geraint Thomas maintained his lead to win the Tour de France; Thomas became the third Briton and the first Welshman to be awarded the yellow jersey, while Chris Froome finished in third place.

INTERNATIONAL AFFAIRS

AFRICA

AUGUST 2017
4. Paul Kagame was re-elected president of Rwanda, with 99 per cent of the vote. **7.** South Sudanese government forces took the rebel stronghold of Pagak, on the Ethiopian border. **8.** Kenya's President Kenyatta was returned to power in the country's general election; within a week, at least 20 people had died in violent clashes after opposition parties claimed that the result was rigged. **12.** Gunmen killed 18 people in an attack on a restaurant in Ouagadougou, Burkina Faso. **14.** A mudslide following heavy rains killed as many as 900 people near Freetown, Sierra Leone. **15.** A suicide bomber killed at least 27 people at a market in north-eastern Nigeria. **25.** US and Somali troops mistakenly killed at least ten people in a raid near Mogadishu that was intended to target al-Shabab terrorists.

SEPTEMBER 2017
1. Boko Haram militants killed at least 18 people in Banki, north-east Nigeria. Kenya's supreme court declared Uhuru Kenyatta's victory in August's presidential election invalid and ordered a new poll within 60 days. **10.** The World Health Organization announced that more than 500 people had died in a cholera epidemic in the Democratic Republic of the Congo. **26.** Joao Lourenco was sworn in as president of Angola, the country's first new president in 38 years.

OCTOBER 2017
1. The World Health Organization promised staff and supplies to Madagascar after an outbreak of plague since late August 2017 had killed 21 people. **4.** Four US soldiers and five Nigerien troops were killed in an ambush in western Niger. Iraqi forces recaptured the last territory held by Islamic State (IS) in the country when they retook Hawija, west of Kirkuk. **14.** At least 500 people were killed in a truck bomb attack in Mogadishu, Somalia; officials believed that al-Shabab was responsible. Human Rights Watch reported that as many as 67 people may have been killed by police at anti-government demonstrations in Kenya. **28.** Somali security forces ended a 15-hour siege of a Mogadishu hotel occupied by armed militants; at least 20 people were killed.

NOVEMBER–DECEMBER 2017
14 November. Troops moved into Harare, Zimbabwe, a day after the army chief warned President Mugabe to stop a purge of rivals; the state media headquarters were seized and President Mugabe was placed under house arrest. **17.** At least five people were killed by Kenyan police at an opposition rally in Nairobi, days before the country's supreme court dismissed two challenges to President Kenyatta's victory in rerun elections on 26 October. **21.** Robert Mugabe resigned as President of Zimbabwe; former vice-president Emmerson Mnangagwa was sworn into office on the 24th. More than 100 Islamist fighters were killed in a US airstrike on an al-Shabab camp in Somalia. A suicide bomber killed at least 50 people at a mosque in Mubi, north-east Nigeria; Boko Haram claimed responsibility on 2 January 2018. **24.** At least 31 migrants died and 40 were missing after trying to make the sea crossing from Libya to Italy; the Libyan coastguard reported that some of the victims were attacked by sharks. **26 December.** Former

footballer George Weah, FIFA World Player of the Year in 1995, was elected president of Liberia.

JANUARY 2018

4. A train collided with a lorry in Free State province, South Africa, killing 21 people and injuring 254. **15.** Fighting broke out between militia and security personnel at Mitiga International Airport, Libya, resulting in at least 20 deaths and 60 wounded. **18.** At least six people were killed and hundreds arrested in a crackdown on anti-government protests in the Democratic Republic of the Congo; it was reported that state agents killed 1,175 people in 2017. **20.** The president of South Africa, Jacob Zuma, was asked to resign by his party the African National Congress (ANC) after growing concerns regarding corruption and his ability to rule; his defiance led to violent clashes between ANC members on 5 February. **22.** Dozens of civilians were killed in US-led airstrikes on al-Shabab in Somalia. **23.** A double car bombing at a mosque in Benghazi, Libya, killed 35; government officials blamed Islamic extremists.

FEBRUARY 2018

7. The Kenyan government arrested and deported the opposition leader, Miguna Miguna, in an ongoing crackdown on political opponents. **8.** Over 300 child soldiers were freed from armed groups in South Sudan, as the civil war in the country continued. **14.** Jacob Zuma resigned as president of South Africa after weeks of political pressure; Cyril Ramaphosa officially succeeded him the next day. The influential Zimbabwe opposition leader Morgan Tsvangirai died of bowel cancer. **15.** The Ethiopian prime minister, Hailemariam Desalegn, resigned after months of demonstrations calling for democratic change, which resulted in hundreds of deaths and tens of thousands of arrests. The French air force killed ten jihadist rebels in northeast Mali; on 21 February, two French soldiers were killed by a roadside explosive in the Gao region. **20.** Around 110 schoolgirls were kidnapped by Boko Haram near the northern village of Dapchi; the Nigerian government falsely claimed a day later to have rescued 76 of them.

MARCH 2018

2. In Ouagadougou, Burkina Faso, Islamist extremists attacked the French embassy and army headquarters, resulting in 16 deaths, including those of the eight gunmen. **6.** At least 180 people died and almost 1,000 were infected in South Africa after an outbreak of listeria, which was blamed on contaminated meat products. **7.** Up to 90 people were reported to have died and around 1,100 infected with Lassa fever in Nigeria, transmitted via infected rats. **30.** Four suicide bombers killed two people in the Borno region of Nigeria; two days later, Boko Haram terrorists and Nigerian forces clashed, killing at least 20 combatants.

APRIL 2018

11. A military plane crashed in Algeria, killing all 257 on board. Protesters laid at least 16 corpses outside the UN headquarters in Bangui, Central African Republic, alleging that UN peacekeepers had killed them during clashes in the PK5 neighbourhood. **19.** King Mswati III of Swaziland declared the country would now be called eSwatini to mark the 50th anniversary of its independence from British rule. **24.** At least 18 people were killed in central Nigeria, including two priests, in an ongoing conflict over land rights between sedentary farmers and nomadic Fulani herdsmen.

MAY 2018

1. Twin suicide bomb attacks at a mosque and market in Mubi, eastern Nigeria, killed 86 people; the attacks were blamed on Boko Haram. **2.** IS militants killed at least 12 people in a raid on Libya's electoral commission in Tripoli. **8.** A public health emergency was issued in the Democratic Republic of Congo

after a renewed outbreak of Ebola. **12.** Twenty-six people were killed in an attack on the rural town of Cibitoke, Burundi, days before a constitutional referendum; government officials blamed militiamen from the neighbouring Democratic Republic of Congo for the deaths (*see* 17 May). **17.** Amid claims of violence and intimidation at the polling booths, over 70 per cent of voters approved changes to Burundi's constitution, including increasing the presidential term from five to seven years and enabling incumbent President Pierre Nkurunziza to stand for a fourth term. **24.** Amnesty International alleged that Nigerian soldiers had starved and raped thousands of women and girls rescued from Boko Haram since 2015. **28.** *The Times* obtained a copy of a leaked UN report alleging workers from over 40 charities, including 15 international aid organisations, had sexually exploited children in refugee camps in west Africa.

JUNE 2018

1. Twenty-three people were killed when cattle rustlers attacked a village in northern Nigeria's Zamfara state; for months, thieves had terrorised herders and farmers in the region, and killed those who resisted. **4.** In Minna, central Nigeria, 210 inmates escaped a medium-security prison when unidentified gunmen attacked the facility. **23.** A failed assassination attempt on Zimbabwe's president Emmerson Mnangagwa during a political rally in Bulawayo killed two people and injured at least 49 others. **27.** Clashes between Fulani nomadic herders and farmers in central Nigeria resulted in at least 200 deaths. In Addis Ababa, two people died and 150 were injured in a grenade attack at a rally organised by the Ethiopian prime minister Abiy Ahmed.

JULY 2018

9. Eritrea and Ethiopia formally ended the border conflict of 1998–2000 and agreed to re-establish trade and diplomatic ties; a week later, the Eritrean embassy in Ethiopia was reopened. **20.** Following months of conflict between English-speaking and Francophone communities in southwest Cameroon, it was estimated at least 400 people had been killed and a further 180,000 people had been displaced in the violence.

THE AMERICAS

AUGUST 2017

8. In the USA, President Trump warned North Korea that threats would 'be met with fire and fury like the world has never seen'; US intelligence officials had earlier concluded that the state had the capability to fire a ballistic nuclear missile. **12.** Legal assistant Heather Heyer, 32, was killed and 19 other people injured when a car was driven into a group of counter-protestors at a white-supremacist rally in Charlottesville, Virginia, USA; President Trump was criticised afterwards for condemning 'violence on many sides'. **16.** At least 37 prisoners were killed in clashes between inmates and security forces at a jail in Amazonas state, Venezuela. Seven people were killed when gunmen stormed a hospital in Guatemala and freed an imprisoned gang member who was undergoing tests. **27–30.** In the USA, Hurricane Harvey killed at least 68 people in Texas and forced 32,000 into shelters; one forecast put the damage estimate at US$125bn.

SEPTEMBER 2017

6. Hurricane Irma, the most powerful storm recorded in the Atlantic Ocean with winds of 185mph, made landfall in Barbuda before travelling over Anguilla, St Martin, St Barts, the Virgin Islands and Puerto Rico, killing at least 44 people; more than two million people were left without power and 600,000 without water in Puerto Rico, while 99 per cent of buildings on the Caribbean islands were damaged. **10.**

Hurricane Irma landed in Florida, where it claimed at least 14 lives, and left more than 2.5 million homes and other premises without power; the cost of damages was expected to be around US$20bn. **15–19.** More than 150 people were arrested in four nights of protests in St Louis, USA, following the acquittal of white police officer Jason Stockley, who shot dead Anthony Lamar Smith, an African American. **19.** More than 360 people were killed when an earthquake struck central Mexico, notably the city of Raboso and nearby Mexico City. Category 5 storm Hurricane Maria hit Dominica, bringing with it winds of up to 155mph and leaving at least 31 people dead; one day later, sustained winds of 155mph struck Puerto Rico, leaving its population of 3.4 million without power and making Maria the strongest storm to hit the US territory since 1928. **23.** At a rally in Alabama, USA, President Trump attacked National Football League players who did not stand for the national anthem; in the preceding year, many athletes had joined the 'take a knee' campaign, initiated by quarterback Colin Kaepernick in protest at racial inequality. **25.** President Trump extended his controversial travel ban to include citizens from Venezuela, Chad and North Korea.

OCTOBER 2017
1. From his hotel room in the Mandalay Bay Hotel, Las Vegas, USA, retired accountant Stephen Paddock opened fire on crowds at a country music festival, killing 58 people and injuring more than 500 others, before shooting himself dead; it was the worst mass shooting in modern US history. **2.** The USA ordered the expulsion of 15 Cuban embassy officials after American diplomats in Havana had been affected by a string of mysterious ailments; Cuba denied any wrongdoing and US investigators and doctors were unable to ascertain the cause of the illnesses. **9–13.** At least 44 people were killed by wildfires in California that forced more than 20,000 people to flee their homes and destroyed at least 3,500 buildings; a state of emergency was declared in the wine regions of Napa, Sonoma and Yuba counties. **30.** In the USA, a foreign policy adviser to the Trump campaign, George Papadopoulos, pleaded guilty to lying to the FBI about his contact with a Kremlin-linked academic; President Trump's former campaign chief Paul Manafort was charged with tax evasion. **31.** Eight people were killed when a pick-up truck was driven into a cycle lane in Lower Manhattan, New York City; a suspect, named as Uzbek national Sayfullo Saipov, was arrested at the scene after he was shot by police.

NOVEMBER 2017
5. In the USA, gunman Devin Patrick Kelley shot dead 26 people and injured 20 more at a church in Sutherland Springs, southern Texas, before police later found him dead in his car; the motive for the attack was unclear. **6.** Authorities in northern Mexico arrested a polygamist sect over the deaths of three young Americans. **24.** More than one week after the Argentinian navy lost contact with the submarine *San Juan*, it was reported that monitoring devices had picked up a sound consistent with a violent explosion on the 15th and all 44 crew were presumed to have perished on board. **10.** In mayoral elections in Venezuela, the government almost won a clean sweep of municipalities following a boycott by the three main opposition parties, who said they did not trust the outcome of the election; President Maduro announced that their non-participation should disqualify the opposition from future elections. **11.** Brooklyn resident Akayed Ullah detonated a pipe bomb in New York's Port Authority bus station in an attack apparently inspired by IS, injuring only himself.

DECEMBER 2017
1. As special counsel Robert Mueller's investigation into Russian interference into the US election gathered pace, President Trump's former national security adviser, Mike Flynn, pleaded guilty to lying to the FBI. **2.** In Honduras, at least four people were killed by police in protests over the country's contested presidential race; incumbent Juan Orlando Hernández was declared the winner on the 16th. **8.** A state of emergency was declared in California as wildfires forced the evacuation of 120,000 people from their homes. **19.** At least 12 people, principally tourists from a cruise ship, were killed when the bus they were travelling in overturned in the state of Quintana Roo, Mexico. **20.** President Trump hailed a US$1.5 trillion tax overhaul in the USA after it was passed by both houses of Congress; it was the most comprehensive reform in decades. **31.** A plane crash in the Guanacaste province of Costa Rica killed all ten US passengers and the two Costa Rican pilots.

JANUARY 2018
1. A prison riot in the Colonia Agro industrial prison in Goias state, Brazil, resulted in 106 escapees and the deaths of nine inmates; the drug trafficker accused of ordering the riot, Stephan de Souza Vieira, was arrested on 6 January. An economic crisis in Venezuela resulting in food shortages led to weeks of looting and mob violence, with hundreds of thousands fleeing into neighbouring Brazil and Colombia. **10.** Mudslides killed at least 17 people and injured 25 others in southern California. **11.** President Trump was accused of making derogatory remarks about African and Central American countries at a meeting in the White House, which drew condemnation from political leaders around the world. **13.** In Hawaii, USA, a missile alert was mistakenly sent to residents after months of tense relations between the US and North Korea, causing panic among the 1.4 million islanders. **15.** At least ten people were killed after one of the world's highest motorway bridges collapsed near Bogotá, Colombia. **21.** *The Guardian* reported that over 29,000 people were murdered in Mexico in 2017, the highest toll in decades; most deaths were blamed on the government's crackdown on drug cartels.

FEBRUARY 2018
6. The world's most powerful rocket for 45 years was successfully launched in Florida, USA, by billionaire entrepreneur Elon Musk's SpaceX company. **7.** Rob Porter, staff secretary and close aide to President Trump, was forced to resign after historic accusations of domestic abuse. **10.** The alleged leader of a major Mexican drug cartel, José María Guízar Valencia, was arrested in Mexico City. **14.** At Marjory Stoneman Douglas High School in Florida, expelled former pupil Nikolas Cruz, 19, killed 17 people with a legally purchased assault rifle; pupils who survived the attack re-invigorated national debates on gun control. **16.** Prosecutors in the USA charged 13 Russian citizens, many of whom were closely tied to Russia's President Putin, with plotting to influence the 2016 presidential election. **23.** Paul Manafort, the former chair of Donald Trump's presidential campaign, was charged with covertly recruiting European politicians to advance the interests of the former pro-Russian government of Ukraine.

MARCH 2018
6. A top US government official, economic adviser Gary Cohn, resigned in protest at President Trump's plans to introduce tariffs on steel and aluminium imports; these were imposed two days later. **13.** President Trump sacked his secretary of state, Rex Tillerson, which increased the turnover of senior White House staff to 43 per cent under Trump, the highest in modern history; on 22 March the president dismissed his national security adviser, Lt.-Gen. H. R. McMaster. **14.** Hundreds of thousands of students walked out of classrooms in 3,000 schools across the USA to protest gun violence (*see* 14 February); on 24 March an estimated 500,000 people joined

800 'March For Our Lives' protests around the country. **15.** Six people died in Florida, USA, after a newly-built pedestrian bridge collapsed; it later emerged that officials had met several hours before the collapse to discuss a crack that had appeared in the structure, deeming it safe for public use. **28.** A fire broke out after a disturbance at a police station in Venezuela, killing at least 78 people while they were locked in cells.

APRIL 2018

2. China responded to US tariffs (*see* 6 March) by placing duties on the importation of US meat, fruit, nuts and other products, stoking fears of a trade war. Costa Rica elected centre-left Carlos Alvarado Quesada as its new president with over 60 per cent of the vote. **7.** A bus crash in the province of Saskatchewan, Canada, killed 15 passengers. **8.** The former president of Brazil, Luiz Inacio Lula da Silva, surrendered to police and began a 12-year prison sentence for corruption. **10.** The co-founder and CEO of Facebook, Mark Zuckerberg, apologised at a US senate judiciary hearing after it emerged 87 million people's personal data was improperly harvested from the website by data analytics firm Cambridge Analytica for the purpose of influencing elections (*see* UK Affairs, 17 March). At least 20 people died in a gunfight with police following an attempted prison breakout in Sao Paulo, Brazil. **13.** In Trinidad and Tobago, a court ruled homosexuality laws were unconstitutional. **17.** Former FBI director James Comey released his memoir, *A Higher Loyalty,* which alleged President Trump was 'untethered to reality'. **18.** Violent protests began in Nicaragua against President Daniel Ortega and his social security reforms; the demonstrations lasted several weeks and resulted in dozens of deaths. **19.** Miguel Díaz-Canel replaced Raúl Castro as president of Cuba, ending almost 60 years of rule by the Castro brothers. **23.** A man killed ten pedestrians and injured 15 after deliberately hitting them with a vehicle in Toronto, Canada; police later named the suspect as 25-year-old Alex Minassian.

MAY 2018

3. Kilauea volcano erupted on Hawaii's Big Island, causing weeks of damage and disruption, and over 2,000 residents were evacuated. **8.** President Trump withdrew the USA from the 2015 Iran nuclear deal and vowed to re-impose stringent sanctions on the country; the move was met with disapproval by most US allies. **11.** In the USA, following the announcement of a 'zero-tolerance' policy against all adult illegal immigrants entering the country at the US–Mexico border, the secretary of homeland security, John Kelly, defended the separation of children from their parents as a 'necessary evil' in the administration's attempts to increase border security (*see* 20 June). **18.** Eight students and two teachers were killed and 13 others wounded in a shooting at Santa Fe High, Santa Fe, Texas; the shooter was taken into custody and later identified as a 17-year-old student at the school. In Cuba, a passenger jet crashed shortly after take-off from Havana, killing 112 of the 113 passengers and crew on board. **21.** Nicolás Maduro was re-elected as president of Venezuela amid international condemnation over claims of electoral fraud and vote buying. **25.** Harvey Weinstein, the disgraced Hollywood mogul whose alleged sexual assaults sparked the #MeToo movement, was charged with rape and several counts of sexual abuse following his arrest in New York City.

JUNE 2018

1. The implementation of tariffs on US imports of European steel and aluminium resulted in threats of retaliation and fears of a trade war. **2.** At least 110 people were killed and thousands displaced after Volcan de Fuego, one of Guatemala's largest volcanoes, erupted; it was the deadliest eruption in the country since 1929. **10.** President Trump clashed with Canada's prime minister Justin Trudeau and other world leaders over trade at the G7 summit, as he called for Russia's readmission into the club of world leaders. **15.** The Nicaraguan government and protest groups agreed to halt violence after weeks of turmoil left 170 dead. **17.** After a long and divisive campaign, conservative Iván Duque won the Colombian presidential election with 53.9 per cent of the vote; it was the country's first peacetime election in 52 years, following the fragile peace deal with Farc rebels in 2016. **19.** Canada's senate passed a bill by a vote of 52 to 29 to legalise recreational marijuana, making it the second nation in the world after Uruguay to permit a nationwide marijuana market. **20.** President Trump signed an executive order suspending his administration's 'zero-tolerance' policy and directing authorities to keep families together while detained at the border; the policy, which sparked a national outcry and international condemnation, had resulted in over 2,000 children being forcibly separated from their parents and placed in federal care in the previous six weeks.

JULY 2018

1. The former mayor of Mexico City, Andrés Manuel Lpez Obrador, won a landslide presidential election victory with 53 per cent of the vote, 30 percentage points ahead of his nearest competitor; Mr Obrador, who ran on an anti-corruption platform and promised to reshape social programmes, became the first left-wing candidate to claim the presidency since one-party rule ended in Mexico in 2000. **16.** Following a joint press conference with President Putin in Helsinki, President Trump faced heavy criticism for siding with the Kremlin over US government agencies regarding Russia's alleged meddling in the 2016 presidential election campaign; three days earlier, 12 Russians were charged with hacking and leaking emails during the campaign. During continued political violence in Nicaragua, police and paramilitary groups loyal to the president killed ten anti-government protesters in Monimbo and the nearby city of Masaya; human rights activists claimed that 350 people had been killed since protests began on 18 April. **20.** During one of California's worst-ever fire seasons, the National Interagency Fire Center reported that wildfires had so far burned more than 5.6 million acres across the USA in 2018, about 27 per cent above the average rate for the time of year. **22.** Cuban lawmakers approved a new constitution that omitted references to communism and accepted the concept of private property; the constitution will need approval by popular referendum, set to take place in early 2019. **26.** Following the Cambridge Analytica scandal, Facebook recorded the biggest ever one-day drop in a company's market value when the US technology firm's shares fell by 18 per cent, a loss of $110bn; on 2 August, Apple became the world's first company to be valued at $1 trillion. **30.** Wildfires continued to rage in California, having claimed eight lives and forced at least 50,000 people to flee their homes.

ASIA

AUGUST 2017

8. An earthquake in China's Sichuan province was believed to have killed up to 100 people and damaged 130,000 homes. **10.** No fewer than 60 infants died in a hospital in the northern Indian city of Gorakhpur when oxygen supplies were allegedly cut off over unpaid bills. **16.** President Duterte praised 'shock and awe' raids in which police killed 32 suspected drug dealers in the Philippines. **18–31.** Monsoon rains killed more than 1,200 people in in Bangladesh, Nepal and India, where 16 million people were affected by floods. **20.** At least 23 people were killed and more than 200 injured when a train crashed about 80 miles north of Delhi. **25.** At least 38 people died in riots after an Indian court found guru Gurmeet Ram Rahim Singh guilty of rape. **31.** An anti-terrorism court in Pakistan declared former president Pervez Musharraf a fugitive after he failed to appear at court, where two high-ranking police officials were sentenced to 17 years in prison over the assassination of Benazir Bhutto in 2007; since 2016, Musharraf had lived in self-imposed exile in Dubai.

SEPTEMBER 2017

1. At least 33 people were killed when an apartment block in Mumbai collapsed following continuing floods in the region. **5.** The UN said that nearly 126,000 Rohingya had crossed to Bangladesh since 25 August, fleeing violence in Myanmar that had left more than 400 people dead; Myanmar security forces had launched retaliation for Rohingya insurgent attacks in the preceding weeks. **17.** New UN figures revealed that 409,000 Rohingya had made the perilous journey to Bangladesh from Myanmar. **19.** Nobel laureate Aung San Suu Kyi gave a televised address denying that there had been any conflict or clearance operations aimed at Rohingya Muslims, despite UN claims that the Myanmar army's actions amounted to 'textbook ethnic cleansing'. **22.** It was revealed that 147 soldiers had lost their lives in nearly five months in the battle to regain the southern Philippine city of Marawi from IS and its Asian affiliates; many of the city's 200,000 displaced residents were living in camps or public buildings on the city's outskirts.

OCTOBER 2017

12. Caitlan Coleman, Joshua Boyle and their three children were freed by Pakistani troops in the Kurram Valley region five years after they had been captured by militants linked to the Taliban. **15.** In Vietnam, landslides and heavy rain triggered by tropical storm Khanun killed 72 people. **16.** Twelve people were killed when a boat carrying Rohingya Muslims to Bangladesh capsized. **17.** The Philippine government declared that the city of Marawi had been liberated from groups linked to IS after a five-month uprising; more than 40 militants died in the final street battles. Analysis of satellite images by Human Rights Watch showed at least 228 villages in Rakhine state, Myanmar, had been completely or partially destroyed by security forces since the end of August; at least 537,000 had fled to Bangladesh in two months. **31.** A Japanese TV news station claimed that more than 200 people had died when a tunnel collapsed at North Korea's nuclear test site.

NOVEMBER 2017

1. A Pakistani bride, Aasia Bibi, was accused along with her lover, Shahid Lashari, of killing 17 members of her extended family in a botched attempt to poison her new husband; ten other family members were left critically ill in hospital. **5.** Floods caused by typhoon Damrey killed at least 100 people in central and southern Vietnam. **19.** Nineteen people, many of them migrant workers, were killed in a fire in an apartment block in Beijing, China. **25.** In Bali, a volcano blew for the first time since 1963, affecting flights to and from the country; 100,000 residents in the vicinity of Mount Agung were told to evacuate. **28.** North Korea fired a missile towards Japan that would have been capable of reaching Washington DC. Pope Francis arrived in Myanmar, but in a speech in the capital, failed to mention directly the plight of the Rohingya.

DECEMBER 2017

1. Taliban militants killed nine people at a college in Peshawar, Pakistan; the gunmen were killed in the attack. **17.** Landslides on the central Philippine island of Biliran killed at least 26 people; 23 more residents were reported missing following tropical storm Kai-Tak. Two suicide bombers killed at least nine people and injured 56 more in an attack on a church in Quetta, Pakistan. **21.** Some 29 people died in a fire in an eight-storey building in Jecheon town, South Korea. **29.** In India, at least 15 people were killed by a fire in Mumbai that started in a restaurant and spread throughout a building in the city's Kamala Mills district.

JANUARY 2018

2. In India, more than 300,000 doctors went on strike in protest at a bill allowing practitioners of alternative therapies to practise Western medicine. **3.** Over 300,000 protesters blocked roads and railway lines into Mumbai, bringing India's largest city to a standstill, triggered by anger at the discrimination suffered by low-caste communities. **6.** A Chinese cargo ship collided with an Iranian oil tanker in the East China Sea, eventually sinking on 14 January and releasing most of the 136,000 tonnes of light crude oil it was transporting; only three bodies from the tanker were recovered from a crew of 32. **13.** North Korea reopened a border telephone hotline with South Korea which had been disconnected for almost two years, marking an improvement in relations between the two nations. **16.** The United Nations demanded access to northwest Myanmar as plans were unveiled to repatriate some of the 700,000 Rohingya Muslims who had fled the country, but on the same day at least nine Buddhist protestors were killed by police in Mrauk-U, Rakhine state; a week later plans were postponed due to fears of coercion. **26.** A fire in a hospital in Miryang, South Korea, killed 40 and injured at least 140.

FEBRUARY 2018

1. India launched what it called the world's largest national healthcare programme, nicknamed Modicare, to provide cover for 500 million people. **4.** A political crisis began in the Maldives when President Yameen defied a supreme court ruling to free political opponents; opposition MPs and political challengers were arrested and parliament was suspended as a 15-day state of emergency was declared. **6.** Two people were killed and over 250 injured after a 6.4-magnitude earthquake hit the east coast of Taiwan. **8.** It was discovered that China had heavily militarised the disputed and uninhabited Spratly Islands in the South China Sea, which the Philippines, Malaysia, Vietnam, Taiwan and Brunei all claim ownership over. The international criminal court launched an inquiry into the president of the Philippines, Rodrigo Duterte, over allegations that he authorised extra-judicial executions and mass murder; on 13 February he ordered soldiers to shoot female communist rebels and two days later offered citizens a bounty for killing them. **9.** The opening ceremony for the Winter Olympic Games in PyeongChang, South Korea, was held and witnessed Korean athletes marching under a unified flag in a thawing of relations between the two countries. **19.** The Associated Press and Reuters claimed that the Myanmar government had bulldozed Rohingya grave sites in an effort to destroy evidence of mass executions in 2017.

MARCH 2018

2. Religious riots between Muslims and Sinhalese Buddhists began in Kandy, Sri Lanka, and lasted over a week; arson attacks were perpetrated on both sides, but predominantly by Buddhists. **5.** North Korea's supreme leader Kim Jong-un met senior South Korean officials in Pyongyang for the first time since taking power in 2011. **11.** China's National People's Congress overwhelmingly voted in favour of abolishing presidential term limits, allowing President Xi Jinping to rule for life. **18.** China's parliament endorsed Wang Qishan, a close ally of President Xi Jinping, as vice-president. **21.** The president of Myanmar and close ally of Prime Minister Aung San Suu Kyi, Htin Kyaw, resigned. Police killed 13 suspected drug dealers and arrested more than a 100 in anti-narcotics raids in the Philippines; *The Guardian* reported over 4,000 Filipinos had been killed during the controversial 20-month war on drugs. **28.** Kim Jong-un indicated his commitment to denuclearisation on an official visit to China; formal discussions with the USA and South Korea began in April.

APRIL 2018

6. The former president of South Korea, Park Geun-hye, was sentenced to 24 years in prison for abuses of power, coercion and corruption; three days later Lee Myung-bak, another former prime minister, was charged with corruption. **21.** After weeks of widespread protests, India's cabinet approved the introduction of the death penalty for child rapists. **22.** Indian armed forces killed at least 37 Maoist rebels in Maharashtra state. A bus crash in North Korea killed 36 people, including 32 Chinese nationals. **26.** At least 18 people died after an illegal oil well caught fire in the Aceh province of Indonesia. **27.** Kim Jong-un visited South Korea to discuss peace and denuclearisation, making him the first North Korean leader ever to visit the country; the talks were heralded as marking 'a new era' for the two nations.

MAY 2018
3. A powerful dust storm killed at least 134 people in northern India; ten days later, further storms killed at least 86 more. **10.** Fifteen years after he stood down from the post, 92-year-old Mahathir Mohamad was re-elected as the Malaysian prime minister, making him the world's oldest leader. North Korea released three US captives, which was a precondition for peace and denuclearisation talks to officially start between the two countries; days before, satellite images indicated that the country's only nuclear test site was being dismantled. **27.** Burkina Faso became the second country in a month, after the Dominican Republic, to switch diplomatic allegiance from Taiwan to China; the move left Taiwan with 18 mostly small and poor diplomatic allies in the Pacific and Caribbean. **28.** A copper smelter closed down in Tamil Nadu, India, days after police killed 13 people and injured 80 more protesting over pollution from the plant and its proposed expansion. At least 86 suspected drug traffickers were killed and 7,000 arrested as police in Bangladesh launched an anti-narcotics crackdown; Prime Minister Sheikh Hasina had approved the campaign in early May to tackle the spread of methamphetamine in the country. **30.** India and Pakistan agreed to a ceasefire in the disputed region of Kashmir after months of skirmishes resulted in the deaths of dozens of soldiers and civilians.

JUNE 2018
12. Kim Jong-un shook hands with President Donald Trump at a historic summit in Singapore, which marked the first ever meeting between a sitting US president and a North Korean leader; both men signed a tentative agreement to work towards peace, and North Korean demilitarisation and denuclearisation. **15.** Afghan and Pakistani officials claimed a US drone strike killed the leader of the Pakistani Taliban, Mullah Fazlullah.

JULY 2018
1. A crowded bus careered off a mountain road in northern India, killing 48 people. **2.** The mayor of Tanauan City, Philippines, who was known for parading suspected drug dealers in public, was shot dead by a sniper during a flag-raising ceremony. **3.** After falling from power in May, former Malaysian prime minister Najib Razak was arrested for embezzling over £500m of government funds in what was reported to be the biggest corruption scandal in Malaysian history. **10.** A multinational rescue mission succeeded in freeing 12 children and their football coach from the flooded Tham Luang cave complex in northern Thailand after they became trapped by a rapidly rising tide on 23 June; a volunteer, former Thai navy diver Saman Gunan, died during the operation on 6 July. **13.** Pakistan's former prime minister Nawaz Sharif was arrested in Lahore as he returned to face a prison sentence; hours before, two suicide bombers killed 132 people at political rallies as election violence escalated. **14.** Over 210 people died following a week of flooding and landslides in Japan. **24.** It was reported that over 210,000 children in China had been given ineffective vaccinations for diphtheria, tetanus and whooping cough; a private company

had reportedly produced the vaccinations. **26.** The centrist party of former cricketer Imran Khan won the Pakistan general election amid widespread political violence, accusations of vote rigging and military interference. **29.** Cambodia's prime minister of 33 years, Hun Sen, won a landslide election victory following an extensive crackdown that destroyed all opposition. An earthquake on the Indonesian island of Lombok killed at least 17 people; a week later, on 5 August, another, larger earthquake claimed at least 430 lives and displaced over 350,000 people.

AUSTRALASIA AND THE PACIFIC

AUGUST–SEPTEMBER 2017
1 August. Scientists in Australia reported that the growing humpback whale population may be attracting more sharks, leading to a rise in attacks on humans. **6.** Three US Marines died after their aircraft crashed into the sea off northern Australia. **18 September.** New Zealand suffered a shortage of aviation fuel after a farm digger struck a supply pipe in Auckland.

OCTOBER–NOVEMBER 2017
13 October. Three people died in a skydiving accident in Queensland. **1 November.** Authorities in Australia announced that, from 2019, climbers would be banned from attempts on Uluru, the sandstone monolith formerly known as Ayers Rock. **7.** Two eight-year-old boys were killed at their school in Greenacre, south-west Sydney, when a car crashed through a wall of their temporary classroom. **13.** Australian MPs were given two weeks to reveal the birthplaces of their parents and grandparents after it was revealed that several MPs had dual nationality; the constitution bans dual citizens from sitting in parliament. **14.** A government-sponsored survey found that more than 61 per cent of Australians supported the legalisation of same-sex marriage in the country; the bill recognising same-sex marriage was passed on 7 December. **29.** In Australia, Victoria state legalised doctor-assisted suicides from mid-2019.

DECEMBER 2017
17. Two female couples were married in Australia's first same-sex weddings. **22.** A man with a history of mental illness was arrested after he drove a car into pedestrians in Melbourne, injuring 19 people. **26.** An Australian government survey estimated that 2,250 adult great white sharks could be found off Western Australia beaches.

JANUARY 2018
22. The Australian government unveiled a AU$60m package of funding to tackle unprecedented bleaching of the Great Barrier Reef; in April a further AU$500m was allocated. **26.** An estimated 60,000 took to the streets of Melbourne and Sydney to protest against Australia Day, labelling it 'invasion day'. **29.** An inter-island ferry which went missing off Kiribati with 50 people on board was located after one week, with seven survivors.

FEBRUARY 2018
20. The remnants of Cyclone Gita hit New Zealand, causing widespread flooding and destruction. **23.** The deputy prime minister of Australia, Barnaby Joyce, resigned after accusations of sexual harassment following revelations of an extramarital affair two weeks earlier; he was replaced two days later by Michael McCormack. **26.** A 7.5-magnitude earthquake hit Papua New Guinea, leaving 67 dead and almost 150,000 people isolated and without food or water.

MARCH–APRIL 2018
18 March. Bushfires in south-eastern Australia forced hundreds to flee and left 20,000 homes without power. **19**

April. A mass evacuation of the entire population of Ambae island, Vanuatu, began after the Manaro volcano erupted for the second time in six months; 11,000 people were likely to be permanently rehoused on either Maewo or Pentecost islands.

MAY–JUNE 2018

11 May. Seven members of a family were killed in a home in Osmington, Western Australia, in the country's first mass shooting since 1996. **13.** A family of suicide bombers carried out coordinated attacks on three churches in Surabaya, Indonesia, killing 13 people; a second family performed a similar attack a day later at a police station, killing only themselves. **22.** The archbishop of Adelaide, Philip Wilson, became the most senior Catholic official in the world to be convicted of concealing child sexual abuse after he failed to report to police the abuse of two altar boys by a priest in the 1970s (*see* 29 June). **21 June.** Jacinda Ardern, the prime minister of New Zealand, became the second world leader in modern history to give birth in office. **29.** Denis Hart, the archbishop of Melbourne, resigned over Australia's mandatory sex abuse reporting law, after he stated that he would rather risk jail than report allegations of child sex abuse given during confession.

JULY 2018

3. At least 34 people drowned off the coast of Indonesia's Selayar Island after a ferry ran aground. **24.** New Zealand became the second nation, after Indonesia, to pass legislation granting victims of domestic abuse 10 days' paid leave to allow them to leave their partners and find new homes.

EUROPE

AUGUST 2017

1. Three members of a gang who allegedly murdered 17 people in road attacks were killed in a struggle with guards at a court near Moscow, Russia. **2.** Two people were killed while sunbathing when a light aircraft made an emergency landing on a beach near Lisbon, Portugal. **9.** A mafia boss, Mario Romito, and his brother-in-law were killed in an attack that also left two bystanders dead in Italy's southern Foggia province. **15.** At least 13 people died when a tree fell on a congregation gathered for a religious ceremony on Madeira. **17.** In an attack claimed by IS, a van was driven into crowds on Barcelona's Las Ramblas, killing 14 people and injuring more than 100, before the driver, Younes Abuoyaaqoub, killed a man for his car and a woman was killed by accomplices in Cambrils; in Cambrils, five members of the cell were shot dead by police after their car rammed a checkpoint, while Abuoyaaqoub was shot dead by police five days later in the Subirats area. **24.** Eight people were killed following landslides in Switzerland's south-eastern Val Bondasca region. **25.** In Belgium, a man who attacked two soldiers in Brussels was shot dead by the army.

SEPTEMBER 2017

3. In Germany, some 60,000 Frankfurt residents were evacuated from their homes when explosives experts defused a 1.8-tonne Second World War bomb. **5.** Danish inventor Peter Madsen was charged with the murder of Swedish journalist Kim Wall aboard his self-built submarine after her headless torso was found floating in the waters off Copenhagen in August 2017. **11.** In Barcelona, up to one million people marched in support of independence on Catalonia's national day. **12.** France's CGT union claimed that 400,000 people took part in protests across the country against President Macron's labour reforms. **20.** Spanish police arrested 14 members of the Catalan government on suspicion of organising an illegal independence referendum. **24.**

Chancellor Angela Merkel's Christian Democratic Union of Germany party won 33 per cent of the votes in the country's general election while the far-right Alternative for Germany (AfD) came third with 13 per cent; at a press conference the following day, AfD co-leader Frauke Petry quit the party, stating that she could not sit with the 'anarchic' group in parliament. **29.** Police in Moscow detained Russian opposition leader Alexei Navalny as he prepared to travel to a presidential election campaign rally in Nizhny Novgorod; on 2 October, he was sentenced to 20 days in jail for calling supporters to an unsanctioned rally.

OCTOBER 2017

1. Spanish riot police clashed with voters taking part in Catalonia's independence referendum, injuring as many as 850 people according to Catalan authorities; organisers claimed that about 90 per cent of the 2.2 million voters who took part in the illegal plebiscite backed secession. **4.** A court in Mugla, south-west Turkey, sentenced 40 people to life in prison on charges related to 2016's failed coup. **16.** Wildfires in northern Portugal and Spain killed 32 people; it was thought that the majority of the blazes had been set deliberately. Journalist Daphne Caruana Galizia, who led the Panama Papers investigation, was killed when a bomb blew up her car in Malta. Two people were killed in bear attacks in eastern Russia, thought to have been provoked by lack of food. **21.** The Spanish government announced that it would invoke article 155 of its constitution and impose direct rule on Catalonia in a move that provoked hundreds of thousands of protestors to take to the streets of Barcelona. **26.** A Russian helicopter with eight people on board crashed into the sea off Svalbard, an extensive search recovered no survivors. **27.** The Catalan government passed a resolution to proclaim an independent Catalan republic before Spain's prime minister Mariano Rajoy was given authority by the senate to sack the regional government and announced regional elections for 21 December. **30.** Catalan leader Carles Puigdemont fled to Brussels with several members of his deposed cabinet hours before Spain's attorney general asked for charges of rebellion, sedition and misuse of public funds to be brought against them.

NOVEMBER 2017

2. Eight members of the ousted Catalan government were arrested on charges of rebellion against Spain. Eight members of the Turkish security forces and 22 militants were killed in clashes in Hakkari and Tunceli provinces, in the south-east of Turkey. **5.** The bodies of 26 migrant women were brought ashore in Italy amid a surge in departures from Libya. **9.** Nurse Niels Hoegel, who was serving a life sentence for two murders and three attempted murders, may have been behind the deaths of 102 patients at two hospitals, police in Germany announced. **22.** Ratko Mladic was found guilty at The Hague on 11 charges including genocide; the Bosnian Serb general ordered the siege of Sarajevo from 1992–6 and the killing of more than 8,000 men and boys at Srebrenica in 1995. **23.** Gunmen seized control of Luhansk, capital of the self-proclaimed Luhansk People's Republic in east Ukraine. **29.** In The Hague, war criminal Slobodan Praljak drank poison in the dock and died, moments after his 20-year jail sentence had been upheld by the court.

DECEMBER 2017

14. Six children were killed when a train struck their school bus at a level crossing near Millas, southern France; the bus driver was later arrested. **20.** Pro-independence parties won a majority in snap regional elections in Catalonia, Spain. **25.** Five people were killed and 15 injured when a bus ploughed into an entrance to Slavyansky Bulvar metro station in Moscow. **24–26.** Three climbers died in three separate avalanches in the Swiss Alps.

JANUARY 2018

6–8. At least 76 migrants drowned over the course of three days after attempting to travel from Libya to Italy in dinghies. **8–12.** One of the worst storms in decades left 13,000 tourists and locals stranded and without electricity across the Alps as 7ft (2.1m) of snow fell in two days. **13.** Robbers stole an estimated £4m of jewellery from a luxury hotel in Paris. **15.** The prime minister of Romania, Mihai Tudose, resigned after his party withdrew support for him; on 29 January Viorica Dancila became the first woman to hold the position and the country's third prime minister in a year. In Greece, a general strike against changes to industrial action law led to clashes between riot police and protesters. **16.** Prominent Kosovan political leader Oliver Ivanovic was assassinated in Mitrovica, Kosovo; his death was widely blamed on Serbian nationalists, but nobody was charged. **21.** An estimated 50,000 protestors marched through Bucharest in opposition to proposed laws which would make it harder to prosecute high-level corruption. **26–27.** The French, Italian and Libyan coastguards rescued over 900 migrants off the coast of Libya over two days, but at least 15 drowned. **28.** The Polish government passed a law criminalising any mention of 'Polish crimes' during the Holocaust, drawing international condemnation led by Israel; the law was eventually weakened in June. **30.** The far-right Czech president Milos Zeman was narrowly re-elected.

FEBRUARY 2018

1. Twenty-two people were injured in Calais, France, after clashes between around 100 Eritrean and 30 Afghan migrants. **2.** A boat destined for Italy capsized off the coast of Libya, and was believed to have killed as many as 90 migrants; The Times reported that over 2,800 people had drowned in similar attempted crossings in 2017. **4.** In Italy, a far-right supporter murdered six African migrants in Macerata. Almost 1 million Greek nationalists were involved in protests over plans to allow Macedonia formal rights to the name, claiming that it would imply that the Balkan nation had a territorial claim over a northern Greek region, also known as Macedonia. **10.** A Russian passenger jet crashed near Moscow, killing all 71 people on board. Ongoing coalition talks in Germany between Chancellor Merkel's Christian Democrats and the Social Democratic Party (SDP) led to calls for Merkel to step down after she had conceded key ministerial positions to the SDP. **18.** Five women were killed by a gunman in a church in Kizlyar, Russia; IS later claimed responsibility. **19.** The World Health Organization reported that over 21,000 people were infected with measles in Europe in 2017, a 400 per cent rise, after an increasing number of parents shunned the vaccine. **21.** In Slovakia, investigative journalist Jan Kuciak was murdered while investigating alleged links between the mafia and Prime Minister Robert Fico's close adviser Maria Troskova, leading to street protests which attracted an estimated 50,000 on 9 March. **25.** In Germany, Chancellor Merkel announced her 'grand coalition' cabinet, ending almost six months of negotiations between the Christian Democratic Union and the SDP; the coalition was formalised on 5 March.

MARCH 2018

1. German politicians denounced a suspected Russian cyber attack on government computers as 'a form of warfare'. Former, exiled Catalan leader Carles Puigdemont withdrew his bid to become president of the region, but announced plans to lead a government in exile. **4.** Thousands of Macedonians joined demonstrations in Skopje to protest plans to change the country's name; the government hoped to end the ongoing political naming dispute with Greece over the use of 'Macedonia'. **6.** A Russian military transport plane crashed in Syria, killing all 39 people on board. **12.** The Slovakian interior minister and deputy prime minister, Robert Kalinak,

quit following anti-corruption protests following the death of journalist Jan Kuciak (see 21 February); Prime Minister Robert Fico also resigned three days later. **15.** France, Germany, the USA and the UK issued a joint statement condemning Russia for its alleged chemical attack in Salisbury, UK, on 4 March; the USA also announced further sanctions for Russia (see 26 March and UK Affairs, 4 March). **18.** Vladimir Putin was re-elected president of Russia with over 76 per cent of the vote, amid claims of vote-rigging and a crackdown on opposition. **21.** Former French president Nicolas Sarkozy was charged with corruption over allegations the late Libyan despot Muammar Gaddafi funded his 2007 election campaign. **23.** A gunman killed three people and injured 14 others in the town of Trebes in south-west France; IS later claimed responsibility for the attack. In the build-up to the 50th anniversary of the May 1968 uprising in France, hundreds of thousands joined protests and a wave of strikes began against the president Emmanuel Macron, which lasted months and were occasionally violent. **25.** Exiled Catalan leader Carles Puigdemont was arrested in Germany, resulting in violent clashes with protesters in Barcelona as 55,000 took to the streets; a German court later denied extradition to Puigdemont, but on 15 April over 300,000 marched in Barcelona to protest his arrest. At least 70 people were arrested in anti-government protests in Minsk, Belarus, including a prominent opposition leader. **26.** Russia expelled western diplomats in retaliation for hundreds of its own diplomats being expelled from 23 ally countries, including the UK, USA, France, Germany and Ukraine; the political dispute arose after UK prime minister Theresa May blamed Russia for the use of a military-grade nerve agent in the UK (see UK Affairs, 4 March).

APRIL 2018

6. A new wave of US sanctions aimed at Russian oligarchs was introduced. **8.** Viktor Orban was re-elected for a third term as prime minister of Hungary, with his Fidesz party claiming a large parliamentary majority. **13.** Protests began in Armenia over an alleged power grab by former president Serzh Sargsyan, who was sworn in as prime minister; after 11 days of demonstrations, Mr Sargsyan resigned on 23 April. **15.** In Montenegro, the pro-EU candidate Milo Djukanovic won the presidential election, putting the country on course for future EU membership. **16.** The militant Basque separatist group ETA, responsible for the deaths of over 800 people over a 40-year campaign, apologised and announced its full dissolution. **23.** Over 1,200 migrants destined for Italy were rescued off the Libyan coast, contributing to around 9,000 attempted crossings since the start of 2018.

MAY 2018

8. Opposition leader Nikol Pashinyan was elected Prime Minister of Armenia, putting an end to weeks of popular unrest. The lower house of the Russian parliament voted to allow Dmitry Medvedev to continue as prime minister for another term. **17.** Catalan nationalist Quim Torra was sworn in as the Catalan president, replacing exiled leader Carles Puigdemont. **24.** An international team of investigators concluded that a Russian missile was responsible for the downing of flight MH17 over Ukraine in 2014, leading to calls from Australia and the Netherlands for Russia to accept responsibility for the incident. **25.** In a historic referendum in Ireland, 66.4 per cent of the turnout overwhelmingly voted to end the country's near-total ban on abortion. **26.** More than 1,800 migrants were rescued in international waters between Italy and Libya over a single weekend. **27.** After two months of political stalemate in Italy following an inconclusive general election, President Sergio Mattarella announced fresh elections, set for August; however, on 31 May a coalition was formed following 88 days of negotiations, with Giuseppe Conte sworn in as prime minister on 1 June. herd of wild European bison were successfully reintroduced to state forest land on the Dutch coast, 80 years after they were hunted to near-extinction in Europe. **30.** The murder of a prominent Russian critic of President Putin in Kiev caused a sensation after it was revealed that Ukraine's secret service had staged the death in order to thwart a genuine plot.

JUNE 2018

1. Spain's prime minister, Mariano Rajoy, was ousted after a vote of no confidence following a corruption scandal; he was replaced by socialist Pedro Sánchez. **12.** The EU committed itself to spending £5bn a year on tackling illegal immigration, including establishing a 10,000-strong standing corp of guards. Spain agreed to allow a rescue ship carrying 629 migrants to dock after both Italy and Malta refused the vessel entry. **16.** In Hungary, four members of a people-smuggling gang were imprisoned for murder after they allowed 71 migrants to suffocate in a lorry. **17.** The Former Yugoslav Republic of Macedonia provisionally agreed to change its name to the Republic of Severna (Northern) Macedonia, ending a 27-year dispute with neighbouring Greece over its contested name; the announcement was met with large protests in both countries. **24.** Having ruled for 16 years, Recep Tayyip Erdogan won Turkey's snap presidential election and returned with sweeping new powers.

JULY 2018

3. Three nights of violent rioting began in Nantes, France, after a police officer shot and killed 22-year-old Aboubakar Fofana during a traffic stop; on 5 July, 1,000 protesters marched through Nantes calling for 'justice for Abou'. **4.** More than 200 migrants drowned in the Mediterranean over three days, while the German chancellor Angela Merkel averted a coalition crisis over immigration by agreeing to create 'transit zones' on the southern border in order to repatriate refugees; meanwhile, many EU nations, including Italy, decided to toughen their policies on immigration. **11.** The sole survivor of a German neo-Nazi terrorist cell, Beate Zschäpe, was sentenced to life imprisonment for the murder of ten people. **12.** In Czechia, almost nine months of political stalemate ended as incumbent prime minister Andrej Babis formed a new coalition government. The government of the Republic of Ireland voted to sell its investment of €8bn (£7.2bn) in fossil fuel companies, making it the first country in the world to pursue the divestment strategy. **15.** France beat Croatia 4–2 in the final of the FIFA World Cup in Moscow. **23.** In Greece, wildfires in the coastal town of Mati, 29km east of Athens, burned for four days and claimed at least 94 lives; there was widespread public anger at the government's insufficient response to the crisis, which also left 200 injured and more than 1,500 homes damaged or destroyed. **26.** About 800 migrants attempted to storm the Spanish–Moroccan border fence, as Spain's migrant crisis mounted.

MIDDLE EAST

AUGUST 2017

1. In Herat, western Afghanistan, a suicide bomber and gunman killed at least 29 people and wounded 63 at a Shia mosque. **5.** A hot air balloon crashed in the Egyptian city of Luxor, killing eight people. **6.** It was reported that Syrian government forces had retaken al-Sukhna, the last stronghold of Islamic State (IS) in Homs province; at least 30 IS fighters were killed in the final days of fighting. **7.** Israeli jets reportedly bombed a Syrian government chemical weapons site near Masyaf. **8.** Six al-Qaeda fighters were killed in an attack on an army camp in south Yemen that left two soldiers dead. **9–10.** Around 120 Somali and Ethiopian teenagers were deliberately drowned by people traffickers in two separate incidents in the Arabian Sea, the UN reported. **11.** In Egypt, at least 43 people

were killed and more than 100 injured when two trains collided east of Alexandria. **25.** A suicide bomber killed at least 20 people inside a Shia mosque in Kabul, Afghanistan.

SEPTEMBER 2017

2–3. Coalition airstrikes killed 85 IS fighters in the Syrian desert. **11.** Militants attacked an armoured police convoy in the Sinai Peninsula in Egypt and killed 18 officers. **14.** IS gunmen and suicide bombers killed at least 74 people in Dhi Qar province, southern Iraq. **25.** Kurds in northern Iraq held a referendum on independence despite the presence of troops, and a land and air blockade; more than 80 per cent of registered voters cast their ballot. **26.** Saudi Arabia's King Salman issued a decree allowing women in the kingdom to drive for the first time. **28.** A new recording released by IS of its leader Abu Bakr al-Baghdadi appeared to contradict claims that he had been killed in a Russian airstrike near Raqqa, Syria, in May 2017.

OCTOBER 2017

1. The Syrian Observatory for Human Rights said that at least 3,000 people, including 955 civilians, had died in Syria's civil war in September, the deadliest month thus far in 2017. **3.** At least 33 people were arrested in Egypt on suspicion of homosexuality in the wake of public shows of support for LGBT rights in the country. **6.** Activists in eastern Syria said that up to 120 civilians had been killed in a week of airstrikes on Deir ez-Zor province; 60 civilians were also said to have died while attempting to flee fighting across the Euphrates. **12.** In Cairo, representatives of Hamas and Fatah signed a preliminary reconciliation deal in an attempt to end ten years of hostility in the Gaza Strip. The World Health Organization reported more than 815,000 suspected cases of cholera in Yemen – the fastest-spreading outbreak of the disease in modern history. **16.** Iraqi soldiers seized the city of Kirkuk from Kurdish forces that had held the city for three years. **17.** Western-backed forces retook Raqqa, Syria, after four years of IS control. **18.** Taliban militants killed at least 69 people in attacks on government targets across Afghanistan. **20.** At least 30 police officers were killed in a raid on a militant hideout in Egypt's western desert. **21.** Government forces in Syria retook the town of al-Qaraytan, in eastern Homs province, and discovered the bodies of 116 civilians who had been executed as spies by IS militants. **30.** Seven Palestinians were killed when Israeli forces blew up a tunnel stretching from the Gaza Strip into southern Israel.

NOVEMBER 2017

5. More than 100 people were killed by a truck bomb near Deir ez-Zor in eastern Syria. More than 200 princes, businessmen, officials and former and present ministers – including Prince Alwaleed bin Talal, one of the world's richest people – were arrested in a fortnight-long anti-corruption drive in Saudi Arabia, with many held at the Riyadh Ritz-Carlton hotel. **9.** Government forces retook the Syrian border town of al-Bukamal from IS. **12.** A magnitude 7.3 earthquake in the border region of Iran and Iraq killed more than 530 people; Kermanshah in Iran was worst hit. **21.** In Iraq, a suicide bomber killed at least 24 people in an attack on a market in Tuz Khurmatu, south of Kirkuk. **24.** Militants allied to IS killed more than 300 people attending prayers in the town of Bir al-Abed in the north of Egypt; government forces immediately launched raids in the Sinai peninsula following the ambush, which involved as many as 40 attackers in trucks. **26.** Syrian government forces killed 23 civilians in the rebel-held eastern Ghouta region outside Damascus, the Syrian Observatory for Human Rights reported.

DECEMBER 2017

2. Dozens were killed after heavy fighting broke out in Yemen's capital, Sana'a, following former president Ali

Abdullah Saleh's call for a ceasefire with Saudi Arabia; Saleh was killed by Houthi fighters the next day as he fled Sana'a; *The Sunday Times* reported on 14 January 2018 that over 5,000 people had been killed in the fighting and 3 million internally displaced. **6–8.** At least two Palestinians were shot dead amid protests after President Trump announced that he planned to move the US embassy from Tel Aviv to Jerusalem. **11.** Russian president Vladimir Putin made an unannounced visit to Syria, proclaiming victory over IS in the country and in the war to save President Assad's regime. **15.** Four Palestinian men were shot dead by Israeli security forces in separate incidents – ranging from a protest in Ramallah to a knife attack on a soldier in the West Bank. **21.** Aid agencies announced that there were one million suspected cases of cholera in Yemen in what had become the world's worst humanitarian crisis. **25.** In Afghanistan, an IS suicide bomb attack on the national directorate of security in Kabul left five people dead. **26.** In Yemen, airstrikes by the Saudi-led coalition on the al-Hayma market and Hodeida killed 68 civilians. **28.** IS claimed responsibility for a suicide bomb attack in the Dashte-Barchi district of Kabul that killed 41 people and wounded more than 90. **31.** Four people were reported to have been shot dead by security forces in the western Iranian city of Drood as the country experienced a third day of protests, initially sparked by economic discontent; at least 25 people died in two weeks of protests, alongside thousands of arrests, and pro-government counter-demonstrations were held on 3 January 2018 after the government blamed Iran's 'enemies' for the unrest.

JANUARY 2018
3. In Israel, Prime Minister Netanyahu ordered the estimated 38,000 African migrants in the country to leave voluntarily or face prison. **4.** A suicide bomber killed at least 11 people, including several police officers, and wounded 25 in Kabul, Afghanistan; IS claimed responsibility. **6.** Violent protests erupted in Tunisia and lasted over two weeks, resulting in an aggressive government crackdown and at least one death, as crowds called for an end to austerity, high taxation and high unemployment; on 13 January the government committed to increasing welfare for the poorest but failed to quell the protests. **7.** Israel banned representatives of 20 foreign non-governmental organisations from visiting the country due to their support for Palestinian-led boycott movements. Saudi Arabian authorities arrested 11 princes who protested after the government suspended state payment of their utility bills. **14.** *The Guardian* reported that over 100,000 people had fled the Syrian city of Idlib since December 2017 due to an assault by President Bashar al-Assad's forces on rebels in the city; over 500,000 had died in the conflict since 2011. **15.** In Iraq, at least 38 people were killed and over 100 injured in a double suicide bombing in Tayaran Square, Baghdad; IS later claimed responsibility. **21.** In Kabul, Afghanistan, 22 people were killed by five Taliban gunmen who stormed a luxury hotel in an attack that lasted 14 hours; on 26 January the Taliban claimed responsibility for a bomb which killed 103 people and injured 235 in Kabul. **23.** In Egypt, President Sisi's main political opponent, Sami Anan, was arrested after being denied permission to run in upcoming elections, leading others also to withdraw. **24.** Five people died in a ten-hour siege in Jalalabad, Afghanistan, after IS gunmen stormed an office occupied by the charity Save the Children; on 29 January, IS gunmen attacked a military academy, killing at least 11 cadets. **30.** Paramilitary separatists from southern Yemen surrounded Prime Minister Ahmed bin Daghr in the country's de facto capital of Aden, after three days of fighting which left at least 36 people dead.

FEBRUARY 2018
1. *The Times* reported that over 270,000 people had fled northwestern Syria in six weeks due to an intensification of

fighting between government and rebel forces. **2.** Police in Iran arrested 29 women for protesting against a law that makes wearing the hijab compulsory. **5.** Syrian government and Russian forces began a major offensive on the Idlib region in the north-west of the country; government forces simultaneously launched a new offensive on eastern Ghouta, a suburb of Damascus, which killed nearly 200 in four days. **8.** A new wave of US airstrikes in Syria killed over 100 opposition soldiers, as Turkey warned that US forces fighting alongside Kurdish rebels would also be attacked. Another assault on rebel-held eastern Ghouta began; ten days later fighting intensified with at least 250 civilians killed by airstrikes, many of them in hospitals. **10.** Tensions between Iran and Israel escalated after an Israeli fighter aircraft was shot down in Syria, resulting in retaliatory airstrikes on Iranian forces in Syria. **13.** Police in Israel recommended charging Prime Minister Netanyahu with bribery, fraud and breach of trust after a year-long corruption investigation; a week later many of his closest aides were arrested on corruption charges, and Netanyahu was questioned by police on 2 March. US airstrikes in eastern Syria reportedly killed up to 200 Russian mercenaries allied to President Assad. Turkey launched an assault on US-backed Kurdish militia forces in Syria, as the USA announced plans to increase its military involvement in the conflict; intense fighting continued for weeks, displacing thousands of civilians. **18.** Two teenagers were shot dead by Israeli soldiers in Gaza, following a car bomb which injured four soldiers; retaliatory airstrikes by Israel also injured two Palestinians. An aircraft crashed in Iran, killing all 65 passengers on board. **19.** At least 27 paramilitary soldiers were ambushed and killed by IS militants in Iraq, two months after the nation claimed victory over the group. **20.** A Turkish military assault on US-backed Kurdish forces in Syria escalated as they also shelled Syrian soldiers, resulting in Kurdish and Syrian forces allying against Turkey. **24.** International efforts for a 30-day ceasefire in eastern Ghouta, Syria, succeeded as the death toll reached 450 in the region, but government forces immediately broke the agreement with bombing and an alleged chemical weapons attack. **28.** *The Times* reported that at least 10,000 people had been killed and many more had died of starvation and disease in Yemen after three years of war.

MARCH 2018
5. The first UN aid delivery reached the besieged area of eastern Ghouta, Syria, after government soldiers removed medical supplies; around 800 had died in the area during a month of fighting (*see* 14 March). **11.** Israeli military intelligence discovered at least ten Iranian military bases in Syria housing thousands of soldiers, which raised the threat of war between the two nations. **12.** Afghan forces, supported by US air strikes, fought to recapture the western province of Farah from Taliban forces, killing 56 insurgents; the Taliban had rejected peace talks earlier in the year. **13.** The Palestinian prime minister, Rami Hamdallah, was the victim of an assassination attempt in Gaza; his convoy had just crossed into the city when an explosive detonated at the roadside, failing to injure him. **14.** It was reported over 1,400 civilians had died, over 20,000 people were displaced and 400,000 were trapped in eastern Ghouta, Syria, as government forces reclaimed half of the rebel-held region; in northern Syria. Turkish forces besieged Kurdish-held Afrin, trapping up to 200,000 inside, before capturing the town four days later. **21.** An IS suicide bomber killed at least 29 Shia Muslims worshipping at a shrine in Kabul, Afghanistan. **29.** President Sisi of Egypt was re-elected with 97 per cent of the vote amid claims of intimidation and after several leading opponents were arrested. **30.** Israeli troops shot and killed at least 16 Palestinians and wounded hundreds more after 30,000 protesters descended on border fences around Gaza; on 6 April, at least six more demonstrators

were killed and over 1,000 people were injured in the ongoing clashes.

APRIL 2018

2. Israel abandoned plans to deport or indefinitely imprison up to 40,000 African migrants, instead agreeing with the UN to deport over 16,000 to various western countries. **8.** At least 70 people died in a suspected chemical attack perpetrated by government forces in Douma, Syria; international condemnation culminated in joint US, UK and French air strikes on chemical weapons facilities on 15 April, which were launched without the support or condemnation of the UN Security Council (*see* UK Affairs, 12 April). **12.** Taliban militants killed at least 15 people, including the local governor, at a government compound in the Khwaja Omari district of Afghanistan. **22.** An IS suicide bomber killed 60 people as they registered to vote in Kabul, Afghanistan; on 30 April, a double suicide bombing killed a further 26 people in the city, and on 6 May, 14 were killed in another attack on a voter registration centre. Saudi Arabian-led air strikes in Yemen killed the rebel Houthi leader along with at least 33 others.

MAY 2018

8. Israeli airstrikes reportedly targeted Iranian forces in Syria just hours after the US withdrew from the 2015 Iran nuclear agreement, resulting in reciprocal attacks over the pursuing days. **14.** The USA opened its new embassy in Jerusalem on the 70th anniversary of the Israeli state, breaking with decades of diplomatic precedent; on the same day, Israeli forces opened fire on tens of thousands of Palestinian protesters on the Gaza border, killing at least 62 and injuring 2,700. **17.** Egyptian security forces killed 19 IS militants; their deaths brought the total killed since a large-scale security operation against insurgents was launched in February to at least 296, including 35 military personnel. **22.** At least 16 people died and 38 were injured in Kandahar, Afghanistan, when a van filled with explosives detonated as security forces tried to defuse it. A US rocket strike in southern Afghanistan killed 50 Taliban leaders. **29.** Israel launched its biggest aerial bombardment of Gaza since the 2014 war following weeks of unrest on the border.

JUNE 2018

3. Israel claimed that Iran was still pursuing its nuclear programme and urged European leaders to end their support for the 2015 nuclear deal. **4.** The prime minister of Jordan, Hani Mulki, resigned after popular protests against planned tax rises. **5.** Saudi Arabia issued its first driving licences to ten women prior to lifting the ban on female drivers on 24 June, despite several activists who had protested the ban remaining under arrest. **7.** At least 17 people were killed in Baghdad, Iraq, after a house storing heavy weapons exploded. **13.** The Saudi-led coalition battling Iran-aligned Houthi rebels in Yemen initiated a large assault on the port of Hodeidah, displacing tens of thousands. **15.** A rare, peaceful anti-government protest in Palestine against the rule of Mahmoud Abbas resulted in security forces launching a violent crackdown on demonstrators. **16.** The first ceasefire between the Taliban and the government of Afghanistan in 17 years was marked by an IS bomb attack in Nangarhar province, which killed 26 people; IS was not part of the ceasefire and government attempts to extend the agreement for more than one week failed. **20.** Taliban militants in western Afghanistan killed 30 Afghan soldiers in the first major attack since the ceasefire. **23.** Iraqi forces claimed to have killed 45 IS militants in the town of Hajin in eastern Syria. **25.** In Tehran, a series of large-scale strikes and demonstrations against spiralling prices and the rising cost of living, due in large part to the collapse of Iran's currency, were met with a strong police crackdown.

JULY 2018

5. Three weeks of regime attacks on towns in western Syria drove 320,000 people to flee their homes and camp near the country's closed western border; Israel and Jordan refused the refugees asylum. **12.** Government forces reclaimed the rebel stronghold of Daraa, southwestern Syria. **14.** Israel launched a further wave of airstrikes in Gaza, the largest of 2018, following rocket attacks from the region and the death of an Israeli soldier. **19.** Israel passed a law declaring that only Jews have the right to self-determination in the country, complicating a two-state solution to the conflict with Palestine; a number of international bodies, including the EU, criticised the law. **23.** After Iran's president Hassan Rouhani cautioned the US against starting a war between the two countries, President Trump warned that such threats would cause Iran to 'suffer consequences the likes of which few throughout history have ever suffered before.' **24.** Israel shot down a Syrian warplane that had entered its airspace, as Syrian forces battled to reclaim the rebel-held Golan Heights region. **25.** More than 220 people were killed in coordinated IS suicide bombings in government-held southern Syria.

OBITUARIES 2017–18

Alaïa, Azzedine, fashion designer, aged 82 – *b*. 26 February 1935, *d*. 17 November 2017

Annan, Kofi, Ghanaian diplomat, UN Secretary-General (1997–2006) and co-recipient of the 2001 Nobel Peace Prize with the UN, aged 80 – *b*. 8 April 1938, *d*. 18 August 2018

Atherton, Candy, Labour MP for Falmouth and Camborne (1997–2005), aged 62 – *b*. 21 September 1955, *d*. 31 October 2017

Bairsto, Air Marshal Sir Peter, KBE, CB, AFC, Deputy C-in-C Strike Command (1981–4), aged 91 – *b*. 3 August 1926, *d*. 24 October 2017

Bannister, Sir Roger, CH, CBE, DM, FRCP, middle-distance athlete and neurologist who first ran the mile in under four minutes (1954), aged 88, *b*. 23 March 1929, *d*. 3 March 2018

Barber of Tewkesbury, Lord, farmer and conservationist; chair of the RSPB (1976–81), aged 99 – *b*. 17 June 1918, *d*. 21 November 2017

Barder, Sir Brian, KCMG, Ambassador to Ethiopia (1982–6), Poland (1986–8) and High Commissioner to Nigeria, and concurrently Ambassador to Benin (1988–91), aged 83 – *b*. 20 June 1934, *d*. 19 September 2017

Barklem, Jill, children's illustrator and author famous for the *Brambly Hedge* series of books, aged 66 –*b*. 23 May 1951, *d*. 15 November 2017

Becker, Roger, tennis player, aged 83 – *b*. 6 February 1934, *d*. 5 November 2017

Bell, Trevor, artist, aged 87 –*b*. 18 October 1930, *d*. 3 November 2017

Bettencourt, Liliane, businesswoman. heiress and philanthropist, aged 94 – *b*. 21 October 1922, *d*. 21 September 2017

Bickerstaffe, Rodney, trade unionist; General Secretary of the National Union of Public Employees (1982–93), UNISON (1996–2001) and president of the National Pensioners Convention (2001–5), aged 72 – *b*. 6 April 1945, *d*. 3 October 2017

Booth, Tony, actor, aged 85 – *b*. 9 October 1931, *d*. 25 September 2017

Carluccio, Antonio, OBE, cook and restaurateur, aged 80 – *b*. 19 April 1937, *d*. 8 November 2017

Carrington (6th) and Carington of Upton (life peerage), KG, GCMG, CH, MC, PC, Lord, First Lord of the Admiralty (1959–63); Minister without Portfolio and Leader of the House of Lords (1963–4); Leader of the Opposition, House of Lords (1964–70; 1974–9); Secretary of State for Defence (1970–4), Energy (1974) and Foreign and Commonwealth Affairs (1979–82), aged 99 – *b*. 6 June 1919, *d*. 9 July 2018

Cassidy, David. singer and actor, aged 67 – *b*. 12 April 1950, *d*. 22 November 2017

Chambers, Emma, actor, aged 53 – *b*. 11 March 1964, *d*. 21 February 2018

Chegwin, Keith, children's TV presenter, aged 60 – *b*. 17 January 1957, *d*. 11 December 2017

Clarke, Simon, rugby player, aged 79 – *b*. 2 April 1938, *d*. 12 October 2017

Clifford, Max, publicist, aged 74 – *b*. 6 April 1943, *d*. 10 December 2017

Cosgrave, Liam, Irish prime minister *Taoiseach* (1973–7), aged 97 – *b*. 13 April 1920, *d*. 4 October 2017

Craig, Sir James, GCMG, Ambassador to Syria (1976–9) and Saudi Arabia (1979–84), aged 93 – *b*. 13 July 1924, *d*. 26 September 2017

Dawn, Liz, MBE, actor, best known for playing Vera Duckworth in *Coronation Street* (1976–2008), aged 77 – *b*. 8 November 1939, *d*. 25 September 2017

Dodd, Sir Ken, OBE, comedian, aged 90 – *b*. 8 November 1927, *d*. 11 March 2018

Domino, Fats, singer-songwriter, aged 89 – *b*. 26 February 1928, *d*. 25 October 2017

Dotrice, Roy, OBE, actor, aged 94 – *b*. 26 May 1923, *d*. 16 October 2017

Dumon, Micheline, GM, French Resistance agent, aged 96 – *b*. 20 May 1921, *d*. 16 November 2017

Esser, Robin, journalist; Editor, *Sunday Express* (1986–9), Executive Managing Editor, *Daily Mail* (1998–2015), aged 84 – *b*. 6 May 1933, *d*. 6 November 2017

Flather, Gary, QC, OBE, judge and disability campaigner, aged 80 – *b*. 4 October 1937, *d*. 9 October 2017

Franklin, Aretha, American singer, songwriter and pianist, aged 76 – *b*. 25 March 1942, *d*. 16 August 2018

Greenbury, Sir Richard, chair (1991–9) and Chief Executive (1988–99) of Marks and Spencer, aged 81 – *b*. 31 July 1936, *d*. 26 September 2017

Hallyday, Johnny, French singer, aged 74 – *b*. 15 June 1943, *d*. 6 December 2017

Hatch Dupree, Nancy, historian and philanthropist, aged 89 – *b*. 3 October 1927, *d*. 10 September 2017

Hawking, Prof. Stephen, CH, CBE, FRS, physicist, cosmologist, and author; Lucasian Professor of Mathematics, University of Cambridge (1979–2009), aged 76 – *b*. 8 January 1942, *d*. 14 March 2018

Hefner, Hugh, founder of *Playboy* magazine, aged 91 – *b*. 9 April 1926, *d*. 27 September 2017

Horton, Tommy, MBE, golfer, aged 76 – *b*. 16 June 1941, *d*. 7 December 2017

Howie of Troon, Lord, life peer; civil engineer; Labour MP for Luton (1963–70); Assistant Whip (1964–6); Lord Commissioner of HM Treasury (1966–7); Comptroller, HM Household (1967–8), aged 94 – *b*. 2 March 1924, *d*. 26 May 2018

Hughes, Sean, comedian, aged 51 – *b*. 10 November 1965, *d*. 16 October 2017

Hurt, Sir John, CBE, actor, aged 77 – *b*. 22 January 1940, *d*. 25 January 2017

Hutchins, Pat, children's author, aged 75 – *b*. 18 June 1942, *d*. 7 November 2017

Hutchinson of Lullington, Lord, QC, criminal barrister, aged 102 – *b*. 28 March 1915, *d*. 13 November 2017

Imbert, Lord, CVO, QPM, Lord-Lieutenant of Greater London (1998–2008); Commissioner, Metropolitan Police (1987–93), aged 84 – *b*. 27 April 1933, *d*. 13 November 2017

John, Helen, peace campaigner, aged 80 – *b*. 30 September 1937, *d*. 5 November 2017

Jowell, Baroness, DBE, PC, Labour MP for Dulwich (1992–7), Dulwich and West Norwood (1997–2015); Secretary of State for Culture, Media and Sport (2001–7); Minister for the Olympics (2005–10); Paymaster General (2007–10); Minister for London (2007–8 and 2009–10); Minister for the Cabinet Office (2009–10), aged 70 – *b*. 17 September 1947, *d*. 12 May 2018

Keeler, Christine, model and showgirl who was one of the key figures in the Profumo Affair of the 1960s, aged 75 – *b*. 22 February 1942, *d*. 4 December 2017

Knightley, Phillip, journalist, aged 87 – *b*. 23 January 1929, *d*. 7 December 2017

Laird, Lord, life peer; Ulster Unionist Party MP for St Anne's, Belfast, Northern Ireland Parliament (1970–3); UUP Member for West Belfast, Northern Ireland Assembly (1973–5), aged 74 – *b.* 23 April 1944, *d.* 10 July 2018

Lassally, Walter, Oscar-winning cinematographer, aged 90 – *b.* 18 December 1926, *d.* 23 October 2017

Leach, Rosemary, actor, aged 81 – *b.* 18 December 1935, *d.* 21 October 2017

Léger, Hervé, French fashion designer, aged 60 – *b.* 30 May 1957, *d.* October 2017

Manduell, Sir John, CBE, founding principal of the Royal Northern College of Music (1971–96) and director of the Cheltenham Music Festival (1969–94), aged 89 – *b.* 2 March 1928, *d.* 25 October 2017

Marks, David, MBE, architect, aged 64 – *b.* 15 December 1952, *d.* 6 October 2017

Mascolo, Toni, OBE, hairdresser, aged 75 – *b.* 6 May 1942, *d.* 10 December 2017

Michie, Bill, Labour MP for Sheffield Heeley (1983–2001), aged 81 – *b.* 24 November 1935, *d.* 22 September 2017

Millett, Kate, Feminist author of *Sexual Politics* (1970), aged 82 – *b.* 14 September 1934, *d.* 6 September 2017

Moonman, Eric, OBE, Labour MP for Billericay (1966–70) and Basildon (1974–9); Senior Vice-President Board of Deputies of British Jews (1985–91 and 1994–9); President Zionist Federation (2001–17), aged 88 – *b.* 29 April 1929, *d.* 22 December 2017

Novotna, Jana, Czech tennis player and 1998 Wimbledon ladies singles champion, aged 49 – *b.* 2 October 1968, *d.* 19 November 2017

O'Brien, HE Cardinal Keith, Roman Catholic Archbishop of St Andrews and Edinburgh (1985–2013), aged 80 – *b.* 17 March 1938, *d.* 19 March 2018

Opie, Iona, CBE, author, anthropologist and folklorist, aged 94 – *b.* 13 October 1923, *d.* 23 October 2017

Petty, Tom. musician, aged 66 – *b.* 20 October 1950, *d.* 2 October 2017

Quirk, Lord, CBE, linguist and life peer, aged 97 – *b.* 12 July 1920, *d.* 20 December 2017

Root, Alan, OBE, wildlife film-maker, aged 80 – *b.* 12 May 1937, *d.* 26 August 2017

Saleh, Ali Abdullah, president of Yemen (North Yemen 1978–90; Yemen 1990–2011), aged 75 – *b.* 21 March 1942, *d.* 4 December 2017

Secondé, Sir Reginald, KCMG, CVO, Ambassador to Chile (1973–6), to Romania (1977–9) and to Venezuela (1979–82), aged 95 – *b.* 28 July 1922, *d.* 26 October 2017

Shepherd, David, CBE wildlife artist and conservationist, aged 86 – *b.* 25 April 1931, *d.* 19 September 2017

Speakman, Bill, VC, awarded the Victoria Cross for bravery (Korea, 1951), aged 90 – *b.* 21 September 1927, *d.* 20 June 2018

Stephen, Rt. Hon. Sir Ninian, KG, GCMG, GCVO, KBE, Justice of High Court of Australia (1972–82); Governor-General of Australia (1982–9), aged 94 – *b.* 15 June 1923, *d.* 29 October 2017

Steyn, Lord, PC, Lord of Appeal in Ordinary (1995–2005), aged 85 – *b.* 15 August 1932, *d.* 28 November 2017

Sulston, Sir John, CH, PHD, FRS, biologist and co-winner of the Nobel Prize in Physiology or Medicine (2002), aged 75 – *b.* 27 March 1942, *d.* 6 March 2018

Swinburn, Lt.-Gen. Sir Richard, KCB, Deputy C-in-C UK Land Forces, Cdr UK Field Army and Inspector-Gen. Territorial Army (1994–5), aged 79 – *b.* 30 October 1937, *d.* 11 October 2017

Talabani, Jalal, Iraqi Kurdish politician; President of Iraq (2005–14), aged 83 – *b.* 12 November 1933, *d.* 3 October 2017

Terry, Air Chief Marshal Sir Peter, GCB, AFC, aged 91 – *b.* 18 October 1926, *d.* 19 December 2017

Thomas of Macclesfield, Lord, CBE, life peer; managing director of the Co-operative Bank (1988–97), aged 80 – *b.* 19 October 1937, *d.* 1 July 2018

Wade of Chorlton, Lord, life peer; farmer and cheese maker, aged 85 – *b.* 24 December 1932, *d.* 7 June 2018

Whitrow, Benjamin, actor, aged 80 – *b.* 17 February 1937, *d.* 28 September 2017

Wiazemsky, Anne, actor, aged 70 – *b.* 14 May 1947, *d.* 5 October 2017

Young, Malcolm, rock musician; founder of AC/DC, aged 64 – *b.* 6 January 1953, *d.* 18 November 2017

ARCHAEOLOGY

Dr Matthew Symonds

It is said that nothing dates so quickly as one person's vision of the future. Looking back at the archaeological discoveries, breakthroughs and publications over the last 12 months, though, it is hard to shake the feeling that visions of the past can date almost as quickly. Both fresh data and new insights gleaned from existing evidence are continually refining or even rewriting our knowledge of past human activity in Britain.

NEOLITHIC NEIGHBOURS?

The arrival of agriculture in Britain around 6,000 years ago spelled doom for established lifestyles. For hundreds of thousands of years, hunter-gatherer bands had tracked migrating prey through the landscape, but their world disappeared as farming took hold. An ability to cultivate crops and control livestock triggered a revolution in human development, because it allowed enough surplus food to be produced to support people who were no longer obliged to spend their days finding something to eat. Freeing up their time permitted ever more complex and sophisticated specialist skills and knowledge to be developed, ultimately bequeathing a modern world where a startling proportion of the population has little idea how to grow, gather, hunt or process food. Even though we still reap the benefits bestowed by the arrival of these first farmers, huge gaps in knowledge remain about the everyday lives of these pioneers in Britain.

Roughly rectangular or square buildings are often seen as something that the Romans introduced to this country, but they were also popular with our Neolithic residents. In areas where timber was plentiful, these residences were typically constructed of wood, meaning that they usually survive as no more than faint stains in the soil where posts or walls once stood. Given the ease with which such fragile traces can be erased by later activity, it is unsurprising that examples remain scarce. Even the modest vestiges available for study today, though, can reveal surprisingly evocative snapshots of past life. Magnetic susceptibility survey of a house excavated at Horton, Berkshire, by Wessex Archaeology in 2012, for instance, revealed an area of enrichment at the entrance, where house-proud Neolithic inhabitants had jettisoned their sweepings out of the door. Horton was also exceptional for revealing multiple Neolithic houses scattered within the 34-hectare area examined by archaeologists.

Now, excavations undertaken by C. R Archaeology in advance of constructing a school at Llanfaethlu on Anglesey have exposed the remains of four houses built much closer together. The importance of this discovery, outlined in *Current Archaeology* 332, is ably illustrated by the fact that the sum total of early Neolithic houses known in Wales prior to this work amounted to three isolated examples. Inevitably, the Llanfaethlu cluster has been proposed as a candidate for the first village in Wales, while initial dates suggest activity from 3800 to 3600 BC. This means it is far from certain that all of the houses stood at the same time, although closely grouped sets of two or three houses were a feature of settlements on the other side of the Irish Sea. Holyhead on Anglesey is still a major ferry port serving Ireland, so the Llanfaethlu houses could testify to the Irish Sea acting as a highway to unite communities as early as the Neolithic period. What does seem certain is that these homes were not just places to live, as contemporary beliefs were carefully woven into their fabric. A possible shrine was set within one house, while the 'death' of these buildings was seemingly marked with the destruction and deposition of prized objects, including an arrowhead and axe.

A more spectacular example of Neolithic ritual activity has been forthcoming from Woodbridge, Suffolk, where Wardell Armstrong has been spearheading archaeological work commissioned by ScottishPower Renewables in order to connect an offshore windfarm to the national grid. The site is one of over 50 investigated along the 37km route taken by new power cables, providing an excellent illustration of how much new knowledge comes from major infrastructure projects. Much of the importance of Woodbridge flows from the presence of natural springs. These may well have attracted Neolithic visitors – watery places were a notoriously popular place for making offerings during the prehistoric period – while the boggy conditions have preserved rare organic remains ever since. These include a 30m wooden trackway and platform dating from *c.*2300 BC. 'Some of the wood is so well preserved, we can clearly see markings made by an apprentice, before a more experienced tradesman has taken over to complete the job', noted Richard Newman, associate director at Wardell Armstrong. 'Initially some of the wooden posts looked like they were maybe 100 years old, and it is incredible to think that they are over 4,000 years old.' Further finds include white pebbles that were deposited beside the track, and the skull of an aurochs (an extinct species of cattle). This had been adapted so that it could be mounted on a totem pole or even worn as a headdress; it was already 2,000 years old when it entered the earth at Woodbridge, suggesting that it was prized by successive generations.

Buildings and rituals entwined to produce the spectacular Ness of Brodgar site, which has been described as the Neolithic heart of Orkney. Long-running excavations by the Ness of Brodgar Trust and the University of the Highlands and Islands Archaeology Institute have exposed multiple structures that require rather less of a feat of imagination to appreciate than the Llanfaethlu houses (on Orkney, stone rather than timber was the building material of choice). Activity at the Ness – a narrow spit of land between the Stenness and Harray lochs – can be traced over millennia, but the site reached its zenith in around 3100 BC. At that time a complex of massive rectangular stone structures with curved corners, set within a stout enclosure wall, created a communal centre that drew visitors from across the island and almost certainly further afield. The buildings were arranged around a paved space that contained a decorated standing stone, which aligns with both a nearby tomb and sunrise on the equinox. Indeed, one of the most remarkable features of the Ness is the wealth of artwork that has been discovered, something that is rarely encountered in Neolithic buildings in Britain. One structure yielded 36 examples in a single week, while styles can range from deeply incised decorative schemes to faint lines. Some such stones were clearly not intended for display, as the embellished faces were concealed within the bulk of the wall. Obscuring this artwork means that it was not seen as simply pleasing to the eye, and it is tempting to wonder if these motifs symbolically strengthened or protected the structure in some way.

By 2900 BC change was underway at the Ness, and a massive, near-square edifice known as 'structure 10' was built over part of one of the earlier structures. Once complete, the excavators believe that this would have been one of the most impressive buildings in the British Isles. The explanation for this extraordinary new style may be even more important than the imposing superstructure, though. It has been suggested that while the earlier rectangular buildings would be well suited to serve whole communities, the new structure could better fit displays of power focused on an individual leader. If the emergence of a new mode of architecture was linked to broader social changes, it seems that it was not long before there was another radical shift. By 2800 BC the heyday of the Ness had passed and the site became a dumping ground for refuse, perhaps because society could no longer muster the resources to sustain such a complex. Whatever the explanation, the Ness was not forgotten, and in around 2400 BC people gathered at structure 10 en masse once more. During what was presumably a memorable feast, some 400 cattle were slaughtered and buried at the site, alongside a number of deer. By the time that these revels were underway, though, the Neolithic period had given way to the early Bronze Age.

BEWARE OF ARCHERS BEARING BEAKERS

Archaeologists usually take pains to stress that the shift from one ancient time period to another did not necessarily mean that everything changed overnight. Those living in Britain on the day that the Bronze Age became the Iron Age would not, for example, have immediately sought to replace existing blades with those forged from a newly plentiful and superior type of metal. It is looking increasingly probable, though, that the earlier transition from the Neolithic to the Bronze Age was accompanied by upheaval on a par with the arrival of farming. The appearance of metal implements in Britain is associated with the arrival of a wider package of desirable goods c.2450 BC, including archery kit and a distinctive pottery vessel known as a bell beaker. These beakers proved phenomenally popular and at their floruit can be found across much of Europe, prompting the term 'beaker people' traditionally used to describe the populations making and using them. Despite the wide currency of the generic bell beaker form, different regions display preferences for different shapes or decorative styles, creating a headache for those attempting to establish how the beaker package spread. Does it signify a mass migration across Europe, or did different local communities simply put their own spin on fashionable commodities that they encountered through trade and social contact with other groups?

Now, a game-changing study (that brought together dozens of specialists to sequence ancient DNA from 400 sets of human remains found at 136 sites across Europe) has been published in *Nature* 555. It is hard to overstate the importance of the results for understanding early Bronze Age Britain. The project sampled 226 sets of remains that could be directly linked to the beaker phenomenon, while further individuals pre- and post-dating the period were targeted in order to establish a baseline with which to compare the DNA of the 'beaker people'. In Europe, the results indicate various processes at work, with Iberian beaker users typically maintaining the same DNA make-up as their Neolithic forebears. The clear implication there, is that the beaker idea travelled without an accompanying influx of people. Not so in Britain, where intriguingly the Neolithic population seems to have been closely related to those Iberian farmers. In this case, though, the arrival of the beakers is accompanied by the arrival of people carrying a different DNA profile. These newcomers probably reached Britain via the Netherlands, where the project detected human remains bearing a very similar genetic signature. Although the DNA reveals that there was some mixing between the local and migrant population, by the close of the beaker period little trace was left of the people whose achievements were discussed in the preceding section. In Britain, at least, their monuments have long outlived their genes. This difference would not just have lain concealed in the incomers' DNA, as their genes reveal that they had much fairer skin than the resident Neolithic population.

Jumping forward to the Iron Age, and technology has also been shining new light on the interior of hillforts in Dorset.

Today, these magnificent monuments constitute some of the most impressive prehistoric sites in Britain, with the most famous example lying just outside modern Dorchester at Maiden Castle. There, serried ranks of gigantic ramparts and ditches were constructed to equip a modest hill with an extraordinary defensive perimeter. Such a transformation could only have been achieved by a community capable of organising labour on a massive scale, but the grandeur of the defences may have been contrived to obscure a critical weakness. As the different banks of ramparts do not intersect, defenders could be isolated during an attack. What precisely such defenders would have been protecting remains disputed, as hillforts have received varying interpretations ranging from full-blown settlements to handy refuges in troubled times. Now, geophysical surveys of many Dorset examples have been published by Dave Stewart and Miles Russell in *Hillforts and the Durotriges*, providing a sense of what lies beneath the turf. The results show that many sites contained large numbers of roundhouses, with the 200 examples at Hod Hill – some overlapping – speaking of a lengthy period of habitation. Internal tracks, drainage systems, storage facilities and industrial areas suggest that these sites were effectively market towns with a permanent resident population. Although the hillforts appear to have been in decline by the 1st century AD, some commanded the attention of the invading Roman army in the AD 40s, who even tucked a fort into a corner of the Iron Age defences at Hod Hill.

BRIDGEHEADS, BORDERS AND BELLEROPHON

While it was the Emperor Claudius who launched the first concerted attempt to conquer Britain in AD 43, Julius Caesar famously led two earlier expeditions against the island in 55 and 54 BC. He also left a detailed account of his actions in a remarkable ancient text describing the Gallic wars. Although Caesar's pretext for the invasion – that the Britons were aiding their Gallic brethren – does not bear detailed scrutiny, the propaganda value of his British adventure was considerable. Back in Rome, Caesar's safe return was celebrated with an unprecedented 20 days' thanksgiving. This rapturous reception stemmed from the Roman belief that the world was bound by an all-encompassing ocean. By projecting military force across it – as represented by the English Channel – Caesar pulled off a feat that has been likened to a Roman equivalent of the moon landing. Until recently, though, Caesar's exploits could only be followed through the written rather than the archaeological record. That changed after lengths of ditch were investigated during excavations by Oxford and Wessex Archaeology for the East Kent access road at Ebbsfleet, which may reveal the site of Caesar's bridgehead during his second British foray in 54 BC.

The ditch was 5m wide and 2m deep, a size that can only mean it was envisioned as some form of defence. Associated pottery dated this earthwork to the 1st century BC, a surprising result as monumental defences were not usually constructed in southern Britain during the late Iron Age. Subsequent investigation by the University of Leicester included geophysical survey – which indicated that an area of at least 20 hectares was bound by the ditch – and excavation that confirmed this earthwork was cut to uniform specifications. While the scale, design and standardised nature of the ditch are a close fit with an element of the siege works constructed by Caesar's army at Alesia in 52 BC, a find from within the Ebbsfleet ditch provides further evidence for a Roman military presence: the tip of a distinctive Roman javelin known as a *pilum*. Investigating a causeway crossing the ditch revealed a jumble of weapons and body parts, at least one of which bore traces of being sliced with a blade. The local terrain fits the sparse descriptions of the landing ground preserved in Caesar's text, but the ditch may not be part of the camp that he established at the beachhead. Instead, his account refers to an unfortunate incident when his anchored invasion fleet was caught in a storm, forcing 800 ships to be dragged up onto the shore while repairs were made. A new defensive perimeter was established to link the boats to the camp, providing a compelling explanation for the enigmatic earthwork. If Caesar's landing ground has indeed been discovered, it should allow more of the sites mentioned in his account to be identified.

Unlike Caesar's landing grounds, the spectacular ruins of (most of) Hadrian's Wall were never truly lost. There, though, the situation is the polar opposite, as a border system that could not be more prominent in the archaeological record passes almost unremarked in the ancient literature. A throwaway comment in a document written 200 years or so after the border was built tells us simply that Hadrian 'was the first to build a wall, 80 miles long, to separate the Romans from the barbarians'. Archaeologists continue to debate what this separation entailed, and over the last four decades scholars have been broadly split between two opposing camps. One sees the wall as effectively a bureaucratic soft border primarily designed to regulate and tax the peaceful movement of people, while the other envisions a hard border capable of repulsing full-scale barbarian invasions. Since 1976, when David J. Breeze and Brian Dobson's *Hadrian's Wall* was published, the regulate-and-tax model has proven most influential. Now, respected scholar Nick Hodgson has offered an alternative reading in a new book, *Hadrian's Wall: Archaeology and History at the Limit of Rome's Empire,* which emphasises the contribution that the wall could make to curtailing punishing assaults on the Roman province. He sees the Roman army firmly on the backfoot when the decision to build the new border was taken, following a humiliating retreat from Scotland and then a devastating war at the beginning of Hadrian's reign. By this reading, the wall was urgently needed to shore up the military defence of northern England as a precarious security situation threatened to spiral out of control.

Your reviewer also waded into Hadrian's Wall studies with the publication of *Protecting the Roman Empire,* which tackled a discrepancy that famously piqued the interest of the German historian Theodor Mommsen in the 19th century. He was intrigued by the striking difference in the scale of the artificial borders erected in Britain and Germany during the Hadrianic period. While Hadrian's Wall was intended to feature a stout 3m-wide stone rampart for most of its course, the contemporary barrier in Upper Germany was a simple timber palisade. Mommsen saw this as a product of the two border systems being geared towards meeting different intensities of threat, but it is possible that the explanation lies in what must surely have been the primary purpose of the borders: controlling the communities already living in the frontier zones. While long stretches of Hadrian's Wall severed established farmland worked by societies that numbered in the tens of thousands, most of the Upper German frontier lay in unpopulated terrain several days' travel from the nearest known settlements. This stark difference in the size of the settled groups living in the shadow of the two borders may well have made a more robust frontier system seem proportionate in Britain and superfluous in Germany. Indeed, the original construction programme for Hadrian's Wall appears to have prioritised posts in major valleys or on the approaches to possible bridges or fords, allowing traffic that was using existing routes through the landscape to be blocked or redirected to authorised crossing points. Such an approach suggests that the Roman army was deadly serious about ending traditional modes of movement into the province.

Despite the existential threat that the wall posed to existing lifestyles along its course, there is every reason to believe that the border did deliver a security dividend for those living more widely within its embrace. An illustration of the prosperity enjoyed by some individuals was recently unearthed at Boxford, Berkshire, where a newly discovered mosaic has been described as the most innovative composition to be found in Britain for 50 years. The lavishly decorated floor was excavated by members of the local community and Berkshire Archaeology Research Group, with professional supervision from Cotswold Archaeology. To date, only a portion of the pavement has been exposed – and even that glimpse is thanks to the long hours worked by the volunteers – but it is ample to demonstrate that the mosaic is crammed with a riot of scenes drawn from Greek mythology. Bellerophon's battle with the monstrous chimera rubs shoulders with Hercules braining a centaur, while elsewhere a seated king is flanked by armed guards. Whether this vigorous medley tells a coherent story is a mystery that can only be solved by excavation of the remainder of the mosaic.

GALVANISING GLOBALISATION

Over 1,000 years later in January 1740, more than 237 passengers and crew onboard the *Rooswijk* would have had opportunities to turn a profit on their mind as they set sail from the Netherlands. But it was not to be. Instead, one day into a journey that should have lasted six to eight months, the *Rooswijk* foundered off the coast of Kent, condemning everyone on board to a watery grave. It was only in the 1990s that the shifting sediments of the Goodwin Sands exposed the debris of the stricken vessel once more, 26m below sea level. Once the ship's timbers shed the cocoon of silt that had protected them for 250 years, they were left at the mercy of wood-boring creatures. Historic England and the Cultural Heritage Agency of the Netherlands decided to join forces to excavate, study and, in some cases, raise the remains of the *Rooswijk* before they were lost forever. She was no ordinary ship, as she belonged to the Dutch East India Company – known by its Dutch initials as the VOC – a powerful outfit that at its height commanded similar resources to a state. As well as ships, the VOC controlled far-flung trading posts and employed soldiers to protect them.

The Rooswijk was en route to what is now Jakarta when she sank, taking an extraordinarily valuable cargo with her. Not only was her hold brimming with the cash and kit needed to resupply, pay for and protect the company's interests, but it is also a safe bet that the passengers and crew were weighed down with quantities of metal – especially silver – stashed about their person. All of those on board would have been keenly aware that the law of supply and demand in a global market allowed them to double their money, simply by sailing to and from Jakarta. 'It was a crazy situation', says Martijn Manders, maritime heritage programme manager at the Cultural Heritage Agency of the Netherlands. 'People were smuggling silver in shoes and belts – probably to hide it from their fellow sailors more than anything – and we think that by the time the Rooswijk went down maybe half of the money being transported on these ships was illegal.' Once at Jakarta, the silver smugglers would sell their contraband to the VOC for a hefty profit, before investing in spices or porcelain. Back in the Netherlands, these commodities were worth twice the value of the original silver. The opportunity to examine an intact VOC cargo is rare – their value usually attracted salvage operations – meaning that the Rooswijk offers an exceptional opportunity to study the archaeology of globalisation.

PRESENT IMPERFECT

Sadly, the desire for personal enrichment continues to drive people to desperate acts, and Hadrian's Wall was also in the news this year for depressing reasons. The appearance of over 50 holes pockmarking a site on the former border was a tell-tale sign that clandestine metal detecting – illegal at a scheduled ancient monument – had been underway, and

Historic England issued an appeal for information about the perpetrators. Frustratingly, the objects themselves are likely to have been of very low value by modern monetary standards, while the much higher potential knowledge yield from them has been lost now that they have been torn from their context without record. This looting of one of our greatest national – and international – archaeological monuments is nothing short of appalling. It also provides a regrettable distraction from the important work being done by the Portable Antiquities Scheme, which allows responsible metal detectorists who are operating legally to register their finds voluntarily and ensure that we can all share in the knowledge that comes from them.

Proposals for a new tunnel within the Stonehenge World Heritage Site (WHS) have proven more contentious. The most recent public consultation on the proposal to upgrade the A303, which passes uncomfortably close to the celebrated Neolithic monument, closed on 23 April. Plenty of stakeholders have voiced concerns about matters ranging from the course and length of the proposed 2.9km tunnel, its impact on the WHS, the destruction of archaeology both within and beyond the WHS, and even the nature of the consultation process. Other commentators believe that the current proposal improves on the original plan, while doubts have been expressed that a perfect solution to the extraordinary range of issues unleashed by this exercise even exists, let alone is attainable. As the integrity of the major Mesolithic site at Blick Mead is jeopardised by the current proposals, though, it must raise questions about whether improving the setting of one key site is really worth sacrificing others for, especially when this particular problem could be alleviated by lengthening the tunnel. On 5 June, a parliamentary debate was held on the matter.

Another example of archaeologists operating in a less-than-perfect world may be found in the review of the *National Planning Policy Framework*. This document is crucial for embedding archaeology within the planning process, a provision that has been vindicated time and again by discoveries of national and international significance. Yet the text that has emerged from the review process has relegated some key policies to footnotes or glossary entries, prompting the Council for British Archaeology to launch a fundraising appeal for its advocacy work. Any dilution of archaeological investigation during the development process would unquestionably result in important new information about our collective heritage being lost without record.

ARCHITECTURE

John Hitchman

UNITED STATES EMBASSY, VAUXHALL, LONDON
Architect: KieranTimberlake

The designers of the new American Embassy, from whose 2010 competition-winning entry has emerged this imposing 12-storey cube encompassing some 48,000m² of accommodation, have had a number of formidable challenges to overcome before arriving at such an apparently simple architectural form. The building occupies a prominent riverside location midway between Vauxhall Bridge and the enormous phoenix project that is Battersea Power Station. With Eero Saarinen's 1960 embassy in Grosvenor Square becoming increasingly unsuitable and unable to satisfy contemporary security requirements, a move had to be made. The new location provides a site area large enough for a substantial stand-alone structure, surrounded by generous landscaping, hard and soft, which even extends to a water feature resembling a partial moat along one side.

Despite the well-publicised misgivings of the 45th US president regarding the lack of a Mayfair address, the new site does present some advantages over its predecessor: it is closer to the seat of government, with a clear line of sight to the Houses of Parliament and Victoria Tower; there are easily accessible links to public transport, with overground and underground rail connections and buses available close by; and the available site area allows for a sufficiently comprehensive security system to be implemented to meet current standards.

The extent of the immediate landscape setting, which links to other adjacent green areas and public parks forming part of a green corridor joining Vauxhall and Battersea, has permitted the required security arrangements to be subtly integrated into the various treatments of soft planting, ground cover and hard features. The building appears neither too defensive or aggressive at first sight, though of course the approaches to and entrances into the building are carefully orchestrated; visitors are vetted on arrival at one of the three gatehouses placed around the perimeter at a distance from the main building itself. Notwithstanding appearances, the embassy necessarily remains something of a fortress – despite being surrounded by public walkways, it is impossible to get closer than the gatehouse pavilions guarding the east, south and west (landside) approaches.

The cubic form of the building presents its own challenges. As a precise, self-contained, pure geometric form it is not easily adaptable to growth and change. As such it can seem isolated and mechanical, unwelcoming perhaps, but also capable of expressing ideas of solidity, permanence and strength, concepts that may be considered relevant for a building aiming to represent a set of cultural values associated with a nation. The embassy is set out on the site with its elevations facing the four cardinal points, an orientation that has generated, for environmental control reasons, a different treatment for the east, south and west elevations compared with the north, river-facing elevation.

All four elevations employ the same primary envelope: a high-performance, thermally broken, triple-glazed curtain wall system utilising laminated glass, rising from a double-height base of externally expressed tapering columns, though as a result of being tight to the recessed lower-level glazing, these do not for the most part form a true colonnade. The floor-to-floor glazing provides good internal daylighting to the deep-plan offices and is just one component among many setting extremely high standards for energy conservation and sustainability throughout. The repetitive simplicity of the glazed skin is relieved by the inclusion of long silvery finish vertical glass strips inset at intervals and staggered vertically to create a loose weave pattern.

This is only openly visible on the north elevation however as the other three facades of the building are partially concealed behind a sculptural brise-soleil, providing solar shading. The strongly modelled screen of stretched ETFE fabric panels projects clear of the main building face, supported by alternating short and long 'hoops', tubular steel outriggers, with each successive vertical rise displaced by a storey height to generate a strong interlocking diagonal pattern. While veiling much of the internal activities of the embassy from prying eyes, the undulating profiles of the screen provide shade and permit extensive views across London to be enjoyed from within. The fine sculpted finish sets the building apart from its more mundane neighbours (predominantly mainstream high-rise residential buildings).

The one visible disruption to the orderly manifestation of the facades occurs at high level at the north-east corner, where the glazed curtain wall and the solar shading elements are cut away to reveal the underlying structure. The resulting void functions as the ambassador's open-air private terrace and enjoys a wide-ranging view across the city to the parliament buildings and Westminster. For security reasons, not much has been revealed about the internal organisation of the embassy, but the interior does feature six differently themed internal garden areas, functioning as break-out spaces from the office floors, some internal, some external, reflecting the many different landscapes of the North American continent. These double-height spaces are themed around specific climatic zones in the United States: Gulf coast, Midwest prairie, Pacific forest, desert canyons, Potomac river valley and Mid-Atlantic.

Each of the three entry pavilions is designated for a different use: the main entrance for dignitaries, official visitors and staff located on the east side; the consulate entrance to the south for those seeking visas and other consular facilities; and the third to the west for servicing, maintenance and deliveries. The double-height main entrance lobby features a large relief of the United States Great Seal accompanied by the engraved names of previous US ambassadors, while the lobby to the consular section features a more interesting art work in the form of Rachel Whiteread's sculpture titled 'US Embassy (Flat pack house; 2013-1015)'. This is a series of wall-mounted casts of a typical American flat pack timber house, separated into discrete sections to represent a kit of parts, the pair of triangulated gable fronts boldly pointing the way in. The route down to the main event space, at basement level, passes an enormous mural by Mark Bradford, an African-American artist, which makes great play with a multi-coloured smorgasbord of snatched words and quotations.

Throughout the building there has been a concentrated effort on achieving an exemplary level of energy performance and sustainability, with the designers working to environmental target ratings of BREEAM 'Outstanding' and LEED 'Platinum'. Many devices help to achieve this, including roof-mounted photovoltaic panels, harvested water for irrigation and toilet flushing, ground-source heat pumps and onsite combined heat and power generation, as well as the solar control measures provided by the external envelope. The substantial water feature on the north side acts as a balancing pond and regulates site water run-off so as not to overload the local drainage system.

While the substantial construction costs (along with the location) have been castigated by President Trump as representing 'a lousy deal', in fact the development has been completed more or less at no cost to the American taxpayer, with the US$1bn price tag being met by the sale of the former embassy in Grosvenor Square to Qatari developers, who plan a hotel conversion. Completed in January 2018, the new building is a dignified, sober and confident replacement of Saarinen's much admired forerunner and one worthy of a more considered and rational judgement.

V&A DUNDEE, SCOTLAND
Architect: Kengo Kuma and Associates

While the Tate Gallery has become well known for its forays into satellite galleries, such as its Liverpool and St Ives outposts, for the Victoria and Albert (V&A) Museum this very unusual and strikingly modern building will be the first time that it has ventured outside its famous London base in Kensington. Dundee, situated on the north bank of the River Tay estuary on Scotland's east coast, became the first UK city to be designated by UNESCO as a 'City of Design', an award recognising the city's many contributions to the world of design. These cover such diverse areas as computer engineering, groundbreaking medical research and comics

(Dundee has long been home to the firm of DC Thomson, publishers of such treasured items as *The Beano*).

Fittingly this new V&A outpost will function as a museum of design, with exhibitions from around the world as well as permanent galleries of Scottish design, installations by up-and-coming designers and exhibits drawn from the collections of the V&A as well as from museums and private collections in Scotland and worldwide.

As has become the pattern in recent decades, the implementation of a major cultural building has been the catalyst for a city-wide regeneration project. In Dundee it has focused around the riverside and docklands, with the intention of reinvigorating these industrial areas and reintegrating the city with its River Tay frontage, as well as attracting further investment and tourism. Winner of an architectural competition held in 2010, the design by Japanese architect Kengo Kuma originally placed the building entirely in the water, but technical difficulties and inevitable cost consequences resulted in it withdrawing to its present largely land-based but nevertheless prominent quayside location, just dipping its toes in the water (*see* Fig. 1). Sited over the former Earl Grey dock, which was infilled in the 1960s when the Tay Bridge was constructed, the building is highly visible not only from the bridge but as the visual termination of the view from Union Street in the city centre and as a striking stand-alone sculptural object in the wider context of the estuary.

Fig. 1 V&A Dundee (section), **Lead Architect:** Kengo Kuma & Associates, *Partners in charge:* Kengo Kuma, Yuki Ikeguchi, Teppei Fujiwara, **Project Architect:** Maurizio Mucciola, **Delivery Architect:** PiM.studio, **Executive Architect:** James F. Stephen Architects

The sharply angular mass of the museum suggests references to the forms of a couple of ship's hulls, but the main thrust of the design concept takes its inspiration from a rocky cliff face, a common feature of Scotland's north-east coastline, layered with myriad striations of rock and with water lapping at its base. This idea is underpinned with a series of dramatic cantilevered structural wall sections constructed in black reinforced concrete, emphasising the underlying notion of a rocky natural outcrop, its faces jutting out over the river.

The structure is extremely complex, not only because of its waterside location but also arising from the underlying form, which is not too dissimilar from that of two interlinked inverted ziggurats, giving rise to a number of outwardly inclined cantilevered walls. Some of these cantilever out by as much as 19.5m while others curve and twist in section, adding further challenges for the contractors. A temporary coffer dam was required during the early construction stages to keep water away from the part of the site where the building juts out into the river. Linking the two primary elements of the structure together at the upper level enabled the engineers to achieve structural stability, with the roof-level trusses used to tie the building together having the fortuitous benefit of enabling largely column-free space for the main gallery spaces at second-floor level.

The cliff-like striations of the exterior are achieved through the use of rough-textured cast stone planks, suspended via metal fixings from the underlying black concrete walls. Some 2,300 planks were used, in varying lengths up to 4m and weighing up to 2.5 tonnes, each plank having two cast-in metal

hooks to enable it to be fixed in place. A stone aggregate was chosen for its similar colouring to Dundee's local stone; the deliberately rough textured finish gives the building a softer, more organic and natural feel. The gaps left between the planks provide opportunities for long horizontal slot windows to be inserted and also generate a dynamic shadow pattern that changes throughout the day.

The building provides approximately 8,000m² of internal space distributed between the two inverted pyramid elements. The main pedestrian approach takes the visitor into the progressively more confined space between the two stone-clad hull-like forms to reveal a clear view of the river through a triangular gap, much like a natural rock arch. The entrance leads into a double-height foyer space, lit from above by small roof-lights and with a number of small slit-like windows cut into the walls. There is also a waterside cafe and shop together with a multi-purpose area that can be adapted to accommodate shows or concerts.

The first-floor accommodation, linking the two building elements, contains a lounge area and four display galleries. Apart from a regular diet of exhibitions, here it is intended to house Charles Rennie Mackintosh's restored Oak Room (designed for Miss Cranston's Ingram Street tea rooms in 1907, it was subsequently saved and has been held in storage, dismantled, for half a century). There is also an auditorium, a creative learning centre, and staff and back-up facilities. The main galleries at the upper level are linked by bridges and the inclusion of some more open glazed areas, as well as the little slot windows, help to maintain a visual connection with the city and surrounding landscape.

As with many such ambitious projects, final costs (at £80m) came in well above the original estimates, but the client, Dundee Design Limited, an amalgam of Dundee City Council, Scottish Enterprise, Abertay University, the University of Dundee and the V&A Museum, is to be congratulated on seeing the project through to completion. Construction work was completed in January 2018 and the building was handed over to the V&A for the fitting out of the galleries, including a first major exhibition on the subject of 'Ocean Liners: Speed and Style', ready for a public opening on 15 September 2018.

WESTON TOWER AND TRIFORIUM GALLERY, WESTMINSTER ABBEY, LONDON

Architect: Ptolemy Dean Architects (Weston Tower)
Architect/Exhibition designer: MUMA (Triforium Gallery)

The chance to make a significant addition to such an important national icon as the 1,000-year-old Grade I listed Westminster Abbey could justifiably be regarded as a once-in-a-lifetime opportunity and a daunting undertaking for any architect. However, the current Surveyor of the Fabric of the Abbey, Ptolemy Dean, has risen to the challenge with a beautifully crafted and sensitively designed insertion that provides access to the hitherto unexploited attic spaces of the triforium that wrap around the upper levels of the chancel apse at the east end. These have now been transformed by the gallery designer MUMA into a complex sequence of interlinked spaces displaying a selection of the abbey's fascinating collection of historical artefacts. The Queen's Diamond Jubilee Galleries, as they are titled, a £23m project overall, opened to the public on 11 June 2018.

The new tower, approximately 27m in height, has been eased into a tight corner between the Chapter House, the apse and the eastern front of the south transept, rising snugly behind the stone flying buttress to the Chapter House inserted by Gilbert Scott in the 19th century. Accessed from a doorway in Poets' Corner, inside the abbey, the Weston Tower (named after the tower's principal benefactor, the Garfield Weston Foundation) is the first significant external addition to the abbey's fabric since the completion of Nicholas Hawksmoor's western towers in 1745. It contains a central lift shaft around which winds a generous oak staircase. Throughout its height, close-up views of the surrounding medieval architecture are obtained through a decorative glazed screen comprising hundreds of small rectangular leaded panes. From the topmost level of the tower, some six storeys above ground level, entry to the galleries is made via an internal bridge whose windows are enlivened by thousands of fragments of medieval stained glass that were unearthed from the rubble below the old floor before work started and the new floor was put in.

The central lift shaft is constructed of concrete and faced with stone, and is the primary support element for the tower, its mass concrete foundation bedded on the Thorney Island gravel nearly 3m down, as were the abbey's original walls. Its square profile on plan is reflected in the outer glazed screen, but here elaborated using two squares overlaid and rotated to create a star-shaped octagon, a motif that appears elsewhere in the abbey. The external glazed screen follows this outline. In seeking to make the supporting mullions and transoms as slender as possible, the structural frame has been suspended from a radiating arrangement of steel beams placed across the top of the lift shaft. From this structural 'top hat', the loads of the glazed panels are transferred onto vertical suspended steel channels placed at the internal and external apex points of the octagonal plan. Using the steel framing in tension, rather than in compression, has enabled the screen structure to achieve minimal visual impact and maximise the area of glass. The delicate glazed infills comprise hundreds of individual rectangular leaded clear-glass panes that break down the reflections and create an intimate, almost domestic, scale.

Alternate supporting piers are faced with decorative patterned leadwork, featuring narrow strips shaped and laid to create a rising pattern of chevrons contained within sections defined by roll-moulded edges. The lead-cased support piers continue above the topmost glazing to create a faceted solid balustrade around the top of the lift shaft, which is crowned by a short octagonal steeple, also clad in lead, an appropriate termination to the formal composition reflected in the piers and capstones of the abbey's gothic elevations. The evident precision of all this work demonstrates, as one might expect in this special context, a level of commitment and immaculate attention to detail coupled with workmanship of the highest order. A further decorative touch has been added in the form of intertwining bands of metal tracery, winding up the outside of each facet of the glazed envelope in a series of leaf-like shapes – a light-hearted softening of the otherwise orthogonal geometry.

The cladding to the lift shaft provides an interesting visual history lesson in the abbey's use of natural stone over the centuries and features layers of all the different types of stone used. Akin to the strata of an exposed cliff face, though far smoother of course, it starts at the base with Purbeck marble and clunch (11th century). Then follows Caen, Reigate and Purbeck grub (12th century), magnesium limestone (15th century), Burford (17th century), Portland (18th century), Kilkenny marble, Ashburton, Chilmark, Cornish granite (19th century), and finally Portland whitbed, Portland basebed and Clipsham limestone (20th century).

The spaces within the triforium, created when Sir Christopher Wren replaced the then-decaying original roof with a flat one and inserted a floor above the gothic vaults spanning the aisles below, have been artfully converted into a wonderful new gallery, lit by the medieval stone traceried windows set into the bulbous protrusions of the east end as well as offering clear views internally down into the body of the nave. The stunning view now afforded from the central point of the gallery back down the nave once inspired Sir John Betjeman to describe the vista as 'the best in Europe'.

Careful control of daylight and the precise placing of display cases followed a painstaking study of sunlight and shadow patterns cast throughout the year, in order to provide maximum protection for the sometimes fragile and light sensitive treasures on display. The angled struts supporting Wren's roof structure remain visible within the gallery and provide a further level of complexity to the sub-division of space, linking the exposed timber roof beams to the smooth new oak flooring.

Deference to the decorative complexity of the new tower's context has been the driving force in the overall design concept, the detailing and subsequent craftsmanship of an unusual but ultimately successful exercise in 'contemporary Gothic'. Its general visual 'busyness' and natural human scale enables it to blend seamlessly into the architectural tour de force that is Westminster Abbey in a way that a more craven pursuit of total modernity would arguably be unlikely to have achieved. As the architect himself has expressed it: 'sometimes more really is less'.

ROYAL BIRMINGHAM CONSERVATOIRE, JENNENS ROAD, BIRMINGHAM

Architect: Feilden Clegg Bradley Studios

The Royal Birmingham Conservatoire, one of the country's leading music teaching colleges, has moved from its previous location in Birmingham's Paradise Circus to this new site in the Eastside 'Learning Quarter' of Birmingham City University's campus, where a state-of-the-art purpose-built facility for musical teaching and performance has been completed. Developed by Birmingham City University under the leadership of renowned cellist and conductor Julian Lloyd

Webber, the conservatoire features five varied performance spaces alongside some 70 practice studios and ensemble rooms for the college's 600 undergraduate and graduate students, as well as administrative and support facilities including a foyer bar and cafe.

The major performance space is the main concert hall, capable of accommodating an audience of nearly 500 and an orchestra of 120 players in a traditional format. There is also a 150-seat recital hall, designed as a flexible space with retractable seating; an experimental black box 'lab' space; a specially designed 100-seat organ studio and recital room; and the Eastside Jazz Club (this innovation being a first for any conservatoire). The club, naturally enough, has been tucked away at low level and given a 'basement' feel to recreate the typical atmosphere of a city centre jazz venue.

The site is an uncompromising one and with the incessant traffic noise generated by Jennens Road, the dual carriageway city approach running alongside, not one best suited to the acoustic demands of musical performance, study and rehearsal. The architect has responded with a robust architectural treatment involving largely blank brick walls relieved by minimal punched window openings. This conservative treatment almost entirely wraps the building, which consequently reads as a single urban block, tight up to its site boundaries, with angled facades and faceted inflections emphasising its defensive nature, protective of internal delights and subtleties.

Approaching the site from the north, one encounters a sharply angled 'prow' rising some 25m above the pavement. This cutting edge marks the junction between the northern edge of the campus, the 'city' side, and the start of a pedestrian route leading down into the park at the centre of the campus. The building is cut into the slope of the site and the landscaped pedestrian route descends by a storey to the main ground level where, turning the corner, it runs past the new main entrance, one of the few points where the brickwork gives way to a generous expanse of glazing that provides daylight to the foyer spaces.

The foyer rises through three levels and is the organisational hub of the building, spacious and visually interesting with its stairs and balconies wrapping round the tall sunlit space. A wide staircase leads up to the first floor, at which point the internal planning becomes clear. Ahead there is the alternative 'main' entrance from the Jennens Road 'city' side, completing a through route across the building which is open to the public and can be used as a shortcut. To left and right, creating an axis along the length of the building, runs the primary central circulation spine (a feature repeated on all upper floors). The spine performs a key function in separating the principal performance spaces from the noise of the dual carriageway, allowing the practice and rehearsal rooms to be placed along the north side to act as an acoustic barrier and shield the performance spaces along the south side. The foyer extends into a bar and cafe area at ground level, from where access is also available to the recital hall, the experimental lab and the jazz club, all three spaces rising through the ground and first-floor levels. Timber finishes predominate, with walls and ceilings lined with timber fins, which form part of an acoustic treatment that can enable the potentially busy public space to cater for occasional musical offerings.

The main concert hall, located immediately above the recital hall and lab, follows the traditional 'shoe-box' layout, thus occupying a large rectangular volume, and is supported on an independent steel structure to create a 'box within a box' and provide complete acoustic isolation. Accessed from the upper foyer balcony, the interior again features extensive timber acoustic panelling in warm honey-brown tones. The stage is sized to permit full-scale performances by symphony orchestras, so the 500-seat capacity is relatively small by conventional standards and will no doubt offer a full-on

experience for the audience. The hall is a model of restrained design, with ribbed plywood panelling in warm natural tones forming a plinth extending around the base of the walls and giving way at upper levels to tall panels of varying widths with dark brown folded infill panels canting forward and back between slender timber fins. Above the platform, an array of curved plywood panels houses down-lighters and provides additional acoustic control.

The acoustic performance is the key driver of the final visual appearance in all the performance spaces, with various forms of faceting, ribbing, rippling and perforation in the mainly timber finishes used to modulate wall and ceiling surfaces to achieve the required levels of absorption, diffusion or reverberation. The largely introspective nature of the conservatoire is the main reason for the lack of significant fenestration with which to leaven the principal elevations, and the consequent blankness and solidity of the relatively simple brick facades has necessitated some decorative interventions in the brickwork detailing to provide a degree of articulation and texture and so soften the 'urban castle' aesthetic.

Along the Jennens Road frontage, repeated vertical lines created by projecting perpends of alternate courses pick up the edges of the windows to the teaching and practice rooms, expanding at the topmost level into larger rectangular panels, textured in the same way with projecting bricks. Rising above a darker brick plinth band, the soft buff brick facade thus acquires a regular quasi-structural rhythm along its length, though this is in fact unrelated to the internal structural frame.

A similar treatment extends into the campus side of the building, with subtle changes in the treatment of the top levels helping to articulate component elements of the massing. The overall effect is of a sober solidity that might in some quarters be regarded as a bit grim, but the effects are subtle and neatly detailed, resisting the temptation to brashness that could have been deemed appropriate for a 'gateway' building. Construction of the £57m project commenced in 2015 and the college opened its doors to its first students in September 2017. Its sophisticated interiors and state-of-the-art acoustics will no doubt serve them well and do much to boost the already flourishing cultural life of Birmingham.

THE MACALLAN DISTILLERY, SPEYSIDE, SCOTLAND
Architect: Rogers Stirk Harbour + Partners (RSHP)

Whisky has been produced at Macallan's Speyside estate distillery since 1824, with its fine single malt long established as one of Scotland's leading brands. Malt whisky as a product has always been intimately linked with the landscape within which it is created and the 150-hectare Macallan site, along with the 18th-century Easter Elchies House, sits within a designated 'Area of Great Landscape Value'. Following the contemporary trend for superbly designed wineries, as have recently been completed at a number of vineyards in France and Spain, the owners of Macallan sought to introduce high-quality architectural design into the development of their own manufacturing facilities.

To this end, in 2012 a competition was organised with a few invited participants. This was won by RSHP with a design that took much inspiration from the surrounding landscape in an attempt to minimise its visual impact and protect views, while still providing a highly efficient and state-of-the-art production unit with the potential to expand in the future if required. The new combined distillery and visitor centre has been cut into the landscape such that roughly half the building is hidden from most viewpoints. The upper parts are surmounted by an undulating green roof featuring five dome-like grassy mounds, suggestive perhaps of a series of ancient tumuli, sloping gently down towards a chunky undulating fascia that overhangs a continuous glazed screen, recessed behind 'the inclined struts of the steel-framed supporting structure.

While the competition brief called for separate facilities for the distillery and visitor centre, the architect instead chose to combine the two functions, thus opening up the whole production process to the visitor experience. In a further innovation, the layout of the various elements involved in whisky production has been rethought, with the introduction of 'still houses' or individual complete 'cells of production', combining fermentation and distillation vessels in a circular layout, repeatable on a modular basis as a number of pods.

The five undulating mounds reflect the linear layout of the production units below, with pod 1 containing the 'mash house' and pods 2, 3 and 4 containing the modular 'still house' units, each centred under one of the four identical grassy domes. The fifth dome rises higher than the others and marks the location of the visitor centre, which is placed at the end nearest to the estate house. From the house an angled pathway, lined with a high retaining wall clad in black polished concrete, leads directly into the lower level of the visitor centre, passing beneath the lie of the land in a tunnel for the final few yards.

The roof form is a direct reflection of the circular production pods on plan and the grassy mounds in section – the mounds are not built up with soil but are a planted skin following the structural profile. The roof is fully expressed internally and takes the form of a continuous glulam and laminated veneered lumber grid-shell, the undulating ribs visible from one end of the building to the other. As is evident from the outside, the grid-shell structure is raised to a higher level over the visitor centre. The curved top surface of the shell is covered with a final skin comprising thermal insulation and a finishing layer of irrigated growing medium with a pre-grown Scottish wildflower meadow blanket.

Curving and interleaving through the downstand ribs of the grid-shell, dark grey tubular steel structural members pick up the loads of the roof, thence to be transferred via sets of triangulated inclined struts or 'trees' down to ground level. The inclined struts are visible around the perimeter where the loads are transferred directly from the roof edge beam down to solid construction.

The one vertical intervention in the length of the new building is a full-height glazed screen installed to separate the visitor centre from the production pods. This performs as a two-hour fire compartment wall (a requirement given the assessed fire risk from the whisky-making process) and was achieved with the use of double-glazed heat-soaked toughened laminated glass units set within a ground slab bearing intumescent coated steel frame and protected on each side by a drencher system. Being fully clear-glazed, its presence does nothing to inhibit the internal views or minimise the impact of the impressive circular arrays of steel tanks, contrasting with the burnished tones of the handmade copper pot stills raised on high in the centre of each pod.

The visitor centre section retains the circular motif in its planning, with a central drum clad in local granite enclosing winding stairs leading up from the entry level to the main viewing level, from where walkways lead down each side of the central space containing the production pods.

Completed in May 2018, the visitor centre is considered capable of receiving 17,000 people a year, while the layout of production units should render future expansion of the distillery operation relatively simple, though having in the process enabled production to be increased fourfold this is not thought to be likely in the short term. There is no doubt that this superb building sets a new benchmark for the whisky industry, displaying an assured feeling for context and traditional materials without unnecessary showmanship, and one that should attract many more visitors to this beautiful part of Scotland.

AWARDS

THE RIBA STIRLING PRIZE 2017
Hastings Pier; dRMM Architects

The Stirling Shortlist
Barretts Grove (housing), Stoke Newington, London; Groupwork + AminTaha
British Museum World Conservation and Exhibitions Centre, London; Rogers Stirk Harbour + Partners
'Command of the Oceans' visitor centre at Chatham Historic Dockyard, Kent; Baynes and Mitchell Architects
City of Glasgow College – City Campus, Scotland; Reiach and Hall Architects and Michael Laird Architects
Photography Studio for Juergen Teller, West London; 6a Architects

RIBA SPECIAL AWARDS 2018
Royal Gold Medal – Neave Brown

RIBA SPECIAL AWARDS 2017–18
RIBA House of the Year 2017 – Caring Wood (private residence), Kent; James Macdonald Wright and Niall Maxwell
The 2017 Manser Medal – House in Coombe Park (private residence), Kingston, London; Eldridge London (Architects)
The Stephen Lawrence Prize – The Houseboat (private residence), Poole Harbour, Dorset; Meredith Bowles (Mole Architects) and Rebecca Granger

BRITISH CONSTRUCTION INDUSTRY AWARDS 2017
Prime Minister's Better Public Building Award – New Scotland Yard, London; Allford Hall Monaghan Morris
Major Project Award (over £50m) – City of Glasgow College – City Campus; Reiach and Hall Architects and Michael Laird Architects
Building Award (£10m–£50m) – Oriam Sports Performance Centre, Scotland; Reiach and Hall Architects
Small Building Award (up to £10m) – Maggie's at the Robert Parfett Building, Manchester; Foster + Partners
Natural and Cultural Heritage Award – Remembrance Centre at the National Memorial Arboretum, Staffordshire; Glenn Howells Architects
Judges' Special Award – British Airways i360 (observation tower), Brighton; Marks Barfield Architects

RIAS AWARDS 2017
RIAS Andrew Doolan Best Building in Scotland Award – Dunfermline Carnegie Library and Galleries; Richard Murphy Architects

CIVIC TRUST SPECIAL AWARDS 2018
Selwyn Goldsmith Award for Universal Design – National Army Museum, London; BDP with Access Design Consultants
Special Award for Community Impact and Engagement – Storyhouse Cultural Centre, Chester; Bennetts Associates with Ellis Williams
Special Award for Sustainability – Sydney Park Water Re-use Project, Sydney, Australia; Turf Design Studio & Environmental Partnership
AABC Conservation Award – Quay Place (regeneration of St Mary at the Quay), Ipswich; Churches Conservation Trust with Molyneux Kerr Architects
National Panel Special Award – Central European University Phase 1, Budapest, Hungary; O'Donnell + Tuomey with Teampannon

ART

Eddy Frankel

OFF TO MARKET

One story overshadowed all other auction and art market news this year: the record-breaking sale of Leonardo da Vinci's *Salvator Mundi*. The *c.*1500 painting by the most masterful of Old Masters is a portrait of Christ holding a crystal orb in his left hand with his right hand raised in the sign of benediction. It sold at Christie's for a staggering $450.3m on 15 November 2017, in the process becoming the most expensive painting ever sold. The previous record holder was Willem de Kooning's *Interchange,* sold privately in 2015 for approximately $300m. But the most expensive painting sold at auction prior to Salvator Mundi was Pablo Picasso's *Les Femmes d'Alger,* sold at Christie's for $179.4m in 2015. That's a difference of over $270m – a breathtaking figure by anyone's standards.

On the one hand, it is almost understandable. *Salvator Mundi* is one of fewer than 20 known paintings still in existence by the great Leonardo, and apparently the last one in private ownership, so it was not unexpected that it would sell for vast amounts when it did eventually hit the market. But on the other hand, this is not a work without its controversies. For years, the painting was thought to be a copy of a long-lost Leonardo original. Even though most specialists now agree that the work is legitimate, there are still plenty of dissenting voices who remain doubtful. And beyond the disagreements, everyone can agree on one thing: the work has been repeatedly – and badly – restored and overpainted. Whatever is left of the original is very well disguised. After much mystery, it was eventually revealed to have been bought by Prince Badr bin Abdullah bin Mohammed Al Farhan on behalf of the Abu Dhabi Department of Culture and Tourism.

Now, that huge headline sale might give the impression that the auction world, and the art market in general, spent 2018 in rude health, but – as ever – the truth is a lot more complex. This year, the main fears about the economics of art regarded the industry's top-heaviness. Back in 2016, sales of works over $10m fell a massive 53 per cent across the auction market – spread across the British big hitters Sotheby's and Christie's, alongside smaller houses like Bonhams – but 2017 saw sales rise again by 125 per cent, according to the UBS/Art Basel market report. That sounds good, but those major sales account for a huge amount of the total sales, leaving big question marks hovering over the medium and lower ends of the spectrum. According to Rachel Pownall of Maastricht University, global auction sales grew 17 per cent in 2017, but if you take away the *Salvator Mundi,* that figure drops to 14 per cent. That's the impact of a single painting; how sustainable is growth in the top end of the market when the rest of it is left to flounder?

Christie's announced annual revenue of £5.1bn for 2017, a 26 per cent increase over the previous year. The Leonardo painting, however, accounted for an estimated 37.5 per cent of that increase (not the total, just the bounce). The growth of online sales can be partly thanked for the rest of the growth. Sotheby's on the other hand posted $118m net income for 2017, a whopping 60 per cent year-on-year increase, helped largely by a 28 per cent increase in private, rather than auction, sales. In the first quarter of 2018, private sales at the auction house increased 70 per cent year-on-year. Compare that to Christie's, where private sales plummeted, and you start to see the impact of non-auction results. Bonhams meanwhile saw its profits rise in 2017 to £4.8m from £1.9m the previous year, a happy state of affairs that has seen advisory group Rothschild

reportedly brought in to oversee a potential sale of the auction house. Sotheby's also launched its inaugural sales in both Dubai and India this year, opening up two huge new potential markets.

If all of this seems at once positive yet not, or at the very least a little confusing, then that is merely a reflection of the lack of transparency in the art market's financial reporting. Every year we see bad news smuggled through in amongst good news in order to appease investors, and are left wondering what the real state of affairs is. It is not until next year that we will really start to get a good understanding of what happened this year.

There were still plenty of headlines made at auction this year beyond Leonardo though. A record was set for a work by Marc Chagall when *Les Amoureux* (1928) sold for $28.4m in November 2017. Abstract painter Joan Mitchell, at one point the most expensive female artist, had a new artist record set when her *Blueberry* (1969) sold for $16.6m in May 2018. Contemporary artist Kerry James Marshall meanwhile set a record for a living African-American artist when *Past Times* (1997) was bought by rapper Sean Combs for $21.1m in May 2018.

This year saw gender imbalance in the workplace make international headlines, and the auction world was no different. At Bonhams, women were found to earn 37 per cent less than men, while the gap at Christie's was 25 per cent and 22 per cent at Sotheby's; the discrepancy was also echoed in bonus pay, where women at Bonhams got 45 per cent less than men, 40 per cent less at Christie's and 17 per cent less at Sotheby's. The problem is just as bad when it comes to top earners, where only 27 per cent of top quartile earners at Bonhams are women, though Sotheby's and Christie's did better at 48 per cent and 43 per cent respectively. It's worth bearing in mind that the median pay gap across all industries in the UK was 9.7 per cent.

But hanging over the future of the art market – as with the rest of the UK – is the cloud of Brexit. Analysts are (still) clamouring to figure out what the impact of the UK leaving the EU will be on the art world. Barrister Carl Islam, among many others, was keen to point out that Brexit will lead to an increased regulatory burden and transaction costs on all sales of art. Pontus Silfverstolpe of search service Barnebys highlighted that leaving the customs union would drastically impact the way that we currently, and freely, sell and move art around the EU – in a wholly negative way. However, Britain is currently a signatory of the Artist's Resale Right, a levy imposed on sales of art by living or not-long-dead artists, which often pushes buyers to places like New York; leaving the EU would allow Britain to walk away from that agreement, potentially attracting buyers who would normally be scared away by it.

The impact of Brexit is not some faraway thing, either: it is already being felt. A general decline in the global art market in 2016 may have masked the impact of the referendum, but there was nothing of the sort to hide behind this year. While UK art exports dropped 2.2 per cent to £4.8bn in 2017, imports slumped 21 per cent to £1.8bn. A weak pound played a large role in that, but general reluctance in Europe (the UK's most regular art trading partner) to send art and antiques over the channel accounts for the rest. Either way, the potential future impact of Brexit has again left the UK art market fearful for another year.

The big headline to take from all of this is that even if the auction world looks to be doing well, it is so reliant on the top end of the market that its future is shrouded in worrying uncertainty – combine that with the all-encompassing fear of a Brexit future and you have a recipe for serious uneasiness.

PLAYING TO THE GALLERIES

Away from the auction houses, the gallery world had its own year of ups and downs, as ever. At first glance, it all seems more down than up, with galleries closing at a similar rate to previous years. British gallerist David Risley shut his Copenhagen space after writing an impassioned letter calling for more support for artists, while the David Roberts Art Foundation – based in a Camden mews since 2012 – decided to shut up shop to concentrate on putting together a programme that was accessible to the rest of the country, a sort of itinerant gallery project. Supplement Gallery in London's East End, run by the people behind Sunday Art Fair, also closed after ten years. These closures are just a small sample of what is happening on a wider scale to the global commercial art scene, with the UBS report *The Art Market 2018* finding that just 0.9 galleries were being opened for every one that closed (down from five openings for every closure just ten years ago).

There are many reasons why this might be happening, but one of the more obvious – in London at least – is skyrocketing rent. The Fine Art Society, for example, has occupied the same Bond Street townhouse for more than 140 years, helping to launch the careers of John Singer Sargent and James McNeill Whistler in the process. Its rent has risen so much that it feels that its hand has been forced and this year the lease was put up for sale. Coming in the wake of galleries fleeing London's former art hub Cork Street, seemingly en masse, this is a tentative time for the city's more traditional galleries.

But on the other hand, there has been an awful lot of good news, too. Galleries have been opening new spaces or moving to fancier digs like it's going out of style. The movers included Peckham's The Sunday Painter, which moved into the far more accessible environs of Vauxhall; Arebyte, which left achingly hip Hackney Wick for a new development in the Docklands; Arcadia Missa, which also left Peckham but for Soho; and Richard Saltoun Gallery, which took its collection of avant-garde feminist photography from the depths of Fitzrovia to the infinitely more civilised Mayfair. There were plenty of secondary spaces added to established galleries, including Stuart Shave's Modern Art opening a new outpost by taking over the old Wilkinson Gallery building on Vyner Street; Herald St taking over a building near the British Museum; Thomas Dane Gallery opening a space in Naples; and Victoria Miro inaugurating its new Venice gallery. There were some brand new galleries too, including Amanda Wilkinson's new Soho space (after last year's breakup of Wilkinson Gallery, which she ran with her husband) and a clever gallery in the rotunda of Piccadilly Circus station called Soft Opening, open 24 hours a day as a sort of art gallery shop front.

On a more international level, gallerist Vanessa Carlos of London's ultra-hip Carlos/Ishikawa gallery took her Condo scheme to new territories. Condo is essentially an art fair where galleries in one city invite international galleries to show in their space for a month (an exchange programme, if you will). Started in London, it moved to New York last year and this summer had great success in Mexico City.

In non-gallery commercial news, two major art fairs also announced new expansion plans. London's Frieze Art Fair declared that it was expecting to open a new annual fair in Los Angeles to accompany its New York and London fairs, and Masterpiece announced that it too would be trying to break into the American market by next year, after MCH Group bought a majority stake in the company. Downturn? What downturn?

FRIGHT AT THE MUSEUMS

Away from all the commercialism of the mainstream art world, the UK's museums and institutions were rocked by a single topic this year: restitution. It is no secret that the nation's great public galleries are filled with objects and treasures that were acquired in a, shall we say, less than ethical manner. This year, the debate around many of those objects finally started coming to the fore – the focus, however, was not on Nazi loot, but rather on postcolonial repatriation. The Victoria and Albert (V&A) Museum, whose former director Martin Roth died this year at just 62, opened a display of Ethiopian artefacts in April. The treasures – which included a gold crown and a royal wedding dress – were plundered by the British during the 1868 capture of Maqdala in the mountains of what was then Abyssinia. Ethiopia first lodged a restitution claim back in 2007, which was refused, but as the furore around the objects reared its head again this year, museum director Tristram Hunt suggested that the treasures could be returned to Ethiopia on long-term loan.

Though that sounds like a step in the right direction, campaigners fear that it is simply not enough, and that all the objects should be returned to the country that they were taken from, a sentiment echoed by the Ethiopian government. This is not as simple as it sounds, however, as the Maqdala treasures are spread across roughly a dozen UK institutions, including a tablet of the ten commandments said to be hidden in Westminster Abbey.

The V&A's openness to the return of these objects caused ripples in the museum world, as the British Museum was forced to consider giving back its collection of Beninese cast brass plaques, or bronzes, to Nigeria, under pressure from a Nigerian consortium. The opening of a new museum in Benin City seems to promise a safe environment for the storage of the objects, which, like the Maqdala artefacts, were looted during a punitive British military expedition.

These cases show that the impact of colonialism is finally being considered on an institutional level, with important questions being asked – and beginning to be answered – about the provenance of much of what fills our great museums.

Closer to home, the lord mayor of London decided to return a Dutch Old Master painting that was looted from the Netherlands by the Nazis. *The Oyster Meal* by Jacob Ochtervelt was on display at Mansion House, the lord mayor's residence, and was handed over to its original owner's granddaughter in a ceremony in November. There was some almost-reverse restitution news this year too, when it was announced that the Bayeux Tapestry would be loaned back to Britain almost 1,000 years after it was created. The 70m work is currently housed in the Bayeux Museum in France, but will tour the UK in 2022 while the museum undergoes refurbishment.

In more contemporary international museum relations news, the British Museum decided to end its ten-year loan and cooperation deal with Abu Dhabi's new Zayed National Museum two years early, after it became clear that the Emirati institution was nowhere near completing construction. The construction of museum projects in the UK similarly took a hit, when it was found that this year only 17 per cent of major museum projects (that is, those costing over £2m) won grants from the Heritage Lottery Fund, down from over 40 per cent in 2016. This is due to funding dropping from £434m in 2016–17 to £305m in the last financial year, with the figure due to drop to £190m in 2018. The reduction represents a huge blow for UK institutions. There was a further setback thanks to Brexit, as the EU parliament pulled the plug on the UK's bid for European Capital of Culture 2023. Another impact of Brexit wrangling came in the form of seemingly ceaseless cabinet reshuffling, with Jeremy Wright becoming the seventh UK culture minister in just eight years.

There was controversy around the opioid crisis, too. Purdue Pharma, the company which makes OxyContin and which came under huge scrutiny for allegedly helping to make millions of people around the world debilitatingly addicted to the pain medication, is run by the Sackler family. Anyone who has ever set foot in a major UK museum or gallery will be familiar with the name; it graces whole rooms at places like the Royal Academy of Arts, and even an entire building at the Serpentine. Institutions in the UK spent the year being forced to answer questions about whether or not they will continue to accept donations from the family.

More bad press came flooding in when 27 educators who had been employed on a freelance basis by the National Gallery (some for decades) were laid off and subsequently took the museum to an employment tribunal, seeking recognition as employees. The gig economy has developed a particularly bad rap lately, and the art world is clearly not immune. There was some truly devastating news in June 2018 when fire once again consumed the Charles Rennie Mackintosh-designed Glasgow School of Art (the building had already been severely damaged by a blaze in 2014). The damage was extensive and the university considered finally knocking the building down, but in the end it decided to rebuild.

The final bit of discouraging news came when the *Art Newspaper* published its annual attendance figures survey. There was just one UK show in the global top 20 most popular exhibitions in 2017 – and that was 'Painters' Painters' at the Saatchi Gallery, an institution which the *Art Newspaper* believes 'augments' its attendance figures. The top ten most popular museums do not make for happy reading either, with the British Museum dropping two places to fifth (5.8 million visitors) and the National Gallery dropping four places to eighth (5.2 million visitors), though the Tate held firm in sixth place (5.6 million visitors). Not a good year for attendance figures at UK art museums, and bearing in mind that many of these institutions rely on high attendances to ensure government funding, that is grim news indeed.

But there were positive developments too, including the National Gallery buying a Bernardo Bellotto and an Artemisia Gentileschi for its collection. There was also a glut of openings, re-openings and refurbishments. The Royal Academy of Arts celebrated its 250th birthday by finally unveiling its new wing, featuring a new gallery, a huge lecture theatre and its first-ever permanent collection display; the Southbank's brutalist icon the Hayward Gallery opened its doors after a two-year refurbishment with a major show of the work of German photographer Andreas Gursky; Tate St Ives similarly got refurbished and then promptly won Museum of the Year; the V&A opened a brand new wing in London as well as finally inaugurating its Chinese outpost in Shenzhen; south London's Horniman Museum opened a gorgeous new 'world' gallery filled with all sorts of fascinating objects; and Westminster Abbey unveiled a brand new museum of its own, hidden in a secret undercroft. In the future, there are refurbishments of the Royal College of Art and the Courtauld Gallery to look forward to. It's not all doom and gloom.

AND THEN THE ARTISTS

Great controversy arose this year when artist Sonia Boyce removed John William Waterhouse's nude painting *Hylas and the Nymphs* from the walls of Manchester Art Gallery. She did so, in collaboration with the institution, with the aim of fostering debate about how our museums are curated. She wanted discussion, but instead engendered a torrent of hatred and countless column inches dedicated to 'political correctness gone mad' and the dangers of censorship.

The Turner Prize nominees this year met with similar reactions. After Lubaina Himid was announced as the winner of the 2017 prize in December, this year's shortlist was seen as too political, and too right-on, by many in the mainstream commentariat. Nominees were Forensic Architecture, Luke Willis Thompson, Naeem Mohaiemen and Charlotte Prodger. There's a lot of conceptual, heavily political, and not-especially-aesthetic art there, but that might just be an accurate reflection of our times. Other winners this year included Helen Cammock, who won the Max Mara Art Prize for Women; Lis Rhodes, who won the Freelands Award; Idris Khan, who was one of the winners of the 2017 American Architecture Prize for his work on an installation in Abu Dhabi; and Richard Long, who was given a knighthood in the Queen's birthday honours list.

There was sadness too as the abstract painter Gillian Ayres died, as did photorealist artist Malcolm Morley, the photographer David Goldblatt and influential American pop artist Robert Indiana. But, ending on a happier note, there was the unveiling of Gillian Wearing's excellent, and very important, statue of the suffragette Millicent Fawcett. This became the first-ever statue of a woman in Parliament Square, and not before time.

ART CRIME AND PUNISHMENT

Where there is money, there is crime, and there is a lot of money in art. Bath's Museum of East Asian Art was burgled in April, with 48 objects stolen. A police statement said that due to the speed and intensity of the crime, they believe that the objects were stolen to order. Over in Canada, an unidentified work of art by notorious British street artist Banksy was also reportedly stolen from a show put on by his one-time manager Steve Lazarides. Earlier in the year, art dealer Jean-David Cahn was accused of selling looted and stolen antiquities at Frieze Masters art fair in Regent's Park after two vases that once belonged to disgraced, and convicted, Italian art dealer Gianfranco Becchina popped up for sale on his stand. All of the above would lead you to think that a police art and antiques squad would be more necessary than ever, but the Metropolitan Police's unit was disbanded after the Grenfell Tower fire last year and seconded to help with the inquiry. Fortunately, in December it was re-formed and rejigged to try and put a stop to all of the UK's art crime shenanigans.

BUSINESS AND FINANCE

Lisa Carden

THE HIGH STREET: AT A CROSSROADS?

While many of the key issues facing the UK's business community over the past year remain unresolved – the country's future relationship with the European Union (EU) chief among them – one thing is certain: the British high street has taken a battering. Well-known names from a dizzying variety of sectors closed their doors for the last time, while others are retrenching. Maplin, Toys R Us, East and Staples are all no more, while chains ranging from Mothercare to Jamie's Italian, Byron Burger, New Look, Carpetright, House of Fraser, Marks & Spencer and even Waitrose, that barometer of middle-class life, have announced plans to shut branches. The high street has been under considerable pressure for some time, so what has caused so many businesses to fold now? A toxic combination of a weak pound, Brexit-related uncertainty and increased regulatory costs (such as the living wage) and business rates has undoubtedly had an impact, but more broadly it is likely that we are witnessing the sharp edge of a massive shift in consumer behaviour. More people than ever are shopping online – particularly for food, clothing and white goods – where they likely have access to greater choice than is available locally, and where most items can be delivered to their homes or a nearby location the next day.

The record global profits posted by Amazon in February 2018, when the company announced that it had pulled in more than £1.4bn during the previous quarter (boosted by the Thanksgiving and Christmas periods), seem to indicate that the high street's future is in more doubt than ever. So what is the way forward? Mergers could become more common, as large companies seek to enjoy benefits provided by economies of scale. Perhaps one of the more surprising mooted mergers over the past 12 months has been that between Sainsbury's and Asda, which ostensibly cater to very different customer bases. Nonetheless, the bold move – announced in May 2018 – would bring together two businesses with combined sales of £51bn, according to *The Grocer* magazine. At the time of writing there was no proposed finalisation date for the deal, and no details about the fine print (including potential closures), but it is thought that stores would keep their existing branding, allowing them to play to their respective regional strengths. It remains to be seen whether the Sainsbury's/Asda axis will be capable of halting the rise of Lidl and Aldi, both of which had an excellent year. In January 2018, Aldi reported its UK and Ireland annual sales had exceeded £10bn for the first time, though this came after its September 2017 results indicated that profits had fallen for the third successive year. Lidl too reported a strong Christmas 2017, with sales up more than 15 per cent on the previous festive season.

TURNING AROUND OR TAKING OVER?

Not all corporate alignment takes place with the consent of both parties, however, as demonstrated by the £8bn hostile takeover of the Redditch-based engineering company GKN by Melrose Industries. A long-established British business, GKN currently operates in the aerospace and automotive industries, where its customers include Boeing, Airbus and Jaguar Land Rover; some 6,000 of the business's 59,000 employees are based in the UK.

Despite its hitherto successful track record, an unexpected profits warning as a result of difficulties at one of its US plants in November 2017 brought GKN to the attention of Melrose Industries, which specialises in 'turning around' struggling companies – typically by cutting costs – and then selling them on. Amid much queasiness at Melrose Industries' tactics among trade unions, and even in the House of Commons, GKN attempted to fend off Melrose's initial £7bn bid by offering its own shareholders cash and shares, only for Melrose to offer another £1bn.

Calls on the secretary of state for business to step in fell on largely deaf ears, and GKN has been left to its fate. Job losses are likely, as is the sale of assets. The shareholders and hedge funds have no doubt prospered, but one has to wonder at what cost.

CAREERING FORTUNES AT CARILLION

One of the biggest business stories of the year under review concerned a firm whose services many of us use on a daily basis, but not many would have been able to name 12 months ago. In January 2018, it was announced that the UK's second-largest construction company and services provider, Carillion, was going into liquidation, after being felled by a debt of £1.5bn. Carillion had actually been in trouble for some time: according to its own figures, its average net borrowing had rocketed from roughly £100m in 2010 to over £800m in 2017. It is thought that major problems and attendant cost over-runs at three major public-sector building projects had finally caused the wheels to fall off the Carillion bus, but the full ramifications of the company's collapse remain unknown.

In June 2018, the National Audit Office estimated that the cost to the public purse would be £148m, and reported that the government had been seemingly unprepared for the company's demise, so much so that even after Carillion announced a profits warning in July 2017, it was awarded another £1.9bn worth of public-sector contracts, according to a report in *The Independent*. As jobs were lost, school children and hospital patients went unfed, and roads went ungritted, the only party to come out unscathed seemed to be the accountancy firm PwC, which had been tasked with settling claims from Carillion's debtors and pensioners. In March 2018, representatives for PwC told the House of Commons Work and Pensions Committee that they planned to charge more than £20m for their first eight weeks' work alone.

FOOD FOR THOUGHT

While the UK's culinary reputation has waxed and waned over the years, food plays an undeniably large role in the nation's finances. According to the Food and Drink Federation, exports of British food and drink raked in more than £10bn during 2017, with the most popular items ranging from whisky and salmon to cheese, chocolate and gin. Four of the top five markets were within the EU – the other being the United States – but other key international markets included China, the United Arab Emirates and Commonwealth countries.

Industry-wide innovation has had a huge impact on the UK food industry, but what of home cooks? Celebrity chefs, offering their take on everything from traditional fare to the current trend for plant-based eating, are hard to miss, and the UK cookbook market continues to thrive: according to *The Bookseller* magazine, Jamie Oliver sold more than 500,000 copies of just one of his books in 2017 alone, and countless recipes can be found online. Keen cooks are not lacking inspiration, then, but they are short on one major ingredient – time. Bearing that in mind, it may come as no surprise that in March 2018, the 'meal kit' company Gousto raised more than £25m from investors as it set out to expand its business. Meal kits provide recipes and ready-prepared ingredients for customers, so that the more time-consuming aspects of everyday cooking are dealt with for them. And these kits are big business: according to a report in the *Daily Telegraph*, by 2020 the meal kit industry is expected to be worth more than £7bn globally.

The contentious concept of 'clean eating' has pretty much reached its peak now, but there is still an increasing interest in healthier foods and cooking. The data- and information-gathering company Nielsen announced in April 2018 that the demand for health-focused products had risen across Europe, with organic and 'free from' items in the vanguard. In the UK, Holland & Barrett benefited from this trend and in May 2018 announced a growth in like-for-like sales for the ninth year in a row, bucking the prevailing high street trend noted above. For some of us, though, on some days, it looks as though only a takeaway will do: also in May 2018, the online delivery service, Just Eat, announced that it had facilitated more than 400m orders in the UK. Indeed orders from British customers increased by a quarter in the first three months of 2018, to just shy of 30 million, no doubt boosted by Just Eat's recent acquisition of one its closest rivals, Hungryhouse.

PUTTING THE BRAKES ON?
The UK's automotive sector is often a barometer of prevailing national concerns, and to date 2018 has been no exception. Concern at the lack of clarity around the UK's exit from the EU ratcheted up during the spring and summer. In June 2018, Jaguar Land Rover (JLR) announced that it would move production of its popular Land Rover Discovery model from Solihull to Slovakia, potentially affecting hundreds of employees. The pill was sweetened somewhat by the news that the Solihull plant would be upgraded significantly, perhaps with a view to making it a hub for electric vehicle production, and that JLR's Halewood factory would become the new home of the Range Rover Evoque, but nerves were rattled nonetheless: 1,000 job losses across the company's UK holdings had already been announced in April. JLR had cited uncertainty about future trading relations with the EU as one of the catalysts for that decision, and the issue raised its head just a few weeks later in July 2018, when the business stated bluntly that its £80bn five-year plan for its British operations could not be guaranteed in the face of a 'hard' Brexit.

JLR was not alone in its concerns: Airbus and BMW also said that they would have to review their UK options if the eventual Brexit deal had a negative impact on their production processes. Tens of thousands of jobs – 85,000 according to the Society of Motor Manufacturers and Traders – rest on the progress of the British government during its negotiations with the EU. Given that the prime minister accepted the resignations of both the secretary of state for exiting the European Union and the foreign secretary on the same day in early July, the way forward will not be easy.

A LESS THAN HAPPY MEAL
Workers at some of the UK's McDonald's restaurants chose May Day, a traditional day of protest, to rail against a host of workplace grievances, including pay, contracts and union recognition. While they were not the first of their colleagues to raise these issues – staff from branches in Cambridge and Crayford had taken a day's strike action to do the same in September 2017 – their action brought these important issues to the public's attention once more.

While zero-hour contracts are seen by most employers (and some staff) as a flexible way of working – the employer is not obligated to provide a set amount of work, and employees are not obligated to accept it – their inherent lack of security can make life very difficult for low-paid or low-skilled workers, adding to financial stress and hardship. The contracts remain a popular option, however, and their numbers rose by 100,000

in the year to November 2017, according to the Office for National Statistics.

While concern about this way of working is not new, working practices and norms are constantly evolving as traditional 'full-time' jobs do not meet the needs of all and the 'gig' economy continues to gain traction; 2018 has seen several precedents set in how people who are notionally self-employed may actually be classed as employees. For example, in June the London plumbing firm Pimlico Plumbers was on the wrong end of a Supreme Court judgment about when subcontractors were deemed to have gained employment status and associated benefits. The same month, a group of Hermes couriers also established that they were employees at an industrial tribunal, and thus were entitled to the minimum wage and holiday pay, and may also be able to recoup pay that had been deducted due to their former classification.

THE SPECIAL RELATIONSHIP?
The election of President Trump in November 2016 was arguably one of the biggest political shocks of the past 30 years. The president's disdain for traditional diplomacy, lack of appreciation for the merits of 'business as usual' and his enthusiastic use of the social media platform Twitter may play well to his base, but all have caused consternation around the world. Perhaps one of his most dramatic moves during 2018 was the decision to levy a 25 per cent tax on imports of steel and aluminium from producers in the EU, Mexico and Canada; if demand drops for these products – as no doubt Mr Trump was hoping, so that US production would be boosted – jobs across the affected areas would soon be put at risk. According to the industry association UK Steel, 350,000 tones of British steel are exported to the US every year, worth £360m.

The UK steel industry could have done without this blow, as the past few years have been rocky. And some have gone to extraordinary lengths to get around the Trump tariff: in June 2018, for example, a UK firm with steel operations across Europe and Australia reopened a mothballed steel plant owned by the company in South Carolina so that the output would not be affected by the levy. It is impossible to guess which sector the unpredictable president might strike next, but one can only hope that his visit to the UK in July 2018 went some way to softening his stance on this particular issue. Mr Trump aside, there was a glimmer of good news in the merger of the Indian-owned Tata Steel and the German Thyssenkrupp company, creating a pan-European steel giant. It is hoped that the new venture will bring much-needed investment to some of Tata's UK operations, including its plant at Port Talbot.

COPYRIGHT
Copyright is an essential plank of intellectual property protection. It is afforded to the creators of original musical, artistic and literary works and gives them alone the right to benefit financially from their creation. They may assign copyright to other parties if they wish (typically if they are paid to do so), but essentially it is up to them to stipulate how the work may be used – or not.

Copyright usually lasts for 70 years after an artist's death, after which time the work can be used by others without payment. However, many tech companies have found ways to avoid paying artists who are still alive, and in early July 2018 they were let off the hook by none other than the EU. For example, online sites such as YouTube allow users to watch music videos for free, paying the artists who had created the songs a nominal sum – less than $1 annually, in some cases.

Content creators and owners — principally music artists and their record companies – have been lobbying for a change in the rules to force the sites to share their revenues (most of which come from advertising) more equitably, but the EU rejected the proposals, though there was a possibility that this could be discussed again during autumn 2018.

Given the vast wealth enjoyed by some of the music stars who had supported the campaign for change, including Sir Paul McCartney, sympathy for their disappointment will no doubt be thin on the ground. Yet in other creative industries, low-earning artists genuinely are missing out on sums that could make a real difference to their financial circumstances. The Oceans of PDF website, for example, features many full-length books that users can download for free: authors, who have not given permission for their works to appear in this way, receive nothing. According to the UK Authors' Licensing and Collecting Society, there has been a 42 per cent real terms drop in authors' earnings since 2005, and the average income of a professional author in 2017 was just £10,500, so the revenues being lost could make a real difference. At the time of writing, complaints have been made about the site by high-profile writers and the Society of Authors, but it remains up and running. It is a sorry tale.

A BAD YEAR FOR THE BANKS
Few have a good word for bankers these days, and while those in lofty perches in the City usually receive the most opprobrium, the UK's high street banks have not covered themselves in glory this year. During May and June 2018, an IT meltdown with TSB's online banking service caused myriad problems for its customers, ranging from the everyday (not being able to withdraw any cash) to the disastrous (house sales falling through due to transfers not being made). More than 1.9 million customers were affected by what was supposed to be a standard service upgrade, and the subsequent attempts to fix the problem dragged on for weeks. Despite attempts by Paul Pester, the bank's CEO, to assuage fears, the Financial Services Authority (FSA) was singularly unimpressed and announced plans to investigate. Mr Pester promised that he would forego a £2m bonus as a result of the fiasco but, if the FSA fines the bank, that may be the least of his worries.

May was also a cruel month for the Royal Bank of Scotland (RBS), which announced plans to shut over 160 branches in England and Wales during 2018, at a cost of 800 jobs. It was likely that rural branches would be the worst hit. Just six months earlier, in December 2017, RBS said that it would be closing 259 branches – at that time a quarter of its network. While the bank said that customers could bank online instead, they seemingly overlooked the fact that broadband is typically very poor away from towns and cities, and furthermore banks have traditionally played an important role in small communities. While the internet offers us many conveniences and advantages, it cannot replicate human contact, and that is already in short supply for many.

A DISTINCT LACK OF FIZZ
Perhaps one of summer 2018's most unexpected business stories was the saga of the CO_2 shortage. How important could a lack of carbon dioxide really be for the UK economy? Very, as it turned out. Carbon dioxide's wide range of uses takes in everything from animal processing to putting the fizz in fizzy drinks and the bubble in crumpets, as well as prolonging the shelf life of many other foods and beverages, not to mention its role in food transportation, medical procedures and even oil production.

So given how important it is, how did stocks become so low? The gas is produced as a byproduct of ammonia production (for use in fertiliser), and several fertiliser plants closed down by chance at the same time for maintenance once their peak

period was over. Those closures coincided with a period of hot weather and the football World Cup, both of which drove up demand for beer and other drinks. The impact was dramatic: bottling plants struggled to meet demand; supermarkets rationed the sale of fizzy drinks and pub supplies ran dry; and some online grocery services had to temporarily halt the dispatch of frozen goods in customers' orders, as they were unable to keep them cool. The Department for Environment, Food and Rural Affairs seemed disinclined to step in despite requests for assistance from the food industry, but the situation would surely serve as an important lesson for CO_2 producers – and their maintenance teams – in future.

MIND THE GAP
The BBC has found itself rather more uncomfortably in the spotlight than it might like in recent months, as discussions about the gender pay gap forced several unpalatable truths out into the open. For example, Carrie Gracie left her role as the BBC's China editor in December 2017 when she discovered how much less she was paid than her male colleagues in similar roles (some earned over 50 per cent more than her). While the BBC offered her a pay rise, it did not offer her equal pay with her peers, and she returned to a role in the BBC newsroom. In July 2018, the BBC apologised to Ms Gracie, and agreed a financial settlement, which she donated to the Fawcett Society so that it could set up a fund for other women seeking to fight equal pay claims.

Ms Gracie's resignation acted as a catalyst at the BBC and beyond for an unflinching look at the reality of women's pay. That said, the broadcaster had already been in hot water for a good six months before her decision, when it was forced to publish a list of stars who earned more than £150,000: it was staggering to see that the highest-paid man, Radio 2 DJ Chris Evans, earned four times more than the highest-paid woman, the presenter Claudia Winkleman. The disparity even in the same Radio 4 programme was startling: John Humphrys earned more than twice as much as his fellow *Today* programme presenter, Mishal Husain. Another female presenter, Sarah Montague, left *Today* completely upon hearing similar news – in an article in the *Sunday Times,* she described herself as being 'incandescent with rage' at the situation – and moved to the *World at One.*

Statistics released in the Government Equalities Office's Gender Pay Gap report – to which all organisations with more than 250 employees had to contribute – in April 2018 gave much to ponder. More than 10,000 responses were received, across a variety of sectors, and few had good news for their female employees. Only 14 per cent of companies that replied paid women more than men; typically men earned more in terms of both basic pay and bonuses. All sectors had a pay gap in favour of men, although that gap ranges dramatically from almost 25 per cent in construction and 20 per cent in education down to less than 5 per cent in arts and entertainment, health, accommodation and food.

According to the Trades Union Congress (TUC), the current average 18 per cent pay gap between men and women is shrinking each year, but at such a meagre level – just 0.2 per cent annually – that it will take four decades for equal pay to be achieved. What really brings home the imbalance is that women in effect work two months per year for free: the TUC marked the day from which women start to earn as 'Women's Pay Day' on 8 March (to align with International Women's Day). Can we really wait 40 years for the gap to close?

CLASSICAL MUSIC AND OPERA

Leonora Dawson-Bowling

ANNIVERSARIES

Celebrations of the anniversaries of Monteverdi and Telemann continued from the previous year into the 2017–18 season. With 2018 itself came commemorations of the 100th anniversary of Bernstein's birth, the 100th anniversaries of Debussy and Parry's deaths and the 350th anniversary of François Couperin's birth.

The Barbican in particular celebrated Bernstein's anniversary throughout the season with the London Symphony Orchestra (LSO) performing his three symphonies and his musical *Wonderful Town* as well as presenting a Bernstein 'anniversary weekend'. The public were able to learn Bernstein's *Chichester Psalms* in a day of choral singing instructed by LSO choral director Simon Halsey and full performances of the piece were given by three very different ensembles over the season: the Choir of King's College Cambridge with the Britten Sinfonia, the Los Angeles Philharmonic with the London Symphony Chorus, and the BBC Singers (performing the chamber version). The Royal Scottish National Orchestra (RSNO) also presented a two-week Bernstein focus and the Southbank Centre mounted an updated version of his *Mass*, which incorporated the National Youth Orchestra of Great Britain, youth choirs drawn from local boroughs, dancers, street singers, a rock band and a brass band.

The Barbican also featured Debussy in his anniversary year: scholar Roger Nichols presented a day of Debussy's piano music and François-Xavier Roth curated a major survey of Debussy's career through three orchestral concerts, each featuring a different French soloist: Edgar Moreau (cello), Cédric Tiberghien (piano) and Renaud Capuçon (violin). Mirga Gražinytė-Tyla, music director of the City of Birmingham Symphony Orchestra (CBSO), also oversaw a significant Debussy festival which included the first performance by the CBSO of his opera *Pelléas et Mélisande.*

The Barbican's Milton Court also presented an eclectic programme in joint celebration of Couperin and Debussy while Les Talens Lyriques and Christophe Rousset explored Couperin's music more comprehensively at the main venue.

Glyndebourne Tour and the London Sinfonietta both celebrated turning 50, the Philharmonia Chorus turned 60, the BBC National Orchestra of Wales turned 90, the Bournemouth Symphony Orchestra celebrated its 125th anniversary while the RSNO Chorus celebrated an impressive 175 years.

OTHER HIGHLIGHTS

The Academy of Ancient Music continued its Purcell opera exploration with *King Arthur* while a strong thread of Bach ran through the RSNO season. The Barbican celebrated Sir John Eliot Gardiner's 75th birthday, inviting him to curate a Bach weekend which incorporated a three-concert cycle of cantatas performed by the Monteverdi Choir and English Baroque Soloists, as well as performances of Bach motets, violin sonatas, cello suites and the *Goldberg Variations*. The Southbank Centre's International Organ Series also celebrated Bach with new works co-commissioned for the Orgelbüchlein Project, a mission to complete Bach's set of organ miniatures. And Bach's music, along with that of his sons and other composers whose work he influenced, were at the centre of the Royal Northern Sinfonia's 'At Home' series.

The Royal Northern Sinfonia also performed its first complete cycle of Mendelssohn symphonies. Wigmore Hall mounted a 17-concert survey of Haydn string quartets as well

as a complete cycle of Beethoven's quartets, the latter performed entirely by Cuarteto Casals. Beethoven also featured in symphonic form as the BBC National Orchestra of Wales commenced a two-year Beethoven symphony cycle under the direction of Xian Zhang and the Britten Sinfonia under Thomas Adès completed theirs, juxtaposed with music by Gerald Barry. Beethoven alongside Brahms was also a central focus for the Bournemouth Symphony Orchestra. The RSNO under Thomas Søndergård explored German Romanticism, continuing its exploration of the worlds of Brahms and Richard Strauss, and commenced a two-year Schumann symphonic cycle with Sir Roger Norrington.

The Bournemouth Symphony Orchestra under Kirill Karabits presented the great symphonies of Schumann, Bruckner and Mahler while the Philharmonia and Esa-Pekka Salonen performed large-scale works including Mahler's third and ninth symphonies and Schoenberg's *Gurrelieder*. The BBC Scottish Symphony Orchestra's 'Composer Roots' series, programmed by Thomas Dausgaard, explored influences on the music of Beethoven, Rachmaninov, Bartók, Nielsen and Sibelius. The London Philharmonic Orchestra and Vladimir Jurowski began their first ever Wagner *Ring Cycle* with a gala concert performance of *Das Rheingold* while the Hallé completed its *Ring Cycle* with *Siegfried.*

Brahms and Wagner also featured in the Scottish Chamber Orchestra's season as Robin Ticciati put Antonín Dvořák at the core, investigating his religious beliefs and his relationship with these two composers and the world of folksong, as well as his eventual journey to the 'New World' and the revelation of native melodies.

The Royal Liverpool Philharmonic's 'From the New World' thread also featured music by European composers who emigrated to America to safeguard themselves and their creative output or who were influenced by America, alongside works by American composers. Similarly, the RSNO featured American artists and composers including works by Jennifer Higdon, John Adams, Copland, Barber, Gershwin and Bernstein.

One hundred years on, multiple concerts marking the Russian Revolution were given by the Philharmonia under Vladimir Ashkenazy, exploring the impact of the revolution on Russian composers and music, and by the BBC National Orchestra of Wales. Welsh National Opera also had a 'Russian Revolution' seam running though its autumn season with performances of Tchaikovsky's *Eugene Onegin* and Mussorgsky's *Khovanshchina*, and the premiere of a new edition of Janáček's *From the House of the Dead*. Russian composers also featured more broadly with the Bournemouth Symphony Orchestra focusing on Tchaikovsky in the context of his contemporaries, including Glinka and the less familiar Kalinnikov. And the Hallé's Russian season presented works within the context of personal and wider cultural associations by Stravinsky, Mussorgsky, Rimsky-Korsakov, Tchaikovsky, Rachmaninov as well as three Shostakovich symphonies, created in the heat of controversy and against a background of great personal danger. Scottish Opera's 'Opera in Concert' series also presented four concerts featuring rarely performed Russian operas, including the Scottish premiere of Rachmaninov's *Francesca da Rimini*. Throughout 2018, Vladimir Jurowski and the London Philharmonic Orchestra's 22-concert 'Changing Faces: Stravinsky's Journey' series celebrated the life and works of Igor Stravinsky, alongside his predecessors and contemporaries.

Both the BBC Symphony Orchestra (BBCSO) under Sakari Oramo and the Philharmonia under Esa-Pekka Salonen marked the centenary of Finnish independence with concerts featuring Finnish composers, particularly Sibelius, the BBCSO mounting his full symphony cycle. A rare performance of Sibelius' choral symphony *Kullervo* was also given by the BBC Scottish Symphony Orchestra while the Southbank Centre's 'Nordic Matters' project, featuring the Philharmonia also under Salonen, explored Nordic arts and culture.

The BBC National Orchestra of Wales and Bournemouth Symphony Orchestra both featured the music of Elgar, the latter also focusing on Walton, while the BBC Scottish Symphony Orchestra concluded its Tippett symphony cycle with the first professional performance of the composer's withdrawn *Symphony in B-flat*. The Scottish Chamber Orchestra premiered works by Scottish composers Sir James MacMillan and Tom Harrold, and the BBC Scottish Chamber Orchestra's 'Scottish Inspirations' project commissioned and performed works by Anna Clyne and William Sweeney, which were inspired by Scottish culture.

Sage Gateshead introduced a new series of solo piano recitals, 'Piano Greats', which Lars Vogt opened with his highly acclaimed *Goldberg Variations*, alongside performances by Imogen Cooper, Anna Fedorova and Peter Donohoe. The Royal Liverpool Philharmonic Orchestra presented 'The Art of the Piano', which explored the huge range of musical styles inspired by the 'world's favourite instrument'. The London Philharmonic Orchestra turned its attentions to choral music with eight concerts showcasing the London Philharmonic Choir in Bach's *Christmas Oratorio*, Rossini's *Stabat Mater* and many works by Stravinsky.

Indian classical music was a major focus for the Southbank Centre with its Darbar Festival, the biggest celebration of Indian classical music outside south Asia, returning for its 12th edition, and also for the Barbican and Milton Court which also hosted an Indian classical music celebration.

Also at the Southbank, the year-long 'Belief and Beyond Belief' festival exploring what it means to be human in the 21st century, featuring the London Philharmonic Orchestra and Vladimir Jurowski, continued with focuses on 'Judgement', 'War and Peace' and 'Rituals and Seasons'. The Orchestra of the Age of Enlightenment started the first of six seasons examining the Enlightenment – the age of radical developments in science, arts and philosophy from which the group took its name. Its first season looked at the notions of 'Visions, Illusions and Delusions', exploring ambiguity and certainty, curiosity and doubt, asking questions related to these themes and presenting different works of music that might provide an answer.

There was also a nod to the centenary of the first (partial) women's suffrage bill of 1918 with Welsh National Opera's *Rhondda Rips It Up!*, composed by Elena Langer to a libretto by Emma Jenkins, telling the story of the Welsh suffragette Margaret Haig Thomas. And Helen Grime, working closely with Wigmore Hall's pioneering learning department, wrote a new song cycle based on the experience of motherhood, from conception and giving birth to the developing relationship between mother and child, which was performed by mezzo-soprano Ruby Hughes and pianist Joseph Middleton.

The Aurora Orchestra and conductor Nicholas Collon were at the heart of the Southbank's 'Ligeti in Wonderland' festival devoted to the Hungarian-Austrian composer's work, curated by artist-in-residence Pierre-Laurent Aimard, while the Philharmonia performed works from the 'Music of Today' project, curated by South Korean composer Unsuk Chin. Similarly, almost half of the concerts in the BBC Philharmonic season contained new music with Rodion Shchedrin's *Dialogues with Shostakovich*, George Walker's *Lilacs*, Anna Clyne's *This Midnight Hour* and Wolfgang Rihm's horn concerto among the

featured UK premieres, and world premieres including Mark Simpson's cello concerto and Arlene Sierra's *Nature Symphony*.

The season also witnessed the launch of the 'Composers' Collective' at the Southbank, an initiative to help composers at the start of their careers, in partnership with the Southbank Centre's resident ensembles and artists. It was also the first full year of the London Philharmonic Orchestra's 'Junior Artists', an 'orchestral experience' programme for talented musicians aged 15–19 from communities and backgrounds currently under-represented in professional UK orchestras. The Bournemouth Symphony Orchestra also initiated its 'Change Makers' project which helped James Rose, a conductor with disabilities, to accelerate his development and create, curate and direct BSO Resound, a professional ensemble made up of disabled musicians.

The major ensembles all continued to develop new ways to reach out to diverse audiences. New initiatives included Sir Simon Rattle and the London Symphony Orchestra offering one-hour 'Half Six Fix' concerts for time-poor music-lovers to fit in at the end of their busy working day. Similarly, Opera North's 'Little Greats' showcase paired two short operas per evening, each with tickets sold separately, leaving audience members free to choose whether to opt for a bite-sized musical evening or to attend both. Scottish Opera meanwhile brought back composer Lliam Paterson's opera for babies, *BambinO*, after its warm reception at several summer festivals. The opera aimed to reinvent operatic language for children while their minds are wide open to new sounds and experiences. The City of Birmingham Symphony Orchestra planned 28 concerts designed for younger audience members as well as performing 'pop-up' concerts around Birmingham at venues such as New Street station. As part of its 'Nordic Matters' series, the Philharmonia's virtual reality presentation '360 Experience' returned to the Southbank, enabling the public, through earphones and a headset, to experience being in the heart of the orchestra performing Sibelius' *Symphony No. 5*. Public participation was also very much at the centre of several new commissions which formed part of 'LS Open', a new festival launched by the London Sinfonietta and Contemporary Music for All. The London Sinfonietta 'RSVP' project also encouraged the public to submit their own pieces sent from anywhere in the world from which the orchestra would pick a selection to play, the only stipulation being that they had to fit onto the back of a postcard. And the Royal Opera collaborated with the Victoria and Albert Museum to bring the public an exhibition covering almost 400 years of operatic history: 'Opera: Passion, Power and Politics'.

FESTIVALS

Among its usual broad and rich offerings, the 2017 BBC Proms celebrated the 70th and 80th birthdays respectively of American composers John Adams and Philip Glass, the first and last night both featuring works by Adams. The 'Proms At...' series returned, matching music to suitable venues, this year travelling beyond London to Stage@TheDock in Hull for a concert inspired by the 300th anniversary of Handel's *Water Music* as well as performances of choral music at Southwark Cathedral and experimental music at the Tanks at Tate Modern among others. The festival also hosted its first-ever 'Relaxed Prom', offering an informal environment for people with autism, sensory and communication impairments and learning disabilities or those hard of hearing, blind or partially sighted. The Proms paid tribute to its former conductor Sir Malcolm Sargent with a recreation of his 500th Prom concert and the John Wilson Orchestra presented Rodgers and Hammerstein's *Oklahoma!* There was also plenty of new music, with 16 world premieres and 14 European premieres.

Opera was at the heart of the 70th Edinburgh International Festival with Verdi's *Macbeth* programmed in recognition of its being the very first opera performed at the inaugural Edinburgh International Festival of 1947. Wagner's *Die Walküre* continued the festival's *Ring Cycle* from the previous year (with the RSNO) and Monteverdi's three surviving operas, *L'Orfeo, Il ritorno d'Ulisse in patria* and *L'incoronazione di Poppea,* were presented in semi-staged performances by Sir John Eliot Gardiner, the Monteverdi Choir and English Baroque Soloists. There were productions of Mark-Anthony Turnage's *Greek* and Puccini's *La bohème* as well as Britten's *Peter Grimes* in concert. There was also a wealth of concert performances from 13 world-class orchestras as well as recitals from performers including pianist Mitsuko Uchida, violinist Joshua Bell and bass-baritone Bryn Terfel with pianist Malcolm Martineau.

In November 2017, the 40th Huddersfield Contemporary Music Festival reflected somewhat on its history and its shift from primarily focusing on contemporary music composed and written down in classical notation to now being centred on non-traditional concert spaces, multimedia, installations, performance art, electronica, improvisation and more experimental work. The London Sinfonietta looked back with performances of its own past commissions, Iannis Xenakis' *Thallein* (1984) and Sir Harrison Birtwistle's *Silbury Air* (1977). Another strand of the festival was realisations and reconstructions, with Berlin's zeitkratzer ensemble performing acoustic arrangements of early Kraftwerk tracks and joining French group Ensemble 2e2m for its realisation of Lou Reed's *Metal Machine Music* (1975). Other highlights included a brand new work, *Tanz/haus: triptych 2017,* by Scottish composer James Dillon; the UK premiere of a major cycle, *Umbrations* by Brian Ferneyhough; and a focus on key works by two important contemporary music figures – the late Pauline Oliveros and American-Canadian composer Linda Catlin Smith.

In June 2018, the Aldeburgh Festival celebrated its 70th year, a key strand being 'The Spirit of 1948' which reflected on the post-war period and the launch of a new cultural life. Another strand was 'Britten in America', which also tied in with Bernstein's centenary and explored the connection between the two composers. The festival was curated by artists-in-residence violinist Patricia Kopatchinskaja, conductor John Wilson and flautist Claire Chase. Programmes included: a Varèse-inspired recital with his own *Density 21.5* and *Poème électronique;* the premiere of Emily Howard's opera *To See the Invisible;* works by Bartók, Stravinsky and Ligeti in a programme considering the boundary between fable and reality, memory and modernity, virtuosity and expression; and two concerts exploring Britten's wartime experiences in America through Colin Matthews' orchestration of Britten's *Seven Sonnets of Michelangelo, Four Sea Interludes* and *Diversions,* Bernstein's *Halil* and Copland's *Billy the Kid.*

The summer of 2018 also saw Garsington Opera present the world premiere of *The Skating Rink* by British composer David Sawyer alongside productions of Verdi's *Falstaff,* Strauss' *Capriccio* and Mozart's *Die Zauberflöte.* Longborough Festival Opera's offering comprised Wagner's *Der fliegende Holländer,* Verdi's *La traviata,* Strauss' *Ariadne auf Naxos* and Monteverdi's *L'incoronazione di Poppea.* Grange Park Opera staged Rodgers and Hammerstein's *Oklahoma!,* Gounod's *Roméo et Juliette* and Verdi's *Un ballo in maschera.* And the Grange Festival mounted productions of Handel's *Agrippina,* Rossini's *The Barber of Seville,* Mozart's *The Abduction from the Seraglio* (in English) and a concert performance of Bernstein's *Candide.*

Candide was also performed at the 74th Cheltenham Music Festival as were *Juliana,* a new chamber opera by Joseph Phibbs, and a retelling of *Hansel and Gretel* by Matthew Kaner. The festival included 20 world premieres and there was a strong choral thread with performances from the King's Singers, the choirs of Keble College Oxford and King's College Cambridge with works by Dupré, Fauré, Duruflé, Berlioz and

various psalm settings. A four-concert series paid tribute to Bach's favoured coffee house, Café Zimmermann, with his music performed alongside that of Buxtehude, Albinoni and Erlebach. Other highlights included the BBC National Orchestra of Wales and Martyn Brabbins' three-day residency which encompassed work by Brahms, Mendelssohn and Elgar; the Hallé performing Elgar's first symphony with Strauss and Mozart songs sung by Louise Alder; and a programme of English song by Dame Sarah Connolly.

The same month, the Buxton Festival staged Verdi's *Alzira,* Mozart's *Idomeneo,* a modern update of Donizetti's *The Daughter of the Regiment* and a concert staging of Brescianello's *Tisbe.* The festival also included an evening of music from operettas, classic musicals and cabaret, hosted by soprano Lesley Garrett, as well as a wealth of performances including those by pianists Christian Blackshaw, Joanna MacGregor and Stephen Kovacevich, flautist Ashley Solomon, local violinist Lizzie Ball, the Fitzwilliam and Consone Quartets, and the Fibonacci Sequence chamber ensemble.

OBITUARIES

Jóhann Jóhannsson, the Icelandic composer renowned for blending classical orchestrations with electronic music to create some of the most acclaimed film soundtracks (including *The Theory of Everything*), died aged 48. Siberian baritone Dmitri Hvorostovsky, known for his Verdi and his portrayals of Eugene Onegin, died aged 55. Caroline Brown, cellist and founder of the Hanover Band (which performed Beethoven's music on 19th-century instruments and recorded his complete symphonies as well as works by Schubert, Schumann, Bach and Weber), passed away aged 64.

Enoch zu Guttenberg, the German conductor of great international repute, died at the age of 71. Derek Bourgeois, English composer and former director of the National Youth Orchestra who wrote 115 symphonies, died aged 75. John Maxwell Geddes, a composer much influenced by the dramatic mountains and seascapes of his native Scotland and with a keen interest in music education, passed away aged 76. Jesús López Cobos, the Spanish conductor with a career that included Deutsche Oper Berlin, Teatro Real Madrid and 15 years with the Cincinnati Symphony Orchestra, died aged 78. José Abreu, Venezuelan conductor and founder of the El Sistema music education programme (which aimed to help impoverished children through music and led to the creation of the Simón Bolívar Symphony Orchestra), died also aged 78.

Michael Tree, violist, violinist and founder member of the Marlboro Trio and Guarneri Quartet, the latter famous for recordings of Bartók and Beethoven string quartets, died aged 84. Gennady Rozhdestvensky, the Russian conductor affectionately known to colleagues as 'Noddy', who managed to work either side of the Iron Curtain and championed the music of both Britain and Russia, died aged 87. Simonetta Puccini, the granddaughter and only known remaining descendant of Puccini, and co-founder of the Institute for Puccini Studies, died aged 89. Wanda Wiłkomirska, Polish violinist and regular soloist with the Warsaw Philharmonic Orchestra who formed the Wiłkomirska Trio with her brother and sister, and later defected from Poland, died aged 89. Composer Pierre Henry, who helped pioneer experimental electronic music, and Barbara Cook, Broadway soprano who premiered several lead roles including Cunégonde in Bernstein's *Candide,* also both passed away aged 89.

Piet Kee, Dutch organist and composer who won first prize at the Haarlem International Competition three years in a row and recorded extensively for Chandos, particularly Baroque organ music, died aged 90. Zuzana Růžičková, the Czech harpsichordist who promoted and recorded Bach's complete keyboard works, also died aged 90. Walter Levin, violinist and founder of the LaSalle Quartet (praised for their Romantic repertoire and champions of the Second Viennese School, recording the complete quartets of Schoenberg, Berg and Webern), passed away aged 92. Robert Mann, violinist and founder of the Juilliard String Quartet, died aged 97.

NEW APPOINTMENTS AND HONOURS

At the start of the 2017–18 season, Sir Simon Rattle took up his much-anticipated role of music director of the London Symphony Orchestra. The BBC Philharmonic's incumbent principal guest conductor John Storgårds graduated to chief guest conductor and Ben Gernon was appointed principal guest conductor. Bramwell Tovey also started his tenure as the BBC Concert Orchestra's principal conductor, and Jakub Hrůša and Santtu-Matias Rouvali were appointed principal guest conductors of the Philharmonia, a post last held by Sir Charles Mackerras until his death in 2010. The BBC Singers appointed Sofi Jeannin as the new chief conductor and the Bournemouth Symphony Orchestra announced Marta Gardolińska as the new BSO Leverhulme young conductor-in-association.

Esa-Pekka Salonen, principal conductor and artistic advisor to the Philharmonia Orchestra, Joshua Bell, music director of the Academy of St Martin in the Fields, and Thomas Dausgaard, chief conductor of the BBC Scottish Symphony Orchestra, all also extended their contracts.

Meanwhile Charles Dutoit, who was originally intended to retire from his positions as artistic director and principal conductor of the Royal Philharmonic Orchestra (RPO) in October 2019 and to be made honorary conductor for life, stepped down early amid allegations of sexual impropriety, a case echoed by James Levine's departure under similar circumstances from the New York Metropolitan Opera. Vasily Petrenko was subsequently announced as the RPO's new music director, a broad role that incorporates Dutoit's former position, beginning his tenure in the 2021–22 season.

Edmund Hunt was named as Wigmore Hall's apprentice composer 2018, the BBC Concert Orchestra announced the appointment of Dobrinka Tabakova as the new composer-in-residence and Alexander Campkin was appointed as the Bournemouth Symphony Orchestra 'Change Makers' composer-in-residence. The English National Opera (ENO) and Grange Park Opera entered into a new collaboration which would see the ENO orchestra playing for most of the festival's opera productions.

In the New Year's and Queen's Birthday Honours, soprano Dame Kiri Te Kanawa was made a member of the order of companions of honour, a prestigious order that only includes 65 people at any time. Baritone Simon Keenlyside was given a knighthood while Jonathan Freeman-Attwood, principal of the Royal Academy of Music, Gillian Moore, director of music at Southbank Centre and composers Thomas Adès and Debbie Wiseman were all made CBEs. MBEs were awarded to violinist Anthony Marwood, Crouch End Festival Chorus director David Temple, London Community Gospel Choir founder Bazil Meade, the Royal Philharmonic Society's outgoing executive director Rosemary Johnson, and Susanna Eastburn and Barry Farrimond, the chief executives respectively of Sound and Music (a charity for new music) and OpenUp Music (a charity that aims to make orchestras more accessible to young disabled musicians). OBEs were awarded to Sarah Alexander, chief executive and artistic director of the National Youth Orchestra, and mezzo-soprano Alice Coote.

COMPETITIONS

At the Wigmore Hall/Kohn Foundation International Song Competition in September 2017, first prize was awarded to baritone Julien Van Mellaerts while second and third prizes went to baritones John Brancy and Josh Quinn, and the pianist's prize was awarded to Ian Tindale.

In April 2018, the Handel Singing Competition was won by mezzo-soprano Helen Charlston while soprano Lauren Lodge-Campbell claimed both the second prize and audience prize.

The same month, the Wigmore Hall International String Quartet Competition was won by the Esmé Quartet with second prize going to the Goldmund Quartett and third prize going to the Viano String Quartet.

Also the same month at Wigmore Hall, bass William Thomas won first prize at the Kathleen Ferrier Awards with second prize going to soprano Josephine Goddard. The song prize was awarded to soprano Catriona Hewitson and the accompanist's prize to Michael Pandya.

In its 40th anniversary year, the BBC Young Musician competition was won by 16-year-old pianist Lauren Zhang who beat cellist Maxim Calver and saxophonist Rob Burton in the final.

OPERA PRODUCTIONS

The list below summarises each opera company's activities and the date in parentheses indicates the year that the current production entered their repertoire.

ROYAL OPERA
Founded 1946
W www.roh.org.uk

REPERTORY: *Les Vêpres siciliennes* (2013), *Cavalleria rusticana/ Pagliacci* (2015), *Lucia di Lammermoor* (2016), *4.48 Psychosis* (2016)

NEW PRODUCTIONS: *La bohème* (Puccini). Conductor, Antonio Pappano; director, Richard Jones. Nicole Car (Mimì), Michael Fabiano (Rodolfo), Mariusz Kwiecień (Marcello), Simona Mihai (Musetta), Florian Sempey (Schaunard), Luca Tittoto (Colline), Jeremy White (Benoît), Wyn Pencarreg (Alcindoro)
Semiramide (Rossini). Conductor, Antonio Pappano; director, David Alden. Joyce DiDonato (Semiramide), Michele Pertusi/ Mirco Palazzi (Assur), Daniela Barcellona (Arsace), Lawrence Brownlee (Idreno), Jacquelyn Stucker (Azema), Bálint Szabó (Oroe), Konu Kim (Mitrane), Simon Shibambu (Nino's Ghost)
Lohengrin (Wagner). Conductor, Andris Nelsons; director, David Alden. Klaus Florian Vogt (Lohengrin), Jennifer Davis (Elsa), Christine Goerke (Ortrud), Thomas J. Mayer (Friedrich von Telramund), Georg Zeppenfeld (Heinrich I), Kostas Smoriginas (Herald)
Carmen (Bizet). Conductor, Jakub Hrůša; director, Barrie Kosky. Anna Goryachova (Carmen), Francesco Meli (Don José), Kostas Smoriginas (Escamillo), Kristina Mkhitaryan (Micaëla), David Soar (Zuniga), Jacquelyn Stucker (Frasquita), Aigul Akhmetshina (Mercédès), Pierre Doyen (Dancaïre), Jean-Paul Fouchécourt (Remendado), Gyula Nagy (Moralès)
From the House of the Dead (Janáček). Conductor, Mark Wigglesworth; director, Krzysztof Warlikowski. Willard W. White (Alexandr Gorjančikov), Pascal Charbonneau (Aljeja), Štefan Margita (Luka Kuzmič), Ladislav Elgr (Skuratov), Johan Reuter (Šiškov/Priest), Alexander Vassiliev (Prison Governor), Nicky Spence (Big Prisoner/Nikita), Grant Doyle (Small Prisoner/Cook), Graham Clark (Elderly Prisoner), Konu Kim (Voice), Jeffrey Lloyd-Roberts (Drunk Prisoner), Peter Hoare (Šapkin), John Graham-Hall (Prisoner/Kedril), Aleš Jenis (Prisoner/Don Juan/Brahmin)

WORLD PREMIERES: *Lessons in Love and Violence* (George Benjamin). Conductor, George Benjamin; director, Katie Mitchell. Stéphane Degout (King), Barbara Hannigan (Isabel), Gyula Orendt (Gaveston/Stranger), Peter Hoare (Mortimer), Samuel Boden (Boy/Young King), Ocean Barrington-Cook (Girl), Jennifer France (Witness 1/Singer 1/Woman 1),

Krisztina Szabó (Witness 2/Singer 2/Woman 2), Andri Björn Róbertsson (Witness 3/Madman) *L'ange de Nisida* (Donizetti) – concert performance. Conductor, Mark Elder. Joyce El-Khoury (Sylvia), David Junghoon Kim (Leone de Casaldi), Vito Priante (King Fernand of Naples), Laurent Naouri (Don Gaspar), Evgeny Stavinsky (Monk)

ENGLISH NATIONAL OPERA
Founded 1931
W www.eno.org

REPERTORY: *The Barber of Seville* (1987), *A Midsummer Night's Dream* (1995), *Satyagraha* (2007), *The Marriage of Figaro* (2011), *Rodelinda* (2014)

NEW PRODUCTIONS: *Aida* (Verdi). Conductor, Keri-Lynn Wilson/Christian Baldini; director, Phelim McDermott. Latonia Moore/Gweneth-Ann Rand (Aida), Gwyn Hughes Jones (Radamès), Michelle DeYoung/Dana Beth Miller (Amneris), Musa Ngqungwana (Amonasro), Brindley Sherratt/Robert Winslade Anderson (Ramfis), Matthew Best (King), Eleanor Dennis (High Priestess)
Iolanthe (Gilbert and Sullivan). Conductor, Timothy Henty/Chris Hopkins; director, Cal McCrystal. Samantha Price (Iolanthe), Ellie Laugharne (Phyllis), Yvonne Howard (Queen of the Fairies), Andrew Shore (Lord Chancellor), Marcus Farnsworth (Strephon), Ben McAteer (Earl Mountararat), Ben Johnson (Earl Tolloller)
La traviata (Verdi). Conductor: Leo McFall/Toby Purser; director, Daniel Kramer. Claudia Boyle (Violetta), Lukhanyo Moyake (Alfredo Germont), Alan Opie (Giorgio Germont), Heather Shipp (Flora Bervoix), Aled Hall (Gastone, Vicomtede Letorieres), Benjamin Bevan (Baron Douphol), Božidar Smiljanić (Marchese d'Obigny), Henry Waddington (Dr Grenvil), Martha Jones (Annina)

WORLD PREMIERE: *Marnie* (Nico Muhly). Conductor, Martyn Brabbins; director, Michael Mayer. Sasha Cooke (Marnie), Daniel Okulitch (Mark Rutland), James Laing (Terry), Diana Montague (Lucy), Alasdair Elliott (Mr Strutt), Kathleen Wilkinson (Marnie's Mother), Eleanor Dennis (Laura Fleet), Lesley Garrett (Mrs Rutland), Matthew Durkan (Malcolm Fleet), Darren Jeffery (Dr Roman)

OPERA NORTH
Founded 1978
W www.operanorth.co.uk

REPERTORY: *Madama Butterfly* (2007), *Don Giovanni* (2012)

NEW PRODUCTIONS ('LITTLE GREATS' SERIES): *Pagliacci* (Leoncavallo). Conductor, Tobias Ringborg; director, Charles Edwards. Elin Pritchard (Nedda), Peter Auty (Canio), Richard Burkhard (Tonio), Joseph Shovelton (Beppe), Phillip Rhodes (Silvio)
L'enfant et les sortilèges (Ravel). Conductor, Martin Andre; director, Annabel Arden. Wallis Giunta (The Child), Ann Taylor (His Mother/Chinese Cup/Squirrel), Fflur Wyn (Fire/Nightingale/Princess), Quirijn de Lang (Grandfather Clock/Tom Cat), John Savournin (Armchair/Tree), John Graham-Hall (Tea Pot/Tree Frog/Arithmetic), Katie Bray (Louis XV Chair/Female Cat/Owl)
Cavalleria rusticana (Mascagni). Conductor, Tobias Ringborg; director, Karolina Sofulak. Giselle Allen (Santuzza), Katie Bray (Lola), Jonathan Stoughton (Turiddù), Phillip Rhodes (Alfio), Rosalind Plowright (Mamma Lucia)
Trial by Jury (Gilbert and Sullivan). Conductor, Oliver Rundell; director, John Savournin. Jeremy Peaker (The Learned Judge), Amy Freston (The Plaintiff), Nicholas Watts (The Defendant), Claire Pascoe (Counsel for the Plaintiff)
Osud (Janáček). Conductor, Martin Andre; director, Annabel Arden. Giselle Allen (Míla Valková), John Graham-Hall

(Živný), Rosalind Plowright (Míla's Mother), Peter Auty (Dr Suda), Richard Burkhard (Lhotský), Ann Taylor (Miss Stuhlá)
Trouble in Tahiti (Bernstein). Conductor, Tobias Ringborg; director, Matthew Eberhardt. Quirijn de Lang (Sam), Wallis Giunta (Dinah)

NEW PRODUCTIONS (OTHER): *Un ballo in maschera* (Verdi). Conductor, Richard Farnes; director, Tim Albery. Rafael Rojas (King Gustavus), Phillip Rhodes (Anckarstroem), Adrienn Miksch (Amelia), Patricia Bardon (Madame Arvindson), Tereza Gevorgyan (Oscar)

CONCERT STAGING: *Salome* (R. Strauss). Conductor, Sir Richard Armstrong. Jennifer Holloway (Salome), Katarina Karnéus (Herodias), Robert Hayward (Jochanaan)

SCOTTISH OPERA
Founded 1962
W www.scottishopera.org.uk

REPERTORY: *La traviata* (2008)

NEW PRODUCTIONS: *Ariadne auf Naxos* (R. Strauss). Conductor, Brad Cohen; director, Antony McDonald. Mardi Byers (Prima Donna/Ariadne), Kor-Jan Dusseljee (The Tenor/Bacchus), Julia Sporsén (The Composer), Jennifer France (Zerbinetta), Alex Otterburn (Harlequin), Elizabeth Cragg (Naiad), Laura Zigmantaite (Dryad), Lucy Hall (Echo), Thomas Allen (The Professor of Composition/Music Master), Simon Hannigan (Butler/Lackey), Jamie MacDougall/Alasdair Elliott (The Producer/Dancing Master), Elgan Llŷr Thomas (Brighella), Daniel Norman (Scaramuccio), John Molloy (Truffaldino), Richard Shaffrey (Officer), Alexey Gusev (The Wig Master/Wig Maker), Eleanor Bron (The Party Planner/Major Domo)
Eugene Onegin (Tchaikovsky). Conductor, Stuart Stratford; director, Oliver Mears. Samuel Dale Johnson (Onegin), Natalya Romaniw (Tatyana), Peter Auty (Lensky), Sioned Gwen Davies (Olga), Alison Kettlewell (Madame Larina), Anne-Marie Owens (Filipyevna), Graeme Broadbent (Prince Gremin)
Greek (Mark-Anthony Turnage). Conductor, Finnegan Downie Dear; director, Joe Hill-Gibbins/Daisy Evans. Alex Otterburn (Eddy), Susan Bullock (Eddy's Mum/Waitress/Sphinx), Allison Cook (Eddy's Sister/Waitress, later Eddy's Wife/Sphinx), Andrew Shore (Eddy's Dad/Cafe Manager/Chief of Police)
Pagliacci (Leoncavallo). Conductor, Stuart Stratford; director, Bill Bankes-Jones. Ronald Samm (Canio/Pagliacci), Anna Patalong (Nedda/Columbina), Robert Hayward (Toni/Taddeo), Samuel Dale Johnson (Silvio), Alasdair Elliott (Beppe/Arlecchino)
Flight (Jonathan Dove). Conductor, Stuart Stratford; director, Stephen Barlow (reimagining his 2015 Opera Holland Park production). James Laing (Refugee), Jennifer France (Controller), Peter Auty (Bill), Stephanie Corley (Tina), Marie McLaughlin (Older Woman), Sioned Gwen Davies (Stewardess), Jonathan McGovern (Steward), Stephen Gadd (Minsk Man), Victoria Simmonds (Minsk Woman), Dingle Yandell (Immigration Officer)

WELSH NATIONAL OPERA
Founded 1946
W www.wno.org.uk

REPERTORY: *From the House of the Dead* (1982), *Tosca* (1992), *Eugene Onegin* (2004), *Khovanshchina* (2007), *Die Fledermaus* (2011), *Don Giovanni* (2011)

NEW PRODUCTION: *La forza del destino* (Verdi). Conductor, Carlo Rizzi; director, David Pountney. Mary Elizabeth Williams (Leonora), Gwyn Hughes Jones (Don Alvaro), Luis Cansino (Don Carlo), Justina Gringytė (Preziosilla), Miklós

Sebestyén (Padre Guardiano/Marquis of Calatrava), Donald Maxwell (Mellitone)

WORLD PREMIERES: *The World's Wife* (Tom Green with libretto by Carol Ann Duffy). Mavron Quartet; director, Ed Madden. Amanda Forbes (soprano)

Rhondda Rips It Up! (Elena Langer). Conductor, Nicola Rose; director, Caroline Clegg. Lesley Garrett (Emcee), Madeleine Shaw (Lady Rhondda), Anitra Blaxhall (Helen Archdale), Rosie Hay (Sybil), Catherine Wood (Lottie), Paula Greenwood (Prid), Meriel Andrew (Edith), Monika Sawa (Birkenhead), Kate Woolveridge (Lord Asquith), Carolyn Jackson (Churchill)

GLYNDEBOURNE
Founded 1934
W www.glyndebourne.com

REPERTORY: *Giulio Cesare* (2005), *Der Rosenkavalier* (2014), *Saul* (2015), *Madama Butterfly* (2016)

NEW PRODUCTIONS: *Pelléas et Mélisande* (Debussy). Conductor, Robin Ticciati; director, Stefan Herheim. Christopher Purves (Golaud), Christina Gansch (Mélisande), Karen Cargill (Geneviève), Brindley Sherratt (Arkel), John Chest (Pelléas), Chloé Briot (Yniold)

Vanessa (Barber). Conductor, Jakub Hrůša/Leo McFall; director, Keith Warner. William Thomas (Nicholas, the Major-Domo), Virginie Verrez (Erika), Emma Bell (Vanessa), Edgaras Montvidas (Anatol), Rosalind Plowright (The Old Baroness), Donnie Ray Albert (The Old Doctor), Romanas Kudriašovas (Footman)

AWARDS

GRAMOPHONE AWARDS 2017
DISC AWARDS
Baroque Instrumental – 'The Italian Job': La Serenissima/ Adrian Chandler (violin)

Baroque Vocal – J. S. Bach *Cantatas Nos 54, 82 & 170*: Iestyn Davies (countertenor), Arcangelo/Jonathan Cohen

Chamber – Grażyna Bacewicz *Complete String Quartets*: Silesian Quartet

Choral – Mozart *Mass in C Minor, K427; Exsultate, Jubilate, K165*: Carolyn Sampson (soprano), Olivia Vermeulen (mezzo-soprano), Makoto Sakurada (tenor), Christian Immler (baritone), Bach Collegium Japan/Masaaki Suzuki

Concerto (Recording of the Year) – Mozart *Violin Concertos Nos 1–5; Adagio, K261; Rondos – K269; K373*: Isabelle Faust (violin), Il Giardino Armonico/Giovanni Antonini

Contemporary – G. Benjamin *Palimpsests*; Ligeti *Lontano*; Murail *Le désenchantement du monde*: Pierre-Laurent Aimard (piano), Bavarian Radio Symphony Orchestra/Sir George Benjamin

Early Music – Dowland *Lachrimae, or Seaven Teares*: Phantasm with Elizabeth Kenny (lute)

Instrumental Award – J. S. Bach *Six French Suites*: Murray Perahia (piano)

Opera – Berg *Wozzeck*: Christian Gerhaher, Gun-Brit Barkmin, Brandon Jovanovich, Chorus of Zurich Opera, Philharmonia Zurich/Fabio Luisi

Orchestral – 'Haydn 2032 – No 4, Il distratto': Riccardo Novaro (baritone), Il Giardino Armonico/Giovanni Antonini

Recital – 'In War & Peace': Joyce DiDonato (mezzo-soprano), Il Pomo d'Oro/Maxim Emelyanychev (harpsichord)

Solo Vocal – Brahms *Lieder und Gesänge, Op 32; Vier ernste Gesänge, Op 121; Lieder nach Gedichten von Heinrich Heine*: Matthias Goerne (baritone), Christoph Eschenbach (piano)

SPECIAL AWARDS
Anniversary Award – Classic FM

Artist of the Year – Vasily Petrenko (conductor)

Label of the Year – Signum Classics

Lifetime Achievement – Dame Kiri Te Kanawa (soprano)

Special Achievement – Colin Matthews (composer and arranger)

Young Artist of the Year – Beatrice Rana (pianist)

BBC MUSIC MAGAZINE AWARDS 2018
Chamber – Debussy *Cello Sonata; Violin Sonata; Sonata for Flute, Viola and Harp; Syrinx; Piano Trio*: Renaud Capuçon (violin), Bertrand Chamayou (piano), Edgar Moreau (cello), Emmanuel Pahud (flute), Gerard Caussé (viola), Marie-Pierre Langlamet (harp)

Choral – *Ein feste Burg ist unser Gott: Luther and the Music of the Reformation*: Vox Luminis/Lionel Meunier, Bart Jacobs (organ)

Concerto – *Fagerlund & Aho*: Bram Van Sambeek (bassoon)

Instrumental – *Bach2 The Future*: Fenella Humphreys (violin)

Opera – Berlioz *Les Troyens*: Joyce DiDonato, Marie-Nicole Lemieux, Michael Spyres, Orchestre philharmonique de Strasbourg, Badischer Staatsopernchor; Choeur de l'Opéra du Rhin/John Nelson

Orchestral (Recording of the Year) – Mahler *Symphony No. 3*: Bavarian Radio Symphony Orchestra/Bernard Haitink

Vocal – *All Who Wander*: Jamie Barton (mezzo-soprano), Brian Zeger (piano)

JURY AWARDS
DVD – *Max Reger: The Last Giant*: Frauke May (mezzo-soprano), Julius Berger (cello), Markus Becker, Rudolf Meister (piano), Graham Barber, Bernard Haas (organ), Aris Quartett, WDR Funkhausorchester/Wayne Marshall

Newcomer – Chopin *24 Preludes, Op 28; Piano Sonata No 2, Op 35 ('Marche funèbre')*: Julien Brocal (piano)

Premiere – Carter *Interventions; Dialogues; Dialogues II; Soundings; Two Controversies and a Conversation; Instances; Epigrams*: Pierre-Laurent Aimard (piano), Colin Currie (percussion), Isabelle Faust (violin), Jean-Guihen Queyras (cello), Birmingham Contemporary Music Group, BBC Symphony Orchestra/Oliver Knussen

ROYAL PHILHARMONIC SOCIETY AWARDS 2018
Audiences and Engagement – 'Classically Yours' (Orchestras Live in partnership with East Riding of Yorkshire Council)

Chamber Music and Song – *Schumann Street* (Spitalfields Music)

Chamber-Scale Composition – James Dillon: *Tanz/haus triptych 2017*

Concert Series and Festivals – 'This is Rattle' (London Symphony Orchestra)

Conductor – Vladimir Jurowski

Creative Communication – *Becoming a Lied Singer: Thomas Quasthoff and the Art of German Song* (BBC Studios for BBC 4)

Ensemble – The Sixteen

Instrumentalist – Igor Levit (piano)

Large-Scale Composition – Mark-Anthony Turnage: *Hibiki*

Learning and Participation – *Calderland – A People's Opera* (509 Arts)

Opera and Music Theatre – *Monteverdi 450 Trilogy* (Monteverdi Choir and Orchestras)

Singer – Allan Clayton (tenor)

Young Artist – Sean Shibe (guitar)

CONSERVATION

NATURAL ENVIRONMENT

Peter Marren

THE GOVERNMENT'S 'GREEN PLAN'

In January 2018 the government published *A Green Future*, a white paper on how it hopes to improve our natural environment within a generation. Universally known as 'the green plan', it sets out a targeted agenda 'to help the natural world regain and maintain good health'. The plan takes in water, air, the soil, climate change and 'protecting and growing natural capital', which is another way of saying 'protecting wildlife'. Much of the plan applies to the UK as a whole, but aspects of it would need to be approved and adopted by the devolved governments in Scotland, Wales and Northern Ireland.

Much of the paper takes the form of a wish-list, with very broad outlines as to how these aims might be achieved. Their implication is that it should be well within the bounds of possibility to enjoy clean air, clean and plentiful water, and thriving 'plants and wildlife', while minimising waste and enhancing natural beauty. To achieve this, the government promises a mass of incentives but, apparently, no new legislation.

The key commitments include embedding an 'environment net gain' principle into development, so that, for example, lost land could be compensated for by the planting of trees. It pledges to restore and protect peatlands, and admits that farming on drained lowland peat is unsustainable. It wishes to expand the use of 'natural' flood management schemes rather than resorting to drainage each and every time. It makes a commitment to developing a Nature Recovery Network, including the establishment of 500,000 hectares of 'additional wildlife habitat' – although the success of this ambitious plan will depend very much on the quality of that habitat. It also revises previous commitments that failed to achieve their targets (for example, ending the use of peat in horticulture by 2020 was not deemed achievable, so the government moved the target to 2030).

Interestingly the government now seems to support the reintroduction of lost native species, notably the beaver and, by implication at least, the lynx too (and possibly even the wolf). A further surprise commitment, apparently the brainchild of environment secretary Michael Gove, is the proposed establishment of a new and independent statutory body 'to hold government to account' in environmental matters. This implicitly recognises that its erstwhile wildlife watchdog, Natural England, is no longer up to the job. A re-shuffle of responsibility for nature conservation in England seems to be on the cards.

The green plan encompasses approaches to a wide range of environmental challenges from the Department for Environment, Food and Rural Affairs (Defra), which until recently seemed to be out of ideas. Its targets are mostly long-term; they generate positive headlines but are aspirations rather than actual policies. They allow a cash-strapped government to sound green while avoiding any commitment to increasing expenditure. Whether the future will be as green as they, and we, hope will depend on whether the government is prepared to follow up the white paper with clearly defined short-term commitments.

NATURAL ENGLAND AND NATIONAL NATURE RESERVES

National Nature Reserves (NNRs) are conservation's top tier of protection. With 380 such sites in the UK, large and small, and 224 of them in England, they protect all of our natural habitats down to the low-water mark, as well as the best geological sites. The oldest NNRs date back to the 1950s. Many are owned, on our behalf, by the state, but most are still private land managed by agreement. Some are managed by a wildlife charity, the Forestry Commission or the National Trust.

Unfortunately nature reserve management is relatively expensive (and requires a man or woman on the spot) at a time when the responsible agencies have been experiencing cuts on an annual basis. Expenditure on NNRs has fallen to half of what it was in 2010, and when the land is state-owned, it does not qualify for agri-environment stewardship payments. Asking whether the Natural Environment and Rural Communities Act 2006 was still fit for purpose, the Lords Select Committee recently concluded that successive cuts have had a 'profound, negative impact on England's biodiversity' and that Natural England is becoming 'unable to fulfil its general purpose'.

In desperation Natural England has taken to handing over NNRs to a third party, as the law allows. Unfortunately NNRs are not much in the public eye; they have no role in the government's 'green plan', and are not much mentioned even in Natural England's own corporate strategy. It is almost as though they have become an embarrassment. Yet privatisation would not only make a mockery of the word 'National' but their upkeep would be beyond the existing resources of the private sector.

Natural England is also responsible for Sites of Special Scientific Interest (SSSIs), the primary means of protecting nature on privately owned land. These places are supposedly monitored to ensure that they remain in reasonably good condition. Yet the under-staffed Natural England was able to monitor only 2 per cent of 'SSSI units' in 2017. At this rate it would need 60 years to monitor the entire network.

THE STATE OF UK BIRDS

Since 1999, the British Trust for Ornithology has published an annual census of breeding birds in the UK and British overseas territories. The latest, for 2017, shows that the impacts of climate change continue, with southern birds extending their range northwards, while many northern birds are in retreat. Migrants are arriving earlier and also nesting earlier. For example, the swallow now arrives 15 days earlier than in the 1960s, and lays its eggs 11 days earlier.

One result of a warming climate is the remarkable number of new species now breeding in Britain. In recent years the little egret, Mediterranean gull and Cetti's warbler have become well established in southern Britain. Also on the increase as breeding birds are the great white egret, garganey, quail, firecrest and honey buzzard. In 2017, the black-winged stilt had its best season yet, with six breeding pairs fledging 13 young. The cattle egret (which bred for the first time only in 2008) nested at a number of new sites and the night heron bred for the first time in Britain.

Among the losers are the turtle dove, whose numbers are falling remorselessly year on year, as well as northern species such as common scoter, capercaillie, Slavonian grebe and whimbrel. Seabirds have experienced mixed fortunes. The most successful are birds that have a varied diet and so can adapt to changing conditions at sea, such as the gannet, great skua and black-headed gull. More vulnerable are birds that depend on stocks of a particular kind of fish, such as the kittiwake and the Atlantic puffin, which depend on a supply of sand-eels to feed their young. Where changing ocean currents and over-fishing reduce sand-eel numbers, the birds must move or starve. More frequent storms are leading to large 'wrecks' of seabirds blown ashore, and the birds face an additional danger in the pollution of the seas by plastic. On the more positive side, several more off-shore islands have been declared rat-free, and so are safer breeding grounds for hole-nesting puffins, Manx shearwaters and storm petrels. The most recent examples are St Agnes and Gugh in the Isles of Scilly in 2016, and the Shiant Isles in the Outer Hebrides in 2018.

LOST BIRDS AND THEIR RE-INTRODUCTION
The great bustard is the world's heaviest flying bird. About the size of a turkey, it is a spectacular bird that competes to attract a female with magnificent feather-puffing displays. It nests on agricultural land among grassy plains and is currently regarded as vulnerable worldwide, although there are still reasonably large populations in Spain, the Ukraine and Russia. It died out in Britain in the 1830s on its last breeding ground on Salisbury Plain.

After a failed attempt to re-introduce the bird in the 1960s, the Great Bustard Group was set up in 1988 to explore ways of re-establishing it here. A ten-year trial began in 2004 using young birds rescued from agricultural operations in Russia. The birds take several years to mature and the survival rate was low (though higher than in the wild), with many falling victim to fox predation. Many of the surviving birds dispersed far from the establishment site.

Better results were achieved from 2012 onwards with birds taken from Spain. These are genetically closer to the lost British bird, and with presumably more similar habits. The survival rate rose and enough birds remained on Salisbury Plain to provide the nucleus of a breeding population which may soon become self-sustaining. During the past three years, numbers have grown from ten adult birds to at least 48. Six nests were found in 2016, and 'at least two chicks and possibly three' successfully fledged. The hope is to reach a population of 100 free-living birds by 2019. In the meantime a great deal has been learned about the ecology and habitat needs of great bustards.

The white-tailed or sea eagle has also had a long reintroduction history. The largest native bird of prey, it too is an extinct British bird, the last one having been shot in 1919. By contrast Norway has a healthy population of sea eagles – the best in the world. Chicks were taken under licence from Norwegian nests from the 1970s onwards for a trial reintroduction based on the Inner Hebrides island of Rum. However the birds take several years to mature and the first successful nesting attempt was not until 1985, on the neighbouring island of Mull. More releases were made in Wester Ross and, from 2007, also in Fife on the east coast of Scotland.

The establishment of a sustainable number of free-living eagles has been slow but steady, and by 2015 the population reached the significant milestone of 100 pairs. The British sea eagle population is now thought to be self-sustaining, and can be expected to increase in numbers to a natural level without further releases. It is thought that the natural 'carrying capacity' could be as many as 900 to 1,000 pairs. Its decline and ultimate loss was entirely due to human persecution.

For a third species of large bird, the common crane, attempts to re-establish it on the Somerset Levels proved easier than expected. Some 93 birds from German stock, hand-reared at the Wildfowl and Wetlands Trust, Slimbridge, were released between 2010 and 2015. The survival rate has been good and, aided by artificial feeding, some ten pairs have made breeding attempts, with as many as 27 chicks hatching in the wild in 2017, of which 11 eventually fledged. The aim is to establish 20 breeding pairs by 2025, by which time it is hoped that the birds will be able to look after themselves. In Norfolk, where the crane established itself naturally, there were 11 pairs and four fledglings in 2016. Altogether about 60 pairs of common cranes currently nest in Britain.

HEN HARRIERS AND GROUSE MOORS
The hen harrier is a bird of open moors which feeds on small mammals and birds. Unfortunately its prey includes a bird for which moorland owners have a commercial interest: red grouse. Large stocks of grouse are maintained by muirburning and zealous trapping of predators such as foxes, stoats and crows. This is perfectly legal. But the presence of a breeding pair of hen harriers can lower the commercial viability of a grouse moor (though the hen harrier is fully protected by law). Hence the burgeoning conflict between birdwatchers and moor owners.

The hen harrier is a popular bird. Its 'sky dances' in the spring, whereby the male attempts to impress its potential mate, are one of the natural world's most wonderful sights. There are about 800 pairs of hen harriers in Britain, mostly in Scotland and the Isle of Man. Ecologists estimate that there should be around 300 pairs of hen harriers in England. But in fact only a handful have succeeded in breeding in recent years, though 2017 was one of the better years with three successful nests in England, all of them on Forestry Commission land in Northumberland, which produced ten fledged nestlings, and in 2018 a pair nested successfully on National Trust property in Derbyshire. The reason why there are not more hen harriers is undoubtedly illegal persecution (very few birds manage to nest successfully on grouse moors). However this is difficult to prove and successful prosecutions are few.

There are two main ways of reconciling the presence of hen harriers and shooting interests. One is diversionary feeding – effectively a bird table of meat situated at some distance from the shoot. This is time-consuming, expensive and not always practicable. Another is so-called brood management, whereby eggs or chicks are located and removed from the moor to be raised in captivity and then released somewhere else. Natural England has licensed a five-year brood management trial on grouse moors in nine counties in northern England. This is opposed by the Royal Society for the Protection of Birds (RSPB), which is preparing to lodge a legal challenge.

Meanwhile birdwatchers organised a petition for the government to ban driven grouse shooting altogether. As well as reducing hen harrier numbers, they point to evidence that intensive management of moors to raise grouse stocks has caused 'significant flood risk, water pollution and environmental damage contributing to global climate change'. The petition gained 48,000 signatures, forcing an official reply from government stating that 'Defra is working with key interested parties to ensure the sustainable management of the uplands, balancing environmental and economic benefits'. Simultaneously, Mark Avery, the former head of conservation at the RSPB, challenged Natural England to explain exactly why the organisation is backing brood management, suspecting that the body had caved in to pressure. The controversy continues.

REINTRODUCED BUTTERFLIES
The large blue, a beautiful butterfly whose bizarre life cycle depends for its success on the kidnapping of its half-grown caterpillars by ants, died out in Britain in 1979. A reintroduction attempt using eggs imported from Sweden began in 1984, and has been judged a complete success. Despite 2016 being a poor summer for butterflies generally, more than 10,000 large blues flew at three sites in Somerset

and Gloucestershire, prompting claims that this was the largest concentration of the species in all of Europe. The success was due to painstaking research and meticulous restoration of the habitat in favour of the butterfly and its favourite ant host, *Myrmica sabuleti*.

Attention has now turned to another lost butterfly, the chequered skipper. Although this species still occurs in a small area of the Scottish Highlands, the English race died out in 1976, probably due to a combination of drought and the over-shading of its favourite woodland rides and glades. In the hopes of restoring a breeding population in its former heartlands, butterflies caught in Belgium were released in a secret location in Rockingham Forest, Northamptonshire, where wide, flowery rides have been re-established. The project is being undertaken by the charity Butterfly Conservation and funded by the National Lottery.

The Belgian butterflies are believed to be closer to the lost English race than the Scottish form. It is hoped that with further releases over the next three years a sustainable population of this attractive little butterfly will result and will spread into other locations in the forest and beyond.

A GOOD YEAR FOR BEAVERS

Once widespread across Britain, the beaver died out in the Middle Ages, probably as a result of over-hunting (high prices were then paid for beaver pelts by hatters). A trial release of four families of Eurasian beavers in a remote corner of Argyll was made in in 2009, which is ongoing. In December 2017, Michael Gove, the environment secretary, approved a release of beavers in the Forest of Dean. As well as aiding the restoration of a lost species, it is hoped that their activities as 'natural water engineers' will help to reduce flooding in the village of Lydbrook, just downstream of the release site. In a similar vein, a Cornish farmer has been allowed to introduce a pair of beavers onto his land in the hope of reducing floods in the nearby village of Ladock.

Eurasian beavers are already naturalised on the River Tay in Scotland and on the River Otter in North Devon. After the Devon animals were captured and given a clean bill of health, they were re-released and are now part of a formal reintroduction plan. New guidelines for reintroducing species are intended to streamline proposals and make it easier to introduce beavers elsewhere in England.

In Wales there is official support for the Wildlife Trusts' proposal for a small-scale release into an unfenced area on the River Cowyn. In Scotland, too, the beaver is to remain after its closely monitored reintroduction site was judged a success, and it is now a formally protected species. More releases are planned at this site to give the current small population a better chance of survival.

The beaver is the first formal reintroduction of a lost native animal in British history. The next may well be the lynx, but an introduction would face greater obstacles, especially from sheep-farming interests. Nonetheless a formal proposal for a five-year trial introduction in Northumberland's Kielder Forest has been made and is currently at the consultation stage.

NATIVE TREES IN TROUBLE

Ash dieback, caused by a fungus known as Chalara *(Hymenoscyphus fraxineus)*, was first detected in Britain in 2012, but only now are its effects becoming noticeable. The symptoms begin with leaf loss and thinning foliage. More and more bare boughs appear, and lesions may appear on the bark. After a few years the tree dies, either directly from Chalara infection or from being weakened to such an extent that the tree becomes prone to other parasites such as honey fungus. Once infected, there is no way back for the tree. The disease spreads more rapidly when the trees grow closely together as in woodland or along road verges. There is some evidence that older trees may have more resistance than younger ones

(probably those with least resistance will be planted trees originating from tree nurseries). The disease is spread from wind-blown spores which ripen on infected leaves.

The full impact on the landscape is yet to become fully apparent. It is likely to devastate woods where ash is a principal component, and dying trees are also appearing along roadsides, stream-sides and hedgerows; roughly half of our roadside trees are ash. In a threatened double whammy, the tree is also vulnerable to attack by the emerald ash borer beetle, which has devastated ash trees in North America and Russia. Fortunately the beetle, which is of Asian origin, has not yet been detected in Britain.

One answer to ash dieback is to cultivate a stock of disease-resistant trees that can be planted to replace the lost trees. Field trials to find such strains are ongoing, but even if successful, it seems unlikely that resources would permit the replacement of millions of mature trees. Furthermore mass tree-planting threatens to perpetuate the problem of disease that is ripping through our native trees.

Other diseases are also getting a grip on British trees, including Massaria, which infects plane trees in streets and parks, and chestnut blight which has devastated chestnut trees in North America and threatens to do the same here. More noticeable is the early browning of many horse chestnuts caused by a recent invader, the horse chestnut leaf-miner moth. Though unsightly, and undoubtedly a cause of weakening to the tree, the moth is not fatal. Unfortunately horse chestnuts are also being damaged by a canker which disfigures and can even kill mature trees.

FEWER FLYING INSECTS

Many have commented on how there seem to be fewer flying insects these days, even in warm weather. The 'snowstorm' of moths in the car headlights on warm nights is almost a thing of the past, while the midsummer hum of bees and grasshoppers is less frequently heard. The best evidence of falling insect numbers comes from Germany, where a group of entomologists has been monitoring insects on a range of nature reserves since 1987. At the beginning of the project, the traps were catching an average of nine grams of insect life each day. Some 30 years later, that had fallen to just one gram per day. The group estimates that flying insect numbers have fallen by 80 per cent in just 30 years. Even more worrying, these losses were on land protected as nature reserves.

Most of these sites are surrounded by agricultural land, which has remained broadly the same throughout the recording period. Possibly some of the nature reserves are too small to sustain their full biodiversity. But the evidence points to the use of systemic insecticides as the main driver, including the neonicotinoid pesticides introduced in the mid-1990s, which are known to be fatal to bees, and probably also to most other insects. Conditions in Germany are broadly similar to those in lowland Britain, and the results are consistent with the known losses of butterflies and moths. Today's agricultural landscape has become a killing ground for insects.

The implications of this research are grim. As the American ecologist E. O. Wilson points out, if we go on like this, the natural environment 'will collapse into chaos'. Plants will disappear through lack of pollinators, dung will cease to be recycled, soil will become infertile unless chemically recharged, and birds and bats will starve. The EU-wide ban on neonicotinoids belatedly introduced in 2018 was one positive step in averting ecological catastrophe – assuming that we can find a less harmful replacement.

ROAD-VERGE REFUGES

The last refuge for wild flowers in intensively farmed areas is on road verges. Some rare and endangered species occur mainly on verges, such as tower mustard, spiked rampion and crested cow-wheat, and nearly half of our native wild flowers can be found within inches of passing traffic. The best examples receive a form of protection as 'roadside nature reserves' marked with posts, but even so they often suffer from road maintenance operations, drainage, too-frequent cutting or simply from neglect. Verges also suffer from nitrogen deposition from vehicles and agricultural run-off, which favours coarse grass and cow-parsley at the expense of more colourful flowers. Ideally, flower-rich verges should be managed like mini-meadows, cut once in late summer, and the grass clippings removed. Cutting too early encourages invasive plants such as docks, nettles and thistles.

'We're erasing summer from our verges', claims the charity Plantlife. It is campaigning to highlight the special interest of road verges and to try to improve the protection for wild flowers. There are plenty of examples provided of what not to do: for example, the mowing of 2,000 bee orchids by Norfolk County Council in June 2018 (the council responded that the verge had looked 'scruffy' and needed tidying up). On the other hand the charity has praise for Dorset County Council for its more restrained mowing, which has saved money as well as helping to make verges more attractive.

Plantlife has published *The Good Verge Guide,* which describes floral diversity and sets out guidelines on how to manage verges for flowers while retaining road traffic safety obligations. Thoughtful maintenance benefits not only flowers but butterflies, bees and other insects. Better, more species-rich verges can be created by removing the topsoil where nitrogen has accumulated, and sowing the ground with yellow rattle, a plant parasite which helps to reduce the vigour of competing grasses. Seed can be harvested by hand and used to create flowery verges elsewhere. Uses for the clippings may be found, for example in biomass generators. Plantlife would like our verges to be managed for wildlife as a matter of course. They are important because, although only a few metres wide, together they comprise nearly half of the natural, flower-rich grassland remaining in the UK.

BUILT HERITAGE

Matthew Saunders

The most dispiriting news of 2018 came on 15 June when, for the second time in four years, fire swept through the Glasgow School of Art, the masterpiece of Charles Rennie Mackintosh and a British work of architecture that is universally accepted as being of European significance. At the time of writing, the prospects for a costly replica reconstruction seemed hopeful.

SPENDING POWER

No other body can compete with the Heritage Lottery Fund (HLF) when it comes to monies for conservation from the public purse, albeit through the 'voluntary taxation' of the National Lottery. Even so, it has faced spectacular retrenchment during the year under review. From a highpoint in 2016–17 of £430m per annum as its grant pot, it plummeted to £190m in 2018–19, on the back of reduced lottery sales and a resolution not to run down reserves. It has announced that those 12 months will be a stringent interim year before a new strategic plan kicks in, during 2019–20. In 2019, no grants over £5m will be offered.

On the verge of a public consultation on the new plan, the HLF declared the closure of the targeted programmes on landscapes, parks and historic townscapes and reiterated the earlier decision to abolish the programme for places of worship. Applicants would henceforward have to apply under the open grant streams. Despite this comparative reduction, it has still been able to offer some significant first-round grants. Recipients included the Old College in Aberystwyth (£10.5m), set to become a major new gallery; Sheerness Dockyard Church in Kent (£4.7m), to create a business and skills hub;

the Maritime Museum in Hull (£15m), to save two historic vessels; Marble Hill in Twickenham (£4.1m) and Belsay Hall in Northumberland (£2.1m) to conserve, respectively, an 18th-century villa and a neoclassical country house, both owned by English Heritage; Walkley Carnegie Library in Sheffield (£1.3m), to underpin the efforts of volunteers in taking on this fine building passed on by the local authority; *The Monarch of the Glen* (£2.7m), to permit the successful purchase of this famous painting by Sir Edwin Landseer by the Scottish National Gallery; Bevis Marks Synagogue in the City of London (£3m); St Nicholas Cathedral in Newcastle upon Tyne (£4.6m); the Black Country Living Museum in Dudley (£9.8m); Brymbo Ironworks in Wrexham (£5m); the Grand Opera House in Belfast (£4.8m); and Leyton Cricket Pavilion in Waltham Forest, London (£1.8m), which will become a permanent indoor food market. Not that every HLF-funded scheme will succeed – Hastings Pier (which received an HLF grant of £12.4m) was declared bankrupt in the year and sold to local businessman Abid Gulzar, while the brave scheme at Wigmore Church in Herefordshire (which received £1.3m) did not get off the ground following the effective refusal of planning permission.

LATEST OPENINGS

HLF grants were also the principal catalysts behind schemes that were opened or re-opened in the year under review. These included Pitzhanger Manor in Ealing, Sir John Soane's 'country house'; the Postal Museum in London; the Temperate House at Kew Gardens (which received £14.7m); Reading Abbey; Kettle's Yard in Cambridge, a modern and contemporary art gallery; Hartlebury Castle in Worcestershire, which also houses the County Museum; and the Garden Museum in Lambeth, based in a converted church, which has undergone a refit and expansion.

There were other good news stories, too. New attractions were made available at the reconstructed ruins of the Roman Temple of Mithras in the City of London; at the Old Chapel Museum in Stonyhurst, Lancashire; and at the new English Heritage museum at Hailes Abbey, Gloucestershire, which also opened full access for the first time to the chapel at Dover Castle. There were promises of more to come – plans were confirmed by Charles Jencks, the critic and theorist, to open to the public his pioneering study in postmodernism, the Thematic House, in London's Kensington. Lanherne in Cornwall, 'the oldest Carmelite monastery in England', is set to become a spiritual centre and museum. Two great country houses, Elveden Hall in Suffolk and Tottenham House at Savernake, Wiltshire, are once again to become the ancestral homes for the aristocratic families which had moved out decades before. One of the most triumphant banks, the former Midland in the City of London, reopened as a restaurant christened 'The Ned' after its architect, Sir Edwin Lutyens. The timber-framed Reader's House (1616) at Ludlow has been passed to the Landmark Trust, which creates holiday accommodation with careful regard for historic fabric. The eccentric Grade II* listed church of St Luke at Blakenhall in Wolverhampton is set to become an antiques emporium, after its closure. The Churches Conservation Trust took into care the Grade I listed redundant church at Gamston in Nottinghamshire.

Uncertainty hangs over the Historic Chapels Trust, which owns 20 historic non-Anglican places of worship. It has gone into a year of careful appraisal, set to end in 2019, in which time efforts are being made to secure its long-term viability. There is a concurrent moratorium on any new vestings.

GOVERNMENT AND LEGISLATION

Money seeped out of central government but at a trickle. The chancellor set aside £4m for Jodrell Bank Observatory in Cheshire, which is being put forward as a World Heritage Site, and £2m apiece was found for countryside stewardship grants towards historic buildings within the national parks and another grant stream towards 'place-making'. Another £1.8m was diverted to two pilots (in Suffolk and Greater Manchester) to build up the capacity of historic churches, at the suggestion of the Taylor Review, which was commissioned by former chancellor George Osborne; £500,000 of that was earmarked to finance a grant stream for minor works. The programme to reimburse the VAT levied on repairs and new works at places of worship (worth some £42m a year) was confirmed until March 2020. Cadw, the public historic buildings agency in Wales, ceased giving any grants at all for a year. Historic England's total budget for grants in 2016–17 was just over £19m, of which £10m was for buildings and monuments, much of it concentrated in the 'heritage action zones' that were declared in areas such as Bishop Auckland, Grimsby, Lowestoft and Dewsbury. Historic Environment Scotland had £14m available in its grant programmes for 2016–17.

The only significant legislative enhancement was the coming into force of the Historic Environment (Wales) Act of 2017 which, uniquely in the UK, provides for the interim protection of structures being considered for statutory listing. Wales also showed the way in compiling a list of historic place names and in re-examining the terms of the ecclesiastical exemption from secular legislation on historic buildings. As part of the latter, the decision of the United Reformed Church in Wales to give up the exemption has been accepted. The Lake District was confirmed as a World Heritage Site, some 12 years after the launch of the campaign to secure that status. Historic England, which compiles the lists of protected structures, introduced its 'Enrich the Lists' initiative, under which members of the public are able to expand the database of facts for each asset.

Other constitutional updating saw the establishment of the Historic Coventry Trust, the launch of the Royal Parks Charity and the rationalisation of the various trusts set up by HRH the Prince of Wales. The Prince's Foundation for Building Community, his Regeneration Trust and the School for Traditional Arts have come together as the Prince's Foundation. This will focus on culture, heritage and community and operate out of Dumfries House, near Cumnock; 2018 also saw the establishment of the Jameel House of Traditional Arts and Building Skills, at the same location.

ADVANCES IN KNOWLEDGE

Scholarship has progressed with new or revitalised websites on everything from church visiting (through the National Churches Trust) and the photographs of Fox Talbot (through the Bodleian Library in Oxford), to historic musical instruments (through the Royal Academy of Music) and other sites on setting, curtilage and historic farmsteads (through Historic England). There were notable biographies of C. F. A. Voysey (Stuart Durant); J. L. Pearson (Historic England); William Butterfield (Victorian Society); Edward Prior (Martin Godfrey Cook); Sir William Fairbairn (Railway and Canal Historical Society); and Sir Frederick Gibberd (Christine Manley).

A major symposium on James Gibbs was organised by the Georgian Group in the autumn. There were celebrations of the bicentenaries of Humphry Repton's death and of Thomas Rickman's publication of An Attempt to Discriminate the Styles of Architecture, and of the tricentenary of James Paine's birth.

A year of celebration of Northamptonshire's historic churches was launched in March. There have been major published works on nonconformist chapels (Christopher Wakeling); the British mosque (Shahed Saleem); cottages ornés (Roger White); the country house library (Mark Purcell); Chinese wallpaper in Britain (Emile de Bruijn); Italian plasterers – or stuccatori – in the UK (Christine Casey); fire stations (Billy Reading); and railway goods sheds and warehouses (John Minnis). A new revised edition of Charles Mynor's Listed Buildings and Other Heritage Assets, the standard text on historic buildings legislation, was published. There was a significant account of Welsh art and architecture from 1400 until 1990 by Peter Lord. In the course of the year there were revised and greatly expanded editions in the Pevsner 'Buildings of Britain' series on Yorkshire West Riding: Sheffield and the South, Oxfordshire North and West, Dorset, and Hampshire: South.

DANCE

Maria Iu

The 2017–18 season was dominated by #MeToo and the fight against sexual misconduct. In dance, the most publicised was New York City Ballet's ballet master Peter Martins, who resigned in January 2018 following accusations of sexual harassment; an investigation later found that the allegations were not corroborated.

#MeToo became part of a wider questioning of abuse of power that is not simply split along gender lines, and so it was with Martins' case, as he was also accused of physical and verbal abuse. British companies have not seen sexual misconduct allegations, but one has been caught up in the debate about power.

In a report in *The Times*, sources accused English National Ballet of verbal abuse and a hostile working environment. Artistic director Tamara Rojo – celebrated as a dancer and praised for transforming ENB – came under fire for her relationship with principal dancer Isaac Hernández and for creating a difficult working culture. There were claims that dancers were leaving in droves because of this environment. Linked or not, principals Cesar Corrales, Aaron Robison and Laurretta Summerscales all left at the end of the 2017–18 season. Rojo has defended her relationship with Hernández in interviews, while saying that she 'didn't recognise' her company in some of the claims. ENB stated that it has made improvements in medical provisions and lines of reporting, while the Arts Council – which provides more than £6m funding to ENB each year – said it was satisfied that 'ENB has appropriate policies and processes in place to handle grievances, complaints and conflicts of interest'.

Perhaps this year's trials and tribulations will finally lead to change. Scottish Ballet's CEO and artistic director, Christopher Hampson, wrote a thoughtful piece on this topic, saying: 'When you are in a position of power and influence, it isn't simply a question of whether you did or you didn't … The questions should be: how do others perceive you and how does your leadership affect them?'

The dance world said goodbye to Dame Gillian Lynne in July 2018. After a classical career at Sadler's Wells Ballet, she later moved to dance, then choreograph, in the West End. Her most famous work is for Andrew Lloyd Webber's *Cats,* and Lynne also had a hand in productions including *Phantom of the Opera, Chitty Chitty Bang Bang* (2002) and, in a return to classical ballet, a reinterpretation of Robert Helpmann's *Miracle in the Gorbals* for Birmingham Royal Ballet in 2014. Lloyd Webber renamed the New London Theatre, the original home of *Cats,* after Lynne shortly before her death.

Dancer and choreographer Scott Ambler, a founding member of New Adventures, died unexpectedly in March. Having trained at Rambert and worked with companies including DV8, Ambler went on to create roles in early New Adventures pieces, while later in his career he worked on West End projects, including *Chariots of Fire* and *Enron.* Ambler will be fondly remembered as the first Prince in Matthew Bourne's groundbreaking *Swan Lake* in 1995.

There were two big vacancies. Mark Baldwin left his post as artistic director at Rambert at the end of the season, having led the company since 2002. David Bintley announced in March 2018 that he was stepping down as artistic director of Birmingham Royal Ballet after the 2018–19 season, following almost a quarter of a century at the helm. The search for his successor began in July.

TOURS AND FESTIVALS

August started with the Opera House stage filled by the Mariinsky Ballet, which presented a selection that could be roughly split into white and red. The former comprised *Swan Lake* (whose famously uniform swans is the standard for which all other companies strive) and *La Bayadère.* The 'red' soubrette roles included *Don Quixote* and the high-camp *Carmen Suite,* accompanied by another heroine in red, *Anna Karenina.* There was also Wayne McGregor's modern classic *Infra* (with even more exaggerated hyperextensions) and imperial glamour in the *Paquita grand pas.*

The 2017 Edinburgh Festival had its usual diverse showing, including Blue Boy Entertainment's Olivier-nominated *Blak Whyte Gray,* National Dance Company Wales's *Folk* by Caroline Finn and a reworking of *King Lear* from John Scott Dance featuring 82-year-old former Merce Cunningham Dance Company member Valda Setterfield. There were two notable all-male works; while *Lady Macbeth: Unsex Me Here* was a bold exploration of the antiheroine, Chicos Mambo's *Tutu: Dance in all its Glory* was a disappointingly uninventive look at dance genres.

The Birmingham International Dance Festival in June 2018 featured established groups, including Birmingham Royal Ballet and Company Wayne McGregor, but also some interesting site-specific works, such as Satchie Noro and Silvain Ohl's ode to human and machine, *Origami. Woyzeck* featured 100 local dancers and performers in 'a tale of woes and peas'. Perhaps most memorable, though, was the sight of Compagnie Didier Theron in pink inflatable suits dancing through England's second city for *Air.*

A more recent tradition is dance companies appearing at music festivals. Latitude has been strong on this front with its Sadler's Wells partnership and in summer 2018 welcomed acts including National Youth Dance Company and Humanhood, while there was an excerpt of ZooNation's *Sylvia,* a musical about Sylvia Pankhurst that opens at the Old Vic in September. BalletBoyz and Phoenix Dance Theatre were among other appearances.

ROYAL BALLET

It was an important year for the Royal Ballet – it has finally replaced its long-complained-about *Swan Lake* with a new production by Liam Scarlett. Aside from the change from notorious tatty skirts to pancake tutus for the swans, there were lovely new sets and other new costumes (mostly gorgeous, even if some still somewhat resembled ornate curtains). Scarlett stuck close to the Peptipa and Ivanov text and the revisions by Sir Frederick Ashton, but created a new *pas de trois* for Act I and new character dances. The quietly tragic tone of the ending, different to most other companies' versions, also stood out. Marianela Nuñez and Vadim Muntagirov possessed the solid technique required of their roles but Nuñez in particular was exquisite in her artistry.

Another important event was the 25th anniversary of the death of Sir Kenneth MacMillan, one of Britain's most important choreographers. The company staged a series of performances to mark this occasion and, in a spirit of collaboration, invited other British classical companies for several mixed programmes. *Elite Syncopations* was a highlight with its mix of companies and all had a sense of playfulness in this ragtime crowd-pleaser. Precious Adams (English National Ballet) was particularly memorable, while Yasmine Naghdi was delightful in the lead role so famously danced by Darcey Bussell.

The MacMillan celebrations included the controversial *Judas Tree*, but its depiction of graphic sexual violence still left many viewers cold, as well as *Jeux*, a short piece by Wayne Eagling inspired by MacMillan's *Nijinsky* recreation. The full-length ballets that MacMillan was equally famous for were not forgotten either, and *Manon* was revived later in the season. Francesca Hayward, with a few days' notice, replaced an injured Laura Morera on opening night and presented a marvellous portrayal unlike others.

Another important occasion was the centenary of the birth of composer and conductor Leonard Bernstein. It was a landmark celebrated worldwide, with the Royal Ballet presenting two new works. Much of the publicity centred on *Corybantic Games*, chiefly because this is where much of the money must have gone: Christopher Wheeldon is very much in demand and costumes were made by high fashion house Erdem (think classy lingerie). And very nice it was, too. The first part comprised only men, like warriors, and they had a vibrancy that the Royal male corps at times lacks, while the women in the middle section were lyrical and elegant, resembling Greek muses.

But it was Wayne McGregor's *Yugen* that was the better received. The music was more uplifting than McGregor's usual choices and the choreography reflected that, moving away from hyperextended shapes. Highlights included a mesmerising sequence of five men in intertwining lifts and a tender male *pas de deux*. The revival of Scarlett's *Age of Anxiety* paled in comparison; none of the characters sufficiently well-drawn to make a proper impact.

Amazingly, there was a third anniversary: Marianela Nuñez's 20th year at the Royal Ballet. The company – where Nuñez has spent her entire career – celebrated with one of her signature roles: Giselle. And Nuñez was glorious, delicate and simply divine.

Elsewhere, the schedule was packed as usual. In a November 2017 bill, Twyla Tharp extended a 1973 piece to create *The Illustrated 'Farewell'* that showed Steven McRae and Sarah Lamb in their full virtuoso glory. Another new piece, Arthur Pita's *The Wind*, was full of strong imagery but didn't quite result in a consistent whole, even if Natalia Osipova, Thiago Soares and Edward Watson gave it everything. The return of Hofesh Shechter's *Untouchable* remained fascinating, with the classically trained dancers in his crowd movements moving in a very different fashion from what would usually be expected.

There were revivals of Wheeldon's *Alice's Adventures in Wonderland* and *The Winter's Tale*, McGregor's *Obsidian Tear* and Ashton's cape-flinging melodrama *Marguerite and Armand*. There was a pleasing alternative Christmas outing in Ashton's *Sylvia;* in an interesting strategy, the Royal Ballet commissioned Alexander Whitley to create a 'response' piece, *Noumena*, at Clore Studio Upstairs.

In another savvy move, the company (along with the National Ballet of Canada) left Covent Garden for the hip venue of Printworks for *The Dreamers Ever Leave You* by Robert Binet. It was billed as 'immersive', which sounded pretentious, but it took the dancers out of their comfort zones and gave the audience a chance to observe up close.

ENGLISH NATIONAL BALLET

The highlight of ENB's year was *Voices in America,* which again showed artistic director Tamara Rojo's eye for interesting programming and attracted rave reviews. It was also a huge coup to have secured William Forsythe to create his first work for a British ballet company in 20 years. *Playlist (Track 1, 2)* was a blast – understated *ports de bras* and *petit allegro* gave way to big jumps, speedy footwork and utter swagger from the 12 men, and the audience felt their joy. It was accompanied by a rework of Azure Barton's surreal *Fantastic Beings,* plus two acquisitions: *The Cage* by Jerome Robbins and Forsythe's *Approximate Sonata 2016,* which saw Alina Cojocaru back on the London stage after maternity leave. Her final *pas de deux* was a fine examination of artistic perfection.

As part of the Kenneth MacMillan celebrations, *Song of the Earth* joined the repertoire. Erina Takahashi was good in her Opera House performance but it was Rojo who made the role come to life in ENB's Coliseum run, far outshining Joseph Caley and Aaron Robison.

This was accompanied by another acquisition, Frank Andersen's *La Sylphide*. Jurgita Dronina (who joined this season as lead principal) and Isaac Hernández led the opening cast, but there was a sense that the company as a whole hadn't quite mastered the Bournonville style yet.

La Sylphide was also performed alongside Roland Petit's *Le Jeune Homme et la Mort,* a Marmite kind of ballet, but guest superstar Ivan Vasiliev made it look like it was created on him.

During the season, Akram Khan's award-winning *Giselle* made a return (and worldwide cinema showings), Rudolf Nureyev's *Romeo and Juliet* turned 40 and MacMillan's sumptuous *Sleeping Beauty* came back. Cojocaru made her classical return as Aurora, one of her best roles, and was confident in the fiendish Rose Adagio and positively glowing in the final act, supported by an excellent Caley. James Streeter was a delicious Carabosse and, happily, was promoted at the end of the season. Rojo also achieved a ballet first by hiring Chase Johnsey, who identifies as gender fluid, to be part of the female corps.

IN THE REGIONS

In their own shows and as part of the Opera House collaboration, Birmingham Royal Ballet performed Sir Kenneth MacMillan's *Elite Syncopations* and *Concerto,* but the men lacked pizzazz in the latter. In BRB's own season, these were performed alongside the iconic *Still Life at the Penguin Café* by David Bintley. *Still Life…* was in a second programme with a revival of Michael Corder's *Le Baiser de la fée* and *Arcadia,* which premiered earlier in 2017, by first artist Ruth Brill.

BRB stepped up in energy for its June 2018 run at Sadler's Wells. The *Polarity & Proximity* programme featured *Embrace* by George Williamson as part of BRB's Ballet Now scheme in partnership with Sadler's Wells, which aims to mentor emerging choreographers to create larger-scale work. Williamson is still relatively new to the game and *Embrace* showed a talent for intimate duets. The bill also included *Kin* by Alexander Whitley and a modern classic, Twyla Tharp's *In The Upper Room*, in which Céline Gittens was a star.

Opening the season with the return of *Aladdin*, the classics were taken care of by *The Nutcracker, Sleeping Beauty* and, fittingly, MacMillan's celebrated *Romeo and Juliet*.

Following 2017's poorly received *The Boy in the Striped Pyjamas,* Northern Ballet had more of a hit in *The Little Mermaid* by artistic director David Nixon. There was inventive, fluid choreography for the underwater world and the production mostly avoided the saccharine Disney path.

Northern's own MacMillan programme featured *Concerto, Las Hermanas* and *Gloria* – the first time the company has performed MacMillan and a rare opportunity for audiences outside the capital to see these works. The pieces differed significantly in tone, and it was only *Concerto* that exposed a relative lack of experience in neoclassical choreography. As a narrative-led troupe, Northern unsurprisingly presented a fine version of *Las Hermanas,* with their taut movements conveying the sense of repression in the household. The company embodied the sense of loss in the powerful First World War-inspired *Gloria* and was even more impressive when they performed this at the Opera House.

Cathy Marston's *Jane Eyre* was revived – a lovely production but one that anyone unfamiliar with the book may have trouble keeping up with. Marston had a good year; separately, she created the vivid and charming *The Suit* for Ballet Black.

In Scottish Ballet's Stravinsky double bill, one half was its contribution to the MacMillan celebrations: the rarely performed *Le Baiser de la fée* from 1960, with new designs by Gary Harris. It was hard to escape the fact that it wasn't vintage MacMillan and the whole thing looked rather flat and unnecessarily dark. It was shown alongside a revival of Christopher Hampson's *Rite of Spring*.

Scottish Ballet, the only company outside New Adventures to present Matthew Bourne's *Highland Fling*, fittingly toured it to remote regions of Scotland. Bourne's brand of physical-comedy-cum-balletic-contemporary-dance did not faze the company and found natural interpreters in Christopher Harrison and Sophie Martin. For the tour, Scottish Ballet even built a mini-theatre that could be set up within sports halls and leisure centres.

CONTEMPORARY

In May 2018, Rambert unveiled its first full-length work since 1979: *Life is a Dream* by Kim Brandstrup. The dancers attacked the sinewy movements and off-centre turns with gusto, but the multiple characters and blurring of dreams and reality did not a clear narrative make – it was all very Lynchian.

At the start of the season, Rambert presented Andonis Foniadakis' *Symbiosis* – a slick, if predictable, piece about the ebb and flow of city life. Another new commission was *Goat* by Ben Duke that was partly inspired by Nina Simone and used a collection of her songs. There was an abundance of ideas – dancers talking, fragments of Simone's life intertwined with the dancers' own, a ritual, a send-up of contemporary dance – and it was confusing but entertaining.

Rambert toured two pieces premiered in the 2017–18 season: Aletta Collins' *The days run away like wild horses* and a guest appearance of Julie Cunningham & Company's *To Be Me* (separately, Cunningham also had a new production at the Barbican: *Sarah Kane's Crave;* one to watch for those missing Merce Cunningham style). These were performed alongside Christopher Bruce's 1981 classic *Ghost Dances* and Itzik Galili's 2007 party piece *A Linha Curva*. In a similar vein to Nederlands Dans Theater 2, Rambert established a 'youth wing'. Rambert2 will embark on its first tour in autumn 2018.

Sir Matthew Bourne's New Adventures busied itself with touring *Cinderella*. Continuing the wartime theme, it presented three new works at each location of the Imperial War Museums, collaborating with elderly people and schoolchildren locally.

Sadler's Wells celebrated 15 years of both the Flamenco Festival and Breakin' Convention, marking a proud tradition of showing dance of all types. The Flamenco Festival hosted no fewer than seven productions. Breakin' Convention partnered jazz collective Jazz re:freshed to bring 15 musicians to Sadler's Wells to accompany five specially commissioned works.

Hofesh Shechter's company bookended its season at Sadler's Wells with *Grand Finale*. It featured ten dancers, six musicians and continued Shechter's approach of combining dance with theatre and live gig elements. Company Wayne McGregor's *Autobiography*, inspired by McGregor's own genetic code, also had two runs. There were 23 sections with their own theme, and the sequence was randomly selected for each performance so no two shows were the same – it doesn't get more McGregor than that. But not everything was typical. McGregor's recognisable style was there, all athletic, angular shapes amid walks and runs, but some classical elements – pirouettes with feet in *retiré, attitudes derrière* – suggested a softening of style. It was a compelling vocabulary, if you didn't try to read too much into the programme notes.

Retired legend Carlos Acosta returned to the stage (albeit in a cameo capacity) in September 2017 with *Acosta Danza* and the young dancers showed real promise. BalletBoyz, now evolved from Michael Nunn and William Trevitt to comprise a line-up of younger male dancers, explored the concept of balance in *Fourteen Days*. Always savvy marketers, for this bill Nunn and Trevitt commissioned four choreographers to create four works, accompanied by new scores, in less than two weeks. Christopher Wheeldon's *Us* stood out, although Javier de Frutos' use of a seesaw was memorable and fun. These were performed alongside a revival of Russell Maliphant's beautiful *Fallen*.

Richard Alston, a pioneer of British contemporary dance, celebrated 50 years as a choreographer with *Mid Century Modern*, matching a new work, *Cut and Run*, with some older pieces. Cloud Gate Theatre of Taiwan premiered *Formosa*, which tackled Taiwan's history. Dresden's Semperoper Ballett chose to show its contemporary side in its Sadler's Wells debut with a William Forsythe programme, including the always stunning *In the Middle, Somewhat Elevated. Neue Suite* was a series of conventional but never traditional duets, while the sharp lines and shadowy shapes in *Enemy in the Figure* made it an evening to remember.

Other visiting companies included Lyon Opera Ballet, which asked Lucinda Childs, Anne Teresa De Keersmaeker and Maguy Marin to create something to the same Beethoven piece, *Trois Grandes Fugues;* Tanztheater Wuppertal Pina Bausch presented the Rome-inspired *Viktor;* and Nederlands Dans Theater. The high point of NDT's London season was Crystal Pite's *The Statement* and its dancers rose to Pite's challenging choreography in this story of political manoeuvres.

One highlight at Sadler's Wells was Akram Khan's *Xenos*. Honouring Indians who fought in the First World War, *Xenos* was a supremely intense hour-long examination of the body in battle and in agony. It was his final solo performance and Khan will be sorely missed as a dancer.

NEW PRODUCTIONS

ROYAL BALLET
Founded 1931 as the Vic-Wells Ballet
Royal Opera House, Covent Garden, London WC2E 9DD

The Illustrated 'Farewell' (Twyla Tharp), 6 November 2017. A one-act work. *Music,* Haydn; *costume realization,* Fay Fullerton; *lighting,* Simon Bennison. Cast led by Sarah Lamb and Steven McRae.

The Wind (Arthur Pita), 6 November 2017. A one-act work. *Music,* Frank Moon; *set design,* Jeremy Herbert; *costume,* Yann Seabra; *lighting,* Adam Silverman. Cast led by Natalia Osipova, Thiago Soares and Edward Watson.

Yugen (Wayne McGregor), 15 March 2018. A one-act work. *Music,* Leonard Bernstein; *set design,* Edmund de Waal; *costume,* Shirin Guild; *lighting,* Lucy Carter.

Corybantic Games (Christopher Wheeldon), 15 March 2018. A one-act work. *Music,* Leonard Bernstein; *set design,* Jean-Marc Puissant; *costume,* Erdem Moralioglu; *lighting,* Peter Mumford.

Swan Lake (Liam Scarlett, Frederick Ashton, Marius Petipa, Lev Ivanov), 17 May 2018. A full-length work. *Music,* Tchaikovsky; *design,* John Macfarlane; *lighting,* David Finn. Cast led by Marianela Nuñez, Vadim Muntagirov and Bennet Gartside.

BIRMINGHAM ROYAL BALLET
Founded 1946 as the Sadler's Wells Opera Ballet
Birmingham Hippodrome, Thorp Street, Birmingham B5 4AU

Embrace (George Williamson), 15 June 2018. A one-act work. *Music,* Sarah Kirkland Snider; *design,* Madeleine Girling; *lighting,* Peter Teigen. Cast led by Brandon Lawrence and Max Maslen.

ENGLISH NATIONAL BALLET
Founded 1950 as Festival Ballet
Markova House, 39 Jay Mews, London SW7 2ES

Song of the Earth (Kenneth MacMillan), 11 October 2017. A one-act work. *Music,* Gustav Mahler; *design,* Nicholas Georgiadis; *lighting,* John Read. Cast led by Tamara Rojo, Joseph Caley and Jeffrey Cirio.

La Sylphide (Frank Anderson and August Bournonville), 11 October 2017. A two-act work. *Music,* Herman Severin Lovenskiold; *design,* Mikael Melbye; *lighting,* Jorn Melin. Cast led by Isaac Hernández and Jurgita Dronina.

Playlist (Track 1, 2) (William Forsythe), 12 April 2018. A one-act work. *Music,* Peven Everett, Lion Babe; *costume,* William Forsythe; *lighting,* Tanja Ruehl.

The Cage (Jerome Robbins), 12 April 2018. A one-act work. *Music,* Igor Stravinsky; *set design,* Jean Rosenthal; *costume,* Ruth Sabotka; *lighting,* Jennifer Tipton and Perry Silvey. Cast led by Begoña Cao and Jurgita Dronina.

Approximate Sonata 2016 (William Forsythe), 12 April 2018. A one-act work. *Music,* Thom Willems; *set design & lighting,* William Forsythe; *costume,* Stephen Galloway.

SCOTTISH BALLET
Founded 1956 as the Western Theatre Ballet, Bristol; moved to Glasgow as Scottish Theatre Ballet 1969
Tramway, 25 Albert Drive, Glasgow G41 2PE

Le Baiser de la fée (Kenneth MacMillan), 6 October 2017. A one-act work. *Music,* Igor Stravinsky; *design,* Gary Harris; *lighting,* Simon Bennison. Cast led by Andrew Peasgood, Constance Devernay and Bethany Kingsley Garner.

NORTHERN BALLET
Founded 1969 as Northern Ballet Theatre
2 St Cecilia Street, Quarry Hill, Leeds LS2 7PA

The Little Mermaid (David Nixon), 21 September 2017. A full-length work. *Music,* Sally Beamish; *set design,* Kimie Nakano; *costume,* David Nixon; *lighting,* Tim Mitchell. Cast led by Abigåail Prudames and Joseph Taylor.

Las Hermanas (Kenneth MacMillan), 7 October 2017. A one-act work. *Music,* Frank Martin *design,* Nico Georgiadis; *lighting,* John Read. Cast led by Dreda Blow, Guilano Contadini, Minju Kang and Victoria Sibson.

Gloria (Kenneth MacMillan), 7 October 2017. A one-act work. *Music,* Francis Poulenc *design,* Andy Klunder; *lighting,*

John Read. Cast led by Antoinette Brooks-Daw, Riku Ito and Javier Torres.

Concerto (Kenneth MacMillan), 7 October 2017. A one-act work. *Music,* Dmitri Shostakovich; *set & costume design,* Deborah MacMillan; *lighting,* John Read. Cast led by Sean Bates, Sarah Chun, Dominique Larose and Alexander Yap.

RAMBERT
Founded 1926 as the Marie Rambert Dancers
944 Chiswick High Road, London W4 1SH

Symbiosis (Andonis Foniadakis), 28 September 2017. A one-act work. *Music,* Ilan Eshkeri; *costume,* Tassos Sofroniou; *lighting,* Sakis Birbilis.

Goat (Ben Duke), 26 October 2017. A one-act work. *Music,* Nina Simone; *design,* Tom Rogers; *lighting,* Jackie Shemesh.

Life is a Dream (Kim Brandstrup), 22 May 2018. A full-length work. *Music,* Witold Lutosławski; *design,* Quay Brothers; *costume,* Holly Waddington; *lighting,* Jean Kalman.

AWARDS

NATIONAL DANCE AWARDS 2017
Best male dancer – Liam Riddick
Best female dancer – Zenaida Yanowsky
Outstanding company – 42nd Street
Best independent company – HeadSpaceDance
Best classical choreography – Akram Khan for *Giselle* (English National Ballet)
Best modern choreography – Michael Keegan-Dolan for *Swan Lake/Loch na hEala* (Teac Damsa)
Emerging talent – Harry Alexander, dancer with Michael Clark and Julie Cunningham companies
Outstanding female performance (classical) – Alina Cojocaru (Giselle), *Giselle* (English National Ballet)
Outstanding male performance (classical) – Marcelino Sambé (Colas), *La fille mal gardée* (Royal Ballet)
Outstanding female performance (modern) – Ashley Shaw (Vicky Page), *Red Shoes* (New Adventures)
Outstanding male performance (modern) – Robert Fairchild (Jerry Mulligan), *An American in Paris*
One Dance UK Industry award – Mary Brennan
De Valois award for outstanding contribution to dance – Lez Brotherston

SKY ARTS AWARD FOR DANCE
maliphantworks by Russell Maliphant Company

FILM

Trevor Johnston

VIVA MEXICO (AGAIN)!

When he held the best director statuette aloft at the 2018 Academy Awards ceremony, Guillermo del Toro became the third Mexican filmmaker in the past five years to win the prize. With his fantasy drama *The Shape of Water* also taking the best picture crown on the night, del Toro followed in the footsteps of his countrymen Alfonso Cuarón (for the space thriller *Gravity* in 2014) and Alejandro González Iñárritu (for the theatre-land character study *Birdman* in 2015); their combined achievements provide continuing evidence that America's neighbours to the south have indeed produced a golden generation of directorial talent.

It did not, of course, go un-noticed that the triumph for *The Shape of Water* was unfolding some 16 months into the first term of US president Donald Trump, who had made a controversial campaign promise to build a wall between America and Mexico to stem the flow of migrant traffic. Notwithstanding its late 1950s setting, the narrative thrust of del Toro's garlanded film – in which a mute cleaner, her female African-American work colleague and her closeted confidant together outfox the combined might of the US military – could easily be read as a defiant counter-blast to the prevailing right-leaning values of Trump and his supporters. It is typical of del Toro's admired oeuvre, however, that a strongly fantastical element plays against the story's historical context, since this is, above all, a love story whose heroine falls for an amphibious humanoid creature retrieved from the swamps of South America. Neither character has a voice and both appear powerless within the US intelligence base setting (in their respective roles as low-level employee and much-abused specimen), yet their unlikely bond gives them the power to make their own destiny. Critics suggested that the film did not quite match the mastery of del Toro's 2006 Spanish production *Pan's Labyrinth* – in which a young boy retreats from 1940s fascist-dominated Spain into his own imaginary world – yet *The Shape of Water* shows del Toro evidently capable of creating distinctive, unusual and deeply felt work within the Hollywood system, thus benefiting from the marketing clout to reach a much wider audience than his earlier subtitled fare.

OSCAR NIGHT FIESTA

In one way or another, the cultural footprint of Latin America loomed large at the 2018 Academy Awards ceremony, with the best foreign film category seeing a first-ever victory for Chile in the form of Sebastián Lelio's *A Fantastic Woman*. This melodrama centres on a young transgender woman whose older male lover dies suddenly, pitching her into conflict with his family and arousing the suspicion of the local police. The result is striking not only for the director's forays into a magical realist register, but also for the emotive central performance from actress Daniela Vega (who became the Oscars' first-ever transgender presenter when she introduced one of the nominees for best song).

With the groundbreaking *Coco* taking the award for best animated feature, the spotlight was firmly back on Mexico. Always known for technical foresight and innovative storytelling (as manifested by popular and critical favourites *Wall-E, Up* and *Inside Out*), production company Pixar surely outdid itself on this occasion, creating a family-friendly fable drawing on the iconography of Mexico's traditional Day of the Dead. At its core is a story of generational separation familiar from previous Pixar triumphs *Finding Nemo* and *Finding Dory*,

yet it is played out as the plucky young hero is whisked away to the land of the dead – whose skeletal forms, familiar from Mexican folk art, are sustained only as long as those remaining on earth continue to remember them. Startling subject matter for a film produced under the umbrella of Pixar's parent company, the entertainment giant Disney, yet the respect it shows a decidedly non-American cultural heritage is indeed a heartwarming act of outreach. Speaking to acknowledge his own Oscar win, Guillermo del Toro said that 'the greatest thing our art does ... is to erase the lines in the sand. We should continue doing that even when the world tells us to make them deeper.' He was, of course, talking about *The Shape of Water*, and referring to the ongoing backdrop of the Trump presidency, but his words could just as easily apply to *Coco*.

AWARDS AND THEIR USES

Thankfully for the organisers, the 90th Academy Awards ceremony witnessed no repeat of the previous year's calamitous erroneous announcement of the best picture (a snarl-up since dubbed 'Envelopegate'). Instead, there was something rather predictable about the way that the key acting prizes all followed 2018's established awards season form. One could hardly begrudge the recognition of perennial scene-stealers Sam Rockwell (the racist junior cop in Southern states drama *Three Billboards Outside Ebbing, Missouri*) and Allison Janney (controlling mother in the ice-skating biopic *I, Tonya*) in the best supporting actor and actress categories, nor indeed a first Oscar and BAFTA in the best actor category for the long-admired Gary Oldman. In *Darkest Hour* he stirringly embodied the resilience and declamatory prowess of Britain's Second World War prime minister, Winston Churchill; Kazuhiro Tsuji, creator of the remarkable prosthetics facilitating Oldman's physical transformation, was quite rightly rewarded by both US and British academies in the make-up and hair category.

If Oldman was expected to win and did, the same could be said for Frances McDormand, who took best actress awards on both sides of the Atlantic for her indomitable turn as the mother seeking justice for her murdered daughter in *Three Billboards Outside Ebbing, Missouri*. This third feature film directed by esteemed Anglo-Irish playwright Martin McDonagh utilised his trademark tart dialogue to lay out an abrasive yet ultimately hopeful story about the impermanence of corrosive prejudice, with McDormand a rock-like presence at the heart of a story that often challenged audience assumptions. A joint production between the UK and US, it also took both best film and outstanding British film at the BAFTAs, thus affirming McDonagh's prestigious status in both film and theatre circles, yet it was McDormand's presence on both award nights which was to capture the news headlines.

THE #METOO EFFECT

On stage at Hollywood's Dolby Theatre, McDormand supplied the abiding image of the Oscar evening when she asked all the women in the room to stand in a gesture of solidarity. This was one of various recent instances where high-profile film industry gatherings have been used as a platform to register female colleagues' disquiet in the wake of the Harvey Weinstein sexual harassment scandal. While an initial report by the *New York Times* in October 2017 featured several actresses going public with allegations against the Oscar-winning mogul's abusive behaviour, social media worldwide – under the MeToo hashtag on Twitter and elsewhere – subsequently exploded with many thousands of women voluntarily sharing their own experiences of sexual violence and inappropriate behaviour. In response, film industry executives created an organisation called Time's Up to campaign against workplace harassment across the board, and more specifically to engage with bodies including the Producers Guild of America and the Directors Guild of America to instigate concrete anti-harassment measures. Hence, while cynics might regard events such as the black dress protests at both the 2018 Golden Globes and BAFTA awards ceremonies – a conscious rejection of the usual finery of awards season designer frocks – as mere publicity-seeking gestures, there are actually industry-changing moves behind these displays. After Frances McDormand ended her Oscar acceptance speech by exhorting the assembled audience to embrace so-called 'inclusion riders', various production companies did indeed later adopt this contractual proviso to commit to gender equality or to the specified representation of minority or LGBT staff within a film crew.

Whether or not this apparent cultural shift within the film industry will affect long-term changes remains to be seen, but it is definitely having an impact in the short term. Harvey Weinstein's eventual surrender to the New York police prompted the bankruptcy and break-up of his Weinstein Company, a previously powerful production and distribution operation, while a growing tally of sexual assault allegations against leading man Kevin Spacey (who denies wrongdoing and is yet to be charged at the time of writing) caused the producers of the film All the Money in the World to remove him from their already-shot kidnap drama. Veteran Christopher Plummer replaced him in rapidly convened reshoots, and editing was swiftly completed for a late 2017 release which gained Plummer an Oscar nomination. In the present climate, mere allegations of past misconduct are proving toxic, prompting, for instance, the resignation of John Lasseter, co-founder of the hugely successful and influential Pixar animation studio responsible for the Toy Story trilogy, with an admission of 'mis-steps' in his treatment of female staff members. Disney also later removed writer-director James Gunn, the creative force behind the two popular and irreverent Guardians of the Galaxy superhero features, from the series' third instalment, when a series of offensive older social media posts were deemed 'inconsistent with our studio's values'.

FRANCHISE POWER

In terms of its overall spreadsheet, Disney's 2009 acquisition of the Marvel Entertainment brand, home to myriad superhero characters, and its later 2013 purchase of Lucasfilm, creator of the Star Wars franchise, continues to place the company in a dominant position regarding global box-office revenues. Topping the figures for the calendar year 2017, with a worldwide take in excess of $1.3bn, stood Star Wars: The Last Jedi, the eighth feature film in the hugely popular intergalactic saga initiated in 1977 by George Lucas. Under the stewardship of writer-director Rian Johnson, The Last Jedi presented a canny blend of old and new, featuring key roles for cast members from the 1977 original and deepening the character development of leading players from the new generation. The passing of actress Carrie Fisher meant that this outing was initially presumed to be her final screen appearance as the story's heroine Leia, but Disney later announced that she would reprise her role in Episode IX using previously unreleased footage. The Last Jedi saw her leading the Resistance against the malign imperial power of the First Order, while her original co-star Mark Hamill also featured as embittered warrior Luke Skywalker, who must be persuaded that the rebels' cause is still worth fighting for. Lined up against them is relative newcomer Adam Driver, a revelation as the volatile Kylo Ren, Leia's errant son, now seemingly consumed by the dark influence of his grandfather Darth Vader – the series' most memorable villain.

Capably achieved combat and chase highlights presumably kept younger viewers in thrall, but for those old enough to have followed the Star Wars saga since its inception, the significant contributions of Fisher and Hamill gave this instalment an elegiac resonance raising it above the throng of effects-driven extravaganzas currently crowding the cinema release schedules.

Somewhat disappointing audience figures for the subsequent Solo: A Star Wars Story, exploring the youthful origins of the devil-may-care Hans Solo character – with Alden Ehrenreich taking over in the role played memorably by Harrison Ford, hinted that the public appetite for over-expanding movie franchises might be approaching its limit, but the parade of screen superheroes continues, leaving film-makers searching for a distinctive selling-point as characters in spandex save the world for the umpteenth time. Deadpool 2, for instance, continued in the spirit of its predecessor by deploying a knowing and determinedly adult black humour. Another approach, pioneered by the X-Men series and amplified by the Avengers movies, has been to package numerous superhero characters within the same movie, which enhances brand recognition but can prove problematic in story terms, what with the logistics of giving everyone something meaningful to do and the challenge of creating an antagonist capable of providing a serious threat against these massed ranks. A troubled production released to a mixed response from fans and critics alike, Justice League brought together the DC Comics big-hitters, including Batman, Superman and Wonder Woman, though the most common assessment was that at least it was livelier and more fun than its gloomy multi-pack predecessor, Batman v Superman: Dawn of Justice.

It was, however, eclipsed in every respect by Avengers: Infinity War, which has now become the first superhero movie to break the $2bn barrier at the global box office. There have been 19 previous movie releases involving the various components of the self-styled Marvel Cinematic Universe, but as in the previous Avengers entries, here no fewer than 28 different superheroes are brought together. Iron Man, Spider-Man, Thor and Captain America are just some of the much-loved characters peopling the 149-minute movie, which is believed to have cost somewhere between $300m and $400m to make. Bear in mind that Infinity War is essentially the prelude to a concluding second instalment due for release in spring 2019, eagerly awaited by audiences traumatised by Infinity War's unexpectedly bleak ending.

SUPER ALTERNATIVES

After the galactic levels of destruction witnessed in Avengers: Infinity War, one wonders where the genre can go next, and it is fair to say that such computer-generated carnage, while superficially eye-catching, does eventually become curiously academic. Perhaps that explains the appreciative critical and commercial welcome given to Mission: Impossible – Fallout, where the physical authenticity of its stuntwork became an actual selling-point. The sixth instalment in the popular espionage series generated much publicity thanks to a production shut-down incurred when agile star Tom Cruise broke his ankle attempting a risky jump between two office buildings on London's riverside. Animated sequel Incredibles 2, on the other hand, delighted audiences with its slyly comic suggestion that super powers had their uses when battling evil adversaries but might not be quite so effective in facing the everyday trials of childcare and housework. Its delightful combination of imaginative spectacle and recognisable home truths boosted its box-office takings, making it the first animated feature ever to pass the billion-dollar mark worldwide.

THE PANTHER STRIKES

Marvel's release, Black Panther, also proved an exception among superhero pictures for the way it determinedly sought out connections to the real world rather than presenting the usual hermetically sealed fantasy environment. As the title suggests, this is a film which engages with the debate around the social status of African-Americans, and the adventures of Chadwick Boseman's African superhero aim to create an iconography of black pride at a time of fractious race relations in the US. Arguably, *Black Panther* is merely serviceable as a superhero flick, though the way its production design plays on African tribal imagery and its score blends hip-hop with traditional African instrumentation shows the degree of thought that writer-director Ryan Coogler and his team have put into it. Moreover, with the story set in a fictional African country called Wakanda, whose technological advances and mystical powers are far in advance of anything else worldwide, the drama sets up a debate about whether its eponymous superhero leader should preserve his people by keeping them hidden from view – or use Wakanda's firepower to overthrow the status quo and liberate other black citizens across the globe. In essence, this is derring-do with strong additional thematic richness, and demonstrates that there is scope to present a specific and provocative African-American point of view within a mass-market entertainment. That feat was also achieved by Jordan Peele's rapturously reviewed horror fantasy *Get Out*. This starts in comic mode as black leading man Daniel Kaluuya worries about how his white girlfriend's parents are going to react to his impending visit, then reaches a pitch of paranoia when his hosts' welcome proves the very stuff of nightmares. Addressing attitudes towards black sexuality and the lingering stain of slavery on America's social fabric, but also delivering shocks to delight even the most jaded horror fan, the film is seemingly set for classic status, and the Academy's award to Peele for best original screenplay was definitely a popular decision.

GREAT SCOTT

There was also a warm response when veteran British cameraman Roger Deakins finally landed the Academy Award for best achievement in cinematography after no less than 13 previous nominations spanning over 20 years. His work on *Blade Runner 2049* brought an otherworldly sense of tone and texture to the film's future-gazing vision of an android-policed high-density Los Angeles, bordered by drought-ravaged landscape and heightened sea levels. The film itself, while an undeniably fascinating attempt to match up to 1982's *Blade Runner* – now regarded as a milestone in cinematic modernism – brought much slow-paced melancholy and the welcome return of Harrison Ford reprising his key role from the original, but appeared to be trying too strenuously to summon up an aura of mystery that Ridley Scott effortlessly achieved first time round. Scott handed over the directorial reins to Canada's Denis Villeneuve (who had proved his skills with egghead sci-fi in the previous year's *Arrival*), and if the somewhat muted commercial fortunes of *Blade Runner 2049* might be judged a disappointment after long years of anticipation, Sir Ridley himself ploughed on regardless. He passed his 80th birthday working full-tilt to reshoot and polish off the now Spacey-free *All the Money in the World* in record time. Months later, the director of *Alien, Thelma & Louise* and *Gladiator* received a richly deserved career tribute BAFTA Fellowship, though in this instance the British film industry's highest honour certainly did not represent the equivalent of a gold watch presented on retirement. Scott, needless to say, continues to beaver away on upcoming projects including a further episode in the Alien series with which he continues to be most strongly associated. His sheer dedication to his craft continues to inspire.

AWARDS

74TH VENICE INTERNATIONAL FILM FESTIVAL
Golden Lion – *The Shape of Water* (Guillermo del Toro)
Grand Jury Prize – *Foxtrot* (Samuel Maoz)

BRITISH ACADEMY FILM AWARDS 2018
Best Film – *Three Billboards Outside Ebbing, Missouri* (Martin McDonagh)
Director – Guillermo del Toro *(The Shape of Water)*
Outstanding British Film – *Three Billboards Outside Ebbing, Missouri* (Martin McDonagh)
Outstanding Debut by a British Writer, Director or Producer – *I Am Not a Witch* (Rungano Nyoni)
Documentary – *I Am Not Your Negro* (Raoul Peck)
Original Screenplay – *Three Billboards Outside Ebbing, Missouri* (Martin McDonagh)
Adapted Screenplay – *Call Me by Your Name* (James Ivory)
Film Not in the English Language – *The Handmaiden* (Park Chan-wook)
Animated Film – *Coco* (Lee Unkrich and Darla K. Anderson)
Leading Actor – Gary Oldman *(Darkest Hour)*
Leading Actress – Frances McDormand *(Three Billboards Outside Ebbing, Missouri)*
Supporting Actor – Sam Rockwell *(Three Billboards Outside Ebbing, Missouri)*
Supporting Actress – Allison Janney *(I, Tonya)*
Fellowship – Sir Ridley Scott
Outstanding Contribution to British Cinema – National Film and Television School

68TH BERLIN INTERNATIONAL FILM FESTIVAL
Golden Bear – *Touch Me Not* (Adina Pintilie)
Grand Jury Prize – *Mug* (Malgorzata Szumowska)
Silver Bear for Best Director – Wes Anderson *(Isle of Dogs)*

90TH ACADEMY AWARDS
Best Picture – *The Shape of Water* (Guillermo del Toro)
Director – Guillermo del Toro *(The Shape of Water)*
Actor in a Leading Role – Gary Oldman *(Darkest Hour)*
Actress in a Leading Role – Frances McDormand *(Three Billboards Outside Ebbing, Missouri)*
Actor in a Supporting Role – Sam Rockwell *(Three Billboards Outside Ebbing, Missouri)*
Actress in a Supporting Role – Allison Janney *(I, Tonya)*
Animated Feature Film – *Coco* (Lee Unkrich and Darla K. Anderson)
Writing (Original Screenplay) – Jordan Peele *(Get Out)*
Writing (Adapted Screenplay) – James Ivory *(Call Me by Your Name)*
Foreign Language Film – *A Fantastic Woman* (Sebastián Lelio)
Documentary Feature – *Icarus* (Bryan Fogel and Dan Cogan)

CANNES FILM FESTIVAL 2018
Palme d'Or – *Shoplifters* (Hirokazu Kore-eda)
Grand Prix – *BlacKkKlansman* (Spike Lee)
Jury Prize – *Capernaum* (Nadine Labaki)
Best Director – Pawel Pawlikowski *(Cold War)*
Best Actor – Marcello Fonte *(Dogman)*
Best Actress – Samal Yeslyamova *(Ayka)*
Best Screenplay – Alice Rohrwacher *(Happy as Lazzaro)*; Jafar Panahi and Nader Saeivar *(3 Faces)*
Caméra d'Or – *Girl* (Lukas Dhont)
Un Certain Regard – *Border* (Ali Abbasi)
Special Palme d'Or – Jean-Luc Godard

LITERATURE

Nick Rennison

FICTION

Despite past controversies and recent debates about opening it up to American writers, the Man Booker Prize remains the UK's most prestigious literary prize. This year it celebrated its 50th anniversary (although the prize was actually first awarded in 1969) by announcing a 'Golden Man Booker' to be given to the novel chosen as the best of all the winners from the last 50 years. Appointed judges selected one title from each of the five decades and the public was then invited to vote for their favourite. The winner was *The English Patient* by Michael Ondaatje, whose new novel *Warlight* (Cape), set in the years immediately following the Second World War, was published in the summer of 2018.

Other past winners of the Man Booker had new novels available in the 12 months under review. *A Long Way from Home* (Faber) by Peter Carey was the story of a 10,000-mile road race around 1950s Australia and its effects on three of the participants; Julian Barnes' *The Only Story* (Cape) was another of the author's carefully crafted analyses of the pleasures and perils of love; and Alan Hollinghurst's *The Sparsholt Affair* (Picador) moved from 1940s Oxford to contemporary London in its chronicle of the interwoven lives of a group of friends and their families. *Smile* (Cape) was a new work by the Dublin-born writer Roddy Doyle, *The Golden House* (Cape) was Salman Rushdie's latest novel and *Mrs Osmond* (Viking) by John Banville was a cleverly realised sequel to Henry James' *The Portrait of a Lady*. Richard Flanagan's *First Person* (Chatto) was a haunting tale of a ghostwriter corrupted by the man whose memoir he has been employed to write.

Although he has been twice shortlisted, Jim Crace has not yet won the Man Booker but his fiction has long been admired. His latest novel, *The Melody* (Picador), was a hypnotic, ecological fable which opened with its protagonist's encounter with a mysterious, nocturnal intruder. In *Dead Men's Trousers* (Cape) Irvine Welsh revisited, not for the first time, the characters from his ground-breaking 1993 novel *Trainspotting*. Samantha Harvey's *The Western Wind* (Cape) was one of the year's finest historical novels – a brilliant evocation of a small village in medieval Somerset and its inhabitants, disturbed by the unexplained death of one of their number. *West* (Granta) by Carys Davies was another work set in the past – a short but compelling tale of an American pioneer and his journey into unknown territory. *So Much Life Left Over* (Harvill Secker) by Louis de Bernières followed the fortunes of a former fighter pilot in the First World War and his extended family in the interwar years.

Other novels which attracted attention during the year under review included Philip Hensher's *The Friendly Ones* (Fourth Estate), Rachel Cusk's *Kudos* (Faber), which completed her much-admired 'Outline' trilogy, and Ali Smith's *Winter* (Hamish Hamilton), which was the second in her planned 'Seasonal Quartet'. Preti Taneja's *We That Are Young* (Galley Beggar Press) was a reworking of the story of King Lear in the setting of contemporary India, and *Kintu* (Oneworld) by Jennifer Nansubuga Makumbi was an epic tale of life in east Africa which began in the 18th century and moved forwards to the modern world.

In American fiction, Andrew Sean Greer's *Less* (Abacus), a satirical story of a gay writer's voyage of self-discovery, was the winner of the 2018 Pulitzer Prize for Fiction. Kevin Powers' second book, *A Shout in the Ruins* (Sceptre), travelled back in time to the American Civil War to provide an unflinching examination of the perennial human capacity for cruelty and violence. Madeline Miller's *Circe* (Bloomsbury) was a further excursion into Greek mythology by the author of the Orange Prize-winning *The Song of Achilles*. *Clock Dance* (Chatto), a story of family and self-discovery, was Anne Tyler's 22nd novel, as rich in its revelations of ordinary lives as the previous 21. Other significant fiction by American women writers included Meg Wolitzer's *The Female Persuasion* (Chatto), *The Mars Room* (Cape) by Rachel Kushner and Amy Bloom's *White Houses* (Granta), which was about the passionate relationship between first lady Eleanor Roosevelt and the journalist Lorena Hickok.

The year under review was a particularly strong one for short stories. William Trevor's *Last Stories* (Viking) and Helen Dunmore's *Girl, Balancing* (Hutchinson) provided welcome reminders of the gifts of two writers who are, sadly, no longer with us. Other rewarding collections included William Boyd's *The Dreams of Bethany Mellmoth* (Viking), Lionel Shriver's *Property* (Borough Press) and Curtis Sittenfeld's *You Think It, I'll Say It* (Doubleday). The Sunday Times EFG Short Story Award was won by the young American writer Courtney Zoffness for her story 'Peanuts Aren't Nuts'.

Fiction in translation rarely receives the attention in Britain that the best of it deserves but there were exceptions this year. The Polish writer Olga Tokarczuk's *Flights* (Fitzcarraldo Editions) won the 2018 Man Booker International Prize. French-Moroccan novelist Leila Slimani combined the pleasures of the psychological thriller with an acute examination of race, gender and class in *Lullaby* (Faber). Other successes included Ahmed Saadawi's *Frankenstein in Baghdad* (Oneworld), Virginie Despentes' *Vernon Subutex 1* (Maclehose Press), and *The Dinner Guest* (Harvill Secker), an autobiographical novel about a terrorist kidnapping in author Gabriela Ybarra's family.

One of the biggest successes in crime fiction of recent years was Jane Harper's debut novel *The Dry*. Harper's second book *Force of Nature* (Little, Brown) was an equally compelling story of a backpacker missing in the Australian bush. Joseph Knox's *The Smiling Man* (Doubleday), a neo-noir tale of a detective investigating the murder of a mysterious stranger, was another novel which repeated the success of a much-acclaimed debut. *Anatomy of a Scandal* (Simon & Schuster) by Sarah Vaughan was a deftly constructed tale of a marriage falling to pieces after the husband is accused of a terrible crime. A. J. Finn's *The Woman in the Window* (HarperCollins) took the familiar plot premise of a woman witnessing something she shouldn't and gave it new life. *Snap* (Bantam) by Belinda Bauer, about a mother's sudden and inexplicable disappearance, was hailed as 'the best crime novel I've read in a very long time' by none other than Val McDermid.

McDermid herself produced *Insidious Intent* (Little, Brown), her tenth novel to feature psychological profiler Tony Hill and DCI Carol Jordan. Further instalments of other long-admired series also appeared. *Dead If You Don't* (Macmillan) provided a new case for Peter James' Brighton-based detective Roy Grace; *Day of the Dead* (Michael Joseph) was the eighth, and reportedly last, outing for Nicci French's criminal psychologist Frieda Klein; and *London Rules* (John Murray) was the fifth spy thriller by Mick Herron to feature his memorable creation, the slobbish and foul-mouthed Jackson Lamb. The daddy of all fictional spies, of course, is James Bond; Anthony Horowitz became the latest writer to bring 007 back to life in *Forever and a Day* (Jonathan Cape).

Historical crime fiction had its stand-out successes. Abir Mukherjee's *Smoke and Ashes* (Harvill Secker) was the third in his intelligent, entertaining series set in the British Raj; *Greeks Bearing Gifts* (Quercus) was Philip Kerr's 13th Bernie Gunther novel, published just before the author's untimely death; and Andrew Taylor was at his best with *The Fire Court* (HarperCollins), set in the aftermath of the Great Fire of London.

Attica Locke has a high reputation among American crime writers, and her latest novel, *Bluebird, Bluebird* (Serpent's Tail), was a page-turning thriller about love, murder, politics and race in a small Texan town. Stephen King appears to have deserted horror fiction for the crime genre but his ability to hold readers' attention remains. *The Outsider* (Hodder) was the story of a man whose apparently unshakeable alibi for a murder charge was contradicted by all the forensic evidence. Other well-known writers published new adventures for their long-running series characters. *Y is for Yesterday* (Mantle) featured Sue Grafton's California-based detective Kinsey Millhone. After Grafton's death in December 2017, the alphabet books look likely to end with 'Y'. Jeffery Deaver's *The Cutting Edge* (Hodder) was his 14th novel about quadriplegic crime-solver Lincoln Rhyme; *The Wanted* (Simon & Schuster) provided another case for Robert Crais' private investigator Elvis Cole; and *Robicheaux* (Simon & Schuster) by James Lee Burke saw the eponymous Louisiana detective waking from a drinking binge to find himself suspected of murder.

The science fiction genre is so varied and flourishing at present that all a review of this kind can do is highlight a few of the many fine novels which fall within its very broad parameters. The British Science Fiction Association Award for best novel of 2017 was won by Nina Allan's *The Rift* (Titan), the story of a teenager who disappears for 20 years and returns with word of her life on another planet. Nick Harkaway's *Gnomon* (Heinemann) was a vastly ambitious novel set in a near-future Britain where the state has unlimited powers of mass surveillance; *Summerland* (Gollancz) by Hannu Rajaniemi provided an alternative history of the 1930s in which both sides in a Cold War have access to the afterlife; Alastair Reynolds combined the science fiction and crime genres in *Elysium Fire* (Gollancz); and *America City* (Corvus) by Chris Beckett, author of the 'Eden' trilogy, was set in a future America where climate change has reshaped society. Lidia Yuknavitch's *The Book of Joan* (Canongate) was a powerful feminist dystopia in which medieval women, including Joan of Arc, were reimagined as participants in a future war. *Artemis* (Del Rey) was Andy Weir's follow-up to his huge bestseller *The Martian*. Interesting debut novels included *Autonomous* (Orbit) by Annalee Newitz, Tristan Palmgren's *Quietus* (Angry Robot), the story of an alien anthropologist's engagement with human beings at the time of the Black Death, and *The Rending and the Nest* (Bloomsbury), Kaethe Schwehn's tales of post-apocalyptic survivors.

Fantasy fiction tends to come in multi-volume sagas and there were plenty of additions to such works in the year. Adrian Tchaikovsky's *The Hyena and the Hawk* (Macmillan) was the latest volume of his 'Echoes of the Fall' sequence; Jen Williams added a second novel entitled *The Bitter Twins* (Headline) to her 'Winnowing Flame' sequence; *Wyntertide* (Jo Fletcher) returned author Andrew Caldecott to the town of Rotherweird that he had created in his previous novel; and *The Stone Sky* (Orbit) was the concluding book of N. K. Jemisin's much-praised and prize-garlanded 'Broken Earth' trilogy. *The Wolf* (Headline) by Leo Carew was the first novel in a new series, 'Under the Northern Sky'. Standalone fantasy novels of interest included Naomi Novik's *Spinning Silver* (Macmillan) and *The Book of M* (Harper Voyager) by Peng Shepherd, in which the

world is turned upside down when people begin to lose both their shadows and their memories.

NON-FICTION

No work of non-fiction this year attracted as much attention – or went further to prove the old adage that truth is stranger than fiction – than Michael Wolff's *Fire and Fury* (Little, Brown). This fly-on-the-wall view of life in the White House proved astonishing even to those who thought that they could no longer be surprised by Donald Trump. Hillary Rodham Clinton, Trump's opponent in the 2016 US elections, had already provided her own version of events in *What Happened* (Simon & Schuster). Another of Trump's bêtes noires, the former director of the FBI, James Comey, weighed in with his own memoir, *A Higher Loyalty* (Macmillan), which was again deeply critical of the president. Meanwhile the rollercoaster ride of recent British politics came under scrutiny in a series of books by high-profile journalists including Tim Shipman's *Fall Out* (Collins), Robert Peston's *WTF?* (Hodder) and *How Britain Really Works* (John Murray) by Stig Abell. Afua Hirsch's *Brit(ish): On Race, Identity and Belonging* (Cape) was an often scathing and deeply personal investigation of the everyday racism which still pervades British society.

History provides a longer perspective than politicians and journalists can and, among many ambitious works published, a few stood out. Keith Thomas' *In Pursuit of Civility* (Yale University Press) was the distinguished social historian's richly detailed examination of what it meant to be 'civilised' in early modern England; David Edgerton's *The Rise and Fall of the British Nation* (Allen Lane) was a bold attempt to reassess the history of the country in the 20th century; and *Arnhem* (Viking) was another of Antony Beevor's much-acclaimed studies of the battles of the Second World War. Two deservedly celebrated popular historians also published new works. Sadly, John Julius Norwich's *France: A History from Gaul to de Gaulle* (John Murray) was his last publication before his death at the age of 88; Antonia Fraser's *The King and the Catholics* (Weidenfeld & Nicolson) was a vivid account of the early 19th-century struggle for Catholic emancipation.

Barracoon (HarperCollins) was a previously unpublished work by Zora Neale Hurston, the author of *Their Eyes Were Watching God*, and told the true story of the last known survivor of the Atlantic slave trade who had, in the 1920s and 1930s, talked to Hurston of his experiences. The period under review had its full share of other remarkable memoirs. *Educated* (Hutchinson) was the extraordinary story of Tara Westover's escape, through education, from the crippling limitations of her upbringing within a fundamentalist Mormon family in Idaho. Viv Albertine's *To Throw Away Unopened* (Faber) was the second volume of unflinchingly truthful autobiography by the punk musician. The novelist Rose Tremain provided what her subtitle called 'Scenes from a Vanished Life' in *Rosie* (Chatto), her account of growing up in post-war England. *The Cost of Living* (Hamish Hamilton) was Deborah Levy's second volume of reflections on her life as a writer and as a woman. Two memoirs paid tribute to the importance of reading in their authors' lives. Laura Freeman's *The Reading Cure* (Weidenfeld & Nicolson) was the story of her recovery from anorexia with the help of the books she enjoyed; *Bookworm* (Square Peg) by Lucy Mangan celebrated the delights of childhood reading. *Calypso* (Little, Brown) was a collection of darkly comic autobiographical tales by David Sedaris. Collected in *Feel Free* (Hamish Hamilton), Zadie Smith's essays ranged from personal responses to Brexit to thoughts on art and other writers.

POETRY

The two major British awards for poetry went to writers from very different backgrounds. Ocean Vuong, born in Vietnam, arrived in the USA as a child and could not read until he was 11. After studying literature at university in New York, he began publishing his poetry in magazines and chapbooks. *Night Sky with Exit Wounds* (Cape), his first collection, was hailed as 'the definitive arrival of a significant voice' and won the T. S. Eliot Prize for 2017. Northern Ireland poet Sinéad Morrissey had already won the same prize three years earlier for a previous collection. Her latest work, *On Balance* (Carcanet), which ranged in subject matter from the first woman to build and fly her own plane to the reconstructed skeleton of Napoleon's horse, was awarded the 2017 Forward Prize.

Major poets produced new work in the period under review. *The Noise of a Fly* (Faber) was Douglas Dunn's first collection for 16 years; Andrew Motion's *Essex Clay* (Faber) revisited subjects, including his mother's early death, which have haunted the former poet laureate's writings throughout his career; *Salt* (Faber) was an interlinked assembly of short poems by David Harsent; Moniza Alvi's collection *Blackbird, Bye Bye* (Bloodaxe) was unified by the theme of birds; and *Europa* (Picador) was Sean O'Brien's ninth collection of his imaginative and intelligent poetry. The ever-popular Wendy Cope played to her strengths in the poems gathered together in *Anecdotal Evidence* (Faber). Robin Robertson mixed verse, prose and the motifs of film noir into an exceptionally original narrative of a man returning from the Second World War in *The Long Take* (Picador).

Three Poems (Faber) provided an acclaimed debut for Hannah Sullivan. Other notable collections included Vahni Capildeo's *Venus as a Bear* (Carcanet); *The Radio* (Cape) by Leontia Flynn; Mark Ford's *Enter, Fleeing* (Faber); and Frieda Hughes' *Out of the Ashes* (Bloodaxe). Sasha Dugdale's *Joy* (Carcanet) took its title from her remarkable monologue in the voice of William Blake's wife, which won the Forward Prize for Best Single Poem two years ago. And, for those who wanted to know how poets of all kinds approach their craft, Don Paterson offered a monumental exposition of the workings of poetry in *The Poem: Lyric, Sign, Metre* (Faber).

CHILDREN'S

The richness and diversity of children's fiction was as much in evidence in these 12 months as in previous years, although the popularity of stories set in fantasy worlds rather than the real one was noticeable. For younger readers, *Nevermoor: The Trials of Morrigan Crow* (Orion) by Jessica Townsend was one of the more inventive children's fantasy novels of recent years and was the winner in the 'Younger Fiction' section of the 2018 Waterstones Children's Book Prize. *Bad Dad* (HarperCollins) and *The World's Worst Children 3* (HarperCollins) were two more titles by the bestselling phenomenon that is David Walliams. *The Light Jar* (Scholastic) was a second novel by Lisa Thompson, author of *The Goldfish Boy*; Maz Evans' *Beyond the Odyssey* (Chicken House) was a third volume in her ongoing series in which she provides a very contemporary take on old stories; and Matt Brown's *Aliens Invaded My Talent Show!* (Usborne) was a strong contender for the oddest, most memorable title of the year.

For older children and young adults, David Almond's *The Colour of the Sun* (Hodder) was the story of a boy growing up in a small Tyneside town for whom the real and the imaginary begin to merge; Juliette Forrest's *Twister* (Scholastic) was a first novel about a young girl's encounters with witchcraft; and *The Storm Keeper's Island* (Bloomsbury) by Catherine Doyle was an inventive tale set on the magical island of Arranmore. *Spark* (Scholastic) was the second volume in Alice Broadway's 'Ink' trilogy and *Station Zero* (Oxford University Press) brought to a conclusion Philip Reeve's much-acclaimed 'Railhead' sequence. Emily Suvada's *This Mortal Coil* (Simon Pulse) was a debut novel by a young Australian writer about a gene-hacker set in the near future; another first-time novelist, Mary Watson, produced an eerie and compelling work of fantasy in *The Wren*

Hunt (Bloomsbury). *Children of Blood and Bone* (Macmillan) by the Nigerian-American writer Tomi Adeyemi, already in development as a movie, was an epic work of the imagination inspired by the mythology of west Africa.

NEWS

It may seem a statement of the obvious but the future of literature lies not with publishers, nor literary agents, nor commissioning editors but with the writers who write books and the readers who read them. In this context, the year under review was not filled with good news stories. A report from Arts Council England, published in December 2017, revealed both dwindling sales of literary fiction and the exceptional difficulties of earning even a modest income through writing. A later report by the Authors' Licensing and Collecting Society, based on a survey of more than 5,500 professional authors, painted an equally gloomy picture: median earnings had plummeted to less than £10,500 a year. It is little wonder that the proportion of authors reporting that their income came solely from their writings fell from 40 per cent in 2005 to just 13 per cent this year. 'The word exploitation comes to mind,' remarked Philip Pullman, author of the 'His Dark Materials' trilogy, and he and other writers pointed the finger of blame at publishers and giant online booksellers like Amazon. Stephen Lotinga, chief executive of the Publishers Association, argued in response that 'these figures will be unrecognisable to the majority of publishers as they just do not reflect the investments they are making in creative talent'.

Readers and writers could take a little comfort from news of Britain's bookshops. The sale of Waterstones in April 2018 to the hedge fund Elliott Advisors raised concerns about its future but it was difficult to see that it would make a significant difference. Recently returned to profit, it looks likely to continue to thrive. Even the word from the independent sector was encouraging. Figures from the Booksellers Association in late 2017 showed that the number of such shops rose rather than fell for the first time since 1995. It went up by one. It may not have seemed much but, after the sector had lost more than 1,000 shops in just over 20 years, it was worth celebrating.

Libraries continued to feel the pitiless effects of government austerity. In Somerset, the county council, struggling to meet its budget, was looking for savings. Nearly half of its libraries were under threat if volunteers could not be found to run them. It was a similar story in other parts of the country. In Northamptonshire, there were protests against plans to make swingeing cuts in the services and concerns were expressed about the future of the collection of the 19th-century poet John Clare's books and manuscripts, which is housed in the central library in Northampton. Local author Alan Moore, renowned worldwide for his graphic novels, was only one of many writers and academics to express their fears for its future.

No year in the literary world would be complete without rows, debates and scandals, and 2017–18 proved no exception. The novelist Lionel Shriver crossed swords with Penguin Random House after the publishing conglomerate had stated that its aim was to mirror UK society by 2025. Its authors and staff would 'reflect the UK population taking into account ethnicity, gender, sexuality, social mobility, and disability'. To some, this might have seemed a progressive, even praiseworthy stance to take, but Shriver was having none of it. In an article in *The Spectator,* she argued forcefully that it meant that 'literary excellence will be secondary to ticking all those ethnicity, gender, disability, sexual preference… boxes'. The publisher defended its position. Other writers such as Hanif Kureishi added their contributions to the developing argument, mostly on the side of Penguin Random House. Shriver, who had courted controversy earlier in the year with suggestions that politically correct censorship was damaging fiction, was dropped from her position on the judging panel of a literary award. The debate about the Man Booker Prize's decision four years ago to make American writers eligible for the award grumbled on. After two successive victories by writers from across the Atlantic, there were suggestions that the prize's distinctiveness was being lost. Many novelists, including such past winners as Peter Carey and Julian Barnes, voiced their concerns.

The biggest scandal of the year was the one that hit the Swedish Academy, the institution which awards the Nobel Prize for Literature. In November 2017, the Swedish newspaper *Dagens Nyheter* reported that more than a dozen women had accused Jean-Claude Arnault, husband of a leading academy member, of sexual harassment. The scandal escalated to such an extent that the award of the 2018 prize was eventually cancelled, with the academy announcing that: 'We find it necessary to commit time to recovering public confidence… before the next laureate can be announced.' How much time needs to be committed has not been revealed but 100 Swedish writers and other cultural figures have banded together to form a 'New Academy'. They will announce an Alternative Nobel Prize in the autumn and the longlist of possible winners, ranging from familiar names like Cormac McCarthy and Margaret Atwood to lesser known writers such as Sofi Oksanen and Nnedi Okorafor, suggests that their choice will be more adventurous than any the old Academy might have made.

Finally, a recent discovery may throw new light on one of the most famous works in world literature. A clay slab unearthed in an archaeological dig at the site of the Ancient Greek city of Olympia was found to have 13 verses of *The Odyssey* inscribed on it. Believed to date back to the 3rd century AD, these could well be the oldest written record of Homer's work yet discovered.

FAREWELLS
Several giants of American literature died in the period under review. With the passing of Philip Roth, author of *Portnoy's Complaint,* Sabbath's Theater and American Pastoral, a particular generation of (largely male) novelists of huge ambition, ego and acclaim came to an end. Tom Wolfe, progenitor of the 'New Journalism' in the 1960s and author of The Bonfire of the Vanities, had been a notable, often controversial, presence on the American literary scene for more than 50 years. Ursula K. Le Guin, with novels such as The Left Hand of Darkness, The Dispossessed and the 'Earthsea' books, was one of the finest of all science fiction and fantasy writers.

Other writers who died during these 12 months included the British science fiction writer Brian Aldiss; the American science fiction authors Harlan Ellison and Julian May; the playwright Ann Jellicoe (The Knack); the American poets John Ashbery, Donald Hall and Richard Wilbur; Kate Millett, the American feminist and author of Sexual Politics; the novelist J. P. Donleavy (The Ginger Man); Iona Opie, folklorist and joint author, with her late husband Peter, of The Lore and Language of Schoolchildren; the American novelists William Gass, John

Ehle and Anita Shreve; the crime novelist Sue Grafton, author of the Kinsey Millhone books; the poet Jenny Joseph ('When I am an old woman, I shall wear purple'); Peter Mayle, author of the bestselling A Year in Provence; the Irish poet Richard Murphy; the publisher Ernest Hecht, founder of Souvenir Press; Michael Green, author of The Art of Coarse Acting; the novelist Penny Vincenzi; the novelist and short-story writer Clive Sinclair; the Australian crime novelist Peter Temple; the American author of science fiction and crime novels Kate Wilhelm; the crime and thriller writer Philip Kerr, author of the Bernie Gunther novels; the historian John Julius Norwich; the chef and writer Anthony Bourdain; and Clive King, the author of the children's classic Stig of the Dump.

AWARDS

MAN BOOKER PRIZE 2017
George Saunders – *Lincoln in the Bardo*

Shortlist
Paul Auster – *4321*
Emily Fridlund – *History of Wolves*
Mohsin Hamid – *Exit West*
Fiona Mozley – *Elmet*
Ali Smith – *Autumn*

COSTA BOOK AWARDS 2017
Book of the Year Award, Helen Dunmore – *Inside the Wave*
Novel Award, Jon McGregor – *Reservoir 13*
First Novel Award, Gail Honeyman – *Eleanor Oliphant is Completely Fine*
Children's Book Award, Katherine Rundell – *The Explorer*
Poetry Award, Helen Dunmore – *Inside the Wave*
Biography Award, Rebecca Stott – *In the Days of Rain*

WOMEN'S PRIZE FOR FICTION 2018
Kamila Shamsie – *Home Fire*

Shortlist
Elif Batuman – *The Idiot*
Imogen Hermes Gowar – *The Mermaid and Mrs Hancock*
Jessie Greengrass – *Sight*
Meena Kandasamy – *When I Hit You*
Jesmyn Ward – *Sing, Unburied, Sing*

CILIP CARNEGIE MEDAL IN CHILDREN'S LITERATURE 2018
Geraldine McCaughrean – *Where the World Ends*

Shortlist
Lissa Evans – *Wed Wabbit*
Will Hill – *After the Fire*
Anthony McGowan – *Rook*
Patrick Ness – *Release*
Marcus Sedgwick – *Saint Death*
Angie Thomas – *The Hate U Give*
Lauren Wolk – *Beyond the Bright Sea*

MEDIA

Steve Clarke

TELEVISION

Television entered a new phase during the year under review. Increasingly, traditional broadcasters assessed how they could best compete with online viewing platforms, principally Netflix and Amazon. As the number of people who owned TV sets connected to the internet grew, the latest front in the battle for viewers' attention was being opened up.

The streaming services were particularly popular with young people. BBC director-general Tony Hall noted that, in a typical week, 16–24-year-olds spend more time with Netflix than with all of the BBC services combined, including the iPlayer. Research published in July by Ofcom revealed that the number of subscribers to streaming services like Netflix and Amazon Prime for the first time had overtaken the number of subscribers to pay TV operators like Sky (which was itself the subject of a fierce and protracted bidding war between Disney and the US cable firm Comcast).

Paradoxically, viewing staples dominated audience choices. The football World Cup, *Blue Planet II*, presented by the evergreen Sir David Attenborough, and *The Great British Bake Off*, featuring a new line-up of presenters as the show debuted on Channel 4, all proved the resilience of traditional television. Coverage of the royal wedding between Prince Harry and Meghan Markle was another ratings winner.

DRAMA KEEPS ON DELIVERING

If there was one single genre that encapsulated the sheer volume of choices available to audiences during 2017–18, it was drama. Viewers might be forgiven for failing to keep up. There was a fiction glut as rivals spent dizzying amounts of money on stars and production budgets to engage viewers. In the autumn, the second season of BBC One's *Doctor Foster* was a ratings hit. Drama was driving binge viewing, with TV box-sets surging in popularity. Over Christmas the BBC loaded up the iPlayer and gave audiences the chance to indulge themselves. The first three series of *Peaky Blinders* were made available alongside the new season. Other box-sets included *Taboo*, starring Tom Hardy; *Wolf Hall*, starring Mark Rylance; all four series of acclaimed crime-thriller *Line of Duty*; and both series of Sally Wainwright's *Happy Valley*. Ryan Murphy's new eight-part series, *Feud: Bette and Joan* – depicting the legendary rivalry between Hollywood sirens Bette Davis and Joan Crawford – was available both online and as a weekly scheduled show on BBC Two. There were nearly 80 million requests to view shows on the iPlayer over the Christmas and New Year period, according to the BBC.

Quantity is not always synonymous with quality. Early in 2018, some critics began to complain over the apparent 'blandness' of much TV drama. 'Why is our TV drama in crisis?' asked the *Daily Telegraph*'s Ben Lawrence. He lambasted shows like *McMafia*, *Hard Sun*, *Liar*, *Next of Kin*, Philip K. Dick's *Electric Dreams*, *SS-GB*, *The Replacement* and *Gunpowder*. Lawrence claimed that 'portentous dialogue and ham acting' was all-pervasive. The journalist may have had a point but, as the year progressed, the very best offerings suggested that TV drama retained the power to delight and innovate in equal measure.

CUMBERBATCH SCORES AGAIN

Reviewers agreed that Benedict Cumberbatch's performance in *Patrick Melrose*, Sky Atlantic's five-part adaptation by David Nicholls of the hard-hitting novels of Edward St Aubyn, was outstanding. In the *FT Weekend Magazine*, its previewer suggested that the series set a new benchmark for TV drama equivalent to Granada's *Brideshead Revisited* in the 1980s. Christopher Hooton agreed in *The Independent:* 'What a fantastic show this was, and one no doubt bound for BAFTAs and Emmys in the mini-series and acting categories.'

The late spring and early summer witnessed a number of other memorable performances in drama. BBC Two's adaptation of *King Lear*, directed by Richard Eyre, was 'a remarkable two hours of TV,' wrote *The Times'* Carol Midgley. Anthony Hopkins was 'superb' as Lear. The acting of Emily Watson, Emma Thompson and Florence Pugh, cast as Regan, Goneril and Cordelia respectively, was also praised.

On BBC One, *A Very English Scandal,* Russell T. Davies' re-telling of Liberal leader Jeremy Thorpe's alleged plot to murder his ex-lover Norman Scott, was widely seen as one of the year's best TV dramas. It was based on John Preston's book of the same name and Hugh Grant excelled as Thorpe. *Guardian* writer Mark Lawson hailed Grant's portrayal of the political leader, driven by a toxic combination of ambition and lust, as 'a total reputational turnaround, one of the finest ever achieved by an actor'. Ben Whishaw, playing Scott, also received plaudits, as did Adrian Scarborough, cast as Thorpe's defence barrister George Carman.

CROWNING GLORY FOR FOY

It wasn't only male actors on TV that attracted a lot of attention during the period under review. The performance of Claire Foy as a young Queen Elizabeth II in the second season of Netflix's *The Crown,* released in December, was regarded as worthy of a BAFTA award. She was nominated for best leading actress. However, on the night she was beaten by Molly Windsor for her role in another acclaimed show, *Three Girls,* the BBC drama inspired by the sexual abuse scandal in Rochdale. Reviewers were split over whether the second series of *The Crown* was better than the first. Most commentators agreed that as the Netflix show made references to rumours regarding Prince Philip's philandering, it would have been difficult for the BBC to screen the series.

DRAMEDY DRAWS ATTENTION

In the era of #MeToo, prompted by prolific allegations of sexual misconduct against the Hollywood producer Harvey Weinstein, commentators alighted on a new style of comedy drama evident in shows such as Channel 4's *Derry Girls,* set in sectarian Northern Ireland during the 1990s. Some opinion formers believed that women had been shut out of TV drama, which was dominated by well-educated males, and so had, in the words of author Joy Press, 'found a side door to sneak through: the hybrid genre of dramedy, which is exactly what it sounds like – comedy shot through with heavier dramatic themes'.

At the opposite end of the comedy spectrum, John Cleese recanted on his decision to never work again for the BBC by accepting a part in *Hold the Sunset,* a six-part series written by Oscar-nominated writer Charles McKeown. The female lead was played by Alison Steadman. Reviews were mixed: the *Daily Telegraph* awarded the show four stars and said it 'fizzed with comic energy'; others reckoned it was 'cringeworthy' and 'boring'. Nonetheless, the show was the BBC's most popular new comedy in three years and more than six million viewers tuned in.

A more left-field comedy, BBC Three's *This Country,* returned for series two and was a big winner at TV awards ceremonies. Critics agreed that the downbeat but rather tender style of *This Country* and *Detectorists* – which returned for a third series in the autumn on BBC Four – brought some welcome originality to the comedy genre. Two of Britain's most popular comedy actors, David Mitchell and Robert Webb, were reunited for Channel 4's *Back,* described by its writer Simon Blackwell as being 'about people stuck where they are and people who want to move, and the differences that come from that. Like *Steptoe and Son* with echoes of Brexit.'

BLUE PLANET II DIGS DEEP

Blue Planet II was the most watched programme of 2017. More than 14 million people saw the first episode. Technological innovations in underwater filming enabled audiences to see life beneath the waves as never before, in what pundits agreed was truly remarkable film-making. 'With the aid of drone cameras, we saw for the first time sea lions hunting tuna by working together to drive them into a shallow cove,' observed the *Daily Telegraph's* Ceri Radford. The final edition of *Blue Planet II* focused on the menace of plastic pollution in the world's oceans. Viewers watched in horror as an albatross chick died from eating a plastic toothpick that pierced its intestine; in another scene, a sperm whale attempts to eat a blue plastic bucket after confusing it for food. Public opinion was outraged. David Attenborough urged us all to act – or face the consequences. 'The future of all life now depends on us,' he said in a rousing closing speech.

BAKE OFF'S BURNT FINGERS

The transfer of *The Great British Bake Off* to Channel 4 in the autumn, with Prue Leith, Noel Fielding and Sandi Toksvig all new to the show, was a success. The final attracted Channel 4's second-largest audience ever, and its biggest for 32 years, as 11 million people watched the contest. This was despite Prue Leith inadvertently tweeting the name of the winner, Sophie Faldo, hours before the final show was broadcast. The celebrity chef, who was in Bhutan at the time, pleaded that she had made the mistake due to confusion over the six-hour time difference.

DOCUMENTARIES AIM HIGH

In 2017–18, documentary and factual programmes remained prominent despite the proliferation of TV drama. Highlights included BBC Two's *A House Through Time* by David Olusoga, which examined the history of an early Victorian house in Liverpool as the fortunes of its various occupants faced different challenges during the last 140 years. Olusoga was also one of three presenters, along with Mary Beard and Simon Schama, of the keenly awaited arts showcase, *Civilisations,* somewhat oversold by the BBC as a successor to Kenneth Clark's superlative BBC Two series, *Civilisation.* Some critics were disappointed. The BBC's arts correspondent Will Gompertz, writing for the corporation's website, complained that the programme was 'more confused and confusing than a drunk driver negotiating Spaghetti Junction in the rush hour'. The *New Statesman's* Rachel Cooke was less damning: 'While its frantic restlessness is undoubtedly wearing – and queasy-making: I might invest in one of those anti-travel sickness wristbands before part two – there is, I think, no doubting the sincerity of its writer-presenters.'

Reviewers agreed that the US documentarian Ken Burns' latest series, *The Vietnam War,* made in tandem with Lynn Novick, provided a definitive statement. It debuted on BBC Four in the autumn before being made available on the iPlayer. There was also approval for two programmes that confronted mental health issues: BBC One's *Alan Shearer: Dementia, Football*

and Me and BBC Two's *Chris Packham: Asperger's and Me.* On Channel 4, a series that raised issues regarding the care of the elderly, *Old People's Home for 4 Year Olds,* was the broadcaster's highest rated new show in 2017 after *Bake Off.* In the series, young children were invited into a care home to see what effect they would have on a group of residents. Critics agreed that it was touching television, which asked some awkward questions regarding British society's treatment of old people.

WORLD CUP'S RECORD RATINGS

England's semi-final against Croatia in the World Cup in early July shattered TV ratings records. ITV's audience for the game peaked at an astonishing 26.6 million people, an audience share of 84 per cent. Throughout the 90 minutes, the average audience was 24.3 million. For ITV, under the new management of ex-Easy Jet boss Carolyn McCall since January, this was a much-needed boost. Brexit was having a negative impact on advertising revenues. However there was criticism that, during the tournament, children were inundated with ITV advertisements for betting companies. Labour's deputy leader, Tom Watson, told *The Guardian:* 'One of the only downsides to this brilliant World Cup has been the bombardment of gambling advertising on TV and social media that thousands of children will have been exposed to.'

For ITV the summer saw another season of *Love Island* engage younger audiences on ITV2, much of the viewing propelled by social media and blanket coverage in the tabloid press. In November, ITV's entertainment show *I'm a Celebrity…Get Me Out of Here!* had again proved its enduring appeal by achieving audiences in excess of 12 million. Unfortunately one of the show's stars, Ant McPartlin, was forced to abandon the latest season of *Ant & Dec's Saturday Night Takeaway* in March after he was involved in a car accident in London. He was arrested and subsequently fined for drink-driving.

CLARKSON DRIVES INTO MILLIONAIRE

In the year under review, ITV and Channel 5 revived two former TV entertainment stalwarts, *Who Wants to Be a Millionaire?* and *Blind Date.* Their news hosts were Jeremy Clarkson and Paul O'Grady, respectively. Unlike the original Cilla Black-presented show, gay couples looking for love participated in the dating series. As for Clarkson replacing Chris Tarrant on *Millionaire,* audiences appeared divided. Wrote viewer Rob Innes on Twitter: 'Jeremy Clarkson is SO wrong for this show. Insulting the contestants and their phone a friend does not give them confidence to answer the questions.'

In May, it was announced that Clarkson's old BBC vehicle, *Top Gear,* would be losing presenter Matt LeBlanc. He said that the show had been 'great fun', but the 'time commitment and extensive travel … takes me away from my family and friends more than I'm comfortable with'. Another BBC presenter who stood down in 2017–18 was the veteran *Question Time* host, David Dimbleby. 'At the end of the year I will have been chairing *Question Time* for a quarter of a century and I have decided that this is the right moment to leave,' said the 79-year-old broadcaster. He added that he wanted to return to his first love – working as a reporter.

The marriage in May of Prince Harry and Meghan Markle generated big audiences for BBC One, which attracted nearly four times as many viewers as ITV. Some 13.1 million people watched the Beeb's wedding coverage, anchored by Kirsty Young, Huw Edwards and Dermot O'Leary. Even republican cynics were moved by the power of the sermon given by Bishop Michael Curry and a rendition of 'Stand by Me' performed by the Kingdom Choir. This was a sharp reminder that live events are more important than ever for broadcasters challenged by the likes of Netflix.

RADIO

Strengthened competition – not least the incursions of the internet, as podcasts assumed a higher profile – and social and cultural shifts asked some difficult questions of BBC Radio during the year under review. Critics said that flagship shows like Radio 4's *Today* were in need of modernisation. They maintained that, overall, the BBC gave too much airtime to established presenters, most of them white, male and over 50.

Was BBC Radio doing all it could to be relevant to younger people? Did it have enough female presenters, and was it truly reflecting the cultural diversity of the UK? Admittedly, the point regarding diversity could equally be made, and was, of the commercial stations, as regulator Ofcom attacked UK radio for being too white.

EDDIE MAIR MOVES TO LBC

Significantly, in June it was announced that the much-respected presenter of Radio 4's *PM*, Eddie Mair, was leaving the BBC to join commercial rival LBC. Writing in the *Radio Times* Mair, who had worked for the BBC for more than 30 years, insisted that it was entirely his own decision to quit. The 'main driving force behind it was a desire to do something a little different after 20 years in one job,' he explained. The corporation's need to cut the pay of its highest earners was not a factor, Mair insisted.

LBC was closing the gap with BBC stations, as its managing editor James Rea said in November: 'A few years ago, 5 Live was way ahead,' he says. 'We now beat them in London and James O'Brien [famous for his tough interviews] levels with them nationally – and they [the BBC] have 20-plus years [of national broadcasting history] on us.' The challenge provided by Radio 4 represents 'a bigger mountain', conceded Rea. 'But right now there are more and more day parts [slots in the schedule] where we are closing the gap. We are in the business of expansion and it's not an impossible dream.'

BBC RADIO LOSES GROUND

Clearly, Mair joining LBC represented a blow for BBC Radio, which in 2017–18 lost some audiences at a time when commercial radio was in the ascendant. Figures released by RAJAR in May showed that commercial radio attracted an average of 35.97 million listeners per week, compared to just over 35 million for the BBC.

As with BBC Television, younger listeners were the ones with little or no loyalty to the national broadcaster. Not that the BBC was unaware of the problem. Its annual report, published in July, noted: 'Over the longer term all broadcast television as well as BBC Radio have trended downwards as new competitors grow significantly. Public service broadcasting will need to work hard to maintain relevance to younger generations.' The report said that 16–34-year-olds spend more than four-and-a-half hours a week with music streaming services – roughly equivalent to the time they spend with BBC Radio.

GRIMSHAW'S BREAKFAST TURNS SOUR

In May, it was revealed that Nick Grimshaw's *Radio 1 Breakfast Show* had lost 600,000 listeners so far in 2018. This was the slot's second-lowest audience total since records began. At the end of the month, the DJ announced that he would stop hosting the show in the autumn. 'Come September, it will be six years ... I've decided it's time for a change, time for a new show and, most importantly, it's going to be time for a new wake-up time ... preferably about 11.30am,' he said. Grimshaw was swapping jobs with Radio 1 drive-time presenter Greg James. In mitigation, Radio 1 bosses pointed to

the industry-wide decline in radio listening by young people. They highlighted the growth in the station's following on Facebook and YouTube as evidence that they were still relevant to younger audiences.

PODCASTS MOVE CENTRE STAGE

Earlier in 2017–18, Radios 1, 2, 3 and 4 had celebrated their 50th anniversaries. Writing in *The Observer,* radio critic Miranda Sawyer wondered if the stations were facing an existential crisis in the age of the internet: 'In a swipe-left-multi-format-binge-watch world, can these old pals continue as they are?' Sawyer pointed out that nowadays a lot of the very best listening could be found on podcasts. One of those making a big impact was Ed Miliband's weekly show, *Reasons to Be Cheerful,* where the former Labour leader sounded 'relaxed and personable', according to *Independent* media writer Ian Burrell. Other politicians who jumped on board the podcast bandwagon during the period under review included Nick Clegg and Jacob Rees-Mogg.

Objective statistics relating to podcast use are difficult to find. However, it was estimated that six million British adults – 11 per cent of the population – download at least one a week from the podcasts app on an Apple iPhone. The BBC was taking the boom seriously. In March it appointed its first commissioning editor for podcasts, Jason Phipps, poached from *The Guardian* where he was head of audio.

CHANGING THE GUARD

Radio 2, with over 14 million listeners, remained far and away the UK's most popular radio station. But even here, there were signs that the old guard was changing. A presenter reshuffle, announced in January, saw the exit of the long-serving Paul Jones. He had presented a blues show for Radio 2 for 30 years. Jones was replaced by Cerys Matthews, whose Sunday morning Radio 6 Music show enjoyed a devoted following.

Being old, or even elderly, is not always a barrier to new opportunities in media. At the beginning of 2017 the doyenne of radio critics, Gillian Reynolds, revealed that she was signing off at the *Daily Telegraph,* for whom she had written for 42 years. She was joining the *Sunday Times.* 'Being offered a new job at age 82 is rather cheering,' Reynolds told *The Oldie.* In her final *Telegraph* column, Reynolds sounded noticeably upbeat regarding radio's future: 'Someone asked me the other day about radio's renaissance. Renaissance?' she wrote. 'This is a medium that attracts 90 per cent of the UK population, has audience loyalty and listening hours TV can only envy, is a major seedbed of talent for journalism, drama, comedy, sports reporting and all kinds of music. It's been like that for ages. There's a healthily even share of audience now between commercial radio and the BBC, plus an interesting interflow of ideas and talent.'

THE PRESS

There were signs during the year under review that a more inclusive and less pro-Brexit press may emerge in the future. Veteran *Daily Mail* editor, Paul Dacre, announced his decision to stand down in June while in February arch-Brexiteer Richard Desmond sold the *Daily Express* to a rival publisher, Trinity Mirror.

A TURNING POINT

Dacre's decision to leave was interpreted by commentators as a pivotal moment in British newspaper history. Simon Kelner writing in *The Independent* suggested that, after 26 years as editor of the *Daily Mail,* the move was 'unquestionably the end of an era, one in which the relationship between the press and the body politic has become increasingly toxic. This serves no one, and he has played a part in that.'

His replacement was the editor of the *Mail on Sunday,* Geordie Grieg, described as a 'Notting Hill Tory,' in other words someone whose views were more socially liberal than Dacre's. Greig, while at the *Mail on Sunday,* had supported remaining in the European Union. In an article published in *The Spectator,* Dacre warned his successor that any weakening of the *Mail*'s virulent anti-EU stance would amount to 'editorial and commercial suicide'. Dacre will stop editing the *Mail* this autumn. In his *Spectator* piece he claimed that he had received 'countless messages from readers worried about whether the *Mail* will continue its support for EU withdrawal'. The editor added: 'Support for Brexit is in the DNA of both *The Daily Mail* and, more pertinently, its readers.'

DAILY EXPRESS CHANGES OWNERSHIP

In September 2017, Richard Desmond, a high-profile donor to UKIP, had confirmed that he was selling the *Daily Express* and *Sunday Express,* the *Daily Star* and *Daily Star Sunday* to rival Trinity Mirror for a reported £127m. With Desmond's Northern & Shell group no longer in control, National Union of Journalists (NUJ) general secretary Michelle Stanistreet said: 'After many years of under-investment and one pay increase in the past decade, journalists working for Richard Desmond have been desperate for a new owner to provide the resources needed to help increase the readership and the success of the titles. However, the NUJ is concerned that Trinity Mirror, with its long record of making cuts to its newspapers, will not be the knight on the white horse they were hoping for. Therefore we will be seeking guarantees that the deal will not result in redundancies and that the titles will be able to thrive.'

In April, the *Daily Express*' new editor Gary Jones told MPs that, under Desmond's ownership, some of the newspaper's past front pages had been 'downright offensive'. Furthermore, they had contributed to an 'Islamophobic sentiment' in the media. He said that he wanted to change the tone of the *Express.* 'It is my responsibility to ensure content is accurate and newspapers don't look at stereotypical views that may or may not be around in the general public. I should be held to account and be answerable,' Jones said when questioned by the Home Affairs select committee.

Much, however, remained predictable regarding the national press as editors from both sides of the political spectrum attempted to engage readers in difficult times. They had to tackle complex topics, including the endless logjam over Brexit, populist movements and the concomitant rise of US and European nationalism.

CORBYN ACCUSED OF SPYING

In February, certain newspapers devoted many column inches to a story allegedly linking the Labour Party leader, Jeremy Corbyn, to a Czech spy, Jan Sarkocy. The *Daily Telegraph* was among several titles that claimed Corbyn had met Sarkocy during Corbyn's previous career as a backbench MP. He refuted the claims. Writing in the *Financial Times,* journalist Henry Mance suggested that covering the story further undermined the credibility of the *Telegraph,* the *Daily Mail* and *The Sun.* Clearly, the days when these once all-conquering papers were essential reading for a significant section of the UK's population were, in the age of Facebook, a thing of the past. The 'freesheet' *Metro* was now the country's biggest circulation paper. Some 1.5 million copies of the apolitical *Metro,* owned by the same group as the *Daily Mail,* were handed out every weekday.

WEDDING MANIA HITS FLEET STREET

The royal wedding between Prince Harry and Meghan Markle inevitably provided rich fodder for the tabloid press. When the couple announced their engagement in November, the *Daily Mail* published 42 pages covering the pair's imminent marriage. On the Sunday following the May wedding, national newspapers devoted an estimated 230 pages to the nuptials. Fortunately for the regal couple, the kind of press intrusiveness

that accompanied the rise and fall of the marriage of Prince Charles and Lady Diana Spencer was largely absent from the coverage. 'That is entirely due to the way in which the royal family has dealt with the media in the post-Diana era. More particularly, it is about how Charles' two sons were sheltered from the press after the death of their mother and then, in their adult years, have sought to protect themselves,' observed *Guardian* media commentator Roy Greenslade. Certain papers, however, did their best to portray Meghan Markle's father in a less-than-flattering light.

While much of the national press struggled to compete effectively with the online world, outside London the fortunes of the local and regional press were of such concern that, in February, Prime Minister Theresa May announced a review looking at the future of the newspaper industry. She warned that the closure of hundreds of titles was a 'danger to our democracy'. May said that the decline of 'credible' news providers left the public 'vulnerable to news which is untrustworthy'. The review would examine sustainable funding models for the printed press at national, regional and local level.

'Good-quality journalism provides us with the information and analysis we need to inform our viewpoints and conduct a genuine discussion,' she said. 'It is a huge force for good. But in recent years – especially in local journalism – we've seen falling circulations, a hollowing-out of local newsrooms, and fears for the future sustainability of high-quality journalism.' She might have added that with the likes of Donald Trump and his supporters rubbishing the 'mainstream media' as 'fake news' whenever it published, broadcast or posted something they disagreed with, the need for objective and well-researched reporting was more important than ever.

In January the death was announced of Peter Preston, the former and highly influential editor of *The Guardian* (itself relaunched in a new tabloid shape the same month). At a subsequent memorial service, Paul Dacre, the outgoing *Daily Mail* editor and well-known *Guardian* basher, surprised those present by paying a fulsome tribute to Preston. 'Peter was a hero of mine,' noted Dacre. 'I always felt – and here you must forgive my presumption – that in his love of, his obsession with, his addiction to journalism, we were kindred spirits.' The cat was out of the bag.

THE INTERNET

Politicians and regulators on both sides of the Atlantic struggled to curb the power of Facebook and other US tech giants during the period under review. As Donald Trump continued to express his opinions via Twitter, and health concerns were expressed by campaigners who claimed that addiction to social media was damaging young people's mental health, Facebook and the other powerful Silicon Valley firms were rarely far from the headlines in 2017–18.

'THE STORY OF THE YEAR'

In March, Facebook became involved in deep controversy when an investigation by *The Observer*'s Carole Cadwalladr revealed that the British data-analytics group, political consultancy Cambridge Analytica, had harvested millions of Facebook profiles in order to target specific voters with fake news. This breach of the company's terms and conditions, which forbids sharing data with third parties, led to Cambridge Analytica closing down. The firm had passed on the data of 50 million Americans so that they could be targeted by political advertisements. Cambridge Analytica's CEO Alexander Nix was filmed by *Channel 4 News* boasting of using manufactured sex scandals, fake news and dirty tricks to influence voters.

The misuse of data was linked to the Brexit 'Leave' campaign, Russian interference in the 2016 US presidential election,

Donald Trump's digital campaign and to Steve Bannon, regarded by many as the ideologue behind Trump. J. K. Rowling suggested in a tweet that the Cambridge Analytica story was 'surely the story of the year, if not the decade'. Bannon, meanwhile, insisted that the effect of handing over the data of US voters was insignificant: people have minds of their own and are not swayed by what they see and hear on the internet, he claimed.

Mark Zuckerberg, Facebook's CEO, was initially reluctant to admit to any wrongdoing, although he had previously conceded that his company needed to act to curb the dissemination of fake news via his website. However, five days after the publication of the Cambridge Analytica story, Zuckerberg apologised: 'We have a responsibility to protect your data, and if we can't then we don't deserve to serve you.' He noted that the company had already changed some of the rules that had enabled the breach, but added: 'We also made some mistakes, there's more to do, and we need to step up and do it.' More than one pundit suggested that the corporate disaster that was the Cambridge Analytica scandal effectively ended Zuckerberg's apparent ambition to one day run for president.

USERS AND THEIR DATA

In London, a House of Commons select committee looking into the phenomenon of fake news invited the Facebook CEO to answer questions but on three separate occasions he declined. If, at times, Facebook appeared to be unaccountable to legislators, some commentators suggested that the public had only themselves to blame for allowing Facebook free access to their data. Writing in the *Financial Times,* columnist Daniel Thomas said: 'Responsibility lies with the user. Tim Berners-Lee, founder of the internet, tweeted: "Any data about me, wherever it is, is mine and mine alone to control." This can easily be twisted into a less kind counterpoint: a fool and their data are soon parted.'

However, the writer John Lanchester insisted that Facebook's ownership of billions of people's data went beyond the company's desire to generate advertising revenue. 'Even more than it is in the advertising business, Facebook is in the surveillance business,' he insisted. The sheer global power of companies like Facebook, Amazon and Netflix was one reason, according to commentators, that Rupert Murdoch announced in December that he was selling his entertainment empire to Disney.

ZUCKERBERG HIT BY FALLING SHARE PRICE

A campaign urging people to delete their Facebook accounts following the revelations over Cambridge Analytica was launched. In July, the company told investors that user growth was slowing because of the scandal; 3 million people in Europe had abandoned Facebook. In a single day, shares plunged dramatically and wiped more than $119bn from the firm's value. Zuckerberg took a $17bn hit. There was some evidence to suggest that teenagers were more likely to use other social networking sites such as Instagram and Snapchat. The former, it should be remembered, is owned by Facebook, although Snapchat rebuffed Zuckerberg's attempt to buy the site.

SILICON VALLEY WOOS CHINA

The lucrative but restricted Chinese market was potentially attractive to all the giant US tech companies. In July, Facebook announced that it was setting up a subsidiary in China, despite the ban on Western websites. Google had announced in December that it was launching an artificial intelligence lab in China.

Google's parent company, Alphabet, posted highly impressive results on Wall Street in the year under review – despite Google being fined a record $5.1bn by the European Union. In quarterly results, announced in July 2018, Google announced revenues of $26.2bn, up from $20.9bn in July 2017. Brussels had imposed the fine because it considered that the company was guilty of abusing its power in the mobile phone market. The EU also ordered the company to change its practices. The aim was to loosen Google's grip on its Android software. Google said it had done nothing wrong and would appeal. 'The severity of the decision against Google was in keeping with Europe's aggressive curtailment of American tech companies in areas including privacy, antitrust and taxes,' opined the *New York Times. The Sun* reported that the $5.1bn fine was equivalent to two weeks' Google revenue. In 2017–18, the EU ordered Apple to return $15.4bn in taxes.

Another tech company facing the wrath of regulators was ride-hailing operator Uber. In September, Transport for London rejected the firm's application to renew its licence because its working practices were not considered fit and proper. This was later overturned after Uber promised to improve working conditions and the vetting of its drivers. In the summer it emerged that the capital's black-cab drivers were considering suing Uber £1bn for loss of earnings.

TWITTER ADDICTS

Throughout the year under review, concerns were expressed that excessive use of social media was damaging people's health. Many researchers suggested that social media's effects on wellbeing were ambiguous, but there was agreement that social media has a more negative effect on people who are socially isolated. As for Donald Trump's use of Twitter, the website TechCrunch argued that while the president's tweets 'may be negative and consequential, unless he thinks he has a problem, there is no basis for asserting pathology'. In other words, the leader of the free world was not addicted to Twitter. Some may beg to differ.

PARLIAMENT

Patrick Robathan

Prime minister Theresa May faced a difficult year in 2017–18, having to negotiate a Brexit settlement acceptable to all sides while only achieving a Commons majority through an agreement with ten Democratic Unionist Party MPs. She managed to get the European Union (Withdrawal) Act into the statute book and claimed to have at least Cabinet agreement to a so-called Chequers' Brexit plan. During the year the Speaker, John Bercow, granted a record number of urgent questions and emergency debates.

Returning after the recess on 9 October 2017, transport secretary Chris Grayling made a statement about support for those affected by the collapse of Monarch Airlines. The prime minister updated MPs on plans for leaving the EU as the fifth round of negotiations began in Brussels: 'we want to take a creative and pragmatic approach to securing a new, deep and special partnership with the EU which spans both a new economic relationship and a new security relationship. I have been clear that when we leave the EU we will no longer be members of its single market or its customs union. The British people voted for control of their borders, their laws and their money, and that is what this government are going to deliver.' On 10 October, the business, energy and industrial strategy (BEIS) minister Claire Perry responded to Mark Hendrick about job losses at BAE Systems military air and information sites. Cabinet Office minister Damian Green published the race disparity audit. BEIS secretary Greg Clark updated MPs on the trade dispute between Boeing and Bombardier. Alistair Carmichael (LD) led an emergency debate on the government's policy of failing to vote in Opposition-day debates. On 11 October universities minister Joseph Johnson replied to Labour spokesperson Angela Rayner on higher education funding. On 12 October justice minister Sam Gyimah replied to Labour spokesperson Richard Burgon on prisons policy and the recent disturbance in HM Prison Long Lartin. Greg Clark published the draft Energy Price Cap Bill and Claire Perry published the Clean Growth Strategy.

On 16 October the minister for the Middle East, Alistair Burt, replied to the shadow foreign secretary Emily Thornberry on the future of the joint comprehensive plan of action with Iran, following President Trump's decision not to recertify the plan. Claire Perry responded to Justin Madders on Vauxhall's decision to move staff in Ellesmere Port from two production shifts to one, resulting in 400 redundancies. On 17 October Greg Clark published a Green Paper on international investment, proposing reforms to the scrutiny of foreign investment to ensure that national security is protected. Brexit secretary David Davis reported back on the fifth round of negotiations with the EU: 'I am confident that we are on the right path'. On 18 October housing minister Alok Sharma issued a call for evidence about protecting consumers in the letting and management agents market. On 19 October the communities and local government secretary Sajid Javid updated Labour spokesperson John Healey on government action following the Grenfell Tower fire: 'we have been working hard to ensure that everyone affected by the fire gets the support they need and that all tall residential buildings across the country are safe'. On 20 October, Labour MP Chris Bryant's Assaults on Emergency Workers (Offences) Bill was given an unopposed second reading.

On 23 October the prime minister reported back on the European Council meeting, which had made 'important progress in moving towards the new, deep and special partnership that we want to see'. On 24 October Alistair Burt updated John Woodcock on the liberation of Raqqa and the counter-Daesh campaign. Labour spokesperson Debbie Abrahams introduced an emergency debate on pausing the full service roll-out of universal credit. On 26 October David Davis updated his shadow Keir Starmer on the government's policy of a meaningful vote in Parliament to agree the final Brexit withdrawal agreement: 'there will be a vote in both Houses of Parliament on the final deal'.

On 30 October, the Speaker made a statement about the culture of sexual harassment at Westminster. The leader of the House, Andrea Leadsom, responded to Harriet Harman about her plan to tackle sexual harassment in Parliament. Policing minister Nick Hurd published Dame Elish Angiolini's independent review of deaths and serious incidents in police custody. Foreign secretary Boris Johnson made a statement on the legacy of the Balfour declaration on its centenary. On 31 October the digital, culture, media and sport (DCMS) minister Tracey Crouch told her Labour shadow Tom Watson that she had published a consultation on proposals for changes to gaming machines and social responsibility measures in the gambling industry. On 1 November the Commons passed a motion asking that impact assessments arising from sectoral analyses be provided to the Brexit select committee. On 2 November Foreign Office minister Sir Alan Duncan updated Hywel Williams on the political situation in Catalonia: 'we want to see the rule of law upheld, the Spanish constitution respected and Spanish unity preserved'. On 3 November, Labour MP Steve Reed's Mental Health Units (Use of Force) Bill received an unopposed second reading.

On 6 November the financial secretary to the Treasury, Mel Stride, replied to shadow chancellor John McDonnell about the government's actions to curb aggressive tax avoidance schemes in the light of the Paradise Papers revelations. Following the vote obliging ministers to provide the Brexit committee with impact assessments, the Speaker ruled that it 'should be done very promptly indeed. Failing that, I expect ministers to explain to the House before we rise tomorrow evening why they have not provided them and when they propose to do so.' Sajid Javid made a statement on the independent recovery task force working with the Royal Borough of Kensington and Chelsea in the wake of the fire at Grenfell Tower. The Commons finally agreed the membership of the liaison select committee. On 7 November Brexit minister Steve Baker told Labour spokesperson Matthew Pennycook that 'it is not the case that there are 58 sectoral impact assessments for Brexit … Our analysis is constantly evolving and being updated, but it is not, and nor has it ever been, a series of impact assessments examining the quantitative impact of Brexit on these sectors. Given this, it will take the government some time to collate and bring together this information in a way that is accessible and informative to the committee … We have made plain to the House authorities that we currently expect this to be in no more than three weeks.' Alistair Burt updated Labour spokesperson Kate Osamor on international development secretary Priti Patel's meetings with a number of people and organisations in Israel earlier in 2017 (Ms Patel subsequently resigned). Mr Burt updated international development committee chairman Stephen Twigg on the impact on the humanitarian situation in

Yemen of the escalation of Saudi Arabia's blockade. Boris Johnson updated MPs on the campaign against Daesh in Iraq and Syria and on the case of Mrs Nazanin Zaghari-Ratcliffe, detained in Iran.

Returning after a short recess, on 13 November Boris Johnson updated Emily Thornberry on the Zaghari-Ratcliffe case. David Davis updated MPs on EU negotiations: 'we need to see flexibility, imagination and willingness to make progress on both sides if these negotiations are to succeed and if we are to realise our new partnership'. On 14 November, Dame Margaret Hodge introduced an emergency debate on systemic issues enabling tax avoidance and evasion uncovered by the Paradise Papers. The European Union (Withdrawal) Bill began eight days in committee of the whole House.

EUROPEAN UNION (WITHDRAWAL) BILL

In total, Parliament spent over 272 hours debating this bill: 112 hours, 33 minutes in the Commons (including eight days in committee, two on report), and 160 hours, 44 minutes in the Lords (including 11 days in committee, six on report).

The government suffered two defeats in the Commons. On 13 December 2017 (committee stage, day 7), an amendment guaranteeing MPs a say on the final Brexit deal was passed by 309 votes to 305, with 12 Conservative rebelling against the government. On 16 January 2018 (report stage, day 1), an amendment was tabled by Dominic Grieve (C.) to allow ministers only to use statutory instruments if Parliament has voted to approve the final terms.

The government suffered fifteen defeats in the Lords in committee and on report between 18 April and 18 June 2018.

The Commons debated the amendments proposed by the Lords on 12 and 13 June 2018: a majority voted to reject 14 of the 15 Lords' amendments and accepted only one, which pertained to the preservation of relations with the EU. The government agreed to accept an amendment encouraging the negotiation of a customs arrangement with the EU and further compromised with amendments concerning the issues of Northern Ireland, scrutiny, the environment and unaccompanied child migrants. An amendment allowing legal challenges on the basis of EU law for the three-year period following Brexit was passed. It was agreed that any withdrawal agreement with the EU would not be implemented without Parliament's approval and if there was no such approval, a minister will make a statement setting out how the government 'proposes to proceed' within 28 days; a potential rebellion by pro-Remain Conservatives over a 'meaningful vote' on the final Brexit deal was avoided after ministers agreed at the last moment to discuss a compromise.

On 18 June the Lords passed another 'meaningful vote' amendment similar to the one rejected by the Commons but reworded so it wouldn't involve only a 'neutral motion'; they did not 'insist' on any other of their amendments. This amendment was defeated by the Commons on 20 June by 319 votes to 303. The same day, the Lords agreed to accept the Bill as it then stood. Royal assent was given on 26 June.

On 15 November 2017, Boris Johnson responded to Kate Hoey on the situation in Zimbabwe. On 16 November health minister Steve Brine responded to Yasmin Qureshi about the publication of a report of the Commission on Human Medicines' Expert Working Group on hormone pregnancy tests. Andrea Leadsom updated MPs on steps to tackle harassment and abuse in Parliament.

On 20 November Joseph Johnson responded to Gordon Marsden on the Student Loans Company. Alistair Burt made a statement on Yemen and the implications of the conflict for regional security.

BUDGET 2017

The Chancellor of the Exchequer, Philip Hammond, delivered the Budget, now moved to the autumn, on 22 November. The main points included:

- the abolition of stamp duty on properties of up to £300,000; plans for 300,000 homes a year to be built by the mid-2020s; local authorities to be able to increase the council tax premium on empty homes from 50% to 100%
- the income tax personal allowance to rise to £11,850, and the higher rate threshold to £46,350
- measures to cut waiting times for universal credit payments
- duty was frozen on beer, cider and spirits, increased on some high-strength drinks, including some white ciders, and additional duty placed on hand-rolling tobacco
- fuel duty was frozen; vehicle excise duty on older diesel cars to be levied one band higher than on petrol cars
- a 'millennial' travel card was introduced
- the state pension was increased by 3%

The Chancellor said: 'I have set out a vision for Britain's future: by getting our debt down, by supporting British families and businesses, by investing in the technologies and the skills of the future and by creating the homes and the infrastructure that our country needs.' Labour leader Jeremy Corbyn was less welcoming: 'The reality test of this Budget has to be how it affects ordinary people's lives. I believe, as this Budget unravels, the reality will be that a lot of people will be no better off, and the misery that many are in will be continuing.'

On 23 November DCMS minister Matt Hancock responded to Wes Streeting on the theft of the personal data of 57 million Uber customers and drivers. Work and pensions secretary David Gauke made a statement on universal credit: 'we will continue to roll out universal credit in a steady and considered manner'.

On 27 November Nick Hurd responded to shadow home secretary Diane Abbott on developments surrounding the alleged manipulation of forensic evidence at the Randox and Trimega laboratories in Manchester. Greg Clark published the industrial strategy White Paper. On 28 November Brexit minister Robin Walker responded to Keir Starmer on the release of the Brexit impact assessments. On 28 November health secretary Jeremy Hunt made a statement about a new strategy to improve safety in NHS maternity services. On 29 November the chief secretary to the Treasury, Liz Truss, responded to Chris Leslie on the expected costs of exiting the EU. Chris Grayling made a statement about future plans for Britain's railways. On 30 November home secretary Amber Rudd responded to Stephen Doughty on the activities of Britain First, online hate speech and the sharing of inflammatory content online by US president Donald Trump. David Gauke published a White Paper on work, health and disability. Conservative MP Andrew Mitchell introduced an emergency debate on Yemen. On 1 December, Labour MP Afzal Khan's Parliamentary Constituencies (Amendment) Bill received a second reading by 229 votes to 44 but was later blocked as the government would not lay a money resolution.

On 4 December minister for families Robert Goodwill responded to Lib Dem leader Sir Vince Cable on the resignation of Alan Milburn as chair of the Social Mobility Commission. On 5 December David Davis updated the House on the progress of the Brexit negotiations. Amber Rudd published David Anderson's report on the terrorist attacks in London and Manchester. On 7 December Alistair Burt responded to Emily Thornberry on the implications of President Trump's decision to move the US embassy from Tel Aviv to Jerusalem and to recognise Jerusalem as Israel's capital. Health minister Jackie Doyle-Price made a statement in response to the Opposition-day debate on social care (on 25 October): 'we want to build consensus on a long-term, sustainable settlement for the future – looking at the quality of care being delivered, the funding of the system, and how it will be paid for in the round'.

On 11 December the prime minister updated MPs on the negotiations with the EU and the publication of a joint UK/ EC report on progress during the first phase: 'This is good news for people who voted leave, who were worried that we were so bogged down in tortuous negotiations that it was never going to happen, and it is good news for people who voted remain, who were worried that we would crash out without a deal.' Boris Johnson reported on the outcome of his visit to Oman, the UAE and Iran. The Finance Bill (No 2) passed its second reading by 313 votes to 269. On 12 December health minister Philip Dunne responded to Harriet Harman on the resignation of Lord Kerslake as chair of the King's College Hospital NHS Foundation Trust.

On 18 December Theresa May reported on the outcome of the European Council meeting, where they had formally agreed that sufficient progress has been made to move on to the second stage of the negotiations: 'an important step on the road to delivering the smooth and orderly Brexit that people voted for'. Sajid Javid updated MPs on the ongoing response to the Grenfell Tower fire and the wider review of building safety. Amber Rudd outlined the government's plan to tackle threats to MPs and harassment in public life. On 19 December Sajid Javid announced the annual local government finance settlement, followed by Nick Hurd's statement on police funding. On 21 December Andrea Leadsom made a statement on the independent complaints and grievance policy: 'we should not rest until everyone working in Parliament can feel safe, valued and respected'. Communities and local government minister Marcus Jones updated MPs on plans for a new funding model for supported housing.

Returning from the Christmas recess on 8 January 2018, Philip Dunne updated Labour spokesperson Jonathan Ashworth on the NHS winter crisis: 'we are lucky to be able to depend on the extraordinary dedication of frontline staff at this highly challenging time'. Joseph Johnson responded to Dawn Butler on the appointment of Toby Young to the board of the Office for Students. On 9 January new DCMS secretary Matt Hancock replied to Hannah Bardell about accusations of unequal pay at the BBC. Justice secretary David Gauke made a statement on the Parole Board's decision to release John Worboys.

On 15 January defence secretary Gavin Williamson replied to defence committee chair Julian Lewis on reductions in conventional military forces proposed by the national security capability review. The minister for the Cabinet Office and Chancellor of the Duchy of Lancaster, David Lidington, made a statement on Carillion plc, a major government supplier, going into liquidation.

On 22 January work and pensions secretary Esther McVey replied to Debbie Abrahams about stopping private-sector pension abuse; on 23 January she replied to Peter Grant about the High Court ruling over the judicial review on the application of personal independence payments to persons with mental health problems. Matt Hancock updated MPs on the interim report by the Competition and Markets Authority on the proposed merger between 21st Century Fox and Sky. On 24 January education minister Anne Milton replied to Jess Phillips about whether David Meller should remain a non-executive director in the Department for Education following revelations about treatment of female staff at the Presidents Club charity dinner. On 25 January Gavin Williamson updated MPs on the programme to modernise defence.

On 29 January Robin Walker replied to Sir William Cash about EU directives setting out its negotiating position on the implementation period for leaving the EU: 'we would be seeking a strictly time-limited implementation period to allow a smooth and orderly exit'. The minister for Asia and the Pacific, Mark Field, responded to Stephen Doughty on Taliban and Daesh attacks on civilians and humanitarian workers in Afghanistan. Cabinet Office minister Chloe Smith replied to Diana Johnson about progress in establishing an inquiry into the contaminated blood scandal. On 30 January Steve Baker replied to Keir Starmer on the government's analysis of the long-term economic impact of Brexit on the economy: 'I can confirm that when we bring forward the vote on the final deal that we agree with the EU, we will ensure that the House is presented with the appropriate analysis that the government have carried out, so that the House can make an informed decision.' The minister for disabled people, Sarah Newton, replied to Marsha De Cordova on the process and timetable for the personal independence payment back payments. On 1 February, Cabinet Office minister Oliver Dowden replied to Rachel Reeves on the risk to public finances and public services as a result of the serious financial concerns about Capita, a major government supplier.

On 5 February, minister for immigration Caroline Nokes replied to Yvette Cooper on the publication of the proposed immigration White Paper: 'we will end free movement and build an immigration system that works in the national interest'. Health minister Stephen Barclay replied to Jonathan Ashworth on the government's response to the resolution of the House of 10 January on the NHS winter crisis. Minister for housing Dominic Raab replied to John Healey on the implications of the withdrawal of the Building Research Establishment's safety test results for insulation materials used at Grenfell Tower. Chris Grayling made a statement on rail franchising and the East Coast main line. On 6 February housing, communities and local government minister Rishi Sunak responded to Philip Hollobone on the potential bankruptcy of Northamptonshire County Council. Minister for women Amber Rudd marked the centenary of women's suffrage. On 7 February BEIS minister Andrew Griffiths updated Labour spokesperson Rebecca Long Bailey on the government's response to the Taylor review of modern working. On 8 February Esther McVey replied to John Mann on executive pay and cash reserves held at Motability. Andrea Leadsom published the report on an independent complaints and grievance policy for Parliament. New health minister Stephen Barclay made a statement on the Kirkup review of Liverpool Community Health NHS Trust. Pensions minister Guy Opperman made a statement following the Opposition-day debate on state pension age about the decision to equalise the state pension age for men and women.

Returning after the half-term recess on 20 February, Nick Hurd replied to Crispin Blunt about the case of Alfie Dingley and access to medical cannabis to treat his epilepsy. Northern Ireland secretary Karen Bradley made a statement on the political situation in Northern Ireland. International development secretary Penny Mordaunt updated MPs on the response to sexual abuse and exploitation perpetrated by charity workers in Haiti in 2011. Education secretary Damian Hinds made a statement on the review of post-18 education and funding. On 21 February Jeremy Hunt set out the government's actions to address public concerns about the safety of medicines and medical devices used by the NHS. On 22 February DEFRA minister Thérèse Coffey replied to Neil Parish about steps to improve air quality after a High Court ruling.

On 26 February, Boris Johnson replied to John Woodcock on the situation inside de-escalation zones in Syria. On 27 February health minister Jackie Doyle-Price replied to Luciana Berger on the Care Quality Commission's report *Monitoring the Mental Health Act in 2016/17*. Universities minister Sam Gyimah responded to Angela Rayner about the appointment of the board of the Office for Students. On 28 February Cabinet Office minister David Lidington replied to Emily

Thornberry on future border arrangements between Northern Ireland and the Republic of Ireland following Brexit. Foreign minister Mark Field replied to Stephen Twigg about the Burmese government's failure to issue visas to members of the International Development Committee. On 1 March Matt Hancock made a statement about the implementation of the Leveson inquiry and freedom of the press.

On 5 March Theresa May made a statement on future economic partnership with the EU: 'as we go forwards, foremost in my mind is this pledge: to act not in the interests of the privileged few, but in the interests of all our people, and to make Britain a country that works for everyone'. Sajid Javid made a statement on the national planning policy framework. On 6 March Boris Johnson replied to Tom Tugendhat on policy towards Russia following the Novochok poisoning incident in Salisbury. Caroline Nokes replied to Diane Abbott on Yarl's Wood immigration removal centre. Thérèse Coffey updated MPs on the water supply situation following the severe weather. On 7 March foreign minister Alistair Burt replied to Sir Vince Cable about relations with Saudi Arabia. On 8 March health minister Steve Brine replied to Barbara Keeley about the Care Quality Commission's review of children and young people's mental health services. Amber Rudd updated MPs on the Salisbury poisoning incident.

On 12 March Home Office minister Victoria Atkins replied to Yasmin Qureshi about hate crime in light of inflammatory letters inciting a 'Punish a Muslim day' on 3 April. Andrea Leadsom replied to Caroline Lucas about the treatment of House of Commons staff. Theresa May updated MPs on the Salisbury poisoning incident. Karen Bradley made a statement on Northern Ireland finances. International trade secretary Liam Fox made a statement on the US imposition of steel and aluminium import tariffs. Alistair Burt updated MPs on the situation in Afrin, Syria.

SPRING STATEMENT

On 13 March Philip Hammond presented the first spring statement. The main points were:

• the 2018 economic growth forecast was revised upwards to 1.5%, the 1.3% growth forecast for 2019–20 was unchanged; inflation was forecast to fall to 2% by the end of 2018
• government borrowing to be £45.2 billion in 2017–18 and to fall every financial year to £21.4 billion in 2021–22
• consultations to be held on: reducing tax on the least polluting vans; tax changes to discourage use of single-use plastic; a new VAT collection mechanism for online sales; extending current training tax relief to self-employed people and employees; the role of cash in the new economy
• the next revaluation of business rates to be brought forward to 2021

He said: 'We are building our vision of a country that works for everyone and an economy where prosperity and opportunity are in reach of all, wherever they live and whatever their gender, colour, creed or background, where talent and hard work alone determine success, as a beacon of enterprise and innovation and an outward-looking, free-trading nation, confident that our best days lie ahead of us, a force for good in the world and a country that we can all be proud to pass on to our children.' John McDonnell was scathing: 'his complacency today is astounding. We face in every public service a crisis on a scale that we have never seen before.'

On 14 March Theresa May gave an update on the response of the Russian government to the Salisbury poisoning incident. Sajid Javid published the integrated communities strategy Green Paper. Mark Field updated MPs on the plight of Burma's Rohingya minority.

On 19 March security minister Ben Wallace responded to John McDonnell about action to address dirty money being laundered in the UK. Financial secretary Mel Stride replied to Brexit committee chair Hilary Benn about customs clearance arrangements at UK ports after Brexit. Matt Hancock replied to DCMS committee chair Damian Collins about alleged breaches of Facebook user data by Cambridge Analytica. On 20 March environment secretary Michael Gove replied to Alistair Carmichael about the progress of negotiations relating to fisheries management arrangements after Brexit. Andrew Griffiths published a consultation paper on corporate governance and insolvency. On 21 March Jeremy Hunt replied to Jonathan Ashworth about the new NHS pay deal. Sajid Javid published the Grenfell Tower independent recovery task force's second report.

On 26 March Caroline Nokes replied to Liz Twist about why the contract for the new UK passport had been awarded to a French-owned company. Theresa May reported back on the European Council meeting: 'The agreements on the withdrawal agreement and the implementation period are proof that, with political will, a spirit of co-operation and a spirit of opportunity for the future, we can find answers to difficult issues together. For whether people voted leave or remain, many are frankly tired of the old arguments and the attempts to refight the referendum.' On 27 March Chris Grayling made a statement about the future of the West Coast main rail line, plans for the integration of track and train on the railways and plans for the transition to the operation of High Speed 2. Sajid Javid updated MPs about the independent inspection report on Northamptonshire County Council. Greg Clark made a statement about the takeover bid by Melrose Industries plc for GKN plc. Lib Dem MP Tom Brake introduced an emergency debate about alleged breaches of electoral law during the EU referendum. On 28 March Ben Wallace replied to Lucy Powell about the Kerslake review of the Manchester arena attack. David Gauke made a statement about the High Court judgment relating to the Parole Board's decision to release John Worboys.

Returning after the Easter recess on 16 April, Amber Rudd replied to David Lammy on the status of Windrush migrants' children in this country: 'there is absolutely no question about their right to remain'. Theresa May made a statement on the actions taken to degrade the Syrian regime's chemical weapons capabilities. Labour MP Alison McGovern introduced an emergency debate on Syria. On 17 April Jeremy Corbyn introduced an emergency debate on Parliament's rights in relation to the approval of military action by British forces overseas. On 18 April Victoria Atkins responded to Harriet Harman on closing the gender pay gap. The Attorney-General, Jeremy Wright, replied to SNP spokesperson Joanna Cherry about the government's position on the Leaving the EU and the Scotland and Wales Continuity Bills.

On 23 April Chloe Smith replied to Cat Smith about piloting voter identity checks in the local government elections on 3 May. Amber Rudd set out urgent measures to help the Windrush generation. On 24 April Harriett Baldwin updated Stephen Twigg on Yemen. Oliver Dowden replied to Sir Vince Cable about Capita. Greg Clark made a statement about Melrose Industries' bid for GKN: 'there are not reasonable and proportionate grounds to make a statutory intervention on the grounds of national security'. On 26 April Amber Rudd replied to Diane Abbott about the use of immigrant removal targets by the Home Office and what she had said about these to the select committee. BEIS minister Margot James published the artificial intelligence sector-support deal. Mel Stride made a statement on the quarterly stamp duty land tax statistics showing the impact of first-time buyers' relief.

On 30 April Andrew Griffiths replied to Rebecca Long Bailey on the proposed merger of Sainsbury's and Asda supermarkets. The new home secretary, Sajid Javid, replied to Diane Abbott about the government's handling of the Windrush scandal, which had led Amber Rudd to resign her post that morning. Penny Mordaunt updated MPs on the UK's support for the people of Syria.

On 1 May the Speaker led tributes to former Speaker Michael Martin. On 2 May Jeremy Hunt informed the House of a serious failure in the national breast screening programme in England.

On 8 May minister for care Caroline Dinenage replied to Barbara Keeley on the learning disabilities mortality review. Victoria Atkins responded to Diane Abbott on the renewal of G4S's contract to run immigration removal centres. On 9 May Boris Johnson made a statement on the future of the Iran nuclear agreement, the joint comprehensive plan of action. On 10 May Andrea Leadsom replied to Afzal Khan about the government's policy on introducing money resolutions for Private Members' Bills. Jeremy Wright made a statement on the settlement of the claim of Abdul Hakim Belhaj and Fatima Boudchar against the government over its alleged compliance in their rendition to Libya in 2004.

On 14 May the Speaker led tributes to former MP and minister Tessa Jowell. Damian Hinds replied to Angela Rayner about the government's response to the 'Schools that work for everyone' consultation. On 15 May Alistair Burt replied to Emily Thornberry about the violence at the Gaza border. On 16 May Chris Grayling made a statement about the future of the East Coast main rail line, terminating the Stagecoach and Virgin Trains franchise from 24 June. On 17 May DCMS minister Tracey Crouch published the government's response to the consultation on proposals for changes to social responsibility requirements in the gambling industry. Housing, communities and local government secretary James Brokenshire published the final report of Dame Judith Hackitt's review of building regulations and fire safety.

On 21 May James Brokenshire replied to John Healey on action taken and planned with respect to residents in tower blocks with dangerous cladding. Alistair Burt responded to Richard Burden about the decision to abstain from voting on the resolution of the UN Human Rights Council calling for an independent investigation into recent violence in Gaza. The Speaker explained why he used the word 'stupid' in the chamber. Afzal Khan introduced an emergency debate on the expectation that the government brings forward a money resolution relating to Private Members' Bills. On 22 May Michael Gove replied to Neil Parish about improving transport emissions in urban areas. Alistair Burt replied to Tulip Siddiq about the case of Nazanin Zaghari-Ratcliffe following the new charges brought against her in Iran.

On 4 June Esther McVey replied to Debbie Abrahams about the withdrawal of the government's appeals in relation to personal independence payment claimants with chronic conditions. Liam Fox made a statement on the US's imposition of steel and aluminium import tariffs. Chris Grayling updated MPs on the recent difficulties arising from the rail timetable changes, in particular on GTR and Northern routes. Greg Clark confirmed that Hitachi and the government had decided to enter into negotiations over the proposed Wylfa Newydd nuclear power plant. On 5 June Chris Grayling laid the final proposal for an airports national policy statement, which included expanding Heathrow airport. Matt Hancock made a statement about the proposed mergers between Comcast and Sky and between 21st Century Fox and Sky. Stella Creasy introduced an emergency debate on the role of the UK Parliament in repealing abortion laws in Northern Ireland. On 7 June transport minister Jesse Norman replied to Justine Greening on the potential taxpayer liabilities in the statement of principles agreement with Heathrow Airport Ltd. Karen Bradley responded to Stella Creasy about whether, following the ruling of the Supreme Court on abortion in Northern Ireland, the current law was incompatible with the European Convention on Human Rights.

On 11 June Alistair Burt replied to Keith Vaz about reports of an imminent attack by the Saudi- and Emirati-led coalition on Hodeidah, Yemen. Theresa May reported on the G7 summit in Quebec: a 'difficult summit with, at times, some very candid discussions, but the conclusion I draw is that it is only through continued dialogue that we can find ways to work together to resolve the challenges we face'. James Brokenshire made a statement about the government's response to the Grenfell Tower fire. On 13 June, during Prime Minister's Questions, the SNP's Westminster leader Ian Blackford was ordered to withdraw from the House for the remainder of the day; all the other SNP MPs also walked out. On 14 June defence minister Guto Bebb replied to Labour spokesperson Nia Griffith about the UK's future participation in development of the Galileo satellite navigation system. On 15 June Christopher Chope objected to the second reading of Wera Hobhouse's Voyeurism (Offences) Bill, despite it having all-party support.

On 18 June Nick Hurd replied to Tonia Antoniazzi about an emergency licence to allow the use of medical cannabis for Billy Caldwell. Justice minister Lucy Frazer replied to Wera Hobhouse about the government plan to legislate on making 'upskirting' a specific sexual offence. Jeremy Hunt made a statement about a new long-term funding plan for the NHS. Ian Blackford introduced an emergency debate on the Sewel convention. On 19 June Sajid Javid reported that he had issued an emergency licence to allow Billy Caldwell's medical team to access cannabis-based medicine. On 20 June Jeremy Hunt published the independent panel report on Gosport Memorial Hospital between 1987 and 2001. On 21 June defence minister Tobias Ellwood replied to Fabian Hamilton about the awarding of the defence fire and rescue contract to Capita. Esther McVey made a statement about universal credit and welfare changes. Caroline Nokes made a statement about the new settlement scheme for resident EU citizens and their family members.

On 25 June Greg Clark replied to Mark Tami following the publication of the Airbus Brexit risk assessment report and its implications for future investment and job security in the UK. Steve Brine replied to Jonathan Ashworth on the publication of the second chapter of the government's childhood obesity strategy. Greg Clark announced his rejection of the proposed Swansea Bay tidal lagoon scheme. MPs approved the national policy statement on new runway capacity and infrastructure at airports in south-east England by 415 votes to 119. On 27 June justice minister Rory Stewart replied to Richard Burgon about plans for more privately financed prisons. On 28 June Sam Gyimah replied to John Woodcock on the launch of the nuclear sector deal. Damian Collins introduced a debate on privilege as a consequence of Dominic Cummings' refusal to appear before the digital, culture, media and sport select committee.

On 2 July Sir Alan Duncan replied to Kenneth Clarke about reinstating the judge-led inquiry, promised by the government in 2012, on detainee mistreatment and rendition. Nick Hurd responded to Jonathan Reynolds about the fires on the Saddleworth and Tameside moors. Theresa May reported back on the European Council, where it was agreed 'we must now urgently intensify and accelerate the pace of negotiations on our future relationship'. David Lidington announced that the infected blood inquiry was to formally begin its work. On 3 July Joseph Johnson updated Andy McDonald on the Govia Thameslink franchise and plans for rail electrification. Minister for women Penny Mordaunt replied to Dawn Butler about the LGBT action plan. Gavin Williamson delivered the regular counter-Daesh update. On 4 July Esther McVey apologised for mistakenly saying that the National Audit Office had asked for the roll-out of universal credit to continue at a faster rate when it had not. Michael Gove published a White Paper, *Sustainable Fisheries for Future Generations*. Esther McVey replied to Frank Field on universal credit. BEIS minister Richard Harrington published the government's construction sector deal. Sajid Javid made a statement on the Novochok poisoning incidents in Amesbury and Salisbury.

On 9 July Theresa May made a statement on leaving the EU – on 6 July at Chequers the Cabinet had 'agreed a comprehensive and ambitious proposal that provides a responsible and credible basis for progressing negotiations with the EU towards a new relationship ... It is a proposal that will take back control of our borders, our money and our laws, but do so in a way that protects jobs, allows us to strike new trade deals through an independent trade policy and keeps our people safe and our Union together'. Unfortunately this had led to the resignation of the Brexit secretary on 8 July and the foreign secretary on 9 July. Sajid Javid updated MPs on the Amesbury and Salisbury poisonings and the death of Dawn Sturgess. MPs passed the Northern Ireland Budget (No. 2) Bill to allow business to continue in Northern Ireland without an executive. On 11 July Gavin Williamson made a statement on Afghanistan. On 12 July Caroline Nokes replied to David Lammy on the decision to pause the hostile environment for immigrants. Nick Hurd replied to Louise Haigh on policing during President Trump's four-day visit. New Brexit secretary Dominic Raab published a White Paper on the UK's future relationship with the EU: 'principled and practical, faithful to the referendum, it delivers a deal that is good for the UK and good for our EU friends'.

On 16 July Theresa May reported back on the NATO summit in Brussels. Liam Fox set out the role of Parliament, the devolved administrations, public, business and civil society in agreeing new international trade agreements to benefit the whole of the UK. New clauses in the Taxation (Cross-border Trade) Bill that enforce the need for consent of the Scottish Parliament and also the prohibition on collection of certain taxes or duties on behalf of a territory without reciprocity were passed by 305 votes to 302. On 17 July an amendment to the Trade Bill to allow for a free trade area for goods was defeated by 307 votes to 301. On 18 July Chloe Smith replied to Chuka Umunna on the findings of the Electoral Commission's investigation into the conduct of the Vote Leave campaign. Gavin Williamson outlined a strategy for the combat air sector. A move by the government to adjourn the Commons early for the summer recess was withdrawn. Joseph Johnson updated Andy McDonald on the performance of the Govia Thameslink franchise. Karen Bradley replied to her Labour shadow Tony Lloyd about the recent violence in Northern Ireland and assistance to the Police Service of Northern Ireland and local community organisations to ensure that violence does not return. Andrea Leadsom replied to Alistair Carmichael about arrangements for MPs on maternity leave and proxy voting. Sam Gyimah made a statement on a key development in UK space policy. Boris Johnson delivered a personal statement on his resignation. On 19 July the DUP MP Ian Paisley made a personal statement following the recommendation to ban him from the Commons for 30 days after the recess for failing to declare two family holidays paid for by the Sri Lankan government. Sarah Newton replied to Marsha De Cordova about employment and support allowance underpayments. Damian Hinds made a statement about the consultation on proposals for relationships education, sex education and health education. MPs approved a new parliamentary independent complaints and grievance policy.

On 23 July Ben Wallace replied to Diane Abbott on the rendition of UK citizens who may be subject to capital punishment. David Lidington replied to Alistair Carmichael on policy and practice with regard to pairing arrangements in Commons' votes. On 24 July Liz Truss responded to her Labour shadow Peter Dowd on the public sector pay announcement: 'the biggest pay rise in almost 10 years for about 1 million public workers'. Sir Alan Duncan replied to

Alison McGovern about steps being taken to save civilian life in Syria. Dominic Raab published a White Paper setting out plans for legislating for the Brexit withdrawal agreement and implementation period. Sajid Javid made a statement on immigration detention and the publication of Stephen Shaw's second independent review. Both Houses then rose for the summer recess, with 26 government Bills having received royal assent in the House of Commons' 177 sitting days.

PUBLIC ACTS OF PARLIAMENT

Public acts included in this list are those which received royal assent after 31 July 2017. The date stated after each act is the date on which it came into operation. For further information see W www.legislation.gov.uk

Finance (No. 2) Act 2017 ch. 32 (16 November 2017) grants certain duties, alters other duties, amends the law relating to the national debt and the public revenue, and makes further provision in connection with finance.

Air Travel Organisers' Licensing Act 2017 ch. 33 (16 November 2017) amends sections 71, 71A and 84 of the Civil Aviation Act 1982.

Northern Ireland Budget Act 2017 ch. 34 (16 November 2017) authorises the issue out of the Consolidated Fund of Northern Ireland of certain sums for the service of the year ending 31 March 2018 and appropriates those sums for specified purposes, authorises the Department of Finance in Northern Ireland to borrow on the credit of the appropriated sums, authorises the use for the public service of certain resources (including accruing resources) for the year ending 31 March 2018, and repeals certain spent provisions.

European Union (Approvals) Act 2017 ch.35 (7 December 2017) makes provision approving for the purposes of section 8 of the European Union Act 2011 draft decisions under Article 352 of the Treaty on the Functioning of the European Union on the participation of the Republic of Albania and the Republic of Serbia in the work of the European Union Agency for Fundamental Rights and on the signing and conclusion of an agreement between the European Union and Canada regarding the application of their competition laws.

Telecommunications Infrastructure (Relief from Non-Domestic Rates Act) 2018 ch. 36 (8 February 2018) makes provision enabling relief from non-domestic rates in England and Wales to be conferred in respect of hereditaments used for the purposes of facilitating the transmission of communications by any means involving the use of electrical or electromagnetic energy.

Armed Forces (Flexible Working Act) 2018 ch. 37 (8 February 2018) makes provision for members of the regular forces to serve part-time or subject to geographic restrictions.

Finance Act 2018 ch. 38 (15 March 2018) grants certain duties, alters other duties, amends the law relating to the national debt and the public revenue, and makes further provision in connection with finance.

Supply and Appropriation (Anticipation and Adjustments) Act 2018 ch. 39 (15 March 2018) authorises the use of resources for the years ending with 31 March 2017, 31 March 2018 and 31 March 2019, authorises the issue of sums out of the Consolidated Fund for the years ending 31 March 2018 and 31 March 2019, and appropriates the supply authorised by this Act for the years ending with 31 March 2017 and 31 March 2018.

Space Industry Act 2018 ch. 40 (15 March 2018) makes provision about space activities and sub-orbital activities.

Northern Ireland (Regional Rates and Energy) Act 2018 ch. 41 (28 March 2018) makes provision about the regional rate in Northern Ireland for the year ending 31 March 2019 and amends the Renewable Heat Incentive Scheme Regulations (Northern Ireland) 2012.

Northern Ireland Assembly Members (Pay) Act 2018 ch. 42 (28 March 2018) confers power on the Secretary of State to determine salaries and other benefits for Members of the Northern Ireland Assembly in respect of periods when there is no Executive.

Northern Ireland Budget (Anticipation and Adjustments) Act ch. 43 (28 March 2018) authorises the issue out of the Consolidated Fund of Northern Ireland of certain sums for the service of the years ending 31 March 2018 and 2019, appropriates those sums for specified purposes, authorises the use for the public service of certain resources for those years, revises the limits on the use of certain accruing resources in the year ending 31 March 2018, and authorises the Department of Finance in Northern Ireland to borrow on the credit of the sum appropriated for the year ending 31 March 2019.

Laser Misuse (Vehicles) Act 2018 ch. 44 (10 May 2018) makes provision creating new offences of shining or directing a laser beam towards a vehicle or air traffic facility.

Financial Guidance and Claims Act 2018 ch. 45 (10 May 2018) makes provision establishing a new financial guidance body (including provision about a debt respite scheme), makes provision about the funding of debt advice in Scotland, Wales and Northern Ireland, provides a power to make regulations prohibiting unsolicited direct marketing in relation to pensions and other consumer financial products and services, and makes provision about the regulation of claims management services.

Secure Tenancies (Victims of Domestic Abuse) Act 2018 ch. 46 (10 May 2018) makes provision about the granting of old-style secure tenancies in cases of domestic abuse.

Data Protection Act 2018 ch. 47 (23 May 2018) makes provision for the regulation of the processing of information relating to individuals and in connection with the Information Commissioner's functions under certain regulations relating to information, and the direct marketing code of practice.

Sanctions and Anti-Money Laundering Act 2018 ch. 48 (23 May 2018) makes provision enabling sanctions to be imposed where appropriate for the purposes of compliance with United Nations obligations or other international obligations or for the purposes of furthering the prevention of terrorism or for the purposes of national security or international peace and security or for the purposes of furthering foreign policy objectives, and for the purposes of the detection, investigation and prevention of money laundering and terrorist financing and for the purposes of implementing Standards published by the Financial Action Task Force relating to combating threats to the integrity of the international financial system.

Smart Meters Act 2018 ch. 49 (23 May 2018) extends the period for the Secretary of State to exercise powers relating to smart metering, provides for a special administration regime for a smart meter communication licensee, and makes provision enabling half-hourly electricity imbalances to be calculated using information obtained from smart meters.

Nuclear Safeguards Act 2018 ch. 50 (26 June 2018) makes provision about nuclear safeguards; and for connected purposes.

European Union (Withdrawal) Act 2018 ch. 51 (26 June 2018) repeals the European Communities Act 1972 and makes other provision in connection with the withdrawal of the United Kingdom from the EU.

Supply and Appropriation (Main Estimates) Act 2018 ch. 52 (19 July 2018) authorises the use of resources for the year ending with 31 March 2019, authorises both the issue of sums out of the Consolidated Fund and the application of income for that year, and appropriates the supply authorised for that year by this Act and by the Supply and Appropriation (Anticipation and Adjustments) Act 2018.

Automated and Electric Vehicles Act 2018 ch. 53 (19 July 2018) makes provision about automated vehicles and electric vehicles.

Haulage Permits and Trailer Registration Act 2018 ch. 54 (19 July 2018) makes provision about the international transport of goods by road and about the registration of trailers.

Northern Ireland Budget Act 2018 ch. 55 (19 July 2018) authorises the issue out of the Consolidated Fund of Northern Ireland of certain sums for the service of the year ending 31 March 2019, appropriates those sums for specified purposes, authorises the Department of Finance in Northern Ireland to borrow on the credit of the appropriated sums, authorises the use for the public service of certain resources (including accruing resources) for the year ending 31 March 2019, and repeals certain spent provisions.

Domestic Gas and Electricity (Tariff Cap) Act 2018 ch. 56 (19 July 2018) makes provision for the imposition of a cap on rates charged to domestic customers for the supply of gas and electricity.

POP MUSIC

Piers Martin

DIVIDE AND CONQUER
The British pop singer Ed Sheeran enjoyed another hugely successful year, ending 2017 with the world's best-selling album. The 27-year-old from Suffolk sold 6.1 million copies of his third album ÷ (known as *Divide*), according to the International Federation of the Phonographic Industry, 2.7 million of which were sold in the UK between its release in March and the end of the year. The album became Spotify's most streamed of the year, with 3.1 billion plays, while its lead single 'Shape of You' was the platform's most streamed track of 2017 both globally and in the UK, with 1.4 billion streams, a total which also made it the most popular song of all time on Spotify.

Upon release, nine of *Divide*'s tracks entered the UK top ten – a record in itself – and by the midpoint of 2017, Sheeran's success had boosted sales of music in the UK by 11.2 per cent, with *Divide* becoming the UK's biggest-selling entertainment product. Sheeran secured the Christmas number one with 'Perfect' and also became the only artist in history to spend a full year in the top ten with three albums (*Divide, Multiply* and *Plus*). By June 2018, *Divide* had racked up more than 3 million sales, making it the UK's 11th best-selling album of the millennium, according to the Official Chart Company (OCC).

The Sheeran phenomenon naturally translated to colossal box office success for his world tour, which began in 2017 and runs until spring 2019. During the first six months of 2018, for example, Sheeran sold more than 2.6 million tickets, including 300,000 in a single day in Ireland, an unprecedented feat by an artist, while in Australia and New Zealand the tour sold over one million tickets, a record for ticket sales in those countries. In the UK, Sheeran played to 1.13 million people across eight stadium shows in May and June, including a run of four at Wembley Stadium. Only Michael Jackson, with seven, has played more shows there. In total, ticket sales for the first six months of 2018 earned Sheeran a gross profit of $213.9m (around £165m), according to industry title *IQ Index*.

Such is the appeal of Sheeran that the New Zealand city of Dunedin planned a week-long festival in honour of the Ipswich singer, who played three shows there over the Easter weekend. The 100,000 'Sheerios', as his fans are sometimes known, doubled the southern city's population. According to *The Guardian,* a mural of the singer's face was painted in the city centre at a cost of NZ$8,000 (£4,100), special licences were granted to allow bars to sell alcohol to fans on Good Friday and Easter Sunday, and a passenger train was renamed the Easter Ed Express as the city decided to 'paint the town Ed'. One Dunedin musician, Martin Phillipps, frontman of The Chills, was quoted in response to the mural: 'I think something like this is better spent celebrating local arts.'

NEW RULERS
Despite the revenue that Sheeran generated for the music industry this year, at the Brit Awards in February he was presented with a solitary trophy, for British global success. There, the focus instead shifted to celebrating new talent, with 22-year-old newcomer Dua Lipa receiving awards for breakthrough act and British female solo artist following the global success of her hits 'Be the One' and 'New Rules' from her self-titled debut album. The singer, whose parents are Kosovan, grew up in London and in August became the first recipient of the key to Kosovo's capital Pristina when she headlined a festival in the city. The event had been organised by her charity, the Sunny Hill Foundation, which aims to promote social equality in the country. For all the attention that Lipa received this year, however, one of the best-selling female artists of 2017 turned out to be Dame Vera Lynn, who celebrated her 100th birthday by releasing a new compilation album. Lynn, best known as the 'forces' sweetheart' during the Second World War, became the oldest living artist to have a top ten album when *Vera Lynn 100* entered the UK charts at number three in March.

At the Brits, the south London rapper Stormzy took home awards for British male solo artist and British album, for his debut *Gang Signs & Prayer,* a compelling mix of grime, rap and gospel, which also won the album award at the Ivor Novello Awards in May. Stormzy, 25, whose real name is Michael Omari, used the Brits as a platform to denounce the government over its handling of the Grenfell Tower tragedy. 'Theresa May, where's the money for Grenfell?' he rapped during a freestyle performance, adding: 'You criminals, and you got the cheek to call us savages? You should all do some jail time, you should pay some damages.' The following day a Downing Street spokesman defended the prime minister, pointing out that the government had committed more than £58m to the community in the aftermath of the fire.

INDUSTRY INCOME IMPROVES
A combination of increased streaming figures and physical sales ensured that industry income in the UK grew by 11 per cent in 2017, its highest annual growth since 1995, according to the British Phonographic Industry (BPI). However, this rise in revenue to £816.5m is only the second year of growth after more than a decade in steady decline – industry turnover peaked in 2001 at £1.2bn – but does illustrate that the industry-wide focus on streaming seems to be paying off. Revenue from streaming platform subscriptions, ad-supported streams and video streams (predominantly via YouTube) was up 41.1 per cent year-on-year to £388.8m, the BPI notes. As of May, the two leading platforms, Spotify and Apple Music, claim to have, respectively, 83 million and 50 million users worldwide, though how much of their profits trickle down to the artists and songwriters still remains unclear. In August, the venerable British musician Peter Frampton expressed his view on social media, tweeting: 'For 55 million streams of "Baby, I Love Your Way", I got $1,700. I went to Washington with [rights agency] ASCAP last year to talk to law makers about this. Their jaws dropped and they asked me to repeat that for them.

While much has been made of the resurgence of vinyl – and this year the format's share of album purchases in the UK rose 6.9 per cent to 4.1 million, its highest peak since the early 1990s – sales of CDs still make up nearly 70 per cent of sales, even though these are at their lowest point since 1994; annual digital sales, meanwhile, slipped to 23.2 per cent. In 2017, Ed Sheeran's *Divide* topped year-end sales charts across all formats, including vinyl, but in 2018 the higher echelons of the album chart reflected the British public's rather more old-fashioned tastes. By mid-April, the soundtrack to the circus musical *The Greatest Showman,* a film starring Hugh Jackman as the American showman P. T. Barnum which was originally released in December, had become the UK's top-selling album of 2018, shifting more than half a million copies. The soundtrack, featuring hits such as 'Rewrite the Stars' and 'This is Me', equalled Adele's record of 11 consecutive weeks at the top of the UK album chart for her *21* album, and come August the album had notched up 21 non-consecutive weeks at number one out of a possible 28, beating the 18 weeks previously held by the *Saturday Night Fever* soundtrack in 1978. By this point, the album's combined sales of physical, digital downloads and streaming units had passed one million. Some industry figures were concerned that the soundtrack's popularity had prevented new albums by the likes of Snow Patrol, Kanye West, Manic Street Preachers, James Bay and Justin Timberlake from reaching number one.

In July, the long-running compilation series *Now That's What I Call Music!* released its centenary edition, 35 years after the first album hit the market and revolutionised the market. Amid much fanfare, *Now! 100* sold 176,000 copies in its opening week, according to the OCC, making it the fastest-selling album of 2018 at the time and bucking the downward trend in compilation sales. The original 1983 edition of the first *Now That's What I Call Music!*, which featured hits by Phil Collins, The Cure and Culture Club, was also reissued and sold 16,537 copies, enough to reach number two in the compilations chart.

ARCTICS ROLL ON
In May, the Sheffield band Arctic Monkeys returned with their sixth album, *Tranquillity Base Hotel + Casino*, a conceptual effort largely composed in Los Angeles by frontman Alex Turner that showed a bold new side to the group. Fans expecting melodic rock in the vein of 2013's *AM* may have been surprised by the album's louche grooves and piano blues, and by the way that Turner had settled into his role as something of a lounge crooner, a persona he had developed in his other group, the Last Shadow Puppets. Released in full without a lead single, the album received broadly positive reviews and went on to sell 86,359 units in its opening week, making it the fastest-selling artist album of 2018 in the UK, according to the OCC. Of those, 24,500 copies were sold on vinyl, helping *Tranquillity Base Hotel + Casino* to become the fastest-selling vinyl record of the last 25 years, beating the 16,000 first-week sales of Liam Gallagher's solo debut *As You Were* in October.

Gallagher, the former frontman of Oasis and Beady Eye, played to the crowd on his first solo album with a set of rousing indie rock that comfortably delivered the success that he felt he deserved after the fallow years of Beady Eye, reaching number one in its week of release. Not to be outdone, his older brother's group, Noel Gallagher's High Flying Birds, released their third album, *Who Built the Moon?*, in November. An adventurous set that touched on psychedelia, Motown and electronic soul, this also topped the UK albums chart upon release.

DRAKE DOMINATES
The Canadian rapper and singer Drake continued to command attention this year with the release at the end of June of his fifth album *Scorpion*, which entered the UK charts at number one and remained there for three weeks. With guest spots from the likes of Jay-Z and Nicki Minaj as well as a posthumous appearance by Michael Jackson, *Scorpion* proved easy to admire but perhaps hard to love, as the melancholy showman exhausted his familiar routine across 25 tracks of hip-hop and R&B that ran to almost 90 minutes. Nevertheless, on its day of release *Scorpion* broke the one-day global records for album streams on Spotify (132 million) and Apple Music (170 million), breaking the previous record on Apple Music set by Drake's 2017 album *More Life*. Released in March 2017, *More Life* ended the year as the eighth best-selling artist album and second-most streamed album in the UK. More than most, Drake understands how to operate as an artist in the digital age: teasing and releasing a steady stream of new music direct to fans, and seldom granting interviews to maintain an air of mystery despite being one of the most successful musicians on the planet.

As hip-hop became the dominant style in contemporary pop – or at least the most-streamed genre, which regularly produced inventive new music, particularly in the US – stories involving rappers captivated the media. A former stripper from the Bronx in New York City named Cardi B broke through with a track called 'Bodak Yellow' that became one of the year's more ubiquitous hits. In April, the Los Angeles rapper Kendrick Lamar was awarded the Pulitzer Prize for music for his third album, *Damn*, a prestigious award typically granted to modern composers. Long heralded as the greatest rapper of his generation, Lamar was a worthy winner of a prize that had previously ignored most forms of popular music and held little cultural currency beyond the classical world. On *Damn*, Lamar continued to examine his place in American society as a young black man with wit, vision and audacious production.

In May, the rapper Childish Gambino – the alter ego of actor Donald Glover – released a powerful video for a song called 'This Is America' which drew attention to the simmering racial tension in modern-day America with a compelling choreographed ensemble piece. As of August, the video had racked up 370 million YouTube views. Elsewhere, the untimely deaths of fast-rising US rappers Lil Peep and XXXTentacion shocked the hip-hop community. Noted for his intimate raps about depression and drugs, Lil Peep – real name Gustav Åhr – died of an overdose in November at the age of 21. Troubled Florida rapper XXXTentacion (Jahseh Onfroy), meanwhile, had his flourishing if notorious career cut brutally short when he was shot dead as he left a motorcycle dealership in Deerfield Beach, Florida, in June. He was 20. The week after his murder, his song 'Sad!' topped the Billboard Hot 100 in the US.

BRITISH JAZZ BLASTS OFF
Often considered unfashionable, jazz enjoyed something of a moment in the UK this year as a new generation of young players and bands across the country fashioned a grassroots movement that drew on grime, dancehall and hip-hop and threatened to spill into the mainstream. Centred in London – in particular around small clubs in the south-eastern districts of Deptford, Catford and Peckham – the movement took no obvious form but involved musicians such as saxophonist Shabaka Hutchings, drummer Moses Boyd and tuba player Theon Cross, who play in or are affiliated with groups such as Sons of Kemet, The Comet is Coming and Ezra Collective. Championed by the likes of BBC DJ Gilles Peterson, their music – jazz with a modern twist – resonated with a young audience who tend to listen without prejudice. In July, Spotify told the BBC that in the first half of 2018, there had been a 108 per cent increase in the number of UK users aged 30 or under listening to their popular Jazz UK playlist, while streaming platforms Deezer and Amazon Music also reported increases. Asked to account for jazz's rise in popularity, Hutchings, 34, the band leader in Sons of Kemet and The Comet is Coming, told *Uncut* magazine: 'Jazz has been re-contextualised so it means a lot of new people are coming to the music and realising it's not actually that far off other stuff they might like.'

In May, Hutchings joined the American saxophonist Kamasi Washington on stage at London's Roundhouse, illustrating the close ties within the international jazz community. Washington, a large man who wears a dashiki and carries a cane, is seen as the figurehead of this new jazz generation. He played on Kendrick Lamar's 2015 album *To Pimp a Butterfly* and, in June, released his fourth solo album, the three-hour cosmic opus *Heaven and Earth*, to mostly glowing reviews.

END OF AN ERA
Two influential British music institutions ceased to exist this year. In March, the iconic music title *New Musical Express* (the *NME*) closed its weekly print edition after 66 years, with its publisher Time Inc UK citing rising production costs and a

difficult advertising market. Launched in 1952, the *NME* came of age during the punk era of the mid-1970s – 'I use the *NME*', Johnny Rotten famously sneered in the Sex Pistols' hit 'Anarchy in the UK' – giving readers access and insight to the most exciting acts and musical trends, and thrived for two further decades. But the magazine had been in decline for a number of years, and in September 2015 the *NME* went free, though by then the editorial quality was compromised by the publisher's commercial imperative. As a brand it still carries some weight but as an online-only newsgathering enterprise its days are surely numbered.

January brought news of the death of Mark E. Smith, the frontman of the cult Manchester post-punk band The Fall, who lost his battle with cancer at the age of 60. A singular talent with a distinctive vocal delivery, idiosyncratic approach to language and a formidable work ethic, Smith founded The Fall in Prestwich in 1976 and went on to release 32 studio albums, the most recent of which, *New Facts Emerge,* came out in July 2017. Smith was the one constant member of The Fall – indeed, he was The Fall – and over the years he hired (and fired) 66 musicians to play in the various incarnations of the band. 'If it's me and your granny on bongos, it's The Fall,' Smith is reported to have said. Every Fall fan has their favourite period of the band, generally determined by which record they heard first, though it is hard to deny the impact that the run of albums The Fall produced in the 1980s – from *Hex Enduction Hour* (1982) to *Perverted by Language* (1983) and *This Nation's Saving Grace* (1985) – had on British pop. The Fall's keenest champion was the late BBC DJ John Peel, who booked them for a record 24 sessions for his radio show. 'Always the same, always different,' he said of the band. Smith still performed during the latter stages of his illness, singing from a wheelchair during the band's final shows in the autumn. With his withering put-downs and pragmatic outlook on life, Smith was a hugely entertaining interviewee who would usually arrange press meetings in the pub.

WELCOME RETURNS

The year saw notable comebacks by artists whose new material found them exploring alternative directions. David Byrne, the former band leader in US art-rockers Talking Heads, returned in March with his seventh solo album, *American Utopia.* Working with a number of younger producers and musicians, including Sampha and Oneohtrix Point Never, as well as his old foil Brian Eno, the album's blend of angular pop and awkward funk received mixed reviews but came alive during Byrne's eye-catching tour for which the 66-year-old and a group of musicians performed a tightly choreographed show which used radical stage design. The album was part of Byrne's broader multimedia project 'Reasons to Be Cheerful', which focuses on positive news stories.

Seven years after their last studio record, and six years after they officially called it a day with a huge hometown show at Madison Square Garden in New York, James Murphy's LCD Soundsystem released their fourth album, *American Dream,* in September. Unlike Byrne, Murphy used his rich new-wave rock to paint a more intimate picture with soul-searching, self-deprecating lyrics that lampoon the travails of the middle-aged rock star. There was a return, too, for the Australian singer Kylie Minogue, who released her 14th solo album, *Golden,* one month before her 50th birthday in May. Largely recorded in Nashville, Tennessee, *Golden* brought a new country sound to Minogue's tales of heartbreak and happiness, and entered the UK album chart at number one.

IN MEMORIAM

Walter Becker (Steely Dan) (1950–2017)
Tom Petty (1950–2017)

Fats Domino (1928–2017)
Dolores O'Riordan (The Cranberries) (1971–2018)
Mark E. Smith (The Fall) (1957–2018)
Jóhann Jóhannsson (composer) (1969–2018)
Tim Bergling (Avicii) (1989–2018)
Aretha Franklin (1942–2018)

AWARDS

BRIT AWARDS 2018
British Male Solo Artist – Stormzy
British Female Solo Artist – Dua Lipa
British Group – Gorillaz
British Single – Rag'n'Bone Man, 'Human'
British Album – Stormzy, *Gang Signs & Prayer*
Critics' Choice – Jorja Smith
International Male Solo Artist – Kendrick Lamar
International Female Solo Artist – Lorde
British Breakthrough Act – Dua Lipa
International Group – Foo Fighters
British Global Success – Ed Sheeran

MERCURY PRIZE 2017
Sampha, *Process*

NME AWARDS 2018
British Band – Alt-J
British Solo Artist – Loyle Carner
Album – J Hus, *Common Sense*
Track – Charli XCX, 'Boys'
Live Artist – Kasabian
New Artist – Stefflon Don
International Solo Artist – Lorde
International Band – Haim
Mixtape – Avelino, *No Bullshit*
Festival – Glastonbury
Godlike Genius – Liam Gallagher
Villain of the Year – Piers Morgan

EUROVISION SONG CONTEST WINNER 2018
Netta, 'Toy' (Israel)

MUSIC OF BLACK ORIGIN (MOBO) AWARDS 2017
Best Male – Stormzy
Best Female – Stefflon Don
Best Song – J Hus, 'Did You See'
Best Album – Stormzy, *Gang Signs & Prayer*
Best International Act – Wizkid
Best Newcomer – Dave
Best Gospel Act – Volney Morgan & New-Ye
Best Jazz Act – Moses Boyd
Best Reggae Act – Damian Marley
Best African Act – Davido
Best R&B/Soul Act – Craig David
Best Hip-Hop Act – Giggs
Best Grime Act – Stormzy

IVOR NOVELLO AWARDS 2018
PRS for Music Most Performed Work – Ed Sheeran, 'Shape of You'
Best Television Soundtrack – Dan Jones, *The Miniaturist*
Best Original Film Score – Mica Levi, *Jackie*
Best Contemporary Song – Dave, 'Question Time'
The Ivors Inspiration Award – Shane MacGowan
Album Award – Stormzy, *Gang Signs & Prayer*
Outstanding Contribution to British Music – Billy Bragg
Best Song Musically and Lyrically – Elbow, 'Magnificent (She Says)'
Songwriter of the Year – Ed Sheeran

SCIENCE AND DISCOVERY

Storm Dunlop

THE VERY EARLIEST GALAXIES

In July 2017, astronomers from Arizona State University announced in *The Astrophysical Journal* that they had managed to detect the earliest galaxies, formed some 800 million years after the universe exploded into being. This is a remarkable achievement, because it was not until a period between about 300 million and 1 billion years after the Big Bang that the universe became transparent, in what is known as the re-ionisation event (caused by the radiation from the first stars and galaxies). Detection of any objects at such an early stage in the life of the universe is extremely difficult, likened to detecting bodies in thick fog. By using the Dark Energy Camera on the 4-metre Blanco Telescope at Cerro Tololo Inter-American Observatory in Chile, together with a sophisticated filter, the researchers were able to detect 23 young galaxies in that fog, and determine that they dated from just 800 million years after the Big Bang.

1,700 MILLION STARS

In April 2018, the European Space Agency (ESA) released the second catalogue of data obtained by the Gaia satellite – it is an immense trove of information. Gathered over 22 months, it includes the positions and distances of 1.3 billion stars, with the positions and brightness of 1.7 billion stars. It also obtained effective temperatures, radii and luminosity for 76 million stars, time-series observations of over 550,000 variable stars, information on half a million quasars and, nearer home, observations of about 14,000 minor planets (asteroids) in the Solar System.

VISITORS FROM AFAR

On 19 October 2017, the Pan-STARRS 1 telescope on Haleakala, Hawaii, discovered an object, initially thought to be a minor planet or comet and known as A/2017 U1. The object, subsequently named 1I/'Oumuamua (which approximately translates from Hawaiian as 'a messenger from afar'), was found to be on a hyperbolic orbit, implying that it came from interstellar space. Although it had already swung around the Sun, and was escaping from the Solar System, it was the subject of intense observation and study. It was thought to be dense, consisting of rock or metals, and thus not a comet. It is dark red in colour, probably as a result of irradiation by cosmic rays during many millions of years in interstellar space. Initially believed to be elongated or cigar-shaped, subsequent analysis of its light-curve, published in *Astrophysical Journal Letters* in March 2018, suggests that it is pancake-shaped.

Also in March 2018, another team of astronomers stated that the object was almost certainly originally ejected from a binary-star system. Calculations suggested that the majority of objects ejected from stellar systems would be icy, and thus cometary in nature. Ejection of a rocky object is more likely to occur from a binary system. However, results published in June 2018 indicate that its observed motion as it passed through the Solar System is best accounted for by assuming that solar radiation irradiated an icy surface, releasing material and causing an acceleration. In this case 'Oumuamua was of cometary origin. As such it possibly formed in the outer region of another planetary system; it would probably have been easier for it to be ejected from such a location than if it had formed closer to its parent star. To eliminate the remote possibility that the object could be an alien artefact, data from the Murchison Widefield Array in Western Australia was examined to check

'Oumuamua for any radio emissions; the negative result was reported in April 2018 in *The Astrophysical Journal*.

Studies suggest that many thousands (possibly even millions) of such objects may pass through the Solar System every year, but are normally undetected. In May 2018, a team from the Université Côte d'Azur in France and the Universidade Estadual Paulista in Brazil reported that the object 2015 BZ509, although a permanent member of the Solar System, probably had an interstellar origin. It has a retrograde orbit, in resonance with that of Jupiter. Calculations indicate that this orbit has been stable for thousands of millions of years, effectively since the formation of the Solar System. The retrograde orbit strongly suggests that it did not condense from the primordial solar nebula and thus originated in another stellar system.

DOES PLANET NINE EXIST?

The controversy over the existence of a distant planet (Planet Nine) in the Solar System has taken a new turn. In 2016, astronomers announced that analysis of the orbits of distant Solar-System objects suggested that a large planetary body existed far from the Sun and exerted its influence on the orbits of bodies in that region. Subsequently, this result was called into question over observational bias. In July 2017, researchers at the Complutense University of Madrid published in *Monthly Notices of the Royal Astronomical Society* their analysis of the orbits of extreme trans-Neptunian objects (ETNOs) with average distances of more than 150 astronomical units (AU) from the Sun (1 AU is roughly the distance from the Earth to the Sun, around 150 million kilometres). New analysis of the orbits revealed the location of the nodes of the orbits (where the orbits cross the main plane of the Solar System). If there were no perturbing body – that is, if there were no Planet Nine – the nodes would be uniformly distributed in space. However, the nodes and orbits of the 28 ETNOs examined, together with a further 24 'extreme centaurs' – asteroids with extremely eccentric orbits – were found to cluster significantly, suggesting that there is indeed a major planetary body in the remote Solar System beyond Pluto (the largest TNO). Indications are that the body lies at a distance of between 300 and 400 AU.

A WATER-RICH LUNAR INTERIOR

A further twist to the problem of the origin of the Moon came with the publication in July 2017 in *Nature Geoscience*, by researchers led from Brown University in the United States, that satellite observations of the lunar surface showed that volcanic deposits contained large amounts of water. Although high water content of surface samples had been determined back in 2008, when observations by the Indian Chandrayaan-1 lunar orbiting satellite showed that water-rich volcanic deposits were widespread on the Moon's surface, the implication is that because the lavas originated in the lunar mantle, the latter must also be water-rich.

The discovery has implications for the question of the Moon's origin, because the generally favoured theory is that the Moon accreted from a ring of particles created around the Earth when a Mars-sized body (known as Theia) collided with the young Earth. Such a collision would have vaporised hydrogen, which would not survive to form water in Earth's orbit. With such a method of formation, any water present on the Moon would have to have been accreted from cometary or meteoritic material before the body had completely solidified.

BOTH PARTICLE AND ANTIPARTICLE

In July 2017, a team of physicists from the University of California and Stanford University announced in *Science* the discovery of a Majorana particle. This came after an 80-year search for the fermion, underway ever since Ettore Majorana's 1937 prediction that a particle that is its own antiparticle should exist. This fermion – of the family that includes the proton, neutron, electron, neutrino and quark – has now been shown to exist. Majorana particles have the property of being their own antiparticles, and it is considered possible that neutrinos may be Majorana particles. Although this current discovery does not have a direct influence on studies of the neutrino, it is hoped that it may offer some insight into the processes at work.

A NEW NEUTRINO?

Details published in early June 2018 on the arXiv website and reported at a conference in Heidelberg by scientists working with the MiniBooNE detector at Fermilab near Chicago suggest that a proposed new variety of neutrino, the sterile neutrino, may have been detected. Three varieties (flavours) of neutrino (electron, muon and tau neutrinos) are already known. The results come from a 15-year run of the experiment, where muon neutrinos are generated and travel underground to the detector. On the way, the muon neutrinos oscillate and some were expected to appear as electron neutrinos. In the event, an excess of electron neutrinos was detected. This suggests that the existence of sterile neutrinos has influenced the production of electron neutrinos.

If confirmed, the existence of a sterile neutrino would be extremely significant, because it would represent physics beyond the accepted standard model of physics. Sterile neutrinos would interact rarely with known particles, but primarily interact with gravity. Their existence would have major implications for cosmology, and they have been suggested as the origin of dark matter. The expectation was that sterile neutrinos would be extremely heavy, but the results reported indicate a very low mass.

Unfortunately, the confidence level of the findings is 4.8 sigma, short of the 5.0 sigma normally taken as implying a definite discovery. When the results are combined with those from a much earlier experiment, the Liquid Scintillator Neutrino Detector, the confidence level reaches 6. However, results from other neutrino experiments, including the IceCube observatory in Antarctica, do not reveal any evidence for sterile neutrinos, so confirmation by other experiments is still required. The field of neutrino physics is in a complex state at present. One experiment, measuring electron neutrinos produced in nuclear reactors, finds fewer interactions than predicted, which may indicate the existence of more than one variety of sterile neutrino.

NEUTRON-STAR MERGER

On 17 August 2017, the LIGO gravitational-wave detectors in the United States and the Virgo detector in Italy both observed an event – the first to be discovered by both systems. Unlike black-hole mergers, where only a gravitational-wave event is seen, the collision of two neutron stars produces signals throughout the electromagnetic spectrum, from radio waves to gamma-ray radiation. The event, the very first of what is known as 'multi-messenger astronomy', opens up a new realm of observational astronomy. About two seconds after the gravitational-wave event, both the ESA INTEGRAL and the NASA Fermi gamma-ray satellites detected a short gamma-ray burst from the same direction, finally confirming that neutron-star mergers are the source of these gamma-ray events.

In October 2017, a whole series of papers were published of observations of this event at various wavelengths and particularly in the visible region, where the event was about 1,000 times as bright as a normal nova eruption (causing such

an event to be named a 'kilonova'). The evolution of the visible light confirmed predictions of the way in which the heaviest elements are forged. Elements up to the atomic number of iron may be created in the cores of stars, particularly those that later explode as supernovae and scatter elements into space. Anything heavier than iron requires an environment where elements are bombarded by free neutrons. This is not found in supernova explosions, but the merger of neutron stars releases neutron-rich material. Visible-light observations of this event first exhibited the signature of light elements, like those seen in supernova explosions, but then showed a behaviour that can be explained only by the presence of the heaviest elements such as gold and platinum. This strongly suggests that such elements have been created in neutron-star mergers.

From the gravitational-wave observations of the event, known as GW170817 in lenticular galaxy NGC 4993, it has been deduced that two stars of about 1.48 and 1.26 solar masses merged. But the true nature of the object that resulted from the merger is equivocal. It has a mass of approximately 2.7 solar masses, meaning that this is either the most massive neutron star known, or the least massive black hole. In a study published in June 2018, a team led by David Pooley (Trinity University, Texas, and Eureka Scientific) used observations from the Chandra X-ray satellite to examine the evolution of X-ray radiation from the event. The X-ray emission grew as the shockwave expanded over the first 100 days after the merger. However the level of radiation was not as great as expected if the remnant were a neutron star, which would itself contribute X-rays in addition to those from the shock. The conclusion is that the remnant is actually a black hole. A definitive answer should be obtained by continuing observations for at least another year. After that time, if the central object were a neutron star, its emission would overtake the radiation from the shockwave and there would be a major brightening in X-rays.

In July 2017 it was announced that major work was underway on the Kamioka Gravitational-wave Detector (KAGRA) on the west coast of Japan. This is the site of the Super-Kamioka neutrino detector; the gravitation-wave detector is being built underground. It is expected that work will be completed by the end of 2018.

EXOPLANETS AND A POSSIBLE 'EXOMOON'

On 18 April 2018, NASA successfully launched the Transiting Exoplanet Survey Satellite which, unlike the previous Kepler mission, is designed to survey the whole sky. It will replace the ailing Kepler satellite, which examined some 150,000 distant stars, and instead survey about 200,000 relatively nearby stars. The satellite is in a lunar-resonant orbit, orbiting the Earth in 13.7 days (half the Moon's orbital period).

In August 2017, a team of astronomers from Columbia University, working in the Hunt for Exomoons with Kepler collaboration, announced that they had probably discovered the existence of an 'exomoon' – a satellite of an exoplanet – from an analysis of data returned by the Kepler spaceprobe, which detected three transits of the body across its parent star, which lies at a distance of 4,000 light years from us. The exomoon appears to be very large, comparable with the planet Neptune in the Solar System, and to orbit a planet (known as Kepler-1625b) that is approximately the size of Jupiter, but has 10 times its mass.

TRULY NEW HORIZONS

In June 2018, NASA announced that the New Horizons spaceprobe (which flew past Pluto and was subsequently placed in hibernation mode) was 'awake' and preparing to pass the Trans-Neptunian Object (486958) 2014 MU$_{69}$, now known by the unofficial name of Ultima Thule, on 1 January 2019. Little is known about this object, which is believed to be about 30km across; it is red in colour and very irregular in shape. It may actually be two bodies in contact, in what is known as a contact-binary asteroid. At the time of the encounter, the asteroid will be at a distance of 43.4 AU from the Sun and thus the most distant object visited by a spaceprobe.

ANOTHER MISSION TO MARS

On 5 May 2018, NASA also launched the InSight mission. Scheduled to arrive at Mars on 26 November 2018, the spacecraft will land and deploy a seismometer, together with a 'mole', designed to penetrate to a depth of 5m. In addition to detecting seismic activity (and thus information about the interior of Mars), it will take heat-flow measurements and use additional instrumentation to determine the exact rotation period and orientation of the rotational axis of Mars.

ASTEROID RETURN MISSIONS

On 27 June 2018, the Japanese probe Hayabusa2 reached its destination, the asteroid 162173 Ryugu. This is a C-type asteroid, consisting of carbonaceous material, and thus considered to be the oldest and most primordial type of asteroid, dating back to the formation of the Solar System. The ambitious mission is expected to spend about 18 months orbiting the asteroid, during which time it will deploy several small landers, including the German-built Mobile Asteroid Surface Scout. The plan is to drive an impactor into the surface to create a crater, from which previously sub-surface material will be sampled. The spacecraft will leave Ryugu in December 2019 and return to Earth with the asteroid sample in 2020. A NASA probe, OSIRIS-REx, is expected to reach the asteroid 101955 Bennu (another C-type asteroid) in 2018 August. It is also a sample-return mission, albeit with a different method of sample collection.

ORGANIC ENCELADUS

In June 2018 it was announced that the Cassini spaceprobe, which was deliberately steered into the cloud-tops of Saturn on 15 September 2017 at the end of its life, had detected complex organic molecules in the material ejected from the 'tiger stripes' near the south pole of the planet's satellite Enceladus. Such compounds have previously been found only on Earth and in a few meteorites. Those detected are thought to have originated in reactions between water and hot rocks at the base of the satellite's sub-surface ocean. Although not a sign of the existence of life on the satellite, they indicate that the body could support living organisms.

ANCIENT MICROORGANISMS

On 18 December 2017, scientists from UCLA and the University of Wisconsin–Madison announced that extremely ancient organisms had been identified in rocks from Western Australia with an age of 3,465 million years. The various microorganisms exhibited different characteristics: two employed a primitive form of photosynthesis; one produced methane gas; and two others consumed methane and used the products to create cell walls. The existence of such diverse activity at such an early stage in the Earth's history, when taken in conjunction with the growing understanding of the prevalence of exoplanets in other systems, suggests that life is common in the universe, because it is exceptionally unlikely that diverse life should form so quickly on Earth, but not arise elsewhere.

EARLY CONTINENTAL CRUST

In April 2018, researchers from the Department of Geophysical Sciences at the University of Chicago announced that investigations of the strontium content of zircon crystals in rocks from northern Canada indicated that continental crust formed hundreds of millions of years earlier than previously thought. The research placed the age of the rocks just 350 million years after the formation of the Solar System. This is contrary to the previously prevailing view that the Earth was hot, dry and unlikely to harbour any life-forms for some 500 million years after its formation, but agrees with the results obtained from early rocks found in Western Australia. The investigation used a new, and so far unique, instrument known as the Chicago Instrument for Laser Ionization, with which they were able to count individual strontium-atom isotopes within the samples.

GREAT PERMIAN EXTINCTION

For many years there has been considerable discussion of the cause (or causes) of the Great Permian Extinction, which occurred approximately 250 million years ago and was the most severe extinction event in Earth's history. About 95 per cent of marine and some 70 per cent of terrestrial life-forms became extinct. In October 2017, a team of scientists from New York University announced in *Scientific Reports* that they had obtained evidence that the event was caused by massive volcanism, most probably the extensive eruptions in Siberia that took place at that time. Using an inductively coupled plasma mass spectrometer to measure the abundance of elements at an atomic level, the researchers determined that anomalous amounts of nickel were present in a wide range of samples from various regions. The conclusion was that nickel-rich lavas were erupted by the volcanism that created the large igneous province known as the Siberian Traps. It was suggested that the magma interacted with existing widespread coal deposits to release large quantities of carbon dioxide and methane, causing the extreme global warming that occurred at the same time on both land and at sea. The circulation of the oceans became sluggish and they were also depleted in oxygen, leading to the mass extinction of marine life.

ESSENTIAL NICKEL

In July 2017, a team of scientists from Vienna University of Technology and Würzburg University announced in *Nature Communications* that their research indicated that rather than the Earth's magnetic field being created by the motion of molten iron, it was essential for a large percentage of the molten interior to consist of nickel. It turns out that the dynamo effect cannot be produced by the Earth's rotation and molten iron alone, but that it is essential for about 20 per cent of the molten material to be nickel. Although conditions in the Earth's deep interior cannot be simulated in the laboratory, the researchers were able to use advanced and highly complex computer simulations of the electron-scattering properties of many alloys of iron and nickel. The techniques employed are likely to find applications in other fields, such as chemistry, biology and technology.

MAGNETIC REVERSALS

In June 2018, researchers at the Universities of Liverpool, Lancaster and Oslo published in *Tectonophysics* details of the correlation that they had established between the motion of tectonic plates in the Earth's crust, flow in the mantle and magnetic reversals in the core. The study suggests that slabs of dense oceanic crust take 120–130 million years to subduct through the mantle and cool the core. This actually causes the molten iron in the outer core to flow more rapidly, leading to a reversal of the magnetic field. The study proved possible because of greatly improved worldwide data regarding subduction rates and the timing of magnetic reversals.

This finding contradicts the results of a study, published in August 2017 by researchers at MIT, that only early in the Earth's history (around 3 billion years ago) would the density of crustal rocks have been sufficiently great and the temperature of the mantle significantly higher – by some 200°C – and thus allow subducted slabs to sink some 2,800km to the bottom of the mantle. It is generally felt that nowadays subducted slabs are able to sink just 670km before the viscosity of the mantle rocks brings them to a halt.

GRAVITY AND EARTHQUAKES

In December 2017, researchers at the Paris Institute of Earth Physics demonstrated that monitoring changes in gravity created by major earthquakes could offer a rapid method of determining an earthquake's magnitude and be superior to conventional seismic techniques. They examined records of the devastating Tohoku earthquake of 2011 in Japan, and the proposed method would have determined the earthquake's magnitude within three minutes. Such an improvement in information would be particularly valuable in warning of a potential tsunami, which was particularly devastating in the case of the Tohoku event.

TOBA ERUPTION

It has long been held that the largest known volcanic eruption in the last 2.5 million years, that of Mount Toba in Indonesia some 74,000 years ago, led to a volcanic winter and reduced the human population to a small remnant, creating a population 'bottleneck'. Later humans were thought to have arisen from this tiny population. In March 2018, an international team of researchers published in *Nature* results of excavations in South Africa that not only positively identified volcanic tephra from Toba at the sites, but also found increased human activity after the eruption, suggesting that populations may have increased, rather than suffered a dramatic decline.

UNEXPECTED RESULT OF GLOBAL WARMING

In July 2017, a team of researchers from the Potsdam Institute for Climate Impact Research and Columbia University, New York, announced that from computer simulations they had discovered that the Sahel, one of Africa's driest regions, could suddenly switch to a wet regime. They identified a self-amplifying mechanism that might become activated if global warming crossed the level of 1.5–2°C that had been stipulated in the Paris Climate Agreement. The research showed that the region might suddenly switch to a monsoon-type regime, with torrential rainfall for part of the year. Although this might seem to be a positive development, the change would be a major challenge to pastoralists in the region. What is noticeable is that the system has a very sensitive 'tipping point'; any change could take place within a few years, once that point had been reached.

REVISING OUR ORIGINS?

Discoveries in recent years have cast considerable doubt upon the generally accepted view that the human species originated in eastern Africa, from whence it spread throughout the world, emerging from the region around 60,000 years ago.

In December 2017, the skeleton of a specimen of *Australopithecus*, known as 'Little Foot', was revealed to science. Although a few foot bones were initially discovered in 1980, it was not until 1992 that serious study of this fossil was initiated. Eventually, a large part of the skeleton was recovered, but it took the team of scientists some 20 years to excavate, conserve and reconstruct it. This proved to be a specimen of *Australopithecus*, somewhat similar to the famous 'Lucy' skeleton *(Australopithecus afarensis)* from Ethiopia, but of a different species. It has been determined that it differs from *Au. afarensis* and from another species, *Au. africanus*, and so the name *Au. prometheus* has been proposed. The specimen has been dated to around 3.67 million years ago, about 500,000 years earlier than *Au. afarensis*, and considerably earlier than *Au. sediba*, another example also discovered in South Africa that has been dated to 2 million years ago. Despite the almost inevitable arguments about the relationship between these species, the implication is that there were a number of them, ancestral to humans, present across a wide area of Africa.

ANCIENT HUMAN LINEAGES

The relationship between modern humans, Neanderthals and Denisovans has been subject to considerable debate. In August 2017, a team from the University of Utah published results of a new method of analysing DNA sequence data. They determined that a major split occurred hundreds of thousands of years ago in which modern humans diverged from the Neanderthal and Denisovan line. Some 744,000 years ago, Neanderthals and Denisovans diverged. The Neanderthal population grew, but they existed as fragmented, isolated populations across Europe as shown by the wide variation in the DNA sequences obtained. The study confirmed that modern Eurasians share about 2 per cent of Neanderthal DNA.

AN EXTREMELY ANCIENT CRANIUM

In June 2018, a team based at the University of the Witwatersrand published the results of a sophisticated examination of a cranium belonging to a specimen of *Australopithecus*, found at the Jacovec Cavern in the Sterkfontein Caves, about 40km north-west of Johannesburg in South Africa. This specimen has an age of about 4 million years and, in 1995, was described as the 'oldest evidence of human evolution'. The recent research, subjecting the fragmentary cranium to modern high-resolution imaging techniques, revealed unexpected similarities to features found in modern humans. The team also imaged material from another extinct hominin relative, *Paranthropus*, dated to approximately 2 million years ago, and found distinct differences, suggesting a completely different biological origin.

MODERN HUMANS' EMERGENCE

In September 2017, a research team consisting of scientists from Uppsala University, Sweden, and the Universities of Johannesburg and the Witwatersrand, South Africa, presented results which suggested that modern humans originated some 300,000 years ago in southern Africa. Although the genomes that they sequenced were from relatively modern individuals, they estimated that the divergence found in modern humans actually emerged some 300,000 years ago. Previously, the fossil record of East Africa suggested that modern humans originated about 180,000 years ago. However, the revised dating coincides with the dates of certain specimens (the Florisbad and Hoedjiespunt fossils) which are considered to be transitional forms to modern humans. These species were contemporary with the relatively recently described hominin, *Homo naledi*. This strongly suggests that a few species of *Homo* existed at the same period in southern Africa. This, in turn, would agree with the idea that various species of *Homo* arose in different regions of Africa at approximately the same time, rather than a single species arising in eastern Africa. It is distinctly possible that modern humans arose in several locations in both northern and southern Africa and that the modern species arose from gene flow between the different populations.

BRAIN SIZE IN ANCIENT HOMININS

Although it has long been held that human evolution was accompanied by an inevitable increase in brain size, this view has been challenged by various discoveries. In particular, research on *Homo naledi* published in May 2018 by researchers from the University of the Witwatersrand, South Africa, and Des Moines University in the USA, revealed that the brain of this species had many 'modern' features. Although the recovered skulls of *Homo naledi* are fragmentary, it was possible to reconstruct endocasts (casts of the skulls' interiors) and from these to examine the structure of the brain. This surprisingly revealed that, although extremely small, the brain's frontal lobes in particular were humanlike, and completely unlike those of the great apes, and also showed considerable difference from the features found in the brains of the primitive hominin *Australopithecus*. Taken with other characteristics of the skeleton of *Homo naledi*, this suggests that the species did indeed exhibit complex and humanlike behaviour, despite its small brain size comparable with that of *Australopithecus*.

THE EARLIEST AUSTRALIANS

A discovery at the Madjedbebe rock shelter, near Kakadu National Park in northern Australia, reveals that humans reached Australia at least 65,000 years ago, some 18,000 years earlier than the previously generally accepted date for any artefacts on the continent. The research was carried out by archaeologists led by Chris Clarkson from the University of Queensland and published in *Nature* in July 2017. Excavations at the rock shelter discovered primitive stone axes – said to be the world's oldest such tools – and 'crayons' of ochre, believed to be used for artistic purposes. The dating of 65,000 years ago has wider implications than just the history of the occupation of Australia because, until very recently, the date at which humans left eastern Africa was considered to be reliably dated at just 60,000 years ago. Discoveries in other parts of the world have cast considerable doubt upon this dating, however, and this is compounded by such an early date for the settlement of Australia at such a vast distance from Africa.

THE EARLIEST AMERICANS

Analysis of the DNA from a female child, found at Upward Sun River in Alaska in 2013, reveals a date of about 11,500 years ago. More significantly, although she is related to modern Native Americans, study of the mutations that occur with time in human DNA suggests that the child was part of a previously unknown population that entered North America some 20,000 years ago. These are believed to be the first group to enter the continent from northern Asia, during the last ice age when sea levels were lower and there was a land bridge across the Bering Strait between Siberia and Alaska. The incomers were thus the ancestors of all Native Americans. The ancestral population appears to have become genetically differentiated from East Asians some 36,000 years ago, with the transition being completed by 25,000 years ago. The group of which the child was part – they have been called Ancient Beringians – remained in Alaska, whereas other humans moved on, possibly through an ice-free 'corridor' between the main ice sheet covering the continental interior and ice on the high coastal ranges, to colonise the rest of North America, subsequently diverging into two distinct genetic groups.

ANCIENT HUMANS IN SOUTHEAST ASIA

In a study, published in *Science* in May 2018, researchers from Harvard Medical School described the first comprehensive analysis of the whole genome of ancient human DNA from Southeast Asia (the area east of India and south of China). This study revealed that there has been at least three waves of human colonisation of the region in the last 50,000 years. Descendants of each of the waves of colonisation still live in the area today, and a particular surprise was the finding that there are still significant traces of the original hunter-gather population.

SPREAD OF THE BEAKER PEOPLE

It has long been assumed that the spread of the practices surrounding the 'Beaker people' and their characteristic pottery was a cultural flow, not a reflection of a migration of individuals. In 2018, however, research carried out under David Reich and Nick Patterson of Harvard Medical School used analysis of DNA from ancient human remains to show that, in Britain for example, Beaker folk replaced an astonishing 90 per cent of the pre-existing population. Earlier work by the same team had established that in the late Neolithic and early Bronze Age, the Yamnaya nomadic steppe pastoralists had migrated west and replaced some 75 per cent of the population already in western Europe.

VACCINES FROM UNUSUAL SOURCES

In July 2017 researchers at the International AIDS Vaccine Initiative and the Scripps Research Institute announced that they had discovered that cows produced antibodies to the HIV virus extremely rapidly. The antibodies were produced within weeks, whereas in humans it would take three to five years to develop the same antibodies. The discovery of an immune system that is capable of neutralising the HIV virus so rapidly offers the possibility that it may be possible to create a vaccine that causes the human immune system to create the same antibodies in a short period of time.

In August 2017, scientists at the John Innes Centre in Norfolk announced that they had made a polio vaccine in plants. They used a relative of the tobacco plant to make 'virus-like' particles that could be used as a vaccine. The particles were sized and shaped like the polio virus, but were empty shells and could thus not cause an infection. The technique began by using the genetic code that creates the outer coat of a polio virus, which was combined with material from viruses that infect plants. The resulting material was inserted into bacteria and used to infect the plants. These then produced the virus-like particles. The research team stated that the method was easy, cheap and rapid, and could be used to produce other forms of vaccine.

DEFEATING HEREDITARY DISEASES

Significant progress has been reported on the treatment of hereditary diseases. In December 2017 it was reported in the *New England Journal of Medicine* that a team from Barts Health NHS Trust and Queen Mary Hospital in London had successfully used genetic techniques to create a treatment for haemophilia. A genetically engineered virus was used to cause the patients' livers to create the missing blood-clotting protein known as factor VIII. Although only a small trial, 11 of the 13 patients are producing near-normal levels of the all-important clotting factor, and all 13 have ceased to require haemophilia medication. Larger trials are being implemented, but the treatment appears to be revolutionary and life-changing.

Preliminary results suggest that a similar breakthrough has been achieved in the treatment of sickle-cell disease. A team at the Necker Children's Hospital in Paris altered the DNA of a teenager so that his blood marrow created only healthy (round) red blood cells. After 15 months the teenager is no longer on any medication and is producing healthy cells.

MODIFYING DNA IN EMBRYOS

In September 2017, a team from Sun Yat-sen University in China reported that they had modified a single 'letter', or base, in the DNA of human embryos to correct an error that leads to the disease of beta thalassaemia. A point mutation – alteration of a single base – is the cause of the disease. The team changed a single instance of the amino acid guanine, converting it to adenine in order to correct the error. The embryos with the corrected genetic structure were not implanted. The procedure demonstrates the feasibility of curing genetic disease by directly editing the bases in DNA. In principle, it should be applicable to a range of diseases, not just beta thalassaemia, but there are, of course, considerable ethical issues to be resolved before any such technique could be employed in practice.

HARNESSING THE IMMUNE SYSTEM

In August 2017, the United States Food and Drug Administration gave approval to a new and potentially revolutionary method of combatting cancer. Treatment is 'tailored' to each individual patient by harvesting white blood cells from the patient's blood. These cells are then genetically reprogrammed to locate and attack cancer. Once re-inserted into the patient, the cells search for their target and then begin to replicate. Initially, the treatment will be used for patients with acute lymphoblastic leukaemia. Although most patients respond to conventional methods, the new treatment will be applied when normal methods fail. Although there are currently known serious and deleterious side-effects to this particular treatment, the method can potentially be applied to other forms of cancer.

THEATRE

Matt Trueman

CHANGING THE TUNE

The West End had to wait for it. Two years after bedding in on Broadway, where tickets had at one point reached re-sale prices of $1,150, Lin-Manuel Miranda's revolutionary musical *Hamilton* reached London. History in hip-hop, it raps through Alexander Hamilton's life – as civil warrior, founding father and cheating husband. It came clutching a Pulitzer, a Grammy and 11 Tony Awards, but there were no guarantees that the British public would go for an American history lesson told in American street-song.

Its host, super-producer Cameron Mackintosh, clearly knew better. He revamped the Victoria Palace Theatre and its 1,550 seats at a cost of £50m, but hit delays over drains installed by George III, Hamilton's colonial nemesis, that pushed opening night back by a fortnight (16 previews were pulled). On opening night, British critics kowtowed, with the *Evening Standard* splashing 'Believe the hype'.

Miranda's music and lyrics were bound to dazzle. Some of hip-hop's biggest stars had taken them to heart, contributing cover versions to *The Hamilton Mixtape*. In the flesh, however, Thomas Kail's staging looked slightly old-fashioned on its timber-frame set. But a British cast shone: recent RADA graduate Jamael Westman made a hunkier Hamilton than Miranda's original brainiac. His hubris loomed large over his chief rival Aaron Burr – a smouldering Giles Terera was the Salieri to Hamilton's Mozart. It swept up awards as it had back home.

But *Hamilton* was not the only game-changing American tuner in town. *Fun Home*, a musical adaptation of Alison Bechdel's autobiographical graphic novel, arrived at the Young Vic to equally universal acclaim. A coming-out tale offset by a closeted father, Jeanine Tesori's book split its protagonist into three: a ten-year-old tomboy, a student stumbling towards sexual awakening and an adult author assessing her life. Lisa Kron's shapeshifting score, including an effervescent hymn to housekeeping, seeped out of the story, and another crack cast – especially Jenna Russell's jittery mother and Zubin Varla's conflicted father – made an innovative, understated musical their own.

America's invention has spurred the Brits on. Handed the keys to Bob Dylan's back catalogue, Conor McPherson fine-tuned the jukebox musical. *Girl from the North Country* left a lot out – no 'Blowin' in the Wind', no 'Knockin' on Heaven's Door' – to catch the timbre of times a-changin'. In a Depression-era guest house in Duluth, Minnesota, down-and-outs drift through Dust Bowl America: two-bit pulpit preachers, convicts on the run, the disabled and the dependent. Heartfelt in hard times, it wrung you out with Sheila Atim's wrenching 'Tight Connection to My Heart', Sam Reid's loving lament 'I Want You' and Shirley Henderson's 'Like a Rolling Stone' as a woman with early-onset dementia. Other musical compilations paled in comparison: *The Band* trotted through Take That's career, while *Tina* and *Dusty* loaded lumpen scripts onto stellar leads: as Turner and Springfield respectively, Adrienne Warren and Katherine Kingsley both had big hair and even bigger voices.

Experiments abounded during the year under review. *Committee* set parliamentary process to song at the Donmar, with Tom Deering scoring a transcript of the tribunal into the collapse of the charity Kids Company. John Tiffany brought giant puppets to *Pinocchio*, turning Disney's film into a commedia-inspired spectacular. Emma Rice turned an obscure French romcom about anxious lovers into a chocolate-box chamber musical, *Romantics Anonymous*. None of them troubled a West End starved of new musicals. The English National Opera revived the overblown Cold War tuner *Chess*, celebrating its score yet losing the plot, while a sumptuous Broadway staging of *The King and I* took up residence in the long-empty Palladium.

By contrast, straight plays have had a revival in town. For the first time in years, new plays premiered in the West End – Simon Stephens' uncertain science play *Heisenberg* launched Marianne Elliott's new commercial company, while James Graham's look at Labour Party history, *Labour of Love*, opened at the Noël Coward Theatre despite losing its lead, Sarah Lancashire. Tamsin Greig stepped in, but Graham won the headlines with three plays in the West End over the course of the year. *Ink*, his story of *The Sun* newspaper, and his take on the *Who Wants to Be a Millionaire?* cheating scandal, *Quiz*, both transferred into town.

Plenty of playwrights did likewise, including Nina Raine's legal drama *Consent* and David Hare's Glyndebourne origin story *The Moderate Soprano*. By contrast, traditional fare faltered. Former Globe boss Dominic Dromgoole presented a season of glitzy Oscar Wilde plays that simply seemed out of keeping with the times, while star vehicles – Orlando Bloom in Tracy Letts' *Killer Joe*, Stockard Channing in *Apologia*, Christian Slater in *Glengarry Glen Ross* – all struggled to make much of a splash. Theatregoers were seeking something new.

In June, Natasha Gordon's *Nine Night* announced a transfer from the National – the first play by a black British woman to reach the West End. Set in a British Jamaican household after a death, over the nine-night wake that tradition demands, it laced a clever examination of first-, second- and third-generation immigrant experiences through a broadly comic script. Even if it followed the formula of funeral dramas too closely, audiences lapped it up. Arinzé Kene's gig-theatre solo show *Misty*, a self-aware critique of the way that black writers address the issue of race, was another unlikely West End transfer – a mark of British theatre opening up to a more diverse range of voices. Recent schemes are bearing fruit. The Eclipse Theatre Company's Black Theatre Live debuted with Testament's lyrical and layered *Black Men Walking*, a tale of three black hikers pacing the moors, while the Bush Theatre's push to revive canonical black plays delivered a gorgeous, long-overdue revival of Winsome Pinnock's 1987 family drama *Leave Taking*.

STATE OF THE NATIONAL

Under Rufus Norris, the National Theatre has blown hot and cold. For every West End transfer, there's been an in-house flop. Rory Mullarkey's somersaulting *Saint George and the Dragon*, a state-of-the-nation spin on a Russian folk play, was the third Olivier misfire on the trot, after an obtuse *Salome* and the bewildering *Common*. It raised questions about how to use the National's main space – it came as no surprise that the surefire hit *War Horse* was recalled to mark ten years of globetrotting success.

Yet, the National's smaller spaces delivered hit after hit. Lucy Kirkwood slammed two sisters together at CERN in *Mosquitoes*, a thrilling exploration of the limits of human and scientific knowledge. David Eldridge's tender will-they-won't-they romcom *Beginning*, set in the wee hours after a housewarming, waited for two heartbroken singletons to rediscover their mojo. Annie Baker's *John* went the other way: a disjointed couple break up in a Gettysburg B&B, watched by an audience of vintage dolls. It asked questions about the ghosts haunting a divided America.

Norris' National has been strong on the subject. Having sent its *Angels in America* to Broadway for a Tony-winning run, theatre's equivalent of selling coals to Newcastle, it imported *Oslo*, J. T. Rogers' dramatisation of the Norwegian negotiations that brought peace to Palestine. Ivo van Hove's staging of Paddy Chayefsky's classic screen satire *Network*, with a real restaurant onstage, asked if fake news wasn't making Americans mad as hell; Bryan Cranston's unanchored anchorman deployed inflammatory tactics reminiscent of one Donald J. Trump. Dominic Cooke, meanwhile, made a superb case for Stephen Sondheim's *Follies* with an opulent, diamante-encrusted staging that set a showgirls reunion against a chorus of ghosts. Its crumbling theatre, all faded former glories, looked like a metaphor for the nation at large.

The Lehman Trilogy offered an explanation. Tracking the history of American capitalism through that of its fourth-biggest bank, Lehman Brothers, it showed expansion and collapse. Sam Mendes turned Stefano Massini's sprawling play into a nimble three-hander told by the German-Jewish brothers – Henry, Emanuel and Mayer – who set up the fabric shop that grew into a giant of global finance. Ben Power's translation accelerated with the markets, as Es Devlin's revolving design span dizzily on. Simon Russell Beale, Ben Miles and Adam Godley trickled down the generations of the Lehman clan, delivering mercurial performances in multiple roles.

Norris' naysayers found a new home upriver. Nicholas Hytner's Bridge Theatre, a mile from his old offices at the National, opened in October 2017. Designed by Haworth Tompkins, the architectural practice doing more for British theatre than anyone since Frank Matcham, it's a beauty: a flexible, 900-seat state-of-the art space. Two galleries wrap around the open auditorium and madeleines are baked, fresh, at the bar. Hytner and his producer Nick Starr have another theatre lined up: a 600-seat studio is set for Kings Cross.

Year one put the Bridge through its paces. *Young Marx* found the father of communism (Rory Kinnear) living his best life in London, boozing and carousing with best buddy Friedrich Engels. Cue Victorian japes and scrapes – but Richard Bean's farce fell quite flat. Hytner fared far better with a *Julius Caesar* that put populist politics in promenade. Starting as a Trump-like rally – Make Rome Great Again – it saw David Calder's balding Caesar dispatched by his liberal elite. Ben Whishaw's studious Brutus was no match for David Morrissey's man of the people, Mark Antony. Rome plunged into a civil war that enveloped the audience.

My Name is Lucy Barton brought stillness instead. Alone on a thrust stage, Oscar-nominee Laura Linney brought Elizabeth Strout's pensive novel to life. Playing a woman in a hospital ward, looking back on her life, she found sadness beneath sunshine. Like *The Lehman Trilogy* and *John*, Richard Eyre's simple staging suggested America as an amalgam nation scarred by the traumas of its wars, both military and cultural.

Barney Norris' *Nightfall* looked at the blemishes of Brexit Britain. Set on a grief-stricken family farm, divided down the middle by an oil pipe, it argued that the trickle of riches had dried up. It was not convincing, though; normally such a careful, humane writer, Norris overloaded the play with bulky Brexit metaphors.

It was one of a harvest of countryside dramas – theatre's attempt to look beyond the so-called liberal elite. The best was the bleakest: Simon Longman's *Gundog*, staged at the Royal Court on mounds of mud, let year blur into unchanging year as a once-proud farming family slowly caved in to crime. Joe

White's rural romcom *Mayfly* offered another look at a young generation leaving the countryside behind. Phil Ormrod's scrapheap-set *Isaac Came Home from the Mountain* suggested otherwise at Theatre503, as an old poacher took a troubled teenager under his wing. Its point – that industrial decline has left Britain broken – was echoed by a spate of industrial plays: Maxine Peake's *Queens of the Coal Age*, Ray Castleton and Kieran Knowles' *Chicken Soup* and National Theatre Wales' *We're Still Here*, made with the steelworkers of Port Talbot.

But it was Mike Bartlett's *Albion* that best summed up the state of the nation. A sprawling Chekhovian character play, it gave us the garden of England: a green and pleasant lawn gone to seed. Victoria Hamilton's grieving mother sought to restore an iconic garden to its former glories, but in the process, effectively privatised public land.

SHAKESPEARE'S WOMEN

In such divisive times, it made sense that, on the Shakespeare front, this was the year of *King Lear*. Ian McKellen began his second stab at the role by slicing up a map of the UK with golden scissors. Dressed in royal ceremonial reds, surrounded by deferent civil servants, McKellen's senile king suggested that the stable, ever-sensible British establishment had lost its marbles. Jonathan Munby's staging was full of ominous imagery, including a cracked white cliff and a once-plush red carpet now soiled. At its centre was McKellen's brilliant portrayal of dementia, never linear in its decay. At Shakespeare's Globe, Kevin McNally's Lear fell foul of that – a plummet from royal pomp to park bench.

Macbeth provided another nation in disarray. At the National, Rufus Norris set it in some nameless fallen state afflicted by civil war. A right witches' brew, his production shot for spectacle but made little sense. With no power structure, Rory Kinnear's nutcase *Macbeth* had little to aim at, no matter how slyly Anne-Marie Duff's Lady Macbeth egged him on. The Royal Shakespeare Company (RSC) countered with a *Macbeth* framed as tight psychological horror, with Christopher Eccleston in the lead as a born solider always primed for attack as a digital clock turned time against him.

Even so, this was not a vintage year for the Bard. Tom Hiddleston's *Hamlet,* directed by Kenneth Branagh, played to just 120 people a night, a fundraiser for the Royal Academy of Dramatic Art with little new to say. Shakespeare, today, has to speak to our world, but his plays can pose a diversity problem. In Liverpool, Golda Rosheuvel played a lesbian Othello – the first actor to play the part as a woman – and an all-black Unicorn production reframed the play's racism as 'shadeism' (discrimination based on degree of skin tone) and xenophobia. Matthew Dunster took *Much Ado About Nothing* to Mexico – the sort of screwball staging that Emma Rice's Globe did best.

Her successor at a still-bright organisation, Michelle Terry, announced an in-house ensemble – a collaborative company where anyone could play any part. Her tenure began with her own *Hamlet* – a mad clown figure – as doubled with a gender-swapped *As You Like It,* which incorporated the British sign language of Nadia Nadarajah's Celia.

The lack of female roles in the folio has led theatres to commission their own women-led historical dramas. Gina McKee played the famous Iceni queen in *Boudica* at Shakespeare's Globe, in Tristan Bernays' attempt to humanise an ancient British icon, while the RSC's *Queen Anne,* as written by Helen Edmundson, ran in the West End with Romola Garai outstanding as her scheming rival Sarah Churchill.

Other theatres turned to the corseted camp of restoration comedy. *The Country Wife*, at Chichester, starred a colourful Susannah Fielding in a bawdy black and white city while, at the Donmar, James Macdonald faithfully dusted off *The Way of the World,* though the production was rocked by the sudden death of comic actor Alex Beckett mid-run. Two extant comedies written by women were put on display: Mary Pix's lost 1700 play *The Beau Defeated* became a misfire foppery retitled *The Fantastic Follies of Mrs Rich* at the RSC, while Hannah Cowley's *The Belle's Stratagem*, a response to George Farquhar's similarly titled play, was artfully over the top at the Lyceum in Edinburgh.

In a year in which women spoke up against sexism in the industry, new writers turned to female stories too. Alan Ayckbourn hardly helped their caused with *The Divide*, a gruelling six-hour sci-fi piece set in a society segregated by sex. The reason? A virus carried by adult women. A Netflix pitch of a play, a poor relation of *The Handmaid's Tale* and Naomi Alderman's novel *The Power*, it was as overblown as it was under-cooked.

It was precisely the sort of drama that Ella Hickson lambasted in her Pirandellian meta-play *The Writer* – an assault on the way that women playwrights are curbed by an industry dominated by men. Following Romola Garai's infuriated playwright, it looped in and out of her work and her life in five scenes that attempted a feminist story-structure. Sharpened by references to the Almeida regime that programmed it, *The Writer* made an impassioned polemic.

That it played as the #MeToo movement was gaining momentum added weight, as it did to Dennis Kelly's solo examination of patriarchal violence *Girls and Boys,* starring a superlative Carey Mulligan as a brilliant filmmaker stuck minding her kids, and to Joe Penhall's recording studio ding-dong *Mood Music*, in which a middle-aged male producer manipulates a young female singer-songwriter. At the Royal Court, artistic director Vicky Featherstone organised a 'day of action' in response to #MeToo, out of which came a new code of conduct. The theatre was itself embroiled, when it was revealed that former artistic director Max Stafford-Clark had left his company Out of Joint over inappropriate remarks made to female staff members. The Court cancelled its run of Out of Joint's touring revival of Andrea Dunbar's *Rita, Sue and Bob Too*, only to restore it after a public outcry – the irony being that a working-class woman's voice would have been silenced.

BEYOND BORDERS

Featherstone's other key initiative was a season of plays by international writers. A response to borders tightening and protectionist politics, the Royal Court's autumn season skipped from Syria to Chile, Ukraine to the US. Guillermo Calderon's *B* cast a surrealist eye on the guerilla revolutionaries dotting Santiago with bombs – or trying to, once they had mastered convoluted codewords. Think Chris Morris' *Four Lions* as written by Joe Orton. Liwaa Yazji's *Goats* had a similar lunacy – a satire on President Assad's policy of compensating martyrs' families with a gift of a kid goat.

None of the plays wholly convinced, but Julia Jarcho's *Grimly Handsome* made a virtue of its strangeness. Twisted and surreal, it watched, unblinking, as two roadside Christmas-tree salesmen embarked on a killing spree. Chloe Lamford's installation-style design spread small-town America across a series of rehearsal rooms.

America's playwrights have hit their peak in recent years – a result, perhaps, of having plenty to write about. Many have crossed the Atlantic, none with more acclaim than Matthew Lopez. His sweeping two-parter *The Inheritance* lifted E. M. Forster's *Howards End* out of Edwardian England and into the gay scene of today's New York City. Admitting its own artistic debts – to Tony Kushner as much as to Forster himself – it asked what each generation owes to the next. It gave space to reflect on the legacy of AIDS and was a shattering day's drama and, in Stephen Daldry's spare staging, a towering achievement.

Christopher Shinn's *Against* cast Ben Whishaw as a tech billionaire – half Mark Zuckerberg, half Elon Musk – atoning for his company's sins with a listening tour of America in the wake of another school shooting. As his messiah complex kicked in, Ian Rickson's sensitive, spare production practised what it was preaching: it was inclusive, progressive and refused representations of violence. Rajiv Joseph's *Describe the Night* tumbled through Russian disinformation, diagnosing a nation detached from reality and turning President Putin's tactics against him with an invented biography. Amy Herzog's *Belleville,* about a fraying expat couple in Paris, was a millennial mental health horror, while *Mr Burns* writer Anne Washburn turned her attention on *The Twilight Zone,*finding worldly fears and paranoia beneath its cult sci-fi stories. What looked like pastiche became a cultural exegesis.

Under new artistic director Ellen McDougall, the tiny Gate Theatre in Notting Hill switched its attention from America to Europe. Her opening adaptation of José Saramago's philosophical fable, *The Unknown Island* served as a manifesto for theatre itself. As its dreaming sailor woke and saw life anew, so, McDougall implied, should theatergoers. Jude Christian's clutter-filled staging of Falk Richter's anti-capitalist critique *Trust* saw the director live in the theatre for the length of the run, while French playwright Magali Mougel's superb *Suzy Storck* sought our empathy for a working-class woman marooned in motherhood, pinned down by the patriarchy. Jean-Pierre Baro's heart-wringing production had audiences on their knees, helping tidy toys off the floor.

International artists provided some of the year's best shows, courtesy of Manchester International Festival and LIFT. The latter brought Anna Deavere Smith back to London for the first time in over 25 years. The verbatim performer's *Notes From the Field* was a stunning staged essay on structural racism and a searing protest against America's schools-to-prison pipeline and police violence. Alongside her, drag artist Taylor Mac offered the first act of a 24-hour song cycle charting the history of post-independence pop music, decade by decade. Always as playful as it was pointed, it built a picture of a nation built on novelty and division. Dries Verhoeven's theatrical ghost train *Phobiarama* took audiences on a rollercoaster ride through the politics of fear, chased by bears, clowns and men of colour.

In Manchester, German director Thomas Ostermeier offered more nuance on the subject in *Returning to Reims,* transforming Didier Eribon's sociological memoir about the rise of the far-right in post-industrial France into a layered theatrical essay. Staged in a recording studio, with Nina Hoss narrating a documentary voiceover, it offered a critique and a deconstruction of a simplistic media narrative; it was at once a reading, a drama, a film and a gig. Today's world, it insisted, needs complex debate instead of simplistic answers.

SIMPLE SOLUTIONS

If populism promises easy answers, it was unpicked onstage again and again. *Effigies of Wickedness*, at McDougall's Gate, gave us a cabaret of songs banned by the Nazis as 'degenerate art'. Conceived by baritone Peter Brathwaite, it ran in chronological order, listening as the bohemia of 1920s Berlin collapsed under the Third Reich. It was an undoing of historical wrongs, restoring songs that had been struck from the record, and a warning from history. *Imperium*, the RSC's adaptation of Robert Harris' Cicero trilogy, offered another, showing the decline of democracy in Rome and the rise of an opportunistic autocrat, Julius Caesar. While epic in scale, it lacked theatrical imagination.

Kneehigh could never be accused of that. The company's staging of *The Tin Drum,* based on Günter Grass' darkly ambiguous satire on Nazism, starred a puppet Oskar who drowned out the Fuhrer with his tiny toy drum. Rita Kalnejais' inventive *This Beautiful Future* preferred to listen, showing a tender romance between a teenage Nazi soldier and a young French girl at the end of the Second World War. In daring to humanise Nazism, it exposed its irrationality.

The refugee crisis also recurred as a theme. Vox Motus shrunk the issue to scale in *Flight*, a story of movement told through a series of stills. A rotating diorama, like a 3D graphic novel, unfolded Caroline Brothers' story of two Afghan brothers making their way to Calais. Its miniatures made you lean in. Theatre Rites' *The Welcoming Party* fused personal testimony with puppetry to capture the enormity of the journey, while David Greig's version of *The Suppliant Women,* staged with a community chorus, found echoes of a contemporary crisis in antiquity.

Written by the founders of the pop-up theatre Good Chance, Joe Murphy and Joe Robertson, *The Jungle* took you into the heart of the Calais migrant camp. Set in its on-site Afghan Flag restaurant, realised in Miriam Buether's immersive design, it recounted the settlement's history – from its impromptu beginnings to its eventual destruction on orders of the French courts. Telling the stories of refugees, traffickers and British volunteers, it humanised an issue often portrayed from afar.

AWARDS

2018 LAURENCE OLIVIER AWARDS

Best Actor – Bryan Cranston for *Network* at the National Theatre

Best Actress – Laura Donnelly for *The Ferryman* at the Royal Court and Gielgud Theatre

Best Actor in a Supporting Role – Bertie Carvel for *Ink* at the Almeida Theatre and Duke of York's Theatre

Best Actress in a Supporting Role – Denise Gough for *Angels in America* at the National Theatre

Best New Play – *The Ferryman* by Jez Butterworth at the Royal Court and Gielgud Theatre

Best Revival – *Angels in America* at the National Theatre

Best Actor in a Musical – Giles Terera for *Hamilton* at the Victoria Palace Theatre

Best Actress in a Musical – Shirley Henderson for *Girl from the North Country* at the Old Vic

Best Actor in a Supporting Role in a Musical – Michael Jibson for *Hamilton* at the Victoria Palace Theatre

Best Actress in a Supporting Role in a Musical – Sheila Atim for *Girl from the North Country* at the Old Vic

Best New Musical – *Hamilton* at the Victoria Palace Theatre

Best Musical Revival – *Follies* at the National Theatre

Best New Comedy – *Labour of Love* at the Noël Coward Theatre

Best New Dance Production – *Flight Pattern* by Crystal Pite at the Royal Opera House

Outstanding Achievement in Dance – Francesca Velicu for her performance in English National Ballet's production of *Le Sacre du Printemps*

Best New Opera Production – *Semiramide* at the Royal Opera House

Outstanding Achievement in Opera – Joyce DiDonato and Daniela Barcellona for their performances in *Semiramide* at the Royal Opera House

Outstanding Achievement in an Affiliate Theatre – *Killology* at the Royal Court

Outstanding Achievement in Music – *Hamilton* at the Victoria Palace Theatre

Best Entertainment and Family – *Dick Whittington* at the London Palladium

Best Director – Sam Mendes for *The Ferryman* at the Royal Court and Gielgud Theatre

Best Theatre Choreographer – Andy Blankenbuehler for *Hamilton* at the Victoria Palace Theatre

Best Set Design – Bob Crowley and 59 Productions for *An American in Paris* at the Dominion Theatre

Best Lighting Design – Howell Binkley for *Hamilton* at the Victoria Palace Theatre

Best Sound Design – Nevin Steinberg for *Hamilton* at the Victoria Palace Theatre

Best Costume Design – Vicki Mortimer for *Follies* at the National Theatre

Special Award – David Lan

CRITICS' CIRCLE AWARDS FOR 2017

Best Actor – Bryan Cranston for *Network* at the National Theatre

Best Actress – Victoria Hamilton for *Albion* at the Almeida Theatre

The John and Wendy Trewin Award for Best Shakespearean Performance – Andrew Scott for *Hamlet* at the Almeida Theatre and Harold Pinter Theatre

The Jack Tinker Award for Most Promising Newcomer – Sheila Atim for *Girl from the North Country* at the Old Vic and John McCrea for *Everybody's Talking About Jamie* at Sheffield Crucible and the Apollo Theatre

Best New Play – *The Ferryman* by Jez Butterworth at the Royal Court and Gielgud Theatre

The Peter Hepple Award for Best Musical – *Hamilton* at the Victoria Palace Theatre

Best Director – Dominic Cooke for *Follies* at the National Theatre

Best Designer – Vicki Mortimer for *Follies* at the National Theatre

Most Promising Playwright – Branden Jacobs-Jenkins for *An Octoroon* at the Orange Tree Theatre

EVENING STANDARD THEATRE AWARDS FOR 2017

Best Actor – Andrew Garfield for *Angels in America* at the National Theatre

The Natasha Richardson Award for Best Actress – Glenda Jackson for *King Lear* at the Old Vic

Best Play – *The Ferryman* by Jez Butterworth at the Royal Court and Gielgud Theatre

Best Musical Performance – Amber Riley in *Dreamgirls* at the Savoy

The Radio 2 Audience Award for Best Musical – *Bat Out of Hell: The Musical* at the Coliseum

The Milton Shulman Award for Best Director – Sam Mendes for *The Ferryman* at the Royal Court and Gielgud Theatre

Best Design – Bunny Christie for *Heisenberg: The Uncertainty Principle* at the Wyndham's, *Ink* at the Almeida and Duke of York's Theatre, and *The Red Barn* at the National Theatre

The Charles Wintour Award for Most Promising Playwright – Branden Jacobs-Jenkins for *An Octoroon* at the Orange Tree Theatre

Emerging Talent Award – Tom Glynn-Carney for *The Ferryman* at the Royal Court and Gielgud Theatre

SPORTS RESULTS

ALPINE SKIING

WORLD CUP 2017–8

MEN
Downhill: Beat Feuz (Switzerland), 682pts
Slalom: Marcel Hirscher (Austria), 874pts
Giant Slalom: Marcel Hirscher (Austria), 720pts
Super G: Kjetil Jansrud (Norway), 400pts
Combined: Peter Fill (Italy), 140pts
Overall: Marcel Hirscher (Austria), 1,620pts

WOMEN
Downhill: Sofia Goggia (Italy), 509pts
Slalom: Mikaela Shiffrin (USA), 980pts
Giant Slalom: Viktoria Rebensburg (Germany), 582pts
Super G: Tina Weirather (Liechtenstein), 461pts
Combined: Wendy Holdener (Switzerland), 150pts
Overall: Mikaela Shiffrin (USA), 1,773pts

AMERICAN FOOTBALL

AFC Championship 2017–18: New England Patriots beat
    Jacksonville Jaguars 24–20
NFC Championship 2017–18: Philadelphia Eagles beat
    Minnesota Vikings 38–7
Super Bowl 52: Philadelphia Eagles beat New England
    Patriots 41–33

ANGLING

NATIONAL CHAMPIONSHIPS 2018
Individual: Andrew Moss
Individual (ladies): Samantha Sim

TEAMS
Division 1: Barnsley and District
Division 2: Sensas Mark One

ASSOCIATION FOOTBALL

LEAGUE COMPETITIONS 2017–18

ENGLAND AND WALES

Premier League
1. Manchester City, 100pts
2. Manchester United, 81pts
3. Tottenham Hotspur, 77pts
4. Liverpool, 75pts
Relegated: Stoke City, Swansea City, West Bromwich Albion

Championship
1. Wolverhampton Wanderers, 99pts
2. Cardiff City, 90pts
Play-off winner and third promotion place: Aston Villa
Relegated: Barnsley, Burton Albion, Sunderland

League One
1. Wigan Athletic, 98pts
2. Blackburn Rovers, 96pts
Play-off winner and third promotion place: Rotherham United
Relegated: Bury, Milton Keynes Dons, Northampton Town,
    Oldham Athletic

League Two
1. Accrington Stanley, 93pts
2. Luton Town, 88pts
3. Wycombe Wanderers, 84pts
Play-off winner and fourth promotion place: Coventry City
Relegated: Barnet, Chesterfield

National League
1. Macclesfield Town, 92pts
Play-off winner and second promotion place: Tranmere Rovers
*Relegated: Chester, Guiseley, Torquay United, Woking
* Relegated teams go down to National League North or South
dependent on location

Welsh Premier League
1. The New Saints, 74pts
2. Bangor City*, 60pts
3. Connah's Quay Nomads, 57pts
Relegated: Bangor City*, Prestatyn Town
* Bangor City were relegated after failing to obtain Tier One and UEFA
licenses for the 2018–19 Welsh Premier League and 2018–19 UEFA
Europa League, respectively

SCOTLAND

Scottish Premiership
1. Celtic, 82pts
2. Aberdeen, 73pts
Relegated: Ross County

Scottish Championship
1. St Mirren, 74pts
Relegated: Brechin City

Scottish League One
1. Ayr United, 76pts
Relegated: Albion Rovers

Scottish League Two
1. Montrose, 77pts

NORTHERN IRELAND

NIFL Premiership
1. Crusaders, 91pts
2. Coleraine, 89pts
3. Glenavon, 69pts

REPUBLIC OF IRELAND
League of Ireland Premier Division: 1. Cork City, 76pts; 2.
    Dundalk, 69pts; 3. Shamrock Rovers, 54pts

FRANCE
Ligue 1: 1. Paris Saint Germain, 93pts; 2. AS Monaco, 80pts;
    3. Olympique Lyonnais, 78pts

GERMANY
Bundesliga: 1. Bayern Munich, 84pts; 2. Shalke 04, 63pts; 3.
    1899 Hoffenheim, 55pts

ITALY
Serie A: 1. Juventus, 95pts; 2. Napoli, 91pts; 3. AS Roma,
    77pts

NETHERLANDS
Eredivisie: 1. PSV Eindhoven, 83pts; 2. Ajax, 79pts; 3. AZ
    Alkmaar, 71pts

SPAIN

La Liga: 1. Barcelona, 93pts; 2. Atlético Madrid, 79pts; 3. Real Madrid, 76pts

CUP COMPETITIONS 2017–18

ENGLAND

FA Cup final 2018: Chelsea beat Manchester United 1–0
League Cup final 2018: Manchester City beat Arsenal 3–0
EFL Trophy Final 2018: Lincoln City beat Shrewsbury Town 1–0
FA Vase final 2018: Thatcham Town beat Stockton Town 1–0
FA Trophy final 2018: Brackley Town beat Bromley 5–4 on penalties (1–1 aet)
Community Shield 2018: Manchester City beat Chelsea 2–0

WOMEN

FA Cup final 2018: Chelsea beat Arsenal 3–1
*Women's Super League 2017–18: 1. Chelsea, 41pts; 2. Manchester City, 35pts
Premier League Cup final 2018: Blackburn Rovers beat Leicester City 3–1
* There was no promotion or relegation at the end of the season due to the league's restructure in the 2018–19 season

WALES

FAW Welsh Cup final 2018: Connah's Quay Nomads beat Aberystwyth Town 4–1
Welsh League Cup final 2018: The New Saints beat Cardiff Metropolitan University 1–0

SCOTLAND

Scottish Cup final 2018: Celtic beat Motherwell 2–0
League Cup final 2017: Celtic beat Motherwell 2–0

NORTHERN IRELAND

Irish Cup final 2018: Coleraine beat Cliftonville 3–1

EUROPE

UEFA Champions League final 2018: Real Madrid beat Liverpool 3–1
UEFA Europa League final 2018: Atlético Madrid beat Marseille 3–0

FIFA BALLON D'OR

2017 – Cristiano Ronaldo (Portugal)
2016 – Cristiano Ronaldo (Portugal)
2015 – Lionel Messi (Argentina)
2014 – Cristiano Ronaldo (Portugal)
2013 – Cristiano Ronaldo (Portugal)
2012 – Lionel Messi (Argentina)
2011 – Lionel Messi (Argentina)
2010 – Lionel Messi (Argentina)

2018 FIFA WORLD CUP

Russia, 14 June–15 July

GROUP A

	P	W	D	L	F	A	GD	PTS
Uruguay	3	3	0	0	5	0	5	9
Russia	3	2	0	1	8	4	4	6
Saudi Arabia	3	1	0	2	2	7	−5	3
Egypt	3	0	0	3	2	6	−4	0

Russia beat Saudi Arabia 5–0
Uruguay beat Egypt 1–0
Russia beat Egypt 3–1
Uruguay beat Saudi Arabia 1–0
Uruguay beat Russia 3–0
Saudi Arabia beat Egypt 2–1

GROUP B

	P	W	D	L	F	A	GD	PTS
Spain	3	1	2	0	6	5	1	5
Portugal	3	1	2	0	5	4	1	5
Iran	3	1	1	1	2	2	0	4
Morocco	3	0	1	2	2	4	−2	1

Iran beat Morocco 1–0
Portugal drew with Spain 3–3
Portugal beat Morocco 1–0
Spain beat Iran 1–0
Spain drew with Morocco 2–2
Iran drew with Portugal 1–1

GROUP C

	P	W	D	L	F	A	GD	PTS
France	3	2	1	0	3	1	2	7
Denmark	3	1	2	0	2	1	1	5
Peru	3	1	0	2	2	2	0	3
Australia	3	0	1	2	2	5	−3	1

France beat Australia 2–1
Denmark beat Peru 1–0
Denmark drew with Australia 1–1
France beat Peru 1–0
Peru beat Australia 2–0
Denmark drew with France 0–0

GROUP D

	P	W	D	L	F	A	GD	PTS
Croatia	3	3	0	0	7	1	6	9
Argentina	3	1	1	1	3	5	−2	4
Nigeria	3	1	0	2	3	4	−1	3
Iceland	3	0	1	2	2	5	−3	1

Argentina drew with Iceland 1–1
Croatia beat Nigeria 2–0
Croatia beat Argentina 3–0
Nigeria beat Iceland 2–0
Argentina beat Nigeria 2–1
Croatia beat Iceland 2–1

GROUP E

	P	W	D	L	F	A	GD	PTS
Brazil	3	2	1	0	5	1	4	7
Switzerland	3	1	2	0	5	4	1	5
Serbia	3	1	0	2	2	4	−2	3
Costa Rica	3	0	1	2	2	5	−3	1

Serbia beat Costa Rica 1–0
Brazil drew with Switzerland 1–1
Brazil beat Costa Rica 2–0
Switzerland beat Serbia 2–1
Brazil beat Serbia 2–0
Switzerland drew with Costa Rica 2–2

GROUP F

	P	W	D	L	F	A	GD	PTS
Sweden	3	2	0	1	5	2	3	6
Mexico	3	2	0	1	3	4	−1	6
Rep. Korea	3	1	0	2	3	3	0	3
Germany	3	1	0	2	2	4	−2	3

Mexico beat Germany 1–0
Sweden beat Rep. Korea 1–0
Mexico beat Rep. Korea 2–1
Germany beat Sweden 2–1
Rep. Korea beat Germany 2–0
Sweden beat Mexico 3–0

GROUP G

	P	W	D	L	F	A	GD	PTS
Belgium	3	3	0	0	9	2	7	9
England	3	2	0	1	8	3	5	6
Tunisia	3	1	0	2	5	8	−3	3
Panama	3	0	0	3	2	11	−9	0

Belgium beat Panama 3–0
England beat Tunisia 2–1
Belgium beat Tunisia 5–2
England beat Panama 6–1
Tunisia beat Panama 2–1
Belgium beat England 1–0

GROUP H

	P	W	D	L	F	A	GD	PTS
Colombia	3	2	0	1	5	2	3	6
Japan	3	1	1	1	4	4	0	4
Senegal	3	1	1	1	4	4	0	4
Poland	3	1	0	2	2	5	−3	3

Japan beat Colombia 2–1
Senegal beat Poland 2–1
Japan drew with Senegal 2–2
Colombia beat Poland 3–0
Poland beat Japan 1–0
Colombia beat Senegal 1–0

LAST 16
France beat Argentina 4–3
Uruguay beat Portugal 2–1
Russia beat Spain 4–3 on penalties (1–1 aet)
Croatia beat Denmark 3–2 on penalties (1–1 aet)
Brazil beat Mexico 2–0
Belgium beat Japan 3–2
Sweden beat Switzerland 1–0
England beat Colombia 4–3 on penalties (1–1 aet)

QUARTER-FINALS
France beat Uruguay 2–0
Belgium beat Brazil 2–1
England beat Sweden 2–0
Croatia beat Russia 4–3 on penalties (2–2 aet)

SEMI-FINALS
France beat Belgium 1–0
Croatia beat England 2–1

3RD PLACE PLAY-OFF
Belgium beat England 2–0

FINAL
France beat Croatia 4–2

ATHLETICS

EUROPEAN CROSS COUNTRY CHAMPIONSHIPS
Samorín, Slovakia, 10 December 2017

SENIOR MEN (10.18KM)
Individual: Kaan Kigen Ozbilen (Turkey), 29min 45sec
Team: Spain, 34pts

U23 MEN (8.23KM)
Individual: Jimmy Gressier (France), 24min 35sec
Team: France, 14pts

JUNIOR MEN (6.28KM)
Individual: Jakob Ingerbrigtsen (Norway), 18min 39sec
Team: Spain, 29pts

SENIOR WOMEN (8.23KM)
Individual: Yasemin Can (Turkey), 26min 48sec
Team: Great Britain, 33pts

U23 WOMEN (6.28KM)
Individual: Alina Reh (Germany), 20min 22sec
Team: Great Britain, 21pts

JUNIOR WOMEN (4.18KM)
Individual: Harriet Knowles-Jones (Great Britain), 13min 48sec
Team: Great Britain, 33pts

ENGLISH NATIONAL CROSS COUNTRY CHAMPIONSHIPS
Parliament Hill, London, 24 February 2018

SENIOR MEN
Individual: Adam Hickey (Southend-on-Sea Athletic Club), 39min 35sec
Team: Tonbridge Athletic Club, 131pts

JUNIOR MEN
Individual: Mahamed Mahamed (Southampton Athletic Club), 31min 26sec
Team: Sale Harriers Manchester, 76pts

SENIOR WOMEN
Individual: Phoebe Law (Kingston Athletics Club & Polytechnic Harriers), 28min 33sec
Team: Milton Keynes Distance Project, 106pts

JUNIOR WOMEN
Individual: Harriet Knowles-Jones (Warrington Athletic Club), 24min 07sec
Team: Sale Harriers Manchester, 31pts

LONDON MARATHON
London, 22 April 2018

Men: Eliud Kipchoge (Kenya), 2hr 04min 17sec
Women: Vivian Cheruiyot (Kenya), 2hr 18min 31sec

BADMINTON

EUROPEAN CHAMPIONSHIPS 2018
Huelva, Spain, 24–29 April

Men's Singles: Viktor Axelsen (Denmark) beat Rajiv Ouseph (England) 2–0
Women's Singles: Carolina Marin (Spain) beat Evgeniya Kosetskaya (Russia) 2–0
Men's Doubles: Kim Astrup and Anders Skaarup Rasmussen (Denmark) beat Mads Conrad-Petersen and Mads Pieler Kolding (Denmark) 1–0 Retired
Women's Doubles: Gabriela Stoeva and Stefani Stoeva (Bulgaria) beat Emilie Lefel and Anne Tran (France) 2–0
Mixed Doubles: Chris Adcock and Gabrielle Adcock (England) beat Mathias Christiansen and Christinna Pederson (Denmark) 2–1

ALL-ENGLAND CHAMPIONSHIPS 2018
Birmingham, March

Men's Singles: Shi Yuqi (China) beat Lin Dan (China) 2–1
Women's Singles: Tai Tzu Ying (Chinese Taipei) beat Akane Yamaguchi (Japan) 2–0
Men's Doubles: Marcus Fernaldi Gideon and Kevin Sanjaya Sukamuljo (Indonesia) beat Mathias Boe and Carsten Mogensen (Denmark) 2–0

Women's Doubles: Kamilla Rytter Juhl and Christinna Pedersen (Denmark) beat Yuki Fukushima and Sayaka Hirota (Japan) 2–0

Mixed Doubles: Arisa Higashino and Yuta Watanabe (Japan) beat Zheng Siwei and Huang Yaqiong (China) 2–1

ENGLISH NATIONAL CHAMPIONSHIPS 2018
High Wycombe, August

Men's Singles: Toby Penty beat Alex Lane 2–1
Women's Singles: Chloe Birch beat Georgina Bland 2–0
Men's Doubles: Matt Clare and Michael Roe beat Greg Mairs and Johnnie Torjessen 2–0
Women's Doubles: Lauren Smith and Jess Pugh beat Elizabeth Tolman and Abi Holden 2–0
Mixed Doubles: Marcus Ellis and Lauren Smith beat Steven Stallwood and Lizzie Holden 2–0

SCOTTISH NATIONAL CHAMPIONSHIPS 2018
Perth, February

Men's Singles: Kieran Merrilees beat Matthew Carder 2–0
Women's Singles: Kirsty Gilmour beat Julie MacPherson 2–0
Men's Doubles: Alex Dunn and Adam Hall beat Martin Campbell and Patrick MacHugh 2–1
Women's Doubles: Julie MacPherson and Eleanor O'Donnell beat Holly Newall and Ciara Torrance 2–0
Mixed Doubles: Alex Dunn and Eleanor O'Donnell beat Martin Campbell and Julie MacPherson 2–1

WELSH NATIONAL CHAMPIONSHIPS 2018
Cardiff, February

Men's Singles: Daniel Font beat Tsung Fong Mo 2–0
Women's Singles: Jordan Hart beat Lowri Jennifer Hart 2–0
Men's Doubles: Daniel Font and Oliver Paul Gwilt beat Joe Sion Cottrill and Matthew Sprake 2–0
Women's Doubles: Gean Sou Mo and Carissa Turner beat Jordan Hart and Lowri Jennifer Hart 2–0
Mixed Doubles: Tsung Fong Mo and Gean Sou Mo beat Ollie Hartery and Carissa Turner 2–1

BASEBALL

American League Championship Series 2017: Houston Astros beat New York Yankees 4–3
National League Championship Series 2017: Los Angeles Dodgers beat Chicago Cubs 4–1
Major League Baseball World Series 2017: Houston Astros beat Los Angeles Dodgers 4–3

BASKETBALL

BRITISH

MEN
BBL Champions 2017–18: Leicester Riders
BBL Play-off final 2018: Leicester Riders beat London Lions 81–60
BBL Trophy final 2018: Leicester Riders beat DBL Sharks Sheffield 90–85
BBL Cup final 2018: Cheshire Phoenix beat Worcester Wolves 99–88

WOMEN
WBBL Champions 2017–18: Sevenoaks Suns
WBBL Play-off final 2017–18: Sevenoaks Suns beat Leicester Riders 69–44
WBBL Trophy 2018: Leicester Riders beat Sevenoaks Suns 68–53

WWBL Cup 2018: Nottingham Wildcats beat Caledonia Pride 70–66

USA – NATIONAL BASKETBALL LEAGUE (NBA)

Eastern Conference final 2018: Cleveland Cavaliers beat Boston Celtics 4–3
Western Conference final 2018: Golden State Warriors beat Houston Rockets 4–3
NBA final 2018: Golden State Warriors beat Cleveland Cavaliers 4–0

BOWLS — INDOOR

WORLD CHAMPIONSHIPS 2018
Great Yarmouth, Norfolk, January

Men's Singles: Mark Dawes (England) beat Robert Paxton (England) 2–1
Women's Singles: Katherine Rednall (England) beat Rebecca Field (England) 2–0
Men's Pairs: Jamie Chestney (England) and Mark Dawes (England) beat Nick Brett (England) and Greg Harlow (England) 1.5–0.5
Mixed Pairs: Jamie Chestney (England) and Lesley Doig (Scotland) beat Darren Burnett (Scotland) and Rebecca Field (England) 2–0

BRITISH ISLES INDOOR BOWLS CHAMPIONSHIPS 2018
Paisley, March

MEN
Singles: Paul Foster (Scotland) beat Scott Baxter (Channel Islands) 21–9
Pairs: Scotland beat England 25–16
Triples: Scotland beat Channel Islands 19–14
Fours: England beat Ireland 23–10

WOMEN
Singles: Caroline Brown (Scotland) beat Alison Merrien (Channel Islands) 21–4
Pairs: Ireland beat England 24–9
Triples: England beat Ireland 15–14
Fours: England beat Wales 21–10

ENGLISH NATIONAL CHAMPIONSHIPS 2018
Melton & District IBC, Melton Mowbray, March–April

MEN
Singles: J. Bird beat R. Whitlock 21–10
Pairs: Blackpool N. H. beat Whiteknights 22–8
Triples: Huntingdon beat Barwell 14–13
Fours: Spalding beat Kingsthorpe 14–10
Liberty Trophy (Inter-County Championship) final: Lincolnshire beat Kent 120–107
Champion of Champions: J. Chestney beat R. Newman 21–17

WOMEN
Singles: J. Gower beat D. Cooper 21–20
Pairs: Spalding beat Swale 16–13
Triples: Adur beat Torquay Utd 17–13
Fours: Swale beat Beccles 20–9
Atherley Trophy (Inter-County Championship) final: Lincolnshire beat Dorset 126–101
Champion of Champions: K. Rednall beat K. Mann 21–10

SCOTTISH NATIONAL CHAMPIONSHIPS 2018
January–February

MEN
Singles: Prestwick beat East Lothian 21–19
Pairs: Midlothian beat Prestwick 16–13
Triples: Inverclyde beat Elgin 22–9

Fours: East Lothian beat Galleon 21–18

WOMEN
Singles: Blantyre beat Balbardie 21–7
Pairs: Balbardie beat Whiteinch 21–16
Triples: Blantyre beat Teviotdale 19–10
Fours: East Fife beat Midlothian 17–14

BOWLS — OUTDOOR

ENGLISH NATIONAL CHAMPIONSHIPS 2018
Royal Leamington Spa, August–September

Singles: Devon A beat Essex A 21–16
Pairs: Somerset B beat Surrey A 19–12
Triples: Lancashire B beat Devon A 18–12
Fours: Wiltshire A beat Lancashire B 17–15

SCOTTISH NATIONAL CHAMPIONSHIPS 2018
Ayr, July

Singles: Whitefield beat Irvine Park 21–15
Pairs: Port Glasgow beat Prestwick 16–15
Triples: Markinch beat Ayr Seafield 13–12
Fours: Carrick Knowe beat Marchmount 19–8

WELSH NATIONAL CHAMPIONSHIPS 2018
Carmarthen, August

Singles: K. James beat M. Weaver 21–12
Pairs: P. Diment and R. Thomas beat I. Mellor and G. Mellor
22–21
Triples: Harlequins beat Ely Valley 17–15
Fours: Beaufort beat Merthyr West End 19–17

BOXING

WORLD CHAMPIONS
as at September 2018

WORLD BOXING COUNCIL (WBC)
Heavy: Deontay Wilder (USA)
Cruiser: Oleksandr Usyk (Ukraine)
Light-heavy: Adonis Stevenson (Haiti / Canada)
Supermiddle: David Benavidez (Mexico / United States)
Middle: Canelo Alvarez (Mexico)
Superwelter: Jermell Charlo (USA)
Welter: Shawn Porter (USA)
Superlight: José Carlos Ramirez (USA)
Light: Mikey Garcia (USA)
Light Diamond: Jorge Linares (Venezuela)
Superfeather: Miguel Berchelt (Mexico)
Feather: Gary Russell Jr (USA)
Superbantam: Rey Vargas (Mexico)
Bantam: vacant
Superfly: Srisaket Sor Runvisai (Thailand)
Fly: Cristofer Rosales (Nicaragua)
Lightfly: Ken Shiro (Japan)
Mini-fly: Wanheng Menayothin (Thailand)

WORLD BOXING ASSOCIATION (WBA)
Heavy: Manuel Charr (Syria)
Cruiser: Oleksandr Usyk (Ukraine)
Light-heavy: Dmitry Bivol (Russia)
Supermiddle: Rocky Fielding (Great Britain)
Middle: Ryota Murata (Japan)
Superwelter: Brian Carlos Castaño (Argentina)
Welter: Manny Pacquiao (Philippines)
Superlight: Kiryl Relikh (Belarus)
Light: Vasyl Lomachenko (Ukraine)
Superfeather: Alberto Machado (Puerto Rico)

Feather (Interim): Jhack Tepora (Philippines)
Superbantam: Daniel Roman (USA)
Bantam: Naoya Inoue (Japan)
Superfly: Khalid Yafai (Great Britain)
Fly: Artem Dalakian (Ukraine)
Lightfly: Carlos Canizales (Venezuela)
Mini-fly: Thammanoon Niyomtrong (Thailand)

WORLD BOXING ORGANISATION (WBO)
Heavy: Anthony Joshua (Great Britain)
Cruiser: Oleksandr Usyk (Ukraine)
Light-heavy: Eleider Alvarez (Colombia)
Supermiddle: Gilberto Ramírez (Mexico)
Middle: Billy Joe Saunders (Great Britain)
Junior-middle: Jaime Munguia (Mexico)
Welter: Terence Crawford (USA)
Junior-welter: Maurice Hooker (USA)
Light: Jose Pendraza (Puerto Rico)
Junior-light: Masayuki Ito (Japan)
Feather: Oscar Valdez (Mexico)
Junior-feather: Isaac Dogboe (Ghana)
Bantam: Zolani Tete (South Africa)
Junior-bantam: vacant
Fly: Sho Kimura (Japan)
Junior-fly: Ángel Acosta Gómez (Puerto Rico)
Mini-fly: Vic Saludar (Philippines)

INTERNATIONAL BOXING FEDERATION (IBF)
Heavy: Anthony Joshua (Great Britain)
Cruiser: Oleksandr Usyk (Ukraine)
Light-heavy: Artur Beterbiev (Russia)
Supermiddle: Jose Uzcategui (Venezuela)
Middle: vacant
Junior-middle: Jerrett Hurd (USA)
Welter: Errol Spence Jr (USA)
Junior-welter: vacant
Light: Miguel Garcia (USA)
Junior-lightweight: Tevin Farmer (USA)
Feather: Josh Warrington(Great Britain)
Junior-feather: T. J. Doheny (Ireland)
Bantam: Emmanuel Rodriguez (Puerto Rico)
Junior-bantam: Jerwin Ancajas (Philippines)
Fly: Moruti Mthalane (South Africa)
Junior-fly: vacant
Mini-fly: vacant

BRITISH CHAMPIONS
Heavy: Hughie Fury
Cruiser: Matty Askin
Light-heavy: Callum Johnson
Super-middle: vacant
Middle: Jason Welborn
Super-welter: vacant
Welter: Bradley Skeete
Super-welter: vacant
Light: Lewis Ritson
Super-feather: Sam Bowen
Feather: Ryan Walsh
Super-bantam: vacant
Bantam: vacant
Super-fly: vacant
Fly: Andrew Selby

CHESS

FIDE Chess World Cup 2017: Aronian Levon (Armenia) beat
Ding Liren (China) 4–2
British Champion 2018: Michael Adams
British Women's Champion 2018: Jovanka Houska

CRICKET

TEST SERIES 2017–18

AUSTRALIA V ENGLAND
Brisbane (23–27 November 2017): Australia beat England by 10 wickets. Australia 328 and 173–0; England 302 and 195

Adelaide (2–6 December 2017): Australia beat England by 120 runs. Australia 442–8 dec and 138; England 227 and 233

Perth (14–18 December 2017): Australia beat England by an innings and 41 runs. Australia 662–9 dec; England 403 and 218

Melbourne (26–30 December 2017): Australia drew with England. Australia 327 and 263–4 dec; England 491

Sydney (4–8 January 2018): Australia beat England by an innings and 123 runs. Australia 649–7 dec; England 346 and 180

NEW ZEALAND V ENGLAND
Auckland (22 March 2018): New Zealand beat England by an innings and 49 runs. New Zealand 427–8 dec; England 58 and 320

Christchurch (29 March 2018): New Zealand drew with England. New Zealand 278 and 256–8; England 307 and 352–9 dec

ENGLAND V PAKISTAN
Lord's (24 May 2018): Pakistan beat England by 9 wickets. Pakistan 363 and 66–1; England 184 and 242 dec

Leeds (1 June 2018): England beat Pakistan by an innings and 55 runs. England 363; Pakistan 174 and 134

SCOTLAND V ENGLAND
Edinburgh (10 June 2018): Scotland won by 6 runs. Scotland 371–5; England 365

ENGLAND V INDIA
Edgbaston (1 August 2018): England won by 31 runs. England 287 and 180; India 274 and 262

Lord's (9 August 2018): England won by an inning and. 159 runs. England 396–7 dec; India 107 and 130

Trent Bridge (18 August 2018): India won by 203 runs. India 329 and 352–7; England161 and 317

Rose Bowl (30 August 2018): England won by 60 runs. England 246 and India 273 and 184

Kia Oval (7 September 2018): England won by 118 runs. England 332 and 423–8 dec; India 292 and 345

ONE-DAY INTERNATIONALS 2017–18

ENGLAND V WEST INDIES
Old Trafford (19 September 2017): England beat West Indies by 7 wickets. England 210–3, West Indies 204–9

Bristol (24 September 2017): England beat West Indies by 124 runs. England 369–9, West Indies 245

Kia Oval (27 September 2017): England beat West Indies by 6 runs. England 258–5, West Indies 356–5

Rose Bowl (29 September 2017): England beat West Indies by 9 wickets. England 294–1, West Indies 288–6

AUSTRALIA V ENGLAND
Melbourne (14 January 2018): England beat Australia by 5 wickets. England 308–5, Australia 304–8

Brisbane (19 January 2018): England beat Australia by 4 wickets. England 274–6, Australia 270–9

Sydney (21 January 2018): England beat Australia by 16 runs. England 302–6, Australia 286–6

Adelaide (26 January 2018): Australia beat England by 3 wickets. Australia 197–7, England 196

Perth (28 January 2018): England beat Australia by 12 runs. England 259, Australia 247

NEW ZEALAND V ENGLAND
Hamilton (25 February 2018): New Zealand beat England by 3 wickets. New Zealand 287–7, England 284–8

Wellington (3 March 2018): England beat New Zealand by 4 runs. England 234, New Zealand 230–8

Dunedin (6 March 2018): New Zealand beat England by 5 wickets. New Zealand 339–5, England 335–9

Christchurch (9 March 2018): England beat New Zealand by 7 wickets. England 229–3, New Zealand 223

SCOTLAND V ENGLAND
Edinburgh (10 June 2018): Scotland won by 6 runs. Scotland 371–5; England 365

ENGLAND V AUSTRALIA
Kia Oval (13 June 2018): England beat Australia by 3 wickets. England 218–7; Australia 214

Cardiff (16 June 2018): England beat Australia by 38 wickets. England 342–8; Australia 304

Trent Bridge (19 June 2018): England beat Australia by 242 runs. England 481–6; Australia 239

Chester le Street (21 June 2018): England beat Australia by 6 wickets. England 314–4; Australia 310–8

Old Trafford (24 June 2018): England beat Australia by a wicket. England 208–9; Australia 205

ENGLAND V INDIA
Trent Bridge (12 July 2018): India won by 8 wickets. India 269–2; England 268

Lord's (14 July 2018): England won by 86 runs. England 322–7; India 236

Leeds (17 July 2018): England won by 8 wickets. England 260–2; India 256–8

TWENTY20 INTERNATIONALS

AUSTRALIA V ENGLAND
Hobart (7 February 2018): Australia beat England by 6 wickets. Australia 161–5, England 155–9

Melbourne (10 February 2018): Australia beat England by 7 wickets. Australia 138–3, England 137–7

NEW ZEALAND V ENGLAND
Wellington (13 February 2018): New Zealand beat England by 12 runs. New Zealand 196–5, England 184–9

Hamilton (18 February 2018): England beat New Zealand by 2 runs. England 194–7, New Zealand 192–4

ENGLAND V AUSTRALIA
Edgbaston (27 June 2018): England beat Australia by 28 runs. England 221–5; Australia 193

ENGLAND V INDIA
Old Trafford (3 July 2018): India beat England by 8 wickets. India 163–2; England 159–8

Cardiff (6 July 2018): England beat India by 5 wickets. England 149–5; India 148–5

Bristol (8 July 2018): India beat England by 7 wickets. India 201–3; England 198–9

ENGLAND AND WALES DOMESTIC COMPETITIONS 2017–18

Specsavers County Championship 2017, Division 1: Essex, 24; *Relegated* Middlesex, 146pts; Warwickshire, 86pts –

Division 2: Promoted Worcestershire, 238pts;
Nottinghamshire, 222pts
Royal London One-Day Cup final 2018: Hampshire beat Kent
by 61 runs. Hampshire 330–7; Kent 269
Vitality T20 Blast 2018: Worcestershire Rapids beat Sussex
Sharks by 5 wickets. Worcestershire Rapids 158–5;
Sussex Sharks 157–6

OTHER INTERNATIONAL DOMESTIC CHAMPIONSHIPS 2017–18

Australia: Sheffield Shield final 2017–18: Queensland beat
Tasmania by 9 wickets. Queensland 516 and 128–1,
Tasmania 477 and 166–1 dec. *JLT One-Day Cup final
2017–18:* Western Australia beat South Australia by 6
wickets. Western Australia 250–4, South Australia 248–9.
Twenty20 Big Bash League final 2017–18: Adelaide Strikers
beat Melbourne Renegades by 1 run; Adelaide Strikers
178–5, Melbourne Renegades 177–4
Bangladesh: BCL 2017–18: South Zone
India: Irani Cup final 2017–18: Vidarbha beat Rest of India by
an innings. Vidarbha 800–7 dec and 79, Rest of India
390. *Deodhar Trophy 2017–18:* India B beat Karnataka by
6 wickets. India B 281–4, Karnataka 279–8. *Duleep
Trophy final 2017–18:* India Red beat India Blue by 163
runs. India Red 483 and 208, India Blue 299 and 229.
Ranji Trophy Elite final 2017–18: Vidarbha beat Delhi by 9
wickets. Vidarbha 547 and 32–1, Delhi 295 and 280.
Syed Mushtaq Ali Trophy 2017–18: Delhi beat Rajasthan by
41 runs. Delhi 153–6, Rajasthan 112–10. *Vijay Hazare
Trophy final 2017–18:* Karnataka beat Saurashtra by 41
runs. Karnataka 253, Saurashtra 212. *Indian Premier League
Twenty20 final 2018:* Chennai Super Kings beat Sunrisers
Hyderabad by 8 wickets. Chennai Super Kings 181–2;
Sunrisers Hyderabad 178–6
New Zealand: Plunket Shield 2017–18: Central Districts 131pts.
Ford Trophy final 2017–18: Auckland beat Central Districts
by 6 wickets. Auckland 201–4, Central Districts 197.
Burger King Super Smash final 2017–18: Northern Districts
Knights beat Central Districts Stags by 9 wickets.
Northern Districts Knights 103–1, Central Districts Stags
99–8
Pakistan: Quaid-e-Azam Trophy final 2017–18: Sui Northern
Gas Pipelines Limited (Sui Gas) beat Water and Power
Development Authority (WAPDA) by 103 runs. Sui Gas
259 and 268, WAPDA 271 and 153UBL 236. *National
T20 Cup final 2017–18:* Lahore Blues beat Lahore Whites
by 7 wickets. Lahore Blues 131–3, Lahore Whites 127–5
South Africa: Sunfoil Series 2017–18: Titans 143.96pts
Momentum One-day Cup final 2017–18: Dolphins and
Warriors in final. Match abandoned. *Ram Slam T20
Challenge final 2017–18:* Titans beat Dolphins by 7
wickets. Titans 101–3, Dolphins 100–10
West Indies: Regional Super50 final 2017–18: Windward Islands
beat Barbados by 3 wickets. Windward Islands 236–7,
Barbados 232–9. *Regional 4-Day Tournament 2017–18:*
Guyana, 166.8 pts. *Caribbean Premier League T20 final
2018:* Trinbago Knight Riders beat Guyana Amazon
Warriors by 8 wickets. Trinbago Knight Riders 150–2;
Guyana Amazon Warriors 147–9

CURLING

MEN'S WORLD CHAMPIONSHIP 2018
Las Vegas, USA, 31 March–8 April

Final: Sweden beat Canada 7–3

WOMEN'S WORLD CHAMPIONSHIP 2018
North Bay, Canada, 17–25 March

Final: Canada beat Sweden 7–6

CYCLING

Vuelta a España 2018: Simon Yates (Great Britain)
Giro d'Italia 2018: Chris Froome (Great Britain)
Tour de France 2018: Geraint Thomas (Great Britain)

BRITISH NATIONAL ROAD RACE CHAMPIONSHIPS 2018
Stamfordham, July

MEN
Road Race: Connor Swift

WOMEN
Road Race: Jessica Roberts

UCI TRACK CYCLING WORLD CHAMPIONSHIPS 2018
Omnisport Apeldoorn, the Netherlands, February–March

MEN
Points Race: Cameron Meyer (Australia)
Sprint: Matthew Glaetzer (Australia)
1km Time Trial: Jeffrey Hoogland (Netherlands)
Individual Pursuit: Filippo Ganna (Italy)
Scratch Race: Yauheni Karaliok (Belarus)
Keirin: Fabian Hernando Puerta Zapata (Colombia)
Team Pursuit: Great Britain
Madison: Roger Kluge and Theo Reinhardt (Germany)
Team Sprint: Netherlands
Omnium: Szymon Sajnok (Poland)

WOMEN
Points Race: Kirsten Wild (Netherlands)
Sprint: Kristina Vogel (Germany)
500m Time Trial: Miriam Welte (Germany)
Individual Pursuit: Chloe Dygert (USA)
Scratch Race: Kirsten Wild (Netherlands)
Keirin: Nicky Degrendele (Belgium)
Team Pursuit: USA
Madison: Katie Archibald and Emily Nelson (Great Britain)
Team Sprint: Germany
Omnium: Kirsten Wild (Netherlands)

DARTS

BDO World Championship 2018: Men: Glen Durrant (England)
beat Mark McGeeney (England) 7–6; *Women:* Lisa Ashton
(England) beat Anastasia Dobromyslova (Russia) 3–1
PDC World Championship 2018: Rob Cross (England) beat
Phil Taylor (England) 7–2

EQUESTRIANISM

Burghley Horse Trials 2018: Tim Price (New Zealand) on
Ringwood Sky Boy
Badminton Horse Trials 2018: Jonelle Price (New Zealand) on
Classic Moet
British Open Horse Trials 2018 (Gatcombe Park): Chris Burton
(Australia) on Polystar I

ETON FIVES

Amateur Championship (Kinnaird Cup) final 2018: S. Cooley and
T. Dunbar beat J. Ho and R. Houlden 3–0
Alan Barber Cup final 2018: Old Olavians beat Old Salopians
2–1
Marsh Insurance Schools' Championship 2018: Boys: St Olaves
beat Eton 3–1; Girls: Shrewsbury 2 beat Shrewsbury 1 3–
1

Preparatory Schools' Tournament 2018: Summer Fields beat Berkhamsted 2–1
National Ladies' Championships 2018: K. Hird and C. Cooley beat A. Lumbard and E. Scoones 3–1

FENCING

BRITISH CHAMPIONSHIPS 2018
London, April

MEN
Individual Foil: Richard Kruse
Individual Épée: Calum Johnston
Individual Sabre: James Honeybone

WOMEN
Individual Foil: Chloe Dickson
Individual Épée: Mary Cohen
Individual Sabre: Caitlin Maxwell

EUROPEAN CHAMPIONSHIPS 2018
Novi Sad, Russia, June

MEN
Individual Foil: Aleksey Cheremisinov (Russia)
Individual Épée: Yannick Borel (France)
Individual Sabre: Max Hartung (Germany)
Team Foil: Russia
Team Épée: Russia
Team Sabre: Hungary

WOMEN
Individual Foil: Inna Deriglazova (Russia)
Individual Épée: Katrina Lehis (Estonia)
Individual Sabre: Sofya Velikaya (Russia)
Team Foil: Italy
Team Épée: France
Team Sabre: Russia

WORLD CHAMPIONSHIPS 2018
Wuxi, China, July

MEN
Individual Foil: Alessio Foconi (Italy)
Individual Épée: Yannick Borel (France)
Individual Sabre: Kim Jung-hwan (South Korea)
Team Foil: Italy
Team Épée: Switzerland
Team Sabre: South Korea

WOMEN
Individual Foil: Alice Volpi (Italy)
Individual Épée: Mara Navarria (Italy)
Individual Sabre: Sofia Pozdniakova (Russia)
Team Foil: USA
Team Épée: USA
Team Sabre: France

FIGURE SKATING

BRITISH CHAMPIONSHIPS 2017
Sheffield, 28 November–8 December 2017

Men: Phillip Harris
Women: Natasha McKay
Pairs: Zoe Jones and Christopher Boyadji
Ice Dance: Penny Coomes and Nicholas Buckland

EUROPEAN CHAMPIONSHIPS 2018
Moscow, Russia, 15–21 January 2018

Men: Javier Fernández (Spain)

Women: Alina Zagitova (Russia)
Pairs: Evgenia Tarasova and Vladimir Morozov (Russia)
Ice Dance: Gabriella Papadakis and Guillaume Cizeron (France)

WORLD CHAMPIONSHIPS 2018
Milan, Italy, 21–25 March

Men: Nathan Chen (USA)
Women: Kaetlyn Osmond (Canada)
Pairs: Aljona Savchenko and Bruno Massot (Germany)
Ice Dance: Gabriella Papadakis and Guillaume Cizeron (France)

GOLF (MEN)

THE MAJOR CHAMPIONSHIPS
US Masters 2018 (Augusta, 5–8 April): Patrick Reed (USA), 273
US Open 2018 (Shinnecock Hills, 14–17 June): Brookes Koepua (USA), 281
The Open Championship 2018 (Carnoustie, 19–22 July): Francesco Molinari (Italy), 276
US PGA Championship 2018 (Bellerive, 9–12 August): Brooks Koepka (USA), 264

WORLD RANKINGS
as at September 2018

1. Dustin Johnson (USA); 2. Brooks Koepka (USA); 3. Justin Thomas (USA); 4. Justin Rose (England); 5. Jon Rahm (Spain)

TEAM CHAMPIONSHIPS 2018
EurAsia Cup (Kuala Lumpur, Malaysia): Europe beat Asia 14–10
Ryder Cup (Hazeltine, Minnesota, USA, 30 September–2 October): USA beat Europe 17–11
World Cup of Golf (Melbourne, Australia): Denmark, 268

PGA EUROPEAN TOUR 2017
KLM Open (The Dutch, Spijk): Romain Wattel (France), 269
Portugal Masters (Dom Pedro Victoria GC, Vilamoura): Lucas Bjerregaard (Denmark), 264
British Masters (Close House GC, Newcastle-upon-Tyne): Paul Dunne (Ireland), 260
Alfred Dunhill Links Championship (Old Course St Andrews, Scotland): Tyrrell Hatton (England), 264
Italian Open (Milano GC, Parco Reale di Monza): Tyrrell Hatton (England), 263
Andalucia Valderrama Masters (Real Club Valderrama, Spain): Sergio Garcia (Spain), 272
WGC-HSBC Champions (Sheshan International GC, China): Justin Rose (England) 274
Turkish Airlines Open (Regnum Carya, Turkey): Justin Rose (England), 266
Nedbank Golf Challenge (Gary Player CC, South Africa): Branden Grace (South Africa), 277
DP World Tour Championship, Dubai (Jumeirah, United Arab Emirates): Jon Rahm (Spain), 269

PGA EUROPEAN TOUR 2018
UBS Hong Kong Open (Hong Kong GC): Wade Ormsby (Australia), 269
Australian PGA Championship (Royal Pines Resort, Queensland): Cameron Smith (Australia), 270
AfrAsia Bank Mauritius Open (Heritage GC, Mauritius): Dylan Frittelli (South Africa), 268
Joburg Open (Randpark GC, South Africa): Shubhankar Sharma (India), 264
BMW South African Open (Glendower GC, City of Ekurhuleni): Chris Paisley (England), 267

Abu Dhabi HSBC Championship (Abu Dhabi GC, UAE): Tommy Fleetwood (England), 266

Omega Dubai Desert Classic (Emirates GC, UAE): Haotong Li (China), 265

Maybank Championship (Saujana G&CC, Malaysia): Shubhankar Sharma (India), 267

NBO Oman Open (Al Mouj Golf, Muscat): Joost Luiten (Netherlands), 272

Commercial Bank of Qatar Masters (Doha GC): Eddie Pepperell (England), 270

Tshwane Open (Pretoria CC, South Africa): George Coetzee (South Africa), 266

WGC-Mexico Championship (Chapultepec GC, Mexico City): Phil Mickelson (USA), 268

Hero Indian Open (DFL G&CC, New Delhi): Matt Wallace (England), 277

WGC-Dell Technologies Match Play (Austin CC, USA): Bubba Watson (USA), 7 & 6

Open de España (Centro Nacional de Golf, Madrid): Jon Rahm (Spain), 268

Trophee Hassan II (Royal Golf Dar Es Salam, Morocco): Alexander Levy (France), 280

Volvo China Open (Topwin GC, China): Alexander Bjork (Sweden), 270

Rocco Forte Open (Sicily, Italy): Joakim Lagergren (Sweden), 268

BMW PGA Championship (Wentworth, England): Francesco Molinari (Italy), 271

Italian Open (Royal Park i Roveri, Turin): Thorbjorn Olesen (Denmark), 262

Shot Clock Masters (Atzenbrugg, Austria): Mikko Korhonen (Finland), 272

BMW International Open (Munich, Germany): Matt Wallace (England), 261

HNA Open de France (Le Golf National, Paris): Alex Noren (Sweden), 277

Irish Open (Ballyliffin, Donegal): Russell Knox (Scotland), 274

Porsche European Open (Winsen, Germany): Richard McEvoy (England), 277

Fiji International (Natadola Bay GC, Sigatoka): Gaganjeet Bhullar (India), 274

Nordea Masters (Gothenburg, Sweden): Paul Waring (England), 266

D+D Real Czech Masters (Prague, Czechia): Andrea Pavan (Italy), 266

Made in Denmark (Silkeborg, Denmark): Matt Wallace (England), 269

Omega European Masters (Crans-Montana, Switzerland): Matthew Fitzpatrick (England), 263

GOLF (WOMEN)

THE MAJOR CHAMPIONSHIPS

ANA Inspiration 2018 (Rancho Mirage, USA, 29 March–1 April): Pernilla Lindberg (Sweden), 273

KPMG WPGA Championship 2018 (Long Grove, Illinois, USA, 28 June–1 July): Park Sung-hyun (Rep. Korea), 278 (USA), 271

US Women's Open 2018 (Shoal Creek, Alabama, 31 May – 3 June): Ariya Jutanugarn (Thailand), 277

Ricoh British Open 2018 (Royal Lytham & St Annes GC, England, 2–5 August): Georgia Hall (England), 271

WORLD RANKINGS
as at September 2018

1. Park Sung-hyun (Rep. Korea); 2. Ariya Jutanugarn (Thailand); 3. Ryu So-yeon (Rep. Korea); 4. Inbee Park (Rep. Korea); 5. Lexi Thompson (USA)

LADIES EUROPEAN TOUR 2017

Oates Vic Open (13th Beach Golf Links, Australia): Melissa Reid (England), 276

World Ladies Championship (Mission Hills, China): Hae Rym Kim (Rep. Korea), 205

Lalla Meryem Cup (Royal Golf Dar Es Salam, Morocco): Klara Spilkova (Czech Republic), 280

Estrella Damm Mediterranean Ladies Open (Terramar GC, Spain): Florentyna Parker (England), 269

Ladies European Thailand Championship (Phoenix Gold G&CC): Atthaya Thitikul (Thailand), 283

Aberdeen Standard Investments Ladies Scottish Open (Gullane GC, Scotland): Mi Hyang Lee (Rep. Korea), 282

The Solheim Cup (Des Moines GC, IA, USA): USA beat Europe $16\frac{1}{2}$–$11\frac{1}{2}$

The Evian Championship (Evian Resort GC, France): Anna Nordqvist (Sweden), 204

Andalucia Costa Del Sol Open De España Femenino (Guadalmina GC, Spain): Azahara Munoz (Spain), 269

Lacoste Ladies Open De France (Golf De Chantaco, France): Cristie Kerr (USA), 263

Fatima Bint Mubarak Ladies Open (Saadiyat Beach GC, UAE): Aditi Ashok (India), 270

Hero Women's Indian Open (Dlf G&CC, India): Camille Chevalier (France), 204

Sanya Ladies Open (Yalong Bay GC, China): Celine Boutier (France), 204

The Queens (Miyoshi CC, Japan): LPGA of Japan beat Korean LPGA, 7–1

Omega Dubai Ladies Classic (Emirates GC, UAE): Angel Yin (USA), 273

LADIES EUROPEAN TOUR 2018

Oates Vic Open (13th Beach Golf Links, Australia): Minjee Lee (Australia), 279

ActewAGL Canberra Classic (Royal Canberra GC, Australia): Jiyai Shin (Rep. Korea), 197

Ladies Classic Bonville (Bonville GR, Australia): Celine Boutier (France), 278

Women's NSW Open (Coffs Harbour GC, Australia): Meghan MacLaren (England), 274

Investec South African Women's Open (Westlake GC): Ashleigh Buhai (South Africa), 207

Lalla Meryem Cup (Royal Golf Dar Es Salam, Morocco): Jenny Haglund (Sweden), 285

Jabra Ladies Open (Evian-les-Bains, France): Astrid Vayson de Pradenne (France), 206

Ladies European Thailand Championship (Pattaya, Thailand): Kanyalak Preedasuttijit (Thailand), 273

Ladies Scottish Open (Gullane GC, East Lothian): Ariya Jutanugam (Thailand), 271

Lacoste Ladies Open de France (Saint-Jean-de-Luz, France): Caroline Hedwall (Sweden), 272

GREYHOUND RACING

2017
Regency (Hove): Slick Strauss
Golden Jacket (Crayford): Boylesports Star
Derby (Towcester): Astute Missile
Grand National (Sittingbourne): Razldazl Raidio

2018
Regency (Hove): Clares Kyletaun
Golden Jacket (Crayford): Shotgun Bullet
Derby (Towcester): Dorotas Wildcat
Grand National (Sittingbourne): Parkers Dynamite

GYMNASTICS

BRITISH CHAMPIONSHIPS 2018
Liverpool, 8–11 March

MEN
All-Around: Brinn Bevan
Floor: Frank Baines
Pommel Horse: Max Whitlock
Rings: Nile Wilson
Vault: Dominick Cunningham
Parallel Bars: Nile Wilson
High Bar: Nile Wilson

WOMEN
All-Around: Kelly Simm
Floor: Amy Tinkler
Beam: Alice Kinsella
Vault: Lucy Stanhope
Uneven Bars: Amy Tinkler

EUROPEAN CHAMPIONSHIPS 2018
Glasgow, Great Britain 2–12 August

MEN
Team: Russia
Floor: Dominick Cunningham (Great Britain)
Pommel: Rhys McClenaghan (Ireland)
Rings: Eleftherios Petrounias (Greece)
Vault: Artur Dalaloyan (Russia)
Parallel Bars: Artur Dalaloyan (Russia)
High Bar: Oliver Hegi (Switzerland)

WOMEN
Team: Russia
Floor: Melanie de Jesus dos Santos (France)
Beam: Sanne Wevers (The Netherlands)
Vault: Boglarka Devai (Hungary)
Uneven Bars: Nina Derwael (Belgium)

HOCKEY

MEN
England Hockey League 2017–18: Premier Division: Wimbledon, 39pts; *Conference East:* Oxted, 42pts; *Conference North:* University of Nottingham, 40pts; *Conference West:* University of Exeter 44pts
England Hockey League Championship final 2018: Reading beat Beeston 2–2 (4–2 pens)

WOMEN
England Hockey League 2017–18: Premier Division: Surbiton, 34pts; *Conference East:* Hampstead & Westminster, 52pts; *Conference North:* Beeston, 51pts; *Conference West:* Stourport, 41pts
England Hockey League Championship final 2018: Surbiton beat Clifton Robinsons 5–0

HORSE RACING

NATIONAL HUNT

HENNESSY GOLD CUP
(1957) Newbury, 3 miles and about 2½ f

2013 Triolo D'Alene (6y), B. Geraghty

2014 Many Clouds (7y), L. Aspell
2015 Smad Place (8y), W. Hutchinson
2016 Native River (6y), R. Johnson
2017 Total Recall (8y), P. Townend

TINGLE CREEK CHASE
(1957) Sandown, 2 miles

2013 Sire de Grugy (7y), J. Moore
2014 Dodging Bullets (6y), S. Twiston-Davies
2015 Sire de Grugy (9y), J. Moore
2016 Un de Sceaux (8y), R. Walsh
2017 Politologue (6y), H. Cobden

KING GEORGE VI CHASE
(1937) Kempton, about 3 miles

2013 Silviniaco Conti (7y), N. Fehily
2014 Silviniaco Conti (8y), N. Fehily
2015 Cue Card (9y), P. Brennan
2016 Thistlecrack (8y), T. Scudamore
2017 Might Bite (8y), N. de Boinville

CHAMPION HURDLE
(1927) Cheltenham, 2 miles and about ½ f

2014 Jezki (6y), B. Geraghty
2015 Faugheen (7y), R. Walsh
2016 Annie Power (8y), R. Walsh
2017 Buveur d'Air (6y), N. Fehily
2018 Buveur D'Air (7y), B. Geraghty

QUEEN MOTHER CHAMPION CHASE
(1959) Cheltenham, about 2 miles

2014 Sire de Grugy (8y), J. Moore
2015 Dodging Bullets (7y), S. Twiston-Davies
2016 Sprinter Sacre (10y), N. de Boinville
2017 Special Tiara (10y), N. Fehily
2018 Altior (8y), N. de Boinville

CHELTENHAM GOLD CUP
(1924) 3 miles and about 2½ f

2014 Lord Windermere (8y), D. Russell
2015 Coneygree (8y), N. de Boinville
2016 Don Cossack (9y), B. Cooper
2017 Sizing John (7y), R. Power
2018 Native River (7y), R. Johnson

GRAND NATIONAL
(1837) Liverpool, 4 miles and about 4 f

2014 Pineau de Re (11y), L. Aspell
2015 Many Clouds (8y), L. Aspell
2016 Rule The World (9y), D. Mullins
2017 One For Arthur (8y), D. Fox
2018 Tiger Roll (8y), D. Russell

BET365 GOLD CUP
(1957) Sandown, 3 miles and about 5 f

2014 Hadrians Approach (7y), B. Geraghty
2015 Just A Par (8y), S. Bowen
2016 The Young Master (7y), S. Waley-Cohen
2017 Henllan Harri (9y), S. Bowen
2018 Step Back (8y), J. Moore

STATISTICS

WINNING NATIONAL HUNT TRAINERS 2017–18

N. Henderson	£2,652,750
P. Nicholls	1,678,614
C. Tizzard	1,309,071
N. Twiston-Davies	1,226,946
D. Skelton	1,085,488
G. Elliott	1,055,844
W. P. Mullins	840,634
D. McCain	578,064
A. King	566,484
T. George	539,036

WINNING NATIONAL HUNT JOCKEYS 2017–18

	1st	2nd	3rd	Unpl.	Total mts
R. Johnson	176	156	118	451	901
B. Hughes	142	131	112	425	810
H. Skelton	131	107	104	270	612
N. Fehily	110	82	62	278	532
S. Twiston-Davies	108	90	83	287	568
A. Coleman	104	73	84	409	670
S. Bowen	82	64	55	281	482
N. de Boinville	77	54	44	192	367
H. Cobden	76	71	67	226	440
T. Scudamore	74	82	79	375	610

The above statistics have been provided by *Timeform*, publishers of the *Racehorses* and *Chasers and Hurdlers* annuals

THE FLAT

THE CLASSICS

ONE THOUSAND GUINEAS

(1814) Rowley Mile, Newmarket, for three-year-old fillies

Year	Winner	Betting	Owner	Jockey	Trainer	Runners
2013	Sky Lantern	9–1	B. Keswick	R. Hughes	R. Hannon	15
2014	Miss France	7–1	Ballymore Thoroughbred	M. Guyon	A. Fabre	17
2015	Legatissimo	13–2	J. Magnier, M. Tabor and D. Smith	R. Moore	D. Wachman	13
2016	Minding	11–10	J. Magnier, M. Tabor and D. Smith	R. Moore	A. O'Brien	16
2017	Winter	9–1	J. Magnier, M. Tabor and D. Smith	W. Lordon	A. O'Brien	14
2018	Billesdon Brook	66–1	Pall Mall Partners	S. Levey	R. Hannon	15

TWO THOUSAND GUINEAS

(1809) Rowley Mile, Newmarket, for three-year-olds

Year	Winner	Betting	Owner	Jockey	Trainer	Runners
2013	Dawn Approach	11–8	Godolphin	K. Manning	J. S. Bolger	13
2014	Night of Thunder	40–1	S. Manana	K. Fallon	R. Hannon Jr	14
2015	Gleneagles	4–1	D. Smith, J. Magnier and M. Tabor	R. Moore	A. O'Brien	18
2016	Galileo Gold	14–1	Al Shaqab Racing	F. Dettori	H. Palmer	13
2017	Churchill	6–4	D. Smith, J. Magnier and M. Tabor	R. Moore	A. O'Brien	10
2018	Saxon Warrior	3–1	D. Smith, J. Magnier and M. Tabor	D. O'Brien	A. O'Brien	14

THE DERBY

(1780) Epsom, 1 mile and about 4 f, for three-year-olds

The first winner was Sir Charles Bunbury's Diomed in 1780. The owners with the record number of winners are Lord Egremont, who won in 1782, 1804, 1805, 1807, 1826 (also won five Oaks); and Aga Khan III, who won in 1930, 1935, 1936, 1948, 1952. Other winning owners are: Duke of Grafton (1802, 1809, 1810, 1815); Mr J. Bowes (1835, 1843, 1852, 1853); Sir J. Hawley (1851, 1858, 1859, 1868); the 1st Duke of Westminster (1880, 1882, 1886, 1899); and Sir Victor Sassoon (1953, 1957, 1958, 1960).

The Derby was run at Newmarket in 1915–18 and 1940–5.

Year	Winner	Betting	Owner	Jockey	Trainer	Runners
2013	Ruler Of The World	7–1	Mrs J. Magnier, M. Tabor and D. Smith	R. Moore	A. O'Brien	12
2014	Australia	11–8	D. Smith, S. Magnier, M. Tabor and T. Ah Khing	J. O'Brien	A. O'Brien	16
2015	Golden Horn	13–2	Anthony Oppenheimer	F. Dettori	J. Gosden	12
2016	Harzand	13–2	A. Khan	P. Smullen	D. Weld	16
2017	Wings of Eagles	40–1	D. Smith, J. Magnier and M. Tabor	P. Beggy	A. O'Brien	19
2018	Masar	16-1	Godolphin	W. Buick	C. Appleby	9

THE OAKS

(1779) Epsom, 1 mile and about 4 f, for three-year-old fillies

Year	Winner	Betting	Owner	Jockey	Trainer	Runners
2013	Talent	20–1	J. L. Rowsell and M. H. Dixon	R. Hughes	R. Beckett	11
2014	Taghrooda	5–1	H. Al Maktoum	P. Hanagan	J. Gosden	17
2015	Qualify	50–1	C. Regalado-Gonzalez	C. O'Donoghue	A. O'Brien	11
2016	Minding	10–11	J. Magnier, M. Tabor and D. Smith	R. Moore	A. O'Brien	9
2017	Enable	6–1	K. Abdullah	F. Dettori	J. Gosden	10
2018	Forever Together	7–1	Mr. M. Tabor, D. Smith and Mrs. J. Magnier	D. O'Brien	A. O'Brien	9

ST LEGER

(1776) Doncaster, 1 mile and about 6 f, for three-year-olds

Year	Winner	Betting	Owner	Jockey	Trainer	Runners
2012	Encke	25–1	Godolphin	M. Barzalona	M. Al Zarooni	9
2013	Leading Light	7–2	D. Smith, S. Magnier and M. Tabor	J. O'Brien	A. O'Brien	11
2014	Kingston Hill	9–4	P. Smith	A. Atzeni	R. Varian	12
2015	Simple Verse	8–1	QRL, Sheikh Suhaim Al Thani and Al Kubais	A. Atzeni	R. Beckett	7
2016	Habour Law	22–1	J. Cornwell	G. Baker	L. Mongan	9
2017	Capri	3–1	D. Smith, J. Magnier and M. Tabor	R. Moore	A. O'Brien	11

RESULTS

CAMBRIDGESHIRE HANDICAP
(1839) Newmarket, 1 mile and 1 f

2013 Educate (4y), J. Murtagh
2014 Bronze Angel (5y), L. Steward
2015 Third Time Lucky (3y), A. Beschizza
2016 Spark Plug (5y), J. Fortune
2017 Dolphin Vista (4y), G. Wood

PRIX DE L'ARC DE TRIOMPHE
(1920) Longchamp, Paris, 1½ miles

2013 Treve (3y), T. Jarnet
2014 Treve (4y), T. Jarnet
2015 Golden Horn (3y), F. Dettori
2016* Found (4y), R. Moore
2017 Enable (2y), L. Dettori
* Ran at Chantilly while Longchamp was closed for redevelopment

CESAREWITCH
(1839) Newmarket, 2 miles and about 2 f

2013 Scatter Dice (4y), S. De Sousa
2014 Big Easy (7y), T. Queally
2015 Grumeti (7y), A. Beschizza
2016 Sweet Selection (4y), S. De Sousa
2017 Withhold (3y), S. De Sousa

CHAMPION STAKES
(1877) Newmarket, 1 mile and 2 f

2013 Farhh (5y), S. De Sousa
2014 Noble Mission (5y), J. Doyle
2015 Fascinating Rock (4y), P. Smullen
2016 Almanzor (3y), C. Soumillon
2017 Cracksman (3y), L. Dettori

DUBAI WORLD CUP
(1996) Dubai, 1 mile and 2 f

2014 African Story (7y), S. De Sousa
2015 Prince Bishop (8y), W. Buick
2016 California Chrome (5y), V. Espinoza
2017 Arrogate (4y), M. E. Smith
2018 Thunder Snow (4y), C. Soumillon

LINCOLN HANDICAP
(1965) Doncaster, 1 mile

2014 Ocean Tempest (5y), A. Kirby
2015 Gabrial (6y), T. Hamilton
2016 Secret Brief (4y), W. Buick
2017 Bravery (4y), D. Tudhope
2018 Addeybb (4y), J. Doyle

JOCKEY CLUB STAKES
(1894) Newmarket, 1½ miles

2014 Gospel Club (5y), R. Moore

2015 Second Step (4y), A. Atzeni
2016 Exosphere (4y), R. Moore
2017 Seventh Heaven (4y), R. Moore
2018 Defoe (4y), A. Atzeni

PRIX DU JOCKEY CLUB
(1836) Chantilly, 1 mile and about 2½ f, for three-year-olds

2014 The Grey Gatsby, R. Moore
2015 New Bay, V. Cheminaud
2016 Almanzor, J. Eyquem
2017 Bramelot, C. Demuro
2018 Study of Man, S. Pasquier

ASCOT GOLD CUP
(1807) Ascot, 2 miles and about 4 f

2014 Leading Light (4y), J. O'Brien
2015 Trip To Paris (4y), G. Lee
2016 Order of St George (4y), R. Moore
2017 Big Orange (6y), J. Doyle
2018 Stradivarius (4y), F. Dettori

IRISH DERBY
(1866) Curragh, 1½ miles, for three-year-olds

2014 Australia, J. O'Brien
2015 Jack Hobbs, W. Buick
2016 Harzand, P. Smullen
2017 Capri. S. Heffernan
2018 Latrobe, D. O'Brien

ECLIPSE STAKES
(1886) Sandown, 1 mile and about 2 f

2014 Mukhadram (5y), P. Hanagan
2015 Golden Horn (3y), F. Dettori
2016 Hawkbill (3), W. Buick
2017 Ulysses (4y), J. Crawley
2018 Roaring Lion (3y), O. Murphy

KING GEORGE VI AND QUEEN ELIZABETH DIAMOND STAKES
(1952) Ascot, 1 mile and about 4 f

2014 Taghrooda (3y), P. Hanagan
2015 Postponed (4y), A. Atzeni
2016 Highland Reel (4y), R. Moore
2017 Enable (3y) F. Detorri
2018 Poets Word (5y) J. Doyle

GOODWOOD CUP
(1812) Goodwood, about 2 miles

2014 Cavalryman (8y), K. Fallon
2015 Big Orange (4y), J. Spencer
2016 Big Orange (5y), J. Spencer
2017 Stradivarius (3y) A. Atzeni
2018 Stradivarius (4y) A. Atzeni

STATISTICS

WINNING FLAT OWNERS 2017

Godolphin	£6,285,003
Mr D. Smith, Mrs J. Magnier and Mr M. Tabor	3,576,197
Mr Hamdan Al Maktoum	2,815,295
Mr K. Abdullah	2,088,684
Mr. M Tabor, D. Smith and Mrs John Magnier	1,800,136
Mrs John Magnier, Mr M. Tabor and Mr D. Smith	1,769,166
Cheveley Park Stud	1,571,127
Sheikh Hamdan Bin Mohammed Al Maktoum	1,404,080
Flaxman Stables Ireland Ltd	1,252,826
Mr A. E. Oppenheimer	1,098,843

WINNING FLAT TRAINERS 2017

A. O'Brien	£8,336,375
J. Gosden	6,188,845
R. Fahey	4,262,096
Sir Michael Stoute	3,856,639
M. Johnston	3,568,123
R. Hannon	2,986,683
W. Haggas	2,704,085
A. Balding	2,576,593
C. Appleby	2,163,247
R. Varian	1,915,308

WINNING FLAT SIRES 2017

	Races won	Stakes
Galileo by Sadler's Wells	67	£7,256,654
Dark Angel by Acclamation	142	3,536,107
Dubawi by Dubai Millennium	128	2,921,597
Frankel by Galileo	46	2,085,379
Kodiac by Danehill	161	2,039,308
Iffraaj by Zafonic	71	1,984,229
Acclamation by Royal Applause	111	1,953,797
Sea the Stars by Cape Cross	50	1,843,306
Nathaniel by Galileo	48	1,700,064
Exceed and Excel by Danehill	126	1,656,629

WINNING FLAT JOCKEYS 2017

	1st	2nd	3rd	Unpl.	Total mts
S. de Sousa	206	157	148	569	1,080
L. Morris	177	157	192	984	1,510
J. Crowley	161	118	83	493	855
A. Kirby	146	128	102	529	905
J. Fanning	140	112	100	497	849
R. Moore	137	82	48	305	572
P. J. McDonald	128	119	100	540	887
O. Murphy	127	122	112	494	855
D. Tudhope	122	103	89	421	735
J. Doyle	110	69	73	250	502

The above statistics have been provided by *Timeform*, publishers of the *Racehorses* and *Chasers and Hurdlers* annuals

ICE HOCKEY

MEN'S WORLD CHAMPIONSHIP 2018
Denmark, 4–20 May

Final: Sweden beat Switzerland 3–2

WOMEN'S WORLD CHAMPIONSHIP 2018
Vaujany, France, 8–14 April

Final: France beat Slovakia 7–1

DOMESTIC COMPETITIONS
Elite League Champions 2017–18: Cardiff Devils
Play-off Champions 2018: Cardiff Devils
Challenge Cup final 2017–18: Belfast Giants beat Cardiff Devils 6–3

NATIONAL HOCKEY LEAGUE
Stanley Cup final 2018: Washington Capitals beat Vegas Golden Knights 4–1

JUDO

EUROPEAN CHAMPIONSHIPS 2018
Tel Aviv, Israel, 26–28 April

MEN
Heavyweight (over 100kg): Lukas Krpalek (Czechia)
Light-heavyweight (100kg): Toma Nikiforov (Belgium)
Middleweight (90kg): Mikhail Igolnikov (Russia)
Welterweight (81kg): Sagi Muki (Israel)
Lightweight (73kg): Ferdinand Karapetian (Armenia)
Junior Lightweight (66kg): Adrian Gomboc (Slovenia)
Bantamweight (60kg): Islam Yashuev (Russia)

WOMEN
Heavyweight (over 78kg): Romane Dicko (France)
Light-heavyweight (78kg): Madeleine Malonga (France)
Middleweight (70kg): Kim Polling (Netherlands)
Welterweight (63kg): Clarisse Agbegnenou (France)
Lightweight (57kg): Nora Gjakova (Kosovo)
Junior Lightweight (52kg): Natalia Kuziutina (Russia)
Bantamweight (48kg): Irina Dolgova (Russia)

BRITISH OPEN CHAMPIONSHIPS 2017
Sheffield, December

MEN
Heavyweight (over 100kg): Andrew Melbourne
Light-heavyweight (100kg): Adam Hall
Middleweight (90kg): Jamal Petgrave
Welter (81kg): Owen Livesey
Lightweight (73kg): Daniel Powell
Lightweight (66kg): Peter Miles
Bantamweight (60kg): Samuel Hall

WOMEN
Heavyweight (over 78kg): Sarah Hawkes
Light-heavyweight (78kg): Shelley Ludford
Middleweight (70kg): Katie-Jemima Yeats-Brown
Welter (63kg): Lucy Renshall
Lightweight (57kg): Acelya Toprak
Lightweight (52kg): Chelsie Giles
Bantamweight (48kg): Kimberley Renicks

MOTORCYCLING

MOTOGP 2017

Aragón (Spain): Marc Márquez (Spain), Honda
Japan (Motegi): Andrea Dovizioso (Italy), Ducati
Australia (Phillip Island): Marc Márquez (Spain), Honda
Malaysia (Sepang): Andrea Dovizioso (Italy), Ducati
Spain (Valencia): Dani Pedrosa (Spain), Honda
Riders' Championship 2017: 1. Marc Márquez (Spain), Honda, 298pts; 2. Andrea Dovizioso (Italy), Ducati, 261pts; 3. Maverick Viñales (Spain), Yamaha, 230pts

MOTOGP 2018

Qatar (Doha): Andrea Dovizioso (Italy), Ducati
Argentina (Termas del Río Hondo): Cal Crutchlow (Great Britain), Honda
USA (Austin): Marc Márquez (Spain), Honda
Spain (Jerez): Marc Márquez (Spain), Honda
France (Le Mans): Marc Márquez (Spain), Honda
Italy (Mugello): Jorge Lorenzo (Spain), Ducati
Spain (Catalonia): Jorge Lorenzo (Spain), Ducati
Netherlands (Essen): Marc Márquez (Spain), Honda
Germany (Sachsenring): Marc Márquez (Spain), Honda
Czech Republic (Brno): Andrea Dovizioso (Italy), Ducati

Austria (Spielberg): Jorge Lorenzo (Spain), Ducati
Great Britain (Silverstone): cancelled
San Marino (Misano): Andrea Dorizioso (Italy), Ducati

MOTO2 2017

Aragón (Spain): Franco Morbidelli (Italy), Kalex
Japan (Motegi): Alex Márquez (Spain), Kalex
Australia (Phillip Island): Miguel Oliveira (Portugal), KTM
Malaysia (Sepang): Miguel Oliveira (Portugal), KTM
Spain (Valencia): Miguel Oliveira (Portugal), KTM
Riders' Championship 2017: 1. Franco Morbidelli (Italy), Kalex,
   308pts; 2. Thomas Luthi (Switzerland), Kalex, 243pts; 3.
   Miguel Oliveira (Portugal), KTM, 241pts

MOTO2 2018

Qatar (Doha): Francesco Bagnaia (Italy), Kalex
Argentina (Termas del Río Hondo): Mattia Pasini (Italy),
   Kalex
USA (Austin): Francesco Bagnaia (Italy), Kalex
Spain (Jerez): Lorenzo Balsassarri (Italy), Kalex
France (Le Mans): Francesco Bagnaia (Italy), Kalex
Italy (Mugello): Miguel Oliveira (Portugal), KTM
Spain (Catalonia): Fabio Quarteraro (France), Speed Up
Netherlands (Assen): Francesco Bagnaia (Italy), Kalex
Germany (Sachsenring): Brad Binder (South Africa), KTM
Czech Republic (Brno): Miguel Oliveira (Portugal),KTM
Austria (Speilberg): Francesco Bagnaia (Italy), Kalex
Great Britain (Silverstone): cancelled
San Marino (Misano): Francesco Bagnaia (Italy) Kalex

MOTO3 2017

Aragón (Spain): Joan Mir (Spain), Honda
Japan (Motegi): Romano Fenati (Italy), Honda
Australia (Phillip Island): Joan Mir (Spain), Honda
Malaysia (Sepang): Joan Mir (Spain), Honda
Spain (Valencia): Jorge Martín (Spain), Honda
Riders' Championship 2017: 1. Joan Mir (Spain), Honda,
   341pts; 2. Romano Fenati (Italy), Honda, 248pts; 3. Aron
   Canet (Spain), Honda, 199pts

MOTO3 2018

Qatar (Doha): Jorge Martín (Spain), Honda
Argentina (Termas del Río Hondo): Marco Bezzecchi (Italy),
   KTM
USA (Austin): Jorge Martín (Spain), Honda
Spain (Jerez): Philipp Ottl (Germany), KTM
France (Le Mans): Albert Arenas (Spain), KTM
Italy (Mugello): Jorge Martin (Spain), Honda
Spain (Catalonia): Erea Bastianini (Italy), Honda
Netherlands (Assen): Jorge Martin (Spain), Honda
Germany (Sachsenring): Jorge Martin (Spain), Honda
Czech Republic (Brno): Fabio di Giannantonio (Italy), Honda
Austria (Spielberg): Marco Bezzecchi (Italy), KTM
Great Britain (Silverstone): cancelled
San Marino (Misano): Lorenzo Dalla Porta (Italy), Honda

ISLE OF MAN TOURIST TROPHY 2018

Senior: Michael Dunlop (Northern Ireland), BMW
Supersport: Race 1 – Michael Dunlop (Northern Ireland),
   Honda; Race 2 – Dean Harrison (England), Kawasaki

WORLD SUPERBIKES 2018

Australia (Phillip Island): Race 1 – Marco Melandri (Italy),
   Ducati; Race 2 – Marco Melandri (Italy), Ducati
Thailand (Buriram): Race 1 – Jonathan Rea (Great Britain),
   Kawasaki; Race 2 – Chaz Davies (Great Britain), Ducati
Spain (Aragón): Race 1 – Jonathan Rea (Great Britain),
   Kawasaki; Race 2 – Chaz Davies (Great Britain), Ducati

Netherlands (Assen): Race 1 – Jonathan Rea (Great Britain),
   Kawasaki; Race 2 – Tom Sykes (Great Britain), Kawasaki
Italy (Imola): Race 1– Jonathan Rea (Great Britain),
   Kawasaki; Race 2– Jonathan Rea (Great Britain),
   Kawasaki
Great Britain (Donington): Race 1 – Michael van der Mark
   (Netherlands), Yamaha; Race 2 – Michael van der Mark
   (Netherlands), Yamaha
Czech Republic (Brno): Race 1 – Jonathan Rea (Great Britain),
   Kawasaki; Race 2 – Alex Lowes (Great Britain), Yamaha
USA (Monterey): Race 1 – Jonathan Rea (Great Britain),
   Kawasaki; Race 2 – Jonathan Rea (Great Britain),
   Kawasaki
Italy (Misano): Race 1 – Jonathan Rea (Great Britain),
   Kawasaki; Race 2 – Jonathan Rea (Great Britain),
   Kawasaki
Portugal (Portimão): Race 1 – Jonathan Rea (Great Britain),
   Kawasaki; Race 2 – Jonathan Rea (Great Britain),
   Kawasaki

MOTOR RACING

FORMULA ONE GRAND PRIX 2017

Malaysia (Sepang): Max Verstappen (Netherlands), Red Bull
Japan (Suzuka): Lewis Hamilton (Great Britain), Mercedes
USA (Austin): Lewis Hamilton (Great Britain), Mercedes
Mexico (Mexico City): Max Verstappen (Netherlands), Red
   Bull
Brazil (São Paulo): Sebastian Vettel (Germany), Ferrari
Abu Dhabi (Yas Marina): Valtteri Bottas (Finland), Mercedes

Drivers' World Championship 2017: 1. Lewis Hamilton (Great
   Britain), Mercedes, 363pts; 2. Sebastian Vettel (Germany),
   Ferrari, 317pts; Valtteri Bottas (Finland), Mercedes,
   305pts

Constructors' World Championship 2017: 1. Mercedes, 668pts;
   2. Ferrari, 522pts; 3. Red Bull, 368pts

FORMULA ONE GRAND PRIX 2018

Australia (Melbourne): Sebastian Vettel (Germany), Ferrari
Bahrain (Sakhir): Sebastian Vettel (Germany), Ferrari
China (Shanghai): Daniel Ricciardo (Australia), Red Bull
Azerbaijan (Baku): Sebastian Vettel (Germany), Ferrari
Spain (Barcelona): Lewis Hamilton (Great Britain), Mercedes
Monaco (Monte Carlo): Daniel Ricciardo (Australia), Red Bull
Canada (Montreal): Sebastian Vettel (Germany), Ferrari
France (Le Castellet): Lewis Hamilton (Great Britain),
   Mercedes
Austria (Speilberg): Valtteri Bottas (Finland), Mercedes
Great Britain (Silverstone): Lewis Hamilton (Great Britain),
   Mercedes
Germany (Hockenheim): Sebastian Vettel (Germany), Ferrari
Hungary (Budapest): Lewis Hamilton (Great Britain),
   Mercedes
Belgium (Spa-Francorchamps): Lewis Hamilton (Great
   Britain), Mercedes
Italy (Monza): Kimi Raikkonen (Finland), Ferrari
Singapore (Marina Bay): Lewis Hamilton (Great Britain),
   Mercedes

INDIANAPOLIS 500 2018
Indianapolis, USA, 27 May

Will Power (Australia), Team Penske

2018 24-HOURS OF LE MANS
Le Mans, France, 16–17 June

Sebastien Buemi (Switzerland), Kazuki Nakajima (Japan),
   Fernando Alonso (Spain), Toyota Gazoo Racing

MOTOR RALLYING

WORLD RALLY CHAMPIONSHIPS 2017

Spain: Kris Meeke (Great Britain), Citroën
Great Britain: Elfyn Evans (Great Britain), M-Sport
Australia: Thierry Neuville (Belgium), Hyundai

Drivers' World Championship 2017: 1. Sébastien Ogier (France), M-Sport, 232pts; 2. Thierry Neuville (Belgium), Hyundai, 208pts; 3. Ott Tänak (Estonia), M-Sport, 191pts

Manufacturers' World Championship 2017: 1. M-Sport, 428pts; 2. Hyundai, 345pts; 3. Toyota, 257pts

WORLD RALLY CHAMIONSHIPS 2018

Monte Carlo: Sébastien Ogier (France), M-Sport
Sweden: Thierry Neuville (Belgium), Hyundai
Mexico: Sébastien Ogier (France), M-Sport
France: Sébastien Ogier (France), M-Sport
Argentina: Ott Tänak (Estonia), Toyota
Portugal: Thierry Neuville (Belgium), Hyundai
Italy: Thierry Neuville (Belgium), Hyundai
Finland: Ott Tänak (Estonia), Toyota
Germany: Ott Tänak (Estonia), Toyota
Turkey: Ott Tänak (Estonia), Toyota

DAKAR RALLY RAID 2018

Peru, Argentina and Bolivia, 6–20 January

Motorcycle: Matthias Walkner (Austria), KTM
Quad: Ignacio Casale (Chile), Yamaha
Car: Carlos Sainz (Spain), Peugeot
Truck: Eduard Nikolaev (Russia), Kamaz
UTV: Reinaldo Varela (Brazil), Can-Am

NETBALL

Superleague Grand Final 2018: Wasps Netball beat Loughborough Lightning 55–51

NORDIC EVENTS

BIATHLON WORLD CUP 2017–18

MEN
Overall: Martin Fourcade (France), 1,116pts

WOMEN
Overall: Kaisa Makarainen (Finland), 822pts

NORDIC COMBINED WORLD CUP 2017–18
World Cup: Akito Watabe (Japan), 1,495pts
Nations' Cup: Norway, 5,033pts

POLO

Prince of Wales Trophy 2018: Monterosso beat Valiente 13–8
Queen's Cup final 2018: La Indiana beat Park Place 9–7
Warwickshire Cup 2018: Monterosso beat Les Lions 10–7
Gold Cup (British Open) final 2018: El Ramanso beat La Bamba de Areco 13–12
Royal Windsor Cup final 2018: La Dolfina beat Park Place 11–7

RACKETS

Noel Bruce Cup 2017: Haileybury beat Cheltenham 5–1
World Singles 2017: J. Stout beat T. Billings 5–0
Ladies British Open Doubles Championship 2017: L. Van Der Zwalmen and J. Garside beat G. Willis and E. Shenkman 3–1
Amateur Singles Championship 2017: B. Cawston beat J. Coyne 3–1

Men's British Open Singles Championship 2018: T. Billings beat A. Duncliffe-Vines 4–0
Ladies British Open Singles Championship 2018: L. Van der Zwalmen beat L. Gooding 3–0
Amateur Doubles Championship 2018: J. Coyne and A. Duncliffe-Vines beat M. Bailey and N. James 4–1
British Open Doubles Championship 2018: T. Billings and R. Owen beat J. Coyne and A. Duncliffe-Vines 4–2

REAL TENNIS

MEN
British Open Singles final 2017: C. Riviere (USA) beat B. Sayers (Great Britain) 3–0
British Open Doubles final 2017: T. Chisholm (USA) and C. Riviere (USA) beat R. Fahey (Australia) and N. Howell (Australia) 3–1
Henry Leaf Cup final 2017 (public schools' old boys' doubles championship): A. Dolman and J. Acheson-Gray beat R. Shenkman and G. Maxwell 2–0
Doubles World Championship 2017: T. Chisholm (USA) and C. Riviere (USA) beat R. Fahey (Australia) and R. Smith (Great Britain) 5–4
World Championship 2018: R. Fahey (Australia) beat C. Riviere (USA) 7–5

WOMEN
Ladies Open Singles Championship final 2018: C. Fahey (Great Britain) beat S. Bollerman (Netherlands) 2–0
Ladies Open Doubles Championship final 2017: C. Fahey (Great Britain) and S. Shuckburgh (Great Britain) beat S. Bollerman (Netherlands) and T. Lumley (Great Britain) 2–0
World Championship 2017: C. Fahey (Great Britain) beat S. Vigrass (Great Britain) 2–0

ROWING

HENLEY ROYAL REGATTA 2018

Grand Challenge Cup: Georgina Hope Rinehart National Training Centre (Australia) beat Clubul Sportiv Dinamo, Bucuresti and Clubul Sportiv al Amatei Steaua (Romania) by $\frac{3}{4}$ length
Stewards' Challenge Cup: Leander Club beat Oxford University and Leander Club by $2\frac{1}{2}$ lengths
Queen Mother Challenge Cup: Leander Club and Agecroft Rowing Club beat Fana Roklubb (Norway) by $\frac{3}{4}$ length
Silver Goblets and Nickalls' Challenge Cup: M. Sinkovic & V. Sinkovic (Croatia) beat C. Watts & A. J. Widdicombe (Australia) easily
Double Sculls Challenge Cup: J. W. Storey & C. W. Harris (New Zealand) beat P. H. Houin & J. A. Azou (France) by $1\frac{1}{4}$ lengths
Diamond Challenge Sculls: A. M. O. Drysdale (New Zealand) beat K. Borch (Norway) by 3 lengths
Remenham Challenge Cup: Georgina Hope Rinehart National Training Centre (Australia) beat Leander Club and University of London by $\frac{2}{3}$ length
Princess Grace Challenge Cup: Cambridge University Women's Boat Club amd Imperial College London beat Christiania Roklub (Norway) by 3 lengths
Princess Royal Challenge Cup: J. R. Gmelin (Switzerland) bear M. C. Edmunds (Australia) by 3 lengths
Ladies' Challenge Plate: Oxford Brookes University beat Oxford University and Edinburgh University by $\frac{1}{2}$ length
Visitors' Challenge Cup: Leander Club beat University of London by 2 lengths

Prince of Wales Challenge Cup: Algemene Amsterdamse che Studenten Roeivereniging Skoll (Netherlands) beat Edinburgh University and Nottingham Rowing Club by 1 length

Thames Challenge Cup: Thames Rowing Club A beat N. S. R. Oslo (Norway) by $2\frac{3}{4}$ lengths

Wyfold Challenge Cup: Molesey Boat A beat Mercantile Rowing Club (Australia) by $1\frac{1}{2}$ lengths

Britannia Challenge Cup: Thames Rowing Club A beat Molesey Boat Club A by $\frac{1}{2}$ length

Temple Challenge Cup: University of Washington (USA) beat Oxford Brookes University A by 1 length

Prince Albert Challenge Cup: Imperial College London beat Goldie Boat Club by $\frac{3}{4}$ length

Princess Elizabeth Challenge Cup: St Paul's School beat Eton College easily

Fawley Challenge Cup: The Windsor Boys' School beat Maidenhead Rowling Club by 3 lengths

Diamond Jubilee Challenge Cup: Y Quad Cities Rowing Association (USA) beat Marlow Rowing Club by $\frac{1}{2}$ length

The Hambleden Pairs Challenge Cup: H. C. Long & H. E. Scott beat R. G. McKellar & H. A. E. Taylor by $\frac{3}{4}$ length

The Town Challenge Cup: University of London and Leander Club beat Molesey Boat Club by $13\frac{1}{2}$ lengths

The Stoner Challenge Trophy: B. C. Donoghue & O. K. Loe (New Zealand) beat M. Oldenburg & R. de Jong (Netherlands) by $4\frac{3}{4}$ lengths

THE 164TH UNIVERSITY BOAT RACE
Putney–Mortlake, 4 miles, 1 f, 180 yd, 24 March 2018

MEN
Cambridge beat Oxford by 3 lengths; 17min 51sec

Cambridge have won 83 times, Oxford 80 and there has been one dead heat. The record time is 16min 19sec, rowed by Cambridge in 1998.

WOMEN
Cambridge beat Oxford by 7 lengths; 19min 06sec

Cambridge have won 43 times, Oxford 30

EUROPEAN ROWING CHAMPIONSHIPS 2018
Glasgow, Great Britain 2–5 August

MEN
Single Sculls: Kjetil Borch (Norway)
Pair: Martin Sinkovic and Valent Sinkovic (Croatia)
Double Sculls: Hugo Boucheron and Matthieu Androdias (France)
Four: Romania
Quadruple Sculls: Italy
Eight: Germany
Lightweight Single Sculls: Michael Schmid (Switzerland)
Lightweight Pair: Mark O'Donovan and Shane O'Driscoll (Ireland)
Lightweight Double Sculls: Kristoffer Brun and Are Strandli (Norway)
Lightweight Four: Italy

WOMEN
Single Sculls: Jeannine Gmelin (Switzerland)
Pair: Madalina Beres and Denisa Tilvescu (Romania)
Double Sculls: Hélène Lefebvre and Élodie Ravera-Scaramozzino (France)
Fours: Russia
Quadruple Sculls: Poland
Eight: Romania
Lightweight Single Sculls: Alena Furman (Belarus)

Lightweight Double Sculls: Marieke Keijser and Ilse Paulis (Netherlands)

OTHER ROWING EVENTS
Wingfield Sculls 2017: Men, R. Clarke (University of London); *Women,* F. Rawlins (Tideway Scullers School)
Oxford Summer Eights 2018: Men, Keble; *Women,* Pembroke
Torpid Races 2018: Men, Oriel; *Women,* Oriel
Head of the River 2018: Oxford Brookes University A and Leander A (dead heat)

RUGBY FIVES

National Open Singles Championship final 2017: D. Tristao beat W. Ellison 2–0
National Ladies' Singles Championship final 2018: K. Briedenhann beat L. Mathias 2–0
National Ladies' Doubles Championship final 2018: M. Raynor and A. Steel beat K. Briedenhann and T. Mills 2–0
National Open Doubles Championship final 2018: D. Grant and D. Tristao beat C. Brooks and W. Ellison 2–1
National Club Championship final 2018: Wessex beat Old Paulines 107–95
National Schools' Singles Championship final 2018: T. Kidner (Winchester) beat C. Low (Whitgift) 2–0
National Schools' Doubles Championship final 2018: Winchester I beat Whitgift 2–0
Varsity Match 2018: Oxford beat Cambridge 260–222

RUGBY LEAGUE

Super League Grand Final 2017: Leeds Rhinos beat Castleford Tigers 24–6
Ladbrokes Challenge Cup final 2018: Catalans Dragons beat Warrington Wolves 20–14
World Club Challenge 2018: Melbourne Storm beat Leeds Rhinos 38–4

AMATEUR COMPETITIONS 2018
National Conference League Premier Division Grand Final: Thatto Heath Crusaders beat Siddal 16–12
Division One Champions: Hunslet Club Parkside
Division Two Champions: Oulton Raiders
BARLA National Cup final: West Hull beat Haydock 31–12
Varsity Match 2018: Oxford beat Cambridge 24–6

RUGBY UNION

SIX NATIONS' CHAMPIONSHIP 2018

3 February	Paris	Ireland beat France 15–13
	Cardiff	Wales beat Scotland 34–7
4 February	Rome	England beat Italy 46–15
10 February	Dublin	Ireland beat Italy 56–19
	Twickenham	England beat Wales 12–6
11 February	Edinburgh	Scotland beat France 32–26
23 February	Marseille	France beat Italy 34–17
24 February	Dublin	Ireland beat Wales 37–27
	Edinburgh	Scotland beat England 25–13
10 March	Dublin	Ireland beat Scotland 28–8
	Paris	France beat England 22–16
11 March	Cardiff	Wales beat Italy 38–14
17 March	Rome	Scotland beat Italy 29–27
	Twickenham	Ireland beat England 24–15
	Cardiff	Wales beat France 14–13

Final standings: 1. Ireland, 26pts; 2. Wales, 15pts; 3. Scotland, 13pts; 4. France, 11pts; 5. England, 10 pts; 6. Italy, 1pts

DOMESTIC COMPETITIONS 2017–18

ENGLAND

Aviva Premiership: Exeter Chiefs 85 pts
Aviva Premiership final: Saracens beat Exeter Chiefs 27–10
RFU Championship: Bristol 103pts
National League: Division 1, Coventry, 134pts; *Promotion from Division 2 (North):* Sale, 127pts; *Promotion from Division 2 (South):* Cinderford, 143pts
British and Irish Cup final: Ealing Trailfinders beat Leinster A 22–7
County Championship final (Bill Beaumont Cup): Lancashire beat Hertfordshire 31–16
County Championship Shield final 2018: Dorset and Wiltshire beat Essex 24–22
136th Varsity Match: Cambridge beat Oxford 20–10
Anglo-Welsh Cup: Exeter Chiefs beat Bath 28–11

SCOTLAND

Premiership champions: Melrose
National League champions: Edinburgh Academical FC
BT Cup final: Melrose beat Stirling County 45–12

WALES

WRU Challenge Cup final: Merthyr beat Newport 41–7

IRELAND

Ulster Bank League Final: Lansdowne beat Cork Constitution 19–17
Guinness Pro 12 final: Leinster beat Scarlets 40–32

SHOOTING

149TH NATIONAL RIFLE ASSOCIATION IMPERIAL MEETING
Bisley, 12 June–28 July 2018

Queen's Prize: D. C. Luckman, 281.29 v-bulls
Grand Aggregate: J. Corbett, 742.102 v-bulls
Prince of Wales Prize: C. A. Evans, 75.14 v-bulls
All Comers' Aggregate: P. D. Sykes, 373.47 v-bulls
Kolapore Cup: Great Britain, 1179.134 v-bulls
Chancellor's Trophy: Cambridge University, 1155.116 v-bulls
National Trophy: England, 2018.197 v-bulls
Musketeers Cup: University of Southampton, 574.52 v-bulls
County Championship Long Range: Surrey, 572.51 v-bulls
Mackinnon Challenge Cup: England, 1085.74 v-bulls
The Albert: A. R. McLeod, 220.29 v-bulls
Hopton Challenge Cup: J. M. B. H. Buchanan, 988.99 v-bulls

SNOOKER

2017–18
2017 Riga Masters: Ryan Day (Wales) beat Stephen Maguire (Scotland) 5–2
China Championship (Guangzhou): Luca Brecel (Belgium) beat Shaun Murphy (England) 10–5
Paul Hunter Classic (Fürth, Germany): Michael White (Wales) beat Shaun Murphy (England) 4–2
Indian Open (Visakhapatnam): John Higgins (Scotland) beat Anthony McGill (Scotland) 5–1
World Open (Yushan, China): Ding Junhui (China) beat Kyren Wilson (England) 10–3
European Masters (Lommel, Belgium): Judd Trump (England) beat Stuart Bingham (England) 9–7
English Open (Barnsley): Ronnie O'Sullivan (England) beat Kyren Wilson (England) 9–2

International Championship (Daqing, China): Mark Selby (England) beat Mark Allen (Northern Ireland) 10–7
Shanghai Masters: Ronnie O'Sullivan (England) beat Judd Trump (England) 10–3
Northern Ireland (Belfast): Mark Williams (Wales) beat Yan Bingtao (China) 9–8
UK Championship (York): Ronnie O'Sullivan (England) beat Shaun Murphy (England) 10–5
Scottish Open (Glasgow): Neil Robertson (Australia) beat Cao Yupeng (China) 9–8
2018 German Masters (Berlin): Mark Williams (Wales) beat Graeme Dott (Scotland) 9–1
Snooker Shoot-Out (Watford, England): Michael Georgiou (Cyprus) beat Graeme Dott (Scotland) 1–0
World Grand Prix (Preston, England): Ronnie O'Sullivan (England) beat Ding Junhui (China) 10–3
Welsh Open (Cardiff): Barry Hawkins (England) beat John Higgins (Scotland) 7–9
Gibraltar Open: Ryan Day (Wales) beat Cao Yupeng (China) 4–0
Players Championship (Llandudno, Wales): Ronnie O'Sullivan (England) beat Shaun Murphy (England) 10–4
China Open (Beijing): Mark Selby (England) beat Barry Hawkins (England) 11–3
World Snooker Championship (Sheffield): Mark Williams (Wales) beat John Higgins (Scotland) 18–16

SPEED SKATING

WORLD ALL-ROUND CHAMPIONSHIPS 2018
Amsterdam, Netherlands, 9–11 March

MEN
Gold: Patrick Roest (Netherlands); *Silver:* Sverre Lunde Pedersen (Norway); *Bronze:* Marcel Bosker (Netherlands)
500m: Patrick Roest (Netherlands), 36.97sec
1500m: Sverre Lunde Pedersen (Norway), 1min 48.33sec
5000m: Sverre Lunde Pedersen (Norway), 6min 33.81sec
10,000m: Nils van der Poel (Sweden), 13min 40.38sec

WOMEN
Gold: Miho Takagi (Japan); *Silver:* Ireen Wüst (Netherlands); *Bronze:* Annouk van der Weijden (Netherlands)
500m: Miho Takagi (Japan), 39.01sec
1500m: Miho Takagi (Japan), 1min 58.82sec
3000m: Ireen Wüst (Netherlands), 4min 15.80sec
5000m: Ireen Wüst (Netherlands), 7min 26.85sec

EUROPEAN ALL-ROUND CHAMPIONSHIPS 2018
Kolomna, Russia, 5–7 January

MEN
500m: Ronald Mulder (Netherlands), 34.80sec
1000m: Pavel Kulizhnikov (Russia), 1min 08.84sec
1500m: Denis Yuskov (Russia), 1min 44.53sec
5000m: Nicola Tumolero (Italy), 6min 16.85sec
Mass Start: Jan Blokhuijsen (Netherlands), 8min 23.19sec
Team Pursuit: Netherlands, 3min 42.79sec
Team Sprint: Russia, 1min 19.38sec

WOMEN
500m: Vanessa Herzog (Austria), 37.69sec
1000m: Yekaterina Shikhova (Russia), 1min 15.34sec
1500m: Lotte van Beek (Netherlands), 1min 55.52sec
3000m: Esmee Visser (Netherlands), 4min 05.31sec
Mass Start: Francesca Lollobrigida (Italy), 8min 38.69sec
Team Pursuit: Netherlands, 2min 59.34sec
Team Sprint: Russia, 1min 26.71sec

EUROPEAN SHORT TRACK CHAMPIONSHIPS 2018
Dresden, Germany, 12–14 January

MEN
500m: Sjinkie Knegt (Netherlands), 41.377sec
1000m: Sjinkie Knegt (Netherlands), 1min 27.898sec
1500m: Sjinkie Knegt (Netherlands), 2min 14.886sec
3000m: Vladislav Bykanov (Israel), 5min 02.882sec
5000m relay: Netherlands, 6min 36.198sec
Overall: Sjinkie Knegt (Netherlands), 107pts

WOMEN
500m: Martina Valcepina (Italy), 42.805sec
1000m: Arianna Fontana (Italy), 1min 31.921sec
1500m: Martina Valcepina (Italy), 2min 36.889sec
3000m: Sofia Prosvirnova (Russia), 5min 47.610sec
3000m relay: Russia, 4min 11.462sec
Overall: Arianna Fontana (Italy), 84pts

WORLD SHORT TRACK CHAMPIONSHIPS 2018
Montréal, Canada, 16–18 March

MEN
500m: Hwang Dae Heon (Rep. of Korea), 40.742sec
1000m: Charles Hamelin (Canada), 1min 22.249sec
1500m: Charles Hamelin (Canada), 2min 12.982sec
3000m: Shaolin Sandor Liu (Hungary), 4min 56.515sec
5000m relay: Rep. of Korea, 6min 44.267sec
Overall: Charles Hamelin (Canada), 81pts

WOMEN
500m: Choi Min Jeong (Rep. of Korea), 42.845sec
1000m: Shim Suk Hee (Rep. of Korea), 1min 29.316sec
1500m: Choi Min Jeong (Rep. of Korea), 2min 23.351sec
3000m: Choi Min Jeong (Rep. of Korea), 4min 58.939sec
3000m relay: Rep. of Korea, 4min 07.569sec
Overall: Choi Min Jeong (Rep. of Korea), 110pts

SQUASH

MEN
World Championships 2017: Mohamed El Shorbagy (Egypt) beat Marwan El Shorbagy (Egypt) 3–2
World Series Finals 2018: Mohamed El Shorbagy (Egypt) beat Ali Farag (Egypt) 3–1
European Individual Championship 2018: Borja Golan (Spain) beat George Parker (England) 3–2
British Open 2018: Miguel Angel Rodriguez (Colombia) beat Mohamed El Shorbagy (Egypt) 3–2
British National Championship 2018: Nick Matthew beat James Willstrop 3–1

WOMEN
World Championships 2017: Raneem El Welily (Egypt) beat Nour El Sherbini (Egypt) 3–1
World Series Finals 2018: Nour El Sherbini (Egypt) beat Raneem El Welily (Egypt) 3–1
European Individual Championship 2018: Millie Tomlinson (England) beat Coline Aumard (France) 3–1
British Open 2018: Nour El Sherbini (Egypt) beat Raneem El Welily (Egypt) 3–0
British National Championship 2018: Tesni Evans beat Alison Waters 3–0

SWIMMING

EUROPEAN AQUATICS CHAMPIONSHIPS 2018
Glasgow, Great Britain 3–12 August

SWIMMING

MEN
50m freestyle: Ben Proud (Great Britain), 21.34sec
100m freestyle: Alessandro Miressi (Italy), 48.01sec
200m freestyle: Duncan Scott (Great Britain), 1min 45.34sec
400m freestyle: Mykhailo Romanchuk (Ukraine), 3min 45.18secsec
800m freestyle: Mykhailo Romanchuk (Ukraine), 7min 42.96sec
1500m freestyle: Florian Wellbrock (Germany), 14min 36.15sec
50m backstroke: Kliment Koleshikov (Russia), 24.00sec
100m backstroke: Kliment Koleshikov (Russia), 52.53sec
200m backstroke: Evgeny Rylov (Russia), 1min 53.36sec
50m breaststroke: Adam Peaty (Great Britain), 26.09sec
100m breaststroke: Adam Peaty (Great Britain), 57.10sec
200m breaststroke: Anton Chupkov (Russia), 2min 06.80sec
50m butterfly: Andriy Gororov (Ukraine), 22.48sec
100m butterfly: Piero Codia (Italy), 50.64sec
200m butterfly: Kristof Milak (Hungary), 1min 52.79sec
200m medley: Jérémy Desplanches (Switzerland), 1min 57.04sec
400m medley: David Verraszto (Hungary), 4min 10.65sec
4x100m freestyle relay: Russia, 3min 12.33sec
4x200m freestyle relay: Great Britain, 7min 05.32sec
4x100m medley relay: Great Britain, 3min 30.45sec
4x100 mixed medley relay: Great Britain, 3min 30.45sec

WOMEN
50m freestyle: Sarah Sjostrom (Sweden), 23.74 sec
100m freestyle: Sarah Sjostrom (Sweden), 52.93sec
200m freestyle: Charlotte Bonnet (France), 1min 54.95sec
400m freestyle: Simona Quadarella (Italy), 4min 03.35sec
800m freestyle: Simona Quadarella (Italy), 8min 16.45sec
1500m freestyle: Simona Quadarella (Italy), 15min 51.61sec
50m backstroke: Georgia Davies (Great Britain), 27.23sec
100m backstroke: Anastasia Fesikova (Russia), 59.19sec
200m backstroke: Margherita Panziera (Italy), 2min 06.18sec
50m breaststroke: Yuliya Yefimova (Russia), 29.81sec
100m breaststroke: Yuliya Yefimova (Russia), 1min 05.53sec
200m breaststroke: Yuliya Yefimova (Russia), 2min 21.32sec
50m butterfly: Sarah Sjostrom (Sweden), 25.16sec
100m butterfly: Sarah Sjostrom (Sweden), 56.23sec
200m butterfly: Boglarka Kapas (Hungary), 2min 07.13sec
200m medley: Katinka Hosszú (Hungary), 2min 10.17sec
400m medley: Fantine Lesaffre (France), 4min 34.17sec
4x100m freestyle relay: Russia, 3min 12.23sec
4x200m freestyle relay: Great Britain, 7min 05.32sec
4x100m medley relay: Great Britain, 3min 30.45sec
4x100 mixed medley relay: France, 3min 22.07sec

DIVING

MEN
1m springboard: Jack Laugher (Great Britain), 414.60pts
3m springboard: Jack Laugher (Great Britain), 525.95pts
3m synchro springboard: Evgeny Kuznetsov and Ilya Zakharov (Russia), 431.16pts
10m platform: Aleksandr Bondar (Russia), 542.05pts
10m synchro platform: Aleksandr Bondar and Viktor Minibaev (Russia), 423.12pts

WOMEN
1m springboard: Maria Poliakova (Russia), 285.55pts
3m springboard: Grace Reid (Great Britain), 329.40pts
3m synchro springboard: Elena Bertocchi and Chiara Pellacani (Italy), 289.26pts
10m platform: Celine van Duijn (Netherlands), 319.10pts
10m synchro platform: Eden Cheng and Lois Toulsen (Great Britain), 289.74pts

MIXED
3m synchro springboard: Lou Massenberg and Tina Punzel (Germany), 313.50pts
10m synchro springboard: Nikita Shleikher and Yulia Timoshinina (Russia), 309.63pts
Team event: Oleh Kolodiy and Sofiya Lyskun (Ukraine), 355.90pts

TABLE TENNIS

MEN'S WORLD CUP 2017
Liège, Belgium, 20–22 October

Dimitrij Ovtcharov (Germany) beat beat Timo Boll (Germany) 4–2

WOMEN'S WORLD CUP 2017
Markham, Canada, 27–29 October

Zhu Yuling (China) beat Liu Shiwen (China) 4–3

WORLD CHAMPIONSHIPS 2018
Halmstad, Sweden 29 April–6 May
Men's: China beat Germany 3–0
Women's: China beat Japan 3–1

ENGLISH NATIONAL CHAMPIONSHIPS 2018

Men's singles: L. Pitchford beat S. Walker 4–1
Women's singles: T. Ho beat K. Sibley 4–1
Men's doubles: P. Drinkhall and D. McBeath beat L. Pitchford beat S. Walker 3–1
Women's doubles: K. Sibley and M. Tsaptsinos beat T. Ho and D. Payet 3–0
Mixed doubles: T. Ho and L. Pitchford beat D. McBeath and K. Sibley 3–2

TENNIS

AUSTRALIAN OPEN CHAMPIONSHIPS 2018
Melbourne, 15–28 January

Men's Singles: Roger Federer (Switzerland) beat Marin Cilic (Croatia) 6–2, 6–7 (5–7), 6–3, 3–6, 6–1
Women's Singles: Caroline Wozniacki (Denmark) beat Simona Halep (Romania) 7–6 (7–2), 3–6, 6–4
Men's Doubles: Oliver Marach (Austria) and Mate Pavic (Croatia) beat Juan Sebastián Cabal (Colombia) and Robert Farah (Colombia) 6–4, 6–4
Women's Doubles: Tímea Babos (Hungary) and Kristina Mladenovic (France) beat Ekaterina Makarova (Russia) and Elena Vesnina (Russia) 6–4, 6–3
Mixed Doubles: Gabriela Dabrowski (Canada) and Mate Pavic (Croatia) beat Tímea Babos (Hungary) and Rohan Bopanna (India) 2–6, 6–4, [11–9]

FRENCH OPEN CHAMPIONSHIPS 2018
Paris, 27 May–10 June

Men's Singles: Rafael Nadal (Spain) beat Dominic Thiem (Austria) 6–4, 6–3, 6–2
Women's Singles: Simona Halep (Romania) beat Sloane Stephens (USA) 3–6, 6–4, 6–1

Men's Doubles: Pierre-Hugues Herbert (France) and Nicolas Mahut (France) beat Olivier Marach (Austria) and Mate Pavic (Croatia) 6–2, 7–6 (7–4)
Women's Doubles: Barbora Krejcikova (Czechia) and Katerina Siniakova (Czechia) beat Eri Hozumi (Japan) and Makoto Ninomiya (Japan) 6–3, 6–3
Mixed Doubles: Latisha Chan (Chinese Taipei) and Ivan Dodig (Croatia) beat Gabriela Dabrowski (Canada) and Mate Pavic (Croatia) 6–1, 6–7 (5–7), 10–8

WIMBLEDON CHAMPIONSHIPS 2018
Wimbledon, 2–15 July

Men's Singles: Novak Djokovic (Serbia) beat Kevin Anderson (South Africa) 6–2, 6–2, 7–6 (7–3
Ladies' Singles: Angelique Kerber (Germany) beat Serena Williams (USA) 6–3, 6–3
Men's Doubles: Mike Bryan (USA) and Jack Sock (USA) beat Raven Klaasen (South Africa) and Michael Venus (New Zealand) 6–3, 6–7 (7–9), 6–3, 5–7, 7–5
Ladies' Doubles: Barbora Krejcikova (Czechia) and Katerina Siniakova (Czechia) beat Nicole Melichar (USA) and Kveta Peschke (Czechia) 6–4, 4–6, 6–0
Mixed Doubles: Nicole Melichar (USA) and Alexander Peya (Austria) beat Victoria Azarenka (Belarus) and Jamie Murray (Great Britain) 7–6 (7–1), 6–3

US OPEN CHAMPIONSHIPS 2018
New York, 27 August–9 September

Men's Singles: Novak Djokovic (Serbia) beat Juan Martin del Potro (Argentina) 6–3, 7–6 (7–4), 6–3
Women's Singles: Naomi Osaka (Japan) beat Serena Williams (USA) 6–2, 6–4
Men's Doubles: Mike Bryan (USA) and Jack Sock (USA) beat Lukasz Kubot (Poland) and Marcelo Melo (Brazil) 6–3, 6–1
Women's Doubles: Ashleigh Barty (Australia) and CoCo Vandeweghe (USA) beat Timea Babos (Hungary) and Kristina Mladenovic (France) 3–6, 7–6 (7–2), 7–6 (8–6)
Mixed Doubles: Bethanie Mattek-Sands (USA) and Jamie Murray (Great Britain) beat Alicja Rosolska (Poland) and Nikola Mektic (Croatia) 2–6, 6–3 (11–9)

TEAM CHAMPIONSHIPS
Davis Cup final 2017: France beat Belgium 3–2
Fed Cup final 2017: USA beat Belarus 3–2

2018 (XXIII) WINTER OLYMPICS

PyeongChang, Rep. of Korea, 9–25 February 2018

ALPINE SKIING

MEN
Downhill: Aksel Lund Svindal (Norway), 1min 40.25sec
Slalom: Andre Myhrer (Sweden), 1min 38.99sec
Giant Slalom: Marcel Hirscher (Austria), 2min 18.04sec
Super-G: Matthias Mayer (Austria), 1min 24.44sec
Combined: Marcel Hirscher (Austria), 2min 06.52sec

WOMEN
Downhill: Sofia Goggia (Italy), 1min 39.22sec
Slalom: Frida Hansdotter (Sweden), 1min 38.63sec
Giant Slalom: Mikaela Shiffrin (USA), 2min 20.02sec
Super-G: Ester Ledecka (Czechia), 1min 21.11sec
Combined: Michelle Gisin (Switzerland), 2min 20.90sec

MIXED
Team: Switzerland

BIATHLON

MEN
10km Sprint: Arnd Peiffer (Germany), 23min 38.8sec
12.5km Pursuit: Martin Fourcade (France), 32min 51.7sec
15km Mass Start: Martin Fourcade (France), 35min 47.3sec
20km Individual: Johannes Thingnes Boe (Norway), 48min 03.8sec
4 x 7.5km Relay: Sweden, 1hr 15min 16.5sec

WOMEN
7.5km Sprint: Laura Dahlmeier (Germany), 21min 06.2sec
10km Pursuit: Laura Dahlmeier (Germany), 30min 35.3sec
12.5km Mass Start: Anastasiya Kuzmina (Slovakia), 35min 23.0sec
15km Individual: Hanna Oeberg (Sweden), 41min 07.2sec
4 x 6km Relay: Belarus, 1hr 12min 03.4sec

MIXED
Relay: France, 1hr 08min 34.3sec

BOBSLEIGH

MEN
Two-man: Canada and Germany (tie), 3min 16.86sec
Four-man: Germany, 3min 15.84sec

WOMEN
Two-woman: Germany, 3min 22.45sec

CROSS COUNTRY SKIING

MEN
15km: Dario Cologna (Switzerland), 33min 43sec
30km Skiathlon: Simen Hegstad Krueger (Norway), 1hr 16min 20.0sec
50km Mass Start: Iivo Niskanen (Finland), 2hr 08min 22.1sec
4 x 10km Relay: Norway, 1hr 33min 04.9sec
Sprint: Johannes Hoesflot Klaebo (Norway), 3min 05.75sec
Team Sprint: Norway, 15min 56.26sec

WOMEN
10km: Ragnhild Haga (Norway), 25min 00.5sec
15km Skiathlon: Charlotte Kalla (Sweden), 40min 44.9sec
30km Mass Start: Marit Bjoergen (Norway), 1hr 22min 17.6sec
4 x 5km Relay: Norway, 51min 24.3sec
Sprint: Stina Nilsson (Sweden), 3min 03.84sec
Team Sprint: USA, 15min 56.47sec

CURLING
Men: USA
Women: Sweden
Mixed doubles: Canada

FIGURE SKATING
Men: Yuzuru Hanyu (Japan), 317.85pts
Women: Alina Zagitova (OAR), 239.57pts
Pairs Mixed: Aljona Savchenko and Bruno Massot (Germany), 235.90pts
Ice Dance Mixed: Tessa Virtue and Scott Moir (Canada), 206.07pts
Team Dance Mixed: Canada, 73pts

FREESTYLE SKIING

MEN
Moguls: Mikael Kingsbury (Canada), 86.63pts
Aerials: Oleksandr Abramenko (Ukraine), 128.51pts
Halfpipe: David Wise (USA), 97.20pts
Slopestyle: Oystein Braaten (Norway), 95.00pts
Ski Cross: Brady Leman (Canada)

WOMEN
Moguls: Perrine Laffont (France), 78.65pts
Aerials: Hanna Huskova (Belarus), 96.14pts
Halfpipe: Cassie Sharpe (Canada), 95.80pts
Slopestyle: Sarah Hoefflin (Switzerland), 91.20pts
Ski Cross: Kelsey Serwa (Canada)

ICE HOCKEY
Men: OAR
Women: USA

LUGE
Men's singles: David Gleirscher (Austria), 3min 10.702sec
Men's doubles: Germany, 1min 31.697sec
Women's singles: Natalie Geisenberger (Germany), 3min 05.232sec
Mixed Relay: Germany, 2min 24.517sec

NORDIC COMBINED
Individual Large Hill: Johannes Rydzek (Germany), 23min 52.5sec
Individual Normal Hill: Eric Frenzel (Germany), 24min 51.4sec
Team 4 x 5km: Germany, 46min 09.8sec

SHORT-TRACK SPEED SKATING

MEN
500m: Wu Dajing (China), 39.584sec
1000m: Samuel Girard (Canada), 1min 24.650sec
1500m: Lim Hyojun (Rep. of Korea), 2min 10.485sec
5km Relay: Hungary, 6min 31.971sec

WOMEN
500m: Arianna Fontana (Italy), 42.569sec
1000m: Suzanne Schulting (Netherlands), 1min 29.778sec
1500m: Choi Minjeong (Rep. of Korea), 2min 24.948sec
3km Relay: Rep. of Korea, 4min 07.361sec

SKELETON
Men: Yun Sungbin (Rep. of Korea), 3min 20.55sec
Women: Lizzy Yarnold (Great Britain), 3min 27.28sec

SKI JUMPING

MEN
Normal Hill: Andreas Wellinger (Germany), 259.3pts
Large Hill: Kamil Stoch (Poland), 285.7pts
Team: Norway, 1098.5pts

WOMEN
Normal Hill: Maren Lundby (Norway), 264.6pts

SNOWBOARDING

MEN
Big Air: Sebastien Toutant (Canada), 174.25pts
Halfpipe: Shaun White (USA), 97.75pts
Slopestyle: Redmond Gerard (USA), 87.16pts
Parallel Giant Slalom: Nevin Galmarini (Switzerland)
Snowboard Cross: Pierre Vaultier (France)

WOMEN
Big Air: Anna Gasser (Austria), 185.00pts
Halfpipe: Chloe Kim (USA), 98.25pts
Slopestyle: Jamie Anderson (USA), 83.00pts
Parallel Giant Slalom: Ester Ledecka (Czechia)
Snowboard Cross: Michela Moioli (Italy)

SPEED SKATING

MEN
500m: Harvard Lorentzen (Norway), 34.41sec
1000m: Kjeld Nuis (Netherlands), 1min 07.95sec
1500m: Kjeld Nuis (Netherlands), 1min 44.01sec
5000m: Sven Kramer (Netherlands), 6min 09.76sec
10km: Ted-Jan Bloemen (Canada), 12min 39.77sec
Mass Start: Seung-Hoon Lee (Rep. of Korea), 60pts
Team Pursuit: Norway, 3min 37.31sec

WOMEN
500m: Nao Kodaira (Japan), 36.94sec
1000m: Jorien ter Mors (Netherlands), 1min 13.56sec
1500m: Ireen Wüst (Netherlands), 1min 54.35sec
3000m: Carlijn Achtereekte (Netherlands), 3min 59.21sec
5000m: Esmee Visser (Netherlands), 6min 50.23sec
Mass Start: Nana Takagi (Japan), 60pts
Team Pursuit: Japan, 2min 53.89sec

MEDAL TABLE

Country	G	S	B	Total
Norway	14	14	11	39
Germany	14	10	7	31
Canada	11	8	10	29
USA	9	8	6	23
Netherlands	8	6	6	20
Sweden	7	6	1	14
Rep. of Korea	5	8	4	17
Switzerland	5	6	4	15
France	5	4	6	15
Austria	5	3	6	14
Japan	4	5	4	13
Italy	3	2	5	10
OAR	2	6	9	17
Czechia	2	2	3	7
Belarus	2	1	0	3
China	1	6	2	9
Slovakia	1	2	0	3
Finland	1	1	4	6
Great Britain	1	0	4	5
Poland	1	0	1	2
Hungary	1	0	0	1
Ukraine	1	0	0	1
Australia	0	2	1	3
Slovenia	0	1	1	2
Belgium	0	1	0	1
Spain	0	0	2	2
New Zealand	0	0	2	2
Kazakhstan	0	0	1	1
Latvia	0	0	1	1
Liechtenstein	0	0	1	1

OAR = Olympic Athletes from Russia

2018 (XXI) COMMONWEALTH GAMES

Gold Coast, Australia, 4–15 April

ATHLETICS

MEN
100m: Akani Simbine (South Africa), 10.03sec
110m Hurdles: Ronald Levy (Jamaica), 13.19sec
200m: Jereem Richards (Trinidad and Tobago), 20.12sec
400m: Isaac Makwala (Botswana), 44.35sec
400m Hurdles: Kyron McMaster (British Virgin Islands), 48.25sec
800m: Wycliffe Kinyamal (Kenya), 1min 45.11sec
1500m: Elijah Motonei Manangoi (Kenya), 3min 34.78sec
3000m St: Conseslus Kipruto (Kenya), 8min 10.08sec
5000m: Joshua Kiprui Cheptegei (Uganda), 13min 50.83sec
10,000m: Joshua Kiprui Cheptegei (Uganda), 27min 19.62sec
4×100m Relay: England, 38.13sec
4×400m Relay: Botswana, 3min 01.78sec
20km Walk: Dane Bird-Smith (Australia), 1hr 19min 34sec
Marathon: Michael Shelley (Australia), 2hr 16min 46sec
Decathlon: Lindon Victor (Grenada), 8,303pts
High Jump: Brandon Starc (Australia), 2.32m
Long Jump: Luvo Manyonga (South Africa), 8.41m
Triple Jump: Troy Doris (Guyana), 16.88m
Discus: Fedrick Dacres (Jamaica), 68.20m
Hammer: Nick Miller (England), 80.26m
Javelin: Neeraj Chopra (India), 86.47m
Shot Put: Tomas Walsh (New Zealand), 21.41m
Pole Vault: Kurtis Marschall (Australia), 5.70m

MEN'S PARA-SPORT
100m (T12): Ndodomzi Ntutu (South Africa), 11.02sec
100m (T38): Evan O'Hanlon (Australia), 11.09sec
100m (T47): Suwaibidu Galadima (Nigeria), 11.04sec
1500m (T54): Alexandre Dupont (Canada), 3min 11.75sec
Marathon (T54): Kurt Fearnley (Australia), 1hr 30min 26sec
Shot Put (F38): Cameron Crombie (Australia), 15.74m

WOMEN
100m: Michelle-Lee Ahye (Trinidad and Tobago), 11.14sec
100m Hurdles: Oluwatobiloba Amusan (Nigeria), 12.68sec
200m: Shaunae Miller-Uibo (Bahamas), 22.09sec
400m: Amantle Montsho (Botswana), 50.15sec
400m Hurdles: Janieve Russell (Jamaica), 54.33sec
800m: Caster Semenya (South Africa), 1min 56.68sec
1500m: Caster Semenya (South Africa), 4min 00.71sec
3000m St: Aisha Praught (Jamaica), 9min 21.00sec
5000m: Hellen Obiri (Kenya), 15min 13.11sec
10,000m: Stella Chesang (Uganda), 31min 45.3sec
4×100m Relay: England, 42.46sec
4×400m Relay: Jamaica, 3min 24.00sec
20km Walk: Jemima Montag (Australia), 1hr 32min 50sec
Marathon: Helalia Johannes (Namibia), 2hr 32min 40sec
Heptathlon: Katarina Johnson-Thompson (England), 6,255pts
High Jump: Levern Spencer (St Lucia), 1.95m
Long Jump: Christabel Nettey (Canada), 6.84m
Triple Jump: Kimberly Williams (Jamaica), 14.64m
Discus: Dani Stevens (Australia), 68.26m
Hammer: Julia Ratcliffe (New Zealand), 68.60m
Javelin: Kathryn Mitchell (Australia), 68.92m
Shot Put: Danniel Thomas-Dodd (Jamaica), 19.36m
Pole Vault: Alysha Newman (Canada), 4.75m

WOMEN'S PARA-SPORT
100m (T35): Isis Holt (Australia), 13.58sec
100m (T38): Sophie Hahn (England), 12.46sec
1500m (T54): Madison de Rozario (Australia), 3min 34.06sec
Marathon (T54): Madison de Rozario (Australia), 1hr 44min 00sec
Long Jump (F38): Olivia Breen (Wales), 4.86m
Javelin (F46): Hollie Arnold (Wales), 44.43m

BADMINTON
Men's Singles: Chong Wei Lee (Malaysia)
Women's Singles: Saina Nehwal (India)
Men's Doubles: Marcus Ellis and Chris Langridge (England)
Women's Doubles: Mei Kuan Chow and Vivian Hoo (Malaysia)
Mixed Doubles: Chris Adcock and Gabrielle Adcock (England)
Mixed Team: India

BASKETBALL
Men: Australia
Women: Australia

BOWLS

MEN
Singles: Aaron Wilson (Australia)
Pairs: Daniel Salmon and Marc Wyatt (Wales)
Triples: Scotland
Fours: Scotland

WOMEN
Singles: Jo Edwards (New Zealand)
Pairs: Emma Firyana Saroji and Siti Zalina Ahmad (Malaysia)
Triples: Australia
Fours: Australia

PARA-SPORT
Mixed Pairs (B2/B3): Australia
Open Triples (B6/B7/B8): Australia

BOXING

MEN
Light flyweight (49kg): Galal Yafai (England)
Flyweight (52kg): Gaurav Solanki (India)
Bantamweight (56kg): Peter McGrail (England)
Lightweight (60kg): Harry Garside (Australia)
Light welterweight (64kg): Jonas Jonas (Namibia)
Welterweight (69kg): Pat McCormack (England)
Middleweight (75kg): Vikas Krishan (India)
Light heavyweight (81kg): Sammy Lee (Wales)
Heavyweight (91kg): David Nyika (New Zealand)
Super heavyweight (91kg+): Frazer Clarke (England)

WOMEN
Light flyweight (48kg): MC Mery Kom (India)
Flyweight (51kg): Lisa Whiteside (England)
Featherweight (57kg): Skye Nicolson (Australia)
Lightweight (60kg): Anja Stridsman (Australia)
Welterweight (69kg): Sandy Ryan (England)
Middleweight (75kg): Lauren Price (Wales)

CYCLING

MEN
Time Trial: Cameron Meyer (Australia), 48min 13.04sec
Cross-country: Samuel Gaze (New Zealand), 1hr 17min 36sec
Sprint: Sam Webster (New Zealand)
Team Sprint: New Zealand
Keirin: Matthew Glaetzer (Australia)
15km Scratch Race: Sam Welsford (Australia)
1000m Time Trial: Matt Glaetzer (Australia), 59.340sec
4000m Individual Pursuit: Charlie Tanfield (England), 4min
    15.952sec
4000m Team Pursuit: Australia, 3min 49.804sec
40km Points Race: Mark Stewart (Scotland), 81pts
Road Race: Steele von Hoff (Australia), 3hr 57min 01sec

MEN'S PARA-SPORT
Sprint (B&VI): Neil Fachie (Scotland)
1000m Time Trial (B&VI): Neil Fachie (Scotland), 1min
    00.065sec

WOMEN
Time Trial: Katrin Garfoot (Australia), 35min 08.09sec
Cross-country: Annie Last (England), 1hr 18min 02sec
Sprint: Stephanie Morton (Australia)
Team Sprint: Australia

Keirin: Stephanie Morton (Australia)
10km Scratch Race: Amy Cure (Australia)
500m Time Trial: Kaarle McCulloch (Australia), 33.583sec
3000m Individual Pursuit: Katie Archibald (Scotland), 3min
    26.088sec
4000m Team Pursuit: Australia, 4min 15.214sec
25km Points Race: Elinor Barker (Wales), 40pts
Road Race: Chloe Hosking (Australia), 3hr 02min 18sec

WOMEN'S PARA-SPORT
Sprint (B&VI): Sophie Thornhill (England)
1000m Time Trial (B&VI): Sophie Thornhill (England), 1min
    04.623sec

DIVING

MEN
1m Springboard: Jack Laugher (England), 438.00pts
3m Springboard: Jack Laugher (England), 519.40pts
10 Platform: Domonic Bedggood (Australia), 451.15pts
3m Springboard Synch: England, 436.17pts
10m Platform Synch: England, 405.81pts

WOMEN
1m Springboard: Grace Reid (Scotland), 275.30pts
3m Springboard: Jennifer Abel (Canada), 366.95pts
10 Platform: Melissa Wu (Australia), 360.40pts
3m Springboard Synch: Australia, 284.10pts
10m Platform Synch: Malaysia, 328.08pts

GYMNASTICS – ARTISTIC

MEN
Team: England, 258.950pts
Individual All-Around: Nile Wilson (England), 84.950pts
Floor: Marios Georgiou (Cyprus), 13.966pts
Horizontal Bar: Nile Wilson (England), 14.533pts
Parallel Bars: Marios Georgiou (Cyprus), 14.533pts
Pommel Horse: Rhys McClenaghan (N. Ireland), 15.100pts
Rings: Courtney Tulloch (England), 14.833pts
Vault: Christopher Remkes (Australia), 14.799pts

WOMEN
Team: Canada, 163.075pts
Individual All-Around: Elsabeth Black (Canada), 54.200pts
Beam: Alice Kinsella (England), 13.700pts
Floor: Alexandra Eade (Australia), 13.333pts
Uneven Bars: Georgia-Mae Fenton (England), 14.600pts
Vault: Shallon Olsen (Canada), 14.566pts

GYMNASTICS – RHYTHMIC
Team: Cyprus, 130.625pts
Individual All-Around: Diamanto Evripidou (Cyprus),
    55.750pts
Ball: Diamanto Evripidou (Cyprus), 13.800pts
Clubs: Sophie Crane (Canada), 13.950pts
Hoop: Diamanto Evripidou (Cyprus), 14.850pts
Ribbon: Kwan Dict Weng (Malaysia), 13.200pts

HOCKEY
Men: Australia
Women: New Zealand

NETBALL
Women: England

RUGBY SEVENS
Men: New Zealand
Women: New Zealand

SHOOTING

MEN

10m Air Pistol: Jitu Rai (India), 235.1pts
10m Air Rifle: Dane Sampson (Australia), 245.0pts
25m Rapid Fire Pistol: Anish (India), 30pts
50m Pistol: Daniel Repacholi (Australia), 227.2pts
50m Rifle Prone: David Phelps (Wales), 248.8pts
50m Rifle 3 Positions: Sanjeev Rajput (India), 454.5pts
Skeet: Georgios Achilleos (Cyprus), 57pts
Trap: Michael Wixey (Wales), 46pts
Double Trap: David McMath (Scotland), 74pts

WOMEN

10m Air Pistol: Manu Bhaker (India), 240.9pts
10m Air Rifle: Martina Lindsay Veloso (Singapore), 247.2pts
25m Pistol: Heena Sidhu (India), 38pts
50m Rifle Prone: Martina Lindsay Veloso (Singapore), 621.0pts
50m Rifle 3 Positions: Tejaswini Sawant (India), 457.9pts
Skeet: Andri Eleftheriou (Cyprus), 52pts
Trap: Laetisha Scanlan (Australia), 38pts
Double Trap: Shreyasi Singh (India), 96pts

QUEEN'S PRIZE

Individual: David Luckman (England)
Pairs: England

SQUASH

Men's Singles: James Willstrop (England)
Men's Doubles: Australia
Women's Singles: Joelle King (New Zealand)
Women's Doubles: New Zealand
Mixed Doubles: Australia

SWIMMING

MEN

50m Backstroke: Mitch Larkin (Australia), 24.68sec
50m Breaststroke: Cameron van der Burgh (South Africa), 26.58sec
50m Butterfly: Chad le Clos (South Africa), 23.37sec
50m Freestyle: Benjamin Proud (England), 21.35sec
100m Backstroke: Mitch Larkin (Australia), 53.18sec
100m Breaststroke: Adam Peaty (England), 58.84sec
100m Butterfly: Chad le Clos (South Africa), 50.65sec
100m Freestyle: Duncan Scott (Scotland), 48.02sec
200m Backstroke: Mitch Larkin (Australia), 1min 56.10sec
200m Breaststroke: James Wilby (England), 2min 08.05sec
200m Butterfly: Chad le Clos (South Africa), 1min 54.00sec
200m Individual Medley: Mitch Larkin (Australia), 1min 57.67sec
200m Freestyle: Kyle Chalmers (Australia), 1min 45.56sec
400m Freestyle: Mack Horton (Australia), 3min 43.76sec
400m Individual Medley: Clyde Lewis (Australia), 4min 13.12sec
1500m Freestyle: Jack McLoughlin (Australia), 14min 47.09sec
4×100m Freestyle Relay: Australia, 3min 12.96sec
4×100m Medley Relay: Australia, 3min 31.04sec
4×200m Freestyle Relay: Australia, 7min 05.97sec

MEN'S PARA-SPORT

50m Freestyle (S7): Matthew Levy (Australia), 28.60sec
100m Backstroke (S9): Brenden Hall (Australia), 1min 04.73sec
100m Breaststroke (SB8): Timothy Disken (Australia), 1min 13.87sec
100m Freestyle (S9): Timothy Disken (Australia), 56.07sec
200m Individual Medley (SM8): Jesse Aungles (Australia), 2min 30.77sec

200m Freestyle (S14): Thomas Hamer (England), 1min 55.88sec

WOMEN

50m Backstroke: Emily Seebohm (Australia), 27.78sec
50m Breaststroke: Sarah Vasey (England), 30.60sec
50m Butterfly: Cate Campbell (Australia), 25.59sec
50m Freestyle: Cate Campbell (Australia), 23.78sec
100m Backstroke: Kylie Masse (Canada), 58.63sec
100m Breaststroke: Tatjana Schoenmaker (South Africa), 1min 06.41sec
100m Butterfly: Emma McKeon (Australia), 56.78sec
100m Freestyle: Bronte Campbell (Australia), 52.27sec
200m Backstroke: Kylie Masse (Canada), 2min 05.98sec
200m Breaststroke: Tatjana Schoenmaker (South Africa), 2min 22.02sec
200m Butterfly: Alys Thomas (Wales), 2min 05.45sec
200m Individual Medley: Siobhan Marie O'Connor (England), 2min 09.80sec
200m Freestyle: Taylor Ruck (Canada), 1min 54.81sec
400m Freestyle: Ariarne Titmus (Australia), 4min 00.93sec
400m Individual Medley: Aimee Willmott (England), 4min 34.90sec
800m Freestyle: Ariarne Titmus (Australia), 8min 20.02sec
4×100m Freestyle Relay: Australia, 3min 30.05sec
4×100m Medley Relay: Australia, 3min 54.36sec
4×200m Freestyle Relay: Australia, 7min 48.04sec

WOMEN'S PARA-SPORT

50m Butterfly (S7): Eleanor Robinson (England), 35.72sec
50m Freestyle (S8): Lakeisha Patterson (Australia), 30.14sec
100m Backstroke (S9): Alice Tai (England), 1min 08.77sec
100m Breaststroke (SB8): Sophie Pascoe (New Zealand), 1min 18.09sec
100m Freestyle (S9): Lakeisha Patterson (Australia), 1min 03.02sec
200m Individual Medley (SM10): Sophie Pascoe (New Zealand), 2min 27.72sec

TABLE TENNIS

Men's Singles: Ning Gao (Singapore)
Men's Doubles: England
Men's Team: India
Women's Singles: Manika Batra (India)
Women's Doubles: Singapore
Women's Team: India
Mixed Doubles: Singapore

PARA-SPORT TABLE TENNIS

Men's Singles (TT6–10): Ross Wilson (England)
Women's Singles (TT6–10): Melissa Tapper (Australia)

TRIATHLON

Men: Henri Schoeman (South Africa), 52min 31sec
Women: Flora Duffy (Bermuda), 56min 50sec
Mixed Team: Australia, 1hr 17min 36sec

PARA-SPORT TRIATHLON

Men (PTWC): Joseph Townsend (England), 1hr 02min 39sec
Women (PTWC): Jade Jones (England), 1hr 11min 07sec

VOLLEYBALL – BEACH

Men: Australia
Women: Canada

WEIGHTLIFTING

MEN

56kg: Muhammad Azroy Hazalwafie Izhar Ahmad (Malaysia), 261kg

62kg: Muhamad Aznil Bidin (Malaysia), 288kg
69kg: Gareth Evans (Wales), 299kg
77kg: Sathish Kumar Sivalingam (India), 317kg
85kg: Venkat Rahul Ragala (India), 338kg
94kg: Steven Kari (Papua New Guinea), 370kg
105kg: Sanele Mao (Samoa), 360kg
105kg+: David Liti (New Zealand), 403kg

WOMEN
48kg: Chanu Saikhom Mirabai (India), 196kg
53kg: Sanjita Chanu Khumukcham (India), 192kg
58kg: Tia-Clair Toomey (Australia), 201kg
63kg: Maude Charron (Canada), 220kg
69kg: Punam Yadav (India), 222kg
75kg: Emily Godley (England), 222kg
90kg: Eileen Cikamatana (Fiji), 233kg
90kg+: Feagaiga Stowers (Samoa), 253kg

PARA-SPORT POWERLIFTING
Men's Lightweight: Roland Ezuruike (Nigeria), 224.3pts
Men's Heavyweight: Abdulazeez Ibrahim (Nigeria), 191.9pts
Women's Lightweight: Esther Oyema (Nigeria), 141.6pts
Women's Heavyweight: Ndidi Nwosu (Nigeria), 110.4pts

WRESTLING

MEN
57kg: Rahul Aware (India)
65kg: Bajrang (India)
74kg: Kumar Sushil (India)
86kg: Muhammad Inam (Pakistan)
97kg: Martin Erasmus (South Africa)
125kg: Sumit (India)

WOMEN
50kg: Vinesh Vinesh (India)
53kg: Diana Weicker (Canada)
57kg: Odunayo Adekuoroye (Nigeria)
62kg: Aminat Adeniyi (Nigeria)
68kg: Blessing Oborududu (Nigeria)
76kg: Erica Wiebe (Canada)

MEDAL TABLE

Country	G	S	B	Total
Australia	80	59	59	198
England	45	45	46	136
India	26	20	20	66
Canada	15	40	27	82
New Zealand	15	16	15	46
South Africa	13	11	13	37
Wales	10	12	14	36
Scotland	9	13	22	44
Nigeria	9	9	6	24
Cyprus	8	1	5	14
Jamaica	7	9	11	27
Malaysia	7	5	12	24
Singapore	5	2	2	9
Kenya	4	7	6	17
Uganda	3	1	2	6
Botswana	3	1	1	5
Samoa	2	3	0	5
Trinidad and Tobago	2	1	0	3
Namibia	2	0	0	2
Northern Ireland	1	7	4	12
The Bahamas	1	3	0	4
Papua New Guinea	1	2	0	3
Fiji	1	1	2	4
Pakistan	1	0	4	5
Grenada	1	0	1	2
Bermuda	1	0	0	1
Guyana	1	0	0	1
British Virgin Islands	1	0	0	1
Saint Lucia	1	0	0	1
Bangladesh	0	2	0	2
Sri Lanka	0	1	5	6
Cameroon	0	1	2	3
Dominica	0	1	1	2
Isle of Man	0	1	0	1
Mauritius	0	1	0	1
Nauru	0	1	0	1
Malta	0	0	2	2
Vanuatu	0	0	2	2
Cook Islands	0	0	1	1
Ghana	0	0	1	1
Norfolk Islands	0	0	1	1
Seychelles	0	0	1	1
Solomon Islands	0	0	1	1

SPORTS RECORDS

ATHLETICS WORLD RECORDS

As at September 2018
All the world records given below have been accepted by the International Amateur Athletic Federation. Fully automatic timing to 1/100th second is mandatory up to and including 400 metres. For distances up to and including 10,000 metres, records will be accepted to 1/100th second if timed automatically, and to 1/10th if hand timing is used.

MEN

TRACK EVENTS	hr	min	sec
100m			9.58
Usain Bolt (Jamaica), 2009			
200m			19.19
Usain Bolt (Jamaica), 2009			
400m			43.03
Wayde van Niekerk (South Africa), 2016			
800m		1	40.91
David Rudisha (Kenya), 2012			
1000m		2	11.96
Noah Ngeny (Kenya), 1999			
1500m		3	26
Hicham El Guerrouj (Morocco), 1998			
1 mile		3	43.13
Hicham El Guerrouj (Morocco), 1999			
2000m		4	44.79
Hicham El Guerrouj (Morocco), 1999			
3000m		7	20.67
Daniel Komen (Kenya), 1996			
5000m		12	37.35
Kenenisa Bekele (Ethiopia), 2004			
10,000m		26	17.53
Kenenisa Bekele (Ethiopia), 2005			
20,000m		56	26
Haile Gebrselassie (Ethiopia), 2007			
21,285m One Hour Race	1	0	0
Haile Gebrselassie (Ethiopia), 2007			
25,000m	1	12	25.4
Moses Mosop (Kenya), 2011			
30,000m	1	26	47.4
Moses Mosop (Kenya), 2011			
Marathon	2	1	39
Eliud Kipchoge (Kenya), 2018			
110m Hurdles (0.84m)			12.8
Aries Merritt (USA), 2012			
400m Hurdles (0.76m)			46.78
Kevin Young (USA), 1992			
3000m Steeplechase		7	53.63
Saif Saaeed Shaheen (Qatar), 2004			

RELAYS		min	sec
4 x 100m			36.84
Jamaica, 2012			
4 x 200m		1	18.63
Jamaica, 2014			
4 x 400m		2	54.29
USA, 1993			
4 x 800m		7	2.43
Kenya, 2006			
4 x 1500m		14	22.22
Kenya, 2014			

FIELD EVENTS	m	ft	in
High Jump	2.45	8	0½
Javier Sotomayor (Cuba), 1993			
Pole Vault	6.16	20	2½
Renaud Lavillenie (France), 2014			
Long Jump	8.95	29	4¼
Mike Powell (USA), 1991			
Triple Jump	18.29	60	0¼
Jonathan Edwards (Great Britain), 1995			
Shot	23.12	75	10¼
Randy Barnes (USA), 1990			
Discus	74.08	243	0
Jürgen Schult (GDR), 1986			
Hammer	86.74	284	7
Yuriy Sedykh (USSR), 1986			
Javelin	98.48	323	1
Jan Zelezny (Czechia), 1996			
Decathlon†			9,126pts
Kevin Mayer (France), 2018			

† Ten events comprising 100m, long jump, shot, high jump, 400m, 110m hurdles, discus, pole vault, javelin, 1500m

WALKING (TRACK)	hr	min	sec
20,000m	1	17	25.6
Bernardo Segura (Mexico), 1994			
30,000m	2	1	44.1
Maurizio Damilano (Italy), 1992			
50,000m	3	35	27.2
Yohann Diniz (France), 2011			

WOMEN

TRACK EVENTS	hr	min	sec
100m			10.49
Florence Griffith-Joyner (USA), 1988			
200m			21.34
Florence Griffith-Joyner (USA), 1988			
400m			47.6
Marita Koch (GDR), 1985			
800m		1	53.28
Jarmila Kratochvilova (Czechoslovakia), 1983			
1000m		2	28.98
Svetlana Masterkova (Russia), 1996			
1500m		3	50.07
Genzebe Dibaba (Ethiopia), 2015			
1 mile		4	12.56
Svetlana Masterkova (Russia), 1996			
2000m		5	23.75
Genzebe Dibaba (Ethiopia), 2017			
3000m		8	6.11
Wang Junxia (China), 1993			
5000m		14	11.15
Tirunesh Dibaba (Ethiopia), 2008			
10,000m		29	17.45
Almaz Ayana (Ethiopia), 2016			
20,000m	1	5	26.6
Tegla Loroupe (Kenya), 2000			
18,517m One Hour Race	1	0	0
Dire Tune (Ethiopia), 2008			
25,000m	1	27	5.9
Tegla Loroupe (Kenya), 2002			
30,000m	1	45	50
Tegla Loroupe (Kenya), 2003			
Marathon	2	15	25
Paula Radcliffe (Great Britain), 2003			
100m Hurdles (0.84m)			12.2
Kendra Harrison (USA), 2016			
400m Hurdles (0.76m)			52.34

Yuliya Pechonkina (Russia), 2003

3000m Steeplechase	8	44.32

Beatrice Chepkoech (Kenya), 2018

RELAYS	*min*	*sec*
4 x 100m		40.82
USA, 2012		
4 x 200m	1	27.46
USA, 2000		
4 x 400m	3	15.17
USSR, 1988		
4 x 800m	7	50.17
USSR, 1984		
4 x 1500m	16	33.58
Kenya, 2014		

FIELD EVENTS	*m*	*ft*	*in*
High Jump	2.09	6	10¼
Stefka Kostadinova (Bulgaria), 1987			
Pole Vault	5.06	16	7¼
Elena Isinbaeva (Russia), 2009			
Long Jump	7.52	24	8¼
Galina Chistyakova (USSR), 1988			
Triple Jump	15.5	50	10¼
Inessa Kravets (Ukraine), 1995			
Shot	22.63	74	3
Natalya Lisovskaya (USSR), 1987			
Discus	76.8	252	0
Gabriele Reinsch (GDR), 1988			
Hammer	82.98	272	3
Anita Wlodarczyk (Poland), 2016			
Javelin	72.28	237	2
Barbora Spotakova (Czechia), 2008			
Decathlon†			8,358pts
Austra Skujyte (Lithuania), 2005			

† Ten events comprising 100m, long jump, shot, high jump, 400m, 110m hurdles, discus, pole vault, javelin, 1500m

WALKING (TRACK)	*hr*	*min*	*sec*
10,000m		41	56.23
Nadezhda Ryashkina (USSR), 1990			
20,000m	1	26	52.3
Olimpiada Ivanova (Russia), 2001			

ATHLETICS NATIONAL (UK) RECORDS

As at September 2018
Records set anywhere by athletes eligible to represent Great Britain and Northern Ireland.
MEN

TRACK EVENTS	*hr*	*min*	*sec*
100m			9.87
Linford Christie, 1993			
200m			19.87
John Regis, 1994			
400m			44.36
Iwan Thomas, 1997			
800m		1	41.73
Sebastian Coe, 1981			
1000m		2	12.18
Sebastian Coe, 1981			
1500m		3	28.81
Mo Farah, 2013			
1 mile		3	46.32
Steve Cram, 1985			
2000m		4	51.39
Steve Cram, 1985			
3000m		7	32.62
Mo Farah, 2016			
5000m		12	53.11

Mo Farah, 2011

10,000m		26	46.57

Mo Farah, 2011

20,000m		57	28.7

Carl Thackery, 1990

20,855m One Hour Race	1	0	0

Carl Thackery, 1993

25,000m	1	15	22.6

Ron Hill, 1965

30,000m	1	31	30.4

Jim Alder, 1970

Marathon	2	7	13

Steve Jones, 1985

3000m Steeplechase		8	7.96

Mark Rowland, 1988

110m Hurdles		12.91

Colin Jackson, 1993

400m Hurdles		47.82

Kriss Akabusi, 1992

RELAYS	*min*	*sec*
4 x 100m		37.47
GB team, 2017		
4 x 200m	1	21.29
GB team, 1989		
4 x 400m	2	56.6
GB team, 1996		
4 x 800m	7	3.89
GB team, 1982		

FIELD EVENTS	*m*	*ft*	*in*
High Jump	2.37	7	9¼
Steve Smith, 1993			
Robbie Grabarz, 2012			
Pole Vault	5.82	19	1
Steven Lewis, 2012			
Long Jump	8.51	27	11
Greg Rutherford, 2014			
Triple Jump	18.29	60	0¼
Jonathan Edwards, 1995			
Shot	21.92	71	11
Carl Myerscough, 2003			
Discus	68.24	223	10
Lawrence Okoye, 2012			
Hammer	80.26	263	3
Nick Miller, 2018			
Javelin	91.46	300	1
Steve Backley, 1992			
Decathlon			8,847pts
Daley Thompson, 1984			

WALKING (TRACK)	*hr*	*min*	*sec*
20,000m	1	23	26.5
Ian McCombie, 1990			
30,000m	2	11	54
Christopher Maddocks, 1989			
50,000m	4	5	44.6
Paul Blagg, 1990			
27,262m – Two Hour Walk	2	0	0
Christopher Maddocks, 1989			

WOMEN

TRACK EVENTS	*min*	*sec*
100m		10.85
Dina Asher-Smith, 2018		
200m		21.89
Dina Asher-Smith, 2018		
400m		49.41
Christine Ohuruogu, 2013		
800m	1	56.21
Kelly Holmes, 1995		

	min	sec
1500m Laura Muir, 2016	3	55.22
1 mile Zola Budd, 1985	4	17.57
3000m Paula Radcliffe, 2002	8	22.2
5000m Paula Radcliffe, 2004	14	29.11
10,000m Paula Radcliffe, 2002	30	1.09
Marathon Paula Radcliffe, 2003	2 15	25
100m Hurdles Tiffany Porter, 2014		12.51
400m Hurdles Sally Gunnell, 1993		52.74
3000m Steeplechase Barbara Parker, 2012	9	24.24

RELAYS	min	sec
4 x 100m GB team, 2016		41.77
4 x 200m GB team, 2014	1	29.61
4 x 400m GB team, 2007	3	20.04
4 x 800m GB team, 2013	8	13.46

FIELD EVENTS	m	ft	in
High Jump Katarina Johnson-Thompson, 2016	1.98	6	6
Pole Vault Holly Bradshaw, 2017	4.81	00	6
Long Jump Shara Proctor, 2015	7.07	23	2
Triple Jump Ashia Hansen, 1997	15.15	49	8½
Shot Judy Oakes, 1988	19.36	63	6¼
Discus Margaret Ritchie, 1981	67.48	221	5
Hammer Sophie Hitchon, 2016	74.54	244	6½
Javelin Goldie Sayers, 2012	66.17	217	1
Heptathlon Jessica Ennis-Hill, 2012			6,955pts

SWIMMING WORLD RECORDS

50m-pool. As at September 2018

MEN

	min	sec
50m Freestyle Cesar Cielo Filho (Brazil), 2009		20.91
100m Freestyle Cesar Cielo Filho (Brazil), 2009		46.91
200m Freestyle Paul Biedermann (Germany), 2009	1	42
400m Freestyle Paul Biedermann (Germany), 2009	3	40.07
800m Freestyle Zhang Lin (China), 2009	7	32.12
1500m Freestyle Sun Yang (China), 2012	14	31.02
50m Breaststroke Adam Peaty (Great Britain), 2017		25.95
100m Breaststroke Adam Peaty (Great Britain), 2018		57.10
200m Breaststroke Ippei Watanabe (Japan), 2017	2	6.67
50m Butterfly Andriy Govorov (Ukraine), 2018		22.27
100m Butterfly Michael Phelps (USA), 2009		49.82
200m Butterfly Michael Phelps (USA), 2009	1	51.51
50m Backstroke Kliment Kolesnikov (Russia), 2018		24
100m Backstroke Ryan Murphy (USA), 2016		51.85
200m Backstroke Aaron Peirsol (USA), 2009	1	51.92
200m Medley Ryan Lochte (USA), 2011	1	54
400m Medley Michael Phelps (USA), 2008	4	3.84
4 x 100m Freestyle relay USA, 2008	3	8.24
4 x 200m Freestyle relay USA, 2009	6	58.55
4 x 100m Medley relay USA, 2009	3	27.28

WOMEN

	min	sec
50m Freestyle Sarah Sjostrom (Sweden), 2017		23.67
100m Freestyle Sarah Sjostrom (Sweden), 2017		51.71
200m Freestyle Federica Pellegrini (Italy), 2009	1	52.98
400m Freestyle Katie Ledecky (USA), 2016	3	56.46
800m Freestyle Katie Ledecky (USA), 2016	8	4.79
1500m Freestyle Katie Ledecky (USA), 2015	15	25.48
50m Breaststroke Lilly King (USA), 2017		29.40
100m Breaststroke Lilly King (USA), 2017	1	4.13
200m Breaststroke Rikke Moeller-Pedersen (Denmark), 2013	2	19.11
50m Butterfly Sarah Sjostrom (Sweden), 2014		24.43
100m Butterfly Sarah Sjostrom (Sweden), 2016		55.48
200m Butterfly Liu Zige (China), 2009	2	1.81
50m Backstroke Zhao Jing (China), 2009		27.06
100m Backstroke Kathleen Baker (USA), 2018		58
200m Backstroke Missy Franklin (USA), 2012	2	4.06
200m Medley Katinka Hosszu (Hungary), 2015	2	6.12
400m Medley Katinka Hosszu (Hungary), 2016	4	26.36
4 x 100m Freestyle relay Australia, 2018	3	30.05
4 x 200m Freestyle relay China, 2009	7	42.08
4 x 100m Medley relay USA, 2017	3	51.55

WEATHER

In the text below, the 'average' refers to the average for the 30-year period 1981–2010, which is the standard reference period ('normal') for 2011–20. Daily rainfall totals are for 24-hour periods ending at 0900 GMT on the day indicated.

The UK's mean air temperature (July 2017–June 2018) was 9.08°C, the 20th warmest. However, the 12-month period prior to this was significantly warmer (9.76°C); the long term average is 8.87°C. Very warm conditions prevailed during May and June. A mean of 12.1°C in May (average 10.4°C) was joint second warmest with 2017 and warmest since 2008. June, 14.8°C (13.1°C), was third warmest and highest since 1976. Scotland's mean temperature was 7.51°C (7.46°C), 33rd warmest; the previous 12-month period was much warmer (8.24°C). May, 10.7°C (8.9°C), was joint warmest on record with 2008. June, 13.0°C (11.4°C), was joint third warmest, with 2003, and highest since 1970 (13.1°C). Wales' 12 month mean was 9.44°C (9.16°C), 21st warmest, and highest since the previous 12-month period (10.03°C). June set a new record with 15.4°C (13.2°C); the previous warmest was 1940 (15.0°C). Northern Ireland with 8.9°C was average. Despite this, May with 11.8°C (10.2°C), was joint third warmest, shared with 1960. June, 14.9°C (12.8°C), set a new record, replacing the previous highest in 1970 (14.6°C). England's 12-month mean was 10°C (9.66°C) and 18th warmest. The previous 12-month period was much warmer (10.63°C). May 2018, with 13.0°C (11.3°C), is a record, a position shared with 2008 and 1992. June, 15.8°C (14.1°C) was 4th warmest, June 2017 was warmer (15.9°C).

The UK rainfall total, over the 12 months (July 2017–June 2018), was 1,126.9mm, slightly drier than average (1,128.6mm); 2016–17 was much drier (961.4mm). Scotland totalled 1,468.6mm (1523.1mm), the driest since 2016–17 (1,371.7mm). The summer (2017) was 5th wettest, 410.8mm (290.2mm), and wettest since 2009 (427.8mm). Wales, 1,455.3 (1,417.2mm), was the wettest since 2015–16 (1,765.8mm). June 2018 was 4th driest (19mm) and lowest since 1942 (15.1mm); the average is 82.7 mm. The 12-month totals for Northern Ireland and England were above average with 1,247.0mm (1,137.2mm) and 854.8mm (843.3mm) respectively. June 2018 was England's 3rd driest, 15mm (61.1mm), and driest since 1925 (4.3mm).

UK sunshine (July 2017–June 2018) totalled 1,470.1 hours, 8th sunniest, and highest since 2014–15 (1,542.5 hours); the average is 1,368.6 hours. February (95.6 hours) and June (239.9 hours) were 2nd and 5th highest respectively and May (246 hours) set a new record replacing the previous highest set in 1989 (241.7 hours). Similar rankings were recorded regionally and a new record for May of 230.8 hours (177 hours) was set in Scotland; the previous highest was in 2000 (229.3 hours). The 12-month totals for the four UK regions were Scotland 1,326.5 hours (1,170.5 hours), its 3rd sunniest, and highest since 1955–56 (1,400.3 hours). Both Wales, 1,447 hours (1,384.5 hours) and Northern Ireland, 1,370 hours (1,228.2 hours), were sunniest since 2014–15. England totalled 1,569.5 hours (1,500 hours), the previous 12-month period was sunnier, 1,590.4 hours.

NEWSWORTHY EVENTS

July was mostly unsettled with short-lived periods of warm settled weather which were confined mainly to south-east England. At times, thunderstorms brought travel disruption and property damage to parts of the country.

August was mostly cool and unsettled with intense thundery showers or longer periods of rain causing localised flooding

and some transport disruption. A brief respite to these conditions prevailed with fine weather during the 17th–23rd and especially the 27th–29th when it was hot in the south-east.

September was unsettled with frequent Atlantic low pressure systems bringing periods of rain and strong winds. The autumn's first named storm, Aileen, affected the country over the 12th–13th leading to localised flooding, power outages and some transport disruption.

After an unsettled start, October was predominantly mild. Ex-hurricane Ophelia brought exceptionally warm conditions on the 16th along with strong winds causing power and travel disruption to the Republic of Ireland and western parts of the UK. Storm Brian brought strong winds on the 21st, however travel disruption was confined mainly to Wales and coastal areas of south-west England.

November was changeable with periods of locally heavy rainfall, particularly over the period 20th–23rd, causing travel disruption. Icy conditions during the 25th–26th caused difficult driving for parts of north Wales and delays on some South Western railway services. North Yorkshire on the 28th and Aberdeenshire on the 29th were affected by snow.

Strong winds associated with Storm Caroline caused power outages and travel disruption in north Scotland and Northern Ireland on 7 December. Snowfall on the 10th gave rise to travel disruption and power cuts across parts of Wales and the West Midlands. Over the next eight days further disruption from snow occurred across central England, Wales and Scotland. It was unsettled between Christmas and New Year with further snowfall and strong winds with Storm Dylan affecting south-west England and Northern Ireland, especially over the 30th–31st.

January began very windy with Storm Eleanor bringing widespread travel disruption and power cuts across the UK over the 2nd–3rd. Between the 16th–22nd the weather was wintry in nature with snowfall first affecting Scotland, Northern Ireland and northern England and later Wales and southern England. Heavy rain and strong winds on the 24th caused some disruption.

February began cold and icy, causing difficult driving across parts of the country. Mild conditions set in during the second and third week. Near month's end a bitterly cold easterly wind, named 'The Beast from the East' by the media, set in across the country. Snowfall across parts of eastern England and Scotland caused travel disruption and power cuts occurred in Aberdeenshire.

Bitterly cold easterly winds continued into March bringing freezing conditions across the UK with daytime temperatures remaining sub-freezing for a time. Snowfall caused difficulties for many parts of the country and atrocious road conditions. Some communities in the north-west were cut off for days. After a brief interlude of mild weather a second spell of cold weather occurred (17th–18th), again bringing disruption for parts of the country, although not as severe as the beginning of the month.

The cold weather of March extended into early April (5th) after which the cold abated. Heavy rain over the 1st–2nd caused some rivers in northern England to flood. Snowfall in the north made some roads impassable. More flooding occurred in parts of the country on the 9th and 10th causing some disruption to travel. Windy weather at the end of the month caused delays for channel crossings and flights in the south-east.

May began very unsettled with heavy rain causing some travel disruption for parts of England and Wales. However, a period of warm weather soon followed giving rise to the warmest early May Bank Holiday on record. Towards the end of the month thunderstorms and torrential downpours caused disruption in parts of England, in particularly the Midlands, due to flash flooding and lightning strikes.

June's weather was mostly mixed with heavy showers giving rise to some localised flooding early in the month. An active low pressure system, named storm Hector, brought heavy rain and strong winds over the 13th–14th. Travel disruption and power outages were confined to Northern Ireland, Scotland and north-west England. Hot weather across the UK later in the month gave rise to depleted rivers, buckling of railway track and the threat to parched grasslands by fire.

THE YEAR 2017

The UK's mean air temperature for 2017 was 9.56°C, 5th warmest, and the warmest year since 2014, the current record (9.91°C). Winter 2016–17, 5°C (average 3.83°C), was 9th warmest and highest since 2016 (5.49°C). Spring, 9.15°C (7.79°C), was a joint record, shared with 2011. Summer, 14.72°C (average 14.41°C), 2016's was warmer (14.91°C). Autumn, 9.88°C (9.48°C), the warmest since 2015 (10.02°C). Regionally, spring was England's joint warmest on record, 10.05°C (8.56°C), shared with 2011. The UK's year as a whole was fourth warmest, 10.43°C, exceeded by 2006 (10.61°C), 2011 (10.58°C), and 2014 (10.78°C). Wales' spring was record breaking, 9.39°C (8.04°C), its previous record was 2011 (9.34°C). The annual mean temperature was 9.93°C, joint third warmest, shared with 2011. Scotland had its joint 8th warmest year, 8.04°C, shared with 1997. Spring and winter ranked fourth warmest with 7.59°C (6.42°C), shared with 2007, and 4.42°C (2.84°C) respectively. Northern Ireland's mean spring temperature of 9.17°C (7.91°C) was a record, beating the previous high set in 1945 (9.13°C). The annual mean temperature was joint 7th warmest, 9.47°C, shared with 1945.

UK rainfall totalled 1,124.4mm, very close to average. Winter 2016–17, 248.2mm (326.7mm), was the driest since 2006 (206.5mm). Spring, 189.0mm (231.3mm), the driest since 2011 (188.2mm). Regionally, Scotland, 1,534.2mm (average 1,516.7mm), Wales 1,415.8mm (1,414.5mm), Northern Ireland, 1,149.7mm (1,135.6mm) and England 826.6mm (842.1mm) all had their wettest year since 2015. Scotland had its second wettest June, 153.3mm (83.7mm), the wettest since 1938 (155mm).

UK Sunshine totalled 1374 hours. An average or close to average figure was recorded for all UK regions. Scotland, 1.183.5 hours, 2016 was sunnier (1,229.0 hours). January, 46.7 hours (average 32.9 hours), was fourth sunniest, the highest since 2001 (52.3 hours). March, 118.8 hours (average 92.5 hours), May, 214.2 hours (177 hours) and November, 55.9 hours (44.7 hours), were all 9th sunniest for their respective months. June, 106.9 hours (149.2 hours), was the second dullest on record and lowest since 1966 (99 hours). Wales, 1,333.4 hours, the dullest since 2012 (1,323 hours).

February, 43.4 hours (69.9 hours) was 6th dullest and lowest since 1980 (38.1 hours). Northern Ireland totalled 1,233.1 hours, 2016 was sunnier (1,254.5 hours). February, 46.2 hours (average 65.1 hours). April, 103.9 hours (143.6 hours). June, 115.5 hours (148.9 hours) and October, 54.1 hours (85.2 hours) were all within the 12 dullest months on record, for their respective months. May was third sunniest, 253.5 hours (180.3 hours), and highest since 1975 (257.5 hours). England totalled 1,509.8 hours; 2016 was sunnier with 1,554.2 hours. November and December were 7th and 12th sunniest respectively with 83.7 hours (average 64.8 hours) and 56.0 hours (47.7 hours).

UK TEMPERATURE

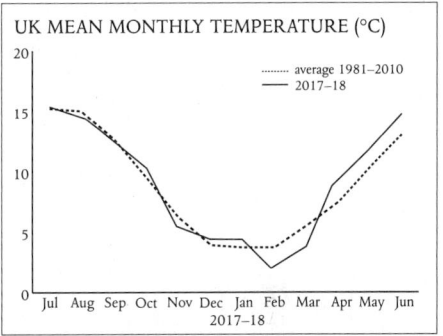

UK MEAN MONTHLY TEMPERATURE (°C)

····· average 1981–2010
—— 2017–18

Jul Aug Sep Oct Nov Dec Jan Feb Mar Apr May Jun
2017–18

The mean summer 2017 temperature was 14.72°C (normal is 14.41°C). The highest site-specific air maximum temperature over the season was 34.5°C at Heathrow (Greater London) on the 21st June. The lowest air minimum was −2.3°C recorded at Altnaharra (Sutherland) on the 8th June.

Autumn 2017, 9.88°C (9.48°C). The highest, site-specific daytime maximum temperature over the season was 24.0°C, recorded at Hawarden Airport (Flintshire) on 4 September. The lowest air minimum temperature of −6.9°C was recorded at Bewcastle (Cumbria) on 30 November.

Winter 2017–18, 3.56°C (3.83°C), the coldest since 2013 (3.34°C). The highest, site-specific maximum daytime temperature was 15.2°C, recorded at Cassley (Sutherland) on the 18th December. The lowest night time air minimum was −13.7°C, recorded on 21 January at Altnaharra and Kinbrace (Sutherland).

Spring 2018, 8.10°C (7.79°C). Spring 2017 was much warmer (9.15°C). The highest site-specific maximum daytime temperature over the season was 29.1°C at London's St James's Park on 19th April. The lowest night time minimum was −10.7°C on 1st March at Cawdor Castle (Nairnshire).

June's mean temperature was 14.8°C, 1.7 degrees above average. The highest site-specific air maximum was 33.0°C recorded at Porthmadog (Gwynedd) on the 28th. The lowest night time air minimum was −1.0°C at Altnaharra (Sutherland) on 6th.

WEATHER STATISTICS 2017

	Mean Temp. °C	Diff. from normal °C*	Rainfall mm	Percentage of normal*	Sunshine hours	Percentage of normal*
England	10.4	+0.7	826.6	98%	1,509.8	101%
Wales	9.9	+0.8	1,415.8	100%	1,333.4	96%
Scotland	8.0	+0.6	1,534.2	101%	1,183.5	101%
Northern Ireland	9.5	+0.5	1,149.7	101%	1,233.1	100%
United Kingdom	9.6	+0.7	1,124.4	100%	1,374.0	100%

* The standard reference period ('normal') for 2011–20 is the average for the 30-year period 1981–2010

UK RAINFALL

Summer 2017 rainfall averaged 315.1mm (normal, 233.7mm), the 13th wettest on record and wettest since 2012 (379.2mm). The highest 24-hour total at a single location (ending at 0900 GMT) was 126.7mm at Bogmuchalls (Banffshire) on 7 June.

Autumn 2017 averaged 328.5mm (normal, 336.5 mm). 2016 was drier (249.2mm). The highest 24-hour total at a single location was 154.4mm at Ennerdale, Black Sail (Cumbria) on the 11 October.

Winter 2017–18 averaged 319.3mm (326.7mm); the previous winter was much drier (248.2mm). The highest 24-hour total at a single location was 212.6mm at Ennerdale, Black Sail (Cumbria) on 25 December.

Spring 2018 averaged 239.2mm (231.3mm), the wettest since 2015 (251.7mm). The highest 24-hour site-specific total for the season, ending at 0900 GMT on 28 May, was 81mm at Winterbourne (W. Midlands).

June's mean UK total was 35.4mm, 50 per cent of normal, and driest since 1995 (29mm). The highest site-specific total over 24 hours, ending on 14th, was 44.6mm at Achnagart (Ross & Cromarty).

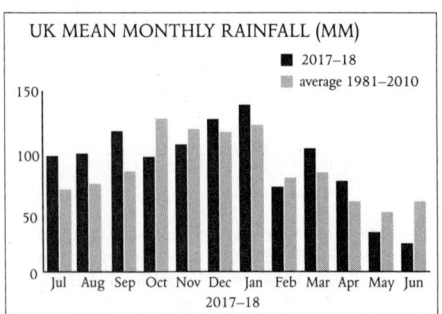

UK MEAN MONTHLY RAINFALL (MM)

UK SUNSHINE

Summer 2017 sunshine totalled 479.9 hours (normal, 505.6 hours), 2016 was duller (474.7 hours).

Autumn 2017, 252.7 hours (273.9 hours), the dullest since 2001 (252.1 hours).

Winter 2017–18, 189.6 hours (155.8 hours) and sunniest since the winter 2014–15 (191.6 hours).

Spring 2018, 463.6 hours (435.7 hours). Spring 2017 was sunnier (486.0 hours).

June's sunshine total amounted to 239.9 hours, the 5th sunniest, and highest since 1975 (245.2 hours).

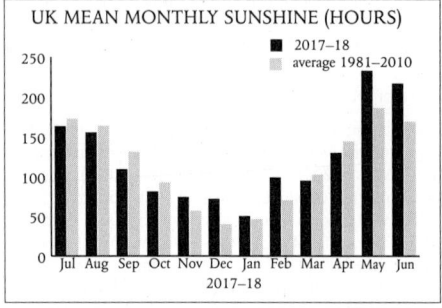

UK MEAN MONTHLY SUNSHINE (HOURS)

UK WEATHER STATIONS

Given below are temperature, rainfall and sunshine at selected climatological stations for July 2017 to June 2018.

Ht height of station above mean sea-level
T. mean monthly air temperature

Rain total monthly rainfall
Sun total monthly sunshine duration

	Ht	July 2017 Temp.	Rain	Sun	August 2017 Temp.	Rain	Sun	September 2017 Temp.	Rain	Sun	October 2017 Temp.	Rain	Sun
	m	°C	mm	hrs	°C	mm	hrs	°C	mm	hrs	°C	mm	hrs
Stornoway	15	13.4	75	166	13.8	115	122	12.4	111	97	10.4	155	57
Nairn	23	14.5	59	152	14.4	91	139	12.6	93	113	11.0	67	84
Leuchars	10	14.7	50	165	14.6	72	165	12.8	64	116	11.5	41	81
Paisley	32	15.1	76	150	14.7	105	134	12.9	105	100	11.1	149	61
Armagh	62	15.5	83	153	15.1	78	131	13.1	92	116	11.7	67	59
Bradford	34	15.9	74	167	15.2	60	170	13.1	97	104	12.0	72	75
Valley	10	15.8	79	195	15.7	60	175	14.1	86	113	13.1	66	61
Shawbury	72	16.9	68	160	15.5	63	130	13.2	114	96	12.2	42	68
Ross-on-Wye	67	17.7	63	203	15.9	50	185	14.0	46	114	13.0	39	92
Lowestoft	18	17.7	73	224	17.2	42	228	14.5	62	136	13.3	24	91
Heathrow	25	19.4	90	178	17.8	59	175	15.1	59	120	13.7	9	85
Hurn	10	17.6	90	200	16.2	52	183	13.8	94	112	12.7	42	81
Camborne	87	16.2	105	136	15.5	70	163	14.0	131	119	13.3	58	69
Eastbourne	7	18.6	78	174	17.5	59	208	15.2	85	65	13.3	20	83
Aberporth	133	15.5	86	165	14.8	99	143	13.5	145	90	12.6	30	58
Waddington	68	17.0	63	169	16.3	54	179	13.9	78	107	12.6	13	80

	Ht	November 2017 Temp.	Rain	Sun	December 2017 Temp.	Rain	Sun	January 2018 Temp.	Rain	Sun	February 2018 Temp.	Rain	Sun
	m	°C	mm	hrs	°C	mm	hrs	°C	mm	hrs	°C	mm	hrs
Stornoway	15	5.5	184	43	4.9	138	17	4.1	167	33	3.7	80	89
Nairn	23	4.9	95	55	4.2	56	27	2.6	49	67	2.7	26	124
Leuchars	10	5.1	38	90	3.7	30	58	3.2	66	60	2.7	26	95
Paisley	32	5.4	91	73	4.1	106	55	3.7	176	39	3.3	56	91
Armagh	62	6.7	63	65	5.3	78	32	4.0	135	50	3.2	52	94
Bradford	34	6.5	40	79	4.5	53	46	4.7	96	45	2.7	37	75
Valley	10	8.7	104	49	6.8	79	35	6.0	89	60	4.5	57	115
Shawbury	72	6.7	51	69	4.5	84	55	5.0	67	56	2.9	28	84
Ross-on-Wye	67	7.2	37	90	5.2	99	60	5.9	70	60	3.8	20	110
Lowestoft	18	7.4	50	90	5.0	106	73	5.6	46	58	3.2	63	108
Heathrow	25	7.8	34	67	5.8	81	44	6.8	58	47	3.7	25	92
Hurn	10	7.0	74	99	5.7	105	59	6.6	71	64	3.0	36	128
Camborne	87	9.6	66	61	8.2	154	35	8.0	176	35	5.0	81	106
Eastbourne	7	8.6	35	72	6.2	122	51	7.3	90	53	3.9	56	138
Aberporth	133	8.7	130	39	6.8	123	32	6.1	116	54	3.8	49	91
Waddington	68	6.9	33	81	4.6	59	72	5.1	55	57	2.5	32	81

	Ht	March 2018 Temp.	Rain	Sun	April 2018 Temp.	Rain	Sun	May 2018 Temp.	Rain	Sun	June 2018 Temp.	Rain	Sun
	m	°C	mm	hrs	°C	mm	hrs	°C	mm	hrs	°C	mm	hrs
Stornoway	15	4.6	72	126	7.9	70	186	10.5	47	203	12.9	38	173
Nairn	23	3.5	39	114	7.9	31	192	11.9	28	241	14.0	23	246
Leuchars	10	3.8	97	89	7.5	48	169	11.8	25	242	13.6	31	207
Paisley	32	4.3	94	87	8.6	66	116	12.9	25	233	15.7	61	252
Armagh	62	4.4	80	94	8.7	70	126	12.9	33	220	15.8	28	250
Bradford	34	4.0	94	76	9.1	83	114	13.2	23	255	15.7	6	234
Valley	10	5.4	88	108	9.4	65	141	12.5	29	232	16.0	11	292
Shawbury	72	4.5	88	60	9.4	71	107	12.8	48	247	16.0	32	247
Ross-on-Wye	67	5.2	141	82	10.4	73	114	13.8	80	243	17.3	9	270
Lowestoft	18	5.2	63	80	10.3	58	148	12.7	13	286	15.5	15	250
Heathrow	25	6.4	85	70	11.7	65	129	15.3	58	248	18.7	0	235
Hurn	10	5.8	124	74	10.6	75	125	13.5	40	266	17.1	0	269
Camborne	87	6.2	148	114	10.0	85	147	12.2	43	215	16.3	9	215
Eastbourne	7	6.2	81	96	10.9	73	172	14.3	38	291	16.4	4	291
Aberporth	133	5.0	91	101	9.3	71	152	11.7	33	219	15.8	10	270
Waddington	68	4.8	74	78	9.8	80	99	13.4	61	256	16.1	34	216

METEOROLOGICAL OBSERVATIONS IN LONDON (St James's Park Weather Station)

Minimum temperature is the lowest air temperature recorded over a 24-hour period ending at 9am on the day indicated; maximum temperature is the highest air temperature recorded over a 24-hour period beginning at 9am on the day indicated. Daily rainfall totals are for 24-hour periods commencing at 9am on the day indicated and include any solid precipitation, such as snow and hail, which is melted and measured in the same way as rainfall. All times are GMT. St James's Park weather station is 5 metres above mean sea-level.

July 2017

Day	Maximum Temperature (°C)	Minimum Temperature (°C)	Daily Total Rainfall (mm)
1	22.0	14.9	0.0
2	23.9	15.4	0.0
3	24.5	15.2	0.0
4	23.9	13.6	0.0
5	28.6	15.7	0.0
6	30.7	18.5	0.0
7	29.4	18.4	0.0
8	27.0	18.4	0.0
9	27.7	17.8	0.0
10	26.5	16.2	0.0
11	19.7	15.3	37.4
12	22.0	14.5	0.0
13	22.2	12.7	0.0
14	21.4	14.5	0.0
15	22.2	15.6	0.0
16	25.2	16.9	0.0
17	26.5	15.3	0.0
18	26.1	17.4	5.4
19	23.1	18.4	1.8
20	21.0	17.2	0.4
21	22.5	13.6	12.4
22	19.4	13.7	6.8
23	20.5	11.3	2.0
24	18.3	13.7	0.0
25	23.0	14.5	0.0
26	22.2	14.5	0.8
27	21.0	14.4	6.6
28	21.5	13.7	0.2
29	20.6	15.9	28.6
30	20.9	14.7	0.0
31	22.8	13.5	0.0

August 2017

Day	Maximum Temperature (°C)	Minimum Temperature (°C)	Daily Total Rainfall (mm)
1	22.8	12.8	0.0
2	19.0	15.2	7.8
3	21.7	15.6	0.0
4	22.2	15.4	0.0
5	20.8	14.5	1.0
6	22.4	10.7	0.0
7	20.9	13.6	0.0
8	18.4	14.7	2.4
9	15.9	13.4	33.2
10	20.8	12.7	0.0
11	22.2	10.5	0.0
12	22.1	16.6	0.0
13	22.8	13.1	0.0
14	24.5	12.1	0.0
15	24.0	15.0	0.0
16	22.8	11.8	3.0
17	24.6	15.6	6.8
18	20.5	15.0	2.4
19	20.5	13.1	0.0
20	21.2	10.5	4.6
21	19.3	14.0	0.0
22	23.0	15.7	0.2
23	22.1	16.9	0.0
24	21.6	13.2	0.0
25	24.2	12.2	0.0
26	25.5	14.3	0.0
27	26.4	16.4	0.0
28	28.0	15.4	0.0
29	25.6	16.9	0.6
30	15.7	13.5	6.0
31	20.9	9.2	0.0

September 2017

Day	Maximum Temperature (°C)	Minimum Temperature (°C)	Daily Total Rainfall (mm)
1	22.0	10.0	0.0
2	21.3	11.0	0.0
3	18.2	12.1	5.2
4	22.4	13.8	0.0
5	20.4	16.6	1.0
6	18.9	11.6	0.0
7	19.8	11.7	2.8
8	18.7	14.5	3.8
9	18.9	10.6	0.2
10	17.2	9.1	0.8
11	19.2	11.6	2.4
12	19.3	10.4	4.8
13	18.4	12.8	1.4
14	18.6	8.5	0.0
15	16.8	7.1	0.2
16	15.9	7.7	0.6
17	17.5	9.8	0.2
18	17.8	10.7	3.8
19	16.0	9.2	0.0
20	17.4	9.3	0.0
21	18.0	13.9	1.0
22	19.0	7.5	0.0
23	19.3	11.4	0.0
24	22.6	12.1	1.6
25	18.8	15.2	0.0
26	21.4	14.6	0.0
27	21.5	13.5	16.8
28	20.5	15.5	3.2
29	19.7	14.2	1.2
30	18.0	11.3	1.8

October 2017

Day	Maximum Temperature (°C)	Minimum Temperature (°C)	Daily Total Rainfall (mm)
1	18.1	13.6	0.2
2	18.1	14.1	0.0
3	16.7	9.0	0.0
4	16.3	9.5	1.4
5	18.0	12.0	0.0
6	16.1	7.6	0.0
7	17.5	10.3	0.8
8	18.0	9.2	0.0
9	18.0	9.7	0.2
10	16.6	11.2	0.0
11	17.1	13.8	1.2
12	18.1	9.6	0.0
13	19.0	11.5	0.0
14	20.1	15.8	0.0
15	20.5	11.8	0.0
16	22.9	13.3	0.0
17	14.8	11.2	0.4
18	15.9	10.9	5.8
19	17.4	12.5	2.4
20	15.4	12.4	2.2
21	16.3	12.4	0.0
22	14.4	9.8	0.0
23	16.9	9.8	0.0
24	18.8	13.3	0.0
25	19.4	14.4	0.0
26	15.8	9.7	1.2
27	15.3	9.4	0.0
28	16.0	5.5	0.2
29	14.0	7.6	0.0
30	12.5	4.6	0.0
31	13.2	6.2	0.0

November 2017

Day	Maximum Temperature (°C)	Minimum Temperature (°C)	Daily Total Rainfall (mm)
1	16.0	8.5	0.0
2	12.8	4.6	0.0
3	15.9	7.0	3.4
4	13.8	9.5	2.4
5	10.8	4.1	0.0
6	11.2	0.8	0.2
7	12.1	3.4	4.6
8	10.3	6.1	0.0
9	13.3	2.2	0.6
10	13.3	7.6	14.2
11	9.8	7.4	2.8
12	8.8	6.6	0.0
13	8.8	3.3	0.2
14	11.7	3.7	0.2
15	11.8	8.8	0.0
16	14.0	9.4	0.2
17	10.7	1.6	0.0
18	9.0	3.2	2.2
19	10.5	2.0	1.0
20	12.9	4.3	0.4
21	14.4	10.4	0.0
22	15.9	12.4	2.6
23	11.6	9.7	0.0
24	8.5	6.2	0.0
25	7.3	0.5	0.0
26	9.9	1.7	3.4
27	10.4	3.0	0.2
28	7.9	2.7	0.0
29	6.6	2.6	0.0
30	4.2	-0.4	0.0

December 2017

Day	Maximum Temperature (°C)	Minimum Temperature (°C)	Daily Rainfall (mm)
1	7.0	0.8	0.0
2	7.8	3.2	0.6
3	10.4	3.9	0.4
4	10.1	3.3	0.0
5	9.7	6.3	0.0
6	11.6	8.1	0.2
7	12.2	9.0	2.4
8	5.3	2.8	0.0
9	4.2	-1.1	11.6
10	3.4	-0.5	12.4
11	3.8	1.0	7.4
12	8.3	-2.5	3.6
13	9.5	-1.6	5.6
14	6.8	3.4	1.4
15	6.3	1.9	0.0
16	5.4	-0.3	1.2
17	9.5	-0.2	3.2
18	8.6	2.2	0.0
19	8.3	0.2	0.4
20	10.7	1.4	0.2
21	12.1	8.2	0.6
22	12.9	9.5	0.4
23	9.7	9.5	0.0
24	11.0	8.4	0.4
25	11.0	8.6	5.2
26	8.2	3.6	9.0
27	4.1	2.8	3.0
28	6.8	-0.3	4.0
29	13.0	-1.0	7.8
30	14.2	4.9	4.2
31	11.6	9.4	2.2

January 2018

Day	Maximum Temperature (°C)	Minimum Temperature (°C)	Daily Total Rainfall (mm)
1	8.3	6.0	0.0
2	12.9	4.0	9.6
3	10.9	5.6	8.2
4	13.0	6.6	2.4
5	9.9	5.2	0.0
6	6.2	2.3	0.0
7	6.2	2.4	0.0
8	5.4	2.5	0.0
9	9.2	4.5	0.2
10	9.5	4.9	0.2
11	8.0	5.4	2.0
12	7.6	6.5	0.0
13	8.1	5.6	0.0
14	8.5	4.5	2.4
15	11.4	4.9	3.4
16	8.0	5.7	0.0
17	12.2	2.6	1.4
18	9.2	4.2	0.0
19	7.0	1.4	0.8
20	4.6	1.9	4.8
21	10.8	1.3	12.0
22	10.6	1.4	0.2
23	13.7	7.9	0.0
24	13.4	9.7	12.4
25	10.9	6.5	0.0
26	8.5	2.9	0.0
27	11.5	4.0	0.8
28	13.5	5.8	0.0
29	12.4	10.7	0.2
30	10.5	0.8	1.8
31	9.3	1.6	1.6

February 2018

Day	Maximum Temperature (°C)	Minimum Temperature (°C)	Daily Total Rainfall (mm)
1	8.0	2.9	0.8
2	7.5	3.8	0.2
3	4.6	3.7	3.6
4	5.7	3.1	0.0
5	4.8	1.9	0.0
6	4.3	1.7	0.0
7	5.8	0.9	0.0
8	7.8	-2.0	6.0
9	6.4	0.9	0.2
10	10.5	-1.2	3.2
11	7.8	2.9	0.0
12	7.6	-0.4	0.0
13	6.1	1.1	2.4
14	8.9	-0.7	5.6
15	10.4	2.0	0.4
16	10.0	0.6	0.0
17	11.3	2.3	0.0
18	11.5	2.7	0.8
19	11.5	5.0	1.4
20	9.8	7.4	0.4
21	7.2	3.1	0.0
22	6.2	2.3	0.0
23	4.2	0.6	0.0
24	6.1	0.3	0.0
25	5.1	0.1	1.0
26	2.2	-1.2	0.4
27	1.1	-2.6	1.4
28	-0.8	-4.7	3.0

March 2018

Day	Maximum Temperature (° C)	Minimum Temperature (° C)	Daily Total Rainfall (mm)
1	0.8	-4.3	0.4
2	1.9	-3.4	0.6
3	6.6	-1.2	1.2
4	9.0	1.8	0.2
5	11.2	4.5	0.4
6	10.0	5.9	2.8
7	11.7	4.8	2.0
8	10.0	4.7	0.0
9	11.6	2.8	7.0
10	14.3	6.4	0.4
11	11.3	7.2	3.8
12	11.5	8.3	3.4
13	11.1	6.1	0.0
14	14.0	4.1	5.2
15	13.3	8.0	0.2
16	14.4	7.8	0.4
17	1.2	0.8	1.0
18	1.5	-0.6	0.4
19	5.5	-0.9	0.2
20	9.1	0.6	0.0
21	11.3	0.2	0.0
22	12.2	4.5	0.0
23	13.4	6.7	1.6
24	10.1	6.8	0.0
25	12.2	7.3	0.0
26	12.5	6.1	4.6
27	15.3	5.4	6.4
28	9.3	4.8	6.8
29	10.1	2.1	3.0
30	8.2	5.0	11.6
31	9.7	4.6	0.8

April 2018

Day	Maximum Temperature (° C)	Minimum Temperature (° C)	Daily Total Rainfall (mm)
1	9.2	4.7	11.2
2	11.8	4.0	3.6
3	14.4	9.2	0.4
4	12.6	8.3	0.6
5	13.3	5.0	0.0
6	17.3	5.5	0.0
7	17.5	9.2	1.2
8	11.8	9.7	7.0
9	9.8	8.5	9.6
10	14.4	8.5	4.4
11	10.5	7.4	0.0
12	11.1	7.4	0.0
13	13.0	6.7	0.0
14	19.3	8.0	0.0
15	15.6	9.8	0.2
16	16.2	8.9	0.0
17	19.9	10.5	0.0
18	25.3	11.5	0.0
19	29.1	11.7	0.0
20	26.5	12.6	0.0
21	24.1	12.0	4.2
22	24.2	13.1	0.0
23	16.3	8.2	0.0
24	18.0	11.7	0.2
25	15.7	8.5	0.6
26	15.9	6.9	2.0
27	12.1	7.5	8.0
28	9.6	8.6	0.2
29	8.5	7.2	5.8
30	10.7	5.5	3.0

May 2018

Day	Maximum Temperature (° C)	Minimum Temperature (° C)	Daily Total Rainfall (mm)
1	14.8	2.9	0.4
2	15.3	8.8	4.8
3	18.0	4.2	0.0
4	21.0	9.5	0.0
5	22.8	8.5	0.0
6	25.0	10.2	0.0
7	28.0	11.3	0.0
8	26.7	11.5	0.0
9	21.4	9.4	2.0
10	17.9	10.3	0.0
11	18.0	8.0	0.0
12	14.9	11.2	6.2
13	18.3	8.5	0.0
14	20.1	10.6	0.0
15	23.2	10.7	0.0
16	15.1	12.2	0.0
17	17.8	7.0	0.0
18	18.7	6.6	0.4
19	21.6	7.5	0.0
20	21.0	8.2	0.0
21	23.0	9.4	0.0
22	22.8	12.5	0.0
23	19.3	11.0	2.4
24	21.5	11.0	0.0
25	20.0	12.8	0.0
26	26.4	15.2	15.2
27	27.6	15.3	0.0
28	25.8	15.6	5.2
29	17.7	14.2	21.2
30	21.4	13.2	0.0
31	23.0	14.5	0.0

June 2018

Day	Maximum Temperature (° C)	Minimum Temperature (° C)	Daily Total Rainfall (mm)
1	22.7	16.2	0.0
2	24.2	15.0	0.0
3	27.1	13.2	0.0
4	19.1	15.4	0.0
5	18.6	12.2	0.0
6	23.2	9.5	0.0
7	21.3	13.0	0.0
8	22.9	14.1	0.0
9	22.7	13.0	0.0
10	23.2	14.6	0.0
11	24.8	12.0	0.0
12	18.5	11.9	0.0
13	21.9	9.3	0.2
14	23.6	14.3	0.0
15	23.8	12.7	0.0
16	19.7	14.5	0.2
17	19.6	13.4	0.2
18	26.0	15.0	0.0
19	25.1	17.6	0.0
20	25.5	15.3	0.0
21	21.1	11.9	0.0
22	22.9	10.2	0.0
23	24.5	11.7	0.0
24	26.0	14.3	0.0
25	30.0	13.4	0.0
26	27.5	14.4	0.0
27	26.1	13.5	0.0
28	28.0	12.9	0.0
29	28.5	13.3	0.0
30	27.9	13.5	0.0

TIME AND SPACE

ASTRONOMY

The following pages give astronomical data for each month of the year 2019. There are four pages of data for each month. All data are given for 0h Greenwich Mean Time (GMT), ie at midnight at the beginning of the day named. This applies also to data for the months when British Summer Time is in operation (for dates, *see* below).

The astronomical data are given in a form suitable for observation with the naked eye or with a small telescope. These data do not attempt to replace the *Astronomical Almanac* for professional astronomers. Positions are given for the equinox of J2000.0 to match the coordinates used in most current atlases.

A fuller explanation of how to use the astronomical data is given on pages 1123–1125.

CALENDAR FOR EACH MONTH

The calendar for each month comprises dates of general interest plus the dates of birth or death of well-known people. As 2019 is the quincentenary of Conquistador Hernán Cortés landing in Mexico, the theme for this edition is 'Latin America'. For key religious, civil and legal dates *see* page 9. For details of flag-flying days *see* page 23. For royal birthdays *see* pages 23 and 24–5. For public holidays *see also* pages 10 and 11.

Fuller explanations of the various calendars can be found under Time Measurement and Calendars.

The zodiacal signs through which the Sun is passing each month are illustrated.

JULIAN DATE

The Julian date on 2019 January 0.0 is 2458483.5. To find the Julian date for any other date in 2019 (at 0h GMT), add the day-of-the-year number on the extreme right of the calendar for each month to the Julian date for January 0.0.

BRITISH SUMMER TIME

British Summer Time is the legal time for general purposes during the period in which it is in operation (*see also* page 1128). During this period, clocks are kept one hour ahead of Greenwich Mean Time. The hour of changeover is 01h Greenwich Mean Time. The duration of Summer Time in 2019 is from March 31 01h GMT to October 27 01h GMT.

SEASONS

The seasons are defined astronomically as follows:

Spring from the vernal equinox to the summer solstice
Summer from the summer solstice to the autumnal equinox
Autumn from the autumnal equinox to the winter solstice
Winter from the winter solstice to the vernal equinox

The time when seasons start in 2019 are:

Northern Hemisphere
Vernal Equinox	March 20d 21h 58m GMT
Summer Solstice	June 21d 15h 54m GMT
Autumnal Equinox	September 23d 07h 50m GMT
Winter Solstice	December 22d 04h 19m GMT

Southern Hemisphere
Autumnal Equinox	March 20d 21h 58m GMT
Winter Solstice	June 21d 15h 54m GMT
Vernal Equinox	September 23d 07h 50m GMT
Summer Solstice	December 22d 04h 19m GMT

The longest day of the year, measured from sunrise to sunset, is at the summer solstice. The longest day in the UK will fall on 21 June in 2019.

The shortest day of the year, measured from sunrise to sunset, is at the winter solstice. The shortest day in the UK will fall on 22 December in 2019.

The equinox is the point at which day and night are of equal length all over the world.

In popular parlance, the seasons in the northern hemisphere comprise the following months:

Spring	March, April, May
Summer	June, July, August
Autumn	September, October, November
Winter	December, January, February

The March equinox can fall as early as 19 March but this has not happened since 1796 and it will not happen again until 2044. This equinox in 2007 was on 21 March, however in 2008 it occurred on 20 March and will not revert to 21 March again until 2102.

In 2008 the June solstice occurred on 20 June, the first time since 1897. The June solstice in 1975 was on 22 June, but it will not occur on this date again until 2203.

January 2019

FIRST MONTH, 31 DAYS. *Janus,* god of the portal, facing two ways, past and future

1	*Tuesday*	The building of the Panama canal begins 1880	day 1
2	*Wednesday*	Sila María Calderón becomes the first woman elected Governor of the Commonwealth of Puerto Rico 2001	2
3	*Thursday*	A prison riot in Venezuela breaks out due to ethnic rivalries, killing 106 people 1994	3
4	*Friday*	Martial law is declared in Honduras to stop riots by workers made redundant by United Fruit 1932	4
5	*Saturday*	The Captaincy General of Guatemala agrees to its annexation to Agustín de Iturbide's Mexican Empire 1822	5
6	*Sunday*	The construction of Angostura Bridge, the first across the Orinoco river in Venezuela, is completed 1967	6

7	*Monday*	The US Reagan Administration lifts the five-year-old embargo on arms sales to Guatemala 1983	week 1 day 7
8	*Tuesday*	Five US missionaries are killed by the Huaorani people of Ecuador 1956	8
9	*Wednesday*	On seeing manatees Christopher Columbus describes 'mermaids' as 'not half as beautiful' as depicted 1493	9
10	*Thursday*	Daniel Ortega is inagurated as president of Nicaragua 1985	10
11	*Friday*	Oswald de Andrade, Brazilian writer and one of the founders of Brazil's Modernist movement *b.* 1890	11
12	*Saturday*	Earthquake strikes Haiti, killing over 200,000 people and destroying much of the capital, Port-au-Prince 2010	12
13	*Sunday*	Salvador Novo, Mexican poet, playwright and theatre director *d.* 1974	13

14	*Monday*	Matthias Zurbriggen becomes the first person to climb Aconcagua in Argentina 1897	week 2 day 14
15	*Tuesday*	The Battle of Miraflores ends in a victory over Peru for Chile 1881	15
16	*Wednesday*	Germany offers help to Mexico to take back Arizona, New Mexico and Texas from the USA 1917	16
17	*Thursday*	The Spanish army defeats rebels at the Battle of Calderón Bridge in the Mexican War of Independence 1811	17
18	*Friday*	The foundation of the city of Lima in Peru's central coast by Spanish conquistador Francisco Pizarro 1535	18
19	*Saturday*	Mexican drug cartel leader Joaquín 'El Chapo' Guzmán escapes from a maximum security prison 2001	19
20	*Sunday*	The Peru-Bolivian Confederation (1836–9) collapses following defeat at the Battle of Yungay 1839	20

21	*Monday*	Indiginous peoples lead a rebellion in Ecuador, demanding the resignation of President Mahuad 2000	week 3 day 21
22	*Tuesday*	Evo Morales assumes the presidency in Bolivia, becoming the country's first leader of indigenous descent 2006	22
23	*Wednesday*	A far-left guerrilla group led by Enrique Gorriarán Merlo seize army barracks outside Buenos Aires 1989	23
24	*Thursday*	Brazilian footballer Leonidas da Silva, who popularised the overhead bicycle kick technique *d.* 2004	24
25	*Friday*	The city of Sao Paulo in Brazil is founded with the opening of a Jesuit church and school 1554	25
26	*Saturday*	Mexican boxer Salvador Sánchez, WBC featherweight champion (1980–2) *b.* 1959	26
27	*Sunday*	Peruvian ambassador to Japan informs the US of a planned Japanese attack on Pearl Harbour 1941	27

28	*Monday*	The first train embarks from the Atlantic to the Pacific Ocean across the Isthmus of Panama 1855	week 4 day 28
29	*Tuesday*	Helio Gracie, co-founder of the martial art of Brazilian jiu-jitsu *d.* 2009	29
30	*Wednesday*	Luc Grimard, Haitian writer, educator and diplomat, who served as the country's consul in Le Havre *b.* 1886	30
31	*Thursday*	Flavio Herrera, Guatemalan writer, whose novels are official reading in schools in the country *d.* 1968	31

ASTRONOMICAL PHENOMENA

d	h	
1	17	Ceres 2° North of the Moon
1	22	Venus 1° South of the Moon
3	5	Earth at Perihelion
5	19	Saturn 0.9° South of the Moon
5	22	Partial Solar Eclipse (East Asia)
6	5	Venus greatest elongation West (47°)
6		Venus brightest morning
8	21	Vesta 2° South of the Moon
13	11	Saturn 2° North of Mercury
17	19	Aldebaran 2° South of the Moon
21	1	Total Lunar Eclipse
22	6	Jupiter 2° South of Venus
29	18	Ceres 2° North of the Moon
31	18	Venus 0.1° South of the Moon

CONSTELLATIONS

The following constellations are near the meridian at

	d	h		d	h
December	1	24	January	16	21
December	16	23	February	1	20
January	1	22	February	15	19

Draco (below the Pole), Ursa Minor (below the Pole), Camelopardalis, Perseus, Auriga, Taurus, Orion, Eridanus and Lepus

THE MOON

Phase, Apsides and Node	d	h	m
● New Moon	6	1	29
◐ First Quarter	14	6	47
○ Full Moon	21	5	17
◑ Last Quarter	27	21	11

	d	h	m
Apogee (406,117 km)	9	4	30
Perigee (357,342 km)	21	20	1

Mean longitude of the ascending node on 1st, 118°

MINIMA OF ALGOL

d	h	d	h	d	h
3	16.7	15	4.0	26	15.3
6	13.5	18	0.8	29	12.1
9	10.4	20	21.6		
12	7.2	23	18.5		

THE SUN Diam. 32.5′

Day	Right Ascension			Dec.	Equation of time		Rise 52°		56°		Transit		Set 52°		56°		Sidereal time			Transit of first point of Aries		
	h	m	s	°	m	s	h	m	h	m	h	m	h	m	h	m	h	m	s	h	m	s
1	18	44	40	−23.0	−3	14	8	08	8	30	12	03	15	59	15	37	6	41	27	17	15	43
2	18	49	05	−23.0	−3	43	8	08	8	30	12	04	16	00	15	38	6	45	23	17	11	47
3	18	53	30	−22.9	−4	11	8	07	8	30	12	04	16	02	15	39	6	49	20	17	07	51
4	18	57	54	−22.8	−4	39	8	07	8	29	12	05	16	03	15	40	6	53	16	17	03	56
5	19	02	18	−22.7	−5	06	8	07	8	29	12	05	16	04	15	42	6	57	13	17	00	00
6	19	06	41	−22.6	−5	33	8	07	8	29	12	06	16	05	15	43	7	01	09	16	56	04
7	19	11	04	−22.4	−5	59	8	06	8	28	12	06	16	06	15	45	7	05	06	16	52	08
8	19	15	27	−22.3	−6	25	8	06	8	27	12	07	16	08	15	46	7	09	02	16	48	12
9	19	19	49	−22.2	−6	51	8	05	8	27	12	07	16	09	15	48	7	12	59	16	44	16
10	19	24	10	−22.0	−7	16	8	05	8	26	12	07	16	11	15	49	7	16	56	16	40	20
11	19	28	31	−21.9	−7	40	8	04	8	25	12	08	16	12	15	51	7	20	52	16	36	24
12	19	32	52	−21.7	−8	04	8	03	8	24	12	08	16	13	15	53	7	24	49	16	32	28
13	19	37	11	−21.6	−8	27	8	03	8	23	12	09	16	15	15	54	7	28	45	16	28	32
14	19	41	30	−21.4	−8	49	8	02	8	22	12	09	16	16	15	56	7	32	42	16	24	36
15	19	45	49	−21.2	−9	11	8	01	8	21	12	09	16	18	15	58	7	36	38	16	20	41
16	19	50	07	−21.0	−9	33	8	00	8	20	12	10	16	20	16	00	7	40	35	16	16	45
17	19	54	24	−20.8	−9	53	7	59	8	19	12	10	16	21	16	02	7	44	31	16	12	49
18	19	58	40	−20.6	−10	13	7	58	8	18	12	10	16	23	16	04	7	48	28	16	08	53
19	20	02	55	−20.4	−10	32	7	57	8	16	12	11	16	24	16	06	7	52	25	16	04	57
20	20	07	10	−20.2	−10	50	7	56	8	15	12	11	16	26	16	07	7	56	21	16	01	01
21	20	11	24	−20.0	−11	08	7	55	8	14	12	11	16	28	16	09	8	00	18	15	57	05
22	20	15	38	−19.8	−11	24	7	54	8	12	12	12	16	29	16	11	8	04	14	15	53	09
23	20	19	50	−19.6	−11	40	7	53	8	11	12	12	16	31	16	13	8	08	11	15	49	13
24	20	24	02	−19.3	−11	56	7	52	8	09	12	12	16	33	16	16	8	12	07	15	45	17
25	20	28	13	−19.1	−12	10	7	50	8	08	12	12	16	35	16	18	8	16	04	15	41	21
26	20	32	24	−18.8	−12	24	7	49	8	06	12	12	16	36	16	20	8	20	00	15	37	26
27	20	36	33	−18.6	−12	37	7	48	8	04	12	13	16	38	16	22	8	23	57	15	33	30
28	20	40	42	−18.3	−12	49	7	46	8	03	12	13	16	40	16	24	8	27	54	15	29	34
29	20	44	50	−18.1	−13	01	7	45	8	01	12	13	16	42	16	26	8	31	50	15	25	38
30	20	48	57	−17.8	−13	11	7	43	7	59	12	13	16	44	16	28	8	35	47	15	21	42
31	20	53	03	−17.5	−13	21	7	42	7	57	12	13	16	46	16	30	8	39	43	15	17	46

DURATION OF TWILIGHT (in minutes)

Latitude	52°	56°	52°	56°	52°	56°	52°	56°
	1 January		11 January		21 January		31 January	
Civil	41	47	40	45	38	43	37	41
Nautical	84	96	82	93	80	90	78	87
Astronomical	125	141	123	138	120	134	117	130

THE NIGHT SKY

Mercury can be seen very low in the south-east the first few mornings of 2019 but is soon lost to view as it heads towards superior conjunction on the 30th. The thin crescent Moon near by on the 4th may aid the search.

Venus (magnitude −4.5) rises four hours before the Sun on the 1st with the Moon in the area both that day and the next. Venus swiftly catches up with Jupiter during the month and they are just over 2° apart on the 22nd. The Moon between the two on the 31st will add to the scene.

Mars (fading from magnitude 0.5 to 0.9) is an evening sky object in Pisces, not setting until the early hours at the beginning of January but by midnight on the 31st.

Jupiter (magnitude −1.8), in Ophiuchus, is rising around three hours before the Sun at the end of January. The Moon is near by on the 3rd and the planet is impressively paired with Venus around the 22nd.

Saturn (magnitude 0.5), in Sagittarius, is at solar conjunction on the 2nd and then moves into the morning sky. It may be spotted fairly low in the south-east during the last week of January.

A partial solar eclipse (magnitude 0.715) on the 6th is visible from NE Asia, Japan, Siberia, and the Aleutians.

A total lunar eclipse on the 21st is visible from the Americas, Europe, the Middle East, Africa, and Arctic regions. It will be seen in its entirety from the UK, in the early morning, from 04:41 to 05:44.

THE MOON

Day	R.A.		Dec	Hor Par	Diam	Sun Co-Long	PA of Br. limb	Ph.	Age	Rise				Transit		Set			
										52°		56°				52°		56°	
	h	m	°	'	'	°	°	%	d	h	m	h	m	h	m	h	m	h	m
1	14	46	−10.7	56.6	30.8	206	111	24	24.0	3	10	3	20	8	21	13	21	13	10
2	15	36	−14.6	56.1	30.6	218	108	15	25.0	4	21	4	36	9	09	13	48	13	33
3	16	27	−17.7	55.6	30.2	230	105	09	26.0	5	30	5	48	9	58	14	20	14	02
4	17	19	−20.0	55.2	30.0	242	101	04	27.0	6	33	6	54	10	47	14	59	14	36
5	18	11	−21.2	54.8	29.8	254	99	01	28.0	7	31	7	53	11	37	15	43	15	20
6	19	03	−21.5	54.5	29.6	266	142	00	29.0	8	20	8	42	12	27	16	35	16	13
7	19	55	−20.8	54.2	29.6	279	259	01	0.5	9	00	9	22	13	15	17	33	17	14
8	20	45	−19.2	54.1	29.4	291	258	03	1.5	9	35	9	52	14	02	18	36	18	19
9	21	34	−16.7	54.0	29.4	303	255	08	2.5	10	02	10	17	14	47	19	40	19	27
10	22	21	−13.6	54.0	29.4	315	252	13	3.5	10	26	10	37	15	31	20	45	20	36
11	23	07	−9.9	54.2	29.6	327	250	20	4.5	10	47	10	54	16	14	21	51	21	46
12	23	52	−5.8	54.5	29.8	340	249	29	5.5	11	06	11	09	16	56	22	58	22	57
13	0	37	−1.5	55.0	30.0	352	248	38	6.5	11	25	11	24	17	39	—		—	
14	1	23	+3.0	55.6	30.4	4	248	47	7.5	11	44	11	39	18	23	0	06	0	09
15	2	10	+7.5	56.4	30.8	16	250	57	8.5	12	05	11	57	19	10	1	16	1	23
16	3	00	+11.8	57.3	31.2	28	252	67	9.5	12	30	12	18	20	00	2	29	2	40
17	3	53	+15.7	58.2	31.8	40	255	77	10.5	13	02	12	44	20	54	3	44	3	59
18	4	50	+18.8	59.2	32.2	52	259	86	11.5	13	40	13	20	21	53	4	59	5	20
19	5	50	+20.8	60.1	32.8	65	265	93	12.5	14	32	14	10	22	54	6	13	6	35
20	6	54	+21.5	60.8	33.2	77	271	98	13.5	15	37	15	15	23	58	7	18	7	40
21	7	58	+20.7	61.2	33.4	89	283	100	14.5	16	54	16	34	—		8	11	8	32
22	9	02	+18.4	61.4	33.4	101	99	99	15.5	18	17	18	03	1	01	8	53	9	10
23	10	04	+14.8	61.1	33.4	113	105	95	16.5	19	42	19	32	2	01	9	28	9	39
24	11	03	+10.3	60.6	33.0	125	108	89	17.5	21	06	21	01	2	57	9	55	10	02
25	11	58	+5.2	59.9	32.6	137	110	80	18.5	22	27	22	26	3	50	10	19	10	22
26	12	52	0.0	59.0	32.2	149	111	70	19.5	23	44	23	49	4	41	10	41	10	39
27	13	43	−5.0	58.1	31.6	162	110	60	20.5	—		—		5	30	11	03	10	57
28	14	34	−9.7	57.3	31.2	174	108	49	21.5	0	59	1	08	6	18	11	26	11	16
29	15	24	−13.7	56.5	30.8	186	106	39	22.5	2	12	2	25	7	06	11	53	11	38
30	16	15	−17.0	55.8	30.4	198	102	29	23.5	3	22	3	39	7	55	12	22	12	05
31	17	07	−19.5	55.2	30.0	210	98	20	24.5	4	27	4	47	8	44	12	59	12	37

MERCURY

Day	R.A.		Dec	Mag.	Diam.	Phase	Rise		Transit		Set	
	h	m	°		"	%	h	m	h	m	h	m
1	17	33.3	−23.2	−0.4	5	89	7	00	10	51	14	43
3	17	46.1	−23.5	−0.4	5	91	7	07	10	56	14	46
5	17	59.0	−23.8	−0.5	5	92	7	14	11	02	14	49
7	18	12.2	−24.0	−0.5	5	93	7	21	11	07	14	53
9	18	25.5	−24.1	−0.5	5	94	7	27	11	12	14	58
11	18	39.0	−24.1	−0.6	5	95	7	33	11	18	15	03
13	18	52.6	−24.1	−0.6	5	96	7	38	11	24	15	10
15	19	06.3	−23.9	−0.7	5	97	7	43	11	30	15	17
17	19	20.1	−23.7	−0.7	5	98	7	47	11	36	15	24
19	19	33.9	−23.4	−0.8	5	98	7	50	11	42	15	33
21	19	47.9	−23.0	−0.9	5	99	7	53	11	48	15	42
23	20	01.8	−22.4	−1.0	5	99	7	56	11	54	15	52
25	20	15.9	−21.8	−1.1	5	99	7	58	12	00	16	02
27	20	29.9	−21.1	−1.2	5	100	7	59	12	06	16	13
29	20	43.9	−20.3	−1.3	5	100	8	00	12	12	16	25
31	20	58.0	−19.4	−1.4	5	100	8	00	12	18	16	37

Rising and setting times are for latitude 54°

VENUS

Day	R.A.		Dec	Mag.	Diam.	Phase	Rise		Transit		Set	
	h	m	°		"	%	h	m	h	m	h	m
1	15	28.0	−15.3	−4.5	28	47	4	04	8	45	13	26
6	15	48.2	−16.5	−4.4	27	50	4	11	8	46	13	20
11	16	09.3	−17.6	−4.4	25	53	4	19	8	47	13	15
16	16	31.2	−18.6	−4.4	24	55	4	28	8	49	13	11
21	16	53.8	−19.5	−4.3	23	57	4	36	8	52	13	08
26	17	17.1	−20.2	−4.3	22	60	4	44	8	56	13	08
31	17	40.9	−20.7	−4.3	21	62	4	52	9	00	13	08

MARS

Day	R.A.		Dec	Mag.	Diam.	Phase	Rise		Transit		Set	
	h	m	°		"	%	h	m	h	m	h	m
1	00	00.3	−0.3	+0.5	7	87	11	15	17	17	23	20
6	00	12.4	+1.1	+0.5	7	88	11	00	17	10	23	20
11	00	24.7	+2.6	+0.6	7	88	10	45	17	02	23	20
16	00	37.0	+4.0	+0.7	7	88	10	31	16	55	23	20
21	00	49.3	+5.4	+0.7	7	89	10	16	16	47	23	19
26	01	01.8	+6.8	+0.8	6	89	10	02	16	40	23	19
31	01	14.3	+8.2	+0.9	6	89	9	47	16	33	23	19

SUNRISE AND SUNSET

d	London 0° 05' 51° 30' Rise	Set	Bristol 2° 35' 51° 28' Rise	Set	Birmingham 1° 55' 52° 28' Rise	Set	Manchester 2° 15' 53° 28' Rise	Set	Newcastle 1° 37' 54° 59' Rise	Set	Glasgow 4° 14' 55° 52' Rise	Set	Belfast 5° 56' 54° 35' Rise	Set
1	8 06	16 02	8 16	16 12	8 18	16 04	8 25	16 00	8 31	15 49	8 47	15 54	8 46	16 08
2	8 06	16 03	8 16	16 13	8 18	16 05	8 25	16 01	8 31	15 50	8 47	15 55	8 46	16 10
3	8 06	16 04	8 15	16 14	8 18	16 06	8 25	16 02	8 31	15 51	8 47	15 56	8 46	16 11
4	8 05	16 05	8 15	16 15	8 18	16 08	8 24	16 04	8 30	15 52	8 46	15 57	8 45	16 12
5	8 05	16 06	8 15	16 16	8 17	16 09	8 24	16 05	8 30	15 54	8 46	15 59	8 45	16 13
6	8 05	16 07	8 15	16 18	8 17	16 10	8 23	16 06	8 29	15 55	8 45	16 00	8 44	16 15
7	8 04	16 09	8 14	16 19	8 16	16 11	8 23	16 08	8 29	15 57	8 45	16 02	8 44	16 16
8	8 04	16 10	8 14	16 20	8 16	16 13	8 22	16 09	8 28	15 58	8 44	16 03	8 43	16 18
9	8 04	16 11	8 13	16 22	8 15	16 14	8 22	16 10	8 28	16 00	8 43	16 05	8 43	16 19
10	8 03	16 13	8 13	16 23	8 15	16 16	8 21	16 12	8 27	16 01	8 43	16 07	8 42	16 21
11	8 02	16 14	8 12	16 24	8 14	16 17	8 21	16 13	8 26	16 03	8 42	16 08	8 41	16 22
12	8 02	16 16	8 12	16 26	8 14	16 19	8 20	16 15	8 25	16 04	8 41	16 10	8 40	16 24
13	8 01	16 17	8 11	16 27	8 13	16 20	8 19	16 17	8 24	16 06	8 40	16 12	8 39	16 26
14	8 00	16 19	8 10	16 29	8 12	16 22	8 18	16 18	8 23	16 08	8 39	16 13	8 39	16 27
15	7 59	16 20	8 09	16 30	8 11	16 23	8 17	16 20	8 22	16 10	8 38	16 15	8 38	16 29
16	7 59	16 22	8 08	16 32	8 10	16 25	8 16	16 22	8 21	16 11	8 37	16 17	8 37	16 31
17	7 58	16 23	8 08	16 33	8 09	16 26	8 15	16 23	8 20	16 13	8 35	16 19	8 35	16 33
18	7 57	16 25	8 07	16 35	8 08	16 28	8 14	16 25	8 19	16 15	8 34	16 21	8 34	16 34
19	7 56	16 27	8 06	16 37	8 07	16 30	8 13	16 27	8 18	16 17	8 33	16 23	8 33	16 36
20	7 55	16 28	8 05	16 38	8 06	16 32	8 12	16 28	8 17	16 19	8 31	16 25	8 32	16 38
21	7 54	16 30	8 04	16 40	8 05	16 33	8 11	16 30	8 15	16 21	8 30	16 27	8 31	16 40
22	7 53	16 32	8 02	16 42	8 04	16 35	8 09	16 32	8 14	16 23	8 29	16 29	8 29	16 42
23	7 51	16 33	8 01	16 43	8 03	16 37	8 08	16 34	8 12	16 25	8 27	16 31	8 28	16 44
24	7 50	16 35	8 00	16 45	8 01	16 39	8 07	16 36	8 11	16 27	8 26	16 33	8 26	16 46
25	7 49	16 37	7 59	16 47	8 00	16 40	8 05	16 38	8 09	16 29	8 24	16 35	8 25	16 48
26	7 48	16 39	7 58	16 49	7 59	16 42	8 04	16 40	8 08	16 31	8 22	16 37	8 23	16 50
27	7 46	16 40	7 56	16 50	7 57	16 44	8 02	16 42	8 06	16 33	8 21	16 39	8 22	16 52
28	7 45	16 42	7 55	16 52	7 56	16 46	8 01	16 43	8 05	16 35	8 19	16 41	8 20	16 54
29	7 44	16 44	7 53	16 54	7 54	16 48	7 59	16 45	8 03	16 37	8 17	16 43	8 19	16 56
30	7 42	16 46	7 52	16 56	7 53	16 50	7 58	16 47	8 01	16 39	8 15	16 46	8 17	16 58
31	7 41	16 47	7 51	16 58	7 51	16 51	7 56	16 49	8 00	16 41	8 14	16 48	8 15	17 00

JUPITER

Day	R.A. h m	Dec °	Mag.	Diam. "	Rise h m	Transit h m	Set h m
1	16 41.4	−21.6	−1.8	32	5 56	9 58	14 01
11	16 50.2	−21.8	−1.8	32	5 27	9 28	13 29
21	16 58.5	−22.1	−1.8	33	4 58	8 57	12 56
31	17 06.4	−22.2	−1.9	34	4 27	8 25	12 24

Equatorial Diam. 32", Polar Diam. 30"

SATURN

Day	R.A. h m	Dec °	Mag.	Diam. "	Rise h m	Transit h m	Set h m
1	18 49.3	−22.5	+0.5	15	8 09	12 06	16 03
11	18 54.4	−22.4	+0.5	15	7 35	11 32	15 29
21	18 59.4	−22.3	+0.5	15	7 00	10 57	14 55
31	19 04.3	−22.2	+0.6	15	6 24	10 23	14 22

Equatorial Diam. 15", Polar Diam. 14"
Rings – major axis 34" minor axis 15", Tilt 25°

URANUS

Day	R.A. h m	Dec °	Mag.	Diam. "	Rise h m	Transit h m	Set h m
1	01 47.1	+10.5	+5.8	4	12 05	19 03	2 04
11	01 47.1	+10.5	+5.8	4	11 26	18 23	1 25
21	01 47.4	+10.5	+5.8	4	10 46	17 44	0 46
31	01 48.0	+10.6	+5.8	4	10 07	17 06	0 08

NEPTUNE

Day	R.A. h m	Dec °	Mag.	Diam. "	Rise h m	Transit h m	Set h m
1	23 02.9	−7.2	+7.9	2	10 53	16 19	21 45
11	23 03.7	−7.1	+7.9	2	10 14	15 40	21 07
21	23 04.7	−7.0	+7.9	2	9 35	15 02	20 29
31	23 05.9	−6.8	+8.0	2	8 56	14 24	19 51

February 2019

SECOND MONTH, 28 or 29 DAYS. *Februa*, Roman festival of Purification

1	*Friday*	An express train crashes into a standing commuter train in the Buenos Aires Province, killing 236 people 1970	day 32
2	*Saturday*	The Treaty of Guadalupe Hidalgo is signed, ending the Mexican-American War 1848	33
3	*Sunday*	Justo de Urquiza defeats Argentine dictator Juan de Rosas at Caseros and forces him to flee into exile 1852	34
4	*Monday*	Hugo Chávez leads hundreds of soldiers in a failed attempt to overthrow the government of Venezuela 1992	week 5 day 35
5	*Tuesday*	Panama ruler Manuel Noriega is indicted in Florida, USA for drug smuggling and money laundering 1988	36
6	*Wednesday*	Óscar Sambrano Urdaneta, Venezuelan writer and literary critic *b*.1929	37
7	*Thursday*	King Philip II of Spain establishes the Inquisition in Spanish America by royal decree 1569	38
8	*Friday*	The Charaña Act is signed, beginning negotiations for a sovereign exit to the Pacific Ocean for Bolivia 1975	39
9	*Saturday*	The city of Valdivia in Chile is founded by Pedro de Valdivia, initiator of the conquest of Chile 1552	40
10	*Sunday*	The Mar del Plata seaside resort in Argentina is founded 1874	41
11	*Monday*	MoMA in New York opens an exhibition devoted exclusively to Brazilian painter Tarsila do Amaral 2018	week 6 day 42
12	*Tuesday*	Supreme Director of Chile, Bernardo O'Higgins, issues the country's Declaration of Independence 1818	43
13	*Wednesday*	Modern Art Week begins in Sao Paulo, a pivotal moment in Modernism in Brazil 1922	44
14	*Thursday*	Dutch expedition arrives in Recife, beginning its conquest of half of Brazil's settled European area 1630	45
15	*Friday*	Gloria Trevi, multi-platinum Mexican singer-songwriter and recipient of the Presidential BMI Award *b*. 1968	46
16	*Saturday*	Fidel Castro is sworn in as Prime Minister of Cuba 1959	47
17	*Sunday*	Passenger ferry *Neptune* overturns near Port-au-Prince, Haiti, with more than 1,000 people killed 1993	48
18	*Monday*	Marlos Nobre, Brazilian composer and Guggenheim Fellow 1985–6 *b*. 1939	week 7 day 49
19	*Tuesday*	Horacio Quiroga, Uruguayan poet, playwright and short-story writer *d*. 1937	50
20	*Wednesday*	Venezuela becomes the first country to launch its own cryptocurrency 2018	51
21	*Thursday*	The ruins of the Great Temple of the Aztec capital Tenochtitlán is discovered in Mexico City 1978	52
22	*Friday*	Indigenous peoples from Peru rebel against Spanish authorities, seizing the city of Huánuco 1812	53
23	*Saturday*	Francisco Vázquez de Coronado's expedition sets off from Mexico in search of the seven cities of gold 1540	54
24	*Sunday*	Juan Domingo Perón, with first lady Eva Perón, is elected President of Argentina, the first of three terms 1946	55
25	*Monday*	The first Pan American Games begin in Buenos Aires, Argentina, with 21 nations participating 1951	week 8 day 56
26	*Tuesday*	Santa Cruz de la Sierra, Bolivia's largest city, is founded by Spanish captain Ñuflo de Chávez 1561	57
27	*Wednesday*	The *Caracazo*, a wave of protests against austerity measures in Venezuela, begins 1989	58
28	*Thursday*	Mexican director Alejandro G. Iñárritu wins his second Academy Award, for *The Revenant*, 2016	59

ASTRONOMICAL PHENOMENA

d	h	
2	7	Saturn 0.6° South of the Moon
5	7	Mercury 0.2° North of the Moon
5	9	Moon furthest 406,555km
6	8	Vesta 1° South of the Moon
7	6	Neptune 3° North of the Moon
13	20	Uranus 1° South of Mars
14	4	Aldebaran 2° South of the Moon
18	14	Saturn 1° South of Venus
19	9	Moon closest 356,761km
19	11	Neptune 0.8° South of Mercury
23	9	Pluto 1° South of Venus
27	1	Mercury greatest elong. E(18°)
27	14	Jupiter 2° South of the Moon

MINIMA OF ALGOL

d	h	d	h	d	h
1	8.9	12	20.2	24	7.5
4	5.8	15	17.0	27	4.3
7	2.6	18	13.9		
9	23.4	21	10.7		

CONSTELLATIONS

The following constellations are near the meridian at

	d	h		d	h
January	1	24	February	15	21
January	16	23	March	1	20
February	1	22	March	16	19

Draco (below the Pole), Camelopardalis, Auriga, Taurus, Gemini, Orion, Canis Minor, Monoceros, Lepus, Canis Major and Puppis

THE MOON

Phase, Apsides and Node	d	h	m
● New Moon	4	21	5
◗ First Quarter	12	22	27
○ Full Moon	19	15	55
◑ Last Quarter	26	11	29

Apogee (406,555 km)*	5	9	30
Perigee (356,761 km)*	19	9	4

* closest and furthest of the year

Mean longitude of the ascending node on 1st, 116°

THE SUN Diam. 32.5′

Day	Right Ascension			Dec.	Equation of time		Rise 52°		Rise 56°		Transit		Set 52°		Set 56°		Sidereal time			Transit of first point of Aries		
	h	m	s	°	m	s	h	m	h	m	h	m	h	m	h	m	h	m	s	h	m	s
1	20	57	09	−17.2	−13	30	7	40	7	55	12	14	16	47	16	32	8	43	40	15	13	50
2	21	01	14	−17.0	−13	38	7	39	7	53	12	14	16	49	16	35	8	47	36	15	09	54
3	21	05	18	−16.7	−13	46	7	37	7	52	12	14	16	51	16	37	8	51	33	15	05	58
4	21	09	21	−16.4	−13	52	7	36	7	50	12	14	16	53	16	39	8	55	29	15	02	02
5	21	13	23	−16.1	−13	58	7	34	7	48	12	14	16	55	16	41	8	59	26	14	58	06
6	21	17	24	−15.8	−14	03	7	32	7	46	12	14	16	57	16	43	9	03	23	14	54	11
7	21	21	25	−15.5	−14	07	7	30	7	44	12	14	16	58	16	46	9	07	19	14	50	15
8	21	25	25	−15.1	−14	10	7	29	7	41	12	14	17	00	16	48	9	11	16	14	46	19
9	21	29	24	−14.8	−14	13	7	27	7	39	12	14	17	02	16	50	9	15	12	14	42	23
10	21	33	22	−14.5	−14	15	7	25	7	37	12	14	17	04	16	52	9	19	09	14	38	27
11	21	37	20	−14.2	−14	16	7	23	7	35	12	14	17	06	16	54	9	23	05	14	34	31
12	21	41	17	−13.9	−14	16	7	21	7	33	12	14	17	08	16	57	9	27	02	14	30	35
13	21	45	13	−13.5	−14	15	7	20	7	31	12	14	17	10	16	59	9	30	58	14	26	39
14	21	49	08	−13.2	−14	14	7	18	7	28	12	14	17	12	17	01	9	34	55	14	22	43
15	21	53	02	−12.8	−14	11	7	16	7	26	12	14	17	13	17	03	9	38	52	14	18	47
16	21	56	56	−12.5	−14	09	7	14	7	24	12	14	17	15	17	05	9	42	48	14	14	51
17	22	00	49	−12.2	−14	05	7	12	7	21	12	14	17	17	17	08	9	46	45	14	10	56
18	22	04	41	−11.8	−14	01	7	10	7	19	12	14	17	19	17	10	9	50	41	14	07	00
19	22	08	32	−11.5	−13	56	7	08	7	17	12	14	17	21	17	12	9	54	38	14	03	04
20	22	12	23	−11.1	−13	50	7	06	7	14	12	14	17	23	17	14	9	58	34	13	59	08
21	22	16	13	−10.7	−13	43	7	04	7	12	12	14	17	25	17	16	10	02	31	13	55	12
22	22	20	03	−10.4	−13	36	7	02	7	10	12	14	17	26	17	18	10	06	27	13	51	16
23	22	23	52	−10.0	−13	29	6	59	7	07	12	13	17	28	17	21	10	10	24	13	47	20
24	22	27	40	−9.6	−13	20	6	57	7	05	12	13	17	30	17	23	10	14	21	13	43	24
25	22	31	28	−9.3	−13	12	6	55	7	02	12	13	17	32	17	25	10	18	17	13	39	28
26	22	35	15	−8.9	−13	02	6	53	7	00	12	13	17	34	17	27	10	22	14	13	35	32
27	22	39	01	−8.5	−12	52	6	51	6	57	12	13	17	35	17	29	10	26	10	13	31	36
28	22	42	48	−8.2	−12	42	6	49	6	55	12	13	17	37	17	31	10	30	07	13	27	41

DURATION OF TWILIGHT (in minutes)

Latitude	52°	56°	52°	56°	52°	56°	52°	56°
	1 February		11 February		21 February		31 February	
Civil	37	41	35	39		38	34	37
Nautical	77	86	75	83	74	81	73	80
Astronomical	117	130	114	126	113	124	112	124

THE NIGHT SKY

Mercury can be found in the evening sky from the second week of February and is best placed when at greatest elongation east on the 27th. It will fade from magnitude −1.2 to −0.2 during the same period. Mercury and Neptune (magnitude 8.0) are less than 1° apart on the 19th but decent optical aid will be needed to glimpse the outermost planet in a twilit sky.

Venus (magnitude −4.2) rises three hours before the Sun at the beginning of February but only 1½ hours beforehand at the end. The planet's eastward motion carries it close to Saturn in Sagittarius mid-month with the gap narrowing to about 1° on the morning of the 18th.

The full Moon on 19th will be the largest and brightest of the year as it is at closest perigee.

Mars (fading from magnitude 0.9 to 1.2) crosses into Aries from Pisces the second week of February. It is in the same low-power binocular field as Uranus (magnitude 5.8) between the 10th and 15th, with the two just 1° apart on the 13th. Mars is setting just a little before midnight all month.

Jupiter (magnitude −1.9) rises during the early hours and lies in southern Ophiuchus. The Moon is near the giant planet on the 27th.

Saturn (magnitude 0.6) gradually becomes better placed for viewing in a darker sky during the month. The Moon is very close on the 2nd with the planet occulted from central and southern Europe, while reappearance only will be seen from the southeast of England. *See also* W www.calsky.com and W http://asa.usno.navy.mil/SecA/occns.html for details of this and other similar events in 2019.

THE MOON

Day	R.A.		Dec	Hor Par	Diam	Sun Co-Long	PA of Br. limb	Ph.	Age	Rise 52°		Rise 56°		Transit		Set 52°		Set 56°	
	h	m	°	'	'	°	°	%	d	h	m	h	m	h	m	h	m	h	m
1	17	58	−21.0	54.8	29.8	222	93	13	25.5	5	26	5	48	9	34	13	40	13	18
2	18	50	−21.5	54.4	29.6	235	87	07	26.5	6	17	6	40	10	23	14	30	14	08
3	19	41	−21.1	54.2	29.6	247	81	03	27.5	7	00	7	22	11	12	15	26	15	06
4	20	32	−19.7	54.0	29.4	259	71	01	28.5	7	37	7	55	11	59	16	27	16	09
5	21	21	−17.4	53.9	29.4	271	307	00	29.5	8	06	8	22	12	45	17	31	17	16
6	22	09	−14.5	53.9	29.4	283	262	01	1.0	8	31	8	43	13	29	18	36	18	25
7	22	55	−10.9	54.0	29.4	296	256	04	2.0	8	52	9	00	14	12	19	42	19	35
8	23	40	−6.9	54.2	29.6	308	253	09	3.0	9	12	9	16	14	54	20	48	20	45
9	0	25	−2.6	54.5	29.8	320	252	15	4.0	9	30	9	31	15	36	21	55	21	56
10	1	10	+1.9	55.0	30.0	332	251	22	5.0	9	49	9	46	16	19	23	03	23	08
11	1	56	+6.3	55.5	30.2	344	252	31	6.0	10	09	10	02	17	04	—	—	—	—
12	2	44	+10.6	56.2	30.6	357	253	40	7.0	10	31	10	20	17	51	0	13	0	23
13	3	34	+14.5	57.0	31.0	9	256	51	8.0	10	59	10	43	18	41	1	25	1	39
14	4	28	+17.8	57.9	31.6	21	260	61	9.0	11	32	11	14	19	36	2	38	2	56
15	5	25	+20.2	58.8	32.0	33	265	72	10.0	12	16	11	55	20	34	3	50	4	11
16	6	25	+21.5	59.8	32.6	45	271	82	11.0	13	13	12	49	21	35	4	56	5	20
17	7	28	+21.3	60.6	33.0	57	278	90	12.0	14	22	14	01	22	38	5	55	6	17
18	8	32	+19.7	61.1	33.4	69	286	96	13.0	15	42	15	24	23	39	6	43	7	01
19	9	35	+16.7	61.4	33.4	82	301	99	14.0	17	08	16	55	—	—	7	21	7	36
20	10	36	+12.4	61.4	33.4	94	77	100	15.0	18	34	18	26	0	38	7	52	8	01
21	11	34	+7.4	61.0	33.2	106	101	97	16.0	19	59	19	57	1	35	8	19	8	23
22	12	30	+2.1	60.3	32.8	118	106	92	17.0	21	22	21	24	2	29	8	42	8	42
23	13	24	−3.2	59.5	32.4	130	107	84	18.0	22	41	22	48	3	20	9	05	9	01
24	14	17	−8.2	58.5	31.8	142	106	75	19.0	23	57	—	—	4	11	9	28	9	20
25	15	09	−12.7	57.6	31.4	154	104	65	20.0	—	—	0	09	5	01	9	54	9	41
26	16	01	−16.3	56.6	30.8	167	101	55	21.0	1	10	1	27	5	50	10	23	10	07
27	16	53	−19.1	55.8	30.4	179	97	45	22.0	2	19	2	38	6	40	10	58	10	37
28	17	45	−20.8	55.2	30.0	191	92	35	23.0	3	21	3	42	7	30	11	37	11	15

MERCURY

Day	R.A.		Dec	Mag.	Diam.	Phase	Rise		Transit		Set	
	h	m	°		"	%	h	m	h	m	h	m
1	21	05.0	−18.9	−1.4	5	100	8	00	12	21	16	44
3	21	19.0	−17.8	−1.4	5	99	8	00	12	28	16	56
5	21	33.0	−16.6	−1.3	5	99	7	59	12	34	17	10
7	21	46.9	−15.3	−1.3	5	98	7	57	12	40	17	23
9	22	00.7	−14.0	−1.3	5	97	7	55	12	46	17	37
11	22	14.4	−12.5	−1.2	5	95	7	53	12	51	17	51
13	22	27.8	−11.0	−1.2	5	92	7	50	12	57	18	05
15	22	41.0	−9.4	−1.2	5	89	7	46	13	02	18	18
17	22	53.6	−7.8	−1.1	6	85	7	42	13	06	18	32
19	23	05.7	−6.2	−1.0	6	80	7	38	13	10	18	44
21	23	17.0	−4.5	−1.0	6	73	7	33	13	13	18	55
23	23	27.3	−3.0	−0.8	6	66	7	27	13	15	19	05
25	23	36.2	−1.5	−0.6	7	57	7	20	13	16	19	12
27	23	43.6	−0.2	−0.4	7	48	7	13	13	15	19	17

Rising and setting times are for latitude 54°

VENUS

Day	R.A.	Dec	Mag.	Diam.	Phase	Rise		Transit		Set	
	h m	°		"	%	h	m	h	m	h	m
1	17 45.8	−20.8	−4.3	21	62	4	53	9	01	13	09
6	18 10.1	−21.1	−4.2	20	64	5	00	9	06	13	11
11	18 34.8	−21.2	−4.2	19	66	5	06	9	11	13	16
16	18 59.7	−21.0	−4.2	18	68	5	10	9	16	13	22
21	19 24.7	−20.6	−4.1	18	70	5	12	9	21	13	30
26	19 49.6	−20.0	−4.1	17	71	5	13	9	27	13	40

MARS

Day	R.A.	Dec	Mag.	Diam.	Phase	Rise		Transit		Set	
	h m	°		"	%	h	m	h	m	h	m
1	01 16.8	+8.4	+0.9	6	89	9	44	16	32	23	19
6	01 29.4	+9.8	+0.9	6	90	9	30	16	24	23	19
11	01 42.1	+11.1	+1.0	6	90	9	16	16	17	23	19
16	01 55.0	+12.3	+1.0	6	90	9	02	16	11	23	20
21	02 07.9	+13.5	+1.1	6	91	8	48	16	04	23	20
26	02 20.9	+14.7	+1.2	5	91	8	35	15	57	23	20

SUNRISE AND SUNSET

d	London 0° 05′ 51° 30′				Bristol 2° 35′ 51° 28′				Birmingham 1° 55′ 52° 28′				Manchester 2° 15′ 53° 28′				Newcastle 1° 37′ 54° 59′				Glasgow 4° 14′ 55° 52′				Belfast 5° 56′ 54° 35′			
	h	m	h	m	h	m	h	m	h	m	h	m	h	m	h	m	h	m	h	m	h	m	h	m	h	m	h	m
1	7	39	16	49	7	49	16	59	7	50	16	53	7	55	16	51	7	58	16	43	8	12	16	50	8	13	17	02
2	7	38	16	51	7	48	17	01	7	48	16	55	7	53	16	53	7	56	16	45	8	10	16	52	8	12	17	04
3	7	36	16	53	7	46	17	03	7	46	16	57	7	51	16	55	7	54	16	47	8	08	16	54	8	10	17	06
4	7	34	16	55	7	44	17	05	7	45	16	59	7	49	16	57	7	52	16	49	8	06	16	56	8	08	17	08
5	7	33	16	56	7	43	17	07	7	43	17	01	7	48	16	59	7	50	16	51	8	04	16	59	8	06	17	10
6	7	31	16	58	7	41	17	08	7	41	17	03	7	46	17	01	7	48	16	53	8	02	17	01	8	04	17	12
7	7	29	17	00	7	39	17	10	7	40	17	05	7	44	17	03	7	46	16	55	8	00	17	03	8	02	17	14
8	7	28	17	02	7	38	17	12	7	38	17	07	7	42	17	05	7	44	16	58	7	58	17	05	8	00	17	16
9	7	26	17	04	7	36	17	14	7	36	17	08	7	40	17	07	7	42	17	00	7	56	17	07	7	58	17	18
10	7	24	17	06	7	34	17	16	7	34	17	10	7	38	17	09	7	40	17	02	7	54	17	09	7	56	17	20
11	7	22	17	07	7	32	17	18	7	32	17	12	7	36	17	11	7	38	17	04	7	52	17	12	7	54	17	22
12	7	21	17	09	7	30	17	19	7	30	17	14	7	34	17	13	7	36	17	06	7	49	17	14	7	52	17	24
13	7	19	17	11	7	29	17	21	7	28	17	16	7	32	17	15	7	34	17	08	7	47	17	16	7	50	17	27
14	7	17	17	13	7	27	17	23	7	26	17	18	7	30	17	17	7	32	17	10	7	45	17	18	7	48	17	29
15	7	15	17	15	7	25	17	25	7	24	17	20	7	28	17	19	7	30	17	12	7	43	17	20	7	46	17	31
16	7	13	17	17	7	23	17	27	7	22	17	22	7	26	17	21	7	28	17	14	7	40	17	23	7	44	17	33
17	7	11	17	18	7	21	17	29	7	20	17	24	7	24	17	23	7	25	17	17	7	38	17	25	7	42	17	35
18	7	09	17	20	7	19	17	30	7	18	17	26	7	22	17	25	7	23	17	19	7	36	17	27	7	39	17	37
19	7	07	17	22	7	17	17	32	7	16	17	27	7	20	17	27	7	21	17	21	7	33	17	29	7	37	17	39
20	7	05	17	24	7	15	17	34	7	14	17	29	7	18	17	29	7	19	17	23	7	31	17	31	7	35	17	41
21	7	03	17	26	7	13	17	36	7	12	17	31	7	16	17	31	7	16	17	25	7	29	17	33	7	33	17	43
22	7	01	17	27	7	11	17	38	7	10	17	33	7	13	17	33	7	14	17	27	7	26	17	36	7	30	17	45
23	6	59	17	29	7	09	17	39	7	08	17	35	7	11	17	34	7	12	17	29	7	24	17	38	7	28	17	47
24	6	57	17	31	7	07	17	41	7	06	17	37	7	09	17	36	7	09	17	31	7	21	17	40	7	26	17	49
25	6	55	17	33	7	05	17	43	7	04	17	39	7	07	17	38	7	07	17	33	7	19	17	42	7	23	17	51
26	6	53	17	35	7	03	17	45	7	02	17	41	7	04	17	40	7	05	17	35	7	17	17	44	7	21	17	53
27	6	51	17	36	7	01	17	47	6	59	17	42	7	02	17	42	7	02	17	37	7	14	17	46	7	19	17	55
28	6	49	17	38	6	58	17	48	6	57	17	44	7	00	17	44	7	00	17	39	7	12	17	48	7	16	17	57

JUPITER

Day	R.A. h m		Dec °	Mag.	Diam. ″	Rise h m		Transit h m		Set h m	
1	17	07.1	−22.3	−1.9	34	4	24	8	22	12	20
11	17	14.2	−22.4	−1.9	34	3	53	7	50	11	47
21	17	20.4	−22.5	−2.0	35	3	20	7	17	11	13

Equatorial Diam. 34″, Polar Diam. 31″

SATURN

Day	R.A. h m		Dec °	Mag.	Diam. ″	Rise h m		Transit h m		Set h m	
1	19	04.8	−22.1	+0.6	15	6	21	10	19	14	18
11	19	09.3	−22.0	+0.6	15	5	45	9	45	13	44
21	19	13.6	−21.9	+0.6	15	5	09	9	10	13	10

Equatorial Diam. 15″, Polar Diam. 14″
Rings – major axis 35″ minor axis 14″, Tilt 24°

URANUS

Day	R.A. h m		Dec °	Mag.	Diam. ″	Rise h m		Transit h m		Set h m	
1	01	48.1	+10.6	+5.8	4	10	04	17	02	0	04
11	01	49.1	+10.7	+5.8	3	9	25	16	23	23	22
21	01	50.3	+10.8	+5.8	3	8	46	15	45	22	45

NEPTUNE

Day	R.A. h m		Dec °	Mag.	Diam. ″	Rise h m		Transit h m		Set h m	
1	23	06.0	−6.8	+8.0	2	8	52	14	20	19	48
11	23	07.3	−6.7	+8.0	2	8	14	13	42	19	10
21	23	08.6	−6.5	+8.0	2	7	35	13	04	18	33

March 2019

THIRD MONTH, 31 DAYS. *Mars,* Roman god of battle

1	*Friday*	The Paraguayan War (1864–70) ends with victory for the Triple Alliance (Argentina, Brazil, Uruguay) 1870	day 60
2	*Saturday*	The Republic of Texas declares its independence from Mexico and until 1845 remains a sovereign state 1836	61
3	*Sunday*	Camila Cabello, Cuban-American singer-songwriter, and former member of the group Fifth Harmony *b.* 1997	62

4	*Monday*	Chile's *A Fantastic Woman* wins Best Foreign Language Film at the 90th Academy Awards 2018	week 9 day 63
5	*Tuesday*	Adriana Barraza, Oscar-nominated actress and film director from Mexico *b.* 1956	64
6	*Wednesday*	Gabriel García Márquez, Colombian novelist, short-story writer and Nobel Laureate (1982) *b.* 1927	65
7	*Thursday*	Argentina's *The Secret in Their Eyes* wins Best Foreign Language Film at the 82nd Academy Awards 2010	66
8	*Friday*	Teófilo Cubillas, Peruvian footballer, nicknamed 'El Nene', the kid *b.* 1949	67
9	*Saturday*	Mexican revolutionary Pancho Villa raids Columbus, New Mexico, killing 17 Americans 1916	68
10	*Sunday*	President of Cuba Carlos Prío Socarrás is deposed by a military coup led by Fulgencio Batista 1952	69

11	*Monday*	Michelle Bachelet is inaugurated as President of Chile, the first woman to hold the position 2006	week 10 day 70
12	*Tuesday*	Moctesuma Esparza, Mexican-American film producer, executive and Oscar nominee *b.* 1949	71
13	*Wednesday*	Argentinian Cardinal Jorge Mario Bergoglio becomes Pope Francis 2013	72
14	*Thursday*	Marielle Franco, Brazilian politician and human rights activist is assasinated 2018	73
15	*Friday*	Brazil's military dictatorship (1964–85) ends when José Sarney's civilian government takes power 1985	74
16	*Saturday*	The Comunero Revolt against taxes imposed by the Spanish authorities in Colombia begins 1781	75
17	*Sunday*	The Uruguay Air Force is founded with the inauguration of a military aviation school 1913	76

18	*Monday*	Paraguy declares war on Argentina in the War of the Triple Alliance 1865	week 11 day 77
19	*Tuesday*	At least 16 people die in a mudslide in Petropolis, 40 miles north of Rio de Janiero 2013	78
20	*Wednesday*	El Salvador's first presidential election following a twelve year civil war 1994	79
21	*Thursday*	Guadalupe Victoria, first President of Mexico *d.* 1843	80
22	*Friday*	Slavery is abolished in Puerto Rico, celebrated as Emancipation Day 1873	81
23	*Saturday*	Paraguay's Vice-President Luis María Argaña is assassinated by gunmen 1999	82
24	*Sunday*	Argentina's *The Official Story* wins Best Foreign Language Film at the 58th Academy Awards 1986	83

25	*Monday*	The BBC ends its Spanish Latin American radio service after 73 years 2011	84
26	*Tuesday*	Earthquake in Caracas, Venezuela, decimates the city 1812	week 13 day 85
27	*Wednesday*	Ten more human skulls are found in a rubbish pile in Port-au-Prince, Haiti, bringing the total to 27 2006	86
28	*Thursday*	Cuba lifts restrictions on private ownership of computers and mobile phones 2008	87
29	*Friday*	El Chichon, a presumed-dormant volcano in Chiapas, Mexico, erupts for the first time in 600 years 1982	88
30	*Saturday*	Three men are publicly lynched in Guatemala after being accused of stealing a truckload of coffee 2011	89
31	*Sunday*	British Summer Time begins. Police gun down 29 civilians in Rio 2005	90

ASTRONOMICAL PHENOMENA

d	h	
1	18	Saturn 0.3° South of the Moon
2	21	Venus 1° North of the Moon
6	14	Neptune 3° North of the Moon
6	18	Vesta 0.5° South of the Moon
13	11	Aldebaran 2° South of the Moon
19	0	Regulus 3° South of the Moon
20	22	Spring equinox
26	8	Ceres 3° North of the Moon
27	2	Jupiter 2° South of the Moon
29	5	Saturn 0.1° North of the Moon

MINIMA OF ALGOL

d	h	d	h	d	h
2	1.2	13	12.4	24	23.7
4	22	16	9.3	27	20.6
7	18.8	19	6.1	30	17.4
10	15.6	22	2.9		

CONSTELLATIONS

The following constellations are near the meridian at

	d	h		d	h
February	1	24	March	16	21
February	15	23	April	1	20
March	1	22	April	15	19

Cepheus (below the Pole), Camelopardalis, Lynx, Gemini, Cancer, Leo, Canis Minor, Hydra, Monoceros, Canis Major and Puppis

THE MOON

Phase, Apsides and Node	d	h	m
● New Moon	6	16	5
◑ First Quarter	14	10	28
○ Full Moon	21	1	44
◐ Last Quarter	28	4	11

	d	h	m
Apogee (406,391 km)	4	11	28
Perigee (359,377 km)	19	19	49

Mean longitude of the ascending node on 1st, 114°

THE SUN Diam. 32.3′

Day	Right Ascension			Dec.	Equation of time		Rise 52°		Rise 56°		Transit		Set 52°		Set 56°		Sidereal time			Transit of first point of Aries		
	h	m	s	°	m	s	h	m	h	m	h	m	h	m	h	m	h	m	s	h	m	s
1	22	46	33	−7.8	−12	31	6	47	6	52	12	12	17	39	17	33	10	34	03	13	23	45
2	22	50	18	−7.4	−12	19	6	44	6	50	12	12	17	41	17	36	10	38	00	13	19	49
3	22	54	03	−7.0	−12	07	6	42	6	47	12	12	17	43	17	38	10	41	56	13	15	53
4	22	57	47	−6.6	−11	55	6	40	6	45	12	12	17	44	17	40	10	45	53	13	11	57
5	23	01	30	−6.2	−11	42	6	38	6	42	12	11	17	46	17	42	10	49	50	13	08	01
6	23	05	14	−5.9	−11	28	6	36	6	40	12	11	17	48	17	44	10	53	46	13	04	05
7	23	08	56	−5.5	−11	15	6	33	6	37	12	11	17	50	17	46	10	57	43	13	00	09
8	23	12	39	−5.1	−11	00	6	31	6	35	12	11	17	52	17	48	11	01	39	12	56	13
9	23	16	21	−4.7	−10	46	6	29	6	32	12	11	17	53	17	50	11	05	36	12	52	17
10	23	20	02	−4.3	−10	31	6	27	6	29	12	10	17	55	17	52	11	09	32	12	48	21
11	23	23	43	−3.9	−10	16	6	24	6	27	12	10	17	57	17	55	11	13	29	12	44	26
12	23	27	24	−3.5	−10	00	6	22	6	24	12	10	17	59	17	57	11	17	25	12	40	30
13	23	31	05	−3.1	−9	44	6	20	6	22	12	10	18	00	17	59	11	21	22	12	36	34
14	23	34	45	−2.7	−9	28	6	17	6	19	12	09	18	02	18	01	11	25	19	12	32	38
15	23	38	25	−2.3	−9	11	6	15	6	16	12	09	18	04	18	03	11	29	15	12	28	42
16	23	42	05	−1.9	−8	54	6	13	6	14	12	09	18	06	18	05	11	33	12	12	24	46
17	23	45	44	−1.5	−8	37	6	10	6	11	12	08	18	07	18	07	11	37	08	12	20	50
18	23	49	24	−1.1	−8	20	6	08	6	08	12	08	18	09	18	09	11	41	05	12	16	54
19	23	53	03	−0.8	−8	02	6	06	6	06	12	08	18	11	18	11	11	45	01	12	12	58
20	23	56	42	−0.4	−7	45	6	04	6	03	12	08	18	13	18	13	11	48	58	12	09	02
21	0	00	20	0.0	−7	27	6	01	6	01	12	07	18	14	18	15	11	52	54	12	05	06
22	0	03	59	+0.4	−7	09	5	59	5	58	12	07	18	16	18	17	11	56	51	12	01	11
23	0	07	38	+0.8	−6	51	5	57	5	55	12	07	18	18	18	19	12	00	48	11	57	15
24	0	11	16	+1.2	−6	33	5	54	5	53	12	06	18	20	18	21	12	04	44	11	53	19
25	0	14	55	+1.6	−6	15	5	52	5	50	12	06	18	21	18	23	12	08	41	11	49	23
26	0	18	33	+2.0	−5	57	5	50	5	47	12	06	18	23	18	25	12	12	37	11	45	27
27	0	22	11	+2.4	−5	39	5	47	5	45	12	05	18	25	18	27	12	16	34	11	41	31
28	0	25	50	+2.8	−5	20	5	45	5	42	12	05	18	26	18	29	12	20	30	11	37	35
29	0	29	28	+3.2	−5	02	5	43	5	39	12	05	18	28	18	31	12	24	27	11	33	39
30	0	33	07	+3.6	−4	44	5	40	5	37	12	05	18	30	18	34	12	28	23	11	29	43
31	0	36	45	+4.0	−4	26	5	38	5	34	12	04	18	32	18	36	12	32	20	11	25	47

DURATION OF TWILIGHT (in minutes)

Latitude	52°	56°	52°	56°	52°	56°	52°	56°
		1 March		11 March		21 March		31 March
Civil	34	37	34	37	34	37	34	38
Nautical	73	80	73	80	74	81	75	84
Astronomical	112	124	113	125	115	128	120	135

THE NIGHT SKY

Mercury fades a little and slips from our sight more quickly each evening as this apparition draws to a close. The planet will be lost to view by the beginning of the second week of March on its way to passing through inferior conjunction on the 15th.

Venus (magnitude −4.0) is now getting lower in the morning sky and by the end of the month it will have only just risen as Civil Twilight begins. The Moon is near by on the 3rd.

Mars (magnitude 1.2 to 1.4) is setting just before midnight all month and crosses from Aries into Taurus during the last week of March. It ends the month within 3° of the Pleiades star cluster when we can contrast the colour of dimmer Mars with the orange-tinted magnitude 0.9 star Aldebaran. The Moon is close to the Red Planet on the 11th.

Jupiter (magnitude −2.0 to −2.2) is rising four hours before the Sun on the 1st with the planet up by 1am at the end of March. Jupiter is at western quadrature mid-month and the Moon is fairly close by on the 27th.

Saturn (magnitude 0.6) rises two hours before the Sun as the month begins and an hour earlier at close. The ringed planet spends the year not far from the 'handle' of the Teapot asterism in Sagittarius. The Moon is near Saturn on the morning of the 1st, between the planet and Venus on the 2nd, and within 1° of Saturn on the 29th.

THE MOON

Day	R.A. h	R.A. m	Dec °	Hor Par '	Diam '	Sun Co-Long °	PA of Br. limb °	Ph. %	Age d	Rise 52° h	Rise 52° m	Rise 56° h	Rise 56° m	Transit h	Transit m	Set 52° h	Set 52° m	Set 56° h	Set 56° m
1	18	37	−21.6	54.7	29.8	203	87	26	24.0	4	15	4	38	8	20	12	25	12	03
2	19	29	−21.4	54.3	29.6	215	82	18	25.0	5	00	5	23	9	09	13	19	12	58
3	20	19	−20.2	54.1	29.4	227	76	12	26.0	5	38	5	57	9	56	14	19	14	01
4	21	09	−18.1	54.0	29.4	240	70	06	27.0	6	09	6	26	10	42	15	22	15	07
5	21	56	−15.3	54.0	29.4	252	62	02	28.0	6	36	6	49	11	27	16	27	16	15
6	22	43	−11.8	54.1	29.4	264	43	00	29.0	6	58	7	07	12	11	17	33	17	25
7	23	29	−7.9	54.2	29.6	276	296	00	0.5	7	18	7	24	12	53	18	40	18	36
8	0	14	−3.6	54.5	29.8	289	264	02	1.5	7	37	7	38	13	36	19	47	19	47
9	0	59	+0.9	54.8	29.8	301	257	05	2.5	7	55	7	53	14	18	20	55	20	59
10	1	45	+5.4	55.2	30.2	313	256	10	3.5	8	14	8	08	15	02	22	04	22	13
11	2	32	+9.7	55.7	30.4	325	256	17	4.5	8	35	8	25	15	48	23	15	23	28
12	3	21	+13.7	56.3	30.6	337	258	25	5.5	9	01	8	46	16	36	—	—	—	—
13	4	13	+17.2	57.0	31.0	349	261	35	6.5	9	30	9	13	17	28	0	27	0	43
14	5	08	+19.8	57.7	31.4	2	265	45	7.5	10	09	9	48	18	23	1	37	1	57
15	6	05	+21.4	58.5	31.8	14	270	56	8.5	10	59	10	35	19	21	2	44	3	07
16	7	05	+21.7	59.2	32.2	26	276	67	9.5	12	01	11	37	20	21	3	44	4	07
17	8	07	+20.7	60.0	32.6	38	282	78	10.5	13	13	12	53	21	21	4	35	4	55
18	9	08	+18.2	60.5	33.0	50	289	87	11.5	14	34	14	18	22	20	5	15	5	32
19	10	08	+14.5	60.9	33.2	62	296	94	12.5	16	00	15	49	23	17	5	48	6	00
20	11	07	+9.8	61.0	33.2	75	307	98	13.5	17	25	17	20	—	—	6	17	6	24
21	12	04	+4.6	60.8	33.2	87	11	100	14.5	18	50	18	50	0	12	6	41	6	44
22	12	59	−0.9	60.3	32.8	99	92	99	15.5	20	13	20	18	1	05	7	04	7	02
23	13	54	−6.3	59.6	32.4	111	101	95	16.5	21	34	21	43	1	57	7	27	7	21
24	14	47	−11.1	58.7	32.0	123	102	88	17.5	22	51	23	05	2	49	7	52	7	41
25	15	41	−15.2	57.8	31.4	135	100	80	18.5	—	—	—	—	3	40	8	20	8	05
26	16	35	−18.4	56.9	31.0	148	97	71	19.5	0	04	0	23	4	32	8	53	8	34
27	17	29	−20.6	56.0	30.6	160	92	62	20.5	1	11	1	33	5	23	9	32	9	10
28	18	22	−21.7	55.3	30.2	172	88	52	21.5	2	09	2	33	6	14	10	18	9	55
29	19	14	−21.8	54.8	29.8	184	83	42	22.5	2	58	3	22	7	04	11	11	10	48
30	20	05	−20.8	54.4	29.6	196	78	33	23.5	3	40	4	00	7	52	12	09	11	49
31	20	55	−18.9	54.1	29.6	209	73	24	24.5	4	13	4	31	8	39	13	12	12	55

MERCURY

Day	R.A. h m	Dec °	Mag.	Diam. "	Phase %	Rise h m	Transit h m	Set h m
1	23 49.2	+1.0	−0.1	8	39	7 05	13 12	19 19
3	23 52.7	+1.9	+0.4	8	30	6 56	13 07	19 18
5	23 54.0	+2.5	+0.9	9	22	6 46	13 00	19 12
7	23 53.2	+2.8	+1.6	9	15	6 36	12 50	19 03
9	23 50.4	+2.7	+2.4	10	9	6 25	12 39	18 51
11	23 45.8	+2.4	+3.3	10	4	6 14	12 26	18 35
13	23 39.9	+1.8	+4.3	11	2	6 04	12 12	18 17
15	23 33.4	+0.9	+4.9	11	1	5 54	11 58	17 58
17	23 26.8	0.0	+4.5	11	1	5 44	11 43	17 39
19	23 20.6	−1.1	+3.8	11	3	5 36	11 30	17 20
21	23 15.4	−2.1	+3.0	11	6	5 28	11 17	17 03
23	23 11.4	−3.1	+2.4	11	10	5 21	11 05	16 47
25	23 08.9	−3.9	+1.9	11	14	5 15	10 56	16 34
27	23 07.8	−4.5	+1.6	10	18	5 10	10 47	16 22
29	23 08.2	−5.0	+1.3	10	23	5 05	10 40	16 13
31	23 09.9	−5.4	+1.0	10	27	5 01	10 34	16 06

Rising and setting times are for latitude 54°

VENUS

Day	R.A. h m	Dec °	Mag.	Diam. "	Phase %	Rise h m	Transit h m	Set h m
1	20 04.6	−19.5	−4.1	17	72	5 13	9 30	13 46
6	20 29.3	−18.5	−4.1	16	74	5 12	9 35	13 58
11	20 53.8	−17.3	−4.0	16	75	5 09	9 40	14 10
16	21 18.0	−15.8	−4.0	15	77	5 05	9 44	14 23
21	21 41.9	−14.2	−4.0	15	78	5 00	9 48	14 37
26	22 05.5	−12.4	−4.0	15	80	4 54	9 52	14 51
31	22 28.8	−10.5	−4.0	14	81	4 47	9 56	15 05

MARS

Day	R.A. h m	Dec °	Mag.	Diam. "	Phase %	Rise h m	Transit h m	Set h m
1	02 28.8	+15.4	+1.2	5	91	8 27	15 53	23 20
6	02 42.0	+16.5	+1.2	5	92	8 14	15 47	23 20
11	02 55.3	+17.5	+1.3	5	92	8 01	15 40	23 20
16	03 08.8	+18.5	+1.3	5	93	7 49	15 34	23 19
21	03 22.3	+19.4	+1.4	5	93	7 37	15 28	23 19
26	03 36.0	+20.2	+1.4	5	93	7 26	15 22	23 18
31	03 49.8	+21.0	+1.4	5	94	7 15	15 16	23 18

SUNRISE AND SUNSET

	London				Bristol				Birmingham				Manchester				Newcastle				Glasgow				Belfast			
	0°	05′	51°	30′	2°	35′	51°	28′	1°	55′	52°	28′	2°	15′	53°	28′	1°	37′	54°	59′	4°	14′	55°	52′	5°	56′	54°	35′
d	h	m	h	m	h	m	h	m	h	m	h	m	h	m	h	m	h	m	h	m	h	m	h	m	h	m	h	m
1	6	46	17	40	6	56	17	50	6	55	17	46	6	58	17	46	6	57	17	41	7	09	17	51	7	14	17	59
2	6	44	17	42	6	54	17	52	6	53	17	48	6	55	17	48	6	55	17	43	7	07	17	53	7	12	18	01
3	6	42	17	44	6	52	17	54	6	50	17	50	6	53	17	50	6	52	17	45	7	04	17	55	7	09	18	03
4	6	40	17	45	6	50	17	55	6	48	17	52	6	51	17	52	6	50	17	47	7	02	17	57	7	07	18	05
5	6	38	17	47	6	48	17	57	6	46	17	53	6	48	17	54	6	48	17	50	6	59	17	59	7	04	18	07
6	6	35	17	49	6	45	17	59	6	44	17	55	6	46	17	56	6	45	17	52	6	57	18	01	7	02	18	09
7	6	33	17	51	6	43	18	01	6	41	17	57	6	44	17	57	6	43	17	54	6	54	18	03	6	59	18	11
8	6	31	17	52	6	41	18	02	6	39	17	59	6	41	17	59	6	40	17	56	6	51	18	05	6	57	18	13
9	6	29	17	54	6	39	18	04	6	37	18	01	6	39	18	01	6	38	17	58	6	49	18	07	6	55	18	15
10	6	27	17	56	6	37	18	06	6	35	18	02	6	37	18	03	6	35	18	00	6	46	18	09	6	52	18	17
11	6	24	17	57	6	34	18	07	6	32	18	04	6	34	18	05	6	33	18	02	6	44	18	11	6	50	18	19
12	6	22	17	59	6	32	18	09	6	30	18	06	6	32	18	07	6	30	18	04	6	41	18	13	6	47	18	21
13	6	20	18	01	6	30	18	11	6	28	18	08	6	29	18	09	6	28	18	05	6	39	18	16	6	45	18	23
14	6	18	18	03	6	28	18	13	6	25	18	10	6	27	18	11	6	25	18	07	6	36	18	18	6	42	18	25
15	6	15	18	04	6	25	18	14	6	23	18	11	6	25	18	12	6	23	18	09	6	33	18	20	6	40	18	27
16	6	13	18	06	6	23	18	16	6	21	18	13	6	22	18	14	6	20	18	11	6	31	18	22	6	37	18	29
17	6	11	18	08	6	21	18	18	6	18	18	15	6	20	18	16	6	17	18	13	6	28	18	24	6	35	18	31
18	6	09	18	09	6	19	18	19	6	16	18	17	6	17	18	18	6	15	18	15	6	25	18	26	6	32	18	33
19	6	06	18	11	6	16	18	21	6	14	18	18	6	15	18	20	6	12	18	17	6	23	18	28	6	30	18	35
20	6	04	18	13	6	14	18	23	6	11	18	20	6	12	18	22	6	10	18	19	6	20	18	30	6	27	18	37
21	6	02	18	14	6	12	18	24	6	09	18	22	6	10	18	24	6	07	18	21	6	18	18	32	6	25	18	39
22	5	59	18	16	6	09	18	26	6	07	18	24	6	08	18	25	6	05	18	23	6	15	18	34	6	22	18	40
23	5	57	18	18	6	07	18	28	6	04	18	26	6	05	18	27	6	02	18	25	6	12	18	36	6	20	18	42
24	5	55	18	20	6	05	18	30	6	02	18	27	6	03	18	29	6	00	18	27	6	10	18	38	6	17	18	44
25	5	53	18	21	6	03	18	31	6	00	18	29	6	00	18	31	5	57	18	29	6	07	18	40	6	15	18	46
26	5	50	18	23	6	00	18	33	5	57	18	31	5	58	18	33	5	55	18	31	6	04	18	42	6	12	18	48
27	5	48	18	25	5	58	18	35	5	55	18	33	5	56	18	35	5	52	18	33	6	02	18	44	6	09	18	50
28	5	46	18	26	5	56	18	36	5	52	18	34	5	53	18	36	5	49	18	35	5	59	18	46	6	07	18	52
29	5	43	18	28	5	54	18	38	5	50	18	36	5	51	18	38	5	47	18	37	5	57	18	48	6	04	18	54
30	5	41	18	30	5	51	18	40	5	48	18	38	5	48	18	40	5	44	18	39	5	54	18	50	6	02	18	56
31	5	39	18	31	5	49	18	41	5	45	18	40	5	46	18	42	5	42	18	41	5	51	18	52	5	59	18	58

JUPITER

Day	R.A.		Dec	Mag.	Diam.	Rise		Transit		Set	
	h	m	°		″	h	m	h	m	h	m
1	17	24.8	−22.6	−2.0	36	2	54	6	50	10	46
11	17	29.3	−22.6	−2.1	37	2	19	6	15	10	10
21	17	32.6	−22.7	−2.2	38	1	44	5	39	9	34
31	17	34.7	−22.7	−2.2	40	1	06	5	02	8	57

Equatorial Diam. 36″, Polar Diam. 34″

SATURN

Day	R.A.		Dec	Mag.	Diam.	Rise		Transit		Set	
	h	m	°		″	h	m	h	m	h	m
1	19	16.7	−21.8	+0.6	16	4	40	8	41	12	42
11	19	20.1	−21.7	+0.6	16	4	04	8	05	12	07
21	19	23.1	−21.6	+0.6	16	3	27	7	29	11	31
31	19	25.4	−21.6	+0.6	16	2	49	6	52	10	55

Equatorial Diam. 16″, Polar Diam. 15″
Rings – major axis 36″ minor axis 15″, Tilt 24°

URANUS

Day	R.A.		Dec	Mag.	Diam.	Rise		Transit		Set	
	h	m	°		″	h	m	h	m	h	m
1	01	51.5	+10.9	+5.9	3	8	15	15	15	22	15
11	01	53.2	+11.1	+5.9	3	7	37	14	37	21	38
21	01	55.1	+11.3	+5.9	3	6	58	14	00	21	02
31	01	57.1	+11.4	+5.9	3	6	20	13	23	20	25

NEPTUNE

Day	R.A.		Dec	Mag.	Diam.	Rise		Transit		Set	
	h	m	°		″	h	m	h	m	h	m
1	23	09.7	−6.4	+8.0	2	7	04	12	34	18	03
11	23	11.2	−6.3	+8.0	2	6	25	11	56	17	26
21	23	12.6	−6.1	+8.0	2	5	47	11	18	16	49
31	23	13.9	−6.0	+8.0	2	5	08	10	40	16	12

April 2019

FOURTH MONTH, 30 DAYS. *Aperire*, to open; Earth opens to receive seed.

1	*Monday*	Seven people, including six police, die in a prison riot in Coatzacoalcos, Mexico 2018	week 14 day 91
2	*Tuesday*	During a drugs raid, police discover $14m in cash in a house in Guatemala City 2003	92
3	*Wednesday*	69 peasants are killed in Lucanamarca, Peru, by Maoist guerrilla group the Shining Path 1983	93
4	*Thursday*	Dominican professional baseball player Sammy Sosa hits 500th home run 2003	94
5	*Friday*	Ecuador expells the US ambassador in Quito after allegations of corruption 2011	95
6	*Saturday*	Controversial Ecuadorian prime minister Rafael Correa *b.* 1963	96
7	*Sunday*	Toussaint Louverture, former slave and leader of the Haitian revolution *d.* 1803	97
8	*Monday*	Mass flooding kills 200 and displaces thousands in Rio de Janeiro 2010	week 15 day 98
9	*Tuesday*	Guatemala bans motorcycle passengers to prevent attacks from motorcycle hitmen 2009	99
10	*Wednesday*	Fernandina Island, a volcano in the Galapagos, erupts 2009	100
11	*Thursday*	Britain imposes naval blockade with 200 mile radius on the Falkland Isles 1982	101
12	*Friday*	Peru revises its estimate of 4,000 artefacts lost from Machu Picchu up to 40,000 2008	102
13	*Saturday*	Cuban journalist Oscar Sanchez is arrested on a charge of 'social dangerousness' 2007	103
14	*Sunday*	Jaime Lopez, a miner, is killed when a tunnel in a Guatemalan gold mine collapses 2017	104
15	*Monday*	Former Mexican state governer Javier Duarte is arrested on charges of corruption 2017	week 16 day 105
16	*Tuesday*	Cuba celebrates 50th anniversary of Bay of Pigs invasion with military parade 2011	106
17	*Wednesday*	Acclaimed Colombian author Gabriel Garcia Marquez *d.* 2014	107
18	*Thursday*	US radifies second treaty agreeing transfer of the Panama Canal to Panama 1978	108
19	*Friday*	Brazilian lawyer, politician and president, Getulio Vargas *b.* 1882	109
20	*Saturday*	The Bay of Pigs invasion is defeated by Cuban armed forces under Fidel Castro 1961	110
21	*Sunday*	Castro's Mariel boatlift begins, depositing 125,000 Cubans on US shores 1980	111
22	*Monday*	Francois 'Papa Doc' Duvalier, president of Haiti, dies after 14 years in office 1971	week 17 day 112
23	*Tuesday*	Spain ignores US call to withdraw from Cuba, initiating the Spanish-American War 1898	113
24	*Wednesday*	Mexican rebels led by Pancho Villa gain ground and launch drive against federal forces 1920	114
25	*Thursday*	Judge Jose Victor Orozco is murdered after ruling against drug gangs 2005	115
26	*Friday*	Human rights campaigner Bishop Juan Geradi is murdered in Guatemala 1998	116
27	*Saturday*	Cuban poet Padilla reads a statement of self-criticism to the Cuban Writers' Union 1971	117
28	*Sunday*	Mexico passes a bill protecting indigenous people's rights; indigenous leaders reject the bill 2001	118
29	*Monday*	US government declares massive oil spill in Gulf of Mexico as emergency 2010	week 18 day 119
30	*Tuesday*	Christopher Columbus lands in Cuba near what is now Guantanamo Bay 1494	120

ASTRONOMICAL PHENOMENA

d	*h*	
2	4	Venus 3° North of the Moon
2	19	Neptune 0.38° South of Mercury
4	4	Vesta 0.2° South of the Moon
10	4	Neptune 0.31° North of Venus
11	20	Mercury greatest elong. W(28°)
22	17	Ceres 3° North of the Moon
23	12	Jupiter 2° South of the Moon
25	14	Saturn 0.4° North of the Moon
25	14	Vesta 3° South of Mercury

MINIMA OF ALGOL

d	*h*	*d*	*h*	*d*	*h*
2	14.2	14	1.5	25	12.8
5	11.0	16	22.3	28	9.6
8	7.8	19	19.1		
11	4.7	22	15.9		

CONSTELLATIONS

The following constellations are near the meridian at

	d	*h*		*d*	*h*
March	1	24	April	15	21
March	16	23	May	1	20
April	1	22	May	16	19

Cepheus (below the Pole), Cassiopeia (below the Pole), Ursa Major, Leo Minor, Leo., Sextans, Hydra and Crater

THE MOON

Phase, Apsides and Node	*d*	*h*	*m*
● New Moon	5	8	52
◑ First Quarter	12	19	7
○ Full Moon	19	11	13
◐ Last Quarter	26	22	19
Apogee (405,577 km)	1	0	15
Perigee (364,205 km)	16	22	6
Apogee (404,582 km)	28	18	21

Mean longitude of the ascending node on 1st, 113°

THE SUN Diam. 32.0′

Day	Right Ascension			Dec.	Equation of time		Rise 52°		Rise 56°		Transit		Set 52°		Set 56°		Sidereal time			Transit of first point of Aries		
	h	m	s	°	m	s	h	m	h	m	h	m	h	m	h	m	h	m	s	h	m	s
1	0	40	24	+4.3	−4	08	5	36	5	32	12	04	18	33	18	38	12	36	17	11	21	51
2	0	44	03	+4.7	−3	51	5	33	5	29	12	04	18	35	18	40	12	40	13	11	17	56
3	0	47	42	+5.1	−3	33	5	31	5	26	12	03	18	37	18	42	12	44	10	11	14	00
4	0	51	21	+5.5	−3	16	5	29	5	24	12	03	18	38	18	44	12	48	06	11	10	04
5	0	55	00	+5.9	−2	58	5	27	5	21	12	03	18	40	18	46	12	52	03	11	06	08
6	0	58	39	+6.3	−2	41	5	24	5	19	12	03	18	42	18	48	12	55	59	11	02	12
7	1	02	19	+6.6	−2	24	5	22	5	16	12	02	18	44	18	50	12	59	56	10	58	16
8	1	05	59	+7.0	−2	07	5	20	5	13	12	02	18	45	18	52	13	03	52	10	54	20
9	1	09	39	+7.4	−1	51	5	18	5	11	12	02	18	47	18	54	13	07	49	10	50	24
10	1	13	19	+7.8	−1	35	5	15	5	08	12	01	18	49	18	56	13	11	46	10	46	28
11	1	17	00	+8.1	−1	18	5	13	5	06	12	01	18	50	18	58	13	15	42	10	42	32
12	1	20	40	+8.5	−1	03	5	11	5	03	12	01	18	52	19	00	13	19	39	10	38	36
13	1	24	21	+8.9	−0	47	5	09	5	01	12	01	18	54	19	02	13	23	35	10	34	41
14	1	28	03	+9.2	−0	32	5	06	4	58	12	00	18	55	19	04	13	27	32	10	30	45
15	1	31	44	+9.6	−0	17	5	04	4	55	12	00	18	57	19	06	13	31	28	10	26	49
16	1	35	26	+9.9	−0	02	5	02	4	53	12	00	18	59	19	08	13	35	25	10	22	53
17	1	39	09	+10.3	+0	12	5	00	4	50	12	00	19	01	19	10	13	39	21	10	18	57
18	1	42	51	+10.7	+0	26	4	58	4	48	11	59	19	02	19	12	13	43	18	10	15	01
19	1	46	34	+11.0	+0	39	4	56	4	45	11	59	19	04	19	14	13	47	15	10	11	05
20	1	50	18	+11.3	+0	52	4	53	4	43	11	59	19	06	19	16	13	51	11	10	07	09
21	1	54	02	+11.7	+1	05	4	51	4	41	11	59	19	07	19	18	13	55	08	10	03	13
22	1	57	46	+12.0	+1	17	4	49	4	38	11	59	19	09	19	20	13	59	04	9	59	17
23	2	01	31	+12.4	+1	29	4	47	4	36	11	58	19	11	19	22	14	03	01	9	55	22
24	2	05	16	+12.7	+1	40	4	45	4	33	11	58	19	13	19	24	14	06	57	9	51	26
25	2	09	02	+13.0	+1	51	4	43	4	31	11	58	19	14	19	27	14	10	54	9	47	30
26	2	12	48	+13.4	+2	02	4	41	4	29	11	58	19	16	19	29	14	14	50	9	43	34
27	2	16	34	+13.7	+2	11	4	39	4	26	11	58	19	18	19	31	14	18	47	9	39	38
28	2	20	22	+14.0	+2	21	4	37	4	24	11	58	19	19	19	33	14	22	44	9	35	42
29	2	24	09	+14.3	+2	30	4	35	4	22	11	57	19	21	19	35	14	26	40	9	31	46
30	2	27	58	+14.6	+2	38	4	33	4	19	11	57	19	23	19	37	14	30	37	9	27	50

DURATION OF TWILIGHT (in minutes)

Latitude	52°	56°	52°	56°	52°	56°	52°	56°
		1 April		11 April		21 April		31 April
Civil	34	38	35	39	37	42	39	44
Nautical	76	84	79	89	83	96	89	106
Astronomical	120	136	127	147	137	165	152	204

THE NIGHT SKY

Mercury is too poorly placed in the morning sky to be seen from the UK during April but may be spotted from lower latitudes mid-month when it lies 5° from Venus.

Venus (magnitude −3.9) hangs in there a little longer but only just clears the horizon before being swamped by the imminent sunrise. The gap between the rise times is down to only 40 minutes at the end of April.

Mars (magnitude 1.4 to 1.6) spends the month in Taurus and sets soon after 11pm. The three day old Moon in the western sky on the evening of the 8th marks the tip of a large triangle anchored at the other corners by Mars and the Pleiades.

Binoculars will show the Red Planet in the same field of view as the star cluster NGC 1746 on the 26th.

Jupiter (magnitude −2.2 to −2.4) is now two months shy of opposition and is up before midnight at the end of April. The planet is stationary in Ophiuchus on the 10th and then begins to retrograde. The Moon is near Jupiter on the 23rd and 24th.

Saturn (magnitude 0.6) rises in the early hours at the beginning of April but not long after midnight by the end. The rings are now at their narrowest for the year (23.5°) but their northern aspect is still very well presented. The planet is at western quadrature in early April and is stationary on the 30th before retrograding. The Moon is near by on the 25th and 26th.

THE MOON

Day	R.A.		Dec	Hor Par	Diam	Sun Co-Long	PA of Br. limb	Ph.	Age	Rise 52°		Rise 56°		Transit		Set 52°		Set 56°	
	h	m	°	'	'	°	°	%	d	h	m	h	m	h	m	h	m	h	m
1	21	44	−16.3	54.1	29.4	221	69	17	25.5	4	40	4	54	9	24	14	16	14	03
2	22	31	−12.9	54.1	29.4	233	64	10	26.5	5	03	5	14	10	08	15	22	15	13
3	23	16	−9.0	54.3	29.6	245	59	05	27.5	5	24	5	31	10	51	16	29	16	23
4	0	02	−4.8	54.6	29.8	257	50	02	28.5	5	43	5	46	11	34	17	36	17	35
5	0	47	−0.3	54.9	30.0	270	18	00	29.5	6	01	6	00	12	16	18	45	18	48
6	1	33	+4.3	55.3	30.2	282	283	00	0.9	6	20	6	15	13	00	19	55	20	02
7	2	20	+8.8	55.8	30.4	294	265	03	1.9	6	40	6	31	13	46	21	06	21	18
8	3	09	+13.0	56.3	30.6	306	262	07	2.9	7	04	6	51	14	34	22	19	22	35
9	4	01	+16.6	56.8	31.0	318	263	13	3.9	7	32	7	15	15	25	23	31	23	50
10	4	55	+19.5	57.3	31.2	331	266	21	4.9	8	07	7	47	16	19	—	—	—	—
11	5	51	+21.4	57.9	31.6	343	270	31	5.9	8	52	8	29	17	15	0	39	1	00
12	6	50	+22.0	58.4	31.8	355	275	41	6.9	9	49	9	24	18	13	1	40	2	03
13	7	50	+21.3	58.9	32.2	7	281	52	7.9	10	56	10	34	19	11	2	32	2	54
14	8	49	+19.3	59.4	32.4	19	286	64	8.9	12	12	11	55	20	08	3	14	3	33
15	9	48	+16.1	59.8	32.6	32	291	75	9.9	13	33	13	20	21	04	3	49	4	03
16	10	46	+11.8	60.1	32.8	44	296	84	10.9	14	57	14	49	21	58	4	17	4	27
17	11	41	+6.8	60.2	32.8	56	300	92	11.9	16	20	16	18	22	50	4	42	4	47
18	12	36	+1.4	60.1	32.8	68	306	97	12.9	17	43	17	46	23	42	5	05	5	05
19	13	30	−4.0	59.7	32.6	80	330	100	13.9	19	05	19	13	—	—	5	27	5	23
20	14	24	−9.2	59.2	32.2	92	75	100	14.9	20	26	20	38	0	34	5	51	5	42
21	15	18	−13.8	58.5	31.8	105	93	97	15.9	21	43	21	59	1	26	6	17	6	04
22	16	13	−17.5	57.7	31.4	117	95	92	16.9	22	54	23	15	2	19	6	47	6	29
23	17	08	−20.1	56.8	31.0	129	92	85	17.9	23	58	—	—	3	12	7	24	7	03
24	18	03	−21.7	56.1	30.6	141	89	77	18.9	—	—	0	22	4	04	8	08	7	44
25	18	57	−22.1	55.4	30.2	153	84	68	19.9	0	53	1	18	4	56	8	59	8	35
26	19	49	−21.5	54.8	29.8	166	80	59	20.9	1	39	2	00	5	46	9	57	9	34
27	20	40	−19.9	54.5	29.6	178	75	49	21.9	2	15	2	35	6	34	10	59	10	39
28	21	29	−17.4	54.2	29.6	190	71	40	22.9	2	45	3	00	7	20	12	03	11	47
29	22	17	−14.2	54.2	29.6	202	68	31	23.9	3	09	3	21	8	04	13	08	12	58
30	23	03	−10.5	54.3	29.6	214	65	23	24.9	3	30	3	38	8	47	14	15	14	08

MERCURY

Day	R.A.		Dec °	Mag.	Diam. "	Phase %	Rise h m	Transit h m	Set h m
	h	m							
1	23	11.2	−5.5	+1.0	9	29	4 59	10 32	16 04
3	23	14.7	−5.6	+0.8	9	33	4 55	10 28	16 00
5	23	19.3	−5.5	+0.7	9	37	4 51	10 25	15 58
7	23	24.8	−5.3	+0.6	8	40	4 48	10 23	15 57
9	23	31.1	−5.0	+0.5	8	44	4 44	10 21	15 58
11	23	38.1	−4.5	+0.4	8	47	4 41	10 21	16 00
13	23	45.8	−3.9	+0.3	8	50	4 38	10 21	16 03
15	23	54.1	−3.2	+0.3	7	53	4 35	10 21	16 08
17	00	02.9	−2.4	+0.2	7	56	4 32	10 22	16 13
19	00	12.2	−1.5	+0.1	7	59	4 29	10 24	16 20
21	00	22.0	−0.6	+0.1	7	61	4 25	10 26	16 27
23	00	32.2	+0.5	0.0	7	64	4 22	10 28	16 35
25	00	42.8	+1.6	−0.1	6	67	4 19	10 31	16 44
27	00	53.9	+2.9	−0.1	6	70	4 16	10 34	16 54
29	01	05.4	+4.1	−0.2	6	72	4 13	10 38	17 04

Rising and setting times are for latitude 54°

VENUS

Day	R.A.		Dec °	Mag.	Diam. "	Phase %	Rise h m	Transit h m	Set h m
	h	m							
1	22	33.4	−10.1	−4.0	14	81	4 45	9 56	15 08
6	22	56.3	−8.0	−4.0	14	82	4 37	10 00	15 22
11	23	19.0	−5.8	−3.9	13	84	4 29	10 03	15 37
16	23	41.5	−3.5	−3.9	13	85	4 20	10 05	15 51
21	00	03.9	−1.2	−3.9	13	86	4 11	10 08	16 06
26	00	26.3	+1.1	−3.9	13	87	4 02	10 11	16 20

MARS

Day	R.A.		Dec °	Mag.	Diam. "	Phase %	Rise h m	Transit h m	Set h m
	h	m							
1	03	52.5	+21.2	+1.4	5	94	7 12	15 15	23 17
6	04	06.4	+21.8	+1.5	5	94	7 02	15 09	23 16
11	04	20.4	+22.5	+1.5	4	94	6 52	15 03	23 15
16	04	34.5	+23.0	+1.5	4	95	6 42	14 57	23 13
21	04	48.6	+23.5	+1.6	4	95	6 34	14 52	23 11
26	05	02.8	+23.8	+1.6	4	95	6 25	14 46	23 08

SUNRISE AND SUNSET

	London				Bristol				Birmingham				Manchester				Newcastle				Glasgow				Belfast			
	0°	05′	51°	30′	2°	35′	51°	28′	1°	55′	52°	28′	2°	15′	53°	28′	1°	37′	54°	59′	4°	14′	55°	52′	5°	56′	54°	35′
d	h	m	h	m	h	m	h	m	h	m	h	m	h	m	h	m	h	m	h	m	h	m	h	m	h	m	h	m
1	5	37	18	33	5	47	18	43	5	43	18	41	5	43	18	44	5	39	18	43	5	49	18	54	5	57	19	00
2	5	34	18	35	5	44	18	45	5	41	18	43	5	41	18	45	5	37	18	45	5	46	18	56	5	54	19	02
3	5	32	18	36	5	42	18	46	5	38	18	45	5	39	18	47	5	34	18	47	5	44	18	58	5	52	19	03
4	5	30	18	38	5	40	18	48	5	36	18	47	5	36	18	49	5	32	18	49	5	41	19	00	5	50	19	05
5	5	28	18	40	5	38	18	50	5	34	18	48	5	34	18	51	5	29	18	51	5	38	19	02	5	47	19	07
6	5	25	18	41	5	35	18	51	5	31	18	50	5	31	18	53	5	27	18	53	5	36	19	04	5	45	19	09
7	5	23	18	43	5	33	18	53	5	29	18	52	5	29	18	55	5	24	18	54	5	33	19	06	5	42	19	11
8	5	21	18	45	5	31	18	55	5	27	18	53	5	27	18	56	5	22	18	56	5	31	19	08	5	40	19	13
9	5	19	18	46	5	29	18	56	5	25	18	55	5	24	18	58	5	19	18	58	5	28	19	10	5	37	19	15
10	5	16	18	48	5	27	18	58	5	22	18	57	5	22	19	00	5	17	19	00	5	25	19	12	5	35	19	17
11	5	14	18	50	5	24	19	00	5	20	18	59	5	20	19	02	5	14	19	02	5	23	19	14	5	32	19	19
12	5	12	18	51	5	22	19	01	5	18	19	00	5	17	19	04	5	12	19	04	5	20	19	17	5	30	19	21
13	5	10	18	53	5	20	19	03	5	15	19	02	5	15	19	05	5	09	19	06	5	18	19	19	5	27	19	23
14	5	08	18	55	5	18	19	05	5	13	19	04	5	13	19	07	5	07	19	08	5	15	19	21	5	25	19	24
15	5	06	18	56	5	16	19	06	5	11	19	06	5	10	19	09	5	04	19	10	5	13	19	23	5	23	19	26
16	5	03	18	58	5	13	19	08	5	09	19	07	5	08	19	11	5	02	19	12	5	10	19	25	5	20	19	28
17	5	01	19	00	5	11	19	10	5	07	19	09	5	06	19	13	5	00	19	14	5	08	19	27	5	18	19	30
18	4	59	19	01	5	09	19	11	5	04	19	11	5	03	19	15	4	57	19	16	5	05	19	29	5	15	19	32
19	4	57	19	03	5	07	19	13	5	02	19	13	5	01	19	16	4	55	19	18	5	03	19	31	5	13	19	34
20	4	55	19	05	5	05	19	15	5	00	19	14	4	59	19	18	4	52	19	20	5	00	19	33	5	11	19	36
21	4	53	19	06	5	03	19	16	4	58	19	16	4	57	19	20	4	50	19	22	4	58	19	35	5	08	19	38
22	4	51	19	08	5	01	19	18	4	56	19	18	4	54	19	22	4	48	19	24	4	56	19	37	5	06	19	40
23	4	49	19	10	4	59	19	20	4	54	19	20	4	52	19	24	4	45	19	26	4	53	19	39	5	04	19	42
24	4	47	19	11	4	57	19	21	4	52	19	21	4	50	19	26	4	43	19	28	4	51	19	41	5	02	19	44
25	4	45	19	13	4	55	19	23	4	49	19	23	4	48	19	27	4	41	19	30	4	48	19	43	4	59	19	46
26	4	43	19	15	4	53	19	25	4	47	19	25	4	46	19	29	4	39	19	31	4	46	19	45	4	57	19	47
27	4	41	19	16	4	51	19	26	4	45	19	27	4	44	19	31	4	36	19	33	4	44	19	47	4	55	19	49
28	4	39	19	18	4	49	19	28	4	43	19	28	4	42	19	33	4	34	19	35	4	41	19	49	4	53	19	51
29	4	37	19	20	4	47	19	30	4	41	19	30	4	39	19	35	4	32	19	37	4	39	19	51	4	50	19	53
30	4	35	19	21	4	45	19	31	4	39	19	32	4	37	19	36	4	30	19	39	4	37	19	53	4	48	19	55

JUPITER

Day	R.A.		Dec	Mag.	Diam.	Rise		Transit		Set	
	h	m	°		″	h	m	h	m	h	m
1	17	34.9	−22.7	−2.2	40	1	03	4	58	8	53
11	17	35.5	−22.7	−2.3	41	0	24	4	19	8	14
21	17	34.8	−22.7	−2.4	42	23	41	3	39	7	34

Equatorial Diam. 40″, Polar Diam. 37″

SATURN

Day	R.A.		Dec	Mag.	Diam.	Rise		Transit		Set	
	h	m	°		″	h	m	h	m	h	m
1	19	25.6	−21.6	+0.6	16	2	46	6	48	10	51
11	19	27.3	−21.5	+0.6	17	2	08	6	11	10	14
21	19	28.2	−21.5	+0.5	17	1	29	5	32	9	35

Equatorial Diam. 17″, Polar Diam. 15″
Rings – major axis 38″ minor axis 15″, Tilt 23°

URANUS

Day	R.A.		Dec	Mag.	Diam.	Rise		Transit		Set	
	h	m	°		″	h	m	h	m	h	m
1	01	57.3	+11.5	+5.9	3	6	16	13	19	20	22
11	01	59.4	+11.7	+5.9	3	5	38	12	42	19	46
21	02	01.6	+11.9	+5.9	3	4	59	12	05	19	10

NEPTUNE

Day	R.A.		Dec	Mag.	Diam.	Rise		Transit		Set	
	h	m	°		″	h	m	h	m	h	m
1	23	14.0	−6.0	+8.0	2	5	04	10	36	16	08
11	23	15.3	−5.9	+8.0	2	4	25	9	58	15	31
21	23	16.5	−5.7	+7.9	2	3	47	9	20	14	53

May 2019

FIFTH MONTH, 31 DAYS. *Maia*, goddess of growth and increase

1	*Wednesday*	Ayrton Senna, Brazilian Formula One driver, is killed in a crash at the San Marino Grand Prix 1994	day 121
2	*Thursday*	Chaiten volcano, southern Chile, erupts for the first time in 9,400 years 2008	122
3	*Friday*	Venezuelan President Hugo Chavez threatens to nationalise banks and steel producers 2007	123
4	*Saturday*	British warship HMS *Sheffield* is sunk by Argentinian fighter bomber 1982	124
5	*Sunday*	First turbines at controversial Amazonian dam Belo Monte go online 2016	125

6	*Monday*	Colombian independence leader Francisco de Paula Santander (1810–19) *d.* 1840	week 19 day 126
7	*Tuesday*	Eva Perón, actor and First Lady of Argentina (1946–52) *b.* 1919	127
8	*Wednesday*	US Congress passes a bill appropriating $50,000 for the relief of earthquake victims in Venezuela 1812	128
9	*Thursday*	18 anti-government protestors are killed by police in El Salvador 1979	129
10	*Friday*	Former Guatemalan dictator Efrain Montt is found guilty of genocide and crimes against humanity 2013	130
11	*Saturday*	Notorious Puerto Rican bank robber Norbeto Gonzales Claudio is arrested by the FBI 2011	131
12	*Sunday*	Former US President Jimmy Carter arrives in Cuba for visit with Fidel Castro 2002	132

13	*Monday*	Brazil is the last country in the world to abolish slavery with the 'Golden Law' 1888	week 20 day 133
14	*Tuesday*	Paraguay gains independence from Spain 1811	134
15	*Wednesday*	First reported Zika virus incident in Brazil in what becomes a national emergency 2015	135
16	*Thursday*	Thousands gather in Bolivia to demand the nationalisation of the energy industry 2005	136
17	*Friday*	Maoist radicals attack polling location on eve of election in Peru 1980	137
18	*Saturday*	45 young Chilean soldiers die during a training mission in the Andes 2005	138
19	*Sunday*	World leaders urge the Bush Administration to close detention camp Guantanamo Bay 2006	139

20	*Monday*	Toussaint Loverture, former slave and Haitian leader, *b.* 1743	week 21 day 140
21	*Tuesday*	Mexican president Venustiano Carranza is executed by army generals 1920	141
22	*Wednesday*	Most powerful earthquake ever recorded hits Chile, with a moment magnitude scale 9.4–9.6 1960	142
23	*Thursday*	Torrential rain begins in Haiti and the Dominican Republic, resulting in devastating floods 2004	143
24	*Friday*	First attempted assasination of Soviet revolutionary Leon Trotsky in Mexico 1940	144
25	*Saturday*	Spanish Viceroy Cisneros is expelled from Buenos Aires during Semana de Mayo 1810	145
26	*Sunday*	Puerto Rican composer Felipe Guiterrez Y Espinosa *d.* 1899	146

27	*Monday*	Central America's largest church opens in Guatemala City; it has 12,500 seats and a helipad 2007	week 22 day 147
28	*Tuesday*	Fidel Castro's Cuban revolutionary group overwhelm army post in El Uvero 1958	148
29	*Wednesday*	Villiagers in Panzos town square are murdered by the Guatemalan Army 1978	149
30	*Thursday*	Gabriel Garcia Marquez's *One Hundred Years of Solitude* is published 1967	150
31	*Friday*	The 13th FIFA World Cup begins in Mexico 1986	151

ASTRONOMICAL PHENOMENA

d	h	
2	12	Venus 4° North of the Moon
2	13	Vesta 0.2° South of the Moon
3	6	Mercury 3° North of the Moon
3	23	Uranus 5° North of the Moon
7	24	Mars 3° North of the Moon
8	8	Uranus 1° North of Mercury
18	8	Uranus 1° North of Venus
19	18	Ceres 1° North of the Moon
20	17	Jupiter 2° South of the Moon
22	22	Saturn 0.5° North of the Moon
28	23	Ceres at opposition (Mag. 7.0)
30	22	Vesta 0.6° South of the Moon

MINIMA OF ALGOL

d	h	d	h	d	h
1	6.4	12	17.7	24	4.9
4	3.2	15	14.5	27	1.8
7	0.0	18	11.3	29	22.6
9	20.9	21	8.1		

CONSTELLATIONS

The following constellations are near the meridian at

	d	h		d	h
April	1	24	May	16	21
April	15	23	June	1	20
May	1	22	June	15	19

Cepheus (below the Pole), Cassiopeia (below the Pole), Ursa Minor, Ursa Major, Canes Venatici, Coma Berenices, Bootes, Leo, Virgo, Crater, Corvus and Hydra

THE MOON

Phase, Apsides and Node	d	h	m
● New Moon	4	22	47
◐ First Quarter	12	1	13
○ Full Moon	18	21	13
◑ Last Quarter	26	16	35
Perigee (369,009 km)	13	21	54
Apogee (404,138 km)	26	13	28

Mean longitude of the ascending node on 1st, 111°

THE SUN Diam. 31.8′

Day	Right Ascension h	m	s	Dec. °	Equation of time m	s	Rise 52° h	m	Rise 56° h	m	Transit h	m	Set 52° h	m	Set 56° h	m	Sidereal time h	m	s	Transit of first point of Aries h	m	s
1	2	31	47	+14.9	+2	46	4	31	4	17	11	57	19	24	19	39	14	34	33	9	23	54
2	2	35	36	+15.2	+2	53	4	29	4	15	11	57	19	26	19	41	14	38	30	9	19	58
3	2	39	26	+15.5	+2	59	4	27	4	13	11	57	19	28	19	43	14	42	26	9	16	02
4	2	43	16	+15.8	+3	05	4	25	4	10	11	57	19	29	19	45	14	46	23	9	12	07
5	2	47	07	+16.1	+3	11	4	24	4	08	11	57	19	31	19	47	14	50	19	9	08	11
6	2	50	59	+16.4	+3	16	4	22	4	06	11	57	19	33	19	49	14	54	16	9	04	15
7	2	54	51	+16.7	+3	20	4	20	4	04	11	57	19	34	19	51	14	58	13	9	00	19
8	2	58	44	+17.0	+3	24	4	18	4	02	11	57	19	36	19	53	15	02	09	8	56	23
9	3	02	37	+17.2	+3	28	4	17	4	00	11	56	19	37	19	54	15	06	06	8	52	27
10	3	06	31	+17.5	+3	30	4	15	3	58	11	56	19	39	19	56	15	10	02	8	48	31
11	3	10	25	+17.8	+3	32	4	13	3	56	11	56	19	41	19	58	15	13	59	8	44	35
12	3	14	20	+18.0	+3	34	4	12	3	54	11	56	19	42	20	00	15	17	55	8	40	39
13	3	18	16	+18.3	+3	35	4	10	3	52	11	56	19	44	20	02	15	21	52	8	36	43
14	3	22	12	+18.5	+3	36	4	08	3	50	11	56	19	45	20	04	15	25	48	8	32	47
15	3	26	08	+18.7	+3	36	4	07	3	48	11	56	19	47	20	06	15	29	45	8	28	52
16	3	30	05	+19.0	+3	35	4	05	3	46	11	56	19	48	20	08	15	33	42	8	24	56
17	3	34	03	+19.2	+3	34	4	04	3	45	11	56	19	50	20	09	15	37	38	8	21	00
18	3	38	01	+19.4	+3	32	4	02	3	43	11	56	19	51	20	11	15	41	35	8	17	04
19	3	42	00	+19.7	+3	30	4	01	3	41	11	57	19	53	20	13	15	45	31	8	13	08
20	3	45	59	+19.9	+3	27	4	00	3	39	11	57	19	54	20	15	15	49	28	8	09	12
21	3	49	59	+20.1	+3	24	3	58	3	38	11	57	19	56	20	16	15	53	24	8	05	16
22	3	54	00	+20.3	+3	20	3	57	3	36	11	57	19	57	20	18	15	57	21	8	01	20
23	3	58	00	+20.5	+3	16	3	56	3	35	11	57	19	58	20	20	16	01	17	7	57	24
24	4	02	02	+20.7	+3	11	3	55	3	33	11	57	20	00	20	21	16	05	14	7	53	28
25	4	06	04	+20.9	+3	05	3	54	3	32	11	57	20	01	20	23	16	09	11	7	49	32
26	4	10	07	+21.0	+3	00	3	52	3	30	11	57	20	02	20	25	16	13	07	7	45	37
27	4	14	10	+21.2	+2	53	3	51	3	29	11	57	20	04	20	26	16	17	04	7	41	41
28	4	18	13	+21.4	+2	46	3	50	3	28	11	57	20	05	20	28	16	21	00	7	37	45
29	4	22	17	+21.5	+2	39	3	49	3	27	11	57	20	06	20	29	16	24	57	7	33	49
30	4	26	22	+21.7	+2	31	3	48	3	25	11	58	20	07	20	30	16	28	53	7	29	53
31	4	30	26	+21.8	+2	22	3	48	3	24	11	58	20	08	20	32	16	32	50	7	25	57

DURATION OF TWILIGHT (in minutes)

Latitude	52°	56°	52°	56°	52°	56°	52°	56°
		1 May		11 May		21 May		31 May
Civil	39	44	41	48	44	53	46	57
Nautical	89	106	97	120	106	141	115	187
Astronomical	152	204	176	TAN	TAN	TAN	TAN	TAN

THE NIGHT SKY

Mercury is at superior conjunction on the 21st but then rapidly moves into the evening sky where it can be picked up the last few days of May. The magnitude −1.2 planet lies almost between the tips of the 'horns' of Taurus on the 31st.

Venus rises the same time as Civil Twilight begins all month so an easy sighting can therefore be discounted from the UK. Southern Hemisphere observers however may catch Uranus (magnitude 5.9) in binoculars about 1° from Venus on the 18th.

Mars fades further from magnitude 1.6 to 1.8 and the disk is now less than four arc-seconds wide. The planet almost bisects the 'horns' of Taurus on the evening of the 6th with the Moon close the next night. Mars crosses into Gemini mid-month to pass near the star cluster M35 on the 19th. It sets before 11pm at the end of May.

Jupiter (magnitude −2.5) is now up mid-evening and slowly makes its way across the backdrop of the Milky Way in Ophiuchus. The shrinking size in the last century of its famous Red Spot is a puzzle for planetary scientists. Jupiter strikingly accompanies the Moon just past Full when it rises on the 20th.

Saturn appears before 11pm by the end of May and brightens from magnitude 0.5 to 0.3 during the month. The Moon is close to Saturn when it rises on the 22nd.

The dwarf planet (1) Ceres is a magnitude 7.0 speck when at opposition in Ophiuchus on the 28th.

THE MOON

Day	R.A.		Dec	Hor Par	Diam	Sun Co-Long	PA of Br. limb	Ph.	Age	Rise				Transit		Set			
										52°		56°				52°		56°	
	h	m	°	'	'	°	°	%	d	h	m	h	m	h	m	h	m	h	m
1	23	48	−6.3	54.6	29.8	227	62	15	25.9	3	49	3	53	9	30	15	22	15	19
2	0	33	−1.8	55.0	30.0	239	60	09	26.9	4	07	4	08	10	12	16	31	16	32
3	1	19	+2.9	55.4	30.2	251	56	04	27.9	4	25	4	22	10	56	17	41	17	46
4	2	06	+7.5	56.0	30.4	263	47	01	28.9	4	44	4	37	11	41	18	53	19	03
5	2	55	+11.9	56.5	30.8	276	336	00	0.4	5	07	4	56	12	29	20	06	20	21
6	3	47	+15.8	57.0	31.0	288	274	01	1.4	5	33	5	17	13	20	21	21	21	39
7	4	41	+19.0	57.5	31.4	300	269	05	2.4	6	07	5	46	14	14	22	32	22	54
8	5	38	+21.2	58.0	31.6	312	271	10	3.4	6	48	6	25	15	10	23	37	0	00
9	6	37	+22.2	58.4	31.8	325	274	18	4.4	7	41	7	17	16	08	—	—	—	—
10	7	37	+21.9	58.8	32.0	337	279	28	5.4	8	46	8	23	17	06	0	32	0	55
11	8	36	+20.1	59.0	32.2	349	284	38	6.4	10	00	9	40	18	03	1	17	1	37
12	9	34	+17.2	59.2	32.2	1	289	50	7.4	11	18	11	04	18	58	1	53	2	09
13	10	31	+13.2	59.4	32.4	13	292	61	8.4	12	39	12	29	19	51	2	22	2	34
14	11	26	+8.5	59.4	32.4	26	295	72	9.4	14	01	13	56	20	43	2	47	2	53
15	12	19	+3.3	59.4	32.4	38	297	82	10.4	15	21	15	22	21	33	3	09	3	11
16	13	12	−2.1	59.2	32.2	50	299	90	11.4	16	42	16	47	22	24	3	30	3	28
17	14	04	−7.3	58.8	32.0	62	301	96	12.4	18	01	18	11	23	14	3	52	3	45
18	14	58	−12.1	58.4	31.8	74	308	99	13.4	19	20	19	35	—	—	4	16	4	05
19	15	52	−16.2	57.8	31.6	86	33	100	14.4	20	35	20	53	0	06	4	44	4	28
20	16	46	−19.3	57.2	31.2	99	85	99	15.4	21	44	22	06	0	59	5	17	4	58
21	17	42	−21.4	56.5	30.8	111	88	95	16.4	22	44	23	08	1	52	5	58	5	34
22	18	37	−22.3	55.9	30.4	123	85	90	17.4	23	34	23	57	2	45	6	46	6	22
23	19	31	−22.0	55.3	30.2	135	81	83	18.4	—	—	—	—	3	37	7	41	7	18
24	20	23	−20.7	54.8	29.8	147	77	75	19.4	0	15	0	36	4	26	8	43	8	22
25	21	13	−18.5	54.5	29.6	160	73	66	20.4	0	47	1	04	5	14	9	47	9	30
26	22	01	−15.5	54.3	29.6	172	70	57	21.4	1	13	1	28	5	59	10	53	10	40
27	22	48	−12.0	54.3	29.6	184	67	47	22.4	1	35	1	46	6	42	12	00	11	50
28	23	33	−7.9	54.4	29.6	196	65	38	23.4	1	55	2	01	7	25	13	06	13	01
29	0	18	−3.5	54.8	29.8	209	64	29	24.4	2	13	2	15	8	07	14	14	14	13
30	1	03	+1.1	55.2	30.0	221	64	20	25.4	2	30	2	29	8	50	15	23	15	26
31	1	49	+5.8	55.8	30.4	233	64	13	26.4	2	49	2	43	9	34	16	34	16	42

MERCURY

Day	R.A.		Dec	Mag.	Diam.	Phase	Rise		Transit		Set	
	h	m	°		"	%	h	m	h	m	h	m
1	01	17.3	+5.5	−0.3	6	75	4	10	10	42	17	16
3	01	29.7	+6.9	−0.4	6	78	4	08	10	47	17	28
5	01	42.6	+8.3	−0.6	6	81	4	05	10	52	17	41
7	01	56.1	+9.8	−0.7	5	84	4	03	10	58	17	55
9	02	10.1	+11.3	−0.9	5	87	4	00	11	04	18	10
11	02	24.7	+12.8	−1.0	5	90	3	58	11	11	18	25
13	02	39.9	+14.4	−1.2	5	93	3	57	11	18	18	42
15	02	55.8	+15.9	−1.4	5	96	3	56	11	27	18	59
17	03	12.2	+17.4	−1.7	5	98	3	56	11	35	19	17
19	03	29.3	+18.8	−2.0	5	99	3	56	11	45	19	35
21	03	47.0	+20.2	−2.3	5	100	3	57	11	55	19	54
23	04	05.0	+21.4	−2.2	5	100	3	59	12	05	20	12
25	04	23.4	+22.5	−1.9	5	98	4	02	12	15	20	30
27	04	41.8	+23.4	−1.7	5	96	4	06	12	26	20	47
29	05	00.2	+24.2	−1.4	5	93	4	11	12	36	21	03
31	05	18.3	+24.8	−1.2	5	89	4	17	12	46	21	17

Rising and setting times are for latitude 54°

VENUS

Day	R.A.		Dec	Mag.	Diam.	Phase	Rise		Transit		Set	
	h	m	°		"	%	h	m	h	m	h	m
1	00	48.7	+3.4	−3.9	12	88	3	52	10	13	16	35
6	01	11.1	+5.7	−3.9	12	89	3	43	10	16	16	50
11	01	33.8	+8.0	−3.9	12	90	3	34	10	19	17	05
16	01	56.7	+10.2	−3.9	12	91	3	25	10	22	17	20
21	02	19.9	+12.3	−3.9	12	92	3	17	10	26	17	35
26	02	43.5	+14.3	−3.9	11	93	3	10	10	30	17	51
31	03	07.5	+16.2	−3.9	11	94	3	03	10	34	18	06

MARS

Day	R.A.		Dec	Mag.	Diam.	Phase	Rise		Transit		Set	
	h	m	°		"	%	h	m	h	m	h	m
1	05	17.0	+24.1	+1.6	4	96	6	18	14	41	23	04
6	05	31.2	+24.4	+1.7	4	96	6	11	14	35	23	01
11	05	45.4	+24.5	+1.7	4	96	6	04	14	30	22	56
16	05	59.7	+24.6	+1.7	4	97	5	58	14	24	22	51
21	06	13.9	+24.5	+1.7	4	97	5	53	14	19	22	45
26	06	28.0	+24.4	+1.7	4	97	5	48	14	13	22	39
31	06	42.1	+24.2	+1.8	4	97	5	44	14	08	22	32

SUNRISE AND SUNSET

	London 0°	05′ | 51° 30′	Bristol 2°	35′ | 51° 28′	Birmingham 1°	55′ | 52° 28′	Manchester 2°	15′ | 53° 28′	Newcastle 1°	37′ | 54° 59′	Glasgow 4°	14′ | 55° 52′	Belfast 5°	56′ | 54° 35′
d	h m	h m	h m	h m	h m	h m	h m	h m	h m	h m	h m	h m	h m	h m
1	4 33	19 23	4 43	19 33	4 37	19 33	4 35	19 38	4 27	19 41	4 34	19 55	4 46	19 57
2	4 31	19 25	4 41	19 35	4 35	19 35	4 33	19 40	4 25	19 43	4 32	19 57	4 44	19 59
3	4 29	19 26	4 39	19 36	4 33	19 37	4 31	19 42	4 23	19 45	4 30	19 59	4 42	20 01
4	4 27	19 28	4 38	19 38	4 32	19 39	4 29	19 43	4 21	19 47	4 28	20 01	4 40	20 03
5	4 26	19 29	4 36	19 39	4 30	19 40	4 27	19 45	4 19	19 49	4 26	20 03	4 38	20 04
6	4 24	19 31	4 34	19 41	4 28	19 42	4 25	19 47	4 17	19 51	4 24	20 05	4 36	20 06
7	4 22	19 33	4 32	19 43	4 26	19 44	4 24	19 49	4 15	19 52	4 21	20 07	4 34	20 08
8	4 20	19 34	4 31	19 44	4 24	19 45	4 22	19 50	4 13	19 54	4 19	20 09	4 32	20 10
9	4 19	19 36	4 29	19 46	4 22	19 47	4 20	19 52	4 11	19 56	4 17	20 11	4 30	20 12
10	4 17	19 37	4 27	19 47	4 21	19 49	4 18	19 54	4 09	19 58	4 15	20 13	4 28	20 14
11	4 15	19 39	4 26	19 49	4 19	19 50	4 16	19 56	4 07	20 00	4 13	20 15	4 26	20 15
12	4 14	19 41	4 24	19 50	4 17	19 52	4 14	19 57	4 05	20 02	4 11	20 17	4 24	20 17
13	4 12	19 42	4 22	19 52	4 16	19 53	4 13	19 59	4 03	20 04	4 09	20 18	4 22	20 19
14	4 11	19 44	4 21	19 53	4 14	19 55	4 11	20 01	4 01	20 05	4 07	20 20	4 21	20 21
15	4 09	19 45	4 19	19 55	4 12	19 57	4 09	20 02	4 00	20 07	4 06	20 22	4 19	20 22
16	4 08	19 47	4 18	19 56	4 11	19 58	4 08	20 04	3 58	20 09	4 04	20 24	4 17	20 24
17	4 06	19 48	4 16	19 58	4 09	20 00	4 06	20 06	3 56	20 11	4 02	20 26	4 15	20 26
18	4 05	19 50	4 15	19 59	4 08	20 01	4 05	20 07	3 55	20 12	4 00	20 28	4 14	20 28
19	4 03	19 51	4 14	20 01	4 07	20 03	4 03	20 09	3 53	20 14	3 59	20 29	4 12	20 29
20	4 02	19 52	4 12	20 02	4 05	20 04	4 02	20 10	3 51	20 16	3 57	20 31	4 11	20 31
21	4 01	19 54	4 11	20 04	4 04	20 06	4 00	20 12	3 50	20 17	3 55	20 33	4 09	20 33
22	4 00	19 55	4 10	20 05	4 02	20 07	3 59	20 13	3 48	20 19	3 54	20 35	4 08	20 34
23	3 58	19 57	4 09	20 06	4 01	20 09	3 57	20 15	3 47	20 21	3 52	20 36	4 06	20 36
24	3 57	19 58	4 07	20 08	4 00	20 10	3 56	20 16	3 45	20 22	3 51	20 38	4 05	20 37
25	3 56	19 59	4 06	20 09	3 59	20 11	3 55	20 18	3 44	20 24	3 49	20 40	4 04	20 39
26	3 55	20 01	4 05	20 10	3 58	20 13	3 54	20 19	3 43	20 25	3 48	20 41	4 02	20 40
27	3 54	20 02	4 04	20 12	3 56	20 14	3 53	20 21	3 41	20 27	3 46	20 43	4 01	20 42
28	3 53	20 03	4 03	20 13	3 55	20 15	3 51	20 22	3 40	20 28	3 45	20 44	4 00	20 43
29	3 52	20 04	4 02	20 14	3 54	20 16	3 50	20 23	3 39	20 30	3 44	20 46	3 59	20 44
30	3 51	20 05	4 01	20 15	3 53	20 18	3 49	20 25	3 38	20 31	3 43	20 47	3 57	20 46
31	3 50	20 07	4 00	20 16	3 52	20 19	3 48	20 26	3 37	20 32	3 41	20 49	3 56	20 47

JUPITER

Day	R.A. h m	Dec °	Mag.	Diam. ″	Rise h m	Transit h m	Set h m
1	17 32.8	−22.7	−2.5	43	22 59	2 58	6 53
11	17 29.5	−22.6	−2.5	44	22 16	2 15	6 11
21	17 25.2	−22.6	−2.6	45	21 32	1 32	5 27
31	17 20.2	−22.5	−2.6	46	20 48	0 47	4 44

Equatorial Diam. 43″, Polar Diam. 41″

SATURN

Day	R.A. h m	Dec °	Mag.	Diam. ″	Rise h m	Transit h m	Set h m
1	19 28.5	−21.5	+0.5	17	0 50	4 53	8 56
11	19 28.1	−21.5	+0.4	17	0 07	4 13	8 17
21	19 27.0	−21.6	+0.4	18	23 27	3 33	7 36
31	19 25.3	−21.6	+0.3	18	22 46	2 52	6 54

Equatorial Diam. 18″, Polar Diam. 16″
Rings – major axis 40″ minor axis 16″, Tilt 24°

URANUS

Day	R.A. h m	Dec °	Mag.	Diam. ″	Rise h m	Transit h m	Set h m
1	02 03.8	+12.1	+5.9	3	4 21	11 27	18 34
11	02 06.0	+12.2	+5.9	3	3 43	10 50	17 58
21	02 08.1	+12.4	+5.9	3	3 05	10 13	17 21
31	02 10.1	+12.6	+5.9	3	2 26	9 36	16 45

NEPTUNE

Day	R.A. h m	Dec °	Mag.	Diam. ″	Rise h m	Transit h m	Set h m
1	23 17.5	−5.6	+7.9	2	3 08	8 42	14 15
11	23 18.4	−5.5	+7.9	2	2 29	8 03	13 37
21	23 19.1	−5.5	+7.9	2	1 50	7 25	12 59
31	23 19.7	−5.4	+7.9	2	1 11	6 46	12 21

June 2019

SIXTH MONTH, 30 DAYS. *Junius,* Roman *gens* (family)

1	*Saturday*	A temperature of −33°C is recorded in Sarmiento, Argentina, the lowest recorded in South America 1907	day 152
2	*Sunday*	Former rebel leader Salvador Sanchez Ceren becomes president of El Salvador 2014	153
3	*Monday*	The Earth Summit, the largest gathering of world leaders, takes place in Rio de Janiero 1992	week 23 day 154
4	*Tuesday*	Juan Perón, founder of the Peronist movement, becomes president of Argentina 1946	155
5	*Wednesday*	Clashes in Peru over oil drilling leave at least 34 dead, including 22 police officers 2009	156
6	*Thursday*	Cuba approves sex change operations and begins to offer them free of charge 2008	157
7	*Friday*	The Treaty of Torsedillas, between Portugal and Spain over South America, is signed 1494	158
8	*Saturday*	Alejandro Dominguez takes office as police chief in Mexico; nine hours later he is killed 2005	159
9	*Sunday*	The largest deep earthquake occurs 400 miles beneath surface of Bolivia 1994	160
10	*Monday*	Mexico announces drug lord 'El Chapo' Guzman's first escape from prison 1993	week 24 day 161
11	*Tuesday*	Pope John Paul II visits Argentina, a majority Catholic country 1982	162
12	*Wednesday*	Cuba adopts the Platt Amendment under pressure from the USA 1901	163
13	*Thursday*	Largest ever show of surrealist artist Frida Kahlo's work opens in Mexico 2007	164
14	*Friday*	The Falklands War ends after ten weeks with Argentina surrendering to the UK 1982	165
15	*Saturday*	The first $50 Panama-Pacific commemorative coin is minted 1915	166
16	*Sunday*	Apache leader Geronimo is born in No-Doyohn Canyon, Mexico 1829	167
17	*Monday*	Cucuta, northeastern Colombia, is founded by Juana Cuellar 1733	week 25 day 168
18	*Tuesday*	Freak torrential rain causes mudslides in Chile, killing 63 people 1991	169
19	*Wednesday*	Notorious Colombian drug lord Pablo Escobar hands himself in to police 1991	170
20	*Thursday*	General assembly in Haiti is dissolved as Henri Namphy mounts a coup 1988	171
21	*Friday*	Skeletal remains exhumed in Brazil are confirmed to be those of Nazi Dr Josef Mengele 1985	172
22	*Saturday*	Eliades Ochoa, Cuban guitarist of Buena Vista Social Club *b.*1946	173
23	*Sunday*	Colombia and Farc guerrillas sign a peace agreement, ending 50 years of war 2016	174
24	*Monday*	Almost 200 people die in Mexico as a train plunges off a bridge into a river 1881	week 26 day 175
25	*Tuesday*	An anti-austerity strike in Argentina brings the country to a standstill 2018	176
26	*Wednesday*	Diplomatic ties between Honduras and El Salvador are dissolved at a FIFA World Cup qualifier game 1969	177
27	*Thursday*	President of Uruguay closes parliament and a coup d'etat begins, which lasts 12 years 1973	178
28	*Friday*	A huge landslide in Quebrada Blanca, Colombia, kills over 150 people 1974	179
29	*Saturday*	Brazil defeats Sweden to win their first World Cup title 1958	180
30	*Sunday*	The Central America Free Trade Agreement (CAFTA) comes into effect 2006	181

ASTRONOMICAL PHENOMENA

d	*h*	
1	18	Venus 3° North of the Moon
4	16	Mercury 4° North of the Moon
5	15	Mars 2° North of the Moon
10	15	Jupiter at opposition (Mag. −2.6)
15	15	Ceres 0.9° South of the Moon
16	19	Jupiter 2° South of the Moon
18	15	Mars 0.24° South of Mercury
19	4	Saturn 0.4° North of the Moon
21	16	Summer solstice
23	23	Mercury greatest elongation East (25°)
28	4	Vesta 1° South of the Moon
30	16	Aldebaran 2° South of the Moon

MINIMA OF ALGOL

d	*h*		*d*	*h*		*d*	*h*
1	19.4		13	6.6		24	17.9
4	16.2		16	3.5		27	14.7
7	13.0		19	0.3		30	11.5
10	9.8		21	21.1			

CONSTELLATIONS

The following constellations are near the meridian at

	d	*h*			*d*	*h*
May	1	24		June	15	21
May	16	23		July	1	20
June	1	22		July	16	19

Cassiopeia (below the Pole), Ursa Minor, Draco, Ursa Major, Canes Venatici, Bootes, Corona, Serpens, Virgo and Libra

THE MOON

Phase, Apsides and Node	*d*	*h*	*m*
● New Moon	3	10	3
◐ First Quarter	10	6	0
○ Full Moon	17	8	32
◑ Last Quarter	25	9	48
Perigee (368,504 km)	7	23	16
Apogee (404,548 km)	23	7	51

Mean longitude of the ascending node on 1st, 110°

THE SUN Diam. 31.6′

Day	Right Ascension			Dec.	Equation of time		Rise 52°		Rise 56°		Transit		Set 52°		Set 56°		Sidereal time			Transit of first point of Aries		
	h	m	s	°	m	s	h	m	h	m	h	m	h	m	h	m	h	m	s	h	m	s
1	4	34	32	+22.0	+2	13	3	47	3	23	11	58	20	09	20	33	16	36	46	7	22	01
2	4	38	38	+22.1	+2	04	3	46	3	22	11	58	20	11	20	34	16	40	43	7	18	05
3	4	42	44	+22.2	+1	55	3	45	3	21	11	58	20	12	20	36	16	44	39	7	14	09
4	4	46	50	+22.4	+1	45	3	45	3	20	11	58	20	13	20	37	16	48	36	7	10	13
5	4	50	57	+22.5	+1	34	3	44	3	20	11	58	20	14	20	38	16	52	33	7	06	17
6	4	55	04	+22.6	+1	24	3	43	3	19	11	59	20	14	20	39	16	56	29	7	02	22
7	4	59	12	+22.7	+1	13	3	43	3	18	11	59	20	15	20	40	17	00	26	6	58	26
8	5	03	20	+22.8	+1	01	3	42	3	18	11	59	20	16	20	41	17	04	22	6	54	30
9	5	07	28	+22.9	+0	50	3	42	3	17	11	59	20	17	20	42	17	08	19	6	50	34
10	5	11	36	+23.0	+0	38	3	41	3	16	11	59	20	18	20	43	17	12	15	6	46	38
11	5	15	45	+23.0	+0	26	3	41	3	16	12	00	20	18	20	44	17	16	12	6	42	42
12	5	19	53	+23.1	+0	14	3	41	3	15	12	00	20	19	20	45	17	20	08	6	38	46
13	5	24	02	+23.2	+0	02	3	41	3	15	12	00	20	20	20	45	17	24	05	6	34	50
14	5	28	11	+23.2	−0	11	3	40	3	15	12	00	20	20	20	46	17	28	02	6	30	54
15	5	32	20	+23.3	−0	23	3	40	3	15	12	00	20	21	20	47	17	31	58	6	26	58
16	5	36	30	+23.3	−0	36	3	40	3	14	12	01	20	21	20	47	17	35	55	6	23	02
17	5	40	39	+23.4	−0	49	3	40	3	14	12	01	20	22	20	48	17	39	51	6	19	07
18	5	44	48	+23.4	−1	02	3	40	3	14	12	01	20	22	20	48	17	43	48	6	15	11
19	5	48	58	+23.4	−1	15	3	40	3	14	12	01	20	22	20	48	17	47	44	6	11	15
20	5	53	08	+23.4	−1	28	3	40	3	14	12	02	20	23	20	49	17	51	41	6	07	19
21	5	57	17	+23.4	−1	41	3	41	3	15	12	02	20	23	20	49	17	55	37	6	03	23
22	6	01	27	+23.4	−1	54	3	41	3	15	12	02	20	23	20	49	17	59	34	5	59	27
23	6	05	36	+23.4	−2	07	3	41	3	15	12	02	20	23	20	49	18	03	31	5	55	31
24	6	09	46	+23.4	−2	19	3	41	3	15	12	02	20	23	20	49	18	07	27	5	51	35
25	6	13	55	+23.4	−2	32	3	42	3	16	12	03	20	23	20	49	18	11	24	5	47	39
26	6	18	04	+23.4	−2	45	3	42	3	16	12	03	20	23	20	49	18	15	20	5	43	43
27	6	22	14	+23.3	−2	58	3	43	3	17	12	03	20	23	20	49	18	19	17	5	39	47
28	6	26	23	+23.3	−3	10	3	43	3	17	12	03	20	23	20	49	18	23	13	5	35	52
29	6	30	31	+23.3	−3	23	3	44	3	18	12	03	20	23	20	49	18	27	10	5	31	56
30	6	34	40	+23.2	−3	35	3	44	3	19	12	04	20	23	20	48	18	31	06	5	28	00

DURATION OF TWILIGHT (in minutes)

Latitude	52°	56°	52°	56°	52°	56°	52°	56°
		1 June		11 June		21 June		31 June
Civil	46	58	48	61	49	63	48	61
Nautical	116	TAN	124	TAN	127	TAN	124	TAN
Astronomical	TAN	TAN	TAN	TAN	TAN	TAN	TAN	TAN

THE NIGHT SKY

Mercury can be seen in the evening sky throughout June and is highest just before mid-month. The Moon is about 35 hours old when near Mercury on the 4th. Mercury then swiftly closes in on Mars and they are just a 0.25° apart on the 18th. The gap has opened to about 2° when Mercury is at greatest elongation east on the 23rd.

Venus is still a struggle to snare just ahead of the approaching sunrise which it precedes by about 50 minutes all month. Any attempt during June has to contend with a rapidly brightening sky.

Mars (magnitude 1.8) is now rather low and is setting just over an hour after the Sun at the end of June when it has just crossed over from Gemini into Cancer. The crescent Moon is close on the 5th.

Jupiter (magnitude −2.6) is at opposition this month in Ophiuchus. That is about a month earlier than Saturn's. Next year the two reach opposition only a week apart in the same month and will have their Great Conjunction in Capricornus during December 2020. Any instrument reveals different aspects of the Jovian system from the nightly changing positions of the Galilean moons to the banded cloud belt system of the planet's atmosphere. The Moon is almost full when near Jupiter on the 16th.

Saturn (magnitude 0.3 to 0.1) rises mid-evening and is on view for the majority of the short night at this time of year. The Moon is near by on the 19th.

THE MOON

Day	R.A.		Dec	Hor Par	Diam	Sun Co- Long	PA of Br. limb	Ph.	Age	Rise				Transit		Set			
										52°		56°				52°		56°	
	h	m	°	'	'	°	°	%	d	h	m	h	m	h	m	h	m	h	m
1	2	38	+10.4	56.5	30.8	245	64	07	27.4	3	09	3	00	10	21	17	47	17	59
2	3	29	+14.5	57.2	31.2	257	63	02	28.4	3	34	3	20	11	11	19	02	19	20
3	4	23	+18.1	57.8	31.6	270	48	00	29.4	4	04	3	46	12	04	20	17	20	38
4	5	20	+20.7	58.4	31.8	282	284	00	0.9	4	43	4	21	13	01	21	27	21	50
5	6	19	+22.2	58.9	32.0	294	275	03	1.9	5	32	5	09	14	00	22	28	22	51
6	7	21	+22.2	59.2	32.2	306	278	08	2.9	6	34	6	11	15	00	23	17	23	39
7	8	22	+20.8	59.4	32.4	319	282	16	3.9	7	47	7	26	15	59	23	56	—	—
8	9	21	+18.1	59.5	32.4	331	286	25	4.9	9	06	8	49	16	55	—	—	0	14
9	10	19	+14.4	59.4	32.4	343	290	36	5.9	10	27	10	15	17	48	0	28	0	41
10	11	14	+9.8	59.3	32.4	355	293	47	6.9	11	48	11	41	18	40	0	53	1	01
11	12	07	+4.7	59.0	32.2	8	294	59	7.9	13	08	13	06	19	30	1	16	1	20
12	12	59	−0.6	58.7	32.0	20	295	70	8.9	14	27	14	30	20	19	1	37	1	36
13	13	50	−5.8	58.4	31.8	32	294	79	9.9	15	45	15	53	21	08	1	58	1	52
14	14	42	−10.7	58.0	31.6	44	293	88	10.9	17	02	17	15	21	58	2	20	2	10
15	15	35	−15.0	57.5	31.4	56	291	94	11.9	18	17	18	35	22	50	2	45	2	31
16	16	28	−18.4	57.0	31.0	69	290	98	12.9	19	28	19	49	23	42	3	15	2	57
17	17	23	−20.8	56.5	30.8	81	302	100	13.9	20	32	20	55	—	—	3	52	3	30
18	18	18	−22.1	55.9	30.4	93	79	100	14.9	21	27	21	51	0	35	4	36	4	13
19	19	12	−22.3	55.4	30.2	105	83	97	15.9	22	12	22	35	1	28	5	29	5	06
20	20	05	−21.4	55.0	30.0	117	80	93	16.9	22	48	23	07	2	18	6	28	6	07
21	20	57	−19.5	54.6	29.8	130	76	87	17.9	23	16	23	32	3	07	7	32	7	14
22	21	46	−16.7	54.3	29.6	142	73	80	18.9	23	40	23	52	3	53	8	38	8	23
23	22	33	−13.3	54.2	29.6	154	70	72	19.9	0	00	—	—	4	37	9	44	9	33
24	23	18	−9.4	54.2	29.6	166	68	63	20.9	—	—	0	08	5	20	10	51	10	44
25	0	03	−5.1	54.4	29.6	178	67	54	21.9	0	18	0	23	6	02	11	57	11	55
26	0	48	−0.6	54.8	29.8	191	66	44	22.9	0	36	0	36	6	44	13	05	13	06
27	1	33	+4.0	55.3	30.2	203	67	35	23.9	0	53	0	50	7	27	14	14	14	20
28	2	20	+8.6	56.0	30.6	215	68	26	24.9	1	12	1	05	8	12	15	26	15	36
29	3	09	+12.9	56.8	31.0	227	70	17	25.9	1	34	1	23	8	59	16	39	16	54
30	4	01	+16.7	57.6	31.4	240	73	10	26.9	2	02	1	45	9	51	17	54	18	14

MERCURY

Day	R.A.		Dec	Mag.	Diam.	Phase	Rise		Transit		Set	
	h	m	°		"	%	h	m	h	m	h	m
1	05	27.2	+25.0	−1.1	5	87	4	20	12	51	21	23
3	05	44.6	+25.3	−1.0	6	83	4	27	13	01	21	34
5	06	01.4	+25.5	−0.8	6	78	4	35	13	09	21	44
7	06	17.4	+25.5	−0.6	6	73	4	43	13	17	21	51
9	06	32.7	+25.3	−0.5	6	69	4	52	13	24	21	57
11	06	47.1	+25.0	−0.3	6	64	5	00	13	30	22	00
13	07	00.7	+24.7	−0.2	7	60	5	09	13	36	22	03
15	07	13.3	+24.2	0.0	7	56	5	17	13	40	22	03
17	07	25.0	+23.6	+0.1	7	52	5	25	13	44	22	02
19	07	35.8	+23.0	+0.2	7	48	5	32	13	46	22	00
21	07	45.5	+22.3	+0.4	8	45	5	38	13	48	21	57
23	07	54.3	+21.6	+0.5	8	41	5	44	13	48	21	52
25	08	02.0	+20.9	+0.6	8	37	5	49	13	48	21	46
27	08	08.7	+20.1	+0.8	9	34	5	52	13	46	21	40
29	08	14.3	+19.4	+0.9	9	30	5	54	13	43	21	32

Rising and setting times are for latitude 54°

VENUS

Day	R.A.		Dec	Mag.	Diam.	Phase	Rise		Transit		Set	
	h	m	°		"	%	h	m	h	m	h	m
1	03	12.4	+16.6	−3.9	11	94	3	02	10	35	18	09
6	03	36.9	+18.2	−3.9	11	95	2	56	10	40	18	24
11	04	02.0	+19.7	−3.9	11	95	2	52	10	45	18	39
16	04	27.4	+20.9	−3.9	11	96	2	50	10	51	18	53
21	04	53.3	+22.0	−3.9	11	97	2	49	10	57	19	06
26	05	19.5	+22.7	−3.9	11	97	2	50	11	04	19	18

MARS

Day	R.A.		Dec	Mag.	Diam.	Phase	Rise		Transit		Set	
	h	m	°		"	%	h	m	h	m	h	m
1	06	44.9	+24.2	+1.8	4	98	5	43	14	07	22	30
6	06	58.9	+23.9	+1.8	4	98	5	39	14	01	22	22
11	07	12.8	+23.6	+1.8	4	98	5	36	13	55	22	14
16	07	26.6	+23.1	+1.8	4	98	5	33	13	49	22	05
21	07	40.3	+22.6	+1.8	4	98	5	31	13	43	21	55
26	07	53.8	+22.1	+1.8	4	99	5	29	13	37	21	45

SUNRISE AND SUNSET

	London 0° 05′ | 51° 30′				Bristol 2° 35′ | 51° 28′				Birmingham 1° 55′ | 52° 28′				Manchester 2° 15′ | 53° 28′				Newcastle 1° 37′ | 54° 59′				Glasgow 4° 14′ | 55° 52′				Belfast 5° 56′ | 54° 35′			
d	h	m	h	m	h	m	h	m	h	m	h	m	h	m	h	m	h	m	h	m	h	m	h	m	h	m	h	m
1	3	49	20	08	3	59	20	17	3	52	20	20	3	47	20	27	3	36	20	34	3	40	20	50	3	55	20	48
2	3	48	20	09	3	59	20	19	3	51	20	21	3	46	20	28	3	35	20	35	3	39	20	51	3	54	20	50
3	3	48	20	10	3	58	20	20	3	50	20	22	3	46	20	29	3	34	20	36	3	38	20	53	3	54	20	51
4	3	47	20	11	3	57	20	21	3	49	20	23	3	45	20	30	3	33	20	37	3	37	20	54	3	53	20	52
5	3	46	20	12	3	57	20	22	3	48	20	24	3	44	20	31	3	32	20	38	3	36	20	55	3	52	20	53
6	3	46	20	13	3	56	20	22	3	48	20	25	3	43	20	32	3	31	20	40	3	36	20	56	3	51	20	54
7	3	45	20	13	3	55	20	23	3	47	20	26	3	43	20	33	3	31	20	41	3	35	20	57	3	50	20	55
8	3	45	20	14	3	55	20	24	3	47	20	27	3	42	20	34	3	30	20	42	3	34	20	58	3	50	20	56
9	3	44	20	15	3	54	20	25	3	46	20	28	3	42	20	35	3	29	20	42	3	34	20	59	3	49	20	57
10	3	44	20	16	3	54	20	26	3	46	20	29	3	41	20	36	3	29	20	43	3	33	21	00	3	49	20	58
11	3	44	20	17	3	54	20	26	3	45	20	29	3	41	20	37	3	28	20	44	3	33	21	01	3	48	20	59
12	3	43	20	17	3	53	20	27	3	45	20	30	3	40	20	37	3	28	20	45	3	32	21	02	3	48	20	59
13	3	43	20	18	3	53	20	28	3	45	20	31	3	40	20	38	3	28	20	46	3	32	21	03	3	48	21	00
14	3	43	20	18	3	53	20	28	3	45	20	31	3	40	20	39	3	27	20	46	3	31	21	03	3	47	21	01
15	3	43	20	19	3	53	20	29	3	45	20	32	3	40	20	39	3	27	20	47	3	31	21	04	3	47	21	01
16	3	43	20	20	3	53	20	29	3	44	20	32	3	40	20	40	3	27	20	47	3	31	21	04	3	47	21	02
17	3	43	20	20	3	53	20	30	3	44	20	33	3	40	20	40	3	27	20	48	3	31	21	05	3	47	21	02
18	3	43	20	20	3	53	20	30	3	44	20	33	3	40	20	41	3	27	20	48	3	31	21	05	3	47	21	03
19	3	43	20	21	3	53	20	30	3	44	20	34	3	40	20	41	3	27	20	49	3	31	21	06	3	47	21	03
20	3	43	20	21	3	53	20	31	3	45	20	34	3	40	20	41	3	27	20	49	3	31	21	06	3	47	21	03
21	3	43	20	21	3	53	20	31	3	45	20	34	3	40	20	42	3	27	20	49	3	31	21	06	3	47	21	04
22	3	43	20	21	3	53	20	31	3	45	20	34	3	40	20	42	3	27	20	49	3	31	21	06	3	47	21	04
23	3	43	20	22	3	54	20	31	3	45	20	34	3	40	20	42	3	28	20	50	3	32	21	07	3	48	21	04
24	3	44	20	22	3	54	20	31	3	45	20	34	3	41	20	42	3	28	20	50	3	32	21	07	3	48	21	04
25	3	44	20	22	3	54	20	31	3	46	20	35	3	41	20	42	3	28	20	50	3	32	21	07	3	48	21	04
26	3	45	20	22	3	55	20	31	3	46	20	34	3	42	20	42	3	29	20	50	3	33	21	06	3	49	21	04
27	3	45	20	22	3	55	20	31	3	47	20	34	3	42	20	42	3	29	20	49	3	33	21	06	3	49	21	04
28	3	45	20	21	3	56	20	31	3	47	20	34	3	43	20	42	3	30	20	49	3	34	21	06	3	50	21	04
29	3	46	20	21	3	56	20	31	3	48	20	34	3	43	20	41	3	31	20	49	3	35	21	06	3	51	21	03
30	3	47	20	21	3	57	20	31	3	48	20	34	3	44	20	41	3	31	20	49	3	35	21	05	3	51	21	03

JUPITER

Day	R.A. h	m	Dec °	Mag.	Diam. ″	Rise h	m	Transit h	m	Set h	m
1	17	19.7	−22.5	−2.6	46	20	43	0	43	4	39
11	17	14.2	−22.4	−2.6	46	19	58	23	55	3	55
21	17	08.8	−22.4	−2.6	46	19	13	23	10	3	11

Equatorial Diam. 46″, Polar Diam. 43″

SATURN

Day	R.A. h	m	Dec °	Mag.	Diam. ″	Rise h	m	Transit h	m	Set h	m
1	19	25.1	−21.6	+0.3	18	22	42	2	48	6	50
11	19	22.9	−21.7	+0.2	18	22	01	2	06	6	08
21	19	20.2	−21.8	+0.2	18	21	20	1	24	5	25

Equatorial – Diam. 18″, Polar Diam. 17″
Rings – major axis 41″ minor axis 17″, Tilt 24°

URANUS

Day	R.A. h	m	Dec °	Mag.	Diam. ″	Rise h	m	Transit h	m	Set h	m
1	02	10.3	+12.6	+5.9	3	2	23	9	32	16	41
11	02	12.1	+12.8	+5.9	3	1	44	8	54	16	05
21	02	13.7	+12.9	+5.8	3	1	06	8	17	15	28

NEPTUNE

Day	R.A. h	m	Dec °	Mag.	Diam. ″	Rise h	m	Transit h	m	Set h	m
1	23	19.7	−5.4	+7.9	2	1	07	6	42	12	17
11	23	20.0	−5.4	+7.9	2	0	28	6	03	11	38
21	23	20.1	−5.4	+7.9	2	23	45	5	24	10	59

July 2019

SEVENTH MONTH, 31 DAYS. *Julius* Caesar, formerly *Quintilis*, fifth month of Roman pre-Julian calendar

1	*Monday*	Rio de Janeiro is awarded UNESCO World Heritage status 2012	week 27 day 182
2	*Tuesday*	Brazil's anti-slavery team frees 1,100 workers from a sugar cane plantation 2007	183
3	*Wednesday*	Former Ecuadorian president Rafael Correa is arrested over kidnapping charges 2018	184
4	*Thursday*	Guatemalan guerilla Fermin Solano is sentenced to 90 years for human rights atrocities 2014	185
5	*Friday*	Venezuela gains independence from Spain 1811	186
6	*Saturday*	Hurricane Dennis moves across Latin America and the USA, killing at least 88 people 2005	187
7	*Sunday*	Footballer Pelé makes his international debut for Brazil against Argentina, aged just 16 1957	188
8	*Monday*	US-backed Castillo Armas takes over Guatemala from communist leadership 1954	week 28 day 189
9	*Tuesday*	Argentina gains independence from Spain 1816	190
10	*Wednesday*	Brazilian rebels gain traction outside San Paulo 1924	191
11	*Thursday*	Mexican drug lord 'El Chapo' Guzman escapes prison for the third time, through a mile-long tunnel 2015	192
12	*Friday*	Chilean president signs much-debated anti-discrimination bill after a young gay man is murdered 2012	193
13	*Saturday*	Celebrated surrealist Mexican artist Frida Kahlo d. 1954	194
14	*Sunday*	The 'Football War' between El Salvador and Honduras begins 1969	195
15	*Monday*	Jean-Bertrand Aristide, the first democratically elected president of Haiti b. 1953	week 29 day 196
16	*Tuesday*	La Paz (Bolivia) declares independence from Spain 1809	197
17	*Wednesday*	Former Mexican governor Javier Duarte is extradited from Guatemala on corruption charges 2017	198
18	*Thursday*	Argentina's deadliest bombing takes place at a Jewish Community Centre 1994	199
19	*Friday*	An arrest warrant for former Guatemalan president Alfonso Cabrera is issued 2005	200
20	*Saturday*	Pancho Villa is assassinated in Mexico	201
21	*Sunday*	Three Ecuadorian journalists are given a prison sentence for libelling President Correa 2011	202
22	*Monday*	Colombian drug lord Pablo Escobar escapes from prison 1992	week 30 day 203
23	*Tuesday*	Agriculture ministers from 34 countries meet in Guatemala 2007	204
24	*Wednesday*	Hiram Bingham rediscovers Machu Picchu and misidentifies it as the 'Lost City of the Incas' 1911	205
25	*Thursday*	Puerto Rico becomes a self-governing commonwealth of the USA 1952	206
26	*Friday*	The 26th of July Movement, a vanguard revolutionary group led by Fidel Castro, begins in Mexico 1953	207
27	*Saturday*	Francisco Pizarro Gonzalez is appointed governor of Peru 1529	208
28	*Sunday*	Gen. Jose de San Martin proclaims Peru independent from Spain after occupying Lima 1821	209
29	*Monday*	The Santa Marta earthquake destroys much of Santiago, killing over 500 people 1773	week 31 day 210
30	*Tuesday*	Last 'old style' Volkswagen Beetle is produced in Mexico 2003	211
31	*Wednesday*	Christopher Columbus is first European to discover Trinidad 1498	212

ASTRONOMICAL PHENOMENA

d	h	
1	22	Venus 2° North of the Moon
2	15	Total Solar Eclipse (S. America)
4	6	Mars 0.1° South of the Moon
4	9	Mercury 3° South of the Moon
4	22	Earth at aphelion
9	17	Saturn at opposition (Mag. 0.1)
13	20	Mars crosses M44
13	20	Jupiter 2° South of the Moon
14	15	Pluto at opposition (Mag. 14.2)
16	7	Saturn 0.2° North of the Moon
16	17	Partial Lunar Eclipse
26	8	Vesta 3° South of the Moon
31	2	Mercury 5° South of the Moon
31	21	Venus 0.6° South of the Moon

MINIMA OF ALGOL

d	h	d	h	d	h
3	8.3	14	19.6	26	6.8
6	5.1	17	16.4	29	3.6
9	2.0	20	13.2		
11	22.8	23	10.0		

CONSTELLATIONS

The following constellations are near the meridian at

	d	h		d	h
June	1	24	July	16	21
June	15	23	August	1	20
July	1	22	August	16	19

Ursa Minor, Draco, Corona, Hercules, Lyra, Serpens, Ophiuchus, Libra, Scorpius and Sagittarius

THE MOON

Phase, Apsides and Node	d	h	m
● New Moon	2	19	17
◑ First Quarter	9	10	56
○ Full Moon	16	21	39
◐ Last Quarter	25	1	19
Perigee (363,726 km)	5	5	1
Apogee (405,481 km)	21	0	0

Mean longitude of the ascending node on 1st, 108°

THE SUN Diam. 31.5′

Day	Right Ascension h	m	s	Dec. °	Equation of time m	s	Rise 52° h	m	Rise 56° h	m	Transit h	m	Set 52° h	m	Set 56° h	m	Sidereal time h	m	s	Transit of first point of Aries h	m	s
1	6	38	49	+23.1	−3	47	3	45	3	20	12	04	20	23	20	48	18	35	03	5	24	04
2	6	42	57	+23.1	−3	58	3	46	3	20	12	04	20	22	20	47	18	39	00	5	20	08
3	6	47	05	+23.0	−4	10	3	46	3	21	12	04	20	22	20	47	18	42	56	5	16	12
4	6	51	13	+22.9	−4	21	3	47	3	22	12	04	20	21	20	46	18	46	53	5	12	16
5	6	55	20	+22.8	−4	32	3	48	3	23	12	05	20	261	20	46	18	50	49	5	08	20
6	6	59	27	+22.7	−4	42	3	49	3	24	12	05	20	20	20	45	18	54	46	5	04	24
7	7	03	34	+22.6	−4	52	3	50	3	25	12	05	20	20	20	44	18	58	42	5	00	28
8	7	07	40	+22.5	−5	02	3	51	3	26	12	05	20	19	20	43	19	02	39	4	56	32
9	7	11	46	+22.4	−5	11	3	51	3	27	12	05	20	18	20	42	19	06	35	4	52	37
10	7	15	51	+22.3	−5	20	3	52	3	29	12	05	20	18	20	41	19	10	32	4	48	41
11	7	19	56	+22.2	−5	29	3	54	3	30	12	06	20	17	20	40	19	14	29	4	44	45
12	7	24	01	+22.0	−5	37	3	55	3	31	12	06	20	16	20	39	19	18	25	4	40	49
13	7	28	05	+21.9	−5	44	3	56	3	32	12	06	20	15	20	38	19	22	22	4	36	53
14	7	32	08	+21.7	−5	51	3	57	3	34	12	06	20	14	20	37	19	26	18	4	32	57
15	7	36	12	+21.6	−5	58	3	58	3	35	12	06	20	13	20	36	19	30	15	4	29	01
16	7	40	14	+21.4	−6	04	3	59	3	37	12	06	20	12	20	35	19	34	11	4	25	05
17	7	44	16	+21.3	−6	09	4	00	3	38	12	06	20	11	20	33	19	38	08	4	21	09
18	7	48	18	+21.1	−6	14	4	02	3	40	12	06	20	10	20	32	19	42	04	4	17	13
19	7	52	19	+20.9	−6	19	4	03	3	41	12	06	20	09	20	31	19	46	01	4	13	17
20	7	56	19	+20.7	−6	23	4	04	3	43	12	06	20	08	20	29	19	49	58	4	09	22
21	8	00	19	+20.6	−6	26	4	06	3	44	12	06	20	07	20	28	19	53	54	4	05	26
22	8	04	19	+20.4	−6	29	4	07	3	46	12	06	20	05	20	26	19	57	51	4	01	30
23	8	08	17	+20.2	−6	31	4	08	3	48	12	07	20	04	20	24	20	01	47	3	57	34
24	8	12	16	+20.0	−6	33	4	10	3	49	12	07	20	03	20	23	20	05	44	3	53	38
25	8	16	13	+19.8	−6	34	4	11	3	51	12	07	20	01	20	21	20	09	40	3	49	42
26	8	20	11	+19.5	−6	35	4	12	3	53	12	07	20	00	20	19	20	13	37	3	45	46
27	8	24	07	+19.3	−6	35	4	14	3	54	12	07	19	58	20	18	20	17	33	3	41	50
28	8	28	03	+19.1	−6	34	4	15	3	56	12	07	19	57	20	16	20	21	30	3	37	54
29	8	31	58	+18.9	−6	33	4	17	3	58	12	07	19	55	20	14	20	25	27	3	33	58
30	8	35	53	+18.6	−6	31	4	18	4	00	12	06	19	54	20	12	20	29	23	3	30	02
31	8	39	47	+18.4	−6	29	4	20	4	02	12	06	19	52	20	10	20	33	20	3	26	07

DURATION OF TWILIGHT (in minutes)

Latitude	52°	56°	52°	56°	52°	56°	52°	56°
		1 July		11 July		21 July		31 July
Civil	48	61	47	58	44	53	42	49
Nautical	124	TAN	117	TAN	107	146	98	123
Astronomical	TAN	TAN	TAN	TAN	TAN	TAN	182	TAN

THE NIGHT SKY

Mercury might be glimpsed after sunset the first few days of July before being lost to view. It moves into the morning sky after inferior conjunction on the 21st and might be spotted accompanying the thin lunar crescent very low down on the 31st.

Venus has now got too close to the Sun to be seen this month.

Mars (magnitude 1.8) crosses the open cluster M44 in Cancer on the 13th but thereafter gets harder to see as it follows the Sun below more quickly each evening. The Moon is very close to Mars on the 4th.

Jupiter (magnitude −2.5) is visible the majority of the night and dominates the summer star groups. The Moon is near by on the 13th.

Saturn (magnitude 0.1) is at opposition on the 9th but the planet's low ecliptic latitude means it is not well placed when on the meridian for observers in the UK. The Moon is close to Saturn on the 15th.

The dwarf planet Pluto (magnitude 14.2) is at opposition in Sagittarius on the 14th. It lies 32.82au distant at this time.

The path of totality for a solar eclipse on the 2nd tracks mostly over the southern Pacific Ocean before crossing the central regions of Chile and Argentina as it concludes. The rest of South America and most of Central America will see a partial.

A partial lunar eclipse (magnitude 0.653) on the 16th will be seen from Europe (including the UK), Asia, Australia, South America, and Antarctica.

THE MOON

Day	R.A. h	R.A. m	Dec °	Hor Par '	Diam '	Sun Co-Long °	PA of Br. limb °	Ph. %	Age d	Rise 52° h	Rise 52° m	Rise 56° h	Rise 56° m	Transit h	Transit m	Set 52° h	Set 52° m	Set 56° h	Set 56° m
1	4	57	+19.8	58.4	31.8	252	77	04	27.9	2	35	2	15	10	46	19	07	19	31
2	5	56	+21.8	59.1	32.2	264	81	01	28.9	3	20	2	58	11	45	20	14	20	39
3	6	58	+22.4	59.7	32.6	276	284	00	0.3	4	18	3	54	12	46	21	10	21	34
4	8	01	+21.5	60.1	32.8	289	278	02	1.3	5	28	5	06	13	48	21	55	22	15
5	9	03	+19.2	60.3	32.8	301	283	07	2.3	6	48	6	29	14	47	22	30	22	45
6	10	03	+15.6	60.2	32.8	313	287	14	3.3	8	11	7	58	15	43	22	58	23	08
7	11	00	+11.1	60.0	32.6	325	290	23	4.3	9	34	9	26	16	36	23	22	23	27
8	11	54	+6.0	59.5	32.4	338	292	34	5.3	10	56	10	53	17	27	23	44	23	44
9	12	47	+0.6	59.0	32.2	350	292	45	6.3	12	16	12	17	18	17	—	—	—	—
10	13	39	−4.6	58.5	31.8	2	292	56	7.3	13	34	13	40	19	06	0	04	0	01
11	14	30	−9.6	57.9	31.6	14	290	67	8.3	14	50	15	01	19	55	0	26	0	18
12	15	22	−13.9	57.3	31.2	26	287	77	9.3	16	05	16	22	20	45	0	50	0	37
13	16	14	−17.6	56.8	31.0	39	284	85	10.3	17	17	17	37	21	37	1	17	1	01
14	17	08	−20.2	56.3	30.6	51	279	92	11.3	18	23	18	46	22	29	1	51	1	30
15	18	02	−21.9	55.8	30.4	63	274	96	12.3	19	20	19	45	23	21	2	32	2	09
16	18	56	−22.4	55.3	30.2	75	267	99	13.3	20	08	20	32	—	—	3	21	2	58
17	19	49	−21.8	54.9	30.0	87	112	100	14.3	20	47	21	08	0	12	4	18	3	55
18	20	41	−20.1	54.6	29.8	100	83	99	15.3	21	19	21	36	1	01	5	20	5	01
19	21	31	−17.6	54.3	29.6	112	78	96	16.3	21	44	21	57	1	48	6	25	6	09
20	22	19	−14.4	54.1	29.6	124	74	91	17.3	22	05	22	15	2	33	7	31	7	19
21	23	05	−10.6	54.1	29.4	136	72	85	18.3	22	24	22	30	3	17	8	38	8	29
22	23	50	−6.4	54.1	29.6	148	70	78	19.3	22	41	22	43	3	58	9	44	9	40
23	0	34	−2.0	54.4	29.6	161	69	70	20.3	22	58	22	56	4	40	10	50	10	50
24	1	18	+2.5	54.7	29.8	173	69	61	21.3	23	16	23	11	5	21	11	57	12	02
25	2	03	+7.1	55.3	30.2	185	70	51	22.3	23	36	23	26	6	04	13	07	13	15
26	2	51	+11.4	56.0	30.4	197	72	41	23.3	—	—	23	46	6	50	14	18	14	31
27	3	41	+15.4	56.8	31.0	210	75	31	24.3	0	01	—	—	7	38	15	31	15	48
28	4	34	+18.7	57.7	31.4	222	79	22	25.3	0	30	0	12	8	31	16	44	17	05
29	5	31	+21.1	58.6	32.0	234	85	13	26.3	1	09	0	47	9	28	17	54	18	18
30	6	32	+22.3	59.5	32.4	246	91	06	27.3	2	00	1	35	10	28	18	55	19	20
31	7	35	+22.1	60.2	32.8	259	101	02	28.3	3	05	2	40	11	30	19	47	20	08

MERCURY

Day	R.A. h m	Dec °	Mag.	Diam. "	Phase %	Rise h m	Transit h m	Set h m
1	08 18.7	+18.7	+1.1	9	27	5 55	13 39	21 24
3	08 21.9	+18.0	+1.3	10	23	5 55	13 34	21 14
5	08 23.9	+17.4	+1.6	10	20	5 52	13 28	21 04
7	08 24.7	+16.8	+1.8	10	17	5 48	13 20	20 53
9	08 24.2	+16.3	+2.1	11	13	5 43	13 12	20 41
11	08 22.4	+15.9	+2.5	11	10	5 35	13 02	20 29
13	08 19.5	+15.6	+3.0	11	7	5 26	12 51	20 16
15	08 15.5	+15.4	+3.5	12	5	5 15	12 38	20 03
17	08 10.7	+15.4	+4.0	12	3	5 03	12 26	19 50
19	08 05.3	+15.4	+4.5	12	2	4 49	12 12	19 37
21	07 59.7	+15.5	+4.8	12	1	4 35	11 59	19 24
23	07 54.2	+15.8	+4.7	11	1	4 20	11 46	19 13
25	07 49.2	+16.1	+4.1	11	2	4 06	11 33	19 03
27	07 45.1	+16.5	+3.5	11	4	3 52	11 22	18 54
29	07 42.2	+16.9	+2.9	10	7	3 39	11 12	18 47
31	07 40.8	+17.4	+2.3	10	11	3 27	11 03	18 41

Rising and setting times are for latitude 54°

VENUS

Day	R.A. h m	Dec °	Mag.	Diam. "	Phase %	Rise h m	Transit h m	Set h m
1	05 46.0	+23.2	−3.9	11	98	2 53	11 10	19 28
6	06 12.6	+23.4	−3.9	11	98	2 59	11 17	19 36
11	06 39.4	+23.3	−3.9	11	99	3 06	11 24	19 42
16	07 06.0	+23.0	−3.9	10	99	3 16	11 31	19 46
21	07 32.5	+22.3	−3.9	10	99	3 27	11 38	19 49
26	07 58.7	+21.4	−3.9	10	100	3 40	11 45	19 49
31	08 24.6	+20.2	−3.9	10	100	3 54	11 51	19 47

MARS

Day	R.A. h m	Dec °	Mag.	Diam. "	Phase %	Rise h m	Transit h m	Set h m
1	08 07.2	+21.4	+1.8	4	99	5 27	13 31	21 34
6	08 20.5	+20.7	+1.8	4	99	5 25	13 24	21 23
11	08 33.7	+20.0	+1.8	4	99	5 24	13 18	21 12
16	08 46.7	+19.2	+1.8	4	99	5 22	13 11	21 00
21	08 59.6	+18.3	+1.8	4	99	5 21	13 04	20 47
26	09 12.4	+17.4	+1.8	4	100	5 20	12 57	20 34
31	09 25.0	+16.4	+1.8	4	100	5 19	12 50	20 21

SUNRISE AND SUNSET

	London				Bristol				Birmingham				Manchester				Newcastle				Glasgow				Belfast			
	0°	05'	51°	30'	2°	35'	51°	28'	1°	55'	52°	28'	2°	15'	53°	28'	1°	37'	54°	59'	4°	14'	55°	52'	5°	56'	54°	35'
d	h	m	h	m	h	m	h	m	h	m	h	m	h	m	h	m	h	m	h	m	h	m	h	m	h	m	h	m
1	3	47	20	21	3	57	20	31	3	49	20	33	3	44	20	41	3	32	20	48	3	36	21	05	3	52	21	03
2	3	48	20	20	3	58	20	30	3	50	20	33	3	45	20	40	3	33	20	48	3	37	21	04	3	53	21	02
3	3	49	20	20	3	59	20	30	3	51	20	33	3	46	20	40	3	34	20	47	3	38	21	04	3	54	21	02
4	3	49	20	20	4	00	20	29	3	51	20	32	3	47	20	39	3	34	20	47	3	39	21	03	3	54	21	01
5	3	50	20	19	4	00	20	29	3	52	20	32	3	48	20	39	3	35	20	46	3	40	21	03	3	55	21	01
6	3	51	20	19	4	01	20	28	3	53	20	31	3	49	20	38	3	36	20	45	3	41	21	02	3	56	21	00
7	3	52	20	18	4	02	20	28	3	54	20	30	3	50	20	38	3	37	20	45	3	42	21	01	3	57	20	59
8	3	53	20	17	4	03	20	27	3	55	20	30	3	51	20	37	3	39	20	44	3	43	21	00	3	58	20	58
9	3	54	20	17	4	04	20	26	3	56	20	29	3	52	20	36	3	40	20	43	3	44	20	59	4	00	20	58
10	3	55	20	16	4	05	20	26	3	57	20	28	3	53	20	35	3	41	20	42	3	45	20	58	4	01	20	57
11	3	56	20	15	4	06	20	25	3	58	20	27	3	54	20	34	3	42	20	41	3	47	20	57	4	02	20	56
12	3	57	20	14	4	07	20	24	3	59	20	27	3	55	20	33	3	43	20	40	3	48	20	56	4	03	20	55
13	3	58	20	13	4	08	20	23	4	00	20	26	3	56	20	32	3	45	20	39	3	49	20	55	4	04	20	54
14	3	59	20	12	4	09	20	22	4	02	20	25	3	57	20	31	3	46	20	38	3	51	20	54	4	06	20	53
15	4	00	20	11	4	11	20	21	4	03	20	24	3	59	20	30	3	47	20	37	3	52	20	53	4	07	20	51
16	4	02	20	10	4	12	20	20	4	04	20	23	4	00	20	29	3	49	20	35	3	54	20	51	4	08	20	50
17	4	03	20	09	4	13	20	19	4	05	20	21	4	01	20	28	3	50	20	34	3	55	20	50	4	10	20	49
18	4	04	20	08	4	14	20	18	4	07	20	20	4	03	20	27	3	52	20	33	3	57	20	49	4	11	20	48
19	4	05	20	07	4	15	20	17	4	08	20	19	4	04	20	26	3	53	20	31	3	58	20	47	4	13	20	46
20	4	07	20	06	4	17	20	16	4	09	20	18	4	06	20	24	3	55	20	30	4	00	20	46	4	14	20	45
21	4	08	20	05	4	18	20	15	4	11	20	17	4	07	20	23	3	56	20	28	4	02	20	44	4	16	20	44
22	4	09	20	04	4	19	20	13	4	12	20	15	4	08	20	22	3	58	20	27	4	03	20	42	4	17	20	42
23	4	11	20	02	4	21	20	12	4	13	20	14	4	10	20	20	3	59	20	25	4	05	20	41	4	19	20	41
24	4	12	20	01	4	22	20	11	4	15	20	13	4	11	20	19	4	01	20	24	4	07	20	39	4	20	20	39
25	4	13	19	59	4	23	20	09	4	16	20	11	4	13	20	17	4	03	20	22	4	08	20	37	4	22	20	37
26	4	15	19	58	4	25	20	08	4	18	20	10	4	15	20	16	4	04	20	21	4	10	20	36	4	24	20	36
27	4	16	19	57	4	26	20	06	4	19	20	08	4	16	20	14	4	06	20	19	4	12	20	34	4	25	20	34
28	4	18	19	55	4	28	20	05	4	21	20	07	4	18	20	12	4	08	20	17	4	14	20	32	4	27	20	32
29	4	19	19	54	4	29	20	03	4	22	20	05	4	19	20	11	4	09	20	15	4	15	20	30	4	29	20	31
30	4	21	19	52	4	31	20	02	4	24	20	03	4	21	20	09	4	11	20	13	4	17	20	28	4	30	20	29
31	4	22	19	50	4	32	20	00	4	25	20	02	4	22	20	07	4	13	20	12	4	19	20	26	4	32	20	27

JUPITER

Day	R.A.		Dec	Mag.	Diam.	Rise		Transit		Set	
	h	m	°		"	h	m	h	m	h	m
1	17	03.7	−22.3	−2.6	45	18	28	22	25	2	27
11	16	59.4	−22.2	−2.5	45	17	43	21	42	1	44
21	16	56.0	−22.1	−2.5	44	17	00	20	59	1	01
31	16	53.9	−22.1	−2.4	43	16	19	20	18	0	20

Equatorial Diam. 45", Polar Diam. 42"

SATURN

Day	R.A.		Dec	Mag.	Diam.	Rise		Transit		Set	
	h	m	°		"	h	m	h	m	h	m
1	19	17.2	−21.9	+0.1	18	20	38	0	42	4	42
11	19	14.1	−22.0	+0.1	18	19	56	23	56	3	59
21	19	10.9	−22.1	+0.1	18	19	15	23	13	3	16
31	19	08.0	−22.2	+0.2	18	18	33	22	31	2	33

Equatorial Diam. 18", Polar Diam. 17"
Rings – major axis 42" minor axis 17", Tilt 24°

URANUS

Day	R.A.		Dec	Mag.	Diam.	Rise		Transit		Set	
	h	m	°		"	h	m	h	m	h	m
1	02	15.1	+13.0	+5.8	3	0	27	7	39	14	50
11	02	16.2	+13.1	+5.8	4	23	48	7	01	14	13
21	02	17.1	+13.2	+5.8	4	23	10	6	22	13	35
31	02	17.6	+13.2	+5.8	4	22	30	5	43	12	56

NEPTUNE

Day	R.A.		Dec	Mag.	Diam.	Rise		Transit		Set	
	h	m	°		"	h	m	h	m	h	m
1	23	20.1	−5.4	+7.9	2	23	05	4	44	10	19
11	23	19.8	−5.4	+7.9	2	22	26	4	05	9	39
21	23	19.3	−5.5	+7.8	2	21	46	3	25	8	59
31	23	18.7	−5.6	+7.8	2	21	07	2	45	8	19

August 2019

EIGHTH MONTH, 31 DAYS. *Augustus*, formerly *Sextilis*, sixth month of Roman pre-Julian calendar

1	*Thursday*	President of Cuba Fidel Castro undergoes gastric surgery, marking the end of his reign 2006	day 213
2	*Friday*	Congress approves a bill lifting the total ban on abortion in Chile 2017	214
3	*Saturday*	A plan to leave oil beneath the Amazon untapped in return for international donations is announced 2010	215
4	*Sunday*	100 killed in earthquake in Dominican Republic 1946	216

5	*Monday*	The Summer Olympic Games opens in Rio de Janeiro 2016	week 32 day 217
6	*Tuesday*	Bolivia gains independence from Spain and is named for the liberator Simon Bolivar 1825	218
7	*Wednesday*	The Esquipulas II Accord is signed by Guatemala, El Salvador, Nicaragua, Honduras and Costa Rica 1987	219
8	*Thursday*	Tomas de Berlanga, discoverer of the Galápagos islands *d.* 1551	220
9	*Friday*	Venezuelan composer Reynaldo Hahn *d.* 1947	221
10	*Saturday*	Ecuador gains independence from Spain 1809	222
11	*Sunday*	Juandel Corral declares independence of Antioquia in Colombia 1813	223

12	*Monday*	Santiago de Liniers retakes Buenos Aires after British invasion 1806	week 33 day 224
13	*Tuesday*	Fidel Castro, Cuban politician and revolutionary, President of Cuba (1976-2008) *b.* 1927	225
14	*Wednesday*	First sighting of the Falkland Islands is reported by John Davis 1592	226
15	*Thursday*	Panama canal is opened 1914	227
16	*Friday*	Ecuador grants WikiLeaks founder Julian Assange political asylum 2012	228
17	*Saturday*	Argentinian racing driver Oscar Alfredo Galvez *d.* 1989	229
18	*Sunday*	Presidential hopeful Luis Carlos Galan is assassinated in Colombia 1989	230

19	*Monday*	Gervasio Antonion de Posadas joins Argentina's Second Triumvirate 1813	week 34 day 231
20	*Tuesday*	Exiled Soviet revolutionary Leon Trotsky is assassinated in Mexico City 1940	232
21	*Wednesday*	Mexian artists Frida Kahlo and Diego Rivera marry in a civil ceremony in Coyoacán 1929	233
22	*Thursday*	Haitian War of Indepence begins with thousands of slaves setting fire to crops 1791	234
23	*Friday*	First voice contact is made with the Chilean miners trapped in the San José mine since 5 August 2010	235
24	*Saturday*	Paulo Coelho, author of *The Alchemist b.* 1947	236
25	*Sunday*	52 people die in a deliberate casino fire in Monterrey, Mexico 2011	237

26	*Monday*	Brazil gives formal approval for the construction of controversial dam Belo Monte 2010	week 35 day 238
27	*Tuesday*	The Ecuadorean government takes state control of all the oil and gas produced by the country 2010	239
28	*Wednesday*	Kaqchikel Maya rebel against Spanish allies during Spanish Conquest of Guatemala 1524	240
29	*Thursday*	Atahuallpa, the last emperor of the Inca is executed by coloniser Francisco Pizarro 1533	241
30	*Friday*	Leonor Fini, Argentinian artist *d.* 1996	242
31	*Saturday*	Brazil's first female president Dilma Rousseff is impeached for breaking budget laws 2016	243

ASTRONOMICAL PHENOMENA

d	h	
1	20	Mars 2° South of the Moon
9	23	Jupiter 3° South of the Moon
9	23	Mercury greatest elongation West (19°)
12	10	Saturn 0.04° North of the Moon
12–13		Perseid meteor shower
17	23	Regulus 0.7° South of Mars
21	4	Regulus 0.96° South of Venus
24	10	Aldebaran 2° South of the Moon
24	13	Mars 0.31° South of Venus
29	3	Regulus 1° South of Mercury
30	1	Mercury 2° South of the Moon
30	10	Mars 3° South of the Moon
30	16	Venus 3° South of the Moon

MINIMA OF ALGOL

d	h	d	h	d	h
1	0.4	12	11.7	23	22.9
3	21.3	15	8.5	26	19.7
6	18.1	18	5.3	29	16.6
9	14.9	21	2.1		

CONSTELLATIONS

The following constellations are near the meridian at

	d	h		d	h
July	1	24	August	16	21
July	16	23	September	1	20
August	1	22	September	15	19

Draco, Hercules, Lyra, Cygnus, Sagitta, Ophiuchus, Serpens, Aquila and Sagittarius

THE MOON

Phase, Apsides and Node	d	h	m
● New Moon	1	3	13
◑ First Quarter	7	17	32
○ Full Moon	15	12	30
◐ Last Quarter	23	14	57
● New Moon	30	10	38

Perigee (359,398 km)	2	7	12
Apogee (406,244 km)	17	10	50
Perigee (357,176 km)	30	15	54

Mean longitude of the ascending node on 1st, 106°

THE SUN Diam. 31.5′

Day	Right Ascension			Dec.	Equation of time		Rise				Transit		Set				Sidereal time			Transit of first point of Aries		
							52°		56°				52°		56°							
	h	m	s	°	m	s	h	m	h	m	h	m	h	m	h	m	h	m	s	h	m	s
1	8	43	41	+18.1	−6	26	4	21	4	03	12	06	19	50	20	08	20	37	16	3	22	11
2	8	47	34	+17.9	−6	22	4	23	4	05	12	06	19	49	20	06	20	41	13	3	18	15
3	8	51	26	+17.6	−6	18	4	24	4	07	12	06	19	47	20	04	20	45	09	3	14	19
4	8	55	18	+17.4	−6	13	4	26	4	09	12	06	19	45	20	02	20	49	06	3	10	23
5	8	59	09	+17.1	−6	08	4	28	4	11	12	06	19	44	20	00	20	53	02	3	06	27
6	9	03	00	+16.8	−6	02	4	29	4	13	12	06	19	42	19	58	20	56	59	3	02	31
7	9	06	50	+16.6	−5	55	4	31	4	15	12	06	19	40	19	56	21	00	56	2	58	35
8	9	10	39	+16.3	−5	48	4	32	4	17	12	06	19	38	19	53	21	04	52	2	54	39
9	9	14	28	+16.0	−5	40	4	34	4	19	12	06	19	36	19	51	21	08	49	2	50	43
10	9	18	16	+15.7	−5	32	4	35	4	21	12	05	19	34	19	49	21	12	45	2	46	47
11	9	22	03	+15.4	−5	22	4	37	4	22	12	05	19	32	19	47	21	16	42	2	42	52
12	9	25	50	+15.1	−5	13	4	39	4	24	12	05	19	31	19	45	21	20	38	2	38	56
13	9	29	37	+14.8	−5	03	4	40	4	26	12	05	19	29	19	42	21	24	35	2	35	00
14	9	33	22	+14.5	−4	52	4	42	4	28	12	05	19	27	19	40	21	28	31	2	31	04
15	9	37	08	+14.2	−4	40	4	43	4	30	12	05	19	25	19	38	21	32	28	2	27	08
16	9	40	52	+13.9	−4	29	4	45	4	32	12	04	19	23	19	35	21	36	25	2	23	12
17	9	44	36	+13.6	−4	16	4	47	4	34	12	04	19	20	19	33	21	40	21	2	19	16
18	9	48	20	+13.3	−4	03	4	48	4	36	12	04	19	18	19	30	21	44	18	2	15	20
19	9	52	03	+12.9	−3	50	4	50	4	38	12	04	19	16	19	28	21	48	14	2	11	24
20	9	55	46	+12.6	−3	36	4	52	4	40	12	03	19	14	19	26	21	52	11	2	07	28
21	9	59	28	+12.3	−3	22	4	53	4	42	12	03	19	12	19	23	21	56	07	2	03	33
22	10	03	10	+11.9	−3	07	4	55	4	44	12	03	19	10	19	21	22	00	04	1	59	37
23	10	06	51	+11.6	−2	52	4	56	4	46	12	03	19	08	19	18	22	04	00	1	55	41
24	10	10	32	+11.3	−2	36	4	58	4	48	12	02	19	06	19	16	22	07	57	1	51	45
25	10	14	12	+10.9	−2	20	5	00	4	50	12	02	19	04	19	13	22	11	54	1	47	49
26	10	17	52	+10.6	−2	03	5	01	4	52	12	02	19	01	19	11	22	15	50	1	43	53
27	10	21	32	+10.2	−1	46	5	03	4	54	12	02	18	59	19	08	22	19	47	1	39	57
28	10	25	11	+9.9	−1	29	5	05	4	56	12	01	18	57	19	06	22	23	43	1	36	01
29	10	28	50	+9.5	−1	12	5	06	4	58	12	01	18	55	19	03	22	27	40	1	32	05
30	10	32	29	+9.2	−0	54	5	08	5	00	12	01	18	52	19	01	22	31	36	1	28	09
31	10	36	07	+8.8	−0	35	5	10	5	02	12	00	18	50	18	58	22	35	33	1	24	13

DURATION OF TWILIGHT (in minutes)

Latitude	52°	56°	52°	56°	52°	56°	52°	56°
		1 August		11 August		21 August		31 August
Civil	41	49	39	45	37	42	35	40
Nautical	97	121	90	107	84	97	79	90
Astronomical	179	TAN	154	210	139	168	128	148

THE NIGHT SKY

Mercury is a tiny spark in the morning sky and remains on view until almost the end of August. It is highest after greatest elongation west on the 9th and brightens as the month goes on. Mercury is a little over 1° from the bright star Regulus in Leo on the 29th but is too close to the Sun by then to be seen.

Venus is at superior conjunction on the 14th and therefore will not be seen this month.

Mars has now got too close the Sun to be seen this month. The planet is at aphelion (1.6661au) on the 26th.

Jupiter (magnitude −2.4 to -2.2) is setting after midnight at the beginning of August but before 11pm by the 31st. The planet is stationary on the 11th when its direct motion on the celestial sphere resumes again. The Moon is close to Jupiter on the 9th.

Saturn (magnitude 0.2 to 0.3) can be found in Sagittarius as soon as the sky darkens. The planet's globe is more bland than that of Jupiter but occasional storm systems erupt. The real draw though is the magnificent ring system and also the half-dozen moons that can be seen in a mid-sized telescope. Titan, the largest, can be picked up in binoculars as a magnitude 8.2 object when at elongation. The Moon is near Saturn on the evenings of the 11th and 12th.

The Perseid meteor shower has to contend with the Moon almost Full when at maximum on August 13th.

THE MOON

Day	R.A. h	R.A. m	Dec °	Hor Par '	Diam '	Sun Co-Long °	PA of Br. limb °	Ph. %	Age d	Rise 52° h	Rise 52° m	Rise 56° h	Rise 56° m	Transit h	Transit m	Set 52° h	Set 52° m	Set 56° h	Set 56° m
1	8	38	+20.3	60.8	33.2	271	147	00	29.3	4	21	4	01	12	31	20	27	20	44
2	9	40	+17.1	61.0	33.2	283	276	01	0.8	5	45	5	29	13	30	20	58	21	11
3	10	40	+12.7	60.9	33.2	295	284	05	1.8	7	11	7	01	14	27	21	25	21	32
4	11	37	+7.6	60.6	33.0	308	288	12	2.8	8	37	8	32	15	21	21	48	21	50
5	12	32	+2.2	60.0	32.8	320	290	21	3.8	10	00	10	00	16	12	22	09	22	07
6	13	25	−3.3	59.3	32.4	332	290	31	4.8	11	21	11	26	17	02	22	31	22	24
7	14	17	−8.5	58.6	32.0	344	288	42	5.8	12	40	12	49	17	52	22	54	22	43
8	15	10	−13.0	57.8	31.4	356	286	53	6.8	13	55	14	10	18	43	23	21	23	05
9	16	02	−16.9	57.0	31.0	9	282	64	7.8	15	08	15	28	19	34	23	53	23	32
10	16	55	−19.8	56.4	30.8	21	278	73	8.8	16	16	16	39	20	25	—	—	—	—
11	17	49	−21.6	55.8	30.4	33	273	82	9.8	17	16	17	40	21	17	0	30	0	08
12	18	43	−22.4	55.3	30.2	45	267	89	10.8	18	06	18	31	22	08	1	17	0	53
13	19	36	−22.0	54.8	29.8	57	260	94	11.8	18	48	19	09	22	57	2	11	1	47
14	20	28	−20.7	54.5	29.8	70	251	98	12.8	19	21	19	40	23	45	3	11	2	50
15	21	18	−18.4	54.3	29.6	82	229	100	13.8	19	48	20	02	—	—	4	15	3	58
16	22	06	−15.3	54.1	29.4	94	102	100	14.8	20	10	20	21	0	30	5	21	5	08
17	22	52	−11.6	54.0	29.4	106	82	98	15.8	20	30	20	37	1	14	6	27	6	18
18	23	37	−7.5	54.0	29.4	118	76	95	16.8	20	47	20	50	1	56	7	34	7	28
19	0	22	−3.1	54.1	29.4	131	73	89	17.8	21	04	21	03	2	38	8	40	8	39
20	1	05	+1.4	54.3	29.6	143	72	83	18.8	21	21	21	17	3	19	9	46	9	49
21	1	50	+5.9	54.7	29.8	155	72	75	19.8	21	40	21	31	4	01	10	54	11	01
22	2	36	+10.3	55.2	30.0	167	74	66	20.8	22	02	21	49	4	44	12	03	12	14
23	3	24	+14.3	55.9	30.4	179	76	57	21.8	22	28	22	11	5	30	13	14	13	30
24	4	15	+17.8	56.7	30.8	192	80	46	22.8	23	02	22	40	6	20	14	26	14	45
25	5	09	+20.4	57.5	31.4	204	84	36	23.8	23	45	23	21	7	14	15	35	15	57
26	6	07	+22.1	58.5	31.8	216	90	26	24.8	—	—	—	—	8	11	16	39	17	03
27	7	08	+22.4	59.4	32.4	228	97	17	25.8	0	41	0	17	9	10	17	34	17	57
28	8	10	+21.3	60.3	32.8	241	104	09	26.8	1	52	1	28	10	11	18	19	18	39
29	9	12	+18.7	60.9	33.2	253	114	03	27.8	3	12	2	54	11	12	18	54	19	09
30	10	14	+14.8	61.3	33.4	265	140	00	28.8	4	38	4	25	12	10	19	24	19	33
31	11	13	+9.8	61.4	33.4	277	264	00	0.3	6	07	5	59	13	07	19	48	19	53

MERCURY

Day	R.A. h	R.A. m	Dec °	Mag.	Diam. "	Phase %	Rise h	Rise m	Transit h	Transit m	Set h	Set m
1	07	40.6	+17.6	+2.0	10	13	3	21	10	59	18	39
3	07	41.7	+18.1	+1.5	9	18	3	12	10	53	18	36
5	07	44.6	+18.5	+1.0	9	24	3	05	10	48	18	34
7	07	49.3	+18.8	+0.6	8	30	3	00	10	46	18	34
9	07	55.8	+19.1	+0.3	8	37	2	57	10	45	18	34
11	08	04.0	+19.2	−0.1	7	44	2	56	10	46	18	36
13	08	14.0	+19.2	−0.3	7	52	2	59	10	48	18	39
15	08	25.4	+19.1	−0.6	7	59	3	03	10	52	18	42
17	08	38.2	+18.8	−0.8	6	67	3	10	10	57	18	45
19	08	52.0	+18.3	−1.0	6	74	3	19	11	04	18	48
21	09	06.7	+17.6	−1.1	6	81	3	31	11	11	18	50
23	09	21.9	+16.8	−1.3	6	87	3	43	11	18	18	52
25	09	37.4	+15.8	−1.4	5	91	3	57	11	26	18	54
27	09	53.0	+14.6	−1.5	5	95	4	12	11	34	18	54
29	10	08.4	+13.3	−1.6	5	97	4	27	11	41	18	54
31	10	23.6	+11.9	−1.7	5	99	4	42	11	48	18	53

Rising and setting times are for latitude 54°

VENUS

Day	R.A. h	R.A. m	Dec °	Mag.	Diam. "	Phase %	Rise h	Rise m	Transit h	Transit m	Set h	Set m
1	08	29.7	+20.0	−3.9	10	100	3	57	11	52	19	46
6	08	55.1	+18.5	−3.9	10	100	4	12	11	58	19	42
11	09	20.0	+16.8	−3.9	10	100	4	28	12	03	19	37
16	09	44.5	+15.0	−3.9	10	100	4	44	12	07	19	30
21	10	08.6	+12.9	−3.9	10	100	5	00	12	12	19	23
26	10	32.2	+10.7	−3.9	10	100	5	16	12	16	19	14
31	10	55.5	+8.4	−3.9	10	100	5	33	12	19	19	05

MARS

Day	R.A. h	R.A. m	Dec °	Mag.	Diam. "	Phase %	Rise h	Rise m	Transit h	Transit m	Set h	Set m
1	09	27.5	+16.2	+1.8	4	100	5	18	12	49	20	19
6	09	40.0	+15.2	+1.8	4	100	5	17	12	41	20	05
11	09	52.3	+14.1	+1.8	4	100	5	16	12	34	19	52
16	10	04.6	+13.0	+1.8	4	100	5	15	12	27	19	38
21	10	16.8	+11.9	+1.8	4	100	5	14	12	19	19	24
26	10	28.8	+10.7	+1.8	4	100	5	12	12	11	19	10
31	10	40.8	+9.5	+1.7	4	100	5	11	12	04	18	56

SUNRISE AND SUNSET

	London 0° 05′ / 51° 30′		Bristol 2° 35′ / 51° 28′		Birmingham 1° 55′ / 52° 28′		Manchester 2° 15′ / 53° 28′		Newcastle 1° 37′ / 54° 59′		Glasgow 4° 14′ / 55° 52′		Belfast 5° 56′ / 54° 35′	
d	h m	h m	h m	h m	h m	h m	h m	h m	h m	h m	h m	h m	h m	h m
1	4 23	19 49	4 34	19 59	4 27	20 00	4 24	20 05	4 15	20 10	4 21	20 24	4 34	20 25
2	4 25	19 47	4 35	19 57	4 29	19 58	4 26	20 04	4 16	20 08	4 23	20 22	4 36	20 23
3	4 26	19 46	4 37	19 55	4 30	19 57	4 27	20 02	4 18	20 06	4 25	20 20	4 37	20 21
4	4 28	19 44	4 38	19 54	4 32	19 55	4 29	20 00	4 20	20 04	4 26	20 18	4 39	20 19
5	4 30	19 42	4 40	19 52	4 33	19 53	4 31	19 58	4 22	20 02	4 28	20 16	4 41	20 17
6	4 31	19 40	4 41	19 50	4 35	19 51	4 32	19 56	4 24	20 00	4 30	20 14	4 43	20 15
7	4 33	19 39	4 43	19 48	4 37	19 49	4 34	19 54	4 25	19 58	4 32	20 12	4 44	20 13
8	4 34	19 37	4 44	19 47	4 38	19 47	4 36	19 52	4 27	19 56	4 34	20 10	4 46	20 11
9	4 36	19 35	4 46	19 45	4 40	19 46	4 38	19 50	4 29	19 54	4 36	20 08	4 48	20 09
10	4 37	19 33	4 47	19 43	4 41	19 44	4 39	19 48	4 31	19 51	4 38	20 05	4 50	20 07
11	4 39	19 31	4 49	19 41	4 43	19 42	4 41	19 46	4 33	19 49	4 40	20 03	4 52	20 05
12	4 40	19 29	4 51	19 39	4 45	19 40	4 43	19 44	4 35	19 47	4 42	20 01	4 53	20 03
13	4 42	19 27	4 52	19 37	4 46	19 38	4 44	19 42	4 37	19 45	4 44	19 59	4 55	20 01
14	4 44	19 25	4 54	19 35	4 48	19 36	4 46	19 40	4 38	19 43	4 46	19 56	4 57	19 59
15	4 45	19 23	4 55	19 33	4 50	19 34	4 48	19 38	4 40	19 40	4 48	19 54	4 59	19 56
16	4 47	19 21	4 57	19 31	4 51	19 32	4 50	19 36	4 42	19 38	4 50	19 52	5 01	19 54
17	4 48	19 19	4 58	19 29	4 53	19 29	4 51	19 34	4 44	19 36	4 52	19 49	5 03	19 52
18	4 50	19 17	5 00	19 27	4 55	19 27	4 53	19 32	4 46	19 34	4 53	19 47	5 04	19 50
19	4 52	19 15	5 02	19 25	4 56	19 25	4 55	19 29	4 48	19 31	4 55	19 45	5 06	19 47
20	4 53	19 13	5 03	19 23	4 58	19 23	4 57	19 27	4 50	19 29	4 57	19 42	5 08	19 45
21	4 55	19 11	5 05	19 21	5 00	19 21	4 58	19 25	4 52	19 27	4 59	19 40	5 10	19 43
22	4 56	19 09	5 06	19 19	5 01	19 19	5 00	19 23	4 53	19 24	5 01	19 37	5 12	19 40
23	4 58	19 07	5 08	19 17	5 03	19 17	5 02	19 20	4 55	19 22	5 03	19 35	5 14	19 38
24	5 00	19 05	5 10	19 15	5 05	19 14	5 04	19 18	4 57	19 19	5 05	19 32	5 15	19 36
25	5 01	19 03	5 11	19 13	5 06	19 12	5 05	19 16	4 59	19 17	5 07	19 30	5 17	19 33
26	5 03	19 01	5 13	19 11	5 08	19 10	5 07	19 14	5 01	19 15	5 09	19 27	5 19	19 31
27	5 04	18 58	5 14	19 08	5 10	19 08	5 09	19 11	5 03	19 12	5 11	19 25	5 21	19 28
28	5 06	18 56	5 16	19 06	5 11	19 06	5 11	19 09	5 05	19 10	5 13	19 22	5 23	19 26
29	5 07	18 54	5 18	19 04	5 13	19 03	5 12	19 07	5 06	19 07	5 15	19 20	5 25	19 24
30	5 09	18 52	5 19	19 02	5 15	19 01	5 14	19 04	5 08	19 05	5 17	19 17	5 26	19 21
31	5 11	18 50	5 21	19 00	5 16	18 59	5 16	19 02	5 10	19 02	5 19	19 15	5 28	19 19

JUPITER

Day	R.A. h m	Dec °	Mag.	Diam. ″	Rise h m	Transit h m	Set h m
1	16 53.7	−22.1	−2.4	43	16 15	20 13	0 16
11	16 53.0	−22.1	−2.4	42	15 35	19 33	23 32
21	16 53.5	−22.2	−2.3	40	14 56	18 55	22 53
31	16 55.4	−22.3	−2.2	39	14 19	18 17	22 15

Equatorial Diam. 43″, Polar Diam. 40″

SATURN

Day	R.A. h m	Dec °	Mag.	Diam. ″	Rise h m	Transit h m	Set h m
1	19 07.7	−22.2	+0.2	18	18 29	22 27	2 29
11	19 05.2	−22.3	+0.2	18	17 48	21 45	1 46
21	19 03.0	−22.4	+0.3	18	17 07	21 04	1 04
31	19 01.5	−22.5	+0.3	18	16 26	20 23	0 23

Equatorial Diam. 18″, Polar Diam. 17″
Rings – major axis 41″ minor axis 17″, Tilt 25°

URANUS

Day	R.A. h m	Dec °	Mag.	Diam. ″	Rise h m	Transit h m	Set h m
1	02 17.6	+13.2	+5.8	4	22 27	5 39	12 52
11	02 17.8	+13.2	+5.8	4	21 47	5 00	12 13
21	02 17.7	+13.2	+5.7	4	21 08	4 21	11 34
31	02 17.3	+13.2	+5.7	4	20 28	3 41	10 54

NEPTUNE

Day	R.A. h m	Dec °	Mag.	Diam. ″	Rise h m	Transit h m	Set h m
1	23 18.6	−5.6	+7.8	2	21 03	2 41	8 15
11	23 17.9	−5.7	+7.8	2	20 23	2 01	7 34
21	23 17.0	−5.8	+7.8	2	19 44	1 21	6 54
31	23 16.0	−5.9	+7.8	2	19 04	0 40	6 13

September 2019

NINTH MONTH, 30 DAYS. *Septem* (seven), seventh month of Roman pre-Julian calendar

1 *Sunday*	Hurricane Gustav weakens after causing an estimated 153 deaths across the Americas 2008		day 244

2 *Monday*	After mounting evidence imbibes him in a customs scandal, Guatemalan president Molina resigns 2015	week 36	day 245
3 *Tuesday*	Hours after his resignation, Guatemalan president Molina is arrested on corruption charges 2015		246
4 *Wednesday*	A massive power cut leaves 70 per cent of Venezuela without electricity 2013		247
5 *Thursday*	Guatemala officially recognises Belize as an independent state 1991		248
6 *Friday*	Argentinian president Hipólito Yrigoyen is deposed in a coup 1930		249
7 *Saturday*	Pedro I, first Emperor of Brazil, declares independence for Brazil 1822		250
8 *Sunday*	A homemade bomb explodes in a Chilean metro station, wounding ten people 2014		251

9 *Monday*	Argentina's congress unanimously approves the women's suffrage act 1947	week 37	day 252
10 *Tuesday*	Simon Bolivar named president of Peru 1823		253
11 *Wednesday*	President of Chile Salvador Allende takes his own life in the face of a coup 1973		254
12 *Thursday*	Abimael Guzman, leader of the Shining Path guerrilla group in Peru, is captured 1992		255
13 *Friday*	Mexico City is captured by American troops during Mexican-American War 1847		256
14 *Saturday*	Jacobo Arbenz, former President of Guatemala *b.* 1913		257
15 *Sunday*	Guatemala, El Salvador, Honduras, Nicaragua, and Costa Rica gain independence from Spain 1821		258

16 *Monday*	The Mexican War of Independence begins 1810	week 38	day 259
17 *Tuesday*	Frida Kahlo suffers near fatal injuries in a bus accident in Mexico City 1925		260
18 *Wednesday*	Chile gains independence from Spain 1810		261
19 *Thursday*	An earthquake in Mexico City kills more than 5,000 people and leaves many homeless 1985		262
20 *Friday*	Jean-Jacques Dessalines, first leader of independent Haiti and former slave *b.* 1758		263
21 *Saturday*	Argentinian Marxist revolutionary Ernesto 'Che' Guevara enters Mexico City 1954		264
22 *Sunday*	Belize joins the United Nations 1981		265

23 *Monday*	Hurricane Jeanne begins in earnest, killing over 3,025 people in Latin America and the USA 2004	week 39	day 266
24 *Tuesday*	Emperor Pedro I, founder of the Empire of Brazil, *d.* 1834		267
25 *Wednesday*	Dominican cricketer Grayson Shillingford *b.* 1944		268
26 *Thursday*	Mexican Benito Vasquez-Hernandez is jailed as a 'material witness'; he is held for 905 days 2012		269
27 *Friday*	Agustin de Iturbide, first Emperor of Mexico *b.* 1783		270
28 *Saturday*	Brazil passes law granting freedom to new children born to slaves 1871		271
29 *Sunday*	Michelle Bachelet, first female president of Chile, *b.* 1951		272

30 *Monday*	Ecuadorian president Rafael Correa is tear-gassed by police and held in hospital 2010	week 40	day 273

ASTRONOMICAL PHENOMENA

d	h	
3	11	Mars 0.7° South of Mercury
6	7	Jupiter 2° South of the Moon
8	14	Saturn 0.04° North of the Moon
10	7	Neptune at opposition (Mag. 7.8)
13	18	Neptune 4° North of the Moon
13	22	Venus 0.34° North of Mercury
17	20	Uranus 5° North of the Moon
20	17	Aldebaran 3° South of the Moon
23	8	Autumnal equinox
28	1	Mars 4° South of the Moon
29	13	Venus 4° South of the Moon

MINIMA OF ALGOL

d	h	d	h	d	h
1	13.4	13	0.6	24	11.9
4	10.2	15	21.4	27	8.7
7	7.0	18	18.2	30	5.5
10	3.8	21	15		

CONSTELLATIONS

The following constellations are near the meridian at

	d	h		d	h
August	1	24	September	15	21
August	16	23	October	1	20
September	1	22	October	16	19

Draco, Cepheus, Lyra, Cygnus, Vulpecula, Sagitta, Delphinus, Equuleus, Aquila, Aquarius and Capricornus

THE MOON

Phase, Apsides and Node	d	h	m
◑ First Quarter	6	3	12
○ Full Moon	14	4	34
◐ Last Quarter	22	2	42
● New Moon	28	18	28

	d	h	m
Apogee (406,377 km)	13	13	34
Perigee (357,802 km)	28	2	25

Mean longitude of the ascending node on 1st, 105°

THE SUN Diam. 31.7′

Day	Right Ascension			Dec.	Equation of time		Rise 52°		Rise 56°		Transit		Set 52°		Set 56°		Sidereal time			Transit of first point of Aries		
	h	m	s	°	m	s	h	m	h	m	h	m	h	m	h	m	h	m	s	h	m	s
1	10	39	45	+8.5	−0	17	5	11	5	04	12	00	18	48	18	55	22	39	29	1	20	18
2	10	43	23	+8.1	+0	02	5	13	5	05	12	00	18	46	18	53	22	43	26	1	16	22
3	10	47	00	+7.7	+0	21	5	14	5	07	11	59	18	43	18	50	22	47	23	1	12	26
4	10	50	37	+7.4	+0	41	5	16	5	09	11	59	18	41	18	48	22	51	19	1	08	30
5	10	54	14	+7.0	+1	01	5	18	5	11	11	59	18	39	18	45	22	55	16	1	04	34
6	10	57	50	+6.6	+1	21	5	19	5	13	11	58	18	37	18	42	22	59	12	1	00	38
7	11	01	27	+6.3	+1	41	5	21	5	15	11	58	18	34	18	40	23	03	09	0	56	42
8	11	05	03	+5.9	+2	02	5	23	5	17	11	58	18	32	18	37	23	07	05	0	52	46
9	11	08	39	+5.5	+2	22	5	24	5	19	11	57	18	30	18	34	23	11	02	0	48	50
10	11	12	14	+5.1	+2	43	5	26	5	21	11	57	18	27	18	32	23	14	58	0	44	54
11	11	15	50	+4.7	+3	04	5	27	5	23	11	57	18	25	18	29	23	18	55	0	40	58
12	11	19	25	+4.4	+3	26	5	29	5	25	11	56	18	23	18	27	23	22	52	0	37	03
13	11	23	00	+4.0	+3	47	5	31	5	27	11	56	18	20	18	24	23	26	48	0	33	07
14	11	26	36	+3.6	+4	08	5	32	5	29	11	56	18	18	18	21	23	30	45	0	29	11
15	11	30	11	+3.2	+4	30	5	34	5	31	11	55	18	16	18	19	23	34	41	0	25	15
16	11	33	46	+2.8	+4	51	5	36	5	33	11	55	18	13	18	16	23	38	38	0	21	19
17	11	37	21	+2.4	+5	13	5	37	5	35	11	55	18	11	18	13	23	42	34	0	17	23
18	11	40	56	+2.1	+5	34	5	39	5	37	11	54	18	09	18	11	23	46	31	0	13	27
19	11	44	31	+1.7	+5	56	5	40	5	39	11	54	18	06	18	08	23	50	27	0	09	31
20	11	48	06	+1.3	+6	17	5	42	5	41	11	54	18	04	18	05	23	54	24	0	05	35
*21	11	51	41	+0.9	+6	38	5	44	5	42	11	53	18	02	18	03	23	58	21	0	01	39
22	11	55	16	+0.5	+7	00	5	45	5	44	11	53	17	59	18	00	0	02	17	23	53	48
23	11	58	52	+0.1	+7	21	5	47	5	46	11	52	17	57	17	57	0	06	14	23	49	52
24	12	02	27	−0.3	+7	42	5	49	5	48	11	52	17	55	17	55	0	10	10	23	45	56
25	12	06	03	−0.7	+8	03	5	50	5	50	11	52	17	52	17	52	0	14	07	23	42	00
26	12	09	39	−1.0	+8	24	5	52	5	52	11	51	17	50	17	49	0	18	03	23	38	04
27	12	13	15	−1.4	+8	44	5	54	5	54	11	51	17	48	17	47	0	22	00	23	34	08
28	12	16	51	−1.8	+9	04	5	55	5	56	11	51	17	45	17	44	0	25	56	23	30	12
29	12	20	27	−2.2	+9	25	5	57	5	58	11	50	17	43	17	41	0	29	53	23	26	16
30	12	24	04	−2.6	+9	44	5	59	6	00	11	50	17	41	17	39	0	33	50	23	22	20

* A second transit of the first point of Aries occurs at 23h 57m 43s on 21 September 2019

DURATION OF TWILIGHT (in minutes)

Latitude	52°	56°	52°	56°	52°	56°	52°	56°
	1 September		11 September		21 September		31 September	
Civil	35	39	34	38	34	37	34	37
Nautical	79	89	76	85	74	82	73	80
Astronomical	127	147	120	136	116	129	113	125

THE NIGHT SKY

Mercury is an evening sky object but is too low to be seen this month.

Venus is also poorly placed for observers in the UK. Although the planet's solar elongation in the evening sky is increasing, the ecliptic's shallow angle relative to the horizon at this time of year compounds the issue.

Mars is at superior conjunction on the 2nd and then moves into the morning sky where the magnitude 1.8 planet should be picked up towards the end of the month in Virgo.

Jupiter (magnitude −2.1) can be found just past the meridian as soon as darkness falls. The planet is at eastern quadrature in Ophiuchus during early September, setting soon after 10pm at the beginning of the month but nearly two hours earlier at the end. The Moon is close to Jupiter on the evenings of the 5th and 6th.

Saturn (magnitude 0.4) is stationary mid-month after which its direct motion resumes. The Moon is close to Saturn on the 8th.

Neptune (magnitude 7.8) is at opposition on the 10th when just over five arc-minutes from the magnitude 4.2 star phi Aquarii. If the region is observed on successive nights then the object that moves is Neptune. A small telescope will show it as a pale blue dot and increasing the power to around 100x reveals a tiny disk.

The Harvest Moon on the 14th is the most distant Full Moon of the year.

THE MOON

Day	R.A. h	m	Dec °	Hor Par '	Diam '	Sun Co-Long °	PA of Br. limb °	Ph. %	Age d	Rise 52° h	m	Rise 56° h	m	Transit h	m	Set 52° h	m	Set 56° h	m
1	12	10	+4.3	61.1	33.2	290	282	04	1.3	7	34	7	32	14	01	20	11	20	11
2	13	05	−1.4	60.5	33.0	302	286	10	2.3	8	59	9	02	14	53	20	33	20	28
3	14	00	−6.9	59.8	32.6	314	286	18	3.3	10	22	10	30	15	45	20	56	20	46
4	14	53	−11.9	58.9	32.0	326	285	28	4.3	11	42	11	54	16	37	21	22	21	08
5	15	47	−16.1	57.9	31.6	338	282	38	5.3	12	57	13	16	17	29	21	53	21	33
6	16	42	−19.3	57.1	31.0	351	278	49	6.3	14	08	14	31	18	21	22	29	22	07
7	17	36	−21.4	56.3	30.6	3	273	59	7.3	15	11	15	36	19	13	23	13	22	49
8	18	30	−22.5	55.6	30.2	15	267	69	8.3	16	05	16	30	20	04	—	—	23	40
9	19	23	−22.3	55.0	30.0	27	262	78	9.3	16	49	17	12	20	54	0	05	—	—
10	20	15	−21.2	54.6	29.8	39	256	85	10.3	17	25	17	44	21	42	1	04	0	41
11	21	06	−19.1	54.3	29.6	52	250	91	11.3	17	52	18	08	22	28	2	07	1	47
12	21	54	−16.2	54.1	29.4	64	243	96	12.3	18	16	18	28	23	13	3	12	2	57
13	22	41	−12.6	54.0	29.4	76	231	99	13.3	18	36	18	44	23	55	4	18	4	08
14	23	26	−8.6	54.0	29.4	88	182	100	14.3	18	54	18	58	—	—	5	25	5	18
15	0	10	−4.2	54.0	29.4	100	95	99	15.3	19	11	19	11	0	37	6	31	6	29
16	0	54	+0.4	54.2	29.6	113	81	97	16.3	19	27	19	24	1	18	7	38	7	40
17	1	39	+4.9	54.5	29.6	125	77	93	17.3	19	45	19	38	2	00	8	45	8	51
18	2	24	+9.4	54.8	29.8	137	76	87	18.3	20	06	19	54	2	42	9	54	10	04
19	3	11	+13.5	55.3	30.2	149	78	80	19.3	20	29	20	14	3	27	11	03	11	18
20	4	01	+17.1	55.9	30.4	161	80	71	20.3	21	00	20	39	4	15	12	14	12	33
21	4	53	+20.0	56.6	30.8	173	84	62	21.3	21	37	21	14	5	06	13	23	13	45
22	5	48	+21.9	57.4	31.2	186	89	51	22.3	22	26	22	03	5	59	14	28	14	52
23	6	47	+22.7	58.2	31.8	198	95	41	23.3	23	29	23	05	6	56	15	25	15	49
24	7	46	+22.1	59.1	32.2	210	101	30	24.3	—	—	—	—	7	55	16	12	16	34
25	8	47	+20.1	59.9	32.6	222	107	20	25.3	0	43	0	22	8	54	16	50	17	07
26	9	47	+16.7	60.6	33.0	234	113	11	26.3	2	06	1	49	9	52	17	22	17	34
27	10	46	+12.2	61.1	33.2	247	121	05	27.3	3	32	3	21	10	49	17	47	17	54
28	11	44	+6.9	61.3	33.4	259	136	01	28.3	5	00	4	55	11	44	18	11	18	13
29	12	40	+1.1	61.1	33.4	271	237	00	29.3	6	27	6	27	12	38	18	33	18	30
30	13	36	−4.7	60.7	33.0	283	276	02	0.7	7	53	7	59	13	31	18	56	18	48

MERCURY

Day	R.A. h	m	Dec °	Mag.	Diam. "	Phase %	Rise h	m	Transit h	m	Set h	m
1	10	31.1	+11.2	−1.7	5	99	4	50	11	52	18	53
3	10	45.8	+9.7	−1.8	5	100	5	05	11	59	18	51
5	11	00.1	+8.2	−1.7	5	100	5	19	12	05	18	49
7	11	14.0	+6.6	−1.5	5	99	5	34	12	11	18	47
9	11	27.5	+5.1	−1.3	5	99	5	47	12	17	18	44
11	11	40.6	+3.5	−1.1	5	98	6	01	12	22	18	41
13	11	53.4	+1.9	−1.0	5	97	6	14	12	26	18	38
15	12	05.9	+0.3	−0.8	5	96	6	26	12	31	18	34
17	12	18.1	−1.2	−0.7	5	95	6	39	12	35	18	31
19	12	30.0	−2.7	−0.6	5	94	6	50	12	39	18	27
21	12	41.7	−4.2	−0.5	5	93	7	02	12	43	18	23
23	12	53.2	−5.7	−0.4	5	91	7	13	12	46	18	19
25	13	04.5	−7.1	−0.4	5	90	7	24	12	50	18	15
27	13	15.6	−8.5	−0.3	5	89	7	34	12	53	18	11
29	13	26.5	−9.9	−0.3	5	87	7	45	12	56	18	06

Rising and setting times are for latitude 54°

VENUS

Day	R.A. h	m	Dec °	Mag.	Diam. "	Phase %	Rise h	m	Transit h	m	Set h	m
1	11	00.1	+7.9	−3.9	10	100	5	36	12	20	19	03
6	11	23.1	+5.5	−3.9	10	99	5	52	12	23	18	54
11	11	45.9	+3.0	−3.9	11	99	6	08	12	26	18	44
16	12	08.6	+0.5	−3.9	11	99	6	24	12	29	18	34
21	12	31.2	−2.1	−3.9	11	98	6	40	12	32	18	24
26	12	54.0	−4.6	−3.9	11	98	6	56	12	35	18	14

MARS

Day	R.A. h	m	Dec °	Mag.	Diam. "	Phase %	Rise h	m	Transit h	m	Set h	m
1	10	43.2	+9.3	+1.7	4	100	5	11	12	02	18	53
6	10	55.1	+8.1	+1.7	4	100	5	10	11	54	18	39
11	11	07.0	+6.8	+1.7	4	100	5	09	11	47	18	24
16	11	18.8	+5.6	+1.8	4	100	5	07	11	39	18	10
21	11	30.6	+4.3	+1.8	4	100	5	06	11	31	17	55
26	11	42.3	+3.0	+1.8	4	100	5	05	11	23	17	41

SUNRISE AND SUNSET

	London				Bristol				Birmingham				Manchester				Newcastle				Glasgow				Belfast			
	0°	05′	51°	30′	2°	35′	51°	28′	1°	55′	52°	28′	2°	15′	53°	28′	1°	37′	54°	59′	4°	14′	55°	52′	5°	56′	54°	35′
d	h	m	h	m	h	m	h	m	h	m	h	m	h	m	h	m	h	m	h	m	h	m	h	m	h	m	h	m
1	5	12	18	48	5	22	18	57	5	18	18	56	5	17	19	00	5	12	19	00	5	21	19	12	5	30	19	16
2	5	14	18	45	5	24	18	55	5	20	18	54	5	19	18	57	5	14	18	57	5	23	19	09	5	32	19	14
3	5	15	18	43	5	26	18	53	5	21	18	52	5	21	18	55	5	16	18	55	5	25	19	07	5	34	19	11
4	5	17	18	41	5	27	18	51	5	23	18	50	5	23	18	52	5	18	18	52	5	27	19	04	5	36	19	09
5	5	19	18	39	5	29	18	49	5	25	18	47	5	24	18	50	5	19	18	50	5	28	19	02	5	37	19	06
6	5	20	18	36	5	30	18	46	5	26	18	45	5	26	18	48	5	21	18	47	5	30	18	59	5	39	19	04
7	5	22	18	34	5	32	18	44	5	28	18	43	5	28	18	45	5	23	18	45	5	32	18	56	5	41	19	01
8	5	23	18	32	5	33	18	42	5	30	18	40	5	30	18	43	5	25	18	42	5	34	18	54	5	43	18	59
9	5	25	18	29	5	35	18	39	5	31	18	38	5	31	18	40	5	27	18	40	5	36	18	51	5	45	18	56
10	5	27	18	27	5	37	18	37	5	33	18	36	5	33	18	38	5	29	18	37	5	38	18	49	5	47	18	54
11	5	28	18	25	5	38	18	35	5	35	18	33	5	35	18	35	5	31	18	35	5	40	18	46	5	48	18	51
12	5	30	18	23	5	40	18	33	5	36	18	31	5	37	18	33	5	33	18	32	5	42	18	43	5	50	18	49
13	5	31	18	20	5	41	18	30	5	38	18	28	5	38	18	31	5	34	18	29	5	44	18	41	5	52	18	46
14	5	33	18	18	5	43	18	28	5	40	18	26	5	40	18	28	5	36	18	27	5	46	18	38	5	54	18	44
15	5	35	18	16	5	45	18	26	5	41	18	24	5	42	18	26	5	38	18	24	5	48	18	35	5	56	18	41
16	5	36	18	13	5	46	18	23	5	43	18	21	5	44	18	23	5	40	18	22	5	50	18	33	5	58	18	39
17	5	38	18	11	5	48	18	21	5	45	18	19	5	45	18	21	5	42	18	19	5	52	18	30	5	59	18	36
18	5	39	18	09	5	49	18	19	5	46	18	17	5	47	18	18	5	44	18	17	5	54	18	28	6	01	18	34
19	5	41	18	06	5	51	18	16	5	48	18	14	5	49	18	16	5	46	18	14	5	56	18	25	6	03	18	31
20	5	43	18	04	5	53	18	14	5	50	18	12	5	51	18	13	5	47	18	11	5	58	18	22	6	05	18	29
21	5	44	18	02	5	54	18	12	5	51	18	09	5	52	18	11	5	49	18	09	5	59	18	20	6	07	18	26
22	5	46	18	00	5	56	18	10	5	53	18	07	5	54	18	09	5	51	18	06	6	01	18	17	6	09	18	23
23	5	47	17	57	5	57	18	07	5	55	18	05	5	56	18	06	5	53	18	04	6	03	18	14	6	10	18	21
24	5	49	17	55	5	59	18	05	5	56	18	02	5	58	18	04	5	55	18	01	6	05	18	12	6	12	18	18
25	5	51	17	53	6	01	18	03	5	58	18	00	5	59	18	01	5	57	17	59	6	07	18	09	6	14	18	16
26	5	52	17	50	6	02	18	00	6	00	17	58	6	01	17	59	5	59	17	56	6	09	18	06	6	16	18	13
27	5	54	17	48	6	04	17	58	6	01	17	55	6	03	17	56	6	01	17	54	6	11	18	04	6	18	18	11
28	5	55	17	46	6	05	17	56	6	03	17	53	6	05	17	54	6	02	17	51	6	13	18	01	6	20	18	08
29	5	57	17	44	6	07	17	54	6	05	17	51	6	06	17	51	6	04	17	48	6	15	17	58	6	21	18	06
30	5	59	17	41	6	09	17	51	6	06	17	48	6	08	17	49	6	06	17	46	6	17	17	56	6	23	18	03

JUPITER

Day	R.A.		Dec	Mag.	Diam.	Rise		Transit		Set	
	h	m	°		″	h	m	h	m	h	m
1	16	55.7	−22.3	−2.2	39	14	16	18	13	22	11
11	16	58.9	−22.4	−2.2	38	13	40	17	37	21	35
21	17	03.3	−22.5	−2.1	37	13	06	17	02	20	59

Equatorial Diam. 39″, Polar Diam. 36″

SATURN

Day	R.A.		Dec	Mag.	Diam.	Rise		Transit		Set	
	h	m	°		″	h	m	h	m	h	m
1	19	01.4	−22.5	+0.3	18	16	22	20	19	0	19
11	19	00.5	−22.5	+0.4	17	15	42	19	38	23	35
21	19	00.4	−22.5	+0.4	17	15	03	18	59	22	55

Equatorial Diam. 17″, Polar Diam. 16″
Rings – major axis 39″ minor axis 17″, Tilt 25°

URANUS

Day	R.A.		Dec	Mag.	Diam.	Rise		Transit		Set	
	h	m	°		″	h	m	h	m	h	m
1	02	17.2	+13.2	+5.7	4	20	25	3	37	10	50
11	02	16.5	+13.1	+5.7	4	19	45	2	57	10	09
21	02	15.4	+13.0	+5.7	4	19	05	2	17	9	28

NEPTUNE

Day	R.A.		Dec	Mag.	Diam.	Rise		Transit		Set	
	h	m	°		″	h	m	h	m	h	m
1	23	15.9	−5.9	+7.8	2	19	00	0	36	6	09
11	23	14.9	−6.0	+7.8	2	18	20	23	52	5	28
21	23	13.9	−6.1	+7.8	2	17	40	23	12	4	47

October 2019

TENTH MONTH, 31 DAYS. *Octo* (eighth), eighth month of Roman pre-Julian calendar

1	*Tuesday*	Battle of Rancagua takes place, in which Spain reclaims Chile four years after independence 1814	week 40 day 274
2	*Wednesday*	Hundreds of students and civilians are killed by government forces at a protest in Mexico City 1968	275
3	*Thursday*	A coup in Panama City is supressed and 11 participants are executed 1989	276
4	*Friday*	Hurricane Flora kills 6,000 in Cuba and Haiti 1963	277
5	*Saturday*	Chile announces the creation of two marine reserves to protect over 1 million sq. km of ocean 2017	278
6	*Sunday*	Mameyes landslide kills almost 200 people in Puerto Rico 1985	279

7	*Monday*	Former Guatemalan president Alfonso Cabrera is extradited from Mexico over money embezzlement 2008	week 41 day 280
8	*Tuesday*	Che Guevara and his rebels are captured in Bolivia 1967	281
9	*Wednesday*	Marxist revolutionary and guerrilla leader Che Guevara is executed in Bolivia 1967	282
10	*Thursday*	Fidel Castro purchases *Granma*, a boat to carry the 26th of July Movement to Cuba 1956	283
11	*Friday*	Alavaro Fernandez, Uruguayan footballer *b.* 1985	284
12	*Saturday*	Emperor Pedro I, founder of the Empire of Brazil *b.* 1798	285
13	*Sunday*	A plane en route from Uruguay to Chile crashes in the Andes; survivors end up eating the victims 1972	286

14	*Monday*	Two Maya tombs from the seventh century are discovered in Guatemala 2016	week 42 day 287
15	*Tuesday*	José Miguel Carrera, Chilean general and politician *b.* 1785	288
16	*Wednesday*	The Cuban Missile Crisis, a confrontation between the USA and the Soviet Union, begins 1962	289
17	*Thursday*	Jean-Jacques Dessalines, first leader of independent Haiti and former slave, is assassinated 1806	290
18	*Friday*	Charles Darwin leaves the Galápagos Islands after five weeks of study towards his theory of evolution 1835	291
19	*Saturday*	Hurricane Wilma passes over Mexico causing eight deaths 2005	292
20	*Sunday*	First cholera outbreak in Haiti for a century begins 2010	293

21	*Monday*	Luis A. Ferré, 3rd governor of Puerto Rico *d.* 2003	week 43 day 294
22	*Tuesday*	Families are told evacuate Guantanamo Bay military base during the Cuban Missile Crisis 1962	295
23	*Wednesday*	Brazil launches its first space rocket 2004	296
24	*Thursday*	Fernando de la Rúa is voted in as Argentina's president with the slogan 'I know I'm boring' 1999	297
25	*Friday*	Jimmy Morales wins the Guatemalan presidency despite no political experience 2015	298
26	*Saturday*	US President George Bush signs the Secure Fence Act, to add fencing along the US–Mexico border 2006	299
27	*Sunday*	British Summer Time ends	300

28	*Monday*	After 13 days, the Cuban Missile Crisis ends 1962	week 44 day 301
29	*Tuesday*	Despite little formal education, Luiz Lula da Silva wins the Brazilian presidential election 2002	302
30	*Wednesday*	Argentinian footballer Diego Armando Maradona *b.* 1960	303
31	*Thursday*	TAM Flight 402 crashes in Brazil, killing 99 people 1996	304

ASTRONOMICAL PHENOMENA

d	h	
3	20	Jupiter 2° South of the Moon
5	21	Saturn 0.3° North of the Moon
10	23	Neptune 4° North of the Moon
17	22	Aldebaran 3° South of the Moon
20	4	Mercury greatest elongation East (25°)
26	17	Ceres 3° South of Jupiter
26	17	Mars 5° South of the Moon
28	8	Uranus at opposition (Mag. 5.7)
29	14	Venus 4° South of the Moon
30	9	Venus 3° North of Mercury
31	14	Jupiter 1° South of the Moon

MINIMA OF ALGOL

d	h	d	h	d	h
3	2.3	14	13.5	26	0.8
5	23.1	17	10.4	28	21.6
8	19.9	20	7.2	31	18.4
11	16.7	23	4.0		

CONSTELLATIONS

The following constellations are near the meridian at

	d	h		d	h
September	1	24	October	16	21
September	15	23	November	1	20
October	1	22	November	15	19

Ursa Major (below the Pole), Cepheus, Cassiopeia, Cygnus, Lacerta, Andromeda, Pegasus, Capricornus, Aquarius and Piscis Austrinus

THE MOON

Phase, Apsides and Node	d	h	m
◗ First Quarter	5	16	48
○ Full Moon	13	21	9
◖ Last Quarter	21	12	40
● New Moon	28	3	40
Apogee (405,899 km)	10	18	30
Perigee (361,311 km)	26	10	40

Mean longitude of the ascending node on 1st, 103°

THE SUN Diam. 32.0′

Day	Right Ascension			Dec.	Equation of time		Rise 52°		Rise 56°		Transit		Set 52°		Set 56°		Sidereal time			Transit of first point of Aries		
	h	m	s	°	m	s	h	m	h	m	h	m	h	m	h	m	h	m	s	h	m	s
1	12	27	41	−3.0	+10	04	6	00	6	02	11	50	17	38	17	36	0	37	46	23	18	24
2	12	31	18	−3.4	+10	23	6	02	6	04	11	49	17	36	17	34	0	41	43	23	14	28
3	12	34	56	−3.8	+10	42	6	04	6	06	11	49	17	34	17	31	0	45	39	23	10	33
4	12	38	34	−4.2	+11	01	6	05	6	08	11	49	17	31	17	28	0	49	36	23	06	37
5	12	42	12	−4.5	+11	20	6	07	6	10	11	49	17	29	17	26	0	53	32	23	02	41
6	12	45	50	−4.9	+11	38	6	09	6	12	11	48	17	27	17	23	0	57	29	22	58	45
7	12	49	29	−5.3	+11	56	6	10	6	14	11	48	17	25	17	21	1	01	25	22	54	49
8	12	53	08	−5.7	+12	13	6	12	6	16	11	48	17	22	17	18	1	05	22	22	50	53
9	12	56	48	−6.1	+12	30	6	14	6	18	11	47	17	20	17	15	1	09	19	22	46	57
10	13	00	28	−6.4	+12	46	6	15	6	20	11	47	17	18	17	13	1	13	15	22	43	01
11	13	04	08	−6.8	+13	02	6	17	6	22	11	47	17	16	17	10	1	17	12	22	39	05
12	13	07	49	−7.2	+13	18	6	19	6	24	11	47	17	13	17	08	1	21	08	22	35	09
13	13	11	31	−7.6	+13	33	6	21	6	26	11	46	17	11	17	05	1	25	05	22	31	13
14	13	15	12	−8.0	+13	48	6	22	6	28	11	46	17	09	17	03	1	29	01	22	27	18
15	13	18	55	−8.3	+14	02	6	24	6	30	11	46	17	07	17	00	1	32	58	22	23	22
16	13	22	38	−8.7	+14	15	6	26	6	33	11	46	17	05	16	58	1	36	54	22	19	26
17	13	26	22	−9.1	+14	28	6	28	6	35	11	45	17	02	16	55	1	40	51	22	15	30
18	13	30	06	−9.4	+14	41	6	29	6	37	11	45	17	00	16	53	1	44	48	22	11	34
19	13	33	51	−9.8	+14	53	6	31	6	39	11	45	16	58	16	50	1	48	44	22	07	38
20	13	37	36	−10.2	+15	04	6	33	6	41	11	45	16	56	16	48	1	52	41	22	03	42
21	13	41	22	−10.5	+15	14	6	35	6	43	11	45	16	54	16	45	1	56	37	21	59	46
22	13	45	09	−10.9	+15	24	6	36	6	45	11	45	16	52	16	43	2	00	34	21	55	50
23	13	48	56	−11.2	+15	33	6	38	6	47	11	44	16	50	16	41	2	04	30	21	51	54
24	13	52	44	−11.6	+15	41	6	40	6	49	11	44	16	48	16	38	2	08	27	21	47	58
25	13	56	33	−11.9	+15	49	6	42	6	51	11	44	16	46	16	36	2	12	23	21	44	03
26	14	00	23	−12.3	+15	56	6	43	6	53	11	44	16	44	16	34	2	16	20	21	40	07
27	14	04	13	−12.6	+16	02	6	45	6	56	11	44	16	42	16	31	2	20	17	21	36	11
28	14	08	04	−12.9	+16	08	6	47	6	58	11	44	16	40	16	29	2	24	13	21	32	15
29	14	11	56	−13.3	+16	13	6	49	7	00	11	44	16	38	16	27	2	28	10	21	28	19
30	14	15	49	−13.6	+16	17	6	51	7	02	11	44	16	36	16	25	2	32	06	21	24	23
31	14	19	42	−13.9	+16	20	6	52	7	04	11	44	16	34	16	22	2	36	03	21	20	27

DURATION OF TWILIGHT (in minutes)

Latitude	52°	56°	52°	56°	52°	56°	52°	56°
		1 October		11 October		21 October		31 October
Civil	34	37	34	37	34	38	35	39
Nautical	73	80	73	80	74	81	75	83
Astronomical	113	125	112	124	113	124	114	126

THE NIGHT SKY

Mercury is too poorly placed to be seen this month from the UK.

Venus (magnitude −3.8) continues to pull away from the Sun but does not become easily visible from the UK until towards the end of October. On the evening of the 29th it is a brilliant lamp hung below the 38-hour old crescent Moon. Venus sets about 45 minutes after the Sun on the 31st.

Mars (magnitude 1.8) is rising two hours before the Sun at the end of October and can be found in Virgo. The waning Moon is in the area on the mornings of the 26th and 27th. The summer solstice falls in the Red Planet's northern hemisphere on the 8th as we stand on the cusp of our winter.

Jupiter (magnitude −2.0) is setting after 8pm at the beginning of the month but is gone from view by early evening on the 31st. The Moon is near Jupiter on the 3rd and 31st.

Saturn (magnitude 0.5) is at eastern quadrature in early October when the globe's shadow may be seen cast on the rings. The Moon is quite close to Saturn on the evening of the 5th. The ringed planet is setting mid-evening by the end of October.

Uranus (magnitude 5.7) is at opposition on the 28th in Aries. The planet can be easily seen in a pair of binoculars and suitable software or charts in the monthly astronomy magazines will help locate it. A small telescope will show the 3.7 arc-second wide disk.

THE MOON

Day	R.A.		Dec	Hor Par	Diam	Sun Co-Long	PA of Br. limb	Ph.	Age	Rise 52°		Rise 56°		Transit		Set 52°		Set 56°	
	h	m	°	'	'	°	°	%	d	h	m	h	m	h	m	h	m	h	m
1	14	31	−10.1	60.0	32.6	296	281	07	1.7	9	17	9	29	14	25	19	20	19	08
2	15	27	−14.8	59.1	32.2	308	280	14	2.7	10	39	10	54	15	18	19	50	19	32
3	16	23	−18.5	58.2	31.8	320	278	23	3.7	11	54	12	16	16	12	20	24	20	03
4	17	19	−21.1	57.2	31.2	332	273	33	4.7	13	02	13	27	17	06	21	07	20	42
5	18	14	−22.5	56.3	30.8	344	268	43	5.7	14	01	14	27	17	59	21	57	21	31
6	19	09	−22.7	55.6	30.2	357	263	53	6.7	14	49	15	13	18	50	22	54	22	30
7	20	02	−21.8	55.0	30.0	9	258	63	7.7	15	28	15	48	19	39	23	57	23	36
8	20	53	−19.9	54.5	29.8	21	253	72	8.7	15	57	16	15	20	26	—	—	—	—
9	21	42	−17.1	54.2	29.6	33	248	80	9.7	16	22	16	36	21	11	1	02	0	45
10	22	29	−13.7	54.1	29.4	45	244	87	10.7	16	43	16	52	21	54	2	08	1	56
11	23	14	−9.7	54.0	29.4	57	240	93	11.7	17	01	17	06	22	35	3	15	3	07
12	23	59	−5.4	54.1	29.4	70	234	97	12.7	17	18	17	19	23	17	4	22	4	18
13	0	43	−0.8	54.3	29.6	82	220	99	13.7	17	34	17	32	23	58	5	29	5	29
14	1	28	+3.9	54.5	29.8	94	143	100	14.7	17	51	17	45	—	—	6	36	6	41
15	2	13	+8.4	54.8	29.8	106	91	99	15.7	18	10	18	01	0	41	7	45	7	54
16	3	00	+12.7	55.2	30.2	118	83	96	16.7	18	32	18	18	1	26	8	55	9	09
17	3	49	+16.5	55.7	30.4	130	82	91	17.7	19	01	18	41	2	13	10	06	10	24
18	4	41	+19.6	56.2	30.6	143	85	84	18.7	19	35	19	13	3	02	11	16	11	38
19	5	35	+21.8	56.7	31.0	155	88	76	19.7	20	20	19	55	3	55	12	22	12	47
20	6	32	+22.9	57.4	31.2	167	93	66	20.7	21	16	20	51	4	50	13	21	13	46
21	7	30	+22.7	58.0	31.6	179	99	56	21.7	22	24	22	02	5	46	14	10	14	34
22	8	29	+21.1	58.7	32.0	191	104	45	22.7	23	41	23	23	6	43	14	50	15	09
23	9	27	+18.2	59.4	32.4	204	109	34	23.7	—	—	—	—	7	40	15	22	15	37
24	10	25	+14.2	60.0	32.6	216	114	23	24.7	1	04	0	51	8	35	15	49	15	58
25	11	21	+9.2	60.4	33.0	228	118	14	25.7	2	28	2	21	9	29	16	12	16	17
26	12	16	+3.7	60.7	33.0	240	122	07	26.7	3	54	3	52	10	22	16	33	16	33
27	13	11	−2.1	60.6	33.0	252	129	02	27.7	5	20	5	23	11	15	16	55	16	50
28	14	06	−7.8	60.4	32.8	265	176	00	28.7	6	46	6	54	12	08	17	18	17	08
29	15	02	−13.0	59.8	32.6	277	267	01	0.2	8	10	8	24	13	03	17	45	17	30
30	15	59	−17.3	59.1	32.2	289	275	05	1.2	9	31	9	50	13	58	18	17	17	58
31	16	56	−20.4	58.2	31.8	301	273	10	2.2	10	46	11	09	14	53	18	57	18	33

MERCURY

Day	R.A.	Dec	Mag.	Diam.	Phase	Rise	Transit	Set
	h m	°		"	%	h m	h m	h m
1	13 37.4	−11.2	−0.2	5	86	7 55	12 59	18 02
3	13 48.0	−12.5	−0.2	5	84	8 04	13 02	17 58
5	13 58.5	−13.7	−0.2	5	82	8 14	13 04	17 54
7	14 08.9	−14.8	−0.1	6	80	8 23	13 06	17 50
9	14 19.1	−15.9	−0.1	6	78	8 31	13 09	17 45
11	14 29.1	−17.0	−0.1	6	76	8 39	13 11	17 41
13	14 38.8	−17.9	−0.1	6	74	8 47	13 12	17 37
15	14 48.3	−18.8	−0.1	6	71	8 54	13 14	17 33
17	14 57.4	−19.7	−0.1	6	68	9 00	13 15	17 29
19	15 06.0	−20.4	−0.1	7	64	9 05	13 15	17 25
21	15 14.1	−21.0	0.0	7	61	9 09	13 15	17 21
23	15 21.4	−21.6	0.0	7	56	9 12	13 14	17 17
25	15 27.8	−22.0	0.0	7	51	9 13	13 12	17 12
27	15 33.0	−22.3	+0.1	8	46	9 12	13 09	17 07
29	15 36.7	−22.4	+0.3	8	40	9 08	13 05	17 02
31	15 38.6	−22.4	+0.5	8	33	9 01	12 58	16 56

Rising and setting times are for latitude 54°

VENUS

Day	R.A.	Dec	Mag.	Diam.	Phase	Rise	Transit	Set
	h m	°		"	%	h m	h m	h m
1	13 16.8	−7.1	−3.9	11	98	7 12	12 38	18 04
6	13 40.0	−9.6	−3.9	11	97	7 28	12 42	17 54
11	14 03.4	−11.9	−3.9	11	96	7 45	12 45	17 45
16	14 27.2	−14.2	−3.9	11	96	8 02	12 50	17 37
21	14 51.5	−16.2	−3.9	11	95	8 18	12 54	17 29
26	15 16.2	−18.2	−3.9	11	95	8 35	12 59	17 23
31	15 41.5	−19.9	−3.9	11	94	8 51	13 05	17 18

MARS

Day	R.A.	Dec	Mag.	Diam.	Phase	Rise	Transit	Set
	h m	°		"	%	h m	h m	h m
1	11 54.1	+1.7	+1.8	4	100	5 03	11 15	17 26
6	12 05.9	+0.4	+1.8	4	100	5 02	11 07	17 12
11	12 17.7	−0.9	+1.8	4	100	5 01	10 59	16 57
16	12 29.5	−2.2	+1.8	4	99	5 00	10 51	16 43
21	12 41.4	−3.5	+1.8	4	99	4 58	10 43	16 28
26	12 53.3	−4.8	+1.8	4	99	4 57	10 36	16 14
31	13 05.3	−6.0	+1.8	4	99	4 56	10 28	16 00

SUNRISE AND SUNSET

	London		Bristol		Birmingham		Manchester		Newcastle		Glasgow		Belfast	
	0° 05′ 51° 30′		2° 35′ 51° 28′		1° 55′ 52° 28′		2° 15′ 53° 28′		1° 37′ 54° 59′		4° 14′ 55° 52′		5° 56′ 54° 35′	
d	h m	h m	h m	h m	h m	h m	h m	h m	h m	h m	h m	h m	h m	h m
1	6 00	17 39	6 10	17 49	6 08	17 46	6 10	17 47	6 08	17 43	6 19	17 53	6 25	18 01
2	6 02	17 37	6 12	17 47	6 10	17 43	6 12	17 44	6 10	17 41	6 21	17 51	6 27	17 58
3	6 04	17 34	6 14	17 44	6 11	17 41	6 13	17 42	6 12	17 38	6 23	17 48	6 29	17 56
4	6 05	17 32	6 15	17 42	6 13	17 39	6 15	17 39	6 14	17 36	6 25	17 45	6 31	17 53
5	6 07	17 30	6 17	17 40	6 15	17 36	6 17	17 37	6 16	17 33	6 27	17 43	6 33	17 51
6	6 08	17 28	6 18	17 38	6 17	17 34	6 19	17 35	6 18	17 31	6 29	17 40	6 35	17 48
7	6 10	17 25	6 20	17 35	6 18	17 32	6 21	17 32	6 20	17 28	6 31	17 38	6 36	17 46
8	6 12	17 23	6 22	17 33	6 20	17 30	6 22	17 30	6 21	17 26	6 33	17 35	6 38	17 43
9	6 13	17 21	6 23	17 31	6 22	17 27	6 24	17 28	6 23	17 23	6 35	17 33	6 40	17 41
10	6 15	17 19	6 25	17 29	6 24	17 25	6 26	17 25	6 25	17 21	6 37	17 30	6 42	17 38
11	6 17	17 17	6 27	17 27	6 25	17 23	6 28	17 23	6 27	17 18	6 39	17 27	6 44	17 36
12	6 19	17 14	6 29	17 24	6 27	17 20	6 30	17 20	6 29	17 16	6 41	17 25	6 46	17 34
13	6 20	17 12	6 30	17 22	6 29	17 18	6 32	17 18	6 31	17 13	6 43	17 22	6 48	17 31
14	6 22	17 10	6 32	17 20	6 31	17 16	6 33	17 16	6 33	17 11	6 45	17 20	6 50	17 29
15	6 24	17 08	6 34	17 18	6 32	17 14	6 35	17 14	6 35	17 09	6 47	17 17	6 52	17 26
16	6 25	17 06	6 35	17 16	6 34	17 12	6 37	17 11	6 37	17 06	6 49	17 15	6 54	17 24
17	6 27	17 04	6 37	17 14	6 36	17 09	6 39	17 09	6 39	17 04	6 51	17 12	6 56	17 22
18	6 29	17 02	6 39	17 12	6 38	17 07	6 41	17 07	6 41	17 01	6 53	17 10	6 58	17 19
19	6 30	16 59	6 40	17 09	6 40	17 05	6 43	17 05	6 43	16 59	6 55	17 08	7 00	17 17
20	6 32	16 57	6 42	17 07	6 41	17 03	6 45	17 02	6 45	16 57	6 57	17 05	7 02	17 15
21	6 34	16 55	6 44	17 05	6 43	17 01	6 46	17 00	6 47	16 54	7 00	17 03	7 03	17 12
22	6 36	16 53	6 46	17 03	6 45	16 59	6 48	16 58	6 49	16 52	7 02	17 00	7 05	17 10
23	6 37	16 51	6 47	17 01	6 47	16 57	6 50	16 56	6 51	16 50	7 04	16 58	7 07	17 08
24	6 39	16 49	6 49	16 59	6 49	16 55	6 52	16 54	6 53	16 47	7 06	16 56	7 09	17 06
25	6 41	16 47	6 51	16 57	6 50	16 52	6 54	16 52	6 55	16 45	7 08	16 53	7 11	17 03
26	6 43	16 45	6 53	16 55	6 52	16 50	6 56	16 49	6 57	16 43	7 10	16 51	7 13	17 01
27	6 44	16 43	6 54	16 53	6 54	16 48	6 58	16 47	6 59	16 41	7 12	16 49	7 15	16 59
28	6 46	16 41	6 56	16 52	6 56	16 46	7 00	16 45	7 01	16 39	7 14	16 46	7 17	16 57
29	6 48	16 40	6 58	16 50	6 58	16 44	7 02	16 43	7 03	16 36	7 16	16 44	7 19	16 55
30	6 50	16 38	7 00	16 48	6 59	16 43	7 03	16 41	7 05	16 34	7 18	16 42	7 21	16 53
31	6 51	16 36	7 01	16 46	7 01	16 41	7 05	16 39	7 07	16 32	7 20	16 40	7 23	16 51

JUPITER

Day	R.A. h m	Dec °	Mag.	Diam. ″	Rise h m	Transit h m	Set h m
1	17 08.7	−22.7	−2.0	36	12 33	16 28	20 24
11	17 15.1	−22.8	−2.0	35	12 01	15 56	19 50
21	17 22.4	−22.9	−1.9	34	11 30	15 23	19 17
31	17 30.3	−23.1	−1.9	33	11 00	14 52	18 45

Equatorial Diam. 36″, Polar Diam. 33″

SATURN

Day	R.A. h m	Dec °	Mag.	Diam. ″	Rise h m	Transit h m	Set h m
1	19 00.9	−22.5	+0.5	17	14 24	18 20	22 17
11	19 02.2	−22.5	+0.5	17	13 46	17 42	21 39
21	19 04.1	−22.5	+0.6	16	13 08	17 05	21 01
31	19 06.7	−22.4	+0.6	16	12 31	16 28	20 25

Equatorial Diam. 17″, Polar Diam. 15″
Rings – major axis 37″ minor axis 16″, Tilt 25°

URANUS

Day	R.A. h m	Dec °	Mag.	Diam. ″	Rise h m	Transit h m	Set h m
1	02 14.2	+12.9	+5.7	4	18 21	1 36	8 47
11	02 12.8	+12.8	+5.7	4	17 41	0 55	8 06
21	02 11.2	+12.7	+5.7	4	17 01	0 15	7 24
31	02 09.6	+12.5	+5.7	4	16 21	23 30	6 43

NEPTUNE

Day	R.A. h m	Dec °	Mag.	Diam. ″	Rise h m	Transit h m	Set h m
1	23 12.9	−6.2	+7.8	2	17 01	22 31	4 06
11	23 12.0	−6.3	+7.8	2	16 21	21 51	3 26
21	23 11.2	−6.4	+7.8	2	15 41	21 11	2 45
31	23 10.6	−6.4	+7.8	2	15 02	20 31	2 05

November 2019

ELEVENTH MONTH, 30 DAYS. *Novem* (nine), ninth month of Roman pre-Julian calendar

1	*Friday*	Antigua and Barbuda gains independence from the United Kingdom 1981	day 305
2	*Saturday*	A million people's homes are estimated to be underwater in the Tabasco floods, Mexico 2007	306
3	*Sunday*	Salvador Allende, the first democratically elected Marxist president, takes office in Chile 1970	307

4	*Monday*	Álvaro Colom is elected Guatemalan president 2007	week 45 day 308
5	*Tuesday*	Salvadoran priest José Delgado rings church bells, launching Independence Movement 1811	309
6	*Wednesday*	First constitution of the Dominican Republic is adopted 1844	310
7	*Thursday*	Dutty Boukman, early leader of the Haitian revolution, is beheaded 1791	311
8	*Friday*	Fifteen bus passengers are shot and set on fire in Guatemala 2008	312
9	*Saturday*	Mexico City legalises same-sex civil unions 2009	313
10	*Sunday*	A law allowing individuals to buy and sell private property in Cuba comes into effect 2011	314

11	*Monday*	Carlos Fuentes, Mexican novelist and essayist *b*. 1928	week 46 day 315
12	*Tuesday*	Law implementing the right to divorce comes into force in Chile 2004	316
13	*Wednesday*	Nevado del Ruiz volcano, Colombia erupts killing over 20,000 people 1985	317
14	*Thursday*	Eliseo Salazar, Chilean racing driver *b*. 1954	318
15	*Friday*	Brazil is declared a republic; the government's motivation is *café com leite* (coffee interests) 1889	319
16	*Saturday*	Lionel Messi, Argentinian footballer, makes his debut for FC Barcelona against Porto 2003	320
17	*Sunday*	Jose Miguel Carrera is sworn in as president of the executive government in Chile 1811	321

18	*Monday*	Chinese president Hu Jintao visits Cuba 2008	week 47 day 322
19	*Tuesday*	Pelé, Brazilian footballer, scores the 1,000 goal of his professional career 1969	323
20	*Wednesday*	The Mexican Revolution begins 1910	324
21	*Thursday*	Two Chilean colonels are imprisoned for torturing the father of President Bachelet 2014	325
22	*Friday*	Guatemalan guerrilla forces massacre 21 residents of El Aguacate 1988	326
23	*Saturday*	Nicolas Maduro, President of Venezuela *b*. 1962	327
24	*Sunday*	Mexican painter and muralist Diego Riveria *d*. 1957	328

25	*Monday*	Cuban revolutionary and Prime Minister Fidel Castro *d*. 2016	week 48 day 329
26	*Tuesday*	Battle of Papudo takes place between Spain and Chile 1865	330
27	*Wednesday*	Russian President Dmitry Medvedev visits Cuba to conclude new trade deals 2008	331
28	*Thursday*	Panama becomes independent from Spain 1821	332
29	*Friday*	Portuguese court flees to Brazil during the Peninsular War 1807	333
30	*Saturday*	Ecuador invites Wikileaks founder Julian Assange to live there 2010	334

ASTRONOMICAL PHENOMENA

d	h	
2	7	Saturn 0.6° North of the Moon
9	12	Jupiter without Galilean satellites
11		Transit of Mercury
12	9	Vesta at opposition (Mag. 6.5)
24	9	Mars 4° South of the Moon
24	14	Jupiter 1° North of Venus
25	3	Mercury 2° South of the Moon
28	10	Mercury greatest elongation West (20°)
28	11	Jupiter 0.7° South of the Moon
28	19	Venus 2° South of the Moon
29	21	Saturn 0.9° North of the Moon
30	12	Ceres 2° South of Venus

MINIMA OF ALGOL

d	h	d	h	d	h
3	15.2	15	2.5	26	13.8
6	12.1	17	23.3	29	10.6
9	8.9	20	20.1		
12	5.7	23	16.9		

CONSTELLATIONS

The following constellations are near the meridian at

	d	h		d	h
October	1	24	November	15	21
October	16	23	December	1	20
November	1	22	December	16	19

Ursa Major (below the Pole), Cepheus, Cassiopeia, Andromeda, Pegasus, Pisces, Aquarius and Cetus

THE MOON

Phase, Apsides and Node	d	h	m
☽ First Quarter	4	10	24
○ Full Moon	12	13	36
☾ Last Quarter	19	21	12
● New Moon	26	15	7
Apogee (405,058 km)	7	8	37
Perigee (366,716 km)	23	7	42

Mean longitude of the ascending node on 1st, 101°

THE SUN Diam. 32.2′

Day	Right Ascension			Dec.	Equation of time		Rise 52°		Rise 56°		Transit		Set 52°		Set 56°		Sidereal time			Transit of first point of Aries		
	h	m	s	°	m	s	h	m	h	m	h	m	h	m	h	m	h	m	s	h	m	s
1	14	23	36	−14.3	+16	22	6	54	7	06	11	44	16	32	16	20	2	39	59	21	16	31
2	14	27	31	−14.6	+16	24	6	56	7	08	11	44	16	30	16	18	2	43	56	21	12	35
3	14	31	27	−14.9	+16	25	6	58	7	10	11	44	16	29	16	16	2	47	52	21	08	39
4	14	35	23	−15.2	+16	25	7	00	7	13	11	44	16	27	16	14	2	51	49	21	04	43
5	14	39	20	−15.5	+16	24	7	01	7	15	11	44	16	25	16	12	2	55	46	21	00	48
6	14	43	18	−15.8	+16	23	7	03	7	17	11	44	16	23	16	10	2	59	42	20	56	52
7	14	47	17	−16.1	+16	20	7	05	7	19	11	44	16	22	16	08	3	03	39	20	52	56
8	14	51	17	−16.4	+16	17	7	07	7	21	11	44	16	20	16	06	3	07	35	20	49	00
9	14	55	18	−16.7	+16	13	7	09	7	23	11	44	16	18	16	04	3	11	32	20	45	04
10	14	59	19	−17.0	+16	08	7	10	7	25	11	44	16	17	16	02	3	15	28	20	41	08
11	15	03	21	−17.3	+16	03	7	12	7	27	11	44	16	15	16	00	3	19	25	20	37	12
12	15	07	24	−17.6	+15	56	7	14	7	29	11	44	16	14	15	58	3	23	21	20	33	16
13	15	11	28	−17.8	+15	49	7	16	7	31	11	44	16	12	15	56	3	27	18	20	29	20
14	15	15	33	−18.1	+15	41	7	17	7	34	11	44	16	11	15	55	3	31	15	20	25	24
15	15	19	39	−18.3	+15	31	7	19	7	36	11	45	16	09	15	53	3	35	11	20	21	28
16	15	23	45	−18.6	+15	22	7	21	7	38	11	45	16	08	15	51	3	39	08	20	17	33
17	15	27	52	−18.9	+15	11	7	23	7	40	11	45	16	07	15	49	3	43	04	20	13	37
18	15	32	01	−19.1	+14	59	7	24	7	42	11	45	16	05	15	48	3	47	01	20	09	41
19	15	36	10	−19.3	+14	47	7	26	7	44	11	45	16	04	15	46	3	50	57	20	05	45
20	15	40	19	−19.6	+14	33	7	28	7	46	11	46	16	03	15	45	3	54	54	20	01	49
21	15	44	30	−19.8	+14	19	7	29	7	48	11	46	16	02	15	43	3	58	50	19	57	53
22	15	48	42	−20.0	+14	04	7	31	7	50	11	46	16	01	15	42	4	02	47	19	53	57
23	15	52	54	−20.2	+13	48	7	33	7	51	11	46	16	00	15	41	4	06	44	19	50	01
24	15	57	07	−20.4	+13	32	7	34	7	53	11	47	15	59	15	39	4	10	40	19	46	05
25	16	01	21	−20.6	+13	14	7	36	7	55	11	47	15	58	15	38	4	14	37	19	42	09
26	16	05	36	−20.8	+12	56	7	37	7	57	11	47	15	57	15	37	4	18	33	19	38	13
27	16	09	51	−21.0	+12	37	7	39	7	59	11	48	15	56	15	36	4	22	30	19	34	18
28	16	14	08	−21.2	+12	18	7	40	8	01	11	48	15	55	15	35	4	26	26	19	30	22
29	16	18	25	−21.4	+11	57	7	42	8	02	11	48	15	54	15	34	4	30	23	19	26	26
30	16	22	42	−21.6	+11	36	7	43	8	04	11	49	15	53	15	33	4	34	19	19	22	30

DURATION OF TWILIGHT (in minutes)

Latitude	52°	56°	52°	56°	52°	56°	52°	56°
	1 November		11 November		21 November		31 November	
Civil	36	40	37	41	38	43	40	45
Nautical	75	84	78	87	80	90	82	93
Astronomical	115	127	117	130	120	134	123	138

THE NIGHT SKY

Mercury transits the Sun on November 11th and then emerges from the dawn glow to gain in altitude as the month progresses. The transit is visible from the Middle East, Europe, Africa, and the Americas. Observers in the UK will miss the latter stages of the event. The Moon is close to Mercury on the 25th.

Venus starts off still very low in the evening sky but closes in on Jupiter the last week of November with the gap less than 2° on the 24th. The two set about 1½ hours after the Sun around this time. Venus is south of the Lagoon Nebula on the 26th with the Moon between Venus and Jupiter on the 28th.

Mars (magnitude 1.8) passes Spica over the mornings of the 10th through 12th. The planet is rising two hours before the Sun on the 1st and three hours beforehand on the 30th. The Moon is near by on the 24th.

Jupiter crosses into Sagittarius mid-month. The planet is without a visible Galilean satellite between 12h 17m and 12h 56m (UT) on the 9th when Io and Ganymede are transiting, Europa is occulted, and Jupiter's shadow eclipses Callisto. This rare event is not visible from the UK unfortunately with the next opportunity for observers located there not occurring until July 2033.

Saturn (magnitude 0.6) is an evening sky object setting nearly three hours after the Sun at the end of November. The Moon is near by on the 2nd and closer on the 29th.

THE MOON

Day	R.A. h	R.A. m	Dec °	Hor Par '	Diam '	Sun Co-Long °	PA of Br. limb °	Ph. %	Age d	Rise 52° h	Rise 52° m	Rise 56° h	Rise 56° m	Transit h	Transit m	Set 52° h	Set 52° m	Set 56° h	Set 56° m
1	17	54	−22.4	57.3	31.2	313	270	18	3.2	11	51	12	17	15	48	19	44	19	19
2	18	50	−23.0	56.5	30.8	326	265	27	4.2	12	45	13	10	16	42	20	40	20	16
3	19	45	−22.5	55.7	30.4	338	260	36	5.2	13	28	13	51	17	33	21	43	21	20
4	20	38	−20.8	55.1	30.0	350	256	46	6.2	14	01	14	21	18	21	22	48	22	30
5	21	28	−18.3	54.6	29.8	2	251	56	7.2	14	28	14	43	19	07	23	55	23	41
6	22	16	−15.0	54.3	29.6	14	248	65	8.2	14	49	15	00	19	51	—	—	—	—
7	23	02	−11.1	54.1	29.6	26	245	74	9.2	15	08	15	15	20	33	1	02	0	52
8	23	46	−6.8	54.2	29.6	39	243	81	10.2	15	25	15	28	21	14	2	09	2	04
9	0	30	−2.3	54.3	29.6	51	241	88	11.2	15	41	15	40	21	56	3	16	3	15
10	1	15	+2.4	54.6	29.8	63	239	94	12.2	15	58	15	53	22	38	4	24	4	27
11	2	00	+7.1	55.0	30.0	75	235	98	13.2	16	16	16	07	23	22	5	33	5	40
12	2	47	+11.6	55.4	30.2	87	220	100	14.2	16	36	16	23	—	—	6	43	6	55
13	3	36	+15.6	55.9	30.4	99	112	100	15.2	17	03	16	45	0	09	7	55	8	12
14	4	27	+19.0	56.3	30.8	111	90	98	16.2	17	34	17	13	0	58	9	07	9	29
15	5	22	+21.5	56.8	31.0	124	89	94	17.2	18	16	17	52	1	50	10	16	10	41
16	6	19	+22.9	57.3	31.2	136	92	88	18.2	19	10	18	43	2	45	11	19	11	44
17	7	17	+23.0	57.8	31.4	148	97	80	19.2	20	14	19	50	3	42	12	11	12	36
18	8	15	+21.8	58.2	31.8	160	102	71	20.2	21	27	21	08	4	39	12	53	13	14
19	9	13	+19.2	58.7	32.0	172	107	60	21.2	22	47	22	31	5	35	13	27	13	43
20	10	10	+15.6	59.1	32.2	184	111	49	22.2	—	—	23	59	6	29	13	53	14	05
21	11	05	+10.9	59.4	32.4	197	114	37	23.2	0	09	—	—	7	21	14	17	14	23
22	11	59	+5.7	59.7	32.6	209	116	27	24.2	1	31	1	27	8	13	14	37	14	39
23	12	52	+0.1	59.8	32.6	221	117	17	25.2	2	54	2	55	9	04	14	58	14	55
24	13	45	−5.6	59.7	32.6	233	118	09	26.2	4	17	4	23	9	55	15	19	15	11
25	14	39	−10.9	59.5	32.4	245	119	04	27.2	5	41	5	52	10	48	15	43	15	30
26	15	35	−15.6	59.1	32.2	257	127	01	28.2	7	03	7	20	11	42	16	12	15	54
27	16	32	−19.3	58.6	32.0	270	251	00	29.2	8	22	8	43	12	38	16	47	16	25
28	17	30	−21.8	57.9	31.6	282	269	02	0.7	9	34	9	58	13	34	17	31	17	06
29	18	28	−23.1	57.1	31.2	294	267	07	1.7	10	35	10	59	14	29	18	24	18	00
30	19	24	−23.0	56.4	30.8	306	263	13	2.7	11	24	11	48	15	23	19	25	19	02

MERCURY

Day	R.A. h m	Dec °	Mag.	Diam. "	Phase %	Rise h m	Transit h m	Set h m
1	15 38.8	−22.3	+0.6	9	29	8 56	12 54	16 53
3	15 37.5	−21.9	+1.0	9	22	8 43	12 44	16 46
5	15 33.7	−21.3	+1.6	9	15	8 27	12 31	16 38
7	15 27.3	−20.4	+2.5	10	8	8 06	12 17	16 29
9	15 18.9	−19.2	+3.7	10	3	7 42	12 00	16 20
11	15 09.2	−17.9	+5.3	10	0	7 17	11 42	16 11
13	14 59.3	−16.5	+4.6	10	1	6 51	11 25	16 02
15	14 50.7	−15.2	+3.0	10	5	6 28	11 09	15 53
17	14 44.2	−14.2	+1.8	9	12	6 08	10 56	15 45
19	14 40.4	−13.5	+1.0	9	20	5 54	10 45	15 38
21	14 39.6	−13.1	+0.4	8	30	5 44	10 37	15 32
23	14 41.4	−13.1	0.0	8	39	5 38	10 32	15 26
25	14 45.5	−13.4	−0.3	7	48	5 37	10 29	15 21
27	14 51.5	−13.9	−0.4	7	56	5 38	10 27	15 16
29	14 59.1	−14.5	−0.5	7	63	5 42	10 27	15 13

Rising and setting times are for latitude 54°

VENUS

Day	R.A. h m	Dec °	Mag.	Diam. "	Phase %	Rise h m	Transit h m	Set h m
1	15 46.6	−20.2	−3.9	11	94	8 54	13 06	17 17
6	16 12.5	−21.7	−3.9	12	93	9 10	13 12	17 14
11	16 38.9	−22.9	−3.9	12	92	9 25	13 19	17 12
16	17 05.6	−23.8	−3.9	12	91	9 38	13 26	17 13
21	17 32.7	−24.4	−3.9	12	91	9 50	13 33	17 16
26	17 59.9	−24.7	−3.9	12	90	10 00	13 41	17 22

MARS

Day	R.A. h m	Dec °	Mag.	Diam. "	Phase %	Rise h m	Transit h m	Set h m
1	13 07.7	−6.3	+1.8	4	99	4 56	10 26	15 57
6	13 19.9	−7.6	+1.8	4	99	4 55	10 19	15 43
11	13 32.1	−8.8	+1.8	4	98	4 54	10 11	15 29
16	13 44.4	−10.0	+1.8	4	98	4 53	10 04	15 15
21	13 56.9	−11.2	+1.7	4	98	4 52	9 57	15 01
26	14 09.5	−12.4	+1.7	4	98	4 52	9 50	14 48

SUNRISE AND SUNSET

	London 0° 05′ / 51° 30′		Bristol 2° 35′ / 51° 28′		Birmingham 1° 55′ / 52° 28′		Manchester 2° 15′ / 53° 28′		Newcastle 1° 37′ / 54° 59′		Glasgow 4° 14′ / 55° 52′		Belfast 5° 56′ / 54° 35′	
d	h m	h m	h m	h m	h m	h m	h m	h m	h m	h m	h m	h m	h m	h m
1	6 53	16 34	7 03	16 44	7 03	16 39	7 07	16 37	7 09	16 30	7 23	16 38	7 25	16 49
2	6 55	16 32	7 05	16 42	7 05	16 37	7 09	16 35	7 11	16 28	7 25	16 35	7 27	16 47
3	6 57	16 30	7 07	16 41	7 07	16 35	7 11	16 33	7 13	16 26	7 27	16 33	7 29	16 44
4	6 58	16 29	7 08	16 39	7 09	16 33	7 13	16 31	7 15	16 24	7 29	16 31	7 31	16 43
5	7 00	16 27	7 10	16 37	7 10	16 31	7 15	16 30	7 17	16 22	7 31	16 29	7 33	16 41
6	7 02	16 25	7 12	16 35	7 12	16 30	7 17	16 28	7 19	16 20	7 33	16 27	7 35	16 39
7	7 04	16 24	7 14	16 34	7 14	16 28	7 19	16 26	7 22	16 18	7 35	16 25	7 37	16 37
8	7 05	16 22	7 15	16 32	7 16	16 26	7 21	16 24	7 24	16 16	7 37	16 23	7 39	16 35
9	7 07	16 20	7 17	16 31	7 18	16 25	7 23	16 22	7 26	16 14	7 40	16 21	7 41	16 33
10	7 09	16 19	7 19	16 29	7 20	16 23	7 24	16 21	7 28	16 12	7 42	16 19	7 43	16 31
11	7 11	16 17	7 21	16 27	7 21	16 21	7 26	16 19	7 30	16 11	7 44	16 17	7 45	16 29
12	7 12	16 16	7 22	16 26	7 23	16 20	7 28	16 17	7 32	16 09	7 46	16 16	7 47	16 28
13	7 14	16 14	7 24	16 24	7 25	16 18	7 30	16 16	7 34	16 07	7 48	16 14	7 49	16 26
14	7 16	16 13	7 26	16 23	7 27	16 17	7 32	16 14	7 36	16 05	7 50	16 12	7 51	16 24
15	7 18	16 12	7 28	16 22	7 29	16 15	7 34	16 13	7 38	16 04	7 52	16 10	7 53	16 23
16	7 19	16 10	7 29	16 20	7 30	16 14	7 36	16 11	7 40	16 02	7 54	16 09	7 55	16 21
17	7 21	16 09	7 31	16 19	7 32	16 12	7 38	16 10	7 42	16 01	7 56	16 07	7 57	16 20
18	7 23	16 08	7 33	16 18	7 34	16 11	7 39	16 08	7 44	15 59	7 58	16 05	7 59	16 18
19	7 24	16 06	7 34	16 16	7 36	16 10	7 41	16 07	7 45	15 58	8 00	16 04	8 01	16 17
20	7 26	16 05	7 36	16 15	7 37	16 09	7 43	16 06	7 47	15 56	8 02	16 02	8 03	16 15
21	7 28	16 04	7 38	16 14	7 39	16 07	7 45	16 04	7 49	15 55	8 04	16 01	8 05	16 14
22	7 29	16 03	7 39	16 13	7 41	16 06	7 46	16 03	7 51	15 53	8 06	15 59	8 06	16 13
23	7 31	16 02	7 41	16 12	7 42	16 05	7 48	16 02	7 53	15 52	8 08	15 58	8 08	16 11
24	7 33	16 01	7 42	16 11	7 44	16 04	7 50	16 01	7 55	15 51	8 10	15 57	8 10	16 10
25	7 34	16 00	7 44	16 10	7 46	16 03	7 52	16 00	7 57	15 50	8 12	15 55	8 12	16 09
26	7 36	15 59	7 46	16 09	7 47	16 02	7 53	15 59	7 58	15 49	8 14	15 54	8 14	16 08
27	7 37	15 58	7 47	16 08	7 49	16 01	7 55	15 58	8 00	15 47	8 15	15 53	8 15	16 07
28	7 39	15 57	7 49	16 07	7 50	16 00	7 57	15 57	8 02	15 46	8 17	15 52	8 17	16 06
29	7 40	15 57	7 50	16 07	7 52	15 59	7 58	15 56	8 03	15 45	8 19	15 51	8 19	16 05
30	7 42	15 56	7 52	16 06	7 53	15 59	8 00	15 55	8 05	15 45	8 21	15 50	8 20	16 04

JUPITER

Day	R.A. h m	Dec °	Mag.	Diam. ″	Rise h m	Transit h m	Set h m
1	17 31.1	−23.1	−1.9	33	10 57	14 49	18 41
11	17 39.7	−23.2	−1.9	33	10 27	14 18	18 10
21	17 48.8	−23.3	−1.9	32	9 57	13 48	17 39

Equatorial Diam. 33″, Polar Diam. 31″

SATURN

Day	R.A. h m	Dec °	Mag.	Diam. ″	Rise h m	Transit h m	Set h m
1	19 06.9	−22.4	+0.6	16	12 27	16 24	20 21
11	19 10.1	−22.3	+0.6	16	11 51	15 48	19 46
21	19 13.8	−22.2	+0.6	16	11 15	15 13	19 11

Equatorial Diam. 16″, Polar Diam. 15″
Rings – major axis 36″ minor axis 15″, Tilt 25°

URANUS

Day	R.A. h m	Dec °	Mag.	Diam. ″	Rise h m	Transit h m	Set h m
1	02 09.5	+12.5	+5.7	4	16 17	23 26	6 38
11	02 07.9	+12.4	+5.7	4	15 37	22 45	5 57
21	02 06.5	+12.3	+5.7	4	14 57	22 04	5 15

NEPTUNE

Day	R.A. h m	Dec °	Mag.	Diam. ″	Rise h m	Transit h m	Set h m
1	23 10.6	−6.4	+7.8	2	14 58	20 27	2 01
11	23 10.1	−6.5	+7.9	2	14 18	19 47	1 21
21	23 09.9	−6.5	+7.9	2	13 39	19 08	0 41

December 2019

TWELFTH MONTH, 31 DAYS. *Decem* (ten), tenth month of Roman pre-Julian calendar

1	*Sunday*	Otto Pérez Molina, Guatemalan president and military officer *b.* 1950	day 335

2	*Monday*	Fidel Castro takes office as president of Cuba 1976	week 49 day 336
3	*Tuesday*	Prudente de Morais, former President of Brazil *d.* 1912	337
4	*Wednesday*	Guatemalan Colonel Marco Sanchez is sentenced to 53 years in prison over forced disappearances 2009	338
5	*Thursday*	Christopher Columbus lands on Haiti and names it Hispaniola, or Little Spain 1492	339
6	*Friday*	Colombian government sends military to supress United Fruit Company strike 1928	340
7	*Saturday*	Former Guatemalan president Arnoldo Aleman is sentenced to 20 years for embezzlement 2003	341
8	*Sunday*	Mexican artists Diego Rivera and Frida Kahlo remarry in San Francisco 1940	342

9	*Monday*	Virgin of Guadalupe first appears to Juan Diego in Mexico City 1531	week 50 day 343
10	*Tuesday*	President of Mexico Felipe Calderon orders 6,500 troops into Michoacán, beginning the War on Drugs 2006	344
11	*Wednesday*	During an address to the UN, two attacks are made on Che Guevara's life 1964	345
12	*Thursday*	President Portillo of Guatemala pays $1.8m compensation to the families of those killed by security forces 2001	346
13	*Friday*	A 24-hour strike in Argentina protesting curbs on bank withdrawals takes place 2001	347
14	*Saturday*	Brazil's first female president Dilma Rousseff *b.* 1947	348
15	*Sunday*	Torrential rain leads to massive landslides in Venezuela, killing over 10,000 people 1999	349

16	*Monday*	Earthquake with estimated magnitude of 8.5 strikes Chile 1575	week 51 day 350
17	*Tuesday*	North American Free Trade Agreement is signed by Mexico, the USA and Canada 1992	351
18	*Wednesday*	Lizmark, Mexican wrestler *b.* 1950	352
19	Thursday	Trotsky is put aboard the oil tanker *Ruth* and deported to Mexico 1936	353
20	*Friday*	Argentina and the UK agree to identify 123 Argentinian soldiers killed in the Falklands war 2016	354
21	*Saturday*	Argentinian president Fernando de la Rúa resigns after protests that leaves 25 dead 2001	355
22	*Sunday*	Gunmen massacre 45 innocent civilians in Chiapas State, Mexico 1997	356

23	*Monday*	More than two months after crashing into an Andean glacier in a plane, 16 are rescued 1972	week 52 day 357
24	*Tuesday*	Eighteen inmates die during a prison revolt outside Guatemala City 2002	358
25	*Wednesday*	The Battle of Tucapel takes place in Chile 1553	359
26	*Thursday*	José Yves Limantour, Mexican Secretary of Finance *b.* 1854	360
27	*Friday*	The Cave of Swallows, largest known cave shaft in the world, is discovered in Mexico 1966	361
28	*Saturday*	More than 2,500 Cuban prisoners are released ahead of a papal visit 2011	362
29	*Sunday*	The Acuerdo de Paz Firme y Duradera peace treaty is signed in Guatemala 1996	363

30	*Monday*	Spanish conquistador Hernán Cortés takes office as the governor of 'New Spain' 1521	week 1 day 364
31	*Tuesday*	Ten people die in a plane crash soon after take off in Costa Rica 2017	365

ASTRONOMICAL PHENOMENA

d	h	
4	12	Neptune 4° North of the Moon
8	11	Uranus 5° North of the Moon
11	5	Saturn 2° North of Venus
11	12	Aldebaran 3° South of the Moon
13–14		Geminid meteor shower
17	5	Regulus 4° South of the Moon
22	4	Winter solstice
23	2	Mars 4° South of the Moon
25	11	Mercury 2° South of the Moon
26	1	Annular Solar Eclipse (Not UK)
26	8	Jupiter 0.2° South of the Moon
27	12	Saturn 1° North of the Moon
29	2	Venus 1° North of the Moon

MINIMA OF ALGOL

d	h	d	h	d	h
2	7.4	13	18.7	25	6.0
5	4.2	16	15.5	28	2.8
8	1.0	19	12.3	30	23.6
10	21.9	22	9.1		

CONSTELLATIONS

The following constellations are near the meridian at

	d	h		d	h
November	1	24	December	16	21
November	15	23	January	1	20
December	1	22	January	16	19

Ursa Major (below the Pole), Ursa Minor (below the Pole), Cassiopeia, Andromeda, Perseus, Triangulum, Aries, Taurus, Cetus and Eridanus

THE MOON

Phase, Apsides and Node	d	h	m
◐ First Quarter	4	6	59
○ Full Moon	12	5	13
◑ Last Quarter	19	4	58
● New Moon	26	5	14
Apogee (404,446 km)	5	4	9
Perigee (370,265 km)	18	20	26

Mean longitude of the ascending node on 1st, 100°

THE SUN Diam. 32.5′

Day	Right Ascension			Dec.	Equation of time		Rise 52°		Rise 56°		Transit		Set 52°		Set 56°		Sidereal time			Transit of first point of Aries		
	h	m	s	°	m	s	h	m	h	m	h	m	h	m	h	m	h	m	s	h	m	s
1	16	27	00	−21.7	+11	15	7	45	8	06	11	49	15	53	15	32	4	38	16	19	18	34
2	16	31	19	−21.9	+10	52	7	46	8	07	11	49	15	52	15	31	4	42	13	19	14	38
3	16	35	39	−22.0	+10	29	7	48	8	09	11	50	15	52	15	30	4	46	09	19	10	42
4	16	39	59	−22.2	+10	06	7	49	8	10	11	50	15	51	15	29	4	50	06	19	06	46
5	16	44	20	−22.3	+9	41	7	50	8	12	11	50	15	51	15	29	4	54	02	19	02	50
6	16	48	41	−22.4	+9	17	7	51	8	13	11	51	15	50	15	28	4	57	59	18	58	54
7	16	53	03	−22.5	+8	52	7	53	8	15	11	51	15	50	15	28	5	01	55	18	54	58
8	16	57	25	−22.7	+8	26	7	54	8	16	11	52	15	49	15	27	5	05	52	18	51	03
9	17	01	48	−22.8	+8	00	7	55	8	17	11	52	15	49	15	27	5	09	48	18	47	07
10	17	06	11	−22.9	+7	33	7	56	8	19	11	53	15	49	15	26	5	13	45	18	43	11
11	17	10	35	−23.0	+7	06	7	57	8	20	11	53	15	49	15	26	5	17	42	18	39	15
12	17	14	59	−23.0	+6	38	7	58	8	21	11	54	15	49	15	26	5	21	38	18	35	19
13	17	19	23	−23.1	+6	11	7	59	8	22	11	54	15	49	15	26	5	25	35	18	31	23
14	17	23	48	−23.2	+5	42	8	00	8	23	11	55	15	49	15	26	5	29	31	18	27	27
15	17	28	13	−23.2	+5	14	8	01	8	24	11	55	15	49	15	26	5	33	28	18	23	31
16	17	32	38	−23.3	+4	45	8	02	8	25	11	55	15	49	15	26	5	37	24	18	19	35
17	17	37	04	−23.3	+4	16	8	02	8	26	11	56	15	49	15	26	5	41	21	18	15	39
18	17	41	30	−23.4	+3	47	8	03	8	26	11	56	15	50	15	26	5	45	17	18	11	43
19	17	45	56	−23.4	+3	17	8	04	8	27	11	57	15	50	15	27	5	49	14	18	07	48
20	17	50	22	−23.4	+2	48	8	04	8	28	11	57	15	50	15	27	5	53	11	18	03	52
21	17	54	48	−23.4	+2	18	8	05	8	28	11	58	15	51	15	27	5	57	07	17	59	56
22	17	59	15	−23.4	+1	48	8	06	8	29	11	58	15	51	15	28	6	01	04	17	56	00
23	18	03	41	−23.4	+1	18	8	06	8	29	11	59	15	52	15	28	6	05	00	17	52	04
24	18	08	08	−23.4	+0	48	8	06	8	30	11	59	15	52	15	29	6	08	57	17	48	08
25	18	12	34	−23.4	+0	18	8	07	8	30	12	00	15	53	15	30	6	12	53	17	44	12
26	18	17	00	−23.4	+0	12	8	07	8	30	12	00	15	54	15	31	6	16	50	17	40	16
27	18	21	27	−23.3	−0	42	8	07	8	31	12	01	15	55	15	31	6	20	46	17	36	20
28	18	25	53	−23.3	−1	11	8	08	8	31	12	01	15	55	15	32	6	24	43	17	32	24
29	18	30	19	−23.3	−1	41	8	08	8	31	12	02	15	56	15	33	6	28	40	17	28	29
30	18	34	45	−23.2	−2	10	8	08	8	31	12	02	15	57	15	34	6	32	36	17	24	33
31	18	39	11	−23.1	−2	39	8	08	8	31	12	03	15	58	15	35	6	36	33	17	20	37

DURATION OF TWILIGHT (in minutes)

Latitude	52°	56°	52°	56°	52°	56°	52°	56°
	1 December		11 December		21 December		31 December	
Civil	40	45	41	47	41	47	41	47
Nautical	82	93	84	96	85	97	84	96
Astronomical	123	138	125	141	126	142	125	141

THE NIGHT SKY

Mercury is on view in the morning sky until the end of the third week of December. It is highest at the beginning of the month but then steadily loses altitude with each passing day.

Venus (magnitude −3.9) is quite prominent in the evening sky during December and telescope users will notice a distinct gibbous phase. It is within 2° of Saturn on the 11th but then quickly pulls clear of the more ponderous planet. The young crescent Moon is near Venus on the 28th.

Mars (magnitude 1.6) is well placed in the morning sky and rises during the early hours. The planet crosses into Libra at the beginning of December and will spend the month in that constellation. The Moon is close to Mars on the morning of the 23rd.

Jupiter is visible the first week of the month but is soon overwhelmed by the solar glare. The planet is at solar conjunction on the 27th.

Saturn (magnitude 0.6) is setting earlier as the month goes on and follows the Sun below the horizon by only an hour at the end of the year. The Moon is near Saturn on the evening of the 27th.

A solar eclipse on the 26th is annular (magnitude 0.970) over Saudi Arabia, India, Sumatra, and Borneo. Parts of eastern Africa, along with most of Asia and Australasia, will see a partial eclipse.

The Geminid meteor shower maximum on the 14th is unfavourable this year as it falls just two days after Full Moon.

THE MOON

Day	R.A.		Dec	Hor Par	Diam	Sun Co-Long	PA of Br. limb	Ph.	Age	Rise				Transit		Set			
										52°		56°				52°		56°	
	h	m	°	'	'	°	°	%	d	h	m	h	m	h	m	h	m	h	m
1	20	19	−21.7	55.7	30.4	318	258	20	3.7	12	01	12	23	16	13	20	31	20	11
2	21	11	−19.5	55.1	30.0	331	254	29	4.7	12	31	12	48	17	01	21	39	21	22
3	22	00	−16.4	54.6	29.8	343	251	38	5.7	12	54	13	07	17	46	22	46	22	35
4	22	47	−12.6	54.3	29.6	355	248	47	6.7	13	14	13	23	18	29	23	54	23	46
5	23	32	−8.4	54.2	29.6	7	246	57	7.7	13	31	13	36	19	10	—	—	—	—
6	0	16	−3.9	54.3	29.6	19	245	66	8.7	13	47	13	48	19	51	1	01	0	57
7	1	00	+0.7	54.5	29.6	31	244	75	9.7	14	04	14	01	20	33	2	07	2	08
8	1	44	+5.4	54.9	29.8	44	245	83	10.7	14	21	14	14	21	16	3	16	3	21
9	2	30	+10.0	55.4	30.2	56	246	89	11.7	14	40	14	29	22	01	4	26	4	36
10	3	19	+14.3	55.9	30.4	68	247	95	12.7	15	04	14	48	22	50	5	38	5	52
11	4	10	+18.0	56.5	30.8	80	248	98	13.7	15	33	15	13	23	42	6	51	7	10
12	5	04	+20.9	57.1	31.2	92	229	100	14.7	16	11	15	47	—	—	8	02	8	27
13	6	01	+22.7	57.7	31.4	104	94	99	15.7	17	02	16	35	0	37	9	10	9	36
14	7	01	+23.2	58.2	31.8	116	95	96	16.7	18	04	17	38	1	35	10	07	10	33
15	8	01	+22.3	58.6	32.0	129	99	91	17.7	19	16	18	55	2	33	10	54	11	17
16	9	00	+20.1	58.9	32.0	141	104	84	18.7	20	35	20	18	3	30	11	31	11	49
17	9	57	+16.6	59.1	32.2	153	108	74	19.7	21	57	21	45	4	26	11	59	12	13
18	10	53	+12.2	59.2	32.2	165	111	64	20.7	23	18	23	12	5	19	12	24	12	32
19	11	46	+7.1	59.2	32.2	177	113	52	21.7	—	—	—	—	6	10	12	44	12	48
20	12	39	+1.6	59.2	32.2	189	114	41	22.7	0	39	0	38	6	59	13	04	13	03
21	13	30	−4.0	59.1	32.2	201	114	30	23.7	2	00	2	04	7	49	13	24	13	18
22	14	23	−9.3	58.9	32.0	214	112	20	24.7	3	21	3	30	8	39	13	46	13	35
23	15	16	−14.1	58.6	32.0	226	110	12	25.7	4	41	4	55	9	31	14	12	13	56
24	16	11	−18.1	58.2	31.8	238	106	06	26.7	6	00	6	20	10	25	14	42	14	22
25	17	08	−21.0	57.7	31.4	250	102	02	27.7	7	14	7	38	11	20	15	22	14	59
26	18	05	−22.8	57.2	31.2	262	103	00	28.7	8	20	8	46	12	16	16	11	15	44
27	19	03	−23.2	56.6	30.8	275	267	01	0.1	9	15	9	40	13	11	17	09	16	43
28	19	58	−22.4	56.0	30.6	287	263	03	1.1	9	57	10	21	14	03	18	13	17	51
29	20	52	−20.5	55.4	30.2	299	259	08	2.1	10	32	10	50	14	53	19	21	19	03
30	21	43	−17.6	54.9	30.0	311	255	14	3.1	10	57	11	12	15	39	20	29	20	16
31	22	31	−14.1	54.5	29.8	323	251	22	4.1	11	19	11	30	16	23	21	37	21	28

MERCURY

Day	R.A.	Dec	Mag.	Diam.	Phase	Rise	Transit	Set
	h m	°		"	%	h m	h m	h m
1	15 07.8	−15.3	−0.6	6	69	5 47	10 28	15 09
3	15 17.4	−16.1	−0.6	6	74	5 54	10 30	15 06
5	15 27.8	−17.0	−0.6	6	78	6 01	10 33	15 04
7	15 38.7	−17.9	−0.6	6	82	6 10	10 36	15 02
9	15 50.1	−18.7	−0.6	5	85	6 19	10 40	15 00
11	16 01.9	−19.6	−0.6	5	87	6 28	10 44	14 59
13	16 14.0	−20.3	−0.6	5	89	6 37	10 48	14 58
15	16 26.4	−21.1	−0.6	5	91	6 47	10 53	14 58
17	16 39.0	−21.8	−0.6	5	93	6 56	10 57	14 58
19	16 51.9	−22.4	−0.6	5	94	7 05	11 02	14 59
21	17 04.9	−23.0	−0.6	5	95	7 14	11 08	15 01
23	17 18.1	−23.5	−0.6	5	96	7 23	11 13	15 03
25	17 31.5	−23.9	−0.7	5	97	7 31	11 18	15 05
27	17 45.0	−24.2	−0.7	5	98	7 39	11 24	15 09
29	17 58.6	−24.4	−0.8	5	98	7 47	11 30	15 13
31	18 12.4	−24.6	−0.8	5	99	7 54	11 36	15 18

Rising and setting times are for latitude 54°

VENUS

Day	R.A.	Dec	Mag.	Diam.	Phase	Rise	Transit	Set
	h m	°		"	%	h m	h m	h m
1	18 27.2	−24.8	−3.9	12	89	10 07	13 48	17 29
6	18 54.4	−24.5	−3.9	13	88	10 13	13 56	17 39
11	19 21.4	−23.8	−4.0	13	87	10 15	14 03	17 51
16	19 48.0	−22.9	−4.0	13	86	10 16	14 10	18 04
21	20 14.2	−21.8	−4.0	13	85	10 14	14 16	18 19
26	20 39.8	−20.3	−4.0	14	84	10 10	14 22	18 34
31	21 04.8	−18.6	−4.0	14	82	10 05	14 27	18 50

MARS

Day	R.A.	Dec	Mag.	Diam.	Phase	Rise	Transit	Set
	h m	°		"	%	h m	h m	h m
1	14 22.3	−13.5	+1.7	4	98	4 51	9 43	14 34
6	14 35.2	−14.6	+1.7	4	97	4 50	9 36	14 21
11	14 48.2	−15.6	+1.7	4	97	4 50	9 29	14 09
16	15 01.5	−16.6	+1.7	4	97	4 49	9 23	13 57
21	15 14.9	−17.6	+1.6	4	96	4 49	9 17	13 45
26	15 28.4	−18.5	+1.6	4	96	4 48	9 11	13 33
31	15 42.2	−19.3	+1.6	4	96	4 47	9 05	13 22

SUNRISE AND SUNSET

d	London 0° 05' 51° 30' rise h m	set h m	Bristol 2° 35' 51° 28' rise h m	set h m	Birmingham 1° 55' 52° 28' rise h m	set h m	Manchester 2° 15' 53° 28' rise h m	set h m	Newcastle 1° 37' 54° 59' rise h m	set h m	Glasgow 4° 14' 55° 52' rise h m	set h m	Belfast 5° 56' 54° 35' rise h m	set h m
1	7 43	15 55	7 53	16 05	7 55	15 58	8 01	15 54	8 07	15 44	8 22	15 49	8 22	16 03
2	7 44	15 54	7 54	16 05	7 56	15 57	8 03	15 54	8 08	15 43	8 24	15 48	8 23	16 02
3	7 46	15 54	7 56	16 04	7 58	15 57	8 04	15 53	8 10	15 42	8 26	15 47	8 25	16 02
4	7 47	15 53	7 57	16 04	7 59	15 56	8 06	15 52	8 11	15 41	8 27	15 47	8 26	16 01
5	7 48	15 53	7 58	16 03	8 00	15 56	8 07	15 52	8 13	15 41	8 29	15 46	8 28	16 00
6	7 50	15 53	8 00	16 03	8 02	15 55	8 08	15 51	8 14	15 40	8 30	15 45	8 29	16 00
7	7 51	15 52	8 01	16 02	8 03	15 55	8 10	15 51	8 16	15 40	8 31	15 45	8 31	15 59
8	7 52	15 52	8 02	16 02	8 04	15 54	8 11	15 50	8 17	15 39	8 33	15 44	8 32	15 59
9	7 53	15 52	8 03	16 02	8 05	15 54	8 12	15 50	8 18	15 39	8 34	15 44	8 33	15 59
10	7 54	15 51	8 04	16 02	8 06	15 54	8 13	15 50	8 19	15 39	8 35	15 44	8 34	15 58
11	7 55	15 51	8 05	16 01	8 08	15 54	8 14	15 50	8 21	15 38	8 37	15 43	8 35	15 58
12	7 56	15 51	8 06	16 01	8 09	15 54	8 15	15 50	8 22	15 38	8 38	15 43	8 37	15 58
13	7 57	15 51	8 07	16 01	8 10	15 54	8 16	15 50	8 23	15 38	8 39	15 43	8 38	15 58
14	7 58	15 51	8 08	16 01	8 11	15 54	8 17	15 50	8 24	15 38	8 40	15 43	8 39	15 58
15	7 59	15 51	8 09	16 02	8 11	15 54	8 18	15 50	8 25	15 38	8 41	15 43	8 40	15 58
16	8 00	15 52	8 10	16 02	8 12	15 54	8 19	15 50	8 26	15 38	8 42	15 43	8 40	15 58
17	8 01	15 52	8 11	16 02	8 13	15 54	8 20	15 50	8 26	15 38	8 43	15 43	8 41	15 58
18	8 01	15 52	8 11	16 02	8 14	15 54	8 21	15 50	8 27	15 39	8 44	15 43	8 42	15 58
19	8 02	15 52	8 12	16 03	8 15	15 55	8 21	15 50	8 28	15 39	8 44	15 44	8 43	15 59
20	8 03	15 53	8 13	16 03	8 15	15 55	8 22	15 51	8 29	15 39	8 45	15 44	8 43	15 59
21	8 03	15 53	8 13	16 03	8 16	15 55	8 23	15 51	8 29	15 40	8 45	15 44	8 44	15 59
22	8 04	15 54	8 14	16 04	8 16	15 56	8 23	15 52	8 30	15 40	8 46	15 45	8 45	16 00
23	8 04	15 54	8 14	16 04	8 17	15 57	8 24	15 52	8 30	15 41	8 46	15 45	8 45	16 00
24	8 05	15 55	8 15	16 05	8 17	15 57	8 24	15 53	8 31	15 41	8 47	15 46	8 45	16 01
25	8 05	15 56	8 15	16 06	8 17	15 58	8 24	15 54	8 31	15 42	8 47	15 47	8 46	16 02
26	8 05	15 56	8 15	16 06	8 18	15 59	8 25	15 54	8 31	15 43	8 47	15 47	8 46	16 02
27	8 06	15 57	8 15	16 07	8 18	15 59	8 25	15 55	8 31	15 44	8 48	15 48	8 46	16 03
28	8 06	15 58	8 16	16 08	8 18	16 00	8 25	15 56	8 31	15 44	8 48	15 49	8 46	16 04
29	8 06	15 59	8 16	16 09	8 18	16 01	8 25	15 57	8 32	15 45	8 48	15 50	8 46	16 05
30	8 06	16 00	8 16	16 10	8 18	16 02	8 25	15 58	8 32	15 46	8 48	15 51	8 46	16 06
31	8 06	16 01	8 16	16 11	8 18	16 03	8 25	15 59	8 31	15 47	8 48	15 52	8 46	16 07

JUPITER

Day	R.A. h m	Dec °	Mag.	Diam. "	Rise h m	Transit h m	Set h m
1	17 58.3	−23.3	−1.8	32	9 27	13 18	17 09
11	18 08.1	−23.3	−1.8	32	8 58	12 48	16 39
21	18 18.1	−23.3	−1.8	32	8 28	12 19	16 10
31	18 28.1	−23.2	−1.8	32	7 58	11 50	15 42

Equatorial Diam. 32″, Polar Diam. 30″

SATURN

Day	R.A. h m	Dec °	Mag.	Diam. "	Rise h m	Transit h m	Set h m
1	19 17.9	−22.1	+0.6	15	10 39	14 37	18 36
11	19 22.4	−22.0	+0.6	15	10 03	14 02	18 02
21	19 27.1	−21.9	+0.6	15	9 27	13 28	17 29
31	19 32.0	−21.7	+0.5	15	8 52	12 53	16 55

Equatorial Diam. 15″, Polar Diam. 14″
Rings – major axis 35″ minor axis 14″, Tilt 24°

URANUS

Day	R.A. h m	Dec °	Mag.	Diam. "	Rise h m	Transit h m	Set h m
1	02 05.2	+12.1	+5.7	4	14 17	21 23	4 34
11	02 04.1	+12.1	+5.7	4	13 37	20 43	3 53
21	02 03.2	+12.0	+5.7	4	12 57	20 03	3 13
31	02 02.7	+11.9	+5.7	4	12 17	19 23	2 33

NEPTUNE

Day	R.A. h m	Dec °	Mag.	Diam. "	Rise h m	Transit h m	Set h m
1	23 09.8	−6.5	+7.9	2	12 59	18 29	0 02
11	23 10.0	−6.5	+7.9	2	12 20	17 49	23 19
21	23 10.4	−6.4	+7.9	2	11 41	17 10	22 40
31	23 11.0	−6.4	+7.9	2	11 02	16 32	22 02

TRANSIT OF MERCURY 11 NOVEMBER 2019

In the present epoch, transits of Mercury occur in May or November. November transits are approximately twice as frequent as May transits. The dates of transits are gradually moving later in the year; in the early 1500s they were in April and October.

The interval between November transits is 7, 13 or 33 years, and May transit intervals are 13 or 33 years. For November transits, Mercury has a diameter of 10″ and occur at the ascending node of Mercury's orbit. For May transits, Mercury has a diameter of 12″ and occur at the descending node.

November transits are more frequent than May transits because during a November transit, Mercury is near perihelion, whereas during a May transit, it is near aphelion.

Previous Mercury transits were in May 2003, November 2006 and May 2016, the next is in November 2032. For reference the next Venus transit is not until 11 December 2117.

The transit is at least partially visible from most of Europe, south-west Asia, North America, South America, Pacific, Atlantic, Indian Ocean and Antarctica.

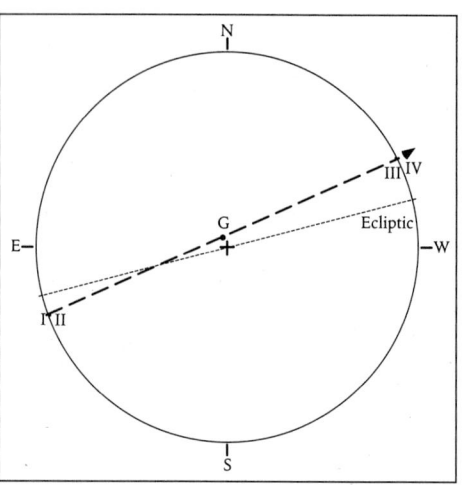

TRANSIT GEOCENTRIC CONTACTS

All times are given in Universal Time. *See* diagram above and map below for positions of I, II, G, III and IV.

I	12:35:26
II	12:37:08
G (Greatest Transit)	15:19:47
III	18:02:33
IV	18:04:14
Duration	5h 28m 47s

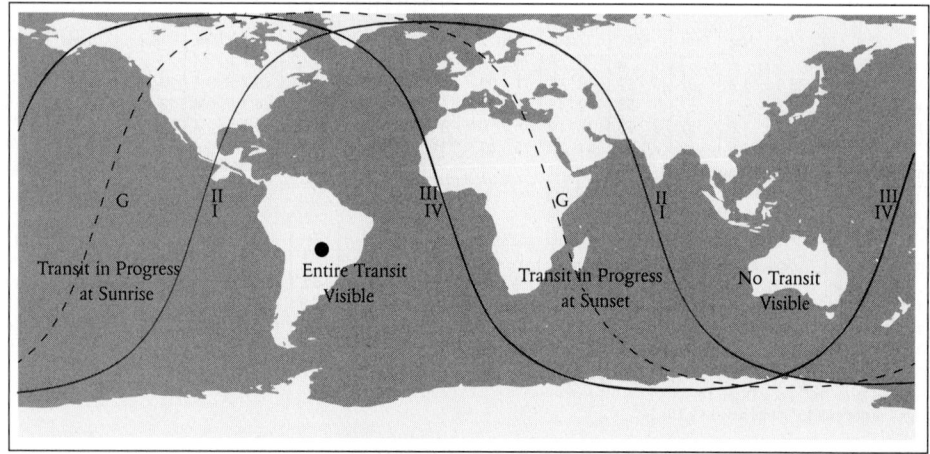

ECLIPSES 2019

During 2019 there will be 5 eclipses, 3 of the Sun and 2 of the Moon.

1. A partial solar eclipse on 5 January will be visible from East Asia.

2. A total lunar eclipse on 21 January will be visible from Europe, western Asia, Africa, North America, South America, the Pacific, Atlantic, Indian Ocean and the Arctic. Details for London are:

Moon enter penumbra	02h 36m
Moon enters umbra	03h 35m
Moon enters totality	04h 42m
Max. eclipse	05h 13m
Moon exits totality	05h 45m
Moon exits umbra	06h 52m
Moon exits penumbra	07h 51m
Penumbral Duration	5h 14.5m
Duration of totality	1h 03.0m
Magnitude	1.195

3. A total solar eclipse on 2 July will be visible from Southern south America, southern Pacific, Chile and Argentina

4. A partial lunar eclipse on 16 July will be visible from much of Europe and Asia, Australia, Africa, South America, western Pacific, Atlantic, Indian Ocean, Antarctica. Details for London are:

Moonrise	20h 07m
Max. eclipse	21h 32m
Moon exits umbra	23h 01m
Moon exits penumbra	00h 21m
Penumbral Duration	4h 13.2m
Umbral duration	2h 53.8m
Magnitude	0.653

5. An annular solar eclipse on 26 December will be visible from most of Asia, north-west Australia, eastern Africa, western Pacific and the Indian Ocean.

MEAN AND SIDEREAL TIME

The length of a sidereal day in mean time is 23h 56m 04s.09. Hence 1h MT = 1h+9s.86 ST and 1h ST = 1h − 9s.83 MT.

Acceleration

h	m	s	m	s	s
1	0	10	0	00	0
2	0	20	3	02	1
3	0	30	9	07	2
4	0	39	15	13	3
5	0	49	21	18	4
6	0	59	27	23	5
7	1	09	33	28	6
8	1	19	39	34	7
9	1	29	45	39	8
10	1	39	51	44	9
11	1	48	57	49	10
12	1	58	60	00	
13	2	08			
14	2	18			
15	2	28			
16	2	38			
17	2	48			
18	2	57			
19	3	07			
20	3	17			
21	3	27			
22	3	37			
23	3	47			
24	3	57			

Retardation

h	m	s	m	s	s
1	0	10	0	00	0
2	0	20	3	03	1
3	0	29	9	09	2
4	0	39	15	15	3
5	0	49	21	21	4
6	0	59	27	28	5
7	1	09	33	34	6
8	1	19	39	40	7
9	1	28	45	46	8
10	1	38	51	53	9
11	1	48	57	59	10
12	1	58	60	00	
13	2	08			
14	2	18			
15	2	27			
16	2	37			
17	2	47			
18	2	57			
19	3	07			
20	3	17			
21	3	26			
22	3	36			
23	3	46			
24	3	56			

To convert an interval of mean time to the corresponding interval of sidereal time, enter the acceleration table with the given mean time (taking the hours and the minutes and seconds separately) and add the acceleration obtained to the given mean time. To convert an interval of sidereal time to the corresponding interval of mean time, take out the retardation for the given sidereal time and subtract.

The columns for the minutes and seconds of the argument are in the form known as critical tables. To use these tables, find in the appropriate left-hand column the two entries between which the given number of minutes and seconds lies; the quantity in the right-hand column between these two entries is the required acceleration or retardation. Thus the acceleration for 11m 26s (which lies between the entries 9m 07s and 15m 13s) is 2s. If the given number of minutes and seconds is a tabular entry, the required acceleration or retardation is the entry in the right-hand column above the given tabular entry, eg the retardation for 45m 46s is 7s.

Example – Convert 14h 27m 35s from ST to MT:

	h	m	s
Given ST	14	27	35
Retardation for 14h		2	18
Retardation for 27m 35s			5
Corresponding MT	14	25	12

For further explanation *see* pages 1126 and 1128.

EXPLANATION OF ASTRONOMICAL DATA

Positions of the heavenly bodies are given only to the degree of accuracy required by amateur astronomers for setting telescopes, or for plotting on celestial globes or star atlases. Where intermediate positions are required, linear interpolation may be employed.

Detailed definitions of the terms used cannot be given here. They must be sought in astronomical literature, the internet or textbooks.

A special feature has been made of the times when the various heavenly bodies are visible in the British Isles. Since two columns, calculated for latitudes 52° and 56°, are devoted to risings and settings, the range 50° to 58° can be covered by interpolation and extrapolation. The times given in these columns are Greenwich Mean Times for the meridian of Greenwich. An observer west of this meridian must add his/her longitude (in time) and vice versa.

In accordance with the usual convention in astronomy, + and − indicate respectively north and south latitudes or declinations.

All data are, unless otherwise stated, for 0h Greenwich Mean Time (GMT), ie at the midnight at the beginning of the day named. Allowance must be made for British Summer Time during the period that this is in operation.

PAGE ONE OF EACH MONTH

The calendar for each month is explained on page 1055.

Under the heading Astronomical Phenomena will be found particulars of the more important conjunctions of the Sun, Moon and planets with each other, and also the dates of other astronomical phenomena of special interest.

Times of Minima of Algol are approximate times of the middle of the period of diminished light.

The Constellations listed each month are those that are near the meridian at the beginning of the month at 22h local mean time. Allowance must be made for British Summer Time if necessary. The fact that any star crosses the meridian 4m earlier each night or 2h earlier each month may be used, in conjunction with the lists given each month, to find what constellations are favourably placed at any moment.

The principal phases of the Moon are the GMTs when the difference between the longitude of the Moon and that of the Sun is 0°, 90°, 180° or 270°. The times of perigee and apogee are those when the Moon is nearest to, and farthest from, the Earth, respectively. The nodes or points of intersection of the Moon's orbit and the ecliptic make a complete retrograde circuit of the ecliptic in about 19 years. From a knowledge of the longitude of the ascending node and the inclination, whose value does not vary much from 5°, the path of the Moon among the stars may be plotted on a celestial globe or star atlas.

PAGE TWO OF EACH MONTH

The Sun's diameter, in arc minutes, is given once a month.

The right ascension and declination (Dec.) is that of the true Sun. The right ascension of the mean Sun is obtained by applying the equation of time, with the sign given, to the right ascension of the true Sun, or, more easily, by applying 12h to the Sidereal Time. The direction in which the equation of time has to be applied in different problems is a frequent source of confusion and error. Apparent Solar Time is equal to the Mean Solar Time plus the Equation of Time. For example, at 12h GMT on August 8 the Equation of Time is −5m 45s and thus at 12h Mean Time on that day the Apparent Time is 12h − 5m 45s = 11h 54m 15s.

The Greenwich Sidereal Time at 0h and the Transit of the First Point of Aries (which is really the mean time when the sidereal time is 0h) are used for converting mean time to sidereal time and vice versa.

The GMT of transit of the Sun at Greenwich may also be taken as the local mean time (LMT) of transit in any longitude. It is independent of latitude. The GMT of transit in any longitude is obtained by adding the longitude to the time given if west, and vice versa.

LIGHTING-UP TIME

The legal importance of sunrise and sunset is that the Road Vehicles Lighting Regulations 1989 (SI 1989 No. 1796) as amended, make the use of front and rear position lamps on vehicles compulsory during the period between sunset and sunrise. Headlamps on vehicles are required to be used during the hours of darkness on unlit roads, on lit roads with a speed limit exceeding 30mph, or whenever visibility is seriously reduced. The hours of darkness are defined in these regulations as the period between half an hour after sunset and half an hour before sunrise.

In all laws and regulations 'sunset' refers to the local sunset, ie the time at which the Sun sets at the place in question. This common-sense interpretation has been upheld by legal tribunals.

MAGNITUDE

Magnitudes of astronomical objects are measured in what may be considered the reverse to the obvious. Magnitude +3 is brighter than +4, magnitude −2 is brighter than magnitude −1. So from brighter to dimmer: −4, −3, −2, −1, 0, +1, +2, +3 etc, with +6 being the dimmest discernible visible with the naked eye in very dark skies. Each magnitude is roughly 2.5 times brighter than the next, so a magnitude +1 object is 100 times brighter than a magnitude +6 object.

SUNRISE AND SUNSET

The times of sunrise and sunset are those when the Sun's upper limb, as affected by refraction, is on the true horizon of an observer at sea-level. Assuming the mean refraction to be 34′, and the Sun's semi-diameter to be 16′, the time given is that when the true zenith distance of the Sun's centre is 90°+34′+16′ or 90° 50′, or, in other words, when the depression of the Sun's centre below the true horizon is 50′.

The upper limb is then 34′ below the true horizon, but is brought there by refraction. An observer on a ship might see the Sun for a minute or so longer, because of the dip of the horizon, while another viewing the sunset over hills or mountains would record an earlier time. Nevertheless, the moment when the true zenith distance of the Sun's centre is 90° 50′ is a precise time dependent only on the latitude and longitude of the place, and independent of its altitude above sea-level, the contour of its horizon, the vagaries of refraction or the small seasonal change in the Sun's diameter; this moment is suitable in every way as a definition of sunset (or sunrise) for all statutory purposes. For further information, *see* Sunrise, Sunset, Moonrise and Moonset on page 1125.

TWILIGHT

Light reaches us before sunrise and continues to reach us for some time after sunset. The interval between darkness and sunrise or sunset and darkness is called twilight. Astronomically speaking, twilight is considered to begin or end when the Sun's centre is 18° below the horizon, as no light from the Sun can then reach the observer. As thus defined twilight may last several hours; in high latitudes at the summer solstice the depression of 18° is not reached, and twilight lasts from sunset to sunrise. The duration of twilight data is given in minutes.

The need for some sub-division of twilight is met by dividing the gathering darkness into four stages.

(1) *Sunrise or Sunset,* defined as above

(2) *Civil twilight,* which begins or ends when the Sun's centre is 6° below the horizon. This marks the time when operations requiring daylight may commence or must cease. In England it varies from about 30 to 60 minutes after sunset and the same interval before sunrise

(3) *Nautical twilight,* which begins or ends when the Sun's centre is 12° below the horizon. This marks the time when it is, to all intents and purposes, completely dark

(4) *Astronomical twilight,* which begins or ends when the Sun's centre is 18° below the horizon. This marks theoretical perfect darkness. It is of little practical importance, especially if nautical twilight is tabulated

To assist observers the durations of civil, nautical and astronomical twilights are given at intervals of ten days. The beginning of a particular twilight is found by subtracting the duration from the time of sunrise, while the end is found by adding the duration to the time of sunset. Thus the beginning of astronomical twilight in latitude 52°, on the Greenwich meridian, on March 11 is found as 06h 24m − 113m = 04h 31m and similarly the end of civil twilight as 17h 57m +34m = 18h 31m. The letters TAN (twilight all night) are printed when twilight lasts all night.

Under the heading The Night Sky will be found notes describing the position and visibility of the planets and other phenomena.

PAGE THREE OF EACH MONTH

The Moon moves so rapidly among the stars that its position is given only to the degree of accuracy that permits linear interpolation. The right ascension (RA) and declination (Dec.) are geocentric, ie for an imaginary observer at the centre of the Earth. To an observer on the surface of the Earth the position is always different, as the altitude is always less on account of parallax, which may reach 1°.

The lunar terminator is the line separating the bright from the dark part of the Moon's disk. Apart from irregularities of the lunar surface, the terminator is elliptical, because it is a circle seen in projection. It becomes the full circle forming the limb, or edge, of the Moon at New and Full Moon. The selenographic longitude of the terminator is measured from the mean centre of the visible disk, which may differ from the visible centre by as much as 8°, because of libration.

Instead of the longitude of the terminator the Sun's selenographic co-longitude (Sun's co-long.) is tabulated. It is numerically equal to the selenographic longitude of the morning terminator, measured eastwards from the mean centre of the disk. Thus its value is approximately 270° at New Moon, 360° at First Quarter, 90° at Full Moon and 180° at Last Quarter.

The Position Angle (PA) of the Bright Limb is the position angle of the midpoint of the illuminated limb, measured eastwards from the north point on the disk. The Phase column shows the percentage of the area of the Moon's disk illuminated; this is also the illuminated percentage of the diameter at right angles to the line of cusps. The terminator is a semi-ellipse whose major axis is the line of cusps, and whose semi-minor axis is determined by the tabulated percentage; from New Moon to Full Moon the east limb is dark, and vice versa.

The times given as moonrise and moonset are those when the upper limb of the Moon is on the horizon of an observer at sea-level. The Sun's horizontal parallax (Hor. par.) is about 9″, and is negligible when considering sunrise and sunset, but that of the Moon averages about 57′. Hence the computed time represents the moment when the true zenith distance of the Moon is 90° 50′ (as for the Sun) minus the horizontal parallax. The time required for the Sun or Moon to rise or set is about four minutes (except in high latitudes). *See also* Sunrise, Sunset, Moonrise and Moonset below.

The GMT of transit of the Moon over the meridian of Greenwich is given; these times are independent of latitude but must be corrected for longitude. For places in the British Isles it suffices to add the longitude if west, and vice versa. For other places a further correction is necessary because of the rapid movement of the Moon relative to the stars. The entire correction is conveniently determined by first finding the west longitude λ of the place. If the place is in west longitude, λ is the ordinary west longitude; if the place is in east longitude λ is the complement to 24h (or 360°) of the longitude and will be greater than 12h (or 180°). The correction then consists of two positive portions, namely λ and the fraction λ/24 (or λ°/360) multiplied by the difference between consecutive transits. Thus for Christchurch, New Zealand, the longitude is 11h 31m east, so λ = 12h 29m and the fraction λ/24 is 0.52. The transit on the local date 14 January 2019 is found as follows:

		d	h	m
GMT of transit at Greenwich	January	13	17	39
λ			12	29
0.52 x (18h 23m − 17h 39m)				23
GMT of transit at Christchurch		14	06	31
Corr. to NZ Standard Time			12	00
Local standard time of transit	January	14	18	31

As is evident, for any given place the quantities λ and the correction to local standard time may be combined permanently, being here 24h 29m.

Positions of Mercury are given for every second day, and those of Venus and Mars for every fifth day; they may be interpolated linearly. The diameter (Diam.) is given in seconds of arc. The phase is the illuminated percentage of the disk. In the case of the inner planets this approaches 100 at superior conjunction and 0 at inferior conjunction. When the phase is less than 50 the planet is crescent-shaped or horned; for greater phases it is gibbous. In the case of the exterior planet Mars, the phase approaches 100 at conjunction and opposition, and is a minimum at the quadratures.

To determine if a planet is visible or not, the transit time should be examined. If the transit time coincides with hours of darkness the planet should be easy to find, provided it is bright enough. If the time of transit is between 00h and 12h the planet should be visible above the eastern horizon; if between 12h and 24h, above the western horizon. The closer the transit time to midnight (0h) the longer it will be visible.

The inner planets – Mercury and Venus can never transit at midnight because they are too close to the Sun. If they transit close to noon (12h) then they will be too close to the Sun to be visible except during a large solar eclipse. The rise or set times should be examined to see if either is near sunrise or sunset. If this also coincides with a large positive declination (Dec.) then conditions are favourable for viewing.

Consulting The Night Sky paragraphs will also help determine observability.

PAGE FOUR OF EACH MONTH

The GMTs of sunrise and sunset for seven cities, whose adopted positions in longitude (W.) and latitude (N.) are given immediately below the name, may be used not only for these phenomena, but also for lighting-up times *(see* page XXXX for a fuller explanation).

The particulars for the four outer planets resemble those for the planets on Page Three of each month, except that, because of the inferior brightness of Uranus and Neptune, these two planets require optical aids such as binoculars or a small telescope. The diameters given for the rings of Saturn are those of the major axis (in the plane of the planet's equator) and the minor axis respectively. The former has a small seasonal change due to the slightly varying distance of the Earth from Saturn, but the latter varies from zero when the Earth passes through the ring plane every 15 years to its maximum opening half-way between these periods. The rings were last open at their widest extent (and Saturn at its brightest) in 2017. The Earth passed through the ring plane in 2009.

SUNRISE, SUNSET, MOONRISE AND MOONSET

The tables have been constructed for the meridian of Greenwich and for latitudes 52° and 56°. They give Greenwich Mean Time (GMT) throughout the year. To obtain the GMT of the phenomenon as seen from any other latitude and longitude in the British Isles, first interpolate or extrapolate for latitude by the usual rules of proportion. To the time thus found, the longitude (expressed in time) is to be added if west (as it usually is in Great Britain) or subtracted if east. If the longitude is expressed in degrees and minutes of arc, it must be converted to time at the rate of 1° = 4m and 15′ = 1m.

The GMT at which the planet transits the Greenwich meridian is also given. The times of transit are to be corrected to local meridians in the usual way, as already described.

TIME

From the earliest ages, the natural division of time into recurring periods of day and night has provided the practical time-scale for the everyday activities of the human race. Indeed, if any alternative means of time measurement is adopted, it must be capable of adjustment so as to remain in general agreement with the natural time-scale defined by the diurnal rotation of the Earth on its axis. Ideally the rotation should be measured against a fixed frame of reference; in practice it must be measured against the background provided by the celestial bodies. If the Sun is chosen as the reference point, we obtain Apparent Solar Time, which is the time indicated by a sundial. It is not a uniform time but is subject to variations which amount to as much as a quarter of an hour in each direction. Such wide variations cannot be tolerated in a practical time-scale, and this has led to the concept of Mean Solar Time in which all the days are exactly the same length and equal to the average length of the Apparent Solar Day.

The positions of the stars in the sky are specified in relation to a fictitious reference point in the sky known as the First Point of Aries (or the Vernal Equinox). It is therefore convenient to adopt this same reference point when considering the rotation of the Earth against the background of the stars. The time-scale so obtained is known as Apparent Sidereal Time.

GREENWICH MEAN TIME

The daily rotation of the Earth on its axis causes the Sun and the other heavenly bodies to appear to cross the sky from east to west. It is convenient to represent this relative motion as if the Sun really performed a daily circuit around a fixed Earth. Noon in Apparent Solar Time may then be defined as the time at which the Sun transits across the observer's meridian. In Mean Solar Time, noon is similarly defined by the meridian transit of a fictitious Mean Sun moving uniformly in the sky with the same average speed as the true Sun. Mean Solar Time observed on the meridian of the transit circle telescope of the Royal Observatory at Greenwich is called Greenwich Mean Time (GMT). The mean solar day is divided into 24 hours and, for astronomical and other scientific purposes, these are numbered 0 to 23, commencing at midnight. Civil time is usually reckoned in two periods of 12 hours, designated am (*ante meridiem,* ie before noon) and pm (*post meridiem,* ie after noon), although the 24 hour clock is increasingly being used.

UNIVERSAL TIME

Before 1925 January 1, GMT was reckoned in 24 hours commencing at noon; since that date it has been reckoned from midnight. To avoid confusion in the use of the designation GMT before and after 1925, since 1928 astronomers have tended to use the term Universal Time (UT) or Weltzeit (WZ) to denote GMT measured from Greenwich Mean Midnight.

In precision work it is necessary to take account of small variations in Universal Time. These arise from small irregularities in the rotation of the Earth. Observed astronomical time is designated UT0. Observed time corrected for the effects of the motion of the poles (giving rise to a 'wandering' in longitude) is designated UT1. There is also a seasonal fluctuation in the rate of rotation of the Earth arising from meteorological causes, often called the annual fluctuation. UT1 corrected for this effect is designated UT2 and provides a time-scale free from short-period fluctuations. It is still subject to small secular and irregular changes.

APPARENT SOLAR TIME

As mentioned above, the time shown by a sundial is called Apparent Solar Time. It differs from Mean Solar Time by an amount known as the Equation of Time, which is the total effect of two causes which make the length of the apparent solar day non-uniform. One cause of variation is that the orbit of the Earth is not a circle but an ellipse, having the Sun at one focus. As a consequence, the angular speed of the Earth in its orbit is not constant; it is greatest at the beginning of January when the Earth is nearest the Sun.

The other cause is due to the obliquity of the ecliptic; the plane of the equator (which is at right angles to the axis of rotation of the Earth) does not coincide with the ecliptic (the plane defined by the apparent annual motion of the Sun around the celestial sphere) but is inclined to it at an angle of 23° 26′. As a result, the apparent solar day is shorter than average at the equinoxes and longer at the solstices. From the

combined effects of the components due to obliquity and eccentricity, the equation of time reaches its maximum values in February (−14 minutes) and early November (+16 minutes). It has a zero value on four dates during the year, and it is only on these dates (approximately April 15, June 14, September 1 and December 25) that a sundial shows Mean Solar Time.

SIDEREAL TIME

A sidereal day is the duration of a complete rotation of the Earth with reference to the First Point of Aries. The term sidereal (or 'star') time is a little misleading since the time-scale so defined is not exactly the same as that which would be defined by successive transits of a selected star, as there is a small progressive motion between the stars and the First Point of Aries due to the precession of the Earth's axis. This makes the length of the sidereal day shorter than the true period of rotation by 0.008 seconds. Superimposed on this steady precessional motion are small oscillations (nutation), giving rise to fluctuations in apparent sidereal time amounting to as much as 1.2 seconds. It is therefore customary to employ Mean Sidereal Time, from which these fluctuations have been removed. The conversion of GMT to Greenwich sidereal time (GST) may be performed by adding the value of the GST at 0h on the day in question to the GMT converted to sidereal time using the Mean and Sidereal Time table on page 1123.

Example – To find the GST at August 8d 02h 41m 11s GMT:

	h	m	s
GST at 0h	21	04	52
GMT	2	41	11
Acceleration for 2h			20
Acceleration for 41m 11s			7
Sum = GST =	23	46	30

If the observer is not on the Greenwich meridian then their longitude, measured positively westwards from Greenwich, must be subtracted from the GST to obtain Local Sidereal Time (LST). Thus, in the above example, an observer 5h east of Greenwich, or 19h west, would find the LST as 2h 04m 52s.

EPHEMERIS TIME

An analysis of observations of the positions of the Sun, Moon and planets taken over an extended period is used in preparing ephemerides. (An ephemeris is a table giving the apparent position of a heavenly body at regular intervals of time, eg one day or ten days, and may be used to compare current observations with tabulated positions.) Discrepancies between the positions of heavenly bodies observed over a 300-year period and their predicted positions arose because the time-scale to which the observations were related was based on the assumption that the rate of rotation of the Earth is uniform. It is now known that this rate of rotation is variable. A revised time-scale, Ephemeris Time (ET), was devised to bring the ephemerides into agreement with the observations.

The second of ET is defined in terms of the annual motion of the Earth in its orbit around the Sun (1/31556925.9747 of the tropical year for 1900 January 0d 12h ET). The precise determination of ET from astronomical observations is a lengthy process as the requisite standard of accuracy can only be achieved by averaging over a number of years.

In 1976 the International Astronomical Union adopted Terrestrial Dynamical Time (TDT), a new dynamical time-scale for general use whose scale unit is the SI second (*see* Atomic Time, below). TDT was renamed Terrestrial Time (TT) in 1991. ET is now of little more than historical interest.

TERRESTRIAL TIME
The uniform time system used in computing the ephemerides of the solar system is Terrestrial Time (TT), which has replaced ET for this purpose. Except for the most rigorous astronomical calculations, it may be assumed to be the same as ET. In June 2019 the difference TT − UT is estimated to be 69.4 seconds. This is known as Delta T.

ATOMIC TIME
The fundamental standards of time and frequency must be defined in terms of a periodic motion adequately uniform, enduring and measurable. Progress has made it possible to use natural standards, such as atomic or molecular oscillations. Continuous oscillations are generated in an electrical circuit, the frequency of which is then compared or brought into coincidence with the frequency characteristic of the absorption or emission by the atoms or molecules when they change between two selected energy levels. Since the 13th General Conference on Weights and Measures in October 1967, the unit of time, the second, has been defined in the International System of units (SI) as 'the duration of 9 192 631 770 periods of the radiation corresponding to the transition between the two hyperfine levels of the ground state of the caesium-133 atom'.

In the UK, the national time scale is maintained by the National Physical Laboratory (NPL), using an ensemble of atomic clocks based on either caesium or hydrogen atoms. In addition the NPL (along with several other national laboratories) has constructed and operates caesium fountain primary frequency standards, which utilise the cooling of caesium atoms by laser light to determine the duration of the SI second at the highest attainable level of accuracy. Caesium fountain primary standards typically achieve an accuracy of around 2 parts in 10 000 000 000 000 000, which is equivalent to one second in 158 million years.

Timekeeping worldwide is based on two closely related atomic time scales that are established through international collaboration. International Atomic Time (TAI) is formed by combining the readings of more than 400 atomic clocks located in more than 70 institutes and was set close to the astronomically based Universal Time (UT) near the beginning of 1958. It was formally recognised in 1971 and since 1988 January 1 has been maintained by the International Bureau of Weights and Measures (BIPM). Civil time in almost all countries is now based on Coordinated Universal Time (UTC), which differs from TAI by 37 seconds and was designed to make both atomic time and UT available with accuracy appropriate for most users. On 1 January 1972 UTC was set to be exactly 10 seconds behind TAI, and since then the UTC time-scale has been adjusted by the insertion (or, in principle, omission) of leap seconds in order to keep it within ±0.9s of UT. These leap seconds are introduced, when necessary, at the same instant throughout the world, either at the end of December or at the end of June. The last leap second occurred immediately prior to 0h UTC on 2017 January 1, and was the 27th leap second. All leap seconds so far have been positive, with 61 seconds in the final minute of the UTC month. The time 23h 59m 60s UTC is followed one second later by 0h 0m 00s of the first day of the following month. Notices concerning the insertion of leap seconds are issued by the International Earth Rotation and Reference Systems Service (IERS).

The computation of UTC is carried out monthly by the BIPM and takes place in three stages. First, a weighted average known as Echelle Atomique Libre (EAL) is calculated from all of the contributing atomic clocks. In the second stage, TAI is generated by applying small corrections, derived from the results contributed by primary frequency standards, to the scale interval of EAL to maintain its value close to that of the SI second. Finally, UTC is formed from TAI by the addition of an integer number of seconds. The results are published monthly in the BIPM Circular T in the form of offsets at 5-day intervals between UTC and the time scales of contributing organisations.

RADIO TIME-SIGNALS
UTC is made generally available through time-signals and standard frequency broadcasts such as MSF in the UK, CHU in Canada and WWV and WWVH in the USA. These are based on national time-scales that are maintained in close agreement with UTC and provide traceability to the national time-scale and to UTC. The markers of seconds in the UTC scale coincide with those of TAI.

To disseminate the national time-scale in the UK, special signals (call-sign MSF) are broadcast by the National Physical Laboratory. From April 1, 2007 the MSF service, previously broadcast from British Telecom's radio station at Rugby, has been transmitted from Anthorn radio station in Cumbria. The signals are controlled from a caesium beam atomic frequency standard and consist of a precise frequency carrier of 60 kHz which is switched off, after being on for at least half a second, to mark every second. The first second of the minute begins with a period of 500 ms with the carrier switched off, to serve as a minute marker. In the other seconds the carrier is always off for at least one tenth of a second at the start and then it carries an on-off code giving the British clock time and date, together with information identifying the start of the next minute. Changes to and from summer time are made following government announcements. Leap seconds are inserted as announced by the IERS and information provided by them on the difference between UTC and UT is also signalled. Other broadcast signals in the UK include the BBC six pips signal, the BT Timeline ('speaking clock'), the NPL telephone and internet time services for computers, and a coded time-signal on the BBC 198 kHz transmitters which is used for timing in the electricity supply industry. From 1972 January 1 the six pips on the BBC have consisted of five short pips from second 55 to second 59 (six pips in the case of a leap second) followed by one lengthened pip, the start of which indicates the exact minute. From 1990 February 5 these signals have been controlled by the BBC with seconds markers referenced to the satellite-based US navigation system GPS (Global Positioning System) and time and day referenced to the MSF transmitter. Formerly they were generated by the Royal Greenwich Observatory. The NPL telephone and internet time services are directly connected to the national time scale.

Accurate timing may also be obtained from the signals of international navigation systems such as the ground-based eLORAN, or the satellite-based American GPS or Russian GLONASS systems.

STANDARD TIME
Since 1880 the standard time in Britain has been Greenwich Mean Time (GMT); a statute that year enacted that the word 'time' when used in any legal document relating to Britain meant, unless otherwise specifically stated, the mean time of the Greenwich meridian. Greenwich was adopted as the universal meridian on 13 October 1884. A system of standard time by zones is used worldwide, standard time in each zone differing from that of the Greenwich meridian by an integral number of hours or, exceptionally, half-hours or quarter-hours, either fast or slow. The large territories of the USA and Canada are divided into zones approximately 7.5° on either side of central meridians.

Variations from the standard time of some countries occur during part of the year; they are decided annually and are usually referred to as Summer Time or Daylight Saving Time.

At the 180th meridian the time can be either 12 hours fast on Greenwich Mean Time or 12 hours slow, and a change of date occurs. The internationally recognised date or calendar line is a modification of the 180th meridian, drawn so as to include islands of any one group on the same side of the line, or for political reasons. The line is indicated by joining up the following coordinates:

Lat.	Long.	Lat.	Long.
90° S.	180°	48° N.	180°
51° S.	180°	53° N.	170° E.
45° S.	172.5° W.	65.5° N.	169° W.
15° S.	172.5° W.	68° N.	169° W.
5° S.	180°	90° N.	180°

Changes to the date line would require an international conference.

BRITISH SUMMER TIME
In 1916 an Act ordained that during a defined period of that year the legal time for general purposes in Great Britain should be one hour in advance of Greenwich Mean Time. The Summer Time Acts 1922 and 1925 defined the period during which Summer Time was to be in force, stabilising practice until the Second World War.

During the Second World War (1941–5) and in 1947 Double Summer Time (two hours in advance of Greenwich Mean Time) was used for the period in which ordinary Summer Time would have been in force. During these years clocks were also kept one hour in advance of Greenwich Mean Time in the winter. After the war, ordinary Summer Time was invoked each year from 1948–68.

Between 1968 October 27 and 1971 October 31 clocks were kept one hour ahead of Greenwich Mean Time throughout the year. This was known as British Standard Time.

The most recent legislation is the Summer Time Act 1972, which enacted that 'the period of summer time for the purposes of this Act is the period beginning at two o'clock, Greenwich Mean Time, in the morning of the day after the third Saturday in March or, if that day is Easter Day, the day after the second Saturday in March, and ending at two o'clock, Greenwich Mean Time, in the morning of the day after the fourth Saturday in October.'

The duration of Summer Time can be varied by Order in Council and in recent years alterations have been made to synchronise the period of Summer Time in Britain with that used in Europe. The rule for 1981–94 defined the period of Summer Time in the UK as from the last Sunday in March to the day following the fourth Saturday in October and the hour of changeover was altered to 01h Greenwich Mean Time.

There was no rule for the dates of Summer Time between 1995–7. Since 1998 the 9th European Parliament and Council Directive on Summer Time has harmonised the dates on which Summer Time begins and ends across member states as the last Sundays in March and October respectively. Under the directive Summer Time begins and ends at 01hr Greenwich Mean Time in each member state. Amendments to the Summer Time Act to implement the directive came into force on 11 March 2002.

The duration of Summer Time in 2019 is:
March 31 01h GMT to October 27 01h GMT

MEAN REFRACTION

Alt.		Ref.	Alt.		Ref.	Alt.		Ref.
°	′	′	°	′	′	°	′	′
1	20	21	3	12	13	7	54	6
1	30	20	3	34	12	9	27	5
1	41	19	4	00	11	11	39	4
1	52	18	4	30	10	15	00	3
2	05	17	5	06	9	20	42	2
2	19	16	5	50	8	32	20	1
2	35	15	6	44	7	62	17	0
2	52	14	7	54		90	00	
3	12							

The refraction table is in the form of a critical table (see page 1123).

ASTRONOMICAL CONSTANTS

Solar parallax	8″.794
Astronomical unit	149597870 km
Annual precession in longitude	50″.288
Precession in right ascension	3ˢ.075
Precession in declination	20″.043
Constant of nutation	9″.202
Constant of aberration	20″.496
Mean obliquity of ecliptic (2018)	23° 26′ 13″
Moon's equatorial hor. parallax	57′ 02″.70
Velocity of light in vacuo per second	299792.5 km
Solar motion per second	20.0 km
Equatorial radius of the Earth	6378.137 km
Polar radius of the Earth	6356.752 km
North galactic pole (IAU standard)	RA 12h 51m (2000.0). Dec + 27°.1 N.
Solar apex	RA 18h 04m Dec. + 30°

Length of year (in mean solar days)

Tropical	365.24219
Sidereal	365.25636
Anomalistic (perihelion to perihelion)	365.25964
Eclipse	346.62003

Length of month (mean values)	d	h	m	s
Synodic (new Moon to new Moon)	29	12	44	02.0
Sidereal	27	07	43	43.2
Anomalistic (perigee to perigee)	27	13	18	51.8

THE EARTH

The shape of the Earth is that of an oblate spheroid or solid of revolution whose meridian sections are ellipses not differing much from circles, while the sections at right angles are circles. The length of the equatorial axis is about 12,756 km, and that of the polar axis is 12,714 km. The mean density of the Earth is 5.5 times that of water, although that of the surface layer is less. The Earth and Moon revolve about their common centre of gravity in a lunar month; this centre in turn revolves round the Sun in a plane known as the ecliptic, that passes through the Sun's centre. The Earth's equator is inclined to this plane at an angle of 23.4°. This tilt is the cause of the seasons. In mid-latitudes, and when the Sun is high above the Equator, not only does the high noon altitude make the days longer, but the Sun's rays fall more directly on the Earth's surface; these effects combine to produce summer. In equatorial regions the noon altitude is large throughout the year, and there is little variation in the length of the day. In higher latitudes the noon altitude is lower, and the days in summer are appreciably longer than those in winter.

The average velocity of the Earth in its orbit is 30km a second. It makes a complete rotation on its axis in about 23h 56m of mean time, which is the sidereal day. Because of its annual revolution round the Sun, the rotation with respect to the Sun, or the solar day, is more than this by about four minutes. The extremity of the axis of rotation, or the North Pole of the Earth, is not rigidly fixed, but wanders over an area roughly 20 metres in diameter.

Perihelion is when the Earth is closest to the Sun, and *aphelion* when the Earth is furthest from the Sun:

Perihelion January 2019   3d 05h 20m
                          (147,099,760km, 0.983301165au)
Aphelion July 2019   4d 22h 11m
                          (152,104,284km, 1.016754345au)

TERRESTRIAL MAGNETISM

The Earth's main magnetic field corresponds approximately to that of a very strong small bar magnet near the centre of the Earth, but with appreciable smooth spatial departures. The origin of the main field is generally ascribed to electric currents associated with fluid motions in the Earth's core. As a result not only does the main field vary in strength and direction from place to place, but also with time. Superimposed on the main field are local and regional anomalies whose magnitudes may in places approach that of the main field; these are due to the influence of mineral deposits in the Earth's crust. A small proportion of the field is of external origin, mostly associated with electric currents in the ionosphere and magnetosphere. The configuration of the external field and the ionisation of the atmosphere depend on the incident particle and radiation flux from the Sun. There are, therefore, short-term and non-periodic as well as diurnal, 27-day, seasonal and approximate 11-year periodic changes in the magnetic field, dependent upon the position of the Sun, the degree of solar activity and the magnetic field embedded in the solar wind.

A magnetic compass points along the horizontal component of a magnetic line of force. These lines of force converge on the 'magnetic dip-poles', the places where the Earth's magnetic field is vertical. These poles move with time, and their present approximate adopted mean positions are 86.4° N., 175.4° E. and 64.2° S., 135.9° E. Compasses do not point directly, ie via great circle routes, to the dip-poles.

There is also a 'magnetic equator', at all points of which the vertical component of the Earth's magnetic field is zero and a magnetised needle remains horizontal. This line runs between 2° and 12° north of the geographical equator in Asia and Africa, turns sharply south in the Atlantic Ocean and crosses South America south of the geographical equator; it re-crosses the geographical equator in mid-Pacific.

Reference has already been made to secular changes in the Earth's field. The following table indicates the changes in magnetic declination (or variation of the compass relative to true north). Declination is the angle in the horizontal plane between the direction of true north and that in which a magnetic compass points. Similar, though much smaller, changes have occurred in 'dip' or magnetic inclination. Secular changes differ throughout the world.

London (Greenwich)

1580	11°	15′	E.	1900	16°	29′	W.
1622	5°	56′	E.	1925	13°	10′	W.
1665	1°	22′	W.	1950	9°	07′	W.
1730	13°	00′	W.	1975	6°	39′	W.
1773	21°	09′	W.	1998	3°	32′	W.
1850	22°	24′	W.				

In Great Britain, lines of equal declination (isogonics) now run approximately north–northeast to south–southwest. Though there are considerable local deviations due to geological causes, a rough value of magnetic declination may

be obtained by assuming that at 50° N. on the meridian of Greenwich, the value in 2019 is 0° 20′ east. Easterly declination is now being sensed for the first time in 350 years as the zero isogonic line (the agonic line) passes by. Allowing for 11′ west for each degree of latitude northwards and one of 26′ west for each degree of longitude westwards. For example, at 53° N., 5° W., declination will be about 0° 20′ east + 33′ west + 130′ west, ie 2° 23′ west. The average annual change at the present time is about 12′ to the east. For navigation by compass using maps with the north lines from the British National Grid (as opposed to lines of equal longitude), account has to be taken of the difference between true north and grid north. This angle can be several degrees.

The number of magnetic observatories is about 170, irregularly distributed over the globe. There are three in the UK, run by the British Geological Survey: at Hartland, north Devon; at Eskdalemuir, Dumfries and Galloway; and at Lerwick, Shetland Islands. Some recent annual mean values of the magnetic elements for Hartland:

Year	Declination West		Dip or inclination		Horizontal intensity	Vertical intensity
	°	′	°	′	nT	nT
1960	9	58.8	66	43.9	18707	43504
1970	9	06.5	66	26.1	19033	43636
1980	7	43.8	66	10.3	19330	43768
1990	6	15.0	66	09.7	19539	43896
2000	4	43.6	66	06.9	19508	44051
2017	1	55.7	65	59.3	19771	44382

nT = nanoTesla

The magnetic field is also observed by a series of specialised satellites, the latest being a mission called Swarm. Three satellites were successfully launched by the European Space Agency in November 2013, each equipped with magnetometers and star cameras for accurate orientation. With the data from these satellites the Earth's magnetic field and its changes in time continue to be mapped to unprecedented accuracy.

Reliance on the Earth's magnetic field for navigation by compass is not restricted to land, maritime or aeronautical navigation (in the latter two usually as a fail-safe back-up system). It also extends underground with the oil industry using magnetic survey tools when drilling well-bores. Very accurate estimates of the local magnetic field are required for this, taking into account the crustal and external fields.

MAGNETIC STORMS

Occasionally, sometimes with great suddenness, the Earth's magnetic field is subject for several hours to marked disturbance. During a severe storm in October 2003 the declination at Eskdalemuir changed by over 5° in six minutes. In many instances such disturbances are accompanied by widespread displays of auroras, marked changes in the incidence of cosmic rays, an increase in the reception of 'noise' from the Sun at radio frequencies, and rapid changes in the ionosphere and induced electric currents within the Earth. These can adversely affect satellite operations, telecommunications and electric power transmission systems. The disturbances are caused by changes in the stream of ionised particles which emanates from the Sun and through which the Earth is continuously passing. Some of these changes are associated with visible eruptions on the Sun, usually in the region of sun-spots. There is some tendency for disturbances to recur after intervals of about 27 days, the period of rotation of the Sun on its axis as seen from the Earth. But the sources of many disturbances are shorter lived than this. Predicting such disturbances with any useful accuracy remains challenging, but the year 2019 is generally expected to be rather quiet.

ELEMENTS OF THE SOLAR SYSTEM

Orb	Mean distance from Sun (Earth = 1)	km 10^6	Sidereal period days	Synodic period days	Incl. of orbit to ecliptic ° '	Diameter km	Mass (Earth = 1)	Period of rotation on axis days
Sun	—	—	—	—	—	1,392,000	332,981	25–35*
Mercury	0.39	58	88.0	116	7　00	4,879	0.0553	58.646
Venus	0.72	108	224.7	584	3　24	12,104	0.8150	243.019r
Earth	1.00	150	365.3	—	—	12,756e	1.0000	0.997
Mars	1.52	228	687.0	780	1　51	6,794e	0.1074	1.026
Jupiter	5.20	778	4,334.4	399	1　18	142,984e / 133,708p	317.83	0.410e
Saturn	9.55	1429	10,787.9	378	2　29	120,536e / 108,728p	95.16	0.426e
Uranus	19.22	2875	30,773.3	370	0　46	51,118e	14.54	0.718r
Neptune	30.11	4504	60,349.2	367	1　46	49,528e	17.15	0.671
Pluto†	39.80	5954	91,708.2	367	17　09	2,390	0.002	6.387

e equatorial, p polar, r retrograde, * depending on latitude, † reclassified as a dwarf planet since August 2006

THE SATELLITES

Name		Star mag.	Mean distance from primary km	Sidereal period of revolution d	Name		Star mag.	Mean distance from primary km	Sidereal period of revolution d
EARTH					SATURN				
I	Moon	—	384,400	27.322	VII	Hyperion	14	1,481,000	21.277
					VIII	Iapetus	11	3,561,300	79.330
MARS					IX	Phoebe	16	12,952,000	550.48r
I	Phobos	11	9,378	0.319					
II	Deimos	12	23,459	1.262	URANUS				
					VI	Cordelia	24	49,770	0.335
JUPITER					VII	Ophelia	24	53,790	0.376
XVI	Metis	17	127,960	0.295	VIII	Bianca	23	59,170	0.435
XV	Adrastea	19	128,980	0.298	IX	Cressida	22	61,780	0.464
V	Amalthea	14	181,300	0.498	X	Desdemona	22	62,680	0.474
XIV	Thebe	16	221,900	0.675	XI	Juliet	21	64,350	0.493
I	Io	5	421,600	1.769	XII	Portia	21	66,090	0.513
II	Europa	5	670,900	3.551	XIII	Rosalind	22	66,940	0.558
III	Ganymede	5	1,070,000	7.155	XIV	Belinda	22	75,260	0.624
IV	Callisto	6	1,883,000	16.689	XV	Puck	20	86,010	0.762
XIII	Leda	20	11,165,000	240.92	V	Miranda	16	129,390	1.413
VI	Himalia	15	11,460,000	250.57	I	Ariel	14	191,020	2.520
X	Lysithea	18	11,717,000	259.22	II	Umbriel	15	266,300	4.144
VII	Elara	17	11,741,000	259.65	III	Titania	14	435,910	8.706
XII	Ananke	19	21,276,000	629.77r	IV	Oberon	14	583,520	13.463
XI	Carme	18	23,404,000	734.17r	XVI	Caliban	22	7,230,000	579.5r
VIII	Pasiphae	17	23,624,000	743.68r	XX	Stephano	24	8,002,000	676.5r
IX	Sinope	18	23,939,000	758.90r	XVII	Sycorax	21	12,179,000	1,283.4r
					XVIII	Prospero	23	16,418,000	1,992.8r
SATURN					XIX	Setebos	23	17,459,000	2,202.2r
XVIII	Pan	20	133,583	0.575					
XV	Atlas	18	137,640	0.602	NEPTUNE				
XVI	Prometheus	16	139,353	0.613	III	Naiad	25	48,230	0.294
XVII	Pandora	16	141,700	0.629	IV	Thalassa	24	50,080	0.311
XI	Epimetheus	15	151,422	0.694	V	Despina	23	52,530	0.335
X	Janus	14	151,472	0.695	VI	Galatea	22	61,950	0.429
I	Mimas	13	185,520	0.942	VII	Larissa	22	73,550	0.555
II	Enceladus	12	238,020	1.370	VIII	Proteus	20	117,650	1.122
III	Tethys	10	294,660	1.888	I	Triton	13	354,760	5.877
XIII	Telesto	19	294,660	1.888	II	Nereid	19	5,513,400	360.136
XIV	Calypso	19	294,660	1.888					
IV	Dione	10	377,400	2.737	PLUTO				
XII	Helene	18	377,400	2.737	I	Charon	17	19,600	6.387
V	Rhea	10	527,040	4.518					
VI	Titan	8	1,221,850	15.945					

The total number of satellites known so far for the outer planets are: Jupiter 79, Saturn 62, Uranus 27, Neptune 14, Pluto 5.

TIME MEASUREMENT AND CALENDARS

MEASUREMENTS OF TIME

Measurements of time are based on the time taken by the Earth to rotate on its axis (day); by the Moon to revolve around the Earth (month); and by the Earth to revolve around the Sun (year). From these, which are not commensurable, certain average or mean intervals have been adopted for ordinary use.

THE DAY

The day begins at midnight and is divided into 24 hours of 60 minutes, each of 60 seconds. The hours are counted from midnight up to 12 noon (when the Sun crosses the meridian), and these hours are designated am *(ante meridiem)*; and again from noon up to 12 midnight, which hours are designated pm *(post meridiem)*, except when the 24-hour reckoning is employed. The 24-hour reckoning ignores am and pm, numbering the hours 0 to 23 from midnight.

Colloquially the 24 hours are divided into day and night, day being the time while the Sun is above the horizon (including the four stages of twilight defined in the Astronomy section). Day is subdivided into morning, ending at noon; afternoon, from noon to about 6pm; and evening, which may be said to extend from 6pm until midnight. Night begins at the close of astronomical twilight (*see* the Astronomy section) and extends beyond midnight to sunrise the next day.

The names of the days are derived from Old English translations or adaptations of the Roman titles.

Sunday	Sol	Sun
Monday	Luna	Moon
Tuesday	Tiw/Tyr (god of war)	Mars
Wednesday	Woden/Odin	Mercury
Thursday	Thor	Jupiter
Friday	Frigga/Freyja (goddess of love)	Venus
Saturday	Saeterne	Saturn

THE MONTH

The month in the ordinary calendar is approximately the twelfth part of a year, but the lengths of the different months vary from 28 (or 29) days to 31.

THE YEAR

The equinoctial or tropical year is the time that the Earth takes to revolve around the Sun from equinox to equinox, ie 365.24219 mean solar days, or 365 days 5 hours 48 minutes and 45 seconds.

The calendar year usually consists of 365 days but a year containing 366 days is called a bissextile (*see* Roman calendar) or leap year, one day being added to the month of February so that a date 'leaps over' a day of the week. In the Roman calendar the day that was repeated was the sixth day before the beginning of March, the equivalent of 24 February.

A year is a leap year if the date of the year is divisible by four without remainder, unless it is the last year of the century. The last year of a century is a leap year only if its number is divisible by 400 without remainder, eg the years 1800 and 1900 had only 365 days but the year 2000 had 366 days.

THE SOLSTICE

A solstice is the point in the tropical year at which the Sun attains its greatest distance, north or south, from the Equator. In the northern hemisphere the furthest point north of the Equator marks the summer solstice and the furthest point south marks the winter solstice.

The date of the solstice varies according to locality. For example, if the summer solstice falls on 21 June late in the day

by Greenwich time, that day will be the longest of the year at Greenwich, but it will fall on 22 June, local date, in Japan, and so 22 June will be the longest day there. The date of the solstice is also affected by the length of the tropical year, which is 365 days 6 hours less about 11 minutes 15 seconds. If a solstice happens late on 21 June in one year, it will be nearly 6 hours later in the next (unless the next year is a leap year), ie early on 22 June, and that will be the longest day.

This delay of the solstice does not continue because the extra day in a leap year brings it back a day in the calendar. However, because of the 11 minutes 15 seconds mentioned above, the additional day in a leap year brings the solstice back too far by 45 minutes, and the time of the solstice in the calendar is earlier, in a four-year pattern, as the century progresses. The last year of a century is in most cases not a leap year, and the omission of the extra day puts the date of the solstice later by about 6 hours. Compensation for this is made by the fourth centennial year being a leap year. The solstice became earlier in date throughout the last century and, because the year 2000 was a leap year, the solstice will get earlier still throughout the 21st century. The date of the winter solstice, the shortest day of the year, is affected by the same factors as the longest day.

At Greenwich the Sun sets at its earliest by the clock about ten days before the shortest day. The daily change in the time of sunset is due in the first place to the Sun's movement southwards at this time of the year, which diminishes the interval between the Sun's transit and its setting. However, the daily decrease of the Equation of Time causes the time of apparent noon to be continuously later day by day, which to some extent counteracts the first effect. The rates of change of these two quantities are not equal or uniform; their combination causes the date of earliest sunset to be 12 or 13 December at Greenwich. In more southerly latitudes the effect of the movement of the Sun is less, and the change in the time of sunset depends on that of the Equation of Time to a greater degree, and the date of earliest sunset is earlier than it is at Greenwich, eg on the Equator it is about 1 November.

THE EQUINOX

The equinox is the point at which the Sun crosses the Equator and day and night are of equal length all over the world. This occurs in March and September.

DOG DAYS

The days about the heliacal rising of the Dog Star, noted from ancient times as the hottest period of the year in the northern hemisphere, are called the Dog Days. Their incidence has been variously calculated as depending on the Greater or Lesser Dog Star (Sirius or Procyon) and their duration has been reckoned as from 30 to 54 days. A generally accepted period is from 3 July to 15 August.

CHRISTIAN CALENDAR

In the Christian chronological system the years are distinguished by cardinal numbers before or after the birth of Christ, the period being denoted by the letters BC (Before Christ) or, more rarely, AC *(Ante Christum),* and AD *(Anno Domini* – In the Year of Our Lord); BCE (Before the Christian Era) and CE (Christian Era) are now also used instead of BC and AD. The correlative dates of the epoch are the fourth year of the 194th Olympiad, the 753rd year from the foundation of Rome, AM 3761 in Jewish chronology, and the 4,714th year of the Julian period.

The system was introduced into Italy in the sixth century. Though first used in France in the seventh century, it was not universally established there until about the eighth century. It has been said that the system was introduced into England by St Augustine (AD 596), but it was probably not generally used until some centuries later. It was ordered to be used by the bishops at the Council of Chelsea (AD 816).

THE JULIAN CALENDAR

In the Julian calendar (adopted by the Roman Empire in 45 BC) all the centennial years were leap years, and for this reason towards the close of the 16th century there was a difference of ten days between the tropical and calendar years; the equinox fell on 11 March of the calendar, whereas at the time of the Council of Nicaea (AD 325), it had fallen on 21 March. In 1582 Pope Gregory ordained that 5 October should be called 15 October and that of the end-century years only the fourth should be a leap year.

THE GREGORIAN CALENDAR

The Gregorian calendar was adopted by Italy, France, Spain and Portugal in 1582, by Prussia, the Roman Catholic German states, Switzerland, Holland and Flanders on 1 January 1583, by Poland in 1586, Hungary in 1587, the Protestant German and Netherland states and Denmark in 1700, and by Great Britain and its Dominions (including the North American colonies) in 1752, by the omission of 11 days (3 September being reckoned as 14 September). Sweden omitted the leap day in 1700 but observed leap days in 1704 and 1708, and reverted to the Julian calendar by having two leap days in 1712; the Gregorian calendar was adopted in 1753 by the omission of 11 days (18 February being reckoned as 1 March). Japan adopted the calendar in 1872, China in 1912, Bulgaria in 1916, Turkey and Soviet Russia in 1918, Yugoslavia and Romania in 1919, and Greece in 1923.

In the same year that the change was made in England from the Julian to the Gregorian calendar, the start of the new year was also changed from 25 March to 1 January.

THE ORTHODOX CHURCHES

Some Orthodox churches still use the Julian reckoning but the majority of Greek Orthodox churches and the Romanian Orthodox Church have adopted a modified 'New Calendar', observing the Gregorian calendar for fixed feasts and the Julian for movable feasts.

The Orthodox Church year begins on 1 September. There are four fast periods and, in addition to Pascha (Easter), twelve great feasts, as well as numerous commemorations of the saints of the Old and New Testaments throughout the year.

EASTER DAYS AND DOMINICAL LETTERS 1500 TO 2040

Dates up to and including 1752 are according to the Julian calendar. For dominical letters in leap years, *see* note below

		1500–1599	1600–1699	1700–1799	1800–1899	1900–1999	2000–2040
March							
d	22	1573	1668	1761	1818		
e	23	1505/16	1600	1788	1845/56	1913	2008
f	24		1611/95	1706/99		1940	
g	25	1543/54	1627/38/49	1722/33/44	1883/94	1951	2035
A	26	1559/70/81/92	1654/65/76	1749/58/69/80	1815/26/37	1967/78/89	
b	27	1502/13/24/97	1608/87/92	1785/96	1842/53/64	1910/21/32	2005/16
c	28	1529/35/40	1619/24/30	1703/14/25	1869/75/80	1937/48	2027/32
d	29	1551/62	1635/46/57	1719/30/41/52	1807/12/91	1959/64/70	
e	30	1567/78/89	1651/62/73/84	1746/55/66/77	1823/34	1902/75/86/97	
f	31	1510/21/32/83/94	1605/16/78/89	1700/71/82/93	1839/50/61/72	1907/18/29/91	2002/13/24
April							
g	1	1526/37/48	1621/32	1711/16	1804/66/77/88	1923/34/45/56	2018/29/40
A	2	1553/64	1643/48	1727/38	1809/20/93/99	1961/72	
b	3	1575/80/86	1659/70/81	1743/63/68/74	1825/31/36	1904/83/88/94	
c	4	1507/18/91	1602/13/75/86/97	1708/79/90	1847/58	1915/20/26/99	2010/21
d	5	1523/34/45/56	1607/18/29/40	1702/13/24/95	1801/63/74/85/96	1931/42/53	2015/26/37
e	6	1539/50/61/72	1634/45/56	1729/35/40/60	1806/17/28/90	1947/58/69/80	
f	7	1504/77/88	1667/72	1751/65/76	1822/33/44	1901/12/85/96	
g	8	1509/15/20/99	1604/10/83/94	1705/87/92/98	1849/55/60	1917/28	2007/12
A	9	1531/42	1615/26/37/99	1710/21/32	1871/82	1939/44/50	2023/34
b	10	1547/58/69	1631/42/53/64	1726/37/48/57	1803/14/87/98	1955/66/77	2039
c	11	1501/12/63/74/85/96	1658/69/80	1762/73/84	1819/30/41/52	1909/71/82/93	2004
d	12	1506/17/28	1601/12/91/96	1789	1846/57/68	1903/14/25/36/98	2009/20
e	13	1533/44	1623/28	1707/18	1800/73/79/84	1941/52	2031/36
f	14	1555/60/66	1639/50/61	1723/34/45/54	1805/11/16/95	1963/68/74	
g	15	1571/82/93	1655/66/77/88	1750/59/70/81	1827/38	1900/06/79/90	2001
A	16	1503/14/25/36/87/98	1609/20/82/93	1704/75/86/97	1843/54/65/76	1911/22/33/95	2006/17/28
b	17	1530/41/52	1625/36	1715/20	1808/70/81/92	1927/38/49/60	2022/33
c	18	1557/68	1647/52	1731/42/56	1802/13/24/97	1954/65/76	
d	19	1500/79/84/90	1663/74/85	1747/67/72/78	1829/35/40	1908/81/87/92	
e	20	1511/22/95	1606/17/79/90	1701/12/83/94	1851/62	1919/24/30	2003/14/25
f	21	1527/38/49	1622/33/44	1717/28	1867/78/89	1935/46/57	2019/30
g	22	1565/76	1660	1739/53/64	1810/21/32	1962/73/84	
A	23	1508	1671		1848	1905/16	2000
b	24	1519	1603/14/98	1709/91	1859		2011
c	25	1546	1641	1736	1886	1943	2038

No dominical letter is placed against the intercalary day 29 February, but since it is still counted as a weekday and given a name, the series of letters moves back one day every leap year after intercalation. Thus, a leap year beginning with the dominical letter C will change to a year with the dominical letter B on 1 March

MOVEABLE FEASTS TO THE YEAR 2040

Year	Ash Wednesday	Easter	Ascension	Pentecost (Whit Sunday)	Advent Sunday
2019	6 March	21 April	30 May	9 June	1 December
2020	26 February	12 April	21 May	31 May	29 November
2021	17 February	4 April	13 May	23 May	28 November
2022	2 March	17 April	26 May	5 June	27 November
2023	22 February	9 April	18 May	28 May	3 December
2024	14 February	31 March	9 May	19 May	1 December
2025	5 March	20 April	29 May	8 June	30 November
2026	18 February	5 April	14 May	24 May	29 November
2027	10 February	28 March	6 May	16 May	28 November
2028	1 March	16 April	25 May	4 June	3 December
2029	14 February	1 April	10 May	20 May	2 December
2030	6 March	21 April	30 May	9 June	1 December
2031	26 February	13 April	22 May	1 June	30 November
2032	11 February	28 March	6 May	16 May	28 November
2033	2 March	17 April	26 May	5 June	27 November
2034	22 February	9 April	18 May	28 May	3 December
2035	7 February	25 March	3 May	13 May	2 December
2036	27 February	13 April	22 May	1 June	30 November
2037	18 February	5 April	14 May	24 May	29 November
2038	10 March	25 April	3 June	13 June	28 November
2039	23 February	10 April	19 May	29 May	27 November
2040	15 February	1 April	10 May	20 May	2 December

NOTES

Ash Wednesday (first day in Lent) can fall at earliest on 4 February and at latest on 10 March

Mothering Sunday (fourth Sunday in Lent) can fall at earliest on 1 March and at latest on 4 April

Easter Day can fall at earliest on 22 March and at latest on 25 April

Ascension Day is forty days after Easter Day and can fall at earliest on 30 April and at latest on 3 June

Pentecost (Whit Sunday) is seven weeks after Easter and can fall at earliest on 10 May and at latest on 13 June

Trinity Sunday is the Sunday after Whit Sunday

Corpus Christi falls on the Thursday after Trinity Sunday

Sundays after Pentecost – there are not less than 18 and not more than 23

Advent Sunday is the Sunday nearest to 30 November

THE DOMINICAL LETTER

The dominical letter is one of the letters A–G which are used to denote the Sundays in successive years. If the first day of the year is a Sunday the letter is A; if the second, B; the third, C; and so on. A leap year requires two letters, the first for 1 January to 29 February, the second for 1 March to 31 December. The dominical letter for 2019, which is not a leap year, is F (*see also* page 9).

EPIPHANY

The feast of the Epiphany, commemorating the manifestation of Christ, later became associated with the offering of gifts by the Magi. The day was of great importance from the time of the Council of Nicaea (AD 325), as the primate of Alexandria was charged at every Epiphany feast with the announcement in a letter to the churches of the date of the forthcoming Easter. The day was also of importance in Britain as it influenced dates, ecclesiastical and lay, eg Plough Monday, when work was resumed in the fields, fell on the Monday in the first full week after Epiphany.

LENT

The Teutonic word *Lent,* which denotes the fast preceding Easter, originally meant no more than the spring season; but from Anglo-Saxon times, at least, it has been used as the equivalent of the more significant Latin term *Quadragesima,* meaning the 'forty days' or, more literally, the fortieth day. Ash Wednesday is the first day of Lent, which ends at midnight before Easter Day.

PALM SUNDAY

Palm Sunday, the Sunday before Easter and the beginning of Holy Week, commemorates the triumphal entry of Christ into Jerusalem.

MAUNDY THURSDAY

Maundy Thursday is the day before Good Friday, the name itself being a corruption of *dies mandati* (day of the mandate) when Christ washed the feet of the disciples and gave them the mandate to love one another.

EASTER DAY

Easter Day is the first Sunday after the full moon which happens on, or next after, the 21st day of March; if the full moon happens on a Sunday, Easter Day is the Sunday after.

This definition is contained in an Act of Parliament (24 Geo. II ch. 23) and explanation is given in the preamble to the Act that the day of full moon depends on certain tables that have been prepared. These tables are summarised in the early pages of the Book of Common Prayer. The moon referred to is not the real Moon of the heavens, but a hypothetical moon on whose 'full' the date of Easter depends, and the lunations of this 'calendar' moon consist of 29 and 30 days alternately, with certain necessary modifications to make the date of its full agree as nearly as possible with that of the real Moon, which is known as the Paschal Full Moon.

A FIXED EASTER

In 1928 the House of Commons agreed to a motion for the third reading of a bill proposing that Easter Day shall, in the calendar year next but one after the commencement of the Act and in all subsequent years, be the first Sunday after the second Saturday in April. Easter would thus fall on the second or third Sunday in April, ie between 9 and 15 April (inclusive). A clause in the bill provided that before it shall come into operation, regard shall be had to any opinion expressed officially by the various Christian churches. Efforts by the World Council of Churches to secure a unanimous choice of date for Easter by its member churches have so far been unsuccessful.

ROGATION DAYS
Rogation Days are the Monday, Tuesday and Wednesday preceding Ascension Day and from the fifth century were observed as public fasts with solemn processions and supplications. The processions were discontinued as religious observances at the Reformation, but survive in the ceremony known as 'beating the parish bounds'. Rogation Sunday is the Sunday before Ascension Day.

EMBER DAYS
The Ember days occur on the Wednesday, Friday and Saturday of the same week, four times a year. Used for the ordination of clergy, these days are set aside for fasting and prayer. The weeks in which they fall are: (a) after the third Sunday in Advent, (b) before the second Sunday in Lent, (c) before Trinity Sunday and (d) after Holy Cross day.

TRINITY SUNDAY
Trinity Sunday is eight weeks after Easter Day, on the Sunday following Pentecost (Whit Sunday). Subsequent Sundays are reckoned in the Book of Common Prayer calendar of the Church of England as 'after Trinity'.

Thomas Becket (1118–70) was consecrated Archbishop of Canterbury on the Sunday after Whit Sunday and his first act was to ordain that the day of his consecration should be held as a new festival in honour of the Holy Trinity.

HINDU CALENDAR

The Hindu calendar is a luni-solar calendar of 12 months, each containing 29 days, 12 hours. Each month is divided into a light fortnight (Shukla or Shuddha) and a dark fortnight (Krishna or Vadya) based on the waxing and waning of the Moon. In most parts of India the month starts with the light fortnight, ie the day after the new moon, although in some regions it begins with the dark fortnight, ie the day after the full moon.

The new year according to the civil calendar begins on the first day of the month of Chaitra (March/April) and ends in the month of Phalgun (March). The financial new year begins on the first day of Kartik (Diwali day). For most Hindus, the first day of Chaitra and the first day of Kartik are equally important.

The 12 months – Chaitra, Vaishakh, Jyeshtha, Ashadh, Shravan, Bhadrapad, Ashvin, Kartik, Margashirsh, Paush, Magh and Phalgun – have Sanskrit names derived from 12 asterisms (constellations). There are regional variations in the names of the months but the Sanskrit names are understood throughout India.

Every lunar month that has a solar transit is termed pure (shuddha). The lunar month without a solar transit is impure (mala) and called an intercalary month. An intercalary month occurs approximately every 32 lunar months, whenever the difference between the Hindu year of 360 lunar days (354 days 8 hours solar time) and the 365 days 6 hours of the solar year reaches the length of one Hindu lunar month (29 days 12 hours).

The leap month, often referred to as Adhik Maas (extra month), may be added at any point in the Hindu year. The name given to the month varies according to when it occurs but is taken from the month immediately following it. There is no leap month in 2019; the next one will occur in 2020.

The days of the week are called Raviwar (Sunday), Somawar (Monday), Mangalwar (Tuesday), Budhawar (Wednesday), Guruwar (Thursday), Shukrawar (Friday) and Shaniwar (Saturday). The names are derived from the Sanskrit names of the Sun, the Moon and five planets, Mars, Mercury, Jupiter, Venus and Saturn.

Most fasts and festivals are based on the lunar calendar but a few are determined by the apparent movement of the Sun, eg Makar Sankranti and Pongal (in southern India), which are celebrated on 14/15 January to mark the start of the Sun's apparent journey northwards and a change of season.

Festivals celebrated throughout India are Chaitra (the New Year), Raksha Bandhan (the renewal of the kinship bond between brothers and sisters), Navratri (a nine-night festival dedicated to the goddess Parvati), Dussehra (the victory of Rama over the demon army), Diwali (a festival of lights), Makar Sankranti, Shivaratri (dedicated to Shiva) and Holi (a spring festival). British Hindus commonly celebrate the festival of Diwali as the start of the financial new year.

Regional festivals are Durga Puja (dedicated to the goddess Durga (Parvati)), Sarasvati Puja (dedicated to the goddess Sarasvati), Ganesh Chaturthi (worship of Ganesh on the fourth day (Chaturthi) of the light half of Bhadrapad), Ram Navami (the birth festival of the god Rama) and Krishna Janmashtami (the birth festival of the god Krishna).

The main festivals celebrated in the UK are Navratri, Dussehra, Durga Puja, Diwali, Holi, Sarasvati Puja, Ganesh Chaturthi, Raksha Bandhan, Ram Navami and Krishna Janmashtami. For dates in 2019, see page 9.

JEWISH CALENDAR

The story of the Flood in the Book of Genesis indicates the use of a calendar of some kind and that the writers recognised 30 days as the length of a lunation. However, after the diaspora, Jewish communities were left in considerable doubt as to the times of fasts and festivals. This led to the formation of the Jewish calendar as used today. It is said that this was done in AD 358 by Rabbi Hillel II, though some assert that it did not happen until much later.

The calendar is luni-solar, and is based on the lengths of the lunation and of the tropical year as found by Hipparchus (c.120 BC), which differ little from those adopted at the present day. The year AM 5779 (2018–19) is the 3rd year of the 305th Metonic (Minor or Lunar) cycle of 19 years and the 11th year of the 207th Solar (or Major) cycle of 28 years since the Era of the Creation. Jews hold that the Creation occurred at the time of the autumnal equinox in the year known in the Christian calendar as 3760 BC (954 of the Julian period). The epoch or starting point of Jewish chronology corresponds to 7 October 3761 BC. At the beginning of each solar cycle, the Tekufah of Nisan (the vernal equinox) returns to the same day and hour.

The hour is divided into 1,080 minims, and the month between one new moon and the next is reckoned as 29 days 12 hours 793 minims. The normal calendar year, called a regular common year, consists of 12 months of 30 and 29 days alternately. Since 12 months such as these comprise only 354 days, in order that each of them shall not diverge greatly from an average place in the solar year, a 13th month is occasionally added after the fifth month of the civil year (which commences on the first day of the month Tishri), or as the penultimate month of the ecclesiastical year (which commences on the first day of the month Nisan). The years when this happens are called Embolismic or leap years.

Of the 19 years that form a Metonic cycle, seven are leap years; they occur at places in the cycle indicated by the numbers 3, 6, 8, 11, 14, 17 and 19, these places being chosen so that the accumulated excesses of the solar years should be as small as possible.

A Jewish year is of one of the following six types:

minimal common	353 days
regular common	354 days
full common	355 days
minimal leap	383 days
regular leap	384 days
full leap	385 days

The regular year has alternate months of 30 and 29 days. In a full year, Marcheshvan, the second month of the civil year, has 30 days instead of 29; in minimal years Kislev, the third month, has 29 instead of 30. The additional month in leap years is called Adar Sheni (Adar II) and follows the month called Adar Rishon; the usual Adar festivals are observed in Adar Sheni. In a leap year Adar I has 30 days, in all other years it has 29. None of the variations mentioned are allowed to change the number of days in the other months, which still follow the alternation of the normal 12.

These are the main features of the Jewish calendar, which must be considered permanent because as a Jewish law it cannot be altered except by a Great Sanhedrin.

The Jewish day begins between sunset and nightfall. The time used is that of the meridian of Jerusalem, which is 2h 21m in advance of Greenwich Mean Time. Rules for the beginning of sabbaths and festivals were laid down for the latitude of London in the 18th century and hours for nightfall are fixed annually by the Chief Rabbi.

JEWISH CALENDAR 5779–80
AM 5779 is a full leap year of 13 months, 55 sabbaths and 385 days. AM 5780 is a full common year of 12 months, 50 sabbaths and 355 days.

Month (length)	AM 5779	AM 5780
Tishri 1 (30)	10 Sep 2018	30 Sep 2019
Marcheshvan 1 (30/30)	10 Oct	30 Oct
Kislev 1 (30/30)	9 Nov	29 Nov
Tebet 1 (29)	9 Dec	29 Dec
Shebat 1 (30)	7 Jan 2019	27 Jan 2020
Adar Rishon 1 (30)	6 Feb	
Adar Sheni 1 (29)	8 Mar	
Nisan 1 (30)	6 Apr	
Iyar 1 (29)	6 May	
Sivan 1 (30)	4 Jun	
Tammuz 1 (29)	4 Jul	
Ab 1 (30)	2 Aug	
Elul 1 (29)	1 Sep	

JEWISH FASTS AND FESTIVALS
For dates of principal festivals in 2019, *see* page 9.

Tishri 1–2	Rosh Hashanah (New Year)
Tishri 3	*Fast of Gedaliah
Tishri 10	Yom Kippur (Day of Atonement)
Tishri 15–21	Sukkot (Feast of Tabernacles)
Tishri 21	Hoshana Rabba
Tishri 22	Shemini Atseret (Solemn Assembly)
Tishri 23	Simchat Torah (Rejoicing of the Law)
Kislev 25	Hanukkah (Festival of Lights) begins
Tebet 10	Fast of Tebet
†Adar 13	§Fast of Esther
†Adar 14	Purim
†Adar 15	Shushan Purim
Nisan 15–22	Pesach (Passover)
Sivan 6–7	Shavuot (Feast of Weeks)
Tammuz 17	*Fast of Tammuz
Ab 9	*Fast of Ab

* If these dates fall on the sabbath the fast is kept on the following day
† Adar Sheni in leap years
§ This fast is observed on Adar 11 (or Adar Sheni 11 in leap years) if Adar 13 falls on a sabbath

MUSLIM CALENDAR
The Muslim era is dated from the *Hijrah,* or flight of the Prophet Muhammad from Mecca to Medina, the corresponding date of which in the Julian calendar is 16 July AD 622. The lunar *hijri* calendar is used principally in Iran, Egypt, Malaysia, Pakistan, Mauritania, various Arab states and certain parts of India. Iran uses the solar hijri calendar as well as the lunar hijri calendar. The dating system was adopted about AD 639, commencing with the first day of the month Muharram.

The lunar calendar consists of 12 months of either 30 or 29 days, with the intercalation of one day at the end of the 12th month at stated intervals in each cycle of 30 years. The object of the intercalation is to reconcile the date of the first day of the month with the date of the actual new moon.

Some adherents still take the date of the evening of the first physical sighting of the crescent of the new moon as that of the first of the month. If cloud obscures the Moon the present month may be extended to 30 days, after which the new month will begin automatically regardless of whether the Moon has been seen. (Under religious law a month must have less than 31 days.) This means that the beginning of a new month and the date of religious festivals can vary from the published calendars.

In each cycle of 30 years, 19 years are common and contain 354 days, and 11 years are intercalary (leap years) of 355 days, the latter being called *kabisah*. The mean length of the Hijrah years is 354 days 8 hours 48 minutes and the period of mean lunation is 29 days 12 hours 44 minutes.

To ascertain if a year is common or kabisah, divide it by 30: the quotient gives the number of completed cycles and the remainder shows the place of the year in the current cycle. If the remainder is 2, 5, 7, 10, 13, 16, 18, 21, 24, 26 or 29, the year is kabisah and consists of 355 days.

MUSLIM CALENDAR 1440–41
Hijrah 1440 (no remainder) and Hijrah 1441 (remainder one) are both common years. Calendar dates below are estimates based on calculations of moon phases.

Month (length)	1440 AH	1441 AH
Muharram 1 (29/30)	12 Sep 2018	1 Sep 2019
Safar 1 (30/29)	11 Oct	1 Oct
Rabi'I 1 (29/30)	10 Nov	30 Oct
Rabi'II 1 (30/29)	9 Dec	29 Nov
Jumada I 1 (30/30)	8 Jan 2019	28 Dec
Jumada II 1 (30/30)	7 Feb	27 January 2020
Rajab 1 (29)	9 Mar	
Sha'ban 1 (30)	7 Apr	
Ramadan 1 (29)	7 May	
Shawwal 1 (30)	5 Jun	
Dhu'l Qa'da 1 (29)	5 Jul	
Dhu'l Hijjah 1 (29)	3 Aug	

MUSLIM FESTIVALS
Ramadan is a month of fasting for all Muslims because it is the month in which the revelation of the *Qur'an* (Koran) began. During Ramadan, Muslims abstain from food, drink and sexual pleasure from dawn until after sunset.

The two major festivals are *Eid-ul-Fitr* and *Eid-ul-Adha*. Eid-ul-Fitr marks the end of the Ramadan fast and is celebrated on the day after the sighting of the new moon of the following month. Eid-ul-Adha, the festival of sacrifice (also known as the great festival), celebrates the submission of the Prophet Ibrahim (Abraham) to God. Eid-ul-Adha falls on the tenth day of Dhu'l-Hijjah, coinciding with the day when those on *hajj* (pilgrimage to Mecca) sacrifice animals.

Other days accorded special recognition are:

Muharram 1	New Year's Day
Muharram 10	Ashura (the day Prophet Noah left the Ark and Prophet Moses was saved from Pharaoh (Sunni), the death of the Prophet's grandson Husain (Shi'ite))
Rabi'u-l-Awwal (Rabi' I) 12	Mawlid ul-Nabi (birthday of the Prophet Muhammad)
Rajab 27	Laylat ul-Isra' wa'l-Mi'raj (The Night of Journey and Ascension)
Ramadan*	Laylat ul-Qadr (Night of Power)

*Moveable feast

For dates of the major celebrations in 2018–19, *see* page 9.

SIKH CALENDAR

The Sikh calendar is a lunar calendar of 365 days divided into 12 months. The length of the months varies between 29 and 32 days.

There are no prescribed feast days and no fasting periods. The main celebrations are Vaisakhi (the new year and the anniversary of the founding of the Khalsa), Diwali Mela (festival of light), Hola Mohalla Mela (a spring festival held in the Punjab), and the Gurpurbs (anniversaries associated with the ten Gurus).

For dates of the major celebrations in 2019, *see* page 9.

THAI CALENDAR

Thailand adopted the Suriyakati calendar, a modified version of the Gregorian calendar, during the reign of King Rama V in 1888, using 1 April as the first day of the year. In 1940 the date of the new year was changed to 1 January. The years are counted from the beginning of the Buddhist era (BE), which is calculated to have commenced upon the death of the Lord Buddha, taken to have occurred in 543 BC, so AD 2019 is BE 2562. The Chinese system of associating years with one of twelve animals is also in use in Thailand. The Chantarakati lunar calendar is used to determine religious holidays; the new year begins on the first day of the waxing moon in November or, if there is a leap month, in December.

CIVIL AND LEGAL CALENDAR

THE HISTORICAL YEAR

Before 1752, two calendar systems were used in England. The civil or legal year began on 25 March and the historical year on 1 January. Thus the civil or legal date 24 March 1658 was the same day as the historical date 24 March 1659; a date in that portion of the year is written as 24 March 1658/9, the earlier date showing the civil or legal year.

THE NEW YEAR

In England in the seventh century, and as late as the 13th, the year was reckoned from Christmas Day, but in the 12th century the Church in England began the year with the feast of the Annunciation of the Blessed Virgin ('Lady Day') on 25 March, and this practice was adopted generally in the 14th century. The civil or legal year in the British dominions (exclusive of Scotland) began with Lady Day until 1751. But in and since 1752 the civil year has begun with 1 January. New Year's Day in Scotland was changed from 25 March to 1 January in 1600.

Elsewhere in Europe, 1 January was adopted as the first day of the year by Venice in 1522, German states in 1544, Spain, Portugal and the Roman Catholic Netherlands in 1556, Prussia, Denmark and Sweden in 1559, France in 1564, Lorraine in 1579, the Protestant Netherlands in 1583, Russia in 1725, and Tuscany in 1751.

REGNAL YEARS

Regnal years are the years of a sovereign's reign and each begins on the anniversary of his or her accession, eg regnal year 68 of the present queen begins on 6 February 2019.

The system was used for dating Acts of Parliament until 1962. The Summer Time Act 1925, for example, is quoted as 15 and 16 Geo. V ch. 64, because it became law in the parliamentary session which extended over part of both of these regnal years. Acts of a parliamentary session during which a sovereign died were usually given two year numbers, the regnal year of the deceased sovereign and the regnal year of his or her successor, eg those passed in 1952 were dated 16 Geo. VI and 1 Elizabeth II. Since 1962 Acts of Parliament have been dated by the calendar year.

QUARTER AND TERM DAYS

Holy days and saints days were the usual means in early times for setting the dates of future and recurrent appointments. The quarter days in England and Wales are the feast of the Nativity (25 December), the feast of the Annunciation (25 March), the feast of St John the Baptist (24 June) and the feast of St Michael and All Angels (29 September).

The term days in Scotland are Candlemas (the feast of the Purification), Whitsunday, Lammas (Loaf Mass) and Martinmas (St Martin's Day). These fell on 2 February, 15 May, 1 August and 11 November respectively. However, by the Term and Quarter Days (Scotland) Act 1990, the dates of the term days were changed to 28 February (Candlemas), 28 May (Whitsunday), 28 August (Lammas) and 28 November (Martinmas).

RED-LETTER DAYS

Red-letter days were originally the holy days and saints days indicated in early ecclesiastical calendars by letters printed in red ink. The days to be distinguished in this way were approved at the Council of Nicaea in AD 325.

These days still have a legal significance, as judges of the Queen's Bench Division wear scarlet robes on red-letter days falling during the law sittings. The days designated as red-letter days for this purpose are:

Holy and saints days
The Conversion of St Paul, the Purification, Ash Wednesday, the Annunciation, the Ascension, the feasts of St Mark, SS Philip and James, St Matthias, St Barnabas, St John the Baptist, St Peter, St Thomas, St James, St Luke, SS Simon and Jude, All Saints, St Andrew.

Civil calendar (for dates, *see* page 9)
Includes the anniversaries of the Queen's accession, the Queen's birthday and the Queen's coronation, the Queen's official birthday, the birthday of the Duke of Edinburgh, the birthday of the Prince of Wales, St David's Day and Lord Mayor's Day.

PUBLIC HOLIDAYS

Public holidays are divided into two categories, common law and statutory. Common law holidays are holidays 'by habit and custom'; in England, Wales and Northern Ireland these are Good Friday and Christmas Day.

Statutory public holidays, known as bank holidays, were first established by the Bank Holidays Act 1871. They were, literally, days on which the banks (and other public institutions) were closed and financial obligations due on that day were payable the following day. The legislation currently governing public holidays in the UK, which is the Banking and Financial Dealings Act 1971, stipulates the days that are to be public holidays in England, Wales, Scotland and Northern Ireland.

If a public holiday falls on a Saturday or a Sunday then another day will be given in lieu, usually the following Monday. For dates of public holidays in 2019 and 2020, *see* pages 10 and 11.

CHRONOLOGICAL CYCLES AND ERAS

SOLAR (OR MAJOR) CYCLE
The solar cycle is a period of 28 years; in any corresponding year of each cycle the days of the week recur on the same day of the month.

METONIC (LUNAR, OR MINOR) CYCLE
In 432 BC, Meton, an Athenian astronomer, found that 235 lunations are very nearly, though not exactly, equal in duration to 19 solar years and so after 19 years the phases of the Moon recur approximately on the same days of the month. The dates of full moon in a cycle of 19 years were inscribed in figures of gold on public monuments in Athens, and the number showing the position of a year in the cycle is called the golden number of that year.

JULIAN PERIOD
The Julian period was proposed by Joseph Scaliger in 1582. The period is 7,980 Julian years, and its first year coincides with the year 4713 BC. The figure of 7,980 is the product of the number of years in the solar cycle, the Metonic cycle and the cycle of the Roman indiction (28 x 19 x 15).

ROMAN INDICTION
The Roman indiction is a period of 15 years, instituted for fiscal purposes about AD 300.

EPACT
The epact is the age of the calendar Moon, diminished by one day, on 1 January, in the ecclesiastical lunar calendar.

CHINESE CALENDAR
A lunar calendar was the sole calendar in use in China until 1911, when the government adopted the new (Gregorian) calendar for official and most business activities. The Chinese tend to follow both calendars, the lunar calendar playing an important part in personal life, eg birth celebrations, festivals, marriages; in rural villages the lunar calendar dictates the cycle of activities, denoting the change of weather and farming activities.

The lunar calendar is used in Hong Kong, Singapore, Malaysia, Tibet and elsewhere in south-east Asia. The calendar has a cycle of 60 years. The new year begins at the first new moon after the sun enters the sign of Aquarius, ie the new year falls between 21 January and 19 February in the Gregorian calendar.

Each year in the Chinese calendar is associated with one of 12 animals: the rat, the ox, the tiger, the rabbit, the dragon, the snake, the horse, the sheep, the monkey, the chicken or rooster, the dog, and the pig.

The date of the Chinese new year and the astrological sign for the years 2019–21 are:

2019	5 February	Pig
2020	25 January	Rat
2021	12 February	Ox

COPTIC CALENDAR
In the Coptic calendar, which is used in parts of Egypt and Ethiopia, the year is made up of 12 months of 30 days each, followed, in general, by five complementary days. Every fourth year is an intercalary or leap year and in these years there are six complementary days. The intercalary year of the Coptic calendar immediately precedes the leap year of the Julian calendar. The era is that of Diocletian or the Martyrs, the origin of which is fixed at 29 August AD 284 (Julian date).

INDIAN ERAS
In addition to the Muslim reckoning, other eras are used in India. The Saka era of southern India, dating from 3 March AD 78, was declared the national calendar of the Republic of India with effect from 22 March 1957, to be used concurrently with the Gregorian calendar. As revised, the year of the new Saka era begins at the spring equinox, with five successive months of 31 days and seven of 30 days in ordinary years, and six months of each length in leap years. The year AD 2019 is 1941 of the revised Saka era.

The year AD 2019 corresponds to the following years in other eras:

Year 2076 of the Vikram Samvat era
Year 1426 of the Bengali San era
Year 1195 of the Kollam era
Year 5120 of the Kaliyuga era
Year 2562 of the Buddha Nirvana era

JAPANESE CALENDAR
The Japanese calendar is essentially the same as the Gregorian calendar, the years, months and weeks being of the same length and beginning on the same days as those of the Gregorian calendar. The numeration of the years is different, based on a system of epochs or periods, each of which begins at the accession of an emperor or other important occurrence. The method is not unlike the British system of regnal years, except that each year of a period closes on 31 December. The Japanese chronology begins about AD 650 and the three latest epochs are defined by the reigns of emperors, whose actual names are not necessarily used:

Epoch
Taisho – 1 August 1912 to 25 December 1926
Showa – 26 December 1926 to 7 January 1989
Heisei – 8 January 1989 to 30 April 2019. Emperor Akihito will abdicate on 30 April 2019, ending the Heisei era.
1 May 2019 – New epoch beings when Crown Prince Naruhito ascends the throne. The name of the new epoch is to be announced on 1 April 2019.

The months are known as First Month, Second Month, etc, First Month being equivalent to January. The days of the week are Nichiyobi (Sun-day), Getsuyobi (Moon-day), Kayobi (Fire-day), Suiyobi (Water-day), Mokuyobi (Wood-day), Kinyobi (Metal-day) and Doyobi (Earth-day).

THE MASONIC YEAR
Two dates are quoted in warrants, dispensations, etc, issued by the United Grand Lodge of England, those for the current year being expressed as *Anno Domini* 2019 – *Anno Lucis* 6019. This *Anno Lucis* (year of light) is based on the Book of Genesis 1:3, the 4,000-year difference being derived, in modified form, from *Ussher's Notation,* published in 1654, which places the Creation of the World in 4004 BC.

OLYMPIADS
Ancient Greek chronology was reckoned in Olympiads, cycles of four years corresponding with the Olympic Games held on the plain of Olympia, in Elis. The intervening years were the first, second, etc, of the Olympiad, which received the name of the victor at the Games. The first recorded Olympiad is that of Choroebus, 776 BC.

ZOROASTRIAN CALENDAR
Zoroastrians, followers of the Iranian prophet Zarathushtra (known to the Greeks as Zoroaster) are mostly to be found in Iran and in India, where they are known as Parsees.

The Zoroastrian era dates from the coronation of the last Zoroastrian Sasanian king in AD 631. The Zoroastrian calendar is divided into 12 months, each comprising 30 days, followed by five holy days of the Gathas at the end of each year to make the year consist of 365 days.

In order to synchronise the calendar with the solar year of 365 days, an extra month was intercalated once every 120 years. However, this intercalation ceased in the 12th century and the new year, which had fallen in the spring, slipped back to August. Because intercalation ceased at different times in Iran and India, there was one month's difference between the calendar followed in Iran (Kadmi calendar) and that followed by the Parsees (Shenshai calendar). In 1906 a group of Zoroastrians decided to bring the calendar back in line with the seasons again and restore the new year to 21 March each year (Fasli calendar).

The Shenshai calendar (new year in August) is mainly used by Parsees. The Fasli calendar (new year, 21 March) is mainly used by Zoroastrians living in Iran, in the Indian subcontinent, or elsewhere.

ROMAN CALENDAR

Roman historians adopted as an epoch the foundation of Rome, which is believed to have happened in the year 753 BC. The ordinal number of the years in Roman reckoning is followed by the letters AUC *(ab urbe condita),* so that the year 2019 is 2772 AUC (MMDCCLXXII). The calendar that we know has developed from one said to have been established by Romulus using a year of 304 days divided into ten months, beginning with March. To this Numa added January and February, making the year consist of 12 months of 30 and 29

days alternately, with an additional day so that the total was 355. It is also said that Numa ordered an intercalary month of 22 or 23 days in alternate years, making 90 days in eight years, to be inserted after 23 February.

However, there is some doubt as to the origination and the details of the intercalation in the Roman calendar. In the year 46 BC Julius Caesar found that the calendar had been allowed to fall into some confusion. He sought the help of Egyptian astronomer Sosigenes, which led to the construction and adoption (45 BC) of the Julian calendar, and, by a slight alteration, to the Gregorian calendar now in use. The year 46 BC was made to consist of 445 days and is called the Year of Confusion.

In the Roman (Julian) calendar, the days of the month were counted backwards from three fixed points, or days, and an intervening day was said to be so many days before the next coming point, the first and last being counted. These three points were the Kalends, the Nones and the Ides. The year containing 366 days was called *bissextilis annus,* as it had a doubled sixth day *(bissextus dies)* before the March Kalends on 24 February – *ante diem sextum Kalendas Martias,* or a.d. VI Kal. Mart.

Present days of the month	March, May, July, October have thirty-one days		January, August, December have thirty-one days		April, June, September, November have thirty days		February has twenty-eight days, and in leap year twenty-nine	
1	Kalendis		Kalendis		Kalendis		Kalendis	
2	VI		IV	ante	IV	ante	IV	ante
3	V	ante	III	Nonas	III	Nonas	III	Nonas
4	IV	Nonas	pridie Nonas		pridie Nonas		pridie Nonas	
5	III		Nonis		Nonis		Nonis	
6	pridie Nonas		VIII		VIII		VIII	
7	Nonis		VII		VII		VII	
8	VIII		VI	ante	VI	ante	VI	ante
9	VII		V	Idus	V	Idus	V	Idus
10	VI	ante	IV		IV		IV	
11	V	Idus	III		III		III	
12	IV		pridie Idus		pridie Idus		pridie Idus	
13	III		Idibus		Idibus		Idibus	
14	pridie Idus		XIX		XVIII		XVI	
15	Idibus		XVIII		XVII		XV	
16	XVII		XVII		XVI		XIV	
17	XVI		XVI		XV		XIII	
18	XV		XV		XIV		XII	
19	XIV		XIV		XIII		XI	
20	XIII		XIII		XII		X	ante Kalendas
21	XII		XII	ante Kalendas	XI	ante Kalendas	IX	Martias
22	XI	ante Kalendas	XI	(of the month	X	(of the month	VIII	
23	X	(of the month	X	following)	IX	following)	VII	
24	IX	following)	IX		VIII		*VI	
25	VIII		VIII		VII		V	
26	VII		VII		VI		IV	
27	VI		VI		V		III	
28	V		V		IV		pridie Kalendas	
29	IV		IV		III		Martias	
30	III		III		pridie Kalendas			
31	pridie Kalendas (Aprilis, Iunias, Sextilis, Novembris)		pridie Kalendas (Februarias, Septembris, Ianuarias)		(Maias, Quinctilis, Octobris, Decembris)			

* Repeated in leap year

CALENDAR FOR ANY YEAR 1780–2040

To select the correct calendar for any year between 1780 and 2040, consult the index below
* leap year

1780 N*	1813 K	1846 I	1879 G	1912 D*	1945 C	1978 A	2011 M
1781 C	1814 M	1847 K	1880 J*	1913 G	1946 E	1979 C	2012 B*
1782 E	1815 A	1848 N*	1881 M	1914 I	1947 G	1980 F*	2013 E
1783 G	1816 D*	1849 C	1882 A	1915 K	1948 J*	1981 I	2014 G
1784 J*	1817 G	1850 E	1883 C	1916 N*	1949 M	1982 K	2015 I
1785 M	1818 I	1851 G	1884 F*	1917 C	1950 A	1983 M	2016 L*
1786 A	1819 K	1852 J*	1885 I	1918 E	1951 C	1984 B*	2017 A
1787 C	1820 N*	1853 M	1886 K	1919 G	1952 F*	1985 E	2018 C
1788 F*	1821 C	1854 A	1887 M	1920 J*	1953 I	1986 G	2019 E
1789 I	1822 E	1855 C	1888 B*	1921 M	1954 K	1987 I	2020 H*
1790 K	1823 G	1856 F*	1889 E	1922 A	1955 M	1988 L*	2021 K
1791 M	1824 J*	1857 I	1890 G	1923 C	1956 B*	1989 A	2022 M
1792 B*	1825 M	1858 K	1891 I	1924 F*	1957 E	1990 C	2023 A
1793 E	1826 A	1859 M	1892 L*	1925 I	1958 G	1991 E	2024 D*
1794 G	1827 C	1860 B*	1893 A	1926 K	1959 I	1992 H*	2025 G
1795 I	1828 F*	1861 E	1894 C	1927 M	1960 L*	1993 K	2026 I
1796 L*	1829 I	1862 G	1895 E	1928 B*	1961 A	1994 M	2027 K
1797 A	1830 K	1863 I	1896 H*	1929 E	1962 C	1995 A	2028 N*
1798 C	1831 M	1864 L*	1897 K	1930 G	1963 E	1996 D*	2029 C
1799 E	1832 B*	1865 A	1898 M	1931 I	1964 H*	1997 G	2030 E
1800 G	1833 E	1866 C	1899 A	1932 L*	1965 K	1998 I	2031 G
1801 I	1834 G	1867 E	1900 C	1933 A	1966 M	1999 K	2032 J*
1802 K	1835 I	1868 H*	1901 E	1934 C	1967 A	2000 N*	2033 M
1803 M	1836 L*	1869 K	1902 G	1935 E	1968 D*	2001 C	2034 A
1804 B*	1837 A	1870 M	1903 I	1936 H*	1969 G	2002 E	2035 C
1805 E	1838 C	1871 A	1904 L*	1937 K	1970 I	2003 G	2036 F*
1806 G	1839 E	1872 D*	1905 A	1938 M	1971 K	2004 J*	2037 I
1807 I	1840 H*	1873 G	1906 C	1939 A	1972 N*	2005 M	2038 K
1808 L*	1841 K	1874 I	1907 E	1940 D*	1973 C	2006 A	2039 M
1809 A	1842 M	1875 K	1908 H*	1941 G	1974 E	2007 C	2040 B*
1810 C	1843 A	1876 N*	1909 K	1942 I	1975 G	2008 F*	
1811 E	1844 D*	1877 C	1910 M	1943 K	1976 J*	2009 I	
1812 H*	1845 G	1878 E	1911 A	1944 N*	1977 M	2010 K	

A

	January	February	March
Sun.	1 8 15 22 29	5 12 19 26	5 12 19 26
Mon.	2 9 16 23 30	6 13 20 27	6 13 20 27
Tue.	3 10 17 24 31	7 14 21 28	7 14 21 28
Wed.	4 11 18 25	1 8 15 22	1 8 15 22 29
Thur.	5 12 19 26	2 9 16 23	2 9 16 23 30
Fri.	6 13 20 27	3 10 17 24	3 10 17 24 31
Sat.	7 14 21 28	4 11 18 25	4 11 18 25

	April	May	June
Sun.	2 9 16 23 30	7 14 21 28	4 11 18 25
Mon.	3 10 17 24	1 8 15 22 29	5 12 19 26
Tue.	4 11 18 25	2 9 16 23 30	6 13 20 27
Wed.	5 12 19 26	3 10 17 24 31	7 14 21 28
Thur.	6 13 20 27	4 11 18 25	1 8 15 22 29
Fri.	7 14 21 28	5 12 19 26	2 9 16 23 30
Sat.	1 8 15 22 29	6 13 20 27	3 10 17 24

	July	August	September
Sun.	2 9 16 23 30	6 13 20 27	3 10 17 24
Mon.	3 10 17 24 31	7 14 21 28	4 11 18 25
Tue.	4 11 18 25	1 8 15 22 29	5 12 19 26
Wed.	5 12 19 26	2 9 16 23 30	6 13 20 27
Thur.	6 13 20 27	3 10 17 24 31	7 14 21 28
Fri.	7 14 21 28	4 11 18 25	1 8 15 22 29
Sat.	1 8 15 22 29	5 12 19 26	2 9 16 23 30

	October	November	December
Sun.	1 8 15 22 29	5 12 19 26	3 10 17 24 31
Mon.	2 9 16 23 30	6 13 20 27	4 11 18 25
Tue.	3 10 17 24 31	7 14 21 28	5 12 19 26
Wed.	4 11 18 25	1 8 15 22 29	6 13 20 27
Thur.	5 12 19 26	2 9 16 23 30	7 14 21 28
Fri.	6 13 20 27	3 10 17 24	1 8 15 22 29
Sat.	7 14 21 28	4 11 18 25	2 9 16 23 30

EASTER DAYS

March 26	1815, 1826, 1837, 1967, 1978, 1989
April 2	1809, 1893, 1899, 1961
April 9	1871, 1882, 1939, 1950, 2023, 2034
April 16	1786, 1797, 1843, 1854, 1865, 1911, 1922, 1933, 1995, 2006, 2017
April 23	1905

B (LEAP YEAR)

	January	February	March
Sun.	1 8 15 22 29	5 12 19 26	4 11 18 25
Mon.	2 9 16 23 30	6 13 20 27	5 12 19 26
Tue.	3 10 17 24 31	7 14 21 28	6 13 20 27
Wed.	4 11 18 25	1 8 15 22	7 14 21 28
Thur.	5 12 19 26	2 9 16 23	1 8 15 22 29
Fri.	6 13 20 27	3 10 17 24	2 9 16 23 30
Sat.	7 14 21 28	4 11 18 25	3 10 17 24 31

	April	May	June
Sun.	1 8 15 22 29	6 13 20 27	3 10 17 24
Mon.	2 9 16 23 30	7 14 21 28	4 11 18 25
Tue.	3 10 17 24	1 8 15 22 29	5 12 19 26
Wed.	4 11 18 25	2 9 16 23 30	6 13 20 27
Thur.	5 12 19 26	3 10 17 24 31	7 14 21 28
Fri.	6 13 20 27	4 11 18 25	1 8 15 22 29
Sat.	7 14 21 28	5 12 19 26	2 9 16 23 30

	July	August	September
Sun.	1 8 15 22 29	5 12 19 26	2 9 16 23 30
Mon.	2 9 16 23 30	6 13 20 27	3 10 17 24
Tue.	3 10 17 24 31	7 14 21 28	4 11 18 25
Wed.	4 11 18 25	1 8 15 22 29	5 12 19 26
Thur.	5 12 19 26	2 9 16 23 30	6 13 20 27
Fri.	6 13 20 27	3 10 17 24 31	7 14 21 28
Sat.	7 14 21 28	4 11 18 25	1 8 15 22 29

	October	November	December
Sun.	7 14 21 28	4 11 18 25	2 9 16 23 30
Mon.	1 8 15 22 29	5 12 19 26	3 10 17 24 31
Tue.	2 9 16 23 30	6 13 20 27	4 11 18 25
Wed.	3 10 17 24 31	7 14 21 28	5 12 19 26
Thur.	4 11 18 25	1 8 15 22 29	6 13 20 27
Fri.	5 12 19 26	2 9 16 23 30	7 14 21 28
Sat.	6 13 20 27	3 10 17 24	1 8 15 22 29

EASTER DAYS

April 1	1804, 1888, 1956, 2040
April 8	1792, 1860, 1928, 2012
April 22	1832, 1984

C

	January	February	March
Sun.	7 14 21 28	4 11 18 25	4 11 18 25
Mon.	1 8 15 22 29	5 12 19 26	5 12 19 26
Tue.	2 9 16 23 30	6 13 20 27	6 13 20 27
Wed.	3 10 17 24 31	7 14 21 28	7 14 21 28
Thur.	4 11 18 25	1 8 15 22	1 8 15 22 29
Fri.	5 12 19 26	2 9 16 23	2 9 16 23 30
Sat.	6 13 20 27	3 10 17 24	3 10 17 24 31

	April	May	June
Sun.	1 8 15 22 29	6 13 20 27	3 10 17 24
Mon.	2 9 16 23 30	7 14 21 28	4 11 18 25
Tue.	3 10 17 24	1 8 15 22 29	5 12 19 26
Wed.	4 11 18 25	2 9 16 23 30	6 13 20 27
Thur.	5 12 19 26	3 10 17 24 31	7 14 21 28
Fri.	6 13 20 27	4 11 18 25	1 8 15 22 29
Sat.	7 14 21 28	5 12 19 26	2 9 16 23 30

	July	August	September
Sun.	1 8 15 22 29	5 12 19 26	2 9 16 23 30
Mon.	2 9 16 23 30	6 13 20 27	3 10 17 24
Tue.	3 10 17 24 31	7 14 21 28	4 11 18 25
Wed.	4 11 18 25	1 8 15 22 29	5 12 19 26
Thur.	5 12 19 26	2 9 16 23 30	6 13 20 27
Fri.	6 13 20 27	3 10 17 24 31	7 14 21 28
Sat.	7 14 21 28	4 11 18 25	1 8 15 22 29

	October	November	December
Sun.	7 14 21 28	4 11 18 25	2 9 16 23 30
Mon.	1 8 15 22 29	5 12 19 26	3 10 17 24 31
Tue.	2 9 16 23 30	6 13 20 27	4 11 18 25
Wed.	3 10 17 24 31	7 14 21 28	5 12 19 26
Thur.	4 11 18 25	1 8 15 22 29	6 13 20 27
Fri.	5 12 19 26	2 9 16 23 30	7 14 21 28
Sat.	6 13 20 27	3 10 17 24	1 8 15 22 29

EASTER DAYS
March 25	1883, 1894, 1951, 2035
April 1	1866, 1877, 1923, 1934, 1945, 2018, 2029
April 8	1787, 1798, 1849, 1855, 1917, 2007
April 15	1781, 1827, 1838, 1900, 1906, 1979, 1990, 2001
April 22	1810, 1821, 1962, 1973

E

	January	February	March
Sun.	6 13 20 27	3 10 17 24	3 10 17 24 31
Mon.	7 14 21 28	4 11 18 25	4 11 18 25
Tue.	1 8 15 22 29	5 12 19 26	5 12 19 26
Wed.	2 9 16 23 30	6 13 20 27	6 13 20 27
Thur.	3 10 17 24 31	7 14 21 28	7 14 21 28
Fri.	4 11 18 25	1 8 15 22	1 8 15 22 29
Sat.	5 12 19 26	2 9 16 23	2 9 16 23 30

	April	May	June
Sun.	7 14 21 28	5 12 19 26	2 9 16 23 30
Mon.	1 8 15 22 29	6 13 20 27	3 10 17 24
Tue.	2 9 16 23 30	7 14 21 28	4 11 18 25
Wed.	3 10 17 24	1 8 15 22 29	5 12 19 26
Thur.	4 11 18 25	2 9 16 23 30	6 13 20 27
Fri.	5 12 19 26	3 10 17 24 31	7 14 21 28
Sat.	6 13 20 27	4 11 18 25	1 8 15 22 29

	July	August	September
Sun.	7 14 21 28	4 11 18 25	1 8 15 22 29
Mon.	1 8 15 22 29	5 12 19 26	2 9 16 23 30
Tue.	2 9 16 23 30	6 13 20 27	3 10 17 24
Wed.	3 10 17 24 31	7 14 21 28	4 11 18 25
Thur.	4 11 18 25	1 8 15 22 29	5 12 19 26
Fri.	5 12 19 26	2 9 16 23 30	6 13 20 27
Sat.	6 13 20 27	3 10 17 24 31	7 14 21 28

	October	November	December
Sun.	6 13 20 27	3 10 17 24	1 8 15 22 29
Mon.	7 14 21 28	4 11 18 25	2 9 16 23 30
Tue.	1 8 15 22 29	5 12 19 26	3 10 17 24 31
Wed.	2 9 16 23 30	6 13 20 27	4 11 18 25
Thur.	3 10 17 24 31	7 14 21 28	5 12 19 26
Fri.	4 11 18 25	1 8 15 22 29	6 13 20 27
Sat.	5 12 19 26	2 9 16 23 30	7 14 21 28

EASTER DAYS
March 24	1799
March 31	1782, 1793, 1839, 1850, 1861, 1907, 1918, 1929, 1991, 2002, 2013
April 7	1822, 1833, 1901, 1985
April 14	1805, 1811, 1895, 1963, 1974
April 21	1867, 1878, 1889, 1935, 1946, 1957, 2019, 2030

D (LEAP YEAR)

	January	February	March
Sun.	7 14 21 28	4 11 18 25	3 10 17 24 31
Mon.	1 8 15 22 29	5 12 19 26	4 11 18 25
Tue.	2 9 16 23 30	6 13 20 27	5 12 19 26
Wed.	3 10 17 24 31	7 14 21 28	6 13 20 27
Thur.	4 11 18 25	1 8 15 22 29	7 14 21 28
Fri.	5 12 19 26	2 9 16 23	1 8 15 22 29
Sat.	6 13 20 27	3 10 17 24	2 9 16 23 30

	April	May	June
Sun.	7 14 21 28	5 12 19 26	2 9 16 23 30
Mon.	1 8 15 22 29	6 13 20 27	3 10 17 24
Tue.	2 9 16 23 30	7 14 21 28	4 11 18 25
Wed.	3 10 17 24	1 8 15 22 29	5 12 19 26
Thur.	4 11 18 25	2 9 16 23 30	6 13 20 27
Fri.	5 12 19 26	3 10 17 24 31	7 14 21 28
Sat.	6 13 20 27	4 11 18 25	1 8 15 22 29

	July	August	September
Sun.	7 14 21 28	4 11 18 25	1 8 15 22 29
Mon.	1 8 15 22 29	5 12 19 26	2 9 16 23 30
Tue.	2 9 16 23 30	6 13 20 27	3 10 17 24
Wed.	3 10 17 24 31	7 14 21 28	4 11 18 25
Thur.	4 11 18 25	1 8 15 22 29	5 12 19 26
Fri.	5 12 19 26	2 9 16 23 30	6 13 20 27
Sat.	6 13 20 27	3 10 17 24 31	7 14 21 28

	October	November	December
Sun.	6 13 20 27	3 10 17 24	1 8 15 22 29
Mon.	7 14 21 28	4 11 18 25	2 9 16 23 30
Tue.	1 8 15 22 29	5 12 19 26	3 10 17 24 31
Wed.	2 9 16 23 30	6 13 20 27	4 11 18 25
Thur.	3 10 17 24 31	7 14 21 28	5 12 19 26
Fri.	4 11 18 25	1 8 15 22 29	6 13 20 27
Sat.	5 12 19 26	2 9 16 23 30	7 14 21 28

EASTER DAYS
March 24	1940
March 31	1872, 2024
April 7	1844, 1912, 1996
April 14	1816, 1968

F (LEAP YEAR)

	January	February	March
Sun.	6 13 20 27	3 10 17 24	2 9 16 23 30
Mon.	7 14 21 28	4 11 18 25	3 10 17 24 31
Tue.	1 8 15 22 29	5 12 19 26	4 11 18 25
Wed.	2 9 16 23 30	6 13 20 27	5 12 19 26
Thur.	3 10 17 24 31	7 14 21 28	6 13 20 27
Fri.	4 11 18 25	1 8 15 22 29	7 14 21 28
Sat.	5 12 19 26	2 9 16 23	1 8 15 22 29

	April	May	June
Sun.	6 13 20 27	4 11 18 25	1 8 15 22 29
Mon.	7 14 21 28	5 12 19 26	2 9 16 23 30
Tue.	1 8 15 22 29	6 13 20 27	3 10 17 24
Wed.	2 9 16 23 30	7 14 21 28	4 11 18 25
Thur.	3 10 17 24	1 8 15 22 29	5 12 19 26
Fri.	4 11 18 25	2 9 16 23 30	6 13 20 27
Sat.	5 12 19 26	3 10 17 24 31	7 14 21 28

	July	August	September
Sun.	6 13 20 27	3 10 17 24 31	7 14 21 28
Mon.	7 14 21 28	4 11 18 25	1 8 15 22 29
Tue.	1 8 15 22 29	5 12 19 26	2 9 16 23 30
Wed.	2 9 16 23 30	6 13 20 27	3 10 17 24
Thur.	3 10 17 24 31	7 14 21 28	4 11 18 25
Fri.	4 11 18 25	1 8 15 22 29	5 12 19 26
Sat.	5 12 19 26	2 9 16 23 30	6 13 20 27

	October	November	December
Sun.	5 12 19 26	2 9 16 23 30	7 14 21 28
Mon.	6 13 20 27	3 10 17 24	1 8 15 22 29
Tue.	7 14 21 28	4 11 18 25	2 9 16 23 30
Wed.	1 8 15 22 29	5 12 19 26	3 10 17 24 31
Thur.	2 9 16 23 30	6 13 20 27	4 11 18 25
Fri.	3 10 17 24 31	7 14 21 28	5 12 19 26
Sat.	4 11 18 25	1 8 15 22 29	6 13 20 27

EASTER DAYS
March 23	1788, 1856, 2008
April 6	1828, 1980
April 13	1884, 1952, 2036
April 20	1924

G

	January	February	March
Sun.	5 12 19 26	2 9 16 23	2 9 16 23 30
Mon.	6 13 20 27	3 10 17 24	3 10 17 24 31
Tue.	7 14 21 28	4 11 18 25	4 11 18 25
Wed.	1 8 15 22 29	5 12 19 26	5 12 19 26
Thur.	2 9 16 23 30	6 13 20 27	6 13 20 27
Fri.	3 10 17 24 31	7 14 21 28	7 14 21 28
Sat.	4 11 18 25	1 8 15 22	1 8 15 22 29

	April	May	June
Sun.	6 13 20 27	4 11 18 25	1 8 15 22 29
Mon.	7 14 21 28	5 12 19 26	2 9 16 23 30
Tue.	1 8 15 22 29	6 13 20 27	3 10 17 24
Wed.	2 9 16 23 30	7 14 21 28	4 11 18 25
Thur.	3 10 17 24	1 8 15 22 29	5 12 19 26
Fri.	4 11 18 25	2 9 16 23 30	6 13 20 27
Sat.	5 12 19 26	3 10 17 24 31	7 14 21 28

	July	August	September
Sun.	6 13 20 27	3 10 17 24 31	7 14 21 28
Mon.	7 14 21 28	4 11 18 25	1 8 15 22 29
Tue.	1 8 15 22 29	5 12 19 26	2 9 16 23 30
Wed.	2 9 16 23 30	6 13 20 27	3 10 17 24
Thur.	3 10 17 24 31	7 14 21 28	4 11 18 25
Fri.	4 11 18 25	1 8 15 22 29	5 12 19 26
Sat.	5 12 19 26	2 9 16 23 30	6 13 20 27

	October	November	December
Sun.	5 12 19 26	2 9 16 23 30	7 14 21 28
Mon.	6 13 20 27	3 10 17 24	1 8 15 22 29
Tue.	7 14 21 28	4 11 18 25	2 9 16 23 30
Wed.	1 8 15 22 29	5 12 19 26	3 10 17 24 31
Thur.	2 9 16 23 30	6 13 20 27	4 11 18 25
Fri.	3 10 17 24 31	7 14 21 28	5 12 19 26
Sat.	4 11 18 25	1 8 15 22 29	6 13 20 27

EASTER DAYS

March 23	1845, 1913
March 30	1823, 1834, 1902, 1975, 1986, 1997
April 6	1806, 1817, 1890, 1947, 1958, 1969
April 13	1800, 1873, 1879, 1941, 2031
April 20	1783, 1794, 1851, 1862, 1919, 1930, 2003, 2014, 2025

I

	January	February	March
Sun.	4 11 18 25	1 8 15 22	1 8 15 22 29
Mon.	5 12 19 26	2 9 16 23	2 9 16 23 30
Tue.	6 13 20 27	3 10 17 24	3 10 17 24 31
Wed.	7 14 21 28	4 11 18 25	4 11 18 25
Thur.	1 8 15 22 29	5 12 19 26	5 12 19 26
Fri.	2 9 16 23 30	6 13 20 27	6 13 20 27
Sat.	3 10 17 24 31	7 14 21 28	7 14 21 28

	April	May	June
Sun.	5 12 19 26	3 10 17 24 31	7 14 21 28
Mon.	6 13 20 27	4 11 18 25	1 8 15 22 29
Tue.	7 14 21 28	5 12 19 26	2 9 16 23 30
Wed.	1 8 15 22 29	6 13 20 27	3 10 17 24
Thur.	2 9 16 23 30	7 14 21 28	4 11 18 25
Fri.	3 10 17 24	1 8 15 22 29	5 12 19 26
Sat.	4 11 18 25	2 9 16 23 30	6 13 20 27

	July	August	September
Sun.	5 12 19 26	2 9 16 23 30	6 13 20 27
Mon.	6 13 20 27	3 10 17 24 31	7 14 21 28
Tue.	7 14 21 28	4 11 18 25	1 8 15 22 29
Wed.	1 8 15 22 29	5 12 19 26	2 9 16 23 30
Thur.	2 9 16 23 30	6 13 20 27	3 10 17 24
Fri.	3 10 17 24 31	7 14 21 28	4 11 18 25
Sat.	4 11 18 25	1 8 15 22 29	5 12 19 26

	October	November	December
Sun.	4 11 18 25	1 8 15 22 29	6 13 20 27
Mon.	5 12 19 26	2 9 16 23 30	7 14 21 28
Tue.	6 13 20 27	3 10 17 24	1 8 15 22 29
Wed.	7 14 21 28	4 11 18 25	2 9 16 23 30
Thur.	1 8 15 22 29	5 12 19 26	3 10 17 24 31
Fri.	2 9 16 23 30	6 13 20 27	4 11 18 25
Sat.	3 10 17 24 31	7 14 21 28	5 12 19 26

EASTER DAYS

March 22	1818
March 29	1807, 1891, 1959, 1970
April 5	1795, 1801, 1863, 1874, 1885, 1931, 1942, 1953, 2015, 2026, 2037
April 12	1789, 1846, 1857, 1903, 1914, 1925, 1998, 2009
April 19	1829, 1835, 1981, 1987

H (LEAP YEAR)

	January	February	March
Sun.	5 12 19 26	2 9 16 23	1 8 15 22 29
Mon.	6 13 20 27	3 10 17 24	2 9 16 23 30
Tue.	7 14 21 28	4 11 18 25	3 10 17 24 31
Wed.	1 8 15 22 29	5 12 19 26	4 11 18 25
Thur.	2 9 16 23 30	6 13 20 27	5 12 19 26
Fri.	3 10 17 24 31	7 14 21 28	6 13 20 27
Sat.	4 11 18 25	1 8 15 22 29	7 14 21 28

	April	May	June
Sun.	5 12 19 26	3 10 17 24 31	7 14 21 28
Mon.	6 13 20 27	4 11 18 25	1 8 15 22 29
Tue.	7 14 21 28	5 12 19 26	2 9 16 23 30
Wed.	1 8 15 22 29	6 13 20 27	3 10 17 24
Thur.	2 9 16 23 30	7 14 21 28	4 11 18 25
Fri.	3 10 17 24	1 8 15 22 29	5 12 19 26
Sat.	4 11 18 25	2 9 16 23 30	6 13 20 27

	July	August	September
Sun.	5 12 19 26	2 9 16 23 30	6 13 20 27
Mon.	6 13 20 27	3 10 17 24 31	7 14 21 28
Tue.	7 14 21 28	4 11 18 25	1 8 15 22 29
Wed.	1 8 15 22 29	5 12 19 26	2 9 16 23 30
Thur.	2 9 16 23 30	6 13 20 27	3 10 17 24
Fri.	3 10 17 24 31	7 14 21 28	4 11 18 25
Sat.	4 11 18 25	1 8 15 22 29	5 12 19 26

	October	November	December
Sun.	4 11 18 25	1 8 15 22 29	6 13 20 27
Mon.	5 12 19 26	2 9 16 23 30	7 14 21 28
Tue.	6 13 20 27	3 10 17 24	1 8 15 22 29
Wed.	7 14 21 28	4 11 18 25	2 9 16 23 30
Thur.	1 8 15 22 29	5 12 19 26	3 10 17 24 31
Fri.	2 9 16 23 30	6 13 20 27	4 11 18 25
Sat.	3 10 17 24 31	7 14 21 28	5 12 19 26

EASTER DAYS

March 29	1812, 1964
April 5	1896
April 12	1868, 1936, 2020
April 19	1840, 1908, 1992

J (LEAP YEAR)

	January	February	March
Sun.	4 11 18 25	1 8 15 22 29	7 14 21 28
Mon.	5 12 19 26	2 9 16 23	1 8 15 22 29
Tue.	6 13 20 27	3 10 17 24	2 9 16 23 30
Wed.	7 14 21 28	4 11 18 25	3 10 17 24 31
Thur.	1 8 15 22 29	5 12 19 26	4 11 18 25
Fri.	2 9 16 23 30	6 13 20 27	5 12 19 26
Sat.	3 10 17 24 31	7 14 21 28	6 13 20 27

	April	May	June
Sun.	4 11 18 25	2 9 16 23 30	6 13 20 27
Mon.	5 12 19 26	3 10 17 24 31	7 14 21 28
Tue.	6 13 20 27	4 11 18 25	1 8 15 22 29
Wed.	7 14 21 28	5 12 19 26	2 9 16 23 30
Thur.	1 8 15 22 29	6 13 20 27	3 10 17 24
Fri.	2 9 16 23 30	7 14 21 28	4 11 18 25
Sat.	3 10 17 24	1 8 15 22 29	5 12 19 26

	July	August	September
Sun.	4 11 18 25	1 8 15 22 29	5 12 19 26
Mon.	5 12 19 26	2 9 16 23 30	6 13 20 27
Tue.	6 13 20 27	3 10 17 24 31	7 14 21 28
Wed.	7 14 21 28	4 11 18 25	1 8 15 22 29
Thur.	1 8 15 22 29	5 12 19 26	2 9 16 23 30
Fri.	2 9 16 23 30	6 13 20 27	3 10 17 24
Sat.	3 10 17 24 31	7 14 21 28	4 11 18 25

	October	November	December
Sun.	3 10 17 24 31	7 14 21 28	5 12 19 26
Mon.	4 11 18 25	1 8 15 22 29	6 13 20 27
Tue.	5 12 19 26	2 9 16 23 30	7 14 21 28
Wed.	6 13 20 27	3 10 17 24	1 8 15 22 29
Thur.	7 14 21 28	4 11 18 25	2 9 16 23 30
Fri.	1 8 15 22 29	5 12 19 26	3 10 17 24 31
Sat.	2 9 16 23 30	6 13 20 27	4 11 18 25

EASTER DAYS

March 28	1880, 1948, 2032
April 4	1920
April 11	1784, 1852, 2004
April 18	1824, 1976

K

	January	February	March
Sun.	3 10 17 24 31	7 14 21 28	7 14 21 28
Mon.	4 11 18 25	1 8 15 22	1 8 15 22 29
Tue.	5 12 19 26	2 9 16 23	2 9 16 23 30
Wed.	6 13 20 27	3 10 17 24	3 10 17 24 31
Thur.	7 14 21 28	4 11 18 25	4 11 18 25
Fri.	1 8 15 22 29	5 12 19 26	5 12 19 26
Sat.	2 9 16 23 30	6 13 20 27	6 13 20 27

	April	May	June
Sun.	4 11 18 25	2 9 16 23 30	6 13 20 27
Mon.	5 12 19 26	3 10 17 24 31	7 14 21 28
Tue.	6 13 20 27	4 11 18 25	1 8 15 22 29
Wed.	7 14 21 28	5 12 19 26	2 9 16 23 30
Thur.	1 8 15 22 29	6 13 20 27	3 10 17 24
Fri.	2 9 16 23 30	7 14 21 28	4 11 18 25
Sat.	3 10 17 24	1 8 15 22 29	5 12 19 26

	July	August	September
Sun.	4 11 18 25	1 8 15 22 29	5 12 19 26
Mon.	5 12 19 26	2 9 16 23 30	6 13 20 27
Tue.	6 13 20 27	3 10 17 24 31	7 14 21 28
Wed.	7 14 21 28	4 11 18 25	1 8 15 22 29
Thur.	1 8 15 22 29	5 12 19 26	2 9 16 23 30
Fri.	2 9 16 23 30	6 13 20 27	3 10 17 24
Sat.	3 10 17 24 31	7 14 21 28	4 11 18 25

	October	November	December
Sun.	3 10 17 24 31	7 14 21 28	5 12 19 26
Mon.	4 11 18 25	1 8 15 22 29	6 13 20 27
Tue.	5 12 19 26	2 9 16 23 30	7 14 21 28
Wed.	6 13 20 27	3 10 17 24	1 8 15 22 29
Thur.	7 14 21 28	4 11 18 25	2 9 16 23 30
Fri.	1 8 15 22 29	5 12 19 26	3 10 17 24 31
Sat.	2 9 16 23 30	6 13 20 27	4 11 18 25

EASTER DAYS

March 28	1869, 1875, 1937, 2027
April 4	1790, 1847, 1858, 1915, 1926, 1999, 2010, 2021
April 11	1819, 1830, 1841, 1909, 1971, 1982, 1993
April 18	1802, 1813, 1897, 1954, 1965
April 25	1886, 1943, 2038

M

	January	February	March
Sun.	2 9 16 23 30	6 13 20 27	6 13 20 27
Mon.	3 10 17 24 31	7 14 21 28	7 14 21 28
Tue.	4 11 18 25	1 8 15 22	1 8 15 22 29
Wed.	5 12 19 26	2 9 16 23	2 9 16 23 30
Thur.	6 13 20 27	3 10 17 24	3 10 17 24 31
Fri.	7 14 21 28	4 11 18 25	4 11 18 25
Sat.	1 8 15 22 29	5 12 19 26	5 12 19 26

	April	May	June
Sun.	3 10 17 24	1 8 15 22 29	5 12 19 26
Mon.	4 11 18 25	2 9 16 23 30	6 13 20 27
Tue.	5 12 19 26	3 10 17 24 31	7 14 21 28
Wed.	6 13 20 27	4 11 18 25	1 8 15 22 29
Thur.	7 14 21 28	5 12 19 26	2 9 16 23 30
Fri.	1 8 15 22 29	6 13 20 27	3 10 17 24
Sat.	2 9 16 23 30	7 14 21 28	4 11 18 25

	July	August	September
Sun.	3 10 17 24 31	7 14 21 28	4 11 18 25
Mon.	4 11 18 25	1 8 15 22 29	5 12 19 26
Tue.	5 12 19 26	2 9 16 23 30	6 13 20 27
Wed.	6 13 20 27	3 10 17 24 31	7 14 21 28
Thur.	7 14 21 28	4 11 18 25	1 8 15 22 29
Fri.	1 8 15 22 29	5 12 19 26	2 9 16 23 30
Sat.	2 9 16 23 30	6 13 20 27	3 10 17 24

	October	November	December
Sun.	2 9 16 23 30	6 13 20 27	4 11 18 25
Mon.	3 10 17 24 31	7 14 21 28	5 12 19 26
Tue.	4 11 18 25	1 8 15 22 29	6 13 20 27
Wed.	5 12 19 26	2 9 16 23 30	7 14 21 28
Thur.	6 13 20 27	3 10 17 24	1 8 15 22 29
Fri.	7 14 21 28	4 11 18 25	2 9 16 23 30
Sat.	1 8 15 22 29	5 12 19 26	3 10 17 24 31

EASTER DAYS

March 27	1785, 1842, 1853, 1910, 1921, 2005
April 3	1825, 1831, 1983, 1994
April 10	1803, 1814, 1887, 1898, 1955, 1966, 1977, 2039
April 17	1870, 1881, 1927, 1938, 1949, 2022, 2033
April 24	1791, 1859, 2011

L (LEAP YEAR)

	January	February	March
Sun.	3 10 17 24 31	7 14 21 28	6 13 20 27
Mon.	4 11 18 25	1 8 15 22 29	7 14 21 28
Tue.	5 12 19 26	2 9 16 23	1 8 15 22 29
Wed.	6 13 20 27	3 10 17 24	2 9 16 23 30
Thur.	7 14 21 28	4 11 18 25	3 10 17 24 31
Fri.	1 8 15 22 29	5 12 19 26	4 11 18 25
Sat.	2 9 16 23 30	6 13 20 27	5 12 19 26

	April	May	June
Sun.	3 10 17 24	1 8 15 22 29	5 12 19 26
Mon.	4 11 18 25	2 9 16 23 30	6 13 20 27
Tue.	5 12 19 26	3 10 17 24 31	7 14 21 28
Wed.	6 13 20 27	4 11 18 25	1 8 15 22 29
Thur.	7 14 21 28	5 12 19 26	2 9 16 23 30
Fri.	1 8 15 22 29	6 13 20 27	3 10 17 24
Sat.	2 9 16 23 30	7 14 21 28	4 11 18 25

	July	August	September
Sun.	3 10 17 24 31	7 14 21 28	4 11 18 25
Mon.	4 11 18 25	1 8 15 22 29	5 12 19 26
Tue.	5 12 19 26	2 9 16 23 30	6 13 20 27
Wed.	6 13 20 27	3 10 17 24 31	7 14 21 28
Thur.	7 14 21 28	4 11 18 25	1 8 15 22 29
Fri.	1 8 15 22 29	5 12 19 26	2 9 16 23 30
Sat.	2 9 16 23 30	6 13 20 27	3 10 17 24

	October	November	December
Sun.	2 9 16 23 30	6 13 20 27	4 11 18 25
Mon.	3 10 17 24 31	7 14 21 28	5 12 19 26
Tue.	4 11 18 25	1 8 15 22 29	6 13 20 27
Wed.	5 12 19 26	2 9 16 23 30	7 14 21 28
Thur.	6 13 20 27	3 10 17 24	1 8 15 22 29
Fri.	7 14 21 28	4 11 18 25	2 9 16 23 30
Sat.	1 8 15 22 29	5 12 19 26	3 10 17 24 31

EASTER DAYS

March 27	1796, 1864, 1932, 2016
April 3	1836, 1904, 1988
April 17	1808, 1892, 1960

N (LEAP YEAR)

	January	February	March
Sun.	2 9 16 23 30	6 13 20 27	5 12 19 26
Mon.	3 10 17 24 31	7 14 21 28	6 13 20 27
Tue.	4 11 18 25	1 8 15 22 29	7 14 21 28
Wed.	5 12 19 26	2 9 16 23	1 8 15 22 29
Thur.	6 13 20 27	3 10 17 24	2 9 16 23 30
Fri.	7 14 21 28	4 11 18 25	3 10 17 24 31
Sat.	1 8 15 22 29	5 12 19 26	4 11 18 25

	April	May	June
Sun.	2 9 16 23 30	7 14 21 28	4 11 18 25
Mon.	3 10 17 24	1 8 15 22 29	5 12 19 26
Tue.	4 11 18 25	2 9 16 23 30	6 13 20 27
Wed.	5 12 19 26	3 10 17 24 31	7 14 21 28
Thur.	6 13 20 27	4 11 18 25	1 8 15 22 29
Fri.	7 14 21 28	5 12 19 26	2 9 16 23 30
Sat.	1 8 15 22 29	6 13 20 27	3 10 17 24

	July	August	September
Sun.	2 9 16 23 30	6 13 20 27	3 10 17 24
Mon.	3 10 17 24 31	7 14 21 28	4 11 18 25
Tue.	4 11 18 25	1 8 15 22 29	5 12 19 26
Wed.	5 12 19 26	2 9 16 23 30	6 13 20 27
Thur.	6 13 20 27	3 10 17 24 31	7 14 21 28
Fri.	7 14 21 28	4 11 18 25	1 8 15 22 29
Sat.	1 8 15 22 29	5 12 19 26	2 9 16 23 30

	October	November	December
Sun.	1 8 15 22 29	5 12 19 26	3 10 17 24 31
Mon.	2 9 16 23 30	6 13 20 27	4 11 18 25
Tue.	3 10 17 24 31	7 14 21 28	5 12 19 26
Wed.	4 11 18 25	1 8 15 22 29	6 13 20 27
Thur.	5 12 19 26	2 9 16 23 30	7 14 21 28
Fri.	6 13 20 27	3 10 17 24	1 8 15 22 29
Sat.	7 14 21 28	4 11 18 25	2 9 16 23 30

EASTER DAYS

March 26	1780
April 2	1820, 1972
April 9	1944
April 16	1876, 2028
April 23	1848, 1916, 2000

GEOLOGICAL TIME

Era	Period	Epoch	Dates*	Evolutionary Stages
Cenozoic	Quaternary	Holocene	11,700 BP†–present	First humans
Cenozoic	Quaternary	Pleistocene	2,588,000–11,700 BP	First humans
Cenozoic	Neogene	Pliocene	5.332–2.588 Mya ‡	Majority of still existing species
Cenozoic	Neogene	Miocene	23.03–5.332 Mya	Majority of still existing species
Cenozoic	Palaeogene	Oligocene	33.9–23.03 Mya	First modern mammals
Cenozoic	Palaeogene	Eocene	55.8–33.9 Mya	First modern mammals
Cenozoic	Palaeogene	Palaeocene	65.5–55.8 Mya	First modern mammals
Mesozoic	Cretaceous		145.5–65.5 Mya	
Mesozoic	Jurassic		199.6–145.5 Mya	First birds
Mesozoic	Triassic		251–199.6 Mya	First mammals
Palaeozoic	Permian		299–251 Mya	First reptiles
Palaeozoic	Carboniferous		359.2–299 Mya	First traces of land-living creatures
Palaeozoic	Devonian		416–359.2 Mya	First traces of land-living creatures
Palaeozoic	Silurian		443.7–416 Mya	
Palaeozoic	Ordovician		488.3–443.7 Mya	First fish
Palaeozoic	Cambrian		542–488.3 Mya	First invertebrates
Precambrian	Proterozoic		2,500–542 Mya	First primitive life forms, eg algae and bacteria
Precambrian	Archaean		3,800–2,500 Mya	Earth uninhabited
Precambrian	Hadean		4,600–3,800 Mya	Earth uninhabited

* approximate † BP = Before Present (1950 = base year) ‡ Mya = million years ago

PALAEOZOIC ('ANCIENT LIFE')

There were two great phases of mountain building in the Palaeozoic era: the Caledonian, characterised in Britain by NE–SW lines of hills and valleys; and the later Hercynian, widespread in west Germany and adjacent areas, and in Britain exemplified in E–W lines of hills and valleys. The end of the era was marked by the extensive glaciations of the Permian period in the southern continents and the decline of amphibians. It was succeeded by an era of warm conditions.

Cambrian – Mainly sandstones, slate and shales; limestones in Scotland. Shelled fossils and invertebrates, eg trilobites and brachiopods, and the earliest known vertebrates (jawless fish) appear

Ordovician – Mainly shales and mudstones, eg in north Wales; limestones in Scotland. First fish

Silurian – Shales, mudstones and some limestones, found mostly in Wales and southern Scotland

Devonian – Old red sandstone, shale, limestone and slate, eg in south Wales and the West Country

Carboniferous – Coal-bearing rocks, millstone grit, limestone and shale. First traces of land-living creatures

Permian – Marls, sandstones and clays. First reptile fossils

MESOZOIC ('MIDDLE FORMS OF LIFE')

Giant reptiles were dominant during the Mesozoic era; marsupial mammals first appeared, as well as *Archaeopteryx lithographica,* the earliest known species of bird. Coniferous trees and flowering plants also developed and, along with the birds and the mammals, were the main species to survive into the Cenozoic era. The giant reptiles became extinct.

Triassic – Mostly sandstone, eg in the W. Midlands; primitive mammals appear

Jurassic – Mainly limestones and clays, typically displayed in the Jura mountains, and in England in a NE–SW belt from Lincolnshire and the Wash to the Severn and the Dorset coast

Cretaceous – Mainly chalk, clay and sands, eg in Kent and Sussex

CENOZOIC ('RECENT LIFE')

From the Miocene through the Pliocene epochs, the Alpine-Himalayan and the circum-Pacific phases of mountain building reached their climax. During the Pleistocene epoch ice-sheets locked up masses of water as land ice, lowering the sea level by 100–200m. The last glacial retreat, merging into the Holocene period, was c.11,700 BP.

Palaeocene/ Eocene – Emergence of new forms of life, including existing species; primates appear

Oligocene – Fossils of a few still existing species

Miocene – Fossils show a balance of existing and extinct species

Piliocene/ Pleistocene – Fossils show a majority of still existing species

Holocene – The present, post-glacial period. Existing species only, except for a few exterminated by humans

HUMAN DEVELOPMENT

All members of the human race belong to one species of animal, *Homo sapiens,* the definition of a species being in biological terms that all its members can interbreed. As a species of mammal it is possible to group humans with other similar types, known as the primates. Amongst these is found a sub-group, the apes, which includes, in addition to humans, the chimpanzees, gorillas, orangutans and gibbons. All lack a tail, have shoulder blades at the back, and a Y-shaped chewing pattern on the surface of their molars, as well as showing the more general primate characteristics of four incisors, a thumb which is able to touch the fingers of the same hand, and finger and toe nails instead of claws. However, there once lived creatures, now extinct, which were closer to modern man than the chimpanzees and gorillas, and which shared with modern man the characteristics of having flat faces (ie the absence of a pronounced muzzle), being bipedal, and possessing large brains.

The debate surrounding evidence for the oldest human ancestors is ongoing. The earliest putative hominin for which there is significant fossil evidence is *Ardipithecus ramidus,* for which an almost complete skeleton, dating to at least 4.4 million years ago (Mya), was discovered in the Afar Rift, Ethiopia in 1992. Analysis of the skeleton suggests the creature had both human and ape characteristics; the ability to climb trees and walk on two feet.

The subsequent Australopithecines have left more numerous remains in south and east Africa, among which sub-groups may be detected. Living between 4.2 and 1.5 Mya, they were relatives of modern humans in the respect that they walked upright, did not have an extensive muzzle and had similar types of pre-molars. The first australopithecine remains were recognised at Taung in South Africa in 1924 and named *Australopithecus africanus,* dating between 3.3 and 2.3 Mya. The most impressive discovery was made at Hadar, Ethiopia, in 1974 when about half a skeleton of *Australopithecus afarensis,* known as 'Lucy', was found. Some 3.2 Mya, 'Lucy' (who is now considered to be male) certainly walked upright.

Also in east Africa, especially at Olduvai Gorge in Tanzania, between 2.5 and 1.8 Mya, lived a hominid group which not only walked upright, had a flat face, and a large brain case, but also made simple pebble and flake stone tools. Due to their distinctive characteristics, they have been grouped as a separate sub-species, now extinct, of the genus *Homo* and are known as *Homo habilis* or 'handy man'.

The use of fire is associated with another group of extinct hominids whose remains, about a million years old, are found in south and east Africa, China, Indonesia, north Africa and Europe. The ability to make fire probably helped the colonisation of the colder northern areas and in this respect the site of Vertesszollos in Hungary is of particular importance. *Homo ergaster* in Africa and *Homo erectus* in Asia are the names given to this group of fossils and they relate to a number of famous individual discoveries, eg Solo Man, Heidelberg Man, and especially Peking Man who lived at the cave site at Choukoutien which has yielded evidence of fire and burnt bone.

The well-known group the Neanderthals, or *Homo neanderthalensis,* is an extinct form of human that lived between *c.*350,000 and *c.*24,000 years ago, spanning the last Ice Age and living alongside modern humans. The Neanderthals' ability to adapt to the cold climate on the edge of the ice-sheets is one of their characteristic features, with remains being found only in Europe, Asia and the Middle East. Complete Neanderthal skeletons were found during excavations at Tabun in Israel, together with evidence of tool-making and the use of fire. Distinguished by very large brains, it seems that Neanderthals were the first to develop recognisable social customs, especially deliberate burial rites. Why the Neanderthals became extinct is not clear but it may be connected with the climatic changes at the end of the Ice Ages, which would have seriously affected their food supplies; possibly they became too specialised for their own good.

The shin bone of Boxgrove Man found in 1993 – *Homo heidelbergensis* – and the Swanscombe skull are the best known early human fossil remains found in England. Some specialists prefer to group Swanscombe Man (or, more probably, woman) together with the Steinheim skull from Germany, seeing both as a separate sub-species.

Anatomically modern humans – *Homo sapiens sapiens* ('doubly wise man') – had evolved to our present physical condition and had colonised much of the world by about 40,000 years ago. There are many previously distinguished individual specimens, eg Cromagnon Man, the first early *Homo sapiens sapiens* of the European Upper Palaeolithic.

The discovery of the structure of DNA in 1953 has come to have a profound effect upon the study of human evolution. For example, it was claimed in 1987 that a common ancestor of all human beings was a person who lived in Africa some 200,000 years ago, thus encouraging the 'out of Africa' theory of hominid migration from east Africa to the Middle East and then throughout the world.

CULTURAL DEVELOPMENT

The Three Age system, whereby prehistory was divided into a Stone Age, a Bronze Age and an Iron Age, was devised by Christian Thomsen, curator of the National Museum of Denmark, in the early 19th century, to facilitate the classification of the museum's collections. The adjectives referred to the materials from which the implements and weapons were made and came to be regarded as the dominant features of the societies to which they related. The Three Age system remains a generally accepted concept in the popular mind. However, it is now seen by archaeologists as an inadequate model for human development. Common sense suggests that there were no complete breaks between one so-called Age and another. Nor can the Three Age system be applied universally. In some areas it is necessary to insert a Copper Age, while in South Africa there would seem to be no Bronze Age at all; in Australia, Old Stone Age societies survived, while in South America, New Stone Age communities exist into modern times.

The concept of the 'Neolithic revolution', associated with the domestication of plants and animals, was a development of particular importance in the human cultural pattern. It reflected a gradual change from hunter-gatherer economies to a more settled agricultural way of life and therefore, so the argument goes, made possible the development of urban civilisation. It appears that the cultivation of wheat and barley was first undertaken, together with the domestication of cattle and goats/sheep, around 10,000 years ago in the Fertile Crescent (the area bounded by the rivers Tigris and Euphrates). There is evidence that sorghum was first domesticated in Africa, rice was first deliberately planted and pigs domesticated in South East Asia, maize first cultivated in Central America and llamas first domesticated in South America. Cultural change took place independently in different parts of the world at different rates and times.

The Neolithic period of cultural development has been difficult to date reliably because it took place long before writing was invented. With the development and refinement of radiocarbon dating and other scientific methods of producing absolute chronologies, it may eventually be possible to obtain a reliable chronological framework, in terms of years, against which the cultural development of any particular area may be set.

TIDES AND TIDAL PREDICTIONS

Tides are the periodic rise and fall of the sea-level caused mainly by the gravitational pull of the Moon and the Sun. This generates the tide raising force (TRF), of which the Moon accounts for approximately 70 per cent and the Sun 30 per cent. When the Moon and the Sun are in line with the Earth they are said to be 'in conjunction' (or syzygy) and their TRFs combine. This produces the largest rise and fall of the tide, known as spring tides; they occur each month just after a full or new Moon. This is amplified when the Moon is at perigee, its closest point to the Earth. When coincident with spring tides (about once every 18 months) this gives rise to very high proxigean tides. The opposite effect, just after the Moon's first and last quarters, when the Sun and Moon are at an angle of 90°, produces neap tides, with a relatively small tidal range between high and low water. There is an 18.6-year interval between the astronomical conditions – the Sun and Moon aligning with the Earth at perigee with zero declination – which generates the maximum TRF. Within this cycle there are times when zero solar declination (equinox) and lunar perigee occur almost simultaneously with zero lunar declination. This last occurred on 27 September 2015 and will occur again on 8 April 2020.

A lunar day is about 24 hours and 50 minutes, giving two complete tidal cycles, with about 12 hours and 25 minutes between successive high waters. These are known as semi-diurnal tides and are applicable in the Atlantic Ocean and around the coasts of north-west Europe. Other parts of the world have diurnal tides, with only one high water and one low water each (lunar) day, or mixed tides which are partly diurnal and partly semi-diurnal.

Land and seabed conditions influence the tides locally. On the south coast of England, for example, double high waters occur between Swanage and Selsey Bill, and low water is much more sharply defined than high water. Tides can also be greatly affected by the Coriolis force, which is induced by the Earth's rotation and, in the northern hemisphere, tends to deflect any moving object to the right. Thus, the easterly flood tidal stream in the English Channel is deflected towards the French coast causing higher high waters; on the ebb the opposite happens causing lower low waters. This, coupled with local geography, means that the mean spring range of the tide at St Malo is nearly 11m while the range on the English coast at Portland, 120 miles to the north, is a mere 2m.

Meteorological conditions such as prolonged strong winds and unusually high (or low) atmospheric pressure can significantly lower (or raise) the height of the tide; the drag of the wind alone (wind stress) can affect the predicted times of high and low water by as much as an hour. Variation of pressure by 34 millibars from the norm can cause a height difference of 0.3m.

STORM SURGES AND SEICHES

On the east and west coasts of the UK there are about 20 events each year when surge levels exceed 0.6m. The semicentennial surge is 1m in the Hebrides and at Land's End but up to 3m in the Thames estuary. Infrequently, surge peaks coincide with high water. The North Sea and the Thames estuary experience the most profound effects, often when a deep depression tracks south–easterly across the UK. Negative surges occur when strong southerly winds in the North Sea may lower tidal levels by 2m below prediction in these areas and the Dover Strait. Intense minor depressions, line squalls, or other abrupt changes in the weather can cause wave oscillations known as seiches. The wave period of a seiche varies from a few minutes to about two hours, with heights of up to a metre. Wick on the north-

east coast of Scotland and Fishguard in south-west Wales are particularly prone to these.

TIDAL STREAMS

Tidal streams are the horizontal movements of water caused by the rise and fall of the tide. They normally change direction about every six hours. Tidal streams should not be confused with ocean currents, such as the Gulf Stream, which run continuously in the same direction. The rate, or set, of the stream at any particular place is proportional to the range of the tide. Thus, the rate during spring tides is greater than that at neaps. In the central English Channel the maximum spring rate is nearly 5 knots while the neap rate at the same position is just 3 knots. As with tidal heights, local geography plays a significant role in the rate of the tidal stream. In the narrow waters of the Pentland Firth between mainland Scotland and the Orkney Islands, rates of 16 knots have been recorded.

The tidal stream does not necessarily turn at the same time as high or low water. In the English Channel the stream turns at approximately high and low water at Dover. However, high water at Dover is at about the same time as low water at Plymouth, and vice versa.

Around the UK, the main flood tidal stream sets eastward up the English Channel, north-east into the Bristol Channel, and north up the west coasts of Ireland and Scotland. However, the flood sets south-east through the North Channel and south into the Irish Sea, where it meets the northerly flood through St George's Channel at the Isle of Man. Off the east coasts of Scotland and England the stream sets south as far as the Thames estuary before meeting the north-going stream from the eastern part of the Dover Strait.

DEFINITIONS

Highest Astronomical Tide (HAT) and **Lowest Astronomical Tide (LAT)** are the highest and lowest tide levels predicted to occur under average meteorological, and any combination of astronomical, conditions. For a given area, **Chart Datum (CD)** is the level, as close as possible to LAT, below which charted depths are given. It is also the reference for tidal predictions: the total depth at a given time being equal to the charted depth plus the height of the tide. **Ordnance Datum (OD)** at Newlyn is the datum level of land survey on mainland England, Scotland and Wales, from which heights on UK land maps are measured. CD depends on the tidal range and varies around the UK from about 5m above OD to 6.5m below. **Duration** of the tide is the interval between low water and the next high water. It can be used to calculate the approximate time of low water when only the time of high water is known. **Mean Sea Level (MSL or ML)** is the average level of the sea's surface over a long period, normally observed over 18.6 years. The **Range** of the tide is the difference in height between successive high and low waters. It is greatest at spring tides, least at neaps. The range may be indicated by **Tidal Coefficients** which are proportional to, but not the same as, the range on a particular day. A coefficient of 95 indicates an average spring tide; 45 is an average neap tide.

TIDAL PREDICTIONS

The following data gives the daily GMT and height of high water at four ports. When BST applies the one hour time difference should be added. The datum of predictions is the difference of height, in metres, of CD from OD.

Compiled with the assistance of Chris Stevens and Perrin Towler.

JANUARY 2019 *High Water* GMT

		LONDON BRIDGE Datum of Predictions 3.2m below						LIVERPOOL (Gladstone Dock) Datum of Predictions 4.93 below						GREENOCK Datum of Predictions 1.62 below						LEITH Datum of Predictions 2.90 below					
		hr	m	hr	m			hr	m	hr	m			hr	m	hr	m			hr	m	hr	m		
Tu	1	09 43	6.4	22 19	6.4			07 20	8.0	19 47	8.2			08 49	3.1	20 44	3.2			10 58	4.8	23 27	5.0		
W	2	10 48	6.4	23 25	6.5			08 22	8.2	20 46	8.3			09 50	3.2	21 52	3.2			11 58	4.9	-	-		
Th	3	11 50	6.6	-	-			09 15	8.5	21 38	8.5			10 41	3.3	22 48	3.3			00 26	5.0	12 52	5.1		
F	4	00 23	6.6	12 44	6.7			10 00	8.7	22 22	8.7			11 27	3.4	23 38	3.3			01 19	5.1	13 38	5.2		
Sa	5	01 11	6.7	13 29	6.8			10 40	8.9	23 02	8.8			12 08	3.5	-	-			02 04	5.2	14 19	5.3		
Su	6	01 52	6.7	14 10	6.9			11 16	9.0	23 38	8.8			00 20	3.3	12 45	3.6			02 45	5.3	14 56	5.3		
M	7	02 28	6.8	14 47	6.9			11 51	9.1	-	-			00 59	3.3	13 19	3.6			03 23	5.3	15 31	5.3		
Tu	8	03 01	6.8	15 21	6.9			00 12	8.8	12 25	9.1			01 34	3.3	13 52	3.7			03 58	5.2	16 04	5.3		
W	9	03 33	6.8	15 54	6.8			00 45	8.7	12 59	9.0			02 09	3.3	14 25	3.6			04 32	5.2	16 38	5.2		
Th	10	04 04	6.7	16 26	6.7			01 18	8.5	13 33	8.8			02 46	3.3	14 59	3.6			05 08	5.1	17 12	5.1		
F	11	04 36	6.6	16 59	6.6			01 52	8.3	14 08	8.6			03 24	3.3	15 35	3.5			05 45	5.0	17 50	5.0		
Sa	12	05 09	6.5	17 34	6.4			02 28	8.1	14 46	8.3			04 03	3.2	16 13	3.4			06 25	4.8	18 30	4.9		
Su	13	05 44	6.3	18 13	6.2			03 08	7.8	15 29	8.0			04 44	3.1	16 55	3.3			07 09	4.7	19 14	4.7		
M	14	06 24	6.2	18 57	6.1			03 56	7.6	16 22	7.8			05 29	3.1	17 44	3.1			07 59	4.5	20 07	4.6		
Tu	15	07 13	6.0	19 55	5.9			04 56	7.4	17 28	7.7			06 19	3.0	18 43	3.0			08 58	4.5	21 12	4.6		
W	16	08 17	5.9	21 15	5.9			06 07	7.4	18 39	7.7			07 20	2.9	19 53	3.0			10 03	4.5	22 24	4.6		
Th	17	09 47	6.1	22 29	6.2			07 20	7.7	19 48	8.0			08 34	3.0	21 08	3.0			11 09	4.7	23 32	4.8		
F	18	10 59	6.4	23 35	6.5			08 24	8.2	20 49	8.5			09 44	3.1	22 16	3.2			12 11	4.9	-	-		
Sa	19	12 02	6.8	-	-			09 20	8.7	21 45	8.9			10 42	3.3	23 15	3.3			00 33	5.1	13 05	5.2		
Su	20	00 35	6.8	12 59	7.1			10 11	9.2	22 37	9.3			11 32	3.5	-	-			01 27	5.4	13 53	5.5		
M	21	01 30	7.0	13 52	7.4			11 00	9.6	23 26	9.6			00 08	3.4	12 19	3.6			02 16	5.7	14 38	5.7		
Tu	22	02 21	7.1	14 43	7.5			11 48	9.8	-	-			01 01	3.5	13 05	3.8			03 03	5.9	15 23	5.9		
W	23	03 09	7.2	15 31	7.6			00 15	9.8	12 36	9.9			01 51	3.5	13 51	3.9			03 50	5.9	16 08	5.9		
Th	24	03 55	7.3	16 18	7.5			01 04	9.7	13 23	9.9			02 39	3.5	14 36	3.9			04 38	5.9	16 55	5.9		
F	25	04 39	7.2	17 05	7.4			01 51	9.5	14 11	9.6			03 26	3.5	15 21	3.9			05 27	5.7	17 45	5.7		
Sa	26	05 24	7.1	17 53	7.1			02 39	9.1	15 00	9.3			04 12	3.4	16 06	3.8			06 17	5.4	18 38	5.5		
Su	27	06 10	6.9	18 43	6.8			03 28	8.6	15 51	8.8			04 58	3.3	16 53	3.6			07 12	5.1	19 39	5.2		
M	28	07 00	6.7	19 36	6.5			04 22	8.2	16 50	8.2			05 47	3.1	17 42	3.4			08 12	4.8	20 45	4.9		
Tu	29	07 58	6.4	20 35	6.3			05 26	7.8	17 59	7.8			06 42	3.0	18 38	3.2			09 16	4.6	21 51	4.7		
W	30	09 02	6.2	21 39	6.1			06 38	7.6	19 15	7.7			07 52	2.9	19 51	3.0			10 21	4.6	23 00	4.7		
Th	31	10 12	6.2	22 52	6.1			07 52	7.7	20 26	7.8			09 14	2.9	21 27	2.9			11 29	4.6	-	-		

FEBRUARY 2019 *High Water* GMT

		LONDON BRIDGE						LIVERPOOL (Gladstone Dock)						GREENOCK						LEITH					
F	1	11 23	6.3	-	-			08 54	8.0	21 24	8.0			10 18	3.1	22 37	3.0			00 09	4.7	12 34	4.8		
Sa	2	00 00	6.3	12 25	6.5			09 44	8.4	22 11	8.3			11 09	3.3	23 29	3.1			01 08	4.9	13 26	5.0		
Su	3	00 53	6.5	13 15	6.7			10 25	8.7	22 50	8.5			11 52	3.4	-	-			01 55	5.0	14 08	5.1		
M	4	01 37	6.6	13 57	6.8			11 02	8.9	23 24	8.7			00 12	3.1	12 31	3.5			02 34	5.1	14 44	5.2		
Tu	5	02 15	6.7	14 34	6.9			11 35	9.1	23 56	8.8			00 49	3.2	13 05	3.6			03 08	5.2	15 16	5.3		
W	6	02 48	6.8	15 06	6.9			12 08	9.1	-	-			01 21	3.2	13 37	3.6			03 39	5.2	15 47	5.3		
Th	7	03 18	6.8	15 36	6.8			00 27	8.8	12 40	9.1			01 53	3.2	14 07	3.6			04 10	5.2	16 18	5.3		
F	8	03 47	6.9	16 05	6.8			00 57	8.8	13 11	9.0			02 25	3.3	14 38	3.5			04 43	5.2	16 50	5.3		
Sa	9	04 17	6.8	16 35	6.7			01 28	8.6	13 42	8.9			02 59	3.3	15 11	3.5			05 17	5.1	17 23	5.2		
Su	10	04 49	6.7	17 08	6.6			01 59	8.4	14 14	8.6			03 33	3.3	15 47	3.4			05 53	5.0	17 58	5.1		
M	11	05 21	6.6	17 44	6.4			02 32	8.1	14 51	8.4			04 09	3.2	16 25	3.3			06 32	4.8	18 37	4.9		
Tu	12	05 58	6.4	18 24	6.2			03 12	8.0	15 35	8.1			04 47	3.2	17 07	3.2			07 16	4.7	19 24	4.8		
W	13	06 41	6.3	19 14	6.0			04 03	7.7	16 35	7.8			05 29	3.0	17 57	3.0			08 09	4.5	20 22	4.6		
Th	14	07 37	6.1	20 24	5.8			05 13	7.5	17 53	7.6			06 21	2.9	19 05	2.9			09 15	4.4	21 40	4.5		
F	15	08 59	6.0	21 54	5.9			06 38	7.5	19 17	7.8			07 32	2.8	20 34	2.9			10 31	4.5	23 02	4.7		
Sa	16	10 28	6.3	23 10	6.3			07 57	7.9	20 31	8.2			09 07	2.9	22 01	3.0			11 43	4.7	-	-		
Su	17	11 40	6.7	-	-			09 02	8.5	21 32	8.8			10 21	3.1	23 06	3.2			00 13	5.0	12 45	5.1		
M	18	00 18	6.6	12 44	7.1			09 57	9.1	22 26	9.3			11 16	3.4	-	-			01 13	5.3	13 36	5.4		
Tu	19	01 16	6.9	13 39	7.3			10 47	9.6	23 15	9.7			00 00	3.3	12 06	3.6			02 05	5.7	14 22	5.7		
W	20	02 07	7.2	14 29	7.5			11 35	10.0	-	-			00 51	3.4	12 53	3.7			02 48	5.9	15 06	6.0		
Th	21	02 53	7.3	15 16	7.6			00 02	9.9	12 21	10.1			01 39	3.5	13 38	3.8			03 33	6.0	15 51	6.0		
F	22	03 37	7.5	16 01	7.6			00 47	9.9	13 05	10.1			02 24	3.5	14 23	3.9			04 19	5.9	16 37	6.0		
Sa	23	04 19	7.5	16 44	7.4			01 30	9.7	13 48	9.8			03 06	3.5	15 06	3.8			05 05	5.7	17 24	5.8		
Su	24	05 01	7.3	17 27	7.1			02 12	9.3	14 31	9.3			03 46	3.4	15 48	3.7			05 52	5.4	18 14	5.5		
M	25	05 42	7.1	18 11	6.7			02 55	8.8	15 16	8.7			04 25	3.3	16 29	3.6			06 40	5.1	19 08	5.2		
Tu	26	06 26	6.8	18 55	6.4			03 42	8.2	16 09	8.1			05 05	3.1	17 12	3.3			07 34	4.8	20 10	4.8		
W	27	07 16	6.4	19 47	6.0			04 39	7.7	17 16	7.5			05 49	3.0	17 58	3.0			08 35	4.5	21 16	4.5		
Th	28	08 18	6.1	20 51	5.8			05 52	7.3	18 40	7.2			06 44	2.8	18 55	2.8			09 40	4.3	22 28	4.4		

MARCH 2019 *High Water* GMT

		LONDON BRIDGE Datum of Predictions 3.2m below						LIVERPOOL (Gladstone Dock) Datum of Predictions 4.93 below						GREENOCK Datum of Predictions 1.62 below						LEITH Datum of Predictions 2.90 below					
		hr	m	ht	hr	m	ht	hr	m	ht	hr	m	ht	hr	m	ht	hr	m	ht	hr	m	ht	hr	m	ht
F	1	09	32	5.9	22	10	5.7	07	17	7.3	20	05	7.3	08	20	2.7	20	58	2.6	10	54	4.3	23	48	4.5
Sa	2	10	53	6.0	23	31	5.9	08	30	7.6	21	08	7.7	09	53	2.9	22	26	2.8	12	11	4.5			
Su	3	12	02	6.3	-	-		09	23	8.1	21	54	8.1	10	47	3.1	23	15	2.9	00	52	4.7	13	08	4.8
M	4	00	29	6.3	12	54	6.6	10	05	8.5	22	32	8.4	11	31	3.3	23	55	3.1	01	39	4.9	13	50	5.0
Tu	5	01	14	6.6	13	36	6.8	10	41	8.8	23	04	8.7	12	10	3.4	-			02	15	5.1	14	25	5.2
W	6	01	52	6.7	14	12	6.8	11	14	9.0	23	34	8.8	00	30	3.1	12	46	3.4	02	47	5.2	14	55	5.3
Th	7	02	26	6.8	14	44	6.8	11	45	9.1				01	02	3.2	13	17	3.4	03	16	5.3	15	25	5.4
F	8	02	56	6.9	15	11	6.9	00	03	8.9	12	16	9.2	01	32	3.2	13	45	3.4	03	45	5.3	15	55	5.4
Sa	9	03	25	7.0	15	40	6.9	00	33	8.9	12	46	9.2	02	01	3.3	14	15	3.4	04	16	5.3	16	25	5.4
Su	10	03	54	7.0	16	10	6.8	01	01	8.9	13	16	9.0	02	31	3.3	14	47	3.5	04	49	5.2	16	57	5.3
M	11	04	25	6.9	16	43	6.7	01	31	8.7	13	47	8.8	03	03	3.4	15	22	3.4	05	25	5.1	17	32	5.2
Tu	12	04	58	6.8	17	18	6.5	02	03	8.5	14	22	8.6	03	36	3.3	15	59	3.3	06	00	5.0	18	11	5.0
W	13	05	35	6.6	17	57	6.3	02	41	8.3	15	06	8.2	04	12	3.3	16	39	3.2	06	42	4.8	18	57	4.9
Th	14	06	17	6.5	18	44	6.0	03	30	7.9	16	04	7.8	04	51	3.1	17	26	3.0	07	31	4.6	19	55	4.6
F	15	07	12	6.2	19	50	5.8	04	38	7.5	17	26	7.5	05	38	3.0	18	29	2.8	08	36	4.4	21	12	4.5
Sa	16	08	31	6.0	21	24	5.8	06	10	7.4	18	57	7.6	06	42	2.8	20	12	2.7	09	59	4.4	22	40	4.6
Su	17	10	05	6.2	22	48	6.1	07	36	7.8	20	17	8.1	08	33	2.8	21	55	2.9	11	20	4.6	23	56	4.9
M	18	11	22	6.6				08	45	8.4	21	20	8.7	10	01	3.1	22	57	3.1	12	25	5.0			
Tu	19	00	00	6.5	12	29	7.0	09	42	9.1	22	12	9.3	10	59	3.3	23	48	3.3	00	56	5.3	13	18	5.4
W	20	00	59	6.9	13	23	7.3	10	31	9.6	22	59	9.7	11	48	3.5	-			01	45	5.6	14	03	5.7
Th	21	01	48	7.2	14	11	7.4	11	16	10.0	23	42	9.9	00	35	3.4	12	36	3.7	02	29	5.8	14	46	6.0
F	22	02	32	7.4	14	56	7.5	12	00	10.1				01	20	3.5	13	21	3.7	03	13	5.9	15	31	6.1
Sa	23	03	14	7.5	15	38	7.5	00	24	9.9	12	42	10.0	02	03	3.5	14	04	3.8	03	56	5.9	16	16	6.0
Su	24	03	54	7.6	16	19	7.3	01	04	9.7	13	23	9.7	02	40	3.5	14	46	3.7	04	40	5.7	17	02	5.8
M	25	04	34	7.4	16	58	7.0	01	43	9.3	14	02	9.2	03	16	3.4	15	25	3.6	05	24	5.4	17	50	5.5
Tu	26	05	14	7.1	17	36	6.6	02	22	8.8	14	44	8.6	03	51	3.3	16	04	3.4	06	10	5.1	18	41	5.1
W	27	05	55	6.8	18	15	6.1	03	05	8.3	15	32	7.9	04	28	3.2	16	45	3.2	06	59	4.8	19	37	4.7
Th	28	06	39	6.3	19	00	5.9	03	57	7.7	16	35	7.3	05	10	3.0	17	29	2.9	07	55	4.5	20	40	4.4
F	29	07	36	5.9	20	00	5.6	05	08	7.2	18	01	6.9	06	00	2.8	18	22	2.7	08	59	4.3	21	50	4.2
Sa	30	08	51	5.7	21	22	5.5	06	34	7.1	19	32	7.0	07	12	2.7	19	45	2.5	10	10	4.2	23	12	4.3
Su	31	10	14	5.7	22	48	5.7	07	53	7.4	20	40	7.5	09	15	2.8	22	00	2.7	11	33	4.3	-	-	

APRIL 2019 *High Water* GMT

		LONDON BRIDGE						LIVERPOOL (Gladstone Dock)						GREENOCK						LEITH					
M	1	11	28	6.1	23	53	6.1	08	51	7.9	21	27	7.9	10	16	3.0	22	47	2.9	00	25	4.5	12	37	4.6
Tu	2	12	23	6.4	-	-		09	35	8.3	22	04	8.3	11	01	3.2	23	26	3.0	01	12	4.8	13	20	4.9
W	3	00	41	6.4	13	06	6.6	10	12	8.7	22	36	8.6	11	41	3.3	-			01	47	5.0	13	55	5.1
Th	4	01	21	6.7	13	42	6.7	10	45	8.9	23	05	8.8	00	01	3.1	12	17	3.3	02	18	5.1	14	27	5.2
F	5	01	56	6.8	14	13	6.8	11	16	9.1	23	35	9.0	00	34	3.2	12	49	3.3	02	47	5.3	14	57	5.3
Sa	6	02	27	6.9	14	42	6.9	11	47	9.2	-			01	05	3.2	13	18	3.3	03	18	5.3	15	28	5.4
Su	7	02	58	7.0	15	13	6.9	00	04	9.0	12	19	9.2	01	33	3.3	13	49	3.4	03	49	5.4	16	00	5.4
M	8	03	29	7.1	15	46	6.9	00	35	9.0	12	51	9.1	02	02	3.4	14	24	3.4	04	22	5.3	16	34	5.4
Tu	9	04	03	7.0	16	20	6.7	01	07	8.9	13	26	8.9	02	34	3.4	15	01	3.4	04	57	5.2	17	11	5.3
W	10	04	38	6.9	16	56	6.5	01	41	8.7	14	04	8.7	03	08	3.5	15	39	3.3	05	34	5.1	17	53	5.1
Th	11	05	17	6.8	17	36	6.3	02	22	8.4	14	51	8.3	03	45	3.4	16	21	3.2	06	17	4.9	18	42	4.9
F	12	06	02	6.5	18	26	6.0	03	13	8.0	15	52	7.8	04	25	3.2	17	10	3.0	07	08	4.7	19	41	4.7
Sa	13	06	59	6.3	19	33	5.8	04	25	7.6	17	14	7.5	05	12	3.1	18	16	2.8	08	12	4.5	20	59	4.6
Su	14	08	20	6.1	21	04	5.8	05	55	7.6	18	44	7.7	06	16	2.9	20	07	2.7	09	38	4.5	22	24	4.7
M	15	09	48	6.3	22	27	6.1	07	17	7.9	20	00	8.1	08	10	2.9	21	43	2.9	10	58	4.7	23	38	4.9
Tu	16	11	03	6.6	23	39	6.5	08	25	8.5	21	02	8.7	09	39	3.1	22	41	3.1	12	03	5.0			
W	17	12	09	7.0	-	-		09	21	9.0	21	52	9.2	10	37	3.3	23	29	3.3	00	36	5.3	12	55	5.4
Th	18	00	37	6.9	13	03	7.2	10	10	9.5	22	37	9.5	11	27	3.5	-			01	24	5.5	13	41	5.7
F	19	01	25	7.2	13	50	7.3	10	54	9.8	23	19	9.7	00	14	3.4	12	14	3.6	02	08	5.7	14	25	5.9
Sa	20	02	08	7.4	14	32	7.3	11	37	9.8	23	59	9.7	00	56	3.4	12	59	3.6	02	50	5.8	15	10	5.9
Su	21	02	48	7.5	15	12	7.3	12	18	9.7	-			01	35	3.5	13	42	3.6	03	33	5.7	15	55	5.8
M	22	03	28	7.5	15	51	7.2	00	37	9.5	12	58	9.4	02	11	3.5	14	23	3.6	04	15	5.6	16	41	5.6
Tu	23	04	08	7.4	16	28	6.9	01	15	9.2	13	36	8.9	02	46	3.4	15	02	3.5	04	58	5.3	17	28	5.3
W	24	04	47	7.1	17	04	6.5	01	53	8.8	14	16	8.4	03	21	3.4	15	40	3.3	05	42	5.1	18	16	5.0
Th	25	05	27	6.7	17	40	6.2	02	34	8.3	15	01	7.8	03	58	3.3	16	21	3.1	06	27	4.8	19	08	4.7
F	26	06	08	6.3	18	20	5.9	03	23	7.8	15	58	7.3	04	38	3.1	17	06	2.9	07	18	4.5	20	04	4.4
Sa	27	06	58	5.9	19	11	5.6	04	28	7.4	17	15	6.9	05	26	2.9	17	59	2.7	08	18	4.3	21	06	4.2
Su	28	08	06	5.6	20	30	5.4	05	47	7.1	18	42	6.9	06	29	2.7	19	09	2.6	09	23	4.2	22	16	4.2
M	29	09	26	5.6	21	55	5.5	07	03	7.3	19	54	7.3	08	09	2.7	20	57	2.6	10	35	4.3	23	32	4.4
Tu	30	10	37	5.9	23	03	5.9	08	06	7.7	20	45	7.7	09	31	2.9	22	01	2.8	11	44	4.5	-	-	

MAY 2019 *High Water* GMT

		LONDON BRIDGE (Datum 3.2m below)				LIVERPOOL (Gladstone Dock) (Datum 4.93 below)				GREENOCK (Datum 1.62 below)				LEITH (Datum 2.90 below)			
		hr	ht m	hr	ht m	hr	ht m	hr	ht m	hr	ht m	hr	ht m	hr	ht m	hr	ht m
W	1	11 37	6.2	23 58	6.3	08 54	8.1	21 25	8.1	10 21	3.1	22 45	3.0	00 27	4.6	12 36	4.7
Th	2	12 24	6.5	-	-	09 34	8.5	22 00	8.5	11 02	3.2	23 24	3.1	01 07	4.9	13 16	4.9
F	3	00 42	6.6	13 04	6.7	10 10	8.8	22 32	8.7	11 39	3.2	-	-	01 42	5.1	13 52	5.1
Sa	4	01 21	6.8	13 39	6.8	10 44	9.0	23 03	9.0	00 00	3.2	12 14	3.3	02 15	5.2	14 26	5.3
Su	5	01 56	7.0	14 13	6.9	11 18	9.1	23 36	9.1	00 32	3.3	12 48	3.3	02 48	5.4	15 01	5.4
M	6	02 31	7.1	14 49	6.9	11 53	9.2	-	-	01 03	3.4	13 24	3.3	03 22	5.4	15 36	5.4
Tu	7	03 07	7.2	15 26	6.9	00 11	9.1	12 31	9.1	01 35	3.5	14 03	3.3	03 57	5.4	16 14	5.4
W	8	03 44	7.1	16 03	6.7	00 48	9.1	13 10	9.0	02 10	3.5	14 43	3.3	04 34	5.3	16 55	5.4
Th	9	04 24	7.0	16 43	6.5	01 28	8.9	13 55	8.7	02 47	3.6	15 26	3.3	05 15	5.2	17 41	5.2
F	10	05 07	6.9	17 26	6.3	02 13	8.6	14 46	8.4	03 26	3.5	16 12	3.2	06 00	5.0	18 32	5.0
Sa	11	05 56	6.6	18 19	6.1	03 09	8.2	15 50	8.0	04 09	3.4	17 06	3.0	06 53	4.8	19 33	4.8
Su	12	06 57	6.4	19 26	5.9	04 21	7.9	17 06	7.8	04 59	3.2	18 19	2.8	08 00	4.7	20 48	4.7
M	13	08 14	6.3	20 48	6.0	05 40	7.9	18 26	7.9	06 06	3.0	19 57	2.8	09 21	4.7	22 05	4.8
Tu	14	09 30	6.4	22 04	6.2	06 55	8.1	19 38	8.2	07 48	3.0	21 18	3.0	10 35	4.8	23 14	5.0
W	15	10 41	6.6	23 12	6.5	08 01	8.5	20 38	8.6	09 12	3.1	22 15	3.1	11 38	5.1	-	-
Th	16	11 46	6.8	-	-	08 57	8.9	21 29	9.0	10 12	3.3	23 04	3.3	00 12	5.2	12 32	5.3
F	17	00 11	6.8	12 41	7.0	09 47	9.2	22 14	9.2	11 03	3.4	23 49	3.4	01 01	5.4	13 20	5.5
Sa	18	01 00	7.0	13 27	7.1	10 32	9.4	22 55	9.4	11 51	3.5	-	-	01 46	5.5	14 06	5.6
Su	19	01 44	7.2	14 09	7.1	11 15	9.4	23 35	9.4	00 30	3.4	12 37	3.5	02 29	5.6	14 52	5.7
M	20	02 25	7.3	14 48	7.1	11 56	9.3	-	-	01 09	3.4	13 20	3.4	03 11	5.5	15 37	5.6
Tu	21	03 05	7.4	15 26	7.0	00 14	9.3	12 36	9.0	01 45	3.5	14 00	3.4	03 53	5.4	16 23	5.4
W	22	03 45	7.2	16 02	6.8	00 51	9.1	13 14	8.7	02 19	3.5	14 39	3.3	04 35	5.3	17 07	5.2
Th	23	04 24	7.0	16 38	6.5	01 29	8.8	13 53	8.3	02 55	3.4	15 18	3.2	05 16	5.1	17 52	5.0
F	24	05 03	6.6	17 12	6.2	02 09	8.4	14 35	7.9	03 32	3.3	16 00	3.0	05 59	4.9	18 38	4.7
Sa	25	05 42	6.3	17 49	6.0	02 54	8.0	15 25	7.5	04 11	3.2	16 45	2.9	06 45	4.7	19 27	4.5
Su	26	06 24	6.0	18 32	5.8	03 49	7.6	16 26	7.1	04 56	3.0	17 36	2.8	07 37	4.5	20 21	4.3
M	27	07 18	5.7	19 32	5.6	04 56	7.4	17 39	7.0	05 51	2.9	18 36	2.7	08 36	4.4	21 19	4.3
Tu	28	08 31	5.7	20 59	5.6	06 05	7.3	18 50	7.1	07 00	2.8	19 46	2.7	09 37	4.3	22 20	4.3
W	29	09 41	5.8	22 09	5.8	07 09	7.5	19 50	7.5	08 22	2.8	20 57	2.8	10 40	4.4	23 22	4.5
Th	30	10 41	6.1	23 08	6.2	08 04	7.9	20 37	7.9	09 26	2.9	21 54	3.0	11 39	4.6	-	-
F	31	11 35	6.4	23 59	6.5	08 50	8.2	21 18	8.3	10 15	3.1	22 41	3.1	00 15	4.8	12 30	4.8

JUNE 2019 *High Water* GMT

		LONDON BRIDGE				LIVERPOOL (Gladstone Dock)				GREENOCK				LEITH			
Sa	1	12 23	6.6	-	-	09 32	8.5	21 56	8.6	10 57	3.1	23 22	3.2	01 00	5.0	13 15	5.0
Su	2	00 44	6.8	13 07	6.8	10 11	8.8	22 33	8.9	11 37	3.2	23 59	3.3	01 41	5.2	13 56	5.2
M	3	01 26	7.0	13 49	6.9	10 51	9.0	23 11	9.1	12 18	3.3	-	-	02 20	5.3	14 36	5.4
Tu	4	02 08	7.1	14 31	6.9	11 32	9.2	23 51	9.2	00 35	3.4	13 01	3.3	02 58	5.4	15 16	5.5
W	5	02 50	7.2	15 13	6.9	12 15	9.2	-	-	01 13	3.5	13 46	3.3	03 36	5.5	15 58	5.5
Th	6	03 32	7.2	15 55	6.8	00 34	9.2	13 01	9.1	01 52	3.6	14 32	3.3	04 17	5.5	16 43	5.5
F	7	04 17	7.2	16 38	6.6	01 20	9.1	13 49	8.9	02 32	3.6	15 19	3.3	05 01	5.4	17 31	5.4
Sa	8	05 03	7.0	17 25	6.5	02 10	8.9	14 43	8.6	03 15	3.6	16 10	3.2	05 49	5.2	18 24	5.2
Su	9	05 55	6.8	18 16	6.3	03 07	8.6	15 43	8.3	04 00	3.5	17 08	3.1	06 43	5.1	19 24	5.0
M	10	06 54	6.6	19 19	6.3	04 11	8.4	16 50	8.1	04 52	3.3	18 15	3.0	07 48	4.9	20 32	4.9
Tu	11	08 02	6.6	20 30	6.3	05 20	8.3	18 01	8.0	05 57	3.2	19 31	2.9	09 01	4.9	21 42	4.9
W	12	09 09	6.6	21 38	6.4	06 28	8.3	19 09	8.2	07 20	3.1	20 43	3.0	10 11	4.9	22 47	4.9
Th	13	10 15	6.6	22 43	6.6	07 34	8.4	20 11	8.4	08 40	3.1	21 44	3.1	11 13	5.0	23 46	5.0
F	14	11 19	6.7	23 44	6.7	08 33	8.6	21 05	8.6	09 45	3.2	22 37	3.2	12 11	5.2	-	-
Sa	15	12 18	6.8	-	-	09 26	8.8	21 52	8.9	10 40	3.3	23 24	3.3	00 39	5.2	13 04	5.3
Su	16	00 37	6.9	13 07	6.8	10 14	8.9	22 35	9.0	11 30	3.3	-	-	01 27	5.3	13 52	5.4
M	17	01 25	7.0	13 51	6.9	10 58	8.9	23 16	9.1	00 07	3.4	12 17	3.3	02 11	5.4	14 39	5.4
Tu	18	02 07	7.1	14 31	6.9	11 39	8.9	23 54	9.1	00 47	3.4	13 00	3.2	02 54	5.4	15 23	5.4
W	19	02 49	7.2	15 08	6.8	12 18	8.8	-	-	01 23	3.4	13 40	3.2	03 35	5.3	16 05	5.3
Th	20	03 28	7.1	15 44	6.7	00 31	9.0	12 55	8.6	01 58	3.5	14 18	3.1	04 15	5.2	16 46	5.2
F	21	04 06	6.9	16 18	6.6	01 08	8.8	13 32	8.3	02 33	3.5	14 57	3.1	04 53	5.1	17 26	5.0
Sa	22	04 43	6.6	16 52	6.4	01 46	8.6	14 10	8.1	03 09	3.4	15 38	3.0	05 32	5.0	18 07	4.7
Su	23	05 19	6.4	17 26	6.2	02 27	8.3	14 52	7.8	03 46	3.3	16 21	3.0	06 13	4.8	18 50	4.7
M	24	05 56	6.2	18 04	6.1	03 12	8.0	15 40	7.5	04 26	3.2	17 07	2.9	06 57	4.7	19 36	4.5
Tu	25	06 37	6.0	18 48	5.9	04 04	7.7	16 35	7.3	05 12	3.0	17 57	2.9	07 48	4.6	20 28	4.4
W	26	07 28	5.8	19 46	5.8	05 04	7.5	17 39	7.2	06 06	2.9	18 51	2.8	08 44	4.5	21 25	4.4
Th	27	08 38	5.8	21 09	5.8	06 06	7.5	18 44	7.3	07 09	2.8	19 50	2.8	09 44	4.5	22 24	4.5
F	28	09 47	5.9	22 17	6.1	07 07	7.7	19 43	7.6	08 18	2.9	20 54	2.9	10 45	4.5	23 24	4.7
Sa	29	10 48	6.2	23 16	6.4	08 04	7.9	20 36	8.0	09 22	2.9	21 53	3.0	11 45	4.7	-	-
Su	30	11 46	6.5	-	-	08 55	8.3	21 23	8.5	10 17	3.1	22 43	3.2	00 20	4.9	12 40	4.9

JULY 2019 *High Water* GMT

LONDON BRIDGE — Datum of Predictions 3.2m below

Day	hr	m	ht	hr	m	ht
M 1	00	10	6.8	12	40	6.7
Tu 2	01	01	7.0	13	29	6.9
W 3	01	49	7.2	14	17	7.0
Th 4	02	37	7.3	15	03	7.0
F 5	03	24	7.4	15	48	7.0
Sa 6	04	10	7.4	16	33	6.9
Su 7	04	58	7.3	17	19	6.8
M 8	05	47	7.1	18	07	6.7
Tu 9	06	42	6.9	19	02	6.6
W 10	07	41	6.7	20	04	6.5
Th 11	08	42	6.5	21	08	6.5
F 12	09	45	6.5	22	13	6.5
Sa 13	10	51	6.4	23	18	6.6
Su 14	11	56	6.5	-	-	
M 15	00	19	6.7	12	51	6.6
Tu 16	01	11	6.9	13	38	6.7
W 17	01	56	7.0	14	19	6.8
Th 18	02	38	7.0	14	55	6.8
F 19	03	16	7.0	15	29	6.8
Sa 20	03	51	6.9	16	01	6.7
Su 21	04	23	6.7	16	32	6.6
M 22	04	54	6.6	17	04	6.5
Tu 23	05	27	6.4	17	37	6.4
W 24	06	01	6.2	18	13	6.2
Th 25	06	42	6.0	18	58	6.0
F 26	07	32	5.8	19	55	5.9
Sa 27	08	47	5.8	21	21	5.9
Su 28	10	06	6.0	22	37	6.2
M 29	11	14	6.3	23	41	6.6
Tu 30	12	16	6.6	-	-	
W 31	00	39	7.0	13	12	6.9

LIVERPOOL (Gladstone Dock) — Datum of Predictions 4.93 below

Day	hr	m	ht	hr	m	ht
M 1	09	43	8.6	22	07	8.8
Tu 2	10	29	8.9	22	52	9.1
W 3	11	16	9.2	23	37	9.4
Th 4	12	03	9.3	-	-	
F 5	00	23	9.5	12	52	9.3
Sa 6	01	12	9.4	13	42	9.2
Su 7	02	02	9.3	14	33	9.0
M 8	02	55	9.1	15	27	8.6
Tu 9	03	51	8.8	16	25	8.3
W 10	04	52	8.5	17	29	8.1
Th 11	05	57	8.2	18	37	8.0
F 12	07	06	8.1	19	44	8.0
Sa 13	08	12	8.2	20	44	8.3
Su 14	09	11	8.3	21	35	8.5
M 15	10	01	8.5	22	20	8.7
Tu 16	10	46	8.6	23	01	8.9
W 17	11	26	8.7	23	38	9.0
Th 18	12	02	8.7	-	-	
F 19	00	14	9.0	12	37	8.6
Sa 20	00	48	8.9	13	10	8.5
Su 21	01	23	8.8	13	44	8.3
M 22	01	58	8.6	14	19	8.1
Tu 23	02	35	8.3	14	57	7.9
W 24	03	16	8.1	15	39	7.6
Th 25	04	03	7.8	16	32	7.4
F 26	05	02	7.6	17	38	7.3
Sa 27	06	11	7.5	18	51	7.5
Su 28	07	21	7.7	19	58	7.8
M 29	08	25	8.1	20	56	8.3
Tu 30	09	22	8.5	21	48	8.8
W 31	10	14	9.0	22	36	9.3

GREENOCK — Datum of Predictions 1.62 below

Day	hr	m	ht	hr	m	ht
M 1	11	07	3.1	23	29	3.3
Tu 2	11	56	3.2	-	-	
W 3	00	12	3.4	12	45	3.3
Th 4	00	55	3.6	13	34	3.3
F 5	01	38	3.7	14	24	3.3
Sa 6	02	22	3.7	15	14	3.3
Su 7	03	06	3.7	16	06	3.2
M 8	03	53	3.6	16	59	3.1
Tu 9	04	42	3.5	17	54	3.1
W 10	05	38	3.3	18	55	3.0
Th 11	06	44	3.2	20	01	2.9
F 12	08	01	3.1	21	10	3.0
Sa 13	09	18	3.0	22	11	3.1
Su 14	10	23	3.1	23	04	3.2
M 15	11	17	3.1	23	50	3.3
Tu 16	12	05	3.1	-	-	
W 17	00	31	3.4	12	48	3.1
Th 18	01	08	3.4	13	25	3.1
F 19	01	41	3.5	14	00	3.1
Sa 20	02	14	3.5	14	35	3.1
Su 21	02	47	3.5	15	13	3.1
M 22	03	21	3.4	15	52	3.1
Tu 23	03	56	3.3	16	32	3.1
W 24	04	36	3.2	17	14	3.0
Th 25	05	21	3.0	18	01	2.9
F 26	06	16	2.9	18	53	2.9
Sa 27	07	22	2.8	19	55	2.9
Su 28	08	36	2.8	21	05	2.9
M 29	09	47	3.0	22	10	3.1
Tu 30	10	48	3.1	23	05	3.3
W 31	11	42	3.2	23	53	3.5

LEITH — Datum of Predictions 2.90 below

Day	hr	m	ht	hr	m	ht
M 1	01	10	5.1	13	29	5.2
Tu 2	01	55	5.3	14	15	5.4
W 3	02	37	5.5	14	59	5.6
Th 4	03	19	5.6	15	44	5.7
F 5	04	02	5.6	16	31	5.7
Sa 6	04	48	5.6	17	19	5.6
Su 7	05	37	5.5	18	11	5.4
M 8	06	29	5.4	19	07	5.2
Tu 9	07	29	5.2	20	09	5.0
W 10	08	37	5.1	21	14	4.9
Th 11	09	45	5.0	22	18	4.8
F 12	10	50	4.9	23	21	4.8
Sa 13	11	53	5.0	-	-	
Su 14	00	20	5.0	12	52	5.0
M 15	01	14	5.1	13	44	5.1
Tu 16	02	00	5.2	14	29	5.2
W 17	02	41	5.3	15	10	5.2
Th 18	03	20	5.3	15	48	5.2
F 19	03	56	5.3	16	24	5.2
Sa 20	04	30	5.2	16	59	5.1
Su 21	05	05	5.2	17	35	5.0
M 22	05	41	5.1	18	14	4.9
Tu 23	06	20	4.9	18	56	4.7
W 24	07	02	4.8	19	42	4.6
Th 25	07	51	4.6	20	35	4.5
F 26	08	50	4.5	21	36	4.5
Sa 27	09	57	4.5	22	41	4.6
Su 28	11	05	4.6	23	44	4.8
M 29	12	10	4.9	-	-	
Tu 30	00	42	5.0	13	08	5.2
W 31	01	33	5.3	13	58	5.5

AUGUST 2019 *High Water* GMT

LONDON BRIDGE

Day	hr	m	ht	hr	m	ht
Th 1	01	33	7.3	14	02	7.0
F 2	02	23	7.4	14	50	7.1
Sa 3	03	11	7.6	15	35	7.2
Su 4	03	58	7.6	16	19	7.3
M 5	04	44	7.4	17	02	7.2
Tu 6	05	30	7.2	17	47	7.0
W 7	06	19	6.9	18	35	6.8
Th 8	07	11	6.6	19	30	6.6
F 9	08	08	6.3	20	33	6.4
Sa 10	09	11	6.2	21	41	6.3
Su 11	10	21	6.1	22	53	6.3
M 12	11	34	6.2	-	-	
Tu 13	00	02	6.5	12	34	6.5
W 14	00	57	6.8	13	22	6.7
Th 15	01	43	6.9	14	03	6.8
F 16	02	23	7.0	14	39	6.8
Sa 17	02	58	6.9	15	10	6.9
Su 18	03	30	6.9	15	40	6.9
M 19	03	58	6.8	16	08	6.8
Tu 20	04	26	6.7	16	38	6.7
W 21	04	56	6.6	17	09	6.6
Th 22	05	29	6.4	17	43	6.4
F 23	06	05	6.1	18	23	6.2
Sa 24	06	49	5.9	19	12	6.0
Su 25	07	49	5.7	20	24	5.9
M 26	09	22	5.7	22	00	6.1
Tu 27	10	44	6.0	23	15	6.5
W 28	11	54	6.5	-	-	
Th 29	00	19	7.0	12	53	6.8
F 30	01	16	7.3	13	44	7.1
Sa 31	02	06	7.5	14	31	7.3

LIVERPOOL (Gladstone Dock)

Day	hr	m	ht	hr	m	ht
Th 1	11	04	9.3	23	24	9.6
F 2	11	52	9.6	-	-	
Sa 3	00	11	9.8	12	40	9.6
Su 4	00	58	9.8	13	27	9.5
M 5	01	46	9.7	14	14	9.3
Tu 6	02	33	9.4	15	02	8.9
W 7	03	23	9.0	15	53	8.4
Th 8	04	19	8.5	16	53	8.0
F 9	05	24	8.0	18	02	7.7
Sa 10	06	39	7.7	19	18	7.7
Su 11	07	56	7.7	20	26	7.9
M 12	09	01	7.9	21	22	8.3
Tu 13	09	53	8.2	22	07	8.6
W 14	10	35	8.5	22	46	8.8
Th 15	11	11	8.6	23	21	9.0
F 16	11	44	8.7	23	53	9.1
Sa 17	12	14	8.8	-	-	
Su 18	00	25	9.1	12	45	8.7
M 19	00	57	9.0	13	15	8.6
Tu 20	01	29	8.8	13	46	8.4
W 21	02	00	8.6	14	18	8.2
Th 22	02	34	8.3	14	54	8.0
F 23	03	15	8.0	15	40	7.7
Sa 24	04	08	7.7	16	43	7.4
Su 25	05	22	7.4	18	07	7.4
M 26	06	47	7.5	19	28	7.7
Tu 27	08	04	7.9	20	35	8.3
W 28	09	07	8.5	21	31	8.9
Th 29	10	01	9.1	22	21	9.4
F 30	10	50	9.5	23	08	9.9
Sa 31	11	36	9.8	23	53	10.1

GREENOCK

Day	hr	m	ht	hr	m	ht
Th 1	12	34	3.3	-	-	
F 2	00	39	3.6	13	25	3.3
Sa 3	01	25	3.7	14	15	3.3
Su 4	02	11	3.8	15	03	3.3
M 5	02	55	3.8	15	50	3.3
Tu 6	03	40	3.8	16	35	3.2
W 7	04	25	3.6	17	21	3.1
Th 8	05	13	3.4	18	10	3.0
F 9	06	06	3.2	19	10	2.9
Sa 10	07	12	2.9	20	30	2.9
Su 11	08	53	2.8	21	48	3.0
M 12	10	17	2.9	22	46	3.1
Tu 13	11	20	3.0	23	43	3.3
W 14	11	58	3.0	-	-	
Th 15	00	15	3.4	12	37	3.1
F 16	00	52	3.5	13	10	3.1
Sa 17	01	24	3.5	13	39	3.1
Su 18	01	53	3.5	14	11	3.1
M 19	02	23	3.5	14	43	3.2
Tu 20	02	54	3.5	15	18	3.2
W 21	03	28	3.4	15	53	3.2
Th 22	04	05	3.3	16	31	3.2
F 23	04	45	3.2	17	14	3.1
Sa 24	05	33	3.0	18	03	3.0
Su 25	06	37	2.8	19	05	2.9
M 26	08	01	2.8	20	24	2.9
Tu 27	09	29	2.9	21	44	3.1
W 28	10	38	3.1	22	45	3.3
Th 29	11	33	3.2	23	36	3.5
F 30	12	23	3.3	-	-	
Sa 31	00	24	3.7	13	11	3.4

LEITH

Day	hr	m	ht	hr	m	ht
Th 1	02	19	5.6	14	44	5.7
F 2	03	02	5.8	15	29	5.9
Sa 3	03	46	5.9	16	15	5.9
Su 4	04	32	5.9	17	02	5.8
M 5	05	19	5.8	17	51	5.6
Tu 6	06	10	5.6	18	43	5.3
W 7	07	06	5.4	19	40	5.0
Th 8	08	10	5.1	20	42	4.8
F 9	09	18	4.8	21	47	4.7
Sa 10	10	27	4.7	22	55	4.6
Su 11	11	38	4.7	-	-	
M 12	00	04	4.8	12	44	4.9
Tu 13	01	03	4.9	13	36	5.0
W 14	01	49	5.1	14	18	5.1
Th 15	02	28	5.3	14	55	5.2
F 16	03	02	5.3	15	27	5.3
Sa 17	03	34	5.4	15	59	5.3
Su 18	04	05	5.4	16	31	5.2
M 19	04	37	5.3	17	04	5.1
Tu 20	05	11	5.2	17	40	5.0
W 21	05	46	5.1	18	18	4.9
Th 22	06	24	4.9	19	00	4.7
F 23	07	09	4.8	19	49	4.6
Sa 24	08	03	4.6	20	49	4.5
Su 25	09	14	4.5	22	02	4.5
M 26	10	33	4.6	23	14	4.7
Tu 27	11	47	4.8	-	-	
W 28	00	19	5.0	12	50	5.2
Th 29	01	13	5.3	13	41	5.6
F 30	01	59	5.7	14	26	5.8
Sa 31	02	42	5.9	15	10	6.0

SEPTEMBER 2019 *High Water* GMT

	LONDON BRIDGE Datum of Predictions 3.2m below				LIVERPOOL (Gladstone Dock) Datum of Predictions 4.93 below				GREENOCK Datum of Predictions 1.62 below				LEITH Datum of Predictions 2.90 below			
	hr m	ht m	hr m	ht m	hr m	ht m	hr m	ht m	hr m	ht m	hr m	ht m	hr m	ht m	hr m	ht m
Su 1	02 53	7.6	15 14	7.4	12 21	9.9	-	-	01 11	3.8	13 58	3.4	03 26	6.1	15 55	6.0
M 2	03 38	7.6	15 57	7.5	00 38	10.1	13 05	9.8	01 56	3.9	14 41	3.4	04 11	6.1	16 40	5.9
Tu 3	04 22	7.5	16 38	7.4	01 23	9.9	13 48	9.4	02 39	3.9	15 23	3.4	04 57	6.0	17 26	5.7
W 4	05 05	7.2	17 20	7.2	02 07	9.5	14 32	9.0	03 22	3.8	16 02	3.3	05 46	5.7	18 15	5.3
Th 5	05 48	6.8	18 03	6.9	02 52	9.0	15 19	8.5	04 03	3.6	16 42	3.2	06 40	5.4	19 08	5.0
F 6	06 34	6.4	18 53	6.6	03 44	8.3	16 14	7.9	04 46	3.4	17 25	3.1	07 42	5.2	20 09	4.7
Sa 7	07 26	6.1	19 54	6.2	04 49	7.7	17 26	7.5	05 32	3.1	18 17	2.9	08 51	4.7	21 15	4.5
Su 8	08 29	5.8	21 07	6.0	06 13	7.3	18 50	7.4	06 28	2.8	19 35	2.8	10 03	4.5	22 27	4.5
M 9	09 47	5.7	22 27	6.0	07 41	7.3	20 07	7.7	08 34	2.6	21 24	2.9	11 21	4.6	23 44	4.6
Tu 10	11 08	5.9	23 41	6.4	08 49	7.7	21 04	8.2	10 10	2.8	22 25	3.1	12 31	4.8	-	-
W 11	12 11	6.3	-	-	09 38	8.1	21 48	8.6	11 00	3.0	23 12	3.3	00 45	4.9	13 22	5.0
Th 12	00 37	6.7	12 59	6.6	10 17	8.5	22 25	8.9	11 40	3.1	23 53	3.5	01 31	5.1	14 00	5.1
F 13	01 22	6.9	13 39	6.7	10 50	8.7	22 58	9.1	12 15	3.1	-	-	02 07	5.2	14 33	5.3
Sa 14	02 00	6.9	14 14	6.8	11 20	8.9	23 29	9.2	00 29	3.5	12 46	3.2	02 39	5.4	15 02	5.3
Su 15	02 33	6.9	14 45	6.9	11 49	8.9	23 59	9.2	01 01	3.5	13 14	3.2	03 09	5.4	15 31	5.4
M 16	03 02	6.9	15 13	7.0	12 17	8.9	-	-	01 29	3.5	13 42	3.3	03 38	5.4	16 01	5.3
Tu 17	03 28	6.9	15 40	7.0	00 29	9.2	12 46	8.9	01 57	3.5	14 12	3.3	04 09	5.4	16 33	5.3
W 18	03 55	6.8	16 10	6.9	00 59	9.0	13 15	8.7	02 28	3.5	14 44	3.4	04 41	5.3	17 07	5.2
Th 19	04 26	6.7	16 42	6.7	01 29	8.8	13 45	8.5	03 02	3.5	15 18	3.4	05 16	5.2	17 43	5.0
F 20	04 58	6.4	17 16	6.6	02 02	8.5	14 20	8.2	03 38	3.4	15 54	3.3	05 54	5.0	18 23	4.9
Sa 21	05 33	6.2	17 55	6.4	02 42	8.2	15 04	7.9	04 17	3.2	16 34	3.2	06 39	4.9	19 10	4.7
Su 22	06 16	6.0	18 45	6.2	03 35	7.8	16 06	7.5	05 01	3.0	17 20	3.1	07 33	4.7	20 10	4.5
M 23	07 12	5.7	19 52	6.0	04 51	7.4	17 36	7.4	06 02	2.8	18 21	3.0	08 44	4.5	21 28	4.5
Tu 24	08 40	5.6	21 30	6.0	06 25	7.4	19 06	7.7	07 36	2.8	19 48	3.0	10 09	4.6	22 49	4.7
W 25	10 15	5.9	22 50	6.5	07 48	7.9	20 17	8.3	09 23	2.9	21 21	3.1	11 27	4.9	23 57	5.0
Th 26	11 29	6.3	23 58	6.9	08 53	8.6	21 14	9.0	10 30	3.2	22 26	3.4	12 30	5.3	-	-
F 27	12 30	6.8	-	-	09 46	9.2	22 03	9.6	11 20	3.3	23 17	3.6	00 51	5.4	13 21	5.6
Sa 28	00 55	7.3	13 21	7.1	10 32	9.7	22 48	10.0	12 06	3.5	-	-	01 37	5.8	14 05	5.9
Su 29	01 45	7.5	14 06	7.4	11 16	9.9	23 32	10.2	00 05	3.7	12 51	3.5	02 20	6.0	14 48	6.0
M 30	02 30	7.5	14 49	7.5	11 58	10.0	-	-	00 52	3.8	13 33	3.5	03 03	6.2	15 31	6.0

OCTOBER 2019 *High Water* GMT

	LONDON BRIDGE				LIVERPOOL (Gladstone Dock)				GREENOCK				LEITH			
Tu 1	03 14	7.5	15 30	7.6	00 15	10.2	12 40	9.8	01 36	3.9	14 14	3.5	03 48	6.2	16 15	5.9
W 2	03 56	7.4	16 11	7.5	00 58	9.9	13 20	9.5	02 19	3.9	14 52	3.5	04 35	6.0	17 00	5.6
Th 3	04 36	7.1	16 52	7.3	01 39	9.4	14 01	9.0	03 00	3.8	15 29	3.5	05 24	5.7	17 47	5.3
F 4	05 16	6.7	17 34	6.9	02 23	8.8	14 45	8.5	03 40	3.6	16 07	3.4	06 16	5.3	18 37	5.0
Sa 5	05 56	6.3	18 20	6.5	03 12	8.1	15 38	7.9	04 21	3.4	16 49	3.2	07 16	4.9	19 35	4.7
Su 6	06 40	5.9	19 15	6.0	04 15	7.4	16 49	7.4	05 06	3.1	17 38	3.0	08 22	4.6	20 41	4.5
M 7	07 38	5.6	20 30	5.8	05 41	7.0	18 16	7.3	06 00	2.8	18 46	2.9	09 32	4.4	21 53	4.4
Tu 8	09 02	5.4	21 52	5.8	07 15	7.1	19 36	7.6	07 38	2.6	20 46	2.9	10 52	4.4	23 11	4.5
W 9	10 27	5.6	23 08	6.1	08 25	7.6	20 35	8.0	09 47	2.8	21 54	3.1	12 06	4.7	-	-
Th 10	11 35	6.0	-	-	09 13	8.0	21 19	8.5	10 33	3.0	22 42	3.4	00 16	4.8	12 56	4.9
F 11	00 06	6.5	12 26	6.4	09 50	8.4	21 56	8.8	11 11	3.2	23 22	3.5	01 02	5.0	13 33	5.1
Sa 12	00 51	6.7	13 07	6.7	10 22	8.7	22 29	9.0	11 44	3.3	23 59	3.5	01 38	5.2	14 04	5.3
Su 13	01 29	6.8	13 42	6.8	10 51	8.9	23 00	9.2	12 15	3.3	-	-	02 10	5.3	14 32	5.4
M 14	02 01	6.8	14 13	6.9	11 20	9.0	23 31	9.3	00 31	3.5	12 45	3.4	02 40	5.4	15 01	5.4
Tu 15	02 29	6.9	14 42	7.0	11 48	9.1	-	-	01 01	3.5	13 13	3.4	03 10	5.5	15 32	5.4
W 16	02 56	6.9	15 12	7.1	00 01	9.2	12 18	9.0	01 31	3.5	13 42	3.5	03 42	5.5	16 04	5.4
Th 17	03 26	6.9	15 44	7.0	00 32	9.1	12 48	8.9	02 04	3.5	14 14	3.6	04 16	5.4	16 38	5.3
F 18	03 59	6.7	16 17	6.9	01 05	8.9	13 20	8.7	02 40	3.5	14 49	3.6	04 52	5.3	17 14	5.2
Sa 19	04 33	6.5	16 54	6.7	01 41	8.6	13 57	8.5	03 18	3.4	15 26	3.5	05 32	5.1	17 55	5.0
Su 20	05 09	6.3	17 36	6.5	02 24	8.3	14 44	8.1	03 57	3.3	16 05	3.4	06 19	5.0	18 42	4.8
M 21	05 52	6.0	18 28	6.3	03 20	7.8	15 49	7.7	04 43	3.1	16 52	3.3	07 15	4.8	19 42	4.6
Tu 22	06 49	5.8	19 36	6.1	04 37	7.5	17 18	7.6	05 45	2.9	17 52	3.1	08 26	4.6	21 02	4.6
W 23	08 12	5.6	21 07	6.2	06 08	7.6	18 44	7.9	07 24	2.8	19 20	3.1	09 50	4.7	22 24	4.7
Th 24	09 47	5.9	22 26	6.5	07 29	8.0	19 55	8.5	09 11	3.0	20 57	3.2	11 06	5.0	23 32	5.1
F 25	11 01	6.3	23 33	6.9	08 33	8.7	20 52	9.1	10 22	3.2	22 03	3.5	12 08	5.3	-	-
Sa 26	12 03	6.8	-	-	09 25	9.2	21 41	9.6	11 00	3.4	22 55	3.7	00 26	5.5	12 58	5.6
Su 27	00 31	7.2	12 55	7.1	10 10	9.6	22 26	9.9	11 44	3.5	23 43	3.8	01 13	5.8	13 42	5.8
M 28	01 21	7.3	13 40	7.3	10 53	9.9	23 10	10.0	12 26	3.6	-	-	01 57	6.0	14 24	6.0
Tu 29	02 06	7.4	14 22	7.5	11 34	9.9	23 52	9.9	00 30	3.8	13 07	3.6	02 42	6.1	15 07	5.9
W 30	02 48	7.4	15 04	7.6	12 15	9.8	-	-	01 15	3.8	13 46	3.6	03 28	6.0	15 50	5.8
Th 31	03 28	7.2	15 45	7.5	00 34	9.7	12 55	9.5	01 58	3.8	14 23	3.6	04 15	5.8	16 35	5.6

NOVEMBER 2019 *High Water* GMT

		LONDON BRIDGE Datum of Predictions 3.2m below					LIVERPOOL (Gladstone Dock) Datum of Predictions 4.93 below					GREENOCK Datum of Predictions 1.62 below					LEITH Datum of Predictions 2.90 below				
		hr	m	ht	hr	m	ht	hr	m	ht	hr	m	ht	hr	m	ht	hr	m	ht		
F	1	04	08	7.0	16	26	7.2	01	16	9.2	13	34	9.0	02	39	3.7	15	00	3.6	05 04 5.5	17 20 5.3
Sa	2	04	45	6.6	17	08	6.8	01	58	8.6	14	16	8.6	03	19	3.5	15	38	3.5	05 55 5.2	18 08 5.0
Su	3	05	22	6.2	17	51	6.4	02	44	8.0	15	06	8.0	04	01	3.3	16	20	3.3	06 50 4.8	19 02 4.7
M	4	06	01	5.9	18	40	6.0	03	42	7.4	16	10	7.6	04	46	3.1	17	08	3.2	07 49 4.6	20 04 4.5
Tu	5	06	49	5.6	19	46	5.7	04	58	7.0	17	29	7.3	05	41	2.8	18	10	3.0	08 53 4.4	21 11 4.4
W	6	08	03	5.4	21	05	5.6	06	26	7.0	18	47	7.5	06	57	2.7	19	41	3.0	10 04 4.4	22 21 4.5
Th	7	09	32	5.4	22	16	5.9	07	41	7.3	19	51	7.8	08	51	2.8	21	07	3.1	11 18 4.5	23 28 4.6
F	8	10	43	5.8	23	19	6.2	08	33	7.8	20	40	8.2	09	48	3.0	22	01	3.3	12 14 4.7	
Sa	9	11	40	6.2		-		09	13	8.2	21	20	8.6	10	30	3.2	22	44	3.4	00 20 4.8	12 54 5.0
Su	10	00	09	6.5	12	27	6.5	09	48	8.6	21	56	8.9	11	07	3.3	23	22	3.5	01 00 5.1	13 28 5.2
M	11	00	50	6.7	13	05	6.7	10	19	8.8	22	30	9.0	11	42	3.4	23	57	3.5	01 36 5.2	14 00 5.3
Tu	12	01	25	6.8	13	40	6.9	10	50	9.0	23	02	9.2	12	14	3.5				02 10 5.3	14 32 5.4
W	13	01	57	6.8	14	13	7.0	11	21	9.1	23	36	9.2	00	31	3.5	12	45	3.6	02 44 5.4	15 05 5.5
Th	14	02	29	6.9	14	47	7.1	11	53	9.2		-		01	06	3.5	13	17	3.6	03 18 5.5	15 39 5.5
F	15	03	04	6.9	15	22	7.1	00	10	9.1	12	27	9.1	01	43	3.5	13	51	3.7	03 55 5.4	16 14 5.4
Sa	16	03	40	6.7	16	00	7.0	00	48	9.0	13	04	8.9	02	22	3.5	14	28	3.7	04 34 5.4	16 52 5.3
Su	17	04	17	6.6	16	41	6.9	01	29	8.7	13	46	8.7	03	03	3.4	15	06	3.7	05 17 5.3	17 34 5.1
M	18	04	56	6.3	17	26	6.7	02	17	8.4	14	37	8.4	03	47	3.3	15	48	3.6	06 06 5.1	18 24 4.9
Tu	19	05	42	6.1	18	20	6.5	03	15	8.0	15	42	8.0	04	36	3.2	16	36	3.5	07 02 4.9	19 23 4.8
W	20	06	39	5.9	19	27	6.3	04	27	7.8	17	01	7.9	05	40	3.0	17	35	3.3	08 11 4.8	20 40 4.7
Th	21	07	55	5.9	20	48	6.3	05	47	7.8	18	19	8.1	07	10	2.9	18	56	3.2	09 28 4.8	21 58 4.9
F	22	09	20	6.0	22	00	6.5	07	03	8.1	19	28	8.5	08	42	3.1	20	27	3.3	10 40 5.0	23 05 5.1
Sa	23	10	32	6.4	23	07	6.8	08	07	8.6	20	27	9.0	09	45	3.3	21	35	3.5	11 41 5.2	
Su	24	11	35	6.7		-		09	01	9.0	21	19	9.3	10	35	3.4	22	31	3.6	00 01 5.4	12 34 5.5
M	25	00	06	7.0	12	29	7.0	09	48	9.3	22	06	9.5	11	21	3.6	23	22	3.7	00 52 5.6	13 20 5.6
Tu	26	00	58	7.1	13	16	7.2	10	32	9.6	22	51	9.6	12	03	3.6		-		01 39 5.8	14 03 5.7
W	27	01	43	7.1	14	00	7.3	11	14	9.6	23	34	9.5	00	10	3.7	12	44	3.7	02 25 5.8	14 47 5.7
Th	28	02	25	7.1	14	43	7.4	11	54	9.6		-		00	56	3.7	13	23	3.7	03 12 5.8	15 30 5.7
F	29	03	06	7.0	15	25	7.3	00	16	9.3	12	34	9.4	01	39	3.6	14	00	3.7	03 59 5.6	16 14 5.5
Sa	30	03	45	6.9	16	06	7.1	00	57	9.0	13	13	9.0	02	20	3.5	14	37	3.7	04 46 5.4	16 57 5.3

DECEMBER 2019 *High Water* GMT

		LONDON BRIDGE						LIVERPOOL (Gladstone Dock)						GREENOCK						LEITH		
Su	1	04	22	6.6	16	47	6.7	01	38	8.5	13	53	8.7	03	01	3.4	15	16	3.6	05 33 5.1	17 42 5.1
M	2	04	57	6.3	17	27	6.4	02	20	8.1	14	38	8.3	03	43	3.2	15	57	3.5	06 21 4.9	18 29 4.8
Tu	3	05	33	6.0	18	10	6.1	03	09	7.6	15	32	7.9	04	28	3.1	16	42	3.3	07 12 4.6	19 22 4.6
W	4	06	12	5.8	18	59	5.8	04	08	7.3	16	36	7.6	05	19	2.9	17	35	3.2	08 06 4.5	20 21 4.5
Th	5	07	04	5.6	20	06	5.7	05	19	7.1	17	46	7.5	06	18	2.8	18	39	3.1	09 05 4.4	21 22 4.5
F	6	08	27	5.5	21	17	5.7	06	32	7.1	18	52	7.6	07	30	2.9	19	55	3.0	10 06 4.4	22 24 4.5
Sa	7	09	45	5.6	22	19	5.9	07	36	7.4	19	50	7.9	08	42	3.0	21	04	3.1	11 07 4.5	23 23 4.6
Su	8	10	46	6.0	23	15	6.2	08	27	7.8	20	38	8.2	09	39	3.1	21	58	3.2	12 01 4.8	
M	9	11	40	6.3		-		09	08	8.2	21	20	8.5	10	27	3.3	22	43	3.3	00 14 4.8	12 46 5.0
Tu	10	00	05	6.5	12	27	6.6	09	46	8.6	21	59	8.8	11	08	3.4	23	24	3.4	01 00 5.0	13 27 5.2
W	11	00	50	6.7	13	08	6.8	10	21	8.9	22	37	9.0	11	46	3.5		-		01 41 5.2	14 05 5.4
Th	12	01	30	6.8	13	48	7.0	10	57	9.1	23	15	9.1	00	04	3.4	12	21	3.6	02 20 5.3	14 41 5.5
F	13	02	10	6.8	14	28	7.1	11	34	9.2	23	55	9.2	00	46	3.4	12	59	3.7	02 59 5.5	15 18 5.5
Sa	14	02	51	6.8	15	09	7.2	12	13	9.3		-		01	27	3.5	13	40	3.8	03 38 5.5	15 56 5.5
Su	15	03	31	6.8	15	51	7.2	00	38	9.1	12	56	9.2	02	10	3.5	14	13	3.8	04 20 5.5	16 36 5.4
M	16	04	12	6.7	16	35	7.1	01	23	9.0	13	42	9.0	02	55	3.4	14	54	3.8	05 06 5.4	17 21 5.3
Tu	17	04	54	6.5	17	23	6.9	02	13	8.7	14	33	8.8	03	41	3.3	15	38	3.7	05 55 5.3	18 10 5.2
W	18	05	40	6.4	18	15	6.7	03	08	8.4	15	32	8.5	04	32	3.2	16	26	3.6	06 49 5.1	19 07 5.1
Th	19	06	33	6.3	19	17	6.5	04	11	8.2	16	39	8.4	05	31	3.1	17	22	3.5	07 52 4.9	20 15 5.0
F	20	07	38	6.2	20	26	6.5	05	19	8.0	17	48	8.3	06	43	3.0	18	30	3.4	09 02 4.9	21 30 5.0
Sa	21	08	53	6.2	21	34	6.5	06	30	8.1	18	57	8.4	08	06	3.0	19	50	3.3	10 14 4.9	22 37 5.0
Su	22	10	02	6.4	22	39	6.6	07	38	8.3	20	02	8.6	09	11	3.2	21	06	3.4	11 13 5.0	23 39 5.2
M	23	11	07	6.6	23	43	6.7	08	37	8.6	20	59	8.8	10	09	3.3	22	09	3.4	12 10 5.2	
Tu	24	12	06	6.8		-		09	29	8.9	21	51	9.0	10	59	3.4	23	05	3.5	00 35 5.3	13 02 5.3
W	25	00	39	6.8	12	59	6.9	10	16	9.1	22	38	9.1	11	44	3.5	23	55	3.5	01 27 5.4	13 48 5.5
Th	26	01	28	6.8	13	46	7.1	10	59	9.3	23	23	9.1	12	27	3.6		-		02 16 5.5	14 33 5.5
F	27	02	12	6.9	14	30	7.1	11	40	9.3		-		00	42	3.5	13	06	3.7	03 02 5.5	15 16 5.5
Sa	28	02	52	6.9	15	12	7.1	00	04	9.0	12	19	9.2	01	26	3.4	13	44	3.7	03 47 5.4	15 58 5.4
Su	29	03	30	6.8	15	52	7.0	00	43	8.8	12	56	9.1	02	06	3.4	14	21	3.7	04 29 5.3	16 38 5.3
M	30	04	05	6.6	16	30	6.7	01	20	8.6	13	33	8.9	02	45	3.3	14	58	3.6	05 10 5.2	17 17 5.2
Tu	31	04	39	6.5	17	06	6.5	01	57	8.3	14	12	8.6	03	24	3.2	15	36	3.5	05 51 5.0	17 57 5.0

INDEX